THE NEW COLUMBIA ENCYCLOPEDIA

THE NEW COLUMBIA ENCYCLOPEDIA

Edited by WILLIAM H. HARRIS
and JUDITH S. LEVEY

COLUMBIA UNIVERSITY PRESS
NEW YORK and LONDON 1975

Library of Congress Cataloging in Publication Data
Main entry under title:
The New Columbia encyclopedia.

Previous editions published under title: The Columbia encyclopedia.

SUMMARY: More than 50,000 alphabetically arranged articles on the humanities, social sciences, life and physical sciences, and geography.

1. Encyclopedias and dictionaries. [1. Encyclopedias and dictionaries] I. Harris, William H., 1927- ed. II. Levey, Judith S., 1936- ed. III. Columbia University.
AG5.C725 1974 031 74-26686
ISBN 0-231-03572-1

THE COLUMBIA ENCYCLOPEDIA
FIRST EDITION 1935
SECOND EDITION 1950
THIRD EDITION 1963
FOURTH EDITION (THE NEW COLUMBIA ENCYCLOPEDIA) 1975

THIRD PRINTING

MANUFACTURED IN THE UNITED STATES OF AMERICA

PREFACE

The New Columbia Encyclopedia is the fourth edition of *The Columbia Encyclopedia.* Compact and ready for instant reference, the encyclopedia offers authentic and accurate information in condensed form. Cross-references enable the reader to locate an article quickly, and bibliographies at the end of many articles provide guides to additional reading matter. Since the development of specialization, no encyclopedia can succeed in presenting the sum of human knowledge. Nevertheless, the editors of *The New Columbia Encyclopedia* have provided the reader with a wide-ranging variety of subjects that fall within the province of a general reference work. There are articles on the arts and literature, geography, the life and physical sciences, and the social sciences.

The tradition of this encyclopedia can be traced back to the year 1935 and the late Clarke Fisher Ansley, the editor of the first edition. In the Preface to that edition, Dr. Ansley wrote:

> One who makes good use of the art of reading needs to have three reference works at hand: a dictionary, an atlas, and an encyclopedia. The dictionary and the atlas for workaday purposes are each in one volume. On the Continent of Europe one-volume encyclopedias have long been in general use. *The Columbia Encyclopedia* has been compiled to serve readers of English in a like way, as the companion of the dictionary and the atlas.

Although the first edition was indeed comprehensive, it did not attempt to provide information for scholars in their own fields. According to Dr. Ansley: "The most that others may have in a specialist's field is first aid; and in the specialties of others, the specialist's need is not less than that of other men."

With these principles in mind, the editors reviewed authoritative sources and summarized generally accepted judgments, not individual interpretations. Insofar as possible, the first edition was a survey of prevailing views, written in language that was clear and intelligible to the general reader.

A second (1950) and a third (1963) edition of *The Columbia Encyclopedia* followed the first, adhering to Dr. Ansley's principle, while at the same time expanding it to meet the needs of contemporary readers. The fourth edition follows the tradition of the first three, of which there are more than 900,000 copies in print, applying it to the world of the 1970s. Between the first and second editions World War II effected enormous sociological and political changes. Between the second and third editions the space age came upon us, school curricula were revised in keeping with the importance of scientific discoveries, and the computer began to reshape our lives. In the years between the third and fourth editions more startling changes occurred: Men traveled more than 200,000 miles from earth and set foot on the moon; study increased in land use, conservation, and environmentalism; and in 1974 for the first time in history a President of the United States resigned from office. *The New Columbia Encyclopedia,* which covers these events, is as up to date as humanly possible as of January, 1975.

The fourth edition in many ways is really new. Although the encyclopedia is still intended primarily for English-speaking readers, its articles cover a wider variety of people, countries, and cultures than ever before. For example, coverage of Africa, Asia, and South America has been greatly expanded. In keeping with the increased knowledge and sophistication of readers, the science entries in this edition include more advanced and detailed technical information than those in previous editions. *The New Columbia Encyclopedia* was set by computer, an innovation that enabled us to include more information on a page than in previous editions. The type of this edition is also easier to read.

For the convenience of the reader, the fourth edition contains certain other improvements. Drawings and maps are now found within or near the articles they illustrate. More information has been organized into charts for easy reference; for example, there are tables listing Shakespeare's plays, constellations, popes, U.S. Presidents and Supreme Court justices, British and Canadian prime ministers, and French, Spanish, and Russian rulers. Also, metric equivalents are given for most measurements in English standard units.

In the preparation of the fourth edition, every article from the third edition was reviewed. Some were revised or replaced; others were found to be more than adequate and remain as they were in the third edition. Also, we retained a special feature of all previous editions: There is an entry for every proper name in the Authorized Version (King James Version) of the Bible, with alternate names and spellings from the revised versions of the Bible whenever possible. As in former editions, because several people were involved in the production of an article, all entries are unsigned.

This encyclopedia is neither an official nor an unofficial publication of Columbia University, but without Columbia University this book would not have been possible. On the following pages is a list of academic consultants, many from the University, who gave unstintingly of their time and knowledge in helping us prepare the article lists, and in some instances the articles themselves, in their fields of specialty.

The population figures are from the most recent sources available at the time the articles were written. For the figures of the People's Republic of China, we are indebted to Kingsley Davis, Ford Professor of Sociology and Comparative Studies and Director of International Population and Urban Research, University of California, Berkeley. We are especially grateful to Hammond Inc. and to Ashley Talbot, Executive Editor, for his generous cooperation in making many of Hammond's vast files of population statistics available to us.

The editors of *The New Columbia Encyclopedia* wish to express our gratitude to Charles G. Proffitt, former President and Director of Columbia University Press, who from the very beginning of the encyclopedia through the third edition and the inception of the fourth edition has been its mentor and guide. Thanks are due to Robert G. Barnes, the present President and Director of the Press, who saw *The New Columbia Encyclopedia* through to its final stages. We wish also to thank Henry H. Wiggins, Assistant Director of the Press, for his dedication to the encyclopedia; a staff editor on the first two editions and consultant on the third, he contributed both experience and scholarship to the fourth edition. In addition, we are grateful to Gerard S. Mayers, who supervised the production of *The New Columbia Encyclopedia,* and to Marshall Lee, who was our consultant on typography and design and was responsible for setting the style of the maps and other illustrations. Finally, we wish to thank Rocappi, the computerized composition division of the Lehigh Press, Inc., who with patience and skill prepared our manuscript for computer typesetting.

HOW TO USE THE NEW COLUMBIA ENCYCLOPEDIA

The New Columbia Encyclopedia is easy to use. All articles are arranged alphabetically, with each article heading in **boldface type.** The headings of biographical articles are inverted and alphabetized by the subject's surname, with the exception of articles on some historical figures. Thus, William Faulkner appears as **Faulkner, William,** but Stephen Báthory and Joan of Arc are listed as **Stephen Báthory** and **Joan of Arc.**

The problem of alphabetizing names that include de, van, von, and the like has been resolved by employing as the heading the most commonly used form of the name. Accordingly, the German statesman Otto von Bismarck is entered as **Bismarck, Otto von,** while the painter Vincent van Gogh is under **Van Gogh, Vincent,** with a cross-reference from **Gogh, Vincent van.**

M', Mc, and Mac are listed as if they were spelled Mac. Thus the political scientist **McBain, Howard Lee** precedes the Scottish king **Macbeth,** who precedes the American author and public official **McCarthy, Charles.** In each instance it is the letter or letters after the Mc or Mac that determine the alphabetical order. Exceptions to this rule are African names beginning with M'; they are listed in strict alphabetical order: M'Ba, Mbandaka, M'Bour, Mdina, etc.

Abbreviations are alphabetized as though they were spelled out (e.g., St. is alphabetized as Saint). Therefore, the heading **St. Clair, Arthur** is listed before **Saint Clair, Lake,** which precedes **St. Denis, Ruth** and the Dutch island **Saint Eustatius.** Again, in each case the first letter of the word after Saint determines the alphabetical order.

When two or more articles have the same heading, entries are alphabetized by category: persons, places, and things. Thus, if one were to look for an article heading with the name Washington, **Washington, George** (person) would precede **Washington,** state (place), and that would precede **Washington, Treaty of** (thing). The order of entry for persons of the same name is determined by rank: saints, popes, emperors, kings, followed by titled nobility, such as crown prince, duke or count, baron, baronet, and so forth. Monarchs of the same name are listed numerically and alphabetically by country: **Charles X,** king of France, appears before **Charles III,** king of Naples, who in turn precedes **Charles III,** king of Spain.

Within some articles in *The New Columbia Encyclopedia,* related material is introduced by subheadings in smaller **boldface type.** For example, in the biographical article **Mond, Ludwig** there is a description of the **Mond process.** The main heading **naval conferences** contains five boldface subheadings: **London Naval Conference** (1908–9), **Washington Conference** (1921–22), **Geneva Conference** (1927), **London Conference** (1930), and **London Conference** (1935). If a reader wishes to have information on any one of these subheadings, he can find it directly without reading the entire article.

This method is also used for family articles. The **Bach** family article contains subheadings for seven members; three of these are cross-references to separate articles on **Johann Sebastian Bach, Carl Philipp Emanuel Bach,** and **Johann Christian Bach.**

Boldface numbers are also used in some multiple entries. For example, when several U.S. cities have the same name, they are listed alphabetically by state in a single article:

> **Jacksonville. 1** City (1970 pop. 19,832), Pulaski co., central Ark. **2** City (1970 pop. 528,865), coextensive (since 1968) with Duval co., NE Fla. **3** City (1970 pop. 20,553), seat of Morgan co., W central Ill. **4** City (1970 pop. 16,289), seat of Onslow co., E N.C.

Because space is limited in a single-volume encyclopedia, information provided in one article is generally not repeated in another. Instead, cross-references are used extensively in the text to guide the reader to various articles containing related material. References to those headings are printed in SMALL CAPITALS. An example of this system may be found in the article **environmentalism,** which has the following definition: "movement to protect the quality and continuity of life through CONSERVATION OF NATURAL RESOURCES, prevention of POLLUTION, and control of LAND USE." All the articles mentioned in SMALL CAPITALS are in the encyclopedia and provide additional information; when read together, they will give the reader a basic understanding of this particular subject. There are many names mentioned in articles that are not indicated as cross-references. However, this does not necessarily mean that there are no separate articles on these persons in the encyclopedia. Cross-references are used only as a means of suggesting that there is further information about the subject matter.

Cross-referencing makes an index in *The New Columbia Encyclopedia* unnecessary. Some boldface entries are cross-references directing the reader to appropriate headings (**mind reading:** see PARAPSYCHOLOGY; TELEPATHY). Others catalog references pertaining to a particular subject; for example, music provides some 70 cross-references while instructing the reader how to locate specific information:

> **music.** For information on types of music, see such articles as ABSOLUTE MUSIC; ALEATORY MUSIC; CHAMBER MUSIC; JAZZ. . . . In addition, see entries on the music of various nations and peoples, including AMERICAN NEGRO SPIRITUALS; ARABIAN MUSIC; BALINESE MUSIC . . . and JEWISH LITURGICAL MUSIC . . . etc.

An additional aid to the reader is the bibliography that appears at the end of many articles. These books have been selected to enable the reader to expand his knowledge on a subject that cannot be treated at great length in a short-entry encyclopedia and, indeed, cannot be treated comprehensively in any encyclopedia. In order to save space not all books have been identified by title. Instead, the kind of work and the author are given. For example, at the end of the article on the French painter **Eugène Delacroix** there are bibliographic references to his journal, selected letters edited by J. Stewart, and studies by L. F. Johnson and G. P. Mras. Although no specific titles are given, such works may be found without difficulty by consulting the card catalog of a library.

Pronunciations have been provided for headings consisting of unfamiliar names or scientific terms; for many foreign names both native and anglicized pronunciation is shown. The key to pronunciation appears on page xi.

In order to conserve space, many abbreviations are used in the text. A list of terms abbreviated in *The New Columbia Encyclopedia* and other common abbreviations begins on page xii.

THE NEW COLUMBIA ENCYCLOPEDIA

Edited by WILLIAM H. HARRIS and JUDITH S. LEVEY

Nathaniel M. Floyd
David V. Forrest
Robert Freeman
Paul Genega
Lois Gilman
Elinor Goettel
Cecil P. Golann
Jesse R. Goodale
Rebecca Greene
Sandra Harner
Elliott Hartman, Jr.
John Henderson
Susan Eva Heuman
Ellis A. Hicks
Thomas A. Horne
Cynthia Insolio
Jo Iwabe
William Jaber
Peter Jacobson
Paul Kalicky
Savak Katrak
Helen Keller
Steven Keller
Nina Kentop
Sandra Kerman
Brenda R. Kissam
Stephen K. Lane
Peter H. Lary
Elsa M. Lattey
Katharine Kyes Leab
Daniel Josef Leab
Mary L. Lee
Jean R. Lewis
Alan Lipkin
Gregory Lombardo
Susan McRory
Catherine Mastny
John May
Ralph Melnick
Michael Meo
Daniel A. Metraux
Carol Migdalovitz
Armand Miranda
Robin O. Motz
Gerda Nette
James R. Newton
Mary Novitski
Nicholas Panagakos
Enid Pearsons
Priscilla Pederson
Marvin R. Pollock
Y. K. Rao
Sara Reguer
Jean Joseph Robinson
Kevin B. Robinson
Harold Rodgers
Patricia Rodriguez
James T. Sabin
Benjamin J. Salzano
Stanley Sawicki
Sister Jean Elizabeth Scanlan
Elena Schmidt
Clara Schrager
Fred Schreiber
Barbara Schwartz
Gary Schwartz
Alison P. Seidel
Robert Seidel
Marta Siegal
Neil Silver
Maurie Sommer
Paulo Sonnino
S. Spotte
J. R. Stander
Jerome Steiner
Richard Steinman
Robert Steinman
Paul Stitelman
Joseph Sullivan
Rachelle Taqqu
C. R. Tinsley
Doris Toumarkine
G. Alberto Traldi
Mark P. Traversa
Eve Vassiliades
Nathaniel Wander
Hanan Watson
S. Weart
Robert Wechsler
Barbara Williams
Viraj Yipintsoi
Gale R. Young

Researchers and Bibliographers

Nora B. Beeson
Nelida Kahan
Janet C. Kvamme
Howard P. Linton
Edyth McKitrick
Ann M. Riotto

Pronunciation

Ann F. Şen

ACADEMIC CONSULTANTS

René Albrecht-Carrié
Professor Emeritus of History
Barnard College
Columbia University

Alexander Alland, Jr.
Professor of Anthropology
Columbia University

Robert Austerlitz
Professor of Linguistics and Uralic Studies
Columbia University

T. R. Bashkow
Professor of Electrical Engineering
Columbia University

Hyman Bass
Professor of Mathematics
Columbia University

C. David Benson
Assistant Professor of English
Columbia University

Sacvan Bercovitch
Professor of English
Columbia University

Kenneth J. Bertrand
Professor of Geography
The Catholic University of America
Washington, D.C.

Raymond L. Bisplinghoff
Deputy Director, National Science Foundation
Washington, D.C.

Joseph L. Blau
Professor of Religion
Columbia University

Walter Bock
Professor of Biology
Columbia University

Stefan Boshkov
Professor of Mining
Columbia University

N. C. Brady
Director, International Rice Research Institute
Manila, Philippines

Ronald Breslow
Professor of Chemistry
Columbia University

Patricia Carpenter
Associate Professor of Music
Barnard College
Columbia University

Lambros Comitas
Professor of Anthropology and Education
Teachers College
Columbia University

Albert P. Crary
Director, Division of Environmental Sciences
National Science Foundation
Washington, D.C.

Robert Gorham Davis
Professor of English
Columbia University

Gabriella de Beer
Associate Professor of Romance Languages
City College of the City University of New York

Edward W. Dempsey
Late Professor of Anatomy
Columbia College of Physicians and Surgeons

Donald J. Dewey
Professor of Economics
Columbia University

Theodosius Dobzhansky
Department of Genetics
University of California, Davis

Patricia Dudley
Professor of Biological Science
Barnard College
Columbia University

David W. Ehrenfeld
Associate Professor of Biological Science
Barnard College
Columbia University

James Marston Fitch
Professor of Architecture
Columbia University

Joseph S. Fruton
Professor of Biochemistry
Yale University

Eldon Gardner
Dean, School of Graduate Studies
Utah State University

Theodor H. Gaster
Professor Emeritus of Religion
Barnard College
Columbia University

Loren R. Graham
Professor of History
Columbia University

James F. Guyot
Resident Associate
Southern Asian Institute
Columbia University

William W. Havens, Jr.
Professor of Physics
Columbia University

Allen T. Hazen
Professor Emeritus of English
Columbia University

John Heilbron
Professor of History of Science
University of California, Berkeley

J. C. Hurewitz
Professor of Government
Director, Middle East Institute
Columbia University

Graham W. Irwin
Professor of History
Columbia University

W. R. Irwin
Professor of English
Director, Graduate Study
Department of English
University of Iowa

Robert Jastrow
Director, Institute for Space Studies (NASA)
New York, New York

Norman Johnson
Chief Clinician, ASPCA
New York, New York

Marshall Kay
Professor Emeritus of Geology
Columbia University

Mark J. Kesselman
Professor of Government
Columbia University

Donald West King, M.D.
Professor of Pathology
Columbia College of Physicians and Surgeons

Herbert S. Klein
Professor of History
Columbia University

Lawrence C. Kolb, M.D.
Professor of Psychiatry
Columbia College of Physicians and Surgeons

Stephen E. Koss
Professor of History
Barnard College
Columbia University

Melvin Kranzberg
Callaway Professor of the History of Technology
Georgia Institute of Technology

Toby Lelyveld
Academic Faculty
The Juilliard School
New York, New York

William E. Leuchtenburg
De Witt Clinton Professor of History
Columbia University

Louis Levine
Professor of Biology
City College of the City University of New York

Robert A. Lewis
Associate Professor of Geography
Columbia University

George Lowy
Director, Social Science Center
Columbia University Libraries

Robert McClintock
Associate Professor of History and Education
Teachers College
Columbia University

Ian R. Manners
Assistant Professor of Geography
University of Texas

Brian Mason
Chairman, Department of Mineral Sciences
Smithsonian Institution
Washington, D.C.

Vojtech Mastny
Assistant Professor of History
Columbia University

Paul A. Meglitsch
Professor of Biology
Drake University

Roy Millward
Department of Geography
University of Leicester
England

James W. Morley
Professor of Government
Columbia University

Richard B. Morris
Gouverneur Morris Professor Emeritus of History
Columbia University

Lloyd Motz
Professor of Astronomy
Columbia University

Charles C. Noel, Jr.
Assistant Professor of History
Columbia University

Michel Oksenberg
Professor of Political Science
University of Michigan

Ellwood C. Parry III
Assistant Professor of Art History
Columbia University

Nunzio Pernicone
Assistant Professor of History
Columbia University

Kathryn Pokorny
Osborn Laboratories of Marine Science
Brooklyn, New York

Peter R. Pouncey
Professor of Greek and Latin
Dean, Columbia College

Homer S. Price
Associate Professor of Geography
Hunter College of the City University of New York

Olga Ragusa
Professor of Italian
Columbia University

Robert A. Reinstein
Institute for Science and Art Research
Little Compton, Rhode Island

Eugene F. Rice, Jr.
William R. Shepherd Professor of History
Columbia University

David Rosand
Professor of Art History
Columbia University

Joseph Rothschild
Professor of Government
Columbia University

Joel Sachs
Assistant Professor of Music
Columbia University

Morris H. Saffron, M.D.
Friends of Columbia Library
Columbia University

Klaus Schröter
Professor of Germanic Languages and Literature
State University of New York at Stony Brook

Harold B. Segel
Professor of Slavic Literature
Columbia University

Karl-Ludwig Selig
Professor of Spanish
Columbia University

Rev. William M. Shea
Professor of Theology
The Catholic University of America
Washington, D.C.

James P. Shenton
Professor of History
Columbia University

Maurice Z. Shroder
Professor of French
Barnard College
Columbia University

J. W. Smit
Queen Wilhelmina Professor of the History, Language, and Literature of the Netherlands
Columbia University

William C. Steere
President, New York Botanical Gardens
The Bronx, New York

Robin H. Strachan
Late Director, McGill-Queen's University Press
Montreal, Quebec, Canada

Andrew P. Vayda
Resident Associate, Anthropology
Columbia University

Kempton E. Webb
Professor of Geography
Columbia University

Robert K. Webb
Adjunct Professor of History
Columbia University
Editor, *The American Historical Revie*

David H. Weinflash
Research Associate, Science
Teachers College
Columbia University

Russell A. White
Associate Professor of Geography
Hunter College of the City University of New York

Rudolf J. Wittkower
Late Professor of Art History
Columbia University

W. Howard Wriggins
Professor of Government
Director, Southern Asian Institute
Columbia University

Cheng-tsu Wu
Associate Professor of Geography
Hunter College of the City University of New York

Warren E. Yasso
Associate Professor of Natural Science
Teachers College
Columbia University

KEY TO PRONUNCIATION

ə	sof*a* (sō'fə), it*e*m (ī'təm), eas*i*ly (ē'zəlē), cann*o*n (kăn'ən), circ*u*s (sûr'kəs)
ă	*a*ct (ăkt), b*a*t (băt)
ā	*a*pe (āp), f*ai*l (fāl), d*ay* (dā)
â	*ai*r (âr), c*a*re (kâr)
ä	*a*rt (ärt), f*a*ther (fä'~~th~~ər)
b	*b*ack (băk), la*b*or (lā'bər), ca*b* (kăb)
ch	*ch*in (chĭn), hat*ch*et (hăch'ət), ri*ch* (rĭch)
d	*d*ock (dŏk), la*d*y (lā'dē), sa*d* (săd)
ĕ	*e*nd (ĕnd), st*ea*dy (stĕd'ē), m*e*t (mĕt)
ē	*e*ve (ēv), cl*ea*r (klēr), s*ee* (sē)
f	*f*at (făt), *ph*ase (fāz), cou*gh* (kôf)
g	*g*et (gĕt), bi*gg*er (bĭg'ər), ta*g* (tăg)
h	*h*and (hănd), a*h*ead (əhĕd')
hw	*wh*eel (hwēl), *wh*ich (hwĭch)
ĭ	*i*t (ĭt), p*i*ll (pĭl), m*i*rror (mĭr'ər)
ī	*i*ron (ī'ərn), *eye* (ī), bu*y*er (bī'ər)
j	*j*am (jăm), *g*in*g*er (jĭn'jər), e*dg*e (ĕj)
k	*k*it (kĭt), ta*ck*le (tak'əl), *c*oo*k* (ko͝ok)
l	*l*itt*l*e (lĭt'əl), ho*ll*y (hŏl'ē), pu*ll* (po͝ol)
m	*m*an (măn), ha*mm*er (hăm'ər), cli*mb* (klīm)
n	*n*ew (no͞o), *kn*ow*n* (nōn), wi*nn*er (wĭn'ər)
ng	si*ng*i*ng* (sĭng'ĭng), fi*n*ger (fĭng'gər), sa*ng* (săng), sa*n*k (săngk)
ŏ	h*o*t (hŏt), b*o*dy (bŏd'e)
ō	*o*ver (ō'vər), h*o*pe (hōp), gr*ow* (grō)
ô	*o*rbit (ôr'bit), f*a*ll (fôl), s*aw* (sô)
o͝o	f*oo*t (fo͝ot), w*o*lf (wo͝olf), p*u*t (po͝ot), p*u*re (pyo͝or)
o͞o	b*oo*t (bo͞ot), l*o*se (lo͞oz), dr*ew* (dro͞o), tr*ue* (tro͞o)
oi	*oi*l (oil), r*oy*al (roi'əl), b*oy* (boi)
ou	*ou*t (out), cr*ow*d (kroud), h*ow* (hou)
p	*p*i*p*e (pīp), ha*pp*y (hăp'ē)
r	*r*oad (rōd), appea*r*ed (əpērd'), ca*r*pente*r* (kär'pəntər)
s	*s*o (sō), *c*ite (sīt), ba*s*te (bāst)
sh	*sh*all (shăl), *s*ure (sho͝or), na*ti*on (nā'shən)
t	*t*igh*t* (tīt), be*tt*er (bĕt'ər), *t*alke*d* (tôkt)
th	*th*in (thĭn), ba*th* (băth)
~~th~~	*th*en (~~th~~ĕn), fa*th*er (fä'~~th~~ər), ba*th*e (bā~~th~~)
ŭ	b*u*t (bŭt), fl*oo*d (flŭd), s*o*me (sŭm)
û	c*u*rl (kûrl), g*i*rl (gûrl), f*e*rn (fûrn), w*o*rm (wûrm)
v	*v*est (vĕst), tri*v*ial (trĭv'ēəl), e*v*e (ēv)
w	*w*ax (wăks), t*w*ins (twĭnz), co*w*ard (kou'ərd)
y	*y*ou (yo͞o), on*i*on (ŭn'yən)
z	*z*ipper (zĭp'ər), ea*s*e (ēz), tread*s* (trĕdz)
zh	plea*s*ure (plĕzh'ər), rou*g*e (ro͞ozh)

Foreign Sounds

ö	as in French p*eu* (pö), German G*oe*the (gö'tə)
ü	as in French Cl*uny* (klünē')
kh	as in German a*ch* (äkh), i*ch* (ĭkh); Scottish lo*ch* (lŏkh)
N	this symbol indicates that the preceding vowel is nasal as in French c*in*q (săNk), *un* (öN), s*an*s (säN), t*om*be (tôNb), *en* (äN)

Accents and Hyphens

'	primary accent, written after accented vowel or syllable: Nebraska (nəbrăs'kə), James Buchanan (byo͞okă'nən)
"	secondary accent: Mississippi (mĭs"əs-sĭp'ē)
-	dash, replacing obvious portion of pronunciation: hegemony (hĭjĕm'ənē, hē-, hĕj'əmō"nē, hĕg'ə-)
-	hyphen, to prevent ambiguity in syllabification: Erlanger (ûr'lăng-ər), dishearten (dĭs-här'tən)

ABBREVIATIONS

The following abbreviations are used in the text of *The New Columbia Encyclopedia*

Å = angstrom
AA = Alcoholics Anonymous
AAA = Agricultural Adjustment Agency; American Automobile Association
A.B. = *Artium Baccalaureus* [Bachelor of Arts]
ABA = American Bar Association
abbr. = abbreviation(s), abbreviated
abr. = abridged
AC = alternating current
Acad. = Academy
ACLU = American Civil Liberties Union
A.D. = *anno Domini* [in the year of the Lord]
AEC = Atomic Energy Commission
AFL = American Federation of Labor
AFTRA = American Federation of Television and Radio Artists
Afrik. = Afrikaans
AIA = American Institute of Architects
AKC = American Kennel Club
ALA = American Library Association
Ala. = Alabama
alt. = altitude
Alta. = Alberta
A.M. = *ante meridiem* [before noon]; *Artium Magister* [Master of Arts]
AM = amplitude modulation
AMA = American Medical Association
amp = ampere(s)
amp-hr = ampere-hour(s)
amu = atomic mass unit(s)
antilog = antilogarithm
AP = Associated Press
Arab. = Arabic
Ariz. = Arizona
Ark. = Arkansas
A.S. = Anglo-Saxon
ASCAP = American Society of Composers, Authors, and Publishers
Assn. = Association
ASSR = Autonomous Soviet Socialist Republic
at. no. = atomic number
at.% = atomic percent
at. wt. = atomic weight
A.U. = atomic unit(s)
Aug. = August
AV = Authorized Version
AVC = American Veterans Committee
avdp. = avoirdupois
Ave. = Avenue
AWOL = absent without leave
b. = born, born in
B.A. = Bachelor of Arts
B.Arch. = Bachelor of Architecture
BBC = British Broadcasting Corporation
B.C. = before Christ
B.D. = Bachelor of Divinity
BEV = billion electron volts
B.Lit. = Bachelor of Literature
B.Mus. = Bachelor of Music
b.p. = boiling point
BPOE = Benevolent Protective Order of Elks
Brig. Gen. = Brigadier General
B.S. = Bachelor of Science
Btu = British thermal unit(s)
Bul. = Bulletin
Bulg. = Bulgarian
C = Celsius (centigrade)
c. = *circa* [about]

CAA = Civil Aeronautics Administration
cal = calorie(s)
Calif. = California
Cant. = Canticles (Song of Solomon)
Capt. = Captain
CARE = Cooperative for American Remittances to Everywhere
cc = cubic centimeter(s)
cd = candela(s)
cent. = century, centuries
CENTO = Central Treaty Organization
cgs = centimeter-gram-second
Chin. = Chinese
Chem.E. = Chemical Engineer
Chron. = Chronicles
CIA = Central Intelligence Agency
CID = Criminal Investigation Department
CIO = Congress of Industrial Organizations
cm = centimeter(s)
cm/sec^2 = centimeter(s) per second per second
co. = county
Col. = Colonel; Colossians
Coll. = Collection
Colo. = Colorado
Comdr. = Commander
COMECON = Council for Mutual Economic Assistance
comp. = compiled, compiler
com. pop. = commune population
Conn. = Connecticut
Cor. = Corinthians
CORE = Congress of Racial Equality
Corp. = Corporation
cos = cosine
cot = cotangent
coul = coulomb(s)
CPA = Certified Public Accountant
Cpl. = Corporal
CPO = Chief Petty Officer
CSC = Civil Service Commission
csc = cosecant
cu = cubic
CVA = Columbia Valley Authority
CWA = Civil Works Administration
d. = died, died in
Dan. = Daniel; Danish
DAR = Daughters of the American Revolution
dB = decibel(s)
DC = direct current
D.C. = District of Columbia
D.C.L. = Doctor of Civil Law
D.D. = Doctor of Divinity
D.D.S. = Doctor of Dental Surgery
DDT = Dichloro-diphenyl-trichloroethane
Dec. = December; declination
Del. = Delaware
dept. = department
Deut. = Deuteronomy
dist. = district
div. = division
Dr. = doctor
dr. = dram(s)
D.Sc. = Doctor of Science
Du. = Dutch
E = east
ECA = Economic Cooperation Administration
Eccles. = Ecclesiastes
Ecclus. = Ecclesiasticus

ECSC = European Coal and Steel Community
ed. = edited, edition, editor(s)
EDC = European Defense Community
E.E. = Electrical Engineer
EEC = European Economic Community
EFTA = European Free Trade Association
e.g. = *exempli gratia* [for example]
emf = electromotive force
emu = electromagnetic unit(s)
Eng. = English
enl. = enlarged
Eph. = Ephesians
ERA = Emergency Relief Administration
ERP = European Recovery Program
ESC = Economic and Social Council (UN)
ESP = extrasensory perception
est. = established; estimated
et al. = *et alii* [and others]
EV = electron volts
Ex. = Exodus
Ezek. = Ezekiel
F = Fahrenheit; farad
F = formal
FAA = Federal Aviation Administration
fac. = facsimile
FAO = Food and Agriculture Organization of the United Nations
FBI = Federal Bureau of Investigation
FCC = Federal Communications Commission
Feb. = February
FDA = Food and Drug Administration
FEPC = Fair Employment Practices Committee
Finn. = Finnish
fl. = *floruit* [flourished]
Fla. = Florida
fl oz = fluid ounce(s)
FM = frequency modulation
FPO = Fleet Post Office
Fr. = French
ft = foot, feet
ft-lb = foot-pound(s)
FTC = Federal Trade Commission
G = gauss
Ga. = Georgia
Gal. = Galatians
gal. = gallon(s)
Gall. = Gallery
Gen. = General; Genesis
Ger. = German
GEV = billion electron volts
GHz = gigahertz
GMT = Greenwich mean time
GNP = gross national product
GOP = Grand Old Party (Republican party)
Gov. = Governor
Gr. = Greek
grad. = graduated, graduated at
^{h} = hour
H = henry
Hab. = Habakkuk
Hag. = Haggai
Heb. = Hebrew; Hebrews (NT)
H.M.S. = His (Her) Majesty's Ship; His (Her) Majesty's Service
Hon. = the Honorable
hp = horsepower
hr = hour(s)

Hung. = Hungarian
Hz = hertz or cycle(s) per second
IADB = Inter-American Defense Board
IAU = International Astronomical Union
ICAO = International Civil Aviation Organization
ICBM = intercontinental ballistic missile
ICC = Interstate Commerce Commission
Icel. = Icelandic
i.e. = *id est* [that is]
IGY = International Geophysical Year
ILA = International Longshoreman's Association
ILGWU = International Ladies Garment Workers Union
Ill. = Illinois
ILO = International Labor Organization
in. = inch(es)
inc. = incorporated
Ind. = Indiana
Inst. = Institute, Institution
introd. = introduction
IQ = intelligence quotient
IRA = Irish Republican Army
IRBM = intermediate-range ballistic missile
Isa. = Isaiah
Ital. = Italian
ITO = International Trade Organization
ITU = International Telecommunications Union
IUPAC = International Union of Pure and Applied Chemistry
IWW = Industrial Workers of the World
J = joule(s)
Jan. = January
Jap. = Japanese
J.D. = *Juris Doctor* [Doctor of Laws]
Jer. = Jeremiah
jg = junior grade
Jr. = Junior
K = Kelvin
kc = kilocycle(s)
kg = kilogram(s)
kg m = kilogram meter(s)
KKK = Ku Klux Klan
kl = kiloliter(s)
km = kilometer(s)
kw = kilowatt(s)
kwh = kilowatt hour(s)
Ky. = Kentucky
£ = *libra* [pound], *librae* [pounds]
La. = Louisiana
Lam. = Lamentations
Lat. = Latin
lat. = latitude
lb = *libra* [pound], *librae* [pounds]
Lev. = Leviticus
L.H.D. = *Litterarum Humaniorum Doctor* [Doctor of Humane Letters]
Lib. = Library
lim = limit
Lith. = Lithuanian
Litt.B. = *Litterarum Baccalaureus* [Bachelor of Literature]
Litt.D. = *Litterarum Doctor* [Doctor of Literature]

LL.B. = *Legum Baccalaureus* [Bachelor of Laws]
LL.D. = *Legum Doctor* [Doctor of Laws]
ln = logarithm, natural
log = logarithm
long. = longitude
LSD = lysergic acid diethylamide
Lt. = Lieutenant
Lt. Col. = Lieutenant Colonel
Ltd. = Limited
Lt. Gen. = Lieutenant General
m = meter(s)
M = molar
m = molal
m = minute(s)
m/sec^2 = meters per second per second
M.A. = Master of Arts
Mac. = Maccabees
Maj. Gen. = Major General
Mal. = Malachi
Man. = Manitoba
Mass. = Massachusetts
mass no. = mass number
Mat. = Matthew
M.D. = *Medicinae Doctor* [Doctor of Medicine]
Md. = Maryland
M.E. = Mechanical Engineer; Middle English
MEV = million electron volts
Mex. = Mexican
mg = milligram(s)
M.H.G. = Middle High German
mi = mile(s)
Mich. = Michigan
min = minute(s)
Minn. = Minnesota
Miss. = Mississippi
mks = meter-kilogram-second
ml = milliliter(s)
Mlle = Mademoiselle [Miss]
mm = millimeter(s)
Mme = Madame [Mrs.]
Mo. = Missouri
Mont. = Montana
m.p. = melting point
mph = miles per hour
Mr. = Mister (always abbreviated)
Mrs. = Mistress (always abbreviated)
MS, MSS = manuscript(s)
M.S. = Master of Science
Msgr = Monsignor
Mt. = Mount, Mountain
mts. = mountains
Mus. = Museum
Mus.B. = *Musicae Baccalaureus* [Bachelor of Music]
Mus.D. = *Musicae Doctor* [Doctor of Music]
MVA = Missouri Valley Authority
N = north; Newton(s)
N = normal (unit of measure)
NAACP = National Association for the Advancement of Colored People
NAM = National Association of Manufacturers
NASA = National Aeronautics and Space Administration
NATO = North Atlantic Treaty Organization
N.B. = New Brunswick
N.C. = North Carolina
NCO = Noncommissioned Officer
N.Dak. = North Dakota
NE = northeast
NEA = National Education Association
Nebr. = Nebraska
Neh. = Nehemiah
Nev. = Nevada
New Lat. = New Latin
N.F. = Newfoundland
N.H. = New Hampshire
N.J. = New Jersey
NLRB = National Labor Relations Board
N.Mex. = New Mexico
no. = *numero* [number]
Nor. = Norwegian
Nov. = November
NRA = National Recovery Administration
NROTC = Naval Reserve Officers' Training Corps
N.S. = New Style; Nova Scotia
Num. = Numbers
NW = northwest
N.Y. = New York
NYA = National Youth Administration
OAS = Organization of American States
Obad. = Obadiah
Oct. = October
O.E. = Old English
OECD = Organization for Economic Cooperation and Development
OEO = Office of Economic Opportunity
OES = Office of Economic Stabilization
O.Fr. = Old French
O.H.G. = Old High German
Okla. = Oklahoma
O.N. = Old Norse
Ont. = Ontario
Op. = *Opus* [work]
OPA = Office of Price Administration
O.S. = Old Style
OSS = Office of Strategic Services
oz = ounce(s)
Pa. = Pennsylvania
PAU = Pan American Union
Pd.D. = *Pedagogiae Doctor* [Doctor of Pedagogy]
P.E.I. = Prince Edward Island
Pers. = Persian
PFC = Private First Class
Ph.B. = *Philosophiae Baccalaureus* [Bachelor of Philosophy]
Ph.D. = *Philosophiae Doctor* [Doctor of Philosophy]
Philip. = Philippians
pl. = plural
P.M. = *post meridiem* [afternoon]
PO = Petty Officer
Pol. = Polish
pop. = population
Port. = Portuguese
Pr. of Manas. = Prayer of Manasses
Prov. = Proverbs
prov(s). = province(s)
Ps. = Psalm
pseud. = pseudonym
Pss. = Psalms
pt = pint(s)
pt. = part(s)
pub. = published; publisher
Pvt. = Private
PWA = Public Works Administration
qt = quart(s)
Que. = Quebec
R = Roentgen
R.A. = right ascension
RAF = Royal Air Force
repr. = reprinted
Rev. = Revelation; the Reverend
rev. = revised
R.I. = Rhode Island
R.N. = registered nurse
RNA = ribonucleic acid
Rom. = Romans
ROTC = Reserve Officers Training Corps
rpm = revolution(s) per minute
RR = railroad
RSFSR = Russian Soviet Federated Socialist Republic
RSV = Revised Standard Version
Rt. Rev. = the Right Reverend
Rum. = Rumanian
Rus. = Russian
RV = Revised Version
S = south
s = second(s)
Sam. = Samuel
Sask. = Saskatchewan
S.C. = South Carolina
Sc.D. = *Scientiae Doctor* [Doctor of Science]
S.Dak. = South Dakota
SE = southeast
SEATO = Southeast Asia Treaty Organization
SEC = Securities and Exchange Commission
sec = second(s); secant
Sept. = September
Ser. = Series
Sgt. = Sergeant
sin = sine
S.J. = *Societas Jesu* [Society of Jesus]
Skt. = Sanskrit
Song = Song of Solomon
SOS = distress signal (not a true abbreviation)
Span. = Spanish
SPCA = Society for the Prevention of Cruelty to Animals
SPCC = Society for the Prevention of Cruelty to Children
sp. gr. = specific gravity
sq = square
Sr. = Senior
S.S. = Steamship
SSR = Soviet Socialist Republic
St. = Saint; Street
S.T.D. = *Sacrae Theologiae Doctor* [Doctor of Sacred Theology]
Ste = *Sainte* [Saint, feminine]
STP = standard temperature and pressure
SW = southwest
Swed. = Swedish
tan = tangent
TASS = Telegraphnoye Agentstvo Sovyetskovo Soyuza (Soviet News Agency)
Tenn. = Tennessee
Thess. = Thessalonians
Tim. = Timothy
TNT = trinitrotoluene, trinitrotoluol
tr. = translated, translation, translator(s)
Turk. = Turkish
TVA = Tennessee Valley Authority
UAW = United Automobile Workers
UCV = United Confederate Veterans
UDC = United Daughters of the Confederacy
UHF = ultrahigh frequency
Ukr. = Ukrainian
UMW = United Mine Workers
UN = United Nations
UNESCO = United Nations Educational, Scientific, and Cultural Organization
UNICEF = United Nations Children's Fund
uninc. = unincorporated
Univ. = University
UNRRA = United Nations Relief and Rehabilitation Administration
UPI = United Press International
U.S. = United States
USA = United States Army
USAF = United States Air Force
USBGN = United States Board on Geographic Names
USCG = United States Coast Guard
USMC = United States Marine Corps
USN = United States Navy
USO = United Service Organizations
U.S.S. = United States Ship
USSR = Union of Soviet Socialist Republics
V = volt(s)
VA = Veterans Administration
Va. = Virginia
var. = variety (in botany)
Ved. = Vedic
VFW = Veterans of Foreign Wars
VHF = very high frequency
VISTA = Volunteers in Service to America
vol. = volume(s)
vs. = versus
Vt. = Vermont
W = west; watt(s)
WAC = Women's Army Corps
Wash. = Washington
WAVES = Women Accepted for Voluntary Emergency Service (United States Women's Naval Reserve)
WCTU = Woman's Christian Temperance Union
WFU = World Federation of Trade Unions
WHO = World Health Organization
Wis. = Wisconsin
WMO = World Meteorological Organization (UN)
WPA = Work Projects Administration
wt. = weight
W.Va. = West Virginia
Wyo. = Wyoming
yd = yard(s)
YMCA = Young Men's Christian Association
YMHA = Young Men's Hebrew Association
YWCA = Young Women's Christian Association
YWHA = Young Women's Hebrew Association
Zech. = Zechariah
Zeph. = Zephaniah

THE NEW COLUMBIA ENCYCLOPEDIA

A

A, first letter of the ALPHABET. Its Greek correspondent is named alpha, symbolizing God. It is a usual symbol for a low central vowel as in *father;* English *ā* is pronounced as a diphthong of *ĕ* and *y.* In MUSICAL NOTATION it is the symbol of a note in the scale.

Aa (ä) [from a word for "water" of the same Indo-European root as Lat. *aqua*], name of many small streams of N Europe and Switzerland. *Aa,* or a derivative of it, is a component part of hundreds of European place names.

aa (ä'ä): see LAVA.

Aabenraa: see ÅBENRÅ, Denmark.

Aachen (ä'khən), **Aix-la-Chapelle** (ĕks-lä-shäpĕl'), or **Bad Aachen** (bät ä'khən), city (1970 pop. 173,473), North Rhine-Westphalia, W West Germany, near the Belgian and Dutch borders. One of the great historic cities of Europe, it is now chiefly important as an industrial center and rail and road junction. Its manufactures include textiles, machinery, rubber goods, metal products, and furniture. Hard coal is mined in the region. The city's hot mineral baths, frequented by the Romans in the 1st cent. A.D., are still used to treat gout, rheumatism, and skin diseases. Charlemagne, who was probably born in Aachen in 742, made the city his northern capital and the leading center of Carolingian civilization. He built a splendid palace and founded the great cathedral, which reputedly contained his tomb. The cathedral, which has an octagonal nucleus modeled on the Church of San Vitale in Ravenna, Italy, received extensive Gothic additions in the 14th–15th cent. From 936 to 1531, German kings were usually crowned at Aachen. Although it later declined in importance, Aachen remained a free imperial city until it was occupied (1794) by French troops and later annexed (1801) by France. It passed to Prussia in 1815. From 1918 to 1930 the city was occupied by the Allies as a result of Germany's defeat in World War I. During World War II approximately two thirds of Aachen was destroyed by aerial bombardment, and the city was the first major German city to fall (Oct., 1944) to the Allies. Treaties ending the War of Devolution (1668) and the War of the Austrian Succession (1748) were signed at Aachen (see AIX-LA-CHAPELLE, TREATY OF). At the Congress of Aix-la-Chapelle (1818) Czar Alexander I of Russia unsuccessfully proposed that the Holy Alliance be tightened. Aachen is the site of a technical university.

Aakjaer, Jeppe (yĕp'ə ôk'yâr), 1866–1930, Danish poet and novelist. He wrote mostly of his native Jutland, and his concern for the poor is reflected in such novels as *The Peasant's Son* (1899) and *Children of Wrath* (1904). Aakjaer's finest work is his poetry; *Songs of the Rye* (1906) and *Heimdal's Wanderings* (1924) reveal his lyric gift.

Aalborg: see ÅLBORG, Denmark.

Aalesund: see ÅLESUND, Norway.

Aalsmeer (äls'mār), town (1970 pop. 18,666), North Holland prov., W central Netherlands, on Westeinder Plassen lake, near Amsterdam. It has one of the largest flower nurseries in Europe.

Aalst (älst), Fr. *Alost,* city (1970 pop. 46,659), East Flanders prov., W central Belgium. It is a commercial and industrial center; manufactures include textiles, clothing, and footwear. Known since the 9th cent., Aalst was held by France from 1667 to 1706 and was the capital of Austrian Flanders in the 18th cent. Of note are the city hall (13th cent.) and the Church of St. Martin (15th cent.), which contains a painting by Rubens.

Aalto, Alvar (ŏl'vär äl'tō), 1898–, Finnish architect and furniture designer. Aalto is considered one of the foremost architects of the 20th cent. Most of his designs were made in collaboration with his wife, Aino Marsio, the celebrated furniture designer, until her death in 1949. Aalto's work adapts Finnish building traditions to modern European techniques and to the specific function of the structure in boldly expressive style. His designs for the municipal library at Viipuri (1927–35; destroyed when it was made part of Russian territory in 1940) and the tuberculosis sanitarium at Paimio (1929–33) are outstanding functionalist works. He gained international fame by his remarkable designs for laminated-wood furniture and by his plans for the Finnish pavilions at the expositions in Paris (1937) and New York (1939). Appointed professor at the Massachusetts Institute of Technology in 1940, he designed there the serpentine Baker House (1947–48). After World War II he was active in reconstruction in Finland. His major postwar works include a number of striking civic buildings in Helsinki, the Maison Carré in Paris (designed in collaboration with Elissa Makkinheimo, his second wife), and the Wolfsburg cultural center in Germany. See his complete works, ed. by Karl Fleig (tr. of 3d ed., 2 vol., 1970–71); studies by F. A. Gutheim (1960) and George Baird, ed. (1971).

Aar, river: see AARE.

Aarau (ä'rou), town (1970 pop. 16,881), capital of Aargau canton, N Switzerland, at the foot of the Jura mts. and on the Aare River. A noted shoe-manufacturing center, it also has factories producing bells, mathematical instruments, electrical and optical goods, and other products. Aarau was founded c.1250; it was the temporary capital (1798) of the HELVETIC REPUBLIC.

aardvark (ärd'värk) [Du.,=ground pig], nocturnal mammal of the genus *Orycteropus,* sole representative of the order Tubulidentata. There are two species, one in central Africa and the other in S Africa. The aardvark, about 6 ft (180 cm) long, has a long snout, large erect ears, an almost naked or sparsely haired body, and a long tail. Its forefeet are adapted for making burrows in the ground and for clawing open the nests of ants and termites in order to capture the insects with its long sticky tongue. Its cylindrical teeth are without enamel and roots. The aardvark resembles the New World ANTEATERS but is not closely related to them. It is also called ant bear and earth pig. Aardvarks are classified in the phylum CHORDATA, subphylum Vertebrata, class Mammalia, order Tubulidentata, family Orycteropodidae.

aardwolf (ärd'wŏŏlf), carnivore of the HYENA family. The aardwolf, *Proteles cristatus,* resembles the true hyena but is smaller and more delicate. It has less powerful teeth and jaws and five instead of four toes on its forepaws. The coat of the aardwolf is yellow-gray with dark stripes; a ridge of hair extends down its sloping back. It is a nocturnal, burrowing animal, inhabiting sandy plain and scrub from South Africa to Angola and Somaliland. A timid beast, it feeds on small animals and insects, especially termites, and defends itself by emitting a foul-smelling fluid from anal scent glands. A litter may include as many as six cubs, but two to four is typical; gestation lasts three months. Aardwolves are solitary, but several females with cubs may share a burrow. In captivity they have been known to live as long as 13 years. Aardwolves are classified in the phylum CHORDATA, subphylum Vertebrata, class Mammalia, order Carnivora, family Hyaenidae.

Aare (är'ə) or **Aar** (är), longest river entirely in Switzerland, 183 mi (295 km) long, rising in the Bernese Alps and fed by several glaciers. The upper Aare emerges from dam-impounded Grimsel Lake and flows generally W through Lake Brienz, past Interlaken (where it is canalized), and through Lake Thun, the head of navigation. The Aare continues northwest, flowing through Bern before turning and flowing generally northeast, past Solothurn and Aarau, to join the Rhine River opposite Waldshut, West Germany. With its chief tributaries, the Reuss and Limmat rivers, the Aare drains most of Switzerland. The Aare is connected with Lake Biel by two canals. Near Meiringen, the Aare flows through a scenic gorge. There are more than 40 hydroelectric power plants on the river.

Aargau (är'gou), Fr. *Argovie,* canton (1970 pop. 433,284), 542 sq mi (1,404 sq km), N Switzerland. AARAU is the capital. It is traversed by the Aare and Reuss rivers, and there are wooded hills and fertile valleys. Cereals and fruit are raised, and cattle grazing is important. Textiles, electrical goods, paper, cement, and metal products are the principal manufactures. BADEN and RHEINFELDEN are noted health resorts. Originally a Celtic settlement, the area was later occupied by the Romans and fell to the Franks in the 6th cent. The territory was taken (1415) by BERN from the house of Hapsburg and was governed by the Swiss cantons until 1798. In 1803, Aargau was admitted as a canton to the Swiss Confederation. Its population is mainly German-speaking and Protestant.

Aarhus: see ÅRHUS, Denmark.

Aaron (âr'ən), in the Bible, first high priest of the Hebrews, the brother of Moses and his spokesman in Egypt. He was the instrument of Jehovah in miracles, as in turning his rod into a serpent and in causing the rod to bud, blossom, and bear almonds. He made the golden calf and took part in the worship of it. Ex. 4.14–16; 6.20; 7.1–12; 28–32; Num. 12; 17; 18; 20; 33.38, 39; Deut. 10.6. His descendants were high priests and priests. The prestige of descent from him was emphasized especially after the Exile.

Aaron, Hank, 1934–, U.S. baseball player, b. Mobile, Ala. His real name is Louis Henry Aaron. A right-handed batter with remarkable bat control, he played most of his major league career with the Braves, first in Milwaukee (1954–65) and then in Atlanta (1966–74). At the end of the 1974 season he was traded to the Milwaukee Brewers. In 1974, Aaron broke Babe Ruth's monumental lifetime record of 714 home runs, closing the season with 733. Also a fine outfielder with an excellent arm, he was the major league lifetime leader in extra-base hits and total bases.

Aaron's-beard, name sometimes applied to several plants usually characterized by some beardlike aspect, as the St.-John's-wort because of its many stamens and the Kenilworth ivy because of its thread-like runners. Aaron's-beard cactus is *Opuntia leucotricha,* a true cactus.

Aaron's-rod, popular name for several tall-flowering, infrequently branching plants, such as goldenrod and mullein. The name is an allusion to the rod that Aaron placed before the ark and that miraculously blossomed and bore almonds (Num. 17.8).

Aba (ä'bä), city (1969 est. pop. 152,000), SE Nigeria. It is an important regional market, a road and rail hub, and a manufacturing center for textiles, pharmaceuticals, processed palm oil, shoes, plastics, soap, and beer. Originally a small IBO village, Aba was developed by the British as an administrative center in the early 20th cent. In 1929, women in Aba rioted against Britain's arbitrary use of indigenous persons as rulers and against direct taxation.

abacá: see MANILA HEMP.

Abaco and Cays (ăb'əkō, kēz, kāz), island group, c.780 sq mi (2,020 sq km), most northerly of the Bahama Islands. It includes Great Abaco (the largest), Little Abaco, and the surrounding islets. The low islands, composed mainly of coral limestone, have native pine forests. Fish and sponges are taken from surrounding waters. Great Abaco was settled by Loyalists from New York City in 1783.

abacus (ăb'əkəs), in architecture, flat slab forming the top member of a capital. In classical orders it varies from a square form having unmolded sides in the Greek Doric, to thinner proportions and ovolo molding in the Greek Ionic, and to sides incurving and corners cut in Roman Ionic and Corinthian examples. In Romanesque work the abacus is heavier in proportion, projects less, and is generally molded and decorated. In Gothic work the form varies, appearing in square, circular, and octagonal forms with molded members.

abacus (ăb'əkəs, əbăk'–), in mathematics, simple device for performing arithmetic calculations. The type of abacus now best known is represented by a frame with sliding counters. An elementary abacus might have ten parallel wires strung between two boards on a frame, with nine beads on each wire. Each bead on a given wire has the same value: either ten or some multiple or submultiple of ten. For example, all of the beads on a particular wire may have a value of 1, making this the units wire, or 10, making this wire the tens wire. Numbers are represented and added together on the abacus by grouping beads together. To represent 155, five beads on the units wire are separated from the others on that wire, five beads on the tens wire, and one bead on the hundreds wire. To add 243 to 155, three more beads on the units wire are slid over to join the group of five, four more beads on the tens wire join the five there, and two more beads on the hundreds wire join the one there. The number 398 is now represented on the abacus. Subtraction can be performed by separating groups of beads. More elaborate processes are used to perform multiplication and division. The abacus is used for calculating in the Middle East, the Orient, and Russia and for teaching children the elements of arithmetic in many countries. An apparatus of pebbles or other movable counters was known in antiquity to the Egyptians, Greeks, Romans, and Chinese. A special merit of the abacus was that it simplified the addition and subtraction of numbers written in Roman numerals. Another type of abacus includes a board covered with sand or wax to facilitate making and erasing marks. See J. M. Pullan, *The History of the Abacus* (1968); P. H. Moon, *The Abacus* (1971).

Abadan (ăbədăn', äbädän'), city (1971 est. pop. 281,000), Khuzestan prov., SW Iran, on Abadan Island, in the delta of the Shatt al Arab, at the head of the Persian Gulf. It is the terminus of major oil pipelines and is an important oil refining and shipping center. There is a large petrochemical complex that produces plastics, detergents, and caustic soda. Abadan is the point of origin of a natural gas pipeline to the USSR. Abadan Island was ceded to Iran by Turkey in 1847. Abadan city was an unimportant village until the discovery (1908) of nearby oilfields. Its oil refinery (commissioned 1913) was the largest in the world until 1951, when it was temporarily closed as a result of the nationalization of the Anglo-Iranian Oil Company. The city is the site of an institute of technology (1938).

Abaddon (əbăd'ən), Hebrew name of APOLLYON. Rev. 9.11. In ancient Jewish tradition it was used for part of Sheol.

Abadeh (äbädā'), town (1966 pop. 16,000), Fars prov., S central Iran. It is the trade center for a grain and fruit-growing region. Sesame oil, castor oil, and opium are also produced there. Woodcarving is a local craft.

Abagtha (əbăg'thə), one of Ahasuerus' seven chamberlains. Esther 1.10.

Abakan (əbəkän'), city (1970 pop. 90,000), capital of the Khakass Autonomous Oblast, in S central Siberian USSR, on the Yenisei River. A commercial center on the South Siberian RR, it produces textiles, furniture, foodstuffs, and metal products. Founded (1707) as a fortress, Abakan was known as Ust-Abakanskoye until 1931. Bronze Age tumuli and Turkic inscriptions have been found in the city.

abalone (ăbəlō'nē), popular name in the United States for a univalve GASTROPOD mollusk of the genus *Haliotis,* members of which are also called ear shells, or sea ears, as their shape resembles the human ear. The shell provides a rooflike covering for the abalone and is perforated by a row of holes on one side through which the animal respires. The iridescent mother-of-pearl shell lining is used to make buttons and other articles. The large, muscular foot is edible, and the animal is taken in large numbers off the coast of California for food. Holding tenaciously to a rock with its foot, the abalone feeds by scraping the substratum with its rasping tongue, or radula. Before protective legislation was enacted, much of the dried flesh and some shells were exported to the Orient. Abalone are classified in the phylum MOLLUSCA, class Gastropoda, order Archeogastropoda, family Haliotidae.

Abana (əbā'nə), river of Damascus. 2 Kings 5.12. It is probably the Barada, flowing near Damascus. See also PHARPAR.

abandonment, in law, voluntary, intentional, and absolute relinquishment of rights or property without conveying them to any other person. Abandonment also means willfully leaving one's spouse or children, intending not to return (see DESERTION). In many states the abandonment of a child is a criminal offense.

Abano, Pietro d' (pyā'trō dä'bänō), 1250?–1316?, Italian physician and philosopher, a professor of medicine in Padua. His famous work *Conciliator differentiarum* was an attempt to reconcile Arabian medicine and Greek speculative natural philosophy and was considered authoritative as late as the 16th cent. His efforts marked the rise of the Paduan school as a center for medical study. He was tried twice by the Inquisition on charges of heresy and practicing magic. Acquitted at the first trial, he was found guilty at the second, after his death.

Abarbanel, Isaac: see ABRAVANEL, ISAAC.

Abarim (ăb'ərĭm), general term for the country E of the Jordan. Num. 27.12; 33.47; Deut. 32.49. The same original term is translated "the passages" in Jer. 22.20.

Abascal, José Fernando de (hōsā' fĕrnän'dō dā äbäskäl'), 1743–1827, Spanish viceroy of Peru (1806–16). During the South American revolt against the colonial rule of Spain, he skillfully reconciled the Spanish officials and the creole colonials of Peru. He promoted educational reforms, abolished the Inquisition, reorganized the army, stamped out local rebellions, and opposed the revolutionists of Buenos Aires and Chile.

Abashiri (ä"bä'shĭrē), city (1970 pop. 43,904), Hokkaido prefecture, E Hokkaido, Japan, on the Sea of Okhotsk and the Abashiri River, lying on the Abashiri plain. It is a fishing center and port.

Abati, Niccolò dell': see ABBATE, NICCOLÒ DELL'.

abattoir (ăb"ətwär') [Fr.], building for butchering. The abattoir houses facilities to slaughter animals; dress, cut and inspect meats; and refrigerate, cure, and manufacture by-products. The largest abattoirs are those of the MEAT-PACKING industry. Plant construction, drainage, water supply, disposal of refuse, and all operations are under government regulation. Abattoirs are also called slaughterhouses.

Abbadids (ă'bədĭdz), Arab dynasty in Spain that ruled SEVILLE from 1023 to 1091. Taking advantage of the disintegration of the caliphate of CÓRDOBA, the cadi [governor] of Seville seized power and became (1023) king of the newly founded state as Abbad I. His son, who succeeded him in 1042 as Abbad II, made Seville the most powerful kingdom in S Spain. He was noted for his cruelty. He was succeeded in 1069 by his son, Abbad III (Abbad al-Mutamid), a poet and a great patron of the arts, but an inept ruler. Seeking military support against ALFONSO VI of León and Castile, Abbad called in the ALMORAVIDS from Morocco. They defeated Alfonso in 1086 but deposed (1091) Abbad, who died in exile.

Abbagmano, Nicolai (nĕkô'lī äb-bägmä'nō), 1901–, Italian philosopher, Ph.D. Univ. of Naples. He taught at the Univ. of Turin from 1936 and became the leading Italian existentialist, criticizing French and German existentialism. He set out his philosophy in *La struttura dell'esistenza* (1939) and called for a change in philosophy's outlook in his 3-volume *Storia della filosofia* (2d ed. 1963). Some of his writings were translated into English in *Critical Existentialism* (ed. by Nino Langiulli, 1969). See Gari Lesnoff-Caravaglia, *Education as Existential Possibility* (1972).

Abbas (ăb'əs, ăb'ăs, äbäs'), d. 653, uncle of Muhammad the Prophet and of Ali the caliph. A wealthy merchant of Mecca, he was at first opposed to the religious movement initiated by his nephew Muhammad. In 629 he became a convert, however, and from then on he was a companion of Muhammad and the chief financial support of Islam. His descendants founded the Abbasid dynasty. The son of Abbas, Ibn Abbas (Abd Allah), was a celebrated authority on Islamic traditions and law.

Abbas I (Abbas the Great), 1557–1629, shah of Persia (1587–1628), of the Safavid dynasty. In 1597 he ended the raids of the Uzbeks, and subsequently (1603–23) he conquered extensive territories from the Turks. He maintained diplomatic contacts with Europe, and with English aid he took (1622) Hormuz from the Portuguese and founded what is now the port of BANDAR ABBAS. He broke the power of the tribal chiefs and established a new tribe, the Shahsavan [friends of the shah]. At his capital at Esfahan, he erected many palaces, mosques, and gardens and did much to improve public works in Persia.

Abbas II (Abbas Hilmi), 1874–1944, last khedive of Egypt (1892–1914); son and successor of TEWFIK PASHA. Nominally he ruled in subordination to the Ottoman Empire, but in fact Egypt was controlled by the British resident—at first Lord CROMER, and later Kitchener. Although he resisted complete British rule, Abbas met with little success; in 1899 he was forced to admit the British claim to rule jointly with Egypt over the Sudan. When Turkey joined the Central Powers in World War I, Britain declared Egypt a British protectorate and deposed Abbas. He lived thereafter in Switzerland, where he died. He wrote *The Anglo-Egyptian Settlement* (1930).

Abbasid (əbă'sĭd, ă'bəsĭd) or **Abbaside** (-sīd, -sĭd), Arabic family descended from ABBAS, the uncle of Muhammad. The Abbasids held the caliphate from 749 to 1258, but they were recognized neither in Spain nor (after 787) W of Egypt. Under the Umayyad caliphs the Abbasids lived quietly until they became involved in numerous disputes, beginning early in the 8th cent. The family then joined with the Shiite faction in opposing the Umayyads, and in 747 the gifted ABU MUSLIM united most of the empire in revolt against the Umayyads. The head of the Abbasid family became caliph as ABU AL-ABBAS AS-SAFFAH late in 749. The last Umayyad caliph, Marwan II, was defeated and killed and the Umayyad family nearly exterminated; one surviving member fled to Spain, where the Umayyads came to rule. Under the second Abbasid caliph, called al-Mansur (see MANSUR, AL-, d. 775), the capital was moved from Damascus to Baghdad, and Persian influence grew strong in the empire. The early years of Abbasid rule were brilliant, rising to true splendor under HARUN AR-RASHID, the fifth caliph, and to intellectual brilliance under his son al-Mamun (see MAMUN, AL-), the seventh caliph. After less than a hundred years of rule, however, the slow decline of the Abbasids began. Long periods of disorder were marked by assassinations, depositions, control by Turkish soldiers, and other disturbances, and from the beginning of their reign there were rival caliphs (see CALIPHATE). In 836 the capital was transferred to Samarra, remaining there until 892. Under the later Abbasids, the power of the caliphate became chiefly spiritual. Many independent kingdoms sprang up, and the empire split into autonomous units. The Seljuk Turks came to hold the real power at Baghdad. The conquests of Jenghiz Khan further lowered the prestige of the Abbasids, and in 1258 his grandson Hulagu Khan sacked Baghdad and overthrew the Abbasid caliphate. The 37th caliph died in the disaster, but a member of the family escaped to Cairo, where he was recognized as caliph (see MAMELUKES). The Cairo line of the Abbasid caliphate, completely subordinated to the Mamelukes, survived until after the Ottoman conquest (1517) of Egypt. See Sir William Muir, *The Caliphate* (1898, repr. 1964); Guy Le Strange, *Baghdad during the Abbasid Caliphate* (1925); P. K. Hitti, *History of the Arabs* (10th ed. 1970); M. A. Shaban, *The Abbāsid Revolution* (1970).

Abbate or **Abati, Niccolò dell'** (nĕk-kōlō' dĕl-läbbä'tä, -bä'tē), 1512?–1571, Italian mannerist painter. From c.1552 he assisted Primaticcio in the decorations at Fontainebleau. He was one of the first in France to paint landscapes. Among them is the *Landscape with Orpheus and Eurydice* in the National Gallery, London.

Abbe, Cleveland (ăb'ē), 1838–1916, American meteorologist, b. New York City; brother of Robert Abbe. He was the first official daily weather forecaster in the United States. Abbe studied astronomy at the Univ. of Michigan, under B. A. Gould at Cambridge, Mass., and in Pulkovo, Russia. As director of the Cincinnati Observatory, he inaugurated daily weather predictions based on telegraphic reports. This work prompted the establishment of the national weather service, under the Signal Corps (1870), which Abbe joined in 1871; from 1891 to 1916 he served in the U.S. Weather Bureau.

Abbe, Ernst (ĕrnst ä'bə), 1840–1905, German physicist. He was appointed professor at the Univ. of Jena in 1870 and director of its astronomical and meteorological observatories in 1878. From 1866 he was associated with the Carl-Zeiss optical works at Jena, of which he became sole owner in 1888. He subsequently reorganized the firm on a cooperative basis. He made his plant a laboratory for the development of model working conditions, created a noncontributory pension fund and a discharge compensation fund, and introduced other advanced ideas that have been influential in shaping thought on the conditions of labor. He invented the Abbe refractometer for determining the refractive index of substances and improved photographic and microscopic lenses.

Abbe, Robert (ăb'ē), 1851–1928, American surgeon, b. New York City, M.D. Columbia, 1874; brother of Cleveland Abbe. He was noted for his skill and resource, especially in plastic surgery, and was a pioneer in the use of catgut sutures. A friend of the Curies, Abbe was also one of the first in the United States to use radium in treating cancer.

Abbeville (äbvēl'), town (1968 pop. 25,072), Somme dept., N France, in PICARDY, on the Somme River. Sugar refining, brewing, and the manufacture of jute and hemp are the chief industries. Abbeville received its commercial charter in 1184 and enjoyed prosperity until the revocation of the Edict of NANTES (1685) caused the Protestants, who constituted the skilled labor, to flee. The closing of the Somme River port because of sedimentation also affected prosperity. Although heavily damaged in World War II,

.he town retains the late Gothic Church of St. Wolfram, with its 13th-century belfry.

.bbeville (ă'bēvĭl), city (1970 pop. 10,996), seat of Vermilion parish, S La., on the Vermilion River, with access to the Intracoastal Waterway; inc. 1850. It is a trade and processing center for a region of dairies and rice and sugarcane fields. In the colorful Teche Cajun country, Abbeville was settled (1843) by descendants of Acadians from Nova Scotia and was laid out like a French town. It grew around the Roman Catholic chapel built in 1845 and preserves much of the early atmosphere in its old buildings.

.bbevillian: see PALEOLITHIC PERIOD.

.bbey, Edwin Austin, 1852-1911, American illustrator and painter, b. Philadelphia, studied at the Pennsylvania Academy of the Fine Arts. Employed by Harper & Brothers, he was sent to England, where he gathered materials for his illustration of Herrick's poems and other works. His illustration of Shakespeare is usually considered his best work. *The Quest of the Holy Grail* (a series of wall panels in the Boston Public Library) is perhaps his most famous painting. He was official painter of the coronation of Edward VII. See biography by E. V. Lucas (1921); catalog by Yale University Art Gallery (1974).

.bbey, monastic house, especially among Benedictines and Cistercians, consisting of not less than 12 monks or nuns ruled by an abbot or abbess. Many abbeys were originally self-supporting. In the Benedictine expansion after the 8th cent., abbeys were often important centers of learning and peaceful arts, and, like FULDA, were sometimes the nuclei of future towns. The buildings surround a church and include a dormitory, refectory, and guest house, all surrounded by a wall. The courtyard, derived from the Roman ATRIUM, was a usual feature, as was the CLOISTER or arcade surrounding the court. Cluniac abbeys were always ornate, Cistercian ones notably bare. The design of the abbey has been radically altered in the modern Benedictine abbey built by Le Corbusier at La Tourette, France. The CARTHUSIANS with their special polity developed an altogether different structure called the charterhouse.

Abbey Theatre, Irish theatrical company devoted primarily to indigenous drama. W. B. Yeats was a leader in founding (1902) the Irish National Theatre Society with Lady Gregory, J. M. Synge, and A. E. (George Russell) contributing their talents as directors and dramatists. In 1904, Annie E. F. Horniman gave them a subsidy and the free use of the Abbey Theatre in Dublin. The theater was bought for them by public subscription in 1910. Among dramatists whose works the Abbey Theatre first presented are Padraic Colum, Lennox Robinson, Sean O'Casey, and Paul Vincent Carroll. The acting company, which included such notable performers as William Fay and Frank Fay, Dudley Digges, Barry Fitzgerald, and Sara Allgood, toured the United States several times. See Lady Gregory, *Our Irish Theatre* (1913), and her journals (ed. by Lennox Robinson, 1946); Robert Hogan and M. J. O'Neill, ed., *Joseph Holloway's Abbey Theatre* (1967); studies by Peter Kavanagh (1950) and Lennox Robinson (1951, repr. 1973).

Abbo of Fleury (ăbō', flörē'), Fr. *Abbon de Fleury,* 945?-1004, French monk at the abbey of Fleury (at present-day Saint-Benoît-sur-Loire, France). Head of the monastery school, he later taught at the abbey in Ramsey, England, and in 988 became abbot at Fleury. He defended his monastery against domination by the high clergy and also served as a diplomat for King Robert II of France. Abbo wrote on grammar, astronomy, mathematics, and philosophy.

Abbot, Charles Greeley, 1872-1973, American astrophysicist, b. Wilton, N.H. He was acting director in 1896 and director in 1907 of the astrophysical observatory of the Smithsonian Institution; he was secretary of the institution from 1928 to 1944, when he became a research associate. Many of his research studies were initiated by S. P. Langley, his predecessor. He completed the mapping of the infrared solar spectrum and carried out systematic studies of variation in solar radiation, its relation to the sunspot cycle, and its effect on weather variation. He also studied intensively the nature of atmospheric transmission and absorption. Abbot perfected various standardized instruments now widely used for measuring the sun's heat, and he invented devices utilizing solar energy. He was the oldest person ever to receive a U.S. patent when his last was issued to him at the age of 99.

Abbot, George, 1562-1633, archbishop of Canterbury. He was one of the collaborators (from Oxford Univ.) on the Authorized Version of the Bible and was an authority on geography. He became archbishop in 1611. His firm Puritan views and antipathy toward the growing High Church party made him unpopular. His accidental killing of a gamekeeper while hunting (1621) was used against him. His steady opposition to William Laud, together with his refusal (1627) to countenance the elevation of the king's prerogative over law and Parliament, led Charles I to force him from active control over church affairs. See biography by P. A. Welsby (1962); bibliography by R. A. Christophers (1966).

Abbott, Berenice, 1898-, American photographer, b. Springfield, Ohio. Abbott turned from sculpture to photography in 1923. She was assistant to Man Ray in Paris (1923-25), where she made an extraordinary series of portraits of the artistic and literary celebrities of the 1920s. She began her great documentation of New York City in 1929. Abbott produced a vast series of photographs of physical phenomena (begun 1958). She discovered the work of Eugène ATGET in 1925 and labored successfully to secure him international recognition. See her *Photographs* (1970).

Abbott, Edith: see ABBOTT, GRACE.

Abbott, Edwin Abbott, 1838-1926, English clergyman and author, b. London. He wrote several theological works and a biography (1885) of Francis Bacon, but he is best known for his standard *Shakespearian Grammar* (1870); see bibliography by R. A. Christophers (1966).

Abbott, George, 1889-, American theatrical producer, director, and playwright, b. Forestville, N.Y. Abbott became celebrated as co-author and director of many hit plays, including *The Fall Guy* (1925) and *Coquette.* With *Three Men on a Horse* (1935) he was acclaimed as a master of farce. His later successes include *On Your Toes, The Boys from Syracuse* (1938), *The Pajama Game* (1954, film 1957), and *Damn Yankees* (1955, film 1958). In 1960 he won a Pulitzer Prize for the musical *Fiorello!* (with Jerome Weidman). See his autobiography (1963).

Abbott, Grace, 1878-1939, American social worker, b. Grand Island, Nebr. She did notable work as director (1921-34) of the Child Labor Division of the U.S. Children's Bureau. *The Child and the State* (2 vol., 1938) is her most important publication. Her sister, **Edith Abbott,** 1876-1957, became dean of the School of Social Service Administration, Univ. of Chicago, in 1924. Her publications include *Women in Industry* (1910) and *The Tenements of Chicago* (1936).

Abbott, Lyman, 1835-1922, American clergyman and editor, b. Roxbury, Mass., son of Jacob Abbott. He was ordained a minister in 1860 and was pastor in several churches before succeeding Henry Ward Beecher at the Plymouth Congregational Church, Brooklyn, in 1888. With Beecher he had begun in 1876 to edit the *Christian Union,* the name of which he changed in 1893 to the *Outlook.* He championed a modern rational outlook in American Christianity. His works include *The Theology of an Evolutionist* (1897), *Henry Ward Beecher* (1903), and *Reminiscences* (rev. ed. 1923). See biography by I. V. Brown (1953, repr. 1970).

Abbottabad (ăb'ətäbäd), town (1961 pop. 31,036), NE Pakistan. It is a popular health resort c.4,000 ft (1,220 m) above sea level in the Himalaya region. It is also an administrative center and a market town for an agricultural and timber area. Founded by Sir James Abbott, a deputy commissioner of British India, it was an important British military post. Nearby are rock inscriptions of Indian emperor Asoka (3d cent. B.C.).

abbreviation, in writing, arbitrary shortening of a word, usually by cutting off letters from the end, as in U.S. and Gen. (General). Contraction serves the same purpose but is understood strictly to be the shortening of a word by cutting out letters in the middle, the omission sometimes being indicated by an apostrophe, as in the word *don't.* Most abbreviations are followed by a period. Usage, however, differs widely, and recently omission of periods has become common, as in NATO and UN. A period is never used when apostrophes appear. A list of abbreviations used in this encyclopedia may be found in the prefatory matter.

Abda (ăb'də). **1** Father of Solomon's officer Adoniram. 1 Kings 4.6. **2** Levite. Neh. 11.17. Obadiah: 1 Chron. 9.16.

Abd al-Aziz (äb"däl-äzēz', Turk. äbdül'äzēz'), 1830-76, Ottoman sultan (1861-76), brother and successor of Abd al-Majid. The reforms enacted under his rule could not outpace the decline of the Ottoman Empire (Turkey). In 1875 his bankrupt government repudiated the interest on the huge loans raised in Western Europe; this act led to foreign control over part of the Ottoman revenues. RUMANIA, SERBIA, and EGYPT gained virtual independence, and revolts broke out in Bosnia and Hercegovina and Bulgaria. Political decay was paralleled, however, by cultural rebirth. Many important schools were founded, and newspapers helped to educate the Turks politically. In 1876, MIDHAT PASHA, foremost among the liberals (known as the Young Turks), overthrew Abd al-Aziz, who died a few days later, probably by suicide. He was succeeded by his nephew, Murad V.

Abd al-Aziz IV, 1880-1943, sultan of Morocco (1894-1908), son of Hassan. His weak control was evident after the death (c.1900) of the regent Ba Ahmed. His submissiveness to foreign influence, his indulgence in European luxuries (which Muslims considered unbefitting his position as religious leader), and his reorganization of the tax system led to widespread unrest. The Franco-British agreement of 1904 furnished a pretext for French demands that led in 1906 to the Algeciras Conference (see MOROCCO). Moroccan disapproval of the settlement led to revolt; Abd al-Aziz was deposed (1908) by his brother Abd al-Hafiz.

Abd al-Aziz ibn Saud: see IBN SAUD.

Abd al-Hafid (äb"däl-häfēd'), 1875?-1937, sultan of Morocco (1908-12). Placed on the throne by the revolution that deposed his brother Abd al-Aziz IV, he was soon confronted with uprisings and the demands of European creditors. Besieged (1911) at Fez by rebels, he was relieved by a French army. On March 30, 1912, he accepted a French protectorate, and on Aug. 12 he abdicated.

Abd al-Hamid I (äb"däl-hämēd', Turk. äbdül'hämēd'), 1725-89, Ottoman sultan (1774-89), brother and successor of Mustafa III. His reign, one of decline for the Ottoman Empire (Turkey), saw the end of the war of 1768-74 and the beginning of the war of 1787-91 with Catherine II of Russia (see RUSSO-TURKISH WARS). The peace terms in 1774 (see KUCHUK KAINARJI, TREATY OF) established Russia as the foremost power in the Middle East and had incalculable effects. In 1775, Austria, jealous of Russian expansion, forced the Turks to cede Bukovina. Abd al-Hamid was succeeded by his nephew, Selim III.

Abd al-Hamid II, 1842-1918, Ottoman sultan (1876-1909). His uncle, Abd al-Aziz, was deposed from the throne of the Ottoman Empire (Turkey) in 1876 by the Young Turks, a liberal reformist group. Abd al-Hamid's brother, Murad V, succeeded as sultan, but was shortly declared insane, and Abd al-Hamid ascended the throne. He at first accepted (1876) the constitution promulgated by MIDHAT PASHA but soon suspended it, dismissed Midhat, and eventually had him strangled. The war with Russia (see RUSSO-TURKISH WARS) led to the Treaty of SAN STEFANO, subsequently modified by the Congress of Berlin (see BERLIN, CONGRESS OF). To save what remained of his empire, the sultan then pursued a policy of friendship with Germany. German officers reorganized the Turkish army, and German business interests obtained concessions, most notably for the construction of the BAGHDAD RAILWAY. For his part in the Armenian massacres of 1894-96, he was called the Great Assassin and the Red Sultan. Ruling as absolute monarch, Abd al-Hamid lived in virtual seclusion. In 1908 the Young Turks, who had penetrated the armed services, revolted and forced the sultan to adhere to the constitution of 1876. He was deposed (1909) when he tried to plot a counterrevolution and was succeeded by his brother, Muhammad V. See study by Joan Haslip (new ed. 1973).

Abd al-Kadir (äb"däl-kädēr'), c.1807-1883, Algerian leader claiming descent from Muhammad. Although born to an anti-Turkish family, he was chosen emir of Mascara to fight the French invaders who had just defeated the Turks. From 1832 to 1839, by alternately fighting and coming to terms with the French, he extended his power over much of N Algeria, subduing hostile tribes and organizing the hinterland. A learned Muslim, he reformed his army along Western lines and finally proclaimed (1839) a holy war. In four years of fighting, General Bugeaud drove Abd al-Kadir into Morocco, where he gained the sultan's support. The Moroccan defeat at Isly (1844) soon forced the sultan to repudiate his ally. Abd al-Kadir surrendered in 1847 and was imprisoned in France until 1852. See Wilfred Blunt, *Desert Hawk* (1947); S. A. Salik, *The Saint of Jilan* (1961).

Abd Allah ibn Yasin: see ALMORAVIDS.

Abd al-Majid (äb"däl-mäjēd', Turk. äbdül' mäjēd'), 1823-61, Ottoman sultan (1839-61), son and successor of Mahmud II to the throne of the Ottoman Empire (Turkey). The rebellion of MUHAMMAD ALI was checked by the intervention (1840-41) of England, Russia, and Austria. Abd al-Majid was influenced by the British ambassador, Viscount STRATFORD DE RED-

CLIFFE, who helped persuade the sultan to introduce Western reforms. Two decrees (1839, 1856) led to many changes but did not have permanent effect. Confident in British and French support, Abd al-Majid resisted (1853) the Russian claim to act as protector of the Orthodox Christians in the Ottoman Empire. This was a primary cause of the CRIMEAN WAR. Turkey received no concrete gains at the Congress of Paris (1856; see PARIS, CONGRESS OF). The sultan was succeeded by his brother, Abd al-Aziz.

Abd al-Malik (äb″do͝ol-mälĭk′), c.646–705, 5th UMAYYAD caliph (685–705); son of Marwan I. At his accession, Islam was torn by dissension and threatened by the Byzantine Empire. With the help of his able general al-Hajjaj, Abd al-Malik overthrew the rival caliphs and united Islam. His battles with Byzantine forces were without final result. An able administrator, he reorganized the government and introduced Arabic coins, improved postal facilities, and made Arabic the official language.

Abd al-Mumin (äb″däl-mo͞o′mĭn), d. 1163, founder of the empire of the ALMOHADS. He was the favorite of the Almohad religious reformer Ibn Tumart and became (1130) his successor. Even before his rise to leadership, he had attacked the ALMORAVIDS. After long campaigns in Morocco and NW Algeria, he was able to destroy (1147) the Almoravid empire. In 1158 he invaded the Muslim states of Tunisia and NE Algeria, which had been weakened by attacks by Arab nomads and Sicilian Normans. By 1160 his rule reached from the Atlantic to Tripoli. The last years of his life were spent fighting the Christians of Spain.

Abd al-Rahman. For Muslim rulers thus named, see ABD AR-RAHMAN.

Abd ar-Rahman (äb″där-rämän′), d. 732, Muslim governor of Spain (721–32). Invading Aquitaine in 732, he won a victory over the Franks at Toulouse but was defeated in the battle of Tours by CHARLES MARTEL.

Abd ar-Rahman, 1778–1859, sultan of Morocco (1822–59). He sought, unsuccessfully, to take advantage of the overthrow of Turkish rule in Algeria in order to extend his territory. Later he allied himself with the emir, ABD AL-KADIR, but after their defeat at Isly (1844), he made peace with France and refused the emir further asylum in Morocco. Abd ar-Rahman was at various times involved in difficulties with Austria, Spain, and Great Britain.

Abd ar-Rahman I, d. 788, first UMAYYAD emir of Córdoba (756–88). The only survivor of the Abbasid massacre (750) of his family in Damascus, he fled from Syria and eventually went to Spain. There he defeated (756) the emir of Córdoba at Alameda and seized power. Despite the jealousy of the Arab aristocracy and the turbulence of the Berbers, he reorganized and consolidated the state and tried to unite the various Muslim races. In 778, CHARLEMAGNE invaded N Spain but was turned back at Saragossa and then defeated at Roncesvalles. The great mosque at Córdoba, which Abd ar-Rahman started, was continued by his son and successor, Hisham I.

Abd ar-Rahman III, 891–961, UMAYYAD emir (912–29) and first caliph (929–61) of Córdoba. When he succeeded to the throne, the Spanish emirate was reduced to Córdoba and its environs and beset with tribal warfare. Abd ar-Rahman recovered the lost provinces, consolidated the central government, and created internal peace and prosperity. He built up a strong army and navy and waged war successfully against the Fatimids in N Africa and the Christian kings of León. He made Córdoba one of the greatest cities in the West.

Abd ar-Rahman Khan (kän, khän), 1844?–1901, emir of Afghanistan (1880–1901); grandson of Dost Muhammad. He opposed his uncle, SHERE ALI, and was forced into exile in 1869. He was, however, recognized by the British as emir in 1880, and he supported British interests as, for example, against Russia.

Abdeel (ăb′dēĕl), father of the Shelemiah sent to arrest Baruch and Jeremiah. Jer. 36.26.

Abd el-Krim (äb′dĕl-krĭm′), 1882?–1963, leader of the Rif tribes of Morocco, called in full Muhammad ben Abd el-Krim. He was an important figure in the administration of the Spanish Zone until 1920, when he took up arms against Spanish rule. In 1921 his small force defeated a disorganized and ill-equipped Spanish army. In the next three years he strengthened his position and in 1924 drove the Spanish back to Tetuán. After capturing his only rival, RAISULI, he advanced into the French Zone in 1925. Defeated by combined Franco-Spanish forces, he surrendered in 1926 and was deported to Réunion. He escaped (1947) to Egypt, was awarded (1958) the title national hero by King Muhammad V of Morocco, and in 1962 announced that he would return to Morocco; but he died before he could carry out his wish. See study by D. S. Woolman (1968).

Abdera (ăbdē′rə) or **Avdira** (ävdē′rä), town, NE Greece, in Thrace, near the mouth of the Mesta River. It is a small agricultural settlement. Founded (c.650 B.C.) by colonists from Clazomenae, it was destroyed by the Thracians (c.550 B.C.) and rebuilt (c.500 B.C.) by refugees from Teos. The town passed to Macedon in 352 B.C. and in 198 B.C. became a free city under Roman rule. The Abderites were considered stupid by the ancient Greeks, and *Abderite* was a term of reproach. However, the philosophers Protagoras, Leucippus, and Democritus lived there.

Abdera, Spain: see ADRA.

Abdi (ăb′dī). **1, 2** Merarite Levites. 1 Chron. 6.44; 2 Chron. 29.12. **3** Israelite married to a foreign wife. Ezra 10.26.

Abdias (ăbdī′əs), Vulgate form of OBADIAH.

abdication, in a political sense, renunciation of high public office, usually by a monarch. Some abdications have been purely voluntary and resulted in no loss of prestige. For instance, Holy Roman Emperor CHARLES V, who abdicated for religious motives, remained influential until his death, and PHILIP V of Spain actually resumed the throne after abdicating. In Japan it has not been uncommon for the ruler to retire voluntarily to a life of religious contemplation, assured of a special title and many honors. However, most abdications have amounted to a confession of a failure in policy and are only the final and formal renunciation of an authority that events have already taken away. In the Chinese Empire forced abdications were frequent, the empire itself ending with the abdication of the boy ruler Hsuan T'ung in 1912 (see PU YI, HENRY). Since 1688, when the English Parliament declared James II to have abdicated by reason of flight and subversion of the constitution, abdication by a British ruler without parliamentary consent has been forbidden. When EDWARD VIII of England abdicated in 1936 in order to marry an American divorcee (his ministers having refused to approve the marriage), the abdication was given legal effect by an act of Parliament. Though several written constitutions contain provisions for abdication, there are few uniformly accepted rules for dealing with it. Defeat and political chaos following World Wars I and II forced the abdication of many rulers, most notably Emperor William II of Germany, Farouk of Egypt, and Leopold III of Belgium.

Abdiel (ăb′dĭəl), in the Bible, a Gadite. 1 Chron. 5.15.

abdomen, in man and other vertebrates, portion of the trunk between the diaphragm and lower pelvis. In man the wall of the abdomen is a muscular structure covered by fascia, fat, and skin. The abdominal cavity is lined with a thin membrane, the peritoneum, which encloses the stomach, intestines, liver, and gall bladder; the pancreas, kidneys, and urinary bladder are located behind the peritoneum. The abdomen of the female also contains the ovaries, fallopian tubes, and uterus. The navel, or umbilicus, an exterior scar on the front of the abdomen, marks the point of attachment of the fetus to the maternal organism before birth. In insects, crustacea, and some other arthropods, the term *abdomen* refers to the entire rear portion of the body.

Abdon (ăb′dŏn). **1** Judge of Israel. Judges 12.13–15. **2** Officer under Josiah. 2 Chron. 34.20. Achbor: 2 Kings 22.12; Jer. 26.22; 36.12. **3, 4** Benjamites. 1 Chron. 8.23,30; 9.36. **5** Unidentified boundary town, NW Palestine. Joshua 21.30; 1 Chron. 6.74. Hebron KJV and Ebron RSV. Joshua 19.28.

Abdubakar Tafawa Balewa, Alhaji Sir: see BALEWA, ALHAJI SIR ABUBAKAR TAFAWA.

Abdül Aziz. For Ottoman sultans thus named, see ABD AL-AZIZ.

Abdül Hamid. For Ottoman sultans thus named, see ABD AL-HAMID.

Abdullah (Abdullah ibn Husayn) (ăbdo͝ol′lä ĭ′bən ho͞osīn′, -sān′), 1882–1951, king of Jordan (1946–51), b. Mecca; son of HUSAYN IBN ALI. During World War I, Abdullah led Arab revolts against Turkish rule and had British support. After the war he unsuccessfully fought against IBN SAUD for the control of the Hejaz. In 1921, Great Britain created Abdullah emir of Trans-Jordan. In World War II, Abdullah strongly opposed the Axis. Following the partition of Palestine (May, 1948) he led the troops of his British-trained force, the Arab Legion, against Israel. He annexed the portions of Palestine not assigned to Israel. His foreign policy was directed toward creation of an Arab federation, preferably under the rule of a member of his family. He was assassinated in Jerusalem in 1951. See his *Memoirs* (1951).

Abdullah, Sheikh Muhammad (shākh mo͞ohäm′-mäd ăbdo͝ol-lä′), 1905–, nationalist leader in Kashmir, known as the Lion of Kashmir. He became active in political reform while a student at Lahore Univ. and was frequently imprisoned from 1931 for urging self-rule for Kashmir, a region now in India but also claimed by Pakistan. He cooperated with Mohandas Gandhi and Jawaharlal Nehru in the movement for India's independence and then became prime minister of Jammu and Kashmir when independence was achieved in 1947. After denouncing (1953) India's treatment of Kashmir, he was removed as prime minister and generally kept in preventive detention by the Indian government, although he was allowed to play a more active role in the early 1970s.

Abdül Mecid. For Ottoman sultans thus named, see ABD AL-MAJID.

Abdul Rahman, Tunku: see RAHMAN, TUNKU ABDUL.

Abdul Razak: see RAZAK, ABDUL.

à Becket, Thomas: see THOMAS À BECKET, SAINT.

Abed-nego (əbĕd′nēgō), one of the THREE HOLY CHILDREN cast into the fiery furnace.

Abel, son of Adam and Eve, a shepherd, killed by his older brother, Cain. Gen. 4.1–8. Mentioned as the first martyr. Mat. 23.35.

Abel, Sir Frederick Augustus, 1826–1902, English chemist, an authority on explosives. He was professor of chemistry at the Royal Military Academy (1851–55) and chemist to the War Dept. and government referee (1854–88). Among his achievements are improvements in the manufacture of guncotton; the invention, with Sir James Dewar, of cordite; a study, in collaboration with Sir Andrew Noble, Scottish physicist, of the behavior of black powder when fired; and the invention of an instrument used in the Abel test, named for him, to determine the flash point of petroleum. He wrote widely on explosives.

Abel, Iorwith Wilbur, 1908–, American labor leader, b. Magnolia, Ohio. In 1925 he went to work in a rolling mill in Canton, Ohio. He soon emerged as a leader of union organization in the steel industry. In 1937 he was appointed staff representative of the Steel Workers Organizing Committee, the progenitor of the United Steelworkers of America. From 1942 to 1952 he was the union's district director for the Canton area. In 1953 he became secretary-treasurer of the union, and in 1965 he succeeded David J. McDonald as third president. In the same year he was also elected a vice president of the AFL-CIO.

Abel, John Jacob, 1857–1938, American pharmacologist, b. Cleveland, grad. Univ. of Michigan, 1883, M.D. Univ. of Strasbourg, 1888. Professor of pharmacology (1893–1932) and director of the laboratory for endocrine research (from 1932) at Johns Hopkins, he is known for the isolation of epinephrine (adrenaline) in 1898 and later of insulin in crystalline form. Other contributions include the isolation of amino acids from the blood. He was a founder and editor (1909–32) of the *Journal of Pharmacology and Experimental Therapeutics.*

Abel, Niels Henrik (nēls hĕn′rĭk ä′bəl), 1802–1829, Norwegian mathematician. While a student at the University of Christiania (Oslo) he did fundamental work on the integration of functional expressions and proved the impossiblity of representing a solution of a general equation of fifth degree or higher by a radical expression. He investigated generalizations of the binomial theorem, pioneered in the general theory of elliptic functions, and showed that elliptic functions are a generalization of trigonometric functions. Commutative groups are also called Abelian groups in his honor. He died of tuberculosis at the age of 26, leaving contributions that rank him as one of the greatest mathematicians of the 19th cent. See Oystein Ore, *Niels Henrik Abel: Mathematician Extraordinary* (1957, repr. 1973).

Abel, Thomas: see ABELL, THOMAS.

Abel. **1** Ostensibly a place name. 1 Sam. 6.18. The RSV text does not give the name. **2** See ABEL-BETH-MAACHAH.

Abelard, Peter (ăb′əlärd), Fr. *Pierre Abélard* (pyĕr äbälär′), 1079–1142, French philosopher and teacher, b. Le Pallet, near Nantes. He went (c.1100) to Paris to study under WILLIAM OF CHAMPEAUX at the school of Notre Dame and soon attacked the ultrarealist position of his master with such success that William was forced to modify his teaching. Abelard became master at Notre Dame but, when deprived of his place, set himself up (1112) at a school on Mont-Ste-Geneviève, just outside the city walls. Abelard's ame as a dialectician attracted great numbers of students to Paris; because of this fact Abelard is usually regarded as the founder of the Univ. of Paris. This part of his career was cut short by his romance with Heloise (d. c.1164), the learned and beautiful niece of Fulbert, canon of Notre Dame, who had hired Abelard as her tutor. After Heloise gave birth to a son, a secret marriage was held to appease her uncle. Fulbert's ill-treatment of Heloise led Abelard to remove her secretly to the convent at Argenteuil. Fulbert, who thought that Abelard planned to abandon her, had ruffians attack and emasculate him. Abelard sought refuge at Saint-Denis, where he became a monk. In 1120 he left Saint-Denis to teach. At the instigation of his rivals, the Council of Soissons had his first theological work burnt as heretical (1121). After a short imprisonment, he returned to Saint-Denis but fell out with the monks and built a hermitage near Troyes. Students sought him out, and to house them he built a monastery, the Paraclete. When he became abbot at Saint-Gildas-en-Rhuys, Brittany, he gave the Paraclete to Heloise, who became an abbess of a sisterhood there. St. BERNARD OF CLAIRVAUX thought Abelard's influence dangerous and secured his condemnation by the Council of Sens (1140). Abelard appealed to the pope, who upheld the council. Abelard submitted and retired to Cluny. He was buried at the Paraclete, as was Heloise; their bodies were later moved to Père-Lachaise in Paris. A Platonist in theology, Abelard emphasized the method of Aristotle's dialectic. His belief that the methods of logic could be applied to the truths of faith was in opposition to the mysticism of St. Bernard. He also opposed the extreme views of William of Champeaux and ROSCELIN on the problems of universals. His own solution, in which universals are considered as entities existent only in thought but with a basis in particulars, is called moderate realism and to some extent anticipates the conceptualism of St. Thomas Aquinas. His most influential work, the *Sic et non*, a collection of contradictory writings of the Fathers of the Church, formed the basis for the widely read *Sentences* of PETER LOMBARD, who may have been Abelard's pupil. Abelard was perhaps most important as a teacher; among his pupils were some of the celebrated men of the 12th cent., including John of Salisbury and Arnold of Brescia. Of Abelard's poetry only Latin hymns survive. He is chiefly remembered for the events of his life as chronicled in his autobiographical *Historia calamitatum* (tr. by J. T. Muckle, 1954; repr. 1964) and revealed in the poignant letters of Heloise and Abelard (tr. by C. K. Scott Moncrieff, 1926). See Joseph McCabe, *Life of Peter Abelard* (1901, repr. 1973); J. G. Sikes, *Peter Abailard* (1932, repr. 1965); E. H. Gibson, *Heloise and Abelard* (tr. 1951, repr. 1960); D. W. Robertson, Jr., *Abelard and Heloise* (1972); Regine Pernoud, *Heloise and Abelard* (tr. 1973).

Abel-beth-maachah (ā'bəl-bĕth-mā'əkə), town, Palestine, the modern Tel Abil (Israel), S of Metulla. It was attacked by Ben-hadad and taken by Tiglath-pileser. 1 Kings 15.20; 2 Kings 15.29. Abel and Beth-maachah: 2 Sam. 20.14. Abel of Beth-maachah: 2 Sam. 20.15. Abel-maim: 2 Chron. 16.4.

Abell, Kjeld (kyĕl ä'bĕl), 1901–61, Danish playwright. Abell's *Melody That Got Lost* (1935, tr. 1939) was an early success. Trained as a stage designer, he was an innovator in stage technique. He later turned to ethical and social drama; *Anna Sophie Hedvig* (1939, tr. 1944), *The Queen Walks Again* (1943), *Silkeborg* (1946), and *Skriget* (1961) are arresting and powerful problem plays concerned with justice and social protest.

Abell or **Abel, Thomas** (both: ā'bəl), d. 1540, English priest, chaplain to KATHARINE OF ARAGÓN. In 1528 he served as Katharine's secret envoy to her nephew, Holy Roman Emperor Charles V, in connection with Henry VIII's proposed divorce. Abell vigorously opposed the divorce both in his sermons and in a book, *Invicta veritas* [truth unconquered] (1532). He was imprisoned for six years in the Tower of London and was finally executed for upholding the validity of Henry's first marriage. See J. E. Paul, *Catherine of Aragon and Her Friends* (1966).

Abel-maim (ā'bəl-mā'ĭm), town, Palestine, the same as ABEL-BETH-MAACHAH.

Abel-meholah (ā'bəl-mēhō'lə), name of towns or districts mentioned in the Bible, probably not all different. **1** Near the Jordan; limit of the Midianites' flight. Judges 7.22. **2** In N central Palestine. 1 Kings 4.12. **3** Home of Adriel. 1 Sam. 18.19. **4** Elisha's home. 1 Kings 19.16. See MEHOLATHITE.

Abel-mizraim (ā'bəl-mĭzrā'ĭm), place "beyond Jordan" where Jacob was mourned. Gen. 50.11.

Abel-shittim: see SHITTIM.

Abenaki Indians: see ABNAKI INDIANS.

Aben Ezra, Abraham ben Meir: see IBN EZRA.

Abengourou (ăbĕng-go͝o'ro͞o), town (1964 est. pop. 18,000), E Ivory Coast. It is the commercial center for a region producing cacao, coffee, kola nuts, plantains, yams, manioc, and timber. The French established an administrative post in Abengourou in 1896.

Åbenrå (ô'bənrô'), city (1970 com. pop. 20,484), capital of Sønderjylland co., S Denmark, at the head of the Åbenrå Fjord. It is a port and the commercial center for a rich agricultural region. The city was chartered in 1335. It was held by Prussia from 1864 to 1920 and was then known as Apenrade. The name was spelled Aabenraa until 1948.

Abeokuta (ä"bēōko͞o'tə, ăb"-), city (1969 est. pop. 217,000), SW Nigeria. It is the trade center for an agricultural region producing cacao, kola nuts, and palm products. Manufactures of the city include beer, cement, dyed textiles, and canned foods. Abeokuta was founded in the 1830s by Egba refugees from the YORUBA civil wars. The city repelled attacks by raiders from Dahomey in 1851 and 1864. It came under British protection in 1893.

Aberavon, Wales: see PORT TALBOT.

Aberbrothock: see ARBROATH, Scotland.

Abercrombie, Lascelles (lăs'əlz), 1881–1938, English poet and critic. Complex and cerebral in style, his poetry often expresses his distaste for 20th-century industrialism. His volumes of poetry include *Interludes and Poems* (1908), *Emblems of Love* (1912), and *Collected Poems* (1930). He also wrote influential critical works, notably *Thomas Hardy* (1912) and *The Theory of Poetry* (1924).

Abercrombie, Sir Patrick, 1879–1957, British architect and town planner. Professor of civil design at the Univ. of Liverpool from 1915 to 1935 and of town planning at the Univ. of London after 1935, he acted as consultant in the rebuilding and planning of London, Edinburgh, Bath, and other British cities. He was knighted in 1945. His voluminous writing has been of considerable influence in the field of city and regional planning. His books include *The Preservation of Rural England* (1926) and *Town and Country Planning* (1933).

Abercrombie, Fort: see FORT ABERCROMBIE.

Abercromby, James, 1706–81, British general in the French and Indian Wars, b. Scotland. He arrived in America in 1756 and in 1758 replaced the earl of Loudoun as supreme British commander. After failing to take Ticonderoga from General Montcalm, Abercromby was replaced (1758) by Jeffrey AMHERST.

Abercromby, Sir Ralph, 1734–1801, British general. He served in the Seven Years War but later retired from active service because he sympathized with the American colonists. Returning in 1793 for service against France, he won a major military reputation by his command of a brilliant retreat in Flanders in the winter of 1794–95. He was (1795–97) commander in chief in the West Indies, where he captured Grenada, St. Lucia, St. Vincent, and Trinidad. In 1800, Abercromby was sent to expel the French from Egypt. He landed at Aboukir in March, 1801, but was mortally wounded in the first engagement (which was successful). He is noted for having renewed the discipline and reputation of the army.

Aberdare (ăbərdâr'), urban district (1971 pop. 37,760), Glamorganshire, S Wales. It is in an anthracite and iron-ore region. Cables are made. In 1974, Aberdare became part of the new nonmetropolitan county of Mid Glamorgan.

Aberdeen, George Hamilton-Gordon, 4th **earl of,** 1784–1860, British statesman. He served (1813) as ambassador extraordinary at Vienna and helped arrange (1814) the peace terms at Paris after Napoleon I's initial defeat. He was foreign secretary (1828–30) in the duke of Wellington's cabinet and secretary for war and the colonies (1834–35) under Sir Robert PEEL. As foreign secretary (1841–46) in Peel's second government, he settled two boundary disputes with the United States, the Northeast Boundary Dispute by the Webster-Ashburton Treaty (1842) and the Oregon controversy by the treaty of 1846. He also improved relations with France. He supported Peel in repealing the corn laws (1846) and resigned with him. As prime minister (1852–55), Aberdeen headed a brilliant coalition ministry and was quite successful in home affairs. He was, however, unable to prevent Viscount PALMERSTON and others in his cabinet from involving England on the side of the Ottoman Empire (Turkey) in the Crimean War. Bad management of the campaigns and unpopularity of the war forced his resignation in 1855. See biography by Lady Frances Balfour (1922); study by W. D. Jones (1958).

Aberdeen, city (1971 pop. 182,006), county town of Aberdeenshire, NE Scotland, on the North Sea at the mouth of the Dee River. Part of the city lies in Kincardineshire. It is Scotland's third largest city and the only industrial center outside the midland belt. Famous as a herring and whitefish port, it is also known for its granite quarries. Other manufactures are paper, textiles, linen, and wool. There are shipyards, engineering and chemical works, and facilities for agricultural research. Aberdeen became a royal burgh in 1176 and was a leading port for trade with England and the Low Countries as early as the 14th cent. The town was burned by the English in 1336. It was a stronghold of royalist and episcopal sentiment in the religious wars of the 17th cent. Aberdeen is noted for its granite Cathedral of St. Machar. The Univ. of Aberdeen includes King's College (founded 1493) and Marischal College (founded 1593). Under the Local Government Act of 1973, Aberdeen became (1975) part of the Grampian region.

Aberdeen. 1 Town (1970 pop. 12,375), Harford co., NE Md., in a farm region; inc. 1892. Just south, on Chesapeake Bay, is the U.S. army's huge Aberdeen Proving Ground, a major research, development, and testing installation and site of the army ordnance center and school. To the northeast, on the Susquehanna River, is a large hydroelectric plant. **2** City (1970 pop. 26,476), seat of Brown co., NE S.Dak.; inc. 1882. The trade and distributing center for a wheat and livestock region, it has flour mills, dairy-processing plants, and a bottling house. Manufactures include fertilizers and feeds, gear boxes, computers, and tools. Northern State College and a junior college are in the city. **3** City (1970 pop. 18,489), Grays Harbor co., W Wash., a port of entry on Grays Harbor, at the confluence of the Chehalis and the Wishkah rivers; inc. 1890. With its adjacent twin city, Hoquiam, it has lumbering, wood-product, fishing, canning, and shipping industries. The two communities, which have grown together and are for all practical purposes one city, are in a region containing some of the world's densest stands of cedar, hemlock, and Douglas fir. They are a gateway to Olympic National Park. A junior college is in Aberdeen, and nearby are many tree farms and two state parks.

Aberdeen Angus cattle: see ANGUS CATTLE.

Aberdeenshire (ăbərdēn'shĭr), county (1971 pop. 319,887), 1,971 sq mi (5,105 sq km), NE Scotland. ABERDEEN is the county town. The terrain varies from the Grampian Mts. in the southwest to the rolling farmlands of the Don valley and the treeless lowlands of Buchan. Oats, barley, turnips, and potatoes are grown. Sheep and the famous Aberdeen Angus cattle are raised. Fishing is carried on from the North Sea ports of Aberdeen, FRASERBURGH, and PETERHEAD. The county played a large role in the Scottish wars of independence (13th cent.) and was a royalist stronghold during the ENGLISH CIVIL WAR. It was the headquarters of the JACOBITE uprising of 1715. BALMORAL CASTLE is the Scottish residence of the British kings and queens. Under the Local Government Act of 1973, Aberdeenshire became (1975) part of the Grampian region.

Aberdeen University, at Aberdeen, Scotland; founded by the bishop of Aberdeen under the authority of a papal bull obtained 1494–95. It has faculties of arts, science, divinity, law, and medicine. Robert Gordon's Institute of Technology and the North of Scotland College of Agriculture are affiliated with the university.

Aberhart, William (ā'bərhärt), 1878–1943, premier of Alberta, Canada, b. Ontario. He was a schoolteacher and a founder and dean of the Calgary Prophetic Bible Institute (opened 1927). About 1932 he became interested in SOCIAL CREDIT, which advocated direct money payments to all citizens. He was an organizer of the Social Credit party of Alberta and was elected (1935) to the provincial legislature with enough supporters to control it. Thus Aberhart became premier (1935–43) of the first Social Credit government in the world. However, many of the legislative attempts to enact his principles were declared invalid by the courts.

aberration, in optics, condition that causes a blurring and loss of clearness in the images produced by lenses or mirrors. Spherical aberration is caused by the failure of a LENS OR MIRROR of spherical section to bring parallel rays of light to a single focus. The effect results from the operation of the laws of optics, not from defects in construction. Spherical aberration can be prevented by using a parabolic rather than a spherical section, but this involves much greater complexity and expense in lens or mirror construction. Chromatic aberration results in the blurred coloring of the edge of an image when

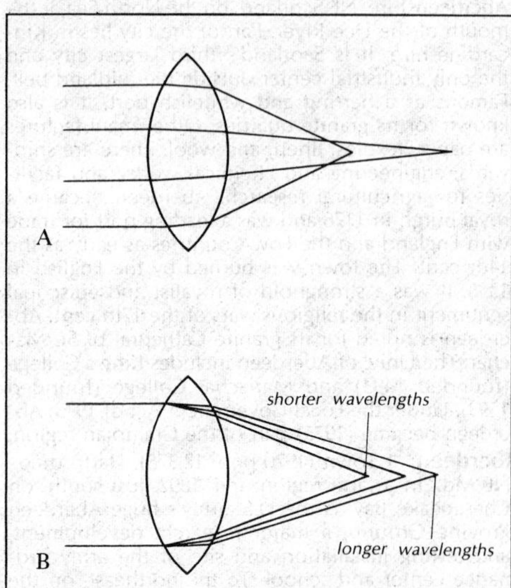

A. *Spherical aberration: Light rays near the edge of the lens are bent more and brought to focus nearer to the lens.*

B. *Chromatic aberration: Shorter wavelengths (higher frequencies) are bent more and focused nearer to the lens.*

white light is sent through a lens. This is caused by the fact that some colors of light are bent, or refracted, more than others after passing through a lens. For example, violet light is bent more than red and thus is brought to a focus nearer the lens than red. No single lens can ever be free of chromatic aberration, but by combining lenses of different types, the effects of the component lenses can be made to cancel one another. Such an arrangement is called an achromatic lens. See REFLECTION; REFRACTION.

aberration of starlight, angular displacement of the apparent path of light from a star, resulting in a displacement of the apparent position of the star from its true position; discovered by the English astronomer James Bradley and explained by him in 1729. The phenomenon is caused by the orbital motion of the earth; in the same way, vertically falling raindrops appear to fall diagonally when viewed from a moving vehicle. The true path of light from a star to an observer is along the straight line from the star to the observer; but, because of the component of the observer's velocity in a direction perpendicular to the direction to the star, the light appears to be traveling along a path at an angle to the true direction to the star. Thus, in order to observe a star the central axis of a telescope must be tilted as much as 20.″5 (seconds of arc) from the true direction to the star, the exact amount of the angle depending on the direction to the star relative to the direction of the earth's motion in its orbit. Because of the earth's orbital motion, the stars appear to move in elliptical paths on the celestial sphere. All these ellipses have the same semimajor axis, 20.″5 of arc, a value known as the constant of aberration. The tangent of the constant of aberration is equal to the ratio of the earth's orbital speed to the speed of light.

Abersychan, Wales: see PONTYPOOL.

Abertawe, England: see SWANSEA.

Abertillery (ăb″ərtĭlâr′ē), urban district (1971 pop. 21,140), Monmouthshire, SE Wales. It is located in an area of coal and iron mines and produces tin plate. In 1974, Abertillery became part of the new nonmetropolitan county of Gwent.

Aberystwyth (ăb″ərĭst′wĭth), municipal borough (1971 pop. 12,672), Cardiganshire, W Wales, on Cardigan Bay. It is a summer resort and a cultural center. Before the construction of railroads, Aberystwyth was a coastal trade center. It is the seat of a constituent college of the Univ. of Wales and of the National Library of Wales, which has an outstanding collection of Welsh manuscripts. In 1974, it became part of the new nonmetropolitan county of Dyfed.

Abez (ā′bəz), city of Issachar. Joshua 19.20.

Abgar, Epistles of: see PSEUDEPIGRAPHA.

Abhidharma (ŭb′ĭdŭr″mə) [Skt.,=further dharma, or doctrine], schools of Buddhist philosophy. Early BUDDHISM classified experience into 5 *skandhas* or aggregates, and alternatively into 18 *dhatus* or elements. Later, different schools developed the process of analysis and listing that was called *Abhidharma;* their treatises were collected in the *Abhidharmapitaka,* one of the three main divisions of the Buddhist canon of scriptures (see BUDDHIST LITERATURE). The categories of analysis were dharmas, or natures, ultimate factors or principles that arise and pass away in irreducible moments of time. Orthodox lists of dharmas varied from 75 to 157, with different classifications of the dharmas into groups. The exact definition of a dharma became the subject of much controversy. The greatest systematizer of Abhidharma thought was Vasubandhu (5th cent. A.D.) who wrote the encyclopedic *Abhidharmakosa* or *Treasury of Abhidharma.* See Herbert Guenther, *Philosophy and Psychology in the Abhidharma* (1957); F. I. Shcherbatskoi, *The Central Conception of Buddhism* (4th ed. 1970).

Abi (ā′bī) [short for ABIJAH], King Hezekiah's mother. 2 Kings 18.2 Abijah: 2 Chron. 29.1.

Abia (əbī′ə): see ABIJAH **2** and ABIJAH **6.**

Abiah (əbī′ə), variant of ABIJAH. **1** Wife of Hezron. 1 Chron. 2.24. **2** Benjamite. 1 Chron. 7.8. **3** Second son of Samuel. 1 Sam. 8.2.

Abi-albon (ā″bī-ăl′bŏn): see ABIEL **2.**

Abiasaph (əbī′əsăf), Levitical family. Ex. 6.24. Ebiasaph: 1 Chron. 6.23; 9.19. Asaph: 1 Chron. 26.1.

Abiathar (əbī′əthär), priest, son of Ahimelech, the only one of his family who escaped massacre by Doeg. He fled to David, to whom he remained loyal. Later he sided with Adonijah against Solomon, who took away his priesthood. 1 Sam. 22.9–23; 2 Sam. 15.29; 1 Kings 1.7; 2.27; Mark 2.26. Name exchanged with his father's. 2 Sam. 8.17; 1 Chron. 18.16; 24.6.

Abida or **Abidah** (both: əbī′də), son of Midian. Gen. 25.4; 1 Chron. 1.33.

Abidan (ăb′ĭdăn, əbī′-), Benjamite chief. Num. 1.11; 2.22; 7.60, 65; 10.24.

Abidjan (ăbĭjän′), city (1973 est. pop. 408,000), capital of Ivory Coast, a port on the Ébrié Lagoon (an arm of the Gulf of Guinea). Abidjan is Ivory Coast's administrative center and largest city. Its modern port is centered on Little Bassam Island, which is linked with the rest of the city by two bridges; a canal through the lagoon bar provides access to the Atlantic Ocean. Coffee, cacao, timber, pineapples, and plantains are the chief items shipped from the port. Abidjan's major industries are food processing, sawmilling, and the manufacture of textiles, chemicals, beverages, and soap. A communications and transportation hub, the city is connected by road or rail with neighboring countries. An international airport is nearby. Abidjan was a small village until the French began to enlarge it in the 1920s. In 1934 it became the capital of France's Ivory Coast colony. Today it is one of Africa's most modern cities. The Univ. of Abidjan, several technical colleges, and the Museum of the Ivory Coast are in Abidjan, which is also a popular tourist spot.

Abiel (ā′bēĕl, əbī′əl, ăb′ēĕl). **1** Grandfather of King Saul. 1 Sam. 9.1; 14.51. **2** One of David's valiant men. 1 Chron. 11.32. Probably erroneously Abi-albon. 2 Sam. 23.31.

Abiezer (ā″bīē′zər). **1** Manassite. 1 Chron. 7.18. Jeezer: Num. 26.30. **2** One of David's captains. 2 Sam. 23.27; 1 Chron. 27.12.

Abigail (ăb′əgāl). **1** The wife of Nabal. She persuaded David not to take vengeance on her husband. When Nabal died, she married David. 1 Sam. 25; 2 Sam. 3.3; 1 Chron. 3.1. **2** David's stepsister, mother of Amasa. 2 Sam. 17.25; 1 Chron. 2.16, 17.

Abihail (ăbəhā′əl). **1** Father of Queen Esther. Esther 2.15; 9.29. **2** Gadite. 1 Chron. 5.14. **3** Merarite woman. Num. 3.35. **4** Wife of Abishur. 1 Chron. 2.29. **5** Mother-in-law of Rehoboam. 2 Chron. 11.18.

Abihu (əbī′hyōō), son of Aaron, destroyed with his brother, Nadab, for offering "strange" fire. Ex. 6.23; 24.1,9; 28.1; Lev. 10.1; Num. 3.2,4; 26.60,61; 1 Chron. 6.3; 24.1.

Abihud (əbī′həd), grandson of Benjamin. 1 Chron. 8.3.

Abijah (əbī′jə). **1** See ABI. **2** Died c.911 B.C., king (c.914–c.911 B.C.) of Judah, the southern kingdom. He succeeded his father, Rehoboam, and King Jeroboam continued warfare against him. 2 Chron. 13. Abijam: 1 Kings 15.1–8. Abia: 1 Chron. 3.10; Mat. 1.7. **3** Son of Jeroboam, whose death was used by a prophet to foreshadow the death of Jeroboam. 1 Kings 14. **4,5** See ABIAH **2,3.** **6** Priestly family. 1 Chron. 24.10. Abia: Luke 1.5. **7,8** Priests in the return to Jerusalem. Neh. 10.7; 12.4,17.

Abijam (əbī′jəm): see ABIJAH **2.**

Abiko (ä″bē′kō), city (1970 pop. 49,240), Chiba prefecture, central Honshu, Japan. It is an important railway junction, a resort town, and a residential suburb NE of Tokyo.

Abildgaard, Nikolaj Abraham (nĭ′kōlī′ ä′bĕlgôrd), 1743–1809, Danish painter of the neoclassical school. He was a student of Eckersberg. Among his own pupils was Thorvaldsen, whom he greatly influenced. Abildgarrd's work may be seen in the House of Representatives in Copenhagen.

Abilene (ăb′ĭlēn). **1** City (1970 pop. 6,661), seat of Dickinson co., central Kansas, on the Smoky Hill River; inc. 1869. It was (1867–71) a railhead for a large cattle-raising region extending SW into Texas. Under the promotion of J. G. McCoy, millions of head of cattle followed the Chisholm Trail into Abilene's stockyards prior to shipment. One of the wildest and toughest cowtowns of the Old West, Abilene once had Wild Bill Hickok as its marshal. The city, now a shipping point for a wheat and farm region, has feed and flour mills. Greyhound racing dogs are bred in Abilene, which is the headquarters of the National Greyhound Association. Former President Dwight D. Eisenhower lived in Abilene in his youth; the Eisenhower Center (completed 1961) includes his old family homestead, a museum, the Eisenhower Library, and his grave. **2** City (1970 pop. 89,653), seat of Taylor co., W central Texas; inc. 1882. Buffalo hunters first settled there; the town, which was founded in 1881 with the coming of the railroad, was named after Abilene, Kansas. Abilene grew as a shipping point for cattle ranches and is now the financial, commercial, and educational center of a large part of W Texas. The city's diversified manufactures include electronic, aircraft, and missile components; oil-field equipment; food and dairy products; cottonseed oil; agricultural equipment; clothing; metals; and musical instruments. Agriculture (cattle, sheep, poultry, cotton, and grain sorghums) and minerals (oil, natural gas, stone, sand and gravel, and clays) are important in the economy of the surrounding area; the headquarters of regional petroleum interests are in Abilene. Hardin-Simmons Univ., Abilene Christian College, and McMurry College are also in the city. Dyess Air Force Base and a Nike missile installation are nearby, as are the ruins of Fort Phantom Hill, an early army post and stagecoach stop. Other points of interest include the ruins of the old frontier town of Buffalo Gap; and Lake Abilene, the city's reservoir, located in a state park.

Abimael (əbĭm′āĕl), descendant of Shem. Gen. 10.28; 1 Chron. 1.22.

Abimelech (əbĭm′əlĕk). **1** Name or title of a king of Gerar who had various dealings with Abraham and Isaac. Gen. 20; 21; 26. **2** See AHIMELECH **1.** **3** Son of Gideon. He murdered his 70 brothers, except Jotham, and became "king." Judges 9.1–57; 2 Sam. 11.21. **4** See ACHISH **1.**

Abinadab (əbĭn′ədăb). **1** Second son of Jesse. 1 Sam. 16.8; 17.13; 1 Chron. 2.13. **2** Son of King Saul, killed at the battle of Mt. Gilboa. 1 Sam. 31.2; 1 Chron. 10.2. **3** Man in whose house the ark remained for 20 years. 1 Sam. 7.1,2; 2 Sam. 6.3,4; 1 Chron. 13.7. **4** Father of one of Solomon's chief officers. 1 Kings 4.11. The officer is called Ben-abinadab in RSV.

Abington. 1 Town (1970 pop. 12,334), Plymouth co., E Mass.; settled 1668, inc. 1713. Chiefly residential, it has some light industry. **2** Township (1970 pop. 62,899), Montgomery co., SE Pa., a residential suburb of Philadelphia; settled 1696, inc. 1906. A junior college campus of Pennsylvania State Univ. is there.

Abinoam (əbĭn′ōəm), father of Barak. Judges 4.6,12; 5.12.

Abiram (əbī′rəm). **1** Levite who died with his brother DATHAN. **2** Son of a rebuilder of Jericho, associated obscurely with its foundations. 1 Kings 16.34.

Abishag (ăb′əshăg), Shunammite woman, David's attendant in his old age and the indirect cause of Adonijah's murder. 1 Kings 1; 2.

Abishai (əbĭsh′āī, ăb′ĭshī), nephew of David. 2 Sam. 2.18–24; 10; 14; 23.18; 1 Sam. 26.6–9.

Abishalom (əbĭsh′əlŏm, əbī′shə-): see ABSALOM.

Abishua (əbĭsh′yōōə). **1** Priest. 1 Chron. 6.4,5,50; Ezra 7.5. **2** Benjamite. 1 Chron. 8.4.

Abishur (ăb′ĭshər, əbī′-), grandson of Jerahmeel. 1 Chron. 2.28.

Abital (ăb′ĭtăl), mother of David's son Shephatiah. 2 Sam. 3.4; 1 Chron. 3.3.

Abitibi Lake (ăbətĭb′ē), irregularly shaped lake, c.60 mi (100 km) long, SW Que. and E Ont., Canada. It is a popular tourist area and the site of the Abitibi

Game Reserve. The Abitibi River drains the lake and flows W and N to the Moose River.

Abitub (ăb'ĭtəb), Benjamite. 1 Chron. 8.11.

Abiud (ăb'īəd) [Gr. for ABIHUD], son of Zerubbabel in Matthew's genealogy. Mat. 1.13.

Abkhaz Autonomous Soviet Socialist Republic (ăbkăz', Rus. äbkhäz'), autonomous region (1970 pop. 487,000), 3,300 sq mi (8,547 sq km), SE European USSR, in Georgia, between the Black Sea and the Greater Caucasus. SUKHUMI (the capital) and GAGRA are the chief cities. Despite some perpetually snowcapped peaks, the region is mainly one of subtropical agriculture. Tobacco is the leading crop; there are also tea and citrus plantations, vineyards, and fruit orchards. Industries include sawmilling, canning, metalworking, and the manufacture of leather goods. Coal is the region's chief mineral. The population is made up of Abkhazians (an Orthodox Christian and Muslim people of the North Caucasian linguistic family), Georgians, Russians, and Armenians. Originally colonized in the 6th cent. B.C. by the Greeks, the region later came under Roman and Byzantine rule. In the 8th cent. a leader of the Abkhaz tribe formed an independent kingdom that became part of Georgia in the 10th cent. In 1578 the Turks conquered the area and gradually converted it to Islam. By a treaty with the Abkhazian dukes, Russia acquired Sukhumi in 1810 and declared a protectorate over all Abkhazia, which was formally annexed in 1864. Abkhazia became an autonomous republic in 1921 and was made part of Georgia in 1930. The region is famous for its health resorts.

Ablative (ăb'lətĭv") [Lat.,=carrying off], in Latin grammar, the CASE used in a number of circumstances, particularly with certain prepositions and in locating place or time. The term is also used in the grammar of some languages (e.g., Sanskrit, Finnish) for a case of separation, e.g., "from the house."

Ablaut (äp'lout) [Ger.,=off-sound], in INFLECTION, vowel variation (as in English *sing, sang, sung, song*) caused by former differences in syllabic accent. In a prehistoric period the corresponding forms of the language (known through scientific reconstruction) had differences in accent, not differences in vowel. See UMLAUT.

ABM: see GUIDED MISSILE.

Abnaki Indians or **Abenaki Indians** (both: ăbnä'kē), North American Indians of the Algonquian branch of the Algonquian-Wakashan linguistic stock (see AMERICAN INDIAN LANGUAGES). The name *Abnaki* was given to them by the French, but properly it should be *Wabanaki,* a word that refers to morning and the east and may be interpreted as those "living at the sunrise." The Abnaki lived mostly in what is now Maine, New Hampshire, and Vermont. Abnaki legend has it that they came from the Southwest, but the exact time is unsure, although archaeological sites do show that they were in the Northeast several thousand years before the beginning of the Christian era. After a series of bloody conflicts with British colonists, the Abnaki and related tribes (the Malecite, the Passamaquoddy, the Pennacook, the Penobscot, and others) withdrew into Canada, where they received protection from the French. The Abnaki were in settled villages, often surrounded by palisades, and lived by growing corn, fishing, and hunting. Their own name for their conical huts covered with bark or mats, WIGWAM, came to be generally used in English.

Abner, relative of Saul and commander in chief of his army. Jealousy and revenge probably caused his death at Joab's hands. 1 Sam. 14.50,51; 17.55; 2 Sam. 2; 8.

Abo, Finland: see TURKU.

abolitionists, in U.S. history, particularly in the three decades before the Civil War, members of the movement that agitated for the compulsory emancipation of Negro slaves. Abolitionists are to be distinguished from free-soilers, who opposed the further extension of slavery, but the groups came to act together politically and otherwise in the antislavery cause. Although antislavery sentiment had existed during the American Revolution, and abolitionist Benjamin LUNDY began his work early in the 19th cent., the abolition movement did not reach crusading proportions until the 1830s. One of its mainsprings was the growing influence of evangelical religion, with its religious fervor, its moral urgency to end sinful practices, and its vision of human perfection. The preaching of Lyman Beecher and Nathaniel Taylor in New England and the religious revivals that began in W New York state in 1824 under Charles G. FINNEY and swept much of the North, created a powerful impulse toward social reform—emancipation of the slaves as well as temperance, foreign missions, and women's rights. Outstanding among Finney's converts were Theodore D. Weld and the brothers Arthur and Lewis TAPPAN. The Tappans and William Lloyd GARRISON, who began publishing an abolitionist journal, *The Liberator,* in 1831, were the principal organizers in Dec., 1833, at Philadelphia, of the American Anti-Slavery Society. The primary concern of the society was the denunciation of slavery as a moral evil; its members called for immediate action to free the slaves. In 1835 the society launched a massive propaganda campaign. It flooded the slave states with abolitionist literature, sent agents throughout the North to organize state and local antislavery societies, and poured petitions into Congress demanding the abolition of slavery in the District of Columbia. The abolitionists were at first widely denounced and abused. Mobs attacked them in the North; Southerners burned antislavery pamphlets and in some areas excluded them from the mails; and Congress imposed the GAG RULE to avoid considering their petitions. These actions, and the murder of abolitionist editor Elijah P. Lovejoy in 1837, led many to fear for their constitutional rights. Abolitionists shrewdly exploited these fears and antislavery sentiment spread rapidly in the North. By 1838, more than 1,350 antislavery societies existed with almost 250,000 members, including many women. Although abolitionists united in denouncing the African venture of the AMERICAN COLONIZATION SOCIETY, they disagreed among themselves as to how their goal might be best reached. Garrison believed in moral suasion as the only weapon; he and his followers also argued that women be allowed to participate fully in antislavery societies, thus disturbing the less radical element. When the Garrisonians passed such a resolution at the 1840 convention, a large group led by the Tappan brothers withdrew and formed the American and Foreign Anti-Slavery Society. The abolitionists were never again united as a single movement. Advocates of direct political action founded (1840) the Liberty party; James G. BIRNEY was its presidential candidate in 1840 and 1844. Writers such as John Greenleaf WHITTIER and orators such as Wendell PHILLIPS gave their services to the cause, while Frederick DOUGLASS and other freed or escaped slaves also took to the lecture platform. An antislavery lobby was organized in 1842, and its influence grew under Weld's able direction. Abolitionists hoped to convert the South through the churches, until the withdrawal of Southern Methodists (1844) and Baptists (1845) from association with their Northern brethren. After the demise of the Liberty party, the political abolitionists supported the FREE-SOIL PARTY in 1848 and 1852, and in 1856 they voted with the Republican party. The passage of more stringent fugitive slave laws in 1850 increased abolitionist activity on the UNDERGROUND RAILROAD. *Uncle Tom's Cabin,* by Harriet Beecher STOWE, became an effective piece of abolitionist propaganda, and the KANSAS question further aroused both North and South. The culminating act of extreme abolitionism occurred in the raid of John BROWN on Harpers Ferry. After the opening of the Civil War insistent abolitionist demands for immediate freeing of the slaves, supported by radical Republicans in Congress, pushed President Lincoln in his decision to issue the EMANCIPATION PROCLAMATION. The abolitionist movement was one of high moral purpose and courage; its uncompromising temper made the slavery question the prime concern of national politics and hastened the demise of slavery in the United States. See SLAVERY. See G. H. Barnes, *The Antislavery Impulse, 1830–1844* (1933, rev. ed. 1957, repr. 1964); D. L. Dumond, *Antislavery: the Crusade for Freedom in America* (1961, repr. 1964); Louis Filler, *The Crusade against Slavery, 1830–1860* (1960); Lawrence Lader, *The Bold Brahmins: New England's War against Slavery* (1961); Martin Duberman, ed., *The Antislavery Vanguard* (1965); Alma Lutz, *Crusade for Freedom: Women in the Antislavery Movement* (1968); Benjamin Quarles, *Black Abolitionists* (1969); A. S. Kraditor, *Means and Ends in American Abolitionism* (1969); Hugh Hawkins, ed., *The Abolitionists* (2d ed. 1972); Lewis Perry, *Radical Abolitionism* (1973).

Abomey (ăbōmā', əbō'mē), town (1970 est. pop. 42,000), S Dahomey. It is the trade center for an agricultural region where grain and palm products are processed. The town is linked by railroad with COTONOU. Abomey was the capital of the kingdom of DAHOMEY, which was founded in the early 17th cent. and conquered by the French between 1892 and 1894. Ruins of the palaces of former Dahomey kings remain, and there is a museum. The city has a fruit research institute.

abominable snowman or **yeti,** manlike creature so named because it is associated with the perpetual snow region of the Himalayas. A figure unknown except through tracks ascribed to it and through alleged encounters, it is described as 6 or 7 ft (1.8 or 2.1 m) tall and covered with long, dark hair. Attempts after the 1950s to verify these tracks (notably by Sir Edmund HILLARY in 1960) have had no results. While many scholars dismiss the existence of the snowman as a myth, others claim that it may be a form of hitherto unclassified ape.

abortion, expulsion of the product of conception before the embryo or fetus is viable. Any interruption of human pregnancy prior to the 28th week is known as abortion. Some authorities restrict the use of this term to the first 12 weeks and refer to the premature termination of pregnancy after the placenta is formed as a miscarriage. Popularly, miscarriage is used to signify accidental premature birth at any period, as opposed to purposely induced abortion. Spontaneous abortion may occur after the death of the fetus and hemorrhage in the uterus. Spontaneous expulsion during the last two thirds of pregnancy may be due to many causes, among them infectious disease (e.g., syphilis and toxemia), endocrine dysfunction (as in hypothyroidism and diabetes), and trauma. Abortion has long been practiced and was used as a form of birth control in ancient Greece and Rome. In the Middle Ages in Western Europe it was generally accepted in the early months of pregnancy. However, in the 19th cent. opinion about abortion changed. In 1869 the Catholic Church prohibited abortion under any circumstances. In England and in the United States in the 19th cent. stringent antiabortion laws were passed. The 20th cent. has generally seen a liberalization of attitudes toward abortion. In the United States on Jan. 22, 1973, the Supreme Court ruled that a state may not prevent a woman from having an abortion during the first six months of pregnancy, thus invalidating abortion laws in some states and overturning restrictive abortion laws in many other states. Abortion was legalized in England in 1967 and is also authorized in the Soviet Union, Japan, various of the Eastern European countries, and Scandinavia. Nevertheless, different groups, because of religious or other convictions, have continued to protest abortions and in the United States have organized, pressing to prohibit them by constitutional amendment. Abortion procedures include vacuum suction, and dilation and curettage—both methods are used in the early stages of pregnancy—as well as saline injection and hysterotomy.

abracadabra (ăb"rəkədăb'rə), magical formula used by the Gnostics (see GNOSTICISM) of the 2d cent. to invoke the aid of benevolent spirits to ward off disease and affliction. It is supposed to be derived from, or similar in origin to, the abraxas, a word highly significant of the Supreme Power, which was engraved on gems and amulets or was variously worn as a protective charm. Handed down through the Middle Ages, the abracadabra gradually lost its occult significance, and its meaning was extended to cover any hocus-pocus.

Abraham [according to Gen. 17.5=father of many] or **Abram** [Heb.,=the father is high], progenitor of the Hebrews. He is the example of a man devoted to God, as in his journey to Canaan from Haran, his treatment of Lot, or his willingness to sacrifice his son. He is principally important as the founder of Judaism, the religion of a covenant. In this function he instituted circumcision and received the promise of Canaan for his people, who are descended from Isaac, the son of his old age. Gen. 11–25. Because of this dual role as founder of a race and its religion, the expression "Abraham's bosom," meaning the bliss awaiting his children, was current among later Jews and has become, for Christians, a synonym for heaven. Luke 16.22–31. His titles, Father of the Faithful and Friend of God (2 Chron. 20.7; Rom. 4.11), are used by Muslims who deem him ancestor, through Ishmael, of the Arabs. The frequent use of his name among Christians and the numerous paintings depicting the story of the sacrifice of Isaac (e.g., by Andrea del Sarto) testify to the universal reverence in which worshipers of God have held this founder of their faith. Modern biblical research tends to accept his historicity. See Sir C. L. Woolley, *Abraham: Recent Discoveries and Hebrew Origins* (1936); A. González, *Abraham, Father of Believers* (tr. 1967); H. Gaubert, *Abraham, Loved by God* (tr. 1968).

Abraham, Plains of, fairly level field adjoining the upper part of the city of Quebec, Canada. There, in 1759, the English under Gen. James Wolfe defeated the French under Gen. Louis Montcalm. The battle decided the last of the FRENCH AND INDIAN WARS and led to British supremacy in Canada. Part of the battle site is now built over, but a part is preserved as a national park. See C. P. Stacey, *Quebec, 1759: The Siege and the Battle* (1959).

Abraham ben Meir ibn Ezra: see IBN EZRA.

Abraham Lincoln Birthplace National Historic Site, 117 acres (47 hectares), central Ky., near Hodgenville; est. 1916. Abraham Lincoln was born in a log cabin in this area on Feb. 12, 1809. The exact location of the original cabin has not been conclusively established, but evidence seems to indicate that it was situated on top of the knoll where the memorial building now stands. Inside of the building is the log cabin traditionally accepted as Lincoln's birthplace.

Abram: see ABRAHAM.

Abramovich, Sholem (or **Solomon) Yakob:** see MENDELE MOCHER SFORIM.

Abramovitz, Max: see HARRISON, WALLACE KIRKMAN.

Abrams, Creighton Williams, 1914–74, U.S. military officer, b. Springfield, Mass. After graduating (1936) from West Point, he served with distinction during World War II, most notably as commander of the 37th Tank Battalion, which relieved Allied forces trapped at Bastogne during the Battle of the Bulge. After service in Korea (1953–54) and in West Germany (1960–62) during the Berlin crisis, he became (1964) vice chief of staff of the U.S. army and was promoted (1964) to the rank of general. Abrams was appointed (1967) deputy commander of U.S. forces in Vietnam under Gen. William Westmoreland and later served (1968–72) as commanding general. From 1972 until his death he was U.S. army chief of staff.

Abrantes (əbrän'tĭsh), town (1970 municipal pop. 48,161), Santarém dist., W central Portugal, in Ribatejo, on the Tagus River. It is the commercial center of a fruit growing region. Historically, Abrantes was a strategic point on the road to Lisbon. Alfonso I took it from the Moors in 1148. John I gathered his army there before the battle of Aljubarrota (1385). In the Napoleonic Wars, the French under Junot won the battle of Abrantes in 1807, but in 1810 they were unable to take the town by siege.

abrasive, material used for grinding, smoothing, cutting, or polishing another substance. Among the important natural abrasives are DIAMOND (in the form of dust and small inferior stones), CORUNDUM, emery, SAND, ground QUARTZ, PUMICE, KIESELGUHR, CHALK, and TRIPOLI. Important artificial abrasives are alundum (see ALUMINA), carborundum (see SILICON CARBIDE), boron carbide, and tungsten carbide, all of which are very hard. Since it was first produced in 1955, synthetic diamond has also become an important abrasive. Tripoli, chalk, and aluminum hydroxide, suspended in water, are efficient polishing agents. Silicon carbide, emery, and corundum are frequently mixed with cement and molded into wheels, blocks, and sticks. The finer powders are dusted on glue paper to produce emery paper, glass paper, and sandpaper. Pumice, finely powdered, is used in some toothpastes. Sand is used to great advantage in sand-blast machines. Automobile cylinders and valves are ground with emery or carborundum powder, mixed with oil, and tools are sharpened on emery wheels. Diamonds are cut by a thin revolving disk of phosphor bronze that has been impregnated with diamond dust. Materials with abrasive qualities can do much damage to machinery, especially to bearings and sliding parts.

Abravanel (əbrä'vənĕl) or **Abarbanel, Isaac** (-bärbə-), 1437–1508, Jewish theologian, biblical commentator, and financier, b. Lisbon. He served as treasurer to Alfonso V of Portugal but fled that country when he was implicated (1483) in a plot. He was then employed by Ferdinand and Isabella of Spain, until they expelled the Jews from their kingdom. He was later employed by the governments of Naples and Venice. His biblical commentaries are notable for their interpretation of the books of the Bible in terms of their various historical and social backgrounds and for their liberal quotations from Christian commentaries. Abravanel attacked the use (by Maimonides) of philosophical allegory, which he believed weakened the faith of many and thus tended to undermine the Jewish community in a precarious time. In his analyses of the Messianic prophecies he specifically denied Christian claims of Jesus as the Messiah (a dangerous position to take at that time), and looked to an impending Messianic age in which the Dispersion would end with Israel's return to the Holy Land and the reign of Messianic rule for all humanity. See study by Benzion Netanyahu (2d ed. 1968).

Abravanel or **Abarbanel, Judah,** c.1460–c.1523, Jewish philosopher, physician, and poet, son of Isaac Abravanel, b. Lisbon; he is also known as Leone Ebreo. He fled (1483) from Portugal to Spain with his father and, after the expulsion (1492) of the Jews from Spain, went to Naples, where he became (1505) physician to the viceroy. Philosophically, Abravanel was influenced by the scholars of the Platonic Academy of Florence, most notably Marsilio Ficino and Giovanni Pico della Mirandola; in addition, there are clear indications of philosophical influence from Maimonides and Ibn Gabirol. In his most celebrated work, the *Dialoghi di Amore* (published posthumously, 1535; tr. *The Philosophy of Love,* with introduction by Cecil Roth, 1937), Abravanel gave a classic exposition of platonic love. Holding love to be the dominating and motivating force within the universe, and seeing as its end a union of the lover with the idea of the beautiful and the good as embodied in the beloved, he posited as the ultimate goal of all creation a union with the sublime goodness and intellect that are contained within God. A "circle of love" is thus formed between the universe and its creator in which all things find sustenance and fulfillment. The work had a profound effect upon philosophers into the 17th cent., most notably upon Giordano Bruno and Baruch Spinoza.

Abruzzi, Luigi Amedeo, duca degli (lwē'jē ämädĕ'ō dōō'kä dä'lyē abrōōt'tsē), 1873–1933, Italian explorer and mountain climber; cousin of Victor Emmanuel III. He led (1897) the first ascent of Mt. St. Elias in Alaska. His polar expedition (1899–1900) reached a point farther north than Nansen's record. He explored (1906) the Ruwenzori range in Africa and unsuccessfully attempted (1909) to reach the peak of Mt. GODWIN-AUSTIN; the southeast ridge of the peak is named in his honor. After 1919 he explored and tried to establish colonies in East Africa. A naval officer, he served in the Italo-Turkish War and World War I. Records of his polar exploration and his Asiatic mountain climbing have been translated.

Abruzzi (äbrōōt'tsē), region (1971 pop. 1,163,334), 4,167 sq mi (10,793 sq km), central Italy, bordering on the Adriatic Sea in the east. L'AQUILA is the capital of the region, which is divided into Chieti, L'Aquila, Pescara, and Teramo provs. (named for their capitals). Abruzzi is mostly mountainous and is crossed by three ranges of the Apennines, which reach their highest point (9,560 ft/2,914 m) there in the Gran Sasso d'Italia group. There is a narrow coastal strip along the Adriatic. The chief rivers are the Pescara, the Sangro, and the Tronto. A generally poor region, Abruzzi has mostly small-scale agriculture and limited, but growing, industry. The main crops are grapes, olives, sugar beets, and tobacco; pigs and sheep are raised. The chief manufactures are processed food, textiles, clothing, and plastics. Tourism is important. Abruzzi was conquered by the Romans in the 4th cent. B.C. Later, it was part of the Lombard duchy of Spoleto (6th–11th cent. A.D.), the Norman kingdom of Sicily (12th–13th cent.), and the kingdom of Naples (13th–19th cent.). From 1948 to 1965 it was included in the region of Abruzzi e Molise. There are universities at Chieti and L'Aquila.

Absalom (ăb'səlŏm), son of David. He murdered his brother Amnon for the rape of their sister Tamar and fled. After a time he returned, but no sooner was he reconciled with his father than he stirred up a rebellion ultimately resulting in his death. 2 Sam. 3.3; 13–39; 2 Chron. 11.20,21. The form Abishalom is used in Kings 15.2,10.

Absalon (äp'sälôn) or **Axel** (äk'səl), c.1128–1201, Danish churchman, archbishop of Lund (1178–1201). He had great influence on political affairs under Waldemar I and Canute VI, warred against the pagan Wends, and in 1184 won a naval victory over Bogislav, duke of Pomerania. He attempted monastic reforms, introduced canon law into Denmark, and was patron of Svend Aagesen and Saxo Grammaticus. In 1167, Absalon was in charge of fortifying Copenhagen.

Absaroka Indians: see CROW INDIANS.

abscess, accumulation of pus in the tissues as a result of INFECTION. Abscesses are characterized by inflammation and swelling, often painful. They occur in the skin, at the root of a tooth, in the middle ear, on the eyelid (see STY), in the mammary glands, in the recto-anal area, and elsewhere in the body . In tuberculosis, abscesses (tubercles) may develop in lung tissue, in the lymph nodes, and in bone. A sinus abscess may result in a FISTULA, and abscess of the appendix in appendicitis. Unless an abscess discharges spontaneously, surgical incision and drainage is required. Many cases respond to treatment with antibiotics. See BOIL; CARBUNCLE.

abscissa: see CARTESIAN COORDINATES.

absentee ownership, system under which a person (or a corporation) controls and derives income from land in a region where he does not reside. Abuses existed in absenteeism in pre-Revolutionary France, in 19th-century Ireland, in E and SE Europe before World War I, and in some oil-producing nations of the Middle East as late as the second half of the 20th cent. Revolution and reform have abolished or greatly reduced the amount of absentee control throughout the world. In the United States the term has been applied to the concentration of economic power through various corporate devices. Chain stores and branch banking are sometimes classified as types of absentee ownership.

absinthe (ăb'sĭnth), an emerald-green, toxic LIQUEUR distilled from wormwood and other aromatics, including angelica root, sweet-flag root, star anise, and dittany, which have been macerated and steeped in alcohol. It was invented by a Dr. Ordinaire, a Frenchman who lived in Switzerland. Genuine absinthe is 70% to 80% alcohol. Because of the harmful effect it has on the nerves, it has been banned in most western countries—Switzerland (1908), the United States (1912), France (1915); an exception is Spain, where absinthe may be legally consumed.

absolute, in philosophy, term used to identify reality; the opposite of *relative.* The term has acquired numerous widely variant connotations in different philosophical systems. It means unlimited, unconditioned, or free of any relation; perfect, complete, or total; permanent, inherent, or ultimate; independent, or valid without reference to a perceiving subject. In logic, absolute means certain or indubitable as opposed to probable or hypothetical. As a substantive, the absolute is the ultimate basis of reality, the principle underlying the universe. Theologically, it is synonymous with, or characteristic of, God. Philosophically, it may be considered as the unknowable, the thing-in-itself; as that ultimate nonrelative that is the basis of all relation; as the ultimate, all-comprehensive principle in which all differences and distinctions are merged. The concept of the absolute was present in Greek philosophy. In modern times, both realists and idealists have used the term, but it is, perhaps, most intimately connected with the idealism of G. W. HEGEL.

absolute differential calculus: see TENSOR.

absolute magnitude: see MAGNITUDE.

absolute monarchy: see MONARCHY.

absolute music, term used for music dependent on its structure alone for comprehension. It is the antithesis of PROGRAM MUSIC. It is not associated with extramusical ideas or with a pictorial or narrative scheme of emotions, nor does it attempt to reproduce sounds in nature. Hence it is always instrumental, although not all instrumental music is absolute. The music of Bach is absolute music.

absolute pitch, the position of a tone in the musical scale determined according to its number of vibrations per second, irrespective of other tones. The term also denotes the capacity to identify any tone upon hearing it sounded alone or to sing any specified tone. Experiments have shown that this ability, a form of memory, can be acquired through practice, but in some individuals it appears to be inborn.

absolute temperature scale: see KELVIN TEMPERATURE SCALE; TEMPERATURE.

absolute value, magnitude of a number or other mathematical expression disregarding its sign; thus, the absolute value is positive, whether the original expression is positive or negative. In symbols, if $|a|$ denotes the absolute value of a number a, then $|a| = a$ for $a > 0$ and $|a| = -a$ for $a < 0$. For example, $|7| = 7$ since $7 > 0$ and $|-7| = -(-7)$, or $|-7| = 7$, since $-7 < 0$.

absorption [Lat.,=sucking from], taking of molecules of one substance directly into another substance. It is contrasted with ADSORPTION, in which the molecules adhere only to the surface of the second substance. Absorption may be either a physical or a chemical process, physical absorption involving such factors as solubility and vapor-pressure relationships and chemical absorption involving chemical reactions between the absorbed substance and the absorbing medium.

absorption spectrum: see SPECTRUM.

abstinence: see FASTING; TEMPERANCE MOVEMENTS.

abstract art: see ABSTRACT EXPRESSIONISM; MODERN ART.

abstract expressionism, movement of abstract painting that emerged in New York City during the mid-1940s and attained singular prominence in American art in the following decade; also called action painting and the New York school. It was the first important school in American painting to declare its independence from European styles and to influence the development of art abroad. Arshile Gorky first gave impetus to the movement. His paintings, derived at first from the art of Picasso, Miró, and surrealism, became more personally expressive. Jackson Pollock's turbulent yet elegant abstract paintings, which were created by spattering paint on huge canvases placed on the floor, brought abstract expressionism before a hostile public. Willem de Kooning's first one-man show in 1948 established him as a highly influential artist. His intensely complicated abstract paintings of the 1940s were followed by images of *Woman,* grotesque versions of buxom womanhood, which were virtually unparalleled in the sustained savagery of their execution. Other important artists were Hans Hofmann and Robert Motherwell. Painters such as Philip Guston and Franz Kline turned to the abstract late in the 1940s and soon developed strikingly original styles—the former, lyrical and evocative, the latter, forceful and boldly dramatic. Abstract expressionism presented a broad range of stylistic diversity within its largely, though not exclusively, nonrepresentational framework. For example, the expressive violence and activity in paintings by de Kooning or Pollock marked the opposite end of the pole from the simple, quiescent images of Mark Rothko. Basic to most abstract expressionist painting were the attention paid to surface qualities, i.e., qualities of brushstroke and texture; the use of huge canvases; the adoption of an approach to space in which all parts of the canvas played an equally vital role in the total work; the harnessing of accidents that occurred during the process of painting; and the glorification of the act of painting itself as a means of visual communication. The movement had an inestimable influence on the many varieties of work that followed it, especially in the way its proponents used color and materials. Its essential energy transmitted an enduring excitement to the American art scene. See articles on individuals (e.g., POLLOCK). See Michael Seuphor, *Abstract Painting: Fifty Years of Accomplishment from Kandinsky to the Present* (1962, repr. 1964); Irving Sandler, *The Triumph of American Painting: A History of Abstract Expressionism* (1970); Maurice Tuchman, ed., *The New York School: Abstract Expressionism in the 40s and 50s* (rev. ed. 1970).

abstract of title, in law, brief history of the title to a piece of land. An account is given of recorded documents, court proceedings, WILLS, MORTGAGES, taxes, previous sales, EASEMENTS, and all other factors that at any time affected the ownership or use of the land. The old rule in England required that an abstract of title should cover the 60 years before the proposed sale. In 1874 this was changed to 40 years. In some U.S. states the title is traced back to the original grant from the government, but in others it is traced only so far back as is necessary to show a present clear title.

Abu al-Abbas as-Saffah (ä'bo͝ol-äbäs' äs-säfä'), d. 754, 1st ABBASID caliph (749-54). Raised to the caliphate by the armed might of ABU MUSLIM, he took the reign name as-Saffah [shedder of blood]. Most of the Umayyad family was exterminated, and the reign was one of massacre and force. He was succeeded by his brother AL-MANSUR.

Abu al-Ala al-Maarri (ä'bo͞o äl-älä' äl-mä-är-rē'), 973-1057, Arabic freethinking poet. He was born and lived most of his life in Maarrah, S of Aleppo. He was blind from childhood. Brilliantly original, he became one of the literary reformers who discarded classicism for a modern intellectual urbanity. After 35 he lived a life of seclusion, and with his advocacy of an utterly ascetic purity, his poetry became more stereotyped. He believed in the ethical teachings of the monotheistic religions.

Abu al-Faraj: see BAR-HEBRAEUS.

Abu al-Faraj Ali of Esfahan (ä'bo͞o äl-färaj' älē', ĕsfähän'), 897-967, Arabic scholar. He is mainly known for his invaluable KITAB AL-AGHANI (book of songs), which provides detailed information about the culture and social life of medieval Islam.

Abu al-Fida (ä''bo͝ol-fē'dä, -fīdä'), 1273-1331, Arab historian, b. Damascus. He fought against the Christians in the last period of the Crusades and later became (1310) governor of Hama in Syria. He was a patron of learning and wrote a descriptive geography and a universal history, which is a superior source for Arabic history from the pre-Islamic period to 1329.

Abu Bakr (ä'bo͞o băk'ər), 573-634, 1st caliph, friend, father-in-law, and successor of Muhammad. He was probably Muhammad's first convert outside the Prophet's family and certainly his most zealous believer. He alone accompanied Muhammad on the hegira. The marriage of Abu Bakr's daughter AISHA to Muhammad made the ties even stronger. On the Prophet's death in 632, UMAR secured Abu Bakr's election over the tribal chiefs and ALI. The two years of his caliphate were critical for Islam. Though he was himself fervent rather than warlike, his party crushed opposition in Arabia and began the remarkable extension of Islam as a world religion. He was succeeded by Umar. See biography by A. Mohy-Nol-Din (1968); Asadul Qadri, *Interested Stories from the Life of Hazarat Abu Bakr Siddiq* (1970).

Abubus (əbyo͞o'bəs), father of the Ptolemy who murdered Simon the Maccabee. 1 Mac. 16.11.

Abu Dhabi (ä'bo͞o thä'bē, zä-, dä-), Arab. *Abu Zabi,* sheikhdom (1968 pop. 46,375), c.26,000 sq mi (67,300 sq km), part of the federation of UNITED ARAB EMIRATES, E Arabia, on the Persian Gulf. The sheikhdom is the largest in the federation; in it is located the town of Abu Dhabi, founded c.1760, which is the temporary capital of the federation pending the construction of a new one on the border between Abu Dhabi and DUBAI. The sheikhdom became a British protectorate in 1892. The history of Abu Dhabi has been marked by violence within the ruling dynasty; few of the rulers died a natural death. Abu Dhabi frequently clashed with the neighboring sheikhdom of Sharjah. There was a long period of tranquillity during the rule (1928-66) of Sheikh Shakhbut ibn Sultan, broken only by a war between Abu Dhabi and Dubai from 1945 to 1948. Oil was discovered in Abu Dhabi in the early 1960s. The oil revenues have been used for development and modernization. Abu Dhabi became part of the United Arab Emirates when it was formed in 1971.

Abu Hanifa (äbo͞o' hänē'fä), 699-767, Muslim jurist. He founded the Hanafite system of Islamic jurisprudence, which gives the judge considerable discretion when the Koran and the Sunna (traditions) are inapplicable (see ISLAM).

Abukir: see ABU QIR, Egypt.

Abulcasis (ä'bo͝olkä'sĭs) or **Abu Khasim** (ä'bo͞o kä'-sĭm), Arabian physician, d. c.1013, b. near Córdoba, Spain. His chief work, a detailed account of surgery and medicine, was for many years the leading surgical textbook. Known as the *Tasrif* [the collection], it consisted of three parts, dealing with cautery, with surgery, and with fractures and dislocations. It was translated many times into Latin and into other languages. His name also appears as Albucasis.

Abulfazl (ä'bo͝olfä'zəl, ə'bo͝olfŭz'əl), 1551-1602, minister of state and adviser to AKBAR, Mogul emperor of India. His *Book of Akbar,* in Persian, recounts the history of the reign, describing the political and religious organization of the empire. He was in part responsible for the development of Akbar's eclectic religion, Din-i-Ilahi. Abulfazl was murdered at the instigation of Akbar's heir, the later emperor Jahangir.

Abu Muslim (ä'bo͞o mo͝os'lĭm), c.728-755, Persian leader of the ABBASID revolution. By political and religious agitation he raised (747) the black banners of the Abbasids against the ruling UMAYYAD family. In 749 he established ABU AL-ABBAS AS-SAFFAH, the head of the Abbasid family, as caliph of Islam. Abu Muslim became governor of Khurasan, but the caliph Mansur feared his power and treacherously murdered him.

Abu Nuwas (ä'bo͞o no͞owäs'), d. c.810, Arabic poet, b. Ahvaz, Persia. He spent most of his life in Baghdad. High in favor with the caliphs Harun ar-Rashid and Amin, he lived a courtier's life; his exquisite lyric poetry echoes the extravagance of this life.

Abu Qir or **Abukir** (both: ä''bo͞okēr', əbo͞o'kər), village, N Egypt, on a promontory in the Nile River delta. Admiral Horatio Nelson's victory over the French fleet off Abu Qir on Aug. 1, 1798 (sometimes called the battle of the Nile), restored British prestige in the Mediterranean region and, with the land victory (1801) led by Sir Ralph Abercromby, cut short the French venture in the Middle East begun by Napoleon I.

Abu Said ibn Abi al-Khair (ä'bo͞o sä'ĭd ĭ'bən äbē' äl-khīr'), 967-1049, Persian poet, a Sufi and a dervish. He was the first to write rubaiyat (quatrains) in the Sufistic strain that Omar Khayyam made famous.

Abu-Simbel (ä''bo͞o-sĭm'bəl) or **Ipsambul** (ĭp'-sämbo͞ol'), village, S Egypt, on the Nile River. Its two temples, hewn (c.1250 B.C.) out of rock cliffs during the reign of Ramses II, were raised over 200 ft (61 m) to avoid the rising waters caused by the construction of the Aswan High Dam. UNESCO solicited funds from 52 nations for the salvage of the Nubian archaeological treasure. The colossal statues of Ramses II and the temples were cut into 950 blocks, raised, and reassembled farther inland. The job was finished in 1966.

Abu Tammam Habib ibn Aus (täm-mäm' häbēb' ĭ'bən ous), c.805-c.845, Arabic poet, compiler of the HAMASA. His poems of valor, often describing historical events, are important as source material.

abutilon (əbyo͞ot'əlŏn): see MALLOW.

Abydos (əbī'dəs), ancient city of Egypt, c.50 mi (80 km) NW of Thebes. Associated in religion with Osiris, Abydos became the most venerated place in Egypt. It was the favorite burial place for the kings of the earliest dynasties, and later kings such as Seti I and Ramses II continued to build temples and sanctuaries there. Its remains date from the I to the XXVI dynasty (3100-500 B.C.). A famous list of kings, found on the wall of the temple built by Seti I, has been valuable in determining the order of succession among the Egyptian kings from Menes to Seti.

Abydos, ancient town of Phrygia, Asia Minor, on the Asiatic side of the Hellespont opposite Sestos, in present-day Turkey. It was originally a Milesian colony. Near there Xerxes built his bridge of boats in 480 B.C., and in 411 the Athenian fleet defeated the Spartans. A free city until it was taken by Philip V of Macedon in 200 B.C., it became a major city of Antiochus III. It was the scene of the story of Hero and Leander.

abyssal plain: see OCEAN.

Abyssinia (ăb''ĭsĭn'ēyə): see ETHIOPIA.

Abyssinian cat: see CAT.

Abzine, mountains, Africa: see SAHARA.

Abzug, Bella Savitsky (səvĭt'skē ăb'zo͝og), 1920-, U.S. Congresswoman (1971-), b. New York City. Admitted to the bar in 1947, she handled many labor, civil rights, and civil liberties cases. Abzug helped found (1961) the Women's Strike for Peace to protest the testing of nuclear weapons and served (1961-70) as its legislative director. A founder (1968) of the reform-oriented New Democratic Coalition, she was elected to the U.S. House of Representatives (1970), where she quickly became a leader of the House antiwar movement. Abzug became known as a sharp critic of the House seniority system and a vigorous proponent of women's rights. See her *Bella! Ms. Abzug Goes to Washington,* ed. by Mel Ziegler (1972).

Ac, chemical symbol of the element ACTINIUM.

AC: see ALTERNATING CURRENT.

acacia (əkā'shə), any plant of the large leguminous genus *Acacia,* often thorny shrubs and trees of the family Leguminosae (PULSE family). Chiefly of the tropics and subtropics, they are cultivated for decorative and economic purposes. Acacias are characteristic of savanna vegetation and are especially numerous in the South African bushveld. The foliage often appears feathery because of the many small leaflets, but in some species leaflike flattened stems contain chlorophyll and take the place of leaves. Various Old World species (especially *A. arabica* and *A. senegal*) yield gum arabic; other species, chiefly *A. catechu,* yield the dye CATECHU. Blackwood (*A. melanoxylon*) is valued in Australia for its hardwood timber. Other members of the genus are valuable for LAC, for perfume and essential oils, and for tannins; some are used as ornamentals. The Australian acacias are commonly called wattles—their pliable branches were woven into the structure of the early wattle houses and fences—and Wattle Day celebrates the national flower at blossoming time. Many wattles are cultivated elsewhere, particularly in California, as ornamentals for their characteristic spherical, dense flowers. The Central American bullhorn acacias (e.g., *A. sphaerocephala*) have large hollow thorns inhabited by ants that are said to feed upon a sweet secretion of the plant and in turn guard it against leaf-eating insects. The most common acacia indigenous to the United States is the cat's-claw (*A. gregii*) of the arid Southwest. The Biblical SHITTIM WOOD is thought to have come from an acacia. Various species of locust are sometimes called acacia, and acacias may be called mimosa; all are of the same family. Acacia is classified in the division MAGNOLIOPHYTA, class Magnoliopsida, order Rosales, family Leguminosae.

academic freedom, right of scholars to pursue research, to teach, and to publish without control or restraint from the institutions that employ them. It is a civil right that is enjoyed, at least in statute, by all citizens of democratic countries. In the case of scholars, whose occupation is directly involved with that right, the concept of academic freedom generally includes the property right of tenure of office (see TENURE, in education). Essential to the acceptance of the concept of academic freedom is the notion that truth is best discovered through the open investigation of all data. A less clearly developed corollary of academic freedom is the obligation of all those who enjoy it to pursue the line of open and thorough inquiry regardless of personal considerations. Historically, academic freedom developed during the Enlightenment. Early cultures, which viewed education as a system of absorbing a well-defined content of subject matter, offered little opportunity for speculation. The medieval universities also operated within a field of definite scope, primarily theological, and any teacher or scholar who extended his inquiry beyond the approved limits was subject to the charge of heresy. The scientific method of analyzing data and establishing hypotheses, a vital concomitant of academic freedom, was initiated during the Enlightenment, mainly by scholars outside university life such as Thomas Hobbes, John Locke, and Voltaire. It was in the Prussia of Frederick the Great that the new freedom first flourished within the university itself. In England, it was laymen like Jeremy Bentham, David Ricardo, Herbert Spencer, Charles Darwin, and Thomas Huxley who demonstrated the value of free investigation. Before the concept of academic freedom could gain general acceptance, however, it was necessary that education become secularized. It was not until 1828 that the first nonsectarian university was established in London. In the United States the early colleges were also religiously controlled, and there are still some denominational schools that define areas of inquiry. The AMERICAN ASSOCIATION OF UNIVERSITY PROFESSORS has been active in establishing standards of academic freedom and has investigated cases in which the right was alleged to have been jeopardized. See Richard Hofstadter and W. P. Metzger, *The Development of Academic Freedom in the U.S.* (1955); R. M. MacIver, *Academic Freedom in Our Time* (1955, repr. 1967); Jack Nelson and Gene Roberts, Jr., *Censors and the Schools* (1963); Louis Joughin, *Academic Freedom and Tenure: A Handbook of the AAUP* (rev. ed. 1969); W. P. Metzger et al., *Dimensions of Academic Freedom* (1969); Sidney Hook, ed., *In Defense of Academic Freedom* (1971).

Académie française: see FRENCH ACADEMY.

academies of art, official organizations of established artists. Lorenzo de' Medici's informal circle of great artists and thinkers was modeled on similar groups formed in classical Greece. The first official academy, the Accademia del Disegno, was founded in Florence by Vasari in 1561. Offshoots of this were the prototypes for the powerful Academie royale de peinture et de sculpture founded in 1648, the first of many French academies. The academies dictated elaborate conventions and aesthetic doctrines for the manufacture of works of art and the term "academic" came to imply derivative rather than creative work. The English Royal Academy, founded in 1768, now serves primarily as an art school and exhibition facility. The AMERICAN ACADEMY IN ROME is a school that embraces many fields including music and classical studies.

Academy, school founded by PLATO near Athens c.387 B.C. It took its name from the garden (named for the hero Academus) in which it was located. Plato's followers met there for nine centuries until, along with other pagan schools, it was closed by Emperor Justinian in A.D. 529. The Academy has come to mean the entire school of Platonic philosophy, covering the period from Plato through Cicero. During this period Platonic philosophy was modified in various ways. These have been frequently divided into three phases: the Old Academy (until c.250 B.C.) of Plato, SPEUSIPPUS, and XENOCRATES; the Middle Academy (until c.150 B.C.) of ARCESILAUS and CARNEADES, who introduced and maintained skepticism as being more faithful to Plato and Socrates; and the New Academy (c.110 B.C.) of Philo of Larissa, who, with subsequent leaders, returned to the dogmatism of the Old Academy.

Acadia (əkā'dēə), region and former French colony, E Canada, centered on Nova Scotia but including also New Brunswick, Prince Edward Island, and the mainland coast from the Gulf of St. Lawrence S into Maine. The first and chief town, Port Royal (now ANNAPOLIS ROYAL, N.S.), was founded by the sieur de Monts in 1605 and was soon involved in the imperial struggle that was to end in America with the FRENCH AND INDIAN WARS. Destroyed by English colonists under Samuel ARGALL in 1613, the town was later rebuilt, and as British claims temporarily lapsed (see NOVA SCOTIA), the colony grew to be fairly prosperous with farmers on their dike-protected fields, fishermen on the shore, and fur traders in the forests. Later, attacks on Port Royal were resumed, and its capture by the British in 1710 was confirmed as permanent in the Peace of Utrecht (1713). The British feared and distrusted their French-speaking, Roman Catholic neighbors, who were friendly with the Indians and, wishing only to remain neutral, refused to swear allegiance to Great Britain. In 1755 the British fell upon the peaceful Acadian farms and, seizing most of the Acadians, deported them to the more southerly British colonies, scattering them along the Atlantic coast from Maine to Georgia and sending some to the West Indies and Europe. The men were sent first, families were separated, farmhouses burned, and some lands abandoned to waste. A second expulsion took place in 1758. Later many exiles returned. Today in Canada, Acadian (French *Acadien*) means a French-speaking inhabitant of the Maritime Provinces. Many exiles who did not return found havens elsewhere, the most celebrated being the region around St. Martinville in S Louisiana, where the Cajuns—as they are popularly called—still maintain a separate folk culture. The sufferings of the expulsion are pictured in Longfellow's *Evangeline*. See G. F. Clarke, *So Small a World: The Story of Acadia* (1958); J. B. Brebner, *New England's Outpost* (1927, repr. 1965); A. H. Clark, *Acadia: The Geography of Early Nova Scotia to 1760* (1968).

Acadia National Park, 41,642 acres (16,853 hectares), SE Maine, on the Atlantic coast; est. 1919. The park occupies a major portion of Mount Desert Island, Isle au Haut and several smaller islands, and the southern tip of Schoodic Peninsula. Almost completely surrounded by the sea, the park is characterized by a rugged, glacier-scoured interior with numerous valleys, lakes, and peaks, and a wave-eroded coastline. A great variety of land and sea life, both plant and animal, as well as several museums and nature centers are found in Acadia. During the 17th and early 18th cent. the region was part of France's New World territory of *La Cadie*.

Acadia University, at Wolfville, N.S., Canada; founded 1838; became Acadia University 1891. It has faculties of arts and science, engineering, home economics, music, theology, education, and business administration. Associated with the university is the Canada-Commonwealth Caribbean Centre.

Acajutla (äkäho͞ot'lä), town (1961 pop. 3,662), SW El Salvador, on the Pacific Ocean. It is a coffee and fishing port and a railroad terminus.

acanthus (əkăn'thəs), common name for a member of the Acanthaceae, a family of chiefly perennial herbs and shrubs, mostly native to the tropics. A few members of the family, many of which have decorative spiny leaves, are cultivated as ornamentals—especially the Mediterranean acanthus, or bear's-breech (genus *Acanthus*), whose ornate leaves were the source of a stylized motif used in Greek and Roman art (see CORINTHIAN ORDER). In Christian art the acanthus symbolizes heaven. Some species of the genus *Ruellia* are native to and cultivated as ornamentals in North America, chiefly in the South. Acanthus is classified in the division MAGNOLIOPHYTA, class Magnoliopsida, order Scrophulariaceae, family Acanthaceae.

Acapulco (äk"əpo͞ol'kō), city (1970 pop. 234,866), Guerrero state, S Mexico. A fashionable resort, it has lavish hotels and facilities for deep-sea fishing and skin diving. Its fine natural harbor, surrounded by cliffs and promontories, served as a base for Spaniards exploring the Pacific and later played a key role in trade with the Philippines. Today, however, the port is little used for commerce. Coconuts, beans, and bananas are grown in the area. Near the city, which was founded in 1550, are the archeological remains of the Ciudad Perdida [lost city], estimated to be 2,000 years old. Acapulco has suffered frequent earthquake and hurricane damage.

Acarnania (ăk"ərnā'nēə), region of ancient Greece, between the Achelous River and the Ionian Sea. The inhabitants maintained their isolation, contributing little to Greek civilization. The chief city was Stratos. The Acarnanians generally sided with Athens, and Athens helped Acarnania to uphold its independence against Corinth and Sparta in the 5th cent. B.C. Later (390–375 B.C.) Sparta controlled the region. The persistent struggle with the Aetolians cost Acarnania national existence for a time, but it was restored and the Acarnanians kept some autonomy under the Roman Empire until the Christian era. When the Byzantine Empire broke up (1204), Acarnania passed to Epirus and in 1480 to the Turks. In 1832 it became part of Greece.

Acarya: see BHASKARA.

Acastus (əkăs'təs), in Greek mythology, son of Pelias, cousin of Jason. He accompanied Jason on the Argonaut expedition, but when Jason and Medea murdered Pelias and usurped the throne of Iolcus, Acastus drove them away. Later, his wife fell in love with Peleus, the father of Achilles, who did not return her affection. Enraged, she falsely accused him of raping her. Acastus took revenge by leaving Peleus unprotected on Mt. Pelion. Rescued by the centaur Chiron, Peleus subsequently captured Iolcus and killed Acastus and his wife.

Accad: see AKKAD.

Accademia della Crusca (äk-kädĕ'mēä dĕl'lä kro͞os'kä) [Ital.,=academy of the chaff], Italian literary society founded in Florence in 1582 to maintain the purity of the language. Leonardo Salviati, influenced by Pietro Bembo, and the poet Grazzini formed the society to unify literary Italian on the model of the vernacular of Tuscany. A comedy by Lorenzino de' Medici, *L'Aridosio*, was chosen as a standard, as were two plays by the artist and poet Michelangelo Buonarroti, first consul of the society. The major work of the society was the compilation of Grazzini's *Vocabulario*, a dictionary of "pure" words, first published in 1612. It has gone through many editions and remains one of the finest Italian dictionaries. The society succeeded in establishing literary purism in Italy for several centuries. Joined with two other academies, it is still in existence.

Acca Larentia (ăk'ə lərĕn'shēə,-shə) or **Acca Larentina** (-tī'nə), in Roman mythology, wife of the shepherd Faustulus and foster mother of Romulus and Remus. Her 12 sons founded the priesthood of the ARVAL BROTHERS. According to one legend she was a wealthy courtesan who left all her money to the people of Rome.

Accaron: see EKRON.

Accault, Michel: see ACO, MICHEL.

acceleration, change in the VELOCITY of a body with respect to time. Since velocity is a VECTOR quantity, involving both magnitude and direction, acceleration is also a vector. In order to produce an acceleration, a FORCE must be applied to the body. The magnitude of the force F must be directly proportional to both the mass of the body m and the desired acceleration a, according to Newton's second law of motion, $F=ma$. The exact nature of the acceleration produced depends on the relative directions of the original velocity and the force. A force acting in the same direction as the velocity changes only the SPEED of the body. An appropriate force acting always at right angles to the velocity changes the direction of the velocity but not the speed. An example of such an accelerating force is the gravitational force exerted by a planet on a satellite moving in a circular orbit. A force may also act in the opposite direction from the original velocity. In this case the speed of the body is decreased. Such an acceleration is often referred to as a deceleration. The following formulas may be used to compute the acceleration a of a body from knowledge of the elapsed time t, the distance s through which the body moves in that time, the initial velocity v_i, and the final velocity v_f:

$$a=(v_f^2-v_i^2)/2s$$
$$a=2(s-v_it)/t^2$$
$$a=(v_f-v_i)/t$$

accelerator: see PARTICLE ACCELERATOR.

accent, in speech, emphasis given a particular sound, called prosodic systems in linguistics. There are three basic accentual methods: stress, tone, and length. In English each word has at least one primary stressed syllable, as in *weath'er;* words of several syllables may also have secondary stress as in *el'e-va"-tor.* In English, vowels in unaccented syllables are often pronounced as ə regardless of the orthographic letter. Thus, the vowels of the second syllables in *cir'cus, na'tion, ther'mos, eas'ily, saun'a,* and *sor'rel* are all pronounced the same. Sentence stress, known as intonation or contour, includes three basic patterns: the statement, *It's a dog,* where the pitch pattern is level-high-low; the yes/no question, *Is it a dog?* where the pattern is level-high pitch; and the command, *Catch him!* which begins high and ends low. Both word stress and sentence stress are obligatory in English. However, emphasis of certain words within a sentence is optional. Tonal languages, such as Chinese and Swedish, have a system of high:low and/or rising:falling tones. Duration or length of sounds (quantity) is used in some languages to create systematic differences. No language uses all three types of accentual systems. In writing, accent is also used to show syllable stress as in Spanish *María* (acute accent) and Italian *pietà* (grave accent). Such written symbols, misleadingly termed accents, are often used only to signal specific pronunciation rather than stress, as in French *élève*. The word *accent* in English is also understood to mean the pronunciation and speech patterns that are typical of a speech community, as foreign accent, hillbilly accent, upper-class accent; it also denotes the particular manner of uttered expression that lends a special shade of meaning, as when one speaks in harsh or gentle accents. See also ABLAUT and PHONETICS.

accessory, in criminal law, a person who, though not present at the commission of a crime, becomes a participator in the crime either before or after the fact of commission. An accessory before the fact is one whose counsel or instigation leads another to commit a crime. An accessory after the fact is one who, having knowledge that a crime has been committed, aids, or attempts to aid, the criminal to escape apprehension. In a MISDEMEANOR and in treason there is no distinction between principals and accessories. In some states the common law distinction between principal and accessory before the fact has been abolished, and the accessory before the fact is prosecuted as a principal. The penalties for being an accessory are usually much less severe than those meted out to the principal. Except where statutes provide differently, an accessory cannot be tried without his consent before the conviction of the principal, unless both are tried together. If an accessory is called as a witness, the court must decide if he is also an accomplice, because the testimony of an accomplice must be corroborated. An accomplice has been defined as any person who could be prosecuted for the crime of which the defendant is accused. This would include principals and accessories before the fact; depending on the jurisdiction and the facts of the case it might also include conspirators (see under CONSPIRACY) and accessories after the fact. See STOLEN GOODS.

Accho (ăk'ō), Old Testament variant of AKKO.

accident, in law, an unusual or unexpected event producing physical injury or loss of property. The term includes events that happen without human agency (see ACT OF GOD) and those that are produced through human agency although without design. When not an act of God, an accident ordinarily involves NEGLIGENCE on the part of the perpetrator. Such terms as "mere accident" or "pure accident," however, connote absence of negligence. An inevitable accident is an act of God or an event produced through human agency that could not be foreseen or prevented. In EQUITY, relief may be given from the effects of an accident that benefits a party; thus, if by accident the boundaries of property are confused, the party injured may seek a judicial determination of the true boundaries. In INSURANCE and in WORKMEN'S COMPENSATION statutes, the term accident has specifically defined meanings.

Accolti, Benedetto (bānādĕt'tō äk-kôl'tē), c.1415–1466?, Italian humanist and historian. From his history of the First Crusade, Tasso supposedly drew the idea for *Jerusalem Delivered*. His son **Bernardo Accolti,** 1465?–1535, was known in his day for extemporaneous poems. Another son, **Pietro Accolti,** 1455–1532, was a cardinal and drew up (1520) the papal bull against Martin Luther.

accomplice: see ACCESSORY.

accordion, musical instrument consisting of a rectangular bellows expanded and contracted between the hands. Buttons or keys operated by the player open valves, allowing air to enter or to escape. The air sets in motion free reeds, frequently made of metal. The length, density, shape, and elasticity of the reeds determine the pitch. The first accordions were made in 1822 by Friedrich Buschmann in Berlin. Bouton added a keyboard 30 years later in Paris, thus producing a piano accordion. The accordion is frequently used in folk music. See CONCERTINA.

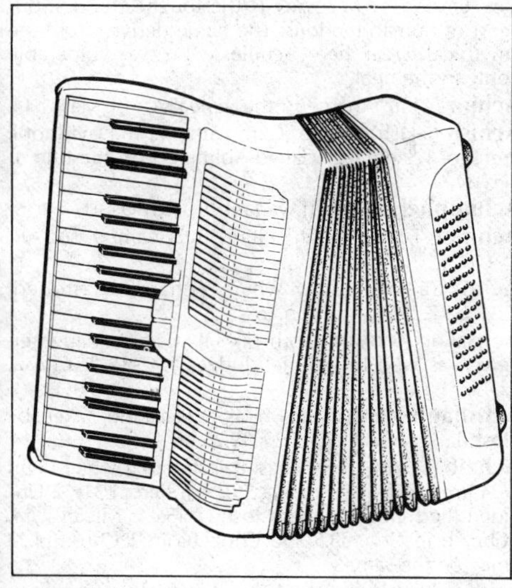
Accordion

accounting, classification, analysis, and interpretation of the financial, or BOOKKEEPING, records of an enterprise. The professional who supplies such services is known as an accountant. The accountant evaluates records drawn up by the bookkeeper and shows the results of his investigation as losses and gains, leakages, economies, or changes in value, so as to reveal the progress or failures of the business and also its future limitations and possibilities. An accountant must also be able to draw up a set of financial records and prescribe the system of accounts that will most easily give the desired information; he must be capable of arriving at a comprehensive view of the economic and the legal aspects of a business, envisaging the effect of every sort of transaction on the profit and loss statement; and he must recognize and classify all other factors that enter into the determination of the true condition of the business, e.g., statistics or memoranda relating to production, and properties and financial records representing investment, expenditures, receipts, fiscal changes, and present standing. Cost accounting shows the actual cost in a certain period of each service rendered or of each article produced; by this system unprofitable ventures, services, departments, and methods may be discovered. Although there were stewards, auditors, and bookkeepers in ancient times, the professional accountant is a 19th-century development. Unlike his precursors, the modern accountant usually does not serve only one employer; instead he offers his services, for a fee, to various individuals and businesses. The profession was first recognized in Great Britain in 1854, when the Society of Accountants in Edinburgh was given a royal charter. Similar societies were later established in Glasgow, Aberdeen, and London. In the United States the first such professional society was the American Association of Public Accountants, chartered by the state of New York in 1887. All the states and also Puerto Rico and the District of Columbia now have laws under which the public accountant who complies with certain educational and experience requirements and passes the required examination may be granted the title Certified Public Accountant (CPA). The holders of such certificates have organized into societies in most of the states. The bodies representing the accounting profession in the United States are the American Institute of Accountants, which succeeded the American Association of Public Accountants in 1916, and the American Accounting Association, also organized in 1916. With the growth of corporate activity in the 20th cent., accounting has increased greatly in importance and has undergone many improvements in theory and techniques. The chief influences on modern accounting have been the increasingly complex income tax structure and the need to keep uniform accounts for possible governmental or public scrutiny. Much of contemporary accounting has taken on managerial functions and is no longer primarily concerned with ascertaining financial condition but rather with how a company can act on this information. AUDITING is an important branch of accounting. See N. A. H. Stacey, *English Accountancy, 1800–1954* (1954); Morton Backer, ed., *Modern Accounting Theory* (1966); Louis Goldberg and V. R. Hill, *The Elements of Accounting* (3d ed. 1966); James D. Edwards, *History of Public Accounting in the United States* (1960); A. J. Briloff, *Unaccountable Accounting* (1972).

Accra (əkrä', ăk'rə), city (1970 pop. 564,194), capital of Ghana, a port on the Gulf of Guinea. It is Ghana's largest city and its administrative, communications, and economic center. The chief manufactures are processed food, beverages, timber and plywood, textiles, clothing, chemicals, and printed materials. A transportation hub, Accra is linked by road and rail with KUMASI, in the interior, and with TEMA, a major seaport. Accra originally was the village-sized capital of a Ga kingdom. It developed into a sizable town around British and Dutch forts built in the 17th cent. In 1876, Accra replaced CAPE COAST as the capital of the British Gold Coast colony. After the completion (1923) of a railroad to the mining and agricultural hinterland, Accra rapidly became the economic center of Ghana. Riots in the city (1948), against high retail prices and European control, led to the rise of Kwame NKRUMAH as a popular leader and marked an important early step in Ghana's road to independence (1957). Today Accra is a sprawling, modern city with wide avenues. It is the site of the national museum and Ghana's central library. Also of note is Christianborg Castle, built by the Danes in the 17th cent. On Accra's outskirts are Achimota School (1927), the country's leading secondary school, and, in Legon, the Univ. of Ghana (1948). The Defense Commission of the Organization of African Unity has its headquarters in Accra.

Accrington, municipal borough (1971 pop. 36,838), Lancashire, NW England. The principal industry is cotton weaving. Textile printing and dyeing and the manufacture of machinery and bricks are also important.

acculturation, the more or less continuous interaction between groups brought about by accommodation and resulting in the intermixture of shared, learned behavior patterns. It may result in almost complete absorption of the CULTURE of one of the groups or a relatively equal merging of traits and patterns from both cultures. Not infrequently, acculturative processes result in considerable social disturbance and individual psychological maladjustment. After World War II one of the most active areas in acculturation study was the one often termed "applied anthropology," in which attention was focused on practical programs aimed at desired changes in societies or subcultures dominated by others.

accusative (əkyōō'zətĭv") [Lat.,=accusing], in Latin grammar, the CASE typically meaning that the noun refers to the entity directly affected by an action. The term is used for similar, but often not identical, features in the grammar of other languages. Thus in English *him,* usually called objective, is also called accusative.

Aceldama (əsĕl'dəmə) [according to Acts 1.18,19= field of blood], potter's field bought with Judas' 30 pieces of silver; it is apparently the place where Judas died. The purchase of this field to bury strangers in is the origin of the term "potter's field" for the paupers' burying ground. Mat. 27.3–10; Acts 1.19,20.

acetaldehyde (ăs"ĭtăl'dəhīd) or **ethanal,** CH_3CHO, colorless liquid ALDEHYDE, sometimes simply called aldehyde. It melts at −123°C, boils at 20.8°C, and is soluble in water and ethanol. It is formed by the partial oxidation of ethanol; oxidation of acetaldehyde forms acetic acid. Acetaldehyde is made commercially by the addition of water to acetylene in the presence of sulfuric acid and mercuric sulfate. It is used as a reducing agent (e.g., for silvering mirrors), in the manufacture of synthetic resins and dyestuffs, and as a preservative. When treated with a small amount of sulfuric acid it forms paraldehyde, $(CH_3CHO)_3$, a trimer, which is used as a hypnotic drug.

acetate, one of the most important forms of artificial cellulose-based fibers. The first patents for the production of fibers from cellulose acetate appeared at the beginning of the 20th cent. During World War I, production of acetylcellulose began on an industrial scale for military applications. Acetate fibers are basically delivered in the form of a continuous textile yarn. Their principal use is in the production of widely used consumer goods, such as men's shirts, women's blouses, underwear, ties, bathing suits, jersey jackets and sweaters, suit fabrics, coats, and sports clothing.

acetic acid (əsē'tĭk), CH_3CO_2H, colorless liquid that has a characteristic pungent odor, boils at 118°C, and is miscible with water in all proportions; it is a weak organic carboxylic acid (see CARBOXYL GROUP). Glacial acetic acid is concentrated, 99.5% pure acetic acid; it solidifies at about 17°C to a crystalline mass resembling ice. Acetic acid is the major acid in VINEGAR; as such, it is widely used as a food preservative and condiment. For industrial use concentrated acetic acid is prepared from acetylene by a reaction yielding ACETALDEHYDE, which is then oxidized to produce acetic acid. Acetic acid is also a product in the destructive distillation of wood. It reacts with other chemicals to form numerous compounds of commercial importance. These include cellulose acetate, used in making acetate rayon, nonflammable motion-picture film, lacquers, and plastics; various inorganic salts, e.g., lead, potassium, and copper acetates; and amyl, butyl, ethyl, methyl, and propyl acetates, which are used as solvents, chiefly in certain quick-drying lacquers and cements. Amyl acetate is sometimes called banana oil because it has a characteristic banana odor.

acetone (ăs'ĭtōn), **dimethyl ketone** (dīmĕth'əl kē'tōn), or **2-propanone** (prō'pənōn), CH_3COCH_3, colorless, flammable liquid. Acetone melts at

−94.8°C and boils at 56.2°C. It is the simplest aliphatic KETONE. Acetone is widely used in industry as a solvent for numerous organic substances and is a component of most paint and varnish removers. It is used in the manufacture of synthetic resins and fillers, smokeless powders (e.g., cordite), and numerous other organic compounds. Acetone is produced commercially chiefly by catalytic dehydrogenation of isopropanol.

acetylcholine (əsēt″əlkō′lēn), organic compound containing carbon, hydrogen, oxygen, and nitrogen. It is liberated at nerve cell endings, and there is strong evidence that it is the transmitter substance that conducts impulses from one cell to another in the ganglia of the autonomic nervous system; from nerve cells to smooth muscle, cardiac muscle, and exocrine glands; and from motor nerve cells to skeletal muscle. Its role in the conduction of nerve impulses elsewhere is still uncertain. The stimulation of skeletal muscle by acetylcholine is inhibited by curare. See NERVOUS SYSTEM.

acetylene (əsĕt′əlēn″) or **ethyne** (ĕth′īn), $HC\equiv CH$, a colorless gas. It melts at −80.8°C and boils at −84.0°C. Offensive odors often noted in commercial acetylene are due to impurities. Acetylene forms explosive mixtures with oxygen or air. It is soluble in acetone, ethanol, and water. When dissolved in acetone it is nonexplosive and so is stored dissolved in acetone under pressure in steel cylinders for commercial use. Since it is explosive in the liquid state, it is not generally stored in this form. Acetylene is usually prepared commercially by the reaction of calcium CARBIDE with water. It is used for cutting and welding metals (see OXYACETYLENE TORCH) and is sometimes used as an illuminant gas. When subjected to high temperatures, it undergoes polymerization; benzene may also be formed. It is used in the production of many organic compounds, e.g., neoprene rubber, plastics, and resins. Acetylene is the simplest ALKYNE.

acetylene series: see ALKYNE.

acetylsalicylic acid (əsēt″əlsăl″ĭsĭl′ĭk), acetate ester of SALICYLIC ACID. See ASPIRIN.

Achaea (əkē′ə), region of ancient Greece, in the northern part of the Peloponnesus on the Gulf of Corinth. It lay between Sicyon and Elis. There the Achaeans supposedly remained when driven from other parts of Greece by the Dorian invasion. The small Achaean cities eventually banded together in the First ACHAEAN LEAGUE. In the late 8th cent. B.C. the Achaeans colonized part of S Italy but were at first of little significance in Greek politics. Later, however, the Second Achaean League became an important factor. After the downfall of the league, the name Achaea, or Achaia, was given to a Roman province in the Peloponnesus.

Achaean League (əkē′ən), confederation of cities on the Gulf of Corinth. The First Achaean League, about which little is known, was formed presumably before the 5th cent. B.C. and lasted through the 4th cent. B.C. Its purpose was mutual protection against pirates. The Achaeans remained aloof from the wars in Greece until they joined the opposition to Philip II of Macedon in 338 B.C. The confederation was dissolved soon after. The Second Achaean League was founded in 280 B.C. Sicyon was freed from the rule of its tyrant in 251 B.C., and it soon joined the confederation under the leadership of ARATUS. Other cities outside Achaea were incorporated on terms of equality, and in 247 B.C. the Macedonians were driven from Corinth. There was some promise of liberating all Greece, but unfortunately the interference of CLEOMENES III of Sparta threatened the Achaean League, and in 227 B.C. he began a war. The Achaean League then requested (224 B.C.) Macedonian aid against Sparta and the Aetolian League. The result was the eclipse of the confederation until the wars between Macedon and Rome. In 198 B.C. the Achaeans went over to Rome and with Roman aid won practically the whole Peloponnesus, forcing Sparta and Messene to join. Later suspecting the Achaeans of again looking toward Macedon, the Romans deported (168 B.C.) many of them (including POLYBIUS) to Italy. Anti-Roman feeling grew, and in 146 B.C. the Achaenas waged a suicidal war. Rome easily triumphed at Corinth, dissolved the confederation, and ended Greek liberty. A smaller Achaean League was formed, but it was powerless.

Achaeans, people of ancient Greece, of unknown origin. In Homer, the Achaeans are specifically a Greek-speaking people of S Thessaly. Historically, they seem to have appeared in the Peloponnesus during the 14th and 13th cent. B.C., and c.1250 B.C. they became the ruling class. There is no sharp line of separation between the earlier MYCENAEAN CIVILIZATION and the Achaean; the cultures seem to have intermingled. The invasions of the DORIANS supposedly forced some of the Achaeans out to Asia Minor; others were concentrated in the region known in classical times as Achaea.

Achaemenids (ăk″əmĕn′ĭdz), dynasty of ancient Persia. They were descended presumably from one Achaemenes, a minor ruler in a mountainous district of SW Iran. His successors, when ELAM declined, spread their power westward. CYRUS THE GREAT established the Persian rule by his conquest of ASTYAGES of MEDIA. The Achaemenids (c.550–330 B.C.) were important for their development of government administration, the appearance of literature written in CUNEIFORM, and the spread of ZOROASTRIANISM; during this period there was also a great flourishing of PERSIAN ART AND ARCHITECTURE. The Achaemenid rulers after Cyrus were Cambyses, the impostor Smerdis, Darius I, Xerxes I, Artaxerxes I, Xerxes II, Sogdianus, Darius II, Artaxerxes II (opposed by Cyrus the Younger), Artaxerxes III, Arses, and Darius III. The dynasty ended when Darius III died in his flight from Alexander the Great.

Achaeus (əkē′əs): see CREUSA **1.**

Achaicus (əkā′ĭkəs), a Christian. 1 Cor. 16.17,18.

Achai of Shabcha: see AHA OF SHABCHA.

Achan (ā′kăn) or **Achar** (ā′kär), Judahite who kept some of the spoil from the city of Jericho. For this he was stoned. Joshua 7; 1 Chron. 2.7.

Achard, Franz Karl (fränts kärl äkh′ärt), 1753–1821, German chemist. He made pioneer use of the discovery by his countryman Andreas Marggraf of sugar in beetroots. The government granted him an estate in Silesia where, in 1806, he succeeded in producing beet sugar. Among his other contributions is the discovery of a method for working platinum.

Achaz (ā′kăz), variant of AHAZ. Mat. 1.9.

Achbor (ăk′bôr), same as ABDON **2.**

Acheampong, Ignatius Kutu (ko͞o′to͞o ăchä′-ämpông), 1931–, government official in Ghana, b. Kumasi. He taught before joining (1959) the army, where he advanced to colonel. In 1972, following a bloodless army coup that overthrew Kofi Abrefa BUSIA, he became chairman of the ruling National Redemption Council.

Achelous: see AKHELÓOS, river, Greece.

Achelous (ăk″əlō′əs), in Greek mythology, river god; son of Oceanus and Tethys. He possessed the power to appear as a bull, a serpent, or a bullheaded man. Hercules defeated him and broke off one of his horns, which, according to one legend, became the CORNUCOPIA. He is sometimes said to be the father of the Sirens.

achene, dry, simple, one-seeded fruit with the seed attached to the inner wall at only one point. Achenes are indehiscent, i.e., they do not split open at maturity. The so-called seed of a sunflower is an achene; the shell is the wall of the fruit, and the true seed lies within. A strawberry consists of many achenes embedded in a fleshy receptacle.

Achenwall, Gottfried (gôt′frēt äkh′ənväl), 1719–72, German statistician and political scientist. He used the term *Statistik* for the first time in his *Staatsverfassung der heutigen vornehmsten europäischen Reiche und Völker im Grundrisse* [the political constitution of the present principal European countries and peoples] (1749). By the term he meant a comprehensive description of the social, political, and economic features of a state.

Achernar (ā′kərnär″), brightest star in the constellation ERIDANUS; Bayer designation α Eridani; 1970 position R.A. $1^h36.6^m$, Dec. −57°23′. A bluish-white white star with apparent MAGNITUDE 0.51, it is one of the 10 brightest stars in the entire sky. Its distance is about 120 light-years, and its luminosity about 600 times that of the sun. Achernar is of SPECTRAL CLASS B5 V. Its name is from the Arabic meaning "end of the river [Eridanus]."

Acheron (ăk′ərŏn): see HADES.

Acheson, Dean Gooderham (ăch′ĭsən), 1893–1971, U.S. Secretary of State (1949–52), b. Middletown, Conn. He was (1919–21) private secretary to Louis D. Brandeis, became a successful lawyer, and served (1933) as Undersecretary of the Treasury until disagreement with President Franklin Delano Roosevelt's fiscal policy caused his resignation. Assistant Secretary of State (1941–45) and Undersecretary of State (1945–47), he was appointed (Jan., 1949) Secretary of State. Under his direction the policy of containment of Communist expansion through foreign economic and military aid was developed. He played an important role in establishing the NORTH ATLANTIC TREATY ORGANIZATION and the security pact with Australia and New Zealand. His attempts to dissociate the United States from the Nationalist Chinese regime in Taiwan drew the relentless attack of many Congressmen of his own party, as well as Republicans. His support of U.S. military commitments to South Korea also aroused much criticism. Acheson's earlier friendly attitude toward Alger HISS became the basis for personal abuse and resulted in attacks on his handling of the loyalty and security policy of the Dept. of State. Returning to private practice in 1953, Acheson remained a spokesman for the Democratic party on foreign policy and exerted considerable influence on the Kennedy administration (1961–63). He wrote *A Democrat Looks at His Party* (1955), *A Citizen Looks at Congress* (1957), *Power and Diplomacy* (1958), *Fragments of My Fleece* (1971), and three autobiographical works, *Morning and Noon* (1965), *Present at the Creation* (1969), and *Grapes from Thorns* (1972). See studies by R. J. Stupak (1969) and Gaddis Smith (1972).

Acheulian (əsho͞o′lēən): see PALEOLITHIC PERIOD.

Achill (ăk′ĭl) [Irish,=eagle], island, 56 sq mi (145 sq km), Co. Mayo, W Republic of Ireland; the largest island of Ireland. It is connected with the mainland by a bridge over Achill Sound. The rugged island is barren, and its inhabitants subsist with great difficulty by fishing and farming. Many of the small villages are resorts; Keel and Doogort are the chief towns. Achill is known for its magnificent cliff scenery; Slievemore, at the north end, rises to 2,204 ft (672 m).

Achilles (əkĭl′ēz), in Greek mythology, foremost Greek hero of the Trojan War, son of Peleus and Thetis. He was a formidable warrior, possessing fierce and uncontrollable anger. Thetis, knowing that Achilles was fated to die at Troy, disguised him as a girl and hid him among the women at the court of King Lycomedes of Skyros. He was discovered there by Odysseus, who persuaded him to go to Troy. One of Lycomedes' daughters, Deidamia, bore Achilles a son, Neoptolemus. According to Homer, Achilles came to Troy leading the 50 ships of the Myrmidons. In the last year of the siege, when Agamemnon stole the captive princess Briseis from him, Achilles angrily withdrew and took his troops from the war. Later he allowed his intimate friend Patroclus to borrow his armor and lead the Myrmidons to aid the retreating Greeks. When Hector killed Patroclus, Achilles was filled with grief and rage and returned to the battle, routed the Trojans, and killed Hector, viciously dragging his body back to the Greek camp. Achilles died of a wound inflicted by Paris. According to one legend, Thetis attempted to make Achilles immortal by bathing him in the river Styx, but the heel by which she held him remained vulnerable, and Paris inflicted a fatal wound in that heel. Other legends state that Achilles was struck from behind and killed by Paris when he went to visit Priam's daughter Polyxena, with whom he had fallen in love. Achilles was the object of widespread hero worship.

Achilles' tendon (*tendo calcaneus*) (tĕn′dō kălkā′-nēəs), sinew prominent at the back of the ankle, connecting the tendons of the calf muscles to the heelbone. When the musculature contracts, the pull on the Achilles' tendon elevates the heel in the springy motion essential to running and jumping. Since the effect is to lift the entire body weight against a severely adverse leverage ratio, the Achilles' tendon by necessity is the toughest and strongest of human tendons. The name derives from the mythical Greek hero Achilles, who was vulnerable only in the heel.

Achim (ā′kĭm), name in the genealogy of Mat. 1.14.

Achish (ā′kĭsh), king of Gath with whom David took refuge. 1 Sam. 27.2. Called Abimelech in the title of Ps. 34.

Achitophel (ăkĭt′əfĕl), variant of AHITHOPHEL.

Achmet. For Ottoman sultans thus named, see AHMED.

Achor (ā′kôr), valley where Achan was stoned. Joshua 7.25,26; 1 Chron. 2.7.

Achsa or **Achsah** (both: ăk′sə), Caleb's daughter, given as wife to Othniel. Judges 1.12–15; 1 Chron. 2.49.

Achshaph (ăk′shăf), town of N Palestine, taken by Joshua. Joshua 11.1; 12.20; 19.25.

Achzib (ăk′zĭb). **1** Seacoast Palestinian town, c.15 mi (24 km) S of Tyre. Joshua 19.29; Judges 1.31. **2** Unidentified city of Judah. Joshua 15.44; Micah 1.14. Chezib in Gen. 38.5 and Chozeba in 1 Chron. 4.22 may be the same.

acid anhydride (ănhī′drĭd, -drəd), chemical compound that reacts with water to form an acid (see

ACIDS AND BASES). Anhydrides of inorganic acids are usually oxides of nonmetallic elements. Carbon dioxide, CO_2, is the anhydride of carbonic acid, H_2CO_3. Nitrogen pentoxide, N_2O_5, is the anhydride of nitric acid, HNO_3. Phosphorus pentoxide, P_2O_5, is the anhydride of phosphoric acid, H_3PO_4. Sulfur dioxide, SO_2, is the anhydride of sulfurous acid, H_2SO_3. Sulfur trioxide, SO_3, is the anhydride of sulfuric acid, H_2SO_4. Anhydrides of organic acids, like the acids themselves, contain the carbonyl group, $>CO$. Organic anhydrides include acetic anhydride or ethanoic anhydride, $(CH_3C{=}O)_2O$, and benzoic anhydride, $(C_6H_5C{=}O)_2O$.

acid-base indicators: see INDICATORS, ACID-BASE.

acidophilus milk (ăs″ĭdŏfĭl′əs): see FERMENTED MILK.

acidosis and alkalosis (ăs″ĭdō′sĭs, ăl″kəlō′sĭs), physiological conditions brought about by a disturbance in the balance of acids and bases, or alkalies, in the body. The acid-base balance is kept normal by three separate regulatory systems. First, a group of buffering compounds in the body fluids can react instantaneously to neutralize any excess acids or alkalies. Secondly, the respiratory system can restore balance in 1 to 3 min if the system is upset: deep, rapid breathing excretes more carbon dioxide and consequently reduces the amount of carbonic acid in the tissues, thereby counteracting acidity; conversely, slow, shallow breathing increases the amount of carbonic acid in the tissues, counteracting alkalinity. The third mechanism, a function of the kidneys, is the most powerful of the regulatory systems; excess acid or alkali is excreted in the urine, but the process requires several hours to a day. Either acidosis or alkalosis follows the disruption of any of these mechanisms. Acidosis depresses the central nervous system, which, in extreme cases, leads to coma and death. It can result from a number of metabolic disturbances, e.g., diabetes, kidney failure, severe diarrhea, severe dehydration, excessive ingestion of acid salts, or liver disease. It is countered by the administration of alkali solutions and by treatment of the original cause of the imbalance. Respiratory acidosis occurs when severely diseased lungs retain too much carbon dioxide and take in too little oxygen; measures must be taken to reduce the carbon dioxide content of the blood and to increase oxygenation. Alkalosis causes overexcitation of the nervous system, which, in extreme cases, causes a state of muscular spasm called tetany. It is usually brought on by ingestion of alkalies in quantities greater than the kidneys can process, or by hyperventilation (rapid breathing) in hysterical or emotional states. Treatment of alkalosis must be addressed to restoring the normal acid-base balance and to removing the original cause of the disturbance.

acids and bases, two related classes of chemicals; the members of each class have a number of common properties when dissolved in a solvent, usually water. Acids in water solutions exhibit the following common properties: they taste sour; turn LITMUS paper red; and react with certain metals, such as zinc, to yield hydrogen gas. Bases in water solutions exhibit these common properties: they taste bitter; turn litmus paper blue; and feel slippery. When a water solution of acid is mixed with a water solution of base, a SALT and water are formed; this process, called NEUTRALIZATION, is complete only if the resulting solution has neither acidic nor basic properties. Acids and bases can be classified as organic or inorganic. Some of the more common organic acids are: CITRIC ACID, CARBONIC ACID, HYDROGEN CYANIDE, salicylic acid, LACTIC ACID, and TARTARIC ACID. Some examples of organic bases are: PYRIDINE and ethylamine. Some of the common inorganic acids are: HYDROGEN SULFIDE, PHOSPHORIC ACID, HYDROGEN CHLORIDE, and SULFURIC ACID. Some common inorganic bases are: SODIUM HYDROXIDE, SODIUM CARBONATE, SODIUM BICARBONATE, CALCIUM HYDROXIDE, and CALCIUM CARBONATE. When an acid or base dissolves in water, a certain percentage of the acid or base particles will break up, or dissociate (see DISSOCIATION), into oppositely charged ions. The Arrhenius theory of acids and bases, named for the Swedish chemist Svante Arrhenius, defines an acid as a compound that can dissociate in water to yield hydrogen ions, H^+, and a base as a compound that can dissociate in water to yield hydroxide ions, OH^-. For example, hydrochloric acid, HCl, dissociates in water to yield the required hydrogen ions, H^+, and also chloride ions, Cl^-. The base sodium hydroxide, NaOH, dissociates in water to yield the required hydroxide ions, OH^-, and also sodium ions, Na^+. Some substances act as acids or bases when they are dissolved in solvents other than water, such as liquid ammonia. The Brönsted-Lowry theory, named for the Danish chemist Johannes Brönsted and the British chemist Thomas Lowry, provides a more general definition of acids and bases that can be used to deal both with solutions that contain no water and solutions that contain water. It defines an acid as a proton donor and a base as a proton acceptor. In the Brönsted-Lowry theory, water, H_2O, can be considered an acid or a base since it can lose a proton to form a hydroxide ion, OH^-, or accept a proton to form a hydronium ion, H_3O^+ (see AMPHOTERISM). When an acid loses a proton, the remaining species can be a proton acceptor and is called the conjugate base of the acid. Similarly when a base accepts a proton, the resulting species can be a proton donor and is called the conjugate acid of that base. For example, when a water molecule loses a proton to form a hydroxide ion, the hydroxide ion can be considered the conjugate base of the acid, water. When a water molecule accepts a proton to form a hydronium ion, the hydronium ion can be considered the conjugate acid of the base, water. Another theory that provides a very broad definition of acids and bases has been put forth by the American chemist Gilbert Lewis. The Lewis theory defines an acid as a compound that can accept a pair of electrons and a base as a compound that can donate a pair of electrons. Boron trifluoride, BF_3, can be considered a Lewis acid and ethyl alcohol can be considered a Lewis base. Each of the three theories has its own advantages and disadvantages; each is useful under certain conditions. Acids, such as hydrochloric acid, and bases, such as potassium hydroxide, that have a great tendency to dissociate in water are completely ionized in solution; they are called strong acids or strong bases. Acids, such as acetic acid, and bases, such as ammonia, that are reluctant to dissociate in water are only partially ionized in solution; they are called weak acids or weak bases. Strong acids in solution produce a high concentration of hydrogen ions, and strong bases in solution produce a high concentration of hydroxide ions and a correspondingly low concentration of hydrogen ions. The hydrogen ion concentration is often expressed in terms of its negative logarithm, or *p*H (see separate article). Strong acids and strong bases make very good electrolytes (see ELECTROLYSIS), i.e., their solutions readily conduct electricity. Weak acids and weak bases make poor electrolytes. See CATALYST; TITRATION; INDICATORS, ACID-BASE; BUFFER.

Acireale (ä″chĕrää′lā), city (1971 pop. 47,086), E Sicily, Italy. Beautifully situated on a volcanic plateau near Mt. Etna and near the Ionian Sea, Acireale has been frequented since Roman times for its warm sulfur springs and today is also a commercial center. The city was damaged by earthquakes in 1169 and 1693.

Acis (ā′sĭs): see GALATEA **1**.

Ackermann von Böhmer: see JOHANNES VON SAAZ.

Acklins Island: see BAHAMA ISLANDS.

acknowledgment, in law, formal declaration or admission by a person who executed an instrument (e.g., a will or a deed) that the instrument is his. The acknowledgment is made before a court, a notary public, or other authorized person. Acknowledgment permits the instrument to be given in evidence without further proof of its execution (e.g., witnesses).

Acmeists (ăk′mēĭsts), school of Russian poets started in 1912 by Sergei M. Gorodetsky and Nikolai Stepanovich GUMILEV as a reaction against the mysticism of the symbolists. The school aspired to concreteness of imagery and clarity of expression. The leading Acmeists were Gumilev, Anna AKHMATOVA, and Osip MANDELSTAM. See L. I. Strakhovsky, *Craftsmen of the Word: Three Poets of Modern Russia.*

acne, common inflammatory disease of the SEBACEOUS GLANDS characterized by blackheads, whiteheads, and pimples and, in the more severe forms, by cysts and scarring. The lesions appear on the face, neck, back, chest, and arms. Acne is most prevalent among adolescents. Although its exact cause is not known, it is undoubtedly related both to genetic predisposition and to the increased hormonal activity that occurs at puberty, which causes an overproduction of sebum, the oily secretion of the sebaceous glands. Cleanliness of the skin is essential when acne is present, and a mild soap and water should be used several times a day. The contents of blackheads and pustular lesions should be evacuated only by a physician under proper aseptic conditions to lessen the possibility of scarring. Astringent lotions may help to counteract the oiliness of the skin usually present in this condition. Foods rich in carbohydrate and fat, such as chocolate and nuts, should be eliminated from the diet. The more severe cases of acne may require antibiotic and hormonal treatment. It is possible to improve the appearance of acne-scarred skin by a method of surgical abrasion in which the skin is frozen and anesthetized and then abraded with fine sandpaper or special brushes.

Aco or **Accault, Michel** (both: mĕshĕl′ ăkō′), fl. 1680–1702, French explorer. He became La Salle's lieutenant, being favored by that explorer because of his courage, prudence, and wide acquaintance with Indian languages. When LA SALLE reached the mouth of the Illinois River on his famous voyage down the Mississippi, he sent Aco with two companions to explore the upper reaches of the Mississippi. One of the companions was Father Louis HENNEPIN, who in his *Nouvelle Decouverte* made himself the hero of the expedition. Near the Falls of St. Anthony, which they were the first Europeans to see, the three were captured by Sioux Indians and were released only through the energy and influence of Daniel Greysolon DULUTH. Little is known of Aco's subsequent life except that he was a trader on the Illinois for many years and that in 1693 he married the daughter of a Kaskaskia chief. His name also appears as Ako.

Acoma or **Ácoma** (both: ăk′əmə), pueblo (1970 est. pop. 2,750), alt. c.7,000 ft (2,130 m), Valencia co., W central N.Mex.; founded c.1100–1250. This "sky city" on top of a steep-sided sandstone mesa, 357 ft (109 m) high and difficult of access, is considered to be the oldest continuously inhabited community in the United States. The residents, who speak a Western Keresan language (see PUEBLO INDIANS), are skilled pottery makers. Below the mesa are the cultivated fields and grazing grounds that help support the community. The pueblo's location has astonished visitors from Fray Marcos de Niza in 1539 and Coronado's men in 1540 to tourists of today. Juan de Oñate was allowed entry in 1598, but the Indians revolted fiercely in 1599 and were subdued only after severe fighting. The missionary Fray Juan Ramírez arrived in 1629. The Acoma people joined in the revolt of the Pueblo Indians in 1680, were forced to submit to Diego de Vargas in 1692, joined in the later uprising of 1696, and were subdued again in 1699. They were later Christianized. Their chief festival is held on Sept. 2, the feast of St. Stephen, their patron saint. See study by L. A. White (1932, repr. 1973).

Acominatus, Michael (əkŏmĭnā′təs) or **Michael Choniates** (kōnēā′tēz), c.1140–1220, Byzantine writer and metropolitan of Athens. Acominatus' speeches, poems, and letters give much information about medieval Athens, which he, a classicist, found barbarous and degenerate. His important history of the Byzantine Empire covers the period 1180 to 1206. After the capture (1204) of Athens by the army of the Fourth Crusade, he retired to the island of Kéa, where he died. His first name is also written as Nicetas.

Aconcagua (äkōnkä′gwä), peak, 22,835 ft (6,960 m) high, Mendoza prov., W Argentina, in the Andes, near the Chilean border. It is the highest peak of the Western Hemisphere. The snow-capped Aconcagua was first scaled in 1897. Uspallata Pass is nearby. See also OJOS DEL SALADO.

aconite (ăk′ənīt), **monkshood,** or **wolfsbane,** any of several species of the genus *Aconitum* of the family Ranunculaceae (BUTTERCUP family), hardy perennial plants of the north temperate zone, growing wild or cultivated for ornamental or medicinal purposes. They contain violent poisons that were recognized from early times and were mentioned by Shakespeare (2 *King Henry IV,* iv:4); more recently they have been used medicinally in a liniment, tincture, and drug, and in India on spears and arrows for hunting. The drug aconite, the active principle of which is the alkaloid aconitine, is used as a sedative, e.g., for neuralgia and rheumatism, and is obtained from *A. napellus.* Aconites are erect or trailing, with deeply cut leaves and, in late summer and fall, hooded showy flowers of blue, yellow, purple, or white. The name wolfsbane derives from an old superstition that the plant repelled werewolves. Winter aconite is a name for plants of the genus *Eranthis,* wild or garden perennials of the same family. Aconites are classified in the division MAGNOLIOPHYTA, class Magnoliopsida, order Ranunculales, family Ranunculaceae.

Acontius (əkŏn′shəs), in Greek mythology, young man who loved Cydippe. He met her at a festival of Artemis and threw before her an apple inscribed, "I swear by the temple of Artemis to marry Acontius." She read the inscription aloud. The goddess accepted her words as an oath and brought about the marriage of the lovers.

Açores: see AZORES, Portugal.

acorn: see OAK.

acorn worm: see HEMICHORDATA.

Acosta, Joaquín (hwäkĕn' äkō'stä), 1800–1852, Colombian historian and scientist. He served under Simón Bolívar in the revolution against Spanish rule and remained active in Colombian politics, holding various political positions. His scientific knowledge was broad, and he wrote about many aspects of Colombia, constituting himself a sort of intellectual publicity agent for his country.

Acosta, José de, c.1539–1600, Spanish Jesuit missionary to Peru. He wrote a well-known history of the Spanish colonial period, *The Natural and Moral History of the Indies* (1590; tr. 1604, 1880, repr. 1970).

Acosta, Uriel (ōōr'yĕl), or **Uriel da Costa,** c.1585–1640, Jewish rationalist, b. Oporto, Portugal. His original name was Gabriel da Costa, and his family had been converted to Roman Catholicism. When he reached manhood, he was restive in the Christian faith and persuaded his family to move to Amsterdam, where all of them returned to Judaism. In a work in 1624, he expressed rationalistic doctrines, criticized rabbinical Judaism, and demanded a return to the teachings of the Sadducees. He was tried, imprisoned, and excommunicated. In 1633 he recanted, but soon he again offended and was excommunicated. After seven years, he once more recanted and was subjected to public humiliation. Rather than endure further trouble he committed suicide. He left an autobiographical sketch, *Exemplar humanae vitae* (1687, tr. *Specimen of Human Life,* 1695). Karl Ferdinand Gutzkow wrote a tragedy about him, *Uriel Acosta.*

acoustics (əkōō'stĭks) [Gr.,=the facts about hearing], the science of SOUND, including its production, propagation, and effects. Various branches of acoustics that deal with different aspects of sound and hearing include bioacoustics, physical acoustics, ULTRASONICS, and architectural acoustics. One important practical application of architectural acoustics is in the designing of auditoriums, which requires a knowledge of the characteristics and behavior of sound WAVES. The most important factors to be considered are reverberation and INTERFERENCE. Reverberation is the persistence of sound in an enclosed space caused by repeated reflections of the sound waves back and forth by the walls. Reflection of sound sometimes causes an ECHO. Some reverberation in auditoriums is desirable, especially where music is performed, to avoid deadening of the sound to a degree that is unpleasant to the human ear. Depending on the location of the listener and the frequency of the sound, varying degrees of interference between the primary sound and its reflections will be produced. In a good auditorium these variations are minimized. Reflection can be reduced by the use of sound-absorbent materials, which are usually soft and porous, such as draperies, upholstery, carpets, acoustic tile, or plaster. In a room reflection is decreased by the presence of people and open windows and doors. See John Backus, *The Acoustical Foundations of Music* (1969); R. B. Lindsay, *Acoustics: Historical and Philosophical Development* (1973).

acquired characteristics, modifications produced in an individual plant or animal as a result of mutilation, disease, use and disuse, or any distinctly environmental influence. Some examples are docking of tails, malformation due to disease, and muscle atrophy. Although belief in inheritability of acquired characteristics was accepted by Lamarck, it was later challenged by Darwin and Mendel. Modern geneticists have affirmed that inheritance is determined solely by the reproductive cells and is unaffected by somatic (body) cells. Belief in the inheritance of acquired characteristics is therefore rejected.

Acre (äk'rə), state (1970 pop. 216,200), 58,915 sq mi (152,590 sq km), W Brazil, on the borders of Peru and Bolivia. RIO BRANCO is the capital.

Acre, Israel: see AKKO.

acre, measure of land area used in the ENGLISH UNITS OF MEASUREMENT. The acre was originally the area a yoke of oxen could plow in a day and therefore differed in size from one locality to another. It is now fixed as 10 square chains or 160 square rods, i.e., 4,840 sq yd, 43,560 sq ft, or 1/640 sq mi. It is equal to about .4047 of a hectare or 4,046.9 sq m.

Acrisius (əkrĭs'ēəs): see DANAË and PERSEUS.

Acrocorinthus (ăk"rōkərĭn'thəs), acropolis, or citadel, of CORINTH, overlooking the ancient city. Some ruins of the acropolis remain. The Acrocorinthus was the site of a temple of Aphrodite. It was strongly fortified in the Middle Ages. Below gushed the fountain of Pirene, from which, in legend, PEGASUS was drinking when captured by Bellerophon.

acromegaly (ăk"rōmĕg'əlē), adult endocrine disorder resulting from hypersecretion of growth hormone produced by the pituitary gland. Since the bones cannot increase in length after full growth is attained, there is a disproportionate thickening of bones, predominantly in the skull and small bones of the hands and feet. Fingers and toes become broadened and spadelike, the skull increases in size, and the cheek bones and jaws protrude. Many of the soft tissues, such as the tongue and liver, enlarge. Frequently glucose metabolism is disturbed, leading to diabetes mellitus. Acromegaly is usually caused by a tumor of the pituitary; treatment consists of irradiation or surgical removal of the tumor. Onset of the disease can also occur in children, before the epiphyses of the bones are closed. In such cases the disorder leads to GIGANTISM.

acropolis (əkrŏp'əlĭs) [Gr.,=high point of the city], elevated, fortified section of various ancient Greek cities. The Acropolis of Athens, a hill c.260 ft (80 m) high, with a flat oval top c.500 ft (150 m) wide and 1,150 ft (350 m) long, was walled before the 6th cent. B.C. by the Pelasgians. Devoted to religious rather than defensive purposes, the area was adorned during the time of Cimon and Pericles with some of the world's greatest architectural and sculptural monuments. The top was reached by a winding processional path at the west end, where the impressive Propylaea (see under PROPYLAEUM) stood. From here, the Sacred Way led past a colossal bronze statue of Athena (called Athena Promachus) and the site of the old temple of Athena to the PARTHENON. To the north was the ERECHTHEUM and to the southwest the temple of Nike Apteros (Wingless Victory). On the southern slope were the Odeum of Herodes Atticus and the theater of Dionysus. Although the Acropolis was laid waste by the Persians in 480 B.C., remains of the Parthenon, Erechtheum, and Propylaea still stand. Many of its treasures are in the national museum of Greece, in Athens. See R. J. Hopper, *The Acropolis* (1971).

acrostic (əkrŏ'stĭk), arrangement of words or lines in which a series of initial, final, or other corresponding letters, when taken together, stand in a set order to form a word, a phrase, the alphabet, or the like. A famous acrostic was made on the Greek for Jesus Christ, God's Son, Savior: *I*esous *Ch*ristos, *Th*eou *U*ios, *S*oter (*ch* and *th* being each one letter in Greek). The initials spell *ichthus,* Greek for fish; hence the frequent use of the fish by early Christians as a symbol for Jesus. There are several alphabetic acrostics (pertaining to the Hebrew alphabet) in the Bible, e.g., in Ps. 119 and LAMENTATIONS. Acrostic verses are common, and very elaborate puzzles have been devised combining several schemes.

Acrux (ā'krəks) [from the Bayer designation α Crucis], brightest star in the constellation CRUX (Southern Cross); 1970 position R.A. $12^h24.9^m$, Dec. $-62°$-56'. Its apparent MAGNITUDE of 0.86 makes it one of the 20 brightest stars in the sky, although its location in the far southern sky prevents it from being seen by most observers in the United States. Acrux is a visual BINARY star, with components of SPECTRAL CLASSES B1 and B3, each component itself being a spectroscopic binary. Its distance is about 400 light-years.

acrylic, man-made fiber made from a special group of vinyl compounds, primarily acrylonitrile. Acrylic fibers are thermoplastic, have low moisture regain, are low in density, and can be made into bulky fabrics. They wash and dry easily and are dimensionally stable. They are resistant to bleaches, dilute acids, and alkalies, and to weathering and microbiological attack.

acrylic plastics: see POLYACRYLICS.

act, in law, anything done by a person, group, or body to which legal consequences attach. The term also refers to decrees, judgments, and awards handed down by an individual in an official position or by an official body (e.g., a judge or a legislature). In this sense it is often synonymous with statute, meaning a bill that has been enacted into law by the legislature. Public acts are those that relate to the entire community, whereas private acts operate only on particular persons or private concerns.

acta (ăk'tə), official texts of ancient Rome, written or carved on stone or metal. Usually acta were texts made public, although publication was sometimes restricted. Acta were first posted or carved for general reading c.131 B.C. They were accounts of general interest and were later called *Acta diurna,* and they have been compared to modern newspapers. There were special acta of municipal, legal, or military content. The *Acta senatus,* according to a Roman administrative tradition, were for many years kept secret so that the public should have no knowledge of senatorial debate. In 59 B.C., Julius Caesar, as consul, ordered their publication along with the *Acta diurna,* but later the publication was censored. Acta was also the term used for the laws themselves, primarily those promulgated by the emperors.

Actaeon (ăktē'ən), in Greek mythology, son of Aristaeus. Because he saw Artemis bathing naked, she changed him into a stag, and his own dogs killed him.

ACTH: see ADRENOCORTICOTROPIC HORMONE.

actin, one of the two major protein constituents of muscle, the other being MYOSIN. Actin occurs in two forms: G-actin (globular actin) and F-actin (fibrous actin). G-actin is a globular protein each molecule of which seems to bind one calcium ion and one ADENOSINE TRIPHOSPHATE (ATP) or adenosine diphosphate (ADP) molecule very tightly. If the ionic strength of a solution of G-actin is raised to a value comparable to that found in muscle, it polymerizes into a high molecular weight protein, F-actin, which has a double-stranded helical structure. The polymerization reaction is accompanied by the hydrolysis of each bound ATP molecule to ADP, releasing an inorganic phosphate. This hydrolysis is not necessary for polymerization, however. Actin and myosin together form the myofibril, which in the presence of ATP is the fundamental contractile unit of muscle.

acting. At its highest levels of accomplishment acting involves an almost total imaginative identification on the part of the actor with the character he is portraying. Only in this way will the full emotional weight of situations on stage be communicated to the audience. The actor must be a sharp observer of life and thoroughly trained in voice projection and enunciation and in body movement. In the ancient Greek theater, acting was stylized; indeed, the large outdoor theaters made subtlety of speech and gesture impossible. The actors, all men, wore comic and tragic masks and were costumed grotesquely, wearing padded clothes and, often, artificial phalluses. Nevertheless, there were advocates of naturalistic acting even at that time, and actors were held in high esteem. In the Roman period actors were slaves, and the level of performance was low, broad farce being the most popular dramatic form. The tragedies of Seneca were probably read in declamatory style, rather than acted on stage. During the Christian period in Rome, acting almost disappeared, the tradition being upheld by traveling mimes, jugglers, and acrobats who entertained at fairs. Nor did the rise of medieval religious drama produce an uplift in the quality of acting. An actor's every gesture and intonation was carefully designated for performance in church, and, as with the later pageants under the auspices of the trade guilds, the actors were amateurs. Modern professional acting began in the 16th cent. with the Italian COMMEDIA DELL'ARTE, whose actors improvised convincing and entertaining situations from general outlines. In England the Elizabethan stage, which featured male actors in all parts, apparently presented a good deal of bombastic acting. During the Restoration period, however, Thomas Betterton and his wife Mary were famous for their naturalness of delivery, as was Edward Kynaston. Their contemporary Charles Hart, however, was well known for his lofty, heroic acting, a style that became dominant in the first third of the 18th cent. Among its chief practitioners were Barton Booth and James Quin. In the mid-18th cent. Charles Macklin and his pupil David Garrick introduced a more naturalistic style, and similar movements took place in France and Germany. However, the old declamatory method never really died out until the early 20th cent., and such great 18th- and 19th-century actors as Lekain, Sarah Siddons, Edmund Kean, and Junius Brutus Booth would probably seem overly histrionic to modern audiences. Part of the reason for the persistence of bombastic acting was the star system that existed until high standards of ensemble playing were set by the MEININGEN PLAYERS in 1874. Important late 19th-century actors, varying considerably in the naturalism of their acting styles, were Edwin Booth, Dame Ellen Terry, Henry Irving, Eleanora Duse, and Sarah Bernhardt. Acting in the 20th cent. has been greatly influenced by the theories of the Russian director Constantin STANISLAVSKY. An advocate of ensemble playing, he believed that an actor must strive for absolute psychological identification with the character he is portraying and that this identification is at least as important as mastery of voice projection or body movement. Stanislavsky's theories were popularized in the United States by the GROUP THEATRE and later by the Actors' Studio, which produced a generation of extremely naturalistic actors, notably Marlon Brando. The emergence of motion pictures and television presented unprecedented opportunities for actors, the sensitivity of camera and microphone making subtlety of voice, expression, and movement absolutely essential. In spite of changing acting styles, however, great acting remains a highly individual achievement. The effectiveness of a performance by Laurence Olivier—whether he be acting Heathcliff in the film *Wuthering Heights,* Othello in Shakespeare's tragedy, or James Tyrone in a television production of O'Neill's *Long Day's Journey into Night*—is dependent on neither the dramatic medium nor any formal theatrical training, but on the extraordinary sensitivity and talent of Olivier the actor. For further information, see DRAMA, WESTERN; ORIENTAL DRAMA; SCENE DESIGN AND STAGE LIGHTING; DIRECTING. See Toby Cole, ed., *Acting: A Handbook of the Stanislavski Method* (1955); Constantin Stanislavski, *Building a Character* (tr. 1962) and *An Actor Prepares* (tr. 1963); J. A. Hamerton, ed., *The Actor's Art* (1969); Toby Cole and H. K. Chinov, ed., *Actors on Acting* (rev. ed. 1970); Tyrone Guthrie, *Tyrone Guthrie on Acting* (1971); Michael Billington, *The Modern Actor* (1973).

actinide series, a series of radioactive metals in group IIIb of the PERIODIC TABLE. Members of the series are often called actinides. ACTINIUM (atomic number 89) is usually considered a member of the series. The series always includes the 14 elements with atomic numbers 90 through 103, which are (in order of increasing atomic number) THORIUM, PROTACTINIUM, URANIUM, NEPTUNIUM, PLUTONIUM, AMERICIUM, CURIUM, BERKELIUM, CALIFORNIUM, EINSTEINIUM, FERMIUM, MENDELEVIUM, NOBELIUM, and LAWRENCIUM. Study of the properties of the actinides is hampered by their instability. It is known, however, that all members of the series resemble actinium in their chemical properties. The actinides are reactive and assume a number of different valences in their compounds. As the atomic number increases in this series, added electrons enter the 5f electron orbital. Elements in this series with atomic numbers greater than that of uranium (92) are called TRANSURANIUM ELEMENTS; they are not found (except in minute amounts) on earth, but have been prepared synthetically. Elements with atomic numbers greater than 103 are not members of the actinide series; element 104 is the first TRANSACTINIDE ELEMENT.

actinium (ăktĭn'ēəm) [Gr.,=like a ray], radioactive chemical element; symbol Ac; at. no. 89; mass no. of most stable isotope 227; m.p. about 1050°C; b.p. 3200°C±300°C; sp. gr. 10.07; valence +3. Actinium is a silver-white metal with a cubic crystalline structure. It is found with uranium minerals in pitchblende. The pure metal can be prepared by reducing its fluoride with lithium vapor at about 1200°C. Actinium-227, the most stable isotope, has a half-life of 21.6 years. All other isotopes of actinium have very short half-lives. Actinium is in group IIIb of the PERIODIC TABLE. Its chemical properties are similar to those of lanthanum and of members of the ACTINIDE SERIES, of which it is usually considered the first member. It reacts with water to form an insoluble hydroxide; with halides to form a trifluoride, trichloride, bromide, or iodide; with oxalic acid to form the oxalate; with oxygen or sulfur to form the sesquioxide or sesquisulfide. Actinium was first recognized in 1899 by André Debierne in uranium residues from pitchblende. It was later found to be identical with an element discovered in 1902 by Fritz Giesel and called by him emanium.

actinium series, natural radioactive decay series beginning with URANIUM-235 (also called actinouranium) and ending with LEAD-207. See RADIOACTIVITY.

actinolite (ăktĭn'əlĭt): see AMPHIBOLE.

actinometer (ăk"tənŏm'ətər), instrument used to measure the heating power of radiation. Actinometers are used chiefly in meteorology to measure solar radiation as transmitted directly by the sun, scattered by the atmosphere, or reflected by the earth. A number of different designs have been developed. In one design a small bimetallic strip is heated by the radiation, and the subsequent bending is measured; from knowledge of such factors as the heat capacity of the strip, its surface area, its reflectivity, and the change in its curvature produced by a given change in temperature, the heating power of the radiation striking it can be found. In another design two bimetallic strips, one blackened and one white, are exposed to the radiation and the difference in their subsequent curvatures measured. In a third design a sheet of photographic paper is exposed to the radiation to provide a measure of the total radiation over a period of time.

actinomycin (ăk"tənōmī'sən), any one of a group of ANTIBIOTICS produced by bacteria of the genus *Streptomyces.* Actinomycin was the first antibiotic reported to be able to halt cancer; however, it is not widely used to treat cancers because it is highly toxic to humans, interfering with the genetic material of cells. It is mainly used as an investigative tool in cell biology.

actinomycosis (ăk"tənōmīkō'sĭs), chronic suppurative fungus infection that occurs around the face and neck. The disease is characterized by the formation of abscesses, or pus-filled cavities, below the surface of the skin. These abscesses spread rapidly and form channels that discharge a yellow granular pus on the surface of the skin. In humans these granules consist of *Actinomyces israelii,* a fungus present in the normal flora of the mouth that becomes pathogenic in association with certain bacteria. Infection typically follows a tooth extraction or other trauma. The disease causes extensive tissue destruction and can prove fatal if it invades the abdomen or lungs. Treatment consists of prolonged massive therapy with penicillin. Actinomycosis also occurs in horses, cattle, and swine; it is caused by *A. bovis* and resembles human actinomycosis.

actinon (ăk'tənŏn"): see RADON.

action, in law: see PROCEDURE.

action painting: see ABSTRACT EXPRESSIONISM.

Actium (ăk'tēəm, -shē -), promontory, NW Acarnania, Greece, at the mouth of the Ambracian Gulf. There are vestiges of several temples and an ancient town. At Actium was fought the naval battle (31 B.C.) in which the forces of Octavian (later Augustus) under Agrippa defeated the sea and land forces of Antony and Cleopatra. The battle established Octavian as ruler of Rome. The Actian games, held at NICOPOLIS every four years, were established to commemorate the event.

activation energy, in chemistry, minimum ENERGY needed to cause a CHEMICAL REACTION. According to the KINETIC-MOLECULAR THEORY OF GASES, the atoms, ions, or molecules of a substance are constantly in motion; the HEAT energy present in a substance is embodied in this motion. A chemical reaction between two substances occurs only when an atom, ion, or molecule of one collides with an atom, ion, or molecule of the other. When the reactants collide, they may form an intermediate product whose chemical energy is higher than the combined chemical energy of the reactants. In order for this transition state in the reaction to be achieved, some energy must enter into the reaction other than the chemical energy of the reactants. This energy, supplied by the heat of the substance, is the activation energy. Once the intermediate product, or activated complex, is formed, the final products are formed from it. The path from reactants through the transition-state activated complex to the final products is known as the reaction mechanism. (Reaction mechanisms for complex reactions may involve several steps analogous to that described here.) If the chemical energy of the final products is greater than that of the reactants, some of the heat energy of the substance will be converted to chemical energy, and the reaction is called endothermic. The activation energy of an endothermic reaction is at least equal to the difference in chemical energy of the reactants and the products. If the chemical energy of the products is less than that of the reactants, some chemical energy will be converted to heat energy in the course of the reaction; such a reaction is called exothermic. If the amount of heat energy in a system is increased, the temperature of the system increases. An exothermic reaction causes the temperature of the reaction system to rise, since the heat energy of the system is increased as the chemical energy is decreased. In general, the activation energies of exothermic reactions are lower than those of endothermic reactions. Because the heat energy of a substance is not uniformly distributed among its atoms, ions, or molecules, some may carry enough heat energy to react while others do not. If the activation energy is low, a greater proportion of the collisions between reactants will result in reactions. If the temperature of the system is increased, the average heat energy is increased, a greater proportion of collisions between reactants result in reaction, and the reaction proceeds more rapidly. A catalyst increases the reaction rate by providing a reaction mechanism with a lower activation energy, so that a greater proportion of collisions result in reaction. The activation energy and rate of a reaction are related by the equation $k=Ae^{-E_a/RT}$, where k is the rate constant, A is a temperature-independent constant (often called the frequency factor), e is the base of natural logarithms, E_a is the activation energy, R is the universal gas constant, and T is the temperature. This relationship was derived by Arrhenius in 1899. Because the relationship of reaction rate to activation energy and temperature is exponential, a small change in temperature or activation energy causes a large change in the rate of the reaction. Activation energies are usually determined experimentally by measuring the reaction rate k at different temperatures T, plotting the logarithm of k against $1/T$ on a graph, and determining the slope of the straight line that best fits the points; the activation energy is a constant multiple of the slope, with the value of the constant depending on the units of measure used.

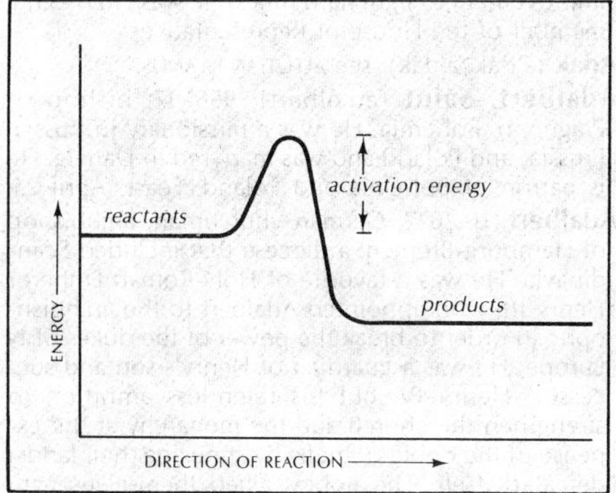

Energy profile of an exothermic reaction: Although the total energy of the products is less than that of the reactants, the activation energy must be added to weaken or break existing bonds before the reaction can take place.

active: see VOICE.

active site: see ENZYME.

act of God, in law, an ACCIDENT caused by the operation of extraordinary natural force. The effect of ordinary natural causes (e.g., that rain will leak through a defective roof) may be foreseen and avoided by the exercise of human care; failure to take the necessary precautions constitutes NEGLIGENCE, and the party injured in the accident may be entitled to damages. An act of God, however, is so extraordinary and devoid of human agency that reasonable care would not avoid the consequences; hence, the injured party has no right to damages. Accidents caused by tornadoes, perils of the sea, extraordinary floods, and severe ice storms are usually considered acts of God, but fires are not so considered unless they are caused by lightning.

Acton, John Emerich Edward Dalberg Acton, 1st **Baron,** 1834–1902, English historian, b. Naples; grandson of Sir John Francis Edward Acton and of Emmerich Joseph, duc de Dalberg. He became (1859) a Liberal member of Parliament and editor of the *Rambler,* a Roman Catholic monthly. William E. Gladstone, his close friend, nominated him to the peerage (1869), and in 1892, Acton was made lord-in-waiting. Acton's genuine and ardent liberalism gave frequent offense to Roman Catholic authorities. His hatred of arbitrary power and all forms of absolutism led him to oppose the syllabus of errors issued by PIUS IX and the promulgation of the dogma of papal infallibility, but, as a sincere Catholic, he accepted them after their pronouncement rather than risk excommunication. In 1895 he was appointed professor of modern history at Cambridge and in the following years planned the *Cambridge Modern History,* of which only the first volume appeared before his death. Acton never completed a book; his influence was felt through his lectures, his writings for periodicals, and his personal contacts with the leading historians of his time. Many articles, essays, and lectures were brought together after his death in *Lectures on Modern History* (1906), *History of Freedom* (1907), and *Historical Essays and Studies* (1907). Some of these were reprinted in *Essays on Freedom and Power* (1948) and *Essays on Church and State* (1952). His impressive personal library, consisting of more than 59,000 volumes, was bought by Andrew Carnegie after his death and donated to Cambridge. See his correspondence with Richard Simpson, ed. by J. L. Altholz (2 vol., 1970–73); studies by Gertrude Himmelfarb (1962) and David Mathew (1968).

Acton, Sir John Francis Edward, 1736?–1811, Neapolitan statesman of British origin, b. Besançon,

France. Called upon by Queen Marie Caroline and King Ferdinand IV of Naples (later FERDINAND I of the Two Sicilies) to reform the Neapolitan army and navy in 1779, Acton also served as minister of finance and as prime minister (1785–1806 with brief interruptions). With the assistance of Emma Lady HAMILTON, the queen's confidante, he rid Naples of Spanish influence and strengthened ties with Great Britain and with Austria. He shared the political vicissitudes of the royal family, going with them into exile in 1798 after Naples had been taken by the French. After the fall of the PARTHENOPEAN REPUBLIC (1799), he played a major role in the bloody reprisals and consolidated absolutism. In 1806, the French reconquest of Naples under Napoleon I forced Acton into exile again.

Acton, town (1970 pop. 14,770), Middlesex co., E Mass., NW of Boston; settled c.1680, inc. 1735. Among its manufactures are electrical machinery and chemicals. Points of interest include the Isaac Davis Home, residence of the first man to die at the battle of Concord during the Revolutionary War. The Acton Minutemen's march to the battle of Concord is reenacted in the town annually.

Actors' Studio, The: see STRASBERG, LEE.

Acts of the Apostles, fifth book of the New Testament, between the Gospels and the Epistles. It is the only contemporary historical account of the expansion of Christianity in its earliest period. It was written in Greek between A.D. 60 and A.D. 80 as a sequel to the Gospel of St. Luke, and Luke is its traditional author. It falls into two divisions: the first 12 chapters, on the Palestinian church from Pentecost until Herod's death, having chiefly to do with St. Peter; and the rest of the book, dealing with the missionary work of St. Paul among the Gentiles (13.1–21.14) and his arrest, trial, and trip as prisoner to Rome (21.15–28). St. Luke was sometimes a companion of St. Paul, and the narrative is then in the first person plural (16.10–17; 20.5–21.18; 27.1–28.16). Three critical events are noteworthy—the descent of the Holy Ghost (2), the martyrdom of St. Stephen (6, 7), and the conversion of St. Paul (9). See H. J. Cadbury, *The Book of Acts in History* (1955); Jacob Jerrell, *Luke and the People of God* (1972); C. W. Cartel and Ralph Earle, *The Acts of the Apostles* (1973).

actuary, one who calculates the probabilities involved in any contingency for which INSURANCE is desired and establishes the premium necessary to cover such contingency. Originally, in England, the term was applied to a clerk or registrar appointed either to record court acts or to manage a joint stock company. Later it came to be used exclusively for managers of insurance companies. As insurance against loss of life is the most common type of policy, actuaries are particularly concerned with studying age, health, and other variables to predict the probable longevity of a person or group. The contingencies involved in fire, accident, or group health policies are also important parts of the actuary's work. An actuary also calculates the probabilities upon which annuities are based and the amount of money, at compound interest, necessary to cover them.

Acuña, Cristóbal de (krēstō'bäl dā ako͞o'nyä), 1597–1676?, Spanish Jesuit missionary and explorer in South America, rector of the Jesuit college at Cuenca, Ecuador. In 1638 he was sent by the viceroy to accompany TEIXEIRA on his return journey down the Amazon River. Acuña's *New Discovery of the Great River of the Amazons* (1639, modern tr. in C. R. Markham's *Expedition into the Valley of the Amazons*, 1859, repr. 1964) was the earliest firsthand description of the Amazon to be printed.

Acuña, Juan de (hwän), 1658?–1734, Spanish-American administrator, viceroy of New Spain (1722–34), marqués de Casa Fuerte, b. Lima, Peru. After a distinguished career in Spain he was sent to Mexico, where his creole origin and his wise government made him popular. He extinguished favoritism and corruption, extended and consolidated Spanish territorial claims, and ordered the construction of many public works. In his term the *Gaceta de México*, Mexico's first newspaper, appeared.

acupuncture, technique of medical treatment, based on traditional Chinese medicine, in which a number of very fine metal needles are inserted into the skin at especially designated points. In China acupuncture has been used, along with herbal medicine, for pain relief and treatment of various ailments. It has often been combined with moxabustion, the burning of leaves of moxa, the Chinese wormwood tree. Today it is widely used in China in the treatment of hay fever, headaches, and ulcers, and some types of blindness, arthritis, diarrhea, and hypertension. Acupuncture has also recently come into use, especially in China, as a general anesthetic during childbirth and some types of surgery. Unlike conventional anesthesia, acupuncture does not reduce blood pressure or depress breathing; in addition, the patient stays fully conscious and there is no postoperative hangover or nausea. In the practice of acupuncture, needles varying in length from ½ in. (1.27 cm) to several inches are inserted in appropriate points of the body, not necessarily near the affected organ. The needles are twirled and vibrated in specific ways; the depth of insertion also affects the treatment. In modern applications, a battery-powered device is often used to provide electrical stimulation through the needles. The traditional acupuncture points (there are about 800) are arranged along 14 lines, or meridians, running the length of the body from head to foot. The traditional Chinese explanation of the effectiveness of acupuncture is based on the Taoist philosophy (see TAOISM), according to which good health depends on a free circulation of T'chi, or life force energy, throughout all the organs of the body; this force is controlled by two forms of energy, yin (negative) and yang (positive). The meridians are the main channels of flow. When energy flow is impeded at any point, e.g., because of a diseased organ or stress, illness in other organs may result. Piercing the channels at the proper points is believed to correct the imbalances. Western researchers have found that the acupuncture points correspond to points on the skin having less electrical resistance than other skin areas. It has been suggested that acupuncture works by stimulating or repressing the autonomic NERVOUS SYSTEM in various ways, and there is some evidence that stimulation of the skin can affect internal organs by means of nerve reflex pathways. In the United States, use of acupuncture has been generally confined to pain relief and anesthesia. In 1974 the National Institutes of Health approved the study of acupuncture for the possible management of chronic pain caused by cancer, neuralgia, and arthritis. See Marc Duke, *Acupuncture* (1972); Felix Mann, *Acupuncture* (rev. ed. 1973).

Ada, city (1970 pop. 14,859), seat of Pontotoc co., S central Okla.; inc. 1904. It is a large cattle market and the center of a rich oil and ranch area. The city is also a center for horsebreeding, and fine quarter horses are raised there. East Central State College and the Sciences and Natural Resources Center of Oklahoma are there, and the Robert S. Kerr Water Research Center (a Federal laboratory) is just south of the city.

Adad: see HADAD.

Adadah (ăd'ədə), town of Judah in the southernmost part of Palestine. Joshua 15.22.

Adah (ā'də). **1** Wife of Esau. Gen. 36.2–20. **2** Wife of Lamech. Gen. 4.19–23.

Adaiah (ədā'yə). **1** Josiah's mother's father. 2 Kings 22.1. **2** Gershomite Levite. 1 Chron. 6.41. Iddo: 1 Chron. 6.21. **3** Benjamite. 1 Chron. 8.21. Shema: 1 Chron. 8.13. **4** Priest. 1 Chron. 9.12; Neh. 11.12. **5, 6** Men who had foreign wives. Ezra 10.29,39. **7** Father of MAASEIAH **2. 8** Ancestor of ASAIAH **4.**

Adair, John, 1757–1840, American pioneer in Kentucky, b. North Carolina. He went into the Kentucky country in 1786 and became famous as an Indian fighter and as a political leader. In the War of 1812 he was a commander of Kentucky volunteers in the battle of New Orleans. As governor of Kentucky (1820–24) he adopted a vigorous program of internal improvement to fight hard times. He was (1831–33) a member of the House of Representatives.

Adak (ā'dăk, ā'däk): see ALEUTIAN ISLANDS.

Adalbert, Saint (ăd'əlbərt), 956–97, bishop of Prague, b. Bohemia. He was a missionary in Russia, Prussia, and Poland and was martyred in Danzig. He is patron of Bohemia and Poland. Feast: April 23.

Adalbert, d. 1072, German churchman, archbishop of Hamburg-Bremen, a diocese that included Scandinavia. He was a favorite of Holy Roman Emperor Henry III, who appointed Adalbert to the archbishopric in order to break the power of the dukes of N Europe. He was a guardian of Henry's son and successor, Henry IV, but his relentless ambition to strengthen the church and the monarchy at the expense of the nobles (chiefly by annexing their lands) defeated itself. The nobles allied themselves with the abbots, who hated him for his efforts to subordinate the abbeys, and with the bishops, who feared his increasing ecclesiastical power. They accomplished his dismissal in 1066, but Henry IV recalled him in 1069. One of the ablest statesmen of his time, Adalbert, though working mainly for selfish aims, helped consolidate the imperial authority. See Adam of Bremen, *History of the Archbishops of Hamburg-Bremen* (tr. 1959).

Adalia (ădəlī'ə), one of Haman's sons. Esther 9.8.

Adalia, Turkey: see ANTALYA.

Adam [Heb., = man], in the Bible, the first man. For the account of his creation, of that of his wife EVE, of their life in the Garden of Eden (see EDEN, GARDEN OF), of their first disobedience, and of their expulsion, see Gen. 1.26–5.5. The opening chapters of Genesis are very interesting to believers of the three principal monotheistic religions; for conceptions derived therefrom, see SIN and GRACE; for examples of the mass of legends that Judaism and Islam have collected about the biblical account, see LILITH and PSEUDEPIGRAPHA. To St. Paul, Adam represented the earthy side of man, as in 1 Cor. 15.20–22, 42–58. The HIGHER CRITICISM has seen in Adam's story an attempt to harmonize Hebrew cosmogonic myths. Critics of that school compare Babylonian myths of creation, which are similar to the biblical account in many features.

Adam, Adolphe Charles (ädōlf' shärl' ädäN'), 1803–56, French composer of the popular song *Cantique de Noël.* He composed more than 50 stage works, including comic operas such as *Le Postillon de Longjumeau* (1836) and the ballet *Giselle* (1841).

Adam, Robert (ăd'əm), 1728–92, and **James Adam,** 1730–94, Scottish architects, brothers. They designed important public and private buildings in England and Scotland and numerous interiors, pieces of furniture, and decorative objects. Robert possessed the great creative talents, with his brother James serving chiefly as his assistant. Robert Adam designed his buildings to achieve the most harmonious relation between the exterior, the interior, and the furniture. His light, elegant, and essentially decorative style was a free, personal reconstitution of antique motifs. He drew upon numerous sources including earlier English Palladian architecture, French and Italian Renaissance architecture, and the antique monuments themselves as he knew them through publications and personal investigation. Adam himself contributed an important study, *Ruins of the Palace of the Emperor Diocletian at Spalatro in Dalmatia* (1764). For decorative painting, Adam employed such artists as Angelica Kauffmann and Antonio Zucchi. The Adam manner gained great favor in his day, and designs in the Adam style have never ceased to appear. Especially interesting examples of Adam planning and decoration are Osterly Park, Middlesex (1761–80); Syon House, Middlesex (1762–69); and Luton Hoo, Bedfordshire (1768–75). The brothers wrote *Works in Architecture of Robert and James Adam* (3 vol., 1778–1822). Robert was architect to the king from 1762 until 1768, when he was succeeded by James. Robert Adam was buried in Westminster Abbey. See John Fleming, *Robert Adam and His Circle* (1962) and D. Stillman, *The Decorative Work of Robert Adam* (1966); Doreen Yarwood, *Robert Adam* (1970).

Adam, town on the upper Jordan. Joshua 3.16.

Adamah (ăd'əmə), Naphtalite city. Joshua 19.36.

Adamawa Massif (ädämäwä', ăd"əmä'wə), plateau, c.26,000 sq mi (67,300 sq km), N central Cameroon and E Nigeria, W central Africa. It is sparsely populated, and grazing is the chief occupation; bauxite is mined there. The Benue River rises on the plateau.

Adam de la Halle (ädäN' də lä äl) or **Adam le Bossu** (lə bōsü'), c.1240–1287, French dramatist and poet-musician, a great TROUVÈRE. Many of his songs and polyphonic motets are preserved, as is the pastoral comedy with music *Le Jeu de Robin et Marion* (c.1283). Another work, *Jeu de la feuillée* (1262), was one of the earliest forerunners of comic opera.

Adami (ăd'əmī) or **Adami-nekeb** (-nē'kĕb), border town of Naphtali. Adami-nekeb in RSV. Two towns, Adami and Nekeb, in AV. Joshua 19.33.

Adam le Bossu: see ADAM DE LA HALLE.

Adams, Abigail, 1744–1818, wife of President John ADAMS and mother of President John Quincy ADAMS, b. Weymouth, Mass. She was born Abigail Smith. A lively, intelligent woman, she was the chief figure in the social life of her husband's administration and one of the most distinguished and influential of the first ladies in the history of the United States. Her detailed letters are a vivid source of social history. The correspondence with her husband was edited in a number of volumes by Charles Francis Adams; her letters, as well as John's, are included in *The Adams-Jefferson Letters*, edited by Lester J. Cappon (1959); letters to her sister, Mary Smith Cranch, are in *New Letters of Abigail Adams, 1788–1801,* edited by Stewart Mitchell (1947, repr. 1973). See biographies by J. Whitney (1947, repr. 1970) and L. E. Richards (1917, repr. 1971); novel by I. Stone, *Those Who Love* (1965). See also bibliography for ADAMS, JOHN.

Adams, Ansel, 1902–, American photographer, b. San Francisco. Adams began taking photographs in the High Sierra and Yosemite Valley, with which his name is permanently associated, becoming professional in 1930. That year he published the first of many books of his photographs, *Taos Pueblo.* With Edward Weston and others he founded the Group *f*/64 in reaction against the painterly aesthetic then current. He specialized in characteristic regional landscape, particularly of the Southwest, emphasizing conservation of nature. Adams wrote numerous technical manuals, including the classic *Basic Photo-Books* series, and helped to found the first photographic art department of a museum at the Museum of Modern Art, New York City. His book *Born Free and Equal* (1944) was an effort to aid Japanese-Americans incarcerated during World War II. He began the first college department of photography (California School of Fine Art, 1946). Adams won two Guggenheim grants to photograph national parks and monuments. He published the first superb portfolio reproductions of his own and others' photographs. See *aperture* monograph (1972).

Adams, Brooks, 1848–1927, American historian, b. Quincy, Mass.; son of Charles Francis ADAMS (1807–86). His theory that civilization rose and fell according to the growth and decline of commerce was first developed in *The Law of Civilization and Decay* (1895). Adams applied it to his own capitalistic age, of which he was a militant critic, but failed to find the universal law that he persistently sought. His ideas greatly influenced his brother Henry ADAMS, whose essays he edited in *The Degradation of the Democratic Dogma* (1919). In *America's Economic Supremacy* (1900), Brooks said that Western Europe had already begun to decline and that Russia and the United States were the only potential great powers left. His other chief works include *The Emancipation of Massachusetts* (1887), *The New Empire* (1902), and *Theory of Social Revolutions* (1913). See biography by A. F. Beringause (1955); J. T. Adams, *The Adams Family* (1930, repr. 1957); T. P. Donovan, *Henry Adams and Brooks Adams* (1961).

Adams, Charles Francis, 1807–86, American public official, minister to Great Britain (1861–68), b. Boston; son of John Quincy ADAMS. After a boyhood spent in various European capitals, he was graduated (1825) from Harvard and studied law under Daniel Webster. He practiced in Boston, looked after his father's business affairs, and wrote articles on American history for the *North American Review.* Adams served (1840–45) in both branches of the state legislature. He founded and edited the Boston *Whig* and became a leader of the Conscience Whigs. In 1848 he was the Free-Soil party candidate for the vice presidency. He represented (1858–61) his father's old district in Congress and assumed prominence as a Republican leader. On Seward's advice, Lincoln appointed him minister to Great Britain. In the face of English sympathy for the Confederacy, he maintained the Northern cause with wisdom and a bold dignity that won British respect, particularly in the serious *Trent* and *Alabama* incidents. He is credited with preventing British recognition of the Confederacy, thus contributing much to the Union victory. He later represented the United States in the settlement of the ALABAMA CLAIMS. He published many political pamphlets and addresses and was an editor of the works (10 vol., 1850–56) of his grandfather, John Adams, and of his father's diary (12 vol., 1874–77). See biography by M. B. Duberman (1961); W. C. Ford, ed., *A Cycle of Adams Letters, 1861–1865* (1920); J. T. Adams, *The Adams Family* (1930).

Adams, Charles Francis, 1835–1915, American economist and historian, b. Boston; son of Charles Francis Adams (1807–86). In the Civil War he fought at Antietam and Gettysburg and was brevetted brigadier general of volunteers. Adams became a railroad expert after the war, writing *Chapters of Erie* (1871), which exposed the corrupt financing of the Erie RR, and *Railroads: Their Origin and Problems* (1878). In 1869 he became a member, and from 1872 to 1879 was chairman, of the Massachusetts Board of Railroad Commissioners, the first such board in the nation. Adams was made chairman of the government directors of the Union Pacific in 1878 and became president in 1884, but he was ousted by the forces of Jay Gould in 1890. His reform of the public schools in the home town of the Adamses, Quincy, Mass., was described in *The New Departure in the Common Schools of Quincy* (1879), and the Quincy system was widely adopted. Adams served 24 years on the Harvard Board of Overseers and was president (1895–1915) of the Massachusetts Historical Society. He wrote *Three Episodes of Massachusetts History* (1892); *Studies: Military and Diplomatic, 1775–1865* (1911); *Trans-Atlantic Historical Solidarity* (1913), which was a collection of lectures he had given at Oxford; and biographies of his father (1900) and Richard Henry Dana (1890). See his autobiography (1916, repr. 1973); W. C. Ford, ed., *A Cycle of Adams Letters, 1861–1865* (1920); J. T. Adams, *The Adams Family* (1930).

Adams, Charles Francis, 1866–1954, U.S. Secretary of the Navy (1929–33), b. Quincy, Mass.; grandson of Charles Francis Adams (1807–86). He practiced law for a brief period in Boston but for most of his life was connected with a wide variety of business enterprises in that city and elsewhere. Adams served in the cabinet of Herbert Hoover.

Adams, Franklin Pierce, pseud. **F. P. A.,** 1881–1960, American columnist and author, b. Chicago. He began (1903) work as a columnist on the Chicago *Journal* and continued it on the New York *Evening Mail,* the *Tribune,* the *World,* the *Herald Tribune,* and the *Post.* His column, "The Conning Tower," consisted of verse and humor by F. P. A. and his contributors, who included Ring Lardner and Dorothy Parker. On Saturdays his columns were accounts of his week's activities that imitated the style of Samuel Pepys. They were republished as *The Diary of Our Own Samuel Pepys: 1911–1934* (1935). Adams's other works included *So There!* (1923), *Christopher Columbus* (1931), and *Nods and Becks* (1944).

Adams, Henry, 1838–1918, American writer and historian, b. Boston; son of Charles Francis Adams (1807–86). He was secretary (1861–68) to his father, then U.S. minister to Great Britain. Upon his return to the United States, having already abandoned the law and seeing no opportunity in the traditional Adams vocation of politics, he briefly pursued journalism. He reluctantly accepted (1870) an offer to teach medieval history at Harvard, but nonetheless stayed on seven years and also edited (1870–76) the *North American Review.* In 1877 Adams moved to Washington, D.C., his home thereafter. He wrote a good biography of Albert Gallatin (1879), a less satisfactory one of John Randolph (1882), and two novels (the first anonymously and the second under a pseudonym)—*Democracy* (1880), a cutting satire on politics, and *Esther* (1884). His exhaustive study of the administrations of Jefferson and Madison, *History of the United States of America* (9 vol., 1889–91; reprinted in a number of editions), is one of the major achievements of American historical writing. Famous for its style, it is deficient, perhaps, in understanding the basic economic forces at work, but the first six chapters constitute one of the best social surveys of any period in U.S. history. Never of a sanguine temperament, Adams became even more pessimistic after the suicide (1885) of his adored wife. He abandoned American history and began a series of restless journeys, physical and mental, in an effort to achieve a basic philosophy of history. Drawing upon the physical sciences for guidance and influenced by his brother, Brooks ADAMS, he found a satisfactory unifying principle in force or energy. He selected for intensive treatment two periods: 1050–1250, presented in *Mont-Saint-Michel and Chartres* (privately printed 1904, pub. 1913), and his own era, presented in *The Education of Henry Adams* (privately printed 1906, pub. 1918). The first is a brilliant idealization of the Middle Ages, specifically of the 13th-century unity brought about by the force of the Virgin, which was dominant then. The second was classified by his publishers as an autobiography, although it was written in the third person and was unrevealing about much of his life. It is, however, a tour de force, and describes his unsuccessful efforts to achieve intellectual peace in an age when the force of the dynamo is dominant. These two books, containing some of the most beautiful English ever written, rather than his monumental *History,* won Adams his lasting place as a major American writer. *The Degradation of the Democratic Dogma* (1919), edited by Brooks Adams and prefaced with a memoir by Henry Adams, contains three brilliant essays on his philosophy of history—"The Tendency of History," "A Letter to American Teachers of History" (pub. separately in 1910), and "The Rule of Phase Applied to History." Friendships, especially those with John HAY and Clarence King, played a large part in Adams's life, and his personal letters reveal a warmer man than one might suspect. See his letters (ed. by W. C. Ford, 2 vol., 1930–38); J. T. Adams, *Henry Adams* (1933, repr. 1970); Ward Thoron, ed., *The Letters of Mrs. Henry Adams, 1865–1883* (1936); H. D. Cater, ed., *Henry Adams and His Friends: A Collection of His Unpublished Letters* (1947); Ernest Samuels, *The Young Henry Adams* (1948), *Henry Adams: The Middle Years* (1958) and *Henry Adams: The Major Phase* (1964); T. P. Donovan, *Henry Adams and Brooks Adams* (1961).

Adams, Herbert Baxter, 1850–1901, American historian, b. Shutesbury, near Amherst, Mass. In 1876, the year he received his doctorate at Heidelberg, he became one of the original faculty of Johns Hopkins Univ. There, in 1880, he began his famous seminar in history, where a large proportion of the next generation of American historians trained. Adams founded the "Johns Hopkins Studies in Historical and Political Science," the first of such series, and brought about the organization in 1884 of the American Historical Association, of which he was secretary until 1900. He wrote *The Germanic Origin of New England Towns* (1882), *Life and Writings of Jared Sparks* (1893), and many articles and reports on the study of the social sciences that were very influential in their day. See W. S. Holt, ed., *Historical Scholarship in the United States, 1876–1901, as Revealed in the Correspondence of Herbert B. Adams* (1938).

Adams, James Truslow (trŭ'slō), 1878–1949, American historian, b. Brooklyn, N.Y. *The Founding of New England* (1921), which brought him the Pulitzer Prize in history for 1922, was followed by *Revolutionary New England, 1691–1776* (1923) and *New England in the Republic, 1776–1850* (1926). Among the best of his many books are *Provincial Society, 1690–1763* (Vol. III in the "History of American Life" series, 1927) and *The Epic of America* (1931), which was widely translated. *The March of Democracy* (2 vol., 1932–33) and *America's Tragedy* (1934) were also popular. *The Adams Family* (1930) and *Henry Adams* (1933) were books on the famous Massachusetts clan, to which he was not related. Adams, who spent much of his time in London as representative of his publishers, Charles Scribner's Sons, also wrote *Building the British Empire: To the End of the First Empire* (1938) and *Empire on the Seven Seas: The British Empire, 1784–1939* (1940). He was editor in chief of *Dictionary of American History* (6 vol., 1940; rev. ed. 1942), *Atlas of American History* (1943), and *Album of American History* (4 vol., 1944–48), three valuable reference works. Some of his later writings reflect his obvious distaste for the New Deal, of which he was a vigorous critic. See biography by Allan Nevins (1968).

Adams, John, 1735–1826, 2d President of the United States (1797–1801), b. Quincy (then in Braintree), Mass., grad. Harvard, 1755. A lawyer, he emerged into politics as an opponent of the Stamp Act and, after moving to Boston, was a leader in the Revolutionary group opposing the British measures that were to lead to the American Revolution. Sent (1774) to the First Continental Congress, Adams distinguished himself, and in the Second Continental Congress he was a moderate but forceful revolutionary. He proposed George Washington as commander in chief of the Continental troops to bind Virginia more tightly to the cause for independence. He favored the DECLARATION OF INDEPENDENCE, was a member of the drafting committee, and argued eloquently for it. As a diplomat seeking foreign aid for the newly established nation, he had a thorny career. Appointed (1777) to succeed Silas Deane as a commissioner to France, he accomplished little before going home (1779) to be a major figure in the Massachusetts constitutional convention. He then returned (1779) to France, where he quarreled with VERGENNES and was able to lend little assistance to Benjamin Franklin in his peace efforts. His attempts to negotiate a loan from the Netherlands were fruitless until 1782. Adams was one of the negotiators who drew up the momentous Treaty of Paris (1783; see PARIS, TREATY OF) to end the American Revolution. After this service he obtained another Dutch loan and then was envoy (1785–88) to Great Britain, where he met with British coldness and unwillingness to discuss the problems growing out of the treaty. He asked for his own recall and ended a significant but generally discouraging diplomatic career. In the United States once more, he was chosen Vice President and served throughout George Washington's administration (1789–97). Although he inclined to conservative policies, he acted somewhat as a balance wheel in the partisan contest between Alexander HAMILTON and Thomas JEFFERSON. In the 1796 election Adams was chosen to succeed Washington as President despite the surreptitious opposition of Hamilton. The Adams administration was one of crisis and conflict, in which the President showed an honest and stubborn integrity, and though allied with Hamilton and the conservative property-respecting Federalists, he was not dominated by them in their struggle against the vigorously rising, more broadly democratic forces led by Jefferson. Though the Federalists were pro-British and strongly opposed to post-Revolutionary France, Adams by conciliation prevented the near war of 1798 (see XYZ AFFAIR) from developing into a real war between France and the United States. Nor did the President wholeheartedly endorse the ALIEN AND SEDITION ACTS (1798), aimed at the Anti-Federalists. He was, however, detested by his Jeffersonian enemies, and in the election of 1800 he and Hamilton were both submerged in the tide of Jeffersonian democracy. After 1801, Adams lived in retirement at Quincy, issuing sober and highly respected political statements and writing and receiving many letters, notably those to and from Jefferson. Their famous correspondence was edited by Lester J. Cappon in *The Adams-Jefferson Letters* (1959). By remarkable coincidence he and Jefferson died on the same day, Independence Day, July 4, 1826. John Adams and his wife, Abigail ADAMS, founded one of the most distinguished families of the United States; their son, John Quincy ADAMS, was also President. A definitive edition of the voluminous writings of the Adams family was begun with four volumes (1961) containing the diary and autobiography of John Adams. Until completion of the definitive edition, see Adams's *Works* (10 vol., ed. by J. Q. Adams and C. F. Adams, 1850-56, repr. 1969; Vol. I is a biography by C. F. Adams); *The Selected Writings of John Adams and John Quincy Adams* (ed. by Adrienne Koch and William Peden, 1946). See also James Truslow Adams, *The Adams Family* (1930); Zoltán Haraszti, *John Adams and the Prophets of Progress* (1952); Manning J. Dauer, *The Adams Federalists* (1953, repr. 1968); Stephen G. Kurtz, *The Presidency of John Adams* (1957, repr. 1961); John R. Howe, Jr., *The Changing Political Thought of John Adams* (1966); biographies by John T. Morse (1884, repr. 1970), Gilbert Chinard (1933, repr. 1964), Page Smith (1962), and J. B. Peabody, ed. (1973).

Adams, John Couch, 1819-92, English astronomer, grad. St. John's College, Cambridge, 1843. By mathematical calculation based on irregularities in the motion of Uranus, he predicted the position of the then unknown planet Neptune. Because of delay in England in making a telescopic search for the planet, the credit for the discovery went to a Frenchman, Leverrier. In 1858, Adams became professor of mathematics at St. Andrews Univ., but he soon returned to Cambridge, to occupy the Lowndean chair of astronomy and geometry until his death. From 1861 he was also director of the university observatory, preferring this post to that of astronomer royal, which was offered to him in 1881. He made valuable studies of the moon's motions, of the Leonids in the great meteor shower of 1866, and of terrestrial magnetism. His collected papers, edited by his brother, were published (1896-1900) at Cambridge.

Adams, John Quincy, 1767-1848, 6th President of the United States (1825-29), b. Quincy (then in Braintree), Mass.; son of John and Abigail Adams and father of Charles Francis Adams (1807-86). He accompanied his father on missions to Europe and gained broad knowledge from study and travel—he even accompanied (1781-83) Francis Dana to Russia—before returning home to graduate (1787) from Harvard and to study law. Washington appointed (1794) him minister to the Netherlands, and in his father's administration he was minister to Prussia (1797-1801). In 1803 he became a U.S. Senator as a Federalist, but his independence of mind led him to approve Jeffersonian policies in the Louisiana Purchase and in the Embargo Act of 1807; the Federalists were outraged, and he resigned (1808). Sent as minister to Russia in 1809, he was well received at court, but the wars of Napoleon eclipsed Russian-American relations. He then helped to draw up the Treaty of Ghent (1814), and his diplomatic training was completed as minister to Great Britain. As Secretary of State (1817-25) under President James Monroe, Adams gained an enduring fame. His best-known achievement was the MONROE DOCTRINE (1823). In 1824, Adams was a candidate for the U.S. presidency. Neither he, Andrew Jackson, nor Henry Clay received an electoral majority, and the election was decided in the House of Representatives. There Clay supported Adams and made him President. Adams then appointed Clay Secretary of State, but the Jacksonians' cry that the appointment fulfilled a corrupt bargain was unfounded in fact. With little popular support and without a party, Adams had an unhappy, ineffective administration, despite his attempts to institute a broad program of internal improvements. After Jackson won the 1828 election, Adams retired to Quincy but returned to win new renown as U.S. Representative (1831-48); he was eloquent in attacking the gag rules and all measures that would extend slavery. His coldness and rather gloomy introspection still kept him from general popularity, but he was respected for his high-mindedness and his great knowledge. His interest in science led him to promote the Smithsonian Institution. His diary (selections ed. by C. F. Adams, 12 vol., 1874-77, repr. 1970; abridged by Allan Nevins, 1928 and 1951) is a valuable document. Most of his writings were edited by W. C. Ford (7 vol., 1913-17), and some appear in *The Selected Writings of John and John Quincy Adams* (ed. by Adrienne Koch and William Peden, 1946). See the definitive biography by Samuel Flagg Bemis (2 vol., 1949 and 1956), other biographies by John T. Morse (1883, repr. 1972) and Bennett Champ Clark (1932); James Truslow Adams, *The Adams Family* (1930).

Adams, Maude, 1872-1953, American actress, b. Salt Lake City, Utah. Her father's name was Kiskadden, but she used her mother's maiden name. She began acting at an early age and became leading lady to John Drew under the management of the Frohmans, an assignment that lasted for five years. In 1897 she had her first starring role in Barrie's *Little Minister.* Other Barrie plays she starred in include *Quality Street* (1901), *Peter Pan* (1905), the play for which she was most loved, and *What Every Woman Knows* (1908). In her retirement after 1918, Adams made valuable contributions to the development of stage lighting; in 1937 she became professor of drama at Stephens College. See biography by Phyllis Robbins (1956).

Adams, Robert McCormick, Jr., 1926-, American anthropologist, b. Chicago, Ill., grad. Univ. of Chicago (Ph.B., 1947; M.A., 1952; Ph.D., 1956). He joined the faculty of the Univ. of Chicago in 1955, and in 1962 he became director of the Oriental Institute there, a post he held until 1968. In 1970 he became dean of social sciences. He has done intensive, regionally oriented studies of long-term patterns of settlement and land-use in the Middle East and comparisons of the early growth of civilization in the Middle East and the New World. Among his writings are *Land Behind Baghdad* (1965), *The Evolution of Urban Society* (1966), and *The Uruk Countryside* (1972; with H. J. Nissen).

Adams, Samuel, 1722-1803, political leader in the American Revolution, signer of the Declaration of Independence, b. Boston, Mass.; second cousin of John Adams. An unsuccessful businessman, he became interested in politics and was a member (1765-74) and clerk (1766-74) of the lower house of the Massachusetts legislature. As colonial resistance to British laws stiffened, Adams spoke for the discontented and replaced James OTIS as leader of the extremists. He drafted a protest against the Stamp Act in 1765 and was one of the organizers of the non-importation agreement (1767) against Great Britain to force repeal of the TOWNSHEND ACTS, and drew up the Circular Letter to the other colonies, denouncing the acts as taxation without representation. More important, he used his able pen in colonial newspapers and pamphlets to stir up sentiment against the British. His polemics helped to bring about the BOSTON MASSACRE. With the help of such men as John Hancock he organized the revolutionary Sons of Liberty and helped to foment revolt through the Committees of Correspondence. He was the moving spirit in the BOSTON TEA PARTY. Gen. Thomas Gage issued (1775) a warrant for the arrest of Adams and Hancock, but they escaped punishment and continued to stir up lethargic patriots. Samuel Adams was a member (1774-81) of the Continental Congress, but after independence was declared his influence declined; the "radical" was replaced by more conservative leaders, who tended to look upon Adams as an irresponsible agitator. He later (1794-97) served as governor of Massachusetts. See writings ed. by H. A. Cushing (4 vol., 1904-8, repr. 1968); biographies by J. C. Miller (1936, repr. 1960), S. Beach (1965), W. V. Wells (2d ed. 1969), and N. B. Gerson (1973).

Adams, Samuel Hopkins, 1871-1958, American author, b. Dunkirk, N.Y., grad. Hamilton College, 1891. He was a reporter for the New York *Sun* (1891-1900) and then joined *McClure's Magazine,* where he gained a reputation as a muckraker for his articles on the conditions of public health in the United States. Adams also wrote a series of articles for *Collier's Weekly,* in which he exposed patent medicines; these pieces were credited with influencing the passage of the first Pure Food and Drugs Act. Adams was a prolific writer, producing both fiction and nonfiction. His best-known novel, *Revelry* (1926), based on the scandals of the Harding administration, was later followed by *Incredible Era* (1939), a biography of Harding and his times. Among his other works are *The Great American Fraud* (1906), *The Harvey Girls* (1942), *Grandfather Stories* (1955), and *Tenderloin* (1959).

Adams, William (Will Adams), 1564?-1620, first Englishman to visit Japan. As pilot of a Dutch ship, he reached there in 1600. He soon became a favorite of the ruler IEYASU, advising him on navigation, trade, and Western affairs. Many of the longer voyages that the Japanese made were in vessels constructed under his direction. Adams attempted to foster trade relations with England, and he himself made trading trips to the Ryukyu Islands, Siam, and Cochin China. He married a Japanese woman, acquired a Japanese name (Anjin Sama, or Mr. Pilot), and was given an estate at Yokosuka. He remained in Japan until his death. See his letters (ed. by Thomas Randall, 1850) and his logbook (ed. by C. J. Purnell, 1916); R. Cocks, *Diary* (1964) and H. H. Gowen, *Five Foreigners in Japan* (1936, repr. 1967).

Adams, town (1970 pop. 11,772), Berkshire co., NW Mass., in the Berkshires, on the Hoosic River; inc. 1778. Its manufactures include lime products and decorative textiles (made there since 1862). The region attracts summer and winter vacationers. A Society of Friends meeting house (built 1782) is the site of annual Quaker meetings. Susan B. Anthony was born in Adams.

Adam's apple: see LARYNX.

Adam's Bridge or **Rama's Bridge,** chain of shoals, c.18 mi (30 km) long, in the Palk Strait between India and Sri Lanka (Ceylon). At high tide it is covered by c.4 ft (1.2 m) of water. A train-ferry links Dhanushkodi, India, with Mannar, Sri Lanka. According to Hindu legend, the bridge was built to transport Rama, hero of the *Ramayana,* to the island to rescue his wife from the demon king Ravanna.

Adams National Historic Site: see NATIONAL PARKS AND MONUMENTS (table).

Adam's-needle: see YUCCA.

Adamson, Robert: see HILL, DAVID OCTAVIUS.

Adam's Peak, Sinhalese *Sri Padastanaya* and *Samanaliya,* mountain, 7,360 ft (2,243 m) high, S central Sri Lanka (Ceylon). It is a sacred mountain, famous as a goal of pilgrimage for Buddhists, Hindus, and Muslims. On its summit is a large flat rock that bears the impression of a gigantic (c.10 sq ft/.93 sq m) human foot. This stone footprint is regarded as Buddha's by Buddhists, Siva's by Hindus, and Adam's by Muslims, who believe this to be the site of Adam's fall from Paradise.

Adana (ä'dänä), city (1970 pop. 351,655), capital of Adana prov., S Turkey, on the Seyhan River. The fourth largest city in Turkey, it is the commercial center of a farm region where cotton, grains, and fruits are grown. Manufactures include processed food, cotton textiles, cement, and soap. The city is a road and rail center. An ancient city probably founded by the Hittites, Adana was colonized (66 B.C.) by the Romans. It prospered under the Romans and then declined. The city was revived (A.D. c.782) by Harun ar-Rashid. In the 16th cent. the city passed to the Ottoman Turks. Nearby is Karatepe, a Hittite archaeological site.

Adana, Plain of (ä'dänä"), fertile region along the Mediterranean coast, S central Turkey. It has a subtropical climate and receives rainfall mainly during the autumn and winter months. The plain, traversed and irrigated by the Seyhan River, is a major agricultural region, producing a large variety of crops including most of the cotton grown in Turkey. The city of Adana is the commercial and marketing center of the region.

Adapazarı (ädä"päzär'ə), city (1970 pop. 101,590), capital of Adapazarı prov., NW Turkey, on the Sakarya River. It is the trade center for a rich agricultural region where tobacco, sugar beets, and grains are produced. The city's manufactures include refined sugar, farm machinery, textiles, and cement.

adaptation, in biology, the adjustment of living matter to environmental conditions and to other living things. This ability is a fundamental property of protoplasm and constitutes a basic difference between living and nonliving matter. Most living things require free oxygen from the air or from water, but yeasts, many bacteria, and some other simple forms obtain the oxygen required for oxidation from molecules of substances that contain the element. Various animals and plants are adapted for securing their food and for surviving the extremes of temperature and of water supply in desert, tropical, and polar regions. For most organisms the optimum temperature is between about 20°C (68°F) and 40°C (104°F). Some algae and protozoa live in hot springs, and some bacteria can survive freezing. The cactus can survive heat and drought. Certain fish and other aquatic animals live in deep water and are so specialized to withstand the great pressure that they burst if lifted to sea level. Animals show anatomical adaptations—e.g., the body of the fish is suited to life in the water; the body of the bird is adapted for flight; the land mammals show wide variation in the structure of limbs and body that enables some to run swiftly, some to climb, some to swing from tree to tree, some to glide through the air, and others to jump. The whale, an aquatic mammal, can adjust to great pressure changes at different levels in the water. The beaks of birds vary in shape and size according to the kinds of food they feed on—e.g., on seeds, on insects, on aquatic animals, and on small mammals. The feet and legs of birds also show modifications that fit them for perching, for wading, and for paddling through the water. Adaptive coloration is observed in many animals (see PROTECTIVE COLORATION). Among communal insects, such as ants and honeybees, the individuals are highly adapted to perform their functions in the community. It is believed by many scientists that life originated in the sea and that through gradual evolutionary changes some forms became adapted to life on land. Variations may arise as a result of MUTATION or of recombinations of the genes in the germ cells. Such variations are inherited (see GENETICS). Those that aid the organism to meet the conditions of a changing environment or help it in its competition with other living things enable it to survive and reproduce, the changes thus being passed on from one generation to another and in this way perhaps producing a new species. See ECOLOGY; EVOLUTION; SELECTION.

adaptive radiation, in biology, the evolution of an ancestral species, which was adapted to a particular way of life, into many diverse species, each adapted to a different habitat. Adaptive radiation has occurred in the evolution of many groups of organisms, and is clearly illustrated by Darwin's finches, 14 species of small land birds of the Galápagos Islands. All the birds on the islands are derived from a single species of ground-dwelling, seed-eating finch that probably emigrated from the South American mainland. Because the environmental niches, or habitats, were unoccupied on the isolated islands, the ancestral stock was able to differentiate into diverse species. Of the 14 species living on the islands, 3 species are ground-dwelling seedeaters, 3 live on cactus plants and are seedeaters, 1 is a tree-dwelling seedeater, and 7 are tree-dwelling insecteaters. See also COMPETITION.

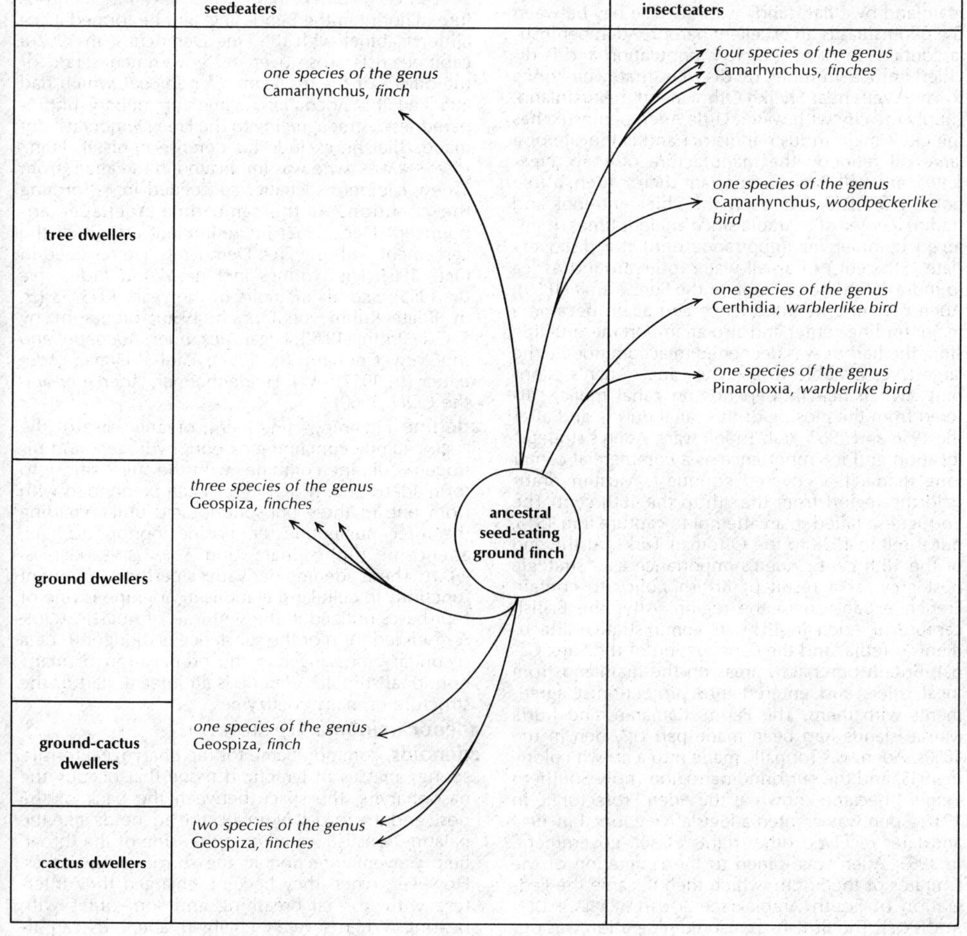

Adaptive radiation in Darwin's finches

Adar (ā'där), in the Bible: see HAZAR-ADDAR.

Adasa (ăd'əsā), town, near Beth-horon, place of encampment of Judas Maccabaeus. 1 Mac. 7.40.

Adbeel (ăd'bēĕl), son of Ishmael. Gen. 25.13; 1 Chron. 1.29.

Adda (äd'dä), river, 194 mi (312 km) long, rising in the Rhaetian Alps, N Italy, and flowing SW through Lake Como, then S into the Po River near Cremona. Its upper course furnishes much electric power; the lower river irrigates the Lombard plain. Many battles have been fought along its course, notably the Battle of LODI (1796).

Addams, Charles Samuel, 1912–, American cartoonist, b. Westfield, N.J. Since 1935, Addams's work has appeared in the *New Yorker* magazine. His cartoons are famed for their wit, fantasy, and sense of the macabre. Members of a ghoulish family are his chief subject matter. His cartoons are collected in *Drawn and Quartered* (1942), *Addams and Evil* (1947), *Monster Rally* (1950), *Home Bodies* (1954), *Black Maria* (1960), *Charles Addams' Mother Goose* (1967), and *My Crowd* (1970).

Addams, Jane, 1860–1935, American social worker, b. Cedarville, Ill., grad. Rockford College, 1881. In 1889, with Ellen Gates Starr, she founded Hull House in Chicago, one of the first social settlements in the United States (see SETTLEMENT HOUSE). Based on the university settlements begun in England by Samuel Barnett, Hull House served as a community center for the neighborhood poor and later as a center for social reform activities. It was important in Chicago civic affairs and had an influence on the settlement movement throughout the country. An active reformer throughout her career, Jane Addams was a leader in the woman suffrage and pacifist movements. She was the recipient (jointly with Nicholas Murray Butler) of the 1931 Nobel Peace Prize. Her books on social questions include *The Spirit of Youth and the City Streets* (1909), *A New Conscience and an Ancient Evil* (1912), and *Peace and Bread in Time of War* (1922). See her autobiographical *Twenty Years at Hull-House* (1910) and *The Second Twenty Years at Hull-House* (1930); biographies by her nephew, J. W. Linn (1935), and A. F. Davis (1973); study by Daniel Levine (1971).

Addan (ăd'ən), unidentified Palestinian town. Ezra 2.59. Addon: Neh. 7.61.

Addar: see ARD.

addax (ăd'ăks), large, desert-dwelling ANTELOPE. It is a single species, *Addax nasomaculatus.* The addax is yellowish-white in color, has a brown mane and throat fringe, and may stand as high as 42 in. (106 cm) at the shoulder. Both sexes bear long, spiraling horns reaching up to 43 in. (109 cm) in length. The addax is native to N African deserts; its short, thick legs and broad hooves are adapted to traveling on sand. It is able to survive only on the water obtained from dew or from forage and can scent grasses newly sprouted by recent rain. Addax are typically found in pairs or in small herds. They have been extensively hunted, and, with much of their habitat destroyed, the species is now much reduced in numbers. Addax are classified in the phylum CHORDATA, subphylum Vertebrata, class Mammalia, order Artiodactyla, family Bovidae.

adder: see VIPER.

adder's-tongue, name for several plants, among them DOGTOOTH VIOLET and a primitive fern genus (*Ophioglossum*). Adder's-tongues are classified in the divisions MAGNOLIOPHYTA and PTERIDOPHYTA, respectively.

Addi (ăd'ī), name in Luke's genealogy. Luke 3.28.

adding machine: see CALCULATING MACHINE.

Addington, Henry: see SIDMOUTH, HENRY ADDINGTON, VISCOUNT.

Addis Ababa (ăd'ĭs ăb'əbə) [Amharic, = new flower], city (1971 est. pop. 795,000), capital of Ethiopia. It is situated at c.8,000 ft (2,440 m) on a well-watered plateau surrounded by hills and mountains. Addis Ababa is Ethiopia's largest city and its administrative and communications center. It is the main trade center for coffee, the country's chief export, and for tobacco, grains, and hides. The major industries produce food, beverages, processed tobacco, textiles, and shoes. Addis Ababa has a large tourist industry. It is the hub of a highway network and a terminus of a railroad that runs to DJIBOUTI, French Territory of the Afars and the Issas. An international airport is near Addis Ababa. In 1886 the city, then known as Finfinnie, was chosen by MENELIK II as the capital of his kingdom of Shoa and was renamed Addis Ababa. In 1889 it was made the capital of Ethiopia. There, in 1896, Italy recognized Ethiopian independence. However, in 1936 (during the Italo-Ethiopian War), Italy captured Addis Ababa and made it the capital of ITALIAN EAST AFRICA. The city was recaptured by the Allies in 1941 and returned to Ethiopian rule. Major growth began after 1945; today the city has many modern buildings. The ORGANIZATION OF AFRICAN UNITY (OAU) and the UN Economic Commission on Africa are headquartered in Addis Ababa, which also hosts numerous international conferences; in 1972 the UN Security Council met in the city. Haile Selassie I Univ., whose Institute of Ethiopian Studies runs an ethnological and traditional arts museum, and Haile Selassie I National Theatre are in Addis Ababa. The OAU center, the imperial palace, the parliament building, and the Coptic and Roman Catholic cathedrals are notable buildings.

Addison, Joseph, 1672–1719, English essayist, poet, and statesman. He was educated at Charterhouse, where he was a classmate of Richard Steele, and at Oxford, where he became a distinguished classical scholar. His travels on the Continent from 1699 to 1703 were recorded in *Remarks on Italy* (1705). Addison first achieved prominence with *The Campaign* (1704), an epic celebrating the victory of Marlborough at Blenheim. The poem was commissioned by Lord Halifax, and its great success resulted in Addison's appointment in 1705 as undersecretary of state and in 1709 as secretary to the lord lieutenant of Ireland. He also held a seat in Parliament from 1708 until his death. Addison's most enduring fame was achieved as an essayist. In 1710 he began his contributions to the *Tatler,* which Richard STEELE had founded in 1709. He continued to write for successive publications, including the SPECTATOR (1711–12), the *Guardian* (1713), and the new *Spectator* (1714). His contributions to these periodicals raised the

English essay to a degree of technical perfection never before achieved and perhaps never since surpassed. In a prose style marked by simplicity, order, and precision, he sought to engage men's thoughts toward reason, moderation, and a harmonious life. His works also include an opera libretto, *Rosamund* (1707); a prose comedy, *The Drummer* (1716); and a neoclassical tragedy, *Cato* (1713), which had an immense success in its own time, but has since been regarded as artificial and sententious. In his last years Addison received his greatest prominence. In 1717 he was made secretary of state, an office he resigned the following year. But the period (1714–19) was also marked by failing health, a supposedly unhappy marriage, and the severing of his relations with his good friend Richard Steele. See biography by P. H. B. O. Smithers (1954, repr. 1968).

Addison, Thomas, 1793–1860, English physician, b. near Newcastle, grad. Univ. of Edinburgh (M.D., 1815). In 1837 he became a physician at Guy's Hospital, London, where he conducted important research on pneumonia, tuberculosis, and other diseases. He was the first to recognize (1855) the disease of the adrenal glands that later became known as Addison's disease, and he is equally famous for his description of pernicious anemia.

Addison, village (1970 pop. 24,482), Du Page co., NE Ill.; inc. 1884. It has some light manufacturing.

Addison's disease [for Thomas Addison], progressive disease brought about by atrophy of the outer layer, or cortex, of the ADRENAL GLAND; it is also called chronic adrenocortical insufficiency. The deterioration of this tissue causes a decrease in the secretion of steroid hormones, many of which are necessary for the maintenance of life. In many cases of Addison's disease the cause of the wasting process is not known; in others the predominant cause is tuberculous destruction, the formation and infiltration of tumors, inflammatory disease, or surgery. Symptoms are increasing weakness, abnormal pigmentation of the skin and mucous membranes, weight loss, low blood pressure, dehydration, and gastrointestinal upsets. Once considered inevitably fatal, Addison's disease can now be treated with injections of adrenocortical hormones that enable its victims to lead a nearly normal life.

addition, fundamental operation of arithmetic. Given two collections, or SETS, of objects having no common members (disjoint sets), the operation of combining all members of both sets into another set is called addition; in terms of set theory, addition is the union of two disjoint sets. The sets combined under addition are known as the addends and the resulting set is called their sum. A name in the form of a cardinal NUMBER is associated with each set; e.g., the number 3 is used to indicate the set $\{x_1, x_2, x_3\}$, the number 4 is used for the set $\{y_1, y_2, y_3, y_4\}$, and the number 7 is used for the set $\{x_1, x_2, x_3, y_1, y_2, y_3, y_4\}$. In arithmetic addition follows the ASSOCIATIVE LAW, the COMMUTATIVE LAW, and, in combination with multiplication, the DISTRIBUTIVE LAW. Addition is also defined for other types of mathematical objects, for example, VECTORS and TENSORS. See also SUBTRACTION.

addition polymers: see POLYMER.

Ad Diwaniyah (äd dēwän'ēyä), city (1965 pop. 60,553), S central Iraq, on a branch of the Euphrates River. It is a market place for dates and grains.

Addon, variant of ADDAN.

addra (ăd'rə): see GAZELLE.

Ade, George, 1866–1944, American humorist and dramatist, b. Kentland, Ind., grad. Purdue Univ., 1887. His newspaper sketches and books attracted attention for their racy and slangy idiom and for the humor and shrewdness with which they delineated people of the Midwestern scene. He is best known for *Fables in Slang* (1899); other volumes include *People You Knew* (1903) and *Hand-made Fables* (1920). Ade also wrote several musical comedies and farcical plays, among them *The County Chairman* (1903) and *The College Widow* (1904). See *The America of George Ade* (selected writings ed. by Jean Shepherd, 1961); *Letters of George Ade* (ed. by Terence Tobin, 1973); study by Lee Coyle (1964).

Adelaide (ăd'əlād) or **Adelheid** (ä'dĕlhīt), c.931–999, empress consort of Holy Roman Emperor Otto I, daughter of King Rudolf II of Arles. After the death (950) of her first husband, King Lothair of Italy, she was about to be forced into a marriage with the son of BERENGAR II, Lothair's successor. She appealed to OTTO I, who rescued and married her in 951. She was sole regent for her grandson, OTTO III, from 991 to 994. She was a great benefactor of religious houses.

Adelaide, city (1971 urban agglomeration pop. 809,466), capital and chief port of South Australia, S Australia, at the mouth of the Torrens River on Gulf St. Vincent. It has automotive, textile, and other industries. Grains, wool, dairy products, and fruit are exported. Named for the consort of William IV, it was founded in 1836 and is the oldest city in the state. The Univ. of Adelaide (1874), a natural history museum (1895), and Anglican and Roman Catholic cathedrals are in the city. The Adelaide Festival of the Arts has been held biennially since 1960.

Adelard of Bath (ăd'əlärd), fl. 12th cent., English scholastic philosopher, celebrated for his study of Arabic learning. He translated Euclid from Arabic into Latin. His major works were *Perdifficiles quaestiones naturales,* which embodied his scientific studies, and *De eodem et diverso,* his principal philosophical work, which attempts a solution to the problems of NOMINALISM and REALISM.

Adelheid: see ADELAIDE, empress.

Adélie Coast (ă'dəlē, ädälē'), region, E ANTARCTICA, between George V Coast and Wilkes Land. It was discovered by Dumont d'Urville, a French explorer who landed in 1840 to collect rock samples; it was explored by an Australian geologist, Douglas Mawson, from 1911 to 1914. The French claim the area, which they call Terre Adélie; this was the first polar claim made without benefit of administration or occupation. The claim, however, was supported in 1950 when France established meteorological stations there.

Adelphi University, at Garden City, N.Y.; coeducational; chartered 1896 as Adelphi College. Originally in Brooklyn, the school moved to its present location in 1929 and in 1963 achieved university status.

Ademar or **Adhémar** (both: ăd'əmär), d. 1098, French prelate, bishop of Le Puy. At the Council of Clermont (1095), he energetically promoted the First Crusade (see CRUSADES) and was designated as papal legate on that expedition. He distinguished himself in the sieges of Nicaea and Antioch and carried the Holy Lance (with which Christ's side had been pierced by a Roman soldier) after its discovery, although he at first doubted its authenticity. He died at Antioch.

Aden, city (1970 est. pop. 250,000), SW Southern Yemen, on the Gulf of Aden near the southern entrance to the Red Sea. It is the capital and chief port of Southern Yemen. Aden consists of two peninsulas, Aden and Little Aden, and an intervening stretch of the mainland. Each peninsula has a high volcanic headland (Aden rises to 1,742 ft/531 m, and Little Aden to 1,147 ft/350 m), which is linked to the mainland by a flat, sandy isthmus. The bay between the peninsulas is an excellent harbor. Aden peninsula contains most of the city's population and is divided into a number of districts that were once towns. Wells near Sheikh Othman, on the mainland, supply the city with water. Little Aden peninsula has the city's main industrial district and is the site of a large oil refinery; the manufacture of soap, cigarettes, and salt is also important there. Aden, a free port since 1850, has been the chief entrepôt and trading center of S Arabia since ancient times. It enjoyed commercial importance until the discovery (late 15th cent.) of an all-water route around Africa to India. With the opening of the Suez Canal (1869), Aden regained its importance and again became a major trading center and also an important refueling stop; the harbor was deepened to accommodate the largest vessels able to use the canal. Aden's economy, which heavily depends on canal traffic, suffered from the closing of the canal during and after the 1956 and 1967 Arab-Israeli wars. Aden's strategic location and its importance as a commercial center long made it a coveted conquest. Muslim Arabs held the region from the 7th to the 16th cent. The Portuguese failed in an attempt to capture it in 1513, but it fell in 1538 to the Ottoman Turks. At the end of the 18th cent., Aden's importance as a strategic post grew as a result of British policy to contain French expansion in the region. After the British capture of Aden in 1839, its administrative attachment to India, and the construction of the Suez Canal, Britain purchased areas on the mainland from local rulers and entered into protectionist agreements with them. The Perim, Kamaran, and Kuria Muria islands had been made part of Aden in the 1850s. Aden was formally made into a crown colony in 1935, and the surrounding region (now Southern Yemen) became known as the Aden Protectorate in 1937. Aden was granted a legislative council in 1944 and later received other rights of self-government. In 1963, Aden was joined to the Federation of the Emirates of the South, which then became the Federation of South Arabia (see SOUTH ARABIA, FEDERATION OF). The British-sponsored federation was opposed by nationalists in Aden who feared domination by the tribal states. They emerged as two rival groups, the National Liberation Front (NLF) and the Front for the Liberation of Occupied Southern Yemen (FLOSY), and they conducted terrorist activities against the British and the federation administration. The NLF, which emerged as the dominant group, forced the collapse of the federal government. With the establishment (1967) of the independent country of Southern Yemen, Aden became the capital along with Madinat ash Shab. In 1970, Aden became the country's sole capital. See Gillian King, *Imperial Outpost, Aden* (1964); Julian Paget, *Last Post: Aden, 1964–67* (1969).

Aden, Gulf of (ä'dən, ā'-), western arm of the Arabian Sea, 550 mi (885 km) long, lying between Southern Yemen and the Somali Republic; connected with the Red Sea by the Bab el Mandeb. The gulf is on the great Mediterranean Sea–Indian Ocean trade route, the importance of which declined following the closing of the Suez Canal in 1967 and the construction of supertankers too large for the canal. After the 16th cent. Portugal, Turkey, and Great Britain were the chief contenders for control of the gulf, but by the 19th cent. Britain dominated the area. In the late 1960s, British military withdrawal E of Suez led to an increased Soviet naval presence in the gulf area.

Adenauer, Konrad (kôn'rät ä'dənou"ər), 1876–1967, West German chancellor. A lawyer and a member of the Catholic Center party, he was lord mayor of Cologne and a member of the provincial diet of Rhine prov. from 1917 until 1933, when he was dismissed by the National Socialist (Nazi) regime. He was twice imprisoned (1933, 1944) by the Nazis. Cofounder of the Christian Democratic Union (1945) and its president from 1946 to 1966, he was elected chancellor of the German Federal Republic (West Germany) in 1949 and was reelected in 1953, 1957, and 1961. He also served (1951–55) as his own foreign minister, negotiating the West German peace treaty (1952) with the Western Allies and obtaining recognition of West Germany's full sovereignty through the Paris Pacts and through an agreement with the USSR in 1955. Adenauer's strong will and political wisdom helped to give *Der Alte* [the old man], as he was known, great authority in West German public life. The political architect of the astounding West German recovery, he saw the solution of German problems in terms of European integration, and he helped secure West Germany's membership in the various organizations of the EUROPEAN COMMUNITY. In 1961 his party lost its absolute majority in the Bundestag, and he formed a coalition cabinet with the Free Democrats. In 1962 a cabinet crisis arose over the government's raid of the offices of the magazine *Der Spiegel,* which had attacked the Adenauer regime for military unpreparedness. After agreeing to the Free Democrats' demands that he exclude his defense minister, Franz Josef STRAUSS, who was implicated in the affair, from a new cabinet, Adenauer succeeded in re-forming the coalition. At the same time Adenauer announced (Dec., 1962) his retirement as part of the agreement with the Free Democrats. He resigned in Oct., 1963. His writings include *World Indivisible* (tr. 1955). See his memoirs of the years 1945–53 (tr. by Beate Ruhm von Oppen, 1966); biography by T. C. F. Prittie (1972); Edgar Alexander, *Adenauer and the New Germany* (tr. 1957); Paul Weymar, *Adenauer* (tr. 1957); A. J. Heidenheimer, *Adenauer and the CDU* (1960).

adenine (ăd'ənĭn, -nīn, -nēn), organic base of the PURINE family containing carbon, hydrogen, and nitrogen. Adenine combines with the sugar ribose to form adenosine, which in turn can be bonded with from one to three phosphoric acid units, yielding the three nucleotides adenosine monophosphate, adenosine diphosphate, and ADENOSINE TRIPHOSPHATE. These adenine derivatives perform important functions in cellular metabolism. Adenine is one of four bases utilized in the synthesis of NUCLEIC ACIDS. A modified form of the substance is thought to be a secondary messenger in the propagation of many hormonal stimuli. Adenine is an integral part of the structure of many coenzymes.

adenocarcinoma: see NEOPLASM.

adenoids, common name for the pharyngeal tonsils, spongy masses of lymphoid tissue that occupy the nasopharynx, the space between the back of the nose and the throat. Normally the adenoids, like the palatine tonsils located on either side of the throat, help prevent infection in the surrounding tissues. However, when they become enlarged they interfere with normal breathing and sometimes with hearing. When severely enlarged, adenoids can affect normal dental development, resulting in an alteration of facial expression. Infection of the adenoids is common, the symptoms resembling those of tonsillitis, with which it is frequently associated. Surgical removal of the adenoids is advisable when enlargement and repeated infection interfere with development and health. See RESPIRATION.

adenoma: see NEOPLASM.

adenosine diphosphate: see ADENINE; ADENOSINE TRIPHOSPHATE.

adenosine monophosphate (AMP) (ədĕn'əsēn mŏn"əfŏs'fāt), organic compound composed of ADENINE, the sugar ribose, and one phosphate unit. AMP is one of the possible products of the hydrolysis of ADENOSINE TRIPHOSPHATE (ATP) and is therefore important in the transfer of chemical energy during anabolism. The action of the enzyme adenyl cyclase on ATP results in the formation of pyrophosphate and cyclic AMP, a very close structural relative of AMP containing an additional ester linkage between the phosphate and ribose units. American biochemist Earl W. Sutherland, Jr., received the 1971 Nobel Prize in Physiology and Medicine for showing that the hormone epinephrine changes the cellular concentration of cyclic AMP and that this change has a regulatory effect on the rates of certain enzymatic reactions. He thus proved that cyclic AMP acts as a secondary messenger for the hormone. Cyclic AMP has since been shown to play similar roles with norepinephrine, glucagon, and adrenocorticotropic hormone. Although the exact chemistry of the steps leading from the arrival of a hormone at a cell's surface to a change in cyclic AMP levels in the cell and finally to a particular change in the cell's metabolism are often obscure, involvement of well-defined enzymes has in a few cases been clearly established. For example, epinephrine has been shown to stimulate adenyl cyclase in the liver. The increased concentration of cyclic AMP produced by this enzyme stimulates protein kinase, an enzyme which catalyzes the first of a complicated series of enzymatic reactions, the last of which results in the splitting of glycogen into its constituent glucose units. Cyclic AMP is converted to AMP by the enzyme phosphodiesterase, which is inhibited by caffeine. This may account in part for the stimulatory effects of this drug.

adenosine triphosphate (ədĕn'əsēn trī"fŏs'fāt), organic compound composed of adenine (containing carbon, hydrogen, and nitrogen), ribose (a sugar containing carbon, hydrogen, and oxygen), and three phosphate units (each containing hydrogen, oxygen, and phosphorus). Adenosine triphosphate (ATP) may undergo cyclic degradation and regeneration within the cell; during this process it is converted to adenosine diphosphate and adenosine monophosphate (with the controlled release of energy) and is returned to the original state by reattachment of the phosphate units. ATP is one of the most important intermediates in the metabolism of living cells; the energy resulting from its degradation may be employed in the synthesis of such macromolecules as polysaccharides, proteins, lipids, deoxyribonucleic acid, and ribonucleic acid. It is also believed to play a role in kidney function, in transmission of nerve impulses, and in MUSCLE contraction.

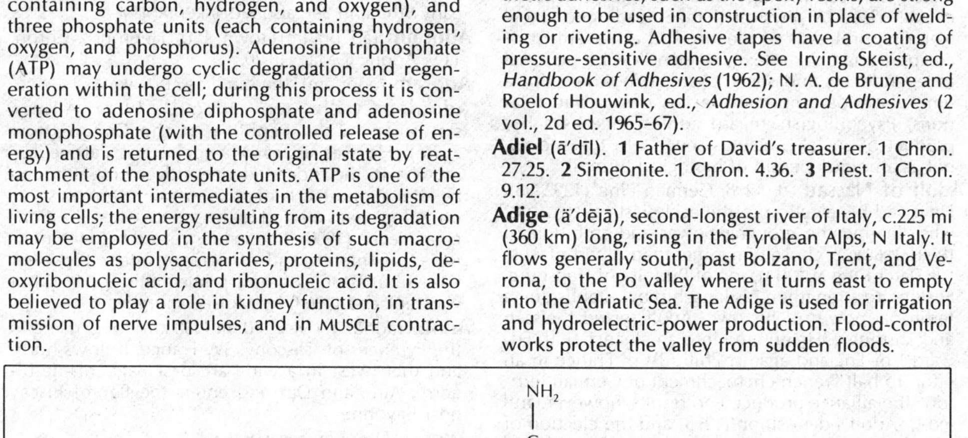

visual BINARY with combined luminosity about 8,000 times that of the sun; its distance is about 700 light-years. The name is from the Arabic meaning "virgin."

Adhémar: see ADEMAR.

adhesion and cohesion, attractive FORCES between material bodies. A distinction is usually made between an adhesive force, which acts to hold two separate bodies together (or to stick one body to another) and a cohesive force, which acts to hold together the like or unlike atoms, ions, or molecules of a single body. However, both forces result from the same basic properties of MATTER. Were it not for adhesion and cohesion, solids and liquids would behave like gases, dispersing freely, since, according to the kinetic theory of matter, the particles making up any material body are in constant motion. In solids and liquids the tendency of all matter to disperse is overcome by the forces of adhesion and cohesion. A number of phenomena can be explained in terms of adhesion and cohesion. For example, SURFACE TENSION in liquids results from cohesion, and CAPILLARITY results from a combination of adhesion and cohesion. The hardness of a diamond is due to the strong cohesive forces between the carbon atoms of which it is made. FRICTION between two solid bodies depends in part upon adhesion.

adhesive, substance capable of sticking to surfaces of other substances and bonding them to one another. The term *adhesive cement* is sometimes used in place of *adhesive,* especially when referring to a synthetic adhesive. Animal glue, a gelatin made from hides, hooves, or bones, was probably known in prehistoric times; it remained the leading adhesive until the 20th cent. It is now used especially in cabinetmaking. Animal glue is sold both as a solid (either ground or in sheets, to be melted in a water-jacketed glue pot and applied while hot) and as liquid glue (an acidic solution). Adhesives from vegetable sources are also important; they include natural gums and RESINS, MUCILAGE, and starch and starch derivatives. They are commonly used for sizing paper and textiles and for labeling, sealing, and manufacturing paper goods. Other adhesives derived from animal and vegetable sources include blood glue, casein glue, fish glue, rubber adhesives, and cellulose derivatives. Adhesives having special properties are prepared from synthetic resins. Some synthetic adhesives, such as the epoxy resins, are strong enough to be used in construction in place of welding or riveting. Adhesive tapes have a coating of pressure-sensitive adhesive. See Irving Skeist, ed., *Handbook of Adhesives* (1962); N. A. de Bruyne and Roelof Houwink, ed., *Adhesion and Adhesives* (2 vol., 2d ed. 1965–67).

Adiel (ā'dĭl). **1** Father of David's treasurer. 1 Chron. 27.25. **2** Simeonite. 1 Chron. 4.36. **3** Priest. 1 Chron. 9.12.

Adige (ä'dējā), second-longest river of Italy, c.225 mi (360 km) long, rising in the Tyrolean Alps, N Italy. It flows generally south, past Bolzano, Trent, and Verona, to the Po valley where it turns east to empty into the Adriatic Sea. The Adige is used for irrigation and hydroelectric-power production. Flood-control works protect the valley from sudden floods.

Adenosine triphosphate (ATP)

Ader (ā'dər), Benjamite. 1 Chron. 8.15.

Adernò: see ADRANO, Italy.

ADH: see ANTIDIURETIC HORMONE.

Adhara, bright star in the constellation CANIS MAJOR; Bayer designation ε Canis Majoris; 1970 position R.A. $6^h57.4^m$, Dec. −28°56′. A bluish-white giant (spectral class B2 II) with apparent MAGNITUDE 1.5, it is one of the 25 brightest stars in the sky. Adhara is a

Adin (ā'dĭn), family that returned from Exile. Ezra 2.15; 8.6; Neh. 7.20; 10.16.

Adina (ăd'ənə, ədī'-), Reubenite captain. 1 Chron. 11.42.

Adino (ăd'ənō, ədī-), the EZNITE, one of David's men. 2 Sam. 23.8.

adipose tissue (ăd'əpōs"): see CONNECTIVE TISSUE.

Adirondack Mountains (ăd"ərŏn'dăk), circular mountain mass, NE N.Y., between the St. Lawrence valley in the north and the Mohawk valley in the south; rising to 5,344 ft (1,629 m) at Mt. Marcy, the highest point in the state. Geologically a southern extension of the Laurentian Plateau, the Adirondacks are sometimes mistakenly included in the Appalachian system. Composed chiefly of metamorphic rock, the Adirondacks were formed as igneous rocks (mainly granite) intruded upward, doming the earth's surface; subsequent faulting of the earth's crust and surface erosion, particularly by the Pleistocene glaciers, have given the mountains a rugged topography. The glaciers also carved scenic gorges, waterfalls, and numerous lakes. The Hudson, Ausable, and Black rivers rise in the Adirondacks. The region is a year-round resort area; most of it has been set aside as Adirondack State Park. Lake Placid and Lake George are major resort centers. Lumbering, once a major occupation in the Adirondacks, declined after a forest preserve was established in 1892. Important mineral products of the mountains include iron ore, titanium, vanadium, and talc.

adit (ăd'ĭt), in mining, underground passage excavated nearly horizontally, with one end open to the earth's surface, usually used to service a mine. The adit end is the furthermost end from the surface, i.e., the location where miners work. The adit collar is the area where an adit opens to the surface and must be reinforced against any surface weakness.

Adithaim (ăd"ĭthā'ĭm), town of Judah, probably c.10 mi (16 km) from the coast. Joshua 15.36.

adjective, English PART OF SPEECH, one of the two that refer typically to attributes. The other is the adverb. These two classes overlap with the form class marked by *-er* and *-est* (or *more . . .* and *most . . .*). They are functionally distinct in that adjectives never occur far from nouns or pronouns, while adverbs are associated primarily with verbs. There is a small class of words (e.g., *very* and *too*) that typically precede adjectives and adverbs; these words are also called adverbs. Many adverbs belong to a form class of words ending *-ly.* Adjective and adverb are typically Indo-European form classes, and probably most other languages lack specialized classes with analogous functions. See Paul Roberts, *Understanding Grammar* (1954) and *Modern Grammar* (1968).

Adlai (ăd'lāī), father of SHAPHAT **4.** 1 Chron. 27.29.

Adler, Alfred (äd'lər), 1870–1937, Austrian psychiatrist, founder of the school of individual psychology. Although one of Freud's earlier associates, he soon rejected the Freudian emphasis upon sex. He maintained that all personality difficulties have their roots in a feeling of inferiority (see INFERIORITY COMPLEX) derived from physical handicaps or from conflict with the environment that restricts an individual's need for power and self-assertion. Thus he saw behavior disorders as overcompensation for deficiencies. In later life he lectured and practiced in the United States. Besides *The Practice and Theory of Individual Psychology* (1923), he wrote *The Neurotic Constitution* (1909) and *Understanding Human Nature* (1927). See biography by Phyllis Bottome (1939); studies by H. H. Mosak, ed. (1973) and Manes Sperber (1974).

Adler, Cyrus, 1863–1940, American Jewish educator, grad. Univ. of Pennsylvania, 1883, Ph.D. Johns Hopkins, 1887. He taught Semitic languages at Johns Hopkins Univ. from 1884 to 1893. He was for a number of years librarian and then secretary of the Smithsonian Institution, was the founder of the American Jewish Historical Society, was one of the editors of the *Jewish Encyclopedia,* and edited the *American-Jewish Year-Book* after 1899. He was president of Dropsie College from 1908 to 1940 and of the Jewish Theological Seminary after 1924. He was a founder of the American Jewish Committee and of the Jewish Welfare Board. His writings include a number of articles on comparative religion, Assyriology, and Semitic philology; *Jews in the Diplomatic Correspondence of the United States* (1906), and, with Allan Ramsay, *Told in the Coffee House* (1898). See biography by A. A. Neuman (1942).

Adler, Elmer, 1884–1962, American bibliophile and printer, b. Rochester, N.Y. From 1930 to 1940 he published *The Colophon,* a highly regarded quarterly of bibliographic research and information for book collectors; it was produced with fine printing. Adler became curator of the graphic arts department of Princeton Univ. in 1940, retiring in 1952.

Adler, Felix, 1851–1933, American educator and leader in social welfare, founder of the ETHICAL CULTURE MOVEMENT, b. Germany. He was brought to the United States as a small child, was graduated from Columbia in 1870, and afterward studied in Germany. In 1876 he established the New York Society for Ethical Culture and, in connection with the Ethical Culture School, the first free kindergarten in New York City. Adler organized the Workingmen's Lyceum, helped to establish the Workingmen's School and the Manhattan Trade School for Girls, and founded (1883) the first child study society in the United States. He was a member (1885) of New York state's first tenement house commission and served for many years as chairman of the National Child Labor Committee. He became professor of political and social ethics at Columbia in 1902 and was Roosevelt professor (1908-9) at the Univ. of Berlin and Hibbert lecturer (1923) at Oxford. Among his books are *Creed and Deed* (1877), *An Ethical Philosophy of Life* (1918), and *The Reconstruction of the Spiritual Ideal* (1924). See H. J. Bridges, *Humanity on Trial* (1971).

Adler, Viktor (vĭk'tôr), 1852-1918, Austrian socialist politician and journalist, founder and leader of the Austrian Social Democratic party. A prominent figure in the Second International of socialist parties, he entered parliament in 1905. When the Austro-Hungarian empire was collapsing, he was named foreign secretary of German Austria, but he died on Nov. 11, 1918, one day before the republic was proclaimed.

Admah (ăd'mə), city destroyed with SODOM.

Admatha (ădmā'thə), counselor of Ahasuerus. Esther 1.14.

Admetus (ădmē'təs): see ALCESTIS.

administration, public: see ADMINISTRATIVE LAW.

administrative law, law governing the powers and processes of administrative agencies. In the United States it deals primarily with questions of the propriety of granting powers to agencies as well as with the judicial checks upon the activities of governmental agencies. Administrative agencies are part of the executive branch of government and are created either by statute, by executive order authorized by statute, or by constitutional provisions. The use of administrative agencies in the United States dates back to 1789, when the original legislative provisions were made for the administration of customs laws, the regulation of oceangoing vessels and the coastal trade, and the payment of pensions to veterans. It was, however, with the growth of public utilities and public transportation that administrative agencies began to play a major role in American life. The passage of the Interstate Commerce Act and the establishment of the INTERSTATE COMMERCE COMMISSION in 1887 marked the start of administrative law in the United States as we know it today. The administrative process involves rule making, adjudication, investigating, supervising, prosecuting, and advising. Agencies have assumed legislative and judicial functions—the day-to-day supervision of details—for which neither Congress nor the courts are adapted. This has resulted in a blurring of the traditional notion of separation of powers that is said to characterize the Federal government. With the growing complexity of modern economic and social life, administrative agencies, having overall knowledge of their fields, are therefore able to deal uniformly and quickly with the numerous complaints referred to them. The principle that Congress cannot delegate its legislative powers has been circumvented by having Congress set a primary standard and allowing the agency to fill in the gaps. As a result of the powers that have been granted the older agencies and the recent proliferation of agencies, administrative agencies have come to participate in nearly every aspect of American life. Administrative agencies affect activities ranging from collective bargaining to television programming. Because of the vast range of subjects dealt with by the agencies the Federal Administrative Procedure Act was enacted (1946) to provide uniform standards of procedure that would be common to all agencies. The act guaranteed the right of judicial review to any person "suffering legal wrong because of any agency action." In general, administrative procedure would be set aside only for abuse of discretion. Under European legal codes, special administrative courts review the activities of administrative agencies. This is in contrast to common law, whereby the ordinary courts have complete jurisdiction over controversies involving the validity of acts of agencies. See FEDERAL COMMUNICATIONS COMMISSION; FEDERAL POWER COMMISSION; FEDERAL TRADE COMMISSION; NATIONAL LABOR RELATIONS BOARD; SECURITIES AND EXCHANGE COMMISSION. See Peter Woll, *Administrative Law, the Informal Process* (1963); M. M. Shapiro, *The Supreme Court and Administrative Agencies* (1968); R. S. Lorch, *Democratic Process and Administrative Law* (1969, repr. 1973).

Admiral's Men, theatrical company of players, officially designated the Admiral's Men in 1585. They were rivals of the CHAMBERLAIN'S MEN and performed at the theaters of Philip HENSLOWE. Their leading actor was Edward ALLEYN.

admiralty, in British government, department in charge of the operations of the Royal Navy until 1964. Originally established under Henry VIII, it was reorganized under Charles II. Five lords commissioners composed the board of admiralty, each gradually developing his own field of specific responsibility, with the first lord responsible to Parliament. In 1832 it absorbed the navy board, previously responsible for the administrative organization. In 1964 the admiralty became the navy department, coequal with the other service departments, of the ministry of defence. The admiralty board still exists within the navy department, but its functions are undefined.

Admiralty Inlet: see PUGET SOUND.

Admiralty Islands, group of 40 volcanic islands (1969 pop. 22,035), c.800 sq mi (2,070 sq km), SW Pacific, in the BISMARCK ARCHIPELAGO and part of Papua New Guinea. Lorengau, the chief port and administrative center of the group, is on Manus, the largest island. Copra, pearls, and marine shells are the principal products. Discovered by the Dutch navigator Willem SCHOUTEN in 1616, the group became part of German New Guinea in 1884 and an Australian League of Nations mandate in 1920.

admiralty law: see MARITIME LAW.

Adna (ăd'nə), name of two Israelites of the returned community. Ezra 10.30; Neh. 12.15.

Adnah (ăd'nə). **1** Deserter from Saul. 1 Chron. 12.20. **2** Officer under Jehoshaphat. 2 Chron. 17.14.

Ado (ä'dō), city (1969 est. pop. 183,000), SW Nigeria. Located in a region where rice and yams are grown, the town has rice mills and also manufactures textiles, bricks, tile, and pottery. Ado was the capital of the YORUBA Ekiti state that was probably founded in the 15th cent. It alternated between independence and subjection to BENIN until the British gained control in 1894. The city is sometimes known as Ado-Ekiti.

adobe (ədō'bē): see RAMMED EARTH.

adolescence, time of life from onset of puberty to full adulthood. The exact period of adolescence, which varies from person to person, falls approximately between the ages 12 and 21. Adolescence is characterized by physical changes leading to sexual maturity; problems of identity and achievement of an appropriate sex role; movement toward personal independence; and social changes in which, for a time, the most important fact is peer group relations. Psychologists regard adolescence as a by-product of social pressures specific to the society, not as a unique period of biological turmoil.

Adolf of Nassau, d. 1298, German king (1292-98). He owed his election to the ecclesiastical ELECTORS, who, fearing the growing power and ambition of the HAPSBURGS, chose him rather than Albert of Austria (later King ALBERT I), son of Rudolf I of Hapsburg. Seeking to strengthen his kingship by establishing a territorial power of his own, Adolf seized Meissen and Thuringia. He entered into an alliance with Edward I of England against Philip IV of France in an effort to halt French encroachment of German territory; the alliance produced no results, however, and led to Adolf's deposition (1298) and the election of Albert. Soon afterward he was defeated and killed by an army commanded by Albert.

Adonai: see GOD.

Adoni-bezek (ădō'nī-bē'zĕk, ăd'-), king of Bezek captured and mutilated by the Judahites. Judges 1.5-7.

Adonijah (ăd"ənī'jə, ədŏn'əjə). **1** Son of David. He sought the throne that David gave to the younger son, Solomon. 2 Sam. 3.4; 1 Kings 1; 2.1-25. **2** Teacher of the law. 2 Chron. 17.7-9. **3** Sealer of the Covenant after the return from the Exile. Neh. 10.16. Perhaps the same as **Adonikam,** a name in the lists of families. Ezra 2.13; 8.13; Neh. 7.18.

Adoniram (ăd"ənī'rəm), tax overseer. 1 Kings 4.6. Adoram: 2 Sam. 20.24; 1 Kings 12.18. Hadoram: 2 Chron. 10.18.

Adonis (ədō'nĭs, ədŏn'ĭs), in Greek mythology, beautiful youth beloved by Aphrodite and Persephone. He was born of the incestuous union of Myrrha (or Smyrna) and Cinyras, king of Cyprus. Aphrodite left Adonis in the care of Persephone, who raised him and made him her lover. Aphrodite later demanded the youth for herself, but Persephone was unwilling to relinquish him. When Adonis was gored to death by a boar, both Persephone and Aphrodite claimed him. Zeus settled the dispute by arranging for Adonis to spend half the year (the summer months) above the ground with Aphrodite and the other half in the underworld with Persephone. Adonis' death and resurrection, symbolic of the yearly cycle of vegetation, were widely celebrated in ancient Greece in the midsummer festival Adonia. As part of this worship, his image was surrounded by beds of plants (the gardens of Adonis), which quickly grew and withered. The worship of Adonis corresponds to the cults of the Phrygian ATTIS and the Babylonian TAMMUZ. See Sir J. G. Frazer, *Adonis, Attis, Osiris* (1907, new ed. 1961).

Adoni-zedec (ădō'nī-zē'dĕk, ăd'-), chief at Jerusalem, leader of the allies routed at Gibeon. Joshua 10.1-27.

adoption, act by which the legal relation of PARENT AND CHILD is created. Adoption was recognized by Roman law but not by COMMON LAW. Statutes first introduced adoption into U.S. law in the mid-19th cent. and today it is allowed in all states of the United States and in Great Britain. Adoption is generally a judicial proceeding, requiring a hearing before a judge. Adoption statutes usually provide that the consent of the parents or guardian of the child—and that of the child, if above a certain age—must be obtained. An adopted child generally assumes the rights and duties of a natural legitimate child. Similarly, the rights and duties accompanying natural parenthood generally accompany adoptive parenthood (e.g., the right of custody and the obligation of support). The natural parents have no right to control an adopted child, nor have they any duties toward it, but in some states the child does not lose the right to inherit from them. Many states permit unmarried adults to adopt. See Margaret Kornitzer, *Adoption* (2d ed. 1967); M. L. Leavy, *Law of Adoption* (3d ed. 1968).

adoptionism, Christian heresy taught in Spain after 782 by Elipandus, archbishop of Toledo, and Felix, bishop of Urgel. They held that Christ at the time of his birth was purely human and only became the divine Son of God by adoption when he was baptized. Variations of this doctrine had been held as early as the 3d cent. by the THEODOTIANS, PAUL OF SAMOSATA, and by the Nestorians. It reappeared in the neo-adoptionist heresy among the followers of Peter Abelard. Elipandus and Felix were condemned at Frankfurt (794). The vigorous refutation of ALCUIN had much to do with the sect's disappearance in the early 9th cent. See also MONARCHIANISM.

Adoraim (ăd"ōrā'ĭm), town, E of Hebron. 2 Chron. 11.9. Adora: 1 Mac. 13.20.

Adoram (ədôr'əm), the same as ADONIRAM.

Adoula, Cyrille (sērĭl' ädōō'lä), 1922-, African statesman in the Republic of the Congo (now Zaïre). He was an early associate of Patrice Lumumba in the independence movement, although he later supported Lumumba's rival, Joseph Kasavubu. Adoula was elected to the senate when the Congo achieved (1960) independence and held the ministries of interior and of defense under President Kasavubu. Adoula became prime minister (1961) but was replaced (1964) by Moise Tshombe.

Adour (ädōōr'), river, 210 mi (338 km) long, rising in the Pyrenees of Gascony, SW France. It flows north and then west in a wide arc past Bagnères-de-Bigorre, Aire, and Dax and enters the Bay of Biscay near Bayonne.

Adowa, Ethiopia: see ADUWA.

Adra (ä'thrä), town (1970 pop. 16, 283), Almería prov., S Spain, in Andalusia, on the Mediterranean Sea. Adra, a port, is the center of a fertile agricultural region. At the foot of a hill below the present town stood Abdera, founded by Phoenician traders and which later became a Roman colony. Adra was the last stronghold of the Moors under Boabdil.

Adrammelech (ədrăm'əlĕk). **1** God of a Samaritan cult. 2 Kings 17.31. **2** One of the two men named as murderers of their father, Sennacherib; Sharezer was the other. Babylonian sources mention one son. 2 Kings 19.37 (the same in Isa, 37.38).

Adramyttium (ăd"rəmĭt'ēəm), place, the modern Edremit, NW Turkey. Here St. Paul's ship was built. Acts 27.2.

Adrano (ädrä'nō), town (1971 pop. 32,270), E Sicily, Italy, at the foot of Mt. Etna, near the confluence of the Simeto and Salso rivers. It is the commercial center for a region where olives and citrus fruit are grown. Adrano was founded c.400 by Dionysius the Elder near a temple of the god Hadranus. Fierce fighting took place in Adrano during World War II. Of note are the ruins of the town's ancient walls and an imposing 11th-century Norman castle. The town was known as Adernò until 1929.

Adrastus (ədrăs'təs), in Greek legend, king of Argos. He organized the ill-fated SEVEN AGAINST THEBES expedition and was the only survivor. Ten years later he successfully assisted the sons of the Seven, the EPIGONI, in their attack on Thebes.

adrenal gland (ədrēn'əl) or **suprarenal gland** (so͞oprərēn'əl), endocrine gland (see ENDOCRINE SYSTEM) about 2 in. (5.1 cm) long situated atop each kidney. The outer yellowish layer (cortex) of the adrenal gland secretes about 30 steroid hormones, the most important of which are ALDOSTERONE and CORTISOL. Aldosterone regulates water and salt balance in the body and its secretion is controlled by the output of ADRENOCORTICOTROPIC HORMONE (ACTH) from the pituitary gland. Cortisol regulates carbohydrate, protein, and fat metabolism; its secretion is only slightly influenced by the pituitary. Steroid hormones also counteract inflammation and allergies and influence the secondary sex characteristics to a limited degree. The adrenal cortex controls metabolic processes that are essential to life and if it ceases to function death ensues within a few days. Artificial synthesis of the steroid hormones has made it possible to treat many conditions related to underactivity of the adrenal cortex, e.g., ADDISON'S DISEASE. The inner reddish portion (medulla) of the adrenal gland, which is not functionally related to the adrenal cortex, secretes EPINEPHRINE (adrenaline) and norepinephrine. The release of these hormones is stimulated when an animal is excited or frightened, causing increased heart rate, increased blood flow to the muscles, elevated blood sugar, dilation of the pupils of the eyes, and other changes that increase the body's ability to meet sudden emergencies.

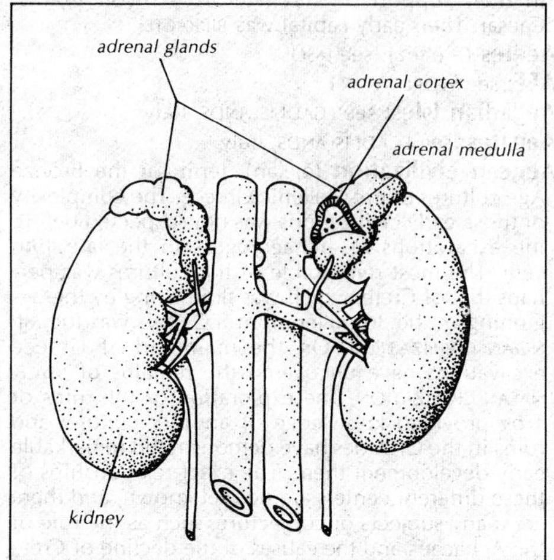

Adrenal glands: The cross-sectioned area shows the adrenal cortex and medulla.

adrenaline (ədrĕn'əlĭn, -lēn): see EPINEPHRINE.

adrenocorticotropic hormone (ədrē'nōkôr"təkōtrŏp'ĭk), polypeptide hormone secreted by the anterior PITUITARY GLAND. Its chief function is to stimulate the cortex of the ADRENAL GLAND to secrete adrenocortical steroids, chiefly CORTISONE. The release of adrenocorticotropic hormone (ACTH), also known as corticotropin, is stimulated by corticotropin-releasing factor (CRF), a secretion of the hypothalamus. ACTH secretion is an excellent example of the regulation of a biological system by a negative-feedback mechanism; high levels of adrenocortical steroids in the blood tend to decrease ACTH release, whereas low steroid levels have the opposite effect. ACTH has the same pharmacologic and clinical effects as cortisone when given intravenously or intramuscularly; however, it has no value when applied externally and cannot be taken orally since it is deactivated by digestive enzymes. The action of ACTH is contingent upon normally functioning adrenal glands and is therefore useless in disorders caused by adrenal insufficiency, e.g., as replacement therapy where both adrenal glands have been removed.

Adria (ā'drēə), ancient name of the Adriatic, extended to mean the central Mediterranean in Acts 27.27.

Adrian I, d. 795, pope (772–95), a Roman; successor of Stephen IV. At Adrian's urging, CHARLEMAGNE crossed the Alps and defeated the Lombard king, DESIDERIUS, who had annexed papal territory. That defeat marked the end of the Lombard kingdom. Charlemagne, during the siege of Pavia, went to Rome (774) and there confirmed the donation of Pepin to the PAPAL STATES and joined additional provinces to it. Adrian in turn confirmed Charlemagne's title of patrician of the Romans, thereby acknowledging Charlemagne's protectorate over all Italy. Adrian supported Empress Irene in her struggle against iconoclasm, and he sent legates to the Second Council of Nicaea. The great Roman water systems were built during his rule. He was succeeded by St. Leo III.

Adrian IV, d. 1159, pope (1154–59), an Englishman (the only English pope), b. Nicholas Breakspear at Langley, near St. Albans. He was successor of Anastasius IV. At an early age he went to France. There he became an Austin canon and later an abbot. Pope Eugene III made him cardinal bishop of Albano and sent him to Scandinavia to organize the church. After his election to the papacy, Adrian defeated (1155) opposition of ARNOLD OF BRESCIA. He crowned (1155) FREDERICK I but fell into conflict with Frederick when the emperor, disregarding the Concordat of Worms, invested (1158 or 1159) imperial favorites in the archbishoprics of Cologne and Ravenna. To make peace (1156) with William of Sicily, who had invaded papal territory, Adrian acknowledged William's titles to Sicily, Apulia, and Capua. This angered Frederick, who had designs on the Two Sicilies, but it served to protect the Papal States against further imperial encroachments. Frederick's expressed intention to assume the government of Rome almost brought him excommunication. Adrian, forced by imperial intrigues to leave Rome, died before he could pronounce sentence. The historicity of Adrian's donation of Ireland, as a papal fief, to Henry II of England has been the subject of scholarly dispute. He was succeeded by Alexander III.

Adrian VI, 1459–1523, pope (1522–23), a Netherlander (b. Utrecht) named Adrian Florensz; successor of Leo X. He was the most recent non-Italian pope. He taught at Louvain and was tutor of the young prince, later Holy Roman Emperor CHARLES V. This was a time when Roman life was most extravagant, papal expenditures on worldly objects were at their height, and the Curia most needed drastic reform. Adrian, an ascetic and a pious man, did his best to curb the abuses he found, but he died after 20 months. He was succeeded by Clement VII.

Adrian, Roman emperor: see HADRIAN.

Adrian, Edgar Douglas Adrian, Baron, 1889–, English physiologist, M.D. Trinity College, Cambridge, 1915. He was research professor (1929–37) of the Royal Society and professor of physiology (1937–51) at Cambridge. In 1951 he became master of Trinity College. His research was chiefly on the physiology of the nervous system. He wrote *The Basis of Sensation* (1928), *The Mechanism of Nervous Action* (1932), and, with others, *Factors Determining Human Behavior* (1937). With Sir Charles S. Sherrington he shared the 1932 Nobel Prize in Physiology and Medicine for work on the function of the neuron. He was awarded a barony in 1955.

Adrian, Gilbert: see under FASHION.

Adrian, city (1970 pop. 20,382), seat of Lenawee co., SE Mich., on the Raisin River; inc. 1836. It is a manufacturing and trading center for a fertile farm region; its many products include automobile and aircraft parts, metalware, chemicals, and paper goods. The city is known for its chrysanthemums and for the beautiful maples that line its streets. It is the seat of Adrian College and Siena Heights College. Numerous lakes are in the area.

Adrianople, Turkey: see EDİRNE.

Adrianople, Treaty of, 1829, peace treaty between Russia and the Ottoman Empire (see RUSSO-TURKISH WARS). Turkey gave Russia access to the mouths of the Danube and additional territory on the Black Sea, opened the Dardanelles to all commercial vessels, granted autonomy to Serbia, promised autonomy for Greece, and allowed Russia to occupy Moldavia and Walachia until Turkey had paid a large indemnity.

Adriatic Sea (ādrēă'tĭk), arm of the Mediterranean Sea, between Italy and the Balkan Peninsula. It extends c.500 mi (800 km) from the Gulf of Venice, at its head, SE to the Strait of Otranto, which leads to the Ionian Sea. It is from 58 to 140 mi (93–225 km) wide, with a maximum depth of c.4,100 ft (1,250 m). The Po and Adige rivers of Italy are the chief affluents. The Italian coast (west and north) is low; Venice and Bari are the principal ports. Trieste, at the northern end of the sea, was once the chief Adriatic port. Yugoslavia and Albania border the irregular eastern shore; Rijeka and Split, Yugoslavia, are the main ports. The Yugoslavian coast (see DALMATIA), which is rugged and has many offshore islands and sheltered bays, is a popular tourist resort. Fishing is an important activity in the Adriatic Sea; lobsters, sardines, and tuna are the chief catch.

Adriel (ā'drĭəl), husband of MERAB. 1 Sam. 18.17–19.

adsorption, adhesion of the molecules of liquids, gases, and dissolved substances to the surfaces of solids, as opposed to ABSORPTION, in which the molecules actually enter the absorbing medium (see ADHESION AND COHESION). Certain solids have the power to adsorb great quantities of gases. Charcoal, for example, which has a great surface area because of its porous nature, adsorbs large volumes of gases, including most of the poisonous ones, and is therefore used in gas masks. Certain finely divided solids have great adsorptive properties; for example, minute particles of platinum attract and hold multitudes of hydrogen molecules on their surfaces. Its ability to adsorb other gases makes platinum very useful in the production of sulfuric acid by the contact process and in the preparation of ammonia. Adsorption occurs also in solutions; colloidal particles suspended in a solution may adsorb much of the solvent (see COLLOID). Bone black and charcoal are used in industry to remove colors from solutions, since they adsorb many coloring materials and carry these with them when separated from the solution. Liquid dye held to the surface of cloth by adsorption permeates the fibers so that when the liquid has evaporated the dye still remains. Adsorption is employed in the hydrogenation of oils, in gas analysis, and in chromatography, a method used in the chemical analysis of closely related substances.

Adullam (ədŭl'əm), border town of Judah, SW of Jerusalem. Joshua 15.35; 2 Chron. 11.7; Neh. 11.30. David hid in the Cave of Adullam when he fled from Saul. From here three of his men went to get him water from the well at Bethlehem. 1 Sam. 22; 2 Sam. 23.13–17; 1 Chron. 11.15–19.

adult education, extension of educational opportunities to those adults beyond the age of general public education who feel a need for further training of any sort, also known as continuing education. Only in the past two centuries has the field of adult education acquired definite organization. Its relatively recent development results from various social trends—the general spread of public education, the intensification of economic competition with its premiums for skills, the complexities of national and international politics demanding constant study, the stimulating effects of urbanization, opportunities offered by increased leisure time, and increased interest in educational activities on the part of many married women. Modern and formal adult education probably originated in European political groups and, after the Industrial Revolution, as vocational classes for workers. Continuation schools for workers in Germany and Switzerland were common. The FOLK HIGH SCHOOL in Denmark, founded by Bishop Brundtvig, stressed intellectual studies, and the Adult Schools of the Society of Friends in England (1845) fostered the education of the poor. Early American forms of adult education were the public lectures given in the LYCEUM (c.1826) and the Lowell Institute of Boston endowed by John Lowell (1836). In 1873 the CHAUTAUQUA MOVEMENT introduced the discussion group and modified lecture system. Free public lectures under the department of education of New York City were inaugurated in 1904. Through the merger (1951) of the American Association for Adult Education and the National Education Association's Department of Adult Education, the Adult Education Association of the U.S.A. was founded. This group, through its publications and its research, has worked to systematize the methods and philosophy of the field. The Economic Opportunity Act (1964) provided funds for adult education, as did the later Adult Education Act (1966). Both of these acts, however, have been designed to help disadvantaged and illiterate adults only. Most important, public schools have been active in furnishing facilities and assistance to private adult education groups in many communities. Contemporary adult education can take on many different forms. Colleges have instituted evening programs, extension work, courses without credit, and correspondence courses; COMMUNITY COLLEGES have been especially active in this area. Organizations designed to relieve ILLITERACY are instrumental in adult education, as are the schools established to teach the English language and American customs to the foreign-born. A large amount of adult education is carried on in the field of worker education by labor unions and in VOCATIONAL EDUCATION programs. Community centers, political and economic action associations, and dramatic, musical and artistic groups are regarded by many as adult education activities. Great Books groups (est. 1947), in which adults read and discuss a specified list of volumes, grew out of great books seminars at Chicago and Columbia universities and St. John's College. In many places the public library sponsors the group. See PARENT EDUCATION. See C. H. Grattan, *In Quest of Knowledge* (1955); *Handbook of Adult Education in the United States* (ed. by Malcolm S. Knowles, 1960); Malcolm S. Knowles, *The Adult Education Movement in the United States* (1962); P. E. Bergevin et al., *Adult Education Procedures* (1963); R. W. Axford, *Adult Education: The Open Door* (1968); Darrell Anderson, *Adult Education and the Disadvantaged Adult* (1969).

adulteration of food: see FOOD ADULTERATION.

Adummim (ədŭm'ĭm), ascent in the Jericho road. Joshua 15.7; 18.17.

Aduwa or **Adowa** (both: ä'dəwä), Ital. *Adua,* town (1970 est. pop. 16,000), Tigre prov., N Ethiopia. Aduwa was the most important commercial center of Tigre in the 19th cent., but declined in the 1870s as a result of the dislocation caused by the fighting between Ethiopia and Egypt. In 1896, Aduwa was the site of the battle in which Menelik II decisively defeated Italian invaders and forced them out of Ethiopia. The name is also spelled Adwa.

advaita: see VEDANTA.

Advent [Lat.,=coming, i.e., of Jesus], season of the Christian ecclesiastical year, lasting in the West from the Sunday nearest Nov. 30 (St. Andrew's) until Christmas. It is a season of penitence, to prepare for the holy day, and its liturgical color is purple. The first Sunday of Advent is the first day of the church calendar. In the Roman Catholic Church it was until recently a period of fasting, but now, as in the Anglican and Lutheran churches, its observance is primarily liturgical.

Advent Christian Church: see ADVENTISTS.

Adventists (ăd'vĕn"tĭsts) [advent, Lat.,=coming], members of a group of related religious denominations whose distinctive doctrine centers in their belief concerning the imminent second coming of Christ (see JUDGMENT DAY). The name Adventism is specifically applied to the teachings of William MILLER (1782–1849), who predicted the end of the world for 1843, then for 1844. When it did not occur, the Millerites, or Second Adventists, at a meeting at Albany, N.Y., in 1845 adopted a statement declaring their belief in the visible return of Christ at an indefinite time, when the resurrection of the dead would take place and the millennium would have its beginning. Later this body took the name Evangelical Adventists. Another and larger branch of the original Adventist group became known in 1861 as the Advent Christian Church. This branch was formed as a result of a controversy over the question of the soul's immortality. The largest Adventist body, the Seventh-Day Adventists, under the leadership of Joseph Bates and James and Ellen White, adopted in 1844 the observance of Saturday as the Sabbath. Formally organized in 1863, they are fundamentally evangelical, taking the Bible as the sole rule of faith and practice. Fundamental to their doctrine is their belief in the imminent, premillennial, personal, and visible return of Christ. The Seventh-Day Adventists carry on worldwide missionary work; they number some 1.6 million. Another Adventist group is the Church of God, which was organized as Churches of God in Christ Jesus in 1888 and then permanently organized as Church of God in 1921; its members number some 75,000. The Advent Christian Church, organized in 1861, has a membership of about 31,000 (the Life and Advent Union, which was organized in 1863, merged with the Advent Christian Church in 1964). See M. E. Olsen, *A History of the Origin and Progress of Seventh-Day Adventists* (1925, repr. 1972); Le Roy E. Froom, *Movement of Destiny* (1972).

adverb: see PART OF SPEECH; ADJECTIVE.

advertising, in general, any openly sponsored offering of goods, services, or ideas through any medium of public communication. At its inception advertising was merely an announcement; for example, entrepreneurs in ancient Egypt used criers to announce ship and cargo arrivals. The invention of printing, however, may be said to have ushered in modern advertising. After the influence of salesmanship began to insert itself into public notice in the 18th cent., the present elaborate form of advertising began to evolve. The advertising agency, working on a commission basis, has been chiefly responsible for this evolution. The largest group of advertisers are the food marketers, followed by marketers of drugs and cosmetics, soaps, automobiles, tobacco, appliances, and oil products. The major U.S. advertising media are newspapers, magazines, television and radio, business publications, billboards, and circulars sent through the mail. Since many large advertising agencies were once located on Madison Avenue in New York City, the term "Madison Avenue" is frequently used to symbolize the advertising business. The major criticisms of advertising are that it creates false values and impels people to buy things they neither need nor want and that, in fact, may be actually harmful (such as cigarettes). In reply, its defenders say that advertising is meant to sell products, not create values; that it can create a new market for products that fill a genuine, though latent, need; and that it furthers product improvement through free competition. The Association of National Advertisers and the American Association of Advertising Agencies, both founded in 1917, are the major associations. See Martin Mayer, *Madison Avenue, U.S.A.* (1958); S. W. Dunn, *Advertising: Its Role in Modern Marketing* (2d ed. 1969); A. W. Frey, *Advertising* (4th ed. 1970); Robert Glatzer, *The New Advertising* (1970).

advocate: see ATTORNEY.

Ady, Endre (ĕn'drĕ ŏ'dē), 1877–1919, Hungarian poet. He abandoned his studies in law for a career in journalism and literature. His first volume of poetry, *Versek,* appeared in 1899. After 1903 he spent most of his time in Paris, where he fell in love with a woman who became the subject of many poems. A lyric poet noted for an original and creative use of language, Ady was influenced by the French SYMBOLISTS. He became a leader of the politically and artistically radical Hungarian writers who attacked the complacent materialism of Hungary's upper classes. Ady's poetry was published in 12 volumes and his prose works in 7. See his poems, ed. by A. N. Nyerges (1969).

Adyge Autonomous Oblast (ədĭgyĕ'), administrative division (1970 pop. 386,000), c.2,935 sq mi (7,600 sq km), Krasnodar Kray, SE European USSR, at the northern foothills of the Greater Caucasus. MAIKOP is the capital. Agriculture is the chief occupation; wheat, maize, and rice are the leading food crops. Valuable forests in the Caucasian foothills have made lumbering a major industry. The Adyge region has rich oil and natural gas deposits. Oil refining, food processing, furniture making, and the production of machinery, machine tools, and building materials are leading industries. The Muslim Adyge people, related to the Circassians, are known for their tapestries and other handicrafts. Russian immigration has made them a minority in their oblast. The region was conquered (1830–64) by the Russians from the Turks, who had introduced Islam. The autonomous oblast was created in 1922.

adze, tool similar in purpose and use to an axe but with the cutting edge at right angles to the handle rather than aligned with it. The details of construction of a particular adze will depend on its intended application. Some types have a single cutting edge with the rear side of the head formed into a hammer or a picklike tool. Other types have a head with two identical cutting edges back to back. The principal use of the adze is in dressing and squaring large timbers. However, since these two processes are now usually performed by machine tools in factories, the adze is no longer commonly used.

Adzhar Autonomous Soviet Socialist Republic (əjär') or **Adzharistan,** autonomous region (1970 pop. 310,000), c.1,160 sq mi (3,000 sq km), SE European USSR, on the Black Sea, bordering Turkey on the south. The capital is BATUMI. Mountainous and forested, the region has a subtropical climate, and there are many health resorts. Tobacco, tea, citrus fruits, and avocados are leading crops; livestock raising and copper mining are also important. Industries include tea packing, tobacco processing, fruit and fish canning, oil refining, and shipbuilding. The Adzhars, a mainly Muslim people of the South Caucasian linguistic family, constitute the bulk of the population; the remainder are Georgians, Armenians, Russians, and Greeks. Colonized by Greek merchants in the 5th and 4th cent. B.C., the region later came under Roman rule and after the 9th cent. A.D. was part of Georgia. The Turks conquered Adzharistan in the late 17th and early 18th cent. and introduced Islam. Acquired by Russia in 1878, the region became an autonomous republic in 1921.

A. E.: see RUSSELL, GEORGE WILLIAM.

Aeacus (ē'əkəs), in Greek mythology, son of Zeus and the nymph Aegina. He was the father of Peleus and Telamon. After a plague had nearly wiped out the inhabitants of his land, Zeus rewarded the pious Aeacus by changing a swarm of ants to men (known as Myrmidons). According to one legend, Aeacus and his people assisted Apollo and Poseidon in building the walls of Troy. After Aeacus' death, Zeus made him one of the three judges of Hades.

Aëdon (āē'dən), in Greek legend, the wife of Zethus, king of Thebes. She had only one son, while her sister-in-law, NIOBE, had many. Her jealousy increased until, in trying to murder Niobe's oldest son, she killed her own child. She was changed to a nightingale, and her song was a mournful call for her son, Itys or Itylus.

Aedui (ĕ'dyo͞oī) or **Haedui** (hĕ'dyo͞oī), Gallic people, occupying in the 1st cent. B.C. a part of what later became Burgundy. Defeated by ARIOVISTUS and at odds with their Gallic neighbors, they were allies of the Romans. The Aedui at first aided Julius Caesar in the GALLIC WARS and later were not wholehearted in their support of Vercingetorix's revolt against Caesar. Their early capital was BIBRACTE.

Aeëtes (ē-ē'tēz): see JASON.

AEF: see WORLD WAR I.

Aegadian Isles: see EGADI ISLANDS, Italy.

Aegates: see EGADI ISLANDS, Italy.

Aegean civilization (ējē'ən), term for the Bronze Age cultures of pre-Hellenic Greece. The complexity of those early civilizations was not suspected before the excavations of archaeologists in the late 19th cent. The most remarkable of the cultures was perhaps that of Crete, which was flourishing by the beginning of the 3d millennium B.C.; this was the MINOAN CIVILIZATION. On the mainland of Greece excavations have uncovered the remains of MYCENAEAN CIVILIZATION. The exploration of the ruins of Troy provided knowledge of another culture, and ruins in the Cyclades have demonstrated remarkable early development there. The exact relationships of these different centers are not yet known, and there are many subjects of conjecture, such as the role of the Achaeans and the causes of the decline of Crete before 1100 B.C. See V. R. d'Arba Desborough, *The Greek Dark Ages* (1972); Colin Renfrew, *The Emergence of Civilisation* (1972).

Aegean Sea, Gr. *Aigaion Pelagos,* Turkish *Ege Denizi,* arm of the Mediterranean Sea, c.400 mi (640 km) long and 200 mi (320 km) wide, off SE Europe between Greece and Turkey; Crete and Rhodes mark its southern limit. Irregular in shape, it is dotted with islands, most of which belong to Greece; they include Évvoia, the Sporades, the Cyclades, Sámos, Khíos, Lesbos, Thásos, and the Dodecanese. The Aegean Sea's greatest depths (more than 6,600 ft/2,010 m) are found off N Crete. The Dardanelles strait connects the Aegean Sea with the Sea of Marmara and the Black Sea. Sardines and sponges taken from the Aegean are economically important; natural gas has been found off NE Greece. The name Aegean has been variously derived from Aegae, a city of Evvoia; from Aegeus, father of Theseus, who drowned himself in the sea believing his son had been slain by the Minotaur; and from Aegea, an Amazon queen who drowned in it. The sea's ancient name, Archipelago, now applies to its islands and, generally, to any island group.

Aegeus (ē'jo͞os,-jēəs): see THESEUS.

Aegina or **Aíyina** (ā'yēnä), island (1971 pop. 5,704), 32 sq mi (83 sq km), off SE Greece, in the Gulf of Aegina or Saronic Gulf, near Athens. Sponge fishing and farming (figs, almonds, grapes, olives, and peanuts) are the most important occupations. The chief town is Aegina on the northwest shore. The island, inhabited from late Neolithic times, was named for the mythological figure Aegina. Its culture was influenced by Minoan Crete. Conquered by Dorian Greeks, it grew rapidly as a commercial state and struck the first Greek coins. In 431 B.C. the Athenians, against whom Aegina sided in the Peloponnesian War, expelled the population of the island, and Aegina fell into insignificance. In the 12th cent. it served as a haven for pirates, and the Venetians, in suppressing the outlaws, conquered the island. Albanians settled there in the 16th cent. During the Greek War of Independence the town of Aegina was (1828–29) the capital of Greece. Points of interest include the temple of Aphaia, where the AEGINETAN MARBLES were discovered in 1811.

Aegina (ējī'nə), in Greek mythology, river nymph, daughter of the river god Asopus. She was abducted by Zeus to the island Oenone, where she bore him a son, Aeacus. Aeacus later renamed the island in her honor.

Aegina, Gulf of: see SARONIC GULF, Greece.

Aegineta, Paulus: see PAUL OF AEGINA.

Aeginetan marbles (ē"jĭnē'tən), archaic Greek sculptures, c.500–480 B.C., from the temple of Aphaia at Aegina, discovered in 1811 and erroneously restored by Thorvaldsen. Now in the Glyptothek at

Munich, they originally decorated the pediments of the temple. They represent scenes from the Trojan War.

aegis (ē'jĭs), in Greek mythology, weapon of Zeus and Athena. It possessed the power to terrify and disperse the enemy or to protect friends. The aegis was usually described as a garment made of goatskin slung over the shoulder or as a piece of armor. The aegis of Athena was a breastplate covered with goatskin and bordered with snakes, bearing in the center the head of the Gorgon Medusa.

Aegisthus (ējĭs'thəs), in Greek mythology, according to most legends the incestuous offspring of Thyestes and his daughter Pelopia. At Thyestes' behest Aegisthus revenged the murder of his brothers by killing his uncle ATREUS. Later, he was known as the paramour of Clytemnestra and aided her in the murdering of her husband, Agamemnon. He was killed in revenge by Clytemnestra's son, Orestes.

Aegospotamos (ē''gəspŏ'təməs), river of ancient Thrace flowing into the Hellespont. At its mouth in 405 B.C. occurred the culminating battle of the PELOPONNESIAN WAR. Lysander and his Spartan fleet had come north to cut the grain supply of Athens. The Athenian fleet under Conon came to Aegospotamos and at first vainly tried to induce the Spartans to fight. Despite the warnings of ALCIBIADES, Conon and his men did not take proper precautions. Lysander fell upon them and completely destroyed the Athenian fleet.

Aegyptus (ējĭp'təs): see DANAÜS.

Aehrenthal, Alois Lexa, Graf von (ä'lōēs lāk'sä gräf fən âr'əntäl), 1854–1912, Austro-Hungarian foreign minister (1906–12). The chief event of his ministry was the Austrian annexation (1908) of BOSNIA AND HERCEGOVINA. The Russian foreign minister, IZVOLSKY, had given his formal agreement to the annexation in a secret meeting at Buchlau, Moravia; in return, Aehrenthal promised Austrian support for the opening of the Dardanelles to Russian warships. The annexation followed promptly, whereas Izvolsky was frustrated in his Dardanelles plan by English opposition. Serbian indignation at the annexation as well as belated Russian opposition almost led to a European war in 1909. Aehrenthal, with difficulty, restrained the Austrian war party led by Conrad von Hötzendorf. At last the crisis was ended by German mediation. The signatory powers of the Congress of Berlin (1878), including Russia, ratified the annexation.

Aeken, Jerom van: see BOSCH, HIERONYMUS.

Ælfric (ăl'frĭk), c.955–1020, English writer and Benedictine monk. He was the greatest English scholar during the revival of learning fostered by the Benedictine monasteries in the second half of the 10th cent. His aim was to educate the laity as well as the clergy. He wrote in English a series of saints' lives and homilies—designed for use as sermons by the preachers who were generally unable to read Latin. Ælfric was also the author of a grammar, a glossary, and a colloquy, which were for many years the standard texts for Latin study in English monasteries. Among his other writings are the *Heptateuch*, a free English version of the first seven books of the Bible. Ælfric is considered the chief prose stylist of the period. His later writings were strongly influenced by the balance, alliteration, and rhythm of Latin prose. See *Selected Homilies* (ed. by Henry Sweet, 1922) and the *Heptateuch and Other Writings* (ed. by Early English Text Society, 1922); study by James Hurt (1972).

Aelian (ē'lēən), fl. 2d cent. A.D., Roman author; his original name was Claudius Aelianus. He lived in Praenesta and taught rhetoric in Rome. His works, all in Greek, include *Historical Miscellanies*, anecdotes about celebrities of the day; and *On the Characteristics of Animals*. Both of these are largely extant. He also wrote *Peasant Letters*, 20 epistles attributed to farmers from Attica.

Aemilian Way: see ROMAN ROADS.

Aeneas (ē'nēəs, ĭnē'-), palsied man whom Peter cured. Acts 9.33,34.

Aeneas (ĭnē'əs), in classical legend, a Trojan, son of ANCHISES and Venus. After the fall of Troy he escaped, bearing his aged father on his back. He stayed at Carthage with Queen Dido, then went to Italy, where his descendants founded Rome. The deeds of the "pious" Aeneas are the substance of the great Roman epic, the *Aeneid* of VERGIL.

Aeneas Silvius Piccolomini: see PIUS II.

Aenesidemus (ēnĕs''ĭdē'məs), Greek skeptic philosopher, fl. probably 1st cent. B.C. Thought to be a native of Knossos, Crete, he taught in Alexandria. Although his writings have been lost, it is known that his main contributions were 10 tropoi (ways to conduct arguments) that appeared in *Pyrrhonian Discourses*. His arguments, which asserted the impossibility of knowledge, made him one of the leading skeptics.

Aenon (ē'nŏn), unidentified place, where John the Baptist baptized people. John 3.23.

Aeolia: see AEOLIS.

Aeolian Islands: see LIPARI ISLANDS, Italy.

Aeolians: see GREECE.

Aeolis (ē'əlĭs) or **Aeolia** (ēō'lēə), ancient region of the west coast of Asia Minor (in present-day Turkey). Aeolis was not a geographic term but a collective term for the cities founded there by the Aeolians, a branch of the Hellenic peoples. The 12 southern cities were grouped in the Aeolian League; these were Temnos, Smyrna, Pitane, Neonteichos, Aegirusa, Notium, Cilla or Killa, Cyme, Gryneum, Larissa, Myrina, and Aegae.

Aeolus (ē'ələs), in Greek mythology. **1** The wind god. He lived on the island of Aeolia, where he kept the winds in a cave. **2** Son of HELLEN and ancestor of the Aeolian branch of the Hellenic race.

Aepinus, Franz Ulrich Theodosius (fränts o͝ol'rĭkh tā''ōdō'zēo͞os āpē'no͞os), 1724–1802, German physicist. He studied at Jena and Rostock and taught mathematics at Rostock from 1747 to 1755. After a brief stay in Berlin he went to St. Petersburg as professor of physics and academician, remaining there until 1798 and rising to a high position as courtier to Catherine the Great. He made experimental and theoretical contributions to the study of electricity, including work on the thermoelectric properties of tourmaline and the invention, with J. C. Wilche, of the air capacitor. A consideration of the implications of this device led him to reject then current mechanical theories of electricity and to elaborate in his *Tentamen Theoriae Electricitatis et Magnetismi* (1759) a theory of electrostatics similar to Newton's gravitational theory.

aerial: see ANTENNA, in electronics.

aerial photography, technology and science of taking still or moving-picture photographs from an aircraft in flight. It was tried before the advent of the airplane by using kites and balloons. World War I demonstrated its tremendous military value, and during the ensuing peacetime years methods were so far perfected for taking still pictures that photogrammetry, the science of measurement from photographs, became an important tool of agencies making any type of surface map. During World War II and subsequent conflicts, aerial photographs were a most important source of intelligence. The quality of these photographs is now so good that the rank of a foot soldier can be determined from photographs taken at altitudes of c.100,000 ft (30,500 m). The pilot sets his aircraft on the correct speed and course before entering the area to be photographed to insure uniformity of speed and altitude. The camera is activated before the area is entered and remains in operation until the plane is well past the area. This is done to insure longitudinal overlapping between this area and any adjacent area to be subsequently photographed so that the photographs may later be joined together. Aerial photographs may be high oblique (including the horizon), low oblique (below the horizon), or vertical (perpendicular to the earth). Only the vertical may be accurately scaled for mapmaking purposes. Often a multilens camera is used to photograph one section vertically and the adjacent areas obliquely. The individual oblique exposures are then corrected, scaled, and joined to the vertical section to form one continuous photograph. A photograph formed by fitting together several overlapping vertical photographs is called a mosaic. By viewing two overlapping photographs through a stereoscope, a three-dimensional image of a region can be obtained. A reproduction of a photograph to which grid lines, place names, and the like have been added is called a photomap. In addition to its military uses, aerial photography has proved valuable in such fields as archaeology, geology, forestry, highway plotting and construction, mapmaking, and land conservation. See W. H. Baker, *Elements of Photogrammetry* (1960); Beaumont Newhall, *Airborne Camera* (1969); Grover Heiman, Jr., *Aerial Photography* (1972).

aerodynamics, study of gases in motion. As the principal application of aerodynamics is the design of aircraft, air is the principal gas with which the science is concerned. One of the phenomena studied in aerodynamics is the lift exerted on an aircraft's wings as they move through the atmosphere. BERNOULLI'S PRINCIPLE, which states that the pressure of a moving gas decreases as its velocity increases, has been used to explain the lift produced by a wing having a curved upper surface and a flat lower surface. Since the flow is faster across the curved surface than across the plane one, a greater pressure is exerted in the upward direction. This principle, however, does not explain how an airplane can fly upside down. A more general explanation accounting for this phenomenon is that the wing of an aircraft in flight intersects the air at an angle that causes air to be deflected downward. It is easily shown that any heavier-than-air craft must divert air downward in order to stay aloft. It is almost as easily shown that a force that retards the forward motion of the aircraft is developed by diverting air in this way. This force is known as drag due to lift. It decreases with gains in speed and loss of altitude; for subsonic flight, i.e., at speeds less than the speed of sound, it decreases with increasing wingspan, while the reverse is true for supersonic flight, i.e., at speeds greater than the speed of sound. This explains the advantage of swept-back wings for supersonic flight and why some planes are designed with wings that can be fully extended for subsonic flight and swept back for supersonic flight. The slowing of air very near to the aircraft's surface results in a drag caused by friction, which can be reduced by making the surface area of the craft as small as possible. As speeds close to the speed of sound, or Mach 1, are approached, the compressibility of the air, negligible at lower speeds, becomes a factor. There is in the neighborhood of Mach 1 a large and sudden increase in drag, which has been called the sonic, or sound, barrier. While the practical problems that made this drag a barrier have been largely solved through the choice of proper shapes and the use of more powerful propulsion systems, the general phenomena associated with these speeds are still of interest to scientists. One of the troublesome phenomena still associated with supersonic flight is the SHOCK WAVE that trails after the craft. Odd as it may seem, no sound from an aircraft at supersonic speed is heard ahead of it; it literally outruns its own sound. It is also true that craft in supersonic flight experience aerodynamic forces in different locations than in subsonic flight. This can greatly alter the effects of controls. Early supersonic craft were often subject to control reversal, a condition in which a control had exactly the opposite effect from what was expected. Modern jet aircraft have been designed so that these conditions do not arise. For flight at hypersonic speeds, i.e., speeds five times or more the speed of sound, aircraft must be built to withstand the extremely high temperatures created by the air flowing along its surface. Aerodynamics is not solely concerned with flight; it is used in designing automobile bodies and trains for minimum drag and in computing wind stresses on bridges, buildings, smokestacks, trees, and the like. It is also used in charting flows of pollutants in the atmosphere and in determining frictional effects in gas ducts. The WIND TUNNEL is one of the aerodynamicist's basic experimental tools. See Theodore Von Kármán, *Aerodynamics* (1963).

aeroembolism: see DECOMPRESSION SICKNESS.

aerolite (âr'əlīt''): see METEORITE.

aeronautical engineering: see ENGINEERING.

aeronautics: see AERODYNAMICS; AIRPLANE; AVIATION.

aerosol (âr'əsōl,-sŏl): see COLLOID.

aerosol dispenser, device designed to produce a fine spray of liquid or solid particles that can be suspended in a gas such as the atmosphere. The dispenser commonly consists of a container that holds under pressure the substance to be dispersed (e.g., paints, insecticides, medications, and hair sprays) and a liquefied-gas propellant. When a valve is released, the propellant forces the substance through an atomizer out of the dispenser in the form of a fine spray. These devices are more properly termed spray dispensers rather than aerosol dispensers because the particles of the dispersed substance are usually larger than the particles of a true aerosol, such as a fog or a smoke.

aerospace medicine: see AVIATION MEDICINE; SPACE MEDICINE.

aerovane (âr'ōvān''), WEATHER VANE with a propeller attached to measure wind speed. By means of a system of synchronous motors and electric circuitry, both wind direction and speed are monitored on a remote indicator. See WIND.

Aertsen or **Aertszen, Pieter** (both: pē'tər ärt'sən), 1503?–1575, Dutch painter, b. Amsterdam. Aertsen painted genre scenes (see GENRE) that are lighthearted in spirit and realistic in style. He also painted religious subjects, including a few surviving altarpieces. Aertsen's works reveal his rich sense of color and attention to homely detail.

Aeschines (ĕ'skĭnēz), c.390-314? B.C., Athenian orator, rival of DEMOSTHENES. Aeschines rose from humble circumstances and became powerful in politics because of his oratorical gifts. At first he opposed Philip II of Macedon, then later changed sides, arguing that resistance to Macedonian power was useless. Both he and Demosthenes were members of the embassy to Philip in 348 B.C., and afterward Demosthenes bitterly and baselessly accused Aeschines of accepting Macedonian bribes. He was to have been joined in his action by Timarchus, but Aeschines prevented this by his oration *Against Timarchus* (345 B.C.). Aeschines defended himself well in his oration *On the False Legation* (342 B.C.)—a title also used by Demosthenes in his accusatory oration. The trouble between the orators grew and culminated in a dispute over a gold crown that the orator Ctesiphon proposed should be given Demosthenes in 330 B.C. Aeschines brought suit with *Against Ctesiphon.* Demosthenes replied with his sturdy defense *On the Crown.* Aeschines lost and was fined, and retired to Asia Minor where, according to Plutarch, he lived as a professional Sophist.

Aeschylus (ĕs'kĭləs, ēs'-), 525-456 B.C., Athenian tragic poet, b. Eleusis. The first of the three great Greek writers of tragedy, he was the predecessor of SOPHOCLES and EURIPIDES. He fought at Marathon and at Salamis. In 476 B.C. he went to Sicily to live at the court of Hiero I, and he died at Gela. He wrote perhaps 90 plays (7 survive in full) and won 13 first prizes at the Greater Dionysia, the spring festival of Dionysus. In each case 4 connected plays were submitted (a tragic trilogy and a lighter satyr play). Aeschylus is often credited with the invention of tragedy, as tragedy previously had been merely a dialogue between a chorus and one actor—a dramatically limited form. Aeschylus added an actor, thus increasing the potentialities of his vehicle immeasurably. (Though only two actors and the chorus appeared on the stage at the same time, an actor often took more than one part.) Aeschylus introduced costumes, decorated his scene, and placed supernumeraries on the stage. By his supreme poetic ability and his piety he made Athenian tragedy more of an artistic and intellectual creation than it had been before. His choral lyrics are, at their best, rivals of the odes of Pindar. The choruses, more important in Aeschylus than in his successors, are both ethical commentaries on the action and the means for its presentation. Vivid in its character portrayal, majestic in its tone, and captivating in its lyricism, Aeschylus' tragic poetry is esteemed among the greatest of all time. He alone of Greek tragedians was honored at Athens by having his plays performed repeatedly after his death. His extant plays are hard to date. The earliest is probably *The Suppliants,* simple in plot (on the marriage of the 50 daughters of Danaüs) and with only one actor besides the chorus. *The Persians* (472? B.C.), glorifying the Athenian victory over Persia at Salamis, has two actors, but the new form is still unpolished. *The Seven against Thebes* can be dated in 467. *Prometheus Bound* (see PROMETHEUS), of uncertain date, is striking for its bald attack on the vengefulness of the gods toward man, but the later two parts of its trilogy, which are lost, may have portrayed Zeus as just. The last three tragedies of Aeschylus compose the only extant ancient trilogy, called the *Oresteia,* a history of the house of Atreus, with which the poet won first prize in 458. The three plays are *Agamemnon, The Choëphoroe* (The Libation Bearers), and *The Eumenides;* in each play three actors are used—an innovation of Sophocles. Because of its scope, complexity, and the profundity of its themes (the significance of human suffering and the true meaning of justice) the *Oresteia* as a whole is considered by many to be the greatest Attic tragedy. Browning's *Agamemnon* is a poetic translation of the first play, and Eugene O'Neill's *Mourning Becomes Electra* is an American version of the trilogy. The translation by David Grene and Richmond Lattimore in *The Complete Greek Tragedies* is one of many English translations of his plays. See studies by Gilbert Murray (1940), J. H. Finley (1955), A. J. Podlecki (1966), and M. H. McCall, ed. (1972).

Aesculapius: see ASCLEPIUS.

Aesir (ĕ'sər): see GERMANIC RELIGION.

Aesop (ē'səp, ē'sŏp), semilegendary Greek fabulist. According to Herodotus, he was a slave who lived in Samos in the 6th cent. B.C. and who was eventually freed by his master. Other accounts state that he was deformed, associate him with many wild adventures, and connect him with such rulers as Solon and Croesus. The fables called Aesop's fables were preserved principally through BABRIUS, PHAEDRUS, and PLANUDES MAXIMUS. The most famous of these fables include "The Fox and the Grapes" and "The Tortoise and the Hare." See FABLE.

aesthetics (ĕsthĕt'ĭks), the branch of philosophy that is concerned with the nature of art and the criteria of artistic judgment. The classical conception of art as the imitation of nature was formulated by Plato and developed by Aristotle in his *Poetics,* while modern thinkers such as Immanuel Kant, F. W. Schelling, Benedetto Croce, and Ernst Cassirer have emphasized the creative and symbolic aspects of art. The major problem in aesthetics concerns the nature of the beautiful. Generally speaking there are two basic approaches to the problem of beauty—the objective, which asserts that beauty inheres in the object and that judgments concerning it may have objective validity, and the subjective, which tends to identify the beautiful with that which pleases the observer. Outstanding defenders of the objective position were Plato, Aristotle, and G. E. Lessing, and of the subjective position, Edmund Burke and David Hume. In his *Critique of Judgment,* Kant mediated between the two tendencies by showing that aesthetic judgment has universal validity despite its subjective nature. Among the modern philosophers interested in aesthetics, the most important are Croce, Robin Collingwood, Cassirer, John Dewey, and George Santayana. See K. E. Gilbert and Helmut Kuhn, *A History of Esthetics* (rev. ed. 1953, repr. 1972); M. C. Beardsley, *Aesthetics from Classical Greece to the Present* (1965); Harold Osborne, *Aesthetics and Art Theory* (1970); George Dickie, *Aesthetics: An Introduction* (1971).

aestivation (ĕs'təvā"shən): see HIBERNATION.

Aeta: see PYGMY.

Æthelbald (ĕ'thəlbôld, ă'-), d. 757, king of Mercia (716-57), grandson of a brother of Penda. He spent many years in exile before he became king. A strong ruler, by 731 he controlled all England S of the Humber River, and he led expeditions into Northumbria (740) and against the Welsh (743). He was murdered by his own bodyguard.

Æthelbert (ĕ'thəlbərt, ă-), d. 616, king of Kent (560?-616). Although defeated by the West Saxons in 568, he later became the strongest ruler in England S of the Humber River. His wife, Bertha, daughter of a Frankish king, was a Christian. Æthelbert received (597) the missionaries sent by Pope Gregory I to England and was converted by St. Augustine of Canterbury. The first Christian king in Anglo-Saxon England, he made his capital, Canterbury, a great Christian center. The code of laws issued by him is the earliest surviving document in the Anglo-Saxon vernacular.

Æthelbert, d. 865, king of Wessex (860-65), son of Æthelwulf. After the death of his father in 858 he ruled Kent, Surrey, Sussex, and Essex, and he reunited them with Wessex when in 860 he succeeded his brother Æthelbald in that kingdom. Throughout his reign the attacks of the Danes were severe, and they continued through the reign of his brother and successor, Æthelred.

Æthelflæd (ĕ'thəlflĕd, ă'thĕlflăd) or **Ethelfleda** (-flē'də), d. 918, daughter of King Alfred the Great of Wessex and wife of Æthelred, ealdorman of Mercia. After her husband's death in 911, she ruled the semi-independent Mercia alone and was known as the Lady of the Mercians. Campaigning with her brother, EDWARD THE ELDER, she helped to recover the Danish-held lands S of the Humber River. After her death Mercia was fully incorporated into the kingdom of Wessex.

Æthelfrith (ĕ'thəlfrĭth, ă-), d. 616, king of Northumbria (c.593-616). He was the first great leader to arise among the northern English, and he ruled over both Bernicia and Deira, uniting them into the kingdom of Northumbria. He repulsed an attack by the Scots in 603 and about 10 years later defeated the Welsh at Chester. During Æthelfrith's lifetime (if not solely as a result of the battle of Chester) the English penetrated to the Irish Sea, thus separating the Welsh in Wales from the Welsh in SW Scotland. Æthelfrith forced his brother-in-law EDWIN, who was heir to the throne in the Deiran line, into a long exile. Edwin found a protector in Rædwald of East Anglia, who fought against Æthelfrith and killed him in battle at the Idle River near the present-day town of Nottingham.

Æthelmar of Valence: see AYMER OF VALENCE.

Æthelred (ĕ'thəlrĕd, ă'-), d.871, king of Wessex (865-71), son of Æthelwulf and brother of ALFRED. He succeeded his brother Æthelbert as king of Wessex and as overlord of Kent and possibly of East Anglia. Æthelred spent much of his short reign gathering forces to oppose the Danes, who occupied York (866) and ravaged much of England. Alfred was important as his second in command in a series of battles (870-71) and succeeded him in April, 871.

Æthelred, 965?-1016, king of England (978-1016), called Æthelred the Unready [from Old Eng. *unrœd*=without counsel]. He was the son of Edgar and the half brother of EDWARD THE MARTYR, whom he succeeded. Æthelred began his reign under a cloud of suspicion because of the murder of Edward. He was a weak king, but his efforts to resist the Danes, who resumed their raids on England in 980, were also considerably hampered by the frequent treachery of his commanders. In 991 he began paying tribute to the Danes, which he raised by the DANEGELD, but his tributary status did not prevent the Danes from returning. In 997 they came not only to raid but to remain and plunder the rich realm until 1000. A massacre of Danes in England in 1002 (possibly on the king's order) provoked another major raid (1003) led by the Danish king SWEYN. Æthelred tried to defend his kingdom: in 1002 he married Emma, sister of Richard II, duke of Normandy, perhaps in an attempt to gain an ally; in 1007 the army was placed under a single commander; by 1009 a navy had been built, but many of its commanders took to piracy. A severe harrying (1009-12) by the Danes left England disorganized and without hope, and when Sweyn returned in 1013 to conquer, he was well received in the DANELAW, and London capitulated with little resistance. Æthelred fled to Normandy. Upon Sweyn's death in 1014, Æthelred's restoration was negotiated in the first recorded pact between an English king and his subjects. Sweyn's son, CANUTE, withdrew, but he returned with a powerful army in 1015. War was in progress when Æthelred died in April, 1016. His son EDMUND IRONSIDE was declared his successor, but after concluding a treaty with Canute, he died in November. Æthelred's heirs were restored to the throne only with EDWARD THE CONFESSOR.

Æthelstan: see ATHELSTAN.

Æthelwulf (ĕ'thəlwo͝olf, ă'-), d. 858, king of Wessex (839-56), son and successor of Egbert; father of Æthelbert, Æthelred, and Alfred. He was lord of Kent, Surrey, Sussex, and Essex before his father's death in 839. As king of Wessex he was compelled to defend his realm against constant Danish attacks, and he won a notable victory over them at Aclea in 851. He also campaigned against the Welsh. A man of great piety, he went with his son Alfred to Rome in 855. In 856 he took as his second wife Judith, daughter of Charles II (Charles the Bald) of France. Learning before his return to England that his son Æthelbald, who had ruled in his absence, would resist his resumption of the kingship, Æthelwulf left his son as king of Wessex and himself ruled only in Kent and its dependencies, where Æthelbert succeeded him.

aether: see ETHER, in physics and astronomy.

Aetius (āē'shēəs), d. 367, Syrian theologian. He became prominent (c.350) as an exponent of the extreme ARIANISM developed mainly by his secretary EUNOMIUS. Members of his party were called Aetians and Anomoeans.

Aetius, c.396-454, Roman general. At first unfriendly to VALENTINIAN III, he later made his peace with Valentinian's mother, GALLA PLACIDIA, and was given a command in Gaul. An ambitious general, he was embroiled in difficulties with his rival BONIFACE, who defeated him near Rimini in 432. Aetius went briefly into exile among the Huns but returned in 433 and rose to be the chief ruler of the Western Empire. He defeated the Germans in Gaul, then crowned his career by commanding (451) Roman and Visigothic troops in the repulse of Attila and the Huns in the battle near the modern Châlons-sur-Marne—a battle generally said to have saved the West. Valentinian, presumably jealous of Aetius' success, had him murdered.

Aetna, volcano: see ETNA, Italy.

Aetolia (ētōl'yə), region of ancient Greece, N of the Gulf of Corinth and the Gulf of Calydon, E of the Achelous River (separating it from Acarnania). Little is known of the early population of Aetolia, but later Aetolians, though they had coastal cities, were primarily an inland farming and pastoral people. They had famous shrines at Calydon (to Artemis) and at Thermum (to Apollo). Aetolia was of little significance in Greek history until the rise of the AETOLIAN LEAGUE. After the downfall of that confederation, Aetolia was absorbed by the Romans into Achaea.

Aetolian League, confederation centering in the cities of Aetolia. It was formed in the 4th cent. B.C.

and began to gain power in the 3d cent. in opposing the ACHAEAN LEAGUE and the Macedonians. At its height, the league stretched across Greece from sea to sea, including Locris, Malis, Dolopes, part of Thessaly, Phocis, and Acarnania. In alliance with the Romans, the Aetolians helped to defeat Philip V of Macedon at Cynoscephalae in 197 B.C. The Aetolians, dissatisfied, turned against Rome and allied themselves with Antiochus III of Syria. His defeat (189 B.C.) spelled the ruin of the league. Although formally it continued, its power had vanished.

Afanasyev, Aleksandr Nikolayevich (əlyĭksän'dər nyĭkəlī'əvĭch əfənä'syəf), 1826–71, Russian folklorist. His collections, published from 1866 on, were instrumental in introducing Russian popular tales to world literature. A selection was translated into English as *Russian Fairy Tales* (1945).

Afars and the Issas, French Territory of the (äf'ärz, ē'säz), overseas territory of France (1970 est. pop. 95,000), c.8,500 sq mi (22,020 sq km), E Africa, on the Gulf of Aden. DJIBOUTI is the capital. It is bounded on the N and W by Ethiopia, on the S by the Somali Republic, and on the E by the Gulf of Aden. Largely a stony desert with isolated plateaus and highlands, it has a generally dry and torrid climate. The territory is economically underdeveloped, and nomadic pastoralism is the chief occupation; exports are hides, cattle, and coffee (transshipped from Ethiopia). Some revenue is derived from the port of Djibouti. Manufacturing is limited to shipbuilding and repair, building and construction, production of compressed or liquid gas, and the manufacture of foodstuffs. The population is almost evenly divided between Somali (Issas and others) and Afars, both of whom are Muslim. Strategically

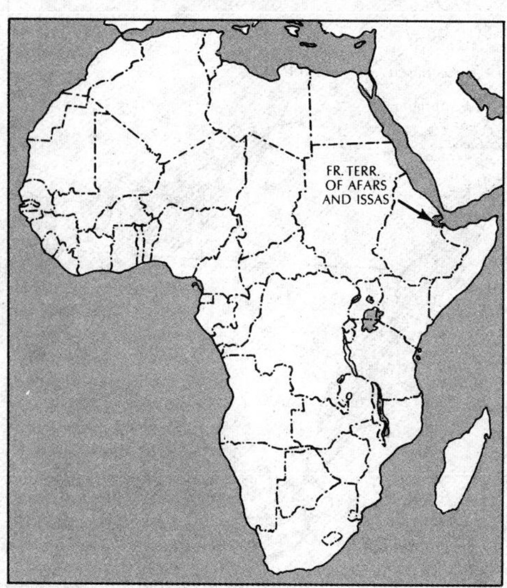

situated, the territory commands the strait between the Gulf of Aden and the Red Sea. France first obtained a foothold there in 1862; French interest centered around Djibouti, the French commercial rival to Aden. By 1896 the present territory was organized as a colony. It remained a colony until 1946, at which time it became a territory within the French Union. Membership in the French Community followed in 1958. The political status of the territory was determined by a referendum in March, 1967, in which the Afar population, until then the group that had the lesser voice in government, gained political ascendancy with French support. The Afars opted for the continuation of the connection with France, whereas the Somali voted for independence and eventual union with the Somali Republic. France retains control of foreign and defense matters. The territory was formerly known as French Somaliland. See V. M. Thompson and Richard Adloff, *Djibouti and the Horn of Africa* (1968); I. M. Lewis, *Peoples of the Horn of Africa* (1969); H. G. Marcus, *The Modern History of Ethiopia and the Horn of Africa* (1972).

affenpinscher (ăf'ənpĭn''shər), breed of TOY DOG perfected in Europe at the end of the 19th cent. It stands from 8 to 10 in. (20.3–25.4 cm) high at the shoulder and weighs about 8 lb (3.6 kg). Its wiry coat is short and dense over most of the body, but grows longer and shaggier on the legs and around the eyes, nose, and chin. It is usually solid black or black with tan, red, or gray markings. Believed by many authorities to have existed as a distinct breed as early as the 17th cent., the affenpinscher is alert and lively and makes a devoted pet. See DOG.

affine geometry: see GEOMETRY.

Afghan hound (ăf'găn), breed of tall, swift hound originating about 5,000 years ago in ancient Egypt. Its modern ancestors were perfected in the northern part of Afghanistan and introduced into England after World War I. The Afghan hound stands between 24 and 28 in. (61–71.1 cm) high at the shoulder and weighs between 50 and 60 lb (22.7–27.2 kg). The long, silky coat is very fine in texture and may be any color. Its unique appearance is partly the result of the position of its hipbones, which are set wider apart and higher than in most other breeds. This hip conformation enables the Afghan to cover uneven country swiftly and contributes to its effectiveness as a sight hunter in the mountainous terrain of its native Afghanistan. Today it is rapidly gaining popularity as a house pet. See DOG.

Afghanistan (ăfgăn'ĭstăn'', ăfgăn''ĭstăn'), republic (1973 est. pop. 18,100,000), 249,999 sq mi (647,497 sq km), S central Asia. The capital is KABUL. Afghanistan is bordered by Iran on the west, by Pakistan on the east and south, and by the USSR on the north. A narrow strip, the Vakhan, extends in the northeast to touch Kashmir and the Sinkiang Uigur Autonomous Region of China. The great mass of the country is steep-sloped with mountains, the ranges fanning out from the towering Hindu Kush (reaching a height of more than 24,000 ft/7,315 m) across the center of the country. There are, however, within the mountain ranges and on their edges, many fertile valleys and plains, with fields of wheat, corn, barley, and rice, and orchards yielding fine fruits, such as the famous peaches and grapes of KANDAHAR. In the south, and particularly in the southwest, are great stretches of desert, including the regions of Seistan and Registan. To the north, between the central mountain chains (notably the Selseleh-ye Kuh-e Baba, or Koh-i-Baba, and the Paropamisus) and the Amu Darya (Oxus) River, which marks part of the boundary with the USSR, are the highlands of Badakhshan (with the finest lapis lazuli in the world), Afghan Turkistan, the Amu Darya plain, and the rich valley of HERAT on the Hari Rud (Arius) River in the northwest corner of the country (the heart of ancient ARIANA). The regions thus vary widely, although most of the land is dry. The rivers are mostly unnavigable; the longest is the Helmand, which flows generally southwest from the Hindu Kush to the Iranian border. Its water has been used since remote times for irrigation, as have the waters of the Hari Rud and of the Amu Darya. The Kabul River, on which the capital stands, is particularly famous because it leads to the Khyber Pass and thus S to India. This has been the traditional route of conquerors, and the incursions of various invaders from prehistoric days until relatively recent times has helped to make the population of present-day Afghanistan almost as variegated as its regions. Tadzhiks live around Herat, Uzbeks and nomadic Turkmen in the Vakhan. In the central mountains are the Hazaras, of Mongolian origin. In the east and south are the Afghans and their almost indistinguishable kinsmen, the Pathans (a name used particularly for those in the North-West Frontier Province of Pakistan). There are many other groups in Afghanistan, but Afghan and Iranian are the country's principal languages. A unifying factor is religion, almost all the inhabitants being Muslim; the large majority are Sunni, the minority (perhaps numbering as many as a million), Shiite. Agriculture is the main occupation, but less than 10% of the land is cultivated. Grazing is also of great importance in the economy; the fat-tailed sheep, a staple of Afghan life, supplies skins and wool for clothing and meat and fat for food. Fine horses are the pride of many tribesmen. Mineral wealth is being developed, and there are deposits of iron ore, coal, copper, and sulfur; oil and natural gas fields are found in the north. Industry is still only in the beginning stages. Cotton and other fabrics, cement, and processed agricultural goods are the main products. Fruits and lambskins (Karakul) are the main exports, manufactured goods and foodstuffs the main imports. Imports greatly exceed exports. The USSR, India, the United States, and Japan are the chief trading partners. Road communications are good, but there are no railroads. There are universities at Kabul (1933) and JALALABAD (1963).

History. The location of Afghanistan astride the land route to India has enticed conquerors throughout history. But its high mountains, while hindering unity, have helped the hill tribes to preserve their independence. It is probable that there were well-developed civilizations in S Afghanistan in prehistoric times, but the archaeological record is not clear. Certainly cultures had flourished in the north and east before Darius I (c.500 B.C.) by conquest annexed these areas to the Persian Empire. Later, Alexander the Great conquered (329–327 B.C.) them on his way to India. After Alexander's death (323 B.C.) the region at first was part of the Seleucid empire. In the north, BACTRIA became independent, and the south was acquired by the MAURYA dynasty. Bactria expanded southward but fell (mid-2d cent. B.C.) to the Parthians and rebellious tribes (notably the Saka). Buddhism was introduced from the east by the Yüechi, who founded the Kushan dynasty (early 2d cent. B.C.). Their capital was PESHAWAR. The Kushans declined (3d cent. A.D.) and were supplanted by the Sassanids, the Mongol Epthalites, and the Turkish Tu-Kuie. The Arab conquest of Afghanistan began in the 7th cent. Several short-lived Muslim dynasties were founded, the most powerful of them having its capital at GHAZNI. MAHMUD OF GHAZNI, who conquered the lands from Khurasan in Iran to the Punjab in India early in the 11th cent., was the greatest of Afghanistan's rulers. Jenghiz Khan (c.1220) and Tamerlane (late 14th cent.) were subsequent conquerors of renown. BABUR, a descendant

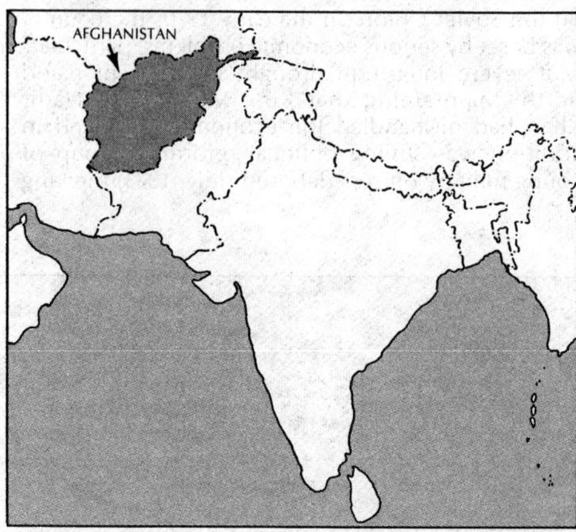

of Tamerlane, used Kabul as the base for his conquest of India and the establishment of the Mogul empire in the 16th cent. In the 18th cent. the Persian NADIR SHAH extended his rule to N of the Hindu Kush. After his death (1747) his lieutenant, AHMAD SHAH, an Afghan tribal leader, established a united state covering most of present-day Afghanistan. His dynasty, the Durani, gave the Afghans the name (Durani) that they themselves frequently use. The reign of the Durani line ended in 1818, and no predominant ruler emerged until DOST MUHAMMAD became emir in 1826. During his rule the status of Afghanistan became an international problem, as Britain and Russia contested for influence in central Asia. Aiming to protect the northern approaches to India, the British tried to replace Dost Muhammad with a former emir, subordinate to them. This policy caused the first Afghan War (1838–42) between the British and the Afghans. Dost Muhammad was at first deposed but, after an Afghan revolt in Kabul, was restored. In 1857, Dost Muhammad signed an alliance with the British. He died in 1863 and was succeeded, after familial fighting, by his third son, SHERE ALI. As the Russians acquired territory bordering on the Amu Darya, Shere Ali and the British quarreled, and the second Afghan War began (1878). Shere Ali died in 1879. His successor, Yakub Khan, ceded the Khyber Pass and other areas to the British, and after a British envoy was murdered the British occupied Kabul. Eventually ABD AR-RAHMAN KHAN was recognized (1880) as emir. In the following years Afghanistan's borders were more precisely defined. Border agreements were reached with Russia (1885 and 1895), British India (the Durand Agreement, 1893), and Persia (1905), although the line with what is now Pakistan remained disputed. The Anglo-Russian agreement of 1907 guaranteed the independence of Afghanistan under British influence in foreign affairs. Abd ar-Rahman Khan died in 1901 and was succeeded by his son Habibullah. Despite British pressure, Afghanistan remained neutral in World War I. Habibullah was assassinated in 1919. His successor, AMANULLAH, attempting to free himself of British influence, invaded India (1919). This third Afghan War was ended by the Treaty of Rawalpindi, which gave Afghanistan full control over its foreign relations. The attempts of Amanullah (who, after 1926, styled himself king) at westernization—including reducing the power of the country's religious leaders and increasing the freedom of its women—provoked opposition that led to his deposition in 1929. A tribal leader, Bacha-i Saqao, held

Kabul for a few months until defeated by Amanullah's cousin, Muhammad Nadir Khan, who became King Nadir Shah. The new king pursued cautious modernization efforts until he was assassinated in 1933. His son Muhammad Zahir Shah succeeded. Afghanistan was neutral in World War II. It joined the United Nations in 1946. When British India was partitioned (1947), Afghanistan wanted the Pathans of the North-West Frontier Province to be able to choose whether to join Afghanistan, join Pakistan, or be independent; the Pathans were only offered the choice of joining Pakistan or joining India—they chose the former. Since then relations between Afghanistan and Pakistan have been embittered. Afghanistan in 1955 urged the creation of an autonomous Pathan state, Pushtunistan (Pakhtunistan). The issue subsided in the late 1960s but was revived by Afghanistan in 1972 when Pakistan was weakened by the loss of its eastern wing (now Bangladesh) and the war with India. In great-power relations, Afghanistan has been neutral, receiving aid from both the United States and the Soviet Union, although it has become increasingly dependent economically on the Soviet Union. In the early 1970s the country was beset by serious economic problems, particularly a severe long-term drought in the center and north. Maintaining that King Muhammad Nadir Khan had mishandled the economic crisis and in addition was stifling political reform, a group of young military officers deposed (July, 1973) the king and proclaimed a republic. Lt. Gen. Muhammad Daud Khan, the former king's cousin and brother-in-law and a former prime minister (1953–63), became president and prime minister. See P. M. Sykes, *A History of Afghanistan* (2 vol., 1940); Arnold Fletcher, *Afghanistan, Highway of Conquest* (1965); W. K. Fraser-Tytler, *Afghanistan* (3d ed. 1967); George Grassmuck et al., ed., *Afghanistan, Some New Approaches* (1969); Vartan Gregorian, *The Emergence of Modern Afghanistan* (1969); H. H. Smith et al., *Area Handbook for Afghanistan* (1969); R. S. Newell, *The Politics of Afghanistan* (1972); R. T. Stewart, *Fire in Afghanistan, 1914–1929: Faith, Hope and the British Empire* (1973); Louis Dupree, *Afghanistan* (1973).

Afinogenov, Aleksandr Nikolayevich (əlyĭksän'-dər nyĭkəlī'əvĭch əfē"nəgyĕ'nəf), 1904–41, Russian playwright. In his early plays he wrote of labor problems and the dangers of straying from the Communist ideal. His later plays concern the difficulties inherent in the development of the new social order. In his most popular work, *Fear* (1931, tr. 1934), a scientist's concept of fear as the Soviet ruling force is refuted by a Bolshevik leader. His other major works include *Dalyokoye* (1935, tr. *Remote*) and *On the Eve* (1941, tr. 1946). Afinogenov was killed in a German air raid.

AFL: see AMERICAN FEDERATION OF LABOR AND CONGRESS OF INDUSTRIAL ORGANIZATIONS.

AFL-CIO: see AMERICAN FEDERATION OF LABOR AND CONGRESS OF INDUSTRIAL ORGANIZATIONS.

Afonso. For rulers thus named, see ALFONSO.

Africa, second largest continent, c.11,677,240 sq mi (30,244,050 sq km) including adjacent islands; 1971 est. pop. 354,000,000. Broad to the north (c.4,600 mi/7,400 km wide), Africa straddles the equator and stretches c.5,000 mi (8,050 km) from Cape Blanc (Tunisia) in the north to Cape Agulhas (South Africa) in the south. It is connected with Asia by the Sinai Peninsula (which is crossed by the Suez Canal) and is bounded on the N by the Mediterranean Sea, on the W and S by the Atlantic Ocean, and on the E and S by the Indian Ocean. The largest offshore island is Madagascar (see MALAGASY REPUBLIC); other islands include St. Helena and Ascension in the S Atlantic Ocean; São Tomé, Príncipe, Annobón, and Fernando Póo in the Gulf of Guinea; the Cape Verde, Canary, and Madeira islands in the N Atlantic Ocean; and Mauritius, Réunion, Zanzibar, Pemba, and the Comoro and Seychelles islands in the Indian Ocean. Most of Africa is a stable, ancient plateau that has been warped into a series of basins, low in the north and west and higher (rising to more than 6,000 ft/1,830 m) in the south and east. The plateau is composed mainly of metamorphic rock that has been overlaid in places by sedimentary rock. The escarpment of the plateau is in close proximity to the coast, thus leaving the continent with a generally narrow coastal plain; in addition, the es-

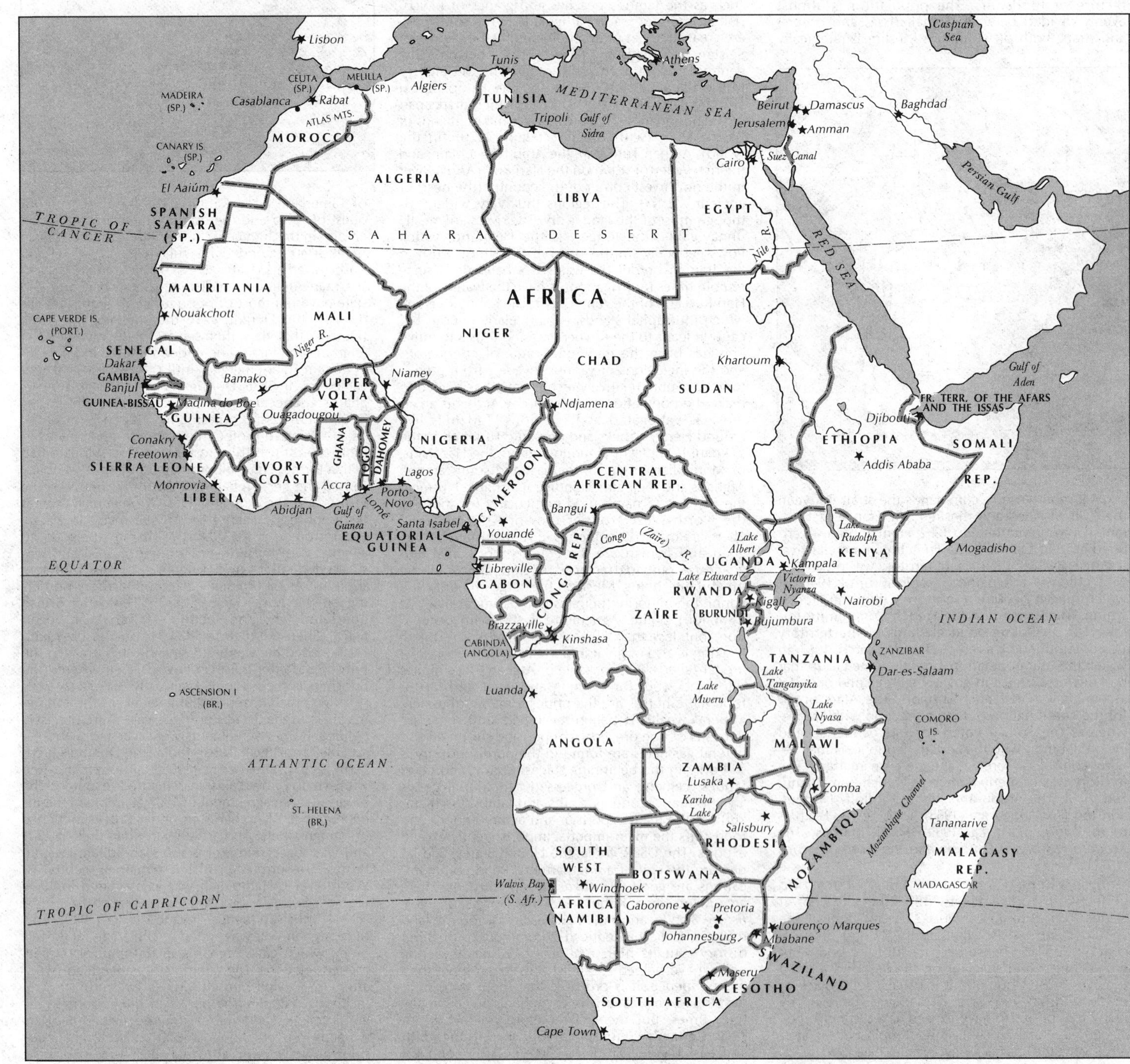

carpment forms a barrier of falls and rapids in the lower course of rivers that impedes their use as transportation routes into the interior. North Africa, a region composed mainly of folded sedimentary rock, is, geologically, more closely related to Europe than to the rest of Africa; the Atlas Mts., which occupy most of the region, are a part of the Alpine mountain system of S Europe. The entire African continent is surrounded by a narrow continental shelf. The lowest point on the continent is 436 ft (133 m) below sea level in the Qattarah Depression, NW Egypt; the highest point is Mt. Kibo (19,340 ft/5,895 m), a peak of Kilimanjaro in NE Tanzania. From north to south the principal mountain ranges of Africa are the Atlas Mts. (rising to more than 13,000 ft/3,960 m), the Ethiopian Highlands (rising to more than 15,000 ft/4,570 m), the Ruwenzori mts. (rising to more than 16,000 ft/4,880 m), and the Drakensberg Range (rising to more than 11,000 ft/3,350 m). The continent's largest rivers are the Nile (the world's longest river), the Congo (or Zaïre), the Niger, the Zambezi, the Orange, the Limpopo, and the Senegal. The largest lakes are Victoria Nyanza (the world's second largest freshwater lake), Tanganyika, Albert, Rudolf, and Nyasa (or Malawi), all in E Africa; shallow Lake Chad, the largest in W Africa, shrinks considerably in the dry season. The lakes and major rivers (most of which are navigable in stretches above the escarpment of the plateau) form an important inland transportation system. Geologically, recent major earth disturbances have been confined to areas of NW and E Africa. Geologists have long noted the excellent fit (in shape and geology) between the coast of Africa at the Gulf of Guinea and the Brazilian coast of South America, and they now have evidence that Africa formed the center of a large ancestral supercontinent known as Pangaea. Pangaea began to break apart in the Jurassic period to form Gondwanaland, from which Africa, the other southern continents, and India were formed. South America was separated from Africa c.76 million years ago, when the floor of the S Atlantic Ocean was opened up by sea-floor spreading; Madagascar was separated from it c.65 million years ago; and Arabia was separated from it c.20 million years ago, when the Red Sea was formed. There is also evidence of one-time connections between NW Africa and E North America, N Africa and Europe, Madagascar and India, and SE Africa and Antarctica. Similar large-scale earth movements (see PLATE TECTONICS) are also believed responsible for the formation of the GREAT RIFT VALLEY of E Africa, which is the continent's most spectacular land feature. From c.40 to c.60 mi (60–100 km) wide, it extends in Africa c.1,800 mi (2,900 km), from the Red Sea to near the mouth of the Zambezi River; the eastern branch of the rift valley is occupied in sections by lakes Nyasa and Rudolf, and the western branch, curving north from Lake Nyasa, is occupied by lakes Tanganyika, Kivu, Edward, and Albert. The lava flows of the recent and subrecent epochs in the Ethiopian Highlands, and volcanoes farther south, are associated with the rift; among the principal volcanoes are Kilimanjaro, Kenya (now extinct), Nyamulagira, Elgon, Meru, and the Virunga range with Mt. Karisimbi. A less spectacular rift, the Cameroon Rift, is associated with volcanic activity in W Africa and trends NE from St. Helena Island to São Tomé, Príncipe, Fernando Póo, and near the Tibesti Massif in the Sahara. Africa's climatic zones are largely controlled by the continent's location astride the equator and its almost symmetrical extensions into the northern and southern hemispheres. Thus, except where altitude exerts a moderating influence on temperature or precipitation (permanently snow-capped peaks are found near the equator), Africa may be divided into six general climatic regions. Areas near the equator and on the windward shores of SE Madagascar have a tropical rain forest climate, with heavy rain and high temperatures throughout the year. North and south of the rain forest are belts of tropical savanna climate, with high temperatures all year and a seasonal distribution of rain during the summer season. The savanna grades poleward in both hemispheres into a region of semiarid steppe (with limited summer rain) and then into true desert conditions in the extensive Sahara (north) and the smaller Kalahari (south). Belts of semiarid steppe with limited winter rain occur on the poleward sides of the desert regions. At the northern and southern extremities of the continent are narrow belts of Mediterranean type climate with subtropical temperatures and a concentration of rainfall mostly in the autumn and winter months. African peoples, who account for about 10% of the world's population, are divided into more than 50 different political units and are further fragmented into a larger (and disputed) number of linguistic and cultural groups. The Sahara forms a great ethnic divide. North of it Caucasoids, mostly Arabs along the coast and Berbers, Tuareg, and Tibbu in the interior regions, predominate. The southern (or sub-Saharan) sections of the continent are occupied by a diverse group of predominantly Negroid peoples, mostly Bantu-speaking (see AFRICAN LANGUAGES). Numerous other groups, of mixed and often disputed origin, occupy transitional areas S of the Sahara and include, among others, the Mossi, Fulani, Yoruba, Ibo, Masai, and Hausa. Europeans are concentrated in areas with subtropical climates or tropical climates modified to temperate by altitude; in the south are persons of Dutch and British descent and in the northwest are persons of French, Italian, and Spanish descent. Indians are an important minority in many coastal towns of S and E Africa. As a whole, Africa is sparsely populated; the highest densities are found in the lower Nile valley, along the Guinea coast, around Victoria Nyanza, along the coast of E Africa S of Mombasa, and along the Mediterranean fringe of NW Africa. The principal cities of Africa are usually the national capitals and the major ports, and they usually contain a disproportionately large percentage of the national populations; Cairo, Alexandria, Johannesburg, Casablanca, and Algiers are the largest cities of Africa. About three quarters of Africa's population is rural, but, except for cash crops, such as cacao and groundnuts (peanuts), agricultural production is low by world standards; Africa produces three quarters of the world's cocoa beans and about one third of its groundnuts, but only small percentages of the world's corn, wheat, meat, and eggs. Rare and precious minerals (including most of the world's diamonds) are abundant in the continent's ancient crystalline rocks, which are found mostly to the south and east of a line from the Gulf of Guinea to the Sinai Peninsula; extensive oil, gas, and phosphate deposits occur in sedimentary rocks to the north and west of this general line. Manufacturing is concentrated in the Republic of South Africa and in N Africa (especially Egypt and Algeria), with only small-scale production in the other countries. Despite Africa's enormous potential for hydroelectric power production, only a small percentage of it has been developed. Africa's fairly regular coastline affords few natural harbors, and the shallowness of coastal waters makes it difficult for large ships to approach the shore; deepwater ports, protected by breakwaters, have been built offshore to facilitate commerce and trade. Major fishing grounds are found over the wider sections of the continental shelf as off NW, SW, and S Africa and NW Madagascar.

Outline of History. Africa's history is long, complex, and only partly known. Man's oldest ancestor, discovered (1959) by Louis S. B. Leaky, the British anthropologist, lived in E Africa's Olduvai Gorge at least 1,750,000 years ago; agriculture, brought from SW Asia, appears to date from the 6th or 5th millennium B.C. Africa's first civilization began in Egypt in 3400 B.C.; other ancient centers were Kush and Aksum. Phoenicians established Carthage in the 9th cent. B.C. and probably explored the northwestern coast as far as the Canary Islands by the 1st cent. B.C. Romans conquered Carthage in 146 B.C., controlled N Africa until the 4th cent. A.D., and, in the 1st or 2nd cent. A.D., were probably the first Europeans to cross the Sahara into tropical Africa. Arabs began their conquest in the 7th cent. and, except in Ethiopia, extended Arabic and the religion of Islam across N Africa and S across the Sahara into the great medieval kingdoms of the W Sudan. The earliest of these kingdoms, which drew their wealth and power from the control of a lucrative trans-Saharan trade in gold, salt, and slaves, was ancient Ghana, already thriving when first recorded by Arabs in the 8th cent. In the 13th cent. Ghana was conquered and incorporated into the kingdom of ancient Mali, famous for its gold and its wealthy capital of Timbuktu. Mali in turn was conquered and incorporated into the Songhai empire in the late 15th cent. There are few written accounts of the interior of the continent before 1500, but it appears from available evidence that the original San, Pygmy, and Azanian inhabitants were displaced beginning in the 1st cent. A.D. by the Bantu, a group of black African peoples speaking related languages. The Bantu spread over most of the continent south of the equator, probably from an original homeland in modern S Zaïre, and established small villages and, in places, powerful kingdoms, such as Kongo, Mwata Yamvo, and Monomotapa. Prior to 1500 pastoralists moved south until they encountered the various Bantu groups and founded the kingdom of Kitara in the 16th cent. and, subsequently, the kingdoms of Bunyoro, Buganda, Rwanda, and Ankole, all of which had elaborate social structures based on a cattle-owning aristocracy with Bantu serfs. The Portuguese began to explore the coasts of Africa in the 15th cent. in an attempt to establish a safe route to India and to tap the lucrative gold trade of the Sudan and the east coast trade in gold, slaves, and ivory conducted for centuries by Arabs, Persians, and Indians. In 1488, Bartolomeu Dias rounded the Cape of Good Hope; in 1498, Vasco da Gama reached the east coast and, the following year, India. In the centuries that followed, coastal trading stations were established by Portugal and later by the Dutch, English, French, and other European maritime powers; under them the slave trade rapidly expanded. At the same time Ottoman Turks extended their control over N Africa and the shores of the Red Sea, and the Omani Arabs established suzerainty over the east coast as far south as Cape Delgado. Before 1800 few Europeans had penetrated the interior of the continent, and Africa was largely controlled by numerous African states, some of whom were weakened and some strengthened by European intervention. Explorations in the 18th and 19th cent. by Mungo Park, James Bruce, John Speke, David Livingstone, Henry Stanley, Heinrich Barth, and others reported the great natural wealth of the continent. Between 1880 and 1912 all of Africa except Liberia and Ethiopia passed under the control or protection of European powers, the boundaries of the new colonies and protectorates often bearing no relationship to the realities of geography or to the political and social organization of the indigenous population. This created a major problem throughout the continent, continuing during independence, when some governments sought to control the movement of peoples across political boundaries in an attempt to assimilate various ethnic groups into national units. This resulted in refugee movements, often of massive proportions, as one group fled the domination of another or as members of a group, scattered throughout a region, sought to concentrate in one area and thereby strained local resources—these movements taking place both within national boundaries and across them. In the northwest and west, France ultimately acquired regions that came to be known as French West Africa, French Equatorial Africa, and the French Cameroons, and established protectorates in Algeria, Morocco, and Tunisia. Other French territories were French Somaliland, French Togoland, Madagascar, and Réunion. The main group of British possessions was in E and SE Africa; it included the Anglo-Egyptian Sudan, British Somaliland, Uganda, Kenya, Tanganyika (after World War I), Zanzibar, Nyasaland, Northern and Southern Rhodesia, Bechuanaland, Basutoland, and Swaziland. Following Britain's victory in the South African War (1899–1902), its South African possessions (Transvaal, Orange Free State, Cape Colony, and Natal) became a dominion within the British Commonwealth of Nations. Gambia, Sierra Leone, the Gold Coast, and Nigeria were British possessions on the west coast. Portugal's African empire was made up of Portuguese Guinea, Angola, and Mozambique, in addition to various enclaves and islands on the west coast. Belgium held the Belgian Congo and, after World War I, Ruanda-Urundi. The Spanish possessions in Africa were the smallest, being composed of Spanish Guinea, Spanish Sahara, Ifni, and the protectorate of Spanish Morocco. The extensive German holdings—Togoland, the Cameroons, German South-West Africa, and German East Africa—were lost after World War I and redistributed among the Allies; Italy's empire included Libya, Eritrea, Italian Somaliland, and, briefly after 1936, Ethiopia. The Union of South Africa was formed and became virtually self-governing in 1910, Egypt achieved a measure of sovereignty in 1922, and in 1925, Tangier, previously attached to Morocco, was made an international zone. Beginning in 1950, in the face of rising nationalism, the former colonies and protectorates were granted independence by all the European powers except Portugal, which began to grant its territories independence in 1974. The sequence of change included independence for Libya in 1951; independence for Eritrea in 1952 in a federation with, and in 1962 merged with, Ethiopia; in 1956 independence for Morocco, Sudan, and Tunisia and the return of Tangier to Morocco; in 1957 independence for Ghana; in 1958 independence for Guinea and the return of Spanish Morocco to Morocco. In 1960 independence was granted to the former French colonies of Cameroon, the Central African Republic, Chad, Republic of the Congo-

Brazzaville (renamed People's Republic of the Congo in 1970), Dahomey, Gabon, Ivory Coast, the Malagasy Republic, Mali (briefly merged in 1959-60 with Senegal as the Sudanese Republic), Mauritania, Niger, Senegal, and Upper Volta; also newly independent in 1960 were the Republic of the Congo (renamed Zaïre in 1971), Nigeria, Somali Democratic Republic, and Togo. In 1961, Sierra Leone and Tanganyika (renamed Tanzania in 1964) became independent, the Portuguese enclave of São João Baptista de Ajudá was seized by Dahomey, the former British Cameroons were divided between Nigeria and the Republic of Cameroon (thereafter the Federal Republic of Cameroon and, in 1972, renamed the United Republic of Cameroon), and the Union of South Africa became a republic. In 1962, Uganda, Algeria, Rwanda, and Burundi became separate and independent nations. Remaining British possessions after 1962 were Zanzibar, which gained independence in 1963 and joined with Tanganyika to form Tanzania in 1964; Gambia and Kenya, which became independent in 1963; Malawi (formerly Nyasaland) and Zambia (formerly Northern Rhodesia), independent in 1964; Lesotho (formerly Basutoland) and Botswana (formerly Bechuanaland), independent in 1966; and Mauritius and Swaziland, independent in 1968. Rhodesia (formerly Southern Rhodesia) unilaterally declared itself independent in 1965, but Great Britain termed the act illegal and imposed trade sanctions against the country; the UN Security Council ordered a trade embargo in 1968. In the mid-1970s Great Britain retained control of the islands of St. Helena, Ascension, and the Seychelles and Dependencies. Remaining French territories included the Comoro Islands, Réunion, and the French Territory of the Afars and the Issas (formerly French Somaliland), which elected in a referendum (1967) to remain French. In 1968, Spain granted independence to Equatorial Guinea, including Río Muni on the mainland and the islands of Fernando Póo and Annobón, and in 1969 returned Ifni to Morocco; it retained the Canary Islands, Spanish Sahara, and Ceuta and Melilla, two small enclaves on Morocco's coast. Portugal retained most of its territories, including Angola, Cabinda, Mozambique, Portuguese Guinea, Cape Verde Islands, and the islands of São Tomé and Príncipe until the early 1970s; in 1974 Portuguese Guinea became independent as Guinea-Bissau, and Mozambique was scheduled to become independent in mid-1975. South West Africa (Namibia) has been administered by South Africa since 1922 under an old League of Nations mandate; South Africa's continued administration of the territory was declared illegal by the UN Security Council in 1970 and by the International Court of Justice in 1971. The African states wield considerable voting power in the UN General Assembly, where, in the mid-1970s, they made up about one third of the membership. Recognition among the new states that greater power was to be found in increased unity and cooperation has aided the cause of Pan-Africanism, and in 1963 at Addis Ababa the Organization of African Unity was established. The most pressing problems facing new African states are their need for aid for the development of natural resources, for education, and for the improvement of living standards; threats of secession and military coups; and shifting alliances among the states and with outside powers. Beginning in the late 1960s and continuing through the mid-70s, a severe drought desiccated the Sahel region S of the Sahara. The drought, along with belated and sporadic heavy rainfall that did more harm than good, had a particularly devastating effect on the people and economy of Senegal, Mauritania, Mali, Upper Volta, Niger, N Nigeria, the Sudan, and Ethiopia. Along with the resulting famine, disease, and poverty, it caused the death of thousands of people and forced the southward migration of additional hundreds of thousands to areas less affected by the drought. See separate entries on individual African states. See Raymond Furon, *Geology of Africa* (tr. 1963); R. I. Rotberg, *A Political History of Tropical Africa* (1965); Basil Davidson, *Africa: History of a Continent* (1966); Anthony Sillery, *Africa: A Social Geography* (2d ed. 1972); J. F. A. Ajayi and Michael Crowder, *History of West Africa* (2 vol., 1972 and 1973); G. S. P. Freeman-Greville, *Chronology of African History* (1974); W. A. Hance, *The Geography of Modern Africa* (rev. ed. 1975).

African art, traditional art created by the peoples S of the Sahara. The predominant art forms are masks and figures, which were generally used in religious ceremonies. The decorative arts, especially in textiles and in the ornamentation of everyday tools, were a vital art in nearly all African cultures. Established forms had evolved long before the arrival (late 15th cent.) of the Portuguese in Africa, but because of its perishable nature little work that is more than 150 years old has survived. No effort was made to preserve these works, as their creators valued them for ritual use rather than for aesthetic accomplishment. Wood—often embellished by clay, shells, beads, ivory, metal, feathers, and shredded raffia—was the dominant material. The discussion here is limited to the works of the peoples of W and central Africa—the regions richest in indigenous art.

Western Sudan and Guinea Coast. Here the style of wood carving is highly abstract. Distortion is often used to emphasize features of cultic significance. The figures of the Dogon tribe of central Mali stress the cylindrical shape of the torso. The Bambara of W Mali are famous for their striking wooden headdresses in the form of stylized antelope heads. The art of the Baga of NW Guinea includes snake carvings, drums supported by small free-standing figures, and spectacular masks. The Poro society of Liberia made ceremonial masks notable for their massiveness, color, and vitality of expression. The Baulé of the Ivory Coast created figurines to house the spirits of the dead or to represent their gods. These have precise renderings in high relief of ornate hairdresses and scarification patterns (see BODY-MARKING). The art of the Guro of the Ivory Coast consists almost entirely of human masks and of weaving pulleys. Guro figures are characterized by slanting eyes and a carved zig-zag design just above the forehead. The southern groups of the Senufu of the Ivory Coast produced an art akin to that of the Baulé, but more simplified and geometric. Senufu masks represent human features with geometric projections and have legs jutting out from each side of the face. The ASHANTI kingdom of Ghana employed (18th and 19th cent.) a system of brass weights based on a unit that was used to weigh gold dust, the state currency. These weights are small figures, mostly less than 2 in. (5.1 cm) high, which were cast in the CIRE PERDUE (lost wax) process indigenous to many W African regions. They portray simplified human and animal forms with a spontaneity unusual in African art. The sculptors of Dahomey also cast (16th-19th cent.) figures in brass by the cire perdue process. Their work is notable for its naturalism and finely chased metal surfaces. Figures are shown in everyday activities. This art was purely aesthetic, and the statues were reserved for the enjoyment of royalty.

Nigeria. From the north, the remarkable Nok terra-cotta heads, most of them fragments of figures, are the earliest African sculpture yet found (c.500-200 B.C.). Characteristic are the impressive simplification of facial features and the pierced pupils of the eyes. The art of S Nigeria reveals considerable contrast. Yoruba work is often brilliantly polychromed. The world-famous Ife portrait heads in bronze and terra-cotta are unique in Africa because of their naturalistic detail, perfection of modeling, and control over the cire perdue process. Nothing certain is known of the artistic sources or, in fact, of the culture that produced them. The art of BENIN arose from the needs of the royal household. It was largely commemorative, ritualistic, and ceremonial in function. Models of human heads were considered to be reincarnations of past kings, or Obas, and held to be divine. Abundant descriptive detail and sharp, precise lines are characteristic of Benin art. The Ibo, Ibibio, Ekoi, and Ijaw of SE Nigeria carved wooden masks for use in their rites and secret societies. Ibo masks were modeled after human skulls, with deep eye sockets, carved exposed teeth, and emaciated faces. On the banks of Middle Cross River are about 300 monolithic carvings, supposedly Ekoi ancestor figures from between 1600 and 1900.

Cameroon. The small tribes of the Cameroon grasslands display a fairly homogeneous style. Sculpture is bold in execution and vital in expression. Wood carvings include large house posts, masks, and other ritual objects.

Gabon. Among the Fang tribes, the decorative motifs on stringed musical instruments, drums, and spoons emphasize the human figure, often elongated with smooth surface planes. Some figures are said to act as guardian spirits over ancestors whose bones are kept in boxes. The art of the Bakota tribes consists almost entirely of highly stylized wood and metal figurines that were placed in reliquaries.

The Congo Region. The sculpture of the Bakongo kingdom is usually characterized by naturalism. Each of the ancestor figures represents a personalized portrait and reveals details of body decoration and dress. The best-known art works of the Bateke of the W Congo are small fetish figures. These asexual figures stand with arms close to the body in a stiff, frontal pose. The Bapende sculptors of the W Congo give a fluid surface to their ivory pendants, which portray human faces. In the Bushongo kingdom statues of royalty were carved (17th to 19th cent.). The king was shown in a pose of static aloofness, wearing a flat crown and often holding a ritual sword. The Basonge of the central Congo carved small, standing fetish figures and masks, bold in proportion and suggestive of cubism. The Baluba of the SE Congo produced bowls and stools supported by slender figures. Small ivory masks and neck rests were made in the E Congo. The art of the Badjokwe of S Congo and Angola consists of free-standing figures, ceremonial staff heads, masks, and carved stools. The dynamic and aggressive figures are particularly outstanding.

Influence. African art came to European notice c.1905, when artists began to recognize the aesthetic value of African sculpture. Such artists as Vlaminck, Derain, Picasso, and Modigliani were influenced by African art forms. In the United States, fine collections of African art can be found in the Museum of Primitive Art, New York; the Natural History Museum, Chicago; the Peabody Museum, Harvard; and the Univ. Museum at the Univ. of Pennsylvania. See general books on African art by Pierre Meauzé (1968), Michel Leiris and Jacqueline Delange (tr. 1968), Frank Willett (1971), Elsy Leuzinger (tr. 1972), M. W. Mount (1973), and W. L. D'Azevedo, ed. (1973).

African buffalo: see CAPE BUFFALO.

African languages, geographic rather than linguistic classification of languages spoken on the African continent. These languages do not belong to a single family, but are divided among several distinct linguistic stocks having no common origin. It is estimated that more than 800 languages are spoken in Africa; however, they belong to comparatively few language families. Some 50 African tongues have more than half a million speakers each, but many others are spoken by relatively few people. Unlike the American Indian languages, which on the whole seem to be dying out, the African tongues appear vigorous. In the last few decades great strides have been made in the study and classification of the African languages, although the results are still far from definitive. The principal linguistic families of Africa are now generally said to be HAMITO-SEMITIC (recently renamed Afroasiatic in some scholarly circles); Niger-Kordofanian (including Niger-Congo); Nilo-Saharan; and Khoisan, or Click; two other stocks, INDO-EUROPEAN and MALAYO-POLYNESIAN, are also represented. Niger-Kordofanian and Nilo-Saharan are the two large families of languages native to about 160 million inhabitants of Africa and spoken exclusively by Negroes. These languages are spoken in all parts of the continent, from the extreme south up to the territory of the Hamito-Semitic languages of N Africa. The Hamito-Semitic, or Afroasiatic, family has both Caucasian and Negro speakers, while the San and Khoikhoi, who are the principal speakers of the Khoisan languages, belong to a different race from that of the Negroes. Some authorities believe that the languages spoken in the Niger-Kordofanian and Nilo-Saharan families are sufficiently similar to suggest that both stocks had the same ancestor language.

Niger-Kordofanian. The largest language stock of the African Negroes, the Niger-Kordofanian family has two branches, Niger-Congo and Kordofanian. The Kordofanian tongues are spoken in the Sudan and form five small groups (Koalib, Tegali, Talodi, Tumtum, and Katla). Niger-Congo is an enormous branch whose languages are found throughout S and central Africa and in most of W Africa below the Sahara. It is generally subdivided into six groups: West Atlantic; Mande; Gur, or Voltaic; Kwa; Benue-Congo; and Adamawa-Eastern. The West Atlantic branch includes many languages, among them Wolof (in Senegal), Temne (in Sierra Leone), and Fulani, the tongue of several million people inhabiting an area from Senegal to a region E of Lake Chad. The Mande group consists of languages prevalent in the Niger valley, Liberia, and Sierra Leone, such as Mende in Liberia and Malinke in Mali. Gur, or Voltaic, is made up of several language groups and includes Mossi, the dominant tongue of Upper Volta, as well as the Dagomba and Mamprusi of N Ghana. The Kwa languages, spoken chiefly in Ghana, Ivory Coast, Dahomey, Nigeria, and Liberia, include Ewe, Yoruba, Ibo, Nupe, Bini, Ashanti, and possibly Ijo (which is sometimes considered a separate branch). Benue-Congo includes the huge Bantu group of hundreds of tongues found throughout central and S Africa (see BANTU LANGUAGES), as well as such non-

Bantu languages as Tiv, Jukun, and Efik, which are spoken in Nigeria and Cameroon. The Adamawa-Eastern branch, to which Banda, Zande, and Sango belong, is composed of a number of languages spoken in Nigeria, Cameroon, and an area north of the Bantu territory to the Sudan. A characteristic feature of most of the Niger-Congo languages is the use of tones. Case inflection is entirely lacking, and sex gender is almost unknown in the Niger-Congo family. The verb root tends to remain unchanged; moods and tenses are denoted either by particles or by auxiliary verbs. For example, in a number of languages the verb "to come" is the auxiliary designating the future. Typical of the Niger-Kordofanian stock as a whole is the division of nouns, which has been compared to the gender system of the Indo-European tongues. However, Indo-European features only three classifications (masculine, feminine, and neuter), whereas some of the Niger-Kordofanian languages have as many as 20 noun classes. The formal basis for these class divisions is not known, except that one class designates human beings, another is used for liquids, and a third class is used for animals. Each class has its own pair of affixes to indicate the singular and the plural.

Nilo-Saharan. The other sizable language stock of Negro Africans, Nilo-Saharan, has six branches: Songhai (spoken in Mali), Saharan (including languages spoken both near Lake Chad, as in Kanuri, and in central Sahara), Maban (a group of tongues found E of Lake Chad), Furian (comprising only Fur, an important language of the Sudan), Coman (a group of languages of Ethiopia and the Sudan), and Chari-Nile, the principal branch of Nilo-Saharan, composed of the Eastern Sudanic languages, the Central Sudanic languages, and two additional tongues, Kunama and Berta; the Chari-Nile tongues are spoken in the Sudan, Zaïre, Uganda, Cameroon, Chad, the Central African Republic, Kenya, mainland Tanzania, and Ethiopia. The Eastern Sudanic subdivision of Chari-Nile itself has ten branches, the two most important of which are Nubian and Nilotic, both found in the Sudan. Nubian is unique among modern African Negro languages in that it has written texts of the medieval period. The Nilotic tongues include Shilluk, Dinka, Nuer, Masai, Turkana, Nandi, and Suk. The Central Sudanic subdivision of Chari-Nile consists of a number of languages, among them Mangbetu, spoken in the Congo, and Efe, used by the pygmies. Like the Niger-Congo languages, most of the Nilo-Saharan languages use tones; some Nilo-Saharan tongues inflect their nouns according to case, and still others have gender. The verb in many Nilo-Saharan languages has a system of verb derivation.

Khoisan. The Khoisan, or Click, linguistic family is made up of three branches: the Khoisan languages of the San (Bushmen) and Khoikhoi (Hottentots), spoken in various parts of S Africa; Sandawe, a language found in E Africa; and Hatsa, or Hadzapi, also spoken in E Africa. Tonality is a common feature of African languages. There are usually two or three tones (based on pitch levels rather than the rising and falling in inflections of Chinese tones) used to indicate semantic or grammatical distinction. All of the Khoisan languages appear to use tones to distinguish meanings. Grammatically, the Khoikhoi languages and some of the San languages inflect the noun to show case, number, and gender. The outstanding characteristic of the Khoisan tongues, however, is their extensive use of click sounds. (Examples of click sounds familiar to speakers of English are the interjection *tsk-tsk* and the click used to signal to a horse.) Click sounds, which are found only in Africa as parts of words, involve a sucking action by the tongue, but the position of the tongue and the way in which air is released into the mouth vary, just as in the formation of other sounds; thus clicks may be dental, palatal, alveolar, lateral, labial, or retroflex; voiced, voiceless, or nasal; and aspirated or glottal. Six types of clicks are known for the San languages as a whole, although no single tongue has all of them. The Khoikhoi languages have dental, palatal, retroflex, and lateral clicks. Some Bantu languages, notably Zulu and Xhosa, which are spoken near the Khoisan area, have borrowed click sounds from the Khoisan languages.

Indo-European and Malayo-Polynesian. Indo-European tongues used in Africa include AFRIKAANS and ENGLISH (native to many people in the Republic of South Africa and Rhodesia). American Negroes coming to Liberia in the 19th cent. introduced English there, and repatriated slaves who settled in Freetown, Sierra Leone, in the 19th cent. used a form of PIDGIN English, from which a creole English (now called Krio) developed. A form of creole Portuguese is current in Guinea-Bissau. Many other African lands employ European languages, particularly French, Portuguese, and English, which is often found in schools and in government as a second language. The Malayo-Polynesian family is represented by Malagasy, which is spoken on the island of Madagascar.

Twentieth-Century Developments. Since the majority of Africans do not know a European tongue, the use of written African languages has become increasingly important for the growing field of mass communication. Most of the Niger-Kordofanian and Nilo-Saharan languages still have no writing except perhaps for translations of the Bible. An exception is Swahili, a Bantu tongue of the Niger-Kordofanian stock that was written before the European conquest of Africa (see SWAHILI LANGUAGE). Vai, a language belonging to the Mande subdivision of Niger-Congo, still employs a native script developed in the 19th cent. The Nilo-Saharan tongue Nubian, the only modern Negro language with early written records (dating from the 8th cent. A.D. to the 14th cent.), is of considerable linguistic interest. Its alphabet was derived from that of COPTIC. Both Arabic and Roman letters are now being used increasingly for languages of the Niger-Kordofanian and Nilo-Saharan stocks, but as yet no standardized writing for these tongues has been universally adopted. The International African Institute has had some success in promoting the use of the written form of native African languages. Many newspapers, magazines, and radio broadcasts now employ various vernaculars, and film theaters can switch sound tracks to accommodate the audience in a given language area. However, Africa's linguistic diversity can be a hindrance to mass communication, and European tongues (especially English and French) are still widely used in the mass media. The modern scientific study of the classification and distribution of African languages has thrown some light on the history of Africa and its inhabitants. More knowledge can be expected from the combined use in the future of evidence from linguistic sources, historical records, reliable traditions, and archaeology. For example, the study of loan words from languages such as Greek, Latin, Punic, Arabic, and Portuguese should reveal much about contacts between African and non-African cultures. The study of loan words of African origin that have been absorbed by English (such as *banjo, jigger, gumbo, okra,* and *voodoo*) has become of increasing interest to American linguists and scholars in the field of black studies. See Diedrich Westermann and I. C. Ward, *Practical Phonetics for Students of African Languages* (1933); M. A. Bryan, *Notes on the Distribution of the Semitic and Cushitic Languages of Africa* (1947), *Distribution of the Nilotic and Nilo-Hamitic Languages of Africa* (1948), and (ed.) *The Bantu Languages of Africa* (1959); J. H. Greenberg, *The Languages of Africa* (2d ed. 1966); E. C. Polomé, *Swahili Language Handbook* (1967); David Dalby, ed., *Language and History in Africa* (1971); W. E. Welmers, *African Language Structures* (1974).

African lion hound: see RHODESIAN RIDGEBACK.

African Methodist Episcopal Church, one of the leading Negro denominations of METHODISM. It was established in 1816 with Richard ALLEN as its first bishop. There are c.1,100,000 members.

African Methodist Episcopal Zion Church, Negro Protestant denomination. It was founded in 1796 by Negro members of the Methodist Episcopal Church in New York City and was organized as a national body in 1821. The church operates in the United States, Africa, South America, and the West Indies and maintains Livingstone College in Salisbury, N.C. The membership of the church is about 900,000, making it one of the largest African Methodist bodies. See D. H. Bradley, *A History of the A.M.E. Zion Church* (2 vol., 1956–70).

African Negro literature. The earliest examples of this literature are to be found in those ancient Muslim religious books written by African Negroes in Swahili and Arabic. A great oral tradition exists in the seemingly inexhaustible folklore of the continent: myths, tales, legends, riddles, and proverbs. Throughout the history of Africa these have been used to instruct the young, and they have been transported to North and South America and to the Carribean. The oral tradition remains strong in the 20th cent., and folktales now often concern contemporary events or political figures. The influence of the oral tradition can also be found in the works of many 20th-century African writers. Modern African Negro literature developed first in areas long in contact with European civilization. It is written in native languages, notably the Bantu languages, and in French, Portuguese, and English. Important 19th-century African Negro writers were Kobe Ntsikana, William W. Gqoba, and, most importantly, Thomas Mofolo, who wrote several novels, the best-known being *Chaka* (tr. 1931), about the famous Zulu chief. In the early 20th cent., Negro writers from the French colonies in Africa made Paris their center. There, during the 1930s, the concept of *négritude* was born. Led by the poet-statesman Léopold Sédar SENGHOR, the major adherents of *négritude* included Aimé CÉSAIRE, Léon DAMAS, Biragio DIOP, and David Diop. These writers rejected the French policy of assimilation and asserted the importance of their African Negro heritage. They also felt their sense of pride, dignity, and racial awareness should extend to Negroes in all parts of the world. In 1947, Césaire and Damas founded the *Présence Africaine,* which became Africa's leading literary journal. Other outstanding writers in French were René Maran, Paul Hazoumé, Camara Laye, Ferdinand Oyono, Mongo Beti, and Edouard Maunick. After World War II certain themes were dominant in the literature of the emerging African nations: pride in being black and African and in becoming part of the modern world; castigation of the Europeans who had subjugated black Africa for so long; foreboding that blacks would now be prey to evils that had long been exclusive to white men; exploration of the conflict between old tribal values and customs and those of the modern Western world; and satire of old and new aspects of African life. During the 1950s and 60s strong national literatures began emerging in several nations, notably Nigeria, Senegal, and Cameroon. In 1966 the World Festival of Negro Arts was held in Dakar, Senegal. It was opened by a performance of the satiric comedy *Kongi's Harvest* by the Nigerian playwright Wole Soyinka. Other important postwar writers include Mário de Andrade and Luis Bernardo Honwana, whose works are in Portuguese; James Mbotela, Omar Shariff, and Robert Shaaban, writing in Swahili; and, numerous writers whose works are in English, including the Nigerians Amos Tutuola, Chinua Achebe, Cyprian Ekwensi, John Pepper Clark, and Gabriel Okara, the South African Ezekiel Mphahlele (author of the now classic autobiography, *Down Second Avenue* (1959), the Gambian Lenrie Peters, the Ruandan J. Saverio Naigiziki, and the Ghanaians Kofi Awoonor and Ama Ato Audoo. See also AFRICAN LANGUAGES; SOUTH AFRICAN LITERATURE. See Langston Hughes, ed., *An African Treasury* (1960); Claude Wauthier, *The Literature and Thought of Modern Africa* (tr. 1967); Wilfred Cartey, *Whispers from a Continent: The Literature of Contemporary Black Africa* (1968); Janheinz Jahn, *Neo-African Literature: A History of Black Writing* (1969); Ruth Finnegan, *Oral Literature in Africa* (1970); O. R. Dathorue, *The Black Mind: A History of African Literature* (1974).

African Negro music. Although its details vary with cultural and linguistic boundaries, sub-Saharan African music has as its distinguishing feature a rhythmic complexity common to no other region. Polyrhythmic counterpoint, wherein two or more locally independent attack patterns are superimposed, is realized by handclaps, xylophones, rattles, and a variety of tuned and nontuned drums. The remarkable aspect of African polyrhythm is the discernible coherence of the resultant rhythmic pattern. Pitch polyphony exists in the form of parallel intervals (generally thirds, fourths, and fifths), overlapping choral antiphony and solo-choral response, and occasional simultaneous independent melodies. In addition to voice, many wind and string instruments perform melodic functions. Common are bamboo flutes, ivory trumpets, and the one-string ground bow, which uses a hole in the ground as a resonator. Scale systems vary between regions but are generally diatonic. Music is highly functional in tribal life, accompanying birth, marriage, hunting, and even political activities. Much music exists solely for entertainment, ranging from narrative songs to highly stylized musical theater. Similarities with other cultures, particularly Indian and Middle Eastern, can be ascribed primarily to the Islamic invasion (7th–11th cent.). How much the American Negro spiritual is indebted to African music is still a subject of inquiry. See JAZZ; AMERICAN NEGRO SPIRITUALS; GOSPEL MUSIC. See E. M. von Hornbostel, *African Negro Music* (1929); Percival Kirby, *Musical Instruments of the Native Races of South Africa* (1953); A. M. Jones, *Studies in African Music* (2 vol., 1959); Rose Brandel, *The Music of Central Africa* (1961); Fred Warren, *The Music of Africa* (1970); J. S. Roberts, *Black Music of Two Worlds* (1972); Ortiz Walton, *Music: Black, White and Blue* (1972).

Africanus, Sextus Julius (sĕk'stəs jo͞ol'yəs afrĭkā'nəs), fl. 221, Christian historian, resident of Palestine. He wrote a history of the world from the creation to 221 (which was used by Eusebius of Caesarea), letters, and an anthology, mostly of materials on magic.

African violet: see GESNERIA.

Afrikaans (ăf"rəkäns'), member of the West Germanic group of the Germanic subfamily of the Indo-European family of languages (see GERMANIC LANGUAGES). Although its classification is still disputed, it is generally considered an independent language rather than a dialect or variant of Dutch (see DUTCH LANGUAGE). Afrikaans is spoken by close to 3 million people, most of whom live in the Republic of South Africa, where it is one of the official languages. It arose from the Dutch spoken by the Boers, who emigrated from the Netherlands to South Africa in the 17th cent., but in its written form it dates only from 1861. The grammar has been considerably simplified. Although its vocabulary is essentially similar to that of Dutch, Afrikaans has absorbed quite a few words from Hottentot and Bantu (such as words designating local flora and fauna) and also from English.

Afro-Asian Bloc: see THIRD-WORLD.

Afroasiatic, another name for the Hamito-Semitic family of languages. See HAMITO-SEMITIC LANGUAGES.

afterdamp: see DAMP.

Afton, uninc. city (1970 pop. 24,898), St. Louis co., E Mo., a suburb of St. Louis. The name is also spelled Affton.

Afyonkarahisar (äfyōn'kä"rähĭsär') [Turkish, = black castle of opium], city (1970 pop. 51,660), capital of Afyonkarahisar prov., W central Turkey, at an elevation of c.3,500 ft (1,070 m). It is the commercial center of a region where opium poppies and grains are grown. Carpets are manufactured in the city, which is a major rail junction.

Afzelius, Arvid August (är'vēd ou'gəst), 1785–1871, Swedish historian, mythologist, and song writer. He made a notable collection of folk material in *Swedish Folk Tunes from Olden Times* (3 vol., 1814–16). His autobiography was published in 1901.

Ag, chemical symbol of the element SILVER.

Agabus (ăg'əbəs), prophet who foretold the famine in the time of Claudius Caesar and the imprisonment of Paul. Acts 11.27,28; 21.10,11.

Agade, ancient Mesopotamian city: see AKKAD.

Agadès (ägädĕs'), town (1963 est. pop. 7,100), W central Niger, in the Aïr Mts. A traditional, picturesque town, Agadès is a trade center visited by TUAREG pastoral nomads. Leather and silver handicrafts are made. Tin, tungsten, uranium, and salt are mined nearby. Founded by the 11th cent., Agadès developed mainly because of its location on trans-Saharan caravan routes linking Egypt and Libya with the Lake Chad area. Agadès was held by the MALI empire during part of the 14th cent., captured by the SONGHAI empire in 1515, and controlled by BORNU in the 17th cent. It remained a trade center until the late 19th cent. During much of this time it was a noted center of Islamic learning. The French occupied the town in the early 20th cent. Agadès has a 16th-century mosque.

Agadir (ägädēr', ăgədēr'), city (1970 est. pop. 34,000), SW Morocco, on the Atlantic Ocean. Agadir has metal-processing industries and exports of fruit and vegetables. While France was engaged in establishing a protectorate in Morocco, the German gunboat *Panther* appeared (1911) in Agadir with the intention of protecting German interests. For a time war seemed imminent, but the Germans agreed to drop their demands when France ceded to them a substantial part of the French Congo. In 1960, Agadir was almost completely destroyed by an earthquake.

Agag (ā'găg). **1** King of the Amalekites who was defeated and spared by Saul, but killed by Samuel. 1 Sam. 15. **2** The allusion is not understood in Num. 24.7.

Agagite (ā'gəgīt), a not necessarily ethnical term used of Haman because of his hatred of the Jews. Esther 3.1.

Aga Khan III (Aga Sir Sultan Mahomed Shah) (ä'gä khän), 1877–1957, Muslim leader, b. Bombay, India. Hereditary ruler of the Muslim Ismaili sect, with followers in India, Pakistan, East Africa, and Central Asia, the Aga Khan was born to great power and wealth. He attempted to secure Muslim support for British rule in India, particularly by founding (1906) the All-India Muslim League, of which he served as president (1909–14). He was chairman of the British Indian delegation to the imperial conference in London in 1930–31. He also represented India at the Geneva disarmament conference (1932) and in the League of Nations (1932, 1934–37), where he was (1937) president of the General Assembly. He was, however, perhaps best known for his fabulous wealth, for his liberal donations to Muslim causes, and for his interest in horse breeding and racing. Early in his rule he took up residence in Europe, where he died. He was succeeded by his grandson, Prince Karim, who became Aga Khan IV. See his memoirs (1954); biography by H. J. Greenwall (1952).

agalloch (əgăl'ək): see ALOES.

Agamedes (ăg"əmē'dēz): see TROPHONIUS.

Agamemnon (ă"gəmĕm'nŏn), in Greek mythology, leader of the Greek forces in the Trojan War; king of Mycenae (or Argos). He and Menelaus were sons of Atreus and suffered the curse laid upon PELOPS. Agamemnon married Clytemnestra, and their children were Iphigenia, Electra, and Orestes. To win favorable winds for the ships sailing against Troy, he sacrificed Iphigenia to Artemis and thus incurred the hatred of Clytemnestra. After arriving at Troy, he quarreled bitterly with Achilles over possession of the captive princess Briseis. Agamemnon was forced to yield the girl to Achilles after the latter withdrew, with his troops, from the war. On his return home, Agamemnon was treacherously murdered by Clytemnestra and her lover, Aegisthus. To avenge his death, Orestes and Electra killed their mother.

Aga Muhammad Khan or **Agha Muhammad Khan** (both: ä'gä mo͞ohäm'mäd khän), 1742–97, shah of Persia, founder of the Kajar, or Qajar, dynasty. He was emasculated by family enemies at the age of five. He was vigorous and able, but his cruelty is proverbial. In 1794, he captured and killed the last ruler of the Zand dynasty and ended his campaign with a wholesale massacre in Kerman. He became shah in 1796. Aga Muhammad resisted a Russian invasion and himself invaded (1795) Georgia. Hated by his subjects, he was finally assassinated. His nephew Fath Ali succeeded him.

Agana (ägä'nyä), city (1970 pop. 2,119), capital of the island of GUAM, W Pacific, in the MARIANAS ISLANDS. It is the administrative center of Guam, and most of the city's economic activities are related to the provision of goods and services to the large U.S. military bases on the island. Completely destroyed in World War II, Agana was subsequently rebuilt.

Aganippe (ăg"ənĭp'ē), in Greek mythology, nymph. Her spring on Mt. Helicon, sacred to the MUSES, gave poetic inspiration to all who drank from it.

Agapemone (ăgəpĕm'ənē) [Gr., = abode of love], English religious community of men and women, holding all goods in common. It was founded (c.1850) at the village of Spaxton, Somerset, by Henry James Prince (1811–99), Samuel Starky, and others. Prince and Starky were clergymen who had left (c.1843) the Church of England after Prince claimed that the Holy Ghost had taken up residence in his body. The Agapemonites proclaimed the imminent second coming of Christ. Riotous conditions at the community caused scandal, and after Prince lost a lawsuit brought by two disenchanted followers in 1860 the community slipped from public notice. There was a period (c.1890) of renewed activity when J. H. Smyth-Pigott, who believed himself to be Jesus Christ reincarnated, conducted meetings at an Agapemonite branch establishment in Clapton, London. He succeeded Prince as leader of the sect, which soon vanished. See Donald McCormick, *Temple of Love* (1962).

Agar (ā'gər), the same as HAGAR.

agar (ä'gär, ā'–, ăg'är), product obtained from several species of red algae, or SEAWEED, chiefly from the Ceylon, or Jaffna, moss (*Gracilaria lichenoides*) and species of *Gelidium*. Although most agar comes from the Far East, California also is a source of supply. Chemically, agar is a polymer made up of subunits of the sugar galactose; it is a component of the algae cell walls. Dissolved in boiling water and cooled, agar becomes gelatinous; its chief uses are as a culture medium (particularly for bacteria) and as a laxative, but it serves also as a thickening for soups and sauces, in jellies and ice cream, for clarifying beverages, and for sizing fabrics. It is conveniently marketed in the form of dried flakes.

Agartala (əgŭr'tələ), city (1971 pop. 59,682), capital of Tripura state, NE India, near the Bangladesh border. It is a market town for rice, tea, jute, and oilseed.

Agasias (ăgā'shēăs), fl. 1st cent. B.C., Greek sculptor, commonly known as Agasias of Ephesus; son of Dositheus. His *Borghese Warrior,* discovered in the 17th cent., is in the Louvre.

Agassiz, Alexander (ăg'əsē), 1835–1910, American naturalist and industrialist, b. Neuchâtel, Switzerland; son of Louis Agassiz, stepson of Elizabeth Cary Agassiz. He came to the United States in 1849 and studied at Harvard, receiving degrees in engineering (B.S., 1857) and natural history (B.S., 1862). Throughout his life he was connected in various capacities with Harvard. In 1871 he consolidated the Calumet and Hecla copper mines on Lake Superior and, as president, developed the combined interests with great success. He adopted safety and welfare measures relating to the mines. Agassiz contributed much of his fortune to science—chiefly in endowments to Harvard and to the Museum of Comparative Zoology founded there through his father's efforts. He also financed expeditions and publications of his own research. In 1877 he began his oceanographic explorations, including detailed observations of the Pacific and the Caribbean. Noting that the deep-sea animals of the two are similar, he suggested that the Caribbean was a bay of the Pacific that had been cut off in the Cretaceous period by the rise of the Panama isthmus. He also developed a theory of the formation of coral atolls that differed from that of Darwin. His chief work is *Revision of the Echini* (2 vol., 1872–74). See study by his son G. R. Agassiz (1913).

Agassiz, Elizabeth Cabot Cary, 1822–1907, American author and educator, b. Boston. In 1850 she married Louis Agassiz, and together they established the pioneering Agassiz School for girls in Boston (1856–65). She accompanied her husband on expeditions to Brazil (1865–66) and along the Atlantic and Pacific coasts of the Americas (1871–72). She was one of a group (along with Arthur Gilman and Alice Longfellow) influential in the founding of Radcliffe College, and was (1894–1903) its first president. Her writings include *A Journey in Brazil* (in collaboration with her husband, 1868); a biography of her husband (1885); and, with her stepson Alexander Agassiz, *Seaside Studies in Natural History* (1865). See study by L. A. Paton (1919); Louise Tharp, *Adventurous Alliance* (1959).

Agassiz, Louis (Jean Louis Rodolphe Agassiz) (zhäN lwē rôdôlf'), 1807–73, Swiss-American zoologist and geologist, b. Môtiers-en-Vuly, Switzerland. He studied at the universities of Zürich, Erlangen (Ph.D., 1829), Heidelberg, and Munich (M.D., 1830). Agassiz practiced medicine briefly, but his real interest lay in scientific research. In 1831 he went to Paris, where he became a close friend of Alexander von Humboldt and studied fossil fishes under the guidance of Cuvier. In 1832 he became professor of natural history at the Univ. of Neuchâtel, which he made a noted center for scientific study. Among his publications during this period were *Recherches sur les poissons fossiles* (5 vol. and atlas, 1833–44), a work of historic importance in the field (although his system of classification by scales has been discarded); studies of fossil echinoderms and mollusks; and *Étude sur les glaciers* (1840), one of the first expositions of glacial movements and deposits, based on his own observations and measurements. Agassiz came to the United States in 1846 and two years later accepted the professorship of zoology and geology at Harvard. His first wife died in Germany in 1848, and in 1850 in Cambridge he married Elizabeth Cabot Cary. In the United States he was primarily a teacher and very popular lecturer. Emphasizing advanced and original work, he gave major impetus to the study of science directly from nature and influenced a generation of American scientists. His extensive research expeditions included one along the Atlantic and Pacific coasts of the Americas from Boston to California (1871–72). His *Contributions to the Natural History of the United States* (4 vol., 1857–62) includes his famous "Essay on Classification," an extension of the theory of RECAPITULATION to geologic time. Despite his own evidences for evolution, Agassiz opposed Darwinism and believed that new species could arise only through the intervention of God. See biographies by Jules Marcou (including letters, 1896), J. D. Teller (1947), and Edward Lurie (1960; repr. 1967); Lane Cooper, *Louis Agassiz as a Teacher* (rev. ed. 1945).

Agassiz, Lake, glacial lake of the PLEISTOCENE EPOCH, c.700 mi (1,130 km) long, 250 mi (400 km) wide, formed by the melting of the continental ice sheet some 10,000 years ago; covered much of present-day NW Minnesota, NE North Dakota, S Manitoba, and SW Ontario. The lake was named in 1879 in memory of Louis Agassiz for his contributions to the theory of the glacial epoch. Lake Traverse, Big Stone Lake, and the Minnesota River are in the channel of prehistoric River Warren, Lake Agassiz's original outlet to the south. As the ice melted, the water drained E into Lake Superior, and after the ice disappeared, N into Hudson Bay, leaving lakes Winnipeg, Manitoba, and Winnipegosis, Red Lake, Lake of the Woods, and many smaller lakes. The bed of the old lake, the Red River valley, has become an important wheat-growing region because of its rich, deep soil. See Warren Upham, *The Glacial Lake Agassiz* (1895; U.S. Geological Survey, Monographs, Vol. XXV).

agate, cryptocrystalline variety of QUARTZ banded in two or more different colors, extensively used as a semiprecious gemstone and in the manufacture of grinding equipment. The banded appearance owes its origin to the fact that agates are built up by the slow deposition of silica from solution into cavities in older rock—often igneous rocks. The layers differ in porosity, and the stones can be artificially stained to produce combinations of color more vivid and pleasing than those found in the natural state. The cutting and staining of agates has long had its center at Idar-Oberstein in Germany. Important sources of agate are Brazil, Uruguay, India, Mexico, and the United States (in the Lake Superior region and in some western states). The moss agate or mocha stone is so called because it contains dendritic inclusions resembling moss. See CHALCEDONY; ONYX; SARD.

Agate Fossil Beds National Monument: see NATIONAL PARKS AND MONUMENTS (table).

Agatha, Saint (ăg'əthə), 3d cent., Sicilian virgin, martyred under Roman Emperor Decius. She is mentioned in the Canon of the Mass and is invoked against outbreaks of fire. She is also the partron saint of bell makers. Feast: Feb. 5.

Agatharchus (ăg"əthär'kəs), fl. 5th cent. B.C., Greek painter of the Athenian school, b. Samos. He is credited with important discoveries in the application of shading and perspective and is said to have been the first painter of scenery for tragedies.

Agathon (ăg'əthŏn), c. 450-c.400 B.C., Athenian tragedian. Plato's *Symposium* has as its scene the celebration of Agathon's first dramatic victory. Less than 40 lines of his work survive.

Agave (əgā'vē): see PENTHEUS.

agave: see AMARYLLIS.

Agawam (ăg'əwäm). **1** Town (1970 pop. 21,717), Hampden co., SW Mass., on the Connecticut River; settled 1636, inc. 1855. Leather goods, machinery, and electronic equipment are produced. **2** Former name of IPSWICH, Mass.

Agboville (ägbōvēl'), town (1964 est. pop. 15,475), S Ivory Coast. Situated in a forest zone, the town is the market center for a region producing plantains, yams, coffee, cassava, manioc, rice, and timber. Fishing is pursued in numerous family ponds nearby. Agboville is on the country's railroad line, which reached the town in 1907.

Agdistis: see ATTIS; CYBELE.

age, in classical mythology, a period of the world's history, especially as systematized by the poets Hesiod and Ovid. The ages were the Golden Age, ruled by Cronus (Saturn), a period of serenity, peace, and eternal spring; the Silver Age, ruled by Zeus (Jupiter), less happy than the preceding, with luxury prevailing; the Bronze Age, a period of strife; and the Iron Age, the present, a time of travail, when justice and piety have vanished. Hesiod also included a Heroic Age before the Iron Age, during which the Trojan War was fought. The division of history into three technological ages (stone, bronze, and iron) was also present in ancient Greek and Roman writings. The sequence became more widely used in the 19th cent. as archaeological evidence confirmed the historical validity of the three stages. Artifacts were first arranged according to the three-age system in 1836 by C. J. Thomsen at the Museum of Northern Antiquities in Copenhagen.

Agee (ăg'ē-ē), father of Shammah, a mighty man. 2 Sam. 23.11.

Agee, James (ā'jē), 1909-55, American writer, b. Knoxville, Tenn., grad. Harvard, 1932. He was a writer for *Fortune* magazine, a movie critic for *Time* and *The Nation,* and a film scriptwriter. His best-known work is the posthumously published novel *A Death in the Family* (1957; Pulitzer Prize), which recounts in poetic prose the tragic impact of a man's death on his wife and family. Agee's other works include *Let Us Now Praise Famous Men* (1941), a prose commentary on the tenant farmer; a novel, *The Morning Watch* (1954); a collection of reviews, comments, and scripts, *Agee on Film* (2 vol., 1958-60); a collection of letters to a former teacher, *Letters of James Agee to Father Flye* (1962); *Collected Poems* (1968); and *Collected Short Prose* (1969). See study by P. H. Ohlin (1966).

age grade or **age set,** in anthropology, differentiation of social role based on age. Entry into a grade may come about by the attainment of a certain biological state, especially puberty, or a socially recognized status change that typically occurs at certain age periods, notably marriage and the birth of a child. Persons of junior grade may give respect and some degree of obedience to those of more senior grade; the seniors expect deference but may also acknowledge obligations to assist, teach, test, or lead their juniors. The practice of age grading is found in some form in every society.

Ageladas (ăj"əlā'dəs), c.540-c.460 B.C., Greek sculptor of the Argive school, famous for his statues of gods and Olympian athletes. A popular tradition, discredited by many authorities, names him as the teacher of the great sculptors, Polykleitos, the Elder; Phidias; and Myron.

Agen (äzhäN'), town (1968 pop. 37,470), capital of Lot-et-Garonne dept., SW France, on the Garonne River, in GUIENNE. It is an agricultural market place in the center of a fruit-growing region and an industrial center where food products, clothing, agricultural machinery, bicycles, tiles, drugs, furniture, and musical instruments are manufactured. Originally a Gallic settlement, Agen was a crossroads in Roman times. It became the capital of the county of Agenois under the CAROLINGIANS. An episcopal see from the 10th cent., it passed (1154) to England with the rest of AQUITAINE. It was reconquered in the HUNDRED YEARS WAR (1337-1453) and incorporated into the province of Guienne. Among the historic structures are chapels from the 13th and 14th cent.; the Church of St. Jacobius (13th cent.), with its Gothic frescoes; the St. Hilaire Church (15th cent.); and the Romanesque and Gothic St. Caprais Cathedral.

Agency for International Development (AID), Federal agency in the State Dept. created by Congress (Sept., 1961) to consolidate U.S. nonmilitary foreign-aid programs. The agency incorporated the International Cooperation Administration, the Development Loan Fund, and related agencies such as the Office of Food for Peace. AID is organized into five divisions—one for each major underdeveloped area—East Asia, Vietnam, Near East and South Asia, Latin America, and Africa. AID offers technical, capital, and commodity assistance and gives priority to programs in agriculture, population-growth control, and education. AID stresses long-run development goals financed through long-term loans and encourages the investment of private capital through liberal investment guarantees. Countries applying for loans are required to show that they have made effective use of their human and material resources and have undertaken policies such as land reform so as to insure that AID benefits will reach the populace as rapidly as possible.

Agenor (əjē'nôr), in Greek mythology. **1** King of Tyre, father of Cadmus and Europa. When Europa disappeared, Agenor sent Cadmus and his other sons in search of her. **2** Trojan hero, son of Antenor.

Ageo (ä'gāō), city (1970 pop. 110, 792), Saitama prefecture, central Honshu, Japan. It is an agricultural and communications center. Raw silk and sake are produced in the city.

age of consent, the age at which, according to the law, persons are bound by their words and acts. There are different ages at which one acquires legal capacity to consent to marriage, to choose a guardian, to conclude a contract, and the like. For marriage, the age may be higher for males than for females if the jurisdiction does not guarantee equal rights to men and women. Age of consent also means the age below which consent of the female to sexual intercourse is not a defense to a charge of RAPE. Under common law this age was 10; state statutes in the United States generally set it between 13 and 18. See also CONSENT.

ageratum (ăj"ərā'təm, əjĕr'ə-) [Gr.,=unaging], any plant of the genus *Ageratum,* tropical American annuals of the family Compositae (COMPOSITE family). The commonly cultivated species is the Mexican *A. houstonianum,* with thick terminal clusters of blue flowers. The similar mistflower, a *Eupatorium* (see BONESET), is a perennial sometimes called hardy ageratum. Ageratum is classified in the division MAGNOLIOPHYTA, class Magnoliopsida, order Asterales, family Compositae.

Agesander (ăj"əsăn'dər): see LAOCOÖN.

Agesilaus II (əjĕ"sĭlā'əs), c.444-360 B.C., king of Sparta. After the death of Agis I (398? B.C.), he was brought to power by Lysander, whom he promptly ignored. After the Peloponnesian War the Greek cities in Asia Minor had not been ceded to Persia despite Sparta's promises, and in 396 B.C. Agesilaus went there to oppose the Persian satraps TISSAPHERNES and PHARNABAZUS by attacking them. He managed to rout Tissaphernes, but Persian naval power drove him back to Greece, where he won (394 B.C.) a hollow victory over the Thebans and their allies at Coronea, but he could not reestablish Spartan hegemony. By the King's Peace (or Peace of Antalcidas) in 386 B.C., the cities of Asia Minor were ceded to Persia. Thebes and Athens entered an alliance against Sparta, and war followed. When Agesilaus deliberately excluded Thebes from the peace talks, Thebes renewed the war and the Theban general Epaminondas won (371 B.C.) a resounding victory at LEUCTRA. Sparta did not recover. Agesilaus took Spartan mercenaries to Asia Minor and Egypt and died on the way back. His rule had seen the ruin of Sparta, although he was lauded by his contemporaries, notably Xenophon.

aggada: see HALAKAH.

Aggeus (ăgē'əs), Vulgate form of HAGGAI.

agglutination, in biochemistry: see IMMUNITY.

agglutination, in linguistics: see INFLECTION.

aggression, a form of behavior characterized by forceful physical or verbal attack. It may be appropriate and self-protective, even constructive, as in healthy self-assertiveness; or inappropriate, destructive, or annihilatory. Aggression may be directed outward, against others, as in explosive personality disorders, or inward, against the self, leading to self-damaging acts or suicide. The directness and degree of hostility may vary from physical assault to gentle verbal criticism, and the means of expression may include deprecation, avoidance, teasing, provocation, and obstructiveness. In ordinary social life aggressive tendencies are restrained except in such ritualized situations as competitive sports. In adults physical aggression that is not a response to a clear threat or unusual provocation is usually considered a symptom of mental illness or character disorder and is attributed to pathological intensity of aggressive drives, weakness of controls, or both. Sadistic or masochistic acts are a combination of aggressive and affectionate behavior. Sigmund Freud postulated in 1920 the potential, present in humans at birth, of an aggressive drive, which together with the opposing sexual, or libidinal, drive contributed to the development of personality and found expression in behavior. However, many psychoanalysts who followed Freud have not accepted aggression as a primary drive and have instead viewed it as a reaction to frustration of primary needs. The ethologist Konrad Lorenz extrapolated from animal data that human aggression is an inborn legacy from man's prehuman primate ancestors. His colleague Nicholas Tinbergen traced this aggressiveness from the time when man ceased to be a vegetarian individualist like most of his primate cousins and became a carnivorous group hunter like the wolf. Tinbergen believes that there is a complex relationship between this innate aggressive potential and a social conditioning that evokes it. Other ethological data also suggest the presence of innate mechanisms to prevent or terminate aggressive behavior destructive to species. Anthropologists such as Montagu have argued that animal data cannot be applied directly to man's special situation, that man is largely instinctless, and that his aggressiveness is wholly a learned form of behavior. Some psychoanalysts share a similar view, holding that aggressive behavior is learned as a maladaptive means of coping with real and symbolic threats to the satisfaction of needs. Interest in the causes of violence, war, and assassination has led to wide inquiry into the social and biological roots of violence as a specific expression of aggression. The contributions of abnormal genetic endowment, learning difficulties, minimal brain damage, brain abnormalities, such as certain forms of temporal lobe epilepsy, and such social factors as crowding and poverty have been suggested in certain cases to have contributed to exaggeratedly aggressive behavior. But even if these factors were proved to be causative, each would have limited applicability to the range of aggressive phenomena in man. See Konrad Lorenz, *On Aggression* (tr. 1966); Alexander Alland, *The Human Imperative* (1972); R. N. Johnson, *Aggression in Man and Animals* (1972).

Agha Muhammad Khan: see AGA MUHAMMAD KHAN.

Aghrim, Republic of Ireland: see AUGHRIM.

agilawood: see ALOES.

Agincourt (äzhăNko͞or'), modern Fr. *Azincourt,* village (1968 pop. 276), Pas-de-Calais dept., N France. There, on Oct. 25, 1415, Henry V of England defeated a much larger French army in the HUNDRED YEARS WAR (1337-1453). His success, which was due mainly to the superiority of the masses of English longbow men over the heavily armored French knights, demonstrated the obsolescence of the methods of warfare of the age of chivalry. The victory enabled the English to conquer much of France. The battle is the central scene of Shakespeare's drama *Henry V.*

Agis (ā'jĭs), name of four Spartan kings. **Agis I,** fl. late 10th cent. B.C., was the traditional founder of the Agiad dynasty, one of the two ruling dynasties of Sparta, which had a dual kingship. The other dynasty, the Eurypontids, fathered the succeeding Agises. **Agis II,** d. 398? B.C., acceded to the throne on the death (c.427) of his father, Archidamus II. Agis led Spartan forces at the battle of MANTINEA (418 B.C.) during the PELOPONNESIAN WAR. Advised by ALCIBIADES, who had fled to Sparta to avoid trial at home, he quickly invaded Attica and established a post there. Later he quarreled with his adviser. Agis aided Lysander in the final Spartan victories of the war. **Agis III,** d. 331 B.C., succeeded his father Archidamus III in 338. He led a revolt of Peloponnesian cities against Alexander the Great, who was in Asia. The rebels were crushed, and Agis was killed at Megalopolis. His death ended Greek revolts against Alexander. **Agis IV,** d. c.240 B.C., son of Eudamidas II, succeeded his father c.244 B.C. He tried to revitalize Sparta by reform and by returning to the constitution of Lycurgus. His efforts failed, and he was murdered.

Aglaia (ăglā'ə): see GRACES.

Aglipay, Gregorio (grāgō'rēō äglēpī'), 1860–1940, Philippine clergyman. A priest who joined the revolutionary forces of Emilio Aguinaldo, he was excommunicated (1902). He took his followers from the Roman Catholic Church to found the PHILIPPINE INDEPENDENT CHURCH. Bishop Aglipay attracted many followers, said to number more than 1 million. His church, which retained many of the forms of the Roman Catholic Church, discarded confession and celibacy for the priesthood. Later it established friendly relations with the Unitarians. After Aglipay's death dissension shook the organization. In 1961, however, full communion was established between the Philippine Independent Church and the American Episcopal Church. Aglipay was defeated by Manuel Quezon in the presidential election of 1935.

Aglipayans: see PHILIPPINE INDEPENDENT CHURCH.

Agnes, Saint, 4th cent., virgin martyr. A noble Roman girl, she was martyred at the age of 13 after rejecting a well-born suitor. She is commemorated in the Canon of the Mass. On her feast two lambs are blessed and from their wool pallia (see PALLIUM) are made. Feast: Jan. 21.

Agnes Scott College, at Decatur, Ga.; Presbyterian, U.S.; for women; founded 1889 as the Decatur Female Seminary, chartered 1906 as Agnes Scott College.

Agnew, Spiro Theodore (spēr'ō), 1918–, 39th Vice President of the United States (1969–73), b. Baltimore, Md. Admitted to the bar in 1949, he entered politics as a Republican and was elected (1961) chief executive of Baltimore co. He later became (1967) governor of Maryland, where he won passage of an open housing law and expanded the state's antipoverty programs. Nominated (1968) for the vice presidency on the Republican ticket with Richard M. Nixon, Agnew campaigned on a tough law-and-order platform. As Vice President, he sharply attacked opponents of the Vietnam War as disloyal, criticized intellectuals and college students for questioning traditional values, and frequently accused the news media of biased news coverage. In the 1970 congressional campaigns, he campaigned vigorously against liberals and antiwar candidates in both parties. Reelected with Nixon in 1972, Agnew was forced to resign on Oct. 10, 1973, after a Justice Dept. investigation uncovered evidence of corruption during his years in Maryland politics; his alleged acceptance of bribes overlapped with his tenure as Vice President. He pleaded no contest to the charge of Federal income tax evasion. He was sentenced to three years' probation and fined $10,000; and he was later disbarred (1974) by the Maryland court of appeals. See biographies by Joseph Alright (1972), Theo Lipmann (1972), and Jules Witcover (1972).

Agni (ăg'nē): see VEDA.

Agnon, Shmuel Yosef (shmo͞oĕl' yōsĕf' ägnōn'), 1888–1970, Israeli novelist and short-story writer, b. Galicia, Poland, as Samuel Josef Czaczkes. He changed his name after settling in Palestine in 1907, where he remained for the rest of his life, except for 10 years in Germany (1913–23). Although he initially wrote in both Hebrew and Yiddish, eventually he wrote in classical Hebrew alone. His works were thus difficult to translate and were not widely appreciated for many years. He is now regarded as the greatest modern writer of fiction in Hebrew. Often containing symbolic and mystical elements, his novels and stories explore various aspects of Jewish life. They frequently focus on the problems of Jews assimilitating into Western culture. His works include the novels *The Bridal Canopy* (1919, tr. 1937), *A Guest for the Night* (1938, tr. 1968), and *The Day Before Yesterday* (1945); the short-story collections *Forsaken Wives* (1908), *Two Tales* (tr. 1966), and *Twenty-One Stories* (tr. 1970); and *In the Heart of the Seas: A Story of a Journey to the Land of Israel* (1966). Agnon shared the 1966 Nobel Prize for literature with the poet Nelly Sachs.

agnosticism (ăgnŏs'tĭsĭzəm), form of skepticism that holds that the existence of God cannot be logically proved or disproved. Among prominent agnostics have been Herbert Spencer, T. H. Huxley (who coined the word *agnostic* in 1869), and Auguste Comte. Immanuel Kant was an agnostic who argued that belief in divinity can rest only on faith. Agnosticism is not to be confused with ATHEISM, which asserts that there is no God.

Agnus Dei (ăg'nəs dē'ī, än'yo͞os dā'ē) [Lat.], the Lamb of God, i.e., Jesus Christ. The lamb of the PASSOVER sacrifice is said to prefigure the crucifixion. Isaiah calls the expected Messiah the Lamb of God, and Jesus is met by John the Baptist with the words, "Behold, the Lamb of God, who takes away the sins of the world." In the MASS the Agnus Dei, or Lamb of God, is said or sung while the communion bread is being broken for distribution. It is usually the final movement of choral masses. In Anglican worship it is sung during communion. In iconography a lamb with halo and cross is called an Agnus Dei.

agora (ăg'ərə) [Gr.,=market], in ancient Greece, the public square or market place of a city. In early Greek history the agora was primarily used as a place for public assembly; later it functioned mainly as a center of commerce. Usually in a readily accessible part of the city, it was often surrounded by the public buildings, such as the royal palace, the law courts, the assembly house, and the jail. A favorite architectural device was the colonnade surrounding the agora. One of the highest honors was to be granted a tomb in the agora. The agora was similar to the Roman FORUM.

Agoracritus (ăg"ōrăk'rĭtəs), fl. 5th cent. B.C., Athenian sculptor born on the island of Paros, said to have been the favorite pupil of Phidias. His best-known work was the colossal *Nemesis* at Rhamnus in Attica, erroneously ascribed by some to Phidias himself. Fragments of this statue and of its pedestal are in the British Museum and in the national museum in Athens.

Agostino di Duccio (ägōstē'nō dē do͞ot'chō), b. 1418, d. after 1481, Florentine sculptor. Agostino worked mainly in other parts of Italy; he carved marble narrative reliefs for the facade of the cathedral at Modena, decorated portions of the so-called Tempio Malatestiana at Rimini, and worked on the facade of San Bernardino at Perugia. Somewhat awkward in his rendering of anatomy, Agostino nevertheless developed a lively style. There are numerous charming reliefs by him of the *Madonna and Child* (Opera del Duomo, Florence; Louvre; National Gall. of Art, Washington, D.C.).

agouti (əgo͞o'tē), name applied to rabbit-sized rodents of the genus *Dasyprocta,* found in Central and South America and in the West Indies. They have slender limbs with five front and three hind toes, rudimentary tails, and coarse rough hair that varies from reddish to dark brown depending upon the species. Agoutis are forest dwellers; they eat leaves, roots, nuts, fruits, and sugarcane. They are good swimmers and fast runners. *Agouti* is occasionally used instead of *Cuniculus* as the generic name of the related paca, or spotted CAVY. Agoutis are classified in the phylum CHORDATA, subphylum Vertebrata, class Mammalia, order Rodentia, family Dasyproctidae.

Agra (ä'grə, ăg'rə), former province, N central India. The presidency, or province, of Agra was created in 1833 when the British partitioned the Bengal presidency. In 1836, Agra was renamed the North West Province. In 1877, Agra and Oudh were placed under one administrator, and in 1902 they became known as the United Provinces of Agra and Oudh. The city of **Agra** (1971 pop. 594,858), Uttar Pradesh state, is on the Jumna River. An important rail junction and commercial center and a district administrative headquarters, it is noted for its shoes, glass products, handicrafts, carpets, and especially its historic architecture. The present city was established (1566) by AKBAR and was for many years a Mogul capital. In the reign of Shah Jehan (1628–58), the magnificent TAJ MAHAL was built. Other notable historic buildings are Akbar's fort, the Pearl Mosque, and the Great Mosque (within the fort). Agra's importance diminished after the Mogul court moved to Delhi in 1658. During the decline of the Mogul empire, the city frequently changed rulers until 1803, when it was annexed by the British. From 1836 to 1858 it was the capital of the North West Province. Agra Univ. is in the city.

Agramonte, Arístides (ärē'stēdās ägrämōn'tā), 1869–1931, Cuban physician and pathologist, M.D. Columbia, 1892. A member of the medical corps of the U.S. army, he was appointed pathologist on the Commission on Yellow Fever in Havana, with Walter Reed and James Carroll, in 1900. He was professor of bacteriology and experimental pathology at the Univ. of Havana. Shortly before his death he undertook the organization of a department of tropical medicine at Louisiana State Univ.

Agramonte, Ignacio (ēgnä'syō), 1841–73, Cuban revolutionist. He played an important part in the Ten Years War. He became (1869) an official of the revolutionary government, but, disagreeing with Carlos Manuel de CÉSPEDES, resigned. For a time commander in chief of the revolutionary forces, Agramonte died in battle.

agranulocytosis (əgrăn"yəlōsītō'sĭs), disease in which the production of granulated white blood cells by the bone marrow is impaired. Although the disease may occur spontaneously it is usually induced by exposure to certain drugs, commonly antithyroid drugs, sulfonamides, and phenothiazines. Granulocytes are necessary to protect the body against infectious agents; their depletion results in severe respiratory infections, ulceration of the mouth and colon, high fever, and prostration. These symptoms may occur suddenly or over a period of days or weeks. Penicillin is usually the drug of choice to combat the bacterial invasion. The fatality rate is high (approaching 80%) in untreated cases, and deaths are common even with antibiotic treatment.

Agrapha of Jesus (ăg'rəfə) [Gr.,=unwritten], sayings attributed to Jesus not found in the Gospels. There are quotations in the New Testament that do not appear in the Gospels (e.g., Acts 20.35), and in early Christian literature there are some Agrapha from oral tradition. Thus the papyri found at OXYRHYNCHUS have given some new Agrapha. Many may be PSEUDEPIGRAPHA.

agrarian laws, in ancient Rome, the laws regulating the disposition of public lands (*ager publicus*). It was the practice of Rome to confiscate part of the land of conquered cities and states, and this was made public land. So long as it remained public land, it was occupied by tenants who paid rent, usually in produce, to the state. From the earliest times the patricians gained the largest part of the public lands, and the holding of public lands tended always in Italy to become the exclusive prerogative of the wealthy. There was also a tendency to consider land long occupied as real property of the occupier. The agrarian laws resulted from the continued efforts of the poorer classes to gain some share in the public lands. Since these lands were occupied without lease, the strictly legal aspects were not difficult; but inasmuch as most agrarian legislation challenged the lucrative privilege of the powerful of retaining the lands they held, the agrarian laws were often flagrantly disobeyed or calmly ignored. In 486 B.C., Spurius CASSIUS Viscellinus tried to pass a law assigning some new lands in Gaul to the poor of Rome and Latium, but Roman jealousy prevented its passage. The most famous of early agrarian laws were the Licinian Rogations (367 B.C.) of Caius Licinius Calvus Stolo (see under LICINIUS), which limited strictly the amount of land any citizen could hold and the number of sheep and cattle he could pasture on public land. These laws fell into disuse. About 233 B.C., Caius Flaminius succeeded in assigning some public lands to poor citizens. The next serious attempt to rectify an increasingly difficult situation was the Sempronian Law of 133 B.C. devised by Tiberius Sempronius Gracchus (see GRACCHI). This reenacted the provisions of the Licinian Rogations and added to the maximum allowance an extra amount for each son. The occupants were to be reduced to the legal maximum and the surplus given to the poor. The occupants were to receive in compensation full title to the land they retained. A commission was set up to execute the law, but the senate by its obstructionist tactics weakened the commission, thus rendering the law ineffective. In 123 B.C., Caius Gracchus revived the Sempronian

Law, but this time the senate ruined the reform by allowing the new tenants to sell their new land, which the wealthy bought up. From time to time newly acquired lands would be assigned to the poor, but as a rule they simply passed into the hands of the wealthy landholders. In the 1st cent. B.C. there were several assignments of public lands to veterans in Italy as well as on the borders of the empire. The wholesale confiscation and reassignment of private lands by Sulla (82 B.C.) and Octavian and Antony (43 B.C.) were called agrarian laws. The first step in the final collapse of the democratic effort that had resulted in the agrarian laws was the edict of Domitian (A.D. c.82) assigning the title of public lands in Italy to those who held them. The poorer classes were thus confirmed in a dependency on the powerful that foreshadowed the greater dependency of FEUDALISM.

agrarian reform, redistribution of the agricultural resources of a country. The traditional conception of agrarian, or land, reform is confined to the redistribution of land; in a wider sense it includes other related changes in agricultural institutions, such as credit, taxation, rents, and cooperatives. Reform of the conditions for land tenure has been one of the recurring themes in history. The history of the Greek city-states is filled with struggles between landowners and the landless. The land reform issue erupted into violence several times in Rome's history and was a major part of the Gracchian AGRARIAN LAWS. During the Middle Ages many peasant rebellions were triggered by demands for land reform; among the more famous were the Peasants' Revolt in England led by John Ball and Wat Tyler in 1381 and the German PEASANTS' WAR of 1524–26. In the 20th cent., with the successful revolution of the Bolsheviks in Russia, a new dimension to the concept of agrarian reform was added. The socialization of agriculture (i.e., the collective ownership of all land, partly through state farming but mainly through collective farming under state control) was regarded by the Marxists as vital to the realization of COMMUNISM. A major element in the success of the Russian Revolution was the desire for land among the peasantry, who formed 80% of the population. Shortly after he assumed power, Vladimir Ilyich Lenin, the Bolshevik leader, published his decree (1917) declaring all land to be state property. The landed estates belonging to the nobility and gentry were seized by peasants, and until 1929 there were approximately 25 million peasant holdings. Government propaganda urging the collectivization of farms had little effect, and, under Joseph Stalin, collectivization was enforced at the cost of much bloodshed. After World War II most of the countries of Eastern Europe under Communist governments experienced similar agrarian reforms. Large landed estates, operated by laborers whose social and economic status was little better than that of serfs, were broken up and redistributed, with a maximum size of 50 to 124 acres (20.2–50 hectares) imposed. Following the pattern established in the Soviet Union, however, this step toward individual small holdings was only a prelude to the introduction of compulsory collectivization, the ultimate goal of Communist land reform. In China, the successful revolution by the Communists in 1949 brought about a fundamentally more agrarian revolution than had occurred in the Soviet Union. Initially, 40% to 50% of the arable land was transferred from landlords and rich peasants to poor peasants and workers. By 1956 more than 95% of the peasant households had been organized into agricultural cooperatives. In 1958 it was decided to amalgamate these cooperatives into the larger people's communes; the main objective of the communes was to establish a collective socialist agriculture prior to mechanization, a decision much criticized by the Soviet Union. World pressure for land reform is most powerful in the underdeveloped areas, particularly in Asia and Latin America. In Asia, especially in densely populated areas such as the Indian subcontinent and Japan, agitation has been mainly for redistribution among landless laborers, for security of tenure, and for the elimination of middlemen rent receivers, oppressive rents, and usurious interest. Agrarian reforms began in Japan during the Meiji Restoration (1868–1912), when feudal fiefs and stipends were abolished and the land tax was revised. From this period until World War II agrarian disputes continued from time to time. After the war the U.S. occupation forces supervised further land reform so that by 1949 over 80% of Japan's tenanted land had been transferred from absentee landlords to tenant cultivators. In India and Pakistan similar programs of agrarian reform were instituted as well as programs of land donation (see BHAVE, Vinoba). In Latin America land reform is a major problem. The agrarian structure in Latin America consists of enormous tracts of land (latifundios) concentrated in very few hands. Because of this degree of concentration, greater than that of any other world region of comparable size, there is a growing demand for expropriation and redistribution. Ownership is often of the absentee type, with laborers no better off than serfs. Although the revolution in Mexico resulted in a land reform (1917), the program of redistribution of land is still only partially completed. A land reform law also followed the Bolivian revolution of 1952, but by 1970 only 45% of the peasant families had received titles to land. One of the most complete agrarian reforms in Latin America has taken place in Cuba, where land reform was one of the main platforms of the revolution of 1959. Nearly all the large holdings subject to expropriation were taken over by the National Institute for Land Reform (INRA), which is responsible not only for administering land reform, but for planning and directing all agricultural policy. The remaining agricultural area is limited to a ceiling of about 166 acres (67 hectares) with the tenants having full ownership rights. Most of the land taken over by INRA has not been distributed to the peasants, but is being managed by officials of INRA or by army personnel. An agrarian reform program was conducted in Chile between 1970 and 1973 under the socialist government of Salvador Allende. All farms of over 198 acres (80 hectares) were expropriated, and redistribution to the peasants was begun; this program ceased (1973) with the downfall of Allende's government. See COLLECTIVE FARM. See United Nations, *Land Tenure, Land Reform: Defects in Agrarian Structure as Obstacles to Economic Development* (1951); Kenneth Parsons, ed., *Land Tenure* (1956); Clarence Senior, *Land Reform and Democracy* (1958); Kuo-chün Chao, *Economic Planning and Organization in Mainland China* (2 vol., 1959–60); J. R. Brown and Sein Lin, ed., *Land Reform in Developing Countries* (1967); Doreen Warriner, *Land Reform in Principle and Practice* (1969); E. H. Jacoby, *Man and Land* (1971).

Agricola (Cneius Julius Agricola) (əgrĭk'ələ), A.D. c.40–A.D. 93, Roman general, the conqueror of Britain. After a distinguished military and political career (partly in Britain), he was made consul (A.D. 77) and was governor (A.D. 78?–A.D. 85?) of Britain. He pacified most of the island, conquering North Wales and advancing far into Scotland. He also circumnavigated the island. An enlightened governor, he sought to Romanize Britain without harshness or oppression. As portrayed in the biography by his son-in-law, Tacitus, Agricola was the finest exemplar of the old Roman virtues in his day. See A. R. Burn, *Agricola and Roman Britain* (1953, repr. 1965).

Agricola, Georgius, Latinized from **Georg Bauer** (gā'ôrk bou'ər), 1494–1555, German physician and scientist, known as the father of mineralogy. He was a pioneer in physical geology and the first to classify minerals scientifically. His celebrated work *De re metallica* (1556) was a standard in metallurgy and mining for over a century and was translated into English (1912) by Herbert C. Hoover and Lou H. Hoover.

Agricola, Johann or **Johannes** (yō'hän, yōhä'nəs), c.1494–1566, German Protestant minister, whose family name was Schnitter (originally Schneider). He was born at Eisleben and is sometimes called Magister Islebius. He had an early association with Martin Luther and was active in the founding of Protestantism. In 1536 he espoused antinomianism, thus breaking with Luther. He was court preacher to Joachim II, elector of Brandenburg and helped draw up the Augsburg Interim. Agricola also made a collection of German proverbs.

Agricola, Rudolphus, 1443–85, Dutch humanist, whose real name was Roelof Huysman. He opposed scholasticism and spread the culture of the Renaissance throughout Germany.

Agricultural Adjustment Administration (AAA), former U.S. government agency established (1933) in the Dept. of Agriculture under the Agricultural Adjustment Act of 1933 as part of Franklin Delano Roosevelt's New Deal program. Its purpose was to help farmers by reducing production of staple crops, thus raising farm prices and encouraging more diversified farming. Farmers were given benefit payments in return for limiting acreage given to staple crops; in the case of cotton and tobacco coercive taxes forced (1934–35) farmers to cut the amounts that they marketed. In 1936 the Supreme Court declared important sections of the act invalid, but Congress promptly adopted (1936) the Soil Conservation and Domestic Allotment Act, which encouraged conservation by paying benefits for planting soil-building crops instead of staple crops. The Agricultural Adjustment Act of 1938 empowered the AAA in years of good crops to make loans to farmers on staple crop yields and to store the surplus produce, which it could then release in years of low yield. Soil conservation was continued and farmers could by two-thirds vote adopt compulsory marketing quotas (as they did for cotton and tobacco). In World War II the AAA turned its attention to increasing food production to meet war needs. It was renamed (1942) the Agricultural Adjustment Agency, and in 1945 its functions were taken over by the Production and Marketing Administration. See E. G. Nourse and others, *Three Years of the Agricultural Adjustment Administration* (1937, repr. 1971); G. S. Shepherd, *Agricultural Price and Income Policy* (3d ed. 1952); V. L. Perkins, *Crisis in Agriculture* (1969).

agricultural subsidies, financial assistance to farmers through government-sponsored price support programs. Since the 1930s most industrialized countries have developed agricultural price support policies to reduce the instability of farm prices and to raise farm income; the programs vary considerably by country. In food-importing countries, such as Great Britain and the nations of the Continent, agricultural price support programs are also aimed at encouraging domestic production to make the economies more self-sufficient. In food-exporting countries, such as the United States and Canada, agricultural subsidy programs are used primarily to increase farm income by raising the long-term level of prices above free-market levels. In the United States the Federal government first assisted agriculture directly in the 1920s. During World War I farmers had been encouraged to increase production, and in the postwar period wartime levels of production were maintained, resulting in an oversupply that caused a disastrous collapse of prices. In Congress, in order to aid the farmer, a nonpartisan farm bloc attempted to promote favorable legislation. The Agricultural Credits Act (1923) expanded Federal credit available to farmers for intermediate loans, but the measure failed to solve the problem. Although President Coolidge vetoed the McNary-Haugen bills (1927, 1928), which featured price fixing of products and direct subsidies, the situation of the farmers had so worsened by 1929, even before the onset of the depression, that President Hoover signed the Agricultural Marketing Act (1929), initiating a program of direct aid to agriculture. The act established the Federal Farm Board with a fund of $500 million to further farming cooperatives and to set up stabilization boards, which by their purchases on the open market were to fix the prices of grain and cotton. The purchases of the Farm Board, however, encouraged farmers to raise still larger crops in expectation of higher prices; the Farm Board failed and sold out its holdings at a loss of $200 million. Between 1929 and 1932 the ratio of prices paid by farmers to that received by farmers fell to the lowest point on record. The Agricultural Adjustment Act of 1933, one of the first pieces of legislation passed under President Franklin Delano Roosevelt's New Deal program, attempted to control farm prices by reducing and controlling the supply of basic crops. Previous attempts to raise farm prices—such as the Farm Board—had failed because of the difficulty in controlling supply. Through the Agricultural Adjustment Administration (AAA) in the Dept. of Agriculture, the Secretary of Agriculture was empowered to fix marketing quotas for major farm products, to take surplus production off the market, and to cut the production of staple crops by offering producers payments for voluntarily reducing their acreage. It was hoped that these measures would not only provide farmers with immediate relief in the form of cash payments but would increase the prices for their products by reducing their surpluses. The Commodity Credit Corporation (CCC), also created in 1933, began making loans to farmers on corn and cotton and, later, on other basic farm commodities. These were nonrecourse loans for which borrowers gave no security except the commodities that were put in storage; if prices advanced above the loan value, the farmers could sell the products and repay the loan, and if they dropped below the loan level the CCC sold the commodities and absorbed the loss. Loans were granted only to farmers who agreed to sign production control agreements. Severe drought and the programs of the AAA led to the curtailment of the surpluses, and farm prices subsequently improved; between 1932 and 1937 the prices for major farm products increased by approximately 85%. In 1936 the Supreme Court declared unconstitutional certain production control features of the Agricultural Adjustment Act. Later in 1936 the Soil Conservation and Domestic Allotment Act was passed; although it made for better land use, it provided inadequate authority for price and income stabilization operations. Heavy crops of wheat and cotton in 1937 led to passage of the Agricultural Act of 1937; in its amended form this act provided the framework for the major farm program since that time. The act made price support loans by the CCC mandatory on the designated basic commodities of corn, wheat, and cotton; optional support was authorized for other commodities. Under this act and related legislation, the CCC has supported more than 100 different commodities, including fruit, vegetables, and various types of seed. From 1941 to 1948, during and just after World War II, surpluses were being rapidly utilized and price supports were used as an incentive to stimulate production of agricultural commodities. The Steagall Amendment of 1941 made supports on many nonbasic commodities mandatory for the duration of the war and for two years after the end of hostilities. In 1948 price support levels were lowered for most of these commodities. By 1949 the agriculture of war-devastated Europe and Asia had recovered to a considerable extent, and demand for American farm products declined considerably. In the meantime, however, crop production in the United States had greatly increased, with the result that farm commodity prices dropped and surpluses began to build up. The Agricultural Act of 1948, which replaced wartime controls, maintained rigid support levels for the basic commodities. The Agricultural Act of 1949 retained mandatory supports for basic commodities and provided flexible support levels for a new list of nonbasic commodities. The Korean War strengthened farm prices, and most CCC stocks were sold; from the creation of the CCC in 1933 to the end of 1952 the CCC showed a profit on basic commodities of over $13 million. The National Wool Act of 1954 provided mandatory price supports for wool and mohair. Mounting surpluses and increased costs of government programs led to the enactment of a flexible price support program in 1954; its objective was to decrease price support levels when large surpluses existed. Large quantities of surplus basic commodities were also moved overseas under the Agricultural Trade Development and Assistance Act of 1954, popularly known as Public Law 480. In 1956 the Soil Bank Program was created, which called for payment to farmers for reducing their acreage of major supported crops and required leaving idle the land removed from production. Price-support operations, as directed by the Congress, are financed by the CCC and constitute its major activity. The largest and probably the most effective programs used were the loan and storage programs of the CCC; in addition to the nonrecourse loan program of the CCC, in some cases direct purchases were made. The desired effect of control programs was largely being negated by the utilization by farmers of improved technology that made it possible to greatly increase yields per acre. In general, the price support levels were set above the market-clearing price and the disequilibrium between prices and quantities that might be offered has been handled by stock accumulation, land withdrawal programs, and export subsidies of various types. In the early 1960s there was a shift in emphasis: The market price supports on major commodities were dropped to or near market-clearing prices, and producer's incomes meanwhile were protected by direct payments on fixed quantities of products. This shift made possible the reduction of export subsidies on major price supported crops without inducing continual stock increases or applying compulsory production controls. Direct payments to farmers greatly increased in the 1960s and 70s. The feed grain, cotton, and wheat programs accounted for most of this increase. Subsidies to maintain prices, once introduced, have proved extremely difficult to end. Representatives of the farm states have fought for their continuation despite the high prices for farm commodities. See O. B. Jesness, *Readings in Agricultural Policy* (1947); M. R. R. Benedict, *Farm Policies of the United States* (1953) and *Can We Solve the Farm Problem?* (1955); Karl Fox, *The Contribution of Farm Price-Support Programs to General Economic Stability* (1954); C. M. Hardin, ed., *Agricultural Policy, Politics, and the Public Interest* (1960); M. C. Campbell, *The Farm Bureau and the New Deal* (1962); G. S. McGovern, ed., *Agricultural Thought in the Twentieth Century* (1967); Marion Clawson, *Policy Directions for U. S. Agriculture* (1968); R. J. Hildreth, ed., *Readings in Agricultural Policy* (1968); Iowa State University Center for Agricultural and Economic Development, *Food Goals, Future Structural Changes and Agricultural Policy: A National Basebook* (1969); V. L. Perkins, *Crisis in Agriculture* (1969); D. F. Hadwiger, *Federal Wheat Commodity Programs* (1970); E. A. Heady, *Future Farm Programs* (1972).

agriculture, science of producing crops and livestock from the natural resources of the earth. The primary aim of agriculture is to cause the land to produce more abundantly and at the same time to protect it from deterioration and misuse. The diverse branches of modern agriculture include AGRONOMY, HORTICULTURE, entomology, animal husbandry, DAIRYING, agricultural engineering, soil chemistry, and agricultural economics. Early man depended for his life on hunting, fishing, and food gathering. To this day, some groups still pursue this simple way of life, and others have continued as roving herdsmen (see NOMAD). However, as various groups of men undertook deliberate cultivation of wild plants and domestication of wild animals, agriculture came into being. Cultivation of crops—notably grains such as wheat, rice, rye, barley, and millet—encouraged settlement of stable farm communities, some of which grew to be towns and city-states in various parts of the world. Early agricultural implements—the digging stick, the HOE, the scythe, and the PLOW—developed slowly over the centuries, each innovation (e.g., the introduction of iron) causing profound changes in human life. From early times, too, men created ingenious systems of irrigation to control water supply, especially in semiarid areas and regions of periodic rainfall, e.g., the Middle East, the American Southwest and Mexico, the Nile Valley, and S Asia. Farming was intimately associated with landholding (see TENURE) and therefore with political organization. Growth of large estates involved the use of slaves (see SLAVERY) and bound or semi-free labor. In the Western Middle Ages the MANORIAL SYSTEM was the typical organization of more or less isolated units and determined the nature of the agricultural village. In the Orient large holdings by the nobles, partly arising from feudalism (especially in China and Japan), produced a similar pattern. As the Middle Ages waned, increasing communications, the commercial revolution, and the steady rise of cities in Western Europe tended to turn agriculture away from subsistence farming toward the growing of crops for sale outside the community (commercial agriculture). In Britain the practice of INCLOSURE allowed landlords to set aside plots of land, formerly subject to common rights, for intensive cropping or fenced pasturage—leading to efficient production of single crops. In the 16th and 17th cent. horticulture was greatly developed and contributed to the so-called agricultural revolution. Exploration and intercontinental trade, as well as scientific investigation, led to the development of horticultural knowledge of various crops and the exchange of farming methods and products, such as the potato, which was introduced from America along with beans and corn (maize) and became almost as common in N Europe as rice is in SE Asia. The appearance of mechanical devices such as the sugar mill and Eli Whitney's cotton gin helped to support the system of large plantations based on a single crop. The Industrial Revolution after the late 18th cent. swelled the population of towns and cities and increasingly forced agriculture into greater integration with general economic and financial patterns. In the American colonies the independent, more or less self-sufficient farm worked by the farmer and his family became the norm in the North, while the plantation, using slave labor, was dominant (although not universal) in the South. The free farm pushed westward with the frontier. In the N and W United States the era of mechanized agriculture began with the invention of such farm machines as the REAPER, the CULTIVATOR, the thresher, and the COMBINE. Other revolutionary innovations, e.g., the TRACTOR, continued to appear over the years, leading to a new type of large-scale agriculture. Modern science has also revolutionized food processing; refrigeration, for example, has made possible the large meat-packing plants and shipment and packaging of perishable foods. Urbanization has fostered the specialties of MARKET GARDENING and TRUCK FARMING. Harvesting operations (see HARVESTER) have been mechanized for almost every plant product grown. Breeding programs have developed highly specialized animal, plant, and poultry varieties, thus increasing production efficiency greatly. In the United States and other leading food-producing nations agricultural colleges and government agencies attempt to increase output by disseminating knowledge of improved agricultural practices, by the release of new plant and animal types, and by continuous intensive research into basic and applied scientific principles relating to agricultural production and economics. These changes have, of course, given new aspects to agricultural policies. Most of the governments of the world face their own type of farm problem, and the attempted solutions vary as much as does agriculture itself. The modern world includes areas, such as Denmark, where specialization and conservation have been highly refined, as well as areas such as N Brazil and parts of Africa where forest peoples still employ "slash and burn" agriculture—cutting down and burning trees, exhausting the ash-enriched soil, and then moving to a new area. In other regions, notably SE Asia, dense population and very small holdings necessitate intensive cultivation, using manpower and animals but few machines; here the yield is low in relation to energy expenditure. In many countries extensive government programs control the planning, financing, and regulation of agriculture. See also DRY FARMING; GRANGER MOVEMENT; GREEN REVOLUTION; RANCH; RANGE.

Agriculture, United States Department of, Federal executive department established in 1862, whose head was made a cabinet member in 1889. The department is charged with administering Federal programs related to food production and rural life. Although the department's principal duty is to aid farmers through research, planning, service, and regulatory agencies, it also serves consumers by inspecting and grading certain products, and administers Federal food programs designed to alleviate hunger. Divisions of the Dept. of Agriculture are: Rural Development (which includes the Farmers Home Administration and the RURAL ELECTRIFICATION ADMINISTRATION); Marketing and Consumer Services (which includes the Food Stamp Program and agencies overseeing government inspection of meat, poultry, and dairy products); International Affairs and Commodity Programs; Conservation, Research and Education (which includes the Agricultural Research Service, the Forest Service, and the Soil Conservation Service); and Agricultural Economics. The publications of the department are of great value to farmers, horticulturists, and others. See Ferdie Deering, *USDA, Manager of American Agriculture* (1945); U.S. Department of Agriculture, *Century of Service* (1963); study by J. U. Terrell (1966).

Ağrı Dağı (ärŭ' dä-ŭ'): see ARARAT.

Agrigento (ägrējän'tō), Lat. *Agrigentum,* city (1971 pop. 49,174), capital of Agrigento prov., S Sicily, Italy, on a hill above the Mediterranean Sea. It is an agricultural market and a tourist center. Sulfur, salt, and gypsum are produced. Founded c.580 B.C. as Acragas (or Akragas) by Greek colonists of GELA, the city became one of the most prosperous in the Greek world, as is indicated by the imposing ruins that remain. It was destroyed c.406 B.C. by Carthage but recovered. During the first of the PUNIC WARS the city suffered at the hands of both the Romans and the Carthaginians. It fell definitively to Rome in 210 B.C. during the Second Punic War. After the fall of Rome, Agrigento passed to the Byzantines and then to the Arabs (9th cent.) and to the Normans (11th cent.). Of note in the city are the remains of several Doric temples (6th–5th cent. B.C.), Roman ruins, Christian catacombs, and archaeological and art museums.

agrimony (ăg'rĭmō"nē), any plant of the genus *Agrimonia,* perennials of the family Rosaceae (ROSE family) native to north temperate zones, to Brazil, and to Africa. They are found wild in the N and central United States. Agrimony is sometimes cultivated in herb gardens for its small yellow flowers and aromatic leaves, used for an astringent tea. Agrimony is classified in the division MAGNOLIOPHYTA, class Magnoliopsida, order Rosales, family Rosaceae.

Agrippa (əgrĭp'ə), in Palestinian history: see HEROD.

Agrippa, Marcus Vipsanius (mär'kəs vĭpsā'nēəs), c.63 B.C.–12 B.C., Roman general. A close friend of Octavian (later Emperor AUGUSTUS), he won a name in the wars in Gaul before becoming consul in 37 B.C. He organized Octavian's fleet and is generally given much credit for the defeat (36 B.C.) of Sextus Pompeius in the naval battles at Mylae and Naulochus (N Sicily). Agrippa took part in the war against Antony, and his naval operations were the basis of Octavian's decisive victory at Actium in 31 B.C. He was perhaps the most trusted of all Augustus' lieutenants and rendered many services, notably in putting down disorders in both the East and West. His third wife was Augustus' daughter Julia. See biography by Meyer Reinhold (1933).

Agrippina I (ăg″rīpī′nə), d. A.D. 33, Roman matron; daughter of Agrippa and Julia and granddaughter of Augustus. She was the wife of GERMANICUS CAESAR and accompanied him on his provincial duties. After her husband's death (A.D. 19), she accused TIBERIUS of having Germanicus poisoned, and thereafter she was consistently on bad terms with the emperor. Exiled to Pandatería Island in the Bay of Naples, she starved herself to death. She is also called Agrippina Major or Agrippina the Elder. Her son Caius Caesar Germanicus became the emperor CALIGULA.

Agrippina II, d. A.D. 59, Roman matron; daughter of Germanicus Caesar and Agrippina I. By her first husband, Cneius Domitius Ahenobarbus, she was the mother of NERO. After her brother Caligula became emperor, she had some power until she was discovered conspiring against him. She achieved her ambitions for her son after her uncle Emperor CLAUDIUS I took her as his third wife. She dominated the emperor and persuaded him to advance the interests of Nero at the expense of his own son, BRITANNICUS. She almost certainly poisoned Claudius, thus bringing Nero to power. She quarreled with Seneca, with Claudius' secretary Narcissus, and with the other ministers. Her son, weary of her intrigues, had her murdered. Colonia Agrippinensis (modern Cologne) was named for her.

agronomy (əgrŏn′əmē), branch of agriculture dealing with soil management and production of major field crops. It embraces a variety of physical and biological disciplines, e.g., soil fertility and conservation, plant breeding and physiology, and climatology. Its aim is to provide food and fiber for mankind, and it thus comprises the world's largest single industry. Agronomy deals primarily with the production of large-scale crops, e.g., wheat, barley, corn, oats, rice, soybeans, and cotton, as opposed to HORTICULTURE, which is concerned with fruits, vegetables, flowers, and ornamental plants.

Agua (ä′wä, ä′gwä), inactive volcano, 12,310 ft (3,752 m) high, S Guatemala. In 1541, climaxing several days of unceasing rain and earthquakes, a wall of water, whose origin is not scientifically explained, swept down from its slopes, completely destroying Ciudad Vieja. Over 1,000 inhabitants were drowned, including the governor, Doña Beatriz de la Cueva. The flood resulted in the founding of Antigua.

Aguadilla (ä″gwädē′yä, ä″wä-), town (1970 pop. 21,031), NW Puerto Rico, a port on Mona Passage. It is the trade center for an agricultural region. Columbus reputedly landed at the site of Aguadilla in 1493.

Aguascalientes (ä″gwäskälyān′tās, ä″wäs-) [Span.,="hot waters"], state (1970 pop. 334, 936), 2,499 sq mi (6,472 sq km), central Mexico, on the Anáhuac plateau, a fertile agricultural region. AGUASCALIENTES is the capital. Cattle are raised on the wide plains and in the foothills, and there is some mining in the mountainous areas, though much of the mineral wealth, especially copper, remains unexploited. Aguascalientes is noted for the warm mineral springs, for which it is named, and for a fine climate.

Aguascalientes, city (1970 pop. 173,126), capital of Aguascalientes state, central Mexico. The city is a pleasant health resort, noted for its mineral waters. Its industries include smelting and the manufacture of textiles. Aguascalientes is built over an ancient, intricate system of tunnels constructed by early, still unidentified, inhabitants. Founded in 1575, the city was long a Spanish outpost against hostile Indians; railroad development in the late 19th cent. gave it commercial importance.

Aguesseau, Henri François d' (äNrē′ fräNswä′ dāgĕsō′), 1668–1751, French lawyer. He became *procureur général* in the Parlement of Paris (1700) and chancellor of France (1717). Because of his opposition to John LAW he was briefly exiled to his estates. He served as chancellor again (1720–22, 1737–50) and devoted himself to judicial reform. The name also appears as Daguesseau.

Aguinaldo, Emilio (āmē′lyō ägēnäl′ dō), 1869–1964, Philippine leader. In the insurrection against Spain in 1896 he took command, and by terms of the peace that ended it he went into exile at Hong Kong. After the outbreak of the Spanish-American War, Aguinaldo returned to the Philippines and led a Philippine insurrection in concert with U.S. attacking forces. He set up a republic with its capital at Malolos and himself as president, and when Philippine independence was brushed aside in the peace treaty that ended the Spanish-American War, he headed (1899–1901) a rebellion against U.S. occupying forces until he was captured by Frederick Funston. Aguinaldo took the oath of allegiance to the United States, was briefly imprisoned, and retired to private life. In 1935 he ran for president but was defeated by Manuel Quezon. Aguinaldo was charged with cooperating with the Japanese occupying the Philippines in World War II; in 1945 he was taken into custody, but he was not tried. With V. A. Pacis he wrote *A Second Look at America* (1957). See his memoirs (tr. 1967); biography by Carlos Quirino (1969).

Aguirre, Lope de (lō′pā thā agē′rā), c.1510–1561, Spanish rebel and adventurer in colonial South America. He was often involved in violence and sedition before joining (1560) the expedition of Pedro de URSÚA down the Marañón and the Amazon. He was one of the men who overthrew and killed Ursúa, then he killed Ursúa's successor, Fernando de Guzmán, and took command himself. He and his men reached the Atlantic—probably by the Orinoco River—and on the way wantonly laid waste Indian villages. In 1561 he seized Margarita island and held it in a grip of terror. He then crossed to the mainland in an attempt to take Panama, openly proclaiming rebellion against the Spanish crown. Surrounded at Barquisimeto, Venezuela, Aguirre in desperation crowned his infamous life by the murder of his own daughter. He surrendered and was shot. See Walker Lowry, *Lope Aguirre, the Wanderer* (1952); A. F. Bandelier, *The Gilded Man* (1893, repr. 1962).

Agulhas, Cape (əgŭ′ləs) [Port.,=needles], W Cape Province, Republic of South Africa; the southernmost point of Africa. Its name refers to the saw-edged reefs and sunken rocks that run out to sea and make navigation hazardous. A powerful lighthouse on the cape alerts ships. The meridian of Cape Agulhas, long. 20° E, is used to divide the Atlantic and Indian oceans.

Agur (ā′gər), unidentified author of Prov. 30.

Agusan (ägo͞o′sän), river, c.240 mi (390 km) long, rising in the mountains of SE Mindanao, the Philippines, and flowing N past Butuan to Butuan Bay. It is navigable for small craft c.160 mi (260 km) upstream. The Agusan valley is very fertile and is one of the Philippines' chief rice-growing regions.

Agustini, Delmira (dĕlmē′rä ägo͞ostē′nē), c.1886–1914, Uruguayan poet. Essentially a poet of ideas, Agustini combined deep spiritual and erotic yearnings in bold and expressive imagery. She abandoned traditional forms in her strongly controlled verses. After a brief and unhappy marriage she was murdered by her estranged husband. *El Rosario de Eros* (1914) is one of her best-known collections; her complete works were published in 1924.

Ahab (ā′hăb), d. c.853 B.C., king of Israel (c.874–c.853 B.C.), son and successor of OMRI **1**. Ahab was one of the greatest kings of the northern kingdom. He consolidated the good foreign relations his father had fostered, and Israel was at peace during much of his reign. His marriage with JEZEBEL helped his friendship with Tyre, and his alliance with JEHOSHAPHAT **1**, king of Judah, made Ahab sure of his less powerful neighbor to the south. Ahab's prestige is seen in Assyrian inscriptions mentioning his alliance against SHALMANESER III, who won an indecisive victory (c.854 B.C.) at Karkar on the Orontes. After this campaign Ahab and BENHADAD **2** of Damascus went to war over the country E of the Jordan. Ahab was killed in battle. The biblical account of Ahab's reign (1 Kings 16.28–22.40) is most interesting in its religious aspects. To the devout, Ahab's foreign wife, with her Tyrian cults and behavior, represented evil. Besides, she was a willful woman and entertained exalted ideas of royal prerogative. She met her match in ELIJAH, the champion of Israel's God. He was an important factor in the discontent that began to develop in Israel at this period. Ahab was succeeded by his sons, first Ahaziah, then Jehoram. The ruins of his palace have been excavated at SAMARIA. The Ahab of Jer. 29.21,22 is a different person, a lying prophet.

Ahad Ha-Am (äkhäd′ hä-äm), 1856–1927, Jewish thinker and Zionist leader, b. Russia. Originally named Asher Ginsberg, he adopted the pen name of Ahad Ha-Am [One of the People] when he published his first and highly controversial essay "The Wrong Way" (1889), in which he criticized those who sought immediate settlement in Palestine, advocating instead Jewish cultural education as the basis for building a strong people for later settlement. At first he received a traditional Hasidic education. His later philosophic and literary studies (in Russian, German, French, English, and Latin) led him to develop a strong rationalist attitude that resulted in his rejection first of Hasidism and then of religion itself. Not a political Zionist, he saw Palestine as the "spiritual center" in which the best in Jewish life would be revived and strengthened, giving strength and direction to Jews in the Diaspora. Since he regarded religion as no longer valid in a modern age, he saw the chief obligation of Jewish life as fulfillment of the ethical demands of the Old Testament prophets. He spent his last years in Palestine and died there. A number of his essays have been anthologized in *Selected Essays of Ahad Ha-Am* (tr. and ed. by Leon Simon, 1912; repr. 1962). See biography by Leon Simon (1960).

Ahaggar, mountains, Africa: see SAHARA.

Aha of Shabcha (ä′hä, shäb′khä) or **Achai of Shabcha** (ä′khī), c.680–c.762, Babylonian rabbi. He settled (c.752) in Palestine after being passed over for appointment as head of the rabbinic academy of Pumbedita for political reasons. His major work, *Sheilthoth* [questions], reflects both the Babylonian Talmud of his earlier years and the influence of the Palestinian Talmud, with which he became familiar at this later period. It is a collection of legal and ethical sermons or treatises intended to be of use to laymen as well as to the scholars for whom most of the learned Jews wrote. Aha is the first scholar after the close of the compilation of the Talmud of whom there is record. His work emphasizes the value of the basic virtues and everyday morals.

Aharah (āhâr′ə), the same as AHIRAM.

Aharhel (əhär′hĕl), Judahite family. 1 Chron. 4.8.

Ahasai (āhăs′āī, āhā′sī), priest. Ahzai RSV. Neh. 11.13. Jahzerah: 1 Chron. 9.12.

Ahasbai (āhăs′bāī, –bī), father of ELIPHELET **3**.

Ahasuerus (āhăs″yo͞oē′rəs), Hebrew form of the name Xerxes, as used in the Bible. The Ahasuerus of Esther is probably Xerxes I. That of Tobit 14.15 may be Cyaxares I, destroyer of Nineveh. The name of the father of DARIUS THE MEDE is also given as Ahasuerus.

Ahava (āhā′və), unidentified place, where Ezra collected one of his expeditions. Ezra 8.15,21,31.

Ahaz (ā′hăz), d. c.727 B.C., king of Judah (c.731–727 B.C.), son of Jotham. His reign marked the end of the real independence of Judah. A coalition of Pekah of Israel and Rezin of Syria attacked him and nearly took Jerusalem. Ahaz appealed for help to Tiglathpileser III of Assyria, who defeated Ahaz's enemies but demanded tribute of Judah. Ahaz sent some Temple gold as payment. The greatest figure of that time in Judah was the prophet Isaiah, who opposed the Assyrian alliance. Ahaz is denounced in the Bible for his heathen abominations and his sacrilege with the Temple gold. In Ahaz's reign Judah lost Elath, its Red Sea port, permanently. Ahaz was succeeded by Hezekiah. 2 Kings 16; 2 Chron. 28; Isa. 7. Achaz: Mat. 1.9. A different Ahaz, otherwise unknown, is mentioned in 1 Chron. 8.35 and 9.42.

Ahaziah (āhəzī′ə). **1** King of Israel, son of Ahab. He was a worthy successor of his father only in that he followed Ahab's religious views. He was succeeded by his brother JEHORAM **1.** 1 Kings 22.51–53; 2 Kings 1; 2 Chron. 20.35–37. **2** King of Judah, son of JEHORAM **2** and ATHALIAH **1.** He was considered a typical descendant of Ahab. He was killed in Jehu's coup d'état while visiting at Jezreel. His mother succeeded him. 2 Kings 8.25–29; 9; 2 Chron. 22. He is called Azariah in 2 Chron. 22.6 and Jehoahaz in 2 Chron. 21.17 and 25.23.

Ahban (ā′băn), Jerahmeelite. 1 Chron. 2.29.

Aher (ā′hər), Benjamite. 1 Chron. 6.12. Perhaps the same as AHIRAM.

Ahi (ā′hī). **1** Gadite. 1 Chron. 5.15. **2** Asherite. 1 Chron. 7.34.

Ahiah (əhī′ə), variant of AHIJAH.

Ahiam (əhī′əm), one of David's men. 2 Sam. 23.33; 1 Chron. 11.35.

Ahian (əhī′ən), Manassite. 1 Chron. 7.19.

Ahidjo, Ahmadou (ämä′dō āhē′jo͞o), 1924–, president of the United Republic of Cameroon (1960–). The son of a Muslim Fulani chief, he served with the French during World War II. Entering politics in the French Cameroons after the war, he became vice premier (1957) and then premier (1958) of the territory. With the independence (1960) of the Cameroon Republic, he was elected its first president. He also became president of the Mouvement d'Union Camerounaise, a political party affiliated with the Rassemblement Démocratique Africain (RDA), both of which favored continued strong ties with France. As a result of his efforts, the British-administered Southern Cameroons voted (1961) to unite with the Cameroon Republic in the Federal Republic of Cameroon. He was reelected president in 1965 and 1970 as the candidate of the country's sole political party. In 1972 he secured adoption of a new unitary constitution, creating the United Republic of Cameroon.

Ahiezer (āhīē'zər). **1** Prince of Dan. Num. 1.12. **2** Chief of David's bowmen. 1 Chron. 12.3.

Ahihud (āhī'həd). **1** Prince of Asher. Num. 34.27. **2** Benjamite. 1 Chron. 8.3.

Ahijah (əhī'jə), common name in the Bible, occasionally spelled Ahiah. **1** Prophet from Shiloh. 1 Kings 11.29; 12.15; 14.1–18; 2 Chron. 10.15. **2** Priest in the time of Saul, perhaps the same as AHIMELECH **1.** 1 Sam. 14.3. **3** One of David's captains. 1 Chron. 11.22. **4** Scribe. 1 Kings 4.3. **5** Father of King BAASHA. **6** Jerahmeelite. 1 Chron. 2.25. **7** Benjamite. 1 Chron. 8.7. Ahoah: 1 Chron. 8.4. **8** Levite. 1 Chron. 26.20. **9** Sealer of the covenant. Neh. 10.26.

Ahikam (əhī'kəm), protector of Jeremiah and the father of Gedaliah. 2 Kings 22.12, 14; 2 Chron. 34.20; Jer. 26.24; 40.5.

Ahilud (əhī'ləd). **1** Father of JEHOSHAPHAT **2.** **2** Father of BAANA **3.**

Ahimaaz (əhĭm'āăz). **1** Father of AHINOAM **1.** **2** One of the men set to spy on Absalom. 2 Sam. 15.27; 17.17–21; 18.19–32. **3** Husband of BASMATH and perhaps the same as **2.**

Ahiman (əhī'mən). **1** Son of ANAK. **2** Family of porters. 1 Chron. 9.17.

Ahimelech (əhĭm'əlĕk). **1** Priest at Nob, brother of, or perhaps the same as, AHIJAH **2.** He befriended David, and Saul had him killed. 1 Sam. 22.9–19. Abimelech: 1 Chron. 18.16. Name reversed with that of his son, Abiathar. 2 Sam. 8.17; 1 Chron. 18.16; 24.6. **2** Hittite in David's camp. 1 Sam. 26.6.

Ahimoth (əhī'mŏth), Merarite Levite. 1 Chron. 6.25.

ahimsa (əhĭm'sä) [Sanskrit,=noninjury], ethical principle of noninjury to both men and animals, common to Buddhism, Jainism, and Hinduism. Ahimsa became influential in post-Vedic India, contributing to the spread of vegetarianism. Political implications of ahimsa were developed in the nonviolence movement of Mohandas GANDHI.

Ahinadab (əhĭn'ədăb), one of Solomon's stewards. 1 Kings 4.14.

Ahinoam (əhĭn'ōəm). **1** A wife of Saul. 1 Sam. 14.50. **2** One of David's early wives. 1 Sam. 25.43; 27.3; 30.5; 2 Sam. 2.2; 3.2.

Ahio (əhī'ō). **1** One of those who drove the cart that carried the Ark. 2 Sam. 6.3, 4; 1 Chron. 13.7. **2** Uncle of Saul. 1 Chron. 8.31; 9.37. **3** Benjamite. 1 Chron. 8.14.

Ahira (əhī'rə), prince of Naphtali. Num. 1.15.

Ahiram (əhī'rəm), son of Benjamin. Num. 26.38. Ehi: Gen. 46.21. Aharah: 1 Chron. 8.1. AHER may be the same.

Ahisamach (əhĭs'əmăk), father of AHOLIAB.

Ahishahar (əhĭsh'əhär, əhī'-), Benjamite. 1 Chron. 7.10.

Ahishar (əhī'shär), royal steward. 1 Kings 4.6.

Ahithophel (əhĭth'əfĕl), David's counselor who joined with Absalom against David. He killed himself when Absalom ignored his counsel. He may have been the grandfather of Bath-sheba. 2 Sam. 15.12; 16.20–17.23; 23.34. The Vulgate form of the name is Achitophel.

Ahitub (əhī'təb). **1** Father of AHIMELECH **1** and AHIJAH **2.** **2** Father, or grandfather, of ZADOK **1.** **3** Father of ZADOK **5.**

Ahlab (ä'lăb), town of Asher. Judges 1.31.

Ahlai (ä'lāī). **1** Jerahmeelitess. 1 Chron. 2.31,34. **2** Father of one of David's men, Zabad. 1 Chron. 11.41.

Ahlin, Lars (lärsh älēn'), 1915–, Swedish novelist. Ahlin's works are marked by great creative vitality, psychological realism, and a concern with spiritual values. Although his novel *If* (1946) was criticized for narrative meandering and excessive religious theorizing, *The Cinnamon Stick* (1953) won him critical acclaim. His baring of human foibles and self-deceptions and his vision of life as bizarre are reminiscent of Dostoyevsky.

Ahmad. For Ottoman sultans thus named, see AHMED.

Ahmad al-Mansur (ä'məd äl-mänsōōr', Arabic äkhmäd') [al-Mansur,=the victorious], d. 1603, emir of Morocco (1578–1603). Proclaimed ruler after his brother's death at the battle of ALCAZARQUIVIR, he gained great prestige from the victory over Portugal. In addition, the ransom of the Portuguese captives made him wealthy. He was able to give Morocco a quarter-century of relative peace and prosperity. His conquest of Timbuktu (1590–91) marked the peak of Morocco's extension into the territory south of the Sahara. The cost of maintaining an army at so great a distance prevented him from gaining any permanent benefit from the conquest. He engaged in a commercial correspondence with Queen Elizabeth I of England and encouraged foreign trade.

Ahmad Khan, Sir Sayyid (sä'yēd äkhmäd' khän), 1817–98, Indian Muslim educator. His family was long connected with the Mogul court, but he entered the service of the British East India Company. Convinced of the futility of revolt, he remained loyal to the British during the Indian Mutiny (1857–58) and saved the lives of many Europeans. Seeking to revitalize the Muslim community by the introduction of Western ideas, Sayyid Ahmad Khan organized societies for the translation of English works into Urdu and for the teaching of civics to the Indian public. In 1875 he established the Muslim Anglo-Oriental College at Aligarh, which later became Aligarh Muslim University. He was knighted in 1888. Among his works are *Loyal Mohammedans of India* (1860–61) and *Causes of the Indian Revolt* (1873). See J. M. S. Baljon, *Reforms and Religious Ideas of Sir Sayyid Ahmad Khan* (1949).

Ahmad Mirza (äkhmäd' mērzä'), 1898–1930, shah of Persia (1909–25), son of Muhammad Ali. The last of the Kajar, or Qajar, dynasty, he came to power as a result of a coup d'etat against his father. A regent initially ruled for him. A weak figure, Ahmad was overthrown in 1921 in a military coup by Reza Khan (later REZA SHAH PAHLEVI). The shah, unable to oppose the new government, left (1923) for Europe, where he died.

Ahmadnagar or **Ahmednagar** (both: ämədnŭg'ər), city (1971 pop. 117,275), Maharashtra state, W central India, on the Sina River. It is a district administrative center and has textile manufacturing and some light industry. Founded in 1490, it was the capital of a kingdom that lasted until 1600. Sivaji, leader of the Mahrattas, was born in Ahmadnagar.

Ahmad Shah, c.1723–1773, Afghan ruler (1747–73), founder of the Durani dynasty. His success in commanding Afghan forces in India for Nadir Shah of Iran won him the rule of Afghanistan on Nadir's death (1747). He invaded India several times and twice (1756, 1760) occupied and sacked Delhi, the capital of the Mogul empire. He conquered a vast territory, extending roughly from the Oxus to the Indus rivers and from Tibet to Khurasan, but he was unable to consolidate this empire and it soon disintegrated. He united and strengthened Afghanistan, however, and is therefore often considered its modern founder. His family retained power until the rise of Dost Muhammad.

Ahmed. For some names beginning thus, see AHMAD.

Ahmed I (ä'mĕd, äkhmĕt'), 1589–1617, Ottoman sultan (1603–17), son and successor of Muhammad III to the throne of the Ottoman Empire (Turkey). The chief event of his reign was the Treaty of Szitvatorok (1606), which supplemented the Treaty of Vienna between Archduke (later Holy Roman Emperor) MATTHIAS and Prince Stephen BOCSKAY of Transylvania. By the treaty, the emperors, as kings of Hungary, ceased to pay tribute to the sultan, and Transylvania was recognized as independent. The treaty also marked the first time the sultan recognized other European rulers as his equals. In the Asian provinces disorders were suppressed by Ahmed's vizier, the Croatian Murad Pasha, but after Murad's death (1611) they broke out again, allowing Shah Abbas I of Persia to retain Tabriz. On becoming sultan Ahmed had not killed his brother Mustafa as was the custom. Therefore Mustafa I succeeded as the oldest male in the ruling family.

Ahmed II, 1642–95, Ottoman sultan (1691–95), brother and successor of Sulayman II to the throne of the Ottoman Empire (Turkey). Soon after his reign began, the Turkish defeat at SLANKAMEN (1691) heralded the start of the conquest of Hungary by Austria. His nephew, Mustafa II, succeeded him.

Ahmed III, 1673–1736, Ottoman sultan (1703–30), brother and successor of Mustafa II to the throne of the Ottoman Empire (Turkey). He gave asylum to CHARLES XII of Sweden and to MAZEPA after Peter the Great of Russia had defeated (1709) them at Poltava. Charles's advice helped to bring about war between Turkey and Russia (1710–11). By the Treaty of the Pruth (1711), Turkey recovered Azov and the surrounding territory from Russia. Ahmed seized (1715) the Peloponnesus and the Ionian Isles (except Corfu) from Venice, but he was defeated by the Austrians under Prince EUGENE OF SAVOY in 1716–18. By the Treaty of Passarowitz (1718), Banat, Lesser Walachia, and N Serbia, including Belgrade, were lost to the Hapsburg emperor. Ahmed's grand vizier (chief executive officer) after 1718 was Ibrahim, who encouraged learning by establishing several notable libraries and favored the rise of Greek Phanariots (see under PHANAR) to high offices. The sultan and his minister were overthrown by the JANISSARIES, who were jealous of the new aristocracy. Ahmed's nephew Mahmud I became sultan, and Ahmed died in prison.

Ahmedabad or **Ahmadabad** (both: ä''mədəbäd'), city (1971 pop. 1,588,378), capital of Gujarat state, NW India, on the Sabarmati River. An industrial center noted for its cotton mills, Ahmedabad is also a transportation hub and a commercial center. Founded in 1412 by Ahmad Shah, it fell to Akbar in 1573 and enjoyed great prosperity under the Mogul empire. The British opened a trading post there in 1619; by the early 19th cent. they controlled the city. The cultural center of Gujarat, Ahmedabad has many outstanding mosques and tombs. It is also sacred to the Jains, who have more than 100 temples there. The Jama Masjid, an ancient Hindu temple converted (15th cent.) to a mosque, is one of the city's most beautiful buildings. Mahatma Gandhi lived for a while in Ahmedabad. Gujarat Univ. (1950) is in the city.

Ahmed Shah: see AHMAD SHAH.

Ahoah (əhō'ə), the same as AHIJAH **7.** The patronymic **Ahohite** suggests this name; it occurs with the names of DODO **2** and ILAI.

Aholah (əhō'lə) and **Aholibah** (əhōl'ĭbə), the sisters in an allegory on Israel's idolatry. Ezek. 23.

Aholiab (əhō'lēăb), specially chosen worker on the Tabernacle. Ex. 31.6; 35.34; 36.1,2; 38.23.

Aholibah: see AHOLAH.

Aholibamah (əhō''lĭbä'mə, ā''həlĭb'ə-). **1** One of Esau's wives. Gen. 36.2. **2** Duke of Edom. Gen. 36.41.

Ahome (äō'mā), city (1970 pop. 165,612), Sinaloa state, W Mexico, on the Pacific Ocean. Ahome lies along the Inter-American Highway and is linked by rail with Mexico City. Sugarcane, grains, and cotton are grown in the region, which is irrigated by the Fuerte River. The city also has an important fishing industry, based mainly on shrimp.

Ahriman (ä'rĭmən): see ZOROASTRIANISM.

Aht Confederacy: see NOOTKA INDIANS.

Ahuachapán (äwächäpän'), city (1968 est. pop. 26,000), W El Salvador, near the Guatemalan border. It is the westernmost city in the country and is the center of an agricultural region producing coffee, sugar, grain, and fruit. There are thermal springs nearby.

Ahumai (əhyōō'māī, -mī), Judahite. 1 Chron. 4.2.

Ahura Mazdah (ä'hōōrə măz'də): see ZOROASTRIANISM.

Ahuzam (əhyōō'zəm), Judahite. 1 Chron. 4.6.

Ahuzzath (əhŭz'ăth), friend of Abimelech of Gerar. Gen. 26.26.

Ahvaz or **Ahwaz** (both: äwäz'), city (1971 est. pop. 215,000), SW Iran, on the Kurun River. It is an oil center, a transportation hub, and an industrial city that has petrochemical, textile, and food-processing industries. An ancient city, Ahvaz was rebuilt (3d cent. A.D.) by Ardashir I, who named it Hormuzd-Ardashir. In the 4th cent. Ahvaz became the seat of a bishopric, and a large church was built there. It was an important Arab trading center in the 12th and 13th cent. but later declined. The discovery of oil nearby in the early 20th cent. restored the city to its former importance. The new part of Ahvaz, the administrative and industrial center, is on the right bank of the Kurun, but the population is still concentrated in the old section on the left bank.

Ahvenanmaa Islands (ä'vĕnänmä'') or **Åland Islands** (ä'lənd, ô'-), Swed. *Ålandsöerna* (ō'läntsû'ûrnä), archipelago (1970 pop. 21,010), 581 sq mi (1,505 sq km), in the Baltic Sea between Sweden and Finland, at the entrance of the Gulf of Bothnia. It belongs to Finland. The archipelago consists of about 7,000 islands, but fewer than 100 are inhabited. The climate is mild. The chief town is MAARIANHAMINA, a port on Åland, the largest of the islands. Shipping, fishing, forestry, farming, and tourism are the chief occupations. Swedish is the main language. The islands, colonized by Swedes, are of strategic importance. With Finland, they were ceded by Sweden to Russia in 1809. In the Crimean War the Russian fortifications were destroyed (1854), and remilitarization was forbidden by the Treaty of Paris (1856). At the end of World War I, the islanders sought to join Sweden. The League of Nations in 1921, however, recognized Finland's sovereignty, but guaranteed the autonomous status of the islands and confirmed their demilitarization. After the Finnish-Russian War (1939–40) Finland and Russia signed a demilitarization agreement that was renewed after World War II. Under pressure from Russia, Finland's parliament renounced the League guarantee of autonomy in 1951 but at the same time accorded the islanders additional rights of self-government. Pro-Swedish sentiment continues, however, and emigration to Sweden has caused a population decline in recent years.

Ai (āˈī). **1** Canaanite royal city, E of Bethel. Abraham pitched his tent there when he arrived in Canaan. It is probably the modern et-Tell, near Bethel (Jordan). Excavations have revealed a strongly fortified city situated there. Ai was in ruins at the time of Joshua's conquest. The account in Joshua 7 possibly refers instead to BETHEL **1**, whose people may have used the nearby ruins of Ai as a bastion against the invading Israelites. Hai: Gen. 12.8; 13.3. Aiath: Isa. 10.28. Aija: Neh. 11.31. **2** City of the Ammorites, near Heshbon. Jer. 49.3.

Aiah (āˈə). **1** Edomite. 1 Chron. 1.40. Ajah: Gen. 36.24. **2** Father of RIZPAH.

Aiath (āˈəth), the same as Ai **1**.

Aichi (īˈchē), prefecture (1970 pop. 5,386,116), 1,962 sq mi (5,082 sq km), central Honshu, Japan. NAGOYA is the capital. Bounded on the E by Ise Bay and on the S by the Philippine Sea, Aichi consists of a coastal plain and a mountainous, forested interior. It is drained by the Kiso River, an important source of hydroelectric power. The major industrial centers are Nagoya, Toyohashi, Okazaki, Ichinomiya, Toyota, Tanjo, and Seto. Agricultural products and raw silk are produced, and lignite and quartz are mined.

aids, in FEUDALISM, type of feudal due paid by a vassal to his suzerain (overlord). Aids varied with time and place, although in English-speaking countries aids were traditionally due on the knighting of the lord's eldest son, on the marriage of the lord's eldest daughter, and for ransom of the lord from captivity. These are the three aids specified in the MAGNA CARTA (1215), which forbade the king to levy aids from the barons on occasions other than these, except by the "common counsel" of the realm. It is difficult to distinguish aids from other feudal dues such as SCUTAGE and TALLAGE. The term had a much wider scope than was indicated in the Magna Carta. In general, aids fell into disuse with the decline of feudalism, although they continued nominally in most places. On the Continent, the aids often became land or justice taxes due the local lords. In France, the aids were converted later into a royal tax that continued until the French Revolution.

Aiea (äˈēäˈä), city (1970 pop. 12,560), Honolulu co., Oahu, Hawaii, a residential suburb of Honolulu, on the eastern shore of Pearl Harbor. Once a quiet sugarcane town with a sugar refinery, it is now the site of numerous housing developments and a shopping center. Many residents work at nearby military installations. Between Aiea and Honolulu are the U.S. Army Tripler General Hospital and U.S. Fort Shafter, headquarters of the Army of the Pacific.

Aiglon, L': see NAPOLEON II.

Aija (āˈjə), the same as AI **1**.

Aijal (īˈjəl), city (1971 pop. 31,436), capital of the union territory of Mizoram, NE India. Situated on a ridge in the Lushai Hills that is 3,500 ft (1,067 m) high, Aijal is an important trade center for the surrounding area.

Aijalon (ăˈjəlŏn, īˈ–, āˈ–). **1** Town, on the border between Philistia and Israel, the modern Yalo (Israel), NW of Jerusalem. Judges 1.35; 2 Chron. 11.10. Ajalon: Joshua 19.42; 2 Chron. 28.18. In the Tel-el-Amarna letters it is called Aialuna. **2** Town in Zabulon. Judges 12.12. **3** Valley over which Joshua commanded the moon to stand still. Joshua 10.12.

Aijeleth Shahar (ăjˈəlĕth shāˈhär), superscription of Ps. 22, probably the tune to which it was to be sung, named from the first words of some other verse set to it. Other superscriptions of similar explanation are: Al-taschith. Pss. 57; 58; 59; 75. Jonath-elem-rechokim. Ps. 56. Mahalath. Ps. 53. Mahalath Leannoth. Ps. 88. Shoshannim. Pss. 45; 69. Shoshannim-Eduth. Ps. 80. Shushan-eduth. Ps. 60.

Aiken, Conrad (āˈkĭn), 1889–1973, American author, b. Savannah, Ga., grad. Harvard, 1912. His writings reveal a concern for the workings of the mind and for the evolution of personal identity. Aiken is best known for his poetry, which is often preoccupied with the sound and structure of music; his volumes of verse include *The Charnel Rose* (1918), *Selected Poems* (1929; Pulitzer Prize), *Brownstone Eclogues* (1942), *Collected Poems* (1953), *A Letter from Li Po* (1956), *A Seizure of Limericks* (1964), and *The Clerk's Journal* (1971). In 1924 he edited Emily Dickinson's *Selected Poems*, which established her literary reputation. Aiken's interest in psychopathology is evident in the novels *Blue Voyage* (1927) and *Great Circle* (1933). His collected critical essays, *A Reviewer's ABC*, appeared in 1958, his collected short stories—including "Mr. Arcularis" and "Silent Snow, Secret Snow"—in 1961. From 1950 to 1952, Aiken held the poetry chair at the Library of Congress. In 1969 he was awarded the National Medal for Literature. See his autobiography, *Ushant* (1952, repr. 1971); studies by Jay Martin (1962) and F. J. Hoffman (1962).

Aiken, city (1970 pop. 13,436), seat of Aiken co., W S.C.; inc. 1835. It is a fashionable resort and polo center located in the midst of sand hills and pine forests. Aiken is also an industrial city, with textile and lumber mills and a large fiberglass plant; kaolin mines are nearby. A branch of the Univ. of South Carolina is located in the city. Nearby is the Atomic Energy Commission's Savannah River Plant, which produces nuclear materials. Aiken State Park is to the east.

ailanthus (ālănˈthəs), any tree of the genus *Ailanthus,* native to the warm regions of Asia and Australia. Ailanthus wood is sometimes used for cabinetmaking and for the manufacture of charcoal. The leaves are a source of food for silkworms, and the bark and leaves are used medicinally. Females of a species called tree of heaven, native to China, are widely grown in European and American cities because of their attractive foliage and their resistance to smoke and soot; the male flowers, however, have a disagreeable odor. Ailanthus is classified in the division MAGNOLIOPHYTA, class Magnoliopsida, order Sapindales, family Simarubaceae.

ailanthus moth: see SILKWORM.

aileron: see AIRFOIL; AIRPLANE.

Ailey, Alvin, 1931–, American modern dancer and choreographer, b. Rogers, Tex. Ailey studied in Los Angeles with Lester HORTON, whose strong, dramatic style influenced his choreography. In the late 1950s he formed his own company, the American Dance Theater, which has been internationally acclaimed. His best-known works include *Creation of the World* (1960), *Roots of the Blues* (1961), *Hermit Songs* (1962), and *Revelations*, as well as works he created for other companies, such as *Macumba* for the Harkness Ballet.

Ailly, Pierre d' (pyĕr dāyēˈ), 1350–1420, French theologian and writer, cardinal of the Roman Catholic Church. He was the teacher of John GERSON and was Gerson's predecessor as chancellor at the Univ. of Paris (1385–95). Ailly figured prominently among the conciliarists working to end the Great Schism (see SCHISM, GREAT). He urged that in order to name a new pope a general council be called as the only means of settling the schism. He seems to have been more concerned with a practical solution than with the implications of the conciliar theory. He participated in both the Council of Pisa (see PISA, COUNCIL OF) and the Council of Constance (see CONSTANCE, COUNCIL OF). In the latter Ailly took part in the trial and condemnation of John Huss. His vast writings embrace theology, philosophy, cosmography, plans for ecclesiastical reform, and French religious verse. His best-known work, the *Imago mundi,* an astronomical compendium, was studied by Columbus. See studies by J. P. McGowan (1936) and Francis Oakley (1964).

Ailsa Craig (ālˈsə), island, c.1 sq mi (2.6 sq km), off SW Scotland, W of Girvan in the Firth of Clyde; it rises to 1,114 ft (340 m). It has granite quarries and a lighthouse and is a sanctuary for sea birds.

Ain (ăN), department (1968 pop. 339,262), E central France, in BURGUNDY, bordering on Switzerland. BOURG-EN-BRESSE is the capital.

Ain (āˈĭn). **1** Town, N Palestine. Num. 34.11. **2** See EN-RIMMON.

Aintab, Turkey: see GAZIANTEP.

Ainu (īˈno͞o), aborigines of Japan who may be descended from the Caucasoid people who once lived in N Asia. The more powerful Oriental invaders from the Asian mainland gradually forced the Ainu to retreat to the northern islands, where today, they reside on the N Japanese island of Hokkaido and in Sakhalin and the Kuril Islands, now part of the Soviet Union. Reduced in number, they live by hunting, fishing, and small-scale farming. On Hokkaido, the Ainu have attracted the attention of tourists, and some now make a living by selling reproductions of their cultural artifacts. Physically, they seem related to European peoples, i.e., they have much more body hair than Orientals, but intermarriage with Asians has introduced Oriental traits among them. Contact with the Orientals has led to culture change and assimilation, which the Ainu have resisted in the past, with decreasing success. Their religion is highly animistic and centers on a bear cult; a captive bear is sacrificed at an annual winter feast and his spirit, thus released, is believed to guard the Ainu settlements. See N. G. Munro, *Ainu Creed and Cult* (1963); Inez Hilger, *Together with the Ainu* (1971).

Aioi (ī-oiˈ), city (1970 pop. 40,657), Hyogo prefecture, W Honshu, Japan, on the Inland Sea and Aioi Bay. It is a major port with a good natural harbor and a flourishing shipbuilding industry.

air: see ATMOSPHERE; LIQUID AIR; VENTILATION.

air, law of the, in the broadest sense, all law connected with the use of the air, including radio and telegraph communications. More commonly, it refers to laws concerning civil aviation. The development of large-scale air transport after World War I brought with it the need for regulation, both national and international. In 1919 a meeting of the victorious nations of World War I resulted in the International Convention for Air Navigation, commonly called the Paris Convention. The convention was a compromise between two contradictory views: some nations held that a state had sovereignty over the air above it; others that there should be freedom of the air comparable to the freedom of the seas. The convention recognized the sovereignty of each state over its own air space without prejudice to innocent passage by aircraft of another state. It further provided that each aircraft (like each ship) must have a registered nationality. Rules were adopted as to the airworthiness of aircraft, certification of pilots as competent, and licensing of pilots. Among the 33 signatory nations were Great Britain, France, Italy, and Japan. The United States signed but did not ratify the convention. Nevertheless U.S. air laws were modeled on it. These laws are administered by the CIVIL AERONAUTICS BOARD and the FEDERAL AVIATION ADMINISTRATION. Other countries adopted legislation modeled on the Paris Convention. There were also many bilateral agreements among nations as well as general conventions—notably the Pan American Convention on Air Navigation (1925). World War II emphasized the need for sounder regulation of international air transport and for uniformity of equipment, laws, and regulations. Even before the war's end an international civil aviation conference met in Chicago in Nov., 1944. Representatives of 52 nations attended, but the USSR did not take part. There was much discussion of the "five freedoms of the air"—freedom to fly across the territory of a state without landing; freedom to land for nontraffic purposes; the right to disembark in a foreign country traffic from the country of registry of the aircraft; the right to pick up in a foreign country traffic destined for the country of registry; and the right to carry traffic between two foreign countries. The first two were accepted, but the fifth was bitterly opposed; only the first two were included in the International Air Services Transit Agreement, which was generally signed. Authorization to carry traffic between two nations is given through an agreement between those two nations. The conference, after considerable debate, set up the Provisional International Civil Aviation Organization, which had its seat at Montreal. In 1947 this organization became the INTERNATIONAL CIVIL AVIATION ORGANIZATION, affiliated with the United Nations. There have been several general conferences since the Chicago Convention to interpret its provisions, and many bilateral agreements have been concluded by parties to the convention. The successful launching of satellites necessitated the development of SPACE LAW.

air bladder, in fish: see SWIM BLADDER.

air brake: see BRAKE.

air cargo: see AVIATION.

air conditioning, mechanical process for controlling the humidity, temperature, cleanliness, and circulation of air in buildings and rooms. Indoor air is conditioned and regulated to maintain the temperature-humidity ratio that is most comfortable and healthful. In the process, dust, soot, and pollen are filtered out, and the air may be sterilized, as is sometimes done in hospitals and public places. Most air-conditioning units operate by ducting air across the colder, heat-absorbing side of a refrigeration apparatus and directing it back into the air-conditioned space (see REFRIGERATION). The refrigeration apparatus is controlled by some form of thermostat. In water-cooled air-conditioning units, the waste heat is carried away by a flow of water. For recirculation in water-cooled units, a cooling tower is used. This apparatus maintains a constant level of water in the system and replaces water lost by evaporation. The development of small, self-contained systems has greatly expanded the use of air conditioning in homes. A portable or window-mounted unit drawing 7.5 amperes or less from a 117-volt power line is usually adequate for one room. Often domestic heating systems are converted to provide complete air conditioning for a home. In the construction of office buildings in the United States, air-conditioning systems are commonly included as integral parts of the structure. First used c.1900 in the textile industry, air conditioning found little use outside of factories until the late 1920s. It is of great importance in chemical and pharmaceutical plants, where air contamination, humidity, and temperature affect manufacturing processes. See A. D. Althouse et al., *Modern Refrigeration and Air Conditioning* (1968); E. P. Anderson, *Air Conditioning* (1969); Ernest Tricomi, *A.B.C.'s of Air Conditioning* (1970).

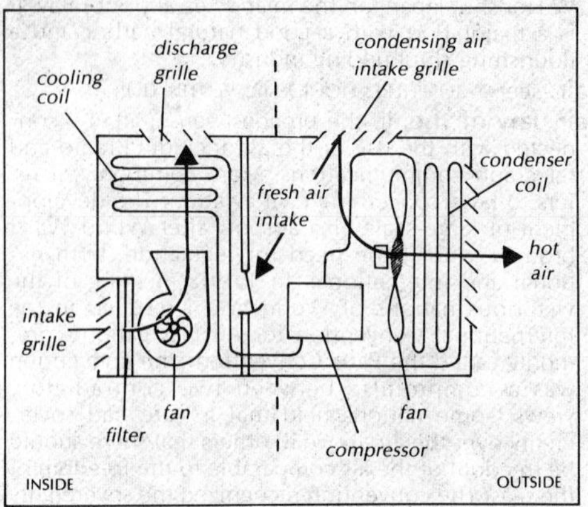

Cross section of air conditioning unit

aircraft carrier, ship designed to carry aircraft and to permit takeoff and landing of planes. The carrier's distinctive features are a flat upper deck (flight deck) that functions as a takeoff and landing field, and a main deck (hangar deck) beneath the flight deck for storing and servicing the aircraft. The aircraft carrier emerged after World War I as an experimentally modified cruiser. The first aircraft carrier built (1925) from the keel up as an aircraft carrier for the U.S. navy was the U.S.S. *Saratoga.* The aircraft carrier remained an experimental and untested war vessel until World War II, when the Japanese destroyed or drove out of the Far Eastern waters the British, Dutch, and U.S. navies with carrier-borne aircraft. By 1942 the aircraft carrier had replaced the battleship as the major unit in a modern fleet, and in World War II it was indispensable in naval operations against a sea- or land-based enemy. The battle of the Coral Sea (1942) was fought by naval aircraft, and the two opposing fleets never came within gunshot range of each other. After World War II aircraft carriers were enlarged and improved by the British and U.S. navies. With the introduction of nuclear-powered carriers in the 1960s, extremely lengthy voyages became possible because such carriers do not need regular refueling. See Norman Polmar, *Aircraft Carriers* (1969); G. L. Pawlowski, *Flat-Tops and Fledglings* (1971).

air-cushion vehicle, abbr. ACV, device designed to travel close to but above ground or water. It is also called a ground effect machine or hovercraft. These vehicles are supported in various ways. Some of them have a specially designed wing that will lift them just off the surface over which they travel when they have reached a sufficient horizontal speed. Others are supported by fans that force air down under the vehicle to create lift. In a plenum chamber vehicle the rate of leakage of this air from underneath the vehicle is reduced by placing a skirt around the lower edge of the craft. In an annular jet vehicle the rate of leakage is reduced by directing the air downward and inward from the outer edges of the vehicle. Air propellers, water propellers, or water jets usually provide forward propulsion. Most early vehicles of this type came into existence in the late 1950s. In 1962 a British vehicle became the first to go into active service on a 19-mi (31-km) ferry run. The maximum size of air-cushion vehicles is now over 100 tons; some of them travel at over 100 mi (160 km) per hr. Ships of several thousand tons and special trains, both employing air cushions, are under development. The advantages expected from air-cushion vehicles include higher speeds than those of ships and most land vehicles and lower power requirements than for helicopters of the same weights. However, a relatively smooth land or water surface below is a necessity; most of these vehicles cannot clear waves higher than 3 to 5½ ft (1–1⅔ m). See *Jane's Surface Skimmer Systems* (annually, 1968–); W. T. Gunston, *Hydrofoils and Hovercraft* (1969); Garry Hogg, *The Hovercraft Story* (1970).

Airdrie (âr'drē), burgh (1971 pop. 37,736), Lanarkshire, S central Scotland. Chemicals and electrical and electronic equipment are produced, and there are facilities for electronic research. Airdrie's free library was the first established in Scotland.

airedale terrier (âr'dāl), breed of dog developed in England in the 19th cent. It is the largest of the TERRIER group, standing about 23 in. (58.4 cm) high at the shoulder and weighing from 40 to 50 lb (18.1–22.7 kg). Its dense, wiry, close-lying coat is a mixture of tan, black, and grizzle in color. Although little can be said with certainty of its history prior to 1850, authorities generally believe the airedale was produced from crosses of the extinct black-and-tan terrier and the otterhound. It has been used to hunt a variety of game, trained as a police dog and dispatch bearer in war, bred for show competition, and kept as a pet. See DOG.

air embolism: see EMBOLUS.

airfoil, surface designed to develop a desired force by reaction with a fluid, especially air, that is flowing across the surface. For example, the fixed wing surfaces of an airplane produce lift, which opposes gravity. Airfoils that are manipulated to produce variable forces are called control surfaces. Ailerons, control surfaces hinged to the trailing edges of wings, can produce rolling, which is rotational motion of the aircraft about a line running through its fuselage, or yawing, which is rotational motion about a line running from the top to the bottom of an aircraft. Modern aircraft have fairly complex arrays of control surfaces, including elevators, a rudder, and flaps. Elevators, which are hinged to the rear of the horizontal airfoil of the tail assembly, are used to produce pitching, which occurs when an airplane in level flight points its nose upward or downward. The rudder, which is hinged to the rear of the vertical airfoil of the tail assembly, is used to produce yawing. Flaps are located near the ailerons to increase lift for takeoff and landing. Spoilers, which can be made to protrude from lifting surfaces to give controlled reduction of lift, often replace ailerons and elevators. In aircraft of the swing-wing type, in which the sweep of the wings is variable, the entire wing can be considered a control surface. Other airfoils include propeller blades and the blades utilized in turbojet engines.

Air Force, United States Department of: see DEFENSE, UNITED STATES DEPARTMENT OF.

air forces. The history of air forces begins with the use of balloons by French forces in Italy in 1859 and by Union forces in the U.S. Civil War. Balloons thereafter proved useful as a means of observation, but air forces in the modern sense date from World War I, when the offensive capabilities of the airplane were first demonstrated. The airplane was first used for war purposes by Italy against the Turks in Tripoli in 1911, but until World War I it had served mainly for reconnaissance. Germany, with a large number of airplanes and airships, established its superiority in the air at the beginning of the war. The German Fokker monoplane, with a fixed machine gun that could fire forward through the propeller blades, quickly assured Germany's superiority and inspired Allied efforts toward better aircraft. Indeed, throughout World War I such development and counterdevelopment accounted for the rapid advance of military aeronautics. The initial use of aircraft for reconnaissance made control of the skies essential to military operations. As a result, aerial combat developed, which in turn led to formation flying, dogfights, and the bombing of enemy lines of communication and munitions depots. Throughout most of the war the air forces were considered an extension of the nations' armies and were mostly employed tactically in support of the ground forces. As the effectiveness of aircraft as a tactical weapon increased, consideration was given to the establishment of air forces independent of a nation's ground forces. Giulio DOUHET, an Italian, was the first to develop a full-scale theory of strategic AIR POWER and to suggest the primacy of an independent air force. Douhet and others, such as Gen. William MITCHELL of the United States, called for the development of strong independent air forces to gain control of the air over an enemy's homeland and to destroy the enemy's means of resistance by intensive aerial bombardment of his industrial centers. Their urgings, combined with the rapid and extensive advance in aeronautical knowledge and technique that followed World War I, brought about a much broader application of air power in World War II. During the 1930s, Germany devoted great efforts to air armament and in the early years of World War II held a marked superiority over the Allies. The first great air battle in history was the BATTLE OF BRITAIN, in which the British Royal Air Force defeated the German Luftwaffe (1940) over Britain. In the Pacific, Japan entered the war with a stunning air attack launched from aircraft carriers (see AIRCRAFT CARRIER) on PEARL HARBOR. The subsequent development of air power greatly altered the nature of warfare, and the use of aircraft to control the air over both land and sea was decisive in nearly all major engagements of World War II. Airplanes were used for strategic and tactical bombing, attacking of naval and merchant ships, transportation of personnel and cargo, mining of harbors and shipping lanes, antisubmarine patrols, photographic reconnaissance, and support of ground, naval, and amphibious operations. Throughout the war the British and U.S. air forces conducted strategical bombardment of Germany, which led to the destruction of the Luftwaffe and the crippling of German industry, transportation, and communications. In the Pacific, U.S. carrier-based aircraft by the end of 1944 had destroyed the Japanese fleet and air force. In the last months of the war Japan itself was subjected to massive strategical bombardment, ending with the dropping of atomic bombs on Hiroshima and Nagasaki. Major developments of World War II included improved techniques of flying and aircraft design and an accumulation of geographical and technological knowledge essential to modern aviation. The development of nuclear weapons, jet propulsion, and the GUIDED MISSILE have combined to widen the concept of air power and the role of air forces. Wars in Korea and Vietnam were limited wars, in which tactical air operations were more important than strategic operations. However, air forces have come to assume a primary strategic role in deterring major war by employing in readiness a second-strike retaliatory force. In the United States this mission is carried by the Strategic Air Command and by the Aerospace Defense Command as well as by the Tactical Air Command. See H. B. Hinton, *Air Victory: The Men and the Machines* (1948); A. P. De Seversky, *Air Power: Key to Survival* (1950); Quentin Reynolds, *They Fought for the Sky* (1957); *Jane's All the World's Aircraft* (pub. annually since 1911); Johnnie Johnson, *Full Circle: The Story of Air Fighting* (1964); Robert B. Casari, *Encyclopedia of U.S. Military Aircraft* (2 vol., 1970).

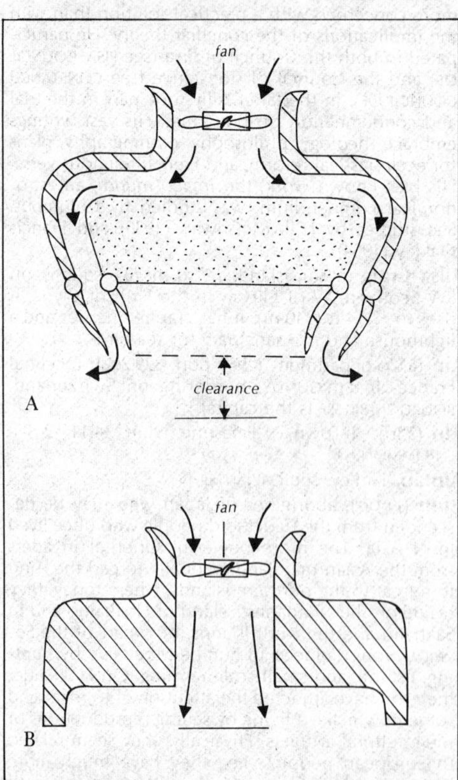

Air-cushion vehicle: In vehicles modified with a trunk or skirt (A), the rate of leakage is reduced and less power is needed to maintain the cushion. Vehicles designed to travel over deep water (B) have sides extending into the water so that the vehicle actually rides on an air bubble.

air gas: see FUEL.

airglow, faint diffuse illumination of the night sky originating in the tenuous upper atmosphere. The energy in the form of visible light is derived from the sun's ultraviolet light, which ionizes atoms and dissociates molecules at heights between 40 and 200 mi (64–322 km) above the earth's surface. When the fragments collide and recombine, some atoms and molecules are left with excess energy, which they release as light at characteristic wavelengths. Most prominent in the visible spectrum are the red and green light of oxygen and the yellow light of sodium. In polar regions the airglow is masked by the aurora; this is caused by charged particles spiraling into the atmosphere along magnetic lines of force.

air lock, compartment connecting two different environments, usually at different pressures, that enables personnel to transfer from one environment to the other. Space capsules have air locks to enable astronauts to move between the pressurized cabin and the near vacuum of space. A more common example is the air lock between the outer atmosphere and the working chamber of a CAISSON. By its means access can be gained to the working chamber without loss of pressure. It is also used at the head of tunnel excavations under water. There is a door at each end. When the outer door of the air lock is opened, men or material may be admitted into the compartment. After the outer door is closed, compressed air is admitted to raise pressure in the air lock to the level of the pressure in the working chamber, and the inner door can be opened. The reverse of this procedure takes place on leaving the working chamber. Great care must be exercised in passing workmen through an air lock, so that the change of atmospheric pressure takes place gradually. Too sudden a change of pressure may cause DECOMPRESSION SICKNESS.

airmail, transport of mail by airplanes. Demonstration flights that showed the feasibility of carrying mail by air were made in Great Britain and in the United States in 1911. In the United States, after money for experimentation was appropriated by Congress in 1918, the first regular airmail service for carrying civilian mail began on May 15, 1918. Army pilots and army equipment were used. The first flight was from Washington, D.C., to New York City; although the pilot got lost and never completed the trip, regular airmail service was soon established. The Post Office Dept. took over operation of the line in 1920, but in 1921 the line was discontinued. In May, 1920, the transcontinental route from New York City to San Francisco was completed. On July 1, 1924, coast to coast service by air was scheduled for the first time (before then the mail had been transferred to trains at night). Transpacific airmail was introduced in 1935 and transatlantic airmail in 1939. The Civil Aeronautics Authority, established in 1938, took over the work of the Bureau of Air Mail (created in the Interstate Commerce Commission in 1934). In the United States today, the Civil Aeronautics Board determines the rates to be paid by the U.S. Postal Service for the carriage of mail by air. Airmail service now extends to most parts of the world.

air mass, large body of air within the earth's atmosphere in which temperature and humidity, although varying at different heights, remain similar throughout the body at any one height. Air masses form over parts of the earth's surface called source regions, which are large, relatively uniform expanses, often ranging hundreds of thousands of square miles in area. Stable atmospheric conditions, e.g., high-pressure systems, are conducive to their formation. When a body of air remains over a source region for days or weeks, it reaches an equilibrium with the surface; radiation and convection exchanges between the earth's surface and the air, as well as evaporation and condensation, determine the air's temperature and humidity distribution. As a result of these exchanges, air masses formed over oceans generally contain more moisture than those formed over continental regions, and air masses formed in polar latitudes are colder than those from the tropics. As an air mass moves away from its source region, it brings its particular weather conditions to the areas over which it travels. At the same time, its characteristic properties are slowly modified by exposure to new environments. The boundaries between air masses, called FRONTS, are, typically, zones of rapid transition from cold to warm or from dry to moist air. This turbulence at the boundary often breeds low-pressure storms.

Aïr Mountains, Africa: see SAHARA.

air navigation, science and technology of determining the position of an aircraft with respect to the surface of the earth and accurately maintaining a desired course (see NAVIGATION). Because of the relatively high speeds of aircraft and the intense congestion of airways, the pilot of an aircraft must be able to determine quickly and accurately his position, course, and speed. The simplest and least sophisticated way in which this can be done is by pilotage, a method in which landmarks are noted and compared with an aeronautical chart. A craft flown by this technique is usually subject to visual flight regulations (VFR). These establish the minimum weather conditions under which navigation by visual reference to points outside the cockpit is permissible. Sometimes pilotage is carried on by means of electronic aids to navigation, e.g., a ground-looking radar, with which landmarks can be observed and later identified by reference to a radar map. Pilotage is not satisfactory for long trips, especially over water or terrain lacking distinctive features. In these cases, or when weather conditions do not permit navigation by visual reference, recourse to instruments is necessary. Air navigation by instruments is governed by instrument flight regulations (IFR), which require that the aircraft be equipped with the necessary instruments and that the pilot be trained in operating those instruments. Also required under IFR is the filing of a flight plan with air traffic control authorities at the departure point. The aircraft is then cleared for a given course and a given altitude. Air traffic controllers monitor the craft until it reaches its destination. Basic to air traffic control are special air routes called AIRWAYS. Airways are defined on charts and are provided with RADIO RANGES, devices that allow the pilot whose craft has a suitable receiver to determine his bearing from a fixed location. This fixed location is the site of a radio transmitter sending a specially modulated signal via a directional antenna. A second type of radio range, the VHF omnidirectional radio range, operates at very high frequencies and emits a signal that varies according to the direction in which it is transmitted. Using a special receiver, an air navigator can obtain an accurate bearing on the transmitter. For long distances LORAN, another electronic navigation system, has been developed. Other electronic aids include the radio ALTIMETER, a radar device that indicates the distance of the plane from the ground, and the ground-speed indicator, which operates by measuring the Doppler shift in a radio wave reflected from the ground. The advent of computers small enough to be airborne has made possible systems that perform astronomical observations automatically and give the pilot a readout of his position. Other similar systems use inertial devices such as free-swinging pendulums and gyroscopes as references in determining position. In addition, computer systems can be used to carry out the position-determining technique called dead reckoning by monitoring all course and speed changes of the aircraft. Pressure-based systems use the difference in reading between a radio altimeter and an aneroid altimeter as a basis for computing the local wind velocity. These automated and semiautomated procedures free the pilot from some of the activities necessary to control the aircraft and thus allow him to concentrate on actual flying of the aircraft. Another device which is useful in this way is the automatic pilot, which interprets data on direction, speed, attitude, and altitude to maintain an aircraft in straight, level flight on a given course at a given speed. Light aircraft, flown by pilotage, may have quite a simple set of navigational instruments. These would include an airspeed indicator (see PITOT STATIC SYSTEM), an aneroid altimeter, and a magnetic compass. An airspeed indicator is included in a sophisticated set of instruments to help the pilot maintain an airspeed above the value at which the airplane stalls. For supersonic and hypersonic aircraft the airspeed indicator is altered to show the airspeed as a Mach number, which is the ratio of the speed of an aircraft to the speed of sound. Advanced aircraft also use electronic systems that give the pilot highly accurate positional information for use during landing. In many cases the pilot is guided by radio communication from a controller observing the plane via ground-based radar. Some systems actually land the plane automatically, although the pilot always has the option of overriding manually.

airplane, aeroplane, or **aircraft,** heavier-than-air vehicle, mechanically driven and fitted with fixed wings that support it in flight through the dynamic action of the air. Early attempts were made to build flying machines according to the principle of bird FLIGHT, but these failed; it was not until the beginning of the 20th cent. that flight in heavier-than-air craft was achieved. On Dec. 17, 1903, Americans Orville and Wilbur WRIGHT produced the first manned, power-driven, heavier-than-air flying machine near Kitty Hawk, N.C. The first flight lasted 12 sec, but later flights on the same day were a little longer; a safe landing was made after each attempt. The machine was a biplane (an airplane with two main supporting surfaces, or wings) with two propellers chain-driven by a gasoline motor. Modern airplanes are monoplanes (airplanes with one wing) and may be high-wing, mid-wing, or low-wing. Airplanes may be further classified as driven by propeller, jet, turbojet, or rocket. The airplane has six main parts—fuselage, wings, stabilizer (or tail plane), rudder, one or more engines, and landing gear. The fuselage is the main body of the machine, customarily streamlined in form. It usually contains control equipment, and space for passengers and cargo. The wings are the main supporting surfaces. The objects, such as fuel tanks and engines, that are carried outside the fuselage are enclosed in structures called nacelles, or pods, to reduce air drag. The lift of an airplane, or the force that supports it in flight, is basically the result of the direct action of the air against the surfaces of the wings, which causes air to be accelerated downward. The lift varies with the speed, there being a minimum speed at which flight can be maintained. This is known as the stall speed. At the trailing edge of the wings are auxiliary hinged surfaces known as ailerons that are used to gain lateral control and to turn the airplane. Directional stability is provided by the tail fin, a fixed vertical AIRFOIL at the rear of the plane. The stabilizer, or tail plane, is a fixed horizontal airfoil at the rear of the airplane used to suppress undesired pitching motions. To the rear of the stabilizer are usually hinged the elevators, movable auxiliary surfaces that are used to produce controlled pitching. The rudder, generally at the rear of the tail fin, is a movable auxiliary airfoil that gives the craft a yawing movement in normal flight. The rear array of airfoils is called the empennage, or tail assembly. Some aircraft have additional flaps near the ailerons that can be lowered during takeoff and landing to augment lift at the cost of increased drag. On some airplanes hinged controls are replaced or assisted by spoilers, which are ridges that can be made to project from airfoils. Until recently, most engines were of the internal-combustion, piston-operated type, which may be air- or liquid-cooled. During and after World War II, duct-type and gas-turbine engines became increasingly important, and since then JET PROPULSION has become the main form of power in most commercial and military aircraft. This has had a major effect upon airplane design, which is closely associated with the ratio between power load (horsepower) and weight. The Wright brothers' first engine weighed about 12 lb (5.4 kg) per horsepower. The modern piston engine weighs about 1 lb (0.4 kg) or less per horsepower, and jet and gas-turbine engines are much lighter. With the use of jet engines and the resulting higher speeds, airplanes have become less dependent on large values of lift from the wings. Consequently, wings have been shortened and swept back so as to produce less drag, especially at supersonic speeds. In some cases these radically backswept wings have evolved into a single triangular lifting surface, known as a delta wing, that is bisected by the fuselage of the plane. Similar alterations have been made in the vertical and horizontal surfaces of the tail, again with the aim of decreasing drag. The lessened lift associated with swept-back designs increases the length of runway needed for takeoffs and landings. To keep runway lengths within reasonable limits the variable-sweep, or swing, wing has been developed. A plane of this type can extend its wings for maximum lift in taking off and landing, and swing them back for travel at high speeds. A proposed variant of the swing wing, in which one wing sweeps to the rear and another forward, produces an arrangement that causes a minimum shock wave at supersonic speeds. It is thought that if this modification is applied to supersonic transport (SST) designs it will somewhat lessen their objectionable noise levels. No solution has been proposed to lessen their high fuel consumption. Recent developments in fan-jet engines, in which a turbine powers a set of vanes that drive air rearward to augment thrust, have made supersonic flight possible at low altitude. Much research has also gone into reducing the noise and air pollution caused by jet engines.The landing gear is the understructure that supports the weight of the craft when on the ground or on the water and that reduces the shock on landing. There are five common types—the wheel, float, boat, skid, and ski types. For certain applications, e.g., short-haul traffic between small airports, it is desirable to have airplanes capable of operating from a runway of minimum length. Two approaches to the problem have been tried. One,

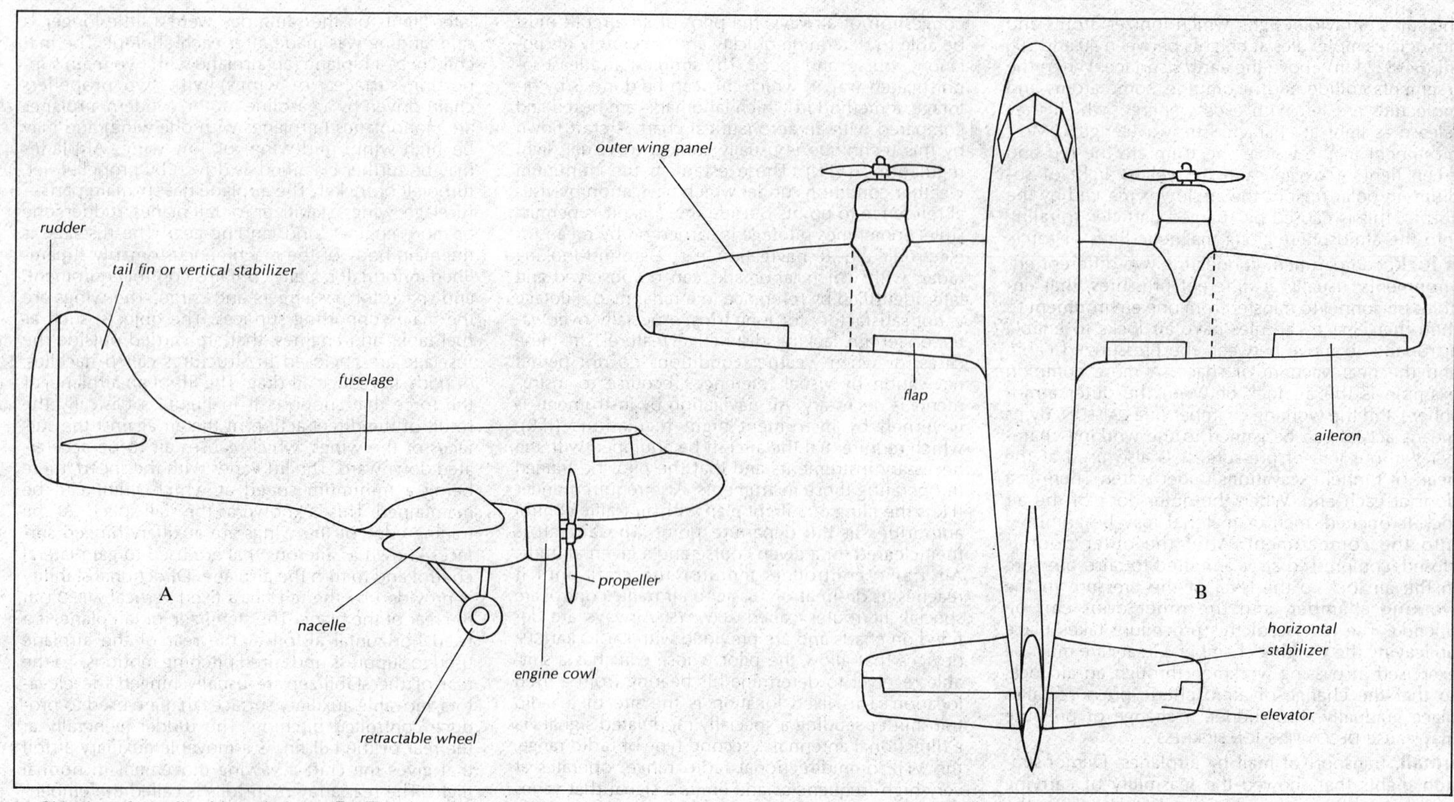

A. *Side view of propeller-driven airplane* B. *Top view of propeller-driven airplane*

the VERTICAL TAKEOFF AND LANDING (VTOL) approach, seeks to produce craft that take off and land like HELICOPTERS, but that can fly much faster. The other approach, SHORT TAKEOFF AND LANDING (STOL), seeks to design more conventional aircraft that have reduced runway requirements. See AERODYNAMICS; AIRPORT; AVIATION; AUTOGIRO; GLIDER; SEAPLANE. See bibliography under AVIATION.

air plant: see EPIPHYTE.

air pollution, contamination of the air by noxious gases and minute particles of solid and liquid matter (particulates) in concentrations that endanger health. The major sources of air pollution are transportation, which is responsible for more than 50% by weight of all air pollution in the United States, power and heat generation, industrial processes, and the burning of SOLID WASTE. The combustion of GASOLINE and other hydrocarbon fuels in AUTOMOBILES, trucks, and jet airplanes produces several primary pollutants: nitrogen oxides, gaseous hydrocarbons, and carbon monoxide, as well as large quantities of particulates, chiefly lead. In the presence of sunlight, nitrogen oxides combine with hydrocarbons to form a secondary class of pollutants, the photochemical oxidants, among them OZONE and the eye-stinging peroxyacetylnitrate (PAN). Nitrogen oxides also react with oxygen in the air to form nitrogen dioxide, a foul-smelling brown gas. In urban areas like Los Angeles where transportation is the main cause of air pollution, nitrogen dioxide tints the air, blending with other contaminants and the atmospheric water vapor to produce brown SMOG. In cities, air may be severely polluted not only by transportation but also by the burning of fossil fuels (oil and coal) in generating stations, factories, office buildings, and homes, and by the incineration of garbage. The massive combustion produces tons of ash, soot, and other particulates responsible for the gray smog of cities like New York and Chicago, along with enormous quantities of sulfur oxides. These oxides rust iron, damage building stone, decompose nylon, tarnish silver, and kill plants. Like photochemical pollutants, sulfur oxides contribute to the incidence of respiratory diseases such as emphysema, bronchitis, asthma, and even influenza and the common cold. When a weather condition known as a TEMPERATURE INVERSION prevents dispersal of smog, inhabitants of the area, especially children and the elderly and chronically ill, are warned to stay indoors and avoid physical stress. The dramatic and debilitating effects of severe air pollution episodes in cities throughout the world—such as the London smog of 1952 that resulted in 4,000 deaths—have alerted governments to the necessity for crisis procedures. But even everyday air pollution may insidiously affect health and behavior. Carbon monoxide, for example, by driving oxygen out of the bloodstream, causes apathy, fatigue, headache, disorientation, and decreased muscular coordination and visual acuity. Air pollution may possibly harm populations in ways so subtle or slow that they have not yet been detected. For that reason research is now under way to assess the long-term effects of chronic exposure to low levels of air pollution—what most people experience—as well as to determine how air pollutants interact with one another in the body and with physical factors such as nutrition, stress, alcohol, cigarette smoking, and common medicines. Another subject of investigation is the relation of air pollution to cancer, birth defects, and genetic mutations. Every industrial process exhibits its own pattern of air pollution. Petroleum refineries are responsible for extensive hydrocarbon and particulate pollution. Iron and steel mills, metal smelters, pulp and paper mills, chemical plants, cement and asphalt plants—all discharge vast amounts of various particulates. Uninsulated high-voltage power lines ionize the adjacent air, forming ozone and other hazardous pollutants. Airborne pollutants from other sources include INSECTICIDES, HERBICIDES, radioactive FALLOUT, and DUST from fertilizers, mining operations, and livestock feedlots. The yearly economic toll exacted by air pollution from all sources has been estimated at more than $16 billion in the United States alone. To combat pollution in the United States, the Clean Air Act Amendments of 1970 gave the Environmental Protection Agency (EPA) the authority to establish and enforce air pollution standards. National "ambient air quality standards" describe the concentrations of various pollutants allowable in the air. To meet those standards, the states are required to regulate the emissions of various pollutants from existing stationary sources, such as power plants and incinerators. The EPA itself determines emission standards for new factories and new motor vehicles and for certain extremely hazardous industrial poisons such as asbestos, beryllium, mercury, and lead. The law then requires that local governments, public utilities, and factories install pollution control devices such as smokestack scrubbers, electrostatic precipitators, and filters that will prevent gases and particulates from reaching the environment. Auto manufacturers must install exhaust controls or develop an improved engine that will not generate gaseous or particulate contaminants. In the long run the most satisfactory solutions to the air pollution problem may well be the elimination of fossil fuels and the ultimate replacement of the INTERNAL COMBUSTION ENGINE. To these ends efforts have begun in the United States, Japan, and Europe to develop alternative energy sources, such as nuclear fusion and solar heat (see ENERGY, SOURCES OF), as well as different kinds of transportation engines, perhaps powered by electricity or steam. See ENVIRONMENTALISM; POLLUTION. See R. G. Bond et al., *Air Pollution* (1972); U.S. Council on Environmental Quality, *Environmental Quality* (3d Annual Report, 1972); S. J. Williamson, *Fundamentals of Air Pollution* (1973).

airport or **airfield,** place for landing and departure of aircraft, usually with facilities for housing and maintaining planes and for receiving and discharging passengers and cargo. The essential requirements in airport construction are that the field be as level as possible; that the ground be firm and easily drained; that approaches to runways be free of trees, hills, buildings, and other obstructions; and that the site be as free as possible of smoke and weather that produces low-visibility conditions. The runways of large airports vary from 2,500 to 12,000 ft (762–3,658 m) in length and 100 to 200 ft (30–61 m) in width. Narrower paved strips called taxiways that connect the runways to other parts of the airport are entered by aircraft as soon as possible after landing, thus freeing the runways for use by other traffic. A taxiway and a runway are usually connected at each end and at several intermediate points. Besides the hangars (buildings for housing and servicing aircraft), airports are usually provided with office and terminal buildings which house administrative, traffic control, communication, and weather observation personnel. The rapid development of aircraft, especially after the introduction of jet propulsion, has created problems for all major airports. Greater speed and weight of aircraft have made longer and more durable runways necessary. The increasing number of high-speed jet aircraft has caused problems of noise control and has led many communities to reject plans to build an airport within their boundaries. Locating airports away from densely populated areas can alleviate noise problems, but this solution makes it difficult for passengers and others to reach the airport. In England airports are sometimes called aerodromes. See B. J. Hurren, *Airports of the World* (1971); G. E. Campbell, *Airport Management and Operation* (1972); E. G. Blankenship, *Airports,* (1974).

air power, concept that achieved progressive importance in military strategy with the rapid development of aviation and the increased use of aircraft in war during the 20th cent. (see AIR FORCES). The somewhat tentative use of scout planes at the beginning of World War I was followed by the creation of small forces of fighter planes that engaged in aerial combat and some bombing. The Germans took the lead in air strategy, but the Allies soon closed the gap. After the war a few Allied strategists, among them Gen. William MITCHELL, Air Chief Marshal Sir Hugh Montague TRENCHARD, and Gen. Giulio DOUHET, fought for the intensive development of air power and pleaded for large air forces, arguing that future wars would be won by strategic bombardment of an enemy's industrial centers, thereby destroying the economic means of conducting a war. Their theories were controversial, and many continued to see air power as merely an adjunct to ground power. However, Great Britain, France, and Italy established separate departments of government for air strategy, and by 1935 the U.S. Air Corps Tactical School had developed and was teaching a full-blown theory of high-level precision bombardment. Adolf Hitler effectively intimidated other nations by the threat of air war, and the early days of World War II seemed to uphold Hitler's boasts of the effectiveness of the Luftwaffe under Hermann Goering. Aircraft were to a great extent responsible for German victories in Poland, Norway, the Low Countries, and France. However, Germany suffered a setback with the failure of the Luftwaffe to destroy the Royal Air Force in the BATTLE OF BRITAIN. The capture of Crete (1941) by air-transported troops seemed to bear out some of the more extreme claims of air power enthusiasts. The effect of air power in revolutionizing naval warfare was demonstrated by the attack by Japanese aircraft, launched from aircraft carriers, on PEARL HARBOR. Extensive use of the AIRCRAFT CARRIER was decisive in the battles of the CORAL SEA and MIDWAY, and thereafter aircraft were employed in all major naval battles. Throughout the war the Allies conducted an intensive campaign of strategic bombardment against Germany and wrought enormous destruction in German cities; postwar studies, however, have cast doubt on the effectiveness of this campaign. Aircraft also provided invaluable support to ground forces throughout the war by attacking enemy troops, transport, and supply bases. And it was, of course, aircraft that delivered the atomic bombs that finally ended World War II. After the war, moderates argued that no major battle had been won by air forces alone, but only by air forces combined with land or naval forces. Air-power advocates argued that air power should have been used as the primary strategic weapon instead of being used mainly to support ground troops seeking to occupy territory. The importance of air power was, however, accepted by all. In Korea air forces of the United Nations Command effectively enveloped the North Korean army and later cut supply arteries to Chinese Communist troops so that an armistice could be negotiated. Similar ground-air tactics were employed by the United States in Vietnam, while the North Vietnamese made effective use of Soviet-built ground-to-air missiles and tactical air support. After World War II the GUIDED MISSILE came to surpass the airplane as a strategic weapon, but manned bombers as well as offensive and antiballistic missiles have had an important role in the building and maintenance of air power by major nations. There is continued controversy over the number and types of strategic missiles and bombers to be designed and built, but the primary role of air power as a deterrent to attack is hardly contested. See Giulio Douhet, *Command of the Air* (1927, tr. 1942); W. F. Craven and J. L. Cate, ed., *The Army Air Forces in World War II* (7 vol., 1948–58); C. K. Webster and Noble Frankland, *The Strategic Air Offensive against Germany, 1939–1945* (4 vol., 1961); S. M. Ulanoff, *True Stories of Strategic Air Power from World War I to the Present* (1971).

airship or **dirigible balloon** (dĭr'əjəbəl), aircraft consisting of a cigar-shaped balloon that carries a propulsion system, a steering mechanism, and accommodations for passengers, crew, and cargo. Although sails, paddles, and flapping wings were tried, propellers proved to be the most suitable means of propulsion. The balloon section is filled with a lighter-than-air gas, either helium or hydrogen, to give the airship its lift; helium, although lesser in lifting power, has the decided advantage of being nonflammable. In the nonrigid type of airship the balloon maintains its form by the internal gas pressure. In the semirigid type the form is maintained in a similar manner with addition of a rigid keel. The rigid type maintains its form by having a balloonlike hull of metal that holds its shape regardless of the internal gas pressure; inside the hull are a number of small balloons called gas cells that hold a lifting gas. The first successful power-driven airship was built by the French inventor Henri Giffard in 1852. Many experimenters, including the Tissandier brothers of France, followed his efforts. In 1884, Charles Renard and Artur Krebs, also of France, built and successfully operated an airship, *La France*, with propulsion obtained from electric storage batteries. The Brazilian Alberto Santos-Dumont was prominent in the early development of the nonrigid airship. This type, sometimes called a blimp, is simple in construction and very light. It proved useful during World War II for coastal patrol and antisubmarine warfare; before the war it was used commercially in such activities as advertising, traffic control, and mail delivery. Blimps were kept in use by the U.S. navy until the early 1960s. Count Ferdinand von ZEPPELIN of Germany invented the first rigid airship, which was completed in 1900. Except for the *Mayfly*, which met with disaster upon completion, the building of rigid airships was not undertaken in England until World War I, when the *R33*, *R34*, and others were built. The *R34* was the first airship to cross (1919) the Atlantic, returning in 75 hr. Postwar airships constructed in England were the *R100* and *R101*, which were built as commercial vessels. The *Graf Zeppelin*, built in Germany in 1926–27, traveled 20,000 mi (32,000 km) around the world in 1929. The first rigid airship built in the United States, the *Shenandoah*, completed in 1923, was the first vessel to use helium as a lifting gas. She was wrecked by a violent storm in 1927. The *Los Angeles*, built by Germany as part of her reparations payment to the United States and completed in 1924, was successfully navigated across the Atlantic late in 1924 by Capt. Hugo Eckener of Germany. The German airship *Hindenburg*, built in 1936, and those aboard burned at its mooring mast at Lakehurst, N.J., in 1937. No rigid airship survived World War II. See M. M. Mooney, *The Hindenburg* (1972); Patrick Abbott, *Airship* (1973); Robert Jackson, *Airships* (1973); D. H. Robinson, *Giants in the Sky* (1973).

airsickness: see MOTION SICKNESS.

airspeed indicator, instrument that indicates the speed of a vehicle, especially an aircraft, relative to the speed of the surrounding air. See AIR NAVIGATION; PITOT STATIC SYSTEM.

air transportation: see AVIATION.

airway, air route between air traffic centers that is over terrain best suited for emergency landings, with landing fields at intervals equipped with aids to air navigation and with a communication system for the transmission of information pertinent to the operation of aircraft. Airways do not always follow a straight line, since it is often advisable to detour in order to avoid mountains or certain localities where weather conditions are generally unfavorable. Definite flying rules have been established that require all aircraft to keep to the right of an airway and to observe regulations governing minimum altitudes, approaching and overtaking other aircraft, and acrobatic flying.

Airy, Sir George Biddell, 1801–92, English astronomer. The son of a poor farmer, he distinguished himself as Senior Wrangler at Cambridge, where he was elected fellow of Trinity College (1824) and appointed professor (1826). As Astronomer Royal and director of the Royal Greenwich Observatory from 1835 to 1881, he organized the efficient and accurate observation of stellar positions. Airy wrote many governmental reports on astronomical and other subjects, published works on celestial mechanics, and made discoveries in theoretical and practical optics, including the cylindrical lens for correcting astigmatism, an eye defect he himself possessed. See his autobiography (1896).

Aisha (ī'shə, ä'ĭshä"), c.614–678, favorite wife of MUHAMMAD the Prophet. She was the daughter of Abu Bakr and was married to the Prophet soon after the hegira. A brilliant, astute woman, she was devoted to her husband and his teachings, and after his death she exerted considerable influence, especially against Ali. She fomented an unsuccessful revolt during Ali's tenure of the caliphate. The name also appears as Ayesha or Aishah. See Nabia Abbott, *Aishah, the Beloved of Mohammed* (1942, repr. 1973).

Aisne (ĕn), department (1968 pop. 526,346), NE France, in ÎLE-DE-FRANCE, PICARDY, and CHAMPAGNE, touching the Belgian border. LAON is the capital.

Aix-en-Provence (ĕk-säN-prôväNs'), city (1968 pop. 93,671), Bouches-du-Rhône dept., in Provence, SE France. It is a commercial center in an area producing olives, grapes, and almonds. Its manufactures include food products, wine-making equipment, and electrical apparatus. Founded (123 B.C.) by the Romans near the site of mineral springs, it has long been a popular spa. There, in 102 B.C., Marius defeated the Teutons. It became an archiepiscopal see in the 5th cent. It has been the capital of Provence since the 12th cent. (except when replaced by Arles), and passed with Provence to the crown in 1487, becoming the seat of a provincial PARLEMENT. A music center since the 11th cent. and a focus of PROVENÇAL LITERATURE, Aix has a university (founded 1409; recently combined with one at Marseilles). A notable structure is the Cathedral of Saint-Sauveur (13th–14th cent.). A picturesque town, Aix has become a favorite sojourn for painters. A music festival is held each summer. Cézanne was born and died there.

Aix-la-Chapelle: see AACHEN, West Germany.

Aix-la-Chapelle, Treaty of (ĕks-lä-shäpĕl'). **1** Compact of May 2, 1668, that ended the French invasion of the Spanish Netherlands (see DEVOLUTION, WAR OF). France kept most of its conquests in Flanders; Cambrai, Aire, Saint-Omer, and the province of Franche-Comté were returned to Spain; and the remainder of Spain's possessions in the Low Countries were guaranteed by the TRIPLE ALLIANCE. **2** Treaty of 1748, ending the War of the AUSTRIAN SUCCESSION. In general, it restored the *status quo ante*, but it awarded Silesia and Glatz to Prussia and conferred the duchies of Parma, Piacenza, and Guastalla on the Spanish infante Philip. It confirmed the PRAGMATIC SANCTION of 1713, and it renewed Britain's privilege (acquired 1713) over transporting slaves to Spanish America, the trade agreements with Britain regarding the Spanish colonies, and the recognition of the Protestant succession in England.

Aix-les-Bains (ĕks-lā-băN'), town (1968 pop. 20,718), Savoie dept., SE France, situated on Lake Bourget at the foot of the Alps. It is a popular resort and spa. The town's alum and sulphur springs have been frequented since Roman times. There are ruins of Roman baths.

Aizu-Wakamatsu (ī'zo͞o-wäkämät'so͞o), city (1970 pop. 101,065), Fukushima prefecture, N Honshu, Japan. Its major products are wooden items, sake, rice, and persimmons. The capture of its castle by imperial forces in 1868 marked the end of civil war in Honshu.

Ajaccio (äyät'chō), town (1968 pop. 42,300), capital of Corsica, France, on the Gulf of Ajaccio, an inlet of the Mediterranean. A fortified seaport, it is an important market town, an active industrial center, and a year-round tourist attraction. Its present site was established by Genoese colonists in 1492. Ajaccio was the birthplace of Napoleon I; the house where he was born is preserved. Other points of interest are the old cathedral (16th cent.) and St. Erasmus Church (17th cent.; restored). In World War II, Ajaccio was occupied by the Italians until the people successfully revolted (Sept., 1943) with the aid of Free French troops.

Ajah (ā'jə), variant of AIAH **1**.

Ajalon (ă'jəlŏn, ā'-), variant of AIJALON.

Ajanta (əjŭn'tə), village, Maharashtra state, W central India, in the Ajanta Hills. The famous Ajanta caves, discovered in 1819, contain remarkable examples of Buddhist art. The caves, carved out of the side of a steep ravine, consist of chapels and monasteries dating from c.200 B.C.–A.D. 650 with magnificent frescoes and sculpture depicting scenes from the life of Buddha.

Ajax (ā'jăks), Gr. *Aias*, in Greek mythology. **1** Hero of the Trojan War, son of TELAMON, thus called the Telamonian Ajax, also called Ajax the Greater. In the *Iliad* he is represented as a gigantic man, slow of thought and speech, but quick in battle and always showing courage. He led the troops of Salamis against Troy and was one of the foremost Greek warriors, fighting both Hector and Odysseus to draws. He and Odysseus rescued the corpse of Achilles from the Trojans, but when the armor of Achilles was awarded to Odysseus, the disappointment of Ajax was so great that he went mad and committed suicide. The *Ajax* of Sophocles deals with the madness and death of the great warrior. Ajax had hero cults at Salamis, Attica, and Troad. **2** Leader of the forces from Locris in the Trojan War, called the Locrian Ajax, Ajax of Oileus (after his father, Oileus), or Ajax the Lesser, because he was not the equal of the Telamonian Ajax. In the sack of Troy he violated Cassandra at the altar of Athena, and Athena caused him to be shipwrecked on the way home. Poseidon saved him, but Ajax, boasting of his own power, defied the lightning to strike him down and was instantly struck by it. Other versions of the story say that he stole the PALLADIUM and that later Poseidon destroyed him for blasphemy.

Ajivika (äjē'vĭkə), religious sect of medieval India, once of major importance. The Ajivikas were an ascetic, atheistic, anti-Brahmanical community whose pessimistic doctrines are related to those of JAINISM. Its founder, Gosala (d. c.484 B.C.), was, it is said, a friend of Mahavira, the founder of Jainism. Gosala denied that a man's actions could influence the process of transmigration, which proceeded according to a rigid pattern, controlled in the smallest detail by an impersonal cosmic principle, *Niyati,* or destiny. After a period of prosperity under Asoka, the sect rapidly declined and only retained local importance in SE India, where it survived until the 14th cent. See A. L. Basham, *History and Doctrines of the Ajivikas* (1951).

Ajman (äjmän'), sheikhdom (1968 pop. 4,245), c.100 sq mi (260 sq km), part of the federation of UNITED ARAB EMIRATES, E Arabia, primarily on the Persian Gulf. The smallest member of the federation, Ajman consists principally of a town (pop. 3,725) of the same name and two mountain villages. Oil production in Ajman began in 1964. A former British protectorate, it joined the United Arab Emirates in 1971.

Ajmer (ăjmēr', əj-), former state, NW India. Now part of Rajasthan state, it formerly consisted of two detached areas surrounded by Rajasthan and was identical with the former British province of Ajmer-Merwara. The city of **Ajmer** (1971 pop. 262,480), the former capital and now a district administrative center, was founded in the 12th cent. The city is a trade center and has cotton mills and railroad shops. Marble is quarried nearby. Ajmer was a Mogul military base; it was there that Jehangir received Sir Thomas Roe, ambassador of James I of England. A Jain temple (constructed 1153; now a mosque), the tomb of the Muslim saint Muin-al-din Hasan Chishti, and a palace of AKBAR are the most notable historic buildings. Mayo Rajkumar College is in Ajmer.

Ajodhya (əjōd'yə) or **Ayodhya** (əyōd'yə), village, Uttar Pradesh state, N India, on the Gogra River. It is a joint municipality with Faizabad. Ajodhya was the capital of the kingdom of Kosala (7th cent. B.C.). Long associated with Hindu legend, the town is a center of pilgrimage and is one of the seven sites sacred to Hindus. It is also called Oudh.

Akaba: see AQABA, Jordan.

Akademgorodok (äkädămgô'rôdôk), city, W central Siberian USSR, near NOVOSIBIRSK. A scientific center begun in 1959, it is the site of 15 institutes of the Soviet Academy of Sciences.

Akan (ā'kăn), descendant of Esau. Gen. 36.27. Jakan: 1 Chron. 1.42.

Akan (əkän', äk'ən), people of W Africa, primarily in S Ghana, E Ivory Coast, and parts of Togo. They speak languages of the Twi branch of the Kwa subfamily. Although patrilineal descent is recognized, matrilineal descent is more important; social organization is through clans. The ASHANTI and the FANTI, both of Akan stock, developed powerful confederacies in the 17th and 18th cent.

Akashi (ä"kä'shē), city (1970 pop. 206,525), Hyogo prefecture, W Honshu, Japan, on the Harima Sea and the Akashi Channel. It is a fishing port and industrial center where electrical machinery is produced.

Akbar (ăk'bär), 1542–1605, Mogul emperor of India (1556–1605); son of Humayun, grandson of Babur. He succeeded to the throne under a regent, Bairam Khan, who rendered loyal service in expanding and consolidating the Mogul domains before he was summarily dismissed (1560) by the young king. Akbar, however, continued the policy of conquest. A magnetic personality and an outstanding general, he gradually enlarged his empire to include Afghanistan, Baluchistan, and nearly all of the Indian peninsula north of the Godavari River. To unify the vast state, he established a uniform system of administration throughout his empire and adopted a policy of religious toleration. Having defeated the Rajputs, the most militant of the Hindu peoples, he allied himself with them, giving their chiefs high positions in his army and government; he twice married Rajput princesses. Although he was himself illiterate, Akbar's courts at Delhi, Agra, and FATEHPUR SIKRI were centers of the arts, letters, and learning. He was much impressed with Persian culture, and because of him the later Mogul empire bore an indelible Persian stamp. At his sumptuous courts, where he reigned as a philosopher-king, Akbar surrounded himself with Muslim divines, Hindu Brahmans, and Jesuits. Apparently disillusioned with orthodox Islam and hoping to bring about religious unity within his empire, he promulgated (1582) the Din-i-Ilahi [divine faith], an eclectic creed derived from Islam, Hinduism, Zoroastrianism, and Christianity. A simple, monotheistic cult, tolerant in outlook, it centered on Akbar as prophet. This religious revolution led to serious rebellions by outraged Muslims. The Din-i-Ilahi never took hold in India and disappeared soon after Akbar's death. Akbar, generally considered the greatest of the Mogul emperors, was succeeded by his son Jahangir. See biographies by Laurence Binyon (1930) and V. A. Smith (2d rev. ed. 1966); R. Krishnamurti, *Akbar, the Religious Aspect* (1961).

Akeldama (əkĕl'dəmə), variant of ACELDAMA.

Akeley, Carl Ethan (āk'lē), 1864–1926, American naturalist, animal sculptor, and author, b. Orleans co., N.Y. He served (1887–95) at the Museum of Milwaukee; from 1895 to 1909 he was at the Field Museum, Chicago (now the Chicago Natural History Museum), and from 1909 he was affiliated with the American Museum of Natural History, New York City. His principal contribution was in the field of taxidermy; his system of mounting specimens by applying the skin to a finely contoured model is still used by museums. His animal sculptures and paintings may be seen in Akeley Hall in the Museum of Natural History and in the Chicago Natural History Museum. The extraordinary realism of Akeley's displays derived from his wide field experience; he made numerous expeditions to Africa to collect specimens. He invented the cement gun for use in his own work, and the Akeley camera is widely used by naturalists. His influence led to the establishment in 1926 of the Albert National Park, an animal sanctuary in Zaïre. He wrote *In Brightest Africa* (1923).

Akenside, Mark (ā'kĭnsīd), 1721–70, English poet and physician. His chief literary work was the didactic poem *The Pleasures of Imagination* (1744). Among his other works are the neoclassical *Odes on Various Subjects* (1745) and the *Epistle to Curio* (1744), a vigorous political satire. Akenside's conversion to Tory principles at the accession of George III earned him the appointment of physician to the queen. See biography by C. T. Houpt (1944).

Akershus (ä'kərs-ho͞os"), county (1972 est. pop. 332,000), 1,895 sq mi (4,908 sq km), SE Norway, bordering on the Oslofjord in the south and on Sweden in the east. The capital is Oslo. The county has productive farms and extensive forests. Manufactures include processed food, textiles, metals, and forest products.

Akhelóos or **Achelous** (äkhĕlô'ôs), river, 137 mi (221 km) long, rising in the Pindus Mts., NW Greece, and flowing generally south, traversing many mountain gorges, and emptying into the Ionian Sea opposite Keffallinía. It is used for floating logs and is an important source of hydroelectric power. It formed a part of the boundary between ancient Aetolia and Acarnania and was formerly called Aspropotamos.

Akhenaton: see IKHNATON.

Akhetaton: see TEL EL AMARNA.

Akhisar (äk"həsär'), city (1970 pop. 47,856), W Turkey. It is in a region where tobacco, cotton, and grapes are grown. The city is noted for its rugs. It is the biblical THYATIRA.

Akhmatova, Anna (än'nə əkhmä'təvə), pseud. of **Anna Andreyevna Gorenko** (əndrā'əvnə gôryĕng'kô), 1888–1966, Russian poet of the ACMEIST school. Her brief lyrics, simply and musically written in the tradition of Pushkin, attained great popularity. Her themes were personal, emotional, and often ironic. Among her most popular volumes are *Chiotki* [the rosary] (1914) and *Iva* [the willow tree] (1940). She was married to the Acmeist poet Gumilev until 1918. Akhmatova remained silent for two decades. She began writing again at the outbreak of World War II, after which her writings regained popularity. She was harshly denounced by the Soviet regime in 1946 and 1957 for "bourgois decadence." See her *Selected Poems* (Fr. 1969) and *Poems of Akhmatova* (tr. 1973); study by S. N. Driver (1972).

Akhmim (ăkhmēm'), city (1966 pop. 44,800), E central Egypt, on the Nile. Textiles and handicrafts are produced. The ancient Chemmis and Panopolis, the city was long noted for its linen and limestone; the temple of Pan is there.

Akiba ben Joseph (əkē'bə), A.D. c.50–A.D. c.135, Palestinian rabbi. He was one of the first Jewish scholars to make a systematic compilation of the Hebrew oral laws. This compilation, known as the *Mishna of Rabbi Akiba,* exercised a profound influence upon the development of Mishnaic doctrines. Akiba believed in the Messianic mission of BAR KOKBA and sided with him in his revolt against Rome. He was idolized by the people, and the facts of his life are obscured with legends. He was incarcerated and, it is said, tortured to death by the Romans; he is one of the martyrs mentioned in the Jewish penitential prayer. See study by Louis Finkelstein (1936, repr. 1970).

Akihito (äkē'hētō), 1933–, Japanese crown prince, son of HIROHITO. In 1952 he was officially proclaimed heir to the throne. A popular figure, he has traveled widely, visiting Great Britain, Canada, the United States, and many countries of South America and Asia. In April, 1959, he married Michiko Shoda, a commoner; it was the first time that an heir to the Japanese throne had wed outside of the court nobility. They have three children; the oldest, a son, was born in 1960.

Akimiski, island: see JAMES BAY, Canada.

Akita (ä'kētä), city (1970 pop. 235,879), capital of Akita prefecture, NW Honshu, Japan, on the Sea of Japan. An oil-refining center, it is also a large port that exports lumber and rice. It became an important feudal town in the 8th cent., and its castle-fort (733) still stands. **Akita** prefecture (1970 pop. 1,241,261), 4,503 sq mi (11,663 sq km), contains Japan's largest oil field and copper mine. The prefecture's mountains have extensive stands of quality timber, and its fertile lowlands yield crops of rice, tobacco, and fruit. Akita (the capital), Noshiro (the chief port), Tsushisoki, and Yokote are centers of population.

Akita (äkē'tə), breed of large dog developed in Japan from ancient ancestry and used originally as a hunter of such game as deer, wild boar, and bear. It stands from 20 to 27 in. (50.8–68.6 cm) high at the shoulder and weighs from 75 to 110 lb (34.1–49.9 kg). Its double coat consists of a thick, furry underlayer and a medium-length, harsh, straight topcoat which may be any shade of cream, brown, red, gray, black, silver, or brindle. A muscular dog with erect ears and tail curved over its back, the Akita has been used in the 20th cent. as a police and war dog and as a companion and watchdog. It is rapidly gaining popularity in the United States and is presently exhibited in the miscellaneous class at the dog shows sanctioned by the American Kennel Club. See DOG.

Akka: see PYGMY.

Akkad (ă'kăd, ä'käd), ancient region of Mesopotamia, occupying the northern part of later Babylonia. The southern part was SUMER. In both regions city-states had begun to appear in the 4th millennium B.C. In Akkad a Semitic language, Akkadian, was spoken. Akkad flourished after SARGON began (c.2340 B.C.) to spread wide his conquests, which ranged from his capital, Agade, also known as Akkad, to the Mediterranean shores. He united city-states into a vast organized empire. Furthermore, he was overlord of all the petty states of Sumer and Akkad, as were his successors, most notably Naramsin. The merit of Sargonic art can be seen in the stele of Naramsin. The naturalistic sculpture, depicting a wide range of mythological scenes, reflected a high achievement in glyptic art. After more than a century the empire declined and was overrun by mountain tribes. When the Akkadian empire had fallen, Mesopotamia was in chaos. Peace was maintained only in the south in the city-state of Lagash under Gudea. Lagash was later absorbed by the 3d dynasty of Ur, which governed both Akkad and Sumer. Toward the end of the 3d millennium Elam took over most of the power as a new wave of Semitic-speaking peoples entered Mesopotamia. It was by defeating the Elamites that Hammurabi was able to create Babylonia. The name Akkad also appears as Accad.

Akkadian (əkā'dēən), language belonging to the Northeast Semitic subdivision of the Semitic subfamily of the Hamito-Semitic family of languages (see HAMITO-SEMITIC LANGUAGES). Also called Assyro-Babylonian, Akkadian (or Accadian) was current in ancient Mesopotamia (now Iraq) from about 3,000 B.C. until the time of Christ. The earliest surviving inscriptions in the language go back to about 2,500 B.C. and are the oldest known written records in a Semitic tongue. Old Akkadian is the earliest period of the language and can be dated from its appearance in Mesopotamia c.3000 B.C. to c.1950 B.C., when the 3d dynasty of Ur fell. Thereafter, Akkadian evolved into two dialects, Assyrian, the tongue of ancient Assyria, and Babylonian, the language of ancient Babylonia. The history of both Assyrian and Babylonian can be roughly divided into three successive periods designated as Old (beginning c.1950 B.C.), Middle (c.1500–c.1000 B.C.), and New or Late (after c.1000 B.C.). Around 1500 B.C., Babylonian began to be widely used, both in the Near East and in international diplomacy. As time went on, Babylonian even replaced Assyrian to a large extent in the written records and literature of the Assyrian civilization. By the beginning of the Christian era, however, Babylonian had died out, and it remained a lost language until modern times, when it was deciphered during the first half of the 19th cent. Unlike the other Semitic languages, which employed an alphabetic writing system, Akkadian and its later forms, Assyrian and Babylonian, were written in CUNEIFORM. The Akkadians adopted cuneiform c.2500 B.C. from the Sumerians, a non-Semitic people who are believed to have invented it. See AKKAD. See I. J. Gelb, *Old Akkadian Writing and Grammar* (2d ed.

1961); Erica Reiner, *A Linguistic Analysis of Akkadian* (1966).

Akkerman: see BELGOROD-DNESTROVSKY, USSR.

Akko (ăk'ō) or **Acre** (ā'kər, ä'-), Fr. *Saint-Jean d'Arce,* Arab. *Acca,* city (1970 est. pop. 33,900), NW Israel, a fishing port on the Bay of Haifa (an arm of the Mediterranean Sea). Its manufactures include iron and steel, chemicals, and textiles. The city was captured (A.D. 638) by the Arabs, who developed its natural harbor. In 1104 it was captured in the First Crusade and was held by Christians until 1187, when it was taken by Saladin. In the Third Crusade it was won back (1191) by Guy of Lusignan, Richard I of England, and Philip II of France, who gave it to the Knights Hospitalers (the Knights of St. John, hence its French name). For the next century it was the center of the Christian possessions in the Holy Land. Its surrender and virtual destruction by the Saracens in 1291 marked the decline of the Latin Kingdom of Jerusalem and the Crusades. Akko was taken by the Ottoman Turks in 1517 and was revived in the late 18th cent. under Dahir al-Umar, the local Ottoman ruler. In 1799, Ottoman forces, with the aid of Great Britain, withstood a 61-day siege by Napoleon I. The city was taken in 1832 by Ibrahim Pasha for Muhammad Ali of Egypt, but European and Ottoman forces won it back for the Ottoman Empire in 1840. British troops captured the city in 1918. Akko was assigned to the Arabs in the 1948 partition of Palestine, but it was captured by Israeli forces in the Arab-Israeli war of that year.

Akkub (ăk'əb). **1** Descendant of David. 1 Chron. 3.24. **2** Levitical family. 1 Chron. 9.17; Ezra 2.42; Neh. 7.45; 11.19; 12.25. **3** One of the Nethinim. Ezra 2.45. **4** One who explained the Law. Neh. 8.7.

Aklavik (ăklä'vĭk), settlement (1971 pop. 677), Mackenzie dist., Northwest Territories, Canada, on the west channel of the Mackenzie River. The unsuitability of the land at the site led to the construction of INUVIK.

Akmolinsk: see TSELINOGRAD, USSR.

Ako, Michel: see ACO, MICHEL.

Ako (äkō'), city (1970 pop. 45,942), Hyogo prefecture, W Honshu, Japan, on the Harima Sea. It is an industrial city where fire bricks, fishing nets, medicine, and cement are produced. Ako is famous for its Oishi (Shinto) shrine and Kogakuji (Buddhist) temple.

Akola (əkō'lə), town (1971 pop. 168,454), Maharashtra state, W central India, on the Morna River. It is a district administrative center and a market town. Cotton and groundnuts are the chief products of the region. A citadel built by the Mogul emperor Akbar Shah II in the 19th cent. stands in Akola.

Akosombo Dam, Ghana: see VOLTA, river.

A-k'o-su (ä-kō-sōō), town, SW Sinkiang Uigur Autonomous Region, China, on the A-k'o-su River. The center of an oasis at the foot of the Tien Shan mts., it is a caravan hub on the Old Silk Road. Industries include textile and carpet manufacturing, jade carving, tanning, and metalworking. Iron deposits are in the area. A-k'o-su has ancient Buddhist statues and caves, but most are in poor condition. The name is sometimes spelled Aksu or Aqsu.

Akrabbim (əkrăb'ĭm): see MAALEH-ACRABBIM.

Akranes (ä'krānĕs"), town (1969 est. pop. 4,245), SW Iceland, on a peninsula in the Faxaflói. It is a fishing port and industrial center, with a huge cement plant.

Akron (ăk'rən), city (1970 pop. 275,425), seat of Summit co., NE Ohio, on the Little Cuyahoga River, on the highest point of the Ohio and Erie Canal; inc. 1825. It is a port of entry, an important industrial and transportation center, and the heart of the country's rubber industry. In addition to its enormous variety of rubber products, its many manufactures range from fishing tackle to plastics, missiles, and heavy machinery; the dirigibles *Akron* and *Macon* were built there. The Ohio and Erie Canal (opened 1827) and later the railroad spurred the city's growth. The first rubber plant was established in 1870. The city is the seat of the Univ. of Akron and the Institute of Rubber Research. It has an art institute, a music center, and a symphony orchestra. Points of interest include a giant dirigible airdock, one of the world's largest buildings without inner supports; the John Brown home, where the abolitionist lived from 1844 to 1846 (now housing a museum); and several old mansions.

Akron, University of, at Akron, Ohio; coeducational; established 1870 as Buchtel College, transferred 1913 as the nucleus of the Municipal Univ. of Akron. In 1967 the school became a state university. During World War II scientists connected with the university worked on the critical development of synthetic rubber; similar scientific programs are now carried on by the Institute of Polymer Science. The university has an extensive adult education system.

Aksakov, Konstantin Sergeyevich, 1817–60, Russian critic and writer, son of Sergei Timofeyevich Aksakov. Like his brother Ivan, he was an ardent Slavophile and strongly idealized the village community as a voluntary association. His literary criticism was devoted mainly to urging writers to seek closer ties with the Orthodox religion and with the peasantry. He wrote *O vnutrennem sostoyanii Rossii* [on the internal situation of Russia] in 1855.

Aksakov, Sergei Timofeyevich, 1791–1859, Russian writer, known for his nostalgic descriptions of the Orenburg region. Aksakov's chief work is *Family Chronicle* (1856, tr. 1924), a picture of country life in the days of serfdom. His *Years of Childhood* (1858, tr. 1960) vividly describes his joyous youth.

Aksu: see A-K'O-SU, China.

Aksum or **Axum** (both: äksōōm'), town (1970 est. pop. 12,800), Tigre prov., N Ethiopia. Aksum was the capital of an empire (c.1st–8th cent. A.D.) that controlled much of what is now N Ethiopia. In the 4th cent. the emperor Ezana was converted to Christianity, and today Aksum is a major center of Ethiopian Christianity. The Ark of the Covenant is said to have been brought there from Jerusalem and placed in the church of St. Mary of Zion, where Ethiopia's emperors were crowned. There are gigantic carved obelisks dating from pre-Christian times.

Akte, Greece: see ATHOS.

Aktyubinsk (əktyōō'bĭnsk), city (1970 pop. 550,000), capital of Aktyubinsk oblast, Kazakhstan, S European USSR, on the Ilek River and the Kazalinsk RR. Aktyubinsk has an important ferroalloy plant and chromium complex based on nearby ore deposits. Founded in 1869, the city grew rapidly with the expansion of metallurgical industries during World War II.

Akure (äkōō'rā), town (1969 est. pop. 82,000), S Nigeria. Timber is cut nearby and processed in Akure. The town is also a cacao marketing center. Akure was a small independent YORUBA kingdom until it was conquered by BENIN in the early 19th cent. Great Britain gained control in 1894. Akure has a school of agriculture.

Akureyri (ä'kürā"rē), city (1970 pop. 10,735), N Iceland, at the head of the Eyjafjörður. The second largest city of Iceland, it is a fishing, commercial, and industrial center. It was settled A.D. c.900 and chartered in 1786. The modern Lutheran Church is a landmark.

Akyab: see SITTWE, Burma.

al-. For some Arabic names beginning thus, see second part of name; e.g., for Anwar al-Sadat, see SADAT, ANWAR AL-.

Al, chemical symbol of the element ALUMINUM.

Alabama (ăləbăm'ə), state (1970 pop. 3,444,165), 51,609 sq mi (133,667 sq km), SE United States, admitted as the 22d state of the Union in 1819. The capital is MONTGOMERY, the largest city is BIRMINGHAM, and the major seaport is MOBILE. Alabama is bounded on the N by Tennessee, on the E by Georgia, on the S by Florida and the Gulf of Mexico, and on the W by Mississippi. Except for the mountainous section in the northeast (the southern end of the Cumberland Plateau) the state is a rolling plain with a mean elevation of c.500 ft (150 m) in two geologic regions—the Appalachian Piedmont above the FALL LINE and the coastal plain below. These plains, drained by the ALABAMA and the TOMBIGBEE rivers and their tributaries, are primarily devoted to agriculture. The central BLACK BELT, formerly a principal cotton-growing area, is now a center for raising cattle and poultry, Alabama's most valuable agricultural products. Cotton, grown in the Tennessee River valley, is still the chief crop. Other important crops are peanuts, soybeans, and hay. Although about half of Alabama's area is devoted to agriculture, manufacturing accounts for a larger share of the state's income. Where the Tennessee River loops across the north, hydroelectric power from the TENNESSEE VALLEY AUTHORITY has been increasingly turning an agricultural land into an industrial section. The mineral riches of coal, oil, stone, and iron also contribute to the state's industries, and Birmingham is a leading U.S. iron and steel center. Other major industries produce chemicals, textiles, paper products, and processed foods. In addition Gulf fishing and lumbering add to the wealth of Alabama; pine plywood is also an important product. Agriculture was known to the four great Indian groups of the region (Creek and Cherokee in the east, Choctaw and Chickasaw in the west) when the Spanish explorers arrived. Cabeza de Vaca (and possibly Pánfilo de Narvaez) visited Alabama in 1528, and Her-

nando De Soto spent some time in the region in 1540. White settlement was begun, however, not by the Spanish but in 1702 by the French under the sieur de Bienville in the Mobile area. The French and British contended for the furs gathered by the Indians, and the region passed (1763) to the British, who were victorious over France and Spain in the French and Indian Wars. At the close of the American Revolution, Great Britain ceded (1783) to the United States all lands E of the Mississippi except the Floridas (see West Florida Controversy). The territory of Mississippi, which included parts of present-day Alabama, was set up in 1798, but the land was still largely wilderness with a considerable fur trade, centered at Saint Stephens, and with only the beginnings of cotton cultivation. Both were interrupted during the War of 1812, when part of the Creek Confederacy began attacking under William Weatherford. Andrew Jackson decisively defeated the Indians at Horseshoe Bend on March 27, 1814. That Jackson victory, coupled with the British demand for cotton, ushered in a period of heavy settlement. New settlers poured into the Alabama region, especially from Georgia and Tennessee. The wealthy newcomers settled in the fertile bottomlands and established great plantations based on slave labor, which helped to produce cotton for the markets of Southern ports. Poorer newcomers took over less fertile uplands, where they eked out a living. The population grew to such an extent that the Territory of Alabama, taking Saint Stephens as its capital, was set up in 1817 with William W. Bibb as governor; two years later it became a state. In Alabama the slave-owning planters were dominant because of the prosperous cotton crop, and as the Civil War loomed closer the support of Southern rights and secession sentiment grew under the urging of "fire-eaters" such as William L. Yancey. Alabama broke away from the Union on Jan. 11, 1861, when its second constitutional convention passed the ordinance of secession. The government of the Confederacy was organized at Montgomery on Feb. 4, 1861. Federal troops held the Tennessee valley after 1862. One of the great naval battles of the war was won by Admiral D. G. Farragut in Mobile Bay in 1864, but most of the state was not occupied in force until 1865. Alabama ratified the Thirteenth Amendment to the U.S. Constitution in 1865, but in 1867 it refused to ratify the Fourteenth Amendment and was placed under military rule. That rule ended the following year when a new state legislature operating under a new constitution approved the Fourteenth Amendment. However, Federal troops did not leave Alabama until 1876. In the RECONSTRUCTION era Alabama's government was filled with CARPETBAGGERS and SCALAWAGS, and corruption was widespread. Few reforms emerged during the period; but the mining of coal and iron was expanded by Daniel Pratt and his successor, H. F. De Bardeleben, marking the rise of industry in Alabama. Railroads built during Reconstruction also encouraged industrialization. BIRMINGHAM was founded in 1870, and its first blast furnace began operations in 1880.

The cotton textile industry developed in the 1880s. At that time farming was still dominant, and the fortunes of the state rose and fell with the market price of cotton; however, constant use and erosion began to exhaust the land. Diversification of crops, much advocated in the 20th cent., was accelerated when the boll weevil invaded the cotton fields and the great demand during World War I brought high prices for food crops. The Great Depression and the agricultural program of President Franklin D. Roosevelt's New Deal caused more farmers to produce subsistence crops and took more land away from the wasting cotton culture. Industrialization was greatly increased during World War II with the appearance of factories producing machines, munitions, powder, and other war supplies. HUNTSVILLE became a center for rocket research, and its population more than quadrupled between 1950 and 1960. Industrialization and commerce increased throughout the state. Adding impetus to that growth was an ambitious development program of Alabama's inland waterways to provide cheap water transportation, more hydroelectric power, and flood-control measures. In 1954 the U.S. Supreme Court handed down a decision ruling racial segregation in public elementary and secondary schools unconstitutional, and the decision was followed by a severe rise in racial tension (see INTEGRATION). Alabama has witnessed many civil rights protests, including a year-long black boycott of public buses in Montgomery in 1955–56 to protest segregated seating and a Freedom March from Montgomery to Selma in 1965. Alabama's constitution, adopted in 1901, provides for an elected governor, who may not succeed himself in office. The legislature is made up of a 35-member senate and a 106-member house of representatives. The state elects 2 Senators and 7 Representatives to the U.S. Congress and has 9 electoral votes. Although Republicans gained in the state in the 1960s, Alabama is still predominantly Democratic. George C. Wallace, a Democrat, was elected governor in 1962 and again in 1970 and entered the U.S. presidential race in 1968 as the candidate of the American Independent party. He ran for the presidency again in 1972 and was reelected governor in 1974. In 1966 his wife, Lurleen Wallace, was elected governor. Alabama contributed such important figures to the country as Hugo L. Black and Helen Keller. Places of interest in the state include Russell Cave National Monument, near Bridgeport, the site of caves that were inhabited almost continuously from 6000 B.C. to A.D. 1650, and Mound State Monument, near Tuscaloosa, the site of numerous early Indian mounds. Among Alabama's educational institutions are the Univ. of Alabama, at University, Auburn Univ., at Auburn; Birmingham-Southern College and Howard College, at Birmingham; Huntingdon College, at Montgomery; the Univ. of Montevallo, at Montevallo; and Tuskegee Institute, at Tuskegee. See W. L. Fleming, *Civil War and Reconstruction in Alabama* (1905); W. T. Jordan, *Ante-bellum Alabama, Town and Country* (1957); T. P. Abernethy, *The Formative Period in Alabama, 1815–1828* (2d ed. 1965); V. B. Haagen, *Alabama, Portrait of a State* (1968); C. P. Denman, *The Secession Movement in Alabama* (1933, repr. 1971); Lucille Griffith, *Alabama: A Documentary History to 1900* (rev. ed. 1972); Federal Writers' Project, *Alabama: A Guide to the Deep South* (1941, repr. 1973).

Alabama, river, 315 mi (507 km) long, formed in central Ala. by the confluence of the Coosa and Tallapoosa rivers N of Montgomery, Ala., and flowing SW to Mobile, Ala., where it joins the Tombigbee to form the Mobile River; drains c.22,600 sq mi (58,500 sq km). In the 1800s the Alabama played an important role in the development of the region's economy as a transporter of goods. It remains an important mover of farm products, lumber, and manufactured goods, especially textiles and iron and steel products. The Cahaba River, its chief tributary, is the source of water for Birmingham, Ala.

Alabama, ship: see CONFEDERATE CRUISERS.

Alabama, University of, mainly at University, near Tuscaloosa; state supported, coeducational; chartered 1820, opened 1831. An experimental station of the U.S. Bureau of Mines, the state natural history museum, the state geological survey, and a business research bureau are there. The university also has a campus at Huntsville and a branch offering medical programs at Birmingham.

Alabama claims, claims made by the U.S. government against Great Britain for the damage inflicted on Northern merchant ships during the American Civil War by the *Alabama* and other CONFEDERATE CRUISERS that had been built, fitted out, and otherwise aided by British interests. William H. Seward failed to reach a settlement while he was Secretary of State. However, his successor, Hamilton Fish, brought about the Treaty of Washington (1871), which provided for arbitration. Charles Francis Adams for the United States, Alexander J. E. Cockburn for Great Britain, and three members from neutral countries constituted the tribunal, which met at Geneva in 1871–72. The arbitrators threw out American claims for indirect losses, but they awarded the United States $15.5 million for all the direct damage done by the *Alabama* and the *Florida* and for most of the damage caused by the *Shenandoah*. The British were absolved of blame in the cases of several less important cruisers. See study by T. W. Balch (1900, repr. 1969).

Alabama Indians or **Alibamu Indians** (ălĭbăm'ōō), North American Indians whose language belongs to the Muskogean branch of the Hokan-Siouan linguistic stock (see AMERICAN INDIAN LANGUAGES). They lived in S Alabama in the early 18th cent. and were members of the Creek confederacy. During the 19th cent. they moved to W Louisiana and E Texas. The state of Alabama takes its name from them. The Alabama share a reservation with the Coushatta Indians in Texas where together they number some 380; they are often referred to jointly as the Alabama-Coushatta Indians.

Alabama Polytechnic Institute: see AUBURN UNIVERSITY.

alabamine (ăl"əbăm'ēn): see ASTATINE.

Alabaster, William, 1567–1640, English theologian and poet. Although he wrote two epic poems in Latin, he is remembered for his theological studies, including *Spiraculum Tubarum* (1633). Alabaster converted to Roman Catholicism in Spain in 1597 and was imprisoned on his return to England in 1598. He reconverted to Protestantism and was chaplain to James I.

alabaster, fine-grained, massive, translucent variety of GYPSUM, pure white or streaked with reddish brown, used in statuary and for other decorative purposes. It is soft enough to be scratched with the fingernail and hence is easily carved, but it is also easily broken, soiled, and weathered. It is quarried in England and also in Italy. Vases and statuettes of Italian alabaster are sold as "Florentine marbles." The alabaster of the ancients, called Oriental alabaster and onyx marble, to distinguish it from true alabaster, is MARBLE, a calcium carbonate, whereas gypsum is a calcium sulphate. The calcium carbonate form occurs both in spring deposits (TRAVERTINE) and in cave formations (see STALACTITE AND STALAGMITE). Important sources of supply are Algeria, Egypt, Iran, and Mexico (from which it is exported under the name Mexican onyx); in the United States there are important sources in Utah and Arizona. Oriental alabaster (marble) was extensively used by the Egyptians in sarcophagi, in the linings of tombs, in the walls and ceilings of temples, and in vases and sacrificial vessels. The Romans worked the Algerian and Egyptian quarries and used the stone for similar purposes. In modern times it was used by Muhammad Ali for his mosque in Cairo. The French make extensive use of alabaster in interior decoration. See R. Webster, *Gems* (1970); J. L. Gillson, *Industrial Minerals and Rocks* (1960).

Alacoque, Margaret Mary: see MARGARET MARY, SAINT.

Alagez, Mount: see ARAGATS, MOUNT, USSR.

Alagoas (älägō'əs) [Port.,=lagoons], state (1970 pop. 1,589,605), 10,707 sq mi (27,331 sq km), NE Brazil, on the Atlantic Ocean. MACEIÓ is the capital.

Alai or **Alay** (both: älī'), mountain range, SW Kirghizstan, Central Asian USSR. A western branch of the Tien Shan system, it extends c.200 mi (320 km) west from the Chinese border and rises to c.19,280 ft (5,880 m) in its western portion. The Alai Valley, south of the range, is a fertile elevated (c.9,800 ft/2,990 m) grassland used for grazing; there is irrigated grain cultivation in the west.

Alain: see CHARTIER, ÉMILE-AUGUSTE.

Alain de Lille (äläN' də lēl), c.1128–c.1202, French scholastic philosopher, a Cistercian, honored by his contemporaries as the Universal Doctor. He was born in Lille; he taught at Paris and Montpellier before retiring to Cîteaux. De Lille attempted to give rational support to the tenets of Christian faith in his writings. He held that the mind unaided by revelation can know the universe, but by faith alone can man know God. Although his thought was largely Neoplatonic, he made use of numerous Aristotelian and neo-Pythagorean elements. The mathematical and deductive method had an important place in the working out of his theology. One of his chief works, *De fide catholica contra haereticos*, was written in order to refute heretics and unbelievers. Alain de Lille was also one of the foremost didactic poets of his day; his chief poem *Anticlaudian* (tr. 1935) is a complicated allegory. He is also called Alanus de Insulis.

Alain-Fournier (äläN-fōōrnyā'), 1886–1914, French novelist, whose real name was Henri Alban Fournier. He was killed in action during World War I. His single full-length work is his poetic novel about a youthful search for the ideal, *Le Grand Meaulnes* (1913, tr. *The Wanderer,* 1928). Set in an imaginary locale called "the domain," it is based partly on Alain-Fournier's own childhood and partly on his mystical experiences and ideas. Its distinctiveness lies in its delicate blend of symbolism and realism.

Alais: see ALÈS.

Alajuela (älähwā'lä), city (1970 pop. 29,171), capital of Alajuela prov., central Costa Rica. On the central plateau, it is a commercial and agricultural center with sugar, coffee, and lumber industries. It was the national capital in the 1830s.

Alam, Assadollah (äs-sädōl"lä' äläm'), 1919–, Iranian political leader, prime minister of Iran (1962–64). He held a variety of governmental posts in the decade following World War II. When Shah Muhammad Reza Pahlevi announced his desire for a democratic party system in Iran, Alam became head of the newly formed People's party (1956). He became prime minister in 1962 and proceeded to support large-scale land reform and a pro-Western foreign policy until his resignation in 1964. One of Iran's largest landholders, he later returned (1966) to government to serve as minister of the imperial court.

Alamán, Lucas (lōō'käs älämän'), 1792–1853, Mexican historian and statesman. As deputy to the Spanish Cortes, he failed to win a hearing for the insurgents in Mexico. Returning to Mexico, he held several public offices and was twice minister of foreign affairs in the government after the fall of Agustín de Iturbide. Alamán founded the Archivo General and the National Museum, in Mexico City. He is chiefly remembered for his magnificent history of Mexico, *Historia de Méjico* (5 vol., 1849–52).

Alamanni or **Alemanni, Luigi** (lōōē'jē älämän'nē, älā-), 1495–1556, Italian poet and patriot. He was a friend of Macchiavelli, who may have encouraged his conspiracy (1522) against Cardinal Giulio de' Medici (later Pope Clement VII). Its failure forced him to flee to the French court. He returned (1527) to Florence to fight the Medici, but after their restoration (1532) he was declared a rebel. Alamanni was versatile and prolific. He wrote plays (*La Flora,* a comedy and *Antigone,* a tragedy) and lively letters to his friends and introduced the epigram into modern Italian poetry.

Alamayn, Al, Egypt: see ALAMEIN, EL.

Alameda (äləmē'də, -mā'də), city (1970 pop. 70,968), Alameda co., W central Calif., on an island just off the eastern shore of San Francisco Bay; settled 1850, inc. as a city 1884. Shipbuilding, ship repairing, and the production of peanut butter are the leading industries. It is primarily residential, however, with excellent beaches, parks, and pleasure-boating facilities. The major employer in the city is the Alameda Naval Air Station, a large U.S. carrier base, which was built from 1938 to 1940. An important Coast Guard base and a junior college are also there. The city is connected with the mainland by four bridges and two tunnels.

Alamein, El (ĕl äləmān', ä-) or **Al Alamayn** (äl älămān'), town, N Egypt, on the Mediterranean Sea. It was the site of a decisive British victory in World War II (see NORTH AFRICA, CAMPAIGNS IN). In preparation for an attack by German Field Marshal Erwin Rommel from Libya (begun May 26, 1942) the British forces retreated into Egypt and by June 30 had set up a defense line extending 35 mi (56 km) from Alamein S to the Qattara Depression, a badland which could neither be crossed nor flanked. If this position had fallen, the British might have lost Alexandria and been forced to withdraw from North Africa. In August, Gen. Bernard L. MONTGOMERY took command of the 8th Army. The British offensive opened on Oct. 23 with tremendous air and artillery bombardments. Montgomery's forces cleared the German minefields and on Nov. 1 and 2 burst through the German lines near the sea and forced a swift Axis retreat out of Egypt, across Libya, and into E Tunisia. Egypt was definitely saved, and with the landing on Nov. 7 and 8 of American troops in Algeria the Axis soon suffered (May, 1943) total defeat in North Africa. The Allies thereafter received more support from Middle Eastern countries, some of which had drawn close to the Axis powers. For his victory Montgomery was made a viscount with the title Montgomery of Alamein. See Michael Carver, *El Alamein* (1962).

Alameth (ăl'əməth), Benjamite. 1 Chron. 7.8.

Alamgir: see AURANGZEB.

Alammelech (əlăm'əlĕk), village of Asher, NW Palestine. Joshua 19.26. The modern Wadi el-Melek near Mt. Carmel perhaps echoes the name.

Alamo, the [Span.,=cottonwood], building in San Antonio, Texas, "the cradle of Texas liberty." Built as a chapel after 1744, it is all that remains of the mission of San Antonio de Valero, which was founded in 1718 by the Franciscans and later converted into a fortress. In the Texas Revolution, San Antonio was taken by Texas revolutionaries in Dec., 1835, and was lightly garrisoned. When Santa Anna approached with an army of several thousand in Feb., 1836, only some 150 men held the Alamo, and confusion, indifference, and bickering among the insurgents throughout Texas prevented any help from joining them, except for 32 volunteers from Gonzales who slipped through the Mexican lines after the siege had already begun. Defying Santa Anna's demands for surrender, the Texans in the fort determined to fight against the hopeless odds. The siege, which began Feb. 24, ended with hand-to-hand fighting within the walls on March 6. William B. TRAVIS, James Bowie, Davy CROCKETT, and some 180 other defenders were dead, but the heroic resistance roused fighting anger among Texans, who six weeks later defeated the Mexicans at San Jacinto, crying, "Remember the Alamo!" The chapel-fort was bought by the state in 1883, the surrounding area was added in 1905, and the whole complex was restored and improved from 1936 to 1939. See A. G. Adair and M. H. Crockett, ed., *Heroes of the Alamo* (2d ed. 1957); Lon Tinkle, *13 Days to Glory* (1958); Walter Lord, *A Time to Stand* (1961).

Alamogordo (ăl"əməgôr'dō, -də), city (1970 pop. 23,035), seat of Otero co., S N.Mex., near the Sacramento mts.; inc. 1912. It is a trade center for a large livestock, irrigated farm, timber, and recreational area. Pressure cookers, wearing apparel, and lumber are among its products. Holloman Air Force Base, headquarters of the 49th Tactical Air Command and site of the White Sands Missile Range, where the first atomic bomb was exploded on June 16, 1945, is located in Alamogordo. The city was founded in 1898 with the arrival of the Southern Pacific RR. New Mexico State Univ. has a branch at Alamogordo. Near the city are White Sands National Monument (see NATIONAL PARKS AND MONUMENTS, table), an Apache Indian Reservation, and Lincoln National Forest.

Alamoth (ăl'əmōth), Hebrew musical term, unknown in meaning, although some have guessed "soprano," connecting it with a word for "maidens." It occurs in 1 Chron. 15.20 and in the title of Ps. 46. The term *Sheminith,* in the titles of Pss. 6 and 12, has been explained as "bass," complementary to Alamoth.

Alanbrooke, Alan Francis Brooke, lst **Viscount,** 1883–1963, British general. He entered the field artillery in 1902 and served with distinction during World War I. In the 1930s he made himself a master of mechanized warfare. At the beginning of World War II he commanded the 2d Army Corps in France and was (1940–41) commander in chief of the British Home Forces. From Dec., 1941, to 1946 he was chief of the imperial general staff and participated in the war conferences of Winston Churchill, Franklin Delano Roosevelt, and Joseph Stalin. He was made Baron Alanbrooke in 1945 and Viscount Alanbrooke in 1946.

Åland Islands, Finland: see AHVENANMAA ISLANDS.

alanine, organic compound, one of the twenty-two alpha AMINO ACIDS commonly found in animal proteins. Only the L-stereoisomer participates in the biosynthesis of proteins (see STEREOCHEMISTRY). Its one-carbon aliphatic side chain confers no special reactivity upon this amino acid when it is included within a protein by two amide bonds, but it does allow the side chain to participate in hydrophobic interactions. Alanine is not essential to the human diet, since it can be synthesized from other cellular metabolites. It was discovered in protein in 1875.

$$H_2N-\overset{\overset{\large CH_3}{|}}{\underset{\underset{\large H}{|}}{C}}-C\begin{matrix}{/\!\!/}O\\ \diagdown OH\end{matrix}$$

alanine

Alarcón, Hernando de (ārnän'dō dā älärkōn'), fl. 1540, Spanish explorer in the Southwest. He was given command of a fleet that was supposed to support the land expedition of Francisco Vásquez de CORONADO. In the summer of 1540 he sailed up the Gulf of California; proved definitely that Lower California was a peninsula, not an island; and discovered the Colorado River. He failed, however, to make contact with Coronado's expedition. He explored the river a few months before García López de CÁRDENAS discovered the Grand Canyon.

Alarcón, Pedro Antonio de (pāth'rō äntō'nyō), 1833–91, Spanish writer and diplomat. Alarcón was active in politics, became editor of a revolutionary journal in Madrid, and was later an ambassador. His first important literary work was a masterful and popular memoir of the Spanish Moroccan campaign (1859–60). He wrote several novels, including *El sombrero de tres picos* (1874, tr. *The Three-cornered Hat,* 1891), on which Manuel de Falla based his popular ballet, and *El capitán Veneno* (1881, tr. *Captain Venom,* 1914). In these works Alarcón shows keen powers of observation and subtle humor. A longer novel is *El escandalo* (1875, tr. *The Scandal,* 1945).

Alarcón y Mendoza, Juan Ruiz de (hwän rōōēth' dā älärkōn' ē mändō'thä), 1581?–1639, Spanish dramatic poet, one of the great literary figures of the Spanish Golden Age, b. Mexico. After practicing law in Spain (1600–1608) and Mexico, he returned (1613) to Spain, where he obtained a minor government post. Like Molière, Alarcón was a comedic moralist; his comedies (2 vol., 1628–34) are notable for brilliant characterization and lively dialogue. Alarcón was a hunchback, and his carefully wrought plays reflect the stoic point of view that this circumstance compelled him to adopt. Best known is *La verdad sospechosa* [the suspicious truth], which was the model for Corneille's *Le Menteur.* Among the others are *Las paredes oyen* [the walls have ears] and *El anticristo.*

Alaric I (ăl'ərĭk), c.370–410, Visigothic king. He headed the Visigothic troops serving Emperor Theodosius I. After the emperor's death (395) the troops rebelled and chose Alaric as their leader (see VISIGOTHS). Alaric devastated Thrace, Macedonia, and Greece. Stopped, but not defeated, by STILICHO, he retired northward, and by an agreement with the Eastern emperor, ARCADIUS, occupied Epirus. In 401 he invaded Italy, where after some indecisive warfare he agreed to withdraw. Stilicho persuaded (407) the Romans to buy Alaric's alliance, but shortly afterward Emperor HONORIUS had Stilicho executed for treason. Alaric again invaded (408) Italy and laid seige to Rome. Raising the seige after an agreement with the Roman senate, Alaric again turned on Rome (409) and forced the city to accept a puppet emperor, Attalus, whom he himself deposed the next year for disregarding his advice. After the failure of renewed negotiations with Honorius (who all the while held out at Ravenna) Alaric stormed and sacked Rome (410) and then marched south to attack Sicily and Africa. A storm destroyed his fleet, and Alaric, having turned back, died of an illness. His brother Ataulf was elected his successor. It is said that Alaric was buried with his treasures near Cosenza in the bed of the Busento River, which was temporarily diverted from its course. That the secret of his burial place might be kept, the slaves employed in the labor were killed. See study by Marcel Brion (tr. 1932).

Alaric II, d. 507, Visigothic king of Spain and of S Gaul (c.484–507), son and successor of Euric. He issued (506) at Toulouse the BREVIARY OF ALARIC for his Roman subjects. Alaric's adherence to Arianism gave CLOVIS I, king of the Franks, an easy pretext for attacking him in the name of orthodoxy. Alaric was defeated and slain at Vouillé (507), and the Visigoths lost all their possessions in Gaul except Septimania.

Alas, Leopoldo (lāōpōl'dō ä'läs), 1852–1901, Spanish novelist, short-story writer, and literary critic who wrote under the pseudonym Clarín, b. Zamora. Although he began his literary career as a journalist, he later was a professor of law at the Univ. of Oviedo. He is best known for his naturalistic novel *La Regenta* (1884–85), a detailed analysis of provincial life. His other works include another novel, *Su único hijo* [his only son] (1890), and several volumes of short stories, which are generally regarded as among the best of the genre. See study by Albert Brent (1951).

Alasco or **à Lasco, Johannes:** see LASKI, JOHN.

Alaşehir (älä'shĕhĕr"), town (1970 pop. 20,313), W Turkey, at the foot of the Tmolus mts. (Boz Dağ). It is the trade center for a region where tobacco, fruit, and mineral water are produced. The town is picturesque, with narrow winding streets and a Byzantine wall. Nearby is the site of ancient PHILADELPHIA.

Alaska, state (1970 pop. 302,173), 586,400 sq mi (1,518,776 sq km), including 15,335 sq mi (39,718 sq km) of water surface, NW North America, admitted 1959 as the 49th state. Nearly one fifth the size of the rest of the United States, Alaska is the largest state in the Union but the least populous one. JUNEAU is the capital, ANCHORAGE the largest city. Alaska is a huge block of land at the northwestern extremity of the North American continent, between the Arctic Ocean on the north and the Gulf of Alaska and the Pacific Ocean on the south. It is bounded on the E by Canada (Yukon and British Columbia) and on the W by the Bering Sea, Bering Strait, and Chukchi Sea. The tip of the Seward Peninsula is only a few miles from Far Eastern USSR; the two are separated by the narrow Bering Strait. Seward Peninsula is chiefly tundra-covered and sparsely inhabited. Nome was founded there when gold was discovered (1898) in the sand on the beaches; but gold mining has greatly declined, and Nome's population is now well under 5,000. The Bering Strait widens in the north to the Chukchi Sea, which slices into Alaska with Kotzebue Sound; in the south the strait widens to the Bering Sea, which cuts into Alaska with Norton Sound and Bristol Bay. The state again extends toward the USSR in the Alaska Peninsula and the Aleutian Islands, reaching out a total of 1,200 mi (1,931 km) toward the Soviet Komandorski Islands; together they divide the Bering Sea from the Pacific. The Aleutian Range, which is the spine of the Alaska Peninsula, is continued in the grass-covered, treeless Aleutian Islands; the climate there is unremittingly bad—foggy and, in the winter, disagreeably damp and cold and subject to violent winds (the williwaws). Once traversed by Russian fur traders hunting sea otters, the Aleutians are now chiefly of strategic importance. The southern shore of Alaska is deeply indented by two inlets of the wide Gulf of Alaska, Cook Inlet and Prince William Sound; the Kenai Peninsula between them extends southwest toward Kodiak Island. The narrow Panhandle dips southeast along the coast from the Gulf of Alaska, cutting into British Columbia. It consists of the offshore islands of the Alexander Archipelago and the narrow coast, which rises steeply to the mountains of the Coast Range and the St. Elias Mts. Winters in the Panhandle are relatively mild, with heavy rainfall and, except on the upper slopes of the mountains, comparatively little snow. The interior of Alaska, on the other hand, has very cold winters and short but very hot summers. In Arctic Alaska, N of the Brooks Range, the temperature in winter reaches −10°F to −40°F (−23.3°C to −40°C). The land there is mostly barren, cut by many short rivers and one long one, the Colville. Alaska's major river is the Yukon, which crosses the state from east to west for 1,200 mi (1,931 km), from the Canadian border to the Bering Sea. The northernmost reach of Alaska is Point Barrow. Alaska's climate and terrain (rough coast and high mountain ranges) divide it into isolated regions; the difficulty of communication is one of the state's most troublesome problems. Air transport is a partial solution, and all Alaskan cities have airports, but they nevertheless remain fundamentally isolated, self-contained units. This is true even in the Panhandle, the most populous region, where the capital and the state's third largest city, KETCHIKAN, are located. The Panhandle's connection with Seattle is by steamships, which ply the INSIDE PASSAGE between the coast and the offshore islands. In S central Alaska, Anchorage is the center for the Alaskan RR and for airways; it is also connected with the Alaska Highway. The port of Seward, having lost its commanding position as terminus of the Alaska RR to Whittier, was forced to construct a road link to the Alaska Highway at Fairbanks. Cordova and Kodiak both depend upon the ocean lanes. In the north, the entire Arctic coast is icebound most of the year; the ground there is permanently frozen. Alaska has very little agriculture; in number of farms and in the value of its farm products, it ranks last in the nation. The Panhandle, which has the best climate, is generally too steep for farming. The state's best farmland is in its S central region, in the Matanuska Valley; farmers from drought-stricken areas of the Midwest were resettled there by the Federal government in 1935. The Tenana Valley (the area around Fairbanks) is also good farmland. Most of Alaska's farms are dairies or poultry ranches, and the state's most valuable farm commodities are dairy products, potatoes, cattle, and eggs. Fishing is a leading industry. Alaska heads the nation in the value of its commercial catch—chiefly salmon, crab, shrimp, halibut, herring, and cod. Its largest manufacturing enterprise is food processing, particularly the freezing and canning of fish. Lumbering and related industries are second. The state has two great national forests. Mining, principally of petroleum, sand and gravel, natural gas, and coal, is the state's most valuable industry. Alaska leads the nation in the production of platinum, is second in production of antimonies, and is a leading producer of tin. Mercury, uranium, and beryllium are also found. Gold, which led to the opening of the area in the 19th cent., is no longer mined in quantity. Fur-trapping, Alaska's oldest industry, still endures, and pelts are obtained from a great variety of animals. The Pribilof Islands are especially noted as a source of sealskins. The seals there are now owned by the U.S. government, and their use is carefully regulated. Government—Federal, state, and local—is Alaska's major source of employment. The state's strategic location has generated considerable defense activity, including the establishment of permanent military bases. However, construction on the Distant Early Warning line and on the Ballistic Missiles Early Warning System is now completed, and Federal employment in the state declined in the early 1970s. Oil and natural gas offer the best hope for Alaska's future. The vast discoveries on the Arctic North Slope indicate that that area, along with the offshore deposits in S central Alaska, may make the state one of the world's greatest petroleum and natural gas producers. The proposed construction of an 800-mi (1,287-km) pipeline from the Arctic North Slope to the ice-free port of Valdez, however, encountered heated opposition from ecologists, but work on it began in 1974. Alaska's tourist industry also has great potential, especially with improvements in transportation. The state abounds in natural wonders. In the Panhandle, the scenic beauty of the mountains and the rugged fjord-indented coast are augmented by such attractions as the MALASPINA GLACIER and the acres of blue ice in GLACIER BAY NATIONAL MONUMENT. In the Alaska Range of S central Alaska stands the highest point in North America, Mt. McKinley (in MOUNT MCKINLEY NATIONAL PARK), while the Alaska Peninsula and the Aleutian Islands have numerous volcanoes; KATMAI NATIONAL MONUMENT contains the Valley of Ten Thousand Smokes, scene of a volcanic eruption in 1912. Alaska was discovered by white men, not from the United States or Canada but from Russia. The disastrous voyage of Vitus Bering and Aleksey Chirikov in 1741 climaxed the march of Russian traders across Siberia. The survivors who returned with sea otter skins started a rush of fur hunters to the Aleutian Islands. Rough, resourceful men, they survived great hardships to bring away fortunes in fur. Grigori Shelekhov in 1784 founded the first permanent settlement in Alaska on Kodiak Island and sent (1790) to Alaska the man who was to dominate the period of Russian influence there, Aleksandr Baranov. A monopoly was granted to the Russian American Company in 1799, and it was Baranov who directed its Alaskan activities. Sitka was founded in 1799 as his capital; it was rebuilt after destruction by the Indians in 1802. Baranov extended the Russian trade far down the west coast of North America and even, after several unsuccessful attempts, founded (1812) a settlement in N California. Rivalry for the northwest coast was strong, and British and American trading vessels began to threaten the Russian monopoly. In 1821 the czar issued a ukase (imperial command) claiming the 51st parallel as the southern boundary of Alaska and warning foreign vessels not to transgress beyond it. British and American protests, the promulgation of the Monroe Doctrine, and Russian embroilment elsewhere resulted (1824) in a negotiated settlement of the boundary at lat. 54°40′ N (the present southern boundary of Alaska). Russian interests in Alaska gradually declined, and, after the Crimean War, Russia sought to dispose of the territory altogether. In 1867, Alaska was sold to the United States for $7,200,000. The U.S. purchase was accomplished solely through the determined efforts of Secretary of State William H. Seward, and for many years afterward the land was derisively called Seward's Folly or Seward's Icebox because of its supposed uselessness. Since Alaska appeared to offer no immediate financial return, it was neglected. The U.S. army officially controlled the area until 1876, when scandals caused the withdrawal of the troops. After a small lapse, during which government was in the hands of customs men, the U.S. navy was given charge (1879). Most of the territory was not even known, although the British (notably Sir John Franklin and Capt. F. W. Beechey) had explored the coast of the Arctic Ocean, and Hudson's Bay Company men had explored the Yukon. It was not until after the discovery of gold in the Juneau region in 1880 that Alaska was given a governor and a feeble local administration (under the Organic Act of 1884). Missionaries, who had come to the region in the late 1870s, exercised considerable influence. Most influential was Sheldon Jackson, best known for his introduction of reindeer to help the Alaska Eskimo, impoverished by the wanton destruction of the fur seals. Sealing was the subject of a long international controversy (see Bering Sea Fur-Seal Controversy under BERING SEA), which was not ended until after gold had permanently transformed Alaska. Paradoxically, the first finds that tremendously influenced Alaska were in Canada. The great KLONDIKE strike of 1896 brought a stampede, mainly of Americans, and most of them came through Alaska. The big discoveries in Alaska itself followed—Nome in 1898-99, Fairbanks in 1902. The miners and prospectors (the sourdoughs) took over Alaska, and the era of the rough mining camps reached its height; this was the Alaska of Jack London. It was lawless, and a criminal code was belatedly applied in 1899. Not until 1906 did Alaska get a territorial representative in Congress. The longstanding controversy concerning the boundary between the Alaska Panhandle and British Columbia was aggravated by the large number of miners traveling the Inside Passage to the gold fields. The matter was finally settled in 1903 by a six-man tribunal, composed of American, Canadian, and British representatives. The decision was generally favorable to the United States, and a period of rapid building and development began. Mining, requiring heavy financing, passed into the hands of Eastern capitalists, notably the monopolistic Alaska Syndicate. Opposition to the "interests" became the burning issue in Alaska and was catapulted into national politics; Gifford Pinchot and R. A. Ballinger were the chief antagonists, and this was a major issue on which Theodore Roosevelt split with President William Howard Taft. A new era began for Alaska when local government was established in 1912 and it became a U.S. territory (Juneau had officially replaced Sitka as capital in 1900 although it did not begin to function as such until 1906). The building of the Alaska RR from Seward to Fairbanks was commenced with government funds in 1915. Already, however, gold mining was dying out, and Alaska receded into one of its quiet periods. The fishing industry, which had gradually advanced during the gold era, became the major enterprise. Alaska enjoyed its greatest economic boom during World War II. The ALASKA HIGHWAY was built, supplying a still weak but much-needed link with the United States. After Japanese troops occupied the Aleutian islands of Attu and Kiska, U.S. forces prepared for a counterattack. Attu was retaken in May, 1943, after bloody fighting, and the Japanese evacuated Kiska in August after intensive U.S. bombardments. Dutch Harbor became a major key in the U.S. defense system. The growth of air travel after the war, the permanent military bases established in Alaska, and the success of arctic farming in Siberia all brightened the hopes for Alaska's growth; between 1950 and 1960 the population nearly doubled. In 1958, Alaskans approved statehood by a 5 to 1 vote, and on Jan. 3, 1959, Alaska was officially admitted into the Union as a state, the first since Arizona in 1912. On Mar. 27, 1964, the strongest earthquake ever recorded in North America occurred in Alaska, taking approximately 114 lives and causing extensive property damage. Some cities were almost totally destroyed, and the fishing industry was especially hard hit, with the loss of fleets, docks, and canneries from the resulting tidal waves. Reconstruction, with large-scale Federal aid, however, was speedily completed. Alaska operates under a constitution drawn up and ratified in 1956 (effective with statehood). Its executive branch is headed by a governor and a secretary of state, both elected (on the same ticket) for four-year terms. Alaska's bicameral legislature has a senate with 20 members elected for four-year terms and a house of representatives with 40 members elected for two years. The state sends 2 Senators and 1 Representative to the U.S. Congress and has 3 electoral votes. Democrats have generally dominated Alaskan politics, but there has been a Republican trend since 1966. William A. Egan, a Democrat, served as Alaska's first governor, from 1959 to 1967. He was succeeded by Walter J. Hickel, a Republican, after whom Egan was returned to office in 1971. In 1974, Alaska voted to move its capital from Juneau to a more central location, but a precise date and place was not set. Alaska has a four-year institution of higher learning, the Univ. of Alaska, at College, near Fairbanks. See W. W. Woollen, *The Inside Passage to Alaska, 1792-1920* (1924); Herbert Hilscher and Miriam Hilscher, *Alaska, U.S.A.* (1959); George Rogers, *The Future of Alaska* (1962); H. Chevigny, *Russian Alaska* (1965); E. H. Gruening, *The Battle for Alaska Statehood* (1967) and *The State of Alaska* (rev. ed. 1969); C. C. Hulley, *Alaska, Past and Present* (3d ed. 1970); Bern Keating, *Alaska* (2d ed. 1971); H. W. Clark, *History of Alaska* (1930, repr. 1972); Bryan Cooper, *Alaska, the Last Frontier* (1973); Federal Writers' Project, *A Guide to Alaska, Last American Frontier* (1940, repr. 1973).

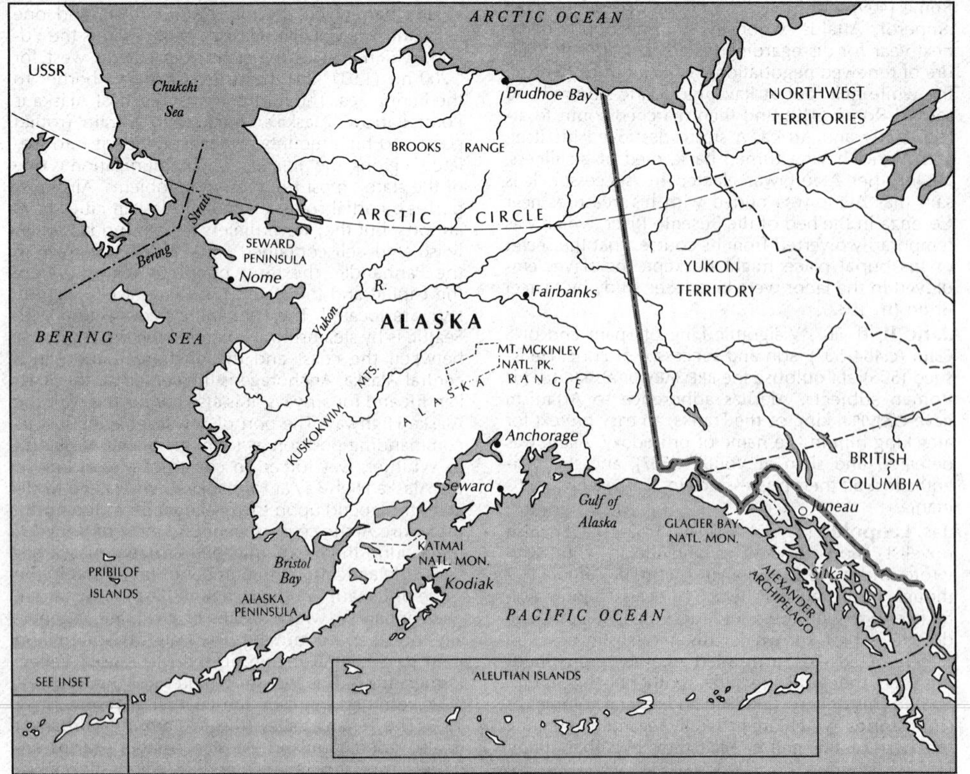

Alaska, University of, at College, near Fairbanks; land-grant and state supported; coeducational; chartered 1917, opened 1922 as Alaska Agricultural College and School of Mines. In 1935 it became a university. There are several two-year branches throughout the state.

Alaska Highway, all-weather graveled road, 1,523 mi (2,451 km) long, extending NW from Dawson Creek, British Columbia, to Fairbanks, Alaska. An extension of an existing Canadian road between Dawson Creek and Edmonton, Alta., the Alaska Highway was constructed (March–Sept., 1942) by U.S. troops as a supply route to military forces in Alaska during World War II. It was a significant engineering feat because of the difficulties of terrain and weather. In the last stretch to Fairbanks the road used the previously built Richardson Highway. The Haines Cutoff connects the Alaska Highway with the Alaska panhandle. In 1946 control of the Canadian part of the road was transferred to Canada. In 1947 the entire highway was opened to unrestricted travel; it is one of the best routes to Alaska. The highway is open throughout the year, and there are roadside facilities along its length. It was formerly known as the Alaskan International Highway and the Alcan Highway.

Alaskan malamute (măl'əmyo͞ot''), breed of strong, compact WORKING DOG believed to be one of the oldest arctic sled dogs. It stands about 23 in. (58.2 cm) high at the shoulder and weighs from 70 to 85 lb (31.75–38.5 kg). Its coarse coat is composed of oily, woolly underhairs and a thick cover coat. It may be colored any shade of gray or black with white markings. Named after the Malamutes, an Inuit tribe of N Alaska, it has been raised for centuries as a sled dog. The malamute is by nature a gentle and devoted companion; claims of wolf ancestry have never been proved. The malamute is often called a "husky," a term which properly applies to one purebred arctic dog, the Siberian husky. See DOG.

Alaska North Slope or **Arctic North Slope,** region, N Alaska, between the Arctic Ocean and the Brooks Range. Large petroleum reserves were found there in the late 1960s.

Alaska Range, S central Alaska, rising to the highest mountain in North America, Mt. McKinley (20,320 ft/6,194 m). The range divides S central Alaska from the great plateau of the interior.

Alastor (əlăs'tər), in Greek mythology, spirit of vengeance. It is an epithet applied to Zeus or any other god in his aspect as avenger and is also sometimes applied to an evildoer who is subject to vengeance.

Ala-Tau (ä'lä-tou) [Turkic,=mottled mountains], several ranges of the Tien Shan system in central Asia. The Ala-Tau ranges are the Dzungarian, the Kungei, the Täläss, the Terskei, and the Trans-Ili; all except the Täläss Ala-Tau rise to more than 16,000 ft (4,880 m). Generally forested, these ranges are chiefly inhabited by Turkic-speaking pastoral tribes. A variety of grains are grown. The Dzungarian Ala-Tau, the northernmost and loftiest branch of the Tien Shan, forms part of the USSR-China border. Silver and lead mines and hot springs are found there (see DZUNGARIA). The Kungei Ala-Tau lies N of Issyk Kul, a huge lake in the Tien Shan. The Trans-Ili Ala-Tau, on the Kirghizia-Kazakhstan border, supports intensive, irrigated agriculture; Alma-Ata, the region's largest city, is on the northern slope.

Alatyr (ələtĭr'), city (1967 est. pop. 43,000), Chuvash Autonomous Republic, E European USSR, at the confluence of the Sura and Alatyr rivers. Founded in 1552, it is a river port and railroad junction with locomotive and food-processing plants.

Alaungpaya (əlông'päyä), 1711–60, Burmese king, founder of the Konbaung dynasty, which ruled until 1885. His name, also given as Alompra, means "the coming Buddha." The son of a village headman, he rallied the Burmese and led them against their Mons rulers. He seized the important town of Ava in 1753 and moved south, uniting upper and lower Burma under his rule. Pursuing the Mons, he invaded Siam but was wounded in a siege of Ayuthia and died while returning to Burma.

Álava: see BASQUE PROVINCES.

Alay: see ALAI, mountains, USSR.

Al Aziziyah (äl äzēzē'yä) or **Azizia** (ăzĭzē'ä), town, NW Libya, near Tripoli. It is a major trade center of the Gefara plain. The hottest recorded temperature on earth, 141°F (60.6°C), was recorded there.

Alba or **Alva, Fernando Álvarez de Toledo, duque de** (äl'bə, ăl'və, Span. both: fārnän'dō äl'-värāth dā tōlā'tho͞o do͞o'kā dā äl'vä), b. 1507 or 1508, d. 1582, Spanish general and administrator. After a distinguished military career in Germany and Italy, Alba returned to Spain as adviser to King Philip II. Advocating a stern policy toward the rebels against Spain in the NETHERLANDS, he was appointed (1567) captain general there, with full civil and military powers. The regent, MARGARET OF PARMA, opposed him and resigned, and Alba became regent and governor general. A religious fanatic and ruthless absolutist, he set out to crush the Netherlands' attempts to gain religious toleration and political self-government. He set up a special court at Brussels, popularly known as the Court of Blood, which spread terror throughout the provinces. Some 18,000 persons were executed (among them the counts of EGMONT and HOORN) and their properties confiscated. Increased taxation also fanned popular resentment, and in 1572 the Netherlanders rebelled again. Alba defeated the invading forces of WILLIAM THE SILENT, but he was unable to recover much of the NW Netherlands, which had been taken by the GUEUX. At the Spanish court he was accused of having compromised the royalist cause, and in 1573 he was recalled to Spain. In 1580, Philip was persuaded to use Alba for the conquest of Portugal. He took Lisbon within a few weeks.

Albacete (älbäthā'tā), city (1970 pop. 93,233), capital of Albacete prov., SE Spain, in Murcia. Under the Moors, Albacete was a part of the Kingdom of MURCIA, with which it was incorporated (1269) into Castile. The city now has a modern aspect and is mainly an agricultural center. It is noted for the manufacture of fine knives and daggers.

albacore: see TUNA.

Alba Iulia (äl'bä-yo͞o'lyä), Hung. *Gyulafehérvár,* Ger. *Karlsburg,* town (1969 est. pop. 84,000), W central Rumania, in Transylvania, on the Mureşul River. It is a rail junction and distribution center for a wine-making region, where grain, poultry, and fruit are raised. The town's light manufactures include soap, furniture, and footwear. Alba Iulia is the site of the ancient Apulum, founded by the Romans in the 2d cent. A.D., and destroyed by Tatars in 1241. It was the seat (16th–17th cent.) of the princes of Transylvania, of a Roman Catholic bishop, and of an Eastern Orthodox metropolitan. From 1599 to 1601, Alba Iulia was the capital of the united principalities of Walachia, Transylvania, and Moldavia. It was the site (1918) of the proclamation of Transylvania's union with Rumania and of the coronation (1922) of King Ferdinand. Points of interest include an 18th-century fortress, built by Emperor Charles VI; a 13th-century Roman Catholic cathedral; and a museum and library housing exhibits from the Roman period and rare manuscripts.

Alba Longa (ăl'bə lông'gə), city of ancient Latium, in the Alban Hills near Lake Albano, c.12 mi (19 km) SE of Rome. It was a city before 1100 B.C. and apparently the most powerful in Latium. Legend says that it was founded by Ascanius, son of Aeneas, and that Romulus and Remus were born there, thus making it the mother city of Rome. Tradition also says that Tullus Hostilius, king of Rome, razed it in 665 B.C. Possibly Rome was founded from Alba Longa, and certainly the Romans destroyed it (c.600 B.C.). The modern Castel Gandolfo occupies the site.

Alban, Saint (ôl'bən), 3d or 4th cent., traditionally the first British martyr. He lived and died at Verulamium, now St. Albans. In 793 an abbey was founded there in his honor. Feast: Roman Catholic Church, June 22; Church of England, June 17.

Albanel, Charles (shärl älbänĕl'), 1616–96, French missionary explorer in Canada, a Jesuit priest. After arriving in Canada (1649), he was stationed many years at Tadoussac where he explored the surrounding wilderness. At the time when the English Hudson's Bay Company was beginning operations, he was a leader of a French party that went (1671–72) by the Saguenay River, Mistassini Lake, and the Rupert River to Hudson Bay. The region was claimed for France. On another journey there he was captured (1674) by the English and taken to England. After returning (1676) to Canada, he served at missions in western Canada and died at Sault Ste Marie.

Albanese, Licia (lē'chēä älbänā'sä), 1913–, Italian-American lyric soprano, b. Bari. Albanese made her debut (1935) in *Madame Butterfly* in Parma. She first sang at the Metropolitan Opera House in 1940. After 1945 she appeared with the NBC Symphony Orchestra and continued to sing at the Metropolitan Opera.

Albania (ălbā'nyə), Albanian *Shqipnija* or *Shqiperia,* independent republic (1970 est. pop. 2,100,000), 11,101 sq mi (28,752 sq km), SE Europe, on the Adriatic Sea coast of the Balkan Peninsula, between Yugoslavia on the north and east and Greece on the south. TIRANË is the capital; other important cities are VLORË, DURRËS, SHKODËR, and KORÇË. Albania is rugged and mountainous, except for the fertile Adriatic coast. Mt. Korab (9,066 ft/2,763 m), on the

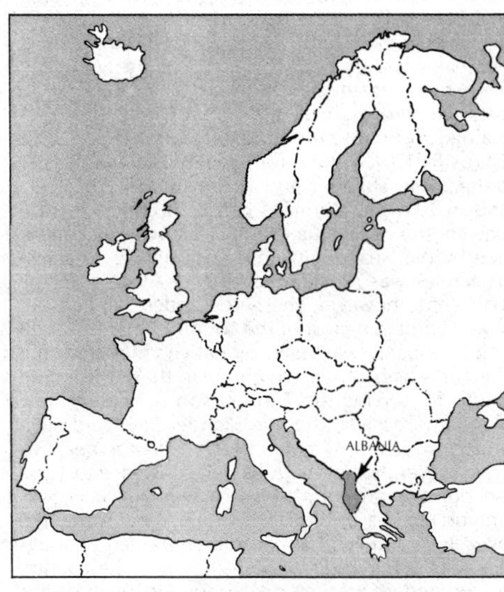

Yugoslav-Albanian border, is the highest point in the country. The coastal climate is typically Mediterranean, with hot, dry summers and mild, wet winters. The mountainous interior, especially in the north, has severe winters and mild summers. The chief rivers of Albania are the Drin, Mat, Shkumbî, Vijose, and Seman, but they are mostly unnavigable. The largest lakes are the Scutari and Ohrid, both shared with Yugoslavia, and the Prespa, on the border with Greece. More than one third of Albania's land is covered by forests and swamps, about one third is pasture, and only about one tenth is cultivated, nearly one half of the cultivated land being given over to vineyards and olive groves. Grains (especially wheat and maize), cotton, tobacco, potatoes, and sugar beets are also grown. Livestock raising (particularly the raising of sheep) is important. Agriculture is socialized in the form of collective and state farms, but small private plots are permitted. Albania is rich in mineral resources, notably oil, lignite, copper, chromium, limestone, salt, and bauxite. Although about two thirds of the population is still engaged in agriculture, mining provides the largest percentage of the national income and employs the highest proportion of the industrial labor force. Industry provides an increasing share of the national income, agricultural processing and the manufacture of textiles and cement and other building materials being among the leading industries; other important products include naphtha, copper, and machinery. Engineering, chemical, and iron and steel plants are being developed, and several hydroelectric stations have been built. All industrial enterprises and mines are nationalized, and the economy is run on the basis of Five-Year Plans. Foreign trade is carried by sea, Durrës and Vlonë (also the terminus of the oil pipeline) being the major ports. Exports include crude oil, coal, chromium, copper, textiles, iron, and agricultural produce. Among the imports are machinery, industrial equipment, and metal, chemical, and rubber products. Almost half of the total foreign trade is with China; Albania's chief trade partner in Eastern Europe is Czechoslovakia and in Western Europe, Italy. The Albanian unit of currency is the lek, which equals 100 qintars. The country's rugged and inaccessible terrain has traditionally isolated Albania from its neighbors, thus helping to preserve its ethnic homogeneity. About 97% of the population is ethnic Albanian, with scattered Greek, Vlach, Bulgar, Serb, and Gypsy minorities. About one million Albanians live in the Kosovo region of Yugoslavia, with which there has long been a border dispute. Albanian is one of the Indo-European languages. The Shkumbî River, which virtually bisects the country, separates speakers of the northern dialect (Gheg) from those of the southern dialect (Tosk). The great majority of the people are Muslim, with Roman Catholic and Greek Orthodox minorities; however, Albania is officially an atheist country.

Historic Albania. The Albanians are reputedly descendants of Illyrian and Thracian tribes that settled the region in ancient times. The area then comprised parts of ILLYRIA and EPIRUS and was known to the ancient Greeks for its mines. The coastal towns,

Epidamnus (Durrës) and APOLLONIA, were colonies of Corcyra (Kérkira) and Corinth, but the interior formed an independent kingdom that reached its height in the 3d cent. A.D. After the division (395) of the Roman Empire, Albania passed to Byzantium. While nominally (until 1347) under Byzantine rule, N Albania was invaded (7th cent.) by the Serbs, and S Albania was annexed (9th cent.) by Bulgaria. In 1014, Emperor Basil II retook S Albania, which remained in the Byzantine Empire until it passed to Epirus in 1204. Venice founded coastal colonies at present-day Shkodër and Lezhë in the 11th cent., and in 1081 the Normans began to contest Byzantine control of Albania. Norman efforts were continued by the Neapolitan Angevins; in 1272, Charles I of Naples was proclaimed king of Albania. In the 14th cent., however, the Serbs under Stephen DUSHAN conquered most of the country. After his death (1355), Albania was ruled by native chieftains until the Turks began their conquests in the 15th cent. In return for serving the Turks, a son of one of these chieftains received the title Skander Bey (Lord Alexander), which in Albanian became Skanderbeg. Later, however, he led the Albanian resistance to Turkish domination and, after his death in 1468, was immortalized as Albania's national hero. Supported by Venice and Naples, Albania continued to struggle against the Turks until 1478, when the country passed under Ottoman rule. Many Albanians distinguished themselves in the Turkish army and bureaucracy; others were made pashas and beys and had considerable local autonomy. In the early 19th cent., ALI PASHA ruled Albania like a sovereign and founded an Egyptian dynasty that lasted until the 1950s. Under Turkish rule Islam became the predominant religion of Albania; but the Albanian highlanders, never fully subjected, were able to retain their tribal organizations. Economically, the country stagnated under Ottoman rule; numerous local revolts flared. A cultural awakening began in the 19th cent., and Albanian nationalism grew in the aftermath of the Treaty of San Stefano (1877), which Russia imposed on the Turks and which gave large parts of Albania to the Balkan Slavic nations. The European Great Powers intensified their struggle for influence in the Balkans during the years that followed.

National Independence. The first of the BALKAN WARS, in 1912, gave the Albanians an opportunity to proclaim their independence. During the Second Balkan War (1913), Albania was occupied by the Serbs. A conference of Great Power ambassadors defined the country's borders in 1913 and destroyed the dream of a Greater Albania by ceding large tracts to Montenegro, Serbia, and Greece. The ambassadors placed Albania under their guarantee and named WILLIAM, PRINCE OF WIED, as its ruler. Within a year he had fled, as World War I erupted and Albania became a battleground for contending Serb, Montenegrin, Greek, Italian, Bulgarian, and Austrian forces. Secret treaties drafted during the war called for Albania's dismemberment, but Albanian resistance and the principle of self-determination as promoted by U.S. President Woodrow Wilson helped to restore an independent Albania. In 1920 the Congress of Lushnje reasserted Albanian independence. The early postwar years witnessed a struggle between conservative landlords led by Ahmed Zogu and Western-influenced liberals under Bishop Fan S. Noli. After Noli's forces seized power in 1924, Zogu fled to Yugoslavia, where he secured foreign support for an army to invade Albania. In 1925, Albania was proclaimed a republic under his presidency; in 1928 he became King ZOG. Italy, whose political and economic influence in Albania had steadily increased, invaded the country in 1939, forcing Zog into exile and bringing Albania under Italian hegemony. The Albanian puppet government declared war on the Allies in 1940; but resistance groups, notably the extreme leftist partisans under Enver HOXHA, waged guerrilla warfare against the occupying Axis armies. In 1943–44, a civil war also raged between the partisans and non-Communist forces within Albania. The only European Communist country that was liberated from the Axis invaders without the aid of the Red Army or of direct Soviet military assistance, Albania received most of its war matériel from the Anglo-American command in Italy. In late 1944, Hoxha's partisans seized most of Albania and formed a provisional government. The Communists held elections (Dec., 1945) with an unopposed slate of candidates and, in 1946, proclaimed Albania a republic with Hoxha as premier. From 1944 to 1948, Albania maintained close relations with Yugoslavia, which had helped to establish the Albanian Communist party. After Marshal TITO of Yugoslavia broke with STALIN, Albania became a virtual satellite of the USSR. Albania's disapproval of de-Stalinization and of Soviet-Yugoslav rapprochement led in 1961 to a break between Moscow and Tiranë. Chinese influence and economic aid replaced Soviet, and Albania became China's only ally in Communist Eastern Europe. Albania ceased active participation in the COUNCIL FOR MUTUAL ECONOMIC ASSISTANCE and, after the Soviet invasion of Czechoslovakia in 1968, withdrew from the Warsaw Pact military alliance (in which it had long been inactive). In the early 1970s continuing Soviet hostility and Albanian isolation led the Hoxha regime to make overtures to neighboring Yugoslavia, Greece, and Italy, as well as to other Western nations. The Albanian constitution (adopted 1946) names the People's Assembly as "the highest organ of state power," but in practice the Communist party (officially the Albania Workers' party) wields complete control. Hoxha is the party's first secretary. Deputies to the unicameral people's assembly (which rubber-stamps party legislative proposals) are elected by universal suffrage for four-year terms. The assembly elects a presidium, whose chairman becomes titular head of state. The country's highest executive body, the council of ministers, is appointed by the assembly. The chairman of the council of ministers serves as premier. Albania is divided into 26 districts; the chief units of local government are the district-level people's councils. See Ferdinand Schevill, *History of the Balkan Peninsula* (1922); E. P. Stickney, *Southern Albania or Northern Epirus in European International Affairs, 1912–1923* (1926); Harry Hamm, *Albania—China's Beachhead in Europe* (tr. 1963); Stavro Skendi, ed., *Albania* (1956) and *The Albanian National Awakening, 1878–1912* (1967); E. K. Keefe et al., *Area Handbook for Albania* (1971).

Albano, Lake (älbä'nō), crater lake, 2 sq mi (5.2 sq km), central Italy, in the Alban Hills SE of Rome. It is c.6 mi (9.7 km) in circumference and c.560 ft (170 m) deep. An underground tunnel built in the 4th cent. B.C. is still its only outlet. ALBA LONGA was located near the lake. Castel Gandolfo, the Pope's summer residence, is located there. South of the lake is Albano Laziale, a small town on the Appian Way, noted for the beautiful villas and several tombs built there by the ancient Romans.

Albany, Alexander Stuart or **Stewart, duke of:** see STUART OR STEWART, ALEXANDER, DUKE OF ALBANY.

Albany, Louisa, countess of (ôl'bənē), 1752–1824, wife of Charles Edward STUART (the Young Pretender), self-styled count of Albany; daughter of a German noble, the prince of Stolberg-Gedern. Married in 1772, she was made unhappy by her dissolute husband, left him after eight years, and became the mistress of the poet Vittorio Alfieri. After his death in 1803, she was mistress of a French painter, François Fabre. Secret marriages with both men were rumored, but not well attested. See biography by Margaret Crosland (1962).

Albany, Robert Stuart or **Stewart,** 1st **duke of:** see STUART OR STEWART, ROBERT, 1ST DUKE OF ALBANY.

Albany, ancient and literary name of Scotland, N of the Firth of Forth and Firth of Clyde. Variants are Alban and Albin.

Albany, town (1971 pop. 12,434), Western Australia, SW Australia. It is a port on Princess Royal Harbour of King George Sound. The town has woolen mills and fish canneries. Founded in 1826 as a penal colony, Albany is the oldest settlement in the state of Western Australia.

Albany. 1 Residential city (1970 pop. 14,674), Alameda co., W Calif., on the eastern shore of San Francisco Bay; inc. 1908. A U.S. Dept. of Agriculture research laboratory and a Univ. of California agricultural experiment station are there. **2** City (1970 pop. 72,623), seat of Dougherty co., SW Ga., on the Flint River; inc. 1841. It is the industrial center of a great pecan and peanut area. Among its many industries are peanut and pecan processing, meatpacking, and cotton milling. Manufactures include airplanes and airplane parts, farm tools, fertilizers, pharmaceuticals, and paper, wood, cotton, and concrete products. In the city are Albany State College, a junior college, the Albany Naval Air Station, and a U.S. marine corps supply center. The Georgia Pecan Festival is held there annually. Nearby are Chehaw State Park and the popular resort, Radium Springs. **3** City (1970 pop. 114,873), state capital and seat of Albany co., E N.Y., on the west bank of the Hudson; inc. 1686. A deepwater port of entry, it handles much shipping and is a major transshipment point. The trading center for a large agricultural and resort area, it has oil tanks, breweries, machine shops, foundries, meat-packing houses, and plants making paper items, felt, textiles, chemicals, brushes, and sports equipment. In 1609, Henry Hudson visited the site, and four years later the Dutch built a fur-trading post, called Fort Nassau, on Castle Island. In 1624 several Walloon families began permanent settlement at the Dutch post of Fort Orange, which was renamed Albany when the English took control (1664). Albany was long important as a fur-trading center and was involved in the French and Indian Wars. In 1754 the ALBANY CONGRESS met there, and after the Revolution the state capital was moved (1797) to Albany from New York City. Albany's trade grew with the development of the state, particularly after the opening of the Champlain and Erie canals in the 1820s. Today it is the seat of the State Univ. of New York at Albany, the schools of pharmacy, law, and medicine of Union Univ., the College of St. Rose, two junior colleges, and the Albany Institute of History and Art. Siena College is in suburban Loudonville. Among the many old buildings are the Schuyler mansion (1762), where Gen. Philip Schuyler's daughter, Elizabeth, was married to Alexander Hamilton; Ten Broeck Mansion (1798); and Cherry Hill (1768), the home of Philip Van Rensselaer and his descendants until 1963. Dominating the city, at the top of State Street hill, is the capitol, built (1867–98) in the French château style. The colonnaded State Education Building contains the state museum and state library. An annual tulip festival is held in the city. In the 1960s a major urban renewal project resulted in the razing of 90 acres (36.4 hectares) in the downtown section for a great complex of state administrative buildings, residences, and parks. Bret Harte was born in Albany. **4** City (1970 pop. 18,181), seat of Linn co., NW Oregon, on the Willamette River; inc. 1864. A metallurgical center in the Pacific Northwest, it is the seat of a U.S. Bureau of Mines experimental station. Many refractory metals are produced there. The city also has important lumbering and paper and wood-product industries. Other manufactures are packaged meats, frozen foods, mobile homes, and seeds. An annual world championship timber carnival is held there. Albany has a junior college.

Albany, river, 610 mi (982 km) long, rising in Lake St. Joseph, W Ont., Canada, and flowing generally E into James Bay, near Fort Albany. The Kenogami and Ogoki rivers are its chief tributaries. The river, named for the duke of York and Albany, later James II, was long an important fur-trading route. Fur-bearing animals are still caught along the river. Gold is found near Lake St. Joseph.

Albany, Fort: see FORT ALBANY, Canada.

Albany Congress, 1754, meeting at Albany, N.Y., of commissioners representing seven British colonies in North America to treat with the Iroquois, chiefly because war with France impended. A treaty was concluded, but the Indians of Pennsylvania were resentful of a land purchase made by that colony at Albany and allied themselves with the French in the ensuing French and Indian War. The meeting was notable as an example of cooperation among the colonies, but Benjamin Franklin's Plan of Union for the colonies, though voted upon favorably at Albany, was refused by the colonial legislatures (and by the crown) as demanding too great a surrender of their powers. See Robert Newbold, *Albany Congress and the Plan of Union of 1754* (1955).

Albany Regency, name given, after 1820, to the leaders of the political machine developed in New York state by Martin VAN BUREN. The name derived from the charge that Van Buren's principal supporters, residing in Albany, managed the machine for him while he served in the U.S. Senate. During the Jacksonian period the Regency controlled the Democratic party in New York. It was one of the first effective political machines, using the SPOILS SYSTEM and rigid party discipline to maintain its control. Notable figures in the Regency were William L. MARCY, Silas WRIGHT, Azariah C. FLAGG, and the elder Benjamin F. BUTLER. After 1842 it split into factions (BARNBURNERS and HUNKERS) over issues of internal improvements and slavery, thereby losing its power. See J. D. Hammond, *The History of Political Parties in the State of New York* (3 vol., 1852); Robert Remini, *Martin Van Buren and the Making of the Democratic Party* (1959).

Al Basrah: see BASRA, Iraq.

albatross (ăl'bətrôs), common name for sea birds of the order of tube-nosed swimmers (Procellariiformes), which includes petrels, shearwaters, and fulmars. The wandering albatross, *Diomedea exulans,* made famous by Coleridge's *Rime of the Ancient Mariner,* has a wingspread of from 10 to 12 ft (305–366 cm), although the wings are only about 9 in. (22.5 cm) wide. Because of their tapering wing design they excel at gliding and flying. Albatrosses eat mainly fish, floating carrion, and refuse. Most albatrosses are found in the South Pacific region, e.g., the wandering and the sooty species; a few, the black-footed (*D. nigripes*), the short-tailed, and the Laysan (*D. immutabilis*) albatrosses, regularly frequent the N Pacific. Albatrosses have unique courtship behavior. They groan, scrape their bills, and dance about awkwardly, before pairing and mating occurs. They are colonial breeders, the female laying her single white egg in crude nests on the ground. Both sexes incubate the egg; incubation takes from two to three months. Albatrosses have few natural enemies, with the exception of man. They were slaughtered for their feathers and wings in the 19th cent., and used in millinery and as "swansdown" pillow stuffings. Albatrosses are somewhat hazardous to aircraft, with many collisions reported between bird and plane, resulting in the bird's death and minor damage to the plane. Albatrosses are classified in the phylum CHORDATA, subphylum Vertebrata, class Aves, order Procellariiformes, family Diomedeidae.

Al-Battani (äl-bät-tä'nē) or **Albatenius** (ăl"bətē'nēəs), b. before 858, d. 929, Arab astronomer and mathematician. He is best known in astronomy for his improvements and corrections of the Ptolemaic tradition. His *Kitab al-Zij,* which in Latin translation was very influential in the Middle Ages and the Renaissance, contains an elaborate set of astronomical tables and discusses a wide range of practical problems in spherical astronomy, some of which were devised for the purpose of solving related astrological problems. He recognized the possibility of an annular eclipse of the sun and obtained the very accurate value of 23°35′ for the obliquity of the ecliptic.

Albay (älbī'), province (1970 pop. 672,285), SE Luzon, on the Bicol peninsula, in the Philippines. Legaspi is the capital, chief port, and largest city. Albay's terrain is rugged, but its fertile volcanic soil and heavy rainfall favor farming, and the province is a major hemp-producing area. It has many small, sheltered harbors for interisland shipping. Major tourist attractions are the beautiful active volcano, Mt. Mayon (c.8000 ft/2,440 m); the church of Cagsawa, half-buried since an eruption of Mayon early in the 19th cent.; and Tiwi Hot Springs. In 1968, Mt. Mayon erupted and engulfed three villages as some 20,000 people fled their homes.

Al Bayda (äl bā'dä) or **Beida** (bā'də), city (1964 pop. 12,799), NE Libya, situated at 2,000 ft (610 m) in the Jabal al Akhdar plateau. Construction of the city began in 1961 on the site of the tomb of Raweifi ibn Thabit, a revered Muslim holy person who was a companion of the prophet Muhammad. It is the seat of an Islamic university and government offices.

albedo (ălbē'dō), reflectivity of the surface of a planet, moon, asteroid, or other celestial body that does not shine by its own light. Albedo is measured as the fraction of incident light that the surface reflects back in all directions. A perfect diffuse reflector by definition has an albedo of unity, i.e., all the incident light is reflected; a body that reflects no light at all would have an albedo of zero. Real surfaces have albedos between these values. The albedos of planets, moons, and asteroids provide valuable information about the structure and composition of their surfaces. The dark regions on the earth's moon give it the very low average albedo of 0.07, while highly reflective clouds give Venus an albedo of 0.85, the highest of any body in the solar system.

Albee, Edward (ăl'bē), 1928–, American playwright, b. Washington, D.C. Considered the major American exponent of the theater of the absurd, Albee is most famous for his clever, satiric, and often vindictive commentaries on American life. *Who's Afraid of Virginia Woolf* (1962), generally regarded as his finest play, presents an all-night drinking bout in which a middle-aged college professor and his wife verbally lacerate each other in scathingly brilliant colloquial language. Albee's other plays include five one-act plays, *The Zoo Story* (1959), *The Death of Bessie Smith* (1960), *The Sandbox* (1960), *Box* (1968), and *Quotations from Chairman Mao Tse-Tung* (1968); a dramatization of Carson McCullers's novella *The Ballad of the Sad Cafe* (1963); *Tiny Alice* (1965); *Malcolm* (1966), a dramatization of James Purdy's novel; *Everything in the Garden* (1967), from a play by Giles Cooper; *A Delicate Balance* (1967; Pulitzer Prize); *All Over* (1971); and *Seascape* (1975).

Albemarle, Arnold Joost van Keppel, 1st **earl of** (ăl'bəmärl), 1669–1718, Dutch adherent and constant companion of William III of England. He accompanied the king to England (1688) and was made an earl in 1696. After William's death (1702), he returned to Dutch service and fought in the War of the Spanish Succession.

Albemarle, George Monck or **Monk,** 1st **duke of:** see MONCK, GEORGE.

Albemarle, city (1970 pop. 11,126), seat of Stanly co., central N.C., in the Piedmont region; inc. 1857. A marketing center in an agricultural and aluminum-mining area, Albemarle has poultry-processing and textile and clothing industries. Pfeiffer College is in nearby Misenheimer. There is also a state park in the vicinity.

Albemarle, island, Ecuador: see GALÁPAGOS ISLANDS.

Albemarle Sound, large inland body of generally fresh water, c.55 mi (90 km) long, from 3 to 14 mi (4.8–22 km) wide, NE N.C. Shallow and tideless, the sound is separated from the Atlantic Ocean by a long, narrow barrier island. The Chowan and Roanoke rivers are the largest of many streams flowing into the sound. Albemarle Sound forms a vital link in the Intracoastal Waterway; canals connect it with Chesapeake Bay. Fort Raleigh National Historic Site on Roanoke Island and Wright Brothers National Memorial at Kitty Hawk are at the western end of the sound (see NATIONAL PARKS AND MONUMENTS, table).

Albéniz, Isaac (ēsäk' älbā'nēth), 1860–1909, Spanish pianist and composer. He made his debut as a pianist at the age of four. When still young, he ran away from home and traveled in North and South America and Spain, supporting himself by playing the piano. As a composer, he was influenced by Liszt and later by Debussy, and studied with D'Indy and Dukas, among others. Filipe Pedrell interested him in Spanish music. Although he wrote operas, songs, and many short piano pieces, he is best remembered for his later piano works (especially *Iberia,* 1906–9), which combine a stylized use of Spanish folk material with a brilliant pianistic idiom.

Alberdi, Juan Bautista (hwän boutēs'tä älbār'dē), 1810–84, Argentine political philosopher, patriot, and diplomat. With other young intellectuals he opposed Juan Manuel de ROSAS, and after 1838 he spent years of exile in Uruguay, Chile, and in Europe writing against Rosas. After the overthrow of Rosas by Justo José de URQUIZA (1852), Alberdi served on a number of diplomatic missions. His most important work, *Bases y puntos de partida para la organización política de la república argentina,* a masterpiece of political science, was published in 1852. Many of the suggestions contained in it were incorporated into the Argentine constitution of 1853. After Urquiza was defeated (1861), Alberdi settled in Paris and wrote political tracts against Bartolomé MITRE and Domingo Faustino SARMIENTO as well as sociological works and essays.

Alberoni, Giulio (jōō'lyō älbārō'nē), 1664–1752, Italian statesman in Spanish service, cardinal of the Roman Catholic Church. Appointed (1713) representative of the duke of Parma at the court of PHILIP V of Spain, Alberoni gained influence and ultimately became de facto prime minister. With the princesse des URSINS he arranged the marriage of the king with ELIZABETH FARNESE. His aims were to strengthen Spain, nullify the Peace of Utrecht (see UTRECHT, PEACE OF), and crush Austrian hegemony in Italy. The expeditions by which he recovered Sardinia from Austria (1717) and Sicily from Savoy (1718) provoked Britain, the Netherlands, France, and Austria to form the QUADRUPLE ALLIANCE. Spain was forced to yield, and Philip dismissed and banished (1719) Alberoni, who retired to Rome. He later became papal legate in the Romagna and in Bologna.

Albers, Josef, 1888–, German-American painter, printmaker, designer, and teacher, b. Bottrop, Germany. After working at the BAUHAUS (1920–23), Albers and his wife, the weaver Anni Albers, emigrated to the United States. He has taught throughout the Americas and Europe, and, as director of the Yale School of Art (1950–58), was responsible for major innovations in art education. An extremely versatile artist, he is best known for his *Homage to the Square,* a series of paintings begun in 1949. These serene works, quasi-concentric squares of subtly related colors, form an extensive examination of color properties. See his *Interaction of Color* (1963); studies by Eugen Gomringer (1968) and Werner Spies (1971).

Albert I, 1875–1934, king of the Belgians (1909–34), nephew and successor of Leopold II. He married (1900) Elizabeth, a Bavarian princess. In World War I his heroic resistance (1914) to the German invasion of Belgium greatly helped the Allied cause. Albert spent the entire war at the head of his army, and in 1918 he led the Allied offensive that recovered the Belgian coast. The king and queen did much to improve social conditions in Belgium and in the Belgian Congo. Albert's democratic and affable ways won him great regard at home and abroad. He died in a rock-climbing accident and was succeeded by his son, Leopold III. His daughter, Marie José, married the crown prince (later King Humbert II) of Italy. See biography by Emile Cammaerts (1935).

Albert I, c.1250–1308, German king (1298–1308), son of RUDOLF I. Albert was invested with Austria and Styria in 1282 by his father, who also hoped to secure the succession as king of the Germans for Albert. However, on Rudolf's death (1291) the ELECTORS rejected Albert's candidacy in order to check the growing power of the Hapsburgs and to prevent the crown from becoming hereditary within the Hapsburg dynasty. They chose ADOLF OF NASSAU as king. Albert later engineered Adolf's deposition and replaced him. As king, Albert attempted to strengthen Hapsburg claims for a hereditary dynasty by allying (1299) with Philip IV of France, by supporting the Rhine towns against the Rhenish imperial electors, and by unsuccessfully attempting (1300) to add Holland and Zeeland to the Hapsburg domains. These actions provoked a revolt (1300–1302) by the Rhenish electors, backed by Pope BONIFACE VIII, which Albert suppressed. He later reached an agreement with Boniface, who recognized his title in 1303. Albert attempted to expand his dominion to the east by preventing WENCESLAUS II of Bohemia from acquiring Hungary, but his campaign was unsuccessful until Wenceslaus's death (1305). Albert's son Rudolf succeeded Wenceslaus III (1306). Albert was assassinated by a band of conspirators that included his nephew. Henry of Luxemburg (HENRY VII) was elected to succeed him.

Albert II, 1397–1439, German king, king of Hungary and Bohemia (1438–39), duke of Austria (1404–38). He was the son-in-law of Holy Roman Emperor Sigismund, whom he aided against the Hussites of Bohemia. Albert was unable to suppress the Bohemian revolts (see HUSSITE WARS) and subsequently died on a disastrous campaign against the Turks. With Albert began the lasting HAPSBURG rule over the Holy Roman Empire.

Albert, 1819–61, prince consort of Victoria of Great Britain, whom he married in 1840. He was of WETTIN lineage, the son of Ernest I, duke of Saxe-Coburg-Gotha, and first cousin to Victoria. As an alien prince he was initially unpopular in England, but, in time, the English came to admire him for his irreproachable character, his devotion to the queen and their children, and his responsible and studious concern with public affairs. His influence was particularly strong in diplomacy, and his insistence on a moderate approach to the TRENT AFFAIR (1861) may have averted war with the United States. See biographies by Hector Bolitho (1932), Roger Fulford (1949), Frank Eyck (1959), and Reginald Pound (1974).

Albert, 1490–1545, German churchman, cardinal of the Roman Catholic Church. A member of the house of Brandenburg, he became (1514) archbishop-elector of Mainz. It was on his authorization that Johann TETZEL began in 1517 to preach an indulgence in Albert's diocese—occasioning Martin Luther's first attack on the church. A patron of Ulrich von HUTTEN, Albert was expected to join the Reformers, but after 1525 he actively opposed them. Later he invited the Jesuits to preach in his diocese. He was a friend of Erasmus.

Albert, Carl Bert, 1908–, U.S. Congressman (1947–), b. McAlester, Okla. Admitted to the bar in 1935, Albert enlisted (1941) in the army as a private, served (1942–46) in the Pacific during World War II, and rose to the rank of lieutenant colonel. Elected (1946) as a Democrat to the House of Representatives from a rural Oklahoma district, he rose to the position of majority whip (1955–62), majority leader (1962–71), and speaker of the House (1971). A loyal member of the farm bloc, Albert was also a reliable supporter of the liberal social and economic policies of the

Democratic party. As presiding officer of the 1968 Democratic National Convention, he kept in check the antiwar supporters of Senators Eugene McCarthy and George McGovern.

Albert, Lake, E Africa: see ALBERT NYANZA.

Alberta (ălbûr'tə), province (1971 pop. 1,627,874), 255,285 sq mi (661,188 sq km), including 6,485 sq mi (16,796 sq km) of water surface, W Canada. EDMONTON is the capital and the largest city. The second largest city is CALGARY; other important cities are Lethbridge, Red Deer, and Medicine Hat. Alberta is bounded on the E by Saskatchewan, on the N by Mackenzie dist., Northwest Territories, on the W by British Columbia, and on the S by Montana. Westernmost of the Prairie Provinces, it lies on a high plateau, rising on the W to the Continental Divide at the British Columbia border. There are the foothills of the Rocky Mts. and the spectacular mountains themselves, with three noted national parks—Jasper, Banff, and Waterton Lakes (the Canadian section of Waterton-Glacier International Peace Park). Although Alberta is known as a Prairie Province, only about one quarter of its area is actually treeless—chiefly the undulating prairie of S Alberta. Central Alberta has parklike, partly wooded country, and the northern stretches bear thousands of acres of virgin timberland. Endowed with many lakes,

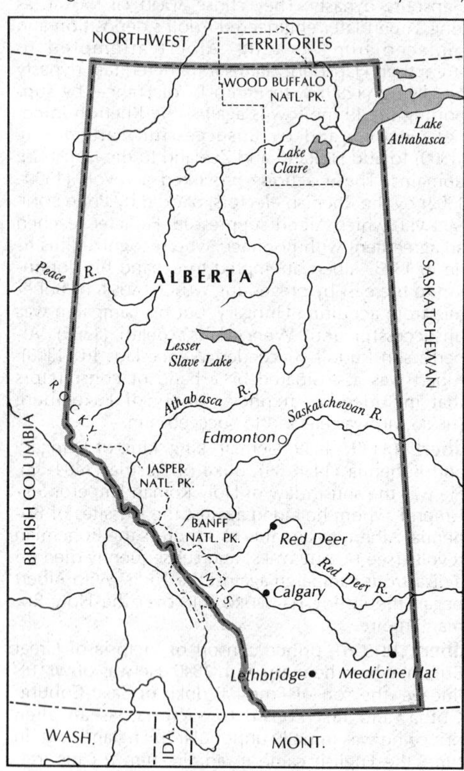

streams, and rivers, the province is drained by the Peace, the Athabasca, the north and south branches of the Saskatchewan, the Red Deer, the St. Mary, the Milk, and many other rivers. The population is concentrated in S and central Alberta, and except for farm centers in the fertile valley of the Peace, the northern portion is sparsely settled; it is still fur-trapping country. Until recently agriculture was Alberta's basic industry. Grain, especially wheat, is the dominant crop, but farming is becoming increasingly diversified. In the south, large irrigation developments, such as the St. Mary-Milk development and those around Calgary, have placed thousands of additional acres under cultivation. In this area is grown a variety of crops, such as vegetables and sugar beets. The province is noted as well for the quality of its livestock. Meat packing, flour milling, dairying, and food processing are important industries. But Alberta's major industry, since the early 1960s, has been the exploitation of its vast petroleum and other mineral resources. Alberta's coal beds contain about one half of Canada's reserves, while the province leads the country in the production of oil; it is believed to have the richest oil deposits in the world, most notably in the famous tar beds of the Athabasca River. Its sources of natural gas are also among the world's greatest. Pipelines radiate from Alberta, carrying crude oil and natural gas to points in E and W Canada and into the United States. The refining of oil and the production of petrochemicals within Alberta itself are growing industries. Other industries include lumbering, textile milling, and the manufacture of iron, steel, and clay products. Alberta's landscape—its rolling wheat fields, huge granaries, sprawling cattle ranches, and vast oil refineries—reminds many visitors of the U.S. Southwest. Annual festivals include the Indian Days Celebration at Banff, which attracts thousands of Indians from a wide area, and the famous Calgary Exhibition and Stampede. Other tourist attractions are Elk Island National Park and the extensive Wood Buffalo National Park, which shelters some 15,000 bison. Alberta was originally part of the territory granted to the HUDSON'S BAY COMPANY by King Charles II in 1670, and its early history was dominated by the fur trade. Traders arrived from the upper Great Lakes before Sir Alexander Mackenzie crossed (1793) the region on his way to the Pacific. In 1794 a Hudson's Bay Company fort was built at the site of present-day Edmonton. Destroyed by Indians in 1807, it was rebuilt 12 years later, and for 50 years it served traders and missionaries within a wide radius. The area remained under the control of the Hudson's Bay Company until 1870 when it was sold, as part of the company's vast domain, to the newly created confederation of Canada. In 1872 mounted police established Fort Macleod in S Alberta, and the following year they built a log fort on the site of present-day Calgary. An act of 1882 created four administrative divisions from the Northwest Territories, and one was named Alberta in honor of Queen Victoria's daughter, Princess Louise Alberta, whose husband was then governor general of Canada. The railroad came through in the mid-1880s, opening up the area to ranchers and homesteaders. To settle the vast fertile land, the Canadian government advertised for immigrants, offering many free acres as inducements. Europeans and Americans began streaming in, and farming began in earnest. The city of Edmonton boomed during the 1898 Klondike gold rush, serving as a supply base, and its growth continued during the early 1900s as immigrants began settling the rich surrounding farmlands. Alberta became a province in 1905. The discovery (1914) of oil in quantity at Turner Valley, near Calgary, presaged a new era for the mineral-rich province, but it was not until 1947, when oil was found in the Leduc fields near Edmonton, that the basic change in Alberta's economy began. By then agriculture had suffered extensively: the 1929 crash, followed by droughts, early frosts, grasshopper plagues, and dust storms, had triggered emigration from the area. Politically, Albertans turned to the SOCIAL CREDIT party in 1935, when William Aberhart became premier of the first Social Credit government. Social Credit administrations were elected for many years after Aberhart's death in 1943, but most attempts to reform banking and money control were declared unconstitutional by the courts. In 1971 the Progressive Conservatives gained control of the provincial government, and Peter Lougheed became premier. In 1974, Ralph Steinhauer, a Cree Indian, was appointed lieutenant governor of Alberta by Canadian Prime Minister Trudeau; Steinhauer was the first Indian to hold such a high executive post. Alberta sends 6 senators (appointed) and 19 representatives (elected) to the national parliament. The Univ. of Alberta is at Edmonton. See W. A. McIntosh, *Prairie Settlement: The Geographical Setting* (1934); P. F. Sharp, *The Agrarian Revolt in Western Canada* (1948); E. J. Hanson, *Dynamic Decade* (1958); C. B. Macpherson, *Democracy in Alberta* (2d ed. 1962); W. F. Schultz, *The People and Resources of Northeastern Alberta* (rev. ed. 1967); Robert Kroetsch, *Alberta* (1968).

Alberta, University of, at Edmonton, Alberta, Canada; provincially supported; coeducational; chartered 1906, opened 1908. It has faculties of arts, engineering, medicine, agriculture, law, dentistry, education, pharmacy and pharmaceutical science, science, graduate studies and research, business administration and commerce, and physical education, as well as schools of dental hygiene, library science, nursing, household economics, and rehabilitation medicine. The Boreal Institute for Northern Studies promotes and supports research in the circumpolar regions.

Albert Achilles, 1414–86, elector of Brandenburg (1470–86); third son of Elector FREDERICK I. He succeeded his brother in 1470. Anxious to consolidate Hohenzollern power in Brandenburg, he issued (1473) the *Dispositio* of Achillea, which decreed that the title of elector should pass to the eldest son. This established the law of primogeniture in Brandenburg. The *Dispositio* remained in force until 1918.

Albert Canal, waterway, c.80 mi (130 km) long N Belgium, from the Meuse River to the Scheldt River; constructed 1930–39. The canal connects the important industrial region around Liège with the port of Antwerp, Belgium.

Alberti, Domenico (dōmā'nĕkō älbĕr'tē), c.1710–c.1740, Venetian singer, harpsichordist, and composer. The Alberti bass (which he used but probably did not invent) is a broken, left-hand chord accompaniment frequently employed in 18th-century keyboard music.

Alberti, Leone Battista (lāō'nā bät-tēs'tä), 1404–72, Italian architect, musician, painter, and humanist, active at the papal court, Florence, Rimini, and Mantua. His treatise *De re aedificatoria* was written c.1450. Though largely dependent upon Vitruvius, it was the first modern work on architecture and influenced the development of Renaissance architectural style. Buildings erected from his designs from c.1450 until his death are among the most dignified and classical of the 15th cent. They include the exteriors of the churches of San Francesco in Rimini, and San Andrea and San Sebastiano in Mantua; part of the facade of Santa Maria Novella, Florence; and the Palazzo Rucellai, Florence, where superimposed orders of architecture adorned the facade for the first time since antiquity. His treatise on painting (1436), the first book in this field to treat theory as well as technique, exercised a great influence on the Renaissance painters and sculptors; in it Alberti discusses the imitation of nature, beauty, perspective, and ancient art. His treatise on sculpture, written c.1464, another first work in its field, dealt, in addition, with human proportions. Other writings include mathematical studies, a treatise on St. Potitus, one on the family, and works on ethics, jurisprudence, and other subjects. See his *On Painting,* tr. by J. R. Spencer (rev. ed. 1966) and study by E. Arntzen (1959).

Alberti, Rafael (räfäĕl'), 1902–, Spanish poet. After abandoning an earlier career as a painter, Alberti published his first book, *Marinero en tierra* (1925), which was widely applauded. His poems show the influence of Juan Ramón Jiménez and of the Spanish classics, especially of Góngora. His poetic brilliance is revealed in *Concerning the Angels* (1929, tr. 1967), a collection of introspective lyrics with surrealist overtones. A Loyalist in the Spanish civil war, Alberti sought exile in Buenos Aires after Franco's triumph. His later poetry is enhanced by an intimate, spiritual lyricism. He edited *A Year of Picasso Paintings* (1969). See his selected poems, ed. and tr. by Mark Strand (1973); studies by C. B. Morris (1966) and Joan Gadol (1969).

Albertinelli, Mariotto (märyôt'tō älbärtēnĕl'lē), 1474–1515, Italian painter. A product of the Florentine school of the High Renaissance, Albertinelli was influenced by Leonardo and Raphael. His best-known works are *The Visitation* (1503; Uffizi) and *The Annunciation* (1510; Accademia, Florence). Albertinelli's works were typical products of his time, revealing an infatuation with classical elegance.

Albert Lea (lē), city (1970 pop. 19,418), seat of Freeborn co., S Minn., near the Iowa line; inc. 1878. It is an important manufacturing and marketing center in a dairy, livestock, and poultry region. Lea College is located there on Lake Chapeau. A state park is nearby.

Albert Nile, river, Uganda: see NILE.

Albert Nyanza (nīăn'zə, nyän'zä) or **Lake Albert,** 2,064 sq mi (5,346 sq km), on the Zaïre-Uganda border, E central Africa. The lake is c.100 mi (160 km) long and c.19 mi (30 km) wide, with a maximum depth of 168 ft (51 m). Lying in the GREAT RIFT VALLEY, 2,030 ft (619 m) above sea level, Albert Nyanza receives the Semliki River and the Victoria Nile and is drained by the Albert Nile, which becomes the Bahr-el-Jebel when it enters the Republic of the Sudan. Albert Nyanza, discovered in 1864 by Sir Samuel Baker, was named for Queen Victoria's consort.

Albert of Brandenburg, 1490–1568, grand master of the TEUTONIC KNIGHTS (1511–25), first duke of Prussia (1525–68); grandson of Elector Albert Achilles of Brandenburg. In 1525 he became a Protestant, and on the advice of Martin LUTHER he secularized the dominions of the Teutonic Knights and became duke of the hereditary duchy of PRUSSIA. The knights' lands had been held as a fief from the king of Poland, and the new duchy remained under Polish suzerainty. On the extinction of Albert's line (1618), Prussia passed to the senior line of Brandenburg, and in 1701 it was made a kingdom.

Alberton, town (1970 pop. 30,322), Transvaal, NE Republic of South Africa, on the WITWATERSRAND; founded 1904. It is an industrial center manufacturing cast iron, machine tools, paints, and abrasives.

Albert the Bear, c.1100-1170, first margrave of Brandenburg (1150-70). He was a loyal vassal of Holy Roman Emperor Lothair II, who, as duke of Saxony, helped him take (1123) Lower Lusatia and the eastern march of Saxony. Albert lost these lands in 1131. He was rewarded (1134) for his share in Lothair's first Italian campaign with the North March. Calling himself margrave of Brandenburg as early as 1136 or 1142, he used the North March as a base for campaigns against the Wends, a pagan Slavic people. Invested (1138) with Saxony by Conrad III, Lothair's successor, he was expelled from the dukedom by HENRY THE PROUD, whom Conrad had deprived of the duchy. Albert later made peace (1142) with HENRY THE LION, son of Henry the Proud. He took part in the Wendish Crusade of 1147, but preferred more conciliatory methods of dealing with his pagan neighbors. As a result he inherited (1150) Brandenburg from its last Wendish prince. Albert's achievements in Christianizing and Germanizing NE Germany were important.

Albertus Magnus, Saint (ălbûr'təs măg'nəs), or **Saint Albert the Great,** b. 1193 or 1206, d. 1280, scholastic philosopher, Doctor of the Church, called the Universal Doctor. A nobleman of Bollstädt in Swabia, he joined (1223) the Dominicans and taught at Hildesheim, Freiburg, Regensburg, Strasbourg, and Cologne before the Univ. of Paris made him doctor of theology in 1245. Later he taught again at Cologne, and he was also briefly (1260-62) bishop of Regensburg. He was a thorough student of Aristotle, and he not only followed Robert Grosseteste in his approach to Aristotelian thought but also did much to introduce Aristotle's scientific treatises and scientific method to Europe. Like Roger Bacon, he had a scientific interest in nature. He made notable botanical observations (recorded in such works as *De vegetabilibus*), was the first to produce arsenic in a free form, and studied the combinations of metals. In philosophy he set out in his *Summa theologiae* to controvert AVERROËS and others and to reconcile the apparent contradictions of Aristotelianism and Christian thought. He wrote many treatises, and many more have been ascribed to him; the problem of determining which are genuinely of his authorship is difficult. He was a strong influence on his favorite pupil, St. Thomas Aquinas. Albertus was canonized in 1931. Feast: Nov. 15. See biography by T. M. Schwertner (1933); D. H. Madden, *A Chapter of Medieval History* (1969).

Albertville, Zaïre: see KALEMI.

Albi (ălbē'), town (1968 pop. 46,613), capital of Tarn dept., S France, in Languedoc, on the Tarn River. A commercial center in an area yielding coal, salt, and sand, it has glassworks, foundries, and food and textile industries. An old Roman city (Albiga), it became an episcopal see in the 5th cent. It was the center of the heresy to which it gave its name (see ALBIGENSES). The old part of the city, known as the *ville rouge* because of its red-brick buildings, is a marvel of medieval architecture. The huge Gothic Cathedral of Sainte-Cécile, begun in 1282, resembles a fortress rather than a church. Other structures include the episcopal palace (13th-15th cent.) and an 11th-century bridge. The birthplace of Toulouse-Lautrec, Albi has an art museum containing much of his work.

Albigenses (ălbĭjĕn'sēz) [Lat.,=people of Albi, one of their centers], religious sect of S France in the Middle Ages. They were officially heretics, but actually they were CATHARI, i.e., not Christians at all, but Provençal adherents of the great Manichaean dualistic system that was endemically popular in the Mediterranean basin for centuries (see MANICHAEISM; BOGOMILS). They held the coexistence of two principles, good and evil, represented by God and the Evil One, light and dark, the soul and the body, the next life and this life, peace and war, and the like. They believed that Jesus only seemed to have a human body (a typically Gnostic idea; see DOCETISM). They were extremely ascetic, bound to absolute chastity, and abstaining from flesh in all its forms, including milk and cheese. They comprised two classes, believers and Perfect, the former much more numerous, making up a catechumenate not bound by the stricter rules observed by the Perfect. The Perfect were those who had received the sacrament of *consolamentum,* a kind of laying on of hands. The Albigenses held their clergy in high regard. One of the most curious practices of the sect was the custom of suicide, preferably by starvation; for, if this life is essentially evil, its end is to be hastened. They had proselyting enthusiasm and preached vigorously. This fact partly accounted for their success, for at that time preaching was unknown in ordinary parish life. In the practice of asceticism as well the contrast between local clergy and the Albigenses was helpful to the new sect. Albigensianism appeared in the 11th cent. and soon had powerful protectors. Local bishops were ineffectual in dealing with the problem, and the pope sent St. Bernard of Clairvaux and other Cistercians to preach in Languedoc, the center of the movement. In 1167 the Albigenses held a council of their own at Toulouse. Pope Innocent III attacked the problem anew, and his action in sending (1205) St. Dominic to lead a band of poor preaching friars into the Albigensian cities was decisive. These missionaries were hampered by the war that soon broke out. In 1208 the papal legate, a Cistercian, Peter de Castelnau, was murdered, probably by an aid of RAYMOND VI of Toulouse, one of the chief Albigensian nobles. The pope proclaimed (1208) the **Albigensian Crusade.** From the first, political interests in the war overshadowed others; behind Simon de MONTFORT, the Catholic leader, was France, and behind Raymond was Peter II of Aragón, irreproachably Catholic. Innocent attempted to make peace, but the prize of S France was tempting, and the crusaders continued to harry the whole region. In 1213 at Muret, Montfort was victor and Peter was killed. The war went on, with the son of Philip II (later Louis VIII) as one of the leaders. Simon's death in 1218 robbed him of victory and left his less competent son to continue the fight. Raymond's son, Raymond VII, joined the war, which was finally terminated with an honorable capitulation by Raymond. By the Peace of Paris (1229), Louis IX acquired the county of Toulouse. The religious result of the crusade was negligible. In 1233, Pope Gregory IX established a system of legal investigation in Albigensian centers and put it into the hands of the Dominicans; this was the birth of the medieval INQUISITION. After 100 years of the Inquisition, of tireless preaching by the friars, and of careful reform of the clergy, Albigensianism was dead. See Steven Runciman, *The Medieval Manichee* (1947, repr. 1961); studies by Edmond Holmes (1925), Jacques Madaule (tr. 1967), J. R. Strayer (1971).

albino (ălbī'nō) [Port.,=white], animal or plant lacking normal pigmentation. The absence of pigment is observed in the body covering (skin, hair, and feathers) and in the iris of the eye. The blood vessels of the retina show through the iris, giving it a pink or reddish color, and the eyes are highly sensitive to light. Albinism is inherited as a Mendelian recessive character in humans and other animals. Through experimental breeding races of albinos have been established among some domestic animals, e.g., mice, rabbits, pigeons, and chickens. Albino animals are sometimes held sacred, for example, white elephants in Siam and white cattle in India. The presence of an excess of black pigment is called melanism.

Albinoni, Tomaso (ălbēnō'nē), 1671-1751, Italian violinist and composer. He wrote nearly 50 operas, as well as instrumental works. His orchestral music was admired by Bach, who used several of Albinoni's themes in his own compositions. Albinoni's surviving works include a violin concerto, two violin sonatas, three oboe concertos, and an adagio for strings and orchestra.

Albinus (ălbī'nəs): see ALCUIN.

Albion (ăl'bēən), ancient and literary name of Britain. It is usually restricted to England and is perhaps derived from the Latin *albus* meaning "white," referring to the chalk cliffs of S England.

Albion, industrial city (1970 pop. 12,112), Calhoun co., S Mich., at the forks of the Kalamazoo River; inc. 1855. Among its manufactures are iron castings, electronic parts, air conditioners, heaters, bakery ovens, and wire products. Albion College is there; it was established in 1835 and the city developed around it. There are many lakes in the area.

Al-Biruni (ăl-bērōō'nē) or **Al Beruni, Abu Rayhan Muhammad ibn Ahmad** (äbōō' rĭhän' məhăm'ĭd ĭb'ən ä'məd ăl bĕrōō'nē), b. 973, d. after 1050, Central Asian scientist. His earlier years were disturbed by political troubles, but after 1017 he was patronized by members of the Ghaznavid dynasty of Turkey. He traveled in Afghanistan and India, making astronomical and geographic observations. The largest part of his writings are on astronomy, astrology, and applied mathematics, but he also wrote on pharmacology, geography, philosophy, history, and other subjects. A taste for precise observation is shown in his determinations of latitudes and the densities of gemstones. His encyclopedic *India* (tr. 1888) and *Chronology* (tr. 1879) provide invaluable information about his time.

albite (ăl'bīt): see FELDSPAR.

Albizu Campos, Pedro (pä'drō älbē'sōō käm'pōs), 1891-1965, Puerto Rican political leader. After service in a Negro unit during World War I he developed a lasting enmity for the United States and became the fiery champion of Puerto Rican independence. His Nationalist party, however, failed to receive popular support in the Puerto Rican elections of 1932, and Albizu Campos turned increasingly to violent action. Convicted of seeking to overthrow the U.S. government, he was imprisoned (1937-43) at Atlanta, then hospitalized in New York City before returning to Puerto Rico in 1947. His party made a poor showing in the 1948 election, and in 1950 Nationalists attacked the governor's mansion in Puerto Rico and Blair House in Washington. Charged with inciting to murder, Albizu Campos was again imprisoned. He was pardoned (1953) because of failing health, but the next year he was implicated in the Nationalist armed attack on the U.S. House of Representatives, and his pardon was revoked. He was sentenced to life imprisonment. He suffered a stroke in 1956 that left him speechless and bedridden. He was again pardoned in 1964 and died the next year.

Alboin (ăl'boin), d. 572?, first Lombard king in Italy (569-572?). With the AVARS he defeated the Gepidae (see GERMANS). He then led (568) an army across the Alps into Italy, took (569) Milan, and after a three-year siege conquered Pavia, which became his capital. He won most of N and central Italy from the Byzantines (see LOMBARDS). According to a legend probably based on fact, he was murdered at the instigation of his wife, ROSAMOND.

Ålborg (ôl'bôrg, ôl'bôr), city (1970 com. pop. 154,343), capital of Nordjylland co., N Denmark, on the Limfjord. It is a major industrial, transportation, and cultural center. Manufactures include cement, machinery, chemicals, liquor, ships, and textiles. Known in the 11th cent., Ålborg was chartered in 1342. Of note are the Cathedral of St. Botolph (12th cent.), a castle (early 16th cent.), and a large cultural hall (1953). The city has two colleges. Until 1948 the name was spelled Aalborg.

Albornoz, Gil Álvarez Carrillo de (hēl äl'värĕth kärē'lyō dā älbôrnôth'), 1310?-1367, Spanish and papal statesman and general, cardinal of the Roman Catholic Church. Under Alfonso XI of Castile he became archbishop of Toledo and distinguished himself fighting the Moors at Tarifa and Algeciras. He also served as chancellor of Castile. Created cardinal in 1350, he left Spain and entered the service of the pope, then at Avignon. He was put in charge of the papal armies and sent (1353) to the Papal States with Cola di RIENZI to restore papal authority. By skillful diplomacy and force of arms, he reduced the communes and petty local tyrants to obedience, thus preparing the way for the return (1378) of the popes from Avignon to Rome. He compiled the law code of the Marches, known as the Constitutions of Aegidius (1357), which was in use until 1816. He died soon after becoming papal legate at Bologna, where he founded a college for Spanish students.

Albrecht. For rulers thus named, see ALBERT.

Albrechtsberger, Johann Georg (yō'hän gā'ôrk äl'brĕkhtsbĕr"gər), 1736-1809, Austrian musical theorist, teacher, and composer. He became (1772) court organist in Vienna and later was chief organist, conductor, and choirmaster of St. Stephen's Cathedral, Vienna. He composed more than 240 works and wrote one of the most important books on counterpoint in the 18th cent. Considered the best teacher of composition in Vienna in his time, he taught Beethoven.

Albret, Jeanne d': see JEANNE D'ALBRET.

Albret (älbrā'), former duchy, SW France, in the LANDES of Gascony. The powerful lords of Albret became kings of NAVARRE by the marriage (1484) of Jean d'Albret with Catherine de Foix, queen of Navarre, who also brought him FOIX and BÉARN. Their son, Henri d'Albret, married (1527) Margaret of Angoulême (MARGARET OF NAVARRE). The marriage added ARMAGNAC to Henri's territories, which now included nearly all of Gascony. In 1550, Albret was raised to a duchy. Henri's daughter and heir, JEANNE

D'ALBRET, married Antoine de BOURBON, and their combined territories were inherited by Henry of Navarre, who in 1589 became king of France as Henry IV. Henry added Albret to the royal domain in 1607 as part of the province of Gascony.

Albright, Ivan Le Lorraine (ôl'brĭt), 1897–, American painter, b. North Harvey, Ill. Allied with the Magic Realist group, Albright developed a style combining American scene painting with surrealist influences. He sought to portray the decadence of mankind and the horror of America during the depression. His compositions, such as *Poor Room* (1942; artist's coll.), contain much realistic detail organized into a fantastic conglomeration. The surfaces of his works are uniform in texture, predominantly gray in tone, and sordid in effect.

Albright, Jacob, 1759–1808, American religious leader, founder of the Evangelical Association (later the Evangelical Church), b. near Pottstown, Pa. A Pennsylvania German and a Lutheran, he was converted c.1790 to Methodism. Preaching and forming classes among his converts in the German settlements, he was ordained a minister (1803) by representatives from these classes and was elected bishop at the first annual conference held by his followers in 1807. The movement, unrecognized by the Methodists, did not take the name Evangelical Association until after Albright's death. A college in Reading, Pa., bears his name. The Evangelical Church united in 1946 with the United Brethren in Christ to form the EVANGELICAL UNITED BRETHREN CHURCH.

Albumazar (ăl"bo͞omä'zər), 805?–885, Arabian astronomer, more fully Abu-Mashar Jafar ibn Muhammad. In his *De magnis conjunctionibus* he claimed that the world had been created when the seven planets were in conjunction in the first degree of the constellation Aries and that its end would come when they should be in conjunction again in the last degree of Pisces. In his astronomical tables he used the Persian calculations of the years and pointed out that they did not follow the Jews' reckoning of time.

albumin (ălbyo͞o'mən) [Lat.,=white of egg], member of a class of water-soluble, heat-coagulating PROTEINS. Albumins are widely distributed in plant and animal tissues, e.g., ovalbumin of egg, myogen of muscle, serum albumin of blood, lactalbumin of milk, legumelin of peas, and leucosin of wheat. Some albumins contain carbohydrates. Separation of serum albumins from other blood proteins can be carried out by electrophoresis or by fractional precipitation with various salts. (A 27% solution of sodium sulfate will precipitate the globulins from blood serum while leaving the albumins in solution). Albumins normally constitute about 55% of the plasma proteins. They adhere chemically to various substances in the blood, e.g., amino acids, and thus play a role in their transport. Albumins and other proteins of the blood aid significantly in regulating the distribution of water in the body. In conditions of shock, heart action may be impaired by a decrease in the volume of circulating blood. Intravenous injection of an albumin solution restores the fluid volume by causing water to flow from the tissues into the circulatory system. In certain types of kidney disease albumin is lost through excretion; as the concentration of blood albumin falls water tends to flow into the tissues, causing edema. Albumins are also used in textile printing, in the fixation of dyes, in sugar refining, and in other important processes.

Albuquerque, Afonso de (əfôN'zō dĭ əlbo͞okĕr'kə, –də ăl"bəkĕr'kə), 1453–1515, Portuguese admiral, the effective founder of the Portuguese Empire in the East. He first went to India in 1503, and in 1506 he set out for India again, carrying a royal commission empowering him to supersede Francisco de ALMEIDA in command. Albuquerque sailed with Tristão da CUNHA along the coasts of Madagascar and E Africa and captured the island of Socotra (Suqutra). Then, leaving da Cunha, he ravaged the Oman coast and took (1507) the island of Hormuz; he attempted to build a fort at Hormuz but had to retire to Socotra when some of his men deserted. Almeida disavowed the conquest and, after Albuquerque had arrived in India, refused to yield command and imprisoned him. When a Portuguese fleet arrived with confirmation of Albuquerque's appointment, Almeida gave way (1509). Albuquerque captured Goa (1510), making it the mainstay of Portuguese power in India; Malacca (1511), extending Portuguese domination to SE Asia; and Hormuz again (1515), thus cutting off the Arab spice trade. While returning from Hormuz to India, Albuquerque learned that he had been replaced. He died at the entrance to Goa harbor. Albuquerque had built forts at Goa, Calicut, Malacca, and Hormuz; reconstructed those of Cannanore and Cochin; begun shipbuilding and other industries in Portuguese India; and established relations with the rulers of SE Asia. The main goals of his policy—control over the spice sources and of the trade routes—were nearly attained during his brief tenure of power. See his *Commentaries* (tr., 4 vol., 1875–84; repr. 1970); biography by Elaine Sanceau (1936).

Albuquerque (ăl'bəkûr"kē), city (1970 pop. 243,751), seat of Bernalillo co., W central N.Mex., on the upper Rio Grande; inc. 1890. The largest city in the state, it is an important commercial, industrial, and transportation center serving a rich timber, livestock, and farm area. It has railroad shops, lumber mills, food-processing plants, and a large electronics industry. A major employer is the huge Atomic Energy Commission installation there, engaged in nuclear research, testing, and weapons development. Kirtland Air Force Base, home of the air force special weapons center, is in Albuquerque. Spanish settlers arrived in the mid-1600s but were driven out (1680) by the Indians. The old town was founded in 1706 and named for the viceroy of New Spain, the duke of Alburquerque. The new town was platted in 1880 in connection with the railroad and grew rapidly, soon enveloping the old town. Albuquerque is a noted health resort with many sanatoriums and hospitals (including a U.S. veterans' hospital and a U.S. Indian hospital). It is the seat of the Univ. of New Mexico, the Univ. of Albuquerque, a U.S. polytechnical institute for Indians, and the headquarters for Cibola National Forest. Tourist attractions in and about the city include the Church of San Felipe de Nerí (1706); the Old Town plaza; numerous museums; the Sandia mts., with caves that contain remains of some of the oldest inhabitants in the western hemisphere; and many Indian pueblos. Coronado State Monument, to the north, is an excavated pueblo near which Coronado camped in 1541. More than one third of the city's residents speak Spanish.

Albury, city (1971 pop. 28,398), New South Wales, SE Australia, on the Murray River at the Victoria border. It is an agricultural market. Among the industries are food processing (including wine) and woolens milling. Albury is also a railroad center.

Alcaeus (ălsē'əs), d. c.580 B.C., Greek poet of Lesbos, a noted early writer of personal lyrics. An aristocrat, he was often embroiled in political battles with the ruling tyrants. The extant fragments of his verse are mostly convivial and light, but his political poetry is sterner. He was, according to tradition, a close associate of SAPPHO. The Alcaic strophe said to have been his invention was much used by Greek lyrists. It was greatly admired by Horace who employed it with slight modification. See C. M. Bowra, *Greek Lyric Poetry* (1936, repr. 1961); Denys Page, *Sappho and Alcaeus* (1955); Hubert Martin, *Alcaeus* (1972).

Alcalá de Henares (älkälä' dā ānä'rās), town (1970 pop. 59,783), Madrid prov., central Spain, on the Henares River, in New Castile. Leather, soap, and china are produced in the town, which is surrounded by an agricultural district that yields wheat. Called Complutum in Roman times, the town is triply famous as the former seat of a great university founded in 1508 and transferred in 1836 to Madrid, as the birthplace of Ferdinand I, Katherine of Aragón, and Cervantes, and as the scene of the Cortes in which ALFONSO XI promulgated the *Ordenamiento de Alcalá.* The town was severely damaged in the Spanish civil war. Among the landmarks are a Gothic collegiate church and the former archiepiscopal palace.

Alcalá la Real (lä rāäl'), town (1970 pop. 21,349), Jaén prov., S Spain, in Andalusia. It has well-known mineral springs. The town played an important part in the conquest of Granada from the Moors (15th cent.). In 1810 it was the site of a French victory in the Peninsular War.

Alcalá Zamora, Niceto (nēthā'tō älkälä' thämō'rä), 1877–1949, Spanish statesman and president of Spain (1931–36). After holding several cabinet posts under the monarchy, he became a republican and was jailed for his political activity in 1930. He helped lead the successful revolution of 1931 and became first provisional and then constitutional president of the Spanish republic. A middle-of-the-road liberal, he was deposed by the Cortes on a Socialist motion (April, 1936) and was succeeded as president by Manuel Azaña. He went into exile first to France and then (1942) to Argentina.

alcalde (ălkăl'dē, Span. älkäl'dā) [Span., from Arab.,=the judge], Spanish official title, in existence at least from the 11th cent. Since the late 19th cent. it has been used for the mayor of a town or village who also acts as justice of the peace. Originally, however, it designated a judge whose scope of jurisdiction varied and who had administrative functions as well. There were, for example, *alcaldes de la hermandad* (judges attached to the tribunals of the town federations formed to assure public order and safety; see HERMANDAD) and *alcaldes de corte* (judges whose jurisdiction extended over the royal residence and the surrounding area). The *alcaldes* were distinguished from the *regidores,* whose functions were primarily administrative. In the 14th cent. the *corregidores,* royal appointees charged with assisting the *regidores* in their duties, encroached upon the judicial functions of the *alcaldes,* depriving them of all but minor civil and criminal jurisdiction. Moreover, *alcaldes* were increasingly chosen by the crown, with only a few towns keeping the right to choose their own *alcaldes* (these being known thereafter as *alcaldes ordinarios*). Since the *corregidores* were often inadequately versed in law, each usually received advice from two trained lawyers, termed *alcaldes mayores,* who specialized in criminal and civil law, respectively. The office was also instituted in the Spanish colonies, but changed its character. There the *alcalde mayor* was the administrator of a provincial division usually smaller than that of a *corregidor;* he also presided over the town *ayuntamiento* (later known as the CABILDO). The *alcalde ordinario* was an elected municipal officer who frequently exercised the powers of mayor and sheriff and was in some villages the sole representative of the law.

Alcamenes (ăl"kəmē'nēz), fl. 5th cent. B.C., Athenian sculptor, said to have been a pupil and rival of Phidias. He worked in gold, ivory, and bronze. His *Aphrodite of the Gardens* at Athens is one of the great masterpieces of antiquity. Pausanias erroneously attributed to him the sculptures of the west pediment of the temple of Zeus at Olympia. He was also well known for his *Hermes Propylaios* [Hermes of the gateway] at the entrance of the Acropolis of Athens. A Roman copy found at Pergamum is in the Turkish Museum of Antiquities in İstanbul.

Alcamo (äl'kämō), city (1971 pop. 41,340), NW Sicily, Italy. It is an agricultural and industrial center and is noted for its white wine. The ruins of the ancient Greek settlement of Segesta are nearby.

Alcántara (älkän'tärä), town (1970 pop. 4,636), Cáceres prov., W Spain, in Estremadura, near the Tagus River. A fine Roman bridge (Arabic *al-kantara*) built in honor of Emperor Trajan and the ruins of the convent and church of the Knights of Alcántara are located in the town. The **Order of Alcántara,** one of the great military religious orders of Spain, established its seat in the town in the 13th cent. after the expulsion of the Moors and enjoyed a period of great splendor (13th–14th cent.). The dignity of grand master passed to the Castilian crown in the 15th cent.

Alcatraz (ăl'kətrăz") [Sp. *Álcatraces*=pelicans], rocky island in San Francisco Bay, W Calif. Discovered by the Spanish in 1769, it was named for its large pelican colony. The Spanish fortified Alcatraz, which, in 1851, came under U.S. control. The island was used as a U.S. military prison from 1859 until 1933, when it became a Federal prison for incorrigible criminals; the prison was closed in 1963. Nicknamed "The Rock," it was a symbol of the impregnable fortress prison with maximum security and very strict discipline. The island became part of Golden Gate National Recreation Area in 1972.

Alcazarquivir (älkä"thärkēvēr'), city (1960 pop. 34,035), N Morocco. The name also appears as Al Qasr al Kabir and Kasr el Kebir. Near the city on Aug. 4, 1578, the Moroccans soundly defeated the Portuguese. King Sebastian of Portugal had invaded Morocco in support of a pretender to the Moroccan throne. Abd al-Malik, ruler of Morocco, King Sebastian, and the Moroccan pretender, Muhammad, all died in the fighting. As a result of the battle, Portugal soon passed (1580) to Philip II of Spain, and the new Moroccan ruler, Ahmad al-Mansur, began his reign with tremendous prestige.

Alcestis (ălsĕs'tĭs), in Greek mythology, daughter of PELIAS. She was won in marriage by ADMETUS, who fulfilled her father's condition that her suitor come for her in a chariot pulled by a wild boar and a lion. So great was her wifely devotion that when Admetus was granted life by the gods if someone would die in his place, she willingly gave her life. In some myths Hercules rescued her from the dead; in others

Persephone was so touched by her devotion that she reunited husband and wife. The legend was dramatized by Euripides in his play *Alcestis*.

alchemy (ăl'kəmē), ancient art of obscure origin that sought to transform base metals (e.g., lead) into silver and gold; forerunner of the science of chemistry. Some scholars hold that it was first practiced in early Egypt and others that it arose in China (in the 5th or 3d cent. B.C.) and was carried westward. It consisted chiefly of experiments with metals and other chemical materials. Alchemical apparatus included the alembic (or *ambix*) for distillation and the *kerotakis* for sublimation. In its beginnings alchemy was essentially a craft and embraced many kinds of metalwork, including the use of alloys resembling gold and silver. Alexandria is generally considered a center of early alchemy, and the art was influenced by the philosophy of the Hellenistic Greeks; the conversion of base metals into gold (considered the most perfect of metals) was part of a general striving of all things toward perfection. Since the early alchemists were mainly artisans, they tried to conceal the secrets of their work; thus, many of the materials they used were referred to by obscure or astrological names. It is believed that the concept of the philosopher's stone (called also by many other names, including the elixir and the grand magistery) may have originated in Alexandria; this was an imaginary substance thought to be capable of transmuting the less noble metals into gold and also of restoring youth to the aged. Alchemy, strongly tinged with magic, reached the Arabs (perhaps in the 8th cent.) and remained for several centuries under Muslim influence; in the 12th cent. it reached parts of Europe through translations of Arab writings (the early Greek treatises were not known in Europe in the Middle Ages). Arabian alchemy was preserved especially in the works of Geber, and the earlier Greek alchemy in those of Zosimus and others. The alchemical writings of the Middle Ages continued to be couched in symbolic and cryptic language. The alchemists became obsessed with their quest for the secret of transmutation; some adopted deceptive methods of experimentation, and many gained a livelihood from hopeful patrons. As a result, alchemy fell into disrepute. However, in the searching experimental quests of the alchemists chemistry had its beginnings; indeed, the histories of alchemy and chemistry are closely linked. TRANSMUTATION OF ELEMENTS has been accomplished in modern chemistry. See Lynn Thorndike, *A History of Magic and Experimental Science* (8 vol., 1923–58); John Read, *Prelude to Chemistry* (2d ed. 1939, repr. 1966); A. J. Hopkins, *Alchemy: Child of Greek Philosophy* (1943); Mark Graubard, *Astrology and Alchemy* (1953); C. A. Burland, *The Arts of the Alchemists* (1967); Jack Lindsay, *The Origins of Alchemy in Graeco-Roman Egypt* (1970).

Alcibiades (ălsĭbī'ədēz), c.450–404 B.C., Athenian statesman and general. Of the family of Alcmaeonidae, he was a ward of Pericles and was for many years a devoted attendant of Socrates. He turned to politics after the Peace of Nicias (421 B.C.), and during the PELOPONNESIAN WAR he was the leader in agitating against Sparta. He was so successful that Athens joined an alliance against Sparta. When Sparta attacked (418 B.C.) Argos, Alcibiades led an Athenian force to help the Argives, but Athens and the allies were beaten at Mantinea. He was (415 B.C.) the chief promoter of the Sicilian campaign and was one of the three leaders (with Nicias and Lamachus) of the Athenian forces. On the night before the expedition sailed, all the statues of Hermes (the hermae) in Athens were mutilated, a sacrilege that caused fear and commotion in the city. Alcibiades was accused—almost certainly falsely—of the crime and was not allowed to have an immediate trial before sailing. When the forces reached Sicily, he proposed an attempt to win allies rather than attacking the hostile cities of Selinus and Syracuse at once. NICIAS carried out this policy to ultimate disaster. Alcibiades had meanwhile been summoned home to stand trial. Instead he fled to Sparta, where he gave advice to King AGIS I, who was successful against Athens. Alcibiades later fell into trouble with the Spartan king, and c.413 he fled to the protection of the Persian satrap TISSAPHERNES and then sought to return to Athens. After the oligarchy of the Four Hundred fell (411), he was recalled at the request of Thrasybulus. Athens had a short era of greatness as Alcibiades directed brilliantly the Athenian fleet in the Aegean and in 410 won a victory over the Peloponnesian fleet off Cyzicus. In command of Athenian forces, he recovered (408) Byzantium and was acclaimed in Athens. A new Spartan commander, however, appeared in Lysander, who defeated the Athenian fleet at Notium in c.406 B.C. Though Alcibiades was absent on another expedition at the time, he was, nevertheless, blamed and exiled. He went to a castle he owned on the western shore of the Hellespont. There in 405 B.C. he attempted to warn the Athenian fleet at AEGOSPOTAMOS against a surprise attack by the Spartans, but his advice was ignored. In 404 at the behest of Lysander, the Persian satrap PHARNABAZUS had Alcibiades murdered. Historians have disagreed in their estimate of Alcibiades from his own day to the present; some have viewed him as a highly competent and unappreciated leader, but most have considered him to be largely responsible for the decline of Athens.

Alcimus (ăl'sĭməs), Hellenizing Jew, appointed to the high priesthood, but opposed by the Maccabees. 1 Mac. 7; 9.1,54–57; 2 Mac. 14.3,13,26.

Alcindor, Lew: see JABBAR, KAREEM ABDUL.

Alcinoüs (ălsĭn'ōəs), in Greek mythology, king of Phaeacia, father of Nausicaä. He aided Odysseus in his journey back to Ithaca. In the story of Jason, he protects Jason and Medea from the Colchians.

Alciphron (ăl'sĭfrŏn, -frən), fl. A.D. c.200?, Greek satirist. His only extant work, in fine Attic style, consists of 122 imaginary letters by common people living in Athens in the 4th cent. B.C. The letters tell much about domestic life of the times.

Alcmaeon (ălkmē'ən), in Greek legend, son of Amphiaraüs and Eriphyle, a leader of the expedition of the EPIGONI against Thebes. He murdered his mother in revenge for his father's death and consequently was haunted by the Erinyes until he found haven on Achelous' island. There he married Callirrhoë, daughter of Achelous, and lived in peace until his wife demanded the sacred robe and necklace of Harmonia, which were in the possession of his former wife Arsinoë. When he tried to regain them from Arsinoë, her brothers killed him.

Alcmaeonidae (ălk"mēŏ'nĭdē), Athenian family powerful in the 7th, 6th, and 5th cent. B.C. Blamed for the murder of the followers of Cylon, the would-be tyrant (c.632 B.C.), they were considered attainted and were exiled. They were again in Athens in the 6th cent. The most prominent members of the family later were CLEISTHENES, PERICLES (whose mother was an Alcmaeonid), and ALCIBIADES.

Alcman (ălk'mən), fl. before 600 B.C., Greek poet of Sparta, founder of the Dorian school of choral lyric poetry. Short choral fragments and a longer one (part of a *parthenion* or choir song for girls) survive. His verse, simple, clear, and musical, was often sung at festivals. See his *Partheneion* (ed. by Denys L. Page, 1951).

Alcmene (ălkmē'nē): see AMPHITRYON.

Alcobaça (əlkōōbä'sə), town (1970 pop. 4,799), Leiria dist., W central Portugal, in Estremadura. The town became a center of the Cistercians in the reign of Alfonso I, and its abbey (building begun 1152) was the greatest of medieval Portugal. The Alcobaça Cistercians exercised enormous influence on education, social conditions, finance, and politics. The early kings of Portugal are buried in the abbey.

alcohol, any of a class of organic compounds with the general formula R—OH, where R represents an alkyl group made up of carbon and hydrogen in various proportions and —OH represents one or more HYDROXYL GROUPS. In common usage the term *alcohol* usually refers to ETHANOL. The class of alcohols also includes METHANOL; the amyl, butyl, and propyl alcohols; the GLYCOLS; and GLYCEROL. An alcohol is generally classified by the number of hydroxyl groups in its molecule. An alcohol that has one hydroxyl group is called monohydric; monohydric alcohols include methanol, ethanol, and ISOPROPANOL.

```
    H   H
    |   |
H — C — C — OH
    |   |
    H   H
```

ethyl alcohol (ethanol)

```
    OH  OH  OH
    |   |   |
H — C — C — C — H
    |   |   |
    H   H   H
```

glycerol or glycerine (1,2,3-propanetriol)

Alcohols

Glycols have two hydroxyl groups in their molecules and so are dihydric. Glycerol, with three hydroxyl groups, is trihydric. The monohydric alcohols are further classified as primary, secondary, or tertiary according to the number of carbon atoms bonded to the carbon atom to which the hydroxyl group is bonded. Many of the properties and reactions characteristic of alcohols are due to the electron charge distribution in the C—O—H portion of the molecule (see CHEMICAL BOND). Chemical reactions involving the hydroxyl group in an alcohol molecule are of two kinds: those in which the hydroxyl group is replaced as a whole, e.g., reaction of ethanol with hydrogen iodide to form ethyl iodide and water; and those in which only the hydrogen in the hydroxyl group is replaced, e.g., the reaction of ethanol with sodium, an active metal, to form sodium ethoxide and hydrogen. Alcohols are generally less volatile, have higher melting points, and are more soluble in water than the corresponding hydrocarbons (in which the —OH group is replaced with hydrogen). For example, at room temperature methanol is a liquid, while methane is a gas.

Alcoholics Anonymous, worldwide organization dedicated to the curing of alcoholics; founded 1935 by two former alcoholics, one a New York broker, the other an Ohio physician. They developed a philosophy of life that has made recovery from alcoholism possible for countless men and women everywhere. It includes psychological principles that have long been recognized as being effective in the reorganization of personality. The organization functions through local groups that have no constitutions, officers, or dues. Anyone who has a drinking problem may become a member. There are presently about 17,000 local groups in the United States, with a total membership of approximately 575,000.

alcoholism, the consumption of alcoholic beverages to a degree that interferes with bodily or mental health or with normal social and occupational behavior. Chronic alcoholism is a condition in which the drinker is physiologically dependent on alcohol; i.e., he is addicted. Alcoholism, either in the form of heavy steady drinking or in the form of occasional periods of intense drinking alternating with sober periods, is the most widespread drug addiction problem; it is estimated that about 9 million of the 95 million social drinkers in the United States are problem drinkers or alcohol addicts (see DRUG ADDICTION AND DRUG ABUSE). Because alcohol can profoundly alter behavior (by blocking inhibitions, for example, and releasing aggressive behavior), it is one of the most dangerous addictive drugs. A large proportion of arrests in the United States are for drunkenness or for drunken driving, and a high proportion of crimes of violence (e.g., child beating, homicide, and suicide) are committed by people who have been drinking. Alcoholics cause one half of all highway fatalities and are responsible for much lost work time and inefficiency on the job. Intoxication is produced by alcohol as it circulates in the blood and acts to depress the central NERVOUS SYSTEM (see DEPRESSANT). Alcohol, which requires no digestion, can pass directly into the bloodstream. The absorption rate depends principally on the concentration of the drug in the stomach and small intestine; the presence of food in the stomach slows the absorption process. Alcohol is not stored in the body or excreted but is metabolized in the liver at a fixed rate of between 0.25 and 0.33 oz (7.1–9.4 grams) per hr, varying with the individual. Thus alcohol is found in the bloodstream and signs of intoxication appear when the rate of alcohol consumption is greater than the rate at which it is metabolized in the liver. At a blood level of about .05%, alcohol lowers alertness, increases appetite, and may relieve fatigue. In increasing doses, it causes exaggerated behavior, impairs muscular coordination and judgment, slows reflexes, and reduces negative feelings such as anxiety and guilt. Definite intoxication occurs at more than .15%, although .10% is frequently considered legal drunkenness. The lethal level, often given as .60%, may be as low as .40% in some people. Death results from respiratory failure as the medulla of the brain is depressed. The rapid ingestion of about a pint of absolute ethyl alcohol or its equivalent would be fatal for most individuals. In practice, most people become unconscious before they drink themselves to death. However, ingestion of adulterated alcoholic beverages containing methyl (wood) alcohol will cause damage to retinal cells and may lead to complete blindness within a few days. The effects of alcohol are similar to those of BARBITURATES, and the combination of the two is particularly dangerous. Like all addictive drugs, alcohol produces tolerance and physical dependence in the habitual user. A hangover, a combination of headache, nausea, fatigue, and depression, may be a mild type of withdrawal from alcohol. Sudden abstinence by the chronic alcoholic produces a severe withdrawal syndrome—including tremors, vomiting, and convulsions resembling those of epilepsy—that is more likely to cause death than withdrawal from narcotic drugs. The final and most dangerous phase in this withdrawal pattern is DELIRIUM TREMENS, a toxic psychosis characterized by insomnia, hallucinations, seizures, and maniacal behavior. Chronic use of alcohol results in loss of brain cells, producing memory lapses, impaired learning ability, motor disturbances, and general disorientation. It is not known whether the deterioration is caused by the alcohol itself or by malnutrition and vitamin deficiencies resulting from the body's decreased ability to use vitamins. Other ailments that can result from prolonged alcoholism include CIRRHOSIS, a liver ailment, diseases of the digestive system, damage to the heart, and lowered resistance to infection. Although anyone who drinks alcohol experiences intoxicating effects, only a small percentage of all drinkers become alcoholics. The steps in the development of chronic alcoholism vary with the individual; it is usually not possible to determine which of a group of drinkers will become addicted. Although there is no such thing as an alcoholic personality, there are certain personality traits common in alcoholics, e.g., feelings of inadequacy and inability to tolerate frustration or deal with the demands of life. Many alcoholics may border on serious mental illness. Nearly half come from broken homes or have an alcoholic parent. Certain cultural groups, e.g., some N European peoples, and some groups where the social structure has been disrupted, e.g., Eskimos and North American Indians, seem to be more susceptible than others. In the United States, although the number of women drinkers has markedly increased in recent years, four out of five alcoholics are male. It is possible that a hereditary component exists, i.e., some people may experience a unique sense of gratification when intoxicated. A typical case of beginning alcoholism resembles ordinary social drinking, although drinking may be more intense and prolonged. Later the drinker may begin to drink in the morning to obliterate his guilt feelings and to relieve the physical discomfort of the hangover from the drinking of the night before. As the alcoholic becomes increasingly unable to control his drinking he becomes antisocial and disorganized. Severe chronic alcoholism may result in loss of job, home, and family. The treatment of alcoholism begins with medical efforts to achieve sobriety. Anti-anxiety drugs such as certain SEDATIVES and barbiturates are used to ease withdrawal and delirium tremens. Medical treatment is usually followed by membership in a supportive group such as ALCOHOLICS ANONYMOUS, in which alcoholics commit themselves to change and work together to solve their drinking problems. Although most therapeutic methods emphasize complete abstinence, some experimental groups try to teach alcoholics to keep drinking under control. Psychoanalysis is not usually helpful. Some alcoholics are helped by hypnotic suggestion, methods of conditioning to avoid alcohol, or self-administration of drugs such as ANTABUSE, which produces severe discomfort if present in the system when alcohol is consumed. An experimental treatment for severe drinking bouts is the use of lithium salts, presently used to treat manic-depressive illness. Increased sensitivity to the problem of alcoholism led to the establishment of the U.S. National Institute on Alcohol Abuse and Alcoholism as part of the National Institutes of Mental Health. The Federal government now sponsors rehabilitation centers, outpatient halfway houses, and much research. See H. M. Trice, *Alcoholism in America* (1966); Henrik Wallgren, *Actions of Alcohol* (2 vol., 1970); Yedy Israel and Jorge Mardones, ed., *Biological Basis of Alcoholism* (1971); P. G. Bourne and Ruth Fox, ed., *Alcoholism: Progress in Research and Treatment* (1973).

Alcor (ălkôr'), in astronomy: see MIZAR.

Alcott, Bronson (Amos Bronson Alcott) (ôl'kət), 1799–1888, American advocate of educational and social reform, b. near Wolcott, Conn. His meager formal education was supplemented by omnivorous reading, while he gained a living from farming, working in a clock factory, and as a peddler in the South. He taught in several places before he opened (1834) his Temple School in Boston. His own records, as well as those made by Elizabeth Palmer Peabody, his assistant, show his concern with the integrated mental, physical, and spiritual development of the child. Yet unfavorable reactions to his advanced and liberal theories forced him to close his school. His disappointment was lessened when he learned of the success of Alcott House, a school founded by his disciples in England. One of the leading exponents of TRANSCENDENTALISM, he wrote for the transcendental periodical *Dial* (the "Orphic Sayings" being his most famous contribution) and was a nonresident member of Brook Farm. He was one of the founders (1843) of a cooperative vegetarian community, "Fruitlands," near Harvard, Mass., but it was abandoned in 1844. Poverty continually plagued the life of the Alcotts until the writings of his daughter, Louisa May Alcott, relieved the family of financial worry. He became superintendent of the Concord public schools, whose reformation he described in his *Reports.* From 1879 he was dean of the Concord School of Philosophy, which annually gathered disciples to hear him and many other speakers. Among his writings are *Observations on the Principles and Methods of Infant Instruction* (1830), *Record of a School* (1835), and *Ralph Waldo Emerson* (1882). See his journals (ed. by Odell Shepard, 1938, repr. 1966) and his letters (ed. by R. L. Herrinstadt, 1969); biographies by F. B. Sanborn (1893, repr. 1965) and D. McCuskey (1969); study by G. E. Haefner (1970); Odell Shepard, *Pedlar's Progress* (1937, repr. 1967).

Alcott, Louisa May, 1832–88, American novelist and writer of children's books, b. Germantown, Pa.; daughter of Bronson Alcott. She is chiefly remembered for *Little Women,* one of the most popular girls' books ever written. Mostly educated by her father, she was also guided by her friends Emerson and Thoreau, and her first book, *Flower Fables* (1854), was a collection of tales originally created to amuse Emerson's daughter. Alcott was determined to contribute to the small family income and worked as a servant and a seamstress before she made her fortune as a writer. By 1860 her poems and short stories were appearing in the *Atlantic Monthly.* Her letters written to her family when she was a Civil War nurse were published as *Hospital Sketches* (1863) and were received with enthusiasm; her first novel, *Moods,* followed in 1864. In 1867 she became editor of a children's magazine, *Merry's Museum.* She first achieved wide fame and wealth with *Little Women,* published in two volumes in 1868–69. The novel, which recounts the adolescent adventures of the four March sisters, is largely autobiographical, the author herself being represented by the spirited Jo March. Her other books for juveniles include *Little Men* (1871) and *Jo's Boys* (1886), both sequels to *Little Women; An Old-Fashioned Girl* (1870); *Eight Cousins* (1875), with its sequel *Rose in Bloom* (1876); and *Under the Lilacs* (1879). They all picture family life in Victorian America with warmth and perception. Another novel, *Work* (1873), draws on Alcott's early experiences as a breadwinner for her family. In her mature years she was active in the abolition and temperance movements, woman suffrage, and other causes. Her letters and journal were edited by E. D. Cheney (1889, repr. 1966). See biographies by M. M. Worthington (1958) and C. L. Meigs (1970).

Alcoy (älkoi'), city (1971 pop. 61,371), Alicante prov., SE Spain, in Valencia, on the Serpis River. An important industrial center with manufactures of paper (especially cigarette paper), matches, and textiles, it also has trade in grain, wine, and oil from the surrounding region.

Alcuin (ăl'kwĭn) or **Albinus** (ălbī'nəs), 735?–804, English churchman and educator. He was educated at the cathedral school of York by a disciple of Bede; he became principal in 766. CHARLEMAGNE invited him (781?) to court at Aachen to set up a school. For 15 years Alcuin was the moving spirit of the Carolingian renaissance. He combated illiteracy with a system of elementary education. On a higher level he established the study of the seven liberal arts, the trivium and quadrivium, which became the curriculum for medieval Western Europe. He encouraged the study and preservation of ancient texts. His dialogue textbook of rhetoric, called *Compendia,* was widely used. He wrote verse, and his letters were preserved. Alcuin's treatise against Felix of Urgel did much to defeat the heresy of ADOPTIONISM. He died as head of the abbey of St. Martin of Tours, where he had one of his most famous schools. See studies by E. J. B. Gaskoin (1904), Eleanor Duckett (1951, repr. 1965), and Gerald Ellard (1956).

Alcyone: see HALCYONE.

Aldan (əldän'), city (1967 est. pop. 67,000), Yakut Autonomous Republic, E Siberian USSR, on the Aldan Plateau. Located on a major north-south highway of the region, it is also in the heart of an important gold-mining area. Nearby, at Emeldzhak, are valuable mica deposits.

Aldan, river, c.1,400 mi (2,250 km) long, rising in the Stanovoy Range, Yakut Autonomous Republic, SE Siberian USSR. It flows north and east, past Tommot and around the Aldan Plateau, before flowing generally northwest to enter the Lena River c.100 mi (160 km) N of Yakutsk. The Amga, Uchur, and Maya rivers are its main tributaries. The Aldan River is navigable c.1,000 mi (1,610 km) upstream. Gold is found in its basin.

Aldana, Francisco de (fränthēs'kō thā äldä'nä), 1537–78, Spanish general, diplomat, and poet, b. Alcántara or Naples. He symbolizes the ideal of the Spanish Renaissance. As a soldier he served Philip II of Spain and Sebastian of Portugal in Europe and Africa. He cultivated many verse forms, and his poetry treats themes such as love and religion. His works were published posthumously by his brother Cosme.

Aldanov, Mark (märk əldä'nəf), pseud. of **Mark Aleksandrovich Landau,** 1886–1957, Russian writer. Aldanov earned degrees in chemistry and law. He took part in the Revolution of 1917, after which he emigrated to France, where he wrote novels about social conflict. These include *The Thinker,* a tetralogy on the events of the era 1793–1821, comprising *The Ninth Thermidor* (1923, tr. 1926), *The Devil's Bridge* (1925, tr. 1928), *The Conspiracy* (1927), and *St. Helena: Little Island* (1921, tr. 1924). *The Tenth Symphony* (1931, tr. 1948) concerns Vienna in Beethoven's time. *The Fifth Seal* (1939, tr. 1943) portrays the decay of revolutionary idealism during the Spanish civil war. Aldanov describes the clash between Soviet and American ideologies in *Nightmare and Dawn* (tr. 1957). Among his last works are *A Night at the Airport* (tr. 1949) and *The Escape* (tr. 1950). He visited the United States in 1941, returning to France shortly before his death.

Aldebaran (ăl"dĕb'ərən), brightest star in the constellation TAURUS; Bayer designation α Tauri; 1970 position R.A. $4^h34.2^m$, Dec. +16°27'. An orange giant star (SPECTRAL CLASS K5 III) with apparent magnitude averaging 0.85, it is one of the 20 brightest stars in the sky. Aldebaran is a visual BINARY STAR and an irregular VARIABLE STAR, with MAGNITUDE ranging from 0.78 to 0.93. Its distance is 68 light-years. The name is from the Arabic meaning "follower (of the Pleiades)."

aldehyde (ăl'dəhīd) [*al*cohol + New Lat. *dehydrogenatus*=dehydrogenated], any of a class of organic compounds that contain the CARBONYL GROUP, >C=O, and in which the carbonyl group is bonded to at least one hydrogen; the general formula for an aldehyde is RCHO, where R is hydrogen or an alkyl or aryl group. Aldehydes are formed by partial oxidation of primary alcohols and form carboxylic acids

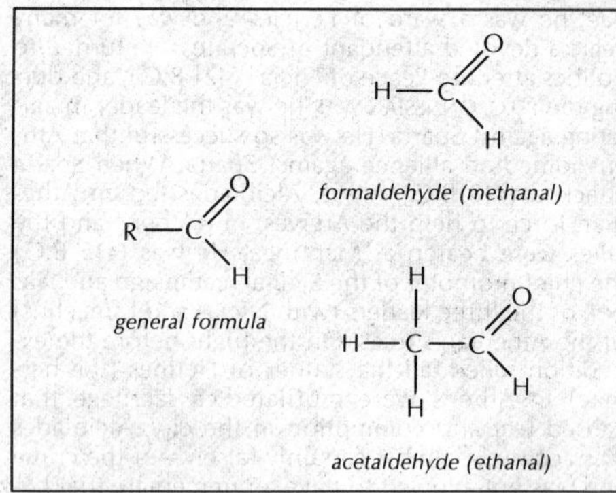

Aldehydes

when they are oxidized. The common name for an aldehyde is often derived from the name of the acid it forms; the IUPAC name is usually derived from the name of the alcohol from which it is formed. Low molecular weight aldehydes, e.g., FORMALDEHYDE and ACETALDEHYDE, have sharp, unpleasant odors; higher molecular weight aldehydes, e.g., BENZALDEHYDE and FURFURAL, have pleasant, often flowery, odors and are found in the ESSENTIAL OILS of certain plants. Aldehydes are important in industry for the manufacture of synthetic resins, e.g., bakelite, and for making dyestuffs, flavorings, perfumes, and other chemicals. Some are used as preservatives and disinfectants.

Alden, Henry Mills (ôl'dən), 1836–1919, American editor, b. Mt. Tabor, Vt. He was editor of *Harper's*

Magazine from 1869 until his death. A highly religious and fastidious man, he directed his efforts toward making *Harper's* a family magazine. His works include *A Study of Death* (1895) and *Magazine Writing and the New Literature* (1908).

Alden, John, c.1599-1687, Puritan settler in Plymouth Colony. He came to America on the *Mayflower* and was prominent as assistant to the governor of the colony. He moved (c.1627) to Duxbury and there was neighbor and friend of Miles STANDISH. Alden's marriage to Priscilla Mullens gave rise to the romantic legend made familiar by Longfellow's poem, *The Courtship of Miles Standish*.

Alder, Kurt (äl'dər), 1902-58, German chemist, educated at Berlin and at Kiel. He was on the research staff of the Bayer Dye Works (1936-40) before becoming (1940) professor of chemistry and director of the chemical institute of the Univ. of Cologne. He shared with Otto Diels the 1950 Nobel Prize in Chemistry for discovering a process for the synthesis of complex organic compounds. The commercial application of the process led to the preparation of various products, including dyes, drugs, insecticides, and plastics.

alder (ôl'dər), name for deciduous trees and shrubs of the genus *Alnus* of the family Betulaceae (BIRCH family), widely distributed, especially in mountainous and moist areas of the north temperate zone and in the Andes. The black alder (*A. glutinosa*) is an Old World species now naturalized in E North America. Its bark, still used for dyes and tanning, was formerly considered medicinal; its wood is useful chiefly as charcoal. *A. rugosa*, the speckled alder, forms extensive swamp thickets in Eurasia and North America. The red alder (*A. rubra*), the largest tree of the genus, is the most important hardwood timber tree in its native region, the Pacific coast of North America. Alder trees are classified in the division MAGNOLIOPHYTA, class Magnoliopsida, order Fagales, family Betulaceae.

alderfly: see DOBSONFLY.

Alderney (ôl'dərnē), Fr. *Aurigny* (ōrēnyē'), anc. *Riduna*, island (1971 pop. 1,686), c.3 sq mi (7.7 sq km), in the English Channel, northernmost of the larger Channel Islands. It is separated from the French coast and from other islands by swift tidal races. The soil is fertile and well cultivated about St. Anne, the principal town; the island's main crops are potatoes and grains. Tourism is important.

Aldershot (ôl'dərshôt), municipal borough (1971 pop. 33,311), Hampshire, S central England. It is the site of the largest military training center (est. 1854) in Great Britain. The minister of defense appoints most of the borough council.

Aldhelm, Saint (ôld'hĕlm), 639?-709, English churchman and scholar. He was abbot of Malmesbury (from 675) and became the first bishop of Sherborne (705). A distinguished student of the classics whose own Latin prose style was widely imitated, he was also a skilled musician and wrote hymns, popular songs, and ballads for the people. He founded several monasteries and built several churches; the one still standing at Bradford-on-Avon is considered a fine example of Saxon architecture. His name also occurs as Ealdhelm. Feast: May 25.

Aldington, Richard (ôl'dĭngtən), 1892-1962, English poet and novelist. While studying at the Univ. of London, he became acquainted with Ezra Pound and H. D. (Hilda DOOLITTLE), whom he married in 1913. He was one of the leading IMAGISTS and helped edit the *Egoist*, the principal imagist organ. His early poems, extraordinary in their verbal precision, were published under the title *Images* (1915). *Images of War* and *Images of Desire* followed in 1919, the latter marking a departure from pure imagism. Aldington's first novel, *Death of a Hero* (1929), was a bitter indictment of war. It was followed by *The Colonel's Daughter* (1931), equally biting in its satiric intent. Aldington was at his best when in an angry state of artistic and intellectual rebellion; experiments with milder satire proved less effective. After World War II he published little poetry. His most important work was in biography—*Wellington* (1946); *Portrait of a Genius, But . . .* (1950), a study of D. H. Lawrence; *Lawrence of Arabia* (1955), a harshly critical portrait of T. E. Lawrence; and *Portrait of a Rebel: the Life and Work of Robert Louis Stevenson* (1957). See his autobiographical *Life for Life's Sake* (1941); study by N. T. Gates (1974).

aldosterone (ăl''dŏstĭrōn'), steroid secreted by the cortex of the adrenal gland. It is the most potent HORMONE regulating the body's electrolyte balance. Aldosterone acts directly on the kidney to decrease the rate of sodium-ion excretion (with accompanying retention of water), and to increase the rate of potassium-ion excretion. The secretion of aldosterone appears to be regulated by two mechanisms. First, the concentration of sodium ions may be a factor since increased rates of aldosterone secretion are found when dietary sodium is severely limited. Second, reduced blood flow to the kidney stimulates certain kidney cells to secrete the proteolytic enzyme renin, which converts the inactive angiotensinogen globulin in the blood into its active form, angiotensin. This peptide in turn stimulates the secretion of aldosterone by the adrenal cortex. Pathologically elevated aldosterone secretion with concomitant excessive retention of salt and water often results in edema.

Aldrich, Nelson Wilmarth, 1841-1915, U.S. Senator from Rhode Island, b. Foster, R.I. He rose in local politics as state assemblyman (1875-76) and U.S. Representative (1879-81) before he served as Senator (1881-1911). Aldrich, after the death of Henry B. Anthony, dominated Republican politics in Rhode Island, and because of his wide interests in banking, manufacturing, and public utilities he was popularly considered the spokesman of big business in the Republican party and the nation. After the controversy of 1888 he was the great proponent of protective tariffs and was successful in saving the Payne-Aldrich Tariff Act of 1909 even against the combined opposition of the Democrats and the Progressives. He took charge of Republican administrative legislation after 1897 and helped force the Silver Republicans out of the party, the Gold Standard Act of 1900 completing the work. As Theodore Roosevelt's sympathies grew increasingly progressive, Aldrich led the Senate opposition to him. Aldrich was deeply concerned with monetary problems, helped shape the Aldrich-Vreeland Currency Act of 1908, and headed the National Monetary Commission to study bank reform. He visited Europe in the course of this study, which he continued after leaving the Senate. The "Aldrich plan," published in 1911, was not made into law, but it did offer information that was used by the Democrats in setting up the Federal Reserve System. See biography by N. W. Stephenson (1930, repr. 1971).

Aldrich, Thomas Bailey, 1836-1907, American author and editor, b. Portsmouth, N.H. His most widely read work was *The Story of a Bad Boy* (1870), a vigorous narrative based on his own boyhood. His short stories, especially those in *Marjorie Daw and Other People* (1873), are noted for their naturalness and craftsmanship. Aldrich also excelled at writing light verse. In 1881 he succeeded W. D. Howells as editor of the *Atlantic Monthly*, a position he held until 1890. See biography by Ferris Greenslet (1908, repr. 1965); Mrs. T. B. Aldrich, *Crowding Memories* (1920); study by C. E. Samuels (1966).

Aldridge-Brownhills, urban district (1971 pop. 88,475), Staffordshire, central England. It was created in 1966 through the merger of two former districts. Aldridge-Brownhills is residential and has extensive areas of open countryside. Chasewater Pleasure Park, in the northern part of the district, has the largest area of open water in the Midlands. The village of Rushall in the district was the site of a battle in 1643 during the English civil war. In 1974, Aldridge-Brownhills became part of the new metropolitan county of West Midlands.

aldrin (ôl'drĭn): see INSECTICIDE.

Aldrovandi, Ulisse (o͞olēs'sä äldrōvän'dē), 1522-1605, Italian naturalist, professor at the Univ. of Bologna. He instigated the establishment (1567) of the Bologna Botanical Garden and wrote an early pharmacopoeia. His chief work was the *Natural History* (14 vol.), of which four volumes (some sources say five) were published before his death; the rest were prepared for publication from his manuscripts.

Aldus Manutius (ăl'dəs mənyo͞o'shəs) or **Aldo Manuzio** (äl'dō mäno͞o'tsyō), 1450-1515, Venetian printer. He was educated as a humanistic scholar and became tutor to several of the great ducal families. One of them, the Pio family, provided him with money to establish a printery in Venice. Aldus was at this time almost 45 years old. He devoted himself to publishing the Greek and Roman classics, in editions noted for their scrupulous accuracy; a five-volume set of the works of Aristotle, completed in 1498, is the most famous of his editions. He was especially interested in producing books of small format for scholars at low cost. To this end he designed and cut the first complete font of the Greek alphabet, adding a series of ligatures or tied letters, similar to the conventional signs used by scribes, which represented two to five letters in the width of one character. To save space in Latin texts he had a type designed after the Italian cursive script; it is said to be the script of Petrarch. This was the first *italic* type used in books (1501). Books produced by him are called Aldine and bear his mark, which was a dolphin and an anchor. Aldus employed competent scholars as editors, compositors, and proofreaders to insure accuracy in his books. Much of his type was designed by Francesco Griffi, called Francesco da Bologna. The Aldine Press was later managed by other members of his family, including a son, Paulus Manutius (1512-74), and a grandson, Aldus Manutius (1547-97), who was best known for his classical scholarship.

ale: see BEER.

Aleandro, Girolamo (jĕrô'lämō äläān'drō), 1480-1542, Italian scholar, cardinal of the Roman Catholic Church. He is also called Hieronymus Aleander. A principal in the Lutheran crisis, he obtained the condemnation of Martin Luther at the Diet of Worms (1521), and he made an outline of policy for the Catholic Reformation. His grandnephew **Girolamo Aleandro,** the younger, 1574-1649, was a humanist, known for his antiquarian studies.

aleatory music (ā'lēətôr''ē), music in which elements traditionally determined by the composer are determined either by a process of random selection chosen by the composer or by the exercise of choice by the performer(s). At the compositional stage, pitches, durations, dynamics, and so forth are made functions of playing card drawings, dice throwings, or mathematical laws of chance, the latter with the possible aid of a computer. Those elements usually left to the performers' discretion include the order of execution of sections of a work, the possible exclusion of such sections, and subjective interpretation of temporal and spatial pitch relations. Also called "chance music," aleatory music has been produced in abundance since 1945 by several composers, the most notable being John CAGE and Iannis XENAKIS.

Alecsandri, Vasile (väsē'lē älĕksän'drē), 1821-90, Rumanian poet, dramatist, and statesman. He was (1858) provisional foreign minister and subsequently served in various diplomatic posts. Besides writing lyric poetry celebrated for the description of his native landscape, he published a notable collection of Rumanian folk songs. His plays include *Ovidiu* (1890). See study by Alexandre Cioranescu (tr. 1973).

Alecto (əlĕk'tō): see FURIES.

Alegría, Ciro (sē'rō älägrē'ä), 1909-67, Peruvian novelist. Imprisoned several times for his political activities, Alegría was exiled to Chile in 1934. He gained fame with his novel *La serpiente de oro* (1935, tr. *The Golden Serpent*, 1943). In 1941 he won the Latin American Novel Prize for *El mundo es ancho y ajeno* (tr. *Broad and Alien Is the World*, 1941), which depicts the exploitation of the Indian by the white man.

Aleichem, Sholom (shō'ləm älā'khəm) [Heb.= Peace be upon you!—a very common form of greeting in Yiddish], 1859-1916, Yiddish author, b. Russia. His real name was Solomon, or Shalom, Rabinowitz. The first part of his pseudonym is also written Sholem or Shalom. He was influential in establishing Yiddish as a literary language. His stories are celebrated for their portrayal of character, and he is perhaps best known for his humorous tales of life among the poverty-ridden and oppressed Russian Jews of the late 19th and early 20th cent. His five novels, many plays, and some 300 short stories, all written in Yiddish, have been translated into Russian, German, and other European languages. English translations of some of his tales include *The Old Country* (1946) and *Tevye's Daughters* (1949). In the last years of his life Sholom Aleichem lived in the United States; he died in New York City where, through his work, he helped to found the Yiddish Art Theater. His autobiographical writings include *Adventures of Mottel* (tr. 1953) and *The Great Fair* (tr. 1955). See biography by his daughter, Marie Waife-Goldberg (1968); Maurice Samuel, *The World of Sholom Aleichem* (1943, repr. 1973); Melech Grafstein, ed., *Sholom Aleichem Panorama* (1949).

Aleijadinho (älāzhädē'nyō) [Port.,=little cripple], 1730-1814, Brazilian sculptor. His real name was Antônio Francisco Lisboa. Although he was maimed in hands and feet, he is known for the brilliance of his church sculpture. His most famous works are the carvings in the Church of São Francisco at OURO PRÊTO and the statues of the Twelve Prophets at Congonhas do Campo. The distinctive baroque style of Aleijadinho's works, carved in wood and indigenous soapstone, has caused much church sculpture in his native Minas Gerais to be attributed to him.

Aleixandre, Vicente (vēthĕn'tā älāhän'drā), 1898–, Spanish lyric poet. He won the national prize for literature for *La destrucción o el amor* (1935). His verse, often free in form, is pessimistic and surrealistic; it expresses the anguish and hope of man. Aleixandre's works are collected in *Poesías completas* (1960) and *Obras completas* (1968). See study by Kessel Schwartz (1970).

Alekhine, Alexander (əlyĕkh'ĕn), 1892–1946, Russian-French chess player, b. Moscow. He became a naturalized French citizen after the Russian Revolution. At the age of 16 he gained the rank of master and in 1927, by a surprising defeat of Capablanca at Buenos Aires, became world champion. In 1930 at San Remo, Italy, he did not lose a single game in a tournament that included all of the major European players. In 1935 he lost the championship to Max Euwe but regained it in 1937 and kept it until his death. His clear and realistic style and the brilliance of his middle-game and end-game combinations are found in his book, *My Best Games of Chess, 1924–1937* (1939). See study by R. G. Eales and A. H. Williams (1973).

Aleks-. For some Russian names beginning thus, see ALEX-; e.g., for Aleksandr, see ALEXANDER.

Aleksandropol, see LENINAKAN, USSR.

Aleksandrov (əlyĭksän'drəf), city (1967 est. pop. 46,000), Russian Republic, E European USSR. It has radio, textile, and food industries. The city came under the control of the Muscovite princes in 1302. Ivan IV resided (1564–81) in Aleksandrov, where he organized his political police, the Oprichnina. The city is also the site of the first printing establishment in Russia, founded during the reign of Ivan IV, and of the famous Uspenski convent (late 17th cent.).

Aleksandrov-Grushevski: see SHAKHTY, USSR.

Aleksandrovsk: see ZAPOROZHYE, USSR.

Aleksandrovsk-Sakhalinski (əlyĭksän'drəfsk-səkhəlyĕn'skē), city on N Sakhalin island, Far Eastern USSR. A port on the Tatar Strait, it is also a coal-mining center and has lumber and fishing industries. The city was founded in 1881 as a place of exile.

Alekseyev, Mikhail Vasilyevich (mēkhəēl'vəsē'-lyəvĭch əlyĭksyā'əf), 1857–1918, Russian general, chief of staff (1915–17) of Czar Nicholas II. With other officers he urged the czar to abdicate in favor of the czarevich in order to save the dynasty prior to the Russian Revolution. Alekseyev was briefly chief of staff in the provisional government headed by Aleksandr Feodorovich Kerensky after the czar was overthrown. After the Bolsheviks took over in Nov., 1917 (Oct., 1917, O. S.), Alekseyev and General KORNILOV organized an anti-Bolshevik movement in the south.

Alema (ăl'əmə), unidentified town, E of the Jordan. 1 Mac. 5.26.

Alemán, Mateo (mätā'ō älämän'), 1547–1614?, Spanish novelist, b. Seville. Alemán studied medicine and practiced accounting. He led a turbulent life, was sent to jail twice for his debts, and at the age of 60 found refuge in Mexico. The first part of his picaresque novel, *Guzmán de Alfarache,* was published in 1599 and the second part in 1604. Written with moralizing overtones, the novel presents a valuable picture of contemporary life and a view of mankind as corrupt but salvable through divine grace. James Mabbe translated it into English as *The Rogue; or, The Life of Guzmán de Alfarache* (1922).

Alemán, Miguel (mēgĕl' älämän'), 1902–, president of Mexico (1946–52). Son of a revolutionary general, Alemán became a highly successful lawyer and a champion of Mexican labor. He was governor of Veracruz from 1936 to 1940 but resigned to manage the presidential campaign of Manuel Ávila Camacho, under whom Alemán held (1940–45) the ministry of the interior. Elected president in 1946, Alemán became the first civilian president of Mexico since Francisco I. MADERO. He changed the name of the official government party from National Revolutionary party to Institutional Revolutionary party (PRI), to indicate the permanent status of the revolution. Alemán's administration was characterized by a vigorous program of modernization. He encouraged foreign investment, developed reclamation and power projects, improved communications and education, and generally raised the standard of living. In his post-presidential years he headed the national tourism council, encouraging the development of Acapulco as a resort and helping to bring the Olympic games to Mexico City in 1968.

Alemanni (ălĭmăn'ī), Germanic tribe, a splinter group of the Suebi (see GERMANS). The Alemanni may have been a confederation of smaller tribes. First mentioned (A.D. 213) as unsuccessfully assaulting the Romans between the Elbe and the Danube, they later settled (3d cent.) in upper Italy. By the 5th cent. they occupied territories on both sides of the Rhine south of its junction with the Main (present Alsace, Baden, and NE Switzerland). Their westward expansion brought them into conflict with the Franks, whose king CLOVIS I defeated them in 496. In 505 he forced them to retire into Rhaetia, and in 536 they passed under Frankish rule. By the 7th cent. they had accepted Christianity. SWABIA is also known as Alamannia, and the High German dialects of SW Germany and Switzerland are called Alemannic. In French speech the name *Allemands* came to signify all Germans.

Alemanni, Luigi: see ALAMANNI, LUIGI.

Alembert, Jean le Rond d' (zhäN lərôN' däläN-bĕr'), 1717–83, French mathematician and philosopher. The illegitimate son of the chevalier Destouches, he was named for the St. Jean le Rond church, on whose steps he was found. His father had him educated. Diderot made him coeditor of the ENCYCLOPÉDIE, for which he wrote the "preliminary discourse" (1751) and mathematical, philosophical, and literary articles. Discouraged, however, by attacks on his unorthodox views, he withdrew (1758) from the *Encyclopédie.* A member of the Academy of Sciences (1741) and of the French Academy (1754; appointed secretary, 1772), he was a leading representative of the ENLIGHTENMENT. His writings include a treatise on dynamics (1743), in which he enunciated a principle of mechanics known as D'ALEMBERT'S PRINCIPLE; a work on the theoretical and practical elements of music (1759); and a valuable history of the members of the French Academy (1787).

Alembert's principle: see D'ALEMBERT'S PRINCIPLE.

Alemeth (ăl'əmĕth). **1** Descendant of Saul. 1 Chron. 8.36; 9.42. **2** Town, NE of Jerusalem. 1 Chron. 6.60. Almon: Joshua 21.18.

Alemtejo: see ALENTEJO, Portugal.

Alençon, François, duc d': see FRANCIS, duke of Alençon and Anjou.

Alençon (äläNsôN'), town (1968 pop. 33, 388), capital of Orne dept., N France, in Normandy, on the Sarthe. A commercial center in a fertile farm area, it is particularly noted for its fine lace work, an industry which dates from the 17th cent. The town also has spinning mills, printing plants, sawmills, and quarries. Alençon was heavily damaged in World War II. Among its surviving structures are Notre Dame Church, with windows and a porch from the 16th cent.; the Gothic St. Leonard's Church (completed in 1505); and the Ozé House (15th cent.).

Alentejo (əläntā'zho͞o), historic province, SE Portugal, now divided into Altro (Upper) Alentejo (4,888 sq mi/12,660 sq km) and Baixo (Lower) Alentejo (5,318 sq mi/13,774 sq km). The capital of Altro Alentejo is ÉVORA, and the capital of Baixo Alentejo is BEJA. The historic province has been further subdivided into the districts of Beja, Évora, and Portalegre. Alentejo, "the granary of Portugal," is drained by the Guadiana River and tributaries of the Sado River. Sheep, horses, cattle, and hogs are raised, and grains, olives, cork trees, and fruits are grown. Alentejo was involved in Portugal's many wars with Castile. The name was formerly spelled Alemtejo.

Aleppo (əlĕp'ō) or **Alep** (əlĕp'), Arabic *Haleb,* city (1970 est. pop. 639,000), capital of Aleppo governorate, NW Syria. It is a commercial center located in a semidesert region where grains, cotton, and fruit are grown. The city is also a market for wool, hides, and fruit. Manufactures include silk, printed cotton textiles, dried fruits and nuts (especially pistachios), and cement. Aleppo is a transportation hub; it has an international airport and is connected by rail with Damascus and the Mediterranean port of Latakia, as well as with Turkey and Iraq. The city was inhabited perhaps as early as the 6th millenium B.C. In the 14th–13th cent. B.C. it was controlled by the Hittites. Later, Aleppo was a key point on the major caravan route across Syria to Baghdad. From the 9th to the 7th cent. B.C. it was mostly ruled by ASSYRIA and was known as Halman. It was later (6th cent. B.C.) held by the Persians and Seleucids. Seleucus I (d. 280 B.C.) rebuilt much of the city, renaming it Berea. The city's commercial importance was enhanced by the fall of Palmyra in A.D. 272, and by the 4th cent. Aleppo was a major center of Christianity. A flourishing city of the Byzantine Empire, it was taken without a struggle by the Arabs in 638; subsequently, in the late 11th cent., it was captured by the Seljuk Turks. Crusaders besieged Aleppo without success in 1118 and 1124, and Saladin captured it in 1183, making it his stronghold. The city was held briefly by the Mongols under Hulagu Khan (1260) and by Tamerlane (1401); in 1517 the Ottoman Empire annexed Aleppo, which then became a great commercial city. From 1832 to 1840 it was held by Muhammad Ali of Egypt. Aleppo's importance declined in the late 19th cent. with the advent of the Suez Canal and other trade routes, but the city revived under French control after World War I and continued to prosper after Syrian independence (1941). The Univ. of Aleppo (1960), Aleppo Institute of Music (1955), and Muslim theological schools are in the city. Points of interest include the Byzantine citadel (12th cent.) and the Great Mosque (715).

Alert, settlement, on Ellesmere Island, extreme N Northwest Territories, Canada, on the Arctic Ocean. It is the most northerly permanent settlement in the world. The settlement has a radio and meteorological station and a landing strip operated jointly by Canada and the United States.

Ales, Alexander: see ALESIUS, ALEXANDER.

Alès (älĕs'), formerly **Alais** (älā', älĕs'), city (1968 pop. 44,607), Gard dept., S France, in Languedoc, at the foot of the Cévennes mts., on the Gardon River. Situated in one of the most important coal basins in SE France, it has iron and steel industries, vehicle-repair facilities, and factories making machinery and hosiery. In the 16th cent. Alais was one of the principal centers of French Protestantism (see HUGUENOTS). The Peace of Alais, signed there (1629), stripped the Huguenots of their political power. Several buildings date from the 17th cent.

Alesia (əlē'zhə), hilltop town of Celtic and Roman Gaul, on the site of Alise-Sainte-Reine, near Dijon. It was held by VERCINGETORIX and his men (52 B.C.) when Caesar besieged it. Caesar prevented Vercingetorix' allies from raising the siege and starved out the town, thereby ending Gallic resistance to Rome.

Alesius (əlē'shəs), **Ales,** or **Aless, Alexander** (both: əlĕs'), 1500–1565, Scottish Protestant theologian. As canon of the collegiate church at St. Andrews he tried to reclaim Patrick HAMILTON from his Lutheran views but was himself persuaded to accept the reformed teachings. In 1532 he escaped to the Continent, where he gained the confidence of Martin Luther and Philip Melanchthon and joined in signing the Augsburg Confession. He was commended to Henry VIII by them, and arriving in England in 1535, he enjoyed friendly association with Archbishop Cranmer, Thomas Cromwell, and others. He lectured on divinity at Cambridge and afterward practiced medicine in London. After Cromwell's fall in 1540, Alesius returned to Germany, where he was professor of theology, first at Frankfurt-an-der-Oder and later at Leipzig.

Alessandri, Arturo (ärto͞o'rō älĕssän'drē), 1868–1950, president of Chile (1920–25, 1932–38). The 1920 presidential candidate of the Liberal Alliance, a coalition of all the enemies of the conservatives, Alessandri was elected on a reform platform. During his first administration, the conservatives were able to block most of his program, and when his cabinet refused to support him, Alessandri went (1924) into voluntary exile. Returning in 1925, he supervised the writing of a new constitution that guaranteed universal male suffrage, granted greater provincial powers, and effectively ended the power of the conservative-clerical oligarchy. During these years, Chile underwent a political reformation that was supported essentially by the middle class and the labor unions. His second term was also stormy, but marked by continued political and social reforms.

Alessandria (äläs-sän'drēä), city (1971 pop. 102,349), capital of Alessandria prov., in Piedmont, NW Italy, at the confluence of the Tanaro and Bormida rivers. It is an industrial center and agricultural market. Manufactures include furniture, machinery, and hats. Alessandria was built (1164–67) as a stronghold of the LOMBARD LEAGUE and was named for Pope Alexander III. At first a free commune, the city passed in 1348 to the duchy of Milan and, in 1707, to the duke of Savoy. Alessandria was the scene of a pro-Mazzini conspiracy in 1833. There are two 13th-century churches and remains of the city's medieval fortifications.

Ålesund (ô'ləso͞on), city (1970 pop. 39,496), Møre og Romsdal county, W Norway, on 3 islands in the Atlantic Ocean at the mouth of the Storfjord. It is a major commercial and fishing port. Products include clothing, processed fish, and dairy goods. Of note is a nearby stone church (early 13th cent.). The name was formerly spelled Aalesund.

Aletsch (ä'lĕch), glacier, 66 sq mi (171 sq km), 16 mi (26 km) long and 1.2 mi (1.9 km) wide, S central Switzerland, largest in the Alps. It lies between the

Jungfrau and the Aletschhorn, one of the highest (13,721 ft/4,182 m) peaks in the Bernese Alps.

Aleut (əlo͞ot′, ăl′ē̄o͞ot″), native inhabitant of the Aleutian Islands and W Alaska. Like the ESKIMO, the Aleuts are racially similar to Siberian peoples. Their language is a member of the ESKIMO-ALEUT family (see AMERICAN INDIAN LANGUAGES). When they were first noted by Vitus Jonassen Bering in 1741, their estimated population was between 20,000 and 25,000. Because of their skill in hunting sea mammals, the Aleuts were exploited by Russian fur traders throughout the coastal waters of the Gulf of Alaska, sometimes as far south as California. The ruthless policies of their masters and conflict with the fierce mainland natives reduced their population by the end of the 18th cent. to one tenth its former size. They now number about 1,000 and continue to live in relative isolation. Most are members of the Russian Orthodox Church. See V. I. Jochelson, *The History, Ethnology and Anthropology of the Aleut* (1933, repr. 1966); Robert Ackerman, *Ethnohistory in Southwestern Alaska and the Southern Yukon* (1970).

Aleutian Islands (əlo͞o′shən), chain of rugged, volcanic islands curving c.1,200 mi (1,900 km) west from the tip of the Alaska Peninsula and approaching the Komandorski Islands, USSR. A partially submerged continuation of the Aleutian Range, they separate the Bering Sea from the Pacific Ocean. The Aleutians are composed of four main groups: Fox Islands, nearest to the mainland, including Unimak, Unalaska, Umnak, and Akutan; Andreanof Islands, including Amlia, Atka, Adak, Kanaga, and Tanaga; Rat Islands, including Amchitka and Kiska; and Near Islands, smallest and westernmost group, including Agattu and Attu. The Semichi Islands, of which Shemya Island is the largest, are nearby. The Aleutians have few good harbors, and the numerous reefs make navigation treacherous. Temperatures are relatively moderate, but heavy rains and constant fog make the climate dreary. Almost completely treeless, the islands have a luxuriant growth of grasses, bushes, and sedges. Sheep and reindeer are raised. Hunting and fishing are the main occupations of the Eskimo population. The Aleutian Islands were discovered in 1741 by Vitus Bering, a Danish explorer employed by Russia. The indigenous Aleuts were exploited by the Russian trappers and traders who, in search of sea otter, seal, and fox fur, established settlements on the islands in the late 18th and early 19th cent. The Aleutian Islands were included in the Alaska purchase in 1867 and at that time became part of the United States. After the purchase, the U.S. government forbade seal trapping off the Aleutians except by the Aleuts. Fishing and fur hunting are now controlled by the Federal government. Dutch Harbor, one of the few good Aleutian harbors, became a transshipping point for Nome in 1900, after the discovery of gold turned Nome into a boom town. The Aleutian Islands were important during World War II; in 1940, a U.S. naval base was established at Dutch Harbor. In 1942 the Japanese bombed the base and later occupied Attu, Kiska, and Agattu islands. From bases on Adak and Amchitka, the United States launched a counterattack and regained the islands in 1943. The Aleutian Islands play an important role in U.S. defense because of their proximity to the USSR. Radar stations (part of the Distant Early Warning Line) and military bases are located on the islands. Most of the islands are incorporated in the Aleutian National Wildlife Reserve. The islands have a population of 8,057. The main settlements are on Unalaska island.

Aleutian Range, volcanic mountain chain, c.1,600 mi (2,600 km) long, SW Alaska, extending W from Anchorage along the Alaska Peninsula, and continuing, partly submerged as the Aleutian Islands, to Attu island. Mt. Redoubt (10,200 ft/3,109 m) is the highest peak. Part of the volcanic belt that rings the Pacific Ocean, the Aleutian Range has been active in recent years, notably at Katmai (see KATMAI NATIONAL MONUMENT).

alewife: see HERRING.

Alex-. For some Russian names beginning thus, see ALEKS-; e.g., for Alexandrov, see ALEKSANDROV.

Alexander III, d. 1181, pope (1159–81), a Sienese named Orlando Bandinelli, successor of Adrian IV. He was a learned canonist who had studied law under Gratian and had taught at Bologna. He came to Rome under Eugene III, was made a cardinal, and became a trusted adviser of Adrian IV. Alexander's election to the papacy was opposed by a few cardinals, who elected an antipope, Victor IV. Although the antipope was supported only by Germany and some Lombards, the schism thus begun continued until 1178 with antipopes Paschal III and Calixtus III. Alexander was forced (1162) by Holy Roman Emperor FREDERICK I into exile in France. In the long struggle with the emperor, the pope was aided by the LOMBARD LEAGUE, which named the town of Alessandria for him. After the battle of Legnano (1176), the emperor was forced to submit. Alexander had already (1174) received the penance of Henry II of England for the murder of St. Thomas à Becket, whom Alexander had canonized in 1173. He convened and presided at the Third LATERAN COUNCIL. One of the great medieval popes, he issued many decretals, established the procedure for canonizing saints, inaugurated the two-thirds rule for papal elections, protected the universities, and was one of the most distinguished champions of ecclesiastical independence in the Middle Ages. He was succeeded by Lucius III. See biography by Cardinal Boso (tr. 1973).

Alexander VI, 1431?–1503, pope (1492–1503), a Spaniard (b. Játiva) named Rodrigo de Borja or, in Italian, Rodrigo Borgia; successor of Innocent VIII. He took Borja as his surname from his mother's brother Alfonso, who was Pope Calixtus III. Rodrigo became cardinal (1456), vice chancellor of the Roman Church (1457), and dean of the sacred college (1476). Cardinal Borgia had four illegitimate children by a Roman woman, Vannozza; among them were Cesare and Lucrezia Borgia. Alexander was elected by a corrupt conclave. The foreign relations during his papacy were dominated by the increasing influence of France in Italy, which culminated in the invasion of Charles VIII in 1494. Alexander prevented Charles from taking the church property in Rome, but he turned over to the French the valuable Ottoman hostage Djem, brother of Sultan BEYAZID II. Alexander's son, Cesare Borgia, was the principal leader in papal affairs, and papal resources were spent lavishly in building up Cesare's power. For his daughter Lucrezia, Alexander arranged suitable marriages. The favoritism shown his children and the lax moral tone of Renaissance Rome as well as the unscrupulous methods employed by Cesare and other papal officials have made Alexander's name the symbol of the worldly irreligion of Renaissance popes. Girolamo SAVONAROLA was an outspoken opponent and critic of Alexander. Recent studies tend to minimize the pope's immorality and stress his solid achievements as a political strategist and church administrator. It was Alexander who proclaimed the line of demarcation that awarded part of the new discoveries in the world to Spain, part to Portugal (see TORDESILLAS, TREATY OF). Alexander was a munificent patron of the arts. He was succeeded by Pius III. See Orestes Ferrara, *The Borgia Pope: Alexander VI* (1940); Michael de La Bedoyère, *The Meddlesome Friar and the Wayward Pope* (1958).

Alexander I, 1777–1825, czar of Russia (1801–25), son of PAUL I (in whose murder he may have taken an indirect part). In the first years of his reign the liberalism of his Swiss tutor, Frédéric César de LA HARPE, seemed to influence Alexander. He suppressed the secret police, lifted the ban on foreign travel and books, made attempts to improve the position of the serfs, and began to reform the backward educational system. In 1805, Alexander joined the coalition against NAPOLEON I, but after the Russian defeats at Austerlitz and Friedland he formed an alliance with Napoleon by the Treaty of Tilsit (1807) and joined Napoleon's CONTINENTAL SYSTEM. Alexander requested M. M. SPERANSKI to draw up proposals for a constitution, but adopted only one aspect of Speranski's scheme, an advisory state council, and dismissed him in 1812 to placate the nobility. During this period Russia gained control of Georgia and parts of Transcaucasia as a result of prolonged war with Persia (1804–13) and annexed (1812) Bessarabia after a war with Turkey (1806–12). Relations with France deteriorated, and Napoleon invaded Russia in 1812. Alexander's defeat of the French made him one of the most powerful rulers in Europe. At first his foreign policy was liberal. He insisted on a constitutional charter and mild treaty terms for France at the Congress of Vienna, and he gave autonomy to Finland (annexed in 1809) and a constitution to Poland, of which he became king in 1815. From 1812 on, Alexander was preoccupied by a vague, mystical Christianity, which contributed to his increasing conservatism. Under the influence of the pietistic Juliana KRÜDENER and others, he created the HOLY ALLIANCE to uphold Christian morality in Europe. Viewing revolutionary movements as challenging to the authority of legitimate Christian monarchs, the czar now supported METTERNICH in suppressing all national and liberal movements. Alexander's religious fervor was partly responsible for the establishment of military colonies, which were agricultural communities run by peasant soldiers. Intended to better the lot of the common soldier, the colonies became notorious for the regimentation and near-serfdom imposed on the soldiers. Alexander abrogated many of his earlier liberal efforts. His policies caused the formation of secret political societies, and when Alexander's brother NICHOLAS I succeeded him the societies led an abortive revolt (see DECEMBRISTS). After Alexander's death, rumors persisted that he escaped to Siberia and became a hermit. His tomb was opened (1926) by the Soviet government and was found empty; the mystery remains unsolved. In Alexander's reign St. Petersburg became a social and artistic center of Europe. Ivan KRYLOV and Aleksandr PUSHKIN dominated the literary scene. An excellent picture of Alexander's period is found in Leo Tolstoy's *War and Peace*. See biographies by Maurice Paleologue (1938, repr. 1969), Allen McConnell (1970), and Alan Palmer (1974).

Alexander II, 1818–81, czar of Russia (1855–81), son and successor of Nicholas I. He ascended the throne during the Crimean War (1853–56) and immediately set about negotiating a peace (see PARIS, CONGRESS OF). Influenced by Russia's defeat in the war and by peasant unrest Alexander embarked upon a modernization and reform program. The most important reform was the emancipation of the serfs (1861; see EMANCIPATION, EDICT OF). This failed, however, to meet the land needs of the newly freed group and created many new problems. In 1864, a system of limited local self-government was introduced (see ZEMSTVO) and the judicial system was partially westernized. Municipal government was overhauled (1870), universal military training was introduced (1874), and censorship and control over education were temporarily relaxed. In Poland, Alexander initially adopted a moderate policy, granting the subject nation partial autonomy. When revolt broke out in 1863, however, Alexander reacted with brutal suppression, imposing severe russification. The Western powers were sharply warned against interference. Prussia's support of Russia during this diplomatic crisis led to a Russo-Prussian rapprochement, and in 1872 the THREE EMPERORS' LEAGUE was formed by Russia, Prussia, and Austria-Hungary. Throughout his reign Alexander promoted vigorous expansion in the East. The conquest of the Ussuri region in the Far East was confirmed by the Treaty of Peking (1860) with China. Central Asia was added to Russia by the conquest of Kokand, Khiva, and Bokhara (1865–76). Alaska, however, was sold (1867) to the United States. In 1877–78 Russia waged war on Turkey, ostensibly to aid the oppressed Slavs in the Balkans (see RUSSO-TURKISH WARS). Meanwhile, in domestic affairs, Alexander's reforms, while outraging many reactionaries, were regarded as far too moderate by the liberals and radicals. Radical activities increased sharply among the intelligentsia, resulting in a reassertion of repressive policies. When the populist, or "to the people," movement arose in the late 1860s (see NARODNIKI), the government arrested and prosecuted hundreds of students. Many radicals responded with terrorist tactics. In 1881, after several unsuccessful attempts, a member of the People's Will, a terrorist offshoot of the populist movement, assassinated Alexander with a hand-thrown bomb; this on the very day (March 13) that Alexander had signed a decree granting the zemstvos an advisory role in legislation. He was succeeded by his son Alexander III. See biography by Stephen Graham (1935, repr. 1968); studies by W. E. Mosse (rev. ed. 1962), E. M. Almedingen (1964), and David Footman (1974).

Alexander III, 1845–94, czar of Russia (1881–94), son and successor of Alexander II. His father's assassination, his limited intelligence and education, his military background, and the influence of such advisers as Konstantin P. POBYEDONOSTZEV and Mikhail N. Katkov all contributed to his reactionary policies. On his accession he discarded the modest proposals for reform made by Count LORIS-MELIKOV. Alexander increased the repressive powers of the police and tightened censorship and control of education. He limited the power of the *zemstvos* [local assemblies] and the judiciary, increased controls over the peasantry, subjected the national minorities to forcible Russification, and persecuted all religious minorities, especially the Jews. Perhaps the only enlightened policy of Alexander's reign was pursued by his energetic minister of finance, Count WITTE, who used governmental pressure and investments to stimulate industrial development and to begin construction of the TRANS-SIBERIAN RR. The czar and his foreign minister, Nikolai K. GIERS, worked for peace in Europe, although Russian expansion in Central

Asia almost led to conflict with Great Britain. In the Balkans, Russia's attempts to make Bulgaria a satellite proved unsuccessful and led to a final break with Austria-Hungary, which also had interests there. The Three Emperors' League of Russia, Austria-Hungary, and Germany was replaced (1887) with a Russo-German alliance. This was not renewed in 1890, and a Franco-Russian entente grew after 1891 (see TRIPLE ALLIANCE AND TRIPLE ENTENTE). Alexander was succeeded by his son Nicholas II.

Alexander, 1893–1920, king of the Hellenes (1917–20), second son of CONSTANTINE I. After his father's forced abdication, he succeeded to the Greek throne with the support of the Allies, who distrusted the sympathies of his elder brother George (later King George II). Alexander died of a monkey bite. His father, Constantine I, was restored to the throne shortly afterward.

Alexander III, king of Macedon: see ALEXANDER THE GREAT.

Alexander I, 1078?–1124, king of Scotland (1107–24), son of Malcolm III and St. Margaret of Scotland. He succeeded his brother Edgar, who had divided the kingdom so that Alexander ruled only N of the Forth and Clyde rivers, while his brother David ruled in the south. Early in his reign he decisively quelled an uprising in N Scotland. Like his mother, Alexander encouraged ecclesiastical conformity with English ways and established several monasteries, including the abbeys at Inchcolm and Scone. David succeeded him as David I.

Alexander II, 1198–1249, king of Scotland (1214–49), son and successor of William the Lion. He joined the English barons in their revolt against King John of England in 1215. Though he made his peace with John's successor, Henry III, in 1221, there was later friction that almost led to war. In 1237, Alexander agreed to give up his claims to overlordship in old Northumbria and to exchange lands he held in central England for lands in the north. At home Alexander was firm in quelling disorder.

Alexander III, 1241–86, king of Scotland (1249–86), son and successor of Alexander II. He married a daughter of Henry III of England and quarreled with Henry, and later Henry's son Edward I, over the old English claims to overlordship in Scotland. The great achievement of Alexander was his final acquisition for Scotland of the Hebrides and of the Isle of Man, which his father had already claimed from Norway. King Haakon IV of Norway attempted to drive the Scots from the islands in 1263, but a storm battered his ships, and he was defeated in the battle of Largs in the Clyde River. In 1266, Alexander signed a treaty with Haakon's successor, Magnus VI, assigning the islands to Scotland. This was followed by an arrangement with Norway providing for the marriage of Magnus's son Eric with Alexander's daughter Margaret. Alexander survived his children, and when he died his only near relative was his little granddaughter MARGARET MAID OF NORWAY. See biography by James Fergusson (1937).

Alexander (Alexander Obrenović) (ōbrĕ'nəvĭch), 1876–1903, king of Serbia (1889–1903), son of King MILAN. He succeeded on his father's abdication. Proclaiming himself of age in 1893, he took over the government, abolished (1894) the relatively liberal constitution of 1889, and restored the conservative one of 1869. He recalled his father in 1897, gave him command of the army, and permitted him to undertake a campaign against the pro-Russian Radical party. In 1900 he married Draga Mašin, the widow of a foreign engineer and a former lady-in-waiting (see DRAGA). The scandal of the marriage exasperated his opposition. In 1903, after Alexander had arbitrarily suspended and then restored the new liberal constitution that he had granted in 1901, he and his queen were assassinated by a clique of officers. Peter Karadjordjević was recalled as King Peter I, and the Obrenović dynasty came to an end.

Alexander, 1888–1934, king of Yugoslavia (1921–34), son and successor of Peter I. Of the Karadjordgević family, he was educated in Russia and became crown prince of Serbia upon the renunciation (1909) of the succession by his brother George. He led Serbian forces in the Balkan War of 1912, became regent in June, 1914, led the Serbian army in World War I, and became (Dec., 1918) regent of the kingdom of the Serbs, Croats, and Slovenes (later Yugoslavia). In 1922 he married Princess Marie of Rumania. After his accession increasing disorder arose from the Croatian autonomy movement. After the assassination (1928) of Stjepan RADIĆ, the Croat Peasant party leader, Alexander in 1929 dismissed the parliament, abolished the constitution and the parties, and became absolute ruler. To emphasize the unity he hoped to give the country he changed (Oct., 1929) its official name to Yugoslavia. Although he announced the end of the dictatorship in 1931 and proclaimed a new constitution, he kept power in his own hands. His authoritarian and centralizing policy brought him the hatred of the separatist minorities, particularly the Croats and Macedonians, as well as the opposition of Serbian liberals. In foreign policy he was loyal to the French alliance and to the LITTLE ENTENTE. In 1934 he debarked at Marseilles on a state visit to France. A member of a Croatian terrorist organization fired on his car, killing the king and fatally wounding the French foreign minister, Louis Barthou. Alexander was succeeded by his young son, Peter II. See Stephen Graham, *Alexander of Yugoslavia* (1939, repr. 1972).

Alexander (Alexander of Battenberg), 1857–93, prince of Bulgaria (1879–86); second son of Prince Alexander of Hesse-Darmstadt and nephew of Alexander II of Russia. He served in the Russian army against the Turks (1877–78) and, backed by the Russian czar, was elected hereditary prince of Bulgaria under Turkish suzerainty. In 1885 the revolutionaries in Eastern RUMELIA, also known as Southern Bulgaria, proclaimed the union of that province with Bulgaria. Alexander accepted the union, thus incurring the wrath of the Russian czar and Serbia. The latter declared war. Alexander was victorious and by an agreement with Turkey became governor of Eastern Rumelia, but he was forced to abdicate by a group of officers. He became an Austrian officer, and Ferdinand was elected to succeed him as prince. See biography by E. C. Corti (1920, tr. 1955).

Alexander (Alexander Karadjordjević) (kărəjôr'jəvĭch), 1806–85, prince of Serbia (1842–58), son of KARAGEORGE (Karadjordje). He was elected to succeed the deposed MICHAEL of Serbia. Weak and vacillating, he did not send troops to aid the Slavic minorities in Hungary during the revolution of 1848–49. He later submitted to Turkish and Austrian pressure in withholding his support from Russia in the Crimean War of 1854–56. Discontent with his ineffective government finally led his subjects to depose him and to recall MILOŠ as king. In 1868, Alexander was condemned to death in absentia by a Serbian court for his alleged part in the assassination of Michael, who had succeeded Miloš. Alexander was the father of Peter I of Yugoslavia.

Alexander, in the Bible. **1** Kinsman of Annas. Acts 4.6. **2** Son of Simon of Cyrene, probably a Christian. Mark 15.21. **3** Heretic condemned by Paul. 1 Tim. 1.20. **4** Coppersmith who did Paul harm. 2 Tim. 4.14. **5** Jew who tried to speak during a riot at Ephesus. Acts 19.33. The last three may be the same man. The Alexanders in the books of the Maccabees are Alexander the Great and ALEXANDER BALAS.

Alexander, Grover Cleveland, 1887–1950, American baseball player, b. St. Paul, Nebr. One of the great right-hand pitchers of the National League, Alexander pitched 696 games, won 373 of them, and compiled a .642 winner percentage. He played for the Philadelphia Phillies (1911–17 and again in 1930), the Chicago Cubs (1918–26), and the St. Louis Cardinals (1926–29). Alexander was elected to the National Baseball Hall of Fame in 1938.

Alexander, Harold Rupert Leofric George, 1st **Earl Alexander of Tunis,** 1891–1969, British field marshal. His long military career began with service in World War I, followed by a period (1934–38) in the North-West Frontier Province, India. In World War II he directed the retreats at Dunkirk (1940) and in Burma (1942). Then, appointed (Aug., 1942) head of the Middle Eastern Command (see NORTH AFRICA, CAMPAIGNS IN), he directed the conquest of Sicily (1943) and the bitter fighting in Italy. In 1944, Alexander was made field marshal and Allied commander in chief in the Mediterranean. In 1946 he was appointed governor general of Canada (holding the post until 1952) and was created viscount. He became minister of defense under Sir Winston Churchill and was raised (1952) to the rank of earl. See his *Alexander Memoirs: 1940–1945* (1962); biography by Nigel Nicholson (1973); study by W. G. F. Jackson (1972).

Alexander, Samuel, 1859–1938, British philosopher, b. Australia. From 1893 to 1924 he was professor of philosophy at Victoria Univ., Manchester. Strongly influenced by the theory of evolution, Alexander conceived of the world as a single cosmic process in which higher forms of being emerge periodically. The basic principle of this process is space-time, and the result is God. His works include *Space, Time, and Deity* (1920), *Spinoza and Time* (1921), *Art and the Material* (1925), and *Beauty and Other Forms of Value* (1933). See studies by J. W. McCarthy (1948), A. P. Stiernotte (1954), and S. R. Dasgupta (1965).

Alexander, Sir William, d. 1640: see STIRLING, WILLIAM ALEXANDER, EARL OF.

Alexander, William, known as **Lord Stirling,** 1726–83, American Revolutionary general, b. New York City. Although the House of Lords rejected his claim to succeed as the 6th earl of Stirling, in America he was generally considered a nobleman. He served in the French and Indian Wars and joined the Continental Army early in the Revolution. Although he fought well at the battle of Long Island (1776), he was captured by the British. After being freed in a prisoner exchange, he saw action at Trenton, Brandywine, Germantown, and Monmouth. In 1778 he helped to expose the CONWAY CABAL. See A. C. Valentine, *Lord Stirling* (1969).

Alexander, in Greek mythology: see PARIS.

Alexander Archipelago (ärkĭpĕl'əgō), island group off SE Alaska. The islands are the exposed tops of the submerged coastal mountains that rise steeply from the Pacific Ocean. Deep, fjordlike channels separate the islands and cut them off from the mainland; the northern part of the Inside Passage threads its way among the islands. The largest islands are Chichagof, Admiralty, Baranof, WRANGELL, Revillagigedo, Kupreanof, Mitkoff, and PRINCE OF WALES. All the islands are rugged, densely forested, and have an abundance of wildlife. The Tlingit Indians are native to the area. Ketchikan (1970 pop. 6,994) on Revillagigedo island, Sitka (1970 pop. 3,310) on Baranof island, and Wrangell (1970 pop. 2,029) on Wrangell island are the largest towns. Lumbering, trapping, fishing, and canning are the main industries. The archipelago was discovered by the Russians in 1741 and was later explored by Britain, Spain, and the United States.

Alexander Balas (bā'ləs), d. 145 B.C., ruler of Syria, putative son of Antiochus IV. He seized power from his uncle Demetrius I (c.152 B.C.); Jonathan the Maccabee supported him. He died in battle against Ptolemy Philometor. 1 Mac. 10–11.

Alexander Bay, town, Cape Prov., NW South Africa, where the Orange River enters the Atlantic Ocean; site of some of the world's richest alluvial diamond deposits.

Alexander City, city (1970 pop. 12,358), Tallapoosa co., E central Ala., in a piedmont farm area; inc. 1874. Nearby Martin Dam supplies power for the city's textile mills, foundries, and mobile home manufactures; the dam also has created Lake Martin, a superb recreational area. A junior college is in Alexander City, and nearby is Horseshoe Bend National Military Park (see NATIONAL PARKS AND MONUMENTS, table), site of a fierce battle (1814) between Andrew Jackson and the Creek Indians.

Alexander John I, prince of Rumania: see CUZA, ALEXANDER JOHN.

Alexander Karadjordjević: see ALEXANDER, prince of Serbia; ALEXANDER, king of Yugoslavia.

Alexander Karageorgevich: see ALEXANDER, prince of Serbia; ALEXANDER, king of Yugoslavia.

Alexander Nevsky (nĕv'skē) [Rus.,=of the Neva], 1220–1263, Russian hero, grand duke of Vladimir-Suzdal. As prince of Novgorod (1236–52) he earned his surname by his victory (1240) over the Swedes on the Neva River. He successfully defended N Russia against its western neighbors by defeating the Livonian Knights (1242) and the Lithuanians (1245). After the Tatar invasion of Russia Alexander submitted to Tatar rule and was appointed (1252) grand duke by the khan. His submissive attitude toward the Tatars and his suppression of the anti-Tatar movements in Novgorod and other cities provoked much resentment among the local princes and the common people. However, he saved the principality from ruin by his cooperation with the invaders. Russian popular tradition made him a national hero, and he was canonized by the Russian Orthodox Church. The order of Alexander Nevsky was instituted (1725) by Catherine I of Russia. Although abolished in 1917, it was revived by the Soviet government in 1942.

Alexander of Aphrodisias (ăfrōdĭsh'ēəs), fl. A.D. 200, Greek Peripatetic philosopher. A celebrated ancient commentator on Aristotle, he was often called the Exegete. During the Renaissance, his interpretations of Aristotle were used to counter those of the church. Two original treatises are extant.

Alexander of Hales, d. 1245, English scholastic philosopher, called the Unanswerable Doctor by his fellow scholastics. He was a Franciscan and a lecturer at the Univ. of Paris. His *Summa universae theologiae* was the first systematic exposition of

Christian doctrine to introduce Aristotle as a prime authority. His eclectic work also contains elements of Neoplatonism and Augustinian and Arabic ideas. Alexander held that all created things, spiritual as well as corporeal, are made up of matter and form. This teaching became the central feature of Franciscan scholasticism and an important influence on St. Thomas Aquinas.

Alexander of Pherae (fēr'ē), d. 358 B.C., tyrant of the city of Pherae in Thessaly after 369 B.C. He was opposed by other Thessalian cities and by the Thebans. PELOPIDAS failed (368 B.C.) in one expedition against him and was briefly imprisoned. Returning in 364 B.C., Pelopidas destroyed Alexander's power in the battle of Cynoscephalae, though he himself was killed. Alexander was murdered by members of his own family.

Alexander Severus (Marcus Aurelius Alexander Severus) (sĭvēr'əs), d. 235, Roman emperor (222–35), b. Syria. His name was changed (221) from Alexius Bassianus when he was adopted as the successor to HELIOGABALUS. He possessed a virtuous and studious character, and during his reign Christians enjoyed a brief immunity from the persecutions of his century. Although he won a triumph in a campaign (232) against Ardashir I of Persia, he could not maintain discipline among his own troops and had to retire from battle. In a mutiny on the Rhine, he and his mother, Julia Mamaea, were murdered by the supporters of MAXIMIN (d. 238).

Alexander the Great or **Alexander III,** 356–323 B.C., king of Macedon, conqueror of much of Asia, one of the greatest leaders of all time. The son of PHILIP II of Macedon and OLYMPIAS, he had Aristotle as his tutor and was given the education of a model prince. Alexander had no part in the murder of his father, although he may have resented him because he neglected Olympias for another wife. He succeeded to the throne in 336 B.C. and immediately showed his brilliance by quieting the restive cities of Greece, then putting down uprisings in Thrace and Illyria. Thebes revolted on a false rumor that Alexander was dead. The young king rushed south and sacked the city, sparing only the temples and Pindar's house. Greece and the Balkan Peninsula secured, he then crossed (334) the Hellespont (now the Dardanelles) and, as head of an allied Greek army, undertook the war on Persia that his father had been planning. The march he had begun was to be one of the greatest in history. At the Granicus River (near the Hellespont) he met and defeated a Persian force and moved on to take Miletus and Halicarnassus. None could stand up against his military skill. For the first time in history Persia faced a united Greece, and Alexander saw himself as the spreader of Pan-Hellenic ideals. Having taken most of Asia Minor, he entered (333) N Syria and there in the battle of Issus met and routed the hosts of DARIUS III of Persia, who fled before him. Alexander, triumphant, now envisioned conquest of the whole of the Persian Empire. It took him nearly a year to reduce Tyre and Gaza, and in 332, in full command of Syria, he entered Egypt. There he met no resistance. When he went to the oasis of Amon he was acknowledged as the son of Amon-Ra, and this may have contributed to a conviction of his own divinity. In the winter he founded Alexandria, perhaps the greatest monument to his name, and in the spring of 331 he returned to Syria, then went to Mesopotamia where he met Darius again in the battle of Guagamela. The battle was hard, but Alexander was victorious. He marched S to Babylon, then went to Susa and on to Persepolis, where he burned the palaces of the Persians and looted the city. He was now the visible ruler of the Persian Empire, pursuing the fugitive Darius to Ecbatana, which submitted in 330, and on to Bactria. There the satrap Bessus, a cousin of Darius, had the Persian king murdered and declared himself king. Alexander went on through Bactria and captured and executed Bessus. He was now in the regions beyond the Oxus River (the present-day Amu Darya), and his men were beginning to show dissatisfaction. In 330 a conspiracy against Alexander was said to implicate the son of one of his generals, PARMENION; Alexander not only executed the son but also put the innocent Parmenion to death. This act and other instances of his harshness further alienated the soldiers, who disliked Alexander's assuming Persian dress and the manners of an Oriental despot. Nevertheless Alexander conquered all of Bactria and Sogdiana after hard fighting and then went on from what is today Afghanistan into N India. Some of the princes there received him favorably, but at the Hydaspes (the present-day Jhelum River) he met and defeated an army under Porus. He overran the Punjab, but there his men would go no farther. He had built a fleet, and after going down the Indus to its delta, he sent Nearchus with the fleet to take it across the unknown route to the head of the Persian Gulf, a daring undertaking. He himself led his men through the desert regions of modern Baluchistan, S Afghanistan, and S Iran. The march, accomplished with great suffering, finally ended at Susa in 324. There he found that many of the officials he had chosen to govern the conquered lands had indulged in corruption and misrule. Meanwhile certain antagonisms had developed against Alexander; in Greece, for instance, many decried his execution of Aristotle's nephew, the historian CALLISTHENES, and the Greek cities resented his request that they treat him as a god. Alexander's Macedonian officers balked at his attempt to force them to intermarry with the Persians (he had himself married ROXANA, a Bactrian princess, as one of his several wives), and they resisted his Orientalizing ways and his vision of the equality of peoples. There was a mutiny, but it was put down. In 323, Alexander was planning a voyage by sea around Arabia when he caught a fever and died at 33. Whether or not he had plans for a world empire cannot be determined. He had accomplished greater conquests than any before him, but he did not have time to mold the government of the lands he had taken, and after his death his generals fell to quarreling about dividing the rule (see DIADOCHI). His only son was Alexander Aegus, born to Roxana after Alexander's death and destined for a short and pitiful life. Incontestably, Alexander was one of the greatest generals of all time and one of the most powerful personalities of antiquity. He influenced the spread of HELLENISM and instigated profound changes in the history of the world. There are many legends about him, e.g., his feats on his horse Bucephalus and his cutting of the Gordian knot. The famous Greek sculptor Lysippus did several studies of Alexander. Arrian and Plutarch wrote biographies of him in ancient times, and the literature of the Middle Ages romanticized his life. See modern biographies by J. W. Snyder (1966), Peter Bamm (tr. 1968), R. D. Milns (1969), Peter Green (1970), C. B. Welles (1970), and R. L. Fox (1974).

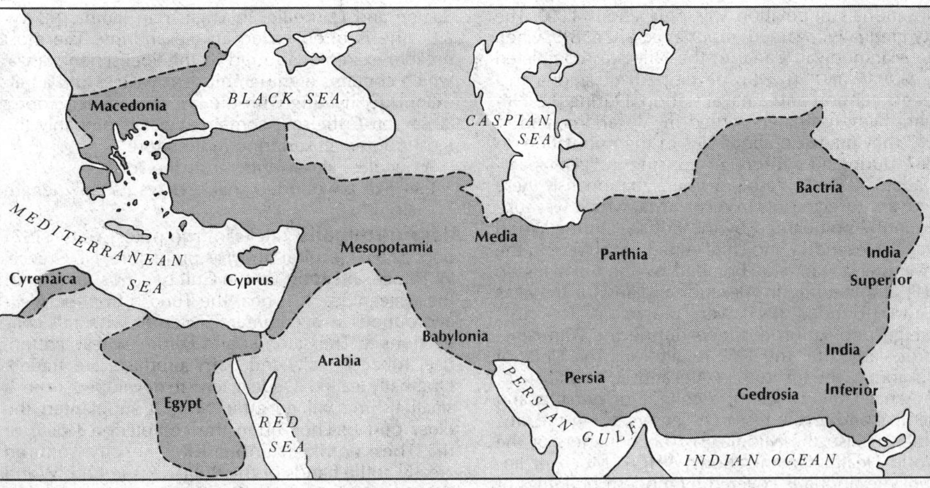

Empire of Alexander the Great (including dependencies)

Alexandra, 1844–1925, queen consort of Edward VII of Great Britain, whom she married in 1863. She was the daughter of Christian IX of Denmark.

Alexandra, Mount, E Africa: see RUWENZORI, mts.

Alexandra Feodorovna (fēô"dərŏv'nə, Rus. fyô'dərəvnə), 1872–1918, last Russian czarina, consort of NICHOLAS II; she was a Hessian princess and a granddaughter of Queen Victoria. Neurotic and superstitious, she was easily dominated by RASPUTIN, who seemingly was able to check the hemophilia of her son. During World War I, when Nicholas took command (Sept., 1915) of the forces at the front, Alexandra Feodorovna assumed control in St. Petersburg and prevailed upon her weak husband to replace independent and liberal ministers with those favored by Rasputin. Her great unpopularity was increased by widespread suspicions that she was pro-German. With her husband and children, she was shot by the Bolsheviks.

Alexandrescu, Grigore (grēgô'rĕ əlĕksəndrĕ'skōō), 1812–85, Rumanian poet. Of a noble family, he was active in secret revolutionary societies. In his fables he commented ironically on the complications of living in a Russian protectorate and tried to encourage pride in the national heritage. In *The Tombs at Drăgăşani* he recalls the greatness of the Rumanian past.

Alexandretta, Turkey: see İSKENDERUN.

Alexandretta, sanjak of (săn"jăk', ăl"ĭgzăndrĕt'ə), former name of Hatay prov. (1970 pop. 596,201), 2,141 sq mi (5,545 sq km), S Turkey, including the cities of Antioch (now Antakya) and Alexandretta (now İskenderun). The population includes many Christians. The sanjak of Alexandretta was awarded to Syria in 1920 and in 1936 became the subject of a complaint to the League of Nations by Turkey, which claimed that the privileges of the Turkish minority in the sanjak were being infringed. The sanjak was given autonomous status in 1937 by an agreement, arranged by the League, between France (then mandatory power in Syria) and Turkey. Rioting by Turks and Arabs resulted (1938) in the establishment of joint French and Turkish military control. In 1939, France transferred the sanjak to Turkey.

Alexandria, Arabic *Al Iskandariyah,* city (1970 est. pop. 2,000,000), N Egypt, on the Mediterranean Sea. It is at the western extremity of the Nile River delta, situated on a narrow isthmus between the sea and Lake Maryut. The city is Egypt's leading port, a commercial and transportation center, and the heart of a major industrial area where refined petroleum, asphalt, cotton textiles, processed food, paper, and plastics are produced. In addition, motor vehicles are assembled and fish are caught. Alexandria, founded in 332 B.C. by Alexander the Great, was (304–30 B.C.) the capital of the Ptolemies. The city took over the trade of TYRE (sacked by Alexander the Great), outgrew CARTHAGE by c.250 B.C., and became the largest city in the Mediterranean basin. It was the greatest center of Hellenistic and Jewish culture. The SEPTUAGINT, a translation by Jews of the Old Testament into Greek, was prepared there. Alexandria had two celebrated royal libraries, one kept in a temple of Zeus and the other in a museum. The collections at their maximum were said to contain, counting duplicates, c.700,000 rolls. A great university grew around the museum and attracted many scholars, including ARISTARCHUS OF SAMOTHRACE, the collator of the Homeric texts; EUCLID, the mathematician; and HEROPHILUS, the anatomist, who founded a medical school there. Julius CAESAR temporarily occupied (47 B.C.) the city while in pursuit of Pompey, and Octavian (later Augustus) entered it (30 B.C.) after the suicide of Antony and Cleopatra. Alexandria formally became part of the Roman Empire in 30 B.C. It was the greatest of the Roman provincial capitals, with a population of about 300,000 free persons and numerous slaves. In the later centuries of Roman rule and under the Byzantine Empire, Alexandria was a center of Christian learning that rivaled Rome and Constantinople. It was (and remains today) the seat of a patriarch of the Eastern Orthodox Church. The libraries, however, were gradually destroyed from the time of Caesar's invasion, and suffered especially in A.D. 391, when THEODOSIUS I had pagan temples and other structures razed. When the Muslim Arabs took Alexandria in 642, its prosperity had fallen severely, largely because of a decline in shipping, but the city still had about 300,000 inhabitants. The Arabs moved the capital of Egypt to Cairo in 969 and Alexandria's decline continued, becoming especially rapid in the 14th cent., when the canal to the Nile silted up. During his Egyptian campaign, NAPOLEON I took the city in 1798, but it fell to the British in 1801. At that time

Alexandria's population was only about 4,000. The city gradually regained importance after 1819, when the Mahmudiyah Canal to the Nile was completed by MUHAMMAD ALI, who developed Alexandria as a deepwater port and a naval station. During the 19th cent. many foreigners settled in Alexandria, and in 1907 they made up about 25% of the population. In 1882, during an antiforeign uprising in Egypt spearheaded by Arabi Pasha, a liberal nationalist, there were antiforeign riots in Alexandria, which was subsequently bombarded by the British. During World War II Alexandria, the chief Allied naval base in the E Mediterranean, was bombed by the Germans. In 1944 at a meeting in Alexandria, plans for the ARAB LEAGUE (founded 1945) were drawn up. The city's foreign population declined during the 20th cent., particularly after the 1952 revolution. The Univ. of Alexandria; the Institute of Alexandria, an affiliate of Al Azhar Univ. in Cairo; a college of nursing; and medical and textile research centers are in the city, which is also the Middle East headquarters of the World Health Organization (WHO). Much of ancient Alexandria is covered by modern buildings or is under water; only a few landmarks are readily accessible, including ruins of the emporium and the Serapeum and a granite shaft (88 ft/27 m high) called Pompey's Pillar. Nothing remains of the lighthouse on the PHAROS (3d cent. B.C.), which was one of the SEVEN WONDERS OF THE WORLD. The Greco-Roman Museum in Alexandria houses a vast collection of Coptic, Roman, and Greek art.

Alexandria. 1 City (1970 pop. 41,557), seat of Rapides parish, central La., on the Red River; inc. 1818. It is a trade, rail, and medical center for a rich agricultural and timber area. Among its many manufactures are valves, lumber, paper, and soaps and cleansers. During the Civil War the city was burned (May, 1864) to the ground by Federal troops. Alexandria is the headquarters for Kisatchie National Forest and the seat of a branch of Louisiana State Univ. Louisiana College is in its neighboring twin city of Pineville. Also in the immediate area are a veterans' hospital, a state mental hospital, and a national cemetery. Several nearby lakes, recreation areas, state parks, and a hot mineral springs resort attract tourists. 2 City (1970 pop. 6,973), seat of Douglas co., W Minn., in a rich farm and timber region surrounded by over 200 lakes; inc. 1877. Its economy is based upon tourism, agriculture, and light manufacturing. The KENSINGTON RUNE STONE is on exhibition at a museum there. Also of interest is a walk-in prehistoric Indian mound. A state park is to the north. 3 City (1970 pop. 110,938), independent and in no county, N Va., a port of entry on the Potomac; patented 1657, permanently settled 1730s, inc. 1779. Primarily a residential suburb of Washington, D.C., it also has extensive railroad yards and repair shops, a sizeable deepwater port, and a great variety of manufactures, including fertilizers, chemicals, and farm equipment. A number of U.S. government buildings and scientific and engineering research firms are there. George Washington helped lay out the streets in 1749. The city was part of the District of Columbia from 1789 to 1847. In May, 1861, it was occupied by Federal troops and was cut off from the rest of the South throughout the Civil War. Its many historic buildings include Gadsby's Tavern (1752), frequented by Washington; Carlyle House (1752), General Braddock's headquarters in the French and Indian War, where Washington received his commission as major; Christ Church (1767–73), where Washington, and later Robert E. Lee, worshiped; and Ramsey House (1749–51). A famous landmark, the George Washington Masonic National Memorial Temple (1923–32), modeled after the ancient lighthouse at Alexandria, Egypt, houses Washington mementos. The Alexandria *Gazette,* believed to be the nation's oldest daily newspaper, was first printed in 1784. Nearby are MOUNT VERNON; Woodlawn, one of the Washington family estates (made a national shrine in 1949); an Episcopal seminary (1823); and U.S. Fort Belvoir, the U.S. Army Engineer Center, with an engineer school and research and development laboratories.

Alexandria Troas (trō'ăs), ancient Greek seaport city, Mysia, NW Asia Minor, called Troas in the Bible. It was important under the Greeks and Romans. (Acts 16.8, 11; 20.5,6; 2 Cor. 2.12; 2 Tim. 4.13.)

alexandrine, in prosody, a line of 12 syllables (or 13 if the last syllable is unstressed). Its name probably derives from the fact that some poems of the 12th and 13th cent. about Alexander the Great were written in this meter. In French, rhyming couplets of two alexandrines of equal length, usually containing four accents, have been the classic poetic form since the time of Ronsard, e.g., in the dramas of Racine and Corneille. In English an iambic HEXAMETER line is often called an alexandrine. The most notable example is found in the Spenserian stanza, which contains eight iambic PENTAMETERS and an alexandrine rhyming with the last pentameter. Pope's "Essay on Criticism" contains what is probably the most quoted alexandrine in literature:

A needless alexandrine ends the song
that like a wounded snake, drags its slow length along.

Alexandroúpolis (ălĕksăndrōō'pôlēs), city (1971 pop. 22,995), capital of Evros prefecture, NE Greece, W Thrace, a seaport on the Gulf of Ainos, an inlet of the Aegean Sea. It is near the Turkish frontier. Alexandroúpolis is a commercial center with rail connections to Thessaloníki and Edirne; wheat, cotton, rice, tobacco, salt, and dairy products are traded. Originally called Dedeagach, it developed from a small fishing village after 1871. It supplanted the older port of Enos upon the completion (1896) of the Thessaloníki-İstanbul RR. The city suffered greatly at the hands of the Bulgarians in both World Wars. It was ceded to Greece in 1919, and it was renamed for King Alexander of Greece.

Alexis (əlĕk'sĭs) (Aleksey Mikhailovich) (əlyĭksyā' mēkhī'ləvĭch), 1629–76, czar of Russia (1645–76), son and successor of Michael. His reign, marked by numerous popular outbreaks, was crucial for the later development of Russia. A new code of laws was promulgated in 1648 and remained in effect until the early 19th cent.; it favored the middle classes and the landowners, but tied the peasants to the soil. The reforms of Patriarch NIKON resulted in a dangerous schism in the Russian Church, and Nikon's deposition (1666) was a prelude to the abolition of the Moscow patriarchate in 1721. In 1654 the Cossacks of Ukraine, led in revolt against Poland by Bohdan CHMIELNICKI, voted for the union of Ukraine with Russia. War with Poland ensued and ended in 1667 with Russia retaining most of Ukraine. A serious revolt against the czar (1670) among the Don Cossacks under Stenka RAZIN was quelled by 1671. Alexis was succeeded by his son Feodor III. A younger son, by a second marriage, became Peter I (Peter the Great).

Alexis (Aleksey Petrovich) (əlyĭksyā' pētrô'vĭch), 1690–1718, Russian czarevich; son of PETER I (Peter the Great) by his first wife, and father of Peter II. Opposing his father's anticlerical policy, Alexis renounced his right of succession and fled (1716) to Vienna. Peter, who feared that Alexis might win foreign backing, enticed him to return; he then had him arrested and tried for treason. Sentenced to death, Alexis died from the effects of torture shortly before his scheduled execution.

Alexius I (Alexius Comnenus) (əlĕk'sēəs, kəmnē'nəs), 1048–1118, Byzantine emperor (1081–1118). Under the successors of his uncle, ISAAC I, the empire had fallen prey to anarchy and foreign invasions. In 1081, Alexius, who had become popular as a general, overthrew Nicephorus III and was proclaimed emperor. The most immediate danger besetting the empire was the Norman invasions (1081–85) under ROBERT GUISCARD and his son, BOHEMOND I. Alexius obtained Venetian help at the price of valuable commercial privileges. This and a truce with the Seljuk Turks enabled him to defend the Balkan Peninsula until the death of Robert Guiscard, when the Normans temporarily withdrew (1085). Next, Alexius secured the alliance of the CUMANS and with their help defeated (1091) the PECHENEGS, who had beseiged Constantinople. He then repulsed the Cumans, who had turned against him, regained territory from the Turks, and suppressed insurrections in Crete and Cyprus. At the same time as Alexius was seeking aid from the West against the Turks, the First Crusade (see CRUSADES) was declared. Faced with the presence of an army of unruly and pillaging Crusaders near his capital, Alexius sought both to rid himself of the Crusaders and to employ them for his own purposes. He furnished them with money, supplies, and transportation to Asia Minor after he had persuaded the leaders to swear him fealty and to agree to surrender to him all conquests of former Byzantine territories. In return, he promised to join the Crusaders, who at first complied. Bohemond, however, seized Antioch for himself, and in 1099 Alexius began operations against him. In 1108, Bohemond was forced to acknowledge Alexius as his suzerain. The last years of Alexius' reign were consumed by fresh struggles with the Turks and by the intrigues of his daughter ANNA COMNENA against his son and heir, John II. Alexius' reign restored Byzantine military and naval power and political prestige, but brought onerous taxation, the depreciation of currency, and the extension of feudalism by grants of estates, draining imperial strength.

Alexius II (Alexius Comnenus), 1168–83, Byzantine emperor (1180–83), son and successor of Manuel I. His mother, Mary of Antioch, who was regent for him, alienated the population by favoring the Latin element in Constantinople. In 1182 Alexius' cousin Andronicus, after instigating a massacre of the Latins, stormed the city, had Alexius sign the death sentence of his mother, and, as Andronicus I, became coemperor. One month later he strangled Alexius and married his widow.

Alexius III (Alexius Angelus) (ăn'jələs), d. after 1210, Byzantine emperor (1195–1203). He acceded to power by deposing and blinding his brother Isaac II. This act served as pretext for the leaders of the Fourth Crusade (see CRUSADES) to attack Constantinople (1203). The Crusaders made Isaac II and his son Alexius IV coemperors, Alexius III having fled. In 1204, Alexius III's son-in-law was briefly emperor as Alexius V. Another son-in-law, Theodore I, became emperor of Nicaea. Alexius died in obscurity.

Alexius IV (Alexius Angelus), d. 1204, Byzantine emperor (1203–4), son of ISAAC II. When his father was deposed, Alexius fled to Italy and then went to Germany. Encouraged by his brother-in-law, Philip of Swabia, he obtained (1202) from the leaders of the Fourth Crusade (see CRUSADES) the promise of help in deposing his uncle, Alexius III. Made joint emperor with Isaac II after the Crusaders entered Constantinople, he was overthrown for his subservience to his allies and was strangled by order of Alexius V.

Alexius V (Alexius Ducas Mourtzouphlos) (dōō'kəs mōōrt'sōōflōs), d. 1204, Byzantine emperor (1204), son-in-law of Alexius III. The head of the Byzantine national party, he overthrew emperors Isaac II and Alexius IV (who had been installed by the Crusaders), thus precipitating the conquest and sack of Constantinople (1204) by the army of the Fourth Crusade (see CRUSADES). He was deposed and executed, and Baldwin I was elected by the Crusaders as Latin emperor of Constantinople.

alfalfa (ălfăl'fə) or **lucern,** perennial leguminous plant (*Medicago sativa*) of the family Leguminosae (PULSE family), the most important pasture and hay plant in North America, also grown extensively in Argentina, S Europe, and Asia. Probably native to Persia, it was introduced to the United States by Spanish colonists. Of high yield, high protein content, and such prolific growth that it acts as an effective weed control, alfalfa is also valued in crop rotation and for soil improvement because of the nitrogen-fixing bacteria in its nodules. The several varieties of the species grow well in most temperate regions except those with acid soil or poor drainage. The alfalfa belt of the United States centers chiefly in the northern and western parts of the country. Young alfalfa shoots have been used as food for humans and have antiscorbutic properties. Carotene and chlorophyll for commercial use are extracted from the leaves. Alfalfa is also called medic, the name for any plant of the genus *Medicago*—Old World herbs with blue or yellow flowers similar to those of the related clovers. Black medic (*M. lupulina*) and the bur clovers (*M. arabica* and *M. hispida*) are among the annual species naturalized as weeds in North America and sometimes also grown for hay and pasture. Alfalfa is classified in the division MAGNOLIOPHYTA, class Magnoliopsida, order Rosales, family Leguminosae.

alfalfa caterpillar, larva of the alfalfa butterfly, *Colias eurytheme*, a member of the family Pieridae. Found throughout most of Mexico, the United States, and S Canada, it is sometimes a serious pest of alfalfa, clover, and other legumes in the SE United States. It usually overwinters as a pupa, the orange adult emerging in early spring, when large numbers of these butterflies may be seen fluttering low over alfalfa fields. The female lays several hundred eggs on the undersides of leaves. The larvae are fully grown in 12 to 15 days; there are two generations each season in the northern part of the range and up to seven in the south. Low cutting of infested alfalfa, which exposes the larvae to sun and predators, aids control. The alfalfa caterpillar is classified in the phylum ARTHROPODA, class Insecta, order Lepidoptera, family Pieridae.

Alfarabius: see FARABI, AL-.

Al-Farghani (ăl-färgä'nē) or **Alfraganus** (ălfrəgā'nəs), d. after 861, Arab astronomer. Al-Farghani was born in Farghana, Transoxania (present-day Pakistan), and died in Egypt. His most important work, written between 833 and 857, is *Elements,* a thorough, readable, nonmathematical summary of Ptolemaic astronomy. The book, which circulated in several Latin editions, was widely studied in Europe from the 12th to the 17th cent. Two treatises on astrolabes by Al-Farghani also survive.

Alfaro, Flavio Eloy (flä'vyō äloi' älfä'rō), 1867–1912, president of Ecuador (1897–1901, 1907–11). Regarded as a champion of liberalism, Alfaro introduced legal and economic reforms that largely undid the clerical privileges granted by Gabriel García Moreno. Exiled by the opposition, he returned to lead a revolt but was defeated, imprisoned, and murdered by an angry mob.

Al-Fasi, Isaac ben Jacob ha-Kohen (äl-fä'sē), 1013–1103, first prominent Jewish Talmudic scholar, following the Gaonic period, b. near Fez, N Africa. His *Halachoth,* a codification of the Talmud, is his greatest work; it contains a simplified exposition of complicated Talmudic passages. It has been reprinted many times, and the edition of 1881 is appended to the regular editions of the Talmud. He is also known for his collection of *Responsa,* a great deal of which was written in Arabic and later translated into Hebrew.

Al Fatah: see ARAFAT, YASIR; PALESTINE LIBERATION ORGANIZATION.

Alfieri, Vittorio, Conte (vĕt-tō'rēō kōn'tā älfyĕ'rē), 1749–1803, Italian tragic poet. A Piedmontese, born to wealth and social position, he spent his youth in dissipation and adventure. From 1767 to 1772 he traveled over much of Europe but returned to Italy fired by a sense of the greatness of his own country. He saw himself as a prophet called to revive the national spirit of Italy and chose tragic drama as his means. The first of his plays, *Cleopatra,* written in a vigorous, harsh, and individual style, was staged in Turin in 1775. From 1776 to 1786 he wrote 19 tragedies, among them *Philip the Second, Saul, Antigone, Agamemnon, Orestes, Sophonisba,* and *Maria Stuart*—all in the tradition of French classical tragedy. He also wrote comedies; a bitter satire against France, the *Misogallo;* and a revealing autobiography (1804, tr. by W. D. Howells, 1877). Alfieri's most productive period coincided with the beginning of his love for the countess of Albany, wife of Charles Edward Stuart, the Young Pretender. The rest of his life was spent with her; they may have married secretly after her husband's death. Alfieri's complete works, which figured in the rise of Italian nationalism, were posthumously edited and published (1805–15) by the countess. His tragedies were translated into English in 1815 and 1876. *Della tirannia* appeared as *Of Tyranny* (1961). See biography by G. Megaro (1930, repr. 1971).

Alfiós: see ALPHEUS, river, Greece.

Alföld (ôl'föld), Hun. *Nagy-Alföld* [Great Alföld], great central plain of Hungary extending into N Yugoslavia and W Rumania. The level region is drained by the Tisza and Danube rivers. Formerly wooded, the Alföld gradually became a steppe region as the Mongol invaders (13th cent.) cut down many trees, exposing the soil to dry winds. Grasslands covered most of the Alföld until the late 19th cent., when extensive irrigation and drainage projects transformed it into fertile farmland; grains, hemp, flax, and livestock are now raised. The Alföld, on a primary invasion route to Europe, has been the scene of many major battles. The Little Alföld (Hun. *Kis-Alföld*) is located in NW Hungary and extends into S Czechoslovakia.

Alfonsine tables or **Alphonsine tables** (ălfŏn'sĭn), compilation of astronomical data tabulating the positions and movements of the planets, completed c.1252 and printed in Venice in 1483. They were a revision and improvement of the Ptolemaic tables and were compiled at Toledo, Spain, by about 50 astronomers assembled for the purpose by Alfonso X of Castile.

Alfonso I (Alfonso the Battler) (ălfŏn'sō, äl-), d. 1134, king of Aragón and Navarre (1104–34), brother and successor of Peter I. The husband of URRACA, queen of Castile, he fought unsuccessfully to extend his authority over her kingdom. He also fought energetically against the Moors, from whom he captured Zaragossa (1118), Calatayud (1120), and many other towns. His raid (1125) into Andalusia bolstered Christian morale, and he encouraged Christians in Muslim lands to settle in his domain. Alfonso was killed in battle against his stepson, Alfonso VII of Castile, and was succeeded by his brother Ramiro II in Aragón and by García IV in NAVARRE.

Alfonso II, 1152–96, king of Aragón (1162–96) and, as Raymond Berengar V, count of Barcelona (1162–96); son and successor of Raymond Berengar IV of Barcelona and Petronilla of Aragón. He inherited Provence (1166), which he successfully defended against the counts of Toulouse, and Roussillon (1172). He conquered (1171) Teruel from the Moors and, after releasing himself from homage to Alfonso VIII of Castile, concluded with him the Treaty of Cazorla (1179), which reserved the reconquest of Valencia for Aragón. He was succeeded in Aragón by his eldest son, Peter II, and in Provence by a younger son.

Alfonso III, 1265–91, king of Aragón and count of Barcelona (1285–91), son and successor of Peter III. He was forced to grant wide privileges to the cortes of the Aragonese nobles. At first he supported the claim to Sicily of his brother James (later JAMES II of Aragón) against CHARLES II of Naples. Later, however, he recognized papal suzerainty over Sicily and pressed James to abandon his claim. He also made war on Castile and on his uncle, JAMES I of Majorca. James II succeeded him.

Alfonso IV, 1299–1336, king of Aragón and count of Barcelona (1327–36), son and successor of James II. Before his accession he conquered (1323–24) SARDINIA, where later a revolt involved him in war with Genoa and Pisa. He was succeeded by his son, Peter IV.

Alfonso V (Alfonso the Magnanimous), 1396–1458, king of Aragón and Sicily (1416–58) and of Naples (1443–58), count of Barcelona. He was the son of Ferdinand I, whom he succeeded in Aragón and Sicily. Queen JOANNA II of Naples sought his aid against LOUIS III, rival king of Naples, and, after Alfonso had defeated (1421) Louis, Joanna adopted Alfonso as her heir. They quarreled in 1423, and when Joanna died (1435), she left her throne to RENÉ of Anjou. Attempting to conquer Naples, Alfonso was captured (1435) by the Genoese, but he was released through the agency of the duke of Milan. In 1442 he defeated René, took Naples, and was recognized (1443) as king by the pope. Leaving his Spanish possessions under the rule of his wife and his brother, Alfonso spent the rest of his life in Naples, where he accorded great privileges to Spanish nobles and tried to introduce Spanish institutions. A patron of arts and letters, he held a splendid court and beautified the city. Alfonso also played a vigorous part in Italian politics. He left Naples to his son Ferdinand I and the rest of his kingdom to his brother John II.

Alfonso I, 1109?–1185, first king of Portugal, son of Henry of Burgundy. After his father's death (1112), his mother, Countess Teresa, ruled the county of Portugal with the help of her Spanish lover, Fernando Pérez. In 1128 young Alfonso, who had allied himself with discontented nobles, defeated her in battle and drove her into León with Pérez (Alfonso did not, despite the popular legend, put her in chains at Guimarãis). Beginning as little more than a quasi-independent guerrilla chief, Alfonso spent his life in almost ceaseless fighting against the kings of León and Castile and against the Moors to increase his prestige and his territories. In 1139 he defeated the Moors in the battle of Ourique (fought not at Ourique, but at some undetermined place). In 1147 he took Santarém by surprise attack and, with the help of the English, Flemish, and German crusaders, captured Lisbon. He began to style himself king in 1139, and in 1143, by the Treaty of Zamora, he placed his lands under papal protection and secured Castilian recognition of his title, which was confirmed (1179) by Pope Alexander III. Alfonso's son SANCHO I ascended an established throne.

Alfonso II (Alfonso the Fat), 1185–1223, king of Portugal (1211–23), son and successor of Sancho I. His reign was spent in struggles with the church and his brothers and sisters, to whom his father had left many of his estates. Alfonso's measures against the church holdings and the bishops led to his excommunication (1219). Though he was himself unwarlike, Alfonso's army took part in the major victory over the Moors at Las Navas de Tolosa (1212) and captured (1217) Alcácer do Sal. He was succeeded by his son Sancho II (reigned 1223–48).

Alfonso III, 1210–79, king of Portugal (1248–79), son of Alfonso II, brother and successor of Sancho II. By his marriage with Matilda, countess of Boulogne, he became count of Boulogne and thus was known as *Alfonso o Bolonhez* [Alfonso of Boulogne]. He seized power after the deposition (1245) of his brother by the pope, becoming king on Sancho's death. Alfonso completed the reconquest of Portugal from the Moors by taking (1249) the rest of the Algarve. This involved him in a long quarrel with Alfonso X of Castile, who had been receiving revenues from Algarve, but the two kings reached an agreement by which Alfonso III married the illegitimate daughter of Alfonso X, and Alfonso X was to relinquish all rights to the Algarve when the heir born of this union (the later King Diniz) should reach the age of seven. Alfonso's second marriage brought the Portuguese king into disfavor with the church because Matilda was still living, but her death ended the conflict. Despite promises he had made at the time of Sancho's deposition, Alfonso seized lands and revenues from the church. This caused another break with the church, which healed shortly before his death. Alfonso called the Cortes of Leiria (1254), the first Portuguese Cortes to include commoners. He also instituted administrative and financial reforms, encouraged commerce and the development of the towns, and commuted many feudal dues into money payments. French and Provençal culture was imported to the court, and the period was one of great intellectual activity. Alfonso was succeeded by Diniz.

Alfonso IV, 1291–1357, king of Portugal (1325–57), son and successor of DINIZ. Disgruntled by the favoritism his father showed toward Alfonso's illegitimate half brothers, Alfonso rose in revolt in 1320. Although peace was arranged twice by his mother, St. Elizabeth (or St. Isabel) of Portugal, he was estranged from Diniz most of the five years before his father's death. He was involved (1337–40) in a fruitless war with Alfonso XI of Castile before joining him in a campaign against the Moors that culminated in the notable victory of Tarifa (Oct., 1340). Alfonso is, however, best remembered for countenancing the murder (1355) of his son's mistress (or wife), Inés de CASTRO, one of the most romantic figures in Portuguese history. His son (later PETER I) promptly led a rebellion, but peace between father and son was restored before Alfonso's death.

Alfonso V, 1432–81, king of Portugal (1438–81), son of Duarte and Queen Leonor. During his minority there was a struggle for the regency between the queen mother and Alfonso's uncle, Dom Pedro, duke of Coimbra. The duke was triumphant (1440) and retained power after Alfonso was declared of age (1446) until the young king fell under the influence of Dom Pedro's illegitimate half brother, Alfonso, duke of BRAGANZA. The dismissal (1448) of Dom Pedro led to a civil war, in which the king's troops killed (1449) his uncle at Alfarrobeira. Alfonso undertook ventures in Morocco and by capturing Alcácer-Seguer (1458) and Tangier (1471) won the name Alfonso the African. Less rewarding was his long attempt to win the throne of Castile after his marriage—never sanctioned by the church—in 1475 to JUANA LA BELTRANEJA, officially the daughter and heiress of Henry IV of Castile, although generally thought to be the child of Beltrán de la Cueva. This claim brought Alfonso into war with ISABELLA I of Castile and her husband, FERDINAND II of Aragón. Alfonso, badly beaten in the battle of Toro (1476), capitulated in 1479. During his reign Prince HENRY THE NAVIGATOR was active. Alfonso was succeeded by his son, John II, who was the effective ruler of Portugal after 1476.

Alfonso VI, 1643–83, king of Portugal (1656–83), son and successor of John IV. Slightly paralyzed and mentally defective, he distinguished himself under the regency of his mother, Queen Luisa, by associating with a group of rowdy youths. After their ringleader was dismissed from court, Alfonso, directed by the count of Castelho Melhor, ousted his mother in 1662. The count of Castelho Melhor then took over the government and ruled ably. Under his direction the army won the series of victories over Spain (1663–65) that finally secured Spanish recognition of Portuguese independence (1668). After Alfonso's marriage (1666) to Marie Françoise of Savoy, daughter of the duc de Nemours, the young queen took a hand in government. She and the king's younger brother (later PETER II) fell in love, and in 1667 they forced Castelho Melhor from power and made Alfonso sign over the government to Peter, who became prince regent. A quick annulment of her marriage to Alfonso enabled Marie Françoise to wed the new regent. Alfonso was confined in the Azores until 1674 and at Sintra thereafter.

Alfonso I (Alfonso the Catholic), 693?–757, Spanish king of Asturias (739–57). He was the son-in-law of the first Asturian king, PELAYO. A Berber rebellion (740–41) against the Moors enabled him to conquer parts of Galicia, León, and Santander.

Alfonso II (Alfonso the Chaste), 759–842, Spanish king of Asturias (791–842), grandson of Alfonso I. He established his capital at Oviedo, which his father, Fruela I, had founded. Continuing the struggle against the Moors, he sought the support of the Frankish emperors Charlemagne and Louis I. Alfonso II built the first church on the site of SANTIAGO DE COMPOSTELA.

Alfonso III (Alfonso the Great), 838?–911?, Spanish king of Asturias (866–911?). He recovered the territory of León from the Moors. The kingdom was consolidated in his reign, but after his forced abdication, it was divided among his sons.

Alfonso V (Alfonso the Noble), 994?–1027, Spanish king of León (999–1027). While he was still a minor, the Moorish ruler al-Mansur died, and the Spanish court recovered the city of León. Alfonso gave (1020) León its *fuero* [charter]. He was killed in the siege of Viseu.

Alfonso VI, 1030–1109, Spanish king of León (1065–1109) and Castile (1072–1109). He inherited León from his father, Ferdinand I. Defeated by his brother SANCHO II of Castile, he fled to the Moorish court of Toledo. After Sancho's assassination (1072) Alfonso succeeded to the throne of Castile and took Galicia from his brother García (1073). He thus became the most powerful Christian ruler in Spain. He encouraged Christians in Muslim lands to migrate north, and he raided Muslim territory, penetrating as far south as Tarifa. After the conquest of strategic Toledo (1085), he took many other cities and reached the line of the Tagus River. Alarmed by his advance, Abbad III (see ABBADIDS) and his Muslim allies called to their aid the Almoravid YUSUF IBN TASHFIN, who defeated Alfonso in 1086. Alfonso was defeated again in 1108, and his only son died in the battle. Alfonso's reign gave a great crusading impulse to the reconquest of Spain and was also notable for the exploits of the CID. Alfonso's court at Toledo became the center of cultural relations between Muslim and Christian Spain. French influence was strong because of the king's many French followers; French monks introduced the Cluniac reform into León during his reign. Alfonso was succeeded by his daughter URRACA.

Alfonso VII (Alfonso the Emperor), 1104–57, Spanish king of Castile and León (1126–57), son and successor of URRACA. He recovered the places in Castile that his stepfather, Alfonso I of Aragón, had occupied and soon gained supremacy over the other Christian states in Spain. In 1135 he had himself crowned emperor in León. His many victories over the Moors had no permanent results; his most famous conquests, Córdoba (1146) and Almería (1147), were soon lost again. Alfonso left Castile to his son Sancho III (reigned 1157–58) and León to his son Ferdinand II.

Alfonso VIII (Alfonso the Noble), 1155–1214, Spanish king of Castile (1158–1214), son and successor of Sancho III. Chaos prevailed during his minority, but he quickly restored order after assuming (1166) the government. Alfonso took (1177) Cuenca from the Moors, but later (1195) he was seriously defeated by them at Alarcos. León and Navarre then invaded Castile, but Alfonso forced them to make peace, annexing Álava and Guipúzcoa from Navarre. Allied with his former Christian enemies, he led them to the great victory over the Almohads at Las Navas de Tolosa (1212). Alfonso was married to Eleanor, daughter of Henry II of England. Their children included Henry, who succeeded his father as Henry I; Blanche, who married Louis VIII of France; and Berenguela, who married Alfonso IX of León and whose son Ferdinand III united Castile and León.

Alfonso IX, 1171–1230, Spanish king of León (1188–1230), son and successor of Ferdinand II. He conquered from the Moors several cities in Estremadura and was frequently at war with Alfonso VIII of Castile. His marriages with Teresa of Portugal and Berenguela of Castile were both annulled by the pope. He defeated (1230) the Moors at Mérida. His son by Berenguela, Ferdinand III, reunited (1230) León and Castile.

Alfonso X (Alfonso the Wise), 1221–84, Spanish king of Castile and León (1252–84); son and successor of Ferdinand III, whose conquests of the Moors he continued, notably by taking Cádiz (1262). His mother, Beatriz, was a daughter of the German king Philip of Swabia, and Alfonso's principal ambition was to become Holy Roman Emperor. In 1257 he was elected by a faction of German princes as antiking to Richard, earl of Cornwall, but because of papal opposition and Spanish antagonism, he did not go to Germany, and in 1275 he finally renounced his claim to the imperial throne. In his domestic policy, Alfonso's assertion of royal authority led to a rebellion of the nobles. His Moorish subjects also rose (1264) against him and were subdued only with the help of James I of Aragón. After the death (1275) of his eldest son, Ferdinand, while fighting the Moors, civil war for the succession broke out between Ferdinand's children and Alfonso's second son, who eventually succeeded him as Sancho IV. Sancho's partisans in the Cortes at Valladolid even declared Alfonso deposed (1282). The king died while the dynastic dispute was still unsettled. Alfonso stimulated the cultural life of his time. Under his patronage the schools of Seville, Murcia, and Salamanca were furthered, and Muslim and Jewish culture flowed into Western Europe. He was largely responsible for the *Siete Partidas,* a compilation of the legal knowledge of his time; for the ALFONSINE TABLES in astronomy; and for other scientific and historical works. See studies by E. E. S. Procter (1951), J. E. Keller (1967), and J. Ribera y Tarragó (1970).

Alfonso XI, 1311–50, Spanish king of Castile and León (1312–50), son and successor of Ferdinand IV. His vigorous campaign against Granada provoked an invasion by the Moors from Morocco; they took Gibraltar in 1333. In 1340, having formed alliances with Portugal, Navarre, and Aragón, Alfonso won the great victory of Tarifa (also called the battle of Salado), and in 1344 he took Algeciras. By the *Ordenamiento de Alcalá,* issued at Alcalá de Henares in 1348, Alfonso enforced the *Siete Partidas* of Alfonso X. He died while besieging Gibraltar and was succeeded by his son, Peter the Cruel.

Alfonso XII, 1857–85, king of Spain (1874–85), son of ISABELLA II. He went into exile with his parents at the time of the revolt of the CARLISTS in 1868 and was educated in Austria and England. In 1870 his mother abdicated her rights in his favor, and in 1874 he was proclaimed king. He entered Madrid in triumph early in 1875 and soon won great popularity. Supported by MARTÍNEZ DE CAMPOS and CÁNOVAS DEL CASTILLO, he consolidated the monarchy, suppressed republican agitation, and restored order. His widow, MARIA CHRISTINA (1858–1929), was regent during the minority of his posthumous son, Alfonso XIII.

Alfonso XIII, 1886–1941, king of Spain (1886–1931), posthumous son and successor of Alfonso XII. His mother, MARIA CHRISTINA (1858–1929), was regent until 1902. In 1906, Alfonso married Princess Victoria Eugénie of Battenberg, granddaughter of Queen Victoria of Great Britain. An attempt was made to kill the couple on their wedding day, the first of several assassination attempts. Although Alfonso enjoyed some personal popularity, the monarchy was threatened by social unrest in the newly industrialized areas, by Catalan agitation for autonomy, by dissatisfaction with the constant fighting in Morocco, and by the rise of socialism and anarchism. In 1909 the government was widely attacked for the execution of the radical publicist Francisco FERRER GUARDIA, following an uprising in Barcelona. After keeping Spain out of World War I, Alfonso, dissatisfied with the functioning of parliamentary government, supported Gen. Miguel PRIMO DE RIVERA in establishing (1923) a military dictatorship. At the fall (1930) of Primo de Rivera, discontent was running high. After the municipal elections of 1931 showed an overwhelming republican majority, Alfonso "suspended the exercise of royal power" and went into exile (April 14, 1931). A few weeks before his death in Rome he renounced his claim to the throne in favor of his third son, Juan (see BOURBON, family).

Alfraganus: see AL-FARGHANI.

Alfred, 849–99, king of Wessex (871–99), sometimes called Alfred the Great, b. Wantage, Berkshire. The youngest son of King Æthelwulf, he was sent in 853 to Rome, where the pope gave him the title of Roman consul. He returned to Rome with his father in 855. His adolescence was marked by ill health and deep religious devotion, both of which persisted for the rest of his life. Little is known of him during the reigns of his older brothers Æthelbald and Æthelbert, but when Æthelred took the throne (865), Alfred became his *secundarius* (viceroy?) and aided his brother in subsequent battles against the Danes, who then threatened to overrun all England. When the Danes began their assault on Wessex in 870, Æthelred and Alfred resisted with varying results: they won a victory at Ashdown, Berkshire; they were defeated at Basing; and they had several indecisive engagements. Upon his brother's death after Easter in 871, Alfred became king of the West Saxons and overlord of Kent, Surrey, Sussex, and Essex. Faced by an enemy too powerful to defeat decisively, Alfred cleared the Danes from Wessex by a heavy payment of tribute (see DANEGELD) in 871. Alfred used the five-year respite that followed to begin building up a fleet. In 876 and 877 the Danes returned to ravage for several months and finally, halted by Alfred's army, swore to leave Wessex forever. However, in a surprise invasion early in 878 they crushed Alfred's forces, and he fled to Athelney in the fens of Somerset, where he organized a series of harassing raids on the enemy. The famous legend in which, unrecognized, he is scolded by a peasant woman for letting her cakes burn probably derives from this period of his life. In May, 878, Alfred rallied his army and won a complete victory over the Danes at Edington. He then dictated the Peace of Chippenham (or Wedmore) by which Guthrum, the Danish leader, accepted Christian baptism and probably agreed to separate England into English and Danish spheres of influence. The Danes moved into East Anglia and E Mercia, and Alfred established his overlordship in W Mercia. Later, Alfred captured (886) London and concluded another treaty with Guthrum that marked off the DANELAW E and N of Thames, Lea, and Ouse rivers, and Watling Street, leaving the south and west of England to Alfred. Security gave Alfred the chance to institute numerous reforms within his kingdom. Against further probable attacks by the Danes, he reorganized the militia, or *fyrd,* about numerous garrisoned forts throughout Wessex. Drawing from the old codes of Æthelbert of Kent, Ine of Wessex, and Offa of Mercia, he issued his own code of laws, which contained measures for a stronger centralized monarchy. He reformed the administration of justice and energetically participated in it, and he reorganized the finances of his court. He came eventually to be considered the overlord of all England, although this title was not realized in concrete political administration. Alfred's greatest achievements, however, were the revival of learning and the establishment of Old English literary prose. He gathered together a group of eminent scholars, including the Welshman Asser. They strengthened the church by reviving learning among the clergy and organized a court school like that of Charlemagne, in which not only youths and clerics but also mature nobles were taught. Alfred himself between 887 and 892 learned Latin and translated several Latin works into English—Gregory the Great's *Pastoral Care,* Orosius's universal history, Boethius's *Consolation of Philosophy,* and St. Augustine's *Soliloquies.* A translation of Bede's *Ecclesiastical History* is also commonly ascribed to him, but there is some doubt since it differs markedly in style from the others. Alfred liberally interpolated his own thoughts into his writings, and the Orosius is particularly interesting for the addition of accounts of voyages made by the Norse explorers OHTHERE and Wulfstan. Although he probably was not directly responsible for the compilation of the ANGLO-SAXON CHRONICLE, his patronage of learning undoubtedly encouraged it. All these pursuits were interrupted, but not ended, by new Danish invasions between 892 and 896. The struggle was severe because Alfred's military reforms had not been completed and because the invading forces were joined by settlers from the Danelaw. He received strong support from his son EDWARD THE ELDER, his daughter Æthelflæd, and her husband, Æthelred of Mercia, and in the critical year of 893 the great Danish fort at Benfleet was successfully stormed. The one Danish attempt to penetrate deeply into Wessex was halted by Edward the Elder. In 896 the Danes slowly dispersed to the Danelaw or overseas, and Alfred's new long ships fought with varying success against pirate raids on the south coast. Alfred's career was later embroidered by many heroic legends, but history alone justifies calling him Alfred the Great. See J. A. Giles, ed., *The Whole Works of King Alfred the Great* (1858, repr. 1969); biographies by E. S. Duckett (1956), P. J. Helm (1963), and H. R. Loyn (1967); F. M. Stenton, *Anglo-Saxon England* (3d ed. 1971).

Alfred University, at Alfred, N.Y.; state and private support; coeducational; opened as a school 1836, chartered 1857 as Alfred University. It is especially known for the College of Ceramics, which is among the few institutions in the United States offering a doctoral program in ceramics. The college is administered by Alfred Univ., although it is a division of the State University of New York.

algae (ăl'jē) [plural of Lat. *alga*=seaweed], group of plants belonging to the most primitive subkingdom of the plant kingdom, the THALLOPHYTES, plants that lack true roots, stems, leaves, and flowers. Unlike the fungi, the other large group of thallophytes, the algae have chlorophyll. They are of world-wide distribution and form the chief aquatic plant life both in the sea and in fresh water. Practically all SEAWEEDS are marine algae. The simplest algae are single cells (e.g., the diatoms); the more complex forms consist of many cells grouped in a spherical colony (e.g., *Volvox*), in a ribbonlike filament (e.g., *Spirogyra*), or in a branching thallus form (e.g., *Fucus*). The cells of the colonies are generally similar, but some are differentiated for reproduction and for other functions. Many algae are microscopic, though the marine thalloid forms, known as kelps, may attain a length of more than 100 ft (30 m). *Euglena* and similar genera are free-swimming one-celled forms that contain chlorophyll but that are also able, under certain conditions, to ingest food in an animallike manner. They are therefore classified either as protozoan animals or as a unique group separate from both plant and animal phyla. The blue-green algae and green algae include most of the freshwater forms. The POND SCUM, a green slime found in stagnant water, is an alga, as is the green film found on the bark of trees. The more complex brown algae and red algae are chiefly saltwater forms; the green color of the chlorophyll is masked by the presence of other pigments. Algae, the major food of fish (and thus indirectly of many other animals), are a keystone in the food chain of life; they are the primary producers of the food that provides the energy to power the whole system. They are also important to aquatic life in their capacity to supply oxygen through photosynthesis; hence algae are a necessary component of a healthy aquarium. Research has investigated the possibility of sea gardening with algae (especially the diatoms, the most numerous of marine plants) as a solution to the problem of insufficient output of land agriculture to meet the needs of the growing world population. In experimental cultivation, algae utilize about 2% of available solar energy for photosynthesis and carbohydrate production, as compared to 0.1% for land plants in general. Algae have also been suggested as a source of oxygen and food for prolonged space travel. Seaweeds (e.g., AGAR) have long been used as a limited source of food, especially in the Orient. Algae are also much used as fertilizer. See the separate algal divisions CHLOROPHYTA, EUGLENOPHYTA, CRYPTOPHYTA, PYRROPHYTA, CHRYSOPHYTA, PHAEOPHYTA, RHODOPHYTA.

Algardi, Alessandro (äläs-sän'drō älgär'dē), 1595–1654, Italian sculptor and designer, b. Bologna. He studied under Lodovico Carracci. In Rome his friend Domenichino obtained his first commissions for him, the *Magdalene* and *St. John* statues for San Silvestro al Quirinale. When Bernini temporarily fell from favor, Algardi replaced him c.1644 as the most important sculptor in Rome under Pope Innocent X and received numerous commissions, including some from Spain. Although greatly influenced by Bernini, he retained the classical inclination of the Bolognese in his work, lacking Bernini's emotional vitality. An example of Algardi's work in relief is *The Meeting of Leo and Attila* (St. Peter's). A few prints in the style of Agostino Carracci are attributed to Algardi.

Algarve (əlgär'və), province (1970 est. pop. 316,200), 1,958 sq mi (5,070 sq km), extreme S Portugal, coextensive with Faro dist. The capital is FARO, and other important cities are Silves, Portimão, and LAGOS. Much fruit (almonds, citrus, grapes, olives, figs, pomegranates) is grown in Algarve, and there are offshore tuna and sardine fisheries. The region was settled by the Phoenicians and later prospered under the Moors, who made it their last stronghold in Portugal. Alfonso III completed its reconquest in 1250.

algebra, branch of MATHEMATICS concerned with operations on sets of NUMBERS or other elements that are often represented by symbols. In elementary algebra letters are used to stand for numbers, e.g., in the EQUATION $ax^2+bx+c=0$, the letters *a, b,* and *c* stand for various known constant numbers called coefficients and the letter *x* is an unknown variable number whose value depends on the values of *a, b,* and *c* and may be determined by solving the equation. Much of classical algebra is concerned with finding solutions to equations or systems of equations, i.e., finding the ROOTS, or values of the unknowns, that upon substitution into the original equation will make it a numerical identity. For example, $x=-2$ is a root of $x^2-2x-8=0$ because $(-2)^2-2(-2)-8=4+4-8=0$; substitution will verify that $x=4$ is also a root of this equation. The equations of elementary algebra usually involve POLYNOMIAL functions of one or more variables (see FUNCTION). The equation in the preceding example involves a polynomial of second degree in the single variable *x* (see QUADRATIC). One method of finding the zeros of the polynomial function $f(x)$, i.e., the roots of the equation $f(x)=0$, is to factor the polynomial, if possible. The polynomial x^2-2x-8 has factors $(x+2)$ and $(x-4)$, since $(x+2)(x-4)=x^2-2x-8$, so that setting either of these factors equal to zero will make the polynomial zero. In general, if $(x-r)$ is a factor of a polynomial $f(x)$, then *r* is a zero of the polynomial and a root of the equation $f(x)=0$. To determine if $(x-r)$ is a factor, divide it into $f(x)$; according to the Factor Theorem, if the remainder $f(r)$ (found by substituting *r* for *x* in the original polynomial) is zero, then $(x-r)$ is a factor of $f(x)$. In many cases a polynomial cannot be separated into simple factors because the roots of the equation are not real; e.g., x^2-9 separates into $(x+3)(x-3)$, which yields two zeros, $x=-3$ and $x=+3$, but x^2+9 does not have simple factors because its zeros are imaginary numbers. The Fundamental Theorem of Algebra states that every polynomial $f(x)=a_nx^n+a_{n-1}x^{n-1}+\cdots+a_1x+a_0$, with $a_n\neq0$ and $n\geq1$, has at least one zero, from which it follows that the equation $f(x)=0$ has exactly *n* roots, which may be real or complex and may not all be distinct. For example, the equation $x^4+4x^3+5x^2+4x+4=0$ has four roots, but two are identical and the other two are imaginary; the factors of the polynomial are $(x+2)(x+2)(x+i)(x-i)$, as can be verified by multiplication. Algebra is a generalization of arithmetic and gains much of its power from dealing symbolically with elements and operations (chiefly addition and multiplication) and relationships (such as equality) connecting the elements. Thus, $a+a=2a$ and $a+b=b+a$ no matter what numbers *a* and *b* represent. Modern algebra is yet a further generalization. It deals with operations that are not necessarily those of arithmetic and that apply to elements that are not necessarily numbers. The elements are members of a SET and are classed as a GROUP, a RING, or a FIELD according to the axioms that are satisfied under the particular operations defined for the elements. Among the important concepts of modern algebra are those of a MATRIX and of a VECTOR space. See Garrett Birkhoff and Saunders Maclane, *A Brief Survey of Modern Algebra* (1965); R. H. Bardell and Abraham Spitz-bart, *College Algebra* (2d ed. 1966).

algebraic geometry, branch of GEOMETRY, based on ANALYTIC GEOMETRY, that is concerned with geometric objects (loci) defined by algebraic relations among their coordinates (see CARTESIAN COORDINATES). In plane geometry an algebraic curve is the locus of all points satisfying the POLYNOMIAL equation $f(x,y)=0$; in three dimensions the polynomial equation $f(x,y,z)=0$ defines an algebraic surface. In general, points in *n*-space are defined by ordered sequences of numbers $(x_1,x_2,x_3,\ldots,x_n)$, where each *n*-tuple specifies a unique point and $x_1,x_2,x_3,\ldots,x_n$ are members of a given FIELD (e.g., the complex numbers). An algebraic hypersurface is the locus of all such points satisfying the polynomial equation $f(x_1,x_2,x_3,\ldots,x_n)=0$, whose coefficients are also chosen from the given field. The intersection of two or more algebraic hypersurfaces defines an algebraic set, or variety, a concept of particular importance in algebraic geometry.

algebraic number: see NUMBER.

Algeciras (älhāthē'räs), city (1970 pop. 81,622), Cádiz prov., S Spain, in Andalusia, on the Bay of Algeciras opposite Gibraltar. A Mediterranean seaport, it has fishing and tourist industries. It was the first Spanish town taken (711) by the Moors. In the naval engagements of July, 1801, near Algeciras, the British defeated the French and Spanish fleets.

Algeciras Conference: see MOROCCO.

Alger, Horatio (ăl'jər), 1834–99, American writer of boys' stories, b. Revere, Mass. He wrote over 100 books for boys, the first, *Ragged Dick,* being published in 1867. By leading exemplary lives, struggling valiantly against poverty and adversity, Alger's heroes gain wealth and honor. His works were all extremely popular. *Silas Snobden's Office Boy,* which ran serially in the *Argosy* magazine in 1889–90, was not published as a book until 1973. See H. R. Mayes, *Alger: A Biography without a Hero* (1928); biography by Frank Gruber (1961); studies by J. W. Tebbel (1963) and R. D. Gardner (1964).

Alger, Russell Alexander, 1836–1907, U.S. Secretary of War (1897–99), b. near Medina, Ohio. After moving to Michigan he engaged in the lumber business, in which he made a fortune. During the Civil War he rose from the ranks to be a brevet major general. Alger was (1885–86) a popular governor of Michigan and was prominent in Republican national affairs. He was made Secretary of War by President McKinley, but the inefficiency of his department, which was highly disorganized when he took charge, and his appointment of William R. SHAFTER as leader of the Cuban expedition were bitterly criticized, and he resigned. He was later (1902–7) Senator from Michigan.

Algeria (ăljēr'ēə), Arab. *Al Djazair,* Fr. *Algérie,* republic (1973 est. pop. 15,200,000), 919,590 sq mi (2,381,741 sq km), NW Africa, bordering on Mauritania, Spanish Sahara, and Morocco in the west, on the Mediterranean Sea in the north, on Tunisia and Libya in the east, and on Niger and Mali in the south. ALGIERS is the capital and largest city of the country, which is divided into 15 departments. Other major cities include ANNABA, BLIDA, CONSTANTINE, MOSTAGANEM, ORAN, SÉTIF, SIBI-BEL-ABBÈS, SKIKDA, and TLEMCEN. Algeria falls into two main geographical areas, the northern region and the much larger Saharan or southern region. The northern region, which is part of the MAGHREB, is made up of four parallel east-west zones: a narrow lowland strip (interspersed with mountains) along the country's 600-mi (970-km) Mediterranean coastline; the Tell Atlas Mts. (highest point: c.7,570 ft/2,310 m), which have a Mediterranean climate and abundant fertile soil; the sparsely populated, semiarid Plateau of the Chotts (average elevation c.3,500 ft/1,070 m), containing a number of shallow salt lakes (*chotts*) and supporting mainly sheep and goat herders; and the Saharan Atlas Mts., a broken series of mountain ranges and massifs (highest point: 7,638 ft/2,330 m), also a semiarid area and used chiefly for pasturing livestock. The arid and very sparsely populated Saharan region has an average elevation of c.1,500 ft (460 m), but reaches greater heights in the Ahaggar Mts. in the south, where Algeria's loftiest point, Mt. Tahat (9,850 ft/3,002 m), is located. Most of the region is covered with gravel or rocks, with little vegetation; there are also large areas of sand dunes in the north (the Great Western Erg) and east (the Great Eastern Erg). In addition, the region contains several oases (including TOUGGOURT, BISKRA, Chenachane, In Zize, and Tin Rerhoh), where date palms are cultivated. The Chéliff River, which flows into the Mediterranean, is the largest of the country's few permanent streams. The great majority of Algeria's inhabitants are Berbers, who, beginning in the late 7th cent. A.D., adopted the Arabic language and Islam from the small number of Arabs who settled in the country. Many Berbers today are partly of Arab descent. About 15% of the population still speaks a Berber language; these inhabitants live mostly in the mountainous regions of the north, but also include the nomadic TUAREG of the Sahara. About 80,000 persons of European descent live in Algeria. Almost all Algerians are Sunni Muslims; Arabic is the official language of the country. About half of Algeria's workers are engaged in farming, but agriculture's contribution to the country's annual domestic product is much less than that of either mining or manufacturing, both of which began their main growth in the mid-1960s. The state plays a leading role in planning the economy and owns many important industrial concerns. Farming is concentrated in the fertile valleys and basins of the north and in the oases of the Sahara. The principal crops are wheat, barley, oats, potatoes, citrus fruit, wine grapes, olives, tomatoes, tobacco, figs, and dates. Large numbers of sheep, poultry, goats, and cattle are raised. Petroleum, found principally in the E Sahara and produced almost exclusively under the auspices of the state-owned SONATRACH corporation, is Algeria's most important mineral resource and its leading export. There are pipelines to the seaports of Arzew and BEJAÏA in Algeria and As Sukhayrah in Tunisia. Much natural gas is also produced. Other minerals extracted in significant quantities include iron, lead, and copper ores; phosphates; zinc; mercury; antimony; kaolin; salt; and coal. The country's leading manufactures are processed food (notably olive oil),

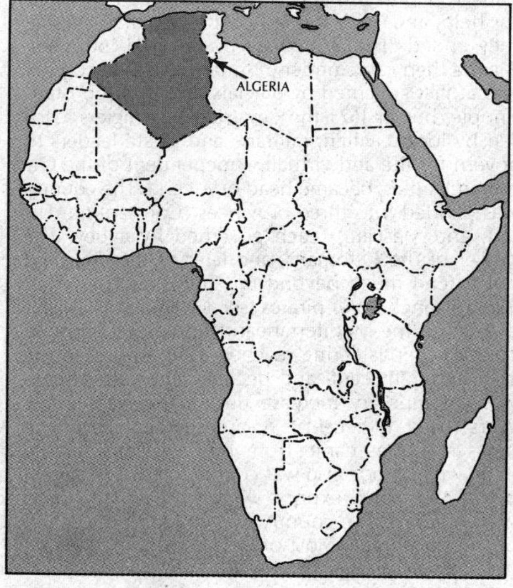

beverages (especially wine), tobacco products, construction materials, chemicals, metals (including steel), refined petroleum, liquefied natural gas, textiles, and clothing. There are small forest-products and fishing industries. Algeria's limited rail and road networks serve mainly the northern region. The annual cost of Algeria's imports is usually slightly higher than the earnings from exports. The chief imports are food, machinery, iron and steel, and transport equipment. The principal exports besides petroleum (which accounts for about 70% of annual foreign exchange earnings) are wine, agricultural goods (especially fruit), and liquefied natural gas. Algeria's main trade partners are France, West Germany, the USSR, and Italy.

History to the early 19th cent. The earliest known inhabitants of Algeria were Berber-speaking nomads, who lived there in small political units by the 2d millennium B.C. In the 9th cent. B.C., CARTHAGE was founded in modern-day Tunisia, and Carthaginians eventually established trading posts at Annaba, Skikda, and Algiers. Coastal Algeria was known as Numidia and was usually divided into two kingdoms, both of which were strongly influenced by Carthage. The kingdoms of Numidia were united by King MASINISSA (c.238–149 B.C.). In 146 B.C., Rome destroyed Carthage, and by 106 B.C., after defeating King JUGURTHA of Numidia, it held coastal Algeria. The Romans also gained control of the Tell Atlas region and part of the Plateau of the Chotts; the rest of present-day Algeria remained under Berber rulers and was outside Roman influence. Under Rome, the cities were built up and impressive public works (including roads and aqueducts) were constructed. Much grain was shipped from Algeria to Rome. By the Christian era, Algeria (divided into Numidia and Mauritania Caesariensis) was an integral, albeit relatively unimportant, part of the Roman Empire. One of its most famous citizens was St. AUGUSTINE (354–430), who was bishop of Hippo (now Annaba) and a leading opponent of DONATISM (which was in part a Berber protest against Roman rule). However, by the 5th cent. Roman civilization in Algeria had been eroded by the incursions of Berbers and Saharan tribes, and the destruction wreaked by the VANDALS (who passed through Algeria on their way to Tunisia) in 430–431 marked the end of effective Roman influence. Algeria again came under the control of numerous small indigenous political units. In the early 6th cent. a temporary veneer of unity and order was forged by the Byzantine Empire, which conquered parts of the North African coast including the region E of Algiers. In the late 7th and early 8th cent. Muslim Arabs conquered Algeria and ousted the Byzantines. Although few Arabs settled in the region, they had a profound influence as most of the Berbers quickly became Muslims and gradually absorbed the Arabic language and culture. In addition, the Arabs interbred with the Berbers. A number of small Muslim states rose and fell in Algeria, but generally the eastern part of the country came under the influence of dynasties centered in Tunisia (notably the Aghlabid of Kairouan) and the western part was controlled by states centered in Morocco (notably the ALMORAVIDS and ALMOHADS). Also, in the 8th and 9th cent. Tlemcen was the center of the Muslim Kharajite sect, and in the early 10th cent. the FATIMID dynasty began its major rise from a base in NE Algeria. In the late 15th cent. Spain expelled the Muslims from its soil and soon thereafter captured the coastal cities of Algeria. Algerians appealed to Turkish pirates (especially the BARBAROSSA brothers) for help, and, with the aid of the Ottoman Empire, they ended Spanish control by the mid-16th cent. Algeria then came under Ottoman rule. The country was at first governed by officials sent from Constantinople, but in 1671 the dey (ruler) of Algiers, chosen by local civilian, military, and pirate leaders to govern for life and virtually independent of the Ottoman Empire, became head of Algeria. The country was divided into three provinces (Constantine, Titteri, and Mascara), each governed by a bey. The power of the Ottomans, and later of the deys, did not extend much beyond the Tell Atlas. The coast was a stronghold of pirates (see BARBARY STATES) who preyed on the Mediterranean shipping of Christian countries. Privateering reached a high point in the 16th and 17th cent. and declined thereafter; there was a temporary increase during the Napoleonic Wars (early 19th cent.). A large percentage of the dey's revenues came from pirates. Considerable trade with Europe also was conducted from Algerian ports; the chief exports were wheat, fruit, and woven goods. The country was in addition a center of the slave trade, most of the slaves being persons captured by pirates.

Algeria in the 19th and 20th cent. In an effort to discourage privateering from Algerian ports, a British fleet bombarded Algiers in 1816. By this time the dey's power was greatly circumscribed by the three beys and by independent-minded Berber groups, and he effectively controlled only a small part of the coastal region. In the 1820s a minor dispute with the French reached a climax that had far-reaching effects: two Algerian merchants had delivered wheat to France in the 1790s but had never been paid for it. The dey unsuccessfully pressed their claim for payment, and, in exasperation, he flicked the French consul in Algeria with a fly whisk during an audience in 1827. To avenge this insult and also to gain glory for his lackluster regime, Charles X of France responded first by instituting a naval blockade of Algeria and then, in June, 1830, by invading the country. The dey capitulated in July, 1830, but most of the country resisted the French, who lapsed into a period of indecision regarding Algeria with the accession of Louis Philippe later in July, 1830. In 1834 the French renewed their drive to occupy Algeria and in 1837 they took Constantine, which had been the last major city to retain its independence. However, the Berber leader, ABD AL-KADIR, whose power was centered in the hinterland of Oran, held out against the French, and it was only in 1847, after a major military campaign against him led by Gen. T. R. BUGEAUD DE LA PICONNERIE, that he capitulated. Until 1910, France faced isolated (but occasionally fierce) resistance, mainly in Kabylia (see KABYLES) and the Sahara region. Colonization by Europeans (half of whom were French and the rest mainly Spanish, Italian, and Maltese) began c.1840 and accelerated after 1848, when Algeria was declared to be French territory. By 1880 persons of European descent numbered about 375,000, and they controlled most of the better farmland. During the 19th cent. Algeria was usually administered under civil departments in Paris, but there were also short periods of military rule. In 1900 the country was given administrative and financial autonomy and placed under a governor general, who was advised by bodies whose membership was two-thirds European and one-third Muslim. By this time the colonists had started large-scale agricultural and industrial enterprises (introducing, among other things, wine and tobacco production) and had built roads, railroads, schools, and hospitals and modernized the cities. These improvements were intended for the Europeans' own use, and the Muslims benefited little from them, being left with scant political or economic power and with few legal rights. Although the official French policy in Algeria was to encourage the Muslims to adapt to European ways and thus to prepare them for full citizenship, very little was done to implement this policy. There was virtually no mixing between the European and Muslim populations. After World War I two types of protest groups were started by the Muslims. One movement called for a fully independent, Muslim-controlled Algeria; an early exponent was Messali Hadj, who in 1924 founded the Star of North Africa movement (later called, successively, the Party of the Algerian People and the Movement for the Triumph of Democratic Liberties, or MTLD). The other faction sought assimilation with France and the equality of Muslims and Europeans in Algeria; its chief exponent was Ferhat Abbas, who, however, after several rebuffs by the French in the 1930s and early 40s, by the mid-40s was calling for Algerian autonomy and by the early 50s advocated complete independence. In World War II, Algeria at first came under the Vichy regime, but later became (1942) Allied headquarters in North Africa; it also served for a time as the seat of Charles de Gaulle's Free French government. The hopes of the nationalists were buoyed by Allied statements during the war concerning self-determination, but the Muslims' actual status improved little. In May, 1945, a spontaneous nationalist uprising in Sétif resulted in the massacre of about 90 Europeans; the French responded by a sweeping crackdown during which at least 1,500 Muslims (and perhaps as many as 10,000) were killed. In 1947 the French national assembly passed the Statute of Algeria, under which the Muslims were to be given some additional political power. However, most of the statute's provisions were not implemented, and the colonists (in partnership with the French government) continued to control Algerian affairs. Despairing of ever gaining meaningful concessions from the colonists or the French government, a radical group of Muslims in 1954 seceded from Messali's MTLD, formed the National Liberation Front (FLN; its military arm was called the National Liberation Army or ALN), and on Nov. 1 attacked police posts and other government offices in the Batna-Constantine region. In the following months the revolt gradually spread to other parts of the country. The FLN called for the establishment of an independent Algerian state controlled by the Muslim majority. The MTLD was reorganized into the Algerian Nationalist Movement, which, led by Messali, unsuccessfully competed with—and at times fought against—the FLN. On Aug. 20, 1955, the FLN carried out more extensive attacks on the colonists (especially in the Skikda area), and the French responded with severe reprisals. By 1956 the FLN had the support of virtually all Algerian nationalists except Messali, controlled much of the countryside, and was organizing frequent terrorist actions in the cities (especially Algiers). In 1957 the French successfully used massive measures to rid the cities of most of the terrorists, and the FLN was forced to concentrate on guerrilla activities in the rural areas; the French also constructed electrified barriers along Algeria's borders with Morocco and Tunisia in order to reduce the infiltration of men and matériel. By this time, about 500,000 French troops, including crack paratroopers, were stationed in Algeria. In May, 1958, there were demonstrations in Algeria by colonists and elements of the French army who feared that the government in France might negotiate a settlement with the Muslims that would undermine the Europeans' position; an ensuing political crisis in France resulted in the return to power of De Gaulle and the establishment of the Fifth French Republic. De Gaulle indicated a willingness to talk with the Muslims, but was imprecise as to the future of Algeria beyond a ceasefire. Fighting continued, and in 1959 the FLN established at Tunis the Provisional Government of the Algerian Republic (GPRA), with Ferhat Abbas as prime minister. By 1960, De Gaulle had come to recognize the inevitability of some form of Algerian independence; the main problem concerned the future status of the almost one million European colonists, many of whom had been born in Algeria. Sensing the direction of French policy, the colonists and army (both of whom aimed for the full integration of Algeria with France) staged major protests in Jan., 1960, and April, 1961, but both were put down by De Gaulle. In mid-1961, Ferhat Abbas resigned as prime minister of the GPRA and was replaced by Ben Yusuf Ben Khedda. Shortly thereafter, negotiations with the French government began at Évian-les-Bains (in France), and in March, 1962, an agreement was signed. The accord provided for an end to the fighting and for the establishment of an independent Algerian state after a transition period; France and Algeria were to cooperate in economic and social affairs and France was to retain for a limited period military bases and the right to test nuclear devices in the Sahara. The people of France overwhelmingly approved the Évian agreement in a referendum held in early April, 1962. Members of the French army in Algeria, banded together in the Secret Army Organization (OAS), launched a terrorist campaign against Muslims in an attempt to prevent the implementation of the accord. However, in late April their leader, Gen. Raoul Salan, was captured and by late June the army revolt had been ended. Already in April the colonists had begun to leave Algeria in large numbers; by October only about 250,000 remained and most of them as well soon left. As a result of the more than seven years' fighting at least 100,000 Muslim and 10,000 French soldiers had been killed; in addition, many thousands of Muslim civilians and a much smaller number of colonists lost their lives. On July 1, 1962, the people of Algeria voted almost unanimously for independence in a referendum, and on July 3 France recognized Algeria's sovereignty. As a result of the fighting and of the exodus of colonists, the Algerian economy lay in ruins by mid-1962. Ben Khedda, the moderate leader of the GPRA, formed the initial Algerian government, but in Sept., 1962, he was replaced as prime minister by Ahmed BEN BELLA, a leftist radical who had the support of the ALN (led by Houari BOUMEDIENNE). A constituent assembly chosen in late 1962 established a strong presidential government, and in Sept., 1963, Ben Bella was elected president. Ben Bella, who increasingly concentrated power in his hands, followed a left-wing domestic policy that included the confiscation of European-held farms and the nationalization of various parts of the economy. There were border disputes with Morocco in 1963–64 that resulted in sporadic fighting; the disputes erupted again in 1967, but were settled by negotiation in 1972. On June 19, 1965, Ben Bella was deposed in a bloodless coup d'etat by Boumedienne, his defense minister, who was angered by the army's greatly reduced influence and by the deterioration of the economy. Boumedienne suspended the constitution and established a revolutionary council, of which he was president, to run the country. During his first years in power Boumedienne faced resistance from students and regional groups, but by the end of 1968 he had a secure hold on Algeria. Algeria gave strong vocal support to the Arabs in the Arab-Israeli wars of 1967 and 1973 and also contributed some soldiers and matériel (especially aircraft). After an initial slowdown Boumedienne increased the pace of state involvement in the economy. In 1971 he nationalized (with compensation) the French oil and natural gas companies active in Algeria; he planned thereby to increase production and thus to augment Algeria's revenues. By 1972 output had reached record levels, and there was a growing emphasis on the export of liquefied natural gas. Price rises for petroleum and natural gas in 1973-74 resulted in considerably higher export earnings. In the early 1970s, Algeria was on good terms with its North African neighbors, and gave moral support (if not much material aid) to the various movements against white minority rule in Africa. See Stéphane Gsell et al., *Histoire d'Algérie* (1929); Edgar O'Ballance, *The Algerian Insurrection 1954-62* (1967); Frantz Fanon, *The Wretched of the Earth* (tr. 1968); W. B. Quandt, *Revolution and Political Leadership: Algeria, 1954-1968* (1969); David Ottaway and Marina Ottaway, *Algeria: the Politics of a Socialist Revolution* (1970); Charles-André Julien, *Histoire de l'Algérie contemporaine, conquête et colonisation, 1827-1871* (1964) and *History of North Africa* (tr. 1970); A. A. Heggoy, *Insurgency and Counterinsurgency in Algeria* (1972).

Algerine War, early 19th-century conflict between Algiers and the United States. The TRIPOLITAN WAR (1801-5) had brought a temporary halt to the pirate activities of the Barbary States. However, during the subsequent Napoleonic Wars and the War of 1812 the Barbary pirates renewed their predatory raids on American Mediterranean commerce, and Algiers actually declared war on the United States. In 1815, Stephen DECATUR was sent to Algiers at the head of a squadron of 10 ships. After two minor engagements he sailed into the harbor of Algiers and forced (June 30) the dey of Algiers to sign a treaty renouncing U.S. tribute and agreeing to release all U.S. prisoners without ransom. Decatur then exacted similar guarantees from Tunisia (July 26) and Tripoli (Aug. 5), and the so-called Algerine War was ended.

Algiers (ăljērz'), Fr. *Alger* (älzhā'), city (1966 pop. 943,142), capital of Algeria, N Algeria, on the Bay of Algiers of the Mediterranean Sea. It is one of the leading ports of North Africa (wine, citrus fruit, iron ore, cork, and cereals are the major exports), as well as a popular winter resort and a commercial center. Industries include metallurgy, oil refining, automotive construction, machine-building, and the production of chemicals, tobacco, paper, and cement. Founded by the Phoenicians and called Icosium by the Romans, the city disappeared after the fall of the Roman Empire. It was reestablished in the late 10th cent. by the Muslims. Many of the Moors expelled from Spain in 1492 settled in Algiers. In 1511 the Spanish occupied an island in the city's harbor, but they were driven out when BARBAROSSA captured Algiers for the Turks. Algiers then became a base for the Muslim fleet that preyed upon Christian commerce in the Mediterranean (see BARBARY STATES). Under the Ottoman Empire, the city's population reached 100,000. The ruling Turkish official in Algeria, the dey of Algiers, made himself virtually independent of Constantinople in the 18th and 19th cent. As European navies repeatedly attacked Algiers, the city's prosperity, which was based on piracy, declined. When French forces captured the port in 1830, Algiers had less than 40,000 inhabitants. Algiers became headquarters for the Allied forces in North Africa in World War II, as well as for Charles de Gaulle's provisional French government. An anti-French uprising in the city in 1954 provided a major spark in the Algerian armed struggle for independence. In May, 1958, Algiers was the principal scene of a revolt that ended the Fourth French Republic and returned De Gaulle to power. During the final months before Algeria won independence (1962), bombings by the French terrorist Organization of the Secret Army (OAS) damaged industrial and communications facilities in Algiers. In 1973 a major conference of nonaligned nations was held there. The city is divided into the newer, French-built sector, with wide boulevards and modern administrative and commercial buildings, and the original Muslim quarter, with narrow streets, numerous mosques, and the 16th century casbah (fortress), which was once the residence of the Turkish deys. Other points of interest in Algiers include the observatory, botanical gardens, the national library and museum, the Basilica of Notre Dame, and the Cathedral of Sacré Coeur, which was designed by Le Corbusier. The Univ. of Algiers dates back to 1909. Only a few thousand permanent European residents remain in the city.

Algoa Bay (ălgō'ə), arm of the Indian Ocean, indenting SE Cape Province, Republic of South Africa. Discovered by the Portuguese in the late 15th cent., it was used as an anchorage. Port Elizabeth is on the shore of the bay.

Algol (ăl'gŏl), famous VARIABLE STAR in the constellation PERSEUS; Bayer designation β Persei; 1970 position R.A. $3^h06.0^m$, Dec. +40°50'. Algol's variation in apparent MAGNITUDE, from 2.06 to 3.28, is due to the fact that it is an eclipsing BINARY STAR, with one component revolving about the other with a period of 2 days, 20 hr, 49 min. Because the plane of revolution is almost parallel to the line of sight, the star dims noticeably when the dimmer component passes in front of, or eclipses, the brighter component, and dims again very slightly when the brighter component eclipses the dimmer one (see ECLIPSE); the primary minimum, when the brighter component is eclipsed, lasts about 10 hr. Algol is of SPECTRAL CLASS B8 V. It is about 105 light-years from the earth. The star is actually a quadruple system, with two other components orbiting but not eclipsing the nearby eclipsing pair. The name *Algol* comes from the Arabic *Ras al Ghul*, which means "demon's head," and the star is sometimes called the Demon Star.

Algonquian (ălgŏng'kēən, -kwēən), branch of the Algonquian-Wakashan linguistic family of North America. See AMERICAN INDIAN LANGUAGES.

Algonquin Indians (ălgŏng'kwĭn, -kĭn), small group of now extinct North American Indians. The name of the Algonquian branch of the Algonquian-Wakashan linguistic stock (to which they belonged) is derived from their name (see AMERICAN INDIAN LANGUAGES). They were among the first Indians with whom the French formed alliances, and their name was used to designate other tribes in the area. Despite French aid, they were dispersed in the 17th cent. by the Iroquois, and the remnants of the tribe found refuge chiefly near white settlements in Quebec and Ontario. The name is also spelled Algonkin.

algorithm (ăl'gərĭth"əm) or **algorism** (-rĭz"əm) [for al-Khowarizimi, 9th-century Persian mathematician], procedure used in calculations to simplify the operation; it involves direct manipulation of the figures without regard for the underlying principles of the operation. Much of ordinary arithmetic as traditionally taught consists of algorithms involving the fundamental operations of addition, subtraction, multiplication, and division. An example of an algorithm is the common procedure for division, e.g., the division of 1,347 by 8, in which the remainders of partial divisions are carried to the next digit or digits; in this case the remainder of 5 in the division of 13 by 8 is placed in front of the 4, and 8 is then divided into 54.

Algren, Nelson, 1909–, American novelist, b. Detroit. He grew up in Chicago, and much of his fiction is laid in the slums. His novels, such as *Never Come Morning* (1942), *The Man with the Golden Arm* (1949), and *A Walk on the Wild Side* (1956), are brutally realistic. In a lighter vein are the personal sketches collected in *Who Lost an American* (1963), *Notes from a Sea Diary* (1965), and *The Last Carousel* (1973).

algum: see ALMUG.

Al-Hakam II: see HAKAM II, AL-.

Alhambra (ălhăm'brə), city (1970 pop. 62,125), Los Angeles co., S Calif., a suburb NE of Los Angeles; inc. 1903. Its many manufactures include aircraft parts, electronic equipment, oil refinery machinery, airconditioners, and felt products.

Alhambra [Arabic, = the red], extensive group of buildings on a hill overlooking Granada, Spain. They were built chiefly between 1230 and 1354 and they formed a great citadel of the Moorish kings of Spain. After the expulsion of the Moors in 1492, the structures suffered mutilation, but were extensively restored after 1828. The Alhambra is a true expression of the once flourishing Moorish civilization and is the finest example of its architecture in Spain. It comprises remains of the citadel, the so-called palace of the kings, and the quarters once used by officials. The halls and chambers surround a series of open courts, which include the Court of Lions containing arcades resting on 124 white marble columns. The interior of the building is adorned sumptuously with magnificent examples of the so-called honeycomb and stalactite vaulting; its walls and ceilings are decorated with geometric ornamentation of minute detail and intricacy, executed with surpassing skill in marble, alabaster, glazed tile, and carved plaster. See Washington Irving, *Legends of the Alhambra* (1832); A. F. Calvert, *The Alhambra* (1907); Stewart Desmond, ed., *The Alhambra* (1974).

Alhazen: see IBN AL-HAYTHAM.

Al Hillah (äl hĭl'lä), city (1965 pop. 84,717), provincial capital, central Iraq, on a branch of the Euphrates River. It was built (c.1100) largely of material taken from the nearby ruins of ancient Babylon. It is a port and the main cereal market of the middle Euphrates area.

Al Hudaydah: see HODEIDA, Yemen.

Al Hufuf: see HOFUF.

Ali (älē'), 600?-661, 4th caliph (656-61). He was the son of Abu Talib, Muhammad's uncle, but was more closely related to the Prophet as the husband of FATIMA. One of the Prophet's most faithful followers, he was expected to become caliph on Muhammad's death, but Abu Bakr was chosen. Ali succeeded only on Uthman's death. He was strongly opposed by AISHA, who incited a revolt in Iraq. Ali put down the disturbance, but he was never able to suppress MUAWIYA. Ali was murdered at Kufa by fanatics (the Kharijites), and his son HASAN abdicated in favor of Muawiya. The division in Islam between the SUNNI and SHIITES began in the time of Ali. He and his son HUSEIN are the great saints of the Shiites.

Ali, Muhammad (məhăm'əd älē'), 1940–, American boxer. Originally named Cassius Marcellus Clay, Jr., he changed his name in 1964 on becoming a Black Muslim. After winning an Olympic gold medal in 1960, he turned professional. In 1964 he defeated Sonny Liston, winning the world heavyweight championship. Although this title was accepted by the public, it was not officially recognized by the World Boxing Association. Nevertheless, Ali twice defended his boxing title in 1965, defeating both Liston and Floyd Patterson. In 1967, however, various state and foreign boxing commissions stripped him of the title when he refused induction into the U.S. armed services on religious grounds. (The U.S. Supreme Court, in June, 1971, upheld Ali's draft appeal on religious grounds.) Prevented from fighting by the professional boxing establishment, he was finally granted a license to fight again in 1970. In 1971 he lost his first fight; it was to Joe Frazier, who was then champion. In 1974, Ali regained the championship by defeating George Foreman in a fight held in Zaïre. See biographies by José Torres (1971) and Budd Schulberg (1972).

Aliah (ălī'ə): see ALVAH.

Aliákmon (äleäk'môn), longest river of Greece, c.200 mi (320 km) long, rising in the mountains near Lake Préspa, N Greece, and flowing SE then NE into the Thermaic Gulf. The river waters an agricultural region; Kastoría and Véroia are along its course. The Aliákmon forms the western portion of the extensive Vardar River delta. It is also known as the Vistrítsa River.

Alian (ălī'ən): see ALVAN.

Alibamu Indians: see ALABAMA INDIANS.

Alibates Flint Quarries and Texas Panhandle Pueblo Culture National Monument: see NATIONAL PARKS AND MONUMENTS (table).

Ali Bey: see BADIA Y LEBLICH, DOMINGO.

Alicante (älĕkän'tā), city (1971 pop. 184,716), capital of Alicante prov., SE Spain, in Valencia. A Mediterranean port and resort, it has exports of wine, oil, cereals, fruit, and esparto from the fertile surrounding region. Textiles and tobacco and clay products are made. The Romans had a naval base on the site. The town was permanently recaptured from the Moors c.1250. The Falangist leader José Antonio Primo de Rivera was executed by the Republicans in 1936 in Alicante.

Alice, city (1970 pop. 20,121), seat of Jim Wells co., S Texas; inc. 1910. Long a cow town at a railroad junction, Alice is still a cattle-shipping center. Oil and natural gas are also important to its economy. Manufactures include oil well equipment and cottonseed oil. Nearby are a wildlife refuge, the great King Ranch, and several Gulf Coast resorts.

Alice Springs, town (1971 pop. 11,118), Northern Territory, Australia. It lies in a pastoral area near the center of the continent and at the terminus of the Central Australian RR. The town became important as a telegraph station on the overland route from Adelaide to Darwin. Gold, copper, wolfram, and mica are mined in the area. An aborigine reservation is nearby. Formerly called Stuart, Alice Springs was (1926-31) the capital of Central Australia, a former subdivision of the Northern Territory.

alien, in law, person residing in one political community while owing ALLEGIANCE to another. A legal procedure known as naturalization permits aliens to become CITIZENS. The attitude toward aliens is a matter of custom, usage, and law. All modern governments have laws covering the rights and privileges of aliens, and there is a large body of international law on the subject. A country has the right to exclude undesirable aliens, and most countries, including the United States, forbid the admission of criminals, paupers, and the diseased. A country has the right to exclude completely certain groups and nationalities, but such discrimination is likely to cause friction. From the right to exclude aliens proceeds the right to establish the conditions upon which they will be admitted and to make special laws concerning them. An alien, while he resides in a country, is subject to the laws of that country and not to those of his own country, except in the case of EXTRATERRITORIALITY jurisdiction. A state distinguishes between aliens who are merely traveling or living there temporarily and those who have come to stay or to earn their livelihood, and wider powers are assumed over the second class. Such aliens are subject to taxation and may even be drafted to serve in the national defense. As a citizen of his own country, an alien may call upon it to intercede if he feels that the country in which he lives has failed properly to protect his person or property. The home state usually points out or protests injustice, but it may threaten reprisals. Such situations have frequently caused international disputes, and there is controversy as to how far a nation is justified in interfering in behalf of its nationals abroad. On the other hand, an alien may find ASYLUM in the country to which he has fled unless treaties of EXTRADITION provide for the DEPORTATION of such refugees. A state also has the right to expel an alien who was once admitted. As population in a state increases and the competition for livelihood becomes more intense, a country may become less hospitable to aliens. This process was seen in the United States in the 20th cent. in more restrictive IMMIGRATION laws and more stringent deportation laws. In time of war the laws governing aliens are stricter, and special restrictions usually govern enemy aliens. Treaties between most governments provide that in case of war a reasonable period should be given enemy citizens in either country to withdraw under supervision. After that time the remaining enemy aliens may be expelled or may be permitted to remain under whatever conditions the government chooses to impose. Thus, in World War II, enemy aliens in the United States were required to register, were excluded from certain areas, and in some cases were interned. Aliens in the United States are required to register each year under the Immigration and Nationality Act of 1952. See NATIONALITY.

Alien and Sedition Acts, 1798, four laws enacted by the Federalist-controlled U.S. Congress, allegedly in response to the hostile actions of the French Revolutionary government on the seas and in the councils of diplomacy (see XYZ AFFAIR), but actually designed to destroy Thomas Jefferson's Republican party, which had openly expressed its sympathies for the French Revolutionaries. Depending on recent arrivals from Europe for much of their voting strength, the Republicans were adversely affected by the Naturalization Act, which postponed citizenship, and thus voting privileges, until the completion of 14 (rather than 5) years of residence, and by the Alien Act and the Alien Enemies Act, which gave the President the power to imprison or deport aliens suspected of activities posing a threat to the national government. President John Adams made no use of the alien acts. Most controversial, however, was the Sedition Act, devised to silence Republican criticism of the Federalists. Its broad proscription of spoken or written criticism of the government, the Congress, or the President virtually nullified the First Amendment freedoms of speech and the press. Prominent Jeffersonians, most of them journalists, such as John Daly Burk, James T. Callender, Thomas COOPER, William DUANE (1760-1835), and Matthew LYON were tried, and some were convicted, in sedition proceedings. The Alien and Sedition Acts provoked the KENTUCKY AND VIRGINIA RESOLUTIONS and did much to unify the Republican party and to foster Republican victory in the election of 1800. The Republican-controlled Congress repealed the Naturalization Act in 1802; the others were allowed to expire (1800-1801). See John C. Miller, *Crisis in Freedom* (1951, repr. 1964); James Morton Smith, *Freedom's Fetters* (1956).

alienation, in property laws: see TENURE.

Aligarh (əlēgŭr'), city (1971 pop. 254,008), Uttar Pradesh state, N central India. A district administrative headquarters and an important agricultural trade center, it also has cotton mills. Aligarh is famous chiefly for its university, opened in 1875 as Anglo-Oriental College, which is the leading school for Indian Muslims. The city, whose native name is Koil, has ancient Buddhist remains and many Muslim buildings.

alimentary canal: see DIGESTIVE SYSTEM.

alimony, in law, allowance for support that, by court order, a husband pays to his wife if she is not living with him. It is based on the COMMON LAW right of a wife to be supported by her husband. Alimony is distinct from the husband's duty to contribute to the support of his minor children. Temporary alimony is allowed pending the outcome of a suit for DIVORCE, for SEPARATION, or for a decree of NULLITY OF MARRIAGE, whether wife or husband initiated the suit. Permanent alimony is the allowance to the wife after the action has been tried and the decree rendered. In the United States, laws regulating alimony awards vary greatly among the states. Generally it may be granted after separations or divorces, but not after annulments. Alimony ceases on the death of the husband, because it is not payable out of his estate unless there are arrears. Although remarriage does not necessarily terminate alimony, the amount may be reduced or cut off at the court's discretion if the second husband is able to support the wife. In all cases the amount of, and the continuing need for, alimony are questions that can always be reopened in a court having jurisdiction over the parties. The rule that the husband cannot obtain alimony from the wife has been changed in a few states but for the most part holds, since the wife generally has no duty to support the husband. A decree awarding alimony is a court order issued to the husband personally, and failure to pay constitutes CONTEMPT OF COURT.

Alingsås (ä"lĭngsōs'), city (1970 pop. 18,761), Älvsborg co., SW Sweden, on Lake Mjörn; chartered 1619. It is an industrial center. Manufactures include textiles, leather goods, processed food, candy, beer, and metal goods.

Aliotta, Antonio (äntô'nyō älyôt'tä), 1881-1964, Italian philosopher, b. Salerno. He taught at the universities of Padua and Naples. He wrote a critical analysis of contemporary philosophy, *The Idealistic Reaction Against Science* (1912, tr. 1914), and then became identified with pragmatism, primarily in opposition to the idealism of Benedetto Croce and Giovanni Gentile. His complete works, in Italian, were published in 7 volumes (1949-54).

Ali Pasha (älē' päshä'), 1744?-1822, Turkish pasha [military governor] of Yannina (now Ioánnina, Greece), a province of the Ottoman Empire (Turkey). He was called the Arslan [lion] of Yannina. His father, governor at Tepelene in S Albania, was murdered, and Ali went to live with the mountain brigands who infested the country. He soon rose to leadership among them, came to the attention of the Turkish government, and as its agent put down the rebellion of a governor at Scutari in Albania. About 1787 he became governor of Yannina, where his power grew until he ruled as a quasi-independent despot over most of Albania and Epirus. He made war on the French along the Adriatic coast and entered an alliance (1814) with Great Britain. Valuing Ali's services, the sultan let him do as he wished until, in 1820, Ali ordered the assassination of an opponent in Constantinople. Sultan Mahmud II ordered Ali deposed. Ali refused to comply, thus keeping Turkish troops engaged against himself while they were needed against the Greeks, who had begun their fight for independence. Ali was assassinated by an agent of the Turks; his head was exhibited at Constantinople. The wild yet cultured court of Ali was described by French and English visitors, notably by Byron in *Childe Harold.*

aliphatic compound (ăl"əfăt'ĭk), any of a large class of organic compounds whose carbon atoms are joined together in straight or branched open chains rather than in rings. The hydrocarbons of the ALKANE, ALKENE, and ALKYNE series are aliphatic compounds, as are FATTY ACIDS and many other compounds. Most compounds containing rings are AROMATIC COMPOUNDS; compounds that contain a ring but are not aromatic compounds are called alicyclic.

Aliquippa (ălĭkwĭp'ə), borough (1970 pop. 22,277), Beaver co., W Pa., in a highly industrialized region along the Ohio River N of Pittsburgh; inc. 1894. Aliquippa grew after the expansion of steel mills in 1909.

Alisal, Calif.: see SALINAS.

alizarin (əlĭz'ərĭn), or 1,2-dihydroxyanthraquinone, mordant vegetable dye obtained originally from the root of the madder plant (*Rubia tinctorum*), in which it occurs as a glucoside. The term also includes a group of synthetic dyestuffs prepared from coal-tar derivatives. A method for the synthesis of alizarin was first discovered (1868) by Karl Graebe and Karl Liebermann, German chemists. With salts of metals the compound forms brilliant LAKES, although by itself it is a poor dye. Turkey red is produced with an aluminum mordant, other shades of red with calcium and tin salts, dark violet with iron mordants, and brownish red with chromium. Purpurin, also used in dyeing, occurs with alizarin in madder and is produced synthetically.

Al-Jadida (äl-jädē'də), city (1960 pop. 40,302), W Morocco, on the Atlantic Ocean. Agricultural products are exported from the port. It was seized by the Portuguese in 1502 and after 1541 was the only place Portugal held in Morocco. Repeatedly besieged by the Moroccans, it was finally captured by them in 1769. The city was formerly called Mazagan.

Al Jazirah (äl jäzē'rä) or **Gazira** (gäzē'rä), region, central Sudan, occupying the tract between the White and Blue Niles south of their convergence at Khartoum. The Arabic word *Jazira* means "island" or "peninsula." WAD MADANI is the region's chief town. The plan to develop the region for irrigated cotton cultivation has made it by far Sudan's leading cotton-producing area. Originally operated by a private company in conjunction with the government, the entire project was nationalized in 1950. The Sannar Dam and the irrigation canals built there since 1925 have put more than 1 million acres (400,000 hectares) into cultivation. Profits from the cotton crop are divided among the government, the board that supervises the project, and the tenant farmers, who provide the labor. The region was under the hegemony of the Funj rulers of Sannar from 1504 to 1821 and later passed to Turco-Egyptian and British control.

Aljubarrota (əlzho͞obər-rô'tə), village, Leiria dist., W central Portugal, in Beira Litoral. On Aug. 14, 1385, it was the site of the momentous battle in which the Portuguese, aided by English archers, defeated the forces of the Spanish King John I of Castile, thus assuring Portuguese independence. Nun'Álvares Pereira was the Portuguese hero of the battle.

alkali (ăl'kəlī) [Arabic, *al-gili*=ashes of saltwort], HYDROXIDE of an ALKALI METAL. Alkalies are readily soluble in water and form strongly basic solutions with a characteristic acrid taste. They neutralize acids, forming salts and water. Strong alkalies (e.g., those of sodium or potassium) are sometimes called caustic alkalies. The term *alkali* originally applied to salts obtained from plant ashes and is sometimes applied to a carbonate of sodium or potassium or to the hydroxide of an ALKALINE-EARTH METAL.

alkali metals, metals found in group Ia of the PERIODIC TABLE. Compared to other metals they are soft and have low melting points and densities. Alkali metals are powerful reducing agents and form univalent compounds. All react violently with water, releasing hydrogen and forming hydroxides. They tarnish rapidly even in dry air. They are never found uncombined in nature. In order of increasing atomic number the alkali metals are LITHIUM, SODIUM, POTASSIUM, RUBIDIUM, CESIUM, and FRANCIUM.

alkaline dry cell: see CELL, in electricity.

alkaline-earth metals, metals constituting group IIa of the PERIODIC TABLE. Generally, they are softer than most other metals, react readily with water (especially when heated), and are powerful reducing agents, but they are exceeded in each of these properties by the corresponding alkali metal. They form divalent compounds. In order of increasing atomic number the alkaline-earth metals are BERYLLIUM, MAGNESIUM, CALCIUM, STRONTIUM, BARIUM, and RADIUM.

alkaline earths (ăl'kəlĭn, -līn), oxides of the ALKALINE-EARTH METALS, especially of calcium, strontium, and barium. They are not readily soluble in water and form solutions less basic than those of alkalies.

alkaloid, any of a class of organic compounds composed of carbon, hydrogen, nitrogen, and usually oxygen that are often derived from plants. Although the name means alkalilike, some alkaloids do not exhibit alkaline properties. Many alkaloids, though poisons, have physiological effects that render them valuable as medicines. For example, curarine, found in the deadly extract CURARE, is a powerful muscle relaxant; ATROPINE is used to dilate the pupils of the eyes; and physostigmine is a specific for certain muscular diseases. Narcotic alkaloids used in medicine include MORPHINE and CODEINE for the relief of pain and COCAINE as a local anesthetic. Other common alkaloids include QUININE, CAFFEINE, NICOTINE, STRYCHNINE, SEROTONIN, and LYSERGIC ACID DIETHYLAMIDE. Aconitine is the alkaloid of ACONITE. Cinchonine and quinine are derived from CINCHONA, coniine is found in poison HEMLOCK, and reserpine is an extract of rauwolfia roots. Emetine is an alkaloid of IPECAC.

alkalosis (ăl″kəlō′səs): see ACIDOSIS.

Alkan, Charles Henri Valentin (shärl äNrē′ välăNtăN′ ălkăN′), 1813–88, French pianist and composer; his original surname was Morhange. He began studying piano at the Paris Conservatory at the age of 6. Throughout his career he was admired for his skill as a performer. Alkan wrote mainly for the piano. His most influential works were the technically formidable *Études* (Op. 35 and 39), which greatly enlarged the piano techniques of the day. Much of his music was program music.

alkane (ăl′kān), any of a group of aliphatic hydrocarbons whose molecules contain only single bonds (see CHEMICAL BOND). Alkanes have the general chemical formula C_nH_{2n+2}. An alkane is said to have

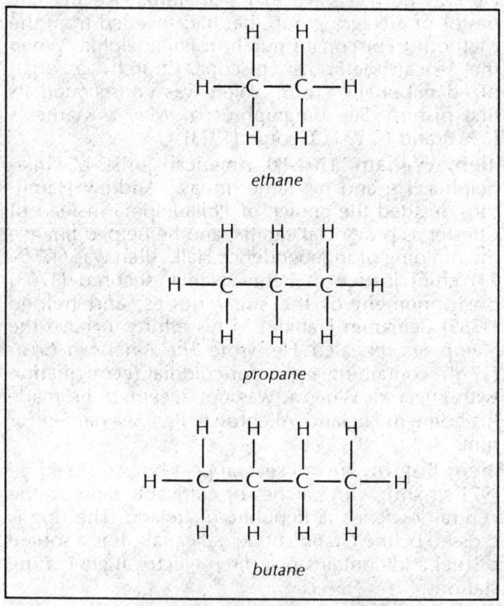

ethane

propane

butane

Alkanes

a continuous chain if each carbon atom in its molecule is joined to at most two other carbon atoms; it is said to have a branched chain if any of its carbon atoms is joined to more than two other carbon atoms. The first four continuous-chain alkanes are METHANE, CH_4; ETHANE, C_2H_6; PROPANE, C_3H_8; and BUTANE, C_4H_{10}. Names of continuous-chain alkanes whose molecules contain more than five carbon atoms are formed from a root that indicates the number of carbon atoms and the suffix *-ane* to indicate that the compound is an alkane; e.g., alkanes with 5, 6, 7, 8, 9, and 10 carbon atoms in their molecules are pentane, hexane, heptane, octane, nonane, and decane, respectively. The name of a branched-chain alkane is formed by adding prefixes to the name of the continuous-chain alkane from which it is considered to be derived; e.g., 2-methylpropane (called also isobutane) is thought of as being derived by replacing one of the hydrogen atoms bonded to the second (2-) carbon atom of a propane molecule with a methyl (CH_3) group, forming $CH_3CH(CH_3)_2$. Chemically, the alkanes are relatively unreactive. They are obtained by fractional distillation from petroleum and are used extensively as fuels. The alkanes are sometimes referred to as the methane series (after the simplest alkane) or as paraffins.

Al Karak (äl kärăk′), town, W central Jordan. It is also known as Krak. It is a road junction and an agricultural trade center. The ancient Kir Moab (also mentioned in the Bible as Kir Hareseth, Kir Haresh, and Kir Heres), it was the walled citadel of the Moabites. Al Karak played an important role in the Crusades. The lordship of Al Karak and Montreal was one of the chief baronies of the Latin Kingdom of Jerusalem. The brigand Reginald of Châtillon was lord of Al Karak and Montreal when, in 1187, he attacked a caravan led by Sultan SALADIN and thus provoked the events leading to the fall of Jerusalem. Al Karak was taken by Saladin in 1188 after a long siege. The town was an archiepiscopal see from the early Christian era until the Christians were massacred or expelled in 1910. A 12th-century castle built by the Crusaders at Al Karak is well preserved.

alkene (ăl′kēn), any of a group of aliphatic hydrocarbons whose molecules contain one or more carbon-carbon double bonds (see CHEMICAL BOND). Alkenes with only one double bond have the general formula C_nH_{2n}. In the International Union of Pure and Applied Chemistry (IUPAC) system of chemical nomenclature, the name of an alkene is derived from the name of the corresponding ALKANE by replacing the *-ane* alkane suffix with *-ene* and, if necessary, adding a prefix to indicate the location of the double bond in the molecule. The IUPAC name of the simplest alkene, $H_2C{=}CH_2$, is ethene, which is derived from ethane. Propene is related to propane. Two alkenes, 1-butene and 2-butene, are related to butane; these two compounds, which differ in the location of the double bond in their molecules, are structural ISOMERS. In addition to these IUPAC names, many of the alkenes have common names, e.g., ethene is called ethylene and propene propylene. The alkenes as a group are sometimes called the ethylene series. Since the carbon-carbon double bond is sometimes called an olefinic linkage, the alkenes are sometimes called the olefins. Many of the reactions in which alkenes take part involve the cleavage of half the carbon-carbon double bond and subsequent formation of two single bonds, one to each of the adjacent carbon atoms. Such reactions include hydrogenation, with the formation of an alkane, and hydrolysis, with the formation of an alcohol.

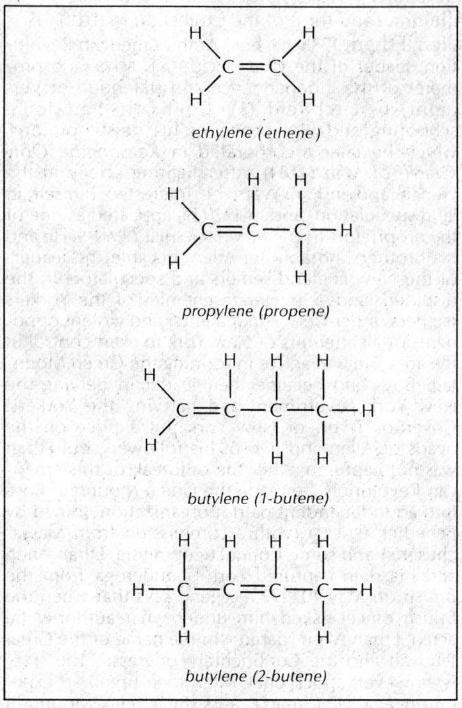

ethylene (ethene)

propylene (propene)

butylene (1-butene)

butylene (2-butene)

Alkenes

Al-Khowarizmi (äl-khōwärē′zmē), fl. 820, Arabian mathematician of the court of Mamun in Baghdad. His treatises on Hindu arithmetic and on algebra made him famous. He is said to have given algebra its name, and the word *algorithm* is said to have been derived from his name. Much of the mathematical knowledge of medieval Europe was derived from Latin translations of his works.

Alkmaar (älk′mär), town (1971 pop. 51,643), North Holland prov., NW Netherlands. It is an important market town and has varied industries. The Edam-cheese market, held weekly in front of the 16th-century weighhouse, is world famous. Alkmaar was chartered in 1254. Its successful defense (1573) against Spanish troops was a turning point in the revolt of the Netherlands.

Al Kufah (äl ko͞o′fä), town (1965 pop. 30,862), S central Iraq. Founded (638) by Caliph Umar I, it was one of the two Muslim centers (the other was BASRA) of the early Ummayad caliphs.

Al Kut (äl ko͞ot), town (1965 pop. 42,116), SE Iraq, on the Tigris River. It is a port and a market center for grains, dates, fruit, and vegetables. Much of the town was destroyed during World War I. Al Kut was taken from the Turks in Sept., 1915, by the British under Gen. Charles Townshend, who then advanced north to attack Baghdad. Defeated by the Turks, he retreated to Al Kut; his small army withstood siege by the Turks for 143 days before surrendering in April, 1916. The town was recaptured by Gen. S. F. Maude in 1917 in his successful advance on Baghdad. It is also called Kut-al-Amara or Kut-el-Amara.

alkyl group (ăl′kĭl), in chemistry, group of carbon and hydrogen atoms derived from an ALKANE molecule by removing one hydrogen atom (see RADICAL). The name of the alkyl group is derived from the name of its alkane by replacing the *-ane* suffix with *-yl*, e.g., methyl, CH_3, from methane, CH_4, and ethyl, C_2H_5, from ethane, C_2H_6. In some cases different alkyl groups can be formed from the same alkane by removing different hydrogen atoms; the alkyl groups are then distinguished by adding a prefix, e.g., 1-propyl or n-propyl, $CH_2CH_2CH_3$, and 2-propyl or isopropyl, $CH(CH_3)_2$, both formed from propane, $CH_3CH_2CH_3$. When a FUNCTIONAL GROUP is joined with an alkyl group, replacing the hydrogen that was removed, a compound is formed whose characteristics depend largely on the functional group.

alkyne (ăl′kīn), any of a group of aliphatic hydrocarbons whose molecules contain one or more carbon-carbon triple bonds (see CHEMICAL BOND). Alkynes with one triple bond have the general formula C_nH_{2n-2}. In the International Union of Pure and Applied Chemistry (IUPAC) system of chemical nomenclature, the name of an alkyne is derived from the name of the corresponding ALKANE by replacing the *-ane* alkane suffix with *-yne* and, if necessary, adding a prefix to indicate the location of the triple bond in the molecule. The IUPAC name of the simplest alkyne, $HC{\equiv}CH$, is thus ethyne, which is derived from ethane. Ethyne is more commonly known as ACETYLENE; it is an extremely important starting material in commercial chemical synthesis. The next simplest alkyne is propyne, $CH_3C{\equiv}CH$. There are two butynes, 1-butyne and 2-butyne, which are structural ISOMERS that differ in the location of the triple bond in their molecule. The alkynes are sometimes referred to as the acetylene series, the higher members of the series being named as derivatives of acetylene, e.g., propyne as methylacetylene, 1-butyne as ethylacetylene, and 2-butyne as dimethylacetylene. The usefulness of the alkynes in chemical synthesis is due both to the reactions of the triple bond itself and to the relative acidity of a hydrogen atom bonded to a triply bonded carbon.

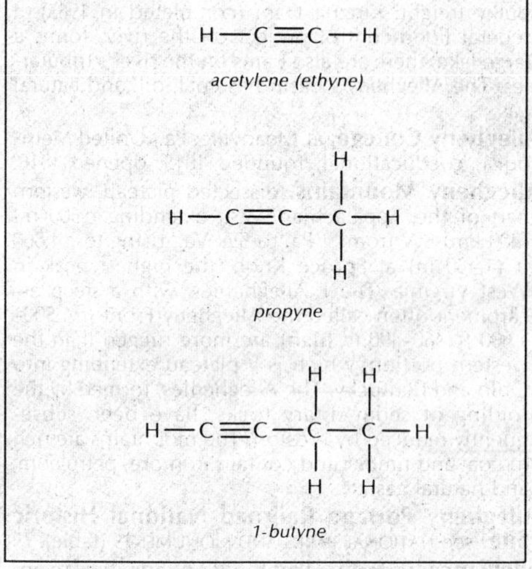

acetylene (ethyne)

propyne

1-butyne

Alkynes

Allah (ăl′ə, ä′lə), Arabic name of GOD. It is used not only in ISLAM but also among Arabic-speaking Christians. The name Allah was well known in pre-Islamic Arabia, when religion there was polytheistic. It was the Prophet Muhammad who emphasized the uniqueness of the god Allah and introduced the idea of monotheism to Arabia. See S. M. Zwemer, *The Moslem Doctrine of God* (1905); F. M. Fitch, *Allah, the God of Islam* (1950, repr. 1967); Daud Rahbar, *God of Justice* (1960).

Allahabad (ăl″əhəbăd′, -bäd′), city (1971 pop. 493,524), Uttar Pradesh state, N central India. On the site of Prayag, an ancient Indo-Aryan holy city, Allahabad is at the junction of two sacred rivers, the Jumna and the Ganges, and is visited by many Hindu pilgrims. The oldest monument is a pillar (c.242 B.C.) with inscriptions from the reign of ASOKA. The city was the scene of much fighting in the INDIAN

MUTINY (1857). Allahabad was the capital of the United Provinces from 1901 to 1949. It is a district administrative headquarters and trading center and has a university.

All-American Canal, 80 mi (129 km) long, SE Calif.; part of the Federal irrigation system of the Hoover Dam. Built between 1934 and 1940 across the Colorado Desert, the canal is entirely within the United States and replaces the Inter-California Canal, which passes through Mexico. The Imperial Dam, NE of Yuma, Ariz., diverts water from the Colorado River into the All-American Canal, which runs W to Calexico, Calif. Smaller canals move water into the Imperial Valley; the Coachella Canal branches NW to the Coachella Valley. This canal system irrigates more than 630,000 acres (254,961 hectares) and has greatly increased crop yield in the area; problems of drainage and salinity exist, however. The All-American Canal also supplies water to San Diego, Calif.

Allan, Sir Hugh, 1810–82, Canadian financier and shipowner, b. Scotland. He emigrated to Canada in 1826, was employed by a large shipbuilding company in Montreal, and later founded the Allan Line of steamships. He was given the contract to build the Canadian Pacific Railway, but the PACIFIC SCANDAL (1873) led to its cancellation.

Allegheny (ăl′əgā″nē, ăl″əgā′nē), river, 325 mi (523 km) long, rising in N central Pa., and flowing NW into N.Y., then SW through Pa. to the Monongahela River, with which it forms the Ohio River at Pittsburgh; drains 11,580 sq mi (29,992 sq km). Before the railroad era, the river was an important commercial route and is still used to transport coal and other bulky freight. Kinzua Dam (completed in 1965), a federal flood-control project on the river, forms a large lake; there are also dams on the river's tributaries. The Allegheny's basin has coal, oil, and natural gas.

Allegheny College, at Meadville, Pa.; United Methodist; coeducational; founded 1815, opened 1816.

Allegheny Mountains, dissected plateau, western part of the Appalachian Mts., extending c.500 mi (800 km) SW from N Pa. to SW Va., rising to c.4,860 ft (1,480 m) at Spruce Knob, the highest peak in West Virginia. The E Alleghenies, with a steep escarpment often called the Allegheny Front (c.1,500–1,600 ft/460–490 m high) are more rugged than the western portion, which is a plateau extending into Ohio and Kentucky. The Alleghenies, formed by the folding of sedimentary rocks, have been subsequently reduced by erosion. The mountains are rich in coal and timber and contain iron ore, petroleum, and natural gas.

Allegheny Portage Railroad National Historic Site: see NATIONAL PARKS AND MONUMENTS (table).

allegiance, formal tie that binds an individual to another individual or institution. The term usually refers to a person's obligation of obedience to a government in return for the protection of that government, although it may have reference to any institution that one is bound to support. Allegiance in strict usage is a legal tie only, but as used in ordinary speech, the term may include supplemental emotional ties that make it loosely synonymous with loyalty. In the United States allegiance is required of both CITIZENS and resident aliens. There are four types of allegiance: natural allegiance, which arises from membership by birth within a political society; express allegiance, which arises from an oath or promise to support a political society and usually results from NATURALIZATION; local allegiance, in which an alien owes temporary allegiance to a government for the protection it offers; and legal allegiance, which arises in certain cases from an oath taken to support a government temporarily, as when a foreign soldier joins its armed forces. Under the customary law of Europe a subject did not have the right to change his allegiance without the consent of his government. In 1868 the United States challenged this notion and declared that it was the right of any citizen to voluntarily expatriate himself, that is, to transfer voluntarily his allegiance to another government. Great Britain provided the same opportunity for its citizens in 1870, and thereafter various other European states followed similar policies. The process of EXPATRIATION, however, is by no means universal.

allegory, in literature, symbolic story that serves as a disguised representation for meanings other than those indicated on the surface. The characters in an allegory often have no individual personality, but are embodiments of moral qualities and other abstractions. The allegory is closely related to the parable, fable, and metaphor, differing from them largely in intricacy and length. A great variety of literary forms have been used for allegories. The medieval morality play *Everyman,* personifying such abstractions as Fellowship and Good Deeds, recounts the death journey of Everyman. John Bunyan's *Pilgrim's Progress,* a prose narrative, is an allegory of man's spiritual salvation. Spenser's poem *The Faerie Queene,* besides being a chivalric romance, is a commentary on morals and manners in 16th-century England as well as a national epic. Although allegory is still used by some authors, its popularity as a literary form has declined in favor of a more personal form of symbolic expression (see SYMBOLISTS).

allele (əlēl′): see GENETICS.

Alleluia, Latin form of the expression HALLELUJAH.

Allen, Ethan, 1738–89, hero of the American Revolution, leader of the GREEN MOUNTAIN BOYS, and promoter of the independence and statehood of Vermont, b. Litchfield (?), Conn. He had some schooling and was proud of his deist opinions, which he later incorporated in *Reason the Only Oracle of Man* (1784). After fighting briefly in the French and Indian Wars, he interested himself in land speculation, and in 1770 he appeared as one of the proprietors in the NEW HAMPSHIRE GRANTS. He and his brothers, notably Ira Allen, became the leaders of the New England settlers and speculators in the disputed lands—inveterate enemies of the Yorkers (settlers under New York patents) and violent opponents of all attempts of New York to exert control in the area. He was active in forming the Green Mountain Boys and became their leader in defying the New York government and harrying the Yorkers. Governor Tryon of New York put a price on the heads of Allen and two of his followers, but Ethan was not captured. After the outbreak of the American Revolution, he made the Green Mountain Boys into an independent patriot organization. Joined by Benedict ARNOLD (with a commission from Massachusetts) and some Connecticut militia, Ethan Allen and his men captured Fort Ticonderoga from the British on May 10, 1775. Legend says that when the British officer asked him under what authority he acted, Ethan Allen roared, "In the name of the Great Jehovah and the Continental Congress!" The story is, however, apocryphal. Allen then urged an expedition against Canada, and the Green Mountain Boys were attached to Gen. P. J. Schuyler's invasion force, but the men chose not Allen, but his cousin Seth WARNER, as leader. Allen went on the expedition and in a rash effort to capture Montreal before the main Continental army arrived was captured (Sept., 1775) by the British. He told his own story of this in the popular *Narrative of Colonel Ethan Allen's Captivity,* which appeared in 1779, a year after he had been exchanged. He returned to Vermont, which had declared its independence but was unrecognized by the Continental Congress. Ethan and his brother Ira then devoted themselves to insuring the new political unit in one way or another. The region remained in danger of British attack, and the British late in 1779 opened negotiations with Ethan Allen in an attempt to attach Vermont to Canada. No conclusion was reached, and the victory at Yorktown ending the American Revolution also ended the talks. Ethan Allen withdrew from politics in 1784. When he died, Vermont was still independent and still dickering with Congress and dealing with internal struggles between the Allen party and their opponents. See biography by C. A. Jellison (1969).

Allen, Frederick Lewis, 1890–1954, American social historian and editor, b. Boston, grad. Harvard (B.A., 1912; M.A., 1913). He is best remembered for his journalistic but nonetheless penetrating works of social history, including *Only Yesterday* (1932), *The Lords of Creation* (1935), *Since Yesterday* (1940), *The Great Pierpont Morgan* (1949), and *The Big Change* (1952). After teaching English at Harvard, he was an assistant editor of the *Atlantic Monthly* (1914–16), then managing editor of *The Century* (1916–17). In 1923 he began working for *Harper's Magazine,* where he remained until 1953, becoming chief editor in 1941.

Allen, Hervey, 1889–1949, American novelist and poet, b. Pittsburgh, grad. Univ. of Pittsburgh, 1915. After service in World War I, he taught English in Charleston, S.C., where, in collaboration with DuBose Heyward, he wrote *Carolina Chansons* (1922), a volume of verse. He wrote other books of poetry but is best known for his excellent biography of Poe, *Israfel* (1926), and the picaresque novel *Anthony Adverse* (1933), which achieved enormous popular success.

Allen, Ira, 1751–1814, political leader in early Vermont, b. Cornwall, Conn. He was the younger brother and the assistant of Ethan ALLEN. Although he was a member of the GREEN MOUNTAIN BOYS, he took little part in their activities. His cool shrewdness, his adeptness in business matters, and his brilliant planning complemented the colorful vigor and rash violence of his brother. He organized the Onion River Land Company and secured the lands around the Winooski River and Lake Champlain that the Allens worked hard to protect. Ira Allen took part in the conventions at Dorset and Westminster that brought about the independence of VERMONT, and he was a leading figure in its political life in the years following, holding many offices. He was involved in the long negotiations with the British and was accused of treason. After Vermont became a state he was forced out of politics. He helped to establish the Univ. of Vermont. In 1798, Allen published his *Natural and Political History of the State of Vermont.* See biography by J. B. Wilbur (1928).

Allen, James Lane, 1849–1925, American novelist, b. Lexington, Kentucky. Among his stylized, "genteel" novels set in his native region are *A Kentucky Cardinal* (1894), *Aftermath* (1895), and *The Choir Invisible* (1897). See studies by W. K. Bottorff (1964) and G. C. Knight (1935, repr. 1967).

Allen, Richard, 1760–1831, American clergyman, founder of the African Methodist Episcopal Church. He was born a slave in Philadelphia. He became pastor of a Negro group that had seceded from the Methodist Episcopal Church in Philadelphia. When the African Methodist Episcopal Church was organized nationally (1816), Allen was consecrated its first bishop. See biographies by M. M. Mathews (1963) and C. V. R. George (1973).

Allen, William, 1704–80, American jurist, b. Philadelphia. He and his father-in-law, Andrew Hamilton, decided the choice of Philadelphia instead of Chester as provincial capital, and he helped finance the building of Independence Hall. Allen was (1750–74) chief justice of Pennsylvania, secured (1763) postponement of the sugar duties, and helped (1765) Benjamin Franklin in his efforts to have the Stamp Act repealed. He wrote *The American Crisis* (1774), containing a plan for colonial reconciliation with England. When it was not accepted, he made his home in England. Allentown, Pa., was named for him.

Allen, Bog of, area of several peat bogs c.375 sq mi (971 sq km), with patches of cultivable land, in the central lowlands, E Republic of Ireland. The bog is crossed by the Grand and Royal canals. It is a source of fuel and contains peat-fired electrical generating stations.

Allen, Lough (lŏkh, lŏk), lake, 8 mi (12.9 km) long and 3 mi (4.8 km) wide, Co. Leitrim and Co. Roscommon, N Republic of Ireland. The upper Shannon River flows through the lake.

Allenby, Edmund Henry Hynman Allenby, 1st Viscount (ăl′ənbē), 1861–1936, British field marshal. Educated at Sandhurst, he saw active service in Bechuanaland (1884–85) and Zululand (1888) and in the South African War (1899–1902). When World War I broke out (1914), he commanded first the cavalry and then (1915–17) the 3d Army in France. Appointed commander of the Egyptian Expeditionary Force in June, 1917, he waged the last of the great cavalry campaigns by invading Palestine, capturing Jerusalem, and ending Turkish resistance after the battle of Megiddo (Sept. 18–21, 1918). He served as British high commissioner for Egypt and the Sudan (1919–25). He was made viscount in 1919. See A. P. Wavell, *Allenby* (1941) and *Allenby in Egypt* (1945); Brian Gardner, *Allenby of Arabia* (1965).

Allende, Ignacio (ēgnä′syō äyān′dā), 1779–1811, Mexican revolutionist. He was a captain in the army when he joined the movement against Spanish domination. He played a prominent part in the revolution and after the great defeat at Calderón Bridge (Jan. 17, 1811) took chief command of the forces. His seizure of power left Miguel HIDALGO Y COSTILLA, with whom he had quarreled, only nominal control. The revolutionists went northward, hoping to reach the United States, but the treachery of one of their leaders led to capture by the royalists. Allende was shot at Chihuahua.

Allende Gossens, Salvador (sälvä*th*ōr′ äyān′dā gō′sāns), 1908–73, president of Chile (1970–73). A physician, he helped found the Chilean Socialist party in 1933 and later served as minister of health (1939–42) and as president of the senate (1965–69). He ran for president several times, and on his fourth try (1970) he won by a narrow plurality, thus becoming the first freely elected Marxist in the Western Hemisphere. Attempting to turn Chile into a socialist state, he nationalized numerous industries (including the giant copper operations) and pushed extensive land reform. However, as a minority president he lacked the popular support necessary for such drastic measures, and much of the nation opposed him. Soaring inflation and widespread shortages sparked a period of crippling strikes and violence, caused at least in part by the undercover activities of the U.S. Central Intelligence Agency. In Sept., 1973, Allende was overthrown in a bloody military coup, during which he apparently committed suicide (his wife asserted that he was murdered). He was succeeded as president by Gen. Augusto Pinochet Ugarte.

Allen Park, city (1970 pop. 40,747), Wayne co., SE Mich., a suburb of Detroit; inc. as a city 1957. Its manufactures include automobiles, tires, liquor, bread, and potato chips. The area was settled in the early 1800s and was named after Lewis Allen, a settler from Detroit.

Allenstein: see OLSZTYN, Poland.

Allentown, city (1970 pop. 109,527), seat of Lehigh co., E Pa., on the Lehigh River; inc. as a borough 1811, as a city 1867. Allentown, situated in the agricultural Lehigh valley and in the Pennsylvania Dutch region, is an industrial and commercial city. Cement, truck and bus bodies, clothing, machinery, small appliances, transistors, tubes, air-reduction equipment, gas-generating equipment, pneumatic loading machinery, and beer are the major products. In the city are Muhlenberg College, Cedar Crest College, Allentown College of St. Francis de Sales, Lehigh County Community College, and a campus of Pennsylvania State Univ. Allentown was founded in 1762 by William Allen, Chief Justice of the Commonwealth of Pennsylvania, and was settled by representatives of various German religious groups. First known as Northampton, it was renamed Allentown c.1836. The Liberty Bell was brought there (1777) for safekeeping during the Revolutionary War, and the city became a munitions center for the Continental Army. Points of interest include the Zion Reformed Church (where the Liberty Bell was kept) and an art museum.

Alleppey (əlĕp'ē), town (1971 pop. 160,064), Kerala state, SW India. It is a district administrative center and port on the Arabian Sea. Copra, coir, rubber, and spices are its chief exports. Fishing is a major industry.

allergy, hypersensitive reaction of the body tissues of certain individuals to certain substances that, in similar amounts and circumstances, are innocuous to other persons. Allergens, or allergy-causing substances, can be airborne substances (e.g., pollens, dust, smoke), infectious agents (bacteria, fungi, parasites), foods (strawberries, chocolate, eggs), contactants (poison ivy, chemicals, dyes), or physical agents (light, heat, cold). It is believed that a person who is hereditarily predisposed toward allergy produces, when sensitized, special weak types of antibodies, called reagins, that give little immune protection but cause local tissue damage during the antibody-antigen reaction (see IMMUNITY). Allergens can affect the respiratory system, the reaction manifesting itself as asthma or hay fever, or they can affect the skin, causing wheals and rashes. Allergens may also act on the gastrointestinal tract, causing nausea and vomiting. Allergic reactions to substances injected into the bloodstream can cause violent and sometimes fatal reactions (see ANAPHYLAXIS; SERUM SICKNESS). The best treatment of allergic reactions is prevention, i.e., elimination of the offending substances from the sensitive person's environment. If this is not possible, desensitization (i.e., deliberate production of the allergic reaction by injecting the allergen, after which the sufferer is no longer susceptible) is sometimes helpful. Antihistamine drugs may give temporary relief. See HISTAMINE.

Allerton, Isaac (ăl'ərtən), c.1586–1659, Pilgrim settler in Plymouth Colony. Possibly a London tailor, he was a merchant in Leiden before going to America on the *Mayflower*. From 1626 to 1631, acting as the agent of PLYMOUTH COLONY, he was often in England. While there he bought up the rights of merchants in the enterprise and in 1630 secured a new patent for the colony. The terms of the new patent, however, were opposed by William Bradford and other colonists. Allerton was at best incompetent and ran up the debt, even if he was not—as his neighbors accused him of being—dishonest. He probably left Plymouth Colony in 1631 and was later at Marblehead, at New Amsterdam, and in the New Haven colony.

Alleyn, Edward (ăl'ĭn), 1566–1626, English actor. He was the foremost member of the ADMIRAL'S MEN, joining the group c.1587, and was the only rival of Richard Burbage. He gained fame for his portrayals in Marlowe's *Tamburlaine, Jew of Malta,* and *Faustus.* He married the stepdaughter of Philip Henslowe and with Henslowe owned the Rose and Fortune theaters. His popularity brought him wealth, which he employed in the founding of Dulwich College in 1613 and in aiding contemporary writers. After his wife's death, he married a daughter of John Donne.

Alliance, city (1970 pop. 26,547), Mahoning and Stark cos., NE Ohio, on the Mahoning River, in a farm area; inc. 1854. It is an industrial, distributing, and rail center, with manufactures of steel, heavy machinery, electric tubing, chinaware, and farm, railroad, and industrial equipment. It is the seat of Mount Union College, where Clarke Observatory is located.

Alliance for Progress (*Alianza para Progreso*), inter-American program of economic assistance begun in 1961. Conceived as an evolutionary plan to relieve Latin American economic and social problems, it was created, in part, to counter the appeal of revolutionary approaches such as the one adopted by Cuba. It is administered by the Inter-American Committee for the Alliance for Progress (CIAP), a permanent committee within the ORGANIZATION OF AMERICAN STATES. The charter of the Alliance, formulated at the Inter-American Economic and Social Council conference at Punta del Este, Uruguay, in Aug., 1961, envisioned a minimum annual increase of 2.5% in per capita income. To achieve this a capital investment of $80 billion over a period of 10 years was pledged by the Latin American countries (excluding Cuba), who in turn agreed to carry out tax and land reforms. The United States agreed to supply or guarantee 60% of an additional $20 billion in outside financing. Private capital was asked to supply a yearly average of $300 million of this amount. Although the increase of 2.5% in per capita income was not achieved by the early 1970s, the United States had already assured (1967) Latin American leaders that the program would be extended beyond the 1971 terminal date. By the early 1970s, criticism of the program was heard across Latin America and in the United States. In 1971 the United States began a reduction in loans to the program, limiting its prospects for future success. See H. K. May, *The Problems and Prospects of the Alliance for Progress* (1968); Harvey S. Perloff, *Alliance for Progress* (1969); Jerome Levinson and Juan de Onis, *The Alliance That Lost Its Way* (1970).

Allier (älyā'), department (1968 pop. 386,533), central France, in BOURBONNAIS. MOULINS is the capital.

alligator, large aquatic reptile of the genus *Alligator,* in the same order as the CROCODILE. There are two species—a large type found in the S United States and a small type found in China. Alligators differ from crocodiles in several ways. They have broader, blunter snouts, which give their heads a triangular appearance; also, the lower fourth tooth does not protrude when the mouth is closed, as it does in the crocodile. The American alligator, *Alligator mississipiensis,* is found in swamps and sluggish streams from North Carolina to Florida and along the Gulf Coast. When young, it is dark brown or black with yellow transverse bands. The bands fade as the animal grows, and the adult is black. Males commonly reach a length of 9 ft (2.7 m) and a weight of 250 lbs (110 kg); females are smaller. Males 18 ft (5.4 m) long were once fairly common, but intensive hunting for alligator leather has eliminated the larger individuals (a specimen over 10 ft/3 m long is now unusual) and threatened the species as a whole. The American alligator is now completely protected by law. Alligators spend the day floating just below the surface of the water or resting on the bank, lying in holes in hot weather. They hunt by night, in the water and on the bank. Young alligators feed on water insects, crustaceans, frogs, and fish; as they grow they catch proportionally larger animals. Large alligators may occasionally capture deer and cows as they come to drink; they are not known to attack humans except in self-defense. Alligators hibernate from October to March. In summer the female builds a nest of rotting vegetation on the bank and deposits in it 20 to 70 eggs, which she guards for 9 to 10 weeks until they hatch. The Chinese alligator, *A. sinensis,* which grows to about 6 ft (1.8 m) long, is found in the Yangtze River valley near Shanghai. This species is nearly extinct. Caimans are members of the alligator family found in Central and South America. There are several species, classified in three genera. The largest grow up to 15 ft (4.8 m) long. Unlike alligators, caimans have bony overlapping scales on their bellies. Baby caimans are often sold in the United States as baby alligators. Alligators and caimans are classified in the phylum CHORDATA, subphylum Vertebrata, class Reptilia, order Crocodilia, family Alligatoridae.

alligator pear: see AVOCADO.

Alliluyeva, Svetlana (svyĕt'länä äl-lĕlo͞o'yəvə), 1926–, only daughter of the Soviet Communist leader Joseph Stalin and his second wife, Nadezhda Alliluyeva. After her father's death (1953) she was a teacher and translator in the Soviet Union. In late 1966, while in India, she defected to the West. She left a grown son and daughter from two earlier marriages in the Soviet Union. She settled in the United States in April, 1967, and published (1967) her memoirs, *Twenty Letters to a Friend.* She also wrote *Only One Year* (1969), an account of her experiences under diverse Soviet regimes. Becoming a U.S. citizen, she married (1970) an American architect, William Peters, but separated from him after having given birth to a daughter.

Allingham, Margery (ăl'ĭng-əm), 1904–66, English detective-story writer, b. London. Most of her novels feature Mr. Albert Campion, a scholarly detective of noble birth, bespectacled, mild, and believable. Her thrillers are intelligently written and noted for their adroit characterization and literate style. Among her more than 25 books are *The Crime at Black Dudley* (1928), *Flowers for the Judge* (1936), *Black Plumes* (1940), *The Tiger in the Smoke* (1952), and *The Mind Reader* (1965), her last.

Allingham, William, 1824–89, English poet, b. Donegal, Ireland. He is best known for his short lyrics, most notably "The Fairies," beginning "Up the airy mountain, Down the rushy glen." See study by Alan Warner (1972).

Allison, William Boyd, 1829–1908, U.S. Senator from Iowa (1873–1908), b. Ashland co., Ohio. He served (1863–71) in the House of Representatives and entered the Senate in 1873. One of the most influential Republican members of Congress, he spoke for the farmers of the Midwest and was considered a political moderate. Allison opposed high tariffs on goods needed in quantity by the farmers and helped to build compromise tariff bills. He changed the bill for "free and unlimited coinage" of silver to allow specified limited coinage and thus gave his name to the BLAND-ALLISON ACT. See biography by Leland Sage (1956).

alliteration (əlĭt"ərā'shən), the repetition of the same starting sound in several words of a sentence. Probably the most powerful rhythmic and thematic uses of alliteration are contained in *Beowulf,* written in Anglo-Saxon and one of the earliest English poems extant. For example:

Pa com of more under mist-hleopum
Grendel gongan; Godes yrre baer. . .
(Then came from the moor, under the misty hills,
Grendel stalking; he God's anger bare).
Beowulf, Book XI

The poet was drawing here on an even older Germanic tradition, just as he was setting a high standard for other poets in Anglo-Saxon, who produced such alliterative works as *Widsith, Deor's Lament, The Wanderer, The Seafarer,* and *The Ruin.* Although the tradition lay dormant for centuries, an alliterative revival occurred in England in the mid-1400s, as evidenced by such masterworks as *Piers Plowman* and *Sir Gawain and the Green Knight* (see LANGLAND, WILLIAM; PEARL, THE). Shakespeare parodies alliteration in Peter Quince's Prologue in *A Midsummer Night's Dream*:

Whereat, with blade, with bloody blameful
blade,
He bravely breach'd his boiling bloody breast.

Modern poets have continually renewed the possibilities of alliteration, e.g., Gerard Manley Hopkins's "Pied Beauty":

Glory be to God for dappled things . . .
Landscapes plotted and pieced—fold, fallow
and plough;
And áll trádes, their gear and tackle
and trim.

Alliterative Morte Arthure: see ALLITERATION.

Alliterative Revival: see ALLITERATION.

Alloa (ăl'lōə), burgh (1971 pop. 14,110), administrative center of Clackmannanshire, central Scotland, on the Forth River. Coal mining, brewing, and bottle making are the principal industries. A 15th-century tower on Mar's Hill marks the seat of the Erskines, earls of Mar. In 1975, Alloa became part of the new Central region.

Allobroges (əlŏ'brəjēz), Celtic tribe in Gaul, inhabiting later Dauphiné and Savoy. They were conquered (121 B.C.) by Quintus Fabius Maximus, who was called Allobrogicus in commemoration of the victory. In the time of Julius Caesar they sided with Rome.

allograft: see TRANSPLANTATION, MEDICAL.

Allon. 1 Simeonite. 1 Chron. 4.37. 2 Naphtalite city. Joshua 19.33.

Allon-bachuth (ăl'ən-băk'əth), place close to Bethel, where they buried Rebecca's nurse. Gen. 35.8.

allotropy (əlŏ'trəpē) [Gr.,=other form]. A chemical element is said to exhibit allotropy when it occurs in two or more forms; the forms are called allotropes. Allotropes generally differ in physical properties such as color and hardness; they may also differ in molecular structure or chemical activity, but are usually alike in most chemical properties. Diamond and graphite are two allotropes of the element CARBON. OZONE is a chemically active triatomic allotrope of the element OXYGEN. PHOSPHORUS, SULFUR, and TIN also exhibit allotropy. Many metals have allotropic crystalline forms that are stable at different temperatures. POLYMORPHISM is an analogous phenomenon observed in chemical compounds.

Allouez, Claude Jean (klōd zhäN älwā'), 1622–89, French Jesuit missionary in Canada and the American Midwest. After arriving (1658) in Canada he served at posts in the St. Lawrence region until 1665, when he went to Lake Superior and founded the Chequamegon Bay mission (near present-day Ashland, Wis.). A canoe trip around Lake Superior in 1667 supplied material for the well-known Jesuit map of the lake. Later he founded several missions, including that at De Pere, made his headquarters at Green Bay, and spent his last years as missionary to the Illinois and Miami Indians. His accurate and informed reports made the Great Lakes country known.

Alloway, Scotland: see AYR.

alloy (ăl'oi, əloi') [from O. Fr.,=combine], substance with metallic properties that consists of a metal fused with one or more metals or nonmetals. Most alloys are solid at room temperature. An alloy may be a homogeneous solid solution, a heterogeneous mixture of tiny crystals, a true chemical compound, or a mixture of these. Alloys generally have properties different from those of their constituent elements: they may be poorer conductors of heat and electricity; harder; or more resistant to corrosion. Because of these and other properties, alloys are used more extensively than pure metals. Alloys of iron and carbon are among the most widely used; they include cast iron and steels. Brass and bronze are important alloys of copper. Nickel is often added to alloys to improve their properties. Because pure gold and pure silver are too soft for many uses, e.g., jewelry and tableware, they are often alloyed either with one another or with other metals, e.g., copper or platinum. Amalgams are alloys that contain mercury.

All Saints Bay, Brazil: see TODOS OS SANTOS BAY.

All Saints' Day, Nov. 1, feast of the Roman Catholic and Anglican churches, the day on which the church glorifies God for all his saints, known and unknown. It is one of the principal feasts of the year in the Roman Catholic Church; all are obliged to hear Mass on it. Its origin probably lies in the common commemoration of martyrs who died in groups or whose names were unknown. In 609, Pope Boniface IV dedicated the Pantheon at Rome to Our Lady and all martyrs, and by 900 All Saints was generally celebrated on Nov. 1. In medieval England the festival was known as All Hallows; hence the name Halloween (Hallows' eve) for the preceding day (Oct. 31). Halloween is associated, in countries where Celtic influence is strong, with age-old customs peculiar to that night. In certain parts of the British Isles bonfires and fortune-telling like those of midsummer night continue. Elsewhere, especially in America, mumming and masquerading are popular, and jack-o'-lanterns are displayed. Tales of witches and ghosts are told, and in remote communities old superstitions are kept. One of the special games, bobbing for apples, is known to date from the Middle Ages. These pagan survivals of Halloween probably represent old Celtic practices associated with Nov. 1, the beginning of winter. Probably All Saints' Day arose apart from Celtic influence, and the customs of Halloween have survived independently of the Christian feast.

All Souls' Day, Nov. 2 (exceptionally, Nov. 3), feast of the Roman Catholic Church on which the church on earth prays for the souls of the faithful departed still suffering in PURGATORY. The proper office is of the dead, and the Mass is a REQUIEM. General intercessions for the dead (e.g., for those of a parish, a city, or a regiment) are very ancient (2 Mac. 12.43–45); but the modern feast was probably first established by an 11th-century abbot of Cluny for his community and later extended throughout the church. In Catholic countries there are many customs peculiar to All Souls' Day (e.g., leaving lights in the cemeteries on the night before). These vary from region to region. They should be distinguished from the customs of Halloween, which were apparently an independent development (see ALL SAINTS' DAY).

allspice: see PIMENTO.

Allston, Washington, 1779–1843, American painter and author, b. Georgetown co., S.C. After graduating from Harvard (1800), where he composed music and wrote poetry (published in 1813 as *The Sylphs of the Seasons*), Allston went to London and there studied painting with Benjamin West. He then spent four years in Rome studying the old masters and began his ambitious religious and allegorical paintings, which at first he rendered with classical reserve. His greatest years were spent in England (1810–18), where his work revealed a sophisticated and controlled, yet romantic mind. An important work of this period was the portrait of his lifelong friend Coleridge. In England and Europe, Allston was the intimate of intellectuals and in frequent contact with the best of Western art. He returned to the United States, where artistic stimulation was lacking, and, as a result, his own work eventually lost its vitality. His allegorical works and his tragic failure, *Belshazzar's Feast*, over which he labored for more than 20 years, were totally overshadowed by his lyric fantasies—his landscapes and seascapes, of which *Moonlit Landscape* (1819; Mus. of Fine Arts, Boston) and *Ship in a Squall* (before 1837; Fogg Art Mus.) are two of the finest. Although he was his own most perceptive critic, Allston persisted in his nostalgic re-creation of monumental neoclassic figure paintings until his death. Samuel F. B. Morse was one of his numerous pupils. See biographies by J. B. Flagg (1892, repr. 1969) and E. P. Richardson (1948).

Alma (älmä', ăl'mə), city (1971 pop. 22,622), S central Que., Canada, on the Saguenay River. In 1954 its name was shortened from St. Joseph d'Alma. There are granite quarries in the region, and the town has pulp and paper and aluminum plants.

Alma-Ata (ăl'mə-ä'tä, Rus. əlmä'-ətä'), city (1970 pop. 730,000), capital of the Kazakh Soviet Socialist Republic, Central Asian USSR, in the foothills of the Trans-Ili Ala-Tau. A terminus of the Turkistan-Siberia RR, Alma-Ata is the industrial and cultural center of Kazakhstan. Leading industries include motion picture production, fruit canning, meat-packing, tobacco processing, and the repair of railroad equipment. The city was founded in 1854 as a Russian fort and trade center known as Verny. Alma-Ata has a university and is the site of the Kazakh Academy of Sciences.

Almagest: see PTOLEMY.

Almagro, Diego de (dyā'gō dā älmä'grō), c.1475–1538, Spanish conquistador, a leader in the conquest of Peru. A partner of Francisco PIZARRO, he took part in the first (1524) and second (1526–28) expeditions and in the bloody subjugation of the Incas after 1532. He aided (1534) BENALCÁZAR in thwarting Pedro de ALVARADO in the conquest of Ecuador. No match for the Pizarro brothers, he lost out in the division of spoils but was granted the lands S of CUZCO. In 1535, Almagro set out on a march that was incredible in its hardships—south through the freezing cordillera of the Andes, probably as far as Coquimbo in present Chile, and then, after finding no gold, back north through the desert wastes of ATACAMA. He believed Cuzco was within his jurisdiction and so seized (1537) the city from Hernando PIZARRO, whom he injudiciously set free. Civil war ensued, and Almagro's forces were defeated. Almagro begged for his life and was promised it; but he was garroted by orders of Hernando Pizarro. Almagro's half-Indian son, **Diego de Almagro** (d. 1542), inherited his rights. Later the youth nominally headed the revolt that began with the assassination of Francisco Pizarro, but in 1542 he was captured and executed by the new governor, VACA DE CASTRO.

Al Mahdiyah (äl mädē'yä) or **Mahdia,** town (1966 pop. 15,900), E Tunisia, on the Mediterranean Sea. It is a fishing port where olive oil and handicrafts are marketed. The town was founded in 912 by the Fatimids on the site of Phoenician and Roman colonies, and it was the Fatimid capital from 921 to 948.

almanac, calendar with notations of astronomical and other data. Almanacs have been known in simple form almost since the invention of writing, for they served to record religious feasts, seasonal changes, and the like. The Roman *fasti*, originally a list of *dies fasti* (days when legal business might be transacted) and *dies nefasti* (days when legal business should not be transacted), were later elaborated into various lists, some of them resembling modern almanacs. The almanac did not become a really prominent type of reading matter until the introduction of printing in Western Europe in the 15th cent. Regiomontanus produced one of the famous early almanacs (his *Ephemerides*), incorporating his astronomical knowledge. Most early almanacs were devoted primarily to astrology and predictions of the future. Prediction of the weather has persisted in many modern almanacs, but the crude and sensational magic began to disappear early, to be replaced by more or less scientific information. There appeared late in the 18th cent. truly scientific almanacs—notably the British Nautical Almanac (founded 1767) (see EPHEMERIS), which was the inspiration for the *American Ephemeris and Nautical Almanac* (founded 1855). The popular almanac, however, developed in the 17th and 18th cent. into a full-blown form of folk literature, with notations of anniversaries and interesting facts, home medical advice, statistics of all sorts, jokes, and even fiction and poetry. The first production (except for a broadside) of printing in British North America was an almanac for the year 1639. One of the best colonial almanacs was the *Astronomical Diary and Almanack* begun by Nathaniel Ames in 1725, and this was the forerunner of the most famous of them all, Benjamin Franklin's *Poor Richard's Almanack* (pub. by him 1732–57), which in its title recalled one of the most popular and long-lasting of English almanacs, that of "Poor Robin" (founded c.1662). The most enduring of all American almanacs was first published in 1793 by Robert Baily Thomas; it came later to be called *The Old Farmer's Almanack*. The best types of present-day almanacs are handy and dependable compendiums of large amounts of statistical information. Noteworthy are *The World Almanac and Book of Facts* (first pub. as a booklet in 1868; discontinued 1884; revived 1885), *Information Please Almanac* (first pub. 1947), and the *Reader's Digest Almanac* (first pub. 1965).

Al Manamah (äl mänäm'ä), town (1971 pop. 89,728), capital of Bahrain, on the Persian Gulf. It has oil refineries and light industries and is a free port. A causeway links it with the island of Al Muharraq.

Alma-Tadema, Sir Lawrence (ăl'mə-tăd'ĭmə), 1836–1912, English painter, b. Friesland. He studied in Belgium, where he lived until 1869. In that year he went to England; there he became a citizen and enjoyed a long popularity and many honors. He is best known for his scholarly and meticulous paintings of scenes from Greek and Roman life.

Almeida, Antonio José de (äNtô'nyo͞o zho͞ozĕ' dĭ älmä'də), 1866–1929, Portuguese statesman. A republican, he was minister of the interior in the provisional government after the overthrow of the monarchy in 1910. As leader of the moderate Evolutionist party, he was premier of a coalition cabinet in World War I and later (1919–23) president of the republic.

Almeida, Francisco de (frənsĕsh'ko͞o), c.1450–1510, Portuguese admiral, first viceroy of Portuguese India. He was first sent to India in 1503 as captain major of a fleet and helped Portuguese forces defeat the ruler of Calicut. In 1505 he was appointed viceroy and set out from Lisbon with instructions to develop Portuguese commerce by building fortifications on the east coast of Africa, concluding alliances with the Indian rulers, and taking control of the spice trade from the Arabs. In Africa he built forts at Kilwa and Sofala and burned Mombasa. After his arrival in India he built further forts but relied mainly on his fleets to secure control of all sea trade. The Egyptians, seeing their commerce threatened, built a fleet (with the help of Venice) and defeated and killed (1508) Almeida's son at Chaul. However, in 1509, Almeida won a great naval battle against them and their Indian allies off Diu. Almeida at first refused to yield his power to Afonso de ALBUQUERQUE and had Albuquerque imprisoned (1509), but he later gave him command. On his way home to Portugal, Almeida was killed by Hottentots near the Cape of Good Hope. See K. G. Jayne, *Vasco da Gama and His Successors* (1910).

Almeida Garrett, João Batista de (zhwouN bətĕsh'tə dĭ älmä'də gərĕt'), 1799–1854, Portuguese dramatist, poet, journalist, and orator, leader of the romantic movement in Portugal. After a period in the Azores he returned to graduate from the Univ. of Coimbra. An ardent liberal democrat, he supported the revolution of 1820 and was twice forced into exile (1823–26, 1828–32). Upon his return he abandoned classicism for a romanticism that he expressed most effectively in the plays *Alfageme de Santarém* and *Frei Luis de Sousa* (tr. *Brother Luiz de Sousa*, 1909), and the long poems *Camões* and *Dona*

Branca. Generally considered the greatest of Portuguese dramatists, he was a significant poet and folklorist as well. Almeida Garrett held numerous political offices, working effectively for the democratic cause. His major works include collections of poetry, *Flores sem fruto* [flowers without fruit] (1844), *Fôlhas caídas* [fallen leaves] (1853); a book of folklore, *Romanceiro* (1843); and the prose *Viagens na minha terra* [journeys in my native land] (1846).

Almelo (äl'məlō), city (1971 pop. 59,426), Overijssel prov., E Netherlands. It is a manufacturing center and has a large textile industry.

Almería (älmärē'ä), city (1970 pop. 114,510), capital of Almería prov., SE Spain, in Andalusia, on the Gulf of Almería. A busy Mediterranean port, it exports the celebrated grapes of the region, other fruits, esparto, as well as iron and other minerals mined nearby. The city has refineries and processing plants and light industries. Probably founded by Phoenicians, Almería flourished from the 13th to the 15th cent. as the outlet of the Moorish kingdom of Granada. Under the Moors it was an important naval base. It fell to the Christians in 1489. There is a Moorish fort, now in ruins, and a Gothic cathedral. In 1937, during the civil war, the city was shelled by German warships.

Almirante Brown (älmērän'tā) or **Adrogué** (ädrōgā'), city (1960 pop. 136,924), Buenos Aires prov., E Argentina. It was settled in 1873 by families fleeing a yellow fever epidemic in the city of Buenos Aires.

Almodad (ălmō'dăd), descendant of Shem. Gen. 10.26; 1 Chron. 1.20.

Almohads (ăl'məhădz), Berber Muslim dynasty that ruled Morocco and Spain in the 12th and 13th cent. It had its origins in the puritanical sect founded by Ibn Tumart, who stirred up (c.1120) the tribes of the Atlas Mts. area to purify Islam and oust the Almoravids. His successors, ABD AL-MUMIN, Yusuf II, and YAKUB I, succeeded in conquering Morocco and Muslim Spain, and by 1174 the Almohads had completely displaced the Almoravids. With time the Almohads lost some of their fierce purifying zeal; Yakub had a rich court and was the patron of Averroës. Yakub defeated (1195) ALFONSO VIII of Castile in the battle of Alarcos, but in 1212 the Almohad army was defeated, and Almohad power in Spain was destroyed by the victory of the Spanish and Portuguese at Navas de Tolosa. In Morocco they lost power to the Merenid dynasty, which took Marrakesh in 1269. See studies by Abd al-Wahid al Marrakushi (1881, repr. 1968) and Roger Le Tourneau (1969).

Almon: see ALEMETH **2.**

almond, name for a small tree (*Prunus amygdalus*) of the family Rosaceae (ROSE family) and for the nutlike, edible seed of its drupe fruit. The "nuts" of sweet-almond varieties are eaten raw or roasted and are pressed to obtain almond oil. Bitter-almond varieties also yield oil, from which the poisonous prussic acid is removed in the extraction process. Almond oil is used for flavoring, in soaps and cosmetics, and medicinally as a demulcent. The tree, native to central Asia and perhaps the Mediterranean, is now cultivated principally in the Orient, Italy, Spain, and (chiefly the sweet varieties) in California. It closely resembles the peach, of which it may be an ancestor, except that the fruit is fleshless. The flowering almonds (e.g., *P. triloba*) are pink- to white-blossomed shrubs also native to central Asia; like the similar and closely related pink-blossomed almond, they are widely cultivated as ornamentals. Several Asian types are known as myrobalan, a name applied also to the cherry plum, with which flowering almonds are sometimes hybridized. The beauty of the almond in bud, blossom, and fruit gave motif to sacred and ornamental carving. In the Middle East the tree breaks into sudden bloom in January, and in Syria and Palestine it came to symbolize beauty and revival. The rod of Aaron in the Bible (see AARON'S-ROD) bore almonds. Almonds are classified in the division MAGNOLIOPHYTA, class Magnoliopsida, order Rosales, family Rosaceae.

Almon-diblathaim (ăl'mən-dĭb"lathā'əm), camping place of the Israelites. Num. 33.46,47. Called Beth-diblathaim in a denunciation of Moab. Jer. 48.22.

Almoravids (ălmôr'əvĭdz), Berber Muslim dynasty that ruled Morocco and Muslim Spain in the 11th and 12th cent. The Almoravids may have originated in what is now the Islamic Republic of Mauritania. The real founder was Abd Allah ibn Yasin, who by military force converted a number of Saharan tribes to his own reformed religion and then advanced on Morocco. After his death (c.1059), YUSUF IBN TASHFIN and his brother ABU BAKR came to power. MARRAKESH was founded in 1062 and was the center of a powerful empire. Called by the Moors in Spain to help stem Christian reconquest, Yusuf entered Andalusia and defeated (1086) Alfonso VI of Castile. He later subdued the local Muslim rulers and governed Muslim Spain and N Morocco (Abu Bakr ruling over S Morocco). The dynasty also pushed south, destroying the ancient state of GHANA. The Almoravids were rough and puritanical, contemptuous of the luxurious Muslim courts in Spain. Their rule was never entirely stable and in the 12th cent. was attacked by the ALMOHADS, who finally (by 1174) won both Morocco and Muslim Spain.

Almquist, Carl Jonas Love (kärl yōō'näs lōō'və älm'kvĭst), 1793–1866, Swedish writer. He has been called the only Swedish novelist of note in the period 1830–50. At first a somewhat bizarre romanticist, inclined toward anarchy, he later became more concerned with realism and democracy. This transition is seen in *The Book of the Thorn Rose* (14 vol., 1832–51), which contains most of his novels, stories, plays, and poems. His novel *Sara Videbecke* (1839) appeared in English in 1919. In his varied career he was civil servant, teacher, clergyman, and socialist. Accused of forgery and suspected of murder, he fled to the United States and after 1865 lived in Bremen as Professor Westermann. See Axel Hemming-Sjöberg, *A Poet's Tragedy* (tr. 1932).

almug or **algum,** precious wood mentioned in the Bible (2 Chron. 2.8; 9.10,11), used in the Temple of Solomon and in his palace, brought from Ophir and Lebanon. It is perhaps a red SANDALWOOD.

Aloadae (əlō'ədē) or **Aloidae** (ălōĭ'dē), in Greek mythology, two giants who warred against the Olympian gods. Their names were Otus and Ephialtes, and they were the sons of Aloeus' wife by Poseidon. They tried to reach heaven to overthrow the gods by piling Mt. Ossa on Mt. Olympus and Mt. Pelion on Mt. Ossa. Some said they were killed by Apollo; others that they killed each other while shooting at a hind sent by Apollo. For their wickedness they were condemned to eternal torture in Tartarus. Thus the phrase "to pile Pelion on Ossa" means to attempt an enormous but fruitless task.

alod (ă'lŏd). In feudal tenure, lands held without obligation to any suzerain (overlord) were termed held in alod. Alodial lands existed in England and on the Continent. They became less common as landowners sought protection by turning their lands over to more powerful lords and receiving the holdings back as fiefs. In modern times the distinction between fee simple (see TENURE) and alod has vanished.

aloe (ăl'ō) [Gr.], any species of the genus *Aloe,* succulent perennials of the family Liliaceae (LILY family), native chiefly to the warm dry areas of S Africa and also to tropical Africa, but cultivated elsewhere. The juice of aloe leaves contains the purgative aloin. Today the various drug-yielding species, e.g., *A. barbadensis* and *A. chinensis,* are still used for their traditional medicinal properties as well as for X-ray-burn treatment, insect repellent, and a transparent pigment used in miniature painting; cords and nets are made from the leaf fiber. In ancient times the juice was used in embalming. A Muhammadan, on his return from his pilgrimage to Mecca, hangs an aloe above his door. The American and false aloes are agaves, a family Amaryllidaceae (AMARYLLIS family) group that is the American counterpart in habit and general appearance to the true aloes. There is evolutionary evidence that the aloes and the agaves should be considered a single separate family, the Agavaceae. The Scriptural aloes is unrelated: Aloe is classified in the division MAGNOLIOPHYTA, class Liliatae, order Liliales, family Liliaceae.

aloes (ăl'ōz), drug obtained from the ALOE; also a biblical name for an aromatic substance of various uses, mentioned in connection with myrrh and spices (Ps. 45.8; Prov. 7.17; Cant. 4.14; John 19.39) and thought to be the fragrant wood of the modern aloeswood (also called eaglewood, agalloch, or agilawood), an *Aquilaria* native to Asia. In the East the aloeswood has been valued for medicinal purposes, as an incense, and for the beautiful grain of its wood, which takes a high polish and was used for setting precious stones. The tree lignaloes of Num. 24.6, sometimes thought to be the aloeswood, may have been a different plant. The aloe and the American aloe, or agave (see AMARYLLIS), are not to be confused with the aloes of the Scriptures.

Aloidae: see ALOADAE.

Alompra: see ALAUNGPAYA.

Alonso, Alicia (Alicia Martinez) (älē'syä älōn'sō, märtē'näs), 1921–, Cuban ballerina and choreographer, b. Havana. Alonso danced in Broadway musicals before becoming a soloist with several leading companies, including the American Ballet Theatre, in 1939. She soon gained acclaim in an enormous variety of starring roles, ranging from classical to modern. She was best known for her work in *Giselle* and in Agnes de Mille's *Fall River Legend.* Her own works include *La Tinaja* (1943), *Ensayos Sinfonicos,* and *Lidia,* all created for her own company in Cuba.

Alonso, Dámaso (dä'māsō älōn'sō), 1898–, Spanish philologist, lyric poet, and literary critic, b. Madrid. He is known for his literary sensitivity and the precision and rigor of his critical approach. His critical works include *La lengua poética de Góngora* [the poetic language of Góngora] (1935) and *Ensayos sobre poesía española* [essays on Spanish poetry] (1944). Among his volumes of poetry are *El viento y el verso* [wind and verse] (1925) and *Hijos de la ira* (1944; tr. *Children of Wrath,* 1970).

alopecia (ăl"əpē'shēə): see BALDNESS.

Alor Setar (ä'lôr sētär') or **Alor Star** (stär), city (1971 pop. 66,179), capital of Kedah, Malaysia, central Malay Peninsula, on the Kedah River. It is a major center for trade in rice and rubber. The residence of the Sultan of Kedah is in the city.

Alost: see AALST, Belgium.

Aloth (ā'lŏth): see BEALOTH.

Aloysius, Saint (ălōĭ'shəs), 1568–91, Italian Jesuit, b. Luigi Gonzaga, heir to the marchese de Castiglione. Highly devout from childhood, he renounced his title and entered (1585) the Society of Jesus under the tutelage of St. Robert Bellarmine. He died of a fever he caught while ministering to victims of the plague. He is the patron of youth. St. Aloysius has been especially extolled for his purity. Feast: June 21.

alpaca (ălpăk'ə), partially domesticated South American hoofed mammal of the CAMEL family. Like the LLAMA, it is probably a descendant of the guanaco. Although the flesh is sometimes used for food, the animal is bred chiefly for its long, lustrous wool, which varies from black, through shades of brown, to white. Flocks of alpaca are kept by Indians in the highlands of Bolivia, Chile, and Peru. They feed on grasses growing close to the snow line, and they require a pure water supply. The Incas had domesticated the alpaca and utilized its wool before the Spanish Conquest. Exporting of alpaca wool to Europe began after Sir Titus Salt discovered (1836) a way of manufacturing alpaca cloth. The name alpaca is sometimes used for materials such as mohair, which do not contain alpaca wool. Alpacas are classified in the phylum CHORDATA, subphylum Vertebrata, class Mammalia, order Artiodactyla, family Camelidae.

Alp Arslan (älp ärslän'), 1029–72, Seljuk sultan of Persia (1063–72). In 1065 he led the Seljuks in an invasion of Armenia and Georgia and in 1066 attacked the Byzantine Empire. The success of his campaign was crowned (1071) by his brilliant victory over Romanus IV at MANZIKERT. After defeating the Byzantines, he wrested Syria from the Fatimids. In Dec. 1072, while campaigning beyond the Oxus River, he was murdered by one of his captives. He was succeeded by his son Malik Shah, who consolidated the victories his father had won.

Alpena (ălpē'nə), city (1970 pop. 13,805), seat of Alpena co., N Mich., on Thunder Bay, an arm of Lake Huron; inc. 1871. Limestone quarried nearby is used to make cement, Alpena's chief manufacture. Other products include hardboard, paper, machinery, and automobile parts. Cement, limestone, and coal are transported on the Great Lakes by way of Alpena's harbor. Alpena lies in a year-round resort area and has an annual winter carnival. Alpena Community College is there.

alpenhorn: see ALPHORN.

Alpes-de-Hautes-Provence (älp"-də-ōt"-prəväNs'), department (1968 pop. 104,813), SE France; formerly Basses-Alpes dept. DIGNE is the capital.

Alpes-Maritimes (älp-märētēm'), department (1968 pop. 722,070), SE France, bounded by Italy on the east and the Mediterranean Sea on the south and surrounding the independent principality of MONACO. NICE is the capital.

alphabet [Gr. *alpha-beta,* like Eng. ABC], system of WRITING, theoretically having a one-for-one relation between character (or letter) and phoneme (see PHONETICS). Few alphabets have achieved the ideal exactness. A system of writing is called a syllabary when one character represents a syllable rather than a phoneme; such is the kana, used in Japanese to supplement the originally Chinese characters normally used. The precursors of the alphabet were the iconographic and ideographic writing of ancient man, such as wall paintings, CUNEIFORM, and the HIEROGLYPHIC writing of the Egyptians. The alphabet of

وتوفى الامير زين الدين هلال بن عبد الله الرومى الطواشى
ARABIC ←

預聞也其國事、猶不盡木参番民一
CHINESE ←↓

В Турции имеются еще сирийско-арабские элементы еще
CYRILLIC

च पुत्रा [illegible] प्रतिदिनं अ
DEVANAGARI

Ἐν ἀρχῇ ἦν ὁ λόγος καὶ ὁ λόγος ἦν πρὸς τὸν θεόν, και θεὸς ἦν ὁ
GREEK

עמי אשר במצרים ואת־צעקתם שבעתי מפני נגשיו כי ידעתי עמי
HEBREW ←

ダイガクノミチハアリアキラ、ン
JAPANESE ←↓

From dust we come, to dust we shall return.
ROMAN

Examples of letters in various alphabets
(arrows indicate the direction of reading)

modern Western Europe is the Roman alphabet, the base of most alphabets used for the newly written languages of Africa and America, as well as for scientific alphabets. Russian, Serbian, Bulgarian, and many languages of the USSR are written in the Cyrillic alphabet, an augmented Greek alphabet. Greek, Hebrew, and Arabic all have their own alphabets. The most important writing of India is the Devanagari, an alphabet with syllabic features; this, invented probably for Sanskrit, is the source of a number of Asian scripts. The Roman is derived from the Greek, perhaps by way of Etruria, and the Greeks had imitated the Phoenician alphabet. The exact steps are unknown, but the Phoenician, Hebrew, Arabic, and Devanagari systems are based ultimately on signs of the Egyptian hieroglyphic writing. This writing was not alphabetic, but in the phonogram it bore the germ of phonemic writing; thus the sign "bear" might (to use an English analogy) mean also the sound *b,* and "dog" *d.* A similar development created the Persian cuneiform syllabary. Two European alphabets of the late Roman era were the RUNES and the OGHAM. An exotic modern system is the Cherokee syllabary created by SEQUOYAH, suggested by, but not based on, the Roman alphabet. Another was the short-lived Mormon Deseret alphabet. See Samuel Mercer, *The Origin of Writing and Our Alphabet* (1959); David Diringer, *The Alphabet* (2 vol., 3d ed. 1968); Oscar Ogg, *The 26 Letters* (rev. ed. 1971).

Alpha Centauri (ăl'fə sĕntôr'ē), brightest star in the constellation CENTAURUS and 3d-brightest star in the sky; also known as Rigil Kent or Rigil Kentaurus; 1970 position R.A. $14^h37.6^m$, Dec. $-60°43'$. It is a yellow main-sequence star of the same SPECTRAL CLASS (G2 V) as the sun and of about the same size and mass; its apparent MAGNITUDE is -0.26. Actually, Alpha Centauri is a triple-star system, the components being designated A, B, and C. Alpha Centauri C is also called **Proxima Centauri** because it is the closest star to the earth (other than the sun), its distance being 4.28 light-years while that of components A and B is 4.34 light-years. Proxima Centauri orbits about the common center of mass of the system with a period of more than 250,000 years, so that in about 125,000 years it will be more distant than A and B.

Alpha Crucis (kro͞o'sĭs): see ACRUX.

Alphaeus (ălfē'əs). **1** See CLEOPHAS. **2** Father of the evangelist Matthew. Mark 2.14.

alpha particle, one of the three forms of natural RADIOACTIVITY. Alpha radiation (or alpha rays) was distinguished and named by E. R. Rutherford, who found by measuring the charge and mass of alpha particles that they are the nuclei of ordinary helium atoms, consisting of two protons and two neutrons (see NUCLEUS).

Alpheus (ălfē'əs), river god: see ARETHUSA.

Alpheus (ălfē'əs) or **Alfiós** (ălfēôs'), river, c.70 mi (110 km) long, rising in the Taygetus mts., S Greece. The longest river in the Peloponnesus, it flows northwest through gorges, past Olympia, and onto the Olympia plains before entering the Ionian Sea. In Greek mythology, its waters were said to pass under the sea and to emerge at Syracuse (Italy) in the fountain of Arethusa. Hercules, to clean the stables of Augeas, turned the Alpheus through them. It is the river Alph of Coleridge's poem *Kubla Khan.* The lower Alpheus was formerly known as Rouphia.

Alphonse (ălfôNs'), 1220–71, count of Poitiers and of Toulouse, brother of King Louis IX of France. By his marriage to the daughter of RAYMOND VII, count of Toulouse, he inherited Raymond's lands in 1249. An able administrator, he did much to heal the wounds of the crusade against the Albigenses. During the absence of Louis in the Holy Land, Alphonse was coregent (1250–52) with his mother, Blanche of Castile, and later (1252–54) with his younger brother, Charles of Anjou (later Charles I, king of Naples and Sicily). Alphonse left no heir, and at his death his lands were incorporated into the holdings of Philip III, king of France.

Alphonsine tables: see ALFONSINE TABLES.

Alphonso. For rulers thus named, see ALFONSO.

Alphonsus Liguori, Saint (ălfŏn'səs lĭgwô'rē), 1696–1787, Italian churchman, Doctor of the Church. He was named Alfonso Maria de' Liguori. In 1732 he founded the Congregation of the Most Holy Redeemer (the Redemptorists) for religious work among the poor, especially in the country. He refused the archiepiscopal see of Palermo but accepted (1762) a poor country diocese near Capua. He labored incessantly until 1775, when sickness forced him to resign. He worked for his order under great difficulties, caused by an anticlerical government and overzealous monks. Goatherds of the mountains were his especial care. St. Alphonsus was an accomplished musician and wrote many hymns and instrumental pieces. His point of view in CASUISTRY, which has become standard, is called equiprobabilism. St. Alphonsus was unusual, even among Roman Catholics, for his great devotion to the Virgin. Feast: Aug. 2. See biography by D. F. Miller and L. X. Aubin (1940).

alphorn or **alpenhorn** [Ger.,= Alps horn], wooden horn from 3 ft to 12 ft (91 cm–3.7 m) long, sometimes curved slightly, with conical bore and a cup-shaped mouthpiece. It produces only the natural

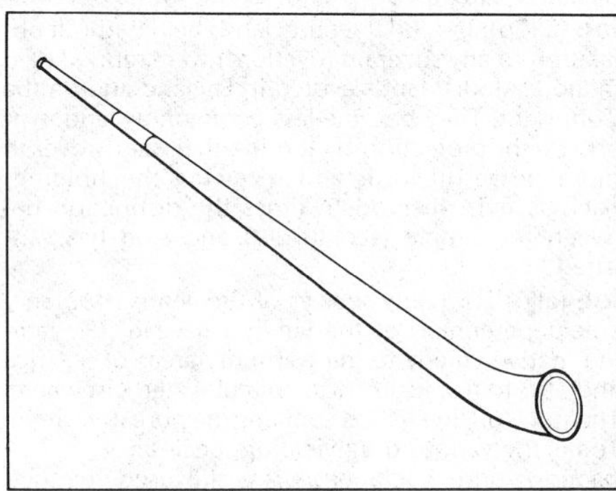

Alphorn

harmonics of the tube, slightly modified, however, by the material of the horn and its somewhat irregular shape. In Switzerland it is used to call cattle and to entertain tourists. The RANZ DES VACHES is played upon it.

alpine plants, high-altitude representatives of various flowering plants (chiefly perennials) that because of their dwarfed form, profuse blooming, and the preference of many for shady places are cultivated in alpine and ROCK GARDENS. Some species require specially constructed gardens duplicating mountain terrain, including systems for supplying cool water underground, comparable to the melting snows of their natural habitat. Others thrive without special care in favorable conditions (e.g., cool climate, short growing season, and sweet, rocky soil). Alpine species of gentians, saxifrages, and stonecrops are among those most commonly planted. Many garden plants (e.g., roses, irises, and primroses) have alpine representatives. The EDELWEISS is a popular alpine.

Alps, great mountain system of S central Europe, c.500 mi (800 km) long and c.100 mi (160 km) wide, curving in a great arc from the Riviera coast on the Mediterranean Sea, along the borders of N Italy and adjacent regions of SE France, Switzerland, S West Germany, and Austria, and into NW Yugoslavia. MONT BLANC (15,771 ft/4,807 m) is the highest peak. Cut by numerous gaps and passes, the Alps do not form a complete climatic or strategic barrier, as is evidenced by the similarities of air, people, and animals on either side of the system. The Alps form the watershed of many of Europe's rivers, including the Rhine, the Rhône, the Po, and the Danube. Geologically, the Alps were formed during the Oligocene and Miocene epochs as a result of the pressure exerted on the Tethyan geosyncline as its Mesozoic and Cenozoic strata were squeezed against the stable Eurasian landmass by the northward moving African landmass. The squeezing action formed great recumbent folds (nappes) that rose out of the sea and pushed northward, often breaking and sliding one over the other to form gigantic thrust faults. Crystalline rocks, which are exposed in the higher central regions, are the rocks forming Mont Blanc, the MATTERHORN, and high peaks in the Pennine Alps and Hohe Tauern; limestone and other sedimentary rocks are predominant (but not continuously present) in the generally lower ranges to the north and south. Permanently snowcapped peaks rise above the snowline—located between 8,000 ft and 10,000 ft (2,440–3,050 m)—and glaciers (the longest being Aletsch glacier) form the headwaters of many Alpine rivers. Glaciation (see GLACIER) was more extensive during the Pleistocene epoch and carved a distinctive mountain landscape—characterized as alpine—of arêtes, cirques, matterhorns, U-shaped and hanging valleys, and long moraine-blocked lakes (such as Garda, Como, and Maggiore in the south and Zürich, Geneva, Thun, and Brienz in the north). Below the snowline is a treeless zone of alpine pastures that have for generations been used for the summer grazing of goats and cattle. Agriculture is confined to the valleys and foothills, with fruit growing and viticulture on some sunny slopes. Hydroelectric power, used for industries in the mountains and in nearby regions, is generated from the many waterfalls and swift-flowing rivers. Tourism, based on the scenic attractions of the Alps and the mountaineering and winter sports they provide, is a major source of income; among the more famous resorts are Chamonix (France); Zermatt, Interlaken, St. Moritz, Davos, and Arosa (Switzerland); Sankt Anton, Innsbruck, Kitzbühel, Salzburg, and Bad Gastein (Austria); Berchtesgaden (West Germany); Cortina d'Ampezzo and Bolzano (Italy); and Bled (Yugoslavia). The Alps are divided by rivers and other topographic features into more than 40 subunits for which local names are commonly used. Well-known groups in the W Alps (from the Riviera to the Great St. Bernard Pass) include the Maritime, Ligurian, Cottian, and Graian alps, the Mont Blanc group, and Valle d'Aosta. The highest western peaks are Mont Blanc, Mont Pelvoux, Monte Viso, and the Gran Paradiso; the chief routes across this section are via the Mont Cénis Tunnel and the Great and Little St. Bernard passes. The Central Alps (between the Great St. Bernard and Brenner passes) include, in the south, the Pennine, Lepontine, Phaetian, and Ötztal alps; and, in the north, the Bernina, Glarus, Allgaü, and Bavarian alps. The principal peaks of the Central Alps are Monte Rosa, the Matterhorn, the Finsteraarhorn, the Jungfrau, and the Wildspitze; the chief routes are the Simplon Tunnel and the St. Gotthard, Grimsel, Furka, Splügen, Bernina, and Brenner passes. The E Alps comprise, in the south, the Dolomites, the Carnic Alps, and the Julian Alps; and, in the north, the Hohe Tauern and Niedere Tauern; the principal eastern peak is Grossglockner. The major routes across the E Alps follow the Brenner and Semmering passes. The Alps were the first mountain system to be extensively studied by geologists, and many of the geologic terms associated with mountains and glaciers originated there. The term *alps* has been applied to mountain systems around the world that exhibit similar traits to the Alps of Europe. See C. E. Engel, *Mountaineering in the Alps: An Historical Survey* (new ed. 1971); *The Alps,* prepared by the National Geographic Society, Washington, D.C. (1973); Ronald Clark, *The Alps* (1973).

Alps, Australian: see AUSTRALIAN ALPS.

Al Qayrawan (äl kīräwän') or **Kairouan** (kīrwän', Fr. kĕrwäN'), city (1966 pop. 46,199), NE Tunisia. It is a sacred city of Islam. Founded in 670 by Okba, an Arab leader, it was the seat of Arab governors in W Africa until 800. Under the Aghlabid dynasty (800–909) it remained the chief center of commerce and learning. It was the first capital (909–21) of the Fatimids. When the city was ruined (1057) by invaders, it was supplanted by Tunis. Of Al Qayrawan's 150 mosques, the most celebrated is the Grand Mosque, started by Okba and completed in the 9th cent. The city is noted for its carpet industry.

Als (äls), Ger. *Alsen,* island, 121 sq mi (313 sq km), Sønderjylland co., S Denmark, in the Lille Baelt, separated from the mainland by the narrow Als Sund. Sønderborg (partly situated on the mainland) is the main city; other towns include Augustenborg and Nordborg. Farming (particularly of apples and grain), fishing, and manufacturing (especially of motor vehicle parts) are the main occupations. The island was held by Germany from 1864 to 1920.

Alsace (älzäs'), Ger. *Elsass,* region and former province, E France. It is separated from West Germany by a part of the Rhine River. It comprises the departments of Bas-Rhin, Haut-Rhin, and the Territory of Belfort (a department created after the Franco-Prussian War when the rest of Alsace was annexed by Germany). Alsace is rich agriculturally (especially in the plain between the Rhine River and the Vosges mts.), geologically (potassium exploitation in the Mulhouse area ranks France third among worldwide producers), and industrially. STRASBOURG is the ancient capital and the leading industrial center. Textile industries are located in the Mulhouse-Colmar area, and wines (notably Riesling) are produced there. Hydroelectric plants are at Kembs and Ottmarscheim. Virtually the whole population speaks French, but a very large majority have also retained their Alemannic dialect. About 75% of the population is Roman Catholic. Of Celtic origin, Alsace became part of the Roman province of Upper Germany (see GAUL). It fell to the Alemanni (5th cent.) and to the Franks (496). The Treaty of Verdun (843; see VERDUN, TREATY OF) included it in Lotharingia; the Treaty of MERSEN (870) put it in the kingdom of the East Franks (later Germany). The 10 chief cities of Alsace gained (13th cent.) virtual independence as free imperial cities. The remainder of the region was divided into fiefs with the exception of Upper Alsace, where the HAPSBURG family consolidated its original holdings. Alsace became a center of the Reformation (although the rural areas remained generally Catholic). The Treaty of Westphalia (1648) transferred all Hapsburg lands in Alsace to France. Lower Alsace was conquered (1680–97) by Louis XIV of France; the Treaty of Ryswick (1697) confirmed French possession. The Edict of Nantes (1685), promulgated before the annexation of Alsace, could not be revoked; therefore religious worship remained free. In 1798 the city of Mulhouse voted to join France. In 1871, as a result of the FRANCO-PRUSSIAN WAR, all Alsace (except Belfort) was annexed by Germany. With part of Lorraine, it formed the "imperial land" of Alsace-Lorraine, held in common by all the German states. Many Alsatians emigrated to France rather than submit to a policy of Germanization. Clamor for the return of Alsace-Lorraine became the chief rallying force for French nationalism and was a major cause of the armaments race that led to World War I. France's recovery (1918) of this territory was confirmed by the Treaty of Versailles (1919). After the decline of early enthusiasm over the reunion with France, a strong particularist movement gained ground, demanding cultural and even political autonomy. The movement received impetus from recurrent efforts by the French government to end the CONCORDAT OF 1801, which had remained valid in Alsace-Lorraine although it had been ended in the rest of France in 1905. In 1940, German troops occupied Alsace; a large part of the population had already been evacuated to central France. Alsace was treated as a part of Germany. French and American troops recovered (Jan., 1945) Alsace for France and were generally hailed as liberators. Alsace retains many old customs such as the wine and harvest festivals.

Alsen: see ALS, Denmark.

alsike (ăl'sīk): see CLOVER.

Alsip, village (1970 pop. 11,141), Cook co., NE Ill., a suburb of Chicago; inc. 1927.

Alsop, Richard (ôl'səp), 1761–1815, American author, b. Middletown, Conn. Best remembered as one of the CONNECTICUT WITS, he collaborated with Theodore Dwight and others in writing light satiric verse for the *Political Greenhouse* and the *Echo.* See biography by K. P. Harrington (1939, repr. 1969).

Alta California, term used by the Spanish to refer to their possessions along the entire Pacific coast north of what is now the Mexican state of Baja California. California was often represented on maps as an island some 3,000 mi (4,800 km) long until the 18th-century explorations of the Jesuit father Eusebio Kino proved conclusively that the southern part of the area was a peninsula and the rest of it mainland. Thereafter the peninsula came to be called Baja (Lower) and the mainland Alta (Upper) California.

Altadena (ăltədē'nə), uninc. residential city (1970 pop. 42,380), Los Angeles co., S Calif., just N of Pasadena, on the slopes of the San Gabriel Mts. and in an orange and avocado area; founded 1887.

Altai or **Altay** (both: ăltī', äl–, ăl'tī, Rus. əltī'), geologically complex mountain system of central Asia; largely in the Gorno-Altai Autonomous Oblast, and in Kazakh SSR, but extending into W Mongolia (where it is called the Mongolian, or Gobi, Altai), and into N China. In the northeast the Kuznetsk Ala-Tau and the Salair Ridge adjoin the Altai and enclose the KUZNETSK BASIN. The Soviet Altai are bounded by the Sayan range in the west, the Mongolian Altai in the south, and the Tannu-Ola range in the east. The highest sections of the Soviet Altai are the Katun, the Chuya, and the Sailyugem ranges. The highest peak in the Soviet Altai, Belukha (14,783 ft/4,506 m), is in the Katun range. Meltwater from more than 230 sq mi (596 sq km) of glaciers feeds many rivers; the Ob and the Irtysh rise in the Altai. Lake Teletskoye, with an area of 90 sq mi (233 sq km) and a depth of 1,066 ft (325 m), is the largest of the Altai's more than 3,000 lakes. Rich deposits of gold, silver, mercury, iron, lead, zinc, and copper are found in the mountains, especially in E Kazakhstan. Located in the center of the great Asian landmass, the Altai have a continental climate with a wide annual temperature range and receive c.40 in. (101.6 cm) of precipitation annually. Dense forests on the lower slopes are used for timber. Bears, martens, musk deer, and mountain goats inhabit the mountains. The first Russians entered the area in the 17th cent., settled in the foothills, and mined silver. In the late 19th cent., piedmont agriculture replaced mining as the main occupation. After the Soviet takeover in the early 20th cent., the area became both an important farming and mining region. UST-KAMENOGORSK and LENINOGORSK are principal mining and industrial centers. The Mongolian Altai support little agriculture and are economically undeveloped.

Altaic (ăltā'ĭk), subfamily of the Ural-Altaic family of languages (see URALIC AND ALTAIC LANGUAGES). Some scholars still consider Altaic an independent linguistic family. Spoken by about 70 million people, who occupy parts of a territory that stretches from E Europe across Russia and Asia to the Pacific Ocean, the Altaic languages fall into three subdivisions: TURKIC, Mongolian (see MONGOLIAN LANGUAGES), and Tungusic. It has also been suggested that Korean and Japanese belong to the Altaic subfamily, but this is still disputed. The Tungusic subdivision has an estimated 300,000 speakers. It includes Manchu, the tongue of 200,000 persons in various parts of Manchuria, and Tungus, native to 15,000 people in eastern Siberia. Like the Uralic languages, the Altaic tongues are characterized by agglutination and vowel harmony. The former involves using suffix upon suffix to express grammatical relationships and meanings. Suffixes are also employed to form derived words. With vowel harmony, the vowel in a suffix corresponds to the vowel of the root to which the suffix is added. The Altaic languages lack grammatical gender. See Nicholas Poppe, *Introduction to Altaic Linguistics* (1965).

Altai Kray, administrative division (1970 pop. 2,766,000), c.102,400 sq mi (265,220 sq km), S central Siberian USSR. BARNAUL is the capital. It is drained by the Upper Ob River and traversed by the Turksib and South Siberian railroads. In the southeast is a subdivision of the region, the GORNO-ALTAI AUTONOMOUS OBLAST, which contains a large portion of the Altai mountain range. The fertile Kulunda steppe, where spring wheat and sugar beets are grown, is in the western part of the territory. Major cities, besides Barnaul, include BIYSK and Chesnokovka.

Altair (ăltā'ĭr), brightest star in the constellation AQUILA (Eagle); Bayer designation α Aquilae; 1970 position R.A. $19^h49.3^m$, Dec. $+8°47'$. Its apparent MAGNITUDE is 0.74, making it one of the 20 brightest stars in the sky, and it is of SPECTRAL CLASS A7 IV,V. Altair is one of the nearest bright stars, its distance being 16.8 light-years.

Altamira: see PALEOLITHIC ART.

Altamirano, Ignacio Manuel (ēgnä'syō mänwĕl' ältämērä'nō), 1834–93, Mexican novelist and poet. Altamirano came from a poor, wholly Indian background, and after gaining his formal education he joined Benito JUÁREZ in the struggle against Maximilian. Afterward he was a key figure in the reconstruction of the republic. He edited the newspaper *Correo de Mexico.* As a poet Altamirano interpreted the Mexican landscape. He is best known for two novels—*Clemencia* and *La Navidad en las Montañas* [Christmas in the mountains], a story sketching Mexican customs.

Altamira y Crevea, Rafaél (räfäĕl' ältämē'rä ē krāvā'ä), 1866–1951, Spanish jurist and historian. He was appointed professor of the history of the law in the universities at Oviedo (1897), Madrid (1914), and Mexico City (1945), and he served (1921–45) as a judge of the Permanent Court of International Justice (the World Court). Among his numerous works on education, social science, literature, law, and history, his *Historia de España y de la civilización española* (5 vol., 1913–29; tr. *A History of Spanish Civilization,* 1930) is the best known; an English adaptation is C. E. Chapman, *A History of Spain* (1931).

Altamont, uninc. town (1970 pop. 15,746), Klamath co., S Oregon, a suburb of Klamath Falls.

Altamura (äl"tämoo'rä), city (1971 pop. 45,865), Apulia, S Italy. It is a commercial and agricultural center. The imposing Romanesque cathedral, with twin campaniles, was begun by Emperor Frederick II in 1232.

altar, table or platform for the performance of religious sacrifice. In its simplest form the altar is a small pile, with a square or circular surface, made of stone or wood. Its features vary according to its purpose. The altar of libation usually has a drain for the liquid, and so does the altar of bloody sacrifice; the altar of burnt offering (including incense) often has a depressed hollow for a fire. Altars in Egypt, in Mesopotamia, in Greece, in Rome, and among the Aztec and the Maya were highly adorned with friezes, cornices, elaborate platforms, and canopies. At Pergamum there was a huge monumental altar 40 ft (12.2 m) high. Altars as a rule were out of doors in the ancient world and in Central America. The Christian altar is the place to celebrate the EUCHARIST, a sacrifice in the traditional view. In the Western Church the altar is a long, narrow table of stone or wood, often reminiscent of a tomb; at its back is a REREDOS, which often bears a canopy. In the Roman rite there are in the middle of the altar a crucifix and a tabernacle to contain the reserved Host, although recent legislation of Roman liturgical reform suggests that the tabernacle be placed elsewhere in the church. There is a recess in each altar containing bones of martyrs; this is even true of tiny portable altars carried by chaplains. In Eastern rites the altar is square and has no backing or reredos; it is away from the wall. Most Protestant denominations have no altar; a typical practice is to have a permanent communion table below and in front of the pulpit.

Al-taschith: see AIJELETH SHAHAR.

Altay: see ALTAI, mountain system, Asia.

altazimuth mounting (ăltăz'əməth): see TELESCOPE.

Altdorf (ält'dôrf), town (1971 pop. 8,647), capital of Uri canton, central Switzerland. Cables and rubber goods are manufactured. Altdorf was the scene of the legendary exploits of William TELL, commemorated by a monument (1895) and by the William Tell theater (1925).

Altdorfer, Albrecht (äl'brĕkht ältdôr'fər), 1480–1538, German painter and engraver. He served as city architect of Regensburg, where much of his life was spent. Although influenced by Dürer, Altdorfer's works are less severe in mood. The forms and lines in his works seem to vibrate with intense movement. These qualities are especially clear in his white-ink drawings of figures and landscapes. Altdorfer may have been the first German to paint pure landscape, of which the *Danube Landscape at Regensburg* (1522–25) is typical. His varied subject matter included allegorical and biblical themes such as *Susannah at the Bath* (1526) and *Birth of the Virgin* (c.1521). The *Battle of Alexander* (1529) displays his penchant for detailed, panoramic vistas. All four works are in the Alte Pinakothek, Munich. Equally skilled at woodcutting and engraving, Altdorfer often executed one subject in a variety of media.

Altenburg (äl'tənbŏŏrk), city (1970 pop. 46,737), Leipzig district, S East Germany, on the Pleisse River. Manufactures include sewing machines, machine tools, textiles, and playing cards. "Skat," the popular German card game, originated there in the 19th cent. Lignite is mined nearby. Built on the site of early 9th-century Slavic fortifications, Altenburg became an important trade center and was made an imperial city in the 12th cent. It formally passed in 1329 to the house of Wettin and later was (1603–72, 1826–1918) the capital of the duchy of SAXE-ALTENBURG. Noteworthy structures include an 11th-century church and the tower of the monastery founded (1172) by Emperor Frederick I.

alternating current, abbr. AC, a flow of electric charge that undergoes periodic reverses in direction. There are certain currents, such as pulsating direct currents, that contain both alternating and direct components. See ELECTRICITY; GENERATOR.

alternation of generations: see GAMETOPHYTE; REPRODUCTION.

alternator: see GENERATOR.

Altgeld, John Peter (ält'gĕlt), 1847-1902, American politician, governor of Illinois (1892-96), b. Germany. He was taken by his immigrant parents to Ohio, where he grew up with little formal schooling. After service in the Union army he spent some years as an itinerant worker on farms, read law, and became county attorney of Savannah, Mo. In 1875 he moved to Chicago, where he wrote *Our Penal Machinery and Its Victims* (1884), arguing that American judicial methods were weighted against the poor. In 1886 he was elected to the Cook co. superior court, and in 1892 he was elected governor. In office he established himself as a champion of labor, reform, and liberal thought. Charging a miscarriage of justice, he pardoned three anarchists imprisoned as parties to the Haymarket riot of 1886. During the PULLMAN STRIKE of 1894, when President Cleveland sent Federal troops into Chicago, Governor Altgeld publicly termed the act unconstitutional. His extreme liberalism, coupled with his espousal of free silver, lost him reelection in 1896. Denounced as a radical in his own day, he was later regarded as a defender of the freedom of the individual against entrenched power. See his writings and speeches, ed. by H. M. Christman (1960, repr. 1970); biography by H. Barnard (1938); study by R. Ginger (1958, repr. 1965).

althaea or **althea:** see MALLOW.

Althing (äl'thĭng) [Icel., = general diet], parliament of Iceland. This assembly, the oldest in Europe, was convened at Thingvellir, SW Iceland, in 930. It was dissolved in 1800, was revived as an advisory body in 1843, and in 1874, when Iceland was granted a constitution, became again a legislative body. Each of the 60 members serves for four years. Its upper house (one third of the members) and lower house (two thirds) sometimes work together in a United Althing. The Althing in 1944 voted the independence of Iceland from Denmark, a decision ratified by popular vote. Since 1959 the Althing has used a complicated system of proportional representation.

Althorp, John Charles Spencer, Viscount: see under SPENCER, GEORGE JOHN SPENCER, 2D EARL.

Altichiero da Zevio (ältēkyā'rō dä tsāv'yō), c.1330–c.1395, early Italian painter, follower of Giotto. He worked in Verona and then Padua. His frescoes in the churches of Sant' Antonio and San Giorgio in Padua are notable as early examples of the use of rational proportions in the treatment of figures and space.

altimeter (ăltĭm'ĭtər, ăl'tĭmē"tər), device for measuring altitude. The most common type is an aneroid BAROMETER calibrated to show the drop in atmospheric pressure in terms of linear elevation as an airplane, balloon, or mountain climber rises. It shows height above sea level, but not above such land features as hills, mountains, and valleys. The radio altimeter, or terrain-clearance indicator, is an absolute altimeter; it indicates the actual altitude over water or over terrain, however uneven. It operates by first sending either continuous or pulse radio signals from a transmitter in an aircraft to the earth's surface. A receiver in the aircraft then picks up the reflection of the signals from the surface. The time it takes for the signals to travel to the earth and back is converted automatically into absolute altitude that can then be read from a calibrated indicator. The radio altimeter is used in the automatic landing systems of aerospace vehicles; systems developed from radio altimeters can automatically control military aircraft flying at high speeds and low altitudes.

altiplano, high plateau (alt. c.12,000 ft/3,660 m) in the Andes Mts., c.65,000 sq mi (168,350 sq km), W Bolivia, extending into S Peru. The altiplano is a sediment-filled depression between the Cordillera Oriental and the Cordillera Occidental. Its lowest point is occupied by Lake Titicaca, the largest high-altitude lake in the world. The lake is drained by the Desaguadero River south across the altiplano into Lake Poopó. The sparsely vegetated region receives little precipitation and has several large salt flats. The bleak plateau has a cool climate throughout the year. Potatoes and hardy grains are the principal crops there. Mining is the chief industry in the mineral-rich plateau. One of the world's most densely populated areas, the altiplano contains most of Bolivia's inhabitants; La Paz, the capital, and Oruro are the largest cities.

altitude, vertical distance of an object above some datum plane, such as mean SEA LEVEL or a reference point on the earth's surface. It is usually measured by the reduction in atmospheric pressure with height, as shown on a barometer or altimeter. In surveying and astronomy, it is the vertical angle of an observed point, such as a star or planet, above the horizon plane. The altitude of a feature of the earth's surface is usually called its ELEVATION.

altitude, in astronomy, angular distance of a heavenly body above the astronomical horizon. The angle used in measuring is that which a line drawn from the eye of the observer to the heavenly body makes with the plane of the horizon. The reading of the apparent altitude, as determined by a telescope attached to a graduated circle, must be corrected for refraction by the atmosphere and for certain other errors to ascertain the true altitude. The altitude of the north celestial pole, which is approximately that of the star POLARIS, is equal to the observer's latitude. In navigation, observations of altitude are made with a sextant.

altitude sickness: see DECOMPRESSION SICKNESS.

alto, singing voice the range of which is lower than the soprano by the interval of a fifth. More generally, the term refers to the register in which this voice sings, i.e., the second highest part in a four-part musical texture, and to instruments utilizing this register. See COUNTERTENOR.

Alto Adige: see TRENTINO-ALTO ADIGE, Italy.

Altoaguirre, Manuel (mänwĕl' ältōägē'rā), 1904–59, Spanish poet, b. Málaga. With his contemporary Emilio PRADOS he founded the literary journal *Litoral.* His poetry is distinguished by its grace, sensitivity, and refinement, treating such themes as love, nature, and solitude. His interest in typography is evident in some of the beautiful editions of his poetry. His works include *Las islas invitadas y otros poemas* [invited islands and other poems] (1920) and *Fin de un amor* [end of a love] (1949).

altocumulus: see CLOUD.

Alton (ôl'tən), city (1970 pop. 39,700), Madison co., SW Ill., on bluffs of the Mississippi River 5 mi (8.1 km) above its confluence with the Missouri; inc. 1837. Alton is a shipping and industrial center, with machine shops, foundries, oil refineries, and a large bottle-making plant. Among its many other manufactures are food products, building materials, and ammunition and explosives. Lewis and Clark built their first camp and spent the winter of 1803-04 just south of what is now Alton. The town was laid out in 1815. During the Civil War it grew as a main supply point for the Union armies. A state penitentiary (built in 1827) served as a prison and hospital for captured Confederate soldiers, many of whom are buried in the Confederate cemetery there. Of interest are a monument to Elijah Lovejoy, who was killed in Alton; a tablet marking the site of the last Lincoln-Douglas debate (1858); and a replica of a huge man-eating bird originally painted by Indians on the face of a bluff above the Mississippi. The Principia (at Elsah) and a state park are nearby.

Altona (äl'tōnä), part of Hamburg, N West Germany, a port on the Elbe River. Its manufactures include chemicals, textiles, and tobacco products. There are fisheries, and the district is a rail center. Founded as a fishing village in the 16th cent. and later one of the first free ports in N Europe, Altona was incorporated into Hamburg in 1937.

Altoona (ăltōō'nə), industrial city (1970 pop. 62,900), Blair co., central Pa., on the eastern slopes of the Allegheny Mts., near the source of the Juniata River; settled c.1769, laid out (1849) by the Pennsylvania RR as a switching point for locomotives preparing to cross the Alleghenies; inc. as a city 1868. It is still a major railroad center with huge construction and repair shops. The city's great variety of manufactures include foundry products, machinery, electrical equipment, paper items, shoes, clothing, and textiles. Bituminous coal is mined nearby. In 1862, Governor Curtin called a conference of governors at Altoona to pledge support of Lincoln's administration. Nearby tourist attractions are the scenic Horseshoe Curve of the Pennsylvania RR, a world-famous engineering feat; Wopsononock Mt. (2,580 ft/786 m high), which offers a magnificent view of six counties; and Fountain Inn, the historic hotel mentioned by Dickens in his *American Notes.* Pennsylvania State Univ. has a junior college campus in Altoona.

altostratus: see CLOUD.

Altrincham (ôl'trĭng-əm), municipal borough (1971 pop. 40,752), Cheshire, W central England. A suburb of Manchester, it has a textile-printing industry and engineering works and is also noted for its market gardens. The town's growth was stimulated by the construction of the Bridgewater Canal in 1760. In 1974, Altrincham became part of the new metropolitan county of Greater Manchester.

altruism (ăl'trōōĭz'əm), concept in philosophy and psychology that holds that the interests of others, rather than of the self, can motivate an individual. The term was invented in the 19th cent. by the French philosopher Auguste Comte, who devised it as the opposite of EGOISM. Herbert Spencer and John Stuart Mill, English contemporaries of Comte, accepted the worth of altruism but argued that the true moral aim should be the welfare of society, rather than that of individuals.

Altus (ăl'təs), city (1970 pop. 23,302), seat of Jackson co., SW Okla.; inc. 1907. The city's agricultural products include cotton, wheat, and cattle. Altus Air Force Base, a large training facility, also contributes to the economy. The city was founded in 1892 as the town of Fraiser, but after floods forced the moving of the city to its present site it was renamed Altus [Lat., = high place]. Wichita Mountain Wildlife Refuge, which is state-operated, is nearby.

Al Ubayyid (äl ōōbäyīd') or **El Obeid** (ĕl ōbād'), city (1969 est. pop. 66,000), central Sudan. It is a rail terminus, a road and camel caravan junction, and the end of a pilgrim road from Nigeria. Al Ubayyid is also a trade and transshipment point. Founded by the Turco-Egyptian pashas in 1821, it fell to the Mahdists in 1883 and was destroyed. Its reconstruction followed the fall of the Mahdist empire in 1898.

alum (ăl'əm), any one of a series of isomorphous double salts that are hydrated SULFATES of a univalent cation (e.g., potassium, sodium, ammonium, cesium, or thallium) and a trivalent cation (e.g., aluminum, chromium, iron, manganese, cobalt, or titanium). The name *alum* commonly refers to potassium aluminum sulfate dodecahydrate, or potash alum, $KAl(SO_4)_2 \cdot 12H_2O$, a colorless-to-white, crystalline compound having a sweetish-sour taste. It is used in water purification, leather tanning, mordant dyeing, as an astringent, and in baking powder; it occurs in nature as the mineral kalunite. Sodium aluminum sulfate, or soda alum, $NaAl(SO_4)_2 \cdot 12H_2O$, is also used in baking powder. Ammonium aluminum sulfate, or ammonia alum, $NH_4Al(SO_4)_2 \cdot 12H_2O$, is used in tanning, in dyeing and fireproofing textiles, in vegetable glues and porcelain cements, and in water purification. Chromium potassium sulfate, or chrome alum, $KCr(SO_4)_2 \cdot 12H_2O$, is used as a mordant in dyeing, in tanning, and in photographic fixing baths to harden gelatin films and plates. Aluminum sulfate, $Al_2(SO_4)_3 \cdot 18H_2O$, is also called alum. A pseudoalum is a double sulfate salt of a divalent cation (e.g., magnesium or calcium) and a trivalent cation (e.g., aluminum).

alumina (əlōō'mīnə) or **aluminum oxide,** Al_2O_3, chemical compound with m.p. about 2000°C and sp. gr. about 4.0. It is insoluble in water and organic liquids and very slightly soluble in strong acids and alkalies. Alumina occurs in two crystalline forms. Alpha alumina is composed of colorless hexagonal crystals with the properties given above; gamma alumina is composed of minute colorless cubic crystals with sp. gr. about 3.6 that are transformed to the alpha form at high temperatures. Alumina powder is formed by crushing crystalline alumina; it is white when pure. Alumina is widely distributed in nature. Combined with silica and other minerals it occurs in clays, feldspars, and micas. It is the major component of BAUXITE and occurs in an almost pure form as CORUNDUM. Alumina is commercially important. A major use is in the production of ALUMINUM metal. It is also used for abrasives; corundum and emery are widely used, as are artificially prepared alumina abrasives. Trade names for alumina abrasives include Alundum and Aloxite. Alumina is also used in ceramics, in pigments, and in the manufacture of chemicals. Clays containing alumina are used in porcelain, pottery, and bricks. Pure alumina is used in making crucibles and other refractory apparatus. Hydrated alumina is used in mordant dyeing to make lake pigments; it is also used in glassmaking, in cosmetics, and in medicine as an antacid.

aluminum (əlōō'mĭnəm), called in British countries **aluminium** (ăl"yōōmĭn'ēəm), metallic chemical element; symbol Al; at. no. 13; at. wt. 26.9815; m.p. 660.37°C; b.p. 2467°C; sp. gr. 2.6989 at 20°C; valence +3. Aluminum is a silver-white metal with a face-centered cubic crystalline structure. It is a member of group IIIa of the PERIODIC TABLE. It is ductile, malleable, and an excellent conductor of heat and electricity. The pure metal is soft, but it becomes strong and hard when alloyed. Although less conductive than copper wire of the same diameter, aluminum wire is often used for high-tension power transmission because it is lighter and cheaper. Although it is chemically very reactive, aluminum resists corrosion by the formation of a self-protecting oxide coating. It is rapidly attacked by alkalies (such as lye) and by hydrochloric acid. Although it is the most abundant metal in the earth's crust (about 8% by weight), aluminum does not occur uncombined but is an important constituent of many minerals, including clay, BAUXITE, mica, feldspar, alum, CRYOLITE, and the several forms of aluminum oxide (alumina) such as emery, corundum, sapphire, and ruby. Commercially, aluminum is prepared by the Hall-Héroult process, which consists essentially of the electrolysis of alumina prepared from bauxite and dissolved in fused cryolite. In an electric furnace an iron tank lined with carbon serves as the cathode and large blocks of carbon serve as the anode; the electric current generates enough heat to keep the cryolite melted. Molten aluminum collects at the bottom of the tank, and oxygen is liberated at the anode. The anode is consumed as it combines with the oxygen to form carbon dioxide. Aluminum foil is used as a wrapping material. Aluminum powder is used in paints. A mixture of powdered aluminum and iron oxide, called THERMITE, is used in welding because of the large amount of heat liberated when it is ignited. The development of methods for coloring aluminum led to its use in jewelry, on wall surfaces, and in colored kitchenware. Important alloys of aluminum include DURALUMIN, aluminum bronze, and aluminum-magnesium; they are used extensively in aircraft and other industries. Although the metal was not isolated until the 19th cent., use of aluminum compounds originated in antiquity. The Romans used various aluminum compounds as astringents; they called these *alum*. Sir Humphry DAVY and other chemists in the early 19th cent. recognized aluminum as the metal and alumina as its oxide. H. C. OERSTED succeeded in obtaining impure aluminum in 1825, but Friedrich WÖHLER had greater success and is usually credited with its first isolation, in 1827. H. E. SAINTE-CLAIRE DEVILLE first prepared inexpensive pure metal in 1854 and set about perfecting a process for its commercial production. However, it was not until 1886 that the process by which aluminum is produced today was discovered independently by C. M. Hall, a student at Oberlin College, and Paul Héroult, a French metallurgist. The process depends critically on the availability of cheap hydroelectric power.

aluminum oxide: see ALUMINA.

alundum: see ALUMINA.

Alush (ā'ləsh), wilderness camping ground of the Israelites. Num. 33.13,14.

Alva, Fernando Álvarez de Toledo, duque de: see ALBA, FERNANDO ÁLVAREZ DE TOLEDO, DUQUE DE.

Alvah (ăl'və), duke of Edom. Gen. 36.40. Aliah: 1 Chron. 1.51.

Alvan (ăl'vən), Horite. Gen. 36.23. Alian: 1 Chron. 1.40.

Alvarado, Juan Bautista (hwän boutēs'tä älvärä'thō), 1809-82, governor of Alta California (1836-42), b. Monterey, Calif. Out of the chaotic times in the neglected Mexican province of Alta California, Alvarado emerged as a brilliant politician. After a small but successful revolt in 1836, he declared California an independent state with himself as governor. He pacified his opponents in San Diego and Los Angeles, but the southern faction continued to view the northern upstart with suspicion until he secured (1838) regular appointment as Mexican governor. He and his uncle, Mariano Guadalupe Vallejo, who acted as military commander, could not accomplish much, and after they disagreed both men were removed in 1842. Alvarado was one of the leaders of a new and successful revolt in 1844-45, but the new government was unable to withstand the Bear Flag revolt and the Mexican War.

Alvarado, Pedro de (pä'thrō dā), 1486-1541, Spanish conquistador. He went to Hispaniola (1510), sailed in the expedition (1518) of Juan de Grijalva, and was the chief lieutenant of Hernán CORTÉS in the conquest of Mexico. He commanded at Tenochtitlán in the absence of Cortés, and his brutality provoked a brief Indian rebellion. Sent out by Cortés in 1523, he conquered Guatemala and Salvador. He was governor of Guatemala until his death. He met with much opposition from the audiencia in Mexico, but strengthening his power on two voyages to Spain (1527-28, 1536-39), he exercised absolute control. He founded many cities and developed the colony. An expedition to Ecuador (1534-35), made in an attempt to share in the booty Francisco PIZARRO was taking from the Incan empire, ended in defeat. In 1540, Alvarado, sailing for the Moluccas, stopped in Mexico. While there he was influenced by the viceroy Antonio de MENDOZA and by the tales of MARCOS DE NIZA to begin a search for the fabled Cibola. When the Indians of Nueva Galicia unexpectedly revolted in 1541, Alvarado took part against them in the Mixtón War. He led a foolhardy attack and was accidentally killed in the subsequent retreat. Juan Rodríguez CABRILLO took command of the maritime expedition. Alvarado's wife, Doña Beatriz de la CUEVA, succeeded him as governor of Guatemala. His letters concerning the conquest of Guatemala have been published. See J. E. Kelly, *Pedro de Alvarado* (1932).

Alvarez, A. (Alfred Alvarez), 1929-, English writer and critic, b. London, grad. Oxford (B.A., 1952; M.A., 1956). He has been theater critic for the *New Statesman*, a writer for the British Broadcasting Corp., and poetry editor and critic for the *Observer*. He writes in a brisk, contemporary style, free of pedantry. His works include *The New Poetry* (1962), edited by him; *Beyond All This Fiddle* (1968), collected essays; and *The Savage God* (1972), a study of suicide in which he treats in detail the suicide of Sylvia PLATH and his own failed suicide attempt; and *Samuel Beckett* (1973), a critical work.

Álvarez, José (José Álvarez de Pereira y Cubero) (hōsā' äl'värĕth dā pārā'rä ē kōōbā'rō), 1768-1827, Spanish neoclassical sculptor. He was a follower of Canova. Álvarez was employed on the decoration of the Quirinal Palace in Rome. On returning to Madrid he became director of the Academy of San Fernando and sculptor to Ferdinand VII. He is best known for his portrait statues of Spanish royalty and for his mythological figures in marble (e.g., *Nestor and Antilochus*, 1818; Modern Art Mus., Madrid).

Álvarez, Juan (hwän äl'väräs), 1780-1867, Mexican general, president of Mexico (1855). An Indian, he distinguished himself in battle under Morelos y Pavón and was later the first governor of Guerrero. In 1854 he led the liberal Revolution of Ayutla, which overthrew (1855) General SANTA ANNA. After two months he yielded the presidency to Ignacio COMONFORT. Álvarez later fought against Maximilian and the French invaders.

Alvear, Carlos María de (kär'lōs märē'ä dā älväär'), 1789-1852, Argentine general and statesman. After distinguished service with the Spanish army in Europe, he returned to Argentina with his friend SAN MARTÍN and became a leader in the domestic revolution of 1812 and a member of the constituent assembly of 1813. He was in command of the patriot army when the Spanish royalists at Montevideo capitulated (1814). In 1815 Alvear was named supreme director of the United Provinces of the Río de la Plata, but was deposed when he attempted to become a dictator. In the war with Brazil he won the decisive battle of Ituazingó (Feb. 20, 1827). From 1838 until his death he was minister to the United States.

Alvear, Marcelo Torcuato de (märsā'lō tōrkwä'tō), 1868-1942, Argentine statesman and diplomat, president of the republic (1922-28). A member of the Radical party, he became minister to France after a victory of the Radicals in 1916 placed IRIGOYEN in the presidency. Succeeding Irigoyen in 1922, Alvear secured enactment of some reforms, especially agricultural measures, but largely because of a split with Irigoyen his administration, on the whole, accomplished little. Later the breach was healed, and Alvear became the leader of the Radicals. In 1931 he was barred from the presidential race, and in 1937 he was defeated by Roberto M. Ortiz.

Alvend or **Elvend** (both: ĕlvĕnd', ĕl'vĕnd), mountain, c.11,600 ft (3,540 m) high, W Iran. It bears cuneiform inscriptions of Darius and Xerxes.

alveolus (ălvē'ələs): see LUNGS.

Alverstone, Richard Everard Webster, 1st **Viscount** (ôl'vərstən), 1842-1915, lord chief justice of England (1900-1913). He served on various international arbitration commissions, including those dealing with the Bering Sea Fur-Seal Controversy (1893) and the Venezuela Boundary Dispute (1898-99). In the Alaska Boundary Dispute (1903), he gave the deciding vote against the Canadian claims. He wrote *Recollections of Bar and Bench* (1914).

Alves, Antônio de Castro: see CASTRO ALVES, ANTÔNIO DE.

Alvin, city (1970 pop. 10,671), Brazoria co., S Texas; inc. 1893. The city is chiefly residential, and many of its citizens work in Houston or at the nearby Lyndon B. Johnson Space Center. There is a petro-chemical industry in the city, and a junior college is there.

Alvord, Clarence Walworth (ăl'vərd), 1868-1928, American historian, b. Greenfield, Mass. He became (1901) an instructor in history at the Univ. of Illinois (Ph.D., 1908) and was full professor there (1913-20) and at the Univ. of Minnesota (1920-23). Alvord was general editor (1906-20) of the *Illinois Historical Collections*, and he edited the *Centennial History of Illinois* (6 vol., 1918-24) and wrote its first volume. The principal founder of *The Mississippi Valley Historical Review*, Alvord served as its managing editor (1914-23). He also wrote *The Mississippi Valley in British Politics* (1917, repr. 1959).

Alvord, Henry Elijah, 1844-1904, American agriculturist, educator, and specialist in dairy husbandry, b. Greenfield, Mass. He pioneered in developing the cooperative creamery system and served (1886-93) as professor and president of various state agricultural colleges. In 1895 he became first chief of the dairy division of the Bureau of Animal Industry, U.S. Dept. of Agriculture.

Alwar (ŭl'vər, -'wər), city (1971 pop. 100,791), Rajasthan state, N central India. On the Delhi-Jaipur railroad, Alwar is a market for grain, oilseed, cotton, and marble. There are textile and oilseed mills, iron foundries, and chemical and porcelain factories. Turban-making is an important handicraft. The city was the capital of the former Alwar state and is now a district administrative center. An old RAJPUT fort dominates the city.

Alyattes (ălēă'tēz), d. 560 B.C., king of Lydia. During his reign, Alyattes expanded the kingdom. While he was warring with Cyaxares of Media, an eclipse of the sun occurred (585 B.C.). The two kings interpreted the event as a warning omen and made peace. Alyattes continued Lydian conquest of the Ionian cities of Asia Minor. The remains of his tomb can still be seen N of Sardis. He was the father of CROESUS.

Alypius or **Alypios** (both: əlĭp'ēəs), fl. c.360, Greek author of *Introduction to Music*, chief source of modern knowledge of Greek musical notation.

alyssum (əlĭs'əm), any species of the genus *Alyssum* of the family Cruciferae (MUSTARD family), chiefly annual and perennial herbs native to the Mediterranean area. A few species, notably the perennial golden tuft (*A. saxatile*), are cultivated as rock-garden or border ornamentals for their masses of yellow or white flowers. The annual sweet alyssum (called *A. maritima* but separated by most botanists as *Lobularia maritima*) is a similar plant with fragrant white or lilac blossoms. The alyssums have been called madwort or heal-bite because of an old belief that they cured hydrophobia. Alyssum is classified in the division MAGNOLIOPHYTA, class Magnoliopsida, order Capparales, family Cruciferae.

Am, chemical symbol of the element AMERICIUM.

AM: see MODULATION; RADIO.

Amad (ā'măd), unidentified city of Asher, NW Palestine. Joshua 19.26.

Amadas or **Amidas, Philip** (both: ăm'ədăs), 1550-1618, English navigator. With Arthur Barlowe he was sent by Sir Walter Raleigh in 1584 to explore the North American coast. Their favorable report on Roanoke Island, N.C., led to the colonizing expedition (1585) under Sir Richard Grenville and Sir Ralph LANE.

Amadeus VIII (ămədē'əs), 1383-1451, count (1391-1416) and duke (from 1416) of Savoy, antipope (1439-49) with the name Felix V. In 1434 he appointed his son regent of Savoy and retired to the hermitage of Ripaille, on Lake Geneva, which he had founded. In 1439 the Council of Basel (see BASEL, COUNCIL OF), which had been pronounced heretical by the pope, declared EUGENE IV deposed and elected Amadeus, much respected for his probity, to the papacy. Although a layman, Amadeus reluctantly accepted, believing that he could bring peace to the church. As Felix V, he received only scattered recognition from the secular powers. When Nicholas V became pope, Felix yielded his claim. He was subsequently made a cardinal. He was the last of the antipopes.

Amadeus, 1845-90, king of Spain (1870-73), duke of Aosta, son of Victor Emmanuel II of Italy. After the expulsion (1868) of Queen ISABELLA II, Juan PRIM urged the Cortes to elect Amadeus as king. He accepted the crown reluctantly. Just before the new king arrived in Spain, Prim was assassinated. The upper classes were opposed to Amadeus, who belonged to the anticlerical house of Savoy, and repeated attempts were made on his life. When a new rebellion by the CARLISTS began, Amadeus abdicated and returned to Italy. A year later Alfonso XII was proclaimed king.

Amadis of Gaul (ăm'ədĭs), Fr. *Amadis de Gaule* (ämädēs' də gōl), famous prose romance of chivalry, first composed in Spain or Portugal and probably based on French sources. Entirely fictional, it dates from the 13th or 14th cent., but the first extant version in Spanish, a revision by García de Rodríguez de Montalvo, was published in 1508. The original inspired innumerable variations and continuations, as well as several translations. It was immensely popular in France and Spain until superseded by *Don Quixote,* and it was, indeed, a sign of inelegance not to be acquainted with its code of honor and knightly perfection. Its influence is apparent in Sir Philip Sidney's *Arcadia.* The story became the subject of a lyric tragedy by Philippe Quinault (1684), with music by Lully, and it inspired the opera *Amadigi* (1715) by Handel.

Amado, Jorge (zhôr'zhĭ əmä'do͞o), 1912–, Brazilian novelist. Amado's works deal largely with the sufferings of the common man. Marked by grim and violent realism, his major works include *Cacau* [cacao] (1933), *Suor* [sweat] (1934), the epic novel *Terras do sem fim* (1942; tr. *The Violent Land,* 1945), *Gabriela, cravo e canela* (1958; tr. *Gabriela, Clove and Cinnamon,* 1962), *Doña Flor* (1966, tr. 1969), and *Tent of Miracles* (tr. 1971). Amado's works are collected as *Obras completas* (18 vol., 1961–69).

Amador Guerrero, Manuel (mänwĕl' ämädôr' gārä'rō), 1833–1909, first president of Panama (1904–8), b. Colombia. A physician, he served as medical officer for the Panama RR and was a leader in the movement for Panamanian independence from Colombia. As the emissary (1903) for the revolutionaries to the United States, he helped obtain U.S. aid for the successful revolution. He was unanimously selected president of the new republic by the constitutional convention despite a stipulation in the constitution that the president be born in Panama.

Amagasaki (ä'mägäsä'kē), city (1970 pop. 553,660), Hyogo prefecture, S Honshu, Japan, a port on Osaka Bay. An important industrial center, with iron and steel factories, chemical plants, and textile mills, it lies on the banks of the Yodo River. Amagasaki has a 16th-century castle.

Amager (ā'mägər), island (1965 pop. 177,818), 25 sq mi (65 sq km), Copenhagen co., E Denmark, in the Øresund. Northern Amager is occupied by a part of Copenhagen city that has important shipbuilding and harbor facilities. Southern Amager includes fishing ports, beach resorts, and farms.

Amagi (ä"mä'gē), city (1970 pop. 43,259), Fukuoka prefecture, N Kyushu, Japan. It is an agricultural center and railway terminus. Textiles are produced in the city.

Amakusa Islands (ämäko͞o'sä), archipelago, c.340 sq mi (880 sq km), Kumamoto and Kagoshima prefectures, in the East China Sea, off W Kyushu, Japan. There are about 70 islands in the group. Shimo, the largest island, is the site of Hondo, which is the chief town. The interior of the islands is rugged; the coastal lowlands are fertile. Rice, camellia oil, fish, porcelain, and coal are the principal products. Amakusa clansmen made the islands a major center of Christianity in the 16th cent. Villages and historical relics of this period are found in Unzen-Amakusa National Park. In 1637, when Christianity was banned in Japan, the islanders, suffering economic hardship, joined in the rebellion at Shimabara. After the revolt was mercilessly suppressed (1638), the islands passed under the control of the Tokugawa shogunate.

Amal (ā'məl), Asherite. 1 Chron. 7.35.

Amalasuntha (ă"mələsŭn'thə), d. 535, Ostrogothic queen in Italy (534–35), daughter of THEODORIC THE GREAT. After her father's death (526) she was regent for her son Athalaric. He died in 534, and she and her husband, Theodahad, became joint rulers of Italy. Her friendly relations with the Byzantine emperor Justinian I alienated her people. In 535 the Ostrogoths revolted; Amalasuntha was exiled and later murdered by order of her husband. Justinian used her murder as his pretext for attacking and reconquering Italy.

Amalekites (ăm'ələkīts), aboriginal people of Canaan and the Sinai peninsula. They waged constant warfare against the Hebrews until dispersed by Saul. Their ancestor, Amalek, for whom they were named, was a duke of Edom and Esau's descendant. Gen. 14.7; 36.12,16; Ex. 17.8–16; Num. 13.29; 14.25,45; 24.20; Judges 3.13; 6.3,33; 7.12; 1 Sam. 15.5–8; 30.1–20; 1 Chron. 1.36; 4.43.

Amalfi (ämäl'fē), town (1971 pop. 6,136), in Campania, S Italy, a small fishing port on the Gulf of Sorrento. Built on a mountain slope, it is also a picturesque seaside resort. According to legend, Amalfi was founded by the Romans; it later became (9th cent. A.D.) an early Italian maritime republic. It rivaled Pisa, Venice, and Genoa in wealth and power and had a population of about 70,000. Amalfi's maritime code, the *Tavole Amalfitane,* had wide influence until the 18th cent. Amalfi reached its zenith in the 11th cent. Thereafter it declined fairly rapidly; it was captured (1131) by the Normans and sacked (1135, 1137) by the Pisans, and in 1343 a storm destroyed much of the town. Of note in Amalfi is the Sicilian-Arab cathedral (11th cent., with numerous later additions), which has an imposing facade, fine bronze doors cast (1066) in Constantinople, and a stunning cloister (*chiostro del Paradiso*). The **Amalfi Coast,** running from Salerno to Sorrento, is famous for its rugged scenery.

amalgam (əmăl'gəm), ALLOY containing MERCURY. The alloy may be liquid or solid, depending on the proportion of mercury, although all naturally occurring amalgams, i.e., those of gold and silver, are solid. Amalgams are widely used. Silver, gold, and copper amalgams are used in dentistry, and tin amalgam is used in making mirrors.

amalgamation process (əmăl"gəmā'shən), method used for the extraction of gold and silver from their ores. The ore is crushed and treated with mercury, in which the metal dissolves. When the resulting amalgam is heated, the mercury evaporates, leaving the pure gold or silver.

Amalia, duchess of Saxe-Weimar: see ANNA AMALIA.

Amalric I (əmăl'rĭk, ă'məlrĭk) or **Amaury I** (əmō'rē, Fr. ämōrē'), c.1137–1174, Latin king of Jerusalem (1162–74); brother and successor of Baldwin III. He spent his reign in attempts to gain and hold the suzerainty of Egypt, but was balked by the Turkish sultan NUR AD-DIN, one of whose lieutenants finally obtained control of the country and left it at his death to SALADIN. During Amalric's frequent absences in Egypt, Nur ad-Din repeatedly raided the increasingly weak Latin states of the East. Amalric was succeeded by his son, Baldwin IV.

Amalric II or **Amaury II,** c.1155–1205, Latin king of Jerusalem (1197–1205) and Cyprus (1194–1205); brother and successor (in Cyprus) of GUY OF LUSIGNAN. His title to Jerusalem was established through his marriage with Isabella, eldest daughter of Amalric I (see JERUSALEM, LATIN KINGDOM OF).

Amalric of Bena (bē'nə), d. 1207?, French professor of philosophy. He taught heretical precepts concerning God, a pantheistic universe, and a progressive Trinity. Before he died, he publicly retracted, but his followers in Champagne formed a heretical sect, the Amalricians. They were condemned by Pope Innocent III and by councils held at Paris (1210) and the Lateran (1215). The heresy resulted in a temporary ban on Aristotle and the Arabic philosophers at the Univ. of Paris.

Amalthaea (ămălthē'ə), in Greek mythology, shegoat or nymph who nursed the infant Zeus. It was said that Zeus made one of her magnificent horns into the CORNUCOPIA and set her image among the stars as the constellation Capricorn.

Amalthea (ăm"əlthē'ə), in astronomy, one of the 12 known moons, or natural satellites, of JUPITER.

Amam (ā'măm), city of Judah. Joshua 15.26.

Aman (ā'măn), the same as HAMAN.

Amana (əmā'nə), unidentified mountains. Cant. 4.8.

Amana Church Society (əmăn'ə), corporate name of a group of seven small villages in E central Iowa, clustered around the Iowa River NW of Iowa City; settled 1855 by members of the Ebenezer Society. The society originated in one of the Pietist religious sects of 17th-century Germany. Led by Christian Metz (1794–1867), 800 members emigrated to the United States in 1842 to escape persecution at home. Settling first near Buffalo, N.Y., they developed a communal way of life that reached its flowering in Iowa. Amana became one of the most successful of such communities in America. In 1932 it was made a cooperative corporation, with separation of religious and economic administration. Long famous for the products of their woolen mills (especially blankets) and farms, the quaint villages also attract many visitors. The name *Amana* is used for a refrigerator and appliance company there; the company is not owned by the society. There are about 700 members of the society today. See B. M. Shambaugh, *Amana That Was and Amana That Is* (1932); Barbara Yambura, *A Change and a Parting: My Story of Amana* (1960).

Amanita (ăm"ənī'tə): see MUSHROOM.

Ama-no-hashidate: see MIYAZU, Japan.

Amanullah (ămənŏŏl'ə), 1892–1960, emir (1919–26) and king (1926–29) of Afghanistan. To win popular support for his rule he invaded India in an attempt to free Afghanistan from British-ruled India. No serious fighting occurred, however, and the Treaty of Rawalpindi was soon signed (1919). He attempted to introduce a number of Western reforms and changed the country from an emirate to a kingdom. His subjects rebelled against his program, and he fled the country in 1929. He remained in exile in Switzerland until his death. See study by L. B. Poullada (1973).

Amapá (əməpä'), federal territory (1970 pop. 114,687), 53,013 sq mi (137,304 sq km), extreme N Brazil, bounded on the N by French Guiana and the Atlantic Ocean. Macapá is the capital.

Amapala (ämäpä'lä), town (1961 pop. 2,368), S Honduras, on Tigre Island, in the Gulf of Fonseca. It is the chief Pacific port of Honduras. Products (coffee, lumber) are shipped from the mainland to Amapala by launch.

Amara (ämä'rä), town (1965 pop. 64,847), SE Iraq, on the Tigris River. A marketplace for dates and grains, it was taken by the British during the Mesopotamian campaign in 1915.

amaranth (ăm'ərănth") [Gr.,=unfading], common name for the Amaranthaceae (also commonly known as the pigweed family), a family of herbs, trees, and vines of warm regions, especially in the Americas and Africa. The genus *Amaranthus* includes several widely distributed species called amaranths, which are characterized by a lasting red pigment in the stems and leaves. They have been a poetic symbol of immortality from the time of ancient Greece. *Amaranthus* also includes such weeds as the green amaranth, *A. retroflexus,* and various species commonly called TUMBLEWEED and PIGWEED, as well as several cultivated plants—e.g., love-lies-bleeding, or tassel flower, and Joseph's coat. Other ornamentals in the family are the globe amaranth (genus *Gomphrenia*), sometimes called bachelor's button, and the cockscomb (*Celosia*), both originally tropical annuals. They can be preserved dry and are used in EVERLASTING bouquets. Amaranth is classified in the division MAGNOLIOPHYTA, class Magnoliopsida, order Caryophyllales.

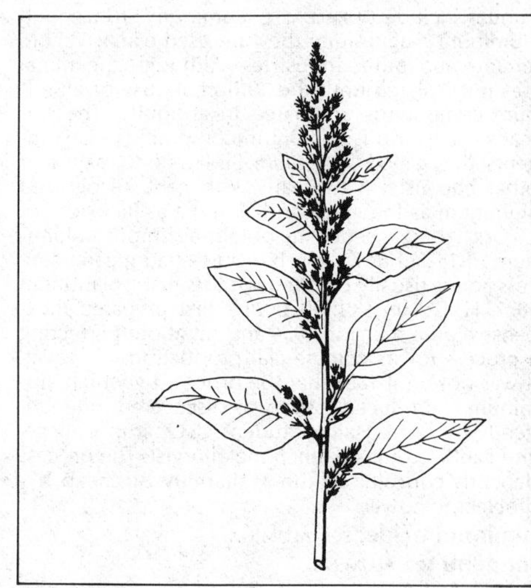

Green amaranth, Amaranthus retroflexus

Amarapura (ŭ"mərăpo͞o'rä), town (1962 est. pop. 71,015), Mandalay division, central Burma, on the Irrawaddy River. It is a silk-weaving center and has varied handicraft industries. Amarapura was founded in 1782 and was twice (1783–1823 and 1837–60) the capital of Burma. Its royal palace, great temples, and fortifications are now in ruins.

Amaravati (ŭ"məravŭ'tē), ancient ruined city, Andhra Pradesh state, SE India, near the mouth of the Kistna River. The former capital of the Buddhist Andhra kingdom, it is a well-known archaeological site. Remains include a beautiful Buddhist stupa (1st cent. A.D.).

Amariah (ăm"ərī'ə). **1** High priest, son of Meraioth. 1 Chron 6.7,52. Perhaps he is the same as **2** and **3.** **2** High priest, son of Azariah. 1 Chron. 6.11. Perhaps he is the same as **1, 3,** and **4.** **3** Ancestor of Ezra. Ezra 7.3. Perhaps he is the same as **1** and **2.** **4** High priest under Jehoshaphat. 2 Chron. 19.11. Perhaps he is the same as **2.** **5** Levite. 1 Chron. 23.19; 24.23. **6, 7** Contemporaries of Ezra, perhaps the same person. Ezra 10.42; Neh. 11.4. **8** A priestly family. 2 Chron. 31.15; Neh. 10.3; 12.2,13. See IMMER **1** and IMRI **1.** **9** Ancestor of the prophet Zephaniah. Zeph. 1.1.

Amarillo (ămərĭl'ō, –'ə), city (1970 pop. 127,010), seat of Potter co., N Texas; inc. 1899. A commercial, banking, and industrial center of the Texas Panhandle, Amarillo is situated in the midst of treeless plains that are swept by summer duststorms and winter blizzards. The city grew after the coming of the railroad in 1887, and at the turn of the century it was a market for wheat farmers. After the discovery of gas (1918) and oil (1921), Amarillo mushroomed into an industrial city. In addition to oil and gas, the city's economy is based on cattle ranching, meatpacking, flour milling, zinc smelting, as well as the production of helicopters, synthetic rubber, and farm and dairy items. Nearby are a U.S. government helium plant; Amarillo Air Force Base, which has a Strategic Air Command wing; and an atomic energy project. The city's educational and cultural facilities include Amarillo College, civic and art centers, a symphony orchestra, and a little theater.

Amarna: see TEL EL AMARNA.

amaryllis (ăm″ərĭl′ĭs), common name for some members of the Amaryllidaceae, a family of mostly perennial plants with narrow, flat leaves and with lilylike flowers borne on separate, leafless stalks. They are widely distributed throughout the world, especially in flatlands of the tropics and subtropics. Many ornamental plants of this family are mistakenly called lilies; they can be distinguished from members of the LILY family by the anatomical placement of the ovary (see FLOWER) and are considered more advanced in evolution than the lilies. Several fragrant, showy-blossomed species are commonly called amaryllis: the true amaryllis (*Amaryllis belladonna*), or belladonna lily, of S Africa, and the more frequently cultivated tropical American species of *Sprekelia, Lycoris,* and especially *Hippeastrum* (e.g., the Barbados lily). The large *Narcissus* genus, including jonquils and daffodils, is native chiefly to the Mediterranean region and the Orient, but it has been naturalized and is now widespread in the United States. Although the common names are sometimes used interchangeably, strictly the daffodil is the yellow *N. pseudo-narcissus,* with a long, trumpet-shaped central corona; the jonquil is the yellow *N. jonquilla,* with a short corona; and the narcissus is any of several usually white-flowered species, e.g., the poet's narcissus (*N. poetica*) with a red rim on the corona. The Biblical ROSE OF SHARON may have been a narcissus. Among many others that have become naturalized and are cultivated in Europe and North America are the snowdrops (any species of *Galanthus*), small early-blooming plants of the Old World whose flowers are symbolic of consolation and of promise; and the tuberose (*Polianthes tuberosa*), a waxy-flowered Mexican plant. Economically, the most important plants of the family are of the nonbulbous genus *Agave,* the tropical American counterpart of the African *Aloe* genus of the family Liliaceae (lily family). Different agaves provide soap (e.g., those called amoles—see SOAP PLANT), food and beverages, and hard fiber. Henequen and SISAL HEMP are among the fibers obtained from agaves; fique and Cuban hemp come from other similar genera. Maguey is the Mexican name for various species (chiefly *A. americana*) called American aloe, or century plant, that contain the sugar agavose, sometimes used medicinally but better known as the source of the popular alcoholic beverages PULQUE and MESCAL. The name "century plant" arises from the long intervals between bloomings—from 5 to 100 years. After blooming, the century plant dies back and is replaced by new shoots. The agave cactus (*Leuchtenbergia principis*) is a true CACTUS that resembles the agave. Amaryllis is classified in the division MAGNOLIOPHYTA, class Magnoliopsida, order Sapindales.

Amasa (ăm′əsə, əmā′sə). **1** Cousin of Absalom, with whom he revolted. Later he became David's commander in chief; he was murdered by Joab. 2 Sam. 17.25; 19.13; 20.4–13; 1 Kings 2.5. **2** Ephraimite chief. 2 Chron. 28.12.

Amasai (āmăs′āī, əmā′sāī). **1** Chief of the deserters from Saul to David. 1 Chron. 12.18. **2** Priest. 1 Chron. 15.24. **3** Levite. 1 Chron. 6.25,35. **4** Levite contemporary with Hezekiah. 2 Chron. 29.12.

Amashai (əmā′shāī), priest contemporary with Nehemiah. Neh. 11.13. Amashai is perhaps the same as MAASIAI.

Amasiah (ăm″əsī′ə), captain in Jehoshaphat's army. 2 Chron. 17.16.

Amasis I (əmā′sĭs), d. c.1545 B.C., king of ancient Egypt (c.1570–1545 B.C.), founder of the XVIII dynasty. He drove the HYKSOS out of the Nile delta and pursued them into Palestine. His name also appears as Ahmose.

Amasis II, d. 525 B.C., king of ancient Egypt (569–525 B.C.), of the XXVI dynasty. In a military revolt he dethroned APRIES. He erected temples and other buildings at Memphis and Saïs and encouraged Greek merchants and artisans to settle at Naucratis. He also established alliances with Greek leaders and maintained his rule partly with the aid of Greek mercenaries. His revision of the laws is said to have influenced the Athenian lawgiver Solon. Amasis II died just before the Persian invasion (525 B.C.) under CAMBYSES. The name also appears as Ahmose II.

amateur, in sports, one who engages in athletic competition solely for the love of sport and without any desire for material gain. Unlike the amateur, a professional athlete is paid for competing. The actual rules governing amateurs differ from sport to sport and from country to country. In the United States, students with athletic scholarships are classified as amateurs, even though they do receive a form of remuneration for their competitive activities. In the Soviet Union a large number of athletes who are classified as amateurs nevertheless receive large subsidies from the state. Such contraventions of the basic amateur rule have generally been disregarded by the International Olympic Committee, sponsor of the quadrennial Olympic Games, the world's most prestigious amateur athletic competitions. Occasionally, however, individuals are punished for violations. Jim THORPE was stripped of his two gold medals from the 1912 Olympics because he had once inadvertently played in a professional baseball league; the Austrian skier Karl Schranz was barred from the 1972 Winter Olympics for his endorsements of a ski manufacturer's products. Critics of the amateur code contend that it is not appropriate to contemporary realities; they point out that it was adopted during an era when amateurs were upper-class gentlemen who could afford to compete without remuneration. The major organizations involved in the supervision of amateur athletics in the United States are the National Collegiate Athletic Association (NCAA), responsible for college and university sports, and the Amateur Athletic Union (AAU), responsible for most other areas of amateur competition.

Amati (āmä′tē), Italian family of violinmakers of Cremona. The founder of the Cremona school was Andrea Amati (c.1520–c.1578), whose earliest violins date from c.1564. His labels bore the name Amadus, and he is credited with the basic design of the modern violin. His sons were Antonio Amati and Girolamo or Geronimo Amati, who worked together and followed closely their father's patterns in making violins of graceful shape and sweet tone. The Amati instruments had a characteristic amber-colored varnish. Niccolò Amati (1596–1684), son of Girolamo, brought the Amati violin to its height after c.1645. Antonio STRADIVARI and Andrea Guarneri were pupils of Niccolò. Niccolò's son, Girolamo (1649–1740), was the last of his line to achieve distinction. The Latin forms of the first names, Andreas, Antonius, Hieronymus, and Nicolaus, were generally used on the violin labels, and the family name was sometimes Latinized as Amatus.

Amato, Giovanni Antonio d' (jōvän′nē äntô′nyō dämä′tō), 1475–1555, Neapolitan painter, called Il Vecchio [the elder]. He imitated the style of Pietro Perugino. Paintings by him are in many churches in Naples, among them the *Holy Family* in a chapel of San Domenico Maggiore.

Amaury. For persons thus named, see AMALRIC.

Amaziah (ăm″əzī′ə). **1** King of Judah, son and successor of Jehoash of Judah. The two incidents of his reign were the conquest of Edom, including the capture of Petra, and an unprovoked attack by Amaziah on King Jehoash of Israel. Jehoash took Amaziah prisoner, entered Jerusalem, and sacked the Temple. Amaziah was assassinated at Lachish, and his son Uzziah succeeded him. 2 Kings 14; 2 Chron. 25. **2** Simeonite. 1 Chron. 4.34. **3** Levite. 1 Chron. 6.45. **4** Priest of Bethel, Amos's enemy. Amos 7.10–15.

Amazon, Port. *Amazonas* (ämäzō′nəs), world's second longest river, c.3,900 mi (6,280 km) long, formed by the junction in N Peru of two major headstreams, the UCAYILI and the shorter MARAÑÓN. It flows across N Brazil before entering the Atlantic Ocean near Belém. The Amazon carries more water than any other river in the world. The gradient of the river is very low: Manaus, c.1,000 mi (1,610 km) upstream, is only c.100 ft (30 m) higher than Belém and is an ocean port; ships with a draft of 14 ft (4 m) can reach Iquitos, Peru, c.2,300 mi (3,700 km) from the sea. Peru, Ecuador, and Colombia have international shipping rights on the Amazon. For most of its course, the river has an average depth of c.150 ft (50 m). The drainage basin is enormous (c.2,500,000 sq mi/6,475,000 sq km; c.35% of South America), gathering waters from both hemispheres and covering not only most of N Brazil but also parts of Bolivia, Peru, Ecuador, Colombia, and Venezuela. In the lowlands stretching E from the Andes is the largest rain forest (selva) in the world—a wet, green land, rich in plant life. The tropical climate is tempered by the heavy rainfall (exceeding 100 in./254 cm annually in parts of the upper and lower regions) and by high relative humidity; the average temperature at Santarém, 400 mi (644 km) upriver, is 78°F (26°C). Geologically, the Amazon basin is a sediment-filled structural depression between crystalline highlands of Brazil and Guiana. The river bed (1-8 mi/1.6-12.9 km wide) is in a wide flood plain that is up to 30 mi (48 km) wide. For much of its course, the Amazon wanders in a maze of brownish channels amid countless islands, but is unobstructed by falls. Its headstreams, however, arise cold and clear in the heights of the Andes. They descend northward before turning east to join and form the Amazon (which is, however, occasionally called the Solimões from the Brazilian border to the junction with the Rio Negro). Of the Amazon's more than 500 tributaries, the chief ones are the Negro, Japurá (Caquetá), Putumayo (Içá), and Napo, which enter from the north; and the Javari, Juruá, Purús, Madeira, Tapajós, and Xingú rivers, which enter from the south. The Casiquiare River, a natural canal, links the Amazon basin (through the Rio Negro) with the Orinoco basin. Below the Xingú the river reaches its delta, with many islands formed by alluvial deposit and submergence of the land. Around the largest of these, MARAJÓ, the river splits into two large streams. The northern stream is the principal outlet and threads its way around many islands. The southern channel, called the Pará River, receives the Tocantins River and has the important port of Belém. The awesome tidal bore (up to 12 ft/3.7 m high) of the Amazon is called *pororoca;* it travels c.500 mi (800 km) upstream. The river's immense silt-laden discharge is visible far out to sea. The Amazon was probably first seen in 1500 by the Spanish commander Vicente Yáñez Pinzón, who explored the lower part. Real exploration of the river came with the voyage of the Spanish explorer Francisco de Orellana down from the Napo in 1540–41; his fanciful stories of female warriors gave the river its name. Not long afterward (1559) the Spanish conquistador Pedro de Ursúa led an expedition down from the Marañón River. In 1637–38 the Portuguese explorer Pedro Teixeira led the voyage upstream that definitively opened the Amazon to world knowledge. The river continued to be of enormous importance to explorers and naturalists, among them Charles Darwin and Louis Agassiz. The valley was largely left to its sparse Indian inhabitants (mostly groups of the Guarani-Tupi linguistic stock and of meager material culture) until the mid-19th cent., when steamship service was regularly established on the river and when some settlements were made. In the late 19th and early 20th cent., the brief wild-rubber boom on the upper Amazon attracted settlers from Brazil's northeastern states, and since the 1930s Japanese immigrants have developed jute and pepper plantations. But the area still remains largely unpopulated and undeveloped, yielding small quantities of forest products (rubber, timber, vegetable oils, Brazil nuts, and medicinal plants) and cacao. The establishment of a health service (chiefly by launch) in World War II was followed by the creation of a UNESCO research institute in 1948, and several developmental programs, both governmental and private, have been set up in Brazil in recent years to foster the valley's development. Oil and manganese resources are exploited near Manaus and in Amapá. In the 1960s the Amazon region began experiencing increased economic development brought on by tax incentives and construction of the Trans-Amazon Highway, the Belém-Brasília Highway, and two rail lines. See C. R. Marham, ed., *Expeditions into the Valley of the Amazon* (1859); W. L. Herndon, *Exploration of the Valley of the Amazon* (1854, repr. 1952); Robin Furneaux, *The Amazon* (1969); Gaspar De Carvajal, *The Discovery of the Amazon* (tr. 1934, repr. 1970); Brian Blaston, *The Last Great Journey on Earth* (1971); J. R. Holland, *The Amazon* (1972).

Amazon (ăm′əzŏn), in Greek mythology, one of a tribe of warlike women who lived in Asia Minor. The Amazons had a matriarchal society, in which women fought and governed while men performed the household tasks. Each Amazon had to kill a man before she could marry, and all male children were either killed or maimed at birth. It was believed that the Amazons cut off one breast in order to shoot and throw spears more effectively. They were celebrated warriors, believed to have been the first to use cavalry, and their conquests were said to have included many parts of Asia Minor, Phrygia, Thrace, and Syria. Several of the finest Greek heroes proved their mettle against the Amazons: Hercules took the golden girdle of Ares from their queen Hippolyte; Theseus abducted Hippolyte's sister Antiope and then defeated a vengeful army of Amazons at Athens. A contingent of Amazons fought with the Trojans under PENTHESILEA.

Amazonas (ămәzō'nәs), state (1970 pop. 955,394), 604,032 sq mi (1,564,445 sq km), NW Brazil. The capital is MANAUS.

amazonite: see FELDSPAR.

Ambala (әmbä'lә), town (1971 pop. 83,649), Haryana state, N central India. It is a district administrative headquarters, a military station, and a transportation center. Automobile parts, pharmaceuticals, scientific instruments, machinery and iron products, porcelain, and glassware are manufactured.

Ambarvalia (ămbәrvăl'yә), in Roman religion, yearly agricultural rite held at the end of May. To insure fertility and disperse evil, each farmer led members of his household and a sacrificial beast in a procession around the boundaries of his fields.

ambassador: see DIPLOMATIC SERVICE.

Ambato (ämbä'tō), city (1970 est. pop. 75,300), capital of Tungurahua prov., central Ecuador, in a high Andean valley. A major commercial and transportation center, Ambato is noted for the variety of fruit grown in its outskirts and is called the "Garden of Ecuador." Sugarcane, grains, and cotton are also raised, and hides are processed. Picturesque Ambato is a favorite resort of the rich. Among its fine buildings is an old cathedral. The city has been frequently damaged by volcanic eruptions and earthquakes and in 1949 was almost totally destroyed.

amber, yellow to brown fossil RESIN exuded by coniferous trees now extinct. Capable of being highly polished, it is used in the manufacture of beads, amulets, mouthpieces, cigar and cigarette holders, pipes, and other small ornamental objects. When rubbed with a cloth, amber becomes charged with static electricity. The chief source of the world's amber is the Baltic coast of Germany; some is found off the coasts of Sicily and England. The empirical formula of amber is thought to be $C_{10}H_{16}O$. When destructively distilled, amber yields acetic, butyric, valeric, and other acids; water; and hydrocarbons. Baltic amber also contains succinic acid and is often called succinite. An ESSENTIAL OIL (amber oil) is obtained from amber. The best amber is transparent, but some varieties are cloudy. Bubbles of air, leaves, bits of wood, and insects are frequently found in amber, the insects sometimes being of extinct species. Amber was known in the Bronze Age and to the Greeks and Romans, who used it extensively in jewelry. Thales was familiar with its electrical properties, and Pliny recounts several instances of its artistic uses. It is connected with many superstitions and is believed to be a preventive against disease and bad luck.

amberfish: see POMPANO.

Amberg (äm'bĕrk), city (1970 pop. 41,522), Bavaria, SE West Germany, on the Vils River, near Czechoslovakia. Its manufactures include precision instruments, machinery, blast furnaces, plastics, and porcelain. Nearby are large iron mines known since the Middle Ages. Until 1810, Amberg was capital of the Upper Palatinate. At Amberg in 1796, Archduke Charles of Austria defeated the French under Marshal Jean Baptiste Jourdan. St. Martin's church (15th cent.) and the town hall (14th–16th cent.) are the city's outstanding buildings.

ambergris (ăm'bәrgrēs), waxlike substance originating as a morbid concretion in the intestine of the sperm whale. Lighter than water, it is found floating on tropical seas or cast up on the shore in yellow, gray, black, or variegated masses, usually a few ounces in weight, though pieces weighing several hundred pounds have been found. Ambergris has been greatly valued from earliest times. It is now used as a fixative in perfumes. Its active principle is ambrein, a crystalline alcohol with the empirical formula $C_{30}H_{51}OH$.

amberjack: see POMPANO.

ambidexterity: see HANDEDNESS.

Ambiorix (ămbī'әrĭks), fl. 54 B.C., Gallic chieftain of the Eburones (in what is now central Belgium). He had been favorably treated by the Romans, but he joined another tribe in attacking Julius Caesar's legates. When he heard of Caesar's approach, he fled across the Rhine.

ambivalence (ămbĭv'әlәns), coexistence of two opposing drives, desires, feelings, or emotions toward the same person, object, or goal. The ambivalent person may be unaware of either of the opposing wishes. The term was coined in 1911 by Eugen Bleuler to designate one of the four symptoms he considered primary to schizophrenia, the others being autism and disturbances of affect (i.e., emotion) and of association. As Bleuler explained it, "by ambivalence is to be understood the specific schizophrenic characteristic, to accompany identical ideas or concepts at the same time with positive as well as negative feelings (affective ambivalence), to will and not to will at the same time the identical actions (ambivalence of the will), and to think the same thoughts at once negatively and positively (intellectual ambivalence)." Closely related to ambivalence is Bleuler's concept of ambitendency, in which "a definite tendency to contrary or opposite action is combined with every impulse." Bleuler felt that there were normal instances of ambivalence and ambitendency, such as the feeling, as soon as one has done something, that it would have been better to have done the opposite; but the normal person, unlike the schizophrenic, is not prevented by his opposing impulses from deciding and acting. The psychoanalytic movement, following Freud, imparted a narrower meaning to the term in specifying that the opposing forces were feelings of love and hate toward the same person. This specific meaning has attained common usage by psychiatrists, whether or not they see the conflicting emotions as derived from postulated instinctual sources of sexual and destructive wishes. Many psychiatrists prefer to reserve the term ambivalence for the simultaneous presence in schizophrenia of strong destructive and erotic wishes toward a major family member. Mixed feelings of lesser intensity are generally said to be evidence of conflict rather than ambivalence. For example, the spells of doubting and brooding and the indecision characteristic of a person with an obsessive personality or neurosis have been traced to a conflict between obedience and defiance.

Ambler, Eric, 1909–, English novelist. A successful advertising executive, he turned exclusively to writing after his novels—realistic suspense stories—became popular. His heroes are usually ordinary men who become accidentally or innocently involved in international intrigues. Included among his thrillers are *A Coffin for Dimitrios* (1939), *Journey into Fear* (1940), *Passage of Arms* (1959), *To Catch a Spy* (1964), *The Levanter* (1972), and *Dr. Frigo* (1974).

Amboina: see AMBON, Indonesia.

Amboise, Georges d' (zhôrzh däNbwäz'), 1460–1510, French statesman, cardinal of the Roman Catholic Church. He became archbishop of Rouen in 1493. In 1498, as an intimate friend of the new king, Louis XII, he became chief minister. Subsequently he was appointed cardinal and papal legate in France. He devoted himself primarily to the furtherance of Louis's ambitions in Italy and was lieutenant general in Italy at the conquest of Milan (1500). His ambitions for the papal crown were disappointed by the election of Pope Pius III (1503), but Pius's successor, Pope Julius II, designated him (1503) papal legate in France for life. He negotiated the treaties of BLOIS (1504) and helped form the League of Cambrai (1508; see CAMBRAI, LEAGUE OF). His domestic administration was beneficent. By his patronage of artists and writers, he contributed to the promotion of the Renaissance in France.

Amboise, Jacques d' (zhäk), 1934–, American dancer and choreographer, b. Dedham, Mass. D'Amboise became a soloist with the New York City Ballet in 1953. He is best known for his roles in such distinctly American dance works as *Filling Station* and *Western Symphony*. He has also danced in several movies, including *Seven Brides for Seven Brothers* (1954) and *Carousel* (1956). His own ballets include *The Chase* (1963), *Quatuor* (1964), and *Irish Fantasy* (1964).

Amboise (äNbwäz'), town (1968 pop. 8,899), Indre-et-Loire dept., N central France, in Touraine, on the Loire. It is a wine and wool market, and its manufactures include precision instruments, shoes, sporting goods, pharmaceuticals, and film and radio equipment. The town is chiefly famous, however, for its Gothic château, a royal residence from the reign of Charles VIII (who was born and died there) to that of Francis II. Leonardo da Vinci, who probably worked on it, is said to be buried in its chapel. Amboise was the scene (1560) of a Huguenot plot against the GUISE family. Other old structures in the town include St. Denis Church (12th, 15th, 16th, and 17th cent.), St. Florentin Church (15th cent.), the town hall (16th cent.; restored), and the Clos-Lucé (15th cent.), where Francis I spent part of his youth and where da Vinci died.

Amboise, conspiracy of, 1560, plot of the Huguenots (French Protestants) and the house of BOURBON to usurp the power of the GUISE family, which virtually ruled France during the reign of the young FRANCIS II. The plan, presumably worked out by Louis I de Bourbon, prince de CONDÉ, provided for a march on the castle of Amboise, the abduction of King Francis II, and the arrest of François, duc de Guise, and his brother Charles, cardinal of Lorraine. The cardinal was forewarned, and the rebels, beaten before they had united their forces, were ruthlessly massacred. For weeks the bodies of hundreds of conspirators were hanging from the castle and from every tree in the vicinity. The Huguenots were enraged. A brief period of conciliation followed under the chancellorship of Michel de L'HÔPITAL, appointed by the king's mother, CATHERINE DE' MEDICI. He temporarily halted Protestant persecution until the outbreak (1562) of the Wars of Religion.

Ambon (ăm'bōn), island, c.1,800 sq mi (4,660 sq km), E Indonesia, one of the Moluccas, in the Banda Sea. It is mountainous, well watered, and fertile. Maize and sago are produced, and hunting and fishing supplement the diet. Nutmeg and cloves, once grown in abundance, are produced in limited quantities, and copra is exported. The chief town and seaport, also called Ambon (1961 pop. 56,037), is capital of Moluccas prov. It is the seat of the Univ. of Maluku and a private college, and it has an airport. The island was discovered (1512) by the Portuguese, who made it a religious and military headquarters. It was captured by the Dutch in 1605. An English settlement there was destroyed (1623) by the Dutch in what is called the Ambon massacre. Ambon was temporarily under British rule from 1796 to 1802 and again from 1810 to 1814. The town was the site of a major Dutch naval base captured (1942) by the Japanese in World War II, and it was the scene (1950) of a revolt against the Indonesian government during the short-lived South Moluccan Republic. The majority of the population is Christian. The island and town are also called Amboina.

Ambracia: see ÁRTA.

Ambridge, industrial borough (1970 pop. 11,324), Beaver co., W Pa., on the Ohio River; inc. 1905. Founded by and named for the American Bridge Co. in 1901, it is still the home of the bridge company and of one of the largest structural steel plants in the world. Manufactures include steel, foundry and machine-shop products, and electrical equipment. On the northwest edge of town are 17 restored buildings and homes from the old village of Economy, a communistic colony established by members of the HARMONY SOCIETY in 1825. The most successful of the society's communities, it thrived until 1906.

Ambrogio Stefani da Fossano: see BERGOGNONE.

Ambrose, Saint (ăm'brōz), 340?–397, bishop of Milan, Doctor of the Church, b. Trier, of Christian parents. Educated at Rome, he became (c.372) governor of Liguria and Aemilia—with the capital at Milan. He was highly regarded in that office, and popular demand caused his appointment (374) as bishop, although he was reluctant and lacked religious training. After much study he became the chief Catholic opponent of Arianism in the West. He was adviser to Emperor GRATIAN, whom he persuaded to outlaw (379) all heresy in the West. He firmly refused the demands of Justina and the young Emperor VALENTINIAN II to surrender a church of his diocese to the Arians. "The Emperor," he preached, "is in the Church, not above it." He excommunicated THEODOSIUS I for the massacre at Salonica (390) and imposed a heavy public penance on him before reinstating him. Ambrose's eloquent preaching spurred the conversion of St. Augustine. His writings, mostly homilies based on Scripture, have come down to us largely from his hearers. They reveal wide classical learning, knowledge of patristic literature, and a Roman bent toward the ethical and practical. Of his formal works, *On the Duties of the Clergy* (*De officiis ministrorum*) shows the influence of Cicero; *On the Christian Faith* (*De fide*) was written at Gratian's request. Ambrose's method of biblical interpretation was allegorical, following Philo and Origen. About 386 he arranged hymns and psalms for the congregation to sing antiphonally. A PLAINSONG called Ambrosian chant is attached to his name. His hymns, written in the iambic dimeter that became standard in Western hymnody, were widely imitated. Only a few are extant. The Ambrosian Rite used in Milan today is probably a development of a liturgy Ambrose introduced. Feast: Dec. 7. See biography by Angelo Paredi (1964); C. Morino, *Church and State in the Teaching of St. Ambrose* (1969).

ambrosia (ămbrō'zhә), in Greek religion, food with which the Olympian gods preserved their immortality. Extraordinarily fragrant, ambrosia was probably conceived of as an idealization of honey. It was accompanied by nectar, wine of the gods.

Ambrosian Library, founded c.1605 in Milan by Cardinal Federigo Borromeo. It became one of the earliest libraries to be opened to the public. The library's collection is rich in classical manuscripts, notably Homer and Vergil, in incunabula, and in Oriental texts. It also contains Leonardo da Vinci's profusely illustrated *Codex Atlanticus*.

Amchitka (ămchĭt'kə), island, 40 mi (64 km) long, off W Alaska; one of the Aleutian Islands. It was selected in 1967 by the Atomic Energy Commission (AEC) as the site for underground tests of nuclear weapons, thus arousing much criticism, especially from ecological groups. The AEC financed the transplanting of much of the island's animal life. In 1971 the use of Amchitka for the detonation of atomic devices without specific presidential approval was banned. The first test, sanctioned by President Richard Nixon, was made on Nov. 6, 1971.

ameba or **amoeba,** common name for certain one-celled organisms belonging to the class Sarcodina of the phylum PROTOZOA. The many genera of amebas were given their common name because of their resemblance to the genus *Amoeba* (order Amoebida), which includes several large, common species of which the freshwater *Amoeba proteus* is the most familiar. Amebas constantly change the shape of their bodies as a result of the phenomenon known as ameboid movement, involving the formation of temporary extensions (pseudopodia, or false feet) of the body. Pseudopodia, used in locomotion and feeding, may be rounded at the tip (lobopodia), pointed (filopodia), branched and fused together (rhizopodia), or somewhat rigid and pointed (axopodia). Most amebas are very small (from 5 to 20 microns in diameter) and contain a single nucleus. *A. proteus* averages 0.25 mm in length. Members of the genus *Pelomyxa*, however, may be well over a millimeter (up to 8 mm) in diameter and may contain hundreds of nuclei. Amebas engulf their prey, or particles of appropriate size, with their pseudopodia, forming food vacuoles. Digestive enzymes, manufactured and secreted by the organism, are then poured into these vacuoles, and the particles are digested. Useful compounds are subsequently absorbed into the ameba's body. Useless residues remain in the vacuoles and are ultimately expelled (egested) as the vacuole comes in contact with the membrane at the body surface. Amebas can distinguish food (e.g., algae, diatoms, bacteria, and other protozoans) from other material and use different tactics in approaching plant and animal food. Freshwater amebas take up water constantly through the process of OSMOSIS, and water content is regulated with a pulsating contractile vacuole. Marine amebas lack a contractile vacuole. Respiration is by diffusion of gases through the cell membrane. Under favorable conditions, amebas divide by binary fission (splitting) to produce two daughter amebas, the nucleus dividing by MITOSIS. When an ameba is divided artificially, the portion containing the nucleus forms a new cell membrane and continues as a whole animal, while the other portion lives only as long as its present food supply lasts, ultimately dying, since it cannot ingest food or reproduce. If conditions are unfavorable, e.g., in the absence of food and water, amebas secrete a firm, protective covering and encyst until conditions are again favorable to active division. Although simple in form, amebas are very successful organisms and are found abundantly in a variety of habitats all over the world. Amebas live in fresh water, the oceans, and in the upper layers of the soil, and many have adapted to a parasitic life on the body surface of aquatic animals or in the internal organs of both aquatic and terrestrial animals. Few animals escape invasion by some type of ameba. Some are harmless, but others are pathogenic and cause serious diseases; e.g., *Entamoeba histolytica* causes amebic dysentery, which is fatal if untreated. Other ameboid protozoans of the class Sarcodina include the marine radiolarians, which form silicate skeletons; their freshwater counterparts, the heliozoans; and the shell-bearing FORAMINIFERANS. Amebas are classified in the phylum PROTOZOA, class Sarcodina, order Amoebida.

amebiasis: see DYSENTERY.

Amecameca (ämä″kämä'kä), town (1970 pop. 21,753), Mexico state, S central Mexico, at the foot of the Popocatépetl and Ixtacíhuatl volcanoes. The sanctuary of El Sacro Monte, the most venerated spot in Mexico after the shrine of Guadalupe, stands on a hill above Amecameca. The town's history dates back to 1200.

Amen: see AMON.

amendment, in law, alteration of the provisions of a legal document. The term usually refers to the alteration of a STATUTE or a CONSTITUTION, but it is also applied in PARLIAMENTARY LAW to proposed changes of a bill or motion under consideration and in judicial PROCEDURE to the correction of errors. A statute may be amended by the passage of an act that is identified specifically as an amendment to it or by a new statute that renders some of its provisions nugatory. Written constitutions, however, for the most part must be amended by an exactly prescribed procedure. The CONSTITUTION OF THE UNITED STATES, as provided in Article 5, may be amended when two thirds of each house of Congress approves a proposed amendment and three fourths of the states thereafter ratify it. Congress decides whether state ratification shall be by vote of the legislatures or by popularly elected conventions. Only in the case of the Twenty-first Amendment (the repeal of prohibition) was the convention system used. The constitutions of many states require that a proposed constitutional amendment be submitted to the voters in a referendum.

Amenemhet I (ä″mĕnĕm'hĕt, ā″-), d. 1970 B.C., king of ancient Egypt, founder of the XII dynasty. The son of a powerful Theban family, he seized the kingship c.2000 B.C. The XII dynasty ushered in the Middle Kingdom of Egypt. Amenemhet centralized the government and subjected the long-powerful nobles to a virtually feudal state. His son and successor, SESOSTRIS I was coregent from 1980 B.C. **Amenemhet II,** d. 1903 B.C., son and successor of Sesostris I, was coregent with his father (1938–1935 B.C.), then sole ruler (1935–1906 B.C.), finally coregent with his son and successor, Sesostris II (see under SESOSTRIS I). He reopened the mines of Sinai. **Amenemhet III,** d. 1801 B.C., was the son and successor of Sesostris III (see under SESOSTRIS I), with whom he had been coregent. He extended the irrigation system. Thousands of acres in the Faiyûm were reclaimed. Under his successor, **Amenemhet IV,** d. 1792 B.C., the power of the dynasty declined, and his successor, a woman, Sebenekfrure, was last of her family. The dynasty of pharaohs named Amenemhet or Sesostris maintained peace throughout their hegemony, thus enabling the arts and sciences to flourish as they never would again in Egypt.

Amenhotep I (ä″mĕnhō'tĕp, ā″-) or **Amenophis I** (ä″mĕnō'fĭs), fl. 1570 B.C., king of ancient Egypt, of the XVIII dynasty; son and successor of Amasis I. His chief exploits were military. He pushed southward into Nubia and reestablished Egypt's boundary at the Second Cataract of the NILE, as previously fixed by Sesostris III. He invaded Syria as far as the Euphrates. His successor, THUTMOSE I, was not his son. **Amenhotep II** or **Amenophis II,** son and successor of Thutmose III (see under THUTMOSE), succeeded (1448 B.C.) as coregent and later ruled alone for 26 years. There are records of his prowess in hunting and horsemanship. He put down a revolt in Syria and maintained his father's conquests. His tomb is at Thebes; he also built extensively at Karnak. On his death (c.1420 B.C.) he was succeeded by his son Thutmose IV (see under THUTMOSE). **Amenhotep III** or **Amenophis III** succeeded his father, Thutmose IV, c.1411 B.C. His reign (until c.1372 B.C.) marks the culmination and the start of the decline of the XVIII dynasty. It was the age of Egypt's greatest splendor; there was peace in his Asiatic empire (in spite of incursions by Bedouins and Hittites) and he invaded Nubia only once. This is the period of extreme elaboration in Egyptian architecture and sculpture. Amenhotep III built extensively at Thebes, Luxor, and Karnak. His wife TIY was given an unprecedented position as queen consort and exerted much influence over her husband and his son and successor, IKHNATON. The sources of the "solar monotheism" of the god Aton, elaborated by Ikhnaton may be traced to the reign of Amenhotep III. Tablets found at Tel-el-Amarna shed light on the sociopolitical conditions in Egypt and Asia Minor in the 14th cent. B.C.

Amenophis: see AMENHOTEP.

America [for Amerigo VESPUCCI], the lands of the Western Hemisphere—North America, Central America (sometimes called Middle America), and South America. In English, *America* and *American* are frequently used to refer only to the United States. Martin Waldseemüller was the first to use the name (1507).

American, river, 30 mi (48 km) long, rising in N central Calif. in the Sierra Nevada near Lake Tahoe and flowing SW into the Sacramento River. Two dams on the river, regulating its flow and generating hydroelectric power, are part of the Central Valley Project. The discovery of gold at Sutter's Mill (see SUTTER, John Augustus) along the river in 1848 led to the California gold rush of 1849 and played an important part in U.S. history.

Americana, defined as all that has been printed about the Americas, printed in the Americas, or written by Americans, but usually restricted to the formative period in the history of the two continents. The Columbus letter (1493), a two-leaf newssheet announcing to the Spanish court the discovery of the islands of the Indies, is the earliest known printing about America. Richard Hakluyt's *Divers Voyages touching the Discovery of America* was published in London in 1582. Early American books were printed by Juan PABLOS, Stephen DAYE, and William BRADFORD (1722–91). The John Carter Brown Library, Providence; the New York Public Library; the Newberry Library, Chicago; and the Huntington Library, San Marino, Calif., all have fine collections of Americana. See Charles Evans, *American Bibliography, 1639–1800* (13 vol., 1903–55, repr. 1941–62); Joseph Sabin et al., *Bibliotheca Americana* (29 vol., 1868–1937, repr. 1961–62); M. B. Stilwell, *Incunabula and Americana* (2d. ed. 1961); J. C. Oswald, *Printing in the Americas* (1937, repr. 1965).

American Academy in Rome, founded in 1894 as the American School of Architecture in Rome by Charles F. McKim and enlarged in 1897 with the founding of the American Academy in Rome for students of architecture, sculpture, and painting. It was incorporated by act of Congress in 1905. In 1913 its charter was amended to include the American School of Classical Studies in Rome. It annually awards to U.S. citizens competitive fellowships bearing a yearly stipend, a travel allowance, and residence in Rome. Fellowships are granted in architecture, painting, sculpture, music, landscape architecture, and art history.

American Academy of Arts and Letters, founded 1904 to further literature and the fine arts in the United States; located in New York City. Its fifty members, who have made notable achievements in art, literature, or music, are selected from the membership of its parent body, the National Institute of Arts and Letters. It gives awards in art, literature, and music, maintains a library (14,000 volumes) and museum, and holds exhibitions of works of art, manuscripts, books, and scores. It also purchases paintings by American artists for distribution to museums.

American architecture. Each group of settlers in North America brought with it the building techniques and the prevailing forms of its home country and thus gave rise to different types of colonial building. But in all areas the differences between American and European conditions and climates, the fact that available building materials were not those of the home country, the dearth of trained architects and craftsmen, and the general poverty of the settlers produced rapid and profound change. Thus in French America, stone building was rare and was often replaced by a sort of stucco over half timber or, in the St. Lawrence valley, by wood; a characteristic low, rectangular plan with high hipped roofs, however, persisted. Only in New Orleans, where the French government sent skilled architects and engineers, was anything produced that approached the sophistication of building in France. The comparatively short Spanish domination of Florida also produced highly complex structures, including the forts at St. Augustine and Matanzas, the St. Augustine cathedral, and several houses; but that building had little enduring influence. In the Southwest, however, the Spanish impress was more permanent; there the settlers borrowed extensively from the Indian techniques of construction in smallstone masonry and in adobe and produced work admirably suited to the environment. Mexican baroque details and church forms appeared in a new and simpler guise, as in the Texas, New Mexico, Arizona, and California missions. The Dutch settling in New Amsterdam, who were traders for the most part, rapidly developed a typical 17th-century Dutch village. But outside the large centers they modified their building types. The English settlements were of two basic types: one, in the South, based on the large mansion house and plantation system; the other, in the North, served small-scale individual activities in farming, fishing, lumbering, and commerce. In both cases the settlers tried first to build as they had at home; they erected many-gabled half-timber houses of late Gothic inspiration. In the South, brick rapidly superseded wood as the chief building material, and the growing formality and classicism of English architecture was almost immediately reflected, as in the official buildings of WILLIAMSBURG, Va. In the North the climate rapidly forced the covering of half-timber houses, the lowering of roof slopes, and the simplification of plans; poverty (except in space and natural resources) prompted simplicity of detail. A type of residence that became popular in the wilderness and on the Western frontier by the mid-18th cent. was the LOG CABIN. During this time a growing prosperity and widening commerce brought a new influx of well-trained craftsmen, and English architectural books became increasingly available. There was a flowering of native craftsmen and designers who adapted the English precedent to American conditions with great skill. The result can be seen especially well in Charleston (S.C.), Annapolis, Philadelphia, Portsmouth (N.H.), Newburyport, Marblehead, and the earlier buildings of Salem (all: Mass.). The same period produced many churches in which the current English types by Christopher Wren and James Gibbs received simple, but elegant, American interpretations (e.g., St. Paul's Chapel, New York). The English Restoration style of Wren was superbly adapted in the Wentworth-Gardner house in Portsmouth, N.H. Toward the end of the colonial period, styles based on a direct study of ancient Roman and Greek structures were beginning to appear in Europe. The Adam trend (see ADAM, ROBERT) was soon translated to American use, especially in interior detail; simplifications of Adam's designs were made popular by the books of Asher BENJAMIN. A more monumental aesthetic, which became known as the Federal Style, is typical of the work of Charles BULFINCH in Boston and of Samuel MCINTIRE in Salem, both among the growing number of native-born designers. Presidents George Washington and Thomas Jefferson gave serious thought to architecture and were deeply involved in the planning and building of WASHINGTON, D.C. Both looked to the ancient classic world as the best source of inspiration, and as a result there evolved an American CLASSIC REVIVAL. Jefferson's conception of Roman ideals of beauty and proportion was elegantly expressed in his own house at Monticello and in the Virginia capitol and the Univ. of Virginia. European architects came to the New World in search of commissions and honor. Benjamin Henry LATROBE initiated the Greek revival in his works in Philadelphia and Washington. The later books of Asher Benjamin and those of Minard Lafever gave impetus to the use of classic detail; examples can be found in Louisiana and Maine, in the Carolinas and Wisconsin. Yet certain regional styles persisted beneath this uniformity. The plantation regions still built great mansions, often with two-story colonnades, and farmhouses of a basic 18th-century type still dominated much of New England. In the port cities classic uniformity was greatest. Temple porticoes decorated churches, banks, and public buildings. In the Southwest the Spanish tradition, occasionally (as in California) modified by Eastern influences, remained supreme until the Mexican War. As early as the end of the 18th cent. romanticism, prevalent in Europe, affected American design. The English "castellated Gothic" style began to have American imitators and became increasingly popular in the United States from 1835 on, especially for churches and cottages; the Gothic work of A. J. Davis, Richard Upjohn, and Minard Lafever won instant acclaim, and the widely distributed books of A. J. DOWNING on domestic architecture and landscape gardening increased the trend. Other historic revivals that won wide popularity at the same time were the Italian villa and the Lombard Romanesque styles. The latter was simple, uncluttered, and relatively inexpensive to produce, major advantages for public building. Just before and during the Civil War, the writings of John Ruskin began to influence American architects profoundly. An epidemic of elaborate American versions of the Victorian Gothic followed but was short-lived. The two decades following the Civil War produced vastly changed building techniques, primarily through industrialization. A new study of the functional basis of house design brought many experimental forms into being. Westward expansion and growing urbanization forced rapid, often crude, building developments. At the same time newly wealthy patrons dictated building in styles characterized by unbridled ostentation. Typical of such work are the designs of Richard Morris Hunt for the sprawling mansions of Newport, R.I. Americans' increased foreign travel brought acquaintance with all types of European building, overwhelming existing local traditions of taste and technique. Under such conditions the development of eclectic taste was inevitable, and in the United States eclecticism dominated architecture from the late 1880s. Many architects went to Paris, if possible to the École des Beaux-Arts, to receive the traditional doctrines. Until the period just before the Civil War, architect and engineer had been one person, or two with closely related goals. This unity of purpose was defeated by the rage for borrowed styles. The engineer designed the structural elements which the architect decorated; in the process both ignored the principle of the oneness of visible form and structure. Technical achievements of this chaotic era included construction innovations in the use of cast iron, steel, and reinforced concrete. The art of planning interior spaces for efficient functioning evolved, and the building industry was reorganized to make possible the swift and economical erection of projects of almost any size. Henry Hobson RICHARDSON designed massive, dignified buildings that contrasted sharply with the ornate edifices that reflected the prevailing tastes of his day. He is considered the father of modern American architecture. The cràft movement implemented by William MORRIS had enormous, lasting influence in the United States. The trend toward functional design, which had been steadily growing, reached its supreme expression in the works of the so-called Chicago school of architecture and in the designs and writings of its arch-prophet, Louis Henry SULLIVAN. Sullivan broke completely with the eclectic aesthetic. He used materials in such a way as to emphasize their function. The commercial buildings of Chicago, built under his influence, were unique in the United States for power and originality. Frank Lloyd Wright, generally acknowledged as one of the greatest architects of the 20th cent., was a student of Sullivan and stands alone in his understanding of Sullivan's concepts and in his ability to grant them the breadth of treatment they warranted. The Columbia World Exposition of 1893, however, further endorsed the neoclassical style and historical eclecticism, and major architectural firms, including that of McKim, Mead, and White, adhered firmly to that tradition. Thus, despite the iconoclastic efforts of Sullivan and Wright, its doctrines remained solidly entrenched for many decades. Not until the end of the 1930s was there general acceptance of the subtle, earthy, and elegant houses of the California school, typified by the works of Richard Neutra, and the pristine New England building of the International school, both types influenced by the designs of the BAUHAUS masters. As a result religious, domestic, and business architecture (including skyscrapers) became streamlined, reflecting innovations in the building methods developed to construct them and an expanded interest in the inherent qualities of texture and color of the materials used. See articles on individual architects, such as Frank Lloyd WRIGHT. See also MODERN ARCHITECTURE. See L. H. Sullivan, *Autobiography of an Idea* (1924); Talbot Hamlin, *The American Spirit in Architecture* (1926) and *Greek Revival Architecture in America* (1944, repr. 1964); J. E. Burchard and Albert Bush-Brown, *The Architecture of America: A Social and Cultural History* (rev. ed. 1966); Edgar Kaufman, Jr., ed., *The Rise of an American Architecture* (1970); S. F. Kimball, *Domestic Architecture of the American Colonies and Early Republic* (1922, repr. 1966) and *American Architecture* (1928, repr. 1970); V. J. Scully, *American Architecture and Urbanism* (1969) and *The Shingle Style and the Stick Style* (rev. ed. 1971); Lewis Mumford, ed., *Roots of Contemporary American Architecture* (2d ed. 1959, repr. 1972); J. M. Fitch, *American Building* (Vol. I, 1966; Vol. II, rev. ed. 1972).

American art. This article deals with the art of the North American colonies and of the United States. There are separate articles on NORTH AMERICAN INDIAN ART, PRE-COLUMBIAN ART AND ARCHITECTURE, MEXICAN ART AND ARCHITECTURE, SPANISH COLONIAL ART AND ARCHITECTURE, and CANADIAN ART AND ARCHITECTURE. The North American colonies in the 17th cent. enjoyed neither the wealth nor the leisure to cultivate the fine arts extensively. The colonial craftsmen working in pewter, silver, glass, or textiles followed closely the European model. The 17th-century LIMNERS, generally unknown by name, turned out crude but often charming portraits in the Elizabethan style, the Dutch baroque manner, or the English baroque court style, with the preferred style depending upon the European background of both the artist and his patron. The portrait painters alternated limning with coach and sign painting or other types of craftsmanship, and even in the 18th cent. it was seldom possible to earn a living by working at art alone. The silversmith Paul Revere turned his talents to commercial engraving and the manufacture of false teeth. The crafts in general followed English, Dutch, and Bavarian models, although in furniture some variations appeared in the work of talented craftsmen such as Samuel McIntire and Duncan Phyfe. In the first half of the 18th cent. a growing demand for portrait painting attracted such artists as John Smibert, Peter Pelham, and Joseph Blackburn from England, Gustavus Hesselius from Sweden, Jeremiah Theus from Switzerland, and Pieter Vanderlyn from Holland. Joseph Badger, Robert Feke, Ralph Earl, John Trumbull, and Charles Willson Peale did not depart widely from the tradition of 18th-century English portraiture, but while their work is more awkward, it is often more vigorous. In the early work of John Singleton Copley this vigor is combined with a great native talent. Another 18th-century American painter, Benjamin West, set up shop in London and became painter to the king and president of the Royal Academy. Although his training and practice were European, his studio became the mecca of American painters who for half a century came to study under him. His teaching of historical painting did not stand them in good stead on their return to America, where no demand existed for such work. Gilbert Stuart, however, emerged from his tutelage a superb portrait painter and after gaining success in England returned to America, where he executed a long series of famous and charming portraits and set a standard rarely surpassed in the United States. Of all the arts, sculpture was, perhaps, the least cultivated in the colonies. Apart from the anonymous carvers of tombstones and ships' figureheads, William Rush is almost the only known native sculptor to have practiced in pre-Revolutionary and early Federalist times. The period from the birth of the republic to the Civil War did not see much increase in the demand for the fine arts. Such early painters as Washington Allston, Samuel F. B. Morse, John Vanderlyn, and John Trumbull, who sought a market in America for historical painting in the classical manner of Jacques Louis David, were quickly disillusioned. Portrait painting alone could provide the patronage enjoyed by such men as Mather Brown, Henry Benbridge, Edward Savage, Thomas Sully, John Neagle, Chester Harding, and the miniaturists Edward G. Malbone and John Wesley Jarvis. None of these men, with the exception of Allston, produced work equal to that of Stuart or Copley, but all of them created paintings that expressed the energy and self-confidence of the builders of the new American nation. The colonial period saw the gradual rise of a number of excellent GENRE painters—Henry Inman, William Sidney Mount, Richard C. Woodville, David G. Blythe, Eastman Johnson, and George Caleb Bingham. These were the earliest painters of the American scene. J. J. Audubon created an extraordinary, detailed series of paintings of American birds. It is significant that he had to go to England for recognition and publication of his work. John Quidor painted scenes and legendary figures from the works of Fenimore Cooper and Washington Irving. The first half of the 19th cent. witnessed development of the first school of American landscape painting. Thomas Doughty and Thomas Cole led the HUDSON RIVER SCHOOL, which was continued by Asher B. Durand, John F. Kensett, and Frederick E. Church. The land and peoples west of the Mississippi were described in paintings by Frederick Remington, George Catlin, Charles M. Russell, and Seth Eastman, and by the panorama painters of the wilderness Albert Bierstadt and Thomas Moran. Despite this tendency toward the panoramic, the better work of these men showed a direct response to nature which has never ceased to be an important factor in American art. The characteristic American passion for objects realistically portrayed found remarkable expression in the paintings of William Harnett and John F. Peto, as well as in the still-life works of Charles Willson Peale and his children. The strain of primitivism, first evident in the limners, was more pronounced and popular in the early 19th cent. with works by Edward Hicks and Erastus Salisbury Field; it was continued by Grandma Moses in the 20th cent. In sculpture, portraiture provided the main source of patronage. John Frazee and Hezekiah Augur with little training produced forceful and original work in marble and wood. Horatio Greenough began the long tradition of the American sculptor trained in Italy, where he was soon followed by Thomas Crawford, Hiram Powers, and Harriet Hosmer. The American sculptors in Italy were greatly influenced by the Danish neoclassicist A. B. Thorvaldsen. Works of greater originality were produced by Clark Mills, Thomas Ball, and particularly by William Rimmer, whose untutored sculpture was enormously powerful. In painting, the post-Civil War period, one of unprecedented patronage for the arts from government and private sources, produced works of enduring worth and striking individuality. Much of the more popular work of the period, such as the historical and mural paintings of Leutze and the vistas of Bierstadt, have relatively little aesthetic interest today. But Whistler, Ryder, Eakins, and Winslow Homer produced works that rank among the finest achievements in American art. The four are strikingly dissimilar. James Whistler, an expatriate, cultivated a delicate art of suggestion in his oils and etchings alike. Albert Pinkham Ryder, a hermit, produced a visionary art of profound emotional impact. Thomas Eakins painted sympathetic portraits of extraordinary psychological insight and uncompromising honesty. Winslow Homer's watercolors are among the strongest realistic interpretations of pure landscape and seascape ever painted. This period also saw the development of the romantic landscape painters George Inness, Alexander H. Wyant, Homer D. Martin, and Ralph Blakelock. In Inness, and perhaps even more in William Morris Hunt, the influence of the Barbizon school was brought to America. Although French influence had begun to supplant German, the work of the portrait painters William M. Chase and Frank Duveneck reflected contemporary currents in Munich, as the earlier genre painters had reflected the influence of artists in Düsseldorf. John La Farge, who studied in Paris, did much to widen the American cultural horizon. His religious murals and stained glass set a new standard for these arts. John Singer Sargent, working chiefly in England, excelled in society portraiture, and Elihu Vedder and Edwin Abbey in illustration. At the close of the century John Twachtman, Childe Hassam, Ernest Lawson, and Mary Cassat worked under the direct influence of French impressionism. Under the same influence, Maurice Prendergast created original, boldly colorful images of passing urban scenes. In sculpture after the Civil War there was an increased demand for commemorative work. In the late 19th cent., John Quincy Adams Ward introduced a strong note of realism into a tradition suffering from the vapid classicism of the Italianates. His student Daniel Chester French also devoted his talents to monumental sculpture. William Rimmer's extensively illustrated *Art Anatomy* (1877) was admired by artists and physicians alike. The workshop of John Rogers produced small figures and genre groups that became popular, and later Frederick Remington's small bronzes extended the subject matter of native realism westward to include the cowboy. Neoclassic tendencies dominated in the work of Olin Warner and Augustus Saint-Gaudens, both of whom studied in Paris. Among the early 20th-century sculptors, Paul Bartlett, Karl Bitter, Frederick MacMonnies, George Barnard, and Lorado Taft exhibited a continuing conflict between naturalistic and idealized modes of representation. A significant cultural development of the era was the founding and expansion of American museums, whose collections were important to the art student and public alike. Museums, together with the rapid growth of art galleries, private collections, and art schools, widened the understanding of the European past and lessened the naïveté of earlier periods. Under the impetus of new techniques of reproduction the art of illustration flourished. The work of Edwin Abbey, Arthur Frost, and Howard Pyle was outstanding, appearing in *Harper's* and numerous other illustrated magazines and books. American art turned in the 20th cent. to exploitation of new techniques and new expression. The functional precision of the machine strongly influenced all the arts. The development of PHOTOGRAPHY forced a reevaluation of the representational nature of painting, while the formal and expressive capacities of modern European art opened fresh fields for the artist. In reflecting the radical European tendencies, American art in general maintained a more constant interest in local color and subject matter. Early in the century a vigorous movement toward realism in subject matter and freedom in technique was headed by Robert Henri, John Sloan, and George Luks. With others they formed the EIGHT, a group that sought to communicate something of the reality of everyday life through art. Dubbed the "Ashcan School," they included in their number William Glackens, Everett Shinn, and George Bellows. At his revolutionary 291 Gallery for contemporary photographs and paintings Alfred STIEGLITZ offered America early glimpses of fauve and cubist work and in addition exhibited abstract paintings by such Americans as Max Weber, Marsden Hartley, and John Marin. The full force of European modern art was presented to shocked Americans in the famous ARMORY SHOW of 1913, organized by Arthur B. Davies, Walt Kuhn, and other artists. Under the influence of this exhibition, the early work of such Americans as Joseph Stella, Yasuo Kuniyoshi, Charles Demuth, and Stuart Davis revealed new abstract tendencies. George Bellows and Rockwell Kent remained popular realists, and Edward Hopper and Charles Burchfield developed a more poignant and intensely personal realism. John Marin caught the imposing breadth of nature in his watercolors, while Georgia O'Keeffe and Charles Sheeler combined realism with varying degrees of precise formal design. Peter Blume, Ivan Albright, and Edwin Dickinson developed differing and complex surrealistic styles. A chauvinistic espousal of the American scene flourished under Thomas Hart Benton and Grant Wood in the early 1930s, while the same decade and the 1940s saw the rise of more personally meaningful, socially conscious art in the work of Ben Shahn, Philip Evergood, Reginald Marsh, Jacob Lawrence, Isabel Bishop, and Raphael and Moses Soyer. Several years later this social awareness was given bitter expression in the paintings of Jack Levine. Government sponsorship of the arts during the years of the Great Depression was the chief means by which many artists were able to continue work. Two independent programs, the Dept. of the Treasury's Section of Fine Arts and the Federal Art Project of the Works Progress Administration, were responsible for the embellishment of many public buildings with murals and the creation of smaller works for display in public institutions. The Farm Security Administration supported the photographic documentation of rural America, a project that employed a number of outstanding photographers and resulted in a dreadful and moving portrait of America in crisis. World War II brought an influx of European painters who were to influence the course of American art. They included Joan Miró, Salvador Dali, Max Ernst, and Yves Tanguy. In painting since 1945 the work of all but the most intensive realists, such as Andrew Wyeth, has tended increasingly toward abstraction. Such artists as Arshile Gorky, Irene Rice Pereira, Morris Graves, and Mark Tobey have developed and employed abstraction in works of highly personal symbolic content, whereas painters such as Jackson Pollock, Willem de Kooning, Adolph Gottlieb, and Franz Kline have created a bold and unique imagery that has made American painting a dominant influence in world art (see ABSTRACT EXPRESSIONISM). The POP ART movement of the 1950s and 60s revealed an aesthetic that made use of the mass-produced artifacts of urban culture and rejected the concepts of beauty and ugliness. Its major practitioners include Andy Warhol, Roy Lichtenstein, Jasper Johns, and Robert Rauschenberg. OP ART was an exercise in pure visual sensation, often exploiting techniques that give the illusion of movement. Developments in painting of the late 1960s and 70s include minimalism, POST-PAINTERLY ABSTRACTION, and photo-realism (see MODERN ART). American sculpture in the 20th cent. produced works in the traditional styles, including Gutzon Borglum's Mt. Rushmore monument, the classicizing figures of Paul Manship, and Mahonri Young's naturalistic athletes and laborers. However, the dominant tendency has been toward abstract design and expressive form, a trend to which William Zorach, Gaston Lachaise, and, more recently, Leonard Baskin contributed figurative work. Alexander Calder pioneered in the use of mobile welded metal forms, adding motion as a new dimension in sculpture. In the 1940s and 50s the free play of abstract forms in light and space and the use of new materials were vigorously exploited by David Smith, Theodore Roszak, Herbert Ferber, Isamu Noguchi, and Richard Lippold. Recent styles in sculptural abstraction have been developed in individual directions by John Chamberlain, Eva Hesse, Carl Andre, Louise Nevelson, and Tony Smith. See articles about individual artists, e.g., Thomas EAKINS. See Holger Cahill and A. H. Barr, *Art in America* (1935); A. T. Gardner, *Yankee Stonecutters* (1945); John Baur, *Revolution and Tradition in Modern American Art* (1958); Oliver Larkin, *Art and Life in America* (rev. ed. 1960); J. C. T. Flexner, *First Flowers of Our Wilderness* (1947) and *That Wilder Image* (1962); Lucy Lippard, *Pop Art* (1967); *The Artist in America* (1967; comp. by ed. of *Art in America*); Sam Hunter, *Modern American Painting and Sculpture* (1959); Wayne Craven, *Sculpture in America* (1968); Barbara Novak, *American Painting of the Nineteenth Century* (1969); Irving Sandler, *Triumph of American Painting: A History of Abstract Expressionism* (1970); John K. Howat, *The Hudson River and Its Painters* (1972).

American Association of University Professors (AAUP), organization of college and university teachers. It was founded (1915) for the purpose of defending faculty rights, most notably ACADEMIC FREEDOM and tenure (see TENURE, in education). Its major activities involve protecting teachers from harassment or arbitrary dismissal for espousing unpopular causes, and assuring due process in those cases where a teacher is charged with incompetence or moral turpitude. See Louis Joughin, *Academic Freedom and Tenure: A Handbook of the AAUP* (1969).

American Ballet Theatre, one of the foremost international dance companies of the 20th cent. It was founded in 1937 as the Mordkin Ballet and reorganized as the Ballet Theatre in 1940 under the direction of Lucia Chase and Rich Pleasant. It became the American Ballet Theatre in 1956. Its repertoire has included newly staged classical ballets and innovative modern dance works, many concerned with specifically American themes. Most of the company's seasons have been presented in New York City, but it has also toured throughout Europe and the Middle East. George Balanchine, Adolph Bolm, Michael Fokine, Léonide Massine, and Bronislava Nijinska have staged works for the company, as has the brilliant British choreographer Antony Tudor, who was introduced to the American public with such works as *Pillar of Fire* (1942) and *Romeo and Juliet* (1943). Agnes de Mille has staged nearly all of her dance works for the company, including *Fall River Legend* (1948). Jerome Robbins's *Fancy Free* (1944) and Michael Kidd's *On Stage* (1945) were also created for the company. Dancers who have gained fame or reached their peak with the American Ballet Theatre include Alicia ALONSO, Alicia MARKOVA, Erik BRUHN, Nora KAYE, and Jenny Workman.

American Bar Association (ABA), voluntary organization of lawyers admitted to the bar of any state. Founded (1878) largely through the efforts of the Connecticut Bar Association, it is devoted to improving the administration of justice, seeking uniformity of law throughout the nation, and maintaining high standards for the legal profession. It is composed of over 25 committees that deal with such diverse legal topics as maritime law, professional ethics, legal education, the judicial system, and legal aid for the indigent. Through its main office in Chicago, the ABA coordinates the activities of state and local bar associations. In 1974 its membership exceeded 170,000. Affiliated organizations include the American Law Student Association, and the American Bar Foundation, a group devoted to legal research and education.

American Civil Liberties Union (ACLU), nonpartisan organization devoted to the preservation and extension of the basic rights set forth in the U.S. Constitution. Founded (1920) by such prominent figures as Jane Addams, Helen Keller, Judah Magnes, Roger Baldwin, and Norman Thomas, the ACLU grew out of earlier groups that had defended the rights of conscientious objectors during World War I. Its program is directed toward three major areas of civil liberties: inquiry and expression, including freedom of speech, press, assembly, and religion; equality before the law for everyone, regardless of race, nationality, political opinion, or religious belief; and due process of law for all. Its most significant and successful activities have involved court tests of important civil liberties issues. Since its founding, the ACLU has participated directly or indirectly in almost every major civil liberties case contested in American courts. Among those are the so-called Scopes monkey trial in Tennessee (1925), the Sacco-Vanzetti case (1920s), the Federal court test (1933) that ended the censorship of James Joyce's *Ulysses,* and the landmark *Brown* vs. *Board of Education* (1954) school desegregation case. The ACLU has about 250,000 members in its state organizations. The national office, located in New York, also supports lobbying and educational activity on behalf of civil liberties issues. See Charles L. Markmann, *The Noblest Cry* (1965).

American Colonization Society, organized Dec., 1816–Jan., 1817, at Washington, D.C., to transport free Negroes from the United States and settle them in Africa. The freeing of many slaves, principally by idealists, created a serious problem in that no sound provisions were made for establishing them in society on an equal basis with white Americans anywhere in the United States. Robert FINLEY, principal founder of the colonization society, found much support among prominent men, notably Henry Clay. Money was raised—with some indirect help from the Federal government when (1819) Congress appropriated $100,000 for returning to Africa Negroes illegally brought to the United States. In 1821 an agent, Eli Ayres, and Lt. R. F. Stockton of the U.S. navy purchased land in Africa, where subsequently Jehudi ASHMUN and Ralph R. Gurley laid the foundations of LIBERIA. The colonization movement came under the bitter attack of the abolitionists, who charged that in the South it strengthened slavery by removing the free Negroes. The Negroes themselves were not enthusiastic about abandoning their native land for the African coast. The colonization society, with its associated state organizations, declined after 1840. More than 11,000 Negroes were transported to Liberia before 1860. From 1865 until its dissolution in 1912, the society was a sort of trustee for Liberia. See P. J. Staudenraus, *The African Colonization Movement* (1961); W. L. Garrison, *Thoughts on African Colonization* (1832, repr. 1968).

American Ephemeris and Nautical Almanac: see EPHEMERIS.

American Federation of Labor and Congress of Industrial Organizations (AFL-CIO), a federation of autonomous labor unions in the United States, Canada, Mexico, Panama, and U.S. dependencies, formed in 1955 by the merger of the American Federation of Labor (AFL) and the Congress of Industrial Organizations (CIO).

American Federation of Labor. In 1881 representatives of workers' organizations, meeting in Pittsburgh, formed the Federation of Organized Trades and Labor Unions in the United States and Canada. In 1886 at another conference in Columbus, Ohio, this group reorganized as the American Federation of Labor. Opposed to the socialistic and political ideals of the KNIGHTS OF LABOR, the AFL was, instead, a decentralized organization recognizing the autonomy of each of its member national craft unions. Individual workers were not members of the AFL but only of the affiliated local or national union, and from its inception it emphasized organization of skilled workers on a craft, or horizontal, basis, as opposed to an industrial, or vertical, basis. The AFL's object was to define and protect separate craft jurisdictions, to encourage legislation favorable to its members, and to provide assistance in organizing workers. The AFL was against the direct entry of organized labor into politics, and, operating under the precepts developed by Samuel GOMPERS, it was relatively static as a force for social change, although it did secure higher wages, shorter hours, workmen's compensation, and laws against child labor. It also helped to secure the 8-hr day for government employees and the exemption of labor from antitrust legislation (see CLAYTON ANTITRUST ACT). Under the leadership of Gompers, that of William GREEN, and then George MEANY, the AFL became the largest labor federation in the United States, with a membership of over 10 million at the time of its merger with the CIO in 1955. Divorced throughout most of its history from the radical element in American labor, the AFL was split in 1935 when dissident elements within the federation protested its conservative organization policies with regard to the mass-production industries. The formation of the Committee for Industrial Organization (later the Congress of Industrial Organizations) by the dissidents resulted in the suspension (1936) and then expulsion (1937) from the AFL of 10 affiliates. Two of these unions later rejoined—the INTERNATIONAL LADIES GARMENT WORKERS UNION (ILGWU) in 1940 and the UNITED MINE WORKERS OF AMERICA (UMW) in 1946. The UMW left again in 1947 because of a difference with the AFL leadership over the filing of non-Communist affidavits as required by the Taft-Hartley Labor Act. The federation maintained its prevailing craft-union philosophy, even in the face of the growth of mass-production industries that made the organization of workers along craft lines more difficult.

Congress of Industrial Organizations. Within the AFL in the early 1930s a strong minority faction evolved advocating the organization of workers in the basic mass-production industries (such as steel, auto, and rubber) on an industry-wide basis. John L. LEWIS of the UMW led this faction in forming a Committee for Industrial Organization in 1935. This group (changing its name in 1938 to Congress of Industrial Organizations) immediately launched organizing drives in the basic industries. The spectacular success of those drives, particularly in auto and steel, enhanced the CIO's prestige to the point where it seriously challenged the AFL's hegemony within U.S. organized labor. After fruitless negotiation the parent body revoked the charters of the 10 dissident international unions. The CIO, under the presidency of Lewis until 1940 and of Philip MURRAY thereafter until his death in 1952, followed more militant policies than the AFL. The CIO's Political Action Committee, headed by Sidney HILLMAN of the Amalgamated Clothing Workers Union, played an active role in the CIO's attempt to urge its membership into more active political participation. The CIO grew rapidly until its affiliated international unions numbered 32 at the time of the 1955 merger, with an estimated membership of five million. Its growth, however, was marked by internal dissension; one such dispute led to the withdrawal in 1938 of one of its original constituent unions, the ILGWU, and that union's reaffiliation with the AFL. Another dispute, this time over Lewis's support of Wendell Willkie in the 1940 presidential election, led Lewis to resign the CIO presidency. Coolness developed between Lewis and Murray and culminated in the withdrawal (1942) of the UMW from the CIO and its subsequent brief reaffiliation (1946–47) with the AFL. In the same period that the AFL was grappling with the problem of gangster-dominated affiliates, the CIO was faced with the problem of the extent to which their affiliates were Communist-dominated. In 1948 after a bitter struggle the CIO barred Communists from holding office in the organization, and in 1949–50 it expelled 11 of its affiliated unions, which were said to be Communist-dominated. During World War II the CIO (like the AFL) pledged a no-strike policy. The CIO joined (1945) the World Federation of Trade Unions (WFTU), exacerbating its relations with the AFL since the latter had refused to participate in the WFTU because of possible Communist domination of that body. This obstacle to U.S. labor unity was removed by the CIO's withdrawal from the WFTU in 1949; and relations were further improved by subsequent cooperation of the AFL and the CIO in helping to form the International Confederation of Free Trade Unions.

Merger. During the entire period of the alienation of the CIO from the AFL, the idea of merger was being considered by elements in both federations. By the early 1950s both federations had proved their sustaining power as labor organizations; it had become evident that craft and industrial unions could exist side by side within the labor movement. Furthermore, labor's concern over the apparent antiunion policies of President Eisenhower's administration (the first Republican administration in 20 years) gave new impetus to the movement for labor unity. The death in 1952 of the presidents of both organizations paved the way for the appointment of leaders more amenable to unity. The AFL chose George Meany, and the CIO picked Walter P. REUTHER. An indication of the possibility of a merger occurred in 1953 when a no-raiding agreement was signed between the two organizations. It was followed in 1955 by a merger agreement. At its first convention the merged organizations, now called the American Federation of Labor and Congress of Industrial Organizations (AFL-CIO), elected Meany as its president. The organization has five operating levels. The first is the biennial convention, in which ultimate authority is vested. The second level is the executive council, which governs between conventions and is composed of the executive officers (president and secretary-treasurer) and 27 vice presidents (17 from former AFL and 10 from former CIO unions). A general board (the convention in microcosm) acts on the third level as an advisory body to the council. On the fourth level the executive officers handle the day-to-day operations of the organization; they are advised on the fifth level by an executive committee consisting of the executive officers and 6 vice presidents (3 from each of the former AFL and CIO organizations). In addition to these levels of authority, the AFL-CIO carried over autonomous departments from the AFL (such as the Building Trades Dept.) and added an Industrial Union Dept. to handle the problems of the former CIO unions. The AFL-CIO also created a series of standing committees to handle problems in specific spheres of the federation's interests; the most notable of these is the Committee on Political Education. The AFL-CIO supported the Democratic presidential candidates in 1956, 1960, 1964, and 1968. In 1972, however, Meany led the AFL-CIO into a neutral stance, supporting neither major candidate. Committed to advancing the welfare of its members, the AFL-CIO has lobbied actively against the so-called right-to-work laws, which outlawed union shops (see CLOSED SHOP), and other legislation deemed inimical to organized labor's interests. In 1957 the AFL-CIO adopted antiracket codes, and the convention expelled the INTERNATIONAL BROTHERHOOD OF TEAMSTERS (which under Dave BECK and James R. HOFFA had gained a notorious reputation) for alleged failure to meet the parent organization's ethical standards. The AFL-CIO took a major step in 1961 in the direction of settling internal disputes by setting up a mandatory arbitration procedure. A submerged dispute between George Meany and Walter Reuther finally erupted in 1968. Reuther, continuously critical in the 1960s of the AFL-CIO's conservative approach to civil rights and social welfare programs, sought a reorganization of the executive council. To apply pressure, he began to withhold the $1 million annual dues of the United Automobile Workers of America (UAW). For this the UAW was suspended. By 1974 the AFL-CIO had 110 national and international unions, with a membership of some 13.5 million. See Samuel Gompers, *Seventy Years of Life and Labor* (1925, repr. 1967); Arthur Goldberg, *AFL-CIO: Labor United* (1956, repr. 1964); Philip Taft, *The A. F. of L. from the Death of Gompers to the Merger* (1959, repr. 1970); Walter Galenson, *The CIO Challenge to the AFL* (1960); Paul Jacobs, *The State of the Unions* (1963); Len De-Caux, *Labor Radical* (1970).

American Federation of State, County, and Municipal Employees (AFSCME), largest union of public employees in the United States. It began as a number of separate locals organized by a group of Wisconsin state employees in the early 1930s. By 1935 there were 30 locals that became a separate department within the American Federation of Government Employees. In 1936, AFSCME received its charter. By 1955, at the time of the AFL-CIO merger, the union had 100,000 members. The following year it merged with the 30,000-member Government and Civil Employees Organizing Committee. The union has over 500,000 members, about two thirds of whom are blue-collar workers. The single largest occupational area is hospital and health workers with about 150,000 members.

American Federation of Teachers (AFT), an affiliate of the AFL-CIO. It was formed (1916) out of the belief that the organizing of teachers should follow the model of a labor union, rather than that of a professional association. In the 1960s and early 70s the AFT experienced a period of rapid growth, expanding from 55,000 to almost 250,000 members. This increase in membership was largely due to an increasing willingness on the part of American teachers to use militant labor union tactics, including strikes and the threat of strikes, in contract negotiations. In 1973–74 the AFT negotiated unsuccessfully for a merger with the NATIONAL EDUCATION ASSOCIATION. See American Federation of Teachers, *Organizing the Teaching Profession* (1955); T. M. Stinnett, *Turmoil in Teaching* (1968); Stephen Cole, *The Unionization of Teachers* (1970); and R. J. Braun, *Teachers and Power* (1972).

American Film Institute, nonprofit organization established in Washington, D.C., in 1967 by the National Endowment for the Arts to preserve and catalog American films and to provide work grants for new and established filmmakers. The institute operates a movie theater at the John F. Kennedy Center for the Performing Arts in Washington, D.C., and provides financial and research assistance to U.S. museums and other organizations that present film programs. It maintains the Center for Advanced Film Studies in Beverly Hills, Calif., where it holds professional seminars and workshops, with a library of more than 3,000 books and film scripts. The institute also publishes detailed catalogs of feature films produced in the United States after 1921.

American foxhound, breed of sturdy, medium-sized HOUND developed in America over 300 years ago. It stands about 23 in. (58 cm) high at the shoulder and weighs between 60 and 70 lb (27–32 kg). The smooth, hard, "hound-marked" coat is usually black, tan, and white. The American foxhound, with its great endurance and keen sense of smell, was once widely used in packs of as many as 15 or 20 dogs to hunt fox and other small game. Today, however, it is more commonly bred for field trial competition. See DOG.

American Fur Company, chartered by John Jacob ASTOR (1763–1848) in 1808 to compete with the great fur-trading companies in Canada—the North West Company and the Hudson's Bay Company. Astor's most ambitious venture, establishment of a post at ASTORIA, Oregon, to control the Columbia River valley fur trade, was made under a subsidiary, the Pacific Fur Company. His early operations around the Great Lakes were under another subsidiary, the South West Company, in which Canadian merchants had a part. The War of 1812 destroyed both companies. In 1817, after an act of Congress excluded foreign traders from U.S. territory, the American Fur Company commanded the trade in the Lakes region. An alliance made in 1821 with the Chouteau interests of St. Louis gave the company a monopoly of the trade in the Missouri River region and later in the Rocky Mts. (see MOUNTAIN MEN). The company was one of the first great American trusts.

It maintained its monopoly by the customary early practice of buying out or crushing any small company that threatened opposition. When Astor withdrew in 1834, the company split and the name became the property of the former northern branch under Ramsey Crooks, but popular usage still applied it to succeeding companies. The American Fur Company strongly influenced the history of the frontier, not only by preparing the way for permanent settlement but by opening Great Lakes commercial fishing, steamboat transportation, and trade in lead. See G. L. Nute, *Calendar of the American Fur Company's Papers* (1945); B. DeVoto, *Across the Wide Missouri* (1948); H. M. Chittenden, *The American Fur Trade of the Far West* (3 vol.; 1902, repr. 1954); J. U. Terrell, *Furs by Astor* (1963); D. S. Lavender, *The Fist in the Wilderness* (1964); P. C. Phillips, *The Fur Trade* (1961, repr. 1967).

American Geographical Society (AGS), oldest geographical society in the United States, founded 1852 in New York City. Its purpose is to advance the science of geography through discussion and publication. The society has the largest private geographical library in the Western Hemisphere. Its archives contain many rare maps and globes, historic letters, and artifacts from explorations. The society is noted for its support of scientific research and exploration, for its research facilities (extensively used by the Federal government during the 1919 Paris Peace Conference and again during World War II), and for its cartographic work. The *Geographical Review* is its quarterly journal. See J. K. Wright, *Geography in the Making: The American Geographical Society 1851–1951* (1952).

American Indian languages, languages of the native peoples of the Western Hemisphere and their descendants. A number of the American Indian languages that were spoken at the time of the European arrival in the New World in the late 15th cent. have become extinct, but many of them are still in use today. The classification "American Indian languages" is geographical rather than linguistic, since those languages do not belong to a single linguistic family, or stock, such as the Indo-European or Hamito-Semitic language families. The American Indian languages cannot be differentiated as a linguistic unit from other languages of the world but are grouped into a number of separate linguistic stocks having significantly different phonetics, vocabularies, and grammars. There is no part of the world with as many distinctly different native languages as the Western Hemisphere. Because the number of American Indian tongues is so large, it is convenient to discuss them under three geographical divisions: North America (excluding Mexico), Mexico and Central America, and South America and the West Indies. It is not possible to determine exactly how many languages were spoken in the New World before the arrival of Europeans, nor how many people spoke these languages. Some scholars estimate that the Western Hemisphere at the time of the first European contact was inhabited by 40 million people who spoke 1,800 different tongues. Another widely accepted estimate suggests that at the time of Columbus more than 15 million speakers throughout the Western Hemisphere used more than 2,000 languages; the geographic divisions within that estimate are 300 separate tongues native to some 1.5 million Indians in America N of Mexico, 300 different languages spoken by roughly 5 million people in Mexico and Central America, and more than 1,400 distinct tongues used by 9 million Indians in South America and the West Indies. Recent studies suggest that some 700 American Indian languages survive, that they are spoken by nearly 12 million people, most of whom live in Central and South America. In the United States no more than 250,000 American Indians currently speak their native languages, which number about 200. By the middle of the 20th cent., as a result of European conquest and settlement in the Western Hemisphere, perhaps two thirds of the many Indian languages had already died out or were dying out, but others flourished. Still other aboriginal languages are only now being discovered and investigated by researchers. Some authorities suggest that about one half of the American Indian languages N of Mexico have become extinct. Of the tongues still in use, more than half are spoken by fewer than 1,000 persons per language; most of the speakers are bilingual. Only a few tongues, like Navaho and Cherokee, can claim more than 50,000 speakers. Mexico and Central America, however, have large Indian populations employing a number of American Indian languages, such as Nahuatl (spoken by 800,000 people) and the Mayan tongues (native to more than one million people). In South America the surviving Quechuan linguistic family accounts for several million people. Another flourishing language stock of South American Indians is Tupí-Guaraní. A language family consists of two or more tongues that are distinct and yet related historically in that they are all descended from a single ancestor language, either known or assumed to have existed. The languages of a family are closely related in phonetics, grammar, and vocabulary. The attempts made to classify American Indian languages into such families have encountered various obstacles. One is the absence of written records of these languages except in the case of Aztec and Maya. Even there the texts are comparatively few in number; the Spanish conquerors destroyed almost all the texts they found. Another problem is that most records of any linguistic value were made after 1850. Also, there are at present insufficient numbers of trained persons able to record many of the American Indian languages and collect data, especially in Mexico and Central and South America. The absence of grammars handed down from the past, owing to either the dearth of writing or the destruction of written texts, has further hampered the study of the American Indian tongues. Linguistic scholars, therefore, have to turn to native informants to gain material for the analysis of these languages. The languages in America N of Mexico are best known; those of Mexico and Central America are less so, and those of South America and the West Indies are the least studied. Systematic investigation has shown the American Indian languages to be highly developed in their phonology and grammar; they are not at all primitive, whether they are the tongues of the sophisticated Aztecs and Incas or of peoples of simpler cultures, such as the Eskimos or Paiutes. There is great diversity among the American Indian languages with respect to phonology and grammar. The tongue of the Greenland Eskimos, for example, has only 17 phonemes, whereas that of the Navahos has 47 phonemes. Some languages have nasalized vowels similar to those of French. Many have the consonant known as the glottal stop. Some American Indian languages have a stress accent reminiscent of English, and others have a pitch accent of rising and falling tones similar to that of Chinese. Still others have both stress and pitch accents. A grammatical characteristic of widespread occurrence in American Indian languages is polysynthesism. A polysynthetic language is one in which a number of word elements are joined together to form a composite word that functions as the sentence does in Indo-European languages. Thus, a sentence or phrase is expressed by one long word unit, each element of which has meaning usually only as part of the sentence or phrase and not as a separate item. In a polysynthetic language, no clear distinction is made between a word and a sentence. For example, a series of words expressing several connected ideas, such as "I am searching for my lost horse," would be merged to form a single word or meaning unit. Edward SAPIR, a major scholar in the field of American Indian languages, first presented the following, much-quoted word unit from Southern Paiute: *wiitokuchumpunkurüganiyugwivantümü*, meaning "they-who-are-going-to-sit-and-cut-up-with-a-knife-a-black-female-(or male-) buffalo." It is thought that the numerous aboriginal tongues showing polysynthesism may originally have been the offshoots of a single parent language. The existence of gender as found in Indo-European languages is encountered only infrequently in American Indian tongues. In the Algonquian languages, nouns are classified as animate and inanimate. Noun cases like those of Latin occur in some languages, but a lack of case distinction similar to English usage is more common (at least N of Mexico). A number of American Indian tongues have a form for the plural of the noun that differs from the singular form, but many others have the same form for both, as in the English noun *sheep*. Asia is generally accepted as the original home of the American Indians, although linguistic investigations have not yet established any definite link between the American Indian languages and those spoken in Asia or elsewhere in the Eastern Hemisphere. Some scholars postulate a connection between the Eskimo-Aleut family and several other families or subfamilies (among them Altaic, Paleosiberian, Finno-Ugric, and Sino-Tibetan). Others see a relationship between members of the Nadene stock (to which Navaho and Apache belong) and Sino-Tibetan, to which Chinese belongs; however, such theories remain unproved.

Languages of North America. The most widely accepted classification of American Indian languages N of Mexico (although some included are also spoken in Mexico and Central America) is that made by Edward Sapir in 1929. Sapir arranged the numerous linguistic groups in six major unrelated linguistic stocks, or families. There are ESKIMO-ALEUT, Algonquian-Wakashan, Nadene, Penutian, Hokan-Siouan, and Aztec-Tanoan. The Algonquian-Wakashan language family of North America was one of the most widespread of Indian linguistic stocks; in historical times, tribes speaking its languages extended from coast to coast. Today the surviving languages of the Algonquian-Wakashan family are native to some 80,000 Indians in Canada, the Great Lakes region, Montana, Wyoming, Oklahoma, and the NE United States. The Algonquian branch of the family once had some 50 distinct tongues, among them Algonquin, Arapaho, Blackfoot, Cheyenne, Cree, Delaware, Kickapoo, Micmac, Ojibwa (or Chippewa), Penobscot, Sac and Fox, Shawnee, and Yurok. Two other important branches of the Algonquian-Wakashan stock are Salishan and Wakashan. Among the tribes speaking Salishan languages are the Bella Coola, Clallam, Coeur d'Alene, Colville, Flathead, Nisqualli, Okanogan, Pend d'Oreille, Puyallup, Shuswap, Spokan, and Tillamook. The Salishan tongues are spoken in British Columbia, Washington, Oregon, Idaho, and Montana. Tribes speaking Wakashan languages (used along the Pacific Northwest coast) include the Nootka, Nitinat, Makah, Kwakiutl, Bella Bella, and Kitamat. Polysynthesism characterizes the Algonquian-Wakashan languages, which are inflected and make great use of suffixes. Prefixes are employed to a limited extent. The Nadene languages form another linguistic family; its branches include ATHABASCAN, Eyak, Haida, and Tlingit. The Eyak, Haida, and Tlingit tongues are spoken in parts of Canada and Alaska. As a whole, the Nadene languages have tones that convey meaning and some degree of polysynthesism. The verb is characterized by a reliance on aspect and voice rather than on tense. The Penutian linguistic stock includes several branches, such as the Maidu, Wintun, and Yokuts language groups, all of which are native to California. Probably also in the Penutian family are the Sahaptin, Chinook, and Tsimshian languages of the Pacific Northwest coast, as well as other tongues in Mexico and parts of Central America. Penutian languages resemble those of the Indo-European family in several ways (for example, they have true cases for the noun). The Hokan-Siouan family is thought to include a number of linguistic groups, but the classification of some of them is still disputed. Among the groups generally considered branches of the Hokan-Siouan stock are Muskogean, whose languages include such tongues as Choctaw, Chickasaw, Creek, and Seminole and are spoken in Oklahoma and Florida; Caddoan, composed of the Caddo, Wichita, Pawnee, and Arikara languages found in Oklahoma and North Dakota; Yuman, with individual languages (such as Cocopa, Havasupai, Kamia, Maricopa, Mohave, Yavapai, and Yuma) in Arizona and California; Iroquoian, to which belong the Seneca, Cayuga, Onandaga, Mohawk, Oneida, Wyandot, and Tuscarora languages spoken in New York, Wisconsin, and Oklahoma, as well as the Cherokee tongue found in Oklahoma and North Carolina; and Siouan, which includes Catawba (in South Carolina), Winnebago (in Wisconsin and Nebraska), Osage (in Nebraska and Oklahoma), Dakota and Assiniboin (in Minnesota, North Dakota, South Dakota, Montana, and Nebraska), and Crow (in Montana). Languages of the Hokan-Siouan stock are also found in Mexico and parts of Central America. These Hokan-Siouan languages tend to be agglutinative; various word elements, each having a fixed meaning and an independent existence, are merged to form a single word. The two principal branches of the Aztec-Tanoan linguistic stock are Uto-Aztecan and Tanoan, and their languages are spoken in areas extending from the NW United States to Mexico and Central America. Uto-Aztecan has such subdivisions, or groups, as NAHUATLAN, whose languages are spoken in Mexico and parts of Central America, and Shoshonean, to which Comanche, Hopi, Paiute, Shoshone, and Ute belong. Ute and Paiute are found in Utah, Nevada, California, and Arizona; Comanche and Shoshone are spoken in Wyoming, Nevada, Utah, California, and Oklahoma; Hopi is found in Arizona. The languages of the Tanoan branch of Aztec-Tanoan are spoken in the Rio Grande valley, New Mexico, and Arizona. Zuñi (found in New Mexico) may be connected with Tanoan. The Aztec-Tanoan languages show a degree of polysynthesism. They differentiate clearly between the noun and the verb.

Languages of Mexico and Central America. Of the languages of Mexico and Central America, about 24 linguistic groups, or stocks, have been identified; it is still not clear which of these can be classified together to reduce the number of groups. Among these groups is Yuman, whose tongues are spoken in Baja California and are related to the Yuman languages found in the United States. In both, Yuman falls within the larger Hokan-Siouan classification, which, in Mexico and parts of Central America, also includes the Coahuiltecan, Guaycuran, and Jicaque stocks, or groups. The Otomian stock (current in central Mexico and including the Otomí language) forms part of the larger Macro-Otomanguean division, in which the Mixtecan and Zapotecan stocks of Mexico are often placed. The Nahuatlan group, as indicated earlier, is classified under Uto-Aztecan, some of whose languages are found in Mexico and parts of Central America. Uto-Aztecan is itself a branch of the greater Aztec-Tanoan stock. Nahuatl, or Aztec, is a language of the Nahuatlan group. Mayan, which is found in Yucatán and parts of Central America and to which the language Maya belongs, is part of the larger Penutian linguistic stock. The Penutian stock also has as members the Huave, Mixe-Zoque, and Totonacan branches, whose languages are spoken in Mexico and Guatemala. In Mexico and parts of Central America, there are still more than one million speakers of the modern dialects of Maya proper, which was the official language of the ancient Mayan empire before the Spanish conquest of the New World. The languages of two South American stocks, Cariban and Chibchan, can also be found in Central America.

Languages of South America and the West Indies. More than 100 distinct linguistic stocks have been proposed for South America, and more than 1,000 separate languages have been discovered on that continent and in the West Indies. The latter had two aboriginal stocks, Arawakan and Cariban, which are also found in South America. When more is known about the South American Indian languages, some of the stocks may turn out to be sufficiently closely related so as to allow linguists to group them together and thus reduce the number of basic stocks. The principal linguistic groups of South America and the West Indies are usually said to be eight: Chibchan, Cariban, Ge, QUECHUA, Aymara, Araucanian, Arawakan, and Tupí-Guaraní. Before the European conquest, Chiban flourished in the areas now designated as Colombia, Ecuador, Panama, Costa Rica, and Nicaragua. It belongs to the larger Macro-Chibchan stock. Some Chibchan languages still survive in Colombia and Central America. Cariban and Ge are families of the greater Ge-Pano-Carib linguistic stock. In the aboriginal period the Cariban languages were important in the West Indies, Brazil, Peru, the Guianas, Venezuela, and Colombia. Today a number of them are still found in N South America and in some of the West Indian islands. Ge languages were spoken in E Brazil in preconquest times. About 50 of them are still in use in that country. Quechua (also called Kechua or Quichua), Aymara, and Araucanian are linguistic families assigned to the Andean branch of the larger Andean-Equatorial stock. Aymara today consists of 14 languages native to about one million people in Peru and parts of Bolivia, where those languages were also current in preconquest times. A number of languages, the most important of which is Mapuche, make up the Araucanian family, which thrives in Chile and Argentina. The Arawakan and Tupí-Guaraní families belong to the Equatorial branch of the Andean-Equatorial languages. Arawakan is considered the most extensive South American linguistic stock. In the aboriginal period (before 1500), Arawakan tongues were spoken in the West Indies and S Brazil and along the eastern side of the Andes. Some Arawakan languages have died out, particularly in the West Indies, but others still survive there and in South America, especially in Venezuela, Colombia, Brazil, the Guianas, Peru, Paraguay, and Bolivia. The Tupí-Guaraní family of languages is next to the Arawakan in extent. The Tupian subdivision reaches from the coast of E Brazil along the Amazon River to the Andes. The Guaranian subdivision is found in Paraguay, Brazil, Argentina, and Bolivia. Some 120 Tupí-Guaraní languages have survived. The two dominant members of this large family are Tupí and Guaraní. Tupí serves as a lingua franca for the Indians in Brazil. Guaraní is co-official with Spanish in Paraguay, and it is spoken by one million people in Paraguay and Brazil. The linguistic diversity of South America is unparalleled. There are many other families and hundreds of additional languages that have yet to be researched and definitely classified. Written literature in the usual sense does not exist in the American Indian languages; however, there are folk literatures. Communication by writing among the American Indians in the aboriginal period was limited to the Maya and the Aztecs. Both cultures used a form of picture writing to represent their ideas. About 800 of the Maya hieroglyphs, or symbols, are known, and in recent years substantial progress has been made in deciphering them. The computer is also expected to be of service in the effort to solve the puzzle of Maya writing. Not many texts of the Maya survive, the most numerous being inscriptions on buildings. The Incas of Peru used a system of knotted cords, ropes, or strings to communicate. Called the quipu, it is considered a form of writing. The color and shape of the knotted cords were the clues to meaning. For instance, green cords signified grain, and red cords, soldiers. One knot stood for the number 10; two knots, 20; a double knot, 100. Among Indians of E North America, beaded wampum belts often contained pictographic symbols for communication. Another means of nonlinguistic communication among many of the North American Indians was SIGN LANGUAGE, consisting of gestures with the hands and arms. One advantage of sign language was that it made communication possible among Indian tribes having different languages. In addition, smoke signals were used by some American Indians to convey information, but they were capable only of giving simple messages, such as "enemies in the area" or some previously agreed-upon message. The American Indian languages have contributed numerous place-names in the Western Hemisphere, especially in the United States, many of whose states have names of Indian origin. The European languages that are official today in countries of the New World, such as English, Spanish, and Portuguese, have borrowed a number of words from aboriginal languages. English, for example, has been enriched by such words as *moccasin, moose, mukluk, raccoon, skunk, terrapin, tomahawk, totem,* and *wampum* from North American Indian languages; by *chocolate, coyote,* and *tomato* from Mexican Indian tongues; by *barbecue, cannibal, hurricane, maize,* and *potato* from aboriginal languages of the West Indies; and by *coca, condor, guano, jaguar, llama, maraca, pampa, puma, quinine, tapioca,* and *vicuña* from South American Indian languages. Some American Indian languages, among them Navaho, Apache, and Cherokee, have been used for wartime communications by the U.S. military to evade enemy decipherment. Navaho Indians cooperated with the American armed forces during World War II as the transmitters of vital messages in their formidably difficult language. Unfortunately, the outlook for the future of the American Indian languages is not good. Most of them will probably die out; perhaps all of them will. At the present time, the aboriginal languages of the Western Hemisphere are gradually being replaced by the Indo-European tongues of the European conquerors and settlers of the New World—English, Spanish, Portuguese, French, and Dutch. Apparently there is no role for the American Indian languages as languages of world importance. Moreover, because of the almost total absence of writing and the earlier destruction of most of what writing did exist, the American Indian languages lack great literatures, although they do possess rich oral traditions. The investigation of these languages contributes much to a scientific knowledge of language in general, since these tongues possess a number of linguistic features not otherwise known. Some groups of native Americans in the United States are working to revitalize the languages of their peoples as a result of recently increased ethnic consciousness and feelings of cultural identity. See Edward Sapir in *Selected Writings in Language, Culture, and Personality,* ed. by D. G. Mandelbaum (1949); J. A. Mason in *Handbook of South American Indians,* ed. by J. H. Stewart (Vol. 6, 1950); Franz Boas, *Handbook of American Indian Languages* (1911–38, repr. 1969); Jesse Sawyer, ed., *Studies in American Indian Languages* (1971); Esther Matteson et al., *Comparative Studies in Amerindian Languages* (1972).

American Indian Movement (AIM), organization of the American Indian civil rights movement. In 1972, members of AIM briefly took over the headquarters of the Federal Bureau of Indian Affairs in Washington, D.C. They complained that the Bureau had created the tribal councils on reservations in 1934 as a way of perpetuating paternalistic control over Indian development. In 1973, about 200 Sioux, led by members of AIM, seized the tiny village of Wounded Knee, S. Dak., site of the last great massacre of Indians by the U.S. cavalry in 1890. Among their demands was a review of more than 300 treaties between the Indians and the Federal government that AIM alleges have been broken. Wounded Knee was occupied for 70 days before the militants surrendered. The leaders were subsequently brought to trial, but the case was dismissed on grounds of misconduct by the prosecution.

Americanization, term used to describe the movement during the first quarter of the 20th cent. whereby the immigrant in the United States was induced to assimilate American speech, ideals, traditions, and ways of life. As a result of the great emigration from E and S Europe between 1880 and the outbreak of World War I (see IMMIGRATION), the Americanization movement grew to crusading proportions. Fear and suspicion of the newcomers and of their possible failure to become assimilated gave impetus to the movement. Joined by social workers interested in improving the slum conditions surrounding the immigrants and by representatives of the business and industrial world some of whom feared the source of cheap labor might be subverted by spread of radical social doctrines, organizations were formed to propagandize and to agitate for municipal, state, and Federal aid to indoctrinate the immigrants into American ways. Leading the drive were the Daughters of the American Revolution, the North American Civic League for Immigrants (a New England group), the Committee for Immigrants in America, and the National Americanization Committee (both with headquarters in New York City). The coming of World War I with the resultant heightening of U.S. nationalism strengthened the movement. The Federal Bureau of Education and the Federal Bureau of Naturalization joined in the crusade and aided the private Americanization groups. Large rallies, patriotic naturalization proceedings, and Fourth of July celebrations characterized the campaign. When the United States entered into the war, Americanization was made an official part of the war effort. Many states passed legislation providing for the education and Americanization of the foreign-born. The anti-Communist drive conducted by the Dept. of Justice in 1919–20 stimulated the movement and led to even greater legislative action on behalf of Americanization. Virtually every state that had a substantial foreign-born population had provided educational facilities for the immigrant by 1921. The passage of this legislation and the quota system of immigration caused the Americanization movement to subside; private groups eventually disbanded. See John Higham, *Strangers in the Land* (1963); M. M. Gordon, *Assimilation in American Life* (1964).

American Labor party, organized in New York by labor leaders and liberals in 1936, primarily to support Franklin Delano Roosevelt's New Deal and the men favoring it in national and local elections. It gathered strength in New York state and particularly in New York City and had considerable weight there in tipping the scales toward chosen Democratic or Republican candidates. After 1939 it was much torn by strife between left-wing and right-wing factions, chiefly concerning policy toward the USSR. In 1944 an anti-Communist group led by David DUBINSKY, defeated in the primaries, dropped out and formed the Liberal party. In 1948 the party polled over 500,000 votes for Henry A. Wallace for President, but many members withdrew in opposition to his candidacy. Failing to poll 50,000 votes in the 1954 New York state election, it lost its place on the New York ballot. In 1956 the party was voted out of existence by its New York state committee.

American Landrace swine, relatively new breed of swine developed from Danish Landrace hogs imported in 1934 by the U.S. Dept. of Agriculture. They are totally white. Noted for their smoothness, length of body, and lean carcasses, these swine are prolific, fast-growing, and sturdy. They are found primarily in the central Corn Belt area.

American Legion, national association of male and female war veterans, founded (1919) in Paris. Membership is open to veterans of World Wars I and II, the Korean War, and the Vietnam War. The preamble to the organization's constitution, adopted at the convention in St. Louis that same year, expresses its purposes in part as "to uphold and defend the Constitution of the United States; to maintain law and order; to foster and perpetuate a one hundred percent Americanism; . . . to safeguard and transmit to posterity the principles of justice, freedom, and democracy; to consecrate and sanctify our comradeship by our devotion to mutual helpfulness." To achieve these ends the American Legion has done much work in social welfare, particularly in the areas of veterans benefits and child care. The largest of the veterans' associations, it is organized into a system of 58 state departments and some 16,000 local posts. Its national headquarters is in Indianapolis, Ind. The annual convention, at which policies are formulated, gains much attention, and the political force of the organization is considerable. The efforts of the American Legion have been bent not only to obtaining benefits for veterans but also to building up the military strength of the United States and to attacking so-called subversive or anti-American teachings and organizations. Although it is organized on a nonpartisan, nonpolitical basis, its policies have been criticized as reactionary by many opponents. There is also a women's auxiliary for the wives, mothers, sisters, and daughters of veterans. See Raymond Moley, *The American Legion Story* (1966).

American Library Association, founded 1876, organization whose purpose is to increase the usefulness of books through the improvement and extension of library services. As the major professional association for librarians and libraries, it seeks to maintain high standards for all branches of library service through functions ranging from the accreditation of library training schools to the recognition of outstanding books. The association was involved in early attempts to expand library services to all people. It supported public access to library shelves, tax-supported libraries, books made available for home loan, and research libraries sponsored by the government and major educational institutions. After the advent of audio-visual equipment, it promoted expansion of library programs to include the new electronic materials. The organization, based in Chicago, consisted of some 37,000 members in the early 1970s.

American literature in English began with the writings of English adventurers and colonists in the New World chiefly for the benefit of readers in the mother country. Some of these works reached the level of literature, as in the robust and perhaps truthful account of his adventures by Captain John Smith and the sober, tendentious journalistic histories of John Winthrop and William Bradford in New England. From the beginning, however, the literature of New England was also directed to the edification and instruction of the colonists themselves, intended to direct them in the ways of the godly. The first work published in the Puritan colonies was the *Bay Psalm Book* (1640), and the whole effort of the divines who wrote furiously to set forth their views—among them Roger Williams and Thomas Hooker—was to defend and promote visions of the religious state. They set forth their visions—in effect the first formulation of the concept of national destiny—in a series of impassioned histories and jeremiads from Edward Johnson's *Wonder-Working Providence* (1654) to Cotton Mather's epic *Magnalia Christi Americana* (1702). Even their poetry was offered uniformly to the service of God. Michael Wigglesworth's *Day of Doom* (1662) was uncompromisingly theological, and Anne Bradstreet's poems, issued as *The Tenth Muse Lately Sprung Up in America* (1650), were pious. The best of the Puritan poets, Edward Taylor, whose work was not published until two centuries after his death, wrote metaphysical verse worthy of comparison with that of George Herbert. Sermons and tracts poured forth until austere Calvinism found its last utterance in the words of Jonathan Edwards. In the other colonies writing was usually more mundane and on the whole less notable, though the journal of the Quaker John Woolman is highly esteemed, and some critics maintain that the best writing of the colonial period is found in the witty and urbane observations of William Byrd, a gentleman planter of Westover, Virginia.

A New Nation and a New Literature. The approach of the American Revolution and the achievement of the actual independence of the United States was a time of intellectual activity as well as social and economic change. The men who were the chief molders of the new state included excellent writers, among them Thomas Jefferson and Alexander Hamilton. They were well supported by others such as Philip Freneau, the first American lyric poet of distinction and an able journalist; the pamphleteer Thomas Paine, later an attacker of conventional religion; and the polemicist Francis Hopkinson, who was also the first American musical composer. The variously gifted Benjamin Franklin forwarded American literature not only through his own writing but also by founding and promoting newspapers and periodicals. Many literary aspirants, such as John Trumbull, Timothy Dwight, Joel Barlow, and the other CONNECTICUT WITS, used English models. The infant American theater showed a nationalistic character both in its first comedy *The Contrast* (1787), by Royall Tyler, and in the dramas of William Dunlap. The first American novel, *The Power of Sympathy* (1789), by William Hill Brown, only shortly preceded the Gothic romance, *Wieland* (1799), by the first professional American novelist, Charles Brockden Brown. Recognition in Europe, and especially in England, was coveted by every aspiring American writer and was first achieved by two men from New York: Washington Irving, who first won attention by presenting American folk stories, and James Fenimore Cooper, who wrote enduring tales of adventure on the frontier and at sea. William Cullen Bryant had by 1825 made himself the leading poet of America with his delicate lyrics extolling nature and his smooth, philosophic poems in the best mode of romanticism. Even more distinctly a part of the romantic movement were such poets as Joseph Rodman Drake, Fitz-Greene Halleck, and Henry Wadsworth Longfellow. Longfellow won the hearts of Americans with glib, moralizing verse and also commanded international respect. Ralph Waldo Emerson and Henry David Thoreau stood at the center of TRANSCENDENTALISM, a movement that made a deep impression upon their native land and upon Europe. High-mindedness, moral earnestness, the desire to reform society and education, the assertion of a philosophy of the individual as superior to tradition and society—all these were strongly American, and transcendentalists such as Emerson, Thoreau, Margaret Fuller, and Bronson Alcott insisted upon such principles. Men as diverse as James Russell Lowell, Boston "Brahmin," poet, and critic, and John Greenleaf Whittier, the bucolic poet, joined in support of the abolitionist cause, while the more worldly and correct Oliver Wendell Holmes reflected the vigorous intellectual spirit of the time, as did the historians William Hickling Prescott, George Bancroft, Francis Parkman, and John Lothrop Motley. The solemn histories were as distinctly American as the broadly humorous writing that became popular early in the 19th cent. This was usually set forth as the sayings of semiliterate, often raffish, and always shrewd American characters like Hosea Biglow (James Russell Lowell), Artemus Ward (Charles Farrar Browne), Petroleum Vesuvius Nasby (David Ross Locke), Josh Billings (Henry Walker Shaw), and Sut Lovingood (G. W. Harris). Far apart from these was Edgar Allan Poe, whose skilled and emotional poetry, clearly expressed aesthetic theories, and tales of mystery and horror won for him a more respectful audience in Europe than—originally, at least—in America. In the 1850s came Nathaniel Hawthorne's novel *The Scarlet Letter* (1850), depicting the gloomy atmosphere of early Puritanism; Herman Melville's *Moby-Dick* (1851), which infused into an adventure tale of whaling days profound symbolic significance; and the rolling measures of Walt Whitman's *Leaves of Grass* (1st ed. 1855), which employed a new kind of poetry and proclaimed the optimistic principles of American democracy.

The Literature of a Reunited Nation. The rising conflict between the North and the South that ended in the Civil War was reflected in regional literature. The crusading spirit against Southern slavery in Harriet Beecher Stowe's overwhelmingly successful novel *Uncle Tom's Cabin* (1852) was matched by the violent anti-Northern diatribes of William Gilmore Simms. While the Civil War was taking its inexorable course, the case for reunion was set forth in the purest and most exact statement of American political ideals, the Gettysburg Address of President Abraham Lincoln. Once the war was over, literature gradually regained a national identity amid expanding popularity, as writings of regional origin began to find a mass audience. The stories of the California gold fields by Bret Harte, the rustic novel of Edward Eggleston, *The Hoosier Schoolmaster* (1871), the rhymes of James Whitcomb Riley, the New England genre stories of Sarah Orne Jewett and Mary E. Wilkins Freeman, the sketches of Louisiana by George W. Cable, even the romance of the Old South woven by the poetry of Henry Timrod and Sidney Lanier and the fiction of Thomas Nelson Page—all were seized eagerly by the readers of the reunited nation. The outstanding example of genius overcoming any regionalism in scene can be found in *Huckleberry Finn* (1884), by Mark Twain. The connection of American literature with writing in England and Europe was again stressed by William Dean Howells, who was not only an able novelist but an instructor in literary REALISM to other American writers. Though he himself had leanings toward social reform, he did encourage what has come to be called "genteel" writing, long dominant in American fiction. The mold for this sort of writing was broken by the American turned Englishman, Henry James, who wrote of people of the upper classes but with such psychological penetration, subtlety of narrative, and complex technical skill that he is recognized as one of the great masters of fiction. His influence was quickly reflected in the novels of Edith Wharton and others and continued to grow in strength in the 20th cent. The realism preached by Howells was turned by some writers away from bourgeois milieus, particularly by Stephen Crane in his poetry and in his fiction—*Maggie: A Girl of the Streets* (1893) and the Civil War story, *The Red Badge of Courage* (1895); these were forerunners of NATURALISM, which reached heights in the hands of Theodore Dreiser and Jack London, the latter a fiery advocate of social reform as well as a writer of Klondike stories. Ever since the Civil War, voices of protest and doubt have been heard. Mark Twain (with Charles Dudley Warner) had in *The Gilded Age* (1873) held the postwar get-rich-quick era up to scorn. By the early 20th cent. Henry Adams was musing upon the effects of the dynamo's triumph over man, and Ambrose Bierce literally abandoned a civilization he could not abide. Poetry, meanwhile, had tended to the pretty-pretty—with the startling exception of the Amherst recluse, Emily Dickinson, whose terse, precise, and enigmatic poems, published in 1890, after her death, placed her immediately in the ranks of major American poets. Drama after the Civil War and into the 20th cent. continued to rely, as it had before, on spectacles, on the plays of Shakespeare, and on some of the works of English and Continental playwrights. A few popular plays such as *Uncle Tom's Cabin* and *Rip Van Winkle* were based on American fiction; others were crude melodrama. Realism, however, came to the theater with some of the plays of Bronson Howard, James A. Herne, and William Vaughn Moody. A revolution in poetry was announced with the founding in 1912 of *Poetry: A Magazine of Verse,* edited by Harriet Monroe. It published the work of Ezra Pound and the proponents of imagism (see IMAGISTS)—Amy Lowell, H. D. (Hilda Doolittle), John Gould Fletcher, and their English associates, all declaring against romantic poetry and in favor of the exact word. Other poets moved along their own paths: Edwin Arlington Robinson, who wrote dark, brooding lines on man in the universe; Edgar Lee Masters, who used free verse for realistic biographies in *A Spoon River Anthology* (1915); his friend Vachel Lindsay; Carl Sandburg, who tried to capture the speech, life, and dreams of America; and Robert Frost, who wrote with evocative simplicity and won universal admiration.

The Lost Generation and After. The years immediately after World War I brought a highly vocal rebellion against established social, sexual, and aesthetic conventions and a vigorous attempt to establish new values. Young artists flocked to Greenwich Village, to Chicago, and to San Francisco, determined to protest and intent on making a new art. Others went to Europe, living mostly in Paris as expatriates. They willingly accepted the name given them by Gertrude Stein: the lost generation. Out of their disillusion and rejection, the writers built a new literature, impressive in the glittering 1920s and the years that followed. Romantic clichés were abandoned for extreme realism or for complex symbolism and created myth. Language grew so frank that there were bitter quarrels over censorship, as in the troubles about James Branch Cabell's *Jurgen* (1919) and—much more notably—Henry Miller's *Tropic of Cancer* (1931). The influence of new psychology and of Marxian social theory was strong. Out of this highly active boiling of new ideas and new forms came writers of recognizable stature in the world: Ernest Hemingway, F. Scott Fitzgerald, William Faulkner, Thomas Wolfe, John Dos Passos, John Steinbeck, e e cummings. Eugene O'Neill became the greatest by far of the dramatists the United States has produced. Other writers also enriched the theater with comedies, social reform plays, and historical tragedies. Among them were Maxwell Anderson, Philip Barry, Elmer Rice, S. N. Behrman, Marc Connelly, Lillian Hellman, Clifford Odets, and Thornton Wilder. The social drama and the symbolic play were further developed by Arthur Miller, William Inge, and Tennessee Williams. By the 1960s the influence of foreign movements was much felt with the development of "off-Broadway" theater. One of the new playwrights who gained special notice was Edward Albee. The naturalism that governed the novels of Dreiser and the stories of Sherwood Anderson was intensified by the stories of the Chicago slums by James T. Farrell and later Nelson Algren. Violence in language and in action was extreme in some of the novels of World War II, notably those of James Jones and Norman Mailer. Not unexpectedly, after World War I, Negro writers came forward, casting off the sweet melodies of Paul Lawrence Dunbar and speaking of social oppression. Countee Cullen, James Weldon Johnson, Claude McKay, and Langston Hughes were succeeded by Richard Wright, Ralph Ellison, James Baldwin, and LeRoi Jones. Poetry after World War I was largely dominated by T. S. Eliot and his followers, who imposed intellectuality and a new sort of classical form that had been urged by Ezra Pound. Eliot was also highly influential as a literary critic and contributed to making the period 1920-60 one that was to some extent dominated by literary analysts and promoters of various warring schools. Among those critics were H. L. Mencken, Edmund Wilson, Lewis Mumford, Malcolm Cowley, Van Wyck Brooks, John Crowe Ransom, Yvor Winters, Lionel Trilling, Allen Tate, R. P. Blackmur, Robert Penn Warren, and Cleanth Brooks. The victories of the new over the old in the 1920s did not mean the disappearance of the older ideals of form even among lovers of the new. Much that was traditional lived on in the lyrics of Conrad Aiken, Sara Teasdale, Edna St. Vincent Millay, and Elinor Wylie. In the later years of the period two poets gained world recognition, though they had been quietly writing before: Wallace Stevens and William Carlos Williams. The admirable novels of Willa Cather did not resort to new devices; the essays of E. B. White were models of pure style, as were the stories of Katherine Anne Porter and Jean Stafford. Humor left the broadness of George Ade's *Fables* (1899) for the acrid satire of Ring Lardner and the highly polished writing of Robert Benchley and James Thurber. The South still produced superb writers, notably Carson McCullers, Flannery O'Connor, and Eudora Welty, whose works, while often grotesque, were also compassionate and humorous. The tension, horror, and meaninglessness of contemporary American life became a major theme of novelists during the 1960s and 70s. While authors such as Saul Bellow, Bernard Malamud, Hortense Calisher, and Philip Roth presented the varied responses of urban intellectuals, usually Jews, and John Updike and John Cheever treated the middle class, William Burroughs and Joyce Carol Oates unsparingly depicted the violence inherent in American life at all levels of society. Irony and so-called "black humor" were the weapons of authors like Roth, Joseph Heller, and Jules Feiffer. However, other writers, notably Donald Barthelme, Jerzy Kosinski, Thomas Pynchon, and Kurt Vonnegut, Jr., expressed their view of the world as unreal, as mad, by writing fantasies that were by turn charming, obscure, exciting, profound, and terrifying. Although the poets Allen Ginsberg, Theodore Roethke, and Lawrence Ferlinghetti gained initial recognition as part of the BEAT GENERATION, their individual reputations were soon firmly established. Writers of "perceptual verse" such as Charles Olson, Robert Creeley, Denise Levertov, and Robert Duncan became widely recognized during the 1960s. One of the most provocative and active poets of the decade was Robert Lowell, who often wrote of the anguish and corruption in modern life. His practice of revelation about his personal life evolved into so-called "confessional poetry," which was also written by such poets as Anne Sexton, Sylvia Plath, and, in a sense, John Berryman. Accomplished poets with idiosyncratic styles were Elizabeth Bishop and James Dickey. The pressure and fascination of actual events during the 1960s intrigued many writers of fiction, and Truman Capote, John Hersey, James Michener, and Norman Mailer wrote with perception and style about political conventions, murders, demonstrations, and presidential elections. For more information, consult the individual entries on any of the authors mentioned in this article. See Robert E. Spiller et al., ed., *Literary History of the United States* (3d ed. 1963); E. H. Emerson, ed., *Major Writers of Early American Literature* (1972); Ihab Hassan, *Contemporary American Literature, 1945-1972* (1973).

American Medical Association (AMA), professional physicians' organization (founded 1847). Its goals are to promote public health, protect the welfare of American physicians, and support the growth of medical science. Among its many activities, the AMA investigates alleged cases of medical quackery, engages in medical research on drugs, foods, cosmetics, and other substances, and sponsors an extensive health education program. The organization helps set standards for American medical schools and in-hospital doctor training programs; it was largely responsible for the upgrading of American medical education that took place in the early 20th cent. The AMA maintains close relationships with the state and county medical societies, and in some areas the societies require all physicians to belong to the AMA. Although the AMA's headquarters is in Chicago, it also maintains an office in Washington, D.C., in order to follow closely legislation that may affect the medical profession. The organization has consistently opposed—since the mid-1930s—proposals for a comprehensive system of national health insurance. The AMA is composed of over 20 different subdivisions that deal with a variety of medical topics, including medical education, maternal and child care, medicolegal problems, and mental health. It also has a section for each of the medical specialities. As of 1974 it had approximately 204,000 members.

American Museum of Natural History, incorporated in New York City in 1869 to promote the study of natural science and related subjects. Buildings on its present site were opened in 1877. Among the buildings since added are the Hayden Planetarium (opened 1935) and the Roosevelt Memorial building (completed 1936). It maintains exhibitions in all branches of natural history, including anthropology and ecology. As a result of its wide explorations and its program of research the museum has acquired specimens and data of great value. Resources are derived from endowment, grants from the city, and a membership fund. Among the facilities for study are an extension library; illustrated lectures; publications; programs for young people; a special school service whereby the museum cooperates with city schools; circulating exhibits; habitat groups of animals and plants; a mineral and gem collection; an unrivaled assemblage of skeletons of extinct animals, especially dinosaurs; and replicas of invertebrates in glass.

American National Theatre and Academy (ANTA), a tax-exempt, nationwide organization, chartered by Congress in 1935 to encourage outstanding theater in the United States. ANTA relies on money raised by popular subscription. Since 1946 it has concentrated its support on independent touring companies; it maintains an information service, an artist and speaker program, and various other activities. As the U.S. center of the International Theatre Institute, it has sponsored the exchange of foreign productions and artists. See their quarterly *Newsletter;* H. H. Taubman, *The Making of the American Theatre* (rev. ed. 1967).

American Negro spirituals, religious folk songs. Beginning in the late 19th cent., when a celebrated chorus from Fisk Univ. traveled throughout the United States and abroad, wide attention was given to the spirituals of the American Negro. This body of song was long thought to be the spontaneous creation of the Negro and the only original folk music of the United States. Research into its origin centered mainly on the nature and extent of its African ancestry. Because Negro slaves were brought to the United States from many parts of Africa, no single musical source is clear. Elements that African music and American Negro spirituals have in common include syncopation, polyrhythmic structure, the pentatonic scale, and a sort of responsive rendition of text. Audience participation increased the improvisatory nature of the spirituals, with the result that tens and even hundreds of versions of a single text idea exist. Early in the 20th cent. Cecil SHARP explored the extent of American folk-song literature, much of which he demonstrated to be of British ancestry. After that discovery G. P. JACKSON traced the considerable influence of revivalist and evangelist songs from the early 19th-century camp meetings of the Southern white population. Jackson claimed, using hundreds of comparative examples, that many Negro spirituals were adapted from or inspired by these white spirituals. Thus it can be assumed that African musical traditions were amalgamated with the religious songs of the white South, which had many sources, to produce a form of folk music that was distinctly Negro in character. The Negro spiritual is, above all, a deeply emotional song. The words are most often related to biblical passages, but the predominant effect is of patient, profound melancholy, even though the condition of slavery is very seldom referred to. The spiritual was directly related to the sorrow songs that were the source material of the blues (see JAZZ). A number of more joyous spirituals influenced the content of gospel songs (see GOSPEL MUSIC). Collections and arrangements have been made by Rosamond Johnson and J. W. Johnson, R. N. Dett, George L. White, John A. Lomax and Alan Lomax, Roland Hayes, and others. See G. P. Jackson, *White Spirituals in the Southern Uplands* (1933), *Spiritual Folk-Songs of Early America* (1937), and *White and Negro Spirituals* (1943); LeRoi Jones, *Blues People* (1963); H. A. Chambers, ed., *Treasury of Negro Spirituals* (1963); H. W. Odum and G. B. Johnson, *The Negro and His Songs* (1925, repr. 1964); W. F. Allen, *Slave Songs of the United States* (1857, repr. 1965).

American party: see KNOW-NOTHING MOVEMENT.

American Philosophical Society, first scientific society in America, founded (1743) in Philadelphia. It was an outgrowth of the Junto formed (1727) by Benjamin Franklin. Franklin was the first secretary of the society, and Thomas Hopkinson the first president. In 1769 it merged with the American Society for Promoting Useful Knowledge. The combined organization elected Franklin its first president, an office he held until his death. David Rittenhouse and Thomas Jefferson were his immediate successors. The society, which has a notable library located in Philadelphia, takes its members from people of distinction in all fields of intellectual and scientific study.

American Red Cross: see RED CROSS.

American Revolution, 1775-83, struggle by which the THIRTEEN COLONIES on the Atlantic seaboard of North America won independence from Great Britain and became the United States. It is also called the American War of Independence. By the middle of the 18th cent., differences in life, thought, and interests had developed between the mother country and the growing colonies. Local political institutions and practice diverged significantly from English ways, while social customs, religious beliefs, and economic interests added to the potential sources of conflict. The British government, like other imperial powers in the 18th cent., favored a policy of MERCANTILISM; the NAVIGATION ACTS were intended to regulate commerce in the British interest. These were only loosely enforced, however, and the colonies were by and large allowed to develop freely with little interference from England. Conditions changed abruptly in 1763. The Treaty of Paris in that year ended the FRENCH AND INDIAN WARS and removed a long-standing threat to the colonies. At the same time the ministry (1763-65) of George GRENVILLE in Great Britain undertook a new colonial policy intended to tighten political control over the colonies and to make them pay for their defense and return revenue to the mother country. The tax levied on molasses and sugar in 1764 caused some consternation among New England merchants and makers of rum; the tax itself was smaller than the one already on the books, but the promise of stringent enforcement was novel and ominous. It was the STAMP ACT, passed by the British Parliament in 1765, with its direct demand for revenue that roused a violent colonial outcry, which was spearheaded by the Northern merchants, lawyers, and newspaper publishers who were directly affected. Everywhere leaders such as James Otis, Samuel Adams, and Patrick Henry denounced the act with eloquence, societies called the SONS OF LIBERTY were formed, and the Stamp Act Congress was called to protest that Parliament was violating the rights of trueborn Englishmen in taxing the colonials, who were not directly represented in the supreme legislature. The threat of boycott and refusal to import English goods supported the colonial clamor. Parliament repealed (1766) the Stamp Act but passed an act formally declaring its right to tax the colonies. The incident was closed, but a barb remained to wound American feelings. Colonial political theorists—not only radicals such as Samuel Adams, Patrick Henry, Josiah QUINCY (1744-75), and Alexander MacDOUGALL but also moderates such as John DICKINSON, John ADAMS, and Benjamin FRANKLIN—asserted that taxation without representation was tyranny. The teachings of 18th-century French philosophers and continental writers on law, such as Emmerich de Vattel, as well as the theories of John LOCKE, were implicit in the colonial arguments based on the theory of NATURAL RIGHTS. The colonials claimed that Parliament had the sovereign power to legislate in the interest of the entire British Empire, but that it could only tax those actually represented in Parliament. Trouble flared when the Chatham ministry adopted (1767) the TOWNSHEND ACTS, which taxed numerous imports; care was taken to levy only an "external" or indirect tax in the hope that the colonials would accept this. The indirect taxes were challenged too, and although the duties were not heavy, the principle was attacked. Incidents came in interrupted sequence to make feeling run higher and higher—the seizure of a ship belonging to John HANCOCK in 1768, the bloodshed of the BOSTON MASSACRE in 1770, the burning of H. M. S. GASPEE in 1772. Even repeal of the Townshend Acts in 1770 did no more than temporarily quiet the turmoil, for the tax on tea was kept as a sort of token of Parliament's supremacy. Indignation in New England at the monopoly granted to the East India Company led to the BOSTON TEA PARTY in 1773. Despite the earnest pleas of William Pitt the elder (see CHATHAM, WILLIAM PITT, 1ST EARL OF) and Edmund BURKE, Parliament replied with coercive measures. These (and the QUEBEC ACT) the colonials called the INTOLERABLE ACTS, and resistance was prompt. The Sons of Liberty and individual colonials were already spreading statements of the colonial cause to win over merchant and farmer, workingman and sailor. Committees of correspondence had been formed to exchange information and ideas and to build colonial unity, and in 1774 these committees prepared the way for the CONTINENTAL CONGRESS. The representatives at this First Continental Congress, except for a few radicals, had not met to consider independence, but wished only to persuade the British government to recognize their rights. A plan of reconciliation offered by Joseph GALLOWAY was rejected. It was agreed that the colonies would refuse to import British goods until colonial grievances were righted; those grievances were listed in petitions to the king; and the congress adjourned. Before it met again the situation had changed. On the morning of April 19, 1775, shots had been exchanged by colonials and British soldiers, men had been killed, and a revolution had begun (see LEXINGTON AND CONCORD, BATTLES OF). On the very day (May 10, 1775) that the Second Continental Congress met, Ethan ALLEN and his Green Mountain Boys, together with a force under Benedict Arnold, took Fort Ticonderoga from the British, and two days later Seth WARNER captured Crown Point. Boston was under British siege, and before that siege was climaxed by the costly British victory usually called the battle of Bunker Hill (June 17, 1775) the Congress had chosen (June 15, 1775) George WASHINGTON as commander in chief of the Continental armed forces. The war was on in earnest. Some delegates had come to the Congress already committed to declaring the colonies independent of Great Britain, but even many stalwart upholders of the colonial cause were not ready to take such a step. The lines were being more clearly drawn between the pro-British LOYALISTS and colonial revolutionists. The time was one of indecision, and the division of the people was symbolized by the split between Benjamin Franklin and his Loyalist son, William FRANKLIN. The Loyalists were numerous and included small farmers as well as large landowners, royal officeholders, and members of the professions; they were to be found in varying strength in every colony. A large part of the population was more or less neutral, swaying to this side or that or else remaining inert in the struggle, which was to some extent a civil war. So it was to remain to the end. Civil government and administration had fallen apart and had to be patched together locally. In some places the result was bloody strife, as in the partisan raids in the Carolinas and Georgia and the Mohawk valley massacre in New York; elsewhere hostility did not produce open struggles. In January, 1776, Thomas Paine wrote a pamphlet, *Common Sense*, which urged the colonial cause. Its influence was tremendous, and it was read everywhere with enthusiastic acclaim. Militarily, however, the cause did not prosper greatly. Delegations to the Canadians had been unsuccessful, and the QUEBEC CAMPAIGN (1775–76) ended in disaster. The British gave up Boston in March, 1776, but the prospects were still not good for the ill-trained, poorly armed volunteer soldiers of the Continental army when the Congress decided finally to declare the independence of the Thirteen Colonies. The DECLARATION OF INDEPENDENCE is conventionally dated July 4, 1776. Drawn up by Thomas Jefferson (with slight emendations), it was to be one of the great historical documents of all time. It did not, however, have any immediate positive effect. The British under Gen. William HOWE and his brother, Admiral Richard Howe, came to New York harbor. After vain attempts to negotiate a peace, the British forces struck. Washington lost Brooklyn Heights (see LONG ISLAND, BATTLE OF), retreated northward, was defeated at Harlem Heights in Manhattan and at White Plains, and took part of his dwindling army into New Jersey. Thomas Paine in a new pamphlet, *The Crisis*, exhorted the revolutionists to courage in desperate days, and Washington showed his increasing military skill and helped to restore colonial spirits in the winter of 1776–77 by crossing the ice-ridden Delaware and winning small victories over forces made up mostly of Hessian mercenaries at Trenton (Dec. 26) and Princeton (Jan. 3). In 1777 the British attempted to wipe out the flickering revolt by a concerted plan to split the colonies with converging expeditions concentrated upon the Hudson valley. Gen. William Howe, instead of taking part in it, moved into Pennsylvania, defeated Washington in the battle of Brandywine (Sept. 11), took Philadelphia, and beat off (Oct. 4) Washington's attack on Germantown. Meanwhile the British columns under Gen. John BURGOYNE and Gen. Barry ST. LEGER had failed (see SARATOGA CAMPAIGN), and Burgoyne on Oct. 17, 1777, ended the battle of Saratoga by surrender to Gen. Horatio GATES. The victory is commonly regarded as the decisive battle of the war, but its good effects again were not immediate. The Continental army still had to endure the hardships of the cruel winter at VALLEY FORGE, when only loyalty to Washington and the cause of liberty held the half-frozen, half-starved men together. Among them were three of the foreign idealists who had come to aid the colonials in their struggle—Johann KALB, Baron von STEUBEN, and the marquis de LAFAYETTE. At Valley Forge, Steuben trained the still-raw troops, who came away a disciplined fighting force giving a good account of themselves in 1778. Sir Henry CLINTON, who had succeeded Howe in command, decided to abandon Philadelphia for New York, and Washington's attack upon the British in the battle of Monmouth (see MONMOUTH, BATTLE OF) was cheated of success mainly by the equivocal actions of Gen. Charles LEE. The warfare in the Middle Atlantic region settled almost to stagnation, but foreign aid was finally arriving. Agents of the new nation—notably Benjamin Franklin, Arthur Lee, Silas DEANE, and later John Adams—were striving to get help, and in 1777 Pierre de BEAUMARCHAIS had succeeded in getting arms and supplies sent to the colonials in time to help win the battle of Saratoga. That victory made it easier for France to enter upon an alliance with the United States, for which Franklin and the comte de Vergennes (the French foreign minister) signed (1778) a treaty. Spain entered the war against Great Britain in 1779, but Spanish help did little for the United States, while French soldiers and sailors and especially French supplies and money were of crucial importance. The warfare had meanwhile shifted from the quiescent North to other theaters. George Rogers CLARK by his daring exploits (1778–79) in the West, climaxed by the second capture of Vincennes, established the revolutionists' prestige on the frontier. Gen. John SULLIVAN led an expedition (1779) against the British and Indians in upper New York. The chief fighting, however, was in the South. The British had taken Savannah in 1778. In 1780, Sir Henry Clinton attacked and took Charleston (which had resisted attacks in 1776 and 1779) and sent Gen. Charles CORNWALLIS off on the CAROLINA CAMPAIGN. Cornwallis swept forward to beat Horatio Gates soundly at Camden (Aug., 1780), and only guerrilla bands under Francis MARION, Andrew PICKENS, and Thomas SUMTER continued to oppose the British S of Virginia. Another low point had been reached in American fortunes. Bitter complaints of the inefficiency of the Congress, political conniving, lack of funds and food, and the strains of long-continued war had increased widespread apathy and disaffection, and the British tried to take advantage of the division among the people. In 1780 occurred the most celebrated of the disaffections, the treason of Benedict ARNOLD. Lack of pay and shortages of clothing and food drove some Continental regiments into a mutiny of protest in Jan., 1781. The dark, however, was already lifting. A crowd of frontiersmen with their rifles defeated a British force at Kings Mt. in Oct., 1780, and Nathanael GREENE, who had replaced Gates as commander in the Carolina campaign, and his able assistant, Daniel MORGAN, together with Thaddeus KOSCIUSKO and others, ultimately forced Cornwallis into Virginia. The stage was set for the YORKTOWN CAMPAIGN. Now the French aid counted greatly, for Lafayette with colonial troops held the British in check, and it was a Franco-American force that Washington and the comte de ROCHAMBEAU led from New York S to Virginia. The French fleet under Admiral de GRASSE played the decisive part. Previously naval forces had been of little consequence in the Revolution. State navies and a somewhat irregular national navy had been of less importance than Revolutionary privateers. Esek HOPKINS had led a raid in the Bahamas in 1776, John BARRY won a name as a gallant commander, and John Paul JONES was one of the most celebrated commanders in all U.S. naval history, but their exploits were single incidents. It was the French fleet—ironically the same one defeated by the British under Admiral Rodney the next year in the West Indies—which bottled up Cornwallis at Yorktown. Outnumbered and surrounded, the British commander surrendered (Oct. 17–19, 1781), and the fighting was over. The rebels had won the American Revolution. The Treaty of Paris (see PARIS, TREATY OF) formally recognized the new nation in 1783, although many questions were left unsettled. The United States was floundering through a postwar depression and seeking not too successfully to meet its administrative problems under the Articles of Confederation (see CONFEDERATION, ARTICLES OF). The leaders in the new country were those prominent either in the council halls or on the fields of the Revolution, and the first three Presidents after the Constitution of the United States was adopted were Washington, Adams, and Jefferson. Some of the more radical Revolutionary leaders were disappointed in the turn toward conservatism when the Revolution was over, but liberty and democracy had been fixed as the highest ideals of the United States. The American Revolution had a great influence on liberal thought throughout Europe. The struggles and successes of this youthful democracy were much in the minds of those who brought about the French Revolution, and most assuredly later helped to inspire revolutionists in Spain's American colonies. Naturally the stirring events of the birth of the country have been often represented in U.S. literature. It has given dramatic material to playwrights from William Dunlap to Maxwell Anderson, to novelists from James Fenimore Cooper and William G. Simms to S. Weir Mitchell, Paul Leicester Ford, and Kenneth Roberts. Older histories, still read for their literary value, are those of George Bancroft, John Fiske, and G. O. Trevelyan. Countless excellent studies have been made of particular aspects and incidents; some examples are H. E. Wildes, *Valley Forge* (1938); R. B. Morris, ed., *The Era of the American Revolution* (1939); Carl Van Doren, *Secret History of the American Revolution* (1941) and *Mutiny in January* (1943); Lynn Montross, *Rag, Tag and Bobtail: The Story of the Continental Army* (1952); Carl Berger, *Broadsides and Bayonets: The Propaganda War of the American Revolution* (1961). For works of more general interest, see C. H. McIlwain, *The American Revolution: A Constitutional Interpretation* (1923, repr. 1973); J. F. Jameson, *The American Revolution Considered as a Social Movement* (1926, new ed. 1961); J. C. Miller, *Origins of the American Revolution* (1943, new ed. 1959); C. R. Ritcheson, *British Politics and the American Revolution* (1954); L. H. Gipson, *The Coming of the Revolution* ("New American Nation" series, 1954); E. S. Morgan, *The Birth of the Republic, 1763–89* (1956); Henry Steele Commager and R. B. Morris, ed., *Spirit of 'Seventy-Six* (1958); Samuel Flagg Bemis, *The Diplomacy of the American Revolution* (rev. ed. 1957); Howard Peckham, *The War for Independence* (1958); R. R. Palmer, *The Age of the Democratic Revolution* (1959); J. B. Mitchell, *Decisive Battles of the American Revolution* (1962); Bernard Bailyn, *The Ideological Origins of the American Revolution* (1967); Richard Morris, *The American Revolution Reconsidered* (1967); J. P. Greene, ed. *The Reinterpretation of the American Revolution* (1968); Merrill Jensen, *The Founding of a Nation* (1968); J. R. Alden, *A History of the American Revolution* (1969); W. C. Stinchcombe, *The American Revolution and the French Alliance* (1969); G. S. Wood, *The Creation of the American Republic, 1776–1787* (1969); Don Higginbotham, *The War of American Independence* (1971); Richard Morris, ed., *The American Revolution, 1763–1783* (1971); Pauline Maier, *From Resistance to Revolution* (1972); S. G. Kurtz and J. H. Hutson, *Essay on the American Revolution* (1973).

American saddle horse, breed of LIGHT HORSE with great beauty, easy gait, and stamina. Also known as the Kentucky saddler, it was developed from the THOROUGHBRED and MORGAN. It is noted for its tremendous showy action in all gaits, its well-formed, swanlike neck with aristocratic arch, and its uplifted tail. It is most popular as a show horse and possesses an exceptional aptitude for training. It has nevertheless been subjected to a variety of cruelties in order to train it to particular gaits. The breed is characterized by a satin coat of brown, black, or chestnut, often with white face and leg markings. It stands 15 to 16 hands (60–64 in./150–160 cm) high and weighs approximately 1,000 lb (450 kg).

American Samoa, unincorporated territory of the United States (1970 pop. 27,159), comprising the eastern half of the SAMOA island chain in the South Pacific. The group (76 sq mi/197 sq km) consists of six major islands: TUTUILA, the MANU'A group (Ta'u, Ofu, and Olosega), Rose and Sand Islands, and SWAINS ISLAND. PAGO PAGO, the capital, is on Tutuila.

Most of the islands are mountainous, heavily wooded, and surrounded by coral reefs. Subsistence agriculture and the export of canned fish, copra, cocoa, and handicrafts became the mainstays of the economy after the U.S. naval base at Pago Pago closed down in 1951. Nearly all the land is owned by the Polynesian natives, who are considered American nationals, although they do not vote in U.S. elections. American Samoa was defined by a treaty in 1899 between the United States, Great Britain, and Germany, which gave the United States control of all Samoan islands east of long. 171° W. American Samoa was under the jurisdiction of the U.S. Navy Dept. until 1951, at which time administration was transferred to the Dept. of the Interior. Executive power rests in the territorial governor, who is appointed by the Secretary of the Interior. There is a bicameral legislature, consisting of a senate (18 members chosen by county councils), and a house of representatives (20 members elected by popular vote, plus one nonvoting member from Swains Island, which is privately owned). The 1967 constitution gave the legislature power for the first time to appropriate funds from local revenues. There is also an independent judiciary.

American Society for the Prevention of Cruelty to Animals (A.S.P.C.A.), founded (1866) in America by Henry Bergh to shelter homeless animals, to assist farmers in caring for their livestock, and to cooperate with law enforcement agencies in the prosecution of game-law violators. The A.S.P.C.A. is patterned on the English organization, the Royal Society for the Prevention of Cruelty to Animals, founded in 1824 through the efforts of Richard Martin (1754–1834), an Irish member of Parliament. See study by Lloyd Alexander (1964).

American University, at Washington, D.C.; United Methodist; founded by Bishop J. F. Hurst, chartered 1893, opened in 1914. It was at first a graduate school; an undergraduate college was opened in 1925. Programs provide for student research at many government institutions.

American University of Beirut, at Beirut, Lebanon; English language; founded 1866 as Syrian Protestant College, rechartered 1920 as the American Univ. of Beirut. It has faculties of arts and sciences, engineering and architecture, and agricultural sciences as well as schools of medicine, nursing, pharmacy, and public health.

American Veterans Committee (AVC), founded in 1943 as an organization of veterans of World War II. It is now open to veterans of the two world wars, the Korean War, and the Vietnam War. The AVC differs from other veterans' groups in its opposition to benefits for veterans beyond those based on service-incurred disabilities or the needs of readjustment to civilian life ("Citizens first, veterans second"). The AVC's interest is not limited to veterans' affairs; it has been active in supporting civil rights legislation and increased government activity to maintain economic prosperity and expand social welfare programs. It is affiliated with the World Veterans Federation, a Paris-based organization concerned with the maintenance of peace and international cooperation.

American Veterans of World War II and Korea (Amvets), founded 1944, organization of veterans of World War II and the Korean and Vietnam wars. The Amvets had posts in every state by 1947, when Congress granted a national charter to the organization. It is mainly concerned with veterans' benefits and rights.

American water spaniel, breed of medium-sized SPORTING DOG developed in the American Midwest. It stands about 17 in. (43.2 cm) high at the shoulder and weighs between 30 and 40 lb (13.6–18.1 kg). Its dense and closely curled coat ranges in color from solid liver to dark chocolate. A sturdy, muscular dog, the American water spaniel is a versatile scent hunter, flushing, or springing, game birds rather than pointing them. It is a strong swimmer and retrieves both on land and water. It is also used for hunting rabbits and other small animals. See DOG.

Americas, University of the, at Cholula, Mexico; founded 1940 as Mexico City College. The school achieved university status in 1963. It publishes several periodicals, including *The Aztec, The Mayan,* and *Meso-American Notes.*

America's Cup: see SAILING.

americium (ămərĭ'shēəm), synthetic, radioactive chemical element; symbol Am; at. no. 95; mass no. of most stable isotope 243; m.p. about 1000°C; b.p. unknown; sp. gr. 13.67 at 20°C; valence +2, +3, +4, +5, or +6. Americium is a silver-white metal thought to have either a loose-packed cubic or a close-packed double hexagonal crystalline structure. The pure metal has been prepared by reduction of americium trifluoride with barium vapor at about 1100°C. It tarnishes slowly in dry air. Americium-243, the most stable isotope, has a half-life of over 7,000 years. Americium-241, which has a half-life of about 460 years, is more often used in chemical investigations since it is easily prepared in a fairly pure form. Americium is a member of the ACTINIDE SERIES in group IIIb of the PERIODIC TABLE. It was discovered in 1944 by G. T. Seaborg, R. A. James, L. O. Morgan, and A. Ghiorso, who bombarded plutonium-239 with neutrons to form plutonium-241, which decays to form americium-241.

Americus (əmĕr'ĭkəs), city (1970 pop. 16,091), seat of Sumter co., SW Ga.; inc. 1855. It is a manufacturing city, a livestock market, and a processing center for the area's timber, crops (peanuts, corn, cotton), and minerals (kaolin and bauxite). Charles Lindbergh made his first solo flight from Souther Field there. Georgia Southwestern College is in Americus. ANDERSONVILLE is nearby.

Amersfoort (ä'mərsfōrt), city (1971 pop. 78,908), Utrecht prov., central Netherlands. It is a transportation and manufacturing center. Points of interest include a 14th-century water gate, the 15th-century Gate of Our Lady, and the old town, which has medieval houses. Johan van Oldenbarneveldt, the Dutch statesman, was born there in 1547.

Ames, Ezra, 1768–1836, American painter, b. Framingham, Mass. Early in his life he worked as a carriage painter, miniaturist, engraver, and decorator, first in Worcester, Mass., and later in Albany, N.Y., where he settled. His portrait of Governor Clinton of New York (1818; Albany Inst. of History and Art) established his renown as a vigorously realistic portraitist. Among his many skillful likenesses are those of Gouverneur Morris (N.Y. Historical Society) and Stephen van Rensselaer (New York State Historical Association). See monograph by Theodore Bolton and I. F. Cortelyou (1955).

Ames, Fisher, 1758–1808, American political leader, b. Dedham, Mass.; son of Nathaniel Ames. Admitted to the bar in 1781, he began political pamphleteering and by a speech in the Massachusetts convention that ratified the Federal Constitution started on the road to becoming a leading Federalist. As a Congressman (1789–97) and after his retirement he was high in party councils, a staunch follower of Hamilton, and a vicious opponent of Jefferson. Of Ames's able speeches perhaps the best known was that made in 1796 when the House was disposed to nullify Jay's Treaty by withholding appropriations; he spoke for the treaty. He was the archetype of the New England conservative of his period, a strong proponent of order and of the rights of property. See biography by W. E. Bernhard (1965).

Ames, James Barr, 1846–1910, American jurist, b. Boston, grad. Harvard Law School, 1873. At Harvard he became associate professor (1873), professor (1877), and dean (1895). A disciple of C. C. LANGDELL, Ames insisted that legal education should require the study of actual cases instead of abstract principles of law. He was instrumental in introducing the case method in the teaching of law, a method in general use by American law schools at the time of his death. Ames's careful historical and legal scholarship is displayed in his *Lectures on Legal History* (1913).

Ames, Joseph, 1689–1759, English bibliographer. He compiled *Typographical Antiquities* (1749), a valuable list of English books printed before 1600.

Ames, Nathaniel, 1708–64, American almanac maker, b. Bridgewater, Mass. His *Astronomical Diary and Almanack,* begun in 1725 and issued annually after c.1732 from Dedham, Mass., was highly popular and served as a model for Franklin's *Poor Richard's Almanack* and later almanacs. It had a circulation of 60,000 copies. After Ames's death it was continued until 1795 by his son Nathaniel, Jr. The elder Ames was a physician and also after 1750 landlord of the Sun Tavern at Dedham. He was the father of Fisher Ames. See Samuel Briggs, ed., *The Essays, Humor, and Poems of Nathaniel Ames* (1891, repr. 1969).

Ames, Oakes, 1804–73, American manufacturer, railroad promoter, and politician, b. Easton, Mass. With his brother Oliver he managed the family's well-known shovel factory at Easton. The business grew under demands from the expanding Midwest frontier and the Western gold diggings. Active in founding the Republican party in Massachusetts, Ames served in the U.S. House of Representatives from 1863 to 1873. Interested in the construction of the Union Pacific RR, Ames secured control of the CRÉDIT MOBILIER OF AMERICA after ousting T. C. DURANT, its founder. The financial scandals of that company brought upon Ames in 1872 public disgrace and the censure of Congress.

Ames, city (1970 pop. 39,505), Story co., central Iowa, on the Skunk River; inc. 1870. Its chief manufactures are electronic equipment and water-analysis and water-treatment equipment. Iowa State Univ. of Science and Technology is located in Ames and contributes significantly to the economy. The National Animal Disease Laboratory and the Iowa State Center, a large cultural, educational, and athletic complex, are also in the city.

Amesbury, rural district (1971 pop. 27,611), Wiltshire, S central England. There are British remains that predate the Roman occupation. In 980 the widow of King Edgar founded Amesbury Abbey, where Queen Guinevere of Arthurian legend is believed to have died. STONEHENGE, the chief megalithic monument in Britain, is nearby.

Amesbury, town (1970 pop. 11,388), Essex co., NE Mass., on the Merrimack River; inc. 1668. Rubber, metal, and vinyl products are manufactured. John Greenleaf Whittier lived there most of his life, and his house is preserved. Josiah Bartlett was born in Amesbury.

amethopterin (ăm"əthŏp'tərĭn), drug used in halting the growth of actively proliferating tissues, e.g., the malignant cells associated with several forms of leukemia. By binding to an ENZYME that controls the metabolism of folic acid, amethopterin interferes with synthesis of NUCLEIC ACIDS and therefore with tissue cell reproduction. It is sold under the trade name Methotrexate.

amethyst (ăm'əthĭst) [Gr.,=non-drunkenness], variety of QUARTZ, violet to purple in color, used as a gem. It is the most highly valued of the semiprecious quartzes. It is associated with a number of superstitions, being regarded as a love charm, as a potent influence in improving sleep, and as a protection against thieves and drunkenness. Brazil, Uruguay, Sri Lanka, Siberia, and parts of North America are important sources of supply. The so-called Oriental amethyst, or purple sapphire, is not quartz but a variety of corundum, a much harder and rarer stone.

Amharic (ămhâr'ĭk), language of Ethiopia belonging to the South Ethiopic group of Ethiopian Semitic languages, which, in turn, belong to the Southeast Semitic subdivision of the Semitic subfamily of the Hamito-Semitic family of languages (see HAMITO-SEMITIC LANGUAGES). The official tongue of Ethiopia since the 14th cent., Amharic is spoken by about 7 million people in that country. Amharic employs a modification of the Ethiopic script (see ETHIOPIC). The earliest extant texts in Amharic go back to the 14th cent. Amharic has been considerably influenced in its grammar and vocabulary by the nearby Cushitic tongues. See Wolf Leslau, *Amharic Textbook* (1968); Charles A. Ferguson, *The Ethiopian Language Area* (1971).

Amherst, Jeffrey Amherst, Baron (ăm'ərst), 1717–97, British army officer. He served in the War of the Austrian Succession and in the early part of the Seven Years War. In 1758 he was sent to America as a major general to lead the Louisburg campaign in the last of the French and Indian Wars. The capture (1758) of the French fortress gave Britain her first important victory in the war, and Amherst replaced James Abercromby as supreme commander in America. The next year (1759), pushing northward from Albany, he took Crown Point and Ticonderoga, but he arrived too late to help General Wolfe take Quebec. He directed (1760) the capture of Montreal and returned (1763) to England. In the American Revolution, Amherst refused to command British troops in New England, but in 1778 he became commander in chief of home defenses. Amherst, for whom Amherst College is named, was created baron in 1776 and was made a field marshal in 1796. See his journal (ed. by J. C. Webster, 1931); biography by J. C. Long (1933).

Amherst, town (1971 pop. 9,966), N central N.S., Canada. Amherst is an industrial center. Its products include steel, aircraft parts, clothing, luggage, and insulating materials. Nearby are salt beds. Across the border in New Brunswick is Fort Beausejour National Historic Park. Sir Charles Tupper, the Canadian statesman, was born in Amherst.

Amherst, town (1970 pop. 26,331), Hampshire co., W Mass., in a fertile farm area; inc. 1759. Named for Lord Jeffrey Amherst, it is a lovely, tree-lined college town. Emily Dickinson was born and lived there all her life. Helen Hunt Jackson was also born there, and Ray Stannard Baker, Eugene Field, Robert Frost, and Noah Webster lived in the town. It is the seat of the Univ. of Massachusetts, Hampshire College, and AMHERST COLLEGE.

Amherstburg, town (1971 pop. 5,169), S Ont., Canada, on the Detroit River. It is the site of Fort Malden National Historic Park. Fort Malden was built (1797–99) to replace the post lost when Detroit was ceded to the United States.

Amherst College, at Amherst, Mass.; for men; founded 1821. A liberal arts institution, Amherst maintains a cooperative program with Smith College, Mount Holyoke College, Hampshire College, and the Univ. of Massachusetts.

Ami (ā'mī), servant of Solomon whose descendants came out of exile. Ezra 2.57. Amon: Neh. 7.59.

Amici, Giovanni Battista (jōvän'nē bät-tēs'tä ämē'chē), 1786–1863, Italian astronomer, mathematician, and naturalist. He became director of the observatory and professor of anatomy at Florence and published papers on various scientific subjects. His most important work was in designing and improving physical and astronomical apparatus, especially the microscope and reflecting telescope.

Amida (ăm'īdə, əmī'də), ancient city, E Asia Minor, on the Tigris River. It became (A.D. 230) a Roman colony and was later (4th cent.) captured by Shapur II of Persia. It is the modern DIYARBAKIR, Turkey.

Amidas, Philip: see AMADAS, PHILIP.

amide (ăm'īd), organic compound formed by reaction of an acid chloride, acid anhydride, or ester with an amine. See AMINO GROUP; CARBOXYL GROUP.

Amidism: see PURE LAND BUDDHISM.

Amiel, Henri Frédéric (äNrē' frādārēk' ämyĕl'), 1821–81, Swiss critic. He was unsuccessful and unnoticed during his life, but the posthumous publication of his *Journal intime* (1883, tr. of augmented ed. 1936) aroused great interest. It is a document of scrupulous self-observation. See Van Wyck Brooks, *Malady of the Ideal* (1913).

Amiens (ämyăN'), city (1968 pop. 122,864), capital of Somme dept., N France, in PICARDY, on the Somme River. It is a rail hub and a large market for the truck farming carried on in the surrounding Somme marshlands. Also an important textile center (since the 16th cent.), it has been particularly famous for its velvet. Other products are chemicals, soap, tires, and electrical equipment. Originally a Gallo-Roman town, it was an episcopal see from the 4th cent. The historic capital of Picardy, it was overrun and occupied by many invaders. It was conquered by Henry IV in 1597. There, in 1802, the treaty of Amiens was signed. It was severely devastated in both World Wars and has been rebuilt since 1945, largely in the medieval style. Of interest is the Cathedral of Notre Dame (begun c.1220), the largest Gothic cathedral in France. It is 470 ft (143 m) long and has a nave 140 ft (43 m) high; the transept dates from the 14th cent.; the spire (370 ft/113 m high) and the large rose window were added in the 16th cent.

Amiens, Treaty of, 1802, peace treaty signed by France, Spain, and the BATAVIAN REPUBLIC on the one hand and Great Britain on the other. It is generally regarded as marking the end of the FRENCH REVOLUTIONARY WAR and setting the stage for the Napoleonic Wars (see NAPOLEON I). By its terms England was to give up most conquests made in the wars and France was to evacuate Naples and restore Egypt to the Ottoman Empire. England retained Ceylon and Trinidad but abandoned its claim to the French throne. The peace, though much acclaimed, lasted barely a year; in 1803, England refused to restore Malta to the Knights Hospitalers, thereby causing a resumption of hostilities.

Amin, Idi (ē'dē amēn'), c.1925–, Ugandan political leader, president of Uganda (1971–). He advanced in the Ugandan armed forces from private (1946) to commander in chief (1966). He seized political power in 1971, toppling the regime of Milton Obote, and soon established dictatorial control. In 1972 he ordered the expulsion of most of Uganda's Asians. He was often at odds with Uganda's neighbors, accusing them of plotting against him.

Aminadab, variant of AMMINADAB.

amine (əmēn', ăm'ēn): see under AMINO GROUP.

amino acid (əmē'nō), any one of a class of simple organic compounds containing carbon, hydrogen, oxygen, nitrogen, and in certain cases sulfur. These

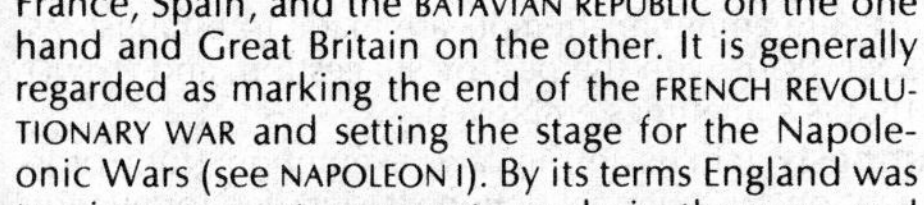

General formula of an amino acid

compounds are distinguished by the presence of two characteristic groups of atoms known as the carboxyl group (COOH) and the amino group

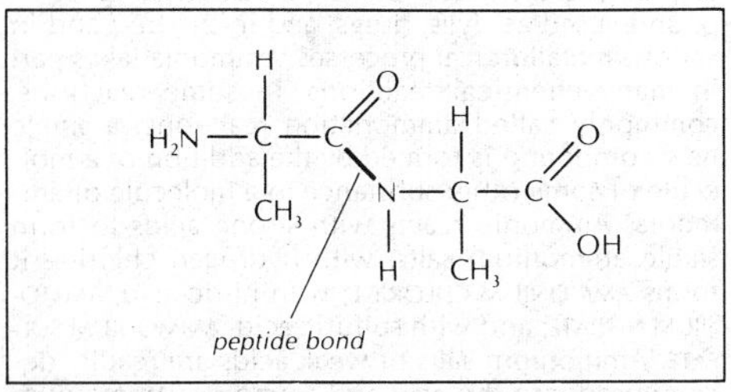

peptide bond

Peptide bond between two molecules of the amino acid alanine

(NH_2). The amino group is said to be α to the carboxyl group when both groups are attached to the same carbon atom. The 22 α-amino acids commonly found in animals are ALANINE, ARGININE, ASPARAGINE, ASPARTIC ACID, CYSTEINE, GLUTAMIC ACID, GLUTAMINE, GLYCINE, HISTIDINE, HYDROXYLYSINE, HYDROXYPROLINE, ISOLEUCINE, LEUCINE, LYSINE, METHIONINE, PHENYLALANINE, PROLINE, SERINE, THREONINE, TRYPTOPHAN, TYROSINE, and VALINE. More than 100 less common amino acids also occur in biological systems, particularly in plants. Every amino acid except glycine can occur as either of two optically active stereoisomers, D or L; the more common ISOMER in nature is the L-form. When the carboxyl carbon atom of one amino acid covalently binds to the amino nitrogen atom of another amino acid with the release of a water molecule, a peptide bond is formed. Two or more amino acids thus linked are known as a peptide. When 2 to 10 amino acids are thus joined in a chain, the resultant molecule is known as an oligopeptide. A chain of more than 10 amino acids can usually be called a polypeptide, and a chain of about 50 or more, a PROTEIN. The chemical and indeed physiological characteristics of a given oligopeptide, polypeptide, or protein are completely determined by the sequence and interactions of its constituent amino acids. Amino acids are released in the intestinal tract by the digestion of food proteins and are then carried in the blood stream to the body cells, where they are used for growth, maintainance, and repair. During cellular anabolism amino acids are linked to form oligopeptides, polypeptides, and proteins; the amino acid sequences of the latter are determined by NUCLEIC ACIDS. Cellular catabolism breaks amino acids down into smaller fragments. Many of the amino acids necessary in metabolism can be synthesized in the human or animal body when needed; these are called nonessential. Others cannot be synthesized in sufficient quantities; these are termed essential and must be provided in the diet.

amino group, in chemistry, FUNCTIONAL GROUP that consists of a nitrogen atom attached by single bonds to hydrogen atoms, ALKYL GROUPS, ARYL GROUPS, or a combination of these three. An organic compound that contains an amino group is called an **amine**. Amines are derivatives of the inorganic compound AMMONIA, NH_3. When one, two, or all three of the hydrogens in ammonia are replaced by an alkyl or aryl group, the resulting compound is known as a primary, secondary, or tertiary amine, respectively. Like ammonia, the amines are weak bases because the unshared electron pair of the nitrogen atom can form a coordinate bond with a proton (see CHEMICAL BOND). Amines will react with a mineral acid to form an amine salt, e.g., with hydrochloric acid to form an amine hydrochloride. A water-insoluble amine can be made to dissolve by adding acid to form its water-soluble amine salt. Amines react similarly with alkyl halides to form alkyl ammonium salts. Amines can be synthesized by reacting ammonia with an alkyl halide and neutralizing the resulting alkyl ammonium salt with an alkali, e.g., sodium hydroxide. This procedure yields a mixture of primary, secondary, and tertiary amines that is easily separated into its three components by fractional distillation. Amines can also be prepared by the reaction of ammonia with an alcohol or by the reduction of any of a variety of compounds containing nitrogen in a higher oxidation state. Amines take part in many kinds of chemical reactions; in particular, they can react with an acid chloride, acid anhydride, or ester to form an amide. All reactions of amines involve bonding of an electron-deficient atom to the amino nitrogen through its unshared electron pair. The most important amine is ANILINE, an aromatic amine.

Aminopterin: see METABOLITE.

Amiot, Joseph: see AMYOT, JOSEPH.

Amis, Kingsley, 1922–, English novelist. His first and best-known novel, *Lucky Jim* (1953), a brilliant comic satire on academic life, classified him as one of England's ANGRY YOUNG MEN. His cultural and social disillusionment, always well laced with a fine sense of comedy, is also apparent in *That Certain Feeling* (1955), *Take a Girl Like You* (1960), and *Ending Up* (1974). Of Amis's other novels *The Anti-Death League* (1966) and *Colonel Sun: A James Bond Adventure* (1968) are espionage novels, while *The Green Man* (1969) is a ghost story, *Girl, 20* (1971) a comedy, and *The Riverside Villas Murder* (1973), a mystery. In addition to several volumes of poetry, Amis has published numerous nonfiction works, including *Socialism and the Intellectuals* (1957), *What Became of Jane Austen?* (1970), and *On Drink* (1972). Amis's wife, **Elizabeth Jane Howard,** 1923–, is also a novelist. Among her works are *The Beautiful Visit* (1950), *After Julius* (1965), and *Odd Girl Out* (1971).

Amish Church: see MENNONITES.

Amistad National Recreation Area: see NATIONAL PARKS AND MONUMENTS (table).

Amisus: see SAMSUN.

amitosis: see MITOSIS.

Amittai (āmĭt'āī), father of Jonah. Jonah 1.1.

Ammah (ăm'ə), hill near Gibeon. 2 Sam. 2.24.

Amman (ämän'), city (1970 est. pop. 570,000), capital of Jordan, N central Jordan, on the Jabbok (Wadi Zerka) River. Jordan's largest city and industrial and commercial heart, it is also a transportation hub, especially for pilgrims en route to Mecca. Amman, which is built on a series of hills and valleys, is noted for its locally quarried colored marble. Industries include the manufacture of textiles, leather and leather goods, cement, marble, tiles, flour, and tobacco products. On a site occupied since prehistoric times, Amman is the biblical Rabbah, or Rabbath-Ammon, capital of the Ammonites. It was conquered by King David in the 11th cent. B.C. but regained independence under Solomon (Deut. 3.11; Joshua 13.25; 15.60; 2 Sam. 11.1; 12.26–29; 17.27; 1 Chron. 20.1; Jer. 49.2,3; Ezek. 21.20; 25.5; Amos 1.14). The city was taken by Assyria in the 8th cent. B.C. and by Antiochus III c.218 B.C. Ptolemy II Philadelphus named it Philadelphia, by which it was known throughout the Roman and Byzantine periods. It belonged to the Decapolis, a commercial league of free cities organized in the 1st cent. B.C. It was also a leading city of Rome's Arabian provinces. After the Arab conquest of 635, the city, which then became known as Amman, experienced a steady decline; it was only a small village when Emir Abdullah (later king) made it the capital of newly created Trans-Jordan in 1921. Growth was particularly rapid after World War II, when Amman absorbed refugees from Palestine. The city is the site of the Univ. of Jordan (est. 1962) and a Muslim college. Historical monuments include a Roman amphitheater (1st cent. B.C.), remains of a temple that was probably built by Hercules, and some tombs and a section of wall that date to the 9th or 8th cent. B.C. Amman suffered some damage during the civil war in Jordan in 1970.

Ammanati, Bartolomeo (bärtōlōmĕ'ō äm-mänä'tē), 1511–92, Italian sculptor and architect. He studied under Bandinelli in Florence and assisted Jacopo Sansovino in his work on the Library of St. Mark's, Venice. Ammanati, whose style was greatly influenced by Michelangelo's Medici tombs, made a colossal statue of Hercules, at Padua. In Rome he collaborated with Vignola and Vasari in their work at the villa of Pope Julius III. His best work here was in the Ruspoli Palace and in the court of the Collegio Romano. Returning to Florence in 1557, he became architect to Cosimo de' Medici. He made the Santa Trinita bridge over the Arno and a number of fountains, among them the Neptune fountain for the Piazza della Signoria. He built the court facade of Pitti Palace, the Guigni Palace, and a cloister of Santo Spirito. Pious in his old age, he wrote a recantation of his secular work and destroyed some of it. The poet Laura Battiferri was his wife.

Ammann, Othmar Hermann (ōt'mär, ō'mŏn), 1879–1965, American civil engineer, b. Switzerland, grad. Federal Polytechnic Institute, Zurich, 1902. He came to the United States in 1904 and was naturalized in 1924. He served (1925–39) with the Port of New York Authority and was its director of engineers from 1937 to 1939. An authority on bridges, he participated in either the designing or the construction of Hell Gate, George Washington, Triborough, Bronx-Whitestone, and Verrazano-Narrows (at its opening in 1964, the longest and heaviest suspension bridge in the world) bridges in New York City, and San Francisco's Golden Gate Bridge.

ammeter (ăm'mē″tər), instrument used to measure the magnitude of an electric current in amperes or units that are multiples or fractions of amperes. An ammeter is usually combined with a voltmeter and an ohmmeter in a multipurpose instrument. Most ammeters are based on the d'Arsonval GALVANOMETER and are of the analog type, i.e., they give current values that can vary over a continuous range as indicated by a scale and pointer. However, digital ammeters, which provide current values that are composed of a group of digits, are becoming increasingly common.

Ammi (ăm'ī), figurative name of Israel after reconciliation with God. Hosea 2.1. See LOAMMI.

Ammianus Marcellinus (ămēā'nəs märsĭlī'nəs), c.330–c.400, Roman historian, b. Antioch. After retiring from a successful military career, he wrote a history of the Roman Empire as a sequel to that of Tacitus, his model. The history, in 31 books, covered the years from A.D. 96 to 378; only Books XIV–XXXI, covering the years A.D. 353–78, survive. Though written in an extremely rhetorical style, his work is reliable and impartial, and his literary ability has been highly esteemed by modern scholars. A pagan and an admirer of Julian the Apostate, Ammianus was not prejudiced against Christianity. See E. A. Thompson, *Historical Work of Ammianus Marcellinus* (1947); *Ammianus Marcellinus* (his work tr. by J. C. Rolfe 1935, repr. 1963).

Ammiel (ăm'ēĕl). **1** Spy. Num. 13.12. **2** Father of MACHIR **2**. **3** Porter of the Temple. 1 Chron. 26.5. **4** See ELIAM **1**.

Ammihud (ăm'ĭhəd, əmī'həd). **1** Ancestor of Joshua. Num. 1.10; 2.18; 7.48,53; 10.22; 1 Chron. 7.26. **2** Simeonite. Num. 34.20. **3** Naphtalite. Num. 34.28. **4** Judahite. 1 Chron. 9.4. **5** Father of a king of Geshur. 2 Sam. 13.37.

Amminadab (əmĭn'ədăb). **1** Aaron's father-in-law. Ex. 6.23; Num. 1.7; 2.3; 7.12; 10.14; Ruth 4.19,20; 1 Chron. 2.10. Aminadab: Mat. 1.4; Luke 3.33. **2** Head of a Levitical family. 1 Chron. 15.10–12. **3** The same as IZEHAR.

Ammi-nadib (ăm″ĭnā'dĭb, əmĭn'ədĭb), word of uncertain significance. Cant. 6.12.

Ammishaddai (ăm″ĭshăd'āī), Danite, father of AHIEZER **1**. Num. 1.12; 2.25; 7.66,71; 10.25.

Ammizabad (əmĭz'əbăd), son of BENAIAH **1**. 1 Chron. 27.6.

Ammon (ăm'ən), in the Bible, people living E of the Dead Sea. Their capital was Rabbath-Ammon, the present-day Amman (Jordan). Their god was Milcom, to whom Solomon built an altar. 1 Kings 11.5; 2 Kings 23.13. A Semitic people, they flourished from the 13th cent. B.C. to the 8th cent. B.C. and were then absorbed by the Arabs. Excavations in Jordan show that they had a highly developed kingdom. They were hostile to the Hebrews, to whom they were related. The ancestor for whom they were named was Lot's son Ben-Ammi. Gen. 19.38; Deut. 2.19,20,37; 23.3,4; Judges 3.13; 1 Sam. 11; 2 Sam. 10–12; 2 Chron. 20; Neh. 2.10; 4.7; Jer. 49.1–6.

Ammon, Egyptian god: see AMON.

ammonia, chemical compound, NH_3, colorless gas that is about one half as dense as air at ordinary temperatures and pressures. It has a characteristic pungent, penetrating odor. It is extremely soluble in water; one volume of water dissolves about 1,200 volumes of the gas at 0°C (90 grams of ammonia in 100 cc of water), but only about 700 volumes at room temperature and still less at higher temperatures. The solution is alkaline because much of the dissolved ammonia reacts with water, H_2O, to form ammonium hydroxide, NH_4OH, a weak BASE. The ammonia sold for household use is a dilute water solution of ammonia in which ammonium hydroxide is the active cleansing agent. It should be used with caution since it can attack the skin and eyes. The vapors are especially irritating—prolonged exposure and inhalation cause serious injury and may be fatal. Water solutions of ammonia are also called ammonium hydrate, aqua ammonia, or ammonia water; the solution may contain up to 30% ammonium hydroxide by weight at room temperature and pressure. Ammonia solutions are used to clean, bleach, and deodorize; to etch aluminum; to saponify oils and fats; and in chemical manufacture. Anhydrous (water-free) ammonia gas is easily liquefied under pressure (at 20°C liquid ammonia has a vapor pressure of about 120 lb per sq in.). It is used in REFRIGERATION because the liquid absorbs a relatively large amount of heat when it evaporates. The major use of ammonia and its compounds is as FERTILIZERS. Ammonia is also used in large amounts in the OSTWALD PROCESS for the synthesis of nitric acid; in the SOLVAY PROCESS for the synthesis of sodium carbonate; in the synthesis of numerous organic compounds used as dyes, drugs, and in plastics; and in various metallurgical processes. Ammonia takes part in many chemical reactions. In some reactions, commonly called ammonation reactions, a single new compound is formed by the addition of a molecule of some other substance to a molecule of ammonia. Ammonia reacts with strong acids to form stable ammonium salts: with hydrogen chloride it forms AMMONIUM CHLORIDE; with nitric acid, AMMONIUM NITRATE; and with sulfuric acid, AMMONIUM SULFATE. Ammonium salts of weak acids are readily decomposed into the acid and ammonia. Ammonium carbonate, $(NH_3)_2CO_3 \cdot H_2O$, is a colorless-to-white crystalline solid commonly known as smelling salts; in water solution it is sometimes called aromatic spirits of ammonia. Ammonia reacts with certain metal ions to form complex ions called ammines. Ammonia also reacts with Lewis acids (electron acceptors), e.g., sulfur dioxide or trioxide or boron trifluoride. Another kind of reaction, commonly called ammonolysis, occurs when one or more of the hydrogen atoms in the ammonia molecule is replaced by some other atom or radical. Chlorine gas, Cl_2, reacts directly with ammonia to form monochloramine, NH_2Cl, and hydrogen chloride, HCl. Products of such ammonolyses include amides, amines, imides, imines, and nitrides. Ammonia also takes part in OXIDATION AND REDUCTION reactions. It burns in oxygen to form nitrogen gas, N_2, and water. In the presence of a catalyst (e.g., platinum) it is oxidized in air to form water and nitric oxide, NO. It reduces hot-metal oxides (e.g., cupric oxide) to the metal. Ammonia forms a minute proportion of the atmosphere; it is found in volcanic gases and as a product of decomposition of animal and vegetable matter. Ammonia is prepared commercially in vast quantities. The major method of production is the HABER PROCESS, in which nitrogen is combined directly with hydrogen at high temperatures and pressures in the presence of a catalyst. It is obtained as a by-product of the destructive distillation of coal. Ammonia is also prepared synthetically by the cyanamide process: nitrogen gas combines with calcium carbide, CaC_2, at high temperatures to form calcium cyanamide, $CaCN_2$, and carbon; the calcium cyanamide reacts with steam to form calcium carbonate, $CaCO_3$, and ammonia. For use in the laboratory, ammonia is prepared by heating an ammonium salt with a strong base. It can also be prepared by reacting a metal nitride with water. Liquid ammonia is used in the chemical laboratory as a solvent. It is a better solvent for ionic and polar compounds than ethanol, but not as good as water; it is a better solvent for nonpolar covalent compounds than water, but not as good as ethanol. It dissolves alkali metals and barium, calcium, and strontium by forming an unstable blue solution containing the metal ion and free electrons that slowly decomposes, releasing hydrogen and forming the metal amide. Compared to water, liquid ammonia is less likely to release protons (H^+ ions), is more likely to take up protons (to form NH_4^+ ions), and is a stronger reducing agent. Because strong acids react with it, it does not allow strongly acidic solutions, but it dissolves many alkalies to form strongly basic solutions. Because ammonia was formerly obtained by destructive distillation of horns and hooves of animals, its water solution was called spirits of hartshorn. Ammonia has also been called alkaline air and volatile alkali.

ammoniac or **gum ammoniac** (əmō'nēăk″), yellowish substance with a sickening, bitter taste, obtained from the milky exudate of the injured stem of a plant (*Dorema ammoniacum*) found in Iran, India, and S Siberia. It is a gum resin, soluble in alcohol and ether. It is used in industry in the manufacture of porcelain cements and in medicine as an expectorant. When gum ammoniac is distilled, it yields a liquid, oil of ammoniac.

ammonite (ăm'ənīt), one of a type of extinct marine CEPHALOPOD mollusk, related to the NAUTILUS and resembling it in having an elaborately coiled and chambered shell. Unlike the interiors of nautilus shells, the chambers of ammonite shells display intricately-shaped septa and sutures. The type included numerous species, which were widely distributed during the Mesozoic era, about 200 million years ago. Ammonites are classified in the phylum MOLLUSCA, class Cephalopoda, subclass Ammonoidea.

ammonium chloride (əmō'nēəm klôr'īd), chemical compound, NH_4Cl, a white or colorless, odorless, water-soluble, cubic crystalline salt with a biting taste, commonly known as sal ammoniac. It is prepared commercially by reacting AMMONIA, NH_3, with hydrogen chloride, HCl, and is used chiefly in the manufacture of electric dry-cell batteries, in soldering fluxes, in textile printing, and in making other compounds. It is also used in certain medical treatments. It occurs in nature in volcanic regions.

ammonium group, in chemistry, a positively charged nitrogen atom joined by single bonds to four other atoms or groups. The simplest ammonium group, NH_4^+, is formed by PROTONATION of AMMONIA, NH_3, e.g., by its reaction with hydrogen chloride, HCl, to form ammonium chloride, NH_4Cl, an ammonium compound. Organic ammonium compounds are formed by the reaction of an alkyl halide with an amine (see AMINO GROUP), for example, ethyl chloride, C_2H_5Cl, reacts with triethylamine, $(C_2H_5)_3N$, to form tetraethyl ammonium chloride, $(C_2H_5)_4N^+Cl^-$. They are also formed by reaction of an amine with a mineral acid or by reaction of an alkyl halide with ammonia.

ammonium nitrate, chemical compound, NH_4NO_3, that exists as colorless, rhombohedral crystals at room temperature but changes to monoclinic crystals when heated above 32°C. It is extremely soluble in water and soluble in alcohol and liquid ammonia. It is prepared commercially by reaction of nitric acid and AMMONIA. Major uses are in FERTILIZERS and EXPLOSIVES. For fertilizers it is in the form of small clay-coated pellets. For explosives it is sometimes mixed with other substances, e.g., TNT, so that it is more easily detonated. It is also used in solid-fuel rocket propellants, in pyrotechnics, and in the production of nitrous oxide.

ammonium sulfate, chemical compound, $(NH_4)_2SO_4$, a colorless-to-gray, rhombohedral crystalline substance that occurs in nature as the mineral mascagnite. It is soluble in water and insoluble in alcohol or liquid ammonia. It is prepared commercially by passing AMMONIA, obtained from destructive distillation of coal, into sulfuric acid and is used as a FERTILIZER, in preparing other ammonium compounds, and for fireproofing.

amnesia [Gr.,=forgetfulness], condition characterized by loss of MEMORY for long or short intervals of time. It may be caused by injury, shock, senility, severe illness, or mental disease. Some cases of amnesia involve the unconscious suppression of a painful experience and everything remindful of it including the individual's identity (see DEFENSE MECHANISM). Retrograde amnesia is loss of memory of events just preceding temporary loss of consciousness, as from head injury; it is evidence that memory proceeds in two stages, short term and long term. One form of the condition known as tropic amnesia, or coast memory, affecting white men in the tropics, is probably a variety of HYSTERIA. APHASIA of the amnesic variety is caused by an organic brain condition and is not to be confused with other forms of amnesia. To cure amnesia, attempts are made to establish ASSOCIATIONS with the past by suggestion, and HYPNOTISM is sometimes employed.

amnesty (ăm'nəstē), in law, exemption from prosecution for criminal action. It signifies forgiveness and the forgetting of past actions. Amnesties are usually extended to a group of persons during a period of prolonged disorder or insurrection. The criminals are offered a promise of immunity from prosecution if they will abandon their unlawful activities. After a revolution or civil war the victorious side will often extend amnesty to the losers; e.g., the United States granted a qualified amnesty to the Confederate forces after the Civil War. An amnesty is distinguished from a PARDON, which is an act of forgiveness after the criminal has already been convicted.

Amnon. **1** David's eldest son. He raped his half sister Tamar and was killed for it by her brother Absalom. 2 Sam. 3.2; 13. **2** Judahite. 1 Chron. 4.20.

amobarbital (ăm″ōbär'bĭtăl), drug that acts as a nervous system DEPRESSANT. See BARBITURATE.

amoeba: see AMEBA.

Amok (ā'mŏk), post-Exilic Jewish family. Neh. 12.7,20.

Amol (āmōl'), city (1966 pop. 40,076), Mazanderan prov., N Iran, near the Caspian Sea. It is an agricultural trade center. Amol was a provincial capital under the Abbasids in the 9th cent.

amole: see SOAP PLANT.

Amon (ā'mŏn). **1** King of Judah, son and successor of Manasseh. He was inattentive to the worship of God, and biblical accounts denounce him strongly. Jeremiah was his contemporary. Amon was murdered, and Josiah succeeded him. 2 Kings 21.19–26;

2 Chron. 33.20-25. **2** Ahab's governor of Samaria. 1 Kings 22.26; 2 Chron. 18.25. **3** See AMI.

Amon (ā'mən, ā'-) or **Ammon** (ă'mən) or **Amen** (ä'mĕn), Egyptian deity. He was originally the chief god of Thebes; he and his wife Mut and their son Khensu were the divine Theban triad of deities. Amon grew increasingly important in Egypt, and eventually he (identified as Amon Ra; see RA) became the supreme deity. He was identified with the Greek Zeus (the Roman Jupiter). Amon's most celebrated shrine was at Siwa in the Libyan desert; the oracle of Siwa later rivaled those of Delphi and Dodona. He is frequently represented as a ram or as a human with a ram's head.

amontillado (əmŏn"tĭlä'dō), dry SHERRY noted for its delicate bouquet, resembling the wine of Montilla, Spain, from which it derives its name. A blend of pale, dry sherries of the *palma* type, it assumes in aging a darker color.

Amor: see EROS.

Amoraim (ä'mōrä'ĭm) [from Heb. *amar*=to interpret], term referring to those Jewish scholars, predominantly in Palestine at Caesarea and Tiberias (A.D. c.200–c.350) and in Babylonia at Sura and Pumbedita (A.D. c.200–c.510), who interpreted the MISHNA and other Tannaitic collections (see TALMUD). They ultimately saw as their chief function the compilation of a final, explanatory text for the HALAKAH. They thus constitute the link between the early tradition of the TANNAIM and their own successors, the Saboraim, who edited the final compilation of the Talmud in the 6th cent. Their authority did not supersede that of the Tannaim, but, as expositors, they were able to make additions to the halakah as contemporary conditions necessitated. These discussions constitute the section of the Talmud known as the Gemara. In addition, they were responsible for much of the nonlegal or aggadic material that appears in the Talmud and in the Midrashim (see MIDRASH). See H. L. Strack, *Introduction to the Talmud and Midrash* (1931); Jacob Neusner, *There We Sat Down* (1972).

Amorites (ăm'ərīts), a people of Canaan. There is evidence of them also in Babylonia, where in the 18th cent. B.C. they established a dynasty at Babylon; their most powerful king was Hammurabi. At the time of Joshua the Amorites were living both E and W of the Dead Sea. They were subdued and gradually absorbed by the Israelites. Gen. 10.16; 14.7; 15.16; Num. 13.29; 21.13,21-32; Deut. 1.4-7; 4.47,48; Joshua 5.1; 10.6.

amortization (ăm"ərtəzā'shən, əmôr'-), reduction, liquidation, or satisfaction of a debt. The term *amortization* may also refer to the sum used for that purpose. The term is commonly used in ascertaining the investment value of securities. Thus, if a security is bought at more than its face value (i.e., at a premium), a part of the premium is periodically charged off in order to bring the value of the security to par at maturity; if the security is bought at less than its face value, the discount is similarly charged off. Paying off a mortgage or any other debt by installments or by a SINKING FUND is amortization. Amortization by paying off a certain number of bonds each year is practiced by public corporations. National governments of limited credit as well as private companies commonly amortize by sinking funds. Governments with stronger credit usually refund debts by issuing new bonds. The satisfying of a debt by a single payment may be termed amortization. Amortization of a fixed asset refers to the DEPRECIATION of a nonmaterial investment over its estimated average life. See H. A. Finney, *Principles of Financial Accounting* (1968).

Amos (ā'məs), book of the Old Testament. Although it is placed third in order of the books of the Minor Prophets, it is chronologically the earliest. The prophet was a shepherd of Tekoa in the southern kingdom of Judah, but he preached in the northern kingdom of Israel under Jeroboam II (reigned c.793–753 B.C.). Israel was at the peak of its political power but was ridden with social injustices; Amos inveighed especially against hypocritical worship, oppression of the poor, and immorality. The book falls into three parts: God's judgment on various Gentile nations and on Judah and Israel (1–2); three sermons on the doom of Israel (3–6); and five visions of destruction (7–9), of which the last promises redemption. The name of another Amos occurs in the genealogy of Luke 3.25. See studies by Erling Hammershaimb (tr. 1970) and H. J. Routtenberg (1971); see also bibliography under OLD TESTAMENT.

Amoy (əmoi') or **Hsia-men** (shēä-mŭn), city (1970 est. pop. 400,000), S Fukien prov., China, on Amoy island, at the mouth of the Chiu-lung River. It has an excellent natural harbor and is connected to the mainland by a railroad (built 1957) that crosses on a dike. Fishing, shipbuilding, and food processing are the major industries; machine tools and chemicals are also manufactured. Opposite Amoy proper, across the inner harbor, is the island of Ku-lang Hsü, the former foreign settlement and a fine residential section. Amoy was one of the earliest seats of European commerce in China, with Portuguese (16th cent.) and Dutch (17th cent.) establishments. It was captured (1841) by the British in the OPIUM WAR and became a TREATY PORT in 1842. It was long a Chinese port of emigration, mainly to SE Asia. Amoy Univ. is there.

Amoz (ā'mŏz), father of the prophet Isaiah. Isa. 1.1.

AMP: see ADENOSINE MONOPHOSPHATE.

ampelopsis (ăm"pĭlŏp'səs) [from Gr.,=looking like a vine], botanically, name for woody ornamental vines of the genus *Ampelopsis*, but from long association also used in horticultural practice for the VIRGINIA CREEPER, BOSTON IVY, and others of related genera of the family Vitaceae (GRAPE family). Species of *Ampelopsis* native to Asia and North America have showy berries of various colors. The pepper-vine (*A. arborea*) is indigenous to the S United States. Ampelopsis is classified in the division MAGNOLIOPHYTA, class Magnoliopsida, order Rhamnales, family Vitaceae.

Ampère, André Marie (ăm'pēr; Fr. äNdrā' mărē' äNpĕr'), 1775–1836, French physicist, mathematician, and natural philosopher. He was professor of mathematics at the École Polytechnique, Paris, and later at the Collège de France. Known for his contributions to electrodynamics, including the formulation of Ampère's law, he confirmed and amplified the work of Oersted on the relationship of electricity and magnetism, and he invented the astatic needle. The ampere was named for him. His writings include *Recueil d'Observations électro-dynamiques* (1822) and *Essai sur la philosophie des sciences* (2 vol., 1834–43, vol. 1 repr. 1838). See his *Correspondance* pub. by L. de Launay (3 vol., 1936–43).

ampere (ăm'pēr), abbr. amp or A, basic unit of electric current. It is the fundamental electrical unit used with the MKS SYSTEM of units of the METRIC SYSTEM. The ampere is officially defined as the current in a pair of equally long, parallel, straight wires 1 meter apart that produces a force of 0.0000002 newton (2×10^{-7} N) between the wires for each meter of their length. Current meters such as ammeters and galvanometers are calibrated in reference to a current balance that actually measures the force between two wires. Until 1948 the ampere was defined as the flow of 1 COULOMB of charge per second, the coulomb being then considered the fundamental unit. The old (International) ampere equals 0.999835 new (absolute) ampere. The milliampere (ma), equal to one-thousandth of an ampere, and the microampere (μa), equal to one-millionth of an ampere, are units often used in measuring small currents.

amphetamine (ămfĕt'əmēn), any one of a group of drugs that are powerful central nervous system STIMULANTS. Amphetamines have stimulating effects opposite to the effects of DEPRESSANTS such as alcohol, NARCOTICS, and BARBITURATES. They raise the blood pressure by causing the body to release EPINEPHRINE, postpone the need for sleep, and can reverse, partially and temporarily, the effects of fatigue. Amphetamines enhance mental alertness and the ability to concentrate, and also cause wakefulness, euphoria, and talkativeness. They have been used for short periods of time in weight-control programs to suppress appetite; in conjunction with some forms of psychotherapy to treat chronic alcoholism; and to treat narcolepsy and certain psychological disorders such as depression. They were used as vasoconstrictors in inhalant therapy to shrink nasal mucous membranes in such conditions as nasal allergies and asthma; now such inhalants have been banned because of their toxicity. Amphetamines have been thought to have a calming effect on some hyperactive children; the use of these drugs to treat such children has been very controversial. Amphetamines are potent drugs that can produce severe systemic effects, including cardiac irregularities and gastric disturbances. Popularly known as bennies, speed, or uppers, they are also addictive and easily abused: users can become psychologically dependent on the drugs and, by developing tolerance for them, can require increasingly large doses (see DRUG ADDICTION AND DRUG ABUSE). Chronic use often results in insomnia, hyperactivity, and irritability. Amphetamine-induced psychosis often mimics schizophrenia. Amphetamine addiction has been common among such diverse groups as truck drivers, students, and athletes, who have used the drugs for increased energy, alertness, or endurance. Addiction to amphetamines can result in psychosis or death from overexhaustion or cardiac arrest. Benzedrine is the trade name for the drug amphetamine; dextroamphetamine is marketed as Dexedrine. Methamphetamine, a potent stimulant marketed as Desoxyn, is the most rapidly acting amphetamine.

Amphiaraüs (ăm"fēərā'əs), in Greek legend, a prophet, one of the ill-fated SEVEN AGAINST THEBES. He foresaw the disaster of the expedition, but his wife, Eriphyle, bribed by Polynices with the magic necklace of Harmonia, compelled him to go. Before setting out he commanded his sons, Alcmaeon and Amphilochus, to avenge his death on Eriphyle and to make a second expedition against Thebes. Amphiaraüs also was one of the Argonauts.

amphibian, in aviation: see SEAPLANE.

amphibian, in zoology, cold-blooded VERTEBRATE animal of the class Amphibia. There are three living orders of amphibians: the FROGS and TOADS (order Anura, or Salientia), the SALAMANDERS and NEWTS (order Urodela, or Caudata), and the CAECILIANS, or limbless amphibians (order Apoda, or Gymnophiona), a little known tropical group. Amphibians, the most primitive of the terrestrial vertebrates, are intermediate in evolutionary position between the FISH and the REPTILES. Typically they undergo a metamorphosis from an aquatic, water-breathing, limbless larva (called a tadpole) to a terrestrial or partly terrestrial, air-breathing, four-legged adult. The eggs are usually deposited in water or in a protected place where their moisture will be conserved; they have neither shells nor the sets of membranes that surround the eggs of reptiles and other higher vertebrates. Some amphibians lay their eggs in dry places, and the young undergo the larval stage within the egg, emerging as small adults; in these the eggs have evolved various protective structures. Adult amphibians differ from reptiles in having moist skins, without scales or with small, hidden scales. All living amphibians are specialized for their way of life, none representing the main amphibian stock from which the reptiles evolved. The salamanders and newts are superficially the most similar to ancestral amphibians, having long tails and front and hind legs of approximately equal size. Frogs and toads are highly modified for jumping, with large, muscular hind legs and no tails, while the caecilians have lost all external traces of limbs.

amphibious warfare (ămfĭb'ēəs), employment of a combination of land and sea forces to take or defend a military objective. The general strategy is very ancient and was extensively employed by the Greeks, e.g., in the Athenian attack on Sicily in 415 B.C. The term is, however, of modern coinage. It is sometimes applied to the joint operations of the Allied army and naval forces in the disastrous Gallipoli campaign (1915) of World War I. Amphibious warfare was widely employed in World War II. When the Japanese entered the war on a large scale in Dec., 1941, they used combined air, land, and naval operations to capture strategic islands such as the Philippines, Java, and Sumatra. However, the Japanese landings, like the Allied landing in N Africa (Nov., 1942), encountered little opposition and did not offer a true illustration of the problems of amphibious warfare. The problem faced by the Allies in the reconquest of Europe and the Pacific islands was how to land their forces on a heavily defended coast line. It was solved by the construction of special vessels called landing craft that were seaworthy and yet capable of allowing tanks and infantry to emerge without difficulty into shallow water for landing. The typical Allied amphibious operation consisted of heavy and continued air and naval bombardment of the enemy defenses, followed by a landing of troops with complete equipment from landing craft; the landing forces were supported in the early stages by naval guns until land artillery could come into action. By use of this method the Allies were able to invade heavily defended Pacific islands such as Tarawa (1943) and Saipan (1944), Iwo Jima (1945), and Okinawa (1945). In Europe the Allies made landings on Sicily (1943) and Italy (1943–44), but the most spectacular example of amphibious warfare was the invasion of Normandy by the Allies from England on June 6, 1944 (see NORMANDY CAMPAIGN). That action was a prime example of combined movements of naval craft, land forces, and aircraft (used for offense, protection of other forces, and transport). The U.S. invasion of Inchon (1950) during the Korean War and the British and French invasion of Egypt during the Sinai crisis (1957) utilized the same basic tactics. More recently research has been conducted to evolve practical amphibious technique for nuclear warfare. See J. A. Isely and P. A. Crowl, *The U.S. Marines and Amphibious War* (1951); Bernard Fergusson, *The Watery Maze: The Story of Combined Operations* (1961).

amphibole (ăm'fəbōl''), any of a group of widely distributed rock-forming minerals, magnesium-iron silicates, often with traces of calcium, aluminum, sodium, titanium, and other elements. The amphibole minerals are closely related in crystal structure, but they crystallize in two different systems, orthorhombic and monoclinic; their close structural relationship is reflected in uniform prism angles of about 56° and 124° and in good cleavages parallel to these prisms. They are commonly green to black, but may be colorless, white, yellow, blue, or brown. The amphibole minerals are found both in igneous and metamorphic rocks. The commonest form is hornblende; other species include anthophyllite, cummingtonite, tremolite, actinolite, riebeckite, and glaucophane. A variety of jade, called nephrite, consists of actinolite in a finely fibrous form.

amphictyony (ămfĭk'tēō''nē, -ō''nē, -ənē''), in ancient Greece, a league connected with maintaining a temple or shrine. There were a number of these, but by far the most important was the Great Amphictyony or Delphic Amphictyony, a league originally of 12 tribes. It had meetings in the spring at the temple of Demeter at Anthela near Thermopylae and in the autumn at Delphi. The Amphictyonic Council passed legislation regarding religious matters and had power to declare a sacred war against an offender. Each tribe had two votes. By the 6th cent. B.C. the religious organization had begun to have political influence. The greater city-states, by using pressure on the lesser, got control of more tribal votes and were able to control laws and policy. The significance of the Amphictyonic Council was shown by Philip II of Macedon, who, after managing to get on the council by securing the votes of the Phocians, used sacred wars as a pretext for furthering his conquests in Greece. This one large unifying organization, therefore, in the end had no real unifying power in divided Greece. The Great Amphictyony continued in existence (but with no power) until late in the Roman Empire.

Amphilochus (ămfĭl'əkəs), in Greek legend, son of AMPHIARAÜS and ERIPHYLE and brother of Alcmaeon. He was one of the EPIGONI and with his brother slew Eriphyle for her treachery in bringing about their father's death.

Amphion (ăm'fēən): see ANTIOPE **1.**

amphioxus: see LANCELET.

Amphipolis (ămfĭ'pəlĭs), ancient city of Macedonia, on the Strymon (Struma) River near the sea and NE of later Thessaloníki. The place was known as Ennea Hodoi [nine ways] before it was settled and was of interest because of the gold and silver and timber of Mt. Pangaeus (Pangaion), to which it gave access. Athenian colonists were driven out (c.464 B.C.) by Thracians, but a colony was established in 437 B.C. Amphipolis became one of the major Greek cities on the N Aegean. This colony was captured by Sparta, and Brasidas and Cleon were both killed in a battle there in 422 B.C. After it was returned to Athens in 421 B.C., it actually had virtual independence until captured (357 B.C.) by Philip II of Macedon. He had promised to restore it to Athens, and his retention of Amphipolis was a major cause of the war with Athens. It was the capital (168–148 B.C.) of Macedonia Prima, one of the Roman republics. Paul, Silas, and Timothy passed through Amphipolis (Acts 17.1). Nearby is the modern Greek village of Amfípolis.

amphitheater, open structure used for the exhibition of gladiatorial contests, struggles of wild beasts, sham sea battles, and similar spectacles. There is no Greek prototype of amphitheaters, which were primarily Roman and were built in many cities throughout the empire. More or less well-preserved examples are at Rome (see COLOSSEUM), Verona, and Capua in Italy; at Nîmes and Arles in France; at Cirencester in England; and at sites in Sicily, Greece, and North Africa. The typical amphitheater was elliptical in shape, with seats, supported on vaults of masonry, rising in many tiers around an arena at the center; corridors and stairs facilitated the circulation of great throngs. The arena itself was usually built over the quarters for gladiators, wild animals, and storage. Until the erection of the Colosseum (A.D. 80), practically all amphitheaters were of wood, the notable exception being that of stone built at Pompeii c.70 B.C. The word *amphitheater* is now applied to modern structures which may bear little resemblance to their ancient prototypes.

Amphitrite (ămfĭtrī'tē), in Greek mythology, queen of the sea; daughter of Nereus. She was the wife of Poseidon and mother of Triton.

Amphitryon (ămfĭ'trēən, -ŏn''), in Greek mythology, son of Alcaeus. While betrothed to Alcmene, he accidentally killed her father, Electryon. Alcmene and Amphitryon fled to Thebes, but she demanded that he defeat Pterelaos, her father's enemy. This Amphitryon did, but on the night of his return Zeus took Amphitryon's form and came into Alcmene's bed. That night she conceived children by both Zeus and Amphitryon. Hercules was the son of Zeus, Iphicles the son of Amphitryon.

amphotericin B (ăm''fətĕr'ĭsĭn), ANTIBIOTIC that halts the growth of several disease-causing fungi. It is produced by bacteria of the genus *Streptomyces.* It is used in lotion or ointment form to treat fungus infections of the skin and is given internally only to patients with potentially fatal fungus infections. Amphotericin B is not effective against bacterial infections.

amphoterism (ăm''fətĕr'ĭzm), in chemistry, the property of certain substances of acting either as acids or as bases depending on the reaction in which they are involved. Many hydroxide compounds are amphoteric. For example, aluminum hydroxide, $Al(OH)_3$, reacts as a base with common acids to form salts, e.g., with sulfuric acid, H_2SO_4, to form aluminum sulfate, $Al_2(SO_4)_3$. It reacts as an acid with strong bases to form aluminates, e.g., with sodium hydroxide, NaOH, to form sodium aluminate, $NaAlO_2$. Organic molecules that contain both acidic (e.g., carboxyl) and basic (e.g., amino) FUNCTIONAL GROUPS are usually amphoteric.

ampicillin (ăm''pĭsĭl'ĭn), ANTIBIOTIC chemically related to PENICILLIN but having a broader spectrum of antibacterial activity. The penicillin antibiotics inhibit the synthesis of bacterial cell wall components.

Amplias (ămp'lēəs) or **Ampliatus** (ămplēā'təs), Christian in Rome to whom Paul sent greetings. Rom. 16.8.

amplifier, device in which a varying input signal controls a flow of energy to produce an output signal that varies in the same way but has a larger amplitude; the input signal may be a current, a voltage, a mechanical motion, or any other signal, and the output signal is usually of the same nature. The most common types of amplifiers are electronic and have ELECTRON TUBES or TRANSISTORS as their principal components. Tube and transistor amplifiers are used in radio and television transmitters and receivers, stereophonic phonographs, and intercoms. Amplifiers in their simplest form have either a single transistor or a single electron tube known as a triode. In the single-triode amplifier, a varying input voltage is fed to the triode, which acts upon the input to produce a larger varying output voltage; the ratio of the output voltage to the input voltage is called the voltage gain. For many purposes a single tube or transistor does not provide the signal with sufficient gain, or amplification, a problem that can be overcome by a cascade, or multistage, amplifier. In a cascade amplifier the output of the first amplifying device (tube or transistor) is fed as input to the second amplifying device, whose output is fed as input to the third, and so on until an adequate signal amplification has been achieved. In a device such as a radio receiver, several amplifiers boost a weak input signal until it is powerful enough to drive a speaker, producing audible sound. Another less common group of electronic amplifiers use magnetic devices as their principal components. There are also many kinds of mechanical amplifiers, e.g., the power steering system of an automobile. See OPERATIONAL AMPLIFIER.

amplitude (ăm'plĭtōōd''), in physics, maximum displacement from a zero value or rest position. In the HARMONIC MOTION of a pendulum, the amplitude of the swing is the greatest distance reached to either side of the central rest position. Amplitude is important in the description of a WAVE phenomenon such as light or sound. In general, the greater the amplitude of the wave, the more energy it transmits (e.g., a brighter light or a louder sound).

amplitude modulation: see MODULATION; RADIO.

amputation, removal of all or part of a limb or other body part. Although amputation has been practiced for centuries, the development of sophisticated techniques for treatment and prevention of infection has greatly decreased its necessity. Surgical amputation is currently performed in cases of bone and tissue cancers, gangrene, and uncontrollable infections of the arm or leg. An amputation is performed as far above the affected area as is necessary to remove all unhealthy tissue and to leave a portion of sound tissue with which to pad the bone stump. Whenever possible amputations are performed at points on the limb that permit the fitting of prosthetic devices (see ARTIFICIAL LIMB). Ceremonial amputation of finger joints has been practiced in parts of Australia and Africa in conjunction with male initiation rites. In some areas of New Guinea females have finger joints amputated to signify mourning.

Amram (ăm'răm). **1** Moses' father; ancestor of a Levitical family. Ex. 6.18,20; Num. 3.19,27; 26.58,59; 1 Chron. 6.2,3,18; 23.12,13; 24.20; 26.23. **2** See HEMDAN. **3** Jew who had married a foreign wife. Ezra 10.34.

Amram ben Scheschna (shĕsh'nä) or **Amram Gaon** (gä'ōn), d. c.875, Hebrew scholar, head of the Jewish academy at Sura in Persia. He is chiefly known as the author of the *Seder Rab Amram,* a compilation of the order of prayers, with their context for the whole year and the liturgical laws governing the ceremonial observances of all the holidays. This book is the oldest surviving Jewish prayer book, serving as a basis for later compilations. See David Hedegård, ed., *Seder R. Amram Gaon* (Vol. I, 1951).

Amraphel (ăm'rəfĕl, ămrā'fəl): see CHEDORLAOMER and HAMMURABI.

Amravati (əmräv'ətē), town (1971 pop. 193,636), Maharashtra state, central India. The town is a district administrative center. It is the site of the Great Stupa (c.A.D. 200) of the Andhra Dynasty.

Amritsar (əmrĭt'sər), city (1971 pop. 432,663), Punjab state, NW India. It is a district administrative center, as well as a trade and industrial city where carpets, fabrics of goat hair, and handicrafts are made. The center of the SIKH religion, Amritsar was founded in 1577 by Ram Das, the fourth guru [Hindustani,= teacher], on land given by AKBAR. The Golden Temple (refurbished 1802), set in the center of a lake, is especially sacred to Sikhs. The city was the center of a Sikh empire in the early 19th cent., and modern Sikh nationalism was founded there. Khalsa College, a branch of Punjab Univ., is in Amritsar. The Amritsar massacre took place in the Jalianwala Bagh, an enclosed park, in April, 1919; hundreds of Indian nationalists were killed and thousands wounded when they were fired upon by the troops under British control.

Amru al-Kais (äm'rōō äl-kīs), fl. 6th cent., Arabic poet. His verse, like much of the poetry of the pre-Islamic period, is intensely subjective and stylistically perfect. He was esteemed by Arabs as the great model for erotic poetry. He is thought to have lived in high favor with the imperial court at Constantinople. Amru al-Kais' work is represented in the MUALLAQAT. His name is also spelled Imru al-Kais.

Amsdorf, Nikolaus von (nē'kōlous fən äms'dôrf), 1483–1565, German Protestant reformer. He became a devoted supporter of Martin Luther. Elector John Frederick I of Saxony appointed Amsdorf bishop of Naumberg in 1541, but after the elector was captured by Holy Roman Emperor Charles V, the office was withdrawn (1547). A zealous defender of Luther's doctrines, Amsdorf attacked all who deviated from them in the slightest, including Melanchthon. He took part in the founding of the Univ. of Jena and superintended the Jena edition of the works of Luther.

Amstelveen (äm'stəlvān), town (1971 pop. 70,202), North Holland prov., W Netherlands, a suburb of Amsterdam. Schiphol international airport is there.

Amsterdam (ăm'stərdăm'', Dutch ämstərdäm'), city (1971 pop. 820,406), constitutional capital and largest city of the Kingdom of the Netherlands, North Holland prov., W Netherlands, on the IJ, an inlet of the IJsselmeer. The city derives its name from the fact that it is situated where the small, bifurcated Amstel River (which empties into the IJ) is joined by a sluice dam (originally built c.1240). A major port, Amsterdam is also the seat of one of the world's chief stock exchanges, a center of the diamond-cutting industry, and one of the great commercial, intellectual, and artistic capitals of Europe. Its manufactures include food products, clothing, printed materials, and metal goods. Amsterdam is connected with the North Sea by the North Sea Canal (opened in 1876), which can accommodate large oceangoing vessels, and by the older North Holland Canal (opened 1824). The Amsterdam-Rhine Canal connects the city with the Rhine delta and thus with industrial NW Germany, with which there is considerable transit trade. Amsterdam is a major road and rail hub and is served by nearby Schiphol airport. Because of the underlying soft ground, Amsterdam is built on wooden and concrete piles. The city is cut by about 40 concentric and radial canals that are flanked by streets and crossed by some 400 bridges. Because of the canals, the city is sometimes called the "Venice of the North." The many old and picturesque houses along the canals, once patrician dwellings, are now mostly offices and warehouses. The main streets of Amsterdam are the Dam, on which stand the Nieuwe Kerk (15th–17th cent.) and the 17th-century Dam Palace (formerly the city hall, since 1808 a royal palace); the Damrak, with the stock exchange (completed 1903); and the Kalverstraat and Leidenschestraat, which are the chief shopping centers. Outstanding buildings are the Oude Kerk [old church], built in 1334; the weighhouse (15th cent.); the city hall (16th cent.); and the Beguinage (Dutch *Begijnenhof*), or almshouses, of the 17th cent. Amsterdam was chartered c.1300 and in 1369 joined the Hanseatic League. Having accepted the Reformation, the people of Amsterdam in 1578 expelled their pro-Spanish magistrates and joined the rebellious Netherland provinces. The commercial decline of Antwerp and Ghent and a large influx of refugees from all nations (notably of Flemish merchants, of Jewish diamond cutters and merchants, and of French Huguenots), contributed to the rapid growth of Amsterdam after the late 16th cent. The Peace of Westphalia (1648), by closing the Scheldt (Escaut) to navigation, further stimulated the growth of Amsterdam at the expense of the Spanish Netherlands. Amsterdam reached its apex as an intellectual and artistic center in the 17th cent., when, because of its tolerant government, it became a center of liberal thought and of book printing. The city was captured by the French in 1795 and became the capital of the Kingdom of the Netherlands, which was ruled by Louis Bonaparte. The constitution of 1814 made it the capital of the Netherlands; the sovereigns are usually sworn in at Amsterdam and now reside in a palace outside the city. However, The Hague is the seat of government. During World War II, Amsterdam was occupied by German troops from 1940 to 1945 and suffered severe hardship, including famine. Most of the city's Jews (c.75,000 in 1940) were deported and killed by the Germans. Rembrandt and the other Dutch masters are best represented in the world famous Rijks Museum, or National Museum, founded in 1808 by Louis Bonaparte. Among the many other notable museums are the municipal museum (with a magnificent Van Gogh collection) and Rembrandt's house. Amsterdam is also famous for the Concertgebouw Orchestra. The Univ. of Amsterdam, which was founded as an academy in 1632 and achieved university status in 1876, is the largest center of learning in the Netherlands. The city is also the site of the Free Univ. (1880; Calvinist). Near Amsterdam is the Bosplan, an enormous man-made national park.

Amsterdam, city (1970 pop. 25,524), Montgomery co., E central N.Y., on the Mohawk River; inc. 1885. It is an industrial city where carpets, rugs, clothing, and novelties are manufactured. The area was settled in 1783 and was named Amsterdam because many of the early settlers were from the Netherlands. Nearby stands Fort Johnson, home of the British colonial leader Sir William Johnson.

Amtrak, federally chartered corporation authorized to operate virtually all intercity passenger railroad routes in the United States. Officially known as the National Railroad Passenger Corporation, Amtrak was created by an act of Congress in Oct., 1970. Its establishment was preceded by more than two decades of continuous operating deficits by privately run passenger railroads. At the time of Amtrak's creation, more than 100 of the nation's 500 passenger railroad lines had filed discontinuation-of-service petitions with the Interstate Commerce Commission. Given an initial funding of $40 million and $100 million in federal loan guarantees, Amtrak was designed to be a profit-making enterprise even though it is quasi-public in structure. Its board of directors is composed of three representatives of the railroad industry, four private investors from among those holding the corporation's preferred stock, and eight officers appointed by the President. Amtrak began operation in 1971 and immediately reduced the number of intercity passenger rail routes by one half, retaining service only in areas of high density travel. In its first year Amtrak had over 180 routes serving some 300 cities. The corporation reported increasing travel and decreasing deficits in its early years of operation. Its government funding also increased in these years.

Amu Darya (ä'mo͞o där'yə, ämo͞o' däryä'), river, c.1,600 mi (2,580 km) long, formed by the junction of the Vakhsh and Pandj rivers, which rise in the Pamir mts. of central Asia. It flows generally northwest, marking much of the USSR-Afghanistan border before flowing through the Kara-Kum desert of Turkmenistan and Uzbekistan, Central Asian USSR, and entering the S Aral Sea through a large delta. The river drains c.180,000 sq mi (466,200 sq km). It flows swiftly until it reaches the Kara-Kum where its course braids into several channels. The Amu Darya is rich in fish and it provides water for irrigation. The Kara-Kum Canal (c.500 mi/800 km long) carries water from the Amu Darya near Kelif across S Turkmenistan to Ashkhabad and supplements the flow of the Tedzhen and Murgab rivers. The Amu Darya is paralleled by the Trans-Caspian RR, which has lessened the river's importance as a transport route. In ancient times the Amu Darya was called the Oxus and figured importantly in the history of Persia and in the campaigns of Alexander the Great.

amulet (ăm'yəlĭt), object or formula that credulity and superstition have endowed with the power of warding off harmful influences. The use of the amulet to avert danger and to dispel evil has been known in different religions and among diverse peoples. Like the talisman and the charm, the amulet is believed to be the source of an impersonal force that is an inherent property of the object rather than the manifestation of a deity working through that object (see FETISH and TABOO). Although amulets are most often worn on the body, hanging from the neck or strapped to the arm or leg, they may also serve as protective emblems on walls and doorways (e.g., the Jewish mezuzah). Sometimes the amulet consists of a spoken, written, or drawn magic formula, such as ABRACADABRA and the MAGIC SQUARE, or of a symbolic figure, such as the wheel of the sun god and the Aryan swastika. In many cultures the teeth, claws, and other parts of an animal are believed to communicate their properties to the wearer. Although belief in amulets is very widespread in primitive societies, it has survived in modern civilization. Common superstition has endowed such things as the rabbit's foot with the property of being able to bring good luck. In some modern religious practices, amulets such as the Jewish phylactery and the Christian cross are more strictly related to ritual and serve as personal reminders to the wearers of their relationship to God.

Amundsen, Roald (rō'äl ä'mo͞onsən), 1872–1928, Norwegian polar explorer; the first man to reach the South Pole. He served (1897–99) as first mate on the *Belgica* (under the Belgian Adrien de Gerlache) in an expedition to the Antarctic, and he commanded the *Gjöa* in the arctic regions in the first negotiation of the NORTHWEST PASSAGE (1903–6); the *Gjöa* was the first single ship to complete the route through the Northwest Passage. His account appeared in English as *Amundsen's North West Passage* (1908). He then purchased Fridtjof Nansen's *Fram* and prepared to drift toward the North Pole and then finish the journey by sledge. The news that Robert E. Peary had anticipated him in reaching the North Pole caused Amundsen to consider going south. He was successful in reaching the South Pole on Dec. 14, 1911, after a dash by dog team and skis from the Bay of Whales (an inlet of Ross Sea). He arrived there just 35 days before Robert F. SCOTT. This story he told in *The South Pole* (tr. 1913). He had added much valuable scientific and geological information to the knowledge of Antarctica. In 1918, back in the arctic regions, he set out to negotiate the Northeast Passage in the *Maud.* After two winters he arrived at Nome, the first after N. A. E. Nordenskjöld to sail along the whole northern coast of Europe and Asia. Amundsen then turned to air exploration. He and Lincoln ELLSWORTH in 1925 failed to complete a flight across the North Pole, but the next year in the *Norge*, built and piloted by Umberto Nobile, they succeeded in flying over the pole and the hitherto unexplored regions of the Arctic Ocean N of Alaska. A bitter controversy followed with Nobile as to the credit for the success. Yet in 1928 when Nobile crashed in the *Italia*, Amundsen set out on a rescue attempt that cost him his life. The story of the ventures with Ellsworth written by the two of them appear in *Our Polar Flight* (1925) and *The First Crossing of the Polar Sea* (1927). See the autobiographical *My Life as an Explorer* (tr. 1927); biographies by Charles Turley (1935) and J. A. Kugelmass (1955).

Amur (ämo͝or'), Chin. *Hei-lung Chiang*, river, c.1,800 mi (2,900 km) long, formed by the confluence of the Shilka and Argun rivers, NE Asia, at the Soviet-Chinese border; the Amur-Shilka-Onon system is c.2,700 mi (4,350 km) long. The Amur flows generally southeast, forming for more than 1,000 mi (1,610 km) the border between the Soviet Union and China, then NE through the Far Eastern USSR before entering the Tartar Strait opposite Sakhalin island. Its chief tributaries are the Ussuri, Sungari, Zeya, and Bureya rivers. One of the chief waterways of Asia, the Amur is navigable for small craft for its entire length during the ice-free season (May–Nov.). The chief ports are the Soviet cities of Khabarovsk (the head of large craft navigation), Komsomolsk, and Nikolayevsk.

Amurath. For Ottoman sultans thus named, see MURAD.

Amvets: see AMERICAN VETERANS OF WORLD WAR II AND KOREA.

amygdalin (əmĭg'dəlĭn): see BENZALDEHYDE.

amylase (ăm'əlās''), ENZYME having physiological, commercial, and historical significance, also called diastase. It is found in both plants and animals. Amylase was purified (1835) from malt by Anselme Payen and Jean Persoz. Their work led them to suspect that similar substances, now known as enzymes, might be involved in biochemical processes. Amylase hydrolyzes STARCH, GLYCOGEN, and DEXTRIN to form in all three instances GLUCOSE, MALTOSE, and the limit-dextrins. Salivary amylase is known as ptyalin; although humans have this enzyme in their saliva, some mammals, such as horses, dogs, and cats, do not. Ptyalin begins polysaccharide digestion in the mouth; the process is completed in the small intestine by the pancreatic amylase, sometimes called amylopsin. The amylase of malt digests barley starch to the disaccharides that are attacked by yeast in the fermentation process.

amyloplast (ăm'əlōplăst''), also called leucoplast, a special organelle, or plastid, occurring in the CYTOPLASM of plant cells. They are nonpigmented. Amyloplasts have the specific abilities to transform glucose, a simple sugar, into starch through the process of polymerization, and to store one or more starch grains within their stretched membranes. Especially large numbers of amyloplasts occur in subterranean storage tissues of some plants, such as those that comprise the tuber of the common potato.

amylopsin (ăm''əlŏp'sĭn): see AMYLASE.

Amyot, Jacques (zhäk ämyō'), 1513–93, French humanist, translator of Heliodorus' *Aethiopica* (1547), of Longus' *Daphnis and Chloë* (1559), and particularly of Plutarch's *Lives* (1559).

Amyot or **Amiot, Joseph** (zhôzĕf'), 1718–1794?, French Roman Catholic missionary in China, a Jesuit. He wrote a long treatise on the history, sciences, and customs of the Chinese (15 vol., 1776–89). He was one of the first Europeans to make Chinese literature, antiquities, and customs known to Europe. He was an early authority on the Manchu language.

Amyraut, Moïse (môēz' ämērō'), or **Moses Amyraldus** (ămĭrăl'dəs), 1596–1664, French Protestant theologian. As pastor of Saumur he won a reputation as a theologian and orator, and he was appointed (1631) to present to Louis XIII the protest of the synod against infractions of the Edict of Nantes. He became professor of theology at Saumur and wrote extensively on theological subjects.

Amytal (ăm'ĭtôl''), trade name for the drug amobarbital, a BARBITURATE.

Amzi (ăm'zī). **1** Levite. 1 Chron. 6.46. **2** One of a priestly family. Neh. 11.12.

Anab (ā'năb), hill town, SW Palestine. Joshua 11.21; 15.50.

Anabaptists (ăn''əbăp'tĭsts) [from Gr., = rebaptizers], name applied, originally in scorn, to certain Christian sects holding that infant baptism is not authorized in Scripture and that baptism should be administered to believers only. A convert if baptized in infancy must be rebaptized. Anabaptists were prominent in Europe during the 16th cent., forming part of the radical wing of the Reformation. Their principal centers were in Germany, Switzerland, Moravia, and the Netherlands. They are to be distinguished from the BAPTISTS, primarily an English group. The religious ideas of the Anabaptists antedate the Reformation. Although they were never united either politically or doctrinally, Anabaptists held certain views in common for which they were persecuted everywhere. Among these were their desire for radical religious, social, and economic reform and their advocacy of the separation of church and state. In their beliefs great stress was placed upon individual conscience and private inspiration. Perhaps their most characteristic and most influential belief was their conception of the church as a voluntary association of believers. Martin Luther regarded them as enemies of the Reformation and added to their persecution. Most of the Anabaptists were peace loving and moderate, but extremists led by Thomas MÜNZER, a Saxon pastor, helped to incite the Peasants' War. Leaders like Melchior Hoffman, a Swabian farmer, spread doctrines of an imminent return of Christ and the "reign of God," without church or dogma. In Münster c.1533 some of the Anabaptists set up a theocracy, first under the direction of Bernard Rothmann, a preacher, and Jan Matthys, a fanatical Dutch baker, then under Bernhard Knipperdollinck. In 1534 JOHN OF LEIDEN proclaimed himself King David and ruled this theocracy in which communal ownership of property and polygamy were practiced. This extreme form of Anabaptism ended with the execution of the leaders in 1535. Another group of Anabaptists, under the leadership of MENNO SIMONS, became MENNONITES. Others, descendants of the followers of Jacob Hutter, moved in 1874 from Russia to South Dakota (see HUTTERIAN BRETHREN). See studies by C. P. Clasen (1972) and K. P. Davis (1974).

Anabasis (ənăb'əsĭs): see XENOPHON.

anabolism: see METABOLISM.

Anacletus, Saint: see CLETUS, SAINT.

Anaconda (ănəkŏn'də), city (1970 pop. 9,771), seat of Deer Lodge co., SW Mont.; inc. 1887. Marcus Daly chose this place (1883) to build the smelter for the Anaconda Copper Mining Company and in the 1890s tried unsuccessfully to make it the state capital. The present high-stacked smelter (585 ft/178 m high), one of the largest in the world, dominates the life of the city and produces copper, zinc, and manganese.

anaconda: see BOA.

Anacreon (ənăk'rēən, -ŏn), fl. c.521 B.C., Greek lyric poet, b. Teos in Ionia. He lived at Samos and at Athens, where Hipparchus patronized him. His poetry, graceful and elegant, celebrates the joys of wine and love. Little of his verse survives. The Anacreontics were poems in the style of Anacreon written from Hellenistic to late Byzantine times.

Anadyr (ənədĭr'), river, c.695 mi (1,120 km) long, rising on the Anadyr Plateau, NE Far Eastern USSR, and flowing S then E into Anadyr Bay, an inlet of the Bering Sea. The Anadyr basin, a lowland between the Anadyr and Koryak ranges, is mostly covered by tundra. There are coal and gold deposits near the river's mouth. The town of Anadyr, capital of Chukchi National Okrug, Khabarovsk Kray, is a port on the bay.

anae-, for words beginning thus, see ANE-.

anagram [Gr.,=something read backward], rearrangement of the letters of a word or words to make another word or other words. A famous Latin anagram was an answer made out of a question asked by Pilate. The question was *Quid est veritas?* [What is truth?], and the answer *Est vir qui adest* [it is the man who is here]. An anagram that reads the same backward as forward is a palindrome, e.g., "Able was I ere I saw Elba."

Anah (ā'nə), name appearing several times in the genealogy of Esau's family. Three persons may be distinguished, but if the genealogy refers to tribes rather than to persons, Anah may be a single tribal name. Gen. 36; 1 Chron. 1.

Anaharath (ăn"əhā'răth), unidentified town of E central Palestine. Joshua 19.19.

Anaheim (ăn'əhīm), city (1970 pop. 166,701), Orange co., S Calif., SE of Los Angeles; inc. 1870. Anaheim was founded by Germans in 1857 as an experiment in communal living. Lying in an area of citrus fruit and walnut groves, the city is an important industrial center and one of the great tourist and convention centers in the United States. In Anaheim are Disneyland (opened 1955), a gigantic amusement park; the Anaheim Stadium, home of the American League's California Angels baseball team; and the Anaheim Convention Center. Among the city's manufactures are electronic equipment, guidance systems, paper converters, metal fabricators, greeting cards, and processed foods.

Anáhuac (änä'wäk) [Aztec,=near the water], geographical term used variously in Mexico before the Spanish Conquest. Today it commonly refers to that part of the central plateau of Mexico comprising the Pánuco and Lerma river systems and the lake basin of the Valley of Mexico.

Anaiah (ăn"ī'ə, ănā'yə), name of two persons who returned from the Exile. Neh. 8.4; 10.22.

Anak (ā'năk), in the Bible, ancestor of the Anakim or Anakims, a race of giants inhabiting Hebron and its vicinity at the time of the conquest of Canaan. ARBA is cited as Anak's father, and his sons are given as Ahiman, Sheshai, and Talmai. Joshua and Caleb practically eradicated the race. Num. 13.22,28,33; Deut. 1.28; 9.2; Joshua 11.21; 14.15; 15.13,14; 21.11; Judges 1.20.

analgesic (ăn"əljē'zĭk), any of a diverse group of drugs used to relieve pain. Analgesic drugs include the nonnarcotics such as the SALICYLATES, the narcotic drugs such as MORPHINE, and synthetic drugs with morphinelike action (see NARCOTIC). ASPIRIN and other salicylates reduce fever and inflammation as well as relieve pain. Salicylate substitutes such as phenacetin or acetaminophen (Tylenol) are often given to individuals sensitive or allergic to salicylates. Phenylbutazone (Butazolidin) and chemically similar drugs reduce pain in diseases associated with inflammation such as rheumatic and arthritic disorders, but these drugs are very toxic and are not used where salicylates alone are effective. Narcotic analgesics depress the central nervous system and alter the perception of pain. They are used to alleviate pain not relieved by the salicylates. Besides morphine and codeine, this group includes the synthetic narcoticlike substances propoxyphene (Darvon) and MEPERIDINE (Demerol).

analog circuit, electronic circuit that operates with currents and voltages that vary continuously with time, having no abrupt transitions between levels. Generally speaking, analog circuits are contrasted with DIGITAL CIRCUITS, which function as though currents or voltages were at one of a set of discrete levels, all transitions between levels being ignored. Since most physical quantities, e.g., velocity and temperature, vary continuously, an analog circuit provides the best means of representing them. However, for rapid calculations in a computer, digital circuits are often preferred. Thus, high-speed convertors are required to change the data from one form to another.

analog computer: see COMPUTER.

analogy, in biology, the similarities in function, but differences in evolutionary origin, of body structures in different organisms. For example, the wing of a bird is analogous to the wing of an insect, since both are used for flight. However, there is no common ancestral origin in the evolution of these structures: While the wings of birds are modified skeletal forelimbs, insect wings are extensions of the body wall. Although insects and birds do have a very remote common ancestry (more than 600 million years ago), the wings of the two groups evolved after their ancestries had separated. See also HOMOLOGY.

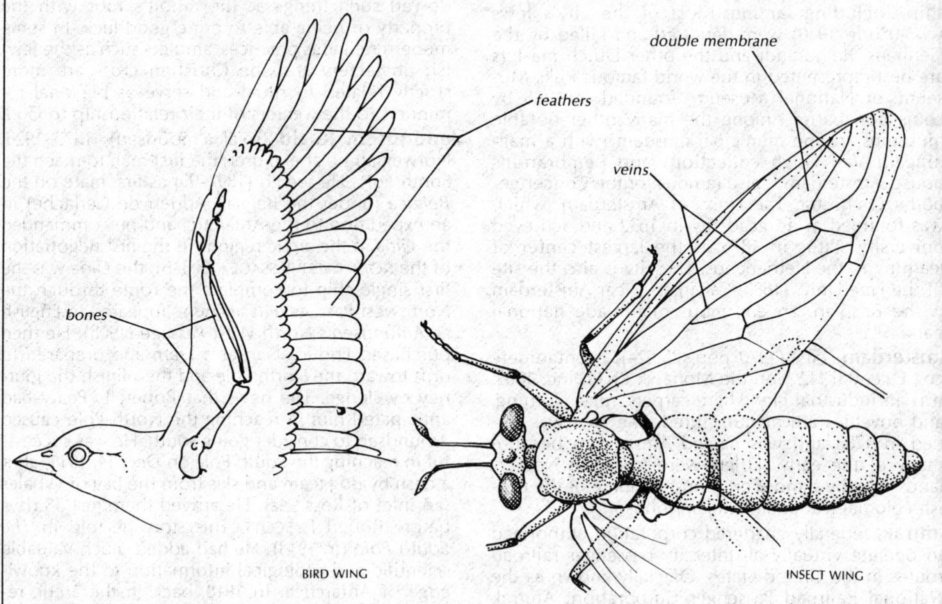

Analogy in bird and insect wings

analysis, branch of MATHEMATICS that utilizes the concepts and methods of the CALCULUS. It includes not only basic calculus, but also advanced calculus, in which such underlying concepts as that of a LIMIT are subjected to rigorous examination; differential and integral equations, in which the unknowns are FUNCTIONS rather than numbers, as in algebraic equations; complex variable analysis, in which the variables are of the form $z=x+iy$, where i is the imaginary unit; VECTOR analysis and TENSOR analysis; DIFFERENTIAL GEOMETRY; and many other fields.

analysis, chemical: see CHEMICAL ANALYSIS.

analysis situs: see TOPOLOGY.

analytic geometry, branch of GEOMETRY in which points are represented with respect to a coordinate system, such as CARTESIAN COORDINATES, and in which the approach to geometric problems is primarily algebraic. Its most common application is in the representation of equations involving two or three variables as curves in two or three dimensions or surfaces in three dimensions. For example, the linear equation $ax+by+c=0$ represents a straight line in the xy-plane, and the linear equation $ax+by+cz+d=0$ represents a plane in space, where a, b, c, and d are constant numbers (coefficients). In this way a geometric problem can be translated into an algebraic problem and the methods of algebra brought to bear on its solution. Conversely, the solution of a problem in algebra, such as finding the roots of an equation or system of equations, can be estimated or sometimes given exactly by geometric means, e.g., plotting curves and surfaces and determining points of intersection. In plane analytic geometry a line is frequently described in terms of its slope, which expresses its inclination to the coordinate axes; technically, the slope m of a straight line is the (trigonometric) tangent of the angle it makes with the x-axis. If the line is parallel to the x-axis, its slope is zero. Two or more lines with equal slopes are parallel to one another. In general, the slope of the line through the points (x_1, y_1) and (x_2, y_2) is given by $m=(y_2-y_1)/(x_2-x_1)$. The conic sections are treated in analytic geometry as the curves corresponding to the general quadratic equation $ax^2+bxy+cy^2+dx+ey+f=0$, where $a, b, \ldots, f$ are constants and a, b, and c are not all zero. In solid analytic geometry the orientation of a straight line is given not by its slope but by its direction cosines, λ, μ, and ν, the cosines of the angles the line makes with the x-, y-, and z-axes, respectively; these satisfy the relationship $\lambda^2+\mu^2+\nu^2=1$. In the same way that the conic sections are studied in two dimensions, the 17 quadric surfaces, e.g., the ellipsoid, paraboloid, and elliptic paraboloid, are studied in solid analytic geometry in terms of the general equation $ax^2+by^2+cz^2+dxy+exz+fyz+px+qy+rz+s=0$. The methods of analytic geometry have been generalized to four or more dimensions and have been combined with other branches of geometry. Analytic geometry was introduced by René Descartes in 1637 and was of fundamental importance in the development of the CALCULUS by Sir Isaac Newton and G. W. Leibniz in the late 17th cent. More recently it has served as the basis for the modern development and exploitation of ALGEBRAIC GEOMETRY.

Anamim (ăn'əmĭm), unidentified tribe of Egypt. Gen. 10.13; 1 Chron. 1.11.

Anammelech (ənăm'əlĕk), god of an otherwise unknown Samaritan cult. 2 Kings 17.31.

Anan (ā'nən), sealer of the convenant. Neh. 10.26.

Anan (än'än), city (1970 pop. 58,467), Tokushima prefecture, E Shikoku, Japan, on the Kii Channel. It is a fishing port and agricultural center.

Anan ben David (änän'), fl. 8th cent., Babylonian Jewish theologian, founder of the Ananites from whom the KARAITES claim spiritual descent. He is said to have been a descendant of BOSTANAI BEN CHANINAI. Anan rejected the Talmudic tradition and in its place sought a return to Scripture as the sole source for God's Law. It is evident from those writings attributed to him that he made use of rabbinic methods of scriptural interpretation in the formulation of legal decisions to meet the needs of his age. These decisions often represent a quite ascetic attitude. See Leon Nemoy, *Karaite Anthology* (1952).

Ananda (ä'nəndə): see PALI LITERATURE.

Anani (ănā'nī), descendant of David. 1 Chron. 3.24.

Ananiah (ă"nənī'ə). **1** Ancestor of AZARIAH **20.** **2** Benjamite town, probably just N of Jerusalem. Neh. 11.32.

Ananias (ăn"ənī'əs) [Gr.,=Heb. ANANIAH and HANANIAH]. **1** Man who, with his wife Sapphira, held back part of a gift to the church and lied about it. They were rebuked by Peter and fell dead. Acts 5.1–11. The name has become a term for liar. **2** High priest at Jerusalem, a Roman sympathizer, hated by most of the Jews for his oppression and his alliance with the Roman interest. He was assassinated between A.D. 60 and 67. Acts 23.2–5; 24. **3** Christian at Damascus who took charge of Paul after his conversion. Acts 9.10–22. **4** One of the THREE HOLY CHILDREN.

Ananites: see ANAN BEN DAVID; KARAITES.

anaphylaxis (ăn"əfəlăk'sĭs), hypersensitive state that may develop after introduction of a foreign protein or other antigen into the body tissues. When an anaphylactic state exists, a second dose of the same protein (commonly an antibiotic such as penicillin, or certain insect venoms) will cause a violent allergic reaction. Anaphylaxis results from the production of specific antibodies in the tissues in very high concentration; the violent reaction is produced by the neutralization of antigens by the antibodies. The histamines released during the reaction are thought to cause the most damage, i.e., severe vasodilation and loss of capillary fluid, resulting in circulatory collapse. Other symptoms include urticaria or edema, choking, coughing, shock, and loss of consciousness. Death may occur within 5 to 10 min if no medical help is available. Anaphylaxis differs from IMMUNITY; in immunity, antibodies circulate in the blood and neutralize antigens without producing a violent reaction. See also ALLERGY; SERUM SICKNESS.

anaplasmosis (ăn"aplăzmō'sĭs), infectious blood disease in cattle, sheep, and goats, caused by a protozoan of the genus *Anaplasma.* The organism parasitizes red blood cells causing their destruction and producing emaciation, anemia, jaundice, and, occasionally, death. The disease is present in the warmer regions of the world and is most prevalent in the United States in the Gulf states, lower plains, and California. Wild ruminants such as deer and antelope may be asymptomatic carriers. Transmission of the disease occurs mainly by the spread of infected blood through insect vectors, especially ticks and biting flies. The incubation period varies from three to four weeks. Infected animals first show a fever, which may rise to 107°F (62°C) in severe cases, and then jaundice and anemia set in. They are often hyperexcitable and may attack attendants just before death. Pregnant cows will frequently abort. Treatment of anaplasmosis consists of antibiotic therapy and blood transfusions. Control is extremely difficult because of the wide range of insects capable of transmitting the disease, the presence of carriers in wild-animal populations, and the difficulty of detecting infected animals. Continuous feeding of antibiotics, segregation of affected animals, and vaccination are the only effective means of control.

Anarajapura: see ANURADHAPURA, Sri Lanka.

anarchism (ăn'ərkĭzəm) [Gr.,=having no government], theory that equality and justice are to be sought through the abolition of the state and the substitution of free agreements between individuals. Central to anarchist thought is the belief that society is natural and that men are good but are corrupted by artificial institutions. Also central in anarchism are the belief in individual freedom and the denial of any authority, particularly that of the state, that hinders man's development. Zeno of Citium, founder of Stoic philosophy, is regarded as the father of anarchism. In the Middle Ages the anarchist tradition was closely linked to utopian, millenarian religious movements such as the Brethren of the Free Spirit of the 13th cent. and the Anabaptists of the 16th cent. The philosophy of modern political anarchism was outlined in the 18th and 19th cent. by William GODWIN, P. J. PROUDHON, and others. Mikhail BAKUNIN attempted to orient the First INTERNATIONAL toward anarchism but was defeated by Karl MARX. Bakunin gave modern anarchism a collectivist and violent tone that has persisted despite the revisionary efforts of Piotr Kropotkin and Leo Tolstoy. Political anarchism in Russia was suppressed by the Bolsheviks after the Russian Revolution. Anarchism's only real mass following was in Latin countries, where its doctrines were often combined with those of SYNDICALISM, especially in Spain. In the United States, early anarchists such as Josiah WARREN were associated with cooperatives and with utopian colonies. After the Haymarket riot in Chicago in 1886 and the assassination of President McKinley in 1901 a law was passed forbidding anarchists to enter the country. The SACCO-VANZETTI CASE attests to the fear of anarchism in the United States. As an organized movement, anarchism is almost dead, but it retains importance as a philosophical attitude and a political tendency. See George Woodcock, *Anarchism* (1962); L. I. Krimerman and L. Perry, ed., *Patterns of Anarchy* (1966); Atindranath Bose, *History of Anarchism* (1967); Roderick Kedward, *The Anarchists* (1971); Gerald Runkle, *Anarchism, Old and New* (1972).

Anasazi culture (ăn"əsä'zē): see BASKET MAKERS; CLIFF DWELLERS; PUEBLO INDIANS.

Anastasia, Saint (ănəstā'shə), 4th cent., Roman noblewoman, kind to the poor, martyred under Diocletian. She is mentioned in the Canon of the Mass. In the Roman Catholic Church, her feast is Dec. 25 and is commemorated in the Christmas Mass at dawn. In the Orthodox Eastern Church her feast is Dec. 22.

Anastasia (Anastasia Nikolayevna) (ănəstā'shə nyĭkəlī'əfnă), 1901–1918, youngest daughter of Czar Nicholas II, last of the Russian czars. It is generally believed that she was killed with the rest of her immediate family after the Russian Revolution; however, several women later claimed to be Anastasia. See study by M. Maurette (1955).

Anastasius I (ănəstā'shəs, -zhəs), c.430–518, Roman emperor of the East (491–518); successor of Zeno, whose widow he married. He broke the power that the Isaurians had enjoyed since Leo I, made peace with Persia, maintained friendly relations with Theodoric the Great, and made Clovis I an ally. He built a wall to protect Constantinople against the Slavs and Bulgars. His reign saw the revision of tax collection and the abolition of gladiatorial contests. His Monophysite inclinations stirred religious unrest throughout the empire. Anastasius was succeeded by Justin I.

Anath (ā'năth), father of SHAMGAR.

anathema (ənă'thĭmə) [Gr.,=set aside, as a devoted object], traditional Christian decree of EXCOMMUNICATION in its severest form. The usual form of a canon of a council is, "If anyone (says such and such or does so-and-so), let him be anathema." References to it appear in 1 Cor. 16.22 and Gal. 1.8–9.

Anathoth (ăn'əthŏth, -thōth). **1** Town, NE of Jerusalem, near the modern Anata, Jordan. It was the home of Jeremiah. Jer. 1.1; 1 Chron. 12.3; 1 Kings 2.26; Neh. 7.27. Its adjective is Antothite, Anetothite, Anathotite. 1 Chron. 27.12; 12.3. **2** Chief of the people. Neh. 10.19. **3** Benjamite. 1 Chron. 7.8.

Anatolia (ăn"ətō'lēə) [Gr.,=sunrise], Asian part of Turkey, usually synonymous with ASIA MINOR.

Anatolian languages (ăn"ətō'lēən), subfamily of the Indo-European family of languages (see INDO-EUROPEAN, table). The progress made in the identification, decipherment, and analysis of the Indo-European Anatolian languages from extant texts owes much to 20th-century scholarship. These Anatolian languages were spoken in Anatolia, or Asia Minor, from about the 2d millennium B.C. and gradually became extinct during the first few centuries A.D. They include Cuneiform Hittite, Hieroglyphic Hittite, Luwian (also called Luvian or Luish), Palaic, Lycian, and Lydian. The Anatolian languages are the tongues of Indo-European-speaking invaders of Anatolia and became mixed to some extent with indigenous languages of the region. Much of the vocabulary of the Anatolian languages was apparently borrowed from these native tongues, but their grammar continued to be essentially Indo-European. The principal known member of the Anatolian division of the Indo-European family is Hittite, the tongue of the HITTITES, who entered and conquered much of Anatolia early in the 2d millennium B.C. The oldest surviving written records of Hittite, dated at about the 15th or 14th cent. B.C., are among the earliest extant remains of any Indo-European language. From c.1500 to 1200 B.C., Hittite was written both in CUNEIFORM (a system of writing taken over from Mesopotamia) and in HIEROGLYPHICS (a form of picture writing unrelated to the hieroglyphics of Egypt). After the fall of the Hittite Empire (c.1200 B.C.) the use of cuneiform ceased, but writing in hieroglyphics continued until the 7th cent. B.C. Cuneiform and Hieroglyphic Hittite are separate but closely related languages. A near relative of Hittite was Luwian, the Anatolian language of the now extinct Luwian people. Dominant in a large part of S Anatolia during the period of the Hittite Empire, Luwian was written in cuneiform, and its surviving documents go back to the 14th cent. B.C. In areas of N Anatolia, Palaic flourished. Also close to Hittite, it was written in cuneiform. Grammatical features common to Hittite, Luwian, and Palaic include: two genders, one of which combines masculine and feminine as a common gender and the other of which is neuter; two moods, indicative and imperative, the first of which has a present and a preterit tense; and two voices, active and middle. Lycian, a language of SW Anatolia for which there are written records dated from about the 5th to 4th cent. B.C., may have been a continuation of Luwian. Lycian was written in a form of the Greek alphabet, as was Lydian. Lydian was spoken in W Anatolia, and the surviving written records date from about the 5th to 4th cent. B.C. The term "Anatolian languages" is also used to refer to all languages, Indo-European and non-Indo-European, that were spoken in Anatolia in ancient times. See E. H. Sturtevant and E. A. Hahn, *A Comparative Grammar of the Hittite Language* (2d ed. 1951); Johannes Friedrich, *Extinct Languages* (tr. 1957, repr. 1971).

anatomy, branch of biology concerned with the study of body structure of plants and animals, including man; the study of plant structures is often called comparative morphology. Comparative anatomy is concerned with the structural differences of various animal forms. The study of similarities and differences in anatomical structures forms the basis for CLASSIFICATION of both plants and animals. Embryology (see EMBRYO) deals with developing plants or animals until hatching or birth (or germination, in plants); CYTOLOGY covers the internal anatomy of the cell, while HISTOLOGY is concerned with the study of aggregates of similarly specialized cells, called tissues. There are four basic types of tissue in the human body: epithelial tissue (see EPITHELIUM), muscular tissue (see MUSCLE), CONNECTIVE TISSUE, and nervous tissue (see NERVOUS SYSTEM). Human anatomy is often studied by considering the individual systems that are composed of groups of tissues and organs; such systems include the skeletal system (see SKELETON), muscular system, cutaneous system (see SKIN), circulatory system (including the LYMPHATIC SYSTEM), respiratory system (see RESPIRATION), DIGESTIVE SYSTEM, REPRODUCTIVE SYSTEM, URINARY SYSTEM, and ENDOCRINE SYSTEM. Little was known about human anatomy in ancient times because dissection, even of corpses, was forbidden. In the 2d cent., Galen, largely on the basis of animal dissection, made valuable contributions to the field that remained authoritative until the 14th and 15th cent., when a limited number of cadavers were made available to the medical schools. A better understanding of the science was soon reflected in the discoveries of Vesalius, William Harvey, and John Hunter.

Anau: see ANNAU, USSR.

Anaxagoras (ăn"əksăg'ərəs), c.500–428 B.C., Greek philosopher of Clazomenae. He is credited with having transferred the seat of philosophy to Athens. He was closely associated with many famous Athenians and is thought to have been the teacher of Socrates. His belief that the sun was a white-hot stone and that the moon was made of earth that reflected the sun's rays resulted in a charge of atheism and blasphemy, forcing him to flee to Lampsacus, where he died. Rejecting Empedocles' four elements (earth, air, fire, and water), Anaxagoras posits an infinity of particles, or "seeds," each unique in its qualities. All natural objects are composed of particles having all sorts of qualities; a preponderance of similar though not identical particles creates the difference between wood and stone. Anaxagoras' universe, before separation, was an infinite, undifferentiated mass. The formation of the world was due to a rotary motion produced in this mass by an all-pervading mind (*nous*). This led to the separating out of the "seeds" and the formation of things. Although Anaxagoras was the first to give mind a place in the universe, he was criticized by both Plato and Aristotle for only conceiving of it as a mechanical cause rather than the originator of order. See D. E. Gershenson and D. A. Greenberg, *Anaxagoras and the Birth of Physics* (1964).

Anaximander (ənăk"sĭmăn'dər), c.611–c.547 B.C., Greek philosopher, b. Miletus; pupil of THALES. He made the first attempt to offer a detailed explanation of all aspects of nature. Anaximander argued that since there are so many different sorts of things, they must all have originated from something less differentiated than water, and this primary source, the boundless or the indefinite (*apeiron*), had always existed, filled all space, and, by its constant motion, separated opposites out from itself, e.g., hot and cold, moist and dry. These opposites interact by encroaching on one another and thus repay one another's "injustice." The result is a plurality of worlds that successively decay and return to the indefinite. The notion of the indefinite and its processes prefigured the later conception of the indestructibility of matter. Anaximander also had a theory of the relation of earth to the heavenly bodies, important in the history of astronomy. His view that man achieved his physical state by adaptation to environment, that life had evolved from moisture, and that man developed from fish, anticipates the theory of evolution. See C. H. Kahn, *Anaximander and the Origins of Greek Cosmology* (1960); Paul Selegman, *The Apeiron of Anaximander* (1974).

Anaximenes (ăn″əksĭm′ĭnēz), Greek philosopher, 6th cent. B.C., last of the Milesian school founded by THALES. With Thales he held that a single element lay behind the diversity of nature, and with ANAXIMANDER he sought a principle to account for diversity. He believed that single element to be air. The principle of diversification he taught was rarefaction and condensation. Different objects were therefore merely different degrees of density of the one basic element. Anaximenes anticipates the spirit of modern scientific practice that seeks to explain qualitative differences quantitatively.

ancestor worship, ritualized propitiation and invocation of dead kin. Closely related to the primitive concept of ANIMISM, ancestor worship is based on the belief that the spirits of the dead continue to dwell in the natural world and have the power to influence the fortune and fate of the living. Ancestor worship has been found in various parts of the world and in diverse cultures. It was a minor cult among the Romans (see MANES). The practice reached its highest elaboration in W Africa and in the ancient Chinese veneration of ancestors. It is also well developed in the Japanese SHINTO cult and among the peoples of Melanesia. See APOTHEOSIS; TOTEM. See J. G. Frazer, *The Belief in Immortality and the Worship of the Dead* (3 vol., 1913–24, repr. 1968).

Anchieta, José de (zhōōzĕ′ dĭ ənshēä′tä), 1530–97, Brazilian Jesuit missionary, b. Canary Islands of Spanish parents. A tireless traveler and pioneer, he spread Portuguese control and settlement and was a founder of the city of São Paulo. He wrote in Spanish, Latin, Portuguese, and Tupi and wrote poetry as well as prose tracts on history, philosophy, and religion. He is usually regarded as the first Brazilian writer. See H. G. Dominian, *Apostle of Brazil* (1958).

An-ch'ing (än-chĭng) or **Anking** (än′kĭng), city (1970 est. pop. 160,000), SW Anhwei prov., China. A port and trading center on the Yangtze River, it was capital of the province until 1949. It was formerly called Hwaining.

Anchises (ănkī′sēz), in Greek mythology, Trojan shepherd. He was seduced by Aphrodite, and from this union Aeneas was born. When Anchises boasted of the goddess's love, Zeus crippled him.

anchor, device cast overboard to secure a ship, boat, or other floating object by means of weight, friction, or hooks called flukes. In ancient times an anchor was often merely a large stone, a bag or basket of stones, a bag of sand, or, as with the Egyptians, a lead-weighted log. The Greeks are credited with the first use of iron anchors, while the Romans had metal devices with arms similar to modern anchors. The ordinary modern anchor consists of a shank (the stem, at the top of which is the anchor ring), a stock (the crosspiece at the top of the shank, either fixed or removable), a crown (the bottom portion), and arms, attached near the base of the shank at a right angle to the stock and curving upward to end in flat, triangular flukes. Other types of anchors include the patent anchor, which has either no stock at all or a stock lying in the same plane as the arms; the stream, or stern anchor, lighter than the regular anchor and used in narrow or congested waters where there is no room for the vessel to swing with the tide; and the grapnel, a small four-armed anchor used to recover lost objects. A sea anchor is a wooden or metal framework covered with canvas and weighted at the bottom; it is a temporary device used by disabled ships. Modern ships have several anchors; usually there are two forward and two aft. Formerly made of wrought iron, anchors are now usually made of forged steel.

Anchorage (ăng′kərĭj), city (1970 pop. 48, 029), Anchorage census div., S central Alaska, a port at the head of Cook Inlet; inc. 1920. It is the largest city in the state, the administrative and commercial heart of S central and W Alaska, one of the nation's key defense centers, and a vital transportation hub. Glenn Highway connects the city to the Alaska Highway, and the international airport there, one of the nation's busiest, is a regular stop on intercontinental and transpolar flights. Adjacent to the city are two huge U.S. military bases, Fort Richardson and Elmendorf Air Force Base; the latter contains the headquarters for the entire Alaska command (including navy and coast guard). Anchorage is also a focus for the state's oil, coal, and natural gas industries; anticipated pipelines from areas where new discoveries have been made are expected to result in the expansion of these industries. Tourism also contributes to the city's economy. Anchorage was founded (1915) as construction headquarters for the Alaska RR and grew as a railroad town. It also became a fishing center, a market and supply point for gold-mining regions to the north, and the metropolis for the coal mining and farming of the Matanuska valley. World War II brought the establishment of the large military bases and the enormous growth of air and rail traffic. The city suffered severe damage in the 1964 earthquake. Points of interest include Earthquake Park and several notable museums. A "Fur Rendezvous" winter carnival is held in Anchorage every year. The city is the seat of Alaska Methodist Univ. Portage Glacier and Lake Hood are nearby, and Mt. McKinley is visible from the city.

anchoret or **anchorite:** see HERMIT.

anchovy: see HERRING.

anchovy pear: see BRAZIL NUT.

Ancohuma (ängkō-ōō′mä), mountain, Bolivia: see ILLAMPÚ.

Ancona (ängkō′nä), city (1971 pop. 110,017), capital of Ancona prov., chief city of Marche region, central Italy, on a promontory in the Adriatic Sea. It is a leading Adriatic port and an industrial and commercial center. Manufactures include ships, musical instruments, and refined sugar. There is a fishing industry and an annual fish fair. Late in the 4th cent. B.C., Greeks from Syracuse took refuge in Ancona. The city prospered under the Romans, and its harbor was enlarged (2d cent. A.D.) by Emperor Trajan. In the 9th cent. it became a semi-independent maritime republic under the nominal rule of the popes, to whose direct control it passed in 1532. The city was badly damaged in World War II. Noteworthy buildings include the Romanesque Cathedral of San Ciriaco (11th–13th cent.) and the Venetian-Gothic Merchants' Loggia (15th cent.).

Ancre, Concino Concini, marquis d': see CONCINI.

Ancren Riwle (äng′krĕn rē′ōōlə) or **Ancrene Wisse** (äng′krĕnə wĭs′ə) [Mid. Eng.,=anchoresses' rule], English tract written c.1200 by an anonymous English churchman for the instruction of three young ladies about to become religious recluses. The work, important as a sample of early Middle English prose, is a charming mixture of realism and humor, didacticism and tenderness. It is also important for its depiction of the manners and customs of the time. French and Latin versions of the work are also extant. See edition by J. R. R. Tolkien (1962); study by Arne Zettersten (1965).

Ancus Martius (ăng′kəs mär′shəs), fourth king of ancient Rome (640?–616? B.C.). This semilegendary king is supposed to have enlarged the area of Rome.

Ancyra, Turkey: see ANKARA.

Åndalsnes (ôn′dälsnās″), town (1960 pop. 2,202), Møre og Romsdal co., W Norway, at the head of the Romsdalfjord. It is a popular tourist resort. In World War II, the town was heavily damaged when the Germans pushed back (1940) an Allied landing.

Andalusia (ăndəlōō′zhə, -shə), Span. *Andalucía* (än″dälōōthē′ä), region (1970 pop. 5,971,277), 33,675 sq mi (87,218 sq km), S Spain, on the Mediterranean Sea, the Strait of Gibraltar, and the Atlantic Ocean. Spain's largest and most populous region, it covers all of S Spain, comprising the provinces of Almería, Cádiz, Córdoba, Granada, Huelva, Jaén, Málaga, and Seville (Sevilla), all named for their chief cities. Andalusia is crossed in the north by the Sierra Morena and in the south by mountain ranges that rise in the snow-capped Sierra Nevada to the highest peak in mainland Spain, Mulhacén (11,417 ft/3,480 m); between the ranges lies the fertile basin of the Guadalquivir River. With its subtropical climate, Andalusia has many affinities with Africa, which it faces. Barren lands contrast with richly fertile regions where cereals, grapes, olives, sugarcane, and citrus and other fruits are produced. Industries, based generally on local agricultural produce, include wine making, flour milling, and olive-oil extracting. Cattle, bulls for the ring, and fine horses are bred. The rich mineral resources, exploited since Phoenician and Roman times, include copper, iron, zinc, and lead. Mediterranean peoples have been attracted to this region since ancient times, and because of this Andalusia is one of Europe's most strikingly colorful regions. In the 11th cent. B.C., the Phoenicians settled there and founded several coastal colonies, notably Gadir (now CÁDIZ) and, supposedly, the inland town of Tartessus, which became the capital of a flourishing kingdom (sometimes identified with the biblical TARSHISH). Greeks and Carthaginians came in the 6th cent. B.C.; the Carthaginians were expelled (3d cent. B.C.) by the Romans, who included S Spain in the province of Baetica. The emperors Trajan, Hadrian, and Theodosius were born in the region. Visigoths ended Roman rule in the 5th cent. A.D., and in 711 the MOORS, crossing the Strait of Gibraltar, established there the center of their western emirate (see CÓRDOBA). Andalusia remained under Moorish rule until most of it was conquered in the 13th cent. by the kings of Castile; the Moorish kingdom of GRANADA survived; it, too, fell to the Catholic kings in 1492. The Moorish period was the golden age of Andalusia. Agriculture, mining, trade, and industries (textiles, pottery, and leather working) were fostered and brought tremendous prosperity; the Andalusian cities of Córdoba, SEVILLE, and Granada, embellished by the greatest Moorish monuments in Spain, were celebrated as centers of culture, science, and the arts. From the 16th cent. Andalusia generally suffered as Spain declined, although the ports of Seville and Cádiz flourished as centers of trade with the New World. Gibraltar was ceded to Britain in 1713, and in 1833 Andalusia was divided into the present eight provinces. With Catalonia, Andalusia was a stronghold of anarchism during the Spanish republic (est. 1931); however, it fell early to the Insurgents in the SPANISH CIVIL WAR of 1936–39. Despite the natural wealth of the region, poverty is widespread; Andalusian farm laborers are among the poorest in Europe, and many unemployed Andalusians have migrated to other Western European countries. The region has seen recurrent demonstrations against the national government of Francisco Franco. Moorish influence is still strong in the character, language, and customs of the people, which may account for the widespread hostility other segments of the Spanish population feel toward Andalusians. However, Andalusian songs, dances, and festivals, influenced by the large groups of gypsies who live in the region, enjoy great popularity.

Andalusia (ăndəlōō′shə, -zhə), city (1970 pop. 10,092), seat of Covington co., S Ala., in a farming and forestry area; inc. 1844. Its manufactures include processed peanuts and pecans, meat products, textiles, lumber, and plywood. Lurleen B. Wallace State Junior College is in Andalusia.

Andaman and Nicobar Islands (ăn′dəmən, nĭk′-ōbär), union territory (1971 pop. 115,090), India, in the Bay of Bengal. Port Blair (1971 pop. 26,212), in the Andamans, is the capital. Comprising the Andaman Islands (2,508 sq mi/6,496 sq km) in the south and the Nicobar Islands (707 sq mi/1,831 sq km) in the north, the territory chiefly exports tropical products and lumber. The territory is administered by the home minister in the central Indian government. Known to Europeans since the 7th cent. A.D., the Andamans, consisting of more than 200 islands, were the site of a British penal colony from 1858 to 1945. An earlier attempt by the British to colonize the islands was abandoned in 1796. The population is made up of native Negritos and settlers from the Indian mainland. The Nicobars, which comprise 19 small islands, are separated from the Andamans by a channel that is 90 mi (145 km) wide. The native population is of Mongoloid stock. The Nicobars became a British possession in 1869. See study by Lidio Cipriani (1966).

Andelys, Les (lāzäNdəlē′), town (1968 pop. 7,438), in Eure dept., N France, Normandy, on the Seine. The twin communities of Grand-Andely and Petit-Andely form a commercial center, with a distillery, metalworks, glassworks, and silk and leather industries. On the border between Normandy proper and the Norman VEXIN, it was of considerable strategic importance in the Middle Ages. The impressive Château Gaillard was built (1197) by Richard I of England.

Anderlecht (än′dərlĕkht), commune (1970 pop. 103,796), Brabant prov., central Belgium, on the

Charleroi-Brussels Canal, an industrial and residential suburb of Brussels. Erasmus lived (1517–21) in Anderlecht, and his house is now a museum.

Andermatt (än'dərmät), village (1970 pop. 1,589), Uri canton, S central Switzerland. It is a road junction, health resort, and sports center. The St. Gotthard Tunnel runs beneath the village. Andermatt has a 12th-century church.

Andernach (än'dərnäkh), city (1970 pop. 27,140), Rhineland-Palatinate, W West Germany, a port on the Rhine River. Its manufactures include chemicals, steel, wood products, and construction materials. Drusus founded a Roman frontier garrison there about A.D. 12. In 939 at Andernach, Emperor Otto I defeated the rebellious dukes Geselbert of Lotharingia and Eberhard of Franconia. From 1167 to 1801 the city belonged to the archbishopric of Cologne. In 1815 it passed to Prussia. Andernach has a Romanesque church (13th cent.), a 16th-century town hall, and parts of its medieval city wall.

Andersen, Hans Christian, 1805–75, Danish poet, novelist, and writer of fairy tales. Reared in poverty, he left Odense at 14 for Copenhagen. He failed as an actor, but his poetry won him generous patrons including King Frederick VI. In 1829 his fantasy *A Journey on Foot from the Holmen Canal to the Eastern Point of Amager* was published, followed by a volume of poetry in 1830. Granted a traveling pension by the king, Andersen wrote sketches of the European countries he visited. His first novel, *Improvisatoren* (1835), was well received by the critics. His sentimental novels were for a time considered his forte. However, with his first book of fairy tales, *Eventyr* (1835), he found the medium of expression that was to immortalize his genius. He produced about one volume a year and was recognized as Denmark's greatest author and as a storyteller without peer. His tales are often tragic or gruesome in plot. His sense of fantasy, power of description, and acute sensitivity contributed to his mastery of the genre. Among his many widely beloved stories are "The Fir-Tree," "The Little Match Girl," "The Ugly Duckling," "The Snow Queen," "The Little Mermaid," and "The Red Shoes." See his *Fairy Tales,* tr. by R. P. Keigwin (4 vol., 1956–60); his autobiography (1855, tr. 1871); *A River—A Town—A Poet,* autobiographical selections by A. Dreslov (1963); biographies by F. Böök (tr. 1962), R. Godden (1955), M. Stirling (1965), and S. Toksvig (1934, repr. 1969).

Andersen Nexø, Martin (mär'tēn än'dərsĕn nĕksö), 1869–1954, Danish novelist. Born one of 11 children in a Copenhagen slum, he spent his impoverished childhood largely on the island of Bornholm. Both locales appear centrally in his novels. His famous proletarian novels *Pelle the Conqueror* (4 vol., 1906–10; tr., in 1 vol., 1930) and *Ditte, Daughter of Mankind* (5 vol., 1917–21; tr., in 1 vol., 1931) relate the struggles of the poor, focusing attention on conditions of poverty in Denmark. Though admittedly a propagandist for communism and social reform, he transcended that role and created a memorable group of tender human portraits. He also wrote about Russia, where he spent many of his later years. The first two volumes of his four-volume autobiography have been translated as *Under the Open Sky* (1938). See Harry Slochower, *Three Ways of Modern Man* (1937).

Anderson, Carl David, 1905–, American physicist, b. New York City, grad. California Institute of Technology (B.S., 1927; Ph.D., 1930). Associated with the institute's physics department from 1930, he became professor in 1939. For his discovery (1932) of the positron, he shared with V. F. Hess the 1936 Nobel Prize in Physics. The MESON (or mesotron) was discovered in cosmic rays in 1936 by Anderson and his associate S. H. Neddermeyer and almost simultaneously by J. C. Street and E. C. Stevenson at Harvard.

Anderson, Elizabeth Garrett, 1836–1917, English physician. A sister of Millicent Garrett Fawcett, Elizabeth also worked for woman suffrage. With difficulty she obtained a private medical education under accredited physicians and in London hospitals; in 1865 she was licensed to practice by the Scottish Society of Apothecaries. In London in 1866 she opened a dispensary, later a small hospital, for women and children, the first in England to be staffed by women physicians; it was known after 1918 as the Elizabeth Garrett Anderson Hospital. Largely as a result of her efforts, British examining boards opened their examinations to women. See biography by Jo Manton (1965).

Anderson, Jack, 1922–, American newspaper columnist, b. Long Beach, Calif. After serving as a Mormon missionary (1941–44) and a term as a war correspondent during 1945, he was hired by Drew Pearson for the staff of his column, "Washington Merry-Go-Round." Anderson took over the column after Pearson's death in 1969. Controversial because of his unorthodox methods of obtaining news stories, Anderson has nonetheless produced vital information, especially concerning the Watergate affair. Anderson and Pearson collaborated on *The Case Against Congress* (1969).

Anderson, John, 1893–1962, Scottish-Australian philosopher, b. Scotland. A graduate of the Univ. of Glasgow, he taught (1918–27) at the universities of Cardiff, Glasgow, and Edinburgh before becoming professor of philosophy at the Univ. of Sydney, Australia (1927–58). His extreme concern for independence of thought led to a controversial academic career because he attacked many institutions (including Christianity, social welfare, and Communism) for encouraging servility. Philosophically he warred against ultimates of every sort, but his philosophy was inclusive rather than negative, stressing the complexity of experience—a complexity not reducible to any ultimate units or wholes—and the limits of any one description of it. His articles were collected in *Studies in Empirical Philosophy* (1962).

Anderson, Dame Judith, 1898–, Australian actress, originally named Frances Margaret Anderson. She made her debut in Sydney in 1915 and by 1924 had become celebrated for her powerful portrayals of classical and modern roles. In 1937 she made her London debut in *Macbeth* with Laurence Olivier. The title role in *Medea* by Robinson Jeffers, which she originated in 1947, was a personal triumph. Anderson's notable films include *Rebecca* (1940) and *Cat on a Hot Tin Roof* (1958). She was made a Dame of the British Empire in 1960.

Anderson, Margaret C., 1886–1973, American author, editor, and publisher, b. Indianapolis, Ind. As editor and publisher of *The Little Review* (1914–29), one of the most famous of the American LITTLE MAGAZINES, she included articles on controversial subjects and pieces by such writers as Vachel Lindsay, William Butler Yeats, Ernest Hemingway, Ezra Pound, and André Breton. From 1917 to 1920, *The Little Review* published excerpts from James Joyce's then unpublished novel *Ulysses* (1922). Because of their alleged obscenity, the U.S. Post Office burned four issues of the magazine containing the excerpts; in 1920, Anderson and her associate Jane Heap were convicted of publishing obscene matter, fined $100, and fingerprinted. After 1923, Anderson lived in France. See her autobiography (3 vol.: 1930, repr. 1971; 1951, repr. 1969; 1969).

Anderson, Marian, 1902–, American contralto, b. Philadelphia. She was the first Negro to be named a permanent member of the Metropolitan Opera Company, and she was also the first Negro to perform at the White House. Anderson first sang in Philadelphia church choirs, then studied with Giuseppe Boghetti. She began her concert career in 1924 and achieved her first great successes in Europe. Her rich, wide-ranged voice was superbly suited to both opera and the Negro spirituals that she included in her concerts and recordings. In 1939 the Daughters of the American Revolution (DAR) forbade her to perform at Constitution Hall in Washington, D.C. Eleanor Roosevelt resigned her DAR membership in protest and sponsored Anderson's concert at the Lincoln Memorial. In 1955 she made her debut with the Metropolitan Opera Company. She was appointed alternate delegate to the United Nations in 1958 and in 1963 was awarded the President's Medal of Freedom. See her autobiography, *My Lord, What a Morning* (1956).

Anderson, Mary, 1872–1964, American labor expert, chief (1919–44) of the Women's Bureau, U.S. Dept. of Labor, b. Sweden. She emigrated to the United States in 1888. After some years as an industrial worker in garment and shoe factories, she became an organizer for the National Boot and Shoe Workers' Union and one of the founders of the National Women's Trade Union League. In 1918 she was appointed assistant to the chief of the Women's Bureau, becoming its chief in 1919. See her autobiography, *Woman at Work* (1951, repr. 1973).

Anderson, Maxwell, 1888–1959, American dramatist, b. Atlantic, Pa., grad. Univ. of North Dakota, 1911. His plays, many of which are written in verse, usually concern social and moral problems. Anderson was a journalist until the successful production in 1924 of *What Price Glory?,* a war drama written with Laurence Stallings. *Winterset* (1935), based on the Sacco-Vanzetti case, is probably Anderson's most successful verse tragedy. He wrote many historical dramas including *Elizabeth the Queen* (1930), *Mary of Scotland* (1933), *Valley Forge* (1934), *Joan of Lorraine* (1947), *Anne of the Thousand Days* (1948), and *Barefoot in Athens* (1951). Among his other plays are *Both Your Houses* (1933), *High Tor* (1937), *The Star Wagon* (1937), *Key Largo* (1939), and *The Eve of St. Mark* (1942). He also wrote the librettos for Kurt Weill's *Knickerbocker Holiday* (1938) and *Lost in the Stars* (1940). A collection of his poetry, *Notes on a Dream,* was published in 1972. See study by M. D. Bailey (1957); bibliography by Martha Cox (1958, repr. 1974).

Anderson, Robert, 1805–71, American army officer, defender of FORT SUMTER, b. near Louisville, Ky., grad. West Point, 1825. He fought in the Black Hawk, Seminole, and Mexican wars and was promoted to major in 1857. In Nov., 1860, he took command of the U.S. force in the harbor of Charleston, S.C., where he distinguished himself in the Fort Sumter controversy. Anderson, made a brigadier general in the regular army (May, 1861), commanded the Dept. of Kentucky (June–Oct.). He retired from active service in Oct., 1863. In Feb., 1865, he was brevetted major general for his gallant service in the defense of Fort Sumter.

Anderson, Sherwood, 1876–1941, American novelist and short-story writer, best known for his novel *Winesburg, Ohio,* b. Camden, Ohio. After serving briefly in the Spanish-American War, he became a successful advertising man and later a manager of a paint factory in Elyria, Ohio. Dissatisfied with his life, however, Anderson abandoned both his job and his family and went to Chicago to become a writer. His first novel, *Windy McPherson's Son* (1916), concerning a boy's life in Iowa, was followed by *Marching Men* (1917), a chronicle about the plight of the working man in an industrial society. In *Winesburg, Ohio* (1919), his greatest novel, he explores the loneliness and frustration of small-town lives. This work contains perhaps the most successful expression of the theme that dominates all Anderson's works—the conflict between organized industrial society and the subconscious instincts of the individual. In his later novels—*Poor White* (1920), *Many Marriages* (1923), and *Dark Laughter* (1925)—he continues to explore, but generally with less skill, the spiritual and emotional sterility of a success-oriented machine age. Anderson's unique talent, however, found its best expression in his short stories. Such collections as *The Triumph of the Egg* (1921), *Horses and Men* (1923), and *Death in the Woods* (1933) contain some of his most compassionate and penetrating writing. In 1927, Anderson moved to Marion, Va., where he bought and edited two newspapers, one Republican and one Democratic. See his autobiographical *Story Teller's Story* (1924) and *Tar: A Midwest Childhood* (1926); memoirs (1942); letters (ed. by H. M. Jones and W. B. Rideout, 1953); biography by Irving Howe (1966); study by W. A. Sutton (1972); P. P. Appel, ed., *Homage to Sherwood Anderson* (1970).

Anderson. 1 City (1970 pop. 70,787), seat of Madison co., E central Ind., on the White River; inc. 1838. It is a manufacturing center in a rich farm area; products include automotive parts, steel tools, and corrugated paper boxes. The city's industrial growth began with the discovery of natural gas in 1887. The automotive industry was established in 1901. Anderson College is there. The city has a fine-arts center and a symphony orchestra. Nearby Mounds State Park has numerous prehistoric mounds. The Moravians operated an Indian mission nearby (1801–6). **2** City (1970 pop. 27,556), seat of Anderson co., NW S.C.; settled in the 17th cent., inc. 1828. The commercial center of a farming and livestock area, its manufactures include textiles, fiberglass products, and sewing machines. A junior college is there.

Anderson, river, c.465 mi (750 km) long, rising in several lakes in NW Mackenzie dist., Northwest Territories, Canada. It meanders north and west before receiving the Carnwath River and flowing north to Liverpool Bay, an arm of the Arctic Ocean. The village of Staton is at its mouth.

Andersonville, village (1970 pop. 274), SW Ga., near Americus; inc. 1881. In **Andersonville Prison,** tens of thousands of Union soldiers were confined during the Civil War under conditions so bad that more than 12,000 soldiers died. It is now a national historic site (see NATIONAL PARKS AND MONUMENTS, table). Andersonville National Cemetery, nearby, contains more than 13,000 soldiers' graves. See study by O. L. Fitch (1968).

Andersson, Dan (dän än'dərsōn"), 1888–1920, Swedish poet, novelist, and short-story writer. Although his entire life was lived in extreme poverty, Andersson dealt in his works with religious and metaphysical rather than social problems. He worked as a laborer and achieved no recognition for his writing during his lifetime. Today he is considered one of the foremost Swedish writers. Among his best-known works are *Kolarhistorier* [the charcoal-burner's tales] (1914), *Kolvaktarens visor* [the charcoal-burner's songs] (1915), and the novel *De tre hemlösa* [three homeless ones] (1918).

Andersson, Karl Johan (yo͞o'hän än'dərsōn''), 1827–67, Swedish explorer in Africa. In 1850 he and Francis Galton set out from Walvis Bay (in South West Africa) to explore Damaraland and Ovamboland, but they were able only to reach the Etosha Pan. On a second trip Andersson reached Lake Ngami, for years the goal of explorers, and penetrated for 60 mi (97 km) beyond it. A subsequent journey (1859) took him to the Kubango River in what is now Botswana. He died while seeking out the upper reaches of the Kunene River. He wrote *Lake Ngami* (1855) and *The Okavango River* (1861). *Notes of Travel in South Africa* is a posthumous account of his last trip and was reprinted in 1969.

Anderton shearer: see COAL MINING.

Andes (ăn'dēz), mountain system, more than 5,000 mi (8,000 km) long, W South America. The ranges run generally parallel to the Pacific coast and extend from Tierra del Fuego northward, across the equator, as the backbone of the entire continent. The Falkland Islands are a continuation of the Andes, and evidence shows that the system is continued in Antarctica. The Andes go through seven South American countries—ARGENTINA, CHILE, BOLIVIA, PERU, ECUADOR, COLOMBIA, and VENEZUELA. A geologically young system, the Andes were originally uplifted in the Cretaceous and Tertiary periods. They are still rising; volcanoes and earthquakes are common. The folded ranges are discontinuous—merging and bifurcating within the system—but as a whole they form one of the world's most important mountain masses. They are loftier than any other mountains except the Himalayas, with many snow-capped peaks more than 22,000 ft (6,700 m) high. Far south in Tierra del Fuego, the mountains run east and west, then turn north between Argentina and Chile. The westernmost of the mountains run into the sea, lining the coast of S Chile with islands. In the Patagonian Andes are high, glacier-fed lakes in both Argentina and Chile. The highest range of the Andes is on the central and northern Argentine-Chilean border; Aconcagua (22,835 ft/6,960 m; highest mountain of the Western Hemisphere) and Tupuncato are there. Between the peaks is Uspallata Pass, with the Transandine Railway and the Christ of the Andes. Other major peaks such as Llullaillaco flank the main range, and in N Chile subandean ranges enclose the high, cold Desert of Atacama. The central Andes broaden out in Bolivia and Peru in multiple ranges (c. 400 mi/640 km wide) with high plateau country (the altiplano) and many high intermontane valleys, where the great civilization of the Inca had its home. High in the mountains on the Peru-Bolivia border is Lake Titicaca. In Bolivia are the notable volcanoes, Illimaní and Illampú, and in S Peru is El Misti. The western or coastal range in Peru has lofty peaks (notably Huascarán) and is crossed by the highest railroad of the Andes (from La Oroya to Lima). The ranges approach each other again in Ecuador, where the N Andes begin. Between two volcanic cordilleras (including the cloud-capped Chimborazo and Cotopaxi) are rich intermontane basins. In Colombia the Andes divide again, the western range running between the coast and the Cauca River, the central between the Cauca and the Magdalena rivers, and the eastern running north parallel to the Magdalena River, then stretching out on the coast into Venezuela. The Andes continue in some of the islands of the West Indies, and in Panama N Andean spurs connect with the mountains of Central America and thus with the Sierra Madre and the Rocky Mts. The Andes have an immense influence on the patterns of communication, climate, weather, and life in South America. Andean waters reach the Orinoco, the Amazon, and the Río de la Plata. The plateaus and valleys of Bolivia, Peru, Ecuador, and Colombia have been peopled since remote times and saw the rise of not only the Inca and the Chibcha but some of the earliest Indian civilizations in the Western Hemisphere. Agriculture was the basis of these cultures (the native llama and alpaca were domesticated later), and the lands there are still tilled mainly for subsistence crops. Commercially the Andes have always been important for great mineral wealth, especially copper, silver, and tin; oil has been found in the foothills of the N Andes. Certain Andean areas have developed a tourist trade. See Isaiah Bowman, *The Andes of Southern Peru* (1916); A. G. Ogilvie, *Geography of the Central Andes* (1922); Claude Arthaud and F. Hébert-Stevens, *The Andes: Roof of America* (tr. 1956); P. E. James, *Latin America* (1969); Takehide Kazami, *The Andes* (1972).

Andhra Pradesh (än'drə prä'dăsh), state (1971 pop. 43,394,951), 106,052 sq mi (274,675 sq km), SE India, on the Bay of Bengal. The capital is HYDERABAD. The state was created in 1956 from the Telugu-speaking portions of Madras and Hyderabad states. It includes the northern portion of the Coromandel Coast of the Bay of Bengal. Although mountainous in the Eastern Ghats, Andhra Pradesh is largely on a plain drained by the Penner, the Krishna, and the Godarvi rivers. Rice, sugarcane, peanuts, and cotton are raised; coal, chrome, and manganese are mined. The state takes its name from the Andhra dynasty (c.230 B.C.–A.D.230), which ruled most of the Deccan plateau. Among the political forces within Andhra Pradesh is a movement advocating separation from India. The state is governed by a chief minister and cabinet responsible to a bicameral legislature with one elected house and by a governor appointed by the president of India.

Andizhan (ăndĭzhăn', Rus. əndyēzhän'), city (1970 pop. 188,000), capital of Andizhan oblast, Uzbekistan, Central Asian USSR, in the Fergana Valley, on the Andizhan-Say River. It is an industrial center in an irrigated area that produces cotton and silk. Andizhan's history dates back to the 9th cent.

Andkhui (əndkho͞o'ē), city (1967 pop. 30,000), N Afghanistan, in Afghan Turkistan, near the USSR border. Wool is its chief product, and it has a noted trade in fruits and karakul (Persian lamb) skins. Andkhui is also known for its handwoven rugs. Legend attributes the city's founding to Alexander the Great (4th cent. B.C.). It was subject to the khanate of Bukhara for some time, until a Russo-Afghan boundary commission assigned it to Afghanistan in 1885.

Andocides (ăndŏs'ĭdēz), c.440–390 B.C., one of the Ten Attic Orators (see ORATORY). In 415 B.C. he was accused of mutilating the hermae (sacred pillars topped by busts of the gods) and, in association with ALCIBIADES, of other sacrilege. He went into exile, and one of his speeches was a plea to be restored to citizenship. After he returned in 403, he was again accused (399) of sacrilege and again successfully defended himself.

Andong (än'dŭng'), city (1970 est. pop. 76,000), E South Korea. It is a railroad junction and commercial center in an agricultural area where rice, hemp, cotton, and tobacco are grown.

Andorra (ăndôr'ə), Fr. *Andorre* (äNdôr'), small state (1970 est. pop. 21,000), 191 sq mi (495 sq km), high in the E Pyrenees between France and Spain, under the joint suzerainty of the president of France and the bishop of Urgel (Spain). It has iron and lead deposits, marble quarries, and extensive pine forests. Drained by the Valira River, Andorra comprises several high mountain valleys that are generally poor in soil but support large flocks of sheep. Livestock raising, the traditional source of livelihood, is being supplemented by a growing tourist trade; the picturesque little state now attracts over 500,000 visitors a year. Smuggling remains an important economic activity. In the 9th cent., Emperor Charles II is reputed to have made the bishop of Urgel overlord of Andorra. The French counts of Foix contested this overlordship, and finally in 1278 an agreement was reached providing joint suzerainty. The rights of the count passed by inheritance through the house of Albret to Henry IV of France, and from the French kings to the French presidents. In actuality Andorra is independent; it pays homage to France and Spain only through nominal yearly gifts—960 francs and 460 pesetas, respectively. A semifeudal state with an ancient communal agrarian organization, Andorra is governed by a council of 24 members, elected by the heads of families and led by a syndic. It has two radio stations, one of them French-controlled. The people, Catalan speaking and Roman Catholic, live in six villages; Andorra la Vella (1971 est. pop. 8,000; Span. *Andorra la Vieja*) is the most important.

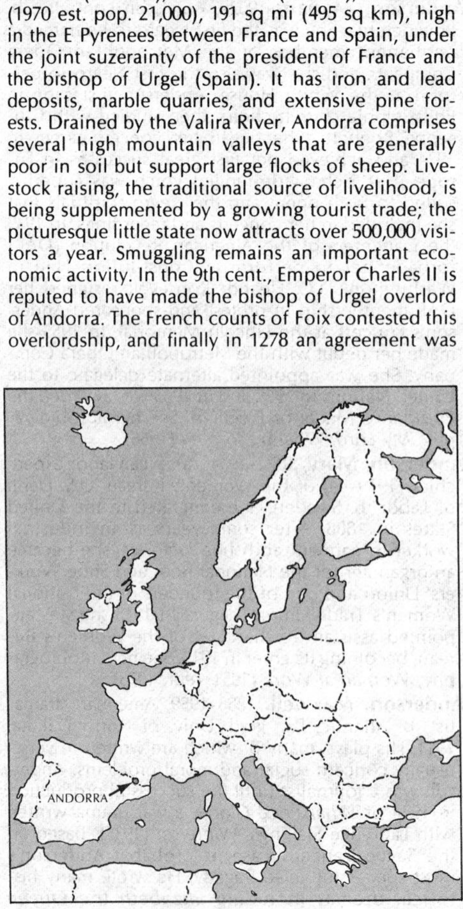

Andover (ăn'dōvər), town (1970 pop. 23,695), Essex co., NE Mass.; inc. 1646. Chiefly a textile producer in the 19th cent., Andover now makes toiletries, electronic equipment, chemicals, rubber products, and other items. Two preparatory schools (Phillips Andover Academy, 1778, for boys; and Abbot Academy, 1829, for girls) are in Andover. The Addison Gallery of American Art and the Robert S. Peabody Foundation archaeological museum are on the Phillips Andover campus. In 1832, Samuel Francis Smith wrote the words for "America" in Andover. Harriet Beecher Stowe lived in the town and is buried there.

Andrada e Silva, José Bonifácio de: see BONIFÁCIO, JOSÉ.

Andrássy, Julius, Count (ŏn'dräsh-shē), 1823–90, Hungarian politician. One of the leading figures in the 1848–49 Hungarian revolution, he supported the liberal program of Louis KOSSUTH and after the Hungarian defeat he went into exile, mostly in Paris and London, until 1858. With Francis DEAK he then rose to prominence in the negotiations leading to the *Ausgleich* [compromise] of 1867, which created the AUSTRO-HUNGARIAN MONARCHY. Andrássy was (1867–71) the first constitutional premier of Hungary. He opposed Austrian interference, attained the creation of a separate Hungarian defense force, put down the opposition led by Kossuth's partisans, and established Magyar supremacy at the expense of Slavic and other minorities of the kingdom. In 1870 his influence was largely responsible for keeping Austria-Hungary neutral in the Franco-Prussian War. As foreign minister of the Dual Monarchy (1871–79) he reversed the anti-Prussian policy of his predecessor, Beust, held Austria-Hungary to the THREE EMPERORS' LEAGUE, and signed (1879) the Dual Alliance with Germany (see TRIPLE ALLIANCE AND TRIPLE ENTENTE). His chief program was to limit Russian expansion in the Balkans and to maintain the status quo among the Slavic peoples. At the Congress of Berlin (see BERLIN, CONGRESS OF) in 1878, he obtained for the Dual Monarchy the right to occupy BOSNIA AND HERCEGOVINA. This step provoked much opposition in Hungary because it further increased the Slavic element in the empire, and Andrássy resigned.

Andrássy, Julius, Count, 1860–1929, Hungarian politician; son of the elder Count Andrássy. He occupied several cabinet posts before becoming (1900) minister of the interior of Hungary in the coalition cabinet under WEKERLE. He opposed the Austrian diplomacy of 1914, and as foreign minister (late in 1918) he severed all connections with Germany in the hope of obtaining a separate peace for Austria-Hungary. In 1921 he was involved in the second attempt of King Charles (Emperor CHARLES I) to regain the Hungarian throne, and he later led the royalist opposition to Admiral Horthy and Count Stephen Bethlen. He wrote a number of political and historical studies, notably, in German, *Bismarck, Andrássy, and Their Successors* (1924, tr. 1927).

André, Brother (äNdrā', än'-), 1845–1937, Canadian Roman Catholic mystic, b. St. Grégoire d'Iberville, Que. His secular name was Alfred Bissette, Bassette, or Bessette. For about 40 years he was a porter at a school in Montreal. His simple, devout life began (c.1900) to attract attention. Many miraculous cures were attributed to him. Through his efforts the Oratory of St. Joseph was built in Montreal. See biographies by H. P. Bergeron (1938), K. K. Burton (1952), and Alden Hatch (1959).

Andre, Carl, 1935–, American sculptor, b. Quincy, Mass. A student of Patrick Morgan and Frank Stella, Andre produces sculptures of elemental, classic form. His works reflect the quarries, shipyards, and islands of his birthplace and his years spent as a freight-train brakeman. His celebrated floor pieces include *144 Pieces of Lead* (Mus. of Modern Art, New York City).

André, John (ändrā', ăn'drē), 1751–80, British spy in the American Revolution. He was captured (1775) by Gen. Richard Montgomery in the Quebec campaign but was exchanged and became adjutant general under Sir Henry Clinton. Major André negotiated with Benedict ARNOLD for the betrayal of West Point and was captured (Sept. 23, 1780), when returning to New York, by John Paulding, David Williams, and Isaac Van Wart, near Tarrytown, N.Y. He was tried, condemned, and hanged at Washington's headquarters at Tappan, despite protests from Clinton. Major André's charming personality and his talents in the arts had won him many American friends, who mourned him as a romantically tragic young man. See studies by J. T. Flexner (1953) and J. H. Smith (1969).

Andrea del Sarto: see SARTO, ANDREA DEL.

Andreanof Islands: see ALEUTIAN ISLANDS.

Andrée, Salomon August (sä'lōōmôn ou'gəst ändrā'), 1854–97, Swedish polar explorer. An aeronautical engineer, he was the first to attempt arctic exploration by air. His first attempt by balloon in 1896 was unsuccessful, owing largely to bad weather. In 1897, however, he set out again in a balloon called the *Eagle*. Beset by mishaps from the start, Andrée and his party reached as far as 82° 56'N, where insufficient food and clothing halted their progress. All three members of the party died of exposure. Search expeditions failed, and it was not until 1930 that a Norwegian scientific expedition accidentally found the remains and diaries of Andrée and his two companions. These diaries are included in *Andrée's Story* (tr. 1930). See G. P. Putnam, *Andrée: the Record of a Tragic Adventure* (1930), and fictionalized life, *The Flight of the Eagle* by P. O. Sundman (1970).

Andreini, Isabella Canali (ē"zäbĕl'lä ändrāē'nē), 1562–1604, Italian actress. Beautiful, elegant, and well-educated, she was one of the most famous performers of her time. She joined the Gelosi troupe, becoming a leading player, and married the troupe's manager, Francesco Andreini, in 1578. She wrote the pastoral *Mirtilla* (1588); her collected letters appeared in 1607. Andreini was lauded by the poets Tasso and Marini. See Rosamond Gilder, *Enter the Actress* (1931).

Andrew, Saint [Gr.,=manly], one of the Twelve Disciples, brother of Peter. Mat. 4.18; 10.2; Mark 3.18; 13.3; Luke 6.14; John 1.40–42; 6.8,9; 12.22; Acts 1.13. According to tradition he was a missionary in Asia Minor, Macedonia, and S Russia and was martyred at Patras in Greece. He is said to have died on an X-shaped cross (St. Andrew's cross). He is patron saint of Russia and Scotland. Feast: Nov. 30.

Andrew II, d. 1235, king of Hungary (1205–35), son of Bela III. He continued his predecessors' policy of transferring crownlands to the magnates, and the lesser nobles forced him to issue a Golden Bull (1222), which served as a charter of feudal privilege. This "Magna Carta," expanded in 1231, extended the old nobility's privileges (immunities from local courts, taxes, and military service abroad) to the lesser nobles, most of whom were freemen in the king's service. It made royal ministers responsible to the diet, which was to meet annually, and gave the right of resistance to the nobles if any of the bull's provisions were violated. Foreigners were not to receive office without consent of the diet, and offices were not to be hereditary. Nobles were also protected against arbitrary arrest or punishment. Andrew took part (1217) in the Fifth Crusade. Initially welcoming the Teutonic Knights to S Transylvania in 1211, he later became alarmed at their growing power and expelled them in 1225. He was the father of St. Elizabeth of Hungary and of Bela IV, his successor.

Andrew, John Albion, 1818–67, Civil War governor of Massachusetts (1861–66), b. Windham, Maine. He practiced law in Boston, but his antislavery sympathies drew him into politics. He was one of the organizers of the Free-Soil party and later of the Republican party. Soon after taking office as governor, he secured both special legislation placing the militia in readiness and an appropriation for transporting it to Washington. When Lincoln's call came, the 6th Massachusetts regiment was the first to reach the capital. The same spirit characterized Andrew's actions throughout the war, and his zeal was imparted to the people. When peace came, he advocated a policy of friendship and leniency toward the South. See biography by H. G. Pearson (1904); W. B. Hesseltine, *Lincoln and the War Governors* (1948).

Andrewes, Lancelot (ăn'drōōz), 1555–1626, Anglican divine, bishop of Chichester (1605), of Ely (1609), and of Winchester (1619). One of the most learned men of his time, he was among the first to be selected to create a new English version of the Bible, the Authorized Version. He was royal chaplain to Elizabeth, James I, and Charles I. His preaching gained him great favor with King James, who was keenly interested in theology. The great theologian of the High Church party of the 17th cent., Andrewes was opposed to Puritanism, his position being somewhat similar to that of LAUD. His outstanding characteristics were his goodness and piety. His contributions to charity were also noteworthy. His *XCVI Sermons* were edited (1629) by bishops Laud and Buckeridge; his *Private Devotions,* translated (1647) from his noble prayers in Greek and Latin, passed through a number of editions. Richard Crashaw, the poet, paid him a beautiful tribute in "Upon Bishop Andrewes' Picture before His Sermons," and Milton, a Puritan, wrote a Latin elegy on his death. See biographies by M. F. Reidy (1955) and P. A. Welsby (1958); T. S. Eliot, *For Lancelot Andrewes* (1928).

Andrew Johnson National Historic Site: see NATIONAL PARKS AND MONUMENTS (table).

Andrews, Charles McLean, 1863–1943, American historian, b. Wethersfield, Conn. He was associate professor at Bryn Mawr (1889–1907) and professor at Johns Hopkins Univ. (1907–10) and Yale (1910–31). Andrews, a leader in the reinterpretation of British colonial policy in America, studied the colonies in the light of the larger imperial problem, and his seminar in colonial institutions at Yale stimulated much able research in this field. His long, distinguished career reached a climax with *The Colonial Period of American History* (4 vol., 1934–38; Vol. I–III, *The Settlements;* Vol. IV, *England's Commercial and Colonial Policy*). This excellently received work won him the 1935 Pulitzer Prize for history and, in 1937, the gold medal for history and biography awarded only every 10th year by the National Institute of Arts and Letters. His other books include *Colonial Self-Government, 1652–1689* (1904, repr. 1968; in the "American Nation" series), *The Fathers of New England* (1919) and *Colonial Folkways* (1919; both in the "Chronicles of America" series), and *The Colonial Background of the American Revolution* (1924, repr. 1961). He also compiled manuscript and bibliographical guides and wrote works on various historical subjects. See biography by A. S. Eisenstadt (1956).

Andrews, Lorrin, 1795–1868, American missionary to the Hawaiian Islands, b. present-day Vernon, Conn., grad. Princeton Theological Seminary, 1825. He founded (1831) on Maui a training school for teachers, offered courses in printing (which he had himself learned from a book), and began (1834) publishing the first Hawaiian newspaper. After 1841 he had posts in the royal Hawaiian government, becoming (1852) an associate justice of the supreme court. His great cultural contribution was his *Dictionary of the Hawaiian Language* (1865; rev. by H. H. Parker, 1922).

Andrews, Roy Chapman, 1884–1960, American naturalist and explorer, b. Beloit, Wis., B.A. Beloit College, 1906, M.A. Columbia Univ., 1913. Connected with the American Museum of Natural History, New York City, from 1906, he was its director from 1935 to 1942. Between 1908 and 1914 he made several trips to Alaska, along the coast of Asia, and in Malayan seas to study aquatic mammals. He later conducted (1917–30) several expeditions into central Asia to study both fossil and living plants and animals; he discovered some of the world's great fossil fields, which have yielded the remains of many ancient animals (including *Baluchitherium,* the largest known land mammal) and plants previously unknown to science. He described these expeditions in several books and discussed them all in *The New Conquest of Central Asia* (1932). His writings also include *Meet Your Ancestors* (1945), *In the Days of the Dinosaur* (1959), and the autobiographical works *Under a Lucky Star* (1943) and *An Explorer Comes Home* (1947).

Andrews Air Force Base, U.S. military installation, 4,279 acres (1,732 hectares), central Md., est. 1943. It is the chief military airport of Washington, D.C., as well as the headquarters for the air force's high-priority airlift command.

Andreyev, Leonid Nikolayevich (lyāənyĕt' nyĭkəlī'əvĭch əndrā'yəf), 1871–1919, Russian writer. Andreyev's early stories were realistic studies of everyday life. Gorky was attracted by the note of social protest in his work and used his influence to obtain publication of Andreyev's first volume of short stories. After an enormous initial success Andreyev turned to more metaphysical themes, frequently employing allegory and symbol. He declared his anti-Bolshevism, and his friendship with Gorky was terminated. Andreyev went to Finland at the Bolshevik accession to power and died there. His strongest dramatic works include *The Red Laugh* (1905) and *King Hunger* (1907), an acerbic portrait of Russian society. Besides the popular drama of a circus clown, *He Who Gets Slapped* (1916, tr. 1921), his best-known plays are *Anathema* (1904, tr. 1910), an allegory on the futility of goodness, and *The Pretty Sabine Women* (1912, tr. 1914), a political satire. The pessimism of his later writings cost Andreyev his popularity. His name also appears as Andreev. See *Letters of Gorky and Andreev,* ed. by Peter Yershov (1958); biographical studies by A. S. Kaun (1924, repr. 1969), J. B. Woodward (1969), and J. M. Newcombe (1973).

Andria (än'drēä), city (1971 pop. 77,514), in Apulia, S Italy. It is an agricultural market, handling wine, olives, and almonds. Andria was founded in the 11th cent. It was a favorite residence of Emperor Frederick II, who built (13th cent.) nearby the imposing Castel del Monte with eight round towers. There is a restored 12th-century cathedral, which has an 8th-century crypt.

Andrić, Ivo (ē'vō än'drĭch), 1892–, Yugoslav novelist, b. Bosnia. As a student Andrić worked for the independence and unity of the South Slavic peoples, and after the formation in 1918 of the Kingdom of the Serbs, Croats, and Slovenes (later Yugoslavia), he served in diplomatic posts. His best-known work is a historical trilogy (1945) on Bosnia: *The Bridge on the Drina* (tr. 1959), *Bosnian Story* (tr. 1959), and *Young Miss.* Andrić's other works include poems and novellas. The misery of man's struggle for existence is his principal theme. Andrić was awarded the 1961 Nobel Prize in Literature. His later stories and novellas include *Devil's Yard* (1954, tr. 1962), *Faces* (1960), *Vizier's Elephant* (tr. 1962), cited in the Nobel Prize presentation, and *The Pasha's Concubine* (tr. 1968).

androgen (ăn'drəjən): see TESTOSTERONE.

Androgeus (ăndrŏj'ēəs): see MINOS.

Andromache (ăndrŏ'məkē), Greek legend, Trojan woman; wife of Hector and mother of Astyanax. After the Trojan War she was carried away by NEOPTOLEMUS, whose father, Achilles, had slain her husband. Neoptolemus died, and she married Hector's brother Helenus. She is mentioned in the *Iliad.* The plays of Euripides and Racine that bear her name tell of her captivity by Neoptolemus.

Andromeda, in astronomy, northern CONSTELLATION located to the NE of Pegasus and to the S of Cassiopeia. Its brightest star, Alpheratz (Alpha Andromedae), marks the northeast corner of the Great Square in Pegasus. The constellation also contains the bright stars Mirach (Beta Andromedae) and Almach (Gamma Andromedae) and the famous Great Nebula, or ANDROMEDA GALAXY, the only galaxy visible to the naked eye in the Northern Hemisphere. Andromeda reaches its highest point in the evening sky in November.

Andromeda (ăndrŏm'ĭdə), in Greek mythology, princess of Ethiopia; daughter of Cepheus, king of Ethiopia, and Cassiopeia. According to most legends Cassiopeia angered Poseidon by saying that Andromeda (or possibly Cassiopeia herself) was more beautiful than the nereids. Poseidon sent a sea monster to prey upon the country; he could be appeased only by the sacrifice of the king's daughter. Andromeda in sacrifice was chained to a rock by the sea; but she was rescued by PERSEUS, who killed the monster and later married her. Cassiopeia, Cepheus, and Andromeda were all set among the stars as constellations.

Andromeda Galaxy, cataloged as M31 and NGC 224, visible to the naked eye as a faint patch in the constellation Andromeda; also known as the Great Nebula in Andromeda. It is the closest spiral galaxy at 2 million light-years distance and is part of the local group of galaxies that includes the Milky Way, which it resembles in shape and composition. The Andromeda Galaxy has a linear diameter of about 120,000 light-years, as compared to about 90,000 light-years for the Milky Way, and contains at least 200 billion stars, or twice as many as the Milky Way. It has a companion satellite galaxy, M32.

Andronicus I (Andronicus Comnenus) (ăndrənī'kəs kŏmnē'nəs), 1120?–1185, Byzantine emperor (1183–85), nephew of John II. He acceded to the throne by strangling his cousin ALEXIUS II. Though notorious in his younger years for his scandalous morals, he was a competent, if cruel, ruler. He took strict measures to protect the peasants against the great landowners, enforced honesty on the tax collectors, and was the terror of corrupt officials. His severity and his failure to stop the rapid advance of WILLIAM II of Sicily against the capital led to his overthrow and the elevation of ISAAC II. Andronicus was tortured to death by the rabble. He was the last of the Comneni to hold the throne of Constantinople.

Andronicus II (Andronicus Palaeologus) (pālēŏl'əgəs), 1258–1332, Byzantine emperor (1282–1328), son and successor of Michael VIII. He devoted himself chiefly to church affairs, renewing the schism by renouncing (1282) the union established at the Second Council of Lyons. He made a treaty with the rising kingdom of Serbia. He also made an unsuccessful alliance with ROGER DE FLOR against the Turks but could not prevent their taking most of Asia Minor. His reign, shared from 1295 to 1320 with his son Michael IX, was cut short by his grandson, who forced him into a monastery and became emperor as Andronicus III.

Andronicus III (Andronicus Palaeologus), c.1296–1341, Byzantine emperor (1328–41), grandson of Andronicus II, whom he deposed after a series of civil wars. His chief minister was John Cantacuzene (later Emperor John VI). During his reign the Ottoman Turks gained almost complete control of Asia Minor, while STEPHEN DUSHAN of Serbia conquered part of Macedonia and Albania. He was succeeded by his son, John V.

Andronicus, apostle at Rome. Rom. 16.7.

Andronicus, Livius: see LIVIUS ANDRONICUS.

Andropov, Yuri Vladimirovich (yo͞o'rē vlədyē'mĭravĭch əndrô'pôf), 1914–, Russian public official. As ambassador to Hungary from 1954 to 1957, he played a major role in the suppression of the 1956 anti-Communist uprising there. In 1957 he was appointed head of liaison between the Communist party of the Soviet Union and its fraternal parties within the Communist bloc. He promoted the idea of regional economic specialization within the bloc and helped to direct the ideological campaign against the Chinese Communists. In 1967 he was appointed chairman of the state security committee, or secret police. In 1973 he was named a member of the Politburo, the ruling body of the Communist party.

Andros, Sir Edmund (ăn'drŏs), 1637–1714, British colonial governor in America, b. Guernsey. As governor of New York (1674–81) he was bitterly criticized for his high-handed methods, and he was embroiled in disputes over boundaries and duties (see NEW JERSEY), going so far as to arrest Philip CARTERET. When James II, partly influenced by Edward RANDOLPH, consolidated all the New England colonies into the Dominion of New England, he named (1686) Andros governor. In 1688, New York and the Jerseys were also put under his control. The suppression of charters and colonial assemblies, interference with local customs and rights, and Andros's overbearing ways caused intense friction. After news of the overthrow of James II in 1688 reached the colonies, the colonials in Boston rebelled (1689), seized Andros and other officials, and sent them to England as prisoners. He was soon released and later was governor of Virginia (1692–97) and governor of Guernsey, (1704–6). See V. F. Barnes, *Dominion of New England* (1923).

Ándros, island (1971 pop. 10,457), 146 sq mi (378 sq km), SE Greece, in the Aegean Sea, the northernmost and second largest of the CYCLADES. Ándros (1971 pop. 1,827) is the capital and chief town. The island produces silk, wine, and lemons and has manganese deposits. Colonized by Athens in the 5th cent. B.C., Ándros rebelled in 410 B.C., became a free state, and later passed successively to Macedon, Pergamum, and Rome. Seized (1204) from the Byzantines by Venice and made a principality, it remained almost entirely under Venetian rule until its conquest (1514) by the Turks. In 1829 it passed to Greece.

Androscoggin (ăndrəskŏg'ĭn), river, c.175 mi (280 km) long, rising in NE N.H., flowing south and east to enter the Atlantic Ocean at Bath, Maine. Hydroelectric plants, using the river's steep gradient, supply power to nearby towns. The area is a major pulp and paper producer; the practice of floating logs downstream has hindered the river's further development for power.

Andros Island: see BAHAMA ISLANDS.

Androuet du Cerceau (äNdro͞o-ā' dü sĕrsō'), family of French architects active in the 16th and 17th cent. It was founded by **Jacques Androuet,** c.1520–c.1584, surnamed du Cerceau [Fr.,=circle] from the emblem of a circle marking his workshop. He is best known for his writings and his fanciful engravings of decorative architectural elements. Attributed to him are designs for two châteaux, Verneuil and Charleval. Of his two sons, who both worked on the Louvre, **Baptiste Androuet du Cerceau,** c.1545–1590, designed the Pont Neuf spanning the Seine at Paris and became supervisor of royal construction in Paris, while **Jacques Androuet du Cerceau,** the younger, c.1556–1614, worked on the Tuileries. Baptiste's son **Jean Androuet du Cerceau,** c.1585–1650, is known for his mansions in Paris, one of which is the Hôtel de Sully.

Andrusov, Treaty of (ăn'dro͞osŏf", Rus. əndro͞o'səf), 1667, signed by Poland and Russia at the village of Andrusov, Russia, (present-day Androsovo, RSFSR). It ended the war of Czar ALEXIS of Russia against JOHN II of Poland. Russia gained the Smolensk and Seversk provinces and the Ukraine E of the Dnepr (left-bank Ukraine), including Kiev.

Andújar (ändo͞o'här), city (1970 pop. 31,464), Jaén prov., S Spain, in Andalusia, on the Guadalquivir River. Its pottery and its water-cooling jars made of porous stone are famous. A painting by El Greco hangs in the 12th-century Gothic Church of Santa María.

anecdote (ăn'ĭkdōt"), brief narrative of a particular incident. An anecdote differs from a SHORT STORY in that it is unified in time and space, is uncomplicated, and deals with a single episode. The literal Greek meaning of the word is "not published," and it still retains some such sense of confidentiality. Sometimes an anecdote is inserted into a novel as an interval in the main plot, as in Laurence Sterne's *Tristram Shandy.* Famous books of anecdotes include the *Deipnosophistae* of Athenaeus and Plutarch's *Lives.*

Anegada: see VIRGIN ISLANDS.

Aneirin: see ANEURIN.

Anem (ā'nĕm), the same as EN-GANNIM **2.**

anemia, condition in which the concentration of hemoglobin in the circulating blood is below normal. Such a condition is caused by a deficient number of erythrocytes (red blood cells), an abnormally low level of hemoglobin in the individual cells, or both these conditions simultaneously. Regardless of the cause, all types of anemia cause similar signs and symptoms because of the blood's reduced capacity to carry oxygen. These symptoms include pallor of the skin and mucous membranes, weakness, dizziness, easy fatigability, and drowsiness. Severe cases show difficulty in breathing, heart abnormalities, and digestive complaints. One of the most common anemias, iron-deficiency anemia, is caused by insufficient iron, an element essential for the formation of hemoglobin in the erythrocytes. In most adults (except pregnant women) the cause is chronic blood loss rather than insufficient iron in the diet, and, therefore, the treatment includes locating the source of abnormal bleeding in addition to the administration of iron. Pernicious anemia causes an increased production of erythrocytes that are structurally abnormal and have attenuated life spans. This condition rarely occurs before age 35 and is inherited, being more prevalent among persons of Scandinavian, Irish, and English extraction. It is caused by the inability of the body to absorb vitamin B_{12} (which is essential for the maturation of erythrocytes) from food and is treated by repeated injections of vitamin B_{12}. There are several conditions that cause the destruction of erythrocytes, thereby producing anemia. Allergic-type reactions to bacterial toxins and various chemical agents, among them sulfonamides and benzene, can cause hemolysis, which requires emergency treatment. In addition, there are unusual situations in which the body produces antibodies against its own erythrocytes; the mechanism triggering such reactions remains obscure. Any disease or injury to the bone marrow can cause anemia, since that tissue is the site of erythrocyte synthesis. Bone marrow destruction can also be caused by irradiation, disease, or various chemical agents. There are several inherited anemias that are more common among dark-skinned people. SICKLE-CELL ANEMIA is inherited as a recessive trait almost exclusively among blacks; the condition is characterized by a chemical abnormality of the hemoglobin molecule that causes the erythrocytes to be misshapen. Thalassemia major (Cooley's anemia) is the most serious of the hereditary anemias that occur more frequently among those of Mediterranean, Middle Eastern, and S Chinese ancestry. The erythrocytes are abnormally shaped and many are nucleated. Symptoms include enlarged liver and spleen and jaundice. Thalassemia major usually causes death before adulthood is reached.

anemometer: see WIND.

anemone (ənĕm'ənē) or **windflower,** any of the perennial herbs, wild or cultivated, of the genus *Anemone* of the family Ranunculaceae (BUTTERCUP family). A rich legendary history has gained the anemone many names and attributes. It is said to have sprung from the blood of Adonis; Romans considered it valuable in preventing fever; it has been applied for bruises and freckles; for some it is tainted with evil; and by the Chinese it has been associated with death. The name windflower is accounted for in several ways, one of which is Pliny's statement that anemone blossoms are opened by the wind. Anemones contain an acrid compound called anemonin. It is poisonous but was formerly used medicinally. Best known of the wild kinds are the white- or purplish-flowered wood anemone (*A. quinquefolia*), sometimes known specifically as windflower, and the greenish-white-flowered tall anemone, or thimbleweed (*A. virginiana*), with thimble-shaped fruit. The most common cultivated kinds include the tall, autumn-flowering Japanese anemone (*A. japonica*) for gardens and the florists' poppy anemones (*A. coronaria*), native to the Mediterranean area. Similar to the anemone is the wild rue anemone of another buttercup-family genus (*Anemonella* or *Syndesmon*). The PASQUEFLOWER is sometimes included in *Anemone.* Anemones are classified in the division MAGNOLIOPHYTA, class Magnoliopsida, order Ranunculales, family Ranunculaceae.

Aner (ā'nər). **1** Ally of Abraham. Gen. 14.13,24. **2** Levitical town, E of the Jordan. 1 Chron. 6.70.

aneroid altimeter: see AIR NAVIGATION.

aneroid barometer: see BAROMETER.

anesthesia (ănĭsthē'zhə) [Gr.,=insensibility], loss of sensation, especially that of pain, induced by drugs. General anesthetics, usually employed in surgical operations of long duration, cause unconsciousness and are usually inhalation anesthetics. These inhalant gases include ether, halothane, and cyclopropane. Anesthesia of short duration may be induced by intravenous injection of sodium pentothal, a procedure used to initiate unconsciousness in most surgical operations. Rectal anesthetics such as tribromoethanol (Avertin) are also used in this manner, usually supplemented later by inhalation anesthetics. Nitrous oxide is used when deep unconsciousness is not required. Local anesthetics (e.g., novocaine and ethyl chloride) are used in dentistry and in minor surgery and affect sensation only in the region of application. Spinal anesthesia is produced by injecting the anesthetic beneath the membrane of the spinal cord. This method is often used in surgery of the abdomen and legs. Caudal anesthesia, used in obstetrics, is produced by injecting the anesthetic into the sacral canal. Muscle relaxants, such as curare and its derivatives, are used to reduce the amount of conventional anesthetic required. Body temperature may be lowered in conjunction with the use of anesthetics. Extensive heart and brain surgery can be carried out at body temperatures which are 10° F or more below normal. The metabolic rate is so much reduced that cells are not damaged by the lack of circulating blood. The various forms of anesthesia are frequently used in combination; in the United States, a skilled anesthetist is present at all major operations. Anesthetics are also used in the treatment of certain types of mental illness. Early experimenters with nitrous oxide (laughing gas) were Sir Humphry Davy of England and Horace Wells of the United States. Ether was used as a general anesthetic in the United States by Crawford W. Long in 1842, but more general use of ether came after a demonstration at the Massachusetts General Hospital in Boston by William T. G. Morton in 1846. Sir James Y. Simpson in 1847 was the first to employ a general anesthetic in obstetrics. Safer and more efficient anesthetics are continually discovered, as anesthesiologists perfect new ways of combining and administering them. See ACUPUNCTURE. See T. E. Keys, *History of Surgical Anesthesia* (rev. ed. 1963); Frederick Prescott, *The Control of Pain* (1965).

anesthesiology (ăn"ĭsthē"zēŏl'əjē), branch of MEDICINE concerned primarily with procedures for rendering patients insensitive to pain, and for supporting life systems under the strains of ANESTHESIA and surgery. The anesthesiologist will induce unconsciousness for various clinical purposes and will perform cardiac and respiratory resuscitation when necessary.

Aneto, Pico de (pē'kō dā änā'tō), Fr. *Pic de Néthou* or *Pic d'Anethou,* peak, 11,168 ft (3,404 m) high, NE Spain, in the Maladetta group near the French border. It is the highest peak of the Pyrenees.

Anetothite (ăn'ĭtōthīt): see ANATHOTH.

Aneurin (ă'nyo͝orĭn, ă'-) or **Aneirin** (ă'nīrĕn), fl. c.600, Welsh bard whose reputed writings are contained in a 13th-century manuscript, *Book of Aneirin.* Included in this manuscript is *Gododin,* a 900-line elegiac poem of a defeat of the Welsh by the Saxons. The poem is one of the oldest extant works of Welsh literature and contains probably the earliest explicit allusion to King Arthur.

neurysm (ăn'yo͞orĭzəm), localized dilatation of a blood vessel, particularly an artery. Dilatation of an artery, and therefore weakness of that portion of the arterial wall, may be congenital, or it may be caused by syphilis, high blood pressure, arteriosclerosis, bacterial and fungus infections, or penetrating injury as from a bullet or knife. An aneurysm may be asymptomatic, or it may cause varying symptoms depending upon its location and on whether the expanding mass is pressing on adjacent nerves or vital organs. The weakened arterial walls of an aneurysm are always in danger of sudden rupture, with resulting hemorrhage and death. Aneurysms occur most commonly in the large arteries; the aorta, the largest vessel in the body, is the one most often affected. They also occur in the arteries within the skull and in other areas of the body. The only treatment is surgical, where feasible, i.e., excision of the dilated saclike portion of the affected artery. This may require replacement by an arterial graft, a portion of vessel similar in size. There has also been successful replacement with tubes made of synthetic material.

NFO, ammonium nitrate and fuel oil. See EXPLOSIVE.

ngara (äng"gərä', Rus. ŭn"gərä'), river, c.1,150 mi (1,850 km) long, SE Siberian USSR, the outlet of Lake Baykal. After leaving the southwestern end of Lake Baykal, it flows north past Irkutsk and Bratsk, then turns west after receiving the Ilim River and flows into the Yenisei River near Strelka. Below its junction with the Ilim River the Angara is known also as the Upper Tunguska (Rus. *Verkhnyaya Tunguska*). The Angara is navigable between Irkutsk and Bratsk; below Bratsk there are many rapids. At Bratsk is a large dam with one of the world's largest hydroelectric power plants (c.4.5 million kw); a smaller hydroelectric station is at Irkutsk. Iron, coal, and gold deposits are found in the Angara basin. The Upper Angara River (Rus. *Verkhnyaya Angara*), c.200 mi (320 km) long, rises NE of Lake Baykal and flows SW through the Buryat Autonomous Republic into the lake; it is partly navigable.

ngara Shield, Asia: see SIBERIAN PLATFORM.

ngel [Gr.,=messenger], bodiless, immortal spirit, limited in knowledge and power, accepted in the traditional belief of Judaism, Christianity, and Islam. Angels appear frequently in the Bible, often in critical roles, e.g., visiting Abraham and Lot (Gen. 18; 19), wrestling with Jacob (Gen. 32.24-32), and guiding Tobit (Tobit 5). In the Gospels an angel announced the Incarnation to the Virgin Mary (Luke 1), and an angel at the empty tomb revealed the Resurrection (Mat. 28.1-7). The Bible also speaks of guardian angels, protecting individuals or nations. Dan. 10.10-21; Mat. 18.10. The hierarchy of angels in three choirs appears early in the Christian era; the classes are, from the highest: seraphim, cherubim, thrones; dominations, virtues, powers; principalities, arch-angels, angels. Eph. 1.21; Col. 1.16. From these two passages Dionysius the Areopagite fixed the number and order of angels in *The Celestial Hierarchy.* Roman Catholics and the Orthodox venerate angels, and the cult of guardian angels is especially extensive in the West (feast of Guardian Angels: Oct. 2). Protestants have generally abandoned the cult of angels. The angels of Hell, or dark angels, or devils, are the evil counterpart of the heavenly host; the chief of them, Satan (or Lucifer), was cast out of heaven for leading a revolt. They are often viewed as the initiators of evil temptations. Job 1-2; Isa. 14.4-23; Mat. 25.41; Luke 10.18; Eph. 6.12; Jude 9. Famous literary treatments of angels are those of John Milton's *Paradise Lost* and Dante's *Divine Comedy.* See ARCHANGEL; CHERUB; SERAPH; GABRIEL; MICHAEL; RAPHAEL; SATAN.

ngel Fall, waterfall, Sp. *Salto Ángel,* 3,212 ft (979 m) high, SE Venezuela, in the Guiana Highlands. Springing from Auyán-Tepuí Mesa, it is the highest uninterrupted waterfall in the world.

ngelfish: see BUTTERFLY FISH.

ngelholm (ĕng"əlhôlm'), city (1970 pop. 18,364), Kristianstad co., SW Sweden, on Skälderviken Bay (an arm of the Kattegat); chartered 1516. It is a beach resort and has tanneries. The city is also known as Engelholm.

ngelica (ănjĕl'ĭkə), any species of the genus *Angelica,* plants of the family Umbelliferae (CARROT family), native to the Northern Hemisphere and New Zealand, valued for their potency as a medicament and protection against evil spirits and the plague, which probably accounts for the name; angelica is a poetic symbol for inspiration. The roots and fruits yield angelica oil, which is used in perfume, confectionery, medicine, and for flavoring liqueurs (such as angelica). The species most often used for these purposes is *A. archangelica,* a subarctic and alpine plant of the Old World once extensively grown but now seldom cultivated outside Germany. This and a few other species are sometimes used as ornamentals. Angelica is classified in the division MAGNOLIOPHYTA, class Magnoliopsida, order Umbellales, family Umbelliferae.

Angelico, Fra (frä änjĕl'ĭkō), c.1400-1455, Florentine painter, b. Vicchio, Tuscany. He was variously named Guido (his baptismal name), or Guidolino, di Pietro; and Giovanni da Fiesole. After his death he was called Il Beato Fra Giovanni Angelico, although he was never officially beatified. Angelico's style is remarkable for its purity of line and color and its spiritual expressiveness. He took his vows c.1425 in the Dominican order. The first painting of certain date (1433) by Angelico is his *Madonna of the Linen Guild* (St. Mark's convent, Florence). It is supposed that his activity began at least 10 years earlier, and that he first painted small pictures, such as *St. Jerome Penitent* (Princeton Univ.) and miniatures. Other works suggested for this period (1423-33) are *Virgin and Child Enthroned with Twelve Angels* (Staedel Inst., Frankfurt); *Virgin and Child with Angels* (National Gall., London); *Madonna of the Star* and *Naming of the Baptist* (both: St. Mark's convent). It is thought that Angelico was first influenced by Gentile da Fabriano, and that he soon adopted Masaccio's advances in spatial conception. Critics have assigned to the 1430s such works as the *Annunciation* (Cortona); *Coronation of the Virgin* (Louvre); *Deposition* and *Last Judgment* (both: St. Mark's convent). In 1436, under the protection of Cosimo de' Medici, the Dominicans of Fiesole moved to St. Mark's convent in Florence. Fra Angelico supervised the fresco decoration of the building. Among the works considered to be by his hand are the *Crucifixion with St. Dominic* (cloisters) and the great *Crucifixion* (chapter house). In the convent also are frescoed *Noli mi Tangere, Annunciation, Transfiguration, Mocking of Christ, Presentation in the Temple, Virgin and Child with Saints,* and others. In 1445 he was summoned to Rome by Pope Eugenius IV to decorate the Cappella del Sacramento in the Vatican. In 1447 he visited Orvieto, where, assisted by his pupil Benozzo Gozzoli, he painted *Christ as Judge* and the *Prophets* in the Cappella Nuova of the cathedral. Returning to Rome, he designed in the following year his greatest and most unified scenes—episodes from the lives of St. Stephen and St. Lawrence. However, the execution of this project was probably carried out mainly by pupils. Fra Angelico treated none but religious subjects. Adapting the artistic innovations of his time (e.g., sculptural clarity of form and spatial depth), he interpreted them in terms of the greatest spirituality. Angelico endowed the new forms with his own incomparable sense of coloring and unity. In the United States he is represented by the *Crucifixion* (Fogg Mus., Cambridge); *Assumption and Dormition of the Virgin* (Gardner Mus., Boston); *Temptation of St. Anthony Abbot* (Mus. of Fine Arts, Houston, Texas);and *Crucifixion* and *Nativity* (both: Metropolitan Mus.).

Angel Island, largest island in San Francisco Bay, W Calif. Discovered by the Spanish in 1775, it came under U.S. control in 1851. The U.S. army used the island as a base from 1863 to 1946; in 1952 a radar and missile site was established. During World War II, enemy prisoners of war were confined on Angel Island. Part of the island is now a state park.

Angell, James Burrill, 1829-1916, American educator, editor, and diplomat, b. Scituate, R.I., grad. Brown, 1849, and studied abroad. He became professor of modern languages at Brown. Resigning in 1860, he served as editor of the Providence *Journal.* Later, as president of the Univ. of Vermont (1866-71) and of the Univ. of Michigan (1871-1909), Angell became known as an administrator. In this period he served also as minister to China (1880-81) and to Turkey (1897-98). See his *Reminiscences and Selected Addresses* (1912, repr. 1971); biography by S. W. Smith (1954).

Angell, James Rowland, 1869-1949, American educator and psychologist, b. Burlington, Vt., grad. Univ. of Michigan (B.A. 1890; M.A. 1891), M.A. Harvard, 1892; son of James B. Angell. After study abroad, he taught at the Univ. of Minnesota, then at the Univ. of Chicago (1894-1920), where he became professor and head of the psychology department (1905), dean of the university faculties (1911), and acting president (1918-19). He served as president of Yale from 1921 until his retirement in 1937; in his administration the physical facilities of Yale were greatly expanded. In 1937 he became educational counselor of the National Broadcasting Company. His writings include several standard psychology textbooks, *Chapters from Modern Psychology* (1912), *American Education* (1937), and articles on psychology and education.

Angell, Sir Norman, 1872?-1967, British internationalist and economist, whose name originally was Ralph Norman Angell Lane. He came to fame with *The Great Illusion* (1910, rev. ed. 1933), in which he posited that the common economic interests of nations make war futile. At the close of World War I he worked for a generous peace and international cooperation. In *Peace with the Dictators?* (1938) he attacked the British Conservative party's policy of condoning Japanese and Italian aggression. After World War II he urged unity among the Western democracies in such works as *Defence and the English-speaking Role* (1958). Knighted in 1931, Norman Angell was awarded the 1933 Nobel Peace Prize. See his autobiography (1951).

Angelus (ăn'jələs), family name and dynasty of three Byzantine emperors (1185-1204): see ISAAC II; ALEXIUS III; ALEXIUS IV.

Angelus [Lat.,=angel], daily prayer of the Roman Catholic Church, said usually three times daily, as announced by a bell, traditionally at six in the morning, at noon, and at six in the evening. It is said in honor of the Incarnation and consists of three repetitions of the Hail Mary together with verses and a prayer. It takes its name from the opening word of the Latin version: *Angelus Domini nuntiavit Mariae* [the angel of the Lord declared unto Mary].

Angelus Silesius (ăn'jələs sīlē'zhəs), pseud. of **Johannes Scheffler** (yōhän'əs shĕf'lər), 1624-77, German poet. He is best known for his pastoral lyric cycles *Heilige Seelenlust* (1657-68) and *Cherubinischer Wandersmann* (1674-75), which can be interpreted as Christian as well as pantheistic. Scheffler's mysticism strongly influenced 18th-century PIETISM. See study by J. L. Sammons (1967).

Ångermanälven (ông'ərmänĕl"vən), river, c.280 mi (450 km) long, rising in Västerbotten prov., W central Sweden, and flowing generally southeast through narrow lakes and past Sollefteå and Kramfors to the Gulf of Bothnia at Härnösand. The Faxeälven is its chief tributary. The river is used to float logs downstream to sawmills. There are numerous hydroelectric power plants on the river. Sandöbridge (866 ft/264 m long; opened 1943), one of the world's longest concrete arch bridges, spans the river.

Angers (äNzhā'), city (1968 pop. 134,959), capital of Maine-et-Loire dept., W France, in Anjou, on the Maine River. A business and trade center, it is known for its wine. It also has glassworks, printing plants, and factories making electronic and photographic equipment, textiles, food, paper products, and tiles. On its outskirts are the largest slate quarries in France. Of pre-Roman origin, Angers became the seat (870-1204) of the powerful counts of ANJOU and the historic capital of the province. There is a fine cathedral (12th-13th cent.) and a museum containing 14th-century tapestries and a large collection of the sculpture of David d'Angers. The 13th-century castle was among the buildings damaged in World War II. Schools of fine arts and medicine are located there.

Angevin (ăn'jəvĭn) [Fr.,=of Anjou], name of two medieval dynasties originating in France. The first ruled over parts of France and over Jerusalem and England; the second ruled over parts of France and over Naples, Hungary, and Poland, with a claim to Jerusalem. The older house issued from one Fulk, who became count of ANJOU in the 10th cent. Fulk V (see FULK) of Anjou, one of his descendants, became (1131) king of Jerusalem. A younger son inherited the kingship of Jerusalem as Baldwin III and was succeeded by Almaric I, Baldwin IV, and Baldwin V, with whom the branch ended (1186). Fulk V's elder son, GEOFFREY IV (Geoffrey Plantagenet), inherited Anjou. He married Matilda of England, daughter of King Henry I of England, and conquered Normandy. Their son became (1154) the first Angevin (or Plantagenet) king of England as Henry II. His successors were Richard I, John, Henry III, Edward I, Edward II, Edward III, and Richard II, after whom the English branch split into the houses of Lancaster and of York. A nephew of Richard I and John became (1196) duke of Brittany as Arthur I. From his sister and her husband, Peter of Dreux, a Capetian noble who became Duke PETER I of Brittany, the subsequent rulers of Brittany issued. The Breton line of the Angevins came to an end with the marriages of Anne of Brittany and her daughter to the kings of France. The second house of Anjou was a cadet branch of the Capetians and originated with Charles, a younger brother of King Louis IX of France. Charles was made count of Anjou by Louis, acquired Provence by marriage, and in 1266 was invested by the pope with the kingdom of Naples and Sicily as Charles I. Charles lost Sicily but retained Naples. His successors were Charles II, Robert, and Joanna I of Naples and Provence. On the death (1382) of Joanna I the succession to Naples was contested by two cadet branches, both descended from Charles II of Naples. The first was represented by Charles of Durazzo (Charles III of Naples), a great-grandson through the male line, and by his children, Lancelot and Joanna II. They retained, for the most part, actual possession of the kingdom, despite the efforts of the rival line, issued from Margaret, a daughter of Charles II. Margaret married Charles of Valois; their son and grandson were kings Philip VI and John II, respectively, of France. John made his younger son, Louis, duke of Anjou; Joanna I of Naples adopted Louis as heir; Louis thus became Louis I of Naples and Provence. His successors were Louis II, Louis III, and René. Although the last two were successively designated as heirs by Joanna II, Naples was seized by King Alfonso V of Aragón and eventually remained in Spanish hands. René became duke of Lorraine by marriage. His nephew and heir, Charles, count of Maine, died in 1481 without issue; and Anjou, Maine, Provence, and the Angevin claim to Naples all passed to the French crown. The theoretical claim to Jerusalem stemmed from Charles I of Naples, whom Pope John XXI invested (c.1276) with the title. René's claim to the title was transmitted to the house of Lorraine. The Hungarian branch of Anjou began (1308) with Charles Robert (King Charles I of Hungary), a grandson of Charles II of Naples. Charles I's son became king of Hungary and Poland as Louis I. Hungary passed to Louis's daughter Mary and to her husband Sigismund (later Holy Roman emperor), and Poland passed to Ladislaus II of Poland, husband of Louis's daughter Jadwiga.

Angilbert, Saint (ăng'gĭlbərt), d. 814, Frankish statesman and courtier under Charlemagne, abbot of Centula (now Saint-Riquier), near Amiens. He was highly regarded in the Carolingian revival as a writer of Latin poetry. Feast: Feb. 18.

angina pectoris (ănjī'nə pĕk'tərĭs), condition characterized by chest pain and caused by occlusion (closure) of the coronary arteries, resulting in insufficient supply of oxygen to the heart muscle; in rare cases, it occurs in the absence of coronary artery disease. The pain is usually experienced under or to the left of the sternum (breastbone) and radiates to the left shoulder and down the upper arm; less frequently, it spreads to the right shoulder. The attack usually subsides without residual discomfort and, when precipitated by physical exertion, is quickly halted when the subject rests. Angina pectoris occurs usually after the age of 50, more often in men than women, and frequently follows exertion, excitement, eating, or exposure to cold. Associated symptoms are faintness and difficulty in breathing. Drugs (e.g., amyl nitrite or nitroglycerine) that dilate the blood vessels of the heart are used in treatment.

angiosperm (ăn'jēəspûrm''), term used for any flowering plant in which the ovules, or young seeds, are enclosed within the ovary (that part of the pistil specialized for seed production), in contrast to the gymnosperms, in which the seeds are exposed during all stages of development. The angiosperms constitute the division MAGNOLIOPHYTA and include all our agricultural crops (including the cereal grains and other grasses), all garden flowers and horticultural plants, all the common broad-leaved shrubs and trees, and all the usual field, garden, and roadside weeds. The angiosperms are the best known and most economically important of all plants.

Angkor (ăng'kôr), site of several capitals of the KHMER EMPIRE, N of Tônlé Sap, NW Cambodia, for five and a half centuries the heart of the empire. Extending over an area of 40 sq mi (104 sq km), the ruins contain some of the most imposing monuments in the world. The first capital was founded by Yasovarman I (889–900) and was centered around the pyramidal temple of Phnom Bak Kheng. To the southeast of the original capital, a new temple complex, **Angkor Wat** [Angkor temple], was created under Suryavarman II (1113–50). Planned as a sepulcher and a monument to the divinity of the monarch, it is probably the largest religious structure in the world. Surrounded by a vast moat, the temple is approached by means of an extensive causeway bordered on either side by balustrades in the form of giant Nagas (divine serpents). This avenue leads to a magnificent entrance gate. The temple proper is reached through three series of galleries separated by paved courts. The middle series has four corner towers; above it, the highest series also has four corner towers and is joined to the central sanctuary by colonnades. The architecture of Angkor Wat, derived from the stupa form, is enormously impressive, but the most remarkable feature of the temple compound is its sculptural ornament, covering thousands of feet of wall space. The decoration is in the form of low relief of impeccable craftsmanship, illustrating scenes from the legends of Vishnu and Krishna, with some historical events from the life of the king. More delicate in proportions than their Indian prototypes, many of the figures, in their elegance of gesture and stateliness of pose, bear a resemblance to modern Cambodian dancers. In 1177, Angkor was sacked by the Chams, and Angkor Wat fell into ruins. Jayavarman VII (1181–c.1218) established a new capital, **Angkor Thom** [the great Angkor], N of Phnom Bak Kheng. The buildings of an already existing city were used as residential palaces and governmental buildings; an excellent system of moats and canals was constructed. At the four entrances of the capital, there are gateways; they open onto four avenues that meet at the Bayon, the temple in the center of the city. Before each gateway is a bridge decorated with a balustrade in the shape of a giant Naga, supported on each side by 27 carved figures. Above the gates are carved imposing stone faces, generally thought to symbolize the Bodhisattva Lokesvara. Under Jayavarman VII the Bayon was used as a Buddhist sanctuary, but it underwent alterations during a later Hindu period. The central tower bears a giant image of Buddha, which has been interpreted as the incarnation of Jayavarman VII. Surrounding the main structure is a forest of more than 50 smaller towers studded with multiple heads of the king as a Buddhist god. The buildings are covered with elaborate decoration, more spontaneously and realistically rendered than that at Angkor Wat and again illustrating historical episodes from the king's life. Angkor was raided in the 14th and 15th cent. by the Thai. It was abandoned in 1434 for Phnom Penh. Overgrown by the jungle, the ruins were discovered by the French in 1861. Many of the monuments were subsequently restored to their former glory. See Madeleine Giteau, *Khmer Sculpture and the Angkor Civilization* (1966); Bernard Groslier and Jacques Arthaud, *The Arts and Civilization of Angkor* (rev. ed. 1966); Jan Myrdal and Gun Kessle, *Angkor: An Essay on Art and Imperialism* (1971); John Audric, *Angkor and the Khmer Empire* (1972).

angle, in mathematics, figure formed by the intersection of two straight lines; the lines are called the sides of the angle and their point of intersection the vertex of the angle. Angles are commonly measured in degrees (°) or in radians. If one side and the vertex of an angle are fixed and the other side is rotated about the vertex, it sweeps out a complete circle of 360° or 2π radians with each complete rotation. Half a rotation from 0° or 0 radians results in a straight angle, equal to 180° or π radians; the sides of a straight angle form a straight line. A quarter rotation (half of a straight angle) results in a right angle, equal to 90° or $\pi/2$ radians; the sides of a right angle are perpendicular to one another. An angle less than a right angle is acute, and an angle greater than a right angle is obtuse. Two angles that add up to a right angle are complementary. Two angles that add up to a straight angle are supplementary. One of the GEOMETRIC PROBLEMS OF ANTIQUITY is the trisection of the angle.

angler, common name for a member of the family Ceratiidae, European and American bottom-dwelling predacious fishes. The angler lies on the bottom and lures its prey with a long, wormlike appendage that extends forward and dangles over its mouth. When the lure is touched, the huge mouth opens automatically. The deep-sea anglers are fantastic fishes, many with luminescent lures, that live at depths of 200 to 600 fathoms. The various species grow from 6 to 40 in. (15–500 cm) long. The parasitic males attach themselves to the females and do not develop eyes and digestive organs. The sargassum fishes, less than 6 in. (15 cm) long, have armlike pectoral fins and mottled coloration adapted to merge with the seaweed in which they live; they are found in warm Atlantic waters, as are the 8- to 12-in. (20–30 cm) batfishes, named for their jointed pectoral fins. The goosefish, the largest angler, reaches 4 ft (120 cm) and 50 lb (23 kg) and is capable of swallowing fish as big as itself. Angler fish are classified in the phylum CHORDATA, subphylum Vertebrata, class Osteichthyes, order Lophiiformes, family Ceratiidae.

Angles: see ANGLO-SAXONS.

Anglesey or **Anglesea** (both: ăng'gəlsē), island (1971 pop. 59,705), 275 sq mi (712 sq km), NW Wales. Beaumaris is the chief town. It is a region of low, rolling hills. The principal industries are agriculture and stock raising. Two bridges over the Menai Strait connect the island to the mainland. The town of Menai Bridge has long been a stock-trading center for NW Wales. Anglesey is said to have been the last refuge of the druids from the Romans in Britain. Penmynydd, at the center of the island, was the home of Owen Tudor, founder of the house of

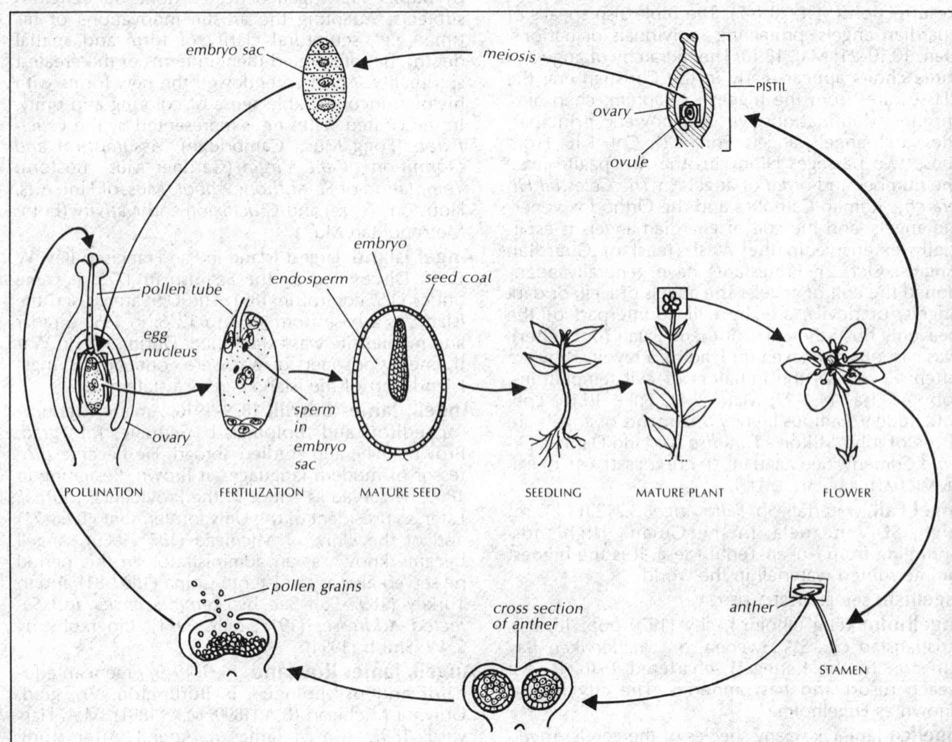

Life cycle of an angiosperm

Tudor. In 1974, Anglesey became part of the new nonmetropolitan county of Gwynedd.

nglesite (ăng'gləsīt), pale green, blue, yellow-to-white, or colorless mineral, a sulfate of lead, $PbSO_4$, that is formed by oxidation of GALENA, crystallizing in the orthorhombic system and occurring also in granular or massive form. It is widely distributed and commonly associated with galena and other lead minerals. It is a minor lead ore.

nglican Communion, the body of churches in all parts of the world that are in communion with the Church of England (see ENGLAND, CHURCH OF). The Communion is composed of regional churches, provinces, and separate dioceses bound together by mutual loyalty as expressed in the Lambeth Conference of 1930. There are 20 national member churches, including the Protestant Episcopal Church of America (see EPISCOPAL CHURCH, PROTESTANT), the Scottish Episcopal Church, the Church in Wales, the Church of Ireland (see IRELAND, CHURCH OF), and the Nippon Sei Ko Kwai (Japan). There are separate dioceses in Jerusalem and Egypt. There are over 46 million baptized members. Worship is liturgical and is regulated by the BOOK OF COMMON PRAYER. See Stephen Neill, *Anglicanism* (3d ed. 1965); C. E. Simcox, *The Historical Road of Anglicanism* (1968).

ngling: see FISHING.

nglo-Catholic movement: see OXFORD MOVEMENT.

nglo-Norman literature, body of literature written in England, in the French dialect known as Anglo-Norman, from c.1100 to c.1250. Initiated at the court of Henry I, it was supported by the wealthy, French-speaking aristocracy who controlled England after the Norman conquest. The dominant literary forms were histories, sacred and secular biographies, and homilies; romance and fiction were relatively scarce. Perhaps the most important historian was Geoffrey Gaimer, whose two-part history of England, *Histoire des Bretons* and *Estorie des Engles,* was written in verse. Philippe of Thaün, the earliest known Anglo-Norman poet, was noted for the moral allegory the *Bestiaire.* Of secular works, Thomas's *Tristan* (c.1170) is notable both artistically and as an early source for the Tristram and Isolde legend. See M. D. Legge, *Anglo-Norman Literature and Its Background* (1963).

nglo-Saxon Chronicle, collective name given several English monastic chronicles in Anglo-Saxon, all stemming from a compilation made from old annals and other sources c.891. Although the work was thought for some time to have been commissioned by King Alfred, there is no positive evidence to substantiate this claim; his encouragement of learning, however, undoubtedly inspired the compilation of the chronicle. The original chronicle was later edited with additions, omissions, and continuations by monks in various monasteries. The account begins with the start of the Christian era and extends to 1154. Much of the very early material is drawn from Bede's history. From the period of the wars between Saxons and Danes onward, most of the annals are original and are the sole source for information about certain events. The writing is generally in sparse prose, but some poems are inserted, notably the stirring "Battle of Brunanburh" (see BRUNANBURH). The four chronicles recognized as distinct are called the Winchester Chronicle, the Abingdon Chronicle, the Worcester Chronicle, and the Peterborough Chronicle. See Charles Plummer, ed., *Two of the Saxon Chronicles Parallel* (1892–99); Dorothy Whitelock et al., ed., *The Anglo-Saxon Chronicle* (1962); Cecily Clark, ed., *The Peterborough Chronicle* (2d ed. 1970).

nglo-Saxon literature, the literary writings in Old English (see ENGLISH LANGUAGE), composed between c.650 and c.1100. There are two types of Old English poetry: the heroic, the sources of which are pre-Christian Germanic myth, history, and custom; and the Christian. Although nearly all Old English poetry is preserved in only four manuscripts—indicating that what has survived is not necessarily the best or the most representative—much of it is of high literary quality. Moreover, the Old English heroic poetry is the earliest extant in all of Germanic literature. It is thus the nearest we can come to the oral pagan literature of Germanic culture, and it is also of inestimable value as a source of knowledge about many aspects of Germanic society. WIDSITH, a 7th-century Old English poem, is one of the earliest and thus of particular historic and linguistic interest. BEOWULF, a complete epic, is the oldest surviving Germanic epic as well as the longest and most important poem in Old English. It originated as a pagan saga transmitted orally from one generation to the next; court poets known as scops were the bearers of tribal history and tradition. The version of *Beowulf* that is extant was composed by a Christian poet probably early in the 8th cent. However, intermittent Christian themes found in the epic, although affecting in themselves, are not integrated into the essentially pagan tale. The epic celebrates the hero's fearless and bloody struggles against monsters and extols courage, honor, and loyalty as the chief virtues in a world of brutal force. The elegaic theme, a strong undercurrent in *Beowulf,* is central to *Deor, The Wanderer, The Seafarer,* and other poems. In these works, a happy past is contrasted with a precarious and desolate present. The *Finnsburgh* fragment, *The Battle of Maldon,* and *The Battle of Brunaburgh* (see MALDON and BRUNABURGH), which are all based on historical episodes, mostly celebrate great heroism in the face of overwhelming odds. In this heroic poetry, all of which is anonymous, greatness is measured less by victory than by perfect loyalty and courage in extremity. Much of the Old English Christian poetry is marked by the simple belief of a relatively unsophisticated Christianity; the names of two authors are known. CAEDMON—whose story is charmingly told by the Venerable BEDE, who also records a few lines of his poetry—is the earliest known English poet. Although the body of his work has been lost, the school of Caedmon is responsible for poetic narrative versions of biblical stories, the most dramatic of which is probably *Genesis B.* CYNEWULF, a later poet, signed the poems *Elene, Juliana,* and *The Fates of the Apostles,* and no more is known of him. The finest poem of the school of Cynewulf is *The Dream of the Rood,* the first known example of the dream vision, a genre later popular in MIDDLE ENGLISH LITERATURE. Other Old English poems include various riddles, charms (magic cures, pagan in origin), saints' lives, gnomic poetry, and other Christian and heroic verse. The verse form for Old English is an alliterative line of four stressed syllables and an unfixed number of unstressed syllables broken by a caesura and arranged in one of several patterns. Lines are conventionally end-stopped and unrhymed. The form lends itself to narrative; there is no lyric poetry in Old English. A stylistic feature in the heroic poetry is the kenning, a figurative phrase, often a metaphorical compound, used as a synonym for a simple noun, e.g., the repeated use of the phrases *whale-road* for *sea* and *twilight-spoiler* for *dragon* (see OLD NORSE LITERATURE). Old English literary prose dates from the latter part of the period. Prose was written in Latin before the reign of King ALFRED (reigned 871–99), who worked to revitalize English culture after the devastating Danish invasions had ended. As hardly anyone could read Latin, Alfred translated or had translated the most important Latin texts. He also encouraged writing in the vernacular. Didactic, devotional, and informative prose was written, and the *Anglo-Saxon Chronicle,* probably begun in Alfred's time as an historical record, continued for over three centuries. Two preeminent Old English prose writers were AELFRIC, Abbot of Eynsham, and his contemporary WULFSTAN, Archbishop of York. Their sermons (written in the late 10th or early 11th cent.) set a standard for homiletics. A great deal of Latin prose and poetry was written during the Anglo-Saxon period. Of historic as well as literary interest, it provides an excellent record of the founding and early development of the church in England, and reflects the introduction and early influence there of Latin-European culture. See also ENGLISH LITERATURE. See G. P. Krapp and E. V. K. Dobbie, ed., *The Anglo-Saxon Poetic Records* (6 vol., 1932–53); G. K. Anderson, *The Literature of the Anglo-Saxons* (1949, repr. 1962); S. B. Greenfield, *A Critical History of Old English Literature* (1965); C. L. Wrenn, *A Study of Old English Literature* (1967).

Anglo-Saxons, name given to the Germanic-speaking peoples who settled in England after the decline of Roman rule there. The Angles (Lat. *Angli*), who are mentioned in Tacitus' *Germania,* seem to have come from what is now Schleswig in the later decades of the 5th cent. Their settlements in the eastern, central, and northern portions of the country were the foundations for the later kingdoms known as EAST ANGLIA, MERCIA, and NORTHUMBRIA. The SAXONS, a Germanic tribe who had been continental neighbors of the Angles, also settled in England in the late 5th cent. after earlier marauding forays there. The later kingdoms of SUSSEX, WESSEX, and ESSEX were the outgrowths of their settlements. The Jutes, a tribe about whom very little is known except that they probably came from the area around the mouths of the Rhine, settled in Kent (see KENT, KINGDOM OF) and the Isle of Wight. The term "Anglo-Saxons" was first used in Continental Latin sources to distinguish the Saxons in England from those on the Continent, but it soon came to mean simply the "English." The more specific use of the term to denote the non-Celtic settlers of England prior to the Norman Conquest dates from the 16th cent. In more modern times it has also been used to denote any of the people (or their descendants) of the British Isles. See P. Hunter Blair, *An Introduction to Anglo-Saxon England* (1954, repr. 1962); F. M. Stenton, *Anglo-Saxon England* (3d ed. 1971); D. M. Wilson, *The Anglo-Saxons* (rev. ed. 1971); D. J. V. Fisher, *The Anglo-Saxon Age, 400–1042* (1973).

Angmagssalik (ängmäg'sälĭk), settlement and trading post (1969 pop. 2,530), E Greenland, on the Denmark Strait just S of the Arctic Circle. It was founded in 1894. Its radio-meteorological station (est. 1925) is the oldest on Greenland.

Angola (ăng-gō'lə) or **Portuguese West Africa,** Portuguese territory (1973 est. pop. 5,850,000), including the exclave of Cabinda, 481,351 sq mi (1,246,700 sq km), SW Africa. LUANDA is the capital; other important cities are NOVA LISBOA, LOBITA, BENGUELA, and MOSSAMEDES. Angola is bounded by the Atlantic Ocean on the west, by Zaïre on the north and northeast, by Zambia on the east, and by South West Africa on the south. The Bié Plateau, which forms the central region of the territory, has an average altitude of 6,000 ft (1,830 m). Rising abruptly from the coastal lowland, the plateau slopes gently eastward toward the Congo and Zambesi basins and forms one of Africa's major watersheds. The uneven topography of the plateau has resulted in the formation of numerous rapids and waterfalls, which are used for the production of hydroelectric power. The territory's principal rivers are the Cuanza and the Cunene. Rainfall in Angola is generally low, and nearly all the land is desert or savanna. The northeast, however, has densely forested valleys that yield hardwoods, and palm trees are cultivated along a narrow coastal strip where precipitation is heavy. Its mineral, power, and agricultural resources make Angola, which is nearly 14 times the size of metropolitan Portugal, the most valuable Portuguese possession in Africa. Diamond mining is the principal industry. Oil has been produced and refined near Luanda since the 1950s, and the exploitation of large reserves off Cabinda began in 1968. Angola's important deposits of copper, iron, and manganese ores remain largely undeveloped. Livestock, notably sheep and goats, is raised in much of the savanna region. Coffee is the most important cash crop of Angola, which is one of the world's major producers. Europeans own most of the coffee plantations. Maize, sisal, and some sugarcane are also raised for export. Fishing is important along the coast. Among Angola's industries are railroad shops, foundries, cereal mills, fish and palm oil processing plants, meat and fish canneries, and enterprises that manufacture jute, cotton textiles, and paper. An important source of revenue is the Benguela railroad, which carries metals from the mines of Zaïre and the Zambian Copperbelt; the railroad extends from Beira, Mozambique, to Angola's port of Lobito. Angola also has several shorter rail lines and a fairly good road network. Luanda and Lobito are among the best shipping ports in Africa. Angola's population is overwhelmingly black African, and most of the people speak a Bantu language; the Mbundu are the

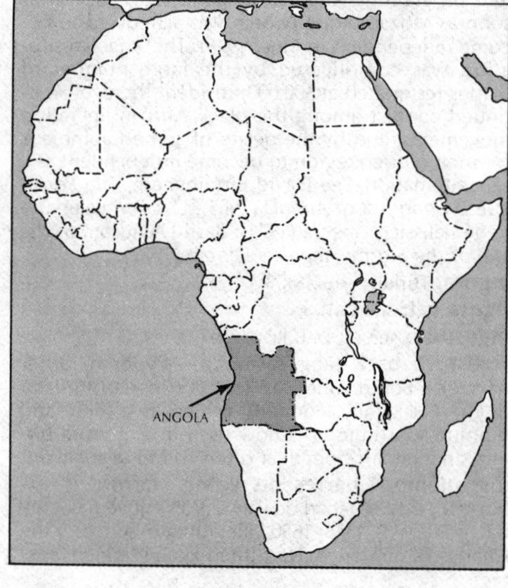

largest ethnic group. The number of Europeans has greatly increased since 1951, when immigration was officially encouraged; there is also a sizable mixed (*mestiço*) population. Most of the Europeans live in urban areas. All Angolans are citizens of Portugal. Although Roman Catholicism is the state religion, Protestant missionaries are active, and various tribal religions are practiced. The Portuguese first explored Angola in the late 15th cent., and except for a short occupation (1641-48) by the Dutch, it has always been under Portugal's control. Although they failed to discover the gold and other precious metals they were seeking, the Portuguese found in Angola an excellent source of slaves for their colony in Brazil. Portuguese colonization of Angola began in 1575, when a permanent colony was founded at Luanda. By this time the Mbundu dynasty had established itself in central Angola. Portugal's attempts to subjugate the Mbundu ended in 1902, when Portuguese troops finally broke the back of the kingdom and captured the Bié Plateau. Construction of the Benguela railroad followed, and white settlers arrived in the Angolan highlands. The modern development of Angola began only after World War II. In 1951 the colony was designated an overseas province, and Portugal initiated plans to develop industries and hydroelectric power. Although the Portuguese professed the aim of a multiracial society of equals in Angola, many Africans still suffered repression. Inspired by nationalist movements elsewhere, they rose in revolt in 1961. When the uprising was quelled by the Portuguese army, many native Angolans fled to Zaïre and other neighboring countries. In 1962 a group of refugees in Zaïre, led by Holden Roberto, organized the Revolutionary Government of Angola-in-Exile (GRAE). It maintains supply and training bases in Zaïre, wages guerrilla warfare in Angola, and, while developing contacts with both Western and Communist nations, obtains its chief support from the Organization of African Unity (OAU). Angola's fragmented liberation movement comprises two other guerrilla groups as well. The Movimento Popular de Libertação de Angola (MPLA) has headquarters in Zambia and is most active among educated Angolan Africans and *mestiços* living abroad. The third rival group is the União Nacional para a Independência Total de Angola (UNITA), which was established in the mid-1960s. In 1972, with Zambian mediation, the heads of GRAE and MPLA assumed joint leadership of a newly formed Supreme Council for the Liberation of Angola, but their military forces did not merge. As a result of the guerrilla warfare, Portugal was forced to keep more than 50,000 troops in Angola by the early 1970s. The four main areas of military activity were along the Zaïre frontier in the north, along the Zambian and South West African borders in the southeast, in the area around Luanda, and in the Cabinda exclave. In 1972 the Portuguese national assembly changed Angola's status from an overseas province to an "autonomous state," with the authority to elect is own governing bodies, draft its own budget, collect its own taxes, and pass legislation concerning internal affairs; Portugal was to retain responsibility for defense and foreign relations and to exercise a supervisory role over the Angolan economy and administration. In 1973 elections were held for a legislative assembly. In April, 1974, the Portuguese government was overthrown in a military uprising. In May of that year the new government proclaimed a truce with the guerrillas in an effort to promote peace talks. By later in the year Portugal seemed intent on granting Angola independence, but not as soon as Mozambique (which was scheduled to become independent in June, 1975). The Angolan situation was complicated by the large number of whites (estimated at 500,000) resident there, by continued conflict among the black African liberation movements, and by the desire of some Cabindians for their oil-rich region to become independent as a separate nation. See David Birmingham, *The Portuguese Conquest of Angola* (1965); D. L. Wheeler and René Pélissier, *Angola* (1971); Basil Davidson, *In the Eye of the Storm: Angola's People* (1972).

Angora, Turkey: see ANKARA.

angora cat: see CAT.

Angostura: see CIUDAD BOLÍVAR.

angostura bark (ăng"gəstŏŏr'ə, -styŏŏr'ə), bitter bark of a South American tree (*Cusparia trifoliata*) of the RUE family. Formerly valued as a tonic and quinine substitute, it is now used in angostura bitters, an aromatic appetizer often added to cocktails.

Angoulême, Charles de Valois, comte d'Auvergne, duc d' (shärl də välwä' kôNt dōvĕrn'yə dük däNgōōlĕm'), 1573-1650, illegitimate son of King Charles IX of France. He turned against King Henry IV, conspired with Henriette d'ENTRAGUES, his half sister, and was imprisoned until 1616. After his release he held military commands. He left memoirs.

Angoulême, Margaret of or **Marguerite d':** see MARGARET OF NAVARRE.

Angoulême, Marie Thérèse Charlotte, duchesse d' (märē' tārĕz'shärlôt'düshĕs'), 1778-1851, wife of Louis Antoine d'Angoulême; daughter of Louis XVI and Marie Antoinette. She was imprisoned (1792-95) during the French Revolution. Energetic and ambitious, she exerted considerable political influence after the restoration of the French monarchy during the reigns of Louis XVIII and Charles X. She died in Frohsdorf, Austria.

Angoulême (äNgōōlĕm'), city (1968 pop. 50,883), capital of Charente dept., W France, on the Charente River. A former river port, it is now a major road and rail center. Its paper industry dates from the 15th cent., and it has copper foundries, and plants making electric motors, soap, and shoes. It was an early episcopal see and became (9th cent.) the seat of the counts of ANGOUMOIS. Ceded (1360) to England, it was reconquered (1373) by Charles V. Its remarkable Cathedral of St. Pierre was begun c.1110.

Angoumois (äNgōōmwä'), region and former province, W France, now coextensive with most of Charente dept. ANGOULÊME is the historic capital and chief city. In the region is the Charente valley, with its excellent vineyards; the brandy made from their grapes is named for Cognac, the chief distillery center. In pre-Roman times the region was occupied by the Santones and Pictones, two Gallic peoples. Part of the kingdom of AQUITAINE under Charlemagne's empire, Angoumois became a county in the 9th cent. and was united with the French crown in 1307. Under the Treaty of Brétigny (1360) Angoumois, then ruled by the counts of Angoulême, was recognized as English territory, but in 1371 it became a fief of the dukes of Berry, a branch of the French royal family. When Francis I, formerly the count of Angoulême, became king in 1515, Angoumois was definitively incorporated into the French crown lands.

Angra do Heroísmo (äng'grə dōō ərōōēzh'mōō), town (1960 pop. 13,929), capital of Angra do Heroísmo dist., Portugal, in the Azores, on Terceira island. It is a port and was until 1832 capital of the Azores. There is an old castle in the town.

Angren (ən-gryĕn'), city (1969 est. pop. 94,000), Uzbekistan, Central Asian USSR. The largest lignite-mining center in Soviet Central Asia, it was developed during and after World War II.

angry young men, term applied to a group of English writers of the 1950s whose heroes share certain rebellious and critical attitudes toward society. This phrase, which was originally taken from the title of Leslie Allen Paul's autobiography, *Angry Young Man* (1951), became current with the production of John Osborne's play *Look Back in Anger* (1956). The word *angry* is probably inappropriate; *dissentient* or *disgruntled* perhaps is more accurate. The group not only expressed discontent with the staid, hypocritical institutions of English society—the so-called Establishment—but betrayed disillusionment with itself and with its own achievements. Included among the angry young men were the playwrights John Osborne and Arnold Wesker and the novelists Kingsley Amis, John Braine, John Wain, and Alan Sillitoe. In the 1960s these writers turned to more individualized themes and were no longer considered a group.

Ångström, Anders Jöns (än'dərs yöns ōng'ström), 1814-74, Swedish physicist. He was educated at the Univ. of Uppsala and in 1839 became a member of its faculty. He is particularly noted for his study of light, especially spectrum analysis. He mapped the solar spectrum, discovered hydrogen in the solar atmosphere, and was the first to examine the spectrum of the aurora borealis. A unit of length used to measure light waves is named for him.

angstrom (ăng'strəm), abbr. Å, unit of length equal to 10^{-10} METER (0.0000000001 meter); it is used to measure the wavelengths of visible light and of other forms of ELECTROMAGNETIC RADIATION, such as ultraviolet radiation and X rays. The angstrom is named in honor of Swedish physicist Anders J. Ångström.

Anguier, François (fräNswä' äNgyā'), 1604-69, French sculptor. He is noted for the monuments of the Longuevilles and of Jacques Souvré (Louvre). His most ambitious work is probably the mausoleum of Henri II, duc de Montmorency, in Moulins. His brother **Michel Anguier,** 1614-86, collaborated in this project. The works of both brothers reflect the classical baroque influence of Algardi, with whom they studied in Rome. In Paris, Michel executed the marble group *The Nativity,* now in the Church of Saint-Roch. He also made decorations for the apartments of Anne of Austria in the Louvre and worked on reliefs for the triumphal arch at Porte Saint-Denis. A third brother, **Guillaume Anguier,** 1628-1708, a painter, was director of the Gobelin tapestry factory.

Anguilla (ăng-gwĭl'ə), island (1971 est. pop. 6,000), 35 sq mi (91 sq km), British West Indies, one of the Leeward Islands. Salt mining, fishing, and stock raising are the mainstays of the economy. In 1967 the British possessions of Anguilla, St. Kitts, Nevis, and Sombrero were united in the self-governing state of St. Kitts-Nevis-Anguilla, associated with Great Britain. Anguilla, claiming political and economic discrimination, seceded in 1967 and returned to British colonial rule in 1971. See SAINT KITTS-NEVIS.

angular momentum: see MOMENTUM.

Angus, earls of: see DOUGLAS, ARCHIBALD.

Angus, county (1971 pop. 97,312), 874 sq mi (2,264 sq km), NE Scotland; formerly (until 1928) called Forfarshire. FORFAR is the county town. The terrain varies from wild rugged mountains (the Sidlaw Hills and part of the Grampians) to the fertile valleys of the North and South Esk and the Isla rivers. Oats, barley, and root crops are grown; cattle, sheep, and horses are raised. The coastal towns engage in fishing and boat building. Angus is a center of the Scottish textile industry; jute and linen are processed at DUNDEE, ARBROATH, BRECHIN, and MONTROSE. Many relics of early Pictish and Roman occupation and the famous GLAMIS Castle are in Angus. Under the Local Government Act of 1973, Angus became part of the Tayside region.

Angus cattle (ăng'gəs), breed of black polled (hornless) beef cattle, originated in Scotland and introduced in 1873 to the United States, where they have become well established. Often called Black Angus or Aberdeen Angus cattle, they have low, compact bodies and are noted for the fine quality of their flesh. As a breed, they lack the size of Shorthorn and Hereford cattle. In recent years, the Red Angus breed of cattle has been derived from red cattle born in registered black herds.

angwantibo: see LORIS.

Anhalt (än'hält), former state, c.900 sq mi (2,330 sq km), central Germany, surrounded by the former Prussian provinces of Saxony and Brandenburg, located in what are now the Halle and Magdeburg districts of East Germany. Dessau, the capital, and Köthen were the chief cities. A level area except for the outliers of the lower Harz mts. in the west, it was drained by the Elbe, Mulde, and Saale rivers. Until 1918, Anhalt was ruled by one of the most ancient houses of Germany, issued from a son of Albert the Bear (12th cent.); it was divided, at most times, into several principalities held by various branches of the family. Reunited into a single duchy in 1863, it joined the German Empire in 1871, became a republic in 1918, and joined the Weimar Republic. Celebrated members of the house of Anhalt were Leopold I, prince of Anhalt-Dessau, and Sophie of Anhalt-Zerbst, who was empress of Russia as Catherine II.

Anhwei (än'hwā') or **An-hui** (än-hwē), province (1968 est. pop. 35,000,000), c.55,000 sq mi (142,450 sq km), E central China. HO-FEI is the capital. Anhwei may be divided into two climatic areas. The northern half, within the N China plain and watered by the Huai and its tributaries (flooding is a common problem), is cold in winter and dry throughout the year. It has a single harvest annually, the chief crops being wheat, kaoliang, corn, soybeans, and cotton. The southern half, through which the Yangtze River flows, is mountainous and has a relatively moist, warm climate. It is a major rice-producing region; two thirds of the cultivated area is double-cropped. Wheat, sweet potatoes, cotton, barley, and tobacco are also grown, and tea is produced in the southeast. Fish culture is important. Coal and iron are abundant throughout the province. Three of China's 34 leading industrial centers are in Anhwei: Ho-fei, the capital, which has textile mills and new iron and steel works; HUAI-NAN, a large coal-mining center, with important chemical manufactures; and Ma-an-shan, a major industrial complex with huge steel works. Railroad building has not had high priority because of the excellent waterways—the Yangtze is open to ocean vessels in the summer, the Huai and its affluents are navigable by junk, and an intricate canal system connects the two rivers. Some single line tracks have been built to link the industrial centers with Ho-fei, and there are rail connections with other provinces, generally radiating from Ho-fei; the ailroad connecting Nanking and Shanghai crosses the province. Road building has been accomplished t the local level, linking marketing and industrial enters. Anhwei Univ. is in Ho-fei.

nhydride (ănhī'drīd, -drĭd) [Gr.,=without water], chemical compound formed by removing water, H_2O, from another compound; the anhydride can also react with water to form the original compound. An acid anhydride reacts with water to form an acid; e.g., sulfur trioxide, SO_3, reacts with water to form sulfuric acid, H_2SO_4. A basic anhydride reacts with water to form a base; e.g., calcium oxide, CaO, reacts with water to form calcium hydroxide, $Ca(OH)_2$. Anhydrides of organic acids have many uses. They react with alcohols to form esters; e.g., acetic anhydride, $(CH_3CO)_2O$, reacts with ethanol, C_2H_5OH, to form ethyl acetate, $CH_3COOC_2H_5$, a useful solvent. They also react with ammonia and primary or secondary amines to form amides. Other important acid anhydrides include maleic anhydride and phthalic anhydride.

nhydrous ammonia, liquefied ammonia that contains 82% nitrogen and is used as an agricultural fertilizer. It is stored under pressure and must be added to the soil at a depth of several inches in order that the ammonia may be absorbed by the soil. See FERTILIZER.

ni (ä'nē), bird: see CUCKOO.

niakchak (ănēăk'chăk), volcano, 4,420 ft (1,347 m) high, in the Aleutian Range, SW Alaska. Its crater is 6 mi (9.7 km) in diameter. Aniakchak was thought to be extinct until it erupted on May 1, 1931.

niam (ənī'əm), Manassite. 1 Chron. 7.19.

niene (ănyā'nā), Lat. *Anio,* river, 61 mi (98 km) long, rising in Latium, central Italy, and flowing generally southwest to empty into the Tiber River near Rome. Two aqueducts have carried water from the Aniene to Rome since ancient times, and now the river also supplies several hydroelectric plants. Below Tivoli, where it forms a celebrated waterfall, it is also called the Teverone.

niline (ăn'əlĭn), $C_6H_5NH_2$, colorless, oily, basic liquid organic compound; chemically, a primary aromatic amine whose molecule is formed by replacing one hydrogen atom of a benzene molecule with an AMINO GROUP. Aniline boils at 184°C and melts at −6°C. It is of great importance in the dye industry, being used as the starting substance in the manufacture of many dyes—e.g., indigo—and as an aid in the manufacture of others. For this reason many dyes have the word *aniline* in their common name, such as aniline black (one of the best black dyes known), aniline red, yellow, blue, purple, orange, green, and others. Today these synthetic dyes have largely replaced the natural ones. Aniline is prepared commercially by the reduction of nitrobenzene, a product of coal tar, or by heating chlorobenzene with ammonia in the presence of a copper catalyst. Sulfonation of aniline yields sulfanilic acid, the parent compound of the sulfa drugs. Aniline is also important in the manufacture of rubber-processing chemicals and antioxidants.

nim (ā'nĭm), town of Palestine, SW of Hebron. Joshua 15.50.

nimal, any member of the animal kingdom (Kingdom Animalia) as distinguished from the PLANT kingdom (Kingdom Plantae). Demarcation between animals and plants is usually based on a fundamental difference in their method of obtaining food. Plants characteristically manufacture their food from inorganic substances (usually by photosynthesis). Animals, on the other hand, must secure food already organized into organic substances. In addition, most animals have specialized means of locomotion, possess nervous systems and sense organs, and are adapted for securing, ingesting, and digesting their food. In all but the simpler forms there is a distinct alimentary canal or digestive system. Almost all animals, unlike most plants, possess a limited scheme of growth; that is, the adults of a given species are nearly identical in their characteristic form and are similar in maximum size. It is easy to distinguish between plants and animals of the higher groups, but among the simpler and microscopic forms it is often difficult. Some single-celled organisms, such as *Euglena,* possess chlorophyll and carry on photosynthesis but have a flexible cell membrane rather than the cellulose wall characteristic of plant cells and swim actively by means of flagella. Such forms are probably descended from the common ancestors of plants and animals that existed in the early stages of evolution. They are classified by zoologists as one-celled animals and by botanists as ALGAE, or simple plants. They may also be classified in a third kingdom, the PROTISTA. Animals and plants are interdependent—green plants provide oxygen as a by-product of photosynthesis and are the ultimate source of all food for animals. Animals (as well as plants) provide carbon dioxide through respiration and the decomposition of their dead bodies (see CARBON CYCLE; NITROGEN CYCLE). In zoological CLASSIFICATION the animal kingdom is divided into the two subkingdoms of PROTOZOA (one-celled animals) and Metazoa (many-celled animals). The Metazoa comprise numerous INVERTEBRATE phyla and the phylum CHORDATA. The distinguishing characteristics of the chordates are a NOTOCHORD (a dorsal stiffening rod) in the embryo; a dorsal, hollow SPINAL CORD; and GILL slits (sometimes present only during embryonic stages, e.g., in the frog and man). The chordates include two primitive subphyla of a few species each, in which these features are present only at certain stages of the life cycle. The fourth and major chordate subphylum is the Vertebrata (see VERTEBRATE), in which the embryonic notochord is replaced by the SPINAL COLUMN of the adult. The scientific study of animals is called ZOOLOGY; the study of their relation to their environment and of their distribution is animal ECOLOGY. For specific approaches to the study of animals and plants, see BIOLOGY.

animal husbandry, domestication of animals especially as a source of food, fuel, power, or raw materials. Maintenance of control over an animal species for several generations has often led to man's dependence upon that animal for his well-being. Domestic animals have functioned as symbols of wealth, prestige, or religious belief, or as accessories to acts of aggression and defense. The domestication of animals influenced settlement patterns, architecture, and equipment, as well as the value placed on the animals and the elaboration of rules governing property rights concerning them. They have also figured importantly in the verbal symbolism of myths and songs, and in the idiomatic vocabularies of the societies possessing them. The first domesticated animal seems to have been the sheep, which was tamed around 9000 B.C. in N Iraq. Around 6500 B.C., domestic goats were kept in the same region; about 6000 B.C. the pig was domesticated in Iraq; about 5500 B.C. there were domesticated cattle in SW Iran, and around 3000 B.C. the horse was domesticated in Russia.

animal jelly: see GELATIN.

animated cartoon: see MOTION PICTURES.

animism, belief that within every object dwells an individual spirit or force that governs its existence. It has been said that upon this concept rests the historic structure of religion. Since primitive man did not distinguish between animate and inanimate objects or between physical and mental processes, everything in the universe was thought to have its own individuality. Men, animals, plants, stones, as well as emotions, dreams, and ideas alike, were regarded as having indwelling spirits. More generalized is the idea of mana, which originated among Melanesians of the South Seas. A kind of transcendental force, mana is thought to be the spirit that pervades all objects and things and is responsible for the good and evil in the universe. In philosophy, the term animism is applied to the doctrine that the principle of life, called the vital force, cannot be reduced to the mechanistic laws of physics and chemistry, but is separate and distinct from matter. See FETISH; TABOO; TOTEM; IDOL; SHAMAN; ANCESTOR WORSHIP; AMULET. See J. G. Frazer, *The Golden Bough* (1890, repr. 1966); E. B. Tylor, *Religion in Primitive Culture* (1871, repr. 1970).

Anio, river: see ANIENE.

anion (ăn'ī''ən), atom or group of atoms carrying a negative charge. The charge results because there are more electrons than protons in the anion. Anions can be formed from nonmetals by reduction (see OXIDATION AND REDUCTION) or from neutral acids (see ACIDS AND BASES) or polar compounds by ionization. Anionic species include Cl^-, SO_4^{--}, and CH_3COO^-. Highly colored intermediates in organic reactions are often radical anions (anions containing an unpaired electron). SALTS are made up of anions and CATIONS. See ION.

anise (ăn'ĭs), annual plant (*Pimpinella anisum*) of the family Umbelliferae (CARROT family), native to the Mediterranean region but long cultivated elsewhere for its aromatic and medicinal qualities. It has flat-topped clusters of small yellow or white flowers that become seedlike fruits—the aniseed of commerce, used in food flavoring. Anise oil is derived from the seeds and sometimes from the leaves; it is also obtained from the star anise, an unrelated woody plant. The oil, composed chiefly of anethole, is used in medicinals, dentifrices, perfumes, beverages, and, in drag hunting, to scent a trail for dogs in the absence of a fox. The anise of the Bible (Mat. 23.23) is dill, a plant of the same family. Anisette is an anise-flavored liqueur. Anise is classified in the division MAGNOLIOPHYTA, class Magnoliopsida, order Umbellales, family Umbelliferae.

Anjo (änjō'), city (1970 pop. 94,307), Aichi prefecture, S central Honshu, Japan. It is an agricultural and poultry center with cotton textile mills and food canneries. There are agricultural and forestry schools in the city.

Anjou (äNzhōō'), region and former province, W France, coextensive roughly with Maine-et-Loire and parts of Indre-et-Loire, Mayenne, and Sarthe depts. ANGERS, the historic capital, and SAUMUR are the chief towns. A fertile lowland, Anjou is traversed by the Loire, Mayenne, Sarthe, Loir, and Maine rivers. It is chiefly an agricultural area with excellent vineyards that produce the renowned Vouvray and Saumur sparkling wines. Occupied by the Andecavi, a Gallic people, the region was conquered by Caesar. Anjou fell to the Franks in the 5th cent. and became a countship under Charlemagne in the 9th cent. By the 10th cent. it was in the hands of the first line of the counts of Anjou (see ANGEVIN dynasty), who expanded their holdings vigorously. Fulk Nerra, who founded the Angevin dynasty, acquired Saumur from the counts of BLOIS. His successor, Geoffrey Martel, won Touraine from Blois (1044) and Maine from Normandy (1051). FULK (d. 1143), the grandson of Fulk Nerra, after protracted wars with Henry I of England over the possession of Maine, married his son Geoffrey (Geoffrey Plantagenet) to Henry's daughter Matilda. Geoffrey ruled Anjou (1129–51) and conquered Normandy, of which he was crowned duke in 1144. His son, later Henry II of England, married Eleanor of Aquitaine and with her inheritance ruled most of W France. When Henry II's grandson, Arthur I, duke of Brittany, rebelled against his uncle, John of England, he won the support of Philip II of France, to whom he paid homage (1199) for Anjou, Maine, and Touraine. After Arthur's death, Philip II seized (1204) all Anjou. In 1246, Louis IX of France gave Anjou in appanage to his brother Charles, count of Provence, who later also became king of Sicily and Naples (see CHARLES I). Charles II of Naples gave Anjou as dowry to his daughter Margaret when she married Charles of Valois, son of Philip III of France. When their son became (1328) King Philip VI of France, Anjou was again reunited to the French crown. John II of France, however, made Anjou a duchy (1360) and gave it to his son Louis (later Louis I of Naples). Louis XI of France inherited Anjou after the death (1480) of René, grandson of Louis I, and the death (1481) of Charles of Maine, René's nephew, the last of the Angevin line. Anjou was definitively annexed to France in 1487. In the 16th cent. Anjou was held as appanage at various times; the last duke was Francis of Alençon and Anjou. The region was devastated during the Wars of Religion (see under RELIGION, WARS OF) (1562–98). During the French Revolution the rising of the VENDÉE, the Royalist revolt against the revolution, occurred in Anjou.

Ankara (ăng'kərə, Turk. äng'kärä), city (1970 pop. 1,208,791), capital of the Republic of Turkey and its Ankara province, W central Turkey, at an elevation of c.3,000 ft (910 m). Turkey's largest city after İstanbul, Ankara is an administrative, commercial, and cultural center. Grains, vegetables, and fruit are grown nearby. Manufactures of the city include food products, farm machinery, and cement. Known in ancient times as Ancyra and later as Angora, the city was an important commercial center at least as early as Hittite times (18th cent. B.C.). In the 1st cent. A.D. it became the capital of a Roman province. It flourished under Augustus; in the ruins of a marble temple dating from his reign (31 B.C.–A.D. 14) was found the *Monumentum Ancyranum,* a set of inscribed tablets valuable as a record of Augustan history. The city was conquered by the Ottoman Turks in the mid-14th cent., and in 1402 Tamerlane defeated and captured Sultan Beyazid I there. In the late 19th cent. Ankara declined and by the early 20th cent. was a small town known only for the production of mohair. In 1920, Kemal Atatürk made the city the seat of his Turkish Nationalist government. In 1923 it replaced İstanbul as the capital of all Turkey, partly to break with tradition and partly to take advantage of its central location. The city grew rapidly from the 1920s; in the 1960s its population almost doubled. There are few historic remains. Ankara's leading modern monument is the Atatürk mausoleum, completed in 1953. The city has numerous museums and is the seat of the Ankara, Hacettepe, and Middle East Technical universities.

Anking: see AN-CH'ING, China.

An Lu-shan (än lo͝o-shän), d.757, Chinese general of the T'ang dynasty. Of mixed Sogdian and Turkish birth, he was appointed regional commander on the northeastern frontier. In 755 he led c.200,000 troops in revolt against the T'ang central government. Emperor HSÜAN TSUNG fled the capital Ch'ang-an for Szechuan, and on the way he was forced by discontented soldiers to execute his concubine YANG KUEI-FEI, who was blamed for demoralizing the court and was even rumored to have had a secret affair with An Lu-shan. An Lu-shan was killed by his son in 757. The rebellion lasted until 763, when foreign troops helped restore the T'ang dynasty to power.

Ann, Cape, NE Mass., N of Massachusetts Bay. It is noted for its old fishing villages, resorts, and artists' colonies, especially Gloucester and Rockport.

Anna (Anna Ivanovna) (än'nə ĭvä'nôvnə), 1693–1740, czarina of Russia (1730–40), daughter of Ivan V and niece of Peter I (Peter the Great). On the death of her distant cousin, Peter II, she was chosen czarina by the supreme privy council, which thus hoped to gain power for itself. Anna signed articles limiting her power, but she soon restored autocratic rule, with support from the lesser nobility and the imperial guards. She made minor concessions to the nobles but restored the security police and terrorized opponents. Distrusting the nobility, she excluded Russians from high positions and surrounded herself with Baltic Germans. Her favorite, Ernst Johann von BIRON, had the greatest influence. Allied with Holy Roman Emperor CHARLES VI, Anna intervened in the War of the POLISH SUCCESSION (1733–35), installed Augustus III as king of Poland, and attacked Turkey in 1736. Charles's separate peace with the Turks at Belgrade forced Russia to make peace in turn, at the price of all recent conquests except Azov. During Anna's reign began the great Russian push into central Asia. She was succeeded by her grandnephew, Ivan VI.

Anna [Gr.,=Heb. HANNAH]. **1** Aged prophetess who hailed Jesus' presentation at the Temple. Luke 2.36–38. **2** In Tobit, the mother of young Tobias.

Anna Amalia, duchess of Saxe-Weimar (ämä'lyä, zăk'sə-vī'mär), 1739–1807, German patron of letters and science; niece of Frederick II of Prussia and mother of CHARLES AUGUSTUS, duke of Saxe-Weimar. As regent for her son (1757–75) she fostered German culture by her patronage of such authors as Herder, Wieland, Goethe, and Schiller. She wrote the music for Goethe's *Erwin und Elmire.*

Annaba (ăn-näb'ə), formerly **Bône** (bōn), city (1966 pop. 168,790), capital of Annaba dept., extreme NE Algeria, a port on the Mediterranean Sea. One of the country's leading ports, the city is also an important administrative, commercial, and industrial center. The large El Hadjar ironworks, built with French and Soviet financial and technical aid, constitutes the chief industry; others include chemical (superphosphate) manufacturing, food canning, cork production, and railway construction. Founded by the Carthaginians, the city became a favorite residence of the Numidian kings. Under the Romans, it was called Hippo Regius and was a center of early Christianity, the episcopal see of St. Augustine. The city was captured by the Vandals in 431. After the Arab conquest of Algeria in the 7th cent., Annaba became an important Muslim city and port. Spanish forces occupied it in the 16th cent. During the 17th and 18th cent., Annaba was a busy center for European trade. The French took the city in 1832. Landmarks include the Great Mosque and the Cathedral of St. Augustine.

Anna Comnena (kŏmnē'nə), b. 1083, d. after 1148, Byzantine princess and historian; daughter of Emperor Alexius I. She plotted, during and after her father's reign, against her brother, JOHN II, in favor of her husband, Nicephorus Bryennius, whom she wished to rule as emperor. Having failed, she retired to a convent. There she wrote the *Alexiad* (finished in 1148), one of the outstanding Greek historical works of the Middle Ages. Covering the reign of Alexius I and the First Crusade, it tends to glorify her father and his family; however, Anna's familiarity with public affairs and her access to the imperial archives give her work great value. There is an English translation by Elizabeth A. S. Dawes (1928, repr. 1967). See biography by Georgina Buckler (1929).

Anna Ivanovna: see ANNA, czarina of Russia.

An Najaf (än nä'jäf), city (1965 pop. 128, 096), S central Iraq, on a lake near the Euphrates River. The city is also called Mashad Ali, after the tomb (in a mosque) of Ali, son-in-law of Muhammad the Prophet. The tomb is an object of pilgrimage by Shiite Muslims and a starting point for the pilgrimage to Mecca.

Annaka (än-nä'kä), city (1970 pop. 40,092), Gumma prefecture, central Honshu, Japan. It is an agricultural and tourist center, noted for its mineral springs.

Anna Leopoldovna (lyä"əpôl'dəvnə) or **Anna Karlovna** (kär'ləvnə), 1718–46, duchess of Brunswick-Wolfenbüttel, regent of Russia (1740–41); daughter of Charles Leopold, duke of Mecklenburg-Schwerin, and of Catherine, sister of Czarina Anna of Russia. She married the prince of Brunswick-Wolfenbüttel, and their son, IVAN VI, succeeded (1740) Anna as czar. After the deposition of Ivan by Czarina ELIZABETH, Anna Leopoldovna and her husband were imprisoned. She died in childbirth.

Annam (ənăm', ă'năm), historic region (c.58,000 sq mi/150,200 sq km) and former state, in central Vietnam, SE Asia. The capital was HUE. In 1954, when Vietnam was divided on a line approximating the 17th parallel, Annam went largely to South Vietnam. The region extended nearly 800 mi (1,290 km) along the South China Sea between Tonkin (now in North Vietnam) on the north and Cochin China (now part of South Vietnam) on the south. The ridge of the Annamese Cordillera separated N and central Annam from Laos on the west; the ridge then swung southeastward and ran along the coast of S Annam, which included the plateaus that stretched to the borders of Cambodia and Cochin China. The narrow coastal plains of N and central Annam were interrupted by spurs of mountains that almost reached the sea, as at Porte d'Annam, a pass important in Annamese history. In addition to Hue, the principal cities in the region were DA NANG (the chief seaport), An Nhon, Quang Tri, and VINH (now in North Vietnam). The origins of the Annamese state may be traced to the peoples of the Red River valley in North Vietnam. After more than 2,000 years of contact with the Chinese, they fell under Chinese rule as the result of a Han invasion in 111 B.C. The region, to which the Chinese gave the name Annam ("Pacified South"; a name resented by the people), comprised all of what later became N Annam and Tonkin. Southern Annam was occupied by the kingdom of the Chams, or Champa, from the late 2d cent. A.D. In 939 the Annamese drove out the Chinese and established their independence, which they maintained, except for one brief period of Chinese reoccupation (1407–28), until their conquest by the French in the 19th cent. Le Loi, who defeated the Chinese in 1428, established the Le dynasty. A long series of wars against the Chams ended in 1471 when the Chams were defeated and the Annamese kingdom was extended southward to the vicinity of Da Nang. The power of the Le dynasty declined, and in 1542, after several rebellions, the dynasty was defeated. By 1558 the kingdom was in effect divided between two great families: the Trinh line, which reinstalled a puppet Le emperor and ruled from Hanoi (then called Tonkin) as far south as Porte d'Annam (this area was called Tonkin by the Europeans who arrived in the 16th cent.), and the Nguyens, who ruled from Hue over the territory extending from Porte d'Annam south to the vicinity of Qui Nhon. In the 17th cent. the lords of Hue pushed further southward into the Cambodian provinces on the lower Mekong. The early 18th cent. saw their control extended into parts of Laos and, at the expense of Cambodia, to the shores of the Gulf of Siam. The ruling dynasties of Hue and Tonkin were overthrown in 1778 and 1786 respectively, and the two domains were reunited (1802) as the empire of Vietnam by Nguyen-Anh, a Hue general, who had procured French military aid by ceding (1787) to the French the port of Da Nang and the Con Son islands. Nguyen-Anh established himself as emperor; his authority was formally recognized by the Chinese in 1803. In 1807 the Vietnamese extended a protectorate over Cambodia, which led in succeeding years to frequent wars against Siam. After the death of Nguyen-Anh, his successor, attempting to withdraw into isolation, mistreated French nationals and Vietnamese Christian converts. This provided an excuse for French military operations, which began in 1858 and resulted in the seizure of southern Vietnam (Cochin China) and the establishment of protectorates (by 1884) over northern Vietnam (Tonkin) and central Vietnam (Annam). The French, who abolished the name Vietnam, received recognition for their protectorates from the Chinese emperor. In 1887, Annam became part of the Union of Indochina. In World War II, Indochina was occupied by the Japanese, who set up the autonomous state of Vietnam, comprising Tonkin, Annam, and Cochin China; Bao Dai, the last emperor of Vietnam, was established as ruler. After the war Annamese and Tonkinese nationalists demanded independence for the new state of Vietnam, and the region was plunged into a long and bloody conflict (see VIETNAM).

Annamese Cordillera (ăn"nāmēz' kôr"dĭlyâr'ə) or **Chaîne Annamitique** (shĕn änämētēk'), principal mountain range of Southeast Asia, extending c.700 mi (1,130 km) from N central Laos SE to S central South Vietnam; Ngoc Linh (8,524 ft/2,598 m) in N South Vietnam is the highest peak. The range forms the divide between rivers draining into the Mekong basin and those flowing into the South China Sea. An igneous massif, the range has a steep eastern face and a gently sloping western section. The Tran Ninh Plateau in the north and the Moi plateaus in the south are extensions of the range.

Annapolis (ənăp'əlĭs), city (1970 pop. 29,592), state capital and seat of Anne Arundel co., central Md., on the south bank of the Severn River. Annapolis is a port of entry and the business and shipping center for the fruit and vegetable farmers of S Maryland. Local industries include the packaging of seafood and the manufacture of small boats and plastics. Annapolis was settled in 1649 by Puritans fleeing Virginia. Hostility between the Puritans and the Roman Catholic governors of Maryland resulted in the battle of the Severn River in 1655, in which the Puritans successfully revolted, only to lose control after the RESTORATION in England. The settlement, originally called Providence, was later known as Anne Arundel Town, after the wife of the 2d Lord Baltimore. In 1694 it became the provincial capital of Maryland and was renamed Annapolis for Princess (later Queen) Anne of England. During the 1700s the city prospered, largely because of its tobacco exports and trade with the West Indies and Europe; it rapidly became an important social and commercial center for the colonies. In 1783–84, Annapolis served as the capital of the United States when the Congress met there. The city was the site of the Annapolis Convention (1786), which led to the FEDERAL CONSTITUTIONAL CONVENTION. Still standing is the statehouse where George Washington resigned as commander in chief of the Continental Army in 1783 and where the treaty that ended the Revolutionary War was ratified in 1784 (see PARIS, TREATY OF). Other notable landmarks are the Old Treasury (c.1695), the oldest original building in Maryland; the library (1737); St. John's College; and St. Anne's Church (1858–59) and graveyard, where the former royal governor of Annapolis Sir Robert Eden (an ancestor of Anthony Eden) is buried. Much 18th-century architecture is preserved in the city. Annapolis is also the site of the United States Naval Academy, founded in 1845.

Annapolis, river, c.75 mi (120 km) long, rising in W Nova Scotia, Canada, and flowing SW past Annapolis Royal to Annapolis Basin, an arm of the Bay of Fundy. The entrance to the basin, bordered by cliffs 500 ft (152 m) high, is known as Digby Gut. The Annapolis valley, an important agricultural area noted for its apples, was the site of Nova Scotia's first successful farming colony.

Annapolis Convention, 1786, interstate convention called by Virginia to discuss a uniform regulation of commerce. It met at Annapolis, Md. With only 5 of the 13 states—Delaware, New Jersey, New York, Pennsylvania, and Virginia—represented, there could be no full-scale discussion of the commercial problems the nation faced as a result of the weak central government under the Articles of Confederation. The main achievement of the convention was the decision to summon a new meeting for the express purpose of considering changes in the Articles of Confederation to make the union more powerful. An address was drawn up by Alexander Hamilton and was sent to all the states, asking them to send delegates to Philadelphia in May, 1787. The move was extraconstitutional, but Congress passed a resolution urging attendance. The call from Annapolis was heeded and delegates from 12 states met. From that Federal Constitutional Convention was to emerge the Constitution of the United States.

Annapolis Royal, town (1971 pop. 758), W N.S. Canada, on the Annapolis River. Founded as Port Royal by the sieur de MONTS in 1605, the settlement was destroyed (1613) by English colonists under Samuel ARGALL but was rebuilt by the French. The fort changed hands between the French and the English five times from 1605 to 1710, when it capitulated to a force of New Englanders under Francis Nicholson. The name was then changed in honor of Queen Anne. Annapolis Royal was the capital of Nova Scotia from 1713 to 1749. Fort Anne Historic

National Park includes the ruins of the fort. The officers' quarters (built 1797–98) have been restored as a museum.

Annapurna (ən-năpo͝or'nə), massif of the Himalayas, N central Nepal, forming a ridge 35 mi (56 km) long, including two of the highest peaks in the world. Having four snow-covered peaks, it rises to Annapurna I (26,502 ft/8,078 m) in the west and Annapurna II (26,041 ft/7,938 m) in the east. Annapurna I was first climbed in 1950 by a French expedition led by Maurice Herzog.

Ann Arbor, city (1970 pop. 99,797), seat of Washtenaw co., S Mich., on the Huron River; inc. 1851. It is a research and educational center, with a large number of government and industrial research and development firms, the huge Univ. of Michigan, and two junior colleges. Products include lasers, computers, hospital and laboratory equipment, scientific instruments, automotive parts, and precision machinery. The city is also a medical center; in addition to the university hospitals and medical school, it has a community hospital, a veterans' hospital, and a neuropsychiatric hospital. There are Indian mounds in the region.

Annas (ăn'əs) [Gr.,=Heb. HANANIAH], Jewish high priest who examined Jesus. Nonbiblical sources say that he was retired high priest. His son-in-law was Caiaphas. John 18.13,24; Acts 4.6–22.

An Nasiriyah (ăn näsĭrī'yä), city (1965 pop. 60,405), provincial capital, SE Iraq, on the Euphrates River. It is the center of a date-growing region. Founded in 1870, the city was captured by the British in 1915. Nearby are the ruins of Ur.

Annau or **Anau** (both: ənou'), village, Central Asian USSR, in Turkmenistan, 5 mi (8 km) SE of Ashkhabad, near the Iranian border. It has a 15th-century mosque, a citadel, ancient burial mounds, and other remains. At Annau, Raphael Pumpelly discovered (1903) traces of habitation dating back to c.3000 B.C. There are indications of ancient cultivation of grain, and beautifully designed pottery has been found. The discovery has been related to other excavations throughout central Asia. See Raphael Pumpelly, *The Prehistoric Civilization of Anau* (1908).

Anne, Saint, in tradition, mother of the Virgin and wife of St. Joachim. She is not mentioned in Scripture, but her cult is very old. In the West she has been especially popular since the Middle Ages. She is patroness of Quebec prov., and Ste Anne de Beaupré is one of the most visited of New World shrines. Brittany, also under her patronage, has the renowned shrine of Ste Anne d'Auray, with its annual pilgrimage. St. Anne is invoked by women in childbirth. In art, she is usually an elderly veiled woman and often appears teaching her daughter to read. Her name also appears as Anna. Feast: July 26.

Anne, 1665–1714, queen of England, Scotland, and Ireland (1702–7), later queen of Great Britain and Ireland (1707–14), daughter of James II and Anne Hyde; successor to William III. Reared as a Protestant and married (1683) to Prince George of Denmark (d. 1708), she was not close to her Catholic father and acquiesced in the GLORIOUS REVOLUTION (1688), which put William III and her sister, Mary II, on the throne. She was soon on bad terms with them, however, partly because they objected to her favorite, Sarah Jennings (later Sarah Churchill, duchess of MARLBOROUGH), who was to exercise great influence in Anne's private and public life. Of Anne's many children the only one to live much beyond infancy—the duke of Gloucester—died at the age of 11 in 1700. Since neither she nor William had surviving children and support for her exiled Catholic half brother rose and fell in Great Britain (see STUART, JAMES FRANCIS EDWARD; JACOBITES), the question of succession continued after the Act of SETTLEMENT (1701) and after Anne's accession. The last Stuart ruler, she was the first to rule over Great Britain, which was created when the Act of Union joined Scotland and England in 1707. Her reign, like that of William III, was one of transition to parliamentary government; Anne was, for example, the last English monarch to exercise (1707) the royal veto. Domestic and foreign affairs alike were dominated by the War of the SPANISH SUCCESSION, known in America as Queen Anne's War (see FRENCH AND INDIAN WARS). In the actual fighting on the Continent, Sarah Churchill's husband, the duke of MARLBOROUGH, won a series of spectacular victories. At home the costs of the fighting were an issue between the Tories, who were cool to the war, and the Whigs, who favored it. Party lines were slowly hardening, but party government and ministerial responsibility were not yet established; intrigues and the favor of the queen still made and unmade cabinets, though the influence of public opinion, shaped by an increasingly powerful press, and elections was growing. Thus it was at least partly through the pressure of the Marlboroughs that Anne was induced, despite her Tory sympathies, to oust Tory ministers in favor of Whigs. The Marlboroughs were even able to force the dismissal of Robert HARLEY in 1708, though the scolding duchess had already lost much of her power to Anne's new favorite, the quiet Abigail MASHAM, kinswoman and friend of Harley. When the unpopularity of the war and the furor over the prosecution of Henry SACHEVERELL showed the power of the Tories (who won the elections of 1710) and made the move feasible, Anne recalled Harley to power, and the Marlboroughs were dismissed. Harley, created earl of Oxford, was political leader until 1714, when he was replaced by his Tory colleague and rival, Viscount Bolingbroke (see ST. JOHN, HENRY). Soon afterward the queen died, and Jacobite hopes were dashed by the succession of GEORGE I of the house of Hanover. Queen Anne was a dull, stubborn, but conscientious woman, devoted to the Church of England and within it to the High Church party. She supported the act (1711) against "occasional conformity" and the Schism Act (1714), both directed against dissenters and both repealed in 1718. She also created a trust fund, known as Queen Anne's Bounty, for poor clerical benefices. During Anne's reign such thinkers as George Berkeley and Sir Isaac Newton and such scholars and writers as Richard Bentley, Swift, Pope, Addison, Steele, and Defoe were at work, while Sir Christopher Wren and Sir John Vanbrugh were at the same time setting in stone and brick the rich elegance of the period. See biographies by M. R. Hopkinson (1934) and David Green (1970); G. M. Trevelyan, *England under Queen Anne* (3 vol., 1930–34); G. N. Clark, *The Later Stuarts* (2d ed. 1955).

Anne (Anne Elizabeth Alice Louise), 1950–, British princess, daughter of Queen Elizabeth II and Prince Philip, duke of Edinburgh. She was educated at Benenden School. An accomplished horsewoman, she represented Britain in various international show-jumping events. In 1973 she married a British army officer, Mark Phillips.

annealing (ənē'lĭng), process in which glass, metals, and other materials are treated to render them less brittle and make them more workable. Annealing consists of heating the material and then cooling it very slowly and uniformly; the time and temperatures required in the process are set according to the properties desired. Annealing increases ductility and lessens the possibility of a failure in service by relieving internal strains.

Anne Boleyn, queen of England: see BOLEYN, ANNE.

Annecy (änsē'), town (1968 pop. 56,689), capital of Haute-Savoie dept., SE France, in SAVOY in the N Alps, on beautiful Lake Annecy. A popular tourist resort, it also has printing plants and factories making jewelry and wood and leather products. The center of the city, traversed by narrow canals, is picturesquely medieval. St. Francis of Sales, who was born in Annecy, was bishop from 1602 to 1622. The city has many fine churches, monasteries, and seminaries. The castle of the counts of Geneva (12th–14th cent.) dominates Annecy from a hill.

Anne de Beaujeu (də bōzhö'), c.1460–1522, regent of France, daughter of the French King Louis XI. With her husband, Pierre de Beaujeu, duc de Bourbon, she acted as regent for her brother, Charles VIII, after the death (1483) of Louis XI. Preserving the royal authority, she put down the rebellious great nobles and subdued Brittany. In 1491 she and her husband arranged the marriage of Charles VIII to ANNE OF BRITTANY, and soon afterward their influence declined.

Annelida (ənĕl'ĭdə) (Lat. *anellus*=a ring), phylum of soft-bodied, bilaterally symmetrical (see SYMMETRY, BIOLOGICAL) segmented animals, known as the segmented, or annelid, worms. The approximately 8,600 known species are grouped in three classes: the EARTHWORMS and freshwater worms (oligochaetes), the LEECHES (hirudineans), and the marine worms (polychaetes). Annelids are found throughout the world, from deep ocean bottoms to high mountain glaciers. They live in protected habitats such as mud, sand, and rock crevices, and in and among other invertebrate animals, such as sponges. Many live in tubes they secrete around themselves. The fundamental characteristic of the phylum is the division of the body into a linear series of cylindrical segments, or metameres. Each metamere consists of a section of the body wall and a compartment of the body cavity with its internal organs. The external divisions, which may be seen in the common earthworm, correspond to the internal divisions. The annelid body consists of a head; a trunk, made up of metameres; and an unsegmented terminal region. In the more primitive members of the phylum the metameres are identical, or very similar to one another, each containing the same structures; in more advanced forms there is a tendency toward a consolidation of some segments and a restriction of certain organs to particular segments. The body wall is covered with epidermis overlaid with a thin, pliant cuticle secreted by the epidermal cells. The body wall consists of well-developed, segmentally arranged muscles, used for crawling and swimming movements. Most annelids possess short external bristles called setae, or chaetae, composed of chitin. Chaetae are used to grip the soil, to hold the animal in a tube, or to increase the surface areas of appendages for swimming. The digestive system of annelids consists of an unsegmented gut that runs through the middle of the body from the mouth, located on the underside of the head, to the anus, which is on the terminal region. The details of the digestive tract are characteristic of each class within the phylum. The gut is separated from the body wall by the body cavity, called the COELOM. The compartments of the coelom are separated from each other by thin sheets of tissue, called septa, which are perforated by the gut and by blood vessels. Except in the leeches, the coelom is filled with an incompressible fluid that serves as a skeleton, providing the animal with rigidity and with the resistance necessary for muscular movement. If the worm is punctured, it loses its ability to move properly, since functioning of the body muscles is dependent on the maintenance of the fluid volume in the coelom. In primitive annelids each compartment of the coelom is connected to the outside by ducts for the release of sex cells, and by paired excretory organs, or nephridia. These openings are closed except when functioning, thus preventing the loss of coelomic fluid. In more advanced species both excretory and reproductive functions are sometimes served by a single type of duct, and ducts may be absent in certain segments. Characteristics of the circulatory system vary within the phylum. The blood usually contains hemoglobin, a red oxygen-carrying pigment; some annelids have a green oxygen-carrying pigment, and others have unpigmented blood. The circulatory system is usually closed, i.e., confined within well-developed blood vessels; in some leeches the circulatory system is partly open, with blood and coelomic fluid mixing directly in the sinuses of the body cavity. Blood flows toward the head through a contractile vessel above the gut and returns to the terminal region through vessels below the gut; it is distributed to each body compartment by lateral vessels. Some of the lateral vessels are contractile and serve as hearts, i.e., pumping organs for driving the blood. Some aquatic annelids have thin-walled, feathery gills, through which gases are exchanged between the blood and the environment. However, most annelids have no special organs for gas exchange, and respiration occurs directly through the body wall. The nervous system typically consists of a primitive brain, or ganglionic mass (see GANGLION), located in the head, connected by a ring of nerves to a ventral nerve cord which runs the length of the body; the cord gives rise to lateral nerves and ganglia in each segment. Sense organs of annelids generally include eyes, taste buds, tactile tentacles, and organs of equilibrium called statocysts. Reproduction is sexual or asexual. Asexual reproduction is by fragmentation, budding, or fission. Among sexually reproducing annelids hermaphrodites are common, but many species have separate sexes. Fertilized eggs of marine annelids develop into free-swimming larvae. Eggs of terrestrial forms are enclosed in cocoons and hatch as miniature versions of the adults. The ability to regenerate lost body parts is highly developed in all annelids except the leeches. Because of the soft nature of the annelid body, there are few fossils of the phylum. Fossils of tube-dwelling polychaetes have been found, but there is scarcely any fossil record for earthworms and none for leeches. The Annelida may be divided on the basis of their anatomical structure into three classes: Polychaeta (marine worms), Oligochaeta (earthworms and freshwater worms), and Hirudinea (leeches).

Class Polychaeta. The vast majority of the 5,300 known species of polychaete worms are marine; a few, however, are found in fresh or brackish water. They are most abundant from the low-tide line to a depth of about 150 to 200 ft (50 m) but some occur in deeper water and many in the intertidal zone. The polychaetes, so-named because of the numerous setae (chaetae) they bear, range in length from less than ⅛ in. to more than 9 ft (2 mm to 3 m), but most are from 2 to 4 in. (5-10 cm) long. Their colors are often brilliant and some species are iridescent.

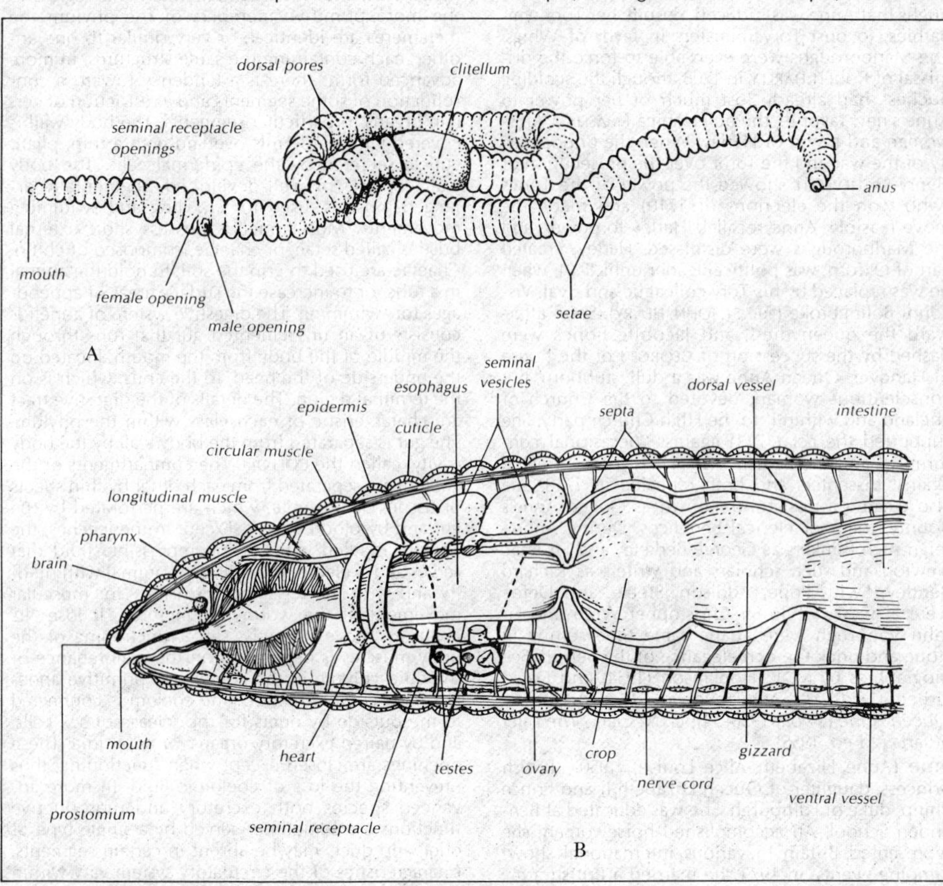

A. *The earthworm,* Lumbricus terrestris, *representative of the phylum Annelida*

B. *Internal anatomy of an earthworm*

The class is usually divided on the basis of mode of existence into two subclasses, the Errantia and the Sedentaria. Members of the Errantia, or errant polychaetes, include actively crawling or swimming forms, which may, however, also spend time in burrows or crevices, or under rocks on the seashore. The Sedentaria, or sedentary polychaetes, are adapted to living permanently in tubes or burrows; some attach themselves to rocks or piers. A familiar errant polychaete is the CLAMWORM, *Nereis*, widely used as bait. Errant polychaetes swim, crawl over the ocean bottom, or tunnel through surface sediments. Most are predators on small invertebrates; some are scavengers. In most, the first few body segments bear sensory projections called cirri, while the remaining body segments bear conspicuous leglike appendages called parapodia. The parapodia, along with undulations of the body, propel the worm in crawling and swimming; they are tipped with bundles of setae, usually made of chitin. Most errant polychaetes have well-developed heads, which bear eyes, sensory tentacles, and a specialized organ, the nuchal organ, thought to detect chemicals. The anterior end of the gut forms a protrusible structure, the proboscis, equipped with strong chitinous jaws and used in feeding. The setae of some polychaetes, e.g., the tropical fireworm, are hollow and contain calcium carbonate rather than chitin. These setae are easily broken off and contain a toxin that produces a painful reaction in humans. In the scaleworms, a series of overlapping scales form an armor on the animal's upper surface. In the SEA MOUSE this armor is completely covered by a feltwork of long, slender setae projecting from the parapodia. Many sedentary polychaetes, like the LUGWORM, *Arinicola*, live in burrows in sand or mud. The majority, however, are tube builders. Tubes of different species vary greatly in their composition and structure. They may be built of sand, shell, or other particles held together with mucus, or made entirely of organic substances, secreted by the worm, that harden on contact with water. The tubes may be straight, branched, spiraled or U-shaped. Most are permanently attached to a substrate, and the worm seldom or never ventures outside; however, the tube worm *Cistenides* moves about the sea floor, dragging along its delicate tube of sand grains. Sedentary polychaetes have greatly modified heads for specialized feeding habits. Many are adapted for feeding on organic matter deposited on the ocean floor. For example, the lugworms have a simple, thin-walled, jawless proboscis, which is used to draw sand into the gut, where organic matter is removed. Other worms have feeding tentacles that extend from the tube opening and creep along the mud or sand, picking up organic deposits. Still others of the Sedentaria are filter feeders: the beautiful feather-duster worms have a crown of feathery, ciliated tentacles that extend from the tube opening to sweep small planktonic organisms from the water. The tentacles are quickly withdrawn if the animal is startled. The parapodia are reduced in the sedentary polychaetes, and the setae of many tube-dwelling forms are hooked, to help the worm hold itself to the wall of its tube. The structure of the digestive tract of polychaetes is variable, reflecting the diversity of feeding types. Respiration is entirely through the body wall in some polychaetes, and partially so in most. Many species have thin-walled extensions of the body surface, i.e., gills, used for gas exchange; most commonly the gills are extensions of the parapodia. The tentacles of feather-duster worms are used for respiratory exchange as well as for feeding. A polychaete may have a single pair of excretory tubes, or a pair in each segment. Sedentary polychaetes have various modifications to insure that wastes will be deposited near the mouth of the tube or burrow, where they are washed away. Most polychaetes reproduce sexually, and the sexes are separate. Sex cells develop from masses of tissue in the metameres and leave by way of tubules or by rupture of the body wall. In most cases fertilization of the eggs by sperm occurs externally in seawater, and results in the formation of free-swimming larvae. Variations include internal fertilization, laying of egg masses that are attached to objects with mucus, and brooding of developing eggs in the worm's body. Some errant polychaetes, including the clamworm, undergo extreme changes in appearance and become active swimmers at the time of year that the sex cells mature; males and females swarm to the surface of the sea to spawn. In some of these species the portion of the body containing the sex cells breaks free and engages in swarming and spawning, leaving the asexual portion behind to regenerate its lost parts. Swarming generally occurs at night and is correlated with particular phases of the moon. Some species perform a kind of nuptial dance, swimming in circles as they spawn. In some species the worms liberate a luminous secretion, which produces circles of light on the ocean surface as they dance. The most famous swarming polychaete is the tropical palolo worm, a name sometimes applied to all swarming polychaetes. Two groups of polychaetes that are sometimes regarded as separate classes are the Archiannelida and the Myzostomaria. The former group includes a variety of minute marine worms living in surface mud, in tide pools near the high-tide line, and in the interstitial spaces of mud and sand in some subtidal areas. All archiannelids are scavengers. They have a ciliated epidermis and only a few body segments; many resemble the larvae of other polychaetes. The Myzostomaria are a small group of marine worms parasitic on certain echinoderms (crinoids, starfish, and brittle stars). They are disk-shaped and flattened, with a series of reduced parapodia with hooked setae; they often match the color pattern of the host.

Class Oligochaeta. This class includes about 3,000 species of earthworms and freshwater worms. The members of the class range in length from about $\frac{1}{32}$ in. to 10 ft (0.5 mm–3 m) but most are comparable to the polychaetes in size. Oligochaetes occur in a variety of habitats throughout the world. Most are burrowers in the soil, but the class also includes worms that inhabit wells, marshes, and swamps. Other species live under rocks on the seashore, in the leaves of tropical trees and vines, on the surface of glaciers, or on the gills of freshwater crayfish. Like the polychaetes, oligochaetes have bodies divided into segments. However, they lack parapodia and, with a few exceptions, have relatively few and inconspicuous setae. The setae are usually arranged in four bundles on each segment; those of aquatic forms are longer than those of land forms. The setae of an earthworm may be felt as a roughness if one rubs a finger along its side. Oligochaetes are less varied in their external form than the polychaetes, but are much more numerous. As many as 4,000 oligochaetes have been counted in one square meter of lake bottom, and about 9,000 in one square meter of meadow soil. In almost all oligochaetes, the head is a simple cone-shaped structure without sensory appendages. Light is detected by photoreceptor cells in the skin, usually concentrated toward the front of the animal. The mouth, located under the head, leads to a relatively simple, straight digestive tract consisting of a pharynx, an esophagus, and an intestine, terminating in an anal opening. Terrestrial oligochaetes tunnel through the ground, swallowing soil as they go. The digestive tract of such a worm is specially modified for this rough diet. Typically it has a thin-walled storage area, or crop, and a muscular gizzard for grinding the soil to remove the organic matter that is the actual food of the worm. Specialized calciferous glands remove excess calcium, magnesium, strontium, and phosphate and regulate the level of these ions in the blood. Solid wastes are egested and plastered against the burrow wall, or ejected from the mouth of the burrow; the ejected material is called castings. Earthworms, through their burrowing and digestive processes, are largely responsible for the mixing and aeration of the soil. Not all oligochaetes have soil diets; some of the small aquatic worms are active predators on other small invertebrates. The circulatory system is that typical of the annelids and has many contractile vessels, or hearts. Although a few aquatic forms have gills for respiration, most oligochaetes lack such specialized structures and use the capillaries of their body walls for respiratory exchange. Oxygen dissolved in the soil water diffuses through the moist epidermis of the worm. If earthworms are forced to the surface, as when their burrows are filled with rainwater, they suffocate as a result of desiccation. Excretion is typically carried out by a pair of tubes in each segment. All oligochaetes are hermaphroditic and nearly all cross-fertilize by copulation. Male and female reproductive organs are located in separate segments. The copulating pair exchange sperm, which are stored in the body of the recipient worm until its eggs are mature. The worm then secretes a cocoon into which it deposits the eggs and the sperm; fertilization and development of the eggs occurs in the cocoon. When the young emerge they are miniatures of the adults. The cocoon is secreted by a glandular region, the clitellum, consisting of several thickened segments. The clitellum of an earthworm is a conspicuous saddle-shaped region near its front end.

Class Hirudinea. This class includes the 300 species of leeches: flattened, predacious or parasitic annelids equipped with suckers used for creeping. Leeches range in length from about ½ in. to 8 in. (1 cm-20 cm); most are under 2 in. (5 cm) long. They are commonly black, brown, green, or red, and may have stripes or spots. The majority of leeches are predators on small invertebrates; most swallow their prey whole, but some suck the soft parts from their victims. Some leeches are parasites rather than predators, and suck the body fluids of their victims without killing them. The distinction is not sharp, as many predatory leeches take blood meals on occasion. Leeches are primarily freshwater annelids, but some live in the ocean and some in moist soil or vegetation. These are the only annelids with a fixed number (34) of body segments; each segment has secondary subdivisions known as annuli. A clitellum, less conspicuous than that of oligochaetes, is present; there are no parapodia. A leech has a small anterior sucker and a larger posterior one; the leech crawls by moving the anterior sucker forward, attaching it, and drawing up the posterior sucker. Most leeches can swim by rapid undulations of the body, using well-developed muscles of the body wall. The coelom differs from that of other annelids in that it is largely filled in with tissue. Coelomic fluid is contained in a system of sinuses, which in some leeches functions as a circulatory system; there is a tendency in this group toward the loss of true blood vessels. The blood of some leeches is red. In others the blood lacks oxygen-carrying pigments and is therefore colorless; the oxygen dissolved directly in the blood is sufficient for respiration. Gas exchange occurs through the body surface of most leeches, although many fish-parasitizing leeches have gills. The sense organs consist of sensory cells of various types, including photoreceptor cells, scattered over the body surface. There are also from 2 to 10 eyes, consisting of clusters of photoreceptor cells and located toward the front of the body. Many leeches have a proboscis used for swallowing the prey or for sucking its fluids; others have jaws for biting. Many parasitic leeches are able to parasitize a wide variety of hosts. Most of the marine and some of the freshwater leeches are fish parasites. The medicinal leech, *Hirudo medicinalis*, is one of a group of aquatic bloodsucking leeches with jaws. Another group of jawed bloodsuckers is terrestrial; these leeches live in damp tropical vegetation and drop onto their mammalian prey. Most parasitic leeches attach to the host only while feeding; a single meal may be 5 or 10 times the weight of the leech and provide it with food for several months. The digestive tract of bloodsuckers produces an anticoagulant, hirudin, which keeps the engorged blood from clotting. A few leeches attach permanently to the host, leaving only to reproduce. Predatory leeches are active at night and hide by day. Like the oligochaetes, leeches are hermaphroditic and cross-fertilizing, although fertilization is internal. In some species the sperm are enclosed in sacs, called spermatophores, that are attached to the outside of the partner; the sperm pass through the body wall to the ovaries, where the eggs are fertilized. In other species, the sperm are not enclosed and are transferred directly into the body of the partner by copulation. A courtship display is seen among some leeches at the time of mating. The fertilized eggs are deposited in a cocoon, secreted by the clitellum; the cocoon is buried in mud or affixed to submerged objects. The young emerge as small copies of the adults.

Annensky, Innokenty Feodorovich (ēnəkĕn'tyē fyô'dərəvĭch ənyĕn'skē), 1856–1909, Russian poet. A classical scholar, he translated Euripides before he began to publish verse in 1904. His highly metrical lyrics concern death, suffering, and beauty. Annensky's scant output is collected in *Quiet Songs* (1904) and *The Cypress Chest* (1910).

Anne of Austria, 1601–66, queen of France, daughter of King Philip III of Spain. Married to the French king Louis XIII (1615), she was neglected by her husband and sought the society of the court intriguer, Mme de CHEVREUSE. Anne's indiscretion, especially her flirtation with the duke of Buckingham, injured her reputation. Her loyalty to Spain and her strong Roman Catholic background made her suspect after France's alliance (1635) with the Protestant nations in the Thirty Years War; she was accused by the French minister of state, Cardinal Richelieu, of treasonable correspondence with Spain but was pardoned (1637). Contrary to the express wish of her husband before his death she was granted (1643) by PARLEMENT full powers as regent for her son LOUIS XIV. She entrusted the government to Cardinal MAZARIN, whom she supported during the wars of the FRONDE in France. After Mazarin's death (1661), her son excluded her from participation in affairs of state. Anne of Austria is a central figure of Alexandre Dumas's *Three Musketeers.*

Anne of Bohemia, 1366–94, queen consort of Richard II of England, daughter of Holy Roman Emperor Charles IV. She was married to Richard early in 1382 and quickly gained popularity in England. It was probably through her entourage that the writings of John Wyclif were introduced into Bohemia, where they gained much prominence through the teachings of John HUSS.

Anne of Brittany, 1477–1514, queen of France as consort of CHARLES VIII from 1491 to 1498 and consort of LOUIS XII from 1499 until her death. The daughter of Duke FRANCIS II of Brittany, she was heiress to his duchy. Shortly before her father's death (1488), a French army under Louis de La Trémoille successfully invaded Brittany and secured the duke's promise that Anne would marry only with the consent of the French crown. Upon becoming duchess, the young Anne's hand and her duchy were eagerly sought. To prevent France from swallowing up the duchy, a coalition including Archduke Maximilian of Austria (later Holy Roman Emperor MAXIMILIAN I), King HENRY VII of England, and King FERDINAND II of Aragón sent forces to Anne's aid. Nevertheless, Anne's situation was perilous and she appealed (1489) directly to Maximilian for protection. In 1490, Maximilian married Anne by proxy but failed to assist her with armed strength. Besieged at Rennes in 1491, Anne was forced by the French to annul her marriage and was quickly married to Charles VIII. It was agreed that if Charles died before Anne without issue, she was to marry his successor. Accordingly, in 1499, she married Louis XII, who had previously obtained a divorce from his first wife. The marriage (1514) of Claude, Anne's daughter by Louis XII, to Francis of Angoulême (later Francis I of France) led to the eventual incorporation (1532) by France of Brittany, which had previously remained theoretically separate. See biography by H. J. Sanborn (1917).

Anne of Cleves (klēvz), 1515–57, fourth queen consort of HENRY VIII of England. The sister of William, duke of Cleves, one of the most powerful of the German Protestant princes, she was considered a desirable match for Henry by those English councilors, most notably Thomas CROMWELL, who wished to ally England with the SCHMALKALDIC LEAGUE. The marriage was agreed upon in 1539, and although Henry tried to break the contract after seeing his bride, they were married in Jan., 1540. Henry found Anne dull and unattractive, and the marriage was never consummated. This and the fact that Anne had previously contracted to marry the duke of Lorraine's son were used as grounds for divorce in July, 1540. Anne gave her consent and, by agreement, lived the rest of her life in England. See biography by M. C. Barnes (1958).

Anne of Denmark, 1574–1619, queen consort of James I of England (James VI of Scotland), daughter of Frederick II of Denmark and Norway. She married James in 1589. Brought up a Lutheran, she became a Roman Catholic some time in the 1590s and at James's English coronation (1603) refused to take Anglican communion. James appeared devoted to her at first, but her extravagance and shallowness came to annoy him, and her Catholicism was an embarrassment to him in England. They lived apart after c.1606. See biography by E. C. Williams (1968).

annexation, in international law, formal act by which a state asserts its sovereignty over a territory previously outside its jurisdiction. Many kinds of territory have been subject to annexation, chief among them those inhabited by settlers of the annexing power, those which already have had the status of protectorates of the annexing state, and those conquered by the force of arms. The consent of other interested powers must be obtained in order that the annexation be generally recognized in international law. Efforts to establish the self-determination of inhabitants as the only grounds for the transfer of territory have been realized in the Charter of the United Nations, which does not recognize annexation as an instrument of national policy. The term *annexation* is also used in municipal government to describe the process by which an incorporated local government may extend its legal control over surrounding areas. Usually this type of annexation requires the consent of the other communities concerned.

An Nhon: see QUI NHON, South Vietnam.

Anniston, city (1970 pop. 31,533), seat of Calhoun co., NE Ala., in a mining region of the Appalachian foothills; inc. 1873. Its many varied manufactures include soil pipes, textiles, microwave ovens, factory-built homes, and vaccines. Founded (1872) as an iron-manufacturing "company town," it was opened to the public in 1883. A local landmark is the beautiful Church of St. Michael and All Angels (Episcopal; 1887). Nearby are the huge Anniston Army Depot and U.S. Fort McClellan, headquarters of the Women's Army Corps (WAC) and of the Chemical Corps Training Command.

annual, plant that germinates from seed, blossoms, produces seed, and dies within one growing season. Annuals propagate themselves by seed only, unlike many biennials and perennials. They are thus especially suited to environments that have a short growing season. Cultivated annuals are usually considered to be of three general types: tender, half-hardy, and hardy. Tender and half-hardy annuals do not mature and blossom in one ordinary temperate growing season unless they are started early under glass and are set outdoors as young plants. Hardy annuals are usually sown where they are expected to bloom. Quite often they reseed themselves year after year. Blooming is prolonged by cutting the flowers before the seeds can form. Typical annual flowers are cosmos, larkspur, petunia, and zinnia; annual vegetables include corn, tomatoes, and wheat. See H. G. W. Fogg, *Dictionary of Annual Plants* (new ed. 1972).

annual rings, the growth layers of WOOD that are produced each year in the stems and roots of trees and shrubs. In climates with well-marked alternation of seasons (either cold and warm or wet and dry) the wood cells that are produced when water is easily available and growth is rapid (in the spring or wet season) are usually noticeably larger and have thinner walls than those produced later in the season when the supply of water has diminished and growth is slower. There is thus a sharp contrast between the small, thick-walled late-season wood cells produced one year, and the large, thin-walled cells of the spring wood of the following year. Where the climate is uniform and growth continuous, as in wet, tropical forests, there is little or no visible contrast between the annual rings, although differences exist. When rings are conspicuous, they may be counted to give a reasonably accurate approximation of the age of the tree. They are also reflective (by their range of thickness) of the climatic and environmental factors that influence growth rates. The science of dendrochronology is based upon the phenomenon of variability in the thickness of annual rings.

annuity: see INSURANCE.

annulment of marriage: see NULLITY OF MARRIAGE.

Annunciation of the Virgin: see MARY.

Annunzio, Gabriele D': see D'ANNUNZIO, GABRIELE.

anoa (ənō'ə): see BUFFALO.

anode, ELECTRODE through which current enters an electric device. In ELECTROLYSIS, it is the positive electrode in the electrolytic cell.

anointing of the sick, SACRAMENT of the Orthodox Eastern Church and the Roman Catholic Church, formerly known as extreme unction. In it a sick or dying person is anointed on eyes, ears, nostrils, lips, hands, feet, and sometimes, in the case of men, the loins, by a priest while he recites absolutions for sins committed. The Roman Catholic Church teaches that through the sacrament the sick and dying receive remission of sins, health of soul, and, if God wills, health of body. The sacrament may be shortened, and it may be given conditionally, as when there is doubt as to whether the recipient is living or as to whether he is baptized. Anointing of the sick is given only to persons seriously ill and in danger of death from internal causes; hence, it is not given before operations or in battle before attack. Anointing of the sick, the last confession, and the VIATICUM are the last rites of the church. The chief biblical text for anointing of the sick is James 5.14,15. In the Eastern churches it is normally given by three priests, and it may be given to the healthy to prevent sickness; it is not so widely used in the Eastern churches as in the West.

Anoka (ənō'kə), city (1970 pop. 13,489), seat of Anoka co., E Minn., on the Mississippi at the confluence of the Rum; inc. 1878. Originally a trading post and lumber town, it grew as a farm trade center. Ammunition and metal products are among its manufactures. A state mental hospital is there.

anole: see CHAMELEON.

anomalistic year (ənŏm"əlĭs'tĭk), time required for the earth to go from the perihelion point once around the sun and back to the perihelion point. It is 365 days, 6 hr, 13 min, 53.0 sec of MEAN SOLAR TIME. The anomalistic year is longer than the SIDEREAL YEAR and the TROPICAL YEAR because of the eastward motion of the line of apsides (see APSIS), which is caused by the slow rotation of the earth's orbit as a whole.

Anopheles: see MOSQUITO.

anorthite (ănôr'thīt): see FELDSPAR.

Anouilh, Jean (zhäN änwē'yə), 1910–, French dramatist. Anouilh's many popular plays range from tragedy to sophisticated comedy. His first play, *L'hermine,* was published in 1932. During the Nazi regime he wrote plays about resistance to oppression in terms of subjects from classical mythology; *Antigone* (1944, tr. 1946) is the most celebrated of these. Several of his later plays have contemporary and historical settings. Anouilh's works frequently contrast the worlds of romantic dreams and harsh reality. His later plays include *The Waltz of the Toreadors* (1952, tr. 1957), *Poor Bitos* (1958, tr. 1964), *The Lark* (1953, tr. 1955), *Becket* (1959, tr. 1960), *The Rehearsal* (1963), and *Dear Antoine* (1969, tr. 1971). See studies by L. C. Pronko (1961), John Harvey (1964), E. O. Marsh (1968), Marguerite Archer (1971), and B. A. Lenski (1973).

Anquetil-Duperron, Abraham Hyacinthe (äbräăm'yäsăNt' äNkətēl' düpĕrôN'), 1731–1805, French Orientalist. He gave up studying for the priesthood to pursue his deep interest in Eastern languages. In India (1755–61) he learned Persian, Sanskrit, Zend, Avestan, and Pahlevi. After studying with the PARSIS, he was forced to return to France as a result of the British conquests in India. He took with him 180 manuscripts, which he gave to the Royal Library. His three-volume translation of the *Zend-Avesta* (1771) introduced Zoroastrian texts to Europe. Anquetil-Duperron also translated the *Upanishads* into Latin (1804) and wrote several works on India.

Ansbach (äns'bäkh), city (1970 pop. 30,603), capital of Middle Franconia, Bavaria, S West Germany, on the Rezat River. Its manufactures include machine tools, electrical products, and chemicals. The city developed around an 8th-century Benedictine abbey. It became the residence of the Franconian branch of the Hohenzollern family in 1331. Ansbach passed to Prussia in 1791 and to Bavaria in 1806. Noteworthy buildings include the 12th-century Romanesque Church of St. Gumbertus, which was redone in baroque style in the 18th cent., and an 18th-century castle.

Anschluss (än'shlo͝os), German term designating the incorporation of Austria into Germany. Prohibited by the 1919 peace treaty of St. Germain in order to prevent a resurgence of a strong Germany, the Anschluss was favored by German nationalists, and by Austrians dissatisfied with their country's diminished status after World War I. Under the threat of military force, Adolf Hitler occupied Austria on March 11, 1938, and incorporated it into Germany as the province of Ostmark. In 1943, the Moscow Declaration of the United States, Great Britain, and the Soviet Union annulled the Anschluss, recognizing Austria's right to independence; an independent government was not set up until the end of World War II.

Anselm, Saint (ăn'sĕlm), 1033?–1109, Italian prelate, archbishop of Canterbury, Doctor of the Church (1720), b. Aosta, Piedmont. After a carefree youth of travel and schooling in Burgundy he became a disciple and companion of LANFRANC, the famed theologian and prior of the monastery at BEC, which Anselm soon joined (1060). Anselm became prior (1063) and abbot (1078) and brought widespread fame to the school there. Monastic holdings in England threw him into English public life, and he won the esteem of William the Conqueror. He was a frequent visitor to Lanfranc at Canterbury, and when the latter died, Anselm succeeded him as archbishop (1093). He disputed the right of WILLIAM II to invest him, reserving this for Pope URBAN II, whom William refused to recognize. Anselm momentarily overcame the king's intransigence and took the pallium from Urban's legate. Anselm's further reform-minded efforts to free the church from secular control met stiff resistance. When he went to Rome for support, William banished him and confiscated the diocesan properties. At the Council of Bari (1098) Anselm ably defended the *Filioque* of the CREED in the East-West controversy on the procession of the Holy Spirit. The new king, HENRY I, recalled Anselm, who proved valuable in arranging Henry's marriage to Matilda of Scotland and in gaining the support of the barons for the king in his dispute with Robert of Normandy. Conflict over lay INVESTITURE again broke out, however, and Anselm refused to consecrate bishops and abbots nominated by the king. He was again banished while appealing in Rome. Anselm eventually won (1107) Henry's agreement to surrender the right of investiture in exchange for homages from church revenues—a compromise that in effect established papal supremacy in the English church. Many consider this Anselm's most important achievement. His writings mark him as the founder of SCHOLASTICISM. A strict Augustinian, operating from the formula *fides quaerens intellectum* (faith seeking understanding), he believed in an essential harmony between revelation and reason. He was the first to incorporate successfully the rationalism of Aristotelian dialectics into theology. Although he wrote no great summa, his precision together with his mystical insight give permanent value to such works as *Cur Deus Homo?* (1094–98), on the ATONEMENT. He constructed rational proofs for God's existence in *Monologium* (c.1070), and in the sequel *Proslogium* he advanced his famous ontological proof, which deduces God's existence from man's notion of a perfect being in whom nothing is lacking. In *De Fide Trinitatis* he defended universals against the nominalist ROSCELIN. He taught the Immaculate Conception of Mary in *De Conceptu Virginali* and is said to have instituted that feast in England. Feast: April 21. See Eadmer's *Life of St. Anselm, Archbishop of Canterbury* (tr. by R. W. Southern, 1962); biographies by R. W. Church (1884), A. C. Welch (1901), and Joseph Clayton (1933); studies by R. W. Southern (1963), Charles Hartshorne (1965), and D. P. Henry (1967).

Ansermet, Ernest (ĕrnĕst' äNsĕrmĕ'), 1883–1969, Swiss conductor. For several years he was a high-school mathematics teacher. He began his conducting career in Germany and toured with Diaghilev's Ballets Russes from 1915 to 1923. In 1918 he founded the Orchestre de la Suisse Romande in Geneva and remained its director until 1967. Ansermet was noted for his interpretations of modern French and Russian music and made many concert tours. He also composed several short pieces.

An-shan or **Anshan** (both: än-shän), city (1970 est. pop. 1,500,000), central Liaoning prov., China, on a branch of the South Manchurian RR. Its huge integrated iron and steel complex is the largest in China and one of the ten largest in the world. It comprises iron and coal mines and numerous blast furnaces, open hearths, and finishing facilities. Many varieties of steel and steel products (including rails and cables) are produced. Other manufactures in An-shan include chemicals, tractors, machinery, alarm clocks, and cement. An-shan was developed as a metallurgical center largely by the Japanese, who occupied the region during World War II. The Soviet Union dismantled much of the steel mill between 1944 and 1946, but by 1956 the facilities had been rebuilt. The city has a mineral-spray sanitarium for the treatment of arthritis and joint diseases.

An-shun or **Anshun** (both: än-sho͞on), town, W central Kweichow prov., SW China. A flourishing town during the opium traffic days, it is known for its green tea. Other industries include sugar refining and machine building. Coal deposits are there.

Ansky, 'Shloime (shloi'mə än'skē) or **Solomon Seinwil Rapoport,** 1863–1920, Russian author who wrote in Yiddish. His last name is also spelled An-ski. He extensively researched regional Jewish folklore and incorporated folk elements into his realistic stories of peasant life and Hasidism. His most famous work is *Tavishn Tsvei Veltn, oder der Dibuk* (1916; tr. *The Dybbuk,* 1926), a story of demonic possession, which he later adapted into a play. It was turned into an opera by Lodovico Rocca (1934) and again by David and Alex Tankin (1949). A modernized version of the play, adapted by Paddy Chayefsky, appeared in New York City in 1960.

Ansley, Clarke Fisher, 1869–1939, American teacher and editor, b. Swedona, near Springfield, Ill., grad. Univ. of Nebraska, 1890. After teaching English at Nebraska, he was professor of English at the State Univ. of Iowa (1899–1917) and dean of its College of Fine Arts (1911–15). Having turned to editing, he conceived the idea of a one-volume general encyclopedia, compact enough and simply enough written to serve as a guide to the "young Abraham Lincoln." This work was started in 1928 as *The Columbia Encyclopedia* with Ansley as its editor in chief. The first edition (1935) and the first supplement (1938) were completed under his direction.

Anson, Adrian Constantine, 1851–1922, American baseball player-manager, known usually as "Cap" Anson, b. Marshalltown, Iowa. For most of his career he played with the Chicago club of the National League and was four times league batting champion. As manager (1879–97), he led the team to five pennants. In 1939 he was elected to the National Baseball Hall of Fame; his lifetime batting average was .339.

Anson, George Anson, Baron, 1697–1762, British admiral. In his famous voyage (1740–44) around the world, Anson, in spite of shipwrecks and scurvy, inflicted great damage on Spanish shipping and returned to England with a rich prize. He was raised to the peerage after his popular naval victory (1747) off Cape Finisterre. Appointed then as first lord of the admiralty, he assisted William Pitt, Lord Chatham, in reorganizing naval administration. See *A Voyage round the World* (comp. by Richard Walter, rev. ed. 1911); biographies by M. V. Anson (1912) and S. W. C. Pack (1960); L. A. Wilcox, *Anson's Voyage* (1970).

Anson, Sir William Reynell, 1843–1914, English jurist. He was a founder of the school of law at Oxford Univ. From 1899 to his death he sat in Parliament as a member for Oxford. His *Principles of the English Law of Contract* (1879) and *The Law and Custom of the Constitution* (2 vol., 1886–92) are frequently consulted standard works. See memoir ed. by H. H. Henson (1920).

Ansonia, city (1970 pop. 21,160), New Haven co., SW Conn., on the Naugatuck River; inc. as a city 1893. Its manufactures include brass and copper products, iron castings, foundry products, plastics, and electronic devices. Settled in 1651 as part of Derby, Ansonia was founded (1844) as an industrial community by Anson G. Phelps, a metals merchant and philanthropist. Ansonia's historical landmarks include the birthplace of David Humphreys, who accepted Gen. Charles CORNWALLIS's sword in surrender after the YORKTOWN CAMPAIGN (1781), and "Pork Hollow," where Revolutionary patriots hid food stores from British raiders.

Anstey, Christopher, 1724–1805, English poet and satirist. He is known chiefly for *The New Bath Guide* (1766), a series of poetical episodes humorously depicting contemporary life at Bath. This work was widely read in its time and may have influenced Tobias Smollet's *Humphrey Clinker.*

Anstey, F., pseud. of **Thomas Anstey Guthrie,** 1856–1934, English author. He relinquished his law practice to write humorous fiction. His best and most successful works are marked by an atmosphere of fantasy and include *Vice Versa* (1882), *The Tinted Venus* (1885), and *The Brass Bottle* (1900). Besides translating several comedies of Molière, he wrote the play *The Man from Blankley's,* successfully produced in 1901. See his autobiography, *A Long Retrospect* (1936).

ant, any of the 2,500 INSECT species constituting the family Formicidae of the order Hymenoptera, to which the bee and the wasp also belong. Like most members of the order, ants have a "wasp waist," that is, the front part of the abdomen forms a narrow stalk, called the waist, or pedicel, that attaches to the thorax. The wings, when present, are also typical of the order; the small hind pair of wings is attached to the rear edge of the front pair. The head has two bent antennae, used both as organs of touch and as chemosensory organs. In most species there are two compound eyes. The jaws are of the biting type and in some species are used for defense. Some ants have stings, and some can spray poison from the end of the abdomen. Most ants are black, brown, red, or yellow. METAMORPHOSIS is complete. A soft, legless, white larva hatches from the egg; in most species it is completely helpless and must be fed and carried by adults. In some species pupation occurs within a cocoon. Ants are cosmopolitan in distribution. All species show some degree of social organization; many species nest in a system of tunnels, or galleries, in the soil, often under a dome, or hill, of excavated earth, sand, or debris. Mound-building ants may construct hills up to 5 ft (1.5 m) high. Other species nest in cavities in dead wood, in living plant tissue, or in papery nests attached to twigs or rocks; some invade buildings or ships. Colonies range in size from a few dozen to half a million or more individuals. Typically they include three castes: winged, fertile females, or queens; wingless, infertile females, or workers; and winged males. Those ordinarily seen are workers. In some colonies ants of the worker type may become soldiers, or members of other specialized castes. Whenever a generation of queens and males matures it leaves on a mating flight; shortly afterward the males die, and each fecundated queen returns to earth to establish a new colony. The queen then bites off or scrapes off her wings, excavates a chamber, and proceeds to lay eggs for the rest of her life (up to 15 years), fertilizing most of them with stored sperm. Females develop from fertilized and males from unfertilized eggs. The females become queens or workers, depending on the type of nutrition they receive. The first generation larvae are fed by the queen with her saliva; all develop into workers, which enlarge the nest and care for the queen and the later generations. It is thought that the production of males by the queen and the rearing of new queens by the workers may be controlled by hormonal secretions of all the members of the colony. There are many variations on the basic pattern of new colony formation. In some species the queen cannot establish a colony herself and is adopted by workers of another colony. Slave-making ants raid the nests of other ant species and carry off larvae or pupae to serve as workers; in a few slave-making species the adults cannot feed themselves. Different species differ widely in their diets and may be carnivorous, herbivorous, or omnivorous. Members of some species eat honeydew from plants infested with APHIDS and certain other insects; others, called dairying ants, feed and protect the aphids and "milk" them by stroking. Harvester ants eat and store seeds; these sometimes sprout around the nest, leading to the erroneous belief that these ants cultivate their food. However, cultivation is practiced by certain ants that feed on fungi grown in the nest. Some of these, called leaf-cutter, or parasol, ants, carry large pieces of leaf to the nest, where the macerated leaf tissue is used as a growth medium for the fungus. Most leaf cutters are tropical, but the Texas leaf-cutting ant is a serious crop pest in North America. The army ants of the New World tropics and the driver ants of tropical Africa are carnivorous, nomadic species with no permanent nests. They travel like armies in long columns, overrunning and devouring animals that cannot flee their path; the African species even consume large mammals. House pests among the North American ants include the yellowish Pharoah ant, the little black ant, the odorous house ant, the Argentine ant of warm climates, and the black carpenter ant. Carpenter ants tunnel in wood, but do not feed on it. The TERMITE is often miscalled "white ant," but belongs to a different insect order. Ants as a group are beneficial to humans. Their tunneling mixes and aerates the soil, in some places replacing the activity of earthworms. Many species feed on small insects that are serious pests of crops. Ants are classified in the phylum ARTHROPODA, class Insecta, order Hymenoptera, family Formicidae. See publications of the U.S. Dept. of Agriculture; P. P. and M. W. Larson, *All about Ants* (1965); L. H. Newman, *Ants from Close Up* (1967); C. L. Hogue, *The Armies of the Ant* (1972).

ANTA: see AMERICAN NATIONAL THEATER AND ACADEMY.

Antabuse (ăn'təbyo͞os), trade name for the drug tetraethylthiuram disulfide, used in the treatment of ALCOHOLISM. Also called sulfiram, Antabuse is nontoxic, but it alters the metabolism of alcohol in the body, making it impossible for one who is taking the drug to drink without experiencing severe discomfort. When alcohol is present the drug increases the concentration of acetaldehyde in the body, causing symptoms resembling those of a bad hangover: the individual feels hot, the face becomes flushed, the neck and head throb, and nausea, vomiting, and headache may follow. Small quantities of alcohol, such as from food sauces and cough medicines, and even inhaled traces from shaving lotions and varnishes, may induce the same symptoms. The drug Temposil, or citrated calcium carbamide, has the same function as Antabuse, but is weaker and safer. The therapeutic use of Antabuse was discovered in the 1930s when workers exposed to tetraethylthiuram disulfide, a chemical used in the rubber industry, became ill after drinking alcoholic beverages.

antacid, any one of several basic substances that counteract stomach acidity (see STOMACH). Antacids are used by physicians to treat peptic ulcers and hyperchlorhydria, i.e., the excessive production of hydrochloric acid by the parietal cells lining the stomach. Commonly used antacid preparations, most sold without prescription, contain sodium bicarbonate, magnesium hydroxide, or aluminum hydroxide. Some preparations contain substances such as magnesium trisilicate that reduce the formation of gas.

Antaeus (ăntē'əs), in Greek mythology, giant; son of Poseidon. He became stronger whenever he touched the earth, his mother, Gaea. He killed everyone with whom he wrestled until Hercules overcame him by lifting him in the air.

Antakya: see ANTIOCH, Turkey.

Antalcidas, Peace of: see CORINTHIAN WAR.

Antalya (äntäl'yä), city (1970 pop. 95,185), capital of Antalya prov., SW Turkey, a seaport on the Mediterranean Sea. Its manufactures include textiles and ships. Nearby are deposits of chrome and manganese. Founded in the 2d cent. B.C. by Attalus II, king of Pergamum, the city was known as Attaleia or Attalia, and later as Adalia. It is mentioned in Acts 14.25 as the port from which Paul and Barnabas sailed to Antioch. It passed under the control of the Seljuk Turks in the 13th cent. and in the 15th cent. was annexed by the Ottoman Empire. Situated on a steep cliff, Antalya is a picturesque city surrounded by an old wall. The city is a popular resort. Nearby are numerous ancient ruins.

Antananarivo: see TANANARIVE, Malagasy Republic.

Antara (äntär'ä), fl. 600, Arabian warrior and poet, celebrated in his own day as a hero because he rose from slave birth to be a tribal chief. His poetry is represented by one poem in the MUALLAQAT. His greatness gave rise to many legends over the centuries, and he became the hero of the popular Arabic epic *Sirat Antar.* In it he represents the ideal of a Bedouin chief, rich, generous, brave, and kind. His name also appears as Antar.

Antarctica (ănt"ärk'tĭkə), the 5th largest continent, c.5,500,000 sq mi (14,245,000 sq km), asymmetrically centered on the South Pole and almost entirely within the Antarctic Circle. It consists of two major regions: W Antarctica (c.2,500,000 sq mi/6,475,000 sq km), a mountainous archipelago that includes the Antarctic Peninsula, and E Antarctica (c.3,000,000 sq mi/7,770,000 sq km), geologically a continental shield. They are joined into a single continental mass by an ice cap thousands of feet thick. The seaward margins of the ice cap are steeply sloping; masses of ice break off and float away as icebergs, leaving ice cliffs. Where the outward creep of the ice is channeled into ice streams (zones of more rapid flowage), great floating ice tongues project into the sea; where mountains retard outward movement, the flow is channeled into great valley glaciers. The two major coastal indentations are the Ross Sea, facing the Pacific Ocean, and the Weddell Sea, facing the Atlantic Ocean. At the head of each sea are great ice shelves, the Ross and the McMurdo ice shelves in the Ross Sea and the Ronne and the Filchner ice shelves in the Weddell Sea. Partly aground but mostly afloat, these nearly level ice shelves are from 600 to 4,000 ft (180–1,220 m) thick. They move steadily toward the sea and are fed by valley glaciers, ice streams, and surface snow accumulations. Smaller ice shelves are found all along the coast. Except for mountain ranges, much of E Antarctica's rock surface is near sea level; however, the continent's domed, snow-covered glacial surface rises to about 13,000 ft (4,000 m). In W Antarctica there is great variation in the subglacial relief, suggesting mountainous islands or submerged ranges separated by deep sounds beneath the ice cover. Less than 5% of Antarctica is free of ice; these areas include mountain peaks, small coastal areas, and islands. The Transantarctic Mts. (c.3,500–14,300 ft/1,100–4,400 m high), which extend from the east side of the Filchner Ice Shelf to the western portal of the Ross Sea, form the inner margin of E Antarctica. Primarily formed by block faulting (see MOUNTAINS), the lower slopes have a complex structure of late Precambrian and early Paleozoic metamorphic rocks. These are overlaid by essentially horizontal sedimentary rock, mainly of continental or near-shore origin and ranging in age from the Devonian period to the early Jurassic, which are similar to rocks found in Australia, S Africa, and E South America; coal-bearing Permian strata are also found there. Distinctive plant, insect, fish, and animal fossils in the Triassic and Jurassic strata strongly indicate that the continents of the Southern Hemisphere are parts of a hypothetical supercontinent, Gondwanaland, which broke up in the late Mesozoic era. The continents have since drifted to their present positions. The ice-drowned, mountainous archipelago of W Antarctica is related to the Andes Mts. of South America and is structurally connected to them by way of the Antarctic Peninsula and the Scotia Arc (South Georgia and the South Orkney and South Sandwich islands). The complex structure consists of highly folded metasedimentary strata from Paleozoic to Pliocene epochs. There has been much volcanism down to the present. Mountains of the Antarctic Peninsula rise to c.11,000 ft (3,350 m); the mountains of Marie Byrd Land have comparable heights. The Ellsworth Mts., at the head of Ronne Ice Shelf, are the highest in Antarctica; Vinson Massif (16,860 ft/5,140 m) is the continent's highest peak. A variety of mineral deposits have been discovered in Antarctica, but the extent of the deposits is largely unknown and their relative inaccessibility makes their utility doubtful. Antarctica is surrounded by the world's stormiest seas. A belt of pack ice surrounds the continent; only a few areas are ice-free at the end of most summers. The physical boundary most widely accepted today for the antarctic region is the Antarctic Convergence, a zone c.25 mi (40 km) wide encircling the earth roughly between the 50th and 60th parallels of latitude. Within this zone the colder and denser north-flowing antarctic surface waters sink beneath warmer and saltier subantarctic waters; the difference in temperature and chemical content of the water on the two sides of the zone is reflected in noticeable differences in air temperature and in marine life. Antarctic climate is characterized by low temperature, high wind velocities, and frequent blizzards. Rapidly changing weather is typical of coastal locations, where temperatures for the warmest month average around freezing. Winter minimums drop as low as −40°F (−40°C). High altitude and continuous darkness in winter combine to make the interior of Antarctica the coldest place on earth. Summer temperatures are unlikely to be warmer than 0°F (−18°C); winter mean temperatures are −70°F (−57°C) and lower. The lowest temperature ever recorded on earth was −126.9°F (−88.3°C) at Vostok, a Russian station. Precipitation is in the form of snow; the annual water equivalent in the interior is c.2 in. (5 cm) and c.10 in. (25 cm) in coastal areas. In the dry, dust-free air one can see for miles in clear weather; distances are deceptive, and mirages are common. Refraction of light on blowing snow or low clouds causes "whiteouts" in which the sky blends with the snow-covered surface, eliminating the horizon; no condition is more feared by aviators. There is no native human population in Antarctica, nor are there any large land animals. Few species are adapted to the antarctic environment, but individuals of these few species are numberless. Life that depends completely on the land is limited to microscopic life in summer meltwater ponds, tiny wingless insects living in patches of moss and lichens, and two types of flowering plants (both in the Antarctic Peninsula). Birds and seals that spend part of their time on land (e.g., emperor and Adélie penguins and the brown skua—the most southerly bird and a notorious predator—and Weddell, crabeater, and Ross seals) are dependent on the surrounding sea for food. Antarctic waters are rich in plankton, which serves as food for krill—small shrimplike crustaceans that are the principal food of baleen whales, crabeater seals, Adélie penguins, and several kinds of fish. Fur and elephant seals, which spend the summers on islands north of lat. 65°S were the basis for 19th-century commercial activity in Antarctica. In the 20th cent., commercial interest shifted to baleen whales. Fur seals, thought to be extinct, have only a few small rookeries, but they are recovering from the slaughter of the 19th cent., as are the elephant seals. Whaling has been declining since the peak year of 1930–31 when the Norwegians dominated the industry; since 1967 only the Japanese and the Russians have continued whaling. International efforts to regulate whaling to preserve the stock have been ineffective, and the baleen whales that spend the summer in a zone up to 300 mi (480 km) north of the pack ice are now in danger of extinction.

History of Exploration. Although there was for centuries a tradition that another land lay south of the known world, attempts to find it were defeated by the ice. Antarctica's frigid nature was revealed by the second voyage (1772–75) of the English explorer Capt. James Cook. He did not see the continent as he circumnavigated the world, but he was the first to cross the Antarctic Circle. British and U.S. seal hunters followed him to South Georgia, an island in the S Atlantic. In 1819 the British mariner William Smith discovered the South Shetland Islands. Returning in 1820, he and James Bransfield of the British navy explored and roughly mapped the Shetlands and part of the shore of the Antarctic Peninsula. Searching for rookeries, sealers explored the coastal and offshore regions of the Antarctic Peninsula. Most notable were the British captains James Weddell, George Powell, and Robert Fildes and the Americans Nathaniel B. Palmer, Benjamin Pendleton, Robert Johnson, and John Davis. Davis made the first landing on the antarctic continent (Feb. 7, 1821) at Hughes Bay on the Antarctic Peninsula. First to spend the winter in Antarctica, on King George Island in 1821, were 11 men from the wrecked British vessel *Lord Mellville.* After 1822 fur sealing declined, but in 1829–30 Palmer and Pendleton led a sealing and exploring expedition that included Dr. James Eights, the first U.S. scientist to visit Antarctica. John Biscoe, a British navigator, circumnavigated Antarctica from 1830 to 1832, sighting Enderby Land in 1831 and exploring the western side of the Antarctic Peninsula in 1832. John Balleny and Peter Kemp were other British sealers who made discoveries in E Antarctica in the 1830s. Four naval

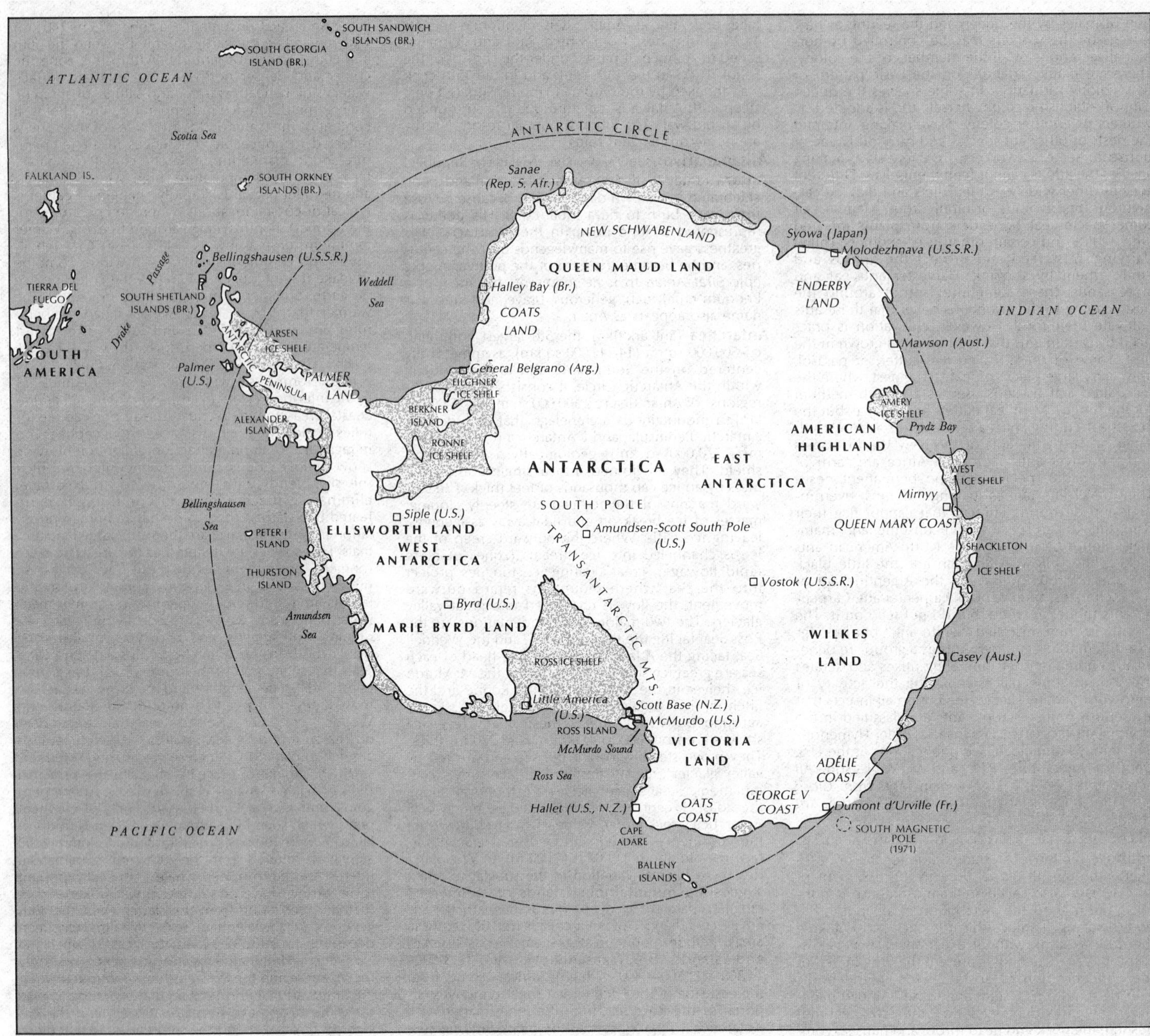

exploring expeditions visited Antarctica in the first half of the 19th cent. Capt. T. T. Bellingshausen was the leader of a Russian expedition that circumnavigated Antarctica (1819–21). He apparently was the first to see (1820) the part of the continent that is now called Queen Maud Land. In W Antarctica he discovered (1820) Peter I Island and Alexander Island. Admiral J. S. C. Dumont d'Urville led a French expedition to the Pacific Ocean that made two visits to Antarctica. He explored in the area of the Antarctic Peninsula in 1838 and in 1840 discovered Clarie Coast and ADÉLIE COAST in E Antarctica. In 1840, Lt. Charles Wilkes, leader of the U.S. Exploring Expedition to the Pacific (1838–42), sailed along the coast of E Antarctica for 1,500 mi (2,400 km), sighting land at nine points. British Capt. James C. Ross commanded two vessels on an expedition (1841–43) that discovered Victoria Land in E Antarctica, the Ross Sea, and the Ross Ice Shelf and explored and mapped the western approaches of the Weddell Sea. In the 1890s, after a half-century of neglect, interest in Antarctica was revived. Norwegian and Scottish whaling firms sent ships (1892–93) to investigate the possibilities of whaling around the Antarctic Peninsula, and a Norwegian vessel examined the Ross Sea area, where a landing was made (1895) on Cape Adare. C. A. Larsen began whaling at South Georgia island in 1904–5, and the seas of the Scotia Arc became the center of Antarctic whaling until after 1926. The 1890s also marked the beginning of a period of extensive Antarctic exploration, during which 16 exploring expeditions from nine countries visited the continent. For the first time, many of them were financed by private individuals and sponsored by scientific societies. It was a period of innovation and hardship in an extremely harsh, little-known environment. The Belgian expedition under Lt. Adrien de Gerlache was beset in the pack ice in March, 1898, and the ship drifted west across the Bellingshausen Sea for a year before it was released. A British expedition led by C. E. Borchgrevink was the first to establish a base for wintering on the continent (Cape Adare, 1899) and the first to make sledge journeys. Different parts of the Antarctic Peninsula and the islands of the Scotia Arc were explored by de Gerlache (1897–98), a Swedish expedition under Dr. Otto Nordenskjold (1901–4), the Scottish National Antarctic Expedition led by W. S. Bruce (1902–4), and two French expeditions led by Dr. Jean B. Charcot (1903–5 and 1908–10). Nordenskjold spent two winters in Antarctica before being rescued after his ship was crushed by ice. Exploration in the Ross Sea area during this period was characterized by long inland journeys. Four British expeditions had bases on Ross Island at McMurdo Sound. British Capt. R. F. Scott headed two expeditions (1901–4 and 1910–13), E. H. Shackleton led another expedition (1907–9), and A. E. Mackintosh headed the Ross Sea Party of Shackleton's unsuccessful Trans-Antarctic Expedition (1914–17). Roald Amundsen, a Norwegian, set up his base at the Bay of Whales, an indentation in the front of the Ross Ice Shelf, and a Japanese expedition (1911–12) was ship-based. The British expeditions carried out extensive exploration and scientific investigation of Victoria Land. Shackleton sledged to within 97 mi (156 km) of the South Pole (Jan., 1909), but it was Amundsen who reached the Pole first, on Dec. 14, 1911. Scott reached it on Jan. 17, 1912, but he and four companions perished on the return trip. The Weddell Sea border of E Antarctica was seen first by Bruce (1904), and it was later explored by the German expedition of Dr. Wilhelm Filchner, discoverer of the Filchner Ice Shelf, whose ship was beset and drifted in the Weddell Sea through the winter of 1912 before being released. Shackleton reached the Weddell Sea in Jan., 1915. He had planned to sledge to McMurdo Sound, via the South Pole, but his ship was beset and crushed in the ice, and his party lived on ice floes until they finally reached Elephant Island in boats. From there Shackleton made his epic voyage of c.800 mi (1,290 km) to South Georgia in an open boat. Two other expeditions explored E Antarctica during the early 20th cent.—Dr. Erich von Drygalski's well-equipped German expedition (1901–3) was cut short on the Wilhelm II Coast when the ship was beset; and Douglas Mawson, leader of the Australasian Expedition (1911–14) established bases at Commonwealth Bay on the George V Coast and on the Queen Mary Coast. Five major sledge journeys were made from Commonwealth Bay; two men perished and Mawson barely survived. In the period following World War I, scientific and technological advances were applied to further antarctic exploration. The first airplane flight in Antarctica (Nov. 26, 1928) was by Sir Hubert Wilkins, an Australian who later flew down the eastern side of the Antarctic Peninsula. However, it was U.S. explorer Richard E. Byrd who most successfully coordinated radios, tractors, airplanes, and aerial cameras for the purposes of exploration. On his first expedition Byrd established his base, Little America, near the site of Amundsen's old base at the Bay of Whales. From Little America he made the first flight over the South Pole on Nov. 29, 1929. On this expedition Marie Byrd Land was discovered and explored from the air. On his second expedition (1933–35) Byrd successfully integrated flights with long sledge and tractor journeys in a more complete exploration of Marie Byrd Land. In 1929–30 three other expeditions were also using aircraft for short flights over the coast. Sir Hubert Wilkins in 1929–30 operated in the Bellingshausen Sea. A Norwegian captain, Hjalmar Riiser-Larsen, explored (1929–30) the coast of E Antarctica from Enderby Land to Coats Land; the area was later claimed by Norway as Queen Maud Land. In Nov., 1935, U.S. explorer Lincoln Ellsworth made the first transantarctic flight, from Dundee Island at the tip of the Antarctic Peninsula to the Bay of Whales, landing four times en route. The British Graham Land Expedition explored the Antarctic Peninsula by sea, air, and dog team from 1935 to 1937, using a different base each winter. Germany made a calculatedly spectacular effort at aerial surveying when two aircraft flying from a catapult ship photographed approximately 135,000 sq mi (350,000 sq km) of Queen Maud Land. The Norwegians had done considerable exploration and mapping during the first two decades of antarctic whaling in the Scotia Arc. In 1925–26 they introduced pelagic whaling with factory ships that could operate in the open sea. Between 1927 and 1937, Lars Christensen led an extensive program of aerial exploration and mapping of the coast of E Antarctica from the Weddell Sea to the Shackleton Ice Shelf. Also allied to whaling were the investigations in physical oceanography, marine biology, and coastal mapping carried out by the Discovery Committee of the British Colonial Office from 1925 to 1939. Their major achievement was the discovery of the Antarctic Convergence. The 1930s were a period of international rivalry in Antarctica, and the map was cut into wedgelike territorial claims that often overlapped. Although the U.S. government did not make a claim nor recognize those of other nations, it supported antarctic exploration. The U.S. Antarctic Service Expedition (1939–41), directed by Byrd, introduced the concept of continuously occupied bases, one of which was set up at the Bay of Whales and another on Stonington Island W of the Antarctic Peninsula. The onset of World War II forced the evacuation of the bases, but before the war ended Great Britain, in order to offset claims by Chile and Argentina, had established permanent bases on the Antarctic Peninsula and off-lying islands. Interest in Antarctica intensified after the war, and several governments established permanent agencies to direct antarctic affairs. Great Britain, Argentina, and Chile continued the system of scientific bases in the Antarctic Peninsula and Scotia Arc. Australia established bases on Heard and Macquarie islands, and France founded one on the Adélie Coast. From 1945 to 1957 the U.S. navy conducted Operation Highjump, the largest expedition ever sent to Antarctica. It involved c.5,000 men, 13 ships including 2 icebreakers, 6 seaplanes, 6 airplanes, 2 small amphibian planes, and 3 helicopters. About 60% of the coastline was photographed, of which about 25% was reported as sighted for the first time. Much of the interior bordering the Ross Ice Shelf was also photographed. The navy's Operation Windmill (1947–48), a part of the larger operation, consisted of two icebreakers equipped with helicopters; it was sent to get ground control for Highjump photography on the coast of Wilkes Land. After World War II, most expeditions were again government-financed. The Ronne Antarctic Research Expedition (1947–48), led by Finn Ronne, was the last privately sponsored U.S. expedition. Using the old U.S. Antarctic Service Expedition Base on Stonington Island, Ronne closed the unexplored gap at the head of the Weddell Sea. Some work was done as a joint effort with the British party that also had a base on the island. A portent of the international cooperation soon to follow, the Norwegian-British-Swedish Antarctic Expedition was organized by the respective governments and scientific societies for exploration and scientific investigation in Queen Maud Land. Although geophysical exploration of the Ross Ice Shelf had been carried out by the Second Byrd Expedition, the Norwegian-British-Swedish Expedition was the first to use geophysical methods inland on a very extensive scale. The International Geophysical Year (IGY), from July 1, 1957, to Dec. 31, 1958, was planned to correspond with a period of maximum sunspot activity. Organized as a cooperative venture by a special committee of the International Council of Scientific Unions, the IGY involved scientists from 56 nations at approximately 2,000 stations on five meridian belts from pole to pole. In a cooperative program, planned and coordinated to avoid duplication and achieve maximum results, 12 nations maintained 65 stations and operational facilities in Antarctica. World data centers were established to collect and organize information and make it available to all scientists. The more difficult logistical problems of establishing inland bases were undertaken by the United States and the USSR. The American effort, beginning in 1955–56, was carried out by Naval Task Force 43 (Operation Deep Freeze). A major base of operations was built on Ross Island, and an airfield was established on the ice. Five other U.S. stations were established, including one at the South Pole that was entirely supplied by air. The Russians concentrated on E Antarctica, building Mirnyy, a station on the Queen Mary Coast, and two relay stations and three bases inland: Komsomolskaya, Vostok (at the Geomagnetic South Pole), and Sovetskaya. There were 14 British stations, 8 Argentine stations, and 6 Chilean stations. France reoccupied the station opened in 1950 on the Adélie Coast and set up another inland near the Magnetic South Pole. Australia, Belgium, Japan, Norway, South Africa, and New Zealand also participated and occupied either insular or coastal sites. From 1951 to 1958, Dr. Vivian Fuchs led the British Commonwealth Trans-Antarctic Expedition's traverse with tractors from the Weddell Sea to McMurdo Sound via the South Pole, conducting a seismic and magnetic profile en route. Although mapping was not part of the IGY program, long-distance flights by U.S. planes covered c.2,000,000 sq mi (5,180,000 sq km) in 1955–56, half of which had never been seen before. These and later support flights, the tractor journeys to build bases, and geophysical traverses by tracked vehicles during the IGY left little of the continent that had not been seen. So outstanding were the results that before the IGY ended it was proposed to continue and broaden the program after 1958. The International Council of Scientific Unions in 1957 established SCAR (Scientific Committee on Antarctic Research) to plan and coordinate the programs that would be carried out in a manner similar to the IGY. Of the 12 nations involved in the IGY, some have dropped their programs, others have suspended and then renewed operations; those that have been continually involved have reduced the size of their programs. Some stations have been closed, new ones have been opened, and old ones have had to be replaced by buildings designed for permanence and comfort. At McMurdo the United States has built a scientific village where people may be housed in summer and winter. The village is heated and lighted by a small atomic power plant that uses waste heat to distill sea water. From McMurdo other U.S. bases are supported by air. Since the IGY the National Science Foundation (NSF) has financed the U.S. program. Logistical support is in the hands of the U.S. navy, and mapping is done by the U.S. Geological Survey. Since 1962, when the NSF introduced a research ship, work on various branches of oceanography in the S Pacific and S Atlantic has been done. In 1968–69 the NSF added a wooden trawler-type vessel especially designed for marine biological investigations in the area of the Antarctic Peninsula. The success of the IGY effort led to the signing (1959) of the Antarctic Treaty by representatives of the 12 nations that had been involved in the IGY. The treaty applied to the area south of lat. 60°S, exclusive of the high seas, and it provided for cooperation and freedom of movement for scientific investigation as well as for the exchange of observers and scientific data. It prohibited military operations, nuclear explosions, and the disposal of radioactive wastes. Previous territorial claims were not prejudiced, nor was any activity during the life of the treaty to be construed as supporting territorial claims. By 1971 six consultative conferences had been held, resulting in amendments relative to cooperation in scientific research, conservation of living resources, contamination of the environment, development of telecommunications, and preservation of historic areas and buildings. In the early 1970s fossil finds and geological studies gave further support to the theory of continental drift. These studies concluded that Antarctica has been frozen for at least 20 million years (not 7 million years as previously thought) and that a tropical environment existed there 250 million years ago. See H. R. Mill, *The Siege of the South Pole* (1905); J. G. Hayes, *The Conquest of the South Pole* (1932); E. W. H. Christie, *The Antarctic Problem* (1951); P. I. Mitterling, *America in the Antarctic to 1840* (1959); Frank Debenham, *Antarctica, the Story of a Continent* (1959); L. P. Kirwan, *A History of Polar Exploration* (1960); Walter Sullivan, *Quest for a Continent* (1957) and *Assault on the Unknown* (1961); A. G. Price, *The Winning of Australian Antarctica* (1962); P. E. Victor, *Man and the Conquest of the Poles* (1963); Raymond Priestley et al., ed., *Antarctic Research* (1964); Trevor Hatherton, ed., *Antarctica* (1965); R. S. Lewis, *A Continent for Science* (1965); L. B. Quartermain, *South to the Pole* (1967); H. G. R. King, *The Antarctic* (1969); L. O. Quam, ed., *Research in the Antarctic* (1971); K. J. Bertrand, *Americans in Antarctica, 1775–1948* (1971); R. S. Lewis and P. M. Smith, eds., *Frozen Future* (1973).

Antarctic Circle, imaginary circle on the surface of the earth at 66½°S lat., i.e., 23½°N of the South Pole. It marks the southernmost point at which the sun can be seen at the summer SOLSTICE (about June 22) and the northernmost point of the southern polar regions at which the MIDNIGHT SUN is visible.

Antarctic Peninsula, glaciated mountain region of W ANTARCTICA, extending c.1,200 mi (1,930 km) N toward South America; in the south, volcanic peaks rise to c.11,000 ft (3,350 m). It is surrounded by numerous islands, including the South Shetlands and the Palmer Archipelago. The tip of the peninsula, 670 mi (1,078 km) from Cape Horn, is Antarctica's farthest point from the South Pole. The continent's only flowering plants are found on the peninsula. The northwest coast of the peninsula was mapped by the British navigator James Bransfield in Jan., 1820, and was explored by sealers in 1820–21. First considered to be part of the continent, the peninsula was later (1928) thought to be a group of islands; the John Rymill expedition (1934–37) proved its peninsularity. It was originally named Palmer Peninsula by Americans for Nathaniel Palmer, a U.S. captain who explored the area in Nov., 1820. In 1832, Britain claimed it and called it Graham Land and Trinity Peninsula. Argentina claimed it in 1940 as San Martin Land and Chile in 1942 as O'Higgins Land. In 1964, by international agreement, the entire feature was called the Antarctic Peninsula; Graham Land, Trinity Peninsula, and Palmer Land are used as local names.

Antares (ăntâr'ēz), brightest star in the constellation SCORPIUS; Bayer designation Alpha Scorpii; 1970 position R.A. $16^h27.6^m$, Dec. −26°22′. A red supergiant of SPECTRAL CLASS M1, Antares has an apparent MAGNITUDE of about 0.9, making it one of the 20 brightest stars in the sky. Its name is from the Greek meaning "rival of Mars," referring both to its color and to its brightness. Antares is a binary star and a semiregular variable, with magnitude ranging from 0.86 to 1.02. Its distance from the earth is about 500 light-years.

ant bear: see AARDVARK.

anteater, name applied to various animals that feed on ants, termites, and other insects, but more properly restricted to a completely toothless group of the order Edentata. There are three genera, all found in tropical Central and South America. The great anteater, or ant bear (*Myrmecophaga*), has an elongated, almost cylindrical head and snout, a long sticky tongue, a coarse-haired body about 4 ft (1.2 m) long, and a long, broad tail. The large, sharp claws on the forefeet are weapons of defense and are used to open the hard earth mounds of termites and ants, which are then picked up on the saliva-coated tongue. The tongue extends to a length of about 2 ft (60 cm). The collared, or lesser, anteater (*Tamandua*), less than half the size of the great anteater, is a short-haired yellowish and black arboreal creature. The arboreal two-toed anteater (*Cyclopes*) is the size of a squirrel and has a prehensile tail and silky yellow fur. Other animals called anteater are members of other groups. The banded anteater of Australia is a marsupial; the spiny anteater, also of Australia, is related to the PLATYPUS. For the scaly anteater, see PANGOLIN. True anteaters are classified in the phylum CHORDATA, subphylum Vertebrata, class Mammalia, order Edentata, family Myrmecophagidae.

Antelami, Benedetto (bānādĕt'tō äntälä'mē), c.1150–c.1225, Italian sculptor. Considered the most important sculptor of the late Romanesque period in N Italy, Antelami was an aesthetic forebear of Nicola and Giovanni PISANO. His relief carvings emphasize rhythmic design by means of drapery details on elongate figures and tight compositions. The faces of his figures are profoundly expressive. Antelami's style, as in his doors for the baptistery at Parma (begun 1196), suggests that he was trained in S France. It is clear that his late work was influenced by French Gothic style.

antelope, name applied to a large number of hoofed, ruminant mammals of the CATTLE family

(Bovidae), which also includes the sheep and goats. The North American PRONGHORN is sometimes called an antelope, but belongs to a separate, related family (Antilocapridae). True antelopes are found only in Africa and Asia. They range in size from pygmy antelopes, 12 in. (30 cm) high at the shoulder, to the giant ELAND, with a shoulder height of over 6 ft (180 cm). Most types stand 3 to 4 ft (90–120 cm) high. The horns of antelopes, unlike the antlers of deer, are unbranched, consist of a chitinous shell with a bony core, and are not shed. Africa is the home of most antelopes. The spiral-horned antelopes are the BUSHBUCKS, (including the nyala and the sitatunga), KUDU, eland, and BONGO. These oxlike animals have patterns of light and dark stripes on the body, and most have them on the face as well. The DUIKERS are a group of small, straight-horned antelopes of forest and thick brush country. MARSH ANTELOPES are deerlike animals of marshes and reedbeds; they include the waterbuck, kob, puka, lechwe, reedbuck, and rhebok. The GNU (or wildebeest) and the closely related HARTEBEEST and DAMALISK are horselike antelopes of the grasslands. The name ORYX is applied to smaller horselike animals of the desert and scrublands, including the gemsbok and the beisa; the ADDAX is a related desert antelope. The sable antelope and the closely related roan antelope have enormous, backward-curved, scimitar-shaped horns. GAZELLE is the name for a number of small, delicate antelopes with spreading horns, inhabiting deserts and grassy plains. The largest of these is the pale brown IMPALA, the kind of antelope best known from motion pictures. The gazelle tribe also includes the gerenuk, dibatag, springbok, and BLACKBUCK, as well as the so-called true gazelles (genus *Gazella*). The blackbuck, found in India, was the first antelope to be described by zoologists, and has the generic name *Antilope.* The delicate pygmy antelopes include the royal antelope, beira, klipspringer, oribi, grysbok, steinbok, dik-dik, and suni. Males have tiny, straight horns. The nilgai and the four-horned antelope are found in SE Asia. More closely related to the goats than to any of the above-named animals, but often called antelopes, are the saiga of central Asia and the chiru of Tibet. Antelopes are classified in the phylum CHORDATA, subphylum Vertebrata, class Mammalia, order Artiodactyla, family Bovidae.

antelope brush, low, deciduous shrub (*Purshia tridentata*) of the family Rosaceae (ROSE family), widely distributed in the W United States where it is a characteristic constituent of the vegetation on arid slopes and desert ranges. One of the most important Western browse plants, it provides abundant forage throughout the year for both cattle and deer. Antelope brush is classified in the division MAGNOLIOPHYTA, class Magnoliopsida, order Rosales, family Rosaceae.

antenna (ăntĕn'ə), in electronics, system of wires or other conductors used to transmit or receive radio or other electromagnetic waves (see RADIO); popularly called an aerial. The idea of using an antenna was developed by Guglielmo Marconi (c.1897). In a transmitting antenna, the signal from an electronic circuit causes electrons in the antenna to oscillate; these moving electric charges generate electromagnetic radiation, which is transmitted through space. Distribution of the waves depends on the design of the antenna; the transmitting antennas of radio stations are designed to emit waves in all directions, while those used for RADAR focus the waves in a single direction. In a receiving antenna electromagnetic waves cause the electrons to oscillate, inducing a signal that can be detected by an electronic circuit. The antenna has a characteristic frequency that depends on the relationship between its physical dimensions and the wavelength of the signal; a wire of a given length is inherently tuned to radio waves whose wavelengths are simple fractions of the length of the wire. In general, a longer antenna is used to transmit or receive signals of longer wavelength. Theoretically, the same antenna can be used both for sending and for receiving signals, but in practice, transmitting antennas are designed differently from receiving antennas, since they must be able to handle higher power loads. Any straight vertical conductor may serve as an antenna and will transmit to or receive from all directions. A horizontal antenna radiates or intercepts energy principally at right angles to itself; the use of horizontal antennas enables transmitters to concentrate or beam their signals into desired areas and enables receivers to select one of several signals having the same frequency but arriving from different directions. Developments in radio circuitry and antenna design have eliminated the need, in most locations, for an external antenna for AM radio reception; however, external antennas are usually needed for FM radio and television reception. Special antennas are employed in transmitting and receiving radar and microwaves and in satellite communications. The radio telescopes used in astronomy are specially designed receiving antennas.

Antenor (ăntē'nôr), fl. last half of 6th cent. B.C., Greek sculptor who executed the bronze statues of the tyrannicides Harmodius and Aristogiton. In 480 B.C., Xerxes carried these statues away from Athens, but they were discovered later at Susa by Alexander and sent back. A marble figure of a woman, signed on the base by Antenor, was found in the ruins of the Acropolis at Athens. See also CRITIUS.

Antenor, in Greek mythology, wise elder of Troy who urged that Helen be returned to Menelaus. The Greeks spared him and his family when they sacked Troy. A later myth portrays Antenor as a traitorous spy who opened the door of the wooden horse. Agenor was his son.

Antequera (äntākä'rä), city (1970 pop. 40,908), Málaga prov., S Spain, in Andalusia. At the foot of the Sierra de los Torcales, it is the center of a fertile agricultural region. The Cueva de Menga, a large prehistoric burial chamber, possibly Celtic, was discovered in the vicinity in 1842. Similar finds were made in 1903 and 1904.

Antequera y Castro, José de (hōsā' dā äntākä'rä ē kä'strō), 1690–1731, Peruvian lawyer, leader of a revolt in Paraguay. A prosecutor of the audiencia of Charcas, he was sent to Asunción to probe charges against the governor of Paraguay, Diego de los Reyes. Antequera sided with the opposition, became governor himself, and upheld the celebrated doctrine that "the authority of the people is superior to that of the king." He led the uprising of the COMUNEROS in a war against the authority of the viceroy and was finally captured and beheaded in 1731. This first struggle for freedom was the forerunner of the Spanish American revolts against Spain.

Anteros: see EROS.

Antheil, George (ăn'tīl), 1900–59, American composer, b. Trenton, N.J. He went to Europe in 1920 and became known for his iconoclastic approach to music. In 1927 a performance of his *Ballet mécanique,* scored for player piano, car horns, airplane propellers, and the like, caused a great stir among critics and concertgoers in New York City. Much of his early work, such as the opera *Transatlantic* (1930), reveals the influence of jazz. Antheil's later compositions include more traditional symphonies and sonatas.

anthelion: see HALO.

anthem [ultimately from ANTIPHON], short nonliturgical choral composition used in Protestant services, usually accompanied and having an English text. The term is used in a broader sense for "national anthems" and for the Latin motets still used occasionally in Anglican services. A full anthem is entirely choral, while a verse anthem includes parts for solo singers. The anthem arose in the Anglican Church, as the English counterpart of the Latin motet, through the work of Christopher Tye (c.1500–1573), Thomas TALLIS, and William BYRD (1543–1623). Early anthems were often in the style of Latin motets, sometimes being merely an English text set to well-known motets. In the late 17th cent. composers such as Henry Purcell and John Blow, under Italian influences, wrote verse anthems with several movements, as in cantatas. George F. Handel's anthems, in the tradition of the full anthem, are, like those of Purcell and Blow, too elaborate for ordinary church use. Since the 19th cent. extracts from oratorios, masses, passions, etc., are commonly used as anthems, but these pieces are not anthems in the original sense of the term. See R. T. Daniel, *The Anthem in New England before 1800* (1966); M. B. Foster, *Anthems and Anthem Composers* (1901, repr. 1970).

anthemion (ănthē'mēən), commonly called a palmette, a radiating, fan-shaped ornament or motif suggestive of a palm leaf or of honeysuckle and found in Egyptian, Assyrian, and Aegean art. It was widely used by the Greeks and Romans on their buildings and on many kinds of decorative objects.

Anthemius of Tralles (ănthē'mēəs, trăl'ēz), fl. 6th cent., Greek architect, engineer, and mathematician. By order of Emperor Justinian and with the aid of Isidorus of Miletus, he built (532–37) the Church of HAGIA SOPHIA in Constantinople.

anther, POLLEN-bearing structure of the stamen of a flower, usually borne on a slender stalk called the filament. Each anther generally consists of two pollen sacs, which open when the pollen is mature. The method of opening, or dehiscence, is uniform in any single species of plant.

anthology, collection of selected literary pieces of varied authorship. The name derives from the Greek word *anthologia,* which means "gathered flowers," and it was first given to the GREEK ANTHOLOGY. Whereas in the past an anthology usually contained short, select poems or epigrams, in modern times an anthology has come to include all forms of literary composition.

Anthony, Saint (ăn'tənē, ăn'thənē), 251?–c.350, Egyptian hermit, called St. Anthony of Egypt and St. Anthony the Abbot. At the age of 20 he gave away his large inheritance and became a hermit. At 35 he went into seclusion and at that time he experienced, says tradition, every temptation the devil could devise, but he repelled them. A colony of hermits grew up about him, and after 20 years he emerged to rule them in a community, the monks being in solitude except for worship and meals. After a few years he went away to the desert near Thebes, where he lived most of the rest of his long life. St. Anthony was the father of Christian MONASTICISM; his community became a model, particularly in the East, but he did not write the rule ascribed to him. His type of community is seen in the West among the Carthusians. He is a patron of herdsmen. St. ATHANASIUS wrote his life. The temptation of St. Anthony has inspired works of literature, particularly a novel by Flaubert, and became a popular theme early in the history of Western art. Feast: Jan. 17.

Anthony, Marc: see ANTONY.

Anthony, Susan Brownell, 1820–1906, American reformer and leader of the woman-suffrage movement, b. Adams, Mass.; daughter of Daniel Anthony, Quaker abolitionist. From the age of 17, when she was a teacher in rural New York state, she agitated for equal pay for women teachers, for coeducation, and for college training for girls. When the Sons of Temperance refused to admit women into their movement, she organized the first woman's temperance association, the Daughters of Temperance. At a temperance meeting in 1851 she met Elizabeth Cady Stanton, and from that time until Stanton's death in 1902 they were associated as the leaders of the woman's movement in the United States and were bound by a warm personal friendship. Susan B. Anthony lectured (1851–60) on woman's rights and on abolition, and, with Stanton, secured the first laws in the New York state legislature guaranteeing to women rights over their children and control of property and wages. In 1863 she was a coorganizer of the Women's Loyal League to support Lincoln's government, especially his emancipation policy. After the Civil War she opposed granting suffrage to freedmen without also giving it to women, and many woman-suffrage sympathizers broke with her on this issue. She and Stanton organized (1869) the National Woman Suffrage Association. In 1890 this group united with the American Woman Suffrage Association to form the National American Woman Suffrage Association, of which Anthony was president from 1892 to 1900. In 1872 she led a group of women to the polls in Rochester, N.Y., to test the right of women to the franchise under the terms of the Fourteenth Amendment. Her arrest, trial, and sentence to a fine (which she refused to pay) were a cause célèbre; other women followed her example until the case was decided against them by the U.S. Supreme Court. From 1869 she traveled and lectured throughout the United States and Europe, seeing the feminist movement gradually advance to respectability and political importance. The secret of her power, aside from her superior intellect and strong personality, was her unswerving singleness of purpose. With Elizabeth Cady Stanton and Matilda Joslyn Gage, she compiled Volumes I to III of the *History of Woman Suffrage* (1881–86), using a personal legacy to buy most of the first edition and present the volumes to colleges and universities in the United States and Europe. The *History* was completed by Ida Husted Harper (Vols. IV–VI, 1900–1922; Susan B. Anthony contributed to Vol. IV.). See *The Life and Work of Susan B. Anthony,* ed. by Ida Husted (3 vol., 1908; repr. 1969); biographies by K. S. Anthony (1954) and R. C. Dorr (1928, repr. 1970).

Anthony of Padua, Saint, 1195–1231, Portuguese Franciscan, Doctor of the Church, b. Lisbon. He was renowned for his eloquence. According to tradition, in a vision he received the child Jesus in his arms and is usually thus represented in art. He was known as a preacher and for his holy life and was canonized the year after he died in Padua. Anthony has a reputation as a miracle worker and is popularly invoked by Roman Catholics to find lost articles. Feast: June 13. See biography by Mary Purcell (1960).

anthophyllite (ăn"thəfĭl'īt): see AMPHIBOLE.

anthracene (ăn'thrəsēn), $C_{14}H_{10}$, solid organic compound derived from coal tar. It melts at 218°C and boils at 354°C. When pure it is colorless and has a violet fluorescence; it darkens when exposed to sunlight. Anthracene is insoluble in water but is quite soluble in carbon disulfide and somewhat soluble in ethanol, methanol, benzene, chloroform, and other organic solvents. It is readily oxidized to form anthraquinone, the parent compound of the ALIZARIN series of dyes. The molecular structure of anthracene consists of three benzenelike rings joined side by side; it is thus an AROMATIC COMPOUND. It is the first member of the anthracene series, a group of aromatic hydrocarbons that are structurally related to it and have the general formula C_nH_{2n-18}.

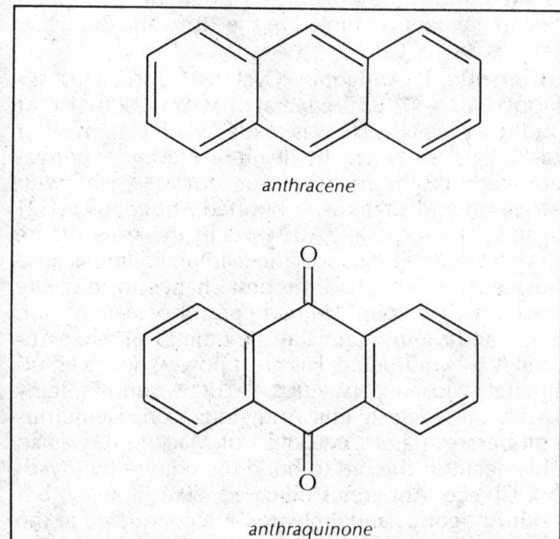

anthracite (ăn'thrəsīt"): see COAL.

anthrax (ăn'thrăks), acute infectious disease of animals that can be secondarily transmitted to humans. It is caused by a bacillus (*Bacillus anthracis*) that primarily affects sheep, horses, hogs, cattle, and goats and is almost always fatal in animals. Transmission to humans normally occurs through contact, but can also occur by breathing air laden with the spores of the bacilli. The disease is almost entirely occupational, i.e., restricted to individuals who handle hides of animals (e.g., farmers, butchers, and veterinarians) or sort wool. In the cutaneous form of the disease, which is not usually fatal to humans, pustules occur on the hands, face, and neck; pulmonary anthrax causes lesions in the lungs and brain. Pure cultures of the anthrax bacillus were obtained in 1876 by Robert Koch, who demonstrated the relationship of the microbe to the disease; confirmation of the bacillus as the cause of anthrax was provided by Louis Pasteur, who also developed a method of vaccinating sheep and cattle against the disease. Anthrax is now relatively uncommon in the United States because of widespread vaccination of animals and disinfection of animal products such as hides and wool.

anthropology, classification and analysis of humans and their society, descriptively, historically, and physically. Its unique contribution to studying the bonds of human social relations has been the distinctive concept of CULTURE. It has also differed from other sciences concerned with human social behavior (especially sociology) in its emphasis on data from nonliterate peoples and archaeological exploration. Emerging as an independent science in the late 18th and early 19th cent., anthropology was associated from the beginning with various other emergent sciences, notably biology, geology, linguistics, psychology, and archaeology. Its development is also linked with the philosophical speculations of the Enlightenment about the origins of human society and the sources of myth. A unifying science, anthropology has not lost its connections with any of these branches, but has incorporated all or part of them and often employs their techniques. It is divided primarily into physical anthropology and cultural anthropology. Physical anthropology focuses basically on the problems of human evolution, including human paleontology and the study of RACE and of body build or constitution (somatology). It uses the methods of ANTHROPOMETRY, as well as those of genetics, physiology, and ecology. Cultural anthropology includes ARCHAEOLOGY, which studies the material remains of prehistoric and extinct cultures; ethnography, the descriptive study of living cultures; ETHNOLOGY, which utilizes the data furnished by ethnography, the recording of living cultures, and archaeology, to analyze and compare the various cultures of humanity; social anthropology, which evolves broader generalizations based partly on the findings of the other social sciences; and LINGUISTICS, the science of language. Applied anthropology is the practical application of anthropological techniques to areas such as industrial relations and minority-group problems. In Europe the term anthropology usually refers to physical anthropology alone. See A. L. Kroeber, *Anthropology* (1948, repr. in 2 vol., 1963); Clyde Kluckhohn, *Mirror for Man* (1949, repr. 1963); M. J. Herskovits, *Cultural Anthropology* (1955, repr. 1963); Margaret Mead and R. L. Bunzel, ed., *The Golden Age of American Anthropology* (1960); B. C. Loring, *The Stages of Human Evolution* (1967); J. O. Brew, ed., *One Hundred Years of Anthropology* (1968); G. M. Foster, *Applied Anthropology* (1969); A. H. Smith and J. L. Fisher, ed., *Anthropology* (1970); Marvin Harris, *The Rise of Anthropological Theory* (1968) and *Culture, Man, and Nature* (1971).

anthropometry (ănthrəpŏm'ətrē), technique of measuring the human body in terms of dimensions, proportions, and ratios such as those provided by the CEPHALIC INDEX. Once the standard approach to racial classification and comparing humans to other primates, the technique is now used for deciding the range of clothing sizes to be manufactured, and determining the nutritional status of people. See Ashley Montagu, *A Handbook of Anthropometry* (1960); Robert McCammon, *Human Growth and Development* (1970).

anthropomorphism (ăn"thrəpōmôr'fĭzəm) [Gr.,= having human form], in religion, conception of divinity as being in human form or having human characteristics. Anthropomorphism also applies to the ascription of human forms or characteristics to the divine spirits of things such as the winds and the rivers, events such as war and death, and abstractions such as love, beauty, strife, and hate. As used by students of religion and anthropology the term is applied to certain systems of religious belief, usually polytheistic. Although some degree of anthropomorphism is characteristic of nearly all polytheistic religions, it is perhaps most widely associated with the Homeric gods and later Greek religion. Anthropomorphic thought is said to have developed from three primary sources: ANIMISM, legend, and the need for visual presentation of the gods.

antiballistic missile: see GUIDED MISSILE.

Antibes (äNtĕb'), resort town (1968 pop. 48,013), in Alpes-Maritimes dept., SE France, on the RIVIERA. It is a seaport and the center of a great flower-growing region; a school of horticulture is there. Nearby is the fashionable resort Cap d'Antibes. The town was founded as a Greek colony in the 4th cent. B.C. A fortified port, it still has the 16th-century Fort Carré. Also of interest is a Grimaldi château (14th and 16th cent.) housing a museum that includes numerous works of Picasso. Roman ruins are to the south.

antibiotic, any of a variety of substances, usually obtained from microorganisms, that inhibit the growth of or destroy certain other microorganisms. Although for centuries preparations derived from living matter were applied to wounds to destroy infection, the fact that a microorganism is capable of destroying one of another species was not established until the latter half of the 19th cent. when Pasteur noted the antagonistic effect of other bacteria on the anthrax organism and pointed out that this action might be put to therapeutic use. Meanwhile the German chemist Paul Ehrlich developed the idea of selective toxicity: that certain chemicals that would be toxic to some organisms, e.g., infectious bacteria, would be harmless to other organisms, e.g., humans. In 1928, Sir Alexander Fleming, a Scottish biologist, observed that *Penicillium notatum,* a common mold, had destroyed staphylococcus bacteria in culture, and in 1939 the American microbiologist René Dubos demonstrated that a soil bacterium was capable of decomposing the starch-like capsule of the pneumococcus bacterium, without which the pneumococcus is harmless and does not cause pneumonia. Dubos then found in the soil a microbe, *Bacillus brevis,* from which he obtained a product, tyrothricin, that was highly toxic to a wide range of bacteria. Tyrothricin, a mixture of the two peptides GRAMICIDIN and tyrocidine, was also found to be toxic to red blood and reproductive cells in humans but could be used to good effect when applied as ointments on body surfaces. PENICILLIN was finally isolated in 1939, and in 1944 Selman Waksman and Albert Schatz, American microbiologists, isolated STREPTOMYCIN and a number of other antibiotics from *Streptomyces griseus.* The mass production of antibiotics began during World War II with streptomycin and penicillin. Now most antibiotics are produced by staged fermentations in which strains of microorganisms producing high yields are grown under optimum conditions in nutrient media in fermentation tanks holding several thousand gallons. The mold is strained out of the fermentation broth, and then the antibiotic is removed from the broth by filtration, precipitation, and other separation methods. In some cases new antibiotics are laboratory synthesized, while many antibiotics are produced by chemically modifying natural substances; many such derivatives are more effective than the natural substances against infecting organisms or are better absorbed by the body, e.g., some semisynthetic penicillins are effective against bacteria resistant to the parent substance. The great number of diverse antibiotics currently available can be classified in different ways, e.g., by their chemical structure, their microbial origin, or their mode of action. They are also frequently designated by their effective range. TETRACYCLINES, the most widely used broad spectrum antibiotics, are effective against both Gram-positive and Gram-negative bacteria, as well as against rickettsias and psittacosis-causing organisms (see GRAM'S STAIN). The medium spectrum antibiotics BACITRACIN, the ERYTHROMYCINS, penicillin, and the CEPHALOSPORINS are effective primarily against Gram-positive bacteria, although the streptomycin group is effective against some Gram-negative and Gram-positive bacteria. Polymixins are narrow spectrum antibiotics effective against only a few species of bacteria. Antibiotics are either injected, given orally, or applied to the skin in ointment form. Many, while potent anti-infective agents, also cause toxic side effects. Some, like penicillin, are highly allergenic and can cause skin rashes, shock, and other manifestations of allergic sensitivity. Others, such as the tetracyclines, cause major changes in the intestinal bacterial population and can result in superinfection by fungi and other microoorganisms. CHLORAMPHENICOL, which is now restricted in use, produces severe blood diseases, and use of streptomycin can result in ear and kidney damage. Many antibiotics are less effective than formerly because antibiotic-resistant strains of microorganisms have emerged (see DRUG RESISTANCE). Antibiotics have found wide nonmedical use. Some are used in animal husbandry, along with vitamin B_{12}, to enhance the weight gain of livestock. However, some authorities believe the addition of antibiotics to animal feeds is dangerous because continuous low exposure to the antibiotic can sensitize humans to the drug and make them unable to take the substance later in the treatment of infection. In addition low levels of antibiotics in animal feed encourage the emergence of antibiotic-resistant strains of microorganisms. Drug resistance has been shown to be carried by a genetic particle transmissible from one strain of microorganism to another, and the presence of low levels of antibiotics can actually cause an increase in the number of such particles in the bacterial population and increase the probability that such particles will be transferred to pathogenic, or disease-causing, strains. Antibiotics have also been used to treat plant diseases such as bacteria-caused infections in tomatoes, potatoes, peppers, and fruit trees. The substances are also used in experimental research. Other antibiotics discussed in this volume are ACTINOMYCIN, AMPHOTERICIN B, AMPICILLIN, LINCOMYCIN, NEOMYCIN, RIFAMPIN, and VANCOMYCIN. See H. M. Böttcher, *Wonder Drugs* (1964); Tadeusz Korzybski, *Antibiotics* (2 vol., 1967); L. P. Garrod et al., *Antibiotics and Chemotherapy* (3d ed. 1971).

antibody, specific protein produced by lymphocyte cells in response to the presence in the body of a foreign agent. Foreign substances, or antigens, may be bacteria, bacterial TOXINS, viruses, or other cells or proteins. The body is capable of making thousands of different antibodies, each specific to a different antigen. Each specific antibody is made by one particular lymphocyte cell and its clone, or descendant cells (see IMMUNITY).

Antichrist (ăn'tĭkrīst), in Christian belief, a person who will represent on earth the powers of evil by opposing Christ, glorifying himself, and causing many to leave the faith. He will be destroyed by Christ at the time of the Second Coming. 1 John 2.18-22; 4.3; 2 John 7; and Rev. 13. Similar ideas are expressed in Judaism (e.g., Ezek. 38.1-39.29), and in Zoroastrianism. Christians have often identified enemies of their faith with the Antichrist; e.g., with early Christians it was Nero, with some Protestants the pope.

anticline: see FOLD.

anticoagulant (ăn″tēkōăg′yələnt), any of several substances that inhibit blood clot formation (see BLOOD CLOTTING). Some anticoagulants, such as the coumarin derivatives bishydroxycoumarin (Dicumarol) and warfarin (Coumadin) inhibit synthesis of prothrombin, a clot-forming substance, and other clotting factors. The coumarin derivatives compete with vitamin K, which is a necessary substance in prothrombin formation (see VITAMIN). They are only effective after the body's existing supply of prothrombin is depleted. Another anticoagulant, heparin, is a POLYSACCHARIDE found naturally in many cells. It acts in several ways: by preventing prothrombin formation; by preventing formation of fibrin, another clotting substance; and by decreasing the availability of a third clotting factor, thrombin. Heparin is obtained by extracting it from animal tissues. Anticoagulants are used to treat blood clots, which appear especially frequently in veins of the legs and pelvis in bedridden patients. Therapy helps to reduce the risk of clots reaching the lung, heart, or other organs. Heparin causes an instantaneous increase in blood-clotting time, and its effect lasts several hours.

Anti-Comintern Pact: see COMINTERN and AXIS.

Anti-Corn-Law League, organization formed in 1839 to work for the repeal of the English CORN LAWS. It was an affiliation of groups in various cities and districts with headquarters at Manchester and was an outgrowth of the smaller Manchester Anti-Corn-Law Association. Richard COBDEN and John BRIGHT were its leading figures. The league won over Sir Robert Peel to its views, and the corn laws were repealed in 1846.

Anticosti (ăntĭkŏs′tē), low, flat island (1971 pop. 419), 135 mi (217 km) long and 10 to 30 mi (16–48 km) wide, E Que., Canada, at the head of the Gulf of St. Lawrence. The island was discovered by Cartier in 1534. Louis XIV granted it to Jolliet as a reward for his discovery of the Mississippi. Jolliet's heirs held it until 1763, when it was annexed to Newfoundland (then a separate colony). It was returned to Canada in 1774 and has been privately owned since 1895. Lumbering for pulpwood is the chief occupation on the island.

anticyclone, region of high atmospheric pressure; anticyclones are commonly referred to as "highs." The pressure gradient, or change between the core of the anticyclone and its surroundings, combined with the CORIOLIS EFFECT, causes air to circulate about the core in a counterclockwise direction in the Northern Hemisphere and a clockwise direction in the Southern Hemisphere. Near the surface of the earth the frictional drag of the surface on the moving air causes it to spiral outward gradually toward lower pressures while still maintaining the rotational direction. This outward movement of air is fed by descending currents near the center of the anticyclone that are warmed by compression as they encounter higher pressures at lower altitudes. The warming, in turn, greatly reduces the relative humidity, so that anticyclones, or "highs," are generally characterized by few clouds and low humidity. Such weather characteristics may extend over an area from a few hundred to a few thousand miles wide. Many low-level anticyclones are swept generally eastward by the prevailing west-to-east flow of the upper atmosphere, usually traversing some 500 to 1,000 mi (800–1,600 km) per day. Other anticyclones are permanent or seasonal features of particular geographic regions. The term *anticyclone* is derived from the fact that the associated rotational direction and general weather characteristics of an anticylone are opposite to those of a CYCLONE.

antidiabetic drug, any of several drugs that control blood sugar level in the treatment of DIABETES. See INSULIN; ORINASE; PHENFORMIN.

antidiuretic hormone (ăn″tēdīyōōrĕt′ĭk), polypeptide hormone secreted by the posterior PITUITARY GLAND. Its principal action is to regulate the amount of water excreted by the kidneys. Antidiuretic hormone (ADH), known also as vasopressin, causes the kidneys to resorb water directly from the renal tubules, thus concentrating the salts and waste products in the liquid, which will eventually become urine. ADH secretion by the pituitary is regulated by neural connections from the hypothalamus, which is believed to monitor either the volume of blood passing through it or the concentration of water in the blood. Dehydration or body stress will raise ADH secretion and water will be retained. Alcohol inhibits ADH secretion. Failure of the pituitary to produce ADH results in diabetes insipidus. In pharmacological doses ADH acts as a vasoconstrictor. The structure and chemical synthesis of ADH was announced (1953) by nobel laureate Vincent Du Vigneaud and others.

Antietam campaign (ăntē′təm), Sept., 1862, of the Civil War. After the second battle of BULL RUN, Gen. Robert E. LEE crossed the Potomac to invade Maryland and Pennsylvania. At Frederick, Md., he divided (Sept. 10) his army, sending Stonewall Jackson to capture the large Union garrison at Harpers Ferry and thus clear his communications through the Shenandoah valley. With the remainder, Lee marched NW toward Hagerstown. Gen. George B. MCCLELLAN learned of this division of forces and moved to attack. In the battle on South Mt. (the Blue Ridge N of the Potomac, 12 mi/19 km W of Frederick) on Sept. 14, 1862, McClellan defeated Lee's rear guard and took the passes of that range. Lee then fell back to Sharpsburg (c.9 mi/14.5 km W of South Mt.), where his position lay behind Antietam Creek. On Sept. 15 the Harpers Ferry garrison capitulated to Jackson, who, with part of his command, joined Lee before McClellan attacked. The battle of Antietam (or Sharpsburg) opened on the morning of Sept. 17. Early assaults on Lee's left were bloody but indecisive, and McClellan failed to press the slight Union advantage with his available reserves. In the afternoon Burnside's corps crossed the Antietam over the bridge on Lee's right and drove the Confederates back, but A. P. Hill's division arrived from Harpers Ferry and repulsed the attack. The battle was not renewed. On Sept. 18–19, Lee recrossed the Potomac into Virginia unhindered. The fighting at Antietam was so fierce that Sept. 17, 1862, is said to have been the bloodiest single day of the war with some 23,000 dead and wounded, evenly divided between the sides. It was a Union victory only in the sense that Lee's invasion was stopped. McClellan has been blamed for not pursuing Lee with his superior forces. The scene of the battle of Antietam has been set aside as a national battlefield site (est. 1890). See K. P. Williams, *Lincoln Finds a General* (Vol. II, 1950); J. Murfin, *The Gleam of Bayonets* (1965).

Antietam National Battlefield Site: see ANTIETAM CAMPAIGN.

Antietam National Cemetery: see NATIONAL PARKS AND MONUMENTS (table).

Anti-Federalists, in American history, opponents of the adoption of the Federal Constitution. Leading Anti-Federalists included George Mason, Elbridge Gerry, Patrick Henry, and George Clinton. Later, many of the Anti-Federalists opposed the policies of the FEDERALIST PARTY and of Alexander HAMILTON. See M. Borden, ed., *The Antifederalist Papers* (1965); C. M. Kenyon, ed., *The Antifederalists* (1966).

antifreeze, substance added to a solvent to lower its freezing point. The solution formed is called an antifreeze mixture. Antifreeze is typically added to water in the cooling system of an internal combustion engine so that it may be cooled below the freezing point of pure water (32°F or 0°C) without freezing. Any substance that dissolves will cause freezing-point depression (see COLLIGATIVE PROPERTIES); a desirable antifreeze also should not corrode metal parts, attack rubber, become viscous at low temperatures, or evaporate readily at the ordinary engine operating temperature. It should be chemically stable, a good conductor of heat, and a poor conductor of electricity. Ethylene GLYCOL is the most widely used automotive cooling-system antifreeze, although methanol, ethanol, isopropyl alcohol, and propylene glycol are also used. Substances that inhibit corrosion are usually added; antifoaming agents are sometimes added as well. In automotive windshield-washer fluids, an alcohol (e.g., methanol) is usually added to keep the mixture from freezing; it also acts as a solvent to help clean the glass. The brine used in some commercial refrigeration systems is an antifreeze mixture; it is typically a water solution of calcium chloride or propylene glycol.

antifriction metal, ALLOY used in plain BEARINGS. Antifriction metals such as BABBITT METAL and white metal are made of tin, lead, antimony, zinc, and copper in various combinations and proportions.

antigen: see IMMUNITY.

Antigone (ăntĭg′ənē), in Greek legend, daughter of Oedipus. She followed her father in his banishment and disgrace. When her brothers Eteocles and Polynices killed each other in the war of the SEVEN AGAINST THEBES, Creon, King of Thebes, forbade the burial of the rebel Polynices. Antigone disobeyed his command and performed the funeral service. In Sophocles' *Antigone* she hangs herself in the tomb where Creon ordered her buried alive. In another version of the story, she is rescued by Creon's son and sent to live among shepherds.

Antigonish (ăn″tĭgōnĭsh′), town (1971 pop. 5,489), N central N.S., Canada, on an inlet of St. Georges Bay. The town was founded in 1784 by disbanded British soldiers and later settled by Highland Scots. It is known for the Antigonish Movement, a cooperative movement promoted in the 1920s and 30s by St. Francis Xavier Univ.

Antigonus I (Antigonus Cyclops) (ăntĭg′ənəs sī′klŏps), 382?–301 B.C., general of ALEXANDER THE GREAT and ruler in Asia. He was made (333 B.C.) governor of Phrygia, and after the death of Alexander he was advanced by the friendship of ANTIPATER, who with PTOLEMY I and Craterus, supported Antigonus in 321 against PERDICCAS and EUMENES. In the wars of the DIADOCHI, Antigonus was the leading figure because he seems to have had the best chance to re-create Alexander's empire. He had control of Asia Minor, Syria, and Mesopotamia at the time (316) when Eumenes was murdered. His great power, however, ultimately caused LYSIMACHUS, SELEUCUS I, and Ptolemy I to unite against him. Antigonus' son, Demetrius Poliorcretes (later DEMETRIUS I of Macedon), was an able agent in the bid to build the empire by invading Greece; Antigonus defeated (306) Ptolemy, but both Antigonus and Ptolemy were conquered at the battle at Ipsus (301). Antigonus was killed.

Antigonus II (Antigonus Gonatas) (gōnā′təs), c.320–239 B.C., king of Macedon, son of Demetrius I. He took the title king on his father's death (283) but made good his claim only by defeating the Gauls in Thrace and by taking Macedon in 276. His rule was very troubled; PYRRHUS attacked him, and so did Ptolemy II. A confederation of Greek cities headed by Athens waged (c.266–c.262 B.C.) the so-called Chremonidean War against him. Antigonus won the war, captured Athens, and restored the Macedonian state. However, the Achaean League, under Aratus, gained power c.251. Nevertheless Antigonus maintained himself and for a brief period united Greece. He was himself a scholar and a patron of philosophy and poetry. Upon his death he was succeeded by his son, DEMETRIUS II.

Antigonus III (Antigonus Doson) (dō′sŏn,-sən), d. 221 B.C., king of Macedon. On the death of Demetrius II he became regent for Demetrius' son Philip (PHILIP V). He married the widow of Demetrius, and in 227 he proclaimed himself king. The attacks of CLEOMENES III on the ACHAEAN LEAGUE caused its leader, Aratus, to request help from Antigonus, who led his troops south in 224. In 222, Antigonus crushed Cleomenes at Sellasia in Laconea and took Corinth as his reward. Meanwhile he had reconstituted the Hellenic League, and when he died he left power in Greece as well as Macedon to Philip.

Antigua (ăntē′gwə, Span. äntē′gwä) or **Antigua Guatemala** (gwätəmä′lə, Span. gwätämä′lä) [Span., =Old Guatemala], town (1964 pop. 21,984), S central Guatemala. Founded in 1542 by surviviors from nearby Ciudad Veija, which had been destroyed by flood and earthquake, Antigua became the capital of Spanish Guatemala. In the 17th cent. it flourished as one of the richest capitals of the New World, rivaling Lima and Mexico City; by the 18th cent. its population had increased to c.100,000. Its university was a center of the arts and learning, and its churches, convents, monasteries, public buildings, and residences were characterized by massive luxury. Antigua, dominated by the volcanoes Agua (12,310 ft/3,752 m high), Acatenango (12,982 ft/3,957 m high), and Fuego (12,854 ft/3,918 m high), was continually subject to disaster from volcanic eruptions, flood, and earthquake. In 1773 two earthquakes leveled the city. The Spanish captain general ordered (1776) the removal of the capital to a plain supposedly free from earthquakes and there founded GUATEMALA city. Antigua is now a major tourist center with many fine Spanish colonial buildings. It is also the commercial center of a rich coffee-growing region.

Antigua (ăntē′gə, -gwə), island (1971 pop. 70,000), 108 sq mi (280 sq km), British West Indies, in the Leeward Islands. SAINT JOHN'S is the capital. With its dependencies of Barbuda and Redonda, Antigua is an associated state of Great Britain and enjoys full internal self-government, with the British responsible for foreign affairs and defense. Hilly, with a much indented coast, Antigua has farms that grow mainly sugarcane and cotton. Tourism is a major industry; the island provides many hunting and fishing resorts. Discovered by Columbus in 1493, Antigua was named for a Spanish church in Seville. Unsuccessful Spanish and French settlements on the island were followed by a fruitful British effort in

1632, when sugarcane was introduced from St. Kitts. After a brief French occupation in 1666, Antigua passed permanently to Britain. The abolition of slav-

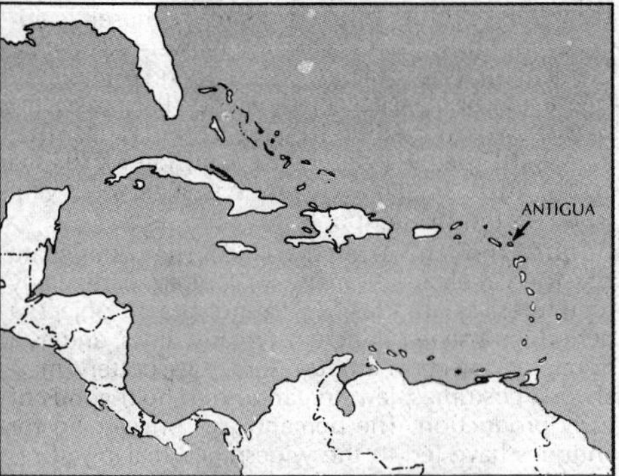

ery in 1834 hurt the sugar industry; in the early 19th cent. cotton was introduced. The United States has a military base on the island.

Antigua Guatemala: see ANTIGUA.

anti-hero, principal character of a modern literary or dramatic work who lacks the attributes of the traditional protagonist or hero. The anti-hero's lack of courage, honesty, or grace, his weaknesses and confusion, often reflect modern man's ambivalence toward traditional moral and social virtues. Literary characters that can be considered anti-heroes are: Leopold Bloom in James Joyce's novel *Ulysses* (1922), Willy Loman in Arthur Miller's play *Death of a Salesman* (1949), the bombardier Yossarian in Joseph Heller's novel *Catch-22* (1961), and the protagonists of many of Philip Roth's and Kurt Vonnegut's novels.

antihistamine (ăn″tĭhĭs′təmēn), any one of a group of compounds having various chemical structures and characterized by the ability to antagonize the effects of HISTAMINE. Their principal use in medicine is in the control of allergies such as hay fever and hives. The antihistamines are also useful as sedatives and for the prevention of motion sickness.

Anti-Lebanon, ancient *Anti-Libanus,* Arabic *Jabal al Sharqi,* mountain range between Syria and Lebanon, rising to Mt. Hermon, 9,232 ft (2,814 m) high. Once noted for its forests of oak, pine, cypress, and juniper, the range is now largely barren and stony. Its name also appears as Anti-Liban.

Antilles: see WEST INDIES.

Antilochus (ăntĭl′əkəs), in Greek mythology, young hero of the Trojan War, a favorite of Achilles. While protecting his father, Nestor, he was killed by Memnon. He was buried with Achilles and Patroclus.

Anti-Masonic party, American political organization that rose after the disappearance in W New York state in 1826 of William Morgan. A former Mason, Morgan had written a book purporting to reveal Masonic secrets. The Masons were said, without proof, to have murdered him, and in reaction local organizations arose to refuse support to Masons for public office. In New York state Thurlow WEED and William H. SEWARD attempted unsuccessfully to use the movement, which appealed strongly to the poorer classes, to overthrow Martin VAN BUREN and the ALBANY REGENCY. Anti-Masonry spread from New York to neighboring states and influenced many local and state elections. At Baltimore, in 1831, the Anti-Masons held the first national nominating convention of any party and issued the first written party platform—innovations followed by the older parties. The vote for their presidential candidate, William WIRT, mostly hurt Henry Clay. Usually the Anti-Masons in national politics acted with the NATIONAL REPUBLICAN PARTY in opposition to Jacksonian democracy, and in 1834 they helped to form the WHIG PARTY. See W. B. Hesseltine, *The Rise and Fall of Third Parties* (1948); Lorman Ratner, *Antimasonry* (1969).

antimatter: see ANTIPARTICLE.

antimetabolite: see METABOLITE.

antimony (ăn′tĭmō″nē) [from Lat. *antimoneum*], semimetallic chemical element; symbol Sb [from Lat. *stibium,*= a mark]; at. no. 51; at. wt. 121.75; m.p. 630.5°C; b.p. 1440°C; sp. gr. (metallic form) 6.69 at 20°C; valence 0, +3, −3, or +5. Antimony exists in two allotropic forms (see ALLOTROPY); the more common is silvery blue-white and has a rhombohedral crystalline structure. It is a poor conductor of heat and electricity and is brittle and easily powdered. It is primarily used in alloys and chemical compounds. It is a member of group Va of the PERIODIC TABLE. Antimony rarely occurs free in nature, but its ores are widely distributed. The principal ore is STIBNITE, a sulfur compound known since early times; there are extensive deposits in China. Antimony is often found in other ores as well, e.g., silver, copper, and lead. The pure element antimony is produced from the ore by roasting it to form the oxide, then reducing the oxide with carbon or iron; often a flux of sodium sulfate or sodium carbonate is used to prevent loss of molten antimony by evaporation. Antimony does not react with air or water at room temperature; it does react with fluorine, chlorine, or bromine, and is soluble in hot nitric or sulfuric acid; at higher temperatures, antimony will ignite and burn in air. It unites with hydrogen to form stibine, a poisonous gas. In combination with metals antimony forms alloys that are hard and brittle and have low melting points. The alloys of antimony include BRITANNIA METAL, TYPE METAL, BABBITT METAL, and sometimes PEWTER; these alloys expand on cooling, thereby retaining fine details of a mold. Alloys and compounds of antimony are used in bearings, storage batteries, safety matches, and as a red pigment in paint. Although antimony and many of its compounds are toxic, TARTAR EMETIC (potassium antimonyl tartrate) is used as a medicine. Small concentrations of antimony can be detected by a method similar to the MARSH TEST for arsenic. Antimony is mixed with soot and other substances to make kohl, used for centuries by women in some countries as an eye cosmetic. A method for the extraction of antimony from stibnite was first described c. 1600 by Basilius Valentinus. Although known to the ancients, the element was first adequately described by Nicolas Lémery in 1707.

antinomianism (ăntĭnō′mēənĭzəm) [Gr.,= against the law], the belief that Christians are not bound by the moral law, particularly that of the Old Testament. The idea was strong among the Gnostics, especially MARCION. Certain heretical sects in the Middle Ages practiced sexual license as an expression of Christian freedom. In the Protestant Reformation theoretical antinomian views were maintained by the Anabaptists and Johann Agricola, and in the 17th cent. Anne Hutchinson was persecuted for supposed antinomianism. Rom. 6 is the usual refutation for antinomianism.

Antinoüs (ăntĭn′ōəs), c.110–130, favorite of Emperor Hadrian, b. Bithynia. He was with the emperor constantly until on a journey in Egypt he was drowned in the Nile—some say in saving Hadrian's life. His beauty was legendary, and Hadrian mourned him greatly, had him deified, founded the city of Antinoöpolis in Egypt in his honor, and seems to have renamed the youth's birthplace Antinoöpolis. A cult was inaugurated in his honor, coins were struck with Antinoüs' head on them, and many busts and statues were made.

Antioch (ăn′tēŏk), ancient town of Phrygia, near the Pisidian border. The site is north of the present-day Antalya, Turkey. It was founded by Seleucus I and became a center of Hellenistic influence. It was visited by St. Paul. (Acts 13.14; 14.21; 2 Tim. 3.11).

Antioch (ăn′tēŏk″) or **Antakya** (äntäk′yä), city (1970 pop. 66,400), capital of Hatay prov., S Turkey, on the Orontes (Asi) River, near the Mediterranean Sea, at the foot of Mt. Silpius. It is the trade center for a farm region where grains, cotton, grapes, olives, and vegetables are grown. The city's few manufactures include processed foods, textiles, and leather goods. Antioch was founded c.300 B.C. by Seleucus I, king of ancient Syria, and named for his father Antiochus, a Macedonian general. Situated at the crossing of north-south and east-west trade routes, the city soon became a rich commercial center. Antioch was occupied by Pompey in 64 B.C. and quickly became an important Roman military, commercial, and cultural center. The Romans built great temples, a forum, a theater, baths, aqueducts, and other public buildings. The two main streets, at right angles to each other, were lined with marble colonnades and adorned with temples, palaces, and statues. Antioch was an early center of Christianity; Peter and Paul preached there. It was in Antioch that the followers of Jesus were first called Christians after having severed themselves from the synagogue about 20 years after Jesus' death (Acts 11.26; 13.1). Antioch is one of the three original patriarchates (see PATRIARCH). Aurelian, who recovered the city from Shapur I of Persia, erected (3d cent.) more magnificent buildings and churches. The city was a great center of Christian learning and played a significant role in the theological controversies of the early Christian church (see CHRISTIANITY). St. John Chrysostom estimated its population (4th cent.) at 200,000, excluding children and slaves. In 526 the city suffered a severe earthquake and in 540 it was captured by Persia. In 637, Antioch was conquered by the Arabs. Nicephorus II reconquered it (969) for the Byzantine Empire, but in 1085 it fell, through treason, to the Seljuk Turks. The army of the First Crusade (see CRUSADES) captured Antioch in 1098, after a half-year siege. Bohemond I was made prince of Antioch. His principality, which extended from İskenderun (Alexandretta) southward beyond Latakia, was one of the most powerful of the Crusaders' states. In 1268 the Mamelukes captured and sacked the city; it was further damaged by Tamerlane in 1401. In 1516, Antioch, by then an unimportant city, was taken by the Ottoman Empire. The city was held (1832–40) by Muhammad Ali of Egypt, and in 1872 it was badly disrupted by an earthquake. After World War I, Antioch was incorporated into the French Syria League of Nations mandate. In 1939 it was restored to Turkey as part of the sanjak of ALEXANDRETTA. Modern Antioch occupies only a fraction of the area of the ancient city, most of which is buried under alluvial deposits. Numerous important archaeological finds have been made in and near Antioch. They include the Great Chalice of Antioch (see CHALICE), held by some to be the Holy Grail, and, at Daphne, Antioch's ancient suburban resort, splendid mosaics (1st–6th cent. A.D.), which are mostly copies of lost paintings. The city has an archaeological museum.

Antioch, city (1970 pop. 28,060), Contra Costa co., W Calif., on the San Joaquin River near the mouth of the Sacramento; inc. 1872. It is a processing and shipping center for the agricultural products of the fertile islands in the delta area between the rivers.

Antioch College, at Yellow Springs, Ohio; coeducational; chartered 1852, opened 1853. Horace Mann, Antioch's first president, envisioned a program stressing the development not only of the intellect but of the whole personality, especially the individual's social conscience and competence. The cooperative work-study program, adopted (1921) during the presidency of Arthur E. Morgan, has been developed in an attempt to achieve this goal. The college years are divided between off-campus work and on-campus study, both full-time. This system usually requires five years. Students are given a voice in community government, college policy formulation, and other administrative affairs. Also, Antioch maintains its own foreign study program. In conjunction with the Universities of Guanajuato (Mexico), Besançon (France), and Tübingen (Germany), Antioch Centers for University Education have been established. Antioch students in different programs, however, attend other foreign schools. On campus the Fels Research Institute for studies in human development, the Charles F. Kettering Research Laboratory for studies in biological science, and other experimental and research centers employ scientists, students, and teachers unaffiliated to the college.

Antiochia Margiana: see MERV.

Antiochus I (Antiochus Soter) (ăntī′əkəs sō′tər), b. c.324 B.C., d. c.262 or 261 B.C., king of Syria (280–261? B.C.), son of SELEUCUS I. He did not, like his father, seek to expand in Europe. The Seleucid holdings were greatly reduced, particularly by the Egyptians under Ptolemy II. Antiochus was famous as a founder of cities.

Antiochus II (Antiochus Theos) (thē′ŏs), d. 247 B.C., king of Syria (261?–247 B.C.), son and successor of Antiochus I. In warfare with Ptolemy II he had sporadic successes, but his marriage to Ptolemy's daughter Berenice sealed the peace, and most of the Syrian possessions his father had lost were restored to Antiochus. On the death of Antiochus, his son by an earlier marriage, SELEUCUS II, and Berenice in behalf of her infant son struggled for the throne; a long war with Ptolemy III ensued.

Antiochus III (Antiochus the Great), d. 187 B.C., king of Syria (223–187 B.C.), son of Seleucus II and younger brother of Seleucus III, whom he succeeded. At his accession the Seleucid empire was in decline. Although Antiochus did not succeed in totally restoring the greatness of the Seleucid dynasty, he did much to revive its glory. He led an expedition (212–205 B.C.) to the eastern provinces and went as far as India. Although he was defeated earlier by the Egyptians at Raphia (modern Rafa), he and Philip V of Macedon undertook (202 B.C.) to wrest Egyptian territories from the boy king, Ptolemy V. Antiochus did not properly appreciate the growing power of Rome. While Philip V was engaged by the Roman armies, Antiochus recovered S Syria and Asia Minor. In 199 he won a decisive victory over the Egyptians; Palestine then reverted to Syria, having been under Egyptian rule for almost a century. In 196 he seized the Thracian Chersonese and thus alarmed the Greeks. They as well as the Egyptians sought the aid of the Romans. Antiochus, who disregarded the advice of Hannibal in 193, waited and then challenged Rome by accepting the invitation of the Aetolian League to interfere in Greece in 192. The Romans crushed him (191) at Thermopylae and again at Magnesia (190). He also lost a number of naval engagements, and in 188 he was forced to give up all his territory W of the Taurus. Thus the Seleucid empire became a purely inland Asiatic state, and dreams of reviving Alexander's empire died.

Antiochus IV (Antiochus Epiphanes) (ĕpĭf'ənēz), d. 163 B.C., king of Syria (175 B.C.–163 B.C.), son of Antiochus III and successor of his brother Seleucus IV. His nephew (later Demetrius I) was held as a hostage in Rome, although still claiming the throne. Antiochus is best known for his attempt to Hellenize Judaea and extirpate Judaism—a policy that instigated the rebellion of the MACCABEES. Antiochus invaded Egypt, which was torn by strife between Ptolemy VI and his brother (later Ptolemy VII), and would probably have conquered that region if the Romans had not intervened in his siege of Alexandria (168). Antiochus was briefly succeeded by his son, Antiochus V, a boy king who was overthrown by Demetrius I.

Antiope (ăntī'əpē), in Greek mythology. **1** Theban princess, daughter of Nycteus. She was seduced by Zeus and bore him twin sons, Zethus and Amphion. Fleeing to Sicyon to escape the wrath of her father, she was forced to abandon her infants on Mt. Cithaeron, where they were raised by shepherds. After Nycteus committed suicide, Antiope was pursued and captured by her uncle Lycus, then king of Thebes, and his wife Dirce, who treated her with great cruelty. Later the sons of Antiope revenged their mother; they dethroned Lycus and punished Dirce by tying her to the horns of a bull. They then erected a wall around Thebes with stones which moved of their own will to the music of Amphion's lyre. Zethus married the nymph Thebe, and after she died he married AËDON. Amphion married Niobe. **2** A queen of the Amazons, sister of Hippolyte. According to one legend she was abducted by Theseus and became the mother of Hippolytus.

antiparticle, ELEMENTARY PARTICLE corresponding to an ordinary particle such as the PROTON, NEUTRON, or ELECTRON, but having the opposite electrical charge and magnetic moment. Antiparticles are also known as charge-conjugate particles. Every elementary particle has a corresponding antiparticle; the antiparticle of an antiparticle is an ordinary particle. In a few cases, such as the PHOTON and the neutral PION, the particle is its own antiparticle, but most antiparticles are distinct from their ordinary counterparts. When a particle and its antiparticle collide, both are annihilated and other particles such as photons or pions are produced. In some cases this represents the total conversion of mass into energy. For example, the collision between an electron and its antiparticle, a positron, results in the conversion of their combined masses into the energy of two or three photons. A proton-antiproton annihilation usually results in several pions. The reverse process, pair production, is the simultaneous creation of a particle and its antiparticle from the combination of the same products that result from their mutual annihilation. The existence of antiparticles was predicted in 1928 by P. A. M. Dirac's relativistic QUANTUM THEORY of the electron. According to the theory both positive and negative values are possible for the total relativistic energy of a free electron. A vacuum is assumed to consist of a sea of electrons that fill all available negative energy levels. These electrons are not detectable by ordinary experiments. However, the absorption of energy by one of the electrons could excite it out of the negative-energy sea to a positive energy level, where it could be observed. The process would result in the appearance of a "hole" in the sea of negative-energy electrons, and the hole would have all the physical properties of a positively charged electron (positron). Thus, the absence of an electron in a negative energy state could be observed as a positron. In 1932, Carl D. Anderson, while studying COSMIC RAYS, discovered the predicted positron, the first known antiparticle. About 23 years passed before the discovery of the next antiparticles—the antiproton was discovered by Chamberlain and Segrè in 1955, and the antineutron was discovered the following year—but the existence of antiparticles for all known particles was by then firmly established in theory. The existence of antiparticles makes possible the creation of antimatter, composed of atoms made up of antiprotons and antineutrons in a nucleus surrounded by positrons. A very simple type of "atom" incorporating antiparticles is positronium, a brief pairing of a positron and an electron that may occur before their annihilation. A few simple nuclei of antimatter have been created in the laboratory, such as the antideuteron (see DEUTERIUM), but any antimatter in our part of the universe is necessarily very short-lived because of the overwhelming preponderance of ordinary matter by which the antimatter is quickly annihilated. Nevertheless, there is no reason in theory why atoms or even entire galaxies of antimatter could not have evolved in a part of the universe far removed from our own. There would be no way to tell from the photons of light and other radiation reaching us from such a galaxy whether the source of the energy was composed of ordinary matter or antimatter, since the same physical laws governing the production of energy apply equally to matter and antimatter and the photon is its own antiparticle.

Antipas (ăn'tĭpăs). **1** See HEROD. **2** Martyr at Pergamum, traditionally its first bishop. Rev. 2.13.

Antipater (ăntĭp'ətər), d. 319 B.C., Macedonian general. He was one of the ablest and most trusted lieutenants of PHILIP II and was a friend and supporter of ALEXANDER THE GREAT. When Alexander went on his Asiatic campaign, Antipater was left as regent (334–323 B.C.) in Macedon. He resisted the attempt of Olympias to gain the regency and governed ably except that his policy of supporting tyrants and oligarchs made him unpopular in Greece. After the death of Alexander he put down a rebellion of many of the Greek cities in the Lamian War and punished Athens. By imposing a more oligarchic form of government on Athens, he drove Demosthenes to commit suicide. Antipater was a leading opponent of the regent, Perdiccas, and after Perdiccas was defeated in 321 by Ptolemy I, Antigonus I, and Craterus, it was Antipater who held the kingdom together. After his death it fell violently apart in the wars of the DIADOCHI.

Antipater, in the Bible: see HEROD.

Antipatris (ăntĭp'ətrĭs), city of Roman Palestine, founded by Herod the Great and named after his father. It was c.10 mi (16.1 km) NE of Joppa, on the north-south road. Paul was taken there on the way to Caesarea. Acts 23.31.

Antiphilus (ăntĭf'ĭləs), fl. 4th cent. B.C., Greek painter, of Alexandrian origin. He invented a grotesque called gryllos, a creature part man, part animal or bird. It is known that he painted portraits of Philip of Macedon and Alexander the Great, though none of his many works have survived.

Antiphon (ăn'tĭfŏn, –fən), c.479–411 B.C., Athenian orator. He rarely spoke in public but wrote defenses for others to speak. Of his 15 extant orations 3 were for use in court, the rest for the instruction of his pupils. A few fragments of other speeches survive, but some may be the work of Antiphon the Sophist, who also lived in Athens in the 5th cent. B.C. Antiphon did much to advance Attic prose writing. His position in politics was with the conservative aristocrats, and he was instrumental in setting up the Four Hundred in 411 B.C. When they fell, Antiphon was among the first to be executed before ALCIBIADES returned.

antiphon (ăn'tĭfən), in liturgical music, generally a short text sung before and after a psalm or canticle. The main use is in group singing of the Divine Office in a monastery. However, introit, offertory, and Communion of the Mass were originally antiphons that later were used independently. Certain festival chants, sung preparatory to the Mass itself, are called antiphons. There are also the four antiphons of the Blessed Virgin Mary, which are in the nature of office hymns and are sung by alternating choirs (i.e., antiphonally), each one belonging to a certain portion of the year. The best known of these is *Salve Regina,* of whose text there are many polyphonic settings. Modern antiphons are set to composed music rather than PLAINSONG. These are independent choral works for which the English term ANTHEM was derived from antiphon.

Antipodes (ăntĭp'ədēz), rocky uninhabited islands, 24 sq mi (62 sq km), South Pacific, c.450 mi (720 km) SE of New Zealand, to which they belong. The Antipodes were discovered by British seamen in 1800 and are so named because they are diametrically opposite Greenwich, England.

antipodes [Gr.,=having feet opposite], people or places diametrically opposite on the globe. Thus antipodes must be separated by half the circumference of the earth (180°), and one must be as far north as the other is south of the equator; midnight at one is noonday at the other. For example, New Amsterdam and St. Paul, small islands nearly midway between S Africa and Australia, are more nearly antipodal to Washington, D.C., than is any other land.

antipope [Lat.,=against the pope], person elected pope whose election was later declared uncanonical and in opposition to a canonically chosen legitimate pontiff. Important antipopes were NOVATIAN; Clement III (see GUIBERT OF RAVENNA); Nicholas V (see RAINALDUCCI, PIETRO); Clement VII (see ROBERT OF GENEVA); Benedict III (see LUNA, PEDRO DE); John XXIII (or by a different count, John XXII; see COSSA, BALDASSARRE); and Felix V (see AMADEUS VIII), who was the last antipope.

antique. The term is used collectively to designate classical Greek and Roman works of art, particularly sculptures; as an adjective to indicate an object, a period, or a style of ancient or early times; and as a noun, for objects of art, furniture, rugs, pottery, metalwork, costumes, jewelry, and household goods of early production. The demand and prices paid for antiques have led to the widespread making of reproductions and reconstructions, some with spurious marks of age. See ANTIQUE COLLECTING. For a description of the characteristics of various styles, see DIRECTOIRE, EMPIRE, LOUIS PERIOD, and RÉGENCE styles.

antique collecting. The term *antique* initially referred only to the pre-classical and classical cultures of the ancient world. It is now applied to old artifacts of all cultures that have historic, aesthetic, and usually monetary value. In 1952 the Florence agreement, sponsored by the United Nations Educational, Scientific, and Cultural Organization, was drawn up to "facilitate the free flow of educational, scientific, and cultural materials." In 1966 the United States tariff regulations were altered to permit duty-free importation of antiques, defined as objects being more than 100 years old at the time of entry. More than 50 countries now have similar regulations. Antique collecting has a venerable history dating from the preservation of valued religious objects in antiquity. By the 16th cent. English and European private collections of rarities flourished. But it was the 18th cent. with its development of the art and science of archaeology that produced the impetus for public and private collecting in earnest. In the United States, collectors, seriously active since the 18th cent., first concentrated on old books, manuscripts, the possessions and mementoes of famous people, and classicial antiquities. State historical societies encouraged the growing interest in colonial history and its artifacts. In the late 1850s an association was founded to restore and preserve MOUNT VERNON, the first of the country's many house museums. Finely crafted household articles such as pewterware and furniture claimed collectors' attention with the opening of the Centennial Exposition of 1876 in Philadelphia, in which reconstructed colonial rooms were exhibited. During the next century many sorts of objects in addition to paintings, books, and furniture excited the collector's lust. Specialty collections grew in such items as quilts, bedspreads, jewelry, glass, coins, postage stamps, china, porcelain, silver and other metalcraft, needlework (including needlepoint, embroidery samplers, lace, and hooked rugs), bottles, stoneware, pill boxes, scrimshaw (expertly carved teeth and bones of sperm whale and walrus tusks of the 18th cent.), snuffboxes, fans, watches, clocks, periodicals, badges, Daguerreotypes, postcards, photographs, toys, posters, military and political souvenirs, objects reminiscent of many forms of public transport (including railroad and ship bells, whistles, lamps, and models), buttons, and many varieties of folk art and memorabilia symbolic of the recent past. Frequently the only value a popular object can claim is that of scarcity. Certain objects (e.g., comic books and fruit-crate labels), more properly called curios, have become collector's items by virtue of nostalgic association or content rather than intrinsic value. Antique dealers, whose number had increased to nearly 20,000 in the United States by 1965, also acquire for sale objects that are characteristic of a particular stylistic current (e.g., ART NOUVEAU and ART DECO) that is experiencing a revival of interest. The sources of many valuable antiques include attics, cellars, barns, and other storage rooms. The objects are sold or traded at auctions, antique fairs, rummage sales, flea markets, and garage sales, all increasing in attendance yearly. The great pleasures of antique collecting are counted as bargain finding; the discovery, after a long search, of a much-desired item; the showing off of a special treasure to others; and, above all, the discovery that an object one has acquired is rarer and of greater worth than one had suspected. The elegant Parke-Bernet auction house in New York City offered in 1974 a week of free appraisals to the public, stimulating 3,500 people to bring possible heirlooms out of their trunks and attics. The estimated ratio of trash to treasure during this week was four to one. With the tremendous growth of interest in antiques, a critical expertise in historical styles and construction methods has developed of necessity for the care and identification of precious objects. Dealers publish extensive directories to provide a basis for consistent appraisal; the fantastic bargain, as a result, has become rarer and rarer. At the same time, museums and private institutions have built up outstanding antique collections. Among the finest of these in the United States are to be seen at the Metropolitan Museum of Art; the Museum of American Folk Art, New York City; the Museum of Fine Arts, Boston; the Yale University Art Gallery, New Haven, Conn.; the Philadelphia Museum of Art; the Winterthur (Delaware) Museum; and the restoration of Williamsburg, Va. See L. G. G. Ramsay, ed., *The Complete Encyclopedia of Antiques* (rev. ed. 1967); Mary Durant, *The American Heritage Guide to Antiques* (1970); M. D. Schwartz and Betsy Wade, *The New York Times Book of Antiques* (1972).

Antirent War, in U.S. history, tenant uprising in New York state. When Stephen Van Rensselaer, owner of Rensselaerswyck, died in 1839, his heirs attempted to collect unpaid rents. Tenants on the estate resisted and an angry mob forcibly turned back a sheriff's posse that tried to evict them. Resistance to landlord authority quickly spread to landed estates throughout the Hudson valley; tenants disguised as Indians harassed landlord agents and sheriffs. When a deputy sheriff of Delaware co., N.Y., was killed (1845), Gov. Silas Wright declared a state of insurrection and called out the state militia. Armed resistance ended and the antirenters turned to politics. They helped elect a Whig, John Young, as governor of New York; the legislature passed ameliorative measures; and the 1846 state constitution outlawed future long-term leases. The Antirent War hastened the breaking up of the large landed estates as worried landlords began selling their holdings. See E. P. Cheyney, *The Anti-Rent Agitation in the State of New York, 1839–46* (1887); Henry Christman, *Tin Horns and Calico* (1945; repr. 1961); D. M. Ellis, *Landlords and Farmers in the Hudson-Mohawk Region, 1790–1850* (1946, repr. 1967).

Anti-Saloon League, U.S. organization working for prohibition of the sale of alcoholic liquors. Founded in 1893 as the Ohio Anti-Saloon League at Oberlin, Ohio, by representatives of temperance societies and evangelical Protestant churches, it came to wield great political influence. Vigorously led by James Cannon, Jr., a Methodist bishop, the League played an important role in securing the passage of the Eighteenth Amendment. Its influence waned, however, especially after the repeal (1933) of prohibition. In 1950 it merged with the National Temperance League. See P. H. Odegard, *Pressure Politics: Story of the Anti-Saloon League* (1928, repr. 1966); biography of Bishop Cannon by Virginius Dabney (1949).

anti-Semitism, form of prejudice against the JEWS, ranging from antipathy to violent hatred. Before the 19th cent., anti-Semitism was largely religious, based on dislike for the Jews who had allegedly crucified Jesus Christ, and was expressed in the later Middle Ages by sporadic persecutions and expulsions—notably the expulsion from Spain under Ferdinand and Isabella—in severe economic and personal restriction (see GHETTO), and in fantastic legends, such as those of ritual murder by Jews of Christian children. However, since the Jews were generally restricted to the pursuit of occupations that were unpopular or taboo, such as moneylending, hence the sentiment was also economic in nature. After the emancipation of the Jews, brought about by the Enlightenment of the 18th cent. and by the French Revolution, religious and economic resentments were gradually replaced by feelings of racial prejudice stemming from the notion of the Jews as a distinct race. This development was due not only to the rising nationalism of the 19th cent. but also to the conscious preservation, especially among Orthodox Jews, of cultural and religious barriers that isolated the Jewish minorities from other citizens. Jewish reaction to the phenomenon of anti-Semitism found political expression in ZIONISM. The unpopularity of the Jews, on whom all evils could be blamed with impunity, was exploited by demagogues, such as Édouard DRUMONT in France, to stir the masses against an existing government, and by reactionary governments, as in Russia, to find an outlet for popular discontent. The millions of Russian and Polish Jews who, after the assassination (1881) of Alexander II, fled the POGROMS and found refuge in other countries contributed to the popular feeling that Jews were aliens and intruders. In addition, a spurious document, the "Protocols of the Wise Men of Zion," purporting to outline a Jewish plan for world domination, emerged in Russia early in the 20th cent. and was subsequently circulated throughout the world. After the Russian Revolution of 1917, the Jews were accused of plotting to dominate the world by their international financial power or by a Bolshevik revolution. Pseudoscientific racial theories of so-called Aryan superiority directed against the Jews emerged in the 19th cent. with the writings of Joseph Arthur GOBINEAU and Houston Stewart CHAMBERLAIN and found their climax in those of Alfred Rosenberg. These theories were incorporated in the official doctrine of German NATIONAL SOCIALISM by Adolf Hitler. Hitler's persecution of the Jews during World War II was unparalleled in history. It is estimated that between 5 and 6 million European Jews were exterminated between 1939 and 1945 (see CONCENTRATION CAMP). The end of persecution did not mean the end of anti-Semitism, as the sporadic attacks on synagogues in many countries since the end of World War II indicate. In the Soviet Union and the countries of Eastern Europe, where anti-Semitism is officially outlawed, it has reappeared in new forms. From the late 1940s until Joseph Stalin's death in 1953, anti-Semitic persecution took the form of deportations, jailings, and the suppression of Jewish publications and cultural institutions. Although anti-Semitism in these countries receded during the 1950s, it reappeared in the 60s and 70s, when synagogues were periodically closed, particularly in the upsurge of anti-Semitism that followed the Arab-Israeli War of 1967. In the 1970s, citizens of the Soviet Union, but particularly Jews, found it increasingly difficult to emigrate to Western countries. In the United States, although anti-Semitism has not been an instrument of national policy, it exists nevertheless; Jews are regularly excluded from membership in certain private clubs, from some schools, and from the rental of certain housing. The problem of anti-Semitism has been analyzed by numerous psychologists and social scientists, most of whom view it as an irrational form of behavior based on the need for a scapegoat to justify aggression or relieve guilt. See Jean Paul Sartre, *Anti-Semite and Jew* (tr. 1948, repr. 1960); E. J. Long, *Two Thousand Years: A History of Anti-Semitism* (1953); Leon Poliakov, *The History of Anti-Semitism* (1965, repr. 1974); Rose Feitelson and George Salomon, *The Many Faces of Anti-Semitism* (1967); Leonard Dinnerstein, *Anti-Semitism in the United States* (1971); Arnold Forster and B. R. Epstein, *The New Anti-Semitism* (1974).

antiseptic, agent that kills or inhibits the growth of microorganisms on the external surfaces of the body. Antiseptics should generally be distinguished from drugs such as antibiotics that destroy microorganisms internally, and from disinfectants, which destroy microorganisms found on nonliving objects. Germicides include only those antiseptics that kill microorganisms. Some common antiseptics are alcohol, iodine, hydrogen peroxide, and boric acid. There is great variation in the ability of antiseptics to destroy microorganisms and in their effect on living tissue. For example, mercuric chloride is a powerful antiseptic, but it irritates delicate tissue. In contrast, silver nitrate kills fewer germs but can be used on the delicate tissues of the eyes and throat. There is also a great difference in the time required for different antiseptics to work. Iodine, one of the fastest-working antiseptics, kills bacteria within 30 sec. Other antiseptics have slower, more residual action. Since so much variability exists, systems have been devised for measuring the action of an antiseptic against certain standards. The bacteriostatic action of an antiseptic compared to that of phenol (under the same conditions and against the same microorganism) is known as its phenol coefficient. Joseph Lister was the first to employ the antiseptic phenol, or carbolic acid, in surgery, following the discovery by Louis Pasteur that microorganisms are the cause of infections. Modern surgical techniques for avoiding infection are founded on asepsis, the absence of pathogenic organisms. Sterilization is the chief means of achieving asepsis.

antislavery movement: see SLAVERY; ABOLITIONISTS.

Antisthenes (ăntĭs'thənēz), b. 444? B.C., d. after 371 B.C., Greek philosopher, founder of the CYNICS. Most of his paradoxical views stemmed from his early Sophist orientation, even though he became one of Socrates' most ardent followers. He believed that man's happiness lay in cultivating virtue for its own sake. To attain virtue, man must reduce his dependence on the external world to a minimum, disregard social convention, shun pleasure, and live in poverty. Antisthenes, like Xenophanes, repudiated polytheism, substituting one god, whom he described as unlike anything known to man. His view that each individual is unique had implications for ethics and for a theory of knowledge.

Anti-Taurus: see TAURUS.

antithesis (ăntĭth'ĭsĭs), a figure of speech involving a seeming contradiction of ideas, words, clauses, or sentences, within a balanced grammatical structure. Parallelism of expression serves to emphasize opposition of ideas. The familiar phrase "Man proposes, God disposes" is an example of antithesis, as is John Dryden's description in "The Hind and the Panther": "Too black for heaven, and yet too white for hell."

antitoxin, any of a group of antibodies formed in the body as a response to the introduction of poisonous products, or TOXINS. By introducing small amounts of a specific toxin into the healthy body, it is possible to stimulate the production of antitoxin so that the body's defenses are already established against invasion by the bacteria or other organisms that produce the toxin. See IMMUNITY.

Antitrust Act: see CLAYTON ANTITRUST ACT; SHERMAN ANTITRUST ACT.

Antium: see ANZIO, Italy.

antler: see HORN.

Antofagasta (äntōfä'gä'stä), city (1970 pop. 126,252), capital of Antofagasta prov., N Chile, a port on the Pacific Ocean. Antofagasta was founded by Chileans in 1870 to exploit nitrates in the Desert of Atacama, then under Bolivian administration. Its occupation by Chilean troops in 1879 sparked the War of the Pacific (see PACIFIC, WAR OF THE), and after the war the city and province were ceded to Chile. Antofagasta has depended primarily on nitrates and copper exports, and its economy has often been affected by sharp fluctuations in world demands. The city is an international commercial center and a major industrial hub with large foundries and ore refineries. Backed by desert hills, Antofagasta enjoys a fine climate but has little rainfall. Water is piped in from the San Pedro River, 280 mi (451 km) away.

Antoine, André (äNdrā' äNtwän'), 1858–1943, French theatrical director, manager, critic. In opposition to the teachings of the Paris Conservatory, he formed his own company, the THÉÂTRE LIBRE, in 1887. There he presented, by means of private subscriptions, the foremost works of the naturalistic school. Financial failure forced him to relinquish the theater in 1894. In 1897 he founded the Théâtre Antoine, where he continued the tradition of his Théâtre Libre for 10 years. From 1906 to 1914 he was director of the Odéon in Paris, and after World War I he became a drama critic and the dean of French theatrical writers.

Antoine, Père (pĕr ăntwän'), 1748–1829, Spanish priest in New Orleans, a Capuchin friar. His family name was Mareno, and the Spanish name given to him by the church was Antonio de Sedella. Through many years of service at St. Louis Cathedral under Spanish, briefly French, and then U.S. rule, he won great love and respect from his French congregation, who had previously regarded his harshness with distaste. He was almost constantly at war with the authorities. The Spanish colonial rulers once sent him back as a prisoner to Spain, and U.S. officials were later highly incensed at his secret dealings with the Spanish. The legend that he was empowered to introduce the Inquisition to Louisiana but refrained from doing so is apparently based on fact.

Antonelli, Giacomo (jä'kōmō äntōnĕl'lē), 1806–76, Italian cardinal and statesman of the Roman Catholic Church, adviser to Pope PIUS IX. He received the red hat of the cardinalate in 1847, presided over the council drafting the constitution for the Papal States, and became the premier of the pope's first constitutional cabinet. After returning (1850) from exile in Gaeta, Pius IX made him secretary of state. His vigorous diplomacy was directed against Italian national unification.

Antonello da Messina (äntōnĕl'lō dä măs-sē'nä), c.1430–1479, Italian painter, b. Messina. Antonello appears to have had early contact with Flemish art. In his deft handling of the oil medium—his rendering of transparent surfaces and minute landscape details—a strong Northern influence can be seen. About 1475 he went to Venice. There he painted the *San Cassiano Altarpiece*, of which only fragments now exist (Vienna). His style affected the art of Bellini and other Venetians. He was also an excellent portrait painter; examples of his portraiture are in the Metropolitan Museum, the Philadelphia Museum, the Louvre, and in Berlin. Other paintings by him are *Ecce Homo* (Metropolitan Mus.); *Madonna* *and Child* (National Gall. of Art, Washington, D.C.); *Pietà* (Venice); *Crucifixion* (Antwerp). See Stefano Bottari's study (1956).

Antonescu, Ion (yôn äntônĕs'kōō), 1882–1946, Rumanian marshal and dictator. He served in World War I and later became chief of staff, but he fell into disfavor with King Carol II because of his pro-Nazi attitude and his suspected intrigues with the IRON GUARD. In World War II, on Sept. 4–5, 1940, Carol, threatened with revolution and German intervention, appointed Antonescu premier with dictatorial powers. On Sept. 6, Antonescu forced the king to abdicate in favor of Carol's son, MICHAEL. In Nov., 1940, Rumania joined the Axis Powers, and Antonescu gave Adolf Hitler virtual control over Rumanian economy and foreign policy, tolerated violent pogroms against the Jews, and declared (June 22, 1941) a "holy war" on the Soviet Union. With two Soviet armies deep in Rumania, King Michael in Aug., 1944, had Antonescu and his cabinet arrested in a dramatic coup. Antonescu was tried (1946) for war crimes, sentenced, and executed.

Antonines (ăn'tənīnz), collective name of certain Roman emperors of the 2d cent., usually listed as ANTONINUS PIUS; his adopted sons, MARCUS AURELIUS and Verus; and COMMODUS.

Antoninus, Saint (ăntōnī'nəs), 1389–1459, Italian churchman, b. Antoninus Pierozzi. He was a Dominican and became archbishop of Florence. He ruled well and was renowned for his charitable work in the city. His *Summa moralis* is a pioneering work in moral theology, of interest for its treatment of commercial ethics and the morality of banking. It is a valuable record of the effect the new economic changes were having on everyday life. Feast: May 10. See Bede Jarrett, *St. Antonino and Medieval Economics* (1914).

Antoninus, Wall of, ancient Roman wall extending across N Britain from the Firth of Forth to the Firth of Clyde. It was built by the Roman governor Lollius Urbicus in the reign of Emperor Antoninus Pius—probably in A.D. 140–42. Intended as a defense against the peoples to the north, it was built out of turf, with a ditch on the north and 19 forts along its southern side. The wall was 37 mi (60 km) long. It was abandoned c.185. See Sir George Macdonald, *The Roman Wall in Scotland* (2d ed., 1934).

Antoninus Pius (Titus Aurelius Fulvus Boionius Arrius Antoninus) (pī'əs), A.D. 86–A.D. 161, Roman emperor (138–161). After a term as consul (120) he went as proconsul to Asia, where he governed with distinction. He was adopted by the emperor Hadrian and, on succeeding him, administered the empire with marked ability and integrity. Italy was embellished with fine buildings, and the provinces were eased of much of their financial burden. During his reign the Wall of Antoninus was built in Britain. His wife was Faustina, aunt of his successor, MARCUS AURELIUS.

Antonioni, Michelangelo (mĕkälän'jälō äntōnyô'nē), 1912–, Italian film director and scriptwriter, b. Ferrara, Italy. In the 1940s he made documentaries that contributed to the development of Italian Neo-Realism. His later films deal with the alienation and loveless eroticism of modern life, with plot and dialogue often subordinate to visual and aural images. His films include *Le Amiche* (1955), *L'Avventura* (1959), *La Notte* (1960), *L'Eclisse* (1961), *The Red Desert* (1964), *Blow-Up* (1966), and *Zabriskie Point* (1969). See study by Ian Cameron and Robin Wood (rev. ed. 1971).

Antony or **Marc Antony,** Lat. *Marcus Antonius,* c.83 B.C.–30 B.C., Roman politican and soldier. He was of a distinguished family; his mother was a relative of Julius CAESAR. Antony was notorious from his youth for riotous living, but even his enemies admitted his courage. Between 58 B.C. and 56 B.C. he campaigned in Syria with Aulus Gabinius and then in Gaul with Caesar, who made a protégé of him. In 52 B.C. he became quaestor and in 49 B.C. tribune. When the situation between POMPEY and Caesar became critical, Antony and Quintus CASSIUS Longinus, another tribune, vetoed the bill to deprive Caesar of his army and fled to him. Caesar crossed the Rubicon, and the civil war began. At the battle of Pharsala, Caesar took the right wing, and Antony gave distinguished service as the leader of the left. After Caesar's assassination (44 B.C.), Antony, then consul, aroused the mob against the conspirators and drove them from the city. When Octavian (later AUGUSTUS), Caesar's adopted son and heir, arrived in Rome, Antony joined forces with him, but they soon fell out. Antony went to take Cisalpine Gaul as his assigned proconsular province, but Decimus BRUTUS would not give it up, and Antony besieged him (43 B.C.) at Mutina (modern Modena). The senate, urged by CICERO, who had excoriated Antony in the *Philippics,* sent the consuls Aulus HIRTIUS and Caius Vibius Pansa to attack Antony. The consuls fell in battle, but Antony retired into Transalpine Gaul. Octavian now decided for peace and arranged with Antony and Marcus Aemilius LEPIDUS the Second Triumvirate, with Antony receiving Asia as his command. In the proscription following this treaty Antony had Cicero killed. Antony and Octavian crushed the republicans at Philippi, and the triumvirate ruled the empire for five years. In 42 B.C. Antony met CLEOPATRA, and their love affair began. While Antony was in Egypt, his wife, Fulvia, became so alienated from Octavian that civil war broke out in Italy. At about the time Antony arrived in Italy, Fulvia died (40 B.C.) and peace was restored between Octavian and Antony, who married Octavian's sister Octavia; she became, thereafter, Antony's devoted partisan and the strongest force for peace between the two. In 36 B.C., Antony undertook an invasion of Parthia. The war was costly and useless, and Antony succeeded only in adding some of Armenia to the Roman possessions. In 37 B.C., Antony settled in Alexandria as the acknowledged lover of Cleopatra. He gave himself up to pleasure, caring neither for the growing ill will in Rome nor for the increasing impatience of Octavian. In 32 B.C. the senate deprived Antony of his powers, thus making civil war inevitable. In 31 B.C., Antony and his fleet met Marcus Vipsanius Agrippa with Octavian's fleet off Actium, and Antony found his large, cumbersome galleys were no match for the swift small craft that Octavian had built. In the middle of the battle Cleopatra retired with her boats, and Antony followed her. His navy surrendered to Octavian. The situation of the two lovers was desperate. Returning to Alexandria, they set about fortifying Egypt against Octavian's arrival. When at length Octavian did come (30 B.C.), Antony committed suicide, under the impression, it is said, that Cleopatra had died already. She killed herself soon afterward. Of the many dramas on the tragedy the best known by far is Shakespeare's *Antony and Cleopatra.* The name also appears as Marc Anthony. See A. E. Weigall, *The Life and Times of Cleopatra* (1968).

Antothijah (ăntəthī'jə), descendant of Benjamin. 1 Chron. 8.24.

Antothite (ăn'tōthīt): see ANATHOTH.

Antrim (ăn'trĭm), county (1971 pop. 352,549), 1,098 sq mi (2,844 sq km), NE Northern Ireland. BELFAST is the county town. The eastern and seaward area of the county is a picturesque region of mountains and glens; to the west, where Antrim borders on Lough Neagh, lie the fertile valleys of the Bann and the Lagan rivers. On the northern coast is the extraordinary basaltic formation known as the GIANT'S CAUSEWAY. The region is chiefly agricultural (oats, flax, potatoes). Fishing and cattle breeding are also important occupations, and there is a significant tourist trade. Belfast is a major British port and the chief industrial center of Northern Ireland. Antrim, BALLYMENA, and CARRICKFERGUS have textile industries; other urban centers include Larne and Lisburn.

Antsirane: see DIÉGO-SUAREZ, Malagasy Republic.

ANTU (ăn'tōō): see PESTICIDE.

Antung (ăn'tŏŏng'), former province (c.24,000 sq mi/62,160 sq km), NE China. The capital was T'unghua (Tunghwa). It was bordered on the SE by the Yalu River, which separated it from Korea, and by the Bay of Korea. A part of Manchuria, it was included in Manchukuo and was created a province in 1945. In 1954, Antung became part of Liaoning prov.

Antung: see TAN-TUNG, China.

Antwerp (ăn'twûrp), Flemish *Antwerpen,* Fr. *Anvers,* province (1970 pop. 1,533,249), 1,104 sq mi (2,859 sq km), N Belgium, bordering on the Netherlands in the north. ANTWERP (the provincial capital) and MECHELEN are the chief cities. The province is largely a flat, cultivated plain, drained by the Scheldt River and its tributaries and served by the Albert Canal. It is mostly Flemish-speaking and was part of the duchy of BRABANT.

Antwerp, Flemish *Antwerpen,* Fr. *Anvers,* city (1970 pop. 224,543), capital of Antwerp prov., N Belgium, on the Scheldt River. It is one of the busiest ports in Europe; a commercial, industrial, and financial center; and a rail junction. The city is linked with industrial E Belgium (especially Liège) by the ALBERT CANAL and also has a large transit trade to and from West Germany (especially the Ruhr district). Manufactures of Antwerp and its surrounding region include refined petroleum, petrochemicals, dyes, photographic supplies, motor vehicles, leather goods, and processed food. In addition, the city is a major international center of the diamond trade and industry, has large shipyards, and is the seat of the world's first stock exchange (founded 1460). Antwerp was a small trading center by the early 8th cent. It was destroyed by the Normans in 836, but by the 11th cent. it was a fairly important port. The city was chartered in 1291. Antwerp was held (13th to mid-14th cent.) by Brabant and then became an early seat of the counts of Flanders. In the 15th cent. it rose to prominence as Bruges and Ghent declined. In 1446 the English Merchant Adventurers and other traders gave the port great impetus by moving their operations from Bruges to Antwerp. By the middle of the 16th cent. Antwerp was Europe's chief commercial and financial center. The diamond industry, established in the 15th cent., had expanded considerably after the arrival (early 16th cent.) of Jewish craftsmen expelled from Portugal. The city's prosperity suffered greatly in 1576 when it was sacked and about 6,000 of its inhabitants killed by Spanish troops (the "Spanish fury") and again in 1584–85 when the city was captured by the Spanish under Alessandro of Farnese after a 14-month siege. Under the Peace of Westphalia (1648), the Scheldt was closed to navigation (as a means of favoring Amsterdam), and Antwerp declined rapidly. The city revived with the opening of the Scheldt by the French in 1795 and with the expansion of its port facilities by Napoleon I. The incorporation (1815) of Belgium in the Netherlands again hindered Antwerp's economic development, a situation that was continued by the Dutch-Belgian treaty of separation (1839), which gave the Netherlands the right to collect tolls on Scheldt shipping. The expansion of Antwerp as a major modern port dates only from 1863, when, by a cash payment, Belgium ended Dutch restrictions on traffic on the Scheldt. Antwerp was seriously damaged in World War I when it was captured (Oct., 1914) by the Germans after a 12-day siege. In World War II, it was again taken (May, 1940) by the Germans, who bombarded it heavily after it had been recaptured (Sept., 1944) by the Allies. The artistic fame of Antwerp dates from the rule (15th cent.) of Philip the Good of Burgundy, who founded an academy of painting there. The painters Quentin Massys and P. P. Rubens resided in the city, and Sir Anthony Van Dyke was born there. Many of their works are in the museums and churches of Antwerp. Christophe Plantin made (16th cent.) the city a center of printing; his house is now a museum. Among Antwerp's many splendid structures are the large Gothic Cathedral of Notre Dame (14th–16th cent.), with a spire c.400 ft (122 m) high; the churches of St. James (containing the tomb of Rubens) and of St. Paul (both 16th cent.); the Renaissance-style city hall (mid-16th cent.); Rubens's house (now a museum); and old guildhalls lining the Groote Markt [market place]. Antwerp is the site of a famous zoological garden and a noted school of music.

Anu (ā'nōō), ancient sky god of Sumerian origin, worshiped in Babylonian religion. The son of Apsu (the underworld ocean) and Tiamat (primeval chaos), Anu was king of the great triad of gods, which included the earth god Enlil and the water god Ea.

An Uaimh, Republic of Ireland: see NAVAN.

Anub (ā'nəb), Judahite. 1 Chron. 4.8.

Anubis (ənōō'bĭs), Egyptian god of the dead. He presided over the embalming of the dead, and is represented as a dog-headed or jackal-headed man.

Anuradhapura (ənōō'rädəpōō'rə) or **Anarajapura** (ənä'räjə-), town (1968 est. pop. 30,000), capital of the North Central prov., Sri Lanka (Ceylon), on the Aruvi River. Rice plantations and vegetable gardens surround the town, which is famous chiefly for its vast Buddhist ruins and as a pilgrimage center. Founded in 437 B.C., it was the capital of a Sinhalese kingdom and a Buddhist center until the 8th cent. A.D., when, after a Tamil invasion, it was abandoned in favor of Pollonarrua. Ruins include several colossal stupas (some larger than the pyramids of Egypt), a temple hewn from rock, and the Brazen Palace (so called from its metal roof). A sacred bo tree at Anuradhapura was grown from a slip of the tree at Bodh Gaya, India, under which Buddha reputedly attained enlightenment.

Anvers: see ANTWERP, Belgium.

Anville, Jean Baptiste Bourguignon d' (zhäN bätēst' bōōrgēnyôN' däNvēl'), 1697–1782, French geographer and cartographer. His maps of ancient geography, characterized by careful, accurate work and based largely on original research, are especially valuable. He left unknown areas of continents blank and noted doubtful information as such; compared to the lavish maps of his predecessors, his maps looked empty. Anville became cartographer to the king, who purchased his maps, atlases, and other geographical material (the largest collection in France); Anville himself made more than 200 maps.

anxiety, anticipatory tension or vague dread persisting in the absence of a specific threat. In contrast to fear, which is a realistic reaction to actual danger, in anxiety the true source of distress is concealed from the individual. Anxiety is characterized physiologically by increased pulse rate, heightened breathing and blood pressure, palpitations, perspiration, muscular tension, dryness of the mouth, and sometimes an increased need to urinate or defecate. Freud first believed that anxiety was the result of repressed, pent-up sexual energy but later viewed it as a danger signal, alerting the ego to excessive stimulation and causing repression. It has been defined as the tension resulting from a sense of failure or disapproval in interpersonal relations, and as an apprehensive reaction to unresolved conflicts or experiences that threaten the personality. DEFENSE MECHANISMS are personality responses to anxiety resulting from frustration and conflict.

An-yang or **Anyang** (both: än-yäng), city (1970 est. pop. 225,000), N Honan prov., China, on the Peking-Canton RR, in a cotton-growing area. It has textile mills, coal mines, and a medium-sized iron and steel complex. An-yang was once a capital of the Shang dynasty and one of the earliest centers of Chinese civilization. Excavations, begun there in 1928, have revealed a rich Bronze Age culture.

Anza, Juan Bautista de (hwän boutēs'tä dā än'sä), 1735–88, Spanish explorer and official in the Southwest and the far West, founder of San Francisco, b. Mexico. Accompanied by Father F. T. H. Garcés and a small expedition, he opened (1774) an overland road from Sonora through present-day Arizona to California, reaching San Gabriel and Monterey. Viceroy A. M. Bucareli, alarmed by the threatened encroachments of the Russians and the British on the Pacific coast, sent (1775) Anza on a new expedition to establish a colony. In 1776 he chose the site of San Francisco, where a presidio was founded by one of his lieutenants and a mission was founded by Father Francisco Palóu under the direction of Father Junípero Serra. Later, as governor of New Mexico (1777–88), Anza built up Spanish frontier defenses and established order. Journals of men on his California journey are in *Anza's California Expeditions* (ed. by H. E. Bolton, 5 vol., 1930, repr. 1966). For his diaries and a study of his administration, see A. B. Thomas, *Forgotten Frontiers* (1932, repr. 1969). See F. Thurman, *The Cahuillas and White Men of San Carlos and Coyote Canyon* (1970).

Anzengruber, Ludwig (lo͞ot'vĭkh än'tsəngro͞o"bər), 1839–89, Austrian writer. An actor and a clerk in the imperial police, Anzengruber had little success as a writer until the production (1870) of his anticlerical play *Der Pfarrer von Kirchfeld* [the parish priest of Kirchfeld]. It was the first of a series of folk plays and was followed by *Der Meineidbauer* (1871, tr. *The Farmer Forsworn,* 1913–15) and *Die Kreuzelschreiber* (1872, tr. *The Crossmakers,* 1958). *Das vierte Gebot* (1878, tr. *The Fourth Commandment,* 1912) is an early example of NATURALISM. Anzengruber also wrote short stories and two novels.

Anzhero-Sudzhensk (ənzhĕ"rə-so͞o'jĕnsk), city (1970 pop. 106,000), SW Siberian USSR, on the Trans-Siberian RR. One of the oldest and largest coal-mining centers of the Kuznetsk Basin, the city was developed as a source of coal for the railroad. Mining equipment, chemicals, and pharmaceuticals are manufactured there.

Anzio (än'tsyō), Lat. *Antium,* town (1971 pop. 23,092), in Latium, central Italy, on the Tyrrhenian Sea. It is a seaside resort with a fishing industry. A Volscian town, it was captured by Rome in 341 B.C. and became a favorite resort of the Romans. Nero and Caligula were born there; among the ruins of Nero's villa two famous statues, the *Apollo Belvedere* and the *Girl of Anzio,* were found. Anzio declined in the Middle Ages, but it revived c.1700 and became a residence of the popes. During World War II, Allied troops landed (Jan., 1944) at Anzio and nearby Nettuno to draw German forces from Cassino, thus effecting a breakthrough (May, 1944) to Rome.

Anzus Treaty, defense agreement signed in 1951, by Australia, New Zealand, and the United States. The name *Anzus* is derived from the initials of the three signatory nations. As a result of the reestablishment of peace between Japan and the United States in 1951, Australia and New Zealand asked for a treaty making it clear that an attack on any of the three signatory countries would be considered an attack upon all. It is also known as the Pacific Security Treaty.

Aomori (äōmô'rē), city (1970 pop. 240,041), capital of Aomori prefecture, extreme N Honshu, Japan, on Aomori Bay. First opened to foreign trade in 1906, Aomori is now the chief port of N Honshu. Rice, textiles, and tobacco are among its exports, many of which are shipped to Hokkaido. A modern city, it was rebuilt after a disastrous fire in 1910 and again after severe air raids in 1945. **Aomori** prefecture (1970 pop. 1,427,430), 3,719 sq mi (9,632 sq km), has rich timber lands and famous apple orchards. Aomori, Hachinoke, and Hirosake are the major cities.

aorist: see TENSE.

aorta (āôr'tə), primary artery of the CIRCULATORY SYSTEM in mammals, delivering oxygenated blood to all other arteries except those of the lungs. The human aorta, c.1 in. (2.54 cm) in diameter, originates at the left ventricle of the HEART. After supplying the coronary arteries that nourish the heart itself, the aorta extends slightly toward the neck to feed branches serving the head and arms. It then arches down toward the waist, directing blood into the arterial system of the chest. Entering the abdomen through the aortic hiatus, an opening in the diaphragm, the aorta next supplies the stomach, kidneys, intestines, gonads, and other organs through extensive arterial networks. It finally divides into the two iliac arteries carrying blood to the legs. The elasticity of the aorta wall permits it to pulse in rhythm with the heartbeat, thus helping to propel blood through the body.

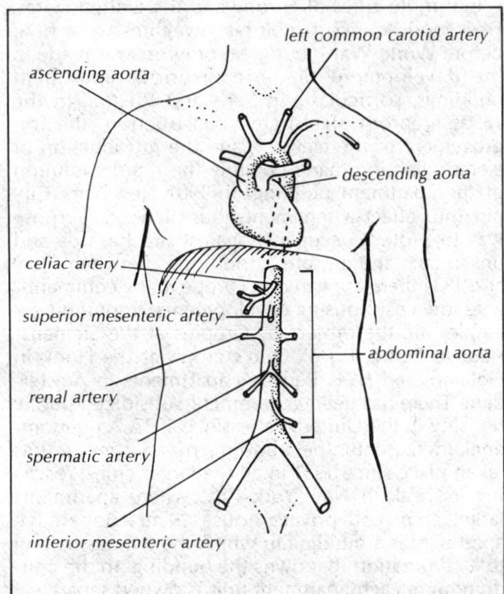

Aorta

Aosta, Emmanuel Philibert of Savoy, duke of (äô'stə, –stä), 1869–1931, Italian general; son of King Amadeus of Spain and cousin of Victor Emmanuel III of Italy. In World War I he held the Piave front after the Italian defeat at Caporetto and later occupied Friuli. He became a marshal in 1926. His son Amadeus (1898–1942), who succeeded to his title, was viceroy of Ethiopia (1937–41). He surrendered to the British during World War II after a valiant defense.

Aosta (äô'stä), city (1971 pop. 36,961), capital of Valle d'Aosta and of Aosta prov., NW Italy, near the junction of the Great and Little St. Bernard roads. Aosta is an industrial and tourist center. Manufactures include iron and steel, aluminum, and chemicals. Emperor Augustus there founded (c.25 B.C.) a colony called Augusta Praetoria, on the site of an older settlement. In the 11th cent. Aosta was given as a fief to Count Humbert I, the founder of the Savoy dynasty; the cadet line of the house bore the title of duke of Aosta. Roman remains in Aosta include walls and gates, a majestic triumphal arch honoring Augustus, a theater, and an amphitheater. There is also a fine cathedral (12th–19th cent.).

Aosta, Valle d' (väldäô'stä), region (1971 pop. 111,239), 1,260 sq mi (3,263 sq km), NW Italy, bordering on France in the west and on Switzerland in the north. AOSTA is the capital of the region and of its only province. A high Alpine country, the Valle d'Aosta includes the Italian slopes of Mont Blanc, the Matterhorn, and Monte Rosa; its highest peak is the Gran Paradiso. The population, much of which is French-speaking, is concentrated in the picturesque valleys of the Dora Baltea River and its tributaries. The Great and the Little SAINT BERNARD roads join in the upper Aosta valley. Farming is the main occupation; cereals and grapes are grown, and dairy cattle are raised. Iron and steel and textiles are the leading manufactures, and there are major hydroelectric facilities. The region has several fashionable resorts, notably Champoluc, Courmayeur, and Cervinia-Breuil. A long vehicular tunnel through Mont Blanc, connecting France and Italy, was opened in 1965; highways feeding it were built in Valle d'Aosta, thus markedly improving the region's transportation network. Rome conquered the region from the Salassi people c.25 B.C. It later was held by the Goths, the Lombards, and the dukes of Burgundy. After passing (11th cent.) to the counts of Savoy, the Valle d'Aosta shared the history of PIEDMONT. Under the Italian constitution of 1947 it was made a region with considerable autonomy, particularly in administrative and cultural affairs. The feudal system long prevailed in the region, and more than 70 castles are still standing.

Apache Indians, North American Indians of the Southwest composed of six culturally related groups. They speak a language that has various dialects and belongs to the ATHABASCAN branch of the Nadene linguistic stock (see AMERICAN INDIAN LANGUAGES), and their ancestors entered the area about 1100. The NAVAHO INDIANS, who also speak an Athabascan language, were once part of the Western Apache; other groups E of the Rio Grande along the mountains were the Jicarilla, the Lipan, and the Mescalero groups. In W New Mexico and Arizona were the Western Apache, including the Chiricahua and the Coyotero. The Kiowa Apache in the early southward migration attached themselves to the Kiowa, whose history they have since shared. Subsistence in historic times consisted of wild game, cactus fruits, seeds of wild shrubs and grass, livestock, grains plundered from settlements, and a small amount of horticulture. The social organization involved matrilocal residence, a rigorous mother-in-law avoidance pattern, and working for the wife's relatives. The Apache are known principally for their fierce fighting qualities. They successfully resisted the advance of Spanish colonization, but the acquisition of horses and new weapons, taken from the Spanish, led to increased intertribal warfare. The Eastern Apache were driven from their traditional plains area when (after 1720) they suffered defeat at the hands of the advancing COMANCHE INDIANS. Relations between the Apache and the settlers gradually worsened with the passing of Spanish rule in Mexico. By mid-19th cent. when the United States acquired the region from Mexico, Apache lands were in the path of the American westward movement. The futile but strong resistance that lasted until the beginning of the 20th cent. brought national fame to several of the Apache leaders—COCHISE, GERONIMO, MANGAS COLORADAS, and VICOTRIO. Remnants of the Apaches now live in reservations in Arizona, where they number some 11,500. See G. C. Baldwin, *The Warrior Apaches* (1965); D. L. Thrapp, *The Conquest of Apacheria* (1967); Keith Basso and Morris Opler, ed., *Apachean Culture and Ethnology* (1971); J. U. Terrell, *Apache Chronicle* (1972).

Apalachee Indians, extinct tribe of North American Indians once centered about Apalachee Bay, NW Florida, belonging to the Muskogean branch of the Hokan-Siouan linguistic stock (see AMERICAN INDIAN LANGUAGES). Prosperous agriculturalists, they fought off the raids of the Creek Indians until early in the 18th cent. Combined Indian and British forces then conquered them, wiping out their villages along with Spanish missions and garrisons. More than 1,000 Apalachee were sold into slavery.

Apalachicola, river: see CHATTAHOOCHEE, river.

APA-Phoenix: see ASSOCIATION OF PRODUCING ARTISTS—PHOENIX.

Aparri (äpär'rē), city (1969 est. pop. 45,700), Cagayan prov., on N Luzon, the Philippines. Situated on the mouth of the Cagayan River on the Babuyan Channel, it is the port for the rich Cagayan valley, the Philippines's leading tobacco-producing area.

apartheid (əpärt'hīt) [Afrik.,=apartness], system of racial segregation peculiar to the Republic of South Africa. Racial segregation and the supremacy of whites had been traditionally accepted in South Africa prior to 1948, but in the general election of that year, Daniel F. MALAN included the policy of apartheid in the Afrikaner Nationalist party platform, bringing his party to power for the first time. While most whites have continued to acquiesce in the policy, there has been bitter and sometimes bloody strife over the degree and stringency of its implementation. The purpose of apartheid is separation of the races: not only of whites from nonwhites, but also of nonwhites from each other, and, among the Africans (known as Bantu), of one group from another. In addition to the Africans, who constitute about 70% of the total population, those regarded as nonwhite include the Coloured (mulatto) and Asiatic (mainly of Indian ancestry) populations. Initial emphasis was on restoring the separation of races within the urban areas. A large segment of the Asiatic and Coloured populations was forced to relocate out of so-called white areas. African townships that had been overtaken by (white) urban sprawl were demolished and their occupants removed to new townships well beyond city limits. Between the passage of the Group Areas Acts of 1950 and 1968, about 500,000 Africans were moved from the cities to rural reservations. Under the prime ministership of Hendrik VERWOERD, apartheid developed into a policy known as "separate development," whereby each of the nine Bantu groups was to become a nation with its own homeland, or Bantustan. An area totaling about 14% of the country's land was set aside for these homelands, the remainder, including the major mineral areas and the cities, being reserved for the whites. The basic tenet of the separate development policy is that within the confines of his designated homeland the black African shall have quite extensive rights and freedoms, the corollary being that outside it his position is akin to that of an alien. His movement to and between other parts of the country is strictly regulated, the location of his residence or employment (if permitted to work) is restricted, and he is not allowed to vote or own land. Thus African urban workers, including those who are third- or fourth-generation city dwellers, are seen as transients, their real homes being the rural reservations from which they or their forefathers migrated. Only those holding the necessary labor permits, which are granted according to the current requirements of the labor market, are allowed to reside within urban areas. Such permits do not automatically include the spouse or family of a permit holder, a fact that has contributed greatly to the breakup of family life among the Africans. Most African urban dwellers must live in the townships on a city's perimeter (an exception is made for domestic servants, who are permitted to live within city limits on the premises of their employers). All Africans living outside the Bantustans are subject to strict curfew regulations and passbook requirements, especially in the cities; if unable to produce these when challenged, they are subject to arrest. In 1962 the South African government established the first of the Bantustans, the Transkei, as the homeland of the Xhosa tribe, and granted it limited self-government in 1963. Since then none of the other tribal groups has succeeded in gaining even this degree of self-government. The reserves are, in general, made up of broken tracts of poor quality land, riddled with erosion and incapable of supporting their large designated populations. Opportunities for employment are few, as there is little or no industry in these areas. Urban wage-earners attempt to contribute to the support of their families in the reserves, but the level of African wages is so low as to make this barely feasible. In 1972, African wages in manufacturing were one fifth or one sixth of those of whites, and in other fields, such as mining, the ratio of discrepancy in cash wages was 20 or more to 1. Despite public demonstrations against apartheid, UN resolutions, and opposition from international religious societies, the policy has been applied with increased rigor, extending to rigid enforcement in the churches and universities. In 1961, South Africa withdrew from the British Commonwealth rather than yield to pressure over its racial policies, and in the same year the three South African denominations of the Dutch Reformed Church left the World Council of Churches rather than abandon their advocacy of apartheid. Although the policy of apartheid was continued under Prime Minister John VORSTER, there are signs of change. After South Africa was barred from the Olympic Games in 1964 and 1968, there were some alterations in the government's policy, so that by the early 1970s international sports events held in South Africa were being viewed and participated in by both blacks and whites. In 1972, a series of antiapartheid protests occurred in both nonwhite and white universities. Probably the most forceful pressures, both internal and external, eroding the barriers of apartheid are economic. African wages are gradually increasing as awareness grows of the market potential of a more highly paid African labor force. There is a chronic shortage of skilled labor, so, over the protests of the white trade unions, an increasing number of more highly rated jobs are being opened up to Africans (for whom trade union membership is illegal). In addition, there are the pressures, political and economic, being exerted by the independent countries of black Africa. Nevertheless there are many who feel that apartheid will only be toppled by force—by political upheaval from within or by violent assault from without. See A. L. Sachs, *South Africa: The Violence of Apartheid* (1969); Jim Hoagland, *South Africa: Civilizations in Conflict* (1972); United Nations Educational, Scientific, and Cultural Organization, *Apartheid: Its Effects on Education, Science, Culture, and Information* (2d rev. ed. 1972).

apartment house, building having three or more dwelling units. Numerous early examples of this form of dwelling have been found in remains of Roman and medieval cities and the 17th-century Pueblo Indian villages of North America. Its most important development came with the Industrial Revolution. After 1850 crowded slums began to develop in the cities of Europe and the United States. Few good, low-cost multiple dwellings were built before World War I, but great progress was made in the development of more luxurious apartment buildings, particularly in Paris and Vienna. In the 1880s fireproof steel-frame construction, the improvement of the elevator, and the introduction of electric lighting made possible the rapid evolution of the apartment building. In 1901 New York City put into effect a tenement-house law; its purpose was to protect occupants against fire hazards and unsanitary and unsafe conditions. Between 1919 and 1934 there appeared in Europe many commendable low-cost housing developments. Important examples are the project by Gropius at the Siemensstadt in Berlin, J. J. P. Oud's group at the Hook in Holland, and H. P. Berlage's apartments in Amsterdam. There has been government-subsidized public housing in the United States since 1937. A phenomenal increase in the building of apartments has taken place since 1921 in all the larger cities, reaching its peak in New York City, where apartments largely replaced private houses. The cooperative apartment is a building in which the tenants belong to a corporation that owns the building. In the condominium each apartment unit is owned separately and owner-tenants generally form an association to provide for apartment maintenance. The apartment hotel combines the accommodations of an apartment, including cooking space, with the services characteristic of a hotel. Apartment houses have now spread to the suburbs of the larger cities, where they often include gardens, tennis courts, and children's playgrounds. Numerous apartment houses are constructed as living complexes for retired persons. A radical experiment in multiple dwellings called Habitat was designed for the Montreal Expo 67 by Moshe SAFDIE. Concrete units were stacked like boxes but in a random-appearing fashion to create a visually exciting housing complex. See F. R. S. Yorke and Frederick Gibberd, *Masterworks of International Apartment Building Design* (1959); Samuel Paul, *Apartments: Their Design and Development* (1967).

apastron (əpăs'trən): see APSIS.

apatite (ăp'ətīt), mineral, a calcium phosphate containing chlorine, fluorine, or both. It is transparent to opaque in shades of green, brown, yellow, white, red, and purple. The yellow-green variety, called asparagus stone, and the blue-green manganapatite are used to a limited extent in jewelry. Large deposits of apatite are mined for use in making phosphatic fertilizers. Apatite is a minor constituent in many types of rock. Commercial deposits are mined in Florida, Tennessee, and Montana, and in N Africa and the USSR.

Apaturia (ăpəchōō'rēə, -tyōō'rēə), in Greek religion, annual festival celebrated by the Ionians and the Athenians. It was held in October or November, in the season when various phratries (clans) met to induct new members, register children born since the previous festival, and pay homage to the gods.

ape, any primate of the family Pongidae (also called Simiidae), closely related to the human family (Hominidae). The small apes, the GIBBON and the siamang, and the smallest of the great apes, the ORANGUTAN, are found in SE Asia. The other great apes, the GORILLA and the CHIMPANZEE, are found in Africa. The term *ape* was formerly applied to certain tailless monkeys as well, and the Pongidae were distinguished as the anthropoid, or manlike, apes. *Ape* and *anthropoid ape* are now used synonymously, although the common names of certain monkeys still contain the word ape; for example, the N African macaque is called the Barbary ape. True apes vary in size from the 3-ft (90-cm), 15-lb (6.8-kg) gibbon to the 6-ft (1.8-m), 500-lb (227-kg) gorilla. All apes are forest dwellers and spend at least some of the time in the trees. They are able, like monkeys, to run along branches on all fours; unlike monkeys, they are also able to move about by brachiation, or arm-over-arm swinging. Gibbons (including siamangs) and orangutans are particularly adept at this type of locomotion and spend most of the time in trees. Gorillas are the most terrestrial of the apes, and chimpanzees also spend much of the time on the ground. The skeleton of an ape is quite similar to that of a human in the structure of the chest and shoulders. Apes have broad, flat chests and arms capable of reaching up and backward from the shoulder; this construction is associated with brachiation. The pelvis, on the other hand, is more like that of a monkey, designed for walking on all fours. Most apes are able to walk on two feet, but only for short distances. The ground-living gorillas and chimpanzees normally walk on the hind feet and knuckles of the hands, with the fingers of the hands curled under. The arms of an ape are longer than the legs. The hands are similar to human hands, but with fingers and thumb of more equal length; the feet are handlike grasping structures. Apes have neither tails nor the cheek pouches found in Old World monkeys; gibbons are the only apes that have the buttock callosities found in Old World monkeys. The face of an ape is quite flat, like that of many monkeys and of humans. The vision is highly developed, with a stereoscopic color image. The brain is similar in structure to the human brain, although smaller, and is capable of fairly advanced reasoning. Apes are classified in the phylum CHORDATA, subphylum Vertebrata, class Mammalia, order Primates, family Pongidae. See Vernon Reynolds, *The Apes* (1967); R. M. Yerkes and A. W. Yerkes, *The Great Apes* (1929, repr. 1970); G. H. Bourne, *The Ape People* (1971).

Apeldoorn (ä'pəldōrn), city (1971 pop. 126,266), Gelderland prov., central Netherlands. Its varied manufactures include paper and paint. The city is a transportation center and attracts many tourists. Nearby is Het Loo, a royal palace and the residence of former Queen Wilhelmina from the time of her abdication in 1948 until her death in 1962.

Apelles (əpĕl'ēz), fl. 330 B.C., Greek painter, the most celebrated in antiquity but now known only through descriptions of his works. He is supposed to have studied under Ephorus of Ephesus and under Pamphilus of Amphipolis at Sicyon. He was court painter to Philip II of Macedon and to Alexander the Great. His portraits of Alexander included one in the Temple of Diana at Ephesus that showed Alexander wielding the thunderbolts of Zeus. Apelles excelled in painting horses, and according to Pliny the portrait of Antigonus Cyclops on horseback was his masterpiece. Most famous, perhaps, was the painting of Aphrodite rising from the sea. A painting made by Botticelli from Lucian's description of Apelles' *Calumny* is in the Uffizi. Apelles is said to have been the first to recognize the talents of PROTOGENES.

Apelles, Christian at Rome. Rom. 16.10.

Apennines (ăp'ənīnz), Ital. *Appennino,* mountain system, running the entire length of the Italian peninsula. It extends south c.840 mi (1,350 km) from the Cadibona Pass in Liguria, NW Italy, where the Apennines join with the Ligurian Alps, to the Strait of Messina; the mountains of Sicily are a southwest continuation of the system. The Apennines are widest (c.80 mi/130 km) in the central section, which also contains the highest peaks, Mt. Corno (9,560 ft/2,914 m high) and Mt. Amaro (9,170 ft/2,795 m high). However, in general the peaks are much lower. The central and southern Apennines have mineral springs, crater lakes, fumaroles, and volcanoes (two, Vesuvius and Etna, are still active). The southern section also experiences many earthquakes. Of the many rivers rising in the Apennines, the few important ones (Arno, Tiber, and Volturno) all flow W into the Tyrrhenian Sea. The N and central Apennines are rich in a great variety of minerals. There are many hydroelectric plants in the mountains. The once heavily forested slopes of the system have been greatly reduced by man through the centuries; attempts at conservation and reforestation have been made. The greatest population concentrations are found in the valleys and the fertile basins. Extensive pasturelands are used for sheep and goat grazing. The Apennines are pierced by many railroad tunnels and highway passes, and by the Appian, Cassian, Flaminian, and Salarian ways (see ROMAN ROADS).

Apharsachites (əfär'səkīts) or **Apharsathchites** (əfär'sāthkīts), Assyrian colonists settled in Samaria. Ezra 4.9; 5.6; 6.6. The **Apharsites** apparently were another group of colonists. Ezra 4.9.

aphasia (əfā'zhə), language disturbance caused by a lesion of the brain, making an individual partially or totally impaired in his ability to speak, write, or comprehend the meaning of spoken or written words. It is distinguished from functional disorders such as stammering or stuttering, and from impaired speech due to physical defects in the organs used for speaking. Treatment consists of reeducation; the oral and lip-reading methods employed in the education of deaf and mute children have been found to be of assistance in therapy.

Aphek (ā'fĕk). **1** Canaanite royal town, the modern Ras el-Ain or Rosh Hayim (Israel). Herod called it Antipatris. It is mentioned in Egyptian documents dating from the 19th cent. B.C. Joshua 12.18. See APHEKAH. **2** Canaanite city in Asher. Joshua 13.4; 19.30. Aphik: Judges 1.31. **3** Place where Ahab defeated Benhadad. 1 Kings 20.26–30; 2 Kings 13.17. **4, 5** Two places where the Philistines encamped, perhaps the same as **1.** 1 Sam. 4.1; 29.1.

Aphekah (əfē'kə), unidentified place, probably the same as APHEK **4.** Joshua 15.53.

aphelion (əfē'lēən, ăp"hē'-), point farthest from the sun in the orbit of a body about the sun. See APSIS.

Aphiah (əfī'ə), ancestor of King Saul. 1 Sam 9.1.

aphid or **plant louse,** tiny, usually green, soft-bodied, pear-shaped insect, injurious to vegetation. It is also called greenfly and blight. Aphids are mostly under 1/4 in. (6 mm) long. Some are wingless; others have two pairs of transparent or colored wings, the front pair longer than the hind pair. In typical aphids (family Aphididae), two tubes called cornicles project from the rear of the abdomen and exude protective substances. Aphids feed by inserting their beaks into stems, leaves, or roots, and sucking the plant juices. Usually they gather in large colonies. Their life cycle is complex and varies in different species. In a typical life cycle, several generations of wingless females, which reproduce asexually (see PARTHENOGENESIS) and bear live offspring, are followed by a generation of winged females, which bears a sexually reproducing, egg-laying generation of males and females. Mating usually occurs in fall and the eggs are laid in crevices of the twigs of the host plant; the first generation of wingless females hatches in spring. Different host plants and different parts of the plant may be used at different stages of the life cycle. Many kinds of aphid secrete a sweet substance called honeydew, prized as food by ants, flies, and bees. This substance consists of partially digested, highly concentrated plant sap and other wastes, and is excreted from the anus, often in copious amounts. Certain aphid species have a symbiotic relationship with various species of ants that resembles the relationship of domestic cattle to humans; hence the name "ant cows" for aphids. The ants tend the aphids, transporting them to their food plants at the appropriate stages of the aphids' life cycle and sheltering the aphid eggs in their nests during the winter. The aphids, in turn, provide honeydew for the ants. Some aphids (e.g., the woolly apple aphid) secrete long strands of waxy material from wax glands, forming a conspicuous woolly coating for their colonies. Gall-making aphids live in GALLS, or swellings of plant tissue, formed by the plant as a reaction to substances secreted by the insects; galls of different aphid species are easily identified (e.g., the cockscomb gall of elm leaves). One group of aphids lives only on conifers (e.g., the eastern spruce gall aphid). The PHYLLOXERA, notorious for its damage to vineyards, is closely related to the aphids. The damage done by aphids is due to a number of causes, including loss of sap, clogging of leaf surfaces with honeydew, and growth of molds and fungi on the honeydew. Leaf curl, a common symptom of aphid infestation, occurs when a colony attacks the underside of a leaf, causing its desiccation. The downward curl provides protection for the colony, but the leaf becomes useless to the plant. Some species also transmit viral diseases of plants. Many larger insects feed on aphids, including ladybird beetles and lacewings. Fungus infection and damp weather also help limit the number of aphids. Among the aphids causing serious damage to food crops are the grain, cabbage, cornroot, apple, woolly apple, and hickory aphids and the alder and beech tree blights. Aphids are classified in several families of the phylum ARTHROPODA, class Insecta, order Homoptera.

Aphik (ā'fĭk): see APHEK **2.**

aphorism (ăf'ərĭz"əm), short, pithy statement of an evident truth concerned with life or nature; distinguished from the axiom because its truth is not capable of scientific demonstration. HIPPOCRATES was the first to use the term for his *Aphorisms,* briefly stated medical principles. Note his famous opening sentence: "Life is short, art is long, opportunity fleeting, experimenting dangerous, reasoning difficult."

aphotic zone: see OCEAN.

Aphrah (ăf'rə), in the punning passage of Micah 1.10, apparently the name of a town. The name meant "dust" in Hebrew or sounded like a word meaning "dust," hence probably the use of the name.

Aphrodite (ăfrədī'tē), in Greek religion, goddess of love and of beauty. Although Homer designated her the child of Zeus and Dione, Hesiod's account of her birth, in which she emerges from the foam of the sea, is more popular. She supposedly rose where Uranus' genitals had fallen after he had been mutilated by Cronus. Although Zeus gave Aphrodite in marriage to Hephaestus, she bestowed her affections on many others. She loved Ares, by whom she bore not only Harmonia but, in some myths, Eros and Anteros. She was the mother of Hermaphroditus by Hermes and of Priapus by Dionysus. Zeus caused her to love the shepherd Anchises, by whom she bore Aeneas. Adonis, in whose legend Aphrodite appears as a goddess of fertility, also won her favors. It was to Aphrodite that Paris awarded the apple of discord, which caused the dispute leading ultimately to the Trojan War. Worshiped throughout Greece, the goddess differed in representation according to her various attributes. As Aphrodite Urania, she was a celestial goddess, the embodiment of pure or spiritual love; as Aphrodite Pandemos, she was a goddess of marriage and family life, the essence of earthly or sensual love. She was also worshiped as a war goddess, as at Sparta, and as a sea goddess and patroness of sailors. Aphrodite had important cults at Cythera on Crete, at Paphos and Amathas on Cyprus, at Corinth, and at Mt. Eryx in Sicily. Probably of Eastern origin, she was similar in many of her attributes to the Oriental goddesses Astarte and Ishtar. The Romans identified Aphrodite with VENUS.

Aphses (ăf'sēz), head of a priestly course. 1 Chron. 24.15.

Apia (äpē'ə), town (1971 est. pop. 30,600), capital of WESTERN SAMOA, on the northern coast of UPOLU island. The economic, social, and political center of Western Samoa, Apia is the nation's only port and city. Through its harbor bananas, copra, and cocoa are exported, and cotton goods, motor vehicles, meats, and sugar are imported. At the western end of the harbor is Mulinu'u, the old ceremonial capital of a Samoan kingdom. Robert Louis STEVENSON is buried on a hill overlooking the city; his former home, Vailima, served as the residence of the New Zealand high commissioner.

Apianus, Petrus (pē'trəs āpēā'nəs), Latinized from **Peter Bienewitz** or **Bennewitz** (pā'tər bē'nəvĭts, bĕn'əvĭts), 1495–1552, German cosmographer and mathematician. He was professor of mathematics at Ingolstadt and was noted for his knowledge of astronomy and his general learning. Best known among his writings is the *Cosmographia* (1524), which has some of the earliest maps of America.

Apicius, Marcus Gabius (əpĭsh'əs), 1st cent., Roman gourmet. He squandered most of his large fortune on feasts and then, anticipating a need to economize, committed suicide. The cookbook called *Apicius* probably dates from a century later.

Apis (ā'pĭs), in Egyptian religion, sacred bull of Memphis, said to be the incarnation of Osiris or of Ptah. His worship spread throughout the Mediterranean world and was particularly important during the time of the Roman Empire. See also SERAPIS.

Apo, Mount (ä'pō), active volcano, 9,690 ft (2,953 m) high, on S Mindanao island, the Philippines. It is the highest peak of the islands. Mt. Apo has a snow-capped appearance but is actually covered with white sulfur. Mt. Apo National Park (281 sq mi/728 sq km; est. 1936) is there.

apocalypse (əpŏk'əlĭps) [Gr.,=uncovering], type of ancient Hebrew and Christian literature dealing with the end of the world. The writing, mostly in the form of visions, is characterized by rich imagery and obscure symbols. In the New Testament the book of REVELATION is often called the Apocalypse. In the Old Testament apocalyptic elements appear extensively in Isaiah, Ezekiel, Daniel, Joel, and Zechariah. The book called 4 ESDRAS is one of the chief Jewish apocalypses; other PSEUDEPIGRAPHA are also apocalyptic. Modern books of this sort are seen among the works of Emmanuel SWEDENBORG. See also FOUR HORSEMEN OF THE APOCALYPSE.

apocrine gland: see SWEAT.

Apocrypha (əpŏk'rĭfə) [Gr.,=hidden things], appendix to the Authorized (or King James) Version of the Old Testament containing the following books and parts of books: First and Second ESDRAS; TOBIT; JUDITH; ESTHER 10.4–16.24; WISDOM; ECCLESIASTICUS; BARUCH; Dan. 3.24–90 (see DANIEL and THREE HOLY CHILDREN); Dan. 13 (see SUSANNA **1**); Dan. 14 (see BEL AND THE DRAGON); the Prayer of Manasses (see MANASSEH **2**); First and Second MACCABEES. The Western canon includes all these except First and Second Esdras and the Prayer of Manasses, which are often given in an appendix to editions of the Vulgate (where the First and Second Esdras of the Apocrypha are called Third and Fourth Esdras). Protestants follow Jewish tradition in treating these books as uncanonical (see OLD TESTAMENT). For Jewish and Christian works resembling biblical books but not included in the Western or the Hebrew canon—sometimes called apocryphal—see PSEUDEPIGRAPHA. See Manuel Komroff, ed., *The Apocrypha* (1936, repr. 1972); E. J. Goodspeed, *The Story of the Apocrypha* (1939, repr. 1962); B. M. Metzger, *An Introduction to the Apocrypha* (1957); L. H. Brockington, *A Critical Introduction to the Apocrypha* (1961).

Apodaca, Juan Ruiz de (hwän rōōēth' dā äpōthä'kä), 1754–1835, Spanish viceroy and military leader. He was sent to London by the Central Junta of Seville to gain English support against Napoleon. After service as governor of Cuba (1812–15), Apodaca, as viceroy of New Spain (1816–21), devoted himself to repressing revolutionary movements. The royalist cause was at first successful, but with the defection of the royalist commander ITURBIDE it failed. Feeling that Apodaca was not making sufficient effort to put down the revolution, a group in Mexico City, headed by the Masons, forced him to surrender his authority. He returned (1821) to Spain where he held various offices. He had the title visconde de Venadito.

apogee (ăp'əjē), point farthest from the earth in the orbit of a body about the earth. See APSIS.

Apollinaire, Guillaume (gēyōm' äpōlēnâr'), 1880–1918, French poet. He was christened Wilhelm Apollinaris de Kostrowitzky. Apollinaire was a leader in the restless period of technical innovation and experimentation in the arts during the early 20th cent. Influenced by the symbolist poets of the previous generation, he developed a casual, lyrical poetic style characterized by a blend of modern and traditional images and verse techniques. His best-known lyrical poems are collected in *Alcools* (1913) and *Calligrammes* (1918). A friend of many avant-garde artists, including Picasso and Braque, Apollinaire is credited with introducing CUBISM with his book *Les Peintres cubistes* (1913, tr. *The Cubist Painters,* 1949). *Les Mamelles de Tirésias* (1918), his only play, was one of the earliest examples of SURREALISM. See biographies by Francis Steegmuller (1963, repr. 1971) and Margaret Davies (1964); studies by Scott Bates (1967) and L. C. Breunig (1969).

Apollinarianism (əpŏlĭnâr'ēənĭzəm), heretical doctrine taught by Apollinaris or Apollinarius (c.315–c.390), bishop of Laodicea, near Antioch. A celebrated scholar and teacher, author of scriptural commentary, philosophy, and controversial treatises, he propounded the theory that Christ possessed the LOGOS in place of a human mind, and hence, while perfectly divine, he was not fully human. Apollinarianism was popular in spite of its repeated condemnation, particularly by the First Council of Constantinople. It anticipated MONOPHYSITISM.

Apollinaris Sidonius (Caius Sollius Apollinaris Sidonius) (əpŏlĭnâr'ĭs sĭdō'nēəs, sĭdō'-), fl. 455–75, Latin writer, b. Lyons. He had a minor role in imperial politics and was bishop of Clermont. Although his panegyric poetry is of little consequence, his letters are an interesting historical source. Canonized by the Roman Catholic Church, he is called St. Sidonius.

Apollo (əpŏl'ō), in Greek religion, one of the most important Olympian gods, concerned especially with prophecy, medicine, music and poetry, archery, and various bucolic arts, particularly the care of flocks and herds. He was a moral god, frequently associated with the higher developments of civilization, such as law, philosophy, and the arts. As patron of music and poetry he was often connected with the Muses. Apollo may have been first worshiped by primitive shepherds as a god of pastures and flocks, but it was as a god of light, Phoebus or Phoebus

Apollo, that he was most widely known. After the 5th cent. B.C. he was frequently identified with Helios, the sun god. Although Apollo was the father of Aristaeus, Asclepius, and, in some legends, Orpheus, his amorous affairs were not particularly successful. Daphne turned into a laurel rather than submit to him, and Marpessa refused him in favor of a mortal. The cult of Apollo was Panhellenic, and the prophecies of his oracles bore great authority. His chief oracular shrine was at Delphi, which he was said to have seized, while still an infant, by killing its guardian, the serpent Python. This event was celebrated every eight years in the festival of the Stepteria, in which a youth impersonating Apollo set fire to a hut (called the palace of Python) and then went into exile to Tempe, where he was purified of his deed. At Delphi, Apollo was primarily a god of purification. He had other notable shrines at Branchidae, Claros, Patara, and on the island of Delos, where, it was said, he and his twin sister, Artemis, were born to Leto and Zeus. In Roman religion, in which he was also known as Apollo, he was worshiped in various forms, most significantly as a god of healing and of prophecy. In art he was portrayed as the perfection of youth and beauty. The most celebrated statue of him is the **Apollo Belvedere,** a marble statue in the Belvedere of the Vatican, Rome; it is a Roman copy, dating from the early empire, of a Greek original in bronze. The right forearm and the left hand were restored by a pupil of Michelangelo. The statue represents the god as a vigorous and triumphant youth, naked except for the chlamys draped over his extended left arm.

Apollo Belvedere: see APOLLO, in Greek religion.

Apollodorus (əpŏl″ōdôr′əs), fl. 430–400 B.C., Athenian painter, called the Shadower, said to have introduced the use of light and shade to model form. Among his few known works are *Ajax Struck by Lightning* and *Priest in the Act of Devotion;* both were at Pergamum in the time of Pliny the Elder; none has survived.

Apollodorus (of Athens), fl. 2d cent. B.C., Greek grammarian and historian. He wrote many works on grammar, history, and mythology. His best-known books, only fragments of which survive, are *On the Gods,* a prose treatise; and *Chronicle,* a verse work treating Greek history from the fall of Troy. He may also have written the *Library,* a valuable work on Greek mythology that may be an abridgment of *On the Gods.*

Apollodorus of Damascus, Roman architect and engineer, fl. late 1st to early 2nd cent. A.D., b. Syria. Apollodorus was responsible for nearly all buildings designed under Trajan, for whom he was official architect. Known for his use of symmetry and axial organization, Apollodorus produced his greatest achievement in the Forum of Trajan (see FORUM) and Trajan's Column (see ROMAN ART), in which he expressed simple grandeur and preserved a marked Hellenic spirit. His treatise *Engines of War* survives.

Apollonia (ăpəlō′nēə) [Gr.,=of Apollo], name of several ancient Greek towns. The most important was a port in Illyria on the Adriatic. It was founded by Corinthians and was later a Greek and a Roman intellectual center. Julius Caesar used it as a base. Octavian (later AUGUSTUS) received news of Julius Caesar's death while stationed at Apollonia. Among the other towns of this name, there was one in Thrace on the Aegean (a town famous for a large statue of Apollo), one in N Sicily, and another in Chalcidice (Khalkidhikí), which was visited by Paul on his way to Salonica (Acts 17.1).

Apollonius (ăp″əlō′nēəs). **1** Governor of Coele-Syria and Phoenicia for Seleucus IV. He oppressed the Jews and was killed by Judas Maccabaeus. 1 Mac. 3.10–24; 2 Mac. 4.4; 5.24. **2** Governor of Coele-Syria under Alexander Balas. 1 Mac. 10.69.

Apollonius of Perga, fl. 247–205 B.C., Greek mathematician of the Alexandrian school. He produced a treatise on conic sections that included, as well as his own work, much of the work of his predecessors, among whom was Euclid. Apollonius introduced the terms *parabola, hyperbola,* and *ellipse.* In his works Greek mathematics reached its culmination.

Apollonius of Tralles: see FARNESE BULL.

Apollonius Rhodius (rō′dēəs), fl. 3d cent. B.C., epic poet of Alexandria and Rhodes. He became librarian at Alexandria. His extant work, the *Argonautica,* is a Homeric imitation in four books on the story of the Argonaut heroes. He and CALLIMACHUS carried on a famous literary quarrel.

Apollos (əpŏl′əs), Alexandrian Jew who became a Christian missionary. Acts 18.24–19.1; 1 Cor. 1.12; 3.4–6; 4.6.

Apollo space program: see SPACE EXPLORATION.

Apollyon (əpŏl′yən), Greek name of the destroying angel. Rev. 9.11. See SATAN; HELL.

apology [from Gr.,=defense), literary work that defends, justifies, or clarifies an author's ideas or point of view. Unlike the ordinary use of the word, the literary use neither implies that wrong has been done nor expresses regret. The most famous ancient example, Plato's *Apology* (3d cent. B.C.), presents Socrates' defense of himself at his trial before the Athenian government. Sir Philip Sidney's *Apologie for Poetrie* and *Defense of Poesie* (both: 1580), which examine the art of poetry and its condition in England, apparently were written to justify the poets' craft after it had been attacked by critics. A third famous example, Cardinal Newman's spiritual autobiography *Apologia pro Vita sua* (1864), was written to clarify the Cardinal's views after they had been misrepresented in an essay by Charles Kingsley.

apoplexy or **stroke,** destruction of brain tissue as a result of intracerebral hemorrhage, THROMBOSIS (clotting), or embolism (obstruction in a blood vessel caused by clotted blood or other foreign matter circulating in the blood stream). Cerebral hemorrhage or thrombosis usually occurs in elderly persons with constricted arteries (see ARTERIOSCLEROSIS) although either may also be caused by inflammatory or toxic damage to the cerebral blood vessels. Cerebral embolism may occur at any age, even in children. Symptoms of stroke develop suddenly. In cases of severe brain damage there may be deep coma, paralysis of one side of the body, and loss of speech, followed by death or by permanent neurological disturbances after recovery. If the brain damage sustained has been slight, there is usually complete recovery. When the stroke has been caused by thrombosis or by an EMBOLUS, anticoagulants are helpful in certain cases; sometimes surgical removal of the clot is possible.

apostle (əpŏs′əl) [Gr.,=envoy], one of the prime missionaries of Christianity. The apostles of the first rank are saints PETER, ANDREW, JAMES (the Greater), JOHN, THOMAS, JAMES (the Less), JUDE (or Thaddaeus), PHILIP, BARTHOLOMEW, MATTHEW, SIMON, and MATTHIAS (replacing JUDAS ISCARIOT). Traditionally the list of the Twelve Disciples includes Judas and not Matthias, and the list of the Twelve Apostles includes Matthias and not Judas. St. PAUL is always classed as an apostle, and so sometimes are a few others, such as St. BARNABAS. The principal missionary to any country is often called its apostle, e.g., St. Patrick is the apostle of Ireland, and St. Augustine of Canterbury the apostle of England. For the Apostles' Creed, see CREED; for the *Teaching of the Apostles,* see DIDACHE; for the earliest account of their activities, see ACTS OF THE APOSTLES. See E. J. Goodspeed, *The Twelve: The Story of Christ's Apostles* (1957, repr. 1962).

Apostle Islands, group of more than 20 wooded islands, in Lake Superior, off N Wis. Madeline, 13 mi (21 km) long, is the largest island and has the group's only settlement, La Pointe. Noted for their wave-eroded cliffs and abundant wildlife, the islands are visited by tourists and hunters. The islands, along with an 11 mi (18 km) strip of the adjacent shoreline, make up Apostle Islands National Lakeshore (see NATIONAL PARKS AND MONUMENTS, table).

Apostolic Constitutions: see CONSTITUTIONS, APOSTOLIC.

apostolic delegate: see LEGATE.

apostolic succession, in Christian theology, the doctrine asserting that the chosen successors of the apostles enjoyed through God's grace the same authority, power, and responsibility as was conferred upon the apostles by Christ. Therefore present-day bishops, as the successors of previous bishops, going back to the apostles, have this power by virtue of this unbroken chain. For the Orthodox, Roman Catholic, and Anglican churches, this link with the apostles is what guarantees for them their authority in matters of faith, morals, and the valid administration of sacraments. Essential to maintaining the apostolic succession is the right consecration of bishops. Apostolic succession is to be distinguished from the Petrine supremacy (see PAPACY). Protestants (other than Anglican) see the authority given to the apostles as unique, proper to them alone, and hence reject any doctrine of a succession of their power. The Protestant view of ecclesiastical authority differs accordingly. See ORDERS, HOLY; CHURCH.

apostrophe: see PUNCTUATION; ABBREVIATION.

apostrophe, figure of speech in which an absent person, a personified inanimate being, or an abstraction is addressed as though present. The term is derived from a Greek word meaning "a turning away," and this sense is maintained when a narrative or dramatic thread is broken in order to digress by speaking directly to someone not there, e.g., "Envy, be silent and attend!"—Alexander Pope, "On a Certain Lady at Court."

apothecaries weight: see ENGLISH UNITS OF MEASUREMENT.

apotheosis (əpŏth″ēō′sĭs), the act of raising a person who has died to the rank of a god. Historically, it was most important during the later Roman Empire. In an emperor's lifetime his genius was worshiped, but after he died he was often solemnly enrolled as one of the gods to be publicly adored. Apotheosis is closely related to ANCESTOR WORSHIP.

Appaim (ăp′āĭm), Jerahmeelite. 1 Chron. 2.30, 31.

Appalachia, region: see APPALACHIAN MOUNTAINS.

Appalachian Mountains (ăpəlā′chən, -chēən, -lăch′-), mountain system of E North America, extending in a broad belt c.1,600 mi (2,570 km) SW from the St. Lawrence valley in Quebec prov., Canada, to the Gulf coastal plain in Alabama. Main sections in the system are the White Mts., Green Mts., Taconic Mts., Catskill Mts., Allegheny Mts., Black Mts., Great Smoky Mts., the Blue Ridge, and the Cumberland Plateau. The Appalachian Mts., much-eroded remnants of a great mountain mass formed by folding (see MOUNTAINS), consist largely of sedimentary rocks. In general the eastern portions are more rugged than the western, which are mainly of horizontal rock structure. Mt. Mitchell (6,684 ft/2,037 m) in the Black Mts. is the highest peak. The Great Appalachian Valley is a chain of lowlands extending along most of the system's length; its main segments are the St. Lawrence Lowland, Lake Champlain Lowland, Lebanon Valley, Cumberland Valley, Shenandoah Valley, the Valley of Virginia, and the Valley of East Tennessee. The Great Valley has long been an important north-south highway and is one of the most fertile areas in the E United States. The Appalachians themselves are rich in mineral resources, including coal, iron, petroleum, and natural gas. The scenic ranges also abound in resorts and recreation areas; Shenandoah and Great Smoky Mts. national parks are in the region, and the APPALACHIAN TRAIL winds 2,050 mi (3,299 km) along the Appalachian crest from Mt. Katahdin, Maine, to Springer Mt., Georgia. Crossed by few passes, the Appalachians, especially their central portion, were a barrier to early westward expansion and played an important role in U.S. history; major east-west routes followed river valleys and gaps (see CUMBERLAND GAP). See N. M. Fenneman, *Physiography of the Eastern United States* (1938); R. H. Brown, *Historical Geography of the United States* (1948); I. R. Ford, ed., *The Southern Appalachian Region* (1962); Eliot Porter, *Appalachian Wilderness* (1970); H. M. Caudill, *Night Comes to the Cumberlands* (1963) and *My Land is Dying* (1971).

Appalachian Trail, world's longest continuous hiking path, 2,050 mi (3,299 km) long, passing through 14 states, E United States. Conceived in 1921 by Benton Mackaye, forester and regional planner, and completed in 1937, the trail extends along the ridges of the Appalachian Mts. from Mt. Katahdin, Maine, to Springer Mt., Ga. It passes through eight national forests and two national parks, but the greatest part of its length is on private property. Hiking and trail clubs maintain shelters and campsites along the path. The trail was designated a national scenic trail in 1968 (see NATIONAL PARKS AND MONUMENTS, table).

Appaloosa horse, breed of LIGHT HORSE developed in the United States by the Nez Percé Indians of Idaho from a horse that originated in Asia and was popular in Europe during the Middle Ages. Lewis and Clark found the breed in the possession of the Nez Percé in 1805. The Appaloosa is characterized by a spotted pattern of markings; it most commonly has solid-colored foreparts and small, dark, round or oval spots over the loin and hips. Famed for its intelligence, speed, stamina, and endurance, it is an outstanding stock and show horse of great popularity. It stands just over 14 hands (56 in./140 cm) and weighs about 1,100 lb (500 kg).

apparent magnitude: see MAGNITUDE.

apparent solar time: see SOLAR TIME.

apparition, spiritualistic manifestation of a person or object in which a form not actually present is seen with such intensity that belief in its reality is created. The ancient and widespread belief in apparitions and ghosts (specters of dead persons) is based on the idea that the spirit of a man, or of any object, is endowed with volition and motion of its own. Apparitions, especially particular shapes attached to certain legends or superstitions, are often considered as premonitions or warnings. They may appear in any form and may manifest themselves to any or all the senses. The most evil apparitions are said to be those of persons who have died violent or unnatural deaths, those with guilty secrets, and those who were improperly buried. However, not all apparitions are believed to be dangerous; many, especially those associated with a particular religion, are thought to be signs of divine intervention. Summoning apparitions by means of incantations, crystal gazing, polished stones, hypnotic suggestion, and various other ways is one of the oldest practices of DIVINATION. See SPIRITISM. See also Andrew MacKenzie, *A Gallery of Ghosts* (1973).

appeal, in law, hearing by a superior court to consider correcting or reversing the judgment of an inferior court, because of errors allegedly committed by the inferior court. The party appealing the decision is known as the appellant, the party who has won the case in the lower court as the appellee. The term is also sometimes used to describe the review by a court of the action of a government board or administrative officer. Appellate procedure is set by statute. There are two types of errors, of fact and of law. An error of fact is drawing a false inference from evidence presented at the trial. An error of law is an erroneous determination of the legal rules governing PROCEDURE, EVIDENCE, or the matters at issue between the parties. Ordinarily, only errors of law may be reviewed in appeal. In an appeal from an action tried in EQUITY, however, the appellate court passes on the entire record, both as to facts and law. Should the appeals court conclude that no error was committed, it will affirm the decision of the lower court. If it finds that there was error, it may direct a retrial or grant a JUDGMENT or DECREE in favor of the party who lost in the lower court. The determinations of appeals courts are usually printed, often with an opinion indicating the basis for the court's decisions. Such opinions are of great utility in guiding the inferior courts and are often cited as precedents in future cases.

Appel, Karel (kä'rəl äp'əl), 1921–, Dutch painter. A member of CoBrA, the European group allied with ABSTRACT EXPRESSIONISM, Appel reacted against the austerity of earlier Dutch abstraction. Characterized by informal brush work, bright, bold color, and a slashing line, Appel's paintings often possess a childlike quality. Examples of his work are in the Boymans-Van Beuningen Museum, Rotterdam.

appendix, small, worm-shaped blind tube, about 3 in. (7.6 cm) long and ¼ in. to 1 in. (.64–2.54 cm) thick, projecting from the cecum (large intestine) on the right side of the lower abdominal cavity. The structure, also called the vermiform appendix, has no function in man and is considered a vestigial remnant of some previous organ or structure, having a digestive function, that became unnecessary to man in his evolutionary progress (see DIGESTIVE SYSTEM). Infection of accumulated and hardened waste matter in the appendix may give rise to appendicitis, the symptoms of which are severe pain in the abdomen, nausea, vomiting, fever, abdominal tenderness, and muscle spasm. A blood count usually shows a rise in the number of white corpuscles. Appendicitis may occur at any age, although it is more prevalent in persons under 40 years of age. The danger in appendicitis is that the appendix can rupture, either spontaneously or because the patient has injudiciously been given laxatives or an enema, and that the infection can spread to the peritoneum (see PERITONITIS). Surgery is indicated in appendicitis, preceded and followed by antibiotic therapy.

Appenzell (ä'pəntsĕl), canton, NE Switzerland. A rural and sparsely populated region, it is mainly a meadowland dotted with small farms. Appenzell retains many ancient customs and has been famous for centuries as a textile and embroidery center. It was ruled after the 11th cent. by the abbots of St. Gall, against whom it revolted in 1403. In 1411, Appenzell allied itself with the Swiss Confederation, which had helped defeat the abbots. It became a Swiss canton in 1513, and in 1597 it was split into two independent half cantons. Ausser-Rhoden or Outer Rhodes (1970 pop. 49,023), 94 sq mi (243 sq km), with its capital at HERISAU, accepted the Reformation; Inner-Rhoden or Inner Rhodes (1970 pop. 13,124), 67 sq mi (174 sq km), with its capital at the town of Appenzell (1970 pop. 5,217), remained Catholic.

Appert, Nicolas (nēkôlä' äpâr'), also known as **François Appert** (fräNswä'), 1750–1841, French originator of a method of CANNING. In 1795 the French government offered a prize of 12,000 francs for a method of preserving food, especially for use by the army and navy. Appert, already an experienced chef, began to experiment in his workshop at Massy, near Paris, and in 1810 was awarded the prize for his method. The method, based on the idea that heat destroys or neutralizes the ferments that cause food spoilage, involved cooking foods in corked jars. Appert published several editions of his results (*The Art of Preserving,* tr. 1920) and with his prize money opened the first commercial cannery in the world.

Apphia (ăf'ēə), Christian woman associated with Philemon. Philemon 2.

Appia, Adolphe (ädôlf' äp'pyä), 1862–1928, Swiss theorist of modern stage lighting and decor. In interpreting Wagner's ideas in scenic designs for his operas, Appia rejected painted scenery for the three-dimensional set; he felt that shade was as necessary as light to link the actor to this setting in time and space. His use of light, through intensity, color, and mobility, to set the atmosphere and mood of a play created a new perspective in SCENE DESIGN AND STAGE LIGHTING. See his *Work of Living Art* and *Man Is the Measure of All Things,* in a single volume, ed. by Barnard Hewitt (tr. 1960); study by W. R. Volbach (1968).

Appian (ăp'ēən), fl. 2d cent., Roman historian. He was a Greek, born in Alexandria. His history of the Roman conquests from the founding of Rome to the reign of Trajan is strongly biased in favor of Roman imperialism, but it reproduces many documents and sources that otherwise would have been lost. Of the 24 books, written in Greek, only Books VI–VII and Books XI–XVII have been fully preserved.

Appiani, Andrea (ändrĕ'ä äp-pyä'nē), 1754–1817, Italian neoclassical painter and Italian court painter of Napoleon I, active in Lombardy. His frescoes include work in churches and palaces of Milan. In his portraits his style anticipated the romantic approach. Portraits of Napoleon (1796; Bellagio) and Canova are among his oils.

Appian Way (ăp'ēən), Lat. *Via Appia,* most famous of the ROMAN ROADS, built (312 B.C.) under Appius Claudius Caecus. It connected Rome with Capua and was later extended to Beneventum (now Benevento), Tarentum (Taranto), and Brundisium (Brindisi). It was the chief highway to Greece and the East. Its total length was more than 350 mi (563 km). The substantial construction of cemented stone blocks has preserved it to the present. Branch roads led to Neapolis (Naples), Barium (Bari), and other ports. On the first stretch of road out of Rome are interesting tombs and the Church of St. Sebastian with its catacombs. In 1784, Pope Pius VI built the new Appian Way from Rome to Albano, parallel with the old.

Appii forum (ăp'ēī) [Lat.,=Appius' market], important stop on the Appian Way, c.40 mi (64 km) E of Rome. It was at the head of a canal through the Pontine Marshes. When Paul arrived here on his way to Rome, he was met by Christians from the city (Acts 28.15). The modern Italian successor is Foro Appio.

Appius Claudius: see CLAUDIUS, Roman gens.

apple, any tree (and its fruit) of the genus *Malus* of the family Rosaceae (ROSE family). Apples were formerly considered species of the pear genus *Pyrus,* with which they share the characteristic pome fruit. The common apple (*M. sylvestris*) is the best known and is commercially the most important temperate fruit. Apparently native to the Caucasus mts. of W Asia, it has been under cultivation since prehistoric times. According to ancient tradition the forbidden fruit of the Garden of Eden was the apple (Gen. 3). In religious painting, the apple represents the fruit of the tree of knowledge of good and evil, as do occasionally the pear and the quince. It was sacred to Aphrodite in classical mythology. The apple is now widely grown in thousands of varieties, e.g., the Golden Delicious, Winesap, Jonathan, and McIntosh. The tree is hardy in cold climates, and the firm fruit is easy to handle and store. Most apples are consumed fresh, but some are canned or used for juice. Apple juice (sweet cider) is partly fermented to produce hard cider and fully fermented to make vinegar. Wastes from fermenting processes are a major source of PECTIN. APPLEJACK is a liquor made from hard cider. Western Europe, especially France, is the chief apple-producing region; in North America, also with an enormous total output, Washington is the leading apple-growing state, but very many areas grow crops at least for local consumption. The tree is subject to several insect and fungus pests, for which the orchards are sprayed. The hardwood is used for cabinetmaking and fuel. The crab apples are wild North American and Asiatic species of *Malus* now cultivated as ornamentals for their fragrant white to deep pink blossoms—e.g., the American sweet, or garland, crab apple (*M. coronaria*), the prairie crab apple (*M. ioensis*), and the Siberian crabapple (*M. baccata*). The small, hard, sour crabapple fruits are used for preserves, pickles, and jelly; in growth and culture these trees are similar to the common apple. Apples are classified in the division MAGNOLIOPHYTA, class Magnoliopsida, order Rosales, family Rosaceae.

Applegarth, Robert, 1834–1924, English trade union leader, a carpenter by trade. A charter member of the Amalgamated Society of Carpenters and Joiners, he became in 1862 its general secretary. Under his leadership the society, with other unions, pressed the fight for legalization of unions and for protection of their funds. The fight was successfully concluded in 1871. See biography by A. W. Humphrey (1913); John Bowditch and Clement Ramsland, *Voices of the Industrial Revolution* (1961).

Applegate, Jesse, 1811–88, American pioneer in Oregon, b. Kentucky. With his family he moved (1821) to Missouri, and there in 1843 he joined the "great emigration" of more than 900 people over the Oregon Trail—a trek pictured in his *Day with the Cow Column in 1843* (ed. by Joseph Schafer, 1934, pub. with *Recollections of My Boyhood* by Applegate's nephew). A leader on the westward journey, he was elected (1845) a member of the legislative committee of the provisional government that ruled Oregon until it became (1849) a U.S. territory. Later he helped organize the new government and, as surveyor general, did much exploring and opened a wagon route to California.

applejack, brandy made by distilling hard cider or fermented apple pomace. Another method of making applejack, now rarely used, is to let fermented cider freeze and then to remove the ice. It was one of the most popular drinks among the early settlers of North America and remained so for a long time in rural areas.

apple maggot, larva of a FRUIT FLY, *Rhagoletis pomonella.*

apple of discord: see PARIS, in Greek mythology.

Appleseed, Johnny: see CHAPMAN, JOHN.

Appleton, Daniel, 1785–1849, American publisher, b. Haverhill, Mass. The owner of a general store in Boston, he moved to New York in 1826, where he established one of the largest publishing houses in the country. The firm was continued by his sons under the name D. Appleton & Company. It eventually was renamed Appleton-Century-Crofts, Inc.

Appleton, Sir Edward Victor, 1892–1965, English physicist, grad. St. John's College, Cambridge. After returning from active service in World War I he became assistant demonstrator in experimental physics at the Cavendish Laboratory in 1920. He was professor of physics at the Univ. of London (1924–36) and professor of natural philosophy at Cambridge Univ. (1936–39). From 1939 to 1949 he was secretary of the Dept. of Scientific and Industrial Research. Knighted in 1941, he received the 1947 Nobel Prize in Physics for his contributions to the knowledge of the ionosphere, which led to the development of radar. See study by R. W. Clark (1971).

Appleton, city (1970 pop. 57,143), seat of Outagamie co., E Wis., on the Fox River near its exit from the northern end of Lake Winnebago, in a dairying and stockraising region; inc. 1857. Waterfalls provide power for the city's industries, which produce paper, wood, metal, concrete, knitted goods, and dairy products. Appleton had the nation's first hydroelectric plant (1882) and the state's first electric streetcar (1886). The city is the seat of Lawrence Univ. Harry Houdini was born there.

apple worm: see CODLING MOTH.

appliqué: see EMBROIDERY; NEEDLEWORK.

Appomattox (ăpəmăt'əks), town (1970 pop. 1,400), seat of Appomattox co., central Va.; inc. 1925. Confederate general Robert E. Lee surrendered to Union general Ulysses S. Grant at nearby **Appomattox Courthouse** on April 9, 1865. After Gen. Philip Sheridan's victory over the Confederates at Five Forks on April 1, Lee abandoned Petersburg and Richmond and retreated westward, planning to unite with the army of Gen. Joseph Johnston near Danville, Va. Grant pursued, pressing Lee's flank and rear, while Sheridan cut off further retreat at Appomattox Courthouse. Severed from supplies and surrounded by Union forces, Lee surrendered the remnants of the Army of Northern Virginia to Grant at the McLean House on April 9. The surrender marked the virtual end of the war, as the remaining Confederate armies, on hearing of Lee's act, followed suit. The site of the surrender has been made a national historical park (see NATIONAL PARKS AND MONUMENTS, table).

Apponaug, R.I.: see WARWICK.

apprenticeship, system of learning a craft or trade from one who is engaged in it and of paying for the instruction by a given number of years of work. The practice was known in ancient Babylon, Egypt, Greece, and Rome, as well as in modern Europe and to some extent in the United States. Typically, in medieval Europe, a master craftsman agreed to instruct a young man, to give him shelter, food, and clothing, and to care for him during illness. The apprentice would bind himself to work for the master for a given time. After that specified time he would become a journeyman, working for a master for wages, or he might set up as a master himself. The medieval guilds supervised the relation of master and apprentice and decided the number of apprentices in a given guild. The Industrial Revolution, with its introduction of machinery, put an end to most of these guilds, but apprenticeship continues in highly skilled trades, at times competing with technical schools. The terms of apprenticeship are regulated by many trade unions, as well as by law. The apprenticeship programs in Europe today differ from those in Great Britain and the United States by providing training in areas other than the skilled crafts. In Great Britain apprenticeship programs sometimes include outside schooling at company expense. In the United States, Wisconsin in the early 1900s established a system of apprenticeships; it proved so successful that the U.S. Congress adopted a similar system in 1937. After a lapse in the 1950s, Congress passed (1962) the Manpower Development and Training Act to encourage apprenticeship programs. See Andrew Beveridge, *Apprenticeship Now* (1963); N. F. Duffy, ed., *Essays on Apprenticeship* (1967).

appropriation, in constitutional law, allotment by a legislature of money for a particular purpose. In the United States, for example, the Constitution provides that no money may be drawn from the Treasury except under appropriations made by law and that no appropriations shall be made for more than two years. In the United States a general appropriation bill is passed at the beginning of each session of Congress; in England, at the end of sessions of Parliament. See also BUDGET.

APRA (ä'prä), or the *Alianza Popular Revolucionaria Americana,* also called the Partido Aprista, reformist political party in Peru. Founded (1924) by Victor Raul HAYA DE LA TORRE while in exile, the party's Peruvian activities were led by Jose Carlos MARIÁTEGUI until Haya de la Torre's return to Peru in 1931. The party's program advocates social reform, particularly the emancipation of the Indian, the betterment of agrarian conditions, and the socialization of some industries. Originally committed to revolutionary change, the party gradually assumed a less radical stance, so that by the late 1960s it was a moderately reformist group, rather than a revolutionary organization. Characterized as rabble rousers and implicated in acts of political terror, the Apristas were outlawed from 1931 to 1945. During the early part of that period the Apristas engaged in continual gun battles with the military, thus creating an enduring enmity between the two groups. In 1945 the party was legalized, and it joined in a coalition government under Jose Luis Bustamente. In 1948, following an abortive revolt of dissident Apristas in the port city of Callao and with the country on the verge of civil war, a military junta headed by General Manuel ODRIA took power, and the party was again outlawed. Gradually becoming less radical, the APRA party was again legalized (1956) when Manuel Prado, a conservative, was elected president with its support. In the 1962 presidential election, Haya de la Torre won a slight plurality, but the military, remembering its earlier feuds with the party and still distrustful of it, immediately seized the government. Civilian rule was restored in the next year, and the Apristas were allowed to function freely. However, the military coup of 1968 led to the outlawing of all political activity, including that of the Apristas. Since the coup, Aprista groups are allowed to meet as social clubs, but they are not permitted to engage in any political organizing. The party continues to enjoy widespread popularity throughout Peru.

Apra Harbor (ä'prä) or **Port Apra,** port on the west coast of the island of GUAM, W Pacific, in the MARIANAS ISLANDS. The only good harbor on the island, it is a port of entry closed to foreign vessels except by permit. There is a large U.S. naval base used for maintenance of the Seventh Fleet and Polaris submarines.

Apraksin, Feodor Matveyevich (fyô'dər mətvyā'əvĭch əpräk'syĭn), 1671–1728, Russian admiral. He helped Peter I (Peter the Great) create the Russian navy and won several naval battles in Peter's wars against Sweden. He was made a count in 1709.

apricot [Arabic from Lat., = early ripe], tree, *Prunus armeniaca,* and its fruit, of the plum genus of the family Rosaceae (ROSE family), native to temperate Asia and long cultivated in Armenia. The fruit is used raw, canned, preserved, and dried. California is the chief place of cultivation in the United States, although by selecting suitable varieties the apricot can be grown in most regions where the peach is hardy. Apricots are used in the making of a cordial and also for apricot brandy. Apricots are classified in the division MAGNOLIOPHYTA, class Magnoliopsida, order Rosales, family Rosaceae.

Apries (ā'prē-ēz), king of ancient Egypt (588–569 B.C.), of the XXVI dynasty; successor of Psamtik II. Apries sought to recover Syria and Palestine. He attacked Tyre and Sidon but failed (586 B.C.) to relieve the siege of Jerusalem by NEBUCHADNEZZAR. A revolt in Egypt caused him to seek assistance from AMASIS II, who assassinated him and seized the throne. Apries is called Pharaoh-hophra in the Bible (Jer. 44.30).

April: see MONTH.

April Fool's Day or **All Fool's Day,** holiday of uncertain origin, consecrated to practical joking and celebrated on the first of April. Prior to the adoption of the Gregorian calendar in 1564, the date was observed as New Year's Day by cultures as varied as the Roman and the Hindu. The holiday is considered to be related to the festival of the vernal equinox, which occurs on March 21. The English gave April Fool's Day its first widespread celebration during the 18th cent.

apse, the termination at the sanctuary end of a church, generally semicircular in plan but sometimes square or polygonal. The apse appeared early in Roman temples and basilicas; it was originally a semicircular recess with a half dome as ceiling and contained the monumental statue of the deity. The motif was adopted in the early Christian churches; in these the apse occupied the eastern end of the building where the altar, the bishop's throne, and the seats of the clergy were placed. A fine example of this early form is in the cathedral of Torcello near Venice. Because of its location and function in the church services, the apse became the architectural climax of the church interior and was richly ornamented. In the early churches, the half-dome ceiling was incrusted with handsome mosaics, the walls were veneered with fine marbles, and the altar and pulpits were also richly decorated. As the apse steadily increased in liturgical and architectural emphasis, chapels were added to it. In English Gothic architecture the apse was in most cases a square termination, and in Italy its form remained a simple semicircle, as the chapels were in another part of the church. In France the entire choir—composed of apse, ambulatory, and radiating chapels (the whole termed a *chevet*)—attained, in the 12th and 13th cent., its great splendor.

Apsheron (əpshĭrôn'), peninsula, c.40 mi (60 km) long, extending into the Caspian Sea, E Azerbaijan, SW USSR. It is a dry, hilly area at the eastern end of the Greater Caucasus mts. and is underlain by rich oil-bearing rock strata. The oil industry developed there in the 1870s, although the presence of oil was known long before. The peninsula, with its Baku oil fields, was once the USSR's chief oil-producing region but now accounts for a small portion of Soviet production. Natural gas wells, salt lakes, mineral springs, and mud volcanoes are also found on Apsheron. BAKU is the region's chief city, and the peninsula falls within the boundaries of Greater Baku.

apsides (ăp"sīdēz'): see APSIS.

apsis (pl. apsides), point in the ORBIT of a body where the body is neither approaching nor receding from another body about which it revolves. Any elliptical orbit has two apsides. At the perigee the moon or other satellite is as close as it ever gets to the earth, and it begins to move away; at the apogee it is as far away as it gets, and it begins to move closer. Similarly, in the orbit of the earth or another planet around the sun, the perihelion is the point of closest approach and the aphelion is the point of farthest recession. In the orbit of the stars in a BINARY STAR system, the periastron is the point of closest approach and the apastron the point of farthest recession. A line connecting the two apsidal points of an elliptical orbit (e.g., the aphelion and perihelion) is called the line of apsides; it is the major axis of the ellipse. This line may precess because of gravitational influences of other bodies or relativistic effects.

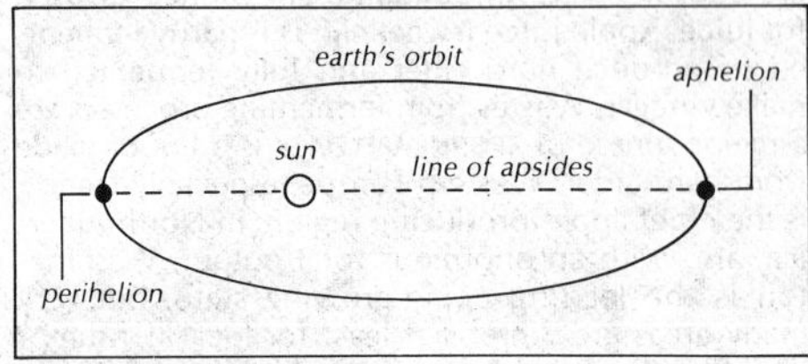

Apsis points, or apsides, in the earth's orbit: At perihelion the earth is closest to the sun and at aphelion it is farthest from the sun.

apteryx (ăp'tərĭks): see KIWI.

Apuleius, Lucius (ă"pyo͞olē'əs), fl. 2d cent., Latin writer, b. Hippo (now Bône, Algeria). His romance *The Golden Ass* or *Metamorphoses* is the only Latin novel to survive in entirety. It tells the story of Lucius of Corinth, who is transformed into an ass by a Thessalian woman and undergoes a series of strange and exciting adventures before he is restored to human form. *The Golden Ass* has been tremendously popular, influencing strongly the history of the novel, e.g., the works of Boccaccio, Cervantes, Fielding, and Smollett. Other works by Apuleius include *The Apology* or *On Magic,* his defense in a suit brought by his wife's family for gaining her affections by magic; *Florida,* an anthology from his own works; and *On the God of Socrates, On the Philosophy of Plato,* and *On the World,* philosophical treatises. See study by H. E. Butler and A. S. Owen (1914).

Apulia (əpyo͞o'lēə), Ital. *Puglia,* region (1971 pop. 3,562,377), 7,469 sq mi (19,345 sq km), S Italy, bordering on the Adriatic Sea in the east and the Strait of Otranto and Gulf of Taranto in the south. Its southern portion, a peninsula, forms the heel of the Italian "boot." BARI is the capital of the region, which is divided into Bari, Brindisi, Foggia, Lecce, and Taranto provs. (named for their capitals). Apulia is mostly a plain; its low coast, however, is broken by the mountainous Garagano Peninsula in the north, and there are mountains in the north central part of the region. Farming is the chief occupation, but industry is expanding. Farm products include olives, grapes, cereals, almonds, figs, tobacco, and livestock (sheep, pigs, cattle, and goats). Manufactures include refined petroleum, chemicals, plastics, fertilizer, and wine. There are saltworks in the north and bauxite mines in the south. Fishing is pursued in the Adriatic and in the Gulf of Taranto. The scarcity of water has long been an acute problem in Apulia, and it is necessary to carry drinking water by aqueduct across the Apennines from the Sele River in Campania. In ancient times only the northern part of the region was called Apulia; the southern peninsula was known as Calabria, a name later used to designate the toe of the Italian boot. The region was settled by several Italic peoples and by Greek colonists before it was conquered (4th cent. B.C.) by Rome. After the fall of Rome, Apulia was held successively by the Goths, the Lombards, and the Byzantines. In the 11th cent. it was conquered by the Normans; ROBERT GUISCARD set up the duchy of Apulia in 1059. After the Norman conquest of Sicily (late 11th cent.), Palermo replaced MELFI (just west of present-day Apulia) as the center of Norman power, and Apulia became a mere province, first of the kingdom of Sicily, then of the kingdom of Naples. From the late 12th to early 13th cent. Apulia was a favorite residence of the Hohenstaufen emperors, notably Frederick II. The coast later was occupied at times by the Turks and by the Venetians. In 1861 the region joined Italy. The feudal system long prevailed in the rural areas of Apulia; social and agrarian reforms proceeded slowly from the 19th cent. and accelerated in the mid-20th cent. The characteristic Apulian architecture of the 11th–13th cent. reflects Greek, Arabic, Norman, and Pisan influences. There are universities at Bari and Lecce.

Apure (äpo͞o'rā), river, c.500 mi (800 km) long, rising in the Andes, N Colombia, and flowing E across W central Venezuela to the Orinoco River. It drains much of the western portion of the Orinoco basin and is navigable by river steamers for c.400 mi (640 km) during the rainy season. There is extensive livestock ranching along the Apure. The Portuguesa River is the chief tributary.

Apurímac (äpo͞orē'mäk), river, c.550 mi (885 km) long, rising in the Andes, S Peru. It flows generally northwest in a narrow valley to join the Urubamba River and form the Ucayali, which is one of the main headstreams of the Amazon.

Aqaba (ä'käbä), town (1964 est. pop. 10,000), SW Jordan, at the head of the Gulf of Aqaba, on the border with Israel. It is the only Jordanian port with direct access to the Red Sea. Phosphates are the chief export. Aqaba is also a popular winter seaside resort. Since at least 1000 B.C., a port has existed continuously on the site to handle trade between Palestine and Syria. Aqaba stands on or near the biblical Elath (Elat). The Roman military post of Aelana later occupied the site. A great road built under Emperor Trajan linked the area with Damascus and Egypt. Occupied and fortified by the Crusaders in 1115, Aqaba was retaken by SALADIN in 1187. During the 19th cent. the town became a staging point on the pilgrim route to Mecca. T. E. Lawrence (Lawrence of Arabia) captured Aqaba for the Allies in World War I; it later became part of the Hejaz but was ceded to Trans-Jordan in 1924. The town's name is sometimes spelled Akaba.

Aqaba, Gulf of, northern arm of the Red Sea, 118 mi (190 km) long and 10 mi (16.1 km) wide, between the Sinai and Arabian peninsulas; a part of the Great Rift Valley. The gulf, which is entered through the Straits of Tiran, has played a major role in the tensions between Israel and the Arab states (Egypt, Jordan, Saudi Arabia) bordering it. Aqaba, with the Israeli port of Elat at its head, has been Israel's only direct access to E Africa, Asia, and Australia since it was barred by Egypt from using the Suez Canal. The Gulf of Aqaba was blockaded by the Arabs from 1949 to 1956 and again in 1967, although it was declared (1958) an international waterway by the United Nations. In the wake of the 1967 Arab-Israeli war, Israel occupied strategic points along the Straits of Tiran to insure open passage of its shipping.

Aqsu: see A-K'O-SU, China.

aquaculture: see HYDROPONICS.

aqua fortis (ăk'wə fôr'tĭs): see NITRIC ACID.

aquamarine (ăk"wəmərēn') [Lat.,=sea water], transparent BERYL with a blue or bluish-green color. Sources of the gems include Brazil, Siberia, Burma, the Malagasy Republic, and parts of the United States. Oriental aquamarine is a transparent crystalline corundum with a bluish tinge. The emerald is similar in composition, differing only in color.

aqua regia (rē'jēə) [Lat.,=royal water], corrosive, fuming yellow liquid prepared by mixing one volume of concentrated nitric acid with three to four volumes of concentrated hydrochloric acid. It was so named by the alchemists because it dissolves gold and platinum, the "royal" metals, which do not dissolve in nitric or hydrochloric acid alone. Its fumes and yellow color are caused by reaction of nitric acid, HNO_3, with hydrogen chloride, HCl, to form nitrosyl chloride, NOCl, chlorine, Cl_2, and water; both chlorine and nitrosyl chloride are yellow-colored and volatile. The nitrosyl chloride further decomposes to nitric oxide, NO, and chlorine. Nitric acid is a powerful oxidizing agent (see OXIDATION AND REDUCTION), but the CHEMICAL EQUILIBRIUM for its reaction with gold, Au, only permits formation of a tiny amount of Au^{+3} ion, so the amount of gold dissolved in pure nitric acid is undetectable. The presence of chloride ion, Cl^-, allows formation of the stable chloraurate COMPLEX ION, $AuCl_4^-$. Because of the high concentration of chloride ion in aqua regia, the Au^{+3} is reacted almost as soon as it is formed, keeping its concentration low; this allows oxidation of more Au to Au^{+3}, and the gold is dissolved. The gold may also react directly with the free chlorine in aqua regia, since chlorine is a powerful oxidizing agent.

aquarelle (ăk"wərĕl'): see WATERCOLOR PAINTING.

Aquarids: see METEOR SHOWER.

aquarium, name for any supervised exhibit of aquatic animals and plants. Aquariums are known to have been constructed in ancient Rome, Egypt, and the Orient. Goldfish have been bred in China for several hundred years and are still the most commonly kept fish in home aquariums, although tropical toy fish, such as guppies, have become increasingly popular. Large public aquariums have been made possible by the development of glass exhibit tanks, capable of holding over 100,000 gal (378,500 liters) of water. The first aquarium known to have been constructed with glass is in Regent's Park, London (1853). The maintenance of an aquarium of any size requires the careful regulation of water flow, temperature, light, food, and oxygen, removal of injurious debris, and attention to the special requirements of the individual species kept. Green aquatic plants are often used in aquariums since, through the process of photosynthesis, they utilize waste carbon dioxide from the animals' respiration and in turn provide oxygen. An aquarium in which the dissolved gases are kept at the proper concentrations by the physiological activities of the plants and animals is called a balanced aquarium. Certain mollusks, such as snails and mussels, are useful as scavengers, as are some species of fish. Large freshwater and saltwater aquariums are often maintained for research and breeding purposes by universities, marine stations, and wildlife commissions, e.g., those in Naples, Italy; Monaco; Plymouth, England; La Jolla, Calif.; and Woods Hole, Mass. There are also many aquariums throughout the world for public exhibition. Among those in the United States are the Fish and Wildlife Service Aquariums at Washington, D.C., and Woods Hole, Mass.; the John G. Shedd Aquarium at Chicago; Marine Studios, Inc., at Marineland, Fla.; the New York Aquarium at Brooklyn; Scripps Institute of Oceanography at La Jolla, Calif.; the Steinhart Aquarium at San Francisco; and the Waikiki Aquarium at Honolulu. See H. R. Axelrod, *Tropical Fish as a Hobby* (rev. ed. 1972); Arne Schiøtz, *A Guide to Aquarium Fishes and Plants* (tr. 1972).

Aquarius (əkwâr'ēəs) [Lat.,=water carrier], large CONSTELLATION located on the ECLIPTIC (the sun's apparent path through the heavens) between Capricornus and Pisces; it is one of the constellations of the ZODIAC. Aquarius is sometimes represented as a man pouring water from a jar. Although it contains no stars of first or second magnitude, it does contain a recurrent nova observed in 1907 and again in 1962. Aquarius reaches its highest point in the evening sky in October.

aquatint (ä'kwətĭnt"), ETCHING technique. The plate is covered with a porous ground, or resist, through which acid bites many tiny pockmarks in the metal. The tones produced resemble those of a wash drawing. The technique is said to have been invented in the 1760s by J. B. Le Prince (1734–84). It is often used in combination with other types of etching. Goya's series of mixed aquatint etchings, *Los Caprichos, Desastres de la Guerra, Tauromaquia,* and *Proverbios,* are considered the supreme examples of this technique. See B. F. Morrow, *The Art of Aquatint* (1935); J. R. Abbey, *Life in England in Aquatint and Lithography, 1770–1860* (1953).

Aquaviva, Claudio (klou'dyō äkwävē'vä), 1543–1615, Italian Jesuit. He was (1581–1615) fifth general of the Society of Jesus and composed the *Ratio,* the basis of Jesuit education.

aqueduct (ăk'wədŭkt) [Lat.,=conveyor of water], channel or trough built to convey water, chiefly for providing a densely populated region with a supply of fresh water. The flow in aqueducts is ordinarily by means of gravity, although pumps are often used. Some aqueducts consist of tunnels cut through rock, while others are conduits made of some sturdy material. For example, the conduit may consist of steel pipe, concrete, wooden staves, sheet-metal flume, or any of these in combination, the flow being controlled by slide gate and needle valves. Aqueducts enable many cities in the United States to obtain water from a considerable distance. Los Angeles, for example, draws much of its water from the Owens River by means of an aqueduct more than 230 mi (370 km) long. Most of the supply for New York City is conducted through the Catskill Aqueduct and the CROTON AQUEDUCT. The topography of the land influences the design of the aqueduct; usually part of the structure is above ground and part below. Where feasible, an aqueduct may generate hydroelectric power as a byproduct of its operation. Typical of such use is the aqueduct system for Springfield, Mass., which generates power at the foot of Cobble Mt. in addition to supplying the city with water. Aqueducts were employed from early times, probably first in Mesopotamia. Their construction reached a peak of skill in Roman times in those around Rome and in Gaul, Spain, and other parts of the empire. Portions of some of the original Roman aqueducts are still standing.

Aquidneck, R.I.: see RHODE ISLAND, island.

aquifer (ăk'wĭfər): see ARTESIAN WELL.

Aquila (ăk'wĭlə, əkwĭl'ə), Christian of Jewish origin from Pontus who lived at Rome. He and his wife, Prisca or Priscilla, were friendly to Paul. Acts 18.2,18,26; Rom. 16.3; 1 Cor. 16.19.

Aquila [Lat.,=the eagle], equatorial CONSTELLATION located N of Sagittarius and Capricornus, lying partly in the Milky Way. It is sometimes depicted as an eagle. It contains the bright star ALTAIR (Alpha Aquilae) and the pulsating variable star Eta Aquilae. The brightest nova ever seen occurred in Aquila in 1918. Other novas were observed in Aquila in 389 and 1899; two were observed there in 1936. Aquila reaches its highest point in the evening sky in late August.

Aquila Ponticus (pŏn'tĭkəs), 2d cent., Jewish translator of the Old Testament from Hebrew into Greek. The characteristic feature of Aquila's version was its extremely literal rendering of the Hebrew. It was much used by Jews, even in the synagogues. No complete specimen exists. Aquila is said to have been a convert from Christianity and a disciple of Akiba ben Joseph.

Aquilegia: see COLUMBINE.

Aquileia (äkwēlĕ'yä), town (1971 pop. 1,938), in Friuli-Venezia Giulia, NE Italy, near the Adriatic Sea. Founded in 181 B.C. by the Romans, it was a stronghold against the barbarians and a trade center. Later, the town was destroyed several times by invaders, notably by Attila (A.D. 452). In the 6th cent. Aquileia became the see of a patriarch. Fleeing the Lombards in 568, the patriarch took refuge in Grado, the island port of Aquileia, and remained there while Aquileia elected its own patriarch. The pope recognized (7th cent.) both patriarchates; in 1445 that of Grado was transferred to Venice. From the 11th cent. Aquileia flourished under the temporal rule of its patriarchs, who acquired Friuli, Carniola, and Istria. Decline began in the 14th cent., and in 1420 Venice occupied Aquileia and Friuli. Aquileia was under Austrian rule from 1509 to 1918, when it passed to Italy. The patriarchate was abolished in 1751. Of particular note in the town is the Romanesque basilica (11th cent., partly restored in the 14th cent.), with an interesting and well-preserved mosaic floor and with frescoes of the 12th and 13th cent. There are also Roman ruins and an archaeological museum. Grado, now joined to the mainland by a bridge, is a popular beach resort as well as a port.

Aquinas, Saint Thomas: see THOMAS AQUINAS, SAINT.

Aquitaine (ăk'wĭtān, ākētĕn'), Lat. *Aquitania,* former duchy and kingdom in SW France. Julius Caesar conquered the Aquitani, an Iberian people of SW Gaul, in 56 B.C. The province that he created occupied the territory between the Garonne River and the Pyrenees; under Roman rule it was extended northward and eastward almost as far as the Loire River. It had been thoroughly Romanized when it was occupied (5th cent.) by the VISIGOTHS, and the persistence of Latin culture made it a rich but indigestible addition to the Frankish realm after the defeat (507) of the Visigoths by the Frankish ruler Clovis I. In the chaotic strife among Clovis's successors, much of Aquitaine escaped Frankish control. After the separation of GASCONY from Aquitaine (7th cent.), the area N of the Garonne was considered Aquitaine proper. From 670, Aquitaine was ruled by semi-independent native dukes, but an Arab invasion (718) forced the Aquitanian duke Eudes to seek the protection of the Frankish ruler Charles Martel, who defeated (732) the Arabs. In 781, CHARLEMAGNE, who subdued the native nobles, made Aquitaine into a kingdom for his son Louis (later emperor of the West LOUIS I). After the death (838) of Louis's son Pepin I, Louis added Aquitaine to the West Frankish kingdom of Neustria (France) and granted it to his youngest son Charles the Bald (CHARLES II, emperor of the West). A group of Aquitanian nobles made Pepin's young son, Pepin II, king, and a struggle for control ensued between Charles and the Aquitanians (840–52; 862–65). Charles was the eventual victor. During this period Aquitaine was subject to attacks by both Normans and Muslims. The repeated invasions, combined with the civil wars, weakened Carolingian control over Aquitaine, despite Charles the Bald's victory over Pepin II. Charles's successors were forced to recognize the hereditary rights of a number of independent noble families, and during the 10th cent. royal influence virtually disappeared. After 973 the counts of Poitou bore the title of duke of Aquitaine; their control beyond Poitou, however, was not realized for many years. In the 11th cent. the dukes of Aquitaine expanded at the expense of their weaker neighbors, establishing themselves over all Aquitaine and Gascony. The new duchy of Aquitaine was one of the most powerful states in western Europe. The marriage (1137) of ELEANOR OF AQUITAINE to the French king Louis VII joined Aquitaine to France. Eleanor's subsequent marriage to Henry II, duke of Normandy, who became king of England in 1154, initiated a long struggle between France and England for possession of Aquitaine. Henry and his successors held Aquitaine in vassalage from the kings of France. Over the years, however, France regained various parts of Aquitaine from England, and in the HUNDRED YEARS WAR France recovered all of Aquitaine. After its recovery, Aquitaine was constituted as the French province of Guienne, a name that had been used interchangeably with Aquitaine for many years.

Ar (är), city of Moab, probably one of the important centers E of the Dead Sea. The Greeks called it Areopolis, and later it was called Rabbath Moab. Num. 21.15,28; Deut. 2.9,18,29; Isa. 15.1. It is the nameless city of Num. 22.36, Deut. 2.36, and Joshua 13.9.

Ar, chemical symbol of the element ARGON.

Ara (ā'rə), Asherite. 1 Chron. 7.38.

Arab (ā'răb), hill town of S Palestine, near Hebron. Joshua 15.52.

Arabah or **Araba** (both: ä'räbä, ăr'əbə), depression, on the Israel-Jordan border, extending c.100 mi (160 km) from the Dead Sea S to the Gulf of Aqaba; part of the Great Rift Valley complex. Limestone, salt, and potash are mined near the Dead Sea. In the Old Testament, Arabah is variously called a wilderness, a plain, and a desert.

arabesque (ărəbĕsk') [Fr.,=Arabian], in art, term applied to any complex, linear decoration based on flowing lines. In Moorish art it was often exploited to cover entire surfaces. The arabesque in modern usage derives from a Renaissance design which was Greco-Roman in inspiration.

Arabia, peninsula (1970 est. pop. 17,000,000), c.1,000,000 sq mi (2,590,000 sq km), SW Asia; called Arabistan in Persian. It is bordered on the W by the Gulf of Aqaba and the Red Sea, on the S by the Gulf of Aden and the Arabian Sea, on the E by the Gulf of Oman and the Persian Gulf, and on the N by Iraq and Jordan. Politically, Arabia consists of Saudi Arabia (the largest and most populous state), Yemen, Southern Yemen (People's Democratic Republic of Yemen), Oman, the United Arab Emirates, Qatar, Bahrain, Kuwait, and several neutral zones. Arabia is mainly a great plateau of ancient crystalline rock, covered with limestone and sandstone. It rises steeply from the narrow Red Sea coastal plain, achieving its greatest height (c.12,000 ft/3,700 m) in SW Arabia, and slopes gently E to the Persian Gulf; the Oman Mts., SE Arabia, rise to c.10,000 ft (3,000 m). The coastal mountains catch what little moisture is carried by the dry winds that cross Arabia, making the interior so arid (4 in./10 cm annual precipitation) that there is not a single perennial stream and large areas lack water. The basin-shaped interior consists of alternating steppe and desert landscape; the Nafud desert in the north is connected with the great Rub al Khali in the south (one of the world's largest sand deserts) by the Dahna, a narrow sand corridor. There is extensive and varied agriculture (coffee, grains, fruits) only in SW Arabia, particularly Yemen [Arabia Felix,=fortunate Arabia], where high coastal mountains intercept the moist southwest monsoon winds during the summer. The northeast coast of Oman has a climate similar to that of Yemen, but in most of Arabia rainfall is cyclonic and occurs only in winter. The coastal lands, however, are much more humid than the interior; fog and dew are common. Except for the inland cities of Riyadh and Hail, in Saudi Arabia, most of Arabia's large urban centers are on or near the coast. Principal cities are Jidda, Mecca, and Medina (Saudi Arabia); Sana (Yemen); Aden and Mukalla (Southern Yemen); Abu Dhabi (United Arab Emirates); Muscat (Oman); Al Manamah (Bahrain); and Kuwait city (Kuwait). Because of their dependence on isolated sources of water, about four fifths of the Arabian population is sedentary, concentrated around oases, notably in the Nejd (central Arabia) and the Hejaz (along the northeast coast of the Red Sea). Agriculture is the main occupation, with dates, grains, and fruits the chief crops. Pastoral nomads raise goats and sheep. Until the mid-20th cent., when oil was discovered in E Arabia, the peninsula's main exports were hides, wool, coffee, spices, and the famed, highly bred Arabian horses. With the exception of Aden, Arabia did not have a good port until after World War II, when modern port facilities were constructed, especially along the Persian Gulf. Arabia has an estimated one third of the earth's petroleum reserves; Kuwait and Saudi Arabia are among the world's leading producers. Europe is the principal customer of Arabian petroleum, consuming more than 50% of the output; the Far East (especially Japan), the United States, and Canada are also large consumers. Until the early 1970s, firms from the United States, Britain, and, to a lesser extent, Japan had a monopoly on drilling concessions. However, the Arabian nations now have much greater control over oil exploration and production and receive far higher payments. Modern technology and the huge wealth generated by oil resources have profoundly altered traditional life in Arabia. Flourishing private enterprise, new transportation links, rapidly growing cities, and rising education and living standards now characterize much of the peninsula. Archaeological evidence points to very early trade between Yemen and the NE African coast. From time to time ancient peoples of Arabian origin invaded and settled the inviting regions of the E Mediterranean basin; possibly they included the HYKSOS, conquerors of Egypt (18th cent. B.C.), and the Israelites who seized Palestine. However, little is definitely known of Arabian history in the period preceding the oldest inscriptions discovered—those dating from c.1000 B.C. In ancient times much of SW Arabia was divided among the domains of Ma'in, SHEBA, and Himyarite. Political unity in Sheba seems to have been hastened by Darius's conquest of N Arabia. No ancient power ever attempted the complete conquest of Arabia, because of the formidable obstacles of crossing the deserts. Rome invaded (24 B.C.) N Arabia but soon withdrew, although for a long period it held N Hejaz. Ethiopia, during its great expansion under the Aksumite kings (see AKSUM), twice (A.D. 300-378 and 525-70) held Yemen and the HADHRAMAUT. In 570, the Sassanids of Persia drove out the Ethiopians and established a short-lived hegemony over the peninsula. Arabia was briefly unified after the founding of ISLAM by MUHAMMAD, the prophet of Mecca, in the 7th cent. His dynamic faith, furthered by his successors, reconciled the warring Arab tribes and soon sent them out on a career of conquest. They subjugated N Africa and SW Asia and gained control of Spain and S France until they were stopped in the west by the Frankish ruler CHARLES MARTEL in 732 and in the east by the Byzantine Empire c.750. However, the tremendous territorial expansion of Islam deprived the religion of its exclusively Arabic character, and the need for a more convenient administrative center led to the transfer of the seat of the CALIPHATE from Medina to Damascus; Arabia was again left without political cohesion, and independent emirates arose in Yemen, Oman, and elsewhere. In the 10th cent. a semblance of unity was imposed by the KARMATHIANS, a Muslim sect, but in the 11th cent. anarchic conditions again prevailed. After the discovery of the route to India around the Cape of Good Hope in 1498, European powers were attracted to Arabia as a site for trading bases. The Portuguese seized Oman in 1508 but were driven out in 1659 by the Ottoman Empire, which attempted, but never with complete success, to control all Arabia. Great Britain established a physical presence in Arabia in 1799 by occupying Perim Island in the Bab el Mandeb; and in 1839 the Ottoman Empire lost Aden to the British. In 1853, Britain and the E Arabian sheikhs signed the Perpetual Maritime Truce by which the Arabs agreed not to harass British shipping in the Arabian Sea and recognized Britain as the dominant foreign power in the Persian Gulf. The truce confirmed the temporary truces of 1820 and 1835; the sheikhdoms were thus called the Trucial States. Arab nationalist opposition to the Ottoman Turks was aroused in the mid-19th cent. by a rekindling of the WAHABI, a reform movement within Islam; it waned toward the end of the century. Just before World War I, IBN SAUD revived the Wahabi, and during the war he signed a military pact with Britain against the Turks. His strongest rival, HUSAYN IBN ALI of the influential Hashemite family, led a successful revolt against the Turks in the Hejaz and set up an independent state there. After the war, however, the Saud family prevailed in a violent struggle against Husayn and other Arab families and founded (1925) Saudi Arabia, which absorbed the state in the Hejaz. Between the World Wars, Britain was the dominant foreign power in Arabia, holding protectorates over the Arab sheikhdoms. The post-World War II era witnessed a gradual decline of Britain's presence, culminating in the withdrawal of British military forces E of Suez in the late 1960s. Both the United States and the USSR sought to fill the vacuum created by Britain's withdrawal from the oil-rich, strategically important peninsula, but in the early 1970s the Arab nations were asserting their independence with growing success. The countries were only peripherally involved in the Arab-Israeli Wars. See D. G. Hogarth, *Arabia* (1922); T. E. Lawrence, *Revolt in the Desert* (1927); C. M. Doughty, *Travels in Arabia Deserta* (new ed. 1936, repr. 1968); Richard H. Sanger, *The Arabian Peninsula* (1954, repr. 1970); Philip K. Hitti, *History of the Arabs* (10th ed. 1970); William B. Fisher, *The Middle East: A Physical, Social and Regional Geography* (6th ed. 1970).

Arabian art and architecture: see ISLAMIC ART AND ARCHITECTURE.

Arabian Desert or **Eastern Desert,** c.86,000 sq mi (222,740 sq km), E Egypt, bordered by the Nile valley in the west and the Red Sea and the Gulf of Suez in the east. It extends along most of Egypt's eastern border and merges into the Nubian Desert in the south. The Arabian Desert is sparsely populated; most of its inhabitants are based around wells and springs. Since ancient times Egypt has used the porphyry, granite, and sandstone found in the desert mountains as building materials. Oil is produced in the north. The name Arabian Desert is also commonly applied to the desert of the Arabian Peninsula.

Arabian Gulf: see PERSIAN GULF.

Arabian horse, breed of LIGHT HORSE developed in Mesopotamia and N Africa, and probably the first true domesticated breed. Prized since earliest times for its superior beauty, spirit, speed, grace of movement, stamina, and intelligence, the Arabian has served as parental stock for such light-weight horses as the AMERICAN SADDLE HORSE, QUARTER HORSE, STANDARD-BRED HORSE, and the THOROUGHBRED. Intercrossings of these and other light and DRAFT HORSE breeds with Arabians is still common. The Arabian's most characteristic color is bay with white markings; grays, chestnuts, and browns are also common. It averages 14 to 15 hands (56-60 in./140-150 cm) high and weighs about 1,000 lb (450 kg).

Arabian music, the music of all the Islamic peoples in Arabia, N Africa, and Persia. Little is known of Arabian music before the Hegira (A.D. 622), but afterwards under the Omayyad caliphs (661-750) a consolidation of Persian and Syrian elements with the native musical style took place in Arabia. Ibn Misjah (d. c.715) devised a system of modal theory that lasted throughout the golden age under the first Abbasid caliphs (750-847). In the 9th cent. at Baghdad many treatises on music theory and history were written by such men as the philosopher Al-Kindi (9th cent.) and the illustrious Al-Farabi (c.870-c.950), who wrote the most important treatise on music up to his time. In the 11th cent. under the last Abbasid caliphs a strong Turkestan influence was brought into Arabian music by the Seljuks, and a gradual decay began in the Arabian art. With the destruction of Baghdad in 1258 came the end of specifically Arabian musical culture, and only a few late examples of this music are extant. The style was preserved in Egypt and Syria because the Arabic language was spoken there, but it had lost its vitality; and even this vestige died when the Ottoman Turks overran Egypt in 1517. The chief characteristics of Arabian music are modal homophony, florid ornamentation, and modal rhythm. The melodic modal system of Ibn Misjah contained, in its final form, eight modes. This system lasted until the 11th cent., when the modes were increased to 12, which were called *maqamat* by the 13th cent. Until this time the Arabian gamut had consisted of 12 tones roughly equal to the chromatic scale of Western music. But in the 13th cent. five more tones were added, each a quarter tone below each diatonic whole tone, i.e., below d, e, g, a, b. A new tuning of the gamut was adopted in the 16th cent., and not only the tones but also the nature of the *maqamat* were changed: instead of scales within which melodies were composed, they became melodic formulas to be used in composition, a system much like the *ragas* of HINDU MUSIC. Ornamentation in Arabian music consisted of shakes and trills, grace notes, appoggiaturas, and the *tarkib,* which was the simultaneous striking of certain notes with their fourth, fifth, or octave. The rhythmic modes were primarily the vocal meters of poetry until the development of instrumental music in the 10th cent. In vocal music often a short melody is repeated for each stanza or verse, each repetition being elaborately ornamented. The principal form of Arabian music is the *nauba,* a "suite" of vocal pieces with instrumental preludes, probably originated at the Abbasid court. The principal Arabian instruments, other than those borrowed from older Semitic cultures, were the short-necked lute called *ud,* from which the European lute derived its form and name, and the long-necked lute called *tanbur.* The introduction of the lute into Europe by the Moors in Spain is a certainty; the extent to which Arabian music has exerted greater influence on the West is still a matter of controversy. See H. G. Farmer, *A History of Arabian Music to the 13th Century* (1929) and *Historical Facts for the Arabian Musical Influence* (1930).

Arabian Nights: see THOUSAND AND ONE NIGHTS.

Arabian Sea, ancient *Mare Erythraeum,* northwest part of the Indian Ocean, lying between Arabia and India. The Gulf of Aden, extended by the Red Sea, and the Gulf of Oman, extended by the Persian Gulf, are its principal arms. The submarine Carlsberg ridge, SE of Socotra Island, is the sea's southern boundary. The Indus River is the largest stream flowing into the sea. The Arabian Sea has long been an important trade route between India and the West; its chief ports are Aden, People's Republic of Yemen; Karachi, Pakistan; and Bombay, India.

Arabic languages, members of the South Semitic group of the Semitic subdivision of the Hamito-Semitic family of languages (see HAMITO-SEMITIC LANGUAGES). The Arabic languages comprise North Arabic (or simply Arabic), which represents the Southwest branch of the South Semitic tongues, and South Arabic (or Himyaritic), which belongs to the Southeast branch of the South Semitic group; South Arabic differs sufficiently from North Arabic to be considered a separate language. North Arabic, or Arabic, was confined largely to the Arabian peninsula until the 7th cent. A.D. Thereafter the spread of Islam took the Arabic language into the Fertile Crescent and across North Africa. Today Arabic is spoken throughout the Arabian peninsula and also in Iraq, Syria, Jordan, Lebanon, Israel, Morocco, Tunisia, Algeria, Libya, Egypt, Sudan, Mauritania, Chad, and Malta. The official language of 17 countries in Africa and Asia and co-official in two other states (Israel and Malta), it is the mother tongue of approximately 100 million people in these two continents. In addition, Arabic reaches the peoples of all countries professing the Muslim religion, for it is the sacred language of Islam and its holy book, the Koran. Thus, Arabic can be considered the most important living Semitic tongue. A great literature has been written in Arabic as well. The Arabic of the Koran and of subsequent Arabic literature is called classical or literary Arabic. It is uniform and standardized. Classical Arabic is still employed today as the written language, but it is restricted to formal usage as a spoken tongue. It differs considerably from its descendant, the modern colloquial Arabic that is the medium of general conversation. Modern colloquial Arabic has three principal groups of dialects: Eastern, Western, and Southern; but the language is becoming standardized owing to the influence of the mass media. Grammatically, Arabic has that distinctive feature of Semitic languages, the triconsonantal root consisting of three consonants separated by two vowels. The basic meaning of the root is furnished by the consonants and is altered by changes in, or omission of, the vowels and by the addition of various affixes. Gender is found in the Arabic verb, as well as in the noun, pronoun, and adjective. The modern Arabic dialects have considerably simplified classical Arabic, as by discarding the declension of the noun and other inflections. Arabic has its own alphabet, which is composed of 28 consonants. Most of the characters have four different forms, one for beginning a word, another for ending a word, still another for a medial position, and a fourth for a letter used by itself. Vowels are shown by symbols above or below the consonants, but they are optional and are often not written. The direction of writing is from right to left. The Arabic alphabet evolved from the Nabataean script, which is a descendant of the Aramaic writing (see ARAMAIC). There are two major styles of the Arabic script, the angular Kufic (well-suited for decorative uses) and the cursive Nashki. Arabic writing is also the basis of a number of scripts used by non-Arab peoples following the Muslim religion and has been adapted for the Persian, Pushtu, Urdu, Malay, Hausa, and Swahili languages, among others. South Arabic in ancient times was the language of people living in the southern Arabian peninsula. It had several known dialects and is closely related to the ETHIOPIC of Ethiopia. Ancient South Arabic had its own South Semitic alphabet, the origin of which is still not clear, although it is generally thought to have had the same source as the North Semitic writing. Surviving inscriptions in ancient South Arabic date from the 8th cent. B.C. or earlier. The coming of Islam in the 7th cent. A.D. brought with it North Arabic, which displaced the ancient South Arabic. Modern South Arabic, which has several dialects, is spoken by about 50,000 people in the southern Arabian peninsula. Its ancestor is probably ancient South Arabic, although not all linguists agree. For grammars see G. W. Thatcher (4th ed. 1942), F. J. Ziadeh and B. B. Winder (1957), and C. P. Caspari (3d ed. 1967); A. G. Chejne, *The Arabic Language, Its Role in History* (1969).

Arabic literature. Numerous peoples have shared in forming the great body of Arabic literature; they include Turks, Persians, Syrians, Egyptians, Indians, Africans, Jews, and Asians, in addition to the Arabs themselves. The first significant Arabic literature was produced during the medieval golden age of lyric poetry, from the 4th to the 7th cent. The poems are strongly personal qasida, or odes, often very short, some longer than 100 lines. They treat the life of the tribe and themes of love, fighting, courage, and the chase. The poet speaks directly, not romantically, of nature and the power of God. The qasida survive only through collections, chiefly the MUALLAQAT, HAMASA, MUFADDALIYAT, and KITAB AL-AGHANI. The most esteemed of the poets are AMRU AL-KAIS, ANTARA, and ZUHAIR. The Prophet Muhammad was not interested in poetry, so Arabic poetry fell into a decline from which it recovered only in far different form. The KORAN supplanted poetry by becoming the chief object of study of the Muslim world. Poetry regained some prestige under the Umayyads, when al-Akhtal (c.640–c.710) and al-Farazdaq (c.640–732) wrote their lyric works. The next great period of Arabic literature was a result of the rise of the new Arabic-Persian culture of Baghdad under the Abbasids in the 8th and 9th cent. Philosophy, mathematics, law, Koranic interpretation and criticism, history, and science were cultivated, and to this period is owed the collections of early Arabic poetry. During the 7th and part of the 8th cent., Arabic poetry had become entirely artificial, refined, and nearly totally inaccessible to the average reader without a scholarly background. At the end of the 8th cent. in Baghdad a group of young poets arose who established a new court poetry. Two of these were ABU AL-ATAHIYA and ABU NUWAS. Typical of the time is the precise, formal, yet exaggerated work of Mutanabbi (murdered in 965). Among the most popular of Arabic poets, he is considered one of the greatest masters of poetic technique. The poet HARIRI (11th cent.) sought to combine "refinement with dignity of style, and brilliancies with jewels of eloquence." ABU AL-ALA AL-MAARRI (d.1057) was an outstanding Syrian poet of great originality. The greatest mystic poet of the age was Omar Ibn al-Faridh (1181–1235). The influence of India and Persia is seen in Arabic prose romance, which had become the principal literary form. The greatest collection is the THOUSAND AND ONE NIGHTS. The major writers of historical and geographical works in Arabic include BUKHARI, AL-TABARI, MASUDI, IBN KHALDUN, Ibn al-Athir (d.1234), and IBN BATUTA. The foremost Arab philosopher was AL-GAZEL; AVICENNA, the great physician, wrote on medicine. In the field of belles lettres, essays and epistles of great wit and erudition known as risalas were composed on subjects as diverse as science, mysticism, and politics. Chief practitioners of the genre include Ibn al-Muqaffa (d.757), the unsurpassed al-Jahiz (d. c.869), and Ibn Qutayba (d.889). The Western center of Arabian culture was Spain, especially Córdoba under the Umayyads. The Spanish Arabs produced fine poets and scholars, but they are dwarfed by the great philosophers—AVEMPACE, AVERROËS, and IBN TUFAYL. Their works became known in Europe chiefly through the Latin translations of Jewish scholars. Since 1200 in Spain and 1300 in the East, there has been little Arabic literature of wide interest. After 1870, with the growth of Western influence on the East, a vernacular literature arose in Syria and in Egypt, which aimed to rouse Arabic national consciousness in literature either by a return to classical models or by an imitation of Western forms. While there has been a reaction to Western models in modern Arabic literature, the novel and the drama, forms never before used, have developed. Notable 20th-century writers in Arabic include the novelist Najib Mafuz, the playwrights Ahmad Shawqi and Tawfiq al-Hakim, the poets Hafiz Ibrahim, Badr Shakir as-Sayyab, and Nazik al-Malaikah, and the short-story writer Mahmud Tymur. See H. A. Gibb, *Arabic Literature, an Introduction* (2d ed. 1963); A. J. Arberry, *Modern Arabic Poetry* (1950, repr. 1967); R. A. Nicholson, *A Literary History of the Arabs* (2d ed. 1969); J. A. Haywood, *Modern Arabic Literature, 1800–1970* (1972).

Arab-Israeli Wars, conflicts in 1948–49, 1956, 1967, and 1973–74 between Israel and the Arab states. Tensions between Israel and the Arabs have been complicated and heightened by the political, strategic, and economic interests in the area of the great powers. Although Israel's independence on May 14, 1948, triggered the first full-scale war, armed conflicts between Jews and Arabs had been frequent since Great Britain received the League of Nations mandate for PALESTINE in 1920. From 1945 to 1948 Zionists waged guerrilla war against British troops and against Palestinian Arabs supported by the ARAB LEAGUE, and they had made substantial gains by 1948. The 1948–49 War reflected the opposition of the Arab states to the formation of the Jewish state of Israel in what they considered to be Arab territory. As independence was declared, Arab forces from Egypt, Syria, Transjordan (later Jordan), Lebanon, and Iraq invaded Israel. The Egyptians gained some territory in the south and the Jordanians took Jerusalem's Old City, but other Arab forces were soon halted. In June the United Nations succeeded in establishing a four-week truce. This was followed in July by significant Israeli advances before another truce. Fighting erupted again in August and continued sporadically until the end of 1948. An Israeli advance in Jan., 1949, isolated Egyptian forces and led to a cease-fire (Jan. 7, 1949). Protracted peace talks resulted in armistice agreements between Israel and Egypt, Syria, and Jordan by July, but no formal peace. In addition, about 400,000 Palestinian Arabs had fled from Israel and were settled in refugee camps near Israel's border; their status became a volatile factor in Arab-Israeli relations. From 1949 to 1956 the armed truce between Israel and the Arabs, enforced in part by the UN forces, was punctuated by raids and reprisals. Among the world powers, the United States, Great Britain, and France sided with Israel, while the Soviet Union supported Arab demands. Tensions mounted during 1956 as Israel became convinced that the Arabs were preparing for war. The nationalization of the Suez Canal by Egypt's Gamal Abdal NASSER in July, 1956, resulted in the further alienation of Great Britain and France, which made new agreements with Israel. On Oct. 29, 1956, Israeli forces, directed by Moshe DAYAN, launched a combined air and ground assault into Egypt's Sinai peninsula. Early Israeli successes were reinforced by an Anglo-French invasion along the canal. Although the action against Egypt was severely condemned by the nations of the world, the cease-fire of November 6, which was promoted by the United Nations with U.S. and Soviet support, came only after Israel had captured several key objectives, including the Gaza strip and Sharm el Sheikh, which commanded the approaches to the Gulf of Aqaba. Israel withdrew from these positions in 1957, turning them over to the UN emergency force after access to the Gulf of Aqaba, without which Israel was cut off from the Indian Ocean, had been guaranteed. After a period of relative calm, border incidents between Israel and Syria, Egypt, and Jordan increased during the early 1960's, with Palestinian guerrilla groups actively supported by Syria. In May, 1967, President Nasser, his prestige much eroded through his inaction in the face of Israeli raids, requested the withdrawal of UN forces from Egyptian territory, mobilized units in the Sinai, and closed the Gulf of Aqaba to Israel. Israel (which had no UN forces stationed on its territory) responded by mobilizing, and escalation of threats and provocations continued until June 5, 1967, when Israel launched a massive air assault that crippled Arab air capability. With air superiority protecting its ground forces, Israel controlled the Sinai peninsula within three days and then concentrated on the Jordanian frontier, capturing Jerusalem's Old City (subsequently annexed), and on the Syrian border, gaining a hold on the strategic Golan Heights. The war, which ended on June 10, is known as the Six-Day War. The Suez Canal was closed by the war, and Israel declared that it would not give up Jerusalem and that it would hold the remaining captured territories until significant progress had been made in Arab-Israeli relations. The end of active fighting was followed by frequent artillery duels along the frontiers and by clashes between Israelis and Palestinian guerrillas. During 1973 the Arab states, believing that their complaints against Israel were going unheeded (despite the mounting use by the Arabs of threats to cut off oil supplies in an attempt to soften the U.S. pro-Israel stance), quietly prepared for war, led by Egypt's President Anwar SADAT. On Oct. 6, 1973, on the Jewish holiday Yom Kippur, a two-pronged assault on Israel was launched. Egyptian forces struck eastward across the Suez Canal and pushed the Israelis back, while the Syrians advanced from the north. Iraqi forces joined the war and, in addition, Syria received some support from Jordan, Libya, and the smaller Arab states. The attacks caught Israel off guard, and it was several days before the country was fully mobilized; Israel then forced the Syrians and Egyptians back and, in the last hours of the war, established a salient on the west bank of the Suez Canal, but these advances were only achieved with a high cost in men and equipment. Through U.S. and Soviet diplomatic pressures and the efforts of the United Nations, a tenuous cease-fire was implemented by October 25. Israel and Egypt signed a cease-fire agreement in November, but Israeli-Syrian fighting continued until a cease-fire was negotiated in 1974. Largely as a result of the diplomatic efforts of U.S. Secretary of State Henry KISSINGER, Israel was prevailed upon to withdraw from the west bank of the canal and to withdraw a further several miles on the east bank (which it had previously controlled) behind a UN-supervised cease-fire zone. On the Syrian front too, territorial gains made in the war were given up. These setbacks, which were attributed largely to Israel's unpreparedness, led to a crisis of leadership that resulted in the retirement in 1974 of Prime Minister Golda MEIR and removal of Dayan as chief of the army. The Arab states had strengthened their political position and gained in military confidence; for the first time they had successfully combined economics with politics, using a petroleum embargo to influence world opinion. After the war Egyptian and Syrian diplomatic relations with the United States, broken since the 1967 war, were resumed, and clearance of the Suez Canal began. The 1973–74 War brought about a major shift of power in the Middle East, but it still failed to resolve the basic problems confronting the area. See Roderick MacLeish, *The Sun Stood Still* (1967); S. L. A. Marshall et al., ed., *Swift Sword* (1967); F. J. Khouri, *The Arab-Israeli Dilemma* (1968); W. Z. Laqueur, *The Road to Jerusalem* (1968); Ibrahim Abu-Lughod, ed., *The Arab-Israeli Confrontation of June 1967: An Arab Perspective* (1970); Dan Kurzman, *Genesis 1948: The First Arab-Israeli War* (1970); S. L. A. Marshall, *Sinai Victory* (rev. ed. 1971); Edgar O'Ballance, *The Sinai Campaign of 1956* (1960) and *The Third Arab-Israeli War* (1972); D. A. Schmidt, *Armageddon in the Middle East* (1974).

Arabistan: see ARABIA.

Arab League, popular name for the League of Arab States, formed in 1945, in an attempt to give political expression to the Arab nations. The original charter members were Egypt, Syria, Lebanon, Trans-Jordan (later Jordan), Iraq, Saudi Arabia, and Yemen. A representative of Palestinian Arabs, although he did not sign the charter because he represented no recognized government, was given full status and a vote in the Arab League. Members later joining the league included Algeria, Bahrain, Kuwait, Libya, Morocco, Oman, Qatar, the Sudan, Tunisia, the Union of Arab Emirates, and the Yemen Arab Republic. The league is organized into a council, special committees, and a permanent secretariat; the secretariat has headquarters in Cairo. The constitution of the league provided for coordination among the signatory nations on education, finance, law, trade, and foreign policy, and it forbade the use of force to settle disputes among members. In 1945 the league supported Syria and Lebanon in their disputes with France and also demanded an independent Libya. The league early announced opposition to the formation of a Jewish state in Palestine and demanded that Palestine as a whole be made independent, with the majority of its population Arab. When the state of ISRAEL was created in 1948 the league countries jointly attacked it, but Israel resisted successfully. The league continued to maintain a boycott of Israel and of companies trading with Israel. Throughout the history of the league, closer political unity has been hampered by a division between pro-Western member countries and neutralist or pro-Soviet ones. On occasion, the league unites, e.g., in 1950 members signed a joint defense treaty, and in 1961 they supported Tunisia in a conflict with France. Typically, however, it is divided. The summit conferences of 1964–65 failed to establish a joint Arab command, and the league has been highly criticized by Arab leaders for failing to redress grievances arising from the Arab-Israeli War of 1967. Among the most important activities of the Arab League have been its attempts to coordinate Arab economic life; efforts toward this aim include the Arab Telecommunications Union (1953), the organization of the Arab Postal Union (1954), and the Arab Development Bank (1959, later known as the Arab Financial Organization). The Arab Common Market was established in 1965 and is open to all Arab League members; by 1973, Iraq, Jordan, Syria, and Egypt had joined. The common market agreement provides for the eventual abolition of custom duties on natural resources and agricultural products, free movement of capital and labor between member countries, and coordination of economic development.

Arabs, name originally applied to the Semitic peoples of the Arabian Peninsula. It now refers to those persons whose primary language is Arabic. They constitute most of the population of Algeria, Bahrain, Egypt, Iraq, Jordan, Kuwait, Lebanon, Libya, Morocco, Oman, Qatar, Saudi Arabia, Sudan, Syria, Tunisia, the United Arab Emirates, the People's Democratic Republic of Yemen, and Yemen; Arab communities are also found elsewhere in the world. The term does not usually include Arabic-speaking Jews (found chiefly in North Africa and formerly also in Yemen and Iraq), Kurds, Berbers, Copts, and Druses, but it does include Arabic-speaking Christians (chiefly found in Syria, Lebanon, Israel, and Jordan). Socially, the Arabs are divided into two groups: the settled Arab [*fellahin*=villagers, or *hadar*=townspeople] and the nomadic BEDOUIN. The derivation of the term Arab is unclear, and the meaning of the word has changed several times through history. Some Arab scholars have equated Joktan (Gen. 10.25) with the ancient Arab patriarch Qahtan whose tribe is thought to have originated in S Arabia. The Assyrian inscriptions (9th cent. B.C.) referred to nomadic peoples inhabiting the far north of the Arabian peninsula; the sedentary population in the south of the peninsula was not called Arab. In classical times the term was extended to the whole of the Arabian peninsula and to all the desert areas of the Middle East, and in the Middle Ages the Arabs came to be called SARACENS. It was the Muslims from Arabia, nomads and settled people alike, whose invasions in the 6th and 7th cent. widely diffused both the Arabic language and ISLAM. They founded a vast empire, which at its height stretched from the Atlantic Ocean on the west, across North Africa and the Middle East, to central Asia on the east. The Arabs became the rulers of many different peoples, and gradually a great Arab civilization was built up. Although many of its cultural leaders were not ethnically Arabs (some were not even Muslims, but Christians and Jews), the civilization reflected Arab values, tastes, and traditions. Education flourished in the Islamic lands, and literature, philosophy, medicine, mathematics, and science were particularly developed by the Arabs. At the same time in all the provinces of the huge empire, except in Persia, Arabic became the chief spoken language. The waves of Arab conquest across the East and into Europe widened the scope of their civilization and contributed greatly to world development. In Europe they were particularly important in Sicily, which they held from the 9th to the late 11th cent., and the civilization of the MOORS in Spain was part of the great Arabic pattern. Christian scholars in those two lands gained much from Islamic knowledge, and scholasticism and the beginnings of modern Western science were derived in part from the Arabs. The emergence of the Seljuk Turks in the 11th cent. and of the Ottoman Turks in the 13th cent. ended the specifically Arab dominance in Islam, though Muslim culture still remained on the old Arab foundations. In the 20th cent., Arab leaders have attempted to form an Arab nation, which would unite the whole Arabic-speaking world from Morocco on the west, across the Middle East, to the borders of Iran and Turkey. Since 1945 most of the Arab nations have combined to form the ARAB LEAGUE, its purpose being to consider matters of common interest, such as policy regarding Israel and colonialism. With 18 member states in the Arab League by the early 1970s (over 120 million people), attempts to forge a unity among the Arabs have continued. Perhaps the most significant economic factor for the Arabs has been the discovery and development of the petroleum industry; two thirds of the world's oil reserves are thought to be in the Middle East. Since World War II a continual problem for the Arab states has been their relations with the Jewish state of Israel, created out of former Arab territory; hostility between them has resulted in four Arab-Israeli wars. See J. B. Glubb, *A Short History of the Arab Peoples* (1969); P. K. Hitti, *History of the Arabs* (10th ed. 1970); Majid Khadduri, *Political Trends in the Arab World* (1972); Menahem Mansoor, *Political and Diplomatic History of the Arab World, 1900–67* (7 vol., 1972); Z. N. Zeine, *The Emergence of Arab Nationalism* (3d. ed. 1973); W. F. Abboushi, *The Angry Arabs* (1974).

Aracaju (ä"rəkəzhōō'), city (1970 pop. 183,333), capital of Sergipe state, E central Brazil, a port on the Sergipe River near the Atlantic Ocean. Mainly a commercial center, the city has cotton-spinning and weaving industries. Aracaju was founded in 1855, when it replaced São Cristovão as state capital.

Arachne (ərăk'nē), in Greek mythology, woman of Lydia who challenged Athena to a trial of skill in weaving. Angered at such presumption, the goddess destroyed Arachne's work, whereupon the woman hanged herself. Athena then turned her into a spider.

arachnid (ərăk'nĭd), mainly terrestrial arthropod of the class Arachnida, including the SPIDER, SCORPION, MITE and tick, DADDY LONGLEGS, and a few minor groups. The body is divided into a cephalothorax with six pairs of appendages, and an abdomen. The first two pairs of appendages are used to kill and crush prey (most arachnids being carnivorous); the remaining four pairs are walking legs. Arachnids have simple eyes and no antennae but are equipped with sensory bristles. Some respire with air tubes, but most possess primitive respiratory organs called BOOK LUNGS. Arachnids are classified in the phylum ARTHROPODA, class Arachnida.

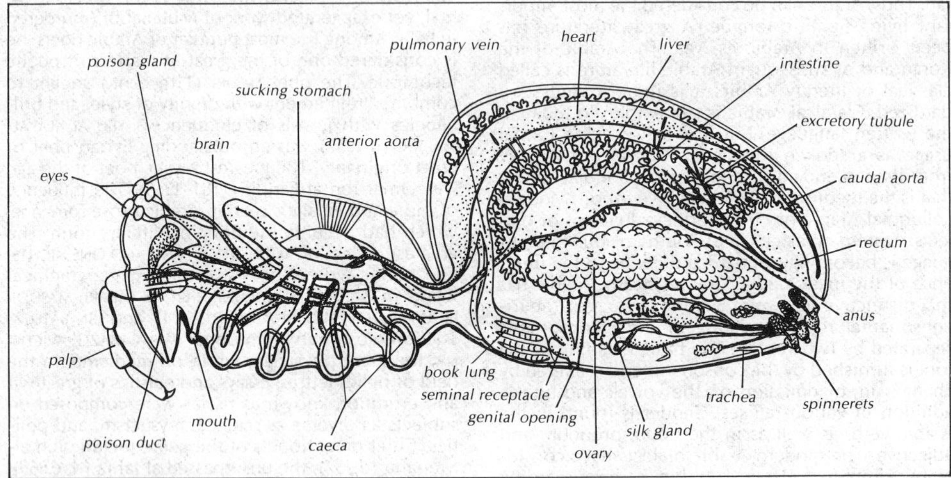

Internal anatomy of a spider, representative of the class Arachnida

Arad (ā'răd). **1** Benjamite. 1 Chron. 8.15. **2** Royal town in the Negev, the modern Tell Arad (Israel), S of Hebron. Joshua 12.14; Judges 1.16. The "king Arad" of Num. 21.1 and 33.40 is a mistranslation for "king of Arad." It is the only tell (mound) in the Negev and indicates the existence of a fortified town in the Bronze Age.

Arad (äräd'), city (1969 est. pop. 115,000), W Rumania, in the Banat, on the Mureşul River, near the Hungarian border. It is an important railroad junction and a leading regional commercial and industrial center. Distilling, sawmilling, and the manufacture of textiles, machine tools, locomotives, electrical goods, and leather products are the chief industries. Long (c.1551–1685) under Turkish rule, Arad passed in 1685 to the Austrians and in 1849 to the Hungarians, who made it the headquarters of their insurrection against the Hapsburg Empire. In 1920, Arad became part of Rumania. The city's educational and cultural institutions include a theological seminary, a teacher training school, a state theatre, a philharmonic orchestra, and a museum containing exhibits on the Hungarian revolution of 1848–49. The 18th-century citadel was built by Empress Maria Theresa. Arad has sizable Hungarian, Serbian, and German minorities.

Aradus (âr'ədəs), islet and town of ancient Phoenicia, the modern Arwad, N of Tripoli off the Syrian coast. It was the most northerly of the important Phoenician centers. In the Old Testament it is Arvad (Gen. 10.18; 1 Chron. 1.16; Ezek. 27.8,11; 1 Mac. 15.23).

Arafat, Yasir (yäsēr' är'äfät), 1929–, leader of the Palestine Liberation Organization (PLO), the coordinating body for anti-Israeli Arab commando groups, and head of Al Fatah, the largest group in the PLO. He was born in Jerusalem. After smuggling arms to Arab forces during the 1948 Arab-Israeli war, Arafat entered Cairo University, where he became chairman of the Palestine Student Federation. He served in the Egyptian Army during the Suez campaign (1956) and the following year moved to Kuwait, where he trained Palestinian commandos and edited *Our Palestine,* an anti-Zionist magazine. Sometime during that period, he joined the Al Fatah commando group, and in 1965, Arafat returned to Egypt to head Al Assifa, the military arm of Al Fatah. He went on to become leader of Al Fatah, and when the group gained control of the PLO (1969), Arafat was named the larger body's chairman. At the 1974 Arab summit conference the Arab leaders unanimously endorsed Arafat as the "sole legitimate" spokesman for the Palestinians.

Arafat (äräfät') or **Arafa** (äräfä'), granite hill, Saudi Arabia, near Mecca. The hill was an ancient pagan sanctuary and is shrouded in many legends. It is now a site for prayers during the annual pilgrimage to Mecca. Atop the hill is a minaret, reached by broad stone steps. On the 60th step is a platform with a pulpit from which the *khutba* (pilgrimage address) is delivered on the Day of Arafa. The hill is also called Jabal ar Rahm [Arabic,=mountain of mercy].

Arafura Sea (ärəfo͞o'rə), shallow part of the Pacific Ocean, between the Timor and Coral seas, separating Australia from New Guinea. It contains several islands of Indonesia. The Torres Strait to the east is a treacherous passage. See CARPENTARIA, GULF OF.

Aragats, Mount (ărəgäts', Rus. ərəgäts') or **Mount Alagez** (ələgyôs'), extinct volcano, 13,435 ft (4,095 m) high, N Armenia, S European USSR, in the Lesser Caucasus. It is the highest peak in Armenia.

Arago, Dominique François (dômēnēk' fräNswä' ärägō'), 1786–1853, French physicist and astronomer. He is noted for his discoveries in magnetism and optics as well as for his astronomical observations. Arago was an ardent supporter of the wave theory of light. In 1811 he invented the polariscope and later developed a polarimeter. His collected works (1854–62) include his well-known *Astronomie populaire* (4 vol.).

Aragon, Louis (lwē ärägôN'), 1897–, French writer. Aragon is considered one of the founders of SURREALISM in literature and a major spokesman for Communism in the West. After a trip to the USSR in 1931, Aragon abandoned surrealism for Marxism. He was a leader of the Resistance during World War II, and he edited the radical Paris daily *Ce Soir* and later the Communist weekly *Les Lettres françaises.* Aragon's early works include the volume of poems *Feu de joie* (1920) and the surrealistic novel *Le Paysan de Paris* (1926, tr. *Nightwalker,* 1970). His cycle of social novels concerning political responsibility are translated as *The Bells of Basel* (1934, tr. 1941), *Residential Quarter* (1936, tr. 1938), *The Century Was Young* (1941, tr. 1941), and *Aurelien* (1945, tr. 1947). *Les Communistes,* the first of his five-volume cycle of realistic novels, appeared in 1949. His later works include a novel about Napoleon, *Holy Week* (1958, tr. 1961); a history of the USSR from 1917 to 1960, *Histoire parallèle* (1962, tr. 1964); the novel *La Mise à mort* (1965); and a two-volume memoir of Matisse (1972). His major works of poetry include *Le Crève-coeur* (1941), war poems; the series of love poems to his wife, the novelist TRIOLET: *Les Yeux d'Elsa* (1954), *Elsa* (1959), and *Le Fou d'Elsa* (1963); and *Les Chambres* (1969). See *Louis Aragon, Poet of the French Resistance* (ed. by Hannah Josephson and Malcolm Cowley, 1945); study by L. F. Becker (1971).

Aragón (âr'əgŏn, Span. ärägōn'), region (1971 pop. 1,152,708), 18,382 sq mi (47,609 sq km), and former kingdom, NE Spain, bordered on the N by France. Comprising the provinces of Huesca, Teruel, and Zaragoza (Saragossa), Aragón includes the southern slopes of the Pyrenees, where the mountains reach their greatest height; a central plain drained by the Ebro River; and the western fringe of the central plateau of Spain. Much of the region is sparsely populated and desertlike. Irrigation works, started by the Moors, were resumed in the 16th cent.; the two lateral canals of the Ebro are the most important. In the oases and irrigated areas cereals, grapes, olives, and sugar beets are grown. Sheep are raised throughout Aragón, and cattle in the Pyrenees. There are iron, sulfur, and lignite deposits, but sugar refining is the only important industry. The Aragonese, mostly poor and deeply religious, have remained secluded in their small towns, jealously preserving the ancient traditions of a region inhabited since prehistoric times. The city of ZARAGOZA was founded by the Roman emperor Augustus. Visigoths conquered the area in the late 5th cent. and Muslims in the early 8th cent. Carolingians pushed out the Muslims (c.850), and Aragón came under the rule of Navarre. At the death (1035) of Sancho III of Navarre, his western territories were organized as the kingdom of Aragón for his illegitimate son, Ramiro I. He and his successors, notably Alfonso I, extended their dominions southward at the expense of the Moorish emirate of Zaragoza, and in the 12th cent. Zaragoza replaced Huesca as the capital. In 1076, Aragón annexed Navarre, and in 1137 it became united, through personal union, with CATALONIA. Both regions preserved their own cortes, laws, languages, and customs and evolved along separate lines; their deep historical, social, and cultural differences at times caused great friction. With the expansion of the house of Aragón (see separate article), the name Aragón came to signify a confederation of its Spanish possessions (Aragón, Catalonia, MAJORCA, and VALENCIA) and several French fiefs. In the bitter struggles (12th–15th cent.) between kings and nobles, the nobles gained more and more privileges until Peter IV defeated them in 1348. The justiciar, a type of magistrate created in the 12th cent., acted as a sort of intermediary between king and nobles; after 1348 he lost most of his political power but gained more juridical importance. Aragón played only a minor role in the expansionist policy of its kings in the Mediterranean. United with Castile after 1479 through the marriage of Ferdinand V (Ferdinand the Catholic) with Isabella, Aragón preserved its cortes and its city privileges. These, however, were gradually limited by the centralizing policies of the Spanish monarchy, and in 1716 Philip V abolished most of the remaining political privileges to punish the Aragonese for siding with Archduke Charles (later Emperor Charles VI) in the War of the Spanish Succession. The passionate attachment of the Aragonese to their liberties was illustrated by the episode of Antonio Pérez under Philip II and by the heroic defense of Zaragoza in the PENINSULAR WAR. In 1833 the administrative unit of Aragón was divided into the three present provinces.

Aragón, house of, family that ruled in Aragón, Catalonia, Majorca, Sicily, Naples, Sardinia, Athens, and other territories in the Middle Ages. It was descended from RAMIRO I of Aragón (1035–63), natural son of SANCHO III of Navarre. Under Ramiro's successors—SANCHO I, PETER I, and ALFONSO I—Navarre was temporarily (1076–1134) united with Aragón. During that period considerable territory was wrested from the Moors. Ramiro II (1134–37) was succeeded by his daughter, Petronilla, and her husband, RAYMOND BERENGAR IV, count of Barcelona. Aragón and CATALONIA (see also BARCELONA) remained united under their descendants—ALFONSO II, PETER II, JAMES I, PETER III, ALFONSO III, JAMES II, ALFONSO IV, PETER IV, JOHN I, and MARTIN; after a brief interregnum (1410–12) they passed to Martin's nephew, FERDINAND I, and from him to ALFONSO V, JOHN II, and FERDINAND II, who after his marriage with Isabella of Castile became joint king of Castile as Ferdinand V or Ferdinand the Catholic. His grandson, Charles I (later Holy Roman Emperor CHARLES V) succeeded him and merged the houses of Aragón and Castile with that of Hapsburg. Through its merger of 1137 with the house of Barcelona, the house of Aragón had acquired various fiefs in S France, notably Roussillon, Provence, and Montpellier, and suzerainty over others. It lost most of these between 1213 and 1246, mainly because Peter II intervened in the ALBIGENSIAN CRUSADE and was defeated (1213) at Muret. In the same period (1229–38), however, James I won the BALEARIC ISLANDS and the region of VALENCIA from the Moors. In 1282, Peter III became king of SICILY, and in the 14 cent., after a long struggle, Alfonso IV conquered SARDINIA. The duchies of ATHENS and Neopatras were under the nominal rule of the family in the 14th cent., and in 1442 the kingdom of Naples (see NAPLES, KINGDOM OF) was conquered by Alfonso V. Only rarely were these possessions united under a single ruler; for the most part they were held by various branches of the house, often at war with each other as well as with other rulers in Spain. The kingdom of MAJORCA, with ROUSSILLON and Cerdagne, was separate from 1276 to 1343; that of Sicily, from 1296 to 1409; and that of Naples, from 1458 to 1501. Even when united under one ruler as they were under Alfonso V, the various possessions retained their distinct institutions, which continued to be important in diminished and varying degrees after the union of the crowns of Aragón and Castile. See NAVARRE. See study by J. L. Shneidman (2 vol., 1971).

Araguaía (ärägwī'ə), river, c.1,300 mi (2,090 km) long, rising in the Serra des Araras, at the border of Goiás and Mato Grosso states, S central Brazil. It flows generally northward into the Tocantins River, forming most of the border between Goiás and the states of Mato Grosso and Pará. Diamonds are washed along its upper tributaries. There are numerous falls on the Araguaía. The island of Bananal (c.200 mi/320 km long; 35 mi/56 km wide), separating the river into two arms, is one of the largest freshwater islands in the world. It is also a national park. The Araguaía region has been made accessible by new highways.

Arah (ā'rə). **1** Asherite. 1 Chron. 7.39. **2** Family in the return from the Exile. Neh. 7.10.

arahant or **arhat:** see BUDDHISM.

Araish, Al: see LARACHE.

Arak (äräk'), city (1966 pop. 71,925), Tehran prov., W central Iran. A center for agricultural trade as well as for road and rail, the city is also known for its rugs and carpets. Founded c.1800, Arak was formerly known as Sultanabad.

Arakan (ărəkăn', äräkän'), division (1969 est. pop. 1,847,000), 14,194 sq mi (36,762 sq km), W Burma, extending along the Bay of Bengal. It lies at the foot of the Arakan Yoma mountain range, which rises to 10,050 ft (3,063 m) at Victoria Peak. The capital is SITTWE. The Arakanese, who are of Burmese stock with strong Indian influences, are mostly engaged in intensive rice cultivation. There is also a large minority of Bengali Muslims. The region, which is geographically isolated, was the seat of a powerful kingdom (after the 15th cent.), famous for a colossal image of Buddha. At various times under Burmese rule, it finally was absorbed into Burma in 1783; it was the first Burmese territory ceded (1826) to the British after the first Anglo-Burmese war. In the 1950s there was a movement in Arakan for secession from Burma. See Maurice Collis, *The Land of the Great Image* (1959).

Arakcheyev, Aleksey Andreyevich (əlĭksyā' əndrā'yəvĭch äräkchā'yĕf), 1769–1834, Russian general, adviser to Czar Alexander I. An exacting officer, he helped organize the bodyguard of Czar Paul I, who made him a count and gave him high offices. Under ALEXANDER I he was made (1808) minister of war and was one of the czar's most powerful advisers. He virtually ruled Russia during Alexander's frequent trips abroad. Although a martinet and cruel, he was an efficient administrator and made valuable military reforms. See biography by Michael Jenkins (1968).

Araks, river, USSR: see ARAS.

Aral Kara-Kum, desert, USSR: see KARA-KUM.

Aral Sea (ăr'əl), Rus. *Aralskoye More,* inland sea and the world's fourth largest lake, c.26,000 sq mi (67,300 sq km), SW Kazakhstan and NW Uzbekistan, Central Asian USSR, E of the Caspian Sea. It is c.260 mi (420 km) long and c.175 mi (280 km) wide. Generally very shallow, it attains a maximum depth of c.220 ft (70 m). The Aral Sea is fed by the Syr Darya and Amu Darya rivers but has no outlet. Because of its geologically recent separation from the Caspian Sea, the Aral Sea's water is only slightly saline. The sea's western and northern shores are the edges of the arid Ustyurt Plateau; the Kyzyl-Kum desert stretches to the southeast. There are many small islands in the sea. Navigation is possible only from Muynak to Aralsk. The sparse population of the region, concentrated mainly near the mouths of the Syr Darya and Amu Darya, engages in fishing (carp, perch, and pike); there is a cannery at Aralsk. Sodium and magnesium sulfate are mined along the shore. Mentioned by the Arabs in the 10th cent., the Aral Sea was called the Khorezm Sea or Khwarazm Sea by later Arab geographers. It was reached by the Russians in the 17th cent. and was known as the Sine (Blue) Sea.

Aram (ā'răm). **1** Ancient people and their country, roughly identifiable with Syria. The Bible records constant contacts between Hebrews and Aram, mentioning states of Damascus, Beth-rehob, Geshur, Maachah, and Zoba. Their language was a form of Aramaic. Gen. 10.22; Num. 13.21; Judges 18.28; 2 Sam. 8.5,6; 10.6–19; 1 Kings 11.23–25; 1 Chron. 19.6; Ps. 60. **2** Descendant of Nahor. Gen. 22.21. **3** Asherite. 1 Chron. 7.34. **4** In the Gospel genealogy: see RAM **1.**

Aram, Eugene (ā'rəm), 1704–59, English philologist, b. Yorkshire. A self-taught linguist, Aram was the first to identify the Celtic languages as Indo-European. In 1758, while at work on an Anglo-Celtic lexicon, he was arrested and later hanged for the murder—14 years earlier—of his friend Daniel Clark. The story of his crime inspired Thomas Hood's poem *The Dream of Eugene Aram,* and Bulwer-Lytton's novel *Eugene Aram.*

Aramaic (ârəmā'ĭk), language belonging to the Northwest Semitic subdivision of the Semitic subfamily of the Hamito-Semitic family of languages (see HAMITO-SEMITIC LANGUAGES). At some point during the second millenium B.C., the Aramaeans abandoned their desert existence and settled in Syria, bringing their language, Aramaic, with them. By the beginning of the 7th cent. B.C., Aramaic had spread throughout the Fertile Crescent as a lingua franca. Still later the Persians made Aramaic one of the official languages of their empire. After the Jews were defeated by the Babylonians in 586 B.C., they began to speak Aramaic instead of Hebrew, although they retained Hebrew as the sacred language of their religion. Although Aramaic was displaced officially in the Near East by Greek after the coming of Alexander the Great, it held its own under Greek domination and subsequent Roman rule. Aramaic was also the language of Jesus. Following the rise of Islam in the 7th cent. A.D., however, Aramaic began to yield to Arabic, by which eventually it was virtually replaced. In the course of its long history the Aramaic language broke up into a number of dialects, one of the most important of which was SYRIAC. Parts of the books of Ezra and Daniel in the Old Testament were written in an Aramaic dialect, as were major portions of the Palestinian and Babylonian Talmuds. Nabataean (the form of Aramaic current among the Nabataean Arabs), Samaritan, and Palmyrene were other significant ancient dialects of Aramaic. Modern forms of the language (including Syriac) are still spoken today, though not by more than a few hundred thousand people scattered in the Near and Middle East. Grammatically, Aramaic is very close to HEBREW. The Aramaic alphabet is a North Semitic script that is first attested in the 9th cent. B.C. After c.500 B.C. its use became widespread in the Middle East. Descended from the Aramaic alphabet are the Square Hebrew alphabet, which is the ancestor of modern Hebrew writing; the Nabataean, Palmyrene, and Syriac scripts; and the Arabic alphabet, among others. It is believed that the alphabetic writing systems of India and Southeast Asia also have the Aramaic script as their source. See Franz Rosenthal, ed., *An Aramaic Handbook* (4 vol., 1967).

Aramburu, Pedro Eugenio (pā'thrō āōōhā'nyō ärämbōō'rōō), 1903–70, president of Argentina (1955–58). An army general, he participated in the overthrow of Juan PERÓN in Sept., 1955, and that November he replaced Gen. Eduardo Lonardi as provisional president. With the vice president, Admiral Isaac Rojas, he ruled by decree, suppressing strikes and revolts and vigorously driving the Peronists from business, government, and military posts. He later returned the country to constitutional democracy and scheduled free elections, in which he ruled out military figures (including himself) as presidential candidates. After Arturo Frondizi was elected president in Feb., 1958, Aramburu retired from the army. He ran unsuccessfully for president in 1963. In May, 1970, he was kidnapped by a Peronist guerrilla group and murdered, allegedly for his part in the execution of 27 Peronist leaders after an unsuccessful coup attempt in 1956.

Aram-naharaim (ā'răm-nā"hărā'ĭm), the same as PADAN-ARAM.

Aram-zobah (ā'răm-zō'bə), the same as ZOBA.

Aran (ā'răn), descendant of Seir the Horite. Gen. 36.28; 1 Chron. 1.42.

Aran (ăr'ən), island (1971 pop. 3,705), 165 sq mi (427 sq km), Buteshire, W Scotland, in the Firth of Clyde. It is largely granitic and is wild and rocky; it rises to 2,866 ft (874 m). Its scenery and its hunting and fishing have made it a resort. Brodick is the chief town. Robert I hid on Aran in 1306–7 and launched his invasion of the mainland from there.

Arana Osorio, Carlos (kär'lōs ärä'nä ōsō'ryō), 1918–, president of Guatemala (1970–74). A conservative army colonel noted for his successes during an antiguerrilla campaign (1966–68), he was elected president on a law-and-order platform. He declared (Nov., 1970) a state of siege, which remained in effect for one year, and directed a vigorous campaign that brought a decline in guerrilla-terrorist activities. He instituted a five-year development plan (1971–75) and promoted social, economic, and land reform, with an emphasis on modernizing and diversifying agriculture.

Aranda, Pedro Pablo Abarca de Bolea, conde de (pā'thrō pä'blō äbär'kä thä bōlā'ä kōn'dā thā ärän'dä), 1718–98, Spanish statesman. He distinguished himself at first as a military commander, serving as director general of artillery and captain general of Valencia and later of Aragón. His aristocratic background and advocacy of enlightened despotism made him ideally suited to play a reforming role in the administration of Charles III. In 1766 he became president of the council of Castile, a position he held until 1773 when he was dismissed because of his failure to hold the Falkland Islands for Spain. Ambassador to France (1773–87), he was one of the signatories to the Treaty of Paris (1783), which recognized the independence of the United States. Under Charles IV he served briefly as foreign minister (1792), but fell into disfavor because of disapproval of war with France following the French invasion of Spain in 1794. Exiled for a short time, he was later permitted to retire to his Aragón estate.

Aranguren, José Luis (hōsā' lōōēs' ärängōō'rān), 1909–, Spanish philosopher, theologian, and essayist, b. Ávila. A professor of ethics and sociology at the Univ. of Madrid, he is concerned with philosophical problems. His works include *La filosofía de Eugenio D'Ors* [the philosophy of Eugenio D'Ors] (1945), *Protestantismo y catolicismo como formas de existencia* [Protestantism and Catholicism as forms of existence] (1952), *La juventud europea y otros ensayos* [European youth and other essays] (1961), and *Human Communication* (tr. 1967).

Aran Islands, 18 sq mi (47 sq km), Co. Galway, W Republic of Ireland, in Galway Bay. The three islands are Inishmore (the largest), Inisheer, and Inishmaan. The islands are barren, and living is primitive; farming and fishing are important. Gaelic is the everyday language of most islanders. There are many early Christian and prehistoric remains. The islands are a tourist attraction.

Aranjuez (äränghwāth'), town (1970 pop. 29,548), Madrid prov., central Spain, in New Castile, on the Tagus River. A market town (the region is known for asparagus and strawberries; horses are bred), it was once a royal residence. The palace burned several times in the 17th cent. but was rebuilt (1727) by Philip V. The Jardín de la Isla is the finest of the several palace gardens.

Arany, János (yä'nôsh ŏ'rŏnyə), 1817–82, Hungarian poet. Arany is considered one of the founders of modern Hungarian poetry. He was an actor, notary, editor, and professor of Hungarian literature at the Nagy-Koros college. His satirical poem *The Lost Constitution* (1845) was followed by his epic *Toldi* (1846, tr. 1914), to which he added *Toldi's Eve* (1854) and *Toldi's Love* (1879). Among his other works are an epic trilogy, *King Buda's Death* (tr. 1936), *Ildiko*, and *Prince Csaba* (both unfinished), and the ballads that are perhaps his finest works. His style, simple and often reminiscent of folk song, is compelling and powerful.

Arao (ärä'ō), city (1970 pop. 55,452), Kumamoto prefecture, W Kyushu, Japan, on Ariake Bay. It is a port and is part of the Omota-Arao industrial region where cement, chemicals, fertilizers, and plastics are produced.

Arapaho Indians (ərăp'əhō), North American Indians whose language belongs to the Algonquian branch of the Algonquian-Wakashan linguistic stock (see AMERICAN INDIAN LANGUAGES). Their own name was Inuna-ina (our people), but they were referred to as "dog eaters" (for the obvious reason) by other Indians. Tradition places their early home in N Minnesota in the Red River valley, but nothing is known of the date or circumstances of their separation from other Algonquian peoples. They are thought to be most closely related to the Cheyenne and to the Blackfoot. However, it is known that the Arapaho divided into two groups after they migrated to the plains. One group, the Northern Arapaho, continued to live on the North Platte River in Wyoming, while the Southern Arapaho moved south to the Arkansas River in Colorado. Traditionally the Southern Arapaho were allied with the Cheyenne against the Pawnee. The Arapaho stressed membership in age-graded societies, mainly for ceremonial purposes. Their annual sun dance was a major tribal event, and later the Arapaho adopted the GHOST DANCE religion. There are three major divisions—the Atsina or GROS VENTRE INDIANS, who were allied with the Blackfoot Indians and now live with the Assiniboin Indians on the Fort Belknap Reservation in Montana; the Southern Arapaho, now living with the Cheyenne in Oklahoma; and the Northern Arapaho, who retain all of the sacred tribal stone articles and are considered by the Indians to represent the parent group. Since 1876 they have lived on the Wind River Reservation in Wyoming with their former enemies, the Shoshone. See G. A. Dorsey and A. L. Kroeber, *Traditions of the Arapaho* (1903, repr. 1974); V. C. Trenholm, *Arapahoes, Our People* (1970).

arapaima (ăr"əpī'mə), tropical fish, *Arapaima gigas*, of the Amazon basin. It is perhaps the largest of the strictly freshwater fishes, reportedly reaching a length of 15 ft (4.5 m), but averaging 7 to 8 ft (2–2.4 m) in length and 200 lb (90 kg) in weight. The dorsal and anal fins of the arapaima are placed so far back that they appear to be part of the tail fin, giving a massive appearance to the posterior region. The scales are olive-green, turning increasingly reddish in the tail region and becoming crimson near the tail fin. The SWIM BLADDER, as in all members of the order Clupeiformes, is open to the pharynx; in the arapaima it is rich in blood vessels and serves as a lung. The arapaima uses its fins to hollow out a nest in clear, shallow, sandy-bottomed areas. It is a graceful swimmer despite its bulk, and it is valued as an aquarium fish as well as for food. It is classified in the phylum CHORDATA, subphylum Vertebrata, class Osteichthyes, order Clupeiformes, family Osteoglossidae.

Ararat (ăr'ərăt), Turkish *Ağrı Dağı*, name of two mountains, Little Ararat (12,877 ft/3,925 m) and Great Ararat (16,945 ft/5,165 m), E Turkey, near the Iranian and Soviet borders. The tradition that Mt. Ararat is the resting place of Noah's ark is based on a misreading of Gen. 8.4, which properly reads "upon the mountains of Ararat," indicating a country or region. The land or the **kingdom of Ararat** (fl. c.9th–7th cent. B.C.), called in Assyrian Urartu, was situated between the river Araks and the lakes Van and Rezaiyeh. It included all the land later called ARMENIA. Its language, written in cuneiform, has no relation to any known language, except perhaps to the Horite. (2 Kings 19.37; Isa. 37.38; Jer. 51.27.)

Aras (äräs'), Rus. *Araks*, river, c.600 mi (970 km) long, rising in the Transcaucasus mts., NE Turkey. It flows generally east, forming parts of the Turkey-USSR and USSR-Iran borders, before entering the Azerbaijan Republic, USSR, where it joins the Kura River at Sabirabad. Much of its upper and middle courses are rapid and tumultuous, and its waters are used for irrigation. The Aras is the chief river of Soviet Armenia, and its valley contains Armenia's greatest concentration of people and industries. The Aras is the Araxes of the ancients.

Arason, Jon: see ARESSON, JON.

Aratus (ərā'təs), fl. 3d cent. B.C., Greek court poet, from Soli in Cilicia. He wrote an astronomical treatise, *Phenomena*, which was quoted by Paul at Athens (Acts 17.28).

Aratus, d. 213 B.C., Greek statesman and general of Sicyon, prime mover and principal leader of the Second ACHAEAN LEAGUE. His objective at first was to free the Peloponnesus from Macedonian domination, and he is credited with bringing into the confederation many of the principal cities of Greece. But he was blamed for the subsequent Macedonian domination of the Peloponnesus, for while fighting Cleomenes III of Sparta and the Aetolian League he changed his policy towards Macedonia and called in ANTIGONUS III. See F. W. Walbank, *Aratos of Sicyon* (1933).

Araucanian Indians (əroukän'ēən), South American people, occupying most of S central Chile at the time of the Spanish conquest (1540). The Araucanians were an agricultural people living in small settlements. They are classified into three major cultural subdivisions, the Huilliche, the Picunche, and the Mapuche, the last being the largest group. The known history of the Araucanians begins with the Inca invasion (c.1448–c.1482) under Tupac Yupanqui, but Inca influence was never strong. Against the Spanish under Pedro de VALDIVIA the Araucanians offered resistance, notably under LAUTARO and CAUPOLICÁN, and their stout fight was immortalized in the epic by Alonso de ERCILLA Y ZÚÑIGA. They were successful in protecting S Chile and by 1598 had destroyed almost all Spanish settlements S of the Bío-Bío River. Their struggle continued intermittently in the 17th and 18th cent. in the uprisings of 1723, 1740, and 1766. White immigration southward brought on the war of 1880–81, which ended with Araucanian submission. Earlier, especially at the beginning of the 18th cent., Araucanians fleeing white encroachment had gone across the Andes into Argentina. Capturing wild horses, they became wanderers on the plains and absorbed the PUELCHE. Gen. Julio A. Roca subjugated them in his campaigns (1879–83). There are many tribes and languages, which make up a separate linguistic family. The Araucanians continue to influence Chilean life, and number over 200,000. See L. C. Faron, *Hawks of the Sun* (1964) and *The Mapuche Indians of Chile* (1968); M. I. Hilger, *Huenun Ñamku* (1966); E. H. Korth, *Spanish Policy in Colonial Chile* (1968).

Araunah (ärô'nə), Jebusite who sold his threshing floor to David so that an altar might be erected there. This site, on Mt. Moriah, was afterward used for the Temple. 2 Sam. 24.15-25. Ornan: 1 Chron. 21.14-30; 2 Chron. 3.1.

Arawak (ä'räwäk), linguistic stock of American Indians who, at the time of the Spanish Conquest, occupied the islands of the Greater Antilles, the Bahamas, and Trinidad. It is believed that the tribes came from South America. Before the arrival of the Spanish they were driven from the Lesser Antilles by the Carib. Most of the Arawak of the Antilles died out after the Spanish conquest. In South America, Arawakan-speaking Indian groups are widespread, from SW Brazil and Paraguay to Colombia and Venezuela, representing a wide range of cultures. They are found mostly in the tropical forest areas N of the Amazon. Contact with white settlement has led to culture change and depopulation among these groups.

Araxes, river, Turkey and the USSR: see ARAS.

Arba or **Arbah** (both: är'bə), eponym of Kirjath-arba, "the city of Arba," usually called HEBRON. Arba is called the father of ANAK. Gen. 35.27; Joshua 14.15; 15.13; 21.11.

Arbela (ärbē'lə), town of ancient Assyria. Its name is sometimes given to the battle fought at Gaugamela, some 60 mi (100 km) away, in which Alexander the Great defeated (331 B.C.) Darius III. Arbela is the modern Irbil (Iraq).

arbitrage: see FOREIGN EXCHANGE.

arbitration, industrial, method of settling disputes between employer and employees by seeking and accepting a decision by a third party. Such arbitration may be compelled by the government, as in New Zealand (since 1894), Australia (since 1904), Canada (since 1907), Italy (since 1926), and Great Britain (since World War II). In other cases, it may be by voluntary agreement, as is often the case in the United States, where the government is occasionally forced to intervene in the case of a strike affecting the public welfare (see TAFT-HARTLEY LABOR ACT) by persuading the parties concerned to accept the decision handed down by the arbitrator. Machinery for that purpose has been set up at both Federal and state levels in the form of mediation and arbitration boards. The American Arbitration Association, founded in 1926, provides the services of over 20,000 skilled arbitrators to help settle labor disputes. In voluntary arbitration a formal agreement is usually made to abide by the decision. See Kurt Braun, *Labor Disputes and Their Settlement* (1955); W. H. McPherson, *Grievance Mediation Under Collective Bargaining* (1956); Frank Elkouri, *How Arbitration Works* (1960).

arbitration, international, judicial process by which international disputes, usually between states, are settled peacefully, generally through the use of a tribunal acting as a court of law. Such a tribunal may consist of an individual (e.g., an impartial monarch, the pope, the secretary general of the United Nations), a neutral country, or an organization such as the United Nations International Court of Justice. The parties to the dispute pick the arbitrating body themselves and are obligated to accept the terms of settlement. If the parties do not agree in advance to follow the decision reached by a third party, but merely agree to consider it, the process is termed conciliation (see MEDIATION). Arbitration was practiced by the Greek city-states, and in the Middle Ages high ecclesiastical authorities were called upon to settle controversies. With the development of the modern system of nation-states, however, arbitration was less frequently used until the 19th cent. when the settlement by arbitration of the famous ALABAMA CLAIMS case between the United States and Great Britain brought this practice back into general use. Great advances have been made since then, most notably in the establishment of a Permanent Court of Arbitration by the HAGUE CONFERENCES. Functions analogous to arbitration were performed by the Permanent Court of International Justice (see WORLD COURT) under the League of Nations and have now been transferred to its successor, the INTERNATIONAL COURT OF JUSTICE. Today many treaties contain clauses providing for arbitration or conciliation of disputes; the most notable of these is the Charter of the United Nations (Article 33). See J. H. Ralston, *International Arbitration from Athens to Locarno* (1929); C. M. Bishop, *International Arbitral Procedure* (1930); Kenneth S. Carlston, *The Process of International Arbitration* (1946); H. W. Briggs, *The Law of Nations* (2d ed. 1952); J. L. Brierly, *The Law of Nations* (6th ed. 1963); Arthur Cox, *Prospects for Peacekeeping* (1967).

Arblay, Madame d': see BURNEY, FANNY.

Arboga (är'bō"gä), town (1970 pop. 11,932), Västmanland co., S Sweden, on the Arboga River, near Lake Hjälmaren. It is a transportation, industrial, and tourist center. Manufactures include metal goods and processed food. Of great importance in the Middle Ages, Arboga was the site of several parliaments, including Sweden's first (1435), and numerous church assemblies. St. Bridget was proclaimed patron saint of Sweden there in 1396. The city has a Franciscan monastery (founded 1285).

Arboleda, Julio (ho͞o'lyō ärbōlä'thä), 1817-61, Colombian poet and politician. A powerful political force, he was for a time imprisoned and then exiled. He returned to lead a revolt (1860) against MOSQUERA, was named president, but shortly thereafter was assassinated. He is best known as the author of the unfinished poem *Gonzalo de Oyón*, an epic of the Spanish conquest.

Arbor Day, in the United States, day specifically designated for the planting of trees. It was first suggested by Julius Sterling MORTON of Nebraska in 1872. It is celebrated at different times in different states because planting seasons vary. The planting of trees by school children is a usual method of celebrating Arbor Day.

arboretum: see BOTANICAL GARDEN.

arborvitae (är"bərvī'tē) [Lat.,=tree of life], aromatic evergreen tree of the genus *Thuja* of the family Cupressaceae (CYPRESS family), with scalelike leaves borne on flattened branchlets of a fanlike appearance and with very small cones. Some of the numerous cultivated varieties are dwarf forms. There are several species, two native to North America, the remainder native to Asia but sometimes cultivated in the United States. *T. occidentalis,* of E North America, called arborvitae, white cedar, or Northern white cedar, has many garden forms and is popular for hedges. The leaves were once used as a remedy for rheumatism, and their oil as a vermifuge. *T. plicata* of W North America, called giant arborvitae, red cedar, or Western red cedar, is much larger and of considerably more importance as lumber; it is primarily used for making shingles and shakes. The wood of both of these species is soft but quite resistant to decay, hence its popularity for fence posts. Arborvitaes are classified in the division PINOPHYTA, class Pinopsida, order Coniferales.

Arbroath (ärbrōth') or **Aberbrothock** (ăb"ərbrəthŏk'), burgh (1971 pop. 22,585), Angus, E central Scotland, on the North Sea at the mouth of the Brothock River. A seaport, it is known for its smoked haddock, shipbuilding, and the processing of flax and jute. There are engineering works, breweries, an iron foundry, and diverse small industries. Arbroath Abbey was founded by WILLIAM THE LION c.1178 and contains his tomb. The Scottish estates met in the abbey in 1320 and called for independence from England. In 1975, Abroath became part of the new Tayside region.

Arbuckle Mountains, range of low, rolling hills, rising c.700 ft (210 m) above the prairie, S Okla.; remnant of mountains formed in the Precambrian era. Interesting geological formations have resulted from the varying erosional rates of the different rock types found in the area. Platt National Park contains many cold mineral springs. Arbuckle National Recreation Area, southwest of the park, surrounds Lake of the Arbuckles, a 2,350-acre (951-hectare) reservoir formed behind Arbuckle Dam (see NATIONAL PARKS AND MONUMENTS, table).

Arbus, Diane, 1923-71, American photographer, b. New York City. For nearly 20 years Arbus operated a successful fashion photography studio with her husband. She studied with Lisette Model and began, in the 1950s, to make the intimate record of life on the freakish margins of society for which she became renowned. Her acceptance of what she saw set her work apart and gave her access to the unapproachable: transvestites, dwarves, prostitutes, nudists, and the everyday ugly. She died a suicide at 48. See *aperture* monograph, *Diane Arbus* (1972).

Arbuthnot, John (ärbŭth'nət, är'bəthnŏt), 1667-1735, Scottish author and scientist, court physician (1705-14) to Queen Anne. He is best remembered for his five "John Bull" pamphlets (1712), political satires on the Whig war policy, which introduced the character John Bull, the typical Englishman. With his friends, Swift, Pope, and Gay, Arbuthnot was a member of the SCRIBLERUS CLUB, organized to ridicule false tastes in learning, and was the principal author of the "Memoirs of . . . Martinus Scriblerus," first published in the quarto edition of Pope's works (1741). He was also the author of several progressive medical works. Greatly admired in his time, Arbuthnot was called an unusual genius by Samuel Johnson, and Pope addressed to him the famous "Epistle to Dr. Arbuthnot." See edition of his works by G. A. Aitken (1892); study by L. M. Beattie (1935).

Arbutus, uninc. town (1970 pop. 22,745), Baltimore co., NE Md., a suburb of Baltimore. A state hospital is nearby.

arbutus, trailing: see TRAILING ARBUTUS.

arc, in electricity, highly luminous and intensely hot discharge of electricity between two electrodes. The arc was discovered early in the 19th cent. by the English scientist Sir Humphry Davy, who so named it because of its shape. An arc is characterized by a high current, low voltage, and indefinite duration. It is usually started when two electrodes carrying an electric current are drawn apart. At the instant the electrodes are parted, strong electric forces draw electrons from one electrode to the other, initiating the arc. The discharge consists of a current composed of these electrons and charged gas particles, called ions, that form between the electrodes. The first practical electric light, the arc lamp, made use of the arc formed between two carbon rods (see LIGHTING). Today the use of the arc lamp is limited to special purposes, e.g., in searchlights and in research applications. The principle of the electric arc is employed in WELDING (as in the hydrogen arc, where hydrogen is introduced between tungsten electrodes) and also in generating heat in the electric furnace. A spark, like an arc, is a discharge of electricity between two points, but it has a high voltage and a short duration. Lightning is an example of a spark.

arc, in geometry, a curved line or any part of it; in particular, a portion of the circumference of a circle. The length s of an arc of a circle of radius r and subtending a central angle of θ radians is $s=r\theta$; if θ is measured in degrees, then the arc is given by $s=2\pi r\theta/360°$.

Arca: see ARKITE.

arcade, series of arches supported by columns or piers. An arcade may stand free; if it is attached to a wall it is called a wall arcade or a blind arcade. The earliest-known arcades were in Roman architecture, in which piers, ornamented with engaged columns carrying an entablature, formed the arch supports. However, in Diocletian's palace at Spalato there are arches supported by columns and resting directly upon their capitals, of the type which was given full development in Romanesque and Gothic architec-

Arcade

ture. In the early Christian basilica columnar arcades separated the nave and side aisles and supported the wall of the clerestory. From this beginning the rich system of bays used in Romanesque and Gothic church interiors was developed, in which lofty arcades extended the full length of the nave. Both freestanding and blind arcades were used in Romanesque facades (notably in N Italy) and in the west fronts of English and French Gothic cathedrals, where the arches were often filled with statues of saints. Richly designed arcades surrounded the enclosed cloisters of the medieval and Renaissance monasteries; they were similarly used in the courts of houses in Italy and Spain and in the courtyards of Muhammadan mosques. The Romanesque structures of Spain, Sicily, and S Italy made frequent use of arcades composed of interlacing arches, in which the arch rings overlap to alternate columns or piers. Continuous arcades, extending over sidewalks, are common in Italian cities, notably in Bologna.

Arcadelt, Jacob (yä'kōp är'kädĕlt), c.1505-c.1560, Flemish composer, b. Liège. He spent much of his time at the Papal court in Rome. After 1555 he was in Paris in the service of the duke of Guise. Arcadelt belonged to the so-called Netherlands school of composition. He wrote madrigals, French chansons, and church music, including several important books of masses.

Arcadia (ärkā'dēə), region of ancient Greece, in the middle of the Peloponnesus, without a seaboard, and surrounded and dissected by mountains. The Arcadians, relatively isolated from the rest of the world, lived a proverbially simple and natural life. By far the largest city was MEGALOPOLIS, founded by Epaminondas. It had some political power, especially in the Arcadian League, but Arcadia as a whole was of little political significance. The independent mountaineers periodically fought against Spartan power, but did not cooperate well. Other cities were Mantinea, Tegea, Orchomenus, and Heraea.

Arcadia, city (1970 pop. 42,868), Los Angeles co., S Calif., a residential suburb of Los Angeles, at the foot of the San Gabriel Mts.; inc. 1903. The city has electronic, aerospace, optical, and camera industries. The Santa Anita racetrack and an arboretum are in Arcadia.

Arcadius (ärkā'dēəs), c.377–408, Roman emperor of the East (395–408), son and successor of Theodosius I. His brother, HONORIUS, inherited (395) the West. Henceforth the division between the Eastern and Western empires became permanent. A weak ruler, Arcadius entrusted the government successively to RUFINUS, EUTROPIUS (d.399), and other ministers and was later greatly influenced by his Frankish wife, EUDOXIA. During his reign, Greece was invaded (395) by ALARIC I who was induced to leave in 397 by STILICHO. Arcadius put down a temporarily successful revolt (399–400) of the Gothic officials and mercenaries in Constantinople. He exiled (404) the patriarch St. JOHN CHRYSOSTOM. His son, Theodosius II, succeeded him.

Arcagnolo: see ORCAGNA.

Arcaro, George Edward (Eddie Arcaro), 1916–, American jockey, b. Cincinnati, Ohio. He began riding at the age of 15, and in his 31-year career he finished first in 4,779 races, a total exceeded in the United States only by Johnny Longden and Willy Shoemaker. Arcaro was one of the two jockeys (Bill Hartack was the other) to win the Kentucky Derby five times (on Lawrin in 1938, Whirlaway in 1941, Hoop Jr. in 1945, Citation in 1948, and Hill Gail in 1952). He also has the exclusive distinction of twice having swept the Triple Crown of racing—the Kentucky Derby, the Preakness, and the Belmont Stakes. Arcaro's mounts won a record $30,039,543 in purses. He retired from racing in 1962.

Arcas: see CALLISTO.

Arc de Triomphe de l'Étoile (ärk də trēôNf' də lātwäl'), imposing triumphal arch in Paris standing on an elevation at the end of the Avenue des Champs Élysées and in the center of the Place de l'Étoile, which is formed by the intersection of 12 radiating avenues. It commemorates the victories of Napoleon I, under whose decree it was built. Construction was begun in 1806 by J. F. CHALGRIN from his own designs and was carried on after his death by L. Goust, J. N. Huyot, and G. A. Blouet successively, who brought the arch to completion in 1836. It is 164 ft (50 m) high, 148 ft (45 m) wide, and 72 ft (22 m) deep, with colossal symbolic groups flanking the arch. The principal sculpture, *La Marseillaise,* was executed by François RUDE. In 1920 the body of an unknown French soldier of World War I was interred beneath the arch, and a perpetual flame was lighted.

Arcesilaus (ärsĕs"ĭlā'əs), c.316–c.241 B.C., Greek philosopher of Pitane in Aeolis. He was the principal figure of the Middle Academy. Despite his position in the ACADEMY, his teachings diverged from Platonic doctrine. By emphasizing the doubt expressed by Socrates as to the possibility of gaining knowledge, he took a position comparable to that of the Skeptics (see SKEPTICISM). As an intellectual agnostic, he taught that knowledge and opinion could not be distinguished from each other. As to behavior in practice, Arcesilaus held that we act on ideas rather than on certain knowledge. Arcesilaus indirectly influenced Carneades and his school. Arcesilaus was, in his day, the great opponent of Stoicism. See M. M. Patrick, *The Greek Skeptics* (1929).

Arch, Joseph, 1826–1919, English labor leader, a Primitive Methodist preacher. He founded the National Agricultural Labourers Union in 1872 and became its president. In 1873, Arch visited Canada and the United States to study labor and immigration problems. He served (1885–86, 1892–1900) as one of the first labor members in Parliament and was instrumental in enfranchising agricultural workers. See his autobiography (ed. by the countess of Warwick, 1898); biography by Pamela Horn (1971).

arch, the spanning of a wall opening by means of separate units (such as bricks or stone blocks) assembled into an upward curve that maintains its shape and stability through the mutual pressure of a load and the separate pieces. The weight of the supported load is thus converted into downward and

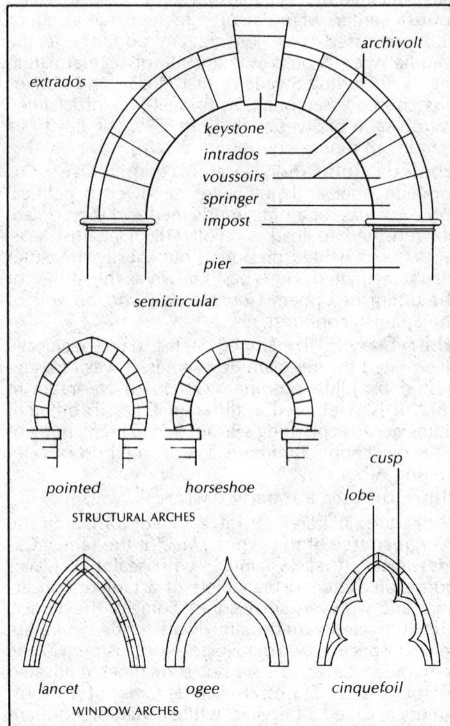

Arches

outward lateral pressures called thrusts, which are received by the solid piers (abutments) flanking the opening. The blocks, called voussoirs, composing the arch usually have a wedge shape but they can be rectangular with wedge-shaped joints between them. The underside of the arch is the intrados or soffit and the upper surface above the crown block (keystone) of the arch is the extrados. The point where the arch starts to curve is the foot of the arch, and the stones there are the springers. The surface above the haunch (just below the beginning of the curve) contained within a line drawn perpendicular to the springing line (from which the arch curves), and another drawn horizontal to the crown is the spandril. In modern fireproof construction the word *arch* is also used for the masonry that fills the space between steel beams and acts as a floor support. The arch was used by the Egyptians, Babylonians, and Greeks, chiefly for underground drains, and also by the Assyrians in the construction of vaulted and domed chambers. In Europe the oldest known arch is the Cloaca Maxima, the huge drain at Rome built by Lucius Tarquinius Priscus c.578 B.C. The Romans developed the semicircular arch, modeled on earlier Etruscan structures, in the vaults and domes of their monumental buildings. Its use was continued in early Christian, Byzantine, and Romanesque architecture. In the 13th cent. the pointed arch (used as early as 722 B.C. in Assyrian drains) came into general use. The contact of Europeans with Saracenic architecture during the Crusades is offered among other theories for its introduction into Europe. But it is likely that the pointed arch may have been independently rediscovered in Europe in the Middle Ages as a device for solving many of the mechanical difficulties of vault construction. Its adoption was an essential element in the evolution of the Gothic system of design. With the Renaissance there was a return to the round arch, which prevailed until the 19th-century invention of steel beams for wide spans relegated the arch to a purely decorative function. Although the circular and pointed forms have predominated in the West, the Muslim nations of the East developed a variety of other arched shapes, including the ogee arch used in Persia and India, the horseshoe arch used in Spain and North Africa, and the multifoil or scalloped arch used especially in the Muslim architecture of Spain. In the 20th cent. arches often take a parabolic shape. They are usually constructed with laminated wood or reinforced concrete, materials that give greater lightness and strength to the structure. See TRIUMPHAL ARCH.

archaeology (ärkēŏl'əjē) [Gr.,=study of beginnings], scientific study of the material remains of human cultures found in deposits dating from the beginnings of human life to the era of modern history. Archaeology provides the material evidence for establishing the history of prehistoric times and supplements documentary evidence in the study of historic periods. To locate, excavate, interpret, record, preserve, and, if necessary, restore finds, the present-day archaeologist requires skilled assistance from a wide variety of experts, including historians, anthropologists, linguists, geologists, chemists, physicists, botanists, architects, engineers, photographers, and climatologists. Materials have been collected since ancient times, notably in the classic period and during the Renaissance. Research into the life and culture of the past was initiated in the 15th cent. in Italy after the introduction of a knowledge of ancient Greece inspired the excavation of Greek sculpture. In the 18th cent. the progress of Greek and Roman archaeology was advanced by Johann WINCKELMANN and Ennio Visconti and by excavations at HERCULANEUM and POMPEII; in the 19th, by the acquisition of the ELGIN MARBLES. The study of ancient cultures in the Aegean region was stimulated by the excavations of Heinrich SCHLIEMANN at Troy and in Greece, and of Arthur EVANS at Crete. The work of Martin Nilsson, Alan Wace, and John Pendlebury was also significant in this area, and the decipherment of the Minoan script by Michael VENTRIS raised new speculations about the early Aegean cultures. The foundations of Egyptology, a prolific branch of archaeology because of the antiquity of Egyptian culture and the wealth of material preserved in the dry Egyptian climate, were laid by the recovery of the Rosetta stone (see under ROSETTA) and the work of French scholars who accompanied Napoleon Bonaparte to Egypt. Investigations that have reconstructed ancient life in the Nile valley and rewritten Egyptian history were carried on in the 19th cent. by Karl Lepsius, Auguste Mariette, and Gaston Maspero, and in the 19th and 20th cent. by W. M. Flinders Petrie, James Breasted, and other scholars. Interest in the Middle East was stimulated by the work of Edward Robinson (1794–1863) on the geography of the Bible and by the decipherment of a cuneiform inscription of Darius I, which was copied (1835) by Henry Rawlinson from the Behistun rock in Iran. The finding of the Dead Sea Scrolls aroused new interest in Biblical studies. Archaeology in Mesopotamia was notably advanced in the 19th cent. by Jules Oppert, Paul Botta, and Austen Layard; in the 20th, by Charles Woolley, Henri Frankfort, and Seton Lloyd. The scientific explanation of prehistoric finds began with the conclusion advanced in 1832 by the Danish archaeologist Christian Thomsen that human industrial culture may be divided into stages of progress based on the principal materials used for weapons and implements. His three-age theory (see STONE AGE; BRONZE AGE; IRON AGE) was essentially based on prehistoric materials from Scandinavia and France. Concerted investigations began in the mid-19th cent. with the stratigraphic excavation of such remains as the LAKE DWELLING, BARROW, and KITCHEN MIDDEN. At first, the sequences of culture change uncovered in Western Europe were generalized to include all of world history, but improved techniques of field excavation and the expansion of archaeological discoveries in Africa, Asia, and the Americas challenged the universality of such rigid classifications. Technological traditions ceased to be regarded as inevitable concomitants of specific cultural stages. Later interpretations of prehistoric human life emphasize cultural responses to particular environments (see ECOLOGY). Thus the PALEOLITHIC, MESOLITHIC, and NEOLITHIC periods are evaluated in terms of food production. Developments in the methods of DATING archaeological remains resulted in many new hypotheses regarding prehistoric migrations and the diffusion of culture. The study of past times was enhanced by the investigation of the life and customs of existent aboriginal groups. Advanced indigenous cultures were ignored until John Stephens published an account of his travels (1839) in Central America, which excited the interest of archaeologists in the MAYA. In the 19th cent. fruitful studies began of the TOLTEC and of the AZTEC who followed them in Mexico and of the INCA in South America. In 1926, discovery of human cultural remains associated with extinct fauna near Folsom, N.Mex., established a depth of prehistory for the New World that is now believed to be at least 25,000 years, and perhaps over 40,000. Among the most important work done in the mid-20th cent. was that of Louis LEAKEY, who located the skeletal remains of humans in East Africa dating back 1.7 million years. Other significant excavations were conducted in the Americas and in China. Important efforts were made to promote systematic research and the scientific study of archaeological materials and to preserve them. Museums with valuable collections include the Metropolitan Museum and the American Museum of Natural History in New York City; the British Museum; the Louvre; national museums in Denmark, Norway, and Sweden, rich in remains of the Iron Age; the Vatican and Capitoline museums, Rome; collections from Pompeii and Herculaneum at Naples; and museums in Athens, Cairo, and Jerusalem. Many universities have established schools and museums of archaeology. Organizations such as the National Science Foundation, the Smithsonian Institution, and the National Geographic Society in the United States promote archaeological studies. See also MAN, PREHISTORIC and STRATIGRAPHY. See Glyn E. Daniel, *A Hundred Years of Archaeology* (1950); Grahame Clark, *Archaeology and Society* (3d ed. 1957, repr. 1968); R. J. Braidwood, *Prehistoric Man* (1961); G. E. Daniel, *The Origins and Growth of Archaeology* (1967); James Deetz, *Invitation to Archaeology* (1967); H. P. Eydoux, *History of Archaeological Discoveries* (1967); Massimo Pallottino, *The Meaning of Archaeology* (1968); Edward Bacon, *Archaeology* (1971); K. W. Marek, *Gods, Graves, and Scholars* (2d ed. 1967) and *The First American* (1971).

archaeopteryx (är"kēŏp'tərĭks) [Gr. *archaeo*= primitive, *pteryx*=wing], primitive bird, two incomplete fossils of which were discovered in the 19th cent. in the late Jurassic limestone of Solnhofen, Bavaria. To date four fossil specimens have been found. Classified as a bird because of the presence of feathers and the structure of the legs and wings, it nevertheless had many characteristics now found only in reptiles or in bird embryos. It was smaller than a crow.

Archangel: see ARKHANGELSK, USSR.

archangel (ärk'ānjəl), chief ANGEL, differing from other angels only in importance. Three are best known, MICHAEL, GABRIEL, and RAPHAEL; they have set functions. According to Tobit 12.15 there are seven archangels, but only Raphael, companion of Tobias, is given a name.

Archelaus (är"kēlā'əs): see HEROD.

Archeozoic era: see PRECAMBRIAN ERA.

Archer, William, 1856–1924, English author, critic, and translator, b. Scotland. Throughout his life he worked as drama critic on several London newspapers, establishing a reputation for integrity and discernment. He influenced the direction of English and American drama through his active interest in the work of the great Norwegian playwright Henrik Ibsen. He translated Ibsen's *Pillars of Society*, and largely through his efforts the play was the first Ibsen play to be produced (1880) in London. Archer subsequently translated several other Ibsen plays; and in 1906–8 he edited Ibsen's collected plays. Archer's writings include *Masks or Faces* (1888), *America To-day* (1900), *Real Conversations* (1904), *The Old Drama and the New* (1923), and several plays, including the highly successful melodrama *The Green Goddess* (1923). His critical reviews for the London *World* were collected and published annually as *The Theatrical "World"* (1893–97). See biography by his brother, Charles Archer (1931).

Archer, The, English name for SAGITTARIUS, a CONSTELLATION.

archerfish, laterally compressed fish, genus *Toxotes*, which catches insects by spitting at and disabling them. The archerfish has a groove in the roof of its mouth that forms a long narrow tube when the tongue is placed against it; the fish propels drops of water along the tube by compressing its gill covers. Some archerfishes can shoot as far as 12 ft (3.5 m), with reasonable accuracy up to about 4 ft (1.2 m). Apparently they are able to correct the trajectory after missing a target. Shooting down insects is an auxilliary method of food-getting for the archerfish, which feeds mostly on insects floating in the water. The five archerfish species inhabit fresh and brackish coastal water in India and SE Asia. The species most often displayed in aquariums is *T. jaculatrix*, a silver fish with black stripes, which grows as long as 8 in. (20 cm). Archerfishes are classified in the phylum CHORDATA, subphylum Vertebrata, class Osteichthyes, order Perciformes, family Toxotidae.

archery, sport of shooting with BOW AND ARROW. An important military and hunting skill before the introduction of gunpowder, it was revived as a sport in England by Charles II. It was introduced into North America in the late 17th cent. Archery became popular in the United States after 1879, when the National Archery Association was formed. Although archery competitions were held in the 1908 and 1920 Olympic Games, it was not until 1972 that it became a certified Olympic event. World championships are held under the auspices of the Fédération Internationale de Tir à l'Arc (FITA; est. 1930). There are four main types of archery competition: target, field, flight, and crossbow shooting. The object in target shooting is to score the highest total of points with a specified number of arrows aimed at the inner circle—the "bull's-eye"—of five concentric colored circles on a padded mat—the target. The value of hits decreases from the bull's eye to the outermost circle. The world's oldest continuous archery tournament is the Ancient Scorton Arrow Contest, established (1673) by King Charles II of England. See D. W. Campbell, *Archery* (1971); E. G. Heath, *The Grey Goose Wing* (1971).

Arches National Park, 82,953 acres (33,571 hectares), E Utah; est. as a national park 1971. Located in red-rock country and overlooking the gorge of the Colorado River, this area contains a vast and unusual array of natural rock formations. Water, frost, and wind have carved giant but graceful arches, windows, spires, and pinnacles.

archetype (är'kĭtīp") [Gr. *arch*=first, *typos*=mold], term whose earlier meaning, "original model," or "prototype," has been enlarged by C. G. JUNG and by several contemporary literary critics. A Jungian archetype is a thought pattern that finds worldwide parallels, either in cultures (for example, the similarity of the ritual of Holy Communion in Europe with the *tecqualo* in ancient Mexico) or in individuals (a child's concept of a parent as both heroic and tyrannic, superman and ogre). Jung believed that such archetypal images and ideas reside in the unconscious level of the mind of every human being and are inherited from the ancestors of the race. They form the substance of the collective unconscious. Literary critics such as Northrop FRYE and Maud Bodkin use the term archetype interchangeably with the term MOTIF, emphasizing that the role of these elements in great works of literature is to unite readers with otherwise dispersed cultures and eras.

Archevites (är'kēvīts), colonists sent into Samaria by the Assyrian government. They were probably natives of Erech. Ezra 4.9.

Archi (är'kī): see ARCHITE.

archil (är'kĭl, -chĭl) or **orchil** (ôr'-), blue, red, or purple dye extracted from several species of LICHEN, also called orchella weeds, found in various parts of the world. Commercial archil is either a powder (called cudbear), a pasty mass (called archil), or a drier paste (called persis).

Archilochus (ärkĭl'əkəs), fl. c.700 or c.650 B.C., Greek poet, b. Paros. As an innovator in the use and construction of the personal lyric, his language was intense and often violent. Many fragments of his verse survive.

Archimedes (ärkĭmē'dēz), 287–212 B.C., Greek mathematician, physicist, and inventor. He is famous for his work in geometry (on the circle, sphere, cylinder, and parabola), physics, mechanics, and hydrostatics. He lived most of his life in his native Syracuse, where he was on intimate terms with the royal family. Few facts of his life are known, but tradition has made at least two stories famous. In one story, he was asked by Hiero II to determine whether a crown was pure gold or was alloyed with silver. Archimedes was perplexed, until one day, observing the overflow of water in his bath, he suddenly realized that since gold is more dense (i.e., has more weight per volume) than silver, a given weight of gold represents a smaller volume than an equal weight of silver and that a given weight of gold would therefore displace less water than an equal weight of silver. Delighted at his discovery, he ran home without his clothes, shouting "Eureka," which means "I have found it." He found that Hiero's crown displaced more water than an equal weight of gold, thus showing that the crown had been alloyed with silver (or another metal less dense than gold). In the other story he is said to have told Hiero, in illustration of the principle of the lever, "Give me a place to stand, and I will move the world." He invented machines of war (Second Punic War) so ingenious that the besieging armies of Marcus Claudius Marcellus were held off from Syracuse for three years. When the city was taken, the general gave orders to spare the scientist, but Archimedes was killed. Nine of Archimedes' treatises, which demonstrate his discoveries in mathematics and in floating bodies, are extant. They are *On the Sphere and Cylinder, On the Measurement of the Circle, On the Equilibrium of Planes, On Conoids and Spheroids, On Spirals, On the Quadrature of the Parabola, Arenarius* [or sand-reckoner], *On Floating Bodies,* and *On the Method of Mechanical Theorems.* Archimedes' many contributions to mathematics and mechanics include calculating the value of π, devising a mathematical exponential system to express extremely large numbers (he said he could numerically represent the grains of sand that would be needed to fill the universe), developing ARCHIMEDES' PRINCIPLE, and inventing ARCHIMEDES' SCREW. See studies by T. L. Heath (1953) and E. J. Dijksterhuis (1956).

Archimedes' principle, principle that states that a body immersed in a fluid is buoyed up by a force equal to the weight of the displaced fluid. The principle applies to both floating and submerged bodies and to all fluids, i.e., liquids and gases. It explains not only the buoyancy of ships and other vessels in water but also the rise of a balloon in the air and the apparent loss of weight of objects underwater. In determining whether a given body will float in a given fluid, both weight and volume must be considered; that is, the relative DENSITY, or weight per unit of volume, of the body compared to the fluid determines the buoyant force. If the body is less dense than the fluid, it will float or, in the case of a balloon, it will rise. If the body is denser than the fluid, it will sink. Relative density also determines the proportion of a floating body that will be submerged in a fluid. If the body is two thirds as dense as the fluid, then two thirds of its volume will be submerged, displacing in the process a volume of fluid whose weight is equal to the entire weight of the body. In the case of a submerged body, the apparent weight of the body is equal to its weight in air less the weight of an equal volume of fluid. The fluid most often encountered in applications of Archimedes' principle is water, and the SPECIFIC GRAVITY of a substance is a convenient measure of its relative density compared to water. In calculating the buoyant force on a body, however, one must also take into account the shape and position of the body. A steel rowboat placed on end into the water will sink because the density of steel is much greater than that of water. However, in its normal, keel-down position, the effective volume of the boat includes all the air inside it, so that its average density is then less than that of air, and as a result it will float.

Archimedes' screw, a simple mechanical device believed to have been invented by Archimedes in the 2d cent. A.D. It consists of a cylinder inside of which a continuous screw, extending the length of the cylinder, forms a spiral chamber. By placing the lower end in water and revolving the screw, water is raised to the top. The principle is applied in machines used for drainage and irrigation, and also in some types of high-speed tools. It can also be applied for handling light, loose materials such as grain, sand, and ashes.

Archipelago (ärkĭpĕl'əgō) [Ital., from Gr.=chief sea], ancient name of the AEGEAN SEA, later applied to the numerous islands it contains. The word now designates any cluster of islands.

Archipenko, Alexander (ärkhĭpĕn'kō), 1887–1964, Ukrainian-American sculptor. As a youth in Paris he began to adapt cubist technique to sculpture. In 1910 he opened his own art school there and later opened schools in Berlin (1921) and New York City (1923). In 1912, Archipenko introduced sculpto-painting, an attempt to unite form and color via mixed media. However, his major contribution to 20th-century sculpture was his realization of negative form. Archipenko recognized the aesthetic value of the void—the hollowed-out shape or perforation as a complement to the bulging mass—as exemplified by his *Madonna* in marble and the bronze *Woman Combing Her Hair* (Mus. of Modern Art, New York City). Archipenko also worked in carved plastic lighted from within. His nearly abstract figures gained him international renown; among them are *Torso in Space* (Whitney Mus., New York City), *Walking Girl* (Honolulu Mus.), and *White Torso* (examples in the Chicago Arts Club and in the Fine Art Association, Phoenix, Arizona). Archipenko was also an engineer, ceramist, and teacher. See his *Archipenko: Fifty Creative Years: 1908–1958* (1960); catalog ed. by D. H. Karshan (1969).

Archipiélago de Colón: see GALÁPAGOS ISLANDS.

Archippus (ärkĭp'əs), Colossian Christian. Col. 4.17.

Archite (är'kīt) or **Archi** (är'kī), clan that owned Ataroth between Bethel and Beth-horon, on the boundary between Ephraim and Benjamin. Joshua 16.2. HUSHAI, David's friend, was a member of the clan. 2 Sam 15.32.

architecture, art of building in which human requirements and construction materials are related so as to furnish a practical and aesthetic solution, thus differing from the pure utility of engineering construction. Modern architecture, however, often approaches actual engineering in its mechanical completeness, and modern works of engineering—airplane hangars, for example—often achieve an undeniable beauty. As an art, architecture is abstract and nonrepresentational and involves the manipulation of the relationships of spaces, volumes, planes, masses, and voids. Time is also an important factor in architecture, since a building is usually comprehended in a succession of experiences rather than all at once. In most architecture there is no one vantage point from which the whole structure can be understood. The use of light and shadow, as well as surface decoration, can greatly enhance a structure. The analysis of architectural types provides an insight into past cultures and eras. The course of architecture has often been considered merely a succession of more or less arbitrary styles. In fact, behind each of the greater styles lies not a casual trend or vogue but a period of serious and urgent experimentation directed toward answering the needs of a specific way of life. Climate, methods of labor, available materials, and economy of means impose their dictates. Each of the greater styles has been given its impetus by the discovery of a new construction method and has arrived laboriously at adequate employment of it. Once developed, it survives tenaciously, giving way only when social changes or new building techniques have reduced it finally to total anachronism. That evolutionary process is exemplified by the history of modern architecture, which developed from the first uses of structural iron and steel in the mid-19th cent. Until the 20th cent. there were three great developments in architectural construction—the post-and-lintel, or trabeated, system; the ARCH system, either the cohesive type, employing plastic materials hardening into a homogeneous mass, or the thrust type, in which the loads are received and counterbalanced at definite points; and the modern steel-skeleton system. In the 20th cent. new forms of building have been devised, with the use of reinforced concrete and the development of geodesic and stressed-skin (light material, reinforced) structures. In Egyptian architecture, to which belong some of the earliest extant structures entitled to be designated as architecture (erected before 3000 B.C.), the post-and-lintel system was employed exclusively and produced the earliest stone columnar buildings in history. The architecture of W Asia from the same era employed the same system; however, arched construction was also known and used. The Chaldaeans and Assyrians, dependent upon clay as their chief material, built vaulted roofs of damp mud bricks that adhered to form a solid shell. After generations of experimentation with buildings of limited variety the Greeks gave to the simple post-and-lintel system the purest, most perfect expression it was to attain (see PARTHENON; ORDERS OF ARCHITECTURE). Roman architecture, borrowing and combining the columns of Greece and the arches of Asia, erected a wide variety of monumental buildings throughout the Western world. Their momentous invention of CONCRETE enabled the imperial builders to exploit successfully the VAULT construction of W Asia and to cover vast unbroken floor spaces with great vaults and domes, as in the rebuilt Pantheon (2d cent. A.D.). The Romans and the early Christians also used the wooden truss for roofing the wide spans of their BASILICA halls. Neither Greek, Chinese, nor Japanese architecture used the vault system of construction. However, in the Asiatic division of the Roman Empire, vault development continued; Byzantine architects experimented with new principles and developed the PENDENTIVE, used brilliantly in the 6th cent. for the Church of HAGIA SOPHIA in Constantinople. The Romanesque architecture of the early Middle Ages was notable for strong, simple, massive forms and vaults executed in cut stone. In Lombard Romanesque (11th cent.) the Byzantine concentration of vault thrusts was improved by the device of ribs and of piers to support them. The idea of an organic supporting and buttressing skeleton of masonry, here appearing in embryo, became the vitalizing aim of the medieval builders. In 13th-century Gothic architecture it emerged in perfected form, as in the Amiens and Chartres cathedrals. The birth of Renaissance architecture (15th cent.) inaugurated a period of several hundred years in Western architecture during which the multiple and complex buildings of the modern world began to emerge, while at the same time no new and compelling structural conceptions appeared. The forms and ornaments of Roman antiquity were resuscitated again and again and were ordered into numberless new combinations, and structure served chiefly as a convenient tool for attaining these effects. The complex, highly decorated baroque style was the chief manifestation of the 17th-century architectural aesthetic. The GEORGIAN STYLE was among architecture's notable 18th-century expressions. The first half of the 19th cent. was given over to the CLASSIC REVIVAL and the GOTHIC REVIVAL. The architects of the later 19th cent. found themselves in a world being reshaped by science, industry, and speed. The needs of a new society pressed them, while steel, reinforced concrete, and electricity were among the new technical means at their disposal. The imitation of dead styles became yearly more futile, and individual architects began the conscious search for adequate new structural and artistic formulas. After more than a half-century of assimilation and experimentation, MODERN ARCHITECTURE has produced an astonishing variety of daring and original structures. See articles under countries, e.g., AMERICAN ARCHITECTURE; styles, e.g., BAROQUE; individual architects, e.g., Andrea PALLADIO; individual stylistic and structural elements, e.g., TRACERY, ORIENTATION; specific building types, e.g., PAGODA, APARTMENT HOUSE. See Talbot Hamlin, *Architecture through the Ages* (rev. ed. 1953); Nikolaus Pevsner, *An Outline of European Architecture* (16th ed. 1960); Banister Fletcher, *A History of Architecture* (17th ed. 1961); F. M. Simpson et al., *History of Architectural Development* (4 vol., rev. ed. 1954–61); H. A. Millon, *Key Monuments of the History of Architecture* (1964); A. E. Richardson and H. O Corfiato, *The Art of Architecture* (3d ed. 1972); S. F. Kimball and G. H. Edgell, *A History of Architecture* (1946, repr. 1972); John Fleming et al., *The Penguin Dictionary of Architecture* (rev. ed. 1973).

architrave (är'kĭtrāv), in architecture, principal beam and lowest member of the classical entablature, the other main members of which are the FRIEZE and the CORNICE. Its position is directly above the columns, and it extends between them, thus carrying the upper members of the order (see ORDERS OF ARCHITECTURE). The term also applies to molding around the sides and top of a door or window frame or around a wainscot or other panel.

archons (är'kŏnz, -kənz) [Gr.,=leaders], in ancient Athens and other Greek cities, officers of state. Originally in Athens there were three archons: the *archon eponymos* (so called because the year was named after him), who was the chief officer of the state; the *archon basileus,* who was primarily connected with sacred rites; and the *archon polemarchos* (the polemarch, or military commander), who—theoretically, at least—had military leadership. Six more archons, the *thesmothetae* (thesmothetes), were later added; they were junior officers, generally in charge of the courts. The archons were elected, and after they had served and their records had been approved, they entered the AREOPAGUS. Solon, Hippias, and Themistocles were archons. After 487 B.C. the archons were chosen by lot; the office, which had previously been limited to the two upper classes, was opened to the third class. Thereafter the archontate declined greatly in importance. The lists of eponymous archons kept after the 7th cent. B.C. are a valuable source of history.

Arcimboldo, Giuseppe (jōōzĕp'pā ärchēmbôl'dō), 1537–93, Italian painter. Court painter to the Hapsburg kings, Arcimboldo is celebrated for his grotesque, realistically rendered symbolic portraits constructed from fruits, vegetables, animals, etc. His *Winter* (1563) is in the Vienna Kunsthistorische Museum. Arcimboldo's fanciful mannerist works were frequently imitated.

Arciniegas, Germán (hĕrmän' ärsēnyā'gäs), 1900–, Colombian historian and diplomat. A leading Latin American intellectual, he gained prominence as a journalist and publisher. He lived in exile in the United States (1942–60) and taught at Columbia. He was appointed Colombian ambassador to Italy in 1960 and later became ambassador to Venezuela. Among his works are *The Knight of El Dorado: The Tale of Don Gonzalo Jiménez de Quesada* (tr. 1942), *The State of Latin America* (tr. 1952), and *Latin America: A Cultural History* (tr. 1967). He edited *The Green Continent* (1944), an interpretation of Latin America by its leading writers.

Arcole (är'kōlā), village (1971 pop. 4,009), Venetia, N Italy. There, in Nov., 1796, Napoleon Bonaparte defeated the Austrians in a three-day battle.

Arcos de la Frontera (är'kōs dā lä frōntā'rä), town (1970 pop. 25,966), Cádiz prov., S Spain, in Andalusia, on a rocky hill above the Guadalete River. A Gothic church and the palace of the duke of Arcos are at the summit. Wine and olive oil are produced. The Moors were driven out in 1250.

Arcot (är'kŏt), town (1971 pop. 30,229), Tamil Nadu state, SE India, on the Palar River. It is an agricultural market and has a weaving industry. It became the capital of the Muslim Nawab of Carnatic in 1712. Arcot was the first important fortified town captured (1751) by Robert Clive in the British-French struggle for S India.

Arctic Archipelago, group of more than 50 large islands, Franklin dist., Northwest Territories, N Canada, in the Arctic Ocean. The southernmost members of the group include Baffin (the archipelago's largest island), Victoria, Banks, Prince of Wales, and Somerset islands; N of Viscount Melville and Lancaster sounds are the Queen Elizabeth Islands, of which Ellesmere is the largest. Tundra and permanent ice cover the islands, on which oil and coal have been discovered. Frobisher Bay, on Ellesmere, is the largest settlement.

Arctic Circle, imaginary circle on the surface of the earth at 66½°N latitude, i.e., 23½° south of the North Pole. It marks the northernmost point at which the sun can be seen at the winter SOLSTICE (about Dec. 22) and the southernmost point of the northern polar regions at which the MIDNIGHT SUN is visible.

Arctic North Slope or **Arctic Slope,** Alaska: see ALASKA NORTH SLOPE.

Arctic Ocean, the smallest ocean, c.5,400,000 sq mi (13,986,000 sq km), located entirely within the Arctic Circle and occupying the region around the North Pole. Once called the Frozen Ocean, it is covered with ice (2–14 ft/.6–4 m thick) throughout the year except in fringe areas. Nearly landlocked, the Arctic Ocean is bordered by Greenland, Canada, Alaska, the USSR, and Norway. The Bering Strait connects it with the Pacific Ocean and the Greenland Sea is the chief link with the Atlantic Ocean. The principal arms of the Arctic Ocean are the Beaufort, Chukchi, East Siberian, Laptev, Kara, Barents, and Greenland seas. The floor of the Arctic Ocean is divided by three submarine ridges—Alpha Ridge, Lomonosov Ridge, and the Arctic Mid-Oceanic Ridge; other submarine ridges, such as the Faeroe-Icelandic Ridge, act to separate the Arctic Ocean from the Atlantic. Svalbard, the Franz Josef group, and Severnaya Zemlya are examples of the islands that are exposed tops of the submarine ridges. The Arctic Ocean has the widest continental shelf of all the oceans; it extends c.750 mi (1,210 km) seaward from Siberia. From the shelf rise numerous islands, including the Arctic Archipelago, Novaya Zemlya, the New Siberian Islands, and Wrangel Island. The continental shelf encloses a deep oval basin (average depth 12,000 ft/3,658 m) that stretches between Svalbard and the Bering Strait; E of Greenland the ring of the continental shelf is broken by the Greenland Sea. The greatest depth (17,850 ft/5,441 m) in the Arctic Ocean is found just N of the Chukchi Sea. Since the Arctic's connection with the Pacific Ocean is narrow and very shallow, its principal exchange of water is therefore with the Atlantic Ocean through the Greenland Sea. Even there, though surface waters communicate freely and a strong subsurface current brings warm water from the Atlantic into the Arctic basin, exchange of deeper waters is barred by submarine ridges. Thus a near stagnant pool of very cold water is found at the bottom of the Arctic basin. Because several major rivers in Siberia (Lena, Yenisei, Ob) and Canada (Mackenzie) bring in much water, and because evaporation is only slight, the outflow through the Greenland Sea is important. It creates the cold East Greenland Current, which flows south along the coast of E Greenland. A weaker current goes through Smith Sound and Baffin Bay and is known as the Labrador Current. Another weak current flows out of Bering Strait. The water that does not flow out by the Greenland Sea seems to be deflected by N Greenland and forms the current that gives rise to a circular current in the Arctic basin itself. This circular current causes the relatively light ice of the Siberian seas, which contrasts with the heavy-pressure ice phenomenon off Greenland and Ellesmere Island (in the Arctic Archipelago). The drift of ice southward and westward has been noted and utilized by explorers. Some of the ice pack remains in the Arctic basin, and some, carried out by the East Greenland Current, melts before going far enough south to reach the regular Atlantic shipping lanes; the icebergs that harass ships are generally brought from the fjords of W Greenland by the Labrador Current. The cold Arctic currents give the shores of NE North America and NE Asia a much colder climate than the northwest shores of Europe and North America, which are warmed by the North Atlantic Drift and the Japan Current. The Arctic currents are also less saline and lighter than these warmer currents, and therefore the Arctic water is at the surface and the Atlantic current beneath, where they are exchanged in the Greenland Sea. It was long thought that no life could exist in the Arctic; however, despite drifting ice, ice packs, vast ice floes, and winter temperatures to −60°F (−51°C), there are hares, polar bears, seals, gulls, and guillemots as far north as 88° and plankton in all Arctic waters. The Arctic basin was almost wholly unexplored until the Amundsen-Ellsworth flight over it in 1926. Arctic research was stimulated when it was recognized that the shortest air routes between the great cities of the Northern Hemisphere cross the Arctic Ocean. Improved technology has also facilitated research, with the development of aerial photography and photogrammetry for precise mapping, radar and the Fathometer for measuring ocean depths, and radio to maintain contact with the rest of the world. Detailed knowledge of drifts and ice floes, water depths, and the ocean floor has been vastly increased. Soviet polar scientists investigated (1948–49) the Lomonosov Ridge, an undersea mountain range that influences the pattern of ice drift and the circulation and exchange of water in the Arctic Ocean. American scientists in 1959 discovered the existence of a submarine plateau rising 8,100 ft (2,469 m) from the ocean floor. One fact of great potential importance is now being studied—the Arctic Ocean is warming. Recorded temperatures, glacial regressions, and the appearance of observed species of fish in larger numbers, at higher latitudes, at earlier seasons, and for long periods prove that over the decades a "climatic improvement" has taken place. Similar changes have been reported in sub-Arctic latitudes. Whether the warming is a phase in a cycle or a permanent development cannot yet be said. For an account of exploration and for bibliography, see ARCTIC REGIONS.

Arctic Red River, c.310 mi (500 km) long, rising in the Mackenzie Mts. of Mackenzie dist., W Northwest Territories, Canada, and flowing generally NW to the Mackenzie River. At its mouth are a post of the Royal Canadian Mounted Police and the village of Arctic Red River.

arctic regions or **the Arctic,** northernmost area of the earth, centered on the NORTH POLE. The arctic regions are not coextensive with the area enclosed by the ARCTIC CIRCLE (lat. 66° 31′N) but are usually defined by the irregular and shifting 50°F (10°C) July isotherm that closely corresponds to the northern limit of tree growth and that varies both N and S of the Arctic Circle. The regions therefore include the ARCTIC OCEAN; the northern reaches of Canada, Alaska, the USSR, Norway, and the Atlantic Ocean; SVALBARD; most of Iceland; GREENLAND; and the Bering Sea. In the center of the arctic regions is a large basin occupied by the Arctic Ocean. The basin is nearly surrounded by the ancient continental shields of North America, Europe, and Asia, with the geologically more recent lowland plains, low plateaus, and mountain chains between them. Surface features vary from low coastal plains (swampy in summer, especially at the mouths of such rivers as the Mackenzie, Lena, Yenisei, and Ob) to high ice plateaus and glaciated mountains. TUNDRAS, extensive flat and poorly drained lowlands, dominate the regions. The most notable highlands are the Brooks Range of Alaska, the Innuitians of the Canadian ARCTIC ARCHIPELAGO, the Urals, and the mountains of E USSR. Greenland, the world's largest island, is a high plateau covered by a vast ice sheet except in the coastal regions. The climate of the Arctic, classified as polar, is characterized by long, cold winters and short, cool summers. Polar climate may be further subdivided into tundra climate (the warmest month of which has an average temperature below 50°F/10°C but above 32°F/0°C) and ice cap climate (all months average below 32°F/0°C and there is a permanent snow cover). Precipitation, almost entirely in the form of snow, is very low, with the annual average precipitation for the regions less than 20 in. (51 cm). Persistent winds whip up fallen snow to create the illusion of constant snowfall. The climate is moderated by oceanic influences, with regions abutting the Atlantic and Pacific oceans having generally warmer temperatures and heavier snowfalls than the colder and drier interior areas. However, except for along its fringe, the Arctic Ocean remains frozen throughout the year. Great seasonal changes in the length of days and nights are experienced N of the Arctic Circle, with variations that range from 24 hours of constant daylight ("midnight sun") or darkness at the Arctic Circle to six months of daylight or darkness at the North Pole. However, because of the low angle of the sun above the horizon, insolation is minimal throughout the regions, even during the prolonged daylight period. A famous occurrence in the arctic night sky is the AURORA BOREALIS, or northern lights. Vegetation in the Arctic, limited to regions having a tundra climate, flourishes during the short spring and summer seasons. The tundra's restrictive environment for plant life increases northward, with dwarf trees giving way to grasses (mainly mosses, lichen, sedges, and some flowering plants), the ground coverage of which becomes widely scattered toward the permanent snow line. There are about 20 species of land animals in the Arctic, including the squirrel, wolf, fox, moose, caribou, reindeer, polar bear, and musk ox, and about six species of aquatic mammals such as the walrus, seal, and whale. Most of the species are year-round inhabitants of the Arctic, migrating to the southern margins as winter approaches. Although generally of large numbers, some of the species, especially the fur-bearing ones, are in danger of extinction. A variety of fish is found in arctic seas, rivers, and lakes. The Arctic's bird population increases tremendously each spring with the arrival of migratory birds (see MIGRATION OF ANIMALS). During the short warm season, a large number of insects breed in the marshlands of the tundra. In parts of the Arctic are found a variety of natural resources, but many known reserves are not exploited because of their inaccessibility. The arctic region of the USSR, the most developed of all the arctic regions, is a vast storehouse of mineral wealth, including deposits of nickel, copper, coal, gold, uranium, tungsten, and diamonds. The North American Arctic yields uranium, copper, nickel, iron, natural gas, and oil. Inaccessibility made the Arctic a relatively unknown area until the wide-scale use of airplanes and snow vehicles in the 20th cent. The arctic region of Europe (including W USSR) benefits from good overland links with southern areas and ship routes that are open throughout the year. The arctic regions of the Asian USSR and North America depend on isolated overland routes, summertime ship routes, and air transportation. Transportation of oil by pipeline from arctic Alaska was highly controversial in the early 1970s, with strong opposition from environmentalists. Because of the extreme conditions of the arctic regions, the delicate balance of nature, and the slowness of natural repairs, the protection and preservation of the Arctic has been a major goal of conservationists who fear irreparable damage to the natural environment from local temperature increases, the widespread use of machinery, the interference with wildlife migration, and oil spills. The Arctic is one of the world's most sparsely populated areas. Its inhabitants, basically of the Mongoloid race, are thought to be descendants of a people who migrated northward from central Asia after the Ice Age and subsequently spread W into Europe and E into North America. The chief groups are now the Lapps of Europe; the SAMOYEDES (Nentsy) of W USSR; the Yakuts, TUNGUS, Yukaghirs, and Chukchis of E USSR; and the ESKIMO of North America. There is a sizable Caucasian population in Siberia, and the people of Iceland are nearly all Caucasian. In Greenland, the Greenlanders, a mixture of Eskimos and northern Europeans, predominate. Because of their common background and the general lack of contact with other peoples, arctic peoples have strikingly similar physical characteristics and cultures, especially in such things as clothing, tools, techniques, and social organization. The arctic peoples, once totally nomadic, are now largely sedentary or seminomadic. Hunting, fishing, reindeer herding, and indigenous arts and crafts are the chief activities. The arctic peoples are slowly being incorporated into the society of the country in which they are located. With the Arctic's increased economic and political role in world affairs, the regions have experienced an influx of personnel charged with building and manning such things as roads, mineral extraction sites, weather stations, and military installations.

History of Exploration. The first explorers in the arctic regions were the Norsemen, the VIKINGS. Much later the search for the NORTHWEST PASSAGE and the NORTHEAST PASSAGE to reach the Orient from Europe spurred exploration to the north. This activity began in the 16th cent. and continued in the 17th, but the hardships suffered and the negative results obtained by early explorers—among them Martin FROBISHER, John DAVIS, Henry HUDSON, Willem BAFFIN, and William BARENTZ—caused interest to wane. The fur traders in Canada did not begin serious explorations across the tundras until the latter part of the 18th cent. Alexander MACKENZIE undertook extensive exploration after the beginnings made by Samuel Hearne, Philip Turnor, and others. Already in the region of NE Asia and W Alaska the Russian explorations under Vitus BERING and others and the activities of the *promyshlennyki* [fur traders] had begun to make the arctic coasts known. After 1815, British naval officers—including John FRANKLIN, F. W. BEECHEY, John ROSS, James ROSS, W. E. PARRY, P. W. DEASE, Thomas SIMPSON, George BACK, and John RAE—inspired by the efforts of John BARROW, took up the challenge of the Arctic. The disappearance of Franklin on his expedition between 1845 and 1848 gave rise to more than 40 searching parties. Although Franklin was not found, a great deal of knowledge was learned about the Arctic as a result, including the general outline of Canada's arctic coast. Otto SVERDRUP, D. B. MACMILLAN, and Vilhjalmur STEFANSSON added significant knowledge of the regions. Meanwhile, in the Eurasian Arctic, FRANZ JOSEF LAND was discovered and NOVAYA ZEMLYA explored. The Northeast Passage was finally navigated in 1879 by Nils A. E. NORDENSKJÖLD. Roald AMUNDSEN, who went through the Northwest Passage (1903–6), also went through the Northeast Passage (1918–20). Greenland was also explored. The race to be first at the North Pole was won by Robert E. PEARY in 1909. Although Fridtjof NANSEN, drifting with his vessel *Fram* in the ice (1893–96), failed to reach the North Pole, he added enormously to the knowledge of the Arctic Ocean. Air exploration of the regions began with the tragic balloon attempt of S. A. ANDREE in 1897. In 1926, Richard E. BYRD and Floyd Bennett flew over the North Pole, and Amundsen and Lincoln ELLSWORTH flew from Svalbard (Spitsbergen) to Alaska across the North Pole and unexplored regions N of Alaska. In 1928, George H. WILKINS flew from Alaska to Spitsbergen. The use of the "great circle" route for world air travel increased the importance of arctic regions, while new ideas of the agricultural and other possibilities of arctic and subarctic regions led to many projects for development, especially by the USSR. In 1937 and 1938 many field expeditions were sent out by British, Danish, Norwegian, Soviet, Canadian, and American groups to learn more about the Arctic. The Soviet group under Ivan Papinin set down and wintered on an ice floe near the North Pole and drifted with the current for 274 days. Valuable hydrological, meteorological, and magnetic observations were made; by the time they were taken off the floe, the group had drifted 19° of latitude and 58° of longitude. Arctic drift was further explored (1937–40) by the Soviet icebreaker *Sedov,* and the existence of Sannikov Island was proved a myth. In 1938 air photographs by Lauge KOCH over N Greenland proved the much-sought Peary Channel to be only a fjord. Before World War II, the USSR had established many meteorological and radio stations in the arctic regions. Soviet activity in practical exploitation of resources also pointed the way to the development of arctic regions. Between 1940 and 1942 the Canadian vessel *St. Roch* made the first west-east journey through the Northwest Passage. In World War II, interest in transporting supplies gave rise to considerable study of arctic conditions. After the war interest in the Arctic was keen. The Canadian army in 1946 undertook a project that had as one of its objects the testing of new machines (notably the snowmobile) for use in developing arctic regions. There was also a strong impulse to develop Alaska and N Canada, but no consolidated effort, like that of the Soviets, to take the natives into partnership for a full-scale development of the regions. Since 1954 the United States and the USSR have established a number of drifting observation stations on ice floes for the purpose of intensified scientific observations. In 1955, as part of joint U.S.-Canadian defense, construction was begun on a c.3,000-mi (4,830-km) radar network (the Distant Early Warning line, commonly called the DEW line) stretching from Alaska to Baffin Island and, subsequently, across Greenland. With the continuing development of northern regions (e.g., Alaska, N Canada, and the USSR), the Arctic is assuming greater importance in the world. During the International Geophysical Year (1957–58) more than 300 arctic stations were established by the northern countries interested in the arctic regions. The Arctic Institute of North America has been prominent in sponsoring studies of the arctic regions. In 1960 the institute set up a permanent year-round station on Devon Island. Atomic-powered submarines have been used for penetrating the arctic regions. In 1958 the *Nautilus,* a U.S. navy atomic-powered submarine, became the first ship to cross the North Pole undersea. Two years later the *Skate* set out on a similar voyage and became the first to surface at the Pole. In the 1960s the Arctic became the scene of an intense search for mineral and power resources. The discovery of oil on the Alaska North Slope (1968) and on Canada's Ellesmere Island (1972) led to a great effort to find new oil fields along the edges of the continents. In the summer of 1969 the SS *Manhattan,* a specially designed oil tanker with ice

PACIFIC OCEAN
Bering Sea
Sea of Okhotsk
ST. LAWRENCE ISLAND
Anadyr
Nome
Bering Strait
ARCTIC CIRCLE
UNITED STATES
Fairbanks
ALASKA
Dawson
Chukchi Sea
WRANGEL ISLAND
East Siberian Sea
Barrow
Verkhoyansk
CANADA
Beaufort Sea
NEW SIBERIAN ISLANDS
UNION OF SOVIET SOCIALIST REPUBLICS
Coppermine
ARCTIC ARCHIPELAGO
BANKS ISLAND
McClure Strait
VICTORIA ISLAND
Viscount Melville Sound
QUEEN ELIZABETH ISLANDS
NORTH MAGNETIC POLE
BATHURST ISLAND
Laptev Sea
Nordvik
TAYMYR PENINSULA
ARCTIC
SEVERNAYA ZEMLYA
NORTH POLE
OCEAN
Lancaster Sound
Arctic Bay
ELLESMERE ISLAND
Hudson Bay
Igarka
FRANZ JOSEF LAND
Kara Sea
Thule
YAMAL PENINSULA
BAFFIN ISLAND
Baffin Bay
NOVAYA ZEMLYA
Pangnirtung
SVALBARD
Barents Sea
GREENLAND
Davis Strait
Greenland Sea
Godthåb
Hammerfest
Murmansk
KOLA PENINSULA
JAN MAYEN
Arkhangelsk
White Sea
Denmark Strait
Norwegian Sea
Reykjavik
ICELAND
FINLAND
Gulf of Bothnia
Helsinki
Leningrad
Moscow
NORWAY
Stockholm
ATLANTIC OCEAN
Oslo
SWEDEN
Baltic Sea
North Sea
GREAT BRITAIN

Cross-references are indicated by SMALL CAPITALS.

breaker and oceanographic research vessel features, successfully sailed from Philadelphia to Alaska by way of the Northwest Passage in the first attempt to bring commercial shipping into the region. In 1971 the Arctic Ice Dynamics Joint Experiment (AIDJEX) began an international effort to study over a period of years arctic pack ice and its effect on world climate. Practically all parts of the Arctic have now been photographed and scanned (by remote sensing devices) from aircraft and satellites. From these sources accurate maps of the arctic regions have been compiled. Classic narratives of arctic exploration include Fridtjof Nansen, *Farthest North* (tr., 2 vol., 1897, repr. 1968) and *In Northern Mists* (tr. 1911); R. E. Amundsen, *The North West Passage* (tr., 2 vol., 1908); R. E. Peary, *The North Pole* (1910, repr. 1969); Vilhjalmur Stefansson, *My Life with the Eskimo* (1913) and *The Friendly Arctic* (1921). For history and geography, see L. P. Kirwan, *A History of Polar Exploration* (1960); P. D. Baird, *The Polar World* (1964); Farley Mowat, comp., *The Polar Passion: The Quest for the North Pole* (1968); Ragnar Thorén, *Picture Atlas of the Arctic* (1969); Richard Perry, *The Polar Worlds* (1973); L. H. Neatby, *Conquest of the Last Frontier* (1966) and *Discovery in Russian and Siberian Waters* (1973).

Arcturus (ärktŏŏr'əs), brightest star in the constellation BOÖTES and 4th-brightest star in the entire sky; Bayer designation Alpha Boötis; 1970 position R.A. $14^h14.3^m$, Dec. +19°20'. An orange giant of SPECTRAL CLASS K2 III, it has an apparent MAGNITUDE of −0.06; its diameter is about 10 times that of the sun and its luminosity about 100 times that of the sun. Arcturus is one of the nearest giant stars, at a distance of about 36 light-years, and has one of the largest PROPER MOTIONS (annual angular shift in position) of the bright stars. Its name is from the Greek meaning "guardian of the bear," and it can be found by following the extension of the curve of the handle of the Big Dipper (Large Bear).

Ard (ärd). **1** Son of Benjamin. Gen. 46.21. **2** Benjamite, perhaps the same as **1.** Num. 26.40. Addar: 1 Chron. 8.3.

Ardashir I (ärdäshĕr') [another form of Artaxerxes], d. 240, king of Persia (226?–240). He overthrew the last Parthian king, Artabanus IV, entered Ctesiphon, and reunited Persia out of the confusion of Seleucid decline. He established the strong SASSANID or Sassanian dynasty and reconquered the old eastern territories. Ardashir established ZOROASTRIANISM as the state religion and gave much power to the priestly caste. His move against Mesopotamia, Armenia, and Cappadocia caused the Roman emperor ALEXANDER SEVERUS to campaign against him. A great battle in 232 cost both armies heavy losses. It was Alexander who had to retire, and though Alexander celebrated a triumph in Rome, Ardashir took Armenia, and Persian power was firmly established. He is sometimes called Ardashir Papakan, for his father, Papak. Shapur I succeeded him.

Ardashir II, king of Persia (379–83), of the SASSANID, or Sassanian, dynasty. A provincial governor under SHAPUR II, he succeeded to the throne. He earned popularity by remitting taxes, but his rule was weak, and he was deposed in favor of his nephew, Shapur III.

Ardebil (ärdəbēl'), town (1971 est. pop. 88,000), NW Iran, near the USSR border. It is a market center for a fertile agricultural region. Carpets and rugs are produced in the town. Ardebil was probably founded in the 5th cent. A.D. It became (10th cent.) the capital of Azerbaijan but was soon superseded by Tabriz. In 1220 it was destroyed by the Mongols. The town quickly regained its importance as the home of Safi ad-Din, the founder of a celebrated Sufi order. The Safavids erected a beautiful shrine there, and the town became a center of pilgrimage. Ardebil also contains the tomb of Shah Ismail. The town was occupied by the Turks in 1725 and by the Russians in 1828. Its fine library was taken to St. Petersburg by the Russians. The name is also spelled Ardabil.

Ardèche (ärdĕsh'), department (1968 pop. 256,927) in VIVARAIS, S France. Privas is the capital.

Arden, John, 1930–, English playwright, b. Barnsly, Yorkshire, educated at Cambridge and at Edinburgh College of Architecture. Although his plays often treat moral problems, Arden does not postulate absolutes, nor does he provide answers to the questions he raises. His plays combine poetry and realism and have had critical rather than commercial success. They include *Sergeant Musgrave's Dance* (1959), *The Workhouse Donkey* (1963), *Armstrong's Last Goodnight* (1967); and two autobiographical plays, *The Ballygombeem Bequest* (1972) and *The Island of the Mighty* (1972).

Arden, uninc. city (1970 pop. 82,492 including Arcade), Sacramento co., N central Calif.

Arden, Forest of, well-wooded area, formerly very extensive, in Warwickshire, central England. It is the setting for Shakespeare's *As You Like It.*

Ardennes (ärdĕn'), department (1968 pop. 309,380), NE France, in Champagne. The capital is CHARLEVILLE-MÉZIÈRES.

Ardennes, wooded plateau, from 1,600 to 2,300 ft (488–701 m) high, in SE Belgium, N Luxembourg, and Ardennes dept., N France, E and S of the Meuse River. The plateau is cut into wild crags and ravines by rapid rivers. Agriculture and cattle raising are the main occupations of this sparsely populated region. Peat bogs are found in shallow depressions. In Germany, the Ardennes is continued by the Eifel. The chief cities (Liège, Namur) are in the Meuse valley. A traditional battleground, the Ardennes saw heavy fighting in both World Wars, notably in the BATTLE OF THE BULGE (Dec., 1944–Jan., 1945).

Ardennes, Battle of the: see BATTLE OF THE BULGE.

Ardigò, Roberto (rōbĕr'tō ärdēgô'), 1828–1920, Italian positivist philosopher. His early life was spent in the priesthood, from which he withdrew in dissatisfaction at the age of 43. Later he was a professor at the Univ. of Padua (1881–1909) and defended his conviction that human knowledge originated in sensation against the philosophical idealism then popular in Italy. Most of his writings were collected in *Opere filosofiche* (12 vol., 1882–1912); he also wrote *La scienza della educazione* (3d ed. 1909).

Ardmore, city (1970 pop. 20,881), seat of Carter co., S Okla.; inc. 1898. It is the commercial center of a rich oil and farm area. Its industries include oil refining, cotton and food processing, and the manufacture of tires, telephone equipment, and electronic and plastic parts. The Goddard Center for the Visual and Performing Arts, the Southern Oklahoma Area Vocational-Technical Center, and Carter Seminary for Indian children are in Ardmore. Adjacent Lake Murray State Park and the nearby Arbuckle Mts. offer recreation.

Ardon (är'dən), Caleb's third son. 1 Chron. 2.18.

area, measure of the size of a surface region, usually expressed in units that are the square of linear units, e.g., square feet or square meters. In elementary geometry, formulas for the areas of the simple plane figures and the surface areas of simple solids are derived from the linear dimensions of these figures. Examples are given in the accompanying table.

Plane figures	*Area**
triangle	$ab/2$
parallelogram	ab
rectangle	ab
square	s^2
circle	πr^2
Solids	*Total surface area**
right circular cylinder	$2\pi r(r+a)$
right circular cone	$\pi r(r+l)$
sphere	$4\pi r^2$

* The abbreviations used are: b = base (length of any side of a plane figure); a = altitude (perpendicular distance from the farthest point of the figure to the extended base); s = side; r = radius (of the base circle in the case of the cylinder or cone); l = slant height (distance from vertex to base of a cone measured on its surface).

The areas of irregular figures, plane or solid, can be computed or closely approximated by the use of integral calculus.

Arecibo (ärəsē'bō), city (1970 pop. 35,484), N Puerto Rico, a port on the Atlantic Ocean at the mouth of the Rio Grande de Arecibo. It is the commercial and industrial center of a region producing coffee, tobacco, sugarcane, and pineapples. Arecibo was founded in 1616.

Arecibo Ionospheric Observatory (är"ĭsē'bō), RADIO-ASTRONOMY facility located at Arecibo, Puerto Rico. It was completed in 1963 and is operated by Cornell Univ. under contract with the U.S. National Science Foundation. The principal instrument is a fixed antenna of spherical section, 1,000 ft (305 m) in diameter, that can be pointed at a source of radio waves by moving the aberration-corrected line feeds to the antenna's focus. As a result of resurfacing of the antenna completed in 1974, observations are possible up to a frequency of 4,000 MHz. A 100-ft (30-m) satellite antenna can be used in conjunction with the large antenna for interferometer observations. In addition there is a wide range of instrumentation for measuring ionospheric conditions. Principal research programs include pulsars, spectral-line and continuous radio emissions, very-long-baseline interferometry, radar studies of planet orbits and surfaces, and a variety of ionospheric studies.

Areli (ârē'lī), son of Gad. Gen. 46.16; Num. 26.17.

Arendal (ä'rəndäl), city (1970 pop. 11,769), capital of Aust-Agder co., SE Norway, a port on the Skagerrak. Manufactures include forest products and electric light bulbs. Chartered in 1723, Arendal has had one of Norway's largest merchant fleets since 1880.

Arendt, Hannah (hän'ä är'ənt), 1906–, German-American political theorist, b. Hanover, Germany, B.A. Königsberg, 1924, Ph.D. Heidelberg, 1928. She emigrated (1941) to the United States and was naturalized in 1950. Arendt was a lecturer and Guggenheim fellow, 1952–53; visiting professor at the Univ. of California at Berkeley, 1955; the first woman appointed to a full professorship at Princeton, 1959; and visiting professor of government at Columbia, 1960. From 1963 to 1967 she was professor at the Univ. of Chicago, and in 1967 she became university professor at the New School for Social Research. With the publication of *Origins of Totalitarianism* (1951) her status as a major political thinker was firmly established. In this book she examined the major forms of 20th-century totalitarianism—National Socialism (Nazism) and Communism—and attempted to trace their origins in the anti-Semitism and imperialism of the 19th cent. Her second major American publication, *The Human Condition* (1958), likewise received wide acclaim. *Eichmann in Jerusalem* (1963), her analysis of the Nazi war crimes based on observation of the trial of Adolf Eichmann, stirred considerable controversy. Arendt also served as research director of the Conference on Jewish Relations (1944–46) and executive director of Jewish Cultural Reconstruction, New York City (1949–52). Her other writings include *On Revolution* (1963), *Men in Dark Times* (1968), *On Violence* (1969), and *Crises of the Republic* (1972).

Arensky, Anton Stepanovich (əntôn' styĭpä'nəvĭch ärĕn'skē), 1861–1906, Russian composer; pupil of Rimsky-Korsakov at the St. Petersburg Conservatory. After 1882 he taught at the Moscow Conservatory and became (1895) conductor of the Imperial Chapel Choir. He wrote operas, including *A Dream on the Volga* (Moscow, 1890), chamber and symphonic music, songs, and piano works.

Areopagite: see DIONYSIUS THE AREOPAGITE, SAINT.

Areopagus (ărēŏp'əgəs) [Gr.,=hill of Ares], rocky hill, 370 ft (113 m) high, NW of the Acropolis of Athens, famous as the sacred meeting place of the prime council of Athens. This council, also called the Areopagus, represented the ancient council of elders, which usually combined judicial and legislative functions from the beginning. The Areopagus represented in the 5th and 6th cent. B.C. the stronghold of aristocracy. Jurisdiction in murder cases had probably been given to it by Draco; Solon gave it various censorial powers over the officers of the state. The change in the method of choosing the archons in 487 B.C. caused the beginning of the decline of the Areopagus. In 480 B.C. the Areopagus enabled the manning of the fleet for the battle of Salamis, and it recovered much of its influence in the war years. But c.462 B.C. a series of attacks began and eventually the august council was reduced to the status of a court of homicide only, although it maintained its religious character. Pericles was a leader in this democratizing movement; Aeschylus was an opponent, and he brought his trilogy of dramas to a close (in *The Eumenides*) with an appeal for the preservation of the ancient traditions of the Areopagus.

Arequipa (äräkē'pä), city (1970 est. pop. 194,700), alt. c.7,800 ft (2,380 m), capital of Arequipa dept., S Peru, on the Chili River. One of Peru's largest cities, it is the commercial center of S Peru and N Bolivia. Leather goods, textiles, and foodstuffs are the chief products. Alpaca wool is graded, sorted, and shipped out through the port of MOLLENDA. Founded in 1540 on the site of an Inca town, Arequipa stands on an oasis in an arid plain and grows crops for local consumption. Although the city was almost totally destroyed by an earthquake in 1868, its lovely examples of Spanish colonial architecture have been restored. The light-colored building stone, sillar, has given Arequipa the name "white city." It has a university and several other institutions of higher education.

Ares (âr'ēz), in Greek mythology, Olympian god of war. He is usually said to be the son of Zeus and Hera; but in some legends he and Eris, his twin sister, were born when Hera touched a flower. A fierce warrior, he loved battle and often took part in conflicts between mortals. Ares killed Halirrhothios, son of Poseidon, when the youth violated his daughter, Alcippe. For this crime Ares was judged by a tribunal of the 12 Olympians and acquitted. The hill on which the trial took place, the Areopagus, was named for him. The worship of Ares was not as important as that of MARS, with whom he was identified by the Romans.

Aresson, Areson, or **Arason, Jon** (all: yōn ä'rĕsôn), 1484?-1550, Icelandic churchman. The last Roman Catholic bishop in Iceland before the Reformation, he was executed together with his sons, Ara and Bjorn, for resisting the new religious ordinances brought about by the Reformation in Denmark. Aresson established the first Icelandic printing press at Holar in 1528. His poetry, secular and sacred, has been preserved.

Aretas (âr'ĭtəs, -tăs), dynastic name of the Nabataean kings of Petra. The best-known Aretas was **Aretas IV,** 9 B.C.-A.D. 49, ruler of S Palestine, most of Trans-Jordan, N Arabia, and Damascus. His daughter was married to HEROD Antipas, who put her away in favor of Herodias. Aretas attacked (A.D. 36) Antipas and defeated him, but Rome took Antipas' part. Tiberius' death (A.D. 37) saved Aretas from the Roman army. He is mentioned in the Bible (2 Cor. 11.32).

Arethusa (ărĭthōō'sə), in Greek mythology, nymph favored by Artemis and loved by the river god Alpheus. While Arethusa was bathing in his stream, Alpheus rose up and tried to abduct her, but she fled under the ocean to the isle of Ortygia. There Artemis changed her into a fountain. But Alpheus followed her, was himself changed into a river and united with her. In ancient times it was believed that the waters of the Alpheus River flowed beneath the sea from Greece and reappeared in the fountain of Arethusa in the harbor of Syracuse.

Arethusa: see ORCHID.

Aretino, Pietro (pyĕ'trō ärātē'nō), 1492-1556, Italian satirist. He led a life of adventure and wrote abusive works for hire. His derisive wit was so feared that the gifts of those who sought either to buy him or buy him off made him very wealthy. He was a friend of Titian, who painted his portrait. His comedies, such as *La cortigiana* and *La talenta,* are lacking in plot and form but are singular, if exaggerated, portraits of his time. His letters, in spite of their impudent coarseness, are full of verve. Ariosto called him the "scourge of princes." See biography by James Cleugh (1966).

Aretinus, Guido: see GUIDO D'AREZZO.

Arezzo (ärĕt'tsō), city (1971 pop. 87,128), capital of Arezzo prov., Tuscany, central Italy. It is an agricultural trade center and has machine and textile industries. Arezzo was an Etruscan town, later became a Roman military station and colony, and was made (11th cent.) a free commune. Siding with the Ghibellines, it was defeated (1289) at Campaldino by Florence, to which it passed definitively in 1384. In Roman times the famous red-clay Arretine vases were made there. Arezzo was a center of learning and the arts in the Middle Ages; Guido d'Arezzo, Petrarch, Aretino, and Vasari were born there. The city retains much of its medieval character. Noteworthy buildings include the Gothic cathedral (1286-1510); the Gothic Church of San Francesco (14th cent.), with frescoes of the Legend of the Holy Cross executed (1452-66) by Piero della Francesca; the Romanesque Church of Santa Maria della Pieve (1330); Bruni Palace (15th cent.), which now houses an art gallery and museum; and Vasari's mansion (decorated by Vasari in 1540).

Argall, Sir Samuel (är'gəl), d. 1626?, English ship captain, prominent in the early settlement of Virginia. He commanded a ship sent to Jamestown in 1609 and had charge of one of the ships Baron De la Warr brought to the failing colony in 1610. He made voyages—supposedly to Bermuda, Cape Cod, and Canada—to get needed supplies for the colonies. In 1613 on a voyage up the Potomac, Argall kidnapped POCAHONTAS. He commanded the Virginia Company expedition that destroyed the rival French colonial settlement on MOUNT DESERT ISLAND in 1613, and in 1614 he led an expedition against Port Royal (now Annapolis Royal, N.S.). As deputy governor of Virginia (1617-18), he governed autocratically, and the accusations of his opponents in the colony that he was unduly harsh with the poor have been credited by most, but not all, modern historians. He was knighted in 1623 and in 1625 as an admiral commanded a fleet off the Spanish coast.

Argelander, Friedrich Wilhelm August (frē'drĭkh vĭl'hĕlm ou'gōōst är'gəländər), 1799-1875, German astronomer. He became director of the observatory at the Univ. of Bonn in 1837 and continued there the work of determining the positions of stars that F. W. BESSEL had begun at Königsberg. The results of his observations appear in the *Bonner Durchmusterung* (1862), which records the positions and brightness of more than 324,000 stars (up to the ninth magnitude) in the northern heavens.

Argenson, Marc Pierre de Voyer de Paulmy, comte d', 1696-1764, French statesman and patron of literature; younger brother of René Louis d'Argenson. As secretary of state for war (1743-57), he assisted Maurice de SAXE in reforming the army, especially the artillery, and founded the École militaire. He was also charged with administrative control of the city of Paris. The Champs Élysées and the Place de la Concorde were planned by him. He was a friend and patron of the philosophes, and Denis Diderot and Jean le Rond d'Alembert dedicated the *Encyclopédie* to him.

Argenson, René Louis de Voyer de Paulmy, marquis d', 1694-1757, French foreign minister (1744-47), brother of Marc Pierre d'Argenson. Well intentioned but impractical, he sought to form a federation of Italian states and to make France the disinterested arbiter of international affairs. After committing numerous blunders he was dismissed and appointed president of the Academy of Inscriptions. A friend of François Marie de Voltaire and the Encyclopedists, he spent the rest of his life in study and in literary pursuits. He left memoirs.

Argenteuil (ärzhäNtö'yə), city (1968 pop. 90,929), Val-d'Oise dept., N France, on the Seine, a suburb of Paris. It has important metalworks and factories making furniture, railroad and airplane parts, and chemicals. It is also famous for its asparagus and grapes. It grew around a convent founded in the 7th cent.; there Heloise was educated and, after her misfortune, became prioress. The convent (later a monastery) was destroyed in the French Revolution; the famous relic, the Seamless Tunic, said to have been worn by Christ, was given by Charlemagne to the convent and is now enshrined in Saint-Denis Basilica (1866).

Argentia: see PLACENTIA BAY.

Argentina (ärjəntē'nə, Span. ärhäntē'nä), republic (1970 pop. 23,364,443), 1,072,157 sq mi (2,776,889 sq km), S South America. The second largest nation of South America, Argentina is composed of 22 provinces, one national territory, and one federal district that is the site of BUENOS AIRES, the country's capital and largest city. Argentina is triangular in shape and stretches c.2,300 mi (3,700 km) from its broad northern region near the Tropic of Capricorn to S TIERRA DEL FUEGO, an island shared with Chile. On the northeast, Argentina fronts on the Río de la Plata (an estuary and one of the major waterways of the Western Hemisphere), which separates Argentina from S Uruguay; its tributaries also act as international boundaries—the Uruguay River, with W Uruguay and S Brazil, and the Paraná and Pilcomayo rivers, with Paraguay. The northwest boundary with Bolivia lies in the GRAN CHACO and the Andes mts. The western boundary with Chile follows the crestline of the Andes. The Atlantic Ocean borders Argentina on the east; there, off S Argentina, are the FALKLAND ISLANDS, and the South Georgia, South Sandwich, and South Orkney islands, all claimed by Argentina but administered by Great Britain. Argentina also claims a sector of Antarctica. The climate of Argentina varies from subtropical in the north to cold and windswept in the south, with temperate and dry areas found throughout much of the country. Precipitation, lowest along the E Andean slopes, increases markedly N and E across Argentina. The chief rivers of Argentina are the Paraná with its tributary, the Salado; the Colorado River; and the Río Negro. Argentina may be divided into six geographical regions—the Paraná Plateau, the Gran Chaco, the Pampa (see under PAMPAS), the Monte, PATAGONIA, and the Andes mts. The Paraná Plateau in the extreme northeast is an extension of the highlands of S Brazil. It is the wettest part of Argentina and has a dense forest cover; tobacco, timber, and yerba maté are the chief products there. The spectacular IGUAÇU FALLS are in a national park located at the point where Argentina, Brazil, and Paraguay meet. In N Argentina the Gran Chaco, with the physiographically similar Mesopotamia (between the Paraná and Uruguay rivers), is a predominantly flat alluvial plain with a subtropical climate. The region is seasonally flooded, and marshlands remain for long periods during the year because of poor drainage. Livestock, cotton, and quebracho are the main products. South of the Gran Chaco is the Pampa, a vast, monotonous natural grassland that extends to the Colorado River (roughly from lat. 30°S to 40°S) and is c.400 mi (640 km) wide from the Atlantic Ocean to the Andean foothills. The Pampa's deep, rich soil is the basic wealth of the country. The "Wet Pampa," the more humid eastern part of the region, is Argentina's principal agricultural area and produces most of the nation's exports. It is the granary of South America, with wheat, alfalfa, corn, and flax the principal crops. Cattle ranching is prevalent throughout the Pampa and especially in the southeast and north; sheep are also raised there. Dairying is important in the vicinity of Buenos Aires. The Pampa has the densest transportation network of roads and railroads in South America. Most of the principal cities of Argentina (containing a majority of the nation's population) and most of its industry are found in the region. Buenos Aires, a port city on the Río de la Plata, is one of the largest cities of South America and the chief industrial center and transportation hub of S South America; it is surrounded by smaller industrial cities. Elsewhere on the Pampa are LA PLATA, the capital of Buenos Aires prov. and a meat-packing and oil-refining center; ROSARIO, the second largest city of Argentina, an iron and steel and oil-refining center, and a huge grain port on the Paraná River; SANTA FE, a northern commercial and industrial center and a major port at the junction of the Salado and Paraná rivers; MAR DEL PLATA, a resort and fishing center on the Atlantic Ocean; and BAHÍA BLANCA, the largest Argentine port directly on the Atlantic Ocean, a gateway to the S Pampa and the oil fields of Nequen prov., and a meat-packing, oil-refining, and wool-processing center. On the western edge of the Pampa is CÓRDOBA, the nation's third largest city, which reflects the transition from the "Dry Pampa" to the Monte, the desolate Andean foothills. The Monte, an arid region in the rain shadow of the Andes, has natural vegetation varying from short grasses in the east to cacti in the west. Scattered throughout the great arid stretches are small but highly productive oases such as JUJUY, SALTA, TUCUMÁN, SAN JUAN, and MENDOZA, which were settled from Peru and Upper Peru (Bolivia) in the second half of the 16th cent. The oases, whose growth and importance greatly increased after they were linked by railroad to the east coast, produce wine, sugar, fruits, and corn; stock raising is also carried on there. The varied mineral deposits of this region (especially oil, lead, zinc, tin, copper, and salt) are being exploited. Mendoza and Tucu-

mán are major industrial areas engaged in food processing, oil refining, and chemical production. Occupying the southern part of Argentina is Patagonia, a vast, bleak, and windswept dissected plateau. Several large rivers flow in deep valleys eastward across Patagonia to the sea. Sheep raising (chiefly for wool) and oil and natural gas production (the area around COMODORO RIVADAVIA is the chief oil-producing region of Argentina) are the principal economic activities of Patagonia; the region also yields coal. The poor soils of Patagonia and its cool and dry climate do not favor cultivation, although irrigated agriculture is practiced in the Negro and Colorado river valleys. Patagonia is sparsely populated and largely undeveloped, with a few small river-mouth ports on the Atlantic coast such as Viedma, Rawson, Puerto Deseado, and Río Gallegos. USHUAIA, S Tierra del Fuego, on Canal Beagle, is the world's southernmost town. The Andes mts. region of Argentina, broad in the north, where it is similar to the Bolivian altiplano, and becoming narrower toward the south, extends along the length of Argentina's western border. The region, which contains some of the world's highest elevations outside of Asia—including Aconcagua (22,835 ft/6,960 m high; the highest point of South America), Bonete, Tupungato, Mercedario, and Llullaillaco—acts as a barrier to the moist westerly winds, thus giving the eastern slopes of the Andes a desert condition that contrasts with the heavy snowfall on the higher elevations. There are timber and mineral resources, but they are not readily exploitable because of the region's inaccessibility. Cattle are raised on the grassy Andean foothills. There are many beautiful lakes in the region, especially where it merges with the Patagonian plateau; Lake NAHUEL HUAPÍ in Nahuel Huapí National Park, adjoining the Chilean lake district, is an attractive resort area. Argentina, unlike most Latin American nations, has a population that is overwhelmingly of European descent, especially of Italian and Spanish origin. The mestizo portion of Argentina's population is very small because there has been little mixture between European and Indian peoples. The Indian population, which has steadily declined since the coming of the Europeans, is still strong only in parts of the Gran Chaco and the Andean highlands. Only in NW Argentina was there an Indian population with a material culture. They were an agricultural people (recalled today by ruins N of Jujuy), but their importance was eclipsed later by the Araucanian Indians from Chile. Elsewhere there were strong and fierce Indian tribes who did much to hamper white settlement but disappeared under European warfare and pressure. Italian, Spanish (including Basque), French, German, British, Swiss, and East European immigrants came to Argentina during the 1880s; other large in-migrations of Europeans occurred in the 1930s and following World War II. The influx of Chileans into Argentina has been historically tied to boundary disputes between the two nations. The GAUCHO, or Argentine cowboy, the nomadic herdsman of the Pampas—depicted in *Martín Fierro*, the great Argentine folk epic by José Hernández—is still a legendary national symbol. By the 1970s, Argentina had a predominantly urban population with nearly three quarters of its people living in places with 2,000 or more inhabitants; nearly a third of the total population lives in and around Buenos Aires. Argentina is overwhelmingly Christian, with about 90% of the population at least nominally Roman Catholic. Spanish is the country's official language. Argentina has one of South America's lowest population growth rates (1.5%) and one of its highest literacy rates (90%). It has a fine education system that is strongly controlled at all levels by the federal government. Argentines have one of the highest per capita incomes in South America, and the wealth is fairly well distributed. However, high inflation rates in the early 1970s cut into the nation's buying power and necessitated sharp cutbacks in imports in order to bring about a more favorable balance of trade. Argentina's economy is based on agriculture, with grains and livestock (cattle and sheep) the bulwark of its wealth. As an exporter of wheat, corn, flax, oats, beef, mutton, hides, and wool, Argentina has traditionally rivaled the United States, Canada, and Australia. Its cattle herds are among the world's finest. Argentina is the world's largest source of tannin and linseed oil. The Pampa is the nation's chief agricultural area; however, since the 1930s there has been a great rise in production in other areas, especially in the oases of the Monte and the irrigated valleys of N Patagonia. Argentina is nearly self-sufficient in its agricultural needs. Although Argentina has a variety of minerals, they are of local importance and are not completely adequate to support the country's industries. Domestic oil and gas production supplies most of the nation's energy; pipelines connect the oil and gas fields with Buenos Aires and other major refining centers. The large coal field of S Patagonia has low-grade coal. All mining operations in the country have been under federal control since 1954. Argentina has a highly developed industrial base. Developed after World War I and protected by a strong nationalistic policy, Argentine industry has made the country virtually self-sufficient in the production of consumer goods and many types of machinery. Food processing (in particular meat packing, flour milling, and canning) is the chief manufacturing industry of Argentina; leather goods and textiles are also major products. Argentina's principal imports are machinery, metals, and manufactured goods. The chief trading partners are the United States, Italy, Brazil, West Germany, and Great Britain. Argentina is governed by the 1853 constitution as modified in 1898 and subsequently amended. It has a federal system of government. The president and the vice president are elected for four-year terms by popular vote. The popularly elected bicameral national congress is composed of 69 senators (three from each province and three from the federal district), who serve four-year terms, and 243 deputies (from each province and the federal district based on proportional representation), who also serve four-year terms. The supreme court of justice, the nation's highest court, has five members. Each province has its own elected governor and legislature and its own judicial system. The chief political parties of Argentina are the Frente Justicia-lista de Liberación (Peronista) and the Unión Cívica Radical.

History. The Europeans probably first arrived in the region in 1502 in the voyage of Amerigo Vespucci. The search for a Southwest Passage to the Orient brought Juan Díaz de Solís to the Río de la Plata in 1516. Ferdinand Magellan entered (1520) the estuary, and Sebastian CABOT ascended (1536) the Paraná and Paraguay rivers. His delight in native ornaments may be responsible for the names *Río de la Plata* [silver river] and *Argentina* [of silver]. Pedro de Mendoza in 1536 founded the first settlement of the present Buenos Aires, but Indian attacks forced abandonment of the settlement, and Asunción became the unquestioned leading city of the Río de la Plata region. Buenos Aires was refounded in 1580 by Juan de GARAY. His son-in-law, Hernando ARIAS DE SAAVEDRA (Hernandarias), secured the division of the Río de la Plata territories, and Buenos Aires achieved (1617) a sort of semi-independence under the viceroyalty of Peru. The mercantilist system, however, severely hampered the commerce of Buenos Aires, and smuggling, especially with Portuguese traders in Brazil, became an accepted profession. While the cities of present W and NW Argentina grew by supplying the mining towns of the Andes, Buenos Aires was threatened by Portuguese competition. By the 18th cent., cattle (which were introduced to the Pampas in the 1550s) roamed wild throughout the Pampas in large herds and were hunted by gauchos for their skins and fat. In 1776 the Spanish government made Buenos Aires a free port and the capital of a viceroyalty that included present Argentina, Uruguay, Paraguay, and (briefly) Bolivia. From this combination grew the idea of a Greater Argentina to include all the Río de la Plata countries, a dream that was to haunt many Argentine politicians after independence was won. A prelude to independence was the British attack on Buenos Aires; Admiral Sir Home POPHAM and Gen. William Carr BERESFORD in 1806 took the city after the Spanish viceroy fled. An Argentine militia force under Jacques de LINIERS ended the British occupation and beat off a renewed attack under Gen. John Whitelocke in 1807. On May 25, 1810 (May 25 is the Argentine national holiday), revolutionists, acting nominally in favor of the Bourbons dethroned by Napoleon (see SPAIN), deposed the viceroy, and the government was controlled by a junta. The result was war against the royalists. The patriots under Manuel BELGRANO won (1812) a victory at Tucumán. On July 9, 1816, a congress in Tucumán proclaimed the independence of the United Provinces of La Plata. Other patriot generals were Mariano MORENO, Juan Martín de PUEYRREDÓN, and José de SAN MARTÍN. URUGUAY and PARAGUAY went their own ways despite hopes of reunion. In Argentina, a struggle ensued between those who wanted to unify the country and those who did not want to be dominated by Buenos Aires. Independence was followed by virtually permanent civil war, with countless coups d'etat by regional, social, or political factions. Rule by the strong man, the caudillo, alternated with periods of democratic rule, too often beset by disorder. Anarchy was not ended by the election of Bernardino RIVADAVIA in 1826. The unitarians, who favored a centralized government dominated by Buenos Aires, were opposed to the federalists, who resented the oligarchy of Buenos Aires and were backed by autocratic caudillos with gaucho troops. The unitarians triumphed temporarily when Argentinians combined to help the Uruguayans repel Brazilian conquerors in the battle of Ituzaingó (1827), which led to the independence of Uruguay. The internal conflict was, however, soon resumed and was not even quelled when Juan Manuel de ROSAS, the most notorious caudillo, established a dictatorship that lasted until 1852. Ironically, this federalist leader, who was nominally only the governor of Buenos Aires, did more than the unitarians to unify the country. Ironically, too, this enemy of intellectuals stimulated his political opponents to write in exile some of the finest works of the Spanish American romantic period; among the writers were Domingo F. SARMIENTO, Bartolomé MITRE, José MÁRMOL, and Esteban ECHEVERRÍA. Rosas was overthrown (1852) by Justo José de URQUIZA, who called a constituent assembly at Santa Fe. A constitution was adopted (1853) based on the principles enunciated by Juan Bautista ALBERDI. Mitre, denouncing Urquiza as a caudillo, brought about the temporary secession of Buenos Aires prov. (1861) and the downfall of the Urquiza plans. Under the administrations of Mitre (1862–68), Sarmiento (1868–74), and Nicolás AVELLANEDA (1874–80), schools were built, public works started, and liberal reforms instituted. The War of the Triple Alliance (see TRIPLE ALLIANCE, WAR OF THE), 1865–70, brought little advantage to Argentina. In 1880 federalism triumphed, and Gen. Julio A. ROCA became president (1880–1886); Buenos Aires remained the capital, but the federal district was set up, and Buenos Aires prov. was given La Plata as its capital. Argentina flourished during Roca's administration. The conquest of the Indians by General Roca (1878–79) had made colonization of the region in the south and the southwest possible. Already the Pampa had begun to undergo its agricultural transformation. The immigration of Europeans helped to fill the land and to make Argentina one of the world's granaries. Establishment of refrigerating plants for meat made expansion of commerce possible. The British not only became the prime consumers of Argentine products but also invested substantially in the construction of factories, public utilities, and railroads (which were nationalized in 1948). Efforts to end the power of the great landowners, however, were not genuinely successful, and the military tradition continued to play a part in politics, the army frequently combining with the conservatives and later with the growing ranks of labor to alter the government by coup d'etat. The second administration of Roca (1898–1904) was marked by recovery from the crises of the intervening years; a serious boundary dispute with Chile was settled (1902), and perpetual peace between the two nations was symbolized in the CHRIST OF THE ANDES. Even before World War I, in which Argentina maintained neutrality, the wealthy nation had begun to act as spokesman for the rights and interests of Latin America as a whole, notably through Carlos CALVO, Luis M. DRAGO, and later Carlos SAAVEDRA LAMAS. Internal problems, however, remained vexing. Electoral reforms introduced by Roque SÁENZ PEÑA (1910–14) led to the victory of the Radical party under Hipólito IRIGOYEN (1916–22). He introduced social legislation, but when, after the presidency of Marcelo T. de ALVEAR, Irigoyen returned to power in 1928, his policies aroused much dissatisfaction even in his own party. In 1930 he was ousted by Gen. José F. Uriburu, and the conservative oligarchy—now with Fascist leanings—was again in power. The administration (1932–38) of Agustín P. JUSTO was opposed by revolutionary movements, and a coalition of liberals and conservatives won an election victory. The Radical leader Roberto M. Ortiz became president (1938), but serious illness caused him to withdraw (1942), and the conservative Ramón S. Castillo succeeded him. In 1943, Castillo was overthrown by a military coup. After two provisional presidents a "palace revolt" in 1944 brought to power a group of army colonels, chief among them Juan PERON. After four years of pro-Axis "neutrality" Argentina belatedly (March, 1945) entered World War II on the side of the Allies and became a member of the United Nations. A return to liberal government momentarily seemed probable, but Perón was overwhelmingly victorious in the election of Feb., 1946. Perón, an admirer of Mussolini, established a type of popular dictatorship new to Latin America, based initially on support from the army, reactionaries, nationalists, and some clerical groups. His regime was marked by curtailment of freedom of speech, confiscation of liberal newspapers such as *La Prensa*, imprisonment of political opponents, and transition to a one-party state. His second wife, the popular Eva Duarte de Perón, helped him gain the support of the trade unions, thereafter the main foundation of Perón's political power. In 1949 the constitution of 1853 was replaced by a new constitution that permitted Perón to succeed himself as president; the Peronista political party was established the same year. To cure Argentina's serious economic ills, Perón inaugurated a program of industrial development—which advanced rapidly in the 1940s and early 50s, but was severely hampered by the lack of power resources and machine tools—supplemented by social welfare programs. Perón also placed the sale and export of wheat and beef under government control, thus undermining the political and economic power of the rural oligarchs. In the early 1950s, with recurring economic problems and with the death (1952) of his wife, Perón's popular support began to diminish. Agricultural production, long the chief source of revenue, dropped sharply, and the economy faltered. The Roman Catholic church, alienated by the reversal of close church-state relations, excommunicated Perón, and, finally the armed forces became disillusioned with him. In 1955, Perón was ousted by a military coup, and the interim military government of Gen. Pedro Aramburu attempted to rid the country of *justicialismo* (Peronism). In 1957, Argentina reverted to the constitution of 1853 as modified up to 1898. In 1958, Dr. Arturo FRONDIZI was elected president. Faced with the economic and fiscal crisis inherited from Perón, Frondizi, with U.S. advice and the promise of financial aid, initiated a program of austerity to "stabilize" the economy and check inflation. Leftists, as well as Peronistas, who still commanded strong popular support, criticized the plan because the burden lay most heavily on the working and lower middle classes. Frondizi later fell into disfavor with the military because of his leniency toward the regime of Fidel Castro in Cuba and toward Peronistas at home, who, in the congressional elections of 1962, scored a resounding victory. Outraged by this resurgence of Peronista strength, the military arrested Frondizi. José María Guido assumed the presidency, but the military remained in power. In 1963, after months of political crisis and control by the military, presidential elections were held. The Peronista and Communist parties were banned before the election, and many persons were placed under arrest. Following the election as president of the moderate liberal Dr. Arturo ILLÍA, many political prisoners were released, and relative political stability returned. The new president was faced, however, with serious economic depression and with the difficult problem of reintegrating the Peronist forces into Argentine political life. In 1964 an attempt by Perón to return from Spain and lead his followers was thwarted when Perón was turned back at Rio de Janeiro by Brazilian authorities. In elections in 1965 and 1966 the Peronists showed that they remained the strongest political force in the country; unwilling to tolerate another Peronist resurgence, a junta of military leaders, supported by business interests, seized power (1966) and placed Gen. Juan Carlos ONGANÍA, a long-time right-wing opponent of Illia, in the presidency. Under Onganía, and with the strong backing of the military, the new government dissolved the legislature, banned all political parties, and exercised unofficial press censorship; Onganía also placed the national universities under government control. Widespread opposition to the rigid rule of the Onganía regime grew, and an antigovernment campaign developed. Faced with labor and student unrest, the military deposed (1970) Onganía and named Gen. Roberto M. Levingston president. Economic problems and increased terrorist activities caused Gen. Alejandro Lanusse, the leader of the coup against Onganía, to dismiss (1971) Levingston and initiate an active program for economic growth, distribution of wealth, and political stability. His direct negotiations with Juan Perón and his call for national elections and a civilian government led to the return of Perón to Argentina in 1972. After failing to achieve unity among the various Peronist groups, Perón declined the nomination from his supporters to run for president in the March, 1973, elections, which were won by Dr. Hector Cámpora, a Peronist candidate who subsequently resigned from office to make way for Perón's return. When new elections were held in Sept., 1973, Perón was elected president and his third wife, Isabel Martínez Perón, vice president. Perón died in July, 1974, and, as provided for in the constitution, was succeeded as president by his widow, the nation's vice president. The government of Isabel Perón, who had only a small personal following, faced an uncertain future complicated by economic troubles, labor unrest, political violence, and deep divisions within the Peronista party. See R. J. Alexander, *An Introduction to Argentina* (1969); H. S. Ferns, *Argentina* (1969); F. P. Munson et al., *Area Handbook for Argentina* (1969); P. H. Smith, *Politics and Beef in Argentina: Patterns of Conflict and Change* (1969); Díaz Alejandro and Carlos Federico, *Essays on the Economic History of the Argentine Republic* (1970); J. A. Fernández, *The Political Elite in Argentina* (1970); Ezequiel Martínez Estrada, *X Ray of the Pampa* (tr. 1971); J. R. Scobie, *Argentina: A City and a Nation* (2d ed. 1971); Marvin Goldwert, *Democracy, Militarism and Nationalism in Argentina, 1930-1966* (1972).

arginine (är'jənīn), organic compound, one of the 22 α-AMINO ACIDS commonly found in animal proteins. Only the L-stereoisomer participates in the biosynthesis of proteins. Its basic side chain often adds a positive charge and hence a greater degree of water-solubility to proteins in neutral solution. Although arginine can be synthesized from cellular metabolites, it is usually considered essential to the diet of children for the maintainance of normal rates of growth. Arginine is the direct metabolic precursor of UREA, the dominant nitrogenous waste product of most mammals. It was discovered in protein in 1895.

arginine

Argirocastro: see GJINOKASTËR, Albania.

Argo (är'gō), in Greek mythology, ship in which JASON and the Argonauts sailed in quest of the Golden Fleece. Most legends say that Argus, son of Phrixus, was the builder, with the help of Athena. Others claim that Argus the Thespian, or Argus the son of Arestor, built the ship. The *Argo* included a beam cut from the divine tree of Dodona, which could foretell the future.

Argob (är'gŏb), region of Bashan, E of the Sea of Galilee. Deut. 3.4,13,14; 1 Kings 4.13. The interpretation of Argob as a person is uncertain. 2 Kings 15.25.

argol (är'gəl): see TARTAR.

Argolis (är'gəlĭs), region of ancient Greece in the NE Peloponnesus. It was roughly identical with the Argive plain and was the area dominated by the city of Argos.

argon (är'gŏn) [Gr.,=inert], gaseous chemical element; symbol Ar; at. no. 18; at. wt. 39.948; m.p. −189.2°C; b.p. −185.7°C; density 1.784 grams per liter at STP (see separate article); valence 0. Argon is a colorless, odorless, tasteless gas occurring in air (of which it constitutes 0.94% by volume) and in some volcanic gases. It is a member of group 0 of the PERIODIC TABLE, a group called the noble or INERT GASES from the mistaken former belief that none of its members could form chemical compounds; in fact, other members of the group, e.g., krypton, xenon, and radon, do form compounds. Argon is prepared by fractional distillation of liquid air. Its extreme inertness has caused it to be substituted for nitrogen in electric light bulbs. It is mixed with neon in so-called neon signs (gas discharge tubes) to produce a green-to-blue glow. It is used as a protective atmosphere in arc welding, in the refining of reactive elements, and in the growing of crystals for use in semiconductor devices. Argon was first obtained by Lord Rayleigh and Sir William Ramsay in 1894. Previously Lord Rayleigh had noticed that a liter of supposedly pure nitrogen drawn from the air weighed more than a liter prepared from a nitrogen compound. This difference in weight led him to conclude that another gas was present in the supposedly pure nitrogen. Actually several unreactive gases were present; the first samples of "argon" also contained HELIUM, NEON, KRYPTON, and XENON. Ramsay obtained pure argon later by evaporating it from liquid air.

argonaut, in zoology: see PAPER NAUTILUS.

Argonauts: see JASON; ARGO; GOLDEN FLEECE.

Argonne (ärgôn'), region of the Paris basin, NE France, in Champagne and Lorraine (Meuse, Marne, and Ardennes dept.), a hilly and woody district centering around the capital, Sainte-Menehould. Thinly populated, with unimportant cultivation and only small industries, its significance has been strategic. There, in 1792, the French repulsed the Prussians. The sector was a battleground throughout World War I. In the Allied victory drive (Sept.-Nov., 1918), the Meuse-Argonne sector was carried by the Americans.

Argonne National Laboratory, nuclear research center, principal facilities located in Argonne, Ill., 27 mi (43 km) SW of downtown Chicago; other facilities located at the National Reactor Testing Station, 50 mi (80 km) W of Idaho Falls, Idaho. This atomic energy research and development establishment was founded in 1946 by the U.S. Atomic Energy Commission. Since 1966 the laboratory has operated under an agreement involving the U.S. Atomic Energy Commission, the Argonne Universities Association, and the Univ. of Chicago. The principal objectives of the laboratory are to carry out multidisciplinary basic research, much of which involves the use of radiation as a tool in the physical and life sciences, and to work on the design and development of nuclear reactors.

Argos (är'gŏs, -gəs), city of ancient Greece, in NE Peloponnesus, 3 mi (4.8 km) inland from the Gulf of Argos, near the modern Nauplia. It was occupied from the early Bronze Age and is mentioned in Homer's *Iliad* as the kingdom of Diomed. Argos was the center of Argolis and in the 7th cent. B.C., under King Pheidon, dominated much of the Peloponnesus. For centuries it was one of the most powerful Greek cities, struggling with Sparta and rivaling Athens and Corinth. Much of Argos' power disappeared after Cleomenes I of Sparta took (c.494 B.C.) the city. Pyrrhus was killed in an attack on Argos in 272. The city joined the Achaean League in 229, and in 146 it was taken by Rome, under whose rule trade flourished. The Heraeum temple, 6 mi (9.7 km) N of Argos, was the principal center for the worship of the goddess Hera. Argos produced important sculptors, including Polycletus, in the 5th cent. There is a small modern town called Argos on the site of the ancient city.

Argos, in Greek mythology: see ARGUS.

Arguedas, Alcides (älsē'thās ärgā'thās), 1879-1946, Bolivian writer and diplomat. His essays and novels, which have social and moralizing tendencies, are a reaction against the romantic idealization of the Indian. His best-known works are *Pueblo enfermo* [a sick people] (1909) and *Raza de bronce* [a race of bronze] (1919), a novel exposing the exploitation of the Indians by the landowners. Some of the Indian folktales he collected are included in the volume *Singing Mountaineers: Songs and Tales of the Quecha People* (tr. and ed. by Ruth Stephen, 1957, repr. 1971).

Arguello, Point (ärgwĕl'ō), promontory, SW Calif., extending W into the Pacific Ocean. A U.S. navy missile-launching complex is nearby.

Argun (är'go͞on'), Mandarin *O-erh-ku-na,* river, 950 mi (1,529 km) long, rising in the Great Khingan mts., Heilungkiang prov., NE China, and flowing W to the USSR border, then NE along the USSR-China frontier, where it joins the Shilka River to form the Amur. The Chinese Eastern RR, a branch of the Trans-Siberian RR, follows the upper Argun valley. Hailar, China, is the largest city on the river. Corn, grains, and sugar beets are grown in the fertile Argun valley. Silver, lead, and coal are found along the river banks.

Argus (är'gəs) or **Argos** (är'gŏs, -gəs), in Greek mythology. **1** Many-eyed monster, also called Panoptes. He guarded Io after she had been changed into a heifer. **2** Builder of the ARGO. He built the ship on which Jason and the Argonauts (of which he was one) sailed in quest of the Golden Fleece.

Argyll, Archibald Campbell, 1st **duke of,** d. 1703, Scottish nobleman; eldest son of the 9th earl of Argyll. Having unsuccessfully sought favor with James II in order to recover the estates forfeited by his father, he supported the cause of William of Orange and formally offered William and Mary the crown of Scotland in 1689. Since his support was important to William, particularly as a basis for encouraging the submission of the clans, he was restored to his estates and made a privy councilor. He remained William's chief adviser on Scottish affairs and was made a duke (1701). Although two companies from his regiment were used to perpetrate the massacre (1692) of the MacDonalds of Glencoe, it is unlikely that he was in any way personally involved.

Argyll, Archibald Campbell, 3d **duke of,** 1682-1761, Scottish nobleman; brother of the 2d duke. As lord high treasurer of Scotland (1705) and a commissioner for the union (1706), he helped negotiate the union (1707) of the kingdoms of Scotland and England. He had been created earl of Islay in 1705, and he sat as a Scottish representative peer in the united Parliament from 1707 until his death. Consistently loyal to the Hanoverian kings, he held high offices in Scotland and promoted the trade, industry, and schools of his native land. He succeeded his brother as duke in 1743.

Argyll, Archibald Campbell, 5th **earl of,** 1530–73, Scottish statesman. He and Lord James Stuart (later earl of Murray) became followers of John Knox in 1556 and led the troops of the Scottish Protestants, the lords of the congregation, against those of the Roman Catholic regent, Mary of Guise. Won over by Mary Queen of Scots when she arrived in Scotland (1561), he supported her until she proposed marrying Lord Darnley. He then tried to enlist the aid of Elizabeth I of England against Mary. Failing in this, he returned to Mary's party and is thought to have had some part in the murder of Darnley (1567). Argyll was in command of Mary's soldiers when they were defeated at Langside in 1568 by the soldiers under Murray, now regent, but he was reconciled with Murray the next year. Becoming a supporter of James VI, he was made lord high chancellor in 1572.

Argyll, Archibald Campbell, 8th **earl** and 1st **marquess of,** 1607–61, Scottish statesman. He became chief of the powerful Campbell clan at the death (1638) of his father, the 7th earl. A staunch Presbyterian, he was a leading opponent of Charles I's attempt to strengthen episcopacy in Scotland. Charles sought to win his support by making him a marquess (1641), but after the outbreak of the English civil war Argyll represented the COVENANTERS in negotiating (1643) the alliance with the English parliamentarians. He commanded the Covenanter army against the earl of MONTROSE and was repeatedly defeated (1644–45). In 1646, Argyll negotiated with both the defeated Charles and the English Parliament, attempting to secure a Presbyterian settlement in England. He later supported Oliver Cromwell but suffered a serious loss of influence because of the revulsion of feeling in Scotland at the king's execution (1649). Hoping that Charles II could be restored as a Presbyterian king, Argyll turned from Cromwell and crowned (1651) Charles II in Scotland. He opposed the disastrous Scottish invasion of England in that year and submitted to the English Commonwealth in 1652. He was executed for treason at the Restoration. See biography by John Willcock (1903).

Argyll, Archibald Campbell, 9th **earl of,** 1629?–1685, Scottish nobleman; son of the 8th earl. An ardent and active royalist and a Protestant, he opposed extreme measures against the COVENANTERS, thereby incurring the enmity of the duke of York (later James II), who in 1680 was high commissioner of Scotland. Argyll was accused of treason and sentenced to death in 1681. He escaped to Holland, was a leader of the rebellion in favor of the duke of MONMOUTH, and was captured and beheaded.

Argyll, John Campbell, 2d **duke of,** 1678–1743, Scottish general; son of the 1st duke, whom he succeeded in 1703. For his ardent support of the union of England and Scotland he was created (1705) earl of Greenwich. He served under the duke of Marlborough in the War of the Spanish Succession (1701–14) and rose to be commander in chief in Spain in 1711. On his return to Scotland he actively supported the succession of George I. He commanded the army that put down the Jacobite rebellion in 1715 and was made duke of Greenwich in 1719. His ambitions brought him high political offices, but he was tactless and too forthright, and his later career was uneven.

Argyllshire (ärgīl'shĭr) or **Argyll,** county (1971 pop. 59,909), 3,124 sq mi (8,091 sq km), W central Scotland. Inveraray is the county town. The county includes numerous islands of the Inner HEBRIDES, including the island of IONA. The coast of the mainland is jagged and deeply indented by lochs; KINTYRE peninsula juts sharply into the North Channel. Wild and mountainous, the county has little arable land. Sheep grazing is the main occupation; crop raising (oats, hay, and barley) is confined to the islands and coastal strips. Fishing and distilling are also important. OBAN and Dunoon are favorite resorts. Argyllshire was settled by Celts from Ireland in the 6th cent. It became the seat of the powerful Campbell clan in the 16th cent. Under the Local Government Act of 1973, Argyllshire was divided between the new Highland and Strathclyde regions.

Argyrokastron: see GJINOKASTËR, Albania.

Århus (ôr'ho͞os), city (1970 com. pop. 237,514), capital of Århus co., central Denmark, on Århus Bay, an arm of the Kattegat. The second largest city in Denmark, it is a commercial, industrial, and shipping center. Manufactures include beer, textiles, machinery, processed food, locomotives, and tobacco products. First mentioned in the mid-10th cent., Århus is one of the oldest cities in Denmark. It developed rapidly after it became an episcopal see in the 11th cent. The city declined after the Reformation (16th cent.) but recovered its prosperity in the 18th cent. Århus is also a cultural center, with a university (opened 1928), a prominent theater, a museum group of early Danish houses, and a large library. Noteworthy buildings include the Cathedral of St. Clemens (12th cent.) and the town hall (1942), made of Norwegian marble. Until 1948 the city's name was spelled Aarhus.

aria (är'ēə), elaborate and often lengthy solo song with instrumental accompaniment. In the 16th cent. it was a melody improvised over a strophic bass line, and a distinction was made between instrumental, vocal, and dance arias. The use of the term to indicate instrumental music was continued by such composers as Froberger, Pachelbel, and J. S. Bach. The first use of the term to indicate solo song was by Giulio Caccini in 1602. Later in the 17th cent. Italian OPERA composers developed the *aria da capo,* a throughcomposed (nonstrophic) three-part structure in which the beginning section is repeated after a contrasting middle section. Though this formal scheme was first used by Monteverdi, he did not designate it *aria da capo.* This type achieved artistic perfection in the operas of Alessandro SCARLATTI and Handel and in the works of J. S. Bach. In the 18th cent. the three main sections were divided into subsections, and there were classifications of many various types of arias. The extreme convention of using as many types as possible, but never the same type in succession, developed in the Neapolitan opera, and the subsequent formal rigidity led to a decline of the *aria da capo.* Later in the 18th cent. prominent virtuoso singers, seeking a means for technical display, caused the development of a type consisting in reality of two separate arias, the first usually dramatic and the second lyrical. Most of the arias of Mozart are of this kind. But in French operas, especially those of Christoph W. von GLUCK, there was a development leading to greater similarity of recitative and aria, which eventually culminated in the complete abandonment of arias in the late operas of Richard WAGNER, who substituted a highly melodic RECITATIVE called *Sprechgesang* [Ger.,=speech-song]. The form continued to be preferred by Italian opera composers, however, and the romantic aria reached its height in the works of Giuseppe VERDI.

Ariadne (ărēăd'nē), in Greek mythology, Cretan princess, daughter of Minos and Pasiphaë. Because of her love for Theseus, she gave him a clue that enabled him to kill the monstrous Minotaur. When Theseus left Crete, he took Ariadne with him, but before they reached Greece, he abandoned her at Naxos. There the god Dionysus consoled and later wedded her. She bore him several children, including Oenopion, whom Dionysus first taught the art of wine making. It was said that Zeus granted Ariadne immortality and that Dionysus set her bridal crown among the stars.

Ariana or **Aryana** (both: ârēā'nə, -ā'nə), general name for the eastern provinces of the ancient Persian Empire. It was used to mean the regions S of the Oxus (modern Amu Darya) River; the regions to the north were called Transoxiana. Ariana is included in present E Iran, N and E Afghanistan, and India NE of the Indus River.

Arianism, Christian heresy founded by ARIUS in the 4th cent. It was one of the most widespread and divisive heresies in the history of Christianity. As a priest in Alexandria, Arius taught (c.318) that God created, before all things, a Son who was the first creature, but who was neither equal nor eternal with the Father. According to Arius, Jesus Christ was a supernatural creature not quite human and not quite divine, but more like a demigod. In these ideas Arius was a disciple of Lucian, who was a disciple of the heretic PAUL OF SAMOSATA. Arius was condemned and deprived of his office. He went to Asia and propagated his doctrine among the masses through popular sermons and songs and among the powerful through the efforts of influential leaders, e.g., EUSEBIUS OF NICOMEDIA and, to a lesser extent, EUSEBIUS OF CAESAREA. The civil as well as the religious peace of the East was threatened, and Roman Emperor Constantine I convoked (325) the first ecumenical council (see NICAEA, FIRST COUNCIL OF). The council condemned Arianism, but the Greek term *homoousios* [consubstantial, of the same substance] used by the council to define the Son's relationship to the Father was not universally popular: it had been used before by the heretical Sabellius. Some, like MARCELLUS OF ANCYRA, in attacking Arianism, lapsed into SABELLIANISM. Eusebius of Nicomedia used this fear of Sabellianism to persuade Constantine to return Arius to his duties in Alexandria. ATHANASIUS, chief defender of the Nicene formulary, was bishop in Alexandria, and conflict was inevitable. The Eusebians managed to secure Athanasius' exile, and when the Arian Constantius II became emperor, Catholic bishops in the East, e.g., EUSTATHIUS, were banished wholesale. The exile of Athanasius to Rome brought Pope JULIUS I into the struggle. A council wholly favorable to Athanasius, convened at Sardica (c.343), was avoided by the Eastern bishops and ignored by Constantius. The Catholics were left dependent on Rome for support. After the West fell to Constantius, the Eusebians reversed the decisions of Sardica in several councils (Arles, 353; Milan, 355; Boziers, 356), and Pope LIBERIUS, St. HILARY OF POITIERS, and HOSIUS were exiled. The victorious Arians, however, had now begun to quarrel among themselves. The Anomoeans [from Gr.,=unlike], followers of EUNOMIUS and AETIUS, were pure Arians and held that the Son bore no resemblance to the Father. The semi-Arian court party were called Homoeans [from Gr.,=similar] from their teaching that the Son was simply like the Father as defined by Scripture. A third party called Homoiousians [from Gr.,=like in substance] were largely prevented from joining the orthodox (Homoousian) party through a misunderstanding of terms. The Arians debated their differences at a series of formularies at Sirmium (351–59). The final formula was an ambiguous Homoean declaration that Constantius imposed (359) upon the church in two councils, Rimini (for the West) and Seleucia (for the East). The voices of orthodoxy, however, were not silent. In the West St. Hilary of Poitiers and in the East St. BASIL THE GREAT, St. GREGORY NAZIANZEN, and St. GREGORY OF NYSSA continued to defend and interpret the Nicene formulary. By 364 the West had a Catholic emperor in Valentinian I, and when the Catholic THEODOSIUS I became emperor of the East (379), Arianism was outlawed. The second ecumenical council was convoked to reaffirm the Nicene formulary (see CONSTANTINOPLE, FIRST COUNCIL OF), and Arianism within the empire seems to have expired at once. However, ULFILAS had carried (c.340) Homoean Arianism to the Goths living in what is now Hungary and Yugoslavia with such success that the Visigoths and other Germanic tribes became staunch Arians. Arianism was thus carried over Western Europe and into Africa. The Vandals remained Arians until their defeat by Belisarius (c.534). Among the Lombards the efforts of Pope St. Gregory I and the Lombard queen were successful, and Arianism finally disappeared (c.650) there. In Burgundy the Catholic Franks broke up Arianism by conquest in the 6th cent. In Spain, where the conquering Visigoths were Arians, Catholicism was not established until the end of the 6th cent. (by Recared), and Arian ideas survived for at least another century. Arianism brought many results—the ecumenical council, the Catholic Christological system, Nestorianism, and, by reaction, Monophysitism. See John Henry Newman, *The Arians of the Fourth Century* (1833, repr. 1968); H. M. Gwatkin, *Studies of Arianism* (2d ed. 1900); Adolf von Harnack, *History of Dogma* (tr. of 3d ed., 7 vol., 1898–1903).

Arias, Arnulfo (ärno͞ol'fō är'yäs), 1901–, president of Panama (1940–41, 1949–51, Oct., 1968). A Harvard-trained physician, he dominated Panamanian politics throughout the 1930s, leading the coup that deposed President Florencio Harmodio Arosemena in 1931 and generally selecting the country's presidents. He held several cabinet and diplomatic posts. In June, 1940, he was elected president by an unprecedented majority. He jailed dissidents, disenfranchised the non-Spanish-speaking portion of the population, and espoused a totalitarian state, which led to his ouster in Oct., 1941. Reelected president in 1949, he was deposed in May, 1951, after organizing his own secret police and suspending the constitution. He ran unsuccessfully for the presidency in 1964, then won election in 1968 after putting together a strong, five-party coalition. Taking office in October, he immediately manuevered to gain absolute control of the national assembly and the supreme court and attempted to restructure the command of the national guard. After only 11 days as president, he was ousted by national guard officers.

Arias de Ávila, Pedro (pä'thrō ä'ryäs dā ä'vēlä), known as **Pedrarias** (pāthrä'ryäs), c.1440–1531, Spanish colonial administrator. He was sent (1514) as governor to Darien (now part of Panama), then under the rule of Vasco Núñez de BALBOA. A long quarrel between the two ended with Balboa's execution. Pedrarias jealously guarded his power and his administration was notoriously harsh and cruel. He sent (1523) Francisco FERNÁNDEZ DE CÓRDOBA to usurp control of Nicaragua, conquered the year before by Gil GONZÁLEZ DE ÁVILA. When Fernández de Córdoba attempted to free himself from Pedrarias' control, Pedrarias captured and executed him. Pedrarias extended the Spanish dominions and founded (1519) Panama City; he first aided, but later hindered, Francisco PIZARRO and Diego de Almagro in their conquest of Peru. Superseded as governor in 1526, he went to Nicaragua, where he retained power until his death. His name also appears as Pedrarias Dávila.

Arias de Saavedra, Hernando (ārnän'dō ä'ryäs dā sävä'drä), known as **Hernandarias** (ārnändä'ryäs), 1561–1634, Spanish colonial governor, b. Asunción, in present-day Paraguay. A remarkable administrator, he was elected (1592) lieutenant governor of Asunción by the CABILDO and was chosen governor of Río de la Plata prov. three times (1597–99, 1602–9, 1614–18). He consolidated the Spanish settlements, pacified and protected the Indians, introduced public schools, and stimulated the growth of Buenos Aires. In 1617 he secured a royal order for the separation of Paraguay (then Guairá) from Río de la Plata, and granted the Jesuits territorial privileges for the religious colonization of the region.

Arias Montanus, Benedictus (bĕnədĭk'təs ā'rēəs mŏntā'nəs), or **Benito Arias Montano** (bānē'tō ä'ryäs mōntä'nō), 1527–98, Spanish Benedictine monk, editor of the Antwerp POLYGLOT BIBLE. He attended the Council of Trent (1562).

Arica (ärē'kä), city (1970 pop. 92,394), N Chile, on the Pacific Ocean, just south of the Peruvian border and at the northern limit of the Desert of Atacama. Peru ceded Arica to Chile after the War of the Pacific (see PACIFIC, WAR OF THE). With the settlement of the TACNA-ARICA CONTROVERSY in 1929, Chile retained sovereignty over the city but was required to furnish complete port facilities to Peru. The district of Arica is now a free zone where both Chile and Peru maintain customs houses. The city is a resort and a port through which the mineral exports (chiefly copper, tin, and sulfur) of both countries are shipped.

Aridai (ərĭd'āī), one of Haman's sons. Esther 9.9.

Aridatha (ərĭd'əthə), son of Haman. Esther 9.8.

Ariège (äryĕzh'), department (1968 pop. 138,478), SW France, in Languedoc, bounded by Spain and Andorra. FOIX is the capital.

Arieh (ārī'ə), one of the two guards murdered with King Pekahiah. 2 Kings 15.25.

Ariel (ā'rēĕl), aide of Ezra. Ezra 8.16. In two other passages AV calls them "lionlike men" ("two ariels of Moab" in RV). 2 Sam. 23.20; 1 Chron. 11.22. Nothing is known of them. Ariel is also used as a symbolic name of Jerusalem. Isa. 29.

Ariel (âr'ēəl), in astronomy, one of the five known moons, or natural satellites, of URANUS.

Aries (âr'ēz) [Lat.,=the ram], CONSTELLATION lying on the ECLIPTIC (the sun's apparent path through the heavens) between Taurus and Pisces; it is one of the constellations of the ZODIAC. It contains the bright star Hamal (Alpha Arietis). About 2,000 years ago the vernal EQUINOX was located at the beginning of Aries and was thus also called the "first point of Aries"; however, the PRECESSION OF THE EQUINOXES has since shifted the vernal equinox into Pisces. Aries reaches its highest point in the evening sky in December.

Arikara Indians (ərĭk'ərə), North American Indians whose language belongs to the Caddoan branch of the Hokan-Siouan linguistic stock (see AMERICAN INDIAN LANGUAGES). Archaeological evidence shows that they occupied the banks of the upper Missouri River since at least the 14th cent. A semisedentary group, they lived in earth-covered lodges. In winter they hunted buffalo, returning to their villages for spring planting; the Arikara were influential in bringing agricultural knowledge from the Southwest to the prehistoric peoples of the upper Missouri River. They traded corn with hunting tribes in return for buffalo hides and meat, and they were active in bartering with early white traders, who frequently called them the Rees. They were closely associated with the MANDAN INDIANS and the HIDATSA INDIANS; these three tribes now share the Fort Berthold Reservation in North Dakota. See D. J. Lehmer, *Arikara Archaeology* (1968).

Arimathaea (ăr"ĭməthē'ə), home of St. Joseph of Arimathea, not otherwise known. It may be the same as RAMATHAIM-ZOPHIM. Mat. 27.57; Mark 15.43; Luke 23.50,51; John 19.38.

Ariminum: see RIMINI, Italy.

Arioch (ā'rēŏk). **1** See CHEDORLAOMER. **2** Captain under Nebuchadnezzar. Dan. 2.14.

Arion (ərī'ən), Greek poet, inventor of the dithyramb. He is said to have lived at Periander's court in Corinth in the late 7th cent. B.C. A legend repeated by Herodotus tells how, having been thrown overboard by pirates, Arion was saved by a dolphin charmed by his music. See A. W. Pickard-Cambridge, *Dithyramb, Tragedy, and Comedy* (1927, repr. 1962).

Ariosto, Ludovico (lo͞odōvē'kō äryôs'tō), 1474–1533, Italian epic and lyric poet. As a youth he was a favorite at the court of Ferrara; later he was in the service of Ippolito I, Cardinal d'Este, and then of the duke of Ferrara. He was never properly rewarded by his patrons. While at the duke's court, he began the *Orlando Furioso,* published in its final form in 1532. This epic treatment of the ROLAND story, theoretically a sequel to the unfinished masterpiece of BOIARDO, greatly influenced Shakespeare, Milton, and Byron. It was intended to glorify the Este family as Vergil had glorified the Julians. Ariosto also wrote lyric verse of unequal merit and several comedies, among them *I suppositi* [the pretenders] and *Il negromante* [the necromancer]. See the famous 16th-century translation of *Orlando Furioso* by Sir John Harington, ed. by Robert McNulty (1972); studies by A. V. Cameron (1930), Benedetto Croce (tr. 1920, repr. 1966), E. G. Gardner (1906, repr. 1968), and Robert Griffin (1974).

Ariovistus (âr"ēōvĭs'təs), fl. 58 B.C., Germanic chieftain, leader of the Suebi. He crossed the Rhine c.71 B.C., defeated the AEDUI, and came to dominate much of Gaul (see GALLIC WARS). In 60 B.C. he was made a friend and ally of Rome, but his power threatened the Romans in Gaul, and Julius Caesar, soon after winning the great victory of Bibracte over the Helvetii, undertook a campaign against him. Caesar defeated Ariovistus somewhere in Upper Alsace in 58 B.C.

Arisai (ərĭs'āī), son of Haman. Esther 9.9.

Arish, Al (äl ärēsh'), town (1970 est. pop. 43,000), NE Egypt, in the Sinai peninsula, on the Mediterranean Sea. It is a fishing port and administrative center. In 1118, King Baldwin I of Jerusalem died in Al Arish on the way back from his Egyptian campaign. In 1800, during the venture of Napoleon I in Egypt, the French signed a convention in the city by which they were to evacuate the country. The British did not ratify the convention, and fighting resumed. Israeli troops briefly held Al Arish during the 1956 Arab-Israeli war and occupied the town in the 1967 war. After the 1967 war an Israeli settlement, Nahal Yam, was established nearby. In 1969, Israel evacuated the civilian population of Al Qantarah, a town on the Suez Canal, to Al Arish.

Arista, Mariano (märyä'nō ärē'stä), 1802–55, Mexican general and president (1851–53). A royalist in the revolt against Spain, he later joined Agustín de Iturbide. He fought in the Mexican army that tried to put down the Texas revolt (1836). In command of the army in N Mexico in the Mexican War, he was defeated by Zachary TAYLOR at Palo Alto and at Resaca de la Palma (1846). Arista succeeded J. J. Herrera as president. His administration sought to bring fiscal stability to the nation. Difficulties in maintaining a loyal cabinet and a conservative revolt in 1852 led to his resignation the following year.

Aristaeus (ărĭstē'əs), in Greek mythology, son of Apollo and Cyrene, especially honored as the inventor of beekeeping. Aristaeus tried to violate Eurydice, wife of Orpheus. Eurydice was fatally bitten by a snake while fleeing him. As punishment, the nymphs, who had previously been his mentors, caused all his bees to die. However, he sacrificed several cattle in atonement, and from their carcasses new swarms of bees were generated. Learned in the arts of medicine and soothsaying, Aristaeus wandered through many lands teaching his skills and curing the sick. He came to be widely worshiped as a beneficent deity.

Aristarchus (ăr"ĭstär'kəs), Macedonian companion of Paul. Philemon 24; Acts 19.29; 20.4; 27.2; Col. 4.10.

Aristarchus of Samos (sā'mŏs), fl. c.310 B.C.–c.230 B.C., Greek astronomer of the Alexandrian school. He is said to have been the first man to propose a heliocentric theory of the universe. Of his writings only a treatise, *The Sizes and Distances of the Sun and Moon,* remains. This does not mention his conclusion that the earth moves around the sun and that the sun is at rest, but a quotation by Archimedes and statements by Copernicus prove that he held this theory. Other conclusions in which he seems to have anticipated later scientists are that the sun is larger than the earth, that the earth rotates upon its axis causing day and night, and that its axis is inclined to the plane of the ecliptic, causing the change of seasons. See T. L. Heath, *Aristarchus of Samos* (1913).

Aristarchus of Samothrace (săm'əthrās), c.217–c.145 B.C., Greek scholar, successor to his teacher, Aristophanes of Byzantium, as librarian at Alexandria. He was an innovator of scientific scholarship, and his critical revision of Homer is responsible for the excellent texts of Homer that survive. Though only fragments of his works survive (he is said to have written more than 800 volumes of commentary and exegesis), frequent quotations by ancient critics provide an insight into his subjects and method. His works cover such writers as Alcaeus, Anacreon, Pindar, Hesiod, and the tragedians.

Aristides, Saint (ărĭstī'dēz), 2d cent., Greek philosopher, author of an early Christian apology. It was presented (c.126 or 136) to the emperor to protest anti-Christian slanders and persecutions. The text is embedded in transcribed versions of the medieval legend BARLAAM AND JOSAPHAT. Feast: Aug. 31.

Aristides (ărĭstī'dēz), d. c.468 B.C., Athenian statesman and general. He was one of the 10 generals who commanded the Athenians at the battle of Marathon (490 B.C.) and in the next year became chief archon. In 483 he was ostracized because he opposed the naval policy of Themistocles. However, in 480 Aristides fought beside his countrymen at Salamis, and the following year he commanded the Athenian army at the battle of Plataea. Later he organized the finances of the Delian League. He is a classic example of probity in public life and was called Aristides the Just.

Aristippus (ărĭstĭp'əs), c.435–c.360 B.C., Greek philosopher of Cyrene, first of the CYRENAICS. He held pleasure to be the highest good and virtue to be identical with the ability to enjoy. His doctrines, comprising the first coherent exposition of HEDONISM, opposed those of the Cynics, although both groups drew upon aspects of Socratic philosophy.

Aristobulus: see MACCABEES.

aristocracy (ăr"ĭstŏk'rəsē) [Gr.,=rule by the best], in political science, government by a social elite. In the West the political concept of aristocracy derives from Plato's formulation in the *Republic.* The criteria on which aristocracy is based may vary greatly from society to society. Historically, aristocracies have usually rested on landed property, have invoked heredity, and, despite frequent conflicts with the throne, have flourished chiefly within the framework of MONARCHY. Aristocracy may be based on wealth as well as land, as in ancient Carthage and medieval Venice, or may be a theocracy like the Brahman caste in India. Other criteria can be age, race, military prowess, or cultural attainment. The best example of a modern landowning aristocracy that conducted government was in England from 1688 to 1832. A resurgence by the French aristocracy in the 18th cent. was ended by the French Revolution, which abolished most of the privileges on which it was based. Inflation, which cut into the fixed income of the aristocracy, the loss of the traditional military role of the aristocracy, and the rise of industry and decline in the importance of landed property have all worked against the aristocracy. Today the political power of traditional western aristocracy has all but disappeared.

Aristogiton: see HARMODIUS AND ARISTOGITON.

Aristophanes (ăr"ĭstŏf'ənēz), b. c.448 B.C., d. after 388 B.C., Athenian comic poet, greatest of the ancient writers of COMEDY. His plays, the only full extant samples of the Greek Old Comedy, mix political, social, and literary satire. The direct attack on persons, the severity of invective, and the burlesque extravagances made the plays fitting for the festival of Dionysus. Aristophanes was conservative in all things, hence he distrusted sophistry and Socrates alike, satirized Euripides' art as degenerate, and deplored the tendency to excessive imperialism that ruined Athens in the Syracusan expedition. The typical plan of an Aristophanic comedy is simple—the protagonist undertakes seriously some preposterous project, and the play is an elaboration of his success or failure. Despite the absurdity of the situation, Aristophanes' characters are real as types; their verisimilitude comes from their perfectly natural behavior in unnatural circumstances. Aristophanes' Greek is exceptionally beautiful, and many of his choruses are among the finest lyric pieces in

Greek literature. His careful diction and his ability to characterize in a few words are remarkable, and he shows himself especially astute in his parodies of Euripides. Eleven of his plays survive: *The Acharnians* (425 B.C.), an attack on the Peloponnesian War; *The Knights* (424), a political satire on the demagoguery of the period; *The Clouds* (423), a satire on the sophists and on Socrates; *The Wasps* (422), a satire on the Athenian passion for litigation; *The Peace* (421), a defense of the Peace of Nicias; *The Birds* (414), an escape into an amazing imaginary kingdom; *Lysistrata* (411), in which the Athenian women boycott their husbands to end a war; *The Thesmophoriazusae* or *The Women at Demeter's Festival* (411), in which the women conspire to ruin Euripides because of his misogyny; *The Frogs* (405), a literary satire involving Aeschylus and Euripides; *The Ecclesiazusae* or *The Women in Politics* (c.392), in which the women take over the government; and *Plutus* (388), in which the blind god of wealth recovers his eyesight and distributes the gifts of fortune more equitably. See his plays (tr. by B. B. Rogers, 3 vol., rev. ed. 1950); studies by V. Ehrenberg (3d ed. 1962), G. Murray (1933, repr. 1964), C. Whitman (1964), K. J. Dover (1972), and Alexis Solomos (tr. 1974).

Aristophanes of Byzantium (bĭzăn'shēəm, -tēəm), c.257–180 B.C., Greek scholar. He was librarian at Alexandria, edited various texts, and reputedly invented the Greek diacritical marks. Aristarchus of Samothrace was his pupil.

Aristotle (âr'ĭstŏt'əl), 384–322 B.C., Greek philosopher, b. Stagira. He is sometimes called the Stagirite. His father, Nicomachus, was a noted physician. Aristotle studied (367–347 B.C.) under Plato at the ACADEMY and there wrote many dialogues that were praised for their eloquence. Only fragments of these dialogues are extant. He tutored (342–c.339 B.C.) Alexander the Great at the Macedonian court, left to live in Stagira, and then returned to Athens. In 335 B.C. he opened a school in the Lyceum; some distinguished members of the Academy followed him. His practice of lecturing in the Lyceum's covered portico or walking place *(peripatos)* gave his school the name Peripatetic. During the anti-Macedonian agitation after Alexander's death, Aristotle fled in 323 B.C. to Chalcis, where he died. His extant writings consist largely of notes made on his lectures by his students and edited in the 1st cent. B.C. Chief among them are the *Organum,* consisting of six treatises on logic; *Physics; Metaphysics; De Anima* [on the soul]; *Nicomachean Ethics* and *Eudemian Ethics,* which are both versions of his *Discourse on Conduct; Politics; De Poetica* [poetics]; *Rhetoric;* and a series of works on biology and physics. In the late 19th cent. his *Constitution of Athens,* an account of Athenian government, was found. Aristotle placed great emphasis in his school on direct observation of nature, and in science he taught that theory must follow fact. He considered philosophy to be the discerning of the self-evident, changeless first principles that form the basis of all knowledge. LOGIC was for Aristotle the necessary tool of any inquiry, and the SYLLOGISM was the sequence that all logical thought follows. He introduced the notion of category into logic and taught that reality could be classified according to several categories—substance (the primary category), quality, quantity, relation, determination in time and space, action, passion or passivity, position, and condition. Aristotle also taught that knowledge of a thing, beyond its classification and description, requires an explanation of CAUSALITY, or why it is. He posited four causes or principles of explanation: the material cause (the substance of which the thing is made); the formal cause (its design); the efficient cause (its maker or builder); and the final cause (its purpose or function). In modern thought the efficient cause is generally considered the central explanation of a thing, but for Aristotle the final cause had primacy. He used this reduction of causes to examine the relation of form to matter, and in his conclusions differed sharply from his teacher, Plato. Aristotle believed that a form, with the exception of the Prime Mover, or God, had no separate existence, but rather was immanent in matter. Thus, in the Aristotelian system, form and matter together constitute concrete individual realities; the Platonic system holds that a concrete reality partakes of a form (the ideal) but does not embody it. Aristotle believed that form caused matter to move and defined motion as the process by which the potentiality of matter (the thing itself) became the actuality of form (motion itself). He held that the Prime Mover alone was pure form and as the "unmoved mover" and final cause was the goal of all motion. Aristotle in ethics reflects Aristotelian metaphysics. Following Plato, he argued that the goodness or virtue of a thing lay in the realization of its specific nature. The highest good for man is the complete and habitual exercise of his specifically human function, which is his rationality. Well-being *(eudaemonia)* is not the pursuit of pleasure (hedonism), but rather is the pursuit of the contemplative life. Aristotle also emphasized the traditional Greek notion of virtue as the mean between extremes. The *Politics* studies man as a political being and holds that in fulfilling the civic function man realizes an intrinsic part of his human virtue. For Aristotle's aesthetic views, which are set forth in the *Poetics,* see TRAGEDY. After the decline of Rome, Aristotle's work was lost in the West. However, in the 9th cent., Arab scholars introduced Aristotle to Islam, and Muslim theology, philosophy, and natural science all took on an Aristotelian cast. It was largely through Arab and Jewish scholars that Aristotelian thought was reintroduced in the West. His works became the basis of medieval SCHOLASTICISM; much of Roman Catholic theology shows, through St. Thomas Aquinas, Aristotelian influence. There has also been a revival of Aristotelian influence on philosophy in the 20th cent. His teleological approach has continued to be central to biology, but it was banished from physics by the scientific revolution of the 17th cent. His work in astronomy, later elaborated by Ptolemy, was controverted by the investigations of Copernicus and Galileo. See edition of his works by Richard P. McKeon (1941); D. J. Allan, *The Philosophy of Aristotle* (1952); Ernest Barker, *The Political Thought of Plato and Aristotle* (rev. ed. 1959); J. H. Randall, *Aristotle* (1960); G. E. R. Lloyd, *Aristotle: The Growth and Structure of his Thought* (1968); John Ferguson, *Aristotle* (1972).

Aristoxenus of Tarentum (ărĭstŏk'sənəs, tərĕn'təm), fl. 4th cent. B.C., pupil of Aristotle. He marks a turning point in Greek musical theory by being the first to base theory on analysis of musical practice. In his two extant treatises, *Elements of Rhythm* and *Elements of Harmony,* he systematized Greek music by clear definitions of terms and orderly arrangement of scales. See H. S. Macran, *The Harmonics of Aristoxenus* (1902).

arithmetic, branch of MATHEMATICS commonly considered a separate branch but in actuality a part of ALGEBRA. Conventionally the term has been most widely applied to simple teaching of the skills of dealing with NUMBERS for practical purposes, e.g., computation of areas, proportions, costs, and the like. The four fundamental operations of this study are addition, subtraction, multiplication, and division. The older teaching arbitrarily divided arithmetic into elementary arithmetic and higher arithmetic. In advanced study the concept of number is greatly generalized to include not only complex numbers, but also quaternions, tensors, and abstract entities with no other meaning than that they obey certain laws (see NUMBER THEORY). This division of arithmetic into the practical and the theoretical dates back to classical Greek times, when the term *logistic* referred to elementary arithmetic and the term *arithmetic* was reserved for the theory. The basic operations of arithmetic were formerly learned largely or even entirely by rote. In the early 20th cent., however, new and more practical methods were adopted, and late in the 1950s there was a turn in elementary education toward utilizing the methods developed by higher mathematics and by the use of computers. For the ordinary purposes of practical figuring the old method survives.

arithmetic progression: see PROGRESSION.

Arius (ərī'əs, âr'ē-), c.256–336, Libyan theologian, founder of the Arian heresy. A parish priest in Alexandria, he advanced the doctrine famous as ARIANISM and was excommunicated locally (321). He was declared orthodox in Asia Minor, where he had fled (323), but he was anathematized by the Council of Nicaea (see NICAEA, FIRST COUNCIL OF) and banished by Roman Emperor Constantine (325). But in the reaction after Nicaea, he came into imperial favor. The emperor had ordered the Athanasians at Alexandria to receive him at communion when he suddenly died.

Arizona, state (1970 pop., 1,770,900), 113,909 sq mi (295,024 sq km), SW United States, admitted as the 48th state of the Union in 1912. The capital and largest city is PHOENIX. Arizona is bounded on the N by Utah; on the W, where the Colorado River forms the border, by S Nevada and California; on the S by Mexico; and on the E by New Mexico. In N Arizona are the Colorado Plateau, an area of dry plains more than 4,000 ft (1,220 m) high, and deep canyons, including the famous Grand Canyon cut out by the Colorado River. Along the Little Colorado River, which runs northwest through the plateau to join

the Colorado, are the Painted Desert, where erosion has left colorful layers of sediment exposed, and the Petrified Forest National Park, one of the world's most extensive areas of petrified wood. South of the Grand Canyon are the San Francisco Peaks, including Humphreys Peak, the highest point (12,655 ft/ 3,857 m) in the state. The southern edge of the Colorado Plateau is marked by an escarpment called Mogollon Rim. The southern half of the state has desert basins broken up by mountains with rocky peaks and extending NW to SE across central Arizona. To the south, the Gila River, a major tributary of the Colorado, flows west across the entire state. This area has desert plains separated by mountain chains running north and south; in the west the plains fall to the relatively low altitude of c.140 ft (43 m) in the region around YUMA. Arizona abounds in minerals, including copper, which has given it the name Copper State. Although some mountain peaks receive an annual rainfall of more than 30 in. (76 cm), precipitation in most of the state is low, and much of Arizona's history has been shaped by the inadequate water supply. Since the early 20th cent. massive irrigation projects have been built in Arizona's valleys. Roosevelt, Horse Mesa, Mormon Flat, and Stewart Mountain dams, with reservoirs and storage lakes, irrigate the Salt River valley. The Gillespie Dam on the Gila River helps irrigate the Yuma vicinity. The Coolidge Dam, with its San Carlos reservoir, serves Indian lands and surrounding farms near CASA GRANDE in the southeast. W Arizona is irrigated by Colorado River dams, which also serve California. These include Hoover, Glen Canyon, Davis, Parker, Imperial, and Laguna dams. Most major dams in the state are associated with hydroelectric power plants as well as irrigation systems. Arizona also obtains water from groundwater pumping stations. The state's principal crops are cotton, hay, lettuce, and sorghum. Cattle, calves, and dairy products are also important farm products. Agriculture is centered in Phoenix, TUCSON, and Yuma. The state's major industries produce machinery, food products, and primary metals. Copper is still the state's most valuable mineral; Arizona produces over half of all copper mined in the United States. Other leading mineral resources are molybdenum, sand and gravel, and cement. The mountains in the north and central regions have 3,180,000 acres (1,286,900 hectares) of commercial forests, chiefly ponderosa pines and other firs, which support the state's lumber and building-materials industries. The U.S. government owns about 95% of the commercial forests in the state. National and state forests attract millions of tourists yearly. Tourism is bolstered in the N by the Grand Canyon, the Painted Desert, the Petrified Forest, meteor craters, ancient Indian ruins, and the Navaho and Hopi Indian reservations that cover nearly all of the state's northeast quadrant. SE Arizona's warm, dry climate, often recommended for people in ill health, also attracts a large tourist trade. Between 1940 and 1960 Arizona's population increased more than 100% and between 1960 and 1970 it increased another 36%. The mountainous, arid north has not shared the population growth of the southern sections of the state. In the 1960s, the population included some 85,000 Indians. In addition to the Navaho, the largest tribe in the state, Arizona Indians include Mohave, Apache, Hopi, Paiute, Papago, Pima, Maricopa, Yavapaí, Hualapai, and Havasupai. Agriculture is the basis of their economy, but the lack of water makes farming difficult, and there is much poverty. Federal and state projects have sought to support Indian education and to introduce modern farm methods on the reservations. Arizona's Indians produce many fine handicrafts, including leather goods, woven items, pottery, and the famous silver and turquoise jewelry of the Navahos. Little is known of the earliest Indian cultures in Arizona, but Indians probably lived in the region as early as 25,000 B.C. A later culture, the Hohokam (A.D. 500-1450) were pit dwellers who constructed extensive irrigation systems. Pueblo Indians flourished in Arizona between the 11th and 14th cent. and built many of the elaborate cliff dwellings that still stand. Apache and Navaho Indians came to the area in c.1300 from Canada. Probably the first Spanish explorer to enter Arizona (c.1536) was Cabeza de Vaca. It is certain that the Franciscan friar Marcos de Niza reached Arizona in 1539, but he encountered hostile Indians and returned to Mexico. He was followed by Francisco Vasquez de Coronado, who led an expedition from Mexico in 1540 in search of seven legendary cities of gold. Coronado's men explored far, with Pedro de Tovar reaching the Hopi villages in the northeast and García López de Cárdenas discovering the Grand Canyon, while an allied expedition under Hernando de Alarcón sailed the lower Colorado. Despite extensive exploration, the region was neglected by the Spanish in favor of the more fruitful area of present-day New Mexico. Antonio de Espejo and Juan de Oñate, both Spaniards, explored the Arizona region in the late 16th cent. and late in the 17th cent. Father Eusebio Kino converted the Indians of Pimería Alta (Sonora and S Arizona) and founded the missions of Guevavi (1692) and Tumacacori (1696), near the present-day Nogales, and San Xavier del Bac (1700), near the present-day Tucson. Father Kino, a Jesuit, not only converted the Indians to Christianity but also introduced cattle and sheep raising among them. However, Jesuits were expelled from the Spanish Empire in 1767, and those in Arizona subsequently lost their control over the Indians. Indian uprisings led the Spaniards to establish a presidio at Tubac in 1752; in 1776 it was moved to Tucson, then an Indian settlement. Also at this time, Juan Bautista de Anza and Father F. T. H. Garcés established missions in the Yuma area. The Arizona region came under Mexican control following the Mexican war of independence from Spain (1810-21). In the early 1800s, U.S. MOUNTAIN MEN, trappers and traders such as Kit Carson, trapped beaver in the area, but otherwise there were few settlers. In the Treaty of GUADALUPE HIDALGO (1848), ending the MEXICAN WAR (1846-48), Mexico relinquished control of the area N of the Gila River to the United States. This area became part of the U.S. Territory of New Mexico in 1850. The United States, wishing to build a railroad through the area S of the Gila River, bought the area between the river and the present-day S boundary of Arizona from Mexico in the GADSDEN PURCHASE (1853). Arizona's minerals, valued even by prehistoric miners, had attracted most of the early explorers, and although the area remained a relatively obscure section of the Territory of New Mexico, mining continued sporadically. Small numbers of prospectors, crossing Arizona to join the California gold rush (1849), found gold, silver, and a neglected metal, copper. By the 1870s mining was flourishing, and by the following decade the Copper Queen Company at Brisbee was exploiting one of the area's largest copper deposits. In 1877 silver was discovered at Tombstone, setting off a boom that drew throngs of prospectors to Arizona but lasted less than 10 years. Tombstone also became famous for its lawlessness; Wyatt Earp and his brothers gained their reputations during the famous gunfight (1881) at the O.K. Corral. In 1861, at the outbreak of the Civil War, conventions held at Tucson and Mesilla declared the area part of the Confederacy. In the only major battle of the war in the Arizona area, Confederate troops were defeated NW of Tucson in the battle of Picacho Pass. In 1863, Arizona was organized as a separate territory, with its first, temporary capital at Fort Whipple. Prescott became the capital in 1865. Charles D. Poston, who had worked to achieve Arizona's new status, was elected as the territory's first delegate to the U.S. Congress. The capital was moved to Tucson in 1867, back to Prescott in 1877, and finally to Phoenix in 1889. When Confederate troops were routed and Union soldiers went east to fight in the Civil War, the territory was almost abandoned to the Indians. Settlement was resumed after the war and encouraged by the Homestead Act (1862), the Desert Land Act (1877), and the Carey Act (1894)—all of which turned land over to settlers and required them to develop it. The region had been held precariously by U.S. soldiers during the intermittent warfare (1861-86) with the Apache Indians, who were led by Cochise and later Geronimo. General George Crook waged a successful campaign against the Apaches in 1882-85, and in 1886 Geronimo finally surrendered to federal troops. Ranching, which had foundered under the Apache attacks on livestock, thrived after their defeat. Cattlemen, who had moved west to open vast grazing areas in the 1870s and 80s, established baronial ranches such as that founded (1872) by Henry Clay Hooker in Sulphur Spring Valley in S Arizona. Sheep raising grew from solely a Navaho occupation to a major enterprise among the white settlers. Grazing land was open to all until the late 1880s, and range wars developed between sheepmen and cattlemen. After 1897, the U.S. Forestry Bureau issued grazing permits to protect public land from depletion. By 1880 the Santa Fe and Southern Pacific railroads both extended into Arizona. In 1912, Arizona, still a raw frontier territory, attained statehood. Its constitution created a storm, with such "radical" political features as initiative, referendum, and judicial recall. Only after recall had been deleted did President Taft sign the statehood bill. Once admitted to the Union, Arizona restored the recall provision. Irrigation, spurred by the Desert Land Act and by Mormon immigration, had promoted farming in the southern part of the territory. By 1900 diverted streams were irrigating 200,000 acres (80,940 hectares). With the opening of the Roosevelt Dam (1911), a federally financed project, massive irrigation projects began to transform Arizona's valleys. Although Arizona's mines were not unionized until the mid-1930s, strikes occurred at the copper mines of Clifton and Morenci in 1915 and at the Bisbee mines in 1917. In the latter strike more than 1,200 miners suspected of being union members were deported by railroad to New Mexico. During World War II defense industries were established in Arizona. Manufacturing, notably electronic industries, continued to develop after the war, especially around Phoenix and Tucson, and in the 1960s manufacturing achieved economic supremacy over mining and agriculture in Arizona. With the development of irrigation and hydroelectric projects along the Colorado River and its tributaries, water rights became a subject of litigation between Arizona and California. In 1963 the U.S. Supreme Court ruled that California's water rights on the Colorado pertained only to the main stream of the river. Arizona was given rights to a share of the water from the Colorado's main stream and sole water rights over the river's tributaries within Arizona's boundaries. The state's constitution provides for an elected governor and bicameral legislature, with a 30-member senate and a 60-member house of representatives. The governor and members of the legislature serve two-year terms. The unit of local government is the county. The state elects two Senators and four Representatives to the U.S. Congress and has six electoral votes. Until the 1950s and 60s the Democratic party predominated in Arizona politics, but Republicans have since gained. In 1964, Senator Barry M. Goldwater of Arizona was the unsuccessful Republican candidate for the U.S. presidency. Stewart L. Udall, an Arizona Democrat, served as Secretary of the Interior under presidents Kennedy and Johnson. In 1974, Raul H. Castro, a Democrat, was elected governor. Arizona's educational institutions include the Univ. of Arizona, at Tucson; Arizona State Univ., at Tempe; Northern Arizona Univ., at FLAGSTAFF; and several private institutions. See E. H. Peplow, Jr., *History of Arizona* (3 vol., 1958); Federal Writers' Project, *Arizona: A State Guide* (4th rev. ed. 1966); *Arizona and Its Heritage* (Univ. of Arizona, 2d ed. 1969); J. J. Wagoner, *Arizona Territory* (1970), and Univ. of Arizona Faculty, *Arizona: Its People and Resources* (rev. 2d ed. 1972).

Arizona, University of, at Tucson; land-grant and state supported; coeducational; chartered 1885, opened 1891. Because of the proximity of Pueblo Indian villages and rich archaeological sites, Indian archaeology and ethnology are important fields of research.

Arizona State University, at Tempe; coeducational; opened 1886 as a normal school, became 1925 Tempe State Teachers College, renamed 1945 Arizona State College at Tempe. Its present name was adopted in 1958.

ark, in the Bible. **1** Boat of NOAH, which he built at God's command to preserve his family and certain creatures from the Flood. Gen. 6-9; Luke 17.27; Heb. 11.7; 1 Peter 3.20. **2** Ark of the Covenant, the sacred wooden chest of the Hebrews, representative of God or identified with Him. It was overlaid with gold inside and out and was always heavily veiled; the high priest alone could look upon its uncovered surface. Especially guarded, it was carried about by staves thrust through rings on its side, for to touch it was a profanation punished by death. Uzza, while escorting the Ark, inadvertently broke this law and so lost his life. As its presence implied victory, it accompanied the warriors into battle, where once it was captured by the Philistines. Restored after many years, the Ark found a resting place in Solomon's Temple. Ex. 25.10-21; Num. 10.33-36; Deut. 10.1-5; Joshua 3.3-17; 1 Sam. 4-7; 2 Sam. 6; 15.24,29; 1 Kings 8.3,9; 1 Chron. 13; 15; 16.6; 2 Chron. 5; Jer. 3.16: Heb. 9.4.

Arkansas (är'kənsô"), state (1970 pop. 1,923,295), 53,104 sq mi (137,539 sq km), central and SW United States, admitted as the 25th state of the Union in 1836. The capital and largest city is LITTLE ROCK; other important cities are FORT SMITH, NORTH LITTLE ROCK, PINE BLUFF, HOT SPRINGS, and WEST MEMPHIS. On the east the Mississippi River separates Arkansas from Tennessee and Mississippi. The state is bounded on the north by Missouri, on the west by Oklahoma and a part of Texas, and on the south by Louisiana. The Arkansas River flows southeast across the state between the Ozark plateaus and the Ouachita Mts. and runs down to the southern and eastern plains to empty into the Mississippi. The other rivers of the state also flow generally SE or S to the Mississippi; these include the Saint Francis (which forms part of the E Missouri line), the White River, the Ouachita, and the Red River (which forms part of the Texas line). The climate of Arkansas is marked by long, hot summers and mild winters. The state's many lakes and streams and its abundant wildlife provide excellent hunting and fishing and bring thousands of sportsmen annually. The mineral springs at Hot Springs also attract many visitors to Arkansas, where tourism is an important industry. The state's transportation network is based on rivers as well as roads, railroads, and air travel. A development project to improve navigation on the Arkansas River and to expand power and flood control facilities promises to stimulate growth in river port cities. A major cotton-producing state in the 19th cent., Arkansas has since diversified its agricultural production and overall economy. Cotton is still an important crop, but it ranked second in value, below soybeans, in 1971. Rice is also important. Livestock (including chickens, cattle, and calves) and dairy products almost equal crops as a source of farm income. Arkansas's most important mineral products are petroleum, bromine and bromine compounds, natural gas, and bauxite. Arkansas is the nation's leading bauxite producer. Lumbering is important in this heavily wooded state, which has large lumbering and wood-processing plants. About three fifths of the state's land area is wooded. Arkansas's major manufactures are food products; electrical equipment; paper, lumber, and wood products; furniture; and fixtures. The state also has a fast-growing chemical industry. A people known as the Bluff Dwellers, who inhabited caves, probably lived in the Arkansas area before 500. They were followed by the MOUND BUILDERS, who received their name from the mounds they constructed, apparently for ceremonial purposes. The first white men to arrive in Arkansas (1541-42) were probably members of the Spanish expedition under Hernando De Soto. Later the French explorers Jacques Marquette and Louis Jolliet came S along the Mississippi to the mouth of

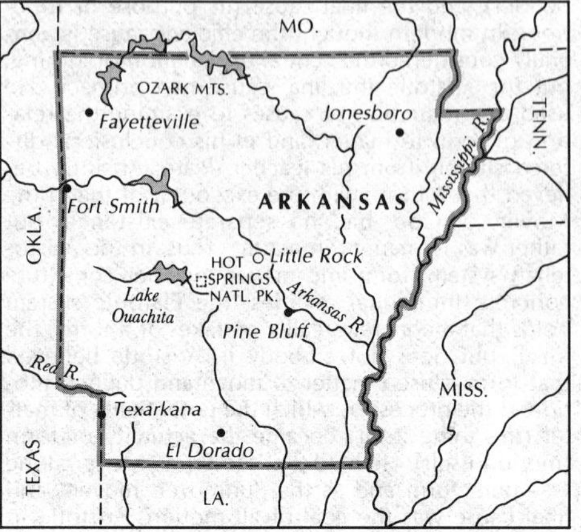

the Arkansas River. Robert Cavelier, sieur de La Salle, en route to the mouth of the Mississippi in 1682, met the friendly Quapaw Indians, who lived at the mouth of the Arkansas River. The Osage and the Caddo Indians also lived in the vicinity. In 1682, La Salle's lieutenant, Henri de Tonti, established Arkansas Post, the first white settlement in the Arkansas area. La Salle claimed the Mississippi valley for France, and the region became part of the French territory of Louisiana. In 1719, John Law, a Scottish financier in France, developed the MISSISSIPPI SCHEME, a colonization plan that brought hundreds of white settlers and Negro slaves to the Arkansas Post area. When Law's financial scheme collapsed in 1720, the settlers abandoned the site. The French ceded the Louisiana territory to Spain in 1762 but regained it again before it passed to the United States with the LOUISIANA PURCHASE (1803). Arkansas became part of the Territory of Missouri in 1812. In 1819 it was made a separate territory, and the first territorial legislature met at Arkansas Post. The capital was moved to Little Rock in 1821. Arkansas achieved statehood in 1836. The cotton boom of 1818 brought the first large wave of settlers, and the Southern plantation system, moving west, fixed itself in the alluvial plains of S and E Arkansas. In the highlands farmers eked out their subsistence. As the Civil War began (1861), the poorer farmers were generally indifferent to questions of slavery and states' rights. The slaveholding planters held the most political power, however, and after some hesitation Arkansas finally seceded (May 6, 1861) from the Union. In the Civil War, Confederate defeats at Pea Ridge (March, 1862), Prairie Grove (Dec., 1862), and Arkansas Post (Jan., 1863) led to Union occupation of N Arkansas, and General Grant's VICKSBURG CAMPAIGN separated states W of the Mississippi from the rest of the Confederacy. In Sept., 1863, Federal troops entered Little Rock, where a Unionist convention in Jan., 1864, set up a government that repudiated secession and abolished slavery. Because the state refused at first to enfranchise Negroes, Arkansas was not readmitted to the Union until 1868, when a new constitution gave Negroes the right to vote and hold office. Reconstruction in Arkansas reached a turbulent climax in the struggle (1874) of two Republican claimants to the governorship, Elisha Baxter and Joseph Brooks. Baxter's apparent success in the election was not accepted by Brooks, and followers of the two men resorted to violence in what became known as the Brooks-Baxter War. After President Ulysses S. Grant declared Baxter to be governor, Baxter called a constituent assembly dominated by Democrats to frame a new state constitution. The convention adopted (1874) the constitution that, in amended form, remains in force today. During Reconstruction the regime of CARPETBAGGERS and SCALAWAGS was detested by most Arkansas whites, but it brought advances in education and (at exorbitant costs caused by corruption) railroad construction. Because of high cotton prices and the failure to give the freed Negroes any economic status, the broken plantation system was replaced by sharecropping and farm tenancy. The lives of the people of the Ozarks remained largely unchanged; they retained the customs, skills, and superstitions that have given the hill folk their distinctive regional characteristics. In 1882, Arkansas farmers protested the nearly monopolistic control of money and transportation for agriculture by forming a new political party called the Agricultural Wheel. Although its gubernatorial candidate was unsuccessful in the election of 1888, most of the party's program was gradually adopted by the state Democratic party. In the late 19th cent., as railroad construction proceeded, Arkansas's population grew substantially, and bauxite and lumbering industries developed. Oil was discovered in Arkansas, near El Dorado, in 1921. Disaster struck in 1927 when the Mississippi River overflowed, flooding one fifth of the state. With the fortunes of the state pegged to the price of cotton, the depression of the early 1930s struck hard. Dispossessed tenants, black and white, formed (1939) the Southern Tenant Farmers Union, which, after trouble with the authorities, moved its headquarters to Memphis, Tenn. A strike called in 1936 spread to other regions before its strength waned. Other impoverished farmers migrated W to California as "Arkies"—like the "Okies" from neighboring Oklahoma. After World War I, blacks moved in a steady stream to the industrial North. World War II brought further loss of population as men left Arkansas for war factories elsewhere. The war, however, also created a boom for new industries in the state, notably the processing of bauxite into aluminum. The decline of industrial output after the war was offset by the vigorous efforts of a state development commission formed in 1955 to attract new industry to Arkansas. Arkansas and landlocked Oklahoma have joined in a project to develop the Arkansas River basin to provide water transportation to the Mississippi. In 1957, Governor Orval Faubus of Arkansas became a center of national and world attention when he resisted the attempted desegregation of public schools in Little Rock (see INTEGRATION). The state constitution (1874) provides for an elected governor and bicameral legislature, with a 35-member senate and a 100-member house of representatives. The governor and representatives serve two-year terms; senators serve for four years. Arkansas sends two Senators and four Representatives to the U.S. Congress and has six electoral votes. Arkansas has long been dominated by the Democratic party, but in 1966 Winthrop Rockefeller was elected the state's first Republican governor since Reconstruction. Although reelected in 1968, Rockefeller lost the governorship to a Democrat, Dale Bumpers, in 1970. Bumpers was reelected in 1972, and in 1974 he succeeded J. William Fulbright as one of Arkansas's U.S. Senators. David H. Pryor, a Democrat, was elected governor in 1974. Among the institutions of higher education in the state are the Univ. of Arkansas, at Fayetteville; Arkansas State Univ., near Jonesboro; Hendrix College and the State College of Arkansas, at Conway; Ouachita Baptist College and Henderson State College, at Arkadelphia; the College of the Ozarks, at Clarksville; Arkansas College, at Batesville; and Harding College, at Searcy. See Federal Writers' Project, *Arkansas: A Guide to the State* (1941); J. G. Fletcher, *Arkansas* (1947); T. S. Staples, *Reconstruction in Arkansas, 1862–1874* (1923, repr. 1964); L. J. White, *Politics on the Southwestern Frontier: Arkansas Territory, 1819–1836* (1964).

Arkansas (ärkăn'zəs, är'kənsô"), river, c.1,450 mi (2,330 km) long, rising in the Rocky Mts., central Colo., and flowing generally SE across the plains to the Mississippi River, SE Ark.; drains 160,500 sq mi (415,700 sq km). The Canadian and Cimarron rivers are its main tributaries. It is the chief waterway for the state of Arkansas, where it drains a broad valley. The upper course of the Arkansas River has many rapids and flows through Royal Gorge, one of the deepest canyons in the United States. More than 25 dams on the river provide flood control, power, and irrigation. During the warm months, because of its extensive use for irrigation, the middle course of the Arkansas is reduced to a trickle. The John Martin dam and reservoir in Colorado is one of the largest water-storage and flood-control units in the river basin. The Arkansas River Navigation System, opened in 1971, makes the river navigable to Tulsa, Okla., c.500 mi (800 km) upstream. The Spanish explorers Coronado and De Soto probably traveled along portions of the river in the 1540s. In 1806, Zebulon Pike, an American army officer, explored the river's upper reaches in Colorado. The Arkansas River was an important trade and travel route in the 19th cent.

Arkansas, University of, mainly at Fayetteville; land-grant and state supported; coeducational; chartered 1871, opened 1872; called Arkansas Industrial Univ. until 1899. The Graduate Institute of Technology, the schools of social work and law, and the medical center are at Little Rock.

Arkansas City (ärkăn'zəs), city (1970 pop. 13,216), Cowley co., S Kansas, at the confluence of the Arkansas and the Walnut rivers, near the Okla. border; inc. 1872. Located in an agricultural and oil region (rich oil fields were discovered there in 1914), it has oil refineries, flour mills, and meat-packing plants. Arkansas City was the starting point for the "run" (1893) of thousands of homesteaders into the Cherokee strip; a marker south of the city commemorates the event. There is a junior college in the city.

Arkansas Indians: see QUAPAW INDIANS.

Arkansas Post (är'kənsô), community on the Arkansas River, SE Ark. Founded by the French in 1686 as a trading post, it is the oldest white settlement in the state; it became the capital of the Arkansas territory in 1819. Once an important port, Arkansas Post was a Confederate stronghold during the Civil War until it was captured by Union troops in 1863. Arkansas Post National Memorial is there (see NATIONAL PARKS AND MONUMENTS, table).

Arkansas State University, near Jonesboro; coeducational; chartered 1909; named State Agricultural and Mechanical College, 1925–1933. In 1933 the school became Arkansas State College, and in 1967 it achieved university status and adopted its present name. There is a branch campus at Beebe.

Arkhangelsk (ərkhän'gĭlsk) or **Archangel** (ärk'ān"-jəl), city (1970 pop. 343,000), NW European USSR, on the Northern Dvina near its mouth at the White Sea. Although icebound much of the year, it is a leading Soviet port and can generally be made usable by icebreakers. Timber and wood products make up the bulk of the exports. The city has factories producing pulp and paper, turpentine, resin, cellulose, building materials, and prefabricated houses. Fishing and shipbuilding are also major industries. Once the site of a Norse settlement, the city was founded (1584) as Novo-Kholmogory; it was renamed (1613) for the monastery of the Archangel Michael (which still stands). Arkhangelsk was Russia's principal port until the founding of St. Petersburg in 1703; it regained importance after the rail line to Moscow was completed in 1898. A supply port during World War I, Arkhangelsk was occupied from 1918 to 1920 by Allied forces (including Americans) and by the White Army; it served as their base for unsuccessful campaigns against the Bolsheviks. During World War II, U.S. and British shipments landed at Arkhangelsk. The city has a maritime school (1771), a regional museum (1859), and institutes of forestry and medicine.

Arkite (är'kīt), Canaanite tribe centered around Arka or Arca, a town near the E Mediterranean Sea NE of Tripoli. Gen. 10.17; 1 Chron. 1.15. Arka, called Arca Caesarea and Caesarea Libani by the Romans, was the birthplace of Alexander Severus; it was vainly besieged by the Crusaders in 1099.

Arklow, urban district (1971 pop. 6,750), Co. Wicklow, E Republic of Ireland, on St. George's Channel at the mouth of the Avoca River. A small fishing port, it has become a popular resort. Irish rebels were defeated at Arklow in 1798. Shelton Abbey nearby is the seat of the earl of Wicklow.

Arkwright, Sir Richard, 1732–92, English inventor. His construction of a machine for spinning, the water frame, patented in 1769, was an early step in the Industrial Revolution. His machines and his gift for organization enabled him and his partner, Jedediah Strutt, to establish huge cotton mills and thus helped to start the factory system. He became very wealthy and was knighted in 1786. See R. S. Fitton and A. P. Wadsworth, *The Strutts and the Arkwrights, 1758–1830* (1958, repr. 1968); The Arkwright Society, *Arkwright and the Mills at Cromford* (1971).

Arlberg (ärl'bĕrk), pass, 5,946 ft (1,812 m) high, W Austria, beside Arlberg peak, on the boundary between Tyrol and Vorarlberg. The Arlberg region forms the water divide between rivers flowing to the North Sea and those flowing into the Black Sea. The Arlberg Tunnel (built 1880–84) is one of the world's longest (6.2 mi/9.9 km) railway tunnels. The Arlberg district is a noted winter sports center.

Arlen, Harold, 1905–, American jazz and popular composer, b. Buffalo, N.Y. as Hyman Arluck. Arlen sang from the age of 7 in the synagogue where his father was cantor, and at 15 he left school to play jazz piano. After coming to New York City in 1925, Arlen achieved fame by writing songs for various reviews and for the Harlem Cotton Club Shows (1930–34). Many of his songs became jazz standards because of their genuine blues feeling and haunting melodies (e.g., "Ill Wind," "Stormy Weather," "Blues in the Night"). In 1939, Arlen won an Academy Award for the song "Over the Rainbow" in the film *The Wizard of Oz*. Among the other films for which he wrote scores are *Cabin in the Sky* (1943) and *A Star Is Born* (1954). He also wrote the music for several Broadway shows, notably *House of Flowers* (1954).

Arlen, Michael, 1895–1956, English novelist, b. Bulgaria as Dikran Kuyumjian. The son of Armenian parents, he was brought to England as a child. In 1922 he became a British subject and changed his name, and in 1928 he married Countess Atalanta Mercati. Arlen is best remembered for his fantastically successful novel (and play) *The Green Hat* (1924), which depicts the licentious postwar life of fashionable London society. His characters are disillusioned, cynical, and witty. Although sophisticated, the novel is ultimately sentimental. Arlen's novels depicted the mood of the 1920s, and by the 30s he was no longer read. His last novel, *Flying Dutchman,* appeared in 1939. See the biography *Exiles* (1970) by his son Michael J. Arlen.

Arles (ärl), city (1968 pop. 46,136), Bouches-du-Rhône dept., S central France, in PROVENCE, on the Rhône River delta. Arles is an important railroad and industrial center with varied manufactures. It was a flourishing Roman town (Arelas) and the metropolis of Gaul in the late Roman Empire. Constantine I convoked (314) a synod at Arles that condemned

DONATISM; Constantine II was born there. Arles was an archiepiscopal see from the 4th cent. until 1790 and the seat of many synods. It became (879) the capital of Provence and (933) of the kingdom of Arles (see separate article). In the 12th cent. it became a free city governed by an elected *podestat*, who appointed the consuls and other magistrates. Arles retained its special status until the French Revolution. Among its noteworthy attractions are a Roman arena (2d cent. A.D.), seating 26,000 and now used for bullfights; a Roman theater (1st or 2d cent. A.D.); the Aliscamps [i.e., Elysian Fields], remains of a Roman cemetery; the Church of St. Trophime (11th–15th cent.; formerly a cathedral); the town hall (17th cent.); and the Museon Arlaten, a museum of Provençal culture and folklore, installed in a 16th-century mansion by Frédéric Mistral, who was born near Arles. Arles has attracted many painters, notably Van Gogh and Gauguin.

Arles, kingdom of, was formed in 933, when Rudolf II, king of Transjurane BURGUNDY, united the kingdom of PROVENCE or Cisjurane Burgundy to his lands and established his capital at Arles. Holy Roman Emperor CONRAD II annexed the kingdom to the Holy Roman Empire in 1034, but few of his successors troubled to be crowned as king of Arles. The imperial rulers exercised little control, and the component parts of the realm (Provence, VIVARAIS, LYONNAIS, DAUPHINÉ, SAVOY, W SWITZERLAND, and FRANCHE-COMTÉ) gradually broke away. In 1378, Holy Roman Emperor Charles IV ceded the realm to the dauphin (later King Charles VI of France), and the kingdom for all practical purposes ceased to exist.

Arlington, Henry Bennet, 1st earl of, 1618–85, English statesman. He fought for the royalists in the English civil war and, after going into exile, served as an envoy in Spain for the future CHARLES II. After the Restoration, Charles made him a secretary of state (1662), and he became one of the king's closest advisers, a member of the CABAL. He knew of the king's secret agreement with Louis XIV in the Treaty of Dover (1670) and seems to have encouraged Charles in promulgating the Declaration of Indulgence (1672) and in instigating the third Dutch War. He was made earl of Arlington in 1672. Impeached (1674) for corruption, betrayal of trust, and pro-Catholic activities, he was acquitted, resigned, and became lord chamberlain (1674). See biography by Violet Barbour (1915).

Arlington, county (1970 pop. 174,284), N Va., across the Potomac River from Washington, D.C. A residential suburb of Washington, the county is governed as a single unit. Within its boundaries are ARLINGTON NATIONAL CEMETERY, ARLINGTON HOUSE NATIONAL MEMORIAL, the PENTAGON, Marymount College of Virginia, and Washington National Airport. Most of the residents are employed by the U.S. government. Arlington, formerly called Alexandria, was ceded to the Federal government by Virginia in 1790 and was part of the District of Columbia until 1847, when it was returned to Virginia. It was named Arlington in 1920.

Arlington. 1 Town (1970 pop. 53,524), Middlesex co., E Mass., a residential suburb of Boston; settled c.1630 as Menotomy, inc. as West Cambridge 1807, renamed Arlington 1867. Menotomy was the scene of fierce fighting after the Lexington and Concord battles in 1775. Some 17th-century buildings remain. **2** Industrial city (1970 pop. 90,643), Tarrant co., N Texas, midway between Dallas and Fort Worth; inc. 1896. The center of a rapidly growing area, it has a huge industrial park with its own railroad. There are steel and iron works, and other industries that produce automobile parts, cans and containers, rubber items, mobile homes, electronic equipment, oil-field equipment, aircraft and parts, insecticides, and paving and road equipment. Six Flags Over Texas (a huge amusement park) and the Pecan Bowl are located there. It is the seat of the Univ. of Texas at Arlington.

Arlington Heights, village (1970 pop. 64,884), Cook and Lake counties, NE Ill., a suburb of Chicago; founded 1836, inc. 1887. Its manufactures include heating and air-conditioning equipment, electronic components, radioactive drugs, and office supplies. Arlington Heights's population more than doubled during the 1960s as a result of large-scale residential construction. Arlington Park racetrack and a missile base are in the village.

Arlington House National Memorial, 3 acres (1 hectare), NE Va., in ARLINGTON NATIONAL CEMETERY; est. 1955. Formerly called the Custis-Lee Mansion, it is a memorial to the Confederate Gen. Robert E. LEE. Arlington house was the home of Lee, inherited by his wife, the daughter of George Washington Parke Custis. It was abandoned by the Lees early in the Civil War and was later used as headquarters for the Union army. The estate was confiscated for nonpayment of taxes, and c.200 acres (80 hectares) were set aside for a national cemetery in 1864.

Arlington Memorial Bridge, granite and concrete bridge across the Potomac River connecting the Lincoln Monument in Washington, D.C., with Arlington National Cemetery, N Va.; built 1926–32.

Arlington National Cemetery, 420 acres (170 hectares), N Va., across the Potomac River from Washington, D.C.; est. 1864. More than 60,000 American war dead, as well as notable Americans including Presidents William Howard Taft and John F. Kennedy, Gen. John J. Pershing, and Admiral Robert E. Peary are interred here. Burial in Arlington is limited to active, retired, and former members of the armed forces, Medal of Honor recipients, high-ranking Federal government officials, and their dependents. There are commemorative monuments, including the Tomb of the UNKNOWN SOLDIER. The cemetery is part of "Arlington," the former estate of the Custis and Lee families, and includes Arlington House, now called the ARLINGTON HOUSE NATIONAL MEMORIAL.

Arliss, George, 1868–1946, English actor. He first appeared on the stage in 1887. In 1901 he came to the United States with Mrs. Patrick Campbell to appear in the Belasco production of *The Darling of the Gods*, and thereafter he became extremely popular for his portrayals of the suave villain. His performance in *The Green Goddess* was especially noted. He also became a favorite in films; his performance in *Disraeli* won him an Academy Award (1930). See his autobiographies, *Up the Years from Bloomsbury* (1927) and *My Ten Years in the Studios* (1940).

Arlon (ärlôN'), Flemish *Aarlen*, town (1970 pop. 13,745), capital of Luxembourg prov., SE Belgium, near the border with Luxembourg. A strategic point since Roman times, the town has suffered numerous attacks in its history. Of note in Arlon are Roman ruins, the Church of Saint-Donat (17th cent.), and the picturesque marketplace.

arm, upper limb in humans. Three long bones form the framework of the arm: the humerus of the upper arm, and the radius (outer bone) and ulna (inner bone) of the forearm. The radius and ulna run parallel but meet at their ends in such a manner that the radius can rotate around the ulna. This arrangement permits turning the forearm to bring the hand palm up (supination) or palm down (pronation). The radius and ulna hinge with the bones of the hand at the wrist, and with the humerus at the elbow. The BICEPS, a muscle of the upper arm, bends the arm at the elbow; the TRICEPS straightens the arm. Movement of the arm across the chest and above the head is accomplished by the pectoral muscles of the chest and deltoid muscles of the shoulder, respectively. In an adult the arm is normally five sixths as long as the leg.

Armada, Spanish (ärmä'də), 1588, fleet launched by PHILIP II of Spain for the invasion of England, to overthrow the Protestant Elizabeth I and establish Philip on the English throne; also called the Invincible Armada. Preparations, under the command of the marqués de Santa Cruz, began in 1586 but were seriously delayed by a surprise attack on Cádiz by Sir Francis DRAKE in 1587. By the time the expedition was ready Santa Cruz had died, and command was given to the duque de MEDINA SIDONIA. The Armada consisted of 130 ships, including transports and merchantmen, and carried about 30,000 men. It was to go to Flanders and from there convoy the army of Alessandro Farnese, duke of Parma, to invade England. It set out from Lisbon in May, 1588, but was forced into Coruña by storms and did not set sail again until July. Medina Sidonia's orders were to proceed straight up the English Channel and refuse battle until he had made junction with Parma. This gave the initiative to the English, whose main fleet, commanded by Charles Howard (later earl of NOTTINGHAM), sailed out from Plymouth to achieve the windward side of the Spanish and attacked at long range. Three minor actions followed, in which the Armada was somewhat damaged but its formation unbroken. On Aug. 6, Medina Sidonia anchored off Calais, from which position he hoped to make contact with Parma. The following night the English sent fire ships into the anchorage, causing the Spanish fleet to scatter, and then attacked (Aug. 8) at close range off Gravelines. Unable to reform, the Armada was severely battered, but a sudden change in the wind enabled most of the ships to escape northward. In attempting to sail home by Scotland and the west coast of Ireland, the Spanish ships were dispersed by storms; their provisions gave out; and many of those who landed in Ireland were killed by English troops. Only about half the fleet reached home. See Garrett Mattingly, *The Armada* (1959); Alexander McKee, *From Merciless Invaders* (1964); Winston Graham, *The Spanish Armadas* (1972).

armadillo (är″mədĭl'ō), New World armored mammal of the order Edentata, a group that also includes the SLOTH and the ANTEATER, characterized by peglike teeth without roots or enamel. Armadillos are found from Argentina to Panama, with one species reaching the southern United States. The head and body of an armadillo are almost completely covered by an armor of plates made of bone and horny material; the plates are separated by soft skin which bears a few hairs. The body armor, or carapace, hangs down on either side of the animal's body and is divided into flexible bands across the back. Members of some armadillo species can roll into a ball for protection. Armadillos are omnivorous, although insects form the bulk of their diet. Most are nocturnal, resting during the day in burrows that they excavate with their strong front feet and enormous claws; they can dig into the ground with amazing speed when threatened. There are 21 armadillo species, classified in 9 genera. The largest is the giant armadillo, *Priodontes giganteus*, which reaches 4 ft (120 cm) in length and may weigh 100 lb (45 kg). Members of this species have almost 100 teeth, more than any other mammal. Despite their great bulk, they are able to stand on their hind feet and sometimes walk in this position. This species inhabits the Amazonian forest; most other armadillos are grasslands dwellers. The smallest armadillos are the fairy armadillos, or pichiagos; the smaller of the two pichiago species (*Chlamyphorus truncatus*) is about 6 in. (15 cm) long and bright pink in color, with plumes of white hair about the face and undersides and between the front and back portions of the shield. The nine-banded armadillo, *Dasypus novemcintus*, is the only species found in the United States; it ranges from Argentina to Texas and Louisiana. It is about 30 in. (76 cm) long and 6 in. (15 cm) high at the shoulder; it weighs about 15 lb (6.4 kg). It normally moves about slowly, but is very swift when threatened. Each animal has several burrows. Females of this species almost always give birth to identical quadruplets. Armadillos are classified in the phylum CHORDATA, subphylum Vertebrata, class Mammalia, order Edentata, family Dasypodidae.

Armageddon (är″məged'ən), great battlefield where, at the end of the world, the powers of evil will fight the powers of good. Rev. 16.16. If the usual etymology is correct, the name alludes to the frequency of battles at MEGIDDO.

Armagh (ärmä'), county (1971 pop. 133,196), 489 sq mi (1,267 sq km), S Northern Ireland. The county town is Armagh. County Armagh rises from boggy, fertile lowlands in the north to barren hills in the south. It is the fruit-growing center of Northern Ireland; cattle, sheep, pigs, and poultry are also raised. Armagh is noted for its fine linen. Granite is quarried there. Other important towns are LURGAN and PORTADOWN.

Armagh, urban district (1971 pop. 12,297), county town of Co. Armagh, S Northern Ireland. Textiles are produced there. Armagh (originally Ard Macha) has been the ecclesiastical capital of all Ireland since the 5th cent., when St. Patrick founded his church there. It is the seat of both Roman Catholic and Protestant archbishoprics. Besides its two cathedrals, the town contains an observatory and St. Patrick Diocesan College. Armagh suffered several Danish raids; it was destroyed by Shane O'Neill in 1566 and was burned in 1642. Nearby is Navan Fort, a large elliptical mound, on the site of Emania (or Emain Macha), the legendary pre-Christian capital of Ulster.

Armagnac (ärmänyäk'), region and former county, SW France, in GASCONY, roughly coextensive with Gers dept. AUCH is the chief town. Armagnac is famous for the brandy bearing the same name. The counts of Armagnac originated in the 10th cent. as vassals of the dukes of Gascony. Their power reached its height with Count Bernard VII, who dominated France in the early 15th cent. Margaret of Angoulême, sister of Francis I of France, married the last count of Armagnac, who died without issue. Armagnac eventually passed to her second husband, Henri d'Albret, king of Navarre, whose grandson became King Henry IV. Henry added Armagnac to the royal domain in 1607.

Armagnacs and Burgundians, opposing factions that fought to control France in the early 15th cent. The rivalry for power between Louis d'ORLÉANS, brother of the recurrently insane King Charles VI, and his cousin JOHN THE FEARLESS, duke of Burgundy, led to Louis's murder in 1407. In the conflicts that followed, the partisans of Charles d'ORLÉANS, son of Louis, were led by Charles's father-in-law, BERNARD VII, count of Armagnac, after whom they were named. The followers of the duke of Burgundy, or Burgundians, were allied with members of the lower classes, notably the CABOCHIENS, who were particularly strong in Paris. Open civil war between the two groups broke out in 1411. John the Fearless at first held control of the government, but in 1413 the Cabochiens were ousted by another Parisian faction and John was forced to flee the city. The Armagnacs came into power and conducted the defense of France against King Henry V of England, who invaded the kingdom in 1415. John gave tacit approval to the invasion. The conflict between Armagnacs and Burgundians thus became part of the HUNDRED YEARS WAR. John took advantage of French defeats to return to Paris and seize the king (1418); in the ensuing massacre of the Armagnacs, Bernard VII and numerous followers were killed. Subsequently John attempted to negotiate with Charles VI's son, the young dauphin (later King Charles VII). During the negotiations John was assassinated (1419). His son and successor, PHILIP THE GOOD of Burgundy, immediately concluded a treaty with the English (see TROYES, TREATY OF), by which he recognized the succession to the French throne of Henry V. This alliance remained in force until 1435 when Philip signed the Treaty of Arras with Charles VII. Although the terms *Armagnacs* and *Burgundians* ceased to have their original meanings, the struggle between the French crown and Burgundy continued until the death (1477) of Charles the Bold of Burgundy.

armature, in art: see SCULPTURE.

armature, in electricity, principal current-carrying member of the electric GENERATOR and electric MOTOR. Essentially it is a coil of wire that rotates in the magnetic field between opposite magnetic poles. In its simplest form the coil is wound around a central core of soft iron, and the whole is rotated. Armatures differ in the way in which the coil is wound about the core, in the shape of the core, and in the number of turns in the coil. Although in general the armature is the rotating part, in some cases it is held stationary and the magnetic field is rotated about it.

Armavir (ärməvēr', Rus. ərməvēr'), city (1970 pop. 146,000), Krasnodar Kray, SE European USSR, on the Kuban River. An important railroad junction, it has machine and tool plants. Armavir was founded in 1848.

Armenia (ärmē'nēə), region and former kingdom of Asia Minor. Greater Armenia lies east of the Euphrates River, and Little, or Lesser, Armenia is west of the river. Armenia is generally understood to include NE TURKEY, the ARMENIAN SOVIET SOCIALIST REPUBLIC, and parts of Iranian AZERBAIJAN. It thus forms a continuation of the Anatolian plateau. Mt. ARARAT, the highest point, is in Turkey, as are the sources of the Euphrates, Tigris, and Aras rivers and Lake VAN. Trabzon, on the Black Sea, Erzurum, and Kars are the chief cities of Turkish Armenia, which, unlike Soviet Armenia, has no official standing. According to tradition, the kingdom was founded in the region of Lake Van by Haig, or Haik, a descendant of Noah. Modern scholars, however, believe that the Armenians crossed the Euphrates and came into Asia Minor in the 8th cent. B.C. Invading the Khaldian state called Urartu by the Assyrians, they intermarried with the indigenous peoples there and formed a homogeneous nation by the 6th cent. B.C. This state was a Persian satrapy from the late 6th cent. B.C. to the late 4th cent. B.C. Conquered (330 B.C.) by Alexander the Great, it became after his death part of the Syrian kingdom of SELEUCUS I and his descendants. After the Roman victory over the Seleucids at Magnesia in 190 B.C., the Armenians declared (189 B.C.) their independence under a native dynasty, the Artashesids. The imperialistic ambitions of King TIGRANES led to war with Rome; defeated Armenia became tributary to the republic after the campaigns of LUCULLUS (69 B.C.) and POMPEY (67 B.C.). The Romans distinguished between Greater Armenia and Lesser Armenia, respectively east and west of the Euphrates. TIRIDATES, a Parthian prince, was confirmed as king of Armenia by Nero in A.D. 66. Christianity was introduced early; Armenia is reckoned the oldest Christian state. In the 3d cent. A.D., ARDASHIR I, founder of the SASSANID, came to power in Persia and overran Armenia. The persecution of Christians created innumerable martyrs and kindled nationalism among the Armenians, particularly after the partition (387) of the kingdom between Persia and Rome. Attempts at independence were short-lived, as Armenia was the constant prey of Persians, Byzantines, White Huns, Khazars, and Arabs. From 886 to 1046 the kingdom enjoyed autonomy under native rulers, the Bagratids; it was then reconquered by the Byzantines, who promptly lost it to the Seljuk Turks following the Byzantine defeat at the battle of Manzikert in 1071. With the Mongol invasion of the mid-13th cent., a number of Armenians, led by Prince Reuben, were pushed westward. In 1080 they established in CILICIA the kingdom of Little Armenia, which lasted until its conquest by the Mamelukes in 1375. Shortly afterward (1386–94) the Mongol conqueror Tamerlane seized Greater Armenia and massacred a large part of the population. After Tamerlane's death (1405) the Ottoman Turks, whom Tamerlane had defeated in 1402, invaded Armenia and by the 16th cent. held all of it. Under Ottoman rule the Armenians, although often persecuted and always discriminated against because of their religion, nevertheless acquired a vital economic role. Constantinople and all other large cities of the Ottoman Empire had colonies of Armenian merchants and financiers. Eastern Armenia was chronically disputed between Turkey and Persia. It was from Persia that Russia, in 1828, acquired the present Armenian SSR. There remains a considerable Armenian minority in NW Iran. The Congress of Berlin (1878; see BERLIN, CONGRESS OF) also assigned the Kars, Ardahan, and Batumi districts to Russia, which restored Kars and Ardahan to Turkey in 1921. The Armenian people underwent one of the worst trials in their history between 1894 and 1915. A systematic plan for their extermination was put into action under Ottoman Sultan Abd al-Hamid II and was sporadically resumed, notably in 1915, when the Armenians were accused of aiding the Russian invaders during World War I. The Armenians rose in revolt at Van, which they held until relieved by Russian troops. The Treaty of Brest-Litovsk (1918) between Soviet Russia and Germany made Russian Armenia an independent republic under German auspices. It was superseded by the Treaty of Sèvres (see SÈVRES, TREATY OF; 1920), which created an independent Greater Armenia, comprising both the Turkish and the Soviet Russian parts. In the same year, however, the Communists gained control of Russian Armenia and proclaimed it a Soviet republic, and in 1921 the Russo-Turkish Treaty established the present boundaries, thus ending Armenian independence. Before 1914 there were about 2.5 million Armenians in Russia, Turkey, and Iran; as of 1974 there were more than four million throughout the world. See also ARMENIAN CHURCH and ARMENIAN LITERATURE. See V. M. Kurkjian, *A History of Armenia* (1959); L. Z. Nalbandian, *The Armenian Revolutionary Movement; the Development of Armenian Political Parties through the Nineteenth Century* (1963); R. G. Hovanisian, *Armenia on the Road to Independence, 1918* (1967) and *The Republic of Armenia: The First Year, 1918–1919* (1971); Sirarpie Der Nersessian, *The Armenians* (1969); D. M. Lang, *Armenia: Cradle of Civilization* (1970); Charles Burney and D. M. Lang, *The Peoples of the Hills* (1971).

Armenia (ärmä'nyä), city (1968 est. pop. 142,200), W central Colombia. Located in a fertile agricultural region (especially for coffee and cattle), Armenia is an industrial center and a transportation hub. It has a university.

Armenian Church, autonomous Christian church, sometimes also called the Gregorian Church. Its head, a primate of honor only, is the catholicus of Echmiadzin, in Soviet Armenia. His rule is shared by the patriarchs of Jerusalem and Constantinople and by the catholicus of Sis (Cilicia). In general, Armenian practices resemble those of other Eastern churches; the priests may marry and communion is distributed in both bread and wine, although the use of unleavened bread is a Western practice. The liturgical language is classical Armenian. Armenia became Christian at the end of the 3d cent. through the missionary work of St. Gregory the Illuminator (see GREGORY THE ILLUMINATOR, SAINT). In the next century the young church made itself autonomous, apparently because of the efforts of the metropolitan bishop of Caesarea, St. Basil the Great, to impose certain reforms. After the Council of Chalcedon the Armenians rejected the orthodox position; this adoption, at least tacit, of MONOPHYSITISM completed the isolation of the Armenian Church from the rest of Christendom. Part of the Armenian Church reunited with Rome temporarily in the 13th and 14th cent., and missionary work by the Roman Church in the 14th cent. resulted in many converts. In 1740 the Catholic Armenian rite was officially organized, in communion with the pope but under its own patriarch. See Papken Catholicos Gulesserian, *The Armenian Church* (tr. 1939, repr. 1970); Donald Attwater, *The Christian Churches of the East* (2 vol., rev. ed. 1961).

Armenian language, member of the Thraco-Phrygian subfamily of the Indo-European family of languages (see INDO-EUROPEAN). There is evidence that in ancient times a distinct subfamily of Indo-European languages existed that is now called Thraco-Phrygian. To it belonged Phrygian (an ancient and now extinct Indo-European language of Anatolia) and Thracian (a now dead Indo-European tongue of the Balkans in antiquity). Modern Armenian may well be a direct descendant of Phrygian. Today Armenian is the mother tongue of more than four million people, of whom two million live in the Armenian Soviet Socialist Republic; one million live elsewhere in the Soviet Union; and the rest are in the Middle East, the Balkans, and the United States. Armenian is an old, rich, and vital language. Although spoken in antiquity, it was not recorded in writing until the early 5th cent. A.D. At that time an alphabet of 36 letters was specially designed for Armenian by St. Mesrop, who used Greek and Iranian letters as a basis. Later, two more letters were added to the alphabet. In its early, or classical, form, Armenian is called *Grabar* or *Krapar*. This was the literary language until the 19th cent. and is still the liturgical language of the Armenian Church (see ARMENIAN LITERATURE). It differed greatly from the spoken language. Grammatically, it has six cases for the noun and nine tenses for the verb, but it has lost gender. The modern form of Armenian, now used for literature as well as for speaking, dates from the 16th cent. and is known as *Ashksarhik* or *Ashksarhabar*. Its grammar is simpler than that of Classical Armenian. The history of the Armenian people is reflected in the sources of the words borrowed by their language. For example, Armenian has absorbed words from Iranian, owing to Parthian domination in the centuries immediately before and after Christ, from Greek and Syriac as a result of Christian influence, from French during the Crusades, and from Turkish in the course of several centuries of Turkish rule. For grammars see S. L. Kogian (1949) and K. H. Gulian (1954).

Armenian literature. The first major work of Armenian literature is a 5th-century translation of the Bible; its language became the standard of classical Armenian. The Armenian Church fostered literature from its inception, and the principal works are religious or hagiographical, most of them translations. They constituted the golden age of Armenian literature. Early Mesopotamian influence resulted in the translations from the Syriac of Aphraates and St. Ephraem Syrus. Armenia then turned westward for literary inspiration and produced fine translations of the works of many religious leaders, e.g., Athanasius, Basil the Great, Gregory of Nyssa, Gregory Nazianzen, and John Chrysostom. Among secular works are renderings of Aristotle and of the romance of Alexander. The original writings of the golden age are confined to saints' lives and histories. The 5th-century history of Moses of Khorni contains practically all that is known of pre-Christian Armenia, its folklore and epics. Later celebrated historians include Thomas Ardzruni (10th cent.), Matthew of Edessa, who described the Crusades, and Stephanos Orbelian (13th cent.), who wrote of the Mongol hordes. A tradition of epic poetry, nationalistic in character and influenced by Muslim form, enriched Armenian literature; the best-known example is *David of Sassoun*. In the 12th cent. many Armenians went to Cilicia to escape the Seljuk Turks, and a new literary period began. Its principal figure is Catholicos Narses IV, prelate and poet, whose literary style is unexcelled in Armenian. After the decline of Armenian cultural centers in the 14th cent., the literature of Armenians abroad was heavily influenced by their host countries. Contemporary forms of the language came into use for writing in many fields—trade, agriculture, medicine, law, and political administration. In 18th-century Constantinople, Mechitar (1676–1749), a monk of the Catholic Armenians (those in communion with the Holy See), founded a community to cultivate Armenian letters. These monks (Mechitarists) now have their headquarters in Venice and are the principal Armenian publishers. The 19th cent. saw a considerable revival of Armenian letters and the establishment of a modern literary language. The major novelists of the 19th cent. were Khachatur Abovian and Hagop Melik-Agopian (called "Raffi"). Currently there is a flourishing Armenian journalism; the chief literary genres are satire and folktales. See Z. C. Boyajian, ed., *Armenian Legends and Poems* (2d ed. 1959).

Armenian Soviet Socialist Republic, constituent republic (1970 pop. 2,493,000), 11,500 sq mi (29,785 sq km), SE European USSR, in the S Caucasus. YEREVAN is the capital. Smallest of the USSR's 15 republics, Armenia is bounded by Turkey on the west, the Azerbaijan Republic on the east, Iran on the south, and the Georgian Republic on the north. The region is one of extinct volcanoes and rugged mountains. Many peaks exceed 10,000 ft (3,048 m); perpetually snowcapped Mt. Aragats (13,432 ft/4,094 m) is the highest point in Armenia. The chief rivers are the Araks and its tributary, the Razdan, which provide hydroelectricity and irrigation water. Lake Sevan supports the important fishing industry and is another source of hydroelectric power. Armenia is rich in mineral resources, notably copper but also molybdenum, zinc, lead, iron, pyrite, manganese, gold, chromite, and mercury. These provide the basis for a flourishing chemical industry. Salts and other minerals have enabled numerous health resorts to thrive in Armenia. Food processing, nonferrous metallurgy, and the manufacture of electrical equipment, machinery, textiles, automobiles, and the famous Armenian cognacs and wines are the republic's other major industries. Agriculture holds a significant place in Armenia's economy, with wine grapes and other fruits, wheat, barley, potatoes, and sugar beets as the major food crops and cotton and tobacco as the foremost industrial crops. Armenia's main cities are Yerevan, LENINAKAN, Kirovakan, and Echmiadzin (seat of the Armenian Church). It is one of the USSR's most densely populated and ethnically homogeneous republics, and has, in addition to its predominant Armenian population, Azerbaijan, Russian, and Kurdish minorities. The republic occupies the eastern part of ancient ARMENIA. It was acquired by Russia from Persia in 1828 and made into a province. After the 1917 Bolshevik Revolution, Russian Armenia joined Azerbaijan and Georgia to form the anti-Bolshevik Transcaucasian Federation, which, however, was dissolved in May, 1918. Armenia then became an independent republic. In 1920 it was occupied by the Red Army and proclaimed a Soviet republic. Two years later, Armenia, Azerbaijan, and Georgia were combined to form the Transcaucasian Soviet Federated Socialist Republic, which became a part of the USSR. With the dissolution of the Transcaucasian SFSR in 1936, Armenia, like Azerbaijan and Georgia, became a separate constituent republic of the USSR.

Armentières (ärməntĕrz', Fr. ärmäNtyĕr'), town (1968 pop. 28,469), Nord dept., N France, in Flanders, on the Lys River. It has foundries, boiler works, breweries, and a large textile industry. During most of World War I it was directly behind the Allied lines. It became known through the song "Mademoiselle from Armentières."

Arminianism: see ARMINIUS, JACOBUS.

Arminius (ärmĭn'ēəs), d. A.D. 21, leader of the Germans, called Hermann in modern German. He was a chief of the Cherusci (in an area of present-day Hanover) when the Romans were pushing E from the Rhine toward the Elbe. Arminius, who had been a Roman citizen and soldier, secretly gathered a great force of allies and set upon Publius Quintilius VARUS by surprise in the Teutoburg Forest in A.D. 9. In the ensuing battle Varus' army was utterly destroyed, and Varus, in disgrace, committed suicide. So great was the shock in Rome that it is said that Emperor Augustus afterward would start up from sleep, crying, "Varus, Varus, bring me back my legions!" The Romans never again made any real effort to absorb the territory E of the Rhine, though GERMANICUS CAESAR (called to aid the father of Arminius' wife, Thusnelda, against Arminius) badly defeated and wounded the German leader in A.D. 16. Arminius was later killed by treachery. Tacitus, the modern source for Arminius, glorified him as the noble barbarian. In the romantic period German nationalists made much of Arminius, who became a major national hero and was sometimes wrongly identified with Siegfried. F. G. Klopstock wrote a trilogy of plays about Arminius, and J. E. von Bandel erected a large monument to him near Detmold.

Arminius, Jacobus (jəkō'bəs), 1560-1609, Dutch Reformed theologian, whose original name was Jacob Harmensen. He studied at Leiden, Marburg, Geneva, and Basel and in 1588 became a pastor at Amsterdam. He undertook to defend the Calvinist doctrine of predestination against the attacks of Dirck Volckertszoon Coornhert, but as a result of the controversy he changed his own views of the doctrine. He was professor of theology at the Univ. of Leiden after 1603, and he engaged in violent theological debates, seeking to win the Dutch Reformed Church to his views. His teaching, known as **Arminianism,** was not yet fully developed, but he asserted the compatibility of divine sovereignty with human freedom, denied John Calvin's doctrine of irresistible GRACE, and thus modified the strict conception of predestination. In this respect his teaching resembled that of the Roman Catholic Council of Trent. Arminianism became a term of abuse among 17th-century Puritans. His ideas were formulated after his death into a definite system by his disciple, Simon Episcopius, who drew up the "Remonstrance" (see REMONSTRANTS). Arminianism later was the doctrine of Charles and John Wesley and most of the Methodist churches.

Armistead, George (är'mĭstĕd), 1780-1818, American artillery officer distinguished in the War of 1812, b. Virginia. He took part in the capture of Fort George on the Niagara frontier but is better remembered as the defender of FORT MCHENRY against British attack (Sept., 1814)—a defense that served as an inspiration for the STAR-SPANGLED BANNER.

Armistead, Lewis Addison, 1817-63, Confederate general, b. New Bern, N.C. He was commissioned (1839) in the U.S. army from Virginia but resigned when that state seceded. In the GETTYSBURG CAMPAIGN, Armistead, commanding a brigade under G. E. PICKETT in the famous charge, accomplished the farthest penetration of the Union lines, but he was mortally wounded. A monument where he fell marks the "high tide" of the Confederacy.

Armoni (ärmō'nī), one of Saul's sons, killed to end the Gibeonite famine. 2 Sam. 21.1-9.

armor, apparatus for defense of persons, horses, and such objects as vehicles, naval vessels, and aircraft. Body armor developed early as protective suits made of such materials as leather, shells, wood, and basketwork. These were later replaced by metal. Such protective coverings were known to the peoples of the ancient Middle East, and out of them Greeks developed the helmet, cuirass, shin guards (greaves), and shield. The armor of the Roman legionary passed through many stages but was characteristically a cuirass and a shield. After the downfall of the Roman Empire defensive garments reinforced by metal strips and plates appeared. Soon chain mail developed and prevailed until c.1300, when it was gradually superseded by protective covering of steel plates. The evolution of warfare, with increased mobility, diminished the importance of personal armor even before firearms speeded its disappearance. Helmets and cuirasses were worn in action as late as the 17th cent.; later they were used only for ceremonial purposes. In the wars of the 20th cent., steel helmets were reintroduced, and there were some experiments with various types of protective clothing. Armor is used also to protect vehicles (see TANK, military). Armor plate forms an important part of the defense of ships and aircraft.

Armory Show, international exhibition of modern art held in 1913 at the 69th-regiment armory in New York City. It was a sensational introduction of modern art into the United States. The estimated 1,600 works included paintings representing avant-garde movements in Europe. Duchamp's *Nude Descending a Staircase* was singled out by the hostile critics as emblematic of the so-called insanity and degeneracy of the new art. One of the most important exhibitions of art ever held in the United States, the Armory Show aroused the curiosity of the public and helped to change the direction of American painting. See Milton Brown, *American Painting from the Armory Show to the Depression* (1955), and *The Story of the Armory Show* (1963).

Armour, Philip Danforth (är'mər), 1832-1901, American meat-packer, b. Stockbridge, N.Y. Armour's Chicago meat-packing plants introduced new principles of large-scale organization, as well as refrigeration, to the industry. He is said to have been one of the first to notice the tremendous waste in the slaughtering of hogs and to take advantage of the resale value of waste products. His prestige was dimmed by the scandals of 1898-99 in which his packing-house was charged with selling tainted beef. See biography by Harper Leech and John C. Carroll (1938).

Arms, John Taylor, 1887-1953, American etcher and draftsman, b. Washington, D.C. He studied architecture, but later he devoted himself to etching and became noted for his excellent studies of medieval architecture. Arms illustrated his wife's *Churches of France* and *Hill Towns and Cities of Northern Italy*. His fine technique and draftsmanship won him numerous awards, and his work is in many principal collections. Arms wrote an excellent *Handbook of Print Making and Print Makers* (1934).

arms, coat of: see BLAZONRY; HERALDRY.

Armstrong, Edwin Howard, 1890-1954, American engineer and radio inventor, b. New York City, grad. Columbia (E.E. 1913). He was associated in research with Michael I. Pupin at Columbia and became professor there in 1934. Armstrong received numerous awards for his contributions to the development of radio, which include the invention of the regenerative circuit (1912); the superheterodyne circuit (1918), the basic circuit of nearly all modern radio receivers; the superregenerative circuit (1920); and FREQUENCY MODULATION (1925-33). In 1947 he received the Medal of Merit for his contributions to military communications during World War II. See biography by L. P. Lessing (1956).

Armstrong, Henry, 1912-, American boxer, b. Columbus, Miss. He was originally named Henry Jackson. He began his professional career in 1931, and soon became known as a strong and tireless puncher. Armstrong won the featherweight championship from Petey Sarron in 1936, the welterweight title from Barney Ross in 1938, and in his next fight (10 weeks later) he defeated Lou Ambers to win the lightweight crown. He thus held three titles simultaneously; this prompted the National Boxing Association to rule that a champion must vacate a title if he wins another. In his career (1931-45), Armstrong won 144 matches, scored 97 knockouts, and lost 19 fights. After his retirement he was ordained a minister and devoted himself to helping underprivileged youth; Youthtown at Desert Wells, Ariz., was built through his efforts. See his autobiography (1956).

Armstrong, John, 1717?-1795, American pioneer, known as the "hero of Kittanning," b. Co. Fermanagh, Ireland. He laid out the town of Carlisle, Pa. In 1756 he led the expedition that destroyed Kittanning, a Delaware Indian town on the Allegheny. Later he was a major general in the American Revolution and a member of the Second Continental Congress.

Armstrong, John, 1758-1843, American army officer, U.S. Secretary of War (1813-14), b. Carlisle, Pa.; son of John Armstrong, "hero of Kittanning." In the American Revolution he was on the staff of Horatio Gates. In 1783, Armstrong wrote the "Newburgh Addresses," or "Newburgh Letters"; these anonymously issued appeals urged the restive Continental officers to force Congress to pay salary arrears and adjust other grievances. General Washington denounced the appeals, and the officers soon followed his lead. After marriage (1789) to Alida, sister of Robert R. Livingston, Armstrong moved to Red Hook, N.Y., and became a political supporter of George and De Witt Clinton. He was U.S. Senator (1800-1802, 1803-4), minister to France (1804-10), and then Secretary of War. In the War of 1812 he was held responsible for the disasters of 1813-14, notably the failure of the expedition to Canada and the British capture of the city of Washington. He resigned in public disfavor. Armstrong wrote *Notices of the War of 1812* (1836-40), biographies of Richard Montgomery and Anthony Wayne, and other books.

Armstrong, Louis "Satchmo" (Daniel Louis Armstrong), 1900-71, American jazz trumpet virtuoso, singer, and bandleader, b. New Orleans. He learned to play the cornet in the band of the Waif's Home in New Orleans, and after playing with Kid Ory's orchestra he made several trips (1918-21) with a Mississippi riverboat band. He joined (1922) King Oliver's group in Chicago, where he met and married the pianist Lilian Hardin. His early playing was noted for improvisation, and his reputation as trumpeter and as vocalist was quickly established. Armstrong was a major influence on the melodic development of jazz in the 1920s; because of him solo performance attained a position of great importance in jazz. He organized several large bands, and beginning in 1932 made numerous foreign tours. Armstrong appeared in Broadway shows, at countless jazz festivals, and in several American and foreign films. See his autobiography (1954); biographies by Max Jones (1971) and H. Panassié (1971).

Armstrong, Samuel Chapman, 1839-93, American educator, philanthropist, and soldier, b. Hawaiian Islands, of missionary parents, grad. Williams, 1862. He served in the Union army in the Civil War, rising to the rank of major general. Appointed an agent of the Freedmen's Bureau in Virginia, he quickly realized the need for vocational training for emancipated slaves and persuaded the American Missionary Association to found, in 1868, the Hampton

Normal and Agricultural Institute, now the Hampton Institute. Because of Armstrong's interest, Indians were later admitted to the institution, which he headed until his death. See biography by E. A. Talbot (new ed. 1969); F. G. Peabody, *Education for Life* (1918), a history of Hampton Institute.

army, armed land force, under regular military organization—distinguished from the horde, the armed mass of all able-bodied men in a tribe. The earliest known army was that of Egypt; like the later Oriental armies of Assyria and Persia, it was a professional body. The Greeks made military service obligatory for citizens, but they also employed large numbers of mercenaries and hired themselves out as such. At first the Roman army was composed of citizen soldiers, but with the growth of Roman power a professional standing army came into being, which was increasingly made up of barbarian mercenaries. The Roman army was divided into units called legions, each of which included heavy and light infantry, cavalry, and a siege train. The method employed by the Germanic tribes, e.g., the Goths, Lombards, and Franks, was the massing of all men of fighting strength into a horde. The army of the Middle Ages depended upon the feudal levy, according to which armed knights and yeomanry owed a set number of days of military service per year to a great lord; the system had limitations, since the knights would often either refuse to serve or desert before the end of the campaign. Alongside the feudal levies grew up bodies of mercenaries, and with the decline of FEUDALISM and the introduction of firearms, which ended the predominance of the knight and the castle, the mercenary became the dominant figure. The CONDOTTIERE hired mercenaries and fought under the prince who was willing and able to pay the most. German and Swiss mercenaries served all over Europe in the 14th and 15th cent. Professional soldiers were also a notable feature of the armies of the Ottoman Turks, who threatened to destroy all the forces of Western Europe in the 15th cent. After the Thirty Years War (1618–48), France emerged as the preeminent European military power. Under Louis XIV and his war minister, the marquis de LOUVOIS, that country organized a national standing army, which was the pattern for all Europe until the French Revolution. A professional body, set apart from civilian life and ruled under an iron discipline, the standing army reached its harsh perfection under Frederick II of Prussia. The introduction of CONSCRIPTION during the French Revolutionary Wars set in motion the development of mass armies built around a professional nucleus. With the advent of hard-surface highway systems and railroads it became possible, in the late 19th cent., to move large concentrations of troops; thus the nations of the world found it increasingly necessary to enlarge their manpower bases by conscription. However, Great Britain and the United States maintained their peacetime armies by voluntary enlistment. The United States traditionally relied for emergencies on its citizen militia (the NATIONAL GUARD), although conscription was used in the Civil War. In 1907, Great Britain organized a militia body, the territorials. These countries also turned to conscription in World War I and, at last, in peacetime—Great Britain in 1939, the United States in 1940. From very early times it was necessary to maintain troops whose major duty was supplying food, quarters, and the like for the troops who actually engaged in fighting—even when the armies simply lived off the land. There was, at first, no formal distinction made between service troops and combat troops; but with the creation of the great citizen armies after the French Revolution formal specialization proliferated, and quartermasters, ordnance troops, engineers, and medical specialists were organized into separate units. The term *army* is still applied to all the armed land forces of a nation, as in "the French army" or "the U.S. army," but it also has other usages. In combat the term came to be used for a self-contained force fighting in a particular region, e.g., the Army of the Potomac in the U.S. Civil War. In the modern armed forces of the United States, the division (usually about 15,000 men) is the smallest self-contained unit (having its own service and supply personnel). Two or more divisions generally form a corps; and an army, with c.100,000 men or more and commanded by a lieutenant general, is composed of two or more corps. In World War II army groups were created, including several armies (sometimes from different allied armed forces). Above the army groups is the command of a theater of operations, which in turn is under the command of the joint chiefs of staff. See STRATEGY AND TACTICS; WARFARE. See L. L. Gordon, *Military Origins* (1971).

Army, United States Department of: see DEFENSE, UNITED STATES DEPARTMENT OF.

armyworm, larva of a moth, *Pseudaletia unipuncta,* found in North America E of the Rocky Mts. When numerous, armyworms move in hordes, traveling by night and devouring grasses, young grains, and some leguminous crops. The full-grown larva is about 2 in. (5 cm) long, dark gray with yellow and green stripes. There are usually two generations in a season, the larvae hatching from eggs in late spring and again in late summer. Pupation (see INSECT) is underground. The moth is grayish brown with a white spot on each fore wing. Armyworms are sometimes serious pests, especially in the second generation of the summer, which occurs when corn and wheat are maturing. Control methods include the use of poisoned bait and toxaphene insecticide and the digging of ditches and holes as traps. Armyworms are classified in the phylum ARTHROPODA, class Insecta, order Lepidoptera, family Noctuidae.

Arnall, Ellis Gibbs, 1907–, governor of Georgia (1943–47), b. Newnan, Ga. A lawyer, he served as a member of the state house of representatives (1933–37), assistant attorney general (1937–39), and attorney general (1939–43) before defeating Eugene TALMADGE in the Democratic primary of 1942. The constitution of 1945 was notable among the many achievements of Arnall's liberal administration as governor. He wrote *The Shore Dimly Seen* (1946) and *What the People Want* (1948).

Arnan (är'năn), descendant of David. 1 Chron. 3.21.

Arnaud, Henri (äNrē' ärnō'), 1641–1721, pastor and leader of the WALDENSES. When Victor Amadeus II, duke of Savoy, in league with the French, set out to expel the Waldenses, Arnaud led (1686) a band of the Waldenses into Switzerland. In 1689 he led some of them back to their Piedmont valleys, where they withstood a combined French-Savoyard attack. In 1690, Victor Amadeus turned against the French, and Arnaud gained the favor of the duke and acted as his agent while the Waldenses fought on the side of the Savoyards and were repatriated. A new political turn sent Arnaud into exile again, and after 1699 he lived in Württemberg. He wrote an account of the return of the Waldenses, *Histoire de la glorieuse rentrée des vaudois dans leurs vallées* (1710, tr. 1827).

Arnauld (ärnō'), French family involved in Jansenism (see under JANSEN, CORNELIS). The name is also spelled Arnaut or Arnault. The leader was a nun, **Marie Angélique de Sainte Madeleine,** 1591–1661, abbess from early youth of PORT-ROYAL, a Cistercian house near Paris. Under the influence of St. Francis of Sales she reformed her abbey. She was interested in Jansenism by DUVERGIER DE HAURANNE, and her introduction of the ideas into Port-Royal was an important step in forwarding the movement. See biography by M. L. Trouncer (1957). Her younger brother, **Antoine Arnauld,** 1612–94, was a leading Jansenist controversialist. He was a priest and a member of the Sorbonne. His best-known work was an attack on the Jesuits, *De la fréquente communion* (1643). He also wrote against Calvinism and the freethinkers. In 1656 he was expelled from the Sorbonne and the faculty of theology. He lived for some years at Port-Royal-des-Champs, where he collaborated on the Port-Royal textbooks. He withdrew to Belgium in 1679. The chief controversy of his later years was with Malebranche on the theology of grace. His elder brother, **Robert Arnauld d'Andilly,** 1588–1674, was a translator of religious writings and a religious poet of originality. He lived for many years in retirement at Port-Royal-des-Champs.

Arndt, Ernst Moritz (ĕrnst mō'rĭts ärnt), 1769–1860, German poet and historian. An ardent nationalist and opponent of Napoleon I, he was forced to flee to Sweden and Russia because of his patriotic and martial verse and his book, *Geist der Zeit* [spirit of the times] (4 vol., 1806–18), which influenced German feelings against the French. He was (1818–20) a professor of history at the Univ. of Bonn but was dismissed because of his liberal ideas and participation in the Burschenschaften, the nationalist students' movement; he was not reinstated until 1840. In 1848, Arndt was elected to the Frankfurt Parliament, the all-German national assembly that attempted to bring about German unification. See A. G. Pundt, *Arndt and the National Awakening in Germany* (1935, repr. 1968).

Arne, Thomas Augustine, 1710–78, English composer. Arne composed the song *Rule, Britannia,* based on an ode by James Thomson. He composed new music for an adaptation of Milton's masque *Comus* (1738) and for some of the songs in Shakespeare's plays. He also wrote operas, oratorios, including *Judith* (1761), instrumental music, and incidental music for plays.

Arnhem (är'nəm), Ger. *Arnheim,* city (1971 pop. 132,330), capital of Gelderland prov., E Netherlands, a port on the Lower Rhine. It is an industrial and transportation center. Textiles, electrical equipment, and metal goods are manufactured. First mentioned in the 9th cent., Arnhem was long the residence of the dukes of Gelderland. During World War II British airborne troops suffered (Sept., 1944) a serious defeat there (see also EINDHOVEN and NIJMEGEN).

Arnhem Land, 31,200 sq mi (80,808 sq km), N Northern Territory, Australia, on a wide peninsula W of the Gulf of Carpentaria. It contains an aboriginal reservation. Bauxite is mined in the area.

arnica (är'nəkə), any plant of the genus *Arnica,* yellow-flowered perennials of the family Compositae (COMPOSITE family), native to north temperate and arctic regions. In North America, arnicas grow in woody areas of the plains region and the Pacific coast, northward to arctic Alaska. Medicinal preparations for the treatment of wounds and bruises are sometimes made from arnica plants, chiefly *A. montana* of the European Alps. Arnica is classified in the division MAGNOLIOPHYTA, class Magnoliopsida, order Asterales, family Compositae.

Arnim, Achim or **Joachim von** (äkh'ĭm, yōäkh'ĭm, fən är'nĭm), 1781–1831, German writer of the romantic school. He is best remembered for his work with his brother-in-law, Clemens BRENTANO, on the folk-song collection *Des Knaben Wunderhorn* [the boy's magic horn] (1806–8). Arnim's novels include *Gräfin Dolores* (1810) and the unfinished *Die Kronenwächter* [the guardians of the crown] (1817). He was at his best in his historical novels, notably in *Isabella of Egypt* (1812, tr. 1927) and *Owen Tudor* (1809). Arnim had a predilection for the fantastic and the supernatural. Like Herder, he helped to create a popular German literary tradition. His wife, **Bettina von Arnim,** 1785–1859, whose maiden name was Elisabeth Brentano, was also a writer. She corresponded with Beethoven and Goethe and published the letters, not as historical documents but in the light of her own highly poetic imagination, as in *Goethe's Correspondence with a Child* (1835, tr. 1837). She was an ardent literary supporter of liberal Young Germany.

Arnim, Mary Annette (Beauchamp), Countess von: see RUSSELL, MARY ANNETTE RUSSELL, COUNTESS.

Arno, Peter, 1904–68, American cartoonist, b. New York City. Arno's satirical cartoons appeared in the *New Yorker* magazine from 1925 until his death. He achieved a distinctive drawing style featuring heavily outlined figures. Notable among his urbane characterizations are the self-important executive and the generously endowed woman. His cartoons have been collected in *Peter Arno's Parade* (1929), *Peter Arno's Hullabaloo* (1930), *Sizzling Platter* (1949), and *Lady in the Shower* (1967).

Arno, river, c.150 mi (240 km) long, rising in the Northern Apennines, Tuscany, central Italy, and flowing south to Arezzo where it turns northwest; it proceeds generally west, through Florence and Pisa, to empty into the Ligurian Sea. The Arno valley is fertile and densely populated. Its upper valley, the Casentino, is famous for its scenery. In 1966 a great flood on the Arno heavily damaged the art treasures of Florence.

Arnold, Benedict, 1741–1801, American Revolutionary general and traitor, b. Norwich, Conn. As a youth he served for a time in the colonial militia in the French and Indian Wars. He later became a prosperous trader. Early in the Revolution, his expedition against Fort Ticonderoga joined that of Ethan ALLEN, and the joint command took the fort. Arnold pushed on to the northern end of Lake Champlain, where he destroyed a number of ships and a British fort. In the QUEBEC CAMPAIGN, he invaded Canada (1775) by way of the Maine forests. The march proved incredibly hard, and the force was exhausted when it reached Quebec. Richard MONTGOMERY arrived from Montreal, and the two small armies launched the unsuccessful assault on Dec. 31, 1775. Arnold was wounded but continued the siege until spring, when Sir Guy Carleton forced him back to Lake Champlain. There he built a small fleet that, although defeated, halted the British advance. In Feb., 1777, Congress, despite General Washington's protests and Arnold's service, promoted five brigadier generals of junior rank to major generalships over Arnold's head. This and subsequent slights by Congress embittered Arnold and may in part have motivated his later treason. Although he soon won his promotion by his spectacular defense (1777) against William Tryon in Connecticut, his seniority was not restored. In the SARATOGA CAMPAIGN, his relief of Fort Stanwix and his brilliant campaigning under Horatio Gates played a decisive part in the American victory. He became (1778) commander of Philadelphia, after the British evacuation, and there married Peggy Shippen, whose family had Loyalist sympathies. In 1779 he was court-martialed because of disputes with civil authorities. He was cleared of all except minor charges and was reprimanded by Washington; nevertheless he was given (1780) command of West Point. He had already begun his treasonable correspondence with Sir Henry CLINTON in New York City, and he arranged to betray West Point in exchange for a British commission and a sum of money. The plot was discovered with the capture of John ANDRE, but Arnold escaped. In 1781 in the British service he led two savage raids—one against Virginia and the other against New London, Conn.—before going into exile in England and Canada, where he was generally scorned and unrewarded. See biographies by Oscar Sherwin (1931) and Malcolm Decker (1932, repr. 1969); Carl Van Doren, *Secret History of the American Revolution* (1941, repr. 1968); J. T. Flexner, *The Traitor and the Spy* (1953).

Arnold, Sir Edwin, 1832-1904, English author. After serving as principal of the government college in Poona, India, he joined (1861) the staff of the London *Daily Telegraph.* He won fame for his blank-verse epic *The Light of Asia* (1879), dealing with the life of Buddha. The poem was attacked for its alleged distortion of Buddhist doctrine and for its tolerant attitude toward a non-Christian religion. Besides other volumes of poetry, he wrote a number of picturesque travel books and translated Oriental literature. See study by Brooks Wright (1957).

Arnold, Henry Harley, 1886-1950, American general, chief of the U.S. Army Air Forces (1942-46), known as "Hap" Arnold, b. Gladwyne, Pa., grad. West Point, 1907. Assigned (1911) to the aviation division of the Signal Corps, Arnold later served almost entirely with the air arm. He was chief of the Air Corps from 1938 to 1940, when he became deputy chief of staff for the air. Chief of the U.S. Army Air Forces throughout World War II, Arnold was made (1944) general of the army and, after the creation of the air force as a separate department, was made (June, 1949) general of the air force; both of these were five-star ranks. He wrote a number of books, several of them with I. C. Eaker. See his autobiography, *Global Mission* (1949, repr. 1972); biography by F. O. Dupre (1972).

Arnold, Matthew, 1822-88, English poet and critic, educated at Rugby, grad. Balliol College, Oxford, 1844, fellow of Oriel College, Oxford, 1845. He was the son of the educator Dr. Thomas Arnold. In 1851, after a period as secretary to the 3d marquess of Lansdowne, Arnold was appointed inspector of schools, a position he held until 1886, two years before his death. During his tenure he went on a number of missions to European schools. He was impressed with some educational systems on the Continent—most particularly the concept of state-regulated secondary education—and wrote several works about them. His first volume of poems, *The Strayed Traveler,* appeared in 1849; it was followed by *Empedocles on Etna* (1852). Dissatisfied with both works, he withdrew them from circulation. *Poems* (1853) contained verse from the earlier volumes and new poems, including "The Scholar Gypsy" and "Sohrab and Rustum." *Poems: Second Series* appeared in 1855 and was followed by *Merope: a Tragedy* (1858) and *New Poems* (1867); the latter volume included "Thyrsis," his famous elegy on Arthur Hugh CLOUGH. His verse is characterized by restraint, directness, and symmetry. Though he believed that poetry should be objective, his verse exemplifies the romantic pessimism of the 19th cent., an age torn between science and religion. His feelings of spiritual isolation are reflected in such poems as "Dover Beach" and "Isolation: To Marguerite." Arnold was one of the most important literary critics of his age. From 1857 to 1867 he was professor of poetry at Oxford, during which time he wrote his first books of criticism, including *On Translating Homer* (1861), *Essays in Criticism* (1865; Ser. 2, 1888), and *On the Study of Celtic Literature* (1867). In *Culture and Anarchy* (1869) and *Friendship's Garland* (1871) he widened his field to include social criticism. His interest in religion resulted in *St. Paul and Protestantism* (1870), *Literature and Dogma* (1873), and *Last Essays on Church and Religion* (1877). In the 1880s he gave several lectures in the United States, which were published as *Discourses in America* (1885). Arnold was the apostle of a new culture, a culture that would pursue perfection through a knowledge and understanding of the best that has been thought and said in the world. He attacked the taste and manners of 19th-century English society, particularly as displayed by the "Philistines," the narrow and provincial middle class. Strongly believing that the welfare of a nation is contingent upon its intellectual life, he proclaimed that the intellectual life is best served by an unrestricted, objective criticism, which is free from personal, political, and practical considerations. See various editions of his letters; his poetical works (ed. by C. B. Tinker and H. F. Lowry, 1950); his complete prose works (ed. by R. H. Super, 1960-1972, 8 vol.); his notebooks (ed. by H. F. Lowry *et al.*, 1950); biographies by E. K. Chambers (1947, repr. 1964) and Lionel Trilling (rev. ed. 1949); studies by J. D. Jump (1955), D. G. James (1961), H. C. Duffin (1963), E. Alexander (1965), A. D. Culler (1966), G. Stange (1967), and D. Bush (1971).

Arnold, Thomas, 1795-1842, English educator, b. Isle of Wight, educated at Winchester school and at Corpus Christi College, Oxford. He was a fellow of Oriel College, Oxford, from 1815 to 1819, was ordained deacon in 1818, and was from 1827 to 1842 headmaster of Rugby school, where he brought about many changes. Mathematics, modern languages, and modern history were added to the traditional classical curriculum, the monitorial system was introduced, and independent thought was encouraged. Arnold's reforms were influential beyond Rugby itself; his changes were adopted by most of the English secondary schools. Through the medium of his weekly sermons to his students in Rugby Chapel, Arnold inculcated the Christian principles and ideals that formed the core of his own religious convictions. An effective preacher, Arnold was an excellent classical scholar and historian as well. An edition of Thucydides (1835), *History of Rome* (3 vol., 1838-43; to the Punic Wars), and *History of the Later Roman Commonwealth* (pub. posthumously, 1845) are among the products of a lifetime of study. Arnold's expression of liberal political and theological views made him unpopular, however, and general recognition was not accorded him until 1841, when he was appointed regius professor of modern history at Oxford. Matthew Arnold was his son and Mary Augusta (Mrs. Humphry) Ward his granddaughter. Thomas Arnold is portrayed in *Tom Brown's Schooldays* (1857), a novel about life at Rugby by Thomas HUGHES. See A. F. Stanley, *The Life and Correspondence of Thomas Arnold, D.D.* (1844); Arnold Whitridge, *Dr. Arnold of Rugby* (1928); N. G. Wymer, *Dr. Arnold of Rugby* (1953, repr. 1970); T. W. Bamford, *Thomas Arnold* (1960); Meriol Trevor, *The Arnolds* (1973).

Arnold of Brescia (brĕsh'ə), c.1090-1155, Italian monk and reformer, b. Brescia. A priest of irreproachable life, Arnold studied at Paris, where according to tradition he was a pupil of Peter Abelard. He first gained prominence in a struggle at Brescia between the bishop and the city government. Arnold became sharply critical of the church, declaring that secular powers only ought to hold property; he opposed the possession of property by the church because he believed it was being tainted by its temporal power. At the Synod of Sens (1140), dominated by St. BERNARD OF CLAIRVAUX, Arnold and Abelard were adjudged to be in error. Abelard submitted, but Arnold continued to preach. Pope Innocent II ordered Arnold exiled and his books burned. In 1145, Pope Eugene III ordered him to go to Rome in penitence. There the people had asserted the rights of the commune and had set up a republic. Arnold was attracted to their cause and became their leader, eloquently pleading for liberty and democratic rights. The republicans under Arnold forced Eugene into temporary exile (1146). Arnold was excommunicated by the pope in 1148 but continued to head the republican city-state even after Eugene III was permitted to reenter Rome. When Adrian IV became pope, however, he took stern measures. By placing Rome under an interdict in Holy Week, 1155, he forced the exile of Arnold. When Holy Roman Emperor Frederick I came to Rome, his forces at the pope's request seized Arnold, who was then tried by the Roman Curia as a political rebel (not a heretic) and executed by secular authorities. To the end he was idolized by the Roman populace. See biography by G. W. Greenaway (1931).

Arnoldson, Klas Pontus (kläs pôn'təs är'nôldsōn), 1844-1916, Swedish journalist and peace advocate. His untiring efforts for peace were rewarded by the 1908 Nobel Peace Prize, which he shared with Fredrik Bajer. A book he wrote on world peace (1900) was widely read. As a member (1882-87) of the Swedish Riksdag, he introduced a motion for permanent neutrality. In the union crisis in 1905, he opposed war with Norway. He founded several societies devoted to peace.

Arnold von Winkelried: see WINKELRIED.

Arnolfo di Cambio (ärnôl'fō dē käm'byō), b. c.1245, d. before 1310, Italian architect and sculptor. He was Nicola Pisano's chief assistant on the Siena pulpit, but he soon began to work independently on important tomb sculpture. He designed admirable monuments to Cardinal Annibaldi (St. John the Lateran, Rome); Pope Adrian V (Viterbo); and Cardinal de Braye (c.1282; Orvieto). These works became the model for Gothic funerary art. Arnolfo is recognized as the foremost architect of his era. In 1296 he was in charge of construction of the cathedral in Florence. He is said to have had a hand in designing other major buildings in Florence, including the baptistery, the Church of Santa Croce, and the Palazzo Vecchio. The monumental character of Arnolfo's work has left its mark on the appearance of Florence.

Arnon (är'nŏn), river of Jordan, entering the east side of the Dead Sea, called today Wadi Mojib. It is frequently mentioned in the Bible as the border between Moab (on the south) and the Amorites and later as the border between Moab and Israel. The city Aroer was on the Arnon. Num. 21.13,14,24,26,28; Deut. 2.24,36; 3.8,12,16; 4.8; Joshua 12.1,2; 13.9,16; Judges 11.13,18,26; 2 Kings 10.33; Isa. 16.2; Jer. 48.20.

Arnstadt (ärn'shtät), city (1970 pop. 28,762), Erfurt district, SW East Germany, on the Gera River. Gloves, shoes, and machinery are manufactured, and fluorspar and manganese are mined nearby. Arnstadt passed to the counts of Schwarzburg in the 14th cent. and later was the capital of the principality of Schwarzburg-Sonderhausen. Noteworthy buildings include the 13th-century Church of Our Lady and an 18th-century palace. J. S. Bach was organist (1703-5, 1706-7) at the Church of St. Boniface there.

Arnulf (är'nəlf), c.850-899, Carolingian emperor (896-99), king of the East FRANKS (887-99), illegitimate son of Carloman of Bavaria. In 887 he led the rebellion of the kingdom of the East Franks (Germany) against his uncle, Carolingian Emperor CHARLES III, and was proclaimed their king. He repulsed the Norse invasions in 891 but campaigned less successfully against the Moravians, with whom he finally negotiated (894) a peace. At the request of Pope Formosus, he invaded (894) Italy, which was then in a state of anarchy, but went no further than Piacenza. He returned in 895, captured Rome, and was crowned (896) emperor, but he was stricken with paralysis and went home. Arnulf, whose personal appearance, energy, and bravery have often caused him to be likened to his great-great-grandfather Charlemagne, was the last Carolingian to be crowned emperor.

Arod (ā'rŏd), son of Gad. Num. 26.17. He is the **Arodi** of Genesis 46.16.

Aroe Islands: see ARU ISLANDS, Indonesia.

Aroer (ăr'ōər). **1** Border town, on the north side of the Arnon River and E of the Dead Sea, the modern Arair (Jordan). Aroer, which changed hands frequently, is mentioned in the Moabite stone. Deut. 2.36; 3.12; 4.48; Joshua 12.2; 13.9; Judges 11.26; 2 Kings 10.33; Jer. 48.19. **2** City of Gad, near Amman. Joshua 13.25; Judges 11.33. **3** City of Judah, the modern Ararah (Israel), near Beersheba. 1 Sam. 30.28. In 1 Chron. 11.44 an Aroerite is mentioned; it is not known which Aroer is meant in this passage or in Isa. 17.2.

aromatic compound, any of a large class of compounds that includes BENZENE and compounds that resemble benzene in certain of their chemical properties. Common aromatic compounds other than benzene include toluene, naphthalene, and anthracene (all of which are present in coal tar). Each of these compounds contains at least one ring that consists of six carbon atoms, each joined to at least two other carbon atoms, and each joined to adjacent carbon atoms by one single and one double bond. The resulting hexagonal structure is characteristic of many aromatic compounds. The distinguishing characteristic of this aromatic structure is that the electrons are delocalized, being shared by all the carbon atoms of the ring; this results in resonance (see CHEMICAL BONDING), the bonds between the carbon atoms being more stable than a pure double bond such as that in an ALKENE. For this reason, the bonds in the aromatic ring are less reactive than ordinary double bonds; aromatic compounds tend to undergo ionic substitution (e.g., replacement of a hydrogen bonded to the ring with some other group) rather than addition (which would involve breaking one of the resonant bonds in the ring). Presence of the six-membered benzene ring is not essential for aromatic compounds; for example, furan, a heterocyclic compound that has a five-membered ring that includes an oxygen atom, has aromatic properties, as does pyridine, a heterocyclic compound whose six-membered ring includes a nitrogen atom.

Aroostook (əro͞os'to͝ok, -tĭk, əro͞os'-), river, c.140 mi (225 km) long, rising in N Maine and winding E to the St. John River in New Brunswick, Canada. The river gives its name to a county famous for potatoes.

Aroostook War, 19th-century border conflict between the United States and Canada. In 1838, Maine and New Brunswick both claimed territory left undetermined on the U.S.-Canadian border, including the valley of the Aroostook River. Maine farmers were interested in the valley's farmlands, and when New Brunswick sent Canadian lumbermen to do logging there, Maine authorities raised a force to eject them. New Brunswick asked for British regular troops and full-scale fighting seemed imminent, but Gen. Winfield SCOTT, who had been sent to the area with a small U.S. force, managed to reach an agreement (March, 1839) that prevented trouble. The boundary was later settled by the WEBSTER-ASHBURTON TREATY (1842).

Arosa (ärō'zä), town (1970 pop. 2,717), alt. c.6,000 ft (1,830 m), Grisons canton, E Switzerland. It is a health resort and sports center.

Arosemena Monroy, Carlos Julio (kär'lōs ho͞o'lyō ärōsāmā'nä mōn'roi), 1919–, president of Ecuador (1961–63). A lawyer and diplomat and the son and grandson of former presidents, he became vice president in 1960 and acceded to the presidency upon the ouster of President Velasco Ibarra. He instituted an austerity program and restored a favorable trade balance. Although he was criticized for his leftist leanings, real opposition to him arose from his immoderate drinking. After two unsuccessful attempts to impeach him, he was overthrown by a military junta.

Arp, Jean or **Hans,** 1887–1966, French sculptor and painter. Arp was connected with the BLAUE REITER in Munich, various avant-garde groups in Paris, including the surrealists, and the Dadaists in Zurich. He consistently created novel and abstract forms in various media—bas-reliefs, collages, painted cutouts, sculpture in the round, and painted wood reliefs. Often given a humorous touch, his works contain elements of organic form while retaining their essential abstraction. Arp finished a monumental wood relief for Harvard Univ. in 1950. See his *Arp on Arp,* ed. by Marcel Jean (1972); catalog of his sculpture by François Arp (1968); study by Herbert Read (1968).

Arpad (ŏr'päd), c.840–907?, chief of the Magyars. He led his people into Hungary c.895. The leaders of the Magyars and the first dynasty of Hungarian kings (St. Stephen I to Andrew III) were of the house of Arpad (see HUNGARY).

Arpad (är'păd), unidentified city, probably in W central Syria. Hamath is always named with it. 2 Kings 18.34; 19.13; Isa. 10.9; Jer. 49.23. It is the **Arphad** of Isa. 36.19; 37.13.

Arphaxad (ärfăk'săd). **1** Median king at Ecbatana, defeated by Nebuchadnezzar. He has not been definitely identified with anyone in other records. Judith 1. **2** Son of Shem. It has been supposed that he was the eponym of the Chaldeans. Gen. 10.22,24; 11.10; Luke 3.36.

Arpino, Cavaliere d': see CESARI, GIUSEPPE.

Arrabal, Fernando (färnän'dō äräbäl'), 1932–, French playwright, b. Melilla, Morocco. He spent his youth in Spain, studying law in Madrid, but moved to Paris in 1954. His plays reflect his aversion to political repression, bourgeois complacency, and war. They are often abstract and employ ironic contrast as a dramatic device. Among his works are the volumes *Théâtre I* (1958; includes the plays *Oraison, Les Deux Borreaux,* and *Le Crime des voitures*) and *Théâtre II* (1961; includes *Guernica, Le Labyrinthe, Le Tricycle,* and *La Bicyclette*). A number of his plays have been translated into English.

arrack (âr'ək), strong spirits distilled chiefly in the Orient from fermented fruits, grains, or sugarcane. The introduction of European spirits led to a decline in the native industry. In the 19th cent., Ceylon became quite noted for palm toddy arrack. Primitive methods of distilling yield raw spirits injurious because of a high content of fusel oil and acids. Other names are rack or raki.

Arrah (ŭ'rə), city (1971 pop. 92,670), Bihar state, NE India, on the Son Canal. It is the administrative center for a district that produces grain, sugarcane, and oilseed. There are limestone deposits in the city's outskirts. Arrah was the scene of fighting during the INDIAN MUTINY (1857).

Ar Ramadi (är rämä'dē), town (1965 pop. 28,723), provincial capital, central Iraq, on the Euphrates River. It is the eastern terminus of a highway across the desert from the Mediterranean Sea. The town was founded in 1869. The British won an important victory over the Turks there in 1917. The name also appears as Ramadie or Rumadiya.

Arran, earls of: see HAMILTON, JAMES, and STUART, JAMES.

Ar Raqqah (är räk'kä) or **El Rashid** (ĕl räshēd'), town (1960 pop. 14,554), capital of Ar Raqqah governorate, N Syria, on the Euphrates River. Carpets are manufactured, and the town has an agricultural experimental station. The ancient Nicephorium, Ar Raqqah was prominent during the early Abbasid caliphate. Caliph Harun ar-Rashid built a summer palace there and used the town as military headquarters against Byzantium. Ar Raqqah was destroyed by the Mongols in the early 13th cent.; some ruins survive. The modern name also appears as Raqqa and Rakka.

Arras (äräs'), city (1968 pop. 53,573), capital of Pas-de-Calais dept., and historic capital of Artois, N France, on the canalized Scarpe River. It is a communications, farm, and industrial center, with oil works and factories making machinery, metal products, and esparto goods. Of Gallo-Roman origin, it became an episcopal see c.500. It was granted (1180) a commercial charter by the crown and enjoyed international importance in banking and trade. By the 14th cent. it had become a center of wealth and culture, renowned particularly for TAPESTRY. It was nearly destroyed during the wars between Burgundy and France (15th cent.), which ended with the Treaty of Arras (1435). Occupied (1492) by the Spaniards, Arras was conquered (1630) by the French; French possession was confirmed (1659) in the Peace of the Pyrenees. Heavy bombardments in World War I destroyed much of the town, and it was further damaged in World War II. Nevertheless it retains much of its old Spanish-Flemish flavor. The town square, bordered by 17th-century buildings, forms a notable ensemble of Flemish architecture. The damaged town hall (16th cent.) and the Abbey of St. Vaast (18th cent.; now housing a museum) have been restored. The house where Robespierre was born still stands. A school of agriculture is there.

Arras, Treaty of. 1 Treaty of 1435, between King CHARLES VII of France and Duke PHILIP THE GOOD of Burgundy. Through it, France and Burgundy became reconciled. Philip deserted his English allies and recognized Charles as king of France. In return, Philip received the Somme towns and was exempted from homage to the crown. Charles also agreed to punish the murderers of Philip's father, Duke John of Burgundy. **2** Treaty of 1482, between King LOUIS XI of France and the local governments of the Netherlands, following the death of MARY OF BURGUNDY. In 1483 Mary's widower, Archduke Maximilian of Austria (later Holy Roman Emperor MAXIMILIAN I), reluctantly accepted the treaty. The acquisition of Burgundy by France was recognized. Maximilian's infant daughter, MARGARET OF AUSTRIA, was to marry the dauphin (later King Charles VIII), bringing Artois and Franche-Comté as dowry. Maximilian's infant son (later King PHILIP I of Castile) was to do homage for Flanders to France. When Charles VIII married ANNE OF BRITTANY, Maximilian forced him to restore Margaret's dowry by the Treaty of Senlis (1493).

Arrebo, Anders (än'ərs ä'rəbō), 1587–1637, Danish poet, bishop of Trondheim. His massive narrative poem, the *Hexaemeron* (written c.1630, pub. 1661), introduced the alexandrine meter to N Europe, where it became the vehicle for serious poetry.

arrest, in law, seizure and detention of a person, either to bring him before a court body or official, or to otherwise secure the administration of the law. A person may be arrested for an alleged violation of civil or criminal law. Civil arrest is most often used when one has been guilty of civil CONTEMPT of court; but in some states of the United States it is also allowed in cases where it is feared the defendant may attempt to flee the court's jurisdiction or otherwise frustrate justice. Arrest is ordinarily accomplished by a WARRANT issued by a court or officer of justice. In civil arrest a warrant must always be issued and generally anyone named may not be apprehended on Sundays or legal holidays. There are no time restrictions on making a criminal arrest. Any pe[illegible] a FELON[illegible] called citize[illegible] even need a wa[illegible] ably suspects of hav[illegible] In all other criminal cas[illegible] before the arrest. Force may [illegible] arrest, even to the extent of ki[illegible] resists arrest for a felony that endang[illegible] If an arrest is contrary to law, the apprehe[illegible] son may procure his release by HABEAS CORPU[illegible] may bring a civil suit for FALSE IMPRISONMENT. In mo[illegible] cases the person detained may be released if he can post BAIL. Diplomatic personnel and members of Congress and of state legislatures during legislative sessions are exempt from arrest.

Arrhenius, Svante August (sfän'tə, ärā'nēəs), 1859–1927, Swedish chemist. He was a professor of physics in Stockholm in 1895 and became director of the Nobel Institute for Physical Chemistry, Stockholm, in 1905. For originating (1884, 1887) the theory of electrolytic dissociation, or ionization, he received the 1903 Nobel Prize in Chemistry. He also investigated osmosis and toxins and antitoxins. His works, translated into many languages, include *Immunochemistry* (1907), *Quantitative Laws in Biological Chemistry* (1915), *The Destinies of the Stars* (tr. 1918), and *Chemistry in Modern Life* (tr. 1925).

arrhythmia, disturbance in the rate or rhythm of the heartbeat. Various arrhythmias can be symptoms of serious heart disorders; however, they are usually of no medical significance except in the presence of additional symptoms. Tachycardia, or heartbeat faster than 100 beats per minute in the adult, can be precipitated by drugs, caffeine, anemia, shock, and emotional upset. Bradycardia, or slow heartbeat, is often present in athletes. Heart murmurs are abnormal sounds (clicks, rumbles, blowing noises) produced by the heart in addition to the normal heartbeat. Premature beats of the atria and ventricles are common and usually of no significance. Murmurs at the various valves sometimes indicate the presence of valvular deformities but also occur in normal hearts. Flutters, and the even faster fibrillations, are rapid, uncoordinated contractions of the atrial or ventricular muscles that usually accompany heart disorders. Ventricular fibrillation is a sign of the terminal stage of heart failure and is usually fatal unless defibrillation is achieved by application of electrical current or mechanical massage. The electrical impulse that is generated to stimulate the heartbeat travels from a clump of tissue on the right atrium called the sinoatrial node to the atria and then to the ventricles. In some cases where there is a disturbance in the conduction of this impulse, called sinoatrial or atroventricular block, rhythm can be maintained by implanted electrodes that act as artificial pacemakers.

Arrian (Flavius Arrianus) (âr'ēən), fl. 2d cent. A.D., Greek historian, philosopher, and general, b. Nicomedia in Bithynia. He was governor of Cappadocia under Emperor Hadrian and in A.D. 134 repulsed a dangerous invasion of the Alans. His chief work is the *Anabasis,* the prime source on Alexander the Great. Modeled on Xenophon's famous book, the *Anabasis* relies chiefly on the writings of two of Alexander's generals (Ptolemy I and Aristobulus) for source material. Other extant works include the *Indica* (an account of a voyage of Alexander's general Nearchus to India) and parts of his edition of and commentaries on the *Discourses of Epictetus.*

Arrow, Kenneth Joseph, 1921–, American economist, b. New York City, grad. City College of New York (B.S. 1940), Columbia (M.A. 1941, Ph.D. 1951). He taught economics at the Univ. of Chicago (1947–49) and Stanford Univ. (1949–68) before serving on the faculty at Harvard (from 1968). A member of the President's Council of Economic Advisers (1962), he has been a consultant for the RAND Corp. since 1948. A specialist in welfare economics and general equilibrium theory, he shared the 1972 Nobel Memorial Prize in economics with Sir John Richard HICKS. Arrow's publications include *Social Choice and Individual Values* (2d ed. 1963), *Aspects of the Theory of Risk-Bearing* (1965), and *General Competitive Analysis* (1972).

arrowhead, any plant of the genus *Sagittaria,* widely distributed marsh or aquatic herbs of the primitive family Alismataceae (water-plantain family). The name derives from the arrowhead-shaped leaves of many species. The North American Indians prepared a potatolike food by roasting or broiling the tubers, particularly of *S. latifolia;* another species has long been cultivated in the Orient for its starchy root. Arrowheads, which have white, buttercuplike flow-

in aquariums, ponds, and bog
rowheads are classified in the division

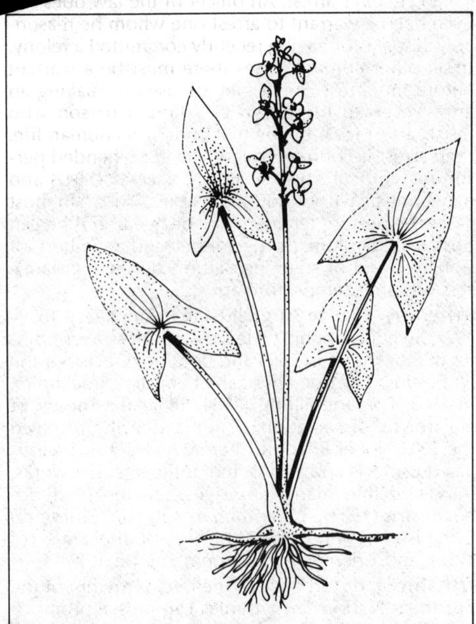

Broad-leaved arrowhead, Sagittaria latifolia

MAGNOLIOPHYTA, class Liliatae, order Alismatales, family Alismataceae.

Arrow Lakes, two expansions of the Columbia River, S British Columbia, Canada. Both lie in narrow valleys bounded by mountain ranges and are noted for their beauty. Upper Arrow Lake has an area of 88 sq mi (228 sq km); Lower Arrow Lake is 59 sq mi (153 sq km). Arrowhead is at the head of the upper lake.

arrowroot, any plant of the genus *Maranta,* usually large perennial herbs, of the family Marantaceae, found chiefly in warm, swampy forest habitats of the Americas and sometimes cultivated for their ornamental leaves. The term *arrowroot* is also used for the easily digestible starch obtained from the rhizomes of *M. arundinacea,* the true, or West Indian, arrowroot, which is naturalized in Florida. Other plants produce similar starches, e.g., East Indian arrowroot (from *Curcuma augustifolia* of the Zingiberaceae, or GINGER family), Queensland arrowroot (from a CANNA of the family Cannaceae), Brazilian arrowroot, or TAPIOCA, of the family Euphorbiaceae (SPURGE family), and Florida arrowroot, or SAGO. True arrowroot is classified in the division MAGNOLIOPHYTA, class Magnoliopsida, family Marantaceae.

Arrowsmith, Aaron, 1750–1823, English cartographer and geographer. He founded the map-making and publishing business carried on by his sons and by his nephew **John Arrowsmith,** 1790–1873. John Arrowsmith's *London Atlas* was famous. He was one of the founders of the Royal Geographic Society. The Arrowsmith maps were among the best of that period.

arrowwood, name for several woody plants, particularly of the family Caprifoliaceae (HONEYSUCKLE family), formerly used for making arrows.

arrowworm: see CHAETOGNATHA.

Arru Islands: see ARU ISLANDS, Indonesia.

Arsaces (är'səsēz), fl. 250 B.C., founder of the Parthian dynasty of the **Arsacids,** which ruled Persia from c.250 B.C. to A.D. 226. Arsaces led a successful revolt against Antiochus II of Syria, when Antiochus was engaged in war with Egypt and trying to put down a revolt in Bactria. Among the other Parthian kings were Tiridates, Mithradates I, Mithradates II, and Phraates IV. Their empire became a formidable rival of the Roman power, but began to decay in the 2d cent. A.D. after Emperor ALEXANDER SEVERUS had invaded the country. The Arsacids were overthrown by a revolt of the Persians under ARDASHIR I, who in A.D. 226 slew Artabanus IV (Ardawan IV), the last of the Arsacids.

arsenic (är'sənĭk), a semimetallic chemical element; symbol As; at. no. 33; at. wt. 74.9216; sublimation point 613°C; sp. gr. (stable form) 5.73; valence −3, 0, +3, or +5. Arsenic appears in several allotropic forms (see ALLOTROPY); the stable form is a silver-gray, brittle crystalline solid that tarnishes rapidly in air, and at high temperatures burns to form a white cloud of arsenic trioxide. A yellow crystalline form and a black amorphous form are also known. Arsenic is a member of group Va of the PERIODIC TABLE. It combines readily with many elements: with hydrogen to form arsine, an extremely poisonous gas; with oxygen to form a pentoxide and the above-mentioned trioxide (As_2O_3 or As_4O_6), a deadly poison also called arsenic (III) oxide, arsenious oxide, white arsenic, or, simply, arsenic; with the halogens; and with sulfur. The element is used with other metals to make hard, strong, corrosion-resistant alloys. Its compounds are used in pigments, animal poisons, insecticides (e.g., PARIS GREEN), and POISON GASES (such as lewisite) for chemical warfare. They are also used in glassmaking, in calico and indigo printing, in tanning and taxidermy (as preservatives), and in pyrotechnics. Small quantities of arsenic added to lead in the manufacture of shot assure perfectly spherical pellets by delaying the solidification of the molten lead, and thereby allowing it to flow more readily; the arsenic also contributes hardness. A small amount of arsenic is added to germanium in the production of semiconductor devices such as transistors and integrated circuits. A number of organic compounds of arsenic are used in medicine; the best known is Salvarsan, formerly used extensively in the treatment of syphilis and yaws. On the other hand, many arsenic compounds are strong poisons. One delicate test for the presence of even microscopic quantities of arsenic in compounds is the MARSH TEST. Arsenic occurs in many ores, including REALGAR, orpiment, and ARSENOPYRITE, the chief commercial source. When it is prepared commercially from sulfide ores, e.g., arsenical pyrites, the ores are roasted (heated in the absence of air); the arsenic sublimes (passes directly from the solid to the gaseous state) and is condensed. In another method, white arsenic is reduced with carbon. Although realgar, orpiment, and other arsenic minerals were known to the Greeks of Aristotle's time, the element itself was not. The "arsenic" so called by them and by the later alchemists was not true arsenic, but probably arsenic trioxide. The element was first described by Albertus Magnus in the 13th cent.

arsenopyrite (är"sĭnōpī'rīt, ärsĕn'ō-) or **mispickel** (mĭs'pĭkəl), silver-white to steel-gray mineral with the metallic luster characteristic of a PYRITE. It is a sulfarsenide of iron, FeAsS, crystallizing in the orthorhombic system and occurring also in massive form. It is widely distributed and is an important source of arsenic. Often it is found associated with other minerals and ores of lead and tin. Saxony, Sweden, Cornwall, and various parts of the United States have important deposits.

arson, at COMMON LAW, the malicious and willful burning of the house of another. Originally, it was an offense against the security of habitation rather than against property rights. Thus, a tenant could not be convicted of arson for burning the house that he rented from his landlord. Although this rule still holds in some states of the United States, in many others statutes have changed the meaning of the offense. Its application has been extended to buildings, structures, and vehicles that are not dwelling places, and greater stress has been placed on protection of property rights. Some statutes distinguish several degrees of arson, e.g., arson committed at night is considered more serious than arson committed in the daytime. In most states setting fire to one's own property to defraud an insurance company is specified as arson.

Arsonval, Arsène d' (ärsĕn' därsôNväl'), 1851–1940, French physicist and physician. He worked under Claude Bernard and under C. E. Brown-Séquard (whom he succeeded in 1897 at the Collège de France) and was professor at the Sorbonne from 1894 to 1932. The D'Arsonval galvanometer is named for him. A pioneer in electrotherapy, he studied the medical application of high-frequency currents. He was also involved in the industrial application of electricity.

art. The major general surveys on topics in the fine arts are PAINTING; SCULPTURE; DRAWING; still PHOTOGRAPHY, and ARCHITECTURE. These articles contain numerous cross-references to specific related subjects. There are articles about individual artists in many fields and about art critics and art historians. The various movements, schools, styles, and particular eras are covered in articles such as ART NOUVEAU, FOLK ART, MANNERISM, MODERN ART, SCHOOL OF PARIS, BAROQUE, and BYZANTINE ART AND ARCHITECTURE. The art of individual countries and peoples is discussed in articles such as DUTCH ART, SPANISH COLONIAL ART AND ARCHITECTURE, and NORTH AMERICAN INDIAN ART. The many types of subject matter are given separate treatment under such headings as CHILDREN'S BOOK ILLUSTRATION, GENRE, LANDSCAPE PAINTING, PORTRAITURE, STILL LIFE, and WATERCOLOR PAINTING. Examples of articles on art media and techniques include FRESCO, GLASS, ILLUMINATION, ILLUSTRATION, METALWORK, PLASTER CASTING, PORCELAIN, RELIEF, STAINED GLASS, and TERRA-COTTA. For the graphic media, see under GRAPHIC ARTS. Topics related to art subjects are also treated. See, for example, MUSEUMS OF ART and articles about individual museums, e.g., LOUVRE. Other related topics include ACADEMIES OF ART, SALON, ART HISTORY, ART CONSERVATION AND RESTORATION, ICONOGRAPHY, ILLUSIONISM, PERSPECTIVE, COMPOSITION, PASSION CYCLE, and FORGERY.

Árta (är'tə), formerly **Ambracia** (ămbrā'shə), city (1971 pop. 19,498), capital of Árta prefecture, W Greece, in Epirus, near the mouth of the Arachtus River. It is a trading and shipping center for agricultural goods including cotton, grain, citrus fruits, almonds, and olives. There is a large fishing industry, and leather goods and cotton and woolen textiles are manufactured. Known as Ambracia, the city was founded (7th cent. B.C.) by Corinthian colonists. It was ceded in 294 B.C. by Macedon to Pyrrhus, who made it the capital of Epirus. It was conquered by Rome in 189 B.C.

Artagnan, Charles de Batz-Castelmore d' (shärl də bäts-kästĕlmôr' därtänyäN'), c.1620–1673, French soldier under King Louis XIV. He fell at the siege of Maastricht. Dumas père used memoirs attributed to him for *The Three Musketeers* and other novels.

Artaphernes (är"təfûr'nēz): see PERSIAN WARS.

Artaud, Antonin (äNtônăN' ärtō'), 1896–1948, French poet, actor, and director. During the 1920s and 30s he was associated with various experimental theater groups in Paris, and he cofounded the Théâtre Alfred Jarry. He was afflicted with mental illness from his childhood, and in 1936 he was declared insane; he spent much of the rest of his life in mental institutions. Artaud's theories of drama, particularly his concept of the "theater of cruelty," greatly influenced 20th-century theater. He related theater to the plague because both destroy the veneer of civilization, revealing the ugly realities beneath and returning man to a primitive state, in which he lacks morality and reason. The aim of the "theater of cruelty" was to disturb the audience and reveal the forces of nature. To achieve this end he emphasized the nonverbal aspects of theater such as color and movement and stressed the importance of violence as a theatrical device. Artaud's most important work is *Le Théâtre et son double* (1938, tr. 1958). His influence can be seen in the works of Jean GENET, Peter WEISS, Peter BROOK, and Julian BECK and Judith Malina. See his *Selected Writings* ed. by Susan Sontag (1971).

Artaxerxes I (är"təzûrk'sēz), d. 425 B.C., king of ancient Persia (464–425 B.C.), of the dynasty of the Achaemenidae. Artaxerxes is the Greek form of the name Ardashir the Persian. He succeeded his father, XERXES I, in whose assassination he had no part. The later weakness of the Persian Empire is commonly traced to the reign of Artaxerxes, and there were many uprisings in the provinces. The revolt of Egypt, aided by the Athenians, was put down (c.455 B.C.) after years of fighting, and Bactria was pacified. The Athenians sent a fleet under CIMON to aid a rebellion of Cyprus against Persian rule. The fleet won a victory, but the treaty negotiated by CALLIAS was generally favorable to Persia. Important cultural exchanges occurred between Greece and Persia during Artaxerxes' reign. He was remembered warmly in the books of Ezra and Nehemiah because he authorized their revival of Judaism. He also befriended the exiled Themistocles. He was succeeded by XERXES II.

Artaxerxes II, d. 358 B.C., king of ancient Persia (404–358 B.C.), son and successor of DARIUS II. He is sometimes called in Greek Artaxerxes Mnemon [the thoughtful]; his Persian name is Ardashir. Early in his reign CYRUS THE YOUNGER attempted to assassinate him and seize the throne. Artaxerxes finally crushed Cyrus' rebellion at the battle of Cunaxa (401 B.C.), where Cyrus was killed. The story of the Greek contingent in the battle was made famous by Xenophon. Artaxerxes was ruled by the will of his wife and mother and relied heavily upon his officials; in addition, the satraps PHARNABAZUS and TISSAPHERNES had real ruling power. They managed by liberal distribution of Persian gold to gain great influence in Greece, and the Peace of ANTALCIDAS (386 B.C.) marked the imposition of Persian control of the Greek city-states. The provinces of the empire eventually became restless. EVAGORAS made himself independent as a ruler of Cyprus but finally (c.381) submitted to the king. Pharnabazus and Iphicrates, sent to reduce Egypt, disagreed and accomplished nothing. A formidable and longlasting revolt of the satraps (among them Mausolus) against the king was put down just before his death. He was eventually succeeded by ARTAXERXES III. The reign of Artaxerxes II also saw a revival of the cult of MITHRA.

Artaxerxes III, d. 338 B.C., king of ancient Persia (358–338 B.C.), son and successor of Artaxerxes II. He was originally named Ochus and is sometimes called Artaxerxes Ochus; his Persian name is Ardashir. He gained the throne by a general massacre of his brother's family, and throughout his reign he continued a policy of terror. An early expedition against Egypt failed (351 B.C.), but he set out again (c.342) and, having destroyed Sidon on his way, reduced Egypt by bloody conquest. He also put down the unruly satraps and centralized and strengthened the empire. One of his ministers, the eunuch Bagoas, finally poisoned the king, put Artaxerxes' son Arses on the throne in 338, then deposed him in 336 in favor of DARIUS III.

art conservation and restoration. Works of art are subject to a variety of disfiguring ills, many of them caused by environmental effects, particularly temperature and humidity changes and pollution. Much modern conservation effort is directed toward producing a stable, favorable situation for the display of art works and maintaining regular inspection and diagnostic procedures to combat deterioration. Techniques for this inspection have become increasingly sophisticated; they currently involve photographic, X-ray, infra red, and other radiation examination, as well as complex chemical analysis. The support (such as wood panel, canvas, paper), the ground (gesso, chalk), and the surface treatment (wax, varnish) of a painting all undergo some form of decay over the years. Frescoed walls absorb moisture from the atmosphere. The moisture carries to the wall surface soluble salts that effloresce and injure the fresco pigments. To halt such injury, water-permeable fixatives may be applied to help stabilize the pigment and prevent it from flaking off. A more drastic treatment is transfer, by which the mural and upper layer of plaster are cut away from the wall altogether and made fast to a new support. A major instance of successful transfer was carried out on many frescoes unearthed at Pompeii. Wood-panel paintings undergo much swelling and shrinking with humidity variations. Wood-boring insects and the dry rot of fungus also attack them. The painting may be transferred to a new support, or the old one may be strengthened by impregnation with a consolidating medium (including several plastics) or given auxiliary support. Insecticides and fungicides may suffice to combat woodworms and dry rot; in cases of advanced destruction, reinforcement by impregnation may be necessary. Canvas supports also absorb and lose moisture, swelling and shrinking, and thereby much pigment is lost. In addition, canvases may be weakened or torn with comparative ease. A method of lining (restretching on a second undercanvas) may be effected whereby the old canvas is attached to the new by means of an adhesive. This may be a thermoplastic wax-resin combination or a water-base glue. The painted surface becomes impregnated with the adhesive and is consequently stabilized. Irregular staining, called foxing, is the bane of print and drawing collectors. In humid conditions, foxing attacks the adhesives and mounts of paper-based art, including watercolors, by producing the nutrients favored by molds present in the atmosphere. The work may sometimes be sterilized and remounted on a support chosen for its mold-repellent quality. It may be further treated with a fungicide. Some foxing stains may be removed by careful bleaching and washing, but this is a difficult technique requiring considerable knowledge of materials. The restorer's greatest problems concern the surface coating of the painting. A decayed or badly discolored varnish may be removed painstakingly by mechanical means or regelled with the judicious use of solvent, often applied as a delicate spray. In other cases, the old varnish may be powdered by rubbing and removed by hand or, more commonly, chemically dissolved. Such techniques are beset by dangers inherent in the variable nature of the original pigments and varnish, and the risk of injury increases with the age of the painting. Repainting and retouching are means by which a damaged work may be restored, but both largely depend for success upon the personal judgment and aesthetic capability of the restorer. Repairs may be necessary where the results of overzealous cleanings of the past have produced injury or revealed a PENTIMENTO that disrupts the composition. Much restorative work of the 19th cent. shows a tendency to "improve" the work of art with arbitrary additions and distortions. Sculpture, especially that which stands out-of-doors, is particularly vulnerable to environmental changes. Placing the sculpture in a temperature- and humidity-controlled situation is the best means by which to preserve it. Stone sculpture requires periodic washing; either steam, spray, or trickled water is used, depending on the porosity of the stone. Soap, but not detergent, may also be applied. Broken sculptures may be mended with clear, cold-setting adhesives, sometimes mixed with a suitably colored filler, or by means of dowelling. Large pieces of sculpture are held together with metal dowels, usually of copper, stainless steel, or brass. Broken wood sculpture is also dowelled, as is ivory. Special cements may also be used to fill cracks. Wood sculpture is also vulnerable to woodworm and dry rot and may be treated with insecticide and fungicide. Badly decayed wood works may sometimes be preserved by means of impregnation with a plastic medium. Metal sculpture may be waxed to protect it from atmospheric corrosives. Bronze acquires a patina, or irregular surface pattern caused by deposits of sulfides and oxides, that is widely considered aesthetically pleasing; patina on lead objects results in eventual decay. Cracks in metal sculpture may be filled with special adhesives. Corrosion may be halted by electrolytic reduction, which, however, destroys patina. Various chemical solvents and mechanical techniques are used to remove specific incrustations. The flood in Florence in Nov., 1966, was among the greatest disasters in modern history in terms of the destruction of works of art. Conservators and restorers from all over the world applied emergency treatment to the treasures of painting, sculpture, and architecture that could be saved. Among those were five panels from the bronze doors of the Baptistry by Ghiberti, which had been ripped apart and ruined by the furious oily waters. In replacing them, experts made use of an exact replica of the doors in San Francisco. In 1972, Michelangelo's *Pietá* in St. Peter's, Rome, was attacked and mutilated by a madman with a hammer. The most delicate restoration work was required to make unobtrusive repairs on this masterpiece of sculpture. All effective art conservation and restoration ultimately depends upon the restorer's understanding of materials, technical craftsmanship, and aesthetic and historical awareness. See also CRAQUELURE. See H. J. Plenderleith and A. E. Werner, *The Conservation of Antiquities and Works of Art* (2d ed. 1971); Francis Kelly, *Art Restoration* (1972).

art deco, style of popular design during the 1920s and 30s. Art deco is characterized by long, thin forms and straight lines. The practitioners of the style attempted to describe the sleekness they thought expressive of modern technology. The style has undergone a resurgence of popularity in the 1970s.

Artem (artyôm'), city (1969 est. pop. 65,000), Primorsky Kray (Maritime Territory), Far Eastern USSR. It is a coal-mining center and has an important thermoelectric station that utilizes local coal deposits.

Artemas (är'tĭməs), companion of Paul. Titus 3.12.

Artemidorus of Ephesus (ärtĕm"ĭdôr'əs, ĕf'əsəs), fl. 103 B.C., Greek geographer quoted by Strabo. He wrote 11 books on his Mediterranean travels. Only fragments remain of his work.

Artemis (är'təmĭs), in Greek religion, Olympian goddess, daughter of Zeus and Leto and twin sister of Apollo. Artemis' early worship, especially at Ephesus, identified her as an earth goddess, similar to Astarte. In later legend, however, she was primarily a virgin huntress, goddess of wildlife and patroness of hunters. Of the many animals sacred to her, the bear was most important. Artemis valued her chastity so highly that she took terrible measures against anyone who even slightly threatened her (e.g., ACTAEON). She was attended by nymphs, whose virginity she guarded as jealously as her own. She was also an important goddess in the life of women, concerned with marriage and with the young of all creatures. As the complement to Apollo, she was often considered a moon goddess and as such was identified with Selene and Hecate. In ancient Greece, the worship of Artemis was widespread. The Romans identified her with Diana.

Artemisia (är"təmĭ'shēə), fl. 4th cent. B.C., ruler of the ancient region of Caria. She was the sister, wife, and successor of MAUSOLUS and erected the MAUSOLEUM at Halicarnassus in his memory. A strong ruler, she conquered Rhodes. She also patronized the arts. An earlier Artemisia ruled part of Caria under Xerxes I of Persia.

artemisia: see WORMWOOD.

Artemisium (är"təmĭsh'ēəm), cape, N Euboea (now Évvoia), Greece, named for a great temple of Artemis. Off the cape in 480 B.C. was fought a naval battle of the Persian Wars. The delay won by the defense of Thermopylae under LEONIDAS helped make it possible for the Greeks to ward off the Persian fleet, although the fighting was indecisive and the Greeks were eventually forced to withdraw.

Artemovsk (artyô'məfsk), Ukr. *Artemivsk*, city (1969 est. pop. 81,000), S European USSR, in the Ukraine. An industrial center of the Donets Basin, it produces metals, mining equipment, glass, bricks, and chemicals. Nearby are salt and dolomite deposits that are utilized in the Donets iron and steel and chemical industries.

arteriosclerosis (ärtĭr"ēōsklərō'sĭs), general term for a condition characterized by thickening, hardening, and loss of elasticity of the walls of the blood vessels. These changes are frequently accompanied by accumulations inside the vessel walls of lipids, e.g., cholesterol; this condition is frequently referred to as atherosclerosis. The deposition of calcium in the fatty material hardens the walls of the vessels. As the vessel walls thicken, the passageways through the vessels narrow, decreasing the blood supply to the affected region. Constriction of the coronary arteries may affect the heart (see HEART DISEASE). Cerebral arteriosclerosis is often responsible for senility in elderly persons. If the leg vessels are affected, there may be loss of movement of the extremities and an onset of gangrene. When there is total clotting of a vessel (THROMBOSIS) the result may be a heart attack (if it occurs in the coronary arteries) or APOPLEXY (if in cerebral arteries). While there is no specific preventive or cure for arteriosclerosis, reduction of body cholesterol to normal levels through a restricted-fat diet, with the substitution of vegetable fats for animal fats is usually prescribed, although the relationship between the level of cholesterol in the bloodstream and arteriosclerosis is not yet fully understood.

artery, blood vessel that conveys blood away from the HEART. Except for the pulmonary artery, which carries deoxygenated blood from the heart to the lungs, arteries carry oxygenated blood from the heart to the tissues. The largest arterial trunk is the AORTA, branches of which divide and subdivide into ever-smaller tubes, or arterioles, until they terminate as minute CAPILLARIES, the latter connecting with the VEINS (see CIRCULATORY SYSTEM). Other important arteries are the subclavian and brachial arteries of the shoulder and arm, the carotid arteries that lead to the head, the coronary arteries that nourish the heart itself, and the iliac and femoral arteries of the abdomen and lower extremities. The walls of the large arteries have three layers: a tough elastic outer coat, a layer of muscular tissue, and a smooth, thin inner coat. Arterial walls expand and contract with each heartbeat, pumping blood throughout the body. The pulsating movement of blood, or PULSE, may be felt where the large arteries lie near the body surface.

Artesia (ärtē'zhə). **1** City (1970 pop. 14,757), Los Angeles co., S Calif.; founded 1875, inc. 1959. Chiefly residential, it serves the surrounding farm area and was named for the many artesian wells in the vicinity. **2** City (1970 pop. 10,315), Eddy co., SE N.Mex., just W of the Pecos River, in an oil, gas, farm, and livestock area; laid out 1903, inc. 1939. Artesian wells, under tremendous pressure from the nearby Sacramento Mts., irrigate a large area. The city's manufactures include petroleum products and fiberglass and plastic pipes.

artesian well, deep drilled WELL through which water is forced upward under pressure. The water in an artesian well flows from an aquifer, which is a layer of very porous rock or sediment, usually sandstone, capable of holding and transmitting large quantities of water. The geologic conditions necessary for an artesian well are an inclined aquifer sandwiched between impervious rock layers above and below that trap water in it. Water enters the exposed edge of the aquifer at a high elevation and percolates downward through interconnected pore spaces. The water held in these spaces is under pressure because of the weight of water in the portion of the aquifer above it. If a well is drilled from the land surface through the overlying impervious layer into the aquifer, this pressure will cause the water to rise in the well. In areas where the slope of the aquifer is great enough, pressure will drive the water above ground level in a spectacular, permanent fountain. Artesian springs can occur in similar fashion where faults or cracks in the overlying impervious layer allow water to flow upward. Water from an artesian well or spring is usually cold and free of organic contaminants, making it desirable for drinking. In

North America, the Dakota sandstone provides aquifers for an artesian system that underlies parts of the Dakotas, Montana, Wyoming, Kansas, Nebraska, and Saskatchewan and supplies great quantities of water to the dry Great Plains region. Many East Coast cities derive their water supplies from aquifers that are exposed along the edge of the Piedmont and dip downward toward the Atlantic coast. The largest artesian system in the world underlies nearly all of E and S Australia. Other important artesian systems serve London, Paris, and E Algeria.

Artevelde, Jacob van (yä'kôp vän är'təvĕldə), c.1290–1345, Flemish statesman, of a wealthy family of Ghent. In 1337 the Flemish cloth industry underwent a severe crisis. The pro-French policy of the count of Flanders in the conflict between Edward III of England and Philip VI of France cut off English wool imports and thus ruined the Flemish merchants and weavers. Ghent rebelled, and Artevelde was given dictatorial powers as head of the city government. He negotiated (1338) a commercial treaty with England and obtained recognition of Flemish neutrality. The other towns of Flanders followed his lead, the count fled to France, and trade revived and prospered. In 1340, Artevelde had Edward III recognized as king of France (and thus suzerain of Flanders) by the Flemish towns. Artevelde's firm leadership and wealthy origin inevitably aroused resentment. Enemies accused him of proposing the lordship of Flanders to Edward the Black Prince (of England). In 1345 a riot broke out in Ghent, and Artevelde was killed by the mob.

Artevelde, Philip van, 1340–82, Flemish popular leader, captain general of Ghent; son of Jacob van Artevelde. In the struggle between the so-called "Goods" (the propertied classes supported by the count of Flanders) and the "Bads" (the workers, led by the weavers), he put himself (1381) at the head of the rebellious weavers. He captured (1382) Bruges and most of Flanders but was defeated and killed at Roosebeke by the French under Olivier de Clisson.

art galleries: see MUSEUMS OF ART.

art history, the study of works of art and architecture. In the mid-19th cent., art history was raised to the status of an academic discipline by the Swiss Jacob BURCKHARDT, who related art to its cultural environment, and the German idealists Alois Riegl, Heinrich WÖLFFLIN, and Wilhelm Worringer. The latter three saw art history as the analysis of forms and viewed art apart from any function it serves in expressing the spirit of its age. Major 20th-century art historians include Henri Focillon, Bernard BERENSON, Aby Warburg, Émile MÂLE, Erwin PANOFSKY, and Ernst GOMBRICH. Modern art history is a broad field of inquiry embracing formal questions of stylistic development as well as considerations of the social function of art. See Arnold Hauser, *The Social History of Art* (4 vol., 1958–60); H. W. Janson, *History of Art* (rev. ed. 1969); Kenneth Clark, *Civilization* (1970).

arthritis, painful inflammation of a joint or joints of the body, usually producing heat and redness. In its various forms, arthritis disables more people than any other chronic disorder. The condition can be brought about by nerve impairment, increased or decreased function of the endocrine glands, or degeneration due to age. Less frequently, it is caused by infection (tuberculosis, gonorrhea, rheumatic fever). The cause of rheumatoid arthritis, the most common and most crippling form, is not known. Women are much more susceptible to it than men. Although rheumatoid arthritis usually appears between the ages of 25 and 50, it also occurs in children. Osteoarthritis, another common type, occurs commonly in those over 50. It tends to be more severe when the joints have been strained by obesity or overwork. GOUT, the third most common form of arthritis, affects men almost exclusively. Aspirin is the usual treatment for the pain of arthritis. Gold salts, cortisone, and adrenocorticotropic hormone (ACTH) are used in treating arthritis but often have undesirable side effects. Hydrocortisone and phenylbutazone, both chemical relatives of cortisone, are among other drugs that have been used. See S. P. Blau and Dodi Schultz, *Arthritis* (1974).

Arthropoda (ärthrŏp'ədə) [Gr.,=jointed feet], largest and most diverse invertebrate animal phylum, including over 80% (about 800,000) of all known animal species. The arthropods include the fossil TRILOBITES, HORSESHOE CRABS, SCORPIONS, SPIDERS, ticks, MITES, SEA SPIDERS, CRUSTACEANS, INSECTS, CENTIPEDES, MILLIPEDES, symphylans, and pauropodans. Arthropods are characterized by a segmented body covered by a jointed external skeleton (exoskeleton), with paired jointed appendages on each segment; a complex nervous system with a dorsal brain, connective nerves passing around the upper end of the digestive tract, and a ventral nerve cord with a ganglion in each body segment; an open circulatory system with a dorsal heart into which blood flows through paired openings (ostia); and a greatly reduced body cavity (coelom). Because the jointed exoskeleton blocks growth of the organism, it must be shed periodically. This phenomenon, called molting, or ecdysis, is a characteristic feature of the phylum; it permits rapid growth in size and significant change in body form until the new exoskeleton, secreted by the animal, has hardened. Arthropods are mainly terrestrial, but aquatic representatives are well known. There are three subphyla, comprising nine classes.

Subphylum Trilobita. The trilobites comprise a wholly extinct, primitive group of marine animals. They were extremely abundant in the Cambrian and Ordovician geologic periods, becoming extinct in the Permian. The flattened, oval body was composed of a head covered by a dorsal shield, a trunk (thorax), and a terminal segment (pygidium). Most of the 4,000 fossil species ranged in length from 1 to 4 in. (2.5–10 cm); some planktonic forms were smaller, and some species were as long as 2½ ft (76 cm). *Triarthrus eatoni* is a fossil trilobite common in the Ordovician seas.

Subphylum Chelicerata. There are three classes of chelicerates, including the living horseshoe crabs (class Merostomata), the arachnids (class Arachnida), and the sea spiders (class Pycnogonida). Chelicerates are characterized by the absence of antennae and jaws and the presence of feeding structures (chelicera), which are modified pincerlike appendages used mainly for grasping and fragmenting food. Nearly all the merostomates are extinct, the only living representative being *Limulus,* the horseshoe crab (subclass Xiphosura), which inhabits the soft bottom mud of shallow, coastal seas. Merostomates have five or six gills, which have been modified from body appendages, and a giant tail (telson) lacking appendages. The extinct giant water scorpions (subclass Eurypterida) belong to this class. Members of class Pycnogonida are commonly known as sea spiders. These exclusively marine carnivores are spiderlike in appearance and range in length from 1 mm to ½ in. (1.3 cm). Some are as large as 2 in. (5 cm); the leg spread is sometimes over 2 ft (61 cm). Sea spiders have four pairs of legs. They are found in oceans all over the world. The largest class of chelicerates, class Arachnida, includes orders Aranaea (spiders), Acarina (ticks and mites), Opiliones (daddy longlegs, or harvestmen), and Scorpionida (scorpions), among the most important. Arachnids are predominantly terrestrial, and most are carnivorous, with the digestion of prey starting outside the body. The body is composed of an unsegmented anterior region (prosoma), with a pair of chelicera, a pair of leglike appendages (pedipalps), four pairs of walking legs, and a posterior region (opisthosoma), equipped with book lungs or tracheae, for respiration. Arachnids are an ancient group, their fossil records dating back to the Carboniferous period.

Subphylum Mandibulata. The mandibulates constitute the largest and most varied arthropod group and are characterized by the presence of modified appendages (mandibles) flanking the mouth and used as jaws. There are six classes, all characterized by various aspects of body form. Members of class Crustacea are characterized by having two pairs of antennae and two pairs of modified appendages (maxillae) used for food handling. There are over 26,000 species of crustaceans, including lobsters, shrimps, crayfish, crabs, copepods, barnacles, and a large number of minute forms making up part of the plankton. Crustaceans are the only arthropods that are mainly aquatic, and most of them are marine. Some have spread to humid areas near water. They bear gills for respiration. The thoracic region typically bears walking legs (pereiopods), also used for capturing prey. The abdominal region often is equipped with swimmerets (pleopods) and a tail fan made up of a pair of appendages (uropods) and the telson. Their excretory organs are modified nephridia, as a rule producing a dilute urine that contains a great deal of ammonia. Crustaceans are herbivores, carnivores, or scavengers and are often vital elements of the food chain. Some are important economically as shellfish, such as lobsters, shrimp, and crayfish. Barnacles are important as fouling organisms of ship bottoms and harbor installations. Some crustaceans are significant parasites of other aquatic organisms. As a rule they pass through a complex set of molts during development, involving a series of larval stages. The characteristic larva is called a nauplius, with three pairs of appendages. More appendages are added as the organism passes through its developmental molts. The cuticle of crustaceans, unlike that of other arthropods, contains calcium deposits. The most familiar subclasses are the Branchiopoda—which includes the orders Notostraca (tadpole shrimps), Diplostraca (clam shrimps and water fleas), Ostracoda (ostracods), Copepoda (copepods), and Cirrepedia (barnacles)—and the Malacostraca, which includes the orders Stomatopoda (mantis shrimps), Mysidacea (opossum shrimps), Isopoda (isopods), Amphipoda (amphipods), and Decapoda (crayfish, lobsters, shrimps, and crabs). Class Chilopoda includes the 5,000 species of centipedes, all of which are terrestrial. Centipedes are carnivorous and predacious, immobilizing their prey, usually consisting of smaller arthropods, with the aid of their fangs. The body is composed of a head region, bearing a pair of antennae, a pair of mandibles, and two pairs of maxillae, and a trunk region, with one pair of legs on each segment. The anterior pair of trunk appendages (maxillipeds) is equipped with poison glands. Juveniles have fewer appendages than adults; new segments are added during developmental molts. Chilopods are found throughout the globe in tropical as well as temperate climates. There are about 8,000 species belonging to class Diplopoda, which comprises the millipedes and is found worldwide. The head region has a pair of antennae, a pair of mandibles, and two pairs of maxillae that are usually fused into a single mouthpart, the chilognatharium. Millipedes possess a tracheal system for respiration. They are herbivores or scavengers on dead plant material. Many are protected by stink glands that produce toxic or unpleasant compounds. There are about 60 known species belonging to class Pauropoda. Pauropods are soft-bodied, small (0.5–2.0 mm long), soil-inhabiting arthropods which are distributed worldwide. They are elongated and have many pairs of legs, but they have no trachea and no heart. Members of class Symphyla are rapid runners that range in length from 1 to 4 in. (2.5–10 cm). The class includes some 60 species. They are mainly scavengers on decayed vegetation, but one species, *Scutigerella immaculata,* is a serious pest of certain crops. Symphylans have twelve pairs of legs and resemble the centipedes. Class Insecta is the largest of the arthropod classes, containing hundreds of thousands of species. Except for a few primitive or highly modified forms, insects are characterized by having one or two pairs of wings attached to the thorax. The head region bears a pair of antennae, a pair of mandibles, and two pairs of modified maxillae forming the mouthparts. The abdomen is well set off from the thorax and has no appendages except reduced ones that are modified as reproductive organs. The typical insect head bears compound eyes and one or more simple eyes and is covered by a continuous exoskeletal armor. The thorax is made up of three segments, each bearing a pair of legs. The last two segments usually bear a pair of wings. Insects are predominantly terrestrial and have tracheae for air-breathing. Insects are also characterized by having unique excretory organs, known as Malpighian tubules, which are useful in conserving water. Members of the class are extremely varied. They have adapted to many different kinds of feeding and play a variety of important roles in their ecological communities. Mouthparts may be adapted to chewing either plant or animal food, for sucking plant sap or blood, or for lapping or swabbing moisture such as fruit juices or animal body fluids. Some burrow and feed in soil or plant tissue, some are runners or jumpers that feed at or near the ground level, and others feed on the wing. Most primitive insects are wingless and have a relatively weak exoskeleton. These are forced to seek humid, protected habitats. Juveniles of primitive insects closely resemble the parents and undergo little change other than growth after hatching. This is called ametaboly. Many of the winged insects undergo paurometabolous development, hatching as nymphs that resemble the parent in many ways but that have small buds instead of wings. With each molt these juveniles change somewhat, and the wings increase in size as the young gradually assume the form of the adult. Some insects have adapted to an aquatic life to a certain extent, and in their juvenile stages they are found in ponds and streams. Some of these are hemimetabolous; the juveniles are naiads, i.e., they resemble the nymphs of paurometabolous insects, but their wings do not grow during the juvenile molts, even though other body changes occur. Instead, the last molt before the adult stage is reached involves full development of the wings, after which the insect takes up a terrestrial existence. The least primitive of the insects are termed holometabolous. In holometaboly, the eggs hatch to release the usually wormlike larvae, which are often equipped with false legs in the abdominal region to aid in locomotion. Wing buds are entirely lacking. Although the larvae grow at each molt, they do not begin to resemble the adult until later. At the end of the larval stage the young insect enters into a quiescent pupal stage. At the end of this stage a major metamorphosis occurs, and the insect emerges with all the adult organs. Insects often cause great losses in agriculture, attack stored products, parasitize humans and domesticated animals and plants, and serve as important carriers of disease organisms. They are also beneficial, producing honey and silk and pollinating the flowers of the majority of flowering plants. A great many important insect orders are recognized, including Collembola (SPRINGTAILS), Thysanura (SILVERFISH), Ephemerida (MAYFLIES), Odonata (DRAGONFLIES), Orthoptera (GRASSHOPPERS, LOCUSTS, KATYDIDS, COCKROACHES, MANTIDS, WALKING STICKS), Dermaptera (EARWIGS), Isoptera (TERMITES), Corrodentia (booklice), Mallophaga (chewing lice, see LOUSE), Anoplura (sucking lice), Thysanoptera (THRIPS), Hemiptera (true BUGS), Homoptera (CICADAS, SCALE INSECTS, LEAFHOPPERS), Neuroptera (lacewings), Hymenoptera (ANTS, BEES, WASPS), Coleoptera (BEETLES), Trichoptera (CADDIS FLIES), Lepidoptera (MOTHS, BUTTERFLIES), Diptera (FLIES), and Siphonaptera (FLEAS). See W. R. Horsfall, *Medical Entomology* (1962); J. D. Carthy, *Behavior of Arthropods* (1965); R. E. Snodgrass, *A Textbook of Arthropod Anatomy* (1952, repr. 1965).

Arthur, king of Britain: see ARTHURIAN LEGEND.

Arthur I, 1187–1203?, duke of Brittany (1196–1203?), son of Geoffrey, fourth son of Henry II of England and Constance, heiress of Brittany. Arthur, a posthumous child, was proclaimed duke in 1196, and an invasion by his uncle King Richard I of England was repulsed with French aid. Subsequently, Arthur was brought up at the court of King Philip II of France. On Richard's death (1199), Arthur's claim to the English crown was passed over in favor of his uncle JOHN, youngest son of Henry II. Arthur allied himself with Philip II, who invested him with all of Richard's fiefs in France. The nobles of Anjou, Maine, and Touraine recognized Arthur as their ruler, but the young duke was captured (1202) by John while attempting to subdue Poitou. He was imprisoned in Rouen; his fate is uncertain, although John was suspected of murdering him in 1203. His story is told in Shakespeare's *King John*. Arthur's sister and heir married Pierre Mauclerc, who later became duke of Brittany as PETER I.

Arthur III, 1394–1458, duke of Brittany (1457–58), known before 1457 as comte de Richemont, constable of France in the Hundred Years War. He led the coalition that overthrew Georges de LA TRÉMOILLE, and by the Treaty of Arras (1435) he reconciled Philip the Good, duke of Burgundy and England's former ally, with King Charles VII of France. He captured Paris from the English in 1436 and later helped to regain Normandy for France. His nephew, Francis II, succeeded him.

Arthur, Chester Alan, 1830–86, 21st President of the United States (1881–85), b. Fairfield, Vt. He studied law and before the Civil War practiced in New York City. In the war he was (1861–63) quartermaster general of New York state. In 1871, President Grant appointed him collector of the port of New York. Although Arthur was a loyal party man and a believer in the spoils system, he administered this office honestly and efficiently. President Hayes, bent on civil service reform, displaced Arthur in 1878, thus defying Senator CONKLING and the New York Republican machine. At the Republican national convention of 1880, Garfield was nominated for President, and the Conkling "Stalwarts," who had supported Grant, were placated by the nomination of Arthur for Vice President. Garfield's assassination soon after his inauguration made Arthur President. He came into office handicapped by a record in machine politics and grave doubt as to his ability and integrity, but his administration proved honest, efficient, and dignified. He effectively supported the civil service reform act of 1883, vetoed a Chinese exclusion bill that violated a treaty with China, and vigorously prosecuted the STAR ROUTE trials. Serious illness kept Arthur from actively seeking renomination in 1884. See biography by George F. Howe (1957).

Arthur, Timothy Shay, 1809–85, American editor and moralist, b. near Newburgh, N.Y. His only successful editorial venture was *Arthur's Home Magazine*, which he edited (1853–85) while producing a stream of books and moral tracts in the cause of temperance. His novel *Ten Nights in a Barroom and What I Saw There* (1854) was successfully dramatized by William W. Pratt in 1858.

Arthurian legend, the mass of legend, popular in medieval lore, concerning King Arthur of Britain and his knights. The battle of Mt. Badon—in which, according to the *Annales Cambriae* (c.1150), Arthur carried the Cross of Jesus Christ on his shoulders—but not Arthur's name, is mentioned (c.540) by Gildas. The earliest apparent mention of Arthur in any known literature is a brief reference to a mighty warrior in the Welsh poem *Gododdin* (c.600). Arthur next appears in Nennius (c.800) as a Celtic warrior who fought (c.600) 12 victorious battles against the Saxon invaders. These and several subsequent references indicate that his legend had already developed into a considerable literature before GEOFFREY OF MONMOUTH wrote his *Historia* (c.1135), in which he elaborated on the feats of King Arthur, representing him as the conqueror of Western Europe. After Geoffrey's *Historia* came Wace's *Roman de Brut* (c.1155), which infused the legend with the spirit of chivalric romance. The *Brut* (c.1200) of Layamon, modeled on Wace's work, gives one of the best pictures of Arthur as a national hero. CHRÉTIEN DE TROYES, a 12th-century French poet, wrote five romances dealing with the knights of Arthur's court. His *Perceval* contains the earliest extant literary version of the quest of the Holy Grail (see GRAIL, HOLY). Two medieval German poets important in the development of Arthurian legend are WOLFRAM VON ESCHENBACH and GOTTFRIED VON STRASSBURG. The latter's *Tristan* was the first great literary treatment of the TRISTRAM AND ISOLDE story. After 1225 no significant medieval Arthurian literature was produced on the Continent. In England, however, the legend continued to flourish. *Sir Gawain and the Green Knight* (c.1370), one of the best Middle English romances, embodies the ideal of chivalric knighthood. The last important medieval work dealing with the Arthurian legend is the *Morte d'Arthur* of Sir Thomas MALORY, whose tales have become the source for most subsequent Arthurian material. Many writers have used Arthurian themes since Malory, notably Tennyson in his *Idylls of the King*. Swinburne, William Morris, and Edwin Arlington Robinson also wrote poetic works based on the legend. T. H. White's trilogy *The Once and Future King* (1958) is a charming and decidedly 20th-century retelling of the Arthurian story. It was thought formerly that the Arthurian legend was the work of inventive poets and romancers of the Middle Ages. The generally accepted theory now is that Arthurian legend developed out of stories of Celtic mythology. The most archaic form in which these occur in British sources is the Welsh MABINOGION, but much of Irish mythology is palpably identical with Arthurian romance. It is probable that traditional Irish hero stories fused in Britain with those of the Welsh, the Cornish, and the Celts of North Britain. The resultant legend with its hero, Arthur, was transmitted to their Breton cousins on the Continent probably by the year 1000. The Bretons, famous as wandering minstrels, followed Norman armies over Western Europe and used for their repertory the stories of the legend. By 1100 therefore, Arthurian stories were well known even in Italy.

The Story. Although there are innumerable variations of the Arthurian legend, the basic story has remained the same. Arthur was the illegitimate son of Uther Pendragon, king of Britain, and Igraine, the wife of Gorlois of Cornwall. After the death of Uther, Arthur, who had been reared in secrecy, won acknowledgment as king of Britain by successfully withdrawing a sword from a stone. MERLIN, the court magician, then revealed the new king's parentage. Arthur, reigning in his court at Camelot, proved to be a noble king and a mighty warrior. He was the possessor of the miraculous sword EXCALIBUR, given him by the mysterious LADY OF THE LAKE. Of his several enemies, the most treacherous were his sister Morgan le Fay and his nephew Mordred. Morgan le Fay was usually represented as an evil sorceress, scheming to win Arthur's throne for herself and her lover. Mordred (or Modred) was variously Arthur's nephew or his son by his sister Morgawse. He seized Arthur's throne during the king's absence. Later he was slain in battle by Arthur, but not before he had fatally wounded the king. Arthur was borne away to the isle of AVALON, where it was expected that he would be healed of his wounds and that he would someday return to his people. Two of the most invincible knights in Arthur's realm were Sir Tristram and Sir Launcelot of the Lake. Both of them, however, were involved in illicit and tragic love unions—Tristram with Isolde, the queen of Tristram's uncle, King Mark; SIR LAUNCELOT with GUINEVERE, the queen of his sovereign, King Arthur. Other knights of importance include the naive Sir Pelleas, who fell helplessly in love with the heartless Ettarre (or Ettard); Sir Gawain, Arthur's nephew, who appeared variously as the ideal of knightly courtesy and as the bitter enemy of Launcelot; Sir Balin and Sir Balan, two devoted brothers who unwittingly slew one another; Sir Galahad, Launcelot's son, who was the hero of the quest of the Holy Grail; Sir Kay, Arthur's villainous foster brother; Sir Percivale (or PARSIFAL); Sir Gareth; Sir Geraint; Sir Bedivere; and other knights of the ROUND TABLE. To modern readers, Arthurian legend has become the mirror of the ideal of medieval knighthood and chivalry. See studies by R. H. Fletcher (2d ed. 1966), R. L. Loomis (1949; 1956; 1927, repr. 1969; 1963, repr. 1970), Leslie Alcock (1972), John Morris (1973), and R. W. Barber (1973); J. L. Weston, tr., *Arthurian Romances Unrepresented in Malory's Morte d'Arthur* (8 vol., 1907; repr. 1971).

artichoke, name for two different plants of the family Compositae (COMPOSITE family), both having edible parts. The French, or globe, artichoke (*Cynara scolymus*) is a thistlelike plant of which the globular flower heads are used in the immature state as a salad or vegetable; only the lower part of the fleshy bracts ("leaves") and the center ("heart") are eaten. The cultivation of this S European plant is now a considerable industry in California. A large part of the yearly crop is canned for export to South America. The edible blanched leaves and leafstalks are called chard. The other artichoke plant is the JERUSALEM ARTICHOKE. Artichokes are classified in the division MAGNOLIOPHYTA, class Magnoliopsida, order Asterales, family Compositae.

artificial elements: see SYNTHETIC ELEMENTS.

artificial insemination, technique of artificially injecting sperm-containing semen from a male into a female to cause pregnancy. The technique is widely used in the propagation of cattle, especially to produce many offspring from one prize bull. The prepared semen can be preserved for more than a year by refrigeration, and it is frequently shipped over great distances. Artificial insemination is sometimes used in humans when normal fertilization cannot be achieved.

artificial languages, languages that are invented by one or more human beings as opposed to languages that develop naturally among peoples. Examples of artificial languages are Volapük, Esperanto, and Ido. See INTERNATIONAL LANGUAGE.

artificial limb, mechanical replacement for a missing limb. An artificial limb, called a prosthesis, must be light and flexible to permit easy movement, but must also be sufficiently sturdy to support the weight of the body or to manipulate objects. The materials used in artificial limbs include willow wood, laminated fibers and plastics, and various metallic alloys. One model of artificial leg is made of layers of stockinette cloth coated with plastic; it has duraluminum joints at the knee and ankle, rubber soles on the feet, and a leather cuff cushioning the stump. The cuff fits around the thigh like a corset, holding the artificial leg firmly in place, and connects to a leather belt around the waist. Often, spring joints are employed on foot pieces to give natural-looking movements. Artificial legs may also be secured by suction between socket and stump. Artificial arms, not having to support the weight of the body, may be made of lighter metals and plastics. They are usually strapped to the trunk and controlled by a shoulder harness. Artificial hands vary in structure and utility; research and development has resulted in devices that are both cosmetic and functional. For example, an artificial hand has been devised that utilizes a split hook resembling a lobster claw; this is enclosed within a flexible plastic glove that can be made remarkably lifelike, even having fingerprints. The biceps muscle can be attached to the prosthesis by a surgical procedure called cineplasty, which permits grasping in the terminal device while dispensing with shoulder harnesses.

artificial respiration, any measure that causes air to flow in and out of a person's lungs when natural breathing is inadequate or ceases, as in respiratory paralysis, drowning, electric shock, choking, gas or smoke inhalation, or poisoning. Respiration can be taken over by mechanical appliances such as the artificial lung (especially in respiratory paralysis), the pulmotor, or any other type of mechanical respirator. See RESUSCITATOR. In emergency situations, however, when no professional help is available, rescuers should undertake the mouth-to-mouth or mouth-to-nose method of artificial respiration (which have been proven far superior to manual methods). First, any foreign material should be swept out of the mouth with the hand, wrapped in a cloth if possible. The victim should be placed on his back, with his head tilted backward and chin pointing upward so that the tongue does not block the throat. The reviver's mouth is then placed tightly over the victim's mouth, with the latter's nostrils kept tightly shut. Alternatively, the reviver's mouth may be placed over the victim's nose, with the victim's mouth kept closed. For a small child or infant, the reviver places his mouth firmly over the mouth and nose. The reviver takes a deep breath and blows into the victim's mouth (or nose). If there is no exchange of air, the reviver should check the position of the head. If there is still no exchange, the victim should be turned on his side and rapped between the shoulder blades to dislodge any foreign matter that may be blocking the air passages. A child can be held by the ankles and rapped between the shoulder blades. The reviver stops blowing when the chest expands, turns his head away, and listens for exhalation. If the victim is an adult, blowing should be vigorous, at the rate of about 12 breaths per minute. For a child the breaths should be shallower, about 20 per minute. For an infant, breaths should come in short puffs. If the victim begins to vomit, the reviver must quickly turn him on his side and wipe out his mouth before continuing artificial respiration. If the victim has had the larynx removed, the above method is used, but the reviver must breathe into the stoma (surgical opening made in front of neck for breathing). Breathing into the subject should be continued until natural breathing resumes or until professional help arrives.

Artigas, José Gervasio (hōsā' härvä'syō ärtē'gäs), 1764–1850, national hero of Uruguay, first leader in the movement toward independence. A typical gaucho of the BANDA ORIENTAL, he joined the revolution against Spain in 1811 and became the leader of the Orientales. In 1813 he instructed the delegates from the Banda Oriental to the Buenos Aires constituent assembly to work for a federation of autonomous La Plata provinces, but they were denied admission to the assembly by the centralist military junta. Artigas then championed Uruguayan independence. After an initial setback in 1813 by Buenos Aires and subsequently the restoration of Spanish power (1816), he still managed to rule much of the territory as protector against Spain, Brazil, and Buenos Aires. Finally in 1820, when Artigas had once again renounced the United Provinces of La Plata (Argentina), the Portuguese captured the territory and annexed it to Brazil. Artigas spent his remaining years in exile in Paraguay. See John Street, *Artigas and the Emancipation of Uruguay* (1959).

artillery, term originally applied to any weaponry (including such ancient engines of war as catapults and battering rams) but later applied only to heavy FIREARMS as opposed to SMALL ARMS. Types of artillery include antiaircraft and antitank guns (which fire at high muzzle velocity through long barrels at flat trajectories) and howitzers (with shorter barrels, lower velocities, and parabolic trajectories). Modern artillery came into use in the mid-14th cent. with the invention of gunpowder. At first used mainly against fortifications, artillery was extensively employed in the field during the Thirty Years War (1618–48); thereafter it played an increasingly important role until the advent of aircraft. Now that few pieces of fixed artillery (e.g., coastal defense guns) still survive, artillery is generally classified as either towed or self-propelled; in Western countries the latter type predominates. Artillery was characteristically smoothbore and muzzle-loaded, firing solid, round shot, until the latter part of the 19th cent., when breech-loaded, rifled, and shell-firing artillery became standard. See study by John Batchelor and Ian Hogg (1972).

Art Institute of Chicago, museum and art school, in Grant Park, facing Michigan Ave. It was incorporated in 1879; George Armour was the first president. Since 1893 the Institute has been housed in its present building, designed in the Italian Renaissance style by Shepley, Rutan, and Coolidge. Among its famous collections are those of early Italian, Dutch, Spanish, and Flemish paintings, including works by El Greco, Rembrandt, and Hals. The Institute is rich in 19th-century American and French paintings; particularly well known is *La Grande Jatte* by Seurat. Modern American and European paintings are also well represented. Other collections include prints and drawings, dating from the 15th cent., and sculpture. The section on decorative arts has porcelains, textiles, glass, and rooms of period furniture. The Institute also has a fine collection of Chinese art. Other features include the Ryerson library for research and a school of drama.

art nouveau (är" no͞ovō'), decorative-art movement centered in Western Europe. It began in the 1880s as a reaction against the historical bombast of mid-19th-century art, but did not survive World War I. Art nouveau originated in London and was variously called *Jugendstil* in Germany, *Sezessionstil* in Austria, and *Modernismo* in Spain. In general it was most successfully practiced in the decorative arts: furniture, jewelry, and book design and illustration. The style was richly ornamental and asymmetrical, characterized by a whiplash linearity reminiscent of twining plant tendrils. Its exponents chose themes fraught with symbolism, frequently of an erotic nature. They imbued their designs with dreamlike and exotic forms. Stylistic descendants of William Blake and of the PRE-RAPHAELITES, the outstanding designers of art nouveau in England include the graphic artist Aubrey Beardsley, A. H. Mackmurdo, Charles Ricketts, Walter Crane, and the Scottish architect Charles R. Mackintosh; in Belgium the architects Henry Van de Velde and Victor Horta; in France the architect and designer of the Paris *métro* entrances, Hector Guimard, and the jewelry designer René Lalique; in Austria the painter Gustav Klimt; in Spain the architect Antonio Gaudí, whose fantastic buildings reveal him to be one of the most original geniuses of the entire movement; in Germany the illustrator Otto Eckmann and the architect Peter Behrens; in Italy the originator of the ornamental *Floreale* style, Giuseppe Sommaruga; and in the United States Louis Sullivan, whose architecture was dressed with art nouveau detail, and the designer of elegant glassware Louis C. Tiffany. The aesthetics of the movement were disseminated through various illustrated periodicals including *The Century Guild Hobby Horse* (1894), *The Dial* (1889), *The Studio* (begun, 1893), *The Yellow Book* (1894–95), and *The Savoy* (1896–98). Liberty, the Regent St. store in London, popularized the style in fabrics. In the 1960s there was a general resurgence of interest in art nouveau masters; in the United States the works of Beardsley and Tiffany were especially popular. See definitive studies by R. Schmutzler (1964), M. Rheims (1966), P. Selz and M. Constantine (1960); N. Pevsner's, *Pioneers of Modern Design* (1960).

Artois (ärtwä'), region and former province, in Pas-de-Calais dept., N France, near the English Channel, between Picardy and Flanders. Arras is the chief city. Slightly hilly, it is largely agricultural and occupies part of the rich Franco-Belgian coal basin. Owned in the Middle Ages by the counts of Flanders, Artois was annexed (1180) to France by Philip II through marriage. Burgundy gained (14th cent.) the territory, also through marriage. Later it was under Austrian rule, and from 1493 until its conquest (1640) by Louis XIII it was under Spanish rule. Confirmation of French possession was made by the Peace of the Pyrenees (1659) and the Treaty of Nijmegen (1678). Renowned for its *états* (assembly), which met until the 18th cent., it declined in political importance thereafter. Of strategic significance in World War I, it was the scene of heavy fighting. The region gives its name to the ARTESIAN WELL, known there for centuries.

arts and crafts, term for that general field of applied designing in which hand fabrication is dominant. The term was invented in England in the late 19th cent. as a label for the current movement directed toward the revivifying of the decorative arts. The chief influence behind this movement was William MORRIS. By the mid-19th cent., factory processes had almost entirely driven handicraftsmen from their ancient trades and obliterated the techniques by which beautiful objects of utility could be produced. The GOTHIC REVIVAL, however, had brought into existence a great body of knowledge concerning the arts of the Middle Ages, and Morris, together with the Pre-Raphaelite painters and a small group of architects and designers, eagerly returned to these arts as a rich source of inspiration. The pupils and followers of Morris multiplied, and numbers of proficient craftsmen developed. Their methods aimed at a practical demonstration not only of Morris's aesthetic creed but also of his ideas concerning socialism and the moral need for integrating beauty with the accessories of daily life. The revival of folk arts has prospered, especially in remote communities and among American Indians of the Southwest (see NORTH AMERICAN INDIAN ART). Handicrafts are widely taught in schools, have been adopted by hobbyists, and are valued in occupational therapy.

Artzybasheff, Boris (ärtsĭbä'shĕf), 1899–1965, American draftsman, illustrator, writer, and cartoonist, b. Kharkov, Russia; son of Mikhail Petrovich ARTZYBASHEV. In 1919 he went to New York City, where he worked in an engraving shop. Later he became noted for his brilliant and imaginative work as an advertising artist and illustrator of books and periodicals, including many covers for *Time* magazine. Grotesque and weirdly humorous drawings appear in his *As I See* (1955).

Artzybashev, Mikhail Petrovich (mēkhəyēl' pētrô'vĭch ärtsĭbä'shĕf), 1878–1927, Russian novelist, playwright, and essayist. Artzybashev's early works were short stories in the manner of Tolstoy. His novel *Sanine* (1907, tr. 1914) created a sensation and was proscribed as pornographic in many countries. When the *Sanine* cult subsided, he tried to maintain his popularity with similar works, e.g., the novel *Breaking-Point* (1912, tr. 1915). Artzybashev bitterly attacked the Bolsheviks from abroad.

Aruba, island (1970 pop. 60,734), 69 sq mi (179 sq km), in the Leeward Islands group of the Netherlands Antilles. Oranjestad is the capital. Tourism and the refining of oil brought in from nearby Venezuela are the major industries.

Aruboth (ăr'yo͞obŏth), part of Solomon's kingdom. Arubboth RSV. 1 Kings 4.10.

Aru Islands or **Aroe Islands** (both: ä'ro͞o), group of about 95 low-lying islands (1961 pop. 29,604), 3,306 sq mi (8,563 sq km), E Indonesia, in the Moluccas, in the Arafura Sea, SW of New Guinea. The largest island is Tanahbesar; Dobo, the chief port of the group, is on Wamar, just off Tanahbesar. Products include sago, coconuts, tobacco, mother-of-pearl, trepang, tortoise shell, and bird of paradise plumes. The inhabitants are of a mixed Papuan and Malay stock. The islands were discovered by the Dutch, who colonized them after 1623. Arru is another spelling.

arum, common name for the Araceae, a plant family mainly composed of species of herbaceous terrestrial plants found in swampy and muddy habitats of the tropics and subtropics; some are native to temperate zones, and a few are epiphytic. The family is characterized by an inflorescence consisting of a single spadix (a fleshy spike bearing small flowers) and a usually showy and flowerlike bract (modified leaf) called a spathe, which surrounds the spadix. The krubi (*Amorphophallus titanum*) of Sumatra, sometimes grown in greenhouses, has the largest plant inflorescence known—the spadix reaches a height of 15 ft (4.6 m) and the spathe a height and upper diameter of some 8 ft (2.5 m). Commonly cultivated for their showy inflorescences are the arum lilies, or callas (genus *Zantedeschia*), native to tropical and S Africa; the common florists' white-spathed calla lily is *Z. aethiopica*. The wild calla, or water arum (*Calla palustris*), of E North America and other northern regions is similar to the calla lily but smaller and is not usually cultivated. Several plants of the arum family are grown (often as house plants)

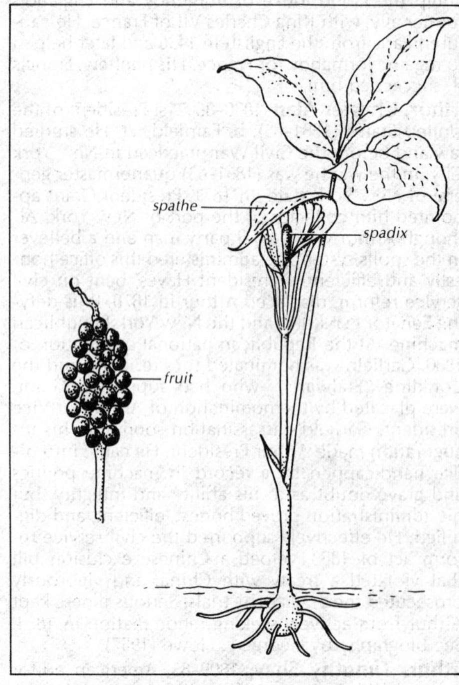

Jack-in-the-pulpit, Arisaema triphyllum, *a member of the arum family*

for their ornamental foliage, e.g., species of the genera *Monstera, Philodendron*, and *Caladium*, all native to the American tropics. Monstera is a vine popular for its perforated and deeply lobed leaves. Philodendron, usually a climbing shrub in the tropics, is now one of the most popular house plants. Caladium, noted for its multicolored foliage, is sometimes mistakenly called elephant's-ear, a name properly applied to *Colocasia esculenta* because of the shape of its large, decorative leaves. *C. esculenta*, with its large, starchy corms or rootstocks (characteristic of the arum family) is a major source of food in the Pacific islands and the Far East; in Hawaii it is the main ingredient of POI. It is now cultivated in many warm regions, including the S United States, in some 1,000 varieties; as a food plant it is known by many local names, the most common being taro and dasheen. Plants of the arum family native to the United States are found chiefly in the eastern and central states; all species are bog or aquatic plants except *Arisaema*, which grows in moist woodlands. The jack-in-the-pulpit, or Indian turnip (*A. triphyllum*), has a spadix (jack) enveloped by a purplish-striped spathe (the pulpit). Its starchy corms were eaten by the American Indians, as were those of the TUCKAHOE or Indian bread, sweet flag (*Acorus calamus*), and skunk cabbage (*Symplocarpus foetidus*). The latter two and the jack-in-the-pulpit are also sources of medicinal substances. Sweet flag, found in many north temperate regions, yields flavorings and calamus, a perfume oil. Skunk cabbage, found in both E Asia and E North America, is one of the most abundant and earliest-blooming northern wild flowers. The unpleasant odor noticeable when the plant is bruised is produced by the acrid sap, which contains needle-shaped crystals of calcium oxalate, called raphides, that are formed as a metabolic by-product. This acridity, characteristic of the arum family, is removed from the corms by cooking. The family is classified in the division MAGNOLIOPHYTA, class Liliatae, order Arales.

Arumah (əro͞o'mə), town of Palestine. Judges 9.41.

Arunachal Pradesh (är"ənächəl prədĕsh'), union territory (1971 pop. 444,744), 31,438 sq mi (81,424 sq km), NE India, bordered on the N by the Tibet region of China and on the E by Burma. The capital is ZIRO. Formerly the North-East Frontier Agency special territory, Arunachal Pradesh became a union territory in 1972. A remote region, it includes part of the E Himalayas and extends through mountainous highlands to the plains of Assam. Its border with Tibet, disputed by China, is known as the MacMahon line. It was established by the British, with the agreement of Tibet, in the early 20th cent.; the Chinese claim more than 90% of the territory. In Oct., 1962, after tentative probings, the Chinese launched a massive offensive against the area, and by November they had advanced far into Indian territory, even threatening the tea plantations and oil fields of the rich Assam plain. On Nov. 21, however, the Chinese proclaimed a unilateral cease-fire, and they soon withdrew behind the disputed MacMahon line. Arunachal Pradesh is inhabited by tribesmen of Mongoloid stock, most of whom practice animism. The territory is administered by the home minister in the central government of India but has an elected advisory council. The states of Assam, Nagaland, Meghalaya, Manipur, and Tripura and the union territories of Mizoram and Arunachal Pradesh have a common governor appointed by the president of India.

Arundel, Henry Fitzalan, 12th **earl of** (ăr'əndəl), 1511?–1580, English statesman. Lord chamberlain under Henry VIII, he was a member of the council appointed by Henry to govern during the minority of Edward VI. After Edward's death (1553), he helped bring Mary I to the throne, foiling the duke of Northumberland's attempt to crown Lady Jane Grey. Arundel was prominent in Mary's reign and remained powerful, though always under suspicion because he was a Catholic, after the accession (1558) of Elizabeth I.

Arundel, Thomas Howard, earl of, 1585–1646, first great English art collector and patron of arts. Educated at Trinity College, Cambridge, he married a goddaughter of Queen Elizabeth and was always closely connected with the court. He held many high offices; in 1616 he was appointed privy councillor and later made earl marshal of England. Both Rubens and Van Dyck painted portraits for Arundel of himself and his wife in addition to other works. Inigo Jones, long in his service, accompanied him to Rome; there Arundel excavated some Roman statues, which with other ancient sculptures, including the *Parian Chronicle*, or *Marmor Chronicon*, were given to Oxford University in 1667 and became known as the Arundel Marbles. Most of his sculpture collection is in Oxford's Ashmolean Museum. His collections also included Flemish, Dutch, German, and Italian paintings of the 16th cent.; Dürer and Holbein were particularly well represented. His library was given to the Royal Society; the manuscripts known as the Arundel Collection were later transferred (1831) to the British Museum. The Arundel Society (1848–97) reproduced works by famous artists in order to promote public interest in art. In 1904 the Arundel Club began to print reproductions of works in private collections. See study by Mary F. Hervey (1921, repr. 1969).

Arusha (əro͞o'shə), city (1967 pop. 32,452), capital of Arusha prov., NE Tanzania. It is an industrial and administrative center, connected by rail with Tanga on the Indian Ocean and with Kenya. Manufactures include textiles, beverages, processed foods, plastics, and electronic equipment. The city is also the headquarters of the East African Community (founded 1967), which regulates aspects of the economy, runs transportation and communications facilities, and sponsors research for Tanzania, Kenya, and Uganda. In Jan., 1967, President Julius Nyerere of Tanzania issued the influential Arusha Declaration, which called for socialism, hard work, and self-reliance in Tanzania. The city is the site of an institute devoted to research in tropical pesticides.

Arvad (är'văd), variant of ARADUS.

Arvada (ärvăd'ə), city (1970 pop. 46,814), Jefferson and Adams counties, N central Colo., a suburb of Denver; inc. 1904. Primarily residential, Arvada manufactures processed foods, beer, chemicals, and wood and metal products.

Arval Brothers, in Roman religion, college of 12 priests chosen from the most distinguished senatorial families. It was said that the original brothers were sons of ACCA LARENTIA. Theirs was chiefly an agricultural cult, but they were also concerned with the well-being of the imperial house. The Roman emperor was necessarily a member of the college. Their most important ceremony, held in May, was in honor of Dea Dia, a goddess of fields and crops.

Arvida (ärvē'də), city (1971 pop. 18,448), S Que., Canada, on the Saguenay River. It has a large aluminum smelter.

Arvika (är'vē"kä), city (1970 pop. 15,509), Värmland co., W Sweden, on Lake Glafsfjorden. It is a commercial and industrial center, with a lake port. Arvika was mentioned in a 13th-century Norse saga.

Aryabhata (är"yəbhŭt'ə), c.476–550, Hindu mathematician and astronomer. He is one of the first known to have used algebra; his writings include rules of arithmetic and of plane and spherical trigonometry, and solutions of quadratic equations.

Aryan [Sanskrit,=noble], term formerly used to designate the Indo-European race or language family or its Indo-Iranian subgroup. Originally a group of nomadic tribes, the Aryans were part of a great migratory movement that spread in successive waves from S Russia and Turkistan during the 2d millennium B.C. Throughout Mesopotamia and Asia Minor, literate urban centers fell to their warrior bands. Archaeological evidence corroborates the text of the VEDA by placing the invasion of India by the Aryans at c.1500 B.C. They colonized the Punjab region of NW India, and absorbed much of the indigenous culture. The resulting Indo-Aryan period saw the flourishing of a pastoral-agricultural economy that utilized bronze objects and horse-drawn chariots. Before the discovery of the Indus valley sites in the 1920s, Hindu culture had been attributed solely to the Aryan invaders. The idealization of conquest pictured in the Vedic hymns was incorporated into Nazi racist literature, in which German descent was supposedly traced back to Aryan forebears.

Aryana: see ARIANA.

Arya Samaj: see SARASWATI, DAYANANDA.

aryl group (âr'ĭl), in chemistry, group of atoms derived from BENZENE or from a benzene derivative by removing one hydrogen that is bonded to the benzene ring (see RADICAL). The simplest aryl group is phenyl, C_6H_5; it is derived from benzene. The tolyl group, $CH_3C_6H_4$, is derived from TOLUENE (methylbenzene). The xylyl group, $(CH_3)_2C_6H_3$, is derived from xylene (dimethylbenzene). Just as several different ALKYL GROUPS may be derived from certain alkanes, so may several aryl groups be derived from certain aromatic compounds; for example, three different tolyl groups can be formed from toluene by removing hydrogen from different locations relative to the methyl group. When a FUNCTIONAL GROUP is joined with an aryl group, replacing the hydrogen that had been removed, a compound is formed whose characteristics depend largely on the functional group.

Arza (är'zə), steward at Tirzah. 1 Kings 16.9.

Arzamas (ərzəmäs'), city (1970 pop. 62,000), E European USSR, on the Tyosha River. A rail junction, it has food-processing plants and industries that produce leather and felt goods and farm implements. An ancient Mordvinian settlement, Arzamas became a fortress after Czar Ivan IV captured it from the Kazan Tatars in 1552.

Aš or **Asch** (both: äsh), city (1970 pop. 11,539), W Czechoslovakia, in Bohemia, near the Bavarian border. It is a textile center and also manufactures lace, woolens, embroidery, and carpets.

As, chemical symbol of the element ARSENIC.

Asa (ā'sə). **1** King of Judah, son and successor of Abijah. He was a good king, zealous in his extirpation of idols. When Baasha of Israel took Ramah (a few miles N of Jerusalem), Asa bought the help of Benhadad of Damascus and recaptured Ramah. His son Jehoshaphat succeeded him. 1 Kings 15.8–24; 2 Chron. 14–16. **2** Levite. 1 Chron. 9.16.

Asada Goryu (äsä'dä gôr'yo͞o), 1734–99, Japanese astronomer who helped to introduce modern astronomical instruments and methods into Japan. Asada spent much of his career in the flourishing commercial city of Osaka, where he practiced medicine for a living. Because of the Japanese government's policy of seclusion, Western scientific theory was generally available only through obsolete Chinese works edited by Jesuit missionaries in China. Yet Asada managed to construct sophisticated mathematical models of celestial movements and is sometimes credited with the independent discovery of Kepler's third law.

Asahel (ă'səhĕl, ăs'ə-). **1** David's nephew. Murdered by Abner, he was avenged by his brother Joab. 2 Sam. 2.18–32; 3.27, 30; 1 Chron. 11.26; 27.7. **2, 3** Levites. 2 Chron. 17.8; 31.13. **4** Priest. Ezra 10.15.

Asahiah (ā"səhī'ə, ăs"ə-), the same as ASAIAH **1**.

Asahigawa (äsähē'gäwä), city (1970 pop. 288,490), W central Hokkaido, Japan, on the Ishikari River. Asahigawa is the commercial, industrial, and rail center of a great agricultural region. Pulp, paper, cotton yarn, lumber, wood products, and sake are among the city's industrial products.

Asaiah (ā"saī'ə, ăs"ə-). **1** One of Josiah's deputation to Huldah. 2 Chron. 34.20–22. Asahiah: 2 Kings 22.12–14. **2** Simeonite. 1 Chron. 4.36. **3** Levite. 1 Chron. 6.30; 15.6, 11. **4** Shilonite. 1 Chron. 9.5. Maaseiah: Neh. 11.5.

Asaka (äsä'kä), city (1970 pop. 67,938), Saitama prefecture, central Honshu, Japan. It is an industrial and residential suburb of Tokyo. There is an important metalworks industry in the city.

Asama, Mount (äsä'mä), or **Asama-yama** (-yä'mä), peak, 8,340 ft (2,542 m) high, central Honshu, Japan, near Komoro. One of the largest and most active volcanoes in Japan, it erupted violently in 1783.

asana: see YOGA.

Asansol (əsənsōl'), city (1971 pop. 157,388), West Bengal state, NE India. It is an industrial center in a coal-mining area.

Asaph (ā'săf). **1** Choirmaster of David's time, or the eponym of a corps of singers. His name is attached to a little collection of psalms: Ps. 50;73–83. 1 Chron. 6.39; 9.15; 25.1; 2 Chron. 20.14; 29.30; Neh. 11.17; 12.46. **2** The same as ABIASAPH. **3** Father of a chronicler. 2 Kings 18.37; Isa. 36.3, 22. **4** King's forester. Neh. 2.8.

Asareel (əsă'rēĕl), son of Jehaleleel. 1 Chron. 4.16.

Asarelah (ăs"ərē'lə), Asaphite. 1 Chron. 25.2. Jesharelah: 1 Chron. 25.14.

Asbestos, town (1971 pop. 9,749), SE Que., Canada. Asbestos is mined in the area and asbestos products are made in the town.

asbestos, common name for any of a group of silicate minerals that are fibrous in structure and more or less resistant to acid and fire. The name was originally given to fibrous forms of actinolite and tremolite, varieties of amphibole. Chrysotile asbestos, a form of SERPENTINE, is the chief commercial asbestos. Important varieties of amphibole are amosite, which is not as strong or as easy to spin as chrysotile but is used in insulating materials; crocidolite, known also as blue asbestos, used because of its high strength for making asbestos-cement products; and tremolite, used in laboratories for filtering acids and other chemicals because of its resistance to chemical action. Varieties of amphibole of lesser commercial importance include anthophyllite and actinolite. Asbestos is usually found comprising veins in other rock; in most cases it appears to be the product of METAMORPHISM. By far the chief asbestos-producing country is Canada; other important producers are the USSR, Rhodesia, Swaziland, the Republic of South Africa, Cyprus, and the United States. Canadian asbestos is mostly chrysotile. South African asbestos, found chiefly in Cape Prov., is largely amosite and crocidolite. In the United States, chrysotile asbestos is produced mainly in Arizona and Vermont. Asbestos is mined both in open quarries and underground. After being crushed, dried, and screened to remove the fibers from the ore, it is graded and sold to manufacturers. The chief products made from it include asbestos yarns and ropes, pipe covering, brake linings, fire-fighting equipment, cloth, shingles, millboard, and plaster and plasterboard. Particles of asbestos are released into the atmosphere by human activity—e.g., when brakes are applied, microscopic asbestos particles are rubbed off the brake linings; larger, visible particles of asbestos are released when asbestos insulation is applied by a spray gun during building construction. Studies have shown that asbestos particles may be carcinogenic. See D. V. Rosato, *Asbestos: Its Industrial Applications* (1959); J. L. Gillson, *Industrial Minerals and Rocks* (1960).

Asbjørnsen, Peter Christian (pä'tər krēs'tyän äs'-byörnsən), 1812–85, Norwegian folklorist, writer, and naturalist. *Norwegian Folk Stories* (4 vol., 1841–44), which he collected with the poet Jørgen MOE, his friend from school days, was acclaimed throughout Europe for its contribution to comparative folklore and literature. In 1845 he published the first series of his *Norwegian Fairy Stories and Folk Legends.* English translations of his works include *Popular Tales from the Norse* (tr. 1858) and *Fairy Tales from the Far North* (tr. 1897). Asbjørnsen was a forester for many years and wrote numerous scholarly papers on the natural sciences.

Asbury, Francis (ăz'bərē, -bĕ-), 1745–1816, Methodist bishop in America, b. England. The Wesleyan conference in London sent him in 1771 as a missionary to America, where he promoted the growth of the CIRCUIT RIDER system that proved so eminently suited to frontier conditions. His powerful preaching, his skill in winning converts, and his mastery of organization had, by the end of the Revolution, established Asbury as the leader of American Methodism. In 1784, John Wesley ordained Dr. Thomas Coke as superintendent of the societies in America; Asbury was to be associate superintendent. At the American conference held that year, however, Asbury was the dominating figure and was made superintendent. He then assumed the title of bishop and took steps to institute a centralized church government. Although tormented by ill health, he maintained personal supervision of the expanding church, traveling on horseback over 5,000 mi (8,047 km) each year and strongly entrenching Methodism over the entire area of the new nation. His journal is valuable for its account of contemporary society as well as of his personal life. See his journal and letters (3 vol., 1958); biography by L. C. Rudolf (1966).

Asbury Park, city (1970 pop. 16,533), Monmouth co., E N.J., on the Atlantic coast; inc. 1897. It is a popular resort with a noted beach, boardwalk, convention hall, and auditorium. The steamship *Morro Castle,* which caught fire at sea in Sept., 1934, was grounded there and continued to burn, with the loss of 125 lives.

Ascalon: see ASHQELON, Israel.

Ascension, island, 34 sq mi (88 sq km), in the S Atlantic, NW of St. Helena and belonging to the British St. Helena colony. Ascension is volcanic and rocky with little vegetation, but it supports considerable livestock (sea turtles, rabbits, wild goats, and partridges), much of which was brought in by the nonindigenous population. The United States maintains a missile and satellite tracking station. Discovered by the Portuguese João da Nova in 1501, Ascension was taken by the British in 1815 and used as a naval station. In 1922 it was made a dependency of St. Helena. Georgetown is the main settlement on the island.

Ascension, name usually given to the departure of Jesus from earth as related in the Gospels according to Mark (16) and Luke (24) and in Acts 1.1–11. The annual commemoration of this is one of the principal feasts in most Christian churches. **Ascension Day,** as it is called, occurs on the 40th day after Easter, being the Thursday of the sixth week of Easter. In early English usage this festival was known as Holy Thursday.

Ascension Island, Caroline Islands: see PONAPE.

Ascensius, Jodocus Badius: see BADIUS, JODOCUS.

asceticism (əsĕt'Ĭsĭzəm), rejection of the world and bodily pleasures through sustained self-denial and self-mortification, with the objective of strengthening spiritual life. Asceticism has been common in Hinduism, Islam, Judaism, and Christianity: all of these have special ascetic cults. It is also known in Buddhism and in other religions. The most common and least severe ascetic practice is prolonged FASTING, used for many purposes—to produce visions, as among the Crow Indians; to mourn the dead, as among various African peoples; and to sharpen spiritual awareness, as among the early Christian saints, such as St. Simeon Stylites. More extreme forms have been flagellation (see FLAGELLANTS) and self-mutilation, usually intended to propitiate or reach accord with a god. Thus the priests of Cybele practiced self-castration. Asceticism has been associated with taboo in primitive societies and in such well-developed religions as Zoroastrianism and Manichaeism. In Greece the Cynics preached the ascetic life. The imposed rules of self-denial in MONASTICISM, both Eastern and Western, are considered rules of austerity rather than asceticism, although individuals may adopt ascetic practices beyond the monastic rules. See ESSENES; FAKIR; HERMIT; RECHABITES. See Owen Chadwick, ed., *Western Asceticism* (1958).

Asch, Sholem or **Shalom** (shō'ləm ăsh, shä'ləm), 1880–1957, Jewish novelist and playwright, b. Poland. He first came to the United States in 1909, was naturalized in 1920, and lived in various parts of Europe and the United States. He settled in Israel in 1956. One of the most widely known Yiddish writers, he won his first success with the play *The God of Vengeance,* produced by Max Reinhardt in Berlin in 1910 and given in many languages and places since then. Among his works available in English translations are the novels *Mottke the Thief* (1917), *Uncle Moses* (1920), *Three Cities* (1933), *The War Goes On* (1935), *The Nazarene* (1939), *The Apostle* (1943), *One Destiny* (1945), *East River* (1946), *Mary* (1949), *Salvation* (1951), *Moses* (1951), *A Passage in the Night* (1953), and *The Prophet* (1955). His two collections of short stories and novelettes are *Children of Abraham* (1942) and *Tales of My People* (1948). Asch's writings often depict Jewish life in Europe and in the United States, and later works reflect the common spiritual heritage of Jews and Christians. Several of his plays were very successful in the Yiddish theater in New York City.

Asch: see AŠ, Czechoslovakia.

Aschaffenburg (äshä'fənbo͝ork), city (1970 pop. 55,193), Bavaria, S central West Germany, on the Main River. Its manufactures include clothing, machinery, precision and optical instruments, and colored paper. Once the location of a Roman garrison and later of a Frankish castle, Aschaffenburg passed to the archbishopric of Mainz in the 10th cent. The imperial diet met there in 1474. It changed hands several times during the Thirty Years War (1618–48) and was stormed in 1672 by the French marshal Henri Turenne. It passed to Bavaria in 1814. Noteworthy buildings include a 12th-century church and a 17th-century castle.

Ascham, Roger (ăs'kəm), 1515–68, English humanist and scholar, b. Yorkshire. Ascham was a major intellectual figure of the early Tudor period. His *Toxophilus* (1545), an essay on archery, proved him a master of English prose; in it he urged the importance of physical recreation for students and scholars. The essay won him the favor of Henry VIII, and Ascham became tutor (1548–50) to Princess Elizabeth. He seems to have been largely responsible for her love of the classics and her proficiency in Greek. As a member of a diplomatic mission Ascham spent several years on the Continent, in contact with other scholars, and in 1553 was appointed Latin secretary to Queen Mary. He continued as secretary and private tutor to Elizabeth I after Mary's death. *The Scholemaster* (1570), his treatise on the teaching of Latin, urged the use of the double translation method. Dr. Johnson's life of Ascham (1761), included in many editions of Ascham's collected works, is a classic. See W. F. Phelps, *Roger Ascham and John Sturm* (1879); study by L. V. Ryan (1963).

Aschelminthes (ăsk-hĕlmĭn'thēz), large phylum of loosely related, wormlike organisms of extremely varied structure and habits. All are covered by a noncellular coat, or cuticle, and have a pseudocoelom, i.e., a fluid-filled cavity separating the body wall from the gut but lacking a peritoneal lining. In many species the digestive, excretory, and reproductive systems join in a cloaca, or discharge chamber, near the posterior end. Many aschelminths also show cell constancy, a condition in which each organ of the adult contains the precise number of cells characteristic of the species.

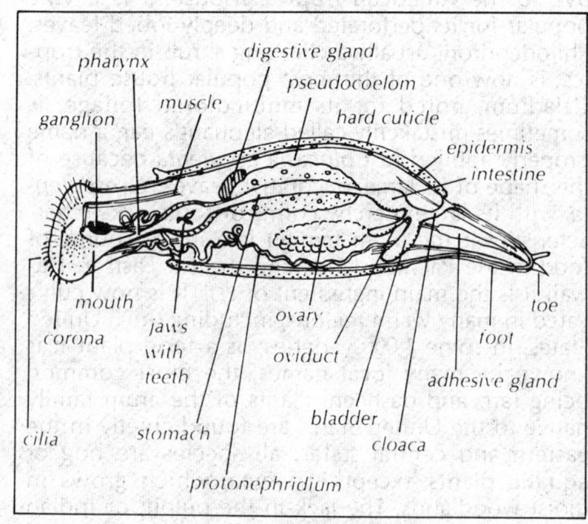

Internal anatomy of a female rotifer, representative of the phylum Aschelminthes

Class Rotifera. Rotifers are predominantly free-living, microscopic, aquatic or semiterrestrial organisms. Each has a head bearing a crown of cilia, the corona, at the anterior end; most rotifers feed with the aid of currents generated by the coronal cilia. A posterior foot, often equipped with two or three toes, contains adhesive glands permitting temporary attachment to objects. Unique grinding jaws are found in the pharynx, and an esophagus, stomach, and intestine can be distinguished. The excretory system consists of ciliated cells, called flame cells, that move collected liquids into two coiled tubes called protonephridia; these tubes open into a contractile bladder. The reproductive system is simple, consisting in the female of ovary, yolk gland, and oviduct, and in the male of testis and sperm duct. The intestine, bladder, and reproductive ducts unite to form a cloaca. Rotifers, of which there are about 2,000 known species, are widely distributed in freshwater and marine habitats; they also live in the soil, in mosses, and associated with lichens on rocks and trees. A few are parasitic. Most feed on bacteria, algal cells, small protozoa, or organic detritus. As a rule, only female rotifers are seen; in some species the males have never been observed. Eggs develop parthenogenetically, i.e., without fertilization, to produce only females. When conditions are unfavorable, haploid male and female eggs are produced; these can unite to form fertilized eggs that have heavy shells and remain dormant until more favorable conditions occur. Many species can survive in a dry form for long periods of time, emerging from a dormant state and becoming active when moisture is available.

Class Gastrotricha. Gastrotrichs are microscopic organisms that live in ponds, lakes, or seashore sands. Most have a definite head, a narrower neck, and a trunk that ends in a pair of projections, or rami, containing adhesive glands. The external surface is covered with bristles or plates except on the ventral (under) surface, which is ciliated. The digestive tract consists of a muscular pharynx and a straight stomach-intestine. In freshwater forms flagellated cells called solenocytes open into two protonephridial (excretory) tubules. Details of the reproductive system are not well known, but the excretory, reproductive, and digestive systems do not unite to form a cloaca. Although some gastrotrichs are hermaphroditic, all freshwater forms are females. They produce eggs that develop without fertilization, and some produce thin-walled and thick-walled eggs, much like rotifers. Most gastrotrichs have a low reproductive potential; since they are never very abundant, they are not influential in their habitats. They feed on bacteria, algae, protozoa, and organic detritus.

Class Kinorhyncha. Containing about 100 species of tiny worms, the class Kinorhyncha is widely distributed in tidal mudflats or shallow, muddy-bottomed marine habitats. The kinorhynch body is divided into 13 or 14 segments, each covered with a heavy cuticle and equipped with characteristic spines. The first segment is a bristly head that can be protruded or withdrawn. Using its head as an anchor, the creature ploughs through the mud pulling its body after it. Kinorhynchs have a relatively complex digestive system, a protonephridial (excretory) system, and a relatively simple reproductive system; no cloaca is formed. Sexes are separate, and the young hatch with three segments, new ones being added as they grow. They feed on mud, extracting its organic content. Nothing is known of their ecological importance.

Class Nematoda. Largest of the aschelminths, the class Nematoda contains thousands of known species, and many more predicted species. Nematodes live in the soil and in other terrestrial habitats as well as in freshwater and marine environments. Many are parasites of plants and animals, including man. The elongated, unsegmented nematode body is covered by a cuticle. The head is poorly developed; either mouth or pharynx may contain parts used to pierce or wound plant or animal tissues. The straight stomach-intestine ends in a short rectum. Nematodes have a unique excretory system consisting, in simpler species, of one or two one-celled glands called renette cells and, in more highly specialized forms, of longitudinal excretory ducts. The excretory physiology of the class is not well understood. The reproductive system is complex, and many parasitic species have a very high reproductive potential. Some nematodes produce live young, the eggs having matured in the female reproductive tract; but most release eggs, the larvae of which molt one or more times before reaching maturity. Nematodes, found in the soil as well as in decaying vegetable and animal matter, are often very abundant. Many of the soil-inhabiting types attack plant roots, making them economically significant. Nematodes are among the most successful of invertebrates in terms of their individual numbers and the number of species. Among the important human parasites are *Ascaris* (roundworms); hookworms; microfilaria, which live in the blood or in the lymphatic system; and *Trichinella,* whose larvae invade muscle tissue.

Class Nematomorpha. The nematomorphs, or horsehair worms, are very slender, elongated creatures found in ponds and streams, whose larvae live as parasites. They emerge as adults for a brief time, then mate and die. Adults are simplified externally and internally; they have no excretory or circulatory systems and only a vestigial digestive tract. The female produces long strings of eggs. After hatching, the larva penetrates any convenient aquatic animal, but its development stops until it has found its way into an appropriate host, typically an insect. The adult nematomorph emerges when the host is in or near water; it molts once after emerging and takes up its brief adult existence. A few species are marine and live as larvae in crabs or shrimps.

Aschersleben (ä'shərslā"bən), city (1970 pop. 37,196), Halle district, W East Germany. An industrial city, it manufactures machine tools, chemicals, iron and steel, and woolen goods. There are lignite, salt, and potash mines nearby. Aschersleben was probably founded in the 11th cent. and passed to Prussia in 1813.

ascidian: see CHORDATA; TUNICATE.

Asclepius (ăsklē'pēəs), Lat. *Aesculapius* (ĕs"kəlā'pēəs), legendary Greek physician; son of Apollo and Coronis. His first teacher was the wise centaur Chiron. When he became so skillful in healing that he could revive the dead, Zeus killed him. Apollo persuaded Zeus to make Asclepius the god of medicine. The worship of Asclepius is believed to have originated in Thessaly. Temples were built to him at Epidaurus, Cos, Pergamum, and many other places, where treatments, including massage and baths, were given to the sick. The serpent and the cock were sacred to Asclepius. People who claimed descent from him and those who followed his teachings were known as Asclepiads.

Ascoli Piceno (ä'skōlē pēchĕ'nō), city (1971 pop. 55,053), capital of Ascoli Piceno prov., Marche region, central Italy, at the confluence of the Castellano and Tronto rivers. It is the market for a rich agricultural area. A Roman settlement with extensive Roman remains, the city became a free republic in the 12th cent. and passed to papal control in the 15th cent.

Ascomycete: see FUNGI.

ascorbic acid: see VITAMIN.

Ascot (ăs'kət), village, Berkshire, S central England. The famous horse races instituted by Queen Anne in 1711 are held annually in June on Ascot Heath.

Asculum (ă'skyŏŏləm), ancient town, Apulia, SE Italy, 18 mi (29 km) S of Foggia, on a branch of the Appian Way. Here Pyrrhus won a hard-fought battle against the Romans in 279 B.C. Modern Ascoli Satriano is in the region. The name also appears as Ausculum.

Asenath (ăs'ənăth), Poti-pherah's daughter, the Egyptian wife of Joseph, mother of Manasseh and Ephraim. Gen. 41.45,50–52; 46.20. Her marriage is the subject of Joseph and Asenath, one of the PSEUDEPIGRAPHA.

Asenovgrad (äsänôv'grät), city (1968 est. pop. 38,100), S central Bulgaria. It is a commercial center, with wineries and tobacco manufactures. An ancient Bulgarian stronghold, it became a trade center under Turkish rule (15th–19th cent.). Asenovgrad has several 16th-century churches and the ruins of a 13th-century castle. The city was formerly known as Stanimaka.

asepsis: see ANTISEPTIC.

Aser (ā'sər), variant of ASHER.

Asfa Wossen (äs'fä wŏŏs'sən), 1916–, Ethiopian crown prince. He was proclaimed crown prince and heir shortly after his father, Haile Selassie, became emperor of Ethiopia in 1930. In Dec., 1960, he was placed on the throne briefly during a coup against his father aimed at establishing a constitutional monarchy. He was absolved of all connection with the coup, which was immediately put down. Partially paralyzed by a stroke in 1972, he was living in Switzerland when Haile Selassie was deposed by the military in 1974.

Asgard (ăs'gärd), in Norse mythology, home of the gods, also known as Aesir. It consisted of luxurious palaces and halls, in which the gods (whose chief was Odin) dwelled, conferred, and banqueted. One of the most beautiful of these halls was VALHALLA. Entrance to Asgard could be gained only by crossing the rainbow bridge Bifrost, which was guarded by Heimdall, the watchman of the gods. See also GERMANIC RELIGION.

Ásgiersson, Ásgeir (äs'kĕr äs'kĕrsôn), 1894–1972, Icelandic statesman, president of Iceland (1952–68). He was a member of the Icelandic parliament from 1923 to 1952, headed the government bureau of education (1926–31, 1934–38), and served as minister of finance (1931–34) and prime minister (1932–34). He was (1946–52) governor of the International Monetary Fund. In 1952 he was elected president of Iceland and was reelected in 1956, 1960, and 1964.

ash, in botany, any plant of the genus *Fraxinus* of the family Oleaceae (OLIVE family), trees and shrubs mainly of north temperate regions. The ashes are characterized by small clusters of greenish flowers and by fruits with long "wings" to aid in wind dispersal. The most valuable of the species used for hardwood timber is the white ash (*F. americana*), ranging from Nova Scotia to Minnesota and Texas. Its strong, durable wood is used for sporting goods, furniture, tool handles, and oars. The bark of the blue ash (*F. quadrangulata*) yields a blue dye; the Mediterranean flowering ash (*F. ornus*) is the source of commercial MANNA. The name flowering ash is also applied to a shrubby species (*F. cuspidata*) of the California canyon chaparral and to the fringe tree (genus *Chionanthus* of the same family) of North America and China. The MOUNTAIN ASH and PRICKLY ASH are not true ashes. Ashes are classified in the division MAGNOLIOPHYTA, class Magnoliopsida, order Scrophulariales, family Oleaceae.

ash, in chemistry, solid residue of combustion. The chemical compositon of an ash depends on that of the substance burned. Wood ash contains metal carbonates (e.g., potassium carbonate) and oxides formed from metals originally compounded in the wood. Coal ash usually has a high content of minerals and is sometimes contaminated with rock; during combustion the mineral matter may become partially fused, forming cinders or clinker. Bone ash is largely made up of calcium phosphate. Seaweed ash (called kelp or varec) contains sodium carbonate, potassium carbonate, and iodine that can be extracted. Fly ash is very fine ash produced during the combustion of many materials.

Ashan (ā'shăn), unidentified town of S Palestine, perhaps the same as CHOR-ASHAN, Joshua 15.42; 19.7; 1 Chron. 4.32; 6.59.

Ashanti (äshăn'tē) or **Asante,** historic and present-day administrative region, central Ghana, W Africa. The region is the source of much of Ghana's cocoa. It is inhabited by the Ashanti, an Akan, matrilineal people, who constitute one of Ghana's major ethnic groups. Before the 13th cent., Akan peoples migrated into the forest belt of present-day Ghana and established small states in the hilly country in the neighborhood of modern Kumasi. By the late 17th cent. the states had been welded by the Oyoko clan into the Ashanti confederation, with the capital at Kumasi and the Oyoko chieftain as king. After subduing neighboring states the confederation came into conflict with the British settlements on the coast, although treaties of friendship had been negotiated in 1817 and 1820. A series of Anglo-Ashanti wars in the 19th cent. culminated in the defeat of the confederation (1896) and the annexation of Ashanti (1901) to the British Gold Coast colony. The British exiled the ruling king, Pempeh I, to the Seychelles and, in spite of great resistance, broke up the confederation. It was restored in 1935. In 1945 the Ashanti were given representation in the executive and legislative councils of the Gold Coast. They supported an unsuccessful attempt to give Ghana a federal constitution in 1954 and resisted the centralizing measures of the Nkrumah government. The Ashanti are noted for the quality of their gold work and their colorful kente cloth, and were long famous for the gold-encrusted stool that was the symbol of their sovereignty. See R. A. Lystad, *The Ashanti* (1958, repr. 1968).

Ashbea (ăshbē'ə), name of either a person or a place. 1 Chron. 4.21.

Ashbel (ăsh'bĕl), son of Benjamin. Gen. 46.21; Num. 26.38; 1 Chron. 8.1.

Ashbery, John, 1927–, American poet and art critic, b. Rochester, N.Y., grad. Harvard, 1949, M.A. Columbia, 1950. His poems are experimental, with logical narrative and a strong visual sense. Among his volumes of poetry are *Some Trees* (1956), *The Double Dream of Spring* (1970), and *Three Poems* (1972). He has also written a play, *The Compromise* (1960). Since 1960, Ashbery has been art critic for the Paris edition of the *Herald Tribune.* He is also editor of the quarterly *Art and Literature.*

Ashburton, Alexander Baring, 1st **Baron:** see BARING, family.

Ashburton, John Dunning, 1st **Baron:** see DUNNING, JOHN, 1ST BARON ASHBURTON.

ashcan school: see EIGHT, THE.

Ashchenaz: see ASHKENAZ.

Ashdod [Heb.,=stronghold], city (1972 pop. 40,500), SW Israel, on the Mediterranean Sea. It is Israel's leading port after Haifa. Construction is Ashdod's main industry; its manufactures include synthetic fibers, woolen yarn, and knitted goods. Nearby is the site of ancient Ashdod, which was settled as early as the Bronze Age. Conquered by the Philistines in the 12th cent. B.C., it became an important city of the Philistine Pentapolis and a center for the worship of Dagon. The city was later ruled by Judah, Egypt, and Assyria. The Jews of Ashdod had been considered idolatrous by other Jews since the time of the return to Jerusalem (6th cent. B.C.), but they were cleansed by Judas Maccabeus in 163 B.C. Jonathan (see JONATHAN **15**), the brother of Judas Maccabeus, took the city in 148 B.C. and destroyed the temple of Dagon. Ashdod was revived by the Romans and was an early Christian center. (1 Sam. 5.1; Joshua 15.47; 2 Chron. 26.6; Neh. 4.7, 13.23; Isa. 20.1; Jer. 25.20; 1 Mac. 5.68, 10.84; Acts 8.40.) The first modern Israeli settlement in Ashdod was made in 1955, and in 1965 the deepwater port was completed.

Ashdoth-pisgah (ăsh'dŏth-pĭz'gə), unidentified portion of Mt. Pisgah. The term occurs three times in AV, translated in RV "slopes of Pisgah." Deut. 3.17; Joshua 12.3; 13.20. The same Hebrew expression is translated in Deut. 4.49 "springs of Pisgah" in AV, but RV translates it again as "slopes of Pisgah."

Ashe, Arthur Robert, 1943–, American tennis player, b. Richmond, Va. The first black American male to reach prominence in tennis, Ashe received a tennis scholarship from UCLA in 1962. In 1968 he was the first black U.S. Open champion, and in 1970 he won the Australian Open. Denied a visa by South Africa on racial grounds in 1970, Ashe forced the issue, appearing before the United Nations and urging the World Tennis Union to expel South Africa because of its apartheid policy. Ashe ultimately competed in South Africa in 1973.

Ashe, John, c.1720–1781, American Revolutionary general, b. Brunswick co., N.C. Speaker of the colonial assembly (1762–65) and a leader of the opposition to the Stamp Act, he was important to the patriot cause in North Carolina. On March 3, 1778, Ashe, a major general commanding North Carolina troops, was defeated by British regulars at Briar Creek, a tributary of the Savannah. The British hold on Georgia was thereby strengthened.

Asheboro (ăsh'bərə), town (1970 pop. 10, 797), seat of Randolph co., central N.C., in the Piedmont; inc. 1796. Its manufactures include hosiery, textiles, clothing, furniture, flashlight batteries, and electric blankets. A prehistoric Keyauwee Indian burial ground is nearby.

Ashendene Press, founded in 1895 at Ashendene, Hertfordshire, England, by Sir C. H. St. John Hornby and moved in 1899 to Chelsea, London. It was a leader (with the KELMSCOTT PRESS and the DOVES PRESS) in the 19th-century revival of fine English printing. Its edition of Dante (1909) is considered an achievement comparable to the Kelmscott Chaucer of William MORRIS. The Subiaco type used by the Ashendene Press was designed by Sir Emery Walker and S. C. Cockerell from an early Italian typeface. The Ashendene Press, which set all of its editions by hand, issued 40 books in the years from 1895 to 1915 and from 1920 to 1935. See Will Ransom, *Kelmscott, Doves, and Ashendene* (1952).

Asher (ăsh'ər) [Heb., = happy, Gen. 30.12,13]. **1** Tribe of Israel. Its eponym was Jacob's eighth son. It occupied the northwestern part of Palestine, and its position laid Asher open to influence from other nations and attacks by them. It seems to have become insignificant early in Jewish history. The name occurs in Egyptian inscriptions. Gen. 30; Deut. 33.24; Joshua 19.24–31; Judges 5.17,18. Aser: Luke 2.36; Rev. 7.6. **2** Unidentified place near Shechem. Joshua 17.7.

Asherah (ăsh'ərə) or **Asheroth** (-rŏth), Canaanite fertility goddess and the symbol that represented her. After the prophets denounced her cult, it was abolished among the Hebrews. By an ancient mistake AV translates the name as "groves." Judges 3.7; 1 Kings 15.13–14; 18.19; 2 Kings 21.7; 23.4; 2 Chron. 15.16; Jer. 17.2.

Asheville, city (1970 pop. 57,681), seat of Buncombe co., W N.C., on the French Broad and the Swannanoa rivers and on a plateau in the Blue Ridge Mts.; inc. 1797. Located near Great Smoky Mountains National Park and Pisgah National Forest, Asheville is a popular mountain resort. Tourism is a major business. The city is also a financial, distribution, transportation, and retail center for W North Carolina; tobacco is processed and marketed, and lumber, electronic equipment, textiles, clothing, and paper, food, and glass products are made in Asheville. Local artisans weave wool and make pottery. Asheville's many points of interest include the magnificent Vanderbilt estate, Biltmore; Colburn Mineral Museum; and numerous recreational and scenic attractions. The writer Thomas Wolfe was born and lived in Asheville; his home is a public memorial. The Univ. of North Carolina at Asheville is in the city.

Ashi or **Asser, Rab** (ä'shē, äs'ər), 352–428, Hebrew scholar of Babylon. He headed the Jewish academy at Sura and devoted his life to editing the Talmud, aided by many of the distinguished scholars he had attracted to Sura. The work was completed by his pupil Rabina II c.500.

Ashikaga (ä"shēkä'gä), city (1970 pop. 156,004), Tochigi prefecture, central Honshu, Japan. An old silk-weaving center, it is famous for its spinning and silk textile industries. The city is also the ancestral home of the Ashikaga shoguns (1336–1568). It has an ancient school (probably founded 9th cent.), which is known for its vast library of Chinese classics. Ashikaga's 12th-century temple is treasured by the Japanese.

Ashima (ăsh'īmə, əshī'mə), god whose cult flourished in Hamath. 2 Kings 17.30.

Ashingdon, battle of: see ASSANDUN, BATTLE OF.

Ashiya (ăshē'yä), city (1970 pop. 70,938), Hyogo prefecture, W central Honshu, Japan, on Osaka Bay. It is a residential and industrial suburb of Osaka.

Ashkelon: see ASHQELON, Israel.

Ashkenaz (ăsh'kĕnăz"), eponym of a people perhaps localized in Armenia. He was grandson of Japheth. Gen. 10.3. Aschchenaz: 1 Chron. 1.6; Jer. 51.27. In modern times the term **Ashkenazim** refers to the German Jews as distinguished from the Sephardim, the Jews of Spain and Portugal.

Ashkhabad (ăsh'kəbăd", ăsh"kəbäd', Rus. əshkhəbät'), city (1970 pop. 253,000), capital of the Turkmen Soviet Socialist Republic, S Central Asian USSR, on the Trans-Caspian RR. The city has textile, motion picture, and machine-building industries. Ashkhabad was founded in 1881 as a fortress. An earthquake in 1948 virtually destroyed the city, which stands in a major fault zone. The Turkmen Academy of Sciences is in Ashkhabad.

Ashland. 1 Uninc. town (1970 pop. 14,810), Alameda co., W Calif. **2** Industrial city (1970 pop. 29,245), Boyd co., E Ky., on terraces along the Ohio River near the influx of the Big Sandy; settled 1786, inc. 1854. In a region yielding coal, clay, natural gas, and timber, it is a river and railroad shipping point, with large repair yards. The city is part of a tri-state metropolitan area (embracing also Ironton, Ohio, and Huntington, W. Va.) that is known for its metallurgical industries. In addition to iron and steel, Ashland's many manufactures include coke, refined oil, chemicals, leather products, clothing, and mining equipment. A junior college is located there. **3** City (1970 pop. 19,872), seat of Ashland co., N Ohio, in a farm area; inc. 1844. Pumps, spray equipment, rubber products, adhesives, printed materials, animal medications, and machine tools are among its manufactures. Ashland College is there. **4** City (1970 pop. 12,342), Jackson co., SW Oregon, near the Calif. line; inc. 1874. A lumbering center and a processing and shipping point for an irrigated dairy, farm, and orchard area, it is also a resort with mineral springs. It is surrounded on three sides by the Rogue River National Forest. Southern Oregon College, a college of art, and a museum of natural history are located in the city. A Shakespeare festival is held each spring and summer.

Ashley, Anthony Ashley Cooper, Baron: see SHAFTESBURY, ANTHONY ASHLEY COOPER, 1ST EARL OF.

Ashley, William Henry, c.1778–1838, American fur trader and politician, b. Virginia. In 1820 he was elected lieutenant governor of Missouri. He sent fur-trading expeditions up the Missouri River to the Yellowstone in 1822 and 1823; the parties included Jedediah Smith and other MOUNTAIN MEN. A detachment of the second party under Thomas Fitzpatrick went through South Pass to the Green River valley. In 1825, Ashley accompanied another expedition that crossed from the upper Platte to Green River and began its exploration. In its valley he held the first rendezvous of the mountain fur traders and trappers. In 1826 he led an expedition that reached the vicinity of Great Salt Lake. Having acquired an ample fortune, he retired from the fur trade and devoted himself to politics. He was defeated for the governorship of Missouri in 1824 and 1836, but from 1831 to 1837 was U.S. Representative and an able advocate of measures favorable to Western development. See H. C. Dale, *The Ashley-Smith Explorations* (1918); Bernard De Voto, *Across the Wide Missouri* (1948).

Ashmodai (ăsh"mōdā'ī), DEMON, probably ASMODEUS.

Ashmole, Elias (ăsh'mōl), 1617–92, English archaeologist and antiquary. He made exhaustive antiquarian studies, especially *The Institution, Laws and Ceremonies of the Order of the Garter* (1672) and *The Antiquities of Berkshire* (3 vol., 1719). In 1677 he donated to Oxford Univ. a collection of curiosities, including his own contributions and those bequeathed to him by a friend. His gift formed the nucleus of the **Ashmolean Museum** (ăshmō'lēən), the first such public institution in England. He later donated his library to Oxford, and the whole was housed in a building erected by Sir Christopher Wren. The collection is now in a 19th-century building and includes European works of art from medieval to present times as well as Oriental works. See his *Autobiographical and Historical Notes and Correspondence,* ed. by C. H. Josten (1967).

Ashmun, Jehudi, 1794–1828, U.S. agent to Liberia, b. Champlain, N.Y. After entering the Congregationalist ministry and spending a few years in teaching and editorial work, he was sent by the AMERICAN COLONIZATION SOCIETY to Liberia. He found the colony ridden with fever, short of supplies, and threatened by native attack. Ashmun with a handful of men repulsed the attacks, and for the next six years, despite severe hardships, he built up the colony. He wrote *History of the American Colony in Liberia from December 1821 to 1823* (1826). See biography by R. R. Gurley (1835, repr. 1971).

Ashmunayn, Egypt: see HERMOPOLIS MAGNA.

Ashnah (ăsh'nə), two unidentified towns of Palestine, W of Jerusalem. Joshua 15.33,43.

Ashokan Reservoir (əshō'kən), 13 sq mi (34 sq km), SE N.Y., completed 1912. It is supplied by the Esopus and Schoharie watersheds and provides part of New York City's water supply. Water is carried to the city via the 92-mi-long (148-km) **Catskill Aqueduct.** Completed in 1917, the aqueduct delivers water to Kensico Reservoir near White Plains and Hillview Reservoir in Yonkers, from where it is distributed to parts of New York City through tunnels cut in solid rock. The aqueduct passes 1,114 ft (340 m) under the Hudson River at Storm King Mt. A steel pipe under the Narrows of New York Bay carries water to Silver Lake, Staten Island, 120 mi (193 km) from Ashokan Reservoir.

Ashpenaz (ăsh'pēnăz), Nebuchadnezzar's chief eunuch. Dan. 1.3.

Ashqelon (ăsh'kəlŏn), city (1972 pop. 43,100), SW Israel, on the Mediterranean Sea. It is a beach resort in an area of citrus groves and cotton plantations. Ashqelon's industries process agricultural products and manufacture cement, wood products, automobile parts, electronic equipment, and watches. Nearby is the site of ancient Ashqelon, or Ashkelon, whose history dates back to the 3d millenium B.C. It was a trade center and port and a seat of worship of the goddess Astarte. Ancient Ashqelon was conquered by the PHILISTINES in the late 12th cent. B.C., completely rebuilt, and made one of the cities of the Philistine pentapolis. (Judges 14.19; Jer. 25.20; Amos 1.8. Askelon: 1 Sam. 6.17. Eshkalon: Joshua 13.3.) Ashkelon flourished under the Greeks and Romans; HEROD, believed to have been born there, greatly enlarged the city. It was taken by the Arabs in A.D. 638, conquered by the Crusaders in 1153 and occupied by RICHARD I in 1191, and completely destroyed by Muslims in 1270. An Israeli settlement was established there in 1948. In 1955 the modern city of Ashqelon was founded when Afridar, a town established by South African Jews in 1952, and Migdal, a former Arab town, were merged. A national park in Ashqelon includes Greek and Roman ruins and the remains of ancient synagogues. A Roman tomb (3d cent.) decorated with frescoes, the ruins of a Byzantine church, and a wall built by Crusaders are also in the city.

Ashtabula (ăsh"təbyōō'lə), city (1970 pop. 24,313), Ashtabula co., NE Ohio, on Lake Erie at the mouth of the Ashtabula River; settled c.1801 by New Englanders, inc. as a village 1831, as a city 1891. It is a port of entry on the St. Lawrence Seaway and receives large amounts of iron ore bound for Pittsburgh. Coal is also shipped. Ashtabula manufactures automobile parts, chemicals, fiberglass products, farm tools, clothing, and electric motors. A campus of Kent State Univ. is in the city.

Ashtaroth (ăsh'tərŏth). **1** Hebrew form of the name of the goddess ASTARTE. **2** City of Bashan, the modern Tell Ashtarah (Syria), E of the Jordan. Joshua 9.10; 12.4; 13.12,31; 1 Chron. 6.71. Astaroth: Deut. 1.4. Beesh-terah, an otherwise unidentified town, was probably the same. Joshua 21.27.

Ashteroth Karnaim (ăsh'tērŏth kärnā'īm), place, E of the Jordan. Gen. 14.5. It is possibly the same as Carnaim in 1 Mac. 5.43,44, and Carnion in 2 Mac. 12.21.

Ashton, Sir Frederick, 1906–, British choreographer and dancer, b. Guayaquil, Ecuador. He studied dance in England with Léonide Massine and Marie Rambert and staged his first work there in 1926. He joined what was later to become the Sadler's Wells Ballet (now the Royal Ballet) in 1935 as chief choreographer, and later became associate director and then director of the company. His mature works are noted for their lyricism, quiet charm, and precision. They include abstract ballets, such as *Symphonic Variations* (1946), short dramatic works, such as *Daphnis and Chloë* and *Tiresias* (both 1951), and full-length traditional ballets, such as *Cinderella* (1948), *Sylvia* (1952), *Ondine* (1958), and *The Dream* (1964). He has also appeared as a dancer in comedy and character roles.

Ashton-under-Lyne, municipal borough (1971 pop. 48,865), Lancashire, NW England, on the Tame River. Its industries include cotton spinning, weaving, and dyeing; coal mining; and the manufacture of diesel, gas, and oil engines. In 1974, it became part of the new metropolitan county of Greater Manchester.

Ashton-Warner, Sylvia, 1905–, British teacher and novelist, b. Stratford, New Zealand. For years a teacher of Maori children, Ashton-Warner developed many stimulating educational methods about which she wrote in the treatise *Teacher* (1963) and her autobiography *Myself* (1967). Her success as a teacher was the result of her thorough commitment to her work and to her conviction that communication, mutual response, is the most important aspect of teaching. *Spearpoint: Teacher in America* (1972) recounts her experiences teaching in an experimental school in the United States. Ashton-Warner's novels are written in an exotic, rather florid style and usually concern strong, passionate women. They include *Spinster* (1958), *Incense to Idols* (1960), *Bell Call* (1964), *Greenstone* (1967), and *Three* (1970).

Ashtoreth (ăsh'tōrĕth), Hebrew form of ASTARTE.

Ashur (ăsh'ər), founder of Tekoa. 1 Chron. 2.24; 4.5.

Ashur (ăsh'ŏŏr), chief god of Assyria. Important as a god of war, he became the omniscient king of the pantheon, replacing the Babylonian Marduk. His name appears variously as Asur, Assur, Ashshur, Asshur, and Ashir.

Ashurbanipal: see ASSURBANIPAL.

Ashurites (ăsh'ərīts), unidentified people mentioned in the Bible. 2 Sam. 2.9. There are two possible interpretations: (1) the Geshurites, as the Vulgate indicates, or (2) the house of Asher.

Ashurnasirpal II (ä'sho͞ornä'zĭrpäl), d. 860? B.C., king of ancient Assyria (884–860? B.C.), also called Ashurnazirpal II and Assurnasirbal II. One of the earliest of the Assyrian conquerors, he gained territory as far west as the Mediterranean. In initiating a system of installing Assyrian governors in conquered lands, Ashurnasirpal helped to create a centralized state. Excavations of the palace and temple built by Ashurnasirpal at CALAH revealed many bas-reliefs portraying the king's conquests in a narrative style. He was succeeded by his son Shalmaneser III.

Ashvath (ăsh'văth), Asherite. 1 Chron. 7.33.

Ash Wednesday, in the Western Church, the first day of LENT, being the seventh Wednesday before Easter. On this day ashes are placed on the foreheads of the faithful to remind them of death, of the sorrow they should feel for their sins, and of the necessity of changing their lives. This practice dates from the early Middle Ages.

Asia, the world's largest continent, 17,139,000 sq mi (44,390,000 sq km), with about 2,044,000,000 people, more than half the world's total population.

Boundaries. Asia's border with Europe—which, geographically, may be regarded as a peninsula of the Eurasian landmass—lies approximately along the Urals, the Ural River, the Caspian Sea, the Caucasus, the Black Sea, the Bosporus and Dardanelles straits, and the Aegean Sea. The connection of Asia with Africa is broken only by the Suez Canal between the Mediterranean Sea and the Red Sea. In the far northeast of Asia, Siberia is separated from North America by the Bering Strait. The continent of Asia is washed on the S by the Gulf of Aden, the Arabian Sea, and the Bay of Bengal; on the E by the South China Sea, East China Sea, Yellow Sea, Sea of Japan, Sea of Okhotsk, and Bering Sea; and on the N by the Arctic Ocean.

Physical Environment. Geologically, Asia consists essentially of ancient Precambrian rocks—the Arabian and Indian peninsulas in the south and the central Siberian plateau in the north—which enclose a central zone of folded ridges. In accordance with this underlying structure, Asia falls into the following major physiographic structures: the northern lowlands covering W central Asia and most of Siberia; the vast central highland zone of high plateaus, rising to c.15,000 ft. (4,570 m) in Tibet and enclosed by some of the world's greatest mountain ranges (the

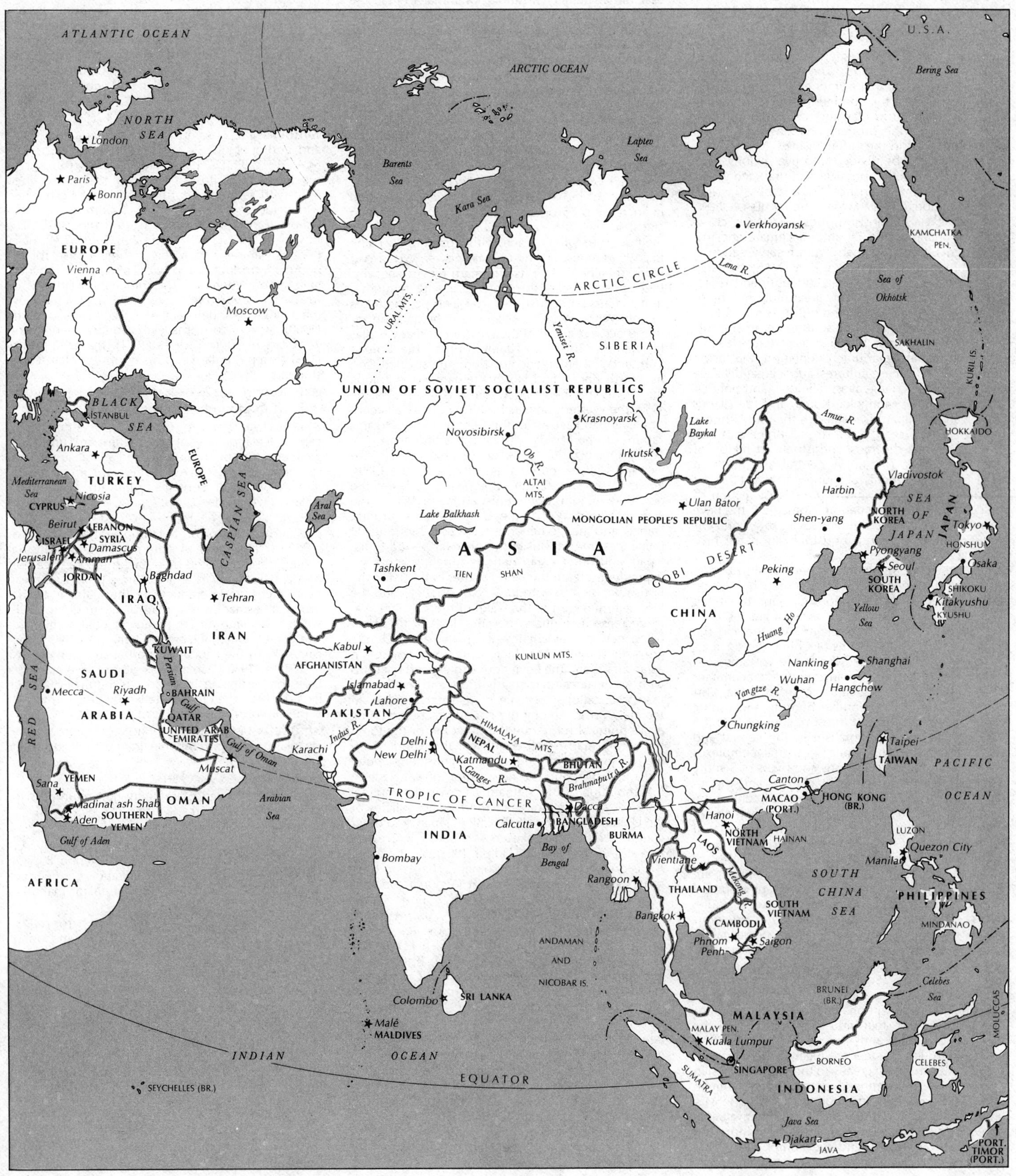

Himalayas, the Karakorum, the Kunlun, the Tien Shan, and the Hindu Kush); the southern peninsular plateaus of India and Arabia, merging, respectively, into the Ganges and Tigris-Euphrates plains; and the lowlands of E Asia, especially in China, which are separated by mountain spurs of the central highland zone. Mt. Everest (29,028 ft/8,848 m), in Nepal, is the world's highest peak; the DEAD SEA (1,292 ft/394 m below sea level) is the world's lowest point. Great peninsulas extend out from the mainland, dividing the oceans into seas and bays, many of them protected by Asia's numerous offshore islands. Asia's rivers, among the longest in the world, generally rise in the high plateaus and break through the great chains toward the peripheral lowlands. They include the Ob, Yenisei, and Lena of Siberia; the Amur, Huang Ho, Yangtze, Si, Mekong, Salween, and Irrawaddy of E and SE Asia; and the Ganges-Brahmaputra, Indus, and Tigris-Euphrates of S and SW Asia. Central Asia has vast areas of interior drainage, including the Amu Darya, Syr Darya, Ili, and Tarim rivers, which empty into inland lakes or disappear into desert sands. The Aral Sea, Lake Baykal, and Lake Balkhash are among the world's largest lakes. Climatically, the continent ranges through all extremes, from torrid heat to arctic cold and from torrential rains (the product of monsoons) to extreme aridity (as in the Tarim Basin).

Regions. Asia can be divided into five regions, each possessing distinctive physical, cultural, economic, and political characteristics. Southwest Asia (Iran and the nations of ASIA MINOR, the FERTILE CRESCENT, and the ARABIAN PENINSULA), long a strategic crossroads, is characterized by an arid climate and irrigated agriculture, great petroleum reserves, and the predominance of Islam. South Asia (Afghanistan and the nations of the Indian subcontinent) is isolated from the rest of Asia by great mountain barriers and was once entirely under British rule. Southeast Asia (the nations of the southeastern peninsula and the East Indian archipelago) is characterized by monsoon climate, maritime orientation, the fusion of Indian and Chinese cultures, and a great diversity of ethnic groups, languages, religions, and politics. East Asia (China, Mongolia, Korea, and the islands of Taiwan and Japan) is located in the mid-latitudes on the Pacific Ocean, has a strong indigenous culture, and forms the most industrialized region of Asia. Soviet Asia (in the W central and northern third of the continent) accounts for about 75% of the area of the USSR and is the largest section of Asia controlled by one nation. Nomadic tribes have been settled and united under Soviet rule, and agricultural settlement and industrialization are progressing steadily.

Population, Economy, and Culture. The distribution of Asia's huge population is governed by climate and topography, with the monsoons and the fertile alluvial plains determining the areas of greatest density. Such are the Ganges plains of India and the Yangtze and northern plains of China, the small alluvial plains of Japan, and the fertile volcanic soils of Java and Indonesia. Urbanization, a concomitant of industrialization, is greatest in Japan, India, China, and Soviet Asia. Primitive hunting and fishing economies prevail in the forest regions of N and S Asia, and nomadic pastoralism in the central and southwestern regions, while industrial complexes are found in the coastal plains and rivers of S and E Asia. Because of extremes in climate and topography, less than 10% of Asia is under cultivation. Rice, by far the most important food crop, is grown for local consumption in the heavily populated countries (e.g., China, India, Bangladesh, and Japan), while countries with smaller populations (Burma, Thailand, Cambodia, and South Vietnam) are generally rice exporters. Other important crops are wheat, soybeans, peanuts, sugarcane, cotton, jute, silk, rubber, and tea. Asia's economy is predominantly agricultural, but regions where power facilities, trained labor, modern transport, and access to raw materials are available have developed industrially. Japan, China, Soviet Asia, India, North and South Korea, Taiwan, and Turkey are distinguished for their industrialization. In most of these countries, an iron and steel industry has grown on the basis of local coal and iron resources; Japan, the world's third largest steel producer, is the major exception. Contributing greatly to the income of Asian countries are vital mineral exports—petroleum in SW Asia, Soviet Asia, and Indonesia and tin in Malaysia, Thailand, and Indonesia. Asia's other valuable mineral exports include manganese from India and chromite from Turkey and the Philippines; China produces great amounts of tungsten and antimony. The development of railroads is greatest in the industrialized countries, with Japan, India, China, and Soviet Asia having the greatest track mileage. Almost two thirds of Asia's indigenous population belongs to the Mongoloid groups. Major religions are Hinduism (in India); Buddhism (in Sri Lanka, Burma, Thailand, Cambodia, and Laos in its purest form; in Tibet and Mongolia as Lamaism, or Tibetan Buddhism; in China as an eclectic mixture with Confucianism and Taoism; in Japan as a mixture with Confucianism and Shinto); Islam (in SW and S Asia, W central Asia, and Indonesia); and Roman Catholicism (in the Philippines and South Vietnam).

Outline of History. Asia was the site of some of the world's oldest civilizations. The empires of Sumeria, Babylonia, Assyria, Media, and Persia and the civilizations of Islam flourished in SW Asia, while in the east the ancient civilizations of India, China, and Japan prospered. Later, nomadic tribes (Huns, Tatars, and Turks) in N and central Asia gave rise to great westward migration. Their tribal, military-state organizations reached their highest form in the 13th–14th cent. under the Mongols, whose court was visited by early European travelers, notably the Italian Marco POLO. The Portuguese explorer Vasco da Gama reached India by sea in 1498, and in N Asia Russian Cossacks crossed Siberia and reached the Pacific by 1640. With the formation of English, French, Dutch, and Portuguese trading companies in the 17th cent., great trade rivalry developed along the coasts of India, SE Asia, and China and resulted in increasing European colonial control of Asian lands. In the 19th cent. China and Japan opened their doors to foreign trade, with Japan rapidly rising to a world industrial and military power. World War II and the conflicts of its aftermath hit Asia heavily. In the postwar years, the center of gravity in international affairs tended to shift from Europe, the focus of both World Wars, to Asia, where the decolonization process resulted in the creation of many unstable nations. The Arab-Israeli conflict, the Korean War, and the emergence of Communist-ruled China, North Korea, and North Vietnam, were among the events that heightened tensions in Asia. In the 1950s the Western powers built up military alliances (the Baghdad Pact—later the Central Treaty Organization—in the Middle East, and the Southeast Asia Treaty Organization—SEATO) to help contain Soviet and Chinese domination of Asia. In the 1960s, however, the Sino-Soviet rift appeared to lessen the possibility of joint Communist efforts in Asia. At the end of World War II the United States, Britain, France, and the Netherlands were the chief outside influences in Asia; but in the postwar period India, Japan, and other Asian nations sought a more independent role on the world scene. In the 1960s the British decision to withdraw "east of Suez" and the U.S. determination in the wake of the Vietnam War to decrease its military presence in Asia foreshadowed new power alignments in the area. China's growing strength and increasing involvement in Asian affairs and the Soviet drive to expand relations with Asian states (particularly India and the Middle East Arab nations) became increasingly evident in the early 1970s. Among the conditions determining Asia's political future are the outcome of the long-simmering Arab-Israeli conflict in the Middle East; the relationships in the Indian subcontinent among India, Pakistan, and the new nation of Bangladesh; the resolution of the Vietnam War, with its implications for all Indochina; and the foreign policies of the United States, the USSR, China, Japan, and other countries with large stakes in Asia. See G. B. Cressey, *Asia's Lands and Peoples* (3d ed. 1963); W. Bingham, *A History of Asia* (1964); J. Romein, *The Asian Century* (1965); L. D. Stamp, *Asia: A Regional and Economic Geography* (rev. ed. 1967); C. A. Buss, *Asia in the Modern World* (1968); G. Wint, *Asia: A Handbook* (1967); R. G. Wilson, *Asia Awakes* (1970); W. G. East, O. K. Spate, and C. A. Fisher, ed., *The Changing Map of Asia* (5th ed. 1971); R. Grousset, *The Empire of the Steppes: A History of Central Asia* (1971); J. K. Fairbank, E. D. Reischauer, and A. M. Craig, *East Asia: Tradition and Transformation* (1973).

Asia Minor, great peninsula, c.250,000 sq mi (647,500 sq km), extreme W Asia, generally coterminous with Asian Turkey, and usually synonymous with Anatolia. It is washed by the Black Sea in the north, the Mediterranean Sea in the south, and the Aegean Sea in the west. The Black and Aegean seas are linked by the Sea of Marmara and the two straits of the Bosporus and the Dardanelles. Near the southern coast of Asia Minor are the Taurus Mts.; the rest of the peninsula is occupied by the Anatolian plateau, which is crossed by numerous mountains interspersed with lakes. In ancient times most Oriental and Occidental civilizations intersected in Asia Minor, for it was connected with Mesopotamia by the Tigris and Euphrates rivers and with Greece by the Aegean and Mediterranean seas. The Hittites established the first major civilization in Asia Minor about 1800 B.C. Beginning in the 8th cent. B.C. Greek colonies were established on the coast lands, and the Greeks thus came into contact with Lydia, Phrygia, and Troy. The conquest (6th cent. B.C.) of Asia Minor by the Persians led to the Persian Wars. Alexander the Great incorporated the region into his empire, and after his death, in the wars of the Diadochi, it was divided into small states. It was reunified (2d cent. B.C.) by the Romans, but was subject to repeated attacks by invaders, notably the Arabs and the Seljuk Turks, while under the Byzantine Empire. After being held by the Crusaders for a short time in the early 13th cent., Asia Minor was gradually (13th–15th cent.) conquered by the Ottoman Turks. It remained part of the Ottoman Empire until the establishment of the Republic of Turkey after World War I.

Asiel (ā'sēĕl), Simeonite. 1 Chron. 4.35.

Asimov, Isaac (ăz'əmŏf), 1920–, American scientist and author, b. USSR, grad. Columbia (B.S., 1939; M.A., 1941; Ph.D., 1948). He became professor of biochemistry at Boston Univ. in 1955 and gained note with serious scientific works, but he reached wider audiences with his much-admired science-fiction stories such as *I, Robot* (1950, repr. 1970), *The Caves of Steel* (1954), and *The Gods Themselves* (1973). Asimov also received high praise for his popular introductions to science written for the layman; among them are *The Intelligent Man's Guide to Science* (2 vol., 1960, rev. ed. 1965), which surveys the fields of modern science; *Wellsprings of Life* (1960), which concerns evolutionary theory; and *The Stars in Their Courses* (1971). *Inside the Atom* (1961) is representative of his books for high school students.

Aske, Robert: see PILGRIMAGE OF GRACE.

Askia Muhammad: see SONGHAI.

Askja (äs'kyä), volcano, c.4,950 ft (1,510 m) high, E central Iceland; one of the highest in Europe. Its great eruption of 1875 devastated a large area; Askja last erupted in 1961. Askja caldera, surrounded by mountains of tuff, contains Öskjuvatn, a crater lake c.550 ft (170 m) deep.

Asmara (äsmä'rä, äz-), city (1971 est. pop. 218,360), capital of Eritrea prov., N Ethiopia, at an altitude of c.7,300 ft (2,225 m). A commercial and industrial center, it is connected by rail with the Red Sea port of Massawa. Textiles and clothing, processed meat, beer, shoes, and ceramics are the major industrial products. Asmara was a small village until the 1880s, when it became an Ethiopian regional administrative center. Occupied by the Italians in 1889, it became (1900) the capital of the Italian colony of Eritrea. In the 1930s, Asmara was rapidly developed as a base for the Italian invasion (1935–36) of Ethiopia; later, in 1941, the city was taken by British forces. It is the site of the Univ. of Asmara (1958).

Asmodeus (ăs"mōdē'əs), DEMON of Hebrew story. He plays an important role in the book of Tobit. Tobit 3.8.

Asmoneans: see MACCABEES.

Asnah (ăs'nə), head of a family that returned with Zerubbabel. Ezra 2.50.

Asnappar: see ASSURBANIPAL.

Asnières-sur-Seine (änyăr'-sür-sĕn), formerly **Asnières,** industrial suburb of Paris (1968 pop. 80,530), Hauts-de-Seine dept., N central France, on the Seine River. Boats and perfumes are the major manufactures.

Asoka (əsō'kə), d. c.232 B.C. Indian emperor (c.273–c.232 B.C.) of the MAURYA dynasty; grandson of CHANDRAGUPTA. One of the greatest rulers of ancient India, he brought nearly all India, together with Baluchistan and Afghanistan, under one sway for the first time in history. However, after his bloody conquest (c.261 B.C.) of the state of Kalinga, Asoka was remorseful for the suffering he had inflicted; he converted from Brahmanism to BUDDHISM and abandoned wars of conquest. Thenceforth he proclaimed his belief in *ahimsa,* or nonviolence. Although tolerant of all faiths, he made Buddhism the state religion of India and erected numerous monasteries and stupas, regulated the slaughter of animals, and softened the harsh laws of his predecessors. He sent Buddhist missionaries throughout India and its adjacent lands and as far as Syria,

Egypt, and Greece. His own son or brother headed the mission to Ceylon. It is said that under his auspices a great Buddhist convocation was held at his capital, Pataliputra; its purpose was probably to suppress heresy and to confirm the Buddhist canon. Knowledge of Asoka's rule is obtained chiefly from the many boulders and pillars inscribed with his pious exhortations; a notable example is at SARNATH. India prospered and art flourished under the reign of Asoka, who, beyond his many imperial accomplishments, is most celebrated for his elevation of Buddhism from a simple Indian sect to a world religion. After his death the Mauryan empire swiftly declined. See studies by V. A. Smith (1909, repr. 1964), Romila Thapar (1961), R. D. Mookerji (3d ed. 1962), and B. G. Gokhale (1966); N. A. Nikam and R. P. McKeon, *Asoka, King of Magadha: Edicts* (1958).

Asopus (əsō'pəs), in Greek mythology, river god. He tried to prevent Zeus from abducting his daughter Aegina, but Zeus drove him off with a thunderbolt.

Aso-san (ä'sō-sän), volcanic mountain, central Kyushu, Japan. Aso-san is topped by one of the world's largest calderas (circumference 75 mi/121 km) that contains five volcanic cones. Taka-dake (5,225 ft/1,593 m) is the highest cone; Naka-dake (4,340 ft/1,323 m) is an active volcano. Cable cars carry people over the caldera. Aso-san is part of Aso National Park (282 sq mi/730 sq km; est. 1934), which also includes Kuju-san (5,866 ft/1,788 m), the highest peak of Kyushu.

asp, popular name for several species of VIPER, one of which, the European asp (*Vipera aspis*), is native to S Europe. It is also a name for the Egyptian COBRA (*Naja haja*). It is believed that the asp Cleopatra used to commit suicide was either that cobra or the horned viper (*Cerastes cornutus*) of N Africa.

Aspadana, Iran: see ESFAHAN.

asparagine (əspâr'əjēn), organic compound, one of the 22 α-AMINO ACIDS commonly found in animal proteins. Only the L-stereoisomer participates in the biosynthesis of mammalian proteins. Its structure is identical to that of the amino acid ASPARTIC ACID, except that the latter compound's acidic side-chain carboxyl group has been coupled with ammonia, yielding an amide. Like GLUTAMINE, asparagine is important in the metabolism of toxic ammonia in the body. The relatively unreactive, neutral amide group on the side chain of asparagine confers no special properties upon this amino acid once it is included within a protein by two peptide bonds. Asparagine is not essential to the human diet, since it can be synthesized from aspartic acid. The first amino acid to be isolated from a natural source, asparagine was purified from asparagus juice in 1806; proof of the occurrence of this amino acid in proteins was finally obtained in 1932.

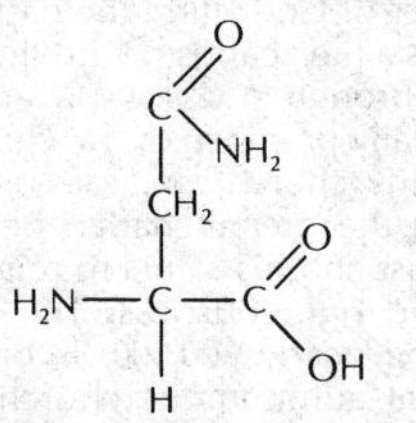

asparagine

asparagus, perennial garden vegetable (*Asparagus officinalis*) of the family Liliaceae (LILY family), native to the E Mediterranean area and now naturalized over much of the world. As in the other species of this Old World genus of succulent plants, the stems are green and function as leaves, while the leaves themselves are reduced to small scales. The tender shoots of asparagus are cut and eaten in the spring. It grows wild in the salt marshes of Europe and Asia, where it has also been under cultivation from antiquity. In early times it was regarded as a panacea. Cato in his *On Farming* gave directions for growing asparagus similar to those in a modern manual of agriculture. The San Joaquin valley is the main asparagus-growing area of the United States; over half the crop is processed, i.e., canned or frozen. The feathery sprays of the mature garden asparagus are sometimes used by florists, but more popular for decorative purposes are other plants of the same genus—the asparagus fern (*A. plumosus,* not a true fern) and the florists' smilax (*A. asparagoides*), both climbing vines native to S Africa. The wild smilax, usually called greenbrier, belongs to the genus *Smilax*. Asparagus is classified in the division MAGNOLIOPHYTA, class Liliatae, order Liliales, family Liliaceae.

aspartic acid, organic compound, one of the 22 α-AMINO ACIDS commonly found in animal proteins. Only the L-stereoisomer participates in the biosynthesis of proteins. Its acidic side chain often adds a negative charge and hence a greater degree of water-solubility to proteins in neutral solution and has been shown to be near the active sites of some enzymes (see PEPSIN). Aspartic acid is not essential to the human diet. It was discovered in protein in 1868.

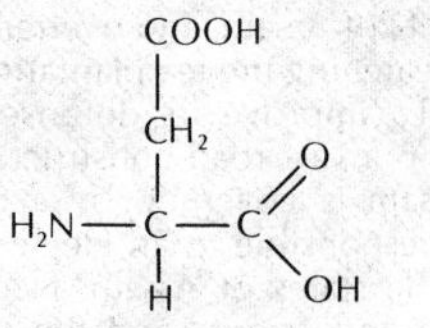

aspartic acid

Aspatha (ăs'pəthə, ăspā'-), one of the sons of Haman. Esther 9.7.

Aspen, city (1970 pop. 2,437), alt. 7,850 ft (2,390 m), seat of Pitkin co., S central Colo., on the Roaring Fork River; founded c.1879 by silver prospectors from Leadville, inc. 1881. Once a booming silver camp (there is still some mining), it has been transformed by the private capital of a Chicago industrialist into a popular, modern, cosmopolitan ski resort. The Aspen Institute for Humanistic Studies and the Aspen Music School (which holds an annual festival) are there.

aspen: see WILLOW.

Aspen Music Festival, annual summer event, held in Aspen, Colo. A former silver-mining boom town, Aspen fell into decline and was culturally revived by Walter Paepcke, who formed the Aspen Institute for Humanistic Studies. The Aspen Music Festival and Music School were founded under the auspices of the Institute in 1949. The Music Festival is held for nine weeks every summer. Artists from all over the world come to teach and to perform in recitals, concerts, and operas. In 1970 the festival presented a Beethoven retrospective concert series under the direction of Jorge Mester.

asperges (əspûr'jəs), ceremonial sprinkling of the people with holy water by the priest before the Sunday High Mass in the Roman Catholic Church. The accompanying antiphon begins, *Asperges me, Domine, hyssopo et mundabor* [Thou shalt sprinkle me with hyssop, O Lord, and I shall be cleansed]. At Easter time the antiphon is different, beginning, *Vidi aquam* [I saw water]; this is based on Ezek. 47.2.

asphalt (ăs'fôlt, -fălt), brownish-black substance used commonly in road making, roofing, and waterproofing. Chemically, it is a natural mixture of hydrocarbons. It varies in consistency from a solid to a semisolid, has great tenacity, melts when heated, and when ignited will burn with a smoky flame leaving very little or no ash. It is found in nature in deposits called asphalt lakes. Natural asphalt was probably formed by the evaporation of petroleum. Asphalt is obtained as a residue in the distillation or refining of petroleum. This is its important commercial source. It occurs also in asphalt rock, a natural mixture of asphalt with sand and limestone, which when crushed is used as road-building material. Asphalt is also used in the manufacture of paints and varnishes, giving an intensely black color.

asphodel (ăs'fədĕl"), name for plants of several genera of the family Liliaceae (LILY family). The true asphodels belong to two small and very similar genera (*Asphodelus* and *Asphodeline*) of the Mediterranean region and India. The showy flower spike of the former is usually white; of the latter, yellow. Both are stemless, hardy herbs. The asphodel (or king's spear) of the ancients, sacred to Persephone and associated with the fields of the dead, was *Asphodeline lutea;* the asphodel of the early French and English poets was a narcissus. The false asphodel is *Tofieldia,* represented in North America by *T. glutinosa* and a few other species. The turkeybeard (*Xerophyllum asphodeloides*) of the Atlantic coastal plains is also called mountain asphodel. Asphodels are classified in the division MAGNOLIOPHYTA, class Liliatae, order Liliales, family Liliaceae.

asphyxia (ăsfĭk'sēə), deficiency of oxygen and excess of carbon dioxide in the blood and body tissues. Asphyxia, often referred to as suffocation, usually results from an interruption of breathing due to mechanical blockage of the breathing passages, paralysis of the respiratory muscles following electric shock, inundation of the lungs as may occur with pneumonia or drowning, or substitution of carbon monoxide for oxygen in the red blood cells. Symptoms of asphyxia vary but may include light-headedness, nausea, and gasping, followed by unconsciousness and death. An area quickly affected is the cerebral cortex, the brain center for speech and other conscious behavior; it can be irreparably damaged by as little as five minutes of oxygen deprivation. Damage to the medulla may result in interference with the heartbeat or other involuntary processes. ARTIFICIAL RESPIRATION is the most practical first-aid procedure for asphyxia. Trained personnel can provide oxygen and employ techniques to maintain the heart rate and respiration (see RESUSCITATOR).

Aspida (äspē'dä, -thä) [Gr.,=shield, an acronym formed by the Greek initials for *Officers, Save the Country, Ideals, Democracy, Meritocracy*], secret organization of Greek left-wing junior army officers founded in the 1960s; it allegedly aimed at deposing King Constantine II, purging the government of rightists and royalists, and establishing a leftist regime. Charges that Aspida members—reportedly led by Andreas PAPANDREOU—had penetrated the Greek army contributed to the downfall of Premier George Papandreou's Central Union government in July, 1965.

Aspinwall: see COLÓN, Panama.

aspirin, acetyl derivative of salicylic acid that is commonly used to lower fever, relieve pain, and reduce inflammation (see SALICYLATE). Aspirin is believed to act by interfering with the synthesis of specific PROSTAGLANDINS in the body. It is used to relieve headache, muscle and joint pain, and the inflammation caused by rheumatic fever and arthritis. Normal dosage may cause nausea, vomiting, diarrhea, or gastrointestinal bleeding. Large doses cause acid-base imbalance and respiratory disturbances. Acetaminophen (Tylenol), which does not cause gastric irritation but does lower fever and relieve pain, is often substituted for aspirin. See ANALGESIC.

Asplund, Erik Gunnar (ä'rĭk gŏŏn'när äs'plənd), 1885–1940, Swedish architect. He designed the central library of Stockholm (completed 1928), but he is best known for the group of pavilions that he planned for the Stockholm Exhibition of 1930. There Asplund employed the forms of the new architecture but added a dynamic line and a dignity of proportion.

Aspropotamos: see AKHELÓOS, river, Greece.

Asquith, Herbert Henry: see OXFORD AND ASQUITH, HERBERT HENRY ASQUITH, 1ST EARL OF.

Asquith, Margot: see under OXFORD AND ASQUITH, HERBERT HENRY ASQUITH, 1ST EARL OF.

Asriel (ăs'rēĕl), descendant of Manasseh. Joshua 17.2; Num. 26.31. Ashriel: 1 Chron. 7.14.

ass, hoofed, herbivorous mammal of the genus *Equus,* closely related to the HORSE. It is distinguished from the horse by its small size, large head, long ears, and small hooves. There are two living species: *Equus hemonius,* the Asian ass, and *E. asinus,* the African ass. The latter species includes the domesticated variety, *E. asinus asinus,* commonly known as the donkey. A male ass is called a jackass and a female, a jenny. Wild asses are swift desert animals that may attain speeds of up to 40 mi (60 km) per hr. They live in herds of up to 1,000 animals. The Asian wild ass typically has a sandy-colored coat with lighter-colored legs and belly, a short erect black mane, a black spinal stripe, and a black tail tuft. Its neigh is shrill. Different races of this species vary in size, but all are smaller than the African ass. They were once widely distributed across Asia, but they have been crowded out of their grazing lands by domestic livestock and have been hunted for their flesh and hides. Each race is now restricted to a very limited territory. Among them are the Persian ass, or ONAGER, of central Asia; the Mongolian ass, or kulan, of NE Asia; the Tibetan ass, or kiang, presently the most numerous Asian wild ass; and the Indian ass, or ghorkhar. All are considered endangered, and the continued survival of the onager and the kulan is particularly threatened. The Syrian wild ass, of SW Asia, is probably already extinct. The two wild races of the African species, called Nubian and Somali wild asses, are also becoming rare. They are found in the mountains and deserts of NE Africa. The African ass averages about 4½ ft (135 cm) in shoulder height; it is grayish in color, with longer ears and mane than the Asian ass, and with a characteristic loud, harsh bray. Its descendant, the donkey, is the oldest domestic beast of burden; it is believed to have been domesticated in Egypt by c.4000 B.C. A variety of the Asian ass was used in ancient Mesopotamia but did not survive as a domestic animal; all modern domestic donkeys are descended from the African species. The donkey is still used widely as a pack and draft animal in underdeveloped regions of the world. Although not as swift or powerful as the horse, it is strong for its size and has great powers of endurance. Donkeys are more surefooted than horses in mountainous country and are cheaper to maintain, as they feed on dry scrub. They may live up to 47 years, about twice as long as a horse. In some regions the donkey is crossbred with the horse to produce a MULE. The donkey was once widely used in Mexico and the SW United States, where it was known by its Spanish name of *burro.* A large population of feral donkeys (wild descendants of domesticated animals) now exists in the deserts of that region. Feral donkeys are also found in the Old World, where they have given rise to some confusion about the number of true wild asses left in existence. Asses are classified in the phylum CHORDATA, subphylum Vertebrata, class Mammalia, order Perissodactyla, family Equidae.

Assab (äsäb'), town (1970 est. pop. 15,000), Eritrea prov., E Ethiopia, a port on the Red Sea. Exports include salt, coffee, oilseeds, and hides and skins. The town has a petroleum refinery. Once the terminus of caravans from the interior of Ethiopia, Assab was acquired by a private Italian shipping company in 1869. In 1882 it was taken over by the Italian government, and in 1890 Assab was included in the colony of Eritrea. The name also is spelled Aseb.

Assad, Hafez al- (häfĕz' äl-äs-säd'), 1928–, president of Syria. He graduated (1953) from the Syrian Military Academy and advanced through the ranks to become a general. He served (1965–70) as Syria's Minister of Defense and commander in chief of the air force. Using that position, Assad was able to become the most powerful figure in Syria, and in 1965 he became the country's president after leading a coup d'etat. He is considered a militant anti-Zionist and a strong supporter of Palestinian commando groups.

As Salamiya (äs-säläm'ēyä), town, W central Syria. It is a transportation center situated in a fertile plain where cereals, vegetables, and cotton are grown. As Salamiya was conquered by the Arabs in the 7th cent. and built up under the early Abbasid caliphate. The Ismailis chose the town as their center c.860. It was later destroyed (903) by the Karmathians and then came under Fatimid control. Taken by the Ottoman Empire in the 16th cent., the town declined until it was resettled by Ismailis in the 19th cent. The name also appears as Selemiya.

Assam (ăsăm'), state (1971 pop. 14,630,422), c.30,000 sq mi (77,700 sq km), extreme NE India. SHILLONG is the capital. Almost completely separated from India by Bangladesh (formerly East Pakistan), Assam is bordered by Burma on the east and China and Bhutan on the north. The terrain consists largely of hill ranges running generally from northeast to southwest and separated by streams and rivers that flow southwest. The river valleys, particularly those of the Brahmaputra and Surma, contain the richest soil and support more than half of the population. The rainfall is often excessive; Cherrapunji in the southwest reputedly has the heaviest precipitation in the world (c.430 in./1,092 cm annually). Tea, grown on large plantations, is by far the principal crop. Rice, citrus fruit, sugarcane, sesame, cotton, and jute are also grown. Industry is mainly limited to the processing of agricultural products. The hills produce abundant timber and some coal and limestone. Assam is an important oil-producing region; there are refineries at Digboi and Nunmati. Rail and road transportation is limited. Calcutta, in West Bengal state, is the nearest large Indian city. Assam has a highly heterogeneous population. Tribal peoples, such as the Nagas, Lushais, and Garos, constitute a large part of the populace. Assamese, a dialect related to Bengali, is the predominant language. The Ahom dynasty (from which the name Assam derives) established its rule in Assam c.1400 and held it intermittently for four centuries. Aurangzeb, the Mogul emperor, conquered Assam in 1661–62 but ruled it for only a short time. The British assisted the Assamese several times in expelling Burmese invaders. By the Treaty of Yandabo (1826), ending an Anglo-Burmese war, Great Britain acquired Assam; it was administered as part of Bengal until 1919, when it became a governor's province. It was made a self-governing province in 1937. A southwest section was incorporated in 1947 into East Pakistan. Education, particularly for the tribal peoples, has been expanded; Assam's first university was opened in 1948. There were serious riots in 1959–60 when Hindu refugees, fleeing from Muslim East Pakistan, settled in Assam. More refugees fled to Assam from East Pakistan in 1971. In 1959 the Chinese invaded the North-East Frontier Agency (now the union territory of Arunachal Pradesh), which is N of Assam, and overran a large part of the area, threatening the tea plantations and oil fields of Assam. To improve its defenses, India then embarked on a vast road-construction program in Assam. Assam is governed by a chief minister and cabinet responsible to an elected unicameral legislature. The states of Assam, Nagaland, Meghalaya, Manipur, and Tripura and the union territories of Mizoram and Arunachal Pradesh have a common governor appointed by the president of India.

Assamese (ăs"əmēz'), language belonging to the Indic group of the Indo-Iranian subfamily of the Indo-European family of languages. See INDO-IRANIAN LANGUAGES.

Assandun, battle of (ă'səndən), a victory by the Danes under CANUTE over the English led by EDMUND IRONSIDE. The battle was fought Oct. 18, 1016, at what is now Ashingdon, in SE Essex.

Assassin (əsăs'ĭn) [Arab.,=user of hashish], European name for the member of a secret order of the Ismaili sect of ISLAM. They are known as Nizaris after Nizar ibn al-Mustansir, whom they supported as caliph. The members of the order were distinguished by their blind obedience to their spiritual leader and by their use of murder to eliminate foes. The order was founded by Hasan ibn al-Sabbah when he gained control (c.1090) of the mountain fortress of Alamut, located S of the Caspian Sea. The order spread over Persia and Syria, gaining control of many strongholds, and it soon inspired terror throughout the Muslim world. The founder took the title Sheikh al-Jabal and was known in Western Europe as the Old Man of the Mountain. Under him members were organized into strict classes, according to degree of initiation into the secrets of the order. The most important of the classes were the devotees, who sought martyrdom and were the instruments of assassination. It is generally believed that they were given hashish and treated to great sensual pleasures in their strongholds as a foretaste of the pleasures of paradise that they were promised if they died at their duties. Hasan and the grand masters who ruled the order after him wielded great political power until the coming of the Mongols. Hulagu Khan attacked and destroyed (1256) their fortresses and massacred most of the Persian branch of the sect. The Syrian branch, with which the Crusaders came in contact, suffered a similar fate at the hands of Baybars, the Mameluke sultan of Egypt. Only scattered groups of the order survived; they are said to persist today, particularly in N Syria. Tales of the Crusaders and the writings of Marco Polo brought the Assassins and the Old Man of the Mountain into European folklore. The term *assassin* came into English and is used today to mean murderer and particularly one who kills for political motives. See Bernard Lewis, *The Assassins* (1967); Enno Franzius, *History of the Order of Assassins* (1969).

assassin bug, common name for members of the family Reduviidae, one of the largest and most varied groups belonging to the order Hemiptera (suborder Heteroptera). Assassin bugs are generally brownish to black, medium-sized to large insects, with heads that are elongate and narrow compared to the thorax. The predaceous front legs are used for grasping prey. Most assassin bugs are found on foliage, and some occasionally enter houses. The majority of species are predaceous on other insects, but a few are bloodsucking and will bite humans if carelessly handled. The bite of some species is painless, while the bite of others is extremely painful, resulting from a venom produced by the bug, the effect of which lasts for months. A painful biter is the common, black, wheel bug (*Arilus cristatus*), easily identified by the semicircular crest resembling a cogwheel on the top of its prothorax. Another is the masked hunter (*Reduvius personatus*), often found in houses where it preys on bedbugs and other insects. The adults often bite humans around the mouth, hence its other common name, the kissing bug. In the Southwest assassin bugs of the genus *Triatoma* are common. Called conenoses or Mexican bedbugs, they also invade houses and may bite man. In Central and South America certain species of this genus are the vectors for a highly fatal TRYPANOSOME disease known as Chagas' disease. Assassin bugs are classified in the phylum ARTHROPODA, class Insecta, order Hemiptera, family Reduviidae.

Assateague Island National Seashore: see NATIONAL PARKS AND MONUMENTS (table).

assault, in law, any unlawful attempt to use violence with the intent and the apparent ability to do bodily harm to another. If there is actual violence, the offense is BATTERY. Every criminal assault is a TORT, for which the party assaulted may sue for damages. At common law, assault was a MISDEMEANOR. Under modern criminal statutes, certain degrees of assault (e.g., assault with intent to kill, to do great bodily harm, to rape) are recognized as aggravated assaults and are felonies, though simple assault is still a misdemeanor. Malevolence and recklessness (e.g., driving a car in reckless disregard of human life) have come to constitute felonious assault in most jurisdictions. See W. L. Prosser, *Handbook of the Law of Torts* (3d ed. 1964).

assaying (əsā'yĭng, ăs'āyĭng), in metallurgy, process of determining the specific metallic content of an ore, alloy, or other substance, especially one containing precious metals. It consists, in some cases, of subjecting the substance to complete chemical analysis and, in others, of simply determining the quantity present of one or more of the metal constituents. An accurate assay depends first upon procuring a representative sample of the ore in question. Since distribution of the ore's components is not uniform, a common method employed in obtaining this sample is to procure several samples, crush and mix them together, and from the final mass take the sample to be assayed. Assays are said to be gravimetric when the weight of the metal is determined and volumetric when the analysis involves the volume of the metal in solution as compared to that in a standardized solution. A wet assay (one which involves the use of liquid reagents) is generally used in a determination of weight. In a dry assay the ore is fused and the metal is finally obtained in a pure state. The U.S. government has assay offices in many cities.

assemblage: see COLLAGE.

Assemblies of God, religious sect, the largest Pentecostal organization in the United States, founded at Hot Springs, Ark., in April, 1914. In doctrine the Assemblies of God affirm the basic teachings of PENTECOSTALISM (i.e., baptism with the Holy Spirit as evidenced through GLOSSOLALIA and divine healing, and the daily presence of the charismatic gifts basic to the early church) and of FUNDAMENTALISM, emphasizing the premillenarian belief in a return of Jesus Christ and his saints to reign over a period of peace and righteousness. The U.S. membership, numbering nearly 600,000, is organized into over 8,500 local autonomous churches with a general council and a general presbytery formulating and administering policies respectively. The sect maintains some 900 missions in 75 countries, the largest number being in Brazil. See Klaude Kendrick, *Promise Fulfilled: A History of the Modern Pentecostal Movement* (1961); W. W. Menzies, *Anointed to Serve* (1971).

assembly, unlawful: see RIOT, ROUT, AND UNLAWFUL ASSEMBLY.

assembly line, manufacturing technique in which a product is carried by some form of mechanized conveyor between stations at which the various operations necessary to its assembly are performed. It is used to assemble quickly large numbers of a uniform product. When its output is high, the cost per unit is relatively low. However, it is somewhat inflexible, as it must be designed and installed for a particular product. Also, the operations on the product must be performed in a sequence that is strictly ordered or very nearly so. A malfunction or shortage of parts that shuts down a single assembly station necessitates shutdown of the entire line. Some automobile manufacturers have found that if full crews are used to assemble cars unit by unit, the decrease in errors and the consequent decrease in rejects more than counterbalance the cost penalty involved in abandoning the assembly line.

Assen (äs'ən), city (1971 pop. 40,471), capital of Drenthe prov., NE Netherlands. It is an administrative and industrial center. Its main growth began in 1945.

Asser (ă'sər), d. 909, Welsh clergyman, monk of St. David's Abbey, Pembrokeshire. He went c.884 to the court of King Alfred, helped Alfred learn Latin, and later was made a bishop. He is remembered for his biography of Alfred to 893, apparently modeled on that of Charlemagne by Einhard. He combined a translation of some text of the *Anglo-Saxon Chronicle* with his original observations on Alfred's life.

Asser, Rab: see ASHI, RAB.

Asser, Tobias Michael Carel (tōbē'äs mē'khäl kä'rəl äs'ər), 1838–1913, Dutch jurist. He was a delegate to many international conferences, including the Hague Conference of 1899, and he wrote on international law. A proponent of international arbitration, he shared the 1911 Nobel Peace Prize with Alfred Fried.

Asshurim (ăshōō'rĭm), unidentified Arabian tribe, whose eponym is named in Gen. 25.3.

Assideans: see HASIDIM.

assignats (ăs'ĭgnăts, äsēnyä'), paper currency issued during the FRENCH REVOLUTION. To redeem the huge public debt and to counterbalance the growing deficit, the revolutionary constituent assembly issued (Dec., 1789) treasury notes, called assignats, to the amount of 400 million livres at 5% interest. These were intended as short-term obligations pending the sale of confiscated crown and church land. They were made legal tender in April, 1790, and subsequent issues bore no interest. Inflation resulted, and early in 1796 the assignats in circulation amounted to less than 1% of their original value; their value did not even cover the cost of printing them. *Mandats territoriaux* [land notes], adopted in 1796 as a new currency also based on confiscated lands, were also soon depreciated. Inflation stopped only when all paper currency was demonetized and redeemed at the rate of 3,000 livres in assignats or 100 francs in land notes to one franc in gold. On May 21, 1797, all unredeemed assignats were declared void. See study by S. E. Harris (1930, repr. 1969).

Assiniboine (əsĭn'əboin), river, 590 mi (950 km) long, rising in S Sask., Canada, and flowing SE into Man. then E to the Red River at Winnipeg; named for the Assiniboin Indians. The Qu'Appelle and Souris rivers are its chief tributaries. The Assiniboine valley is one of Canada's leading wheat growing areas. The river was discovered by the Vérendrye family in 1736, and forts were built at its mouth and near the site of Portage la Prairie. Settlement spread westward along the river from the Red River valley to the plains.

Assiniboine, Mount, 11,870 ft (3,618 m) high, on the British Columbia-Alta. line, Canada, on the Continental Divide in the Rocky Mts. It is the focal point of Mt. Assiniboine Provincial Park (20 sq mi/52 sq km; est. 1922).

Assiniboin Indians (əsĭn'əboin"), North American Indians whose culture is that of the N Great Plains; their language belongs to the Siouan branch of the Hokan-Siouan linguistic stock (see AMERICAN INDIAN LANGUAGES). At the time of the first contact with European settlers they had no permanent village sites; they moved about as their search for food required. They were a branch of the Yanktonai Dakota, who moved north and westward prior to the 17th cent. to the region of Lake Winnipeg; later they went to the upper Saskatchewan and the upper Missouri rivers. After the acquisition of horses and firearms in the 18th cent. they became a typical Plains tribe. They were allied with the Cree against the Blackfoot. The Assiniboin in the United States now live in the Fort Belknap and Fort Peck reservations in Montana, where they number more than 4,000; another 1,000 live in Canada. See M. S. Kennedy, ed., *The Assiniboines* (new ed. 1961); Dan Kennedy, *Recollections of an Assiniboine Chief*, ed. by J. R. Stevens (1972).

Assinie (äsēnē'), town, SE Ivory Coast, on a lagoon off the Gulf of Guinea. Because of its location on the coast and its contacts with the interior, Assinie became an early stopping place for European traders who sought gold and ivory. Portuguese merchants came to Assinie in the late 16th cent. French missionaries established a temporary post there in 1637, and a French fort and merchant community were maintained from 1701 to 1703. French traders returned in the early 19th cent. In 1842–43 the French gained treaty rights in the town and built a new fort. Assinie became a center of the palm oil trade, and coffee plantations were established nearby. The first European school in the Ivory Coast was opened there in 1887. In the 20th cent. the town declined as trade shifted to nearby Abidjan.

Assir (ăs'ĭr). **1** Son of Korah. Ex. 6.24; 1 Chron. 6.22. **2** Ancestor of Samuel. 1 Chron. 6.23,37. **3** Son of Jeconiah, according to AV and RV; translated as "Jeconiah, the Captive" in RSV. 1 Chron. 3.17.

Assis, Joaquim Maria Machado de: see MACHADO DE ASSIS, JOAQUIM MARIA.

Assisi (äs-sē'zē), town (1971 pop. 23,777), Umbria, central Italy. A religious and tourist center, it is situated on a hill in the Apennines with a magnificent view of the plains below. Although a well-known town in Roman times and throughout the Middle Ages, it owes its modern fame chiefly to St. Francis of Assisi (see FRANCIS, SAINT), who was born there in 1182 and died there in 1226. Above the saint's tomb are two Gothic churches (both consecrated 1253)—the lower church and the upper church; they are decorated with frescoes depicting the life of St. Francis and other scenes, executed by CIMABUE, GIOTTO, MARTINI, and others. The Franciscan convent nearby has a valuable library. Other landmarks in Assisi are the Cathedral of San Rufino (begun 1140), the Church of Santa Chiara (1257–65), and a 14th-century castle. In the plain below the town is the imposing late-Renaissance Church of Santa Maria degli Angeli (1569–1679), built around the little chapel of Porziuncola, where St. Francis relinquished active leadership of his order. Also near the town are the Carcieri Hermitage (15th cent.) and the Convent of San Damiano (begun 11th cent.).

Associated Press: see NEWS AGENCY.

association, in psychology, a connection between two sensations, feelings, or ideas by virtue of their previous occurrence together in experience. When an association has been formed, one member of the pair tends to remind an individual of its partner. The concept of association, developed by Plato and Aristotle, entered contemporary psychology through the empiricist philosophers Locke, Berkeley, Hume, and Hartley, and the British associationist school of psychology of James Mill, J. S. Mill, and others (see ASSOCIATIONISM). Translated into the stimulus-response terms of BEHAVIORISM, association has been thought of as the basis of learning, conditioning, and creative thinking. The frequency of occurrence of paired experience and the principle of reinforcement are often invoked to explain associative learning; however, GESTALT psychologists, who believe that association between items is dependent on the relation of the items to each other, interpret association as an aftereffect of perceptual organization. In a basic technique in psychoanalysis known as free association, the patient voices his thoughts exactly as they occur to him, even though they may seem trivial, absurd, or shocking. This procedure is designed to reveal the areas of basic conflict in the patient and to bring into consciousness traumatic events and desires that have been repressed. It rests on the assumption that the originally repressed material and distorted derivatives may be brought to awareness by relating contemporary thoughts to earlier experiences.

associationism, theory that all consciousness is the result of the combination, in accordance with the law of ASSOCIATION, of certain simple and ultimate elements derived from sense experiences. It was developed by David HARTLEY and advanced by James MILL. Associationistic principles continue to be important in the psychology of learning.

Association of Producing Artists—Phoenix (APA-Phoenix), a coalition of a theatrical touring company (APA) and a producing organization (Phoenix) formed to present theater classics off-Broadway. The APA was founded by Ellis Rabb in New York City in 1960. Two years later it became affiliated with the Professional Theatre Program of the Univ. of Michigan. Among the major productions mounted by the APA-Phoenix were *Pantagleize, The Misanthrope,* and *You Can't Take it with You.*

associative law, in mathematics, law holding that for a given operation combining three quantities, two at a time, the initial pairing is arbitrary; e.g., using the operation of addition, the numbers 2, 3, and 4 may be combined $(2+3)+4=5+4=9$ or $2+(3+4)=2+7=9$. More generally, in addition, for any three numbers a, b, and c the associative law is expressed as $(a+b)+c=a+(b+c)$. Multiplication of numbers is also associative, i.e., $(a\times b)\times c=a\times(b\times c)$. In general, any binary operation, symbolized by $\circ$, joining mathematical entities A, B, and C obeys the associative law if $(A\circ B)\circ C=A\circ(B\circ C)$ for all possible choices of A, B, and C. Not all operations are associative. For example, ordinary division is not, since $(60\div12)\div3=5\div3=5/3$, while $60\div(12\div3)=60\div4=15$. When an operation is associative, the parentheses indicating which quantities are first to be combined may be omitted, e.g., $(2+3)+4=2+(3+4)=2+3+4$.

assonance: see RHYME.

Assos (ăs'ŏs) or **Assus** (-əs), ancient city, Mysia, NW Asia Minor, on the Gulf of Adramyttium E of Point Lectum, westernmost point of Asia. St. Paul passed through Assos (Acts 20.13,14).

Assuan: see ASWAN, Egypt.

Assumption of the Virgin: see MARY.

Assur: see ASSYRIA.

assurance: see INSURANCE.

Assurbanipal (ä"sōōrbä'nēpäl) or **Ashurbanipal** (ä'shōōr-), d. 626? B.C., king of ancient Assyria (669–633 B.C.), son and successor of ESAR-HADDON. The last of the great kings of Assyria, he drove Taharka out of Egypt and firmly established NECHO in power there only to have Necho's son PSAMTIK revolt in 660 B.C. and wrest Egypt permanently from Assyria. The uprising took place during a campaign by Assurbanipal against the Elamites and Chaldaeans. His brother, in command at Babylon, also headed a serious revolt by the enemies of the king. This insurgence was suppressed, though not without difficulty, and in retaliation, Assurbanipal took Babylon and slaughtered (648 B.C.) many of the inhabitants. He then defeated Elam and sacked Susa; Elamite power disappeared. Under Assurbanipal, Assyria reached the height of sumptuous living. The famous lion-hunt reliefs in the royal palace at Nineveh date from his reign and are among the finest examples of ancient sculpture. Assurbanipal was interested in learning; excavations at Nineveh have uncovered 22,000 clay tablets from his library—the chief sources of knowledge of ancient Mesopotamia. Among the tablets were found copies of the Babylonian flood and creation stories as well as historical and scientific literature. His reign ended the greatness of the empire (although two of his sons ruled briefly after his death), and Assyria succumbed to the Medes and the Persians only a few years later. His great expenditures in wars to preserve the state contributed somewhat to its collapse. Assurbanipal is probably the Asnappar or Osnapper of Ezra 4.10. He is identified with, but only faintly resembles, the SARDANAPALUS of the Greeks.

Assurnasirbal II: see ASHURNASIRPAL II.

Assus, variant of ASSOS.

Assyria (əsĭr'ēə), ancient empire of W Asia. It developed around the city of Ashur, or Assur, on the upper Tigris River and south of the later capital, Nineveh. The nucleus of a Semitic state was forming by the beginning of the 3d millennium B.C., but it was overshadowed by the greatness of Sumer and Akkad. Ashur was Assyria's chief god, but the gods of the Babylonians and HITTITES were also honored. In the 17th cent. B.C., Assyria expanded briefly, but it soon relapsed into weakness. The 13th cent. B.C. saw Assyria threatening the surrounding states, and under TIGLATHPILESER I Assyrian soldiers entered the kingdom centered about Urartu (Ararat; see ARMENIA), took Babylonia, and crossed N Syria to reach the Mediterranean. This empire was, however, only ephemeral, and Assyrian greatness was to wait until the 9th cent., when ASHURNASIRPAL II came into power. He was not only a vigorous and barbarously cruel conqueror who pushed his conquests N to Urartu and W to Lebanon and the Mediterranean, but he was also a shrewd administrator. Instead of merely making conquered kings pay tribute, he installed Assyrian governors so that he could have more control over the empire. Shalmaneser III (see under SHALMANESER I) attempted to continue this policy, but, although he exacted heavy tribute from Jehu of Israel and claimed many victories, he failed to establish hegemony over the Hebrews and their Aramaic-speaking allies. The basalt obelisk, called the Black Obelisk (British Mus.), describes the expeditions and conquests of Shalmaneser III. Raids from Urartu were resumed and grew more destructive after the death of Shalmaneser. CALAH, the capi-

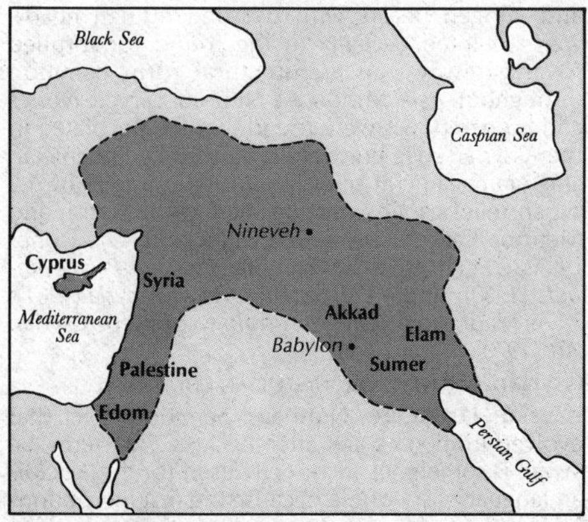

Assyrian Empire (c.650 B.C.)

tal of Assyria during the reigns of Ashurnasirpal II and Shalmaneser III, has been excavated. In the 8th cent. B.C. conquest was pushed by TIGLATHPILESER III. He subdued Babylonia, defeated the king of Urartu, attacked the Medes, and established control over Syria. As an ally of Ahaz of Judah (who became his vassal), he defeated his Aramaic-speaking enemies centering at Damascus. His successor, Shalmaneser V, besieged Samaria, the capital of Israel, in 722–721 B.C., but is was SARGON, his son, who completed the task of capturing Israel. Sargon's victory at Raphia (720 B.C.) and his invasions of Armenia, Arabia, and other lands made Assyria indisputably one of the greatest of ancient empires. His son SENNACHERIB devoted himself to retaining the gains his father had made. He is particularly remembered for his warfare against his rebellious vassal, Hezekiah of Judah. Sennacherib's successor, ESAR-HADDON, defeated the Chaldaeans, who threatened Assyria, and carried his conquests (673–670) to Egypt, where he deposed Tirhakah and established Necho in power. Under ASSURBANIPAL, Assyria reached its zenith and approached its fall. When Assurbanipal was fighting against the Chaldaeans and Elamites, an Egyptian revolt under Psamtik I was successful. The rapid decline of Assyria had begun, but the reign of Assurbanipal saw the Assyrian capital of NINEVEH at its height of splendor. The library of cuneiform tablets he collected ultimately proved to be one of the most important historical sources of antiquity. The magnificent Assyrian bas-reliefs reached their peak. The royal court was luxurious. Assyrian culture owed much to earlier Babylonian civilization, and in religion Assyria seems to have taken much from its southern neighbor and subject (see MIDDLE EASTERN RELIGIONS). The military aspect of the empire was its most prominent feature, for Assyria was prepared for conflict from beginning to end. Because of the ever-present need for men to fight the incessant battles, agriculture suffered and ultimately the Assyrians had to import food. The division of society into a fairly rigid three-class system was not unlike that of other early western Asiatic peoples (see BABYLONIA), but it did not supply a solid base for the overgrown Assyrian state. The lavish expenditures of Assurbanipal on warfare and building drained the resources of the empire and contributed to its weakness. The king of the Medes, Cyaxares, and the Babylonian ruler Nabopolassar, joined forces and took Nineveh in 612 B.C. Under the son of Nabopolassar, NEBUCHADNEZZAR, Babylonia was renewed in power, and the great-grandson of Cyaxares, Cyrus the Great, was to establish the Persian Empire, which owed much to the earlier Assyrian state. See A. T. E. Olmstead, *History of Assyria* (1923, repr. 1960); D. D. Luckenbill, *Ancient Records of Assyria and Babylonia* (2 vol., 1926–7, repr. 1968).

Assyrian art. An Assyrian artistic style distinct from that of Babylonian art (see SUMERIAN AND BABYLONIAN ART), which was the dominant contemporary art in Mesopotamia, began to emerge c.1500 B.C. and lasted until the fall of NINEVEH in 612 B.C. The characteristic Assyrian art form was the polychrome carved stone relief. The precisely delineated reliefs concern royal affairs, chiefly hunting and war making. Predominance is given to animal forms, particularly horses and lions, which are magnificently represented in great detail. Human figures are comparatively rigid and static but are also minutely detailed, as in triumphal scenes of sieges, battles, and individual combat. Among the best known of Assyrian reliefs are the lion-hunt alabaster carvings showing Assurnasirpal II (9th cent. B.C.) and Assurbani-pal (7th cent. B.C.), both of which are in the British Museum. Guardian animals, usually lions and winged beasts with bearded human heads, were sculpted partially in the round for fortified royal gateways, an architectural form common throughout Asia Minor. At Nimrud carved ivories and bronze bowls were found that are decorated in the Assyrian style but were produced by Phoenician and Aramaean craftsmen. Exquisite examples of Assyrian relief carving may be seen at the British and Metropolitan museums. See C. J. Gadd, *The Stones of Assyria* (1936); R. D. Barnett, *Assyrian Palace Reliefs* (1960); André Parrot, *The Arts of Assyria* (1961); T. A. Madhloom, *The Chronology of Neo-Assyrian Art* (1970).

Assyrian Church: see NESTORIAN CHURCH.

Assyrian language, Northeast Semitic dialect that evolved from AKKADIAN after 1950 B.C. The term *Assyrian* is sometimes incorrectly used for the Akkadian language as a whole because the first inscriptions in Akkadian to be found in modern times were discovered in the region that was Assyria in antiquity.

Assyrian religion: see MIDDLE EASTERN RELIGIONS.

Astacus: see NICOMEDIA.

Astaire, Fred, 1899–, American dancer, actor, and singer, b. Omaha, Nebr. His original name was Frederick Austerlitz. After 1911 he and his sister Adele formed a successful Broadway vaudeville team. After his sister retired, Astaire became a film actor (1933). He became known as a debonair song-and-dance man, particularly in the films he made with Ginger Rogers, which elevated the tap dance to an elegant, disciplined art. Among his most notable films are *The Gay Divorcée* (1934), *Top Hat* (1935), *Swing Time* (1936), *Funny Face* (1956), and *On the Beach* (1959). See his autobiography, *Steps in Time* (1959).

Astaroth (ăs'tərŏth), variant of ASHTAROTH.

Astarte (ăstär'tē), Semitic goddess of fertility and love. She was the most important goddess of the Phoenicians and corresponds to the Babylonian Ishtar and the Greek Aphrodite. She took a dominant place in Eastern religions, and the Jews strictly forbade use of her name. In the Bible she is referred to (with condemnation) first as Ashtaroth and later as Ashtoreth (Judges 2.13; 10.6; 1 Sam. 12.10; 31.10; 1 Kings 11.5, 33; 2 Kings 23.13).

astatine (ăs'tətēn,-tĭn) [Gr.,=unstable], semimetallic radioactive chemical element; symbol At; at. no. 85; at. wt. of most stable isotope 210; m.p., b.p., and density unknown; valence believed to be +1, +3, +5, or +7. Astatine is the heaviest known HALOGEN (group VIIa of the PERIODIC TABLE). Its chemical properties are believed to be similar to those of IODINE. The most stable isotope, astatine-210, has a half-life of 8.3 hr. More than 20 isotopes of astatine have been identified. Small amounts of astatine exist in equilibrium with uranium and thorium in the earth's crust, but the total amount of astatine is probably less than 1 oz. Astatine-211 (half-life 7.21 hr) is sometimes used as a radioactive tracer; like iodine, it collects in the thyroid gland. The discovery of astatine (first called alabamine) was announced in 1931 by Fred Allison and E. J. Murphy. In 1940, Emilio Segré, D. R. Corson, and K. R. Mackenzie produced astatine-211 by bombarding bismuth-209 with alpha particles in the cyclotron at the Univ. of California.

Astell, Mary (ăs'təl), 1666–1731, English author and feminist. Her *Serious Proposal to the Ladies* (2 parts, 1694–97) offered a scheme for a women's college, an idea far in advance of the time. The project was not realized, and her ideas were ridiculed in the *Tatler*, possibly by Swift and Addison. See study by Florence M. Smith (1916).

aster [Gr.,=star], in North America, name for plants of the genus *Aster*, sometimes called wild asters, and for a related plant more correctly called China aster *(Callistephus chinensis)*, all members of the family Compositae (COMPOSITE family). In North America, where most species are native, plants of the genus *Aster* are regarded as wild flowers, but in Europe they are cultivated as garden flowers and often called Michaelmas daisy (they usually bloom at Michaelmas). Most species of *Aster* are perennial and fall-blooming. They have small daisylike or starlike flower heads on leafy, often tall, stems. Their colors vary from white to pink, blue, and purple. Among the more showy native species cultivated in North American gardens are the purple New England aster *(A. novae-angliae)* and the violet or blue New York aster *(A. novi-belgii)*. The New England aster was used by Shakers as an application for skin disorders. The China aster is the common aster of florists and flower gardens. It is an Asian plant that in cultivation has a very full head of ray flowers, varying from white and pink to deep purple. Other related genera with similar flowers are sometimes called asters, e.g., the golden asters *(Chrysopsis)*. Asters are classified in the division MAGNOLIOPHYTA, class Magnoliopsida, order Asterales, family Compositae.

Asterabad: see GORGAN, Iran.

Asteria (ăstēr'ēə), in Greek mythology, daughter of the Titans Coeus and Phoebe, mother of Hecate by Perses. To escape Zeus' amorous advances, she turned into a quail, jumped into the sea, and became the isle of Ortygia (quail island).

asteroid, planetoid, or **minor planet,** small body orbiting the sun. More than 2,000 asteroids have been tracked and cataloged; thousands more exist. Most asteroids are irregularly shaped, unlike the major planets, which are spherically shaped. The largest asteroid, CERES, has a diameter of c.470 mi (750 km); the three next largest are PALLAS, VESTA, and JUNO. Only Vesta can be seen with the naked eye. The other asteroids are so small that their sizes cannot

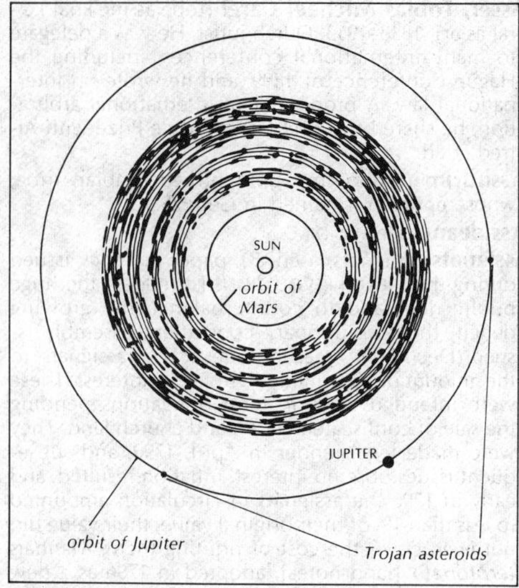

The asteroid belt lies between the orbits of Mars and Jupiter. Gaps where no asteroids are found are called Kirkwood gaps. The Trojan asteroids share Jupiter's orbit with the planet.

be measured directly by telescope; in many cases their sizes have been estimated from their brightnesses and distances. The ORBITS of most asteroids lie at least partially between the orbits of Mars and Jupiter; the orbit of ICARUS is most eccentric, and that of Hidalgo has the greatest inclination to the plane of the ecliptic. The average orbital distance of the asteroids from the sun is about 2.9 astronomical units (or A.U.; 1 A.U. is the mean distance from the earth to the sun). Toward the end of the 18th cent. astronomers were searching for a planet whose orbit should, according to BODE'S LAW, have an average distance from the sun of 2.8 A.U. On Jan. 1, 1801, G. Piazzi discovered Ceres while studying the sky in the constellation Taurus; Ceres was later found to have an orbit very near that predicted by Bode's law. Pallas was discovered in 1802, Juno in 1804, and Vesta in 1807. Astrea, discovered in 1845, was the fifth asteroid to be found; its discovery followed 15 years of searching by K. Hencke. By 1890 more than 300 asteroids had been discovered by visual means. In 1891, Max Wolf introduced the method of identifying an asteroid by the record of its path on an exposed photographic plate; it appears as a short line in a time exposure, rather than the sharp point of a star. Brucia was the first asteroid discovered by this method. Asteroids sometimes come very close to the earth; HERMES, discovered in 1937, comes within 485,000 mi (780,000 km), and EROS comes within 14 million mi (22 million km). The TROJAN ASTEROIDS, two groups of asteroids in Jupiter's orbit, are interesting as a phenomenon predicted by one solution of the three-body problem of mathematics. The origin of asteroids is unclear; one theory claims that they are fragments of a planet that occupied approximately their present position and met with some disaster in the remote past; another theory proposes that the asteroids were formed from material that, because of perturbation effects, could not condense into a single planet; a third theory suggests that they are material from the nuclei of old comets.

asthenosphere (ăsthĕn'əsfēr), region in the upper mantle of the earth's interior, characterized by low-density, semiplastic rock material with little strength. The upper part of the asthenosphere, called the plastic layer, at a depth of 60 to 100 km, is believed to be the zone upon which the great lithospheric plates of the earth's crust move about (see PLATE TECTONICS). Although its presence was suspected as early as 1926, the worldwide occurrence of the plastic zone was confirmed by analyses of earthquake waves from the Chilean earthquake of May 22, 1960. Because earthquakes caused by faulting do originate in this zone and deeper, it is thought that the semiplastic rocks of the asthenosphere behave in a brittle fashion when subjected to sudden forces, yet yield by flowage to long-term stresses. It may also be that crustal plates sinking into the mantle are responsible for earthquakes originating in the asthenosphere. See LITHOSPHERE.

asthma, chronic respiratory disorder characterized by wheezy breathing that may be continuous and paroxysmal. A cough producing sticky mucoid sputum is symptomatic. Asthma usually results from an allergic reaction, and in many cases exhibits a hereditary pattern (see ALLERGY). Such psychogenic factors as mental or emotional stress may precipitate an attack. Reactions to specific allergens (commonly pollen, house dust, animal dander, common foodstuffs) is characteristic of childhood asthma, also known as extrinsic asthma. In adults asthma is often related to respiratory infections, and there is sometimes no clear-cut allergen. This form of the disease is called intrinsic asthma. Treatment of asthma usually includes an attempt at identifying and avoiding contact with the specific allergen. Injections of epinephrine bring immediate relief; ACTH and cortisone injections provide longer-lasting relief in chronic cases, especially when there is no response to other measures.

Asti (ä'stē), city (1971 pop. 76,048), capital of Asti prov., in Piedmont, NW Italy, on the Tanaro River. It is a commercial and industrial center, noted for its sparkling wine (Asti spumante). The city, which retains its medieval appearance, has a fine Gothic cathedral (14th cent.).

astigmatism, type of faulty vision caused by a nonuniform curvature in the refractive surfaces—usually the cornea, less frequently the lens—of the eye. As a result, light rays do not all come to a single focal point on the retina. Instead, some focus on the retina while others focus in front of or behind it. The condition may be congenital, or it may result from disease or injury; it can occur in addition to NEARSIGHTEDNESS or FARSIGHTEDNESS. The spherical lenses used to correct nearsightedness and farsightedness must be specially adapted to correct the out-of-focus plane of vision of the astigmatic eye. When the patient observes a pattern of straight lines placed at various angles, those running in one direction appear sharp while those in other directions (particularly at right angles to the sharp lines) appear blurred. A special cylindrical lens is placed in the out-of-focus axis to correct the condition. In many cases contact lenses are the most effective means of correcting astigmatism.

Aston, Francis William, 1877–1945, English physicist and chemist. He was affiliated with the Cavendish Laboratory, Cambridge, from 1910. In 1922 he received the Nobel Prize in Chemistry mainly for his discovery, by means of a mass spectrograph of his own invention, of a number of isotopes in nonradioactive elements. His writings include *Isotopes* (1922) and *Mass-Spectra and Isotopes* (1933).

Astor, John Jacob, 1763–1848, American merchant, b. Waldorf, near Heidelberg, Germany. At the age of 16 he went to England, and five years later, in 1784, he arrived in Baltimore, penniless. He later went to New York City, where in a few years he entered into business with a small shop for trade in musical instruments and furs. Shrewdness, driving ambition, and stolid concentration brought him to a commanding position in the burgeoning economy of the United States. He became a leader of the China trade and was an astute investor in lands, principally in and around New York City, but he is perhaps best remembered as a fur trader. He chartered the AMERICAN FUR COMPANY (1808) and founded subsidiary companies—the Pacific Fur Company (see ASTORIA, Oregon) and the South West Company (operating around the Great Lakes). His firm exercised a virtual monopoly of the trade in U.S. territories in the 1820s and still did when he retired from it in 1834. The wealthiest man in the United States at his death, he left a fortune that has continued to make the family name prominent. Part of his money went to found the Astor Library (see NEW YORK PUBLIC LIBRARY). His Astor House was a forerunner of family hotel properties that much later included the Astor Hotel and the Waldorf-Astoria. See biographies by J. U. Terrell (1963) and K. W. Porter (1936, repr. 1966).

Astor, John Jacob, 1822–90, American financier, b. New York City, educated at Columbia and Göttingen universities and at Harvard law school; son of William Backhouse Astor (1792–1875). The third Astor in the United States, he served in the Peninsular campaign in the Civil War and later took a minor part in New York civic and political affairs. His son was William Waldorf Astor.

Astor, John Jacob, 1864–1912, American financier, b. Rhinebeck, N. Y.; son of William Backhouse Astor (1829–92). The fourth of the name in the United States, he served in the Spanish-American War. Drowned in the *Titanic* disaster, he left two sons, Vincent, the son of his first marriage, and John Jacob Astor, fifth of the name in America, the son of his second marriage.

Astor, Nancy Witcher (Langhorne) Astor, Viscountess, 1879–1964, British politician, b. Virginia. She was first married to Robert Gould Shaw, and after her divorce (1903) from him she went to England. There she was married (1906) to Waldorf Astor. When he succeeded his father as viscount and had to give up his seat in the House of Commons as member for Plymouth, she was elected in his place and became the first woman to sit in Parliament. In her years as a Conservative member (1919–45) her sharp tongue in debate, her passionate espousal of temperance and of reforms in woman and child welfare, and her cheerful lack of reverence for any and all won respect and attention. In the 1920s she and her husband were leaders in the "gradual" reform program of "Tory democracy." In the late 1930s their pleas for settlement and peace with the fascist powers in Europe were interpreted as treasonable by their enemies. At their country house, Cliveden (given to the government in 1942), the Astors brought together great literary figures and leaders of all political persuasions. See biographies by Maurice Collis (1960) and Christopher Sykes (1972); Elizabeth Langhorne, *Nancy Astor and Her Friends* (1974).

Astor, William Backhouse, 1792–1875, American financier, b. New York City; son of John Jacob Astor (1763–1848). Educated in Germany, he was associated with his father in business after 1818. Later called the landlord of New York, he also inherited money from his uncle Henry Astor and left an immense fortune.

Astor, William Backhouse, 1829–92, American financier and sportsman, b. New York City. The son of William Backhouse Astor (1792–1875), he was a retiring man, notable principally for his wealth and for his marriage to Caroline Schermerhorn. With the assistance of Ward McAlister, she became famous as the Mrs. Astor of modern folklore, queen of New York City society's legendary Four Hundred. Their son was John Jacob Astor (1864–1912).

Astor, William Waldorf Astor, 1st **Viscount,** 1848–1919, American-British financier, b. New York City, educated in Germany and in Italy and at the Columbia law school; son of John Jacob Astor (1822–90). He served as a state assemblyman and senator, but his political career was halted by his failure to win an election to the U.S. Congress. He was then appointed minister to Italy (1881–85). In 1890 he moved to England, where he acquired control of a newspaper and several magazines. He also founded—mainly to forward the literary ambition he had shown in two mediocre novels—*Pall Mall Magazine.* His estates, Cliveden and Hever Castle, were magnificent, his entertainments extravagant, his contributions to public causes—especially in World War I—munificent. He was made a baron in 1916 and a viscount in 1917. His elder son, Waldorf Astor (1879–1952), succeeded him as viscount and was a leader of "Tory democracy." His wife was Nancy, Lady Astor. The younger son, John Jacob Astor (1886–1971), bought a major share of *The Times* of London and was made 1st Baron Astor of Hever.

Astoria (ăstôr'ēə). **1** Commercial, industrial, and residential section of NW Queens borough of New York City, SE N.Y.; settled in the 17th cent. as Hallet's Cove. It was renamed for John Jacob Astor in 1839. Several 18th-century houses remain. **2** City (1970 pop. 10,244), seat of Clatsop co., NW Oregon, on the Columbia River estuary; inc. 1876. A port of entry, Astoria is the trading center for the lower Columbia basin. Its principal industries are fishing and fish processing, lumbering, and tourism; agriculture and shipbuilding are also important. The LEWIS AND CLARK EXPEDITION spent the winter of 1805–6 at a nearby encampment, Fort Clatsop (rebuilt in 1955 and now a national memorial). Fort Astoria, a fur-trading post established in 1811 by John Jacob Astor's Pacific Fur Company, was the first permanent U.S. settlement on the Pacific coast. Although the post was sold to the British in 1813, its vigorous activities helped to establish American claims to the Oregon country and contributed much to the exploration of the continent. Fort Astoria was formally restored to the United States in 1818, but trade remained in British hands until the mid-1840s, when American pioneers followed the Oregon Trail to the fort. In the late 18th cent., Astoria grew as a coastal and river port; it later attracted Scandinavian settlers, whose descendants make up most of its present-day population. Points of interest include the Astoria Column, 125 ft (38 m) high, built in 1926 to commemorate the region's early history. A junior college is in the city.

Astrabad: see GORGAN, Iran.

Astraea (ăstrē'ə), in Greek religion, goddess of justice; daughter of Zeus and Themis. Because of the wickedness of man, she withdrew from the earth at the end of the Golden Age and was placed among the stars as the constellation Virgo.

Astraeus (ăstrē'əs): see EOS.

Astrakhan (ăs'trəkăn, Rus. ä'strəkhənyə), city (1970 pop. 411,000), capital of Astrakhan oblast, SE European USSR. A Caspian Sea port on the Volga River's southern delta, it is a center for river transport and has shipyards, repair docks, and fish-processing plants. Astrakhan is also an important rail junction and a major transshipment center for oil, fish, grain, and wood. The capital of the khanate of Astrakhan (see TATARS) from the 1460s, it was conquered by Ivan the Terrible in 1556. Astrakhan had a flourishing trade with Persia, Khiva, and Bukhara until 1917. It has a kremlin (1587–89) and a cathedral (1700–1710).

astrakhan (ăs'trəkən) [from Astrakhan], pelt of the newborn Persian lamb, used like fur in garments, and also the woolen fabric woven to resemble real astrakhan. The cloth is woven on a cotton base entirely covered by a pile of closely curled mohair. Before being woven the mohair is wound on spindles and steamed to produce a tight, permanent curl.

astringent (əstrĭn'jənt), substance that shrinks body tissues. Astringent medicines cause shrinkage of mucous membranes or exposed tissues and are often used internally to check discharge of serum or mucous secretions in sore throat, hemorrhage, diarrhea, or peptic ulcer. Externally applied astringents, which cause mild coagulation of skin proteins, dry, harden, and protect the skin. Mildly astringent solutions are used in the relief of such minor skin irritations as those resulting from superficial cuts, allergies, insect bites, or athlete's foot. Astringent preparations include silver nitrate, zinc oxide, calamine lotion, tincture of benzoin, and vegetable substances such as tannic and gallic acids, catechu, and oak bark. Some metal salts and acids have also been used as astringents.

astrobleme, large, circular geologic structure ranging from c.½ mi to 40 mi (.8–64 km) in diameter. Astroblemes are found at numerous places on the earth's surface, e.g., Barringer Crater in Arizona, Brent Crater in Ontario, and Vredefort Ring in South Africa. The presence of meteor fragments, strange conical fracture patterns (called shatter cones), and coesite (a superdense, high-pressure form of quartz) in the rocks at astroblemes suggest an impact, rather than volcanic, origin to these circular structures.

astrolabe (ăs'trəlāb), instrument probably used originally for measuring the altitudes of heavenly bodies and for determining their positions and movements. Although its origin is ancient and obscure, its invention is frequently ascribed either to Hipparchus or to Apollonius of Perga. For many centuries it was used by both astronomers and navigators. A simple astrolabe consisted of a disk of wood or metal with the circumference marked off in degrees. It was suspended by an attached ring. Pivoted at the center of the disk was a movable pointer called by Arabian astronomers the alidade. By sighting with the alidade and taking readings of its position on the graduated circle, angular distances could be determined. Mariners, if sufficiently skilled in navigation, could use the astrolabe to determine latitude, longitude, and time of day and as an aid in making other calculations. It was much used on voyages of discovery in the 15th cent. and was important until the invention of the sextant in the 18th cent. The more elaborate astrolabes bore a star map (the planisphere, a circular map, was added by Hipparchus), a zodiacal circle, and various other useful or decorative devices.

astrology, form of DIVINATION based on the theory that the movements of the celestial bodies—the stars, the planets, the sun, and the moon—influence human affairs and determine the course of events. Celestial phenomena have been the object of religious sentiment since earliest times (see MOON WORSHIP; SUN WORSHIP). The Chaldaeans and the Assyrians were the first to discard their sky gods in favor of a nondeistic system of divination founded upon astronomy and numerology. They saw the heavenly bodies as exerting an influence upon the lives of individuals and the destinies of empires. Generally, all future events were believed determined beforehand by a universal order that was a result of the motions of the planets and stars. The practices of astrology spread throughout the ancient Middle

East, Asia, and Europe, but with the rise of Christianity, which emphasized divine intervention and free will, interest in astrology subsided, although astrologers continued to flourish. During the European Renaissance astrology as a form of divination regained popularity, due in part to the rekindled interest in science and astronomy. The European astrologer, considered a scholar exploring the mysteries of the universe through science and reason, was held in high esteem in the community for many centuries. However, in the 16th and 17th cent., Christian theologists waged an all-out war against astrology. In 1585 astrology was officially condemned in a bull of Pope Sixtus V, and in 1631, Pope Urban VIII reinforced this with another bull. At the same time the astronomical work of such men as Copernicus, Tycho Brahe, Kepler, and Galileo was undermining the tenets of astrology. Astrology, however, continued to be practiced. All of the aforementioned scientists remained practicing astrologers, as did other great thinkers such as Descartes and Newton; moreover, Copernican theory did not find sudden and widespread acceptance. Gradually, however, astrology declined, although this form of divination is still very much alive, especially in India. One's horoscope is a map of the heavens at the time of one's birth, showing the position of the heavenly bodies in relation to the 12 "houses" or signs through which they pass (see ZODIAC) and their positions in relation to each other. Each house has as its "lord" one of the heavenly bodies; the one in the "ascendant" is the one of greatest significance to the inquirer, supposedly endowing him with his temperamental qualities, his tendencies to particular diseases, and his liability to certain fortunes or calamities. See Ellen McCaffery, *Astrology: Its History and Influence in the Western World* (rev. ed. 1942); Lynn Thorndike, *History of Magic and Experimental Science* (rev. ed. 1958); Michel Gauquelin, *The Cosmic Clocks* (1967); Christopher McIntosh, *The Astrologers and their Creed* (1969).

astrometry: see ASTRONOMY.

astronaut, crew member on a U.S. manned spaceflight mission; the Soviet term is *cosmonaut*. Candidates for manned spaceflight are carefully screened to meet the highest physical and mental standards, and they undergo rigorous training. The early astronauts had all previously been test pilots, but later astronauts have included scientists and physicians. As far as is possible, all conditions to be encountered in space are simulated in ground training. Astronauts are trained to function effectively in cramped quarters while wearing restrictive spacesuits; they are accelerated in giant centrifuges to test their reactions to the inertial forces experienced during liftoff; they are prepared for the physiological disorientation they will experience in space arising from WEIGHTLESSNESS; and they spend long periods in isolation chambers to test their psychological reactions to solitude. Using trainers and mock-ups of actual spacecraft, astronauts rehearse every maneuver from liftoff to recovery, and every conceivable malfunction and difficulty is anticipated and prepared for. In addition to flight training, astronauts are required to have thorough knowledge of all aspects of SPACE SCIENCE, such as celestial mechanics and rocketry. Concurrent with all other preparation, astronauts must maintain a physical condition equal to that of first-class athletes. Manned spaceflight began on April 8, 1961, when the Soviet cosmonaut Yuri Gagarin orbited the earth. Other prominent cosmonauts included Vladimir Komarov, commander of the first Voskhod spacecraft, Alexis Leonov, first man to walk in space, and Valentina Terechkova, first woman cosmonaut. American astronauts participated in four major programs between 1960 and 1973: Mercury, Gemini, Apollo, and Skylab (see SPACE EXPLORATION). Many astronauts participated in more than one program. The first American astronaut was Alan B. Shepard, Jr., who made a suborbital flight on May 5, 1961. John H. Glenn, Jr., was the first American to orbit the earth, and Edward H. White, 2d, was the first American to walk in space. The first lunar landing was accomplished by the crew of Apollo 11: Neil A. Armstrong, Jr., Edwin E. Aldrin, Jr., and Michael Collins, in 1969. See D. C. Knight, ed., *American Astronauts and Spacecraft* (1972); Michael Collins, *Carrying the Fire* (1974).

astronautics: see SPACE SCIENCE.

astronomical coordinate systems. A coordinate system is a method of indicating positions. Each coordinate is a quantity measured from some starting point along some line or curve, called a coordinate axis. There are four basic systems of astronomical coordinates: the EQUATORIAL COORDINATE SYSTEM, the altazimuth or HORIZON COORDINATE SYSTEM, the celestial or ECLIPTIC COORDINATE SYSTEM, and the GALACTIC COORDINATE SYSTEM. These systems are based on three common principles: (1) all stars are considered to be located on the inner surface of the CELESTIAL SPHERE, the imaginary sphere centered on the earth and representing the entire sky; (2) each coordinate axis is a great circle on the celestial sphere; and (3) coordinate measurements of an object to be located are made along two great circles, one a coordinate axis and the other perpendicular to it and passing through the object. Measurements are made either in degrees or in hours. Since there are 24 hours or 360 degrees in a circle, 1 hour is equal to 15 degrees ($1^h = 15°$). The stars are so distant that their apparent annual motion relative to one another is very small. In a coordinate system that is constructed so that it ignores the daily rotation and annual revolution of the earth, the coordinates of any star remain nearly constant. However, it is impossible to construct a coordinate system, centered at the earth, that gives constant coordinates for another body that orbits the sun.

Astronomical Ephemeris: see EPHEMERIS.

astronomical unit (A.U.), mean distance between the earth and sun; one A.U. is c.92,960,000 mi (149,604,970 km). The astronomical unit is the principal unit of measurement within the solar system, e.g., Mercury is just over ⅓ A.U. and Pluto is about 39 A.U.

astronomy, branch of SCIENCE that studies the motions and natures of celestial bodies, such as PLANETS, STARS, and GALAXIES; more generally, the study of MATTER and ENERGY in the UNIVERSE at large. Astronomy is perhaps the oldest of the pure sciences. It is difficult to fix the exact date when systematic observations of the heavens began. In many primitive civilizations the regularity of celestial motions was recognized, and attempts were made to keep records and predict future events. The first practical function of astronomy was to provide a basis for the CALENDAR, the units of month and year being determined by astronomical observations. Later, astronomy served in navigation and timekeeping. The Chinese had a working calendar as early as the 13th cent. B.C. About 350 B.C., Shih Shen prepared the earliest known star catalog, containing 800 entries. Chinese astronomy is best known today for its observations of SUPERNOVAS, or "guest stars," as they were called. The Babylonians, Assyrians, and Egyptians were also active in astronomy. The earliest astronomers were priests, and no attempt was made to separate astronomy from the pseudoscience of ASTROLOGY. In fact, an early motivation for the detailed study of planetary positions was the preparation of horoscopes. The highest development of astronomy in the ancient world came with the Greeks in the period from 600 B.C. to A.D. 400. The methods employed by the Greek astronomers were quite distinct from those of earlier civilizations, such as the Babylonian. The Babylonian approach was numerological and ad hoc, best suited for studying the complex lunar motions that were of overwhelming interest to the Mesopotamian peoples. The Greek approach, on the contrary, was geometric and schematic, best suited for complete cosmological models. Thales, an Ionian philosopher of the 6th cent. B.C., is credited with introducing geometrical ideas into astronomy. Pythagoras, about a hundred years later, imagined the universe as a series of concentric spheres in which each of the seven "wanderers" (the sun, the moon, and the five known planets) were embedded. The spheres rotated independently, producing the "music of the spheres." Euxodus developed the idea of rotating spheres by introducing extra spheres for each of the planets to account for the observed complexities of their motions. This was the beginning of the Greek aim of "saving the appearances," that is, providing a theory that would account for all observed phenomena. The theoretical models of the universe did not necessarily correspond to absolute truth or reality, which, according to Plato, was inaccessible to man and could only be approached or approximated. This Greek attitude toward scientific knowledge mirrors modern positivism. Aristotle (384–322 B.C.) summarized much of the Greek work before him and remained absolute authority until late in the Middle Ages. Although his belief that the earth does not move was to have a retarding effect on astronomical progress, he gave the correct explanation of lunar eclipses and a sound argument for the spherical shape of the earth. The apex of Greek astronomy was reached in the Hellenistic period by the Alexandrian school. Aristarchus (c.310–c.230 B.C.) determined the sizes and distances of the moon and sun relative to the earth and advocated a heliocentric (sun-centered) cosmology. Although there were errors in his assumptions, his approach was truly scientific; his work was the first serious attempt to make a scale model of the universe. The first accurate measurement of the actual (as opposed to relative) size of the earth was made by Eratosthenes (284–192 B.C.). His method was based on the angular difference in the sun's position at the high noon of the summer SOLSTICE in two cities whose distance apart was known. The greatest astronomer of antiquity was Hipparchus (190–120 B.C.). He developed TRIGONOMETRY and used it to determine astronomical distances from the observed angular positions of celestial bodies. He recognized that astronomy requires accurate and systematic observations extended over long time periods. He therefore made great use of old observations, comparing them to his own. Many of his observations, particularly of the planets, were intended for future astronomers. He devised a geocentric system of cycles and epicycles (a compounding of circular motions) to account for the movements of the sun and moon. Ptolemy (A.D. 85–165) applied the scheme of epicycles to the planets as well. The resulting PTOLEMAIC SYSTEM was a geometrical representation of the SOLAR SYSTEM that predicted the motions of the planets with considerable accuracy. Among his other achievements was an accurate measurement of the distance to the moon by a PARALLAX technique. His 13-volume treatise, the *Almagest,* summarized much of ancient astronomical knowledge and, in many translations, was the definitive authority for 14 centuries. During this period European astronomy was largely dormant, and the only significant work was carried out by the Muslims and the Hindus. It was by way of Moorish Spain that Greek astronomy reached medieval Europe. One of the great landmarks of the revival of learning in Europe that brought about the scientific revolution of the 16th and 17th cent. was the publication (1543) by Nicolaus Copernicus (1473–1543) of his *De revolutionibus orbium coelestium* (*On the Revolutions of the Celestial Spheres*). According to the COPERNICAN SYSTEM, the earth rotates on its axis and, with all the other planets, revolves around the sun. The assertion that the earth is not the center of the universe was to have profound philosophical and religious consequences. Copernicus's principal claim for his new system was that it made calculations easier. He still retained the epicycles and uniform circular motion of the Ptolemaic system; but by placing the sun at the center, he was able to reduce the number of epicycles. Copernicus also determined the sidereal periods (time for one revolution around the sun) of the planets and their distance from the sun relative to the sun-earth distance (see ASTRONOMICAL UNIT). The next great astronomer, Tycho Brahe (1546–1601) was principally an observer; a conservative in matters of theory, he rejected the notion that the earth moves. Under the patronage of King Frederick II, Tycho established Uraniborg, a superb observatory on the Danish island of Hveen. Over a period of 20 years (1576–97), he and his assistants compiled the most accurate and complete astronomical observations the world had seen. At his death his records passed to Johannes Kepler (1571–1630), who had been his last assistant, in Prague. Kepler spent nearly a decade trying to fit Tycho's observations, particularly of Mars, into an improved system of heliocentric circular motion. At last, he conceived the idea that the orbit of Mars was an ellipse with the sun at one focus. This discovery led him to the three laws of planetary motion that bear his name (see KEPLER'S LAWS). Galileo Galilei (1564–1642) made fundamental discoveries in both astronomy and physics; he is perhaps the single man best described as the founder of modern science. Galileo was the first to make astronomical use of the TELESCOPE. His discoveries of the four largest moons of Jupiter and the phases of Venus were persuasive evidence for the Copernican cosmology. His discoveries of craters on the moon and blemishes on the sun (SUNSPOTS) discredited the ancient belief in the perfection of the heavens. These findings were announced in *The Sidereal Messenger,* a small book published in 1610. Galileo's *Dialogue on the Two Chief Systems of the World* (1632) was an eloquent argument for the Copernican system over the Ptolemaic. However, the new astronomical ideas had fallen into increasing disfavor with the church. Galileo was called before the Inquisition and forced to abjure all doctrines considered contrary to Scripture. His writings joined those of Kepler and Copernicus on the Papal Index. Isaac Newton (1642–1727), possibly the greatest scientific genius of all time, succeeded in uniting the sciences of astronomy and PHYSICS. His laws of motion and theory of universal GRAVITATION provided a physical, dynamic basis for the merely descriptive laws of Kepler. Until well into the 19th cent., all progress in astronomy was essentially an extension of Newton's work. Among the many triumphs of Newtonian theory was the beginning of an adequate theory of the TIDES. In the 18th cent. the work of many astronomers vindicated the Newtonian world system, which became the basis of all physical science. In 1728, James Bradley measured the periodic shifts in stellar positions due to the ABERRATION of light. Edmund Halley's prediction that the comet of 1682 would return in 1758 was refined by A. C. Clairault, who included the perturbing effects of Jupiter and Saturn on the orbit to calculate the nearly exact date of the return of the comet. Nevil Maskelyne measured the earth's mean density, which was essential for computing the masses of the earth and other bodies in the solar system. In 1781, William Herschel accidentally discovered a new major planet, eventually named Uranus. Discrepancies between the observed and theoretical orbits of Uranus indicated the existence of a still more distant planet that was affecting Uranus's motion. J. C. Adams and U. J. J. Leverrier independently calculated the position where the new planet, Neptune, was actually discovered (1846). (Similar calculations led in 1930 to the discovery of the most distant known planet, Pluto.) By the early 19th cent., the science of CELESTIAL MECHANICS had reached a highly developed state at the hands of Leonhard Euler, J. L. Lagrange, P. S. Laplace, and others. Powerful new mathematical techniques allowed solution of most of the remaining problems in classical gravitational theory as applied to the solar system. It was demonstrated that the present configuration of the planetary orbits will remain stable for the indefinite future. In 1801, Giuseppe Piazzi discovered Ceres, the first of many ASTEROIDS. When Ceres was lost to view, C. F. Gauss applied the advanced gravitational techniques to compute the position where the asteroid was subsequently rediscovered. In 1838, F. W. Bessel made the first measurement of the distance to a star; using the method of parallax with the earth's orbit as a baseline, he determined the distance of the star 61 Cygni to be 60 trillion mi (about 10 LIGHT-YEARS), a figure later shown to be 40% too large. Astronomy was revolutionized in the second half of the 19th cent. by the introduction of techniques based on photography and SPECTROSCOPY. Interest shifted from determining the positions and distances of stars to studying their physical composition (see STELLAR STRUCTURE and STELLAR EVOLUTION). The dark lines in the solar SPECTRUM that had been observed by W. H. Wollaston and Joseph von Fraunhofer were interpreted in an elementary fashion by G. R. Kirchhoff on the basis of classical physics, although a complete explanation came only with the QUANTUM THEORY. Between 1911 and 1913, Ejnar Hertzsprung and H. N. Russell studied the relation between the colors and luminosities of typical stars (see HERTZSPRUNG-RUSSELL DIAGRAM). With the construction of ever more powerful telescopes (see OBSERVATORY), the boundaries of the known universe constantly increased. Harlow Shapley determined the size and shape of our galaxy, the MILKY WAY. E. P. Hubble's study of the distant galaxies led him to conclude that the universe is expanding (see HUBBLE'S LAW). Various rival theories of the origin and overall structure of the universe, e.g., the big bang and steady state theories, were formulated (see COSMOLOGY). Albert Einstein's theory of RELATIVITY plays a central role in all modern cosmological theories. Most recently, the frontiers of astronomy have been expanded by SPACE EXPLORATION and observations in new parts of the spectrum (see SATELLITE, ARTIFICIAL; RADIO ASTRONOMY; X-RAY ASTRONOMY). The new observational techniques have led to the discovery of strange new astronomical objects, such as PULSARS, QUASARS, and BLACK HOLES. See Arthur Berry, *Short History of Astronomy* (1961); John L. Dreyer, *History of Astronomy from Thales to Kepler* (2d ed. 1953); G. O. Abell, *Exploration of the Universe* (2d ed. 1969); Nigel Calder, *Violent Universe* (1970); Lloyd Motz and Anneta Duveen, *Essentials of Astronomy* (1971); Zdeněk Kopal, *Man and His Universe* (1972); Robert Jastrow and M. H. Thompson, *Astronomy* (1972); Alexandre Koyré, *The Astronomical Revolution* (1973).

astrophysics, application of the theories and methods of physics to the study of STELLAR STRUCTURE, STELLAR EVOLUTION, the origin of the SOLAR SYSTEM, and related problems of COSMOLOGY.

Asturias, Miguel Ángel (mēgĕl' äng'hĕl ästo͞o'ryäs), 1899–1974, Guatemalan novelist, short-story writer, and poet. He worked as a journalist, foreign correspondent, and diplomat, serving as ambassador to El Salvador and later to France. His best-known works include *Las leyendas de Guatemala* [the legends of Guatemala] (1930), dealing with the early legends and folklore of Guatemala; *El señor presidente* (1946, tr. 1963), a novel about a Latin American dictatorship; *Viento fuerte* (1950; tr. *Strong Wind,* 1968), *El papa verde* (1954; tr. *The Green Pope,* 1971), and *Los ojos de los enterrados* (1955; tr. *The Eyes of the Interred,* 1973), a grim trilogy about banana exploitation in the Caribbean. Among his other works are *Week-end in Guatemala* (1956), a collection of short stories; *Mulata de tal* (1963; tr. *Mulata,* 1967), a mystical novel about the Guatemalan Indians; *The Talking Machine* (tr. 1971), a book for children about a frog; and *The Bejeweled Boy* (tr. 1972), a complex allusive novel replete with mysticism and Guatemalan legends. In 1967, Asturias was awarded the Nobel Prize in Literature. See study by R. J. Gallan (1970).

Asturias (ästo͞o'ryäs), region (1970 pop. 1,045,635) and former kingdom, NW Spain, S of the Bay of Biscay and E of Galicia, and coextensive with Oviedo prov. Drained by numerous swift rivers, it is crossed by the Cantabrian Mts. The coal mines, exploited since Roman times, are the richest in Spain. Iron, zinc, lead, and manganese are also mined. The steel mills and metallurgical industries have been important since the late 19th cent., although production and transportation costs are high. Cattle are raised on the broad mountain pastures. The extensive forests are favored by abundant rainfall. Along the coast, apple orchards are the source of a world-famous cider. Gijón is the chief port, and fishing is a major occupation. Most of the population, however, is engaged in mining. The name Asturias is derived from an Iberian people that lived there before the Roman conquest (2d cent. B.C.). When the Moors overran the peninsula, Christian nobles fled into the Asturian mountains. They created the first Christian kingdom of Spain (see PELAYO) and defended themselves at the battle of COVADONGA. From Asturias came the Christian reconquest of Spain, as the successors of King Alfonso I extended their control over Asturias, Galicia, León, and parts of Castile, Navarre, and Vizcaya. Astorga was one of the chief cities of the Asturian kingdom in the 9th cent. In the 10th cent. the capital was moved from Oviedo to León, and the kingdom of Asturias became the kingdom of Asturias and León, which three centuries later was united with the kingdom of Castile. In 1388, John I of León and Castile made his son prince of the Asturias—the title borne from that time on by the heir to the throne. The Asturians are noted for their stubborn courage and independence—traits shown in the warfare against Napoleon, in various uprisings against the Spanish government, in the civil war of 1936–39, and in the general strike of 1962.

Astyages (ăstī'əjēz), fl. 6th cent. B.C., king of the Medes (584–c.550 B.C.), son and successor of Cyaxares. His rule was harsh, and he was unpopular. His daughter is alleged to have married the elder Cambyses and was said to be the mother of CYRUS THE GREAT, who rebelled against Astyages and overthrew him (c.550 B.C.), thus creating the Persian Empire.

Astyanax (əstī'ənăks), in Greek mythology, son of Hector and Andromache. When the Greeks captured Troy, they killed him out of fear that he would avenge his father and his city. He was also known as Scamandrius.

Asunción (äso͞onsyōn'), city (1970 est. pop. 437,000), S Paraguay, capital of Paraguay, on the Paraguay River. It is the principal port and chief industrial and cultural center of Paraguay. Meat-packing is the main industry. From the east bank of the river, the city spreads out on gentle hills in a pattern of rectangular blocks. Asunción is one of the oldest cities in South America and has a decidedly colonial aspect, enhanced by red-tiled roofs, colorful patios, and flowering trees. Its outstanding structures are the government buildings, the Godoi Museum, the Church of La Encarnación, and the Panteón Nacional, a smaller version of Les Invalides in Paris, where many of the nation's heroes are entombed. The city's botanical gardens are notable. The site of the city may have been visited by the conquistador Juan de Ayolas, but the town, called Nuestra Señora de la Asunción [Our Lady of the Assumption], was founded in Aug., 1536 or 1537, by Juan de Salazar and Gonzalo de Mendoza. It became a trading post on the route to Peru and flourished under the governorship of Domingo Martínez de Irala, who founded there the first cabildo in South America. As the most important town in the Río de la Plata region, Asunción became the center of the Jesuits' activities in converting the Indian population. The city developed further under the great Creole governor Hernando Arias de Saavedra (first elected 1592). In 1731 the uprising of *comuneros* under José de Antequera y Castro was one of the first major rebellions against Spanish colonial rule. The eminence of Asunción was ended by the growth of Buenos Aires, which was separated from Asunción's jurisdiction in 1617. After the War of the Triple Alliance (1865–70), Asunción was occupied by Brazilian troops until 1876. The National Univ. and several colleges are in the city.

Asuppim (əsŭp'ĭm). KJV in 1 Chron. 26.15 reads "the house of Asuppim"; RSV reads more correctly "the storehouse."

Aswan or **Assuan** (both: äswän', ăswăn'), city (1970 est. pop. 206,000), capital of Aswan governorate, S Egypt, on the Nile River at the First Cataract. Long famous as a winter resort and commercial center, the city has become an important industrial center since the start nearby of hydroelectricity production in 1960. A chemical fertilizer plant is the largest of the new industries. Iron ore and hematite are mined in the vicinity. The city was called Syene or Seveneh in the Bible and is described as the southern limit of Egypt. It was a trade center, serving as the gateway to the Sudan and Ethiopia, and was the place where the annual Nile flood was first sighted in Egypt. From the syenite quarries nearby came stone for the temples and statuary of the Pharaohs. On ELEPHANTINE island, in the Nile opposite Aswan, and PHILAE island (submerged by the Aswan High Dam complex), south of the city, are found ancient Egyptian and Roman ruins. Aga Khan III (1877–1957), leader of the Muslim ISMAILIS, is buried in Aswan. The **Aswan Dam,** 3 mi (4.8 km) south of the city, was built by the British and completed in 1902. It and the barrages at Asyut in central Egypt were the chief means of storing irrigation water for the Nile valley before the completion of the Aswan High Dam (see below). After being enlarged in 1934, the dam added c.1 million acres (404,700 hectares) of cropland along the Nile. In 1960 a hydroelectric station with an annual capacity of 2 million kilowatt hours was opened at the dam. The **Aswan High Dam,** about 4 mi (6.4 km) S of the Aswan Dam, was constructed from 1960 to 1970, and was dedicated in 1971. Plans for the dam as the cornerstone of Egyptian President Gamal Abdal Nasser's economic development program were announced in 1953. Construction was delayed, however, until 1960 by disputes with Sudan over water rights and by the withdrawal in 1956 of U.S. and British financial aid. After 1956 the Soviet Union took over much of the financing (contributing ultimately about one third of the total cost of more than $1 billion) and technical supervision of the project. Built of earth and rock fill with a core of clay and cement, the High Dam is 375 ft (114 m) high and 11,811 ft (3,600 m) long. Lake Nasser (c.2,000 sq mi/5,180 sq km), the dam's reservoir and one of the world's largest artificial lakes, has a storage capacity of c.204 billion cu yd (157 billion cu m). The water of Lake Nasser has a potential for expanding agriculture in Egypt by c.2 million acres (809,400 hectares)—two thirds of which would be former desert land and one third of which would be former one-crop land planted with two crops yearly. By 1970, c.650,000 acres (263,000 hectares) of land had been reclaimed. In addition, water from Lake Nasser has a potential for increasing cropland in the Sudan by 5 million acres (2 million hectares). There are plans for a large fishing industry based on Lake Nasser. The High Dam's 12 turbines have an annual hydroelectricity capacity of 10 billion kilowatt hours, more than enough to satisfy Egypt's current needs, and enough to power considerable industrial expansion in the country. The creation of Lake Nasser required the relocation of 90,000 people, most of whom lived in Sudan, and of many archaeological treasures. Under UNESCO auspices, the Nubian temples at ABU SIMBEL were moved (1963–68) to a cliff 200 ft (61 m) above the old site and reconstructed. In return for its financial assistance in this project, the United States was given the Roman temple of Dendur, which was disassembled and shipped to the Metropolitan Museum of Art in New York City for reconstruction.

asylum (əsī'ləm), extension of hospitality and protection to a fugitive and the place where such protection is offered. The use of temples and churches for this purpose in ancient and medieval times was known as SANCTUARY. In modern international law, the granting of asylum to refugees from other lands is the right of a state by virtue of its territorial sovereignty. A fugitive, however, has no right to demand asylum from the state to which he flees; that state makes its own determination in each case. Between most nations there are treaties of EXTRADITION providing for the mutual surrender of fugitives from justice, and there is a tendency to confine the granting of asylum to political refugees and victims of apparent discrimination and intolerance. A situation causing many international disputes is the use of embassies and legations, by virtue of their status of EXTRATERRITORIALITY, as places of refuge in times of disorder and conflict. Most countries do not offer this type of asylum except when it seems necessary for the preservation of human life.

asymmetric carbon atom: see ISOMER.

Asyncritus (əsĭn'krĭtəs), Roman Christian. Rom. 16.14.

Asyut (äsyo͞ot'), city (1970 est. pop. 175,700), E central Egypt, on the Nile. An industrial and trading center and also the seat of a university, it is famed for its pottery, carved ivory and wood, leatherwork, and silk shawls. Nearby is the Asyut barrage, which helps to regulate the flow of the Nile and impounds water for irrigational use. Asyut was the ancient Greek city of Lycopolis and later a station of the caravan trade. The city has a large Coptic Christian population.

At, chemical symbol of the element ASTATINE.

Atabrine: see QUINACRINE.

Atacama, Desert of (ätäkä'mä), arid region, c.600 mi (970 km) long, N Chile, extending south from the border of Peru. The desert itself, c.2,000 ft (610 m) above sea level, is a series of dry salt basins flanked on the W by the Pacific coastal range, averaging c.2,500 ft (760 m) high, and on the E by the Andes. There is practically no vegetation; rain has virtually never been recorded in some localities. Of the streams descending from the Andes only the Loa River reaches the Pacific. Antofagasta and other regional ports are without protected anchorages and are subject to frequent and severe earthquakes. The Atacama has been a source of great nitrate and copper wealth. The first European to cross the forbidding waste was Diego de Almagro, the Spanish conquistador, in 1537. From then until the middle of the 19th cent. it was largely ignored, but with the discovery of the use of sodium nitrate as a fertilizer and later with the invention of smokeless powder using nitroglycerin, the desert had a mining boom. Although the southern half of Atacama belonged to Bolivia, the companies exploiting the deposits were Chilean. Differences arose, and in the ensuing war (see PACIFIC, WAR OF THE), Chile won the entire area. When synthetic nitrates were developed after World War I, the boom collapsed. Economically, the Atacama is declining, as reserves are depleted and the desert expands southward into once arable land.

Atad (ā'tăd), name of the unidentified threshing floor where Joseph and his brethren mourned the death of Jacob. Gen. 50.10,11.

Atahualpa (ätäwäl'pä), d. 1533, favorite son of Huayna Capac, Inca of Peru. At his father's death (1525) he received the kingdom of Quito while his half brother, the legitimate heir HUÁSCAR, inherited the rest of the Inca empire. Shortly before the arrival (1532) of Francisco PIZARRO, Atahualpa invaded the domains of Huáscar, whom he defeated and imprisoned, and made himself Inca. On Nov. 16, 1532, Pizarro met Atahualpa at Cajamarca. Invited into the city, Atahualpa was seized and imprisoned. He offered a room full of gold as ransom and at the same time secretly ordered the death of Huáscar. He was tried for his brother's murder and for plotting against the Spanish and was executed. He is also known as Atabalipa.

Atalanta (ătəlăn'tə), in Greek mythology, huntress famous for her speed and skill. She took part in the Calydonian hunt and was rewarded by Meleager with the pelt of the boar. Later, warned by an oracle not to marry, she demanded that each suitor run a race with her, on the condition that the winner would marry her and the losers would die. Hippomenes won the race by dropping three golden apples which Atalanta stopped to retrieve. Later, because Hippomenes and Atalanta made love in a temple sacred to Cybele, they were turned into lions and yoked to Cybele's chariot. Another version of the legend makes Milanion Atalanta's successful suitor.

Atami (ätä'mē), city (1970 pop. 51,281), Shizuoka prefecture, central Honshu, Japan. It is a major resort, famed for its scenery and its hot springs. Atami was once the site of a geyser which, according to tradition, wrought destruction until moved by Buddhist prayers. After an earthquake in 1923 the geyser stopped erupting.

Atarah (ăt'ərə), one of Jerahmeel's wives. 1 Chron. 2.26.

Atargatis (ătärgā'tĭs), ancient Syrian goddess. Of obscure origin, she probably belongs to the general pattern of mother goddesses that were worshiped throughout W Asia and Greece. In Rome she was called Dea Syria.

Ataroth (ăt'ərŏth). **1** Town of Gilead. Num. 32.3,34. **2** Unidentified place, E central Palestine. Joshua 16.7. **3** See ATAROTH-ADAR. **4** Place or family of Judah. 1 Chron. 2.54.

Ataroth-adar (ăt'ərŏth-ā'där), unidentified town, N of Jerusalem. Joshua 18.13. Ataroth: Joshua 16.2. Ataroth-addar: Joshua 16.5.

Ataroth-addar, the same as ATAROTH-ADAR.

Atascadero (ətăskədâr'ō), uninc. town (1970 pop. 10,290), San Luis Obispo co., SW Calif., on the Salinas River; founded 1913 as a model community. It is a residential and farming town. A state mental hospital is located there.

Atatürk, Kemal (kĕmäl' ätätürk'), 1881–1938, Turkish leader, founder of modern Turkey. He took the name in 1934 in place of his earlier name, Mustafa Kemal, when he ordered all Turks to adopt a surname; it is made up of the Turkish words Kemal [the perfect] and Atatürk [father of the Turks]. Born at Thessaloníki, he secretly applied to a military academy, where his excellence at mathematics won him the surname Kemal. As a military officer he joined the Young Turks, a liberal movement that sought to establish a constitutional government for the Ottoman Empire (Turkey). However, he disagreed with its pro-German policy, because he considered Turkish interests to be paramount. In 1908 he took part in the successful Young Turk revolution as chief of staff of ENVER PASHA, whom he later opposed over the German issue. He served in Libya (1911–12) and in the Second Balkan War (1913). In World War I his efficient work in the Dardanelles, on the Armenian front, and in Palestine, though it merely helped to postpone disaster, won him the title pasha. After the Ottomans capitulated to the Allies, Sultan MUHAMMAD VI sent Kemal to E Anatolia in an effort to curb his influence. Arriving in May, 1919, Kemal organized the Turkish Nationalist party and began to form an army. When the Turks were aroused by the Greek landing at Smyrna (now IZMIR) he convoked nationalist congresses at Erzurum (July, 1919) and Sivas (Sept.). Outlawed by the sultan, who was in the hands of the Allies in Constantinople, he set up a rival government at Ankara. The signing of the Treaty of SÈVRES by the Constantinople government made the split with Ankara final. With the tacit consent of Soviet Russia, Kemal retook Kars and Ardahan from Armenia (1920). Then, taking advantage of disagreements among the Allies, he expelled the Greeks from Anatolia in a brilliant campaign (1921–22). For his victory he received the official name Ghazi [victorious]. On Nov. 1, 1922, Kemal proclaimed the abolition of the sultanate, and Sultan Muhammad VI fled to a British warship. The Treaty of Lausanne (1923; see LAUSANNE, TREATY OF) was a triumph for the nationalist cause; an independent and sovereign Turkey was recognized by the European powers. Kemal was elected president (1923) of the newly founded Turkish republic and reelected in 1927, 1931, and 1935—all four times by a unanimous parliament. With astounding energy he set out on a program of internal reform and "Westernization"; 15 years of his rule changed Turkey profoundly in the most essential as well as the most minute aspects of its life (see TURKEY). Although a dictator, Kemal was prepared to tolerate limited opposition, but he was ruthless toward those he considered extremists. Regarding Islam as a conservative influence, he abolished (1924) the CALIPHATE (thereby in effect disestablishing Islam as the state religion) and broke all religious opposition to reform. Abroad, he pursued a policy of conciliation and neutrality. He established friendly relations with all neighbors, particularly Russia, helped to bring about the BALKAN ENTENTE, and freed Turkey from foreign influence, even though he had to refuse capital for industrialization of the country. On his death he was succeeded as president by İsmet İnönü. In 1953 his remains were transferred to a new mausoleum in Ankara. See biographies by Dagobert von Mikusch (tr. 1931), H. E. Wortham (1931), Hanns Froembgen (tr. 1937), and Lord Kinross (1966); D. E. Webster, *Turkey of Ataturk* (1939).

Ataulf (ăt'äəlf), d. 415, Visigothic king (410–15). Succeeding his brother-in-law, ALARIC I, he abandoned Alaric's scheme of southward expansion and led the Visigoths out of Italy into S Gaul (France) in 412. He sought the alliance of the Western emperor, HONORIUS, whose sister GALLA PLACIDIA he married in 414. However, the general Constantius (later Emperor CONSTANTIUS III), jealous of Ataulf, turned Honorius against him. Constantius blockaded the Gallic ports, and Ataulf, cut off from supplies, led his people into N Spain (see VISIGOTHS). He was assassinated at Barcelona.

atavism (ăt'əvĭzəm), the appearance in an individual of a characteristic not apparent in the preceding generation. Originally this phenomenon was thought to be a reversion to a hypothetical ancestral prototype. Mendelian law and the findings of GENETICS demonstrate that abnormal characteristics result from random recombinations of the recessive traits (masked in the intervening generations) that determined the characteristics of the earlier individual. So-called reversion to type may also be produced by disease or by aberrations in embryonic development.

ataxia (ətăk'sēə), lack of coordination of the voluntary muscles resulting in irregular movements of the body. Ataxia can be brought on by any injury, infection, or degenerative disease of the central nervous system, e.g., syphilis, encephalitis, brain tumor, or multiple sclerosis. The term is also used to designate a specific type of CEREBRAL PALSY.

Atbara (ăt'bärä), river, NE Africa, rising in NW Ethiopia and flowing c.500 mi (800 km) to the Nile in Sudan. There are few permanent settlements along its banks. The Atbara's water level is very low, except during the rainy season (from June to October). The river is called the Takazze in its early stages in Ethiopia and the Setit in W Ethiopia and E Sudan.

Atbarah (ătbä'rə), town (1969 est. pop. 53,000), NE Sudan, at the junction of the Atbara and Nile rivers. An important rail junction, it is also the headquarters of the Sudan railway system and has large railroad workshops. Most of the town's workers are connected with service and maintenance jobs on the rail lines. Sudanese trade unionism originated in Atbarah in 1946 with the founding of a workers' association among railroad employees.

Atchafalaya (əchă'fəlī"ə), navigable river, c.170 mi (270 km) long, S central La. The Atchafalaya meanders south, in a former channel of the Mississippi, to the Gulf of Mexico. A distributary of the Red and Mississippi rivers, the Atchafalaya flows to the Gulf through an extensive system of guide levees and floodways. The system serves as a flood control for the lower Mississippi, especially around New Orleans.

Atchison, David Rice, 1807–86, U.S. Senator, b. Frogtown, Ky. A lawyer and politician in Missouri, he served in the Senate from 1843 to 1855. As a proslavery Democrat, Atchison was instrumental in having the KANSAS-NEBRASKA ACT passed. After his defeat for reelection in 1855, he was a leader of the border ruffians in the raids into Kansas (1855–56). He supported the Confederacy in the Civil War. Atchison, Kansas, is named for him. See biography by W.E. Parrish (1961).

Atchison, city (1970 pop. 12,565), seat of Atchison co., NE Kansas, on the Missouri River; inc. as a city 1881. It is a trade and industrial center in a rich farm area. Steel castings and grain products are produced there. Atchison was founded (1854) near a military post, established (1818–19) on Cow Island in the Missouri River. The Atchison, Topeka & Santa Fe RR was chartered there in 1859, and the city boomed as an important wagon-train, river, and railroad terminal, one of the outfitting points for westward travel. Benedictine College is located in the city.

Ate (ā'tē), in Greek mythology, personification of the rash temper that leads men to folly and misfortune. She was the daughter of Zeus, who, angered by her mischief, cast her from Olympus. In Greek tragedy she was an avenger of evil deeds and thus was similar to Nemesis and the Furies.

Ater (ā'tər). **1** Ancestor of a family that returned with Zerubbabel. Ezra 2.16; Neh 7.21; 10.17. **2** Ancestor of a family of porters. Ezra 2.42; Neh. 7.45.

Atget, Eugène (özhĕn' ätzhĕ'), 1857–1927, French photographer. After working as a sailor and then as an actor for many years, Atget became a photographer at the age of 42. He began at once to produce his detailed visual record of Paris and its environs, particularly St. Cloud and Versailles. Atget made his living by selling his images of the city to painters for use as source material, and later to the Parisian historical monuments society. In making his photographs of the parks, lakes, shop windows, vendors, prostitutes, ragpickers, buildings, flower markets, sculpture gardens, doorways, bridges, and street scenes of Paris, Atget went beyond documentation. His quiet, reflective, and poetic images are dramatic with the force of time gone by. A large number of his many thousands of pictures are in the Museum of Modern Art, New York City. Atget's work was published and brought to international attention by the photographer Berenice ABBOTT. See A. D. Trottenberg, ed., *A Vision of Paris: the Photographs of Eugène Atget* (1963); Berenice Abbott, *The World of Atget* (1964).

Athabasca (ăthəbăs'kə), river, 765 mi (1,231 km) long, rising in the Columbia snowfield of the Canadian Rockies near the Alta.-British Columbia line and flowing N through Jasper National Park, then NE and N across central Alta. to Lake Athabasca. It is the southernmost headstream of the Mackenzie River. Its chief tributaries are the Pembina, Lesser Slave, and Clearwater rivers. The Athabasca River has long been the main route to the Mackenzie valley. There are extensive deposits of oil-bearing sand along the river near McMurray.

Athabasca, Lake, fourth largest lake of Canada, c.3,120 sq mi (8,100 sq km), c.200 mi (320 km) long and from 5 to 35 mi (8-56 km) wide, NE Alta., and SW Sask., at the edge of the Canadian Shield. A part of the Mackenzie River system, the lake receives the Athabasca River from the south and drains N into Great Slave Lake by way of the Slave River. Gold and uranium are found nearby. Fort Chipewyan was built (1788) at the west end of the lake by Roderick McKenzie of the North West Company and has been maintained. Steamers of the Hudson's Bay Company ply the lake in summer between Chipewyan and Fond du Lac, from where the canoe route runs by way of Wollaston and Reindeer lakes to the Churchill River. Philip Turnor, the British surveyor, surveyed and mapped the lake between 1790 and 1792.

Athabasca, Mount, 11,452 ft (3,491 m) high, W Alta., Canada, in the Canadian Rockies at the headwaters of the Athabasca River. It is on the edge of the Columbia snowfield, and the Saskatchewan and Athabasca glaciers flow around it.

Athabascan (ăthəbăs'kən), **Athapascan,** or **Athapaskan** (both:-păs'-), group of related North American Indian languages forming a branch of the Nadene linguistic family or stock. In the preconquest period, Athabascan was a large and extensive group of tongues. Its speakers lived in what are now Canada, Alaska, Oregon, California, Arizona, New Mexico, Texas, and parts of Mexico. Today the surviving Athabascan languages include Chipewyan, Kutchin, Carrier, and Sarsi (all in Canada); Chasta-Costa (in Oregon); Hoopa or Hupa (in California); Navaho (in New Mexico, Arizona, and Utah); and Apache (in Oklahoma, Arizona, New Mexico, Texas, and Mexico). These and other Athabascan languages are the mother tongues of about 100,000 Indians. The speech communities of most Athabascan languages today are small, with the exception of Navaho, which has roughly 80,000 speakers, most of whom can also speak English. The Navaho is one of the largest Indian tribes in the United States. A feature of the Navaho language, perhaps the best-known tongue in the Athabascan group, is its tonal quality. There are high tones, low tones, rising tones, and falling tones. Another important Athabascan tongue, Apache, is spoken in its various dialects by about 5,000 Indians. According to some authorities, the Athabascan languages face extinction relatively soon. See AMERICAN INDIAN LANGUAGES. See Harry Hoijer et al., *Studies in the Athapaskan Languages* (1963).

Athabasca Pass, 5,736 ft (1,748 m) high, W Alta. and E British Columbia, Canada, leading from the headwaters of the Athabasca River across the Continental Divide to the Columbia River. It was discovered by David Thompson, a Canadian fur trader, or one of his agents c.1811, and for the next 50 years it was the chief route of the Hudson's Bay men on their journeys to and from the Columbia River country.

Athach (ā'thăk), place in S Palestine, visited by David. 1 Sam. 30.30.

Athaiah (ăthā'yə), Judahite. Neh. 11.4. Uthai: 1 Chron. 9.4.

Athaliah (ăth"əlī'ə). **1** The only queen to occupy the throne of Judah, daughter of AHAB of Israel, wife of JEHORAM **2** of Judah, and mother of AHAZIAH **2** of Judah, whom she succeeded. She had the males of the royal family murdered, but her stepdaughter Jehosheba hid away a baby son of Ahaziah. Some years later, Jehosheba and her husband JEHOIADA **1** effected a coup d'etat in favor of this baby, JEHOASH **2.** Athaliah they killed. These events are the subject of Racine's *Athalie.* 2 Kings 11; 2 Chron. 22-23. **2** Benjamite. 1 Chron. 8.26. **3** Father of one who returned with Ezra. Ezra 8.7.

Athamas (ăth'əmăs), in Greek mythology, king of Boeotia. He married Nephele, who bore him Phrixus and Helle, but he later fell in love with INO, who bore him Learchus and Melicertes. According to one legend, Athamas went mad, killed Learchus and forced Ino, who was fleeing with Melicertes, to leap to her death in the sea.

Athanagild (əthăn'əgĭld), d. 567, Visigothic king of Spain (554-67). Having deposed his predecessor, Agila, with the aid of an army sent by Byzantine Emperor Justinian I, he ceded a large portion of S Spain to the Byzantines and was unable to prevent them from further extending their territory. Although throughout his rule he had to fight the Byzantines, the Franks, and the Basques, Athanagild strengthened his kingdom internally by conciliating the Catholics, whom his Arian predecessors had oppressed. His court at Toledo was famed for its splendor. Athanagild was the father of the Frankish queens Brunhilda and Galswintha. He was succeeded by his brothers Liuva and Leovigild.

Athanaric (əthăn'ərĭk), d. 381, Visigothic chieftain. He led the VISIGOTHS against Emperor VALENS and negotiated a favorable peace in 369. A pagan, he persecuted the Christians, and, possibly for that reason, he was involved in a civil war with FRITIGERN. Defeated by the Huns in 376, he fled to Transylvania and later (381) to Constantinople. There he was received with royal honors by Theodosius I, but he died two weeks later.

Athanasian Creed (ăthənā'zhən), exact, elaborate Roman Catholic statement on the Trinity and the Incarnation. It is no longer believed to have been written by Athanasius, but rather by an unknown Western author of the 6th cent. An English translation appears in the English Book of Common Prayer. It is sometimes called *Quicumque* or *Quicumque Vult* [whoever wishes (to be saved)].

Athanasius, Saint (ăthənā'zhəs), c.297-373, patriarch of Alexandria (328-73), Doctor of the Church, great champion of orthodoxy during the Arian crisis of the 4th cent. (see ARIANISM). In his youth, as secretary to Bishop Alexander, he took part in the christological debate against Arius at the Council of Nicaea (see NICAEA, FIRST COUNCIL OF), and thereafter became chief protagonist for Nicene orthodoxy in the long struggle for its acceptance in the East. He defended the formulary known as *homoousion,* which holds that Christ is of the same substance as the Father, against the various Arian parties who held that Christ was not identical in substance with the Father. The term itself, however, is not particularly his. Made bishop of Alexandria upon the death of his superior, he faced a conspiracy led by EUSEBIUS OF NICOMEDIA to return the condemned Arius to Egypt. When Athanasius refused, a pro-Arian council held at Tyre (335) found him guilty of sacrilege, the practice of magic, dishonest grain dealings, and even murder. Athanasius appealed to Constantine who demanded a retrial, then unaccountably ordered Athanasius into exile—the first of five. Reinstated (337) and exiled again (339), he fled to the West where, under Pope JULIUS I, the Council of Sardica vindicated him (343). To placate his Catholic brother Constans, the Arian Constantius permitted Athanasius to return to his see in 346. There he reigned, a beloved pastor, for ten fruitful years, strengthening orthodoxy in Egypt and composing some of his greatest works, including his *Defense Against the Arians* (348). When Constans died, Constantius procured the condemnation of Athanasius (Arles, 357), again forcing him into exile. It was during this period of hiding with the hermit monks of the Egyptian desert, whom he admired greatly, that he wrote his best exposition of Nicene christology, *Discourses Against the Arians,* attacking both the Arians and the views of MARCELLUS OF ANCYRA. By now a conservative reaction in the East issued in the strongly anti-Arian Lucianic creed promulgated at the Council of Seleucia (359), a step which led to the final victory of Nicene orthodoxy at the Council of Constantinople in 381. Athanasius was restored briefly in 362, only to be quickly exiled by Julian and again by Valens (365). The climate was changing, however, and by 366 Athanasius was secure in his see, where he remained the spokesman for orthodoxy until his death. After him, St. BASIL THE GREAT secured the victory of orthodoxy in the East. Selected works appear in collections of patristic literature—particularly his *De Incarnatione* (c.318). Feast: May 2.

Athapascan or **Athapaskan:** see ATHABASCAN; AMERICAN INDIAN LANGUAGES.

Atharva-Veda (ətär'və-vā'də,-vē-): see VEDA.

atheism, denial of the existence of God or gods and of any supernatural existence, to be distinguished from AGNOSTICISM, which holds that the existence cannot be proved. The term *atheism* has been used as an accusation against all who attack established orthodoxy, as in the trial of Socrates. There were few avowed atheists from classical times until the 19th cent., when popular belief in a conflict between religion and science brought forth preachers of the gospel of atheism, such as Robert G. Ingersoll. There are today many individuals and groups professing atheism.

Athelney, Isle of (ăth'əlnē), small area formerly surrounded by marshland, Somerset, SW England. King Alfred took refuge from the Danes there in 878 and founded a Benedictine abbey in 888. Relics have been found, including the Alfred Jewel, now in the Ashmolean Museum at Oxford.

Athelstan or **Æthelstan** (both: ăth'əlstən, ăth'-ĕlstăn), d. 939, king of Wessex (924-39), son and successor of Edward the Elder. As a youth he lived in the household of his aunt, Æthelflæd, Lady of the Mercians. After coming to the throne, he vigorously built up his kingdom on the foundations laid by his grandfather ALFRED. He made himself overlord of all England, establishing his hegemony firmly by victory over a coalition of his enemies at BRUNANBURH in 937. He was popular as well as able, was generous to the church, and issued laws that attempted to impose royal authority on customary law. Athelstan married his sisters to Charles III of France, the French duke Hugh the Great, Otto I of Germany, and Louis, king of Arles. He was succeeded by his brother Edmund. See F. M. Stenton, *Anglo-Saxon England* (2d ed. 1947).

Athena (əthē'nə), or **Pallas Athena** (păl'əs), in Greek religion, one of the most important Olympian deities. According to myth, after Zeus seduced Metis he learned that any son she bore would overthrow him, so he swallowed her alive. Later Hephaestus split Zeus' skull with an ax, and out sprang Athena, fully armed. Athena was a deity of diverse functions and attributes. Her most conspicuous role was perhaps that of a goddess of war, the female counterpart of Ares. However, she was also a goddess of peace, noted for her compassion and generosity. Like Minerva, with whom the Romans identified her, she was a patron of the arts and crafts, especially spinning and weaving. In later times she was important as a goddess of wisdom. Athena was also a guardian of cities, notably Athens, where the Parthenon was erected as her temple. In a contest with Poseidon concerning dominion over Attica, Athena made an olive tree grow on the Acropolis while Poseidon caused a saltwater stream to gush from the Acropolis. The other Olympians, asked to judge the contest, decided in favor of Athena. Her statue, the PALLADIUM, was supposed to protect the city that possessed it. It was said that because she accidentally killed PALLAS she set the name Pallas before her own. Although a virgin goddess, she was concerned with fertility, and at Athens and Elis her worship was notably maternal. Athena is represented in art as a stately figure, armored, and wielding the AEGIS. Her most important festival was the PANATHENAEA.

Athenaeus (ăth"ənē'əs), fl. c.200, Greek writer, b. Naucratis, Egypt. His anthological work, the *Deipnosophistae* (Banquet of the Sophists), is valuable because of the wealth of information it contains on Greek manners and customs.

Athenodorus: see LAOCOÖN.

Athens (ăth'ĭnz), Gr. *Athínai,* city (1971 pop. 867,023), capital of Greece, E central Greece, on the plain of Attica, between the Kifisós and Ilissus rivers, near the Saronic Gulf. Mt. Aigáleos (1,534 ft/468 m), Mt. Parnis (4,633 ft/1,412 m), Mt. Pendelikón (3,638 ft/1,109 m), and Mt. Hymettus (3,370 ft/1,027 m) rise in a semicircle around the city. The capital of Attica prefecture, Athens is Greece's largest city and its administrative, economic, and cultural center. Greater Athens, which includes the port of PIRAIÉVS and numerous suburbs, has a population of more than 2.5 million and accounts for most of Greece's industrial output. Manufactures include silk, wool, and cotton textiles, machine tools, steel, ships, food products, beverages, chemicals, pottery, printed materials, and carpets. Greater Athens is a transportation hub, served by rail lines, major roads, airlines, and ocean-going vessels. There is a large tourist industry. Water for the city is supplied by the Marathón reservoir (1931), formed by a dam made of Pentelic marble.

The cultural legacy of ancient Athens to the world is incalculable; to a great extent the references to the Greek heritage that abound in the culture of Western Europe are to Athenian civilization. Athens, named after its patron goddess Athena, was inhabited in the Bronze Age. Its citizens later proudly claimed that their ancestors had lived in the city even before the settlements of Attica were molded into a single state (according to legend, by THESEUS). According to tradition, Athens was governed until c.1,000 B.C. by Ionian kings, who had gained suzerainty over all Attica. After the Ionian kings Athens was rigidly governed by its aristocrats through the archontate (see ARCHONS), until SOLON began to enact liberal reforms in 594 B.C. Solon abolished serfdom, modified the harsh laws attributed to DRACO (who had governed Athens c.621 B.C.), and altered the economy and constitution to give power to all the propertied classes, thus establishing a limited democracy. His economic reforms were largely retained when Athens came under (560–511 B.C.) the rule of the tyrant PISISTRATUS and his sons HIPPIAS and HIPPARCHUS. During this period the city's economy boomed and its culture flourished. Building on the system of Solon, CLEISTHENES then established (c.506 B.C.) a democracy for the freemen of Athens, and the city remained a democracy during most of the years of its greatness. The PERSIAN WARS (500–449 B.C.) made Athens the strongest Greek city-state. Much smaller and less powerful than SPARTA at the start of the wars, Athens was more active and more effective in the fighting against Persia. The Athenian heroes MILTIADES, THEMISTOCLES, and CIMON were largely responsible for building the city's strength. In 490 B.C. the Greek army defeated Persia at MARATHON. A great Athenian fleet won a major victory over the Persians off the island of Salamis (480 B.C.). The powerful fleet also enabled Athens to gain hegemony in the DELIAN LEAGUE, which was created in 478–477 B.C. through the confederation of many city-states; in succeeding years the league was transformed into an empire headed by Athens. The city arranged peace with Persia in 449 B.C. and with its chief rival, Sparta, in 445 B.C., but warfare with smaller Greek cities continued. During the time of PERICLES (443–429 B.C.) Athens reached the height of its cultural and imperial achievement. Under Pericles, the philosopher SOCRATES and the dramatists AESCHYLUS, SOPHOCLES, and EURIPIDES were active. The incomparable Parthenon was built, and sculpture and painting flourished. Athens became a center of intellectual life; probably never again in the history of the West (unless perhaps in Renaissance Florence) was so much creative genius gathered in one place. However, the rivalry with Sparta had not ended, and in 431 B.C. the PELOPONNESIAN WAR between Sparta and Athens began. It went badly for Athens from the start. The Long Walls built to protect the city and its port of Piraiévs saved the city itself as long as the fleet was paramount, but the allies of Athens fell away and the land empire Pericles had tried to build already had crumbled before his death in 429 B.C. The war dragged on under the leadership of CLEON and continued even after the collapse of the expedition against Sicily, urged (415 B.C.) by ALCIBIADES. The Peloponnesian War finally ended in 404 B.C. with Athens completely humbled, its population cut in half, and its fleet reduced to a dozen ships. Under the dictates of Sparta, Athens was compelled to tear down the Long Walls and to accept the government of an oligarchy called the THIRTY TYRANTS. However, the city recovered rapidly. In 403 B.C. the Thirty Tyrants were overthrown by THRASYBULUS, and by 376 B.C. Athens again had a fleet, had rebuilt the Long Walls, had re-created the Delian League, and had won a naval victory over Sparta. Sparta also lost power as a result of its defeat (371 B.C.) by Thebes at LEUCTRA; and, although Athens did not again achieve hegemony over Greece, it did have a short period of great prosperity and comfort. However, the growth of Macedon's power under Philip II heralded the demise of Athens as a major power. Despite the pleas by DEMOSTHENES to the citizens of Athens to stand up against Macedon, Athens was decisively defeated by Philip at Chaeronea in 338 B.C. The city did not dare dispute the mastery of Philip's son and successor, Alexander the Great. After his death Athens revolted (323–322 B.C.) against control by Macedon, but the revolt was quashed, and Athens lost its remaining dependencies and declined into a provincial city. Its last bid for greatness (266–262 B.C.) was firmly suppressed by ANTIGONUS II, king of Macedon. Through the troubled times of the Peloponnesian War and the wars against Philip, Athenian achievements in philosophy, drama, and art had continued. ARISTOPHANES wrote comedies, PLATO taught at the Academy, ARISTOTLE compiled an incredible store of information, and Thucydides wrote a great history of the Peloponnesian War. As the city's glory waned in the 3d cent. B.C., its earlier contributions were spread over the world in Hellenistic culture. Athens became a minor ally of growing Rome, and a period of stagnation was broken only when the city unwisely chose to support Mithridates VI of Pontus against Rome. As a result, Athens was sacked by the Roman general Sulla in 86 B.C. Nevertheless, Athens sent out many teachers to Rome and retained a certain faded glory as a moderately prosperous small city in the backwash of the empire. It remained so until the time when the Eastern Empire began to fall to the barbarians. Athens was captured in A.D. 395 by the Visigoths under Alaric I. It became a provincial capital of the Byzantine Empire and a center of religious learning and devotion. Following the creation (1204) of the Latin Empire of Constantinople (see CONSTANTINOPLE, LATIN EMPIRE OF), Athens passed (1205) to Othon de la Roche, a French nobleman from Franche-Comté, who was made *megaskyr* [great lord] of Athens and Thebes. His nephew and successor, Guy I, obtained the ducal title, and the duchy of Athens, under Guy I and his successors, enjoyed great prosperity while becoming thoroughly French in its institutions. In 1311 the duchy was captured by a band of Catalan soldier-adventurers who offered (1312) the ducal title to King Frederick II of Sicily, a member of the house of Aragón. Members of the house of Aragón carried the title, but Athens was in fact governed by the "Catalan Grand Company," which also acquired (1318) the neighboring duchy of Neopatras. The French feudal culture disappeared, and Athens sank into insignificance and poverty, particularly after 1377, when the succession was contested in civil war. Peter IV of Aragón assumed sovereignty in 1381, but ruled from Barcelona. On his initiative, the devastated duchy was settled by Albanians. Athens again prospered briefly after its conquest in 1388 by Nerio I Acciajuoli, lord of Corinth, a Florentine noble. Under the Acciajuoli family's rule numerous Florentine merchants established themselves in Athens. However, the fall of the Acropolis to the Ottoman Turks in 1458 marked the beginning of nearly four centuries of Ottoman rule, and Athens once more declined. Venice, which had held Athens from 1394 to 1402, recovered it briefly from the Turks in 1466 and besieged it in 1687–88. During the siege the Parthenon, used by the Turks as a powder magazine, was largely blown up in a bombardment. Modern Athens was constructed only after 1834, when it became the capital of a newly independent Greece. OTTO I, first king of the Hellenes (1832–62), rebuilt much of the city, and the first modern Olympic games were held in Athens in 1896. The population of Athens grew rapidly in the 1920s, when Greek refugees arrived from Turkey. The city's inhabitants suffered extreme hardships during the German occupation (1941–44) in World War II, but the city escaped damage in the war and in the country's civil troubles of 1944–50. The main landmark of Athens is the ACROPOLIS (412 ft/126 m), which dominates the city and on which stand the remains of the PARTHENON, the PROPYLAEA, and the ERECHTHEUM. Occupying the southern part of Athens, the Acropolis is ringed by the other chief landmarks of the ancient city—the Pnyx, where the citizens' assemblies were held; the AREOPAGUS; the Theseum of Hephaesteum, a well-preserved Doric temple of the 5th cent. B.C.; the old Agora and the Roman forum; the temple of Zeus or Olympieum (begun under Pisistratus in the 6th cent. B.C. and completed in the 2d cent. A.D. under Hadrian, whose arch stands nearby); the theatre of Dionysius (oldest in Greece); and the Odeum of HERODES ATTICUS. There are many Roman remains in the "new" quarter, built east of the original city walls by Emperor Hadrian (1st cent. A.D.); there the modern royal palace and gardens also stand. The STADIUM is E of the Ilissus River. Parts of the ancient city walls are still visible, particularly at the Dipylon, the sacred gate on the road to Eleucis (Eleusis); however, the Long Walls connecting Athens and Piraiévs have almost entirely disappeared. The most noteworthy Byzantine structures are the churches of St. Theodora and of the Holy Apostles, both built in the 12th cent. Athens is the see of an archbishop who presides over the Synod of the Greek Orthodox Church. The city is the seat of the National and Capodistrian University (1837), a polytechnic institute, an academy of sciences, several schools of archaeology, and many museums and libraries. A nuclear research center is nearby, at Aghia Paraskevi. The Greek geographer PAUSANIAS wrote an extensive description of Greece. HERODOTUS, THUCYDIDES, XENOPHON, and POLYBIUS were great Greek historians. Modern general works on ancient Greece include those of J. B. BURY and Michael ROSTOVTZEFF. See A. H. M. Jones, *Athenian Democracy* (1957); C. A. Robinson, *Athens in the Age of Pericles* (1959); P. L. MacKendrick, *The Athenian Aristocracy* (1967); J. C. Hill, *The Ancient City of Athens, Its Topography and Monuments* (rev. ed. 1969); G. Giannelli, *The World of Classical Athens* (1970); C. M. Bowra, *Periclean Athens* (1971); Russell Meiggs, *The Athenian Empire* (1972). See also bibliography under GREECE.

Athens. **1** City (1970 pop. 14,360), seat of Limestone co., N Ala., near the Tenn. line, in a farm area; inc. 1818. It has food-processing industries and plants that make textiles, thermostats, stoves, and chemicals. Sacked and occupied by Federals in 1862, it was recaptured by Gen. N. B. Forrest in 1864. Fine antebellum buildings remain. Athens College is there, and a nuclear power plant is nearby. **2** City (1970 pop. 44,342), seat of Clarke co., NE Ga., on the Oconee River, in a piedmont area; inc. 1806. The city was founded as the site of the Univ. of Georgia. Its industries include poultry processing and the manufacture of clocks, watches, radios, and textiles. Numerous Georgia statesmen have lived in Athens, and some of their houses are among the city's many fine examples of classic revival style—the Howell Cobb house (1850), the T. R. R. Cobb house (1830–43), and the Joseph H. Lumpkin house (c.1845). **3** City (1970 pop. 23,310), seat of Athens co., SE Ohio, on bluffs overlooking the Hocking River, in a coal-mining area of the Appalachian foothills; inc. 1811. There are diverse industries in the city. Athens was surveyed in 1795–96 by the Ohio Company of Associates as the site of a university and was settled shortly thereafter. It is the seat of Ohio Univ. and of a state mental hospital. Wayne National Forest is to the north. **4** City (1970 pop. 11,790), seat of McMinn co., E. Tenn., in a farm and resort area; inc. 1829. Furniture, plastics, farm implements, dairy products, and insecticides are made. Tennessee Wesleyan College is there.

atherosclerosis (ăth″ərōsklərō′sĭs): see ARTERIOSCLEROSIS.

Atherton, Gertrude Franklin (Horn), 1857–1948, American writer, b. San Francisco. She wrote a series of historical novels about California, which include *The Californians* (1898), *Rezánov* (1906), and *The Ancestors* (1907). Her most popular books are *The Conqueror* (1902), which is a fictionalized biography of Alexander Hamilton, and the sensational novel *Black Oxen* (1923), concerning a woman who is rejuvenated by a glandular operation and based on Atherton's own experience of glandular therapy. See her autobiography *The Adventures of a Novelist* (1932).

Athlai (ăth′lī, ăthlā′ī), Israelite. Ezra 10.28.

athlete's foot: see RINGWORM.

athlete's heart, common term for an enlarged HEART associated with repeated strenuous exercise. As a result of the increased workload required of it, the heart will stretch, or hypertrophy, enlarging the size of the chambers and increasing the volume of blood pumped per stroke. Consequently, the heart has to contract less frequently and at rest will beat as few as 40 times per minute as compared with an average number of 70 beats in a normal heart. The condition is not pathological, and there is probably no danger of cardiac disability arising from it.

Athlone, Godart van Ginkel, Ist **earl of:** see GINKEL, GODART VAN.

Athlone (ăthlōn′), urban district (1971 pop. 9,821), Co. Westmeath, central Republic of Ireland, on the Shannon River. It is an important road and rail junction and a busy inland port, reached by the river and two canals. Industries include the production of cotton textiles, woolens, mineral water, and furniture. The English occupied the town in the 13th cent. and built Athlone Castle. Possession of the town was disputed during succeeding centuries, and the castle was often besieged. Athlone fell to the forces of William III of Great Britain in 1691. It is an important military station and the main transmitting station of the Irish National Radio.

Athol (ăth′əl), town (1970 pop. 11,185), Worcester co., N Mass.; inc. 1762. Its manufactures include tools, drills, shoes, and toys. The area was settled in 1735.

Atholl (ăth′əl), successively an earldom, a marquisate, and a dukedom of Scotland, See STUART, JOHN, and MURRAY, JOHN.

Athor: see HATHOR.

Athos (ăth'ŏs, ā'thŏs) or **Akte** (ăk'tā), easternmost of the three peninsulas of KHALKIDHIKÍ, c.130 sq mi (340 sq km), NE Greece, in Macedonia. At the southern tip of the peninsula is the virtually independent state of the monks of **Mount Athos,** also called Hagion Oros [Gr.,=Holy Mountain], which rises to c.6,670 ft (2,030 m). Mount Athos is a community of about 20 monasteries of the Order of St. Basil of the Orthodox Eastern Church and includes c.30 sq mi (80 sq km) of territory. The first monastery was founded c.963. The community of monks (see MONASTICISM) enjoyed administrative independence under the Byzantine and Ottoman empires and under the modern Greek government. In 1927 it was made a theocratic republic under Greek suzerainty, ruled by the patriarch of Constantinople. Karyai, the chief town of Athos, is the seat of the Holy Community, a committee made up of one representative from each monastery, which governs the monks of Mount Athos. No woman or female animal is allowed in the religious community. The icons from Mount Athos are celebrated; the libraries contain a great wealth of Byzantine manuscripts.

Atitlán (ätētlän'), volcanic lake, 53 sq mi (137 sq km), 17 mi (27.3 km) long and 11 mi (17.7 km) wide, SW Guatemala. One of the most magnificent lakes of Central America, it is set among lofty mountains with three inactive volcanoes nearby; Atitlán volcano (11,565 ft/3,525 m) is the tallest. The fertile lakeshore is densely populated by subsistence farmers. Through the principal towns on the lake, Santiago Atitlán, San Lucas Tolimán, and Panajachel, the Indians, paddling dugouts, transport produce to and from the Pacific coast and the highlands.

Atkinson, Brooks (Justin Brooks Atkinson), 1894–, American journalist, b. Melrose, Mass. He began his career as a reporter for the Springfield, Mass., *Daily News* and later worked for the Boston *Transcript.* After serving as an editor for the New York *Times,* he became its drama critic in 1925. Except for his service as a foreign correspondent during World War II, he held the position as critic until 1960. His critical opinion had much influence on the success or failure of Broadway plays. Upon his retirement as drama critic, a New York theater was named for him. Atkinson's books include *Henry Thoreau, the Cosmic Yankee* (1927), *Broadway Scrapbook* (1947), and *Broadway* (1970). An ardent naturalist and conservationist, he wrote *This Bright Land: A Personal View* (1972).

Atkinson, Henry, 1782–1842, American army officer, b. North Carolina. After service as a colonel in the War of 1812, he was a commander in the West and led two expeditions (1819, 1825) to the Yellowstone River. He was general commander of forces in the BLACK HAWK WAR and later superintended removal of the Winnebago Indians to Iowa. Jefferson Barracks (near St. Louis) and Fort Leavenworth were begun under his direction. See biography by R. L. Nichols (1965).

Atlanta (ətlăn'tə, ăt-), city (1970 pop. 497,421), state capital and seat of Fulton co., NW Ga., near the Appalachian foothills; inc. as a city 1847. It is the largest city and the cultural, industrial, transportation, financial, and commercial center of the state; a port of entry; a busy air traffic hub; and one of the leading cities of the South. Manufactures include textiles, furniture, chemicals, glass, paper, lumber, steel, and leather, electrical, and aluminum products. There are flour mills, automobile and aircraft assembly plants, and printing and publishing houses. Hardy Ivy, the first settler, built a cabin there (1833) on what had been Creek Indian land. The town, founded (1837) as Terminus, the end of a railroad line, was incorporated as Marthasville in 1843 and renamed Atlanta in 1845. It became a railroad and marketing hub and in the Civil War was an important communication and supply center; it fell to Gen. W. T. Sherman on Sept. 2, 1864 (see ATLANTA CAMPAIGN). Most of the city was burned on Nov. 15, before Sherman began his march to the sea. The city was rapidly rebuilt and thrived as a commercial and industrial center. It was chosen temporary state capital in 1868 and became permanent capital following a popular vote in 1877. A number of conventions and expositions in the 19th and 20th cent. drew attention to Atlanta's strategic distributory position. Points of interest include the capitol (1899), housing the state library; the city hall (1929); the High Museum of Art; the state archives building, containing an historical museum and library; the building housing the huge *Cyclorama of the Battle of Atlanta;* Oakland Cemetery, containing Civil War dead; "Underground Atlanta," a four-block tract covered for 50 years by a vast viaduct system, now being restored; the grave of Martin Luther King, Jr.; and Grant Park, with the municipal zoo and Confederate Fort Walker (restored). The Federal penitentiary there (est. 1899) is one of the most widely known prisons in the United States. Many departments of the Federal government have branches in Atlanta; also there are Fort McPherson, headquarters of the U.S. 3d Army, and a naval air station. The city's numerous parks are famous for their dogwood blooms, and in the area are Stone Mountain Park, with enormous relief carvings of Confederate figures, and Kennesaw Mountain National Battlefield Park (see NATIONAL PARKS AND MONUMENTS, table). Atlanta is the seat of Emory Univ., Georgia Institute of Technology, Georgia State Univ., Oglethorpe Univ., Beulah Heights College, the Atlanta School of Art, and Atlanta Univ., with its adjacent and affiliated schools, Clark College, Morehouse College, Morris Brown College, and Spelman College. There is a symphony orchestra, and the Atlanta stadium is home for the city's professional football and baseball teams.

Atlanta campaign, May–Sept. 1864, of the U.S. Civil War. In the spring of 1864, Gen. W. T. SHERMAN concentrated the Union armies of G. H. Thomas, J. B. McPherson, and J. M. Schofield around Chattanooga. On May 6 he began to move along the railroad from Chattanooga to Atlanta against Dalton, Ga., c.30 mi (48 km) southeast, where Gen. J. E. JOHNSTON had a smaller Confederate force. Sherman had a twofold objective: the destruction of Johnston's army and the capture of Atlanta, c.140 mi (225 km) southeast. Since Johnston was strongly entrenched, Sherman turned his left flank, forcing him back to Resaca, c.12 mi (19 km) south. The campaign continued in this way—Sherman outflanking Johnston, who withdrew to previously fortified positions—until June 27, when Sherman tried a direct attack at Kennesaw Mt., c.25 mi (40 km) NW of Atlanta, and was repulsed. He then reverted to flank operations. By July, Johnston had withdrawn to the south bank of the Chattahoochee River, where he prepared to fight on his own terms. On July 17, the day Sherman crossed the Chattahoochee, John Bell HOOD replaced Johnston. Following Johnston's plan, Hood unsuccessfully attacked Sherman's divided army (July 20) as it crossed Peach Tree Creek, a small tributary of the Chattahoochee. In the battles of Atlanta (July 22) and Ezra Church (July 28), Hood again failed to stop the Union advance; he then retired behind the strong works of Atlanta, which Sherman soon had under bombardment. The Union lines were gradually extended until the Confederate line of communications south of the city was broken on Sept. 1. Hood abandoned Atlanta that night and Sherman occupied it on Sept. 2, 1864. See A. A. Hoehling, *Last Train from Atlanta* (1958); Samuel Carter, *The Siege of Atlanta, 1864* (1973).

Atlanta University Center, at Atlanta, Ga.; coeducational. It was organized in 1929 when Atlanta Univ. (chartered 1867), Morehouse College (1867), and Spelman College (1881) became affiliated in a university plan, in which Atlanta Univ. was to be devoted exclusively to graduate education, with the other two colleges providing undergraduate programs. In 1947 the Atlanta Univ. School of Social Work (1920) merged with Atlanta Univ. Later Clark College (chartered 1877), Interdenominational Theological Center, and Morris Brown College (1885) also joined the university center's affiliation agreement.

atlantes (ătlăn'tēz) [Latin plural of ATLAS], sculptured male figures serving as supports, or apparent supports, in place of a column or pier. The earliest (c.480–460 B.C.) and most important example from antiquity is in the Greek temple of Zeus at Agrigento, Sicily. The baroque architecture of the 17th cent. made considerable use of atlantes, and they were a frequent decorative motif in mantelpieces and doorways of the classical revival in the early 19th cent.

Atlantic cable: see CABLE.

Atlantic Charter, joint program of peace aims, enunciated by Prime Minister Winston Churchill of Great Britain and President Franklin Delano Roosevelt of the United States on Aug. 14, 1941. Britain at that time was engaged in World War II, and the United States was to enter the war four months later. The statement, which was not an official document, was drawn up at sea, off the coast of Newfoundland. It supported the following principles and aims: renunciation of territorial aggrandizement; opposition to territorial changes made against the wishes of the people concerned; restoration of sovereign rights and self-government to those forcibly deprived of them; access to raw materials for all nations of the world and easing of trade restrictions; world cooperation to secure improved economic and social conditions for all; freedom from fear and want; freedom of the seas; and abandonment of the use of force, as well as disarmament of aggressor nations. In the United Nations declaration of Jan. 1, 1942, the signatory powers pledged adherence to the principles of the charter.

Atlantic City, city (1970 pop. 47,859), Atlantic co., SE N.J., an Atlantic resort and convention center; settled c.1790, inc. 1854. Situated on Absecon Island, a sandbar that is 10 mi (16.1 km) long, Atlantic City was a fishing village until the construction of a railroad in 1854, when it became a fashionable resort for Philadelphians and New Yorkers. The first boardwalk was built in 1870. Atlantic City's chief industry is tourism; about 15 million visitors come annually. The present boardwalk, lined with hotels, shops, and amusements, is 6 mi (9.7 km) long and from 40 to 60 ft (12.2–18.3 m) wide. Rolling chairs, introduced in 1884, provide pleasant rides along the boardwalk. Five amusement piers, including the famous Steel Pier (1898), run out to sea from the boardwalk. Atlantic City has a large convention hall; football games are played in its main arena and the Democratic national convention took place there in 1964. The Miss America Pageant is held in Atlantic City every September. Absecon Lighthouse, in operation from 1854 to 1932, is now a tourist attraction. The first Ferris wheel was built in Atlantic City in 1869. The board game Monopoly, which makes use of the city's street names, was invented there in 1930. Saltwater taffy, developed in Atlantic City, is the chief manufacture.

Atlantic Ocean [Lat.,=of Atlas], second largest ocean (c.31,800,000 sq mi/82,362,000 sq km; c.36,000,000 sq mi/93,240,000 sq km with marginal seas), extending in an S shape from the arctic to the antarctic regions between North and South America on the west and Europe and Africa on the east. It is connected with the Arctic Ocean by the Greenland Sea and Smith Sound; with the Pacific Ocean by Drake Passage, the Straits of Magellan, and the Panama Canal; and with the Indian Ocean by the Suez Canal and the expanse between Africa and Antarctica. The shortest distance across the Atlantic Ocean (c.1,600 mi/2,575 km) is between SW Senegal, W Africa, and E Brazil, E South America. The principal arms of the Atlantic Ocean are (in the west) Hudson and Baffin bays, the Gulf of Mexico, and the Caribbean Sea; (in the east) the Baltic, North, Mediterranean, and Black seas, the Bay of Biscay, and the Gulf of Guinea; and (in the south) Weddell Sea. The continental shelf of the Atlantic Ocean is generally narrow, with the widest sections found off NE North America, SE South America, and NW Europe. The Atlantic has relatively few islands, with the greatest concentration found in the Caribbean region. Most of the islands are structurally part of the continents, such as the British Isles, Falkland Islands, Canary Islands, and Newfoundland. Islands such as Iceland, the Azores, the Cape Verde Islands, Ascension, the South Sandwich Islands, the West Indies, and Bermuda are exposed tops of submarine ridges. The Bahamas are low coral islands, while the Madeiras are high volcanic islands. The floor of the Atlantic has an average depth of c.12,000 ft (3,660 m). It is separated from that of the Arctic Ocean by a submarine ridge extending from SE Greenland to N Scotland; part of the floor (c.3,000 ft/910 m deep) is known as "telegraph plateau" because of the network of cables laid there. A shallow submarine ridge across the Strait of Gibraltar separates the Mediterranean basin from the Atlantic and limits the exchange of water between the two bodies. The Mid-Atlantic Ridge (c.300–600 mi/480–970 km wide), a submarine mountain range extending c.10,000 mi (16,100 km) from Iceland to near the Antarctic Circle, generally follows the trend of the coastlines of the continents. It rises to an average height of c.10,000 ft (3,050 m), and a few peaks emerge as islands. The ridge, which is the center of volcanic activity and earthquakes, has a great rift that is constantly widening (see SEA-FLOOR SPREADING) and filling with molten rock from the earth's interior. As a result the Western Hemisphere and Europe and Africa are moving away from each other. The Mid-Atlantic Ridge divides the floor of the Atlantic Ocean into eastern and western sections that are composed of a series of deep-sea basins (abyssal plains). The greatest depth (c.28,000 ft/8,530 m) is the Milwaukee Deep, in the Puerto Rico Trench, N of Puerto Rico. More large rivers, including the Mississippi, the Congo, and the Amazon, drain into the

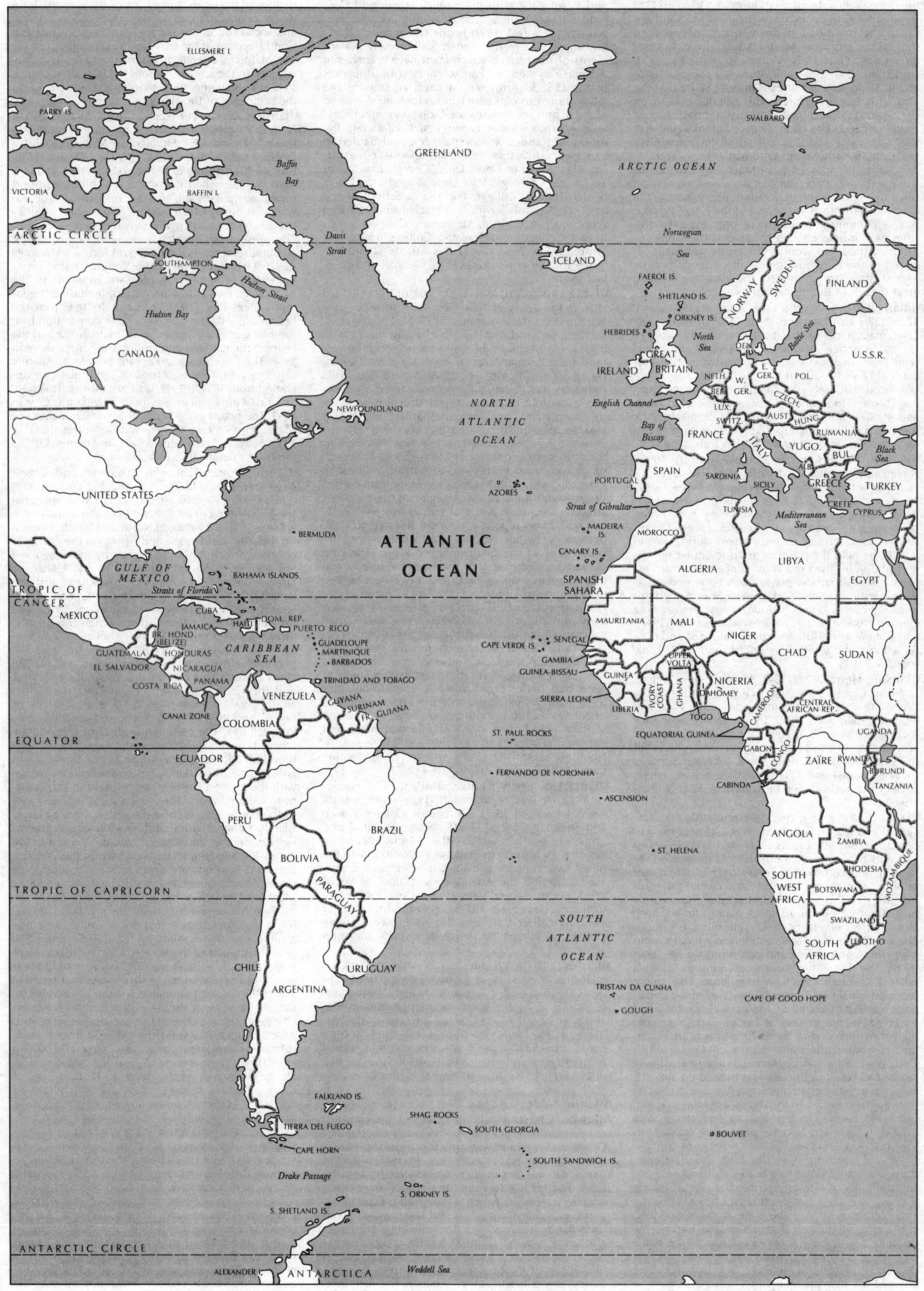

Cross-references are indicated by SMALL CAPITALS.

Atlantic than into any other ocean. The surface waters in the Atlantic's trade wind belts attain the highest salinity known in ocean water. Because of its shape, the Atlantic may be divided into two basins—North Atlantic Ocean and South Atlantic Ocean—each with a distinct circulation system. The clockwise-moving currents of the North Atlantic (North Equatorial Current, Antilles Current, Gulf Stream, North Atlantic Drift, Canaries Current) and the counterclockwise-moving currents of the South Atlantic (South Equatorial Current, Brazil Current, West Wind Drift, Benguela Current) are separated from each other by the Equatorial Counter Current; the Guinea Current off W Africa is a link between the two systems. At the Grand Banks off Newfoundland heavy fogs form along the front where the warm Gulf Stream meets the cold Labrador Current. The Grand Banks along with the Dogger Banks of the North Sea contain some of the world's best commercial fishing grounds. The North Atlantic Ocean has the world's busiest shipping lanes; the northern lanes are patrolled for icebergs. Commerce between the Mediterranean Sea and the NE Atlantic Ocean was initiated by the Carthaginians. From the 7th cent. A.D., Scandinavians navigated the Atlantic; they probably reached North America c.1000. Trade routes along the coast of Africa were opened by Portugal in the 15th cent. and to the Western Hemisphere by Spain after the voyages of Columbus. Scientific knowledge of the ocean floor dates from the CHALLENGER EXPEDITION (1872–76). See A. J. Villiers, *Wild Ocean: The Story of the North Atlantic and the Men Who Sailed It* (1957); B. C. Heezen et al., *The Floors of the Ocean: The North Atlantic* (1959); John Murray and Johan Hjort, *The Depths of the Ocean* (1912, repr. 1965); M. V. Klenova, ed., *Oceanographic Research in the Atlantic* (tr. 1967); V. H. Cassidy, *The Sea Around Them: The Atlantic Ocean, A.D. 1250* (1968).

Atlantic Provinces, term used since 1949 to designate the Canadian provinces of Newfoundland, Nova Scotia, New Brunswick, and Prince Edward Island.

Atlantis, in Greek legend, large island in the western sea. Plato, in his dialogues the *Timaeus* and the *Critias,* tells of the high civilization that flourished there before the island was destroyed by an earthquake. The legend has persisted, and societies for the discovery of Atlantis are perennially active. Plato described Atlantis as an ideal state, and the name is considered synonymous with UTOPIA. Francis Bacon called his account of the ideal state *The New Atlantis.* See N. F. Zhirov, *Atlantis* (tr. 1970); J. S. Bowman, *The Quest for Atlantis* (1971).

Atlas (ăt'ləs), in Greek mythology, a Titan; son of Iapetus and the nymph Clymene and the brother of Prometheus. He joined with Cronus and led the Titans in their defense against the Olympians. (See TITAN.) When the Titans were defeated, Atlas was condemned to hold the sky on his shoulders for all eternity—a mythical explanation of why the sky does not fall. He is identified with the Atlas mountains in NW Africa.

atlas, in geography, collection of maps or charts. It usually includes data on various features of a country, e.g., its topography, natural resources, climate, and population, as well as its agriculture and main industries. In astronomy, a star atlas is a collection of maps or photographs covering much or all of the celestial sphere and showing the locations of stars and other objects. Although the first known atlas was compiled by the Greek geographer Ptolemy in the 2d cent. A.D., its modern form was introduced in 1570 with the publication of *Theatrum orbis terrarum* by the Flemish geographer Abraham Ortelius. In 1595 his close friend Gerardus Mercator published *Atlas sive cosmographicae.* Its frontispiece was a figure of the titan Atlas holding a globe on his shoulders. The name *Atlas* subsequently came to be applied to volumes of maps and information in this format.

Atlas Mountains, system of ranges and plateaus in NW Africa, extending c.1,500 mi (2,410 km) from SW Morocco, through N Algeria, to N Tunisia; Jebel Toubkal (13,671 ft/4,167 m), in SW Morocco, is the highest peak. The Atlas Mts., predominantly folded mountains of sedimentary rock, were uplifted during the late Jurassic period. Geologically related to the Alpine system of Europe, they are separated from the Sierra Nevada of Spain by the Strait of Gibraltar and from Sicily and the Apennines of Italy by the Mediterranean Sea; the Canary Islands are a westward extension. The Atlas system is most rugged in Morocco, where, from north to south, the Rif Atlas, Middle Atlas, High or Grand Atlas (the highest part of the system), and Anti-Atlas are found; fertile lowlands separate the ranges. In Algeria the system becomes a series of plateaus, with the Tell Atlas and the Saharan Atlas rimming the extensive Plateau of the Chotts before converging in Tunisia. The Atlas Mts. are a climatic barrier between the Mediterranean basin and the Sahara Desert. The slopes facing north are generally well watered and have important farmland and forests; on these slopes are the headwaters of many streams used for irrigation. The slopes facing south and the drier areas of the system are generally covered with shrub and grasses and have salt lakes and salt flats; sheep grazing is important there. The Atlas Mts. are rich in minerals, especially phosphates, coal, iron, and oil.

atlatl (ät'lätəl), throwing stick used to give a spear greater propulsion. Archaeological evidence indicates that it was employed extensively by Indians of North and South America prior to A.D. 1200, when it was superseded by the bow and arrow.

Atli: see ETZEL.

Atlin Lake (ăt'lĭn), long, irregular mountain lake, c.300 sq mi (780 sq km), NW British Columbia, Canada, touching the Yukon Territory boundary. It is the source of the Yukon River. The town of Atlin is on the east shore and is the headquarters of the Atlin dist., a region in which there is both placer and quartz gold mining. The region is noted for its scenery and its hunting.

atmometer: see EVAPORIMETER.

atmosphere [Gr.,=sphere of air], the mixture of gases surrounding a celestial body with sufficient gravity to maintain it. Although some details about the atmospheres of Mars and Venus are known, and various remote measurements have hinted at the atmospheric properties of other planets, a complete description is available only for the earth's atmosphere, the study of which is called meteorology. The gaseous constituents of the atmosphere are not chemically combined, and thus each retains its own characteristic properties. Within the first 40 to 50 mi (64–80 km) above the earth the mixture is of uniform composition, except for a high concentration of ozone at 30 mi (50 km). This whole region contains more than 99% of the total mass of the earth's atmosphere. Calculated according to their relative volumes, the gaseous constituents are nitrogen, 78.09%; oxygen, 20.95%; argon, 0.93%; carbon dioxide, 0.03%; and minute traces of neon, helium, methane, krypton, hydrogen, xenon, and ozone. Above this well-mixed region is a narrow layer extending to about 72 mi (120 km) and containing nitrogen and oxygen. It is covered by an atmosphere consisting primarily of oxygen, extending to an altitude of about 600 mi (970 km). Helium predominates in the next higher region, which reaches to an altitude of about 1,500 mi (2,400 km). The outermost layer of atmosphere is composed mainly of hydro-

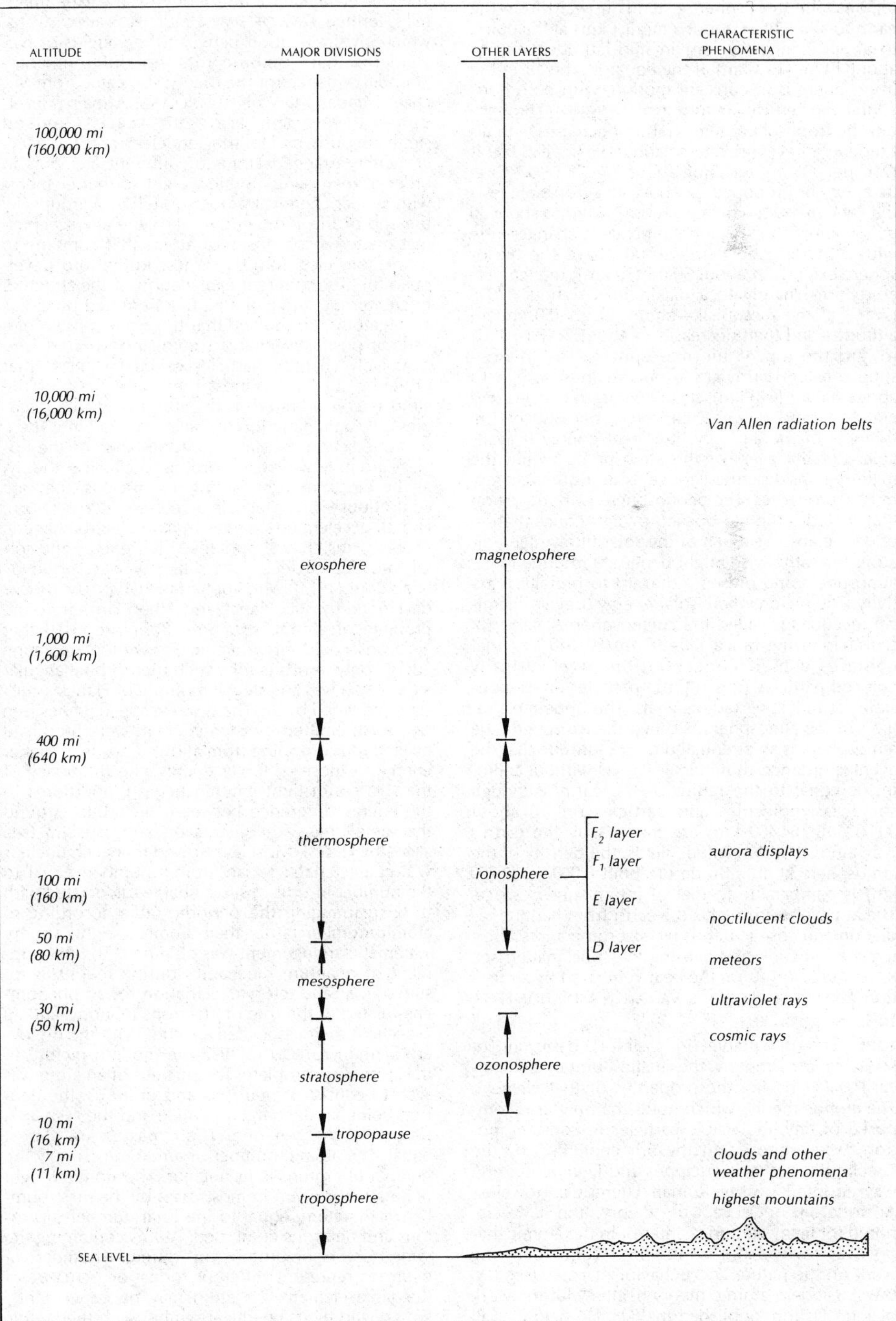

Atmosphere

gen. The diffusion of these gases into such distinct layers is caused by the floating of lighter gases to the outer layers of the atmosphere. The lower atmosphere also contains varying amounts of water vapor, which determine its HUMIDITY. Condensation and sublimation within the atmosphere cause clouds or fog, and the resulting liquid water droplets or ice crystals may precipitate to the ground as rain, sleet, snow, hail, dew, or frost. The air also carries many kinds of DUST, including some of meteoric as well as terrestrial origin, and microorganisms, pollen, salt particles, and various gaseous and solid impurities resulting from human activity (see POLLUTION). The earth's atmosphere is the environment for most of its biological activity and exerts a considerable influence on the ocean and lake environment, where the remainder of biological activity occurs (see BIOSPHERE). WEATHER consists of the day-to-day fluctuations of environmental variables, and CLIMATE is the normal or long-term average state of the atmospheric environment (as determined in spans of about 50 years). Because of the pull of gravity the density of the atmosphere and the pressure exerted by air molecules are greatest near the earth's surface (about 1 gram per 10^3 cc and about 10^6 dynes per sq cm, respectively). Air pressure decreases quickly with altitude, reaching one half of its sea-level value at about 18,000 ft (5,500 m). The instrument used to measure air pressure is called a BAROMETER. The earth's atmosphere is composed of certain distinct regions. The troposphere extends upward from the earth to a height of about 5 mi (8.1 km) at the poles, to about 7 mi (11.3 km) in mid-latitudes, and to about 10 mi (16.1 km) at the equator. The air in the troposphere is in constant motion, with both horizontal and vertical air currents (see WIND). Throughout the troposphere temperature decreases with altitude at an average rate of about 3.6°F per 1,000 ft (2°C per 305 m), reaching about −70°F (−57°C) at its apex, the tropopause. Above the troposphere is the STRATOSPHERE, which extends upward to about 30 mi (50 km); in this region temperature changes little with altitude. Above the stratosphere the mesosphere extends to about 50 mi (80 km); the temperature rises sharply to a maximum of about 170°F (77°C) at the mesopeak—about 30 mi (50 km) in altitude—and then decreases to about 28°F (−2°C) toward the top of the mesosphere. The thermosphere extends upward from the mesosphere to about 400 mi (640 km); its temperature reaches several thousand degrees, although, because of the thinness of the air, very little heat energy is available. Certain layers of the atmosphere within the main regions described above exhibit other characteristic properties. The ozonosphere is in the region that includes the mesopeak; its high concentration of ozone absorbs much of the solar ultraviolet radiation that otherwise might penetrate into the lower atmosphere and present a hazard to biological activity. The region where solar energy triggers chemical reactions is called the chemosphere. The IONOSPHERE is in the range (50–400 mi/80–640 km) that contains a high concentration of electrically charged particles (ions); these particles are responsible for reflecting radio signals. The uppermost region of the atmosphere is called the exosphere; the atmosphere is so attenuated at this altitude that the average distance air molecules travel without colliding is equal to the radius of the earth. Although some gas molecules and particles out to about 40,000 mi (64,400 km) are trapped by the earth's gravitational and magnetic fields, the density of the atmosphere at an altitude of about 6,000 mi (9,700 km) is comparable to that of interplanetary space. The atmosphere protects the earth from harmful radiation and cosmic debris by absorbing and scattering the radiation and causing the solid matter (see METEOR) to burn from the heat generated by air friction. See AURORA BOREALIS; VAN ALLEN RADIATION BELTS.

atoll: see CORAL REEF.

atom [Gr.,=uncuttable (indivisible)], basic unit of MATTER; more properly, the smallest unit of a chemical ELEMENT having the properties of that element. The atomic theory, which holds that matter is composed of tiny, indivisible particles in constant motion, was proposed in the 5th cent. B.C. by the Greek philosophers Leucippus and Democritus and was adopted by the Roman Lucretius. However, Aristotle did not accept the theory, and it was ignored for many centuries. Interest in the atomic theory was revived during the 18th cent. following work on the nature and behavior of gases (see GAS LAWS). Modern atomic theory begins with the work of John Dalton, published in 1808. He held that all the atoms of an element are of exactly the same size and weight (see ATOMIC WEIGHT) and are in these two respects unlike the atoms of any other element. He stated that atoms of the elements unite chemically in simple numerical ratios to form compounds.

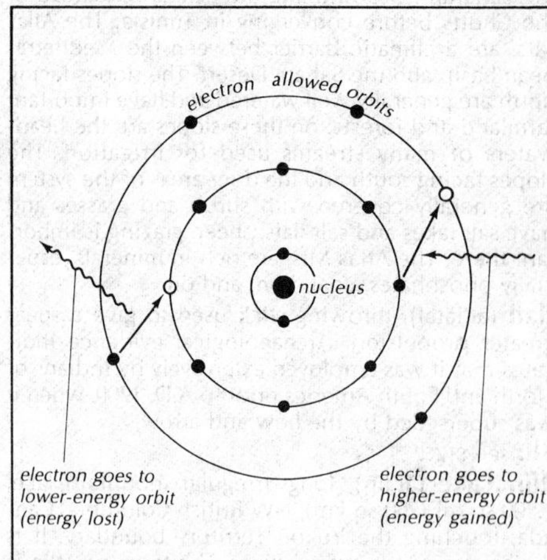

Bohr-Rutherford atom

The best evidence for his theory was the experimentally verified LAW OF SIMPLE MULTIPLE PROPORTIONS, which gives a relation between the weights of two elements that combine to form different compounds. Evidence for the theory also came from Michael Faraday's law of ELECTROLYSIS. A major development was the PERIODIC TABLE, devised simultaneously by Dmitri Mendeleev and J. L. Meyer, which arranged atoms of different elements in order of increasing atomic weight so that elements with similar chemical properties fell into groups. By the end of the 19th cent. it was generally accepted that matter is composed of atoms that combine to form molecules. In 1911, Ernest Rutherford developed the first coherent explanation of the structure of an atom. Using alpha particles emitted by radioactive atoms, he showed that the atom consists of a central, positively charged core, the NUCLEUS, and negatively charged particles called ELECTRONS that orbit the nucleus. Almost the entire mass of the atom is concentrated in the nucleus, which occupies only a tiny fraction of the atom's volume. There was one serious obstacle to acceptance of the nuclear atom, however. According to classical theory, as the electrons orbit about the nucleus, they are continuously being accelerated (see ACCELERATION), and all accelerated charges radiate electromagnetic energy. Thus, they should lose their energy and spiral into the nucleus. This difficulty was solved by Niels Bohr (1913), who applied the QUANTUM THEORY developed by Max Planck and Albert Einstein to the problem of atomic structure. Bohr proposed that electrons could circle a nucleus without radiating energy only in orbits for which their orbital angular MOMENTUM was an integral multiple of Planck's constant h divided by 2π. The discrete spectral lines (see SPECTRUM) emitted by each element were produced by electrons dropping from allowed orbits of higher energy to those of lower energy, the frequency of the PHOTON of light emitted being proportional to the energy difference between the orbits. Around the same time, experiments on x-ray spectra (see X RAY) by H. G. J. Moseley showed that each nucleus was characterized by an atomic number, equal to the number of unit positive charges associated with it. By rearranging the periodic table according to atomic number rather than atomic weight, a more systematic arrangement was obtained. The development of quantum mechanics during the 1920s resulted in a satisfactory explanation for all phenomena related to the role of electrons in atoms and all aspects of their associated spectra. With the discovery of the NEUTRON in 1932 the modern picture of the atom was complete. The nucleus of an atom was seen to consist of neutrons and protrons, the neutron being an uncharged particle and the PROTON a positively charged one. Their masses are almost equal. The atomic number of an atom is simply the number of protons in its nucleus. The atomic weight of an atom is given in most cases by the mass number of the atom, equal to the total number of protons and neutrons combined. Atoms containing the same number of protons but different numbers of neutrons represent different forms, or ISOTOPES, of the same element. An atom may be conveniently symbolized by its chemical symbol with the atomic number and mass number written as subscript and superscript, respectively. For example, the symbol for uranium is U (atomic number 92); the isotopes of uranium with atomic weights 235 and 238 are indicated by ${}^{235}_{92}U$ and ${}^{238}_{92}U$. Surrounding the nucleus of an atom are its electrons; for a neutral atom, the number of electrons is equal to the atomic number. The outermost electrons of an atom determine its chemical and electrical properties. An atom may combine chemically with another atom in various ways, either by giving up or receiving electrons, thus setting up an electrical attraction between the atoms (see ION), or by sharing one or more pairs of electrons (see CHEMICAL BOND). Because metals have few outermost electrons and tend to give them up easily, they are good conductors of electricity or heat (see CONDUCTION). The electrons are often described as revolving about the nucleus as the planets revolve about the sun. However, this picture is misleading. The quantum theory has shown that all particles in motion also have certain wave properties. For a particle the size of an electron, these properties are of considerable importance. As a result, the electrons in an atom cannot be pictured as localized in space but rather should be viewed as smeared out over the entire orbit so that they form a cloud of charge. The electron clouds around the nucleus represent regions in which the electrons are most likely to be found. The shapes of these clouds can be very complex, in marked contrast to the simple elliptical orbits of planets. Another discovery is that the sizes of all atoms are comparable, in spite of the large differences in the number of electrons they contain. With many of the problems of individual atomic structure and behavior now solved, attention has turned to both smaller and larger scales. On a smaller scale, the nucleus itself is being studied in order to determine the details of its structure and to develop sources of energy from nuclear fission and fusion (see NUCLEAR ENERGY), for the atom is not at all indivisible, as the ancient philosophers thought, but can undergo a number of possible changes. On a larger scale, new discoveries about the behavior of large groups of atoms are being made (see SOLID STATE PHYSICS). The question of the basic nature of matter has been carried beyond the atom and now centers on the nature of and relations between the hundreds of ELEMENTARY PARTICLES that have been discovered in addition to the proton, neutron, and electron. Some of these particles have been used to make new types of "atoms" such as positronium (see ANTIPARTICLE) and muonium (see MUON). See George Gamow, *The Atom and Its Nucleus* (1961); H. A. Boorse and Lloyd Motz, ed., *The World of the Atom* (2 vol., 1966).

atomic bomb, weapon deriving its explosive force from the release of atomic energy through the fission (splitting) of heavy nuclei (see NUCLEAR ENERGY). The first atomic bomb was produced at the Los Alamos, N.Mex., laboratory and successfully tested near Alamogordo, N.Mex., on July 16, 1945. This test was the culmination of a mammoth program of U.S. scientific research and technological development that began in 1940, soon after the discovery of fission in uranium in 1939 by the German scientists Otto Hahn and Fritz Strassman. On Aug. 6, 1945, an atomic bomb was dropped on Hiroshima with an estimated equivalent explosive force of 20,000 tons of TNT, followed three days later by a second, more powerful, bomb on NAGASAKI. Both caused widespread death, injury, and destruction. Atomic weapons were developed also by the USSR (1949), Great Britain (1952), France (1960), China (1964), and India (1974), with other nations also engaged in nuclear research. Practical fissionable nuclei for atomic bombs are the isotopes uranium 235 and plutonium 239, which are capable of undergoing CHAIN REACTION. If the mass of the fissionable material exceeds the critical mass (a few pounds), the chain reaction multiplies rapidly into an uncontrollable release of energy. An atomic bomb is detonated by bringing together very rapidly (e.g., by means of a chemical explosive) two subcritical masses of fissionable material, the combined mass exceeding the critical mass. An atomic bomb explosion produces, in addition to the shock wave accompanying any explosion, intense neutron and gamma radiation, both of which are very damaging to living tissue. The neighborhood of the explosion becomes contaminated with radioactive fission products. Some radioactive products are borne into the upper atmosphere as dust or gas and may subsequently be deposited partially decayed as radioactive FALLOUT far from the site of the explosion. The proliferation of nuclear weapons has been an increasing cause of concern throughout the world. Treaties have been signed limiting certain aspects of nuclear testing and development, and there have been continued efforts to negotiate additional restraints. See also DISARMAMENT, NUCLEAR. See Stéphane Groueff, *Manhattan Project* (1967); Michael Blow, *The History of the Atomic Bomb* (1968).

atomic clock, electric or electronic timekeeping device that is controlled by atomic or molecular oscillations. A timekeeping device must contain or be connected to some apparatus that oscillates at a uniform rate to control the rate of movement of its hands or the rate of change of its digits. Mechanical clocks and watches use oscillating balance wheels, pendulums, and tuning forks. Much greater accuracy can be attained by using the oscillations of atoms or molecules. Because the frequency of such oscillations is so high, it is not possible to use them as a direct means of controlling a clock. Instead, the clock is controlled by a highly stable crystal oscillator whose output is automatically multiplied and compared with the frequency of the atomic system. Errors in the oscillator frequency are then automatically corrected. Time is usually displayed by an atomic clock with digital or other sophisticated readout devices. The error between a pair of atomic clocks, i.e., the difference in indicated time if both are started at the same instant and later compared, is typically about one part in one trillion. This extremely low error has allowed their use in an experiment confirming an important prediction of Einstein's theory of relativity. The first atomic clock, invented in 1948, utilized the vibrations of ammonia molecules.

atomic energy: see NUCLEAR ENERGY.

Atomic Energy Agency, International, intergovernmental organization established in 1957 under the aegis of the United Nations to promote the peaceful uses of atomic energy. Its headquarters are in Vienna. The agency is authorized to purchase and sell fissionable materials and to offer nuclear fuels, technical assistance, and other services for the peaceful application of nuclear energy. It may establish and administer safeguards designed to ensure that its services do not further military purposes or endanger public health. The organization is made up of a general conference, consisting of representatives of all member states, a board of governors of 25 members, and a secretariat headed by a director general. In 1973 there were 103 members.

Atomic Energy Commission (AEC), U.S. government commission created by the Atomic Energy Act of 1946 and charged with the development and control of the U.S. atomic energy program. The explosion of the atomic bombs at the end of World War II demonstrated the cataclysmic possibilities of the use of atomic energy. To channel that use to peaceful rather than destructive ends became a national problem. The U.S. Congress set about creating a national control body, with debate centering around the question of whether it should be a predominantly military or civilian commission. A special committee on atomic energy, chaired by Senator Brien McMahon, conducted an investigation and prepared the McMahon Bill in Dec., 1945. This bill, which provided for a full-time commission whose members were to have no conflicting military or business interests, became the basis of the Atomic Energy Act of 1946. Amendments provided for a military liaison committee, which the AEC was directed to advise and consult with on all atomic energy matters that related to military applications. The act provided for a five-member commission appointed by the President with the advice and consent of the Senate, and it further provided for a permanent joint Congressional committee on atomic energy that was to be kept advised of the commission's activities. Finally, it created the General Advisory Committee (GAC), composed of nine members appointed from civilian life by the President to advise the commission on scientific and technical matters relating to materials, production, and research. From 1946 to 1952 the chairman of the GAC was J. Robert OPPENHEIMER, who had directed the development of the atomic bomb but who opposed the manufacture of the hydrogen bomb. The AEC became the center of a nation-wide controversy in 1954 as a result of Oppenheimer's suspension (1953) as a consultant to the commission on the alleged grounds that he was a security risk. The activities of the AEC include the production of fissionable materials, the manufacture and testing of nuclear weapons, the development of nuclear reactors for military and civilian use, and research in biological, medical, physical, and engineering sciences. The Atomic Energy Act of 1954 provided for private participation in such programs as research, development, and production of atomic energy and nuclear materials, and the commission is responsible for the licensing and regulation of such civilian activities. Although the bulk of the AEC's work has been in the field of atomic weaponry, projects relating to the peaceful uses of atomic energy (e.g., the development of atomic power plants for the production of electricity) have become increasingly prominent in the commission's activities. See G. E. Dean, *Report on the Atom* (2d ed. 1957); R. G. Hewlett and O. E. Anderson, Jr., *A History of the United States Atomic Energy Commission* (2 vol., 1962–69); Harold Orlans, *Contracting for Atoms* (1967); Corbin Allardice and Edward Trapnell, *The Atomic Energy Commission* (1974).

atomic mass, the mass of a single ATOM, usually expressed in ATOMIC MASS UNITS (amu). Most of the mass of an atom is concentrated in the protons and neutrons contained in the nucleus. Each proton or neutron weighs about 1 amu, and thus the atomic mass is always very close to the MASS NUMBER (total number of protons and neutrons in the nucleus). Atoms of an ISOTOPE of an ELEMENT all have the same atomic mass. Atomic masses are usually determined by mass spectrography (see MASS SPECTROGRAPH). They have been determined with great relative accuracy, but their absolute value is less certain.

atomic mass unit or **amu,** in chemistry and physics, unit defined as exactly $1/12$ the mass of an atom of carbon-12, the ISOTOPE of carbon with six protons and six neutrons in its nucleus. One amu is equal to approximately 1.66×10^{-24} grams. Before the adoption of the carbon-12 standard, two different definitions of the amu existed. The discrepancy arose for historic reasons. Before the 20th cent., atomic theory held that all atoms of an element have the same mass, and when naturally occurring oxygen was chosen as the basis for the scale of atomic weights it was assigned an atomic weight of exactly 16. Isotopes of radioactive elements were discovered early in the 20th century, and in 1929 oxygen was shown to have three isotopes. Physicists subsequently chose oxygen-16 as the basis of a scale of atomic weights. Under this definition, the ATOMIC WEIGHT of oxygen was 16.0045 amu, since naturally occurring oxygen is a mixture of oxygen-16 (over 99%) and traces of oxygen-17 and oxygen-18. Chemists, however, continued to use the older scale. The discrepancy was eliminated when the International Union of Pure and Applied Physics, in 1960, and the International Union of Pure and Applied Chemistry, in 1961, decided to adopt the carbon-12 scale. The scale went into effect on Jan. 1, 1962.

atomic number, often represented by the symbol *Z*, the number of PROTONS in the nucleus of an ATOM. Atoms with the same atomic number make up a chemical ELEMENT. Atomic numbers were first assigned to the elements c.1913 by H. G. J. Moseley; he arranged the elements in an order based on certain characteristics of their X-ray spectra and then numbered them accordingly. The elements are now arranged in the PERIODIC TABLE in the order of their atomic numbers. Mendeleev's PERIODIC LAW was originally based on ATOMIC WEIGHTS. See MASS NUMBER.

atomic weight, mean (weighted average) of the masses of all the naturally occurring ISOTOPES of a chemical ELEMENT, as contrasted with ATOMIC MASS, which is the mass of any individual isotope. Atomic weight is usually expressed in ATOMIC MASS UNITS. Most naturally occurring elements have one principal isotope and only insignificant amounts of other isotopes. The atomic mass of any isotope is very nearly a whole number, so most atomic weights are nearly whole numbers, e.g., hydrogen has atomic weight 1.00797 and nitrogen has atomic weight 14.007. However, some elements have more than one principal isotope, and the atomic weight for such an element is not close to a whole number. The two principal isotopes of chlorine have atomic masses very nearly 35 and 37 and occur in the approximate ratio 3 to 1, so the atomic weight of chlorine is about 35.5. Some other common elements whose atomic weights are not nearly whole numbers are antimony, barium, boron, bromine, cadmium, copper, germanium, lead, magnesium, mercury, nickel, strontium, tin, and zinc. Atomic weights were formerly determined directly by chemical means; now a MASS SPECTROGRAPH is usually employed. The atomic mass and relative abundance of the isotopes of an element can be measured very accurately and with relative ease by this method, whereas chemical determination of the atomic weight of an element requires a careful and precise quantitative analysis of as many of its compounds as possible.

History. J. L. Proust formulated (1797) what is now known as the law of definite proportions, which states that the proportions by weight of the elements forming any given compound is definite and invariable. John Dalton proposed (c.1810) an atomic theory in which all atoms of an element have exactly the same weight. He made many measurements of the COMBINING WEIGHTS of the elements in various compounds. By postulating that simple compounds always contain one atom of each element present, he assigned relative atomic weights to many elements, assigning a weight of 1 to hydrogen as the basis of his scale. He thought that water had the formula HO, and since he found by experiment that 6 weights of oxygen combine with 1 weight of hydrogen, he assigned an atomic weight of 6 to oxygen. Dalton also formulated the law of multiple proportions, which states that when two elements combine in more than one proportion by weight to form two or more distinct compounds, their weight proportions in those compounds are related to one another in simple ratios. Dalton's work sparked an interest in determining atomic weights, even though some of his results were soon shown to be incorrect. While Dalton was working on weight relationships in compounds, J. L. Gay-Lussac was experimenting with the chemical reactions of gases, and he found that when under the same conditions of temperature and pressure, gases react in simple whole-number ratios by volume. Avogadro proposed (1811) a theory of gases that holds that equal volumes of two gases at the same temperature and pressure contain the same number of particles, and that these basic particles are not always single atoms. This theory was rejected by Dalton and many other chemists. P. L. Dulong and A. T. Petit discovered (1819) a specific-heat method for determining the approximate atomic weight of elements. Among the first chemists to work out a systematic group of atomic weights (c.1830) was J. J. Berzelius, who was influenced in his choice of formulas for compounds by the method of Dulong and Petit. He attributed the formula H_2O to water and determined an atomic weight of 16 for oxygen. J. S. Stas later refined many of Berzelius's weights. Stanislao Cannizzaro applied Avogadro's theories to reconcile atomic weights used by organic and inorganic chemists. The availability of fairly accurate atomic weights and the search for some relationship between atomic weight and chemical properties led to J. A. R. Newlands's table of "atomic numbers" (1865), in which he noted that if the elements were arranged in order of increasing atomic weight "the eighth element, starting from a given one, is a kind of repetition of the first." He called this the law of octaves. Such investigations led to the statement of the PERIODIC LAW, which was discovered independently (1869) by D. I. Mendeleev in Russia and J. L. Meyer in Germany. T. W. Richards did important work on atomic weights (after 1883) and revised some of Stas's values. After the discovery of isotopes by F. Soddy (c.1913), the atomic mass of many individual isotopes was determined, leading eventually to the adoption of the current atomic mass unit.

atomism, philosophic concept of the nature of the universe, holding that the universe is composed of invisible, indestructible material particles. The theory was first advanced in the 5th cent. B.C. by Leucippus and was elaborated by Democritus. Epicurus restated the doctrine, giving the atoms weight. Atomism, nearly forgotten in later antiquity and the Middle Ages, was revived in the 17th cent. by Pierre Gassendi and was given consideration by Robert Boyle, Isaac Newton, and John Locke.

atom smasher: see PARTICLE ACCELERATOR.

atonality, in music, systematic avoidance of reference to tonal centers by harmonies and melodies that imply a keynote (see KEY). The term *atonality*, like *modality* (see MODE), has been used in contrast to TONALITY. Often the term has been applied in an aesthetic sense to 20th-century music in which the user of the term is unable to distinguish the tonal centers that are present. A precise technical use of the term designates a method of composition in which the composer has deliberately rejected a principle of musical organization. This principle is tonality, and it involves a clear distinction between consonance and dissonance, a definite classification of harmonic results as more and less dissonant, and arrangement of tones in a scale which implies harmonic and melodic functions. The gradual rejection of this principle has been apparent since the mid-19th cent., when greatly increased use of chromatic harmonies in the music of Wagner and Richard

Strauss and the use of nonfunctional harmonies in the music of Debussy almost completely obscured whatever basic tonalities are present in their music. The abandonment of the principle of tonality in the early 20th cent. by SCHOENBERG, IVES, and many other composers was the next logical step in the evolution of musical style. To compensate for this lack of one principle of order, another had to be substituted. The most successful one proposed thus far is that of dodecaphony, or 12-tone music (see SERIAL MUSIC). See Rudolph Reti, *Tonality in Modern Music* (1962); Graham George, *Tonality and Musical Structure* (1970); George Perle, *Serial Composition and Atonality* (3d ed. 1972); Allen Forte, *The Structure of Atonal Music* (1973).

atonement, in Christian theology, the reconciliation of sinful man with God. The conception of the atonement most widely held in traditional theology is often called vicarious atonement. It was first explicitly stated by St. ANSELM in *Cur Deus Homo?* His doctrine, slightly altered or elaborated, has become part of Roman Catholic theology and of that of many Protestant churches. God, desiring the reconciliation of man, offers man pardon for his sins if man will make satisfaction for them. But man's offense to God's majesty is greater than any conceivable satisfaction he can give. Therefore, God sent Jesus Christ to earth to reconcile man. As God, Jesus Christ can satisfy God, and as man He can take on the sins of man. By His life on earth, by His sufferings, and especially by His death on the cross, He satisfied God for the sins of man, and man, accepting his Redeemer, may enjoy the atonement Christ has bought. In modern Catholic and Protestant theology this understanding has been superseded by one that places emphasis on God's mercy and on a gradual growth toward union with God and the overcoming of sin. The juridical concept has been replaced by an organic and social concept.

Atonement, Day of, Heb. *Yom Kippur,* the most sacred Hebrew holy day, falling at the end of September or the beginning of October (on the 10th day of the 7th month, Tishri). It is a day of prayer for forgiveness for sins committed during the year. The Jews gather in synagogues on the Eve of Yom Kippur, when the fast begins, and return the following morning to continue confessing, doing penance, and praying for forgiveness. The most solemn of the prayers, Kol Nidre, is chanted on the Eve of Yom Kippur.

ATP: see ADENOSINE TRIPHOSPHATE.

Atrato (äträ'tō), river, c.375 mi (600 km) long, rising in the Cordillera Occidental, W Colombia. It meanders north, across the base of the Isthmus of Panama, to the Gulf of Urabá. Quibdo is the head of navigation. The Atrato drains a region of rain forests. Its headwaters are in Colombia's chief platinum-producing area. Cartagena is the chief outlet for the products of the valley.

Atreus (ā'trēəs), in Greek mythology, the son of Pelops and the father of Agamemnon and Menelaus. He vied with his brother Thyestes for the throne of Mycenae. When Thyestes seduced Atreus' wife, Aerope, in order to attain the golden ram whose possession signified kingship, Atreus, in retaliation, murdered the sons of Thyestes and served them to him at a feast. Thyestes thereupon laid a curse upon the house of Atreus. Thyestes' son Aegisthus, who was not involved in the mass murder, killed Atreus and restored the kingdom to Thyestes.

atrium (ā'trēəm), term for an interior court in Roman domestic architecture and also for a type of entrance court in early Christian churches. The Roman atrium was an unroofed or partially roofed area with rooms opening from it. In early times its center held a cooking hearth. After the 2d cent. B.C., when the hearth was placed elsewhere, the center of the atrium held a tank (impluvium) to receive rain water falling through the opening, which also furnished light to the surrounding rooms. In more luxurious and complex Roman dwellings, the private apartments had a court of their own, called the peristyle, and the atrium served merely as a semipublic reception hall. The ruins of Pompeii contain remains of atria in their various forms. In early Christian churches, the atrium was a large arcaded or colonnaded open court, serving as a general meeting place, in front of the church itself, with a fountain used for ablutions in its center. The basilican churches of Sant'Ambrogio, Milan, and San Clemente, Rome, have noteworthy atria. This type of large forecourt is also a characteristic element of the Muslim mosque.

Atropatene: see AZERBAIJAN, region, Iran.

atrophy (ăt'rəfē), diminution in the size of a cell, tissue, or organ from its fully developed normal size. Temporary atrophy may occur in muscles that are not used, as when a limb is encased in a plaster cast. Interference with cellular nutrition, as through starvation; diseases affecting the nerve supply of tissues, e.g., poliomyelitis and muscular dystrophy; and prolonged disuse may cause a permanent wasting away of tissue. Atrophy may also follow HYPERTROPHY.

atropine (ăt'rəpēn, -pĭn), alkaloid drug derived from BELLADONNA and other plants of the family Solanaceae (nightshade family). Available either as the tincture or extract of belladonna, or as the pure substance atropine sulfate, it is a DEPRESSANT of the parasympathetic NERVOUS SYSTEM. It has some chemical similarity to the body substance ACETYLCHOLINE and interferes with nerve impulses transmitted by that substance. Atropine produces rapid heart rate, dilated pupils, dry skin, and anesthetizes the nerve endings in the skin. Because it relaxes smooth muscle and suppresses gland and mucous secretions, it is widely used to treat peptic ulcer by reducing the production of stomach acid. Atropine is given before general anesthesia to keep the air passages clear and is an ingredient in various preparations for symptomatic relief of colds and asthma. It also acts as an antidote in poisoning from such agents as mushrooms, morphine, prussic acid, and nerve gas, but overdosage causes delirium, convulsions, and coma. A related alkaloid, SCOPOLAMINE, is used mainly as a SEDATIVE.

Atropos (ă'trəpŏs"): see FATES.

Atroth (ăt'rŏth), unidentified town, E of the Jordan. Num. 32.35. Atroth should probably be spelled with the name, Shophan: thus, RV has Atroth-shophan.

Atsina Indians: see GROS VENTRE INDIANS.

Atsugi (ät"sōō'gē), city (1970 pop. 82,888), Kanagawa prefecture, E central Honshu, Japan, on the Sagami River. It is an industrial and agricultural center. An air force base is nearby.

Attai (ăt'āī). **1** Descendant of Jerahmeel. 1 Chron. 2.35,36. **2** One of David's Gadite warriors. 1 Chron. 12.11. **3** Son of Rehoboam. 2 Chron. 11.20.

Attaleia or **Attalia,** Turkey: see ANTALYA.

Attar: see FARID AD-DIN ATTAR.

attar of roses or **rose oil,** fragrant essential oil obtained from roses and used in making perfume. It is one of the most valuable of the volatile oils. Rose water is water in which a small amount of the oil is dissolved.

Attawapiskat (ăt"əwəpĭs'kăt), river, c.465 mi (750 km) long, flowing E from Attawapiskat Lake, N Ontario, Canada, then N and E into James Bay. The trading posts of Attawapiskat and Lansdowne House are on the river.

Attica (ăt'ĭkə), region of ancient Greece, a triangular area at the eastern end of central Greece, around ATHENS. According to Greek legend, the four Attic tribes were founded by Ion; in later legend Theseus combined 12 townships into a single state. This process of unification, which probably occurred over a period of time, was in all likelihood completed c.700 B.C. Cleisthenes (fl. 510 B.C.) reclassified the people into 10 tribes. By the 5th cent. B.C. Athens was dominant, and thereafter the history of Attica was that of its chief city.

Atticus Herodes: see HERODES ATTICUS.

Attila (ətĭl'ə, ăt'ələ), d. 453, king of the HUNS (445–53). After 434 he was coruler with his brother, whom he murdered in 445. In 434, Attila obtained tribute and great concessions for the Huns in a treaty with the Eastern Roman emperor Theodosius II, but, taking advantage of Roman wars with the Vandals and Persians, he invaded the Balkans in 441. Peace was made and Attila's tribute was tripled. In 447 he again attacked the empire, and the following three years were spent negotiating a new peace. In 450, however, the new Eastern emperor, MARCIAN, refused to render further tribute as did VALENTINIAN III, emperor of the West. In a bid for power, and without her brother's knowledge, Valentinian's ambitious sister, Honoria, jeopardized his peaceful relations with Attila by attempting an alliance with the Hun. Attila took her proposal as a marriage offer and made a demand of half of the Western Empire as a dowry, a demand that was refused. Leaving Hungary with an army of perhaps half a million Huns and allies, Attila invaded Gaul but was defeated (451) by AETIUS at Maurica. Attila turned back and invaded (452) N Italy but abandoned his plan to take Rome itself. His withdrawal, often ascribed to the eloquent diplomacy of Pope LEO I, appears instead to have been motivated largely by a shortage of provisions and the outbreak of pestilence in the Hun army. Soon afterward in Hungary, Attila died of a nasal hemorrhage suffered while celebrating his marriage to Ildico. The fear Attila inspired is clear from many accounts of his savagery but, though undoubtedly harsh, he was a just ruler to his own people. He encouraged the presence of learned Romans at his court and was far less bent on devastation than other conquerors before and after him. Often called the Scourge of God, he appears in many legends, particularly as Etzel in the Nibelungenlied (see under NIBELUNGEN). See E. A. Thompson, *History of Attila and the Huns* (1948); C. D. Gordon, *The Age of Attila* (1960); Otto Manchen-Helfen, *The World of the Huns* (1973).

Attis (ă'tĭs) or **Atys** (ā'-), in Phrygian religion, vegetation god. When Nana ate the fruit of the almond tree, which had been generated by the blood of either Agdistis or of CYBELE, she conceived Attis. Later, Agdistis or Cybele fell in love with Attis, and so that none other would have him, she caused him to castrate himself. Like Adonis, Attis came to be worshiped as a god of vegetation, responsible for the death and rebirth of plant life. Each year at the beginning of spring his resurrection was celebrated in a festival. In Roman religion he became a powerful celestial deity. See Sir J. G. Frazer, *Adonis, Attis, Osiris* (1907, new ed. 1961).

Attleboro (ăt'əlbərə), industrial city (1970 pop. 32,907), Bristol co., SE Mass., near the R.I. line; settled 1634, inc. as a city 1914. Its jewelry industry began in 1780; silverware, scientific instruments, and fabricated metal products are also made.

Attlee, Clement Richard Attlee, Ist **Earl** (ăt'lē), 1883–1967, British statesman. Educated at Oxford, he was called to the bar in 1905. His early experience as a social worker in London's East End led to his decision to give up law and devote his life to social improvement through politics. In 1907 he joined the Fabian Society and soon afterward the Independent Labour party. He was a lecturer in social science at the London School of Economics, and, after service in World War I, he became (1919) the first Labour mayor of Stepney. He entered Parliament in 1922. In 1927 he visited India as a member of the Simon commission and was converted to views that strongly favored Indian self-government. He joined the Labour government in 1930 but resigned in 1931 when Ramsay MacDonald formed the National government. As leader of the Labour party from 1935, Attlee was an outspoken critic of Conservative foreign policy, objecting particularly to the government's failure to intervene in the Spanish civil war. During World War II he served (1940–45) in Winston Churchill's coalition cabinet, and on Labour's electoral victory in 1945 he became prime minister. Under Attlee's leadership, the Bank of England, the gas, electricity, coal, and iron and steel industries, and the railways were nationalized. His government also enacted considerable social reforms, including the National Health Service. Independence was granted to Burma, India, Pakistan, Ceylon, and Palestine, and Britain allied itself closely with the United States in the cold war confrontation with the Soviet Union. The postwar economic crisis required stringent economic and financial controls, which reduced support for the government. Labour won the 1950 general election by a narrow margin, but in 1951, Attlee decided to go to the country again and was defeated. He was leader of the opposition until his retirement in 1955, when he received the title of Earl Attlee. See his autobiography, *As It Happened* (1954), and his memoirs, as recorded by Francis Williams, *Twilight of Empire* (1962).

attorney, agent put in place of another to manage particular affairs of the principal. An attorney in fact is an agent who conducts business under authority that is controlled and limited by a written document called a letter, or power, of attorney granted by the principal. An attorney at law is an officer of a court of law authorized to represent the person employing him (the client) in legal proceedings. England retains the distinction between the attorney as agent, the SOLICITOR, who deals directly with the client but does not act as an advocate in court, and the attorney as pleader, the barrister (called advocate in Scotland), who presents the case in court. Most senior and distinguished barristers are designated King's (Queen's) counsel. The distinction between agent and pleader also exists in Europe. In the United States, a similar distinction was formerly made in some states between a counselor at law, who argued the case in court, and an attorney, who prepared the case but did not argue it; but that distinction has now generally disappeared. Today an attorney at law is authorized to exercise all the functions of a practicing lawyer. The growth of large business corporations, beginning in the 19th cent., has brought into existence a large group of attorneys who rarely or never act as trial lawyers yet are among the most influential members of the profession. They work directly for corporations or are members of large law firms and specialize in areas of commercial law. All of them must, however like the ordinary attorney, be admitted to the bar. The term *attorney* is also used for county, state, and Federal prosecuting officers, as county attorney, district attorney, and Attorney General (see JUSTICE, UNITED STATES DEPARTMENT OF). See Albert Blaustein and C. O. Porter, *The American Lawyer* (1954); Martin Mayer, *Lawyers* (1967).

Attu, island: see ALEUTIAN ISLANDS.

Atuona (ätwō'nä) or **Atuana,** town, in the MARQUESAS ISLANDS, South Pacific, in FRENCH POLYNESIA. Situated on the southern coast of the island of HIVA OA, Atuona overlooks the Bay of Traitors. GAUGUIN lived in Atuona Valley and is buried there.

Atwater, Wilbur Olin, 1844-1907, American agricultural chemist, b. Johnsburg, N.Y. He was professor at several American universities and helped to set up and later became director of the first state agricultural experiment station (in Connecticut) in the United States. Along with Edward Bennett Rosa, he developed the respiration calorimeter, determined the calorific value of many foods, and prepared calorie tables widely used today. In 1888 he founded and headed the Office of Experiment Stations for the U.S. Dept. of Agriculture.

Atwater, city (1970 pop. 11,640), Merced co., central Calif., in the San Joaquin valley; inc. 1922. It is the processing and commercial center of an irrigated farming area. Castle Air Force Base and a state park are nearby.

Atys: see ATTIS.

Au, chemical symbol of the element GOLD.

Aub, Max (mäks oup), 1903-72, Spanish author, b. Paris. He was educated in Spain where he lived until 1942, when he emigrated to Mexico. His style combines realism with fantasy. He used the Spanish civil war and its consequences as the theme for his most important work, a trilogy of novels—*Campo cerrado* [closed field] (1943), *Campo de sangre* [bloody field] (1945), and *Campo abierto* [open field] (1951). His other works include *Jusep Torres Campalans* (1958) and *La calle de Valverde* [Valverde street] (1961).

Aube (ōb), department (1968 pop. 270,325), NE France, in Champagne. TROYES is the capital.

Auber, Daniel François Esprit (dänyĕl' fräNswä' ĕsprē' ōbĕr'), 1782-1871, French operatic composer. His greatest successes resulted from his collaboration with the librettist Scribe. Their first success together was *Le Maçon* (1825), and among the long succession that followed were *Fra Diavolo* (1830), *Le Domino noir* (1837), and *La Part du diable* (1843), witty, tuneful, sophisticated works that were very popular in their time. *La Muette de Portici* (1828, also known as *Masaniello*) was the model of the French grand opera of the 1830s.

Auberjonois, René Victor (rənā' vĕktôr' ōbăzhônwä'), 1872-1957, Swiss artist. Auberjonois settled in Lausanne in 1914 and created costumes for Stravinsky's *Histoire du Soldat* (1917). His paintings, characterized by muted colors and geometric forms, reveal an independent spirit influenced by CUBISM.

Aubert de Gaspé, Philippe: see GASPÉ, PHILIPPE AUBERT DE.

Aubervilliers (ōbervēlyā'), town (1968 pop. 73,808), Seine-Saint Denis dept., N central France, NE of Paris. It is an important industrial center where chemicals, pharmaceuticals, metals, and leather goods are produced. Aubervilliers was a pilgrimage site from the 14th cent. onward. The Church of Notre-Dame-des-Vésus dates from the 15th to the 16th cent.

Aubigné, Jean Henri Merle d': see MERLE D'AUBIGNÉ, JEAN HENRI.

Aubigné, Théodore Agrippa d' (tāōdôr' ägrēpä' dōbēnyā'), 1552-1630, French poet and Huguenot soldier. A devoted follower of Henry of Navarre (Henry IV) from 1568, he was later associated with Henri de Rohan in an abortive plot and fled (1620) France to live in Geneva. His *Histoire universelle* (1616-18) is an account of the Huguenots from 1553-1602. D'Aubigné's reputation rests on *Les Tragiques* (1616), a long poem on many subjects—astrology, magic, natural science, mathematics, military tactics, and political theory.

Aubrey, John, 1626-97, English antiquary and miscellaneous writer, b. Kingston, Wiltshire, educated at Trinity College, Oxford. He knew most of the famous people of his day and left copious memorandums as well as letters. His most celebrated work, *Lives of Eminent Men,* was originally compiled for the use of Anthony Wood in his *Athenae Oxonienses.* The *Lives* first appeared in print in 1813. Only his *Miscellanies* (1696), a collection of stories and folklore, was published in his lifetime. Extremely interested in antiquities, he wrote the *Natural History of Wiltshire* (ed. by John Britton, 1847) and *Perambulation of Surrey,* which was included in the *Natural History and Antiquities of Surrey* (1719). See study by Anthony Powell (1948, 2d ed. 1964).

Aubry de Montdidier (ōbrē' də môNdēdyā'), in French legend, a French courtier of King Charles V, murdered c.1371 near Montargis by one Macaire. The animosity of Aubry's dog toward Macaire was so great that the king ordered trial by combat between the dog and Macaire, armed with a cudgel. The dog won; Macaire confessed and was hanged. It is thought that the account of this event in medieval works was based on an older story.

Auburn. 1 City (1970 pop. 22,767), Lee co., E Ala.; inc. 1839. The city's economy centers around Auburn Univ. Lumber products are also made. **2** City (1970 pop. 24,151), seat of Androscoggin co., SW Maine, on the Androscoggin River (there crossed by several bridges) opposite Lewiston; settled 1765 on the site of an Indian village, inc. 1842. It is a major shoe-manufacturing center; its huge shoe industry dates from c.1835. With Lewiston, Auburn forms one of the most important industrial complexes in Maine; abundant water power has spurred a great variety of manufactures. Nearby Mt. Apatite is a source of apatite and feldspar. **3** Town (1970 pop. 15,347), Worcester co., S central Mass.; inc. 1778. Its industries include warehousing and the manufacture of electronic equipment, motors, cement products, plastics, and musical instruments. **4** City (1970 pop. 34,599), seat of Cayuga co., W central N.Y., in the Finger Lakes region, on the outlet of Owasco Lake; settled 1793, inc. 1848. Its manufactures include diesel engines, rope, shoes, rugs, electronic parts, and air conditioners. It is the site of Auburn State Prison (built 1816), in which Thomas Mott Osborne, the prison reformer (who was born in Auburn), served a voluntary term. The city's museum has collections of historical documents and Indian relics. The houses of William H. Seward and Harriet Tubman are preserved, and a junior college is in the city. **5** City (1970 pop. 21,817), King co., W Wash., on the Green and White (Stuck) rivers, between Seattle and Tacoma; settled 1855, inc. 1914. It is a railroad junction and farm trade center, with large aircraft industries. Wood products are also made. A junior college is there.

Auburn University, main campus at Auburn, Ala.; land-grant and state supported; opened 1859 as East Alabama Male College, reorganized 1872 as the Agricultural and Mechanical College of Alabama; became coeducational 1892; renamed Alabama Polytechnic Institute 1899, Auburn University 1960. It has technical and engineering schools as well as a liberal arts college. A large agricultural experiment station system is maintained by the university. In 1967 the Nuclear Science Center was completed.

Aubusson, Pierre d' (pyĕr dōbüsôN'), 1423-1503, French soldier, a cardinal of the Roman Catholic Church, and grand master of the KNIGHTS HOSPITALERS (1476-1503). In 1480 he valiantly defended Rhodes against Ottoman Sultan Muhammad II. After the accession (1481) of Sultan BEYAZID II, Aubusson gave shelter to Jem, Bayazid's brother. However, he soon sent Jem to France as a virtual prisoner and obtained a truce and a large annual pension from Bayazid in exchange for keeping Jem confined. In 1489 Aubusson ceded his valuable hostage to Pope Innocent VIII, who made Aubusson a cardinal and granted new privileges to his order.

Aubusson (ōbüsôN), town (1968 pop. 6,761), Creuse dept., central France, in the former province of Marche, on the Creuse River. Its famous tapestry and carpet manufactures date from the 15th cent. Aluminum, electric lamps, and rubber goods are also made. Aubusson is the seat of a school of decorative arts and a museum of tapestry.

Auch (ōsh), town (1968 pop. 23,718), capital of Gers dept., SW France, in Gascony, on the Gers River. It is a farm market and commercial center with a variety of manufactures and an important trade in Armagnac brandy, and in wine and grain. One of the chief towns of Roman Gaul, it was an archiepiscopal see, the capital of Armagnac (10th cent.), and the capital of Gascony (17th cent.). The old part of town, steep and hilly, is topped by a flamboyant-style Gothic cathedral (15th-16th cent.).

Auchincloss, Louis (ô'kĭnklŏs), 1917–, American novelist, b. New York City. A practicing lawyer, Auchincloss writes polished novels of manners about the white, Anglo-Saxon, Protestant, American upper class. His fictional works include *Venus in Sparta* (1958), *Portrait in Brownstone* (1962), *The Rector of Justin* (1965), *The Embezzler* (1966), and *The Partners* (1974). He has also written *Reflections of a Jacobite* (1961), on Henry James; *Edith Wharton: A Biography* (1971); and *Richelieu* (1972).

Auchinleck, Sir Claude John Eyre (âr ô"kĭnlĕk', ô"khĭn-), 1884–, British field marshal. A long army career led to command of the 1933 and 1935 operations based in the North-West Frontier Prov., India. In World War II he commanded briefly (1940) at Narvik, Norway, then in building defenses in England and in India (1940-41). After succeeding (July, 1941) Gen. Sir Archibald P. Wavell in the Middle East Command, he launched, in Nov., 1941, a campaign into Libya, but in June, 1942, his forces were thrust back into Egypt. In June, 1943, he once more became commander in chief in India, remaining so until 1947. He was made field marshal in 1946. See biography by J. H. Robertson (1959); Correlli Barnett, *The Desert Generals* (1960).

Auchmuty, Sir Samuel (ôkmyōō'tē, ôk'-, ä'mətē), b. 1758 (not, as commonly stated, 1756) in New York City, d. 1822, British general. A Loyalist soldier in the American Revolution, he went to England at the end of the war. Successful service in India (1783-97) and in Egypt (1801-3) brought him popularity and a knighthood (1803). He served under John WHITELOCKE in the unsuccessful attack (1807) on Buenos Aires. He became (1810) commander in chief at Madras and captured (1811) Java from the Dutch. In 1821 he was appointed commander in chief in Ireland. See Annette Townsend, *The Auchmuty Family of Scotland and America* (1932).

Auckland (ôk'lənd), city (1971 pop. 151,580; urban agglomeration pop. 698,400), NW North Island, New Zealand. It is situated on an isthmus and is the largest city and chief port of the country. The chief exports are frozen meats, dairy products, wool, hides, and wood pulp. Petroleum, iron and steel, wheat, sugar, and fertilizers are the leading imports. Auckland is also New Zealand's leading industrial center. The chief industries are engineering (including shipbuilding and boilermaking), automobile and chemical manufacturing, and food processing. It is also a fishing port and the chief base of the New Zealand navy. Auckland was founded in 1840 and was formerly (1841-65) the capital of New Zealand. Educational institutions include the Univ. of Auckland and the Auckland Technical Institute. There are Anglican and Roman Catholic cathedrals. The War Memorial Museum has a collection of Maori art. In the area of the city are many extinct volcano cones, including Mt. Eden (within the city) and Rangitoto (offshore).

Auckland Islands, small uninhabited group (234 sq mi/606 sq km), S Pacific, c.300 mi (480 km) S of South Island, New Zealand, to which they belong. There is some sealing. The islands were discovered in 1805.

auction bridge: see BRIDGE.

Aude (ōd), department (1968 pop. 278,323), S central France, in Languedoc. CARCASSONNE, its capital, and NARBONNE are the chief cities.

Auden, W. H. (Wystan Hugh Auden), (ô'dən), 1907-73, Anglo-American poet, b. York, England, educated at Oxford. A versatile, vigorous, and technically facile poet, Auden ranks among the major literary figures of the 20th cent. Often written in everyday language, his poetry ranges in subject matter from politics to modern psychology to Christianity. During the 1930s he was the leader of a left-wing literary group, which included Christopher Isherwood and Stephen Spender. With Isherwood he wrote three verse plays, *The Dog beneath the Skin* (1935), *The Ascent of F6* (1936), and *On the Frontier* (1938), and also *Journey to a War* (1939), a record of their experiences in China. Auden lived in Germany during the early days of Nazism, and he was a stretcher-bearer for the Republicans during the Spanish Civil War. His first volume of poetry appeared in 1930. Later volumes include *Spain* (1937), *New Year Letter* (1941), *For the Time Being, a Christmas Oratorio* (1945), *The Age of Anxiety* (1947; Pulitzer Prize), *Nones* (1951), *The Shield of Achilles* (1955), *Homage to Clio* (1960), *About the House* (1965), *Epistle of a Godson and Other Poems* (1972), and *Thank You, Fog* (1974). His other works include *Letters from Iceland* (with Louis MacNeice, 1937), librettos, with Chester Kallman, for Stravinsky's opera *The Rake's Progress* (1953) and Mozart's *Magic*

Flute (1957), and *A Certain World: A Commonplace Book* (1970). In 1939, Auden moved to the United States, and he became a citizen in 1946. Subsequently he lived in various places, including Italy and Austria, and in 1971 he returned to England. From 1956 to 1961 he was professor of poetry at Oxford. He was awarded the National Medal for Literature in 1967. See his *Collected Poetry* (1945), *Collected Shorter Poems, 1927–1957* (1967), and *Collected Longer Poems* (1969); studies by M. K. Spears (1968), John Fuller (1970), and Francois Duchene (1972); bibliography by B. C. Bloomfield and Edward Mendelson (2d ed. 1972).

Audenarde: see OUDENAARDE, Belgium.

audiencia (oudyän'syä), royal court of justice in Spain and the Spanish Empire, varying greatly in its form and function but having some administrative as well as judicial capacity. Use of the term also extended to the court's jurisdictional area. Originally a court of appeal primarily, the audiencia had evolved by the late 15th cent. into a tribunal of two chambers, one for civil and the other for criminal jurisdiction. Generally at least four *oidores* (judges or auditors) exercised judicial power within a district. The system of territorial and regional audiencias was instituted in Spanish America in the early 16th cent. to help counterbalance the independence and haphazard administration of the conquistadors. The colonial *audiencia pretorial,* however, differed widely from its peninsular counterpart in exercising executive and legislative, as well as judicial functions, and serving in a sense as the core of Spanish colonial government. As a chief organ of royal authority with the right of appeal to the Council of the Indies, it kept close watch on the acts of the civil administrators. The courts were at first powerful enough to uphold the rights of private individuals, but in the course of the 17th and 18th cent. they became corrupt and inefficient.

audio frequency, frequency at which a longitudinal mechanical wave is audible to the human ear as sound. The range of audio frequencies is not the same for every individual, but is approximately from 15 to 20,000 HERTZ. See SOUND; RADIO.

audio-visual education, term denoting the use of nonverbal materials to enrich learning experiences. It applies particularly to pictures, sounds, and other materials that develop sense perception. The successful use of visual aids in the U.S. armed forces during World War II demonstrated the effectiveness of this medium as a tool of instruction. The use of nonverbal materials—formerly confined to maps, graphs, textbook illustrations, and museum and field trips—now includes all the developments of the photographic and film industries as well as radio, sound and video-tape recordings, and television. The field of PROGRAMMED INSTRUCTION also employs computers and other types of audio-visual teaching machines. Many local school systems in the United States have their own film libraries that are often supplemented by films rented from universities and government offices. The growth of educational television has been exceedingly rapid. In 1952 the Federal Communications Commission reserved over 240 channels for educational purposes. By the end of the 1960s approximately 185 such channels were in operation. The Public Broadcasting Act (1967) set up the Corporation for Public Broadcasting, an independent agency responsible for the distribution and support of educational television programs. Another important aspect of educational television has been the development of closed-circuit and cable television systems. By using coaxial cables, such systems allow for simultaneous communication between the teacher in a studio and students receiving a program at home. See W. A. Wittich and C. F. Schuller, *Audio-Visual Materials: Their Nature and Use* (4th ed. 1967); Paul Saettler, *A History of Instructional Technology* (1968); Caleb Gattegno, *Towards a Visual Culture: Educating Through Television* (1969); Sloan Commission on Cable Communications, *On the Cable: The Television of Abundance* (1971).

auditing, examination and statement of accounts and of other documents connected with accounts by persons who have had no part in their preparation. Systems of financial inspection have long been used, especially in connection with public accounts. In Italy the elaboration of commerce considerably increased the duties of an auditor in the late Middle Ages, but the auditing of business accounts did not become common until the 19th cent., when there were an increasing number of businesses continually growing in size and complexity. Corporate charters usually came to be granted only on condition that licensed experts conduct annual audits. Such audits are particularly useful to the owners (partners or stockholders); executives (managers, officers, and directors); creditors or prospective creditors (investors, note brokers, and commercial and investment bankers); and receivers, trustees, and creditors' committees of a business. Audits are also useful to the vendors of a firm's merchandise, the owners of patents and other recipients of profit shares or royalties, governmental regulatory bodies, and prospective donors to institutions. An audit settles certain categories of questions. It must determine whether all assets and liabilities shown are actual, and that they are properly incurred, valued, and recorded. A check must be made of the surplus, income, and capital-stock accounts, verified by the examination of the authorizations for stock issues and by comparing the amounts issued with the amounts authorized. Finally, auditing constitutes an independent check on the tendency to overstate assets and understate liabilities. The duties of auditors have even expanded into a comprehensive survey and analysis of the entire conduct of the financial and accounting branches of an enterprise. Thus the auditor needs, in addition to his knowledge of ACCOUNTING, a broad understanding of business and finance. The accountant records the facts of a business; the auditor must determine whether or not such recording has been accurately and honestly done and then interpret and judge the facts, perhaps adding to his report recommendations for the future conduct of the business. In many countries, auditors are now established as a separate profession, requiring government licensing. In the United States, private audits are usually performed by certified public accountants; auditing of the Federal government's accounts is conducted by the General Accounting Office (established 1921). The Internal Revenue Service periodically audits individual and corporate tax returns. See W. A. Staub, *Auditing Developments during the Present Century* (1942); H. F. Stettler, *Auditing Principles* (3d ed. 1970); A. W. Holmes, *Auditing: Principles and Procedure* (7th ed. 1971).

Audley of Walden, Thomas Audley, Baron, 1488–1544, lord chancellor of England (1533–44) under Henry VIII. He was made speaker of the House of Commons in 1529 and lord keeper of the great seal in 1532. A loyal servant of Henry VIII, he supported the king's divorce (1533) from Katharine of Aragón and as chancellor presided (1535) over the trials of Sir Thomas More and John Fisher. He also aided in the prosecution of Anne Boleyn (1536), Sir Thomas Cromwell (1540), and other notables. He was created baron in 1538.

Audubon, John James (ô'dəbŏn), 1785–1851, American ornithologist, b. Les Cayes, Santo Domingo (now Haiti). The son of a French naval officer and a Creole woman, he was educated in France and in 1803 came to the Audubon estate, "Mill Grove," near Philadelphia. There he spent much time observing birds and making the first American bird-banding experiments. In 1808 he married Lucy Bakewell, whose faith and support were factors in his eventual success. Between 1808 and 1820 he lived mostly in Kentucky, frequently changing his occupation and neglecting his business to carry on his bird observations. He began painting portraits for a livelihood and descended the Mississippi to New Orleans, where for a time he taught drawing. From 1823 to 1828 his wife conducted a private school, in which he taught for a short time, in West Feliciana parish, La. In 1826 he went to Great Britain in search of a publisher and subscribers for his bird drawings, meeting with favorable response in Edinburgh and London. *The Birds of America,* in elephant folio size, was published in parts between 1827 and 1838, with engravings by Robert Havell, Jr. The accompanying text, called the *Ornithological Biography* (5 vol., 1831–39), was prepared largely in Edinburgh in collaboration with the Scottish naturalist William MacGillivray, who was responsible for its more scientific information. Extracts from Audubon's contributions, edited in 1926 by F. H. Herrick as *Delineations of American Scenery and Character,* reveal his stylistic qualities and furnish many pictures of American frontier life. Audubon worked on a smaller edition of his great work and also, in collaboration with John Bachman, began *The Viviparous Quadrupeds of North America,* which was completed by his sons Victor Gifford Audubon and John Woodhouse Audubon (plates, 30 parts, 1842–45; text, 3 vol., 1846–54). During these years his home was on the Hudson River in the northern part of Manhattan island. While his drawings and paintings of bird life may not wholly satisfy both the critical artist and the meticulous scientist, their achievement in both areas is considerable. They remain one of the great achievements of American intellectual history and have gained wide popularity, having been reprinted many times. See his journal (1929) and letters (1930, repr. 1969), both ed. by Howard Corning; studies by A. J. Tyler (1937), S. C. Arthur (1937), A. E. Ford (1964), A. B. Adams (1966), F. H. Herrick (2d ed. 1938, repr. 1968), and K. H. Proby (1974).

Audubon, borough (1970 pop. 10,802), Camden co., SW N.J., a suburb of Camden; inc. 1905. Audubon is mostly residential. It was named after John James Audubon, the ornithologist, who studied the birds of the area in 1829.

Audubon Society, National, one of the oldest and largest organizations in the Americas devoted to the conservation of wildlife and the natural environment; founded 1905 by George Bird Grinnell and named for John James Audubon. The society, a nonprofit organization with a membership of over 325,000, maintains numerous wildlife sanctuaries, a few of which are open to the public, as well as camps and nature centers and provides various forms of educational services. The organization is actively at work on a wide range of critical issues affecting the natural environment, including strip mining, land use control, resource (land, water, and air) conservation, and, on an international level, protection of endangered species. Its publications include *American Bird* and *Audubon* (formerly *Bird Lore*), the society's official magazine.

Aue, Hartmann von: see HARTMANN VON AUE.

Auenbrugger, Leopold (lä'ōpôlt ou'ənbro͝ogər), 1722–1809, Viennese physician. His findings on the use of percussion in diagnosing chest diseases were published in 1761 (tr. *On Percussion of the Chest,* 1936). Although ignored for some 40 years, his method, revived by Jean Nicolas Corvisart, was ultimately generally adopted.

Auer, Leopold (ou'ər), 1845–1930, Hungarian violinist and teacher, studied at the conservatories of Budapest and Vienna and with Joseph Joachim in Hanover. He taught at the St. Petersburg Conservatory, 1868–1917. Among his pupils were Mischa Elman, Jascha Heifetz, and Nathan Milstein. In 1918 he came to the United States, where he taught at the Institute of Musical Art, New York City, and the Curtis Institute of Music, Philadelphia. He became an American citizen in 1926. He was tremendously successful as a concert violinist and conductor. See his autobiography (1923).

Auerbach, Berthold (bĕrt'hōlt ou'ərbäkh), 1812–82, German novelist. He fought in the Revolution of 1848 and in the Franco-Prussian War. As a result of his *Schwarzwälder Dorfgeschichten* (1843–53, tr. of Vol. I *Village Tales from the Black Forest,* 1846–47), somewhat stylized pictures of peasant life that were much imitated, he became the virtual founder of the peasant-story genre in German. Typical of his use of the novel are *Die Frau Professorin* (1846, tr. *The Professor's Wife,* 1850), *Diethelm von Buchenberg* (1852), and *Barfüssele* (1856, tr. *The Barefooted Maiden,* 1857). Of his longer works (some of them stories of Jewish life), the best known is *Auf der Höhe* (1865, tr. *On the Heights,* 1867). A dramatization of *Die Frau Professorin* by Charlotte Pfeiffer held the stage for 50 years in Germany.

Auerstedt (ou'ərshtĕt), village, Erfurt dist., SW East Germany. At Auerstedt on Oct. 14, 1806 (the same day Napoleon I triumphed at Jena), French Marshal Louis Nicholas Davout defeated the Prussians under Duke Charles of Brunswick.

Augeas (ôjē'əs), in Greek mythology, son of Helios and king of Elis. He kept his huge herds of cattle in the Augean Stables. As his sixth labor, Hercules cleaned the stables in one day by diverting the course of a river (possibly the Alpheus) through them.

auger (ô'gər): see DRILL.

Augereau, Pierre François Charles (pyĕr fräNswä' shärl ōzhərō'), 1757–1816, marshal of France. He fought in the French Revolutionary and Napoleonic wars and was a principal in the coup d'état of 18 FRUCTIDOR (Sept. 4, 1797). For his heroism in the Italian campaign he was made duke of Castiglione. After the restoration of the Bourbons in 1814, Augereau rallied to Louis XVIII.

Aughrim or **Aghrim** (ôg'rĭm, ôkh-), village, Co. Wicklow, SW Republic of Ireland. It was the scene of a battle (July 12, 1691) in which the forces of William III of Great Britain won a decisive victory over those of James II.

Augier, Émile (Guillaume Victor Émile Augier) (gēyōm' vĕktôr' āmēl' ōzhyā'), 1820–89, French dramatist. His plays, early examples of realism, satirize the social foibles of his time and uphold the values of bourgeois family life. His chief work, *Le Gendre de M. Poirier* (1854, tr. 1915), was written with Jules Sandeau.

Augsburg (ouks'bo͝ork), city (1970 pop. 211,566), capital of Swabia, Bavaria, S West Germany, an industrial center on the Lech River. The major industries include the manufacture of textiles, clothing, machinery, motor vehicles, and airplanes. The city is an important rail junction. Augsburg was founded (c.14 B.C.) by Augustus as a Roman garrison called *Augusta Vindelicorum.* In early medieval times it was controlled by the Frankish kings. It was made a free imperial city in 1276 and was later a powerful member of various Swabian leagues, including the SWABIAN LEAGUE of 1488-1534. Augsburg was one of Europe's most important commercial and banking centers in the 15th and 16th cent. and was a rallying point of German science and art. The city was the home of the FUGGER and WELSER families and was the birthplace of Hans Holbein the Elder, Hans Holbein the Younger, and Hans Burgkmair. Several important agreements, including the Augsburg Confession (1530), were concluded there during the Reformation. Augsburg suffered greatly in the Thirty Years War (1618-48). In 1806 it became part of Bavaria. Augsburg's many noteworthy structures include the cathedral (begun in the 9th cent.); the 16th-century Fuggerei, an enclosed settlement for poor persons founded by the Fugger family; and the 17th-century town hall. Bertolt Brecht was also born in Augsburg.

Augsburg, League of, defensive alliance formed (1686) by Holy Roman Emperor Leopold I with various German states, including Bavaria and the Palatinate, and with Sweden and Spain so far as their German interests were concerned. It was an acknowledgment of a community of German feeling against French expansion. The war that broke out after the French attack on the Palatinate in Oct., 1688, is sometimes designated the War of the League of Augsburg. In 1689 a new coalition against the French, the Grand Alliance, was formed by Austria, England, and the Netherlands. Savoy and Spain later joined the Alliance and the war of 1688-97 is more properly known as the War of the Grand Alliance (see GRAND ALLIANCE, WAR OF THE).

Augsburg, Peace of, 1555, temporary settlement within the Holy Roman Empire of the religious conflict arising from the REFORMATION. Each prince was to determine whether Lutheranism or Roman Catholicism was to prevail in his lands (*cuius regio, eius religio*). Dissenters were allowed to emigrate, and the free cities were obligated to allow both Catholics and Lutherans to practice their religions. Calvinists and others were ignored. Under a provision termed the ecclesiastic reservation, the archbishops, bishops, and abbots who had become Protestant after 1552 were to forfeit their offices and incomes.

Augsburg Confession: see CREED **4.**

Augsburg Interim: see REFORMATION.

Augur, Hezekiah, 1791-1858, American sculptor. After a business failure he devoted himself to art and was encouraged by Samuel F. B. Morse. His bust of Washington and the statuette group *Jephtha and His Daughter* (Yale Univ.) are among his best-known works.

augur: see OMEN.

August: see MONTH.

Augusta (ougo͞o'stä), city (1971 pop. 34,709), E Sicily, Italy, on an island (formerly a peninsula) in the Ionian Sea, connected by bridge with the Sicilian mainland. It is an important port and a fishing and industrial center. Manufactures include refined petroleum, chemicals, textiles, and fertilizer. The city was a Greek settlement and then a Roman military base. It was refounded by Emperor Frederick II in 1232 and later (15th-early 16th cent.) was a thriving banking town. Augusta was badly damaged by earthquakes in 1693 and 1848. Of note is Frederick II's castle (now a penitentiary).

Augusta (ôgŭs'tə, əgŭs'-). **1** City (1970 pop. 59,864), seat of Richmond co., E Ga.; inc. 1798. At the head of navigation on the Savannah River and protected by levees, Augusta is the trade center for a broad band of counties in Georgia and South Carolina known as the Central Savannah River Area. It is also an important industrial center, manufacturing textiles, chemicals, bricks and tiles, fertilizers, cleansers, hospital supplies, tools, and wood, paper, metal, and plastic products. The city is a popular resort, noted especially for its golf tournaments. Augusta grew from an old river trading post existing as early as 1717 and was named by James Oglethorpe in 1735 after the mother of George III. In the American Revolution, Augusta changed hands several times and was finally taken by Continental forces in 1781 under Andrew Pickens and Light-Horse Harry Lee. It was the capital of Georgia from 1785 to 1795, and the U.S. Constitution was ratified there. Augusta boomed after the American Revolution, during the rapid expansion of the tobacco industry, followed by the growth of the cotton industry. By 1820 the city was the terminus for river boats, wagon trains, and traders, all carrying the produce of the interior to the sea. Manufacturing began in 1828, when Augusta's first textile plant began operation with machinery brought laboriously from Philadelphia. During the Civil War, Augusta housed the largest Confederate powder works. The city's historical attractions include a boyhood home of Woodrow Wilson, a U.S. arsenal (1815-1955), whose surviving buildings are now part of Augusta College, and old homes of Georgian and classic-revival styles. Paine College, Georgia Medical College, and two large veterans hospitals are also in Augusta. Nearby is Fort Gordon, with training schools for military police, the signal corps, and the corps of engineers. **2** City (1970 pop. 21,945), state capital and seat of Kennebec co., SW Maine, on the Kennebec River; inc. as a town 1797, as a city 1849. Shoes, fabrics, and paper products are manufactured there. Traders visited the site, long known as Cushnoc, even before 1628, when the Plymouth Company established a trading post. Fort Western was built in 1754, and Benedict Arnold's expedition to Quebec gathered at the fort in 1775. (The garrison house was restored as a museum in 1921.) The settlement around the fort developed with the shipping and shipbuilding on the Kennebec, and manufacturing began in 1837, when a dam was built across the river. The capitol building (1829) was designed by Charles Bulfinch but has been considerably enlarged and remodeled. James G. Blaine's early 19-century home is the governor's mansion. A junior college (a branch of the Univ. of Maine), a veterans hospital, and a U.S. arsenal are also in Augusta.

Augustenburg, Christian Augustus, Herzog von: see SCHLESWIG-HOLSTEIN.

Augustine, Saint (ô'gəstēn, -tĭn; ôgŭs'tĭn), Lat. *Aurelius Augustinus*, 354-430, Doctor of the Church, one of the four Latin fathers, bishop of Hippo (near present-day Annaba, Algeria), b. Tagaste (c.40 mi/60 km S of Hippo). His mother, St. Monica, was a great influence in his life. She brought him up as a Christian, but he gave up his religion when he went to school at Carthage. There he became adept in rhetoric. In his *Confessions* he repents of his wild youth in Carthage, during which time he fathered an illegitimate son. At some time in his youth he became a convert to Manichaeism. After 376 he went to Rome, where he taught rhetoric with success; in 384, at the urging of the Manichaeans, he went to Milan to teach. His years at Milan were the critical period of his life. Already distrustful of Manichaeism, he came to renounce it after a deep study of Platonism and skepticism. Augustine, troubled in spirit, was greatly drawn by the eloquent fervor of St. Ambrose, bishop of Milan. After two years of great doubt and mental disquietude, Augustine suddenly decided to embrace Christianity. He was baptized on Easter, 387. Soon afterward he returned to Tagaste, where he lived a monastic life with a group of friends. In 391, while he was visiting in Hippo, he was chosen against his will to be priest of the Christians there. For the rest of his life he remained in Hippo, where he became auxiliary bishop in 395 and bishop soon after. He died in the course of the siege of Hippo by the Vandals. St. Augustine's influence on Christianity is thought by many to be second only to that of St. Paul, and theologians, both Roman Catholic and Protestant, look upon him as the founder of theology. His *Confessions* is considered a classic of Christian mysticism. This work (c.400), the prime source for St. Augustine's life, is a beautifully written apology for the Christian convert. Next to it his best-known work is the *City of God* (after 412)—a mammoth defense of Christianity against its pagan critics, and famous especially for the uniquely Christian view of history elaborated in its pages. Augustine regarded all history as God's providential preparation of two mystical cities, one of God and one of the devil, and to one or the other of which all mankind will finally belong. His greatest purely dogmatic work is *On the Trinity,* a systematization of Christian doctrine, but much of his theological teaching comes from his polemic writings. His works against the Manichaeans, especially *Against Faustus* (his Manichaean teacher), are important for the light they throw on this religion. Against DONATISM St. Augustine directed two works, *On Baptism* and *On the Correction of the Donatists,* in which he formulated the idea, since then become part of Roman Catholicism, that the church's authority is the guarantee of the Christian faith, its own guarantee being the APOSTOLIC SUCCESSION. The most spectacular controversy in which St. Augustine was involved was his battle against PELAGIANISM. The Pelagians denied original sin and the fall of man. The implication of this, that God's grace was unnecessary for the first step toward salvation, aroused Augustine, who held that man was corrupt and helpless. He wrote many treatises in this controversy and continued to elaborate his ideas afterward. From his writings the great controversies on grace proceed, and as professed followers of Augustine, John Calvin and the Jansenists developed predestinarian theologies. Though revering Augustine, many theologians have refused to accept his more extreme statements on grace itself. Another of St. Augustine's important treatises, *On the Work of Monks,* has been much used by monastics. He also composed works on biblical exegesis. One of his most interesting treatises is called *Retractions,* composed late in life, a kind of review of his works, in which he revised some of his views. He was a master of style. His letters are numerous and revealing. His most important works are available in translation. Feast: Aug. 28. See biographies by Jacques Chabannes (tr. 1962) and P. R. L. Brown (1967); R. W. Battenhouse, ed., *A Companion to the Study of St. Augustine* (1955); H. A. Deane, *The Political and Social Ideas of St. Augustine* (1963); R. A. Markus, *Saeculum: History and Society in the Theology of St. Augustine* (1970); Eugene Teselle, *Augustine the Theologian* (1970).

Augustine of Canterbury, Saint, d. c.605, Italian missionary, called the Apostle of the English, first archbishop of Canterbury (from 601). A Roman Benedictine monk, he was sent to England, as the head of some 40 monks, by Pope St. Gregory I. Arriving in 597, they were well received by King ÆTHELBERT, who was converted by Augustine, thus making him the first Christian king in Anglo-Saxon England. Æthelbert gave the monks land at Canterbury, and a church was built on the site of the present cathedral. A monastery was also founded. Augustine's mission, introducing the more indulgent Roman ways, was resented by Celtic monks of the British isles, whose austerities were more severe and who kept a different date of Easter. Their differences were eventually settled in 663 at the Synod of Whitby, when England abandoned Celtic practices. Feast: May 28 (May 26 in England and Wales). See Bede's *Ecclesiastical History;* biographies by F. van der Meer (1961) and J. Gnalloor (1965); studies by R. W. Battenhouse (1955) and T. Prosper (1963).

Augustinians, religious orders in the Roman Catholic Church. The name is derived from the Rule of St. Augustine, an old, rather generalized monastic rule. The canons regularly adopted this rule in the 11th cent. and became known as Augustinian, or Austin, canons. Subsequent orders of canons regular, such as the Premonstratensians, are outgrowths. The Austin friars are an entirely different group of religious, dating from the 13th cent. (see FRIAR). Officially known as Hermits of St. Augustine, they now exist in three independent branches—the Calced Augustinian Hermits, the more austere and less numerous Discalced Augustinian Hermits, and the Recollects of St. Augustine. There are also congregations of women corresponding to both canons and friars.

Augustus (ôgŭs'təs, əgŭs'-), 63 B.C.-A.D. 14, first Roman emperor, a grandson of the sister of Julius CAESAR. Named at first Caius Octavius, he became on adoption by the Julian gens (44 B.C.) Caius Julius Caesar Octavianus (Octavian); Augustus was a title of honor granted (27 B.C.) by the senate. When Octavius was a youth, Caesar took a great interest in his education and made him his heir without the boy's knowledge. Octavius was in Illyricum when Caesar was killed, and he promptly set out for Rome to avenge the dictator's death. Before he reached the city, he heard that he was Caesar's heir. At Rome, ANTONY was in control, and Octavian was recognized by Cicero and the senate as a leader against him. Antony went north to take Gaul and was defeated (43 B.C.) at Mutina (modern Modena). Octavian, now dominant in Rome, secured the consulship and made an alliance with Antony and LEPIDUS (d. 13 B.C.) as the Second Triumvirate. Having proscribed the enemies of the triumvirate, Octavian and Antony went east and defeated (42 B.C.) the army of Marcus Junius BRUTUS and Caius CASSIUS Longinus at Philippi. Octavian's forces then attacked Sextus POMPEIUS, who controlled Sicily and

Sardinia, and Marcus Vipsanius AGRIPPA defeated (36 B.C.) Pompeius at Mylae. Meanwhile, at Rome, Octavian had been consolidating his power. He was helped by the growing impatience of Rome with Antony's intrigue with Cleopatra, and he had himself appointed (31 B.C.) general against Antony. After the naval battle off ACTIUM, which Agrippa won over Antony and Cleopatra, Octavian controlled all Roman territories. He set about at once to reform the city and the provinces. He purged the senate of unworthy members, restored and built temples, and fostered a revival of Roman tradition. Augustus had no court, and he considered himself, at least publicly, not the ruler, but rather the first citizen, of the republic. The senate delighted to honor him: in 29 B.C. he was made imperator [Lat.,=commander; from it is derived *emperor*], in 28 B.C. princeps [leader; from it is derived *prince*], in 27 B.C. augustus [august, reverend], in 12 B.C. pontifex maximus [high priest], and a month (Sextilis) was renamed Augustus (August) in his honor. His reforms were prudent and far-reaching, and he was responsible for Rome's return from a military dictatorship to a constitutional rule. He divided the provinces into two classes—senatorial, ruled by a proconsul chosen by the senate with a term of one year, and imperial, in charge of a governor solely responsible to Augustus with an indefinite term. To control the provinces Augustus spread the army throughout the empire; before this Italy had been burdened with a huge standing army. Augustus desired no further conquest, and his consequent policy was to hold the borders set by Caesar. His attempt to make a buffer state of the German territory between the Rhine and the Weser (or the Elbe) led to a rebellion by ARMINIUS in which Varus was defeated; this was the only real reverse Augustus suffered. Augustus studied the plans of Caesar for colonization throughout the empire. He made taxation more equitable and had general censuses taken. Knowing that the roads were the arteries of the empire, he lavished expenditures on them. He built a new forum, beautified the streets, improved housing conditions, and set up adequate police and fire protection. He was munificent to arts and letters, and he was a close friend of MAECENAS and a patron of Vergil, Ovid, Livy, and Horace. Augustus established the concept of the Pax Romana [Roman peace], which strengthened the imperial government. He was succeeded by his stepson TIBERIUS. See Victor Ehrenberg and A. H. M. Jones, *Documents Illustrating the Reigns of Augustus and Tiberius* (2d ed., 1955); H. T. Rowell, *Rome in the Augustan Age* (1962); G. W. Bowersock, *Augustus and the Greek World* (1965); A. H. M. Jones, *Augustus* (1971).

Augustus II, 1670–1733, king of Poland (1697–1733) and, as Frederick Augustus I, elector of Saxony (1694–1733). He commanded the imperial army against the Turks (1695–96), but had no success and was replaced by Prince Eugene of Savoy as soon as he competed for the Polish throne, left vacant by the death of John III. By becoming a Catholic and granting the Polish nobility unprecedented privileges he was elected king with the support of the Holy Roman emperor and the pope. With help from PATKUL, Augustus allied himself (1699) with PETER I of Russia and FREDERICK IV of Denmark for an attack on young CHARLES XII of Sweden. In the resulting conflict (see NORTHERN WAR) Augustus invaded LIVONIA with his Saxon troops but was defeated (1702) by Charles XII. The Treaty of Altranstädt (1706) forced him to renounce the Polish crown in favor of STANISLAUS I and to give up his alliance with Russia. After Charles's defeat by the Russians at Poltava (1709), Augustus revived the alliance and recovered Poland. In Poland, where he kept a Saxon force, Augustus was highly unpopular. After his death, the ascension of his son and successor in Saxony, Augustus III, to the Polish throne was unsuccessfully contested by Stanislaus I, who was backed by France. Among Augustus's many mistresses was Maria Aurora KÖNIGSMARK; her son, Maurice de SAXE, was one of Augustus's innumerable illegitimate offspring. A patron of the arts, Augustus greatly embellished Dresden and created the MEISSEN china manufactures. He is also called Augustus the Strong.

Augustus III, 1696–1763, king of Poland (1735–63) and, as Frederick Augustus II, elector of Saxony (1733–63); son of Augustus II, whom he succeeded in Saxony. Elected king of Poland by a minority, he allied himself with Empress Anna of Russia and Holy Roman Emperor CHARLES VI in the War of the POLISH SUCCESSION (1733–35) and secured the throne from STANISLAUS I. In the War of the AUSTRIAN SUCCESSION (1740–48), Augustus at first offered to support Maria Theresa in return for a corridor between Poland and Saxony. He was refused and entered the coalition against her, claiming rights as a son-in-law of her uncle, Holy Roman Emperor Joseph I. He changed sides in 1742. When the SEVEN YEARS WAR began (1756) with a surprise attack on Saxony, Augustus fled to Poland; he returned to Dresden only after the war was over (1763). He was a patron of the arts, and his indolence and sensuality kept him from state affairs, which he left to his ministers, notably Count BRÜHL. Augustus's death ended the union of Saxony and Poland. His grandson became elector of Saxony (and later, as FREDERICK AUGUSTUS I, king), but STANISLAUS II was elected king of Poland with Russian support.

auk (ôk), common name for a member of the family Alcidae (alcid family), swimming and diving birds of the N Atlantic and Pacific, which includes the guillemots and puffins. Their legs are set far back on their bodies, making them clumsy on land, where they seldom venture except to nest. The extinct, flightless great auk, *Pinguinus impennis,* or garefowl, represents the largest species. It was about the size of a goose, black above and grayish white below, and was formerly abundant in the N Atlantic. Slaughtered in its breeding grounds for its flesh, feathers, and oil, it became extinct c.1844. The least auklet (about 6½ in./16.3 cm), common in the Bering Sea region, is the smallest of the family, and the razor-billed auk, *Alca torda* (16–18 in./40–45 cm), is the largest surviving member. The Eskimos hunt the dovekie (*Plautus alle*), or little auk, for food and use its feathered skin for clothing. Auks return to the same breeding grounds every year, and each individual goes to the very same nesting site. The single egg is laid on bare rock on cliff ledges, and incubation duties are shared by both parents. Auks are classified in the phylum CHORDATA, subphylum Vertebrata, class Aves, order Charadriiformes, family Alcidae.

Aukrust, Olav (ō'läv ou'kro͝ost), 1883–1929, Norwegian lyric poet. Aukrust's work, which contains strong religious and nationalist sentiment, draws much of its inspiration from Norway's peasant life, traditions, and majestic landscape. His best-known volumes of poetry include *Himmelvarden* [the mountain cairn] (1916) and *Solrenning* [sunrise] (1930). Aukrust writes symbolically of the individual's struggle against dark, elemental powers and his redemption through Christian faith. He uses this theme as a metaphor for Norwegian national development.

Aulard, Alphonse (älfôNs' ōlär'), 1849–1928, French historian. He was the first professional historian of the French Revolution, and he devoted his life to this study. A professor at the Univ. of Paris, he founded the Société de l'Histoire de la Révolution and the monthly review *Révolution française.* Aulard regarded the conservative interpretation of Taine as prejudiced; nevertheless, he himself clearly represented the republican, bourgeois, and anticlerical concept of the Revolution. He concentrated on political history. Some of his students, notably Albert MATHIEZ, broke with his emphasis and turned to social and economic issues. Aulard's works include *Études et leçons sur la Révolution française* (9 vol., 1893–1924); *Histoire politique de la Révolution française* (1901; tr. *The French Revolution: A Political History,* 4 vol., 1910, repr. 1965); *Les Grands Orateurs de la Révolution: Mirabeau, Vergniaud, Danton, Robespierre* (1914); and *La Révolution française et le régime féodal* (1919).

Aulis (ô'lĭs), small port of ancient Greece, in Boeotia, E central Greece. From there the Greek fleet sailed against Troy after the sacrifice of IPHIGENIA. Its ancient temple of Artemis is in ruins.

Aulus Gellius: see GELLIUS, AULUS.

Aunis (ōnēs'), small region and former province, W France, on the Atlantic coast. It is now part of the Charente-Maritime and Deux-Sèvres depts. and includes the islands of Ré and Oléron. La Rochelle, the historic capital and one of the leading ports of the region, and Rochefort are the chief cities. A part of Aquitaine, it was recovered from England in 1373 and incorporated into the French crown lands.

aura: see SPIRITISM.

Aurangabad (ourŭng"gäbäd'), town (1971 pop. 150,514), Maharashtra state, W India. A district administrative center, it also carries on trade in cotton and wheat. Silverware is produced. Aurangabad, founded in 1610, is the home of Marathwada Univ. Nearby is the great mausoleum (1711) of Aurangzeb's empress.

Aurangzeb (ôr'əngzĕb") or **Aurangzib** (-zĭb"), 1618–1707, Mogul emperor of India (1658–1707), son and successor of SHAH JAHAN. He served (1636–44, 1653–58) as viceroy of the Deccan but was constantly at odds with his father and his eldest brother, Dara Shikoh, the heir apparent. When Shah Jahan fell ill in 1658, Aurangzeb seized the opportunity to fight and defeat Dara and two other brothers in a battle for succession. He imprisoned his father for life and ascended the throne of Delhi with the reign title Alamgir [world-shaker]. A scholarly, austere man, fanatically devoted to Islam, he persecuted the Hindus, destroying their temples and monuments. He executed the guru of the SIKHS when he refused to embrace Islam. Such measures produced a fierce Hindu reaction. Thus, although the Mogul empire reached its greatest extent under Aurangzeb, it was also fatally weakened by revolts of the Sikhs, Rajputs, and Jats in the north and the rebellion of the Mahrattas in the Deccan. From 1682, Aurangzeb concentrated all his energies on crushing the Mahrattas, but his costly campaigns were only temporarily successful and further weakened his authority in the north. The Mogul empire fell apart soon after his death. His name also appears as Aurungzebe, Aurungzeb, and Aureng-Zebe. See biography by Sir Jadunath Sarkar (5 vol., 1912–24); study by Stanley Lane-Poole (1964).

Auray (ôrā'), town (1968 pop. 8,639), Morbihan dept., NW France, in Brittany, on the Auray River estuary. Oysters are bred, food is canned, and there is some light manufacturing. Nearby the decisive battle of the War of the BRETON SUCCESSION took place (1364). On the Champ des Martyrs, also near Auray, some 800 royalists, who had landed at Quiberon, were massacred (1795). North of the town is the famous Basilica of Sainte-Anne-d'Auray, built in Renaissance style in the 19th cent. Pilgrimages to the shrine have occurred every July 26 since the 17th cent., when a peasant, Yves Nicolazic, claimed to have seen a vision of St. Anne.

Aurelian (Lucius Domitius Aurelianus) (ôrē'lēən), c.212–275, Roman emperor (270–75). Rising in the ranks, he became consul under Valerian. He succeeded CLAUDIUS II, whose victory over the Goths had begun the territorial rehabilitation of the empire. Aurelian conceded Dacia to the Goths but consolidated the Danubian provinces and held the barbarians beyond the Rhine in check. His most brilliant exploits were in the East—especially in Palmyra, where he captured ZENOBIA and destroyed her kingdom. Aurelian went to Gaul, where he received the submission of the independent "emperor," Tetricus. One of Rome's greatest emperors, Aurelian regained Britain, Gaul, Spain, Egypt, Syria, and Mesopotamia and removed for a while the barbarian threat to the eastern provinces. He fortified Rome with a wall some 12 mi (19 km) in circumference, averaging more than 40 ft (12.2 m) in height. Much of it still remains. Aurelian was murdered, and Marcus Claudius TACITUS succeeded him.

Aurelius, Marcus: see MARCUS AURELIUS.

aureole (ôr'ēōl"), in art: see NIMBUS.

aureole, in physics, luminous circle seen when the sun or other bright light is observed through a diffuse medium, i.e., smoke, thin cloud, fog, haze, or mist. It sometimes occurs as a series of concentric circles. The aureole results from the dispersion of light by particles of dust or water. Because of the refraction of the light waves, it exhibits color in varying intensity.

Aureomycin (ôr"ēōmī'sĭn), trade name for chlortetracycline, a broad spectrum ANTIBIOTIC. See TETRACYCLINE.

Auriga (ôrī'gə) [Lat.,=the charioteer or wagoner], northern CONSTELLATION traditionally represented as a man, possibly Vulcan, carrying a goat on his shoulder while driving a chariot. It lies E of Perseus and N of Gemini and Taurus. Auriga contains CAPELLA, a bright, yellow giant star, and Epsilon Aurigae, an eclipsing binary in which a small star orbits a cool supergiant star. The constellation reaches its highest point in the evening sky in early February.

Aurignac (ôrēnyäk'), village (1968 pop. 1,149), Haute-Garonne dept., S France, at the foot of the Pyrenees. Its caves, excavated in 1860, contain relics of prehistoric man of the Aurignacian period (see PALEOLITHIC PERIOD).

Aurigny: see ALDERNEY, island, England.

Aurillac (ôrēyäk'), town (1968 pop. 31,143), capital of Cantal dept., S central France, in Auvergne, on the Jordanne River. An industrial, communications, and market center, it is noted for its furniture, footwear, umbrellas, and Cantal cheese. It has an 18th-century church and picturesque old houses.

Auriol, Vincent (văNsäN' ôryôl'), 1884–1966, French statesman, first president (1947–54) of the Fourth Republic. A Socialist deputy after 1914, he was finance minister under Léon BLUM (1936–37) and minister of justice in the cabinet of Camille CHAUTEMPS (1937–38). He refused (1940) to vote plenary powers to Marshal PÉTAIN and was held in custody by the Vichy government. Released in 1941, he worked in the French underground and in 1943 left France to join Gen. Charles de Gaulle. A member of the provisional government (1945), he was elected (1946) president of the national assembly. He was president of the republic from 1947 to 1954. In 1958 he aided de Gaulle's return to power, but he later protested (1960) against what he considered de Gaulle's arbitrary rule. He resigned from the Socialist party in 1959.

Aurobindo, Sri: see GHOSE, AUROBINDO.

aurochs (ôr'ŏks), extinct European wild ox, *Bos primigenius,* believed to be the chief ancestor of European domestic cattle. Also called urus, it was a large, horned, dark brown animal, standing up to 7 ft (2 m) at the shoulder. It existed in the Pleistocene period and was apparently domesticated by Neolithic (New Stone Age) man. It is mentioned in the writings of Julius Caesar. Hunting and the clearing of forests resulted in its extermination; the last known survivor died in 1627 in Poland. The animal now commonly called aurochs in Europe is actually the WISENT, or European bison. The aurochs is classified in the phylum CHORDATA, subphylum Vertebrata, class Mammalia, order Artiodactyla, family Bovidae.

Aurora, in mythology: see EOS.

Aurora. 1 City (1970 pop. 74,974), Adams and Arapahoe counties, N central Colo., a residential suburb of Denver; inc. 1903. It is the trade center for a large farming and livestock-raising area. Electrical products, aircraft parts, and oil field equipment are manufactured. Tourism and construction are also important. Nearby are Lowry Air Force Base and Fitzsimmons Army General Hospital. **2** City (1970 pop. 74,182), Kane co., NE Ill., on the Fox River; inc. 1837. It has large railroad yards and a great variety of manufactures, including construction and highway equipment, electric tools, pumps, and heavy steel products. It was one of the first cities to use electricity for street lighting (1881). It is the seat of Aurora College and of a notable historical museum in a 20-room house built in 1857.

aurora borealis (bôr"ēăl'ĭs) and **aurora australis** (ôstrā'lĭs), luminous display of various forms and colors seen in the night sky. The aurora borealis of the Northern Hemisphere is often called the northern lights, and the aurora australis of the Southern Hemisphere is known as the southern lights. Each is visible over an area centering around the geomagnetic pole of its own hemisphere. The aurora borealis is said to occur with greatest frequency along a line extending through N Norway, across central Hudson Bay, through Point Barrow, Alaska, and through N Siberia. It is often visible in Canada and the N United States and is seen most frequently at the time of the EQUINOXES. Among the most magnificent of natural phenomena, auroral displays appear in shades of red, yellow, green, blue, and violet and are usually brightest in their most northern latitudes. The aurora is seen in a variety of forms, e.g., as patches of light, in the form of streamers, arcs, banks, rays, or resembling hanging draperies. The aurora occurs between 35 mi and 600 mi (56 km–970 km) above the earth. It is thought to be caused by high-speed electrons and protons from the sun, which are trapped in the Van Allen radiation belt high above the earth and then channeled toward the polar regions by the earth's magnetic field. These electrically charged particles enter the atmosphere and collide with air molecules (chiefly oxygen and nitrogen), thus exciting them to luminosity; near the 600-mile level, the light may be given off by electrons and protons combining to form hydrogen atoms. The auroras coincide with periods of greatest sunspot activity and with magnetic storms (disturbances of the ionosphere which interfere with long-distance radio communication). Much was learned about the aurora during the 1957–58 International Geophysical Year, when it was studied intensively by means of balloons, radar, rockets, and satellites.

Aurungzebe: see AURANGZEB.

Ausable Chasm (ôsā'bəl), gorge, 2 mi (3.2 km) long, from 20 to 50 ft (6–15 m) wide, from 100 to 200 ft (30–61 m) deep, NE N.Y. The chasm, with its rapids, waterfalls, and curious rock formations, is a popular tourist attraction; Rainbow Falls, 75 ft (23 m) high, is at the southern end of the gorge. The **Ausable,** a river rising in the Adirondack Mts. and flowing NE to Lake Champlain, continues to carve out the gorge as it passes over the sandstone bedrock.

Auschwitz: see OŚWIĘCIM, Poland.

Ausgleich: see AUSTRO-HUNGARIAN MONARCHY.

Ausonius (Decimus Magnus Ausonius) (ôsō'nēəs), c.310–c.395, Latin poet and man of letters, b. Bordeaux. He tutored Gratian, who, when he ascended the throne, made Ausonius prefect of Gaul, Italy, and Africa, and finally consul (379). When Gratian died, Ausonius returned to Bordeaux. His work gives a detailed picture of contemporary people and places. *Mosella,* a description of his journey on the Moselle River, contains his best verse. Among his other works are *Parentalia,* verse sketches of dead relatives, and *Ordo nobilium urbium,* a description of 20 leading cities of the Roman world. Ausonius was nominally a Christian, although his works reveal many pagan beliefs. See T. R. Glover, *Life and Letters in the Fourth Century* (1901, repr. 1968).

Aussig: see ÚSTÍ NAD LABEM, Czechoslovakia.

Aust-Agder (oust"-äg'dər), county (1972 est. pop. 82,000), 3,610 sq mi (9,350 sq km), S Norway, bordering on the Skagerrak in the east. Arendal is the capital. The SETESDAL comprises the county's northern section. The Otra is the main river. Major industries include fishing, shipping, agriculture, tourism, and forestry. The county was formerly called Nedenes.

Austen, Jane, 1775–1817, English novelist. The daughter of a clergyman, she spent the first 25 years of her life at "Steventon," her father's Hampshire vicarage. Here her first novels, *Pride and Prejudice, Sense and Sensibility,* and *Northanger Abbey,* were written, although they were not published until much later. On her father's retirement in 1801, the family moved to Bath for several years and then to Southampton, settling finally at Chawton Cottage, near Alton, Hampshire, which was Jane's home for the rest of her life. *Northanger Abbey,* a satire on the GOTHIC ROMANCE, was sold to a publisher for £10 in 1803, but as it was not published, was bought back by members of the family and was finally issued posthumously. The novels published in Austen's lifetime were *Sense and Sensibility* (1811), *Pride and Prejudice* (1813), *Mansfield Park* (1814), and *Emma* (1816). *Persuasion* was issued in 1818 with *Northanger Abbey.* The author's name did not appear on any of her title pages, and although her own friends knew of her authorship, she received little public recognition in her lifetime. Jane Austen's novels are comedies of manners that depict the self-contained world of provincial ladies and gentlemen. Most of her works revolve around the delicate business of providing husbands for marriageable daughters. She is particularly noted for her vivid delineations and lively interplay of character, her superb sense of comic irony, and her moral firmness. She ridicules the silly, the affected, and the stupid, ranging in her satire from light portraiture in her early works to more scornful exposures in her later novels. Her writing was subjected to the most careful polishing. She was quite aware of her special excellences and limitations, comparing herself to a miniaturist. Today she is regarded as one of the great masters of the English novel. Her minor works include her *Juvenilia,* the novel *Lady Susan,* and the fragments *The Watsons* and *Sanditon.* See her letters (ed. by R. W. Chapman, 2d ed. 1965); biographies by Elizabeth Jenkins (1939) and J. A. Hodge (1972); studies by Mary Lascelles (1939), A. H. Wright (1953), A. W. Litz (1965), F. W. Bradbook (1966), A. M. Duckworth (1971), K. Kroeber (1971) F. B. Pinion (1973), and S. M. Tave (1973).

Austerlitz (ô'stərlĭts, Ger. ou'–), Czech *Slavkov u Brna,* town, S Czechoslovakia, in Moravia. An agricultural center, the town has sugar refineries and cotton mills. It became a seat of the Anabaptists in 1528. At Austerlitz, in the "battle of the three emperors," Napoleon I won (Dec. 2, 1805) his most brilliant victory by defeating the Russian and Austrian armies under Czar Alexander I and Emperor Francis II. The "sun of Austerlitz" (it was a cloudless day) became synonymous with the peak of Napoleon's fortunes. An armistice with Austria, concluded (Dec. 4) at Nikolsburg (now Mikulov), was followed by the Treaty of Pressburg. Russia continued the war but had to withdraw all troops from Austria. There is a famous description of the battle in Tolstoy's *War and Peace.* The town has an 18th-century castle, a 13th-century church, the Renaissance Church of the Resurrection, and the Monument of Peace (built 1910–11).

Austin, Alfred, 1835–1913, English author, b. Leeds. Originally trained for a legal career, he eventually turned to writing and politics. From 1883–95 he edited the *National Review.* Although in 1896 he succeeded Tennyson as poet laureate, his poetry is negligible, and he was the butt of many critics who attacked his snobbishness, tastelessness, and lack of poetic talent. His best work is *A Garden That I Love* (1894, 1907), a miscellany in diary form. See his autobiography (1911, repr. 1973); study by N. B. Crowell (1953).

Austin, John, 1790–1859, English jurist. He served (1826–32) as professor of jurisprudence at the Univ. of London, and his lectures were published (with additional material) as *The Province of Jurisprudence Determined* (1832; repr. 1967, 3 vol.) and *Lectures on Jurisprudence* (1869, 5th ed. 1911). These books presented a comprehensive analysis of the principles underlying all legal systems. Austin argued that law was the expression of the will of the sovereign authority and was not to be confused with the dictates of religion and ethics. Austin's work—in part stemming from that of Jeremy BENTHAM—had a strong influence on many later legal theorists, including John Stuart MILL. His wife, Sarah Taylor Austin, was a well-known translator. See Jethro Brown, ed., *The Austinian Theory of Law* (1906).

Austin, John Langshaw, 1911–60, British philosopher. A graduate of Oxford, he was a fellow of All Souls (1933–35) and Magdalen (1935–52) colleges before he became White's professor of moral philosophy (1952–60) also at Oxford. He strongly influenced analytic philosophy, urging that the use of words be closely examined and holding that the distinctions of ordinary language are more subtle than is usually realized. His writings include *Philosophical Papers* (1961), *Sense and Sensibilia* (1962), and *How to Do Things with Words* (1962). See studies by Mats Furberg (1971) and Sir Isaiah Berlin et al. (1973).

Austin, Moses, 1761–1821, American pioneer, b. Durham, Conn. After developing lead mines in SW Virginia, he went to inspect (1796–97) prospects in Missouri, then Spanish territory. In 1798 he founded Potosi, Mo. and became a miner and trader there. Hard times caused him to go to Texas in 1820 and get the Spanish governor's permission to settle 300 families in Texas. The grant was confirmed in 1821, but Moses Austin died without realizing his settlement plans. His son, Stephen F. Austin, took up the plans.

Austin, Stephen Fuller, 1793–1836, American leader of colonization in Texas, known as the Father of Texas, b. Wythe co., Va.; son of Moses Austin. He grew up in Missouri, studied at Transylvania Univ. in Kentucky, served (1814–20) in the Missouri territorial legislature, and was studying law in New Orleans when his father died. Stephen took up the plans to colonize Texas and on a journey there (1821) selected the area between the Brazos and Colorado rivers. In January, 1822, he planted the first legal settlement of Anglo-Americans in Texas. He later went to Mexico City to have his grant cleared and confirmed by the newly independent Mexican government. Austin's settlements, with the towns of San Felipe de Austin and Brazoria, prospered. Other American colonists poured in. As friction developed over the years with the Mexican government, Austin opposed illegal efforts at Texan independence. He was sent in 1833 to Mexico City to present the settlers' grievances, to ask that Texas be separated from Coahuila, and to get the Mexican immigration law modified. He was accused of treason and imprisoned. On his return to Texas in 1835 he opposed the government of SANTA ANNA and so forwarded the Texas Revolution. He was sent as one of the commissioners (1835–36) of the provisional government to obtain aid in the United States, was defeated (1836) by Samuel HOUSTON for the presidency of Texas, and served briefly until his death as secretary of state. See *The Austin Papers, 1765–1837* (1924–28); biographies by S. Glassock (1951) and E. G. Barker (1925, repr. 1968).

Austin. 1 City (1970 pop. 25,074), seat of Mower co., SE Minn., on the Cedar River, near the Iowa line; inc. 1868. The industrial and commercial center of a rich farm region, it has a large meat-packing industry. Shipping and metal containers are also made. In Austin are a junior college and an arboretum and nature center. **2** City (1970 pop. 251,808), state capital and seat of Travis co., S central Texas, on the Colorado River and two of the Highland Lakes; inc. 1839. It is the commercial heart of a large ranching, poultry, dairy, cotton, and grain area, with a great variety of manufactures. It is also a major convention city and an educational center—the main campus of the Univ. of Texas, St. Edward's Univ., Huston-Tillotson College, two theological seminaries, and a junior college, as well as numerous electronic and scientific research firms, are located there. The site was selected in 1839 for the capital of the independent Texas republic and named by the legislature in honor of Stephen F. Austin. Fear of the Mexicans and the Indians drove government officials to Houston in 1842; they returned in 1845 when Texas was admitted to the Union, and in 1870, following a referendum, Austin was made permanent capital. It remained a small commercial, governmental, and educational center until its industrial growth was spurred by the development of power and flood control projects on the Colorado River (beginning in the 1930s) and by the urgencies of World War II. The massive capitol (completed 1888), set on a hill, is the most prominent of the many state buildings; on its grounds are the state library, the old land office (1857), and two state historical museums. Also of interest are the governor's mansion (1856), the old French embassy (1840; dating from the republic), the house in which O. Henry lived, and the former studio of Elisabeth Ney. A state mental hospital is in Austin. In the hills outside the city are many scenic and recreational areas, notably Barton Springs. Bergstrom Air Force Base adjoins the city.

Austin canons: see AUGUSTINIANS.

Australasia (ôstrəlā'zhə, -shə), islands of the South Pacific, including AUSTRALIA, NEW ZEALAND, NEW GUINEA, and adjacent islands. The term is sometimes used to include all of Oceania.

Australia, smallest continent, between the Indian and Pacific oceans. It extends from east to west some 2,400 mi (3,860 km) and from north to south nearly 2,000 mi (3,220 km). With the island state of TASMANIA to the south, the continent makes up the Commonwealth of Australia (1973 est. pop. 13,100,000), 2,967,877 sq mi (7,686,810 sq km). There are five continental states (QUEENSLAND, NEW SOUTH WALES, VICTORIA, SOUTH AUSTRALIA, and WESTERN AUSTRALIA) as well as the NORTHERN TERRITORY and the AUSTRALIAN CAPITAL TERRITORY (an enclave within New South Wales, containing CANBERRA, the federal capital). Australia's external territories include Norfolk Island, Christmas Island, the Cocos (Keeling) Islands, and the Australian Antarctic Territory.

Geography. The Australian continent is on the whole exceedingly flat and dry. Less than 20 in. (50.8 cm) of precipitation falls annually over 70% of the land area. From the narrow coastal plain in the west the land rises abruptly in what, from the sea, appear to be mountain ranges but are actually the escarpments of a rough plateau that occupies the western half of the continent. It is generally from 1,000 to 2,000 ft (305-610 m) high but several mountain ranges rise to nearly 5,000 ft (1,520 m); there are no permanent rivers or lakes. In the southwest corner of the continent there is a small moist and fertile area, but the rest of Western Australia is arid, with large desert areas. The northern region fronts partly on the Timor Sea, separating Australia from Indonesia; it also belongs to the plateau, with tropical temperatures and a winter dry season. Its northernmost section, Arnhem Land (principally given over to reservations for aborigines), faces the Arafura Sea in the north and the huge Gulf of Carpentaria on the east. On the eastern side of the gulf is the Cape York Peninsula, which is largely covered by rainforest. Off the coast of NE Queensland is the Great Barrier Reef, the world's largest coral reef. In E Australia are the mountains of the Eastern Highlands, which run down the entire east and southeast coasts. The rivers on the eastern and southeastern slopes run to the Coral Sea and the Tasman Sea through narrow but rich coastal plains; the rivers on the western slopes flow either N to the Gulf of Carpentaria or W and SW to the Indian Ocean. The longest of all Australian river systems, the Murray River and its tributaries, drains the southern part of the interior basin that lies between the mountains and the great plateau. The rivers of this area are used extensively for irrigation and hydroelectric power. Australia, remote from any other continent, has many distinctive forms of plant life—notably species of giant eucalyptus—and of animal life, including the kangaroo, the koala bear, the flying opossum, the wallaby, the wombat, the platypus, and the spiny anteater; it also has many unusual birds. Foreign animals, when introduced, have frequently done well. Rabbits, brought over in 1788, have done entirely too well, multiplying until by the middle of the 19th cent. they became a distinct menace to sheep raising. In 1907 a fence 1,000 mi (1,610 km) long was built from the north coast to the south to prevent the rabbits from invading Western Australia.

Economy and People. Most of the rich farmland and good ports are in the east and particularly the southeast, except for the area around PERTH in Western Australia. MELBOURNE, SYDNEY, BRISBANE, and ADELAIDE are the leading industrial and commercial cities. Australia is highly industrialized, and manufactured goods account for about two thirds of the total value of production. The leading manufactures are iron and steel products, transportation equipment, and machinery. Australia is one of the world's great trading nations, with one quarter to one third of its export income derived from the sale of wool, meat, and wheat. Other leading exports are flour, iron ore, and nonferrous ores . The leading imports are metals and metal products, petroleum, machinery, and textiles. The country is self-sufficient in food, and the raising of sheep and cattle and the production of grain have long been staple occupations. Tropical and subtropical produce—citrus fruits, sugarcane, and tropical fruits—are also important, and there are numerous vineyards and dairy and tobacco farms. Some lumbering is done in the east and southeast. Australia has valuable mineral resources, including

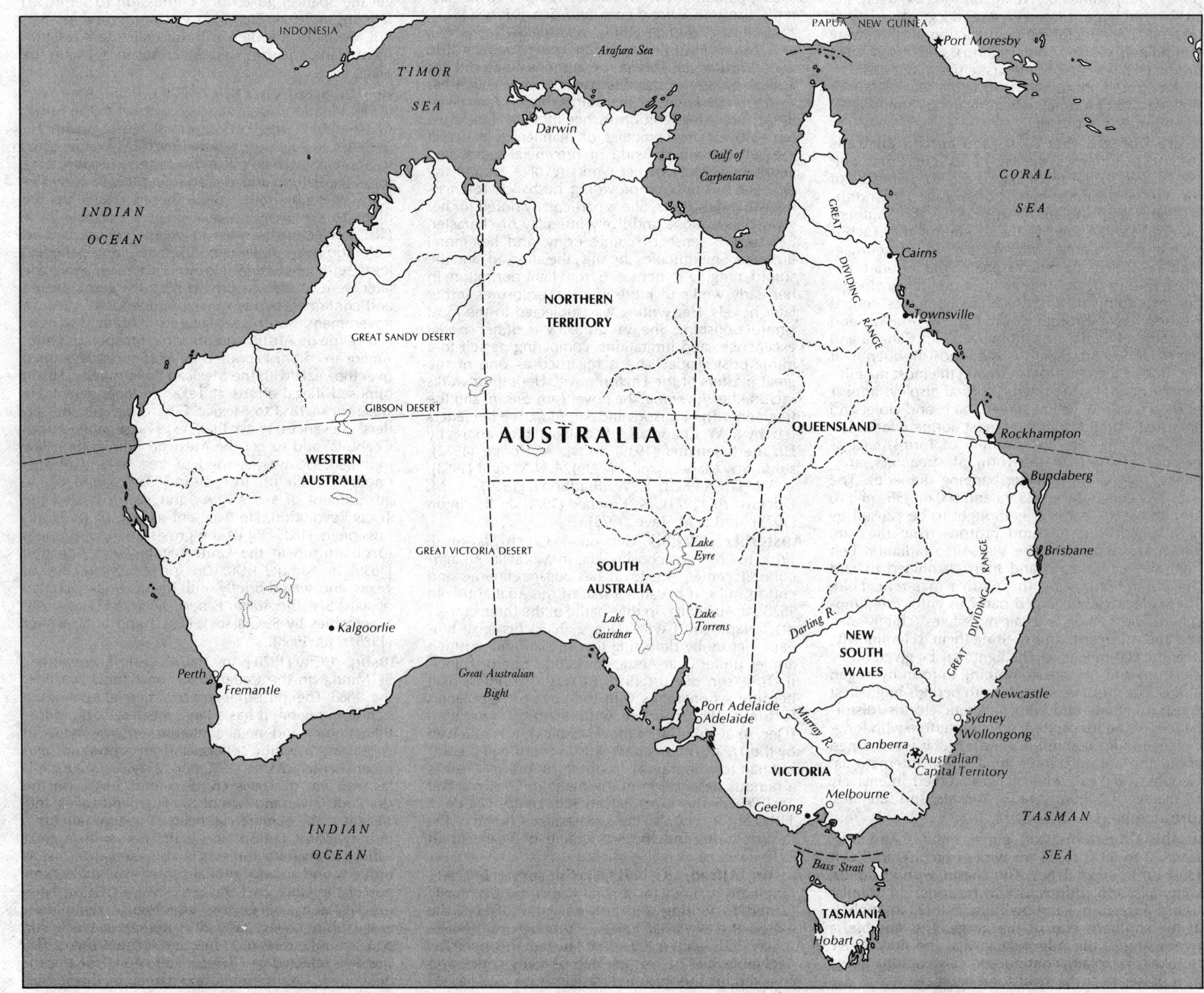

coal, iron, bauxite, uranium, and gold. The country is highly urbanized: about three fifths of the population live in cities of more than 100,000. Since World War II the government has been encouraging immigration, and permanent arrivals have been averaging more than 100,000 annually. The population has increased by more than 60% since the end of World War II. In the 19th cent., Australia enacted strong measures to prevent immigration by nonwhites. Although laws and attitudes have been liberalized somewhat in recent years, the disposition against nonwhite immigration remains. The indigenous population, the aborigines, estimated to number as many as 350,000 at the time of the Europeans' arrival, now numbers about 100,000, although the decline has been reversed in the past few decades. Most live on reservations. In Tasmania the aboriginal population was wiped out in the 19th cent. There is no state religion in Australia. The largest denominations are the Anglican, Roman Catholic, Methodist, and Presbyterian.

History. The groups comprising the aborigines are thought to have migrated from Southeast Asia c.20,000 years ago. They spread throughout Australia and remained isolated from outside influences until the arrival of the Europeans. It seems probable that Australia was first sighted by a Portuguese, Manuel Godhino de Eredia, in 1601 and may have been sighted by a Spaniard, Luis Vaez de Torres around 1605–6. It was later visited by the Dutch, who named it New Holland. In 1688 the Englishman William Dampier landed at King Sound on the northwest coast. Little interest was aroused, however, until the fertile east coast was observed when Capt. James Cook reached Botany Bay in 1770 and sailed N to Cape York, claiming the coast for Great Britain. In 1788 the first British settlement was made—a penal colony on the shores of Port Jackson, where Sydney now stands. By 1829 the whole continent was a British dependency. Exploration, begun before the first settlement was founded, was continued by such men as Matthew Flinders (1798), Count Paul Strzelecki (1839), Ludwig Leichhardt (1848), and John McDouall Stuart (first to cross the continent, 1862). Australia was long used as a dumping ground for criminals, bankrupts, and other undesirables from the British Isles. Sheep raising was introduced early, and before the middle of the 19th cent. wheat was being exported in large quantities to England. A gold strike in Victoria in 1851 brought a rush to that region. Other strikes were made later in the century in Western Australia. With minerals, sheep, and grain forming the base of the economy, Australia developed rapidly. By the mid-19th cent. systematic, permanent colonization had completely replaced the old penal settlements. Confederation of the separate Australian colonies did not come until a constitution, drafted in 1897–98, was approved by the British Parliament and was put into operation in 1901; under its terms the colonies of New South Wales, Victoria, Queensland, South Australia, Western Australia, and Tasmania, all of which by then had been granted self-government, were federated. The Northern Territory was added to the federation in 1911. Australia fought on the side of Great Britain in both world wars. Darwin, Port Jackson, and Newcastle were bombed or shelled by the Japanese in World War II. The Allied victory in the battle of the Coral Sea (1942) probably averted a full-scale attack on Australia. After the war Australia became increasingly active in world affairs, particularly in defense and development projects with its Asian neighbors; it furnished troops to aid the U.S. war effort in South Vietnam in the 1960s and early 70s. Australia is a member of the Commonwealth of Nations, the United Nations, and the Southeast Asia Treaty Organization.

Government. The executive power of the Commonwealth is vested in a governor general (representing the British sovereign) and a cabinet, presided over by the prime minister, which represents the party, or a coalition, holding a majority in the lower house of Parliament. The Parliament consists of two houses. The distribution of federal and state powers is roughly like that in the United States. From its early years the federal government has been noted for its liberal legislation, such as woman suffrage (1902), old-age pensions (1909), and maternity allowances (1912). There are four main political parties: Liberal, Labor, Country, and Democratic Labor. The Liberal and Country parties usually form a coalition. In parliamentary elections in 1974, the Labor party under Prime Minister Gough Whitlam won a narrow victory over the Liberal party. Although education is not a federal concern, government grants have aided in the establishment of state universities including the Univ. of Sydney (1852), the Univ. of Melbourne (1854), the Univ. of Adelaide (1874), and the Univ. of Queensland (in Brisbane, 1909). See D. J. Mulvaney, *The Prehistory of Australia* (1969), R. M. Crawford, *Australia* (3d rev. ed. 1970), E. H. Feeken et al., *The Discovery and Exploration of Australia* (1970), J. D. Miller and Brian Jinks, *Australian Government and Politics* (4th ed. 1971), Frederick Alexander, *Australia Since Federation* (2d. ed. 1972), M. K. Morcombe, *Wild Australia* (1972), Sir Archibald Price, *Island Continent: Aspects of the Historical Geography of Australia and its Territories* (1972), A. G. Shaw, *The Story of Australia* (4th ed. 1972), A. M. Learmonth, *The Australians* (1973).

Australian aborigines, native people of Australia whose origin is uncertain. At present about 125,000 aborigines, 45,000 of pure stock and 80,000 of mixed stock, live on the Australian mainland. In the semidesert northern region they maintain much of their original culture. The largest reservation is ARNHEM LAND. The dark-skinned aborigines are a physically homogeneous group, with regional variations. They have been classified as a distinct stock, the Australoid, and are related to ethnic groups in S India and Sri Lanka. It is probable that they migrated to Australia from S Asia thousands of years ago. Before the European colonization of Australia, the aboriginal population was about 300,000. Contact with white settlers has led to cultural and genetic change, depopulation, and extinction for some groups of aborigines. Many of the natives have been assimilated into rural and urban Australian society, mostly as low-paid laborers with limited economic and legal rights. The aboriginal material culture is adapted to hunting and gathering food and includes the noted boomerang. The religious and social structure of the aborigines is very complex, involving totemic rituals and an intricate classification system defining kinship relations and regulating marriages. The best-known tribes are the Aranda, or Arunta, the Murngin, and the Kariera. See W. L. Warner, *A Black Civilization* (rev. ed. 1958, repr. 1964); A. P. Elkin, *The Australian Aborigines* (4th ed. 1964); Daisy Bates, *The Passing of the Aborigines* (2d ed. 1967); R. M. and C. H. Berndt, *The World of the First Australians* (1967); A. A. Abbie, *The Original Australians* (1969); N. B. Tinsdale, *Aboriginal Tribes of Australia* (1974).

Australian Alps, chain of mountain ranges, SE Australia, making up the southern part of the Eastern Highlands and forming the watershed between the Murray River system and streams flowing into the Tasman Sea. It is the site of the Snowy Mts. hydroelectric project. Mt. Kosciusko (7,316 ft/2230 m) in the Australian Alps is the highest peak in Australia.

Australian bear: see KOALA.

Australian Capital Territory (1971 pop. 143,843), 939 sq mi (2,432 sq km), SE Australia, an enclave within New South Wales, containing CANBERRA, capital of Australia. It was called the Federal Capital Territory until 1938. Most of the territory consists of an area formerly known as Yass-Canberra, which was ceded to the commonwealth by New South Wales in 1911. The remainder was added in 1915, when New South Wales ceded a part of the JERVIS BAY area, providing a potential port for Canberra. The federal government is the largest employer in the territory, and nearly all of the population lives in Canberra. The Royal Australian Naval College is located in the territory.

Australian cattle dog, breed of medium-sized herding dog developed in Australia. It stands from 18 to 20 in. (45.7–50.8 cm) high at the shoulder and weighs about 33 lb (15 kg). Its double coat consists of a soft, dense underlayer and a moderately short, straight topcoat that forms a fringe of slightly longer hair on the back of the forelegs and thighs. The coat may be blue, blue mottle, or red speckled in color. Believed to be the product of crosses among the Australian kelpie, the dingo, and the smooth collie, the Australian cattle dog ranks among the world's best herding dogs. It is sometimes called the Australian heeler, a name derived from the dog's habit of nipping at the heels of stray cattle to direct them back to the herd. The breed is exhibited in the miscellaneous class at dog shows sanctioned by the American Kennel Club. See DOG.

Australian football: see under FOOTBALL.

Australian kelpie, breed of medium-sized sheep-herding dog originating in Australia c.1870. It stands from 17 to 20 in. (43.2–50.8 cm) high at the shoulder and weighs from 25 to 30 lb (11.3–13.6 kg). Its short, dense, straight coat is harshly textured and may be any of a variety of colors, e.g., black, black and tan, red, red and tan, fawn, chocolate, or smoke blue. It has generally been accepted that the border collie and probably the dingo were ancestors of the kelpie. Trained to respond both to hand signal and whistle, this rugged sheep dog is equally adept in pens or on the open plain and has proven indispensable to the Australian herder. The kelpie is exhibited in the miscellaneous class at dog shows sanctioned by the American Kennel Club. See DOG.

Australian languages, aboriginal languages spoken on the continent of Australia. The Australian languages do not appear to be related to any other linguistic family. The exact number of these languages is not known and has been variously estimated at 100 to 600. Perhaps 200,000 persons speak them. Many of the Australian languages have already died out, and the rest appear to be on the way to extinction. Although their respective grammars exhibit a great degree of variation, the Australian languages show a number of similarities. All of them inflect the noun, some having as many as nine cases. The verb lacks a passive voice. Postpositions are used instead of the prepositions typical of Indo-European languages. Most of the Australian languages have three numbers: singular, dual, and plural. Word order tends to follow a similar pattern in the different tongues. They also show considerable similarity phonetically and have a small common vocabulary. Because of so many shared phonetic and grammatical characteristics some scholars believe that the Australian languages have all evolved from a single ancestor language and therefore belong to the same linguistic family. Others, however, feel that the term "Australian languages" constitutes a geographical rather than a linguistic classification. To date, few of these languages have been studied intensively; classification and other matters remain uncertain. Recent studies seem to indicate that there are six major groups of Australian languages, possibly all branches of a single family. The Australian languages have no writing of their own. See Arthur Capell, *Linguistic Survey of Australia* (1963); S. A. Wurm, *Languages of Australia and Tasmania* (1972).

Australian literature. Australian literary works of the early 19th cent. were colonial offshoots of English literature and were written for an English audience. The work of such early poets as W. C. Wentworth, author of *Australasia, an Ode* (1823), is minor and imitative. Australian literature of some consequence can be said to have begun with the interpretive nature poetry of Charles Harpur (1813–68) and Henry Kendall (1839–82) and with the novels of Henry Kingsley (brother of Charles Kingsley), who wrote about pioneer life. The bush ballad, begun by Adam Lindsay GORDON, flowered in the work of Henry Lawson (1867–1922) and A. B. ("Banjo") Paterson (1864–1941), whose *Man from Snowy River and Other Verses* (1895) is famous and whose song "Waltzing Matilda" was nominated, in 1973, to replace "God Save the Queen" as the Australian national anthem. A classic Australian novel is *For the Term of His Natural Life* (1874), a compelling account of life in a penal colony written by Marcus Clarke. Less powerful, but true to life in the bush, were the novels of Rolfe Boldrewood (pseud. of Thomas A. BROWNE). Other important 19th-century novelists were Miles Franklin (1879–1954), whose *My Brilliant Career* (1901) is often designated the first authentically Australian novel, and diarist-novelist Tom Collins (pseud. of Joseph Furphy, 1843–1912). Poets of note include Hugh McCrae (1876–1958), and Dame Mary Gilmore (1865–1962). The increasing industrialization of the early 20th cent. rendered the pastoral nature of most Australian literature anachronistic, and it eventually produced greater sophistication and diversity among writers. Probably the most important Australian writer of the early 20th cent. was Henry Handel RICHARDSON (pseud. of Ethel Richardson Robertson), whose autobiographical trilogy *The Fortunes of Richard Mahoney* (1930) presents a compelling portrait of Australian life. Richardson's reputation was matched at mid-century by Patrick WHITE, whose strong, somber novels, Australian in setting yet universal in theme, reveal the author's ambivalence toward his native land. Other notable 20th-century novelists are Brian Penton, Leonard Mann, Christina STEAD, Arthur William Upfield (1888–1964), John O'Grady, and Morris WEST. After emigrating to Australia in 1950, the English novelist Nevil SHUTE subsequently produced novels with Australian settings and themes. Major Australian poets include C. J. Brennan, R. D. Fitzgerald, Judith WRIGHT, J. P. McAuley, Kenneth Slessor, Vance Palmer, and Max Harris. A controversial Australian with an international reputation as a feminist is Germaine Greer, author of *The Female Eunuch* (1971). The Swedish Academy's awarding of the 1973 Nobel Prize in Literature to Patrick White was perhaps the best evidence that Australian literature has become worthy of world attention. See H. M. Green, *A History of Australian Literature* (2 vol., 1961, repr. 1968); Charles Higham, ed., *Australian Writing Today* (1968); Grahame Johnston, *Annals of Australian Literature* (1970); T. I. Moore, *Social Patterns in Australian Literature* (1972); Barry Argyle, *An Introduction to the Australian Novel, 1830–1930* (1972).

Australian terrier, breed of small, hardy TERRIER perfected in Australia c.1885. It stands about 10 in. (25.4 cm) high at the shoulder and weighs from 12 to 14 lb (5.5–6.4 kg). Its weather-resistant double coat consists of a soft, short underlayer and a straight, harsh outercoat about 2.5 in. (6.4 cm) long. It is silver black or blue black in color with rich tan markings on the head and legs. The Australian terrier is descended from the now extinct broken-hair, or rough-coated, terrier, a dog of widespread popularity in the early 18th cent. and believed to be the progenitor of many terrier breeds. For show purposes the rough-coated terrier was crossed with several British sporting terriers, probably the cairn, Dandie Dinmont, Irish, and Skye, producing the Australian terrier of today. Originally used to guard mines and herd sheep, it is now primarily raised as a pet. See DOG.

Austral Islands (ô'strəl), volcanic island group, South Pacific, part of FRENCH POLYNESIA. They are sometimes known as the Tubuai Islands. The group comprises seven islands, with a total land area of c.115 sq mi (300 sq km). Tubuai, the largest island (c.17 sq mi/44 sq km), was visited by Capt. James COOK in 1777 and was annexed by France in 1880. European diseases and slavers had very nearly wiped out the native Polynesian population of the islands, especially on Rapa, when French authorities imposed strict regulations (1938) on immigration and tourism. Coffee, arrowroot, tobacco, and copra are produced on the islands.

Australopithecus (ôstrā"lōpĭth'əkəs, -pəthē'kəs), an extinct genus of the hominid family, generally considered to be a relative or possible ancestor of modern man. *Australopithecus* fossils have been discovered at various sites in South Africa since 1925 by the anthropologists Raymond Dart, Robert Broom, J. T. Robinson and others. Fossils have also been uncovered at several E African sites since 1959, when the husband and wife team L. S. B. and Mary LEAKEY found a fossil that they termed *Zinjanthropus* at Olduvai Gorge, Tanzania. Fossils that are probably early *Australopithecines* were discovered in the 1960s in the Omo basin of Ethiopia by an international team of anthropologists led by F. C. Howell. Most *Australopithecus* fossils are from 1 million to 2.5 million years old, but remains found in the mid-1960s in Kenya by Bryan Patterson may be 4 million and 5 million years old. The genus *Australopithecus* now generally includes fossil species previously classed *Paranthropus, Plesianthropus* and *Zinjanthropus*, but there is some uncertainty and disagreement whether such fossils as *Homo habilis* and *Telanthropus* of Africa and *Meganthropus* of Java should be included with *Australopithecus* or the later genus *Homo erectus*. *Australopithecus* was under 5 ft tall and could stand and walk erect, although with less dexterity than later predecessors of modern man. The skeletal features of *Australopithecus* fossils have many similarities to modern man, but the size and shape of the skull indicate that the Australopithecine brain was less developed than in the later genus *Homo*. *Australopithecus* may have used simple stone tools. See MAN, PREHISTORIC. See R. A. Dart, *Adventures with the Missing Link* (1959); W. E. LeGros Clark, *Man-Apes or Ape-Men?* (1967).

Austrasia (ôstrā'zhə), eastern portion of the Merovingian kingdom of the FRANKS in the 6th, 7th, and 8th cent., comprising, in general, parts of E France, W Germany, and the Netherlands, with its capital variously at Metz, Rheims, and Soissons. It originated in the partition (511) of the realm of the Frankish king CLOVIS I among his sons. Austrasia was constantly troubled by dynastic rivalries between its rulers and those of the neighboring kingdom of NEUSTRIA. These struggles reached their climax in the fierce fights between Queen BRUNHILDA of Austrasia and Queen FREDEGUNDE of Neustria. During the reigns of CLOTAIRE I, CLOTAIRE II, and DAGOBERT I, Austrasia was temporarily reunited with Neustria. With the decline of the royal power in Austrasia, the office of mayor of the palace developed into the real seat of power and finally became hereditary in the family of the CAROLINGIANS. Austrasia became part of the Carolingian empire.

Austråt (oust'rôt), castle at the mouth of the Trondheimsfjord, central Norway. It was built (1611–74) by Ove Bjelke, chancellor of the kingdom. It is the setting of Henrik Ibsen's historic play *Lady Inger of Ostrat*.

Austria, Ger. *Österreich* [eastern march], federal republic (1973 est. pop. 7,550,000), 32,374 sq mi (83,849 sq km), central Europe. It is bounded by Yugoslavia and Italy in the south, Switzerland and Liechtenstein in the west, West Germany and Czechoslovakia in the north, and Hungary in the east. Its nine provinces (Ger. *Bundesländer*) are VORARLBERG, TYROL, SALZBURG, CARINTHIA, STYRIA, UPPER AUSTRIA, LOWER AUSTRIA, BURGENLAND, and the capital, VIENNA. The Alps traverse Austria from west to east and occupy three fourths of the country. The highest peak in Austria is the Grossglockner (12,460 ft/3,798 m) in the Hohe Tauern group. The scenic beauty of Tyrol, the Salzkammergut, and Salzburg city, and the attractions of Vienna and other cultural centers have made Austria one of the major tourist centers of Europe. The country is drained by the Danube River and its tributaries, the Inn, the Enns, the Mürz, and the Mur. Forestry, cattle raising, and dairying are the main sources of livelihood in the alpine provinces; Vorarlberg has an ancient textile industry. In Upper and Lower Austria and in Burgenland, tillage agriculture predominates: the chief crops are potatoes, sugar beets, barley, wheat, rye, and oats. Manufacturing and mining employ nearly half of the labor force. More than half of the industries are concentrated in the Vienna basin; LINZ, STEYR, GRAZ, LEOBEN, INNSBRUCK, and Salzburg are the other chief industrial centers. Many of the country's industries were nationalized after World War II, together with the largest commercial banks. The chief manufactures are chemicals, foodstuffs, textiles, machinery, iron and steel, and metal goods. Many minerals necessary for industry (graphite, iron, magnesium, copper, zinc, and lignite) are found in Austria. The country also has deposits of natural gas, salt, and uranium, and is rich in hydroelectric power. Austria is governed under the revised 1929 constitution. It has a mixed presidential-parliamentary form of government. The president, elected by popular vote for a six-year term, may issue decrees. The cabinet, headed by the prime minister, is responsible to the lower house (*Nationalrat*) of parliament, which is popularly elected according to proportional representation. The upper house (*Bundesrat*) is chosen by the provincial assemblies. The main parties are the People's party and the Socialist party. The population is predominantly Roman Catholic and German-speaking. Since 1945, Austria has received nearly 1.5 million refugees from elsewhere in Europe. There are universities in Vienna, Salzburg, Innsbruck, and Graz.

History. During the past 10 centuries, the term *Austria* has designated a variety of geographic and political concepts. In its narrowest sense *Austria* has included only the present-day provinces of Upper and Lower Austria, including Vienna; in its widest meaning the term has covered the far-flung domains of the imperial house of Hapsburg. Its present connotation—German-speaking Austria—dates only from 1918. This article deals mainly with the history of German-speaking Austria. For wider historical background, see HOLY ROMAN EMPIRE; HAPSBURG; AUSTRO-HUNGARIAN MONARCHY; HUNGARY; BOHEMIA; and NETHERLANDS, AUSTRIAN AND SPANISH.

The Rise of Austria. Austria is located at the crossroads of Europe; Vienna is at the gate of the Danubian plain, and the Brenner Pass in W Austria links Germany and Italy. From earliest times Austrian territory has been a thoroughfare, a battleground, and a border area. It was occupied by Celts and Suebi when the Romans conquered (15 B.C.–A.D. 10) and divided it among the provinces of Rhaetia, NORICUM, and Upper PANNONIA. After the 5th cent. A.D., Huns, Ostrogoths, Lombards, and Bavarians overran and devastated the provinces. By c.600, Slavs from the east had occupied all of modern Styria, Lower Austria, and Carinthia. In 788, Charlemagne conquered the area and set up the first Austrian (i.e., Eastern) March in the present Upper and Lower Austria, to halt the inroads of the Avars. Colonization was encouraged, and Christianity (which had been introduced under the Romans) was again spread energetically. After Charlemagne's death (814) the march soon fell to the Moravians and later to the Magyars, from whom it was taken (955) by Emperor OTTO I. Otto reconstituted the march and attached it to BAVARIA, but, in 976, Otto II bestowed it as a separate fief on Leopold of BABENBERG, founder of the first Austrian dynasty. Emperor Frederick I raised (1156) Austria to a duchy, and, in 1192, Styria also passed under Babenberg rule. The 11th and 12th cent. saw the height of Austrian feudalism and also witnessed the marked development of towns as the Danube was converted to a great trade route. After the death (1246) of the last Babenberg, King OTTOCAR II of Bohemia acquired (1251–69) Austria, Styria, Carinthia, and CARNIOLA. Fearing his power, the German princes elected (1273) Rudolf of Hapsburg German king. RUDOLF I asserted (1282) his royal prerogative to reclaim the four duchies from Ottocar and incorporate them in his domains. After the murder (1308) of Rudolf's son, ALBERT I, the German princes balked at electing another member of the ambitious family. Albert's ducal successors enlarged the Hapsburg holdings by acquiring Tyrol (1363) and Trieste (1382) and extended their influence over the ecclesiastic states of Salzburg, TRENT, and Brixen (see BRESSANONE), which, however, remained independent until 1803. Marriage brought ALBERT II to the position of being elected German king in 1438. Beginning with Albert II, the rulers of the Holy Roman Empire were always chosen from the Hapsburg dynasty. Despite their vast imperial preoccupations, the emperors always considered German Austria the prized core of their dominions. During the long reign of Frederick III (1440–93), the protracted Hapsburg wars with France began. In 1526, Austria, Bohemia, and Hungary were united under one crown (see FERDINAND I, emperor). In the same year Vienna was besieged for two weeks by troops of the Ottoman Empire under Sulayman the Magnificent, who had made a forceful advance into Europe. The Turkish threat to Austria ebbed and then climaxed again in the second siege of Vienna in 1683. The patterns of medievalism were weakening in Austria, especially as a money economy spread, and in the 16th cent. the COMMERCIAL REVOLUTION diminished the importance of Austrian trade routes and of the ancient gold and silver mines of Tyrol and Carinthia. Economic and political instability in the 16th cent. precipitated the spread of the Protestant Reformation, which the Hapsburg rulers attempted to counter by nurturing the Catholic Reformation. The alliance then formed between church and state continued throughout the history of the monarchy. The Austrian peasantry, especially in Tyrol, had gained some advantages in the PEASANTS' WAR of 1524–26; in general, however, the rising, backed by some Protestants but not by Luther, was defeated. Suppression of Protestantism was at first impossible, and, under Maximilian II, Lutheran nobles were granted considerable toleration. Rudolph II and Matthias pursued policies of partial Catholicization, and, under Ferdinand II, anti-Protestant vigor helped to precipitate the THIRTY YEARS WAR (1618–48). Protestant Bohemia and Moravia, defeated by the Austrians at the White Mt. (1620), became virtual Austrian provinces. Austria proper remained relatively unscathed in the long holocaust; after the Peace of Westphalia the Hapsburg lands emerged as a distinct empire, whereas the Holy Roman Empire drifted into a mere shadow existence.

The Austrian Empire. The monarchy, although repressive of free speech and worship, was far from absolute; taxation and other powers rested with the provincial estates for a further century. Emperor CHARLES VI (1711–40), whose dynastic wars had drained the state, secured the succession to the Hapsburg lands for his daughter, MARIA THERESA, by means of the PRAGMATIC SANCTION. Maria Theresa's struggle with FREDERICK II of Prussia in the War of the Austrian Succession (see AUSTRIAN SUCCESSION, WAR OF THE) and the SEVEN YEARS WAR opened a long struggle for dominance in the German lands. Except for the loss of Silesia, Maria Theresa held her own. The provincial estates were reduced in power, and an efficient centralized bureaucracy was created; as the nobles were attracted to bureaucratic service their power as a class was weakened. Maria Theresa's husband, FRANCIS I, became emperor in 1745, but his position

CZECHOSLOVAKIA
WEST GERMANY
Munich
Inn R.
Danube R.
Linz
Vienna
Salzburg
SALZKAMMERGUT
Neusiedler See
Enns R.
TYROL
Innsbruck
AUSTRIA
Graz
HUNGARY
SWITZ.
ÖTZTAL ALPS
CARNIC ALPS
Klagenfurt
ITALY
YUGOSLAVIA

was largely titular. The major event of Maria Theresa's later reign was the first partition of Poland (1772; see POLAND, PARTITIONS OF); in that transaction and in the third partition (1795) Austria renewed its eastward expansion. JOSEPH II, who succeeded her, impetuously carried forward the reforms which his mother had cautiously begun. His attempts to further centralize and germanize his scattered and disparate dominions met stubborn resistance; his project to consolidate his state by exchanging the Austrian Netherlands for Bavaria was balked by Frederick II. An exemplar of "benevolent despotism" and a disciple of the ENLIGHTENMENT, Joseph also decreed a series of revolutionary agrarian, fiscal, religious, and judicial reforms; however, opposition, especially from among the clergy and the landowners, forced his successor, LEOPOLD II, to rescind many of them. In Joseph's reign the Austrian bourgeoisie began to emerge as a social and cultural force. Music and architecture (see VIENNA) flourished in 18th-century Austria, and modern Austrian literature (see GERMAN LITERATURE) emerged early in the 19th cent. In the reign of FRANCIS II, Austria was drawn (1792) into war with revolutionary France (see FRENCH REVOLUTIONARY WARS) and with NAPOLEON I. The treaties of CAMPO FORMIO (1797) and Lunéville (1801) preluded the dissolution (1806) of the Holy Roman Empire, and in 1804, Francis II took the title "Francis I, emperor of Austria." His rout at Austerlitz (1805) led to the severe Treaty of Pressburg (see PRESSBURG, TREATY OF). An upsurge of patriotism resulted in the renewal of war with Napoleon in 1809; Austria's defeat at Wagram led to the even more humiliating Peace of Schönbrunn (see under SCHÖNBRUNN). Austria was forced to side with Napoleon in the Russian campaign of 1812, but in 1813 it again joined the coalition against Napoleon; an Austrian, Prince Karl Philipp von Schwarzenberg, headed the allied forces. The Congress of Vienna (1814–15; see VIENNA, CONGRESS OF) did not restore to Austria its former possessions in the Netherlands and in Baden but awarded it Lombardy, Venetia, Istria, and Dalmatia. As the leading power of both the GERMAN CONFEDERATION and the HOLY ALLIANCE, Austria under the ministry of METTERNICH dominated European politics. Conservatism and the repression of nationalistic strivings characterized the age. Nevertheless, the Metternich period was one of great cultural achievement, particularly in music and literature. The REVOLUTIONS OF 1848 shook the Hapsburg empire but ultimately failed because of the conflicting economic goals of the middle and lower classes and because of the conflicting nationalist aspirations that set the revolutionary movements of Germans, Slavs, Hungarians, and Italians against each other. Revolts were at first successful throughout the empire (see RISORGIMENTO; GALICIA; BOHEMIA; HUNGARY); in Vienna the revolutionists drove out Metternich (March, 1848). Emperor FERDINAND granted (April) a liberal constitution, which a constituent assembly replaced (July) with a more democratic one. After a new outbreak Vienna was bombarded, and the revolutionists were punished by troops under General WINDISCHGRÄTZ. Prince Felix zu SCHWARZENBERG became premier and engineered the abdication of Ferdinand in favor of FRANCIS JOSEPH. Absolutism returned with the dissolution of the constituent assembly. Austrian leadership in Germany was reasserted at the Convention of Olmütz in 1850. Alexander BACH intensified (1852–59) Schwarzenberg's centralizing policy, thus heightening national tensions within the empire. But economic prosperity was promoted by the lowering of internal tariff barriers, and several reforms dating from 1848 were upheld, notably the complete abolition of feudal dues. The military and political weakness of the empire was demonstrated by the Austrian loss of Lombardy in the Italian War of 1859. Attempts to solve the nationalities problem—the "October Diploma" (1860), which created a central legislature and gave increased powers to the provincial assemblies of nobles, and the "February Patent," which transferred many of these powers to the central legislature—failed. Prussia seized the opportunity to drive Austria out of Germany. After involving Austria in the war over SCHLESWIG-HOLSTEIN in 1864, BISMARCK found an easy pretext for attacking. Overwhelmingly defeated by Prussia at Sadová (Sadowa) in 1866 (see AUSTRO-PRUSSIAN WAR), Austria was forced to cede Venetia to Italy. With this debacle Austria's political role in Germany came to an end. A reorganization of the government of the empire became inevitable, and in 1867 a compromise (Ger. *Ausgleich*) with Hungarian moderate nationalists established a dual state, the AUSTRO-HUNGARIAN MONARCHY. But the realm, a land of diverse peoples ruled by a German-Magyar minority, increasingly became an anachronism in a nationalistic age. Failure to provide a satisfactory status for the other nationalities, notably the Slavs, played a major role in bringing about WORLD WAR I. Important developments in Austrian society during this period were the continued irresponsibility of the nobility and the backwardness of the peasantry, the growth of a socialist working class, widespread anti-Semitism stimulated by the large-scale movement to Austria of poor Jews from the eastern provinces, and extraordinary cultural creativity in Vienna. The disastrous course of the war led to the breakup of the monarchy in 1918. CHARLES I renounced power; after a peaceful revolution staged by the Socialist and Pan-German parties, German Austria was proclaimed (Nov. 12) a republic and a part of Greater Germany.

Modern Austria. The Treaty of SAINT-GERMAIN (1919) fixed the present Austrian borders and forbade (as did the Treaty of Versailles) any political or economic union (Ger. *Anschluss*) with Germany. Observation of these clauses was insisted upon by France, Italy, and Czechoslovakia. This left Austria a small country with some 7 million inhabitants, one third of whom lived in a single large city (Vienna) that had been geared to be the financial and industrial hub of a large state. The Dual Monarchy had been virtually self-sufficient economically; its breakup and the consequent erection of tariff walls deprived Austria of raw materials, food, and markets. In the postwar period, starvation and influenza exacted a heavy toll, especially in Vienna. These ills were followed by currency inflation, ended only in 1924 by means of League of Nations aid, following upon chronic unemployment, financial scandals and crises, and growing political unrest. "Red" Vienna, under the moderate socialist government of Karl SEITZ, became increasingly opposed by the "Black" (i.e., clericalist) rural faction, which won the elections of 1921. The cabinet of Social Democrat Karl RENNER was succeeded by Christian Socialist and Pan-German coalitions under SCHOBER, SEIPEL, and others. Unrest culminated, in 1927, in violent riots in Vienna; two rival private militias—the *Heimwehr* of the monarchist leader E. R. von STARHEMBERG and the *Schutzbund* of the socialists—posed a threat to the authority of the state. Economic crisis loomed again in the late 1920s. NATIONAL SOCIALISM, feeding in part on anti-Semitism, gained rapidly and soon absorbed the Pan-German party. Engelbert DOLLFUSS, who became chancellor in 1932, though irreconcilably opposed to *Anschluss* and to National Socialism, tended increasingly toward corporative FASCISM and relied heavily on Italian support. His stern suppression of the socialists precipitated a serious revolt (1934), which was bloodily suppressed by the army. Soon afterward a totalitarian state was set up, and all independent political parties were outlawed. In July, 1934, the National Socialists assassinated Dollfuss but failed to seize the government. Kurt von SCHUSCHNIGG succeeded Dollfuss. German pressure on Austria increased; Schuschnigg was forced to legalize the operations of the National Socialists and to appoint members of that party to cabinet posts. Schuschnigg planned a last-minute effort to avoid *Anschluss* by holding a plebiscite, but Hitler forced him to resign. In March, 1938, Austria was occupied by German troops and became part of the Reich. Arthur SEYSS-INQUART became the Nazi governor. In 1943, the Allies agreed to reestablish an independent Austria at the end of World War II. In 1945, Austria was conquered by Soviet and American troops, and a provisional government was set up under Karl Renner. The pre-Dollfuss constitution was restored with revisions; the country was divided into separate occupation zones, each controlled by an Allied power. Economic recovery was hindered by the decline of trade between Western and Eastern Europe and by the division into zones. Austria was formally recognized by the Western powers in 1946, but because of Soviet disagreement with the West over reparations, the occupation continued. On May 15, 1955, a formal treaty between Great Britain, France, the United States, the USSR, and Austria restored full sovereignty to the country. The treaty prohibited the possession of major offensive weapons and required Austria to pay heavy reparations to the USSR. Austria proclaimed its permanent neutrality. In 1955 it was admitted to the United Nations. By the 1960s unprecedented prosperity had been attained. Austria had joined the European Free Trade Association in 1959, but association with the Common Market was held back by Soviet opposition. Politically, a nearly equal balance of power between the conservative People's party and the Socialist party resulted in successive coalition cabinets until 1966, when the People's party won a clear majority. They were ousted by the socialists in the 1970 elections and Bruno KREISKY became chancellor. A long-standing dispute with Italy over the German-speaking population of the TRENTINO-ALTO ADIGE region of Italy was dealt with in a treaty ratified in 1971. See R. A. Kann, *The Multinational Empire: Nationalism and National Reform in the Habsburg Monarchy, 1848–1918* (1950, repr. 1970); K. R. Stadler, *Austria* (1971); V. L. Tapie, *The Rise and Fall of the Habsburg Monarchy* (tr. 1971); F. R. Bridge, *From Sadowa to Sarajevo* (1972); W. M. Johnston, *The Austrian Mind: An Intellectual and Social History, 1848–1938* (1972); Kurt Steiner, *Politics in Austria* (1972); W. T. Bluhm, *Building an Austrian Nation* (1973); Leo Valiani, *The End of Austria-Hungary* (tr. 1973); Kurt Waldheim, *The Austrian Example* (tr. 1973); Ernest Wangermann, *The Austrian Achievement, 1700–1800* (1973).

Austrian literature: see GERMAN LITERATURE.

Austrian Succession, War of the, 1740–48, general European war that broke out when, on the strength of the PRAGMATIC SANCTION of 1713, the Austrian archduchess MARIA THERESA succeeded her father, Holy Roman Emperor Charles VI, as ruler of the Hapsburg lands. The elector of Bavaria, Charles Albert, advanced counterclaims to the succession while PHILIP V of Spain and AUGUSTUS III of Poland and Saxony advanced weak claims of their own. FREDERICK II of Prussia, who on even less tenable grounds claimed part of SILESIA, began the war by invading and rapidly occupying that province. His cynical offer of support to Maria Theresa if she would cede Silesia was rejected. Victorious at Mollwitz (1741), Frederick obtained the alliance of France, Spain, Bavaria, and Saxony. Charles Albert of Bavaria, who was promised the imperial election, advanced on Vienna. In Oct., 1741, however, Prussia agreed to a truce in exchange for most of Silesia. This armistice was soon broken but gave the Austrians an opportunity to regroup their forces. The French were unwilling to permit the Bavarians too much power and ordered them to attack Bohemia, which was relatively unimportant, instead of Vienna. Joined by France and Saxony, Bavaria took Prague (Nov., 1741), and Charles Albert was elected emperor as CHARLES VII. Meanwhile Maria Theresa had obtained full support from the Hungarian diet and the promise of aid from Great Britain, which had been at war with Spain since 1739 (see JENKINS'S EAR, WAR OF). Early in 1742 Austrian troops overran Bavaria and laid siege to Prague, and in July, Maria Theresa made peace with Prussia by ceding most of Silesia (Treaty of Berlin). This ended what is sometimes called the First Silesian War. Saxony also made peace and joined Austria as an ally in 1743. The epic retreat from Prague of the French under Marshal BELLE-ISLE (winter, 1742–43) was followed by the victory of GEORGE II of Britain over the French at Dettingen (1743). In 1744 Frederick II, fearing the rising power of Austria, started the Second Silesian War by invading Bohemia, but he was soon expelled by Austrian and Saxon forces. On the death (1745) of Emperor Charles VII, Bavaria, once more overrun by Austrian troops, was forced out of the war. These Austrian successes were balanced by the great French victory (1745) of Fontenoy, where Maurice de SAXE defeated the British. Anxious for peace, George II concluded (1745) the Convention of Hanover with Frederick II, who promised to support the imperial candidacy of Maria Theresa's husband (shortly afterward elected as Francis I) in return for her cession of Silesia guaranteed by Europe. Defeated at Hohenfriedberg and at Kesselsdorf, Maria Theresa accepted the compromise in the Treaty of Dresden with Prussia (Dec., 1745). The war continued in N Italy, in the Low Countries, in North America (see FRENCH AND INDIAN WARS), and in India. The chief belligerents (Austria, Britain, Holland, and Sardinia on the one side, France and Spain on the other) grew weary of the war. Although Maria Theresa secured (1748) the alliance of Russia, the other nations were determined to restore peace, and late in 1748 the Treaty of Aix-la-Chapelle (see AIX-LA-CHAPELLE, TREATY OF, **2**) was signed. Prussia gained Silesia and thus emerged as a major European power; the Hapsburgs thenceforth looked to the east for resources to develop their state. See biography by Edward Crankshaw, *Maria Theresa* (1970); C. A. Macartney, *Maria Theresa and the House of Austria* (1969).

Austro-Hungarian Monarchy or **Dual Monarchy,** the Hapsburg empire from 1867 until its fall in 1918. The reorganization was made possible by the *Ausgleich* [compromise] of 1867, a constitutional compromise between Hungarian aspirations for independence and Emperor Francis Joseph's desire for a strong, centralized empire as a source of power after Austria's defeat in the AUSTRO-PRUSSIAN WAR of 1866. The Hungarians gained control of their internal affairs in return for agreeing to a centralized foreign policy and continued union of the Austrian and Hungarian crowns in the Hapsburg ruler. The agreement, which was worked out primarily by the Austrian foreign minister, Count BUEST, and two Hungarians, the elder Count ANDRÁSSY and Francis DEAK, divided the Hapsburg empire into two states. Cisleithania [Lat., = the land on this side of the Leitha River] comprised Austria proper, Bohemia, Moravia, Austrian Silesia, Slovenia, and Austrian Poland; it was to be ruled by the Hapsburg monarchs in their capacity as emperors of Austria. Transleithania [Lat., = the land on the other side of the Leitha River] included Hungary, Transylvania, Croatia, and part of the Dalmatian coast; it was to be ruled by the Hapsburg monarchs in their capacity as kings of Hungary. Croatia was given a special status and allowed some autonomy but was subordinated to Transleithania, which also nominated the Croatian governor. Austria-Hungary was the greatest recent example of a multinational state in Europe; however, of the four chief ethnic groups (Germans, Hungarians, Slavs, and Italians) only the first two received full partnership. The Hapsburg-held crown of Bohemia was conspicuously omitted in the reorganization. Both Cisleithania and Transleithania elected independent parliaments to deliberate on internal affairs and had independent ministries. A common cabinet, composed of three ministers, dealt with foreign relations, common defense, and common finances. It was responsible to the emperor-king and to the delegations of 60 members each (chosen by the two parliaments), which met to discuss common affairs. The regular armed forces were under unified command and currency was uniform throughout the empire, but there were separate customs regimes. The strength of the Dual Monarchy lay in its vastness, its virtual economic self-sufficiency, its opportunities for commercial intercourse from the Swiss border to the Carpathians. Its weakness was less in its ethnic diversity than in the unequal treatment accorded to its minorities in the spirit of the maxim, "Divide and rule." Of the Slavic elements the Czechs and Serbs were the most disaffected. The efforts of the TAAFFE ministry to satisfy Czech demands failed. The Italian minority was won to the Italian nationalist cause (see IRREDENTISM). The Rumanians of Transylvania had bitter grievances against their Hungarian masters. As nationalist movements gained within the empire they enlarged their demands from cultural autonomy to full independence and ultimately broke up the monarchy. These movements existed not only in the oppressed provinces, but also among Hungarian extremists, who desired total independence, and among Austrian Pan-Germans, who advocated the union of German-speaking Austria with Germany. The greatest danger to the monarchy probably was PAN-SLAVISM, spreading from Serbia and encouraged by Russia among the South Slavs. Archduke FRANCIS FERDINAND, heir to the throne, apparently had a project by which Croatia was to become the nucleus of a third, South Slavic, partner in the monarchy; his assassination (1914) at Sarajevo cut short this hope and precipitated World War I. In external policy, Austria-Hungary early became reconciled with Germany and joined the THREE EMPERORS' LEAGUE. At the Congress of Berlin (1878; see BERLIN, CONGRESS OF) Count Andrássy, the foreign minister, secured a mandate over BOSNIA AND HERCEGOVINA. In 1879 he entered an alliance with Germany, joined also by Italy in 1882 (see TRIPLE ALLIANCE AND TRIPLE ENTENTE). The formation of the Triple Entente (France, England, Russia) to oppose this alliance led to the tense diplomatic situation that preceded WORLD WAR I. The foreign policy of Graf von AEHRENTHAL led to the Bosnian crisis of 1908–9, and the reckless demands that his successor, Graf von BERCHTOLD, made on Serbia after the assassination of Francis Ferdinand helped to precipitate the cataclysm. The internal weakness of the empire became immediately obvious. Czech regiments deserted wholesale from the beginning; Italy and Rumania, eying their respective minorities in Austria and Hungary, joined the Allies; Croats and Slovenes, won by Serbian propaganda, joined (1917) in agreement with the Serbs to found a South Slavic state (see YUGOSLAVIA). Abroad, the Czechs under Thomas Masaryk were the best known of several legions fighting on the Allied side, and in Oct., 1918, Poland, Czechoslovakia, and Hungary proclaimed their independence. The Austrian defeat at VITTORIO VENETO was followed by unconditional surrender; on Nov. 11, Emperor CHARLES I abdicated; on Nov. 12, German Austria was proclaimed a republic. The treaties of Versailles, Trianon, and Saint-Germain fixed the boundaries of the successor states. The breakup of the Dual Monarchy fulfilled the 19th-century liberal ideal of national self-determination; at the same time, the creation of small, strongly nationalist states, cut off from each other by tariff walls, has been criticized as representing a "Balkanization of Europe." See O. Jázi, *Dissolution of the Habsburg Monarchy* (1929, repr. 1961); H. Kohn, *The Hapsburg Empire: 1804–1918* (1961); A. J. May, *The Passing of the Hapsburg Monarchy, 1914–1918* (2 vol., 1966) and *The Hapsburg Monarchy, 1867–1914* (1951, repr. 1968); Z. A. B. Zeman, *The Twilight of the Hapsburgs* (1970); Leo Valiani, *The End of Austria-Hungary* (1973).

Austronesian (ôs″trōnē′zhən, -shən), name sometimes used for the MALAYO-POLYNESIAN LANGUAGES.

Austro-Prussian War or **Seven Weeks War,** June 15–Aug. 23, 1866, between Prussia, allied with Italy, and Austria, seconded by Bavaria, Württemberg, Saxony, Hanover, Baden, and several smaller German states. It was deliberately provoked by BISMARCK, over the objections of his king, in order to expel Austria from the GERMAN CONFEDERATION as a step toward the unification of Germany under Prussian dominance. The pretext for precipitating the conflict was found in the dispute between Prussia and Austria over the administration of SCHLESWIG-HOLSTEIN. When Austria brought the dispute before the German diet and also decided to convene the Holstein diet, Prussia, declaring that the Gastein Convention (see under GASTEIN) had thereby been nullified, invaded Holstein. When the German diet responded by voting for a partial mobilization against Prussia, Bismarck declared that the German Confederation was ended. With an efficient military machine that amazed Europe, Prussia overran the German states allied with Austria and crushed (July 3) the Austrians at Sadowa (Königgrätz), in E Bohemia. However, Bismarck had no intention of weakening Austria, a potential ally, more than necessary. The preliminary treaty of Nikolsburg (July 26) was followed (Aug. 23) by the Treaty of Prague. Against Italy, the Austrians had won victories on the land, at Custozza, and on the sea, at Lissa. Nevertheless, the peace treaty forced Austria to cede Venetia to Italy. Prussia, satisfied with the exclusion, acknowledged in the treaty, of Austria from German affairs, demanded no territory from Austria, but annexed Hanover, Hesse, Nassau, and Frankfurt, in addition to Schleswig-Holstein. The German Confederation was replaced by the Prussian-led NORTH GERMAN CONFEDERATION. Thus the war paved the way for the establishment (1871) of the German Empire and the reorientation of Austria (reorganized in 1867 as the Austro-Hungarian Monarchy) toward the east. The moderate peace terms facilitated the Austro-German alliance of 1879. See Heinrich Friedjung, *The Struggle for Supremacy in Germany, 1859–1866* (10th ed. abr., tr. 1935, repr. 1966); G. A. Craig, *The Battle of Königgrätz* (1964); E. A. Pottinger, *Napoleon III and the German Crisis, 1865–66* (1966).

Auteuil (ōtö′yə), old town between the Seine and the Bois de Boulogne, absorbed (1860) into Paris, France. A favorite resort for writers (Molière, La Fontaine, Boileau) in the 17th cent., it is now the site of a popular steeplechase track.

Authari (ô′thârī), d. 590, Lombard king (584–90). Elected by the Lombard dukes to end the anarchy that prevailed in Italy after the murder (572?) of Alboin (see LOMBARDS), Authari consolidated Lombard power in N Italy and repelled several Frankish invasions instigated by the popes.

authentic modes: see MODE, in music.

autism (ô′tĭzəm), in psychology, a form of PSYCHOSIS characterized by an inability to relate to and perceive the environment in a realistic manner. Autistic thinking is characterized by withdrawal and detachment from reality, fantasies, delusions, and hallucinations. Childhood, or infantile, autism, which begins during infancy, is characterized by delay in the acquisition of speech, withdrawal from normal activity, abnormalities in the use of language, resistance to changes of any kind, and obsessive and stereotyped body movements. Authorities do not always agree on the distinction between infantile autism and forms of SCHIZOPHRENIA. Evidence suggests that infantile autism arises in association with a perceptual disorder, frequently a disorder in language comprehension (i.e., thoughts do not correspond to reality). Treatment for autism is still experimental, and relatively few autistic children show significant remission of symptoms. Shaping the child's behavior by operant conditioning has had some success (see LEARNING).

autobiography: see BIOGRAPHY.

autogiro (ôtōjī′rō) or **gyroplane** (jī′rəplān), type of aircraft supported in the air by a horizontally mounted airfoil similar to that of a helicopter but unpowered. Invented by the Spaniard Juan de la Cierva, it was first flown successfully in Jan., 1923, in Spain. Most of the lift is supplied by large airfoils which are mounted horizontally above the craft and rotated by the airflow created by the craft's forward movement. The autogiro has fixed wings that are smaller than those of an ordinary airplane; the body and tail assembly is of conventional design. Thrust is supplied by an ordinary engine and propeller and control is maintained by a rudder, elevators, and ailerons. In one type, fixed wings are absent, and the rotor provides all the lift. Control of pitch and roll are accomplished by tilting the rotor forward, backward, or to either side. Some advantages of the machine are that its descent will be slowed by the turning of the rotor if the engine fails; that it becomes airborne with a very short takeoff run and can land in small areas; and that with a moderate headwind it can virtually hover with zero ground speed. However, it cannot match the vertical climbing performance of the helicopter. Although its development was halted at one point, interest in it has renewed because of its ability to make short takeoffs and landings.

autograft: see TRANSPLANTATION, MEDICAL.

autoimmune disease, any of a number of abnormal conditions caused when the body produces ANTIBODIES to its own substances. In rheumatoid ARTHRITIS, a group of antibody molecules called collectively RF, or rheumatoid factor, is complexed to the individual's own gamma globulin blood proteins; the circulating complex apparently causes tissue inflammation and muscle and bone deformities. In Hashimoto's thyroiditis, an inflammatory disease of the thyroid gland, antibodies are produced against the thyroid protein thyroglobulin. In some blood disorders, antibodies may be produced against the body's own red and white blood cells. Myasthenia gravis, a disease characterized by weakened muscles, is thought to have an autoimmune origin. In systemic lupus erythematosus it has been shown that individuals have antibodies to certain of their own body substances that for some reason are acting as antigens; these substances include the individual's own nucleic acids and cell organelles such as ribosomes and mitochondria. Lupus can cause dysfunction of many organs, including the heart, kidneys, and joints. Because lupus and certain diseases of probable autoimmune origin, e.g., scleroderma and dermatomyositis, result in pathological changes in COLLAGEN, they are often called connective tissue, or collagen, diseases. In rheumatic fever, the individual produces antibodies to antigens of streptococcal bacteria; it is believed that the streptococcal antigens are structurally similar to antigens of the heart and that antistreptococcal antibodies, combining with antigenic sites on the heart, damage the muscle. Diseases of the immune system are currently treated by a variety of nonspecific IMMUNOSUPPRESSIVE DRUGS and STEROIDS.

Autolycus (ôtŏl′ĭkəs), fl. 4th cent. B.C., astronomer and mathematician of Pitane in Aeolis. Of his two extant works, that on the revolving sphere is said to be the oldest completely preserved Greek treatise on a mathematical subject. The other deals with the apparent rising and setting of the fixed stars.

Autolycus, in Greek mythology, celebrated rogue. He was the son of Hermes, from whom he received special powers in thieving and trickery. According to one legend Autolycus stole from Sisyphus, who revenged himself by seducing Autolycus' daughter Anticlea.

automatic direction finder: see RADIO RANGE.

automatic frequency control: see AUTOMATIC TUNING CONTROL.

automatic pilot: see AIR NAVIGATION.

automatic tuning control, method or device applied to a radio or television receiver by means of which it is automatically kept tuned to a desired frequency or channel. Usually the system is called automatic frequency control (AFC) when applied to frequency modulation (FM) receivers and automatic tuning control (ATC) when applied to television receivers. In either case the operation is similar. Assuming that the receiver is at least approximately tuned to the desired frequency, a circuit in the receiver develops an error voltage proportional to the degree to which the receiver is mistuned. This error voltage is then applied to some component in the tuning circuit whose value depends on applied voltage in such a way that the tuning error is reduced. In most FM detectors an error voltage of this type is easily available; in television receivers extra circuits may be used to develop it. In an FM receiver AFC may make it difficult to receive a weak signal located near in frequency to a strong one. If sufficient care is taken in tuner design, such devices can often be made unnecessary.

automation, automatic operation and control of machinery or processes by devices that can make and execute decisions without human intervention. The principal feature of such devices is their use of self-correcting CONTROL SYSTEMS that employ FEEDBACK, i.e., they use part of their output to control their input. Human participation involves little more than maintenance and repair of the equipment. In a typical automated manufacturing process, the feeding in of materials, the machine operation, the transfers from one machine to another, the final assembly, the removal, and the packing are all done automatically. At various stages in the operation are inspection devices that reject substandard products and adjust the machinery to correct any malfunction. Since electronic COMPUTERS are able to store, select, record, and present data systematically, they are widely employed to direct automated systems. For example, information recorded on tape and fed to a computer activates a series of tooling operations to produce a complex machined metal part. Automation is applied in industry to the manufacture of foodstuffs, chemicals, and pharmaceuticals and is used in steel mills, automobile plants, and coal mines. Another application is its use in the launching, aiming, and guidance of military rockets. Automation has also been applied to information handling, resulting in automatically prepared bills and reports. It offers high quality products together with great savings in costs. See G. H. Amber and P. S. Amber, *Anatomy of Automation* (1962); E. M. Grabbe et al., ed., *Handbook of Automation: Computation and Control* (3 vol., 1958–61); H. R. Bowen and G. L. Mangum, ed., *Automation and Economic Progress* (1966); Otto Mayr, *The Origins of Feedback Control* (1970).

automaton: see ROBOT.

automobile, self-propelled vehicle used for travel on land. The modern automobile is usually driven by the water-cooled, piston-type INTERNAL-COMBUSTION ENGINE, mounted in the front of the vehicle; its power is transmitted to the rear wheels by means of a drive shaft. Some automobiles use air-cooled engines, but these are generally less efficient than the liquid-cooled type. In some models the engine is carried at the rear and in some at the middle of the vehicle. This latter arrangement, while wasteful of space, gives advantages of weight distribution. Diesel engines are employed chiefly for heavy vehicles, i.e., trucks and buses. Other engines are also being studied and developed as possibly superior to the conventional piston type. Steam engines, which were once more common than gasoline engines, are being experimented with now because they give off few noxious emissions. However, the major American auto manufacturers show little enthusiasm for mass producing them, claiming they are too bulky and complicated. Some electric motors have recently been designed for experimental cars. However, these motors restrict the cars to short trips at low speed because of limitations of the storage batteries that power the motors. Also, their widespread use might generate more air pollution than the gasoline engines that they would replace, because additional electric power plants would be needed to recharge their batteries. Two of the most promising replacements for conventional auto engines are the gas TURBINE and the Wankel engine. The gas turbine has drawn interest because of its low output of noxious emissions. However, problems of excessive fuel consumption, high initial costs, and uncertain durability under stop-and-go driving conditions must be solved before the gas turbine can be mass-produced. A rotary engine developed (c.1954) by a team of engineers headed by Felix Wankel of Germany appears very promising because of its low exhaust emissions and feasibility for mass production. In this engine a three-sided rotor revolves within an epithrochoidal drum (combustion chamber) in which the free space contracts or expands as the rotor turns. Fuel is inhaled, compressed, and fired by the ignition system. The expanding gas turns the rotor and the spent gas is expelled. The Wankel engine has no valves, pistons, connecting rods, reciprocating parts, or crankshaft. It develops a high horsepower per cubic inch and per pound of engine weight, and it is essentially vibrationless. Automotive pollutants have begun to pose environmental problems of considerable magnitude. It has been calculated, for example, that 60% to 70% of the air pollution in the United States can be traced directly or indirectly to automobile exhausts. In addition, asbestos, ground from brakes in normal use, and rubber, which wears away from tires, accumulate on roadways and are washed into streams, with effects nearly as serious as those of untreated sewage. A problem also exists in disposing of the automobiles themselves when they are no longer operable. In an effort to improve the situation, the U.S. government has enacted severe regulations on the use of the constituents of automobile exhaust gas that are known to cause air pollution. These constituents fall roughly into three categories: hydrocarbons that pass through the engine unburned and escape from the crankcase, carbon monoxide, also a product of incomplete combustion, and nitrogen oxides, which are formed when nitrogen and oxygen are in contact at high temperatures. Besides their own toxic character, hydrocarbons and nitrogen oxides undergo reactions in the presence of sunlight to form noxious SMOG. Carbon monoxide and hydrocarbons are rather easily controlled by the use of high combustion temperatures, leaner fuel mixtures, and lower compression ratios in engines. Unfortunately, the conditions that produce minimum emission of hydrocarbons tend to raise emission of nitrogen oxides. To some extent this difficulty is solved by adding recycled exhaust gas to the fuel mixture, thus avoiding the oversupply of oxygen that favors formation of nitrogen oxides. The use of reaction chambers external to the engine may provide a technique for burning off hydrocarbon and carbon monoxide emissions. However, effective operation of such reactors appears to depend on the use of expensive catalysts that are easily rendered inactive by the lead compounds used in gasoline to prevent engine knock. The Wankel engine has advantages in this direction, as it runs easily on low-lead fuel and produces a minimum of nitrogen oxides. However, its fuel consumption is somewhat high under these conditions, although not as high as that of the turbine. The problem of automotive pollution is largely unsolved; progress has been made, but it is still an area requiring much research. Unfortunately, all currently practicable solutions tend to increase consumption of fuel, placing increasing burdens on energy supplies. Fatalities due to automobile accidents have stimulated automotive safety design. Safety design requires a wide-ranging systematic approach; many seemingly obvious solutions to safety problems either compound the problems or move them elsewhere. For example, one approach to passenger safety involves increasing the mass and rigidity of the vehicle, but this makes the vehicle so designed a hazard to light vehicles. The use of heavily padded interiors, collapsing steering columns, and other means of lessening the impact between passengers and the vehicle during a collision have met with some success, but one of the most effective systems, involving seat belts and harnesses to hold occupants in place, is largely ineffective because frequently they are not worn. Therefore attention has been turned to devices that either require no attention or disable the vehicle if they are not correctly deployed. Various systems have been devised whereby electronic sensors indicate if any passenger is not wearing a belt and either sound a warning or prevent the vehicle from starting. Another system simply envelops each passenger in a harness as his door is closed. More controversial is a system in which a sensor detects a collision, and rapidly, in a few hundredths of a second, inflates an air bag in front of each passenger to cushion his impact. Subsequently the bag deflates. The defects in the system are two: The bag, if falsely triggered, may cause an accident where one would not have occurred, and the system does not prevent contact with the vehicle roof in case of a rollover. Other aspects of vehicle safety include making it difficult for a driver to start a car

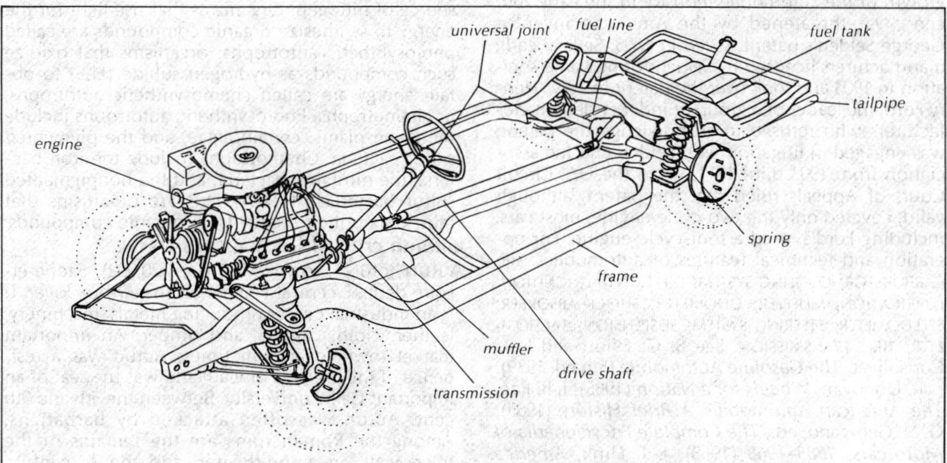

Automobile chassis

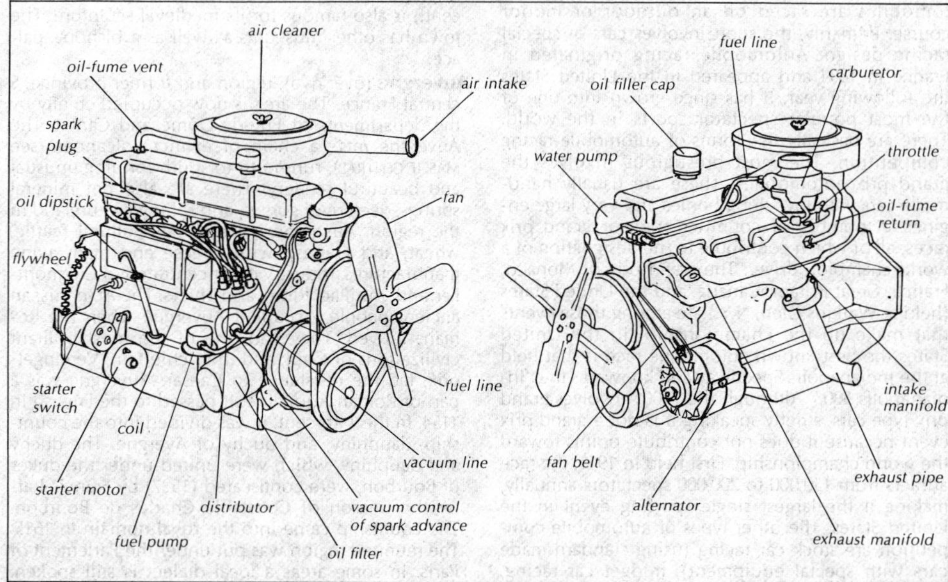

Two views of a six-cylinder automobile engine

while under the influence of alcohol (over half of all vehicle fatalities involve at least one driver who has used alcohol) and designing vehicles so that they are capable of emergency maneuvers. The French engineer Nicolas Joseph Cugnot is generally conceded to have built the first self-propelled vehicle (Paris, 1789), a heavy, three-wheeled, steam-driven carriage with a boiler that projected in front; its speed was c.3 mi per hr (5 km per hr). In 1801 the English engineer Richard Trevithick also built a three-wheeled steam-driven car; the engine drove the rear wheels. Many more vehicles were developed in England, and attempts were made to operate them on regular schedules. However, they were banned from the road, and development was retarded for decades by excessive road and bridge tolls and short-sighted legislation; e.g., speed was limited to 4 mi per hr (6.4 km per hr). In accordance with the Red Flag Act, which was in effect from 1836 to 1896, a man was required to walk in front of a self-propelled vehicle, carrying a red flag by day and a red lantern by night. The development of the automobile was accelerated by the introduction of the internal-combustion engine. Probably the first vehicle of this type was the three-wheeled car built in 1885 by the engineer Karl Benz in Germany. Another German engineer, Gottlieb Daimler, built an improved internal-combustion engine c.1885. The Panhard car, introduced in France by the Daimler company in 1894, had many features of the modern car. In the United States, internal-combustion cars of the horseless buggy type were manufactured in the 1890s by Charles Duryea and J. Frank Duryea, Elwood Haynes, Henry Ford, Ransom E. Olds, and Alexander Winton. Many of the early engines had only one cylinder, with a chain-and-sprocket drive on wooden carriage wheels. The cars generally were open, accommodated two passengers, and were steered by a lever. The Stanley brothers of Massachusetts, the most well-known American manufacturers of steam-driven autos, produced their Stanley Steamers from 1897 until after World War I. The free growth of the automobile industry in the early 20th cent. was threatened by the American inventor George Selden's patent issued in 1895. Several early manufacturers licensed by Selden formed an association in 1903 and took over the patent in 1907. Henry Ford, the leader of a group of independent manufacturers who refused to acknowledge the patent, was engaged in litigation with Selden and the association from 1903 until 1911, when the U.S. Circuit Court of Appeals ruled that the patent, although valid, covered only the two-cycle engine; most cars, including Ford's, used a four-cycle engine. For operation and technical features of automobiles, see CARBURETOR; COOLING SYSTEM; DIFFERENTIAL; IGNITION; LUBRICATION; MUFFLER; ODOMETER; SHOCK ABSORBER; SPEEDOMETER; STEERING SYSTEM; SUSPENSION; TACHOMETER; TIRE; TRANSMISSION. See B. G. Elliott and E. L. Consoliver, *The Gasoline Automobile* (5th ed. 1939); F. R. Donovan, *Wheels for a Nation* (1965); J. B. Rae, *The American Automobile: A Brief History* (1965); G. N. Georgano, ed., *The Complete Encyclopedia of Motorcars: 1885-1968* (1968); J. J. Flink, *America Adopts the Automobile, 1895-1910* (1970); William Crouse, *Automobile Emission Control* (1971).

automobile racing, sport in which high-speed automobiles are raced on an outdoor or indoor course. Primarily, the sport involves cars of special racing design. Automobile racing originated in France in 1894 and appeared in the United States the following year. It has since grown into one of the most popular spectator sports in the world. There are basically five forms of automobile-racing competition. The most prestigious involves the grand prix automobiles. These are usually handmade cars with low-slung bodies and very large engines. A number of countries sponsor grand prix races, all of which contribute to the designation of a world champion driver. The grand prix of Monaco, France, Great Britain, Canada, and the United States (held at Watkins Glen, N.Y.) are among those events that make up the championship. In the United States the best-known automobile race is that held at the Indianapolis Speedway and known as the "Indianapolis 500." Although the "500" involves grand prix type cars, strictly speaking it is not a grand prix event because it does not contribute points toward the world championship. First held in 1911, the race attracts from 150,000 to 200,000 spectators annually, making it the largest single sporting event in the United States. The other types of automobile competition are stock car racing (using standard-made cars with special equipment), midget car racing, sports car racing, and drag racing. The racing of sports cars developed after World War II, and the major races now include Sebring (Florida), Monza (Italy), and the 24-hour endurance event at Le Mans (France). Drag racing, which grew out of the often illegal races held among American teenagers during the mid-20th cent., involves acceleration tests among extremely powerful cars over ¼-mi (.4025-km) tracks. A number of organizations supervise the various types of automobile competition, including the U.S. Automobile Club, the Sports Car Club of America, and the International Automobile Federation, the governing body for world automobile racing. See studies by Richard Hough (1961 and 1965), Griffith Borgeson (1966), and A. R. Bochroch (1974); Robert Cutter and Bob Fendell, *Encyclopedia of Auto Racing* (1973).

autonomic nervous system: see NERVOUS SYSTEM.

autonomy (ôtŏn′əmē) [Gr.,=self-rule], in a political sense, limited self-government, short of independence, of a political state or, more frequently, of some subdivision of a political state. The term is also used for other self-governing units, such as a parish, a corporation, or a religious sect. The objective test of any autonomy is the recognition that the group may legislate or make the rules governing its internal affairs. Political autonomy is frequently based on cultural and ethnic differences. Autonomy within empires has frequently been a prelude to independence, as in the case of the evolution of the British Empire into the Commonwealth of Nations, containing both autonomous and completely sovereign states. The USSR includes among its political units several "autonomous regions." This autonomy is meant to allow groups along the borders to retain their ethnic and cultural distinctiveness, while at the same time they are brought under the political control of the Soviet government.

autopsy: see POST-MORTEM EXAMINATION.

autotroph, in biology, an organism capable of synthesizing its own organic substances from inorganic compounds. Autotrophs produce their own sugars, lipids, and amino acids using carbon dioxide as a source of carbon, and ammonia or nitrates as a source of nitrogen. Organisms that use light for the energy to synthesize organic compounds are called photosynthetic autotrophs; organisms that oxidize such compounds as hydrogen sulfide (H_2S) to obtain energy are called chemosynthetic autotrophs, or chemotrophs. Photosynthetic autotrophs include the green plants, certain algae, and the pigmented sulfur bacteria. Chemotrophs include the iron bacteria, the nitrifying bacteria, and the nonpigmented sulfur bacteria. HETEROTROPHS are organisms that must obtain their energy from organic compounds.

autumn crocus: see MEADOW SAFFRON.

Autun (ōtöN′), town (1968 pop. 20,002), Saône-et-Loire dept., E central France, on the Arroux River. It is an industrial center producing metals, machinery, leather, cloth, carpets, and timber. An important market town in ancient times, Autun was a residence of the prefects of Gaul and was the seat of an important Gallic university. Between the 5th and 9th cent. Autun was often attacked by barbarians. Among the Roman ruins are the remains of the town wall, an amphitheater, and the 3d-century gates of SS. André and Arroux. The Hotel Rolen (15th cent.), with the 12th-century sculpture of Eve, is now a museum. The Cathedral of St. Lazare (12th cent.) is also famous for its medieval sculpture. The town has other museums as well as a bishop's palace.

Auvergne (ōvĕr′nyə), region and former province, S central France. The area is now occupied chiefly by the departments of Puy-de-Dôme and Cantal. The Auvergne mts., a chain of extinct volcanoes (see MASSIF CENTRAL), run north to south forming unusual and beautiful scenery. There are also hot mineral springs, deep river gorges, and rolling pastureland in the region. Auvergne is largely agricultural (cattle, wheat, and grapes), with cheese and many wine manufactures. Industry is concentrated in Clermont-Ferrand, Aurillac, Riom, and Thiers. The Arvennis, an ancient people, occupied Auvergne when the Romans arrived. They had one of the most brilliant civilizations of Gaul, and their chieftain, Vercingetorix, led the resistance to Caesar. Auvergne was a part of Roman Aquitaine. It passed to the English in 1154. In the 14th cent. it was divided into the countship, dauphiny, and duchy of Avergne. The duchy and dauphiny, which were united under the dukes of Bourbon, were confiscated (1527) by Francis I after the treason of Constable Charles de Bourbon. The countship came into the royal domain in 1615. The reunited region was put under the Parlement of Paris. In some areas a local dialect is still spoken. There are many folk fetes, and much Romanesque architecture remains.

Aux Cayes (ō kā), **Cayes,** or **Les Cayes** (lā kā), town (1971 pop. 22,065), SW Haiti, on the Caribbean Sea. Haiti's chief southern port, it handles exports, mainly sugar and coffee. There are liquor distilleries in the town.

Auxerre (ōsĕr′), town (1968 pop. 38,066), capital of Yonne dept., N central France, in Burgundy, on the Yonne River. A commercial and industrial center, it has a great variety of manufactures and an important trade in Chablis wines. Auxerre gave its name to the medieval county of Auxerrois. It became part of Burgundy with the Treaty of Arras (1435). St. Germanus of Auxerre was bishop there in the 5th cent. The former abbatial church of St. Germain (13th cent.) is built on crypts dating back to the 6th cent. The abbey (now a hospital) has a fine Romanesque clock tower. The cathedral (13th-16th cent.) is in the Gothic flamboyant style. An air force school was established at Auxerre in 1965.

auxin (ôk′sĭn), plant hormone that regulates the amount, type, and direction of plant growth. Auxins include both naturally occurring substances and related synthetic compounds that have similar effects. Auxins are found in all members of the plant kingdom. They are most abundantly produced in growth areas (meristem), e.g., root and shoot tips, but are also produced elsewhere, e.g., in the stems and leaves. The method of dispersal throughout the plant body is not yet fully understood. Auxins, through their amount of concentration, affect numerous plant processes, e.g., cell division and elongation, autumnal loss of leaves, and the formation of buds, roots, flowers, and fruit. They are also responsible for many forms of TROPISM. It is known that phototropism is due to the inhibition of auxins by light; the cells on that side of a plant exposed to light do not divide or grow as quickly as those on the shaded side, and thus the plant grows toward the light source. Auxins are widely used commercially to produce more vigorous growth, to promote flowering and fruiting and also root formation in plants not easily propagated by stem cuttings, to retard fruit drop, and to produce seedless varieties (e.g., of tomatoes) by parthenogenetic fruiting. Only minute amounts of auxins occur naturally, and synthetic auxins (e.g., 2,4-D) must be administered in carefully prescribed doses, since excessive concentration produces usually fatal abnormalities. However, different species of plants react to different amounts of auxins, a fact used to advantage as a method of WEED control. The principal natural auxin is indoleacetic acid; other common but less frequent plant hormones include the gibberellins, lactones, and kinins.

Ava (ā′və), in the Bible, unidentified city of Mesopotamia, perhaps the same as IVAH. 2 Kings 17.24. Its inhabitants are called Avites: 2 Kings 17.31.

Ava (ä′və), village, central Burma, on the Irrawaddy River, 10 mi (16 km) S of Mandalay. Founded in 1364, it was the capital of a dynasty of Burmese kings until 1783 (when it was replaced by Amarapura) and again from 1823 to 1837. Only ruins remain of its former greatness.

Avacha (əvä′chə) or **Avachinskaya Sopka** (əvä′-chĭnskīə sôp′kə), active volcano, 8,965 ft (2,733 m) high, Far Eastern USSR, on S Kamchatka peninsula. It has a permanent snow cap.

Avadana: see PALI LITERATURE.

Aval: see BAHRAIN.

avalanche, rapidly descending mass of snow and ice loosened from mountain slopes. Loose debris, such as soil and rock, and trees or other vegetation may be picked up as the mass roars downslope. Avalanches result from the addition of a heavy snowfall to an insecure mass of ice and snow, from the removal of part of the base of the mass, which is caused by melting and eroding, or from sudden shocks such as those caused by explosions or earth tremors. The action of an avalanche is often destructive, since it is sudden, unanticipated, and violent.

Avalon (ăv′əlŏn), in Celtic mythology, the blissful otherworld of the dead. In medieval romance it was the island to which the mortally wounded King Arthur was taken, and from which it was expected he would someday return. Avalon is often identified with Glastonbury in Somerset, England.

Avalon Peninsula, 3,579 sq mi (9,270 sq km), SE N.F., Canada. It is nearly divided at its center by Conception Bay and St. Mary's Bay. The peninsula is the most densely populated part of Newfoundland; St. John's is the chief town. A lighthouse and radio direction-finding station are at Cape Race.

Avalos, Ferdinando Francesco d': see PESCARA, FERDINANDO FRANCESCO D'AVALOS, MARCHESE DI.

Avars (ä'värz), mounted nomad people who in the 4th and 5th cent. dominated the steppes of central Asia. Dislodged by stronger tribes, the Avars pushed west, increasing their formidable army by incorporating conquered peoples into it. Reaching their greatest power in the late 6th cent., they plundered all of present S Russia and the Balkans. Their siege (626) of Constantinople was unsuccessful, but they continued to dominate the Hungarian plain until Charlemagne defeated them. The Avars were not mentioned after the 9th cent. The modern Avars, a pastoral, Muslim people of the Dagestan Autonomous Soviet Socialist Republic, number about 280,000. It is doubted that they are descended from remnants of the old Avars.

avatara (äv"ətärə) [Skt.,=descent], incarnations of Hindu gods, especially VISHNU. The doctrine of avatara first occurs in the BHAGAVAD-GITA, where KRISHNA declares: "For the preservation of the righteous, the destruction of the wicked, and the establishment of dharma [virtue], I come into being from age to age." Vishnu is believed to have taken nine avatara, in both animal and human form, with a tenth yet to come. The avatara of SHIVA are imitations of those of Vishnu.

Avdira, Greece: see ABDERA.

Avebury, John Lubbock, 1st **Baron:** see LUBBOCK, SIR JOHN.

Avebury (ā'bərē), village, Wiltshire, S central England. The village, with a medieval church and Elizabethan manor house, lies within **Avebury Circle,** a Neolithic circular group of upright stones that are older and larger than STONEHENGE but not so well preserved. The village and the circle have belonged to the nation since 1943 and are administered by the National Trust.

Aveiro (ävā'rō), town (1960 pop. 16,430), capital of Aveiro dist., NW Portugal, on the lagoon of Aveiro and at the mouth of the Vouga River, in Beira Litoral. Intersected by numerous canals, one of which connects with the Atlantic, the town is a fishing port and salt-producing center. João Alfonso, one of the discoverers of the Newfoundland fisheries, was born there. A convent (now a museum) contains the tomb of the daughter of Alfonso V, St. Joana.

Avellaneda, Alonso Fernández de (älôn'sō färnän'dāth dā ävělyänä'thä), pen name used by the unknown Spanish writer who published a spurious second part of *Don Quixote* in 1614, before Cervantes's own second part appeared (1615). The book is usually referred to as *El Quijote apócrifo* [the spurious Don Quixote], and its author is unidentified, although various attributions have been made.

Avellaneda, Gertrudis Gómez de: see GÓMEZ DE AVELLANEDA, GERTRUDIS.

Avellaneda, Nicolás (nēkōläs' äväyänä'thä), 1837-85, Argentine statesman, president of the republic (1874-80). As minister of justice, religion, and public instruction under Domingo F. SARMIENTO (1868-74), he introduced many reforms. After his election as president, he suppressed a revolt led by Bartolomé Mitre, the defeated candidate. His administration was notable for economic growth and for the conquest of the Indian frontier southwest of Buenos Aires. An expedition under Gen. Julio A. Roca (1878-79) drove the Indians beyond the Río Negro, opening the territory of Patagonia for colonization. Much of the new land, however, went in large tracts to speculators, influential politicians, and the great landowners. Avellaneda was chiefly responsible for the plan, approved in 1880, by which the city of Buenos Aires was federalized, thereby settling the political tensions that had long existed between the city and Buenos Aires prov.

Avellaneda (äväyänä'thä), city (1970 pop. 337,538), Buenos Aires prov., E central Argentina, across the Riachuelo River from the Buenos Aires federal district. It is one of the most important industrial, commercial, and transportation centers in the country. The city, which grew in the first half of the 19th cent., was formerly called Baracas al Sud but was renamed (1904) after Nicolás Avellaneda, an Argentine president.

Avellino (äväl-lē'nō), city (1971 pop. 52,576), capital of Avellino prov., Campania, S Italy. It is an agricultural and manufacturing center. Although damaged by an earthquake in 1930, the city has retained much of its medieval aspect. Of note are the 12th-century cathedral and the ruins of a castle (9th-10th cent.). Near Avellino is the Benedictine convent and pilgrimage shrine of Monte Vergine (founded early 12th cent.).

Ave Maria (ä'vā märē'ä) [Latin,=hail, Mary], prayer to the Virgin Mary universal among Roman Catholics, also called the Ave, the Hail Mary, and the Angelic Salutation. The words in English are: "Hail Mary, full of grace, the Lord is with thee; blessed art thou amongst women, and blessed is the fruit of thy womb, Jesus. Holy Mary, Mother of God, pray for us sinners now and at the hour of our death. Amen." The first part is from Luke 1.28,42. The prayer is much used in private as well as in public devotions, e.g., in the ROSARY. It has many musical settings, the compositions by Franz Schubert and Charles Gounod being especially popular.

Avempace (ā'vəmpās, ä"vĕmpä'thā), Arabic *Ibn Bajja,* d. 1138, Spanish-Arabian philosopher. Little is known of his life, but he was born in Saragossa and died in Fez, Morocco. He was an outstanding representative of the Islamic Aristotelian-Neoplatonic tradition. This tradition had been established in the east by al-FARABI on whose commentaries Avempace depended. He is important for his influence on AVERROËS and for his concept of the solitary mystic as opposed to the more social concept of Islam held by al-GHAZALI.

Aven (ā'vĕn), in the Bible, abusive name applied to towns: to Bethel (see BETH-AVEN); to Heliopolis in Egypt in Ezek. 30.17; and to some other place, traditionally Baalbek, in Amos 1.5.

Avenasar: see FARABI, AL-.

Avenches (äväNsh'), anc. *Aventicum,* town (1970 pop. 2,235), Vaud canton, W Switzerland. During the 1st and 2d cent. A.D., Avenches flourished under the Romans as the chief town of HELVETIA.

Aventine, hill: see *Rome before Augustus* under ROME.

average, number used to represent or characterize a group of numbers. The most common type of average is the arithmetic MEAN. See MEDIAN; MODE.

Averescu, Alexander (ävĕrĕs'ko͞o), 1859-1938, Rumanian general and political leader. He served as a volunteer in the 1877-78 war against the Ottoman Empire and rose to become minister of war in 1907. He distinguished himself as a commander in World War I, especially in the 1916 Dobruja campaign, and gained a great popular following. In late Jan., 1918, he was chosen to form a cabinet to negotiate peace with the Central Powers. Averescu founded (1918) the People's league (later the People's party), which sought moderate land reform and suppression of the left. He was premier in 1920-21 and again in 1926-27 and was made a marshal in 1930.

Averno (ävĕr'nō), anc. *Avernus* (əvûr'nəs) [from Gr.,=without bird], small crater lake, .6 mi (.9 km) wide, Campania, S Italy, between Cuma and Puteoli, near the Tyrrhenian Sea. Its intense sulphuric vapors, caused by volcanic activity (now extinguished), supposedly killed the birds flying over it, hence its name. The ancient Romans, impressed by its vapors and its gloomy aspect, regarded it as the entrance to hell; later the name was used for hell itself. Near the lake its personification, the *deus Avernus,* was worshiped.

Averroës (əvĕr'ōēz), Arabic *Ibn Rushd,* 1126-98, Spanish-Arabian philosopher. He was far more important and influential in Jewish and Christian thought than in Islam. He was a lawyer and physician of Córdoba and lived for some time in Morocco in favor with the caliphs. He was banished for a period, probably for suspected heresy. Averroës's greatest work was his commentaries on Aristotle. The Averroistic interpretation of Aristotle remained influential long after his death and was a matter of intellectual speculation well into the Renaissance. He attempted to delimit the separate domains of faith and reason, pointing out that the two need not be reconciled because they did not conflict. He declared philosophy the highest form of inquiry. He had the same Neoplatonic cast to his metaphysics as Avempace, to whom he was certainly indebted for his ideas on the intellect. Averroist doctrines on personal immortality and the eternity of matter were condemned by the Roman Catholic Church. St. Thomas Aquinas was respectful of Averroës, but he attacked the Averroist contention that philosophic truth is derived from reason and not from faith. See SCHOLASTICISM. Averroës's works in English translation include *Incoherence of the Incoherence,* ed. by Simon Van Den Bergh (1955); *On Aristotle's De Generatione et Corruptione,* ed. by Samuel Kurland (1958); *Commentary on Plato's Republic,* ed. by E. I. J. Rosenthal (1956, repr. 1966); and *On the Harmony of Religion and Philosophy,* ed. by G. F. Hourani (1961).

Aversa (ävĕr'sä), city (1971 pop. 47,366), Campania, S Italy. It is an agricultural and transportation center, noted for its sparkling white wine. In the early 11th cent. the county of Aversa became the first possession of the Normans in Italy; it later was made part of the kingdom of Naples.

Avery, Milton, 1893-1965, American painter, b. Altmar, N.Y. Avery moved to New York City in 1925. Bold massing of forms is characteristic of his figurative work, such as *Poetry Reading* (1957; Munson-Williams-Proctor Inst., Utica, N.Y.). His landscapes, including *Green Sea* (1954; Metropolitan Mus.), verge on complete abstraction. Avery's paintings display qualities of fantasy and poetic gaiety within the tradition of Matisse. See study by Hilton Kramer (1962); exhibition catalog ed. by A. D. Breeskin (1969).

Avery Island, salt dome, c.200 ft (60 m) high and 2 mi (3.2 km) in diameter, S La., in an area of sea marshes and swamps. The island's former owner, Edward Avery McIlhenny, author of *Bird City,* created Jungle Gardens, which contains many rare plants, trees, and flowers. The island also has a bird sanctuary. All the cayenne peppers grown in the United States are produced on Avery Island. Rock salt has been mined there since 1791.

Avesta: see ZOROASTRIANISM.

Avesta (ä'vəstä"), city (1970 pop. 10,191), Kopparberg co., S central Sweden, on the Dalälven River. Aluminum and high quality steel are manufactured there. Formerly a copper mining and refining center, Avesta was the seat of copper minting in Sweden from 1644 to 1831.

Avestan (əvĕs'tən), language belonging to the Iranian group of the Indo-Iranian subfamily of the Indo-European family of languages. One of the earliest forms of the Iranian languages to survive, Avestan is also the tongue of the *Avesta,* or scriptures of ZOROASTRIANISM. See INDO-IRANIAN LANGUAGES. See A. V. W. Jackson, *An Avestan Grammar in Comparison with Sanskrit* (1968).

Aveyron (ävärôN'), department (1968 pop. 281,568), S central France, in Guienne. RODEZ is the capital.

aviary (ā'vēārē), structure for confining birds. It usually refers to an outdoor screened area within which environmental conditions are suitable to the birds. Aviaries must provide food, shelter, perches and flying space, nesting sites and materials, as well as protection against vermin and predators. For tropical species, heated indoor quarters are often provided for the winter. Aviaries are maintained privately as well as for public exhibit, research, and the breeding of wild birds. The construction of aviaries for exhibition, known since early Roman times, was spurred by the collection of unusual bird specimens by 15th-century explorers and the introduction of the canary into Europe. Aviaries are now found chiefly in public gardens, on private estates, and in many zoological parks. Among the aviaries in the United States are the Parrot Jungle, Miami; the Tracy Aviary, Salt Lake City; and the World of Birds, New York Zoological Park, New York City. Wild birds may be observed in their natural habitat in sanctuaries and on wildlife refuges.

aviation, operation of heavier-than-air aircraft and related activities. Aviation can be conveniently divided into military aviation, air transport, and general aviation. Military aviation includes all aviation activity by the armed services, such as combat, reconnaissance, and military air transport. Air transport consists mainly of the operation of commercial airlines, which handle both freight and passengers. General aviation consists of agricultural, business, charter, instructional, and pleasure flying; it includes such activities as the operation of air taxis, as well as aerial surveying and mapping. The detailed observations, explanations, and drawings preserved in the notebooks of Leonardo da Vinci mark the beginning of scientific studies of FLIGHT. Leonardo's work in this field centered around studies of birds, with observations of bats and other flying creatures. Flight was first successfully accomplished (1783) in a lighter-than-air device (see BALLOON). A number of investigators contributed to an early understanding of the principles involved in achieving flight in heavier-than-air machines. Among them were the Englishman W. S. Henson, who patented (1842) a design for a machine that closely foreshadowed the modern monoplane; the Englishman John Stringfellow, who developed a model plane said to be the first power-driven machine to fly; and F. H. Wenham, who in England devised the first wind-tunnel experiments. Alphonse Penaud, in France, made successful flying models of airplanes and wrote on the theory of flight. Clément Ader, a French engineer, achieved flight (over a distance of about 150 ft/46 m in 1890 and about 300 yd/280 m in 1897) in his power-driven monoplane fashioned after a bat. In 1894 a plane built in England by Sir Hiram S. Maxim, operated by steam engines and carrying a crew of three, rose into the air from the track on which it was being tested. In the United States, S. P. Langley, Octave Chanute, and Otto Lilienthal made notable contributions to the early development of the airplane. The first successful flight in a man-carrying airplane powered by a motor was near Kitty Hawk, N.C., on Dec. 17, 1903, by Orville Wright; later on the same day his brother Wilbur bettered the length of flying time. Glenn H. Curtiss made improvements in the design of airplanes and engines and constructed the first successful flying boat or seaplane (1911–12). Stimulated by awards of trophies and prizes of money, aviators demonstrated, during the early 1900s, the feasibility of air travel to various parts of the world. World War I provided additional motivation for aviation research and development (see AIR FORCES and AIR POWER). During the first decade after the war, progress in air transport in Europe far outstripped that in the United States, but later the United States forged ahead. The cessation of hostilities made available a large number of aircraft that could be bought cheaply. This surplus occasioned a great deal of aviation activity; barnstorming and stunt-flying were the order of the day. The result was a more airplane-conscious public. Private companies in America were permitted to contract for carrying AIRMAIL after 1925; they thus obtained funds for expansion. During the 1930s aviation continued to expand. Technological improvements in wind-tunnel testing, engine and airframe design, and maintenance equipment combined to provide faster, larger, and more durable airplanes. The transportation of passengers became profitable, and routes were extended to include several foreign countries. Transpacific airmail service, begun by the Pan American Airways (later Pan American World Airways) system in 1934, was followed by the first transoceanic aviation service for passengers, on the *China Clipper*, from San Francisco to Manila (to Hong Kong in 1937). In 1939 the first transatlantic service to carry both mail and passengers was inaugurated. World War II interrupted much commercial air service, but with the cessation of the war air transportation was gradually resumed until air routes penetrated to all parts of the globe. The late 1940s saw the development of JET PROPULSION and a corresponding major change in aviation development. In the United States, design and construction of jet aircraft was speeded up by the Korean War, during which a majority of combat missions were flown by jet aircraft. The application of jet propulsion to commercial air transportation began in 1952 when British Overseas Airways Company opened the world's first regular jet passenger service with a flight from London to Johannesburg. Despite the fact that this service was short-lived, several major airlines began to show interest in commercial jet aircraft and today virtually all long-distance commercial air routes are flown by jet-powered aircraft. While jet propulsion has been a boon to the aviation industries it has created some major problems. The jet plane uses more fuel than conventional aircraft and requires longer runways, and its speed makes necessary more durable construction materials and creates special problems of air-traffic control. In addition, the takeoff and landing of jet aircraft over populated areas has created locally dangerous levels of noise POLLUTION. See AIR NAVIGATION; AIRPLANE; AIRSHIP; AIR, LAW OF THE. See Antoine de Saint Exupéry, *Wind, Sand, and Stars* (tr. 1939); J. L. Nayler, *Aviation: Its Technical Development* (1965); J. W. Benkert, *Introduction to Aviation Science* (1971); N. D. van Sickle, ed., *Modern Airmanship* (1971); Enzo Angelucci, *Airplanes from the Dawn of Flight to the Present Day* (1973); J. W. R. Taylor and Kenneth Munson, *History of Aviation* (1973).

aviation medicine, scientific study of the biological effects of aviation, especially on human beings. Although aviation medicine is concerned with such problems as the spread of diseases by persons traveling by air and the harmful effects of noise and air pollution, its principal concern is with stresses applied to the passengers or crew of aircraft in flight. These stresses can include exposure to extreme temperatures, large inertial forces occurring when an aircraft undergoes acceleration, oxygen deprivation, and air sickness, as well as pilot fatigue and psychological disturbances. As the biological problems of space flight exceed considerably those of atmospheric flight, aviation medicine has become a special branch of SPACE MEDICINE, the latter study having largely absorbed the former.

Avicebron: see IBN GABIROL, SOLOMON BEN JUDAH.

Avicenna (ăvĭsĕn'ə), Arabic *Ibn Sina,* 980–1037, Islamic philosopher and physician, of Persian origin, b. near Bukhara. He was the most renowned philosopher of medieval Islam and the most influential name in medicine from 1100 to 1500. His medical masterpiece was the *Canon of Medicine.* Avicenna's interpretation of Aristotle followed to some extent that of the Neoplatonists. He saw God as emanating the universe from himself in a series of triads formed of mind, soul, and body. This process terminated in the Aristotelian "active intellect," which governs directly all earthly regions and transmits to all things their appropriate forms. Man's soul is also derived from it and is immortal. He was not an absolute pantheist as he believed matter to exist independently of God. Avicenna fixed the classification of sciences used in the medieval schools of Europe. See S. M. Afnan, *Avicenna, His Life and Works* (1958); Henry Corbin, *Avicenna and the Visionary Recital* (tr. 1960); Parviz Morewedge, *The Metaphysics of Avicenna* (1973).

Avignon (ävēnyôN'), city (1968 pop. 88,958), capital of Vaucluse dept., SE France, on the Rhône River. It is a farm market with a wine trade and a great variety of manufactures. Located in (but never a part of) the Comtat Venaissin, it was the papal see during the Babylonian captivity, from 1309 to 1378 (see PAPACY), and the residence of several antipopes from 1378 to 1408 (see SCHISM, GREAT). Pope Clement VI bought (1348) full title to Avignon from the countess of Provence. After the Great Schism, Avignon was nominally ruled by papal legates, but the citizens actually governed themselves. The city became an archiepiscopal see in 1475. In 1791, after a plebiscite, it was incorporated into France. One of the loveliest of French cities, Avignon is surrounded by ramparts (12th and 14th cent.) and has many old churches. The beautiful Gothic papal palace was built (14th cent.) atop a hill to serve as residence, fortress, and church. A fragment of a 12th-cent. bridge across the Rhône remains. Avignon was celebrated by Petrarch, who resided at the court of Clement VI.

Ávila, Gil González de: see GONZÁLEZ DE ÁVILA.

Ávila (ä'vēlä), town (1970 pop. 30,983), capital of Ávila prov., central Spain, in Old Castile, on the upper Adaja River. It attracts many tourists. One of the great religious centers of Spain, Ávila has preserved much medieval architecture. Up against its turreted wall (built 11th cent.) is the imposing Cathedral of San Salvador. The Basilica of San Vicente is one of the finest Romanesque buildings in Spain. In the convent of Encarnación lived St. Theresa, who was born at Ávila.

Ávila Camacho, Manuel (mänwĕl' ä'vēlä kämä'chō), 1897–1955, president of Mexico (1940–46). As a young man, Ávila Camacho joined the revolutionary forces. Later he became brigadier general. Under Lázaro CÁRDENAS he became (1938) minister of national defense. As president he followed a middle-of-the-road policy based on the agricultural, industrial, and educational reforms begun by Cárdenas. During World War II, he cooperated with the United States in programs of hemisphere defense, reciprocal trade, and agricultural labor exchange and sent (1945) a token Mexican air squadron to fight in the Pacific.

Avilés (ävēlās'), town (1970 pop. 81,710), Oviedo prov., NW Spain, in Asturias, on the Bay of Biscay. Coal is exported, and there are metalworks and textile mills.

Avim (ā'vĭm), unidentified town of Benjamin. Joshua 18.23.

Avims (ā'vĭmz), the same as AVITES **1.**

Avites (ā'vīts). **1** People of SW Palestine, probably assimilated by the Philistines. Joshua 13.3. Avims: Deut. 2.23. **2** People of AVA.

Avith (ā'vĭth), city of unknown site, E of the Dead Sea. Gen. 36.35; 1 Chron. 1.46.

Avitus (əvī'təs), d. 456?, Roman emperor of the West (455–56). He was proclaimed emperor in Gaul with the support of the Visigoths but was deposed by RICIMER. He was elected bishop of Placentia but died soon afterward.

Aviz (ävēzh'), village, Portalegre dist., central Portugal, in Altro Alentejo. The Castilian order of the Knights of Calatrava assisted in driving the Moors from Portugal and in 1166 settled at ÉVORA. Alfonso II granted (1211) them Aviz, and this branch of the order became separate and was known as the Order of Aviz, a strictly Portuguese organization. The knights played an important part in Portuguese history. After the death of Ferdinand I in 1383, his illegitimate brother, John, who was master of the Order of Aviz, led a revolution to prevent the crown from going to Beatriz of Castile. He himself became king as John I. Thus the house of Aviz was established on the throne. It was the most distinguished of Portuguese dynasties, reigning until 1580, when Portugal passed for a time under Spanish rule (see PORTUGAL). Aviz is sometimes spelled Avis.

Avoca or **Ovoca** (both: əvō'kə), river, c.15 mi (24 km) long, formed by the union of the Avonmore and Avonbeg rivers, in Co. Wicklow, E Republic of Ireland. It flows SE to the Irish Sea at Arklow. The river is celebrated by Thomas Moore's poem "Meeting of the Waters."

avocado (ä'vəkä'do, ăv'-), tropical American broad-leaved evergreen tree of the genus *Persea* of the family Lauraceae (LAUREL family). The fruit, called avocado, alligator pear, or, in Spanish, *aguacate,* has a high oil content. It is eaten fresh, chiefly in salads. The avocado was cultivated by the Aztecs. Avocados are classified in the division MAGNOLIOPHYTA, class Magnoliopsida, order Magnoliales, family Lauraceae.

avocet (ăv'əsĕt), common name for a long-legged wading bird about 15 to 18 in. (37.5–45 cm) long, related to the snipe and belonging to the same family as the stilt. The American avocet, *Himantopus mexicanus,* and the Australian avocet have black and white bodies and brown heads; the African and Eurasian species are black and white and are strikingly visible at distances. Avocets, like stilts, are wetland inhabitants. By sweeping their long, thin, upwardly curved bills through shallow water and mud, they capture small water animals, such as crustaceans, mollusks, amphibians, fishes, and insects; other insects are caught on the wing. Avocets have shrill calls, but also have a soft flutelike song. They breed gregariously. The female lays from three to five eggs per clutch in a shallow depression in the ground, which may be lined with small stones and grass. Avocets are classified in the phylum CHORDATA, subphylum Vertebrata, class Aves, order Charadriiformes, family Recurvirostridae.

Avogadro, Amadeo, conte di Quaregna (ämädā'ō kôn'tā dē kwärā'nyä ävōgä'drō), 1776–1856, Italian physicist, b. Turin. He became professor of physics at the Univ. of Turin in 1820. In 1811 he advanced the hypothesis, since known as Avogadro's law, that equal volumes of gases under identical conditions of pressure and temperature contain the same number of molecules. Since then, through the work of other physicists, the number of molecules in the gram molecular volume has been determined and found to be the same for all gases. This number (6.02×10^{23}) has been called AVOGADRO'S NUMBER. Avogadro's hypothesis, though not accepted for some fifty years after its introduction, is now one of the fundamental concepts of the atomic theory of matter.

Avogadro's number [for Amedeo Avogadro], number of particles contained in one MOLE of any substance; it is equal to 602,252,000,000,000,000,000,000, or in scientific notation, 6.02252×10^{23}. For example, 12.011 grams of carbon (one mole of carbon) contains 6.02252×10^{23} carbon atoms, and 180.16 grams of glucose, $C_6H_{12}O_6$, contains 6.02252×10^{23} molecules of glucose. Avogadro's number is determined by calculating the spacing of the atoms in a crystalline solid through X-ray methods and combining this data with the measured volume of one mole of the solid to obtain the number of molecules per molar volume.

avoirdupois weights (ăv"ərdəpoiz'): see ENGLISH UNITS OF MEASUREMENT.

Avon, 1st **earl of:** see EDEN, SIR ANTHONY.

Avon, nonmetropolitan county (1972 est. pop. 902,000), SW England, created under the Local Government Act of 1972 (effective 1974). It is composed of the county boroughs of BATH and BRISTOL and parts of the former counties of Gloucestershire and Somerset.

Avon (ā'vən, ăv'ən) [Celtic, = river], name of several rivers in England. **1** Also called **Bristol Avon** or **Lower Avon,** rising in SW England at Tetbury, Gloucestershire, and flowing 75 mi (121 km) E, S, and then NW through Bath and Bristol to the Severn River at Avonmouth. It is navigable for large vessels to Bristol, an important port. **2** Also called **East Avon,** rising at Devizes, Wiltshire, S England, and flowing 48 mi (77 km) S past Salisbury to the English Channel at Christchurch. It is navigable for small craft below Salisbury. **3** Also called **Upper Avon,** the most famous of the Avon rivers, sometimes known as Shakespeare's Avon. It rises near Naseby, Northamptonshire, S central England, and flows 96 mi (154 km) SW to the Severn River near Tewkesbury, passing Rugby, Warwick, and Stratford-upon-Avon.

Avon Lake, city (1970 pop. 12,261), Lorain co., NE Ohio, on Lake Erie; inc. 1917. It is chiefly a residential suburb of the Cleveland-NE Ohio industrial area. The city has an electric power plant and factories that make plastics and aluminum castings. Several beaches are there.

Avranches (ävräNsh'), town (1968 pop. 11,102), Manche dept., NW France, in Normandy, on the English Channel. Because of its proximity to the rocky island of MONT-SAINT-MICHEL, Avranches has a large tourist trade. A Roman town, it became an intellectual center in the early Middle Ages; Lanfranc taught there. It was devastated in the Hundred Years War, the Wars of Religion, and World War II.

Awaji-shima (äwä'jē-shē'mä), island, 32 mi (52 km) long and from 3 to 17 mi (4.8-27 km) wide, Hyogo prefecture, Japan, in the Inland Sea. Sumoto, on Osaka Bay, is the chief city and port. A relatively flat, fertile island, it produces grain and flowers and has commercial fisheries. It was to Awaji-shima that the Empress Shotoku banished (764) the Emperor Junnin.

Awami League, political organization in Pakistan and Bangladesh. It was founded in 1949 as an opposition party in Pakistan and had a moderately socialist ideology. The Awami [people's] League, with cofounder Sheikh MUJIBUR RAHMAN as its leader from 1953, called in 1966 for a federation of East and West Pakistan, an arrangement that would have given much greater autonomy to East Pakistan. The league's candidates won a majority in the 1970 elections, but the central government in West Pakistan banned the league after war between East and West Pakistan erupted in early 1971. When Bangladesh (formerly East Pakistan) won its independence in late 1971, the league was the nation's dominant political force.

Awe, Loch (lŏkh ô), lake, 25 mi (40 km) long, Argyllshire, W Scotland; 118 ft (36 m) above sea level. The hydroelectric power facility at Cruachan (completed 1967) has a 400,000-kw capacity.

awl: see DRILL.

Awolowo, Obafemi (ôbäfä'mē äwōlō'wō), 1909–, Nigerian statesman, a Yoruba chief, commonly known as "Awo." His first political activity (1940) was in the Nigerian Youth Movement, and he was one of the founders (1943) of the Nigerian Trades Union Congress. In 1950 he founded a new political party, the Action Group. Elected (1959) to the house of representatives of Nigeria, he became leader of the opposition. Awolowo and other Action Group officials were placed (1962) under restriction but he later regained influence and became chancellor of the Univ. of Ife and commissioner of finance.

Axel: see ABSALON.

Axel Heiberg Island (ăk'səl hī'bərg), 13,583 sq mi (35, 180 sq km), in the Arctic Ocean, N Northwest Territories, Canada, W of Ellesmere Island. It was named by the Norwegian explorer Otto Sverdrup (who explored it 1898-1902) for one of his patrons. The island's plateau surface (3,000-6,000 ft/915-1,830 m high) is deeply indented by fjords. A McGill University expedition has carried out glaciological studies there since 1959.

axiom, in mathematics and logic, general statement accepted without PROOF as the basis for logically deducing other statements (theorems). Examples of axioms used widely in mathematics are those related to equality (e.g., "Two things equal to the same thing are equal to each other"; "If equals are added to equals, the sums are equal") and those related to operations (e.g., the ASSOCIATIVE LAW and the COMMUTATIVE LAW). A postulate, like an axiom, is a statement that is accepted without proof; however, it deals with specific subject matter (e.g., properties of geometrical figures) and thus is not so general as an axiom. It is sometimes said that an axiom or postulate is a "self-evident" statement, but the truth of the statement need not be evident and may in some cases even seem to contradict common sense. Moreover, a statement may be an axiom or postulate in one deductive system and may instead be derived from other statements in another system. A set of axioms on which a system is based is usually assumed to be independent; i.e., no one of its members can be deduced from any combination of the others. (Historically, the development of non-Euclidean geometry grew out of attempts to prove or disprove the independence of the parallel postulate of Euclid.) The axioms should also be consistent; i.e., it should not be possible to deduce contradictory statements from them. Completeness is another property sometimes mentioned in connection with a set of axioms; if the set is complete, then any true statement within the system described by the axioms may be deduced from them.

Axis, coalition of countries headed by Germany, Italy, and Japan, 1936-45 (see WORLD WAR II). The expression "Rome-Berlin axis" originated in Oct., 1936, with an accord reached by HITLER and MUSSOLINI. The Axis was solidified by an Italo-German alliance in May, 1939. This was extended (Sept., 1940) by a military alliance among Germany, Italy, and Japan—the so-called Berlin Pact, to which Hungary, Rumania, Bulgaria, Slovakia, and Croatia adhered later. The related Anti-Comintern Pact (see COMINTERN), originally concluded between Germany and Japan in 1936, later had as adherents, besides the Berlin Pact nations, Spain, Denmark, Finland, and the puppet governments of Manchukuo and Nanking.

axolotl (ăk'səlŏt"əl), a SALAMANDER, *Siredon mexicanum,* found in certain lakes in the region of Mexico City, which reaches reproductive maturity without losing its larval characteristics. This phenomenon is called neoteny; in salamanders it is apparently caused by certain environmental conditions, particularly a low level of iodine in the water, which affect the functioning of the thyroid gland. Axolotls are permanently aquatic, never undergoing the metamorphosis to a terrestrial form characteristic of amphibians. They grow larger than ordinary larval salamanders and develop sexually, but they retain external gills and a well-developed tail. The axolotl was not recognized as a salamander until 1865, when several specimens at the Jardin des Plantes in Paris suddenly underwent metamorphosis. After some experimentation it was discovered that when their pools were dried up most of the animals changed into the adult form. Axolotls will also mature normally if fed thyroid gland extract. The related North American tiger salamander, *Abystoma tigrinum,* often exhibits neoteny in the Rocky Mts., where the iodine content of the water is low. The axolotl has a broad head and bushy gills; its skin is a black-speckled dark brown. It may grow as long as 13 in. (33 cm). In Mexico City, axolotls are sometimes cooked and eaten as delicacies. They are classified in the phylum CHORDATA, subphylum Vertebrata, class Amphibia, order Urodela, family Abystomidae.

axon: see NERVOUS SYSTEM; SYNAPSE.

Axum, Ethiopia: see AKSUM.

Ayabe (äyä'bā), city (1970 pop. 44,983), Kyoto prefecture, W central Honshu, Japan, on the Yura River. It is an agricultural and communications center where raw silk and silk fabrics are manufactured.

Ayacucho (äyäkōō'chō), city (1969 est. pop. 27,900), capital of Ayacucho dept., S central Peru. It is a commercial center in a rich mining region that produces gold, silver, and nickel. Tourism is also important, and there is some agricultural production. On the plains of Ayacucho, near the city, Antonio José de SUCRE crushingly defeated (Dec. 9, 1824) Spanish forces under Viceroy José de la SERNA. The battle not only secured Peruvian independence from Spain but also marked the triumph of the revolutionary forces in all South America. Known as Huamanga since the 16th cent., the city was renamed after the battle. It has a university and many fine examples of Spanish colonial architecture.

Ayala, Pedro López de: see LÓPEZ DE AYALA.

Ayala, Ramón Pérez de: see PÉREZ DE AYALA.

Aydın (īdŭn'), city (1970 pop. 50,551), capital of Aydın prov., W Turkey, on the Büyük Menderes River. It is the trade center for a farm region where olives, figs, cotton, and tobacco are grown. The city was destroyed by fire in 1922 and has been completely rebuilt. Nearby are the ruins of the ancient Greek city of Tralles.

aye-aye (ī'ī'), name for an aberrant primate, *Daubentonia madagascariensis,* related to the LEMURS but distinguished by its specialized teeth and fingers. A nocturnal, arboreal animal, it is found in dense bamboo forests in two isolated regions of Madagascar. The aye-aye is about the size of a house cat. It has silver and black fur with reddish underparts, a long, bushy tail, and a small, round head with large eyes and rounded, naked ears. Its fingers and toes are extremely long and end in claws; the thumb and big toes are opposable. The aye-aye uses its exceedingly slender third finger to dig into bark for wood-boring insect larvae, which it detects by means of its acute hearing. It feeds on larvae, other small animals, eggs, and fruit, as well as on bamboo and sugarcane. Its teeth are adapted for gnawing and it was formerly thought to be a rodent because of its large, chisel-shaped, continuously growing incisors. The aye-aye has no fear of humans and will strike at them if annoyed. It has been the object of superstitious fear. It is classified in the phylum CHORDATA, subphylum Vertebrata, class Mammalia, order Primates, family Daubentoniidae.

Ayer, Sir Alfred Jules, 1910–, British philosopher, b. London, grad. Oxford, 1932. From 1933 to 1944 he was lecturer and research fellow at Oxford's Christ Church College and then was fellow (1944-45) and dean (1945-46) of Wadham College. From 1946 to 1959 Ayer was Grote professor of the philosophy of mind and logic at the Univ. of London, and in 1959 he became Wykeham professor of logic at Oxford. His extremely influential *Language, Truth, and Logic* (1936) brought LOGICAL POSITIVISM to the attention of British and American philosophers. Among his other works are *The Foundations of Empirical Knowledge* (1940), *Philosophical Essays* (1954), *The Problem of Knowledge* (1956), and *The Concept of a Person* (1963). He was knighted in 1970. See studies by F. M. Bak (1970) and Suresh Chandra (1970).

Ayesha: see AISHA.

Aylesbury (ālz'bərē), city (1971 pop. 41,288), Buckinghamshire, central England. It is an agricultural market for the upper Thames valley and is famous for its ducks. There are printing works and other light industries, developed under a government program undertaken to disperse London's population and industry to surrounding counties. The radical John Wilkes represented Aylesbury in Parliament during the late 18th cent.

Ayllón, Lucas Vásquez de (lōō'käs väs'kāth dā īlyōn'), c.1475-1526, Spanish explorer. He emigrated in 1502 to Santo Domingo, where he became a public official. In 1521, Francisco Gordillo, sent by Ayllón to explore northward, seems to have landed in either Florida or South Carolina. Ayllón secured title and permission to colonize. In 1526 he sailed with three ships and about 500 settlers, landing probably in North Carolina, though some authorities claim it was on the site of the later Jamestown, Va. Fever and other hardships plagued the settlers, and when Ayllón died of fever, the survivors returned to Santo Domingo.

Aylmer, John (āl'mər), 1521-94, bishop of London. His name is also spelled Ælmer or Elmer. He was briefly chaplain to the duke of Suffolk and tutor to his daughter, Lady Jane Grey. In 1553 he was deprived of his church preferments for opposing the doctrine of transubstantiation, and he fled to Switzerland. There he aided John Foxe in making a Latin translation of the *Book of Martyrs* and wrote *An Harborowe for Faithfull and Trewe Subjects* (1559) in answer to a tract by John Knox. Returning to England after the accession of Elizabeth I, he rose in the Church of England to be (1577) bishop of London. Though he was a man of great learning, his harsh treatment of his foes made him generally disliked.

Aymara (īmärä'), South American Indians inhabiting the Lake Titicaca basin in Peru and Bolivia. They are believed to have been the originators of the great culture represented by the ruins of TIAHUANACO. Although subjugated by the INCA in the 15th cent. after a long struggle, the Aymara continue to dominate the region. The Aymara languages make up a separate unit; they are spoken in Peru and Bolivia in the Titicaca region. The Aymara, conquered (1538) by Hernando and Gonzalo Pizarro, retained their pastoral and agricultural civilization. In general, social organization was, and still is, based on the patrilineal family unit. Contemporary Aymara and the related Quechua peasant culture is a blend of aboriginal, Spanish colonial, and modern elements. See Harold Osborne, *Indians of the Andes, Aymaras and Quechuas* (1952); Julian Steward, ed., *Handbook of South American Indians,* Vol. II (1963); Hans and Judith-Maria Buechler, *The Bolivian Aymara* (1971).

Aymé, Marcel (märsĕl' āmā'), 1902-67, French writer. Aymé's *La Table aux crevés* (1929), a story of peasant life, typifies the satirical tone of his works. *La Jument verte* (1933, tr. *The Green Mare,* 1955) and *Les Tiroirs de l'inconnu* (1960, tr. *The Conscience of Love,* 1962) contain elements of fantasy and biting commentary on modern values. Aymé wrote several superb volumes of tales for children, including *Les Contes du chat perché* (1934, tr. *The Wonderful Farm,* 1951). Among his plays are *Clérambard* (1949, tr. 1952) and *La Tête des autres* (1952). Two collections of his short stories are *Across Paris* (tr. 1958) and *The Proverb* (tr. 1961). See study by D. R. Brodin (1968).

Aymer of Valence (ā'mər, vəlĕns', väläNs'), d. 1260, bishop of Winchester; son of Isabella (widow of

King John of England) and Hugh X, count of La Marche. He was thus half brother of King Henry III of England. He is sometimes called Æthelmar. With his French brothers he went to England in 1247. Henry forced the chapter of Winchester to elect Aymer bishop in 1250, but his youth and ignorance, combined with his disinclination to assume the responsibilities along with the revenues of office, delayed his consecration. He was one of the king's 12 delegates in formulating the PROVISIONS OF OXFORD. However, he refused to swear to them, and hostility toward him and his brothers was an important factor in the BARONS' WAR. Later he and his brothers had to flee to the Continent. But although the Winchester chapter had chosen a new candidate, Aymer was consecrated by the pope in 1260 and was on his way back to England when he died in Paris.

Aymer of Valence, earl of Pembroke: see PEMBROKE, AYMER DE VALENCE, EARL OF.

Ayolas, Juan de (hwän dā äyō'läs), d. 1537?, Spanish conquistador, explorer of the Río de la Plata country. He accompanied Pedro de MENDOZA on his expedition of 1535–36. Sent to look for provisions, he sailed up the Paraná River and founded a fort called Corpus Christi. Later, leaving Domingo Martínez de Irala at a port called Candelaria, he went up the Paraguay River in search of a route to Peru. He fought the Guaraní Indians, possibly at the site of Asunción, crossed the Chaco plain to the mountains, and is said to have been killed by the Indians on his return to Candelaria.

Ayr (âr), burgh (1971 pop. 47,884), county town of Ayrshire, SW Scotland, at the mouth of the Ayr River on the Firth of Clyde. Ayr is a sea resort and a port for fishing and the export of coal. It manufactures farm and mining machinery, carpets, asphalt, and shoes. Oliver CROMWELL built a 12-acre (5-hectare) fort around St. John's Church when he garrisoned Ayr in 1652. In the heart of the Robert BURNS country, Ayr has various Burns memorials, as well as associations with Sir William WALLACE and Robert I of Scotland. In 1975, Ayr became part of the new Strathclyde region.

Ayrshire (âr'shĭr, -shər) or **Ayr,** county (1971 pop. 361,074), 1,132 sq mi (2,932 sq km), SW Scotland, on the Firth of Clyde. AYR is the county town. N Ayrshire, lying in the midland industrial belt, has iron and oil deposits and varied industries. There is a nuclear power station at Hunterston. Farming is pursued in central and S Ayrshire, where potatoes and the famous Ayrshire cattle are raised. Ayrshire belonged to the kingdoms of STRATHCLYDE and NORTHUMBRIA and was the scene of the early exploits of the Scots leaders Sir William WALLACE and ROBERT I. The poet Robert Burns was born in Alloway, now part of Ayr. Under the Local Government Act of 1973, Ayrshire became (1975) part of the Strathclyde region.

Ayrshire cattle (âr'shēr, -shər), breed of dairy cattle originated in Scotland in the latter part of the 18th cent.; they are of medium size and vary in body color from almost pure white to nearly solid cherry-red or brown, as well as any combination of these colors. Ayrshires have excellent grazing qualities, are good, uniform producers of milk, and rank high among the dairy breeds as veal and beef producers. They are raised in Canada, the NE United States, Europe, South Africa, Australia, New Zealand, and Central America. First imported in 1837, there are now an estimated 150,000 registered Ayrshire cattle in the United States.

Ayton or **Aytoun, Sir Robert** (both: ā'tən), 1570–1638, English poet and courtier. He was private secretary to the queens of James I and Charles I, besides holding other posts of honor. He wrote poems in French, Greek, and Latin, of which only the latter are preserved. His verse in English is marked by courtly elegance and delicacy.

Aytoun, William Edmonstoune (ā'to͞on), 1813–65, Scottish poet. He was (1845–64) professor of belles-lettres at Edinburgh Univ. The *Bon Gaultier Ballads* (written with Sir Theodore Martin, 1845) parodied poems by Macaulay, Tennyson, and others. His best-known poem, *Firmilian* (1854), burlesqued the chaotic, bombastic poetry being written in his day.

Ayub Khan, Muhammad (məhăm'ĭd ä'yo͝ob kän), 1907–74, military leader and president (1958–69) of Pakistan. He was commissioned in the British Indian army in 1928 and saw active service as a battalion commander in World War II. After 1947, when the state of Pakistan was created, he assumed command of military forces in East Pakistan (now Bangladesh), and in 1951 he became commander in chief of the Pakistan army. He served (1954–56) as defense minister. In 1958, after a military coup d'etat and the abrogation of the constitution, Ayub Khan became president; he was confirmed in office by a referendum (Feb., 1960). Ayub Khan launched a vigorous program of land reform and economic development. He also inaugurated a system of what he called "basic democracies," tiers of local government councils that also served as electoral colleges. Martial law was lifted in 1962, and a new constitution of that year gave the executive enormous powers. Ayub Khan was reelected in 1965, defeating Fatimah Jinnah, daughter of the founder of Pakistan. In the same year he led the nation in war with India, but the conflict was ended by the Tashkent Declaration of Jan., 1966. Despite considerable economic growth, continuing economic and social inequalities, the disadvantaged position of East Pakistan, and limitation of civil liberties provoked increasing discontent with Ayub Khan's regime. Early in 1969, Ayub Khan apparently bowed to the pressure of opposition in announcing that he would not seek re-election in 1970. Unrest continued, however, and in March, 1969, he resigned power to a martial law government headed by Gen. Muhammad Yahya Khan. See his *Speeches and Statements* (8 vol., 1959–66) and *Friends, Not Masters: A Political Autobiography* (1967); study by Lawrence Ziring (1971).

Ayuthia: see AYUTTHAYA, Thailand.

Ayutla (äyo͞ot'lä), town (1970 pop. 23,668), Guerrero state, S Mexico. Its full name is Ayutla de los Libres [Ayutla of the free]. It is the commercial center for an agricultural, cattle-raising, and lumbering area. The Plan of Ayutla, drawn up in 1854, was a reform program directed toward removing the dictator Santa Anna and convening a constituent assembly to frame a federal constitution. Preparing the way for the War of Reform (1856–61), the plan and the subsequent Revolution of Ayutla (which exiled Santa Anna and established a liberal government) was initially supported by Juan Álvarez, Ignacio Comonfort, Miguel and Sebastián Lerdo de Tejada, and Benito Juárez.

Ayutthaya (äyo͞otī'ə) or **Phra Nakhon Si Ayutthaya** (prä näkôn' sē), city (1965 est. pop. 40,000), capital of Ayutthaya prov., S central Thailand, on the Chao Phraya River. It is the trade center for a prosperous rice-growing region. Ayutthaya was the capital of a Thai kingdom founded c.1350 and was located on the site of a Khmer settlement. Destroyed by the Burmese in 1559, it was rebuilt by the Siamese in the late 16th cent. but was again devastated by the Burmese in 1767, after which the capital was moved to Thon Buri and then to Bangkok. Ayutthaya has some of the few monuments of early Siamese civilization, notably the royal palace (16th cent.) and numerous temples and pagodas.

Azal (ā'zăl), name of uncertain meaning in an apocalyptic passage. Zech. 14.5.

azalea (əzāl'yə) [Gr.,=dry], any species of the genus *Rhododendron*, North American and Asian shrubs of the family Ericaceae (HEATH family) that are distinguished by the usually deciduous leaves. Azaleas are handsome shrubs with large clusters of pink, red, orange, yellow, purple, or white flowers. The better-known native American azaleas, often cultivated, include the flame azalea (*R. calendulacea*) of the Appalachians; the pinxter flower (*R. nudiflora*) and the fragrant white azalea, or swamp honeysuckle (*R. viscosa*), of the E United States; and the Western azalea (*R. occidentalis*) of California and Oregon. Most azaleas grow in damp, acid soils of hills or mountains. The rose-purple *R. canadense*, a rare species with an unusually northerly range (from Pennsylvania to Newfoundland) is the rhodora immortalized by Emerson. Many of the brilliantly flowered garden varieties are native to China and Japan, where the genus is most abundantly represented. The popular Ghent azaleas are hybrids. Dwarf azaleas are grown by florists as pot plants. Azaleas are classified in the division MAGNOLIOPHYTA, class Magnoliopsida, order Ericales, family Ericaceae.

Azaliah (ăzəlī'ə), father of SHAPHAN **1.** 2 Kings 22.3; 2 Chron. 34.8.

Azaña, Manuel (mänwĕl' äthä'nyä), 1880–1940, Spanish statesman. An author and critic, he gained prominence as president (1930) of the Madrid Ateneo, a literary and political club, and came to the fore as a revolutionary political leader in 1931. He was minister of war in the first republican cabinet, and premier (1931–33) under President Alcalá Zamora. While premier, he pressed for social, military, and educational reforms. After the victory of the Popular Front in the Feb., 1936, elections, he again became premier, and in May, 1936, after the ousting of Alcalá Zamora, he was elected president. He headed the Loyalist government through the civil war, in which he did not, however, play an important role. In Feb., 1939, he fled to France just before organized Loyalist resistance in Spain collapsed.

Azaniah (ăz"ənī'ə), Levite. Neh. 10.9.

Azanza, Miguel José de (mēgĕl' hōsā' dā äthän'thä), 1746–1826, Spanish general and colonial administrator. After brief service in the cabinet of Charles IV, he was sent to the colonies and became viceroy of Mexico (1798–1800). He returned to Spain, served under Joseph Bonaparte, and fled to France after the fall of the Bonaparte regime.

Azarael (āzăr'āĕl), musician. Neh. 12.36.

Azareel (āzăr'ēĕl). **1** One of David's warriors. 1 Chron. 12.6. **2** Musician. 1 Chron. 25.18. Uzziel: 1 Chron. 25.4. **3** Prince. 1 Chron. 27.22. **4** Jew married to a foreign wife. Ezra 10.41. **5** Priest. Neh. 11.13.

Azariah (ăzərī'ə), common name in ancient Israel, especially among the priests. The following are not necessarily all different persons. **1** Chief officer under Solomon. 1 Kings 4.2; 1 Chron. 6.9. **2** Chief officer under Solomon. 1 Kings 4.5. **3,4** Judahites. 1 Chron. 2.8,38,39. **5** Kohathite Levite. 1 Chron. 6.36. Uzziah: 1 Chron. 6.24. **6** High priest. 1 Chron. 6.10,11. **7** Father of SERAIAH **2.** 1 Chron. 6.13,14. **8** Prophet who stirred King Asa to reform. 2 Chron. 15. **9** King of Judah: see UZZIAH **1**. **10** Same as AHAZIAH **2.** **11** High priest who withstood King Uzziah. 2 Chron. 26.17–20. **12** High priest under Hezekiah. 2 Chron. 31.10–13. **13,14** Levites. 2 Chron. 29.12. **15,16** Sons of King Jehoshaphat. 2 Chron. 21.2. **17,18** Aides of Jehoiada in the conspiracy against Athaliah. 2 Chron. 23.1. **19** Ephraimite leader. 2 Chron. 28.12. **20** Worker on the wall of Jerusalem. Neh. 3.23,24. **21** Same as SERAIAH **7**. **22** Interpreter of the law. Neh. 8.7. **23** Sealer of the covenant. Neh. 10.2. **24** Priest in postexilic Jerusalem. 1 Chron. 9.11. Seraiah: Neh. 11.11. **25** See JAAZANIAH. **26** One of the THREE HOLY CHILDREN. Azarias is the Greek form of his name.

azathioprine: see METABOLITE.

Azay-le-Rideau (äzā'-lə-rēdō'), village (1968 pop. 2,755), Indre-et-Loire dept., N central France, in Touraine. It is the center of a wine-producing area and has a canning industry. Its famous Renaissance château (1518–29), set in a beautiful park on the Indre River, now houses a museum of Renaissance furniture and art.

Azaz (ā'zăz), descendant of Reuben. 1 Chron. 5.8.

Azazel (əzā'zəl, ăz'əzĕl), in the Bible, an obscure term of the ritual of the scapegoat. Lev. 16 RSV. Azazel may be the name of the scapegoat or of a desert demon to whom the scapegoat was sent. The name was later applied to one of the fallen angels. KJV translates Azazel as "the scapegoat."

Azaziah (ăz"əzī'ə). **1** Musician. 1 Chron. 15.21. **2** Ephraimite. 1 Chron. 27.20. **3** Overseer of the Temple. 2 Chron. 31.13. **Azbuk** (ăz'bək), father of Nehemiah. Neh. 3.16.

Azbuk (ăz'bək), father of Nehemiah. Neh. 3.16.

Azcapotzalco (äskäpōtsäl'kō), city (1970 pop. 545,513), S Mexico, in the Federal District. An important rail center, with railroad yards, it is the terminus of mail and cargo traffic. Cereals and beans are grown in the area. Azcapotzalco's cattle industry supplies the bulk of Mexico City's dairy products. Other industries include auto assembling, oil refining, and the manufacture of textiles, paper, and records. The city was a leading cultural center in the pre-Columbian period. During Mexico's War of Independence, it was the site (1821) of a major battle in which loyalist troops were forced to retreat by the revolutionary soldiers. Azcapotzalco is noted for its baroque colonial architecture and its 18th-century churches.

Azeglio, Massimo Taparelli, marchese d' (mäs'sēmō täpärĕl'lē märkā'zā dädzā'lyō), 1798–1866, Italian premier and author, b. Turin. He studied painting, then turned to literature and wrote two historical novels, *Ettore Fieramosca* (1833) and *Niccolò de Lapi* (1841). In 1845 he became a leader of the movement for national liberation. He urged a more unified policy but strongly opposed secret conspiracies and violent outbreaks. In his pamphlets he denounced the papal government and condemned Austria's ruthless repression of Italian liberals. He influenced King Charles Albert of Sardinia and fought (1848) against Austria, being wounded at Vicenza. In 1849 the new king, Victor Emmanuel II, made him premier, a post he held until 1852, when he was succeeded by the more radical Cavour. His autobiography throws much light on the Risorgimento.

Azekah (əzē'kə), ancient city of Palestine, lying W of Jerusalem. Joshua 10.10,11; 1 Sam. 17.1; 2 Chron. 11.9; Neh. 11.30; Jer. 34.7.

Azel (ā'zĕl), descendant of Saul. 1 Chron. 8.37,38; 9.43,44.

Azem (ā'zĕm), unidentified town of S Palestine. Joshua 15.29; 19.3. Ezem: 1 Chron. 4.29.

Azerbaidzhan: see AZERBAIJAN SOVIET SOCIALIST REPUBLIC, USSR.

Azerbaijan (ä"zĕrbījän', ă"zər-), region, c.41,160 sq mi (106,600 sq km), NW Iran, divided into the provinces of **East Azerbaijan** (1966 pop. 2,596,439) and **West Azerbaijan** (1966 pop. 1,087,182). The chief cities include TABRIZ (the capital of East Azerbaijan), REZAIYEH (the capital of West Azerbaijan), ARDEBIL, MARAGHEH, and KHVOY. The region is bounded in the N by the Armenian and Azerbaijan Soviet Socialist Republics (from which it is separated by the Aras River) and in the W by Turkey and Iraq. Azerbaijan, which includes Lake Rezaiyeh, is mountainous, with deep valleys and fertile lowlands. Grains, fruits, cotton, and tobacco are grown, and wool is produced. The region has deposits of copper, lead, and iron. There is little modern industry. In ancient times Azerbaijan was dominated by the kings of Van and Urartu (in ARMENIA). By the 8th cent. B.C. it had been settled by the Medes (see MEDIA), and it later formed the province of Media Minor in the Persian Empire. Azerbaijan is the traditional birthplace (7th cent. B.C.) of Zoroaster, the religious teacher and prophet. After Alexander the Great conquered Persia, he appointed (328 B.C.) as governor the Persian general Atropates, who eventually established an independent dynasty. Later, the region, which came to be called Atropatene or Media Atropatene, was much disputed. In the 2d cent. B.C. it was taken by the Parthian Mithradates I, and c.226 A.D. it was captured by the Sassanian Ardashir I. Shapur II enlarged Azerbaijan by adding territory in the north. Heraclius, the Byzantine emperor, briefly held the region in the 7th cent., just before the Arabs conquered it, and he converted most of its people to Islam and made it part of the caliphate. The Seljuk Turks dominated the region in the 11th and 12th cent., and the Mongols under Hulagu Khan established (13th cent.) their capital at Maragheh. After being conquered by Tamerlane in the 14th cent., Tabriz became an important provincial capital of the Timurid empire. It was out of Ardebil that the Safavid dynasty arose (c.1500) to renew the state of Persia. There was fierce fighting between the Ottoman Empire and Persia for Azerbaijan. After brief Ottoman control, Abbas I, shah of Persia, regained control of the region in 1603; it remained entirely in the possession of the shahs until the northern part was ceded to Russia in the treaties of Gulistan (1813) and Turkmanchai (1828). The remainder was organized as a province of Persia; in 1938 the province was divided into two parts. In 1941, Soviet troops occupied Iranian Azerbaijan; they were withdrawn (May, 1946) after a Soviet-supported autonomous local government had been created. Iranian troops occupied the region in Nov., 1946, and the autonomous movement was suppressed. The majority of the people of Azerbaijan are Turkic-speaking Azers, or Azerbaijani, who are Shiite Muslims. There are also some Armenians, Kurds, Jews, and Persians.

Azerbaijan Soviet Socialist Republic or **Azerbaidzhan** (both: ä"zərbījän', ă"zər-, Rus. äzĭrbījän'), constituent republic (1970 pop. 5,111,000), 33,428 sq mi (86,579 sq km), SE European USSR, in Transcaucasia. BAKU is the capital; other major cities include KIROVABAD and SUMGAIT. Strategically situated at the USSR's gateway to SW Asia, Azerbaijan is bounded by Iran on the south, where the Aras (Araks) River divides it from Iranian Azerbaijan; by the Caspian Sea on the east; by the Dagestan Autonomous Republic on the north; and by the Armenian Republic on the west. The republic includes the Nakhichevan Autonomous Republic (separated from Azerbaijan proper by Armenia) and the Nagorno-Karabakh Autonomous Oblast. Azerbaijan occupies the western ranges of the Greater and Lesser Caucasus and the Kura River valley, which is the region's chief agricultural zone. Wheat, barley, corn, fruits, wine grapes, and potatoes are the leading food crops, and cotton, silk, and tobacco the foremost industrial crops. The subtropical Lenkoran lowland supports tea and rice. The Apsheron peninsula is one of the richest oil regions of the world. The republic's other mineral resources include natural gas, iron, copper, lead, zinc, limestone, pyrites, cobalt, and alunite. Widespread salt springs have enabled health resorts to flourish. Among the republic's chief manufactures are machinery, electrical equipment, building materials (especially cement), steel, aluminum, chemicals, and textiles. The old craft of carpet weaving is still practiced. The Azerbaijani, a Turkic-speaking, Shiite Muslim people of Persian culture, make up more than half the republic's population; Russians and Armenians are the largest minorities. The Azerbaijan SSR comprises the Transcaucasian or northern part of the historic region called AZERBAIJAN. Known to the ancients as Albania, the area was linked to the history of Armenia and Persia, particularly after its conquest (4th cent.) by Shapur II. Overrun later by Mongols, it was divided after the fall (15th cent.) of Tamerlane into several principalities (notably Shirvan). The territory of the present Azerbaijan SSR was acquired by Russia from Persia through the treaties of Gulistan (1813) and Turkamanchai (1828). Soon after the Bolshevik Revolution of 1917, Russian Azerbaijan joined Armenia and Georgia to form the anti-Bolshevik Transcaucasian Federation. After its dissolution (May, 1918), Azerbaijan proclaimed itself independent but was conquered by the Red Army in 1920 and made into a Soviet republic. In 1922, Azerbaijan joined the USSR as a member of the Transcaucasian Soviet Federated Republic. With the administrative reorganization of 1936, it became a separate republic. Immediately after World War II, Azerbaijan was used as a base for Communist rebels in Iranian Azerbaijan. The republic's educational institutions include Baku Univ. and the Azerbaijan Academy of Sciences.

Azgad (ăz'găd), family in the return to Palestine. Ezra 2.12; 8.12; Neh. 7.17; 10.15.

Aziel (ā'zēĕl), in the Bible, shorter form of JAAZIEL.

Azikiwe, Benjamin Nnamdi (näm'dē äzē'kwä), 1904–, Nigerian statesman, popularly known as Zik. He undertook (1925) advanced studies in the United States and eventually returned to Nigeria, where he founded a chain of newspapers and became one of the country's leading Ibo nationalists. He led a general strike in 1945 and later held a number of important posts, including the premiership (1954–59) of E Nigeria. Always a controversial figure, he was involved in financial and political scandals. During the 1959 elections he made an alliance with the National Peoples Congress, and, although the coalition won, he was appointed (1960) to the largely honorary office of governor general. In 1963 he became the first president of the republic of Nigeria, serving until his retirement in 1966.

Azilian: see MESOLITHIC PERIOD.

azimuth (ăz'əməth), in astronomy, one coordinate in the HORIZON COORDINATE SYSTEM. It is the angular distance of a body measured westward along the celestial horizon from the observer's south point.

azine (ăz'ēn), IUPAC name for PYRIDINE.

Aziza (əzī'zə), Jew who had a foreign wife. Ezra 10.27.

Azizia: see AL AZIZIYAH, Libya.

Azmaveth (ăzmā'vĕth). **1** One of David's mighty men. 2 Sam. 23.31; 1 Chron. 11.33. **2** David's treasurer, perhaps the same as **1**. 1 Chron. 27.25. **3** Father of two of David's warriors. 1 Chron. 12.3. He may be the same as **1** or **2**, or the name may refer to **5**. **4** Descendant of Saul. 1 Chron. 8.36; 9.42. **5** Town, S Palestine. Ezra 2.24; Neh. 12.29. Beth-azmaveth: Neh. 7.28.

Azmon (ăz'mŏn), town of S Palestine. Num. 34.4,5; Joshua 15.4.

Aznoth-tabor (ăz'nŏth-tā'bər), place, on the boundary of Naphtali, probably N of Mt. Tabor. Joshua 19.34.

Azor (ā'zôr), man in the Gospel genealogy. Mat. 1.13.

Azores (əzôrz', ā'zôrz), Port. *Açores* [Port.,=hawks], islands (1970 est. pop. 336,100), 905 sq mi (2,344 sq km), in the Atlantic Ocean, c.900 mi (1,448 km) W of mainland Portugal. Administratively a part of Portugal, they are divided into three districts named after their capitals: Ponta Delgada (on São Miguel), Angra do Heroísmo (on Terceira), and Horta (on Fayal). The nine main islands are São Miguel (the largest) and Santa Maria in the southeast; Terceira, Pico, Fayal, São Jorge, and Graciosa in the center; and Flores and Corvo in the northwest. Ponta Delgada is the largest city. The fertile soil yields many crops and supports vineyards. The islands are also a resort area. The Azores may have been known to the ancients and were included on a map in 1351. Portuguese sailors reached them in 1427 or 1431, but colonization did not begin until 1445 under Diogo de Sevilha or Gonçalo Velho Cabral (who may have been there in 1431). The islands were used as a place of exile and were also the site of naval battles between the English and the Spanish. In the 19th cent. they were used by supporters of Maria II against Dom Miguel. The United States maintains air bases on the islands.

Azorín: see MARTÍNEZ RUIZ, JOSÉ.

Azov (əzôf'), city (1970 pop. 59,000), SE European USSR, a port on the Don River delta near the Sea of Azov. It is a rail junction and a fishing center and has fish-processing plants. Founded as the Greek colony of Tanaïs (3d cent. B.C.), it was a trading center and fortress. It came under Kievan Russia in the 10th cent., was taken by the Cumans in the 11th cent., became a Genoese colony in the 13th cent., and passed to the Turks in 1471. The Don Cossacks held the city (1637–42), but were driven out by the Turks. Peter the Great won the city in 1696 and thus opened southern routes for Russia; he was forced to cede it back to Turkey in 1711. Russia took it again in 1736, but was forced by the Treaty of Belgrade to dismantle the fortress in 1739. Russia secured Azov definitively by the Treaty of Kuchuk-Kainarji in 1774.

Azov, Sea of, Gr. *Maiotis,* Lat. *Palus Maeotis,* ancient Rus. *Surozhskoye,* northern arm of the Black Sea, c.14,000 sq mi (36,300 sq km), S European USSR, in SE Ukraine. The shallow sea (maximum depth 50 ft/15 m) is connected with the Black Sea by the Kerch Strait. Its chief arms are the Gulf of Taganrog (in the northeast) and the Sivash Sea (in the west), which is nearly isolated from the Sea of Azov by Arabat Tongue, a narrow sandspit. The Don and Kuban rivers flow into the sea, supplying it with an abundance of fresh water but also depositing much silt that tends to make the sea more shallow. The Sea of Azov has important fisheries and accounts for a large portion of the Soviet freshwater catch. The major ports are Rostov-na-Donu, Taganrog, Zhdanov, Kerch, and Berdyansk. The sea's importance increased with the opening of the Volga-Don Canal; the Manych Canal connects the Sea of Azov with the Caspian Sea.

Azrael (ăz'rāĕl) [Heb.,=help of God], in the Koran, angel of death, who severs the soul from the body. The name and the concept were borrowed from Judaism.

Azriel (ăz'rēĕl). **1** Manassite. 1 Chron. 5.24. **2** Naphtalite. 1 Chron. 27.19. **3** Father of SERAIAH **9**.

Azrikam (ăz'rīkăm). **1** Man of the house of David. 1 Chron. 3.23. **2** Descendant of Saul. 1 Chron. 8.38; 9.44. **3** Levite. 1 Chron. 9.14; Neh. 11.15. **4** Chief of the royal household. 2 Chron. 28.7.

Aztec (ăz'tĕk"), Indian people dominating central Mexico at the time of the Spanish conquest. Their language belonged to the Nahuatlan subfamily of Uto-Aztecan languages. They arrived in the Valley of Mexico from the north toward the end of the 12th cent. and until the founding of their capital, TENOCHTITLÁN (c.1325) were a poor, nomadic tribe absorbing the culture of nearby states. For the next century they maintained a precarious political autonomy while paying tribute to neighboring tribes, but by alliance, treachery, and conquest during the 15th and early 16th cent. they became a powerful political and cultural group. To the north they established hegemony over the HUASTEC, to the south over the MIXTEC and ZAPOTEC and even ventured as far as Guatemala. Their subjugation of the people of Tlaxcala in the mountains to the east was bloody but only intermittent, and the Tlaxcala people later became allies of the Spanish against the Aztec. Only in the west, where the TARASCAN Indians severely defeated them, did the Aztec completely fail to conquer. By absorption of other cultural elements and by conquest the Aztec achieved a composite civilization, based on the heritage of TOLTEC and Mixteca-Puebla. They attained a high degree of development in engineering, architecture, art, mathematics, and astronomy. The Aztec calendar utilized a 260-day year and a 52-year time cycle. Aztec skill in engineering was evident in the fortifications of their island capital. The Aztec further developed sculpture, weaving, metalwork, ornamentation, music, and picture writing for historical records. Agriculture was well advanced and trade flourished. The political and social organization was based on three castes—nobility, priesthood, and military and merchant. The priesthood was a powerful political as well as religious force. Aztec government was relatively centralized, although many conquered chiefs retained political autonomy; they paid tribute and kept commerce open to the Aztec. The Aztec had a large and efficient army. Prisoners of war were used for human sacrifice to satisfy the many gods of the Aztec pantheon, notably HUITZILOPOCHTI, the chief god, who was god of war. When the Spaniards, under Hernán CORTÉS, arrived in 1519, the Aztec civilization was at its height. However, many subject Indian groups, rebellious against Aztec rule, were only too willing to join the Spanish. Initially, the invaders were aided by the fact that the Aztec believed them to be descendants of the god QUETZALCOATL. MONTEZUMA II, the last of the independent Aztec rulers, received Cortés, who made him prisoner and attempted to rule through him. The Aztec revolted, Montezuma was killed, and Tenochtitlán was razed (1521). CUAUHTÉMOC, last of the emperors, was murdered (1525) and the Spanish proceeded to subjugate Mexico. See Bernal Diaz del Castillo, *The Discovery and Conquest of Mexico* (tr. by A. P. Maudsley, 1928, repr. 1965); Alfonso Caso, *The Aztecs, People of the Sun* (tr. 1958, repr. 1967); Laurette Sejourné, *Burning Water: Thought and Religion in Ancient Mexico* (1961); Jacques Soustelle, *The Daily Life of the Aztecs on the Eve of the Spanish Conquest* (tr. 1961, repr. 1970); G. C. Vaillant, *The Aztecs of Mexico* (rev. ed. 1962); B. C. Brundage, *A Rain of Darts: The Mexican Aztecs* (1973).

Aztec Ruins National Monument, 27 acres (11 hectares), NW N.Mex., near Farmington; est. 1923. The ruins there of a 12th-century PUEBLO INDIAN town contain interesting KIVAS, one of which has been completely restored. Pueblo Indian culture reached a high level of achievement in this area. The ruins were named by early settlers who mistakenly believed that they were built by the Aztec Indians.

Azubah (əzyo͞o'bə). **1** Wife of Caleb. 1 Chron. 2.18. **2** Mother of Jehoshaphat. 1 Kings 22.42; 2 Chron. 20.31.

Azuela, Mariano (märyä'nō äswā'lä), 1873–1952, Mexican novelist. Azuela began his medical practice in 1899, writing short stories and novels in his spare time. In 1915 he joined Francisco Villa's revolutionary forces as a surgeon. From this experience came his modern classic, *Los de abajo* (1915, tr. *The Underdogs,* 1929), which depicts the military exploitation of the Indian. The novel is composed of linked sketches that are starkly realistic. After Villa's defeat Azuela took refuge in Texas. Returning to Mexico in 1916, he resumed his medical practice and his writing, taking little interest in politics. Among his later novels are *María Luisa* (1907); *Los fracasados* [the defeated] (1908); *Mala yerba* (1909); *Los caciques* (1917, tr. *The Bosses,* 1956); *Las moscas* (1918, tr. *The Flies,* 1956); and *San Gabriel de Valdivias* (1938).

Azur (ā'zər). **1** Father of HANANIAH **2.** **2** Father of JAAZANIAH **4.**

azurite (ăzh'ərīt), blue mineral, the basic carbonate of copper, occurring in monoclinic crystals or masses that range from transparent to translucent and opaque. It is usually associated with MALACHITE, which it resembles except in color; when the two minerals are very closely associated, the stone is called azurmalachite. Beautiful crystals of azurite are found in the United States in Arizona and New Mexico and in France at Chessy (for which the mineral is sometimes called chessylite); they are used for ornamental purposes. The mineral is an important ore of copper.

Azusa (əzo͞o'sə), city (1970 pop. 25,217), Los Angeles co., S Calif., in the San Gabriel valley; inc. 1898. It is a residential and industrial city in a citrus-fruit growing area. Its manufactures include aircraft components, electronic equipment, chemicals, lawn mowers, bicycles, and beer. Azusa has a large Mexican-American population. Azusa Pacific College and Citrus College are in the city.

Azzah (ăz'ə), variant of GAZA.

Azzan (ăz'ăn), man of Issachar. Num. 34.26.

Azzur (ăz'ər), sealer of the covenant. Neh. 10.17.

B

B, second letter of the ALPHABET. Its Greek correspondent is named beta. It is a usual symbol for a voiced bilabial stop. In MUSICAL NOTATION it is used to represent a note in the scale. In chemistry B is the symbol of the element BORON.

Ba, chemical symbol of the element BARIUM.

Baade, Walter (väl'tər bä'də), 1893–1960, German astronomer. From 1919 to 1931 he was on the staff of the Hamburg observatory; from 1931 to 1958, at the Mt. Wilson observatory. He presented evidence for the existence of two different STELLAR POPULATIONS of older and newer stars. After observations through the 200-in. reflecting telescope at the Mt. Palomar Observatory, his recalculations showed that it was necessary to double the cosmic-distance scale, i.e., the distances between extragalactic bodies and the MILKY WAY but not the distances within the Milky Way itself.

Baal (bā'əl), plural **Baalim** (bā'əlĭm) [Semitic,=possessor], name used throughout the Old Testament for the deity or deities of Canaan. The term was originally applied to various local gods, but by the time of the Ugarit tablets (14th cent. B.C.; see UGARIT), Baal had become the ruler of the universe. The Ugarit tablets make him chief of the Canaanite pantheon. He is the source of life and fertility, the mightiest hero, and the lord of war. There were many temples of Baal in Canaan, and the name Baal was often added to that of a locality, e.g., Baal-peor, Baal-hazor, Baal-hermon. The Baal cult penetrated Israel and at times led to a syncretism. The practices of holy prostitution and child sacrifice were especially abhorrent to the Hebrew prophets, who denounced the cult and its "high places" (temples). This abhorrence probably explains the substitution of Ish-bosheth for Esh-baal, of Jerubbesheth for Jerubbaal (a name of Gideon), and of Mephibosheth for Merib-baal. The substituted term probably means "shame." The final detestation of the term is seen in the use of the name Beelzebub (see SATAN), probably the same as Baal-zebub. 1 Kings 11.4–8; 2 Kings 1. The Baal of 1 Chron. 4.33 is probably the same as RAMAH **3.** As cognates of Baal in other Semitic languages there are Bel (in Babylonian religion) and the last elements in the Tyrian names Jezebel, Hasdrubal, and Hannibal.

Baalah (bā'ələ) [Heb., fem. of Baal]. **1** The same as BILHAH **2.** **2** The same as KIRJATH-JEARIM. **3** Unidentified mountain, in the vicinity of Jamnia. Joshua 15,11.

Baalath (bā'əlăth) [Heb., fem. of Baal]. **1** Town of Dan. Joshua 19.44. **2** Unidentified city. 1 Kings 9.18; 2 Chron. 8.6.

Baalath-beer (bā'əlăth-bē'ər), apparently the same as RAMAH **3.**

Baalbek (bäl'bĕk), ancient city, now in Lebanon, 35 mi (56 km) NW of Damascus. Originally it was probably devoted to the worship of Baal or Bel, the Phoenician sun god, although no traces of an early Phoenician settlement have survived. The Greeks called the city Heliopolis [city of the sun]. It became very prominent in Roman days and was made a separate colony by Augustus. Both Greek and Roman architects employed their genius on Baalbek's buildings. Among the most imposing Roman remains are the temple of Bacchus and the temple of Jupiter. The city was sacked by invaders and was destroyed by an earthquake in 1759.

Baal-berith (bā'əl-bē'rĭth), local god of Shechem. Judges 8.33; 9.4. Berith: Judges 9.46.

Baale (bā'əlē) [Heb., fem. of Baal], the same as KIRJATH-JEARIM.

Baal-gad (bā'əl-găd'), place at the foot of Mt. Hermon. It represented the northern limit of Joshua's conquest. Gad apparently refers to a god of fortune. Joshua 11.17; 12.7; 13.5.

Baal-hamon (bā'əl-hā'mŏn), location of Solomon's vineyard. Song 8.11.

Baal-hanan (bā'əl-hā'năn). **1** King of Edom. Gen. 36.38,39; 1 Chron. 1.49,50. **2** One of David's officers. 1 Chron. 27.28.

Baal-hazor (bā'əl-hā'zôr), holy place where Absalom's servant killed Amnon. 2 Sam. 13.23.

Baal-hermon (bā'əl-hûr'mən): see HERMON, MOUNT.

Baali (bā'əlī), title of God that is to be used no longer by Israel. Hosea 2.16,17.

Baalim (bā'əlĭm), plural of BAAL.

Baalis (bā'əlĭs), king of the Ammonites, contemporary with Jeremiah. Jer. 40.14.

Baal-meon: see BETH-BAAL-MEON.

Baal-peor (bā'əl-pē'ôr), local divinity of Peor. One of the apostasies of Israel involved this god; apparently the cult was orgiastic, and the name became symbolic of all shameful apostasies. Num. 25; Deut. 4.3; Ps. 106.28; Hosea 9.10. Peor: Num. 25.18; 31.16; Joshua 22.17. The god's name appears in BETH-PEOR. Under the form Belphegor, the name became that of a devil in the Middle Ages; Machiavelli used it in his *Belfagor.*

Baal-perazim (bā'əl-pĕr'əzĭm), unidentified place where David defeated the Philistines. 2 Sam. 5.20; 1 Chron. 14.11. Perizim of Isa. 28.21 is probably the same.

Baal-shalisha (bā'əl-shăl'ĭshə), place perhaps in SHALISHA. 2 Kings 4.42.

Baal-Shem-Tov (bäl-shĕm-tôv), c.1698–1760, Jewish founder of modern HASIDISM, b. Russia. His life is the subject of many legendary tales, which circulated even before his death and which may be based in part upon a fictional collection of tales published in Yiddish in the 17th cent. Originally named Israel ben Eliezer, he is said to have been born of elderly, poor parents and to have been orphaned at an early age. He later supported himself variously as an assistant in a heder (Hebrew religious school), as a synagogue watchman, as a quarry worker, and as an innkeeper. He gained a reputation as a miracle healer; hence the name Baal-Shem-Tov [Heb.,=master of the good name, i.e., the Name of God]. Central to his teachings was the notion that one must worship and adhere to God in all activities, both in acts of prescribed religious observance and in the affairs of daily life. He further held that not in sorrow but in joy must one worship God, and that repentance is always possible. It appears that his reputation as a miracle healer and his basic orientation to religious life, which allowed the unschooled as well as the scholar to experience a sense of his redemption, gained for him a large circle of followers, out of which developed the several communities of contemporary Hasidim. See Martin Buber, *Legend of the Ba'al Shem* (tr. 1955, repr. 1969) and *Tales of the Hasidim* (tr., 2 vol., 1947–48, repr. 1961); D. Ben Amos and J. R. Mintz, ed., *In Praise of the Baal Shem Tov* (tr. 1970).

Baal-tamar (bā'əl-tā'mär), unidentified place near Gibeah. Judges 20.33.

Baal-zebub (bā'əl-zē'bəb), god of Ekron: see BAAL and SATAN.

Baal-zephon (bā'əl-zē'fŏn), place near the Israelites' crossing of the Red Sea: Ex. 14.2, 9; Num. 33.7.

Baana or **Baanah** (both: bā'ənə). **1** Murderer of Ish-bosheth. 2 Sam. 4.1–12. **2** Father of HELEB. **3** Officer under Solomon. 1 Kings 4.12. **4** Officer under Solomon. 1 Kings 4.16. **5** One who returned with Zerubbabel, apparently the father of ZADOK **6.** Ezra 2.2; Neh. 7.7; 10.27.

Baara (bā'ārə), wife of SHAHARAIM.

Baarle-Hertog (bär'lə-hĕr'tōkh), Fr. *Baerle-Duc,* town (1970 pop. 2,146), Antwerp prov., N Belgium. A Belgian possession since 1479, it is now an enclave (3 sq mi/7.8 sq km) in S Netherlands. The sovereignty of its outlying districts was disputed by the Dutch, but was settled (1959) in favor of Belgium by the International Court of Justice.

Baaseiah (bā"əsē'yə), Levite. 1 Chron. 6.40.

Baasha (bā'āshə), king of Israel. He made himself king by the murder of King Nadab and the royal family. According to the Bible he was a wicked man; he fought against ASA of Judah, who won with the aid of Benhadad of Syria. Baasha was succeeded by his son Elah. 1 Kings. 15.27–34; 16.1–13; 2 Chron. 16.

Ba'ath party (bä'äth), Arab political party, in Syria and Iraq. Its main ideological objectives are socialism and pan-Arab union. Founded in Damascus in 1941 and reformed, with the name Ba'ath, in the early 1950s, it rapidly achieved political power in Syria. In 1958—with one of its founders, Salah al-Din Bitar, as foreign minister—it led Syria into the ill-fated United Arab Republic (UAR) with Egypt. The Ba'athists, like most other Syrians, quickly came to resent Egyptian domination, and the Ba'athist members of the union government resigned in Dec., 1959. Syria withdrew from the UAR in 1961. In 1963 a military coup d'etat restored the Ba'ath to power, and it embarked on a course of large-scale nationalization. From 1963 the Ba'ath was the only legal political party in Syria, but factionalism and splintering within the party led to a succession of governments and new constitutions. In 1966 a military junta representing the more radical elements in the party displaced the more moderate wing in power, purging from the party its original founders, Michel Aflaq and Bitar. Subsequently the main line of division was drawn between the so-called progressive faction, led by Nureddin Atassi, which gave priority to the firm establishment of a one-party state and to neo-Marxist economic reform, and the so-called nationalist group, led by Gen. Hafez al-ASSAD, which was less doctrinaire about socialism but favored a militant posture on Arab union and hostility toward Israel. Despite constant maneuvering and government changes, the two factions remained in an uneasy coalition of power until 1970, when, in another coup, Assad succeeded in ousting Atassi as prime minister. In Iraq the Ba'athists first came to power in the coup d'etat of Feb., 1963, when Abdal Salem Arif became president. Interference from the Syrian Ba'athists and disputes between the moderates and extremists, culminating in an attempted coup by the latter in Nov., 1963, served to discredit the extremists. However, the moderates continued to play a major role in the succeeding governments. In July, 1968, a bloodless coup brought to power the Ba'athist general Ahmad Hassan al-BAKR. Wranglings within the party continued, and the government periodically purged its dissident members. Relations between the Ba'athist regimes of Syria and Iraq have frequently been strained. See IRAQ; SYRIA.

Bab: see BABISM.

Babar: see BABUR.

Babbage, Charles (băb'ĭj), 1792–1871, English mathematician and inventor. He devoted most of his life and expended much of his private fortune and a government subsidy in an attempt to perfect a mechanical calculating machine that foreshadowed present-day machines. He was a founder of the Royal Astronomical Society. He wrote *Tables of Logarithms* (1827) and an autobiography (1864). See biographies by Maboth Moseley (1970) and Dan Halacy (1970).

Babbitt, Irving, 1865–1933, American scholar, b. Dayton, Ohio. At Harvard as professor of French literature from 1912 until his death, he was a vigorous critic of romanticism, deprecating especially the influence of Rousseau on modern thought and art. He and Paul Elmer MORE initiated a movement, called New Humanism, that advocated a forceful doctrine of moderation and restraint, looking to classical traditions and literature for inspiration. His works include *Literature and the American College* (1908), *The New Laokoön* (1910), *The Masters of Modern French Criticism* (1912), and *On Being Creative* (1932). See F. E. McMahon, *The Humanism of Irving Babbitt* (1931); *Irving Babbitt* (ed. by Frederick Manchester and Odell Shepard, 1941, repr. 1969).

Babbitt, Milton, 1916–, American composer, b. Philadelphia. Babbitt turned to music after having begun the study of mathematics. He was a composition pupil of Roger Sessions at Princeton. Babbitt has attempted to apply 12-tone principles to all the elements of composition: dynamics, timbre, and rhythm, as well as melody and harmony. He calls this "total serialization" (see SERIAL MUSIC). In 1959, Babbitt became one of the directors of the new Columbia-Princeton Electronic Music Center in New York City. His works include *Three Compositions for Piano* (1947), three string quartets (1942, 1954, 1969-70), *Composition for Synthesizer* (1961), and *Philomel* (1964) for soprano, taped soprano, and synthesizer.

Babbitt metal, an antifriction metal first produced by Isaac Babbitt in 1839. In present-day usage the term is applied to a whole class of silver-white bearing metals, or "white metals." These alloys usually consist of relatively hard crystals embedded in a softer matrix, a structure important for machine bearings. They are composed primarily of tin, copper, and antimony, with traces of other metals added in some cases and lead substituted for tin in others.

babbler, common name for some members of the large, diversified family Timaliidae, passerine birds found primarily in wooded areas of Asia, Africa, and Australia. Babblers have soft, fluffy plumage and vary in coloring; various species resemble other birds, and five of the seven groups of babblers are named on this basis—the wren babblers, the tit babblers, the laughing thrushes, and the crow tits, or parrotbills. The wrentit, the only American babbler (found W of the Rockies), is believed to be an offshoot of the crow tits. Other groups are called ground babblers, found in Australia; jungle babblers, distributed in the Philippines; and rock fowl, found in W Africa. Babblers are insectivorous and, as their name suggests, are noisy birds. They are classified in the phylum CHORDATA, subphylum Vertebrata, class Aves, order Passeriformes, family Timaliidae.

Babcock, Stephen Moulton, 1843-1931, American agricultural chemist, b. Bridgewater, N.Y., grad. Tufts College (B.A., 1866), Univ. of Göttingen (Ph.D., 1879). He was, from 1887 to 1913, professor of agricultural chemistry at the Univ. of Wisconsin and chief chemist of the Wisconsin Agricultural Experiment Station. He is known chiefly for the Babcock test (perfected in 1890) for determining the percentage of butterfat in milk. The test advanced the modern dairy industry since it permits the rapid and accurate grading of milk at markets, discourages adulteration and thinning practices, and, by making practical the testing of the milk of individual cows, promotes the development of better dairy strains. His experimental studies in the food requirements of animals paved the way for the work of the American chemist E. V. McCollum on vitamin A. He invented an apparatus to determine the viscosity of liquids. The last two decades of his life were spent in basic research on the nature of matter and its relation to energy.

Babel, Isaac Emmanuelovich (ē'säk əmänōōā'ləvĭch bä'bəl), 1894-1941, Russian short-story writer and playwright. Babel won fame with *Odessa Tales* (1923-24), written in a Russo-Jewish jargon, and *Red Cavalry* (1926, tr. 1929), dramatic stories based on his life in the army and employing the racy slang of the Kuban Cossacks. A brilliant stylist, he combined astringent Jewish irony with Russian caricature. He turned to drama in *Sunset* (1928) and *Maria* (1935) and in the novel *Benia Krik* (1927, tr. 1935) about a famous Jewish bandit. He was criticized during the 1930s by the Communist party and was arrested in 1938. A victim of Stalin's purges, Babel died in a concentration camp. After Stalin's death, some of his works were republished in censored form in the Soviet Union. Translations of his best stories appear in *Collected Stories* (1955) and *You Must Know Everything* (1969).

Babel (bā'bəl), in the Bible, Babylonian city where Noah's descendants (who spoke one language) tried to build a tower to reach to heaven. For this presumption their words were made incomprehensible. Gen. 11.1-9. Some see in this an etiological story on the diversity in speech and also a reminiscence of the ziggurats in Mesopotamia.

Bab el Mandeb (băb ĕl măn'dĕb) [Arabic, = gate of tears], strait, 17 mi (27 km) wide, linking the Red Sea with the Gulf of Aden and separating the Arabian Peninsula from E Africa. It is an important passage on the Indian Ocean-Mediterranean Sea shipping route via the Suez Canal. Control of the strategically located strait was long contested by Britain and France. The island of Barim is in the strait.

Babenberg (bä'bənbĕrk), ruling house of Austria (976-1246). It possibly descended from, or succeeded, a powerful Franconian family of the 9th cent. from whose castle the city of Bamberg probably took its name. Holy Roman Emperor Otto II created Count Leopold of Babenberg margrave of the Eastern March (i.e., Austria). Among Leopold's successors were LEOPOLD III; Leopold IV and Henry II, also dukes of Bavaria (1139-56); and Henry II, called Jasomirgott ("if God will") for his favorite phrase. Henry II became (1156) the first duke of Austria. In 1192 the Babenbergs inherited Styria. Duke Leopold V took part in the Third Crusade and later made RICHARD I of England a prisoner. Leopold VI, called the Glorious, brought the house to its greatest power. His son, Frederick II, called the Quarrelsome, died childless in 1246, and Austria passed (1251) to OTTOCAR II of Bohemia, who married Frederick's sister. Under Babenberg rule Austria was extended through eastward colonization, and relative peace was maintained through intermarriage with the ruling families of Bohemia and Poland. As a result the Babenbergs were in part responsible for the multinational character of the later Hapsburg empire.

Baber: see BABUR.

Babeuf, François Noël (fräNswä' nôĕl' bäböf'), 1760-97, French revolutionary, organizer of a communist uprising against the DIRECTORY. Of petty bourgeois origin, he was an enthusiastic supporter of the French Revolution. He settled in Paris in 1794 and founded a political journal, the *Journal de la liberté de la presse* (later the *Tribun du peuple*). In it he argued that the Revolution had not gone far enough merely by establishing political equality. He was imprisoned (Feb.-Sept., 1795) for his writings, but emerged an even more violent enemy of economic injustice. Calling himself Gracchus Babeuf, he organized an egalitarian group that included discontented artisans and soldiers. The Directory halted his journal and banned the organization. He then formed a secret society that plotted to overthrow the government; it became known as the Conspiracy of the Equals. It distributed propaganda and announced a program of economic equality—common ownership of the land and the right of all men to work and to share in the products of the economy. The form of communism desired by the conspirators referred mainly to the distribution of goods rather than to means of production. The plot was betrayed to the government, and after a long trial Babeuf was executed. His doctrines, however, known as Babouvism, were kept alive, largely by secret revolutionary societies. See his *Defense of Gracchus Babeuf before the High Court of Vendôme*, tr. and ed. by J. A. Scott with an essay by H. Marcuse (1967); studies by D. Thomson (1947), F. M. Buonarroti (tr. 1965), and E. B. Bax (1911, repr. 1971).

Babington, Anthony (băb'ĭngtən), 1561-86, English conspirator. A member of the Roman Catholic gentry, he served as a youth in the household of the earl of Shrewsbury at Sheffield Castle, where MARY QUEEN OF SCOTS was imprisoned. In 1586 he became involved in a plot to murder Queen Elizabeth I, to free Mary, and to make England a Catholic realm. The plot was discovered, Babington was executed, and the evidence against him was also used to convince Elizabeth that it was necessary to behead Mary.

Babism (bä'bĭzəm), system of doctrines of a Muslim sect of 19th-century Persia. In 1844 the disciples of a movement within Shiite Islam recognized Sayyid Ali Muhammad of Shiraz as a prophet and thus the successor of Moses, Christ, and Muhammad. They granted Sayyid the title of Bab [gate], and missionaries were sent throughout Persia. Babism took its beliefs especially from Sufism, Gnosticism, and Shiite Islam. It advocated the abrogation of some Koranic laws. The movement placed special emphasis on the coming of the Promised One, who would embody all the tenets of the new religion. In 1845 oppression of Babism began, and in 1848 the movement declared its complete secession from Islam and all its rites. Upon the accession of a new shah in 1848, the Bab's followers, rising in insurrection, were defeated. Many of the leaders were killed, and the Bab was executed at Tabriz in 1850. Two years later, after an attempt had been made on the life of the shah, there were more persecutions. In 1863 the Babists were removed to Constantinople and later to Adrianople and Cyprus. After 1868 a division had its center in Acre under the leadership of BAHA ULLAH, the originator of BAHAISM, who had declared himself the Promised One. See E. G. Browne, ed. and tr., *A Traveller's Narrative Written to Illustrate the Episode of the Bab* (1891) and *Materials for the Study of Babi Religion* (1918); H. M. Balyuzi, *The Bab* (1973).

Babol (bäbōl'), town (1971 est. pop. 52,000), N Iran, near the Caspian Sea, NE of Tehran. It is the region's chief commercial center and was once the major trading center of N Iran. Processed food and textiles are produced, and fruits, tobacco, and cotton are raised nearby. Founded in the 16th cent., it was built on the site of the ancient city of Mamter. Ruins of a palace of Abbas I are there. Located in the Caspian littoral, the city receives abundant rainfall. It was formerly called Barfrush.

baboon, any of the large, powerful, ground-living MONKEYS of the genus *Papio,* also called dog-faced monkeys. Baboons are found in Africa, with one species extending into Asia. They have close-set eyes under heavy brow ridges, long, heavy muzzles, powerful jaws, and sharp, tusklike upper canine teeth. Their fur is thick, and in some species there is a mane about the head and shoulders. The heavy tail is of moderate length. The buttock pads, or ischial callosities, are thick and brightly colored. Baboons have cheek pouches for storing food. They live in grassland, brush, or rocky country, foraging on the ground and sleeping in trees or on rock outcroppings. They travel in troops of up to 100 individuals, led by a dominant male and having a highly developed social structure. They feed on roots, fruits, insects, and small animals, including other monkeys. Powerful fighters, baboons show little fear of larger animals, including humans, and can successfully battle leopards, their worst enemies. They can be nuisances in villages and suburbs, where they sometimes conduct foraging raids into houses. They are considered among the most intelligent of monkeys. The hamadryas baboon (*Papio hamadryas*) of NE Africa and SW Arabia was the sacred baboon of Egypt. It has silvery brown fur and an impressive mane. Several other species, differing in size and color, are found in different parts of sub-Saharan Africa. The gelada (*Theropithecus gelada*) of Ethiopia is closely related to the baboon. It has olive-brown fur, a bright pink face and buttock pads, an enormous mane, and a tufted tail. Also closely related are the fantastically colored MANDRILL and the drill, both forest-dwellers. Baboons are classified in the phylum CHORDATA, subphylum Vertebrata, class Mammalia, order Primates, family Cercopithecidae.

Babrius (bā'brēəs), fl. 2d cent.?, Greek fabulist, versifier of the fables of AESOP. Many of the medieval prose collections of Aesop were based on Babrius. He may have been a Hellenized Roman.

Babson, Roger Ward, 1875-1967, American businessman and statistician, b. Gloucester, Mass. In 1904 he founded the Babson Statistical Organization, Inc., whose business and financial statistics, published in *Babson's Washington Service,* are widely sold in the United States, Great Britain, and Canada. In 1919 he established Babson Institute (now Babson College), in Massachusetts, and in 1927 he founded Webber College, in Florida. He was the Prohibition party's 1940 presidential candidate, polling 57,812 votes. He was the author of many books on finance and investment, among the best known of which are *Business Barometers* (1909, 10th ed. 1961), *Investment Fundamentals* (1930, 4th ed. 1948), and *If Inflation Comes* (1937). See his autobiography, *Actions and Reactions* (1937, rev. ed 1949).

Babur (bä'bər) [Turk., = lion], 1483-1530, founder of the MOGUL empire of India. His full name was Zahir ud-Din Muhammad. A descendant of Tamerlane and of Jenghiz Khan, he succeeded (1494) to the principality of Fergana in central Asia. His early life was spent in an ultimately unsuccessful struggle to retain his inheritance and to recover Samarkand (Tamerlane's capital) from the Uzbeks. In 1504, however, he captured Kabul and established a kingdom in Afghanistan. After the failure of his final attempt (1512) on Samarkand, Babur began raids southward into India. In 1525, responding to an invitation from the governor of the Punjab to overthrow the sultan of Delhi, Babur launched a serious invasion. Although his force was small, he defeated the sultan at Panipat in 1526 and captured Agra and Delhi. He finally conquered nearly all of N India. Babur was also a distinguished poet. His autobiography (tr. by A. S. Beveridge, 1922) is his most important work. His son Humayun succeeded him. Babur's name is also transliterated Baber and Babar. See biography by Fernand Grenard (tr. 1930, repr. 1971); study by R. D. Palsokar (1971).

Babylon (băb'əlŏn), ancient city of Mesopotamia. One of the most important cities of the ancient Near East, it was on the Euphrates River and was north of the cities that flourished in S Mesopotamia in the 3d millennium B.C. It became important when HAMMURABI made it the capital of his kingdom of BABYLONIA. The patron god of Babylon, Marduk (identical with Bel), became a leading deity in the Neo-Babylonian pantheon. The city was destroyed (c.689 B.C.) by the Assyrians under SENNACHERIB, and its real spendor belongs to the later period of Babylonia after the city was rebuilt. The brilliant color and luxury of Babylon became legendary from the days of Nebuchadnezzar (d. 562 B.C.). The Hanging Gardens were one of the SEVEN WONDERS OF THE WORLD. The walls of Babylon, its palace, and the processional way with the famous Ishtar Gate were decorated with colorfully glazed brick. Among the Hebrews (who suffered the BABYLONIAN CAPTIVITY under Nebuchadnezzar) and the later Greeks the city was famed for its sensual living. Under the rule of Nabonidus the city was captured (538 B.C.) by Cyrus the Great and was used as one of the administrative capitals of the Persian Empire. In 275 B.C. its inhabitants were removed to SELEUCIA, which replaced Babylon as a commercial center.

Babylon, residential and resort village (1970 pop. 12,588), Suffolk co., SE N.Y., on Long Island, on Great South Bay; settled 1689, inc. as a village 1893.

Babylonia (băbĭlō'nēə), ancient empire of Mesopotamia. The name is sometimes given to the whole civilization of S Mesopotamia, including the states established by the city rulers of Lagash, Akkad (or Agade), Erech, and Ur in the 3d millennium B.C. Historically it is limited to the first dynasty of Babylon established by HAMMURABI (c.1750 B.C.), and to the Neo-Babylonian period after the fall of the Assyrian Empire. Hammurabi, who had his capital at BABYLON, issued the code of laws for the management of his large empire—for he was in control of most of the Tigris and Euphrates region even before he defeated the Elamites. Babylonian CUNEIFORM writing was derived from the Sumerians. The quasi-feudal society was divided into classes—the wealthy landowners and merchants and the priests; the less wealthy merchants, peasants, and artisans; and the slaves. The Babylonian religion (see MIDDLE EASTERN RELIGIONS) was inherited from the older Sumerian culture. All these Babylonian institutions influenced the civilization of ASSYRIA and so contributed to the later history of the Middle East and of Western Europe. The wealth of Babylonia tempted nomadic and seminomadic neighbors; even under Hammurabi's successor Babylonia was having to stave off assaults. Early in the 18th cent. B.C. the Hittites sacked Babylon and held it briefly. The nomadic Kassites (Cassites), a tribe from Elam, took the city shortly thereafter and held it precariously for centuries. Babylonia degenerated into anarchy c.1180 B.C. with the fall of the Kassites. As a subsidiary state of the Assyrian Empire (after the 9th cent. B.C.), Babylonia flourished once more. It was the key area in the attempted uprising against the Assyrian king, SENNACHERIB, and Babylon was sacked (c.689 B.C.) in his reign. After the death of Assurbanipal, the last great Assyrian monarch, Nabopolassar, the ruler of Babylonia, established (625 B.C.) his independence. He allied himself with the Medes and Persians and helped to bring about the capture of Nineveh (612 B.C.) and the fall of the Assyrian Empire. He established what is generally known as the Chaldaean or New Babylonian Empire. Under his son, NEBUCHADNEZZAR, the new empire reached its height (see BABYLON). The recalcitrant Hebrews were defeated and punished with the BABYLONIAN CAPTIVITY. Egypt had already been defeated by Nebuchadnezzar in the great battle of Carchemish (605) while Nabopolassar was still alive. The empire seemed secure, but it was actually transitory. The steady growth of Persian power spelled the end of Babylonia, and in 538 B.C. the last of the Babylonian rulers surrendered to CYRUS THE GREAT (see also BELSHAZZAR). Babylonia became an important region of the Persian Empire. See R. W. Rogers, *A History of Babylonia and Assyria* (6th ed. 1915); D. D. Luckenbill, *Ancient Records of Assyria and Babylonia* (1926–27); G. R. Driver, et al., *The Babylonian Laws* (1952–55); H. W. F. Saggs, *Everyday Life in Babylonia and Assyria* (1965); J. A. Brinkman, *A Political History of Post-Kassite Babylonia* (1968); L. W. King, *A History of Babylonia* (1915, repr. 1969); James Wellard, *Babylon* (1972).

Babylonian art: see SUMERIAN AND BABYLONIAN ART.

Babylonian captivity, in the history of Israel, the period from the fall of Jerusalem (586 B.C.) to the reconstruction in Palestine of a new Jewish state (after 538 B.C.). After the capture of the city by the Babylonians some thousands, probably selected for their prosperity and importance, were deported to Mesopotamia. The number of those who remained is disputed by scholars. Such deportations were commonplace in Assyrian and Babylonian policy. The exiles maintained close links with their kinsmen at home, as is clear from Ezekiel, the prophet of the early years of the Exile. In 538 B.C., Cyrus the Great, the new master of the empire, initiated a new attitude toward the nations and decreed the restoration of worship at Jerusalem. The century following this decree was critical in the history of the Jews, for it is the time of their reintegration into a national and religious unit. For parts of the period, Ezra and Nehemiah are the best sources. The prophesied 70 years of captivity were fulfilled when the new Temple was completed in 516 B.C. (Jer. 25.11; Dan. 9.2; Zech. 7.5.) For the papal captivity at Avignon, which is also called the Babylonian Captivity, see PAPACY.

Babylonian religion: see MIDDLE EASTERN RELIGIONS.

baby's breath, name for a plant of the family Caryophyllaceae (PINK family) and for several other flowers, e.g., white bedstraw of the family Rubiaceae (MADDER family) and grape hyacinth of the family Liliaceae (LILY family). The pink and madder families are classified in the division MAGNOLIOPHYTA, class Magnoliopsida, orders Caryophyllales and Rubiales, respectively. The lily family is classified in the class Liliatae, order Liliales.

Baca (bā'kə), allegorical name of a valley. Ps. 84.6. The English expression "vale (or valley) of tears" may be a translation of this, through the Vulgate.

Bacabal (bəkəbäl'), city (1970 pop. 69,384), Maranhão state, NE Brazil, on the Mearim River. Babassu nuts, rice, and cotton are its principal products.

Bacău (bäkŭ'o͞o), city (1969 est. pop. 66,000), E Rumania, in Moldavia, on the Bistrita River. The administrative and industrial center of an oil-producing region, Bacău has industries that manufacture oil-field equipment. Other important products include textiles, leather and wood items, and light machinery. Although probably settled in the 5th cent., Bacău did not become important until oil was discovered there in the 20th cent. It has a regional museum and ruins of a 15th-century princely court.

Baccaloni, Salvatore (sälvätô'rā bäk-kälō'nē), 1900–70, Italian operatic bass, b. Rome. Baccaloni studied architecture before he made his singing debut in Rome in 1921. In 1926 he joined La Scala in Milan under Arturo Toscanini. In 1940 he joined the Metropolitan Opera Company, where he specialized in comic roles such as Bartolo in *The Barber of Seville.* Known for his large repertory, Baccaloni sang nearly 170 roles in five languages.

baccarat (bă'kərä", băk'-, Fr. bäkärä'), French card game formerly widely played in European casinos but now supplanted in popularity by CHEMIN DE FER. The banker plays against the hands he deals to two other players called punters. The winning hand is the one whose point total has the number closest to 9 as its last digit, face cards and tens counting nothing. Two cards are dealt to a hand with the privilege of a one-card draw. The term *baccarat* is supposed to mean "nothing" and is applied to hands whose point total ends with a cipher.

bacchae: see MAENADS.

Bacchanalia (băkənā'lēə), in Roman religion, festival in honor of Bacchus, god of wine. Originally a religious ceremony, like the LIBERALIA, it gradually became an occasion for drunken, licentious excesses and was finally forbidden by law (186 B.C.).

bacchantes: see MAENADS.

Bacchus (băk'əs), in Greek and Roman mythology, god of wine, identified with Dionysus. He was also a god of vegetation and fertility, and his worship was orgiastic. He was the protector of vines. Many legends connected with Dionysus were also used in the cult of Bacchus.

Bacchylides (băkĭl'ĭdēz), fl. c.470 B.C., Greek lyric poet, b. Ceos; nephew of Simonides of Ceos. A contemporary of Pindar, he was patronized by Hiero I. Although a competent craftsman capable of elegant lyrics, Bacchylides lacked the inspiration of Pindar. A number of Bacchylides' epinicia and dithyrambs were among the verses recovered from an Egyptian papyrus (text published by F. G. Kenyon, *The Poems of Bacchylides,* 1897). See R. C. Jebb, *Bacchylides: The Poems and Fragments* (1905).

Bach (bäkh), German family of distinguished musicians who flourished from the 16th through the 18th cent., its most renowned member being **Johann Sebastian Bach** (see separate article). **Johannes,** or **Hans, Bach,** 1580–1626, was a Thuringian carpetweaver and a musical performer at festivals. His sons and descendants were noted organists and composers. One of his grandsons was **Johann Ambrosius Bach,** 1645–95, violinist, town musician at Eisenach, and father of Johann Sebastian Bach. Johann Sebastian's eldest brother, **Johann Christoph Bach,** 1671–1721, was organist at Ohrdruf. When his parents died he took his youngest brother, Johann Sebastian, into his home and taught him. Of the 20 children of Johann Sebastian, several were well known as musicians. The eldest son, **Wilhelm Friedemann Bach,** 1710–84, was made organist at the Sophienkirche in Dresden in 1733 and later (1746–64) organist and musical director at the Liebfrauenkirche in Halle. He was a brilliant organist and well-known composer, but he did not live up to his father's hopes and, after a dissolute life, he died in misery. A younger son was **Carl Philipp Emanuel Bach** (see separate article), and the youngest son was **Johann Christian Bach** (see separate article). See Karl Geiringer and I. S. Geiringer, *The Bach Family* (1954); Percy Young, *The Bachs* (1970).

Bach, Alexander, 1813–93, Austrian politician. A well-known lawyer and liberal, he took part in the REVOLUTION OF 1848 in Vienna, but after its suppression he joined the forces of reaction. He became minister of justice (1848) and of the interior (1849–59), and after the death (1852) of Prince Schwarzenberg was the chief figure in the ministry. He was created baron in 1854. Bach instituted the **Bach system** of bureaucratic control of the Hapsburg lands. Centralization and Germanization were its chief aims; stringent control by secret police was the method of enforcing them. This program was accompanied, however, by measures promoting economic prosperity, notably the abolition of internal tariff barriers, and by agricultural reforms implementing the emancipation of the serfs. Through the Concordat of 1855 the Roman Catholic Church gained wide powers. The Bach system met with opposition, especially in Hungary, and after the Austrian defeat in the Italian War of 1859 its author was dismissed and new systems introduced.

Bach, Carl Philipp Emanuel (fē'lĭp ĕmä'no͝oĕl), 1714–88, German composer; second son of J. S. Bach, his only teacher. While harpsichordist at the court of Frederick the Great, where his chief duty for 28 years (1738–67) was to accompany the monarch's performances on the flute, he wrote an important work on technique, *Essay on the True Art of Playing Keyboard Instruments* (1753, tr. 1949). After this artistically unsatisfying service with Frederick, Bach succeeded his godfather, Georg Philipp Telemann, as musical director at Hamburg. His 2 volumes of sonatas (1742–43) and his 12 symphonies established the typical classical forms of such works and powerfully influenced both Haydn and Beethoven. He also composed other keyboard music and sacred choral music. His craftsmanship was outstanding in the period between the baroque and classical periods.

Bach, Johann Christian (krĭs'tyän), 1735–82, German musician and composer; son of J. S. Bach. He went to Italy in 1754, became a Roman Catholic, and composed church music and operas. In 1760 he became organist of the Milan Cathedral. Two years later he went to England, where he became music master to the royal family. A popular and highly prolific composer in the rococo style, he influenced the young Mozart.

Bach, Johann Sebastian (säbäs'tyän), 1685–1750, German composer and organist, b. Eisenach; one of the greatest and most influential composers of the Western world. He brought polyphonic baroque music to its culmination, creating masterful and vigorous works in almost every musical form known in his period. Born into a gifted family (see separate article), Bach was devoted to music from childhood; he was taught by his father and later by his brother Johann Christoph, and was a boy soprano in Lüneberg. His education was acquired largely through independent studies; he had an insatiable curiosity about music and sometimes walked great distances to hear the organists Johann Adam Reinken (at Hamburg) and Buxtehude (at Lübeck). In 1703 he became violinist in the private orchestra of the prince at Weimar but left within a year to become organist at Arnstadt. He went to Mühlhausen as organist in 1707. There he married his cousin Maria Barbara Bach, who was to bear him seven children. In 1708 he was made court organist and chamber musician at Weimar, and in 1714 he became concert master. Prince Leopold of Anhalt engaged him as musical director at Cöthen in 1717. Three years later his wife died, and in 1721 he married Anna Magdalena Wülken, a woman of considerable musical cultivation who eventually bore him 13 children. In

1723 he left Weimar to take the important post of music director of the church of St. Thomas, Leipzig, and of its music school; he remained in Leipzig until his death. Since few of Bach's many works were published in his lifetime, exact dates cannot be fixed for all of them, but most can be placed with some certainty in the periods of his life. At Arnstadt and Mühlhausen he began a series of organ compositions that culminated in the great works of the Weimar period: the Passacaglia and Fugue in C Minor, most of the great preludes and fugues, and the 45 chorale-preludes gathered in *Das Orgelbüchlein* [the little organ book]. At Cöthen he concentrated on instrumental compositions, especially keyboard works: the Chromatic Fantasy and Fugue; the English Suites; the French Suites; the Two-Part and Three-Part Inventions, written for the education of his son Wilhelm Friedemann; and Book I of the celebrated *The Well-Tempered Clavier.* He also wrote several unaccompanied violin sonatas and cello suites, and the Brandenburg Concertos, recognized as the best concerti grossi ever composed. The *St. John Passion* was performed (1723) at Leipzig, when Bach was a candidate for the position of musical director at St. Thomas. His *Magnificat* was presented shortly after he assumed that post. Many more of his superb religious compositions followed: the *St. Matthew Passion* (1729), the *Christmas Oratorio,* the sonorous Mass in B Minor, and the six motets. The principal keyboard works of this period were Book II of *The Well-Tempered Clavier* and the four books of clavier pieces in the *Clavierübung,* which includes: six partitas (1726-31); the Italian Concerto and the Partita in B Minor (1735); the Catechism Preludes, the Prelude and Fugue (St. Anne) in E Flat (1739), and four duets; and the Goldberg Variations (more formally Aria with Thirty Variations, 1742). His last notable compositions were the *Musical Offering* composed (1747) for Frederick the Great and *The Art of the Fugue* (1749). In all his positions as choir director, Bach composed sacred cantatas—a total of some 300, of which nearly 200 are extant. There are also over 30 secular cantatas, composed at Leipzig, among them *Phoebus and Pan* (1731). The bulk of his work is religious—he made four-part settings of 371 Lutheran chorales, also using many of them as the bases of organ preludes and choral works. In addition, he composed an astonishing number of instrumental works, many of them designed for the instruction of his numerous pupils. In his instrumental and choral works he perfected the art of polyphony, displaying an unmatched combination of inventiveness and control in his great, striding fugues. During his lifetime, Bach was better known as an organist than as a composer. For decades after his death his works were neglected, but in the 19th cent. his genius came to be recognized, particularly by romantic composers such as Mendelssohn and Schumann. Since that time his reputation has grown steadily. The classic study of his life and music is that by Phillip Spitta (tr. 1884-85, repr. 1972), and Albert Schweitzer's study (tr. 1911, repr. 1962) has attracted much attention. See also biographies by C. S. Terry (1928, repr. 1962), Imogen Holst (1965), and Karl and Irene Geiringer (1966); studies by J. N. Forkel (tr. 1920, repr. 1970) and R. L. Marshall (2 vol., 1972); H. T. David and Arthur Mendel, *The Bach Reader* (1945).

Bacharach, Burt (băk'ərăk''), 1929–, American composer, b. Kansas City, Mo. He began his career playing piano in nightclubs. With the lyricist Hal David, Bacharach has produced a number of popular songs; they include "Don't Make Me Over," "What the World Needs Now," and "Do You Know the Way to San Jose." The team also provided words and music for the successful Broadway musical *Promises, Promises* (1968) and the film *Butch Cassidy and the Sundance Kid* (1969). Bacharach's music utilizes Latin, rock, and gospel styles and is marked by unexpected chord changes.

Bache, Benjamin Franklin (bāch), 1769-98, American journalist, b. Philadelphia; son of Richard Bache and grandson of Benjamin Franklin. In 1790 he founded the Philadelphia *General Advertiser* (later the *Aurora*). As the champion of the Jeffersonians, Bache's paper denounced the Federalists bitterly, and he was arrested under the Sedition Act (see ALIEN AND SEDITION ACTS) but was released on parole. He died soon afterward of yellow fever.

Bache, Jules Semon, 1861-1944, American banker and art collector, b. New York City. He made an immense fortune on Wall St., organized the banking firm of J. S. Bache and Company, and was director of 12 other firms. In 1937 he opened his magnificent art collection to the public, and in 1944 the collection was given permanently to the Metropolitan Mus. It includes famous works by Raphael, Titian, Rembrandt, Velázquez, and other masters.

Bache, Richard, 1737-1811, American merchant, b. Yorkshire, England. He came to New York City in 1765 to join an older brother in the mercantile business. Bache soon moved to Philadelphia in the interest of the firm, which had built up a large West Indian trade. In 1767 he married Sarah, daughter of Benjamin Franklin. He served on many committees in the American Revolution, including the Board of War. He succeeded Franklin as Postmaster General in 1776 and held office until 1782.

Bachelard, Gaston (gästôN' bäshlär'), 1884-1962, French philosopher. He held degrees in physics, mathematics, and philosophy and taught at Dijon (1930-40) and the Univ. of Paris (1940-54). Bachelard regarded knowing as a result of the interaction between reason and experience. Disagreeing with the Cartesian concept of scientific truths as immutable elements of a total truth, he also rejected the notion of the empirical world as random or senseless. He characterized his position as a "philosophy of saying no" because scientific insights are, as he saw it, always open to reformulation on the basis of new experience. This reformulation does not involve the rejection but the recasting of previous positions as resulting from the dialectic of reason and experience. Bachelard was not, despite his scientific orientation, a thorough-going rationalist; he considered imagination and reverie as well as reason to be creative forces in knowing. Among his books are *La Psychanalyse du feu* (1932; tr. *Psychoanalysis of Fire,* 1964), *Lautréamont* (1939), *La Philosophie du non* (1940; tr. *The Philosophy of No,* 1968), and *On Poetic Imagination and Reverie* (tr. 1971).

Bacheller, Irving, 1859-1950, American novelist, b. Pierpont, N.Y., grad. St. Lawrence Univ., 1882. In 1884 he founded the first newspaper syndicate in the United States. His novels, chiefly concerned with early American life, include *Eben Holden* (1900), *D'ri and I* (1901), and *A Man for the Ages* (1919). See his autobiographical works.

bachelor's-button, popular name for several plants usually characterized by rounded flowers, such as the CORNFLOWER and globe AMARANTH.

Bache Peninsula (bāch), on E Ellesmere Island, in N Northwest Territories, Canada. U.S. explorer Robert Peary proved this area to be a peninsula when he explored (1898) the region. From 1926 to 1933 the Royal Canadian Mounted Police had a post there, c.800 mi (1,290 km) from the North Pole, that was the most northerly habitation in the world.

Bachrites (băk'rīts), descendants of BECHER **2.**

Bach system: see BACH, ALEXANDER.

Baciccio, Il: see GAULLI, GIOVANNI BATTISTA.

bacillus (bəsĭl'əs): see BACTERIA.

bacitracin (băs''ĭtrā'sĭn), ANTIBIOTIC produced by a strain of the bacterial species *Bacillus subtilis.* It is widely used for topical therapy such as for skin and eye infections; it is effective against gram-positive bacteria including strains of staphylococcus that are resistant to PENICILLIN (see GRAM'S STAIN). Bacitracin is toxic to humans and therefore it is used internally only in severe illness where the infecting bacteria are resistant to other drugs.

Back, Sir George, 1796-1878, British explorer in N Canada. He accompanied Sir John Franklin on arctic expeditions in 1818, 1819-22, and 1824-27. On an expedition (1833-35) to search for the missing John Ross, Back explored the Great Fish River (now Back River) and Montreal Island in the present Northwest Territories. His *Narrative of the Arctic Land Expedition* appeared in 1836. On a later journey (1836-37) he explored the arctic coast of Canada.

Back, river, c.600 mi (970 km) long, rising in lakes, E Mackenzie dist., Northwest Territories, Canada, and flowing northeast across the tundra to Chantry Inlet. There are numerous lakes along its course. It is named for Sir George Back, the first person to descend the river (1834).

backbone: see SPINAL COLUMN.

Backbone Mountain, peak, 3,360 ft (1,024 m) high, NW Md., in the Allegheny Mts.; highest elevation in the state.

backgammon (băk'găm''ən, băk''găm'ən), game of chance and skill played by two persons upon a specially marked board divided by a space called the bar into two tables (inner table and outer table), each of which has 12 alternately colored points, or triangular spaces. The moves permitted each player are dictated by the throws of two dice, and the object is to remove one's 15 pieces, or disks, from the board first according to the rules. The game was played by the ancients; a backgammon board with dice and pieces was found in Babylonian excavations. Backgammon was also played in Greece and Rome, and after the 10th cent. A.D. it became popular in Europe. In England the game was known as tables. Parcheesi, which probably originated in India, is a form of backgammon that permits four to play. See Oswald Jacoby and J. R. Crawford, *The Backgammon Book* (1970).

Backhuysen or **Bakhuyzen, Ludolf** (lo͞o'dôlf băk'hīzən), 1631-1708, Dutch marine painter. He is best known for his scenes of stormy seas. Peter the Great is said to have been instructed by him in drawing. In later years Backhuysen also did some etching and engraving of marine views. He was the foremost follower of Willem van de Velde II, but his works lack his master's poetic vision.

backshore: see BEACH.

backswimmer, common name for WATER BUGS of the cosmopolitan family Notonectidae, so named because they swim upside down, usually near the surface of the water. They resemble the upright-swimming water boatmen, having oval bodies and long, oarlike hind legs, with which they swim rapidly, but their backs are more convex than those of the water boatmen. The exposed belly is yellowish to black. Backswimmers, 1/8 to 1/2 in. (3-12 mm) long, feed on small crustaceans, insect larvae, snails, and sometimes on small fish and tadpoles from which they suck the body juices. They can inflict a painful bite on a human being. Most of the 50 North American species overwinter as adults. The eggs are usually laid on submerged plants or rocks and development to the adult stage takes 40 to 60 days. Backswimmers are classified in the phylum ARTHROPODA, class Insecta, order Hemiptera, family Notonectidae.

Backus, Isaac, 1724-1806, American clergyman, leader among New England Baptists and a champion of religious freedom, b. Norwich, Conn. Converted in the Great Awakening, he joined the separatists or "New Light" faction. He became pastor in 1748 of a Congregational church in Middleboro, Mass.; after his adherence to the Baptist faith, he organized and became minister of a Baptist church there, which he served from 1756 until his death. According to his calculations, Backus traveled over 68,000 mi (109,435 km) on his evangelistic tours, mostly on horseback. His *History of New England with Particular Reference to the ... Baptists* (3 vol., 1777-96) is a major source for the religious history of the region and the period.

Bacolod (bäkō'lōd, -lōth), city (1970 est. pop. 165,000), capital of Negros Occidental prov., NW Negros island, the Philippines. It is an important seaport, the shipping and processing center of the country's major sugarcane-producing area. The Univ. of Negros Occidental-Recoletos is there.

Bacon, Francis, 1561-1626, English philosopher, essayist, and statesman, b. London, educated at Trinity College, Cambridge, and at Gray's Inn. He was the son of Sir Nicholas Bacon, lord keeper to Queen Elizabeth I. Francis Bacon was a member of Parliament in 1584 and his opposition to Elizabeth's tax program retarded his political advancement; only the efforts of the earl of Essex led Elizabeth to accept him as an unofficial member of her Learned Council. At Essex's trial in 1601, Bacon, putting duty to the state above friendship, assumed an active part in the prosecution—a course for which many have condemned him. With the succession of James I, Bacon's fortunes improved. He was knighted in 1603, became attorney general in 1613, lord keeper in 1617, and lord chancellor in 1618; he was created Baron Verulam in 1618 and Viscount St. Albans in 1621. In 1621, accused of accepting bribes as lord chancellor, he pleaded guilty and was fined £40,000, banished from the court, disqualified from holding office, and sentenced to the Tower of London. The banishment, fine, and imprisonment were remitted. Nevertheless, his career as a public servant was ended. He spent the rest of his life writing in retirement. Bacon belongs to both philosophy and literature. He projected a large philosophical work, the *Instauratio Magna,* but completed only two parts, *The Advancement of Learning* (1605), later expanded in Latin as *De Augmentis Scientiarum* (1623), and the *Novum Organum* (1620). Bacon's contribution to philosophy was his application of the inductive method of modern science as opposed to the a priori method of medieval scholasticism. He urged full investigation in all cases, avoiding theories based on insufficient data. He has been widely censured for being too mechanical, failing to carry his investigations to their logical ends, and not staying abreast of the scientific knowledge of his own day. In the 19th cent., Macaulay initiated a movement to restore Bacon's prestige as a scientist. Today his contributions are regarded with considerable respect. In *The New Atlantis* (1627) he describes a scientific utopia that found partial realization with the organization of the Royal Society in 1660. His *Essays* (1597-1625), largely aphoristic, are his best-known writings. They are noted for their style and for their striking observations about life. See his works (14 vol., 1857-74, repr. 1968); studies by F. H. Anderson (1948, repr. 1971), A. W. Green (1966), and J. G. Crowther (1960); D. W. Davies and E. S. Wrigley, eds., *Concordance to the Essays of Francis Bacon* (1973).

Bacon, Francis, 1910-, English painter, b. Dublin. A self-taught artist, Bacon became the center of a storm of controversy with his *Three Studies* for the base of *Crucifixion* (1944; Tate Gall., London). He painted a series of variations on diverse themes, e.g., *Van Gogh Goes to Work, Velázquez's Innocent X.* Bacon's works are satirical, emphasizing the repulsive, the terrible, and the hallucinatory in human life. See study by John Russell (1974).

Bacon, Henry, 1866-1924, American architect, b. Watseka, Ill. He began his professional career with the firm of McKim, Mead, and White, but after 1903 he practiced independently. Among the important structures designed by him are the Lincoln Memorial at Washington, D.C. (completed 1917), and the World War Memorial at Yale Univ.

Bacon, Leonard, 1802-81, American Congregational minister, b. Detroit, Mich. He served for 41 years as pastor of the First Church of New Haven, one of the leading Congregational churches in the country. Bacon was a noted antislavery leader, although not an abolitionist. His *Slavery Discussed in Occasional Essays* (1846) made a great impression upon Lincoln. He was a founder and editor of the *Independent* and author of the widely known *Pilgrim Hymn* (1833) and *The Genesis of the New England Churches* (1874). See biography by T. D. Bacon (1931).

Bacon, Nathaniel, 1647-76, leader of BACON'S REBELLION in colonial Virginia. An aristocrat (he was kin to Francis Bacon, had been educated at Cambridge and Gray's Inn, and was a member of the governor's council), Bacon nevertheless became the champion of the discontented frontiersmen after only two years' residence in the colony. When he died suddenly from the effects of malaria, the revolt collapsed.

Bacon, Sir Nicholas, 1509-79, English jurist. Called to the bar in 1533, he was made attorney of the court of wards and liveries in 1546 and, although a staunch Protestant, held this office through the reign of Mary I. On the accession (1558) of Elizabeth I, he was appointed lord keeper of the privy seal, possibly through the influence of William Cecil, later Lord Burghley (whose wife's sister Bacon married). In 1559 he was authorized to exercise the jurisdiction of the lord chancellor. He regarded Mary Queen of Scots as a menace to English peace and opposed any measure of compromise with her. He was the father of Francis Bacon.

Bacon, Peggy, 1895-, American illustrator, caricaturist, and etcher, b. Ridgefield, Conn. Bacon has illustrated more than 60 books including works by George Ade, Carl Sandburg, and Louis Untermeyer, as well as her own poems and her stories for children. Her shrewd and caustic observations have found expression in her writings and in her graphic work. *Socialist Meeting* (Metropolitan Mus.) is characteristic. Among her published works are *Off with Their Heads* (1934); *Cat-Calls* (1935), a volume of light verse; and, for children, *The Ghost of Opalina* (1967) and *Magic Touch* (1968). Bacon was married (1920-40) to the painter Alexander BROOK.

Bacon, Robert, 1860-1919, American banker and government official, b. Jamaica Plain, Mass. He embarked upon a career in business and in 1894 accepted a partnership with J. P. Morgan and Company. He participated in the formation (1901) of the U. S. Steel Corp. and the Northern Securities Company. Bacon later served (1905-9) as Assistant Secretary of State under President Theodore Roosevelt, and was briefly (1909) Secretary of State. He was (1909-12) also ambassador to France. An outspoken proponent of U. S. entry into World War I, he served (1917-19) in the U. S. army. He wrote *For Better Relations with Our Latin American Neighbors* (1915). See biography by J. B. Scott (1923).

Bacon, Roger, c.1214-1294?, English scholastic philosopher and scientist, a Franciscan. He studied at Oxford as well as at the Univ. of Paris and became one of the most celebrated and zealous teachers at Oxford. Bacon was learned in Hebrew and in Greek and stressed the value of knowing the original languages in the study of Aristotle and of the Bible. He may also have known Arabic; his own philosophy drew upon Arabian Aristotelianism as well as upon St. Augustine. He had an interest far in advance of his times in natural science, in controlled experiments, and in the accurate observation of phenomena. "It is the intention of philosophy," he said, "to work out the natures and properties of things." He declared that mathematics was the gateway to science, and experience, or verification, the only basis of certainty. This belief in experience as a guide to the outer world was, however, not divorced from theology; wisdom and faith were to him one. His writings were numerous. Three of his most important works were written for Pope Clement IV in one year (1267-68)—the *Opus majus* (tr. 1928), the *Opus minor*, and the *Opus tertium.* He was deeply interested in alchemy, an interest that may account for his being credited by his contemporaries with great learning in magical practices. He was long credited with the invention of gunpowder (because of a formula for gunpowder that appeared in a work attributed to him). A manuscript in cipher, discovered in the 20th cent. and attributed to him, would make Bacon the first man to have observed spiral nebulae through a telescope and to have examined cells through a microscope; but considerable doubt has been cast on the original date and the authenticity of the manuscript. Earlier editions of his major works were supplemented by an edition of his hitherto unedited works in various fascicles by Robert Steele and others (1909-35). See A. G. Little, ed., *Roger Bacon Essays* (1914, repr. 1972); biography by F. Winthrop Woodruff (1938); studies by Theodore Crowley (1950) and Stewart C. Easton (1952, repr. 1971).

bacon, flesh of hogs—especially from the sides, belly, or back—that has been preserved by being salted or pickled and then dried with or without wood smoke. In early agricultural communities the curing of meat was an important household industry; the process consisted of soaking the pork in brine or rubbing it in a salt mixture by hand, then smoking the sides in smoke from an open chimney. It sometimes took three or four months. From ancient times bacon has been a major part of the diet of poor people, and many references to it are found in proverbs and phrases. Bacon is still home cured in some rural communities, but the bulk of its manufacture is carried on in large industrial meat-packing plants equipped to slaughter, dress, cure, smoke, and sell on a large scale. Bacon refers to different cuts in different countries. In the United States it usually means the side between the fifth rib and the hipbone. In Europe, the word *bacon* generally refers to one half of a fattened pig. The high fat content of bacon makes it a valuable energy food.

Bacon's Rebellion, popular revolt in colonial Virginia in 1676, led by Nathaniel BACON. High taxes, low prices for tobacco, and resentment against special privileges given those close to the governor, Sir William BERKELEY, provided the background for the uprising, which was precipitated by Berkeley's failure to defend the frontier against Indian attacks. Bacon commanded two unauthorized but successful expeditions against the Indians and was then elected to the new house of burgesses, which Berkeley had been forced to convene. When he attempted to take his seat, Berkeley had him arrested. Soon released, Bacon gathered his supporters, marched on Jamestown, and coerced Berkeley into granting him a commission to continue his Indian campaigns. A circumspect assembly then passed several reform measures. The governor, having failed to raise a force against Bacon, fled to the Eastern Shore. He gathered enough strength to return to Jamestown, where he proclaimed Bacon and his men rebels and traitors. After a sharp skirmish Bacon recaptured the capital (Berkeley again took flight) but, fearing that he could not hold it against attack, set fire to the town. Bacon now controlled the colony, but he died suddenly (Oct., 1676), and without his leadership the rebellion collapsed. After a few months Berkeley returned to wreak a bloody vengeance before he was forced to return to England. Berkeley's removal and the end of Indian attacks were the only benefits the yeomen had won in the rebellion, and the tidewater aristocracy long maintained its power. See T. J. Wertenbaker, *Torchbearer of the Revolution* (1940, repr. 1965) and *Bacon's Rebellion, 1676* (1957); W. E. Washburn, *The Governor and the Rebel* (1957, repr. 1967).

bacteremia: see SEPTICEMIA.

bacteria [pl. of bacterium], microscopic unicellular organisms classified either as plants of the class Schizomycetes of the division SCHIZOPHYTA of the thallophytes or as a separate phylum (Schizomycophyta) comprised of heterogeneous types most nearly resembling the blue-green algae. Three forms are typical—rod-shaped (bacillus), round (coccus, e.g., streptococcus), and spiral (spirillum). The cytoplasm and plasma membrane of most bacterial cells is surrounded by a cell wall; the nucleus contains the universal genetic agent DNA (see NUCLEIC ACID) but lacks the nuclear membrane typical of higher plants and animals. Many, chiefly the bacillus and spirillum forms, are motile, swimming about by whiplike movements of flagella. Reproduction is chiefly by transverse fission, but bacteria are also capable of specialized types of sexual reproduction and genetic RECOMBINATION involving the transfer of nucleic acid by individual contact (conjugation), by exposure to nucleic acid remnants of dead bacteria (transformation), or by a viral agent, the BACTERIOPHAGE (transduction). Under unfavorable conditions some bacteria form highly resistant spores with thickened coverings, within which the living material remains dormant in altered form until conditions improve. Some bacteria (those known as aerobic forms) can function metabolically only in the presence of free or atmospheric oxygen; others (anaerobic bacteria) cannot grow in the presence of free oxygen but obtain oxygen from compounds; and a third group, called facultative anaerobes, can grow with or without free oxygen. By their metabolic processes, different types of bacteria are capable of innumerable chemical, metabolic transformations involving enzyme production, including photosynthesis and the conversion of free nitrogen and sulfur into amino acids, organic compounds that can then be used by other plants and animals to synthesize proteins for their own protoplasm. Bacteria are remarkably adaptable to diverse environmental conditions: they are found in the bodies of all living organisms and on all parts of the earth—in land terrains and ocean depths, in arctic ice and glaciers, in hot springs, and even in the stratosphere. There are more bacteria, as separate individuals, than any other type of organism; there may be as many as 100 million bacteria in one gram of fertile soil. Harmless and beneficial bacteria far outnumber harmful varieties. Because they are capable of producing so many enzymes necessary for the building up and breaking down of organic compounds, bacteria are employed extensively by man—for soil enrichment with leguminous crops (see NITROGEN CYCLE), for preservation by pickling, for fermentation (as in the manufacture of alcoholic beverages, vinegar, and certain cheeses), for decomposition of organic wastes (in septic tanks, in some sewage disposal plants, and in agriculture for soil enrichment), and for curing tobacco, retting flax, and many other specialized processes. Bacteria frequently make good objects for genetic study: large populations grown in a short period of time facilitate detection of MUTATIONS, or rare variations. Bacterial parasites that cause disease are called pathogenic forms, or pathogens. Among bacterial plant diseases are leaf spot, fire BLIGHT, and wilts; animal diseases caused by bacteria include TUBERCULOSIS, CHOLERA, SYPHILIS, TYPHOID FEVER, and TETANUS. Some bacteria attack the tissues directly; others produce poisonous substances called toxins. Natural defense against harmful bacteria is provided by antibodies (see IMMUNITY). Certain bacterial diseases, e.g., tetanus, can be prevented by injection of ANTITOXIN or of serum containing antibodies against specific bacterial antigens; immunity to some can be induced by VACCINATION; and certain specific bacterial parasites are killed by ANTIBIOTICS. Bacteria were first observed by Leeuwenhoek in the 17th cent.; bacteriology as an applied science began to develop in the late 19th cent. as a result of research in medicine and in fermentation processes, especially by Louis Pasteur and Robert Koch. See Kenneth Thimann, *The Life of Bacteria* (2d ed. 1963); William Hayes, *The Genetics of Bacteria and their Viruses* (1964) .

bacteriophage (băktēr'ēəfāj"), VIRUS that infects bacteria and sometimes destroys them by lysis, or dissolution of the cell. Bacteriophages, or phages, have a head composed of protein, an inner core of NUCLEIC ACID, either deoxyribonucleic acid (DNA) or ribonucleic acid (RNA), and a hollow protein tail. A particular phage can usually infect only one or a few related species of bacteria; for example, coliphages are DNA-containing viruses that infect only the bacterium *Escherichia coli.* A virus infects a bacterial cell by first attaching to the bacterial cell wall by its tail. In coliphages the tail is a complex protein structure consisting of a hollow contractile sheath, with a plate at the base that contains long protein fibers. The tail fibers fix the base plate to the specific receptor site on the bacterial cell wall, and the tail sheath contracts like a syringe, forcing the DNA that is inside the virus through the cell wall and cell membrane. The entire virus protein coat remains outside the bacterium. The injected nucleic acid is the viral genetic material; it makes use of the bacterium's chemical energy and biosynthetic machinery to produce viral enzymes that an uninfected bacterium does not make, as well as more phage nucleic acid. The viral proteins and nucleic acid molecules within the bacterial host assemble spontaneously into up to a hundred new phage particles. Eventually the bacterium lyses, and the particles are released. Lysis can be readily observed in bacteria growing on a solid medium, where groups of lysed cells appear as clear areas, or plaques. Some DNA phages, called temperate phages, have a more complex relationship with the host than simple lysis. Temperate phages only lyse a small fraction of bacterial cells; in the remaining majority of the bacteria, the phage DNA becomes integrated into the bacterial chromosome and replicates along with it. In this state, known as lysogeny, the information contained in the viral nucleic acid is not expressed. A lysogenic culture, i.e., a bacterial culture infected with temperate phages, can be treated with radiation or mutagens, either of which induces the cells to begin producing viruses and lyse. Lysogenic phages resemble bacterial genetic particles known as EPISOMES. The bacteriophage was discovered independently by the microbiologists F. W. Twort (1915) and Félix d'Hérelle (1917). The phages have been much used in the study of bacterial genetics and cellular control mechanisms largely because the bacterial hosts are so easily grown and infected with phage in the laboratory. There have also been unsuccessful attempts to use phages to destroy such pathogenic bacteria as those causing typhoid and cholera.

Bactria (băk'trēə), ancient Greek kingdom in central Asia. Its capital was Bactra, present-day Balkh in N Afghanistan. Before the Greek conquest, the region had been taken by the Persians and was an eastern province of the Persian Empire. It became prosperous as the area for transmitting Siberian and Indian metals and goods to the Persians. When Alexander the Great invaded the Persian Empire, the defeated Darius III fled to Bactria, where he was murdered (330 B.C.) by the Bactrian satrap, Bessus. The Bactrians, under Bessus, resisted Alexander stoutly, but they were subdued in 328. Bactria took on Greek culture and became quasi-independent. Theoretically it remained part of the Seleucid empire. In 256 B.C., Diodotus I was made satrap, and a little later he assumed complete independence. His successor, Euthydemus, successfully resisted the attempts (208–206 B.C.) of Antiochus III to bring Bactria back into the empire. Euthydemus' son Demetrius made Bactria a powerful state. He was overlord of part of Chinese Turkistan and carried his conquests deep into N India, taking Patna. The Seleucid ruler, Antiochus IV, sent Eucratidas into Bactria, and Eucratidas in 167 B.C. brought about the death of Demetrius but was himself slain in 159 B.C. Menander, Demetrius' general, continued to exercise power until his death in 145 B.C. A little later (c.130 B.C.) Bactria fell to the nomadic Sakas and did not rise again as a state. See H. G. Rawlinson, *Bactria: The History of a Forgotten Empire* (1912, repr. 1969); W. W. Tarn, *The Greeks in Bactria and India* (2d ed. 1951); A. K. Narain, *The Indo-Greeks* (1957, repr. 1962).

Badagri (bädä'grē), town, SW Nigeria, on a lagoon off the GULF OF GUINEA. Jute bags are made there. Badagri was founded c.1730 and became an important shipping point for black African slaves. In the 1840's it became a center for British Christian missionaries, and in 1863 it was annexed by Britain. Badagri declined with the end of the slave trade.

Badajoz (bäthähōth'), city (1970 pop. 101,710), capital of Badajoz prov., SW Spain, in Estremadura, on the Guadiana River. It is situated in a fertile agricultural region where food processing is the main industry. Strategically located near the border of Portugal, it has an active trade with that country. Badajoz was an ancient fortress city that rose to prominence under the Moors as the seat (1022–94) of a vast independent emirate. Alfonso IX of León liberated it in 1228. Thereafter Badajoz was repeatedly attacked by the Portuguese and was consequently strongly fortified. The city has often been besieged; in the Peninsular War the French failed to take it in a long siege (1808–9) and succeeded in 1811 only to be driven out by Wellington in 1812 after bitter fighting. In the civil war of 1936–39 the capture (1936) of Badajoz by the Insurgents after a bloody battle was followed by hundreds of executions. Notable landmarks are the massive cathedral (begun in the 13th cent.) and the remains of the Moorish citadel. Charles IV's favorite, Manuel de Godoy, and the painter Luis de Morales were born in Badajoz.

Badakhshan (bädäkhshän'), province (1970 est. pop. 344,500), 16,844 sq mi (43,626 sq km), extreme NE Afghanistan, between the Hindu Kush Mts. and the Amu Darya River. The capital is FAIZABAD. Renowned for its mineral wealth, it is the world's chief source of lapis lazuli, a semiprecious stone. The deposits have been worked for more than 3,000 years. Rubies, emeralds, amethysts, and gold have also been mined in Badakhshan. Mountain goats and the famed Marco Polo wild sheep are hunted in the province (Marco Polo visited the area in 1272). Some agriculture and sheep and goat herding are also practiced. Badakhshan, part of the ancient Greek kingdom of Bactria, may once have been ruled by Alexander the Great. Its strategic location astride the trade routes from Europe and the Middle East to China and from central Asia and the Indian subcontinent made Badakhshan an international pawn for centuries. In 1859 it became an integral part of Afghanistan. Many of its inhabitants are Tadzhiks who speak an archaic form of Persian.

Badakhshan: see GORNO-BADAKHSHAN AUTONOMOUS OBLAST, USSR.

Badalona (bäthälō'nä), city (1971 pop. 162,888), Barcelona prov., NE Spain, in Catalonia. It is a Mediterranean port and an important industrial suburb of Barcelona, with textile, chemical, and glass manufactures. Nearby there are ancient tombs, possibly Phoenician, and the 15th-century monastery of San Jerónimo de la Murtra.

Bad Blankenburg: see BLANKENBURG, East Germany.

Bade, Josse: see BADIUS, JODOCUS.

Bad Ems, West Germany: see EMS.

Baden (bä'dən), former state, SW West Germany. KARLSRUHE was the capital. Stretching from the Main River in the northeast across the lower Neckar valley and along the right bank of the Rhine to the Lake of Constance (Bodensee), the former state of Baden bordered on France and the Rhenish Palatinate in the west, Switzerland in the south, Hesse in the north, and Bavaria and Württemberg in the east. It included the cities of Mannheim, Pforzheim, Heidelberg, Baden-Baden, Freiburg, and Rastatt and, in the south, most of the Black Forest. Until the French Revolution the area was a confusing jigsaw puzzle of petty margraviates and ecclesiastical states (the bishoprics of Mainz, Speyer, Strasbourg, and Konstanz). The BREISGAU belonged to the Hapsburgs, the Mannheim-Heidelberg area to the Rhenish PALATINATE. In 1771 the margraviates of Baden-Baden and Baden-Durlach were united as Baden under the same branch of the house of ZÄHRINGEN. Margrave Charles Frederick of Baden, raised to the rank of elector at the beginning of the 19th cent., joined the Confederation of the Rhine in 1806 with the title of grand duke and by 1810 had acquired, with the aid of Napoleon I of France, the entire state of Baden. Despite the liberal constitution of 1818 the grand duchy was severely shaken by the Revolution of 1848, which was suppressed with the help of Prussian troops. Among the revolutionary leaders in Baden was Friedrich Hecker. Baden sided with Austria in the Austro-Prussian War (1866), but joined the German Empire in 1871. It became a republic in 1918 and joined the Weimar Republic. After World War II, Baden was divided into two parts—in the south, the state of Baden (3,842 sq mi/9,951 sq km), occupied by France, and in the north, the state of Württemberg-Baden (1,984 sq mi/5,139 sq km), including part of Württemberg, occupied by U.S. armed forces. In 1952 the two states were merged with Württemberg-Hohenzollern to form the new state of BADEN-WÜRTTEMBERG.

Baden (bä'dən) or **Baden-bei-Wien** (-bī-vēn'), city (1971 pop. 22,600), Lower Austria province, E Austria, on the Schwechat River, near Vienna. The hot sulfur springs of this picturesque city have been frequented since Roman times. From 1945 to 1955, Baden served as the Soviet military headquarters for Austria.

Baden, anc. *Aquae Helveticae*, town (1970 pop. 14,115), Aargau canton, N Switzerland, on the Limmat River. A noted spa since ancient times, the town has hot sulfur springs. It is also a manufacturing center known for aluminum ware and electrical machinery. The Swiss diet met at Baden from c.1425 to 1712. The Treaty of Baden (1714) complemented the Peace of Utrecht (see UTRECHT, PEACE OF). Baden was the capital (1798–1803) of Baden canton under the HELVETIC REPUBLIC. The castle of Stein, now in ruins, was once a Hapsburg residence.

Baden-Baden (bä'dən-bä'dən), city (1970 pop. 37,537), Baden-Württemberg, SW West Germany, in the Black Forest. It is one of Europe's most fashionable spas. The city has many parks and a large casino (built 1821–24). Baden-Baden was founded as a Roman garrison in the 3d cent. Its hot mineral springs were used by the Romans, and remains of Roman baths have been found in the city. It was the residence of the margraves of Baden until the early 18th cent.

Badenoch (băd'ənŏkh"), highland district, 45 mi (72 km) long and 19 mi (31 km) wide, Inverness-shire, N central Scotland. It is a wild, densely wooded, mountainous region, cut by the river Spey; Loch Laggan is there. Kingussie is the main town and tourist center.

Baden-Powell of Gilwell, Robert Stephenson Smyth Baden-Powell, 1st Baron (bā'dən-pō'əl), 1857–1941, British soldier, founder of the BOY SCOUTS. He saw much active service in India and Africa prior to the South African War, in which he defended Mafeking for seven months (1899–1900) and subsequently organized the South African constabulary. For his enduring work in organizing (1908) the Boy Scout and Girl Guide movements, he received a peerage in 1929. His writings include *Scouting for Boys* (1908), *Rovering to Success* (1922), and *Scouting and Youth Movements* (1929). See biographies by E. E. Reynolds (1942, 2d ed. 1957) and William Hillcourt and O. S. Baden-Powell (1964).

Baden-Württemberg (bä'dən-wûr'təmbûrg, Ger. vür'təmbĕrk"), state (1970 pop. 8,895,000), 13,803 sq mi (35,750 sq km), SW West Germany. STUTTGART is the capital. It was formed in 1952 by the merger of WÜRTTEMBERG-BADEN, WÜRTTEMBERG-HOHENZOLLERN, and postwar Baden, all of which came into being after 1945. It includes the historic states of Baden and Württemberg, the former principality of HOHENZOLLERN, and the former district of LINDAU, Bavaria. The state borders on Switzerland in the south, France and the Rhineland-Palatinate in the west, Hesse in the north, and Bavaria in the east. Drained by the Rhine (which forms its border on the west), the upper Danube, and the Neckar, Baden-Württemberg includes the Black Forest in the southwest, the Lake of Constance in the south, and the Swabian Jura in the southeast. Although it is a forested and fertile land (the Rhine plain is one of the most fertile areas in Germany), industry is the main occupation. Industries (chiefly the manufacture of electrical power, chemicals, textiles, and machinery and the assembly of motor vehicles) are centered at Stuttgart, Mannheim, Karlsruhe, Heidelberg, Freiburg, and Ulm. Agriculture, forestry, and livestock raising are also important. One of the largest and most varied tourist areas of Germany, Baden-Württemberg has the picturesque Neckar valley, the idyllic forests and lakes of the south, and the famous spas of Baden-Baden and Wildbad. Freiburg and Heidelberg have noted universities. The history of Baden-Württemberg is the history of BADEN and of WÜRTTEMBERG.

Badger, Joseph, 1708–65, American painter, b. Charlestown, Mass. By trade a glazier and house and sign painter, he turned his hand to portraiture. Generally uninspired, his work appears at its best in his numerous portrayals of young children, such as Jeremiah Belknap (Mus. of Art, Cleveland). See Cuthbert Lee, *Early American Portrait Painters* (1929).

badger, name for several related members of the WEASEL family. Most badgers are large, nocturnal, burrowing animals, with broad, heavy bodies, long snouts, large, sharp claws, and long, grizzled fur. The Old World badger, *Meles meles*, is found in Europe and in Asia N of the Himalayas; it is about 3 ft (90 cm) long, with a 4-in. (10-cm) tail, and weighs about 30 lb (13.6 kg). Its unusual coloring, light above and dark below, is unlike that of most mammals but is found in some other members of the family. The head is white, with a conspicuous black stripe on each side. European badgers live, often in pairs, in large burrows called sets, which they usually dig in dry slopes in woods. They emerge at night to forage for food; their diet includes rodents, young rabbits, insects, and plant matter. The American badger, *Taxidea taxus*, is about 2 ft (60 cm) long, with a 5-in. (13-cm) tail and weighs 12 to 24 lb (5.4–10.8 kg); it is very short-legged, which gives its body a flattened appearance. The fur is yellowish gray and the face black, with a white stripe over the forehead and around each eye. It is found in open grasslands and deserts of W and central North America, from N Alberta to N Mexico. It feeds largely on rodents; an extremely swift burrower, it pursues ground squirrels and prairie dogs into their holes, and may construct its own living quarters 30 ft (9.1 m) below ground level. American badgers are solitary and mostly nocturnal; in the extreme north they sleep through the winter. Several kinds of badger are found in SE Asia; these are classified in a number of genera. Badgers are classified in the phylum CHORDATA, subphylum Vertebrata, class Mammalia, order Carnivora, family Mustelidae.

Bad Godesberg (bät gō'dəsbĕrk), part of BONN, North Rhine-Westphalia, W West Germany, on the Rhine River. It is the site of numerous foreign embassies and government agencies as well as residences of diplomats and government officials. It is also a resort noted for its radioactive mineral springs. In Sept., 1938, Adolf Hitler and British Prime Minister Neville Chamberlain met there (see MUNICH PACT). Bad Godesberg was incorporated into Bonn in 1969.

Bad Homburg vor der Höhe (bät hôm'bo͝ork fôr dĕr hö'ə), **Bad Homburg,** or **Homburg,** city (1970 pop. 41,598), Hesse, central West Germany, at the foot of the Taunus mts. It is a famous spa and resort. Manufactures include foodstuffs and machinery. Chartered in the early 14th cent., Bad Homburg was from 1622 to 1866 the capital of the landgraviate of Hesse-Homburg.

Badía y Leblich, Domingo (dōmēng'gō bäthē'ä ē läblēk'), 1766–1818, Spanish traveler, known as Ali Bey. Posing as a Muslim, he set out from Cádiz (1803) and traveled through N Africa, Syria, and Arabia, reaching Mecca, of which he fixed the position astronomically. He wrote *Voyage d' Ali Bey en Asie et en Afrique* (1814). See D. G. Hogarth, *The Penetration of Arabia* (1904, repr. 1967).

Badings, Henk (hĕngk bä'dĭngz), 1907–, Dutch composer, b. Bandung, Java (now Indonesia). Badings studied with Willem Pijper after working as a mining engineer. An extremely prolific composer, he started writing electronic music in the 1950s. Some of his music utilizes scales of alternating whole and half steps and pluritonality. Badings's first symphony was written in 1930; other works are the electronic ballet *Evolutions* (1958) and the opera *Salto Mortale* for voices and electronic accompaniment.

Bad Ischl (bät ĭsh'əl) or **Ischl,** city (1971 pop. 12,700), in Upper Austria prov., W Austria, in the center of the SALZKAMMERGUT. It is a famous spa. After 1822 it was the summer residence of the Austrian imperial family. Emperor Francis Joseph signed (1914) his declaration of war on Serbia there.

Badius, Jodocus (jōdō'kəs bā'dēəs), 1462–1535, French printer, b. Asche, near Brussels. His original name was Josse Bade, and he is sometimes called for his birthplace Jodocus Badius Ascensius. He taught Greek and edited classics in Lyons before he became a printer, gaining recognition as a scholar and as an author; his writings include a life of Thomas à Kempis. In 1503 he went to Paris where he established the Ascensian press, which printed over 400 books, mainly Greek and Latin texts. His printer's marks are early pictures of a printing press. See A. F. Johnson, *French Sixteenth Century Printing* (1928).

Bad Kreuznach (bät kroits'näkh), city (1970 pop. 42,146), Rhineland-Palatinate, W West Germany, on the Nahe River. Its manufactures include precision instruments, tires, glass, and leather. Bad Kreuznach was probably settled in the Stone Age. Its radioactive salt baths have been frequented since Roman times, when it was a garrison town.

badlands, area of severe erosion, usually found in semi-arid climates and characterized by countless gullies, steep ridges, and sparse vegetation. Badland topography is formed on poorly cemented sediments that have few deep-rooted plants because short, heavy showers sweep away surface soil and small plants. Depressions gradually deepen into gullies. The term *badlands* was first applied to the arid, dissected plateau region of SW South Dakota by Indians and fur trappers who found the area difficult to cross. South Dakota's Big Badlands, also known as the Badlands of the White River, are the world's best and most extensive (c.2,000 sq mi/5,180 sq km) example of this topography. Gullies have cut as deep as 500 ft (152 m) below the plateau's surface, and differences in rock type have created colorful and spectacular formations. The Big Badlands are famous for fossils of prehistoric animals. Badlands National Monument occupies most of the region (see NATIONAL PARKS AND MONUMENTS, table).

badminton (băd'mĭntən), game played by volleying a shuttlecock (called a "bird")—a small, cork hemisphere to which feathers are attached—over a net. Light, gut-strung rackets are used. Badminton, which is generally similar to tennis, is played by two or four persons. A badminton court for singles play measures 17 ft (5.18 m) by 44 ft (13.40 m) and for doubles 20 ft (6.10 m) by 44 ft (13.40 m). The net is 5 ft (1.52 m) high at the center and 5 ft 1 in. (1.55 m) at the posts. The game probably originated in India (where it was called poona), although it may have been known earlier in China. It was popular in the 1870s in England, taking its name from Badminton, the Gloucestershire estate of the duke of Beaufort. The game was introduced into the United States in the 1890s and grew in popularity in the 1930s. The International Badminton Association (founded 1934) sponsors the Thomas Cup for men's teams and the Woer Cup for women's teams, the world championships of badminton.

Bad Nauheim (bät nou'hīm), town (1970 pop. 14,242), Hesse, central West Germany, in the Taunus mts. It is a world-famous resort, noted for its salt springs, which are used to treat heart and nerve diseases.

Badoglio, Pietro (pyā'trō bädō'lyō), 1871–1956, Italian soldier and public official. After serving in World War I, he was governor of Libya (1929–33) and succeeded Gen. Emilio de Bono as commander in chief in the Ethiopian conquest, which he brought (1936) to a victorious end. Created duke of Addis Ababa, he was briefly viceroy of Ethiopia, then chief of the Italian general staff until 1940. After the fall of Mussolini, he was made (1943) premier by King Victor Emmanuel III. He negotiated an armistice with the Allies, whom he joined in the war against Germany. Meeting with much opposition in Italy, he resigned in 1944. He wrote *Italy in the Second World War* (tr. 1948).

Bad Reichenhall (bät rī'khənhäl) or **Reichenhall,** town (1970 pop. 13,042), Bavaria, SE West Germany, on the Saalach River, near the Austrian border. It is a year-round health resort. Salt has been mined there since Roman times.

Badrinath (bŭd'rĭnät), peak, 23,210 ft (7,074 m) high, in the central axis of the Himalayas, Uttar Pradesh state, N India. The peak has several glaciers. At a height of c.10,000 ft (3,050 m), is an 8th-century monastery and a temple to the Hindu god Shiva, a popular pilgrimage center built by the great Indian scholar and teacher Sankaracharya.

Baduila: see TOTILA.

Baeck, Leo (lā'ō bĕk), 1873–1956, German rabbi and scholar. He studied at the conservative Jewish Theological Seminary of Breslau and then at the liberal Hochschule für die Wissenschaft des Judentums in Berlin, also attending the universities of Breslau and Berlin; at Berlin he studied philosophy under Wilhelm Dilthey. He held positions as rabbi in Oppeln (1897–1907), Düsseldorf (1907–12), and Berlin (1912–43). In 1943 he was sent to the Theresienstadt concentration camp. After being liberated in 1945, he moved to London, becoming president of the World Union for Progressive Judaism; he also taught on occasion at the Hebrew Union College in Cincinnati. Baeck's works in English translation include *The Essence of Judaism* (1905, tr. 1936), *The Pharisees and Other Essays* (1947), and *Judaism and Christianity* (1958). In *This People Israel* (1955, tr. 1965), he propounded his belief in the eternal dialectical polarity between "mystery" and "command," the latter being the divine instructions that give concrete expression to the "mystery" in terms of man's obligations to others, which he defined as piety. See A. H. Friedlander, *Leo Baeck, Teacher of Theresienstadt* (1968).

Baeda: see BEDE, SAINT.

Baedeker, Karl (bā'dĕkər), 1801–59, German publisher, founder of the Baedeker guidebooks. His printing establishment was at Koblenz, but his son Fritz, who continued the business, moved it to Leipzig. Printed in several languages, the guidebooks provided valuable historical information and ran into many editions, especially for European countries. Although the firm's files were destroyed during World War II, the business was revived after the war by a great-grandson of Baedeker. In 1950 the firm began publishing automobile touring guides.

Baekeland, Leo Hendrik (bāk'lănd), 1863–1944, American chemist, b. Belgium, grad. Univ. of Ghent, 1882. In 1889 he emigrated to the United States. He founded (1893) and conducted, until 1899, when he sold the rights to Eastman, a company for producing a photographic paper of his own invention. In 1909 he announced his invention of BAKELITE, and from 1910 to 1939 he served as president of the Bakelite Corp. He wrote *Some Aspects of Industrial Chemistry* (1914).

Baer, George Frederick (bâr), 1842–1914, American financier, b. Somerset co., Pa. Baer became legal adviser to J. Pierpont Morgan and held many posts as a key figure in the railroad-and-coal empire. He is remembered for his refusal to arbitrate in the strike of the anthracite-coal miners in 1902.

Baer, Karl Ernst von, 1792–1876, Estonian biologist. He was a professor at Würzburg and Königsberg and from 1834 at St. Petersburg. Considered a founder of modern embryology, he discovered the notochord as well as the mammalian ovum. In his *History of the Development of Animals* (2 vol., 1828–37) he presented the theory of embryonic germ layers (the development of body tissues and organs from definite layers of cells formed in the early embryonic stages) and showed that the development of the embryo in different animals is similar in its early stages. He made these ideas a basis for a general evolutionary theory.

Baerle-Duc: see BAARLE-HERTOG, Belgium.

Baeyer, Adolf von (Johann Friedrich Wilhelm Adolf von Baeyer)(ä'dôlf fən bā'yər; yōhän' frē'drĭkh vĭl'hĕlm), 1835–1917, German chemist. He taught at Berlin and Strasbourg and in 1875 succeeded Liebig at Munich. For his work in organic chemistry, especially that on organic dyes and the hydroaromatic compounds, he received the 1905 Nobel Prize in Chemistry. His discovery of the molecular structure of indigo and his research on many other organic substances did much to develop the chemical industry of Germany. His collected works were published in German (1905).

Báez, Buenaventura (bwä"nävänto͞o'rä bä'ās), c.1810–1884, president of the Dominican Republic (1849–53; 1856–58; 1865–66; 1868–73). Like his bitter rival, SANTANA, Báez was unscrupulous and selfish; he gained and lost the presidency by revolution and counterrevolution. With his country in a condition of financial ruin and recurrently gripped by anarchy, he negotiated (1869) a treaty with the United States providing for U.S. annexation of the Dominican Republic. A Dominican plebiscite (1870) confirmed the treaty, but the U.S. Senate, ignoring President Grant's wishes, failed to ratify it. Báez lost his popular support and was overthrown.

Baez, Joan (bä'ĕz, bīz), 1941–, American folk singer and political activist, b. New York City. Baez began singing folk ballads, blues, and spirituals in Cambridge, Mass., coffeehouses, singing traditional folk songs such as "Donna, Donna," "Mary Hamilton," and "All My Trials" in a clear soprano voice with a three-octave range. She made folk music popular where it had been largely ignored. Baez's folk records were the first complete albums to become best-sellers. Her later albums include several of her own compositions, e.g., "Song for David" and "Blessed Are." Among the first performers to urge social protest, she sang and marched for civil and student rights and peace. Since the late 1960s she has devoted most of her time to her school for nonviolence in California. See her autobiography, *Daybreak* (1968).

Baffin, William, c.1584–1622, British arctic explorer. He was pilot on two expeditions (1615–16) sent out to search for the NORTHWEST PASSAGE under command of Robert Bylot, who was formerly with Henry Hudson. The first expedition vainly tried to find a channel in Hudson Bay N of Southampton Island. The second attempt, NW through Davis Strait, led to exploration of what was later called Baffin Bay and the northeast shore of Baffin Island. The existence of Baffin Bay was discredited until 1818 when Sir John Ross confirmed Baffin's discovery and observations. Baffin's conviction that the Northwest Passage did not exist discouraged arctic exploration for a time. His narratives were edited by Sir Clements Markham in 1881.

Baffin Bay, ice-clogged body of water, c.700 mi (1,130 km) long, between Greenland and NE Canada. It connects with the Arctic Ocean to the north and west and with the Atlantic Ocean to the south by way of Davis Strait. Although more than 9,000 ft (2,740 m) deep, navigation in the bay is made hazardous by many icebergs brought there by the Labrador Current. In the 1800s the bay was an important whaling station. The British explorer John Davis was first (1585) to enter the bay, which is named for William Baffin, who explored it in 1616.

Baffin Island, 183,810 sq mi (476,068 sq km), c.1,000 mi (1,610 km) long and from 130 to 450 mi (210–720 km) wide, in the Arctic Ocean, E Northwest Territories, Canada. It is the fifth-largest island in the world and the easternmost member of the Arctic Archipelago. Baffin Island is geographically and geologically a continuation of Labrador, from which it is separated by Hudson Strait. The western side of the island is covered largely by tundra. There are many freshwater lakes, including Nettilling (1,956 sq mi/5,066 sq km) and Amadjuak. In the east, snow-covered mountain ranges rise more than 8,000 ft (2,440 m). Baffin Island has a deeply indented coastline with many fjords. Most of the island's inhabitants are Eskimos who live mainly at coastal trading posts. Whaling, fur trading, and fishing are the chief occupations. The posts have stores, post offices, police stations, schools, and occasionally hospitals. Martin Frobisher visited the island between 1576 and 1578, and Frobisher Bay, in the southeast, is the principal town. The island is named for William Baffin, the British explorer who explored the Arctic in 1616.

Baffin Island National Park, c.8,290 sq mi (21,470 sq km), SE Franklin dist., Northwest Territories, Canada, on E Baffin Island near Pangnirtung; est. 1972. Located on the Cumberland Peninsula, it was the first Canadian national park to be created N of the Arctic Circle. The park includes scenic fjords, glaciated mountains, numerous glaciers, and the extensive Penny Ice Cap.

Bagdad: see BAGHDAD, Iraq.

Bagehot, Walter (băj'ət), 1826–77, English social scientist. After working in his father's banking firm, he edited (1860–77) the *Economist* (which had been founded by his father-in-law) and helped establish its high reputation as a financial journal. From these activities came his noted study of the English banking system, *Lombard Street* (1873). Bagehot's classic *English Constitution* (1864) distinguished between the effective institutions of government and those, like the House of Lords, that had entered decay. His other important books include *Literary Studies* (1879) and *Economic Studies* (1880). In *Physics and Politics* (1875) he made a pioneer analysis of the interrelationship between the natural and the social sciences. Bagehot was also a noted literary critic of his day. See his collected works (10 vol., 1915); biography by William Irvine (1939, repr. 1970); studies by Alistair Buchan (1960) and Norman St. John-Stervas (1963).

Baggesen, Jens (yĕns băg'əsən), 1764–1826, Danish poet and satirist, b. Zealand. Although a Germanophile, Baggesen was considered the leading Danish poet of his day. His elegant, imaginative poems include *Comic Tales* (1785) and the satirical *The Ghost and Himself; or, Baggesen on Baggesen. The Labyrinth* (2 vol., 1792–93), his outstanding prose work, is a vivid and witty account of his journeys.

Baghdad or **Bagdad** (both: băg'dăd, bägdäd'), city (1970 est. pop. 2,183,760), capital of Iraq, central Iraq, on both banks of the Tigris River. Most of Iraq's industries are in Baghdad; they include the making of carpets, leather, textiles, cement, and tobacco products and the distilling of arrack. The present city was founded (762) on the west bank of the Tigris by the Abbasid caliph MANSUR, who made it his capital. Its commercial position became generally unrivaled and under the caliph HARUN AR-RASHID it rose to become one of the greatest cities of Islam. Baghdad was the home of eminent scholars and artists and enjoyed great wealth from the sale of its silks and tiles. Its many gardens gave added justification to its claim to be the "Abode of Peace." This period of its greatest glory is reflected in the *Thousand and One Nights,* in which many of the tales are set in Baghdad. After the death (809) of Harun the seat of the caliph was moved to Samarra; when the caliphate was returned later in the century, Baghdad had already been weakened by internal struggles. In 1258 the Mongols sacked the city and destroyed nearly all of its splendor. It revived but was captured again by Tamerlane (1400) and by the Persians (1524). It was repeatedly contested by Persians and Turks until 1638, when it definitively became part of the Ottoman Empire. By that time the city's population had dwindled from a peak of about 2,000,000 to only a few thousand. Baghdad was captured by the British in 1917. In 1920 it became the capital of the newly constituted kingdom of Iraq. The city was the scene of a coup in 1958 that overthrew the monarchy and established the Iraqi republic. Baghdad is rich in archaeological remains and has several museums. There are three universities in Baghdad; the largest is the Univ. of Baghdad (1958).

Baghdad Pact: see CENTRAL TREATY ORGANIZATION.

Baghdad Railway, railroad of international importance linking Europe with Asia Minor and the Middle East. The line runs from İstanbul, Turkey, to Basra, Iraq. The railroad was initially financed chiefly by German capital; its Anatolian sections were completed in 1896. The ambitious project was then formed to extend the railroad to Baghdad, and a company, again backed chiefly by German capital, was organized for the purpose. Immediate protests were made to Turkey by France, Russia, and, particularly, Great Britain, which saw in the projected line a direct threat to its empire in India. Operations were held up for several years by these international representations and by engineering difficulties, but in 1911 work was resumed. By playing on imperialistic rivalries, the construction of the railroad was a factor in bringing about World War I. By the end of the war only a stretch between Mosul and Samarra remained to be completed on the main line. See E. M. Earle, *Turkey, the Great Powers, and the Bagdad Railway* (1923, repr. 1966); J. B. Wolf, *The Diplomatic History of the Bagdad Railroad* (1936, repr. 1973).

Baghlan (băg'län), city (1971 pop. 105,944), N Afghanistan, on the Kunduz River. A center of beet sugar production, it has industries producing cotton and fabrics.

Bagley, William Chandler, 1874–1946, American educator and editor, b. Detroit, grad. Michigan State College, 1895, M.S. Univ. of Wisconsin, 1898, Ph.D. Cornell Univ., 1900. He taught in elementary schools before becoming (1908) professor of education at the Univ. of Illinois. He was professor of education at Teachers College, Columbia, from 1917 to 1940. An opponent of pragmatism and progressive education, Bagley insisted on the value of knowledge for its own sake, not merely as an instrument, and he criticized his colleagues for their failure to emphasize systematic study of academic subjects. Of his many works, *Education and Emergent Man* (1934) contains the clearest exposition of his educational philosophy. His other writings include *The Educative Process* (1905), *Educational Values* (1911), and *Determinism in Education* (1925). Bagley was editor in chief of the *Journal of the National Education Association* (1920–25) and *School and Society* (1939–46), which he founded in 1915. See biographies by F. B. Stratemeyer (1939) and I. L. Kandel (1961).

Bagnères-de-Luchon (bänyĕr"-də-lüshôN'), town (1968 pop. 4,139), Haute-Garonne dept., S France, at the foot of the Maladetta Mts. It is an important resort in the Pyrenees. Its warm sulfur springs have been known since Roman times.

Bagnold, Enid, 1889–, English novelist and playwright, b. Rochester, Kent, England. She was a nurse in a military hospital in World War I. In 1920 she married Sir Roderick Jones, head of Reuters news agency. Bagnold's works combine wit, charm, sophistication, and wisdom. Her best-known novel is *National Velvet* (1935), the story of a teenage girl who wins a horse in a raffle and rides it to victory in the famed Grand National race. Bagnold's other works include the novels *Serena Blandish* (1924) and *The Loved and the Envied* (1951), and the plays *The Chalk Garden* (1955) and *The Chinese Prime Minister* (1964). See her autobiography (1969).

Bagot, Sir Charles (băg'ət), 1781–1843, British diplomat. As minister to the United States (1815–20) he negotiated the RUSH-BAGOT CONVENTION, which limited armaments along the U.S.-Canadian border. As governor general of Canada (1841–43), he was instructed by the British cabinet to resist Canadian demands for responsible government along the lines proposed by the earl of DURHAM. Bagot, however, allowed Robert BALDWIN and Sir Louis LaFONTAINE to form a ministry on the basis of their parliamentary majority. See G. P. Glazebrook, *Sir Charles Bagot in Canada* (1929).

Bagotville (băg'ətvĭl), town (1971 pop. 6,041), S Que., Canada, on Ha Ha Bay, an arm of the Saguenay River. It is the port for the area's industries.

bagpipe, musical instrument whose ancient origin was probably in Mesopotamia from which it was carried east and west by Celtic migrations. It was used in ancient Greece and Rome and has been long known in India. Some form of bagpipe was later used in nearly every European country; it was particularly fashionable in 18th-century France, where it was called the musette. Its widest use and greatest development was in the British Isles, particularly Northumberland, Ireland, and Scotland. The island of Skye was the home of a school for pipers. The Highland pipe of Scotland, the most well-known type, was a martial instrument and from it comes the modern great pipe; but at least six other

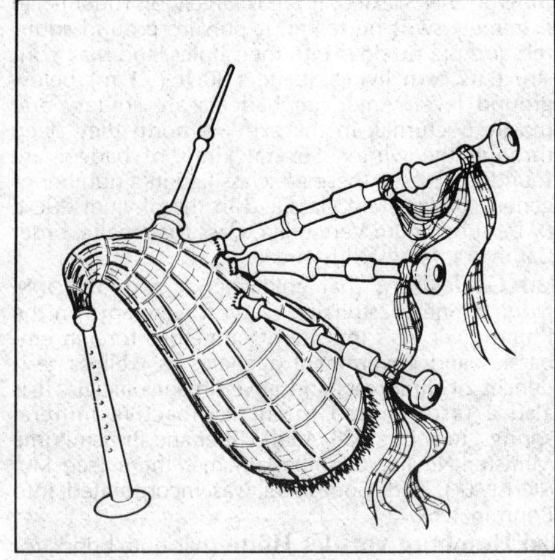

Scottish bagpipe

types were once used in the British Isles. The basic construction of a bagpipe consists of a bag, usually leather, which is inflated either by mouth through a tube or by a bellows worked by the arm; one or two chanters (or chaunters), melody pipes having finger holes and fitted usually with double reeds; and one or more drones, which produce one sustained tone each and usually have single reeds, though the musette drones have double reeds (see REED INSTRUMENT). Associated with folk and military music, it has been neglected by composers, possibly because of its short range. See Anthony Baines, *Bagpipes* (1960); T. H. Podnos, *Bagpipes and Tunings* (1974).

Bagration, Piotr Ivanovich, Prince (pyô'tər ēvä'-nəvyĭch bägrätēôn'), 1765–1812, Russian general in the French Revolutionary and Napoleonic Wars. He fought under Field Marshal SUVOROV in the Italian and Swiss campaigns of 1798–99 and at Austerlitz, Eylau, and Friedland. In 1808 he captured the Aland Islands from Sweden; in 1809 he fought against the Turks in the Russo-Turkish War of 1806–12; and in 1812 he commanded an army against Napoleon and was mortally wounded at Borodino.

Bagrationovsk (bəgrŭ"tyĕô'nəfsk), town, NW European USSR, formerly in East Prussia, on the Polish border. Its German name was Eylau or Preussisch Eylau. It is a rail terminus and has meat-processing and dairy industries. The town was founded in 1336. In Feb. 1807, it was the site of a bloody, indecisive battle between Napoleon I and the allied Russian and Prussian forces that checked Napoleon's movement toward the Russian frontier. The town is named in honor of Gen. P. I. Bagration, who distinguished himself during the battle.

Baguio (bă'gēō, Sp. bägyō'), city (1970 pop. 84,538), Mountain prov., NW Luzon, the Philippines. Baguio is the summer capital of the country, with many government buildings. It is also a noted mountain resort situated in beautiful pine forests and is the center of a major gold-producing area. The city is noted for the wood carvings of its Igorot aborigines. Nearby, at Lepanto, are important copper mines, and there is a major hydroelectric development on the Agno River. Originally settled by the Spanish, Baguio developed only after the American occupation, when a modern city was laid out (1909) by Daniel H. Burnham and roads were built (the first in 1913) to connect it with the main highways. The city was captured early (Dec., 1941) in World War II by Japanese land forces. U.S. Camp John Hay is now maintained there by the U.S. military for recreational purposes. Baguio is the seat of the national Philippine Military Academy, the Univ. of Baguio, and St. Louis Univ.

bagworm, common name for the larva of small moths of the family Psychidae. The larva spins a silken cocoon as it travels, hence the term bagworm. When fully grown, the bagworm fastens its covering to a twig and pupates within it. Some species weave bits of leaves or twigs into their bags. During mating season the wingless, footless adult female perforates the lower end of the bag, crawls in, and soon after laying about a thousand overwintering eggs, dies. The larvae develop slowly, requiring several months to reach maturity. Bagworms prefer arborvitae and juniper trees, but practically all trees are attacked. The best known of these small moths is *Thyridop-*

teryx ephemeraeformis, occurring throughout the E United States and regions adjacent to the Gulf of Mexico. Control of the pests is through use of insecticides or by handpicking the cocoons before the eggs hatch at the end of May. Bagworms are classified in the phylum ARTHROPODA, class Insecta, order Lepidoptera, family Psychidae.

Bahadur Shah II (bähä'do͝or shä), 1775–1862, last Mogul emperor of India (1837–57). A political figurehead, he was completely controlled by the British East India Company, who found it convenient to maintain the fiction of Mogul rule. He was an old man of 82 at the time of the INDIAN MUTINY (1857–58), but implicated by rebel proclamation he was convicted of complicity and exiled to Rangoon for life.

Bahaism (bä'häĭzəm, bəhä'īzəm), religion founded by BAHA ULLAH and promulgated by his eldest son, Sir Abdul Baha Bahai (1844–1921). It is a doctrinal outgrowth of BABISM, with Baha Ullah as the Promised One of the earlier religion. Bahaism holds that God can be made known to man through manifestations, which have come at various stages of human progress; the prophets include Abraham, Moses, Christ, Muhammad, the Bab, and Baha Ullah. Bahaists believe in the unity of all religions, in universal education, in world peace, and in the equality of men and women. An international language and an international government are advocated. Emphasis is laid upon simplicity of living and upon service to suffering fellow men. The teachings spread across the world in the 20th cent. The center of the faith in the United States is the great house of worship at Wilmette, Ill. The administrative center of the world faith is in Haifa, Israel, and in recent years the movement has made progress throughout the world, particularly in Africa.

Bahama Islands, officially **Commonwealth of the Bahamas** (bəhä'məz), country (1970 pop. 168,209), 4,403 sq mi (11,404 sq km), in the Atlantic Ocean, consisting of some 700 islands and islets and about 2,400 cays, beginning c.50 mi (80 km) off SE Florida and extending c.600 mi (970 km) SE almost to Haiti. The country does not include the TURKS AND CAICOS ISLANDS, to the southeast, which, although geo-

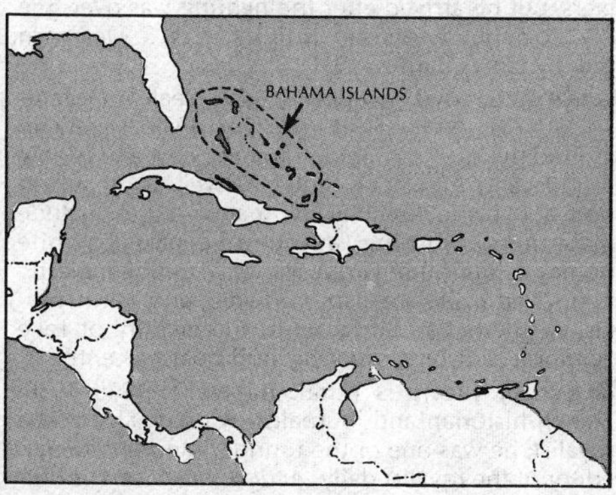

graphically part of the archipelago, have been separately administered by Great Britain since 1848. Until 1973, when they became independent, the Bahamas were administered as a British crown colony. The capital and principal city is NASSAU, on New Providence island. Other chief islands, known as "out islands," are Grand Bahama, Great and Little Abaco (see ABACO AND CAYS), the BIMINIS, Andros, Eleuthera, Cat Island, SAN SALVADOR, Great and Little Exuma (Exuma and Cays), Long Island, Crooked Island, Acklins Island, Mayaguana, and Great and Little Inagua (see INAGUA). The islands, composed mainly of limestone and coral, rise from a vast submarine plateau. Most of the islands are generally low and flat, riverless, with many mangrove swamps, brackish lakes (connected with the ocean by underground passages), and coral reefs and shoals. Fresh water is obtained from rainfall and from the desalinization. Navigation is hazardous, and many of the outer islands are uninhabited and undeveloped, although in recent years steps have been taken to improve transportation facilities. Hurricanes occasionally cause severe damage, but the climate is generally excellent. The islands' vivid subtropical atmosphere—brilliant sky and sea, lush vegetation, flocks of bright-feathered birds, and submarine gardens where multicolored fish swim among white, rose, yellow, and purple coral—as well as rich local color and folklore, has made the Bahamas one of the most fashionable and popular winter resorts in the hemisphere. Tourism, which has grown rapidly since the end of World War II, is by fa[r the] most important industry, employing a la[rge part] of the population and accounting for mos[t] foreign exchange. Crawfish, lumber, cement, agricultural products, and handicraft curios are ex[-] ported. Sugar and oil refining industries have been introduced to diversify the economy and to increase the Bahamas' export trade. The country's population is about 85% black and mulatto. English is the official language. The Bahamas have a relatively low illiteracy rate. The government provides free education through the secondary level; there is a branch of the Univ. of the West Indies at Nassau. The Bahamas are governed by the constitution of 1973 and have a parliamentary form of government. There is a bicameral legislature consisting of a 16-seat Senate and a 38-seat House of Assembly. The prime minister is the head of government, and the monarch of the United Kingdom, represented by an appointed governor-general, is the titular head of state.

History. Christopher Columbus first set foot in the New World in the Bahamas (1492), presumably at San Salvador, and claimed the islands for Spain. Although the aborigines, a gentle people called the Lucayos, were soon exterminated, the Spanish did not in fact colonize the islands. The first settlements were made in the mid-17th cent. by the English, who later imported blacks to work cotton plantations. In 1670 the islands were granted to the lords proprietors of Carolina, who did not relinquish their claim until 1787, although Woodes ROGERS, the first royal governor, was appointed in 1717. Under Rogers the pirates and buccaneers, notably Blackbeard, who haunted the Bahama waters, were driven off. The Spanish attacked the islands several times, and an American force held Nassau for a short time in 1776. After the American Revolution many Loyalists settled in the Bahamas. In 1781 the Spanish captured Nassau and took possession of the whole colony, but under the terms of the Treaty of Paris (1783) the islands were ceded to Great Britain. Plantation life gradually died out after the emancipation of slaves in 1838. Blockade-running into Southern ports in the U.S. Civil War enriched some of the islanders, and during the prohibition era in the United States the Bahamas became a base for rum-running. The United States leased areas for bases in the Bahamas in World War II and in 1950 signed an agreement with Great Britain for the establishment of a proving ground and a tracking station for guided missiles. In the 1950s black Bahamians, through the Progressive Liberal party (PLP), began to oppose successfully the ruling white-controlled United Bahamian party; but it was not until the 1967 elections that they were able to win control of the government. The Bahamas were granted limited self-government in 1964, broadened (1969) through the efforts of Prime Minister Lynden O. PINDLING. The PLP, campaigning on a platform of immediate independence, won an overwhelming victory in the 1972 elections, and negotiations with Britain were begun, and on July 10, 1973, the Bahamas became a sovereign state within the Commonwealth of Nations. See W. A. Roberts, *The Caribbean* (1940, repr. 1969); Timothy Severin, *The Golden Antilles* (1970); H. P. Mitchell, *Caribbean Patterns* (2d ed. 1970).

Baharampur (bəhä'rəmpôr) or **Berhampore** (bûr'-əmpôr), town (1971 pop. 73,380), West Bengal state, E central India. Jute and rice are traded. Its industries include silk weaving, ivory carving, and the production of bell metal. An early uprising in the INDIAN MUTINY occurred there.

Baharumite (bəhä'rəmīt): see BAHURIM.

Bahasa Indonesia (bähä'sä), another name for Indonesian, one of the MALAYO-POLYNESIAN LANGUAGES.

Baha Ullah or **Baha Allah** (bähä' o͞ol'ä), 1817–92, Persian religious leader originally named Mirza Husayn Ali Nuri. One of the first disciples of the Bab (see BABISM), he and his half-brother Subhi Azal became the leaders of the Babi faith. In 1863, shortly before being exiled to Constantinople, he declared himself the manifestation of God, the Promised One, as fortold by the Bab. He then founded BAHAISM and wrote its fundamental book, *Kitabi Ikan* (tr. *The Book of Certitude,* 1943). He spent most of his adult life in prison or under close surveillance. He died in Acre; his tomb there is one of the monuments of the Bahai faith. See J. E. Esslemont *Bahaullah and the New Era* (3d rev. ed. 1970).

Bahawalpur (bəhä'wəlpo͞or"), city (1969 est. pop. 146,800), capital of Bahawalpur division, Punjab prov., E central Pakistan, on the Sutlej River. It is a commercial center, trading in wheat, rice, dates, and cotton. Major manufactures are textiles, machinery,

B[...] mi [...] SALVAD[OR] [...]

Bahia, city, [...]

Bahía Blanca [...] 191,624), Buenos [...] near the head of th[e] [...] Atlantic Ocean. It is t[...] and principal shipping poi[nt] [...] as well as a rail terminus an[d] [...] huge import and export trade [...]. Founded as a fortress town in 182[...] [Bla]nca grew with the economic expansion of [...] [sou]thern Pampa in the early 20th cent. The Bernard[in]o Rivadavia library, founded in 1882, is a city landmark.

Bahr, Hermann (hĕr'män bär), 1863–1934, Austrian dramatist and critic. His essay *Zur Kritik der Moderne* (1890) established *modernism* as a literary term, and his study *Expressionismus* (1916, tr. 1925) defined that literary trend. Bahr's plays include the comedies *Das Konzert* (1909, tr. 1910) and *Der Meister* (1914, tr. 1918).

Bahraich (bärīch'), town (1971 pop. 73,925), Uttar Pradesh state, NE India, on the Saryu River. A district administrative center, Bahraich also carries on a trade in rice, maize, sugar, jute, timber, and herbs. The mausoleum of Saiyud Salar Masud (d. c.1050), a famous Muslim soldier and teacher, is in the town.

Bahrain or **Bahrein** (both: bärān', bə-), sheikhdom and archipelago (1973 est. pop. 225,000), 231 sq mi (598 sq km), in the Persian Gulf. The two main islands are Bahrain, or Aval, and Al Muharraq, connected by a causeway. The capital and chief port is AL MANAMAH, on Bahrain. The islands are flat and sandy, with a few low hills. The climate is hot and humid. There is intensive cultivation of dates and alfalfa; cereals, fruits, and vegetables are also grown, and there are poultry and dairy industries. Oil was found in 1931, and oil revenues have financed extensive modernization projects, particularly in

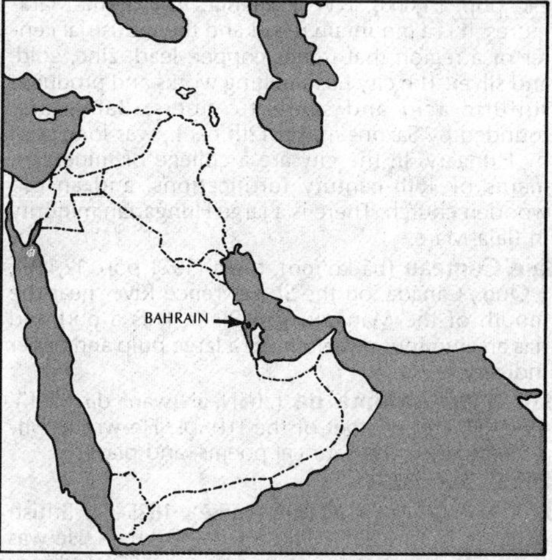

health and education. However, Bahrain is expected to be the first Persian Gulf nation to run dry of oil, and steps are being taken to diversify the nonagricultural sector of the economy. Ship-repair, aluminum, and turbine-manufacturing industries have been started or planned. The population is predominantly Arabic. Bahrain was ruled in the 16th cent. by Portugal and intermittently from 1602 to 1783 by Persia. The Persians were expelled by an Arabian family that established the presently ruling dynasty of sheikhs. In 1861, Bahrain became a British protectorate. There were demonstrations and strikes in the 1950s and 60s demanding greater popular participation in government. Iran claimed the islands in 1970 after the UN reported that the inhabitants desired independence. In 1971, after Britain withdrew from the Persian Gulf area, Bahrain became independent. Bahrain is a member of the United Nations and the Arab League. A council of state, constituting the executive, was appointed by the sheikh in 1970. In June, 1973, a constitution was adopted limiting the powers of the sheikh and granting women the right to vote. See Fereydum Adamīyat, *Bahrein Islands* (1955); A. M. Abu Hakima, *History of Eastern Arabia, 1750–1800: The Rise and Development of Bahrein and Kuwait* (1965).

see WHITE NILE.

Sudan: see BLUE NILE.

zal (bär-ĕl-gäzäl′), region and prov- SW Sudan. The region takes its name from a river that flows E to the Bahr-el-Jebel to form the White Nile. An area of swamps and ironstone plateaus, the region is inhabited mainly by pagan tribes, notably the Nilotic-speaking Dinka. Subsistence agriculture, cattle raising, and game hunting are carried on. Turco-Egyptian and European penetration of the region in the 19th cent. was followed by the development of slave trading. With the suppression of the slave trade in 1864 by the Egyptian Khedive, European traders withdrew and local merchant-princes, independent of the Khedive's authority, took over the trade. In 1873, al-Zubayr, the most powerful of the native merchant-princes defeated a Turco-Egyptian force sent to reinforce the ban on slave trading. The Khedive then made Bahr-el-Ghazal a nominal province of Egypt, with al-Zubayr as governor. A Mahdist force captured the region in 1884 but failed to maintain control. Anglo-Egyptian troops occupied Bahr-el-Ghazal in 1900.

Bahr el-Huleh: see HULA, LAKE.

Bahr-el-Jebel (bä'hər-ĕl-jĕb'ĕl), river, 594 mi (956 km) long, section of the White Nile, S Sudan, Africa. The name is usually used for the White Nile between Nimule, where it enters the Sudan (as the Albert Nile), and Lake No, where it joins with the Bahr-el-Ghazal to form the Bahr-el-Abiad, also a section of the White Nile. As the river passes through the Sudd swamps it loses much of its volume through evaporation and dispersal. The river is navigable to Juba.

Bahurim (bāhyo͝o′rĭm), town, NE of Jerusalem. 2 Sam. 3.16; 16.5; 17.18; 19.16; 1 Kings 2.8. Azmaveth of Bahurim is called once a Baharumite, once a Barhumite. 1 Chron. 11.33; 2 Sam. 23.31.

Baia (bī′ä), Lat. *Baiae,* village, in Campania, S Italy, on the Bay of Naples. In Roman times it was a celebrated spa and a favorite imperial residence, with sumptuous villas (1st cent. B.C.). There are remains of the huge Roman baths.

Baia-Mare (bī′ä-mä′rĕ), Hung. *Nagybánya,* city (1969 est. pop. 51,000), NW Rumania, in Crişana-Maramureş. It is a mountain resort and the industrial center of a region that mines copper, lead, zinc, gold, and silver. The city has smelting works and produces sulfuric acid and synthetic fibers. Baia-Mare, founded by Saxons in the 12th cent., was long held by Hungary. In the city are a college of mines, remains of 16th-century fortifications, and an old wooden church. There is a large Hungarian minority in Baia-Mare.

Baie Comeau (bā kō′mō), town (1971 pop. 12,109), E Que., Canada, on the St. Lawrence River near the mouth of the Manicouagan River. It is a port and has an aluminum smelter and a large pulp and paper industry.

Baïf, Jean Antoine de (zhäN äNtwän′ də bäēf′), 1532–89, French poet of the PLÉIADE. He wrote sonnets, didactic and satirical poems, and plays.

Baikal: see BAYKAL.

Baikie, William Balfour (bā′kē), 1825–64, British explorer in Africa, b. Kirkwall, the Orkneys. He was the surgeon of a Niger expedition in 1854 and succeeded to the command on the death of the leader. In 1856 he published an account of the expedition. Returning to Nigeria as leader of a second expedition, he established himself (1859) at LOKOJA. Under his leadership the town became an unofficial British settlement and thriving commercial center. He compiled valuable information about N Nigeria, including vocabularies of nearly 50 African dialects.

bail, in law, procurement of release from prison of a person awaiting trial or an appeal, by the deposit of security to insure his submission at the required time to legal authority. The monetary value of the security—known also as the bail, or, more accurately, the bail bond—is set by the court having jurisdiction over the prisoner. The security may be cash, the papers giving title to property, or the bond of private persons of means or of a professional bondsman or bonding company. Failure of the person released on bail to surrender himself at the appointed time results in forfeiture of the security. Bail is usually granted in a civil ARREST. Courts have greater discretion to grant or deny bail in the case of persons under criminal arrest, e.g., it is usually refused when the accused is charged with homicide. The Eighth Amendment to the Constitution of the United States provides that "excessive bail shall not be required," but it does not provide any absolute right to bail.

Baile Átha Cliath: see DUBLIN, county borough, Republic of Ireland.

Bailén (bīlān′), city (1970 pop. 13,233), Jaén prov., S Spain, in Andalusia. In 1808, early in the Peninsular War, a French army was surrounded and forced to surrender near Bailén by the Spanish under Castaños, who was made duke of Bailén.

Bailey, Anne, 1742–1825, American frontier heroine, b. Anne Hennis in Liverpool, England. She emigrated to Virginia c.1761. After her first husband, Richard Trotter, was killed at the battle of Point Pleasant (1774), she donned male attire and became a noted scout and messenger. At that time she married John Bailey. According to legend, Indians besieged Fort Lee, on the present site of Charleston, W. Va., in 1791, and Anne Bailey rode 100 mi (161 km) through the mountain wilderness to Fort Savannah (Lewisburg) and returned with enough ammunition to raise the siege. See biography by V. A. Lewis (1891).

Bailey, Gamaliel, 1807–59, American abolitionist editor, b. Mt. Holly, N.J. In 1837 he succeeded James Birney as editor and publisher of the *Philanthropist* at Cincinnati. Three times his office was attacked by proslavery mobs, and once the entire establishment was destroyed. From 1847 until his death Bailey ably edited the influential *National Era,* an abolitionist weekly published in Washington, D.C. Harriet Beecher Stowe's *Uncle Tom's Cabin* first appeared in that journal.

Bailey, Liberty Hyde, 1858–1954, American botanist and horticulturist, b. South Haven, Mich., grad. Michigan Agricultural College (now Michigan State College of Agriculture and Applied Science), 1882. At Cornell Univ. he was professor of horticulture (1888–1903) and dean of the agricultural college and director of the agricultural experiment station (1903–13). Through numerous writings and as chairman of President Theodore Roosevelt's Commission on Country Life (1908), he worked for the improvement of rural life. Bailey was influential in establishing horticulture as a respected science. He wrote many basic works on botany and horticulture, edited *The Standard Cyclopedia of Horticulture* (6 vol., 1914–17; new ed. 1935) and *Cyclopedia of American Agriculture* (4 vol., 1907–9), and compiled (with E. Z. Bailey) *Hortus* (1930, rev. ed. 1935) and *Hortus Second* (1941). See biographies by Philip Dorf (1956) and A. D. Rodgers (1949, repr. 1965).

Bailly, Jean Sylvain (zhäN sēlvăN′ bāyē′), 1736–93, French astronomer and politician. His works on astronomy and on the history of science (notably the *Essai sur la théorie des satellites de Jupiter*) were distinguished both for scientific interest and literary elegance and earned him membership in the French Academy, the Academy of Sciences, and the Academy of Inscriptions. He was elected (1789) from Paris to the States-General and was chosen president of the National Assembly. Mayor of Paris from 1789 to 1791, he lost favor with the popular elements that pushed the French Revolution onward. He permitted the national guard to fire upon a demonstrating crowd (July 17, 1791). Bailly retired from Paris, but in 1793 he was seized, taken to Paris, convicted of having contrived the July massacre, and guillotined. His lengthy *Essai sur l'origine des fables et des religions anciennes* was published in 1799.

Baily, Edward Hodges, 1788–1867, English sculptor. He studied under Flaxman. One of his best works is the statue of Admiral Nelson in Trafalgar Square, London. Other works include decorations for Buckingham Palace; numerous portrait busts and statues; and *Eve at the Fountain, Psyche,* and *Helen and Paris.*

Bailyn, Bernard, 1922–, U.S. historian, b. Hartford, Conn. After receiving his Ph.D. from Harvard in 1953, he taught (1953–) U.S. colonial history there, becoming full professor in 1961. His most noted work, the Pulitzer Prize winning *Ideological Origins of the American Revolution* (1967), challenged long-standing interpretations of the causes of the American Revolution. His other books include *The New England Merchants in the Seventeenth Century* (1955), *Education in the Forming of American Society* (1960), *The Origins of American Politics* (1968), and *The Ordeal of Thomas Hutchinson* (1974).

Baily's beads: see ECLIPSE.

Bain, Alexander, 1818–1903, Scottish philosopher and psychologist. He was educated at Marischal College, Aberdeen, where he later taught for three years. He taught one year (1845) at Anderson's Univ., Glasgow, but resigned to do free-lance work in London. There he joined a brilliant circle including George Grote and John Stuart Mill, with whom he already had close literary relationships. From 1860 to 1880 he held the chair of logic and English at the Univ. of Aberdeen (which had absorbed Marischal College), where he worked for educational reform. After his retirement he was twice elected lord rector of the university. His major contributions were in the field of psychology. Although he remained firmly in the associationalist tradition of the Mills and shared their distrust of metaphysics, he nevertheless developed the current psychology in several directions. The most important of these was toward a greater recognition of the importance of the will and emotions. He considered physiological factors but refused to make any materialistic assumptions. Besides being the founder of the first psychological journal, *Mind,* in 1886, Bain was the author of *The Senses and the Intellect* (1855), *The Emotions and the Will* (1859), *Mental and Moral Science* (1868), *Education as a Science* (1879), *James Mill* (1882), *John Stuart Mill* (1882), and an autobiography (pub. posthumously with a bibliography of his works, 1904).

Bainbridge, William, 1774–1833, American naval officer, b. Princeton, N.J. An experienced sea captain, he joined (1798) the navy when war with France threatened. His ship, the *Retaliation,* was captured by two French frigates, and he and his crew were imprisoned on Guadeloupe. Released, he returned to America and in 1800, as commander of the *George Washington,* he carried U.S. tribute money to the dey of Algiers (see TRIPOLITAN WAR). The dey forced him to proceed under the Turkish flag to Constantinople—an insult that contributed to the American decision to declare war against the BARBARY STATES. In 1803, assigned to the troubled Mediterranean area, Bainbridge's ship, the *Philadelphia,* ran aground in the harbor of Tripoli and was captured. He was freed at the end of the Tripolitan War. In the war of 1812, as commander of the CONSTITUTION, Bainbridge captured the British frigate *Java* off the Brazilian coast in Dec., 1812. In 1815, a commodore, he went out in the *Independence* to aid Stephen Decatur in the operations against Algiers, but he arrived after the fighting was over. See his biography written in 1816 by H. A. S. Dearborn (ed. by James Barnes, 1931).

Bainbridge, city (1970 pop. 10,887), seat of Decatur co., SW Ga., on the Flint River; inc. 1829. It grew up around the site of an Indian trading post and is now a trade and industrial center as well as an inland port and barge terminal. Its manufactures include machinery, clothing, automotive parts, mobile homes, aluminum windows, and molded plastic items. Fertilizers are also produced, and salt is processed there. Bainbridge is in the vicinity of Lake Seminole, a fishing, hunting, and boating center.

Bainville, Jacques (zhäk băNvēl′), 1879–1936, French historian and journalist. A nationalist and a royalist, he was one of the founders and the foreign editor of the royalist daily, *Action française.* His brilliant and concise *History of France* (1924, tr. 1926), although highly debatable in its nationalist thesis, is an eloquent apology for the monarchic tradition in France. His other writings include *Napoleon* (tr. 1934), *The French Republic, 1870–1935* (tr. 1936), and *Dictators* (tr. 1937, repr. 1967).

Baird, John Logie, 1888–1946, Scottish inventor. In 1926 he gave the first demonstration of true television with a televisor of his own invention that differed from later instruments in being partially mechanical rather than wholly electronic. He accomplished transatlantic television in 1928 and demonstrated color television in the same year. He also invented (1926) the noctovisor, an instrument for making objects visible in the dark or through fog by means of infrared light.

Baird, Spencer Fullerton, 1823–87, American zoologist, b. Reading, Pa., grad. Dickinson College, 1840. He was professor of natural history at Dickinson from 1846 to 1850. While at the Smithsonian Institution (from 1850; as secretary from 1878) he supervised the building of a museum to house the great collection of North American fauna that had been amassed under his guidance. In 1871, Congress established the U.S. Fish Commission with Baird as its head. Baird set up the Marine Biological Station at Woods Hole, Mass., organized the expeditions of the research ship *Albatross,* and initiated valuable studies on wildlife preservation. His publications (over 1,000 titles) show a phenomenal range of scientific work. His books on birds inaugurated the so-called Baird school of ornithological description, emphasizing accurate observation of each individual. Among other major studies were the *Catalogue of North American Reptiles* (with Charles Girard, 1853) and the *Catalogue of North American Mammals* (1857). See biography by W. H. Dall (1915).

Bairnsfather, Bruce (bârnz'fäthər), 1888–1959, English illustrator and author, b. India. He served with the British forces in World War I and created the cartoon character "Old Bill" to typify the spirit of the British infantryman. During World War II, Bairnsfather was cartoonist with the U.S. forces in Europe. His works include *Fragments from France* (1916), *Bullets and Billets* (1917), and *Jeeps and Jests* (1943).

Baius (bā'yəs) or **Bajus** (bā'jəs), **Michael,** 1513–89, Flemish Roman Catholic theologian, also known as Michel de Bay. He was chancellor of the Univ. of Louvain and was sent to the Council of Trent. Baius was the center of a subtle controversy on GRACE, in which he is said to have been the forerunner of Jansenism (see under JANSEN, CORNELIS). His position was peculiar in giving original sin an important place while at the same time making man partly instrumental in his own redemption. His doctrines were condemned several times (especially by the bull of St. Pius V, *Ex omnibus afflictionibus,* 1567), but Baius abjured, or recanted, each time, and he died in the church.

Baixada Fluminense (bīshä'də floomĕnēNn'sə), coastal lowland region, Rio de Janeiro state, SE Brazil. It extends c.250 mi (400 km) from Sepetiba Bay to the Paraíba River between the Serro do Mar and the Atlantic Ocean. Intensive farming, especially near Rio de Janeiro, is practiced there. Formerly marshy and disease breeding, much of the region was drained in the 1930s.

Baja (bŏ'yŏ), city (1970 pop. 34,360), S Hungary, on the Danube River. It is a river port and a road and rail hub, where agricultural products of the surrounding region are traded. Baja has textile, woodworking, and agricultural-processing industries. A fine 18th-century town hall is in the city.

Baja California (Span.: bä'hä kälēfôr'nyä) or **Lower California,** peninsula, c. 760 mi (1,220 km) long and from 30 to 150 mi (48–241 km) wide, NW Mexico, separating the Gulf of California from the Pacific Ocean. The peninsula is divided at lat. 28° N into the state of **Baja California** (1970 pop. 856,773), 27,655 sq mi (71,626 sq km), in the north, and the state of **Baja California Sur** (1970 pop. 123,786), 27,979 sq mi (72,466 km), in the south. The capitals of the states are, respectively, MEXICALI and LA PAZ. Except for two large coastal plains on the Pacific side, the peninsula consists largely of rugged mountain ranges averaging 5,000 ft (1,524 m), with one peak, San Pedro Martir, more than 10,000 ft (3,048 m) high. The land is generally desolate and arid. The only naturally cultivable areas are isolated mountain valleys. The mineral yield is considerable, especially silver, lead, gold, and copper. The state is by far more commercially advanced than the territory, and its population has increased rapidly. Irrigation systems on the Colorado River have made possible the development of a rich farming area around Mexicali. Baja California is a leading national producer of cotton and wheat. Fruits and vegetables are also important. There are fisheries and fish canneries at Ensenada, which is also developing as a resort. Wealthy Mexicans, who have bought large estates and established resort ranches on the scenic coasts, have done much to stir tourist interest in regions other than the border towns and to open up hitherto inaccessible areas. Hunting and deep-sea fishing are favorite sports. Communications are generally poor, particularly in the south. Baja California Sur is not economically prosperous, although there is pearl fishing around La Paz and the city itself is very popular with Mexican vacationers. Indians constitute a sizable percentage of Baja California's population. The coasts were first explored by Francisco de Ulloa and other Spaniards in the 1530s. Attempts to colonize the forbidding interior, even those made by the intrepid mission fathers, were largely unsuccessful. U.S. forces occupied (1847–48) Baja California during the Mexican War, and William Walker attempted (1853–54) to wrest it from Mexico in his first disastrous filibustering expedition. In 1911 the area was the scene of an abortive uprising against Porfirio Díaz—the so-called desert revolution led by Ricardo Flores Magón, a liberal anarchist, who was a precursor of Francisco Madero and Emiliano Zapata. The state of Baja California was created in 1952. The peninsula and surrounding waters are a paradise for naturalists and archaeologists, offering unparalleled opportunities for the study of marine life, plants and animals, and Indian artifacts. In 1962 remarkable mural paintings were discovered in a steep coastal cliff. See John Steinbeck, *The Log from the Sea of Cortez* (1951); Leonard Wibberley, *Yesterday's Land* (1961); Joseph Wood Krutch, *Baja California and the Geography of Hope* (1969); F. J. Clavijero, *The History of Lower California* (tr. 1937, repr. 1971).

Bajah (bäjä') or **Béja** (bāzhä'), town (1966 pop. 28,145), N Tunisia. It is on the site of ancient Vacca or Vaga, a Punic town and later a Roman colony. It became a military and administrative center under the Turks. The town has a sugar refinery.

Bajazet: For Ottoman sultans and princes thus named, see BEYAZID.

Bajer, Fredrik (frāth'rĭk bī'ər), 1837–1922, Danish pacifist and writer. He helped found the International Peace Bureau at Berne in 1891, and he shared the 1908 Nobel Peace Prize with K. P. Arnoldson.

Bajith (bā'jĭth), term of unknown significance. Isa. 15.2.

Bajus, Michael: see BAIUS, MICHAEL.

Bakacs, Thomas: see BAKOCZ, THOMAS.

Bakbakkar (băkbăk'ər), Levite. 1 Chron. 9.15.

Bakbuk (băk'bək), family that returned with Zerubbabel. Ezra 2.51; Neh. 7.53.

Bakbukiah (băk"bəkī'ə). **1** Levite with Zerubbabel. Neh. 11.17; 12.9. **2** Porter. Neh. 12.25.

Bakelite (bā'kəlīt) [for its inventor, L. H. Baekeland], synthetic thermosetting RESIN. It is widely used both alone, to form whole objects, and in combination with other materials, as a laminate or a surface coating. It is used as a substitute for hard rubber, amber, or celluloid; for insulating electrical apparatus (since it is a nonconductor); and for the manufacture of certain machinery gears, phonograph records, and many other articles useful and ornamental and as diverse in character as buttons, billiard balls, pipestems, and umbrella handles. Bakelite is a condensation POLYMER of FORMALDEHYDE and PHENOL. In practice, the phenol and formaldehyde are first polymerized to a small extent by using the proper choice of catalyst and temperature. The resulting prepolymer, called a resol, is a low-melting, soluble material, which can then be combined with a filler (usually cotton linters or wood fibers) and a pigment and heated under pressure in a mold to yield an object of the desired shape. The pure resin is colorless or amber-colored and very brittle; the various fillers and other additives give it the desired properties depending on its application. Heating of the prepolymer results in extensive cross-links between the polymer chains, resulting in a tightly bound three-dimensional network. A Bakelite-type resin can also be formed using FURFURAL in place of the formaldehyde.

Baker, Sir Benjamin, 1840–1907, English civil engineer. He helped build London's underground railway, Tower Bridge, and the Blackwall Tunnel, and with Sir John Fowler he designed and built the bridge over the Firth of Forth in Scotland. In Egypt he assisted with the first Aswan dam. Baker also designed the cylindrical ship used to carry the obelisk Cleopatra's Needle from Egypt to London.

Baker, George Fisher, 1840–1931, American financier and philanthropist, b. Troy, N.Y. Baker was one of the founders of the First National Bank of New York in 1863 and became (1877) its president and then (1909) chairman of its board of directors. Largely through his efforts this bank became one of the strongest financial institutions in the United States. Baker was closely associated with the interests of the house of Morgan; he helped finance James J. Hill in building his railroad empire and backed him in the fight to control the Northern Pacific RR. Baker himself became a leading figure in the world of railroad organization and finance and gained a commanding influence in insurance, utilities, and the steel and rubber industries. His philanthropic bequests were many. The most notable were $6 million to found and support the Harvard graduate school of business administration; $2 million to Cornell Univ.; $1 million to build the Baker Memorial Library at Dartmouth; and the money for Baker Field of Columbia.

Baker, George Pierce, 1866–1935, American educator, b. Providence, R.I., grad. Harvard, 1887. He taught (1888–1924) in the English department at Harvard and there conceived and instituted (1906) the 47 Workshop, a class on playwriting techniques and a laboratory of experimental productions. The first of its kind, the workshop was an inspiration to many young dramatists and gave impetus to the movement toward campus theater. In 1925 he went to Yale, where as professor of the history and technique of drama and director of the university theater he continued his work. Baker wrote *The Development of Shakespeare as a Dramatist* (1907, repr. 1965) and *Dramatic Technique* (1919) and edited the works of his students. See memorial by John Mason Brown and others (1939); W. P. Kinne, *George Pierce Baker and the American Theatre* (1954, repr. 1968).

Baker, Janet, 1933–, English mezzo-soprano. She made her singing debut in 1956 with the Glyndebourne Chorus. In 1966 she made her American debut at Town Hall in New York City, winning critical acclaim for the sensitivity, style, and intelligence of her singing. Baker was for many years regarded as primarily an oratorio and lieder singer. However, in 1969 she made a triumphal appearance as Dido in the Scottish Opera's production of Berlioz's *The Trojans,* repeating her performance later that year at Covent Garden in London. She soon was regarded as a great interpreter of Berlioz and began to take on more operatic roles.

Baker, Newton Diehl, 1871–1937, U.S. Secretary of War (1916–21), b. Martinsburg, W.Va. He practiced law and politics in Cleveland as a protégé of Tom L. Johnson. As city solicitor (1902–12) he opposed the powerful public utilities; as mayor (1912–16) he instituted notable tax reforms. Woodrow Wilson appointed him Secretary of War in March, 1916, just before the United States sent a punitive expedition into Mexico to oppose Francisco VILLA. An avowed pacifist, Baker suffered merciless criticism of his conduct of the War Dept. during the early months of World War I and was subjected to a congressional investigation in late 1917. His devotion to his task and the achievements of his department were later praised by all. He retired (1921) to private law practice in Cleveland but remained a public figure. An ardent advocate of peace, he urged U.S. entry into the League of Nations as late as 1924; in 1928, Coolidge appointed him to the Permanent Court of Arbitration (Hague Tribunal). See biographies by Frederick Palmer (1931, repr. 1969) and C. H. Cramer (1961); study by D. R. Beaver (1966).

Baker, Oliver Edwin, 1883–1949, American economic geographer, grad. Heidelberg College, Tiffin, Ohio. He studied forestry at Yale and agriculture and economics at the Univ. of Wisconsin (Ph.D., 1921). He served (1912–42) with the U.S. Dept. of Agriculture, largely in research on land utilization. Besides many articles and reports, he wrote with V. C. Finch *Geography of the World's Agriculture* (1917), and he edited the *Atlas of American Agriculture.*

Baker, Ray Stannard, pseud. **David Grayson,** 1870–1946, American author, b. Lansing, Mich., grad. Michigan State College, 1889. At first a Chicago newspaper reporter, he joined the staff of *McClure's Magazine* in 1897, for which he wrote some famous muckraking articles. With other *McClure's* contributors he purchased the *American Magazine* in 1906 and helped edit it. The first book of quiet country sketches by "David Grayson," *Adventures in Contentment,* appeared in 1907; the series continued with *Great Possessions* (1917), *The Countryman's Year* (1936), and others. An intimate of Woodrow Wilson, Baker was sent to Europe in 1918 as one of the President's special agents to study the war situation. At the peace conference at Versailles, Baker was director of the press bureau of the American peace commission. Afterward he wrote *Woodrow Wilson and World Settlement* (3 vol., 1922), a history of the peace conference based largely on the Wilson papers. With W. E. Dodd he edited Wilson's *Public Papers* (6 vol., 1925–26). His authoritative biography of Wilson (8 vol., 1927–39), for which he used the President's personal papers, won the Pulitzer Prize for biography in 1940 for the last two volumes. See his autobiographical works, *Native American: The Book of My Youth* (1941) and *American Chronicle* (1945).

Baker, Sir Samuel White, 1821–93, English explorer in Africa. He explored the Nile tributaries in Ethiopia in 1861–62. Going up the Nile from Cairo, he reached Gondokoro in 1863. He continued his journey southward in spite of the opposition of Arab slave traders and discovered Albert Nyanza, or Lake Albert, on March 14, 1864. In 1869, with the authority of the khedive of Egypt, he returned to the region and, creating an administration in the Lado Enclave, he suppressed the slave trade and opened up the lake areas to commerce.

Baker Island, uninhabited island (1 sq mi/2.6 sq km), central Pacific, near the equator, c.1,650 mi (2,660 km) SW of Honolulu. The arid coral island was discovered in 1832 by Capt. Michael Baker, an American, and was claimed by the United States in 1856. Like JARVIS ISLAND and HOWLAND ISLAND, Baker was worked for guano by both American and British companies during the 19th cent. In 1935 it was colonized by Americans from Hawaii in order to establish U.S. control against British claims. The colonists were removed during World War II. Baker Island is administered under the U.S. Dept. of the Interior.

Baker Lake, c.1,000 sq mi (2,590 sq km), Keewatin dist., Northwest Territories, Canada, W of Chesterfield Inlet of Hudson Bay. It has a post of the Royal Canadian Mounted Police at its western end.

Bakersfield, city (1970 pop. 69,515), seat of Kern co., S central Calif., at the southern end of the San Joaquin valley; inc. 1898. It is an oil, mining, and agricultural center. Almost all of the major oil companies have refineries in Bakersfield. Cotton, citrus fruits, potatoes, and roses are grown in the area. Among the city's manufactures are plastics, pharmaceuticals, and processed foods. Gold was discovered in the region in 1855 and petroleum in 1899. Silver, borax, and tungsten mines are also in the vicinity. A branch of California State College and a junior college are there. Kern River State Park is nearby.

Baker vs. Carr, case decided in 1962 by the U.S. Supreme Court. Tennessee had failed to reapportion the state legislature for 60 years despite population growth and redistribution. Charles Baker, a voter, brought suit against the state (Joe Carr was a state official in charge of elections) in Federal district court, claiming that the dilution of his vote as a result of the state's failure to reapportion violated the equal protection clause of the Fourteenth Amendment to the Constitution. The court dismissed the complaint on the grounds that it could not decide a political question. Baker appealed to the Supreme Court, which ruled that a case raising a political issue would be heard. This landmark decision opened the way for numerous suits on LEGISLATIVE APPORTIONMENT.

Bakewell, Robert, 1725–95, English livestock breeder and agriculturist. He successfully bred livestock for meat rather than appearance, developing new breeds, which included the Leicestershire sheep and the Dishley, or New Leicestershire, longhorn cattle. He introduced the progeny test for selective breeding and also improved methods of housing stock, cultivating grass, and manuring.

Bakhchisaray (bäkh"chēsərī') [Turkish, = garden palace], city, SE European USSR, in the Ukraine. From the early 15th cent. until 1783 it was the capital of the khanate of Crimea, or Little Tatary. The palace of the khans, celebrated by Pushkin and Mickiewicz for its beauty, notably for its white marble fountains, was built in the 16th cent. and is now a museum. In the city are many mosques and the tombs of the khans. Nearby are the ruins of Chufut-Kale.

Bakhtegan (bäkhtĕgän'), salt lake, c.60 mi (100 km) long, in the Zagros mts., S Iran; fed by the Kur River. The town of Niriz was once on its shores, but because of the lake's shrinkage is now to the southeast. Ancient accounts of the region do not refer to the lake, suggesting that it is of relatively recent origin. The lake is also called Niriz.

Bakhtiari (bäkh"tēä'rē, –ärē', băkh"–), ethnic group (1966 est. pop. 400,000), living in SW Iran, in a mountainous region (c.25,000 sq mi/64,750 sq km) located in Khuzistan and Esfahan provs. They herd sheep and cattle and grow wheat and barley. In the past they were chiefly nomadic, but today only about one third are nomads. The Bakhtiari are Shiite Muslims and are famed for their courage and independence. Women enjoy a high position in their patrilineal society. The group can be divided into two large branches, the Haftlang, with about 55 tribes, and the Charlang, with about 25. The Bakhtiari originally migrated (10th cent.) from Syria to Iran, and until the 15th cent. were known as the Great Lurs. In the early 20th cent., after the discovery of oil in the region they inhabit, their chiefs were courted by the British and were paid to protect oil pipelines. The Bakhtiari played a decisive part in the deposition of Muhammad Ali Shah in 1908–9. Reza Shah Pahlevi forced many of them to abandon their nomadic ways and to settle in permanent communities; after his deposition in 1941, however, some Bakhtiari returned to nomadism. Muhammad Reza Shah was married (1951–58) to Soraya, the daughter of a Bakhtiari chieftain.

Bakhuyzen, Ludolf: see BACKHUYSEN, LUDOLF.

baking soda: see SODIUM BICARBONATE.

Bakocz or **Bakacs, Thomas** (bŏ'kôts, bŭ'kŏch), Hung. *Bakócz* or *Bakács Tamás* (tŏ'mäsh), c.1442–1521, Hungarian politician, cardinal of the Roman Catholic Church. He is often called the Hungarian Wolsey. Of unbounded ambition, he rose from servile origin, was secretary to King Matthias Corvinus, and under Uladislaus II, whom he dominated, became chancellor, archbishop of Esztergom, and papal legate. Although he was expected by many to succeed Julius II as pope, Leo X was elected. Leo in 1514 charged him as primate of Hungary with a crusade against the Turks. The nobles did not heed Bakocz's call, and the peasants who had volunteered revolted against the aristocracy. The rebellion was crushed with great cruelty by John Zapolya (see JOHN I), and the few remaining liberties of the peasants were abolished. After Uladislaus's death Bakocz retired to Esztergom, where he died, leaving an enormous fortune.

Bakr, Ahmad Hasan al- (äkhmäd' häsän' äl-bäk'ər), 1914–, president of Iraq. He served as an officer in the Iraqi army but was forced to retire (1958) because of his participation in revolutionary activities. A member of the Ba'ath party, an ultranationalist left-wing group, he became prime minister after the Ba'athists seized power in 1963. He left the government later in that same year when conservative military leaders forced the Ba'athists from power. Bakr became president in 1968 after leading another Ba'athist coup d'etat.

Bakst, Lev Nikolayevich (lyĕf nyĭkəlī'əvyĭch bäkst), 1868–1924, Russian scene designer and painter. His original, imaginative style and brilliant color exerted a wide influence on costume, stage setting, and the decorative arts. His set and costume designs made for Diaghilev's ballets *Cleopatra* and *Scheherazade* from 1910 to 1912 gained him considerable fame. He was also a fine portrait painter, including among his subjects Diaghilev and Ida Rubinstein. See study by Charles Spencer (1973).

Baku (bäkōō', Rus. bəkōō'), city (1970 pop. 1,261,000), capital of the Azerbaijan Soviet Socialist Republic, SE European USSR, on the Caspian Sea. Greater Baku includes almost the whole Apsheron peninsula, on which Baku proper is situated. The city is a leading Soviet industrial and cultural center and until World War II was the country's chief petroleum center. It handles one of the greatest volumes of freight (mainly oil and oil products) of any Soviet port. Oil drilling (especially on the Apsheron peninsula and offshore) is the major economic activity, and Baku has many oil refineries and factories that produce oilfield equipment. Other important industries include shipbuilding and the processing of food and tobacco. Most of Baku's people are Azerbaijani, Russians, and Armenians. The city was first mentioned in a 9th-century chronicle; but as early as the 6th cent. B.C. oil and gas wells in the area were worshipped, and shrines were made of constantly burning fires. Baku was a great medieval trade and craft center. It flourished in the 15th cent. under the independent Shirvan shahs and from 1509 to 1723 under Persian rule. Captured by Peter I in 1723, it was returned to Persia in 1735. Russia annexed it definitively in 1806. Oil production began in the late 19th cent. Taken by the Bolsheviks in 1917, the city was occupied during the next two years by the White Army and its foreign allies (mainly Britain). From 1918 to 1920, Baku belonged to the independent, anti-Bolshevik Azerbaijan republic. The Old City, comprising the 13th-century fortress of Bad-Kube, has narrow, winding streets, several mosques, and the 17th-century palace of the khans of Baku, who were vassals of the Persian shahs. The mosque of Synyk-Kala dates from the 11th cent. and the Maiden's Tower from the 12th. In the European-style New City are the university (est. 1920), the Azerbaijanian Academy of Sciences, and many other educational and cultural institutions.

Bakunin, Mikhail (mēkhəyēl' bəkōō'nyĭn), 1814–76, Russian revolutionary and leading exponent of ANARCHISM. He came from an aristocratic family but entered upon revolutionary activities as a young man. He took part (1848–49) in the revolutions in France and Saxony and was sent back to Russia and exiled to Siberia. Escaping (1861), he went to London, where he worked with Aleksandr HERZEN. In 1868, Bakunin became active in the First INTERNATIONAL, where, with his militant anarchist doctrines, he had great influence. These doctrines, however, brought him into conflict with Karl MARX, and he was expelled (1872). Bakunin believed that man is inherently virtuous and deserving of absolute freedom obtained through extreme individualism. He advocated violent overthrow of existing states and institutions as a necessary step to achieving such freedom. His writings include *God and the State* (1882, tr. 1893). See biography by E. H. Carr (1937, repr. 1961); studies by G. P. Maximoff (1953) and G. Alfred (1971).

Bakwanga, Zaïre: see MBUJI-MAYI.

Balaam (bā'ləm), prophet hired by Balak, king of Moab, to curse the Jews, encamped in the Jordan valley. For a recounting of the way every curse became a blessing see Num. 22–24. Later, Balaam seduced the Israelites to evil practices, an act for which he was killed. See Num. 31.8,16; Micah 6.5; 2 Peter 2.15,16; Jude 11; Rev. 2.14.

Balac (bā'lăk), Greek form of BALAK.

Baladan: see MERODACH-BALADAN.

Baladhuri, al- (äl-bälä'thōōrē), d. c.892, Arab historian. One of the most important Arab historians, he spent most of his life in Baghdad and enjoyed great influence at the court of the caliph al-Mutawakkil. He traveled in Syria and Iraq, compiling information for his major works. He is regarded as a reliable source for the history of the early Arabs and the history of Muslim expansion. See his major work, *The Origins of the Islamic State* (tr., 2 vol., 1916–24).

Balaguer, Joaquín (hwäkēn' bälägār'), 1907–, president of the Dominican Republic (1960–62, 1966–). A lawyer, he held many important government posts under the dictator Rafael TRUJILLO MOLINA. He served as vice president (1957–60) and assumed the presidency (1960) upon the resignation of President Hector Trujillo (the dictator's brother). Real power rested, however, with Rafael Trujillo until his assassination in May, 1961. Balaguer ruled during the chaos that followed and exiled members of the Trujillo family. Unable to pacify opposing factions, he was ousted by the military in Jan., 1962. He lived in exile until 1965. Elected president in 1966, he was reelected in 1970 and 1974. His administration restored financial stability and promoted economic development, but political chaos, terrorism, and guerrilla activity led him to resort to repressive measures. His 1974 victory climaxed a violent campaign characterized by strikes and bloody clashes. A scholar and poet, Balaguer is the author of numerous books on a wide range of subjects.

Balah (bā'lə), the same as BILHAH **2.**

Balak (bā'lăk), king of Moab who hired Balaam to curse Israel. Num. 22–24. Balac is a Greek form. Rev. 2.14.

Balakirev, Mili Alekseyevich (me'lyĭ əlyĭksyā'yəvĭch bəlakē'ryĕf), 1837–1910, Russian composer and conductor, leader of the group called the FIVE. He founded (1862) the Free School of Music in St. Petersburg and conducted (1867–69) the Russian Music Society and (1883–94) the Imperial Chapel Choir and Imperial Music Society. His works include the symphonic poems *Tamara* and *Russ* (or *Russia*); a piano fantasy, *Islamey;* incidental music for *King Lear;* and songs. His music combined romanticism with Russian and Oriental folk songs. See M. O. Zetlin, *The Five* (tr. 1959).

Balaklava (bələklä'və), section of the city of SEVASTOPOL, SE European USSR, in the Ukrainian Republic, on the Crimean peninsula. Fishing and limestone quarrying are carried on. In ancient times it was an important Greek commercial city. In the Middle Ages it belonged to the Genoese until it was taken (1475) by the Turks, who gave it its present name. In the CRIMEAN WAR, Balaklava became famous for an allied victory (Oct., 1854) over the Russians and particularly for the charge of the Light Brigade, celebrated by Tennyson. On Oct. 25, through a disputed error in orders, the earl of CARDIGAN led an English light cavalry brigade of some 670 in a hopeless charge on a heavily protected Russian position, and more than two thirds of his men were killed or wounded. Balaklava was the capital of the former Balaklava dist. in the Crimean oblast until 1957, when it was incorporated into Sevastopol. There are ruins of a Genoese fortress (14th–15th cent.) in Balaklava.

balalaika (băləlī'kə), Russian stringed musical instrument, with a triangular body and a long fretted neck (see FRETTED INSTRUMENT). Usually there are three strings, which are generally plucked with a pick. The balalaika is made in various sizes, and several may be combined to make a band or orchestra. A similar instrument, the bandura, is found in the Ukraine and Russia, and other types are to be found in the countries of the Middle East, where the balalaika almost certainly originated. The instrument did not appear in Russia until c.1700. Like the guitar, it has

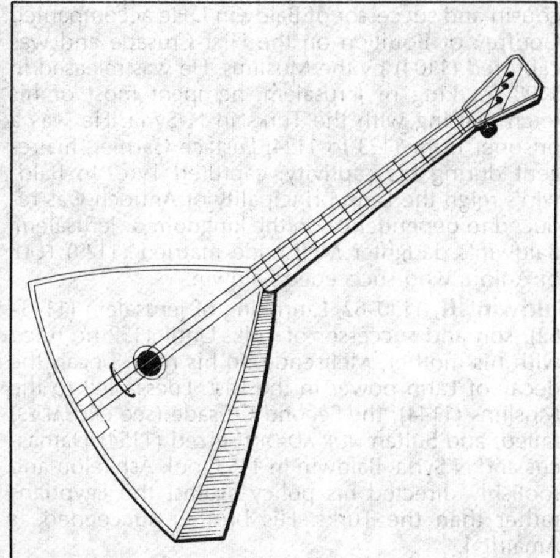

Balalaika

been much used to accompany folk songs and country dances.

balance, instrument used in laboratories and pharmacies to measure the mass or weight of a body. A balance functions by measuring the force of gravity that the earth exerts on an object, i.e., its weight. Since the mass of an object is directly proportional to its weight, a balance can also be used to measure mass. The simplest type of balance, the equal-arm, or beam, balance, is an application of a LEVER. A uniform bar, the beam, is suspended at its exact center upon a knife-edge set at right angles to it. The point of support is called the fulcrum. Two pans of equal weight are suspended from the beam, one at each end, at points equidistant from the fulcrum. Since the center of gravity of a uniform bar is at its midpoint, the beam supporting the pans will be in equilibrium, i.e., will balance upon the knife-edge. A long pointer attached at right angles to the beam at the fulcrum indicates zero on a scale when the beam is at rest parallel to a level surface. It shows also the extent of swing of the beam on one side or the other, acting somewhat as a pendulum, when the beam is coming to rest. The object to be weighed is placed upon one pan and standard weights are added to the other until the balance of the beam is established again. The unknown weight can then be determined by adding up the standard weights in the pan. One balance of this type, the analytical balance, is used for delicate weighing in quantitative chemical analysis and in preparing pharmaceutical prescriptions. It is kept in a glass case, since its accuracy is easily affected by dust and moisture. The platform balance is a form of equal-arm balance in which two flat platforms are attached to the top side of the beam, one at each end. Such a balance has a rider, or weight, mounted upon a bar which has a calibrated scale, is parallel to the beam, and connects the supports of the two platforms. This rider is moved along the bar, its edge marking decimal fractions of the unit weight. On the unequal-arm balance the beam is suspended at a point a very short distance from one of its ends. The object to be weighed is placed on this end, and a small known weight is moved out along the longer arm until balance is obtained. The unknown weight is then determined by using a formula involving the known weight and the distance of each weight from the fulcrum. One example of this type of balance is the Roman steelyard. A spring balance consists of a coiled spring fixed to a support at one end, with a hook at the other to which the body to be weighed is applied. Within the spring's limit of elasticity, the distance through which it is stretched is directly proportional to the weight of the applied body. A pointer and graduated scale attached to the spring convert this distance into a weight reading. Such a balance does not retain its accuracy permanently, for no matter how carefully it is handled, the spring very gradually uncoils even though its limit of elasticity has not been exceeded. Although extremely accurate results can be obtained in measuring the weights of minute objects, it is physically impossible to construct any balance perfect enough to yield absolutely accurate determinations. For ordinary purposes the errors are so small that they are considered insignificant, but in chemical analysis it has been necessary to develop methods by which they can be further minimized. A so-called TORSION BALANCE, which depends upon the twisting of a wire or thread, is employed for weighing, but the term is commonly used to indicate a device for measuring minute electrical and magnetic forces. See SCALE.

Balance, The, English name for LIBRA, a CONSTELLATION; also called The Scales.

balance of payments, relations between all payments out of a country within a given period and all payments into the country. The concept of the balance of payments is an outgrowth of the mercantilist one of BALANCE OF TRADE. Balance of payments includes all payments between a country and its trading partners and includes the balance of trade (known as the current account), private foreign loans and their interest, loans and grants by governments or international organizations, and movements of gold. An unfavorable balance of payments (that is, when remittances exceed receipts), if serious and chronic, may affect the stability of the nation's currency. After World War II the INTERNATIONAL MONETARY FUND was established to deal with problems relating to the balance of payments, particularly with foreign exchange. Since the late 1950s the United States has generally experienced an unfavorable balance of payments due to sizable U.S. investment in Europe, foreign spending by American tourists, large-scale foreign aid, and large expenditures on U.S. military forces abroad. In the early 1970s the United States took action to create a more favorable balance of payments by twice announcing (1971,1973) a DEVALUATION of the U.S. dollar with respect to other currencies. However, the increase in the cost of petroleum from the Arab states in 1973–74 had a deleterious effect on the U.S. balance of payments, as it did on those of most countries of Western Europe. See R. M. Stern, *The Balance of Payments:Theory and Economic Policy* (1973); H. R. Heller, *International Monetary Economics* (1974).

balance of power, system of international relations in which nations seek to preserve international order by maintaining an approximate equilibrium of power among many rivals, thus preventing the preponderance of any one state. Crucial to the system is a willingness on the part of individual national governments to change alliances as the situation demands in order to maintain the balance. Intimations of this idea can be found in Thucydides' description of Greece in the 5th cent. B.C. and Guicciardini's description of 15th-century Italy. Its modern development began in the mid-17th cent., when it was directed against the France of Louis XIV. Balance of power was the stated British objective for much of the 18th and 19th cent., and it characterized the European international system, for example, from 1815–1914. After World War I the balance of power system was attacked by those who sought a system characterized by cooperation and a community of power. International relations were changed radically after World War II by the predominance of two superpowers, the United States and the Soviet Union, with major ideological differences between them. However, in the 1960s the revival of Europe and the emergence of China as a potential great power seemed to indicate a possible return to the traditional balance of power system. See H. J. Morgenthau, *Politics Among Nations* (1960); Ludwig Dehio, *The Precarious Balance* (tr. 1962); Herbert Butterfield and Martin Wright, eds., *Diplomatic Investigations* (1966).

balance of trade, relation between the merchandise exports and imports of a country. The concept first became important in the 16th and 17th cent. with the growth of MERCANTILISM. Mercantilist theorists believed that a country should have an excess of exports over imports (i.e., a favorable balance of trade) to bring money, which they confused with wealth, into the country. They urged legislation to restrict the use of foreign goods, encourage exports, and—in some cases—forbid the export of bullion. The importance of a favorable balance of trade remained unchallenged until David Hume, Adam Smith, David Ricardo, and John Stuart Mill concerned themselves with theories of the international adjustment of the balance of trade. The classical theory of the adjustment mechanism is that a country whose exports fall short of its imports must export part of its stock of gold, thereby affecting its price structure and its ability to compete on the world market. Today the balance of trade is regarded as only one of several elements that make up the BALANCE OF PAYMENTS of a nation. See Imanuel Wexler, *Fundamentals of International Economics* (2d ed. 1972).

Balanchine, George (băl'ənchēn"), 1904–, American choreographer and ballet dancer, b. Russia as Georgi Balanchivadze. Balanchine attended the Imperial Ballet School, St. Petersburg, and performed in Russia. In 1924 he toured Europe and joined Diaghilev's Ballet Russe as a principal dancer and choreographer (1924–28). After moving to the United States (1933), he became director of ballet for the Metropolitan Opera House (1934–37) and a founder of the School of American Ballet (1934). Since 1948 he has been artistic director and principal choreographer for the New York City Ballet. Balanchine's choreography of more than 90 compositions includes *Serenade, Concerto Barocco, Bourrée Fantasque, Seven Deadly Sins, Agon,* and *Don Quixote.* He has done choreography for films, operas, and musicals; he created the original *Slaughter on Tenth Avenue* in the musical *On Your Toes.* Most of his works emphasize patterns of pure dance rather than plot. See study by Bernard Taper (1963, rev. ed. 1974).

Balasore (bŭ'ləsôr), town (1971 pop. 46,279), Orissa state, E central India, near the Bay of Bengal. Settled by the British in 1651, it was the first British settlement in what was then known as Bengal. Goods were unloaded there for transport up the Hooghly River. Balasore was a resort in the 18th cent., with French, Dutch, and Danish, as well as British, settlements. The Dutch and Danish areas were ceded to Great Britain in 1846. A French settlement remained until the French administration of Chandernagore was relinquished to the Indians in 1947. It is a district administrative center and a mining and rice-trading town.

balata (băl'ətə), nonelastic natural RUBBER obtained as a LATEX from the South American tree *Manikara bidentata* and from related trees. Its properties are similar to those of GUTTA-PERCHA, and its processing and uses are essentially the same. It is sometimes called gutta balata.

Balaton (bă'lətŏn, Hung. bŏ'lŏtôn), lake 230 sq mi (596 sq km), W central Hungary, at the foot of the Bakony Forest. The Zala River is its main tributary; the lake is drained by the Sió River. It is the largest lake in Central Europe with many tourist and health resorts. Its shallow waters abound in fish, and along the shores are fine vineyards.

Balbo, Cesare (chā'zārā bäl'bō), 1789–1853, Italian premier, historian, and author. He held various posts during the Napoleonic occupation of Italy and became involved in the liberal revolution of 1821 in Piedmont. He joined with Count Cavour in founding (1847) the review the *Risorgimento.* King Charles Albert of Sardinia made (1848) him premier of his first constitutional cabinet, but Balbo resigned after three months. His works include *Sommario della storia d'Italia* (1846), *Le Speranze d'Italia* (1844), and a life of Dante (2 vol., 1839; tr. 1852).

Balbo, Italo (ē'tälō), 1896–1940, Italian Fascist leader and aviator. After serving in World War I, he joined the Fascist movement and in 1922 was one of the four top leaders of the March on Rome, which brought Mussolini to power. A general of the Fascist militia, he held several cabinet posts and was (1929–33) minister of aviation. He efficiently developed aviation in Italy and led mass flights, the most notable being Rome–Rio de Janeiro and Rome–Chicago (1933). As governor general of Libya (1933–40) he attempted to gain Muslim support for Fascism. He was killed when his plane was brought down over Tobruk, Libya, apparently shot down accidentally by Italian antiaircraft artillery.

Balboa, Vasco Núñez de (bălbō'ə, Span. väs'kō nōō'nyāth dā bälbō'ä), c.1475–1519, Spanish conquistador, discoverer of the Pacific Ocean. After sailing with BASTIDAS in 1501, Balboa probably went to Hispaniola. In 1510, fleeing from creditors, he hid on the vessel that took ENCISO to Panama. After reaching DARIEN, Balboa took command, deposed the incompetent Enciso, and sent him to Spain as a prisoner. Balboa showed only rarely the rapacity and cruelty characteristic of the conquistador. He won the friendship of the Indians, who accompanied him on his epic march across the isthmus. Toward the end of Sept., 1513, he discovered the Pacific and claimed it and all shores washed by it for the Spanish crown. His discovery came too late to offset Enciso's complaints at the court of Spain. Balboa was replaced by Pedro ARIAS DE ÁVILA, and while preparing an expedition to Peru, he was summarily seized, accused of treason and beheaded. See C. L. G. Anderson, *Life and Letters of Vasco Núñez de Balboa* (1941, repr. 1971).

Balboa, town (1970 pop., including Balboa Heights, 2,801), Panama Canal Zone, on the Gulf of Panama. The port for Panama City, Balboa is the largest town in the Canal Zone and the administrative headquarters of the zone and the canal. It is also the site of a U.S. navy base.

Balbus (Lucius Cornelius Balbus) (băl'bəs), fl. 1st cent. B.C., Roman statesman, b. Gades (now Cádiz, Spain). He won notice for brilliant service against Sertorius, and Pompey brought him to Rome and had him made a citizen. Balbus helped to bring about the creation of the First Triumvirate (Pompey, Caesar, and Crassus) in 60 B.C. and thereafter was a friend and protégé of Julius Caesar. In 56 B.C. the conservative party, to embarrass Pompey and Crassus in Caesar's absence, charged Balbus with obtaining citizenship illegally. When the case came to trial, CICERO at Pompey's request made a brilliant oration in Balbus' defense and secured an acquittal. Balbus at first was neutral, then openly favored Caesar in the struggle with Pompey. After Caesar's death he supported Octavian (later Augustus) and in 40 B.C. was made the first foreign-born Roman consul.

Balch, Emily Greene (bŏlch), 1867–1961, American economist and sociologist, b. Jamaica Plain, Mass., grad. Bryn Mawr, 1889. International secretary of the Women's International League for Peace and Freedom (1919–22), she shared with John R. Mott the 1946 Nobel Peace Prize.

Balchen, Bernt (bârnt bäl'kən), 1899–1973, Norwegian-American aviator. He headed one of the search expeditions for Amundsen and Ellsworth in 1925 and was a member of their 1926 expedition to the Arctic. Richard E. Byrd, meeting Balchen at Spitsbergen in 1926, brought him to the United States. He was second pilot on Byrd's transatlantic flight in 1927 and was the hero of the forced night landing of Byrd's plane in the surf on the Normandy coast. He was the chief pilot on Byrd's expedition to Antarctica (1928–30), which included the first flight (1929) over the South Pole. Serving in the U.S. air force during World War II, Balchen again distinguished himself. See his autobiography, *Come North With Me* (1958).

Balch Springs, town (1970 pop. 10,464), Dallas co., NE Texas, a residential suburb of Dallas; inc. 1953.

bald cypress, common name for members of the Taxodiaceae, a small family of deciduous or evergreen conifers with needlelike or scalelike leaves and woody cones. Most species of the family are trees of the Far East; almost all are cultivated for ornament (and are often erroneously called firs or pines). The big trees and redwoods (see SEQUOIA) and the bald cypresses are the only species native to North America. The bald cypresses (genus *Taxodium*) were widely distributed in earlier times (as were the other trees in the family) but are now restricted to the SE United States and Mexico. They are called "bald" because of their deciduous character, unusual in conifers. The common bald cypress (*T. distichum*) forms dense forests in the southeastern swamplands and is a common tree of the Everglades. It produces "knees" which project from the root system upward above water level. Because its wood is resistant to wood-rotting fungi, it is valued as softwood lumber for shingles, trim, and especially for greenhouse benches and racks. *T. mucronatum*, the big cypress or Mexican bald cypress, is a larger tree with a more western range. The true CYPRESSES belong to a separate family. The bald cypress family is classified in the division PINOPHYTA, class Pinopsida, order Coniferales.

Balder (bôl'dər, bäl–), Norse god of light; son of Odin and Frigg. He was the most beautiful and gracious of the gods of Asgard. His mother extracted oaths from all things in nature not to harm her son, but neglected the mistletoe. According to one legend Loki gave a dart of mistletoe to the blind god Hoder and aimed it for him at Balder, who was killed by it. The gods grieved inconsolably over his death. It was prophesied, however, that after RAGNAROK (the doom of the gods) Balder would return to heaven. See GERMANIC RELIGION.

Baldinucci, Abate Filippo (äbä'tä fēlĭp'pō bäldēnōōt'chē), 1624–96, Italian art historian and philologist. Baldinucci was a pioneer in research techniques and among the first to emphasize the aesthetic importance of the print. An artistic adviser to the Medici court, he also wrote the first dictionary of art terminology. His three-volume lives of the artists from Cimabue to the 17th-century masters remains a valuable historical source.

baldness, thinning or loss of hair as a result of illness, functional disorder, or hereditary disposition, also known as alopecia. Male pattern baldness, a genetic trait, is the most common cause of baldness among white males. It is carried by females, but they are rarely susceptible inasmuch as it develops under the influence of testosterone, a male sex hormone. Hair loss begins at the forehead and crown and is slowly progressive. It is irreversible but may be cosmetically disguised by hair-follicle transplants. Diseases characterized by high fever (e.g., scarlet and typhoid fevers), malnutrition, drug poisoning, and glandular disorders can all cause balding. Treatment of the disease or dysfunction will usually halt the loss of hair, and if the scalp and hair follicles are not severely damaged, hair will usually regrow spontaneously. Scalp infection, oiliness or dirtiness of the scalp and hair, and excessive teasing and lacquering of hair are also conducive to baldness. Alopecia areata is a disease of unknown origin characterized by noninflamed bald patches in the scalp hair and beard. It is recurrent but is usually of short duration.

Baldovinetti, Alesso (äläs'sō bäldōvēnĕt'tē), c.1425–1499, Italian painter and decorative artist of the early Florentine Renaissance. He was probably trained in the workshop of Domenico Veneziano, whose influence is evident in his early works. These paintings include an altarpiece for the Medici villa at Cafaggiolo and an *Annunciation* (both: Uffizi). In 1462 he completed the *Nativity* in the Annunziata. This scene and his decoration of the Portuguese chapel in San Miniato have deteriorated because of Baldovinetti's unfortunate experiments with the technique of fresco. He painted several Madonnas (Louvre and Uffizi) in a serene, rather mellow style. Baldovinetti was considered the foremost designer in mosaics of his day. He also worked in other media such as stained glass, inlaid wood, shields, and coats of arms. See study by R. W. Kennedy (1938).

Baldung or **Baldung-Grien, Hans** (häns bäl'dōōng,-grēn), c.1484–1545, German painter and printmaker, active mainly at Strasbourg. He was surnamed Grien or Grün because of his fondness for the color green. Although he probably studied with Dürer, he evolved a personal style revealing his interest in brilliant color, effects of light, and expressively contorted forms. He is best known as a painter of such disturbing subjects as *Death and the Maiden* (Basel) and for drawings and prints of witches and allegorical or mythological scenes. The high altar of the cathedral at Freiburg in Breisgau, with depictions of the *Coronation of the Virgin,* the *Crucifixion,* and other subjects (c.1515) is his most famous work. Baldung was also esteemed as a portrait painter and designer for stained glass.

Baldwin I, 1171–1205, 1st Latin emperor of Constantinople (1204–5). The count of Flanders (as Baldwin IX), he was a leader in the Fourth Crusade (see CRUSADES). After the seizure of Constantinople (1204), the Crusaders elected him emperor (see CONSTANTINOPLE, LATIN EMPIRE OF). He was captured (1205) in battle by the Bulgarians and died in captivity, probably by poison. He was succeeded by his brother, Henry of Flanders.

Baldwin II, 1217–73, last Latin emperor of Constantinople (1228–61), brother and successor of ROBERT OF COURTENAY. He began his personal rule only after the death (1237) of his father-in-law, JOHN OF BRIENNE. Baldwin traveled in Western Europe seeking financial and military aid for his precarious throne (see CONSTANTINOPLE, LATIN EMPIRE OF). To obtain funds he sold a large part of the True Cross and other sacred relics to Louis IX of France and at one time pawned his son to the Venetians. In 1261, MICHAEL VIII, Greek emperor of Nicaea, stormed Constantinople. Baldwin escaped to Italy and ultimately transferred his claims on the throne to CHARLES I of Naples.

Baldwin I (Baldwin of Boulogne), 1058?–1118, Latin king of Jerusalem (1100–1118), brother and successor of GODFREY OF BOUILLON, whom he accompanied on the First Crusade (see CRUSADES). Separating from the main army after the successful siege of Nicaea, Baldwin followed TANCRED into Cilicia and seized (1097) Tarsus from him. He wrested (1097) Edessa from the Muslims and as count of Edessa defended the city until elected ruler of Jerusalem. His election marked the triumph of the military faction of the Crusaders over the ecclesiastical faction. Taking the title of king, he consolidated the Latin states of the East. With the help of crusading fleets from the West and, more important, the Genoese and the Venetians, to whom he made large concessions, he gained possession of the chief ports of Palestine. He helped the Latin rulers of Antioch, Edessa, and Tripoli against the Muslims and fought against the Egyptians. He died on his return from an expedition into Egypt. His cousin, Baldwin II, succeeded him.

Baldwin II (Baldwin of Le Bourg), d. 1131, Latin king of Jerusalem (1118–31), count of Edessa (1100–1131); cousin and successor of Baldwin I. He accompanied Godfrey of Bouillon on the First Crusade and was captured (1104) by the Muslims. He was released in 1108. As king of Jerusalem, he spent most of his reign warring with the Turks in N Syria. He was a prisoner from 1123 to 1124; Eustace Garnier, his regent during his captivity, captured Tyre. In Baldwin's reign the Latin principality of Antioch was reduced to dependence on the kingdom of Jerusalem. Baldwin's daughter Melisende married (1129) FULK of Anjou, who succeeded Baldwin.

Baldwin III, 1130–62, Latin king of Jerusalem (1143–62), son and successor of Fulk. Until 1152 he ruled with his mother, Melisende. In his reign began the decay of Latin power in the East. Edessa fell to the Muslims (1144); the Second Crusade (see CRUSADES) failed; and Sultan NUR AD-DIN seized (1154) Damascus and N Syria. Baldwin in 1153 took Ashkelon and foolishly directed his policy against the Egyptians rather than the Turks. His brother succeeded as Amalric I.

Baldwin IV (Baldwin the Leper), c.1161–1185, Latin king of Jerusalem (1174–85), son and successor of Amalric I. RAYMOND, count of Tripoli, was regent from 1174 to 1176. Baldwin was constantly engaged, except for a truce (1180–82), in defending his kingdom against SALADIN. In 1183 his leprosy began to spread very rapidly; he appointed GUY OF LUSIGNAN as his regent, but in the same year he withdrew the commission and had his five-year-old nephew crowned king as **Baldwin V** (d. 1186). Raymond was regent for Baldwin V, who was succeeded as king by Guy of Lusignan.

Baldwin, Abraham, 1754–1807, American political leader, b. Guilford, Conn. After serving as a chaplain in the American Revolution, he studied law and in 1784 was admitted to practice in Georgia. He was a member (1785–88) of the Continental Congress and the leading Georgia delegate to the U.S. Constitutional Convention in 1787. His change of vote in that convention on the issue of the mode of representation in Congress brought about a tie between the large and small states. Baldwin served on the committee appointed to solve this problem. The compromise system of representation that it proposed (by population in the House of Representatives and by states in the Senate) was adopted. Baldwin was elected to the first House of Representatives and served until 1799. He then served in the Senate until his death. He was an industrious member of many committees and supported Jeffersonian policies. Earlier, while in the Georgia assembly, Baldwin wrote the charter of Franklin College, which later developed into the Univ. of Georgia. See biography by H. C. White (1926).

Baldwin, James, 1924–, American author, b. New York City. He spent an impoverished boyhood in Harlem and at 14 became a preacher in the Fireside Pentecostal Church. After graduating from high school he decided to become a writer, and the receipt of several grants enabled him to live in France for nine years. His first novel, *Go Tell It on the Mountain* (1953), which reflects his experience as a storefront preacher, was well received. Also critically acclaimed was *Another Country* (1962), a bitter novel about sexual relations and race relations. With the publication of the perceptive essays in *The Fire Next Time* (1963), Baldwin was recognized as an extremely articulate spokesman for the feelings and attitudes of American Negroes. His other works include the play *Blues for Mr. Charlie* (1964); a volume of short stories, *Going to Meet the Man* (1964); the novels *Giovanni's Room* (1956), *Tell Me how Long the Train's Been Gone* (1968), and *If Beale Street Could Talk* (1974); collections of essays, including *Notes of a Native Son* (1955), *Nobody Knows My Name* (1961), and *No Name in the Street* (1972). See studies by Stanley Macebuh (1973), and Keneth Kinnamon, ed. (1974).

Baldwin, James Mark, 1861–1934, American psychologist, b. Columbia, S.C., grad. Princeton (B.A., 1884; Ph.D., 1889). He taught philosophy at the Univ. of Toronto (1889–93), psychology at Princeton (1893–1903), and philosophy and psychology at Johns Hopkins (1903–9) and the National Univ. of Mexico (1909–13). Internationally known as a philosopher and psychologist, he was the author of numerous works in these fields, many of which were translated into European languages. Among his books are *Elements of Psychology* (1893), *Story of* *the Mind* (1898), and *Dictionary of Philosophy and Psychology* (1901-6).

Baldwin, Matthias William, 1795-1866, American industrialist and philanthropist, b. Elizabethtown (now Elizabeth), N.J. After earlier business successes, Baldwin became interested in steam-engine production and completed in 1832 the locomotive *Old Ironsides*—one of the first successful American models—for the Philadelphia, Germantown, and Norristown RR. The Baldwin Locomotive Works subsequently prospered and maintained a leading position in the industry. Baldwin made many contributions to the Franklin Institute for the Promotion of Mechanical Arts, of which he was a charter member.

Baldwin, Robert, 1804-58, Canadian statesman, leader of the movement for representative government in Canada, b. York (now Toronto), Ont. His father, William Warren Baldwin (1775-1844), was a leader of the Reform party and a supporter of the principle of responsible (i.e., cabinet) government in the colonies. In 1836, as a recognized leader of reform in Upper Canada, Robert Baldwin was appointed by Sir Francis Bond Head to the executive council, but he resigned in a few weeks when it became apparent that the governor had no intention of acceding to the demands of the reformers. In England, in 1836, Baldwin sent to the colonial secretary a memorandum that was the first clear enunciation of the tenet of responsible government for Canada. Shortly after his return to Canada in 1837, he served as mediator between Head and the rebels; as a moderate reformer, he had opposed the faction of William Lyon Mackenzie in the rebellion of that year. Again (1841) he hopefully accepted appointment to the executive council under Lord Sydenham, only to resign when the governor showed no disposition to grant responsible government. As a member of the assembly, Baldwin led the opposition group and increased his influence, particularly by effecting an alliance with the French in Lower Canada, whom Sydenham had ignored in forming his council. After the reunion of Upper and Lower Canada in 1841, Baldwin and Louis Hippolyte LAFONTAINE were allowed to form their first coalition government (1842) under Sir Charles Bagot. With Bagot's death and the arrival (1843) of Sir Charles Metcalfe as governor, the first Baldwin-LaFontaine government resigned, but in the elections of Dec., 1847, the reformers won an overwhelming vote. As a consequence, the second Baldwin-LaFontaine ministry (1847-51) was formed; it is often called "the great ministry." Outstanding among its accomplishments were the Municipal Corporations Act, commonly called the Baldwin Act, for the reformation of local government in Ontario; an act to revise the judicial system; and an act to transform King's College into the nonsectarian Univ. of Toronto (over the violent opposition of Bishop John STRACHAN). See biography by G. E. Wilson (1933); Stephen Leacock, *Mackenzie, Baldwin, LaFontaine, Hincks* (rev. ed. 1926); R. W. Langstone, *Responsible Government in Canada* (1931).

Baldwin, Simeon Eben, 1840-1927, American jurist and politician, b. New Haven, Conn., grad. Yale, 1861. He taught at Yale from 1869 to 1919, serving as a professor of law after 1872. His teaching and financial aid helped to increase the prestige and quality of the law school. He was appointed (1893) associate justice of the supreme court of Connecticut and in 1907 became chief justice. In the year of his compulsory retirement from judicial office (1910) he was elected governor of Connecticut and was reelected in 1912. See biography by Frederick H. Jackson (1955).

Baldwin, Stanley, 1867-1947, British statesman; cousin of Rudyard Kipling. The son of a Worcestershire ironmaster, he was educated at Harrow and at Trinity College, Cambridge, and entered the family business. In 1908 he was elected to Parliament as a Conservative. In 1916 he became parliamentary private secretary to Andrew Bonar LAW, who made him (1917) joint financial secretary to the treasury. He was made president of the Board of Trade in 1921 but in 1922 played an important role in the decision of the Conservative party to withdraw from David Lloyd George's coalition government. When the Conservatives won the ensuing election, Baldwin became chancellor of the exchequer and in 1923 succeeded Bonar Law as prime minister. His government fell (1924) when he failed to obtain support for a protectionist tariff policy, but he returned to office within the year. Baldwin's second period of office (1924-29) was marked by rising unemployment and by a general strike (1926), following which he secured passage of the Trade Disputes Act (1927) to restrict the power of the labor unions. In 1931, Baldwin became lord president of the council in the National government. Although under the nominal leadership of Ramsay MACDONALD, the coalition was dominated by Baldwin, and in 1935 he again became prime minister. Although he won the general election of 1935 on a platform of support for the League of Nations, Baldwin approved the Hoare-Laval pact (see TEMPLEWOOD, SAMUEL JOHN GURNEY HOARE, 1st VISCOUNT), which greatly discredited his government. As international relations continued to deteriorate, with the German reoccupation of the Rhineland and the beginning of the Spanish civil war, Britain finally began to rearm. Baldwin steadfastly opposed the proposed marriage of EDWARD VIII to Wallis Warfield Simpson and secured the king's abdication (1936). He retired in 1937 and shortly thereafter was created Earl Baldwin of Bewdley. Although an able politician, Baldwin has been much criticized for his indolence and particularly for his apparent complacency in the face of the mounting threats to peace in Europe. See biographies by G. M. Young (1952), A. W. Baldwin (1956), and Keith Middlemas and John Barnes (1969).

Baldwin. 1 Uninc. city (1970 pop. 34,525), Nassau co., SE N.Y., on the south shore of Long Island, on Baldwin Bay; settled 1640s. A fishing center and summer resort, it has varied manufactures. **2** Borough (1970 pop. 26,729), Allegheny co., SW Pa., a suburb just S of Pittsburgh, on the Monongahela River, in a bituminous coal region; inc. 1952. Tools, wood products, flooring, and metal goods are manufactured.

Baldwin of Bewdley, Stanley Baldwin, 1st Earl: see BALDWIN, STANLEY.

Baldwin Park, city (1970 pop. 47,285), Los Angeles co., S Calif., a residential suburb of Los Angeles, in the fertile San Gabriel valley; settled 1870, inc. 1956. It has varied manufactures.

Bale, John, 1495-1563, English dramatist and clergyman. An ardent proponent of the Reformation, he used the stage as a vehicle for his views. His most famous play, *King John* (written c.1535), shows the transition from the medieval morality play to the Renaissance historical drama by allegorical treatment of the fate of England rather than of the fate of man's soul. Bale's *Illustrium . . . Scriptorum* (1548) is one of the first bibliographies of English literature. See Honor McCusker, *John Bale, Dramatist and Antiquary* (1942, repr. 1971).

Bâle, Switzerland: see BASEL.

Balearic Islands (bălēăr'ĭk), Span. *Baleares* (bäläā'rās), archipelago, off Spain, in the W Mediterranean, forming Baleares prov. (1970 pop. 558,287) of Spain. Palma is the capital. The chief islands are Majorca, Minorca, and Ibiza. Noted for their scenery and their mild climate, the Balearics are a major tourist center. After tourism, agriculture and fishing are the chief economic activities; fruit, wine, olive oil, majolica ware, and silver filigree are exported. Inhabited since prehistoric times—there are numerous Cyclopean remains—the islands were occupied by Iberians, Phoenicians, Greeks, Carthaginians, Romans, and Byzantines. The Moors, who first came in the 8th cent., established (11th cent.) an independent kingdom, which became the seat of powerful pirates, harassing Mediterranean coastal cities and trade. James I of Aragón conquered (1229-35) the islands. They were included (1276-1343) in the independent kingdom of Majorca and reverted to the Aragonese crown under Peter IV. At the outbreak of the Spanish civil war (1936), Majorca and Ibiza were seized by Insurgent forces—Majorca becoming a base of the Italian fleet—while Minorca remained in the hands of the Loyalists until 1939.

baleen: see WHALE.

Balen, Hendrik van (hĕn'drĭk vän bä'lən), 1575-1632, Flemish painter, b. Antwerp. Van Balen usually provided the figures for scenes in which another painter, frequently Jan Brueghel, designed the landscape settings. A minor artist, van Balen is noted mainly for his mythological scenes, of which *Landscape with Two Nymphs* (Munich) is typical.

Balenciaga, Cristóbal: see under FASHION.

baler: see HAY BALER.

Balewa, Alhaji Sir Abubakar Tafawa (älhä'jē äbo͝o'bäkär' täfä'wä bälä'wä), 1912-66, Nigerian political leader. He was born Mallam Abubakar. After studying to become a teacher, he held a series of posts in education and then became a member of the Northern Region house of assembly in 1947. Later (1951), he was elected to the federal house of representatives. He was appointed the first prime minister of the Federation of Nigeria in 1957. When the federation became independent (1960), he retained his office. He was a founder and deputy president general of the country's largest political party, the Northern People's Congress. He was knighted by Queen Elizabeth II. In 1966, he was killed in a military coup d'etat.

Balfe, Michael William, 1808-70, Irish composer. Of his many operas, very popular in their time, the best known was *The Bohemian Girl* (1843).

Balfour, Arthur James Balfour, 1st earl of (băl'fo͝or), 1848-1930, British statesman; nephew of the 3d marquess of SALISBURY. He entered parliament as a Conservative in 1874 and served as secretary to his uncle at the Congress of Berlin (1878). Although associated with the "Fourth Party" of Lord Randolph CHURCHILL, he remained close to Salisbury, serving as president of the Local Government Board (1885-86) and secretary for Scotland (1886). As chief secretary for Ireland (1887-91) Balfour was a resolute opponent of the Home Rule movement and suppressed riots, but he worked for agrarian reform. In 1891 he became Conservative leader in the House of Commons and served (1891-92, 1895-1902) as first lord of the treasury. He succeeded his uncle as prime minister in 1902. His government achieved educational reform (1902), passed the Irish Land Purchase Act (1903), created the Committee of Imperial Defence (1904), and inaugurated the Franco-British Entente (1904). However, the Conservative party split over tariff protection advocated by Joseph CHAMBERLAIN. Balfour resigned in 1905, and his party was overwhelmingly defeated in the 1906 election. He continued as leader of the Conservatives during the disputes over the 1909 budget and the reform of the House of Lords but resigned in 1911. Balfour was first lord of the admiralty (1915-16) in Herbert Asquith's coalition government and became (1916) foreign secretary under David Lloyd George. In this capacity he issued the Balfour Declaration (1917), pledging British support to the Zionist hope for a Jewish national home in Palestine, with the proviso that the rights of non-Jewish communities in Palestine would be respected (see ZIONISM). He attended the Versailles peace conference and, as lord president of the council (1919-22), represented Britain at the first meeting of the League of Nations in 1920 and at the Washington Conference on limiting naval armaments in 1921-22. Created earl of Balfour in 1922, he was again lord president of the council (1925-29). Balfour was a brilliant intellectual and an effective public official, devoted to the cause of international peace. His philosophical writings, which explore the problems of modern religion, include *The Foundations of Belief* (1900), *Theism and Humanism* (1915), *Theism and Thought* (1923), and *Opinions and Arguments* (1927). See biographies by Blanche Dugdale (2 vol., 1936), Kenneth Young (1963), and S. H. Zebel (1973).

Balfour, Francis Maitland, 1851-82, Scottish embryologist; brother of A. J. Balfour. He was an early exponent of RECAPITULATION. His *Treatise on Comparative Embryology* (2 vol., 1880-81) is a classic treatment of the evolution of the egg and embryo. Professor of animal morphology at Cambridge Univ., Balfour did research there and at the zoological station at Naples.

Balfour, Sir James, d. 1583, Scottish judge and politician. Captured (1547) at St. Andrews after the murder of Cardinal Beaton, he served a sentence in the French galleys and on his release (1549) abjured Protestantism. He became an adviser to MARY QUEEN OF SCOTS and was deeply involved in the murder of Lord Darnley. He was made governor of Edinburgh Castle, but when the Scottish lords rose against the queen, he surrendered it to them. Balfour repeatedly changed his political allegiance in the conflicts of the succeeding years. Eventually he withdrew to France, but he returned to Scotland (1580) to help secure the conviction of the earl of Morton for Darnley's murder. He was long a jurist, but, despite its name, the early law text, *Balfour's Practicks of Scots Law,* is only partially of his authorship.

Bali (bä'lē), island and (with two offshore islets) province (1970 est. pop. 2,247,000), c.2,200 sq mi (5,700 sq km), E Indonesia, westernmost of the Lesser Sundas, just E of Java across the narrow Bali Strait. The capital is Denpasar. Although Bali is relatively small, it is densely populated and culturally and economically one of the most important islands of Indonesia. Largely mountainous, with active volcanoes, it rises to 10,308 ft (3,142 m) at Mt. Agung; there is a great fertile plain to the south. Fauna include tigers and deer. Bali is known for its giant waringin trees, sacred to the inhabitants. The Balinese (a Malayan group closely related to the Javanese) are skillful farmers; rice, the chief crop, is grown with the aid of elaborate irrigation systems. Vegetables, fruits, coffee, and coconuts are also produced. Livestock is important; pigs and cattle are major export items. Industries include food processing, tourism, and handicrafts. The people are noted for their artistic skill (especially wood carving), their physical beauty, and their high level of culture, which includes advanced forms of music, folk drama, dancing, and architecture. They are Hindu in a nation that is overwhelmingly Muslim; their unique ritualistic culture, as well as the island's scenic beauty, has made Bali one of the great tourist attractions of the Far East. An international airport was opened in 1969. Bali was converted to Hinduism in the 7th cent., and was under Javanese rule from the 10th to the late 15th cent. It was a refuge (1513–28) for the Hindus of Java fleeing the advance of Islam. The Dutch first landed in 1597 and the Dutch East India Company began its trade with the island in the early 17th cent. Dutch sovereignty was not firmly established until after a series of colonial wars (1846–49), and the entire island was not occupied until 1908, after the quelling of two rebellions. Klungklung, NE of Denpasar, was the capital of the native rulers from the 17th cent. until 1908. Bali was particularly hard hit during the nationwide purge of Communists in 1965; more than 40,000 people were killed, and entire villages were destroyed. A state univ. is in Denpasar. See *Bali* (Vol. V and VIII of *Selected Studies on Indonesia,* publ. by W. van Hoeve, 1960 and 1970); Jane Belo, *Trance in Bali* (1960) and *Traditional Balinese Culture* (1970).

Balıkesir (bälŭk"ĕsĕr'), city (1970 pop. 85,032), capital of Balıkesir prov., NW Turkey. It is a rail junction and the center of a fertile agricultural region.

Balikpapan (bä'lĕkpä'pän), city (1961 pop. 91,706), E Borneo (Kalimantan), Indonesia, on an inlet of Makasar Strait. An important seaport and oil center with refineries, it is connected by pipeline with the oil fields of Samarinda. Timber is also exported.

Balinese music represents, to a large extent, a survival of the pre-Islamic music of Java. It was taken to Bali by Hindu Javanese in the 15th cent. and uses the tonal systems of JAVANESE MUSIC, of which *pelog* is by far the more important in Bali. Balinese music sounds impetuous and noisy, in contrast to the soft, tranquil music heard currently in Java. Few *gamelans,* the orchestras of tuned percussion instruments, play in Java today but they flourish, their archaic forms preserved, in modern Bali. The *gamelans* of the princes are no longer important in Bali, but have left their influence on the village societies for music making. There are also the ceremonial *gamelans* of the temples. The most important instruments are xylophones, which may be made of bronze or bamboo. Bronze xylophones are of two basic types—*gangsa,* whose keys are supported over a wooden resonance box, and *g'ndér,* whose keys have individual bamboo resonators. These instruments sometimes play the melody and sometimes they provide a brilliant figuration. Gongs, suspended singly, are used for metrical accentuation; there are also gong chimes, which are of two types. The *trompong,* a set of 10, is a solo instrument, and the *réyong,* a set of 12, is played by four men, supplying figuration. Flutes, in two sizes, are made of bamboo and are used in theatrical music. Although the name of the *rebab,* a two-string spike fiddle, is Persian-Arabic, the instrument probably originated in S China and is used in the music of the *gambuh* play. Cymbals, bell rattles, and drums supply the all-important, elaborate rhythmic background. The *anklung* is an archaic, tuned bamboo rattle. It is not known in all parts of Bali, but gives its name to the *anklung gamelan,* a ceremonial *gamelan* which may at one time have always included *anklungs.* The instrumentation and the repertory of a particular *gamelan* depend on its function. Each of the various forms of dance and drama has a *gamelan* which specializes in its music. The most recent musical development is *kebyar,* a restless, explosive music which discards the highly developed, balanced forms of the older music. *Kebyar* clubs compose their own music, often taking themes from older music. The wealthier clubs include a dancer—a young man who performs seated on the ground, dancing from the waist up. Balinese notation was invented by the Javanese who brought the music to Bali. It gives no indication of the rhythm and is little used. Music is learned by rote; it is not improvisation, however, but a sophisticated, composed art form. See D. A. Lentz, *The Gamelan Music of Java and Bali* (1965); C. McPhee, *Music in Bali* (1965).

Baliol, Edward de (bāl'yəl), d. 1363, king of Scotland, son of John de Baliol (d. 1315). Having secured English support for his claim to the Scottish throne, he invaded Scotland in 1332 and was crowned at Scone. He was soon driven out, but EDWARD III of England came to his active support, and together they defeated forces of the young DAVID II at Halidon Hill in 1334. Baliol then ceded several southern Scottish counties to Edward. He was driven out again, and David, who had been in France, returned in 1341 as king. In 1356 Baliol retired on an English pension, surrendering his title as king to Edward.

Baliol, John de, 1249–1315, king of Scotland (1292–96), son of John de Baliol (d. 1269). He became head of the family after the death of his elder brothers in 1278. At the death of Margaret Maid of Norway (1290), he claimed the Scottish throne through his grandmother, eldest daughter of David of Huntingdon, brother of King William the Lion. His principal rival was Robert the Bruce, of the celebrated BRUCE family, son of David of Huntingdon's second daughter and hence one generation closer to his royal ancestor, although through a younger line. The laws of succession not being firmly established, the question was referred to EDWARD I of England, who first demanded and secured (1291) recognition as feudal overlord of Scotland. Edward decided in favor of Baliol, who was then crowned king (1292) and did homage to Edward for the kingdom. Baliol, after some hesitation, accepted Edward's asserted right to hear appeals from Scottish courts. However, when he attended Edward's Parliament at Westminster in late 1293, he refused to answer such an appeal. The Scottish council subsequently disregarded Edward's summons for help against France and formed (1295) an alliance with Philip IV of France. Early in 1296 the Scots invaded England, and as Edward marched north to take Berwick, Baliol renounced his oath of fealty to the English king. However, after defeat in a brief campaign, in which he took no active part, Baliol surrendered to Edward. He was imprisoned in England until 1299 and ended his days on his estates in France, ignoring the continuing struggle for Scottish independence.

Baliol, John de, d. 1269, nobleman with lands in both England and Scotland; founder of Balliol College, Oxford. The name is also spelled Balliol. In 1249 he became a member of the Scottish council of regency and a guardian of Alexander III. However, he was apparently disliked by the young king and was discharged and heavily fined in 1255. He fought for Henry III of England in the BARONS' WAR and was taken prisoner at the battle of Lewes (1264). His third son, another John, became king of Scotland.

Balkan Entente, loose alliance formed in 1934 by Yugoslavia, Rumania, Greece, and Turkey to safeguard their territorial integrity against Bulgarian revisionism. It thus was in harmony with the LITTLE ENTENTE (formed by Yugoslavia, Rumania, and Czechoslovakia chiefly against Hungarian revisionism). The events of World War II caused the dissolution of the Balkan Entente.

Balkan Peninsula, southeasternmost peninsula of Europe, c.200,000 sq mi (518,000 sq km), bounded by the Black Sea, Sea of Marmara, Aegean Sea, Mediterranean Sea, Ionian Sea, and Adriatic Sea. Although there is no sharp physiographic separation between the peninsula and Central Europe, the line of the Sava and Danube rivers is commonly considered as the region's northern limit; it therefore includes Albania, continental Greece (including the Peloponnesus), Bulgaria, European Turkey, most of Yugoslavia, and SE Rumania. These six countries, successors to the Ottoman Empire, are called the Balkan States. Historically and politically the region extends north of this line to include all of Yugoslavia and Rumania. The peninsula is very mountainous; the main ranges are the Dinaric Alps, the Balkans, the Rhodope Mts., and the Pindus. Except for the barren Karst plateau of Yugoslavia and the eroded highlands of Greece, the mountains are densely forested. The Morava, Vardar, Strimón, Mesta, and Maritsa are the largest rivers. The Morava and Vardar river valleys form the chief corridor across the peninsula. The mild Mediterranean-type climate, with its dry summer period, is limited to the southern and coastal areas. Covering a greater area are the humid subtropical climate in the northwest and the harsher humid continental climate in the northeast. The region as a whole is largely agricultural; fruits, grains, and grazing are important. A variety of mineral deposits are found there, including iron ore, coal, manganese, copper, lead, and zinc. The peoples of the Balkan Peninsula make up several racial groups. However, linguistic and religious differences are more distinct than the racial divisions. The peninsula, at the crossroads of European and Asian civilizations, has a long history; Ancient Greece, the Byzantine Empire, and the Ottoman Empire flourished there.

Balkans, Bulg. *Stara Planina* (stä'rä plä"nĕnä'), major mountain range of the Balkan Peninsula and Bulgaria, extending c.350 mi (560 km) from E Yugoslavia through central Bulgaria to the Black Sea. It rises to 7,794 ft (2,376 m) at Botev, the highest peak. The Balkans are a continuation of the Carpathian Mts. The forested range is sparsely populated and rich in a variety of minerals. It acts as a climatic barrier, preventing the inland penetration of Mediterranean influences. There are numerous trans-Balkan passes including Shipka Pass (alt. c.4,000 ft/1,220 m).

Balkan Wars, 1912–13, two short wars, fought for the possession of the European territories of the Ottoman Empire. The outbreak of the Italo-Turkish War for the possession of Tripoli (1911) encouraged the Balkan states to increase their territory at Turkish expense. Serbia and Bulgaria accordingly concluded (1912), with the aid of Russian secret diplomacy, a treaty of alliance. In a secret annex, the treaty provided for joint military action and the division of prospective conquests. The outbreak of the war (Oct., 1912), in which Greece and Montenegro joined the original allies, was followed by the speedy expulsion of the Turks from all of European Turkey, except the Constantinople area. After the conclusion of hostilities Serbia showed intentions of annexing a large part of Albania, in order to gain an outlet on the Adriatic, but this step toward a "Greater Serbia" was opposed by Austria-Hungary and Italy and by the Albanians, who had proclaimed their independence. Conferences of the ambassadors of the Great Powers at London created (1913) an independent Albania of fair size, thus cutting Serbia off from the sea. Dissatisfied with these terms, Serbia demanded of Bulgaria a greater share of Macedonia. Bulgaria thereupon attacked (June, 1913) Serbia, only to be attacked by Rumania, Greece, and Turkey. As a result of this Second Balkan War, Bulgaria lost territory to all her enemies by the Treaty of Bucharest (Aug., 1913). The Balkan Wars prepared the way for World War I by satisfying some of the aspirations of Serbia and thereby giving a great impetus to the Serbian desire to annex parts of Austria-Hungary; by alarming Austria and stiffening Austrian resolution to crush Serbia; and by giving causes of dissatisfaction to Bulgaria and Turkey. See George Young, *Nationalism and War in the Near East* (1915, repr. 1970); E. C. Helmreich, *The Diplomacy of the Balkan Wars, 1912–1913* (1938, repr. 1969).

Balkar: see KABARDINO-BALKAR AUTONOMOUS SOVIET SOCIALIST REPUBLIC.

Balkh (bälkh), town (1967 pop. 15,000), N Afghanistan, on a dried-up tributary of the Amu Darya River. One of the world's oldest cities, it is the legendary birthplace of the prophet ZOROASTER. Alexander the Great reputedly founded a Greek colony at the site c.328 B.C. The city later attained great wealth and importance as Bactra, capital of the independent kingdom of Bactria. In the early centuries A.D., Balkh, a prominent center of Buddhism, was renowned for its Buddhist monasteries and stupas. Conquered by the Arabs in 653, it became important in the world of Islam as the original home of the Barmecides (see HARUN AR-RASHID). Under the Abbasid caliphate its fame as a center of learning earned Balkh the title "mother of cities." The city was sacked in 1221 by Jenghiz Khan and lay in ruins until Tamerlane rebuilt it (early 16th cent.). It passed to the Uzbeks and then briefly to the MOGUL empire before falling (18th cent.) to Nadir Shah. In 1850, Balkh became part of the unified kingdom of Afghanistan. The old city, sections of whose walls remain, is now mostly in ruins; the new city, some distance away, is an agricultural and commercial center, inhabited chiefly by Uzbeks. Excavations in the area have uncovered some objects of the early Muslim period.

Balkhash (bəl-khäsh'), city (1969 est. pop. 77,000), W Central Asian USSR, in Kazakhstan, on the north shore of Lake Balkhash. A railroad terminus, port, and copper-smelting center, it was founded as Bertys in 1929 and was renamed in 1936.

Balkhash, lake, 6,562 sq mi (16,996 sq km), c.350 mi (560 km) long, maximum width c.45 mi (70 km), Kazakhstan, Central Asian USSR. The lake, which has an average depth of 20 ft (6 m), stretches from the Kazakh Hills in the northeast to desert steppes in the southwest. The eastern half of the lake is saline; the western half, separated from the eastern section by a sandbar and fed by the Ili River, is fresh. Lake Balkhash, which has no outlet, is slowly shrinking from evaporation. There are valuable copper deposits along the northern shore, and the city of Balkhash has a large copper smelter.

Ball, George Wildman, 1909–, American lawyer and diplomat, b. Des Moines, Iowa. Admitted to the bar in 1934, he served (1942–44) as counsel in the Lend Lease Administration and the Foreign Economic Administration. An expert on foreign economic policy, Ball became (1961) Undersecretary of State for Economic Affairs and then served (1961–66) as Undersecretary of State. During that period he played a major role in formulating U.S. foreign aid and foreign trade policy and was the chief architect of the Trade Agreements Act of 1962. A persistent critic of U.S. military involvement in Vietnam, Ball left the State Department to become (1966–68) chairman of Lehman Brothers, a major investment banking firm. After briefly serving (1968) as U.S. representative to the United Nations, he returned to Lehman Brothers as a senior partner. Ball is the author of *The Discipline of Power* (1968).

Ball, John, d. 1381, English priest and social reformer. He was one of the instigators of the Peasant's Revolt of 1381 (see under TYLER, WAT). He was an itinerant for many years, acting independently of the influence of John WYCLIF and advocating ecclesiastical poverty and social equality. Excommunicated in 1376, he was in prison at Maidstone when the rebels released him in 1381. After the dispersal of the rebels, Ball was captured at Coventry. He was taken to St. Albans, where he was hanged, drawn, and quartered. He is perhaps best remembered for giving currency to the couplet "When Adam delved and Eve span/Who was then the gentleman?" William Morris wrote one of his works on utopian socialism under the title *The Dream of John Ball.* See Charles Oman, *The Great Revolt of 1381* (1906).

Ball, Thomas, 1819–1911, American sculptor, b. Charlestown, Mass.; son of a house and sign painter. Thomas Ball was also a singer of reputation, the first in the United States to sing the title role in Mendelssohn's *Elijah.* Although he lived many years in Florence, Ball's work remained distinctly American. He made portrait busts of many distinguished people. Among his works are the mounted figure of Washington in the Boston Public Gardens and a statue of Daniel Webster in Central Park, New York. His autobiography, *My Three Score Years and Ten,* appeared in 1890.

ballad, in literature, short, narrative poem usually relating a single, dramatic event. Two forms of the ballad are often distinguished—the folk ballad, dating from about the 12th cent., and the literary ballad, dating from the late 18th cent. The first form, the anonymous folk ballad (or popular ballad), was composed to be sung. It was passed along orally from singer to singer, from generation to generation, and from one region to another. During this progression a particular ballad would undergo many changes in both words and tune. The medieval or Elizabethan ballad that appears in print today is probably only one version of many variant forms. Primarily based on an older legend or romance, this type of ballad is usually a short, simple song that tells a dramatic story through dialogue and action, briefly alluding to what has gone before and devoting little attention to depth of character, setting, or moral commentary. It uses simple language, an economy of words, dramatic contrasts, epithets, set phrases, and frequently a stock refrain. The familiar stanza form is four lines, with four or three stresses alternating and with the second and fourth lines rhyming. For example:

It was ín and abóut the Mártinmas tíme,
When the gréen léaves were a fálling,
That Sír John Gráeme, in the Wést Countrý,
Fell in lóve with Bárbara Állan
"Bonny Barbara Allan"

It was in the 18th cent. that the term *ballad* was used in England in its present sense. Scholarly interest in the folk ballad, first aroused by Bishop Percy's *Reliques of Ancient English Poetry* (1765), was significantly inspired by Sir Walter Scott's *Minstrelsy of the Scottish Border* (1802). Francis Child's collection, *English and Scottish Popular Ballads* (5 vol., 1882–98), marked the high point of 19th-century ballad scholarship. More than 300 English and Scottish folk ballads are extant, dating from the 12th to the 16th cent. Although the subject matter varies considerably, five major classes of the ballad can be distinguished—the historical, such as "Otterburn" and "The Bonny Earl o' Moray"; the romantic, such as "Barbara Allan" and "The Douglas Tragedy"; the supernatural, such as "The Wife of Usher's Well"; the nautical, such as "Henry Martin"; and the deeds of folk heroes, such as the Robin Hood cycle. Ballads, however, cannot be confined to any one period or place; similar subject matter appears in the ballads of other peoples. Indigenous American ballads deal mainly with cowboys, folk heroes such as Casey Jones and Paul Bunyan, the mountain folk of Kentucky and Tennessee, the Southern Negro, and famous outlaws, such as Jesse James:

Jésse had a wífe to móurn for his lífe,
Three chíldren, théy were bráve;
But the dírty little cóward that shót Mister Hóward
Has láid Jesse Jámes in his gráve.
"Ballad of Jesse James"

During the mid-20th cent. in the United States there was a great resurgence of interest in folk music, particularly in ballads. Singers such as Joan Baez and Pete Seeger included ballads like "Bonny Barbara Allan" and "Mary Hamilton" in their concert repertoires; composer-performers like Woody Guthrie and Bob Dylan wrote their own ballads. The literary ballad is a narrative poem created by a poet in imitation of the old anonymous folk ballad. Usually the literary ballad is more elaborate and complex; the poet may retain only some of the devices and conventions of the older verse narrative. Literary ballads were quite popular in England during the 19th cent. Examples of the form are found in Keats's "La Belle Dame sans Merci," Coleridge's "The Rime of the Ancient Mariner," and Oscar Wilde's "The Ballad of Reading Gaol." In music a ballad refers to a simple, often sentimental, song, not usually a folk song. See D. C. Fowler, *A Literary History of the Popular Ballad* (1968); B. H. Bronson, *The Ballad as Song* (1969); James Kinsley, ed., *The Oxford Book of Ballads* (1971); T. F. Henderson, *The Ballad in Literature* (1912, repr. 1973).

ballade (bəläd'), in literature, verse form developed in France in the 14th and 15th cent. The ballade usually contains three stanzas of eight lines with three rhymes and a four-line envoy (a short, concluding stanza). Also popular was the ten-line stanza with four rhymes and a five-line envoy. The envoy is used primarily as a summary or as a dedication or direct address to an important person. The ballades of Charles d'Orléans, François Villon, and Geoffrey Chaucer are well known.

ballad opera, in English drama, a play of comic, satiric, or pastoral intent, interspersed with songs, most of them sung to popular airs. First and best was *The Beggar's Opera* (1728) by John GAY. The vogue for these operas lasted until c.1750.

Ballanche, Pierre-Simon (pyĕr-sēmôN' bäläNsh'), 1776–1847, French philosopher. A frequenter of Mme Récamier's salon, he was elected to the Académie française in 1842. He is regarded as the precursor of both liberal Catholicism and ROMANTICISM. In *Palingénésie* (1827–32) he historically documents his belief in cyclical cultural rebirth. In addition to essays, Ballanche wrote didactic fiction, including a Christianized *Antigone* (1813) and *L'Homme sans nom* [man without a name] (1820).

ball-and-socket joint, in engineering, mechanical connection used between parts that must be allowed some relative angular motion in nearly all directions. As the name implies, the joint consists essentially of a spherical knob at the end of a shaft, with the knob fitting securely into a mating socket. Like other mechanical joints, a ball-and-socket joint must have some provision for lubrication and is normally provided with a seal to prevent loss of the lubricant. Joints of this type are commonly used in mounting the front wheels of automobiles, allowing these wheels movement sufficient for steering. In this application they are usually called ball joints.

Ballantyne, James (băl'əntīn), 1772–1833, Scottish editor and publisher. Ballantyne and his brother John set up a publishing business in Edinburgh with the aid of Sir Walter SCOTT. The firm published Scott's works, beginning in 1802 with *Minstrelsy of the Scottish Border.* Although the firm failed in 1826, it still continued to operate under the creditors' trustees, and Ballantyne remained its manager.

Ballarat (băl'ərăt'), city (1971 pop. 39,606; urban agglomeration pop. 58,434), Victoria, SE Australia. It is an industrial center; clothing, food products, paper, brick and tile, and other goods are made. The city flourished during the gold rush (1860s), then declined. There are Anglican and Roman Catholic cathedrals in Ballarat.

ball bearing: see BEARING.

ballet (băl'ā, bălā') [Ital. *ballare*=to dance], classic, formalized solo or ensemble dancing of a highly controlled, dramatic nature performed to music. Foreshadowed in earlier mummeries and lavish masquerades, ballet emerged as a distinctive form in Italy before the 16th cent. The first ballet that combined movement, music, decor, and special effects was presented in France at the court of Catherine de' Medici in 1581. Organized by the violinist Balthasar de Beaujoyeux, it was entitled *Le Ballet comique de la Reine.* This production was the first *ballet de cour,* the ancestor of the modern ballet, which influenced the English court *masque,* a 16th-century entertainment with dance interludes. The first treatise on ballet dancing was the *Orchésographie* of Thoinot Arbeau (1588). The 17th cent. saw the major development of ballet in France. At first a court entertainment, the simple entrées were extended c.1610 and joined together to form scenes, called divertissements, which culminated in a *grand ballet.* Louis XIV, who performed in ballets himself for nearly 50 years, founded the Royal Ballet Academy (1661), the Royal Music Academy (1669), and the first National Ballet School (1672). All parts were performed by male dancers; boys in wigs and masks took the female roles. The first ballet using trained women was *The Triumph of Love* (1681), with music by Lully. Ballet remained a court spectacle and included opera or drama until about 1708, when the first ballet was commissioned for public performance. Thereafter the form, infused with new ideas, developed as a separate art (although the court ballet continued its historic traditions). Choreographic notation came into being, and for the first time mythological themes were explored. With the increased influence of the Italian school of ballet, movement became elevated and less horizontal, and the five classic positions of the feet, which form the base for the dancer's stance and movement, were established by Pierre Beauchamps. The costumes, which had been cumbersome with decoration, long skirts, and high heels (for both men and women) were newly designed to allow greater freedom of movement. The virtuosa dancer Marie Camargo, who introduced the entrechat (elevation) for women, shortened her skirt to the middle of the calf, wore tights and what were to be the first ballet slippers (heelless shoes). Her rival, Marie Salle (who was also the first female choreographer), was the first dancer to wear a filmy, liberating Grecian-style costume, made popular two centuries later by Isadora Duncan. Jean Georges Noverre, a revolutionary *maître de ballet,* established the determining principles of the ballet d'action, which he described in his *Lettres sur la danse et les ballets* (1760). He wanted the ballet to tell a story, aided by the music, decor, and dance; he wanted the performer to interpret his role through the dance and through his own body and facial expression. In stressing naturalism, Noverre simplified the costume and c.1773 abolished the mask. Other innovations came from the great artists of the period, Gaetano and Auguste Vestris, Salvatore Vigano, and Charles Didelot. Technical innovation in dance movement was increased after further modification of the ballet costume. In Milan in 1820, Carlo Blasis first set down the technique of ballet as we know it today—with its stress on the turned-out leg, which permits great variety of movement. With the production of *La Sylphide* (1832) the romantic period formally began, ushering in a new era of brilliant choreography that emphasized the beauty and virtuosity of the prima ballerina. In this production Maria Taglioni first wore the filmy, calf-length costume that was to become standard for classical ballet. The great ballerinas of the era included Taglioni, Fanny Elssler, Carlotta Grisi, and Fanny Cerrito. In keeping with the literature and art of the romantic movement, the new ballet concerned the conflicts of reality and illusion, flesh and spirit. Love stories and fairy tales replaced mythological subjects. At the same time dancing sur les pointes [on the toes] had come into favor. By the end of the century the blocked toe had appeared, and the tutu, a very short, buoyant skirt that completely freed the legs, had come into use. The male dancer functioned as partner to support the ballerina, the central focus of the dance and drama. Ballet declined progressively after 1850 with the ballet d'action giving way entirely to divertissements; finally the great stars had retired, and the sets, costumes, and choreography had become stereotyped and uninteresting. The naturalistic trend in the theater had all but destroyed the imaginative touch necessary to ballet. The renaissance in romantic ballet began in Russia after 1875. The Russian Imperial

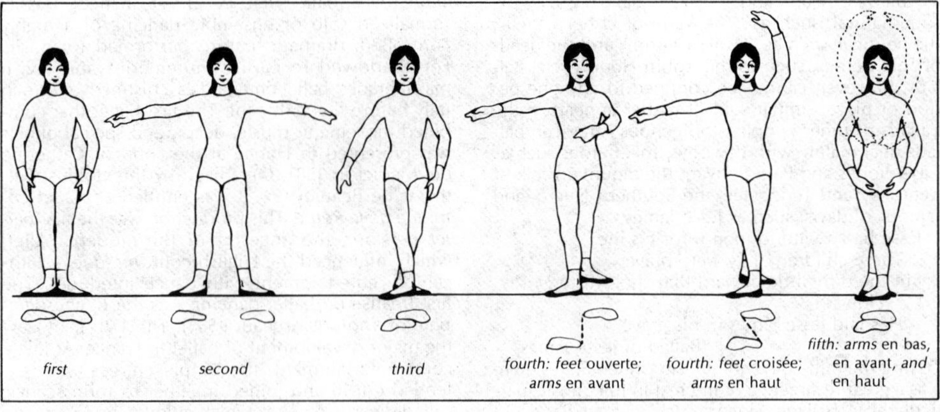

The five classical positions in ballet

SOME IMPORTANT BALLET TERMS

arabesque: graceful posture in which one leg is raised and extended behind the body, which is bent forward from the hip; the arms are held in one of five basic positions.

attitude: posture derived from Giovanni Bologna's *Mercury;* the body is bent slightly forward, one leg raised and bent behind the body with the corresponding arm raised and curved forward, and the opposite arm extended downward and back or to the side.

entrechat: elevation step in which the position of the feet is changed in midair. Nijinsky could perform the *entrechat dix* (ten changes).

glissade: sliding step performed to the side.

grand jeté: great jump, in elevation, performed as an advancing or turning movement.

pas de deux: dance performed by two partners, usually a romantic duet between a ballerina and a danseur. Famous *pas de deux* form part of the great classical ballets.

plié: bending of the knees from any of the five positions of the feet; a movement basic both to ballet performance and exercise.

port de bras: carriage of the arms; the eight basic graceful changes in arm position performed with rounded elbows. They are generally accompanied by complementary movements of the legs and body.

premier danseur: the principal male dancer of the ballet company.

prima ballerina: the principal female dancer of the ballet company; if she is termed *assoluta,* she is considered a great dancer.

School of Ballet had been founded in 1738. During the early 19th cent. the Imperial Theatre housed more than 40 ballet productions staged by the celebrated Swedish master Charles Didelot. Marius Petipa, who created a powerful sense of unity by rigorously training his corps de ballet as had not been done before, and Nicholas Legat indicated in their choreography the direction of intensified romantic drama that the newly revived art was to take. Petipa contributed many of the classic ballets still considered to be the greatest expressions of the form, including *Don Quixote, La Bayadère, The Sleeping Beauty, Raymonda, Harlequinade,* and restagings of *Giselle, Coppélia, La Sylphide,* and *Swan Lake.* In 1909 the celebrated impresario Sergei Diaghilev took his Russian company to Paris, and for 20 years it dominated the world of dance, displaying the creative talents of such choreographers and dancers as Michel Fokine, Léonide Massine, Vaslav Nijinsky, Bronislava Nijinska, Anna Pavlova, and George Balanchine. In 1931 the company merged with the Ballet Russe de Monte Carlo of René Blum and Col W. de Basil, which nurtured the talents of Alexandra Danilova, André Eglevsky, and Igor Youskevitch. Russian dancing has been maintained at the highest level of excellence to the present day. The Moscow Bolshoi Ballet, which brought fame to Galina Ulanova and Maya Plisetskaya, and the Leningrad Kirov Ballet, whose dancers have included Rudolf Nureyev, Natalia Makarova, and Mikhail Baryshnikov, are the two foremost Soviet companies and are ranked among the finest in the world. In England in about 1918, Enrico Cecchetti, who had taught many great dancers including Pavlova, Nijinsky, Massine, and Danilova, set down his method of training (which is still in practice) in collaboration with Cyril Beaumont, proprietor of "Under the Sign of the Harlequin," a world-famous bookstore specializing in the dance. The Cecchetti Society was founded in 1922 to preserve and protect that system. In 1930, Marie Rambert founded the Ballet Club, the first permanent ballet school and company in England, and in 1931, Ninette de Valois established Sadler's Wells Ballet (now the Royal Ballet), which has drawn international attention to the work of Alicia Markova, Anton Dolin, Frederick Ashton, Margot Fonteyn, Robert Helpmann, Rudolf Nureyev, Antoinette Sibley, Svetlana Beriosova, and Anthony Dowell. Nureyev, both a choreographer and dancer, has been instrumental in changing the traditional supportive role of the male dancer to a far more significant, dynamic, and athletic place in the ballet; many other contemporary choreographers have similarly given their male dancers a more flamboyant showcase. In the United States, Lincoln Kirstein and Edward Warburg founded the American Ballet company in 1934. Under the direction of George Balanchine, its chief choreographer, the company established the first major school of ballet in the country, developed the talents of many notable American dancers (including Maria Tallchief, Todd Bolender, Suzanne Farrell, Patricia McBride, Jacques d'Amboise, Arthur Mitchell, and Edward Villella), and influenced enormously the evolution of an American ballet style as parent company to the New York City Ballet (founded 1948), one of the world's outstanding companies. Among the celebrated choreographers (other than Balanchine) who designed ballets for the New York City Ballet are Eugene Loring, Merce Cunningham, Jerome Robbins, and Antony Tudor. The other major American company, the American Ballet Theatre (formerly the Ballet Theatre), was founded in 1939 as an offshoot of the smaller Mordkin Ballet. The company's principal dancers have included Lucia Chase, Anton Dolin, Nora Kaye, Alicia Alonso, Michael Kidd, Schott Douglas, Royes Fernandez, and Sallie Wilson, performing in works designed for them by Michel Fokine, Léonide Massine, Antony Tudor, Jerome Robbins, Michael Kidd, Agnes De Mille, Herbert Ross, Eugene Loring, Glen Tetley, and many others. Through numerous tours both companies have earned international reputations of a high order. Other American companies of note include the Robert Joffrey Ballet (founded 1956), the Harkness Ballet (1964), and the Dance Theatre of Harlem. In addition to these, there are many active regional ballet companies throughout the United States. Using the traditional formal training and movement, the American choreographers have designed a new sort of pure, abstract ballet, far less dependent on literary plot, often using modern rock and electronic music, and have developed greatly simplified decor and costuming (e.g., Balanchine's *Agon,* Robert Joffrey's *Astarte,* and Glen Tetley's *Chronochromie*). Many modern choreographers have also designed dances for stage and film musicals (e.g., Jerome Robbins's *West Side Story* and Agnes De Mille's *Oklahoma!*). See articles about individuals, e.g., Dame Margot FONTEYN, and companies, e.g., BOLSHOI BALLET. See also DANCE; MODERN DANCE. See Serge Lifar, *A History of Russian Ballet* (tr. 1955); Ferdinando Reyna, *A Concise History of Ballet* (tr. 1965); A. L. Haskell, *Ballet Retrospect* (1965); Anatole Chujoy, *The Dance Encyclopedia* (1945, rev. ed. 1967); Walter Terry, *The Ballet Companion* (1968); Lincoln Kirstein, *Movement and Metaphor* (1972) and *The New York City Ballet* (1973); Mary Clarke and Clement Crisp, *Ballet: An Illustrated History* (1973).

Ballia (bŭl'yə), town (1971 pop. 47,080), Uttar Pradesh state, N central India. Situated on a rich alluvial plain, Ballia is a district administrative center and an important market for rice, sugarcane, and oilseed. Changes in the course of the Ganges River destroyed the old town in the years from 1873 to 1877, and a new town was created in 1900. The annual Dadri fair, held on the full moon of Kartik (October-November) attracts about one million people.

Ballinger, Richard Achilles (băl'ĭnjər), 1858–1922, U. S. Secretary of the Interior (1909–11), b. Boonesboro (now in Boone), Iowa. He was mayor of Seattle (1904–6) and commissioner of the General Land Office (1907–9); in 1909, Taft appointed him Secretary of the Interior. While Secretary, he was accused by L. R. Glavis of the Land Office of having halted investigation into the legality of certain private coal-land claims in Alaska. With Taft's approval, Glavis was dismissed from service. Glavis took his case to the public in a series of articles in *Collier's Weekly* that roused the conservationists. Led by Gifford Pinchot, they demanded an investigation. A congressional committee exonerated Ballinger, but the questioning of committee counsel Louis D. Brandeis made the Secretary's anticonservationism clear; he resigned in March, 1911. The incident split the Republican party and helped turn the election of 1912 against Taft. See A. T. Mason, *Bureaucracy Convicts Itself* (1941); J. L. Penick, *The Ballinger-Pinchot Affair* (1968).

Balliol, Scottish family: see BALIOL, EDWARD DE; BALIOL, JOHN DE.

Balliol, Edward de: see BALIOL, EDWARD DE.

Balliol, John de: see BALIOL, JOHN DE.

ballistics (bəlĭs'tĭks), science of projectiles. Interior ballistics deals with the propulsion and the motion of a projectile within a gun or firing device. Its problems include the ignition and burning of the propellant powder, the pressure produced by the expanding gases, the movement of the projectile through the bore, and the designing of the barrel to resist resulting stresses and strains. Exterior ballistics is concerned with the motion of a projectile while in flight and includes the study not only of the flight path of bullets but also of bombs, rockets, and missiles. All projectiles traveling through the air are affected by wind, air resistance, and the force of gravity. These forces induce a curved path known as a trajectory. The trajectory varies with the weight and shape of the projectile, with its initial velocity, and with the angle at which it is fired. The general shape of a trajectory is that of a parabola. The total distance traveled by a projectile is known as its range. A ballistic missile in the first stage of its flight is powered and guided by rocket engines. After the engines burn out, the warhead travels in a fixed arc as does an artillery shell. In criminology the term ballistics is applied to the identification of the weapon from which a bullet was fired. Microscopic imperfections in a gun barrel make characteristic scratches and grooves on bullets fired through it. See E. D. Lowry, *Interior Ballistics* (1968).

Ballivián, José (hōsā' bäyēvyän'), 1805–52, president of Bolivia (1841–47). An able military commander who had served in the war against Spain, Ballivián was proclaimed president after the breakup of the Peru-Bolivia confederation under SANTA CRUZ. At Ingavi (1841) he defeated President Gomarra of Peru, who had attempted to seize La Paz. Ballivián thus insured Bolivian autonomy. Promulgating (1841) a new constitution, he energetically but arbitrarily instituted public reforms. Intense opposition forced him to resign.

balloon, lighter-than-air craft without a propulsion system, lifted by inflation of one or more containers with a gas lighter than air or with heated air. During flight, altitude is gained by discarding ballast (e.g., bags of sand) and is lost by releasing some of the lifting gas from its container. In some late designs using air heated by a small gas-fired burner, the altitude is controlled by varying the temperature of the heated air. Although interest in such a craft dates from the 13th cent., the balloon was not actually invented until the late 18th cent., when two French brothers, Joseph and Jacques Étienne Montgolfier, experimented with inverted paper and cloth bags filled with heated air and, in 1783, caused a linen bag about 100 ft (30 m) in diameter to rise in the air. In the same year the Frenchman Pilatre de Rozier made one of the first balloon ascents by man, rising in a hot-air-filled captive balloon (i.e., one made fast by a mooring cable to prevent free flight) to a height of 84 ft (26 m). In 1766 the English scientist Henry Cavendish had shown that hydrogen was seven times lighter than air, and the usefulness of this gas in balloon ascension was demonstrated in Dec., 1783, by J. A. C. Charles of France, who with his associates successfully ascended in a hydrogen-filled balloon and traveled 27 mi (43 km) from the starting point. The first ascent in England was made by James Tytler, a Scottish writer, in 1784, and in 1793 the French balloonist J. P. Blanchard made an ascent at Philadelphia. Blanchard, with Dr. John Jeffries, an American physician, also made the first sea voyage by balloon, crossing the English Channel in 1784. Among the noted balloon voyages of the 19th cent. was that made by the Swedish engineer S. A. Andree, who, in 1897, attempted unsuccessfully to reach the North Pole by balloon. In the American Civil War and World War I, captive balloons were used to observe troop movements and to direct gunfire. Captive balloons, called barrage balloons, were used as obstacles against low-flying aircraft in World War II. The helplessness of the free balloon in controlling direction led to the development of the dirigible balloon (see AIRSHIP). In 1932 the Belgian physicist Auguste Piccard, one of the major figures in 20th-century ballooning, ascended in a balloon with a sealed spherical gondola to a height of 55,500 ft (16,920 m). His brother, Jean, in 1934 reached an altitude of 58,000 ft (17,680 m). Increasingly high ascents followed, with manned balloons exceeding heights of 100,000 ft (30,480 m) and unmanned balloons exceeding 140,000 ft (42,670 m). Today balloons are used primarily as aids to scientific studies, principally meteorology and the study of cosmic rays. Unmanned meteorological balloons carry aloft radios and other instruments, which at regular intervals during the ascent transmit readings to ground stations. Balloons have also been used by the United States to photograph the atmospheres of other planets in the clear air of the stratosphere. Balloon racing has become a popular sport. The gas bags of modern balloons are generally made of synthetic material; as a lifting gas, hydrogen has lost favor to helium because the latter is nonflammable. See L. T. C. Rolt, *The Aeronauts: A History of Ballooning* (1966); Eric Norgaard, *Book of Balloons* (1972).

ballot, means of voting for candidates for office. The choice may be indicated on or by the ballot forms themselves—e.g., colored balls (hence the term *ballot*, which is derived from the Italian *ballotta*, meaning "little ball"), printed tickets, or mechanical devices—or by the depositories into which the ballots are put. The ballot was used in Athens in the 5th cent. B.C. by the popular courts and, on the question of ostracism, by the people as a whole; in India before 300 B.C.; and in Rome by the popular assemblies and occasionally by the senate. Like other institutions of popular government, it was largely abandoned during the Middle Ages, but its use reappeared in the Italian communes and in elections to the papacy during the 13th cent. In the 16th and 17th cent. the ballot appeared in English borough and university elections. The General Court of Massachusetts elected governors by ballot after 1634; corn and beans were occasionally used as ballots, following Indian custom. Early American ballots were known as "papers": the name ballot does not occur in America before 1676. The British colonies in America were the first to elect representatives by secret ballot, and its use was made obligatory in all but one of the state constitutions adopted in the United States between 1776 and 1780. In the 19th cent. the use of the ballot became widespread in local and national elections in Europe. Groups wishing to exert undue influence, intimidation, or force upon the voter have opposed the ballot. The effort to reform election abuses led to the widespread use of the Australian ballot, which was adopted in Victoria in 1857 and in Great Britain in 1872, and grew increasingly popular in the United States after 1888. In the latter country it gradually replaced earlier methods of voting such as the lengthy "tickets" distributed by political parties. In the Australian system all candidates' names are printed on a single ballot and placed in the polling places at public expense, and the printing, distribution, and marking of the ballot are protected by law, thus assuring a secret vote. The Australian ballot is now used in many European countries and in almost all sections of the United States. Separate ballots are frequently distributed for referendums and constitutional propositions. In the United States the office-group, or Massachusetts, ballot, on which the candidates' names are listed under the headings of the offices for which they are running, is less used than the party-column, or Indiana, ballot. The VOTING MACHINE is increasingly used to ensure electoral honesty. The institution of official ballots has helped bring political parties under the scope of the law. In Great Britain and Canada, party designations are left off the ballot, elective offices are few, and local and national elections are separate; hence the ballot is a short one, easy to use intelligently. Some critics denounce the excessive length of the ballot in the United States and the combination of many items on one ballot, claiming that the voter is thus too pressed for time in his decisions. See H. M. Bain and D. S. Hecock, *Ballot Position and Voter's Choice* (1957); L. E. Fredman, *Australian Ballot: The Story of an American Reform* (1968).

Ballou, Adin (bălōō'), 1803-90, American Universalist clergyman, b. Cumberland, R.I. He was prominent in the movement that resulted in the Massachusetts Association of Universal Restorationists (1831-41). In 1841 he organized near Milford, Mass., the Hopedale Community, one of the religious utopian communities of the period. He was its president and edited its periodical, the *Practical Christian.* The Hopedale Community, whose dissolution as a communal enterprise began c.1857, merged (1868) with the Unitarian Hopedale Parish, of which Ballou was pastor until 1880. His writings include *Practical Christian Socialism* (1854), *Primitive Christianity and Its Corruptions* (1870), and *History of the Hopedale Community* (1897). See his autobiography, edited by his son-in-law, W. S. Heywood (1896).

Ballou, Hosea, 1771-1852, American clergyman, foremost among expositors of Universalism in the United States, b. Cheshire co., N.H. From 1818 until his death he was pastor of the Second Universalist Society in Boston. One of the founders (1819) of the *Universalist Magazine*, he was its editor until 1828; from 1830 he edited the *Universalist Expositor.* His works include *Notes on the Parables* (1804), *A Treatise on the Atonement* (1805), and a number of hymns.

Ballou, Hosea, 2d, 1796-1861, American Universalist clergyman, b. Guilford, Vt.; grandnephew of Hosea Ballou (1771-1852). He was one of the founders and the first president (1853-61) of Tufts College. His *Ancient History of Universalism* (1829) is the earliest American monograph dealing with the history of the doctrine.

Balls Bluff, hill on the south bank of the Potomac River, near Leesburg, Va. In the Civil War, Union troops who had crossed the river were severely repulsed there on Oct. 21, 1861. Dissatisfaction with that defeat and with the general inactivity of the Union armies led to the organization of a joint congressional committee on the conduct of the war.

Ball State University, at Muncie, Ind.; coeducational; founded 1918 as a state institution. In 1929 it became Ball State Teachers College and in 1965 achieved university status.

Ballwin, city (1970 pop. 10,656), St. Louis co., E Mo., a suburb of St. Louis; settled 1803 as Ballshow, renamed 1837, inc. 1950. It is mainly residential with some light industry.

Ballymena (bălēmē'nə), municipal borough (1971 pop. 16,487), Co. Antrim, NE Northern Ireland, on the Braid River. Linen, woolen goods, carpets, and tobacco products are produced there. According to tradition, St. Patrick worked as a herdsman at Slemish Mt., 5 mi (8.1 km) from Ballymena.

balm, name for any BALSAM resin and for several plants, e.g., the BEE BALM.

Balmaceda, José (hōsā' bälmäsā'thä), 1840-91, president of Chile (1886-91). A leader of a liberal, anticlerical group, he was sent as minister (1878) to Argentina, where he successfully prevented Argentina from entering the War of the Pacific. He later served as foreign minister under Domingo Santa María. As president, Balmaceda instituted a wide reform program, but his rule was unparliamentary. A resultant quarrel with congress came to a head in 1890. A disastrous civil war broke out in Jan., 1891, led by Jorge MONTT. After vigorous fighting the revolutionists triumphed. Balmaceda took refuge in the Argentine legation. Rather than surrender for a trial, he committed suicide.

Balmerino, Arthur Elphinstone, 6th Baron (ĕl'fĭnstən, băl"mĕr'ĭnō), 1688-1746, Scottish nobleman. He resigned a command in the English army to join the Jacobite rising of 1715, escaping after its suppression to France. He returned and took part in the 1745 rising, was captured at the battle of Culloden, and was executed.

Balmer series: see SPECTRUM.

balm of Gilead (gĭl'ēəd), name for several plants belonging to different taxonomic families. The historic Old World balm of Gilead, or Mecca balsam, is a small evergreen tree (*Commiphora opobalsam*) of the family Burseraceae (INCENSE-TREE family) native to Africa and Asia and the source of the commercial balm of Gilead; it is referred to in the Bible in Jer. 8.22. The Ishmaelites from Gilead were bearing balm when they bought Joseph from his brothers. Balm of Gilead is still in high repute for healing in some countries. The American balm of Gilead is a species of poplar (*Populus candicans*) of the family Salicaceae (WILLOW family) which has large balsamic and fragrant buds. The tree is seldom seen in the wild but was formerly a favorite dooryard tree of the northern states. The buds were used in domestic medicine. This poplar is closely related to, and sometimes considered a variety of, the balsam poplar (*P. tacamahaca*), which has also been called balm of Gilead and tacamahac. The name balm of Gilead has also been used for the balsam fir and for a herbaceous aromatic, shrubby plant (*Dracocephalum canariense* or *Cedronella canariensis*) of the family Labiatae (MINT family) native to the Canary Islands and cultivated in parts of the United States.

Balmont, Konstantin Dmitrieyevich (kənstəntyĕn' dəmē'trēəvĭch bäl'mônt), 1867-1943, Russian poet and translator. After first hailing the Bolshevik revolution, he repudiated it and lived chiefly in France, where he died destitute and forgotten. Although his early verse was revolutionary in content, after 1894 it revealed the influence of the SYMBOLISTS. He translated Shelley, Ibsen, Poe, Calderón, and Whitman. His major work began with *Under Northern Skies* (1894). *Let Us Be Like the Sun* (1903) and *Love Alone* (1903) are typical of his melodious and inventive verse. His verse written after 1910 is considered mediocre.

balsa: see BOMBAX.

balsam, fragrant RESIN obtained from various trees. The true balsams contain benzoic or cinnamic acid; these include Peru balsam and tolu balsam (both obtained from varieties of the South American tree *Myroxylon balsamum* of the PULSE family), BENZOIN, and STORAX. Other resins called balsams include Mecca balsam (BALM OF GILEAD), CANADA BALSAM, and COPAIBA. Balsams are often used in medical preparations and perfumes.

balsam, garden, common name for the species *Impatiens balsamina,* a member of the JEWELWEED family.

balsam fir, common name for the evergreen tree *Abies balsamea* of NE North American boreal forests. It has small needles and cones and is used for lumber. It is also called CANADA BALSAM, as is the resin it produces, which is used as an adhesive in optical lenses and glass slides. Balsam fir is classified in the division PINOPHYTA, class Pinopsida, order Coniferales, family Pinaceae.

Balsamo, Giuseppe: see CAGLIOSTRO, ALESSANDRO.

Balsas, Río (rē'ō bäl'säs), river, c.450 mi (720 km) long, rising in the state of Puebla, E central Mexico. One of Mexico's longest rivers, it flows in a curve from south to northwest through Puebla and Guerrero states, where it waters a fertile valley, to Michoacán state, forming most of the boundary between the last two states. Then it turns southwest, passing through a hot, dry region before emptying into the Pacific Ocean. It is also known as the Río Mescala.

Balta, José (hōsā' bäl'tä), 1816-72, president of Peru (1868-72). In 1865 he helped Mariano I. Prado to seize the presidency and served in his government, but in 1867 Balta led in overthrowing the dictatorship. As president, he reestablished constitutional rule and undertook vast schemes for internal improvement. He granted a monopoly of guano export to a French company and obtained large loans in Europe, yet the lavish expenditures of his administration plunged Peru deep in debt. Balta was deposed and shot. He was succeeded by Manuel PARDO.

Balthazar (bălthā'zər): see WISE MEN OF THE EAST.

Baltic languages, a subfamily of the Indo-European family of languages. The Indo-European subfamily to which the Baltic languages appear to be closest is the Slavic. Because of this, some linguists regard Baltic and Slavic as branches of a single Balto-Slavic division of the Indo-European family. The Baltic tongues are thus named because they are spoken in an area bordering on the Baltic Sea. The principal ones are Lettish (or Latvian) and Lithuanian (together native to about 5 million people in Eastern Europe) and Old Prussian (which ceased to be a living language during the 17th cent.). The early common ancestor of the various Baltic languages, both living and dead, is traditionally referred to as Proto-Baltic. It is thought that Proto-Baltic broke off from the other Indo-European languages before 1000 B.C. A further division into East Baltic (to which Lettish and Lithuanian belong) and West Baltic (which claims Old Prussian) is believed to have taken place before 300 B.C. The Baltic languages are said to be the closest of the living Indo-European languages to Proto-Indo-European—the original parent of all the Indo-European tongues—both phonologically and grammatically. They show a high degree of inflection in both the noun and verb systems. The earliest surviving text in a Baltic language may be dated c.1400, but by the 16th cent. documents had become fairly numerous. See also LETTISH, LITHUANIAN, INDO-EUROPEAN. See T. F. Magner and W. R. Schmalstieg, ed., *Baltic Linguistics* (1970).

Baltic provinces, historic regions of COURLAND, LIVONIA, ESTONIA, and INGERMANLAND bordering on the eastern coast of the Baltic Sea. They were conquered by Russia from Sweden in the 18th cent. and made into provinces. Ingermanland was included into Russia proper, and the three independent republics of Estonia, LATVIA, and LITHUANIA were established in 1918. See also BALTIC STATES.

Baltic Sea, arm of the Atlantic Ocean, c.163,000 sq mi (422,170 sq km), including the Kattegat strait, its northwestern extension. The Øresund, Store Baelt, and Lille Baelt connect the Baltic Sea with the Kattegat and Skagerrak straits, which lead to the North Sea; the Kiel Canal, across the Jutland peninsula, is a more direct connection with the North Sea. The Gulf of Bothnia, the Gulf of Finland, and the Gulf of Riga are the chief arms of the Baltic Sea. Of the many islands in the sea, the principal ones are Sjaelland, Fyn, Lolland, Falster, and Bornholm (Denmark); Öland and Gotland (Sweden); the Åland Islands (Finland); Sarema (USSR); and Rügen (East Germany). Most of the Baltic is shallow, and its tides are less pronounced than those of the North Sea. The salinity of the sea is reduced by the many rivers that enter it (the Oder, Vistula, Dvina, Tornälven, Umeälv, Angermanälven, and Dalälven), and parts of the sea freeze over in winter. The Baltic was frequented from ancient times, especially because of the amber found along the coast. In the late Middle Ages commerce on the Baltic was dominated by the Hanseatic League. Copenhagen, Szczecin, Gdańsk, Riga, Leningrad, Helsinki, and Stockholm are the chief ports. The Baltic Sea is connected with the White Sea by the White Sea–Baltic Canal, and with the Volga River by the Volga-Baltic Waterway.

Baltic Shield, the continental core of Europe, composed of Precambrian crystalline rock, the oldest of Europe. The tectonically stable region was not affected by the Caledonian, Hercynian, and Alpine mountain periods of Europe, although mountains did rise along the edges. The exposed portion of the Baltic Shield, Fennoscandia, is found in Finland, Sweden, and Norway. During the Pleistocene epoch, great continental ice sheets scoured and depressed the shield's surface, leaving a thin covering of glacial material and innumerable lakes and streams. The ancient rocks have yielded a rich variety of minerals, especially iron and copper. In W USSR the Russian Platform is that portion of the Baltic Shield buried beneath a great thickness of sedimentary rock.

Baltic states, the countries of ESTONIA, LATVIA, and LITHUANIA, bordering on the eastern coast of the Baltic Sea. Formed in 1918, they remained independent republics until their incorporation in 1940 into the USSR. Finland is usually classed with the Scandinavian rather than with the Baltic states. See also BALTIC PROVINCES.

Baltimore, Cecilius Calvert, 2d **Baron:** see CALVERT, CECILIUS.

Baltimore, Charles Calvert, 3d **Baron:** see CALVERT, CHARLES.

Baltimore, George Calvert, 1st **Baron:** see CALVERT, GEORGE.

Baltimore (bôl'tĭmôr, -mər), city (1970 pop. 905,759), N Md., surrounded by but politically independent of Baltimore co., on the Patapsco River estuary, an arm of Chesapeake Bay; inc. 1745. The largest city in the state and the seventh largest in the country, it is a port of entry, a commercial and industrial center, an important railroad point, and a great seaport with extensive anchorages and dock and storage facilities. Large amounts of coal and grain, and iron, steel, and copper products are exported. Among Baltimore's leading industries are shipbuilding, sugar and food processing, copper and oil refining, and the manufacture of chemicals, steel, clothing, aerospace equipment, fertilizer, and tin cans. The site was first settled in the early 17th cent., but the city was not founded until 1729, when the provincial assembly authorized the building of a town. The excellent harbor soon made Baltimore an important center for the shipping of tobacco and grain. Shipbuilding, an early industry, flourished during the Revolution and the War of 1812 with the fitting out of many privateers, and in the early 1800s the famous Baltimore clippers were built. The nation's wars have played a large role in the city's history. When the British occupied (1777) Philadelphia, Baltimore became the meeting place of the Continental Congress. In the War of 1812 the gallant defense of FORT MCHENRY inspired Francis Scott Key to write "The Star-spangled Banner." After the War of 1812, Baltimore experienced a phenomenal growth, largely because of the NATIONAL ROAD. When the Erie Canal (completed in 1825) endangered the city's hold on the trans-Allegheny traffic, Baltimore businessmen chartered (1827) the BALTIMORE & OHIO RAILROAD to meet the competition of New York as a new ocean outlet for the West. During the Civil War, Baltimore was strongly pro-Southern in sentiment; the 6th Massachusetts Regiment, passing through the city in April, 1861, was attacked by a mob. In World Wars I and II, Baltimore was an important shipbuilding and supply-shipping center. A disastrous fire in 1904 destroyed almost the entire downtown section but enabled the emergence of a more beautiful and better-planned city. Today it is famous for its residential streets of red brick row houses with scrubbed white steps. An important cultural and educational center, Baltimore is the seat of The Johns Hopkins Univ., the Univ. of Baltimore, St. Mary's Seminary and Univ., Goucher College, Loyola College, College of Notre Dame of Maryland, Coppin State College, a branch of the Univ. of Maryland and its schools of medicine, dentistry, pharmacy, nursing, law, and social work, and two junior colleges. Also in Baltimore are the Peabody Conservatory of Music, the Maryland College of Art, the Maryland Academy of Sciences, the Walters Art Gallery, and the Baltimore Museum of Art. The Enoch Pratt Free Library and the municipal symphony orchestra are well known. The city's many historical attractions include Flag House; the first Roman Catholic cathedral in the United States (1806–21; designed by B. H. Latrobe); a Unitarian church (1817); the Edgar Allan Poe House (c.1830); Westminster Churchyard, where Poe is buried; Fort McHenry National Monument and Historic Shrine (see NATIONAL PARKS AND MONUMENTS, table); the Baltimore and Ohio Transportation Museum; and numerous colonial homes. The U.S.S. *Constellation,* a national historic shrine, is docked in Baltimore; it was the first U.S. navy ship (1797) and is the oldest navy ship still afloat. Other landmarks are the historic square Mt. Vernon Place, which contains the Washington Monument (1815–42; designed by Robert Mills); Druid Hill Park, with a zoo and a natural history museum; Baltimore's Memorial Stadium, home of the city's professional baseball (Orioles) and football (Colts) teams; and Pimlico Race Course, site of the famous Preakness, held annually since 1873. Baltimore-Washington International Airport is nearby. H. L. Mencken is one of the many famous people born in Baltimore. See A. M. Sioussat, *Old Baltimore* (1931); Hamilton Owens, *Baltimore on the Chesapeake* (1941); F. F. Beirne, *The Amiable Baltimoreans* (1951, repr. 1968) and *Baltimore: A Picture History* (rev. ed. 1968); J. F. Waesche, *Baltimore Today* (1969); J. T. Scharf, *History of Baltimore* (1881; repr. in 2 vol., 1971) and *The Chronicles of Baltimore* (1874, repr. 1972).

Baltimore & Ohio Railroad (B&O), first U.S. public railroad, chartered in 1827 by a group of Baltimore businessmen to regain trans-Allegheny traffic lost to the newly opened Erie Canal. Construction began in 1828, and the first division opened in May, 1830, between Baltimore and Ellicott's Mills, Md. Horses were the first source of power, but the successful trial run of Peter Cooper's *Tom Thumb* in Aug., 1830, brought the change to steam locomotives. The B&O expanded steadily and reached St. Louis in 1857. During the Civil War the railroad moved Union troops and supplies. By the end of the 19th cent. the B&O had achieved most of its present 5,800 mi (9,334 km) of track and connected with Chicago, Philadelphia, and New York City. By the mid-1900s it had become mainly a freight carrier. Faced with financial difficulties, the B&O merged with the Chesapeake & Ohio in 1965. The B&O was the first railroad to publish a timetable, to use electric locomotives and specialty cars (e.g., dining and baggage), and to run fully air-conditioned trains.

Baltimore oriole: see ORIOLE.

Baltimore-Washington Parkway: see NATIONAL PARKS AND MONUMENTS (table).

Balts, peoples of the east coast of the Baltic Sea. They include the Latvians, the Lithuanians, and the now extinct Old Prussians. Their original home was farther east, but from the 6th cent. they were pushed westward by the Slavs. In the 13th cent. the TEUTONIC KNIGHTS and the LIVONIAN BROTHERS OF THE SWORD conquered the region later comprising Estonia and Latvia and forced Christianity on the inhabitants. Pressed by the Teutonic Order, the Lithuanians formed (13th cent.) a unified state of LITHUANIA, which successfully resisted annexation and became one of the largest states of medieval Europe. In 1387, under Grand Duke Jagiello (King Ladislaus II of Poland), Lithuania officially adopted Christianity. The Teutonic Order lost (15th cent.) all but East Prussia, but descendants of the German knights and settlers continued to control land and commerce in Latvia and Estonia until the 20th cent. After the union (1569) of Lithuania with Poland, the Lithuanian nobility became thoroughly Polish in language and politics. The Estonians, a Finnic rather than a Baltic people, came under Swedish rule in 1561 and in 1721 passed to Russia, which by 1795 acquired all the Baltic lands. The incorporation of the Baltic nations of Lithuania, LATVIA, and ESTONIA into the Soviet Union since 1940 has been a source of political disputes. For earliest history to the 13th cent. see Marija Gimbutas, *The Balts* (1963).

Baluchi (bəlo͞o'chē), language belonging to the Iranian group of the Indo-Iranian subfamily of the Indo-European family of languages. See INDO-IRANIAN languages.

Baluchistan (bəlo͞o'chĭstăn), region and province (1969 est. pop. 1,484,000), c.134,000 sq mi (347,000 sq km), Pakistan. It is bounded by Iran on the west, by Afghanistan on the north, and by the Makran coast of the Arabian Sea on the south. QUETTA is the capital. Lying outside the monsoon zone and with few rivers usable for irrigation, Baluchistan is largely desert land with inarable hills and mountains. Pastoral nomads, such as the Baluchi and Pathans, who speak languages related to Persian, constitute the bulk of the sparse population. Some cotton is raised and processed, and natural gas is exploited. On the coast there is trade in fish and salt.

baluchitherium (bəlo͞ochĭthēr'ēəm), extinct primitive rhinoceros, belonging to the genus *Baluchitherium,* of the Oligocene epoch, fossilized bones of which were found in central Asia. It had an estimated shoulder height of nearly 18 ft (5.5 m) and a weight of about 10 tons, and is believed to have been the largest land mammal of all time. The baluchitherium is classified in the phylum CHORDATA, subphylum Vertebrata, class Mammalia, order Perissodactyla, family Rhinocerotidae.

Balue, Jean (zhäN bälü'), c.1421–1491, French statesman, cardinal of the Roman Catholic Church. A trusted adviser of the French king LOUIS XI, he saved Paris for the king during the revolt of the League of the Public Weal (1465). Subsequently he conspired with Charles the Bold of Burgundy against Louis and arranged the meeting of the two rulers at Péronne (1468), where Charles made Louis a prisoner. After his release Louis held Balue prisoner from 1469 to 1480, when the pope intervened. The legend that Balue was kept in an iron cage is unproved. Balue went to Rome, but in 1484 he returned temporarily to France as a papal legate.

Balzac, Honoré de (băl'zăk, bôl-, Fr. ōnōrā' də bälzäk'), 1799–1850, French novelist, b. Tours. Balzac ranks among the great masters of the novel. Of a bourgeois family, he himself later added the "de" to his name. Neglected in childhood, he was sent to a grammar school at Tours and later to a boarding school at Vendôme, where he was a dull student but a voracious reader. In 1816 he began studying law at the Sorbonne, but after receiving his license in 1819 he decided to abandon law for literature. Half starving in a Paris garret, Balzac began writing sensational novels to order, publishing them under a pseudonym. Throughout his life he worked with feverish activity, sleeping a few hours in the evening and writing from midnight until noon or afternoon of the next day. He was ridden with debts, which were increased rather than relieved by his business ventures. Balzac's first success, *Les Chouans* (1829, first published as *Le Dernier Chouan*), was followed by *La Peau de chagrin* (1831). In the next 20 years he produced the vast collection of novels and short stories called "La Comédie humaine." This, his greatest work, is a reproduction of the French society of his time, picturing in precise detail individuals of every class and every profession. The chief novels in "La Comédie humaine" are *Louis Lambert*

(1832), *Eugénie Grandet* (1833), *La Recherche de l'absolu* (1834), *Le Père Goriot* (1835), *Les Illusions perdues* (1837), *César Birotteau* (1837), *La Cousine Bette* (1847), and *Le Cousin Pons* (1847). Outweighing Balzac's faults—his lack of literary style, his moralizing, his tendency toward melodrama—are his originality, his great powers of observation, and his vivid imagination. His short stories include some of the best in the language, but his attempts at drama failed. Though an unattractive, awkward man, Balzac formed several famous liaisons. Only a few months before his death he married the Polish Countess Evelina Hanska, with whom he had conducted a romantic correspondence for 18 years. See *The Human Comedy* (with introductions by George Saintsbury, 40 vol., 1895–98); Balzac's *Letters to His Family*, 1809–1850 (ed. by W. S. Hastings, 1934); biographies by H. J. Hunt (1957, repr. 1969), A. Maurois (1966), and V. S. Pritchett (1973); studies by E. J. Oliver (1959, repr. 1964), P. Bertault (1963); bibliography and index comp. by W. H. Royce (1929, repr. 1969).

Balzac, Jean Louis Guez de (zhäN lwĕ gā), 1597?–1654, French writer. His *Lettres* (1624, tr. 1634) and other writings were a great influence in reforming French prose. Their style was marked by their orderly, Latinate sentence structure.

Bamah (bā'mə) [Heb.,=high place], term elsewhere translated, but in Ezek. 20.29 given in the original. The word is translated earlier in the same verse. There is a pun on the verb "to go" that had in Hebrew a sound much like the word Bamah.

Bamako (bämäkō'), city (1970 est. pop. 170,000), capital of Mali and of its Bamako region, SW Mali, on the Niger River. It is the nation's administrative center, as well as a river port, a junction on the Dakar-Niger RR, and a major regional trade center. Manufactures include textiles, processed meat, and metal goods. Bamako ships shea-nut oil, kapok, cotton, and peanuts. There is commercial fishing on the Niger. Bamako was a leading center of Muslim learning under the Mali empire (c.11th–15th cent.) but by the 19th cent. had declined into a small village. In 1883 it was occupied by French troops under Joseph S. GALLIENI. In 1908, Bamako became the capital of the French Sudan (see MALI) and began to develop into a major city. As a result of a conference of Africans from French West and Equatorial Africa, held in Bamako in 1946, the Rassemblement démocratique africain, an important regional political party, was founded. Bamako is a picturesque city, with a botanical and zoological park and many decorative gardens. Residential areas often consist of mud huts arranged in a star or checkerboard pattern and enclosed by a wall. Bamako's educational institutions include schools of administration, medicine, and engineering. The city also has an international airport.

Bamberg (băm'bĕrk), city (1970 pop. 70,581), Bavaria, S West Germany, a port on the Regnitz River. It is an industrial and commercial center; its manufactures include textiles, clothing, electrical equipment, machinery, and beer. Bamberg was the capital of a powerful ecclesiastical state from 1007 to 1802. In 1803 it passed to Bavaria. Noteworthy buildings in the picturesque city include the cathedral (built mostly in the 13th cent.), which includes the tombs of Emperor Henry II and Pope Clement II; a Gothic church (14th cent.); and two episcopal residences (16th and 18th cent.). It is the seat of a Roman Catholic archbishopric and has a museum of natural history.

Bamberger, Ludwig (lo͝ot'vĭkh bäm'bĕrgər), 1823–99, German economist, politician, and journalist. An ardent liberal, he took part in the Revolution of 1848 and was forced to live in exile until 1866. He worked for the unification of Germany, and as a leader of the National Liberals he supported Otto von Bismarck until he was alienated by the chancellor's turn to protection and state socialism. In 1880, Bamberger led a group out of the party. As a member of the Reichstag (1871–93), he was chiefly responsible for the adoption of the gold standard in Germany and for the founding of the Reichsbank.

Bamboccianti: see LAER, PIETER VAN.

Bamboccio, Il: see LAER, PIETER VAN.

bamboo, plant of the family Gramineae (GRASS family), chiefly of warm or tropical regions, where it is an extremely important component of the vegetation. It is most abundant in the monsoon area of E Asia. Many species are among the largest grasses, sometimes reaching 100 ft (30 m). The stalks are round (rarely square), jointed, and hollow or solid with evergreen or deciduous leaves. Some types die after flowering and some do not flower until they are about 30 years old. In many places bamboo is used as wood, for construction work, furniture, utensils, fiber, paper, fuel, and innumerable small articles. Bamboo sprouts are eaten as a vegetable, and the grains of some species are also utilized for food. The bamboo has long been used for decorative purposes, both in gardens and in art. In the United States the native bamboo is a CANE. The most common bamboo is *Bambusa arundinacea*. Bamboo is classified in the division MAGNOLIOPHYTA, class Liliatae, order Cyperales, family Gramineae. See F. A. McClure, *The Bamboos* (1966).

Bamburgh, village, Northumberland, NE England, on the North Sea. It was the capital of ancient BERNICIA and for a time of NORTHUMBRIA. In the 6th cent. a castle was erected above a tall cliff on the site of a Roman fort. Restored in the 18th cent., it is still used as a residence and contains the 14,000-volume Crewe Library.

Bamford, Samuel, 1788–1872, English weaver, poet, and social reformer. Always sympathetic toward the working class, he was jailed in 1819 for his part in the Peterloo massacre. His dialect verses were popular among the Lancashire workers. Besides his poetry, Bamford is noted for *Passages in the Life of a Radical* (2 vol., 1840–43, repr. 1967).

Bamian (bəmyän'), town (1969 est. pop. 48,000), N central Afghanistan, on the Kunduz River. It was long a major caravan center on the route between India and central Asia. By the 7th cent. the town was a prominent center of Buddhism; the Bamian valley is lined with cave dwellings cut out of the cliffs by Buddhist monks. Particularly interesting are two great Buddha figures (probably 6th or 7th cent.) carved from rock and finished in fine plaster. In the same area are grottoes decorated with well-preserved wall paintings in Greco-Buddhist styles. Bamian was invaded by the Saffarids in 871, and many Buddhist idols were carried off to Baghdad. A Muslim fortress town from the 9th to the 12th cent., Bamian was sacked by Jenghiz Khan in 1221 and never regained its former prominence.

Bamian, valley, E Afghanistan, NW of Kabul; site of the ancient commercial and cultural center of Bamian. This major archeological area is noted for its two gigantic statues of Buddhist saints, 174 ft (53 m) and 115 ft (35 m) high, carved in the valley's rock walls. Many of the rock sanctuaries and cells are still in use.

Bamoth (bā'mŏth) [Heb.,=pl. of BAMAH], unidentified place, E of the Dead Sea. Num. 21.19,20. It is probably the same as **Bamoth-baal** (-bā'əl), Joshua 13.17. Bamoth-baal is translated in Num. 22.41.

Bampton, John, 1689–1751, English clergyman, founder of an Oxford lectureship on religious subjects. The Bampton Lectures, given annually, have frequently given rise to lively controversy.

Bampton, Rose, 1909–, American operatic soprano, b. Cleveland. Bampton studied at the Curtis Institute of Music, Philadelphia. She made her debut at the Metropolitan Opera in 1932 in the leading contralto role in Ponchielli's *La Gioconda* and sang contralto and mezzo-soprano roles until 1936, when she retrained her voice to soprano range and made her first European tour. She made her soprano debut at the Metropolitan in 1937.

Banaba: see OCEAN ISLAND.

Banach, Stefan (stĕ'făn bä'näkh), 1892–1945, Polish mathematician. He was educated at the Institute of Technology in Lvov; his doctoral thesis laid the foundations of modern functional analysis, which he continued to work at throughout his life. He also made fundamental contributions to general topology, set theory, the theory of measure and integration, and the general theory of linear spaces, or vector spaces, e.g., *Théorie des opérations linéaires* (1932). He introduced and developed the concept of complete normed linear spaces, now called Banach spaces.

banana, name for several species of the genus *Musa* and for the fruits these produce. The banana plant—one of the largest herbaceous plants—is said to be native to tropical Asia, but is now cultivated throughout the tropics. Used to a minor degree for its leaf fiber, the banana is of the same genus as the extremely valuable fiber plant MANILA HEMP, or abaca, and is also related to the BIRD-OF-PARADISE FLOWER. Along with the banana, these are economically the most important plants of the banana family (the Musaceae), a group of large monocotyledonous tropical herbs. The banana is of palmlike aspect and has very large leaves, the overlapping bases of which form the so-called false trunk. As the plant reaches maturity its true stem rises from the ground and pushes through the center of the false trunk to emerge from the top of the plant, there becoming pendent and bearing the male and female flowers. The female flowers develop into bananas, the clusters of upturned fruits being called "hands" and each banana a "finger." The plants are cut down to harvest the fruit, since they bear only once. Their seeds are sterile; shoots from the rhizomes are used for propagation. The banana fruit (botanically a berry) is a staple food in the tropics and is used in many forms, raw or cooked, and grown in many varieties, e.g., the plantain. Dried bananas are eaten as "banana figs" and inferior fruits serve as a stock feed. Banana oil is a synthetic product, so named because of its odor. Although the banana has long been cultivated in Asia—Alexander the Great encountered it in India—the large international traffic began only in the late 19th cent. with the development of refrigerated transport. The most common banana of North American commerce is *M. sapientum* (or *M. paradisiaca sapientum*). Bananas are classified in the division MAGNOLIOPHYTA, class Liliatae, order Zingiberales, family Musaceae.

banana fish: see BONEFISH.

Bananal Island, Brazil: see ARAGUAIA, river.

Banat (bä'nät), region extending across W Rumania, NE Yugoslavia, and S Hungary. The term *banat* originally referred to any of several frontier provinces of Hungary and Croatia that were ruled by bans (governors). The Banat region is bordered on the E by Transylvania and Walachia, on the W by the Tisza River, on the N by the Mureşul River, and on the S by the Danube. Except for some eastern mountains, it is primarily an agricultural area of fertile, rolling plains. Inhabited since prehistoric times, the Banat was occupied successively by Romans, Goths, Gepidae, Huns, and Avars. Slavs began to settle there in the 5th cent. and Magyars in the 9th cent. In 1233, King Andrew II of Hungary established the Banat of Severin, a frontier province whose defense was entrusted to the Knights Hospitalers. In the aftermath of the Turkish victory over the Serbs at Kossovo (1389) and the Turkish occupation of Serbia (1459), many Serbs emigrated to the Banat, which itself became a Turkish sanjak (province) around 1552. By the Treaty of Passarowitz (1718), the Banat was made an Austrian military frontier zone known as the **Banat of Temesvar**. Empress Maria Theresa put the region under civilian government in 1751 and brought in thousands of German colonists. In 1779 the Banat passed to Hungary, to which it belonged until 1918, except for a brief period as an Austrian crownland. Although the Allies in World War I had promised through a secret agreement to give the Banat to Rumania, it was divided by the Treaty of Trianon (1920) between Rumania and newly independent Yugoslavia, with the Szeged district reserved for Hungary.

Banbury, municipal borough (1971 pop. 29,216), Oxfordshire, central England, on the Cherwell River. It is an agricultural market and manufactures aluminum, fabricated steel, farm machinery, electrical apparatus, and furniture. The town still produces the spiced currant cakes for which it has been famous since the 17th cent. The Banbury Cross of the nursery rhyme was destroyed by the Puritans in 1602; a new one was installed in 1859.

Bancroft, Anne, 1931–, American actress, b. New York City as Anne Italiano. Her New York stage debut in *Two for the Seesaw* (1958) was a major triumph. She was acclaimed for her performance in *The Miracle Worker* (1959) and won an Academy Award for the 1962 film version. In the mid-1960s she appeared in *Mother Courage, The Devils*, and *A Cry of Players*. Bancroft's films include *The Pumpkin Eater* (1964), *The Graduate* (1968), and *Young Winston* (1972).

Bancroft, Edward, 1744–1821, spy in the American Revolution, b. Westfield, Mass. While living in London, he became a friend of Benjamin Franklin and in the Revolution began to operate as an American secret agent. He reported to the American commissioners in France, but, unknown to them, he was a double agent and reported their movements to the British. Bancroft in 1778 gave advance information of the Franco-American alliance to the British. Evidence of his duplicity was revealed by Paul L. Ford in 1891. See Lewis Einstein, *Divided Loyalties* (1933).

Bancroft, George, 1800–1891, American historian and public official, b. Worcester, Mass. He taught briefly at Harvard and then for eight years at the Round Hill School in Northampton, Mass., of which he was a founder and proprietor. He then turned definitely to writing. His article (Jan., 1831) in the *North American Review* attacking the Bank of the United States delighted Jacksonian Democrats, and in 1834 Bancroft became an avowed apostate from New England Federalism, "a traitor to his class." In that year also appeared the first volume of his monumental work, *A History of the United States* (10 vol., 1834-74; revised into 6 vol. by the author in 1876 and 1883-85). As a reward for his speeches and writings for the Democratic cause he was appointed (1837) collector of the port of Boston by President Martin Van Buren, and as the dispenser of the patronage of that office Bancroft was the Democratic boss in Massachusetts. He was defeated for the governorship in 1844, but President Polk, whom he had helped nominate, made him Secretary of the Navy. In that post (March, 1845-Sept., 1846) he established the U.S. Naval Academy at Annapolis and issued the standing orders under which Capt. John D. Sloat, commanding the Pacific squadron, seized California ports on the outbreak of the Mexican War. That conflict formally began in May, 1845, when Bancroft, then serving also as acting Secretary of War, gave the order that sent Gen. Zachary Taylor into Mexico. While minister to Great Britain (1846-49), he diligently collected materials for his *History* in British and French archives. Bancroft, an antislavery Democrat, came to support Abraham Lincoln in the Civil War and on Feb. 12, 1866, delivered the official memorial address on Lincoln before the Congress (he had also been the official eulogist of Andrew Jackson in 1845). He is assumed to have written President Andrew Johnson's first message to Congress, and in 1867 Johnson appointed him minister to Prussia. He held the post until 1874. Although his famous *History* is little read today, it was an important landmark in American historiography, hitherto burdened with Federalist myths, and it remains valuable for its extensive use of source materials. The *History* is violently anti-British and intensely patriotic and leaves no doubt that the author was passionately sincere in his devotion to democracy. Acknowledged partisan that he was, Bancroft, the first American trained in the so-called scientific school of German historical scholarship, nevertheless insisted that his was an objective interpretation; the high praise his work won from the great Leopold von Ranke as the best history ever written from the democratic point of view annoyed as well as gratified him. His literary style was sonorous and rather ponderous, although some passages still have an emotional appeal. See biographies by M. A. De Wolfe Howe (1908) and R. B. Nye (1944, repr. 1964); study by R. H. Canary (1974).

Bancroft, Hubert Howe, 1832-1918, American publisher and historian, b. Granville, Ohio. Bancroft began his career as a bookseller in San Francisco in 1852. Soon he had his own firm, the largest book and stationery business W of Chicago. He also developed a passion for collecting materials on the western regions of North and South America, from Alaska to Patagonia. After toying with the idea of compiling an encyclopedia, he settled on the publication of a prodigious history (39 vol., 1874-90), reissued (1882-90) as *The Works of Hubert Howe Bancroft*. The *Works* cover the history and to some extent the anthropology of Central America, Mexico, and the Far West of the United States. The first 5 volumes concern the native races, the next 28 the Pacific states, and the last 6 are essays. *Literary Industries*, the 39th volume, contains autobiographical material and an account of Bancroft's historical method. About a dozen assistants—out of hundreds Bancroft had tried out in his "history factory"—did the actual writing of the *Works*; Bancroft personally wrote very little. Because his assistants were not given credit lines and because of Bancroft's rather unethical business practices, Bancroft and the *Works* were at first severely attacked. However, his enormous contribution soon received just recognition. When Bancroft presented his library to the Univ. of California (1905) it contained about 60,000 items, including rare manuscripts, maps, books, pamphlets, transcripts of archives made by his staff, and personal narratives of early pioneers as recorded by his reporters. Known as the Bancroft Library, the collection remains an outstanding repository of the history of the West. See biography by J. W. Caughey (1946, repr. 1970).

Bancroft, Marie Effie Wilton, Lady, 1839-1921, English actress and manager. She made her debut (1856) at the Lyceum Theatre, London, and in 1865 became joint manager of the Prince of Wales's Theatre, London, with **Sir Squire Bancroft**, 1841-1926, whose entire name was Squire Bancroft White Butterfield. They were married in 1867. With their production of *Caste* in the same year, the Bancrofts, as co-stars, began an association with its author, Tom ROBERTSON, that was to prove most successful. Their presentations of his plays, which were more true to life than the current melodramas, and their utilization of the reforms of Mme VESTRIS introduced realism to the 19th-century English stage. They continued their work at the Haymarket theater in London (1880-85). The Bancrofts appeared together until 1886, when Mrs. Bancroft retired. Squire Bancroft was knighted in 1895. See their joint memoirs, *Mr. and Mrs. Bancroft, on and off the Stage* (1888) and *Recollections of Sixty Years* (1909); Sir Squire Bancroft, *Empty Chairs* (1925).

Bancroft, village (1971 pop. 2,276), SE Ont., Canada, on the York River. Uranium mines are in the area.

band, in music, a group of musicians playing principally on wind and percussion instruments, usually outdoors. Such grouping of loud instruments characterized Saracen military bands participating in the Crusades. About 1300 similar groups, often including the SHAWM (a type of oboe), trumpet, and drum, appeared in the courts and towns of Europe. Town bands were manned by members of the watch and were integral to both the civic and social life of the community. These musicians participated in processions, dances, weddings, and feasts and provided incidental music for dramatic representations. During the 16th cent. the practice of playing instruments of the same family in consort (as in a shawm band) became popular, and new families of wind instruments added variety. As the town band began to decline at the end of the 17th cent., its official duties gradually shifted to the military band, which had assumed classical proportions in the early Renaissance. A vestige of the extravagant, almost ritualistic affectations of the instrumentalists has survived in the routines of present-day drum majors and majorettes. For several centuries the general composition of the military band remained static, the fife and drum being associated with the infantry and the trumpet and kettledrum with the cavalry. France introduced the oboe in the latter half of the 17th cent., and a gradual merger with the full wind contingent of the town band ensued. Important developments in instrument-making affected the composition of bands in the 19th cent. A Prussian bandmaster, Wilhelm Wieprecht (1802-72), introduced (c. 1830) valve trumpets and horns into the military band. The saxhorns and saxophones of Adolphe Sax were incorporated into French military bands at midcentury. The sarrusophone was added in the 1860s, thus completing the ensemble that in most respects is known today. Two outstanding European bands are the British Royal Artillery Band (founded 1762) and the band of the French Garde Républicaine, playing under that name since 1872. The U.S. Marine Band, founded in 1798, was the first important band in the United States and remains outstanding. The first U.S. band devoted exclusively to the presentation of public concerts was that of P. S. Gilmore, founded in 1859. His successor as America's leading bandmaster was John Philip SOUSA (1854-1932). In 1911, Edwin Franko Goldman organized the Goldman Band, which continues to give outdoor concerts in New York City in the summer. Modern bands usually include the PICCOLO, FLUTE, CLARINET, OBOE, ENGLISH HORN, BASSOON, SAXOPHONE, CORNET, TRUMPET, FRENCH HORN, TROMBONE, TUBA, flügelhorn, euphonium, and various PERCUSSION INSTRUMENTS. Concert bands may add the cello, bass viol, and harp. The band repertory has traditionally included flourishes, marches, and music transcribed from other mediums. As town bands once provided music for social dancing, so do modern jazz and rock bands of numerous descriptions (see ROCK MUSIC). Prior to the 18th cent., the term *band* was frequently applied in a generic sense to cover the combinations of instruments employed by kings and nobles. The term is also used for an ensemble of any one type of instrument, as brass band, wind band, marimba band. See R. F. Goldman, *The Band's Music* (1938) and *The Concert Band* (1946).

Banda, Hastings Kamuzu (kämo͞o'zo͞o bän'də), 1902?-, African political leader, president of Malawi (1966-). Overcoming the disadvantages of his peasant background, he received a medical degree in the United States and established a prosperous practice in London after World War II. He returned to Africa (1953) and then to his homeland, Nyasaland (1958), to campaign against the federation of Nyasaland (now Malawi) with Rhodesia. In a 1961 general election Banda's Malawi Congress party won a sweeping victory. Nyasaland, led by Banda as prime minister, became an independent member of the British Commonwealth as Malawi in 1964. Banda instituted constitutional changes in 1966, making himself life president and eliminating political opposition. In 1971 he became the first black African leader to visit South Africa. See biography by Philip Short (1974).

Banda Islands, group of 10 volcanic islands, c.70 sq mi (180 sq km), E Indonesia, in the Banda Sea, in the Moluccas. The capital and commercial center is Bandanaira, a seaport on Bandanaira island. The largest island in the group is Bandalontar. Nutmeg and mace are the chief products. The islands were discovered and claimed by the Portuguese in 1512. The Dutch ousted the Portuguese in the early 1600s, and the Dutch East India Company assumed control in 1619. Conflict with the English led to the so-called Ambon massacre. Many inhabitants are Christian.

Banda Oriental (bän'dä ōryäntäl') [Span.,=eastern shore, i.e., of the Río de la Plata], region, S Uruguay. An alluvial plain, it is Uruguay's principal livestock-raising and wheat-growing region. In the Spanish colonial period Banda Oriental was the term applied to Uruguay.

Bandar, India: see MASULIPATAM.

Bandar Abbas (bändär' äb-bäs'), town (1971 est. pop. 38,000), S Iran, on the Strait of Hormoz at the mouth of the Persian Gulf. A port of strategic and commercial importance, it is the focal point of the trade routes of S Iran. It was long noted for its trade with India. The town has food processing and textile industries; cotton, rugs, nuts, and dates are exported. Early in the 16th cent. the Portuguese established themselves in the region, seizing the islands in the strait and using the town, which they fortified and called Gamru, as a mainland port. Shah Abbas I recaptured (c.1615) the town and later the islands. The Dutch (without the shah's consent) and the English (with the shah's approval) subsequently set up trading stations there; they called the town Gombroon. In 1622, Shah Abbas renamed the town Bandar Abbas (port of Abbas) and developed it into a major port. Bandar Abbas began to lose importance in the late 1800s, especially after the opening of the Trans-Iranian RR terminal at the head of the Persian Gulf.

Bandaranaike, Sirimavo (sērēmä'vō bändrānī'kē), 1916-, prime minister of Sri Lanka (formerly Ceylon). Of an aristocratic family, she was educated at a Roman Catholic convent. In 1940 she married S. W. R. D. Bandaranaike, also a Christian. She was converted to Buddhism, as was her husband, before he became (1956) prime minister. After her husband was assassinated (1959) she led his Sri Lanka Freedom party to victory in the 1960 elections and became prime minister. She remained in office until 1965, pursuing a nationalist program; was defeated in the 1965 elections; but returned as prime minister in 1970. In 1972 she was the guiding force behind the adoption of a new constitution that proclaimed a republic and officially changed the country's name to Sri Lanka.

Bandaranaike, Solomon West Ridgeway Dias, 1899-1959, prime minister (1956-59) of Ceylon (later Sri Lanka); husband of Sirimavo Bandaranaike. A lawyer educated in England, he entered politics and rose to hold a cabinet position. He resigned, however, in 1951 to form what became the Sri Lanka Freedom party. In 1956 he organized a leftist coalition that came to power with the 1956 elections. As prime minister, he took a neutralist stance in foreign affairs; domestically, he was faced by economic problems and disputes over languages. He was assassinated by a dissident Buddhist monk.

Bandar-e Pahlavi (bändär-ā päləvē'), city (1966 pop. 41,785), Gilan prov., NW Iran, a port on the Caspian Sea. It has fisheries and exports food products, cotton, fish, and caviar. The city is also called Pahlevi and was formerly known as Enzeli.

Bandar-e Shah (shä), town (1966 pop. 13,000), Mazanderan prov., N Iran, on the Caspian Sea. The town has fisheries and serves as the northern terminus of the Trans-Iranian Railway, which runs to the Persian Gulf.

Bandar-e Shahpur (shäpo͝or'), town (1966 pop. 6,000), Khuzestan prov., SW Iran, a port at the head of the Persian Gulf. It is the southern terminus of the Trans-Iranian Railway, which runs to the Caspian Sea.

Banda Sea (băn'də, bän'dä), section of the Pacific Ocean, c.600 mi (970 km) long and c.300 mi (480 km) wide, E Indonesia, outlined by the South Molucca islands. The deepest point is c.21,000 ft (6,400 m). Reefs and currents near the sea's islands are a hazard to shipping.

Bandeira (bəndēē'rä), highest peak of Brazil, 9,462 ft (2,884 m) high, in the Serra do Caparaó, situated on the border between Minas Gerais and Espírito Santo states, SE Brazil.

Bandelier, Adolph Francis Alphonse (băndəlēr'), 1840–1914, American archaeologist, b. Bern, Switzerland. His pioneering studies on ancient Mexican civilizations and his important excavations in Peru and Bolivia laid the foundations for later research in American archaeology. He is well known for his popular books *The Delight Makers* (1890, repr. 1954) and *The Gilded Man* (1893).

Bandelier National Monument: see NATIONAL PARKS AND MONUMENTS (table).

Bandello, Matteo (mät-tĕ'ō bändĕl'lō), 1485–1561, Italian storywriter, a Dominican priest. He is famous for his novellas, short tales in imitation of Boccaccio, that provided themes for several 17th-century plays. Often coarse, they have considerable vitality and occasional tragic force. His version of an earlier *Romeo and Juliet* is probably the source of Shakespeare's play. An edition of his novellas was translated into English by Sir Geoffrey Fenton in 1567 and reprinted in 1924.

bandicoot, small marsupial mammal native to Australia and nearby islands. Bandicoots have long, pointed, shrewlike faces; gray or brown fur; and long, bushy, ratlike tails. They range in size from that of a rat to that of a rabbit. Their feet are equipped with sharp claws, used for digging food; they feed nocturnally on insects, worms, roots, and vegetables dug from the ground. The second and third toes of the hind legs are bound together and the paired claws are used as a comb for grooming the fur. Bandicoots are able to hop about like rabbits on their strong hind legs, but they also commonly creep on all fours. Bandicoots are classified in the phylum CHORDATA, subphylum Vertebrata, order Marsupialia, family Peramelidae.

bandicoot rat, giant rat of southern Asia, unrelated to true bandicoots. It is an agricultural pest in the grain crops and gardens of India and Sri Lanka and is known for the piglike grunts it emits when attacked. Bandicoot rats are classified in the phylum CHORDATA, subphylum Vertebrata, class Mammalia, order Rodentia, family Muridae.

Bandinelli, Bartolomeo (bärtōlōmā'ō bändēnĕl'lē) or **Baccio** (bät'chō), 1493?–1560, Florentine sculptor and painter; son of a goldsmith. He attempted to emulate Michelangelo, and derived from him a strong interest in musculature. Although his drawings are forceful, his sculpture tends toward a somewhat petrified rendering of the human form. Among his works are a statue of St. Peter and an altar screen in the cathedral at Florence. *Hercules and Cacus* and the monument to Giovanni delle Bande Nere are also in Florence. Together with his assistants, he is responsible for the execution of the tombs of popes Leo X and Clement VII in Santa Maria sopra Minerva, Rome.

bandit: see BRIGANDAGE.

Bandjarmasin (bän''jərmä'sĭn), city (1961 pop. 214,096), capital of South Kalimantan prov., S Borneo (Kalimantan), Indonesia, on a delta island near the junction of the Barito and Martapura rivers. An important deep-water port, it is the trade center of the rich Barito basin; exports include rubber, pepper, timber, oil, coal, gold, and diamonds. There is a large oil refinery, and coal mines and sawmills are in the vicinity. In the 14th cent. Bandjarmasin was part of the Hindu kingdom of Madjapahit, but it passed to Muslim rulers in the late 15th cent. The Dutch opened trade there in 1606. The British controlled the city for several brief periods, and in 1787 it became a Dutch protectorate. There is much flooding, and many of the inhabitants live on raftlike dwellings. A state university is in the town. It is also spelled Banjermasin or Bandjermasin.

Bandjermasin: see BANDJARMASIN, Indonesia.

Bandoeng: see BANDUNG, Indonesia.

Bandung or **Bandoeng** (both: bän'do͝ong), city (1971 est. pop. 1,114,000), capital of West Java prov., W Java, Indonesia, near the Guntur volcano. Formerly the administrative and military headquarters of the Netherlands East Indies, it is the third largest city in Indonesia, an industrial hub, a famous educational and cultural center, and a tourist resort known for its cool, healthful climate. Bandung is a textile center and the site of the country's quinine industry, which uses the cinchona grown on nearby plantations. Other manufactures include ceramics, chemicals, rubber products, and machinery. The city is the seat of a textile institute, the Pasteur Institute, a technological institute, a state university, two private universities, and a nuclear research center. Nearby is Malabar radio station, one of the most powerful in SE Asia. Founded by the Dutch in 1810, Bandung became important with the arrival of the railroad in the late 19th cent.

Bandung Conference, meeting of representatives of 29 African and Asian nations, held at Bandung, Indonesia, in 1955. The aim—to promote economic and cultural cooperation and to oppose colonialism—was more or less achieved in an atmosphere of cordiality. Communist China played a prominent part and strengthened its friendly relations with other Asian peoples. Not invited to the conference were South Africa, Israel, Nationalist China, the Republic of Korea, and the People's Republic of Korea. In the 1960s and 1970s, conflicts between the African and Asian nations eroded the solidarity expressed at Bandung. See AFRO-ASIAN BLOC. See Carlos P. Romulo, *The Meaning of Bandung* (1956).

baneberry, any plant of the small genus *Actaea,* north temperate perennials of the family Ranunculaceae (BUTTERCUP family) sometimes cultivated for the handsome (though poisonous) berrylike fruits. Native species, formerly used medicinally by both Indian and white man and also called cohosh, are the red baneberry (with a stalk of red berries) and the white baneberry (with a stalk of white berries). The plant is also one of several plants called herb Christopher, particularly the dark-fruited European species. The baneberry is similar to the related bugbane, one species of which is also called cohosh. Baneberry is classified in the division MAGNOLIOPHYTA, class Magnoliopsida, order Ranunculales, family Ranunculaceae.

Banér, Johan (yo͞o'hän bänâr'), 1596–1641, Swedish field marshal in the THIRTY YEARS WAR. He served (1626–29) in Poland and Russia and accompanied (1630) Gustavus II of Sweden to Germany. At Gustavus's death (1632) Banér was a leading officer, and after the major Swedish defeat at Nördlingen he became the chief Swedish general in Germany. Banér reestablished Sweden's military prestige at Wittstock (1636), where he defeated the Saxon and imperial forces. After recovering (1638) Pomerania and Mecklenburg and winning (1639) a victory over the Saxons at Chemnitz, he penetrated (1639) into Bohemia but was forced to retreat.

Banerjea, Sir Surendranath (so͞orĕn'drənät bä'nərjē), 1848–1926, Indian nationalist. One of the first Hindus to join the Indian civil service, he was dismissed (1874) for a minor error and was considered by many to be the victim of discrimination. He became a teacher in Calcutta and editor of the nationalist paper *Bengalee,* and in 1876 he founded the nationalist Indian Association, a predecessor of the Indian National Congress. He served twice (1895, 1902) as president of the latter organization but withdrew in 1918 to espouse a more moderate nationalism that called for Hindu-Muslim cooperation and gradual reform. Knighted in 1921, he served (1921–24) as minister for local self-government in Bengal. He was a founder (1882) of Ripon College in Calcutta, which in 1947 was renamed Surendranath College. See his autobiography, *A Nation in Making* (1925); Daniel Argov, *Moderates and Extremists in the Indian Nationalist Movement, 1883–1920* (1967).

Banff (bămf, bănf), town (1971 est. pop. 3,500), SW Alta., Canada, on the Bow River in the Rocky Mts. A famous tourist center and a winter resort, it is the administrative headquarters of Banff National Park. The Banff School of Fine Arts is a branch of the Univ. of Alberta.

Banff National Park, 2,564 sq mi (6,641 sq km), W Alta., Canada, in the Rocky Mts.; est. 1885. Noted for its mountain scenery and hot mineral springs, the park is a year-round resort area. Banff and Lake Louise are the chief resort centers.

Banffshire or **Banff,** county (1971 pop. 43,501), NE Scotland. Banff is the county town. The terrain slopes from the Cairngorm mts. in the south to a fertile farm belt near the Moray Firth. Oats and barley are the staple crops, and sheep and cattle are raised. The distilling industry is mainly around Dufftown; Glenlivet is also famous for whiskey. Fishing villages dot the coast; Buckie and Banff are important cod and herring ports. There is also a boatbuilding industry. Fine woolens are manufactured at Keith. The county has granite, limestone, and marble quarries. Banffshire was torn by religious strife after the Reformation, and troubles continued through the period of the ENGLISH CIVIL WAR. After the GLORIOUS REVOLUTION (1688–89), the county was strongly Jacobite. In 1975, Banffshire became part of the new Grampian region.

Bangalore (băng-gəlôr'), city (1971 pop. [illegible] capital of Karnataka state, S central India, [illegible] (914 m) above sea level. A major industrial cente[illegible] and transportation hub of S India, Bangalore has electronics and aircraft industries, textile mills, and varied manufactures. Coffee is traded. A well-planned city with numerous parks and wide streets, it is famous as a place of retirement. It was founded in 1537, taken by Haidar Ali (c.1760), but was restored to the original rulers of Bangalore after the British defeated Tippoo Sahib, the son of Haidar Ali, at Srirangapatna in 1799. Bangalore became the administrative seat of Mysore in 1831. The remains of the palace of Tippoo Sahib and several institutes of learning, notably the Tata Institute of Science, are the outstanding landmarks of the city.

Bangka or **Banka** (both: băng'kä, băng'kə), island (1961 pop. 251,639), c.4,600 sq mi (11,910 sq km), Indonesia, in the Java Sea, SE of Sumatra, from which it is separated by the narrow Strait of Bangka. Pangkalpinang is the largest town, and Muntok is the principal port. Since c.1710, when tin was discovered there, Bangka has been one of the world's principal tin-producing centers. Tin production is a government monopoly; there is a smelter at Muntok. Pepper is also produced on the island. The majority of the inhabitants are Chinese; they are mostly employed as mine laborers. Bangka was ceded to Britain by the sultan of Palembang in 1812, but in 1814 it was exchanged with the Dutch for Cochin in India.

Bangkok (băng'kŏk''), Thai *Krung Thep,* city (1970 pop. 2,132,000), capital of Thailand and of Phra Nakhon prov., SW Thailand, on the east bank of the Chao Phraya River, near the Gulf of Siam. Thailand's largest city and one of the leading cities of Southeast Asia, Bangkok lies in the heart of the country's major commercial rice-growing region. The metropolitan area includes Bangkok proper, the industrial city of THON BURI on the west bank of the river, and Klongtoi Wharf, c.5 mi (8 km) downstream, which, along with Bangkok's man-made harbor, handles the bulk of Thailand's foreign trade. The city is the hub of a continental Southeast Asian railroad network and has modern highways. Nearby Don Muang international airport is one of the busiest in Asia. Despite these transportation facilities, Bangkok depends mainly on its numerous canals to carry the commercial produce of the surrounding area. Rice, tin, teak, rubber, gold, silver, hides, and processed fish are the leading exports of the city's port. Industrial plants include rice mills, cement factories, sawmills, oil refineries, and shipyards. Textiles, motor vehicles, electrical goods, and food products are also manufactured. The city is a famous jewelry trading center, dealing in silver and bronze ware and precious stones. Ethnic Chinese dominate both commerce and industry in Bangkok, whose population includes sizable Indian, Pakistani, European, and American communities. The city began as a small trading center and port community serving Ayutthaya, the capital of Siam until its destruction by Burmese invaders in 1767. Thon Buri became the capital in 1769, but in 1782, King Rama I, founder of the present ruling Chakkri dynasty, built his royal palace on the east bank of the river and made Bangkok his capital. The vast, walled Grand Palace complex encompasses the Wat Phra Kaew (the royal chapel housing the sacred image of the Emerald Buddha). There are more than 400 other Buddhist temples in Bangkok. During World War II the city was occupied by the Japanese and was a target of Allied bombing raids. Bangkok's educational and cultural facilities include four universities, a fine arts academy, the national theater, and the national museum, which has a large collection of Thai antiquities. Of particular interest is the daily floating market, in which merchandise is sold aboard boats on canals.

Bangladesh (băng-lädĕsh', băng-) [Bengali, = Bengal Nation], republic (1972 est. pop. 75,000,000), 55,126 sq mi (142,776 sq km), S Asia. DACCA is the capital. Bangladesh was formerly East Pakistan, which had been called East Bengal until 1955 and was constituted from the eastern portion of BENGAL and the former Sylhet district of Assam. Bangladesh proclaimed its independence from Pakistan on March 26, 1971; it achieved sovereignty in Dec., 1971, following the war between India and Pakistan. Bangladesh borders on the Bay of Bengal in the south, the Indian states of West Bengal in the west and Assam in the north, and Burma in the southeast. A humid, low-lying, alluvial region, Bangladesh is composed mainly of the great combined delta of the Ganges, Brahmaputra, and Meghna rivers. Except for the

Chittagong Hills along the Burma border, most of the country is no more than 300 ft (90 m) above sea level. Bangladesh is laced with numerous streams,

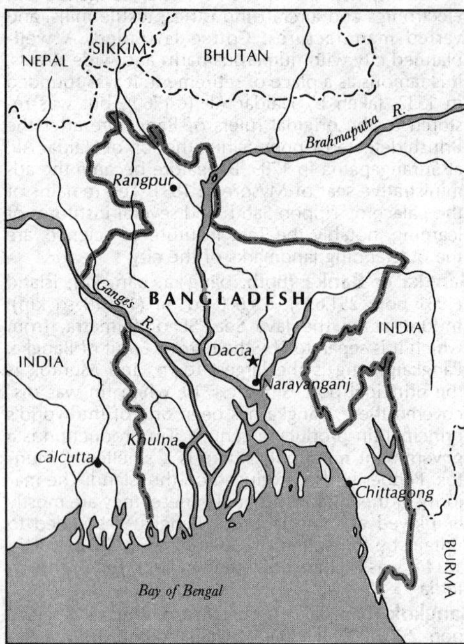

distributaries, and tidal creeks, forming an intricate network of waterways that constitutes the country's chief transportation system. Along the southeastern coast is the Sundarbans, a heavily forested swamp area with numerous low islands. Bangladesh has a tropical monsoon climate with a short dry season in the winter. It receives an average annual rainfall of 80 in. (203 cm), with most falling during the summer monsoon period: the Sylhet district in the northeast is the wettest part of the country, having an annual average rainfall of 140 in. (356 cm). The low-lying delta region is subject to severe flooding from monsoon rains, cyclones, and tidal waves and usually suffers major crop damage and high loss of life. The cyclone and tidal wave of Nov., 1970, devastated the southern delta region and caused an estimated 300,000 deaths. Monsoon rains in mid-1974 caused much damage. Bangladesh, one of the world's ten most populated countries, has the highest population density (more than 1,300 people per sq mi/500 people per sq km) of any nation on earth; its yearly growth rate is a very high 3%. The great majority of Bangladesh's population is Bengali; the Biharis, a non-Bengali Muslim group, form a large minority that has not been assimilated into the national social structure. About 80% of the population is Sunni Muslim; there are Hindu, Buddhist, and Christian minorities. Bengali is the nation's official language, but English is in wide use. Bangladesh has a predominantly rural population, with about 80% of the people engaged in agriculture. Dacca and CHITTAGONG are the largest cities. Bangladesh has several universities, including those at Chittagong, Dacca, MYMENSINGH, and RAJSHAHI. Except for natural gas (found along its eastern border) and oil (in the Bay of Bengal), Bangladesh is lacking in minerals. The country's economy is based on agriculture, with about 65% of the territory under cultivation. Jute, rice, sugarcane, tea, tobacco, and wheat are the chief crops. Bangladesh produces more than half of the world's raw jute. Fishing is also an important economic activity. Dacca and Chittagong (the country's chief port) are the principal industrial centers of Bangladesh; jute products, textiles, paper, processed food, and leather goods are manufactured. Raw jute and jute products account for about 90% of the country's exports, which also include tea, leather, and fish. Since the country is unable to feed itself, the most important of Bangladesh's imports is food. Raw cotton, transportation equipment, and consumer goods are other major imports. Bangladesh is governed by the constitution of 1972 (amended in 1975) and has a presidential system of government. The president is the head of state, and the prime minister is the head of government. There is a 315-seat national assembly. The Awami League is the chief political party, and in the country's first general election (March, 1973) it won virtually all the seats in the national assembly.

History. Until 1757, when Robert CLIVE, the British statesman who laid the basis of the British Empire in India, defeated the Nawab, Suraj-ud-daulah, at Plassey, the area that is now Bangladesh was ruled by Afghan or Mogul dynasties or by independent Muslim kings. Baber, who took Kabul in 1504 and thence advanced through the northwest, established the Mogul empire in India in 1526. Thereafter, with interruptions, the Mogul empire united India until 1857. Like India and Pakistan, the territory that is now Bangladesh was part of imperial British India from 1857 until 1947, when India and Pakistan achieved independence; for nearly 25 years afterward, Bangladesh existed as East Pakistan, the eastern province of Pakistan (for pre-1970 history see PAKISTAN). The two provinces of Pakistan, which differed considerably in natural setting, economy, and historical background, were separated from each other by more than 1,000 mi (1,610 km) of India. The East Pakistanis, who comprised 56% of the total population of Pakistan, were discontented under a government centered in West Pakistan; the disparity in government investments and development funds given to each province also added to the resentment, especially since the eastern province's jute and tea sales supplied two-thirds of the country's foreign earnings. Efforts over the years to secure increased economic benefits and political reforms proved unsuccessful, and serious riots broke out in 1968 and 1969. The movement for greater autonomy gained momentum when, in the Dec., 1970, general elections, the Awami League under the leadership of Sheikh MUJIBUR RAHMAN won practically all of East Pakistan's seats and thus achieved a majority in the Pakistan National Assembly. President Muhammad Agha YAHYA KHAN, hoping to avert a political confrontation between East and West Pakistan that might have led to East Pakistan's regional autonomy and control of its foreign exchange and trade, twice postponed (March, 1971) the opening session of the national assembly. The government's attempts to forestall the autonomy bid led to general strikes and nonpayment of taxes in East Pakistan and finally to civil war on March 25. On the following day the Awami League's leaders proclaimed the independence of Bangladesh. Yahya Khan's government outlawed the Awami League, imprisoned Sheikh Mujibur Rahman on treason charges, and imposed strict press censorship. During the months of conflict an estimated one million Bengalis were killed in East Pakistan and another ten million fled into exile in India. Fighting raged in Dacca, Chittagong, COMILLA, SYLHET, JESSORE, BARISAL, RANGPUR, and KHULNA. Finally India allied itself with Bangladesh, which it had recognized on Dec. 6, and during a two-week war (Dec. 3–16) defeated the Pakistani forces in the east. The Awami League leaders of Bangladesh's provisional government returned from exile in Calcutta, India. Sheikh Mujibur Rahman, who had been chosen president while in prison in West Pakistan, was released and allowed to return to Bangladesh in early Jan., 1972. He set up a government and assumed the premiership; Abu Sayeed Choudhury became president. Rejecting Pakistan's call for a reunited country, the Sheikh embarked upon the tremendous job of rehabilitating an economy devastated by months of warfare. Relations with Pakistan were hostile; Pakistan withheld recognition from Bangladesh, and Bangladesh and India refused to repatriate more than 90,000 Pakistani prisoners of war who had surrendered at the end of the conflict. Armed Bengali "freedom fighters" fought Bihari civilians in Bangladesh, particularly after Indian troops withdrew from Bangladesh in March, 1972. In addition, Bangladesh announced its intention to bring to trial a number of captured civilians and soldiers on war crime charges. Tensions were eased in July, 1972, when President Zulfikar Ali BHUTTO of Pakistan (who assumed power after the fall of the Yahya Khan government) and Prime Minister Indira Gandhi of India agreed during a meeting in Simla, India, to peacefully settle the differences between their countries. In the summer of 1973 the Pakistan national assembly authorized President Bhutto to extend recognition to Bangladesh when he deemed it in the national interest, and he did so in Feb., 1974, prior to the start of a summit conference of Islamic nations in Lahore, Pakistan. Subsequently, India and Pakistan reached consensus on the release of Pakistani prisoners of war and the exchange of hostage populations—between 150,000 and 400,000 Bengalis were permitted to leave Pakistan for Bangladesh, and about 260,000 Biharis were allowed to resettle in Pakistan—but the actual transfer procedures were very slow. Bangladesh was gradually recognized by most of the world's nations. It joined the British Commonwealth in April, 1972, but its first bid for membership in the United Nations was vetoed (Aug., 1972) by China. Widespread famine has been averted through massive international aid, but a smallpox epidemic claimed about 7,000 lives in early 1972. In March, 1972, the country's major industries, banks, and shipping and insurance firms were nationalized. The high rate of inflation has hampered rehabilitation efforts and has triggered open criticism of the government's economic policies. Bangladesh has signed treaties of friendship and trade agreements with India and the Soviet Union. The constitutional amendment of 1975 made Sheikh Mujib president and greatly increased his powers. For bibliography of preindependent Bangladesh see under PAKISTAN; see Mohamed Ayoob and K. Subrahmanyam, *The Liberation War* (1972); Subrata Roy Chowdhury, *The Genesis of Bangladesh* (1972); A. R. Khan, *The Economy of Bangladesh* (1972); Prabhat Srivastava, *The Discovery of Bangla Desh* (1972); *Bangladesh: Documents*, prepared by the Ministry of External Affairs, India (1973); P. S. Payne, *Massacre* (1973).

Bangor (băng'gər), municipal borough (1971 pop. 35,178), Co. Down, E Northern Ireland, on Belfast Lough. It is a seaport, resort, and yachting center (site of an annual regatta), with some light industry. The Elizabethan Bangor Castle is in the borough. There are also remains of an abbey founded c.555 by St. Comgall and destroyed by the Danes in the 9th cent. Rebuilt in 1120, it was taken over by Franciscans in 1469. The missionary abbey was dissolved in 1542.

Bangor (băng'gôr, băn'-, băng'gər), city (1970 pop. 33,168), seat of Penobscot co., S Maine, at the confluence of the Penobscot and Kenduskeag rivers; inc. as a town 1791, as a city 1834. It is a port of entry, commercial center, and gateway to an extensive resort and lumber region. Major industries include the production of shoes and paper, food and lumber processing, and printing. The city was settled in 1769 and was known as Sunbury. During the War of 1812 it was occupied by the British. In the 19th cent. Bangor was a shipbuilding center that carried on an extensive coastal and overseas trade in lumber, stone, and ice. The city has a theological seminary, a conservatory of music, and a community college. Bangor International Airport, part of which was once Dow Air Force Base, has one of the largest runways in the United States.

Bangor (băng'gôr), municipal borough (1971 pop. 14,526), Caernarvonshire, NW Wales, at the northern end of Menai Strait. Slate is shipped from adjacent Port Penrhyn. The cathedral, on the site of a 6th-century church, dates from the 11th cent. and has been rebuilt several times. In 1974, it became part of the new nonmetropolitan county of Gwynedd. Bangor is the seat of the University College of North Wales.

Bangorian Controversy (băng-gô'rēən), religious dispute in the Church of England during the early part of the reign of George I. Benjamin HOADLY, bishop of Bangor, Wales, delivered a sermon (1717) before the king in which he denied that the church had any doctrinal or disciplinary authority. Advocates of ecclesiastical authority (among them William LAW) attacked Hoadly's position, and a sharp controversy ensued, in which some 50 writers participated and about 200 pamphlets were issued. Attacks on Hoadly in convocation, the church assembly, led the king to suspend that body in 1717; it was not allowed to meet again until 1852.

Bangs, John Kendrick, 1862–1922, American humorist, b. Yonkers, N.Y., grad. Columbia, 1883. He was the editor of *Puck* (1904–5) and other magazines and wrote over 30 books of humorous stories, verse, and plays, including *Three Weeks in Politics* (1894), *The Idiot* (1895), and *A Houseboat on the Styx* (1896).

Bang's disease: see BRUCELLOSIS.

Bangui (bäng-gē'), city (1971 est. pop., with suburbs, 187,000), capital of the Central African Republic, a port on the Ubangi River, near the Zaïre border. Bangui is an administrative, trade, and communications center. Its manufactures include textiles, food products, beer, shoes, and soap. Bangui's port handles most of the country's international trade; the chief exports are cotton, timber, coffee, and sisal. Bangui is at the hub of the nation's road network, which connects the city with Cameroon, Chad, and Sudan. The city was founded in 1889 by an aide of the French explorer Savorgnan de BRAZZA. Jean Bédel Bokassa University (1970) is located there.

Bangweulu (băng"wōō'lōō) or **Bangweolo** (-wēō'lō), lake and swamps, c.3,800 sq mi (9,840 sq km), NE Zambia. The lake is c.50 mi (80 km) long and 25 mi

(40 km) wide. Commercial fishing is pursued in the lagoons of the swamps. The swamps are formed largely by the flooding of the lower Chambezi River, which enters Lake Bangweulu from the east. The lake is drained in the S by the Luapula River, a tributary of the Congo.

Banha (băn'hä) or **Benha** (bĕn'-), city (1970 est. pop. 72,500), capital of Qalyubiyah governorate, N Egypt, in the Nile River delta. A rail junction and trade center, Banha has cotton-ginning, rug-weaving, and food-processing industries.

Bani (bā'nī). **1** One of David's mighty men. 2 Sam. 23.36. **2** Musician. 1 Chron. 6.46. **3** Levites. Neh. 3.17; 9.4; 11.22. **4** Family in the return from exile. Ezra 2.10; 10.29; Neh. 10.14. Binnui: Neh. 7.15. **5** The same as BINNUI **1**. **6** Judahite. 1 Chron. 9.4. **7** Jew married to a foreign wife. Ezra 10.38.

Bani Hasan (bä'nē häsän'), village, E central Egypt, on the Nile near Al Minya. There are 39 tombs, carved out of solid rock in the XII dynasty of ancient Egypt. The name is also spelled Beni Hasan.

banishment: see EXILE.

Bani Suwayf (bä'nē swāf) or **Beni Suef** (bĕ'-), city (1970 est. pop. 99,400), capital of Bani Suwayf governorate, N central Egypt, on the Nile River. Situated in an intensely cultivated farming region, Bani Suwayf has cotton mills and sugar refineries. Alabaster is quarried near the city.

Banja Luka (bän'yä lo͞o'kä), city (1971 pop. 157,515), W Yugoslavia, in Bosnia, on the Vrbas River. It has varied manufactures, including iron goods and electrical equipment. Banja Luka was captured by the Turks in 1528 and was (1583-1638) the seat of the pashas of Bosnia. Later (1878-1918) a part of Austria-Hungary, it passed to Yugoslavia after World War I. The city has Roman ruins and a 16th-century mosque.

Banjermasin: see BANDJARMASIN, Indonesia.

banjo, stringed musical instrument, with a body resembling a tambourine. The banjo consists of a hoop over which a skin membrane is stretched; it has a long, often fretted neck and four to nine

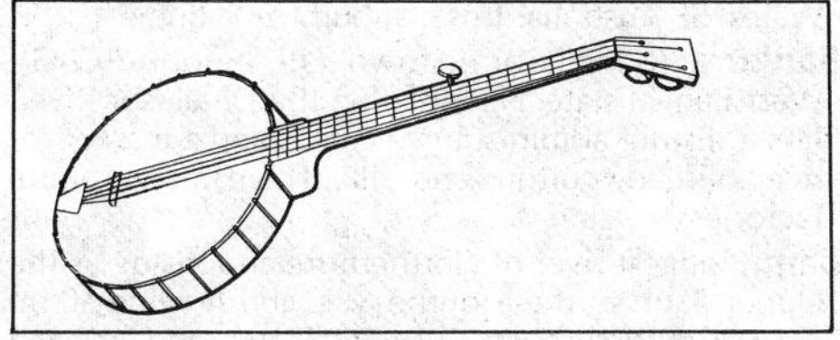

Banjo

strings, which are plucked with a pick or the fingers (see FRETTED INSTRUMENT). Negro slaves brought it to America (by 1688) from W Africa, to which it may have come from Europe or Asia. It is used frequently in hillbilly and Southern folk music. Because of an incisive, percussive quality, it is often used as a rhythm or a solo instrument in Dixieland bands.

Banjoewangi: see BANJUWANGI, Indonesia.

Banjul (băn'jo͝ol), formerly **Bathurst** (băth'ərst), port city (1971 est. pop. 45,000), capital of The Gambia, W Gambia, situated on St. Mary's Island where the Gambia River enters the Atlantic Ocean. It is the only large urban area in The Gambia and is the country's economic and administrative center. Its port handles oceangoing ships. Banjul's chief export is peanuts; beeswax, palm kernels and oil, and skins and hides are also shipped. Peanut processing is the chief industry. The city was founded by the British on the site of an anchorage in 1816 as a trading post and a base for suppressing the slave trade. A vocational school is in the city.

Banjuwangi (bän"yo͞owäng'ē), city (1961 pop. 54,408), E Java, Indonesia, opposite Bali on Bali Strait. It is a railroad terminus and the seaport for shipment of passengers and goods to Bali. It is also spelled Banyuwangi or Banjoewangi.

Banka: see BANGKA, Indonesia.

Bank for International Settlements (BIS), financial institution established (1930) in Basel, Switzerland, by bankers and diplomats of Europe and the United States. Chartered under Swiss laws, the BIS was originally designed to conduct a limited banking business and to administer German war reparations payments according to the provisions of the Hague Agreements. Since then it has become one of the world's foremost international banks. As a meeting place for the governors of West European central banks, the BIS serves to promote international financial cooperation. It is the representative of several important West European financial enterprises, holding the accounts of the European Coal and Steel Community and serving as agent for the European Monetary Agreement. Its professional staff and its publications, especially the *Annual Report,* are important sources of economic data and analysis. The BIS is run by a board composed of eight West European central bank governors and five other financiers. By the early 1960s American interests in the bank had become minimal, with most of the original U.S. shares having been sold to European groups. BIS has holdings of about 30 billion francs (approximately 6 billion dollars).

Bankhead, John Hollis, 1872-1946, American politician, b. Moscow, Alabama; brother of William Brockman Bankhead. He was elected to the Alabama legislature in 1903 and served in the U.S. Senate from 1931 until his death. Bankhead was a leader of the farm bloc in the Senate and strongly supported the New Deal. He sponsored (with his brother) the Bankhead Cotton Control Act of 1934.

Bankhead, Tallulah Brockman, 1903-68, American actress, b. Huntsville, Ala.; daughter of William Brockman Bankhead. After her debut in 1918, Bankhead had great success on the London stage (1923-30). She was acclaimed for her Broadway performance as Regina in *The Little Foxes* (1939). Her best-known film performance was in *Lifeboat* (1944). Bankhead's beauty, wit, and uninhibited behavior made her a legend. See her autobiography (1952); biographies by Brendan Gill (1972), Lee Israel (1972), and Kieran Tunney (1973).

Bankhead, William Brockman, 1874-1940, U.S. Representative from Alabama (1917-40), b. Lamar co., Ala. Chairman of the House rules committee (1934-35), Democratic floor leader (1935-36), and speaker of the House (1936-40), he was one of the outstanding New Deal legislative leaders. The Cotton Control Act of 1934 was largely the work of Bankhead and his brother, Senator John H. Bankhead. He was also interested in monetary legislation and was considered one of the ablest parliamentarians in the House.

bank holidays, days when the law requires that banks be closed. In the United States the list varies from state to state but generally includes, besides the major holidays, many days that are observed only by the banks and such government institutions as post offices. In England since 1871 bank holidays have had special significance as secular and perpetual holidays. The days include Christmas, Boxing Day (the first weekday after Christmas), Good Friday, Easter Monday, Whitmonday (the day after Pentecost), and the special banking day on the first Monday in August.

banking, primarily the business of dealing in money and instruments of credit. Banks are usually differentiated from other financial institutions by their principal functions of accepting deposits—subject to withdrawal or transfer by check—and of making loans. A simple form of banking was practiced by the ancient temples of Egypt, Babylonia, and Greece, which loaned at high rates of interest the gold and silver deposited for safekeeping. Private banking existed by 600 B.C. and was considerably developed by the Greeks, Romans, and Byzantines. Medieval banking was dominated by the Jews and Levantines because of the strictures of the Christian Church against INTEREST and because other occupations were largely closed to Jews. The forerunners of modern banks were frequently chartered for a specific purpose, e.g., the Bank of Venice (1171) and the BANK OF ENGLAND (1694), in connection with loans to the government; the Bank of Amsterdam (1609), to receive deposits of gold and silver. Banking developed rapidly throughout the 18th and 19th cent., accompanying the expansion of industry and trade, with each nation evolving the distinctive forms peculiar to its economic and social life. In the United States the first bank was the Bank of North America, established (1781) in Philadelphia. Congress chartered the first BANK OF THE UNITED STATES in 1791 to engage in general commercial banking and to act as fiscal agent of the government, but failed to renew its charter in 1811. A similar fate attended the second Bank of the United States, chartered in 1816 and closed in 1836. Prior to 1838 a bank charter could be obtained only by a specific legislative act, but in that year New York adopted the Free Banking Act, which permitted anyone to engage in banking, upon compliance with certain charter conditions. Free banking spread rapidly to other states, and from 1840 to 1863 all banking business was done by state-chartered institutions. In many Western states it degenerated into "wildcat" banking because of laxity and abuse of state laws. Bank notes were issued against little or no security, credit was overexpanded, and depressions brought waves of bank failures. In particular, the multiplicity of state bank notes caused great confusion and loss. To correct such conditions, Congress passed (1863) the National Bank Act, which provided for a system of banks to be chartered by the Federal government. In 1865, by granting national banks the authority to issue bank notes and by placing a prohibitive tax on state bank notes, an amendment to the act brought all banks under Federal supervision. Most banks in existence did take out national charters, but some, being banks of deposit, were unaffected by the tax and continued under their state charters, thus giving rise to what is generally known as the "dual banking system." The number of state banks expanded rapidly with the increasing use of bank checks and has exceeded the number of national banks since 1892. Recurrent banking panics caused by overexpansion of credit, inadequate bank reserves, and inelastic currency prompted Congress in 1908 to create the National Monetary Commission to investigate the field of banking and currency and recommend legislation. Its suggestions were embodied in the Federal Reserve Act (1913), which provided for a central banking organization, the FEDERAL RESERVE SYSTEM. Aside from their type of charter, banks may be distinguished according to their primary functions. Commercial banks, which include national and state banks, trust companies, stock savings banks, and industrial banks, render a wide range of services in addition to their primary functions of making loans and investments and handling demand as well as savings and other time deposits. Mutual savings banks, which are exclusively state-chartered institutions, accept only savings and other time deposits, and the types of loans made and services rendered are limited. The fact that commercial banks are able to expand or contract their loans and investments in accordance with changes in reserves and reserve requirements further differentiates them from mutual savings banks, where the volume of loans and investments is governed by changes in customers' deposits. (See SAVINGS BANK.) Since the establishment of the Federal Reserve System, Federal banking legislation has been limited largely to detailed amendments of the National Bank and Federal Reserve acts. The Banking Act of 1933 was an extensive reform measure designed to correct the abuses that had led to numerous bank crises in the years following the stock market crash of 1929. It strengthened the powers of supervisory authorities, increased controls over the volume and use of credit, and provided for the insurance of bank deposits under the Federal Deposit Insurance Corporation (FDIC). The Banking Act of 1935 strengthened the powers of the Federal Reserve Board of Governors in the field of credit management, tightened existing restrictions on certain banking operations, and enlarged the supervisory powers of the FDIC. Membership in the FDIC is compulsory for all Federal Reserve member banks but optional for other banks. The Federal Savings and Loan Insurance Corporation insures deposits in all federally chartered—and in many state-chartered—savings and loan associations, or corporations that make real estate loans and accept savings deposits. Types of financial institutions that are not subject to the supervision of state or Federal banking authorities but that perform one or more of the traditional banking functions are building and loan associations, mortgage companies, finance companies, insurance companies, credit agencies owned in whole or in part by the Federal government, credit unions, brokers and dealers in securities, and investment bankers. Such organizations operate under state or Federal laws, and most of them are under the jurisdiction of the Dept. of Agriculture or the Federal Loan Agency. Other credit institutions operating under Federal laws include the Federal Housing Authority and the Veterans Administration. Building and loan associations, which are state institutions, provide home-building loans to members with funds obtained from savings deposits and from the sale of shares to members. Finance companies make small loans with funds obtained from invested capital, surplus, and borrowings. CREDIT UNIONS, which are institutions owned cooperatively by groups of persons having a common business, fraternal, or other interest, make small loans to their members out of funds derived from the sale of shares to members. The primary functions of investment bankers are the purchase of new issues of securities from public bodies or corporations and their sale to institutional and individual investors and the distribution of blocks of outstanding securities from large holders to the investing public. Investment bankers usually act as intermediaries between the issuers of securities and investors in supplying long-term capital funds, as distinguished from commercial banks, which primarily make short-term loans to finance the production and distribution of goods. After World War II banking institutions were established to advance credit and further investment on an international scale. The International Bank for Reconstruction and Development (World Bank) was organized (1945) to make loans both to governments and to private investors. The discharge of debts between nations has been simplified and facilitated through the International Monetary Fund, which also provides members with technical assistance in international banking. The European Monetary Agreement also makes possible the rapid discharge of debts and balance of payments obligations between nations. See B. H. Beckhart, ed., *Banking Systems* (1954, repr. 1969); R. G. Thomas, *Our Modern Banking and Monetary System* (4th ed. 1964); R. E. Cameron, *Banking in the Early Stages of Industrialization* (1967); Roger Orsingher, *Banks of the World* (tr. 1967); G. C. Fischer, *American Banking Structure* (1968); H. V. Prochnow and H. V. Prochnow, Jr., eds., *The Changing World of Banking* (1974).

Bank of England, central bank and note-issuing institution of Great Britain. Popularly known as the Old Lady of Threadneedle Street, its main office stands on the street of that name in London. The bank has eight branches, all of which are located in the British Isles. Although Bank of England notes are legal tender throughout the United Kingdom, banks in Scotland and Northern Ireland also issue notes that may be either used as currency themselves or exchanged for Bank of England issues. In all matters beside note issue, the Bank of England has sole central banking functions in Great Britain. It was founded (1694) as a commercial bank by William PATERSON with a capital of £1,200,000, which was advanced to the government in return for banking privileges, including the right to issue notes up to the amount of its capital. In 1709 the capital was doubled; the charter was renewed in 1742, 1764, and 1781. The bank's facilities proved a great asset in English commercial, and later industrial, expansion. The bank's functions were both public and private; it safeguarded the English pound and also operated for private profit. Efficient regulation was assured by the Bank Charter Act of 1844, which laid the basis for the bank's modern structure. The issue department, which handles the issuing of bank notes for general circulation, was separated from the banking department, which handles the remaining banking functions, including the management of the public debt, and serves as the depository of government funds and as the staple bank of England. The affairs of the bank are controlled by a governor, a deputy, and 16 directors. It was privately owned until 1946, when an act of Parliament provided for its nationalization. The stockholders were recompensed with government bonds to the value of more than £58 million, and the bank subsequently dropped virtually all its private business. See J. H. Clapham, *The Bank of England: A History* (2 vol., 1944; repr. 1966); John Giuseppi, *The Bank of England* (1966).

Bank of the United States, name for two national banks established by the U.S. Congress to serve as government fiscal agents and as depositories for Federal funds; the first bank was in existence from 1791 to 1811 and the second from 1816 to 1836. The first bank was established under the auspices of the Federalists as part of the system proposed by Alexander HAMILTON to establish the new government on a sound economic basis. Congress approved a charter for the bank despite the argument that the Constitution did not give Congress power to establish a central bank and the charge that the bank was designed to favor mercantile over agrarian interests. The bank had a head office in Philadelphia and branches in eight other cities. The government subscribed one fifth of the capital of $10 million, but a loan of $2 million was immediately made to the government. In addition to acting as a fiscal agent for the government, the bank conducted a general commercial business. It was well managed and paid good dividends, but its conservative policies and its restraining influence on state banks, through its refusal to accept state bank notes not redeemable in specie, antagonized more exuberant business elements, especially in the West. These interests combined with agrarian opponents of the bank to defeat its rechartering, despite the support given the bank by the Madison administration. The bank concluded its affairs and repaid its shareholders. Later, financing the War of 1812 proved difficult because of the lack of a central bank, and by the end of the war the financial system of the country was in chaos. Enough support was secured to charter a new bank for 20 years. The second bank, capitalized at $35 million, operated much as did the first one, 25 branches being established. After an initial period of difficulty during the presidency (1816-19) of William Jones, the bank was placed on a sound basis by Langdon CHEVES (1819-22). It became especially prosperous under the management of Nicholas BIDDLE, but aroused criticism by state banks and frontiersmen on the grounds that it was too powerful and that it operated in the interests of the commercial classes of the East. The opponents of the bank came into power with the election (1828) of Andrew JACKSON. Although the bank's charter did not expire until 1836, Henry CLAY persuaded Biddle to apply to Congress for a renewal in 1832. President Jackson vetoed the bill for its recharter and the bank became a leading issue in his fight for reelection against Clay. Interpreting his victory at the polls as an expression of popular will on the subject, Jackson did not wait for the expiration of the bank's charter but began in 1833, through his new Secretary of the Treasury Roger B. TANEY, to deposit government moneys in state banks, known to his opponents as "pet banks." Under Martin Van Buren's administration the INDEPENDENT TREASURY SYSTEM was established to handle the government's funds. See R. C. H. Catterall, *The Second Bank of the United States* (1902, repr. 1960); W. B. Smith, *Economic Aspects of the Second Bank of the United States* (1953); J. A. Wilburn, *Biddle's Bank* (1967).

bankruptcy, in law, settlement of the liabilities of a debtor who is wholly or partially unable to meet his obligations. The purposes of bankruptcy laws are to distribute, through a court-appointed receiver, the bankrupt's assets equitably among his creditors and, in most instances, to discharge him from further liability. The U.S. Constitution authorizes Congress to enact uniform bankruptcy legislation for the entire United States. The present Federal law was adopted in 1898 and has been amended several times, especially in 1938 by the Chandler Act. Bankruptcy proceedings may be voluntary (instituted by the debtor) or involuntary (instituted by creditors). Ordinarily the debtor must be insolvent, i.e., unable to pay all his debts even if the full value of his assets were realized. Bankruptcy is also permitted when the discharge of debts would otherwise be unduly delayed, e.g., if the debtor has fraudulently transferred property to put it out of a creditor's reach. When a person has been adjudged bankrupt, preferred creditors (e.g., unpaid employees or the Federal government) are paid in full, and the other creditors, who manage the estate through a committee, share, usually pro rata, in the remaining assets. Unless a debtor was discharged from debt by bankruptcy proceedings within the previous six years or was guilty of fraud in becoming bankrupt, the effect of bankruptcy proceedings is to wipe out his indebtedness. The law also permits courts, instead of ordering the liquidation of all the assets of a business threatened with insolvency, to reorganize it on a sound basis. In the United States the bankrupt receives perhaps more lenient treatment than in any other country; this practice reflects the belief that business initiative should not be unduly stifled by the threat of criminal or civil penalties for unintentional commercial failure.

Banks, Sir Joseph, 1743-1820, British naturalist and patron of the sciences. He accompanied Capt. James Cook on his voyage around the world and made large collections of biological specimens, most of which were previously unclassified. Botany Bay was named on this voyage. In 1772, Banks went on an expedition to Iceland. From c.1762 until his death he was the chief influence in inaugurating and directing the policies that made Kew Gardens an important botanical center for encouraging exploration and experimentation. In 1766 he was elected to the Royal Society, and he served as its president from 1778 until his death. The plant genus *Banksia* was named for him. See studies by H. C. Cameron (1952, repr. 1966) and A. M. Lysaght (1971).

Banks, Nathaniel Prentiss, 1816-94, American politician and Union general in the Civil War, b. Waltham, Mass. After serving in the Massachusetts legislature (1849-53), Banks entered Congress as a Democrat, was returned in 1855 as a Know-Nothing and became speaker of the House, and was reelected in 1857 as a Republican. He resigned from Congress in Dec., 1857, and served as Republican governor of Massachusetts (1858-60). In the Civil War he was given command in the Dept. of the Shenandoah, where he was defeated by T. J. (Stonewall) JACKSON at Front Royal and Winchester and then at Cedar Mt. during the second battle of Bull Run. Late in 1862, Banks replaced B. F. Butler at New Orleans and cooperated with Grant in opening up the Mississippi by capturing Port Hudson in July, 1863, and in participating in the Red River expedition of 1864. After the war he again served as Representative from Massachusetts (1865-73, 1875-79, 1889-91). See biography by F. H. Harrington (1948); L. H. Johnson, *Red River Campaign* (1958).

Banks, Thomas, 1735-1805, English neoclassical sculptor, studied at the Royal Academy. A traveling scholarship enabled him to study in Rome from 1772 to 1779. In 1781 he went to Russia, where Catherine II bought his *Cupid Catching a Butterfly* and commissioned his *Armed Neutrality.* On his return to England he executed numerous monuments and portrait busts; many are in English churches. Monuments to Isaac Watts, Sir Eyre Coote, and William Woollett are in Westminster Abbey. See his *Annals* (ed. by C. F. Bell, 1938).

banksia [for Sir Joseph Banks], popularized name of a genus of Australian evergreen trees and shrubs of the same family as the macadamia and sometimes cultivated in America. Banksias are also called honeysuckle trees or Australian honeysuckle. Banksia is classified in the division MAGNOLIOPHYTA, class Magnoliopsida, order Proteales, family Proteaceae.

Banks Island, c.26,000 sq mi (67,340 sq km), NW Northwest Territories, Canada, in the Arctic Ocean, in the Arctic Archipelago. It is the westernmost of the group and is separated from the mainland by Amundsen Gulf. Banks Island, which has many lakes, is a hilly plateau rising to c.2,000 ft (610 m) in the south. There is a small Eskimo population. British explorer Sir Robert McClure discovered that it was an island in 1851. Canadian explorer Vilhjalmur Stefansson spent much time (1914-17) there and explored the interior.

Bankstown, city (1971 pop. 162,310), New South Wales, SE Australia. It is a suburb of Sydney.

Bankura (băng'ko͝orə), town (1971 pop. 79,243), West Bengal state, NE India, on the Dhalkisor River. It is a district administrative center and a market for rice, oilseed, cotton, and silk. There are cigarette factories.

Bann, longest river of Northern Ireland, rising as the Upper Bann in the Mourne Mts. and flowing 40 mi (64 km) NW through Counties Down and Armagh to the southern end of Lough Neagh. It leaves the lake at its north shore as the Lower Bann and flows 40 mi (64 km) north, forming the border between Counties Antrim and Londonderry, past Coleraine to the Atlantic Ocean. It has important salmon fisheries.

Bannack, ghost town, SW Mont. Founded in 1862 when gold was discovered along Grasshopper Creek, Bannack was the first town in Montana and was the first territorial capital (1864-65). It declined when many miners left the thin deposits for the richer gold of Virginia City. Bannack is now a state park.

Bannatyne, George (băn'ətīn), 1545-1608?, collector of Scottish poems. He compiled the Bannatyne MS (1568), the chief collection of Scottish verse of the 15th and 16th cent. The Bannatyne Club was founded in his honor in 1823 for the purpose of publishing old Scottish works.

banner system, Manchu conscription system. Companies of MANCHU warriors were grouped (1601) into brigades, each with a distinctive banner. The banner system integrated former tribal units into a bureaucratic war machine that enabled the Manchus to conquer and rule China as the CH'ING dynasty (1644-1912). Banners (brigades) and their component companies did not live and fight as units but were garrisoned at various places and contributed a certain quota of men to make up a fighting force when needed. Later, banners of Mongol and Chinese adherents were also organized. About 1.5 million bannermen and their families were garrisoned at strategic points and major population centers throughout China. By the 19th cent. corruption and inefficiency pervaded the banner system, forcing the Ch'ing government to rely increasingly on provincial militia.

Banning, resort city (1970 pop. 12,034), Riverside co., S Calif., in a fruit-growing area between Mt. San Jacinto and Mt. San Gorgonio; inc. 1913. Electronic equipment, wearing apparel, plastics, and metal products are manufactured. An annual stagecoach day festival is held, and the city has a stagecoach museum. Nearby are San Bernardino National Forest, a state park, and a Univ. of Southern California art complex.

Bannister, Roger Gilbert, 1929–, British athlete, b. Harrow, England. A physician, on May 6, 1954, at Oxford's Iffley Road track, Bannister became the first man to run the mile in less than 4 min. His time was 3 min 59.4 sec (the old record set by Gunder Haegg of Sweden in 1945 was 4:01.4). John LANDY of Australia bettered the record, as did New Zealand's Peter SNELL. At the British Empire and Commonwealth Games at Vancouver, Canada, on Aug. 7, 1954, Bannister clocked 3:58.8 when defeating Landy in a thrilling race. Bannister retired from active competition in 1954. See his book, *The Four Minute Mile* (1955).

Bannockburn, moor and parish, Stirlingshire, central Scotland, on the Bannock River. Textiles are manufactured in the parish. In 1314 on the moor, a 10,000-man Scots army led by Robert BRUCE routed 23,000 Englishmen under Edward II, thus climaxing Robert's struggle for Scottish independence and establishing him as king of the Scots.

Bannock Indians, North American Indians who formerly ranged over wide territory of the N Great Plains and into the foothills of the Rocky Mts. They were concentrated in S Idaho. Their language belonged to the Uto-Aztecan branch of the Aztec-Tanoan linguistic stock (see AMERICAN INDIAN LANGUAGES). Their culture was typical of the Plains Indians. In 1869, Fort Hall Reservation was established for them and for the Northern SHOSHONE INDIANS, with whom the Bannock were closely associated. Loss of hunting lands, disappearance of the buffalo, and lack of assistance from the U.S. government led to a Bannock outbreak in 1878, which was suppressed. The Bannock and the Shoshone at Fort Hall Reservation today number some 3,000. See B. D. Madsen, *The Bannock of Idaho* (1958); R. F. Murphy, *Shoshone-Bannock Subsistence and Society* (1960).

Bannu (bən'no͞o), town (1961 pop. 31,623), N Pakistan. It is a district administrative center and an important road junction and market town. The major industries are wool milling and the production of sandals and wooden articles. Bannu, noted for its weekly fair, also has a college affiliated with Peshawar Univ. Founded by Sir Herbert Edwardes in 1848, the town was formerly called Edwardesabad and was a leading British military base, especially against Afghan border tribes. Still an important military station, Bannu is enclosed by a 12 ft (3.7 m) earth wall with 10 iron gates that are closed at sunset.

Banská Bystrica (bän'skä bĭs'trĭtsä"), city (1970 pop. 46,846), E central Czechoslovakia, in Slovakia, at the junction of the Bystrica and Hron rivers. It is an industrial center noted for the large plywood, pulp, and veneer factories nearby. An ancient town, Banská Bystrica became well known in the Middle Ages for its surrounding mines. The city was the heart of the Slovak national uprising against German occupation in 1944.

Banstead, urban district (1971 pop. 44,986), Surrey, SE England, on the North Downs. The district is mainly residential and contains some highly regarded landscapes. There is a church from the Norman period and an excavated Roman villa. The area is mentioned in the Domesday Book.

Bantam fowl: see POULTRY.

Banting, Sir Frederick Grant, 1891–1941, Canadian physician, M.D. Univ. of Toronto, 1922. From 1923 he was professor of medical research at Toronto. Working with C. H. Best under the direction of J. J. R. Macleod, he succeeded in isolating (1921) from the pancreas the hormone later called insulin. For this he shared with Macleod the 1923 Nobel Prize in Physiology and Medicine. He was knighted in 1934. Besides his work on insulin, he made valuable studies of the cortex of the adrenal glands, of cancer, and of silicosis and stimulated research in aviation medicine. He was killed in a plane crash while en route to England on a medical war mission. See Seale Harris, *Banting's Miracle* (1946).

Bantry Bay, inlet of the Atlantic Ocean, 21 mi (34 km) long and 4 mi (6.4 km) wide, Co. Cork, SW Republic of Ireland. It is one of Europe's best natural anchorages. At the head of the bay is Bantry, site of a modern facility for unloading oil tankers. Bear and Whiddy islands are in the bay.

Bantu (băn'to͞o"), ethnic and linguistic group of Africa, numbering about 70 million. The Bantu inhabit most of the continent S of the Congo River except the extreme southwest. Physically the Bantu are similar to the Negroes, and there is a wide range of types, from the near Hamite to the near Negro; the classification is primarily linguistic, and there are almost a hundred Bantu languages, including Luganda, Zulu, and Swahili. Few cultural generalizations concerning the Bantu can be made. Before the European conquest of Africa the Bantu tribes were either pastoral and warlike or agricultural and usually pacific. There were some highly developed Bantu states, including Buganda in present-day Uganda. Possibly under the fear of European encroachment, several additional Bantu confederations developed in the 19th cent., notably the Zulu and the Basuto (in Basutoland). Other well-known Bantu tribes include the Matabele and the Mashona. In South Africa, the term *Bantu* is commonly used to refer to the native African population, which is there subject to the policies of APARTHEID. See W. M. MacMillan, *Bantu, Boer, and Briton* (rev. ed. 1963); M. F. Perham, *Ten Africans* (2d ed. 1964); W. C. Willoughby, *The Soul of the Bantu* (1928, repr. 1970).

Bantu languages, group of African languages forming a subdivision of the Benue-Niger division of the Niger-Congo branch of the Niger-Kordofanian language family (see AFRICAN LANGUAGES). Bantu contains hundreds of tongues that are spoken by 70 million Africans in the Congo Basin, Angola, the Republic of South Africa, Mozambique, Rhodesia, Zambia, Malawi, Tanzania, and Kenya. The total number of Bantu languages, however, is uncertain. In addition to SWAHILI, its most important member, Bantu has among its significant languages Zulu, Xhosa, and Sotho, which are spoken respectively by 4 million, 2 million, and 4 million persons, all living in the Republic of South Africa; Makua and Thonga, the languages respectively of 2 million and 1 million people in Mozambique; Bemba, the tongue of 900,000 in Zambia; Shona, reaching 2 million in Rhodesia and Mozambique; Kikuyu, native to 1 million in Kenya; Ganda, the language of 2 million in Uganda; Ruanda, spoken by 5 million in Rwanda and Zaïre; Rundi, the tongue of 2 million in Zaïre and Burundi; Mbundu, native to 2 million in Angola; Luba, reaching 3 million in Zaïre; Kongo, the language of 1 million in both the Congo and Zaïre; and Lingala, spoken by 700,000 in Zaïre. The word *Bantu* means "the people" and is made up of the stem *-ntu* ("person") and the plural prefix *ba-*. All of the Bantu languages are tonal, except perhaps Swahili. Tones are used to indicate differences in meaning. Grammatically, nouns belong to a number of classes, each of which has its pair of prefixes, one to denote the singular and the other the plural. Linguists have not yet discovered a logical basis for most of the many different noun classes. Although they are not based on sex, these classes have been compared to the genders of Indo-European tongues. The class prefix of a noun is attached to every word that is connected grammatically with this noun, whether adjective, verb, or other part of speech. The following example from Swahili illustrates the nature of such agreement: *m-thu m-zuri*, "handsome man," but *wu-thu wu-zuri*, "handsome men." The Bantu verb consists of a stem to which are added one or more prefixes (with the exception of the imperative) and also one or more suffixes. The verbal suffixes relate to person, number, negation, tense, voice, and mood. Suffixes added to certain stems can form nouns and verbs, especially of a derivational nature. At present Bantu languages are being used to a considerable extent in primary and secondary schools and are developing literatures. See M. A. Bryan, ed., *The Bantu Languages of Africa* (1959); Malcolm Guthrie, *The Classification of the Bantu Languages* (1948, repr. 1967) and *Comparative Bantu* (4 vol., 1967–71).

Banu Musa (băno͞o' mo͞osä'), family of Arab mathematicians and astronomers of the 9th cent. A.D. The name means "sons of Musa" and refers to the three brothers, Muhammad, Ahmad, and al-Hasan. They supervised the translation of Greek scientific works into Arabic and helped to found the Arabic school of mathematics. The most important work ascribed to them is the geometrical treatise *Book on the Measurement of Plane and Spherical Figures*.

Banville, Théodore de (tāōdôr' də bäNvēl'), 1823–91, French poet. He was one of the group known as the PARNASSIANS. His many volumes of verse, including *Odes funambulesques* (1857) and *Les Exilés* (1866), are characterized by expert technique.

banyan (băn'yən), species of fig (*Ficus bengalensis*) of the family Moraceae (MULBERRY family), native to India, where it is venerated. Its seeds usually germinate in the branches of some tree where they have been dropped by birds. The young plant puts forth aerial rootlets, which, on reaching the ground, take root to form secondary trunks to support the giant horizontal limbs. Branches from these trunks ultimately send down more such prop roots until the banyan crowds out the host tree and becomes grovelike in appearance, often covering large areas. This undergrowth is sometimes trimmed to form arbors. Alexander the Great is said to have camped under a banyan tree that was big enough to shelter his whole army of 7,000 men. The seeds frequently germinate on walls and buildings, causing considerable damage as does the related strangling fig of tropical America. Banyan is classified in the division MAGNOLIOPHYTA, class Magnoliopsida, order Urticales, family Moraceae.

Banyuwangi: see BANJUWANGI, Indonesia.

baobab (bä'ōbăb", bā'ō-), gigantic tree of India and Africa, exceeded in trunk diameter only by the sequoia. The trunks of living baobabs are hollowed out for dwellings; rope and cloth are made from the bark and condiments and medicines from the leaves; the gourdlike fruit (monkey bread) is eaten. The botanic name is *Adansonia digitata*. An Australian baobab is also called sour gourd. In spite of the enormous girth of the trees, they are not particularly tall, and thus have a bottlelike appearance. Baobab is classified in the division MAGNOLIOPHYTA, class Magnoliopsida, order Malvales, family Bombacaceae.

Bao Dai (bou dī), 1913–, emperor of Annam (1932–45) and chief of state of Vietnam (1949–55). Born Prince Nguyen Vinh Thuy, he was the son of Emperor Khai Din and succeeded to the throne in 1926, but did not occupy it until 1932. Bao Dai cooperated with both the Vichy French and Japanese during World War II but resigned in 1945 when the Viet Minh nationalists under Ho Chi Minh gained widespread acceptance. After extracting concessions from the French, the emperor returned in 1949 as head of state of Vietnam, which included Annam plus Tonkin and Cochin China. Bao Dai was unable to establish an effective government, however, and following Vietnam's partition (1954) he accepted Ngo Dinh DIEM as prime minister. In 1955 Diem engineered a referendum that abolished the monarchy and assumed control. Bao Dai subsequently lived in exile, primarily in France.

Baphomet (băf'əmĕt), idol or mystical figure that the KNIGHTS TEMPLARS were accused of worshiping in the 14th cent. Apparently the name was unknown before that time in Western demonology. Its origin is disputed: It may have been a distorted form of Mahomet; it may have been of Greek origin.

baptism [Gr., =dipping], in most Christian churches a SACRAMENT. It is a rite of purification by water, a ceremony invoking the grace of God to regenerate the person, free him or her from sin, and make that person a part of the church. Thus, baptism is usually required for membership in the church. In Roman Catholic and Anglican theology baptism is also held to confer an indelible character on the person, requiring him or her to worship. Formal baptism is performed by immersion (as among the BAPTISTS) or by pouring or sprinkling water on the person to be baptized. This ceremony is accompanied, in churches that accept the dogma of the Trinity, by a formula asking the blessing of Father, Son, and Holy Ghost. In some churches the child is baptized soon after birth and has sponsors (godfather and godmother) who make declarations of faith in his name. The rite is sometimes called christening, and this term is applied especially to the giving of a baptismal name. Other churches withhold baptism until the person is relatively mature. Some Protestant groups, such as the Religious Society of FRIENDS, reject all outward baptismal rites. Similar customs are known in many non-Christian cultures. The baptism of Jesus himself can be considered part of the founding of the Christian Church (Mat. 3; Mark 1:1–11; Luke 3:1–22, John 3:22,23).

baptistery (băp'tĭstrē), part of a church, or a separate building in connection with it, used for administering baptism. In the earliest examples it was merely a basin or pool, set into the floor. Later, the Christian Church set aside a separate structure for the ceremony. The earliest such structure still extant is in the Lateran basilica at Rome, in which, by tradition, Emperor Constantine was baptized (337). Octagonal in plan, it formed a model for many subsequent baptisteries, most of which were octagonal or circular. In the center of the chamber was the sunken pool, often surrounded by columns, with curtains to screen the neophyte during immersion. Early baptisteries are chiefly found in Italy and Asia Minor. In Hagia Sophia there is a 6th-century example still extant. When immersion was no longer practiced, a separate structure became unnecessary and was supplanted by a place within the church itself, set aside for the purpose. The standing fonts of the Middle Ages and the Renaissance were often objects of superb artistry. In Italy separate baptisteries continued to be built in the 12th to the 15th cent., notably the beautiful Romanesque structures at Florence, Pisa, Siena, and Parma. The baptistery at Florence contains the celebrated bronze doors of Andrea Pisano and of Lorenzo Ghiberti, that at Pisa the pulpit by Nicola Pisano.

Baptists, denomination of Protestant Christians holding a distinctive belief with regard to the ordinance of BAPTISM. There are over 31 million Baptists worldwide. Since 1644 the name has been applied to those who maintain that baptism should be administered to none but believers and that immersion is the only mode of administering baptism indicated in the New Testament. The doctrine and practices of some earlier bodies, such as the Anabaptists and Mennonites, were similar. In Holland a group of English SEPARATISTS, led by John SMYTH, came under Mennonite influence and formed c.1608 in Amsterdam the first English Baptist congregation. Smyth baptized first himself, then the others. In 1611 certain members of this congregation returned to London and established a church there. This was the first of the churches afterward known as General Baptists, since they held the Arminian belief that the atonement of Christ is not limited to the elect only but is general. In 1633 the Particular Baptists were founded. They were a group whose Calvinistic doctrine taught that atonement is particular or individual. Immersion was not yet insisted upon in these churches; but in 1644 seven Particular Baptist churches issued a confession of faith requiring that form of baptism, and Baptist was thenceforth the name given to those who practiced it. In 1891, General and Particular Baptists united into a single body called the Baptist Union of Great Britain and Ireland. In America it was Baptists of the Particular type that first gained influence among the Puritans and Calvinists, when Roger Williams and his companions in Rhode Island rejected infant baptism and established a church in 1639 based on the individual profession of faith. Baptists were later persecuted in New England for opposing infant baptism, and one group emigrated c.1684 from Maine to Charleston, S.C. A group of Separate Congregationalists from New England under Shubael Stearns and Daniel Marshall established (1755) the Separate Baptists in Sandy Creek, N.C. In the Southeast the General Baptist views found acceptance, but the stricter Calvinistic ideas suited the pioneers who settled the Southern mountains after the Revolution. Their opposition to mission work gave them the name Anti-Mission. They were also called Hard Shell or Primitive Baptists. Baptist churches are congregational in matters of government. Such general associations as are formed do not have control over the individual churches. Early missionary activity extended the Baptist movement to the Continent and elsewhere. In the United States the American Baptist Missionary Union (under a longer title) was formed in 1814 to support workers in foreign lands. In 1832 the American Baptist Home Mission Society was organized. When the question of slavery became a dividing wall, the Southern Baptist Convention was established (1845), with its various boards for missions and other activities; it is the largest body, with about 11.6 million members. The American Baptist Convention, organized in 1907, is a delegated body operating through many agencies (until 1950 it was called the Northern Baptist Convention); it has about 1.5 million members. Both support a number of educational institutions and periodicals. The original national organization of black Baptist churches is the National Baptist Convention of the United States of America; it has about 5.5 million members. Separated from that body is the largely black National Baptist Convention of America; this body has about 2.7 million members. Another large body is the National Primitive Baptist Convention, Inc., with about 1.5 million members. The principal conventions agree in doctrine and ecclesiastical order. Some attempts at mergers of these groups (and numerous other, smaller Baptist groups) have been successful. The Baptist World Alliance (formed 1905) holds international congresses regularly. See H. C. Vedder, *Baptist History* (1907); G. F. D. Dobbins, *Baptists* (1958); R. G. Torbet, *A History of the Baptists* (1963); Samuel Hill, *Baptists North and South* (1964); J. E. Tull, *Shapers of Baptist Thought* (1972); Lawrence Davis, *Immigrants, Baptists, and the Protestant Mind in America* (1973).

bar, offshore: see BEACH.

Bar, Confederation of, union formed in 1768 at Bar, in Podolia (now in W Ukraine, USSR), by a number of Polish nobles to oppose the interference of Catherine II of Russia in Polish affairs. Headed by the Pulaski family and supported by the Roman Catholic clergy, it sought to defend Polish independence, the Polish constitution, the rights of the landed gentry, and Roman Catholicism. Further, it endeavored to impose Roman Catholicism, as opposed to Orthodox Eastern beliefs, on the serfs of right-bank Ukraine (W of the Dnepr), which was then under Polish rule. Working against the confederation's policies was the Polish king, STANISLAUS II, whose election (1764) had been sponsored by Catherine and who at her request had conceded to non-Catholics the rights of freedom of worship and participation in the Polish government. Incensed by the confederation's hostile intentions toward them, the right-bank Ukrainians rose up (1768) in the rebellion of the Koliyivshchyna (see UKRAINE). Catherine sent Russian forces to suppress the rebellion, however, in the fear that it might spread among serfs under her control. In 1770, the confederation declared King Stanislaus deposed. Supported to a minor degree by France and more effectively by Turkey, which declared war on Catherine, the confederation fought a bitter war against Russia until 1772, when its effective resistance was ended by the First Partition of Poland.

bar, the, originally, the rail that enclosed the judge in a court; hence, a court or a system of courts. The persons qualified and authorized to conduct the trial of cases are also known collectively as "the bar." From late medieval times in England the INNS OF COURT acted as training schools for men who were to plead causes in the courts, and when a student was judged to be trained in competence, he was "called to the bar" of the Inn; automatically he was then judged competent to plead at the bar of the courts. Modern bar associations, through which the legal profession regulates itself, derive from the Inns of Court. ATTORNEYS must be admitted to the bar before they can practice law in the United States. The requirements for admission vary among the states, but generally an applicant must be of good moral character, have completed a stated course of study at a law school, and have passed a bar examination. The last two requirements were once satisfied by clerking and "reading law" with a practicing attorney. A lawyer can be prohibited from practicing law (disbarred) for conduct impeding justice, criminal acts involving moral turpitude, and unethical professional conduct. The first state to allow women admission to the bar was Iowa (1869), and Great Britain admitted women to law practice in 1919. There are about 150 law schools in the United States, the oldest being Harvard Law School, founded in 1817.

Baraba Steppe (bərəbä'), agricultural district, SW Siberian USSR, between the Ob and the Irtysh rivers. **Barabinsk,** on the Trans-Siberian RR, is the region's chief town. It was founded in the 19th cent.

Barabbas (bərăb'əs), bandit held in jail at the time of Jesus' arrest. Pontius Pilate, who annually released a prisoner at Passover, offered to release Jesus, but the people demanded his death and Barabbas' delivery. Mat. 27.15–18; Mark 15.6–15; Luke 23.13–25; John 18.39,40.

Barabinsk: see BARABA STEPPE.

Barachel (băr'əkĕl, bərā'kəl), father of ELIHU **2.** Job 32.2.6.

Barachias (bărəkī'əs), the same as BERECHIAH.

Baracoa (bäräkō'ä), city (1970 pop. 20,926), Oriente prov., SE Cuba, a port near the eastern extremity of the island. Bananas and coffee are exported. Founded c.1512 by the Spanish explorer Diego de Velázquez, Baracoa is the oldest settlement in Cuba.

Barada (băr'ədə), ancient *Abana* (ăb'ənə), river, 52 mi (84 km) long, rising in the Anti-Lebanon mts. and flowing S to marshy Lake Al Utaybah, SE Syria; forms the Ghutah oasis, site of the city of Damascus. The Barada's waters have been used for irrigation for centuries; fruit orchards, wheat, and vineyards thrive there. Two dams on the Barada generate hydroelectricity and store water for irrigation. See ABANA.

Baradla Caves (bŏ'rŏdlŏ), three large caves, NE Hungary and SE Czechoslovakia, c.25 mi (40 km) NW of Miskolc, Hungary. Aggtelek and Josvafő caves are in Hungary; Dobšiná is in Czechoslovakia. They are noted for their huge stalactites. Two underground rivers and a lake are found there.

Baraga, Frederic (bâr'əgə), 1797–1868, Roman Catholic missionary to the Indians of Upper Michigan, b. Slovenia. He received (1821) a law degree from the Univ. of Vienna, and after study at the Laibach seminary he was ordained (1823). As a missionary, he reached (1831) Cincinnati, where he was later (1853) consecrated bishop of Upper Michigan. The seat of that bishopric was Sault Ste Marie, and in 1865 he was given authority also over the see of Marquette. His authoritative grammar and dictionary of the Ojibwa language are still used by scholars. See biographies by Edward Jacker (1957) and B. J. Lambert (1967).

Baragaon (bŭ'rəgoun), village, Bihar state, E central India. It was the site of Nalanda Univ., which from the 4th to the 12th cent. A.D. was the most famous center of Buddhist learning in India. There are extensive ruins of stupas, monasteries, and temples.

Barahona (bäräō'nä), city (1970 pop. 37,889), SW Dominican Republic, on Neiba Bay, an arm of the Caribbean Sea. Barahona is a provincial capital. It has a lumber industry and is a commercial and processing center for an agricultural region.

Barak (bā'răk), leader from N Canaan who fought, with DEBORAH, against Jabin and Sisera. Judges 4.1–24. See also BEDAN.

Baranagar (bŭr'ənəgər), city (1971 pop. 131,431), West Bengal state, NE India, on the Hooghly River. It is a suburb of Calcutta.

Baranov, Aleksander Andreyevich (əlyĭksän'dər əndrā'əvyĭch bərä'nôf), 1747–1819, Russian trader, chief figure in the period of Russian control in Alaska. When his Siberian business faltered, Baranov accepted (1790) an offer to become managing agent of a Russian fur-trading company on Kodiak Island. The organization of the RUSSIAN AMERICAN COMPANY in 1799 made him virtual governor of all Russian activities in North America until 1817, except for a brief challenge by Rezanov. Baranov's dogged determination to keep the settlement going despite Indian attacks and challenges by British and American trading vessels brought steady profits to the company. He was supplanted in 1817 and died en route to Russia. See Hector Chevigny, *Lord of Alaska* (1942); S. R. Tompkins, *Alaska: Promyshlennik and Sourdough* (1945); Clarence Hulley, *Alaska: Past and Present* (rev. ed. 1953).

Baranovichi (bərŭn'ôvyĕchē), Pol. *Baranowicze* (bäränôvē'chĕ), city (1970 pop. 107,000), Belorussia, W European USSR. It is a major railway junction and has industries that manufacture machinery, metalware, and textiles. Founded as a railway station in 1870, Baranovichi passed from the Soviet Union to Poland in 1920. In 1939, Baranovichi again was incorporated into the USSR.

Barante, Amable Guillaume Prosper Brugière, baron de (ämä'blə gēyōm' prôspĕr' brüzhyĕr' bärôN' də bäräNt'), 1782–1866, French statesman and historian. He held numerous administrative and diplomatic posts but retired with the downfall of Louis Philippe (1848). Of his historical works, the best known is a history of the duchy of Burgundy (1824). His *Souvenirs* (8 vol., 1890–1901), published posthumously, have considerable charm and some value as historical source material.

Barany, Robert (rō'bĕrt bä'rănē), 1876–1936, Austrian physician. For his work on the physiology and pathology of the vestibular apparatus of the ear he received the 1914 Nobel Prize in Physiology and Medicine. From 1917 until his death he was professor at the Univ. of Uppsala.

Barataria Bay (bărətâr'ēə), SE La., separated from the Gulf of Mexico by Grand and Grand Terre islands. It is linked to the Intracoastal Waterway by a navigable channel. The bay is the center of the Louisiana shrimp industry and is trapped for muskrat furs. Oil and natural gas are found in the area, and the bay region is a major source of sulfur. In the early 19th cent. the bay was the headquarters of Jean Laffite and his pirates.

Barbados (bärbā'dōz), island state (1970 pop. 238,141), 166 sq mi (430 sq km), in the West Indies. The capital is BRIDGETOWN. The island, E of St. Vincent, in the Windward Islands, is low and rises gradually toward its highest point at Mt. Hillaby (1,104 ft/336 m). Although there is ample rainfall from June to December, there are no rivers, and water must be pumped from subterranean caverns. The porous soil and moderate warmth are excellent for the cultivation of sugarcane, long the island's major occupation. Other exports include molasses and rum. Commercial fishing is also important. The population of Barbados, about 90% of black African descent, is mostly rural. The healthful and equable climate makes it a very popular tourist resort and tourism is the country's largest source of foreign exchange. Although it was probably discovered by the Portuguese and named Los Barbados for the bearded fig trees they found, the first definite settle-

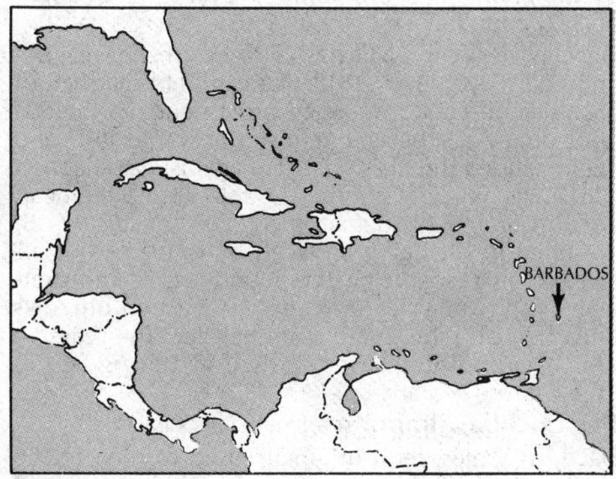

ment was made by English expeditionaries in 1627 (1605, according to local tradition). Barbados remained a British colony until independence was granted in 1966. During the 19th cent. it was the administrative headquarters of the Windward Islands, but in 1885 it became a separate colony. It was a member of the short-lived Federation of the West Indies (1958-62). The island has a parliamentary form of government. It is a member of the Commonwealth of Nations, the Organization of American States, the Caribbean Free Trade Area, and the United Nations. See O. P. Starkey, *The Economic Geography of Barbados* (1939, repr. 1971); R. H. Schomburgk, *The History of Barbados* (1848, repr. 1971).

Barbara, Saint, fl. 3d or 4th cent., virgin martyr, whose life is shrouded in contradictory legends. Her father is said to have shut her up in a tower and then to have killed her for being a Christian. He was struck down by lightning, and by an extended analogy St. Barbara became the patroness of makers and users of firearms and fireworks. She is invoked for a happy death. Feast: Dec. 4.

Barbarelli, Giorgio: see GIORGIONE.

Barbari, Jacopo de' (yä'kōpō dā bärbä'rē), c.1440-1516, Germano-Dutch painter and engraver, b. Venice. Barbari was a major link between North European and Italian art; his and Dürer's works reveal a mutual influence. After 1500 he was court painter to rulers in principalities in Germany and the Netherlands, painting portraits, GENRE scenes, and complex allegorical works. He also showed great skill as an engraver, often treating mythological subjects and the nude. Barbari's still life *Dead Bird* (1504) is in Munich. His name is also given as Jacob Walch.

Barbarossa (bär"bərŏs'ə) [Ital.,=red-beard], surname of the Turkish corsair Khayr ad-Din (c.1483-1546). Barbarossa and his brother Aruj, having seized (1518) Algiers from the Spanish, placed Algeria under Turkish suzerainty. He extended his conquests to the rest of the Barbary States. Between 1533 and 1544, as admiral of the Turkish fleet under Sulayman I, he twice defeated Andrea DORIA and ravaged the coasts of Greece, Spain, and Italy. His able son Hasan (d. 1572) succeeded him in Algeria. See biography by E. D. S. Bradford (1969).

Barbarossa, Frederick: see FREDERICK I, Holy Roman Emperor.

Barbary ape: see MACAQUE.

Barbary Coast, waterfront area of San Francisco, Calif., in the years after the 1849 gold rush. Gamblers, gangsters, prostitutes and confidence men flourished, and the brothels, saloons, and disreputable boardinghouses made the Barbary Coast—named after the pirate coast of North Africa—notorious throughout the world.

Barbary States, term used for the North African states of TRIPOLITANIA, TUNISIA, ALGERIA, and MOROCCO. From the 16th cent. Tripolitania, Tunisia, and Algeria were autonomous provinces of the Turkish Empire. Morocco pursued its own independent development. The corsair BARBAROSSA and his brothers led the Turkish conquest to prevent the region from falling to Spain. A last attempt by Holy Roman Emperor Charles V to drive out the Turks failed in 1541. The piracy carried on thereafter by the Muslims of North Africa began as part of the wars against Spain. In the 17th and 18th cent., when the Turkish hold on the area grew weaker, the raids became less military and more commercial in character. The booty, ransom, and slaves that resulted from attacks on Mediterranean towns and shipping and from occasional forays into the Atlantic became the main source of revenue for local Muslim rulers. All the major European naval powers made attempts to destroy the corsairs, and British and French fleets repeatedly bombarded the pirate strongholds. Yet, on the whole, countries trading in the Mediterranean found it more convenient to pay tribute than to undertake the expensive task of eliminating piracy. Toward the end of the 18th cent. the power of the piratical states diminished. The United States and the European powers took advantage of this decline to launch more attacks. American opposition resulted in the TRIPOLITAN WAR. After the Napoleonic wars, European opinion clearly favored destroying the pirates. In 1816 Lord EXMOUTH with an Anglo-Dutch flotilla all but ended the naval power of the dey of Algiers. An ultimatum from the European Congress of Aix-la-Chapelle (1819) compelled the bey of Tunis to give up piracy. The Tunisian fleet was subsequently sent to help the Ottomans in Greece and was destroyed (1827) at the battle of Navarino. In 1830, France, after a three-year blockade of Algiers, began the conquest of Algeria. The Ottoman Turks were able to reassert (1835) direct control over Tripolitania and end piracy there. About the same time the sultans of Morocco who had occasionally encouraged piracy were forced by France, Great Britain, and Austria to give up plans to rebuild the Moroccan fleet, and North African piracy was at an end. See BLAKE, ROBERT; and DUQUESNE, ABRAHAM.

Barbauld, Anna Letitia (Aikin) (bär'bôld), 1743-1825, English poet and editor. In 1774 she married Rochemont Barbauld and with him opened a boarding school. Her *Hymns in Prose* for children, widely read and translated into several languages, was followed by *Early Lessons* (both 1781). She edited works of Collins, Akenside, and Richardson and the 50-volume edition of *British Novelists* with short biographies and critical notes.

Barbazan, Arnaud Guillaume, seigneur de (ärnō' gēyōm' sānyör' də bärbäzäN'), c.1360-1431, French general in the Hundred Years War. He was called *le chevalier sans reproche* [the knight without blame]. A leader of the Armagnacs (see ARMAGNACS AND BURGUNDIANS) and a staunch supporter of the dauphin, the future King Charles VII, Barbazan defended (1420) Melun against the English and was held prisoner by them from 1420 to 1430. After his release he fought successfully against the English and Burgundians and was made governor of Champagne and Brie. He died fighting in Lorraine.

barbecue [West Indian or South American], in the United States, traditionally an open-air gathering, political or social, where an ox or a hog is roasted whole over a pit of glowing embers and food and drink are liberally enjoyed. The term *barbecue* also refers to the meat being roasted. In the modern barbecue smaller cuts of meat dipped in or basted with a highly seasoned sauce may be used. As an American institution it seems to be of Southern origin, the word having been used in Virginia prior to 1700.

barbed wire, wire composed of two zinc-coated steel strands twisted together and having barbs spaced regularly along them. The need for barbed wire arose in the 19th cent. as the American frontier moved westward into the Great Plains and traditional FENCE materials—wooden rails and stone—became scarce and expensive. Of the many early types of barbed wire, that invented in Illinois in 1873 by Joseph F. Glidden proved most popular. The advent of barbed-wire fences on the plains transformed the cattle industry, ending the open range to a large extent and making possible the introduction of blooded cattle. The transformation was not without protests, which often led to bloodshed. In the 20th cent. barbed wire gained importance as an instrument of defense through its use in wartime for entanglements and obstacles. Barbed-wire fences have been replaced in some applications by other types, e.g., woven-wire fences.

barbel: see CARP.

Barbé-Marbois, François, marquis de (fräNswä' märkē' də bärbā'-märbwä'), 1745-1837, French statesman. He held diplomatic posts in Europe and, during the American Revolution, in the United States. After holding a governmental post in Saint-Domingue (Santo Domingo), he returned to France and was active in the French Revolution. Suspected of royalist sympathies, he was deported (1797) to French Guiana. He was released by Napoleon I, who made him director and then minister of the treasury. Barbé-Marbois negotiated the treaty by which Louisiana was ceded to the United States. Under the Bourbon restoration he was briefly (1815-16) minister of justice and keeper of the seals. See E. W. Lyon, *The Man Who Sold Louisiana* (1942).

Barber, John Warner, 1798-1885, American engraver, b. East Windsor, Conn. He opened (1823) a business in New Haven, where he produced religious and historical books, illustrated with his own wood and steel engravings. He is best known for books on state, national, and local history, in which his vivid engravings caught the flavor and appearance of city, town, and countryside in his day.

Barber, Samuel, 1910-, American composer, b. West Chester, Pa. Barber studied at the Curtis Institute of Music, Philadelphia. His music is lyrical and generally tonal; his later works are more chromatic and polytonal with striking contrapuntal elements. Among his outstanding works are a setting of Matthew Arnold's "Dover Beach" for voice and string quartet (1931); an overture to *The School for Scandal* (1931); *Adagio for Strings* (1936); two symphonies (1936, 1944); Capricorn Concerto for flute, oboe, and trumpet (1944) and a piano concerto (1963; Pulitzer Prize); a ballet, *Medea* (1946); *Knoxville: Summer of 1915,* for soprano and orchestra (1947), derived from a segment of James Agee's novel *A Death in the Family;* a modern oratorio, *Prayers of Kierkegaard* (1954); and two operas, *Vanessa* (1956; Pulitzer Prize) and *Antony and Cleopatra* (1966), commissioned to open the new Metropolitan Opera House. See biography by Nathan Broder (1954).

Barberini, Francesco (fränchās'kō bärbärē'nē), 1597-1679, Italian prelate and Orientalist, a cardinal of the Roman Catholic Church. He was a founder of the library at Rome noted for rare manuscripts; many of these are now in the library of the Vatican.

Barberini vase: see PORTLAND VASE.

barberry, common name for the family Berberidae, and specifically for the spiny barberries (*Berberis* species). The family includes perennial herbs and

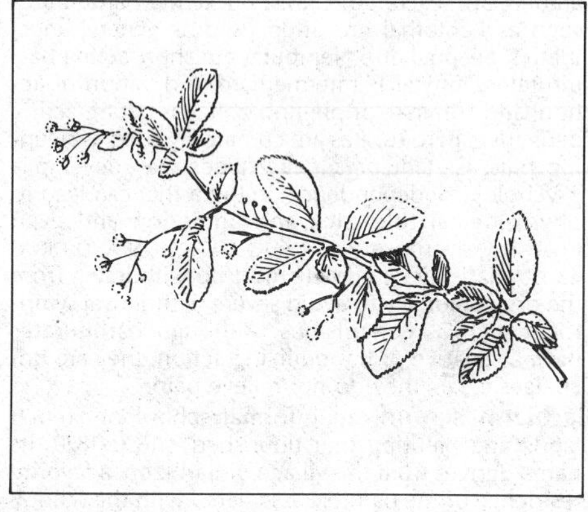

Barberry, Berberis vulgaris

shrubs found in the Northern Hemisphere. The fruit is often a colorful, winter-persistent berry. The spiny barberries are primarily Asian in origin. *B. vulgaris,* the common barberry, is naturalized in the United States and is often cultivated for hedges, but it is a host for one stage of wheat RUST, a pathogen that destroys the plant. The Japanese barberry (*B. thunbergii*) is resistant. Other members of the family are the blue cohosh or papooseroot (*Caulophyllum thalictroides*), the May apple (genus *Podophyllum*; the common American wild flower is *P. peltatum*), and the Oregon grape (*Mahonia aquifolium*), an evergreen shrub that is the floral emblem of Oregon. The edible berries of these three are sometimes used for condiments and jellies. The barberry family is classified in the division MAGNOLIOPHYTA, class Magnoliopsida, order Ranunculales.

Barberton, city (1970 pop. 33,052), Summit co., NE Ohio, an industrial suburb of Akron, on the Tuscarawas River; inc. 1892. Automobile tires and other rubber products are among its manufactures. Lake Anna is in the city.

Barbey d'Aurevilly, Jules Amédée (zhül ämädā' bärbā' dōrvēyē'), 1809?-1889, French writer and critic. An aristocrat and monarchist, he supported himself by journalism; his output of critical and polemical articles was enormous. He favored Balzac, early admired Baudelaire, and harshly criticized naturalism. His novels and stories, set in his native Cotentin, are notable portrayals of provincial life and tragic struggle. Perhaps best remembered is *Les Diaboliques* (1874, tr. 1925), hallucinatory tales with a Satanic motif.

Barbier, Antoine Alexandre (äNtwän' älĕksäN'drə bärbyā'), 1765–1825, French bibliographer and government librarian. Barbier was one of a committee appointed to collect works suppressed by the Revolution. He later became librarian to Napoleon I. His outstanding work was a great bibliography of anonymous and pseudonymous works in French and Latin (1806–8, 3d ed. 1872–79).

Barbieri, Giovanni Francesco: see GUERCINO.

Barbirolli, Sir John (bär"bərō'lē), 1899–1970, English conductor and cellist, b. London. After being cellist (1920–24) in the International String Quartet, he organized the Barbirolli String Orchestra. Barbirolli held positions as conductor of the British National Opera Company (1926), the Covent Garden Opera Company (1930–33), the Scottish Orchestra, and the Leeds Symphony (1933–36). In 1937 he succeeded Toscanini as conductor of the New York Philharmonic-Symphony Orchestra (1937–42). After 1943, Barbirolli conducted the Halle Orchestra, Manchester, and was knighted in 1949. He became conductor of the Houston Symphony Orchestra in 1961. Barbirolli was noted for sensitive musical interpretation and for his transcriptions of early music for the modern orchestra. See biographies by Charles Reid and Michael Kennedy (both 1971).

barbiturate (bärbĭch'ərāt"), any one of a group of drugs that act as DEPRESSANTS on the central NERVOUS SYSTEM. High doses depress both nerve and muscle activity and inhibit oxygen consumption in the tissues. In low doses barbiturates act as SEDATIVES, i.e., they have a tranquilizing effect; increased doses have a hypnotic or sleep-inducing effect, and still larger doses have anticonvulsant and anesthetic activity. The mechanism of action on the central nervous system is not known. The barbiturates are all derivatives of barbituric acid, which was first prepared in 1864 by the German organic chemist Adolf von Baeyer. The drugs differ widely in the duration of their action, which depends on the rapidity with which they are distributed in body tissues, degraded, and excreted. Ultrashort-acting barbiturates such as Pentothal are often used as general anesthetics. Seconal and Nembutal are short-acting barbiturates, Amytal is intermediate in duration of action, and Luminal, or phenobarbital, is a long-acting derivative. Barbiturates are commonly used as sleeping pills. Certain personality types may develop a psychological dependency on them that can lead to physiological tolerance and addiction and even death by overdose (see DRUG ADDICTION AND DRUG ABUSE). Barbiturate addicts must be withdrawn from the drug gradually to avoid severe withdrawal symptoms such as convulsions. Although barbiturates have a sedative or tranquilizing action, they are not analgesic, i.e., they do not relieve pain.

Barbizon school, an informal school of French landscape painting that flourished c.1830–1870. Its name derives from the village of Barbizon, a favorite residence of the painters associated with the school. Theodore Rousseau was the principal figure of the group, which included the artists Jules Dupré, Diaz de la Peña, Constant Troyon, and Charles Daubigny. These men reacted against the conventions of classical landscape and advocated a direct study of nature. Their work was strongly influenced by 17th-century Dutch landscape masters including Ruisdael, Cuyp, and Hobbema. Corot and Millet are often associated with the Barbizon group, but in fact Corot's poetic approach and Millet's humanitarian outlook place them outside the development of the school. The Barbizon painters, with their insistence on a relatively straightforward rendering of landscape, helped prepare for the subsequent development of the impressionist schools. Paintings of the Barbizon school were very popular with American collectors of the late 19th and early 20th cent. and influenced American painters of this period. The school is well represented in American collections, notably the Corcoran Gallery, the Isaac Delgado Museum of Art, New Orleans, the Metropolitan Museum, and the Museum of Fine Arts, Boston. See American Art Assn., *Master Prints of the Barbizon School* (1970); study by Jean Bouret (tr. 1973).

Barbon, Praise-God: see BAREBONE, PRAISE-GOD.

Barbosa, Ruy (rōō'ē bärbō'sä), 1849–1923, Brazilian jurist, writer, and statesman. He was largely responsible for the republican constitution of Brazil and was the champion of law and liberty under recurrent dictatorships. A noted internationalist, he distinguished himself as head of the Brazilian delegation to the 1907 peace conference at The Hague and was elected (1908) to the World Court. As a writer, Barbosa has been regarded as the greatest stylist in the Portuguese language. See C. W. Turner, *Ruy Barbosa* (1945).

Barbour, John (bär'bər), c.1316?–1395, Scottish poet. He was archdeacon of Aberdeen from 1355 until his death. His romance, *The Bruce* (1375), celebrating Scotland's emancipation from England, recounts the heroic deeds of Robert I and Sir James Douglas. The poem was meant to be read as history and shows remarkable accuracy. Barbour's authorship of a fragmentary *Troy-Book* and the *Buik of Alexander* is disputed.

Barbuda, British West Indies: see ANTIGUA.

Barca, surname, probably meaning lightning, given members of a powerful Carthaginian family: see HAMILCAR BARCA; HANNIBAL; HASDRUBAL.

Barcelona (bärsəlō'nə, Span. bärthälō'nä), city (1970 pop. 1,745,142), capital of Barcelona prov. and chief city of Catalonia, NE Spain, on the Mediterranean Sea. Situated on a plain between the Llobregat and Besós rivers and lying between mountains and the sea, Barcelona is the second largest city of Spain, its largest port, and its chief commercial and industrial center. It is also the seat of a university (founded 1430) and many other educational institutions. Textiles, machinery, automobiles, locomotives, airplanes, and electrical equipment are the chief manufactures. It was founded by the Carthaginians, and, according to tradition, it supposedly derives its name from the great BARCA family of Carthage. The city flourished under the Romans and Visigoths, fell to the Moors (8th cent.), and was taken (801) by Charlemagne, who included it in the Spanish March. In the 9th to 10th cent. the march became independent under the leadership of the powerful counts of Barcelona, who wrested lands to the south from the Moors, thus acquiring all Catalonia. The counts also won suzerainty over several fiefs in S France. The marriage of Count Raymond Berengar IV to the heiress of Aragón united (1137) the two lands under one dynasty; the title count of Barcelona was subsequently borne by the kings of Aragón, who made the city their capital, and later the kings of Spain. Under its strong municipal government Barcelona vastly expanded both its Mediterranean trade, becoming a rival of Genoa and Venice, and its cloth industry and flourished as a banking center. Reaching its peak around 1400, the city later shared in the general decline of Catalonia, but enjoyed a period of prosperity as the embarkation point of the armies of Emperor Charles V. It was repeatedly (1640–52, 1715, 1808–14) occupied by the French. Barcelona was always the stronghold of Catalan separatism and was the scene of many insurrections. It was the center of the Catalan revolt (1640–52) against Philip IV of Spain. Later it also became the Spanish center of socialism, anarchism, syndicalism, and other radical political beliefs. It was the capital of the Catalan autonomous government (1932–39) and the seat of the Spanish Loyalist government from Oct., 1938, until its fall to Franco on Jan. 26, 1939. Barcelona remains a center of separatism and political liberalism; in the 1950s, it was the scene of sporadic demonstrations against the Franco regime. Present-day Barcelona is the cultural center of Spain. A handsome modern city, it has broad avenues, bustling traffic, and striking new buildings. Its old city, with winding, narrow streets (Roman walls are still visible), has many historic structures, including the imposing Cathedral of Santa Eulalia (14th–15th cent.) with its fine cloisters, the Church of Santa María del Mar, the city hall, and the *Lonja* or exchange. Also notable is the Church of the Sagrada Familia (begun 1882), designed by Antonio Gaudí.

Barclay, Alexander (bär'klā), 1475?–1552, Scottish clergyman and poet. Although the first to write pastoral eclogues in English, he is best known for *The Ship of Fools* (1509), a translation and elongation of Sebastian Brant's widely popular poem *Das Narrenschiff.*

Barclay, John, 1734–98, minister of the Church of Scotland and founder of the BEREANS or Barclayites. His *Without Faith, without God* (1769) and other works were not acceptable to his presbytery, and he was prohibited from preaching. His adherents then united in independent congregations, and Barclay became minister of the one at Edinburgh. Later he organized a Berean congregation in London.

Barclay, Robert, 1648–90, Scottish apologist for the Society of Friends (Quakers). He wrote many controversial works but is best known for his great treatise *An Apology for the True Christian Divinity,* which appeared in Latin in 1676 and in English two years later. The duke of York (later James II) granted a patent of the province of East Jersey to 12 members of the Society of Friends; Barclay was nominal governor (1682–88), but he never went to America. His collected works were published in 1692 as *Truth Triumphant.* See biographies by M. C. Cadbury (1912) and D. E. Trueblood (1967).

Barclay de Tolly, Mikhail, Prince (mēkhəyēl', bərklī' də tô'lyē), 1761–1818, Russian field marshal, of Scottish descent. He gained prominence in the Napoleonic Wars, became minister of war in 1810, and commanded the Russian forces against Napoleon in 1812. His policy of continuous retreat into the heart of Russia and his defeat at Smolensk (Aug. 17–18) resulted in his being replaced by Kutuzov, but his successor, recognizing the soundness of the strategy, followed the same policy. After Kutuzov's death (1813) he again commanded the Russian forces and distinguished himself at Leipzig and in the capture of Paris.

Bar Cochba, Simon: see BAR KOKBA, SIMON.

bard, in Wales, term originally used to refer to the order of minstrel-poets who composed and recited the poems that celebrated the feats of Celtic chieftains and warriors. The term *bard* in present-day usage has become synonymous with poet, particularly a revered poet.

Bard College, at Annandale-on-Hudson, N.Y.; founded 1860 as St. Stephen's College for men, rechartered 1935 as Bard College; became coeducational in 1944; affiliated with Columbia Univ. 1928–44. A small, progressive college, Bard stresses independent study.

Bardeen, John, 1908–, American physicist, b. Madison, Wis., grad. Univ. of Wisconsin (B.S., 1928; M.S., 1929), Ph.D. Princeton, 1936. He was a research physicist at the Bell Telephone Laboratories from 1945 to 1951. In 1951 he became professor of electrical engineering and physics at the Univ. of Illinois. He is known for his studies of semiconductivity and other aspects of solid state physics. He shared with Walter H. Brattain and William Shockley the 1956 Nobel Prize in Physics for their work in developing the transistor. He also shared the 1972 Nobel Prize in physics with Leon Cooper and John Schreiffer for development of a theory of SUPERCONDUCTIVITY, becoming the first person to win a Nobel Prize twice in the same field.

Bardesanes (bärdəsā'nēz), 154?–222?, Christian philosopher and poet of Syria, missionary among the Armenians. Conflicting traditions report him both as defender of the faith against various Gnostic sects and as a heretic and founder of BARDESANISM.

Bardia: see BARDIYAH, Libya.

Bardiyah or **Bardia** (both: bärdē'ä, bär'dēä), town, NE Libya, a port on the Mediterranean Sea, near the Egyptian border. During World War II it was the most strongly defended Italian position in the British campaign (Dec., 1940–Feb., 1941) in Libya. The town changed hands several times before being captured permanently by the British in Nov., 1942.

Bardstown, city (1970 pop. 5,816), seat of Nelson co., central Ky., SE of Louisville, in a rich farm area; settled 1775, inc. 1788. The city has distilleries, flour and lumber mills, and clothing factories. It was a center for early missionary work in the Mississippi valley and the seat of religious institutions founded by Bishop J. B. M. David, a French missionary. The monument to the American inventor John Fitch, whose grave is there, was erected by the U.S. Congress. Nearby is "Federal Hill" (built 1795–1818), the manor house of John Rowan; it is said that his cousin, Stephen Foster, wrote *My Old Kentucky Home* there. Other places of interest in the area include the Cathedral of St. Joseph (1816–19), which has paintings said to have been given by Louis Philippe of France, and the Abbey of Our Lady of Gethsemane, a Trappist monastery founded in 1848. In the Civil War the city was occupied (Sept., 1862) by Gen. Braxton Bragg's invading Confederate army. The city has wide, tree-lined streets and many early-19th-century houses.

Barebone or **Barbon, Praise-God** (both: bâr'bōn), 1596?–1679, English lay preacher and leather merchant. Soon after 1630 he became leader of half of a Baptist congregation that had split over the issue of infant baptism. Barebone favored this practice and wrote a treatise arguing its legitimate scriptural basis. An effective preacher, he attracted large congregations to his house in Fleet Street and acquired a reputation for rabble rousing. He was referred to by his many detractors variously as a Brownist, Anabaptist, and Fifth Monarchy man, but his actual religious beliefs are unclear. In April, 1653, the army dissolved the Rump Parliament, and in July Oliver

Cromwell and his provisional council assembled 140 "godly men" from amongst the nominees of the independent congregations. Barebone was London member in this Nominated Parliament, which was called in derision Barebone's Parliament. Actually his part in the proceedings was insignificant. The body was composed largely of religious reformers who initiated a series of measures regarded as radical by most of their compatriots. The Parliament met from July until December, when the moderate members willingly and the radical members under compulsion resigned their powers into Cromwell's hands. They had accomplished little. Barebone actively opposed the Restoration in 1660 and remained a staunch republican.

Bareilly (bərā'lē), city (1971 pop. 299,629), Uttar Pradesh state, N central India, on the Ramganga River. It is a district administrative headquarters and a sugar-refining and cotton-trading center. Founded in 1657, Bareilly was the capital (1707–20) of the Hindu Rohilla kingdom. It was ceded to Great Britain in 1801.

Barentsburg (bä'rəntsbo͝org), town, Spitsbergen island, Svalbard. A coal-mining settlement, it was established (1912) by a Norwegian company. Its mines have been worked by the Dutch (1921–26) and since 1932 by the USSR. It was totally destroyed (Sept., 1943) by German battleships but quickly rebuilt.

Barentsøya (bä'rənts-ö"yä) or **Barents Island,** island of Svalbard, 513 sq mi (1,329 sq km), in Barents Sea between Spitsbergen and Edgeøya. The island rises to 1,302 ft (397 m).

Barents Sea, arm of the Arctic Ocean, N of Norway and E USSR, partially enclosed by Franz Josef Land on the north, Novaya Zemlya on the east, and Svalbard on the west. Its waters are warmed by the remnants of the North Atlantic Drift, so that its ports, including Murmansk and Vardö, are ice-free all year. The sea was named for Willem Barentz, the Dutch navigator.

Barentz or **Barents, Willem** (both: vĭ'ləm bä'rənts), d. 1597, Dutch navigator. He made three voyages (1594, 1595, 1596–97) in search of the Northeast Passage to Asia. He reached Novaya Zemlya on the first two expeditions. On the third he accidentally discovered Spitsbergen, rounded the north point of Novaya Zemlya, and was caught in the ice. After the arctic winter the crew started for the mainland in two small boats. Barentz died on the way. The extent of his explorations and the accuracy of his charts made him one of the most important of all arctic explorers. The meteorological data that Barentz collected is still consulted today.

Barère de Vieuzac, Bertrand (bĕrtrăN' bärĕr' də vyözäk'), 1755–1841, French revolutionary. A member of the Revolutionary National Assembly and of the Convention, he moved from a moderate to a radical stand, voting for the execution of King Louis XVI. He was a member of the Committee of Public Safety, the dictatorial body that ruled France for a time during the Revolutionary Wars. When the moderates in the Convention turned against Maximilien ROBESPIERRE, one of the leaders of the committee and perpetrator of the REIGN OF TERROR (June, 1794), Barère deserted his colleague. Nevertheless, Barère was imprisoned for his role in the Terror. Escaping from prison, he remained in hiding for several years but reappeared as a secret agent of Emperor Napoleon I. Banished (1815) after the Bourbon restoration, he returned in the reign of Louis Philippe. He left memoirs. See biography by Leo Gershoy (1962).

Baretti, Giuseppe Marc'Antonio (jo͞ozĕp'pā märkäntô'nyō bärĕt'tē), 1719–89, Italian writer and lexicographer. Baretti held various official positions in several Italian cities while making regular contributions to periodicals. In 1751 he went to London, where he was active in literary and cultural circles and where he wrote an Italian grammar and a biographical dictionary of Italian authors. His *Dictionary of the English and Italian Languages* (1760) remained the best of its kind until the 20th cent. Returning to Italy in 1760, Baretti published a bimonthly iconoclastic review of books, *La Frusta letteraria* [the literary scourge]. The Venetian government eventually suppressed the journal, and Baretti returned to London, where he published amusing and perceptive descriptions of his travels. He is considered largely responsible for the popularity of Italian literature in England in the 18th cent.

Barfrush: see BABOL, city, Iran.

barge, large boat, generally flat-bottomed, used for transporting goods. Most barges on inland waterways are towed, but some river barges are self-propelled. There are also sailing barges. On the Great Lakes and in the American coastal trade, huge steel barges are used for transporting bulk cargoes such as coal. Large flat-bottomed barges called *lighters* are used for transporting cargo to or from a vessel that cannot be berthed at a pier or dock; LASH (for lighter-aboard ship) vessels are equipped to receive and unload lighters on board and thus reduce the time spent in port. Barge towing, done in the past by men or by horses or mules, is now accomplished mostly by steam or motor tugboat or by other, self-propelled barges. In use since the dawn of history, barges were common on the Nile in ancient Egypt. Some were highly decorated and used for carrying royalty; use of such state barges persisted in Europe until modern times.

Bargello (bärjĕl'lō), 13th-century palace in Florence, Italy, which houses the national museum. Once the residence of the highest city official but later used as a prison and as the office of the chief of police (*bargello*), it was restored in 1859 to receive the art treasures of the city. The Bargello is famous for its courtyard and its Renaissance sculptures, including works by Michelangelo, Verrocchio, Donatello, the Della Robbias, Cellini, and others.

Barham, Richard Harris (bär'əm), pseud. **Thomas Ingoldsby** (ĭng'gəlzbē), 1788–1845, English humorist, grad. Oxford. Ordained a minister in 1813, he became a minor canon of the Chapel Royal in 1824. In 1837 he began in *Bentley's Miscellany*, under his pseudonym, a series of parodies of country superstitions, medieval legends, and contemporary foibles. Barham had a lively invention, a gift of creating suspense, and an unusually discerning sense of the ludicrous. *The Ingoldsby Legends* were first published in book form in 1840.

Bar Harbor, town (1970 pop. 3,716), SE Maine, on MOUNT DESERT ISLAND and on Frenchman Bay; settled 1763, inc. 1796. It was one of the most famous resorts in New England during the 19th cent. Bar Harbor is a port of entry, with ferry connections to Yarmouth, N.S., during the summer. In Oct., 1947, a large part of the town was destroyed by a forest fire. Acadia National Park, which covers most of Mount Desert Island, is nearby.

Bar-Hebraeus, Gregorius (bär-hēbrē'əs), 1226–86, Syrian scholar, bishop of the JACOBITE CHURCH. Partly Jewish in ancestry, his original name was Abu-l-Faraj. His most celebrated work is a chronicle in Syriac of the world from Adam down. His commentaries (in Arabic and Syriac) on Aristotle were widely known among Arabic-speaking scholars.

Barhumite (bärhyo͞o'mīt, bär'hyo͞o-): see BAHURIM.

Bari (bä'rē), city (1971 pop. 356,733), capital of Bari prov. and of Apulia, S Italy, on the Adriatic Sea. It is a major seaport and an industrial and commercial center. Manufactures include chemicals, textiles, printed materials, and petroleum. Probably of Illyrian origin, Bari became a Greek and then a Roman colony. It later was controlled by the Goths, the Lombards, and the Byzantines. The Normans conquered Bari in 1071. The city became the chief city of Apulia, and many Crusaders sailed from there. Enfeoffed to the kingdom of Naples, Bari, during the Middle Ages, was a duchy ruled by powerful lords, including the Hohenstaufens and the Sforzas of Milan. It was badly damaged in World War II. Noteworthy buildings include the Romanesque basilica (1087–1197), a major place of pilgrimage, with relics of St. Nicholas of Bari (see NICHOLAS, SAINT); the Romanesque cathedral (12th cent.); and the Hohenstaufen castle (1233). The city has a university founded in 1924.

Bariah (bărī'ə), one of the house of David. 1 Chron. 3.22.

Barim, island, Arabia: see PERIM.

Baring, British family of bankers. Sir Francis Baring (1740–1810) founded (1763) the John and Francis Baring Company, which he renamed Baring Brothers and Company in 1806. At first the firm acted as import and export agents for others, but it soon became an independent merchant bank. Sir Francis, a close associate of William Pitt the Younger, helped finance the Napoleonic Wars and underwrote marine insurance. He was succeeded by his son Alexander Baring (later 1st Baron Ashburton; 1774–1848), who was a pioneer in the financing of United States trade. He was (1834) president of the Board of Trade in the first administration of Sir Robert Peel and was raised to the peerage in 1835. He was the British commissioner sent to the United States in 1842 to negotiate the WEBSTER-ASHBURTON TREATY. The family continued to manage the firm and by 1890 its importance to the British government was such that the Bank of England guaranteed their debts to save them from bankruptcy when Argentina defaulted (1890) on bond payments. Members of the Baring family were also notable public servants. The more important members of the family include Thomas George Baring, 1st earl of Northbrook (1826–1904), a Liberal statesman who served as a successful viceroy of India (1872–76); Evelyn Baring, 1st earl of CROMER; Maurice BARING (1874–1945), author; and George Rowland Stanley Baring, 3d earl of Cromer, (1918–), governor of the Bank of England (1961–66) and ambassador to the United States (1971–74). The family still controls Baring Brothers and Company. See R. W. Hidy, *The House of Baring in American Trade and Finance, 1763–1861* (1949).

Baring, Maurice (bâr'ĭng), 1874–1945, English author. After a career in the diplomatic service, he turned to journalism in 1904. A war correspondent during the Russo-Japanese War, he wrote several books on Russia, including *A Year in Russia* (1905–6) and *The Russian People* (1911). In 1919, following service as staff officer in World War I, he began writing novels. His chief books include *C* (1924), *Daphne Adeane* (1926), and *Tinker's Leave* (1927). He also wrote poetry and plays.

Barisal (bərĭsäl'), city (1969 est. pop. 79,300), S Bangladesh, on the Ganges River delta. It is an important river port, a transshipment point for jute and rice, and a market for betel nuts and fish. There are also flour, rice, oilseed, and jute mills. Barisal has three colleges affiliated with the Univ. of Dacca. The "Barisal guns," unexplained sounds resembling distant thunder or cannon, are a curious local phenomenon; they may have a seismic origin.

Barisan (bärēsän'), volcanic mountain range, c.1,000 mi (1,600 km) long, paralleling the western coast of Sumatra island, Indonesia. It rises to Mt. Kerintji (12,467 ft/3,800 m high). Numerous lakes are found in the mountains, including Toba, the largest in Indonesia.

barite (bâr'īt), **barytes** (bərī'tēz) [New Lat., from barium], or **heavy spar**, a white, yellow, blue, red, or colorless mineral. It is a sulfate of barium, $BaSO_4$, found in nature in tabular crystals or in granular or massive form. The mineral is abundant and is found widely distributed throughout the world. It occurs often mixed with other minerals in veins. It is insoluble in water, and this property is made use of in testing for the SULFATE radical. It is practically insoluble under ordinary conditions in all the usual chemical reagents. Barite is used as a commercial source of barium and many of its compounds. Ground barite is used as a filler in the manufacture of linoleum, oilcloth, rubber, and plastics. Finely ground barite is used to make a thixotropic mud for sealing oil wells during drilling. Prime white, a bleached barite, is used as a pigment in white paint but is not as satisfactory as blanc fixe, a chemically precipitated barium sulfate, or LITHOPONE, a mixture of barium sulfate, zinc sulfide, and zinc oxide.

Barito (bärē'tō), river, c.550 mi (890 km) long, rising in the mountains of central Borneo, Indonesia, and flowing generally S to the Java Sea. Banjermasin is the head of oceangoing navigation. The wide floodplain of the lower Barito is intensely cultivated and contains one of Indonesia's largest rubber plantations.

baritone or **barytone** (both: băr'ĭtōn), male VOICE, in a lighter and higher range than a bass but lower than a tenor. The term is also an alternate name for the viola da gamba.

barium (bâr'ēəm) [Gr.,=heavy], metallic chemical element; symbol Ba; at. no. 56; at. wt. 137.34; m.p. probably about 850°C; b.p. probably about 1140°C; sp. gr. 3.5 at 20°C; valence +2. Barium is a soft, silver-white, chemically active, poisonous metal with a face-centered cubic crystalline structure. It is an ALKALINE-EARTH METAL in group IIa of the PERIODIC TABLE. Its principal ore is BARITE (barium sulfate); it also occurs in the mineral witherite (barium carbonate). The pure metal is obtained by the electrolysis of fused barium salts or, industrially, by the reduction of barium oxide with aluminum. Barium is often used in barium-nickel alloys for spark-plug electrodes and in vacuum tubes as a drying and oxygen-removing agent. Barium oxidizes in air, and it reacts vigorously with water to form the hydroxide, liberating hydrogen. In moist air it may spontaneously ignite. It burns in air to form the peroxide, which produces hydrogen peroxide when treated with water. Barium reacts with almost all of the nonmetals; all of its water-soluble and acid-soluble compounds are poisonous. Barium carbonate is used in glass, as a pottery glaze, and as a rat poison. Chrome yellow (barium chromate) is used as a paint pigment and in safety matches. The chlorate and nitrate are used in pyrotechnics to provide a green color. Barium oxide strongly absorbs carbon dioxide and water; it is used as a drying agent. Barium chloride is used in medicinal preparations and as a water softener. Barium sulfide phosphoresces after exposure to light; it is sometimes used as a paint pigment. Barite, the sulfate ore, has many industrial uses. Because barium sulfate is virtually insoluble in water and acids, it can be used to coat the alimentary tract to increase the contrast for X-ray photography without being absorbed by the body and poisoning the subject. Barium salts give a characteristic green color in the FLAME TEST. Barium metal was first isolated in 1808 by Sir Humphry Davy by electrolysis.

barium sulfate: see BARITE.

Bar-jesus, called **Elymas** (ĕl'ĭmăs), Jewish sorcerer at Paphos who tried to divert a prospective Christian convert and was cursed with blindness. Acts 13.6–12.

Bar-jona (bär-jō'nə), patronymic of St. Peter. Mat. 16.17. Peter's father is called Jonas (KJV) and John (RSV). John 21.15,16,17. He is called Jona (KJV) in John 1.42.

bark, outer covering of the stem of woody plants, composed of waterproof cork cells protecting a layer of food-conducting tissue—the phloem or inner bark (also called bast). As the woody stem increases in size (see CAMBIUM) the outer bark of inelastic dead cork cells gives way in patterns characteristic of the species: it may split to form grooves; shred, as in the cedar; or peel off, as in the sycamore or the shagbark hickory. A layer of reproductive cells called the cork cambium produces new cork cells to replace or reinforce the old. The phloem (see STEM) conducts sap downward from the leaves to be used for storage and to nourish other plant parts. "Girdling" a tree, i.e., cutting through the phloem tubes, results in starvation of the roots and, ultimately, death of the tree; trees are sometimes girdled by animals that eat bark. The fiber cells that strengthen and protect the phloem ducts are a source of such textile fibers as hemp, flax, and jute; various barks supply tannin, cork (see CORK OAK), dyes, flavorings (e.g., cinnamon), and drugs (e.g., cocaine and quinine). The outer bark of the paper birch was used by the American Indians to make baskets and canoes.

bark or **barque** (both: bärk), sailing vessel with three masts, of which the mainmast and the foremast are square-rigged while the mizzenmast is fore-and-aft-rigged. Although the word was once used to mean any small boat, later barks were sometimes quite large (up to 6,000 tons). In addition to the standard three-masted bark there are also four-masted barks (fore-and-aft-rigged on the aftermast) and barkentines, or three-masted vessels with the foremast square-rigged and the other masts fore-and-aft-rigged. Large numbers of barks were employed in carrying wheat from Australia to England before World War I; and in 1926 the bark *Beatrice* sailed from Fremantle, Western Australia, to London in 86 days.

bark cloth, primitive fabric made in tropical and subtropical countries from the soft inner bark of certain trees. It has been made and used in parts of Africa and India, the Malay Peninsula, Samoa, the Hawaiian Islands, and the Fiji Islands and perhaps reached its highest perfection in Polynesia and parts of Central America. Lengths of branches or of young stems are cut from trees, such as the fig, the breadfruit, or the paper mulberry. The outer bark is removed; the inner bark is cut in narrow strips and then alternately soaked and beaten with a grooved or carved wooden mallet, or beetle, until the fibers are well matted and become thin and flexible. Gum is sometimes added, and pieces may be joined and beaten together to form large sheets. The peeling and beetling are usually done by the men; the decorating, by the women. Patterns, often elaborate, may be sketched or may be applied by block printing or by leaves dipped in dye and pressed on the cloth. The cloth may be gummed or oiled to make it waterproof. Tapa cloth is a fine variety made in the Pacific islands. Bark cloth is used for loincloths, skirts, draperies, and wall hangings; in thick layers it makes an excellent bed. So ancient is the art of making the cloth that it is deeply involved in religious and ceremonial life. In Borneo a strip of the cloth signifies mourning. In Malawi it has traditionally formed the initiation dress of girls. In India some sects prescribe bark cloth as the dress of a religious recluse.

Barker, Eugene Campbell, 1874–1956, American historian, b. Walker co., Texas. His distinguished teaching career, begun in 1899, was almost entirely at the Univ. of Texas. An outstanding social historian, Barker wrote about the period of American settlement in Texas and about the Texas Revolution. Notable among his works are a biography of Stephen F. Austin (1925, repr. 1968), *Mexico and Texas 1821–1835* (1928, repr. 1965), and an edition (with Amelia W. Williams) of the writings of Sam Houston (8 vol., 1938–43, repr. 1969). See biography by W. C. Pool (1971).

Barker, George (George Granville Barker), 1913–, English poet, b. Essex, England. He has taught in Japan and the United States as well as in England. His highly dramatic poems are often concerned with themes of remorse and pain. Barker's published works include *30 Preliminary Poems* (1933), *Eros in Dogma* (1944), *News of the World* (1950), *The True Confession of George Barker* (1950), *Collected Poems* (1957), *The View From a Blind I* (1962), *Thurgarton Church* (1969), and *The Alphabetical Zoo* (1972).

Barker, Harley Granville-: see GRANVILLE-BARKER.

Barker, James Nelson, 1784–1858, American playwright, b. Philadelphia. In 1838, Van Buren appointed him comptroller of the Treasury, and with slight interruptions he worked in the Treasury Dept. until his death. He wrote 10 plays, five of which have survived in print. The best were *The Indian Princess* (1808), *The Court of Love* (1836; pub. in 1817 as *How to Try a Lover*), and *Superstition* (1824), a tragedy set in colonial New England. His dramatization (1812) of Scott's *Marmion* had extraordinary success on the stage for 30 years. Aside from his merits as a dramatist, Barker is important for his use of American material and themes, unusual in his period. See biography by P. H. Musser (1929, repr. 1970).

Barking, borough (1971 pop. 160,499), Greater London, SE England. Barking was created in 1965 by the merger of portions of the municipal boroughs of Barking and Dagenham. The borough has a power plant and a Ford Motor Company plant as well as engineering, chemical, paint, wood, and other industries. The remains of a Benedictine abbey (c.670) are there.

Barkla, Charles Glover (glŭ'vər bär'klə), 1877–1944, English physicist. He was professor of natural philosophy at Edinburgh from 1913. For his discovery of the characteristic X rays of elements he received the 1917 Nobel Prize in Physics. He evolved the laws of X-ray scattering and the laws governing the transmission of X rays through matter and excitation of secondary rays.

Barkley, Alben William, 1877–1956, Vice President of the United States (1949–53), b. Graves co., Ky. After being admitted (1901) to the bar, he served as prosecuting attorney (1905–9) and judge (1909–13) for McCracken co., Ky., and was U.S. Representative (1913–27) and U.S. Senator (1927–49) from Kentucky. A loyal Democrat, he was majority leader in the Senate from 1937 to 1946. He became Vice President under Truman in 1948. In 1954, Kentucky returned him to the Senate. See his autobiography, *That Reminds Me* (1954).

Bar Kokba, Simon, or **Simon Bar Cochba** (kōk'bə) [Heb.,=son of the star], d. A.D. 135, Hebrew hero and leader of a major revolt against Rome under Hadrian (132–135). He may have claimed to be a Messiah; the Talmud relates that Akiba ben Joseph credited him with this title. His personality and the facts of his life are surrounded by legend. He is sometimes called Simon the Prince of Israel. At first he successfully defeated the Roman armies, but the tide turned against him with the victories of the Roman general Julius Severus, and he was killed at Bether. Israeli archaeologists have found a number of letters in his handwriting.

Barkos (bär'kŏs), ancestor of a family of Nethinim. Ezra 2.53; Neh. 7.55.

Barlaam and Josaphat (bär'lāəm, jō'səfăt), legend popular in medieval times. It corresponds in part to the legend of Buddha. Versions of the story have been found in nearly every language. At the birth of Josaphat (or Joasaph), the son of the Indian king Abenner, it was prophesied that the young prince was destined for greatness not as a royal leader but as a holy man. The king did all that was possible to stop the prophecy from coming true, but the prince, through the teachings of the monk Barlaam, was converted to religion (according to Western legend, Christianity). After the death of Abenner, Josaphat abdicated the throne and lived out the remainder of his days with Barlaam, as a religious recluse. See the standardized Greek text with translation by G. R. Woodward and Harold Mattingly (1914).

Barlach, Ernst (ĕrnst bär'läkh), 1870–1938, German expressionist sculptor, graphic artist, and writer. After studying at the Dresden Art Academy he lived in Paris (1895–96) and in Berlin, Hamburg, and other German cities. A trip to Russia in 1906 gave new impetus to his art. Barlach pioneered in the introduction of expressionism into Germany. Through the power of his simple, angular, and compact forms, he communicated intense emotion and compassion. From clay modeling he turned to wood carving and woodcutting. Many of his works were destroyed by the Nazis; however, some remain in Lüneberg and the Busch-Reisinger Museum, Cambridge, Mass. Barlach illustrated some of his poems and plays. See his *Three Plays* (tr. 1964); study by Carl D. Carls (1969).

Bar-le-Duc (bär-lə-dük'), town (1968 pop. 20,384), capital of Meuse dept., NE France, in Lorraine. It has textile mills, iron foundries, printing plants, and metallurgical and food-processing industries. Situated in the picturesque Ornain valley, Bar-le-Duc has preserved many old houses (16th, 17th, and 18th cent.). It has a 15th-century church and one from the 13th and 14th cent. It was the capital of the county (later duchy) of Bar, an irregularly shaped area stretching from the Marne to the Luxembourg frontier. The duchy passed (15th cent.) to René of Anjou, later also duke of Lorraine. Bar thereafter shared the history of Lorraine, with which it passed to France in 1766.

Barletta (bärlĕt'tä), city (1971 pop. 75,329), Apulia, S Italy, on the Adriatic Sea. It is a seaport and a commercial and industrial center. Salt is mined nearby, and wine is produced. Barletta passed to the Goths after the fall of the Roman Empire. Later controlled by the Byzantines and the Lombards, it became a Norman city in the later 12th cent. and prospered (14th–15th cent.) with its large merchant fleet. Noteworthy buildings include the Romanesque-Gothic cathedral (12th–14th cent.), the Church of Santo Sepolcro (13th cent.), and a castle (mainly 13th cent.).

barley, annual cereal plant (*Hordeum vulgare* and sometimes other species) of the family Gramineae (GRASS family), cultivated by man probably as early as any cereal. It was known to the ancient Greeks, Romans, Chinese, and Egyptians and was the chief bread material in Europe as late as the 16th cent. It has a wide range of cultivation and matures even at high altitudes, since its growing period is short; however, it cannot withstand hot and humid climates. Today barley is typically a special-purpose grain with many varieties rather than a general market crop. It is a valuable stock feed (often as a corn substitute) and is used for malting when the grain is of high quality. It is a minor source of flour and breakfast foods. Pearl barley is often used in soups. In the Middle East a limited amount of barley is eaten like rice. In the United States most spring barley comes from the western states and most winter barley is grown in the southeastern states for autumn and spring pasture and as a cover crop. Barley is subject to several diseases including smut and rust. Barley is classified in the division MAGNOLIOPHYTA, class Liliatae, order Cyperales, family Gramineae.

Barlow, Joel, 1754–1812, American writer and diplomat, b. Redding, Conn., grad. Yale, 1778. He was one of the CONNECTICUT WITS and a major contributor to their satirical poem *The Anarchiad* (1786–87). His own epic, *The Vision of Columbus* (1787), brought him fame in America and Europe and was revised later as *The Columbiad* (1807). Inspired by his friend Thomas Paine, he wrote *Advice to the Privileged Orders* (1792), urging that the state must represent not a class but the people and must be responsible for the welfare of the individual. His *Letter to the National Convention of France on the Defects in the Constitution of 1791* won him French citizenship. His best-known lighter work is a mock eulogy, *The Hasty-Pudding* (1793). Appointed U.S. consul to Algiers in 1795, Barlow succeeded in releasing many American prisoners and in negotiating treaties with Algiers, Tunis, and Tripoli. Sent to Europe in 1811 to negotiate a commercial treaty with Napoleon I, he was caught in the disastrous retreat of the armies from Moscow and died from exposure. See biography by J. L. Woodress (1958, repr. 1969).

Barmecides: see HARUN AR-RASHID.

Bar Mitzvah (bär mĭts'və) [Aramaic,=son of the Commandment], Jewish ceremony in which the young male is initiated into the religious community and performs his first act as an adult, the reading in the synagogue of a part of the weekly portion of the Torah. According to a tradition dating to the Talmudic period, this is to be done at the age of 13 years and a day. Today the ceremony consists of two parts, the religious rite that surrounds the reading and the social celebration that follows it, which is considered a Seudat Mitzvah, a feast in celebration of the fulfillment of a commandment. The 20th cent. has seen the introduction of the Bas, or Bat, Mitzvah, a comparable ceremony for the young female, by the Reform and Conservative groups and to a much lesser extent by the Orthodox. The exact nature of both the Bar and Bas Mitzvah ceremonies varies from community to community according to local traditions (e.g., Ashkenazic, Sephardic, Oriental).

barn, abbr. b, in physics, unit of nuclear cross section, i.e., the effective target presented by a NUCLEUS for collisions leading to nuclear reactions; it is equal to 10^{-24} square centimeters. The barn is approximately the size of the geometric cross section of an atomic nucleus; the term was coined because an effective cross section that large would present a target "as big as a barn," i.e., an easy target for nuclear bombardment. In practice, effective cross sections of nuclei for many reactions are measured in millibarns (10^{-3} barn) because, for most interactions, only a small fraction of collisions cause reactions.

Barnabas, Saint (bär'nəbəs), Christian apostle. He was a Cypriot and a relative of St. Mark; his forename was Joses (or Joseph). Barnabas was a founder of the church at Antioch and was the companion of St. Paul on his first missionary journey. Acts 4.36,37; 9.27; 11.22–30; 12.25; 13–15; 1 Cor. 9.6; Gal. 2.1,9,13; Col. 4.10. He is said to have been martyred in Cyprus. One of the oldest Christian PSEUDEPIGRAPHA is an epistle attributed to Barnabas. Feast: June 11.

barnacle, common name of the sedentary crustacean animals constituting the subclass Cirripedia. Barnacles are exclusively marine and are quite unlike any other crustacean because of the permanently attached, or sessile, mode of existence for which they are highly modified. Typical barnacles attach to the substrate by means of an exceedingly adhesive cement, produced by a cement gland, and secrete a shell, or carapace, of calcareous (limestone) plates, around themselves. Colonies of such barnacles form conspicuous encrustations on wharves, boats, pilings, and rocky shores. They range in length from under 1 in. (2.5 cm) to 30 in. (75 cm). Their shells are commonly yellow, orange, red, pink, or purple, sometimes with striped patterns. Because of their sedentary life and enclosing shells, barnacles were thought to be mollusks until 1830, when their larval stages were discovered. Much of what is known about barnacles is the result of research by Charles Darwin, who published a monumental work on the subject in the 1840s. Barnacles with a calcareous shell (order Thoracica) include the gooseneck barnacles, which are attached to the substrate by means of a stalk, or peduncle, and the acorn, or rock, barnacles, which are attached directly to the substrate. The stalk of gooseneck barnacles is simply an elongation of the attached end of the animal's body. In some gooseneck barnacles the stalk as well as the body is covered by calcareous plates; in others it is a naked leathery or horny structure. A gooseneck barnacle found in large numbers on ships and pilings is *Lepas,* which has a leathery stalk and flattened shell and looks rather like a small clam attached by its siphon. *Balanus* is an acorn barnacle commonly found on rocks; it has a thick conical shell attached at its wide base, with an opening at the top. As in many of the acorn barnacles, the plates of the surrounding carapace form an impenetrable wall, and the opening is equipped with two movable plates that can be pulled down to close off the body completely. In both gooseneck and acorn barnacles the feathery legs of the animal may sometimes be seen protruding through the carapace opening. When the animal feeds, these jointed legs, called cirri, sweep organic particles and minute planktonic organisms toward the mouth, which is located deeper inside the shell. The attached end of the animal is its anterior, or head region: the barnacle has been described as a shrimplike animal standing on its head in a limestone house and kicking food into its mouth with its feet. Barnacles lack gills; gas exchange occurs through the cirri and the body wall. Some shelled barnacles are commensal, attaching themselves to living animals, such as whales, porpoises, turtles, crustaceans, and echinoderms. The gooseneck barnacle *Conchoderma* may be found growing on the acorn barnacle *Coronula,* which grows on the skin of whales. Besides the shelled barnacles there are naked barnacles (orders Ascothoracica and Rhizocephala), which live on, and in some cases parasitize, other invertebrate animals. There are also shell-less boring barnacles (order Acrothoracica), which live inside holes that they drill in shells and corals. Although nearly all other crustaceans have separate sexes, most barnacles are HERMAPHRODITES, with cross-fertilization between adjacent individuals being the rule. Some species, however, have dwarf males, which are parasitic on female or hermaphroditic individuals. The fertilized egg develops into a free-swimming larva, called a nauplius larva, of the basic crustacean type, with paired antennae. This form then molts to become a cypris, or bivalve, larva, which eventually attaches itself to a suitable substrate by its first pair of antennae and undergoes METAMORPHOSIS into an adult. Barnacles are economically significant because they settle on ship hulls and harbor installations; the resulting encrustation of the ships greatly increases friction, diminishing speed and increasing fuel consumption. Ships are treated with plastic coating or with antifouling paints containing copper or mercury to prevent or diminish encrustation. Barnacles are classified in the phylum ARTHROPODA, class Crustacea, subclass Cirripedia.

Barnard, Christiaan Neething, 1923–, South African surgeon. The son of a Dutch Reformed minister, Barnard studied medicine at the Univ. of Cape Town (M.B. 1946, M.D. 1953), then came to the United States in 1955 to improve his surgical technique under Owen H. Wangensteen at the Univ. of Minnesota. While in Minneapolis he performed his first heart operation. Returning to Cape Town, he was appointed director of surgical research at the Groote Schuur Hospital, where he made medical history on Dec. 3, 1967, when he completed the first human heart transplant. Barnard designed artificial heart valves, wrote extensively on the subject of congenital intestinal atresia, and developed surgical procedures relating to organ transplants. See Peter Hawthorne, *The Transplanted Heart* (1968) and L. E. Leopold, *Dr. Christiaan N. Barnard, The Man With the Golden Hands* (1971).

Barnard, Edward Emerson, 1857–1923, American astronomer, b. Nashville, Tenn., grad. Vanderbilt Univ., 1887. From 1887 to 1895 he was astronomer at Lick Observatory in California, and from 1895 he was professor of practical astronomy at the Univ. of Chicago and astronomer at Yerkes Observatory. The discoverer of 16 comets, Jupiter's fifth satellite (1892), and BARNARD'S STAR (1916), he was given distinguished recognition by the Academy of Sciences of France and the Royal Astronomical Society of Great Britain. His photographs of comets, planets, nebulae, and the Milky Way are notable contributions to astronomy.

Barnard, Frederick Augustus Porter, 1809–89, American educator and mathematician, b. Sheffield, Mass., grad. Yale, 1828. After tutoring at Yale and teaching in institutions for the deaf and mute, he joined the faculty of the Univ. of Alabama, serving as professor of mathematics and natural philosophy (1837–48) and as professor of chemistry and natural philosophy (1848–54). From 1854 to 1856 he was professor of mathematics and natural philosophy at the Univ. of Mississippi. He served there as president (1856–58) and chancellor (1858–61), but resigned at the outbreak of the Civil War to return to the North. After a period of research in astronomy and after work as head of the map and chart department of the U.S. Coast Survey, he was selected to succeed Charles King as president of Columbia College (now Columbia Univ.). During his long administration (1864–89), Columbia grew from a small undergraduate college of 150 students into one of the nation's great universities, with an enrollment of 1,500. He was instrumental in expanding the curriculum, adding departments and fostering the development of the School of Mines (founded 1864; now included in the School of Engineering). He extended the elective system and advocated equal educational privileges for men and women. Barnard College, the woman's undergraduate unit of Columbia, was named for him and opened shortly after his death. Barnard was active in founding the American Association for the Advancement of Science and the National Academy of Sciences. He edited *Johnson's New Universal Cyclopaedia* (1876–78) and wrote many addresses, articles, books, and pamphlets in the fields of mathematics, physics, economics, and education. His annual reports on Columbia, outstanding discussions of the significance of current educational progress, were edited by W. F. Russell in *The Rise of a University,* Vol. I (1937). See memoirs by John Fulton (1896).

Barnard, George Grey, 1863–1938, American sculptor, b. Bellefonte, Pa. He studied engraving, then sculpture, first at the Art Institute of Chicago, then in the École des Beaux-Arts, Paris. A strong Rodin influence is evident in his early work, such as *Two Natures* (Metropolitan Mus.). In 1912 he completed several figures for the new state capitol at Harrisburg, Pa. A colossal statue of Lincoln in 1917 was the subject of heated controversy because of its rough-hewn features and slouching stance. It is now in Manchester, England, and a replica is in Cincinnati. Interested in medieval art, Barnard gathered discarded fragments of Gothic works from French villages. He established this collection near his home in Washington Heights, New York City, in a building that he called the CLOISTERS. Others of Barnard's sculptures are *The God Pan* (Columbia Univ.), *The Hewer* (Cairo, Ill.), and *Rising Woman* and *Adam and Eve* (both: Rockefeller estate, at Pocantico Hills, N.Y.). At the time of his death he was at work on the 100-ft (30-km) *Rainbow Arch,* a memorial to peace.

Barnard, Henry, 1811–1900, American educator, b. Hartford, Conn., grad. Yale, 1830. He studied law and was admitted to the bar in 1835. As a member (1837–39) of the Connecticut legislature, he originated and secured the passage in 1838 of an act to provide for the better supervision of the common schools. Horace Mann had carried through a similar reform in Massachusetts in 1837, and the two men became leaders in the movement to reform the common schools of the country. Barnard was secretary of the Connecticut board of commissioners of common schools from 1838 to 1842. He performed pioneer work in school inspection, recommendation of textbooks, organization of teachers' institutes and associations of parents and teachers, and the framing of additional legislative measures on education. He also edited the *Connecticut Common School Journal* and made valuable reports, including a survey of the existing school system. A political reversal in Connecticut in 1842 abolished his office and entire program. In 1843, Barnard was selected to survey the common school system of Rhode Island and instituted similar reforms there, as well as starting school libraries and revising examination methods. In 1849 he returned to Connecticut, where his program had been reestablished, to serve as superintendent of schools and principal of the new state normal school at New Britain. Ill health compelled his resignation in 1855. In 1858 he accepted the chancellorship of the Univ. of Wisconsin, and in two years there he did much for the state's common school system. He became president of St. John's College, Annapolis, in 1866, but resigned in 1867 to become the first U.S. commissioner of education. Barnard had long urged the establishment of a Federal agency to gather and disseminate educational information and statistics, which had been collected for the first time in the census of 1840. As commissioner he planned and organized the work of this agency and prepared extensive reports on education in this country and abroad and on school legislation. Barnard resigned in 1870. He continued the publication of the *American Journal of Education* (31 vol., 1855–81; reissued in 1902 with an additional volume dated 1882). This journal, subsidized by Barnard, included translations of many previously unavailable European educational classics. Approximately 50 of these treatises were reprinted as Barnard's "Library of Education." See his *Memoirs on Teachers and Educators* (1861, repr. 1969); R. C. Jenkins and G. C. Warner, *Henry Barnard: An Introduction* (1937); and J. S. Brubacher, ed., *Henry Barnard on Education* (1931, repr. 1965).

Barnard College: see COLUMBIA UNIV.

Barnardo, Thomas John, 1845–1905, British social reformer. Pioneering in the care of destitute children, he founded (1867) in London the East End Juvenile Mission. In 1870, with the aid of the 7th earl of Shaftesbury, he opened a boys' home, the first of his famous Dr. Barnardo Homes. These soon spread throughout Great Britain and the British possessions. There are presently over 100 homes in Britain and others in Australia and Canada. Barnardo was instrumental in securing the passage (1891) of parliamentary legislation for child welfare. See biographies by Arthur Williams (3d ed. 1966) and Gladys Williams (1966).

Barnard's star, star with the largest observed PROPER MOTION (annual angular shift in position); located in the constellation Ophiuchus; 1970 position R.A. 17^h56^m, Dec. +4°36′. The star's large proper motion, 10.28″, is due in part to the fact that it is the second-nearest star, being at a distance of 5.98 light-years. Barnard's star, discovered in 1916 by E. E. Barnard, is a faint red dwarf star of SPECTRAL CLASS M5, lying near the bottom of the main sequence in the HERTZSPRUNG-RUSSELL DIAGRAM. Its apparent MAGNITUDE is

9.5. Slight oscillations in its motion indicate that it has one or possibly two unseen companions, which would have to be planets rather than dim stars because the mass of each is small—at most equal to that of Jupiter.

Barnato, Barnett (bärnä'tō), 1852-97, South African financier, b. London. Of Jewish origin, his name originally was Barney Isaacs; he first called himself Barney Barnato when he performed as a comedian. He went to South Africa in 1873 and made a fortune by buying worked-out diamond mines in the Kimberley area and mining the abandoned blue earth. He increased his fortune by speculation in diamond and gold mines until he was maneuvered by Cecil Rhodes into merging the Kimberley interests with Rhodes's De Beers interests. He was also plunged into Cape politics and served in the Parliament there. He committed suicide. See biography by Richard Lewinsohn (tr. 1938).

Barnaul (bərnəo͞ol'), city (1970 pop. 439,000), capital of Altai Kray, SW Siberian USSR, on the Ob River. A port and major railway junction, Barnaul is in the heart of the Kulunda steppe, an agricultural area where wheat, corn, and sugar beets are grown. The city's chief industries produce cotton textiles, artificial fibers, and machinery. Barnaul was founded in 1771 as a silver-smelting center.

Barnave, Antoine Pierre Joseph Marie (äNtwän' pyĕr zhōzĕf' märē' bärnäv'), 1761-93, French revolutionary. A member of the States-General of 1789, he was a brilliant spokesman of the JACOBINS. When King Louis XVI and the queen fled in 1791, Barnave was one of those sent to bring him back from Varennes to Paris. This experience awakened royalist sympathies in Barnave and led to his correspondence with MARIE ANTOINETTE. Seeking to establish a constitutional monarchy, he broke with the Jacobins and became a leader of the FEUILLANTS. Condemned by the Revolutionary Tribunal, he was guillotined. His *Introduction à la révolution française* (in *Œuvres,* 1843) explains the Revolution as the result of the evolution of the bourgeoisie. See biography by E. D. Bradby (1915); O. G. von Heidenstam, ed., *The Letters of Marie Antoinette, Fersen, and Barnave* (1913, tr. 1926).

Barnburners, radical element of the Democratic party in New York state from 1842 to 1848, opposed to the conservative HUNKERS. The name derives from the fabled Dutchman who burned his barn to rid it of rats; by implication, the Barnburners would destroy corporations and public works to do away with the abuses they foster. Among their leaders were C. C. Cambreleng, Silas Wright, Azariah C. FLAGG, and Samuel J. TILDEN. Opposed to the extension of slavery, the Barnburners seceded from the Democratic state organization when the Hunkers captured the state convention at Syracuse in 1847. Refused recognition at the Democratic national convention of 1848, they nominated Martin VAN BUREN for President and endorsed the FREE-SOIL PARTY candidate, Charles Francis ADAMS (1807-86), for Vice President. Largely because of this Democratic split, the Whig candidate, Zachary Taylor, defeated the regular Democrat, Lewis CASS. After 1848 some Barnburners joined the Free-Soilers, who merged with the new Republican party; others returned to the Democratic party. See H. D. A. Donovan, *The Barnburners* (1925).

Barnegat Bay (bär'nəgăt), arm of the Atlantic Ocean, c.30 mi (50 km) long, E N.J., entered through Barnegat Inlet between Long Beach Island and Island Beach Peninsula. A lightship off the coast replaced the Barnegat Lighthouse in 1930.

Barnes, Albert, 1798-1870, American Presbyterian clergyman, b. Rome, N.Y. From 1830 he was pastor of the First Church in Philadelphia, mother church of the Presbyterian denomination in America. In the schism (1837-70) in Presbyterianism between the strict Calvinists and those whose views had become tinged with New England liberalism, Barnes's opinions and writings placed him with the liberal wing. His commentaries on biblical books, published as *Notes: Explanatory and Practical* (rev. ed., 6 vol., 1872), attracted wide attention.

Barnes, Barnabe, 1569?-1609, English poet. His major work is *Parthenophil and Parthenophe* (1593), a collection of sonnets, madrigals, elegies, and odes. He also wrote *A Divine Century of Spiritual Sonnets* (1595) and *The Devil's Charter* (1607), a tragedy on the life of Pope Alexander VI.

Barnes, Djuna (jo͞on'ə), 1892-, American author, b. Cornwall, N.Y. She is best known for her novel *Nightwood* (1936), which, in its sense of horror and decay, has been likened by T. S. Eliot to an Elizabethan tragedy. Barnes also wrote several one-act plays produced by the Provincetown Players in 1919-20. Her other works include *Ryder* (1928), a novel; collections of short stories and poems including *A Night Among Horses* (1929) and *Selected Works* (1962); and *The Antiphon* (1958), a tragedy in verse.

Barnes, Harry Elmer, 1889-1968, American historian and sociologist, b. Auburn, N.Y. He received his Ph.D. from Columbia in 1918 and taught economics, sociology, and history at various institutions of higher learning, notably at the New School for Social Research. His wide interests generally centered on the main themes of the development of Western thought and culture. His ability to synthesize information from various fields into an intelligible pattern showing human development profoundly affected the teaching of history. Notable among the works that show his remarkable scope are *Social History of the Western World* (1921), *Psychology and History* (1925), *History and Social Intelligence* (1926), *History of Western Civilization* (1935), *An Intellectual and Cultural History of the Western World* (with some contributions from others, 1937, 3d rev. ed. 1965), and *Social Thought from Lore to Science* (with Howard Becker, 3d ed. rev. and enl. 1961). See Arthur Goddard, ed., *Harry Elmer Barnes* (1968).

Barnes, Juliana: see BERNERS, JULIANA.

Barnes, William, 1801-86, English poet and philologist. After a career as a schoolmaster, he took holy orders in 1847. He is best known for his poems in Dorset dialect, which began to appear in local newspapers in 1833. His *Poems of Rural Life in the Dorset Dialect* were published in three series between 1844 and 1862. Besides a *Philological Grammar* (1854), he wrote other books on the English language. See his *Selected Poems* (ed. by Geoffrey Grigson, 1950); study by Giles Dugdale (1953).

Barnes, former municipal borough, SE England. See RICHMOND UPON THAMES.

Barnet, borough (1971 pop. 303,578) of Greater London, SE England. The borough was created in 1965 by the merger of the urban districts of Barnet, East Barnet, and Friern Barnet, and the municipal boroughs of Finchley and Hendon. Although mainly residential, the borough manufactures automobile and aircraft parts, electrical components, and beverages. At the battle of Barnet (1471) during the Wars of the Roses, Edward IV of the House of York defeated the Lancastrian Richard Neville, earl of Warwick. Warwick died in the fighting.

Barnett, Samuel Augustus (bär'nĕt), 1844-1913, English clergyman and social worker. As vicar of St. Jude's, Whitechapel, in the slums of London, he pioneered in the social settlement movement. Toynbee Hall, the first SETTLEMENT HOUSE, was opened in 1884 with Barnett as its first warden. He was also active in the university extension movement. In 1894 he was made a canon. His wife, **Henrietta Octavia Barnett,** 1851-1936, was especially interested in housing and helped found a model garden suburb at Hampstead. She collaborated in some of her husband's books, notably *Practicable Socialism* (1888) and wrote his biography (1918). In 1924 she was created Dame Commander of the British Empire.

Barneveldt, Johan van Olden: see OLDENBARNEVELDT, JOHAN VAN.

Barney, Joshua, 1759-1818, American naval officer and privateer, b. Baltimore. He entered the navy early in the American Revolution, engaged in many feats of daring, and was captured by the British three times; his most famous exploit was the capture (1782) of the *General Monk* in Delaware Bay. From 1796 to 1802 he served with distinction in the French navy. In the War of 1812 he engaged in large-scale privateering. In July, 1814, he was given the task of checking the British advance up Chesapeake Bay. For several weeks he slowed the drive on Washington, and when the British did disembark, he rushed with some 400 sailors to Bladensburg, where Gen. William Winder was in command. In the battle on Aug. 24, the American lines quickly broke; Barney and his men stayed behind to cover the retreat. Their gallant defense was soon broken, and Barney was wounded and captured. See biographies by W. F. Adams (1912), R. D. Paine (1924), and Hulbert Footner (1940).

Barnfield, Richard, 1574-1627, English poet. His entire output consists of three small books of poetry written before he was 25: *The Affectionate Shepherd* (1594), *Cynthia* (1595), and *The Encomion of Lady Pecunia* (1598). The lyric "As it fell upon a day" is perhaps his most notable work.

Barnsley, county borough (1971 pop. 75,330), West Riding of Yorkshire, N England. It is the railroad center of a coal region and has ironworks, linen mills, and other industries. In 1974, Barnsley became part of the new metropolitan county of South Yorkshire.

Barnstable (bärn'stəbəl), town (1970 pop. 19,842), seat of Barnstable co., SE Mass.; inc. 1639. It is a resort town on Cape Cod. Candles are produced there. Barnstable is made up of seven villages, including Hyannis. Points of interest include the home of the Revolutionary War patriot James Otis, in West Barnstable; the John F. Kennedy Memorial, in Hyannis; and several 18th-century buildings. From colonial times until the middle of the 19th cent. Barnstable had a prosperous coastal and overseas shipping trade.

Barnstaple (bärn'stəpəl), municipal borough (1971 pop. 17,342), Devonshire, SW England, on the Taw River estuary. The river is spanned there by a 16-arch stone bridge dating from the 13th cent. Barnstaple is the chief marketing town of North Devon and a tourist center. Gloves, pottery, bricks, tiles, furniture, and lace are manufactured. Barnstaple once carried on a large woolen export trade with the American colonies. John Gay, famous for *The Beggar's Opera,* was born in Barnstaple.

Barnum, Phineas Taylor, 1810-91, American showman, b. Bethel, Conn. As a youth Barnum worked at diverse sales jobs and managed a boarding house. He made his first sensation in 1835 when he bought and exhibited Joice Heth, a slave who claimed she was 161 years old (she was about 80) and had been the nurse of George Washington. In 1842 he opened the American Museum in New York City and immediately became famous for his extravagant advertising and his exhibits of freaks. Among his great attractions were the Fiji Mermaid (formed by joining the upper half of a monkey to the stuffed lower half of a fish), "General TOM THUMB," who was viewed by over 20 million people, and the original Siamese Twins, Chang and Eng. In 1850, Barnum managed the American tour of the Swedish singer Jenny LIND and, with his talent for publicity, made it a huge financial success for her and for himself. In 1855 he retired from show business; he served as mayor of Bridgeport, Conn., and in the Connecticut legislature. Driven into bankruptcy by unwise business ventures, he reopened the American Museum and then organized his famous circus, "The Greatest Show on Earth," which opened in Brooklyn, N.Y., in 1871. In 1881 he merged with his most successful competitor, James A. Bailey, and under the name Barnum and Bailey the circus continued for a generation after Barnum's death. The stellar attraction of the circus was Jumbo, the 6½-ton African elephant that Barnum purchased from the London Zoo despite the furious protests of English elephant fanciers, including Queen Victoria. The elephant was stuffed and is on exhibit at the Barnum Museum of Natural History (est. 1883 at Tufts Univ. in honor of Barnum, who was one of its trustees). His autobiography was published in 1855 and went through many editions. He also wrote *Humbugs of the World* (1865), *Struggles and Triumphs* (1869), and *Money Getting* (1883). See his autobiography, ed. by W. R. Browne (1927, repr. 1961); biographies by Raymund Fitzsimons (1970) and Neil Harris (1973).

Barocchio, Giacomo: see VIGNOLA, GIACOMO DA.

Barocci or **Baroccio, Federigo** (fādārē'gō bärôt'chē,-chō), c.1530-1612, Italian painter, b. Urbino, where he was continually employed throughout his life. In the 1550s he traveled to Rome and was influenced by the art of Raphael, Michelangelo, and Taddeo Zuccaro. His mature works reflect baroque tendencies. Noted for his skill as a portraitist, he also executed a small number of important engravings. Among his more notable achievements are *Saint Sebastian* (c.1557; cathedral, Urbino), frescoes (1561-63) in the Vatican, and *The Last Supper* (1592-99; Santa Maria sopra Minerva, Rome). A large collection of his drawings is in the Uffizi. See monograph by Harald Olsen (repr., 1962).

Baroda (bərō'də), former native state, now incorporated in Gujarat state, W central India. It is a prosperous area on a fertile alluvial plain. Its chief city, **Baroda** (1971 pop. 467,422), a district administrative center on the Vishvamitri River, has cotton-textile, chemical, and metal industries; an oil refinery; and a fertilizer plant. There are several colleges.

barograph, instrument used to make a continuous recording of atmospheric pressure. The pressure-sensitive element, a partially evacuated metal cylinder, is linked to a pen arm in such a way that the vertical displacement of the pen is proportional to the changes in the atmospheric pressure. The pen traces a record of pressure versus time on a chart, which is mounted on a drum rotated by a clockwork. Each chart usually provides one week's record. See BAROMETER.

Baroja y Nessi, Pío (pē'ō bärō'hä ē näs'sē), 1879–1956, Spanish novelist from the Basque Provinces, member of the group of writers known as the GENERATION OF '98. He left medicine to devote himself to literature and came to be the most popular Spanish novelist of the 20th cent. Of his several trilogies, the most widely read abroad concerns the underworld of Madrid—*La lucha por la vida* [the struggle for existence] (1904), comprising *La busca* (tr. *The Quest,* 1922), *Mala hierba* (tr. *Weeds,* 1923), and *Aurora roja* (tr. *Red Dawn,* 1924). The longest cycle (22 vol.) has a historical background and is known as *Memórias de un hombre de acción* [memoirs of a man of action]. Baroja's novels are forceful though loosely constructed, characterized by a spare yet lyrical style and an undercurrent of social discontent.

barometer (bərŏm'ətər), instrument for measuring atmospheric pressure. It was invented in 1643 by the Italian scientist Evangelista Torricelli, who used a column of water in a tube 34 ft (10.4 m) long. This inconvenient water column was soon replaced by

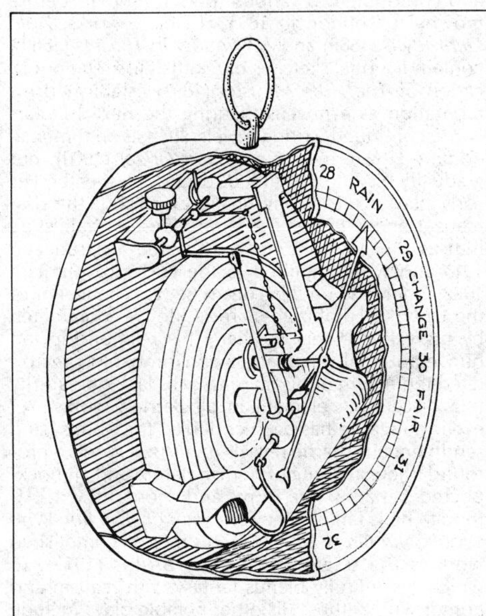

Aneroid barometer

mercury, which is denser than water and requires a tube about 3 ft (0.9 m) long. The mercurial barometer consists of a glass tube, sealed at one end and filled with pure mercury. After being heated to expel the air, it is inverted in a small cup of mercury called the cistern. The mercury in the tube sinks slightly, creating above it a vacuum (the Torricellian vacuum). Atmospheric pressure on the surface of the mercury in the cistern supports the column in the tube, which varies in height with variations in atmospheric pressure and hence with changes in elevation, generally decreasing with increases in height above sea level. Standard sea-level pressure is 14.7 lb per sq in. (1,030 grams per sq cm), which is equivalent to a column of mercury 29.92 in. (760 mm) in height; the decrease with elevation is approximately 1 in. (2.5 cm) for every 900 ft (270 m) of ascent. In WEATHER forecasting, barometric readings are plotted on base maps so that analyses of weather-producing pressure systems can be made. At a given location a storm is generally anticipated when the barometer is falling rapidly; when the barometer is rising, fair weather may usually be expected. The aneroid barometer is a metallic box so made that when the air has been partially removed from the box the surface depresses or expands with variation of air pressure on it; this motion is transmitted by a train of levers to a pointer which shows the pressure on a graduated scale. A BAROGRAPH is a self-recording aneroid barometer in which a pen traces a continuous pressure record on a cylindrical chart which revolves by clockwork. An ALTIMETER, an instrument for measuring altitude, is often an aneroid barometer calibrated to indicate altitude.

Baron or **Boyron, Michel** (mēshĕl' bärôN' or bwärôN'), 1653–1729, one of the first great French actors. A protégé of Molière, he acted at the Hôtel de Bourgogne and at the Comédie Française. He brought a naturalness to the bombastic acting style established by Montfleury. In 1691 he retired at the height of his power only to return (1720) in perfect form to act with Adrienne LECOUVREUR. He wrote several plays, of which *L'Homme à bonnes fortunes* (1686) was the most popular.

Baron, Salo Wittmayer (sä'lō vĭt'mīər bärôn'), 1895–, Jewish historian and educator, b. Galicia. He was taken as a child to Vienna, where he later studied at the university, earning doctorates in philosophy (1917), political science (1922), and law (1923), and where he was ordained at the Jewish Theological Seminary (1920). He taught history at the Jewish Teachers College in Vienna (1919–26) before going to the United States to teach at the Jewish Institute of Religion (1927–30). From 1930 to 1963 he taught at Columbia, holding the first professorship of Jewish history in an American university. Among his works are *The Jewish Community* (3 vol., 1942), *Modern Nationalism and Religion* (1947), and *Jews of the United States, 1790–1840: A Documentary History* (ed. with J. L. Blau, 3 vol., 1963). In his monumental and as yet uncompleted *A Social and Religious History of the Jews* (Vol. I–XV, 2d ed., 1952–73), Baron stresses the social history of the Jewish people in the wider context of world history rather than their history as seen through the lives of its most prominent figures.

Baronius, Caesar (bərō'nēəs), 1538–1607, Italian ecclesiastical historian, cardinal of the Roman Catholic Church. He went to Rome c.1557 and soon came under the tutelage of St. PHILIP NERI. His chief work is *Annales ecclesiastici a Christi nato ad annum 1198* [ecclesiastical annals from the Nativity to 1198]. It is erudite and complete, revealing the author as a remarkably honest scholar; although it was directed against the Protestant arguments, Protestants as well as Catholics concede that Baronius never suppressed a fact. He was a strong defender of the Holy See. He was largely responsible for the Roman martyrology. Baronius became superior of the Oratory (1593) on St. Philip Neri's death, cardinal (1596), and librarian of the Vatican; he was confessor to Pope Clement VIII. It is said that only the hostility of the Spanish, aroused when Baronius questioned the authenticity of their claims to Sicily, prevented Baronius from becoming pope.

Barons' War, in English history, war of 1263–67 between King HENRY III and his barons. In 1261, Henry III renounced the PROVISIONS OF OXFORD (1258) and the Provisions of Westminster (1259), which had vested considerable power in a council of barons, and reasserted his right to appoint councilors. The barons led by Simon de MONTFORT, earl of Leicester, finally resorted to arms in 1263 and forced the king to reaffirm his adherence to the Provisions. In 1264 a decision in favor of the crown by Louis IX of France as arbitrator led to a renewal of war, but Montfort defeated Henry's forces in the battle of Lewes, and the king once again submitted to government by council. Early in 1265, Montfort summoned his famous representative PARLIAMENT to strengthen his position, which was threatened by the possibility of an invasion by Henry's adherents abroad. The invasion did not take place, but an uprising against Montfort of the Welsh "Marchers" (Englishmen along the Welsh border) led to his defeat by the king's son (later EDWARD I) at Evesham. Montfort was killed in the battle, but some baronial resistance continued until 1267. The barons had failed to establish their own control over the crown, but they had helped prepare the way for the constitutional developments of the reign of Edward I. See R. F. Treharne, *The Baronial Plan of Reform* (1932, repr. 1972); F. M. Powicke, *King Henry III and the Lord Edward* (1947).

baroque (bərōk'), in art and architecture, style developed in Europe, England, and Latin America during the 17th and early 18th cent. Although the restrained and classical works created by most French and English artists look very different from the exuberant style favored elsewhere, both trends share to varying degrees certain characteristics. Essential among these is an emphasis on unity, a balance achieved among diverse parts. Through the technical brilliance of its artists, the baroque revealed a remarkable harmony of media wherein architecture took on the fluid, plastic aspects of sculpture and both buildings and sculpture employed the CHIAROSCURO effects of painting. During the baroque there was also in art an extraordinary emphasis on grand scale or the superhuman quality of massive figures. Works of the baroque age engage the beholder in physical and emotional participation. In painting and sculpture this was achieved by means of highly developed ILLUSIONISM. This device served to enhance an unequaled sense of drama, energy, and movement of forms. These characteristics are clearly embodied in the works of three of the giants of the baroque, Pietro da Cortona, Bernini, and Rubens. In architecture the interest in size, impressiveness, and the overwhelming ordering of a dignified environment is most clearly seen at Versailles or in Bernini's elliptical piazza in front of St. Peter's in Rome. Sweeping and multiple rhythms abound in the art of Italy, Germany, Austria, Spain, and Latin America. Buildings of the period are composed of great curving forms with undulating facades or ground plans of unprecedented complexity, as in the churches of Borromini and Wren. Some are created with intricate views through layers of architecture and alternations of light and shade, as in the buildings of Guarini and Hardouin-Mansart. The movement of water was exploited, and fountains, hitherto thin streams, became exciting forms, issuing forth joyous geysers and cascades. The effects of deep space interested many artists including Ruisdael, Guercino, Baciccia, Pozzo, and Claude Lorrain. In their paintings space is deepened in interior scenes by representing long files of rooms, with extended views outside through open doors or windows, as in the works of Velázquez and de Hooch. Dramatic effects are achieved both with highly contrasting areas of light and shadow in the works of Caravaggio, Zurbarán, Georges de la Tour, and Rembrandt and with masses defined by color in either the clear calm tones of Vermeer and Philippe de Champaigne or the warm and shimmering colors of Rubens, Claude Lorrain, and Pietro da Cortona. In no other period is light so important for suggesting supernatural illusions in painting and sculpture. Light effects are exploited in architecture to heighten sculptural qualities, most conspicuously in Venetian churches and in buildings in Spain and Portugal and their colonies. Baroque sculptors felt free to combine different materials within a single work and often used one material to simulate another. Bernini's St. Theresa succumbs on a dull-finished marble cloud in an alabaster and marble niche in which bronze rays descend from a hidden source of light. Many figures of the mourning Virgin in Spain and Latin America cry glass tears. A fascination with emotional states permeates baroque art. The Carracci, Poussin, and Georges de la Tour portrayed restrained feeling, in accordance with the academic principles of dignity and decorum; after 1625, others, including Bernini, Puget, Rembrandt, Montañes, and Cano, depicted religious ecstasy, anguish, or individual psychology. Although history painting, allegories, and portraits were still considered the most noble subjects, landscape painting was practiced by Annibale Carracci, Ruisdael, Hobbema, Rembrandt, Claude Lorrain, and Rosa. Genre scenes and still life became the major preoccupation of van Laer, Steen, de Hooch, Terborch, Vermeer, and the Le Nain family. Caravaggio and his early followers are especially significant for their naturalistic treatment of unidealized, ordinary people. For convenience the baroque period is divided into three parts.

Early Baroque, c.1590–c.1625. The early style was preeminent in Rome where the Carracci and Caravaggio diverged decisively from the preceding late-mannerist artificialities. The Carracci painted heroic figures, modeled from nature and classical antiquity. Caravaggio's dramatic narratives were implemented by a forceful, economic style, remarkable for the use of chiaroscuro. The Carracci school anticipated the opulent excitement of works by Lanfranco and Guercino as well as the markedly classical works of Domenichino and Reni. Caravaggio's followers, including Ribera, Terbrugghen, and Vouet, spread interest in realism and dramatic light throughout Europe. Rubens's early work reveals profound Italian influence. Bernini's early mannerism opened out to express a new vigor, freeing him to render with stunning precision realistic details and textures.

High Baroque, c.1625–c.1660. Italian art was dominated by Bernini, Borromini, and Pietro da Cortona, exemplifying the exuberant trends, while Poussin, Claude Lorrain, Sacchi, and Duquesnoy represented the classicist trends. This period produced an astonishing number and variety of artists of the first rank, including Rembrandt, Rubens, Velázquez, Vermeer, Hals, Van Dyck, Ruisdael, and Zurbarán.

Late Baroque, c.1660–c.1725. In Italy and Spain after c.1660, sculptors and painters, e.g., Murillo and Preti, used lighter, softer colors and replaced the clearly organized forms and volumes of the high baroque with flickering patterns and figures. Italy lost its position of artistic dominance to France, and gradually the massive forms of the baroque yielded to the lighter, more graceful outlines of the ROCOCO. See articles about individual artists, e.g., BERNINI. See Rudolf Wittkower, *Art and Architecture in Italy, 1600–1750* (1958); Sir Anthony Blunt, *Art and Architecture in France, 1500–1700* (1953); J. W. P. Bourke, *Baroque Churches of Central Europe* (1962); E. Hempel, *Baroque Art and Architecture in Central Europe* (1965); H. Busch and B. Lohse, ed., *Baroque Sculpture* (tr. 1965); M. Kitson, *The Age of the Baroque* (1966); S. Sitwell, *Baroque and Rococo* (1967); G. Bazin, *The Baroque* (1968); C. Ripa, *Baroque and Rococo Pictorial Imagery* (1758–60, tr. 1971).

baroque, in music, a style that prevailed from the last decades of the 16th cent. to the first decades of the 18th cent. Its beginnings were in the late 16th-century revolt against POLYPHONY that gave rise to the accompanied RECITATIVE and to OPERA. With opera and recitative came the FIGURED BASS, used consistently in ensemble music throughout the baroque era. Renaissance polyphony persisted, however, being called the *stile antico* and considered more appropriate to the church than the *nuove musiche.* The baroque period was thus one of stylistic duality; it was an era that displayed emotional extremes (see ROMANTICISM). By the end of the era major and minor TONALITY had replaced the church MODES. Contrapuntal writing was resumed in the middle baroque period, but it now had a harmonic basis. Idiomatic writing, taking account of the individual character and capacities of instruments and voices, was characteristic of baroque music. Originating in Italy, opera, ORATORIO, and CANTATA were the principal vocal forms. In instrumental music the SONATA, CONCERTO, and OVERTURE were creations of the baroque. In France and Italy the baroque had by 1725 been overshadowed by its outgrowth, the ROCOCO, and it remained for Germany, where the baroque saw the flowering of Protestant church music, to bring the era to culmination in the works of J. S. BACH. The FUGUE, chorale prelude, and TOCCATA were important forms of the late baroque. See M. F. Bukofzer, *Music in the Baroque Era* (1947); Friedrich Blume, *Renaissance and Baroque Music* (1967); C. V. Palisca, *Baroque Music* (1968); Robert Donington, *A Performer's Guide to Baroque Music* (1974).

Barotseland, Zambia: see WESTERN PROVINCE.

Barozzi, Giacomo: see VIGNOLA, GIACOMO DA.

barque: see BARK.

Barquisimeto (bärkēsēmä'tō), city (1970 est. pop. 291,000), capital of Lara state, NW Venezuela, on the PAN AMERICAN HIGHWAY. Surrounded by good grazing country, the city is a commercial center that ships cattle, coffee, cacao, sugar, and sisal. There are industries producing cigarettes, rope, foodstuffs, and lumber. Founded in 1552, the city was the site of the surrender and execution (1561) of the Spanish rebel and adventurer Lope de AGUIRRE. Barquisimeto was rebuilt after an earthquake in 1812.

Barr, Alfred Hamilton, Jr., 1902–, American art historian, b. Detroit. Barr taught art history at several colleges and since 1929 has been associated with the Museum of Modern Art, New York City. He organized more than 100 museum exhibitions and wrote a number of standard art history texts. These include *Cubism and Abstract Art* (1936); *Picasso: Fifty Years of His Art* (1946); *Matisse: His Art and His Public* (1951).

Barrackpur (băr'əkpôr), town (1971 pop. 97,169), West Bengal state, NE India, on the Hooghly River. The town is a military station. Fifteen miles (24 km) from Calcutta, it was formerly the suburban residence of the British viceroys of India. There is a well-known park. Bengali troops in Barrackpur mutinied in 1824 when ordered to participate in the Burmese War. The INDIAN MUTINY of 1857 also began there.

barracuda, slender, elongated fish of tropical seas. Barracudas have long snouts and projecting lower jaws armed with large, sharp-edged teeth. They are ferocious, striking at anything that gleams, and are considered excellent game fishes. The largest of the group, the great barracuda, averages 5 ft (1.5 m) in length but may reach 10 ft (3 m); it is dangerous to swimmers wearing shiny objects. Other species are the Pacific barracuda (4 ft/1.2 m long) and the smaller Northern barracuda, which is not dangerous. Barracudas are classified in the phylum CHORDATA, subphylum Vertebrata, class Osteichthyes, order Sphyraenoidei, family Sphyraenidae.

Barranquilla (bärängkē'yä), city (1971 est. pop. 656,100), Atlántico dept., N Colombia, on the Magdalena River, 8 mi (12.9 km) from the Caribbean Sea. Colombia's chief port, it also has shipbuilding, textile, glass, perfume, beer, sugar, publishing, and other industries. Founded in 1629, Barranquilla was a sleepy tropical town until the middle of the 19th cent., when steamboats began navigating the river and a port was built. The port was enlarged in the 1920s, and the city gradually surpassed its old rival, CARTAGENA. Barranquilla's carnivals attract many tourists.

Barras, Paul François Jean Nicolas, vicomte de (pōl fräNswä' zhäN nēkōlä', vēkôNt' də bärä'), 1755–1829, French revolutionary. Although of a noble family, he joined the JACOBINS in the Revolution and was a member of the Convention, the revolutionary national assembly. He participated in the reprisals against counterrevolutionaries in Toulon after the recapture of the city from the British (1793). Having turned against the revolutionary dictator Maximilien ROBESPIERRE, Barras was a leader of the coup d'etat against him on 9 THERMIDOR (July 27, 1794). As commander of Paris, he suppressed a royalist uprising on 13 VENDÉMIAIRE (Oct. 5, 1795) by turning the troops over to a young officer, Napoleon Bonaparte. Subsequently, Barras became (1795) a member of the DIRECTORY. He was notorious for his corruption, ostentation, and immorality. During Napoleon's coup d'etat of 18 BRUMAIRE (Nov. 9, 1799), Barras consented to resign from the Directory, thus contributing to Napoleon's success. After the coup, he lost prominence.

Barrault, Jean-Louis (zhäN-lwē bärō'), 1910–, French actor and director. Barrault was a pupil of Dullin in 1930, and from 1940 to 1947 he worked with the Comédie Française. After World War II he organized his own company at the Théâtre Marigny, presenting many outstanding plays and making many successful tours abroad. He is best remembered as Hamlet in the translation by André Gide and as the mime in the film *Children of Paradise* (1944). Barrault wrote *Reflections on the Theatre* (tr. 1951) and *The Theatre of Jean-Louis Barrault* (tr. 1961).

Barré, Isaac (bâr'ē), 1726–1802, British soldier and politician. He served under Gen. James Wolfe in the French and Indian War and was wounded at Quebec (1759). Entering Parliament in 1761, he was adjutant general and governor of Stirling (1763–64), vice treasurer of Ireland (1764–68), treasurer of the navy in the 2d Rockingham ministry (1782), and paymaster general under Lord Shelburne (1782–83). He was less effective in office than as an opposition orator in Parliament. He constantly condemned the taxing and repression of the American colonists. His advocacy of their cause is commemorated in the names of Barre, Mass., and Wilkes-Barre, Pa., the latter named also for John Wilkes, another supporter of the Americans.

Barre (bă'rē), city (1970 pop. 10,209), Washington co., central Vt., SE of Montpelier; settled late 18th cent., inc. 1894. Granite quarrying, which began in the region in the early 19th cent., is still the largest industry.

Barre des Ecrins (bär dāzākrăN'), peak, 13,461 ft (4,103 m) high, in the Pelvoux group, SE France, tallest of the Dauphiné Alps.

barrel: see ENGLISH UNITS OF MEASUREMENT.

barrel organ, mechanical musical instrument requiring nothing but the regular rotary motion of a handle to keep it going. It probably originated at the beginning of the 18th cent., and was once used extensively in English churches. A revolving cylinder is fitted with pegs that open valves, permitting air to enter a set of organ pipes. Some larger ones have several sets of pipes and various couplers. They can be operated by clockwork, by weights, and by electric motors. A portable type of barrel organ whose cylinder is turned by a hand crank has been mistakenly called HURDY-GURDY, from which it is fundamentally different.

Barrère, Georges (zhôrzh bärĕr'), 1876–1944, French-American flutist and conductor, grad. Paris Conservatory, 1895. In Paris he was solo flutist (1897–1905) of the Colonne Concerts and the Paris Opera, and he taught at the Schola Cantorum. He was solo flutist (1905–28) of the New York Symphony Orchestra. He joined the faculty of the Institute of Musical Art in 1905 and of the Juilliard School of Music in 1930. The Barrère Ensemble, which he founded in 1910, was expanded (1914) into the Barrère Little Symphony. His virtuosity increased the importance of the flute as a solo instrument.

Barrès, Maurice (mōrēs' bärĕs'), 1862–1923, French novelist and nationalist politician. As an advocate of the supremacy of the individual self, he wrote the trilogy of novels *Le Culte du moi* (1888–91). Finding that cultivation of the ego called for action as well as analysis, Barrès turned to a nationalism that grew into vengeful hatred of Germany, fanned by strong racist feeling and by love for his native Lorraine. The trilogy *Le Roman de l'énergie nationale* (1897–1902) embodied his nationalistic views. *The Sacred Hill* (1913, tr. 1929) is a symbolic story showing Catholicism as a bar to nationalism. After World War I, Barrès remained a patriotic extremist. His reputation as a literary artist rests on his graceful, lyrical prose and his powers of analysis and description.

Barrett, Elizabeth: see BROWNING, ELIZABETH.

Barrett, Lawrence, 1838–91, American actor, b. Paterson, N.J. An excellent romantic actor, he is best remembered for his portrayal of Cassius to the Brutus of Edwin Booth. Barrett made his New York debut (1856) in *The Hunchback* and appeared (1858–59) with the Boston Museum Company. He was associated with Booth from 1866 to 1889. A dignified actor, tall, with classic features, Barrett excelled in Shakespeare. He wrote a biography of Edwin Forrest (1881). See biography by A. E. Barron (1889).

Barrie, Sir James Matthew, 1860–1937, Scottish playwright and novelist. He is best remembered for his play *Peter Pan,* a supernatural fantasy about a boy who refused to grow up. The son of a weaver, Barrie studied at the Univ. of Edinburgh. He took up journalism, worked for a Nottingham newspaper, and contributed to various London journals before moving to London in 1885. His early works, *Auld Licht Idylls* (1889) and *A Window in Thrums* (1889), contain fictional sketches of Scottish life. The publication of *The Little Minister* (1891) established his reputation as a novelist. During the next 10 years Barrie continued writing novels, such as *Sentimental Tommy* (1896) and *Tommy and Grizel* (1900), but gradually his interest turned toward the theater. His early plays were mostly unsuccessful, but the dramatization in 1897 of *The Little Minister* established him as a playwright. He was created a baronet in 1913 and was appointed to the Order of Merit in 1922. From 1930 until his death he was chancellor of the Univ. of Edinburgh. Barrie's life was dominated by his extraordinary mother. This relationship left him emotionally immature and probably precipitated the failure of his marriage. His lack of maturity is a discernible element in all Barrie's works. Yet even though he has been criticized for whimsy and sentimentality, Barrie reveals in his best works a profound understanding of human nature and an unexpected capacity for irony and mordant wit. Although he is famous for *Peter Pan; or, The Boy Who Would Not Grow Up* (1904), his most accomplished work is the tragicomedy *Dear Brutus* (1917), in which he skillfully blends fantasy with realism and humor with pathos. His other notable plays include *Quality Street* (1901), *The Admirable Crichton* (1902), *What Every Woman Knows* (1908), and the one-act *The Twelve-Pound Look* (1911). Barrie's collected plays were published in 1928. See his letters (ed. by Viola Meynell, 1947); biographies by Janet Dunbar (1970), Denis Mackail (1941, repr. 1972), and Lady Cynthia Asquith (1955, repr. 1972).

Barrie, city (1971 pop. 27,676), S Ont., Canada, on the west shore of Lake Simcoe. The city is in a mixed farming and dairying district. Leather goods, packaged meats, electrical appliances, and other goods are made. A large military base is nearby.

Barrientos Ortuño, René (rānā' bär-ryān'tōs ōrtōō'nyō), 1919–69, Bolivian political leader. Commander of the Bolivian air force, he supported the National Revolutionary Movement (MNR), the majority political party, and was elected vice president in 1964 on the MNR ticket. He soon broke with President Paz, however, and, after joining other army officers in a coup (Nov., 1964), was installed as head of a military junta. In May, 1965, Alfredo Ovando Candia joined him as copresident, but Barrientos became sole president after winning the July, 1966, elections. He launched a moderate (albeit military) administration, retaining the reforms instituted by his predecessors. He was killed in a helicopter crash and was succeeded by Vice President Luis Adolfo Siles Salinas.

Barrington, George, 1755–c.1804, notorious English pickpocket, b. Ireland. His family name was Waldron. Arriving in London in 1773, he became a professional pickpocket and, obtaining introductions in society, robbed many wealthy persons. After serving several jail terms, he was sentenced in 1790 to seven years' transportation to Australia. For his aid in suppressing a mutiny aboard the transport ship, he was released in 1792 and later became superintendent of convicts. He is supposed to have written *A Voyage to Botany Bay* (1801) and a history of New South Wales (1802).

Barrington, town (1970 pop. 17,554), Bristol co., E R.I., on the Barrington River; settled c.1670, included in Massachusetts until 1746, inc. 1770. It is a residential and resort area. Barrington College is in the town.

Barrios, Eduardo (āthwär'thō bär'yōs), 1884-1963, Chilean novelist, short-story writer, and playwright. He was director of libraries and minister of education in Chile. As a writer he was interested in the inner workings of his characters, especially the unstable or abnormal, whom he analyzed with sympathy. His works include *El niño que se enloqueció de amor* [the child who went mad because of love] (1915) and *Gran señor y rajadiablos* [big operator and hellraiser] (1948). See study by N. J. Davison (1970).

Barrios, Justo Rufino (hōō'stō rōōfē'nō bär'yōs), c.1835-1885, president of Guatemala (1873-85). He took part in the successful revolution of 1871 and was elected to office by the liberals. He imposed reforms on the country: the religious orders were suppressed and Roman Catholic schools and universities were replaced by secular institutions. Barrios dreamed of reestablishing the Central American Federation and, failing in his attempts to bring about the union by constitutional means, he resorted to dictatorial methods and brute force. He was killed in a battle with the Salvadorean army.

barrister: see ATTORNEY.

Barron, Clarence Walker, 1855-1928, American financial editor, b. Boston. He worked on the Boston *Daily News,* then on the *Evening Transcript,* and in 1887 founded the Boston News Bureau, to supply financial news to brokers. In 1897 he founded the Philadelphia News Bureau and in 1901 became publisher of the *Wall Street Journal. Barron's Financial Weekly* was founded by him in 1921. His notes of conversations with leading financiers, edited by Arthur Pound and S. T. Moore, are published as *They Told Barron* (1930) and *More They Told Barron* (1931).

Barron, James, 1769-1851, U.S. naval officer, b. Hampton, Va. Of a seafaring family, he served in the Virginia navy in the Revolution, entered the U.S. navy as a lieutenant in 1798, and held commands in the Mediterranean at the time of the Tripolitan War. Promoted to commodore in 1807, he had just left Norfolk, Va., when his flagship, the CHESAPEAKE, was halted and then bombarded by the British warship *Leopard* on June 22, 1807. The incident, notable in the troubles over the right of the British to search American vessels, aroused American anger. Barron was court-martialed, found guilty of "neglecting, on the probability of an engagement, to clear his ship for action" and suspended (1808) from duty for five years. Later, embittered and convinced (perhaps with justice) that Stephen DECATUR was barring his return to honorable standing in the navy, Barron challenged him to a duel, in which Decatur was mortally wounded (March 22, 1820). Though reinstated to duty (1821) Barron never regained his earlier status. He retired in 1848. See biography by W. O. Stevens (1969).

Barros, João de (zhwouN dĭ bä'rōōsh), 1496-1570, Portuguese historian. Of noble family, he early entered the service of the prince who became King John III. The most important office he held (1533-67) was that of factor, or crown administrator, for Guinea and the Indies. His position gave him access to the documents of the Portuguese Empire in Asia and Africa and to the military and colonial officials that staffed it; he used this knowledge to produce his brilliantly written *Décadas da Ásia* (4 vol., 1552-53, 1563, 1615), a stirring narrative of the building of the Portuguese Empire.

Barrot, Camille Hyacinthe Odilon (kämē'yə yäsăNt' ōdēlôN' bärō'), 1791-1873, French political leader. An opponent of the Bourbon restoration, he aided the JULY REVOLUTION (1830), but he was disappointed in the bourgeois monarchy of Louis Philippe. He became a leader of the opposition to the July Monarchy and participated in banquets and other devices used to spread propaganda against the conservative government. He was a moderate in the February Revolution of 1848, which deposed Louis Philippe and established a republic. During the presidency of Louis Napoleon (later Emperor Napoleon III), he briefly headed (1849) the cabinet but was dismissed when Louis Napoleon replaced his legislative advisers with a personal cabinet. Under the Third Republic he was (1872-73) president of the council of state. Some of his writings were collected as *Mémoires posthumes* (4 vol., 1875-76).

Barrow, Errol, 1920-, prime minister of Barbados (1961-). After serving as a British Royal Air Force pilot and navigator (1940-47), he obtained (1949) a law degree in London, returned to Barbados, and entered politics. He was named finance minister in 1959 and became prime minister in 1961. His position in power was confirmed in elections in 1966 and again in 1971. As prime minister, he led his country to independence within the British Commonwealth (1966). He encouraged foreign investment, promoted agricultural diversification and industrial development, and furthered tourism. He also advocated close ties with other Caribbean nations.

Barrow, Isaac, 1630-77, English mathematician and theologian. His method of finding tangents prefigured the differential calculus developed by Isaac Newton. He was professor of mathematics at Cambridge from 1663 to 1669 and was succeeded by Newton. Barrow became master of Trinity College in 1672 and vice chancellor of Cambridge in 1675. His theological works were edited by Alexander Napier (1859) and his mathematical works by William Whewell (1860).

Barrow, Sir John, 1764-1848, British geographer, promoter of arctic exploration. His early travels as secretary to Earl Macartney (who was ambassador to China and governor of the Cape of Good Hope colony) were recorded in *Travels in China* (1804) and *Travels into . . . Southern Africa* (1806). As second secretary of the admiralty (1804-6, 1807-48), he promoted numerous voyages to further knowledge of geography and navigation. He instigated many arctic expeditions, notably those of John Ross and William Parry. He was a principal founder of the Royal Geographical Society in 1830. Point Barrow, Cape Barrow, and Barrow Strait were named in his honor. He wrote *Voyages of Discovery and Research in the Arctic Regions* (1846). See his autobiography (1847); biography by Christopher Lloyd (1970).

Barrow, city (1970 pop. 2,104), N Alaska; inc. 1958. It is the main trade center of N Alaska, and its population is predominantly Eskimo. Hunting of whales and polar bears, basketry, carving in ivory and bone, and the production of mukluks (sealskin or reindeer-skin boots worn by Eskimos) are important. The U.S. Bureau of Indian Affairs runs a school in Barrow. A U.S. navy arctic research laboratory is in the city, and a U.S. air force installation, part of the Distant Early Warning Line, is nearby. Points of interest in the area include the Will Rogers-Wiley Post monument and Birnirk, the site of an ancient Eskimo cultural and trade center.

Barrow, river, c.120 mi (190 km) long, rising in the Slieve Bloom mts., Co. Laoighis, central Republic of Ireland. It flows east to the Co. Kildare line, then south along the borders of several counties, past Athay (the head of navigation), Carlow, and New Ross, to Waterford Harbour. It receives the Nore and the Suir rivers.

barrow, in archaeology, a burial mound. Earth and stone or timber are the usual construction materials; in parts of SE Asia stone and brick have entirely replaced earth. A barrow built primarily of stone is often called a CAIRN. Barrows occur in many parts of the world; they were built during the Neolithic period in Western Europe and in recent times in Buddhist countries. In European prehistory the characteristic barrows are either long or round. The long ones are from the Neolithic period and often contain several burial chambers. They may have been intended to simulate cave burials. The stone chambers were placed at one end of the mound and were approached by a passage, sometimes over 300 ft (90 m) in length. Round barrows, usually dating from the Bronze Age, normally contain a single burial. The round barrow was commonly bell shaped; another type had a low central mound that invariably contained cremated remains and was surrounded by a walled ditch or a circle of standing stones, usually about 150 ft (50 m) in diameter. Barrow building in Europe continued until the Christian era. Roman, Saxon, and Viking barrows are known, though such burials were apparently reserved for important personages. The erection of mounds over burials has been widespread (see TOMB). The round barrow or STUPA of Asia is usually a shrine for relics of Buddha. See MEGALITHIC MONUMENTS and MOUND BUILDERS.

Barrow-in-Furness (-fûr'nĭs), county borough (1971 pop. 63,998), Lancashire, NW England, on the tip of the Furness peninsula. The borough includes four adjacent islands. The port of Barrow has c.300 acres (120 hectares) of docks, and shipbuilding is the largest single industry. Barrow is also one of the principal engineering cities of Britain. There are immense steelworks, diesel-engine factories, armaments plants, smelting works, sawmills, and flour and paper mills. Deposits of iron ore, discovered in the late 19th cent. and responsible for the city's growth, are now much depleted. The ruins of the medieval Furness Abbey, England's second-largest abbey, are nearby. In 1974, Barrow-in-Furness became part of the new nonmetropolitan county of Cumbria.

Barrows, Samuel June, 1845-1909, American clergyman and reformer, b. New York City. He was a pastor in Dorchester, Mass., and later edited (1880-96) the *Christian Register,* a Unitarian weekly. In 1895 he was appointed by President Cleveland to represent the United States on the International Prison Commission. The following year he was elected to Congress, where he worked for prison and civil service reform. Especially interested in obtaining better treatment of prisoners, he helped draft and secure passage of New York state's first probation law (1901). He wrote many reports and articles and several books. See biography by his wife, Isabel C. Barrows, *A Sunny Life* (1913).

Barry, Sir Charles, 1795-1860, English architect. A leader in the revival of the Renaissance style of architecture, he designed the Travellers Club and the Reform Club in London. He planned one of the most important works of the period, the Houses of Parliament (1840-65). In this project he designed a basically classical structure with neo-Gothic detail contributed largely by his assistant, A. W. N. Pugin. See biography by Alfred Barry (1870).

Barry, Elizabeth, 1658-1713, English actress. She gained entrance to the stage through the patronage of the earl of Rochester. From the time of her appearances at the Theatre Royal (1682-95) until her last performance at the Haymarket in 1710, she was Betterton's leading lady and reigned as the greatest tragic actress of the Restoration stage. She created the heroines in the tragedies of Thomas OTWAY, who all his life nourished a hopeless love for her.

Barry, John, 1745-1803, U.S. naval officer in the American Revolution, b. Co. Wexford, Ireland. He went as a youth to Philadelphia, where he was a trader and a shipmaster. In the Revolution he commanded the brig *Lexington* when she captured (1776) the British tender *Edward*—first British ship taken by a commissioned American ship. He fulfilled later commands with gallantry: in the *Raleigh* he fought against superior forces until compelled to beach the vessel to save it and the crew from capture; in the *Alliance* he took (1781) two British vessels after a hard fight. His renown as a naval hero of the Revolution was second only to that of John Paul Jones. See biographies by Joseph Gurn (1933) and W. B. Clark (1938).

Barry, Philip, 1896-1949, American dramatist, b. Rochester, N.Y., grad. Yale, 1919, and studied under George Pierce Baker at Harvard. He is primarily known for his satirical, somewhat unconventional comedies of manners, such as *Holiday* (1928), *Tomorrow and Tomorrow* (1931), *The Animal Kingdom* (1932), and *The Philadelphia Story* (1939). His serious, symbolic plays—*Hotel Universe* (1930) and *Here Come the Clowns* (1938)—are clouded with mystical overtones. Barry's last play, *Second Threshold,* left unfinished at his death, was completed by Robert Sherwood and produced in 1951.

Barry, municipal borough (1971 pop. 41,578), Glamorganshire, S Wales, on the Bristol Channel. It is one of Great Britain's great coal-exporting ports; cement, flour, and steel products are also exported. The leading imports are timber, grain, sand, and oil. Barry has large storage and ship-repair facilities. Other industries are flour milling, mechanical engineering, and the manufacture of clothing, plastics, and silicone. Barry is also a seaside resort especially noted for the beaches on Barry Island (now linked to the mainland). In 1974, Barry became part of the new nonmetropolitan county of South Glamorgan.

Barrymore, Anglo-American family of actors. The first of the name, **Maurice Barrymore,** 1847-1905, whose original name was Herbert Blythe, was born in Agra, India. He graduated from Cambridge, took a law degree, but renounced law for the stage. After appearing in the provinces in England he went to the United States (1875) and joined Augustin Daly's company, making his first appearance in Daly's melodrama, *Under the Gaslight.* In 1876 he married Georgiana Drew. A handsome actor, he was leading man to many of the famous actresses of the period. His wife, **Georgiana Drew Barrymore,** 1856-93, b. Philadelphia, began her career in the company of her parents, John and Louisa Lane DREW. She then appeared in Daly's company in New York City, and after her marriage to Maurice Barrymore she acted with him in Mme Modjeska's company. One of the great comediennes of her day, she appeared under the management of the Frohmans and acted with Lawrence Barrett and Edwin Booth. The Barrymores' older son, **Lionel Barrymore,** 1878–1954, b. Philadelphia, first appeared in minor roles in the company of Louisa Lane Drew, his grandmother, and John Drew, his uncle. A much admired character actor, he is best remembered for his work in films, e.g., *Dinner at Eight* (1933), *You Can't Take It with You* (1938), and in 15 Dr. Kildare films. He received an Academy Award in 1931 for his performance in *A Free Soul.* His portrayal of Scrooge in Dickens's *Christmas Carol* won him a wide radio audience from 1936. In later life, crippled and confined to a wheelchair, he became known for his portrayals on radio. A man who loved art and music more than the theater, he composed over 100 unpublished musical pieces and was a member of the American Society of Etchers. He also wrote a novel, *Mr. Cantonwine: a Moral Tale* (1953). See his autobiography, *We Barrymores* (1951). His sister, **Ethel Barrymore,** 1879–1959, b. Philadelphia, also began her career under the auspices of her relatives. After an engagement with Henry Irving in London she returned to New York City, where, under the Frohman banner, she appeared in Clyde Fitch's *Captain Jinks of the Horse Marines* (1901) and achieved instant success. Although her original desire was to become a concert pianist, she made the theater her home and gained a reputation as an actress of dignity and warmth. Her most endearing portrayal was in *The Corn Is Green* (1940–42). Her work in films was limited, although in 1944 she won an Academy Award for best supporting actress in *None But the Lonely Heart.* A theater bearing her name was opened in 1928 in New York City. See her autobiography, *Memories* (1955). Their younger brother, **John Barrymore,** 1882–1942, b. Philadelphia, tried his hand at painting and cartooning before turning to the stage. After his debut in 1903, he became a matinee idol to millions of playgoers and movie fans because of his dashing nature and good looks. His portrayal of Hamlet in 1922 electrified the public. After 1912 most of his work was confined to films and radio; his last appearance, in 1939, was on the stage in *My Dear Children,* a pathetic burlesque of his baroque private life. He was four times married; his tempestuous personality passed on to two of his four children, Diana and John, Jr. (John Drew Barrymore), who also became actors. Diana died at the age of 38, shortly after the publication of her autobiographical *Too Much Too Soon* (1958). See John Barrymore's autobiography, *Confessions of an Actor* (1926); biography by Alma Powers-Waters (1941); Gene Fowler, *Good Night, Sweet Prince* (1943). Lionel, Ethel, and John Barrymore appeared together only once, in the movie *Rasputin and the Empress* (1932). *The Royal Family* (1934), a play by Edna Ferber and George S. Kaufman, is based, to some extent, on the Barrymore family. See Hollis Alpert, *The Barrymores* (1964).

Barsabas (bär'səbəs), surname of JOSEPH BARSABAS and JUDAS BARSABAS.

Barstow, city (1970 pop. 17,442), San Bernardino co., SE Calif., on the dry Mojave River; founded in the 1880s as a silver-mining town, inc. 1947. Railroad shops, the Goldstone interplanetary tracking station, and nearby U.S. marine corps supply centers are major employers. Barstow is an outfitting point for expeditions into Death Valley. A junior college is there.

Bart, Jean (zhäN bär), 1650–1702, French naval hero, b. Dunkirk. Of a seafaring family, he enlisted in the Dutch navy but entered French service as a privateer at the outbreak of the Dutch War (1672). In 1686 he was commissioned a navy captain. As a reward for his spectacular exploits, particularly in the War of the Grand Alliance, he was ennobled (1694) and made a rear admiral (1696) by King Louis XIV.

Bartas, Guillaume de Salluste Du: see DU BARTAS.

Barth, Heinrich (hīn'rĭkh bärt), 1821–65, German explorer in British service. After traveling (1845–47) through the Levant and N Africa, he entered the service of the British government. He joined (1849) an expedition to the W Sudan. He visited the Fulani and the Hausa and discovered the upper Benue River. After exploring the Chad region he turned westward and made his way through Kano and Sokoto to Gwandu, in N Nigeria. Barth's interest in the Islamic culture of W Africa led him on to Timbuktu where he stayed eight months before returning (1855) to England. His *Travels and Discoveries in North and Central Africa* (5 vol., 1857–58, in English and German) is a masterpiece of narrative and geographic research.

Barth, John, 1930–, American novelist, b. Cambridge, Md., grad. Johns Hopkins (B.A. 1951, M.A. 1952). He has been professor of English at the State University of New York at Buffalo since 1965. Barth's novels, experimental and often comic, reflect his anger and despair with the ludicrous, meaningless world of the 20th cent. He has a particular genius for parody. *The Sot-Weed Factor* (1960) is a deft parody of historical novels. *Giles Goat-Boy* (1966) is a massive satirical allegory in which the world is a large university. Barth's other works include the novels *The Floating Opera* (1956) and *The End of the Road* (1958); and *Chimera* (1972), three novellas.

Barth, Karl, 1886–1968, Swiss Protestant theologian, one of the leading thinkers of 20th-century Protestantism. He taught in Germany, where he early opposed the Nazi regime. In 1935 when he refused to take the oath of allegiance to Adolf Hitler, he was retired from his position at the Univ. of Bonn and deported to Switzerland. There he continued to expound his views, known as dialectical theology or theology of the word. Barth's primary object was to lead theology back to the principles of the Reformation. For Barth, modern theology with its assent to science, immanist philosophy, and general culture and with its stress on feeling, was marked by indifference to the word of God and to the revelation of God in Jesus Christ, which he thought should be the central concern of theology. In the confrontation between man and God, which was Barth's fundamental concern, the word of God and His revelation in Christ is His only means of revealing Himself to humans; he argued that people must listen in an attitude of awe, trust, and obedience. This theological position is also related to those of Emil BRUNNER, Friedrich GOGARTEN, and Rudolf Bultmann, although Barth's position is the more orthodox. Barth's writings include *Der Römerbrief* (1918; tr. *The Epistle to the Romans,* 1933), *Das Wort Gottes und die Theologie* (1924; tr. *The Word of God and the Word of Man,* 1928), *Credo* (1935; tr. 1936), and *Die Kirchliche Dogmatic* (Vol. I—IV, 1932–1962; tr. *Church Dogmatics,* Vol. I-IV, 1936–62). See Wilhelm Pauck, *Karl Barth, Prophet of a New Christianity?* (1931); Herbert Hartwell, *The Theology of Karl Barth: An Introduction* (1965); J. F. Andrews, comp., *Karl Barth* (1969); J. S. Bowden, *Karl Barth* (1971); R. E. Willis, *The Ethics of Karl Barth* (1971).

Barthélemy, Auguste Marseille (ōgüst' märsā'yə bärtālmē'), 1796–1867, French poet. With his friend Joseph Méry he wrote several brilliant and popular political satires, including *La Villéliade* (1827), *Napoléon en Égypte* (1828), and *Le Fils de l'homme* (1829), a poem on Napoleon II, for which Barthélemy was briefly imprisoned. A political chameleon, he celebrated the Revolution of 1830 in *L'Insurrection,* only to attack the July Monarchy in his short-lived (1831–32) journal *Némésis.*

Barthélemy, François, marquis de, 1747?–1830, French statesman. While minister to Switzerland, he negotiated the Treaties of Basel (1795), which took Prussia and Spain out of the French Revolutionary Wars. Elected to the DIRECTORY (1797), he was arrested in the coup d'etat of 18 FRUCTIDOR (Sept. 4, 1797) and was deported to French Guiana. He soon escaped, returned to France, and supported Napoleon. In 1814 he went over to the Bourbons, who raised him to the peerage.

Barthelme, Donald (bär'thĕlm), 1931–, American writer, b. Philadelphia. He has been ranked by critics with those modern writers who, like Kafka, have found the actual world so unreal that traditional modes of fiction can no longer reflect or describe it. Hence Barthelme uses language and symbol to fit his own private vision of an absurd reality. His stories are replete with parodies of advertising jargon and hip talk, counterfeit footnotes, typographical extravagances, telegrammic sketches, and interviews. Barthelme's works include the novel *Snow White* (1967); the short-story collections, *Unspeakable Practices, Unnatural Acts* (1968), *City Life* (1970), *Sadness* (1972); and a collection of non-fiction pieces, *Guilty Pleasures* (1974).

Bartholdi, Frédéric Auguste (frādārĕk' ōgüst' bärtōldē'), 1834–1904, French sculptor, b. Colmar, Alsace. He studied painting under Ary Scheffer but turned to sculpture. Among his many works is a colossal group, *Switzerland Succoring Strasbourg,* presented by France to Switzerland and now at Basel. His monuments and statues include those of Martin Schongauer at Colmar, Vercingetorix at Clermont-Ferrand, and Lafayette and Washington at Paris. Union Square, New York City, has his sculpture of Lafayette. Bartholdi's colossal *Lion of Belfort* commemorates the heroic defense of BELFORT in 1870–71 and is carved from the rock flanking the citadel. His best-known work is *Liberty Enlightening the World* (see LIBERTY, STATUE OF), erected on Bedloe's Island, New York Bay, and dedicated in 1886.

Bartholin (bär'tōlēn), renowned Scandinavian family. **Kaspar Bartholin,** 1585–1629, b. Sweden, was a Danish physician. He was professor of medicine and later of theology at the Univ. of Copenhagen and author of a textbook of anatomy, *Institutiones anatomicae* (1611). His son, **Thomas Bartholin,** 1616–80, physician, naturalist, and philologist, was professor of mathematics and of anatomy at the Univ. of Copenhagen. He was the first to describe the entire lymphatic system. **Kaspar Bartholin,** 1655–1738, a son of Thomas Bartholin, also a professor at the Univ. of Copenhagen, is credited with discovering the glands of Bartholin (a pair of glands of the vagina) and an accessory duct of the sublingual salivary gland.

Bartholomaeus Anglicus: see BARTHOLOMEW DE GLANVILLE.

Bartholomew, Saint (bärthŏl'əmyōō), one of the Twelve Disciples, usually identified with NATHANAEL. Nathanael is a given name, Bartholomew an Aramaic patronymic meaning "son of Talmai." Mat. 10.3; Mark 3.18; Luke 6.14; Acts 1.13. Tradition makes N India his missionary field and Armenia the place of his martyrdom, either by flaying, beheading, or crucifixion. Feast: Aug. 24.

Bartholomew de Glanville or **Bartholomaeus Anglicus** (bärthŏl"əmē'əs ăng'glĭkəs), fl. c.1250, English Friar Minor. He taught theology at Paris, and he was the author of *De proprietatibus rerum* (first pub. c.1470), a famous medieval encyclopedia of natural history.

Barthou, Louis (lwē bärtōō'), 1862–1934, French cabinet minister and man of letters. He held portfolios in numerous cabinets after 1894 and was briefly premier in July–August, 1913. His government was responsible for the law that increased military service from two to three years. In 1934 he became foreign minister in the cabinet of Gaston Doumergue. Barthou sought to strengthen the French position in Eastern Europe. He was welcoming King Alexander of Yugoslavia at Marseilles when a Croatian nationalist assassinated (Oct., 1934) both the king and Barthou. A man of culture and learning, Barthou was the author of several biographies, notably one of Victor Hugo (tr. 1919). See Allen Roberts, *The Turning Point* (1970).

Bartimaeus (bärtĭmē'əs), blind man to whom Jesus restored sight. Mat. 20.29–34; Mark 10.46–52; Luke 18.35–43.

Bartlesville, city (1970 pop. 29,683), seat of Washington co., NE Okla., on the Caney River; inc. 1897. It is a distribution center for a ranching and rich oil-producing area. Petroleum production, marketing, and research have been major enterprises since the first well was tapped in 1897. Of interest are the Price Tower, a concrete and glass building with cantilevered floors, designed by Frank Lloyd Wright; and the Nellie Johnstone oil well, a replica of the first commercial oil well in the state. A U.S. Bureau of Mines energy research center is in the city.

Bartlett, John, 1820–1905, American compiler and publisher, b. Plymouth, Mass. While he worked in his university book store in Cambridge, he compiled the invaluable *Familiar Quotations* (1855), which ran through nine editions in his lifetime and has been revised and enlarged several times since. Bartlett joined the publishing firm of Little, Brown & Company in 1863 and in 1878 became senior partner. His Shakespeare concordance (1894) is still a standard work.

Bartlett, Josiah, 1729–95, political leader in the American Revolution, signer of the Declaration of Independence, b. Amesbury, Mass. He practiced medicine in Kingston, N.H., and was a delegate to the provincial assembly (1765–75) and the provincial congress (1775) before serving in the Continental Congress (1775–76; 1778). He returned to New Hampshire, held judicial posts, advocated (1788) the adoption of the Federal Constitution, and was chief executive of the state (1790–94). Bartlett, N.H., is named for him.

Bartlett, Robert Abram, 1875–1946, American arctic explorer, b. Brigus, near St. John's, N.F., Canada. He accompanied Robert E. PEARY on the expeditions of 1897–98 and 1905–6, and in 1908–9 he accompanied Peary to lat. 87° 47′ N and was the last white man from whom Peary parted to make his dash for the North Pole. Bartlett commanded the *Karluk* on the expedition headed by Vilhjalmur Stefansson in 1913–14. The vessel was frozen in ice near Point Barrow and drifted until it was crushed by ice near Wrangel Island. Bartlett crossed to Siberia for help and returned to rescue 13 members of the party. Later he commanded on many arctic voyages of his own, making an annual cruise from 1925 to 1941. His exploring and scientific work in Greenland was especially notable, and he was widely known and admired. See his *Log of Bob Bartlett* (1928); biography by Paul Sarnoff (1966).

Bartlett, Samuel Colcord, 1817-98, American Congregational clergyman and educator, b. Salisbury, N.H., grad. Dartmouth College, 1836. He studied at Andover Theological Seminary and was ordained in 1843. He was professor (1858-77) of biblical literature and sacred theology at the Chicago Theological Seminary and from 1877 to 1892 was president of Dartmouth.

Bartlett, William Henry, 1800-1854, English painter and illustrator. After four visits to the United States, Bartlett illustrated a book, *American Scenery* (1840), with panoramic vistas of the American landscape. During his travels, he also executed drawings of Jerusalem for a book about the Holy Land. See study by A. M. Ross (1973).

Bartók, Béla (bä'lə bär'tŏk, Hung. bä'lô bôr'tōk), 1881-1945, Hungarian composer and collector of folk music. He studied (1899-1903) and later taught piano at the Royal Academy, Budapest. In 1905 he and Zoltán Kodály began to collect folk music of Eastern Europe, and throughout his life Bartók devoted much attention to folk music of varied origin. As a composer he gained his first success with his mime play *The Wooden Prince* (1914-16). An opera, *Duke Bluebeard's Castle* (1911), and a ballet, *The Miraculous Mandarin* (1919), also gained notice. He became better known, however, for his compositions for piano, for violin, and for orchestra. Among his piano works are a set of progressive studies called *Mikrokosmos* (1926-27) and a concerto for two pianos and orchestra (1938), which he performed with his second wife, Ditta, in New York in 1943. Bartók's important orchestral works include *Music for Strings, Percussion and Celesta* (1936) and *Concerto for Orchestra* (1943). Utilizing in varying degrees folk elements, atonality, and traditional techniques, Bartók achieved an original modern style, which has had a great influence on 20th-century music. In 1940 he emigrated to the United States and was commissioned by Columbia Univ. to transcribe a large collection of Yugoslav folk melodies. He spent his last years in poverty and neglect, but after his death his fame grew steadily. Among his studies of folk music that have been published in English are *The Hungarian Folk Song* (tr. 1931) and *Serbo-Croatian Folk Songs* (with A. B. Lord, 1951). See his letters, ed. by Janos Demeny (1971); biographies by Halsey Stevens (rev. ed. 1964), Agatha Fassett (1958, repr. 1971), and Josef Ujfalussy (tr. 1972); studies by Emil Haraszti (1938) and Serge Moreux (tr. 1953).

Bartolini, Lorenzo (lōrĕn'tsō bärtōlē'nē), 1777-1850, Italian neoclassical sculptor, studied in Florence and Paris. His most imposing creation is the Niccolò Demidoff monument in Florence. Napoleon commissioned many works from him. Among these was a colossal portrait bust of the emperor (Bastia), which is typical of Bartolini's prodigious output in this field.

Bartolommeo di Pagholo del Fattorino, Fra (frä bärtōlōmĕ'ō dē pä'gōlō dĕl fät''tōrē'nō), 1475-1517, Italian painter, also called Baccio della Porta. Under the influence of Savonarola, he joined (1500) the Dominican order. He abandoned art for a while, but resumed practice in 1504, becoming the leading Florentine master for a number of years. He visited Venice (1508) and Rome (1514). Influenced by the art of Raphael, he adapted the classic equilibrium of composition and harmony of color typical of the High Renaissance. He executed a number of paintings together with Albertinelli. Among his works are *Annunciation* (cathedral, Volterra); *Vision of St. Bernard* (Florence Acad.); *God the Father Adored by Mary Magdalen and St. Catherine* (Lucca); two panels of the *Marriage of St. Catherine* (Louvre and Pitti Palace, Florence).

Bartolozzi, Francesco (fränchĕs'kō bärtōlôt'sē), 1727-1815, Italian engraver. In Florence he studied drawing and painting and formed a lifelong friendship with Cipriani, most of whose plates he later engraved. In 1764 he went to London, where he became one of the original members of the Royal Academy. He was responsible for the vogue in England of the stipple technique of engraving, which greatly improved methods of reproduction.

Barton, Benjamin Smith, 1766-1815, American physician and botanist, b. Lancaster, Pa., studied at the College of Philadelphia, at Edinburgh, and at Göttingen (M.D., 1789). He taught at the College of Philadelphia and, after it merged with the Univ. of Pennsylvania, succeeded Benjamin Rush. Barton's chief works were *Elements of Botany* (1803), the first botanical textbook published in the United States, and *Collections for an Essay toward a Materia Medica of the United States* (1798-1804).

Barton, Clara, 1821-1912, American humanitarian, organizer of the American Red Cross, b. North Oxford (now Oxford), Mass. She taught school (1839-54) and clerked in the U.S. Patent Office before the outbreak of the Civil War. She then established a service of supplies for soldiers and nursed in army camps and on the battlefields. She was called the Angel of the Battlefield. In 1865 President Lincoln appointed her to search for missing prisoners; the records she compiled also served to identify thousands of the dead at ANDERSONVILLE Prison. In Europe for a conference at the outbreak of the Franco-Prussian War (1870), she went to work behind the German lines for the International Red Cross. She returned to the United States in 1873 and in 1881 organized the American National RED CROSS, which she headed until 1904. She worked for the President's signature to the Geneva treaty for the care of war wounded (1882) and emphasized Red Cross work in catastrophes other than war. Among her writings are several books on the Red Cross. See biographies by Ishbel Ross (1956) and W. E. Barton (1969).

Barton, Sir Edmund, 1849-1920, Australian jurist and statesman. He held high political offices in New South Wales, was a leader in the movement for Australian federation, and became the first prime minister of the Commonwealth of Australia in 1901. He was knighted in 1902 and the next year was appointed justice of the High Court.

Barton, Elizabeth, 1506?-1534, English prophet, called the Maid of Kent or the Nun of Kent. She was a domestic servant. After a period of illness, she began (c.1525) to go into trances and to utter prophecies, which were claimed to be of divine origin. She entered a convent in Canterbury, and, under the influence of Edward Bocking, her prophecies became increasingly dangerous politically. In particular she foretold dire consequences to King Henry VIII should he divorce Katharine of Aragón and marry Anne Boleyn. Bocking probably hoped to stir an uprising against the king; but his protégée was arrested (1533) and brought to confess herself an impostor. She and her accomplices were put to death. See biography by Alan Neame (1971); study by E. J. Devereux (1966).

Bartow, city (1970 pop. 12,891), seat of Polk co., central Fla.; inc. 1882. The economy is based on the production of phosphate and the raising of citrus fruit and cattle. Bartow was established in 1853 on the site of a fort built in the Seminole War (see SEMINOLE INDIANS).

Bartram, John, 1699-1777, pioneer American botanist, b. near Darby, Pa. He had no formal schooling but possessed a keen mind and a great interest in plants. In 1728 he purchased land along the banks of the Schuylkill River near Philadelphia and planted there the first botanical garden in the United States; it still exists as a part of the Philadelphia park system. He made journeys in the Alleghenies and the Catskills and in the Carolinas and Florida in search of new plants. Among his correspondents were nearly all the great European botanists of the day. By exchanging specimens with them, Bartram introduced many American plants into Europe and established some European species in the New World. To his home and gardens came the famous Americans of his day and many distinguished European travelers. His *Observations* (1751) records a trip to Lake Ontario, and the journal of his Florida trip (1765-66) was published in William Stork's *Description of East Florida* (3d ed. 1769). His name is commemorated in a genus of mosses, *Bartramia*. See Ernest Earnest, *John and William Bartram* (1940) and Ann Sutton, *Exploring with the Bartrams* (1963).

Bartram, William, 1739-1823, American naturalist, b. Philadelphia; son of John Bartram. He is known chiefly for his *Travels* (1791), in which he describes his journey (1773-77) through the Carolinas, Georgia, and Florida and the Indian country to the west. His book vividly portrays the plants and wildlife of the country and lists 215 native birds, the most complete list of that time. Bartram's influence is seen in the works of Wordsworth, Coleridge, Chateaubriand, and other writers who found his book an unexcelled source of descriptions of the American wilderness and its inhabitants.

Bartsch, Adam von (Johann Adam Bernhard von Bartsch) (ä'däm fən bärch), 1757-1821, Austrian engraver, etcher, and writer. His critical catalogue, *Le Peintre Graveur* (21 vol., 1803-21), is still authoritative. Bartsch executed over 500 plates from his own designs and from those of others.

Baruch (bā'rək). 1 Jeremiah's scribe, for whom the book of BARUCH is named. 2 Judahite. Neh. 11.5. 3 Builder of the wall. Neh. 3.20. 4 Signer of the Covenant. Neh. 11.5.

Baruch, Bernard Mannes (bərōōk'), 1870-1965, U.S. financier and government adviser, b. Camden, S.C. He grew rich through stock-market speculation before he was 30. In World War I he advised on national defense and was (1918-19) chairman of the War Industries Board. In World War II he became (1942) special adviser to James F. Byrnes and wrote the report (1943) on post-war conversion. As U.S. Representative to the U.N. Atomic Energy Commission (1946) he formulated plans for international control of atomic energy. See his autobiography *Baruch* (2 vol., 1957-60); biography by W. L. White (1950, repr. 1970).

Baruch, biblical book included in the Old Testament of the Western canon and Septuagint, but not included in the Hebrew Bible and placed in the Apocrypha in the Authorized Version. It is named for a Jewish prince Baruch (fl. 600 B.C.), faithful friend of JEREMIAH the prophet and editor of his book. Jer. 32.12-16; 36; 43.3,6; 45. Baruch contains the following parts: a message from the exiled Jews to the Jews still at home (1-3.8), including a prayer for Palestinian Jews to use, confessing sin and asking divine mercy; an exhortation to wisdom (3.9-4.4), including a famous messianic allusion (3.37); a consolation of Jerusalem (4.5-5.9) containing a lament; finally chapter 6, which is a letter of Jeremiah (sometimes called the Epistle of Jeremy) warning the exiles against idolatry. The extant ancient versions of Baruch are in Greek, but Hebrew was probably the original language. Critics disagree greatly over the dates of Baruch; some see it as a collection of works by several authors. For the Apocalypse of Baruch, see PSEUDEPIGRAPHA. For bibliography, see APOCRYPHA.

Baruch College, division of the City University of New York; coeducational; founded 1919 as the school of business administration of City College. Its name was changed to the Bernard M. Baruch School of Business and Public Administration in 1953. In 1968 it became a separate liberal arts college within the City University of New York (see NEW YORK, CITY UNIVERSITY OF).

Bary, Heinrich Anton de: see DE BARY.

Barye, Antoine Louis (äNtwän' lwē bärē'), 1796-1875, French animal sculptor. Son of a Parisian goldsmith, he followed his father's trade as a youth. In 1832 he exhibited at the Salon his *Lion and Serpent* (Tuileries), which won him recognition; but only late in life did he achieve fame and free himself from debt. His simple, romantic, and forceful studies of animals or groups of animals were often small and designed for commercial reproduction in bronze. They enjoyed an international popularity and are still highly prized. Well-known examples of his work are *Tiger and Gavial, Jaguar and Hare, Theseus and the Minotaur* (all: Louvre), and *Centaur and Lapith* (Tuileries). He is also represented in the Metropolitan Museum and in the Brooklyn Museum. See Charles S. Smith, *Barbizon Days* (1902, repr. 1969).

baryon (bâr'ēŏn'') [Gr.,=heavy], class of ELEMENTARY PARTICLES that includes the PROTON, the NEUTRON, and a large number of unstable, heavier particles, known as hyperons. From a technical point of view, baryons are strongly interacting fermions; i.e., they experience the strong nuclear FORCE and are described by the Fermi-Dirac statistics, which apply to all particles obeying the Pauli EXCLUSION PRINCIPLE. All members of the baryon family of particles adhere to the law of conservation of baryon family number (see CONSERVATION LAWS, in physics); the baryon family number is $+1$ for ordinary baryons and -1 for antibaryons (see ANTIPARTICLE). In any particle interaction, the sum of the baryon family numbers of the interacting particles must equal the sum for the resulting particles. In reactions involving only nucleons, this law requires that the total number of nucleons be the same before and after the reaction. In addition to the nucleons (protons and neutrons), other members of the baryon family include the lambda (Λ), sigma (Σ), delta (Δ), xi (Ξ), and N particles, as well as a series of higher-mass recurrences of each of these particles. These recurrences may be considered excited states of the lowest-mass member of the series.

barytes: see BARITE.

barytone: see BARITONE.

Barzillai (bärzĭl'āī). **1** Chief in Gilead who was friendly to David. 2 Sam. 17.27–29; 19.31–39; 1 Kings 2.7; Ezra 2.61; Neh. 7.63. **2** The father-in-law of Saul's daughter MERAB.

Barzun, Jacques (zhäk bär'zən), 1907–, American writer and educator, b. France, grad. Columbia (B.A., 1927; Ph.D., 1932). Barzun moved to the United States in 1919. A student of law and history, he began teaching history at Columbia in 1928. He was appointed professor in 1945 and dean of the graduate faculties in 1955. In 1958 Barzun was made dean of faculties and provost. He has written and edited critical and historical studies on a wide variety of subjects; they include *Race: a Study in Modern Superstition* (1937), *Darwin, Marx, Wagner* (1941), *Romanticism and the Modern Ego* (1945), *The Teacher in America* (1945), *The House of Intellect* (1959), *Classic, Romantic, and Modern* (1961), *Science: The Glorious Entertainment* (1964), *The American University* (1968), *Berlioz and the Romantic Century* (3d ed. 1969), and *The Use and Abuse of Art* (1974).

basal metabolism: see METABOLISM.

basalt (bəsôlt', băs'ôlt), fine-grained ROCK of volcanic origin, dark gray, dark green, brown, or black in color. Basalt is an igneous rock, i.e., one that has congealed from a molten state. It is the most abundant rock in volcanic LAVA. Most of the world's great lava flows, e.g., the Deccan trap in India, the Iceland flows, and the Columbia River plateau of the NW United States, are basaltic rock. Basalt contains a high percentage of iron and magnesium. Some basalts are porphyritic, i.e., they contain large crystalline structures called phenocrysts embedded in a matrix called a groundmass (see PORPHYRY). Phenocrysts are usually formed in the molten lava before eruption and are often composed of the minerals olivine and PYROXENE. Where molten basalt cools rapidly, as at the earth's surface, fine-grained rocks are formed; if chilling and solidification are very rapid, the groundmass may even be glassy. Basalt may be compact or vesicular, i.e., porous because of gas bubbles contained in the lava while it is solidifying. If the vesicles become filled subsequently with secondary minerals, e.g., quartz or calcite, the rock is called amygdaloidal basalt. Igneous rocks of basaltic composition called gabbros are coarse-grained rocks formed by slow cooling in large underground masses. They are common in the Adirondack Mts. of New York State. Diabase, sometimes called dolerite, is a dark-colored igneous rock intermediate in texture between gabbros and basalt. It is common in formations such as SILLS, which are bodies of igneous rock that when molten ascended into a vertical fissure, and DIKES, which are bodies of igneous rock that when molten filled a bedding plane, or horizontal fissure. Diabase sills make up such Triassic period formations as the Palisades of the Hudson River and similar bodies of the Connecticut River valley (see TRIASSIC PERIOD). When subjected to metamorphism, i.e., very high temperatures and very great pressures, basalt is transformed into various kinds of SCHISTS including hornblende schist. Basalt universally underlies the sediment cover in the world's oceans as evidenced by the basaltic makeup of such midocean islands as the Hawaiian Islands and Iceland, and by samples of lava flows found in drill cores recovered by vessels of the DEEP SEA DRILLING PROJECT and the now defunct Project Mohole. Seismic studies indicate that an irregular layer of basaltic rock underlies the granite-like rocks of the earth's continents. Crystalline rocks returned from the moon by Apollo astronauts were similar in many respects to terrestrial basalts. Fine-grained basaltic lunar rocks were vesicular, with glass-lined pits on exposed surfaces that have been interpreted as micrometeorite impact scars. Coarse-grained basaltic rocks were also found. Lunar rocks differed from terrestrial basalts in lacking water and ferric iron, and were significantly higher in titanium and iron content.

Bascama (băs'kəmə), unidentified town, E of the River Jordan, where Jonathan the Maccabee was killed. 1 Mac. 13.23–26.

Bascom, Henry Bidleman, 1796–1850, American Methodist minister and college president, b. Hancock, N.Y. At the age of 17 he became a preacher in the Ohio Methodist Conference and was a frontier circuit rider. Bascom was chaplain (1824–26) in the U.S. Congress; president (1827–29) of Madison College, Uniontown, Pa.; professor (1832–42) of moral science at Augusta College, Augusta, Ky.; and president (1842–49) of Transylvania Univ., Lexington, Ky. He played an important role at the convention of 1844, which split the Methodist Church over the question of slavery and resulted in the organization of the Methodist Episcopal Church, South. In 1850 he was elected a bishop of that church. He is the author of *Methodism and Slavery* (1847).

base: see ACIDS AND BASES.

baseball, the "national game" of the United States. It derives its name from the four bases on the wide, flat (except for a slight rise at the pitcher's mound) playing field (the diamond). Horsehide-covered hard balls, wooden bats, and padded gloves (the catcher and chief umpire wear additional protective material) constitute the basic equipment. A game is played by two opposing teams of nine players each—a pitcher, a catcher, four infielders, and three outfielders. Once replaced in a particular game, a player may not again take part in that contest. The umpires rule on the plays of the game. To win, a team must score more runs in nine innings than its opponent, a run being made when a player completes a circuit of the bases. If the score is tied at the end of nine innings, play continues until one team has scored more runs than the other in an equal number of innings. Although earlier rules existed, the American and National leagues adopted joint playing rules in 1904, amendments having been introduced since then. A form of baseball, doubtless derived from the English games of cricket and rounders, was played in the early 19th cent., and the children's game "one old cat" existed before that time. Baseball was played largely in the northeastern states before the Civil War, and Alexander Cartwright, who set (c.1845) bases at 90 ft (27.43 m) apart, and Henry Chadwick, who wrote (1858) the first rule book, were important in the development of the game. The report (1907–8) of a commission headed by A. G. Mills declaring that Abner Doubleday created the modern game in 1839 at Cooperstown, N.Y., has been refuted by some authorities. Baseball made great headway in New York City and the neighboring regions, and in 1845 the Knickerbocker Baseball Club, the first organized team, was formed in New York. The National Association of Baseball Players, the first governing body of the sport, was formed in 1858. The sport was popular with Union soldiers during the Civil War, and after the war professional teams banded together in associations. Today there are two main professional baseball associations that together form the major leagues, along with approximately 20 associations of lesser teams that make up the minor leagues. The older of the two major leagues, the National League (organized 1876), is at present made up of the Atlanta Braves, Chicago Cubs, Cincinnati Reds, Houston Astros, Los Angeles Dodgers, Montreal Expos (the first major league team outside the United States), New York Mets, Philadelphia Phillies, Pittsburgh Pirates, St. Louis Cardinals, San Diego Padres, and San Francisco Giants. In 1900 the Western League regrouped as the American League and three years later gained recognition as the second major league. The American League is composed of the Baltimore Orioles, Boston Red Sox, California Angels, Chicago White Sox, Cleveland Indians, Detroit Tigers, Kansas City Royals, Milwaukee Brewers, Minnesota Twins, New York Yankees, Oakland Athletics, and Texas Rangers. The locations of major league franchises were stable for 50 years until 1953, when the Boston Braves moved to Milwaukee and became the first major league team W of Chicago and St. Louis. During the rest of the 1950s a number of other teams continued the westward migration, largely made possible by the expansion of intercity air travel. The 1960s were another period of change. At the beginning of that decade there were eight teams in each of the major leagues; by 1969 each league had grown to include two divisions of six teams each, for a total of 24 teams. Since 1903 the National and American league champion teams have met in an annual series of games, known as the world series, to decide the world's championship. The winners of the world series were: 1903, Boston Red Sox; 1904, no series because the New York Giants of the National League refused to play the Boston Red Sox of the American League; 1905, New York Giants; 1906, Chicago White Sox; 1907–8, Chicago Cubs; 1909, Pittsburgh Pirates; 1910–11, Philadelphia Athletics; 1912, Boston Red Sox; 1913, Philadelphia Athletics; 1914, Boston Braves; 1915–16, Boston Red Sox; 1917, Chicago White Sox; 1918, Boston Red Sox; 1919, Cincinnati Reds; 1920, Cleveland Indians; 1921–22, New York Giants; 1923, New York Yankees; 1924, Washington Senators; 1925, Pittsburgh Pirates; 1926, St. Louis Cardinals; 1927–28, New York Yankees; 1929–30, Philadelphia Athletics; 1931, St. Louis Cardinals; 1932, New York Yankees; 1933, New York Giants; 1934, St. Louis Cardinals; 1935, Detroit Tigers; 1936–39, New York Yankees; 1940, Cincinnati Reds; 1941, New York Yankees; 1942, St. Louis Cardinals; 1943, New York Yankees; 1944, St. Louis Cardinals; 1945, Detroit Tigers; 1946, St. Louis Cardinals; 1947, New York Yankees; 1948, Cleveland Indians; 1949–53, New York Yankees; 1954, New York Giants; 1955, Brooklyn Dodgers; 1956, New York Yankees; 1957, Milwaukee Braves; 1958, New York Yankees; 1959, Los Angeles Dodgers; 1960, Pittsburgh Pirates; 1961–62, New York Yankees; 1963, Los Angeles Dodgers; 1964, St. Louis Cardinals; 1965, Los Angeles Dodgers; 1966, Baltimore Orioles; 1967, St. Louis Cardinals; 1968, Detroit Tigers; 1969, New York Mets; 1970, Baltimore Orioles; 1971, Pittsburgh Pirates; and 1972–74, Oakland Athletics. Some of the minor leagues—notably the International League, the Pacific Coast League, and the Texas League—also hold postseason play-offs. The "Black Sox" scandal, involving eight Chicago White Sox players charged with bribery in the 1919 world series, led the committee of baseball executives to appoint (1921) Judge Kenesaw M. Landis to the new post of baseball commissioner. Landis replaced the three-man National Commission, which had ruled professional organized baseball since 1903. Albert B. (Happy) Chandler was elected (1945) to succeed Landis, who had died in office. Other commissioners were Ford C. Frick (1951–65) and William D. Eckert (1965–69). In 1969, Bowie K. Kuhn was elected to a seven-year term. Night baseball games, introduced in the major leagues in 1935, are now scheduled more frequently than day games. The all-time major league single-game attendance record of 84,587 was set by the Cleveland Indians in 1954. Since the 1960s baseball's position as the national game has eroded. Many minor league teams have disbanded, average attendance at major league games has declined, and the sport has suffered from the criticism that it is too slow, especially in comparison to football, basketball, and ice hockey, the other major professional sports in the United States. In response, baseball executives have promulgated certain reforms in an effort to revitalize interest in the game. Most notable among these has been the tenth player, or designated hitter, experiment introduced into the American League during the 1973 season. Changing social conditions have also forced major league baseball to make changes. In 1947, Jackie Robinson of the Brooklyn Dodgers became the first Negro to play in the major leagues. Prior to that time, Negro ballplayers had been restricted to playing in the segregated Negro Leagues. Baseball's reserve clause, the contractual stipulation that binds a player to his club for as long as the latter desires, has been the subject of three Supreme Court cases (1922, 1953, 1972). In all three cases the Court refused to overturn the reserve clause, ruling that baseball is a sport and not a business, and as such is not subject to Federal antitrust laws. In 1973 major league baseball experienced the first strike in its history. Stemming from a dispute over the size of the players' pension fund, the strike delayed the season's start by 13 days and forced the cancellation of 86 games. Baseball is also played by semiprofessional, amateur, club, college, and school teams. It has achieved considerable popularity in Japan as well as Cuba, Puerto Rico, Mexico, and other Latin American countries. Softball, a form of baseball in which a larger ball and a smaller infield are required, is also popular among amateurs. A number of professional baseball's greatest figures have been elected to the National Baseball Hall of Fame, built (1939) at Cooperstown, N.Y. Among the more famous names in the history of professional baseball are Henry L. Aaron, Grover C. Alexander, Adrian C. (Cap) Anson, John F. (Home Run) Baker, Lawrence P. (Yogi) Berra, Frank L. Chance, Tyrus R. (Ty) Cobb, Gordon S. (Mickey) Cochrane, Edward T. Collins, Joseph E. Cronin, Jerome H. (Dizzy) Dean, William M. (Bill) Dickey, Joseph P. (Joe) DiMaggio, Robert W. A. (Bob) Feller, James E. (Jimmy) Foxx, Frank R. Frisch, Henry L. (Lou) Gehrig, Joshua Gibson, Henry B. (Hank) Greenberg, Robert M. (Lefty) Grove, Rogers Hornsby, Carl O. Hubbell, Miller J. Huggins, Walter P. Johnson, Willie Keeler, William F. Klem, Sanford (Sandy) Koufax, Napoleon (Larry) Lajoie, Walter J. V. (Rabbit) Maranville, Joseph V. McCarthy, Cornelius McGillicuddy (Connie Mack), John J. McGraw, Mickey Mantle, Roger Maris, Christopher (Christy) Mathewson, Willie Mays, Stanley F. (Stan) Musial, Melvin T. (Mel) Ott, Satchel Paige, Jackie Robinson, George H. (Babe) Ruth, George H. Sisler, Warren E. Spahn, Tristram E. (Tris) Speaker, Charles D. (Casey) Stengel, William H. (Bill) Terry, John S. Vander Meer, John P. (Honus) Wagner, Paul G. (Big Poison) Wan-er, Theodore S. (Ted) Williams, and Denton T. (Cy) Young. See Douglass Wallop, *Baseball* (1969); Roger Angell, *The Summer Game* (1972); Leonard Koppett, *All About Baseball* (rev. ed. 1974); *Baseball Encyclopedia* (rev. ed. 1974).

Basedow, Johann Bernhard (yōhän' bĕrn'härt bä'-zədō), 1723–90, German educator, b. Hamburg, educated in Hamburg and at the Univ. of Leipzig. Later he taught in Denmark (1753) and Germany (1761) but became involved in controversies aroused by his unorthodox religious writings. In 1774 his *Elementarwerk* was published with funds raised by popular subscription, and Basedow opened at Dessau a school called the Philanthropinum, where the methods of elementary education outlined in this text were employed. Drawing upon the writings of Comenius, Locke, and Rousseau, Basedow emphasized realistic teaching and introduced nature study, physical education, and manual training. He resigned in 1778 because of disagreements with his staff, and the school closed in 1793. His reforms were widely influential, however, and similar institutions were established throughout Germany and Switzerland.

Basel (bä'zəl) or **Basle** (bäl), Fr. *Bâle*, canton, N Switzerland, bordering on France and West Germany. It is bounded in the N by the Rhine River (which becomes navigable in the canton) and in the S by the Jura mts. Although it has industries, Basel is mainly a region of fertile fields, meadows, orchards, and forests. Its inhabitants are German-speaking and Protestant. The canton has been divided since 1833 into two independent half cantons—**Basel-Land** (1970 pop. 240,889), 165 sq mi (427 sq km), generally comprising the rural districts, with its capital at Liestal, and **Basel-Stadt** (1970 pop. 234,945), 14 sq mi (36 sq km), virtually coextensive with the city of **Basel** (1970 pop. 212,857) and its suburbs. Divided by the Rhine, the city consists of Greater Basel (left bank), which is the commercial and intellectual center, and Lesser Basel, where industry is concentrated. Basel is a major economic center and the chief rail junction and river port of Switzerland. It is also a financial center. The city is the seat of the Swiss chemical and pharmaceutical industry and of the Swiss Industries Fair; it also has an important publishing industry. Other products are metal goods, foodstuffs, and silk textiles. Founded by the Romans (and named Basilia), it became an episcopal see in the 7th cent. It passed successively to the Alemanni, the Franks, and to Transjurane Burgundy. In the 11th cent. it became a free imperial city and the residence of prince-bishops. The celebrated Council of Basel (see separate article) met there in the mid-15th cent. Basel joined the Swiss Confederation in 1501 and accepted the Reformation in 1523. Although expelled from the city, the bishops continued to rule the bishopric of Basel (including PORRENTRUY and DELÉMONT, which in 1815 became part of Bern canton). The oppressive rule of the city's patriciate over the rest of the canton led to revolts (1831–33) and the eventual split into two cantons. One of the oldest intellectual centers of Europe, Basel has through its university (founded 1460 by Pius II) attracted leading artists, scholars, and teachers. It was the residence of Froben, Erasmus, Holbein the Younger, Calvin, Nietzsche, and the Bernoulli family. Jakob Burckhardt and Leonhard Euler were born there. Among the city's noted structures are the cathedral (consecrated 1019), in which Erasmus is buried; the medieval gates; several guild houses; the 16th-century town hall; and an art gallery with a valuable collection of Holbein's works.

Basel, Council of, 1431–49, first part of the 17th ecumenical council in the Roman Catholic Church. It is generally considered to have been ecumenical until it fell into heresy in 1437; after that it is regarded as an anticouncil. Its chief importance lies in the contest between council and pope for supremacy. The Council of Constance had seen the rise of the conciliar theory, the doctrine that the ultimate authority in the church rests upon the general council, to which the pope must be subject. It had been the plan to have frequent councils, but that of Basel was the first of importance to follow Constance, that of Pavia-Siena (1423–24) having accomplished little. Pope Martin V convoked the council but died soon afterward, and it was his successor, EUGENE IV, who confirmed the convocation. Various problems were brought before the council: the settlement of the difficulties with the HUSSITES; reform in the church, particularly financial reform; and the matter of negotiations for the union of the Eastern church and the Western church. Even though he had convened it, Eugene was suspicious of the council, fearing that in the question of the Hussites it might reawaken doctrinal questions already regarded as settled. Therefore, he ordered the council dissolved almost immediately. This marked the outbreak of trouble between the council and the pope that was not to end until the council did. Holy Roman Emperor SIGISMUND, who desired the settlement of Hussite disputes from the council and desired coronation at the hands of the pope, acted as mediator. The council pronounced its supremacy over the pope and in 1433 reached the zenith of its power. Fearing schism, Eugene was driven to granting more and more concessions, but any compromise reached was temporary. The continual assertion of the conciliar supremacy led to the institution of a process against the pope for disobedience and ultimately to the papal denunciation of the council in the bull *Doctoris gentium* (1437). The council, which thus became heretical, had accomplished a good deal. The Compactata had marked a compromise with the Hussites; the annates and various papal taxes had been declared illegal; church organization and finance had been reformed. In order to meet with delegates from the East on the question of reunion, Eugene summoned the council to Ferrara (see FERRARA-FLORENCE, COUNCIL OF). The council at Basel continued to function as an anticouncil. Finally the process against Eugene was carried through, and the council elected AMADEUS VIII of Savoy pope (called Antipope Felix V). The allegiance of most temporal rulers was still given to Eugene; although the reforms of Basel were adopted by the French at Bourges and incorporated into the Pragmatic Sanction of Bourges, the council was not itself approved. The German king Frederick III (who was later crowned Holy Roman emperor) remained neutral, but in 1448 his pressure upon the city forced the delegates to retire to Lausanne. Felix, with only scattered support, abdicated in 1449, submitting to Eugene's successor, Nicholas V. The council recognized the legitimate pope and dissolved itself, thus ending the threat of antipapal conciliarism.

base line: see GEODESY.

Basel-Land and **Basel-Stadt:** see BASEL, Switzerland.

basenji (bəsĕn'jē), breed of medium-sized HOUND whose origins can be traced back several thousand years to Africa and the courts of the Egyptian pharaohs. It stands about 17 in. (43.2 cm) high at the shoulders and weighs about 23 lb (10.4 kg). Its short, silky coat may be colored chestnut red, black, or black and tan, with white chest, feet, and tip of tail. The basenji has two unique characteristics: it does not bark but utters a sound that has been described as a chortle or whine, and, in the manner of a cat, it cleans its own body. Possessing a keen sense of smell, the basenji was used in its native Africa as a hunter but is now commonly kept as a house pet. See DOG.

Bashan (bā'shän), fertile region E of the Jordan from the latitude of Haifa northward to that of Tyre. It was conquered by the Israelites and given to the half tribe of Manasseh. Scholars believe the Bashan culture, essentially Amorite, shows traces of Indo-Iranian and Horite influence. Now occupied by the Druses, it forms a part of Syria. Deut. 3.11; Num. 21.33; 2 Kings 10.33; Ps. 22.12; 68.15; Amos 4.1.

Bashan-havoth-jair: see HAVOTH-JAIR.

Bashemath (băsh'əmăth), wife of Esau. Gen. 26.34; 36.2.3.

Bashkir Autonomous Soviet Socialist Republic (băshkēr') or **Bashkiria** (băshkēr'ēə), autonomous region (1970 pop. 3,819,000), 55,444 sq mi (143,600 sq km), E European USSR, in the S Urals, occupying the Belaya River basin. UFA is the capital; other important cities are STERLITAMAK, BELORETSK, and ISHIMBAY. The Trans-Siberian and South Siberian railroads cross the republic. Bashkiria forms the eastern part of the Volga-Ural petroleum region and also has natural gas, coal, salt, iron, gold, copper, zinc, bauxite, and manganese deposits. The drilling, refining, and processing of oil is the predominant economic activity. About 40% of the land is forested, and sawmilling and the production of plywood and paper are important. Grains (especially wheat, rye, and oats) are the chief agricultural products. The republic's population is made up mainly of Bashkirs (about 25%), Russians (constituting a majority), and Tatars. The Bashkirs, a mixture of Finno-Ugric, Turkish, and Mongolian tribes, are a Muslim people who speak a Turkic language very close to Tatar. Historically, the Bashkirs were controlled by the Volga Bulgars and the Golden Horde, and later by the khanates of Kazan, Nogai, and Siberia. In 1557, during the reign of Ivan IV, they came under Muscovite rule. The Russians founded Ufa in 1574 and began colonization, dispossessing the Bashkirs, who revolted numerous times during the next two centuries (notably under Pugachev in 1773–75). In 1917 a Bashkir national government was formed, but the region experienced heavy fighting between the Red and White armies in the aftermath of the Russian Revolution. In 1919, Bashkiria was made the first autonomous Soviet republic.

basic oxygen process, method of producing STEEL from a charge consisting mostly of pig iron. The charge is placed in a furnace similar to the one used in the BESSEMER PROCESS of steelmaking except that pure oxygen instead of air is blown into the charge to oxidize the impurities present. One desirable feature of this process is that it takes less than an hour, and is thus much faster than the open-hearth process, another important method of steelmaking. A second advantage is that a major by-product is carbon monoxide, which can be used as a fuel or in producing various chemicals, such as acetic acid. The basic oxygen process also produces less air pollution than methods using air.

Basidiomycete: see FUNGI.

Basie, Count (William Basie), 1904–, American jazz pianist, band-leader, and composer, b. Red Bank, N.J. After working in dance halls and vaudeville in New York City, Basie moved to Kansas City, a major jazz center. There he joined Walter Page's Blue Devils in 1927, moving to Bennie Morton's band in 1929. He formed his own band in 1935, and for 40 years it has produced a distinctive sound marked by a powerful yet relaxed attack. Basie's provocative piano style is characterized by a predominant right hand. Among the many pieces he has composed for his band is "One O'Clock Jump."

Basil, Saint: see BASIL THE GREAT, SAINT.

Basil I (Basil the Macedonian), c.813–886, Byzantine emperor (867–86). His ancestors probably were Armenians or Slavs who settled in Macedonia. He became (c.856) the favorite of Emperor MICHAEL III. In 886, Basil, with the aid of Michael, assassinated Michael's uncle and chief minister, Bardas, and was made coemperor. Michael's feeling toward Basil began to change and in 867 Basil had him murdered and had himself proclaimed emperor. Thus the Macedonian dynasty of the East, which lasted until 1056, was founded. A capable ruler, Basil reformed the finances, modernized the law of Justinian I by introducing a new code, the Basilica, protected the poorer classes, and restored the military prestige of the empire. Byzantine art and architecture entered their second golden age during his rule. A major event of his reign was the dissension between the Roman and the Eastern churches. In order to prevent an open break, Basil restored (867) to the patriarchate IGNATIUS OF CONSTANTINOPLE, who had been deposed in favor of PHOTIUS. On Ignatius' death, Basil reinstated (877) Photius, causing strained relations but not a full break with Rome. Basil in 865 had divorced his wife and married the mistress of Michael III. He was succeeded by his son Leo VI.

Basil II, c.958–1025, Byzantine emperor (976–1025), surnamed Bulgaroktonos [Bulgar slayer]. With his brother, Constantine VIII, he nominally succeeded his father, Romanus II, in 963, but had no share in the government during the rule of the usurping generals NICEPHORUS II (963–69) and JOHN I (969–76). Primarily a soldier, Basil exercised virtually sole rule from 976, while his debauched brother was emperor only in name. Basil suppressed (976–89) a series of revolts of the great landowners led by Bardus Sclerus and revived and strengthened the laws directed against them by ROMANUS I. He annexed (1018) Bulgaria, although leaving it some measure of autonomy, and later extended the eastern frontier of his empire to the Caucasus. During his reign the schism between the Roman and the Eastern churches widened. Basil was succeeded by Constantine VIII (reigned 1025–28) and by Constantine's daughter Zoë.

Basil III, Russian ruler: see VASILY III.

basil (băz'əl), any plant of the genus *Ocimum,* tender herbs or small shrubs of the family Labiatae (MINT family), mostly of Old World warm regions and cultivated for the aromatic leaves. The basil of Keats's "Isabella" (and of Boccaccio's story) is the common or sweet basil (*O. basilicum*), once considered medicinal. This is the species usually used for seasoning; it is grown commercially chiefly in the Mediterranean area. There are also the holy basil, venerated in India, the bush basil, and related plants sometimes called basil. Basil is classified in the division MAGNOLIOPHYTA, class Magnoliopsida, order Lamiales, family Labiatae.

Basilan (bäsē'län), island, 494 sq mi (1,279 sq km), northernmost and largest of the Sulu Archipelago, the Philippines. It is closely associated with the city of Zamboango on Mindanao island, just across the 10-mi (16-km) wide Basilan Strait. Major sources of income are sea products, coconut, timber, and rubber. The Univ. of the Philippines maintains a vast rubber plantation there. With neighboring islets, Basilan forms the Basilan island group. The inhabitants are chiefly Muslim.

Basildon, urban district (1971 pop. 129,073), Essex, E England. The southern portion is Basildon New Town, a planned community with many factories. There are light engineering, chemical, and joinery works, milk-bottling and printing plants, and clothing and carbon-black factories.

Basile, Giovanni Battista (jōvän'nē bät-tēs'tä bäsē'-lā), 1575–1632, Italian writer. Basile held several important official positions, devoting his spare time to the study of folklore. He is known for his *Lu Cunta de li cunti* [the tale of tales] (1634–36), a collection of folk and fairy tales written in the Neopolitan dialect in a vigorous, exuberant style. The collection, usually referred to as *Il Pentamerone* because its framework is similar to Boccaccio's *Decameron,* recounts 50 tales told to a prince and his bride by ten women during a five-day period. Cinderella, Rapunzel, Snow White, and many other fairy-tale characters make their first appearance in its pages.

Basilian monks (bəzĭl'ēən), monks of the Eastern Church. They follow the Rule of St. BASIL THE GREAT, which has been universal among them since the 7th cent. They have no centralized government; the rule treats proper monastic living, not organization. Their monasteries are collections of small cells, the whole group being called a laura. The chief monastery is the Great Laura of Mt. Athos; another famous Orthodox monastery is St. Catherine on Mt. Sinai. There are Basilians in communion with the pope. The chief figure of Basilian history is the reformer St. THEODORE OF STUDIUM. See also MONASTICISM.

basilica (bəsĭl'ĭkə), large building erected by the Romans for transacting business and disposing of legal matters. Often rectangular in form with a roofed hall, the building usually contained an interior colonnade, with an apse at one end or at each end. The central aisle tended to be wide and was higher than the flanking aisles, so that light could penetrate through the clerestory windows. The oldest known basilica was built in Rome in 184 B.C. by the elder Cato. Other early examples are the Basilica Porcia in Rome and one at Pompeii (late 2d cent. B.C.). Probably the most splendid Roman basilica is the one constructed during the reign of Maxentius and finished by Constantine after 313. In the 4th cent. Christians began to build edifices for worship that were related to the form of the basilicas. These had a center nave with one aisle at each side and an apse at one end: on this platform sat the bishop and priests. Basilicas of this type were built not only in Western Europe but in Greece, Syria, Egypt, and Palestine. A good example of the Oriental basilica is the Church of the Nativity at Bethlehem (6th cent.). The finest basilicas in Rome were St. John Lateran and St. Paul's-outside-the-Walls (4th cent.), and San Clemente (6th cent.). Gradually there emerged the massive Romanesque churches, which still retained the fundamental plan of the basilica.

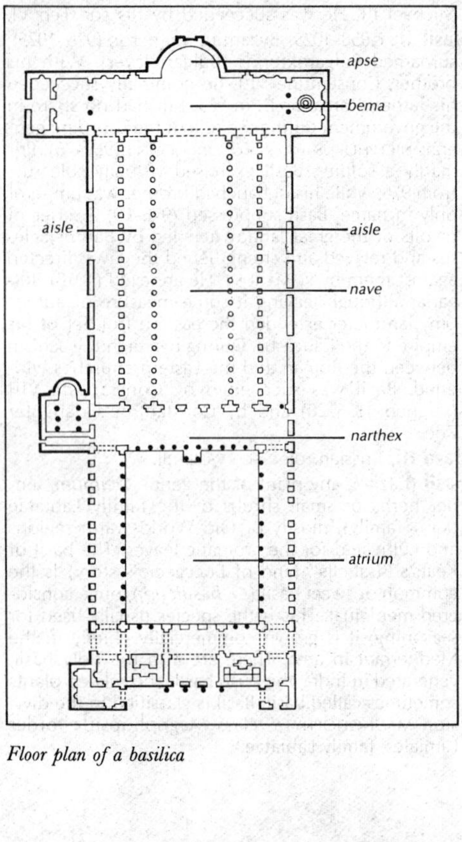

Floor plan of a basilica

Basilicata (bäzēlēkä'tä), region (1971 pop. 602,389), 3,856 sq mi (9,987 sq km), S Italy, bordering on the Tyrrhenian Sea in the southwest and on the Gulf of Taranto in the southeast. It forms the instep of the Italian "boot." POTENZA is the capital of Basilicata, which is divided into Potenza and Matera provs. (named for their capitals). The region is crossed by the Lucanian Apennines; its main river is the Bradano. Because of a dry climate and a scarcity of ground water, farming is difficult, although it is the occupation of most inhabitants of the generally poor region. Olives, plums, and cereals are grown, and sheep and goats are raised. There is also some fishing. The transportation network is very limited, and commerce and industry are minimal. Basilicata corresponds to most of ancient LUCANIA and to part of ancient SAMNIUM. Rome took the region in 272 B.C.; it later passed in turn to the Lombards, to the Byzantines, and (11th cent.) to the Norman duchy of Apulia, of which MELFI (now in Basilicata) was the capital. Although later a part of the kingdom of Naples, Basilicata was controlled by virtually independent feudal lords. Malaria, still a scourge on the coasts, caused the flourishing coastal towns to be abandoned in the early Middle Ages. In the 20th cent. there have been reclamation works and social and land reforms in Basilicata, but many of the inhabitants have emigrated to foreign countries (especially the United States) or have taken jobs in the industrial cities of N Italy. The region has suffered numerous earthquakes.

Basilides (băsĭl'ĭdēz), fl. 120–145, Gnostic teacher of Alexandria. He wrote *Exegitica* (his personal gospel with 24 books of commentary) and poems. He claimed to possess a secret tradition handed down from St. Peter and St. Matthias. The Basilidean sect of GNOSTICISM attracted many followers.

Basilikon Doron (bəsĭ'lĭkən dô'rən) [Gr.,=royal gift], book written by James VI of Scotland (subsequently James I of England) as a guide for the conduct of his son Henry when he became king. The work was completed in manuscript in 1598 and published the following year. James warned Henry of meddlesome ministers and expounded the doctrine of the divine right of kings. Henry died in 1612 and did not ascend the throne. See edition by James Craigie (1944–50).

Basiliscus (bă''sĭlĭs'kəs), d. c.477, usurper at Constantinople (475–76). He was responsible for the failure of the expedition sent (468) against the Vandals by his brother-in-law LEO I. He usurped the throne during the reign of ZENO, but his extortions and Monophysite tendencies led to his overthrow and execution when Zeno recovered his throne.

basilisk: see IGUANA.

Basil the Great, Saint (bă'zĭl, bā'-), c.330–379, Greek prelate, bishop of Caesarea in Cappadocia, Doctor of the Church and one of the Four Fathers of the Greek Church. He was a brother of St. Gregory of Nyssa. In his student days at Athens he knew Julian, later Roman emperor, and began his lifelong friendship with St. GREGORY NAZIANZEN. Converted to the religious life by his sister, St. Macrina, he withdrew (c.357) to a retreat in Pontus. There he wrote much of the *Longer Rule* and of the *Shorter Rule*; on these the life of the BASILIAN MONKS is based. Through his rules Basil was a spiritual ancestor of St. Benedict. As counselor (365) and successor (370) of Eusebius, bishop of Caesarea and head of most of the church in Asia Minor, Basil established Nicene orthodoxy over ARIANISM in the Byzantine East. His revision of the liturgy is occasionally used in the Byzantine rite. His works *On the Holy Ghost* and *Against Eunomius* are elegant, acute defenses of the Catholic system. In the West his feast is June 14. See his letters tr. by R. J. Deferrari (4 vol., 1926–34); studies by G. L. Prestige (1956), E. Amand de Mendieta (1965), and M. G. Murphy (1971).

Basingstoke (bā'zĭngstōk), municipal borough (1971 pop. 52,502), Hampshire, S central England, on the North Downs. Formerly a market town trading in silk and woolens, it now has several industries, including the manufacture of agricultural machinery, precision tools and instruments, leather, clothing, and drugs. The borough is growing rapidly, largely because of a spillover from London's population. In 871, Alfred defeated the Danes at nearby Basing. Basingstoke is mentioned as a royal manor in the Domesday Book. Oliver Cromwell won a victory at Basing in 1645.

Baskerville, John, 1706–75, English designer of type and printer. He and CASLON were the two great type designers of the 18th cent. in England. He began his work as printer and publisher in 1757 and in 1758 became printer to Cambridge Univ. Baskerville's first volume was a quarto edition of Vergil. His type faces introduced the modern, pseudoclassical style, with level serifs and with emphasis on the contrast of light and heavy lines. This style influenced that of the DIDOT family in France and that of BODONI in Italy. Books printed by Baskerville are typically large, with wide margins, made with excellent paper and ink. His masterpiece was a folio Bible, published in 1763. The first wove paper used for printing books was made to his order. After his death his wife operated the press until 1777. Then most of his types were purchased by Beaumarchais and were used in his 70-volume edition of Voltaire. The matrices, long lost, were rediscovered and in 1953 were presented to the Cambridge Univ. Press. Among Baskerville's publications in the British Museum are *Aesop's Fables* (1761), the Bible (1763), and the works of Horace (1770). See biographies by William Bennett (1939) and Henry Evans (1953); bibliography by Philip Gaskell(1959).

basketball, game played generally indoors by two opposing teams of five players each. At each end of the court—usually about 92 ft (28 m) long and 50 ft (15 m) wide—is a bottomless basket made of white cord net and suspended from a metal ring, 18 in. (.46 m) in diameter, which is attached 10 ft (3.05 m) above the floor (usually hardwood) to a backboard. Players may pass, throw, bat, roll, or dribble (bounce) the ball but may not run with it. Players of one team seek to advance the ball into position for shooting it through one basket (the ball must enter from above) and to keep the opposition from scoring through the other basket. Each field goal, or basket, scores two points. Illegal body contact is penalized by awarding free throws—counting one point for each made—to players fouled. There is a limit—five in amateur, six in professional play—to the number of fouls a player may commit before he is disqualified from a game. International and collegiate basketball games are played in two 20-min halves. Basketball was originated in the United States, in 1891, by Dr. James NAISMITH, then a physical education instructor at the YMCA college in Springfield, Mass. Today it is one of the leading American sports, attracting well over 30 million spectators a year, and has been enthusiastically adopted throughout the world. In 1937 one of the most important and far-reaching rule changes was made, when the center jump after each score was eliminated. This greatly speeded up the game, increased scoring, and reduced some of the advantage enjoyed by taller players. Another measure designed to reduce the importance of height is the rule (adopted 1968) against "dunking," or ramming the ball directly into the basket from above, in intercollegiate play. Height, however, continues to be an important asset in basketball. The game is a major sport in American colleges, and such postseason collegiate tournaments as the National Invitation Tournament (begun 1938) and the National Collegiate Athletic Association championships (begun 1939) attract wide attention. The latter tournament, held to determine the nation's best collegiate basketball team, was dominated by the University of California at Los Angeles during the late 1960s and early 1970s. Between 1967 and 1973, UCLA won a record-setting seven straight national championships, and had over 60 consecutive victories in regular competition. Another important factor in the popularizing of basketball was the presentation of college games in large public arenas, begun (1934) with double-headers in Madison Square Garden, New York City. The popularity of college basketball continued to grow until serious scandals hit the sport in 1951. Investigations disclosed that in games in Madison Square Garden and elsewhere college players had been bribed by gamblers to "fix" games (i.e., arrange the final scores to a gambler's advantage). Within the next ten years further investigations resulted in the conviction of more than 100 athletes from colleges throughout the country. Since the scandals college basketball has been able to cultivate a more positive image and has grown in popularity. Although an exhibition basketball game was played at the 1904 Olympics, it was not until 1936 that the sport became a regular part of the games. International competition differs from American collegiate and professional basketball in that the area directly in front of the basket, known as the free throw lane or the three-second area, is cone-shaped rather than rectangular. International basketball is also considered rougher and involves more physical contact than the American game. The United States dominated almost every major international basketball competition until 1972, when the Soviet Union defeated the U.S. team for the Olympic gold medal, in spite of official American protests that the Soviet team was illegally allowed to score a basket after the game had ended. Professional basketball was begun (1896) in New York City and has since grown very popular. The merger (1949) of the National Basketball League and its rival the Basketball Association of America into the National Basketball Association (NBA) led to great development of the game. The NBA consists of 18 teams in four divisions. The teams are: Atlanta Hawks, Boston Celtics, Buffalo Braves, Chicago Bulls, Cleveland Cavaliers, Detroit Pistons, Golden State Warriors, Houston Rockets, Kansas City-Omaha Kings, Los Angeles Lakers, Milwaukee Bucks, New York Knickerbockers, New Orleans Jazz, Philadelphia 76ers, Phoenix Suns, Portland Trail Blazers, Seattle SuperSonics, Washington Bullets. Professional basketball's popularity led to the establishment (1967) of the American Basketball Association (ABA), a rival league to the NBA. The ABA is composed of ten teams in two divisions. The ABA teams are: Carolina Cougars, Denver Rockets, Indiana Pacers, Kentucky Colonels, Memphis Tams, New York Nets, San Antonio Spurs, San Diego Conquistadors, Utah Stars, and Virginia Squires. Economic competition between the two leagues resulted in lucrative first-year contracts for many college stars, some of whom were signed for as much as one million dollars. The expense of this bidding war led NBA and ABA owners to seek congressional approval for a merger, although such a plan is opposed by the players, who expect to gain much from interleague competition. The professional game, with 12-min quarters, has adapted its rules, adding a 24-sec time limit for the offensive team to make a shot. A time limit has long been a feature of international competition. The most famous of all the professional teams were the Original Celtics of New York City, the Boston Celtics between 1957 and 1965, and the Harlem Globetrotters, an independent touring team. There are modifications in basketball rules for high school and women's play. See W. R. Alheim, *Beginning Basketball for Men* (1968); Leonard Koppett, *24 Seconds to Shoot* (1968); Bob Cousy, *Basketball* (1970); Pete Axthelm, *The City Game* (1971); Dale Hanson, *Basketball* (1972); B. L. Webb, *The Basketball Man: James Naismith* (1973); Zander Hollander, ed. *The Modern Encyclopedia of Basketball* (rev. ed. 1973).

basket makers, name given to the members of an early North American Indian culture in the Southwest, predecessors of the PUEBLO INDIANS. Because of the cultural continuity from the basket makers to the Pueblos, they are jointly referred to by archaeologists, as the Anasazi culture. They are so called because of their extensive practice of basketmaking; by covering the baskets with clay and baking them hard they created fireproof containers. One system of dating places their arrival in the area as early as 1500 B.C. They seem to have been at first nomadic hunters, using wooden clubs, hunting sticks, and the ATLATL. They lived chiefly in houses with adobe floors and learned to grow corn and squash, probably from southern neighbors in Mexico. As they developed a more extensive agriculture, they dug pits and lined them with stone for grain storage and later built substantial dwellings lined with slabs of stone. At some time, perhaps c.500 B.C., they were succeeded in the area by the ancestors of the Pueblo Indians, who probably absorbed many of them. Some basket makers may have moved and may have been the ancestors of other Indian tribes. Archaeologists divide the time of their culture into the Basket Maker and Modified Basket Maker periods; in the latter period they turned increasingly to agriculture. See INDIANS, NORTH AMERICAN.

basketry, art of weaving or coiling and sewing flexible materials to form vessels or other commodities. The materials used include twigs, roots, strips of hide, splints, osier willows, bamboo splits, cane or rattan, raffia, grasses, straw, and crepe paper. Discoveries in the W United States indicate that the use of clay-covered baskets for cooking probably led to making pottery, while in the Andaman islands pottery was evidently made first. In Egypt baskets used for storing grain in 4000 or 5000 B.C. have been excavated. The tombs of Etruria have yielded ancient specimens, and these, as well as much later Roman baskets, display weaving strokes still in use. Basketry has been employed by primitive peoples for rude huts, which they daubed with clay, and for articles of dress and adornment, granaries, traps, boats, cooking utensils, water vessels, and other utilities. There are two types of baskets—woven and coiled or sewn—but variety is afforded by the many different strokes, forms, and methods of decoration. There are many large commercial basket-weaving establishments, but basketry is still a popular home industry and is taught in schools and as occupational therapy in hospitals.

Baskin, Leonard, 1922–, American sculptor, graphic artist, and teacher, b. New Brunswick, N.J. In sculptural and graphic works that are figurative in style, Baskin's images of a corrupt, bloated mankind retain an element of sardonic humor. His woodcuts are celebrated for their power and expressiveness. Among his notable prints are *Mid-Century Monster* and *The Poet Laureate;* his sculpture *Man with a Dead Bird* is in the Museum of Modern Art, New York City. Since 1953 Baskin has taught at Smith College. His works, often reproduced, are represented in many of the world's major museums. Baskin founded the Gehenna Press, noted for fine typography, in Northampton, Mass. See his *Sculpture, Drawings and Prints* (1970).

basking shark, large, plankton-feeding shark, *Cetorhinus maximus,* inhabiting many oceans of the world, especially in temperate regions. Found singly or in schools of up to 100, it spends much of its time on or just below the surface, cruising slowly with its dorsal fin breaking water. It reaches a length of 40 ft (12 m) and weighs up to 8,500 lb (3,900 kg)—among fishes it is second in size only to the whale shark. It feeds by filtering out plankton as water passes into its mouth and out of the gills. Its gill openings are greatly enlarged to accommodate a large volume of water, and its throat is lined with numerous slender structures called gill rakers. These rakers, which are attached to the inside of the gill arches, form a fine mesh that serves as a strainer. The basking shark has a torpedo-shaped body, a nearly symmetrical tail fin, and long, conspicuous gill slits. Its color ranges from gray to black or brown. It is fished commercially, mostly by harpooning; its flesh is used for fish meal and its liver oil for certain tanning processes. It is classified in the phylum CHORDATA, subphylum Vertebrata, class Chondrichthyes, order Selachii, family Cetorhinidae.

Basle, Switzerland: see BASEL.

Basmath (băs'măth), daughter of Solomon. 1 Kings 4.15.

Basque language (băsk), tongue of uncertain relationship spoken by about 800,000 people, most of whom live in NE Spain and some of whom reside in SW France. The language has eight dialects. Speakers of Basque are, for the most part, bilingual, and the chances for the survival of the language are not good. Basque is definitely not an Indo-European tongue. Some scholars believe it is descended from Aquitanian, which was spoken on the Iberian peninsula and in S Gaul in ancient times. Other linguists think Basque is akin to the CAUCASIAN LANGUAGES and suggest that its speakers came from Asia Minor to Spain and Gaul c.2000 B.C. However, no relationship between Basque and any other language has been established with certainty. The alphabet used for Basque employs Roman letters. The first printed book in Basque appeared in the 16th cent. Basque is both agglutinative and polysynthetic. In an agglutinative language, different linguistic elements, each of which exists separately and has a fixed meaning, are often joined to form one word. In a polysynthetic language, a number of word elements are joined together to form a composite word that functions like a sentence or phrase in Indo-European languages, but each element has meaning usually only as part of the sentence or phrase and not as a separate item. See William J. Entwistle, *The Spanish Language, Together with Portuguese, Catalan, and Basque* (2d ed. 1962).

Basque Provinces, Basque *Euzkadi,* Span. *Vascongadas,* comprising the provinces of Álava, Guipúzcoa, and Vizcaya (1970 pop. 1,876,787), N Spain, S of the Bay of Biscay and bordering on France in the northeast. The region includes the W Pyrenees and is bounded in the southwest by the Ebro River. It is crossed by the Cantabrian Mts. (In a wider sense the name also applies to other territories largely inhabited by Basques: Spanish Navarre and Basses-Pyrénées dept. in France.) Bilbao, capital of Vizcaya prov., is the largest Basque city and one of the chief industrial centers of Spain. Other cities include San Sebastián, capital of Guipúzcoa prov; Vitoria, capital of Álava prov.; and historic Guernica. In the densely populated coastal provinces of Vizcaya and Guipúzcoa the chief occupations are the mining of iron, lead, copper, and zinc, and metalworking, shipbuilding, and fishing. The minerals are exported mainly to England. Álava is primarily agricultural; corn and sugar beets are grown, and wine and apple cider are made. For the history of the three provinces up to 1936, see BASQUES. Shortly after the outbreak of the Spanish civil war in 1936 the central government granted the three provinces autonomy. The Basque nationalist leader, José Antonio de Aguirre, was elected president of the autonomous government. The Basques defended their newly won status with their customary heroism and fervor, but a large part of their territory was soon in insurgent hands. The fighting was over by Sept., 1937. The new Franco regime abolished Basque autonomy, but to this day Basque nationalism remains strong. Protests and strikes are common, and terrorists, operating from headquarters in other European countries, stage frequent attacks.

Basques (băsks), people of N Spain and SW France. There are about 1,774,000 Basques in the three Basque provs. and Navarre, Spain; over 100,000 in Labourd, Soule, and Lower Navarre, France; and communities of various sizes in Central and South America and other parts of the world. Many preserve their ancient language, which is unrelated to any other tongue. They have guarded their ancient customs and traditions, although they have played a prominent role in the history of Spain and France. The origin of the Basques, almost certainly the oldest surviving ethnic group in Europe, has not yet been determined, but they antedate the ancient Iberian tribes of Spain, with which they have been erroneously identified. Genetically and culturally, the Basque population has been relatively isolated and distinct, perhaps since Paleolithic times. Primarily free peasants, shepherds, fishermen, navigators, miners, and metalworkers, the Basques have also produced such figures as St. Ignatius of Loyola, St. Francis Xavier, and Francisco de Vitoria. Before Roman times, the Basque tribes, little organized politically, extended further to the north and south than at present. But the core of the Basque country resisted Romanization and was only nominally subject to Roman rule. Christianity was slow in penetrating (3d-5th cent.). Once converted, the Basques remained fervent Roman Catholics, but they have retained a certain tradition of independence from the hierarchies of Spain and France. The Basques withstood domination by the Visigoths and Franks. Late in the 6th cent. they took advantage of the anarchy prevailing in the Frankish kingdom and expanded northward, occupying present-day Gascony (Lat. *Vasconia*), to which they gave their name. The duchy of Vasconia, formed in 601 and chronically at war with the Franks, Visigoths, and Moors, was closely associated with, and at times dominated by, Aquitaine. In 778 the Basques, who had just been reduced to nominal vassalage by Charlemagne, destroyed the Frankish rearguard at Roncesvalles, but they subsequently recognized Louis the Pious, king of Aquitaine, as their suzerain. The duchy of Gascony continued, but the Basques early in the 9th cent. concentrated in their present habitat and in 824 founded, at Pamplona, the kingdom of Navarre, which under Sancho III (1000-1035) united almost all the Basques. Although Castile acquired Guipúzcoa (1200), Álava (1332), and Vizcaya (1370), the Castilian kings recognized the wide democratic rights enjoyed by the Basques. GUERNICA was the traditional location of Basque assemblies. With the conquest (1512) of Navarre by Ferdinand the Catholic, the Basques lost their last independent stronghold. After the 16th cent., Basque prosperity declined and emigration became common, especially in the 19th cent. Basque privileges remained in force under the Spanish monarchy, but in 1873 they were abolished because of the Basques' pro-Carlist stand in the Carlist Wars. To regain autonomy, the Basques supported nearly every political movement directed against the central authority. In the civil war of 1936-39, the Basque Provinces, not including Navarre, defended the republican government, under which they had autonomous status. The Basques of Navarre supported the Franco forces. The Franco government, once in power, for the most part discouraged Basque political and cultural autonomy, although Basque nationalism has retained its appeal to the Basques. The trial of Basque nationalists in

1970 caused serious political conflicts in Spain, and the years following have been increasingly marked by unrest and violence by and against the Basque separatist organization. See Rodney Gallop, *A Book of the Basques* (1930, repr. 1970).

Basra (bŭs'rə), Arabic *al Basrah,* city (1965 pop. 313,327), SE Iraq, on the Shatt al Arab. Basra is the only port in Iraq. Its commercially advantageous location, near oil fields and 75 mi (121 km) from the Persian Gulf, has made it prosperous. Since 1948 many oil refineries have been built in the city. Petroleum products, grains, wool, and dates are exported. Basra was founded (A.D. 636) by the caliph Umar I. It was a cultural center under Harun ar-Rashid and declined with the decay of the Abbasid caliphate. Its possession was long contested by the Persians and the Turks. After World War I the construction of a rail line to Baghdad and the building of a modern harbor restored the city's importance. It is the seat of a branch of the Univ. of Baghdad. The name also appears as Bassora, Bussora, and Busra.

Bas-Rhin (bä-răN'), department (1968 pop. 827,367), E France, in N Alsace. STRASBOURG is the capital and the commercial and industrial center.

Bass, Sam, 1851-78, American desperado, b. near Mitchell, Ind. He went (c.1870) to Denton, Texas, where he worked at various jobs before he became an outlaw. He was a road agent and train robber around Deadwood, S. Dak., for a time, then returned to Texas, where he gained notoriety as a train robber. One of his gang informed on him, and when Bass arrived to rob the bank at Round Rock he was mortally wounded by the Texas Rangers. His career and especially his death provided material for frontier ballads. See biographies by Wayne Gard (1936, repr. 1969) and C. L. Martin (1880, repr. 1956, 1968).

bass, common name applied to various fishes of the families Serranidae (sea basses) and Centrarchidae (black basses and sunfishes). The sea basses are a large, diverse, and important family of perchlike fishes with oblong, rather compressed bodies. All basses are carnivorous and most are marine, although several species are found in fresh water (see SUNFISH). Sea basses inhabit warm and temperate seas throughout the world and are highly valued as game and food fishes. Along the Atlantic coast as far north as Cape Cod is found the common, or black, sea bass, a sluggish bottom fish averaging 6 lb (2.7 kg) in weight and 18 in. (45 cm) in length. Offshoots of the sea basses and classified with them are the white basses, including the striped bass (or rockfish) and the white perch, both found in fresh and brackish waters from Florida to Canada; the white bass of the Mississippi valley and the Great Lakes; and the similar but smaller yellow bass, found in the same range. The Pacific sea basses include the giant sea bass, or Pacific jewfish, a bulky bottom fish that reaches a weight of 600 lb (270 kg) and a length of 7 ft (2.1 m), as well as the 2-ft (60-cm) kelp and sand basses. The GROUPERS are an important genus of large tropical sea basses. Very closely allied to the sea basses are the tripletail, with prominent anal and dorsal fins, and the robalo, or snook, widely distributed in tropical American salt waters. Basses are classified in the phylum CHORDATA, subphylum Vertebrata, class Osteichthyes, order Perciformes, families Serranidae and Centrarchidae.

bass (bās), in musical harmony, the part of lowest pitch. The term is used for the lowest-pitched male VOICE and for instruments of low pitch, such as bass clarinet, bass drum, French horn, bassoon (bass oboe), and bass trombone.

Bassano, Jacopo (yä'kōpō bäs-sä'nō), c.1515-1592, Venetian painter, whose original name was Jacopo, or Giacomo, da Ponte, b. Bassano, Italy. Bassano first studied with his father, Francesco da Ponte, and then went to Venice. There he was influenced by Titian and Lorenzo Lotto, but he soon evolved a more turbulent mannerist style. Returning to Bassano c.1540, he established a thriving workshop producing works primarily on biblical themes. Into his paintings, which were characterized by a dramatic intensity, he introduced vignettes of country life. He was among the first Italian painters to depict animals, farmhouses, and landscapes. Jacopo's works include *Jacob's Return to Canaan* (Ducal Palace, Venice); *Dives and Lazarus* (Cleveland Mus.); *Acteon and the Nymphs* (Art Inst., Chicago); *Annunciation to the Shepherds* (National Gall. of Art, Washington, D.C.). See study by Pietro Zampetti (tr. 1958). Of Jacopo's four sons, his most worthy followers were **Francesco Bassano,** 1549-92, whose biblical and pastoral scenes were similar in style to his father's, and **Leandro Bassano,** 1558-1623, who painted altarpieces and portraits as well as pastoral GENRE. The Cleveland Museum of Art has his *Pietà.*

Bassano del Grappa (bäs-sä'nō dĕl gräp'pä), city (1971 pop. 35,187), Venetia, NE Italy, on the Brenta River. It is an agricultural, commercial, and industrial center. First mentioned c.998, the city came under several lords before passing to Venice in 1404. In Sept., 1796, Napoleon I defeated the Austrians there. The Da Ponte family of painters, called the Bassano family after the city, had a flourishing school there in the 16th cent., and many of their works remain in the city. In the 17th and 18th cent. the Remondini printing plant was famous throughout Europe. Of note are a 13th-century castle, a wooden covered bridge (13th cent., rebuilt numerous times including 1945), and a number of fine old churches and villas.

Bassein (bəsēn', -sān'), town (1969 est. pop. 175,000), S Burma, on the Bassein River. Lying at the western edge of the Irrawaddy delta, Bassein is accessible to large vessels; it is also the terminus of a branch of the main railroad line. The town is a rice-milling and export center; teak and bamboo are also handled. The British established a fort at Bassein in 1852. It was occupied by the Japanese during World War II.

Basses-Alpes: see ALPES-DE-HAUTES-PROVENCE.

Basses-Pyrénées: see PYRÉNÉES-ATLANTIQUE.

Basse-Terre (bästĕr'), town (1969 est. pop. 16,000), capital of GUADELOUPE dept., French West Indies. It is a port that ships the products of the surrounding agricultural area. Founded by the French in 1643, it retains its French colonial atmosphere; but its commercial prosperity passed to Pointe-à-Pitre in the late 18th cent.

Basseterre, town (1970 est. pop. 14,000), capital of SAINT KITTS-NEVIS, on St. Kitts island, British West Indies. It is one of the chief commercial depots of the Leeward Islands. Sugar refining is the leading industry. Basseterre was founded by the French in 1627.

basset hound, breed of short-legged, long-bodied HOUND developed centuries ago in France. It stands from 12 to 15 in. (30.1-38.1 cm) high at the shoulder and weighs from 25 to 50 lb (11.3-22.7 kg). The short, dense coat is usually black, tan, or white or any combination of these colors. The basset was perfected to hunt such game as rabbits, fox, squirrels, and pheasant in very heavy ground cover; the shortness of its legs allows it to keep its head to the scent with a minimum of difficulty. It has also been trained to hunt raccoons and opossum and to retrieve. Renowned for its scenting ability, which is second only to that of its close relative the bloodhound, the basset is still popular as a slow but efficient hunter. It is also raised as a pet. See DOG.

Bassett, James, 1834-1906, American Presbyterian missionary, b. Canada. In 1872, under the auspices of the American Board, he founded the first American mission at Teheran, Persia. Under his supervision other mission stations were founded, and in 1882 he became senior missionary and head of the Eastern Mission of Persia. He wrote *Persia, the Land of the Imams* (1886) and *Persia, Eastern Mission* (1890).

Bassett, John Spencer, 1867-1928, American historian, b. Tarboro, N.C. He was professor of history at Trinity College (now Duke Univ.) from 1893 to 1906 and then at Smith from 1906 to 1928. His first writings were mostly monographs on North Carolina history. Bassett founded (1902) the *South Atlantic Quarterly.* Chief among his writings are *The Federalist System, 1789-1801* (1906, repr. 1968; Vol. II in the "American Nation" series), *The Life of Andrew Jackson* (1911, repr. 1967), and *The Middle Group of American Historians* (1917). He also edited much original material, including *The Writings of "Colonel William Byrd . . ."* (1901), *Selections from the Federalist* (1921), *The Southern Plantation Overseer as Revealed in His Letters* (1925, repr. 1968), and *The Correspondence of Andrew Jackson* (7 vol., 1926-35).

Bassompierre, François, baron de (fräNswä' bärôN' də bäsôNpyĕr'), 1579-1646, marshal of France. Under King Henry IV he distinguished himself in the army and as a courtier, and after Henry's death he remained loyal to the queen, Marie de' Medici, during her regency. Subsequently he was ambassador to Spain, to England, and to Switzerland, and he fought against the HUGUENOTS in 1621-22 and 1627-28. Because of his opposition to Cardinal Richelieu and his alleged part in an intrigue he was imprisoned (1631) in the Bastille until after the cardinal's death (1643). During his captivity he wrote valuable memoirs.

bassoon (bəso͞on'), double-reed woodwind instrument that plays in the bass and tenor registers. Its 8-ft (2.4-m) conical tube is bent double, the instrument thus being about 4 ft (1.2 m) high. It evolved from earlier double-reed instruments in the 16th cent. and by 1600 was common throughout Europe. When the orchestra developed in the 17th cent., the bassoon was one of the original woodwinds included and has been indispensable ever since. It was much improved in the 19th cent. in both France and Germany; the French and German bassoons have since differed from each other appreciably in tonal quality and construction. Although used in chamber music, the bassoon has only a small literature as a solo instrument. When played staccato it can have a humorous effect that has been frequently exploited by composers. The contrabassoon, also called double bassoon, is pitched an octave below the bassoon. Fingering is the same for both. The contrabassoon's tube, more than 16 ft (4.9 m) long, is doubled back upon itself four times. First made by Hans Schreiber of Berlin in 1620, it was used by Handel, Haydn, and Beethoven. Technical imperfections hindered any extensive use until a German, Wilhelm Heckel, in the late 19th cent. improved its construction and intonation, producing the model in general use today.

Bassoon

Bassora: see BASRA, Iraq.

Bass Strait (băs), channel, 80 to 150 mi (129-241 km) wide, between Tasmania and Victoria, SE Australia, connecting the Indian Ocean and Tasman Sea; Port Phillip Bay and Melbourne are on the northwest coast. Bass Strait is an important fishing area. The discovery of the strait by English explorer George Bass in 1798 proved that Tasmania was not a part of the Australian continent.

bass viol (bās vī'əl), properly, the largest instrument of the VIOL family. The term now refers most often to the DOUBLE BASS.

basswood: see LINDEN.

Bast (băst), ancient Egyptian cat goddess. At first a goddess of the home, she later became known as a goddess of war. The center of her cult was at Bubastis. Her name also appears as Ubast.

bast: see BARK.

bastard, person born out of wedlock whose legal status is illegitimacy. In CIVIL LAW countries and in about half the states of the United States, the union of the parents in marriage after birth makes the child legitimate. Unlike civil law, which granted bastards certain rights, English COMMON LAW treated them almost as persons outside the law and left their care to poorhouses. At common law a bastard has no right to inherit property from his mother or father except by specific designation (e.g., in a will). Recently their condition has been much improved by statute. It is presumed that any child born to a married woman, or within competent time after termination of the marriage, is the child of her husband. If, however, it can be proved that it was physically impossible for the husband to have been the father (e.g., because of nonaccess to the wife), he may bring action to establish the illegitimacy of the child. For the status of children born to annulled marriages, see NULLITY OF MARRIAGE; HUSBAND AND WIFE. See also LEGITIMATION.

Bastenaken: see BASTOGNE, Belgium.

Bastia (bästē'ä), city (1968 pop. 50,100), NE Corsica, France, on the Tyrrhenian Sea. It is the island's largest city and chief commercial center. It has a thriving export industry, sawmills, and cigarette and food-processing plants. Founded (14th cent.) as a fort by the Genoese, it was the capital of Corsica until 1791. Its citadel (16th–17th cent.) and its many 18th-century buildings are tourist attractions.

Bastian, Adolf (ä'dôlf bäs'tyän), 1826–1905, German anthropologist. Often called the father of ethnography, he recorded his observations of peoples and cultures in *Der Mensch in der Geschichte* [man in history] (1860). His concept of "elemental ideas" as common to mankind but varying in form according to "folk ideas" of a given area foreshadows the culture-area theory of modern anthropology. His influence was transmitted through the works of Franz BOAS and others. Bastian's important studies appeared in the *Zeitschrift für Ethnologie,* which he helped to found and edit, and in *Ethnologische Forschungen* (1871–73).

Bastiat, Frédéric (frädārĕk' bästyä'), 1801–50, French economist. In his *Harmonies of Political Economy* (1850, tr. 1860) he developed the classical theories of economic individualism and laissez-faire. A popular and controversial writer, he vigorously supported free trade. There are several translations of his essays called *Sophismes économiques* (1847–48). See studies by Dean Russell (1959 and 1965) and G. C. Roche, 3d (1971).

Bastidas, Rodrigo de (rôthrē'gō dā bästē'thäs), c.1460–1526, Spanish conquistador in Colombia. In 1501, accompanied by BALBOA and Juan de la COSA, he discovered the mouths of the Magdalena River. Because of difficulties with the Spanish crown, it was 1525 before he returned to found SANTA MARTA. He prohibited exploitation of the Indians and so dissatisfied his followers that they tried to murder him. Wounded, he fled to Santo Domingo, but bad weather forced him to land in Cuba, where he died.

Bastille (băstēl') [O.Fr.,=fortress], fortress and state prison in Paris, located, until its demolition (started in 1789), near the site of the present Place de la Bastille. It was begun c.1369 by Hugh Aubriot, provost of the merchants [mayor] of Paris under King Charles V. Arbitrary and secret imprisonment by LETTRE DE CACHET gave rise to stories of horror, but actually the Bastille was generally used for persons of influence, and its regime for most political prisoners was mild. As a symbol of absolutism the Bastille was hated. It had strategic importance, for its guns commanded one of the gates of Paris. On July 14, 1789, a Parisian mob stormed the Bastille in the hope of capturing ammunition. The governor, the marquis de Launey, was killed; the seven inmates, none of them political prisoners, were freed. This first spontaneous act of the people of Paris opened the way for the lower classes in the French Revolution. The event acquired symbolic significance, and July 14—Bastille Day—became the national holiday of republican France.

Bastogne (bästô'nyə), Flemish *Bastenaken,* town (1970 pop. 6,816), Luxembourg prov., SE Belgium, in the Ardennes and near the border of the duchy of Luxembourg. It is a market town noted for its hams and is a rail junction. In World War II during the Battle of the Bulge (Dec., 1944–Jan., 1945) it was held mainly by a U.S. division, against intensive bombardment by the Germans and generally overwhelming odds, until relieved by the U.S. 3rd Army. Nearby are military cemeteries and the Mardesson monument to the U.S. soldiers who died in battle.

Bastrop (băs'trŏp"), city (1970 pop. 14,713), seat of Morehouse parish, NE La.; founded c.1845. An industrial city in a cattle, farm, and timber area, Bastrop is the center of the huge Monroe natural gas field (discovered 1916). Its principal manufactures are paper, wood pulp, wood products, and chemicals.

Basutoland: see LESOTHO.

bat, winged mammal of the order Chiroptera, which includes between 1,000 and 2,000 species classified in about 200 genera and 17 families. Bats range in size from a wingspread of over 5 ft (150 cm) to a wingspread of less than 2 in. (5 cm). They are found in nearly all parts of the world but are most numerous in the tropics; there are about 30 species in the United States. Bats are the only mammals capable of true flight, that is, flight powered by muscular movement as distinct from gliding. The wing is a double membrane of skin stretched between the enormously elongated bones of four fingers and extending along the body from the forelimbs to the hind limbs and from there to the tail. The thumb is small, clawed, and free from the membrane. The hind limbs are small and may be rotated in such a way that the knees bend backward rather than forward, as in other mammals; this is presumably an adaptation for take off and flight. The body of the bat is mouselike and usually covered with fine fur. The face varies greatly from one species to another; many species have complex appendages on the snout and projections, or false ears, in front of the true ears; the ears themselves are often very large and elaborately convoluted. These facial structures are part of the sensory apparatus that receives sound vibrations. Nearly all bats are nocturnal and many live in caves; although they see well, they rely primarily on their highly developed hearing, using echolocation (sonar) to avoid collisions and to capture insects in flight. The bat emits high-pitched sounds (up to 50,000 hertz) that echo from any object it encounters; the echo provides the bat with information about the size, shape, and distance of the object. The rate at which bats emit these squeaks is sometimes as high as 200 per sec. Blinded bats easily find their way through complex obstacle courses, but deafness leaves them helpless. Bats at rest hang head down, grasping a twig or crevice with their clawed feet; they take off into flight from this position. Some bats are solitary, living in caves, crevices, hollow trees, or attics; other species are communal, with thousands or even millions of bats roosting together in a cave or on branches in a section of forest. In some species of communal bats, the entire colony leaves the roost together in the evening and returns together in the morning; in others, individuals come and go at different times. Bats of northern regions migrate, hibernate, or both in winter. In most species, males and females do not associate except during the mating season. Females of most species bear a single young in the summer of each year. The young are then carried by the mothers for a few days, after which they are left in the roost when not nursing; they begin to fly in a few weeks. The life span of some bats is 20 years in captivity. The bat order is divided on anatomical grounds into two major divisions, or suborders: the Megachiroptera, or FRUIT BATS, found only in the Old World tropics, and the Microchiroptera, or insect-eating bats, with a worldwide distribution. The fruit bats include the largest species of bat, the flying foxes, which may weigh 2 or 3 lbs (.9 to 1.4 kg). Their diet is confined almost entirely to fruit, nectar, and pollen. The insect-eating bats include the smallest bat species. Despite the name, some of these bats live wholly or largely on fruit; a large number eat insects and, in some cases, larger animals. Members of several species catch fish as they skim over water, and the South American VAMPIRE BATS feed exclusively on blood. The most common bats of the temperate Northern Hemisphere are the Old World horseshoe bats (*Rhinolophus*), characterized by one or two horseshoe-shaped facial appendages, the cosmopolitan little brown bats (*Myotis*), big brown bats, or serotines (*Eptesicus*), and pipistrelles (*Pipistrellus*). The last three, all represented by species in North America, belong to the plain-nosed bat family (Vespertilionidae), characterized by a lack of appendages on the snout. There are over a dozen species of *Myotis* in North America; the common little brown bat, *M. lucifugus,* is distributed over the entire continent from Alaska and Labrador to the S United States. A colonial bat, it is found in many habitats, including houses. It is about 2½ in. (6.3 cm) long without the tail and weighs about ¼ oz (7 grams). The North American big brown bat, *Eptesicus fuscus,* of similar distribution, is about three times as heavy, with a wingspread of 12 in. (30 cm). Large, solitary North American bats of wide distribution are the hoary bat, *Lasiurus cinereus,* yellow-brown with silver frosting, and the red bat, *L. borealis,* which is a striking brick-red color. Both have soft, thick fur and roost in trees. The freetail bats (family Molossidae) are a cosmopolitan group of communal bats characterized by a long tail extending well beyond the end of the wing membrane. Among them are the guano bats (*Tadarida*), which live in enormous colonies. Their excrement, called GUANO, accumulates in great quantities in their roosting places and is commercially valuable as fertilizer. Most New World freetail bats are tropical, but several are found in the S United States. One of these, the Mexican freetail bat (*Tadarida brasiliensis*), is noted for its colonies in the Carlsbad Caverns of New Mexico, numbering an estimated 9 million individuals. When these bats leave the caves together it takes about 20 min for the entire column to make its exit. This family also includes the mastiff bats (*Eumops*), largest of the North American bats, with a wingspread of 18 in. (46 cm). Most bats are economically valuable because of the large number of insects they consume. Bats are classified in the phylum CHORDATA, subphylum Vertebrata, class Mammalia, order Chiroptera. See R. W. Barbour and W. H. Davis, *Bats of America* (1969); W. A. Wimsatt, ed., *Biology of Bats* (2 vol., 1970).

Bataan (bătăn', -tän', bătä-än'), peninsula and province (1970 pop. 214,131), W Luzon, the Philippines, between Manila Bay and the South China Sea. Balanga is the provincial capital. A mountainous, thickly jungled region, it has some of the best bamboo forests in the Philippines. There is a pulp and paper mill, a large fertilizer plant, and an oil refinery (established there in 1961). Subsistence farming is carried on. Early in World War II (Dec., 1941–Jan., 1942), the U.S.-Filipino army withdrew to Bataan, where it entrenched and, despite the lack of naval and air support, fought a gallant holding action that upset the Japanese timetable for conquest. The army was crippled by starvation and disease when it was finally overwhelmed on April 9, 1942. The U.S. and Filipino troops captured there were subjected to the long, infamous "Death March" to the prison camp near Cabanatuan; thousands perished. Homage is annually paid these victims on Bataan Day, a national holiday, when large groups of Filipinos solemnly rewalk parts of the death route. The battleground of Bataan is now a national shrine. See also CORREGIDOR. See S. L. Falk, *Bataan: The March of Death* (1962); Robert Conroy, *The Battle of Bataan: America's Greatest Defeat* (1969).

Batalha (bətä'lyə) [Port.,=battle], town (1970 municipal pop. 6,673), W central Portugal, just S of Leiria, in Estremadura. It has a magnificent Dominican monastery and church (Santa Maria da Vitória), built by John I of Portugal to commemorate his victory (1385) over John I of Castile at nearby Aljubarrota. The monastery is now a national museum.

Batalpashinsk: see CHERKESSK, USSR.

Batanes, the Philippines: see BATAN ISLANDS.

Batangas (bätän'gäs), city (1970 pop. 927,290), capital of Batangas prov., SW Luzon, the Philippines. An important port on the Calumpan River near its mouth on Batangas Bay, it has a large oil refinery and serves a fertile farm area noted for its fruits, cacao, and coffee. Tourist attractions in Batangas province include Lake Taal, with its active volcano (which erupted in 1965, causing extensive damage and many deaths), and the popular summer resort city of Tagaytay.

Batan Islands (bätän'), island group (1970 pop. 11,425), 76 sq mi (197 sq km), northernmost of the Philippine islands. They include the islands of Itbayat, Batan, Sabtang, and a number of islets, and comprise the province of Batanes. Basco is the provincial capital. The Batan Islands are separated from Taiwan by the Bashi Channel (50 mi/80 km wide). Coal is mined, and fishing is an important industry. In World War II, Batan Island was the site of the first Japanese landing in the Philippines (Dec. 8, 1941).

Batavi (bətā'vī), ancient Germanic tribe that settled (1st cent. B.C.) in the Rhine delta. Batavian regiments served under Rome, although this relationship was interrupted in A.D. 70 by the anti-Roman conspiracy of CIVILIS, one of their leaders. The tribal name was revived in 1795 to designate Holland, particularly the BATAVIAN REPUBLIC.

Batavia: see DJAKARTA, Indonesia.

Batavia, city (1970 pop. 17,338), seat of Genesee co., W N.Y.; inc. 1915. It was laid out in 1801 by Joseph Ellicott, agent for the Holland Land Company. Situated in a farm area, Batavia has industries producing television sets, die castings, shoes, road equipment, paper boxes, and heating equipment. The city was a center of the Anti-Masonic movement in the 19th cent.

Batavian Republic, name for the Netherlands in the years (1795–1806) following conquest by the French during the FRENCH REVOLUTIONARY WARS. The United Provinces of the Netherlands were reconstituted as the Batavian Republic in 1795 and remained under French occupation and tutelage. In 1801, Napoleon imposed a new constitution on the republic, which was financially drained by French requisitions, and in 1806 he transformed Batavia into the kingdom of Holland under the domain of his brother Louis BO-

NAPARTE. *Batavia,* which derives from the BATAVI, an ancient Germanic tribe, is still used occasionally as a name for Holland.

Bate, William Brimage, 1826–1905, U.S. politician and Confederate general, b. Castalian Springs, Tenn. He served in the Mexican War and was involved in Tennessee politics before entering the Confederate army in 1861. In a spectacular career Bate rose from private to major general and served with distinction in six major campaigns. He was elected governor of Tennessee in 1882 and reelected in 1884. He served in the U.S. Senate from 1887 to 1905. See biography by Park Marshall (1908).

Bates, H. E. (Herbert Ernest Bates), 1905–74, English author, b. Rushden, Northamptonshire. During World War II he served with the Royal Air Force. A good storyteller, Bates had the ability to render the sense of a particular place and time and was noted for his descriptions of the English countryside. Among his many novels are *Fair Stood the Wind for France* (1944), *The Jacaranda Tree* (1949), and *The Triple Echo* (1970). See his autobiography (3 vol., 1969, 1971, 1971).

Bates, Henry Walter, 1825–92, English naturalist and explorer. In 1848 he went with A. R. Wallace to Brazil, where he explored the upper Amazon, returning in 1859 with some 8,000 new zoological species. He was the first to state a plausible theory of MIMICRY. His great work was *The Naturalist on the River Amazon* (1863). From 1864, Bates was assistant secretary of the Royal Geographical Society.

Bates, Katharine Lee, 1859–1929, American author, b. Falmouth, Mass., grad. Wellesley, 1880. She was professor of English literature at Wellesley (1891–1925). Her hymn, "America the Beautiful," first appeared in the *Congregationalist* magazine on July 4, 1895. Besides several books of poems, she wrote scholarly works and books for children. See biography by D. W. B. Burgess (1952).

Bates College, at Lewiston, Maine; coeducational; founded 1855 as Maine State Seminary, chartered as a college 1864. It was the first Eastern college to admit women students.

batfish: see ANGLER.

Bath, city (1971 pop. 84,545), Somerset, SW England, in the Avon River valley. Since 1974, it has been part of the new nonmetropolitan county of Avon. Britain's leading winter resort, Bath has the only natural hot springs in the country. There are also engineering, printing, bookbinding, wool-weaving, and clothing industries. In the 1st cent. A.D., the Romans discovered the natural springs and named the site Aquae Solis ("waters of the sun"), and built elaborate lead-lined baths with heating and cooling systems (first excavated in 1755). In Saxon times the city was destroyed and the baths buried. From the time of Chaucer until the Tudor era, Bath had a flourishing wool and cloth industry. In the 18th cent. Richard (Beau) Nash, establishing social standards equal to those of London society, and the architect John Wood and his son transformed Bath into England's most fashionable spa. The Woods, using Bath stone from nearby quarries, built Queen Square, the Circus, and the Royal Crescent, all excellent examples of Georgian architecture. The Assembly Rooms, of the same period, were destroyed by air raids in World War II but later restored. Near Bath is a museum of American arts and crafts.

Bath, city (1970 pop. 9,679), seat of Sagadahoc co., SW Maine, on the west bank of the Kennebec River near its mouth on the Atlantic; settled c.1670, inc. as a city 1847. It is a port of entry, with a fine harbor. Once a great shipbuilding center, it still has active shipyards and marine manufactures, but summer tourism is becoming increasingly important. Champlain and others visited or passed near this site when exploring the Kennebec River, and at nearby Popham Beach a short-lived colony was established (1607) by George Popham. Shipbuilding began early; many clipper ships were constructed in the 19th cent., and the Bath Iron Works began producing steel warships and commercial vessels in the 1880s. The city flourished, particularly during World Wars I and II, when a large number of destroyers were built. There is a marine museum, and many fine old mansions remain.

batholith, enormous mass of intrusive igneous ROCK, that is, rock made of once-molten material that has solidified below the earth's surface. Batholiths usually are granitic in composition, have steeply inclined walls, and are without any visible floors; they commonly extend over areas of thousands of square miles. One of the larger single batholiths in North America is the Coast Range batholith of W Canada and Alaska, encompassing an area of about 73,000 sq mi (182,500 sq km). Important batholiths in the United States include the Idaho batholith, 18,000 sq mi (45,000 sq km), and the Sierra Nevada batholith, 16,000 sq mi (40,000 sq km). In New England, the White Mountain and Sterling batholiths encompass a total of 1,200 sq mi (3,000 sq km). Batholiths are formed in mountain regions at great depth in the earth's crust and thus are exposed at the surface only after considerable erosion of the overlying mountain mass. The formation and emplacement of batholiths is one of the most perplexing and controversial subjects in geology. Some batholiths appear to have been emplaced by a process called magmatic stoping, in which liquid magma works its way upward in the crust by shattering and breaking large blocks of the roof of the magma chamber by means of thermal or mechanical wedging. These blocks of country rock may sink and ultimately be melted into the hot magma, or they may survive and be incorporated into the batholith as xenoliths. Other batholiths appear to have formed by the alteration of earlier-formed sedimentary or metamorphic rocks into granite without melting. This theoretical process, called granitization, has many supporters, since field studies sometimes show a close relationship between structures found in the granite and the surrounding country rock in many batholiths.

Báthory (bä'tôrē), Pol. *Batory,* Hungarian noble family. **Stephen Báthory,** 1477–1534, a loyal adherent of JOHN I of Hungary (John Zápolya), was made (1529) voivode [governor] of TRANSYLVANIA. His youngest son became (1575) king of Poland (see STEPHEN BÁTHORY, king of Poland) and was succeeded as prince of Transylvania by his brother, **Christopher Báthory,** 1530–81. Christopher married Elizabeth, sister of Stephen BOCSKAY. His son and successor, **Sigismund Báthory,** 1572–1613, was mentally unbalanced. At first a loyal vassal of the Hapsburg king of Hungary (Holy Roman Emperor Rudolf II), he crushed (1594) the pro-Turkish faction of nobles and was recognized by Rudolf as hereditary prince. In 1597, he abdicated in favor of Rudolf but returned to assume power in Aug., 1598. The following March he abdicated in favor of his cousin, Andrew Cardinal Báthory (d. 1599), but again reversed his decision and, with the help of Stephen Bocskay, returned to power as a vassal of Sultan Muhammad III. He abdicated definitively in 1602 (in favor of Rudolf) and retired to Silesia. **Elizabeth Báthory,** d. 1614, a niece of Stephen Bathory, is celebrated in legend and history as a female werewolf. She is said to have slaughtered more than 600 virgins in order to renew her youth by bathing in their blood. She was incarcerated in 1610 and died in prison. See biography by Valentine Penrose (tr. 1970); Baring Gould, *Book of Werewolves* (1865). **Gabriel Báthory,** 1589–1613, a nephew of Andrew Cardinal Báthory, became prince of Transylvania in 1608. His harsh regime provoked a rebellion by the nobles, and he was murdered. By the marriage of his niece Sophia (d. 1680) to George II Rákóczy, the two families were united.

Bath-rabbim (băth-răb'ĭm), gate in Heshbon. Song. 7.4.

baths, in architecture. Ritual bathing is traceable to ancient Egypt, to prehistoric cities of the Indus River valley, and to the early Aegean civilizations. Remains of bathing apartments dating from the Minoan period exist in the palaces at Cnossus and Tiryns. The ancient Greeks devised luxurious bathing provisions, with heated water, plunges, and showers. Bathing in public facilities, or thermae, was developed by the Romans to a unique degree. Thermae, probably copied after the Greek gymnasia, had impressive interiors, with rich mosaics, rare marbles, and gilded metals. Water, brought by aqueducts, was stored in reservoirs, heated to various temperatures, and distributed by piping to the bath apartments. Certain rooms were kept heated by means of furnaces which sent hot air into lines of flues beneath floors and in the walls. There are ruins of public baths in Pompeii, and in Rome there exist extensive remains of the thermae of Titus (A.D. 80), of Caracalla (A.D. 212–35), and of Diocletian (A.D. 302).

Bath-sheba (băth'-shēbə, -shē'bə), wife of Uriah the Hittite. David seduced her, effected the death of her husband, and then married her. Her second son by David was Solomon. 2 Sam. 11;12; 1 Kings 1; 2; Mat. 1.6. Bath-shua: 1 Chron. 3.5.

Bath-shua (băth-shōō'ə), same as BATH-SHEBA.

Bathurst, city (1971 pop. 17,169), New South Wales, SE Australia, on the Macquarie River. It is an agricultural market with food processing and other light industries and railroad workshops. Founded in 1815 and named for the earl of Bathurst, then British colonial secretary, it was the first settlement on the western side of the Blue mts. Bathurst is the seat of Roman Catholic and Anglican bishoprics.

Bathurst, city (1971 pop. 16,674), N N.B., Canada, on Chaleur Bay at the mouth of the Nepisiguit River. A popular beach resort, it is also the center of an area of lead, zinc, and copper mines and has large pulp, paper, and lumber mills.

Bathurst: see BANJUL, Gambia.

Bathurst Island, c.1,000 sq mi (2,590 sq km), Northern Territory, N Australia, near Melville Island, between the Timor and Arafura seas. There is an aboriginal reservation on the island.

Bathurst Island, 7,609 sq mi (19,707 sq km), in the Arctic Archipelago, Franklin dist., Northwest Territories, N Canada. It is the present site of the North Magnetic Pole.

batik (bətēk'), method of decorating fabrics practiced for centuries by the natives of Indonesia. It consists of applying a design to the surface of the cloth by using melted wax. The material is then dipped in cool vegetable dye; the portions protected by the wax do not receive the dye, and when the wax is removed in hot water the previously covered areas display a light pattern on the colored ground. Remains of clothing found in Java indicate that the same or similar patterns have been in use for about 1,000 years and are handed down in families. Certain designs were traditionally reserved for royalty and high officials. Motifs are geometric or are based on conventionalized natural objects. Cotton cloth is generally used, and some silk. Batik was first brought into Europe by Dutch traders. In the 19th cent., Western craftsmen adopted the art.

Batista y Zaldívar, Fulgencio (fōōlhĕn'sēō bätē'stä ē säldē'vär), 1901–73, president of Cuba (1940–44, 1954–58). An army sergeant, Batista took part in the overthrow of Gerardo MACHADO in 1933 and subsequently headed the military and student junta that ousted Carlos Manuel de CÉSPEDES and installed Ramón GRAU SAN MARTÍN. Made chief of staff of the army, he increased its size and power and soon became de facto ruler, launching a three-year plan of economic and social rehabilitation. In 1940, with support from the extreme left, he was elected president and subsequently ruled with a considerable degree of democratic equity. He accepted the defeat of his candidate when Grau won in the election of 1944. However, in 1952, when Batista was a presidential candidate, he seized power through a coup just prior to the election. An election was held in 1954 and Batista, unopposed and employing dubious methods, won easily. Discontent with his regime led to several uprisings, notably that of Fidel CASTRO. Pressed by the rebels and after a mock election (1958) had failed to calm the populace, Batista fled Cuba (Jan., 1959) for the Dominican Republic and thence to Portugal and Madeira. He died in Spain.

Batley, municipal borough (1971 pop. 42,004), West Riding of Yorkshire, N central England. In 1974, it became part of the new metropolitan county of West Yorkshire. Heavy woolens, shoddy, and other textiles are the chief manufactures; tiles, carpets, mattresses, felt, biscuits, and machinery are also produced. The Bagshaw Museum in Batley illustrates the history of clothmaking. Joseph Priestley, the radical minister and scientist, attended Batley Grammar School.

Batlle y Ordóñez, José (hōsā' bät'yā' ē ōrdō'nyās), 1856–1929, president of Uruguay (1903–7, 1911–15). A journalist and the head of the Colorado party, Batlle was a campaigner for political reform. In his second term he initiated radical legislation to increase public welfare and substitute government for the anarchism that had plagued Uruguay since the winning of independence. Among his most significant proposals were universal adult suffrage, labor reforms, and the decentralization of the executive into a junta modeled after the Swiss federal council. The constitution of 1917, framed under his influence, curbed the power of the executive and provided for socialist government, a trend not interrupted until TERRA became president in 1931. See study by M. I. Vanger (1963).

Batoche (bătōsh'), historic site, central Sask., Canada, on the South Saskatchewan River. During Riel's Rebellion, Louis Riel made his headquarters there, and the rebels were routed on May 12, 1885.

Batoni, Pompeo Girolamo (pōmpĕ'ō jērō'lämō bätō'nē), 1708–87, Italian painter. Batoni studied and worked in Rome. His paintings tend toward the neoclassical, a style foreshadowing that of Mengs. Among his notable works are *The Education of Achilles* (Uffizi), *Aeneas and His Family Fleeing Troy* (Turin), and *Mary Magdalen* (Louvre). Batoni is noted also for his portraits, including many of the reigning popes of his day.

Baton Rouge (băt'ən ro͞ozh) [Fr.,=red stick], city (1970 pop. 165,963), state capital and seat of East Baton Rouge parish, SE La., on a bluff along the eastern bank of the Mississippi River; inc. 1817. It is a busy deepwater port of entry; an important transportation, distributing, and commercial center for a large oil, natural gas, and farm area; and a major oil-refining hub. There are large petrochemical industries, food-processing plants, machine shops, foundries, and ironworks. Baton Rouge was founded in 1719 when the French built a fort on that strategic spot along the river. The settlement was ceded to Great Britain in 1762, captured by the Spanish in 1779, and acquired by the United States in 1815 (following a brief period when it was a part of Spanish Florida). It became state capital in 1849. In the Civil War it was captured by Farragut after the fall of New Orleans (May, 1862); a Confederate attempt to recover it failed (Aug., 1862). It has notable antebellum houses. The old capitol (1882), built in the Gothic style of the original that was burned in the Civil War, still stands; a new 34-story capitol was occupied in 1932. Also of interest are the governor's mansion, the old arsenal museum, and the Huey Long grave and memorial. The city has an arts and science center with a planetarium; several museums; a zoo; and a symphony orchestra. It is the seat of Louisiana State Univ. and Agricultural and Mechanical College and of Southern Univ. and Agricultural and Mechanical College.

Batory: see STEPHEN BÁTHORY and BÁTHORY, family.

Battambang (băt'əmbăng), city (1967 est. pop. 43,000), capital of Battambang prov., W Cambodia, in a great rice-growing area. The second largest city in Cambodia, it is a market center with numerous rice mills. Textiles are also made. The city is on both the highway and railroad linking Phnom Penh with Thailand; after the outbreak (1970) of civil war in Cambodia, the Battambang–Phnom Penh road was a prime target of the Khmer Rouge insurgents, who, by capturing it, severed Phnom Penh from its major source of rice. Battambang was acquired by Thailand in 1809 and returned to Cambodia in 1907. A technical university is located in the city.

Battenberg (băt'ənbûrg), German princely family, issued from the morganatic union of Alexander, a younger son of Louis II, grand duke of Hesse-Darmstadt, and Countess Julia von Hauke, who was created (1858) princess of Battenberg. Their oldest son, Louis (1854–1921), an admiral in the British navy, was created marquess of Milford Haven and married a granddaughter of Queen Victoria. During World War I he renounced (1917) his German title and anglicized his name as Mountbatten. His daughter Louise married Gustavus VI, king of Sweden. Another daughter, Alice, married Prince Andrew of Greece, third son of King George I of Greece; their son Philip was created duke of Edinburgh and married (1947) Princess Elizabeth of England (later Queen Elizabeth II). Louis MOUNTBATTEN is the son of the 1st marquess of Milford Haven. The second son of Prince Alexander of Hesse-Darmstadt was (1879–86) prince of Bulgaria (see ALEXANDER). A third son, Henry, married Beatrice, daughter of Queen Victoria of England; their daughter, Victoria, married Alfonso XIII of Spain. See Alden Hatch, *The Mountbattens* (1965) and Edward Spiro, *From Battenberg to Mountbatten* (1966).

Battery, the, park, 21 acres (8.5 hectares), southern tip of MANHATTAN island, New York City; site of Dutch and English fortifications. Castle Clinton, a fort built in 1808 for the defense of New York harbor, was ceded to the city in 1823 and renamed Castle Garden. It was remodeled and served as a noted amusement hall and opera house; Swedish soprano Jenny Lind made her U.S. debut on its stage in 1850. From 1855 to 1892 it served as an immigration station, and from 1896 to 1914 it housed an aquarium. After World War II the park was remodeled, and Castle Clinton became a national monument (see NATIONAL PARKS AND MONUMENTS, table). The park also contains a war memorial and a statue of Giovanni da Verrazano, who discovered New York harbor. Boats to Liberty Island leave from the park.

battery, in law, the unpermitted touching by an aggressor, or by some force put in motion by an aggressor, of any part of the person of another or of anything worn or carried by another. Every consummated ASSAULT is a battery. To be the basis for a suit, contact must be intended by the aggressor, it must be such that a reasonable man would consider it offensive, and there must be no consent on the part of the one affected. Consent is assumed for the ordinary and customary contacts that are necessary in everyday life. Gross negligence may be considered by the court as providing the intention necessary to constitute a battery. Actual physical injuries need not be sustained in order to support an action (e.g., a doctor who performs an operation without consent can be sued for battery, even though the patient is benefited by the operation). The term "assault and battery" refers to a criminal offense, the unlawful touching of another with the intention of committing an injury.

battery, electric, term commonly used for an electric CELL such as the dry-cell flashlight battery but more correctly for a group of cells connected to act as a source of direct electric current at a given voltage. A cell consists of two ELECTRODES immersed in

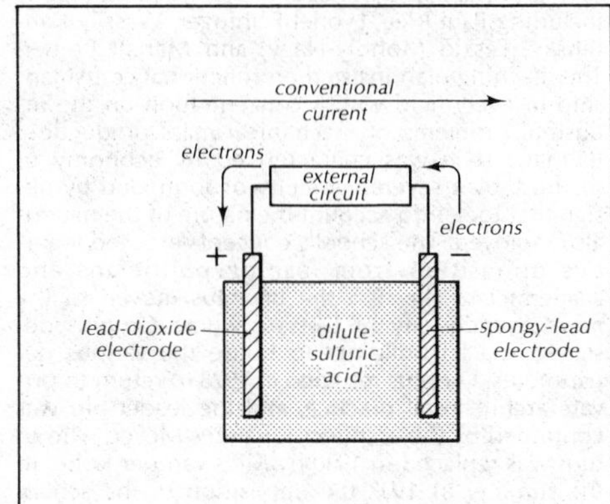

Lead storage cell: At the lead-dioxide electrode, electrons from the circuit combine with lead dioxide and sulfuric acid to form lead sulfate and water. At the spongy-lead electrode, lead reacts with sulfate ions to form lead sulfate and release electrons.

an ELECTROLYTE, which acts chemically upon the electrodes to produce current. Batteries consisting of carbon-zinc dry cells connected in various ways (as well as batteries consisting of other types of dry cells) are used to power such devices as lanterns, transistor radios, and portable public-address systems. A battery called the **storage battery** is generally of the wet-cell type; i.e., it uses a liquid electrolyte and can be recharged many times, unlike the ordinary dry-cell battery, which uses a paste electrolyte and can be recharged few times, if at all. The storage battery consists of several cells connected in series. Each cell contains a number of alternately positive and negative plates separated by the liquid electrolyte. The positive plates of the cell are connected to form the positive electrode; similarly, the negative plates form the negative electrode. In the process of charging, the cell is made to operate in reverse of its discharging operation; i.e., current is forced through the cell in the opposite direction, causing the reverse of the chemical reaction that ordinarily takes place during discharge, so that electrical energy is converted into stored chemical energy. The storage battery's greatest use is in the automobile. In the United States the lead storage battery is commonly used; the nickel-cadmium battery, although far more costly, is also in wide use. The cell of the lead storage battery consists of alternate plates of lead (negative electrode) and lead coated with lead dioxide (positive electrode) immersed in an electrolyte of sulfuric acid solution; when fully charged, it produces a voltage of between 2.0 and 2.5 volts. In the discharging process lead sulfate is deposited on both the negative and the positive electrodes, while the sulfuric acid electrolyte becomes weaker. Another type of storage cell, called the Edison cell, has a nickel oxide positive plate and an iron negative plate suspended in a solution of potassium and lithium hydroxides. Because of its capacity to withstand abuse and its longer effective life, the Edison cell is preferred to the lead cell for railroad signal and lighting service. See FUEL CELL; SOLAR CELL.

Battle, rural district (1971 pop. 33,563), East Sussex, SE England. The town grew up on the site (then a moorland) of the battle of HASTINGS (1066). The victorious William the Conqueror built **Battle Abbey** to commemorate the event. The abbey is now a girls' school, but ruins can be seen.

battle, wager of: see ORDEAL.

Battle above the Clouds: see CHATTANOOGA CAMPAIGN.

Battle Creek, city (1970 pop. 38,931), Calhoun co., S Mich., at the confluence of the Kalamazoo and Battle Creek rivers; settled 1831, inc. as a city 1859. It is an agricultural trade center and is known for its cereals, pet foods, and biscuits. Other manufactures include valves, pumps, farm equipment, trucks, registers, paper products, and brass and wire goods. Battle Creek Sanitarium (founded by Dr. J. H. Kellogg in 1866 as the Health Reform Institute), a natural history museum, a bird sanctuary, a state park, and Kellogg Community College are in or near the city. There is also a civil defense staff college, the training center for U. S. civil defense directors.

Battleford, town (1971 pop. 1,803), N central Sask., Canada, at the confluence of the Battle and North Saskatchewan rivers. Battleford is one of the oldest towns in the central part of the province. It served as the capital (1876–83) of the Northwest Territories and figured prominently in Riel's Rebellion of 1885.

Battle of Britain, in World War II, series of air battles between Great Britain and Germany, fought over Britain from Aug. to Oct., 1940. As a prelude to a planned invasion of England, Germany attacked British coastal defenses, radar stations, and shipping. On Aug. 24 the attack was shifted inland to Royal Air Force installations and aircraft factories in an effort to gain control of the air over S England. Failing to destroy the RAF, the Germans began (Sept. 7) the night bombing, or blitz, of London. Heavy night bombings of English cities continued into October, when the attack was shifted back to coastal installations. The Germans gradually gave up hope of invading England, and the battle tapered off by the end of October. Though heavily outnumbered, the RAF put up a gallant defense; radar, used for the first time in battle, played an important role. The Germans lost some 2,300 aircraft; the RAF lost some 900. The Battle of Britain was the first major failure of the Germans in World War II. See Derek Wood and Derek Dempster, *The Narrow Margin* (1961, repr. 1967); Alexander McKee, *Strike from the Sky* (1960, repr. 1971); Richard Collier, *Eagle Day* (1966); Telford Taylor, *The Breaking Wave* (1967); Peter Townsend, *Duel of Eagles* (1970).

Battle of the Bulge, popular name in World War II for the German counterattack in the Ardennes, Dec., 1944–Jan., 1945. It is also known as the Battle of the Ardennes. On Dec. 16, 1944, a strong German force, commanded by Marshal von Rundstedt, broke the thinly held American front in the Belgian Ardennes sector. Taking advantage of the foggy weather and of the total surprise of the Allies, the Germans penetrated deep into Belgium, creating a dent, or "bulge," in the Allied lines and threatening to break through to the N Belgian plain. Simultaneously, the main Allied supply port of Antwerp was subjected to intensive bombardment by V-2 rockets. An American force held out at Bastogne, even though surrounded and outnumbered. The U.S. 1st and 9th armies, temporarily under Field Marshal Montgomery, attacked the German salient from the north, while the U.S. 3d Army attacked it from the south. Improved flying weather (after Dec. 24) facilitated Allied counterattacks. By Jan. 16, 1945, the German forces were destroyed or routed, but not without some 77,000 Allied casualties. See J. S. D. Eisenhower, *The Bitter Woods* (1969); P. Elstob, *Hitler's Last Offensive* (1971).

Battle of the Spurs. 1 Fought in 1302 near Courtrai, Belgium, between the rebellious Flemish towns, led by Bruges, and an army sent by Philip IV of France, who had annexed Flanders in 1301. The French were totally defeated. The spurs taken from the fallen French knights formed so huge a trophy that they gave the battle its name. **2** Won in 1513 by the English under Henry VIII over the French, at Guinegate, N France. This second battle received its name possibly because of the speedy flight of the French cavalry.

battleship, large, armored warship equipped with the heaviest naval guns. The battleship evolved from the ironclad warship of the mid-19th cent. By 1872 the French were building iron and steel warships, and in 1876 the British started construction of two all-steel war vessels. Development continued in range, size, and accuracy of armament. The H.M.S. *Dreadnought,* which was completed in 1906, was the first modern battleship and introduced the "all-big-gun" class of warship. She was armed with ten 12-in. (30.5-cm) guns and was powered by steam turbines, which developed a speed of 21 knots. The battleship became the major capital unit in modern navies and in World War I and at the beginning of World War II was extensively employed in naval engagements. However, with the development of new aerial tactics, such as dive bombing, and the introduction (1941) of aircraft carriers as the major unit of a naval attack force, battleships became nearly obsolete. The fate of the battleship as a major weapon in modern warfare was sealed on Dec. 7, 1941, when Japanese carrier-borne aircraft attacked and sank the greater part of the U.S. navy's battleships at Pearl Harbor. Shortly after the Korean War the last battleships of the British and American navies were decommissioned. The U.S. navy, during part of the Vietnam War, used one battleship, the *New Jersey,* for shore bombardment and antiaircraft defense. See Siegfried Breyer, *Battleships and Battle Cruisers, 1905–1970* (tr. 1973).

Batu Khan (bä'to͞o kän), d. 1255, Mongol leader; a grandson of Jenghiz Khan. In 1235, Batu became commander of the Mongol army assigned to the conquest of Europe; his chief general was Subutai. Batu crossed the Volga, sending part of his force to Bulgaria but most of it to Russia. By 1240 he had Moscow and Kiev in his grasp, and in the following two years he conquered Hungary and Poland and invaded Germany. His recall to Karakorum in 1242 to participate in the election of a grand khan is sometimes said to have saved Europe from subjection to the Mongols. Batu died while preparing additional campaigns. The domain he established is known as the Kipchak khanate. In Russia it came to be known as the GOLDEN HORDE, because of the gorgeous tents in which the army camped.

Batumi (bäto͞o'mĭ) or **Batum** (bəto͞om'), city (1970 pop. 101,000), capital of Adzhar Autonomous Republic, SE European USSR, in Georgia, on the Black Sea near the Turkish border. A major port and trade center, it is also the terminus of the Trans-Caucasian RR, the Crimean-Caucasian steamship line, and an oil pipeline. Batumi is an important petroleum-shipping port and has oil refineries, shipyards, and food-processing plants. Site of the ancient Greek colony of Batis, the city belonged to Georgia in the Middle Ages, fell to the Turks in the late 16th cent., and passed to Russia in 1878.

Batwa: see PYGMY.

Bat Yam (bät yäm), city (1972 pop. 99,800), W central Israel, on the Mediterranean Sea, near Tel Aviv-Jaffa. It is a seaside resort and an industrial center. The city was founded in 1926 and originally called Bayit VeGan [Heb., =home and garden].

Baucis: see PHILEMON AND BAUCIS.

Baudelaire, Charles (shärl bōdlâr'), 1821–67, French poet and critic. His poetry, classical in form, introduced symbolism (see SYMBOLISTS) by establishing symbolic correspondences among sensory images (e.g., colors, sounds, scents). The only volume of his poems published in his lifetime, *Les Fleurs du mal* (1857, enlarged 1861, 1868; several Eng. tr., *The Flowers of Evil*), was publicly condemned as obscene, and six of the poems were suppressed. Later recognized as a masterpiece, the volume is especially remarkable for the brilliant phrasing, rhythm, and expressiveness of its lyrics. Baudelaire's erratic personality was marked by moodiness, rebelliousness, and an intense religious mysticism. His life was burdened with debts, misunderstanding, illness, and excesses, and his work unremittingly reflects inner despair. The main theme is the inseparable nature of beauty and corruption. A collection of poetic prose pieces was published posthumously as *Petits Poèmes en prose* (1869). As poet and critic Baudelaire earned distinction in literary circles. Believing criticism to be a function of the poet, he wrote perceptive appraisals of his contemporaries. His criticism was collected posthumously in *Curiosités esthétiques* (1868) and *L'Art romantique* (1869). He felt a great affinity to Poe, whose works he translated and brought to the attention of the French public. One of the great figures of French literature, Baudelaire has also been a major influence in other Western poetry. See his letters (tr. by S. Morini and F. Tuten, 1970), his intimate journal (tr. by Christopher Isherwood, 1947), and selected letters (tr. and ed. by L. B. and F. E. Hyslop, 1957); biography by Enid Starkie (rev. ed. 1958), studies by Jean-Paul Sartre (1950, repr. 1972) and M. A. Ruff (1965).

Baudouin (bōdo͞oăN'), 1930–, king of the Belgians (1951–), son of LEOPOLD III. He joined his father in exile (1945–50) in Switzerland. After their return to Belgium his father's unpopularity led to Baudouin's appointment (1950) as regent, and on Leopold's abdication (1951) Baudouin ascended the throne. In 1960 he married Fabiola de Mora y Aragón, a Spanish noblewoman.

Bauer, Georg: see AGRICOLA, GEORGIUS.

Bauer, Harold, 1873–1951, Anglo-American pianist. He was first a successful violinist, but in 1892 he studied the piano with Paderewski and then earned international recognition as a pianist. He also promoted chamber music and exercised a strong influence on American musical life. See his memoirs (1948).

Baugh, Samuel Adrian (Sammy Baugh) (bô), 1914–, American football player, b. Temple, Texas. An All-American backfield star at Texas Christian Univ., he turned professional (1937) to play with the Washington Redskins. Baugh's precision passing gained for him the nickname of "Slinging Sammy." He established many professional passing and punting records before retiring in 1952. Baugh coached the New York Titans of the American Football League in 1960 and 1961, and in 1964 the Houston Oilers of the same league.

Bauhaus (bou'hous), school of art and architecture in Germany. The Bauhaus revolutionized art training by combining the teaching of the pure arts with the study of crafts. It was founded at Weimar in 1919 and headed by Walter GROPIUS, with a faculty including Paul Klee, Lyonel Feininger, Wassily Kandinsky, László Moholy-Nagy, and Marcel Breuer. The teaching plan insisted on functional craftsmanship in every field with a concentration on the industrial problems of mechanical mass production. Bauhaus style was characterized by economy of method, by a severe geometry of form, and by design that took into account the nature of the materials employed. The school's concepts aroused vigorous opposition from leading politicians and academicians. In 1925 the Bauhaus moved to the more friendly city of Dessau, where Gropius designed special buildings to house the various departments. Gropius resigned in 1928 to return to private architectural practice, and the leadership was continued by the architect Johannes Meyer, who in turn was replaced in 1930 by Miës van der Rohe. In the summer of 1932 the opposition to the school had increased to such an extent that the city of Dessau withdrew its support. The school was then moved to Berlin, where the faculty endeavored to carry on their ideas, but in 1933 the Nazi government closed the school entirely. The Bauhaus ideas, enveloping design in architecture, furniture, weaving, and typography, among others, had by this time found wide acclaim in many parts of the world and especially in the United States, where many of the instructors went to encourage and practice further work with the same ideals. The Chicago Institute of Design, founded by MOHOLY-NAGY, most completely carried on the teaching plan of the Bauhaus. See Walter Gropius, *The New Architecture and the Bauhaus* (rev. ed. 1955); H. M. Wingler, *The Bauhaus,* ed. by Joseph Stein (1969); Marcel Franciscono, *Walter Gropius and the Creation of the Bauhaus* (1971).

Bauhin, Gaspard (gäspär' bōăN'), 1560–1624, Swiss botanist and doctor of medicine, of French descent. His early classification of plants by genus and species in his chief work, the *Pinax theatri botanici* (1623), anticipated the binomial arrangement of Linnaeus. Bauhin reformed anatomical nomenclature, especially that of muscles. His elder brother, **Jean Bauhin,** 1541–1613, was also a botanist and doctor of medicine. A genus of plants, *Bauhinia,* was named for the brothers.

Bauld, Cape: see GREAT NORTHERN PENINSULA, Canada.

Baum, Lyman Frank (bôm), 1856–1919, American journalist, playwright, and author of juvenile stories, b. Chittenango, N.Y. While working as a newspaperman in South Dakota he wrote his first book, *Father Goose: His Book* (1899), which became an immediate best-seller. In 1900 he published his most famous work, *The Wonderful Wizard of Oz,* a story about a little girl carried by a cyclone to the magical land of Oz. His dramatization of the book was produced in 1902; the story was also made into an extraordinarily popular motion picture in 1938. Baum published 13 other stories of Oz, including *Ozma of Oz* (1907) and *The Scarecrow of Oz* (1915). See *The Annotated Wizard of Oz,* ed. by M. P. Hearn (1973).

Baumann, Oskar (ôs'kär bou'män), 1864–99, Austrian explorer in Africa. He traveled up the Congo River to Stanley Falls (1885) and the following year explored Fernando Po, in the Gulf of Guinea. After accompanying a party to Mt. Kilimanjaro in 1888, he explored (1890) East Africa for the German East Africa Society. He took a party (1892–93) to Lake Victoria where he found the Kagera River to be the chief tributary of the lake and the ultimate source of the Nile.

Baumeister, Willi (vĭl'ē bou'mīshtər), 1889–1955, German artist. Influenced by primitive art and Miro's SURREALISM, Baumeister created abstractions that contain mechanical and organic forms. In later works (e.g., *Reddish Relief with Sand,* 1950; Baumeister Coll., Stuttgart) he included ideographic signs in his compositions.

Bäumeler, Joseph Michael: see BIMELER, JOSEPH MICHAEL.

Baunsgård, Hilmer (hĭl'mər bouns'gôr), 1920–, Danish politician. A businessman, he was president of the youth organization of the Social-Liberal party (1948–50) and a member of the executive of the Social-Liberal party (1948–57), serving (1954–57) as its vice-president. He was elected to parliament in 1957. From 1961 to 1964, Baunsgård headed the ministry of commerce. He became prime minister in 1968; he resigned in 1971 when his center-right coalition lost its parliamentary majority over economic issues, especially inflation, taxation, and balance of payment deficits.

Baur, Ferdinand Christian (fĕr'dĭnänt krĭs'tēän bour), 1792–1860, German Protestant theologian. He was from 1826 on the theological faculty of Tübingen. He became convinced of Hegel's philosophy of history and studied Christian history and doctrines and the Bible from that point of view. In New Testament criticism he rejected the authenticity of most of the books, using philosophical and literary criteria. His methods and disciples were referred to as the Tübingen School. See study by P. C. Hodgson (1966).

Bautzen (bou'tsən), city (1970 pop. 43,670), Dresden district, SE East Germany, on the Spree River. It is an industrial city, a rail junction, and the center of a kaolin-quarrying region. Manufactures include machinery, textiles, chemicals, leather and paper goods, and railroad cars. Bautzen was founded in the 10th cent. and was contested in the 11th and 12th cent. by Poland, Meissen, Brandenburg, and Bohemia. It eventually passed to Bohemia, was burned (1634) in the Thirty Years War, and passed (1635) with LUSATIA to Saxony. Noteworthy landmarks include a 13th-century church and numerous 18th-century buildings. In 1813, Napoleon I defeated a Russo-Prussian army nearby.

Baux, Les (lā bō), village (1968 pop. 91), Bouches-du-Rhône dept., SE France, in Provence. Nearby are the ruins of a medieval town. The once flourishing town, carved out of dazzling white limestone, was the seat of a powerful feudal family. Destroyed by gunfire in 1632 as a stronghold of enemies of the crown, its ruins are a great tourist attraction. Bauxite, first discovered (1821) there and named accordingly, is mined in the vicinity.

bauxite, mixture of hydrated aluminum oxides usually containing oxides of iron and silicon in varying quantities. A noncrystalline substance formerly thought to be a mineral, bauxite is claylike and earthy and ranges in color from white to deep brown or red according to the nature and quantity of its components. Bauxite occurs characteristically in pisolitic form, i.e., composed of small, round concretions. Its composition varies, alumina constituting from about 50% to about 70%. Bauxite is widely distributed, important deposits occurring in Africa, South America, the USSR, the West Indies, France (notably at Baux, where it was first discovered and from which it received its name), and the United States (Alabama, Arkansas, and Georgia). It is the chief source of aluminum and of its compounds, including alumina, alums, and alundum. It is used in the preparation of abrasives and as a refractory for spark plugs and furnace linings.

Bavai (băv'āī, bävä'ī), the same as BINNUI **1.**

Bavaria, Ger. *Bayern,* state (1970 pop. 10,479,000), 27,239 sq mi (70,549 sq km), S West Germany. MUNICH is the capital. The largest state of West Germany, Bavaria is bordered by Czechoslovakia on the east, by Austria on the southeast and south, by Baden-Württemberg on the west, by Hesse on the northwest, and by East Germany on the north. A region of rich, softly rolling hills, it is drained by several rivers (notably the Main, Danube, Isar, and Inn) and is bounded by mountain ranges (especially the Bavarian Alps and the Bohemian Forest). Bavaria is divided into seven administrative districts: Upper and Lower Bavaria; Upper, Middle, and Lower FRANCONIA; SWABIA; and the Upper PALATINATE. Until the early 19th cent. Bavaria did not include Swabia and Franconia, which have separate histories. Upper Bavaria, with Munich as its capital, rises to the Bavarian Alps, along the Austrian border, and culminates in the ZUGSPITZE, West Germany's highest peak. Between the Alps and the BOHEMIAN FOREST, which forms the border with Czechoslovakia, lies the Franconian Jura plateau, traversed by the Danube. Lower Bavaria comprises part of this plateau and part of the Bohemian Forest. Franconia, in N Bavaria, includes the Frankenwald, the FICHTELGEBIRGE, and the

Main valley. Swabia, in SW Bavaria, is part of the Danubian plateau. The Upper Palatinate, in NE Bavaria, is separated from Czechoslovakia by the Bohemian Forest. The population of Bavaria is about 70% Catholic. Forestry and agriculture are important occupations; wheat, barley, sugar beets, and dairy goods are the leading products. Industry is centered in Munich, Nuremberg, Augsburg, Hof, Ingolstadt, Erlangen, and Schweinfurt. Major industrial products include glass and ceramics, iron and steel, paper, chemicals, machinery, textiles, clothing, optical instruments, petroleum, and motor vehicles. Bavarian beer is world famous. Toys and musical instruments are made by craftsmen. Salt, graphite, iron ore, and lignite are the chief mineral resources. The scenic beauties and the picturesque local customs and costumes of the Bavarian Alps attract many tourists. Among the resorts are Garmisch-Partenkirchen, Berchtesgaden, and the spas Bad Kissingen and Bad Reichenhall. Bayreuth is a cultural center, and Augsburg, Nuremberg, Bamberg, and Würzburg are historic and artistic centers. There are universities at Munich, Regensburg, Würzburg, and Erlangen-Nuremberg.

From the Romans to the Wittelsbachs. The borders of Bavaria have varied considerably in its history. The region was inhabited by Celts when Drusus conquered it (15 B.C.) for Rome. The Baiuoarii (see GERMANS) invaded it (6th cent. A.D.) and set up the duchy to which they gave their name. It was one of the five basic or stem duchies of medieval Germany. Irish and Scottish monks began the Christianization of the area, and it was completed (8th cent.) by St. Boniface. In 788, Charlemagne defeated Duke Tassilo III and added Bavaria to his empire. From 817 to 911, Bavaria was ruled by the Carolingians LOUIS THE GERMAN, CARLOMAN (d. 880), ARNULF, and LOUIS THE CHILD. In 911 the duchy (then comprising, roughly, Bavaria proper, present-day Austria, and part of the Upper Palatinate) came under indigenous rulers. Frequent Magyar inroads were stopped (955) by Emperor OTTO I, who in 947 had given Bavaria to his brother Henry. Henry's grandson was duke of Bavaria when he was elected (1002) German king as Henry II. After his accession Bavaria was ruled by various houses, but in 1070 Emperor Henry IV gave the fief to Welf, or Guelph, d'Este IV (see ESTE), who began the dynasty of the GUELPHS. From the 9th to the 12th cent. the Bavarian dukes, of whatever house, were at the center of the rebellions of the great German princes against the imperial authority. To reduce their power Emperor OTTO II in 976 stripped the duchy of all but present-day Upper and Lower Bavaria and the Tyrol. When in 1137 the Guelph HENRY THE PROUD acquired Saxony in addition to Bavaria, CONRAD III deposed him and gave Bavaria to the BABENBERG rulers of Austria. Frederick II restored (1156) Bavaria to HENRY THE LION but in 1180 deposed the rebellious Guelph and bestowed the duchy (from which he detached considerable territory in what is now Austria) on Otto of Wittelsbach. The political history of Bavaria, much reduced in importance, became that of the WITTELSBACH family, which ruled until 1918.

Bavaria under the Wittelsbachs. The Wittelsbach fiefs, including the Rhenish Palatinate (acquired in 1214), were almost always divided among the numerous branches of the dynasty. Under the Wittelsbach emperor Louis IV (reigned 1328–47), Bavaria was briefly reunited. Duke Albert IV (1467–1508), who again united Bavaria (except the Rhenish Palatinate), introduced the law of primogeniture; thus Bavaria entered the Reformation period much strengthened. The triumph of Catholicism in Bavaria proper was crucial for its later history. Duke Maximilian I (1597–1651) headed the Catholic League in the Thirty Years War and was rewarded with the Upper Palatinate and the rank of elector. The agricultural wealth and the strategic position of Bavaria made it a coveted prize and a frequent battleground then and later. Bavaria was overrun by foreign armies, notably in the War of the SPANISH SUCCESSION, the War of the AUSTRIAN SUCCESSION, the War of the Bavarian Succession (1778, by which Bavaria lost the Inn Quarter to Austria), and the French Revolutionary Wars. Elector Maximilian IV Joseph, who in 1799 united all Wittelsbach lands, allied himself with Napoleon I, joined the CONFEDERATION OF THE RHINE, and in 1806 was proclaimed king of Bavaria as MAXIMILIAN I. In 1813, Maximilian abandoned Napoleon and joined the allies, who at the Congress of Vienna (1814–15) left him in possession of virtually all of present-day Bavaria, including the Rhenish Palatinate. During the period of reaction that followed in Europe, Bavaria stood out for its relatively liberal government. The liberal constitution of 1818 lasted exactly a century. King Louis I (1825–48), dethroned by the mild revolution of 1848, was succeeded by the able MAXIMILIAN II (1848–64) and the brilliant but insane LOUIS II (1864–86). All three rulers had a passion for the arts, science, and architecture. The reputation of Bavaria, particularly Munich, as a cultural center dates from their reigns. The abolition in 1848 of guild restrictions opened the way for industrialization. At the same time, the rural prosperity of Bavaria and the strong influence of the Catholic Church (which predominates except in the Upper Palatinate and in Middle Franconia) accented the hostility of Bavaria toward the rising power of Prussia. Bavaria sided with Austria in the Austro-Prussian War (1866). Defeated in that war, it acknowledged Prussian leadership, sided with Prussia against France in 1870–71, and joined (1871) the German Empire. As the chief German state after Prussia, Bavaria retained separatist tendencies.

Bavaria since World War I. King LOUIS III, successor to the mad OTTO I, was dethroned in Nov., 1918, by Kurt EISNER, who established a socialist republic. The assassination (Feb., 1919) of Eisner led to a Communist revolution (April, 1919), which was bloodily suppressed by the German army. Bavaria then joined the Weimar Republic. In the early 1920s, Munich became the center of the National Socialist (Nazi) movement; in 1923 the National Socialists made an abortive attempt (Beer Hall Putsch) in that city to seize power. Catholic Bavaria as a whole gave little support to the movement until Adolf Hitler came to national power in 1933. Under the National Socialist regime Bavaria lost its autonomy. After World War II the Rhenish Palatinate was separated from Bavaria and was later made part of the state of Rhineland-Palatinate. A new constitution for Bavaria was drawn up in 1946. Since the founding of the Federal Republic of Germany in 1949, the conservative Christian Social Union, allied nationally with the Christian Democratic Union, has been the strongest Bavarian political party.

Bavarian Succession, War of the, between Austria and Prussia, 1778–79. With the extinction of the Bavarian line of the house of WITTELSBACH on the death of Elector Maximilian Joseph in 1777, the duchy of Bavaria passed to the elector palatine, Charles Theodore, of the Sulzbach line. However, by a secret treaty with Holy Roman Emperor Joseph II, who wished to strengthen imperial and Austrian influence in Germany, Charles Theodore ceded Lower Bavaria to Austria and Austrian troops occupied the area. Charles Theodore had no legitimate issue, but his heir presumptive, Duke Charles of Zweibrücken, on the advice of Frederick II of Prussia, protested the transfer of this portion of his inheritance. Prussia, allied with Saxony, declared war on Austria and invaded Bohemia. No serious engagement took place, and the war ended with the Congress of Teschen (1779). Austria renounced its claims but retained the Inn quarter, a small but fertile and densely populated triangle of land along the border between Bavaria and Austria. Prussia's claims to Ansbach and Bayreuth were recognized, and Saxony received monetary compensation. The conflict has been called the Potato War because Prussian troops spent time picking potatoes in the fields.

Bax, Sir Arnold, 1883–1953, English composer, studied at the Royal Academy of Music, London. His early works, in an elaborately chromatic style, did not find great favor with the public, but works in a simpler style, composed after 1910, brought him recognition as an outstanding composer. French impressionism, Celtic folklore, and the work of Richard Wagner all influenced his compositions, which include seven symphonies, many tone poems, chamber music, concertos, ballets, songs, and choral works. He was knighted in 1937 and became Master of the King's Music in 1941. See his autobiography, *Farewell My Youth* (1943).

Bax, Ernest Belfort, 1854–1926, English socialist philosopher. He studied music and philosophy in Germany. In England, influenced by Marxist and other radical thought, he became active in socialist groups, especially the Social Democratic Federation. He left this to help found (1885), with William Morris, the Socialist League, but returned when the League veered toward anarchism. With Morris he wrote *Socialism: Its Growth and Outcome* (1893). His other writings include *The Problem of Reality* (1893, rev. ed. 1914), *The Fraud of Feminism* (1913), and *The Real, the Rational, and the Alogical* (1920). See his autobiography (1918).

Baxter, Richard, 1615–91, English nonconformist clergyman. Ordained in 1638, he began his ministry at Kidderminster in 1641. He sided with Parliament when the civil war broke out and served (1645–47) as a chaplain in Cromwell's army, where he urged moderation in both religious and political opinions. At the Restoration, Baxter was chosen by Charles II as one of the royal chaplains. He took a leading part at the Savoy Conference (1661), where he tried to provide means that would permit moderate dissenters to stay in the Church of England. He declined an offer of the bishopric of Hereford, and with the passage of the Act of Uniformity (1662) he left the Church of England. Despite the persecution of nonconformist ministers, Baxter continued to preach; his followers were known as Baxterians. After a trial conducted with great brutality by Judge Jeffreys, he was imprisoned for 18 months on the charge of having libeled the Church of England in his *Paraphrase of the New Testament* (1685). Among Baxter's voluminous works are *The Saints' Everlasting Rest* (1650), *Gildas Salvianus, the Reformed Pastor* (1656), and *A Call to the Unconverted* (1657). His autobiographical *Reliquae Baxterianae* (1696) was edited (1925) by J. M. L. Thomas. See biography by F. J. Powicke (2 vol., 1924–27); study by Hugh Martin (1954).

bay: see LAUREL; MAGNOLIA.

Bayamo (bäyä'mō), city (1970 pop. 71,660), Oriente prov., SE Cuba. Its economy is based on sugarcane and cattle. Founded in 1513, Bayamo was an inland port until the 19th cent. A former center of revolutionary movements, it gave its name to the Cuban national anthem, *el Himno Bayamés*. Both the Ten Years War (1868–78) and the successful revolt of 1895 began in Bayamo. Carlos Manual de Céspedes and Tomás Estrada Palma were born in the city.

Bayamón (bäyämōn'), town (1970 pop. 147,552), NE Puerto Rico, a residential and industrial suburb of San Juan. Founded in 1772, it is one of the oldest settlements on the island.

Bayar, Celâl (jĕläl' bä'yär), 1884–, Turkish statesman. The son of a religious leader and teacher, Bayar joined the nationalist movement after the Young Turk revolution. Kemal Atatürk's colleague after World War I, he held several ministerial positions (1921–37); he supervised the Greek-Turkish exchange of population (1923). In 1937 he became premier, but he resigned the post after Atatürk's death (1938). In 1946 he founded with Adnan Menderes and others the Democratic party, which came to power in 1950. He then became president of the republic and was reelected in 1954 and 1957. Ousted in 1960 by Cemal Gürsel, he was tried for violating the constitution and sentenced to death. The sentence was commuted to life imprisonment in 1961. Bayar was released because of ill health in 1964 and pardoned in 1966.

Bayard, James Asheton (bī'ərd), 1767–1815, U.S. Representative (1797–1803) and Senator (1805–13) from Delaware, b. Philadelphia. Admitted to the bar in 1787, he began practice at Wilmington, Del. Bayard, a prominent Federalist, played a leading part in securing Thomas Jefferson's election as President over Aaron Burr in 1801. Of an independent mind, he, unlike other Federalists, supported the Nonimportation Act of 1806 and the War of 1812, although he had used all his influence to prevent hostilities. In 1814 he served on the commission that negotiated the Treaty of Ghent (see GHENT, TREATY OF) ending the War of 1812. His papers were edited (1915, repr. 1970) by Elizabeth Donnan. See Morton Borden, *The Federalism of James A. Bayard* (1954).

Bayard, James Asheton, 1799–1880, U.S. Senator from Delaware (1851–64, 1867–69), b. Wilmington, Del.; son of James Asheton Bayard (1767–1815). His Unionist sentiments led him into the new Republican party, but he bitterly opposed the dominant radical Republicans and in 1864 he resigned. He was elected again, however, and served (1867–69) as a Democrat and supporter of President Andrew Johnson's Reconstruction policy. His son, Thomas Francis Bayard, was elected to succeed him in the U.S. Senate.

Bayard, Pierre du Terrail, seigneur de (bā'ərd; pyĕr dü tĕrī'yə sänyör' də bäyär'), c.1474–1524, French military hero, called *le chevalier sans peur et sans reproche* [the knight without fear or blame]. He exhibited bravery and genius as a commander in all the important battles of the ITALIAN WARS, from Fornovo (1495) to the Sesia, in which he was killed. His defense of Mézières (1521) saved central France from an imperial invasion. See biography by Samuel Shellabarger (1928, repr. 1971).

Bayard, Thomas Francis, 1828–98, U.S. statesman, b. Wilmington, Del.; son of James Asheton Bayard (1799–1880). He began his law practice at Wilmington (1851). An active Democrat, Bayard was elected U.S. Senator (1869) to succeed his father and was reelected in 1875 and 1881. He became Secretary of

State during Cleveland's first administration. Bayard was much concerned with Anglo-American relations. He became ambassador to Great Britain during Cleveland's second term. See study by C. C. Tansill (1940, repr. 1969).

Bayard (bā'ərd), Ital. *Baiardo* (bäyär'dō), in chivalric romance, a bay horse, remarkable for his spirit and for his unique ability to fit his size to his rider. He appears in the 12th-century French epic *Renaud de Montauban* and in later tales of ROLAND by Boiardo, Ariosto, and Tasso.

bayberry, common name for the Myricaceae, a family of trees and shrubs with aromatic foliage, found chiefly in temperate and subtropical regions. The waxy gray berries of the North American wild or cultivated bayberry shrubs (chiefly *Myrica cerifera*) are used to make fragrant bayberry candles, scented soap, and sealing wax; bayberry is also called candleberry and wax myrtle. Sweet gale (*M. gale)*, a bog plant, yields tannic acid. Sweet fern (*Comptonia peregrina)* is a North American shrub found chiefly in the E United States and cultivated elsewhere in dry, sandy areas. Its foliage is used for medicines and tea. Bayberry is classified in the division MAGNOLIOPHYTA, class Magnoliopsida, order Myricales.

Bay City. **1** City (1970 pop. 49,449), seat of Bay co., S Mich., a port of entry on the Saginaw River at its mouth on Saginaw Bay (an inlet of Lake Huron); inc. 1859 with the consolidation of several settlements along the river. Its harbor handles considerable Great Lakes and ocean shipping. Bay City is the industrial, marketing, and shipping center of a rich farm area that yields sugar beets, potatoes, and dairy products. It grew as a great lumbering center, and when the forests were depleted (after 1890) it turned to diversified manufacturing. Delta College is in nearby University Center. The vicinity is rich in Indian relics. A state park and two state forests are in the area. **2** City (1970 pop. 11,733), seat of Matagorda co., S Texas, near the Colorado River and the Gulf of Mexico; inc. 1894. It is a shipping and industrial center for a region that produces oil, gas, sulfur, beef cattle, rice, cotton, soybeans, and grain sorghums. There are petrochemical plants and grass and turf farms in the city. The county museum is there, and Matagorda Bay and several Gulf beaches are nearby.

Bayer process, procedure for obtaining alumina from the aluminum ore bauxite. The alumina can then be used for various industrial purposes or smelted to provide aluminum. The first step in the process is the mixing of ground bauxite into a solution of sodium hydroxide. By applying steam and pressure in tanks containing the mixture, the bauxite slowly dissolves. The alumina released reacts with the sodium hydroxide to form sodium aluminate. After the contents of the tank have passed through other vessels where the pressure and temperature are reduced and impurities are removed, the solution of sodium aluminate is placed in a special tank where the alumina is precipitated out. The precipitate is removed from the tank, washed, and heated in a kiln to drive off any water present. The residue is a commercially pure alumina.

Bayes, Thomas, 1702-61, English clergyman and mathematician. The son of a Nonconformist minister, he was privately educated and earned his livelihood as a minister to the Nonconformist community at Tunbridge Wells. Although he wrote on theology, e.g., *Divine Benevolence* (1731), Bayes is best known for his two mathematical works, *Introduction to the Doctrine of Fluxions* (1736), a defense of the logical foundations of Newton's calculus against the attack of Bishop Berkeley, and "Essay Towards Solving a Problem in the Doctrine of Chances" (1763). The latter, a pioneering work, attempts to establish that the rule for determining the probability of an event is the same whether or not anything is known antecedently to any trials or observations concerning the event.

Bayeux (bäyōō', Fr. bäyö'), town (1968 pop. 12,871), Calvados dept., N France, in Normandy, near the English Channel. It is a farm and communications center, noted for its lace industry. A Roman town and episcopal see from the 4th cent., it was burned (1105) by Henry I of England. Sections of its Romanesque church withstood the fire and form a part of the remarkable Gothic cathedral built for the most part in the 13th cent. The town is particularly famous for its museum containing the Bayeux tapestry. In World War II, Bayeux was the first French city liberated by the Allies (June 8, 1944).

Bayeux tapestry. This so-called tapestry is in fact an embroidery that chronicles the Norman conquest of England by William the Conqueror in 1066. It is a long, narrow strip of coarse linen, 230 ft by 20 in. (70 m by 51 cm), embroidered in worsteds of eight colors in couching and stem stitch. The embroidery is a valuable document on the history and the costumes of the time. Its prominence and date have long been disputed. Tradition attributes it to Queen Matilda, wife of William the Conqueror, and her handmaidens; but it is now thought to be of somewhat later origin and possibly the work of English embroiderers. The embroidery is preserved in the Bayeux Museum. See Sir Eric Maclagan, *The Bayeux Tapestry* (1945); Frank Stenton and others, *The Bayeux Tapestry* (1957, repr. 1965).

Bayh, Birch Evans (bī), 1928–, U.S. Senator (1963–), b. Terre Haute, Ind. A Democratic member of the Indiana state assembly (1955–62), he served as minority leader (1957–58, 1961–62) and as speaker (1959–60). Elected (1962) to the U.S. Senate, Bayh became (1963) chairman of the subcommittee on constitutional amendments of the Judiciary Committee. He was credited with formulating the 25th Amendment to the Constitution on presidential succession, which was ratified in 1967. In 1969 and 1970, Bayh led the successful fight against confirmation of the nominations of Clement F. Haynsworth and G. Harrold Carswell to the Supreme Court. He is the author of *One Heartbeat Away* (1968).

Bay Islands, Span. *Islas de la Bahía,* archipelago, 144 sq mi (373 sq km), off the north coast of Honduras, in the Caribbean Sea. The archipelago makes up a department of Honduras. Of the three principal islands (Roatán, Guanaja, and Utila), Roatán is the largest and the port of entry. Guanaja was visited by Columbus in 1502. The climate is sultry. The chief products are fruits and logwood, which English logcutters exploited as early as the 17th cent. British garrisoning of the islands in 1848 led to unrest, which was partially settled by the CLAYTON-BULWER TREATY (1850) and relinquishment of British rights (1859) to Honduras. Dissatisfied, the English islanders sided with the American filibuster William WALKER. The population today retains many English characteristics.

Baykal or **Baikal** (both: bīkäl'), lake, 12,160 sq mi (31,494 sq km), SE Siberian USSR. It is the largest freshwater lake of Eurasia, with a width up to 50 mi (80 km) and a length of c.395 mi (640 km). Its maximum depth is 5,714 ft (1,742 m), making Baykal the world's deepest lake. There are numerous feeder streams (notably the Selenga), but the only outlet is the Angara River, whose great volume is harnessed by a hydroelectric station at nearby Irkutsk. Lake Baykal is navigable and is used to float timber. Surrounded by beautiful mountain scenery, it is rich in fish, including many unusual species. Although it is known for its crystal-clear waters, the lake is now in danger of pollution because of recent industrial development in Siberia. The Trans-Siberian RR skirts the lake's southern shores. Between Lake Baykal and the upper Amur River lies the region known as Transbaykalia.

Bayle, Pierre (pyĕr bāl), 1647–1706, French rationalistic philosopher. Born a Huguenot, he converted to Roman Catholicism and then returned to Protestantism. To avoid French intolerance of Protestants, he moved in 1681 to Rotterdam, where he lived for most of the rest of his life. Trained as a philosopher and with a strong background in theology, Bayle supported Calvinism but was also an advocate of religious toleration, contending that morality was independent of religion. His chief work was *Dictionnaire historique et critique* (1697), a compendium of biographies with comprehensive and detailed criticisms by Bayle. His views had a profound influence on the French and German ENLIGHTENMENT, especially on the authors of the *Encyclopédie* and on the English deists. See K. C. Sandberg, *At the Crossroads of Faith and Reason* (1966); H. E. Smith, *The Literary Criticism of Pierre Bayle* (1971).

bayleaf: see LAUREL.

Baylis, Lilian: see OLD VIC.

Bayliss, Sir William Maddock (bā'lĭs), 1860–1924, English physiologist. At University College, London, he investigated the mechanism of heart action, circulation, and digestion. With E. H. Starling he discovered, in 1902, secretin, a hormone produced in the small intestine, and developed a theory of hormone action. He wrote *Principles of General Physiology* (1914) and *The Vaso-Motor System* (1923).

Baylor, Robert Emmett Bledsoe, 1793?–1873, American jurist, founder of Baylor Univ.; b. Kentucky. He served in the War of 1812, studied law, and served in the Kentucky legislature. Moving (1820) to Alabama, he served in the Alabama legislature and was (1829–31) a U.S. Representative from Alabama before moving again (1839), this time to Texas. He was a district and supreme court judge in the Republic of Texas and was prominent in drafting the state constitution, which became operative upon the annexation of Texas. He became a state judge under the new constitution. Baylor was also a Baptist preacher and is chiefly remembered because he drew up and secured passage of a charter for a college that became Baylor Univ.

Baylor University, mainly at Waco, Texas; coeducational; chartered and opened 1845 by Baptists (see BAYLOR, ROBERT E. B.) at Independence, moved 1886 and absorbed Waco Univ. (chartered 1861). The library has a noted Robert Browning collection. Frank Lloyd Wright designed a theater center at Dallas for the graduate school. The university's medical school was founded (1900) as part of the Univ. of Dallas, and it became affiliated with Baylor in 1903. In 1943 it moved to Houston, and in 1969 it became a separate corporation under the title of Baylor College of Medicine. It was in connection with the Baylor Univ. medical school that Michael De Bakey did his pioneer work in artificial heart implantation and heart transplantation. Baylor Univ. maintains a medical center at Dallas, but there is no medical school.

Bayne, Stephen Fielding, Jr.: see LAMBETH CONFERENCE.

Bay of Pigs Invasion, 1961, an unsuccessful invasion of Cuba by Cuban exiles, supported by the U.S. government. On April 17, 1961, an armed force of about 1,500 Cuban exiles landed in the Bahía de Cochinos (Bay of Pigs) on the south coast of Cuba. Trained since May, 1960, in Guatemala by members of the Central Intelligence Agency (CIA) with the approval of the Eisenhower administration, and supplied with arms by the U.S. government, the rebels intended to foment an insurrection in Cuba and overthrow the Communist regime of Fidel Castro. The Cuban army easily defeated the rebels and by April 20, most were either killed or captured. The invasion provoked anti-U.S. demonstrations in Latin America and Europe and further embittered U.S.-Cuban relations. Poorly planned and executed, the invasion subjected President Kennedy to severe criticism at home. Cuban exile leader José Miró Cardona, president of the U.S.-based National Revolutionary Council, blamed the failure on the CIA and the refusal of Kennedy to authorize air support for the invasion. In Dec., 1962, Castro released 1,113 captured rebels in exchange for $53 million in food and medicine raised by private donations in the United States. See K. E. Meyer and Tad Szulc, *The Cuban Invasion* (1962); H. B. Johnson, *The Bay of Pigs* (1964).

Bay of Whales: see ROSS SEA; ANTARCTICA.

Bayonne (bäyôn'), town (1968 pop. 45,175), Pyrénées-Atlantiques dept., SW France, in Gascony, on the Adour River near its entrance into the Bay of Biscay. Despite a shifting sandbar at the mouth of the Adour, it is a seaport, exporting sulfur. The town also has metallurgical, chemical, aeronautical, leather, and wood industries. French and Spanish, as well as Basque, are spoken there. At Bayonne, Napoleon I forced Charles IV and Ferdinand VII of Spain to abdicate (1808). At the end of the Peninsular War, Bayonne successfully resisted a British siege. Bayonne gives its name to the bayonet, invented there in the 17th cent. The Cathedral of Bayonne (13th cent.) is copied from those of Soissons and Rheims. There is a Basque museum and a fine arts museum, left to the city by the painter Bonnat, who was born there. Parts of the town's Roman and medieval walls are preserved, as are Vauban's fortifications (17th cent.).

Bayonne (bāyōn'), city (1970 pop. 72,743), Hudson co., NE N.J., on a 3-mi (4.8-km) peninsula; inc. 1869. It has oil and chemical industries. Its huge oil refineries (operating since 1875) are supplied by a branch of the oil pipeline from the Southwest. On Bayonne's 9-mi (14.5-km) waterfront is a large U.S. naval dry dock and supply depot. Dutch traders came to this site c.1650; the British gained possession in 1664. The city is connected to Staten Island by Bayonne Bridge (1,675 ft/511 m long; opened 1931).

bayou (bī'ō, bī'ōō) [Louisiana Fr.; from Choctaw *bayuk*=small stream], term used mainly in U.S. Gulf states, especially Louisiana and Mississippi, to describe a stationary or sluggishly moving body of water that was once part of a lake, river, or gulf and is swampy or marshy in nature. *Bayou* is sometimes used as a synonym for *oxbow lake.*

Bay Psalm Book, common hymnal of the Massachusetts Bay colony. Written by Richard Mather,

John Eliot, and Thomas Weld, it was published in 1640 at Cambridge as *The Whole Book of Psalms Faithfully Translated into English Metre.* The announced effort of the authors to make a literal rendering at the expense of elegance is successful if the crudity of the verse be a criterion. This was the first book published in the Thirteen Colonies. See Zoltán Haraszti, *The Enigma of the Bay Psalm Book* (1956).

Bayreuth (bīroit'), city (1970 pop. 64,536), capital of Upper Franconia, Bavaria, S West Germany, on the Red Main River. It is an industrial center; its manufactures include textiles, metals, and machinery. Founded in the mid-12th cent., Bayreuth belonged to a branch of the Hohenzollern family from 1248 to 1791, when it was annexed by Prussia. It was taken by France in 1807 and passed to Bavaria in 1810. Richard Wagner lived in Bayreuth from 1872 to 1883, and annual music festivals of international importance are held in the Festspielhaus, an opera house designed by Wagner and built in 1872-76. Wagner and Franz Liszt are buried in Bayreuth.

Bayreuth Festival, also called the Richard Wagner Festival, annual season of performances of Wagner's works, held in the Bavarian town of Bayreuth. In about 1851, Wagner began to visualize a festival theater that would be devoted to the performance of great German works for the theater. In 1876 the Wagner Festival Theatre (the Festspielhaus) was completed at Bayreuth, and the first festival took place. Planned by Wagner himself, the Festspielhaus is an amphitheater with many notable features, including a sunken, covered orchestra pit and unusually fine acoustics. Despite the composer's original intention, the Bayreuth Festival presents performances only of Wagner's works, usually *Parsifal,* the "Ring" cycle, and one other work. The festivals were interrupted for seven years after World War II but resumed in 1951.

bay rum, aromatic liquid used chiefly as a cosmetic and a perfume. It originated in the West Indies, where it was prepared by distillation from rum and bay leaves. It is now commonly a mixture of oil of bay (from a bayberry), alcohol, water, oil of pimento, and oil of orange peel.

Bayrut: see BEIRUT, Lebanon.

Bay Shore, uninc. city (1970 pop. 11,119), Islip township, Suffolk co., SE N.Y., on the south shore of Long Island, at the widest point of Great South Bay; founded 1708. It is noted as a fishing and duck-hunting center and has some light industry. A ferry runs from there to Fire Island.

Baytown, city (1970 pop. 43,980), Harris co., S Texas, at the head of Galveston Bay, on the Houston ship channel; inc. 1948 after the consolidation of Goose Creek, Pelly, and Baytown. Large volumes of oil are produced in the area, refined in Baytown, and shipped throughout the world. The city also has chemical, synthetic-rubber, and steel industries. A junior college is there.

Bay Village, city (1970 pop. 18,163), Cuyahoga co., NE Ohio, a suburb of Cleveland; inc. 1903. It is a residential community with some light industry.

Baza (bä'thä), town (1970 pop. 19,990), Granada prov., S Spain, in Andalusia. It is a food-processing center for a fertile farm area noted especially for its cattle. Baza has flour mills, tanneries, and textile industries. An important city of the Moorish kingdom of Granada, it fell to the Spaniards in 1489 after a year-long siege.

Bazaine, Achille François (äshēl' fräNswä' băzăn'), 1811-88, French army officer. He served in Algeria, Crimea, Lombardy, and Mexico, and in the FRANCO-PRUSSIAN WAR he was given (Aug., 1870) the supreme command by Emperor Napoleon III. Unequal to the task, Bazaine allowed his army, which was entrenched at Metz, to be surrounded by the Prussians. The attempt of Marshal MACMAHON to rescue him led to the disaster of Sedan. Bazaine then entered questionable diplomatic intrigues with the Germans, which led to his capitulation at Metz (Oct. 27). Convicted of treason in 1873, he was sentenced to 20 years of seclusion but escaped. He spent the rest of his life in Italy and Spain. See Philip Guedalla, *The Two Marshals: Bazaine, Pétain* (1943).

Bazán, Álvaro de: see SANTA CRUZ, ÁLVARO DE BAZÁN, MARQUÉS DE.

Bazán, Emilia Pardo: see PARDO BAZÁN.

Bazard, Saint-Amand (săNtämäN' băzär'), 1791-1832, French socialist. He founded (1818) a republican society, *Les Amis de la vérité* [Friends of Truth], and was a member of the CARBONARI. Bazard plotted (1821-22) for the overthrow of the monarchy but was unsuccessful. He adopted the socialistic doctrines of Claude Henri de SAINT-SIMON and, with ENFANTIN, headed the Saint-Simonian movement until 1831.

Bazargic: see TOLBUKHIN, Bulgaria.

Baziotes, William (băzēō'tēz), 1912-64, American painter, b. Pittsburgh. Baziotes's works of the 1940s and 50s are largely abstract images, usually with brooding, primitive qualities encompassed in rich and muted colors. He taught in New York City at several schools including the Brooklyn Museum Art School and New York Univ. Representative works are *Dragon* (Metropolitan Mus.) and *The Dwarf* and *Pompeii* (both: Mus. of Modern Art, New York City).

Bazlith (băz'lĭth), family in the return from exile. Neh. 7.54. This is the **Bazluth** of Ezra 2.52.

bazooka, in warfare, portable, lightweight metal tube from which rockets are launched, usually operated by two men. It is used by infantry as an antitank weapon and also for attacking pillboxes and bunkers. In general, the bazooka is a short-range weapon with low accuracy; however, it gives the individual soldier the means of destroying heavily armored vehicles and fortified positions. An American invention, it was widely used in World War II—first by the Allies and later by the Germans—and in the Korean War by the UN forces. Since then, bazookas have largely been replaced by recoilless weapons and antitank missiles. In modern warfare, the first major use of the rocket as a weapon was in the bazooka. See ROCKET.

Bazzi, Giovanni Antonio: see SODOMA, IL.

BCS theory: see SUPERCONDUCTIVITY.

bdellium (dĕl'ēəm), aromatic gum RESIN obtained from trees of the genus *Commiphora* (or *Balsamodendron*). It is similar to myrrh. Bdellium is used in medicines and perfumes.

Be, chemical symbol of the element BERYLLIUM.

Beach, Mrs. H. H. A., 1867-1944, American composer and pianist, b. Henniker, N.H. Her maiden name was Amy Marcy Cheney. She received her piano training in the United States, and she toured both there and in Europe. In composition she was largely self-taught. Her *Gaelic Symphony* (1896) was the first symphony by an American woman. She composed more than 150 works, including a piano concerto, chamber music, choral pieces, and well-known songs such as "Ah, Love but a Day" and "The Year's at the Spring." Her music is in the traditional romantic style of the 19th cent.

Beach, Moses Yale, 1800-1868, American journalist, b. Wallingford, Conn. As a young man he invented a rag-cutting machine and a gunpowder engine. In 1838 he bought the New York *Sun* from his brother-in-law, Benjamin Day, for whom he had been working as production manager. The *Sun's* chief competitor in the penny-paper field was the New York *Herald,* edited by James Gordon BENNETT. The two rival papers used ingenious means to get news fast—the *Sun* even kept carrier pigeons in a special house atop its building. Costs, especially during the Mexican War, mounted so much that at a conference in Beach's office the editors of a number of New York newspapers established the New York Associated Press to cooperate in securing the news. Beach is credited with the first European edition of an American paper, the weekly *American Sun* (1848), and with starting the newspaper syndicated article. In 1848 he turned the New York *Sun* over to his sons, Moses Sperry Beach and Alfred E. Beach. See F. M. O'Brien, *The Story of the Sun* (1928, repr. 1968).

beach, mobile deposit of sediment subject to wave action at the shore of an ocean or lake. Most beaches are composed of SAND OR GRAVEL and extend from the level of the surf at lowest tide landward to the effective limit of wave action that marks the edge of the COAST. Essentially rivers of sediment moved by waves and currents, beaches display many common features. Seaward of the surf is the offshore zone, which commonly contains a trough and an offshore bar. The foreshore is a seaward-sloping surface extending from the low tide limit of the beach to the crest of a ridge, called the berm, that is formed by storm waves. The foreshore is the active portion of the beach affected by breaking waves that send water running up and down it, called swash and backwash, respectively. The slope angle of the foreshore is related to the size of the beach material and the vigor of the waves. The backshore extends landward from the berm as a broad terrace or gently landward-sloping surface, perhaps broken by one or more beach ridges. The presence of a cliff or dune complex landward of the backshore permits a clear demarcation of the edge of the coast. Most of the sediment making up a beach is supplied by rivers or by the erosion of cliffs along the coast. Beaches undergo a cyclical migration of sand between the beach and the offshore zone caused by the changing character and the direction of approach of the waves. During the summer, waves cause the beach to extend seaward, while in the winter they cut it back, creating a winter berm high on the beach. In addition, the action of tides causes shorter cycles of cut and fill. Along low sandy coasts, such as the Eastern and Gulf coasts of the United States, a long, narrow beach is commonly separated from the coast by a narrow lagoon. This configuration is called a barrier beach. Where the beach extends from land and terminates in open water it is called a spit or a hook. Waves approaching the shore obliquely move the sediment along the beach in a zigzag pattern called longshore transport. It is estimated that an average of 200,000 to 800,000 cubic yards (150,000 to 600,000 cubic meters) of sand are moved per year along beaches in this fashion. Since beaches are mobile deposits, they owe their existence to a constant replenishment of sand. In many coastal areas of the United States a deficiency in the supply of sand is resulting in serious erosion problems. Artificial replenishment by pumping sand onto the beach from offshore is one solution to erosion problems.

beach grass or **marram grass,** any species of the genus *Ammophila,* perennial grasses used to control the shifting of sand dunes, thereby protecting sandy coastal areas. The European beach grass (*A. arenaria*) has been used to hold dunes in Europe and was early planted at Cape Cod to bind the sands; later it was used at Golden Gate Park and elsewhere in the United States. The American beach grass (*A. breviligulata*) is native to dunes of the Great Lakes and much of the eastern seacoast. Beach grasses have creeping rootstocks which rapidly form an extensive root system. Beach grasses are classified in the division MAGNOLIOPHYTA, class Liliatae, order Cyperales, family Gramineae.

Beachy Head, high chalk cliffs (575 ft/175 m), on the south coast of East Sussex, S England. The battle of Beachy Head, in the War of the Grand Alliance, was fought (1690) between an Anglo-Dutch fleet under the earl of Torrington and the French fleet under the comte de Tourville. Although the French won, they failed to exploit their victory over the damaged opponent to deal a decisive blow to Anglo-Dutch seapower. Torrington, meanwhile, was court-martialed for retreating but, arguing that his action prevented an invasion, was acquitted.

Beacon, city (1970 pop. 13,255), Dutchess co., SE N.Y., on the east bank of the Hudson River opposite Newburgh; settled 1663, inc. as a city in 1913 when Fishkill Landing and Matteawan villages were united. Beacon has textile and related industries, other varied manufactures, and a large industrial research firm. An incline railway ascends Mt. Beacon, site of a towering monument to the Revolutionary soldiers who built signal fires there to warn of the coming of the British. A state hospital for the criminally insane is in the city. Beacon's historic buildings include the Madam Brett homestead (1709).

Beaconsfield, Benjamin Disraeli, 1st **earl of:** see DISRAELI, BENJAMIN.

beaded lizard: see GILA MONSTER.

Beadle, George Wells, 1903–, American geneticist, b. Wahoo, Nebr., grad. Univ. of Nebraska (B.S., 1926; M.S., 1927), Ph.D. Cornell, 1931. Beadle taught (1931-36) biology at the California Institute of Technology, where he also began genetic research on the fruit fly, *Drosophila,* in T. H. Morgan's laboratory. He was later chairman (1946-61) of the biology department there, and in 1961 he became chancellor of the Univ. of Chicago. Beadle shared with Joshua Lederberg and E. L. Tatum the 1958 Nobel Prize in Physiology for work with Tatum on the bread mold *Neurospora crassa,* which showed that genes control the cell's production of enzymes and thus the basic chemistry of the cell. See George Beadle and Muriel Beadle, *The Language of Life* (1966).

bead test, test used in the identification of certain metals. Some metallic ions that cannot be identified by a FLAME TEST are identified by a bead test. The test can also be used to confirm the results of a flame test. The borax bead test is the most common. A small loop is formed at the end of a platinum wire. The loop is cleaned with concentrated hydrochloric acid and dipped in powdered borax, then heated in the flame of a Bunsen burner until the borax melts, forming a bead. The bead is dipped into a tiny amount of the compound to be tested and is reheated in the flame. The metal borate that is formed colors the bead. Some metals and the colors they produce in an oxidizing flame are: chromium, green; cobalt, blue; copper, blue-green; iron, yellow to brown; manganese, violet; nickel, reddish-brown. If too much of the unknown compound is used, the bead may be opaque and the color difficult to determine. A different color is often obtained in a reducing flame. Several metals may give the same color. Some metals give only colorless or gray beads. A test similar to the borax bead test is often made using microcosmic salt. Results of the bead test may be confirmed by other methods of CHEMICAL ANALYSIS.

beagle, breed of small, compact HOUND developed over centuries in England and introduced into the United States in the 1870s. It stands between 10 and 15 in. (25.4–38.1 cm) high at the shoulder and weighs between 20 and 40 lb (9.1–18.1 kg). The breed is divided into two varieties on the basis of size: those under 13 in. (33 cm) in height and those between 13 and 15 in. (33–38.1 cm). The beagle's short, close-lying, harsh coat is usually colored black, tan, and white. Once widely used, either singly or in packs, to hunt hares, today it is more popular as a field-trial competitor and pet. See DOG.

Beagle, naval vessel: see DARWIN, CHARLES ROBERT.

Beale, Edward Fitzgerald, 1822–93, American frontiersman, b. District of Columbia. During the Mexican War, Beale was in California, where he aided Stephen W. Kearny in the battle of San Pasqual by crawling through the lines with Kit CARSON to get help. Later, during one of several trips across the continent, Beale was the first to bring east the news of the California gold strike. Appointed (1852) superintendent of Indian affairs in California and Nevada, he served well. In the Southwest, he is best remembered for a curious experiment in 1857 with camel transportation while doing one of many surveys. Beale was briefly (1876–77) also minister to Austria-Hungary. See biography by Stephen Bonsal (1912); L. B. Lesley, ed., *Uncle Sam's Camels* (1920).

Bealiah (bēalī'ə), warrior who joined David at Ziklag. 1 Chron. 12.5.

Bealoth (bē'əlŏth) [Heb.,=fem. pl. of BAAL], town, S Judah. Joshua 15.24. At 1 Kings 4.16 RSV has Bealoth, but KJV translates "in Aloth."

Bean, Roy, c.1825–1903, legendary American frontier judge, b. Mason co., Ky. He left Kentucky in 1847 to seek his fortune in California. Soon, however, he was managing a trading post in Chihuahua, Mexico. In 1849 he was chased back into U.S. territory for cattle rustling. During the Civil War, Roy Bean aided the Confederate cause by joining a band of lawless irregulars. After the war he followed the construction camps of the Southern Pacific RR as a saloonkeeper and gambler. In 1882, Bean settled at the Texas camp of Vinegaroon, had it renamed Langtry (for the English actress Lily Langtry), named himself justice of the peace (to which he added the title "the law west of the Pecos"), and set up court in his saloon, the Jersey Lily. He there began to dispense justice with the aid of one law book and a six-shooter. As a judge, Bean rendered arbitrary and unorthodox decisions, usually tempered with wit and common sense. See biographies by C. L. Sonnichsen (1943, repr. 1953) and E. Lloyd (rev. ed. 1967).

bean, name applied to the seeds of leguminous trees and shrubs and to various leguminous plants of the family Leguminosae (PULSE family) with edible seeds or seed pods (legumes). The genera and species encompassed by the term *bean* are many and variable. The broad beans (*Vicia faba,* of the vetch genus), the SOYBEAN types (*Glycine max*), and a few lesser species were the only beans known to the Old World before the discovery of America, by which time the Indians had already developed most of the bean types still used today, e.g., the lima beans, kidney beans, string beans, shell beans, and pea beans. All these are species and varieties of *Phaseolus,* the "true" bean genus; the hereditary history of most is unknown, and hence the taxonomic distinctions are often still uncertain. In general, beans are warm-season annuals (although the roots of tropical species tend to be perennial) that grow erect (bush types) or as vines (pole or running types). The plants are easily cultivated but susceptible to several diseases, e.g., rusts, blights, wilts, and bean anthracnose (a fungus). Field beans are mostly the bush type and are used as stock feed. This has also become the principal use of the ancient large-seeded broad bean (called also the horse or Windsor bean), still widely grown in Europe but seldom as food for man. The common garden beans comprise several bush types and most of the pole types; the most often cultivated and most varied species, *P. vulgata,* is familiar as both types. *P. vulgata* is the French haricot and the Spanish FRIJOLE. String beans, snap beans, green and yellow wax beans, and some kidney beans are eaten as whole pods; several kidney beans, pinto beans, pea beans, and many other types are sold as mature dry seeds. The lima or butter beans (*P. lunatus,* including the former *P. limensis*), usually pole but sometimes bush types, have a long history; they have been found in prehistoric Peruvian graves. The sieva is a type of lima. The scarlet runner (*P. multiflorus*), grown in Europe for food, is mainly an ornamental vine in North America. The tepary (*P. acutifolius latifolius*), a small variety long grown by Indians in the SW United States, has been found better suited to hot, arid climates and more prolific than the frijole. Other beans are the hyacinth bean or lablab (*Dolichos lablab*), grown in the Orient and the tropics for forage and food and cultivated in North America as an ornamental vine; the asparagus bean or yard-long bean (*Vigna sesquipedalis*), grown as a curiosity; and the velvet bean (*Stizolobium*), cultivated in the S United States as a forage and cover crop. The CAROB, the COWPEA or black-eye bean, and the CHICK-PEA or garbanzo are among the many other legumes sometimes considered beans. The sacred bean of India is the seed of the Indian lotus (of the WATER LILY family). Because seeds contain much protein, beans are useful as a meat substitute, and in different parts of the world are a characteristic item—often a staple—of the national fare. Baked beans, cooked for hours with pork or molasses or both, are a traditional New England dish. The Greeks and Romans used the broad bean for balloting—black seeds to signify opposition and white seeds agreement. This custom lingered in England in the election of the king and queen for Twelfth Night and other celebrations and was taken to the New World colony at Massachusetts Bay, where Indian beans were used. Beans are classified in the division MAGNOLIOPHYTA, class Magnoliopsida, order Rosales, family Leguminosae.

bean beetle, common name for a destructive beetle, *Epilachna varivestris,* of the LADYBIRD BEETLE family. Although nearly all other members of this family are beneficial carnivores, the bean beetle attacks leguminous plants, especially beans. Both larva and adult feed on the undersides of leaves and sometimes on the pods. The adult is yellow, with black spots; the yellow, oval-bodied larva has forked spines. Bean beetles overwinter as adults and in early spring lay masses of 10 to 50 eggs on the undersides of leaves. One to four generations occur annually, each requiring about a month to mature. Since most damage occurs during July and August, early-maturing beans suffer the least damage. Removing old bean plants helps to destroy overwintering beetles, although many escape to nearby sheltered areas. Chemical insecticides are used for control. Before 1920 the bean beetle, also called Mexican bean beetle, was found only in the SW United States, but it now occurs throughout most of the United States, except on the Pacific coast. It is classified in the phylum ARTHROPODA, class Insecta, order Coleoptera, family Coccinellidae.

bean weevil, common name for a well-known cosmopolitan species of beetle (*Acanthoscelides obtectus*) that attacks beans and is thought to be native to the United States. It belongs to the family Bruchidae, the seed beetles. The bean weevil is small, about ⅙ in. (0.4 cm) long, and stout-bodied, with a short broad snout and shortened wing covers (elytra). The adults attack legumes either in storage or in the field and may even completely destroy them. The grubs, or larvae, hatch from eggs laid in holes that have been chewed by the female into stored beans or into pods in the field. In heavy infestations there may be two dozen or more newly hatched larvae in one bean. When full-grown, the larvae form pupae in the eaten-out cavity. As many as six generations are produced in a single season, and in storage breeding continues as long as there is available food left in the beans and a warm temperature. The larvae can be killed by fumigation or by heating the seeds to 145°F (63°C) for two hours. Bean weevils are classified in the phylum ARTHROPODA, class Insecta, order Coleoptera, family Bruchidae.

Bear, river, 350 mi (563 km) long, rising in the Uinta Mts., NE Utah, and flowing in a U-shaped course NW through Wyoming and Idaho, then S into Utah to enter Great Salt Lake. A perennial stream, the Bear played an important role in the development of the region by the Mormons in the mid-1800s. The Bear irrigates c.50,000 acres (20,230 hectares). At the river's mouth is Bear River National Wildlife Reserve.

bear, large mammal of the family Ursidae in the order Carnivora, found almost exclusively in the Northern Hemisphere. Bears have large heads, bulky bodies, massive hindquarters, short, powerful limbs, very short tails, and coarse, thick fur. They walk on the entire sole of the foot and normally move with a slow, ambling gait. However, they are capable of moving with great speed when necessary and some achieve bursts of 35 mi (56 km) per hr. Most bears can climb trees and swim well. They stand on the hind feet to reach objects with their paws. They have large, strong, non-retractile claws, used for catching prey and for digging. Their teeth are adapted to grinding as well as tearing. Nearly all species are omnivorous, feeding on fruits, roots and other plant matter, honey, carrion, insects, fish, and small mammals. Adult bears are solitary except during the mating season. Groups may feed together where quantities of food are available, but there is little social contact. In cold climates bears sleep through most of the winter in individual dens made in caves or holes in the ground. This sleep is not a true hibernation, as the bear's metabolism remains in a normal state and it may wake and emerge during warm spells. The young, usually twins, are born during winter in a very immature state. Cubs stay with their mothers for about a year, and females usually mate only every other year. Bears are not generally subject to predation, unless they are in a weakened condition. A bear is a formidable adversary and may attack a human if it is injured or startled. The brown bear of Eurasia, *Ursus arctos,* is extinct in much of Western Europe, but small numbers survive in some wooded sections of that region and larger numbers in Russia and N Asia. The Russian variety was the bear most often trained to dance and box by traveling showmen in the past. The North American brown bears, including the Kodiak bear and GRIZZLY BEAR, are regarded by many authorities as varieties of *U. arctos.* Brown bears are dish-faced; i.e., their muzzles curve upward in profile. Their shoulders are humped. They range in color from yellow-brown to nearly black, with much color variation among different varieties, local populations, and individuals. Most varieties do not climb well. The Kodiak bear, or big brown bear, is the largest living member of the Carnivora, sometimes reaching a length of 9 ft (2.7 m), a shoulder height of 4½ ft (140 cm), and a weight of over 1,600 lb (730 kg). It is found along the south coast of Alaska and, like the Siberian brown bear, eats large numbers of salmon during salmon runs. The most widespread and numerous North American bear is the so-called black bear, *U. americanus,* found in Alaska, Canada, the Great Lakes region, mountainous areas of the United States, and on the Gulf Coast. American black bears range in color from light brown to black; in northern regions there are gray and nearly white forms. Their muzzles are always cinnamon brown and are straight in profile. They are further distinguished from brown bears by their smaller size and by their hindquarters, which are higher than their shoulders. Males are usually about 6 ft (190 cm) long and weigh about 500 lb (230 kg). The Asian black bear, or moon bear, *Selenarctos thibetanus,* is found in forests from central Asia and the Himalayas to Japan. The sun bear, *Helarctos malayanus,* is found in tropical forests of SE Asia. Smallest of the bears, it is about 4 ft (120 cm) long and weighs about 100 lb (45 kg). It spends much time in trees and is fond of honey; it is sometimes called honey bear (a name also applied to the KINKAJOU). The sloth bear, *Melursus ursinus,* is a medium-sized bear of the forests of S India and Sri Lanka. The POLAR BEAR, *Thalarctos maritimus,* is an almost exclusively carnivorous species of the arctic regions. The only bear of the Southern Hemisphere is the spectacled bear, *Tremarctos ornatus,* of the Andes mts.; it is so called from the light-colored circles around its eyes. Bears are classified in the phylum CHORDATA, subphylum Vertebrata, class Mammalia, order Carnivora, family Ursidae. See Richard Perry, *Bears* (1970).

bearberry, any plant of the northern and alpine genus *Arctostaphylos* of the family Ericaceae (HEATH family), especially *A. uvaursi,* a trailing evergreen sometimes cultivated as a ground cover. The small, leathery leaves yield a medicinal astringent and a dye. They were used for tobacco by the Indians, who also utilized the mealy red berries for food and beverages. This Northern Hemisphere genus is most abundant in arid areas, where many of the shrubby species (called manzanita in the West) are common chaparral plants. Other plants are also sometimes called bearberry. Bearberry is classified in the division MAGNOLIOPHYTA, class Magnoliopsida, order Ericales, family Ericaceae.

Beard, Charles Austin, 1874-1948, American historian, b. near Knightstown, Ind. A year at Oxford as a graduate student gave him an interest in English local government, and after further study at Cornell and Columbia universities he wrote, for his doctoral dissertation at Columbia, *The Office of Justice of the Peace in England* (1904, repr. 1962). While teaching (1904-17) history and politics at Columbia, he joined James Harvey ROBINSON in promoting the teaching of history that would encompass all aspects of civilization, including economics, politics, the intellectual life, and culture. Together they wrote *The Development of Modern Europe* (1907) and compiled an accompanying book of readings. Beard was especially concerned with the relationship of economic interests and politics. His study of the conservative economic interests of the men at the Federal Constitutional Convention, *An Economic Interpretation of the Constitution* (1913), caused much stir; he also wrote *Economic Origins of Jeffersonian Democracy* (1915, repr. 1965) and *The Economic Basis of Politics* (1922). His interest in city government led to *American City Government* (1912) as well as the long standard *American Government and Politics* (1910). After resigning from Columbia in World War I, he helped to found the New School for Social Research, was director (1917-22) of the Training School for Public Service in New York City, and was an adviser on administration in Tokyo after the disastrous Japanese earthquake of 1923. Beard wrote *A Charter for the Social Sciences in the Schools* (1932), which had an enormous influence on the teaching of history. He became widely known to the general reading public through *The Rise of American Civilization* (2 vol., 1927, repr. 1933) and its sequels (Vol. III and Vol. IV), *America in Midpassage* (1939) and *The American Spirit* (1943), all written in collaboration with his wife, Mary Ritter Beard (1876-1958). This panoramic work is an example of the broad historical view that Beard championed; the great store of fact is laid open with easy and graceful literary style. With his wife he also later wrote a brief survey, *The Beards' Basic History of the United States* (1944, rev. ed. 1960). Mary R. Beard, a historian in her own right, was particularly interested in feminism and the labor movement and wrote a number of works on the subjects, notably *Women's Work in Municipalities* (1915), *A Short History of the American Labor Movement* (1920), *On Understanding Women* (1931), and *Woman as Force in History* (1946). Charles A. Beard, much criticized as a radical in his earlier years, was just as much criticized by the liberals in his later years for his violent opposition to Franklin D. Roosevelt's administration, especially in the struggle over the Supreme Court and in foreign policy. Beard's last work was *President Roosevelt and the Coming of the War, 1941* (1948, repr. 1968). See studies by B. C. Borning (1962) and Richard Hofstadter (1968, repr. 1970).

Beard, Daniel Carter, 1850-1941, American illustrator and naturalist, b. Cincinnati, Ohio, studied at the Art Students League, New York City. He illustrated many books (among them the first edition of Mark Twain's *Connecticut Yankee at King Arthur's Court*) and taught animal drawing. He became interested in work for boys, and his best-known book, *The American Boys' Handy Book*, was published in 1882. One of the founders (1910) of the Boy Scouts of America, he served for the remainder of his life as national scout commissioner. To boys all over the country he was known as Uncle Dan. Mt. Beard, adjoining Mt. McKinley, is named for him. In addition to many articles on woodcraft and nature study, Beard wrote *Boy Pioneers and Sons of Daniel Boone* (1909), *American Boys' Book of Wild Animals* (1921), and *Wisdom of the Woods* (1927). See his autobiography, *Hardly a Man Is Now Alive* (1939).

beard, hair on the lower portion of the face. The term *mustache* refers to hair worn above the upper lip. Attitudes toward facial hair have varied in different cultures. In ancient Egypt, as well as Turkey and India, the beard was regarded as a sign of dignity and wisdom. Beards were continued into the Greek civilization until the 4th cent. B.C., when Alexander the Great ordered his soldiers shaved. The Romans, however, actually introduced the practice of regular shaving. The belief that the beard denotes wisdom was widespread in ancient China, and the cult of the beard has been dominant in Middle Eastern cultures from ancient times to the recent past. As a symbol of virility and status, the beard has often acquired religious significance. Muhammad enjoined his followers to grow beards; the Sikhs of India are not permitted to remove a single hair from their bodies; and the patriarchs of the tribes of Israel were bearded. Hindus, on the other hand, have traditionally been clean-shaven. Prior to the 7th cent., most Anglo-Saxons wore beards, but with the spread of Christianity, beards were discouraged. However, since that time beards of all sizes and shapes have appeared and disappeared with the cycles of fashion. The guardsman's mustache of the 18th and early 19th cent. was the sign of an army man, and after 1830 the beard became the emblem of the French radicals. In the 20th cent. beards and mustaches were generally out of fashion until the 1960s when, together with long hair, they became popular with young people. See Reginald Reynolds, *Beards* (1950).

Bearden, Romare, 1914-, American painter, b. Charlotte, N.C. Bearden grew up in Harlem and, in his work, has attempted to come to terms with everyday experiences of blacks in America. His themes are frequently religious and are rendered in vibrant, flat planes of color combined with photographic elements. His work is represented in the Museum of Modern Art, New York City.

Beardsley, Aubrey Vincent, 1872-98, English illustrator and writer, b. Brighton. One of the foremost of modern illustrators, Beardsley exemplifies the aesthetic movement in English art of the 1890s (see DECADENTS). Largely self-taught and at first inspired by the Pre-Raphaelites, he was later influenced by art forms ranging from Greek vase painting and Japanese woodcuts to the French ROCOCO. In his short working span of only six years, he developed a superbly artificial and graphic manner, expressed in flat, linear black and white designs. His works were often macabre in subject matter, by turns erotic and cruel in emphasis. The art editor of the famous *Yellow Book* quarterly (1894-96), Beardsley also edited and contributed some of his best work to Leonard Smithers's periodical, *The Savoy*, and illustrated many books including Wilde's *Salomé* (1894), Pope's *Rape of the Lock* (1896), Aristophanes' *Lysistrata* (privately pub., 1896), and Jonson's *Volpone* (1898). His fiction, distinguished by an elaborate and erudite prose style, was collected and published in 1904 as *Under the Hill*. Criticized for the erotic character of his work and condemned for his association with Oscar Wilde, Beardsley fell from public favor. Ravaged by tuberculosis, he died at the age of 26. Beardsley had many imitators but his work remains unique. See his *Early Works* (1899, repr. 1967) and *Later Works* (1901, repr. 1967); his letters, ed. by J. L. Duncan and W. G. Good (1970); study by B. Reade (1967).

beardtongue: see FIGWORT.

bearing, machine part designed to reduce FRICTION between moving parts. It is also used to support moving loads. There are two main kinds of bearings: the antifriction type, such as the roller bearing and the ball bearing, operating on the principle of rolling friction; and the plain, or sliding, type, such as the journal bearing and the thrust bearing, employing the principle of sliding friction. Roller bearings are either cylindrical or tapered (conical), depending upon the application; they overcome frictional resistance by a rolling contact and are suited to large, heavy assemblies. Ball bearings are usually found in light precision machinery where high speeds are maintained, friction being reduced by the rolling action of the hard steel balls. In both types the balls or rollers are caged in an angular grooved track, called a race, and the bearings are held in place by a frame, commonly called a pillow block or plummer block. Ball bearings or roller bearings reduce friction more than sliding bearings do. Other advantages of antifriction bearings include ability to operate at high speeds and easy lubrication. A journal bearing usually consists of a split cylindrical shell of hard, strong metal held in a rigid support and an inner cylindrical part of soft metal, which holds a rotating shaft, or journal. A self-aligning journal bearing has a spherically shaped support that turns in a socket to adjust to movements of the shaft. Slight misalignment of the shaft can be accommodated in the ordinary journal bearing by wearing of the soft bearing material, often an alloy of tin or lead. Less frequently used are aluminum alloys, steel, cast iron, or a thin layer of silver covered with a thin coating of a soft bearing material. Ideally, a film of lubricant, normally oil, separates journal and bearing so that contact is prevented (see LUBRICATION). Bearings that are not split are called bushings. A thrust bearing supports an axial load on a shaft, i.e., a force directed along a shaft's length. It may be a plate at the end of a shaft or a plate against which the collar on the shaft pushes. Large thrust bearings, such as those used to transmit the motive force of a ship's propeller from the shaft to the hull, have blocks that are separated from the collar on the shaft by wedge-shaped spaces. Oil swept up by these spaces separates the metal surfaces. Graphite bearings are used in high-temperature situations. Certain plastics make satisfactory self-lubricating bearings for low speeds and light loads and, if additionally lubricated, work at higher speeds and carry greater loads. Rubber and a naturally oily wood, lignum vitae, are used in water-lubricated bearings. Watches and other precision instruments have glass or sapphire pivot bearings. In gas-lubricated bearings a film of gas separates the bearings from the moving machine parts.

Bear Island, Svalbard: see BJØRNØYA.

Bear Mountain, peak, 1,284 ft (391 m) high, SE N.Y., overlooking the Hudson River. The Bear Mt. section of the Palisades Interstate Park, with facilities for both summer and winter sports, is popular among New York City residents. The remains of Fort Clinton, dating from the Revolutionary War, are there. The Bear Mt. Bridge crosses the Hudson River. This suspension bridge, 2,257 ft (688 m) long, was opened in 1924 and was acquired by the state of New York in 1940.

Béarn (bäärn'), former province, SW France, in the Pyrenees. It is now the inland part of Pyrénées-Atlantiques dept. Its valleys are well cultivated, and cattle are bred. Pau replaced Orthez as the capital in the 15th cent. The Bearnese are related to the Basques but speak French. Béarn was part of Roman Aquitania. It came (6th cent.) under the control of GASCONY, and was made (9th cent.) a county. In 1290 it passed to the counts of Foix, who later became kings of Navarre, and in 1484 to the house of ALBRET. Protestantism was imposed by Jeanne d'Albret. When her son became Henry IV of France, Béarn passed to the crown. However, it remained autonomous until 1620, when Louis XIII annexed it as an anti-Protestant measure. With the Basque districts of French or Lower Navarre, it became a French province under the jurisdiction of the parlement of Navarre, which sat at Pau.

bear's-breech: see ACANTHUS.

Beas (bē'äs), river, 250 mi (402 km) long, rising in the Himalayas and flowing generally southwest through the fertile Kulu valley and the Siwalik Hills to join the Sutlej River, S of Amritsar, N India; the easternmost of the "five rivers" of the Punjab. The Beas marked the eastern limit of Alexander the Great's invasion of India in 326 B.C.

beast epic: see BESTIARY.

beat generation, term applied to certain American artists and writers who were popular during the 1950s. Essentially anarchic, members of the beat generation rejected traditional social and artistic forms. They sought immediate expression in multiple, intense experiences and beatific illumination like that of some Eastern religions (e.g., Zen Buddhism). In literature they adopted rhythms of simple American speech and of so-called progressive jazz. Among those associated with the movement are the novelists Jack Kerouac and Chandler Brossard, numerous poets (e.g., Kenneth Rexroth, Allen Ginsberg, Lawrence Ferlinghetti, and Gregory Corso), and others, many of whom have worked in and around San Francisco. Perhaps the only true nihilist of the group is William Burroughs. During the 1960s "beat" ideas and attitudes were absorbed by other cultural movements, and those who practiced the "beat" life style were called "hippies."

beatification: see CANONIZATION.

Beatitudes [Lat.,=blessing], eight blessings uttered by Jesus at the opening of the Sermon on the Mount (Mat. 5.3-12). Some, counting verses 11-12 apart from verse 10, say there are nine. In the parallel passage, Luke 6.20-26, only four of the blessings appear, with four corresponding woes. See also Mat. 11.6; Luke 7.23; John 20.29.

Beatles, The, English rock music group formed in the late 1950s and disbanded in 1970. The members were John Lennon (1940-) guitar and harmonica; Paul McCartney (1942-) guitar and piano; George Harrison (1943-) guitar and sitar; and Ringo Starr (Richard Starkey) (1940-) drums. All were born in Liverpool, England. Influenced by such American performers as Chuck Berry, Little Richard, and Elvis PRESLEY, The Beatles dominated ROCK MUSIC in the 1960s, eventually disbanding when they felt their possibilities as a group were exhausted. The lyrics and music for most of their songs were written by Lennon and McCartney. The group burst on the international rock music scene in 1961. Their initial appeal derived as much from their wit, Edwardian clothes, and moplike haircuts as from their music.

By 1963 they were the objects of wild adoration and were constantly followed by crowds of shrieking adolescent girls. By the late 1960s, "Beatlemania" had abated somewhat, and The Beatles were highly regarded by a broad spectrum of music lovers. From 1963 to 1970 the group released 18 record albums that clearly document its musical development. The early recordings, such as *Meet The Beatles* (1964), are remarkable for their solid rhythms and excitingly rich, tight harmony. The middle albums, like *Rubber Soul* (1965) and *Revolver* (1966), evolved toward social commentary in their lyrics ("Eleanor Rigby," "Taxman") and introduce such instruments as the cello, trumpet, and sitar. In 1967, *Sgt. Pepper's Lonely Hearts Club Band* marked the beginning of The Beatle's final period, which is characterized by electronic techniques and allusive, drug-inspired lyrics. The group acted and sang in four films: *A Hard Day's Night* (1964), *Help!* (1965), *Magical Mystery Tour* (1967), and *Let It Be* (1970); all of these are outstanding for their exuberance, slapstick, and satire. The Beatles also supplied voices for the full-length animated cartoon, *Yellow Submarine* (1968). After they disbanded, all The Beatles continued to compose and record songs. See Hunter Davies, *The Beatles* (1968); Richard DiLello, *The Longest Cocktail Party* (1972); Wilfred Mellers, *Twilight of the Gods* (1974).

Beaton, Cecil Walter Hardy, 1904–, English scenery and costume designer, photographer, writer, and painter. Since designing his first stage show in 1935, Beaton has worked on numerous productions, including *Lady Windermere's Fan*, *Vanessa* (opera), *Gigi* (film, 1951), *My Fair Lady* (stage, 1956; film, 1964), and *Coco* (1969). He has also written and illustrated many books. See his autobiographical *The Wandering Years* (1962) and *Memoirs of the 40s* (1973).

Beaton or **Bethune, David** (both: bē'tən), 1494–1546, Scottish churchman, cardinal of the Roman Catholic Church. He was the nephew of James Beaton, archbishop of St. Andrews. He was made cardinal in 1538 and succeeded his uncle as archbishop and primate of Scotland in 1539. Beaton arranged the marriage of James V and Mary of Guise and tried to assume the regency for Mary Queen of Scots (1542), but James HAMILTON, 2d earl of Arran, seized power. The following year Arran renounced Protestantism and sided with Beaton, who crowned Mary. Beaton became chancellor of Scotland and ably opposed the designs of HENRY VIII of England. Beaton's relentless persecution of Scottish reformers led to the execution of George WISHART in 1546, and in reprisal the cardinal himself was murdered in his castle two months later.

Beatrice (bēă'trĭs), city (1970 pop. 12,389), seat of Gage co., SE Nebr., on the Big Blue River; inc. as a city 1873. It is on the old OREGON TRAIL and is the trading and industrial center for a grain, dairy, and livestock area. Its manufactures include metal goods, farm and garden equipment, fertilizers, hardware and electric products, store fixtures, and dairy products. John J. Pershing College is in Beatrice. Nearby is the Homestead National Monument (see NATIONAL PARKS AND MONUMENTS, table).

Beatrice Portinari (bē'ətrĭs, Ital. bāätrē'chā pōrtēnä'rē), 1266–90, Florentine woman believed to be the Beatrice of the *Divine Comedy* and *Vita nuova* of DANTE. He first saw Beatrice when he was nine years old and she remained his ideal and inspiration until his death in 1321. Her identity has been the cause of much controversy.

Beatrix, 1938–, crown princess of the Netherlands. The oldest daughter of Queen Juliana of the Netherlands and of Prince Bernhard of Lippe-Biesterfeld, she received a law degree from the Univ. of Leyden in 1961. In 1966 she married a German, Claus von Amsberg, and the following year she gave birth to a son, Willem Alexander Claus, the first prince of Orange in the line of succession since 1884. She now has two other sons.

Beattie, James (bā'tē), 1735–1803, Scottish poet and essayist. Educated at Marischal College, Aberdeen, he later became professor of moral philosophy there. His fame in his own lifetime rested on two works, *Essay on the Nature and Immutability of Truth* (1770), an attack on Hume, and an autobiographical poem, written in Spenserian stanzas, entitled *The Minstrel* (1771–74). In describing the formation of a poet's mind, *The Minstrel* places particular emphasis on the effect of nature; the poem influenced the 19th-century romantics, particularly Lord Byron.

Beatty, David Beatty, 1st **Earl** (bē'tē), 1871–1936, British admiral. He served with distinction in Egypt and the Sudan (1896–98) and in the Boxer Uprising (1900) in China. Made rear admiral in 1910, he commanded successful naval actions early in World War I at Helgoland Bight (1914) and at Dogger Bank (1915). His battle cruiser squadron lured the German fleet into position for an engagement with the British grand fleet under Admiral John Jellicoe at the battle of JUTLAND (1916). Beatty commanded (1916–19) the fleet and was (1919–27) first sea lord of the navy. He was created Earl Beatty in 1919.

Beauce (bōs), region, in Orléanais, N France, in the Paris Basin, between the Seine and Loir rivers. It now comprises Eure-et-Loir dept. and parts of Loiret and Loir-et-Cher depts. It is the "granary of France"—a vast, limestone plateau covered with wheat fields. Beets, potatoes, barley, and oats are also grown. The region shared the history of the countship of Chartres; Chartres is its only important city. **Little Beauce**, between the Loir and the Loire rivers, is also a rich wheat area; Vendôme is the center.

Beauchamp, Guy de: see WARWICK, GUY DE BEAUCHAMP, EARL OF.

Beauchamp, Richard de: see WARWICK, RICHARD DE BEAUCHAMP, EARL OF.

Beauchamp, Thomas de: see WARWICK, THOMAS DE BEAUCHAMP, EARL OF.

Beaufort, Edmund: see SOMERSET, EDMUND BEAUFORT, 2D DUKE OF.

Beaufort, François de Vendôme, duc de (fräNswä' də väNdōm' dük də bōfôr'), 1616–69, French courtier and politician; grandson of King Henry IV of France and his mistress Gabrielle d'ESTRÉES. Implicated in the conspiracy of the Marquis de CINQ MARS against Louis XIII's minister Cardinal Richelieu, he fled (1642) to England but returned after Richelieu's death. He was one of the Importants, a clique opposing Richelieu's successor, Cardinal Mazarin, and was imprisoned from 1643 to 1648. A leader of the FRONDE, he was nicknamed King of the Markets because of his popularity with the Parisian mob. Exiled in 1652, he was later recalled and given command (1666) of the French fleet against the Turks and the Barbary pirates.

Beaufort, Henry (bō'fərt), 1377?–1447, English prelate and statesman. The son of John of Gaunt, duke of Lancaster, and his mistress (later wife) Catherine Swynford, he was half brother to Henry IV. He was declared legitimate (1397) and made bishop of Lincoln (1398) by Richard II, and under Henry IV, served as chancellor (1403–4) and became (1404) bishop of Winchester. On the accession of his friend Prince Henry as Henry V, Beaufort again was chancellor (1413–17). At the Council of Constance, Beaufort swung (1417) English influence to help elect Pope Martin V, but Henry refused to let him accept the pope's reward of a cardinalate. When in 1422 the infant HENRY VI succeeded to the throne, Beaufort became involved in a vigorous struggle for power with Humphrey, duke of GLOUCESTER. Beaufort's enormous wealth (he loaned money to the government for the war in France) and political skill gave him the advantage, and he served again as chancellor (1424–26). Made a cardinal (1426) and papal legate, he preached a crusade against the Hussites in Bohemia in 1429, but the troops he raised were diverted to join the English army in France. In 1431 he crowned Henry VI as king of France in Paris. Beaufort defeated (1432) an attempt by Gloucester to remove him from the see of Winchester and by 1437 enjoyed complete ascendancy. He and his faction, which was later led by William de la Pole, 4th earl and 1st duke of Suffolk (see under POLE, family), sought to end the French wars.

Beaufort, Margaret, countess of Richmond and Derby (bō'fərt, där'bē), 1443–1509, English noblewoman, mother of Henry VII. She was the daughter and heiress of John, 1st duke of Somerset, and great-granddaughter of John of Gaunt, duke of Lancaster. She was married three times: to Edmund Tudor, earl of Richmond, who was Henry's father; to Henry Stafford; and to Thomas, Lord Stanley, afterwards earl of Derby. Renowned for her philanthropy, she endowed professorships of divinity at Oxford and Cambridge and with the help of her confessor, John Fisher, founded Christ's College and St. John's College, Cambridge. She was the patron of many religious houses and of William Caxton and Wynkyn de Worde.

Beaufort Sea (bō'fərt), part of the Arctic Ocean, N of Alaska and Canada, between Point Barrow, Alaska, and the Canadian Arctic Archipelago. The Mackenzie River flows into the sea, which is always covered with pack ice. It was first explored by the Canadian Vilhjalmur Stefansson in 1914.

Beaufort's scale: see WIND.

Beaufort West (bō'fərt), town (1970 pop. 17,730), Cape Province, S Republic of South Africa, in the Great KARROO. The town has some light industry and is the trade and distribution center for nearby farms where sheep, grain, and fruit are raised. It is also a resort. Beaufort West was founded in 1818 and in 1837 became the first municipality in South Africa.

Beauharnais, Alexandre, vicomte de (älĕksäN'drə vĕkôNt' də bōärnā'), 1760–94, French general, b. Martinique. He fought with the colonials in the American Revolution and, as a supporter of the French Revolution, was a commander in the French Revolutionary Wars. A moderate member of the National Assembly, he was guillotined in the REIGN OF TERROR. His widow later became the empress JOSEPHINE.

Beauharnais, Eugène de (özhĕn'), 1781–1824, French general; son of Alexandre and Josephine de Beauharnais (Empress JOSEPHINE). He served ably in the campaigns of his stepfather, NAPOLEON I, distinguishing himself at Marengo and Lützen, where he rallied the outnumbered troops. The emperor made him viceroy of Italy in 1805 and officially adopted him the following year. His court at Milan was brilliant, his administration in Italy capable. Beauharnais married a Bavarian princess, and after Napoleon's downfall he lived in Munich under the titles of duke of Leuchtenberg and prince of Eichstätt.

Beauharnais, Hortense de (ôrtäNs'), 1783–1837, queen of Holland (1806–10), daughter of Alexandre and Josephine de Beauharnais and wife of Louis BONAPARTE. She was the mother of Napoleon III and—by her lover, the comte de Flahaut—of the duc de MORNY. See Constance Wright, *Daughter to Napoleon* (1961).

Beauharnais, Josephine de: see JOSEPHINE.

Beauharnois, Charles de la Boische, marquis de (shärl də lä bwäsh märkē' də bōärnwä'), 1670–1749, French governor of New France (1726–46). Despite the loss in 1745 of Louisburg to the British, which caused his replacement, Beauharnois's rule was generally peaceful and prosperous. He returned to France in 1747 and served as a naval official.

Beauharnois (bōhär'nwä), city (1971 pop. 8,704), S Que., Canada, on Lake St. Louis, a broadening of the St. Lawrence River. Furniture, metal alloys, and chemicals are produced in the city. Beauharnois is at the eastern outlet of the Beauharnois Canal, part of the St. Lawrence Seaway System, and is the site of a large hydroelectric development.

Beaujeu, Anne de: see ANNE DE BEAUJEU.

Beaujolais (bōzhôlā'), hilly region, Rhône dept., E central France, W of the Saône between Mâcon and Lyons. It is one of the great wine areas of France, famous for its red wine. Villefranche-sur-Saône, the historic capital, is a leading textile center. Lyons is the industrial hub of the region. Beaujolais was once the fief of the powerful lords of Beaujeu (a small town which gave the region its name). Annexed to the crown in 1531, it was incorporated into Lyonnais prov.

Beaumanoir, Philippe de Remi, sire de (fēlēp' də rəmē' sēr də bōmänwär'), c.1250–1296, French poet and jurist, a writer of medieval law texts. He was a judicial officer at Clermont and Senlis. His *Coutumes de Beauvoisis* [customary laws of the region of Beauvais] is an important source for medieval French law and social customs.

Beaumarchais, Pierre Augustin Caron de (pyĕr ōgüstăN' karôN' də bōmärshā'), 1732–99, French dramatist. Originally a watchmaker with a scant education, he adopted his title from his first wife, and rose to wealth and position among the nobility. His two successful comedies were *Le Barbier de Séville* (1775), which was the basis of an opera by Rossini, and *Le Mariage de Figaro* (1784), which was the source of an opera by Mozart. Brilliant in their clever dialogue and intricate plots, they satirize the privileges and foibles of the upper class. Beaumarchais was famous as a litigant, and the pamphlets he wrote about his cases were witty and effective. One of them (1774) narrated an incident about his sister, which served as the basis of Goethe's *Clavigo*. Beaumarchais's employment as a secret agent by the monarchy led to his involvement in the American Revolution as a supplier of arms. The payment expected in return was never forthcoming, and the claims of Beaumarchais against the Americans were settled only in 1835 through a grant by Congress to his heirs. Another costly venture was a 70-volume edition of Voltaire (pub. 1785–90, though volumes bear dates 1784–89). See biographies by Paul Frischauer (tr. 1935, repr. 1970) and Cynthia Cox (1963); study by J. B. Ratermanis (1961).

Beaumont, Francis (bō'mŏnt), 1584?-1616, English dramatist. Born of a distinguished family, he studied at Oxford and the Inner Temple. His literary reputation is inseparably linked with that of John FLETCHER, with whom he began collaborating about 1606. It is generally agreed that of the two, Beaumont possessed the superior poetic gift and talent for comedy. The plays usually ascribed to him as sole author are *The Woman Hater* (published 1607) and the burlesque *Knight of the Burning Pestle* (c.1607). After his marriage in 1613 he retired to his estate in Kent and ceased writing for the stage.

Beaumont, William, 1785-1853, American physician and army surgeon, b. Lebanon, Conn. He was privately educated and in 1812 was licensed to practice in Vermont. His *Experiments and Observations on the Gastric Juice and the Physiology of Digestion* (1833; fac. ed. 1929, with biographical essay by Sir William Osler; repr. 1941) was an exhaustive account of a case famous in medical history. In 1822, while serving as post surgeon on Mackinac Island, Beaumont was called to treat Alexis St. Martin, a youth of 19 whose abdomen had been torn open by an accidental gunshot at close range. All efforts to close the wound failed, although St. Martin recovered his health and strength. Later, when he realized what a unique opportunity this was to study the digestive process, Beaumont, with the assent of his sometimes rebellious patient, began a series of experiments that completely revolutionized the knowledge of the subject. In all, about 238 experiments were reported, starting at Mackinac Island in 1825 and continuing at intervals over a number of years at Plattsburgh, N.Y., at Fort Crawford (Prairie du Chien, Wis.), and at Washington, D.C. See J. S. Myer, *Life and Letters of Dr. William Beaumont* (1912, new ed. 1939).

Beaumont, city (1970 pop. 115,919), seat of Jefferson co., Texas, a port of entry on the Sabine-Neches Waterway; inc. 1838. A ship channel (completed 1916, reconstructed 1927) provides the facilities of a modern deepwater port, with shipyards and large storage tanks. Beaumont is an important industrial and shipping center and a great oil city, with giant refineries and petrochemical complexes. Other industries are based on the forests and vast farmlands of the area. There are rice mills, granaries, lumber and paper plants, meat-packing houses, and huge metal works. The lush pine forests were the base of the lumbering that began there before the Civil War. Shipbuilding followed, and as livestock raising and rice farming spread in the surrounding area, Beaumont became an important processing and transportation center. Its life was revolutionized in 1901 when the world's first great oil gusher came in at nearby Spindletop; a 58-ft (18-m) granite shaft marks the spot, now a national historic site. The city is the seat of Lamar Univ. It has a pioneer museum, an oil museum, and an art center. Annual events include a horse show, a river festival, and a rodeo.

Beaune (bōn), town (1968 pop. 17,377), Côte-d'Or dept., E France, in Burgundy. It is a noted center for Burgundy wines, with a wine school and wine research facilities. Its manufactures include winemaking equipment. Beaune flourished as a residence of the dukes of Burgundy. Its textile industry was ruined when the revocation of the Edict of Nantes expelled (1685) the Protestant craftsmen. Beaune, a circular city with 15th-century ramparts, has a Romanesque church (12th cent.) with 15th-century Flemish tapestries. Its famous *hôtel Dieu* was founded (1443) by Chancellor Nicolas Rolin, a patron of Roger van der Weyden, whose *Last Judgment* it contains.

Beauport (bōpôr'), city (1971 pop. 14,681), S Que., Canada, on the St. Lawrence River. It is a suburb of Quebec city. Settled in 1634, it is one of the oldest communities in Canada.

Beauregard, Pierre Gustave Toutant (bō'rĭgärd), 1818-93, Confederate general, b. St. Bernard parish, La., grad. West Point, 1838. As engineer on the staff of Winfield Scott in the Mexican War, he figured prominently in the taking of Mexico City. He later did engineering work in Louisiana, and for five days in Jan., 1861, he was superintendent of West Point. Beauregard, resigning from the army in February, was soon made a Confederate brigadier general and was given command at Charleston, where he ordered the firing on FORT SUMTER. Assuming command of the army in NE Virginia (June), he was second in command to J. E. JOHNSTON at the first battle of BULL RUN (July 16, 1861) and was promoted to full general. He was sent to the West in 1862 and succeeded to the command of the Army of Tennessee upon the death of A. S. Johnston at the battle of SHILOH. He retreated to Corinth, which he shortly abandoned to Halleck's superior army. Ill health and friction with Jefferson Davis, whom he had criticized after Bull Run, resulted in his removal from command. After a rest he was charged with the defense of the South Carolina and Georgia coast, which he ably held against Union attacks, particularly those on Charleston in 1863. In May, 1864, Beauregard reinforced Lee in Virginia. He defeated B. F. Butler at DREWRYS BLUFF and held Petersburg against Grant until Lee arrived. In the closing months of the war he was in the Carolinas with J. E. Johnston. After the war Beauregard was a railroad president, manager of the Louisiana state lottery, and for many years adjutant general of that state. His superior engineering abilities overshadowed his deficiencies as a field commander. See his Mexican War reminiscences ed. by T. H. Williams (1956, repr. 1969); A. Roman, *Military Operations of General Beauregard* (1884); biographies by H. Basso (1933) and T. H. Williams (1955).

Beauséjour, Fort: see FORT BEAUSÉJOUR, N.B., Canada.

Beauvais (bōvā'), town (1968 pop. 49,347), capital of Oise dept., N France. Tractors, ceramic tiles, textiles, and musical instruments are among its many manufactures. A Roman town and an early episcopal see, it flourished in the Middle Ages and again after the 17th cent., when Colbert established the state tapestry industry there. It was the center of the Jacquerie revolt in 1358, and in 1472 its citizens resisted Charles the Bold of Burgundy. Jeanne Hachette, who earned her surname for the hatchet with which she helped to repel the Burgundians, is commemorated in a yearly celebration. Beauvais was severely damaged in both World Wars; in June, 1940, its tapestry factory was destroyed, and the industry was moved to Paris. The city still retains its Cathedral of St. Pierre, begun in 1227 as the highest building in Christendom but never completed. Its choir vault (154 ft/47 m), the highest of all Gothic vaults, was reinforced after it fell in 1284; the transept was completed in 1548.

Beauvoir, Simone de (sēmôn' də bōvwär'), 1908–, French author. A leading exponent of the existentialist movement, she is closely associated with Jean-Paul SARTRE. Beauvoir taught philosophy at several colleges until 1943, after which she devoted herself to writing. Her novels *All Men Are Mortal* (1946, tr. 1955), *The Blood of Others* (1946, tr. 1948), and *The Mandarins* (1955, tr. 1956) are interpretations of the existential dilemma. Among her most celebrated works is the profound analysis of the status of women, *The Second Sex* (1949-50, tr. 1953). Her study *The Marquis de Sade* (tr. 1953), is a brilliant, perceptive portrait. Her monumental treatise *The Coming of Age* (1970, tr. 1972) is an exhaustive historical consideration of the social treatment of the aged in many cultures. Beauvoir's autobiographical writings include *Memoirs of a Dutiful Daughter* (1958, tr. 1959), *The Prime of Life* (tr. 1962), *Force of Circumstance* (1963, tr. 1964), *A Very Easy Death* (1964, tr. 1966), and *All Said and Done* (tr. 1974). See study by Elaine Marks (1973).

Beaux, Cecilia (bō), 1863-1942, American figure and portrait painter, b. Philadelphia, studied in Philadelphia under William Sartain and Eakins, in Paris in the Julian and Lazar schools. A skilled technician, she won many honors through her long career. She painted, among other celebrities, Henry James, Clemenceaux, and Cardinal Mercier. Well-known paintings include *The Dancing Lesson* (Art Inst., Chicago), *Sita and Sarita* (Corcoran Gall.), *Portrait of Mrs. Dupont* (Mus. of Fine Arts, Boston), and self-portrait (Uffizi). See her autobiography, *Background with Figures* (1930).

Beaux-Arts, École des: see ÉCOLE DES BEAUX-ARTS.

beaver, large aquatic RODENT, *Castor fiber*, known for its engineering feats. It was once widespread in N and central Eurasia except E Siberia, and in North America from the arctic tree line to the S United States. It is the largest living rodent except the capybara, and is distinguished by its extremely broad, horizontally flattened tail. Beavers are 3 to 4 ft (91-120 cm) long, including the tail (12 in./30.5 cm long, 6 in./15.2 cm wide), and about 15 in. (38 cm) high at the shoulder; they usually weigh about 60 lb (27 kg). Their long, dense fur is reddish brown to nearly black; the naked, scaly tail is black. Both sexes have scent glands, located in a pouch in the anal region. The musky secretion, castoreum, which may function as a sexual attractant, was once believed to have medicinal properties, and the glands, or castors, were of commercial value. Beavers build lodges up to 3 ft (91 cm) high and 5 ft (1.5 m) wide of sticks and mud; the entrances are below water level, with ramps leading to the living quarters, located on a platform above water level. They may also build burrows in banks with underwater entrances. They create deep ponds, or maintain the water level in old ones, by building dams across streams. These are made of sticks and logs, and the upper surfaces are reinforced with stones and mud. Materials are gathered by collecting wood and felling small trees by gnawing; often the beavers dig canals for floating these to the right spot. Most, if not all, of these activities are done mechanically, as a result of instinct; captive animals persist in building useless dams, and even in the wild beavers will attempt to reinforce solid, manmade dams with sticks. Although they form monogamous families and live in colonies, there is little social contact among beavers and they work independently. A colony consists of a cluster of lodges, each occupied by a family of the parents and their last two litters. The beavers sleep by day and spend the night foraging for food and building or repairing their structures. They feed on a variety of aquatic and shore plants, surviving in winter largely on bark. Sticks for winter food are stored in the lodges and under water. Excellent swimmers, they can stay under water for up to fifteen minutes. When alarmed, a beaver slaps the water with its tail, making a loud noise that sends other beavers hurrying to the safety of deep water. Females give birth to two to eight young in the spring; these mature in two years. Beavers are responsible for creating many of the woodland ponds that support lush vegetation and eventually become meadows. They have been extensively trapped for their pelts, once considered the most valuable of furs, and were exterminated over a large part of their range. However, because of their great importance in maintaining the natural environment, they have been reintroduced in many areas of North America and Russia, and are now increasing in numbers. The MOUNTAIN BEAVER of W North America is not a true beaver, but a nonaquatic rodent of a different family. Beavers are classified in the phylum CHORDATA, subphylum Vertebrata, class Mammalia, order Rodentia, family Castoridae. See Lars Wilsson, *My Beaver Colony* (tr. 1968), Grey Owl, *Pilgrims of the Wild* (1935, repr. 1971).

Beaverbrook, William Maxwell Aitken, 1st **Baron,** 1879-1964, British financier, statesman, and newspaper owner, b. Canada. The son of a Scottish Presbyterian clergyman, he grew up near Beaverbrook, N.B. He made a fortune in business and was probably a millionaire when he went to England in 1910. There he immediately entered political life as a member of Parliament and secretary to a fellow Canadian, Conservative leader Andrew Bonar Law. Politically ambitious, he was involved in the intrigues that led to the replacement (1916) of Herbert Asquith as prime minister by David Lloyd George. He was not given a place in the new cabinet, but he received a peerage (1917). Beaverbrook obtained control of the *Daily Express* (1916) and the *Evening Standard* (1923) and began the *Sunday Express* (1918). Both in Parliament and in his newspapers he advocated strong imperial ties and free trade within the empire, regardless of commercial agreements with other countries, but he never succeeded completely in his attempts to have his imperial isolationist policies adopted by the Conservative party. In World War II, Lord Beaverbrook was prominent in Winston Churchill's coalition government as minister of aircraft production (1940-41), minister of supply (1941-42), minister of war production (Feb., 1942), special envoy to the United States on supplies (1942), and lord privy seal (1943-45). After the fall of the Churchill government in 1945, he continued his supervision of his newspapers. His books include *Success* (1922), *Politicians and the War 1914-1916* (1928), *Men and Power: 1917-1918* (1956), and *Friends* (1959). See biographies by Thomas Driberg (1956) and A. J. P. Taylor (1972).

Beaver Dam, city (1970 pop. 14,265), Dodge co., SE Wis., on Beaver Dam Lake, in a productive farm and dairy area; inc. 1856. There is a foundry in Beaver Dam. Stoves, metal goods, and shoes are made, and peas and sweet corn are canned there.

Beaver Falls, city (1970 pop. 14,375), Beaver co., W Pa., on falls of the Beaver River near its junction with the Ohio; settled c.1793, inc. 1868. A steel center in an area of coal mines, natural gas deposits, and clay pits, it is known especially for its cold-drawn steel. The plates for U.S. currency are manufactured there. The city was founded on an Indian trail that later became a pioneer road. It is the seat of Geneva College.

Beaver Island, 14 mi (23 km) long, from 3 to 6 mi (4.8-9.6 km) wide, off N Mich., in Lake Michigan. It is the largest island of the Beaver Archipelago and has forests, lakes, beaches, and a harbor at St. James village. The island's permanent inhabitants are mostly fishermen. James J. Strang had a Mormon settlement there from 1847 to 1856.

Beaverton, city (1970 pop. 18,577), Washington co., NW Oregon, a residential suburb of Portland, in a farm area; inc. 1893. It has some electronic manufactures.

Bebai (bēbā'ī), head of a family in Zerubbabel's return. Ezra 2.11; 8.11; 10.28; Neh. 7.16; 10.15.

Bebel, August (ou'gŏost bā'bəl), 1840–1913, German Socialist leader. A wood turner by trade, he became a Marxian Socialist under the influence of Wilhelm LIEBKNECHT. At a congress at Eisenach (1869) he was instrumental in founding the German Social Democratic party, which he later represented in the Reichstag and which he led virtually single-handedly for many years. His antimilitarism and his social program earned him the hatred of Bismarck. In 1872, Bebel and Liebknecht, tried on false charges of treason, were sentenced to two years' imprisonment, but Bebel's prison sentence only solidified his control over the Social Democrats, and he was reelected to the Reichstag. In 1875 he helped to unite the Lassalle group with the Social Democrats. Among his writings are *Women and Socialism* (1883, tr. 1910), which was highly influential among German workers, and his autobiography (1910–14, abr. tr. 1912, repr. 1973).

Bebington (bĕb'ĭngtən), municipal borough (1971 pop. 61,488), Cheshire, W central England. In 1974, it became part of the new metropolitan county of Merseyside. Its frontage on the Mersey River is part of the Port of Liverpool. The borough includes Bromborough and Eastham, both of great antiquity, and Port Sunlight, an industrial area with soap factories. Bebington also has freestone quarries and manufactures chemicals and margarine. The Church of St. Andrew, on a site occupied since Saxon times, dates from the 14th and 16th cent.

Bec (bĕk), former Benedictine abbey, near the village of Bec-Hellouin, Eure dept., N France, in Normandy. Founded in the 11th cent. by LANFRANC, and later directed by ANSELM, who became (1078) the abbot, it was one of the most famous medieval schools. It declined after the Hundred Years War, was suppressed in the French Revolution, and fell into ruin.

Beccafumi, Domenico di Pace (dōmĕ'nēkō dē pä'chā bāk-käfōō'mē), 1486–1551, Italian mannerist painter and sculptor, also called Il Meccherino. He studied painting in Siena and Rome and was a versatile engraver and sculptor. He is best known for his frescoes in the city hall in Siena and for his designs of scenes from the Old Testament for the pavement of Siena Cathedral. Among his other works are *Holy Family* (Pitti Palace, Florence) and some fine sculptural work for the Siena Cathedral. *Nativity of the Virgin, Descent into Limbo,* and *St. Michael* (all in Siena) exemplify the peculiar spatial and lighting effects of mannerism. *Holy Family with Angels* is in the National Gallery of Art, Washington, D.C.

Beccaria, Cesare Bonesana, marchese di (chĕ'zärā bōnāzä'nä märkā'zā dē bĕk-kärē'ä), 1738–94, Italian criminologist, economist, and jurist, b. Milan. Although of a retiring disposition, he held, in the Austrian government, several public offices, the highest being counselor of state. Through these and through his writings he influenced local economic reforms and stimulated penal reform throughout Europe. As a young man he published (1764) his famous *Essay on Crimes and Punishments* (tr. 1767; 2d American ed. 1819, repr. 1953). The book, widely acclaimed in Western Europe, was one of the first arguments against capital punishment and inhuman treatment of criminals. His ideas especially influenced Jeremy Bentham and the utilitarians. He made original contributions to economic theory, applying mathematics to economics, analyzing population problems, and anticipating the wage and labor theories of Adam Smith. Much of this work appears in *Elementi di economia publica* (1804), a posthumous collection of his lectures (1768–70) in political economy at Milan. See Marcello Maestro, *Caesare Beccaria and the Origins of Penal Reform* (1973).

Beccaria, Giambattista (jäm"bät-tē'stä bāk-kärē'ä), 1716–81, Italian physicist. He joined the Piarist order in 1732 and studied in Rome and Narni. After teaching at various Italian universities he became professor of physics at Turin in 1748. Against the Cartesians there, he upheld Franklin's electrical theories, which he systematized and disseminated in his important *Dell' elettricità* (1753). His contributions include a classification of luminous discharges, the invention of the electrical thermometer, and the collection of data on atmospheric electricity.

Béchar (bāshär'), formerly **Colomb-Béchar** (kôlôN'-), town (1966 pop. 46,505), capital of La Saoura dept., W Algeria. It is an important administrative center in a mining (coal, copper, magnesium, iron) and industrial region. Béchar also serves as a major shipping point for coal. The town was established in 1905 as a French military post to control the then-turbulent Algerian-Moroccan border.

bêche-de-mer (bĕsh-də-mâr'): see SEA CUCUMBER.

Becher (bē'kər). **1** Son of Benjamin. Gen. 46.21; 1 Chron. 7.6,8. In 1 Chron. 8.1 "his first-born" should perhaps be read "Becher"; cf. BOCHERU. See BICHRI. **2** Son of Ephraim. His descendants are called Bachrites. Num. 26.35. Bered: 1 Chron. 7.20.

Becher, Johannes Robert (yōhän'əs rō'bĕrt bĕkh'ər), 1891–1958, German poet and essayist. Becher's anti-imperialist poetry, notably *Der Leichnam auf dem Thron* [the corpse on the throne] (1925), led to exile (1935–45) in the USSR. There he continued to write, producing such volumes of poetry as *Wiedergeburt* [rebirth] (1940) and *Deutschland ruft* [Germany calls] (1942). After the war his writings on socialist humanism and the artist's responsibility to society contributed to the literature of East German socialism. They include *Heimkehr* [homecoming] (1946), *Neue deutsche Volkslieder* [new German folk songs] (1950), *Macht der Poesie* [poetic power] (1955), and *Das poetische Prinzip* [poetic principle] (1957).

Bechet, Sidney (bəshā'), 1897–1959, American jazz musician, b. New Orleans, La. He began his professional career with his brother Leonard's band in 1911. Later he played with many other bands, including that of King OLIVER. Although Bechet played clarinet with vigorous elegance, his most remarkable achievement was his approach to the most difficult of the saxophones, the soprano. His style was marked by a trumpetlike attack, a broad, flaring tone, and a rich vibrato. He lived in Europe for the last 20 years of his life. See his autobiography, *Treat It Gentle* (1959).

Bechorath (bēkō'răth), ancestor of Saul. 1 Sam. 9.1.

Bechuanaland: see BOTSWANA.

Beck, Dave, 1894–, American labor leader, president of the TEAMSTERS UNION (1952–58), b. Stockton, Calif. A laundry-truck driver, Beck began his union career in 1924 and was a vice president (1940–47) and then executive vice president (1947–52) of the International Brotherhood of Teamsters. He was elected president of the teamsters in 1952, and by virtue of his office he became a vice president and member of the executive council of the AFL and of its successor, the AFL-CIO. In 1957, after Beck was called before a Senate committee investigating labor racketeering, the AFL-CIO conducted its own investigation and found Beck guilty of misuse of union funds. Expelled from the AFL-CIO, he did not seek another term as president of the international union and was succeeded by James R. HOFFA. In 1957 a Washington state court found Beck guilty of stealing union funds, and in 1959 he was also found guilty of Federal income tax evasion. Beck served a prison term of two years, from 1962 to 1964.

Beck, Julian, 1925–, American theatrical director, actor, and producer, b. New York City. He married **Judith Malina,** 1926–, also an American theatrical director, actor, and producer, b. Germany. Together they founded the Living Theater in 1947. Their productions are highly imaginative and often involve improvisation. Perhaps their most controversial work is *Paradise Now* (1968), an orgiastic critique of American life that involves nudity and audience participation. Their other productions include *The Connection* (1959), *The Brig* (1963), *Faust Foutu* (1960), *In the Jungle of the Cities* (1960), and *Antigone* (1968). See Judith Malina's autobiography, *The Enormous Despair* (1972); Renfreu Neff, *The Living Theatre: USA* (1970).

Beck, Ludwig (lōōt'vĭkh bĕk), 1880–1944, German general, leader of resistance to Hitler. A highly cultivated career soldier, he served on the general staff during World War I and by 1933 had become in effect head of the army general staff. He opposed Hitler's plans for aggression and his attempts to destroy the independence of the army. In 1938 he resigned in protest against the planned attack on Czechoslovakia. With Carl F. GOERDELER he thereafter conspired to overthrow the regime. Their efforts were repeatedly frustrated until July 20, 1944, when a bomb was placed in Hitler's conference room. Hitler escaped. Beck was arrested and shot. See Allen W. Dulles, *Germany's Underground* (1947).

Becker, Carl Lotus, 1873–1945, American historian, b. Blackhawk co., Iowa. He taught history at Dartmouth College (1901–02), at the Univ. of Kansas (1902–16), and at Cornell Univ. (1917–41). After retirement he was professor emeritus and university historian at Cornell. Among his early works were monographs such as his *History of Political Parties in the Province of New York, 1760–1776* (1909), but his real forte was the analysis of thought and philosophy in action, exemplified by his studies on the American Revolutionary period (e.g., *The Declaration of Independence,* 1922, repr. 1942) and in the broader study, *The Heavenly City of the Eighteenth-Century Philosophers* (1932). His deep concern with the use of history for the betterment of international relations and of mankind was shown in his *How New Will the Better World Be?* (1944). His works are remarkable as much for the quiet originality of his thought as for the purity and lucidity of his impeccable literary style. See collection of his letters (ed. by Michael Kammen, 1974); biographies by C. W. Smith (1956, repr. 1973) and B. T. Wilkins (1961, repr. 1967); Cushing Strout, *The Pragmatic Revolt in American History* (1958, repr. 1966).

Becket, Thomas: see THOMAS À BECKET, SAINT.

Beckett, Samuel, 1906–, Anglo-French playwright and novelist, b. Dublin. Beckett studied and taught in Paris before settling there permanently in 1937. He has written primarily in French, frequently translating his works into English himself. His first novel, *Murphy* (1938), typifies his later works: It portrays with precision an individual's entrapment by increasingly grotesque situations in his apparently normal world. The oddity of these situations is intensified in Beckett's subsequent novels including *Watt* (1942–44); the trilogy *Molloy* (1951), *Malone Dies* (1951), and *The Unnamable* (1953); *How It Is* (1961); and *The Lost Ones* (1972). In his theater of the absurd, Beckett combines poignant humor with an overwhelming sense of anguish and loss. Best-known and most controversial of his dramas are *Waiting for Godot* (1952) and *Endgame* (1957), which have been performed throughout the world. Beckett's other works include a major study of Proust (1931); the plays *Krapp's Last Tape* (1959) and *Happy Days* (1961); a screenplay, *Film* (1969); short stories, *Breath* (1966) and *Lessness* (1970); collected shorter prose in *Stories and Texts for Nothing* (tr. 1967) and *No's Knife* (1967); volumes of collected writings, *More Pricks than Kicks* (1970) and *First Love and Other Shorts* (1974); and *Poems* (1963). Beckett was awarded the 1969 Nobel Prize in Literature. His *Collected Works* (16 vol.) was published in 1970. See studies by Martin Esslin, ed. (1965), John Fletcher (1967, 2d rev. ed. 1970), Ruby Cohn (1972 and 1973), and High Kenner (1968 and 1973).

Beckford, William, 1760–1844, English author. A wealthy dilettante, Beckford had a great desire to ascend to the nobility. Unfortunately his erratic and strange behavior often worked against his ambitions. About 1796 he built in Wiltshire an extravagant Gothic castle, Fonthill Abbey, where he lived in mysterious seclusion and earned himself the reputation of an eccentric. Although not deeply interested in politics, he served in the House of Commons from 1784 to 1794 and from 1806 to 1820. Beckford is chiefly remembered today for the Oriental romance *Vathek,* a bizarre tale about the adventures of the shockingly cruel Caliph Vathek. The book was written in French but was first published (1786) in English translation. He was also the author of several books of travel and two burlesques on the sentimental novels of his day, *The Elegant Enthusiast* (1796) and *Azemia* (1797). See biography by P. Summers (1966); study by A. Boyd (1962).

Beckley, city (1970 pop. 19,884), seat of Raleigh co., S W.Va.; inc. 1927. Its major industries are coal mining, agriculture, tourism, and the production of electronic equipment. A state park is nearby. The city holds an annual Appalachian Arts and Crafts Festival.

Beckmann, Max (mäks bĕk'män), 1884–1950, German painter. A member of the Berlin SECESSION from 1908 to 1911, he was impressionistic in his early style. A subsequent expressionistic phase was altered c.1917 by the savage NEW OBJECTIVITY of George Grosz. Beckmann developed a richer, more personal, and more symbolic art in the 1920s. The power of his allegorical expression increased through the war years, which he spent in Amsterdam. Beckmann spent his last three years in New York City where he taught at the Brooklyn Museum School. His well-known triptych, *Departure* (1932–35), is in the Museum of Modern Art, New York City.

Becque, Henry François (äNrē′ fräNswä′ bĕk), 1837–99, French dramatist. His plays, which portrayed Parisian life in realistic detail, influenced French naturalistic drama. Among them are *Les Corbeaux* (1882) and *La Parisienne* (1885), translated in the volume *The Vultures, The Woman of Paris, The Merry-go-round* (1913).

Bécquer, Gustavo Adolfo (goōstä′vō ädôl′fō bā′kĕr), 1836–70, Spanish poet and writer of romantic tales. Bécquer's work is considered to be among the best 19th-century lyric poetry. Orphaned at 10, unhappy in love and marriage, and living in poverty for most of his brief life, he came to be lonely and introspective. His celebrated *Rimas* (1860, tr. 1908) is a suite of poems characterized by the melancholy and resigned bitterness of the romantics. His finest prose works include the tale *Los Ojos Verdes* [the green eyes], a collection of legends, *Leyendas* (1860–64), and a group of literary letters, *Desde mi celda* [from my cell] (1864). Bécquer died of pneumonia and hepatitis at 34. See Angel Flores, *Anthology of Spanish Poetry* (1961); study by Enrique Ruiz Fornells (1970).

Becquerel (bĕkərĕl′), family of French physicists. **Antoine César Becquerel,** 1788–1878, was a pioneer in electrochemical science. He was professor of physics at the Muséum d'Histoire naturelle from 1838 until his death. Becquerel made a special study of the voltaic cell, telegraphy, and magnetism and wrote several books on these subjects. His second son, **Alexandre Edmond Becquerel,** 1820–91, succeeded his father, in 1878, as professor at the Muséum d'Histoire naturelle. Known for his studies in light, photochemistry, and phosphorescence (for which he invented the phosphoroscope), Alexandre wrote *La Lumière, ses causes et ses effets* (1867–68). His son, **Antoine Henri Becquerel,** 1852–1908, was professor at the École polytechnique, Paris, from 1895. He studied atmospheric polarization and the influence of the earth's magnetism on the atmosphere. In 1896 he discovered RADIOACTIVITY in URANIUM; the Curies made further investigations of the phenomenon and shared with Becquerel the 1903 Nobel Prize in Physics (see CURIE, family).

bed. Article of furniture used for sleeping upon. A litter of dried grasses and animal skins placed on the floor or in a shallow depression or chest was used for sleeping by prehistoric and primitive peoples. In ancient Babylonia, Assyria, and Egypt, people of wealth slept on ornate bedsteads of wood, stone, ivory, or metal, laced with wickerwork or other resilient material on which rested rush mattresses. The Greeks used couches and mattresses that were often stuffed with wool or feathers. The Romans developed different types of beds for sleeping and for reclining. In Europe during the Middle Ages only the nobility used bedsteads; these were light frames easily carried on expeditions or sojourns in the lord's various residences. Canopies were suspended from wall or ceiling; covers and draperies were of the richest fabrics. In the 15th cent., separate bedchambers became common; bedsteads with high, ornately carved headboards had elaborate canopies supported on four posts and were enclosed with rich hangings. Children and servants often slept in cradles or on low pallets or trundle beds, which were concealed by day under the principal bed. In England especially, monumental beds came into fashion in the 15th cent.: the Great Bed of Ware (c.1580) measured 10 by 11 ft (3.1 by 3.4 m). The 17th cent. saw the development of a variety of forms—luxurious great beds with testers (or canopies) of many sizes and shapes, couches with adjustable headpieces, beds that turned up against the wall, cupboard beds concealed by doors or shutters. In the 18th cent. both beds and hangings became lighter and more graceful. In the 19th cent. the sleigh bed with curved ends was popular, and in the latter half of the century cast-iron and brass bedsteads and woven wire, link, and vertical coil springs were common. Modern developments include the inner-spring mattress, a number of space-saving varieties (such as sofa beds), and hospital beds with adjustable parts for raising and lowering patients. An invention of the 1970s is the water bed, which consists of a frame holding a puncture-proof mattress filled with water. In parts of the Orient, rugs piled on the floor serve as beds; the Japanese sleep between quilts spread on the floor matting. Ceremonial beds have been used since ancient Egyptian times. In the 17th cent. it became customary to receive guests while lying in bed. The "Bed of Justice" was a cushioned seat used by the kings of France in the parliament chamber.

Bedad (bē′dăd), father of HADAD 2.

Bedan (bē′dăn). 1 Otherwise unknown deliverer of Israel. 1 Sam. 12.11. The Septuagint reading, Barak, may be correct. 2 Manassite. 1 Chron. 7.17.

Bedaresi or **Bedersi, Yedayah ben Abraham** (yĕdīä′, bädärä′sē, bädĕr′-), 1270–1340, Jewish poet and philosopher, b. Béziers, France. His most successful poem was the didactic *Examination of the World,* of which many translations have been made, among them one in English by Rabbi Tobias Goodman (London, 1806).

bedbug, any of the small, blood-sucking BUGS of the family Cimicidae, which includes about 30 species distributed throughout the world. Bedbugs are flat-bodied, oval, reddish brown, and about 1/4 in. (6 mm) long. They emit an unpleasant-smelling oily secretion from two glands on their undersurface. All are parasites of warm-blooded animals. The common human bedbug of temperate regions, *Cimex lectularis,* is largely nocturnal, spending the day in crevices in walls and furniture and in bedding. Its bite causes irritation in many individuals, but it is not known to transmit diseases. It will feed on other mammals and poultry when humans are not available and can live up to a year without feeding. Maturation from egg to adult takes about two months in warm conditions; there may be three or four generations a year. Control methods include steaming, spraying, and fumigating. Another parasite of humans, *C. hemipterus,* is common in the Old World tropics. A North American species, *Haematosiphon inodora,* parasitizing poultry, will also bite humans. Other species attack bats and various kinds of bird. Bedbugs are classified in the phylum ARTHROPODA, class Insecta, order Hemiptera, family Cimicidae. See publications of the U.S. Dept. of Agriculture.

Beddoes, Thomas Lovell, 1803–49, English poet and dramatist. After graduating from Oxford, he studied medicine and anatomy at Göttingen. His writings, inclined toward the macabre and grotesque, include *The Improvisatore* (1821; three stories in verse) and two plays, *The Bride's Tragedy* (1822) and *Death's Jest-Book* (1850). The first collected edition of his poems appeared posthumously in 1851. See his complete works (ed. with an introduction by H. W. Donner, 1950).

Bede, Saint (bēd), or **Baeda** (bē′də), 673?–735, English historian, a Benedictine monk, called the Venerable Bede. He spent his whole life at the monasteries of Wearmouth (at Sunderland) and Jarrow and became probably the most learned man in Western Europe in his day. His writings, virtually a summary of the learning of his time, consist of theological, historical, and scientific treatises. Like a modern scholar, he consulted many documents, discussed their relative reliability, and duly cited them as sources—practices then most unusual. His theological works are commentaries on the Scriptures in the light of the interpretations of the Church Fathers. He wrote biographical works such as the life of St. Cuthbert (in prose and verse) and the *History of the Abbots* (of Wearmouth and Jarrow). His *Ecclesiastical History of the English Nation,* written in Latin prose, remains an indispensable primary source for English history from 597 to 731. It gives the most thorough and reliable contemporary account of the triumph of Christianity and of the growth of Anglo-Saxon culture in England. He also relates the political events that had bearing on these developments. The *Ecclesiastical History* has been many times translated; the best edition of the text is in *Bedae opera historica* (ed. by Charles Plummer, 1896). The best known of Bede's scientific treatises are those on chronology, held as standard for many years. Long venerated in the church, Bede was officially recognized as a saint in 1899 and was named Doctor of the Church, the only Englishman so honored. Feast: May 27. See the collection of essays, *Bede: His Life, Times, and Writings* (ed. by A. Hamilton Thompson, 1935, repr. 1966); E. C. Duckett, *Anglo Saxon Saints and Scholars* (1967); study by P. H. Blair (1970).

Bedeiah, Jew married to a foreign wife. Ezra 10.35.

Bedersi, Yedayah ben Abraham: see BEDARESI.

Bedford, Brian, 1935–, English actor. Bedford has performed on stage in England and the United States, notably in *Five Finger Exercise* (1958, New York debut), *The Knack, The Misanthrope* (1969), *Private Lives* (1969), *Hamlet* (1970), *School for Wives* (1972), and *Jumpers* (1974). His few films include *The Pad* (1966) and *Grand Prix* (1967).

Bedford, Francis Russell, 5th **duke of:** see RUSSELL, family.

Bedford, Francis Russell, 2d **earl of:** see RUSSELL, family.

Bedford, Francis Russell, 4th **earl of:** see RUSSELL, family.

Bedford, Gunning, Jr., 1747–1812, American political leader, b. Philadelphia. Settling in Delaware, Bedford became a member of the local legislature, attorney general (1784–89), and a delegate to the Continental Congress (1783–85). At the Federal Constitutional Convention (1787) he opposed a strong central government and was a vigorous champion of the rights of small states.

Bedford, John of Lancaster, duke of, 1389–1435, English nobleman; third son of Henry IV of England and brother of Henry V. At the death (1422) of his brother and succession of his 9-month-old nephew, Henry VI, Bedford was designated as regent of France and protector of England. While he was in France his duties in England were to be performed by his younger brother Humphrey, duke of GLOUCESTER. Bedford devoted himself to the affairs of France. In his attempt to make permanent the English occupation of France, he gave the country an able, if severe, administration, but his position was undermined by the waverings of his ally, PHILIP THE GOOD, duke of Burgundy, and by the victories of JOAN OF ARC, whose execution during his term of office has injured his reputation. He died shortly after the conclusion of a separate peace between Philip and King Charles VII of France, a major setback to the English. His death deprived England of the only man powerful and respected enough to keep balance between the court's hostile factions.

Bedford, John Robert Russell, 13th **duke of:** see RUSSELL, family.

Bedford, John Russell, 4th **duke of:** see RUSSELL, family.

Bedford, John Russell, 1st **earl of:** see RUSSELL, family.

Bedford, Sybille, 1911–, English writer, b. Charlottenberg, Germany. She has worked as a legal reporter for various publications, covering such events as the Auschwitz trials and the trial of Jack Ruby. Her novels can be called socio-historical and usually concern the interaction between character and events. They include *A Legacy* (1956), *A Favorite of the Gods* (1963), and *A Compass Error* (1968). Bedford was for 35 years a close friend of Aldous Huxley and is the author of his official biography (Vol. I, 1973).

Bedford, William Russell, 5th **earl** and 1st **duke of:** see RUSSELL, family.

Bedford, municipal borough (1971 pop. 73,064), county town of Bedfordshire, central England, on the Ouse River. It is an important industrial center; diesel engines, pumps, turbines, agricultural machinery, electrical equipment, and transistors are the chief manufactures. Bedford, a battlefield for Britons and Saxons in the 6th cent., was the scene of an important Saxon defeat in 571. St. Peter's Church contains examples of Saxon stone carvings. John Bunyan is commemorated by a chapel on the site of a building where he preached in the 17th cent. Bedford School, in existence since the 12th cent., is one of the largest public schools in England. In 1974, Bedford was included in the new nonmetropolitan county of Bedfordshire.

Bedford. 1 City (1970 pop. 13,087), seat of Lawrence co., S Ind.; inc. 1889. Bedford limestone, which is shipped all over the world, is quarried there. The city also has several small industrial plants and a foundry. Beside the limestone quarries, points of interest include old stone buildings and houses and many carvings. Nearby is a state fish hatchery. 2 Town (1970 pop. 13,513), Middlesex co., E Mass., a residential suburb of Boston; settled c.1637, inc. 1729. Several pre-Revolutionary houses remain. 3 City (1970 pop. 17,552), Cuyahoga co., NE Ohio, a suburb of Cleveland; settled c.1813 on the site of a Moravian settlement (1786), inc. as a city 1931. Although chiefly residential, it also has plants manufacturing office furniture, china, rubber goods, auto parts, processed foods, tools, and fixtures. 4 City (1970 pop. 10,049), Tarrant co., N Texas; settled c.1843, inc. 1954.

Bedford Heights, city (1970 pop. 13,063), Cuyahoga co., N Ohio, a suburb of Cleveland; inc. 1951.

Bedfordshire or **Bedford,** county (1971 pop. 463,493), 473 sq mi (1,225 sq km), central England. It is also called Beds. The county town is BEDFORD. The terrain is generally flat, with low chalk hills in the south. The region, drained by the Ouse River, is fertile, and more than four fifths of the area is under cultivation; agriculture is the chief occupation. The production of cereals, especially wheat, and the raising of livestock are of equal importance with market gardening for London. Bedford, LUTON, and

DUNSTABLE are the chief manufacturing towns (hats, automobiles, electrical equipment, precision instruments, machinery, and ball bearings). The county was a refuge for Protestants from the European continent during the ENGLISH CIVIL WAR. The Puritan writer and preacher John Bunyan preached at Bedford. Bedfordshire was reorganized (1974) as a nonmetropolitan county.

Bédier, Joseph (zhôzĕf' bādyā'), 1864–1938, French authority on medieval literature. He was professor at the Collège de France and a member of the French Academy. His reconstruction, in modern French, of the *Roman de Tristan et Iseult* (1900) brought him fame for its scholarship and beauty. His theory of the origin of the medieval epic, developed in *Les Légendes épiques* (4 vol., 1908–13), was widely accepted until recent years.

Bedlam: see BETHLEM ROYAL HOSPITAL.

Bedlingtonshire, urban district (1971 pop. 28,167), Northumberland, NE England. The district includes the towns of Bedlington, Netherton, and West Sleekburn and part of the port of Blyth. Coal mining, brickmaking, and the manufacture of concrete products, shirts, and gloves are the chief industries. There is also some agriculture. The Bedlington terrier is bred in the district.

Bedlington terrier, breed of long-legged, lithe TERRIER developed in the eastern Border districts of England in the 19th cent. It stands about 16 in. (40.6 cm) high at the shoulder and weighs from 22 to 24 lb (9.9–10.8 kg). Its thick, wiry outercoat is trimmed back to the fleecy undercoat for exhibition. The hair when trimmed is no longer than 1 in. (2.5 cm) on the body, absent on the ears except for a fringe on the tips, and, on the head, formed into a topknot that gradually tapers to the nose. The overall appearance when clipped for show resembles that of a sheep. In color the coat may be solid blue, liver, sandy, or any of these marked with tan. Most authorities believe the Bedlington was produced by crossing the old rough-coated terrier with the whippet. Originally raised to hunt vermin, badger, and fox, and often used in organized dogfights, the Bedlington was later taken into the home as companion and pet. See DOG.

Bedloe's Island: see LIBERTY ISLAND.

Bedny, Demyan (dyĭmyän' byĕd'nyē), 1883–1945, Soviet verse writer, whose original name was Yefim Pridvorov. He wrote a vast number of widely acclaimed topical poems and propaganda jingles, exhorting the peasantry to hate foreign enemies and religious traditions. In 1936, *The Heroes,* his satire on Russian legendary figures, cost him his popularity.

Bedouin (bĕd'ŏŏĭn) [Arab.,=desert dwellers], primarily nomad Arab peoples of the Middle East, where they form about 10% of the population. They are of the same Semitic stock as their sedentary neighbors (the fellahin; see ARABS) and share with them a devout belief in ISLAM and a distrust of any but their own local traditions and way of life. Camel and sheep breeding provide their main livelihood. Land is divided into recognized tribal orbits within which are roving family groups. The tribe is a community of equals headed by a sheikh. Among the Bedouin, hospitality and simple, immediate justice are first rules of conduct. Although Bedouin have traditionally avoided agricultural work, settlement policies of the various Middle Eastern states in the 20th cent. have forced many of them into a sedentary life. See Emanuel Marx, *Bedouin of the Negev* (1967); Edward Nevins and Theon Wright, *World Without Time* (1969).

Beds, England: see BEDFORDSHIRE.

bedstraw: see MADDER.

Bedworth, urban district (1971 pop. 40,535), Warwickshire, central England. It is a residential and industrial area. Coal mining and brickmaking are the major economic activities. George Eliot was born nearby at Arbury.

Będzin (bĕN'jĕn), Ger. *Bendzin* (bĕn'tsĭn), town (1970 pop. 42,787), SE Poland, on the Czarna Przemsza River, a tributary of the Vistula. It is a coal-mining center and has industries producing metal products, machinery, chemicals, and electrical equipment. Founded in the 14th cent., Będzin was situated on the Wrocław-Kraków trade route. The first coal mine in the Upper Silesian basin opened at Będzin in 1785. The town passed to Prussia in 1795 and to Russia in 1815; it was returned to Poland in 1919. In Będzin are the ruins of a 13th-century castle.

bee, name for flying INSECTS of the superfamily Apoidae, in the same order as the ants and the wasps. Bees are characterized by their enlarged hind feet, typically equipped with pollen baskets of stiff hairs for gathering pollen. They usually have a dense coat of feathery hairs on the head and thorax. In many, the lip forms a long tube for sucking nectar. Bees feed on pollen and nectar; the latter is converted to HONEY in the bee's digestive tract. There are about 20,000 species of bees. They may be solitary, social, or parasitic in the nests of other bees. The solitary bees (which do not secrete wax) are called carpenter, plasterer, leaf-cutting, burrowing, and mason bees according to the material or method used to construct nests for their young. The groups of social bees, including altogether about 400 species, are the bumblebees, the stingless bees, and the honeybees. Bumblebees belong to the genus *Bombus.* In the tropics, bumblebee colonies continue for many years, but in temperate regions the workers and the drones die in the fall. Only the young, fertilized queens live through the winter, in hibernation. In the spring they begin new colonies, often laying their eggs in the deserted nests of field mice and chipmunks. The stingless bees are chiefly tropical. Some species release a caustic liquid that burns the skin. The honeybee commonly raised for production of honey and WAX in many parts of the world is *Apis mellifera,* of Old World origin. Honeybees build nests, or combs, of wax, which is secreted by glands in the abdomen. They store honey for future use in the hexagonal cells of the comb. In the wild the nests are made in caves or hollow trees, but beekeepers provide nesting boxes, called hives. Beekeeping is called apiculture. A typical colony consists of three castes: the large queen, who produces the eggs, many thousands of workers (sexually undeveloped females), and a few hundred drones (fertile males). At the tip of a female bee's abdomen is a strong, sharp lancet, or sting, connected to poison glands. In the queen, who stings only rival queens, the sting is smooth and can be withdrawn easily; in the worker bee the sting is barbed and can rarely be withdrawn without tearing the body of the bee, causing it to die. The workers gather nectar; make and store honey; build the cells; clean, ventilate (by fanning their wings), and protect the hive. They also feed and care for the queen and the larvae. They communicate with each other (for example, about the location of flowers) by performing dances in specific patterns. The workers live for only about six weeks during the active season, but those that hatch (i.e., emerge from the pupa stage) in the fall live through the winter. The drones die in the fall. A newly hatched queen is followed aloft in a nuptial flight by the drones, only one of which impregnates her, depositing millions of sperm that are stored in a pouch in her body. The drone dies, and the queen returns to the hive, where for the rest of her life (usually several years) she lays eggs continuously in the cells. A developing bee goes through the larva and pupa stages in the cell and emerges as an adult. The larva is fed constantly by the worker bees; the pupa is sealed into the cell. Fertilized eggs develop into workers; unfertilized eggs become drones. A fertilized egg may also become a queen if the larva is fed royal jelly, a glandular secretion thought to contain sex hormones as well as nutrients, until she pupates. Worker larvae receive this food only during the first three days of larval life, afterward receiving beebread, a mixture of pollen and honey. When a hive becomes overcrowded a swarm may leave with the old queen and establish a new colony. The old colony in the meantime rears several new queens. The first queen that hatches stings the others to death in their cells; if two emerge at once, they fight until one is killed. Mating then occurs. Bees are of inestimable value as agents of cross-pollination, and many plants are entirely dependent on particular kinds of bees for their reproduction (such as red clover, which is pollinated by the bumblebee, and many orchids). In many cases the use of insecticides for agricultural pest control has had the unwelcome side effect of killing the bees necessary for maintaining the crop. Bee venom has been found to have medicinal properties. Toasted honeybees are eaten in some parts of the world. Bees are classified in the phylum ARTHROPODA, class Insecta, order Hymenoptera, superfamily Apoidae. See Maurice Maeterlinck, *The Life of the Bee* (1913); E. W. Teale, *The Golden Throng* (1940); Karl von Frisch, *The Dance Language and Orientation of Bees* (1965, tr. 1967); Martin Lindauer, *Communication Among Social Bees* (rev. ed. 1971).

bee balm, name for several herbs, especially *Melissa officinalis* and *Monarda didyma,* both typical perennials of the family Labiatae (MINT family) named for their aromatic fragrance, attractive to bees and hummingbirds. *Melissa* [Gr.,=bee] *officinalis,* called bee balm or lemon balm, was introduced to North America from the Mediterranean area, where it has long been cultivated for its lemonlike odor and flavor and, formerly, as a curative for many ailments. The leaves and the oil distilled from them (known as melissa or balm) are widely used for seasonings and beverages. *Monarda didyma,* called bee balm, or Oswego tea, is native to E North America and was used, along with other species of *Monarda,* by the Indians and colonists for tea. It is also cultivated as an ornamental for its terminal cluster of red blossoms (sometimes pink in garden varieties). Oswego tea is similar and closely related to wild BERGAMOT. The names bergamot and balm are also used for other plants. Bee balm is classified in the division MAGNOLIOPHYTA, class Magnoliopsida, order Lamiales, family Labiatae.

Beebe, Charles William (bē'bē), 1877–1962, American ornithologist, explorer, and author, b. Brooklyn, N.Y., B.S. Columbia, 1898. He became (1899) curator of ornithology and later (1919) director of the department of tropical research at the New York Zoological Society, retiring in 1952. He made expeditions to Central and South America, the Orient, and the West Indies, and in 1934 he made a record descent of 3,028 ft (923 m) in a bathysphere. Among his numerous books are *Galapagos* (1923), *Beneath Tropic Seas* (1928), *Half Mile Down* (1934), and *Unseen Life of New York* (1953).

beech, common name for the Fagaceae, a family of trees and shrubs mainly of temperate and subtropical regions in the Northern Hemisphere. The principal genera—*Castanea* (CHESTNUT and CHINQUAPIN), *Fagus* (beech), and *Quercus* (OAK, including the

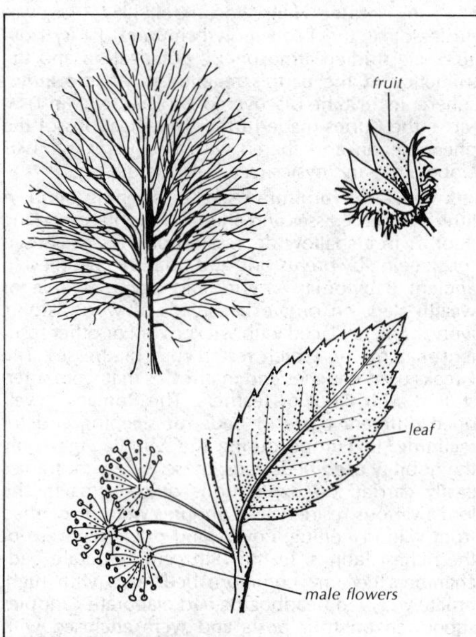

American beech, Fagus grandifolia

cork oak)—form a dominant part of temperate woodland vegetation and are highly valued throughout the world for hardwood timber. Some of their species are also cultivated for their edible fruits and as ornamental and shade trees. The beeches have distinctive smooth, silvery gray bark and pale green leaves that turn golden in autumn and are often winter-persistent. The tough, strong, easily worked wood is used for furniture, flooring, crating, and woodenware. Beechnuts have a sweet flavor but are now seldom eaten except locally in poorer areas of Europe. Swine are often loosed in beech forests to fatten on the nuts (called mast). The American beech (*F. grandifolia*) grows in rich soil over much of the NE United States and Canada. A slow-growing tree, it is declining in abundance through lumbering and through beech bark disease, a fungus infection that attacks the tree through holes bored in its bark by a scale insect. The blue, or water, beech is an American HORNBEAM of the birch family. The European beech (*F. sylvatica*) is an important forest tree, especially in S and Central Europe, and is valued for its wood and for an oil extracted from the nuts. Several of its varieties have reddish brown or purplish leaves and are cultivated in America as ornamentals, e.g., the purple and copper beeches. The beeches of the Southern Hemisphere, mostly of the antarctic regions, belong to the small genus *Nothofagus;* several are also used for timber or grown as ornamentals. The beech family is classified in the division MAGNOLIOPHYTA, class Magnoliopsida, order Fagales.

Beecham, Sir Thomas, 1879–1961, English conductor. Beecham was educated at Oxford but did not attend any formal music school. Early in his career as conductor and producer, he introduced his fellow countrymen to the operas of Richard Strauss, many Russian operas, and the Russian ballet. In 1932 he organized the London Philharmonic Orchestra, forging it into one of the world's finest orchestras, and in 1933 he became artistic director of Covent Garden Opera, London. A frequent conductor, until 1942, of the Hallé Orchestra, Manchester, he later appeared (1942–43) with the New York Philharmonic-Symphony Orchestra and with the Metropolitan Opera, New York. In 1946 he organized the Royal Philharmonic Orchestra, London. He wrote a biography (1960) of Delius, whose music he championed, and he also excelled at interpreting Mozart, Handel, and Berlioz. For his services to British music, Beecham was knighted in 1915; he also had enormous international influence. His versatility and high standards of excellence are attested to by numerous recordings. See his autobiography (1943); biography by Charles Reid (1962).

Beecher, Catharine Esther, 1800–1878, American educator, b. East Hampton, N.Y.; daughter of Lyman Beecher. She first taught in New London, Conn., and in 1824 founded a girls' school in Hartford. Later she organized the Western Female Institute in Cincinnati (1832) and similar institutions in Quincy, Ill., Milwaukee, and Burlington, Iowa. Author of works on religion, health, and domestic science (which she introduced in her schools), Beecher was indefatigable in the promotion of liberal education for women, although she opposed woman suffrage. See biographies by M. E. Harveson (1932, repr. 1969) and K. K. Sklar (1973).

Beecher, Henry Ward, 1813–87, American Congregational preacher, orator, and lecturer, b. Litchfield, Conn.; son of Lyman Beecher and brother of Harriet Beecher Stowe. He graduated from Amherst in 1834 and attended Lane Theological Seminary, Cincinnati. After two pastorates in Indiana, he accepted a call in 1847 to the newly organized Plymouth Church (Congregational) in Brooklyn, N.Y. Every important issue of the day was discussed on his platform. He was a leader in the antislavery movement, a proponent of woman suffrage, and an advocate of the theory of evolution. Beecher became editor of the *Independent* in 1861 and of the *Christian Union* in 1870. In 1863 he visited England, where his lectures were influential in gaining a more sympathetic understanding of the Union cause. Enthusiasm, imaginative insight, a strong interest in his fellow man, ready wit, and an easy command of English produced a convincing eloquence. The sensational lawsuit brought against him by Theodore TILTON for adultery ended after a long trial (1875) with disagreement of the jury. Beecher's friends acclaimed him victor. Despite the trial, Beecher remained influential for the rest of his life. His published works include *The Life of Jesus, the Christ* (1871) and *Evolution and Religion* (1885). See biographies by Lyman Abbott (1904, repr. 1969) and Paxton Hibben (1942, repr. 1973); study by W. G. McLoughlin (1970).

Beecher, Lyman, 1775–1863, American Presbyterian clergyman, b. New Haven, Conn., grad. Yale, 1797. In 1799 he became pastor at East Hampton, N.Y. While serving (1810–26) in the Congregational Church at Litchfield, Conn., he published his six sermons on intemperance, which passed through many American and English editions. Beecher helped to found (1816) the American Bible Society. In 1826 he was called to the Hanover St. Church, Boston, where his revival services created excitement. He was president of Lane Theological Seminary, Cincinnati, from 1832 to 1852. His liberal views not infrequently placed him in sharp opposition to the conservative group in the Presbyterian Church. Of his 13 children, Henry, Charles, Edward, Thomas, Harriet Beecher Stowe, and Catharine Esther Beecher won wide recognition. See his *Collected Works* (1852–53) and his *Autobiography* ed. by B. M. Cross (1864, new ed. 1961); biography by S. C. Henry (1974).

Beechey, Frederick William, 1796–1856, British admiral and Arctic explorer. He accompanied an expedition N of Spitsbergen in 1818 and wrote an account of it in his *Voyage of Discovery towards the North Pole* (1843). He accompanied W. E. PARRY to the Canadian arctic regions in 1819, and in 1825–28 he commanded the *Blossom* in its explorations of the NW Alaska coast and search for the Northwest Passage. On this voyage he reached Point Barrow and explored Hotham inlet. He also surveyed the North African, South American, and Irish coasts.

Beech Grove, city (1970 pop. 13, 468), Marion co., central Ind.; inc. 1906. Primarily residential, it has some manufacturing.

Beeckman, Isaac (bāk'mən), 1588–1637, Dutch physicist. An early proponent of mathematical reasoning and experimental verification in natural philosophy, he contributed to the modern conception of inertia and free fall and discovered an important hydrodynamic law concerning the rate of flow of water from a vessel. Although his recorded scientific work is largely confined to his *Journael* (diary) and notes, he influenced scientific development through his personal acquaintance with such famous contemporaries as René Descartes, Pierre Gassendi, and Marin Mersenne, and through his rectorship of the Latin school at Dordrecht.

bee-eater, any of the brightly colored, insect-eating birds of the family Meropidae. They range in length from 6 to 14 in. (15–36 cm). The plumage of many species is predominantly green but usually includes a variety of other bright colors. Many species have a black stripe running from the eye to the base of the long, sharp bill. They are found throughout the tropical and warm-temperate Old World but are most numerous in the tropical regions of Africa and Asia. Some species are migratory, and the few that breed in temperate areas, such as *Merops apiaster*, the common, or European, bee-eater, winter in the tropics. Most of the Meropidae are gregarious, and the birds of some species travel in flocks of hundreds or thousands of individuals. The nests of most species are colonial burrows, excavated in the sand of riverbanks or road grades. Bee-eaters catch insects on the wing; they subsist primarily upon bees and wasps. They are classified in the phylum CHORDATA, subphylum Vertebrata, class Aves, order Coraciiformes, family Meropidae.

beef, flesh of mature cattle prepared for food. It is an excellent source of protein, minerals, and vitamins. It has become one of the chief products of the MEATPACKING industry and is sold either chilled, frozen, or cured. The leading beef consumers, as well as exporters, are Argentina, Australia, Canada, New Zealand, and the United States. The carcasses, after being dressed, are split in half along the back and then cut into fore- and hindquarters. In the United States, beef usually reaches local dealers in this form and is cut by them into portions, e.g., shank, round, rump, loins (roasts and steaks), flank, rib (roasts), chuck, plate, and brisket. In addition, the heart, kidneys, liver, tongue, stomach wall (tripe), and tail are edible. The best beef comes from steers (castrated males) and heifers (females that have not calved). The meat should be a clear, light-red color, firm and well marbled with fat. Beef from older cattle is converted into various products, such as beef extract, sausage, corned beef, and canned or potted products.

Beefeaters, popular name for the YEOMEN OF THE GUARD and for the warders of the Tower of London. Both wear colorful uniforms modeled after those of the Elizabethan period.

bee fly, name for the small to medium sized FLIES of the family Bombylidae, many of which resemble bees in appearance and behavior. This MIMICRY provides bee flies with some measure of protection against predators that have learned to avoid the sting of true bees. A bee fly has a stout, hairy body and long proboscis. In many species the body and wings are strikingly marked in yellow and brown. Most are very swift fliers and buzz loudly like a bee if caught in a net. They seek heat and are often found flying close to the ground in dry, sandy regions. The adults feed on nectar and hover above flowers like bees. The larvae feed on larvae or pupae of other insects; they are beneficial as parasites of harmful species. Beelike flies are also found in other families. The syrphid flies (family Syrphidae), also called hover flies and flower flies, are a large, cosmopolitan group of beelike and wasplike flies. Many syrphid flies bear a very close resemblance to a particular bee or wasp species. Many of the robber flies (family Asilidae) resemble bumblebees. All of these are true flies; they are classified in the phylum ARTHROPODA, class Insecta, order Diptera.

Beefmaster cattle: see BRAHMAN CATTLE.

Beehive (star cluster): see PRAESEPE.

Beeliada (bē"ĕlī'ədə), the same as ELIADA **1**.

Beelzebub (bēĕl'zəbəb), in the Bible: see SATAN.

bee moth, greater wax moth, or **honeycomb moth,** common name for an insect pest of honeycombs. Bee moths do damage during their larval stages, injuring combs and honey. The moth *Galleria mellonella* belongs to the subfamily Galleriinae of the family Pyralidae, in which the females characteristically lay their eggs in beehives. The adult moths have brownish front wings with wing-spans of about 1 in. (2.5 cm). Eggs are laid in masses in the crevices of the hive. The newly hatched larvae tunnel into the combs, leaving a complex of silken galleries behind; they also puncture the wax caps of honey cells causing honey leakage and making the punctured comb honey unmarketable. Normally, the moths attack only abandoned beehives, or active ones in which the bee colony has been weakened, e.g., as a result of disease or starvation. Another well-known but smaller member of the subfamily is the lesser wax moth, *Achroia grisella*, which has the same type of scavenging habits as the greater wax moth. Bee moths are classified in the phylum ARTHROPODA, class Insecta, order Lepidoptera, family Pyralidae, subfamily Galleriinae.

Beer, George Louis, 1872–1920, American historian, b. Staten Island, N.Y. He was a tobacco importer for 10 years but also lectured on European history at Columbia from 1893 to 1897. After 1903 he devoted himself to continuing his economic historical studies of British colonial policy. His works revolutionized history-writing about the American colonies. These were, notably, *The Commercial Policy of England toward the American Colonies* (1893, repr. 1948), *British Colonial Policy, 1754–1765* (1907), *Origins of the British Colonial System, 1578–1660* (1908, repr. 1959), and *The Old Colonial System,* Part I (1912). He was also a practical expert on colonial problems, and he is sometimes credited with the first employment of the word *mandate* in its modern usage. He was one of the corps of U.S. experts at the Paris Peace Conference and was a member of the League of Nations mandates commission.

Beer, Thomas, 1889–1940, American author, b. Council Bluffs, Iowa, grad. Yale, 1911, and studied law at Columbia, 1911–13. He is best remembered for his biographies of Stephen Crane (1923) and Marcus (Mark) Hanna (1929) and his witty study of American manners in the 1890s, *The Mauve Decade* (1926). Some of his realistic short stories were collected by Wilson Follett in *Mrs. Egg and Other Barbarians* (1947).

Beer (bē'ər). **1** Unidentified place, to which Gideon's son Jotham fled. Judges 9.21. **2** Unidentified place, E of the Dead Sea between the Arnon and the Jordan, where Israel camped and dug a well. Num. 21.16–18. The little song quoted is one of the oldest poetic pieces in the Bible. See BEER-ELIM.

beer, alcoholic beverage made by brewing and fermenting cereals, especially malted barley, usually with the addition of HOPS as a flavoring agent and stabilizer. One of the oldest of alcoholic beverages, beer was well known in ancient Egypt. At first brewed chiefly in the household and monastery, it became in late medieval times a commercial product and is now made by large-scale manufacture in almost every industrialized country, especially Great Britain, West Germany, Czechoslovakia, and the United States. It is less popular in southern or wine-producing areas. Although British, European, and American beers differ markedly in flavor and content, brewing processes are similar. A mash, prepared from crushed malt (usually barley), cereal adjuncts such as rice and corn, and water, is heated and rotated in the mash tun to dissolve the solids and permit the malt enzymes to convert the starch into sugar. The solution, called wort, is drained into a copper vessel, where it is boiled with the hops (which provide beer with its bitter flavor), then run off for cooling and settling. After cooling, it is transferred to fermenting vessels where yeast is added, converting the sugar into alcohol. Modern beers, lighter than ancient, contain about 3% to 6% alcohol. The term *ale,* once used for a beer made without hops, is now applied in Great Britain to any light-colored beer. In the United States, ale is a pale, strongly hopped malt beverage. Most American beers are stored for several weeks or months before marketing, hence the name lager beer [Ger. *Lager*= storage place]. Bock beer, said to take its name from Einbeck, Prussia, where it was first made, is a heavier, darker beer commonly drunk in the spring. Porter is a strong, dark ale brewed with the addition of roasted malt to give flavor and color. Stout, darker and maltier than porter, has a more pronounced hop aroma and may attain an alcoholic content of 6% to 7%.

Beera (bē-ē'rə), Asherite. 1 Chron. 7.37.

Beerah (bē-ē'rə), Reubenite. 1 Chron. 5.6.

Beerbohm, Sir Max (bēr'bōm), 1872–1956, English essayist, caricaturist, and parodist. He contributed to the famous *Yellow Book* while still an undergraduate at Oxford. In 1898 he succeeded G. B. Shaw as drama critic for the *Saturday Review*. A charming, witty, and elegant man, Beerbohm was a brilliant parodist and the master of a polished prose style. His works include *A Christmas Garland* (1912), a collection of parodies on such authors as Joseph Conrad and Thomas Hardy; *Zuleika Dobson* (1911), an amusing satire on Oxford; *Seven Men* (1919), stories; and *And Even Now* (1920) and *Mainly on the Air* (1947), essays. Beerbohm was accomplished at drawing, and he published several volumes of excellent caricatures, including *The Poet's Corner* (1904) and *Rossetti and His Circle* (1922). He was knighted in 1939 on his return from Italy, where he had lived from 1910. See collections ed. by S. C. Roberts (1962) and Lord David Cecil (1971); biographies by S. N. Behrman (1960) and Lord David Cecil (1964); studies by John Felstiner (1972) and Bohun Lynch (1974).

Beer-elim (bē'ər-ē'lĭm), unidentified place, perhaps the same as BEER 2 and certainly in the same region. Isa. 15.8.

Beeri (bē-ē'rī). **1** Father of Esau's wife, Judith. Gen. 26.34. **2** Father of Hosea, the prophet. Hosea 1.1.

Beer-lahai-roi: see LAHAI-ROI.

Beernaert, Auguste (ōgüst' bârnärt', bâr'närt), 1829–1912, Belgian statesman. A member of the liberal wing of the Catholic party, he served in several cabinets and was premier from 1884 to 1894. Beernaert promoted electoral reform and legislation to improve labor conditions. He was a delegate to the Hague Peace conferences (1899, 1907), and he shared the 1909 Nobel Peace Prize with Estournelles de Constant.

Beeroth (bē-ē'rŏth, bē'ĭ-). **1** City important as a road station, now Bireh (Jordan). Joshua 9.17; 18.25; 2 Sam. 4.2; 23.37; Ezra 2.25; Neh. 7.29. **2** Same as BENE-JAAKAN.

Beers, Clifford Whittingham, 1876–1943, American founder of the mental hygiene movement, b. New Haven, Conn., grad. Sheffield Scientific School, Yale, 1897. After the publication of *A Mind That Found Itself* (1908), an autobiographical account of his confinement in a mental institution, he had the support of the medical profession and others in the work to prevent mental disorders. He was a leader in the field until his retirement in 1939.

Beersheba (bērshē'bə, bēr'shēbə) [Heb.,=seven wells or well of the oath], city (1972 pop. 84,100), S Israel, principal city of the Negev Desert. It is the trade center for surrounding settlements and for BEDOUINS, who hold a weekly market in Beersheba. Construction is the city's main industry. Manufactures include chemicals, textiles, ceramics, glass, plastics, and food products. Beersheba is an important rail and road hub for S Israel. The city was one of the southernmost towns of biblical Palestine; hence the expression "from Dan to Beersheba," meaning the whole of Palestine. It is especially connected, in the Bible, with Abraham, Hagar, Isaac, Jacob, and Elijah. A well believed to have been dug by Abraham when he made his covenant with Abimelech is in the city. Beersheba flourished during the late Roman and Byzantine eras but was deserted soon thereafter. It was merely a group of wells for Bedouin flocks when the Ottoman Turks reestablished it c.1900 as an administrative center for Negev tribes. Beersheba was the first city taken by the British in the Palestine campaign (1917) of World War I. Under the British mandate (1922–48) it was a city (Bir-es-Seba) inhabited by about 4,000 Muslim Arabs. Given to the Arabs in the partition of Palestine (1948), it was retaken by Israel in the Arab-Israeli War of 1948 and grew rapidly thereafter. Beersheba is the seat of the Arid Zone Research Institute; a biological institute and museum concerned with desert plant and animal life; and a municipal museum devoted to the history of the city. Remnants of a fortress and shards of the Bronze Age have been found nearby at Tell el-Sheba, the most ancient site of Beersheba.

Beer's law [for August Beer], physical law stating that the quantity of light absorbed by a substance dissolved in a nonabsorbing solvent is directly proportional to the concentration of the substance and the path length of the light through the SOLUTION; the law is sometimes also referred to as the Beer-Lambert law or the Bouguer-Beer law. Beer's law is commonly written in the form $A=\varepsilon cl$, where A is the absorbance, c is the concentration in moles per liter, l is the path length in centimeters, and ε is a constant of proportionality known as the molar extinction coefficient. The law is accurate only for dilute solutions; deviations from the law occur in concentrated solutions because of interactions between molecules of the solute.

Beesh-terah: see ASHTAROTH.

Beeson, Jack, 1921–, American composer, b. Muncie, Ind. Beeson studied at the Eastman School of Music and privately in New York with Béla Bartók. Since 1967 he has been MacDowell Professor of Music at Columbia Univ. Beeson has written songs and choral pieces; piano sonatas; a symphony (1959); and several operas, including *Hello Out There!* (1954), *The Sweet Bye and Bye* (1957), *Lizzie Borden* (premiered by the New York City Opera in 1965), and *My Heart's in the Highlands* (premiered on television in 1970). His vocal works, set to a catholic choice of texts, are marked by a varied stylistic approach unified by attention to contrapuntal lines and instrumental color.

Beeston and Stapleford, urban district (1971 pop. 63,498), Nottinghamshire, central England. There are large pharmaceutical plants and factories that produce boilers, telecommunication equipment, fluorescent lights, textiles, pencils, cardboard boxes, and clothing. The Stapleford churchyard has an ancient Saxon cross, thought to be the oldest Christian memorial in the country.

beeswax: see WAX.

beet, biennial or annual root vegetable of the family Chenopodiaceae (GOOSEFOOT family). The beet (*Beta vulgaris*) has been cultivated since pre-Christian times. Among its numerous varieties are the red, or garden, beet, the sugar beet, Swiss chard, and several types of mangel-wurzel and other stock feeds. Both the roots and the foliage of the red beet are edible, as is the foliage of Swiss chard and similar varieties. The easily stored roots of the mangel-wurzel [Ger.,=beet root] are much used for fodder in Europe and Canada and to a lesser extent in the United States. The biennial beet is one of the root crops most often used in crop rotation. The foliage of the sugar beet and of several other beet varieties is also used as feed. The sugar beet, cultivated commercially throughout the temperate zone, today provides about one third of the world's sugar. Since the 18th cent. selective breeding has raised the root's sucrose content from 2 or 4% to 15 and even 20% and has increased its resistance to disease. In the United States the sugar beet is grown extensively in the West from Michigan to Idaho and California, and mechanical harvesting has reduced production costs sufficiently for beet sugar to compete with cane sugar. The solution of extracted beet sugar in water is treated similarly to cane juice for refinement and granulation, but it has no valuable by-products. Beets are classified in the division MAGNOLIOPHYTA, class Magnoliopsida, order Caryophyllales, family Chenopodiaceae.

Beethoven, Ludwig van (lŭd'wĭg văn bā'tōvən, Ger. lo͝ot'vĭkh fän bāt'hōfən), 1770–1827, German composer. He is universally recognized as one of the greatest composers who ever lived. Beethoven's work crowned the classical period and also effectively initiated the romantic era in music. He is one of the few artists who genuinely may be considered revolutionary. Born in Bonn, Beethoven showed remarkable talent at an early age. His father, a court musician, subjected him to a brutal regimen, hoping to exploit him as a child prodigy. While this plan did not succeed, young Beethoven's gifts were recognized and nurtured by his teachers and by members of the local aristocracy. In 1787, Beethoven first visited Vienna, at that time the center of the music world. There he performed for Mozart, whom he greatly impressed. In 1792, Haydn invited him to become his student, and Beethoven returned to Vienna, where he was to remain permanently. However, Beethoven's unorthodox musical ideas offended the old master, and the lessons were terminated. Beethoven studied with several other eminent teachers, including Antonio Salieri, but was developing according to his own singular genius and could no longer profit greatly from instruction. Both his breathtaking piano virtuosity and his remarkable compositions won him favor among the enlightened aristocracy congregated at Vienna, and he enjoyed their generous support throughout his life. They were tolerant, too, of his notoriously boorish manners, careless appearance, and towering rages. His work itself was widely accepted, if controversial, and from the end of the 1790s Beethoven was not dependent on patronage for his income. The year 1801 marked the onset of Beethoven's tragic affliction, his deafness, which became progressively worse and, by 1817, total. Public performance eventually became impossible; but his creative work was not restricted. Beethoven never married; however, he was stormily in and out of love all his life, always with women unattainable because of marriage or station. His personal life was further complicated when he was made the guardian of his nephew Karl, who caused him much anxiety and grief but to whom he nevertheless remained fondly attached. Beethoven's work may be divided into three fairly distinct periods. The works of the first period include the First (1800) and Second (1802) Symphonies; the first three piano concertos (1795–1800); the first group of string quartets (1800); and a number of piano sonatas, among them the Pathétique (1798) and the Moonlight Sonata (1801). Although the compositions of the first period have Beethoven's unmistakable breadth and vitality, they are dominated by the tradition of Haydn and Mozart. Beginning about 1802, Beethoven's work took on new dimensions. The premiere in 1805 of the massive Third Symphony, known as the Eroica (composed 1803–4), was a landmark in cultural history. It signaled a definitive break with the past and the birth of a new era. The length, structure, harmonies, and orchestration of the Eroica all broke the formal conventions of classical music; unprecedented too was its intention—to celebrate human freedom and nobility. The symphony was originally dedicated to Napoleon, who at first symbolized to Beethoven the spirit of the French Revolution and the liberation of mankind; however, when Napoleon proclaimed himself emperor, the disillusioned composer renamed his work the "Heroic Symphony to celebrate the memory of a great man." The works of Beethoven's middle period, his most productive, include the Piano Concertos No. 4 (1806) and No. 5 (Emperor Concerto, 1809); the Razumovsky Quartets (1806); his Ninth Sonata for violin, the Kreutzer Sonata (1803), and his one Violin Concerto (1806); the Fourth through Eighth Symphonies (1806–12); a number of piano sonatas, among them the Waldstein and the Appassionata (both 1804). His sole opera, *Fidelio*, was produced in its first version in 1805 and in its final form in 1814. Beethoven wrote four overtures for the opera, three of them known as the Leonore Overture. He also composed overtures to Collin's *Coriolan* (1807) and to Goethe's *Egmont* (1810). From about 1813 to 1820 there was some slackening in Beethoven's productivity, probably due in part to difficulties concerning his nephew. Beethoven's final period dates from about 1816 and is characterized by works of greater depth and complexity. They include the demanding, nearly symphonic Hammerklavier sonata (1818) and the other late piano sonatas; the monumental Ninth Symphony (1817–23) with its choral finale based on Schiller's *Ode to Joy;* and the *Missa Solemnis* (1818–23). The last five string quartets and the Grosse Fuge (also for quartet), composed in his last years, are considered by many music lovers to be Beethoven's supreme creations, and by some the most sublime music ever composed. Beethoven died, after a long illness, in the midst of a fierce thunderstorm, and legend has it that the dying man shook his fist in defiance of the heavens. A prolific composer, Beethoven produced, in addition to the works mentioned, sonatas for violin and piano and for cello and piano; string and piano trios; music for wind instruments; miscellaneous piano works, including the popular bagatelle *Für Elise* (1810); over 200 songs; a number of shorter orchestral works; and several choral pieces. His influence on subsequent composers was immeasurable. Aside from his architectonic innovations and expansion of the classical sonata and symphony, he brought to music a new depth and intensity of emotion which was emulated by later romantic composers but probably never surpassed. See his letters, ed. by Emily Anderson (3 vol., tr. 1961); biographies by A. F. Schindler (tr. 1966) and Martin Cooper (1970); studies by D. F. Tovey (1945) and W. S. Newman (1971); Elliot Forbes, ed., *Thayer's Life of Beethoven* (2 vol., rev. ed. 1967); H. C. R. Landon, ed., *Beethoven: A Documentary Study* (1970); Denis Arnold and Nigel Fortune, ed., *The Beethoven Reader* (1971).

beetle, common name for INSECTS of the order Coleoptera, which, with over 250,000 described species, is the largest of the insect orders. Beetles have chewing mouthparts and well-developed antennae. They are characterized by a front pair of hard, opaque, waterproof wings called elytra, which usually meet in a straight line down the middle of the back. The elytra cover the rear pair of membranous flight wings, protecting them and the body from mechanical damage and desiccation. Beetles are poor flyers compared with many other insects, but they are well adapted for surviving rigorous conditions. They are found everywhere except in oceans and near the poles, and they occupy nearly every kind of habitat. Most are terrestrial, but some are underground tunnelers and some live in water. These WATER BEETLES are often confused with water bugs, but the latter all have sucking mouthparts. Beetles range in size from under 1 mm (1/32 in.) to over 15 cm (6 in.) long; tropical species are the largest. Most are dull, but members of several beetle families are brilliantly colored, some with a metallic or iridescent sheen. The majority of beetles are plant eaters, but there are also many predators and scavengers and a few parasites. Many beetles are highly destructive pests of crops and gardens (e.g., JAPANESE BEETLE, POTATO BEETLE, BOLL WEEVIL), but others are beneficial predators of harmful insects (e.g., LADYBIRD BEETLES). The largest of the many beetle families is the SCARAB BEETLE family, with over 20,000 species; among these are the dung beetles, which are invaluable scavengers. WEEVILS are plant-eating beetles with mouthparts elongated into snouts bearing jaws at their ends. The FIREFLIES are luminescent beetles. BLISTER BEETLES, including the so-called Spanish fly, produce irritating secretions. Beetles are classified in the phylum ARTHROPODA, class Insecta, order Coleoptera.

Beets, Nicolaas (nē'kōläs bāts), 1814–1903, Dutch author. He translated Byron into Dutch and was fairly well known as a poet when his *Camera Obscura* (1839), published under the pseudonym Hildebrand, won great popularity. This series of nostalgic sketches of everyday life reflected Beets's wide powers of observation.

beet sugar: see BEET; SUCROSE.

Beeville, city (1970 pop. 13,506), seat of Bee co., S Texas; settled in the 1830s, inc. 1908. Long a cow town, Beeville is the trade center of an agricultural county. A junior college is there, and a naval air training station is nearby.

Beggars of the Sea: see GUEUX.

beggar-tick: see BUR MARIGOLD.

beggarweed or **tick trefoil,** leguminous plant (*Desmodium purpureum*) native to the West Indies and sown in the S United States for green manure and for forage; it has high nutritive value and is palatable to stock. The pods are covered with tiny hooked hairs and cling as burs. Other species of the genus are weeds often called by the same names, as are some other weeds with burs. Beggarweed is classified in the division MAGNOLIOPHYTA, class Magnoliopsida, order Rosales, family Leguminosae.

Beghards (bĕg'ərdz), religious associations of men in Europe, organized similarly to the BEGUINES. They resembled a Franciscan group, with whom they were later often confused. Of unknown origin, they first appeared at Louvain in 1220 and soon spread throughout the Netherlands and into Germany, France, and Italy. Although they survived into the 15th cent., they were from the beginning unpopular and mistrusted. The Beghards were condemned by the Council of Vienne (1311), allegedly for teaching that those who gain perfection in this life cannot commit sin and therefore cannot be blamed for any act. This idea was foreshadowed in the Albigensian teachings. The Beghards were also influenced by the pantheism of a mystical sect, the Brothers of the Free Spirit, which flourished about Cologne.

begonia (bĭgōn'yə), any plant of the large genus *Begonia* and common name for the family Begoniaceae, mostly succulent perennial herbs of the American tropics cultivated elsewhere as bedding or pot plants and easily propagated by stem and leaf cuttings as well as by seed. Some kinds are grown as house plants for their showy, variously colored leaves—rex begonias—and some for their white, pink, red, or yellow flowers, sometimes double. There are a large number of hybrids. Begonias are classified in the division MAGNOLIOPHYTA, class Magnoliopsida, order Violales, family Begoniaceae.

Begovat: see BEKABAD, USSR.

Beguines (bāgēnz'), religious associations of women in Europe, established in the 12th cent. The members, who took no vows and were not subject to the rules of any order, were usually housed in individual cottages and devoted themselves to charitable works; their community was called a beguinage. Until the 14th cent., numerous women of high social standing went into the communities. From Belgium and the Netherlands the movement extended across France and Germany. During the earlier years, their services to society brought the Beguines favor and protection from secular and church authorities; but in the 13th and 14th cent. accusations of heresies and immorality among them as well as among the BEGHARDS, the corresponding bands of men, led to the scattering of the members. The character of the surviving communities eventually changed, in some localities taking the form of almshouses for needy spinsters. See study by E. W. McDonnell (1954, repr. 1969).

Behaim, Behem, or **Boeheim, Martin** (all: bā'hīm), b. 1436? or 1459?, d. 1506?, German traveler and cosmographer. He studied (possibly under Regiomontanus) astronomy, navigation, and mathematics. He went to Portugal as a merchant c.1480 and may have gone on an expedition along the west coast of Africa. In 1486 he went to Fayal in the Azores. He is believed to have developed an astrolabe and other devices for the use of navigators, but is best known for the terrestrial globe that he made in 1492 and gave to his native city Nuremberg (it is now in the Germanic Museum there). The globe is inaccurate and does not represent the best geographical information of the period.

Beham (bā'häm) or **Peham** (pā–), name of two German Renaissance artists, brothers, who were both influenced by Dürer and later by Italian art. **Hans Sebald Beham,** 1500–1550, engraver, etcher, and miniaturist, with his brother was banished from Nuremberg for freethinking in 1525. After some vicissitudes he settled in Frankfurt c.1532. His rare paintings have less interest than his engravings, of which he executed about 300, together with hundreds of etchings and woodcuts in a delicate technique. The subject matter varies from a *Virgin and Child* (1520) to the *Labors of Hercules* and *Farmers' Dances.* His brother, **Barthel Beham,** 1502–40, painter, engraver, and woodcut designer, worked, as did Hans Sebald for a time, for the dukes of Bavaria. His painted portraits are well known; that of Leonhard von Eck is in the Metropolitan Museum. His mature prints show clear composition and excellent technique. They include *Virgin at the Window* and portraits of King Ferdinand I and his brother, Emperor Charles V.

Behan, Brendan (bē'hăn), 1923–64, Irish dramatist. A notoriously outspoken and uninhibited man, he joined the Irish Republican Army in 1937 and was twice imprisoned for political offenses. His first play, *The Quare Fellow* (1956), a somewhat somber drama of prison life, was followed by *The Hostage* (1958), a wild and joyous farce set in a brothel. *Brendan Behan's Island: an Irish Sketch-Book* (1962) is a miscellaneous collection. See his autobiographical *Borstal Boy* (1958); biographies by his brother Dominic Behan (1966) and Ulick O'Connor (1971).

Behar, India: see BIHAR.

behavior, in biology: see ETHOLOGY.

behavior group therapy: see GROUP PSYCHOTHERAPY.

behaviorism, school of psychology seeking to explain animal and human behavior entirely in terms of observable and measurable responses to stimuli. Introduced by the American psychologist J. B. WATSON in 1913, it is based on the early mechanistic concepts of Democritus and Epicurus and the later beliefs of Hobbes. Behaviorism is modern, however, in its subjection of psychology to the laboratory technique. Watson, in his insistence that behavior is a physiological reaction to environmental stimuli, denied the value of introspection and of the concept of consciousness as unscientific and saw mental processes as bodily movements, even when unperceived; in this view, thinking is subvocal speech. The conditioned-reflex experiments of the Russian physiologists Pavlov and Bekhterev had a central place with the behaviorists, who considered that all emotions—aside from rage, fear, and love—were conditioned by habit and could be learned or unlearned. Behaviorism became influential in the United States between World War I and World War II, and was an important antidote to philosophical speculation. The American behaviorist B. F. Skinner rejects the unobservable completely and concerns himself purely with the relationship of observable behavior patterns to stimuli or rewards. See J. B. Watson, *Behaviorism* (1930) and *Behavior* (1967); B. F. Skinner, *The Behavior of Organisms* (1938), *Walden Two* (1948), *Beyond Freedom and Dignity* (1971), and *About Behaviorism* (1974); B. B. Wolman, ed., *Dictionary of Behavioral Science* (1973).

Behem, Martin: see BEHAIM, MARTIN.

behemoth (bē'hĭmŏth, bĭhē'–) [Heb.,=plural of *beast*], animal mentioned in Job 40.15–24; probably the hippopotamus.

Behistun Inscription (bāhĭstōōn', bə–, bēhĭs'tōōn) or **Bisutun Inscription** (bēsōōtōōn', bēsə–), cuneiform text, the decipherment of which was the key to all cuneiform script and opened to scholars the study of the written works of ancient Mesopotamia. The inscription in Old Persian, in Susian (the Iranian language of Elam), and in Assyrian is chiseled on the face of a mountainous rock c.300 ft (90 m) above the ground at Behistun, Persia (modern W Iran). A bas-relief depicting Darius I with a group of captive chiefs is carved together with the inscription. Although the rock was known in ancient times (Diodorus attributed the carvings to Semiramis), it was not until 1835 that Sir Henry RAWLINSON scaled it and copied the inscriptions. Rawlinson translated the Persian section of the inscription, which later led to the entire decipherment of the Assyrian text.

Behmen, Jakob: see BOEHME, JAKOB.

Behmenites: see BOEHME, JAKOB.

Behn, Aphra (ăf'rə bān, bēn), 1640–89, first professional female English author. Little is known of her early life, but there is evidence that c.1658 she married a London merchant of Dutch descent named Behn. After the death of her husband, Aphra Behn became an English spy in the Dutch Wars (1665–67), adopting the pseudonym Astrea, under which she later published much of her verse. Her career as a secret agent was unsuccessful, and she returned to England exhausted and penniless, forced even to serve time in debtors' prison. By 1670 her first play had been performed, and by 1677 she gained her much desired fame with the eminently successful production of *The Rover.* All her plays are noted for their broad, bawdy humor. Despite her success as a playwright, however, her best literary achievement can be found in her novels. The most notable of these is *Oroonoko* (1688), a heroical love story, the first philosophical novel in English. Aphra Behn was famous for her life style as well as her works; her denial of woman's subservience to man and her high-living, bohemian existence has led critics to describe her as the George Sand of the Restoration and a forerunner of the feminist movement. Her literary reputation declined rapidly in the 18th cent., but Montague Summers's collected edition of her work (6 vol., 1915) revived an interest in her. See study by G. Woodcock (1948) and biography by F. M. Link (1968).

Behrens, Peter (pā'tər bā'rəns), 1868–1940, German architect, influential in Europe in the evolution of the modern architectural style. He established before World War I a predominantly utilitarian type of architecture that at the same time achieved qualities of clarity and impressiveness. His factory buildings were among the earliest European works to base a simple and effective style upon the frank terms of modern construction. Behrens is known also for residences, for workers' apartment houses in Vienna, for the Abbey of St. Peter at Salzburg, and for his pioneering work in industrial design. Among his pupils were the Swiss architect Le Corbusier and the Germans Walter Gropius and Ludwig Miës van der Rohe.

Behring, Emil Adolph von (ā'mēl ä'dōlf fən bâr'ĭng), 1854–1917, German physician. He worked with Kitasato at Koch's laboratory in Berlin and from 1895 was professor of hygiene at Marburg. A pioneer in serum therapy, following the work of P. P. É. Roux, he demonstrated immunization against diphtheria (1890) and tetanus (1892) by injections of antitoxins (a word he introduced) that he developed with Kitasato. For this work he received the 1901 Nobel Prize in Physiology and Medicine.

Behrman, S. N. (Samuel Nathaniel Behrman) (bâr'mən), 1893–1973, American dramatist, b. Worcester, Mass., grad. Harvard 1916. His sophisticated comedies often reflect the turbulence of 20th-century society. They include *The Second Man* (1927), *Serena Blandish* (1928), *Rain from Heaven* (1934), *No Time for Comedy* (1939), *Fanny* (1954) with Joshua Logan, and *Lord Pengo* (1962). His books include an autobiography, *The Worcester Account* (1954), and a biography of Max Beerbohm (1960).

Beida: see AL BAYDA, Libya.

Beiderbecke, Leon Bismarck (Bix Beiderbecke), (bī'dərbĕk), 1903–31, American jazz cornetist, pianist, and composer, b. Davenport, Iowa. Mainly self-taught, he was influenced by recordings of the Original Dixieland Jazz Band and by the music of King Oliver, Louis Armstrong, and Jimmie Noone. His cornet playing, noted for its brilliant phrasing and its clarity of tone, soon won him a reputation. A sensitive, lonely man driven by artistic ambition, he was forced to play in the large commercial bands. Unhappy and restless, he changed jobs often, drank heavily, was frequently ill, and finally died of pneumonia. His piano compositions, including *In a Mist,* were influenced by Debussy. See C. H. Wareing and George Garlick, *Bugles for Beiderbecke* (1958); biographies by Burnett James (1961) and R. M. Sudhalter and P. R. Evans (1974).

Beira (bā'rə), region and former province, N central Portugal, S of the Douro River. The old capital was COIMBRA. The province extended to the Atlantic coast between the Douro and the Mondego and SE of the Mondego to the upper Tagus. The region is now occupied by the provinces of Beira Alta (capital VISEU), Beira Baixa (capital Castelo Branco) and part of Beira Litoral (capital Coimbra) and is further subdivided into the districts of Aveiro, Viseu, Coimbra, Guarda, and Castelo Branco. The region is traversed by the Serra da Estrela, Portugal's highest mountain range. Grains, fruits, and olives are grown. Industries include fishing and the manufacture of textiles and forest products. The area had been recovered from the Moors even before Portugal was formed, but Moorish attacks continued into the 13th cent. Later Beira was contested in the incessant Portuguese-Castilian wars.

Beira (bāy'rä), city (1960 pop. 58,970), capital of Manica e Sofala district, E central Mozambique, a seaport on the Mozambique Channel (an arm of the Indian Ocean), at the mouth of the Púngoè River. A commercial center, the city grew (beginning in 1891) as the terminus of a railroad into the interior, and it handles the foreign trade of Rhodesia and Malawi as well as of Mozambique. It is also a popular beach resort.

beira: see ANTELOPE.

Beirut (bāro͞ot'), Arab. *Bayrut,* Fr. *Beyrouth,* city (1972 est. pop. 720,000), W Lebanon, capital of Lebanon, on the Mediterranean Sea, at the foot of the Lebanon Mts. Beirut is an important port and financial center with food processing industries. It was a Phoenician city and was called in ancient times Berytus. It became known after 1500 B.C. as a trade center. Beirut was prominent under the Seleucids but became more important under the Romans, when it was not only a commercial town—with a large trade in wine and linens—but also a colony with some territory. In the 3d cent. A.D. Beirut had a famous school of Roman law. It declined after an earthquake in 551. Beirut was captured by the Arabs in 635. The Crusaders under Baldwin I took the city in 1110, and it was part of the Latin Kingdom of Jerusalem until 1291, despite a siege by Saladin and the Egyptians in 1182. After 1517 the Druses controlled the city under the Ottoman Empire. In the 19th cent. it was one of the centers of the revolt of Muhammad Ali of Egypt against the Turks. Ibrahim Pasha took it for the Egyptians (1830), but in 1840 the French and British bombarded and captured the city, enabling the Turks to return. It was taken (1918) by French troops in World War I. Beirut became the capital of Lebanon in 1920 under the French mandate. It is the seat of the American Univ. of Beirut (1866) and Lebanese Univ. (1951).

beisa: see ORYX.

Beisan: see BET SHEAN, Israel.

Beissel, Johann Conrad (yō'hän kôn'rät bī'səl), 1690–1768, founder of the Seventh-Day Baptist community at Ephrata, Pa. Emigrating (1720) from Germany, he settled first with the German Baptists, or Dunkards, in Germantown, Pa. He soon moved to the Conestoga Valley, where he preached to the German settlers. Beissel published (1728) a tract on his conviction that Saturday was the true Sabbath. With his followers he established (c.1728–1733) at EPHRATA a semimonastic religious community that became well known in colonial times. Over 400 of Beissel's hymns were printed, most of them in the *Turtel-Taube* (1747), the Ephrata hymnal. See biography by W. C. Klein (1942).

Beit, Alfred (bīt), 1853–1906, South African financier, b. Hamburg. He went to South Africa in 1875, grew rich from the development of diamond mines, and was a colleague and lieutenant of Cecil Rhodes in Rhodesia. A philanthropist, he founded a chair for colonial history at Oxford Univ. and made many gifts for educational purposes in London, Hamburg, and South Africa.

Beja (bā'zhə), town (1970 municipal pop. 37,205), S Portugal, capital of Beja dist. and Baixa Alentejo. It is an important trade and manufacturing center. Beja was important under the Romans, who called it Pax Julia. The Moors used it as a fortress city, until the Portuguese recovered it in 1162. Notable landmarks are the 14th-century citadel and the 15th-century Monastery of the Conception.

Bejaïa (bějī'ə), formerly **Bougie** (bo͞ozhē'), city (1966 pop. 49,930), N Algeria, a port on the Gulf of Bejaïa (an arm of the Mediterranean Sea). The northern terminus of the Hassi Messaoud oil pipeline from the Sahara, Bejaïa is the principal oil port of the W Mediterranean. Exports, aside from crude petroleum, include iron, phosphates, wines, dried figs, and plums. The city also has textile and cork industries. A minor port in Carthaginian and Roman times, Bejaïa was the Roman Saldae. It became the capital of the Vandals in the 5th cent. It later disappeared but was refounded by the Berbers in the 11th cent. and became an important port and cultural center. After Spanish occupation (1510–55), the city was taken by the Ottoman Turks. Until it was captured by the French in 1833, Bejaïa was a stronghold of the Barbary pirates (see BARBARY STATES). City landmarks include a 16th-century mosque and a casbah (fortress) built by the Spanish in 1545.

Béjart or **Béjard** (both: bāzhär'), French family of actors associated with MOLIÈRE, who joined their amateur company, Les Enfants de Famille. Their professional debut in Paris (1643) was as the Illustre-Théâtre; this failed (1645) and the company returned to the provinces only to triumph on their return in 1658. The eldest of the family was **Joseph Béjart,** c.1616–1659. His sister **Madeleine Béjart,** 1618–72, a fine actress and virtually the manager of the company, was Molière's mistress. Their sister, **Geneviève Béjart,** 1624–75, and brother, **Louis Béjart,** 1630–78, were also actors in the company. Louis retired in 1670, and was the first of Molière's actors to receive a pension. **Armande Grésinde Béjart,** c.1640–1700, Madeleine's sister or daughter, married Molière in 1662 and, trained by him, played most of his heroines. The death of Molière (1673) caused a momentary collapse of the King's Troupe, as the company was called, but Molière's widow and the actor La Grange procured the absorption by their group of one of the two rival Parisian companies, the troupe of the Théâtre du Marais. At the same time they lost the Palais Royal, the theater they had had since 1660. From its new quarters the company was known as the Hôtel Guénégaud troupe. In 1680 the troupe was merged with its only rival, the company of the HÔTEL DE BOURGOGNE. The resultant company was called the COMÉDIE FRANÇAISE. See Rosamond Gilder, *Enter the Actress* (1931).

Bekabad (byěkäbäd'), formerly **Begovat** (byěgōvät'), city (1969 est. pop. 60,000), Tashkent oblast, Uzbekistan, Central Asian USSR, on the Syr Darya River. It is an important industrial center, with large iron and steel mills and cement works. The Farkhand dam and hydroelectric plant, just upstream from Bekabad, is a major source of electricity and irrigation water for Uzbekistan.

Bek-Budi, USSR: see KARSHI.

Beke, Charles Tilstone (bēk), 1800–1874, English explorer and author. In Ethiopia in 1840–43 he mapped c.70,000 sq mi (181,300 sq km) of the country, determined the approximate course of the Blue Nile, and compiled vocabularies of 14 languages and dialects. He wrote *Origines Biblicae* (1834), *The Sources of the Nile* (1860), and *The British Captives in Abyssinia* (1865). His *Discoveries of Sinai in Arabia and of Midian* appeared posthumously, and his widow published (1874) a summary of his works.

Békéscsaba or **Csaba** (bā'kāshchŏ"bŏ), city (1970 pop. 55,408), SE Hungary. The commercial center for a silk-raising, tobacco-growing, and hog-breeding region, Békéscsaba has meat-packing plants and flour and hemp mills. Other industries produce textiles, farm implements, and cement. The city is also a road and rail hub. It was founded in the 13th cent. but later destroyed by the Turks. In the 18th cent. Slovak settlers helped restore Békéscsaba, and the city still has a large Slovak population. Landmarks include a 13th-century Roman Catholic church, a Lutheran cathedral (testifying to the city's tradition of Lutheranism), and a museum.

Bekesy, Georg von (gā'ôrk fən běk'ĭshē), 1899–1972, American biophysicist, b. Budapest, Hungary, grad. Univ. of Budapest (Ph.D. 1923). He was (1923–46) a physicist in the research laboratory of the Hungarian telephone system and also taught (1932–46) at the Univ. of Budapest. From 1947 to 1949 he was a research professor at the Caroline Institute, Stockholm. In 1949 he became senior research fellow in the psychoacoustic laboratory at Harvard. He was awarded the 1961 Nobel Prize in Medicine and Physiology for his work on the physical mechanism of stimulation within the cochlea, a snail-shaped cavity of the inner ear.

Bel (bāl, běl), deity of the MIDDLE EASTERN RELIGIONS. The name is a cognate of that of BAAL. For Bel in the Bible, see BEL AND THE DRAGON.

Bela IV (bā'lə, bē'lə), 1206–70, king of Hungary (1235–70), son and successor of Andrew II. He tried to curtail the power of the magnates and set out to recover the crownlands his father had given to supporters. Confronted by the menace of the Mongol invasion, he sent unheeded appeals to Pope Gregory IX and Holy Roman Emperor Frederick II, but he was crushingly defeated at Mohi on the Sajo River in 1241. Returning after the withdrawal of the invaders, he repopulated the country by inviting foreign colonization. In a battle (1246) with the last Babenberg duke of Austria, the duke was killed but the Austrians were victorious. Bela's long struggle with OTTOCAR II, king of Bohemia, for Austria and Styria ended (1260) in defeat. His last years were disturbed by the rebellion of his son, later King STEPHEN V.

Bela (bē'lə). **1** First king of Edom. Gen. 36.32; 1 Chron. 1.43. **2** Benjamin's first son. Num. 26.38; 1 Chron. 7.6; 8.1. Belah: Gen. 46.21. **3** Reubenite. 1 Chron. 5.8. **4** City later called ZOAR.

Belah (bē'lə), the same as BELA **2.**

Béla Kun: see KUN, BÉLA.

Belalcázar, Sebastián de: see BENALCÁZAR, SEBASTIÁN DE.

Bel and the Dragon, customary name for Dan. 14, a chapter placed in the Apocrypha in the Authorized Version of the Bible (see DANIEL). Verses 1–22 tell of the Babylonian idol Bel, ministered to by priests who secretly consume food left for it, thus deceiving the king and the people; Daniel reveals the fraud, and priests and idol are destroyed by the king. Verses 23–42 tell of a dragon, i.e., a great beast or monster, worshiped as a god; Daniel kills him and is thrown to the lions. The prophet Habakkuk is brought miraculously to the den by an angel to minister to him; Daniel is preserved, and the Babylonian king recognizes the power of the God of Daniel.

Belasco, David, 1853–1931, American theatrical manager and producer, b. San Francisco. He was actively connected with the theater from his youth, and while associated with Dion Boucicault in Virginia City, Nev., he was first exposed to scenic realism. At 19 he became stage manager of the Baldwin Theatre in San Francisco. His first venture as a playwright was when, in 1880, in association with James A. Herne, he toured the country in *Hearts of Oak,* a play adapted by them from an old melodrama. Connections with the Frohmans brought him to New York City in association (1882–84) with the Madison Square Theatre and later (1886–90) as stage manager of the Lyceum. He became an independent producer in 1895. Known for his minutely detailed and spectacular stage settings, Belasco showed inventiveness in his use of stage lighting. A creator of stars, he was lucratively associated with Mrs. Leslie CARTER, David Warfield, Blanche Bates, Frances Starr, Ina Claire, and Lenore Ulric. His plays, mostly adaptations, were vehicles for his actors and for his lavish settings. His most successful writing combinations were with Herne, Franklyn Fyles, Henry C. De Mille, and John Luther LONG. In 1907 he built the Stuyvesant Theater, later known as the Belasco, during his fight against the Theatrical Syndicate of the 1890s. The New York Public Library has his collection of theatrical materials. He wrote *The Theatre through Its Stage Door* (1919, repr. 1969). See his plays, ed. by R. H. Ball (1940, repr. 1965); biographies by Craig Timberlake (1954) and William Winter (2 vol., 3d ed. 1925, repr. 1972).

Belaúnde Terry, Fernando (fārnän'dō bäläo͞on'dā tä'rē), 1912–, president of Peru (1963–68). A successful architect, he served in the chamber of deputies (1945–48), formed the Popular Action party in 1956, and ran unsuccessfully for president the same year. In the 1962 elections, he ran a close second behind Victor Raúl HAYA DE LA TORRE; the elections were annulled and rescheduled for 1963, at which time Belaúnde won. Despite an opposition congress, he effected social, educational, and land reforms; opened up the rich interior to settlement by constructing a vast highway system across the Andes; established a self-help program for the Indians; and encouraged industrial development. However, an inflationary spiral set in, and Belaúnde antagonized nationalistic army leaders by failing to expropriate U.S.-controlled oil fields and operations. Deposed by an army coup in 1968, he fled to the United States, where he subsequently taught architecture at Harvard and Columbia. See his autobiography, *Peru's Own Conquest* (1959, tr. 1965).

Belaya (byěl'əyə) [Rus.,=white], river, c.880 mi (1,420 km) long, Bashkir Autonomous Republic, E European USSR. It rises in the Ural mts. and winds generally NW past Beloretsk, Sterlitamak (where it becomes navigable), and Ufa to join the Kama River. There are important oil fields in the Belaya River valley near Ufa.

Belaya Tserkov (tsĕr'kəf), Ukrainian *Bila Tserkva*, city (1970 pop. 109,000), W central European USSR, in the Ukraine, on the Ros River. It is a rail junction and an industrial and commercial center. Industries include food processing and the manufacture of machinery, shoes, and building materials. The city was founded in 1032 and was the headquarters of the Ukrainian Cossacks in the 17th cent. It passed to Russia in 1793.

Belcher Islands, c.1,110 sq mi (2,870 sq km), in E Hudson Bay, SE Keewatin dist., Northwest Territories, Canada, off W Quebec. Flaherty Island is the largest of the tundra-covered group.

Belém (bəlāN') or **Pará** (pərä'), city (1970 pop. 603,267), capital of Pará state, N Brazil, on the Pará River. Belém, the chief commercial center and port of the vast Amazon River basin, handles the Amazonian produce (chiefly rubber, Brazil nuts, cacao, and timber) and has processing plants. An airport and a coastal railroad enhance the trade of Belém, which is also connected with Brasília by a railroad and highway. Belém [Port.,=Bethlehem] was founded by Portuguese in 1616 as Santa Maria de Belém do Grão Pará and was a military post for the defense of N Brazil against French, English, and Dutch pirates. It reached a peak of feverish prosperity during the wild-rubber boom in the late 19th and early 20th cent., then suffered a depression that was alleviated by diversification and planned development in the 1930s. Prosperity increased also after World War II with the improvement of communications within the Amazon region. The city is known for its Goeldi museum, with ethnological and zoological collections of the Amazon basin. It also has an open air market, a botanical garden brilliant with exotic flowers, a modern leprosarium, and a state university. The government palace and the cathedral were built in the 18th cent., and there is a 17th-century Jesuit church.

Belfast (bĕlfăst'), county borough (1971 pop. 360,150), capital of Northern Ireland, county town of Co. Antrim, mainly in Co. Antrim but partly in Co. Down. It is on Belfast Lough, an inlet of the North Channel of the Irish Sea, and at the mouth of the Lagan River. The harbor, 8.5 mi (13.7 km) long, is navigable to the largest ships. The great shipyards of the Harland and Wolff Company in Belfast have built some of the world's largest ocean liners. The city is also the center of the Irish linen industry; other industries include tobacco and food processing, packaging, and the manufacture of rayon, aircraft, tools and machinery, yarn, clothing, carpets, and rope. Agricultural and livestock products are the chief exports. Belfast was founded in 1177 when a castle in defense of a ford over the Lagan was built, but the present city is a product of the Industrial Revolution. French HUGUENOTS, coming there after the revocation of the Edict of NANTES (1685), stimulated the growth of the town's linen industry. Serious rioting between Catholics and Protestants has scarred the city many times since the 19th cent. Belfast and the surrounding country were subjected to heavy air raids in 1941. Queen's Univ. (founded 1845); a college of technology; and Victoria College (founded 1859), a pioneer in women's education, are in Belfast. The Protestant Cathedral of St. Anne is notable. The Parliament House of Northern Ireland is at Stormont, a suburb of Belfast.

Belfort (băfôr', bĕ-, bĕl-), city (1968 pop. 55,833), capital of the Territory of Belfort (a department), E France, in Alsace. An important industrial and transportation center, it has large cotton mills and metalworks. A major fortress town since the 17th cent., it commands the Belfort Gap, or Burgundy Gate, between the Vosges and the Jura mts., thus dominating the roads from France, Switzerland, and Germany. An Austrian possession, Belfort passed to France by the Peace of Westphalia (1648) and was fortified by Vauban. During the Franco-Prussian War (1870–71) the garrison withstood a siege of 108 days. Partly in acknowledgment of this heroism, the Germans left Belfort and the surrounding territory to France when they annexed the rest of Alsace. The many Alsatians who then took refuge in the town contributed significantly to its industrial growth. The siege is commemorated by a huge statue, the *Lion of Belfort*, by Bartholdi.

Belfort, Territory of, department (1968 pop. 118,450), E France, in Alsace, on the Swiss border. The city of BELFORT is the capital.

Belgae: see GAUL.

Belgaum (bĕlgoum'), town (1971 pop. 213,830), Karnataka state, SE India. It is an educational and district administrative center and agricultural market that trades in food grains, sugarcane, cotton, tobacco, oilseed, and milk products. Belgaum also has a military cantonment.

Bel Geddes, Norman: see GEDDES, NORMAN BEL.

Belgian Congo: see ZAÏRE.

Belgian horse, one of the largest breeds of DRAFT HORSES of pure European descent. It has a long history, antedating the Christian era, but became especially popular during the Middle Ages. In the 15th and 16th cent. the breed was exported from Belgium to many European countries and became popular as a general working horse. It was not imported to the United States until the 1800s and it was slow to gain favor there because of its ungainly appearance. The breed is characterized by a husky, barrellike appearance and brute strength. It is generally sorrel or chestnut in color, stands just under 17 hands (68 in./170 cm) and weighs over 2,000 pounds (900 kg).

Belgian literature. For literature in Flemish (Dutch), see DUTCH AND FLEMISH LITERATURE. The writings of French-speaking Belgians, of whom the chief are MAETERLINCK and VERHAEREN, belong to FRENCH LITERATURE. See also WALLOONS.

Belgian Malinois (mălĭnwä'), a breed of medium-sized WORKING DOG developed in Belgium at the turn of the 20th cent. It stands from 22 to 26 in. (55.9–66 cm) high at the shoulder and weighs from 50 to 60 lb (22.6–27.2 kg). The smooth, straight coat is short except for longer hair around the neck, on the back of the thighs, and on the tail. It is brindled fawn in color with a black mask. One of three closely related types of sheepherding dogs from Belgium, the Malinois is distinguished from the other two, the Belgian sheepdog and the Belgian Tervuren, by coat and color only. In addition to being used for its herding abilities, the Malinois has frequently been trained as a police dog. See DOG.

Belgian sheepdog, sometimes called Groenendael, breed of sturdy WORKING DOG developed from a wide assortment of sheepherding dogs in Belgium in the early 20th cent. It stands from 22 to 26 in. (55.9–66 cm) high at the shoulder and weighs from 50 to 60 lb (22.6–27.2 kg). Its long, straight coat is black, sometimes with white markings on the chin, forechest, and feet. As a result of such developments as the widespread use of fencing, the increasing availability of rail transportation, and a decline in the threat of marauding animals, the necessity for sheepherding dogs began to decline in Belgium toward the end of the 19th cent. Dog breeders began to turn their attention to the show ring. Of the widely divergent types of herding dogs in existence, three varieties differing only in coat and color were finally bred true, i.e., the Belgian Malinois, Belgian sheepdog, and Belgian Tervuren. All were shown under the name "Belgian sheepdog" until 1959 when they were designated separate breeds by the American Kennel Club. See DOG.

Belgian Tervuren (təvûrn'), breed of medium-sized WORKING DOG perfected in Belgium in the early 20th cent. It stands from 22 to 26 in. (55.9–66 cm) high at the shoulder and weighs from 50 to 60 lb (22.6–27.2 kg). Its long, straight, dense coat may vary in shade from fawn to russet mahogany; the hair tips are always black. Developed from a widely interbred stock of Belgian sheepherding dogs, the Tervuren emerged as one of several distinct varieties, differing from the Groenendael BELGIAN SHEEPDOG in color only. It is a relatively rare breed in the United States today. See DOG.

Belgium (bĕl'jəm), Flemish *België,* Fr. *La Belgique,* constitutional kingdom (1970 pop. 9,694,991), 11,781 sq mi (30,513 sq km), NW Europe. BRUSSELS is the capital. ANTWERP is the chief commercial center and one of the world's great ports. Other important cities are GHENT and LIÈGE. Belgium is bordered on the N by the Netherlands and the North Sea, on the E by West Germany and the Grand Duchy of Luxembourg, and on the W and SW by France. The terrain is low lying except in the Ardennes mts. in the south. Belgium comprises two ethnic and cultural regions, generally called Flanders and Wallony—Flanders embracing the northern provinces of EAST FLANDERS, WEST FLANDERS, ANTWERP, LIMBURG, and part of BRABANT, and Wallony comprising the remainder of Brabant, HAINAUT, LIÈGE, LUXEMBOURG, and NAMUR. The dividing line runs roughly east-west just S of Brussels. Flemish (a Dutch dialect) is the official language in Flanders, while French is official in the south. The French-speaking people are now commonly called WALLOONS, although the term once referred chiefly to those people in the Liège area who spoke Walloon, a French dialect. Brussels is bilin-

gual, and German is spoken in a small section of Liège prov., notably at Eupen and Malmédy. Belgium is one of the most densely populated and highly industrialized areas in Europe; emphasis is on heavy industry. Coal mining and the production of steel, chemicals, and cement are concentrated in the Sambre and Meuse valleys, in the BORINAGE around Mons, Charleroi, Namur, and Liège, and in the Campine coal basin. Liège is a great steel center. Iron and steel constitute Belgium's largest single export item (in 1972 the country ranked ninth in world production of crude steel). Belgium also has an old, established metal-products industry; manufactures include bridges, heavy machinery, industrial and surgical equipment, motor vehicles, rolling stock, machine tools, and munitions. Shipbuilding is centered in Antwerp. Chemical products include fertilizers, dyes, pharmaceuticals, and plastics; the petrochemical industry, concentrated near the oil refineries of Antwerp, has mushroomed since World War II. Textile production, which began in the Middle Ages, now includes cotton, linen, wool, and synthetic fibers; carpets and blankets are important manufactures. Ghent, KORTRIJK, TOURNAI, and VERVIERS are all textile centers; MECHELEN, BRUGES, and Brussels are celebrated for their lace. Other old and important industries include diamond cutting (Antwerp is the world's largest diamond center), glass production, and the processing of leather and wood. Belgian industry is heavily dependent upon imports for its raw materials. Some iron is mined in the southeast, but most is imported, especially from the Lorraine basin in France and its extension in Luxembourg. Zinc deposits once supported an active nonferrous metal industry, but the deposits have been exhausted, and the industry now utilizes imported materials. Other nonferrous metal products, made from imported raw materials, include copper, lead, and tin. Coal is Belgium's only significant mineral resource, but production has recently declined in favor of other fuels and cheaper imported coal. Native limestone supports the cement industry. Industrial centers are linked with each other and with the main ports of Antwerp and Ghent by the Meuse and Scheldt rivers and their tributaries, by a network of canals (notably the ALBERT CANAL), and by the densest railroad net of continental Europe. In shipping and transit trade Belgium is among the world's leading countries; the economy depends upon its exports. Agriculture, while engaging only a small percent of the working force, is important. Except in the marshy Campine and in the heavily forested Ardennes there is much fertile and well-watered soil. The chief crops are cereals (oats, rye, wheat, barley). Sugar beets, potatoes, and flax are also grown, and there is truck farming near the large cities. Cattle raising and dairying (especially in Flanders) are important. Flowers and chicory, grown as a winter vegetable, are valuable crops. Processed foods include beet sugar, cheese and other dairy items, and canned vegetables. Beer is made from rich hops. Many cities (most notably Bruges and Ghent) have preserved their medieval architecture and art, which attract thousands of tourists annually. The North Sea coast is also popular in summer, but the once fashionable spas in the Ardennes are less frequented now.

The Beginnings of Belgium. Belgium takes its name (in general use only since the late 18th cent.) from the Belgae, a people of ancient GAUL. The Roman province of Belgica was much larger than modern Belgium. There the FRANKS first appeared in the 3d cent. A.D. The Carolingian dynasty had its roots at HERSTAL, in Belgium. After the divisions (9th cent.) of Charlemagne's empire Belgium became part of LOTHARINGIA and later of the duchy of Lower Lorraine, which occupied all but the western part of the LOW COUNTRIES. In the 12th cent. Lower Lorraine disintegrated; the duchies of Brabant (see BRABANT, DUCHY OF) and LUXEMBOURG and the bishopric of Liège took its place. The histories of these feudal states and of FLANDERS and Hainaut constitute the medieval history of Belgium. The salient development was the rise of the cities (e.g., Ghent, Bruges, and Ypres) to virtual independence and to economic prosperity through their wool industry and their trade. In the 15th cent. all of present Belgium passed to the dukes of BURGUNDY, who strove to curtail local liberties. At the same time the wool industry declined, mainly because of English competition. With the death (1482) of MARY OF BURGUNDY a period of foreign domination began (see NETHERLANDS, AUSTRIAN AND SPANISH for the period from 1477 to 1794). Belgium was occupied by the French during the FRENCH REVOLUTIONARY WARS and transferred from Austria to France by the Treaty of CAMPO FORMIO (1797). After the defeat (1815) of Napoleon at Waterloo, just S of Brussels, Belgium was given to the newly formed kingdom of the Netherlands (the decision had been made at the Congress of Vienna; see VIENNA, CONGRESS OF). Under King WILLIAM I of the Netherlands, the Belgians resented measures that discriminated against them in favor of the Dutch, especially in the areas of language and religion. A rebellion broke out in Brussels in 1830, and Belgian independence was declared. William I invaded Belgium but withdrew when France and England intervened in 1832. *The Kingdom of Belgium.* Belgian independence was approved by the European powers at the London Conference of 1830–31 (see under LONDON CONFERENCE). In 1831, Prince Leopold of Saxe-Coburg-Gotha was chosen king of the Belgians and became LEOPOLD I. A final Dutch-Belgian peace treaty was signed in 1839, and the "perpetual neutrality" of Belgium was guaranteed by the major powers, including Prussia, at the London Conference of 1838–39. The new country was among the first in Europe to industrialize and soon led the continent in the development of railways, coal mining, and engineering. Under the rule (1865–1909) of LEOPOLD II rapid industrialization and colonial expansion, notably in the Congo, were accompanied by labor unrest and by the rise of the Socialist party in opposition to the reactionary and clerical groups. Social conditions improved under ALBERT I (reigned 1909–34), who also granted universal and equal male suffrage (the vote was extended to all women only in 1948). After the outbreak of World War I (Aug., 1914), Germany invaded Belgium in order to attack France by the easiest route; this flagrant violation of Belgian neutrality shocked much of the world and brought Great Britain, as one of Belgium's guarantors, into the war. The unexpected resistance of the Belgians against heavy odds won widespread admiration, and German atrocities in Belgium, publicized by the Allies, played an important part in consolidating U.S. opinion against Germany. All of Belgium except a small strip in West Flanders, which served as a battle front throughout the war (see, e.g., YPRES), was conquered by Oct. 10, 1914, and the people suffered under a harsh occupation regime. The Belgian army, under the personal leadership of Albert I, fought in West Flanders and France throughout the war. Under the Treaty of Versailles after the war, Belgium received the strategically important posts of Eupen, Malmédy, and Moresnet, and a mandate over the northwestern corner of former German East Africa. In World War II, Germany, which in 1937 had guaranteed Belgian neutrality, attacked and occupied Belgium in May, 1940. King LEOPOLD III (reigned 1934–51) surrendered unconditionally on May 28, but the Belgian cabinet, in exile at London, continued to oppose Germany. German occupation inaugurated a reign of terror. Liberation by British and American troops, aided by a Belgian underground army, came in Sept., 1944. The unsuccessful German counteroffensive of Dec., 1944–Jan., 1945 (see BATTLE OF THE BULGE), caused much destruction, adding to damage previously wrought by invasion and by Allied air raids. However, the industrial plant remained relatively intact, enabling the Belgian economy to recover far more rapidly than the others of Western Europe. The immediate political issue after the war was the return of Leopold III, who was barred from Belgium until July, 1950. Popular discontent following his return led to his abdication (July, 1951) in favor of his eldest son, BAUDOUIN. In 1960 the Belgian Congo was given its independence, with subsequent economic and political turmoil in Belgium, especially after the eruption of violence in the Congo. Long-standing tensions between the Flemish- and French-speaking elements also flared into crises throughout the 1960s, toppling several governments and making it increasingly difficult to form new ones. Sweeping constitutional reform in 1971 in effect federalized the country by creating three regions—Flanders, Wallony, and Brussels—with a degree of autonomy in each and provisions for equal political power. The country remains culturally and linguistically divided, but unifying factors include the monarchy, which is widely respected and liked, and the Roman Catholic church, which embraces virtually the entire population and plays a powerful part in Belgian life, especially in education. There are universities in Brussels, Ghent, Liège, Louvain, Mons, and Antwerp. The country also has numerous colleges, and schools of music, architecture, and art. An economic union between Belgium and Luxembourg, formed in 1921 (the first of its kind in 20th-century Europe), has been largely superseded by the BENELUX ECONOMIC UNION, which also includes the Netherlands. An early proponent of a united Europe and a firm advocate of collective security, Belgium is headquarters for the European Common Market, for Supreme Headquarters Allied Powers Europe (SHAPE), and for the North Atlantic Treaty Organization (NATO). See Adrien de Meeus, *History of the Belgians* (tr. 1962); Henri Pirenne, *Early Democracies in the Low Countries* (tr. 1963); Theo Aronson, *The Coburgs of Belgium* (1969); F. E. Huggett, *Modern Belgium* (1969); Vernon Mallinson, *Belgium* (1969); Robert Senelle, *The Political, Economic and Social Structures of Belgium* (1970); Margot Lyon, *Belgium* (1971); D. O. Kieft, *Belgium's Return to Neutrality* (1972).

Belgorod (byĕl'gərəd), city (1970 pop. 151,000), capital of Belgorod oblast, Ukraine, S central European USSR, on the Northern Donets River. It is a railway junction and one of the chief centers in the USSR for the manufacture of cement and construction materials. These industries are based on nearby limestone deposits; one of the world's largest iron ore deposits is also located in the area. Known since the 13th cent., Belgorod was the center of the Muscovite southern defense against Crimean Tatar attacks in the 17th cent.

Belgorod-Dnestrovsky (byĕl'gərət-dənyĕstrôf'skē), city (1967 est. pop. 29,000), SW European USSR, in the Ukraine, a port at the mouth of the Dnestr River. It is also a rail junction and a trade center for wine. Industries include fishing and fish processing, winemaking, and meat and dairy processing. Founded by Greek colonists in the 6th cent. B.C., it later passed to Rome and Byzantium. In the 9th cent. it was a Slavic trade and political center called Belgorod. The city belonged to the duchy of Galich-Volhynia in the 13th cent., to Genoa in the 14th cent., and to Moldavia in the 15th cent. The Turks acquired it in 1484 and renamed it Akkerman. It was ceded to Russia in the early 19th cent., but was held by Rumania from 1918 to 1940 and by the Germans during World War II. It has been called by its old Slavic name since its liberation by the Soviet army in 1944. The city has medical and pedagogical institutes, a 15th-century church, and the remains of a medieval fortress.

Belgrade (bĕl'grăd), Serbo-Croatian *Beograd,* city (1971 pop. 793,072), capital of Yugoslavia and of its republic of Serbia, at the confluence of the Danube and Sava rivers. It is the commercial, industrial, political, and cultural center of Yugoslavia, as well as a transportation and communications hub. Belgrade's industries include the manufacture of metals, textiles, chemicals, machine tools, and food products. Strategically situated athwart land and river routes between Central Europe and the Balkans, Belgrade has been the target of numerous conquerors throughout history. The city grew around fortresses built by the Celts (3d cent. B.C.), Illyrians, and Romans. Under the name of Singidinum it served as the harbor for much of Rome's Danubian fleet. Captured by the Huns, Goths, Sarmathians, and Gepids, who destroyed its forts, the city was retaken by the Eastern Roman, or Byzantine, emperor Justinian in the 6th cent. A.D. It was held in the late 8th cent. by the Franks and from the 9th to 11th cent. by the Bulgars, who refortified it and named it Beligrad ("white fortress"). It was then ruled again by Byzantium before becoming the capital of Serbia in the 12th cent. Before it fell to the Ottoman sultan Sulayman I in 1521, it was under Hungarian control. The Ottoman Turks made Belgrade their chief strategic fortress in Europe. Although the Austrians stormed it in 1688, 1717, and 1789, they were able to hold onto it only from the Treaty of Passarowitz (1718) until the Treaty of Belgrade (1739). Liberated by Karageorge and Miloš Obrenović during the Serbian uprising of 1806, Belgrade was recaptured by the Turks in 1813. The Turks finally left in 1815 but kept their garrison in the fortress until 1867. Belgrade became the capital of the kingdom of Serbia in 1882. Occupied by Austrian troops during World War I, the city was made the capital of the new kingdom of the Serbs, Croats, and Slovenes (Yugoslavia from 1929) after the war. During World War II, Belgrade suffered much damage and extreme hardship under the German occupation. It was liberated by Yugoslav partisans, with Soviet aid, in 1944. Belgrade is noted for its fine parks, palaces, museums, and churches. The former Kalemegdan citadel is now a military museum. The 16th-century Barjak Mosque was built by Sulayman I. The city is the home of the Serbian Academy of Sciences, a university (founded 1863), a Roman Catholic archbishop, and an Orthodox Eastern patriarch.

Belgrano, Manuel (mänwĕl' bĕlgrä'nō), 1770–1820, Argentine revolutionist. Important as a political figure, he was appointed secretary of the commercial tribunal of Buenos Aires in 1794. He vigorously championed popular education and proposed economic reforms. Belgrano contributed to *Telégrafo mercantil,* the first periodical (founded 1801) of the Río de la Plata, and published (1810–11) *Correo de comercio.* He served under LINIERS against the British invaders (1806–7). A leader in the revolution of May, 1810, he was a member of the first patriot governing junta and commander of the unsuccessful expedition to Paraguay. In 1812 he succeeded Pueyrredón as commander of the Army of the North and won decisive battles at Tucumán (1812) and Salta (1813). Later in 1813 he invaded Upper Peru (now Bolivia), but after defeats at Vilcapugio and Ayohuma he was superseded (1814) by San Martín. In 1815 Belgrano was in Europe on an unsuccessful diplomatic mission. He again commanded the Army of the North from 1816 to 1819.

Belgravia (bĕlgrā'vēə), fashionable residential section of Westminster, London, England. Belgravia surrounds stately Belgrave Square and touches Grosvenor Place on the east.

Belial (bē'lēəl), name applied to SATAN.

Belidor, Bernard Forest de (bĕrnär' fôrĕ' də bālēdôr'), 1693–1761, French engineer. He wrote numerous books dealing with mathematics, artillery, and hydraulic, civil, and military engineering. One of his engineering works, a manual of rules and tables, was reprinted until 1830. His four-volume *Architecture hydraulique* (1737–53) was the first work of its kind to apply integral calculus to practical problems; its influence for the next hundred years was international in scope.

belief, in philosophy, commitment to something, involving intellectual assent. Philosophers have disagreed as to whether belief is active or passive; René Descartes held that it is a matter of will, while David Hume thought that it was an emotional commitment, and C. S. Peirce considered it a habit of action. Compared to faith and probability, the concept of belief has received little attention from philosophers. See Jaakko Hintikka, *Knowledge and Belief* (1962).

Belinsky, Vissarion Grigoryevich (vĭsəryôn' grĭgôr'-yəvĭch byĭlyĭn'skē), 1811–48, Russian writer and critic. He was prominent in the group that believed Russia's hope to lie in following European patterns. Under Hegel's influence he condoned czarism and reaction for a time but returned in the 1840s to his early liberalism and repudiated the doctrine of art for art's sake. As critic for four major reviews he became the principal champion of the realistic and socially responsible new Russian literature. His emphasis on the use of literature to express social and political ideas is the basis of present-day Soviet literary criticism. Among the authors whose talents he recognized and encouraged were Gogol, Lermontov, and Dostoyevsky. A selection of his philosophical and sociological works was published in English in 1948. It includes *Letter to Gogol* (1847), a summation of his beliefs. Belinksy lived in profound poverty and died at 37 of tuberculosis. See studies by Herbert Bowman (1954, repr. 1969) and Victor Terras (1973).

Belisarius (bĕlĭsâr'ēəs), c.505–565, Byzantine general under JUSTINIAN I. After helping to suppress (532) the dangerous Nika riot (see BLUES AND GREENS), he defeated (533–34) the Vandals of Africa, and captured their king. In 535 he was given command of the expedition to recover Italy from the Ostrogoths. He took Naples and Rome (536) and, after some delays occasioned by a conflict of authority with NARSES, captured Milan and Ravenna (540). He fought an indecisive campaign (541–42) against KHOSRU I of Persia, and in 544 was sent back to Italy against the Goths led by TOTILA. Handicapped by Justinian's jealousy and distrust, he could do little more than hold his enemies in check; he was recalled in 548 and replaced by Narses. In 559 he emerged from retirement to drive the Bulgarians from Constantinople. He was accused (562) of a conspiracy and temporarily imprisoned but was shortly restored to favor.

Belitung (bĕlē'tŏng), island (1961 pop. 102,375), 1,866 sq mi (4,833 sq km), Indonesia, in the Java Sea midway between Sumatra and Borneo. It has valuable tin mines (government-owned), worked chiefly by Chinese labor. Belitung is also known for its pepper. Ceded to the British by the sultan of Palembang in 1812, it later became a Dutch possession. The chief town and port is Tandjungpandan. It was formerly called Billiton.

Belize (bəlēz'), city (1970 pop. 39,257), capital of British Honduras (Belize), at the mouth of the Belize River, on the Caribbean Sea. The river flows c.180 mi (290 km) generally west and is navigable almost to Guatemala; outlying cays exclude deep-draft vessels from its good harbor. Timber and wood products are exported from Belize city. Fish packing is the main industry. The city was devastated by hurricanes in 1931 and 1961.

Belknap, Jeremy (bĕl'năp), 1744–98, American historian, b. Boston. A Congregational minister, he wrote history out of antiquarian interest, but showed great diligence and skill in research and considerable ability in writing. His *History of New Hampshire* (3 vol., 1784–92; repr., 2 vol., 1970) was a model of early local history. He was a leader in the founding (1794) of the Massachusetts Historical Society, the first such organization in the United States.

Belknap, William Worth, 1829–90, U.S. Secretary of War (1869–76), b. Newburgh, N.Y. After practicing law in Iowa, he served in the Civil War, was a division commander under Sherman in Georgia and the Carolinas, and became a major general in 1865. An internal revenue collector in Iowa (1865–69), he was made Secretary of War by Grant. In 1876 a political scandal broke when a House committee found evidence that Belknap had indirectly received annual bribes from the trader at an Indian post. Impeachment was unanimously voted. Grant accepted Belknap's resignation. At the Senate trial, the vote was 35 "guilty," 25 "not guilty"—falling short of the two thirds necessary to convict. Of the 25, 22 declared that they voted "not guilty" on the ground that the Senate lacked jurisdiction after Belknap's accepted resignation. He later practiced law in Washington, D.C.

Bell, Alexander Graham, 1847–1922, American scientist, inventor of the telephone, b. Edinburgh, Scotland, educated at the Univ. of Edinburgh and University College, London; son of Alexander Melville Bell. He worked in London with his father, whose system of visible speech he used in teaching the deaf to talk. In 1870 he went to Canada, and in 1871 he lectured, chiefly to teachers of the deaf, in Boston and other cities. During the next few years he conducted his own school of vocal physiology in Boston, lectured at Boston Univ., and worked on his inventions. His teaching methods were of lasting value in the improvement of education for the deaf. As early as 1865, Bell conceived the idea of transmitting speech by electric waves. In 1875, while he was experimenting with a multiple harmonic telegraph, the principle of transmission and reproduction came to him. By March 10, 1876, his apparatus was so far developed that the first complete sentence transmitted, "Watson, come here; I want you," was distinctly heard by his assistant. The first demonstration took place before the American Academy of Arts and Sciences in Boston on May 10, 1876, and a more significant one, at the Philadelphia Centennial Exposition the same year, introduced the telephone to the world. The Bell Telephone Company was organized in July, 1877. A long period of patent litigation followed in which Bell's claims were completely upheld by the U.S. Supreme Court. With the 50,000 francs awarded him as the Volta Prize for his invention, he established in Washington, D.C., the Volta Laboratory, where the first successful phonograph record was produced. Bell invented the photophone, which transmitted speech by light rays; the audiometer, another invention for the deaf; the induction balance, used to locate metallic objects in the human body; and the flat and the cylindrical wax recorders for phonographs. He investigated the nature and causes of deafness and made an elaborate study of its heredity. The magazine *Science,* which became the official organ for the American Association for the Advancement of Science, was founded (1880) largely through his influence. He was president of the National Geographic Society from 1896 to 1904 and was made a regent of the Smithsonian Institution in 1898. After 1895 his interest was occupied largely by aviation. He invented the tetrahedral kite. The Aerial Experiment Association, founded under his patronage in 1907, brought together G. H. Curtiss, F. W. Baldwin, and others, who invented the aileron principle and developed the hydroplane. See biographies by C. D. Mackenzie (1928, repr. 1971) and R. V. Bruce (1973).

Bell, Alexander Melville, 1819–1905, Scottish-American educator, b. Edinburgh. Bell worked out a physiological or visible alphabet, with symbols that were intended to represent every sound of the human voice. He taught elocution in Edinburgh (1843–65), lectured at the Univ. of London and in Boston, and engaged in the education of deaf-mutes in Washington, D.C. He wrote about education and the science of speech. Alexander Graham Bell was his son.

Bell, Andrew, 1753–1832, British educator, b. St. Andrews, Scotland. After seven years in Virginia as a tutor, he returned to England, was ordained a deacon, and later (1789) became superintendent of an orphan asylum in Madras, India. Here he developed the MONITORIAL SYSTEM, which he described in a pamphlet, *Experiment in Education,* published upon his return to London (1797). Joseph Lancaster, a Quaker, established a school on similar principles, which was copied by large numbers of nonconformists. Bell organized a system of monitorial schools that taught the principles of the Established Church. See biography by Robert Southey and C. C. Southey (3 vol., 1844); J. M. D. Meiklejohn, *An Old Educational Reformer* (1881).

Bell, Clive, 1881–1964, English critic of art and literature. He was a member of the Bloomsbury group. His works include *Art* (1914), *Since Cézanne* (1922), *Landmarks in Nineteenth-Century Painting* (1927), and *Proust* (1929). Bell's wife Vanessa was the sister of Virginia Woolf. See his *Old Friends* (1956).

Bell, Sir Charles, 1774–1842, Scottish anatomist and surgeon. He became professor of anatomy and surgery at the Royal College of Surgeons, London, in 1824 and was professor of surgery at the Univ. of Edinburgh from 1836. He was the first to distinguish between the motor and the sensory functions of the nerves; this work was confirmed and elaborated by Magendie in 1822. Among Bell's works is *The Nervous System of the Human Body* (1830). See his letters (ed. by his wife, 1870); biographies by Edwin Bramwell (1935) and Sir Gordon Gordon-Taylor and E. W. Walls (1958).

Bell, Gertrude Margaret Lowthian, 1868–1926, English traveler and author, one of the builders of modern Iraq, grad. Oxford, 1887. From 1899 she journeyed extensively in Persia, Anatolia, and Syria and early in 1914 reached Haïl in the Arabian Desert. In World War I she placed her unmatched knowledge of Middle Eastern conditions at the disposal of the British government and in 1915 was appointed to the intelligence service. As liaison officer of the Arab Bureau in Iraq and assistant political officer, her aid was invaluable. She knew and worked with T. E. Lawrence and was largely responsible for the selection of Faisal I as king of Iraq. She founded and directed the national museum of Baghdad. Her writings include *Poems from the Divan of Hafiz* (1897), *The Desert and the Sown* (1907), *Amurath to Amurath* (1911), *Palace and Mosque at Ukhaidir* (1914), *The Arab of Mesopotamia* (1917), and *Persian Pictures* (1928; pub. anonymously as *Safar Nameh,* 1894). See her *Letters* (new ed. 1947); *Earlier Letters* (ed. by Elsa Richmond, 1937); biographies by Josephine Kamm (1956) and Anne Northgrave (1958).

Bell, John, 1797–1869, American statesman, b. near Nashville, Tenn. A leading member of the Nashville bar, he served in the U.S. House of Representatives (1827–41), was speaker in 1834, and for a few weeks in 1841 was Secretary of War under President William Henry Harrison. At first a Jacksonian, Bell broke with Jackson in the fight over the Bank of the United States and ultimately became the chief leader of the Whigs in Tennessee, dominating state politics for nearly two decades. As U.S. Senator (1847–59), he was the leader of the conservative Southern element that, though supporting slavery, placed the Union first. He admitted the right of Congress to prohibit slavery in the territories, supported the Compromise of 1850, objected to the Kansas-Nebraska Bill, and opposed the admission of Kansas under the Lecompton Constitution. In 1860, Bell was the presidential candidate of the moderate CONSTITUTIONAL UNION PARTY and won the electoral votes of Tennessee, Kentucky, and Virginia. The lower South seceded with Lincoln's election, but Bell held Tennessee in the Union until after the firing on Fort Sumter. Bell counseled resistance to the Union invasion, but, disheartened and in ill health, he took no active part in the Civil War. See biography by J. H. Parks (1950).

Bell, John Joy, 1871–1934, Scottish author. He wrote a number of humorous stories and plays, frequently in dialect, of life in Glasgow, but is best remembered for his story *Wee Macgreegor* (1902).

Bell, city (1970 pop. 21,836), Los Angeles co., S Calif.; inc. 1927. It is chiefly residential, with many small businesses and some light manufacturing.

bell, in music, a percussion instrument consisting of a hollow metal vessel, often cup-shaped with an outward-flaring rim, damped at one end and set into vibration by a blow from a clapper within or from a hammer without. A portable set of bells, usually not more than 15 in number, tuned to the intervals of the major scale, is today called a chime. A carillon is a larger stationary set with chromatic intervals and as many as 70 bells, which are played from a keyboard. Harmonies and effects of shading, not possible on a chime, are part of the art of carillon playing—an art for which there is a school in Belgium. The bells of a carillon must be tuned with more accuracy than those of a chime; the best modern craftsmen can tune the fundamental (known as the hum note), the octave (known as the strike note), the twelfth, and the fifteenth with perfect accuracy. An interesting and unexplained illusion manifest in bells is their apparent pitch (strike note): the pitch the observer hears can often be scientifically proved to be different from any of the pitches produced by the bell. Bells have been known in all metal-using cultures and civilizations and have been used in connection with all major religions except Muhammadanism. Many legends and traditions are associated with bells, which have been used for signaling, in dancing, and as protective charms. Apparently originating in Asia, bells were early employed for religious purposes and by the 6th cent. were used in Christianity. Early bells were baptized, in the belief that dedication to Christian service gave power to ward off lightning. A set of bells tuned to a musical scale and called *cymbala* were used in the Middle Ages for musical instruction and to accompany chant in churches. In the 13th cent., tower bells were attached to clocklike mechanisms to strike the hours; the carillon developed out of the Belgian *voorslag* of the 15th cent., a set of bells attached to a large tower clock that played a tune before striking the hour. In the Low Countries, where the making and playing of carillons centered, the principal cities vied over the size and complexity of their instruments. A peak in carillon making was reached in the work of the brothers Frans (1609–67) and Pieter (1619–80) Hemony of Amsterdam. The carillonneur's art flourished until the 18th cent., declining during the French Revolution, when many carillons were melted to make armaments. In England carillon playing was overshadowed by the science of change ringing, which became popular in the 17th cent. In this practice a group of ringers, using a peal (or set) of bells tuned to the diatonic scale, ring the bells in various stated

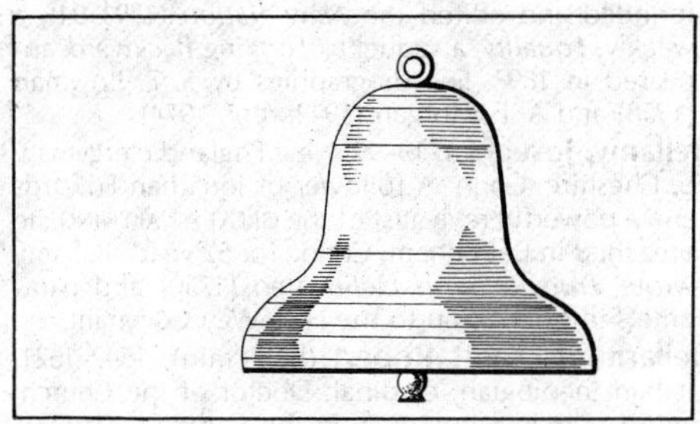

Bell

orders, not repeating any order. The result is a complex but not melodious sound. The bell is swung full circle, being sounded by a clapper within, thus giving a more resonant sound than in carillon playing, wherein a hammer strikes a stationary bell. Toward the end of the 19th cent. English bellmakers rediscovered the secrets of tuning that had been used by the 17th-century Dutch and Flemish craftsmen. This, with improvements in methods of striking, in placement of the bells, and in action of the keyboard, has made 20th-century carillons the finest in existence. Active in a renaissance of carillon music was Jef Denijn (1862-1941), carillonneur of Mechlin. Since World War I many carillons have been installed in the United States; outstanding is that of the Riverside Church, New York (1930), whose 20.5-ton bourdon bell is the largest ever cast in England. The largest bell in the world was the Great Bell of Moscow; cast in 1734, it was broken in a fire in 1737. See R. P. Price, *The Carillon* (1933); P. D. Peery, *Chimes and Electric Carillons* (1948); W. G. Wilson, *Change Ringing* (1965); S. N. Coleman, *Bells* (1928, repr. 1971).

Bella, Stefano della (stāfä'nō dĕl'lä bĕl'lä), 1610-64, Italian engraver, b. Florence. First copying the manner of Jacques Callot, his style changed somewhat when he traveled to Rome, Paris, and the Netherlands. He was adept at landscapes, battle pieces, and animal portraits, although most of his numerous works were designs for festivities and ballets. French theatrical design was considerably influenced by his light, sophisticated style. His drawings are well represented in the Royal Library at Windsor.

belladonna (bĕlədŏn'ə) or **deadly nightshade,** poisonous perennial plant, *Atropa belladona*, of the family Solanaceae (NIGHTSHADE family), which also includes the potato. Native to Europe and now grown in the United States, the plant has reddish, bell-shaped flowers and shining black berries. Extracts of its leaves and fleshy roots act to dilate the pupils of the eye and were once used cosmetically by women to achieve this effect. (The name *belladonna* is from the Italian meaning "beautiful lady".) The plant extract contains the alkaloids ATROPINE, SCOPOLAMINE, and hyoscyamine. Belladonna has also been used since ancient times as a poison and as a sedative; in medieval Europe large doses were used by witchcraft and devil-worship cults to produce hallucinogenic effects (see PSYCHOTOMIMETIC DRUGS). Other species of the potato family such as henbane (*Hyoscyamus niger*), mandrake (*Mandragora officinarum*), and Jimson weed (*Datura stramonium*) also contain one or more of the alkaloids present in belladona. The active substances act physiologically to depress the parasympathetic NERVOUS SYSTEM. Belladonna is classified in the division MAGNOLIOPHYTA, class Magnoliopsida, order Polemoniales, family Solanaceae.

belladonna lily: see AMARYLLIS.

Bellaire (bĕl"âr'), city (1970 pop. 19,009), Harris co., SE Texas; inc. 1918. It is a suburb of Houston.

Bellamy, Edward (bĕl'əmē), 1850-98, American author, b. Chicopee Falls (now part of Chicopee), Mass. After being admitted to the bar he tried his hand at journalism and contributed short stories of genuine charm to various magazines. These were later collected as *The Blind Man's World and Other Stories* (1898). His novels—*Dr. Heindenhoff's Process* (1880), *Miss Ludington's Sister* (1884), and *The Duke of Stockbridge* (1900)—were followed by *Looking Backward, 2000-1887* (1888), which overshadowed his other work and brought him fame. This utopian romance pictured the world in A.D. 2000 under a system of state socialism. Much of the book's appeal lies in its unpretentious style and its vivid picture of the imagined society. The work sold over a million copies in the next few years and resulted in the formation of "Nationalist" clubs throughout the nation and the founding of the *Nationalist* monthly (1888-91). Bellamy himself founded and edited the *New Nation* (1891-94), a weekly. *Equality*, a sequel to *Looking Backward*, appeared in 1897. See biographies by S. E. Bowman (1958) and A. E. Morgan (1944, repr. 1974).

Bellamy, Joseph, 1719-90, New England clergyman, b. Cheshire, Conn. A follower of Jonathan Edwards and a powerful revivalist of the GREAT AWAKENING, he preached in Bethlehem, Conn., for 52 years. Bellamy wrote *True Religion Delineated* (1750) and pamphlets in opposition to the Half-Way Covenant.

Bellarmine, Saint Robert (bĕlär'mĭn), 1542-1621, Italian theologian, cardinal, Doctor of the Church, and a principal influence in the Catholic REFORMATION. His full name was Roberto Francesco Romolo Bellarmino. He joined the Jesuits (1560) and taught at Louvain (1569-76) and at the Roman College (1576). In 1599 he was made cardinal and from 1601 to 1605 he was archbishop of Capua. His theological works (in Latin) were polemical and widely noticed. One, the most lucid modern exposition of Catholic doctrine, called forth many Protestant replies. In another, a reply to the work of William Barclay, Cardinal Bellarmine uses the analogy, taken from THOMAS AQUINAS, of body and soul to show the relative interdependence and importance of the state and the church. As Jesuits nearly always were, Cardinal Bellarmine was uncompromisingly ultramontane (see ULTRAMONTANISM). He was an admirer of Galileo and a moderating influence at his trial. His devotional works have been translated frequently into English. Pope Pius XI canonized him in 1930 and declared him a Doctor of the Church the following year. Feast: May 13. See biography by James Brodrick (rev. ed. 1966).

Bellary (bəlär'ē), town (1971 pop. 125,127), Karnataka state, SE India. It is a district administrative center. Iron and manganese deposits are nearby. Its manufactures include cotton textiles, brassware, and agricultural implements. Until the 16th cent. it was the center of the Hindu kingdom of Vijayanagar.

Bellatrix, bright star in the constellation ORION; Bayer designation Gamma Orionis; 1970 position R.A. $5^h23.5^m$, Dec. +6°19′. A bluish-white giant of SPECTRAL CLASS B2 III, its apparent MAGNITUDE of 1.63 makes it one of the 25 brightest stars in the sky. Its distance from the earth is about 500 light-years. Bellatrix marks the left shoulder of Orion. The name is Latin for "female warrior."

Bellay, Du: see DU BELLAY.

bellbird: see COTINGA.

Belle-Alliance (bel'-älyäNs'), village, central Belgium, near Waterloo. The battle of Waterloo (see WATERLOO CAMPAIGN), where Napoleon I was defeated in June, 1815, is sometimes known, particularly in Germany, as the battle of Belle-Alliance.

Belleau, Remy (rāmē' bĕlō'), 1528-77, French poet of the Pléiade (see under PLEIAD). His *Bergerie* (1565), a collection of poems in a framework of prose, celebrates nature in sonnets, odes, eclogues, and hymns.

Belleau Wood (bĕl'ō, bĕlō'), forested area in Aisne dept., N France, E of Château-Thierry. The scene of a victory over the Germans after hard fighting (June 6-25, 1918), involving chiefly U.S. troops, it was dedicated in 1923 as a permanent memorial to the American war dead.

Belleek ware (bəlēk'), pottery with a highly lustrous and often iridescent glaze. It is made at Belleek, Co. Fermanagh, Northern Ireland.

Bellefontaine (bĕlfoun'tĭn, -fŏn'tĭn), city (1970 pop. 11,255), seat of Logan co., W central Ohio; settled 1818, inc. 1835. It is a trade and rail center for a farm area. Its industries include printing and the manufacture of automobile bearings, small motors, tools, and electrical equipment. East of the city is Campbell Hill, the highest point in Ohio (1,550 ft/472 km).

Bellefontaine Neighbors, city (1970 pop. 13,987), St. Louis co., E Mo., a residential suburb of St. Louis; founded c.1819, inc. 1950.

Belle Fourche (bĕl fo͞osh), river, c.290 mi (470 km) long, rising in NE Wyo., flowing NE and then E to the Cheyenne River in W S.Dak. The Belle Fourche project provides flood control and recreation facilities as well as irrigating c.57,000 acres (23,070 hectares) in South Dakota. DEVILS TOWER NATIONAL MONUMENT overlooks the Belle Fourche River in Wyoming.

Bellegarde, Heinrich, Count von (hīn'rĭkh, fən bĕlgärd'), 1756-1845, Austrian soldier and statesman. He fought against the French in the French Revolutionary and Napoleonic Wars in Germany, Italy, and Switzerland, rising to general of cavalry in 1800. In 1806 he was made field marshal. From 1809 to 1813, Bellegarde was governor general of Galicia. He commanded (1813-15) Austria's armies in Italy and also served (1814-15) as governor of Lombardy and Venetia. From 1820 to 1825 he was president of the Austrian council of war and minister of state.

Belle Glade, city (1970 pop. 15,949), Palm Beach co., SE Fla., near the southern tip of Lake Okeechobee; inc. 1928. Belle Glade is a trade and processing center for a truck farm, sugarcane, and cattle area. An agricultural experiment station is nearby.

Belle-Isle, Charles Louis Auguste Fouquet, duc de (shärl lwē ōgüst' fo͝okā' dük də bĕl-ēl'), 1684-1761, marshal of France and diplomat; grandson of Nicolas Fouquet. His support of the claims of Charles of Bavaria (Holy Roman Emperor Charles VII) was in part responsible for France's entry into the War of the AUSTRIAN SUCCESSION. The war's outcome made him unpopular, although his masterly retreat from Prague had saved the French army from surrender (1742-43). As minister of war (1758-61) he did much to reorganize the army.

Belle Isle, Strait of (bĕlīl'), c.35 mi (60 km) long and from 10 to 15 mi (16-24 km) wide, between the island of Newfoundland and Labrador, Canada. The northern entrance to the Gulf of St. Lawrence, it is deep and free of rocks and shoals; ice blocks it from November to June. There is a strong tidal current. The tiny rock island Belle Isle (700 ft/213 m high), at the Atlantic entrance, has a lighthouse and is the first land sighted by ships from Europe.

Bellerophon (bəlĕr'əfŏn, -fən), in Greek mythology, son of Glaucus; originally called Hipponoüs. He changed his name after he murdered a countryman and was forced to flee to exile. He became a suppliant at the court of King Proetus of Argos, whose wife fell in love with him. When he rejected her advances, she vengefully told Proetus that Bellerophon had tried to seduce her. Proetus sent him to Iobates, king of Lycia, with a sealed message requesting the death of its bearer. Iobates gave Bellerophon the seemingly impossible task of killing the Chimera, a beast that was part lion, part goat, part dragon. Bellerophon, however, with the aid of the flying horse Pegasus, killed the monster. Iobates sent him on other difficult missions, but finally decided that Bellerophon was favored by the gods and gave him his daughter in marriage. At the height of his prosperity, however, Bellerophon tried to ride Pegasus to the throne of the gods atop Mt. Olympus, and Zeus in anger caused Pegasus to throw him to the ground. Bellerophon then wandered alone, crippled, blind, and humiliated, until he died.

belles-lettres [from the French for literature, literally "fine letters"], literature that is appreciated for the beauty, artistry, and originality of its style and tone rather than for its ideas and informational content. Earlier the term was synonymous with *literature*, referring particularly to fiction, poetry, drama, criticism, and essays. However, *belletristic literature* has come to mean light, artificial writing and essays extolling the beauties of literature.

Belleville, city (1971 pop. 35,128), SE Ont., Canada, on Lake Ontario. Machinery, automotive accessories, optical lenses, and cheddar cheese are made there. Belleville is the seat of Albert College and the Ontario School for the Deaf.

Belleville. 1 City (1970 pop. 41,699), seat of St. Clair co., SW Ill.; inc. 1819. Coal mines there produce more than 5 million tons a year. Belleville also has farm-related industries and a great variety of manufactures, including mining equipment, industrial furnaces, machinery, dies and castings, beer, stoves, and clothing. It is the seat of a junior college. Scott Air Force Base (est. 1917 for flight instruction; now headquarters of the Military Air Transport Service) is to the northeast. **2** Town (1970 pop. 34,643), Essex co., NE N.J., on the Passaic River; settled c.1680, set off from Newark 1839, inc. 1910. Electrical equipment, fire extinguishers, water pumps, and precision instruments are among its manufactures. John Stevens's boat, built there in 1798 for the run to New York, contained one of the country's first steam engines.

Bellevue (bĕl'vyo͞o). **1** City (1970 pop. 19,449), Sarpy co., E Nebr., a suburb of Omaha, on the Missouri River; inc. 1855. It has a meat-packing plant. The oldest city in the state, Bellevue was a trading post in the early 1800s and the site of a Presbyterian Indian mission in the 1840s and '50s. The Strategic Aerospace Museum is in the city. **2** Borough (1970 pop. 11,586), Allegheny co., SW Pa., a residential suburb of Pittsburgh, on the Ohio River; settled 1802, inc. 1867. **3** City (1970 pop. 61,102), King co., W Wash., opposite Seattle on Lake Washington; inc. 1953. Concrete and gravel, control systems, food products, and electronics parts are manufactured there. It is connected with Seattle by two four-lane floating bridges. A junior college is there.

Bellevue Hospital, municipal; in New York City. Bellevue developed from a "Publick Workhouse and House of Correction" commissioned in 1734. The establishment changed sites several times before 1811, when the site upon which it now stands was purchased. In 1860 the Bellevue Hospital Medical College, the first of its kind in the United States, was founded. The first nurses' training school in the United States was established there in 1873 and grew into one of the best-known nursing schools in the nation. The largest U.S. city hospital, Bellevue is a noted psychiatric therapy and research center. Other programs of note include radiation therapy and physical and occupational rehabilitation programs. Until 1968, Bellevue was affiliated with the medical schools of Columbia Univ. (from 1882), New York Univ. (1882), and Cornell Univ. (1898); in that year Columbia and Cornell withdrew, leaving the hospital in sole affiliation with the New York Univ. Medical Center. See Page Cooper, *The Bellevue Story* (1948).

Bellflower, city (1970 pop. 51,454), Los Angeles co., S Calif.; inc. 1957. It is mainly residential with some light industry.

bellflower or **bluebell,** name commonly used as a comprehensive term for members of the Campanulaceae, a family of chiefly herbaceous annuals or perennials of wide distribution, characteristically found on dry slopes in temperate and subtropical areas. Members of the largest genus (*Campanula*), predominantly of the Northern Hemisphere, are called campanulas, bellflowers (for the delicate, bell-shaped blossoms), or bluebells (for the prevailing color of the flowers). Among the most popular cultivated species are the harebell, or bluebell of Scotland (*C. rotundifolia*), native to Eurasia and North America, and the Canterbury bells (*C. medium*), native to S Europe. (The names bluebell and harebell are also used for *Scilla nonscripta* of the lily family.) Venus's looking-glass (genus *Specularia*) is found in the Mediterranean area and throughout North America. The giant bellflower (*Ostrowskya magnifica*), native to central Asia, attains a height of 8 ft (2.4 m); it is cultivated in the Puget Sound region. The family Lobeliaceae (lobelia family) is sometimes grouped with the bellflower family as a single taxonomic unit. The bellflower family is classified in the division MAGNOLIOPHYTA, class Magnoliopsida, order Campanulales.

Bell Gardens, city (1970 pop. 29,308), Los Angeles co., S Calif., a suburb of Los Angeles; inc. 1961. Manufactures include paper products and electrical equipment.

Belli, Giuseppe Gioacchino (jōozĕp'pā jōäk-kē'nō bĕl'lē), 1791-1863, Italian poet. Born in Rome into poverty, Belli earned his living as a government clerk. He drew from his knowledge of plebeian life in writing more than two thousand humorous and satirical sonnets. Belli described the vast panorama of Roman society in colorful dialect. His poetry is noted for its vigorous realism. Little known outside Rome, Belli's work was not published during his lifetime.

belligerency (bəlĭj'ərənsē), in international law, status of parties legally at war. Belligerency exists in a WAR between nations or in a civil war if the established government treats the insurgent force as if it were a sovereign power. The rules of international law as formulated at the HAGUE CONFERENCES require that belligerency between states be preceded by an absolute declaration of war or an ultimatum prescribing the terms on which the issuing power will refrain from war. When belligerency has been established, the relations between the warring powers are determined by the laws of war (see WAR, LAWS OF). In civil wars if the insurgent force is granted belligerency rights, neutral nations generally abstain from supplying or helping either the established government or its opponent. An example of this practice is found in the NEUTRALITY proclamations issued by European powers in the American Civil War. Neutral nations may refuse to recognize the belligerency of an insurgent, however, and in this way preserve the right to claim any damages that accrue against the established government for having failed to suppress the rebellion without delay. Under its charter, the United Nations recognizes as legitimate only wars that are fought in self-defense, or for the collective enforcement of the UN Charter. All other wars are regarded as illegal acts of aggression. The United Nations also considers civil wars as threatening to international peace, and, when possible, takes measures to end such hostilities (e.g., Kashmir, Palestine, Korea, Congo, Cyprus). See W. L. Gould, *An Introduction to International Law* (1957).

Bellingham. 1 Town (1970 pop. 13,967), Norfolk co., S Mass., in a farm region; inc. 1719. **2** City (1970 pop. 39,375), seat of Whatcom co., NW Wash., a port of entry on Bellingham Bay, one of the best landlocked harbors on the Pacific coast, near Canada; inc. 1904. It is an important shipping point for lumber, pulp, paper, and canned and frozen fruit. Settled in 1852 as Whatcom, it merged with three adjoining towns to form Bellingham in 1903. Western Washington State College, Bellingham Technical School, and Whatcom Museum of History and Art are in the city, which also has many scenic parks. An Indian reservation is nearby, and Moran State Park is on Orcas Island in Bellingham Bay.

Bellini (bĕl-lē'nē), illustrious family of Venetian painters of the Renaissance. **Jacopo Bellini** (yä'kōpō), c.1400-1470, was a pupil of Gentile da Fabriano. He worked in Padua, Verona, Ferrara, and Venice. Many of his greatest paintings, including the enormous *Crucifixion* for the Cathedral of Verona, have disappeared. Several of his Madonnas (Uffizi; Louvre; Academy, Venice) are still extant. Jacopo's sketches in two notebooks (Louvre and British Mus.) are his most important legacy. They reveal a variety of interests, including problems of perspective, landscapes, and antiquity. His son **Gentile Bellini** (jāntē'lā), 1429-1507, studied with him and with Mantegna, working in Padua and then in Venice. He excelled in portraiture and in depicting ceremonial processions. His paintings, such as *The Procession in the Piazza of San Marco* and *The Miracle of the True Cross* (both: Academy, Venice), are valued for their faithful representation of contemporary Venetian life. In 1479 Gentile was sent by the state to the court of Muhammad II in Constantinople. Subsequently an Oriental flavor appeared in several of his paintings, including the portrait of Muhammad II (National Gall., London); the portrait of a Turkish artist (Gardner Mus., Boston); and *St. Mark Preaching at Alexandria* (Brera, Milan). The last was completed by his brother, **Giovanni Bellini** (jōvän'nē), c.1430-1516, who was first active in Padua where he worked with his father and brother. Also influenced by Mantegna, who became his brother-in-law in 1454, Giovanni painted the *Agony in the Garden* (National Gall., London), the *Crucifixion* (Correo Mus., Venice), and several Madonnas (Philadelphia Mus. and Metropolitan Mus.). Whereas Mantegna and Jacopo and Gentile Bellini were known chiefly as admirable draftsmen, Giovanni developed another style. His sumptuous coloring and fluent, atmospheric landscapes had a great effect upon Venetian painting, especially upon his pupils Giorgione and Titian. He created several imposing altarpieces; best known are those of the Frari and San Zaccaria in Venice and the *St. Job* (now in the Academy, Venice). Other examples of his art are several fine portraits such as the *Doge Loredano* (National Gall., London). He painted *St. Francis in Ecstasy* (Frick Coll., New York City) and *St. Jerome* (National Gall. of Art, Washington, D.C.), as well as some allegorical fantasies such as the *Restello* series (Academy, Venice). He also created mythological scenes, including *The Myth of Orpheus* and *The Feast of the Gods* (both: National Gall. of Art, Washington, D.C.). The zestful *Feast,* one of his last pictures, was painted in 1514 for Isabella d'Este, with finishing touches added by Titian. See Giles Robertson, *Giovanni Bellini* (1968); Hans Tietze, *The Drawings of the Venetian Painters* (1944, repr. 1970).

Bellini, Vincenzo (vēnchān'tsō bĕl-lē'nē), 1801-35, Italian opera composer. He acquired his musical training from his grandfather and father, and began composing religious and secular music in his childhood. His first opera, *Adelson e Salvini,* was successfully performed in 1825. His most celebrated works are the operas *La Sonnambula* and *Norma* (both 1831). In their profusely melodic style they exemplify the bel canto tradition of the 18th cent., and their roles demand great virtuosity of the singers. Bellini's last opera, *I Puritani* (1835), was influenced by the dramatic style of French grand opera.

Bellinzona (bĕl-lēntsō'nä), town (1970 pop. 16,979), capital of Ticino canton, S Switzerland, on the Ticino River, near the Italian border. It is a picturesque old town and a hub of transalpine traffic. Beverages and linoleum are produced. Possibly a Roman settlement, Bellinzona belonged at times to Lombardy, Como, Milan, France, and the Four Forest Cantons. In 1798 it became the capital of the Bellinzona canton under the HELVETIC REPUBLIC and the capital of Ticino in 1803. The town is dominated by three castles (13th-15th cent.) of the dukes of Milan.

Bell Island, island (1971 pop. 658), SE N.F., Canada, in Conception Bay. The island is 6 mi (9.7 km) long and 3 mi (4.8 km) wide. Its famous undersea iron mines were closed in 1966 after having been worked for 72 years.

Bellman, Carl Michael (mē'käēl bĕl'män), 1740-95, Swedish poet; protégé of Gustavus III. His early poetry was chiefly religious. His dithyrambic odes in *Fredmans Epistlar* (1790) and *Fredmans Sånger* (1791) include bacchanals, pastorals, and comic pieces. Sometimes Bellman wrote music for his verse, but more often he borrowed French melodies and music from contemporary plays. See H. W. Van Loon and Grace Castagnetta, *The Last of the Troubadours* (1939).

Bellmawr (bĕlmär'), residential borough (1970 pop. 15,618), Camden co., SW N.J.; inc. 1926.

bell metal: see BRONZE.

Bellmore, uninc. residential town (1970 pop. 18,431), Nassau co., SE N.Y., on SW Long Island.

Bello, Andrés (ändrās' bā'yō), 1781-1865, South American intellectual leader, b. Venezuela. In 1810 he was sent with Bolívar on a mission to London, where he remained for 19 years as a diplomat, teacher, and writer. Politically, he was influenced by Jeremy Bentham. He reflected a new attitude in Hispanic-American letters, initiating the movement for intellectual independence from Europe. Called to a governmental post in Chile, he soon became a leader in Chilean education and reorganized the university at Santiago, becoming (1843) its rector. Many of his learned works, such as *Gramática de la lengua castellana* (1847) and *Principios de derecho internacional* (1844; revised from an earlier work), became textbooks, and he was author of a code of civil law for Chile. He wrote many poems in the neoclassical style.

Belloc, Hilaire (Joseph Hilaire Pierre Belloc) (bĕl'ŏk), 1870-1953, English author, b. France. He became a British subject in 1902, and from 1906 to 1910 was a Liberal member of Parliament for South Salford. Poet, essayist, satirist, and historian, he wrote from the Roman Catholic viewpoint. Among his works are *The Bad Child's Book of Beasts* (1896), *The Path to Rome* (1902), *Marie Antoinette* (1910), *The Jews* (1922), *The Cruise of the Nona* (1925), and *Napoleon* (1922). He was a close friend of G. K. CHESTERTON and with him founded the *New Witness,* a weekly political newspaper. Christened "the Chesterbelloc" by G. B. Shaw, the two were the inventors and propagators of distributism, a medieval, anticapitalist, and anti-Fabian socialist philosophy.

Bellomont, Richard Coote, earl of, 1636-1701, colonial governor of New York, Massachusetts, and New Hampshire, b. Ireland. He arrived (1698) in New York at a time when a more unified administration of colonial affairs was being attempted. His administration was uneventful, but his endeavors to enforce the trade laws and to suppress piracy brought him the enmity of the aristocratic party in New York. He was noted for his arrest of William KIDD, whom he had originally commissioned as a pirate hunter.

Bellona: see MARS.

Bellotto, Bernardo (bĕrnär'dō bäl-lôt'tō), 1720-80, Venetian architectural and landscape painter, also called Canaletto, after his uncle and teacher CANALETTO. His paintings, at first resembling those of his master, are numerous and may be seen in most of the leading European museums. They usually depict scenes in the cities in which Bellotto resided. In 1747 he was appointed court painter at Dresden and in 1770 painter to Stanislaus II at Warsaw. See Stefan Kozakiewicz, *Bernardo Bellotto* (tr., 2 vol. 1972).

Bellow, Saul, 1915-, American novelist, b. Lachine, Que., grad. Northwestern Univ., 1937. Born of Russian-Jewish parents, he grew up in the slums of Montreal and Chicago. His writings, reflecting an intellectual and moral approach to life, are marked by a concern for the struggles of the individual in an indifferent society. His best-known novels include *The Adventures of Augie March* (1953), *Herzog* (1964), and *Mr. Sammler's Planet* (1970). Among his other works are the novels *Dangling Man* (1944), *The Victim* (1947), *Seize the Day* (1956), *Henderson the Rain King* (1959), and a play, *The Last Analysis* (1964). See studies by K. M. Opdahl (1967), J. J. Clayton (1968), and Irving Malin (1969).

Bellows, George Wesley, 1882-1925, American painter, draftsman, and lithographer, b. Columbus, Ohio; son of an architect and builder. In his senior year he left Ohio State Univ. to study painting under Robert Henri in New York City. Bellows never visited Europe and seemed uninfluenced by the currents affecting his European contemporaries, but he actively supported independent art movements in New York City. His work has a direct, unselfconscious realism and has survived because of its humanity and sincere conviction. *Forty-two Kids* (Corcoran Gall., Washington, D.C.); *Up the River* (Metropolitan Mus.); *Stag at Sharkey's* (Mus. of Art, Cleveland); and a portrait of the artist's mother (Art Inst., Chicago) are characteristic paintings. Bellows revived lithography in the United States, and his prints are as important as his paintings. *Billy Sunday, Dance in a Mad House,* and *Dempsey and Firpo* are

American classics. He was a noted teacher at the Art Students League, New York City. See collection of his lithographs by Emma S. Bellows (1927); studies by Peyton Boswell, Jr. (1942), C. H. Morgan (1965), and M. S. Young (1973).

Bellows, Henry Whitney, 1814–82, American clergyman, b. Boston. From 1839 until his death he was pastor of the First Congregational Society, Unitarian (later Church of All Souls) in New York City. Bellows organized and administered the U.S. Sanitary Commission, which served the sick and wounded of the Civil War. He was one of the founders of Antioch College. Among his books are *The Treatment of Social Diseases* (1857) and *Restatements of Christian Doctrine* (1860).

bellows, expansible, gas-tight chamber used to pump or store a gas. One of the simplest and most familiar types of bellows is the manual one used for providing a forced draft to a fire. The expansible chamber consists of a leather bag with pleated sides. The bag is fixed between handles in such a way that they can be used to make it expand and contract. The inlet and outlet vents are provided with valves so that air must enter through the first and leave through the second. The device thus comprises a simple air pump. One of the major uses of the bellows has been to provide a draft for fires that are used to help extract a metal from its ore. In a device such as an aneroid barometer a small bellows is filled with a known amount of gas that expands and contracts in response to changes in external pressure. This small bellows is coupled to some form of indicating or recording device. Another use of the bellows has been to provide wind for such musical instruments as the accordion and older pipe organs.

Belluno (bĕl-lōō'nō), city (1971 pop. 34,520), capital of Belluno prov., Venetia, NE Italy, on the Piave River at the foot of the Dolomites. It is an agricultural and manufacturing center. A Roman town, it later belonged to various lords and was a free commune before voluntarily submitting to Venetian rule (1404–1797). The city has a 16th-century cathedral with a beautiful baroque bell tower and a Renaissance city hall.

Belluschi, Pietro (pyĕ'trō bəlōō'skē), 1899–, Italian-American civil engineer, designer, and architect. Belluschi served as dean and professor at the Massachusetts Institute of Technology's school of architecture and planning (1951–65). He has designed numerous residential and office buildings, including the Equitable Building in Portland, Ore. (1948) and the Juilliard School of Music, part of the LINCOLN CENTER FOR THE PERFORMING ARTS in New York City. The latter reveals an interesting use of dark glass.

Bellville, town (1970 pop. 48,494), Cape Prov., S South Africa, a suburb of Cape Town. Situated in a major wheat-growing region, the city ships wheat and manufactures processed lumber and synthetic textiles. Bellville was founded in 1861 and named for Charles Bell, surveyor general of Cape Colony (1848–72). The Univ. of the Western Cape and Peninsula Technical College there are primarily for Coloured students.

Bellwood, village (1970 pop. 22,096), Cook co., NE Ill.; inc. 1900. Among its manufactures are electrical equipment and metal and asphalt products.

Belmondo, Jean-Paul (zhäN-pōl bĕlmôNdō'), 1933–, French film actor, b. Neuilly-sur-Seine. He was an amateur boxer before turning to acting. Belmondo first gained fame in *Breathless* (1960), playing a restless, flippant young hoodlum. His other films include *Moderato Cantabile* (1960), *That Man from Rio* (1964), *Pierrot le Fou* (1965), *The Mississippi Mermaid* (1968), *Borsolino* (1970), and *Stavisky* (1974).

Belmont. 1 City (1970 pop. 23, 667), San Mateo co., W Calif., a residential suburb midway between San Francisco and San Jose; laid out 1851, inc. 1926. The College of Notre Dame (est. 1851) is there. **2** Town (1970 pop. 28,285), Middlesex co., E Mass., a residential suburb of Boston; settled 1636, inc. 1859. James Russell Lowell often visited the region.

Belmonte, Juan (hwän bĕlmōn'tā), 1892–1962, Spanish matador, b. Seville. He is generally considered the greatest matador of all time, as remarkable for the poetry of his motion in the bullring as for his speed and dexterity. He is said to have "invented" modern bullfighting with his daring, revolutionary style, which kept him almost constantly within a few inches of the bull. Between 1913 and 1936, when he finally retired (he had retired twice before, in 1922 and 1934), he was gored and slashed innumerable times. In 1919 he fought 109 *corridas*, a record number. His years of rivalry (1914–20) with the great JOSELITO, known as the Golden Age of Bullfighting, ended with Joselito's fatal goring. See his autobiography (as told to Manuel Chaves Nogales; tr. 1937); biography by Henry P. B. Baerlein (1934).

Belo Horizonte (bəl"ōorĕzôN'tĭ) [Port.=beautiful horizon], city (1970 pop. 1,235,001), capital of Minas Gerais state, E Brazil. The distributing and processing center of a rich agricultural and mining region, Belo Horizonte is the nucleus of a burgeoning industrial complex; its chief manufactures are steel, steel products, and textiles. Gold, manganese, and precious stones (including diamonds) of the surrounding region are processed in the city. Belo Horizonte is also a transportation hub, with direct highway connections with Brasília, São Paulo, and Rio de Janeiro. One of the most important inland cities of the republic, it was Brazil's first planned metropolis and was built (1895–97) to replace Ouro Prêto as the state capital. With its wide, tree-lined avenues, skyscrapers, and spacious parks, and with its beautiful surroundings and bracing climate, Belo Horizonte is a fashionable resort. It is also a leading cultural center, with a historical museum, three universities, and numerous libraries and sports stadiums. The Chapel of São Francisco, with paintings by Candido Portinari, is famous.

Beloit (bĭloit'), city (1970 pop. 35,729), Rock co., S Wis., on the Rock River; inc. 1846. It lies in an agricultural area. Beloit's manufactures include shoes, papermaking machinery, diesel engines, desalinization equipment, electrical equipment, and pumps. A trading post was established on the site in 1824 for trade with the Winnebago Indians, and in 1837 the first permanent settlers arrived from New England. Beloit College, founded in 1846, is in the city. Roy Chapman Andrews, the U.S. naturalist and explorer, was born in Beloit.

Belon, Pierre (pyĕr bəlôN'), 1517–64, French naturalist. Besides an account of his travels in the Middle East, he wrote monographs on fishes and other aquatic animals, on conifers, and on birds. In *L'Histoire . . . des oyseaux* (1555) his comparison of the skeletons of birds and man foreshadows comparative anatomy.

Belopolsky, Aristarkh Apollonovich (ərĭ'stärkh əpəlôn'əvĭch byələpôl'skē), 1854–1934, Russian astrophysicist, grad. Univ. of Moscow (1877). He worked at the Moscow Observatory and from 1888 at the Pulkovo Observatory, where he became vice director in 1908. He was among the first Russians to study the sun and stars spectroscopically. He discovered important features of pulsating stars and studied the rotation of Jupiter and of Saturn's rings. A tireless observer, he determined the nature of various binary star systems and the radial velocities of many stars.

Beloretsk (byĕlərĕtsk'), city (1969 est. pop. 66,000), W Siberian USSR, in the Urals and on the Belaya River. One of the oldest industrial cities of the Urals region, Beloretsk is a metallurgical center, with industries that produce steel wire and cables. The city was founded in 1762.

Belorussia (byĕ"lərōō'sēə) or **Belorussian Soviet Socialist Republic,** constituent republic (1970 pop. 9,003,000), c.80,150 sq mi (207,600 sq km), W central European USSR. MINSK is the capital; other important cities are Gomel, Vitebsk, Mogilev, Bobruysk, Grodno, and Brest. Belorussia borders on Poland in the west, on the Lithuanian and Latvian republics in the north, on the Russian Soviet Federated Socialist Republic in the east, and on the Ukraine in the south. Much of Belorussia is a hilly lowland, drained by the Dnepr, Western Dvina, and Neman rivers. The climate is moderate humid continental, with warm summers and cold winters. More than one third of the land is covered with peat and other swampy soils, notably in the Pripyat Marshes in the south; peat, the republic's most valuable mineral resource, is used for fuel, for fertilizer, and in the chemical industry. Belorussia also has deposits of limestone, clay, sand, chalk, dolomite, phosphorite, and rock and potassium salt. Forests cover another third of the land, and lumbering is an important occupation. Potatoes, flax, hemp, sugar beets, rye, oats, and wheat are the chief agricultural products. The main branches of industry produce machinery, motor vehicles, chemicals, textiles, and electrical equipment. About 80% of the population are Belorussians; Russians, Poles, Jews, Ukrainians, and Lithuanians are the republic's largest minorities. Eastern Orthodoxy is the predominant religion, but there are some Roman Catholics. The region now constituting Belorussia was colonized by East Slavic tribes from the 5th to the 8th cent. It fell (9th cent.) under the sway of Kiev and was later (12th cent.) subdivided into several Belorussian principalities forming part of the Kievan state. Kiev's destruction by the Mongols in the 13th cent. facilitated the conquest (early 14th cent.) of Belorussia by the dukes of Lithuania. The region became part of the grand duchy of Lithuania, which in 1569 was merged with Poland. The large Jewish population (later decimated by the Germans during World War II) settled in Belorussia in the 14th cent. The region flourished under Lithuanian rule; but after the Polish-Lithuanian union Belorussia lost its relative importance, and its ruling classes became thoroughly polonized. Through the Polish partitions of 1772, 1793, and 1795, all Belorussia passed to the Russian Empire. It suffered greatly during the wars (16th–18th cent.) between Poland and Russia and in the Napoleonic invasion of 1812 (during which it was laid waste by retreating Russian forces). Great poverty under Russian rule, notably among the Jews, led to mass emigration to the United States in the 19th cent. A battlefield in World War I and in the Soviet-Polish War of 1919–20, Belorussia experienced great devastation. In March, 1918, the Belorussian National Rada in Minsk proclaimed the region an independent republic; but in Jan., 1919, the Soviet government proclaimed a Belorussian Soviet Socialist Republic at Smolensk, and soon the Red Army occupied all of Belorussia. In 1921 the Treaty of Riga, which ended the Soviet-Polish War, awarded W Belorussia to Poland. The eastern and larger part formed the Belorussian SSR, which joined the USSR in 1922. In Sept., 1939, the Soviet army overran W Belorussia and incorporated it into the Belorussian SSR. Occupied by the Germans during World War II, Belorussia was one of the most devastated areas of the USSR. In 1945 its western border was adjusted slightly in favor of Poland, but the 1939 frontier remained essentially unchanged. The republic has a separate seat in the United Nations. Its name also appears as Byelorussia or Bielorussia, and it is sometimes called White Russia.

Belovo (byĕlô'və), city (1970 pop. 108,000), S central Siberian USSR. One of the largest industrial centers of the Kuznetsk Basin, it has a zinc plant and a thermal power station. There are coal mines nearby.

Belphegor: see BAAL-PEOR.

Belshazzar (bĕlshăz'ər), according to the Bible, son of NEBUCHADNEZZAR and last king of Babylon. Dan. 5.1. At his feast, handwriting appeared on the wall, and Daniel interpreted it as a prophecy of doom; that night Babylonia fell to Cyrus. Dan. 5.

Belt, Great, and **Little Belt,** straits: see STORE BAELT, strait, Denmark.

belt, girdle or band worn around the body, originally to confine loose garments. Later the girdle became a decorative accessory and was used to carry belongings. The Greeks and Romans wore ornamental cords and bands of many materials, including metal. The medieval belt displayed brilliant goldwork and gems; it carried the purse, dagger, sword, and other personal belongings of the wearer. Since then the belt has varied in style and importance. It has been symbolic of strength, of alertness, and of integrity. In folklore belts have often been accorded supernatural power.

Belteshazzar (bĕltəshăz'ər), in the book of DANIEL, Babylonian name of the prophet Daniel.

Beltraffio, Giovanni Antonio: see BOLTRAFFIO.

Beltrami, Eugenio (āōōjĕ'nyō bälträ'mē), 1835–99, Italian mathematician. He is famous for his work on non-euclidean geometry, electricity, and magnetism.

Beltsville swine, two breeds of swine developed at the agricultural research center of the U.S. Department of Agriculture in Beltsville, Md. The breeds are designated Beltsville No. 1 and Beltsville No. 2. Beltsville No. 1 was developed by crossing Danish Landrace and Poland China swine. It is black in color with uniformly distributed white markings. Beltsville No. 2 was developed from crosses using Danish Yorkshire, Duroc, Landrace, and Hampshire breeds. Its color is solid red with a white underline and occasional black spotting; its length is about the same as that of a Yorkshire.

beluga (bəlōō'gə) or **white whale,** small, toothed northern WHALE, *Delphinapterus leucas.* The beluga may reach a length of 19 ft (5.8 m) and a weight of 4,400 lb (2,000 kg). It has a small, round head, with a short, broad, beaklike snout, and a flexible neck; its flippers are short, broad, and rounded, and it lacks a dorsal fin. It produces a variety of noises and is sometimes called a sea canary. The young are born with dark fur but become almost pure white in maturity. Belugas winter in the Arctic Ocean, feeding upon crustaceans, fish, and squid; they are often found in groups of several hundred individuals. They mate in spring, and in summer they enter northern rivers. The young are born after a gestation period of 14 months, one calf every second year. The beluga is hunted by the Eskimo for food and by commercial whalers for its hide, which is known as porpoise hide. Beluga is also the common name of the largest of the STURGEONS. Beluga whales are classified in the phylum CHORDATA, subphylum Vertebrata, class Mammalia, order Cetacea, family Monodontidae.

Belvedere (bĕl'vədēr, Ital. bālvādĕ'rā), court of the Vatican named after a villa built (1485–87) for Innocent VIII. The villa was decorated with frescoes by Pinturicchio and others; a chapel painted by Mantegna was demolished when the villa was made part of the Museo Pio-Clementino at the end of the 18th cent. The Belvedere court, connecting the villa and the Vatican, was designed (1503–4) by Bramante for Julius II to include an architectural garden, a permanent theater, a museum building, and a statue court. The *Laocoön*, discovered in 1506, was placed in the statue court; in 1511 the *Apollo Belvedere* (see under APOLLO, in Greek religion) was installed in a special niche. When Bramante died in 1514, only a portion of the Belvedere was completed; many modifications were made under a succession of architects including Giuliano Sangallo, Raphael, Peruzzi, and Antonio Sangallo. Now a museum, the Belvedere still contains the *Laocoön* and the *Apollo* as well as other rare works of classical antiquity. See study by James S. Ackerman (1954).

Belvidere (bĕl'vĭdēr"), city (1970 pop. 14,061), seat of Boone co., N Ill., on the Kishwaukee River; inc. 1847. It is a farm trade center with food-processing industries, machine shops, and a huge automobile assembly plant.

Bely, Andrei (əndrā' byĕ'lē), pseud. of **Boris Nikolayevich Bugayev,** 1880–1934, Russian writer. A leading SYMBOLIST, he had a close but stormy relationship with Aleksandr BLOK. His poems are collected in the four-volume *Symphonies* (1901–8); his best prose is in the novels *The Silver Dove* (1910) and *Petersburg* (1912, tr. 1959) and in *Kotik Letayev* (1920), an autobiographical novel in the manner of James Joyce. He was an experimenter—his involved style often mixes realism and symbolism in complex forms. In his later years Bely was influenced by Rudolph STEINER's anthroposophy. He accepted the Soviet regime, but his works were not well received by Soviet critics. By the mid-1970's Western critics had discovered Bely, and several proclaimed him the most important Russian writer of the 20th cent. In 1974 new translations of *The Silver Dove* and *Kotik Letayev* were published in the United States, and a section of the International Slavic Conference, held in Banff, Canada, was devoted to Bely's works.

Belzoni, Giovanni Battista (jōvän'nē bät-tēs'tä bĕltsō'nē), 1778–1823, Italian archaeologist. He lived (1803–12) in England and there invented a hydraulic machine, which he introduced into Egypt in 1815. Becoming interested in archaeology, he opened (1817) the rock temple of Abu-Simbel, and he discovered (1817) the tomb of Seti I at Thebes. His discoveries are recorded in his *Narrative* (1820). See biography by Stanley Mayes (1961).

Bembo, Pietro (pyā'trō bĕm'bō), 1470–1547, Italian humanist, cardinal of the Roman Catholic Church. A favorite of the Medici, he was secretary to Pope Leo X and was made a cardinal by Paul III. Bembo was for many years the arbiter of Italian letters, insisting that classical traditions be preserved. He was responsible for editions of Petrarch and Dante and helped establish the language of Tuscany as the standard literary Italian. He wrote the *History of Venice* (1551); a disquisition on platonic love, *Gli Asolani* (1505, tr. 1954), inspired by Plato's *Symposium*; a book of lyric verse (*Rime*, 1530) in Latin and Italian; and *Prose della volgar lingua* [prose in the vernacular] (1525).

Bemidji (bəmĭj'ē), city (1970 pop. 11,490), seat of Beltrami co., N central Minn., on lakes Bemidji and Irving, through which flows the Mississippi River; inc. 1896. It is in a summer and winter resort and sport fishing area; tourism is the major industry. The city is also a trade and marketing center for the dairy farms of the region, and has lumber, wood-product, and boat manufactures. On the lakeshore stands an 18-ft (5.5-m) figure of Paul Bunyan and his ox. Bemidji State College is in the city.

Bemis, Samuel Flagg, 1891–1973, American historian, b. Worcester, Mass. He received his Ph.D. from Harvard in 1916 and taught history at various schools before becoming Farnum professor of diplomatic history at Yale (1935). In 1945 he was appointed Sterling professor of history and international relations. Considered one of the nation's leading diplomatic historians he twice received the Pulitzer Prize, once for history, *Pinckney's Treaty* (1926, rev. ed. 1960), and once for biography, *John Quincy Adams and the Foundations of American Foreign Policy* (1950). His other works include *Jay's Treaty* (1923, 2d ed. 1962), *The Diplomacy of the American Revolution* (1935), *A Diplomatic History of the United States* (1936, 5th ed. 1965), *The Latin American Policy of the United States* (1943), and *John Quincy Adams and the Union* (1956). He was the editor of *The American Secretaries of State and Their Diplomacy* (18 vol., 1963–72).

Bemis Heights, battle of: see SARATOGA CAMPAIGN.

Ben, Levite porter under David. 1 Chron. 15.18.

Ben-abinadab (bĕn-əbĭn'ədăb): see ABINADAB **4.**

Benaiah (bēnā'yə). **1** One of David's warriors, faithful in David's old age to Solomon. 2 Sam. 8.18; 20.23; 23.20–23; 1 Kings 1; 2; 1 Chron. 11.22–25; 18.17; 27.5,6. **2** Warrior under David. 2 Sam. 23.30; 1 Chron. 11.31; 27.14. **3** Levite. 1 Chron. 15.18,20; 16.5. **4** Priest. 1 Chron. 15.24; 16.6. **5** Simeonite. 1 Chron. 4.36. **6** Asaphite. 2 Chron. 20.14. **7** Levite of the reign of Hezekiah. 2 Chron. 31.13. **8** Father of Pelatiah. Ezek. 11.1,13. **9, 10, 11, 12** Jews who had married foreign wives. Ezra 10.25,30,35,43.

Benalcázar or **Belalcázar, Sebastián de** (sābästyän' dā bänälkä'thär, bäläl-), c.1479–1551, Spanish conquistador. After accompanying Columbus on his third voyage (1498), Benalcázar served in Darien and Nicaragua before joining Francisco PIZARRO in the conquest of Peru (1532). Setting out from PIURA, he forestalled Pedro de Alvarado in support of Diego de ALMAGRO, the elder, and entered (1533) the Indian stronghold of Quito, founded Guayaquil, and marched (1535) into SW Colombia in search of EL DORADO. While in Colombia he founded Pasto and Cali. In 1539 he tried unsuccessfully to ally himself with FEDERMANN against JIMÉNEZ DE QUESADA. Journeying to Spain with them to settle accounts, Benalcázar returned (1541) as governor of Popayán prov. Between 1541 and 1548 he aided Vaca de Castro against Diego de Almagro, the younger, and then helped Nuñez Vela and Pedro de la Gasca against Gonzalo Pizarro. For executing the leader of a neighboring province that he claimed as his, Benalcázar was tried (1550) and convicted. On his way to appeal to the Council of the Indies he died of fever in Cartagena.

Ben-ammi (bĕn-ăm'ī), son of Lot by his younger daughter; eponym of the Ammonites. Gen. 19.38.

Benares, India: see VARANASI.

Benavente y Martínez, Jacinto (häthēn'tō bä"nävān'tä ē märtē'nĕth), 1866–1954, Spanish dramatist, b. Madrid. He was awarded the 1922 Nobel Prize in Literature. His best-known play is *Los intereses creados* (1907, tr. *Bonds of Interest,* 1917), a farce written on the pattern of the Italian *commedia dell' arte.* In 1916 he wrote a second part to this play, *La ciudad alegre y confiada* [the gay and confident city]. *La malquerida* (1913, tr. *The Passion Flower,* 1920), on the Phaedra theme, was popular with the public and the critics. His plays fall into four classes: social satires, psychological dramas, children's plays, and allegorical-morality plays. He was at his best in sparkling satires of aristocratic and upper middle-class life. See study by Marcelino Peñuelas (tr.1969).

Ben Bella, Ahmed (äkhmĕd' bĕn bĕl'lä), 1919–, Algerian statesman. After World War II he joined the Algerian nationalist movement and soon became a leader of its terrorist faction. He later (1952–56) served as director of the movement. Imprisoned (1956–62) for his activities, he became Algeria's first premier after independence was declared in 1962. In 1965, Ben Bella's government was toppled in a coup led by Houari BOUMEDIENNE.

Benbow, John (bĕn'bō), 1653–1702, English admiral. Some of the stories of his exploits seem to be legendary, but he did command the fleet and successfully fight the French at Saint-Malo (1693) and Dunkirk (1696) and the Spanish in the West Indies (1698). In 1702 he engaged in a four-day running fight with a French fleet in the Caribbean off Santa Marta. During this battle his flagship, the *Breda,* was deserted by all but one of his fleet, and Benbow himself was fatally wounded. Several of the disobedient captains were later court-martialed and shot.

Benchley, Robert Charles, 1889–1945, American humorist, b. Worcester, Mass., grad. Harvard, 1912. He was drama critic of *Life* (1920–29) and of the *New Yorker* (1929–40). Benchley was known for a series of short satirical films that he wrote, directed, and acted in himself. His books, which are rich in anecdotes and clever interpretations of everyday situations, include *Of All Things* (1921), *My Ten Years in a Quandary* (1936), and *Benchley beside Himself* (1943).

Bend, city (1970 pop. 13,710), seat of Deschutes co., W central Oregon, on the Deschutes River, at the eastern foot of the Cascade Range; inc. 1904. Lumbering is the primary industry, and tourism is also important. It is the seat of a junior college and the headquarters for Deschutes National Forest. A U.S. silviculture laboratory is in Bend, and nearby pumice fields offer moon-like terrain for a lunar base research facility, which carries on study and training projects there.

Benda, Georg Franz (gā'ôrkh fränts bĕn'dä), 1722–95, Bohemian composer. Benda, whose Bohemian name was Jiří Antonín Benda, came from a musical family that moved to Prussia in 1742. His brother, the violinist Franz (in Bohemian, František) Benda, became a favorite of Frederick II. Benda is best known for his melodramas—dramatic works in which a speaking part is set against orchestral music—and singspiels.

Benda, Julien (zhülyăN' băNdä'), 1867–1956, French novelist and critic. A humanist and rationalist, he led a sustained attack against the romantic philosophy of his time, especially that of Bergson. The novel *The Yoke of Pity* (1912, tr. 1913) won him recognition. In *The Treason of the Intellectuals* (1927, tr. 1928) he accused his contemporary thinkers of abandoning truth and succumbing to political passions. *La Jeunesse d'un clerc* (1936) and *Un Regulier dans le siècle* (1938) recapitulate his intellectual life.

Benda, Wladyslaw Theodor (vlădĭ'slăf), 1873–1948, Polish American painter and illustrator, b. Poland. He studied at the Art Academy in Cracow and in Vienna, San Francisco, and New York City. In addition to decorative works and many illustrations for magazines and books, he created modern masks, used in the theater; they were first seen in *Greenwich Village Follies* (1920). Benda wrote *Masks* (1945).

Ben Day, or **Benday, process:** see PRINTING.

Bendery (bĭndyĕ'rē), city (1969 est. pop. 68,000), SW European USSR, in Moldavia, a port on the Dnestr River. It is a rail hub and a trade center for timber, fruits, and tobacco. Industries include the production of foodstuffs, electrical apparatus, footwear, and textiles. Historically important as the gateway of Bessarabia, the city was founded on the site of a 14th-century Genoese colony that the Rumanians called Tigin. Captured from Moldavia by the Turks in 1538 and renamed Bendery, it became a fortress on the Dnestr. It was captured by Russia in 1812. Between the world wars, Bendery belonged to Rumania; it was transferred to the USSR in 1940 but was occupied by Rumanian troops from 1941 to 1944.

Bendigo (bĕn'dĭgō), city (1971 pop. 31,927), Victoria, SE Australia. Founded in 1851 during the gold rush, Bendigo was the center for the greatest goldfield in Victoria. Mining continues, but the city is now an industrial, railroad, and commercial center in a livestock and dairy-farming region. Textiles, bricks, and pottery are manufactured in Bendigo.

bends: see DECOMPRESSION SICKNESS.

Bene-berak (bē'nē-bē'răk), town, central Israel, near Tel Aviv. Joshua 19.45. It was famous for its academy under Rabbi Akiba's direction; today it has six Talmudic academies. The name is also spelled Bene Beraq.

Benedek, Ludwig von (lo͝ot'vĭkh fən bā'nədĕk"), 1804–81, Austrian general. Entering the army in 1822, he served in the suppression of the Polish insurrection of 1846, in the Austrian campaigns of 1848–49 in Italy and Hungary, and in the Italian War of 1859. In the Austro-Prussian War (1866), he reluctantly accepted, under imperial pressure, an appointment to command the army of the North, although he felt inadequately prepared to direct troops in the unfamiliar territory of Bohemia. He suffered a crushing defeat at the battle of Königgrätz (Sadowa). After his court-martial was stopped by imperial command, von Benedek was permitted to retire to Graz, provided he would make no attempt to rehabilitate himself.

Benedetti, Giovanni Battista (jōvän'nē bät-tēs'tä bänādĕt'tē), 1530–90, Italian mathematician and physicist. An important forerunner of Galileo, Benedetti had diverse interests, including mechanics, music, hydrostatics, astronomy, astrology, and gnomonics (the science of sundials). His work on falling bodies, first outlined in 1552, helped lay the basis for the overthrow of Aristotelian physics in the 17th cent. Like Galileo, he held that bodies of the same material fall through a given medium at the same speed, regardless of their weight. His most important scientific work is the *Diversarum speculationum* (1585).

Benedetti, Vincent (văNsäN'), 1817–1900, French diplomat, b. Corsica, made a count by Napoleon III. He was ambassador to Prussia from 1864 to 1870. In an interview (1870) at Ems with King William I (later German emperor), he asked the king to disapprove formally and permanently the candidacy of a Hohenzollern prince for the Spanish throne. The episode was so altered in Bismarck's version of the EMS DISPATCH that it became an immediate cause of the Franco-Prussian War.

Benedetto da Majano (bānādĕt'tō dä mäyä'nō), 1442–97, Italian sculptor and architect of the Florentine school. His pulpits, altarpieces, and other church furniture are beautifully executed. Examples of his work are in Santa Croce and the Palazzo Vecchio, Florence, and in San Domenico, Siena. He completed the tomb of Mary of Aragón (Naples), begun by Antonio Rossellino.

Benedict, Saint, d. c.547, Italian monk, founder of the BENEDICTINES, called Benedict of Nursia, b. Norcia (E of Spoleto), Italy. He went to Rome to study, then withdrew to Subiaco to live as a hermit; after three years he was renowned for his holiness. He started an establishment of monks, a set of cells of 13 monks each. This he finally left, and at MONTE CASSINO, in an old pagan holy place, he started the first truly Benedictine monastery. The product of Benedict's experience appears in the Rule of St. Benedict (in Latin), the chief rule in Western MONASTICISM, used always by Benedictines and by Cistercians as well. Its 73 chapters (with Prologue) are original, personal, and full of a spirit of common sense. They set forth the central ideas of Benedictine monasticism. St. Benedict's sister, St. Scholastica, was a religious also. Feast: March 21. See St. Gregory I, *Life and Miracles of St. Benedict* (tr. by O. J. Zimmerman and B. R. Avery, 1969); Dom John Chapman, *Saint Benedict and the Sixth Century* (1929, repr. 1971); Paul Delatte, *The Rule of St. Benedict* (tr. 1950); Theodore Maynard, *Saint Benedict and His Monks* (1954); Leonard von Matt, *Saint Benedict* (1961).

Benedict XI, d. 1304, pope (1303–4), an Italian (b. Treviso) named Niccolo Boccasini; successor of Boniface VIII. Prior to his election he had been master general of the Dominican order. As pope he was able to conciliate many of the enemies Boniface had made, chiefly Philip IV of France, whose excommunication he rescinded. However, he would not yield on the excommunication of Boniface's assaulters, Sciarra Colonna and Philip's emissary, Nogaret. The Colonna faction controlled Rome, and Benedict withdrew to Perugia, a prelude to the flight of the papacy to Avignon under Benedict's successor, Clement V, in 1309. Benedict was beatified in 1638.

Benedict XIII, antipope: see LUNA, PEDRO DE.

Benedict XIV, 1675–1758, pope (1740–58), an Italian (b. Bologna) named Prospero Lambertini; successor of Clement XII. Long before his pontificate he was renowned for his learning. In 1728 he became a cardinal. He was much interested in the Eastern churches and began (with the bull *Etsi pastoralis,* 1742) the modern papal legislation that favors the Eastern rites and prohibits activity that is likely to Latinize them. He beautified Rome and restored monuments, and he was munificent to Bologna. He patronized learning and welcomed scholars and artists to his court. He denounced the cruelty to the Indians in the disbanding of the Paraguay REDUCTIONS. He was succeeded by Clement XIII.

Benedict XV, 1854–1922, pope (1914–22), an Italian (b. Genoa) named Giacomo della Chiesa; successor of Pius X. He was made archbishop of Bologna in 1907 and cardinal in 1914, two months before his election as pope. His conduct in World War I was one of the strictest neutrality, and he had the respect of all belligerents. He originated several proposals for peace. Benedict was lavish in charity toward war victims, and he founded the Vatican service for prisoners of war. During his pontificate France and England resumed diplomatic relations with the Holy See. He was succeeded by Pius XI. See biography by W. H. Peters (1959).

Benedict, Ruth Fulton, 1887–1948, American anthropologist, b. New York City, grad. Vassar, 1909, Ph.D. Columbia, 1923. She was a student and later a colleague of Franz Boas at Columbia, where she taught from 1924. She did fieldwork among American Indians and studied contemporary European and Asian cultures. Her works emphasize the concepts of cultural configuration, national character, and the role of culture in individual personality formation. Her widely read books helped popularize the concept of CULTURE and attacked racism and ethnocentrism. She is the author of *Concept of the Guardian Spirit in North America* (1923), *Patterns of Culture* (1934), *Zuni Mythology* (1935), *Race: Science and Politics* (rev. ed. 1943), and *The Chrysanthemum and the Sword: Patterns of Japanese Culture* (1946). A collection of her work and biographical data was edited by Margaret Mead under the title *An Anthropologist at Work* (1959, repr. 1966). See biography by Margaret Mead (1974).

Benedict Biscop (bĭs'kəp), c.628–690, English monk. He founded the monasteries of Wearmouth (at Sunderland) and Jarrow, and he was abbot of St. Peter's, Canterbury. Bede was his pupil.

benedictine (bĕnədĭk'tēn), sweet LIQUEUR originated in 1510 by Benedictine monks at Fécamp, France, and now manufactured by a secular concern on the grounds of the old abbey. Every bottle bears the initials of the Latin dedication *Deo Optimo Maximo* [to God most good, most great]. The exact formula of benedictine remains a secret.

Benedictines, monks of the Roman Catholic Church, following the rule of St. BENEDICT [Lat. abbr., = O.S.B.]. Their first establishment was at MONTE CASSINO, Italy, which came to be regarded as the symbolic center of Western MONASTICISM. St. Benedict's rule was novel in monastic life in replacing austerity by moderation. The monastery, or ABBEY, was conceived as a devout Christian family of men, with the abbot as father. The monks swore to live in the house until death. The whole of Benedictine life was experienced in common, the waking hours being devoted principally to worship and work, especially manual labor. The greatest of the early Benedictines was Pope St. Gregory I, whose espousal of the life had great influence. He sent St. Augustine of Canterbury to convert Anglo-Saxon England to Christianity and to introduce Benedictine life. In the 8th cent. the English Benedictines St. Willibrord and St. Boniface evangelized Frisia and Germany. In this expansion of Christendom the abbey served as an outpost, a unit of both Latin culture (including Western agricultural methods) and Christian religion. The Benedictines were also active within the area that had been Latin for centuries—their preservation of books was a critical service. In the 10th cent. a reform began at the abbey of Cluny, France; although this led to the setting up of a separate organization (see CLUNIAC ORDER), it deepened the long-standing Benedictine tendencies to emphasize the liturgy, study, and education. A Benedictine reform, or reaction, in 1098, resulted in a new foundation, the CISTERCIANS. Throughout the centuries, however, the Benedictine houses have occupied a central position in Western religious orders. They are organized as a loose federation of congregations, each congregation being a collection of geographically related abbeys or monasteries that are mainly autonomous. Benedictine work in liturgy has been outstanding. The abbeys at Solesmes and Beuron in particular have established a spiritual life centered around sung liturgy. They are responsible for the restoration of Gregorian melodies (plain chant) and their universal use today in the Roman Catholic Church. Permanent Benedictine establishments in the United States began in the 1840s. There are presently over 10,000 male Benedictines, with some 2,300 living in 42 foundations in the United States. There are also Benedictine nuns. See E. C. Butler, *Benedictine Monachism* (2d ed. 1924, repr. 1962); L. J. Daly, *Benedictine Monasticism* (1965).

benediction [Lat., = blessing], solemn blessing usually administered in the name of God by a priest or a minister. The temple worship at Jerusalem had fixed forms of benedictions, and Christians have always given them an important place in ceremony, especially at the end of a ritual. Protestants have abandoned many of the blessings of the Roman Catholic Church, such as the apostolic benediction by the pope and his delegates and benediction of the dying. **Benediction of the Blessed Sacrament,** a popular extraliturgical service of Roman Catholics, consists of a blessing of the people by the priest with the Host exposed in a monstrance.

Benedict's solution, deep-blue alkaline solution used to test for the presence of the ALDEHYDE functional group, −CHO. The substance to be tested is heated with Benedict's solution; formation of a brick-red precipitate indicates presence of the aldehyde group. Since simple sugars (e.g., glucose) give a positive test, the solution is used to test for the presence of glucose in urine, a symptom of diabetes. One liter of Benedict's solution contains 173 grams sodium citrate, 100 grams sodium carbonate, and 17.3 grams cupric sulfate pentahydrate. It reacts chemically like FEHLING'S SOLUTION; the cupric ion (complexed with citrate ions) is reduced to cuprous ion by the aldehyde group (which is oxidized), and precipitates as cuprous oxide, Cu_2O.

Benedict the Black, Saint, d. 1589, Sicilian Negro friar. Born a slave, he became a hermit and later a Franciscan lay brother. Although illiterate, his humility and extraordinary powers as spiritual director caused him to be made Superior. He has erroneously been called Benedict the Moor. He was canonized in 1807. Feast: April 4.

Benedictus (bĕnədĭk'təs), hymn of Zachary, taken from Luke 1.68–79. It begins in Latin, "Benedictus Dominus Deus Israel" [blessed be the Lord God of Israel]. It is used at funerals and at lauds in the Roman Catholic Church and at morning prayer in the Church of England. Part of the SANCTUS is also called *Benedictus.*

Benediktsson, Bjarni (bĭyär'nē bĕnĕdĭkt'sōn), 1908–70, Icelandic statesman. A lawyer, he was a vocal advocate of Iceland's independence from Denmark, and became a member of the central committee of the Independence party in 1936. Elected mayor of Reykjavík in 1940, he held a number of important government and diplomatic posts after World War II: He was minister of foreign affairs and justice (1947–53), minister of justice and education (1953–56), and minister of justice (1959). The head of the Independence party from 1961, he served as prime minister from 1963 until 1970, when he was killed in a fire.

benefice, in canon law, a position in the church that has attached to it a source of income; also, more narrowly, that income itself. The occupant of a benefice receives its revenue (temporalities) for the performance of stipulated duties (spiritualities), e.g., the celebration of Mass. He receives the free use of such revenue but is expected to convert into good works any income in excess of his personal needs. Benefices are normally bestowed for life. Canon law forbids plurality of benefices, i.e., the holding of more than one benefice, but papal dispensations have made many exceptions to this rule. Benefices were originally in the form of land donations made to the church by wealthy laymen. Today the revenue of a benefice may come also from government salaries, investments, or the offerings of the faithful. Benefices are common in Europe but are practically unknown in the United States. The Church of England makes extensive use of the beneficiary system; the benefice in England is also called a living. The value of benefices led to many abuses (see SIMONY) and frequent conflict between secular and ecclesiastical authorities in the Middle Ages.

benefit of clergy, term originally applied to the exemption of Christian clerics from criminal prosecution in the secular courts. The privilege was established by the 12th cent., and it extended only to the commission of felonies. The ecclesiastical courts did not inflict capital punishment except in rare cases, in which event those adjudged guilty were turned over to local secular authorities for enforcement of the sentence (see CANON LAW). In the ecclesiastical courts the severest sentences usually were degradation and the imposition of penances. Many criminals posed as clerics to obtain benefit of clergy. In England the privilege was soon extended to all clerks, i.e., literate persons. Since the first verse of Psalm 51 was the test of literacy, violators of the law would memorize the text. The ecclesiastical courts lost all jurisdiction over criminal acts in 1576, and thereafter clerics were tried by the secular courts and, under statute law, were either discharged or sentenced to a year's imprisonment. Early in the 18th cent. the reading test was abolished and all persons were allowed to claim this privilege for the first conviction of felony; later the privilege was extended generally to peers and women. Benefit of clergy thus mitigated the severities of English criminal law, which imposed the death penalty for many offenses now deemed trivial. Criminal law was ameliorated in the early 19th cent., and in 1827 benefit of clergy was abolished as being no longer necessary. In the United States it was abolished in 1790 for all Federal crimes, and c.1850 it disappeared from the state courts. The term "benefit of clergy" has come in popular usage to mean sanction of the clergy, particularly in the phrase "marriage without benefit of clergy." See L. C. Gabel, *Benefit of Clergy in England in the Later Middle Ages* (1929, repr. 1969); Lincoln Bouscaren and A. C. Ellis, *Canon Law* (1946); J. R. Cameron, *Frederick William Maitland and the History of English Law* (1961).

Bene Israel or **Beni Israel** (both: bā'nē) [Heb.,= sons of Israel], Jewish community of India, numbering some 12,000 persons living mostly in and near Bombay city and about 12,000 who have settled in Israel since 1948. According to their own legend, they are descended from Jews who fled persecutions in Palestine in the 2d cent. B.C. Some scholars believe, however, that they are descended either from Babylonian Jews who migrated for reasons of trade or from Yemenite Jews who fled the persecutions of Muhammad; the latter hypothesis would explain the use of the name Bene Israel, which is found in the Koran as a favorable reference to Jews. The Bene Israel are referred to in the travel accounts of Benjamin of Tudela (10th cent.) and Marco Polo (13th cent.). When the Bene Israel were rediscovered by Westerners in the late 18th cent. their customs were substantially like those of the Hindus except that they kept the Sabbath and several Jewish festivals and circumcised boys on the eighth day after birth. The only Hebrew they were said to know was the prayer, "Hear, O Israel, the Lord our God, the Lord is one!" Wealthy Jews established schools to instruct the Bene Israel in Hebrew and Judaism, and in time their religious practices became similar to those of Jews throughout the world. See Schifra Strizower, *The Bene Israel of Bombay* (1971).

Bene-jaakan (bĕn'ē-jā'əkăn), halting place in the wilderness. Num. 33.31,32. Beeroth: Deut. 10.6.

Benelux Economic Union, economic treaty among Belgium, Luxembourg, and the Netherlands, established in 1958 by a 50-year treaty. The treaty represented years of efforts aimed at establishing an economic union among these countries. As early as 1922, the Belgium-Luxembourg Economic Union was formed. In 1944 these two countries and the Netherlands concluded a customs union that went into force in 1948. The treaty of 1958 brought together all of the previous agreements, and in 1960, when it took effect, a fully integrated Benelux was formed. The goal of the union was the free movement of workers, capital, goods, and services among the countries involved.

Beneš, Eduard (ĕ'do͝oärt bĕ'nĕsh), 1884-1948, Czechoslovakian president (1935-38, 1946-48). As a student at Prague Univ. he adopted the political and social philosophy of T. G. MASARYK. Later he studied in France, taught sociology and economics at Prague, and joined (1915) Masaryk in exile in Paris to work for Czechoslovak independence. After the breakup of the Austro-Hungarian Monarchy at the end of World War I, he represented Czechoslovakia at the Paris Peace Conference of 1919. As foreign minister (1918-35), premier (1921-22), leader of the Czech National Socialist party (a liberal and nationalist party, unlike its German namesake), and right-hand man of Masaryk, Beneš influenced both national and European politics. The LITTLE ENTENTE and the Czech alliance with France were essentially his work. He became (1935) president of Czechoslovakia at Masaryk's retirement but resigned (1938) after the dismemberment of his country by the MUNICH PACT and went into exile. After the outbreak of World War II he resumed (1940) the title president and headed, in London, a provisional government at war with Germany. Returning to Prague in 1945, he was confirmed in office and was reelected (1946) president. After the Communist coup of Feb., 1948, he reluctantly endorsed the new regime, but resigned in June on the ground of illness, refusing to sign the new constitution. He died shortly afterward. Among his writings are *My War Memoirs* (tr. 1928, repr. 1971), *Democracy: Today and Tomorrow* (1939, in English), and *Memoirs of Dr. Eduard Beneš* (tr. 1954, repr. 1972).

Benét, Stephen Vincent (bĕnā'), 1898-1943, American poet and author, b. Bethlehem, Pa., grad. Yale, 1919; brother of William Rose Benét. Benét is most famous for *John Brown's Body,* a long narrative poem of the Civil War, which won a Pulitzer Prize in 1929. By the time he left college Benét had already published several volumes of verse. After graduation he rapidly produced more poetry—*Heaven and Earth* (1920), *A Ballad of William Sycamore* (1923), and other volumes—and several novels, of which *Jean Huguenot* (1923) and *The Spanish Bayonet* (1926) are the best. In 1928 he published *John Brown's Body.* A vivid, impressionistic, patriotic poem, it reveals not only Benét's mastery of the ballad form but also his detailed knowledge of Civil War history. Later volumes of verse include *Ballads and Poems* (1931) and *The Burning City* (1936). His short stories, particularly "The Devil and Daniel Webster," are among the best of their time. Although much of Benét's work has been criticized for its unevenness and lack of depth, his writings exhibit a genuine passion for America and a deep interest in its folklore and history. *Western Star,* a long narrative poem about the westward migration left unfinished at his death, was published in 1943 (Pulitzer Prize, 1944). See his selected works (2 vol., 1942); letters, ed. by C. A. Fenton (1960); biographies by C. A. Fenton (1958) and P. E. Stroud (1962).

Benét, William Rose, 1886-1950, American poet and editor, b. Brooklyn, grad. Yale, 1907; brother of Stephen Vincent Benét. He was associated as editor or assistant editor with the *Century Magazine,* the Literary Review of the New York *Evening Post,* and the *Saturday Review of Literature* (which he helped found in 1924). His books include such collections of poetry as *Merchants from Cathay* (1913), *The Great White Wall* (1916), and *Man Possessed* (1927); a novel, *The First Person Singular* (1922); a volume of essays, *Wild Goslings* (1927); and an anthology, *The Reader's Encyclopedia* (1948). He also coedited *The Oxford Anthology of American Literature* (1938). His autobiographical verse-narrative, *The Dust Which Is God* (1941), won the 1942 Pulitzer Prize in poetry. His second wife was the poet, Elinor Wylie, whose poems he edited in 1932.

Benevento (bānāvān'tō), city (1971 pop. 59,016), capital of Benevento prov., in Campania, S Italy. It is a trade center for wine and tobacco. Farm machinery, optical instruments, liqueur, and nougat are manufactured. A leading town of Samnium, Benevento became under the Romans an important trade center on the Appian Way. It was the capital of a powerful Lombard duchy (6th-11th cent.) that extended over much of S Italy. Except for short periods of foreign occupation, the city was under papal rule from the 11th cent. to 1860. In 1266, Charles of Anjou defeated Manfred, King of Sicily, near Benevento. Noteworthy structures of the city include the cathedral (11th-13th cent., restored after being severely damaged in World War II); a triumphal arch erected (114 A.D.) for Trajan; a Roman theatre (2d cent. B.C.); and the Church of Santa Sofia, with a 12th-century cloister.

Benevoli, Orazio (ōrä'tsyō bānāvô'lē), 1605-72, Italian composer. From 1646 until his death Benevoli was *maestro di cappella* at the Vatican. He wrote a large quantity of sacred music, much of it scored for many vocal parts—a mass (1628) for Salzburg Cathedral has 52 vocal parts. Benevoli was strongly influenced by Palestrina in his use of harmony.

Ben Ezra: see IBN EZRA, ABRAHAM BEN MEIR.

Bengal (bĕng-gôl', bĕn-), region, 77,442 sq mi (200,575 sq km), E India and Bangladesh, on the Bay of Bengal. The inland sections are mountainous, with peaks up to 12,000 ft (3,660 m) high in the northwest, but most of Bengal is the fertile land of the Ganges-Brahmaputra alluvial plains and delta. Along the coast are richly timbered jungles, swamps, and islands. The heavy monsoon rainfall and predominantly warm weather make possible two harvests a year. In the 3d cent. B.C., Bengal belonged to the empire of ASOKA. It became a political entity in the 8th cent. A.D. under the Buddhist Pala kings. In the 11th cent. the Hindu Sena dynasty arose from the remnants of the Pala empire. Bengal was conquered (c.1200) by Muslims of Turki descent. When the Portuguese began their trading activities (late 15th cent.), Bengal was a part of the Muslim MOGUL empire. The British East India Company made its first settlement in 1642 and extended its occupation by conquering the native princes and expelling the Dutch and French. Muslim control of Bengal ended with the defeat of Siraj-ud-Daula by British forces under Robert CLIVE at the Battle of Plassey in 1757. Under British control, Bengal was a presidency of India. At various times the neighboring provinces of Assam, Bihar, and Orissa were administered under the Bengal presidency. The population, which speaks mainly Bengali, is ethnically quite homogeneous but is almost equally divided between Muslims and Hindus. When India was partitioned in 1947, the presidency was divided along the line approximately separating the two main concentrations of the religious communities. **West Bengal** (1971 pop. 44,440,095), 33,928 sq mi (87,874 sq km), with its capital at CALCUTTA, became a state of India. It is bordered by Bangladesh and the state of Assam on the east, Bhutan and Sikkim on the north, the states of Bihar and Orissa on the west, and the Bay of Bengal on the south. A highly industrialized region, it has jute mills, steel plants, and chemical industries, all mainly centered in the Hooghlyside industrial complex. Coal is mined and petroleum is exploited. In 1950, West Bengal absorbed the state of Cooch Behar. In more recent years, disputes between Hindus and Muslims, further complicated by droves of refugees from Bangladesh (formerly East Pakistan) and agitation by Maoist groups called Naxalites, have created political instability. West Bengal is governed by a chief minister and cabinet responsible to a bicameral legislature with one elected house and by a governor appointed by the president of India. In the 1972 local elections Prime Minister Gandhi's New Congress party ended the decade-old dominance of the Communist Party of India-Marxist, also known as the Left Communists, who broke away from the more conservative and pro-Soviet Communist party. **East Bengal,** overwhelmingly Muslim in population, became East Pakistan in 1947 and the independent nation of Bangladesh in 1971.

Bengal, Bay of, arm of the Indian Ocean, c.1,300 mi (2,090 km) long and 1,000 mi (1,610 km) wide, bordered on the W by Sri Lanka (Ceylon) and India, on the N by Bangladesh, and on the E by Burma and Thailand; the Andaman and Nicobar Islands separate it from the Andaman Sea, its eastern arm. The bay receives many large rivers including the Irrawaddy, Ganges-Brahmaputra, Mahanadi, Godavari, Kristna, and Cauvery, all forming fertile, heavily populated deltas. Sediment from the rivers has made the bay a shallow sea, and the waters have reduced the salinity of surface waters along the shore. Monsoon rains and destructive cyclone storms have caused great loss of life along the bay's northern coast. The main ports are Visakhapatnam, Madras, and Calcutta, India; Chittagong, Bangladesh; and Sittwe, Burma.

Bengali (bĕngäl'ē), language belonging to the Indic group of the Indo-Iranian subfamily of the Indo-European family of languages. See INDO-IRANIAN LANGUAGES.

Bengasi or **Benghazi** (both: bĕngä'zē), city (1970 est. pop. 170,000), capital of Bengasi district, NE Libya, the main city of Cyrenaica and a port on the Mediterranean Sea. It is primarily an administrative and commercial center. Manufactures include processed food, beverages, textiles, and cement. On the site of Bengasi the Greeks founded (7th cent. B.C.) the colony of Hesperides, which was later (3rd cent. B.C.) renamed Berenice after the wife of Ptolemy III of Egypt. Under the Romans, who conquered it in the mid-1st cent. B.C., Bengasi had a large Jewish colony. In the 5th cent. A.D. the Vandals severely damaged the city, and in the 7th cent. it was captured by the Arabs. The Ottoman Turks took the city in the mid-16th cent., and they held it until it was captured by Italy in 1911. The Italians modernized the city and enlarged its port. At the start of World War II, Bengasi had about 22,000 Italian inhabitants, but they were evacuated before the city fell to the British in late 1942. From 1951 to 1972 Bengasi was the cocapital (with Tripoli) of Libya. The city is the site of the Univ. of Libya, founded in 1955.

Bengel, Johann Albrecht (yō'hän äl'brĕkht bĕng'əl), 1687-1752, German Lutheran theologian and biblical scholar. He was appointed (1713) professor in charge of a theological training school at Denkendorf and remained there for 28 years. In this period he produced his most important works—a carefully prepared Greek text of the New Testament (1734), with an *Apparatus criticus,* which formed the point of departure for modern New Testament textual criticism, and his *Gnomon Novi Testamenti* (1742), an exegetical commentary, later translated into German and English.

Benghazi: see BENGASI, Libya.

Benguela (bĕngĕl'ə, bĕng-), city (1969 est. pop. 35,000), W Angola, on the Atlantic. It is a rail terminus, an export point, and a commercial and fishing center. A fort was built on the site in the late 16th cent., and the city was founded in 1617. Benguela's port played an important role in slave trading.

Ben-Gurion, David (bĕn-go͞o'rēōn), 1886-1973, Israeli statesman, b. Poland as David Grün. He settled in Palestine in 1906. He was an active Zionist and during World War I helped to organize the Jewish Legion in support of the British. In the struggle to found an independent Jewish state in Palestine he followed a policy of cooperation with the British during World War II. After the war, however, he led the political struggle against them, authorizing the sabotage activities of the Hebrew resistance movement. During the struggle for independence (1947-48) he headed the defense effort. A founder and leader of the Mapai party and an early leader of the Histadrut, he was made (1948) the first prime minister of the newly created state of Israel, holding the post until 1953. In 1955 he returned to the cabinet as defense minister under Moshe Sharett and later that year again became prime minister. His replacement of Sharett reflected the shift in Israeli policy toward confrontation with Israel's hostile Arab neighbors. Amid growing controversy he resigned the premiership in Feb., 1961, but was quickly returned to office. He again resigned in June, 1963. In retirement Ben-Gurion continued to be politically active, forming a splinter party from the dominant labor party, Mapai, in 1965. A selection of his writings was published as *Rebirth and Destiny of Israel* (1954); he also wrote *Israel: Years of Challenge* (1965), *Israel's Security* (1960), *The Jews in their Land* (1966), *Memoirs* (1970), *Israel: A Personal History* (1971), and *My Talks with the Arabs* (1973). See biographies by Maurice Edelman (1964), Michael Bar-Zohar (tr. 1967), Ohad Zmora, ed. (1967), and Robert St. John (rev. ed. 1971).

Benha: see BANHA, Egypt.

Benhadad (bĕnhā'dăd), kings of Damascus. **1** The son of Tabrimon, ally of ASA of Judah against Baasha of Israel. 1 Kings 15.17-20. **2** Probably the son and successor of **1,** leader of the coalition that withstood Shalmaneser III of Assyria at Karkar on the Orontes; he continued the traditional enmity of his kingdom with Israel and defeated AHAB and Jehoshaphat. He was murdered and succeeded by Hazael. 1 Kings 20, 22; 2 Kings 8.15. **3** Son of Hazael and contemporary of Jehoash of Israel, who defeated him in war. He also was Assyria's vassal. 2 Kings 13.25; Amos 1.4.

Ben-hail (bēn-hā'ĭl), one of Jehoshaphat's princes. 2 Chron. 17.7.

Ben-hanan (bĕn-hā'năn), Judahite. 1 Chron. 4.20.

Ben-hur: see HUR **4.**

Beni Hasan: see BANI HASAN, village, Egypt.

Beni Israel: see BENE ISRAEL.

Benin (bĕnĕn'), city (1969 est. pop. 117,000), S Nigeria, a port on the Benin River. Rubber, palm nuts, and timber are produced nearby and processed in Benin. Furniture and carpets are also made in the city. Benin served as the capital of a black African kingdom that was probably founded in the 13th cent. and flourished from the 14th through the 17th cent. The kingdom was ruled by the *oba* (to whose family human sacrifices were made) and a sophisticated bureaucracy. From the late 15th cent. Benin traded slaves as well as ivory, pepper, and cloth to Europeans. In the early 16th cent. the *oba* sent an ambassador to Lisbon, and the king of Portugal sent missionaries to Benin. The kingdom of Benin declined after 1700, but revived in the 19th cent. with the development of the trade in palm products with Europeans. Britain conquered and burned the city in 1898 following conflicts between black African and European traders. The iron work, carved ivory, and bronze portrait busts made (perhaps as early as the 13th cent.) in Benin rank with the finest art of Africa. CIRE PERDUE casting is still practiced there. Examples of Benin art are displayed in museums in the city.

Benin, Bight of, northern arm of the Gulf of Guinea, c.550 mi (885 km) wide, W Africa, between Cape Three Points, S Ghana, and the Niger River delta, SW Nigeria.

Beninu (bēnī'nyo͞o), Levite sealer of the covenant. Neh. 10.13.

Beni Suef: see BANI SUWAYF, Egypt.

Benjamin. **1** Youngest son of Jacob and Rachel and ancestor of one of the 12 tribes of Israel. His mother, dying, named him Benoni (bĕnō'nī) [Heb.,=son of my sorrow]. He was the favorite of his family. The tribe of Benjamin was allotted the plateau of E central Palestine lying W of the Jordan between Jerusalem and Bethel. The tribesmen were famous archers. The name survived in the High Gate of Benjamin of the Temple at Jerusalem. Saul was the most noted man of the house of Benjamin. Gen. 35.18; 42-46; 49.27; Num. 1.36; 13.9; 26.38-41; 34,21; Deut. 33.12; Joshua 18.11-28; Judges 3.15; 20-21; 1 Chron. 8.40; 12.2; 2 Chron. 14.8; 17.17. **2** Descendant of Benjamin. 1 Chron. 7.10. **3** One who was separated from a foreign wife. Ezra 10.32. **4** Repairer of the wall. Neh. 3.23. **5** Dedicator of the wall. Neh. 12.34. He may be the same person as **3** and as **4.**

Benjamin, Asher, 1773-1845, American architect, b. Greenfield, Mass. His *Country Builder's Assistant* was published in 1797 and *The American Builder's Companion,* with Daniel Reynard, in 1806. Benjamin designed houses and churches in many New England towns, but his greater influence was through his books, which popularized the details of the late colonial style. His later books, *The Rudiments of Architecture* (1814) and *The Practical House Carpenter* (1830), show more Greek design.

Benjamin, Judah Philip, 1811-84, Confederate statesman and British barrister, b. Christiansted, St. Croix, Virgin Islands, of Jewish parents. His family moved (c.1813) to Wilmington, N.C., and finally settled (1822) in Charleston, S.C. A precocious youth, Benjamin entered Yale at the age of 14 but left (1827) early in his junior year. He went to New Orleans in 1828, worked for a notary, taught English, and studied French and the law in his spare time. Admitted to the bar in Dec., 1832, he published (1834), with his friend Thomas Slidell, a digest of Louisiana appeal cases that enhanced his reputation as a rising young lawyer. His practice soon made him rich enough to become a sugar planter as well. Benjamin, a prominent Whig, served in both branches of the state legislature, was a delegate to two state constitutional conventions, and in 1852 was elected to the U.S. Senate. On the dissolution of the Whig party because of the slavery issue, he publicly proclaimed himself a Democrat (May 2, 1856), and two years later he was reelected Senator. One of the ablest defenses of Southern policy was presented in the Senate by Benjamin on Dec. 31, 1860. On Feb. 4, 1861, after Louisiana's secession, he resigned his seat. In the new Southern government, Benjamin first served as attorney general, was appointed secretary of war in Nov., 1861 (he had been acting secretary since September), and from March, 1862, to the end of the Civil War was secretary of state. Though not popular with the public, he was an intimate friend of Jefferson DAVIS and was known in the North as "the brains of the Confederacy." As secretary of war he was an able administrator, but was severely criticized—for the most part unjustly—for Confederate defeats early in 1862, particularly the loss of Roanoke Island, N.C. After Davis promoted him to head the state department, Benjamin worked unceasingly but unsuccessfully to secure European recognition of the Confederacy. In Feb., 1865, he proposed that slaves who willingly joined the Confederate ranks be freed. Upon the collapse of the Confederacy, Benjamin escaped by way of Florida and the West Indies to England and there established a new career in the law. He was called to the bar in 1866 and won immediate recognition with *A Treatise on the Law of Sale of Personal Property* (1868). On his retirement early in 1883 he was universally acknowledged to have been in the front rank of his profession. He died and was buried in Paris, where his wife, who was a Louisiana Creole, and his daughter had made their home since the 1840s. See biography by R. D. Meade (1943); A. L. Goodhart, *Five Jewish Lawyers of the Common Law* (1949, repr. 1971).

Benjamin, Park, 1809-64, American journalist, b. British Guiana. As owner and editor of the *New England Magazine,* he merged it (1835) with the *American Monthly Magazine* of New York and became associate editor with C. F. Hoffman. A prominent journalist of his day, he is best known as the founder (1839) of the *New World,* a weekly periodical that ran until 1845. See biography by M. M. Hoover (1948).

Benjamin Constant, Paul Henri: see ESTOURNELLES DE CONSTANT.

Benjamin Franklin National Memorial, Pa.: see NATIONAL PARKS AND MONUMENTS, table.

Benjamin of Tudela (to͞odā'lä), d. 1173, Jewish traveler, b. Tudela, Spain. He traveled from 1159 to 1173 and is considered to be the first European to have reached China. His account, *Massaoth Schel Rabbi Benjamin,* sheds light on the history of the times. An English translation was published in 1840 as *The Itinerary of Rabbi Benjamin of Tudela.* See the critical text, tr. and ed. by M. N. Adler (1964).

Ben Macdhui (măkdo͞o'ē), peak, 4,296 ft (1,309 m) high, SW Aberdeenshire, Scotland, in the Cairngorm mts.; second highest peak in Scotland.

Benn, Anthony Wedgwood, 1925-, British politician. After working as a producer for the British Broadcasting Corporation (1949-50), he was elected a Labour member of Parliament in 1950. He inherited the title of Viscount Stansgate (1960) after two unsuccessful attempts to disclaim it in order to retain his seat in the House of Commons. With the passage of the Peerage Act (1963), for which he was largely responsible, he was able to renounce the title for his lifetime and regain his seat in the Commons. In Harold Wilson's first Labour government he served as postmaster general (1964-66) and minister of technology (1966-70), and he was opposition spokesman on trade and industry (1970-74). In the 1974 Labour government he was made secretary of state for industry and minister of posts and telecommunications. See his *Regeneration of Britain* (1965) and *The New Politics* (1970).

Benn, Gottfried (gôt'frēt bĕn), 1886-1956, German poet and critic, a physician. His early verse and poetic dramas, such as *Der Vermessungsdirigent* [the surveyor] (1919), were strongly expressionistic and even nihilistic. His later poems, among them the collection *Statische Gedichte* (1948), and his autobiography, *Doppelleben* [double life] (1950), reflect the agony and conflict of the National Socialist era. Benn's essays on aesthetics and politics are well known, and his fictional works, including *Der Ptolemäer* (1949), are more philosophical prose than tales. See study by J. M. Ritchie (1973).

Bennet, Henry: see ARLINGTON, HENRY BENNET, 1ST EARL OF.

Bennett, Arnold (Enoch Arnold Bennett), 1867-1931, English novelist and dramatist. One of the great 20th-century English novelists, Bennett is famous for his realistic novels about the "Five Towns," an imaginary manufacturing district in northern England. Bennett's early career included editing the fashionable magazine *Woman* and writing literary reviews and articles. About 1900 he began to devote himself industriously to his own work, producing a series of excellent regional novels. Influenced by the NATURALISM of Zola, he depicted in great detail the grim, sometimes sordid, lives of shopkeepers and potters. His attitude toward his characters was one of affectionate sympathy, and he always managed to make their mundane lives interesting. Bennett's best work is contained in his novels of the "Five Towns," which include *Anna of the Five Towns* (1902), *The Old Wives' Tale* (1908), the trilogy *Clayhanger* (1910), *Hilda Lessways* (1911), and *These Twain* (1916). Bennett also achieved considerable success as a playwright, most notably with *Milestones* (1912), written with Edward Knoblock, and *The Great Adventure* (1913). See his journal (3 vol., 1932-33); biography by Margaret Drabble (1974); studies by John Wain (1967), K. E. Roby (1972), and James G. Hepburn (1963; repr. 1973).

Bennett, Hugh Hammond, 1881-1960, American soil scientist, b. near Wadesboro, N.C. Known as the father of soil conservation, he first proposed the theory of sheet erosion of soils in 1905. He directed national programs of soil and water conservation and wrote many articles on the subject, laying the groundwork for consideration of soil conservation by Congress. His books include *Soil Conservation* (1939) and *This Land We Defend* (1942).

Bennett, James Gordon, 1795-1872, American newspaper proprietor, b. Keith, Scotland. He came to America in 1819 and won a reputation as Washington correspondent of the New York *Enquirer* and later (1829-32) as assistant editor of the combined *Courier and Enquirer.* On May 6, 1835, he launched his New York *Herald,* a new penny paper of four four-column pages. His capital totaled $500 and his office was a Wall St. cellar, yet in less than a year the paper sold almost 15,000 copies daily. Bennett's innovations made the *Herald* a landmark in the history of American journalism: in his brief editorials he criticized all political parties; he included new fields of news, notably that of Wall St. finance; he first established (1838) European correspondents for his paper; he first used the telegraph extensively in newspaper work; and he first used illustrations for news articles. Although the *Herald* initially gained an audience by playing up sensational and cheap news, it later earned a reputation as a full and accurate paper, particularly in the period of the Civil War, when Bennett employed 63 war correspondents and spent $525,000 on war reporting. See Oliver Carlson, *The Man Who Made News: James Gordon Bennett* (1942).

Bennett, James Gordon, 1841-1918, American newspaper proprietor, b. New York City; son of James Gordon Bennett. Educated mostly in France, he took over (1867) from his father the management of the New York *Herald* and maintained the paper's reputation as a news gatherer. In 1869-71 he financed Henry Stanley's expedition into Africa to find David Livingston, and from 1879 to 1881 he supported the ill-fated expedition of G. W. De Long to the arctic region. In reporting international news the *Herald* scored repeated triumphs. Its staff of brilliant reporters was famous. After 1877, Bennett lived mostly in Paris, directing his newspapers by cable, and with John W. Mackay he organized (1883) the Commercial Cable Company to handle European dispatches. He established London and Paris daily editions of the *Herald;* the Paris paper was an unprofitable, sincere attempt to promote international good will. Bennett was fond of sports, especially of yachting, and established the James Gordon Bennett cup as a trophy in international yacht races and similar cups for balloon and airplane races. See Richard O'Connor, *The Scandalous Mr. Bennett* (1962); D. C. Seitz, *The James Gordon Bennetts* (1928, repr. 1973).

Bennett, Richard Bedford, 1870-1947, Canadian prime minister, b. Hopewell, N.B. In 1927 he succeeded Arthur Meighen as leader of the Conservative party; upon the defeat of the Liberals in 1930, he became prime minister. At the imperial conference in London in 1930, he strongly urged a preferential tariff for the empire; at the conference held in Ottawa in 1932, over which he presided, his policy was partly adopted with the signing of 12 separate trade agreements of Great Britain with the dominions and of the dominions with each other. As prime minister during the depression, Bennett proposed social legislation in 1934 to lessen the widespread dissatisfaction with his government. Nevertheless, his Conservative party was defeated in 1935 and Bennett resigned. He was leader of the opposition until 1938, when he retired from politics and went to live in England. In 1941 he was raised to the peerage as 1st Viscount Bennett of Calgary, of Mickleham, and of Hopewell.

Bennett, Sir William Sterndale, 1816-75, English musician. Bennett was a friend of Mendelssohn and Schumann, both of whom influenced his work. Besides composing, he was active as a pianist and conductor. He founded the Bach Society and in 1854 gave the first public British performance of the St. Matthew Passion. Bennett's compositions include a symphony, four piano concertos, and much solo piano music.

Ben Nevis (nē'vĭs, nĕv'ĭs), peak, 4,406 ft (1,343 m) high, Inverness-shire, W Scotland, overlooking Glen Nevis; highest peak of Great Britain. Ruins of an observatory are on the summit, from which there is an impressive view, especially on the northeastern side with its precipice of more than 1,450 ft (442 m).

Bennewitz, Peter: see APIANUS, PETRUS.

Bennigsen, Rudolf von (ro͞o'dôlf fən bĕn'ĭksən), 1824-1902, German political leader. A liberal and a nationalist from Hanover, he favored German unification under a democratic Prussian state. After Bismarck's initial successes in unifying Germany, however, he supported the chancellor and helped found (1867) the National Liberal party. President of the party until 1898, he was an important figure in the Reichstag and in the Prussian lower house.

Bennington, town (1970 pop. 14,586), seat of Bennington co., SW Vt.; chartered 1749, settled 1761. It includes the villages of North Bennington and Old Bennington. Major manufactures of the town are automotive batteries, paper products, electronic components, air-conditioning equipment, lubricating equipment, furniture, and lithographic products. The surrounding area has dairy farms and several ski resorts. Points of interest in Bennington include a monument that is 300 ft (91 m) high commemorating the Revolutionary War battle of Bennington (see SARATOGA CAMPAIGN); the site of the first schoolhouse in Vermont; Catamount Tavern, meeting place of the Green Mountain Boys; the site of abolitionist William Lloyd Garrison's printing shop; the Old First Church (1805); and the Walloomsac Inn, opened in 1763. Bennington College is in the town.

Bennington College, at Bennington, Vt.; coeducational (originally for women); chartered 1925, opened 1932. Its curriculum is based on individual interests and needs. All students are required to devote part of their time to off-campus employment, usually relating to their course of study. Many faculty members are practicing artists, and a close relationship between students and faculty is encouraged.

Benno, Saint, d. 1106, German prelate. He was bishop of Meissen and an ardent supporter of Pope Gregory VII against Holy Roman Emperor Henry IV, and the emperor had him deposed. He was reinstated on Gregory's death by GUIBERT OF RAVENNA (the antipope Clement III). He later shifted his allegiance to Guibert's adversary, Pope Urban II. Luther was greatly displeased at the canonization (1523) of Benno. St. Benno is a patron of Munich. Feast: June 16.

Beno (bē'nō), Levite. 1 Chron. 24.26,27.

Benoît de Sainte-More or **Benoît de Sainte-Maure** (bĕnwä' də săNt-môr'), 1154-73, French trouvère. He was the author of the *Roman de Troie,* a romance in 30,000 verses based on historical accounts by Dares and Dictys. It became a primary source of medieval versions of the Trojan legend, notably the story of TROILUS. At the order of Henry II of England, Benoît also wrote a rhymed *Chronique des ducs de Normandie.*

Benoni (bĕnō'nī): see BENJAMIN **1.**

Benoni (bənō'nē), town (1970 pop. 149,563), Transvaal, NE South Africa, on the WITWATERSRAND. It is the distribution center for a gold-mining district. The chief manufacture is electrical equipment. Benoni was founded in 1904. During the violent Witwatersrand miners' strike of 1922, through which white miners sought in vain to prevent mine owners from employing cheaper black African labor, heavy fighting occurred in the town between miners and the South African military. Benoni has commercial and technical schools.

Benozzo Gozzoli: see GOZZOLI, BENOZZO.

Bensenville, village (1970 pop. 12,833), Cook and Du Page counties, NE Ill., a suburb of Chicago; inc. 1894. It has varied light manufactures. O'Hare International Airport is nearby.

Benson, Arthur Christopher, 1862-1925, English author; eldest son of Archbishop Benson. He was master at Eton (1885-1903) and at Magdalene College, Cambridge (1915-25). His works include poetry; novels; essays, notably *From a College Window* (1902); critical studies; and biographies of his father and brother Hugh. See his *Memories and Friends* (1924); selections from his diary (ed. by Percy Lubbock, 1926).

Benson, Edward Frederic, 1867-1940, English author; 3d son of Archbishop Benson. He wrote several biographies and reflections on contemporary society, but he is chiefly remembered for his lightly satirical novels, notably *Dodo* (1893) and the series about Lucia Pillson, the first of which was *Queen Lucia* (1920). His archaeological work in Athens (1892-95) resulted in two novels on Greece, *The Vintage* (1898) and *The Capsina* (1899).

Benson, Edward White, 1829-96, archbishop of Canterbury, educated at Trinity College, Cambridge. He was appointed (1877) the first bishop of Truro, and in 1882 he was appointed archbishop of Canterbury. His clerical writings include *Cyprian* (1897) and *Apocalypse* (1900). Three of his four sons became notable literary figures—A. C. Benson, E. F. Benson, and R. H. Benson. See biography by A. C. Benson (1899).

Benson, Ezra Taft, 1899-, U.S. Secretary of Agriculture (1953-61), b. Whitney, Idaho. An extension economist and marketing specialist at the Univ. of Idaho (1930-38) and executive secretary of the National Council of Farmer Cooperatives (1939-44), he was chairman of the board of trustees of the American Institute of Cooperatives when appointed Secretary of Agriculture. His policies—among other things he opposed rigid price supports at 90% of parity in favor of flexible price supports—brought him much criticism, even from Republican Congressmen. In 1959 farm belt members of the Republican National Committee sought Benson's resignation. He refused, stating that he would continue to fight to oust government from agriculture. A devout Mormon, he became (1943) a member of the Council of Twelve (the Apostles). Benson wrote *Farmers at the Crossroads* (1956), *Freedom to Farm* (1960), *Title of Liberty* (1964), and *An Enemy Hath Done This* (1969). See his *Cross Fire: The Eight Years with Eisenhower* (1962); biography by Wesley McCune (1958).

Benson, Robert Hugh, 1871-1914, English author and clergyman; 4th son of Archbishop Benson. He was converted to Roman Catholicism in 1903 and ordained the next year. In 1911, as a monsignor, he became privy chamberlain to Pope Pius X. His works include the novels *By What Authority?* (1904) and *Richard Raynal* (1906), and *Paradoxes of Catholicism* (1913). See biography by A. C. Benson (1915).

Bent, Charles, 1799-1847, American frontiersman, b. St. Louis. He entered the fur trade of the Missouri River and became one of the mountain men. His interests turned to the Southwest, and he led expeditions on the Santa Fe Trail. Charles Bent was the senior partner of a trading firm that included Ceran St. Vrain as well as William Bent and others of the seven Bent brothers. The company was one of the most prominent on the frontier, and BENT'S FORT was one of the most famous American trading posts. Because of his high standing, Charles Bent was chosen as governor of New Mexico after the American occupation in the Mexican War. He was murdered at Taos in an uprising of Indians and Mexicans.

Bent, James Theodore, 1853-97, English explorer and archaeologist. He engaged in archaeological research on the coast of Asia Minor (1888-89), the Bahrein Islands (1889), Cilicia Trachia (1890), Mashonaland (1891), Ethiopia (1893), and the Arabian peninsula (1893-97), where he mapped the Hadramaut region. He wrote *The Ruined Cities of Mashonaland* (1892), *The Sacred City of the Ethiopians* (1893), and *Southern Arabia* (1900).

Bent, William, 1809-69, American frontiersman, b. St. Louis. One of the younger brothers of Charles Bent, he was for many years the manager of BENT'S FORT, while Charles Bent lived mainly in Taos. William Bent was one of the most widely known and highly respected traders in the West. He scouted for Stephen W. Kearny and Sterling Price in the Mexican War. In 1849 he destroyed the fort, building another farther down the Arkansas River (1853).

bent grass, any species of the genus *Agrostis* of the family Gramineae (GRASS family), chiefly slender, delicate plants native to cool climates. Many are used for forage or lawns. Important species naturalized from Europe include the creeping bent (*A. palustris*), a lawn and putting-green grass; colonial bent (*A. tenuis*), frequently used in lawn mixtures; and especially, redtop (*A. alba*), called also fiorin and herd's-grass. Redtop, a perennial with reddish panicles, is much used (often mixed with clover) for pasture and hay in NE America; it is also effective in erosion control. The cloud grass (*A. nebulosa*), native to Spain, is cultivated for use as an EVERLASTING. Bent grass is classified in the division MAGNOLIOPHYTA, class Liliatae, order Cyperales, family Gramineae.

Bentham, George (bĕn'thəm), 1800-1884, one of the greatest of English systematic botanists; nephew of Jeremy Bentham. He wrote *Handbook of British Flora* (1858) and (with W. J. Hooker) *Genera Plantarum* (1862-83) and handbooks on the flora of several British possessions.

Bentham, Jeremy, 1748-1832, English philosopher, jurist, political theorist, and founder of UTILITARIANISM. Educated at Oxford, he was trained as a lawyer and was admitted to the bar, but he never practiced; he devoted himself to the scientific analysis of morals and legislation. His greatest work was his *Introduction to the Principles of Morals and Legislation* (1789), which shows the influence of Helvétius and won Bentham recognition throughout the Western world. His utilitarianism held that the greatest happiness of the greatest number is the fundamental and self-evident principle of morality. This principle should govern our judgment of every institution and action. He identified happiness with pleasure and devised a moral arithmetic for judging the value of a pleasure or a pain. He argued that self-interests, properly understood, are harmonious and that the general welfare is bound up with personal happiness. Bentham's contribution to theoretical ethics has had less lasting effect than his thorough application of utilitarian principles to economics, jurisprudence, and politics. Devoting himself to the reform of English legislation and law, he demanded prison reform, codification of the laws, and extension of political franchise. The 19th-century reforms of criminal law, of judicial organization, and of the parliamentary electorate owe much to the influence of Bentham and his disciples. See his *Correspondence,* ed. by T. L. Sprigge and L. R. Christie (3 vol., 1968-71); John MacCunn, *Six Radical Thinkers* (1964); studies by M. P. Mack (1963) and David Lyons (1973).

benthos: see MARINE BIOLOGY.

Bentinck, William: see PORTLAND, WILLIAM BENTINCK, 1ST EARL OF.

Bentinck, Lord William Cavendish (bĕn'tĭngk, -tĭk), 1774-1839, British administrator in India. He served in the Napoleonic Wars and was (1803-7) governor of Madras. He was appointed governor general of Bengal in 1827, assuming the title governor general of India in 1833. Bentinck was strongly influenced by British utilitarianism and introduced many reforms in the interest of the people. He admitted Indians to important office, fostered communication and education, and revised the system of landholding. He also abolished SUTTEE and began suppression of the THUGS. See biography by John Rosselli (1974).

Bentinck, Lord William George Frederick Cavendish, 1802-48, English politician and sportsman, known as Lord George. Although he entered Parliament in 1826, he was known primarily for his horse-racing activities until in 1846 he emerged as a leading opponent of the repeal of the corn laws. His brilliant leadership, with DISRAELI, of the protectionists was cut short by his sudden death.

Bentinck, William Henry Cavendish: see PORTLAND, WILLIAM HENRY CAVENDISH BENTINCK, 3D DUKE OF.

Bentivoglio (bän'tēvō'lyō), Italian noble family, one of several powerful clans in the struggle for control of BOLOGNA during most of the 15th cent. Its greatest member was Giovanni II, who was lord—in fact if not in name—from 1462 until 1506, when Pope Julius II took Bologna. Giovanni II maintained a splendid court and beautified his city. After its exile from Bologna the family resided in Ferrara and produced several important prelates.

Bentley, Eric, 1916–, American critic, editor, and translator, b. England, grad. Oxford, 1938, Ph.D. Yale, 1941. A highly regarded critic, particularly of the drama, Bentley is the author of *A Century of Hero-Worship* (1944), *The Playwright as Thinker* (1946), *Bernard Shaw* (1947), *What Is Theatre?* (1956), *The Importance of Scrutiny* (1964), and *Theatre of War* (1972). He is also known for his translations of plays of Bertolt Brecht and Luigi Pirandello and for his editions of collected plays, including *The Classic Theatre* (4 vol., 1958-61). He was drama critic for the *New Republic* from 1952 to 1956. From 1953 to 1969 he was Brander Matthews professor of dramatic literature at Columbia.

Bentley, Richard, 1662-1742, English critic and philologist. He was largely responsible for the high standards of textual criticism in the work of his many followers, and he is generally considered the greatest of English classical scholars. His exposure of a 14th-century forgery, *The Epistles of Phalaris,* is his most celebrated work. See biography by Adam Fox (1954).

Bentley, William, 1759-1819, American Unitarian clergyman, b. Boston. From 1783 until his death he was pastor of East Church, Salem, Mass. His *Diary* (4 vol., 1905-14), covering the years 1784-1819, is a valuable historical source.

Benton, Thomas Hart, 1782-1858, U.S. Senator (1821-51), b. Hillsboro, N.C. He moved to Tennessee in 1809, was admitted to the bar in 1811, and served (1809-11) in the state senate. In 1815, Benton went to St. Louis, where he became editor of the *Missouri Enquirer,* established a thriving law practice, and won political prestige. He entered the U.S. Senate on Missouri's admission to the Union in 1821 and was four times reelected. A supporter from 1824 of Andrew Jackson, with whom he had been at odds, Benton was a power in the administrations of Jackson and Martin Van Buren. He played one of the most prominent parts in the successful war on the Bank of the United States. A rigid "hard money" man (he delighted in the sobriquet "Old Bullion"), Benton had the ratio of silver to gold revised from 15 to 1 to 16 to 1 in 1834 and thus brought gold into circulation again. Congress defeated his resolution requiring that the public lands be paid for in hard money only, but Jackson immediately legalized the idea in an executive order (1836), the famous Specie Circular, which Benton drew up. His currency measures, intended to discourage continued land speculation and thereby encourage actual settlement of the West, were supported by Eastern workingmen, who wished to be paid in specie rather than in notes of uncertain value. Benton also supported all legislation that aided settlers and favored the development of the West, including reduction in the price of government lands, suppression of land speculation, westward removal of the Indians, and internal improvements. He advocated government support of Western exploration, with which he was intimately connected through the expeditions of John Charles FRÉMONT, who married one of his four daughters, Jessie Benton FRÉMONT. The Oregon country especially interested him, and he protested the joint occupation with Britain. Yet he insisted that the 49th parallel (the line established) was the only boundary the United States could rightfully claim and deplored the Democratic campaign slogan of 1844—"Fifty-four forty or fight." As to Texas, although he had protested the 1819 treaty with Spain as one in which the United States gave up its rights to that region, he could not acquiesce in the intrigues that led to the annexation of Texas and the Mexican War. Benton had early come to favor the gradual abolition of slavery, and with the ascendancy of the proslavery Democrats he lost influence in the party. His antislavery sentiments ran counter to majority opinion in Missouri at that time, and with his opposition to the proslavery features of the Compromise of 1850 he was defeated for a sixth term. He returned to Congress as a U.S. Representative (1853-55) but after voting against the Kansas-Nebraska Act in 1854 he was again defeated for reelection. In 1856 he was also defeated for the governorship of Missouri. He compiled *An Abridgment of the Debates of Congress from 1789 to 1856* (16 vol., 1857-61) and wrote the autobiographical *Thirty Years' View* (2 vol., 1854-56). See biographies by Theodore Roosevelt (1886, repr. 1968), W. N. Chambers (1956, repr. 1970), and W. M. Meigs (1904, repr. 1970).

Benton, Thomas Hart, 1889-1975, American regionalist painter, b. Neosho, Mo.; grandnephew of Sen. Thomas Hart Benton and son of Congressman Maecenas E. Benton. In 1906 and 1907 he attended the Art Institute of Chicago and at 19 went to Paris, where he remained five years. On his return to the United States, he designed movie sets, managed an art gallery, and continued to paint. The best-known American muralist of the 1930s and early 40s, he executed murals for the New School of Social Research and the Whitney Museum, both in New York City; the Missouri statehouse, Jefferson City, Mo.; and the Post Office Dept. and Dept. of Justice buildings, Washington, D.C. He is noted for his dramatization of American themes. His style is graphic, strong in color, repetitious and insistent in the use of rhythmic line. *July Hay* (1943) is in the Metropolitan Museum. Benton taught painting at several colleges and art schools. See his autobiographical *An Artist in America* (1951, rev. ed. 1968) and *An American in Art* (1969).

Benton, city (1970 pop. 16,499), seat of Saline co., central Ark.; founded 1836. Its chief industry, aluminum mining and refining, is based on the extensive high-grade bauxite deposits found in the area. Nearby is a state hospital.

Benton Harbor, city (1970 pop. 16,481), Berrien co., SW Mich., on Lake Michigan at the mouth of the St. Joseph River and opposite its twin city, St. Joseph; inc. 1869. Its temperate climate has made it the center of Michigan's fruit industry. Fruit is canned and shipped, and home appliances, metal products, cranes, and machine tools are made. The nearby lake and beaches attract vacationers, and the city itself is a popular health resort. The House of David, a religious colony founded there in 1903, has numerous business and farm holdings. The city is the seat of a junior college. A fish hatchery and Warren Dunes State Park are nearby.

bentonite (bĕn'tənīt"): see CLAY.

Bent's Fort, trading post of the American West, on the Arkansas River in present-day SE Colorado, E of Rocky Ford and La Junta and several miles above the mouth of the Purgatoire. The trading company headed by Charles BENT and Ceran St. Vrain, one of the most successful in the West, also included William BENT and two other Bent brothers. They had their first post in the area in 1826 and in 1833 moved to the completed fort, often called Bent's Old Fort. Because William Bent was the manager and chief trader in all the years of its prosperity, it is also sometimes called Fort William. Within its adobe walls came all the famous mountain men of the later period, as the fort on the mountain branch of the Santa Fe Trail came to dominate the trade of all the Indian tribes S of the Black Hills as well as that of the Mexicans and the arriving Americans. Kit Carson was a hunter there from 1831 to 1842. S. W. Kearny and Sterling Price each briefly used the fort for their troops in the Mexican War. According to the generally accepted story, the Indian trade fell off and William Bent attempted to sell the fort to the U.S. government; he reached no satisfactory conclusion and in anger abandoned the fort and set the powder in it on fire, partially destroying it. In any case the fort was abandoned by 1852. William Bent erected a new establishment farther down the Arkansas in 1853. That post (Bent's New Fort) he leased to the government in 1860. Fort Lyon was afterward built around it. See D. S. Lavender, *Bent's Fort* (1954, repr. 1968).

Bent's Old Fort National Historic Site: see NATIONAL PARKS AND MONUMENTS (table).

Benue (bānwā'), river, W Africa, chief tributary of the Niger. It flows c.670 mi (1,080 km) W from the United Republic of Cameroon into the Niger River at LOKOJA, Nigeria. The Benue, which carries much commercial traffic, is almost entirely navigable by power-driven boats in August and September, the height of the rainy season. In 1854, William B. Baikie piloted a steamer c.400 mi (640 km) upstream from Lokoja.

Ben Yehudah, Eliezer (ĕlĭĕ'zər bĕn yĕho͞o'dä), 1858-1922, Jewish scholar and leader, b. Lithuania. He settled in Palestine as early as 1881, where he dedicated himself to the revival of Hebrew as the national language. His outstanding scholarly achievement is the *Dictionary of Ancient and Modern Hebrew* (16 vol.), which includes all the Hebrew words used throughout the various periods of Hebrew literature, omitting the words of Aramaic and foreign origin and adding new words that he coined to meet modern needs. He also founded the Hebrew Language Council, an institution devoted to promoting and regulating the development of the Hebrew language. In 1953 it was transformed into the Academy of Hebrew Language. See Robert St. John, *Tongue of the Prophets: the Life Story of Eliezer Ben Yehuda* (1952).

Benz, Karl (bĕnts), 1844-1929, German engineer, credited with building the first automobile powered by an internal-combustion engine. The car, driven in Mannheim in 1885 and patented in 1886, had three wheels, an electric ignition, and differential gears and was water-cooled. As a result of a merger in 1926, Benz's company became Daimler-Benz AG, the manufacturer of the Mercedes-Benz automobile. See St. J. C. Nixon, *The Invention of the Automobile (Karl Benz and Gottlieb Daimler)* (1936); Eugen Diesel, *From Engine to Autos* (tr., 1960).

benzaldehyde (bĕnzăl'dəhīd) or **benzenecarbonal** (bĕn"zēnkär'bənəl), C_6H_5CHO, colorless liquid ALDEHYDE with a characteristic almond odor. It boils at 180°C, is soluble in ethanol, but is insoluble in water. It is formed by partial oxidation of benzyl alcohol, and on oxidation forms benzoic acid. It is called oil of bitter almond, since it is formed when amygdalin, a glucoside present in the kernels of bitter almonds and in apricot pits, is hydrolyzed, e.g., by crushing the kernels or pits and boiling them in water; glucose and hydrogen cyanide (a poisonous gas) are also formed. It is also prepared by oxidation of toluene or benzyl chloride or by treating benzal chloride with an alkali, e.g., sodium hydroxide. Benzaldehyde is used in the preparation of certain aniline dyes and of other products, including perfumes and flavorings.

Benzedrine (bĕn'zĭdrēn"), trade name for the drug AMPHETAMINE.

benzene (bĕn'zēn, bĕnzēn'), colorless, flammable, toxic liquid with a pleasant aromatic odor. It boils at 80.1°C and solidifies at 5.5°C. Benzene is a HYDROCARBON, with formula C_6H_6. The simplest picture of the benzene molecule, proposed by the German chemist Friedrich Kekulé (1865), is a hexagon of six carbon atoms joined by alternating single and double bonds and each bearing one hydrogen atom, symbolized by ⌬. However, modern studies have shown that the six carbon-carbon bonds are all of equal strength and distance; thus the double-bond electrons do not belong to any particular bonds but rather are delocalized about the ring, with the result that the strength of each bond is between that of a single bond and that of a double bond (see CHEMICAL BOND). Benzene is the parent substance of the AROMATIC COMPOUNDS, a large and important group of organic compounds. It is the first of a series of hydrocarbons known as the benzene series, formed by the substitution of methyl groups, CH_3, for the hydrogen atoms of the benzene molecule. The second member of the series is TOLUENE, $C_6H_5CH_3$, from which TRINITROTOLUENE is derived, and the third member is XYLENE, $C_6H_4(CH_3)_2$, a solvent. In xylene and other benzene derivatives in which two of the hydrogens have been replaced, there are three possible arrangements of the substitution groups; in the *ortho* (*o*) configuration the groups are on adjacent carbon atoms, in the *meta* (*m*) configuration the groups are separated by one carbon atom, and in the *para* (*p*) configuration the groups are on opposite sides of the ring. The three forms of xylene (dimethylbenzene) are shown below:

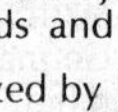

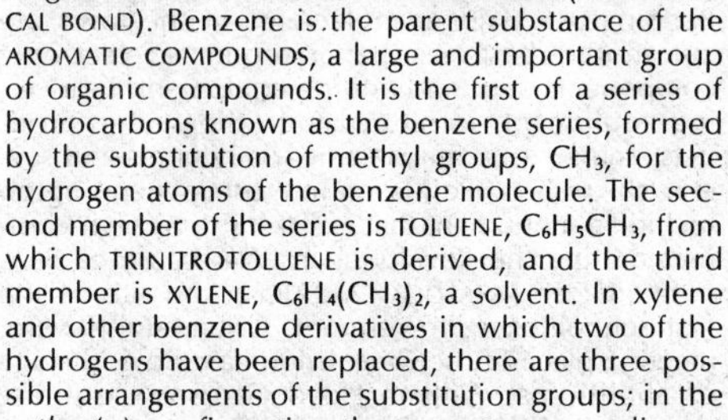

CH_3 CH_3 CH_3 CH_3 CH_3 CH_3

ortho-*xylene* meta-*xylene* para-*xylene*

In addition to derivatives formed by the substitution of other groups for one or more of the hydrogen atoms of the benzene ring, two or more rings may be joined together, as in NAPHTHALENE, ANTHRACENE, and phenanthrene; or other atoms, such as nitrogen, may be substituted for carbon atoms in the ring, as in PYRIDINE (C_5H_5N) and PYRIMIDINE ($C_4H_4N_2$). Among the important derivatives of benzene are PHENOL, ANILINE, and PICRIC ACID. Benzene and the other aromatic hydrocarbons are obtained for industrial purposes from the distillation of coal tar, a by-product in the manufacture of coke, and from petroleum by special cracking methods. They are used in the manufacture of plastics and synthetic rubber and of dyes and drugs.

benzene, dimethyl: see XYLENE.

benzene, 1,2,3-trihydroxy-, IUPAC name for pyrogallol. See GALLIC ACID.

benzenecarbonal, IUPAC name for BENZALDEHYDE.

benzene hexachloride: see INSECTICIDE.

benzine (bĕn'zēn, bĕnzēn'), colorless, highly flammable liquid. It is used as a cleaning agent because it is a solvent for organic substances such as fats, oils, and resins and is also used in the preparation of certain dyes and paints. Benzine is a mixture of hydrocarbons, chiefly alkanes such as pentane and hexane. It is obtained by the fractional distillation of PETROLEUM.

benzoate of soda: see SODIUM BENZOATE.

Ben-zoheth (bĕn-zō'hĕth), Judahite. 1 Chron. 4.20.

benzoic acid (bĕnzō'ĭk), $C_6H_5CO_2H$, crystalline solid organic acid that melts at 122°C and boils at 249°C. It is the simplest aromatic carboxylic acid (see ARYL GROUP and CARBOXYL GROUP). In addition to being synthesized from a variety of organic compounds (e.g., benzyl alcohol, benzaldehyde, toluene, and phthalic acid), it may be obtained from resins, notably gum BENZOIN. It is used largely for making its salts and esters, most notably sodium benzoate, which is widely used as a preservative in foods and beverages and as a mild antiseptic in mouthwashes and toothpastes.

benzoic acid, 2-hydroxy-, IUPAC name for SALICYLIC ACID.

benzoic acid, 3,4,5-trihydroxy-, IUPAC name for GALLIC ACID.

benzoin (bĕn'zoin, -zōĭn) or **benzoinum** (bĕnzoin'əm), balsamic RESIN, the dried exudation from the pierced bark of various species of the benzoin tree (*Styrax*) native to Sumatra, Java, and Thailand; appearing as red-brown to yellow-brown tears. Because of its fragrant odor it is used in perfume and sometimes in incense. The benzoic acid present in it gives it value in medicine as an antiseptic, as a stimulant, and, in certain respiratory diseases, as an inhalant. Among the several varieties are Siam benzoin and Sumatra benzoin. Siam benzoin is considered finer, since it has a high content of benzoic acid; Sumatra benzoin contains cinnamic acid.

Ben-Zvi, Yizhak (yĭtsh'häk bĕn-tsvē), 1884–1963, president of Israel (1952–63), b. Russia, originally named Issac Shimshelevitz. A Zionist, he fled Russia in 1905 because of his activities in the Jewish self-defense movement and settled (1907) in Palestine. With David Ben-Gurion and other Zionist leaders he helped create the Jewish state. In 1952 he succeeded Chaim Weizmann as president of Israel; he was reelected in 1958 and again in 1962. He died in office in 1963. He was a historian and a scholar of note in the field of Jewish ethnology. His writings include *The Moslem World and the Arab World* (1937), *The Exiled and the Redeemed* (new ed. 1961), and *The Hebrew Battalions: Letters* (1969).

Beograd: see BELGRADE, Yugoslavia.

Beolco, Angelo (änjĕ'lō bāōl'kō), 1502–42, Italian actor and playwright. While managing farms belonging to his family, Beolco had much contact with Paduan peasants, with whom he was deeply sympathetic. Their way of life formed the background for his rustic comedies featuring the peasant "Ruzzante," the name commonly given Beolco himself. Using the Paduan dialect, he brought great descriptive powers to his witty depiction of country life.

Beon (bē'ən): see BETH-BAAL-MEON.

Beor (bē'ôr). **1** Father of Balaam. Num. 22.5. Bosor: 2 Peter 2.15. **2** Father of BELA **1**.

Beowulf (bā'əwo͝olf), oldest English epic, probably composed in the early 8th cent. by an Anglian bard in the vicinity of Northumbria. It survives in only one manuscript, written A.D. c.1000 by two scribes and preserved in the British Museum in the collection of Sir Robert Cotton. The materials for the poem are derived mainly from Scandinavian history, folk tale, and mythology. Its narrative consists of two parts: the first relates Beowulf's successful fights with the water monster Grendel and with Grendel's mother; the second narrates the hero's victory in his old age over a dragon and his subsequent death and funeral at the end of a long life of honor. These events take place entirely in Denmark and Sweden. The poem contains a remarkable fusion of pagan and Christian elements and provides a vivid picture of old Germanic life. It is written in a strongly accentual, alliterative verse. See *The Beowulf Poet: A Collection of Critical Essays,* ed. by D. K. Fry (1968); studies by Kenneth Sisam (1965), J. C. Pope (rev. ed. 1966), E. B. Irving (1968), and Ritchie Girvan and Rupert Bruce-Mitford (1971).

Beppu (bāp'po͞o), city (1970 pop. 123,786), Oita prefecture, NE Kyushu, Japan, on Beppu Bay. It is a major fishing port and a tourist resort noted for its numerous hot springs.

Beqa, El: see BIQA, AL.

bequest: see LEGACY.

Bera (bē'rə), king of Sodom. Gen. 14.2.

Berachah (bērā'kə). Beracah RSV. **1** One who joined David at Ziklag. 1 Chron. 12.3. **2** Valley, N of Hebron, running roughly east-west. 2 Chron. 20.26.

Berachiah (bĕr″əkī'ə), variant form of BERECHIAH.

Berachya ben Natronai ha-Nakdan: see BEREKHIAH.

Beraiah (bĕr″aī'ə), Benjamite. 1 Chron. 8.21.

Béranger, Pierre Jean de (pyĕr zhäN də bāräNzhā'), 1780–1857, French lyric poet. He was a protégé of Lucien Bonaparte and a friend of some of the most eminent men of his day. His first collection of songs, published in 1815, was immediately popular. He fitted his verse to popular melodies, and he used his poems largely to express republican and Bonapartist ideas, for which he was twice imprisoned. Some of his most popular pieces are "Le Roi d'Yvetot," "Ce n'est plus Lisette," "Le Grenier," and "Le Dieu des bonnes gens." See translations by William Walsh (1888) and Béranger's autobiography (1857).

Berar, India: see MADHYA PRADESH.

Berat (bĕrät') or **Berati** (bĕrä'tē), town (1970 pop. 25,700), capital of Berat prov., S central Albania. It is a commercial center (producing foodstuffs, textiles, and leather products) and the seat of a bishop of the Albanian Orthodox Church. There is an oil field nearby. Built probably on the site of ancient Antipatrea, Berat fell to the Serbs in 1345 and to the Turks in 1440. A citadel, rebuilt by the Byzantines in the 13th cent., overlooks the town, which has a 15th-century mosque and several old churches. The autocephalic Albanian Orthodox Church was proclaimed there in 1922.

Berbera (bûr'bərə), city (1963 est. pop. 12,000), N Somalia, a port on the Gulf of Aden. The city, which was first described in the 13th cent. by Arab geographers, was taken in 1875 by the rulers of Egypt; when they withdrew in 1884 to fight the Mahdi in Sudan, Britain took Berbera. It served until 1941 as the winter capital of British Somaliland.

Berbers, aboriginal Caucasoid peoples of N Africa. They inhabit the lands lying between the Sahara and the Mediterranean Sea and between Egypt and the Atlantic Ocean. The Berbers form a substantial part of the populations of Libya, Algeria, and Morocco. Except for the nomadic TUAREG, the Berbers are small farmers, living under a loose tribal organization in independent villages. They have developed local industries (iron, copper, lead, pottery, weaving, and embroidery). The Berbers are Sunni Muslims, and their native languages are of the Hamitic group, but most literate Berbers also speak Arabic, the language of their religion. Berber languages are spoken by over 10 million people, not all of whom are considered ethnic Berbers. Despite a history of conquests, the Berbers have retained a remarkably homogeneous culture, which, on the evidence of Egyptian tomb paintings, derives from earlier than 2400 B.C. The alphabet of the only partly deciphered ancient Libyan inscriptions is close to the script still used by the Tuareg. The origins of the Berbers are uncertain, although many theories have been advanced relating them to the Canaanites, the Phoenicians, the Celts, the Basques, and the Caucasians. In classical times the Berbers formed such states as MAURETANIA and NUMIDIA. Until their conquest in the 7th cent. by Muslim Arabs, most of the Berbers were Christian (also, a sizable minority had accepted Judaism), and many heresies of the early African church, particularly Donatism, were essentially Berber protests against the rule of Rome. Under the Arabs, the Berbers became Islamized and soon formed the backbone of the Arab armies that conquered Spain. However, the Berbers repeatedly rose against the Arabs, and in the 9th cent. they supported the FATIMID dynasty in its conquest of N Africa. After the Fatimids withdrew to Egypt, N Africa was plunged into an anarchy of warring Berber tribes that ended only when the Berber dynasties, the ALMORAVIDS and the ALMOHADS, were born. With the disintegration of these dynasties, the Berbers of the plains were gradually absorbed by the Arabs, while those who lived in inaccessible mountain regions, such as the Aurès, the Kabylia, the Rif, and the Atlas, retained their culture and warlike traditions. When the French and the Spanish occupied much of N Africa, it was the Berbers of these mountainous regions who offered the fiercest resistance. In more recent times the Berbers, especially those of the Kabylia, assisted in driving the French from Algeria. See Ernest Gellner, *Saints of the Atlas* (1969); Ernest Gellner and Charles Micaud, ed., *Arabs and Berbers* (1972); John Waterbury, *North for the Trade* (1972).

Berbice: see GUYANA.

Berceo, Gonzalo de (gōnthä'lō thā bārthā'ō), c.1198–1265?, earliest known Spanish medieval poet. He was a religious in a Benedictine monastery who wrote prolifically on saints and other figures important in the history of the church. His devotion to the Virgin is expressed in 25 poems entitled *Milagros de Nuestra Señora* [miracles of Our Lady] (c.1245–60). See study by J. E. Keller (1972).

Berchem (bĕr'khəm), city (1970 pop. 50,241), Antwerp prov., N Belgium, an industrial suburb of Antwerp.

Berchet, Giovanni (jōvän'nē bĕrkĕt'), 1783–1851, Italian patriot and poet. He conspired to free Lombardy from Austria and was exiled. He wrote stirring patriotic ballads of a romantic type and rhymed romances, such as *Giulia* and *Matilde.*

Berchtesgaden (bĕrkh'təsgä″dən), town (1970 est. pop. 4,300), Bavaria, SE West Germany, in the Bavarian Alps. It is a popular winter and summer resort. Salt has been mined there since the 12th cent. At the nearby Obersalzberg is the site of Hitler's residence, the Berghof.

Berchtold, Leopold, Graf von (lā'ōpôlt gräf fən bĕrkh'tôlt), 1863–1942, Austro-Hungarian foreign minister (1912–15). During the BALKAN WARS he successfully worked for the creation of an independent Albania to block Serbian access to the Adriatic Sea. After the assassination (June 28, 1914) of Archduke Francis Ferdinand at Sarajevo, he directed the reckless policy that precipitated World War I. Although Serbia made a conciliatory reply to his harsh ultimatum, Berchtold pressed for full acceptance; he probably even magnified a border incident in order to secure Emperor Francis Joseph's signature to the declaration of war on Serbia. See S. B. Fay, *The Origins of the World War* (2d ed. 1936).

Berdichev (byĭrdyĕ'chĭf), Ukrainian *Berdychiw,* city (1969 est. pop. 61,000), SW European USSR, in the Ukraine, on the Gnilopyat River. It is a rail junction and the industrial and trade center of an area where sugar beets are raised. Engineering, sugar refining, tanning, and the manufacture of foodstuffs are the major industries. Founded in the 14th cent., Berdichev passed to Lithuania in 1546 and to Poland in 1569; Russia acquired it in 1793. During the 18th cent., Berdichev was an important Ukrainian commercial city and a center of Jewish Hasidism. Landmarks include a fortified Carmelite monastery (17th cent.) that is now a museum.

Berdyaev, Nicholas (bĕrdyī'əf), 1874–1948, Russian theologian and religious philosopher, b. Kiev. After an early period as a Marxist, Berdyaev became prominent in a brilliant circle of Russian intellectuals famous in their time for their interest in Russian Orthodoxy. Forced into exile in 1922, Berdyaev attracted similar circles in Berlin and Paris. He wrote prolifically and gained wide recognition. He decried the dehumanization of man by modern technology and believed that man fulfills himself in the free, creative act. Fond of dichotomies, Berdyaev discussed history in terms of eschatology and the human in terms of the divine. He believed in the ideal of the Godmanhood. Among his many works are *The End of Our Time* (tr. 1933); *The Destiny of Man* (tr. 1937); *Slavery and Freedom* (tr. 1944); *Dream and Reality: an Essay in Autobiography* (tr. 1950); *Truth and Revelation* (tr. 1953). See biographies by Donald Lowrie (1960), Michael Vallon (1960), and M. M. Davy (1964, tr. 1967); studies by Fuad Nucho (1966) and C. S. Calian (1968).

Berdyansk (bĕr″dyänsk'), city (1970 pop. 100,000), S European USSR, in the Ukraine on the Berdyansk Gulf of the Sea of Azov. It is a port and a rail terminus. Industries include fishing and fish processing, flour milling, oil refining, and the production of machinery, cables, and clothing. Berdyansk is also a health and seaside resort. The city was founded in 1827. From 1939 to 1958 it was called Osipenko. Medical and teachers colleges are in the city.

Berea or **Beroea** (both: bērē'ə). **1** Town, near Jerusalem. 1 Mac. 9.4. It is probably identical with BEEROTH **1. 2** See VÉROIA, Macedonia. **3** See ALEPPO, Syria.

Berea (bərē'ə), city (1970 pop. 22,396), Cuyahoga co., NE Ohio, a suburb of Cleveland; settled 1809, inc. as a city 1930. Berea was once famous for its sandstone quarries. Baldwin-Wallace College is in the city.

Berea College, at Berea, Ky.; coeducational; founded 1855 by John G. Fee as a one-room district school, chartered 1866 and became a college in 1869. Each student works a minimum of 10 hours a week to help pay expenses. The school owns and the students operate a bakery, laundry, printing shop, and hotel. The campus includes extensive farm and forest lands.

Bereans or **Beroeans** (both: bərē'ənz) , members of a Protestant religious sect founded in Scotland by John BARCLAY c.1773. They took their name from the community mentioned in Acts 17.10–13. They held the main Calvinist doctrines and placed great emphasis on the study of the Scriptures. The sect is almost extinct.

Berechiah (bĕr"əkī'ə). **1** Son of Zerubbabel. 1 Chron. 3.20. **2** Father of MESHULLAM **5. 3,4** Levites, perhaps the same person. 1 Chron. 9.16; 15.23. **5** Important Ephraimite. 2 Chron. 28.12. **6** Father of Asaph the psalmist. 1 Chron. 15.17. Berachiah: 1 Chron. 6.39. **7** Father of Zechariah the Minor Prophet. Zech. 1.1,7. In Mat. 23.35 the name Barachias is probably a textual insertion, for the Zechariah being referred to is almost certainly ZECHARIAH **2,** not Zechariah the Minor Prophet.

Bered (bē'rĕd). **1** Unidentified place, S Palestine. Gen. 16.14. **2** See BECHER **2.**

Berekhiah ben Natronai ha-Nakdan (bĕrəkī'ə bĕn nätrōnī' hä-näk'dän), fl. 12th or 13th cent., French Jewish fabulist, biblical commentator, philosopher, grammarian, and translator. His first name also appears as Berachya. He is best known for his collection of fables in rhymed prose, *Mishlei Shualim* (tr. by Moses Hadas, *Fables of a Jewish Aesop*, 1967), derived from the French collection *Ysopet* of Marie de France (c.1170), from the now lost Latin translation of Aesop, *Romulus*, and from several oriental sources. His *Sefer Mazref* (tr. by Sir Herman Gollancz, *The Ethical Treatises of Berachya*, 1902) is a summary of the ethical views of Saadia and several other GAONIM.

Berengar II (bĕr'ĭng-gər), d. 966, marquis of Ivrea. In 950 he made himself and his son joint kings of Italy, but his great unpopularity and his attempt to force ADELAIDE, his predecessor's widow, to marry his son, brought the intervention (951) of OTTO I of Germany. Berengar swore fealty to Otto in 952. Later he ravaged Italy and intrigued with Pope JOHN XII against Otto, who captured and imprisoned Berengar in 963.

Berengar of Tours (bĕ'rĭng-gər), c.1000–1088?, French theologian, also called Bérenger and Berengarius, b. Tours. He was archdeacon of Angers (c.1040–1060). After studying at Chartres, he returned to Tours to become head of its cathedral school. Berengar is said to have denied the Real Presence in the EUCHARIST. His defiance of authority angered his contemporaries, particularly LANFRANC. Berengar was defended by Pope GREGORY VII and Peter Damian. He wrote a reply to Lanfranc, *De Sacra Coena,* which was condemned. He was declared a heretic, but became reconciled with the church before his death. Berengar's controversy with the church brought about a more explicit formulation of the doctrine of the Eucharist. See A. J. Macdonald, *Berengar and the Reform of Sacramental Doctrine* (1930).

Berenice (bĕrənī'sē), b. c.340 B.C., d. 281 or 271 B.C., consort and half sister of Ptolemy I, king of ancient Egypt. A Macedonian, she was the widow of Philip, one of the officers of Alexander the Great, and was by this marriage the mother of Magas, king of Cyrene; Antigone, wife of Pyrrhus of Epirus; and Theoxena, wife of Agathocles, ruler of Syracuse. She was a niece of Ptolemy's first wife, Eurydice, whom she accompanied to Egypt and soon supplanted in Ptolemy's affections. Berenice, whose portrait appears with that of Ptolemy on many medals, was the mother by him of Ptolemy II and Arsinoë II.

Berenice, c.273–221 B.C., queen of ancient Cyrene and Egypt. She was the daughter and successor of King Magas of Cyrene. Objecting to her mother's choice of a husband for her after her father's death, Berenice led a successful revolt and put her suitor to death. In 247 B.C. she married Ptolemy III, thereby effectively annexing Cyrene to Egypt. According to Callimachus and Catullus, he named a constellation after her, Berenice's Hair (Coma Berenices). After her husband's death she ruled jointly with their son, Ptolemy IV, until he had her put to death.

Berenice, c.280–246 B.C., queen-consort of ancient Syria; wife of Antiochus II. She was called Berenice Syra. She was the daughter of Ptolemy II, and her marriage (252) to Antiochus II marked a temporary cessation in the wars between the Egyptian monarchs and the Seleucids. On the death of Antiochus, however, Laodice, the king's divorced first wife, brought about the death of Berenice and her infant son before Berenice's brother, Ptolemy III, could arrive. New war resulted.

Berenice, fl. 6 B.C., Jewish princess; daughter of Costobarus and Salome, sister of Herod the Great. She was married to her cousin Aristobulus and bore him a son, Herod Agrippa I. She was accused of having instigated the murder of her husband by Herod the Great in 6 B.C. Later she married Theudion, a brother-in-law of Herod the Great. After Theudion was put to death for plotting against Herod, she married Archelaus.

Berenice, b. A.D. c.28, Jewish princess; daughter of Herod Agrippa I. A very beautiful woman, she was often involved in intrigue. After her first husband died, she was married to her uncle Herod of Chalcis. After his death (A.D. 48) she lived in incest with her brother, Herod Agrippa II, causing some scandal. Her third husband was Polemon II, a king in Cilicia, whom she abandoned, returning to Herod Agrippa II. It was before her and Agrippa that Paul appeared at Caesarea (Acts 25.23). In the struggle between Rome and Judaea both she and her brother espoused the Roman cause. She attracted the attention of the emperor Titus, and after the destruction of Jerusalem (A.D. 70) he apparently planned to marry her. The great unpopularity of the Jews with the Romans forced him to withdraw from the match. Titus' dilemma is the subject of Racine's play *Bérénice.*

Berenice, city of ancient Cyrenaica: see BENGASI.

Berenice, ancient city of Egypt, on the Red Sea. Founded by Ptolemy II and named in his mother's honor, it commanded the trade with Arabia.

Berenson, Bernard (bĕr'ənsən), 1865–1959, American art critic and connoisseur of Italian art, b. Lithuania, grad. Harvard, 1887. An expert and an arbiter of taste, he selected for art collectors innumerable paintings, many of which are now in museums. A testament to his taste may be seen in the Gardner Museum in Boston. He was associated for many years with the British art dealer Lord Duveen as chief art adviser. Berenson settled (c.1900) in Settignano, near Florence, Italy, where he built up a fine art collection and library. He was noted as a brilliant conversationalist and wit. His home, I Tatti, became a mecca for European and American intellectuals and was willed to Harvard Univ. Some of Berenson's early publications are still used in the study of art history, though later scholars have criticized many of his judgments. Among his many writings are *Venetian Painters of the Renaissance* (1894), *Lorenzo Lotto* (1895), *Florentine Painters of the Renaissance* (1896), *Central Italian Painters of the Renaissance* (1897), *Drawings of the Florentine Painters* (1903), *North Italian Painters of the Renaissance* (1907), *Sketch for a Self-Portrait* (1949), *Rumor and Reflection* (1952), *The Passionate Sightseer* (1960), *Sunset and Twilight . . . Diaries 1947–1958,* ed. by Nicky Mariano (1963), and *Italian Pictures of the Renaissance* (repr. 1972). See biographies by Sylvia Sprigge (1960) and Nicky Mariano (1966).

Beresford, John (bĕr'ĭzfərd, -ĭs-), 1738–1805, Anglo-Irish Protestant politician. He entered the Irish Parliament in 1760, became a privy councillor (1768), a commissioner of revenue (1770), and chief revenue commissioner (1780). Committed to the continued political dominance of his own class in Ireland, he was a strong supporter of and chief adviser on Irish affairs to William Pitt. He advocated both a commercial treaty that emphasized economic dependence on England and the parliamentary union of England and Ireland, the eventual passage (1800) of which he steered through the Irish Parliament. The extent of his personal power and patronage provoked his brief dismissal (1795) by the 2d earl of FITZWILLIAM, who was attempting to reassert the role of the lord lieutenant, but Fitzwilliam was recalled and Beresford reinstated. He sat in the united British Parliament until 1802.

Beresford, William Carr Beresford, Viscount, 1768–1854, British general. He served with distinction in Egypt (1801–3) and participated (1806) in the capture of Cape Colony (Cape Province, South Africa) from the Dutch. He captured Buenos Aires in 1806 but held it only briefly before it was retaken by Jacques de LINIERS. Beresford occupied Madeira (1807) and for a time was governor of the island. Joining Arthur Wellesley (later duke of Wellington) in Portugal (1808), he successfully reorganized the Portuguese army and was prominent throughout the PENINSULAR WAR. Created viscount in 1823, he was master general of ordnance in Wellington's cabinet from 1828 to 1830.

Berezina (byĕrăzēnä'), river, c.380 mi (610 km) long, rising in NW Belorussia, E central European USSR. It flows generally S past Borisov and Bobruysk into the Dnepr River. It is navigable for most of its length. The heroic retreat across the Berezina of the remnants of Napoleon's Grand Army took place near Borisov from Nov. 26 to Nov. 29, 1812. Despite the loss of more than 20,000 men, the crossing—effected under heavy Russian attack—saved Napoleon and his forces from capture.

Berezniki (bĭryĕznyĭkē'), city (1970 pop. 145,000), E European USSR, a port on the Kama River. Situated in an area rich in potassium salts, Berezniki is one of the main industrial centers of the Urals and contains a huge chemical combine. The city was founded as a sodium plant in 1883.

Berg, Alban (äl'bän bĕrk), 1885–1935, Austrian composer. In his youth he taught himself music but in 1904 he became the pupil and close friend of Arnold Schoenberg. Later Berg himself taught privately in Vienna. He adopted atonality and later the 12-tone technique of Schoenberg, although he tempered it with the lyric and dramatic qualities of the Viennese romantic tradition. His masterpiece, the opera *Wozzeck* (based on the play by Georg Büchner; Berlin, 1925), aroused strenuous protest, but it has since been acclaimed as a major work of the 20th-century musical stage. He left unfinished another symbolic and erotic opera, *Lulu* (based on two plays by Wedekind; Zürich, 1937), which adhered more strictly to the 12-tone principle than did *Wozzeck.* His Violin Concerto (Barcelona, 1936) was his last completed work. He also wrote songs and chamber music. See his letters to his wife, ed. and tr. by Bernard Grun (1971); biographical studies by H. F. Redlich (1957) and Willi Reich (tr. 1965).

Berg (bĕrk), former duchy, W West Germany, along the right bank of the Rhine River between the Ruhr and Sieg rivers. Düsseldorf was its chief city. A county in the 12th cent., Berg passed (1348) to the dukes of JÜLICH and in 1380 was made a duchy. In 1423 the duchies of Berg and Jülich were united. On the extinction (1511) of the Berg-Jülich line, Berg passed to Duke John III of Cleves (see CLEVES, DUCHY OF), whose line died out in 1609, setting off a virulent struggle over succession that contributed to the outbreak of the Thirty Years War (1618–48). In 1614, Berg was awarded to the Palatinate-Neuburg branch of the Bavarian house of Wittelsbach; the award was confirmed in the Treaty of Cleves (1666). Ceded to France in 1806, Berg was raised to a grand duchy by Napoleon I in favor of Joachim Murat. The Congress of Vienna assigned (1815) the duchy to Prussia.

Bergamo (bĕr'gämō), city (1971 pop. 127,181), capital of Bergamo prov., in Lombardy, N Italy, in the foothills of the Alps. It is an industrial center and an agricultural market. Manufactures include machinery, textiles, and cement. Originally a Gallic town, Bergamo became an independent commune in the 12th cent. It came under the rule (1329–1427) of the Visconti and then of Venice until 1797, when it was included in the Cisalpine Republic. Bergamo is divided into two sections: the old, hilltop town and the modern, lower sector. Noteworthy buildings in the old town include a Romanesque church (12th cent.), the beautiful Renaissance Colleoni chapel (15th cent.), and a 14th-century baptistery.

bergamot (bûr'gəmŏt") [from Bergamo, Italy], citrus tree (*Citrus bergamia*) grown chiefly in Italy, belonging to the family Rutaceae (RUE family). From the rind of the bergamot orange is extracted an essential oil used in perfumes and eau de Cologne. Various North American plants of the Labiatae (MINT family) are also called bergamot because of their bergamotlike fragrance. Chief among these is *Monarda fistulosa*, or wild bergamot, closely related to the Oswego tea, or BEE BALM, which it resembles. The name bergamot is also applied to a variety of pear. True bergamot is classified in the division MAGNOLIOPHYTA, class Magnoliopsida, order Sapindales, family Rutaceae.

Bergen, East Germany: see RÜGEN.

Bergen (bĕr′gən), city (1970 pop. 113,351), capital of Hordaland co., SW Norway, situated on inlets of the North Sea. It is Norway's third largest city and a major shipping and shipbuilding center. Other manufactures include processed food, textiles, steel, machinery, and electrical equipment. Founded c.1070 by Olaf III (Olaf Kyrre), Bergen soon became the largest city of medieval Norway. It was often the royal seat, and the earliest coronations took place there. The city became an establishment of the HANSEATIC LEAGUE in the mid-14th cent. The Hansa merchants, enjoying extraterritorial privileges, imposed their unpopular rule on Bergen until 1560, and thereafter continued to have influence until the late 18th cent. During the disturbances accompanying the Reformation (16th cent.), most of the city's old churches and monasteries were destroyed. However, Bergen remained Norway's leading city until the rise of Oslo in the 19th cent. The center of Bergen was rebuilt after a severe fire in 1916. Nevertheless, the city retains many impressive monuments of its medieval past. One of its most famous buildings is Bergenhus fortress, which contains Haakon's Hall (1261); it was rebuilt after being heavily damaged in World War II. Other old buildings include the Quay, a group of wooden quayside houses rebuilt in their medieval style after a fire in 1702; St. Mary's Church (12th cent.); Fantoft Stavkirke (12th cent.); and, just south of Bergen, the 12th-century ruins of Norway's first Cistercian monastery. One of the chief cultural and educational centers of Norway, Bergen has a university (founded 1948), a school of economics and business administration, several scientific institutes, and a Hanseatic museum. Bergen's theater was founded (1850) by the composer and violinist Ole Bull and gained international recognition under such directors as Ibsen and Bjørnson. The dramatist Ludvig Holberg (1684) and the composer Edvard Grieg (1843) were born in Bergen.

Bergen, N.J.: see JERSEY CITY.

Bergenfield, borough (1970 pop. 33,131), Bergen co., NE N.J.; inc. 1894. It is mainly residential with some light industry. Its Old South Church was built in 1799.

Bergen op Zoom (bĕr′gən ôp zōm′), town (1971 pop. 39,612), North Brabant prov., SW Netherlands, on the Zoom River near its confluence with the Eastern Scheldt. It is a commercial and fishing port and its industries manufacture chemicals, machinery, and refined sugar. Bergen op Zoom was chartered c.1260 and was a major commercial rival of Antwerp until the 16th cent. It was repeatedly besieged by the Spanish and French in the wars that took place from the 16th to the 18th cent. and by the English in 1814. There are several historic buildings, notably the town hall (14th cent.), a 15th-century church (*Groote Kerk*), and the Markiezenhof palace.

Berger, Victor Louis, 1860–1929, American Socialist leader and Congressman, b. Austria-Hungary. After studying at the universities of Budapest and Vienna, he emigrated (1878) to the United States and settled in Milwaukee. After 1892 he devoted himself to Socialist politics and journalism, editing the Milwaukee *Vorwärts!* (1892–98) and a weekly that became (1911) the influential Milwaukee *Leader.* With Eugene V. Debs he pioneered in creating the American Socialist party. His leadership brought (1910) the Socialists control of Milwaukee for many years and made Berger the first Socialist member of Congress (1911–13). Reelected twice (1918, 1919), he was excluded by Congress on grounds of sedition, for which he was sentenced (1918–19) to a 20-year prison term. The decision was reversed by the U.S. Supreme Court in 1921, and he was allowed to take his seat when reelected in 1922. Again elected in 1924 and 1926, he was defeated in 1928. *Voice and Pen* (1929) is a collection of his speeches and editorials. See U.S. Congress, House, Special Committee on Victor L. Berger Investigation, *Case of Victor L. Berger of Wisconsin: Hearings* (1919 and 1921, repr. 1972); study by S. M. Miller (1973).

Bergerac, Cyrano de: see CYRANO DE BERGERAC.

Bergerac (bĕrzhəräk′), town (1968 pop. 28,015), Dordogne dept., SW France, in Périgord, on the Dordogne River. It is a farm-trade and processing center. It also has boiler works, foundries, and shoe and clothing plants. Possessed by the English in the 14th cent., it was recovered in 1450 by the French. It became a Protestant stronghold and was taken (1621) by Louis XIII. A tobacco museum and an experimental tobacco institute are there.

Bergh, Henry, 1811–88, American philanthropist, b. New York City. His abhorrence of human cruelty toward animals led him to found (1866) the American Society for the Prevention of Cruelty to Animals. This organization, the first of its kind in the country, was granted the authority to enforce local animal protection laws by the New York state legislature in the same year. In 1875, with Elbridge T. GERRY and others, he helped form the Society for the Prevention of Cruelty to Children. See Zulma Steele, *Angel in Top Hat* (1942).

Bergisch-Gladbach (bĕr′gĭsh-glät′bäkh″), city (1970 pop. 49,558), North Rhine-Westphalia, W West Germany; chartered 1856. Manufactures of this industrial city include paper and metal goods, wool, pharmaceuticals, and electrical equipment.

Bergman, Hjalmar (yäl′mär bĕr′yəmän), 1883–1931, Swedish novelist, dramatist, and short-story writer. A popular and prolific writer, Bergman wrote from the background of an unhappy childhood and chronic mental depression. His works are characterized by insight into the ambivalence of human emotions. Bergman's individual style combines a basically pessimistic view with ironic humor, as in the play *Swedenhielms* [the Swedenhielm family] (1925) and the novels *God's Orchid* (1919, tr. 1924) and *The Head of the Firm* (1924, tr. 1936). See his *Four Plays* (tr. 1968).

Bergman, Ingmar (ĭng′mär bĕr′yəmän), 1918–, Swedish film and stage writer, director, and producer. Bergman is esteemed as creator of numerous films remarkable for their Nordic expressionism, sensuous imagery, and irony. Not long after his first filmscript, for *Torment* (1945), he was allowed complete creative control over his films, working within small budgets. He assembled a group of players and technicians whom he used repeatedly in films and stage works. Although his films are largely concerned with man's search for God and the triumph of evil, none of them is without humor. Some, like *The Devil's Eye* (1960), treat the comic vagaries of love. His foremost films include *The Seventh Seal* (1956), *Wild Strawberries* (1957), *The Virgin Spring* (1959), and the trilogy *Through a Glass Darkly* (1961), *Winter Light* (1962), and *The Silence* (1963). Later films, *Persona* (1965), *Shame* (1968), *The Passion of Anna* (1970), *Cries and Whispers* (1972), and *Scenes from a Marriage* (1974), reflect a growing pessimism, an emphasis on personal relationships, and an increasingly lyric and personal visualization. See *Four Screenplays of Ingmar Bergman* (tr. 1960); *Ingmar Bergman's Trilogy* (1968); biography by Birgitta Steene (1967); study by Vernon Young (1971).

Bergman, Ingrid, 1915–, Swedish actress, b. Stockholm. Bergman acted first in Sweden, then in Hollywood after 1939. She specialized in portrayals of strong, dignified, and sophisticated women. Her performance in *Joan of Lorraine* (1946) on stage was widely acclaimed. After 1949 she appeared in Italian, German, and French films. Her most notable films include *Intermezzo* (1939), *Casablanca* (1942), *For Whom the Bell Tolls* (1943), *Notorious* (1946), and *The Visit* (1964). She won Academy Awards for *Gaslight* (1944) and *Anastasia* (1956). Bergman was married to Roberto ROSSELLINI. See L. J. Quirk, *Films of Ingrid Bergman* (1970).

Bergman, Torbern Olof (to͝or′bərn o͞o′lôv bĕr′yəmän), 1735–84, Swedish chemist, physicist, and mineralogist. A professor at the Univ. of Uppsala from 1758, he developed a theory of chemical affinity, made improvements in the methods of chemical analysis (especially blowpipe analysis) and in the classification of rocks, and did important research in crystallography. He wrote *A Dissertation on Elective Attractions* (1775, tr. 1785). His collected works, *Essays, Physical and Chemical,* appeared in six volumes (1779–81, tr. 1791).

Bergognone (bĕrgōnyō′nā) or **Borgognone** (bôr-), fl. 1450–1523, Italian painter, known also as Ambrogio Stefani da Fossano. His most important works are the frescoes in the Certosa of Pavia. His luminous and often charming paintings are in the National Gallery, London; the Louvre; the Metropolitan Museum; and the National Gallery of Art, Washington, D.C. Other works have remained in the churches of Bergamo, Lodi, Milan, and Pavia.

Bergson, Henri (äNrē′ bĕrgsôN′), 1859–1941, French philosopher. He became a professor at the Collège de France in 1900, devoted some time to politics, and, after World War I, took an interest in international affairs. He is well known for his brilliant and imaginative philosophical works, which won him the 1927 Nobel Prize in Literature. Among his works that have been translated into English are *Time and Free Will* (1889), *Matter and Memory* (1896), *Laughter* (1901), *Introduction to Metaphysics* (1903), *Creative Evolution* (1907), *The Two Sources of Morality and Religion* (1932), and *The Creative Mind* (1934). Bergson's philosophy is dualistic—the world contains two opposing tendencies—the life force (*élan vital*) and the resistance of the material world against that force. Man knows matter through his intellect, with which he measures the world. He formulates the doctrines of science and sees things as entities set out as separate units within the stream of becoming. In contrast with intellect is intuition, which derives from the instinct of lower animals. Intuition gives us an intimation of the life force which pervades all becoming. Intuition perceives the reality of time—that it is duration directed in terms of life and not divisible or measurable. Duration is demonstrated by the phenomena of memory. See H. W. Carr, *The Philosophy of Change* (1914, repr. 1970); H. M. Kallen, *William James and Henri Bergson* (1914); Ben-Ami Scharfstein, *Roots of Bergson's Philosophy* (1943); I. W. Alexander, *Bergson, Philosopher of Reflection* (1957); Thomas Hanna, ed., *The Bergsonian Heritage* (1962); P. A. Y. Gunter, *Bergson and the Evolution of Physics* (1969).

Berhampur (bär′həmpo͞or), town (1971 pop. 117,635), Orissa state, E central India. Rice, sugarcane, silk, gold-embroidered turbans, and leather goods are the main products. Berhampur was formerly a British military post.

Beri (bē′rī), Asherite. 1 Chron. 7.36.

Beria, Lavrenti Pavlovich (ləvrĕn′tyē päv′ləvĭch bâ′rēə), 1899–1953, Russian Communist leader, b. Georgia (now Georgian SSR). He rose to prominence in the Cheka (secret police) in Georgia and the Transcaucasus, became party secretary in these areas, and in 1938 became head of the secret police. As commissar (later minister) of internal affairs, Beria wielded great power, and he was the first in this post to become (1946) a member of the politburo. After Stalin's death (March, 1953), Beria was made first deputy premier under Premier Malenkov, but the alliance was shaky; in the ensuing struggle for power Beria was arrested (July) on charges of conspiracy. He and six alleged accomplices were tried secretly and shot in Dec., 1953. See biography by Thaddeus Wittlin (1972).

Beriah (bērī′ə). **1** Son of Asher, eponym of the Beriites. Gen. 46.17; Num. 26.44,45; 1 Chron. 7.30. **2** Son of Ephraim. 1 Chron. 7.23. **3** Benjamite. 1 Chron. 8.13,16. **4** Levite. 1 Chron. 23.10,11.

beriberi (bĕr′ēbĕr′ē), deficiency disease occurring when the human body has insufficient amounts of thiamine (vitamin B_1). The deficiency may result from improper diet (e.g., ingestion of highly refined grains instead of the whole kernels), from poor absorption of thiamine (as in chronic diarrhea), from conditions which increase the vitamin requirements of the body (e.g., hyperthyroidism, pregnancy, fever), or from poor utilization (as in liver disease). In some instances (e.g., alcoholism) the deficiency arises from a combination of several or of all of these factors. Since thiamine is essential for the proper metabolism of carbohydrate and fat and for the normal functioning of enzymes and nervous tissue, the symptoms of the disorder are primarily those of neurological and gastrointestinal disturbances. In severe cases the heart becomes affected, and the nervous disorder may lead to paralysis and death. The disorder is rarely found in the West, occurring only among alcoholics and other groups who exist on grossly inadequate diets. It is a common malady in parts of Asia where the diet consists mainly of polished white rice. The usual treatment is administering dosages of thiamine.

Bering, Vitus Jonassen (vē′to͞os yō′näsən bâr′ĭng), 1681–1741, Danish explorer in Russian employ. In 1725 he was selected by Peter I to explore far NE Siberia. Having finally got men and supplies across Siberia, Bering in 1728 sailed N through Bering Strait but sighted no land and did not recognize the importance of the strait. Later in 1728, setting out from Kamchatka, he was driven from his course and discovered the southern route around Kamchatka. He returned to St. Petersburg, arriving in 1730. Bering then drew up a large scheme of exploration, which gained the support of the government. Under his general command various units of a huge expedition set out to map the far reaches of the Siberian arctic regions. Much was accomplished, but at great expense and with no immediate prospects of profit. Bering himself headed an expedition across the sea to Alaska. In 1741 he commanded the *St. Peter* while Aleksey Ilich Chirikov (d.1748) commanded the *St. Paul.* They set out, rounded Kamchatka, founded the town of Petropavlovsk, and then sailed west. The vessels were separated. Bering sighted the St. Elias Mts. in Alaska on July 16, and the scientist Georg Wilhelm STELLER led a landing party. Bering then sailed W past the Aleutian Islands. The weather was bad, and almost all the crew had scurvy when the ship was wrecked on the shore of Bering Island, which they mistook for the coast of Kamchatka. There on Dec. 8 Bering died. The few survivors of his crew repaired a small vessel from the *St. Peter* and managed to reach Kamchatka in the summer of 1742. The *St. Paul* under Chirikov had also sighted land and had halted on the way westward at one of the Aleutian Islands, possibly Attu, before returning to Kamchatka in Oct., 1741. See F. A. Golder, *Bering's Voyages* (2 vol., 1922–25; Vol. II is a translation of Steller's journal); studies by C. Goodhue (1944), R. W. Murphy (1961), and P. Lauridsen (tr. 1969).

Bering Island (bēr'ĭng, bâr'-), Rus. *Beringa,* largest of the Komandorski Islands, c.55 mi (90 km) long and up to c.15 mi (20 km) wide, off Kamchatka peninsula, E Far Eastern USSR, in the Bering Sea. It is low and treeless and is subject to severe windstorms. Nikolskoye is the chief town. Vitus Bering, sailing in the *St. Peter,* was shipwrecked and died there.

Bering Sea, c.878,000 sq mi (2,274,020 sq km), northward extension of the Pacific Ocean between Siberia and Alaska. It is screened from the Pacific proper by the Aleutian Islands. The Bering Strait connects it with the Arctic Ocean. The sea's largest embayments are the Gulf of Anadyr, Norton Sound, and Bristol Bay. The Anadyr River enters the sea from the west and the Yukon River from the east. The warm Japan Current has little influence on the Bering Sea, which has much ice; it can usually be traversed only from June to October. The sea has many islands, notably Nunivak, St. Lawrence, Hall, St. Matthew, and the Pribilof Islands (all owned by the United States) and the Komandorski Islands (USSR). The sea was explored by the Russian Dezhnev in the 17th cent., but not until after the voyages of Vitus Bering (1728, 1741) was the fur-seal wealth of the Bering Sea made widely known. The whole region was under the control of the Russian American Company, but it proved impossible to prevent mariners from other nations from getting the skins of the seals and the sea otters. The question of protecting the seals became (1886) the subject of a bitter international incident called the **Bering Sea Fur-Seal Controversy.** The seal herd that summered in the Pribilof Islands wintered farther south; when returning north in the spring they could be taken in the open sea. The pelagic (open-sea) sealing, practiced by Canadian and other sealing vessels, greatly reduced the herd and threatened its extinction. The Alaska Commercial Company, which had a U.S. monopoly on the sealing, protested to the U.S. government, and in 1886 several Canadian vessels were seized and were condemned by a court at Sitka, Alaska. The legal basis for such action was the claim that Russia had controlled all the Bering Sea and that the control had passed to the United States with the purchase of Alaska in 1867; by claiming to exercise jurisdiction beyond the three-mile limit the United States had invoked the doctrine of *mare clausum* (closed sea) for the first time. This was not accepted by the British, and a move to settle the matter of protection by international agreement was blocked by the Canadians. The matter was referred to an international court of arbitration, which, meeting in Paris, declared in 1893 against the U.S. claim and awarded $473,151 in damages to the owners of the seized vessels. It also imposed some restrictions on pelagic sealing, but these were ineffective. In 1911, Great Britain, Russia, Japan, and the United States agreed to prohibit pelagic sealing; sealing in the Pribilofs was put completely under U.S. supervision. For several years sealing was stopped completely, and then it was resumed but only under careful restrictions. Gradually the herd has been built up again. The 1911 agreement also prohibited the killing of sea otters, which are, however, almost extinct today.

Bering Strait, c.55 mi (90 km) wide, between extreme NE Asia and extreme NW North America, connecting the Arctic Ocean and the Bering Sea. It is usually completely frozen over from October to June. The Diomede Islands are in the strait. The narrowness of the strait makes it possible for small boats to cross from Chukchi Peninsula, NE USSR, to Seward Peninsula in Alaska. Since Alaska and Siberia were connected in the distant past, the usual theory is that the ancestors of the American Indians crossed the land bridge to North America. The strait is named for the Danish explorer Vitus Bering, who traversed it in 1728.

Berio, Luciano (lo͞ochä'nō bĕr'yō), 1925–, Italian composer, b. Oneglia. After studying at the Milan Conservatory and working as coach and conductor in Italian opera houses, Berio was introduced to SERIAL MUSIC by Luigi DALLAPICCOLA in 1952. A nondoctrinaire use of serialism pervades all of his music for traditional instruments. In 1954, Berio began working in ELECTRONIC MUSIC at the Milan Radio with Bruno MADERNA. Among his works are *Sequenzas I–VI* (1958–70), each for a different solo instrument; *Circles,* for mezzo, harp, and percussion to poems of e e cummings; several pieces with texts by James Joyce; *Visage* (1961), for electronically manipulated voice; *Sinfonia* (1968), for orchestra and voices; and *Opera* (1970), for mixed media.

Berites (bē'rīts): see BICHRI.

Berith (bē'rĭth), abbreviation of BAAL-BERITH.

Berkeley, George (bär'klē, bûr-), 1685–1753, Anglo-Irish philosopher and clergyman, b. Co. Kilkenny, Ireland. Educated at Trinity College, Dublin, he became a scholar and later a fellow there. Most of Berkeley's important work in philosophy was done in his younger years. His *Essay Towards a New Theory of Vision* (1709), *A Treatise Concerning the Principles of Human Knowledge* (1710), and the famous *Three Dialogues Between Hylas and Philonous* (1713) are among his more important works. At considerable personal sacrifice he organized a movement to establish a college in the Bermudas to convert the American Indians, going to Rhode Island in 1728 to wait for promised support. This support never came, and after three years he returned to England. He was made bishop of Cloyne in 1734. Berkeley in his subjective idealism went beyond Locke, who had argued that such qualities as color and taste arise in the mind while primary qualities of matter such as extension and weight have existence independent of the mind. Berkeley held that both types of qualities are known only in the mind and that therefore there is no existence of matter independent of perception (*esse est percipi*). The observing mind of God makes possible the continued apparent existence of material objects. God arouses sensations in us in a regular coherent order. Selves and God make up the universe. Berkeley felt that his argument constituted a complete disproof of atheism. He believed that qualities, not things, are perceived and that the perception of qualities is relative to the perceiver. See edition of his works by A. A. Luce and T. E. Jessop (9 vol., 1948–57); biography by A. A. Luce (1949); studies by D. M. Armstrong (1960) and I. C. Tipton (1974).

Berkeley, John, 1st **Baron Berkeley of Stratton,** 1602–78, English army officer and courtier. A royalist, he fought in numerous engagements in the English civil war and later, through association with the duke of York (later James II), won great political advancement. Raised to the peerage in 1658, he was appointed lord president of Connaught for life in 1661 and one of the proprietors of NEW JERSEY in 1664. From 1670 to 1672 he was lord lieutenant of Ireland.

Berkeley, Sir William, 1606–77, colonial governor of Virginia. Appointed governor in 1641, he arrived in Virginia in 1642. Berkeley defeated the Indians and the Dutch, extended explorations, and encouraged agriculture, but so persecuted dissenters that many of them left the colony. An uncompromising royalist, he made Virginia a haven for supporters of Charles I and declined to recognize the Commonwealth. Berkeley was deposed by a Puritan force from England in 1652 and lived quietly on his Virginia plantation until the Restoration in 1660, when he was reappointed governor. His second term as governor was marred by great domestic discontent and strife. A drop in tobacco prices brought great economic suffering to the colony. At the same time it was charged that Berkeley was showing favoritism toward a small group of friends and depriving the freemen of their rights. When, in addition, Berkeley refused to take the measures demanded by the frontiersmen for protection against the Indians, BACON'S REBELLION broke out. Temporarily forced to flee, Berkeley regained power after Bacon's premature death and ordered the hanging of many of Bacon's followers. The executions were carried out in defiance of a royal commission that had arrived with pardon for all except Bacon. Finally he yielded to the commission's order that he return to England, where he died discredited. See T. J. Wertenbaker, *Virginia under the Stuarts, 1607–1688* (1914); Wilcomb Washburn, *The Governor and the Rebel* (1957).

Berkeley (bûrk'lē). **1** City (1970 pop. 116,716), Alameda co., W Calif., on the eastern shore of San Francisco Bay; inc. 1878. Originally part of the Rancho San Antonio granted to the Peralta family in 1820 by the Spanish crown, the site was purchased by Americans in 1853. The settlement, at first called Oceanview, was named Berkeley in 1866. The city's industries include food processing and the manufacture of chemicals, pharmaceuticals, and metal products. A campus of the Univ. of California and several divinity schools are in Berkeley. Points of interest include a marina; Tilden Park; University Museum; Lawrence Hall of Science; and Zellerbach Hall, an auditorium. Lawrence Radiation Laboratory, an atomic research center, is nearby. **2** City (1970 pop. 19,743), St. Louis co., E Mo.; inc. 1937. Its manufactures include aircraft, truck bodies, and brake fluid. The first International Air Meet in the United States was held in Berkeley in 1910.

berkelium (bûr'klēəm) [from Berkeley], synthetic, radioactive chemical element; symbol Bk; at. no. 97; mass no. of most stable isotope 247; m.p. and b.p. unknown; sp. gr. 14 (estimated); valence +3 or +4. Because pure berkelium has not been isolated in significant quantities, its physical properties are not known. It is believed to be similar to the other members of the ACTINIDE SERIES and to TERBIUM, its homolog in the lanthanide series. It is found in group IIIb of the PERIODIC TABLE. Nine isotopes of berkelium are known. Berkelium-247, the most stable isotope (half-life about 1,400 years), is difficult to produce; berkelium-249 (half-life 314 days) is more easily produced in weighable quantities and is used in studies of berkelium chemistry. The chloride, fluoride, sulfide, nitrate, sulfate, perchlorate, oxide, and dioxide have been produced. Berkelium was discovered late in 1949 by G. T. Seaborg, S. G. Thompson, and Albert Ghiorso, who produced it by bombarding americium-241 with alpha particles in the cyclotron of the Univ. of California at Berkeley. Weighable quantities of the pure element were first isolated by B. B. Cunningham and S. G. Thompson in 1958.

Berkhamstead, formerly also **Great Berkhampstead** (both: bûrk'əmstĕd, bärk'-), urban district (1971 pop. 15,439), Hertfordshire, central England. Berkhamstead is mainly residential but has clothing, timber, and chemical industries. It is the site of an 11th-century royal castle in which Edgar Atheling, a claimant to the throne, submitted to William the Conqueror; Thomas à Becket lived in the castle, and Henry II held court there. John II of France was briefly imprisoned in the castle after the battle of Poitiers (1356) in the Hundred Years War. Berkhamstead also has a 16th-century grammar school.

Berkley, city (1970 pop. 22,618), Oakland co., SE Mich., a residential suburb of Detroit; inc. 1932.

Berkman, Alexander, 1870?–1936, anarchist, b. Vilna (then in Russian Poland). He emigrated to the United States c.1887. At the time of the Homestead, Pa., strike (1892) Berkman attempted to kill Henry Clay Frick, but succeeded only in wounding him. He served 14 years of a 22-year sentence imposed for this attack. His association with Emma GOLDMAN, begun before his imprisonment, was resumed after his release. In 1917 they were arrested for obstructing the draft and in 1919 were deported to Russia. Disappointed in his hope of finding under the Bolshevik government the freedom that he sought, Berkman left Russia and in various European cities supported himself by translation. He committed suicide in Nice. His writings include *Prison Memoirs of an Anarchist* (1912, repr. 1970), *The Bolshevik Myth* (1925), *The Anti-Climax* (1925), and *Now and After: the A.B.C. of Communist Anarchism* (1929).

Berkovits, Eliezer (ĕl''ēä'zər bûr'kōvĭts), 1908–, rabbi, theologian, and educator, b. Rumania. He served in the rabbinate in Berlin (1934–39), in Leeds, England (1940–46), in Sydney, Australia (1946–50), and in Boston (1950–58). In 1958 he became chairman of the department of Jewish philosophy of the Hebrew Theological College in Chicago. His writings touch upon the tensions created in the thought of a modern Orthodox Jew and Zionist between the claims of religious tradition and secular nationalism; among them are *Towards Historic Judaism* (1943), *God, Man, and History* (1959), and *A Jewish Critique of the Philosophy of Martin Buber* (1962).

Berkshire (bärk'shĭr, -shər, bûrk'-) or **Berks** (bärks, bûrks), county (1971 pop. 633,457), S central England. The county town is READING. Berkshire lies almost entirely in the basin of the Thames River, which forms its northern border. It is largely agricultural; the Vale of the WHITE HORSE in the north and the Vale of Kennet in the south are the most productive areas. Chalk downs extend across the center of the county. Dairying and poultry farming are important, and Berkshire hogs are famous. Barley is the chief crop; wheat, oats, potatoes, cabbage, and kale for fodder are also raised. Industry in Berkshire has grown rapidly since World War II. There are nuclear-research centers at Harwell and Aldermaston. Berkshire has been a transportation hub since Roman times. Modern highways run W from London through Berkshire. Part of the ancient kingdom of WESSEX, Berkshire was the birthplace of King Alfred. At Windsor is the famous Windsor Castle, chief residence of English monarchs for centuries. Berkshire was reorganized (1974) as a nonmetropolitan county.

Berkshire Festival, summer music festival, held since 1937 at "Tanglewood," a former estate in the adjoining towns of Stockbridge and Lenox, Mass. The Berkshire Festivals were begun in 1934 at a farm in Stockbridge. Henry Hadley conducted an orchestra composed largely of members of the New York Philharmonic-Symphony for two summers. In 1936, Serge Koussevitzky and the Boston Symphony Orchestra took over the festival. Charles Munch became musical director of the festival in 1951 and was followed by William Steinberg who conducted there through the summer of 1969. In 1974 the artistic director was Seiji Ozawa.The music shed at Tanglewood, designed by Eliel Saarinen, was opened in 1938. It seats 6,000 people and accommodates thousands of additional listeners on its vast lawns. In 1940 a summer school, the Berkshire Music Center, was begun in combination with the festival. See M. A. De Wolfe Howe, *The Tale of Tanglewood* (1946); J. R. Holland, *Tanglewood* (1973).

Berkshire Hills, region of wooded hills with many small lakes and streams, W Mass. The Berkshires are a southern extension of the Green Mts., but the name is generally applied to all highlands in W Massachusetts. Mt. Greylock, 3,491 ft (1,064 m), is the highest point in the hills and in the state. The Berkshire Hills have numerous summer and winter resorts, state parks, and forests. The Housatonic, Hoosic, and Westfield rivers drain the region and supply water power to manufacturing towns. Pittsfield, North Adams, Great Barrington, and Lenox are the largest towns in the Berkshires.

Berkshire swine, one of the oldest of the improved breeds of swine, originating in the county of Berkshire in S central England. The breed was imported to the United States in large numbers between 1830 and 1850 and has adapted itself to all parts of the country. Berkshires are of medium size, generally smooth, and somewhat longer in proportion to depth than other breeds. Their ears stand erect, their noses are short, and their color is black with white feet, nose, and tail.

Berlage, Hendrik Petrus (hĕn'drək pā'trüs berlä'-gə), 1856–1934, Dutch architect. In both his writings and architectural practice, Berlage advocated a return to simplicity of form and clarity of structure. In his Amsterdam Stock Exchange (1898–1903) and the Diamond Workers' Union Bldg. (Amsterdam, 1899–1900), he introduced a flat wall surface within a Romanesque framework suggestive of the works of H. H. Richardson. Berlage took part in city planning projects for the Hague (1908) and Amsterdam (1915). His publications, e.g., *Gedanken über den Stil in der Baukunst* (1905), won his ideas great favor with the rising generation of modern architects, including the Amsterdam school and the architects of *de Stijl.*

Berle, Adolf Augustus, Jr. (bûr'lē), 1895–1971, American lawyer and public official, b. Boston. Admitted to the bar in 1916, he served in World War I and was a member of the American delegation to the Paris Peace Conference. Resigning in protest against the terms of the Versailles Treaty, Berle returned to practice law in New York City and later became (1927) professor of corporate law at Columbia. As a specialist in corporation law and finance, he was a member of Franklin Delano Roosevelt's Brain Trust and helped shape much of the banking and securities legislation of the New Deal. As Assistant Secretary of State for Latin American affairs (1938–44), Berle attended many inter-American conferences and acted as spokesman for Roosevelt's Good Neighbor Policy. After serving (1945–46) as ambassador to Brazil, he resumed his professorship at Columbia and was a founder and chairman (1952–55) of the Liberal party. In 1961, Berle headed a task force for President John F. Kennedy that recommended the Alliance for Progress. His well-known writings include the classic study *The Modern Corporation and Private Property* (with G. C. Means, 1933, rev. ed. 1968), *The 20th Century Capitalist Revolution* (1954), *Tides of Crisis* (1957), *Power without Property* (1959), and *Power* (1969). A selection of his papers was edited by B. B. Berle and T. B. Jacobs (1973).

Berlichingen, Götz von (göts' fən bĕr'lĭkhĭng-ən), 1480–1562, German knight and adventurer. The head of a band of free soldiers, he lost (1504) his right hand in the battle of Landshut and wore an iron one in its place. His forays against various cities earned him popular fame. He reluctantly agreed to lead the peasants of Franconia during the Peasants' War (1524–26) but deserted them before their defeat. In 1542 he served with Holy Roman Emperor Charles V against the Turks and two years later fought against the French. His memoirs inspired Goethe's drama *Götz von Berlichingen* (1773).

Berlin, Irving, 1888–, American songwriter, b. Russia. Berlin's surname was originally Baline. Of his nearly 1,000 songs, *Alexander's Ragtime Band* (1911) was his first outstanding hit. In 1918, while he was in the army, he wrote, produced, and acted in *Yip, Yip, Yaphank,* which he rewrote in 1942 as *This Is the Army.* Berlin wrote songs for several of the *Ziegfeld Follies* and the *Music Box Revue* (1921–24) as well as the Broadway musicals *As Thousands Cheer* (1933), *Annie Get Your Gun* (1946), *Miss Liberty* (1949), *Call Me Madam* (1950), and *Mr. President* (1962). He was the composer of numerous film scores, and several of his stage musicals were filmed. Among the best known of his songs are "God Bless America" and "There's No Business Like Show Business." See biography by Michael Freedland (1974).

Berlin, Sir Isaiah, 1909–, English political scientist, b. Latvia. He was educated at Oxford, where he became (1932) a fellow and was later (1957–67) professor of social and political theory. In 1966 he was appointed president of Wolfson College, Oxford. In *The Hedgehog and the Fox* (1953) Berlin explored Leo Tolstoy's view of irresistible historical forces, and in *Historical Inevitability* (1954) he attacked both determinist and relativist approaches to history as superficial and fallacious. His other works include *Karl Marx* (3d ed. 1963) and *Four Essays on Liberty* (1969). He was knighted in 1957.

Berlin (bûr"lĭn', Ger. bĕrlēn'), city, former capital of Germany and of Prussia, NE Germany, on the Spree and Havel rivers. It is located within the German Democratic Republic (East Germany). In 1945 it was divided into four occupation zones. The Soviet sector, known as East Berlin, is now the capital of the German Democratic Republic. The zones assigned to the British, American, and French occupation forces now constitute West Berlin. The French occupied the northwestern part of the city, and the Americans and the British occupied the southern districts.

Historic Berlin. Berlin had its beginning in two Wendish villages, Berlin and Kölln, which were chartered in the 13th cent. and merged in 1307. It assumed importance as a Hanseatic town in the 14th cent. and became the seat of the electors of Brandenburg (after 1701, kings of Prussia) in 1486. Berlin suffered severely from the Thirty Years War (1618–48), but Frederick William (reigned 1640–88), the Great Elector, restored and improved the city. Occupied in the Seven Years War by Austrian (1757) and Russian (1760) troops and in the Napoleonic Wars by the French (1806–8), Berlin emerged from the conflicts as a center of German national feeling and an increasingly serious rival of Vienna. From the 18th and early 19th cent. date many of the distinguished monuments and buildings of the city (chiefly by Andreas SCHLÜTER and Karl Friedrich SCHINKEL); nearby POTSDAM became famous as the favorite residence of Frederick II (Frederick the Great, reigned 1740–86). The monumental Brandenburg gate, a triumphal arch in classical style, was erected during his reign. Frederick William Univ. was founded in 1810 and attracted many outstanding scholars, including Humboldt, Fichte, Hegel, and Ranke. Berlin was the center of the Revolution of 1848 against King Frederick William IV. The construction of railroads (1840–61) gave Berlin additional importance as an industrial and commercial center. In 1866 it became the seat of the North German Confederation. After Berlin was made the capital of the German Empire in 1871, it prospered and expanded rapidly and became one of the great cities of the world. The city's population had increased from 201,000 in 1819 to 914,000 in 1871; by 1900 it was 2,712,000. The German military defeat of 1918 brought on a period of social and political unrest. After the establishment (Nov., 1918) of a Socialist government, Berlin was the scene of the abortive uprising of the communist SPARTACUS PARTY (Jan., 1919) and of the conservative putsch of 1920 (see KAPP, WOLFGANG). As the capital of the Weimar Republic, Berlin suffered severe economic crises in the 1920s, but it was also a brilliant cultural capital. After the Nazis came to power in 1933, German culture declined. Berlin remained, however, the second largest city of Europe, a notable economic, political, and educational center, and a huge inland port with a flourishing world trade. Textiles and clothing, iron and steel, chemicals, and electrical machinery were among its chief industries. It was also a large publishing center and the major communications hub of Central Europe, with six railroad stations and the airfield at Tempelhof. A suburban railroad system and a large subway system facilitated internal communication. During World War II, Berlin was repeatedly bombed from the air by the Allies, but the heaviest destruction was caused by a Soviet artillery barrage of unprecedented intensity that preceded the capture (May 2, 1945) of the city by Marshal Zhukov. On May 8, Germany's unconditional surrender to the Allies was signed in Berlin.

Divided Berlin. The division of the city into sectors by the Potsdam Conference resulted in severe tension between the Soviet Union and the Western powers. The joint Allied military government (*Kommandatura*) was not successful and virtually ceased to function when the USSR informally withdrew in 1948. The status of Berlin became a major cold war issue, and attempts at international agreement ended in deadlock (see FOREIGN MINISTERS, COUNCIL OF) as the USSR sought to remove all Western (including West German) control from West Berlin and the Western powers maintained that settlement of the Berlin problem depended on reunification of Germany. In 1948, Soviet authorities established a blockade on all land and water communications between West Berlin and West Germany. The Western powers, foremost among them the United States, successfully undertook to supply West Berlin by a large-scale airlift through three air "corridors" left open to them. The blockade was withdrawn in May, 1949, and the airlift ended in Sept., 1949. In that year East Berlin was proclaimed the capital of the new German Democratic Republic, and in 1950 West Berlin was established as one of the states of the Federal Republic of Germany (of which Berlin is the de jure capital and Bonn the de facto capital). Workers rioted in East Berlin in June, 1953, and were suppressed by Soviet tanks. In the following years there were several Berlin crises, as the USSR in unilateral declarations, often accompanied by harassing actions, contested the legal basis for the Western powers' presence in and access to West Berlin. Meanwhile better living conditions in the western zone had led to a massive exodus of refugees from East to West Berlin, which was both a great embarrassment for the Communists and a serious drain on the East German labor supply. To stop the flow, the Communists in Aug., 1961, gave the division of the city a shockingly physical form by erecting a 29-mi (47-km) fortified wall along the partition line, leaving only a few closely guarded crossing points. The Western powers protested vigorously but ineffectively. East German border guards killed dozens of persons attempting to break through the barrier. War seemed near as Soviet and American tanks faced each other at the border crossings, but after 1962 the crisis eased. In Dec., 1963, the first of several agreements was reached permitting West Berliners to visit relatives in the eastern zone. Visits across the wall and access to West Berlin from West Germany were finally regularized in the Berlin accords reached among the four powers and the two Germanys in 1972.

West Berlin. A state of West Germany, West Berlin (1971 est. pop. 2,130,000; 185 sq mi/479 sq km) is situated more than 100 mi (161 km) inside East Germany. Although it is theoretically the West German capital, all the institutions of government are in Bonn and its representatives in the federal parliament have no vote. West Berlin's recovery from World War II, with American and West German aid, has been impressive and has far outpaced that of East Berlin. The chief manufactures are electrical equipment, foodstuffs, clothing, and machinery. There is a large tourist industry. At the center of the city, on the elegant street the Kurfürstendamm, is the gutted tower of the Kaiser Wilhelm Memorial Church, left unrestored as a reminder of the war. To the northeast, the large Tiergarten park contains the famous Reichstag building and the Berlin zoo and the American-designed Kongress Halle. Nearby is the concert hall of the Berlin Philharmonic. West of the Tiergarten is Potsdam Square, with the new opera house and Schiller Theater. To the south is John F. Kennedy Plaza, with the Schöneberg Rathaus, housing the city government offices, and the Freiheitsglocke, a copy of the Liberty Bell. Among West

Berlin's many museums is the Dahlem Gallery in the Charlottenberg Palace, which has the bust of Nefertiti and many Rembrandts. The Free University of Berlin was founded in 1948, and many of old Berlin's educational institutions have reopened in West Berlin.

East Berlin. The capital of East Germany, East Berlin (1970 est. pop. 1,085,441; 156 sq mi/404 sq km) has been far slower than West Berlin in recovering from wartime damage and achieving prosperity. Electrical goods are the leading products, and chemicals, machinery, and clothing are also produced. An extensive rebuilding program was begun in the 1960s. At the border with West Berlin, opposite the Tiergarten, is the imposing Brandenburg gate. It is the western terminus of the famous tree-lined avenue, Unter den Linden. To the E along Unter den Linden are the state opera, Humboldt Univ. (the old Frederick William Univ.), and St. Hedwig's Cathedral. At its eastern end is the immense Marx-Engels Square, where formerly stood the Royal Palace. The square is often the scene of political rallies. Across the Spree River, radiating from the Alexander Square, are Karl-Marx-Allee and Frankfurter-Allee (until 1961 Stalin-Allee), lined with ornate Moscow-style apartment buildings with shops at street level. To the south, in Treptow, is the Soviet Military Cemetery, with a massive statue of a Soviet soldier built partly from the ruins of Hitler's Chancellery. East Berlin also has a fine zoo (at Friedrichsfelde) and many museums. The Pergamum Museum, on Museum Island in the Spree, has an outstanding collection of classical art. See Philip Windsor, *City on Leave, a History of Berlin, 1945–1962* (1963); Henry Vizetelly, *Berlin under the New Empire* (2 vol., 1879; repr. 1968); W. H. Nelson, *The Berliners, Their Saga and Their City* (1969); Gerhard Masur, *Imperial Berlin* (1971); Otto Friedrich, *Before the Deluge: A Portrait of Berlin in the 1920s* (1972); Anne Armstrong, *Berliners: Both Sides of the Wall* (1973).

Berlin. **1** Town (1970 pop. 14,149), Hartford co., central Conn., an industrial suburb of Hartford; settled 1686, inc. 1785. Tools, metal products, and lacquers are among its manufactures. The first tinware in the United States was made there in 1740. Emma Hart Willard was born in the town. **2** (bûr′lĭn) City (1970 pop. 15,256), Coos co., NE N.H., in the White Mts. at falls of the Androscoggin; inc. 1829. In a heavily forested region, it early became the site of pulp and paper mills. Rubber products are also made. Berlin, a winter sports center, has the first ski club organized (1872) in the United States. Nearby are White Mountain National Forest, several state parks, and a U.S. fish hatchery.

Berlin, Conference of, 1884–85, international meeting aimed at settling the problems connected with European colonies in Africa. At the invitation of the German chancellor Otto von Bismarck, representatives of all European nations, the United States, and Turkey met at Berlin to consider problems arising out of European penetration of W Africa. The stated purpose of the meeting was to guarantee free trade and navigation on the Congo and on the lower reaches of the Niger. In fact, the territorial adjustments made among the powers were the important result. The sovereignty of Great Britain over S Nigeria was recognized. The claims of the International Association, a private corporation controlled by King Leopold II of Belgium, were more or less recognized; these applied to the greater part of the Congo. These territorial awards ignored French claims to parts of the Congo and of Nigeria and the historical claim of Portugal to the mouth of the Congo. The attempts to guarantee free trade and the neutrality of the region in wartime and to set up rules for future colonial expansion in Africa were hailed, but soon the agreements proved too vague to be workable. See S. E. Crowe, *The Berlin West African Conference* (1942).

Berlin, Congress of, 1878, called by the signers of the Treaty of Paris of 1856 (see PARIS, CONGRESS OF) to reconsider the terms of the Treaty of SAN STEFANO, which Russia had forced on the Ottoman Empire (Turkey) earlier in 1878. Great Britain and Austria-Hungary were the powers most insistent on revision; Russia submitted the treaty to revision only after Great Britain threatened war and Bismarck had offered to mediate as "honest broker." He was chairman of the congress. Disraeli represented Great Britain; Count Andrássy, Austria-Hungary; William Henry Waddington, France; Aleksandr Gorchakov, Russia; Count Corti, Italy; and Alexander Karatheodori, Turkey. The agreements reached in the Treaty of Berlin and the accompanying British-Turkish pact deeply modified the Treaty of San Stefano. Montenegro, Serbia, and Rumania were recognized as independent states; Rumania, however, was forced to cede S Bessarabia to Russia in return for the less favored Dobruja. Greater Bulgaria, which had been created at San Stefano, was divided into N Bulgaria, a principality under nominal Turkish suzerainty; Eastern RUMELIA, to be governed, with certain autonomous rights, by a Christian appointee of the Ottoman emperor; and Macedonia (including Adrianople), under unrestricted Turkish sovereignty. BOSNIA AND HERCEGOVINA, original cause of the Russo-Turkish War of 1877–78, were assigned to Austria-Hungary for administration and military occupation. In Asia, Russia acquired Ardahan, Batum, and Kars from Turkey. Cyprus was to be under temporary occupation by Great Britain through a separate agreement, and Crete was promised constitutional government. Other provisions included an important rectification of the Greco-Turkish boundary, the demilitarization of the lower Danube, and the protection of the Armenians and other religious minorities in Turkey. Russia was antagonized by Bismarck's handling of the conference, thereby bringing to an end the first THREE EMPERORS' LEAGUE. See C. D. Hazen, W. R. Thayer, and R. H. Lord, *Three Peace Congresses of the 19th Century* (1917); R. Albrecht-Carrié, *The Concert of Europe* (1968).

Berlin airlift, 1948–49, supply of vital necessities to West Berlin by air transport primarily under U.S. auspices. It was initiated in response to a land and water blockade of the city that had been instituted by the Soviet Union in the hope that the Allies would be forced to abandon West Berlin. The massive effort to supply the 2 million West Berliners with food and fuel for heating began in June, 1948, and lasted until Sept., 1949, although the Russians lifted the blockade in May of that year. During the around-the-clock airlift some 277,000 flights were made, many at 3-min intervals. By spring, 1949, an average of 8,000 tons was being flown in daily. More than 2 million tons of goods—of which coal accounted for about two thirds—were delivered.

Berlin Decree, 1806, decree issued in Berlin by Napoleon I on Nov. 21 in answer to the British blockade. Claiming that the British blockade of purely commercial ports was contrary to international law, Napoleon retaliated by declaring the British Isles under blockade and forbidding any trade to or from them. The Berlin Decree initiated the CONTINENTAL SYSTEM.

Berlin Wall, 29-mi (47-km) fortified concrete and wire barrier along the border between East and West Berlin; it was erected in Aug., 1961, by the East German government to halt the vast numbers of East Berliners defecting to the West and to prevent East Berliners from commuting to jobs in West Berlin, thus depleting the supply of labor in the East. The building of the wall came at a time of increased tension between the United States, Great Britain, France, and West Germany on one side, and the USSR and East Germany on the other, concerning the future status of the divided city of Berlin. Thousands of families were separated as a result of the border closing; after 1963, however, limited passage between East and West Berlin was allowed by the East German government on various holidays.

Berlioz, Louis-Hector (lwē ĕktôr′ bĕrlyôz′), 1803–69, French romantic composer. He abandoned medical study to enter the Paris Conservatory as a composition student. In 1830 his *Symphonie fantastique* was first performed in Paris, marking a bold new development in program music. This work, with its recurring basic theme, departed from traditional symphonies in its loose form and highly emotional, personal style. That same year Berlioz won the coveted Prix de Rome. During the next decade in Paris he wrote the symphonies *Harold in Italy* and *Romeo and Juliet,* the opera *Benvenuto Cellini,* and a requiem. In 1842–43 he conducted concerts in Germany, Austria, England, and Russia. His outstanding "concert opera" *The Damnation of Faust* (1846) met with failure in his lifetime but is now considered a masterpiece. Another dramatic work is the gigantic opera *The Trojans,* first performed in its entirety in 1890 and successfully revived after 1920. The nonliturgical oratorio *The Childhood of Christ,* for which he also wrote the text, was completed in 1854, and it was performed with great success for almost a century. Some of Berlioz's works are scored for large numbers of instruments, not only for volume but for richness of tone color even in delicate passages. His ideas of orchestration influenced many later composers. A passionate and impetuous man, Berlioz had several love affairs and was twice married, first to Harriet Smithson, an Irish actress. He was librarian at the Paris Conservatory, and wrote music criticism, his memoirs (ed. by David Cairns; 1969), and *Evenings with the Orchestra* (tr. 1956). His treatise on instrumentation (1844) was widely recognized as a text. See his letters, ed. by Jacques Barzun (1954); his memoirs, ed. by David Cairns (1973); biographies by J. H. Elliot (rev. ed. 1967) and Jacques Barzun (2 vol., 3d ed. 1969); studies by Ernest Newman (1910, repr. 1969), T. S. Wotton (1935, repr. 1969), and Brian Primmer (1973).

berm: see BEACH.

Bermuda (bûrmyo͞o′də), British crown colony (1970 pop. 52,700), 20 sq mi (52 sq km), comprising some 300 coral rocks, islets, and islands (of which some 20 are inhabited), in the Atlantic Ocean, c.570 mi (920 km) SE of Cape Hatteras, North Carolina. The capital is HAMILTON, on Bermuda (or Great Bermuda), the largest island. Smaller islands are Somerset, Ireland, and St. George. Bermuda, with its fine beaches, excellent climate, and picturesque sites, is a fashionable and popular year-round resort. Its coral reefs are the northernmost in the world. Although tourism is the economic mainstay, ship repairing and light industries are also important. Perfume concentrates, pharmaceuticals, textiles, and cut flowers are the chief exports. The population is about three-quarters black. Reputedly the first person to set foot on the islands was the Spanish navigator Juan de Bermúdez (1515), but they remained uninhabited, despite visits by Spaniards and Englishmen, until Sir George Somers and a group of colonists on their way to Virginia were shipwrecked there in 1609. This incident was known to Shakespeare when he wrote *The Tempest.* Long called Somers Islands, the Bermudas were first governed by chartered companies but were acquired by the crown in 1684. The harbor of St. George was a base for privateers during the War of 1812, and the island was a center for Confederate blockade runners during the American Civil War. During World War II the islands played an important strategic role. The United States, under a 99-year lease, operates a naval and air force base. Internal self-government was granted in 1968. See William Zuill, *Bermuda Journey* (1959); Richard Joseph, *Bermuda* (1967); H. C. Wilkinson, *Adventures in Bermuda* (1933), *Bermuda in the Old Empire* (1950), and *Bermuda from Sail to Steam* (2 vol., 1973).

Bermuda chub: see RUDDERFISH.

Bermuda grass, perennial pasture, lawn, and hay grass (*Cynodon dactylon*) of the family Gramineae (GRASS family), native to Africa and Asia and now common in warm regions of both hemispheres. It is the standard pasture grass in the S United States. It is heat- and drought-resistant and grows in almost any soil that is not too wet or shady, spreading rapidly and often becoming a weed. Bermuda grass is classified in the division MAGNOLIOPHYTA, class Liliatae, order Cyperales, family Gramineae.

Bermuda Hundred, fishing village, on the peninsula at the confluence of the Appomattox and James rivers, SE Va., NE of Petersburg; founded 1613. During the Civil War the Union Army of the James was bottled up there after its defeat at Drewrys Bluff.

Bern or **Berne** (bĕrn), canton (1970 pop. 983,296), 2,658 sq mi (6,883 sq km), W central Switzerland. The second most populous canton of the country, Bern comprises three sections—the Bernese Alps, or Oberland [Ger.,=highlands], with many resorts and peaks, notably the Finsteraarhorn and Jungfrau, and with meadows and pastures in the valleys; the Mittelland [midlands], in the fertile northern foothills of the Alps, and including the Emmental; and the Seeland [lake country], in the northwest, with BIEL and the Bernese Jura mts. Crop and cattle raising, dairying, and tourism are the chief means of livelihood in the Oberland and the Mittelland; the Seeland is more industrialized and has manufactures of watches, wood and metal products, and textiles. The population of the canton (except in the Jura) is predominantly Protestant and German-speaking; the Jura is mostly Roman Catholic and French-speaking. The history of the canton is largely that of its capital, **Bern** or **Berne** (1970 pop. 162,405), which is also the capital of Switzerland. Situated within a loop of the Aare River, the city is a university, administrative, transportation, and industrial center. Its manufactures include precision instruments, textiles, machinery, chemicals and pharmaceuticals, and chocolate. It is also the seat of numerous international agencies, notably the Universal Postal Union (since 1875), the International Telecommunication Union (since 1869), and the International Copyright Union (since 1886). Bern was founded, according to tradition, in 1191 by Berchtold V of ZÄHRINGEN as a military post. It was made (1218) a free imperial city by Emperor Frederick II when Berchtold died without an heir. Bern grew in power and population and in 1353 joined the Swiss Confederation, of which it became the leading member. Its conquests included AARGAU (1415) and VAUD (1536), besides numerous smaller territories. The area was governed until 1798 by an autocratic urban aristocracy. Bern accepted the Reformation in 1528. When Switzerland was invaded (1798) by the French during the French Revolutionary Wars, Bern was occupied, its treasury pillaged, and its territories dismembered. At the Congress of Vienna (1815), Bern failed to recover Vaud and Aargau, but received the Bernese Jura (the former Bishopric of BASEL). A liberal constitution was adopted in 1831, and in 1848 Bern became the capital of the Swiss Confederation. The city is largely medieval in its architecture. It has a splendid 15th-century town hall, a noted minster (begun 15th cent.), and numerous other historic structures. There are many picturesque patrician houses and old guild halls. An elaborate medieval clock tower and a pit in which bears (Bern's heraldic animal for seven centuries) are kept are well known to tourists. More modern buildings include the 19th-century federal parliament building, many fine museums, and the university (1834).

Bernadette, Saint (bûrnədĕt'), 1844–79, French peasant girl who claimed to see the Virgin Mary in apparitions at a grotto near Lourdes, her home, in 1858. She was born Marie Bernarde Soubirous. The authorities, skeptical of her visions, subjected her to severe examinations and abuse. After years of unpleasantness at the hands of the curious, the skeptical, and the powerful, she was allowed to enter the convent of Notre-Dame de Nevers. There Bernadette, her health steadily worsening, spent her last days. She was canonized in 1933. Feast: April 16. See biographies by L. Cristiani (1965) and A. Stafford (1967).

Bernadotte, Count Folke (fôl'kə bĕrnädôt', bûr'nədŏt), 1895–1948, Swedish internationalist; nephew of King Gustavus V. He was active in the Swedish Red Cross and became its president in 1946. Early in 1945 he arranged the evacuation of Danish and Norwegian prisoners from German concentration camps and conveyed a peace offer from Heinrich Himmler to the British and U.S. authorities. Appointed (1948) United Nations mediator in Palestine, he was assassinated by Jewish extremists; Ralph Bunche succeeded him. Bernadotte wrote several autobiographical books. See biography by Ralph Hewins (1950).

Bernadotte, Jean Baptiste Jules: see CHARLES XIV, king of Sweden and Norway.

Bernanos, Georges (zhôrzh bĕrnänōs'), 1888–1948, French novelist and polemicist. Profoundly Catholic, Bernanos attacked modern materialism and advocated a moral and ethical order based on the teachings of the Church. His novels *The Star of Satan* (1926, tr. 1940) and *The Diary of a Country Priest* (1936, tr. 1937) are powerful accounts of intense spiritual struggle and reflect his mysticism. *Dialogue des Carmelites* (1949) was adapted for the stage in 1952. A believer in monarchy, Bernanos was active in Royalist causes until the Spanish civil war. In 1938, after the Munich pact, which he considered a shameful instance of appeasement, he settled in Brazil and remained there until 1945. His political writings include *Les Grands Cimetières sous la lune* (1938, tr. *A Diary of My Times,* 1938), indicting Franco's policies in the Spanish civil war, and *Lettre aux Anglais* (1942, tr. *Plea for Liberty,* 1944). See studies by T. S. Molnar (1960), G. R. Blumenthal (1965), Peter Hebblewaite (1965), W. S. Bush (1969), and Robert Speaight (1974).

Bernard, Saint: see BERNARD OF CLAIRVAUX, SAINT; BERNARD OF MENTHON, SAINT. For the two Alpine passes, see SAINT BERNARD.

Bernard VII, d. 1418, count of Armagnac, constable of France. As father-in-law of Charles d'ORLÉANS he led the Armagnac faction (see ARMAGNACS AND BURGUNDIANS) and from 1415 to 1418 was virtual ruler of France. His oppression of the Parisians, intended to check Burgundian power, caused the betrayal of Paris to John the Fearless of Burgundy; in the ensuing massacre Bernard was killed.

Bernard, Claude (klōd bĕrnär'), 1813–78, French physiologist. He turned from literature to medicine, working in Paris under Magendie and teaching at the Collège de France and at the Sorbonne. One of the great scientific investigators, he is known as the founder of experimental medicine because of his work on digestive processes, especially the discovery of the glycogenic function of the liver and of the action of pancreatic juice, and on the vasomotor mechanism. He wrote *An Introduction to the Study of Experimental Medicine* (1865, tr. 1927). See J. M. D. Olmsted and E. H. Olmsted, *Claude Bernard and the Experimental Method in Medicine* (1952); Reino Virtanen, *Claude Bernard and His Place in the History of Ideas* (1960).

Bernard, Sir Francis (bûrn'ərd), 1712–79, British colonial governor. He was educated at Oxford and was called to the bar in 1737. As colonial governor of New Jersey (1758–60), he did much to promote colonial solidarity and to build defense in the French and Indian Wars. Transferred to the governorship of Massachusetts, he lost popularity there because he felt it his duty to enforce the Stamp Act and other laws the colonists found objectionable. In 1769 he was recalled to England. An amateur architect, he was the designer of Harvard Hall at Harvard.

Bernardes, Diogo (dyō'gō bərnär'dĭsh), c.1530–c.1600, Portuguese poet. A follower of Sá de Miranda, he wrote melodious pastoral verse, and was one of the chief poets of the Portuguese Renaissance. The official poet on the tragic expedition that ended at Alquazarquivir, he was later pensioned.

Bernardin de Saint-Pierre, Jacques Henri (zhäk äNrē' bĕrnärdăN' də săN-pyĕr'), 1737–1814, French naturalist and author. He was a friend of Rousseau, by whom he was strongly influenced. His chief work, *Études de la nature* (1784), sought to prove the existence of God from the wonders of nature; it is rich in descriptive passages, and it added specific color terms and plant names to the French language. A section of this was the sentimental prose idyll *Paul et Virginie* (1788), which attained immense vogue and influenced the French romanticists.

Bernardine of Siena, Saint (bûr'nərdĭn, sēĕn'ə), 1380–1444, Italian preacher. He was a Franciscan of the Observant congregation and one of the most effective and most widely known preachers of his day. His popular, lively sermons still make good reading. He was vicar general of his congregation, and he repeatedly refused ecclesiastical preferment. St. Bernardine was one of the great promoters of devotion to the Holy Name of Jesus. His principal companion was St. John Capistran. Feast: May 20.

Bernardo del Carpio (bĕrnär'dō dĕl kär'pyō), hero of medieval Spanish legend. He was supposedly the nephew of Alfonso II of Asturias, against whom he strove to secure his father's release from prison. Spanish legend has him a counterpart of the French Roland and in some versions the slayer of Roland at Roncesvalles.

Bernard of Clairvaux, Saint (klârvō'), 1090?–1153, French churchman, mystic, Doctor of the Church. Born of noble family, in 1112 he entered the Cistercian abbey of Cîteaux, taking along 4 brothers and some 25 friends. In 1115 he headed the group sent to found a house at Clairvaux. There he remained abbot all his life, despite many efforts to move him higher. A holy life, a reputation for miraculous cures, and unusual eloquence made Bernard renowned, and he became the most powerful religious influence in France and, in time, in all Western Europe. His example and mystical theology had decisive influence on the Cistercian order, and he is sometimes called its second founder. During his lifetime 68 houses were founded out of Clairvaux alone. It was he who led the long struggle to seat Innocent II, the canonically elected pope, and persuaded Lombardy to accept Holy Roman Emperor Lothair II. He procured the condemnation of Peter ABELARD and ARNOLD OF BRESCIA (1140), and he preached the Second Crusade (1146). He was the adviser of popes, especially of his friend EUGENE III. He was tireless in journeys to make peace, and he would undertake any mission of charity, however arduous or apparently trivial; thus he stopped a wave of pogroms in the Rhineland (1146), and he repeatedly saved luckless peasants from the powerful. Through his writings, St. Bernard exerted a profound influence on Roman Catholic spirituality. His deep devotion to the Virgin Mary and to the Infant Jesus is said to have founded a new strain of spirituality known as *devotio moderna.* His works consist of about 330 sermons, some 500 known letters, and 13 treatises. His style, strong and eloquent, full of biblical allusions, and intensely personal and direct, has gained him the name Mellifluous Doctor. Among his sermons, the series of 86 on the Canticles have been favorites (*St. Bernard on the Song of Songs,* tr. 1952). The most important treatises are *On the Steps of Humility and Pride* (c.1125; tr. by Geoffrey Webb and Adrian Walker, 1957) and *On the Love of God* (c.1127; tr. by T. L. Connolly, 1951). He was canonized in 1174. Feast: Aug. 20. See Watkin Williams, *Saint Bernard of Clairvaux* (1952); E. H. Gilson, *The Mystical Theology of Saint Bernard* (tr. 1940); Thomas Merton, *The Last of the Fathers* (1954, repr. 1970); Henry Daniel-Rops, *Bernard of Clairvaux* (tr. 1964); O. J. Egres, *Saint Bernard, His Life and Teaching* (1971).

Bernard of Cluny (klo͞o'nē) or **Bernard of Morlaix** (môrlā'), fl. 1150, French Cluniac monk, of English parentage. He wrote *De contemptu mundi* [on contempt for the world], a poem in 3,000 hexameters. On it Horatio Parker based his oratorio *Hora novissima,* and from it John Mason Neale drew the words of *Jerusalem the Golden.*

Bernard of Menthon, Saint (măNtôN'), d. 1081?, Italian churchman, founder of the Alpine hospices of SAINT BERNARD. His life was spent working among the people of the Val d'Aosta. Also known as Bernard of Montjoux, he is the patron of mountaineers. Feast: May 28.

Bernburg (bĕrn'bo͝ork), city (1970 pop. 45,322), Halle dist., central East Germany, on the Saale River. Located in a salt-mining region, it has industries that produce food products and farm machinery. There is a 16th-century castle in the city.

Bern Convention: see COPYRIGHT.

Berne, Switzerland: see BERN.

Berners, John Bourchier, 2d Baron (bou'chər, bûr'nərz), 1467–1533, English diplomat and man of letters. A member of Parliament from 1495 to 1529, he later became chancellor of the exchequer (1516) and ambassador to Madrid (1518). He was English governor of Calais from 1520 until his death. Berners's literary work includes such translations as Froissart's *Chronicles* (2 vol., 1523–25); *Huon of Bordeaux* (1534?); and *The Golden Book of Marcus Aurelius* (1535; from a French version of Guevara's work).

Berners, Bernes, or **Barnes, Juliana** (bŭr'nərz, bärnz), supposed early 15th-century author of a popular verse treatise on hunting. The treatise is included in *The Book of St. Albans* (1486), a collection treating the arts of heraldry, hawking, and field sports. If Juliana was the author, she is one of the earliest women writers in English; although tradition designates her the prioress of a nunnery in Hertfordshire, nothing is actually known of her life. See facsimile edition with introduction by William Blades (1881).

Bernese mountain dog (bərnēz'), breed of sturdy WORKING DOG first brought to Switzerland by the invading Roman armies over two millennia ago. It stands from 23 to 27 in. (58–69 cm) high at the shoulder and weighs from 50 to 70 lb (23–32 kg). Its long, silky, slightly wavy coat is jet black with a white blaze up the face, white on the chest, feet, and tip of tail, and russet-brown or tan markings on all four legs and above the eyes. For hundreds of years in its native canton of Berne, the Bernese mountain dog was used as a draft animal by the local merchants to haul cartloads of goods to market. Today it is raised principally for show competition and as a pet. See DOG.

Bernhardi, Friedrich von (frē'drĭkh fən bĕrnhär'dē), 1849–1930, German general and military writer. His book *Germany and the Next War* (1912, tr. 1912) was widely publicized by the Allies as an example of Pan-Germanism and German ambition.

Bernhard of Saxe-Weimar (săks'-wī'mär, zäks'ə-vī'mär), 1604–39, Protestant general in the THIRTY YEARS WAR, duke of Weimar. Under Ernst von MANSFELD and the margrave of Baden, Bernhard fought against the imperial forces in defense (1622) of the Palatinate. He served in the Netherlands and later allied himself (1631) with King Gustavus Adolphus of Sweden, after whose death at Lützen (1632) he took command. In 1633, Bernhard became joint commander of the army of the Heilbronn Confederation, created under Swedish auspices. The Swedish government also granted him the newly created duchy of Franconia, formed out of the captured German bishoprics of Würzburg and Bamberg. His capture of Regensburg (1633) made him the hero of the Protestants. In 1634 he suffered a crushing defeat by the imperial army at Nördlingen and soon afterward lost Franconia. Bernhard and his army were taken into French pay in 1635. Victories at Breisgau and Breisach (1638) brought him control over Alsace and the Upper Rhine. He died suddenly of a fever.

Bernhardt, Sarah (bûrn'härt, Fr. bĕrnär'), 1844–1923, stage name of Rosine Bernard, French actress, b. Paris. She was brought up in a convent until she was 13, when she entered the Paris Conservatory. In 1862 she made an unsuccessful debut at the Comédie

Française. During her appearances at the Odéon (1866–72) she attracted attention, first in Coppée's *Le Passant* (1869). With the Comédie (1872–80) she attained full stature with her superb portrayals of Phèdre (1874) and of Doña Sol in Hugo's *Hernani* (1877). Renowned for her golden voice, she was considered the queen of French romantic and classical tragedy. Oscar Wilde called her "the divine Sarah," a designation by which she became universally known. In 1880 she began her tours of Europe, England, and the United States, in such plays as *Adrienne Lecouvreur, La Dame aux camélias,* and *Froufrou.* Long associated with the works of Sardou, she starred in his *Fédora, Théodora,* and *La Tosca.* She managed several theaters in Paris before leasing the Théâtre des Nations, renaming it the Théâtre Sarah Bernhardt. Here she revived some of her former successes and appeared in the title role of *Hamlet* (1899) and in Rostand's *L'Aiglon,* which was written for her in 1901. In 1912 she appeared in the silent films *La Dame aux camélias* and *Queen Elizabeth.* Her leg was amputated in 1915, but her career continued and she made numerous "farewell tours." An accomplished painter, poet, and sculptor, she also wrote plays in which she appeared. Among them were *L'Aveu* (1898) and *Un cœur d'homme* (1909). See her memoirs (tr. 1907); biographies by Jules Huret (1899), Maurice Baring (1934), Louis Verneuil (1942), A. W. Row (1957), Cornelia Otis Skinner (1967), and Gerda Taranow (1972).

Berni, Francesco (frănchās'kō bĕr'nē), 1497?–1535, Italian humorous poet, a priest. He was noted for his burlesque *capitoli,* light, often ribald verses in terza rima. He revised Boiardo's *Orlando Innamorato,* adding humorous touches and what he considered stylistic improvements. For many years Berni's rendering of Boiardo was the standard version; it has been generally discarded. For refusing to help murder Cardinal Salviati, Berni is thought to have been poisoned. One genre of satirical poetry is called *bernesco* after him.

Bernice (bûr'nĕs, bərnēs'), form of the name Berenice. Bernice has been commonly used in English-speaking countries in modern times.

Bernicia (bərnĭsh'ə), Old English kingdom. Established in 547, it later extended from the Tees River to the Forth. In the late 6th cent. it was united with Deira to form NORTHUMBRIA.

Bernina (bĕrnē'nä), mountain group, part of the Rhaetian Alps on the Swiss-Italian border, SE Switzerland. Piz Bernina is the highest (13,304 ft/4,055 m) peak. The group has many glaciers; Morteratsch Glacier is the largest. The Bernina Pass, 7,645 ft (2,330 m) high, from the Upper Engadine Valley, Switzerland, to the Valtellina, Italy, is crossed by a road (built 1842–65) and a railroad (built 1907–10).

Bernini, Giovanni Lorenzo or **Gianlorenzo** (jōvän'nē lōrĕn'tsō, jänlōrĕn'tsō bĕrnē'nē), 1598–1680, Italian sculptor and architect, b. Naples. He was the dominant figure of the Italian BAROQUE. After receiving early training from his father, Pietro (1562–1629), an accomplished Florentine sculptor, Bernini worked mainly in Rome. Many of his early statues, such as the *David* (before 1620), *Rape of Proserpine* (1622), and *Apollo and Daphne* (1625), were done for Scipione Cardinal Borghese, one of the most important patrons of the period. These are all in the Borghese Gallery, Rome. In these masterful early works, Bernini broke with the traditions of MANNERISM. Popes Urban VIII, Innocent X, and Alexander VII gave him unparalleled opportunities to design churches, chapels, fountains, monuments, tombs, and statues. In 1629, Bernini was appointed architect of St. Peter's. He designed the ornate baldachin under the dome, the *Cathedra Petri* (the monument enshrining St. Peter's chair), and the exuberant marble decorations of the chapels and nave. From 1656 onward he worked on the great elliptical piazza and the vast, embracing arms of the colonnades in front of the church. During Innocent's papacy Bernini worked frequently for private patrons. In 1655 he was commissioned to do the magnificent fountains in the Piazza Navona. For the Vatican he created the royal staircase and the heroic equestrian statue of Constantine. He was assisted by a host of sculptors in these vast enterprises. Between 1658 and 1670 he designed three churches: San Tomaso di Villanova at Castelgandolfo, Santa Maria dell' Assunzione at Ariccia, and Sant' Andrea al Quirinale in Rome. He established a new mode, dynamically linking sculpture and architecture. In 1665, Louis XIV invited him to Paris to finish the designing of the Louvre, but Bernini's plans failed to win approval. Returning to Italy, he continued to work on St. Peter's. Much of Bernini's sculpture combines white and colored marbles with bronze and stucco, most effectively used in Santa Maria della Vittoria, Rome, where he represented the *Ecstasy of St. Teresa.* This work exemplifies Bernini's ability to grasp the most dramatic moment from his subject's life. Often inspired by classical forms, Bernini transformed the marble block into a vital, almost breathing figure. A self-portrait drawn c.1665 (Royal Coll., Windsor) is an example of his superb draftsmanship. As a painter he was also noteworthy, although very few of his paintings survive. Bernini was known as a wit; he wrote comedies and made numerous caricatures. All of his important work is in Rome, with the exception of the *Neptune and Triton* (Victoria and Albert Mus.) and the bust of Louis XIV (Versailles). See biography by F. Baldinucci (1682, tr. 1966), studies by H. Hibbard (1965), R. Wittkower (2d ed. 1966), and I. Lavin (1968).

Bernoulli or **Bernouilli** (both: bĕrnōōyē'), name of a family distinguished in scientific and mathematical history. The family, after leaving Antwerp, finally settled in Basel, Switzerland, where it grew in fame. **Jacob, Jacques,** or **James Bernoulli,** 1654–1705, became professor at Basel in 1687. One of the chief developers both of the ordinary CALCULUS and of the CALCULUS OF VARIATIONS, he was the first to use the word *integral* in solving Leibniz's problem of the isochronous curve. He wrote an important treatise on the theory of probability (1713) and discovered the series of numbers that now bear his name, i.e., the coefficients of the exponential series expansion of $x/(1-e^{-x})$. He was succeeded at Basel by his brother, **Johann, Jean,** or **John Bernoulli,** 1667–1748, who earlier had been professor at Gröningen and who was famous for his work in the field of integral and exponential calculus and was also a founder of the calculus of variations. He also contributed to the study of geodesics, of complex numbers, and of trigonometry. His collected works were published under the title *Johannis Bernoulli opera omnia.* His son, **Daniel Bernoulli,** 1700–1782, was a mathematician, physicist, and physician and has often been called the first mathematical physicist. He received his doctorate in medicine but became professor of mathematics at the St. Petersburg Academy in 1725. He was professor of anatomy and botany at Basel from 1733, later becoming professor of natural philosophy (physics). His greatest work was his *Hydrodynamica* (1738), which included the principle now known as BERNOULLI'S PRINCIPLE, and anticipated the law of conservation of energy and the KINETIC-MOLECULAR THEORY OF GASES developed more than 100 years later. He also made important contributions to probability theory, astronomy, and the theory of differential equations (solving a famous equation proposed by Riccati). Among the other noted members of the family are Nicolaus Bernoulli, 1662–1716, brother of Jacob and Johann, who was professor of mathematics at St. Petersburg; Nicolaus Bernoulli, 1695–1726, son of Johann and brother of Daniel, also a mathematician; Johann Bernoulli, 1710–90, another son of Johann (1667–1748) and brother of Daniel, who succeeded his father in the chair of mathematics at Basel and also contributed to physics; his son, Johann Bernoulli, 1746–1807, who was astronomer royal at Berlin and also studied mathematics and geography; and Jacob Bernoulli, 1759–89, another son of Johann (1710–90), who succeeded his uncle Daniel in mathematics and physics at St. Petersburg but met an early death by drowning.

Bernoulli's principle, physical principle formulated by Daniel Bernoulli that states that as the speed of a moving fluid (liquid or gas) increases, the pressure within the fluid decreases. The phenomenon described by Bernoulli's principle has many practical applications; it is employed in the carburetor and the atomizer, in which air is the moving fluid, and in the aspirator, in which water is the moving fluid. In the first two devices air moving through a tube passes through a constriction, which causes an increase in speed and a corresponding reduction in pressure. As a result, liquid is forced up into the air stream (through a narrow tube that leads from the body of the liquid to the constriction) by the greater atmospheric pressure on the surface of the liquid. In the aspirator air is drawn into a stream of water as the water flows through a constriction. Bernoulli's principle can be explained in terms of the law of conservation of energy (see CONSERVATION LAWS, in physics). As a fluid moves from a wider pipe into a narrower pipe or a constriction, a corresponding volume must move a greater distance forward in the narrower pipe and thus have a greater speed. At the same time, the work done by corresponding volumes in the wider and narrower pipes will be expressed by the product of the pressure and the volume. Since the speed is greater in the narrower pipe, the kinetic energy of that volume is greater. Then, by the law of conservation of energy, this increase in kinetic energy must be balanced by a decrease in the pressure-volume product, or, since the volumes are equal, by a decrease in pressure.

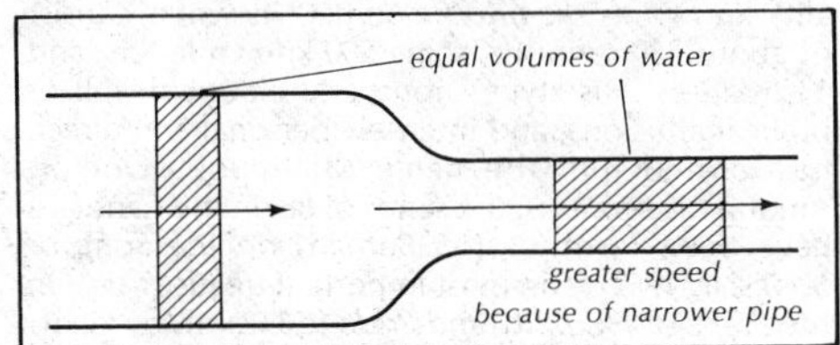

Bernoulli's principle

Bernstein, Eduard (ā'dōōärt bĕrn'shtīn), 1850–1932, German socialist. From 1872 he was actively associated with the Social Democratic party. In 1878 he left Germany because of antisocialist legislation and spent over 20 years in exile, chiefly in England. In 1898 he aroused great discussion among German socialists by his criticisms of Marxist theories, denying the inevitability of intensification of the class struggle and the resultant collapse of the social order ending in world revolution. Returning to Berlin in 1901 he became the leader of revisionism, opposed by Karl Johann KAUTSKY. After World War I, Bernstein was unsuccessful in his attempts to unify the various factions of German socialists. The most important of his several books setting forth criticisms of Marxism is *Evolutionary Socialism* (1898, tr. 1909). See his reminiscences, *My Years of Exile* (1921); Peter Gay, *The Dilemma of Democratic Socialism* (1954); J. W. Hulse, *Revolutionists in London* (1970).

Bernstein, Leonard (bûrn'stīn), 1918–, American composer, conductor, and pianist, b. Lawrence, Mass., grad. Harvard, 1939, and Curtis Institute of Music, 1941. A highly versatile musician, he is the composer of symphonic works (the *Jeremiah* Symphony, 1944; *Age of Anxiety,* 1949; *Kaddish* Symphony, 1963), song cycles, chamber music, ballets (*Fancy Free,* 1944), musicals (*On the Town,* 1944; *Wonderful Town,* 1953; *Candide,* 1956; *West Side Story,* 1957), opera (*Trouble in Tahiti,* 1952), and choral music (*Chichester Psalms,* 1965). His *Mass* (1971), a "theater piece for dancers, singers, and players," was performed at the opening of the John F. Kennedy Cultural Center in Washington, D.C. From 1951 to 1956 he taught at Brandeis Univ. He has been soloist and conductor with many orchestras in the United States and abroad. He first conducted the New York Philharmonic-Symphony Orchestra in 1943, and from 1958 to 1970 was its musical director. Upon his retirement he was named Laureate Conductor, and now frequently appears with the Vienna Philharmonic and the Israel Philharmonic. See his *The Joy of Music* (1959) and *The Infinite Variety of Music* (1966); biographies by John Briggs (1961) and John Gruen (1968).

Bernstorff, Andreas Peter (ändrā'äs pā'tər bĕrns'tôrf), 1735–97, Danish politician; nephew of Johann Hartwig Ernst BERNSTORFF. Made (1773) foreign minister after Struensee's fall from power, he obtained from Russia the final ratification of the exchange treaty negotiated by his uncle in 1767. Removed from office in 1780 to pacify Russia, he was recalled in 1784 and was chief minister until 1797. He sought friendly relations with Sweden, kept Denmark neutral in the French Revolutionary Wars, and undertook a liberal program of social, economic, and educational reform.

Bernstorff, Johann Hartwig Ernst (yōhän' härt'vĭkh), 1712–72, Danish politician, of German (Hanoverian) origin. As minister of foreign affairs (1751–70) under FREDERICK V and Christian VII, he successfully kept Denmark at peace. In 1767 he negotiated with Russia a provisional treaty by which the Danish crown was to cede OLDENBURG to Catherine II of Russia in exchange for ducal HOLSTEIN. In 1770, Christian VII, under the influence of STRUENSEE, dismissed Bernstorff.

Bernstorff, Johann Heinrich, Graf von (hīn'rĭkh gräf fən), 1862–1939, German diplomat. As ambassador to the United States (1908–17), he tried to conciliate American feelings toward Germany and repeatedly warned his government that unrestricted submarine warfare would bring the United States into World War I. A member of the Reichstag from 1921 to 1928 and a delegate to the League of Nations disarmament conference (1926–31), he went into exile at Geneva after Hitler took power in Germany. His memoirs were published in 1936.

Berodach-baladan: see MERODACH-BALADAN.

Beroea (bērē'ə), the same as BEREA **1.**

Beroeans: see BEREANS.

Berossus (bərŏ'səs), 3d cent. B.C., Babylonian priest-historian; contemporary of MANETHO. His work, in Greek, preserved Mesopotamian myths regarding creation and history. It survives in fragments quoted by Josephus and Eusebius of Caesarea.

Berothah (bērō'thə), city of Syria. Ezek. 47.16. Berothai may be the same.

Berothai (bĕr'ōthī), city of Syria, perhaps the same as Berothah. 2 Sam. 8.8. Chun: 1 Chron. 18.8.

Berothite (bĕr'ōthīt), inhabitant of the city Beeroth. 1 Chron. 11.39.

Berra, Yogi (Lawrence Peter Berra), 1925–, American baseball player and manager, b. St. Louis, Mo. An outstanding catcher with the New York Yankees (1946–63), he also played briefly with the New York Mets (1965). Berra was elected the American League's most valuable player in 1951, 1954, and 1955, hit 358 home runs and batted .285. In 1964 he managed the Yankees, leading them to the pennant. He managed the Mets (1972–). He was elected to the Baseball Hall of Fame in 1972. See biography by Phil Pepe (1974).

Berrettini, Pietro: see CORTONA, PIETRO DA.

Berrigan, Daniel, 1921–, American Jesuit priest, poet, and political activist, b. Syracuse, N.Y.; brother of Philip Berrigan. Upon his ordination in 1952, he traveled to France, where he developed admiration for militant workers and supported their efforts. Returning to the United States, he taught at Brooklyn Preparatory School and Le Moyne College until, after a second trip to France (1963), he devoted his time to civil rights and antipoverty and antiwar work. Convicted in 1970 and sentenced to three years imprisonment for destroying selective service files in Catonsville, Md., in 1968, Berrigan became a fugitive but eventually was captured and sent to prison; he was granted parole in Jan., 1972. His works include a play, *The Trial of the Catonsville Nine* (1970); *The Dark Night of Resistance* (1971); his prison memoirs, *Lights On in the House of the Dead* (1974); and several volumes of poems. See biography by Richard Curtis (1974); Stephen Halpert and Tom Murray, ed., *Witness of the Berrigans* (1972).

Berrigan, Philip Francis, 1923–, American Roman Catholic priest and political activist, b. Two Harbors, Minn.; brother of Daniel Berrigan. In 1950 he graduated from Holy Cross College and was ordained. Throughout the 1960s Berrigan was active in civil rights and antiwar groups; during that time he founded the Catholic Peace Fellowship. He was convicted and imprisoned for destroying selective service files in 1967 in Baltimore and in 1968 in Catonsville, Md. In 1970, while in prison, Berrigan was convicted on charges of smuggling mail out of the federal penitentiary at Lewisburg, Pa. His wife, Sister Elizabeth McAlister, whom he married secretly in 1969, was also convicted on similar charges. In 1972 the convictions were overturned. Berrigan was paroled in December of that year. See his prison writings, *Prison Journals of a Revolutionary Priest* (1970) and *Widen the Prison Gates* (1973).

Berruguete, Alonso (ālōn'sō bĕr-rōōgā'tā), c.1480–1561, Spanish mannerist sculptor. Probably the first in Spain to break away from the High Renaissance balance of form, he is noted for the expressive torsion of his figures. He studied with his father, Pedro Berruguete, a painter at the Spanish court. In Italy (c.1504–c.1517) he was strongly influenced by Michelangelo. On Berruguete's return to Spain he was appointed (1518) court painter and sculptor to Charles V. The carved altar screens for San Benito el Real (1527–32; Valladolid Mus.) and the choir stalls of the cathedral at Toledo (1539–43) are among his masterpieces. Berruguete brought the influence of Michelangelo to Spain, but his vigorous and highly original art is essentially Spanish. His work is best seen in Valladolid.

Berry, Caroline Ferdinande Louise, duchesse de (kärôlēn' fĕrdēnäNd lwēz, düshĕs' də bĕrē'), 1798–1870, wife of the French prince, Charles Ferdinand, duc de Berry; daughter of Francis I of the Two Sicilies. She went into exile from France after the overthrow of King Charles X, her father-in-law. Returning secretly in 1832, she organized a small, unsuccessful uprising in an attempt to win the throne for Berry's posthumous son, Henri, later known as the comte de CHAMBORD. For these activities she was imprisoned. However, when it became obvious that the duchesse was pregnant, she was forced to reveal her secret second marriage to an Italian count. This marriage alienated her royalist supporters, and the French government released her from prison.

Berry, Charles Ferdinand, duc de (shärl fĕrdēnäN', dük), 1778–1820, younger son of Charles, comte d'Artois (later Charles X of France). He served in the prince de Condé's army against the French Revolution. His assassination during the reign of King LOUIS XVIII—an attempt to extinguish the Bourbon line—gave the ultraroyalists the opportunity to turn Louis XVIII against the liberals. Berry's posthumous son was Henri, comte de Chambord.

Berry, Martha McChesney, 1866–1942, American educator and philanthropist, b. near Rome, Ga., Ph.D. Univ. of Georgia, 1920. Determined to provide educational opportunities for underprivileged mountain children, Berry opened (1902) a log-cabin school with five pupils. She developed this at Mt. Berry, Ga., into an institution comprising four units: a boys' school (1902), a girls' school (1909), Berry College (1926; coeducational), and a model practice school. See biography by Tracy Byers (1932, repr. 1971); H. T. Kane and I. W. Henry, *Miracle in the Mountains* (1956).

Berry (bĕrē'), former province, central France. Bourges, the capital, and Châteauroux are the chief towns. Cattle are raised on the Champagne Berrichonne, a semiarid plateau that covers most of the region. The valleys of the Indre and the Cher rivers are rich farming areas. A part of Roman Aquitaine, Berry was made a county in the 8th cent., and was purchased (1101) by the French crown. In 1360 it was made a duchy. It was held as an appanage by various royal princes until 1601, when it reverted to the crown.

berry: see FRUIT.

Berryman, John, 1914–72, American poet and critic, b. McAlester, Okla., grad. Columbia, 1936. From 1955 until his death he was on the faculty of the Univ. of Minnesota. Although he had published several volumes of poetry and a highly regarded biography of Stephen Crane (1950), his literary reputation was not established until the appearance of *Homage to Mistress Bradstreet* (1956), a long dialogue in verse between Berryman and the ghost of Anne BRADSTREET. The volumes *77 Dream Songs* (1964; Pulitzer Prize) and *His Toy, His Dream, His Rest* (1968) can be considered a two-part novel in verse in which the only speaker is a middle-aged teacher and lover named Harry, who is the universal voice of an anguished and trivial age. Berryman committed suicide in 1972. *Delusions* (1972), a volume of poems, and *Recovery* (1973), a novel, were published posthumously; in both the poet examines himself and his life—as it slips away—in intimate and harrowing detail. Berryman's other volumes of poetry include *Poems* (1942), *The Dispossessed* (1948), *Berryman's Sonnets* (1967), and *Love and Fame* (1971). See study by J. M. Linebarger (1974).

Bersimis: see BETSIAMITES, river, Canada.

Bertha of the Big Foot: see BERTRADA.

Berthelot, Pierre Eugène Marcelin (pyĕr ûzhĕn' märsəlăN' bĕrtəlō'), 1827–1907, French chemist. He was professor at the École Supérieure de Pharmacie (1859) and at the Collège de France from 1865. In 1900 he became a member of the French Academy. A founder of modern organic chemistry, he was the first to produce organic compounds synthetically (including the carbon compounds methyl alcohol, ethyl alcohol, benzene, and acetylene), at the same time dispelling the old theory of a vital force inherent in organic compounds. He also did valuable work in thermochemistry and in explosives. His writings include *Chimie organique fondée sur la synthèse* (1860) and *Leçons sur la thermochimie* (1897).

Berthier, Louis Alexandre (lwē älĕksăN'drə bĕrtyā'), 1753–1815, marshal of France. He served in the American Revolution and in the French Revolutionary Wars, distinguishing himself under Napoleon in Italy, where he served as chief of staff. He was twice minister of war and from 1805 was chief of staff of the *Grande Armée.* The emperor made him prince of Neuchâtel and Wagram and arranged his marriage with a Bavarian princess. Berthier accommodated himself to the return of the Bourbons in 1814. Torn by divided allegiance when Napoleon returned from Elba, he withdrew to Bavaria, where he killed himself or was killed on June 1, 1815.

Berthollet, Claude Louis, Comte (klōd lwē, kôNt bĕrtōlā'), 1748–1822, French chemist. His contributions to chemistry include the analysis of ammonia and prussic acid and the discovery of the bleaching properties of chlorine. He collaborated with Antoine Lavoisier in his researches and in reforming chemical nomenclature and supported him in his theory of combustion. His greatest contribution was in his *Essai de statique chimique* (1803), in which he presented his speculations on chemical affinity and his discovery of the reversibility of reactions.

Bertillon system (bərtĭl'yən), first scientific method of criminal identification, developed by the French criminologist Alphonse Bertillon (1853–1914). The system, based on the classification of skeletal and other body measurements and characteristics, was officially adopted in France in 1888 and soon after in other countries. Fingerprinting, added later as a supplementary measure, has largely replaced the system. See biography of Alphonse Bertillon by Henry Rhodes (1956, repr. 1969).

Bertoia, Harry (bĕrtoi'yə), 1915–, American sculptor and furniture designer, b. Italy. Bertoia emigrated to the United States in 1933 and joined Knoll International (1950). There he designed chairs that brought him wide acclaim. Important examples of his sculptural works are a structural screen for the Manufacturers Hanover Trust Company, New York City, and a bronze panel at Dulles International Airport, Washington, D.C.

Bertoldo di Giovanni (bärtôl'dō dē jōvän'nē), c.1420–91, Italian sculptor. A pupil and assistant to Donatello and later the teacher of Michelangelo, Bertoldo was employed by the Medici to supervise instruction in sculpture and care for their collection of antique sculpture. His own works, often small bronzes, include battle scenes and mythological episodes (e.g., *Orpheus,* Bargello, Florence).

Bertrada, d. 783, Frankish queen, wife of Pepin the Short and mother of Charlemagne. She tried without success to reconcile Charlemagne and his brother Carloman. Also called Bertha of the Big Foot or Queen Goosefoot, she figures in Carolingian legend.

Bertrand de Born (bûr'trənd də bôrn) or **Bertran de Born** (bĕrträN'), c.1140–c.1214. French TROUBADOUR of Limousin. Some of his 40 surviving poems (in Provençal) tell of his part in the struggles between Henry II of England and his sons. For his warlike role in these quarrels, Bertrand is named as a "sower of schism" in Dante's *Inferno.*

Berwald, Franz (fränts bĕr'väld), 1796–1868, Swedish composer. Unable to support himself entirely by music, for a time Berwald directed an orthopedic clinic and ran a glassworks. His music, which is highly original in its use of rhythm, harmony, and orchestration, had little popular success. Berwald's orchestral music is reminiscent of work by Berlioz, although his thematic ideas are generally more concise. He wrote six symphonies and several concertos, chamber works, and operas. See Robert Layton, *Berwald* (1959).

Berwick, James FitzJames, duke of (bĕr'ĭk), 1670–1734, marshal of France; illegitimate son of King James II of England and Arabella Churchill, sister of the duke of Marlborough. Born and educated in France, he fought in Hungary against the Ottoman Turks. In 1687, his father, who had ascended the English throne in 1685, created him duke of Berwick. When his father was dethroned (1688), Berwick took part in the invasion of Ireland (1689) against James's successor William III; the effort was supported by King Louis XIV of France, James's ally. After the defeat in Ireland, Berwick fought for France in the War of the Grand Alliance and became (1703) a naturalized Frenchman. He subsequently helped suppress the Protestant CAMISARDS. In the War of the Spanish Succession (see SPANISH SUCCESSION, WAR OF THE), he won the decisive victory of Almansa (1707) for King Philip V of Spain, Louis XIV's grandson. In 1709 he campaigned against Prince EUGENE OF SAVOY in defense of the southeastern frontier of France, and his capture of Barcelona (1714) was the closing event of the war. During the War of the Polish Succession, he commanded (1733) the French army of the Rhine; he was killed at Philippsburg.

Berwick (bĕr'ĭk) or **Berwickshire** (bĕr'ĭkshĭr), county (1971 pop. 20,750), 457 sq mi (1,194 km), SE Scotland. The county town is Duns. Berwick is separated from England by the Tweed River. The coastline (along the North Sea) is rocky and inhospitable. The county is divided into three geographical regions: the Merse, in the southeast, one of the most productive valleys in Scotland; the Lammermuirs, a pastoral mountainous region in the northwest; and Lauderdale, a cultivated hilly region along Leader Water in the west. The Eye is Berwick's major river. Sheep grazing, the cultivation of grains, sugar beets, and potatoes, and fishing are the chief occupations. Berwick was part of the ancient Saxon kingdom of

Northumbria. For many centuries it was the scene of border strife between England and Scotland. Dryburgh Abbey, in Berwick, is the burial place of Sir Walter Scott, the writer, and Earl Haig, the general. In 1975, Berwick became part of the Borders region.

Berwick (bûr'wĭk), industrial borough (1970 pop. 12,274), Columbia co., E Pa., on the Susquehanna River, in a forest and farm area; inc. 1818. Clothing and mobile homes are produced in the city. The region abounds in fish and game.

Berwick upon Tweed (bĕr'ĭk), municipal borough (1971 pop. 11,644), Northumberland, NE England, at the mouth of the Tweed River. It is a market town and seaport and is famous for its salmon fishing. Grain is the chief export; oil and timber are imported. Other industries are shipbuilding, engineering, sawmilling, fertilizer production, and the manufacture of tweed and hosiery. The principal border town between Scotland and England, Berwick changed hands more than 13 times between 1147 and 1482, when Edward IV finally claimed it for England. It did not become officially English until 1885. Of interest are the Royal Border Bridge, the old barracks, and the walls surrounding the city that were especially designed to utilize artillery guns.

Berwyn (bûr'wĭn), city (1970 pop. 52,502), Cook co., NE Ill., a residential suburb of Chicago, on the Chicago Sanitary and Ship Canal; inc. 1891. It has varied light manufactures.

beryl (bĕr'ĭl), mineral, a silicate of beryllium and aluminum, $Be_3Al_2Si_6O_{18}$, extremely hard, occurring in hexagonal crystals that may be of enormous size and are usually white, yellow, green, blue, or colorless. Beryl is commonly used as a gemstone. The refractive index is low, and the stones have little or no fire. The most valued variety of beryl is EMERALD. An AQUAMARINE is a blue to sea-green beryl; morganites are rose-red beryls. It is the principal raw material for the element beryllium and its compounds.

beryllium (bərĭl'ēəm) [from *beryl*], rarely **glucinum,** metallic chemical element; symbol Be; at. no. 4; at. wt. 9.0122; m. p. about 1285°C; b. p. 2970°C (estimated); sp. gr. 1.85 at 20°C; valence +2. Beryllium is a strong, extremely light, high-melting, silver-gray metal with a close-packed hexagonal crystalline structure. It is an ALKALINE-EARTH METAL in group IIa of the PERIODIC TABLE. Beryllium is resistant to corrosion; weight for weight, it is stronger than steel, and because of its low density (about 1/3 that of aluminum) it has found extensive use in the aerospace industry. Beryllium is soluble in hot nitric acid, dilute hydrochloric and sulfuric acids, and sodium hydroxide. Like aluminum and magnesium, which it resembles chemically, it readily forms compounds with other elements; it is not found free in nature. However, like aluminum, it is resistant to oxidation in air, even at a red heat; it is thought to form a protective oxide film that prevents further oxidation. The compounds of beryllium are sweet-tasting and highly toxic; this toxicity has limited the use of beryllium as a rocket fuel, even though it yields more heat on combustion for its weight than any other element. Beryllium transmits X rays much better than glass or other metals; this property, together with its high melting point, makes it desirable as a window material for high-intensity X-ray tubes. Because beryllium resists attack by liquid sodium metal, it is employed in cooling systems of nuclear reactors that use liquid sodium as the heat-transfer material; because it is a good reflector and absorber of neutrons, it is also used as a shield and as a moderator in nuclear reactors. The addition of 2% to 3% of beryllium to copper makes a nonmagnetic alloy six times stronger than pure copper. This alloy is used to make nonsparking tools for use in oil refineries and other places where sparks constitute a fire hazard; it is also used for small mechanical parts, such as camera shutters. When beryllium is alloyed with other metals such as aluminum or gold it yields substances with a higher melting point, greater hardness and strength, and lower density than the metal with which it is alloyed. Beryllium aluminum silicates, especially BERYL (of which emerald and aquamarine are varieties), constitute the chief sources of the metal. Although its ores occur widely in North America, Europe, and Africa, the cost of extracting the metal limits its commercial use. Beryllium may be prepared by electrolysis of its fused salts; it is prepared commercially by reduction of the fluoride with magnesium metal. Beryllium was discovered in 1798 as the oxide beryllia by L. N. Vauquelin, a French chemist. Vauquelin analyzed beryl and emerald at the urging of R. J. Haüy, a French mineralogist, who had noted that their optical properties were identical. Beryllium was first isolated in 1828 independently by F. Wöhler in Germany and W. Bussy in France by fusing beryllium chloride with metallic potassium.

Berytus: see BEIRUT, Lebanon.

Berzelius, Jöns Jakob, Baron (bərzē'lēəs; Swed. yöns yä'kôp bĕrsā'lĭəs), 1779–1848, Swedish chemist, M.D. Univ. of Uppsala, 1802. He was noted for his work as teacher at the medical school and other institutions in Stockholm and for his discoveries in diverse fields of chemistry. He developed the modern system of symbols and formulas in chemistry, prepared a remarkably accurate table of atomic weights, analyzed numerous chemical compounds, and discovered the elements selenium, thorium, and cerium. Silicon in the amorphous form was first prepared by Berzelius, and he was the first to isolate zirconium. Berzelius coined the words *isomerism, allotropy,* and *protein.* He also contributed to the science of electrochemistry and wrote numerous books. See study by J. Eric Jorpes (tr. 1971).

Besai (bē'sā), family that returned with Zerubbabel. Ezra 2.49; Neh. 7.52.

Besançon (bəzäNsôN'), city (1968 pop. 119,471), capital of Doubs dept., E France, in Franche-Comté, on the Doubs. An industrial town with metallurgical, textile, and food-processing industries, it is especially famous for its clock and watch manufactures; its watch school is world renowned. Of Gallo-Roman origin, Besançon was an archiepiscopal see from the 5th cent. Although part of the kingdom of Burgundy, it was made (by Emperor Frederick I) a free city, with special privileges for its archbishops. It maintained its independence, with interruptions, until 1648, when it passed under Spanish rule through its incorporation with Franche-Comté. After Louis XIV's second conquest of Franche-Comté (1674), Besançon became (1676) the capital of his new province. Although bombed during World War II, many old monuments remain: Roman ruins, a cathedral (12th–16th cent.), and numerous buildings in Spanish Renaissance style, notably the Palais Granvelle (birthplace of Cardinal Granvelle, now housing a museum) and the imposing town hall. An intellectual center, Besançon is the seat of a university (founded 1422 in Dôle and moved to Besançon in 1691), a music academy (founded 1726), and an international music festival.

Besant, Annie (bĕz'ant), 1847–1933, English social reformer and theosophist, b. Annie Wood. She steadily grew away from Christianity and in 1873 separated from her husband, a Protestant clergyman. In 1879 the courts deprived her of her children because of her atheism and alleged unconventionality. As a member of the National Secular Society she preached free thought and, as a member of the Fabian society, socialism. With Charles BRADLAUGH she edited the *National Reformer* and with her reprinted an old pamphlet on birth control, *The Fruits of Philosophy,* for which they were tried (1877) on a charge of immorality and acquitted. In 1889 she embraced THEOSOPHY, becoming a disciple of Mme Blavatsky and, later, her biographer. She pursued her mission to India, where she soon became involved in nationalist politics. She founded the Central Hindu College at Benares (Varanasi) in 1898 and in 1916 established the Indian Home Rule League and became its president. She was president of the Indian National Congress in 1917, but later split with Gandhi. She traveled (1926–27) in England and the United States with her protégé Jiddu KRISHNAMURTI, whom she announced as the new Messiah. President of the Theosophical Society from 1907, she wrote an enormous number of books and pamphlets on theosophy. Her works include her autobiography (1893), *Four Great Religions* (1897), *The Ancient Wisdom* (1897), and a translation of the *Bhagavad Gita* (1905). See Theodore Besterman, *Mrs. Annie Besant* (1934); A. H. Nethercot, *The First Five Lives of Annie Besant* (1960) and *The Last Four Lives of Annie Besant* (1963).

Besant, Sir Walter (bĭzănt'), 1836–1901, English novelist and humanitarian, grad. Christ's College, Cambridge, 1859. He taught at the Royal College of Mauritius from 1861 to 1867. After his return to England he devoted himself to writing and to various causes, among them the improvement of the copyright laws. His first novels (in collaboration with James Rice) won immediate popularity. Romantic and somewhat florid in style, they include *The Golden Butterfly* (1876) and *Ready-Money Mortiboy* (1872). Many of Besant's novels, written after the collaboration with Rice, dealt with social problems; among them were *All Sorts and Conditions of Men* (1882) and *Children of Gibeon* (1886). Besant was one of the most widely read novelists of the late 19th cent. He was knighted in 1895. See his autobiography (1902, repr. 1971).

Beskids (bĕs'kĭdz), Czech and Slovak *Beskydy,* Pol. *Beskidy* (bĕskē'dē), mountain range of the Carpathians, extending c.200 mi (320 km) along the Polish-Czechoslovakian border. The highest peak, Babia Góra (Slovak *Babí Hora*) rises to 5,658 ft (1,725 m). The Dunajec River divides the range into eastern and western sections. The Vistula River rises in the Western Beskids. Several passes, notably Jablunkov, Dunka, and Vlara, cross the range. The Beskids are heavily forested. Rich in coal and once having large deposits of iron ore, the Beskids became an iron and steel center in the 18th cent.; the largest plants are now located at Ostrava, Třinec, and Kladno, in Czechoslovakia. There are numerous tourist attractions and winter resorts in the mountains.

Besnard, Paul Albert (pôl älbĕr' bänär'), 1849–1934, French painter, studied with Legros and Cabanel and in Italy. He enjoyed many official honors and was the last important academic painter. His *Woman Warming Herself* (1866) is in the Louvre. He is best known for his many mural decorations in schools and public buildings in Paris.

Besodeiah (bĕsōdē'yə, bēsōdē'ə), the father of MESHULLAM **6.**

Besor (bē'sôr), stream, S Palestine. 1 Sam. 30.9, 10.21.

Bessarabia (bĕsərā'bēə), historic region, c.17,600 sq mi (45,600 sq km), SW European USSR, largely in the Moldavian Soviet Socialist Republic and in the Ukraine. It is bounded by the Dnestr River on the north and east, the Prut on the west, and the Danube and the Black Sea on the south. Consisting mainly of a hilly plain with flat steppes, it is an extremely fertile agricultural area, especially for wine grapes, fruits, corn, wheat, tobacco, sugar beets, and sunflowers. Dairy cattle and sheep raising are also important. Agricultural processing is the chief industry. There are some stone quarries and lignite deposits. Bessarabia's leading cities are KISHINEV and TIRASOPOL in Moldavia and IZMAIL and BELGOROD-DNESTROVSKY in the Ukraine. The population consists of Moldavians (about two thirds), Ukrainians, Russians, Jews, and Bulgarians. As the gateway from Russia into the Danube valley, Bessarabia has been an invasion route from Asia to Europe. Greek colonies were planted on the Black Sea coast of Bessarabia as early as the 7th cent. B.C. The region was later part of Roman DACIA; but after the 4th cent. A.D. it was subject to incursions by Goths, Huns, Avars, and Magyars. Slavs first settled in Bessarabia in the 7th cent. in the midst of these incursions. From the 9th to the 11th cent., the area was part of Kievan Russia, and in the 12th cent. it belonged to the duchy of Galich-Volhynia. Cumans and later Mongols overran Bessarabia; after the latter withdrew it was included (1367) in the newly established principality of Moldavia. The region probably derives its name from the Walachian princely family of Bassarab, which once ruled S Bessarabia. In 1513 the Turks and their vassals, the khans of the Crimean Tatars, conquered Bessarabia. After the Russo-Turkish wars, the region was ceded to Russia by the Treaty of Bucharest (1812). The Crimean War resulted (1856) in Russia's cession of S Bessarabia to Moldavia; but the Congress of Berlin (1878) returned the district to Russia. After the Bolshevik Revolution (1917) the anti-Soviet national council of Bessarabia proclaimed the region an autonomous republic; however, in 1918, Bessarabia renounced all ties with Soviet Russia and declared itself an independent Moldavian republic, later voting for union with Rumania. Although the Treaty of Paris (1920) recognized the union, Russia never accepted it, and in 1940 Rumania was forced to cede Bessarabia to the USSR. The larger part of the region was merged with the Moldavian Autonomous Soviet Socialist Republic, thus forming the Moldavian SSR; the southern and northern sections, with a predominantly Ukrainian-speaking population, were incorporated into the Ukraine. The Rumanian peace treaty of 1947 confirmed Bessarabia as part of the USSR.

Bessarion (bĕsâr'ēən), 1395?–1472, Byzantine humanist, cardinal of the Roman Catholic Church. He was a leading figure at the Council of FERRARA-FLORENCE, which he attended as metropolitan of Nicaea. He favored ending the schism between East and West, and when the Orthodox Church refused, he joined the Roman Catholic Church and remained in Italy. He was made a cardinal in 1439, and in 1463 the pope named him patriarch of Constantinople. A projected translation into Latin of Ptolemy was completed by his protégés, Purbach and REGIOMONTANUS. His fine collection of Greek manuscripts was the nucleus of St. Mark's library, Venice.

Bessel, Friedrich Wilhelm (frēd'rĭkh vĭl'hĕlm bĕs'əl), 1784–1846, German astronomer and mathematician. He became (1810) director of the new observatory at Königsberg and professor of astronomy at the Univ. of Königsberg. Among his many achievements the most noted is his discovery of the parallax of the fixed star 61 Cygni. Announced in 1838, it was officially recognized in 1841 as the first fully authenticated measurement of the distance of a star. His observations had, by 1833, increased the number of accurately determined stars to 50,000. This work was continued and extended by his pupil ARGELANDER. Through observing the variations of the proper motions of Sirius and Procyon, he concluded that they possessed dimmer companions, which was verified a century later by astronomers. Bessel's works on astronomy include *Fundamenta Astronomiae* (1818) and *Astronomische Untersuchungen* (1841–42). Bessel also introduced a class of mathematical functions, named for him, which he established as a result of work on perturbation of the planets and which are widely used in applied mathematics, physics, and engineering.

Bessemer, city (1970 pop. 33,428), Jefferson co., N central Ala.; inc. 1887. Founded as a mining town, it was named after Sir Henry Bessemer, inventor of the Bessemer process. The surrounding area is rich in minerals, and the manufacture of iron and steel is still the city's major industry.

Bessemer process [for Sir Henry Bessemer], industrial process for the manufacture of steel from molten pig iron. The principle involved is that of oxidation of the impurities in the iron by the oxygen of air that is blown through the molten iron; the heat

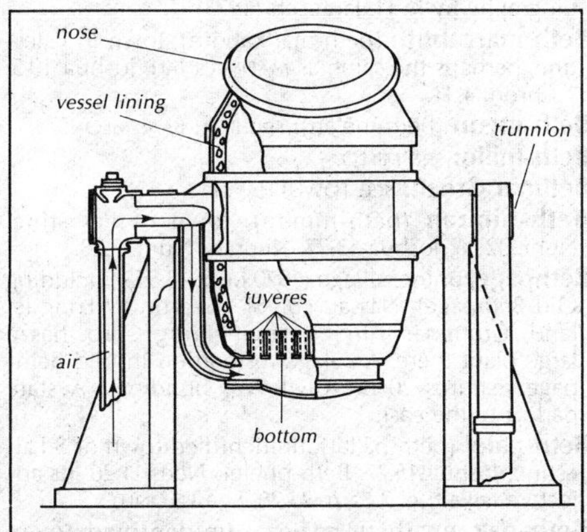

Bessemer converter

of oxidation raises the temperature of the mass and keeps it molten during operation. The process is carried on in a large container called the Bessemer converter, which is made of steel and has a lining of silica and clay or of dolomite. The capacity is from 8 to 30 tons of molten iron; the usual charge is 15 or 18 tons. The converter is egg-shaped. At its narrow upper end it has an opening through which the iron to be treated is introduced and the finished product is poured out. The wide end, or bottom, has a number of perforations (tuyeres) through which the air is forced upward into the converter during operation. The container is set on pivots (trunnions) so that it can be tilted at an angle to receive the charge, turned upright during the "blow," and inclined for pouring the molten steel after the operation is complete. As the air passes upward through the molten pig iron, impurities such as silicon, manganese, and carbon unite with the oxygen in the air to form oxides; the carbon monoxide burns off with a blue flame and the other impurities form slag. Dolomite is used as the converter lining when the phosphorus content is high; the process is then called basic Bessemer. The silica and clay lining is used in the acid Bessemer, in which phosphorus is not removed. In order to provide the elements necessary to give the steel the desired properties another substance (often spiegeleisen, an iron-carbon-manganese alloy) is usually added to the molten metal after the oxidation is completed. The converter is then emptied into ladles from which the steel is poured into molds; the slag is left behind. The whole process is completed in 15 to 20 min. Bessemer steel is used for making machinery, tools, wire, and nails and is the essential modern structural steel used in steel-framework buildings. See METALLURGY.

Bessenyei, György (dyör'dyə bĕ'shĕnyā), 1747–1811, Hungarian dramatist and writer. In Vienna he came in contact with French rationalism and was an ardent follower of Voltaire and the Encyclopedists. Bessenyei's major importance lay in his encouraging the revival of the Hungarian language, rather than in the merits of his own works. His play *The Philosopher* (1777) was among the first modern comic works written in Hungarian. Bessenyei has been called the father of modern Hungarian literature.

Best, Charles Herbert, 1899–, Canadian physiologist, b. West Pembroke, Maine. With F. G. Banting he discovered (1921) the use of insulin in the treatment of diabetes. He was appointed professor of physiology at the Univ. of Toronto in 1929, served as associate director of the Connaught Laboratories from 1932 to 1941, and became director of the Banting and Best department of medical research at the Univ. of Toronto in 1941. With N. B. Taylor he wrote *The Living Body* (rev. ed. 1946), *The Physiological Basis of Medical Practice* (4th ed. 1946), and *The Human Body and Its Functions* (3d ed. 1956).

bestiary (bĕs'chēĕr"ē), a type of medieval book that was widely popular, particularly from the 12th to 14th cent. The bestiary presumed to describe the animals of the world and to show what human traits they severally exemplify. The bestiaries are the source of a bewildering array of fabulous beasts and of many misconceptions of real ones. They were the artist's guide to animal symbolism in religious building, painting, and sculpture. *Physiologus* (the naturalist), an ancient work of the type, was probably the chief source of the bestiaries. A Middle English version is translated in J. L. Weston, *The Chief Middle English Poets* (1914). Variations of the genre remain popular. Modern authors who have written bestiaries include Lewis Carroll, James Thurber, T. H. White, and Jorge Luis Borges.

Bestuzhev, Aleksandr Aleksandrovich (əlyĭksän'dər əlyĭksän'drəvĭch byĭstōō'zhəf), pseud. **Cossack Marlinsky**, 1797–1837, Russian novelist and poet. He wrote popular romantic tales in the Byronic manner. As an officer in the guards he joined the DECEMBRISTS and was exiled to Siberia. He was later transferred to the Caucasus, where he found the material for his best novel, *Ammalat Bek* (tr. 1843).

Bestuzhev-Ryumin, Aleksey Petrovich, Count (əlyĭksyā' pĕtrô'vĭch byĭstōō'zhĕv-rēōō'myĭn), 1693–1766, Russian statesman. With the accession (1741) of Czarina Elizabeth, he was appointed vice chancellor and (1744) grand chancellor. Directing Russian foreign policy, he attempted to unite Russia, Austria, Great Britain, and Saxony against France and Prussia, which he viewed as Russia's natural enemies. Alliances were sealed with Great Britain (1742, 1747) and Austria (1746). The Anglo-Prussian alliance of Jan., 1756, and the outbreak of the Seven Years War that summer virtually nullified Bestuzhev-Ryumin's efforts. Over his strenuous objections, Russia joined (1757) a counteralliance with France and Austria. Removed (1758) from office and banished to his estate, he was recalled (1762) by Catherine II, who made him a field marshal.

Beta Centauri (bā'tə sĕntôr'ī): see HADAR.

Beta Crucis (krōō'sĭs): see MIMOSA, in astronomy.

Betah (bē'tə), the same as TIBHATH.

Betancourt, Rómulo (rō'mōōlō bĕtänkōōr'), 1908–, Venezuelan political leader, president of Venezuela (1945–48, 1959–64). Following a stormy career as a leader of radical student groups, he founded (1935) the *Oganización Venezolana,* which later became the party *Acción Democrática.* In 1945, Betancourt, placed in power by a military coup, declared universal suffrage, instituted social reforms, and secured for Venezuela 50% of the profits reaped by oil companies. Forced into exile in 1948 when Marcos Pérez Jiménez overthrew the constitutionally elected Rómulo Gallegos, he returned (1958) after Pérez Jiménez was ousted, and was elected president. In spite of serious opposition from extremists and disaffected army units, he continued to advance a program of economic and educational reform. He was succeeded by Raúl Leoni. In 1973, Betancourt was awarded a lifetime senate seat.

beta particle, one of the three forms of natural radioactivity. Beta radiation (or beta rays) was identified and named by E. Rutherford, who found that it consists of high-speed ELECTRONS. Unlike alpha and gamma particles, whose energy can be explained as the difference of the energies of the radioactive nucleus before and after emission, beta particles emerge with a variable energy. This apparent violation of the law of conservation of energy (see CONSERVATION LAWS) led to the hypothesis that a second undetected particle, the NEUTRINO, is emitted along with the electron and shares the total available energy. In some forms of induced, or artificial, radioactivity, the electron's ... emitted from the exci... this case is also called ... by β^+ (the ordinary b...

Beta Persei (pûr'sēī") ...

betatron: see PARTICL...

betel (bē'təl), mastic... palm seeds (called ... pepper leaf togeth... and lime paste and ... *catechu*) and the ... PEPPER family) are native to ... S Asia, where betel has been chewed ... times and is an article of considerable commerce. Betel contains a narcotic stimulant and may have some medicinal value. Habitual chewing stains the teeth.

Betelgeuse (bĕt'əljōōz"), bright star in the constellation ORION; Bayer designation α Orionis; 1970 position R.A. $5^h53.5^m$, Dec. $+7°24'$. A red supergiant with a luminosity about 13,000 times that of the sun, it is of SPECTRAL CLASS M2 Iab. Betelgeuse is a semiregular VARIABLE STAR with apparent MAGNITUDE ranging from 0.06 to 0.75; thus, at maximum brightness it is one of the 10 brightest stars in the sky. Betelgeuse marks the right shoulder of Orion; its distance is about 500 light-years.

Beten (bē'tĕn), village of N Palestine. Joshua 19.25.

Bethabara (bĕthăb'ərə), place, on the Jordan, traditionally located at a ford just above the Dead Sea, where John was baptizing when Jesus came to him. RSV: Bethany, following some ancient texts. John 1.28.

Beth-anath (bĕth-ā'năth), town of N Palestine. Joshua 19.38; Judges 1.33.

Beth-anoth (bĕth-ā'nŏth), town, probably the modern Bayt Anun (Jordan), not far NE of Hebron. Joshua 15.59.

Bethany (bĕth'ənē). **1** Village, at the southeastern foot of the Mount of Olives, the modern Al Ayzariyah (Jordan), 2 mi (3.2 km) E of Jerusalem. Home of Lazarus, Martha, and Mary, it was frequently visited by Jesus. It is closely associated with the final scenes of his life, and the Ascension took place near Bethany. Mat. 21.17; 26.6; Mark 11.1,11; 14.3; Luke 19.29; 24.50; John 11. **2** See BETHABARA.

Bethany, city (1970 pop. 21,785), Oklahoma co., central Okla.; inc. 1910. Its manufactures include small airplanes and tires. Bethany was settled in 1906 by members of the Nazarene church. Bethany Nazarene College is in the city.

Bethany College. 1 At Lindsborg, Kansas; Lutheran Church in America; coeducational; chartered 1881 as Bethany Academy. Its present name was adopted in 1886. **2** At Bethany, W.Va.; Disciples of Christ; coeducational; chartered 1840.

Beth-arabah (bĕth-ăr'əbə), town, in the Jordan valley near Jericho. Joshua 15.6,61; 18.22.

Beth-aram (bĕth-ā'răm), the same as BETH-HARAN.

Beth-arbel (bĕth-är'bĕl), unidentified town of Palestine. Hosea 10.14.

Beth-aven (bĕth-ā'vĕn), town of S central Palestine, between Bethel and Michmash. Joshua 7.2; 1 Sam. 13.5; 14.23. It is probably used as an abusive name for Bethel in Hosea 4.15, 5.8, and 10.5. The prophet seems to use Aven (for Beth-aven) also in the same way. Hosea 10.8.

Beth-azmaveth: see AZMAVETH.

Beth-baal-meon (bĕth-bā'əl-mē'ən), town of Moab, E of the Jordan, now called Main (Jordan), 12 mi (19 km) SW of Hisban. Joshua 13.17. Baal-meon: Num. 32.38; Ezek. 25.9; 1 Chron. 5.8. Beth-meon: Jer. 48.23. Beon in Num. 32.3, an otherwise unidentified place, is probably the same. Beth-baal-meon is mentioned on the Moabite stone.

Beth-barah (bĕth-bā'rə), unidentified town, near Beth-shan. Judges 7.24.

Beth-birei (bĕth-bĭ'rēī), unidentified town. 1 Chron. 4.31. See BETH-LEBAOTH.

Beth-car, town, generally west of Jerusalem. 1 Sam. 7.11.

Beth-dagon (bĕth-dā'gŏn). **1** Unidentified town of SW Palestine. Joshua 15.41. **2** Unidentified town of N Palestine. Joshua 19.27.

Beth-diblathaim: see ALMON-DIBLATHAIM.

Bethe, Hans Albrecht (bā'tə), 1906–, American physicist, b. Strassburg, Germany (now Strasbourg, France), educated at Frankfurt and Munich universities. In 1935 he came to the United States to teach at Cornell Univ., where he became professor in 1937. He was director (1943–46) of the theoretical physics division of the Los Alamos Atomic Scientific Labora-

...8 was scientific adviser to the United ... nuclear test ban talks in Geneva. He is ...is brilliant theories on atomic properties ...67 was awarded the Nobel Prize in Physics ... work on the origin of solar and stellar energy ...NUCLEOSYNTHESIS).

...hel (bĕth'əl). **1** Ancient city, central Palestine, ...he modern Baytin (Jordan), N of Jerusalem. According to the Bible, where it is frequently mentioned, it was originally called Luz (see LUZ **1**). Abraham built his first Palestinian altar here. The name Bethel was given to Jacob's sacred stone and was then transferred to the town itself. At the time of the Judges it was a national shrine; it temporarily harbored the Ark of the Covenant. Bethel lost its preeminence as a Jewish shrine to Jerusalem; Jeroboam's attempt to establish Bethel as a rival religious capital failed. Bethel thereafter became increasingly associated with heathen worship—hence the denunciations by Amos and by Hosea, who called it BETH-AVEN by way of insult. Modern excavations have disclosed a temple wall, water gate, and palace complex, indicating the site was once a flourishing Canaanite cultic center. See Gen. 12.8; 35.1–15; Judges 20.26,27; 1 Kings 12.26–33; Amos 3.14. **2** Unidentified place, S Palestine. Joshua 12.16; 1 Sam. 30.27. Chesil: Joshua 15.30. Bethul: Joshua 19.4. Bethuel: 1 Chron. 4.30.

Bethel, town (1970 pop. 10,945), Fairfield co., SW Conn.; inc. 1855. Bethel is noted for its hat industry, which was founded c.1800. Other manufactures include garment leather, clothing, chemicals, rubber goods, metal products, power saws, and game equipment. P. T. Barnum, the showman, was born there.

Beth-emek (bĕth-ē'mĕk), unidentified town of NE Palestine. Joshua 19.27.

Bether (bē'thər), in the Bible, word or name of unknown significance. It has been suggested that it may mean the spice malobathron. Song 2.17.

Bethesda (bəthĕz'də, -thĕs'-), pool in Jerusalem, perhaps the one discovered under the Crusaders' Church of St. Anne near St. Stephen's Gate in the northeast corner of the city. Its healing properties, which made it the resort of the sick, were said to have been the result of an angel's visits. John 5.2–9.

Bethesda, uninc. city (1970 pop. 71,621), Montgomery co., W central Md., a residential suburb of Washington, D.C. The area was settled in the late 17th cent. by the Scottish, English, and Irish. In 1820 they built Bethesda Presbyterian Church, from which the district takes its name. The biblical pool of Bethesda, mentioned in St. John, was a healing place. The National Institutes of Health, the National Cancer Institute, and the Naval Medical Center are in Bethesda.

Beth-ezel (bĕth-ē'zĕl), unidentified town. Micah 1.11.

Beth-gader (bĕth-gā'dər), unidentified town. 1 Chron. 2.51. The Geder of Joshua 12.13, otherwise unidentified, is perhaps the same. See GEDOR **3.**

Beth-gamul (bĕth-gā'məl), unidentified town of Moab. Jer. 48.23.

Beth-haccerem (bĕth-hăk'ərĕm), town, probably the modern En Kerem (Israel), SW of Jerusalem. Neh. 3.14; Jer. 6.1.

Beth-haran (bĕth-hā'rən), town, E of the Jordan, not far northeast of its mouth into the Dead Sea. Num. 32.36. Beth-aram: Joshua 13.27.

Beth-hogla or **Beth-hoglah** (both: bĕth-hŏg'lə), town, the modern Ayn Hajalah (Jordan), W of the Jordan, SE of Jericho. Joshua 15.6; 18.19,21.

Beth-horon (bĕth-hō'rən), name of two neighboring towns on the northerly road from Lod to Jerusalem. They are the modern Beit Ur at Tahta and Beit Ur al Fawga, Jordan. In this strategic locality two historic Jewish victories were gained, by Joshua and by Judas Maccabaeus (Joshua 10; 1 Mac. 3). See also Joshua 16.3,5; 18.13,14; 21.22; 1 Kings 9.17; 1 Chron. 6.68; 7.24; 2 Chron. 8.5.

Beth-jeshimoth (bĕth-jĕsh'ĭmŏth), town, NE of the Dead Sea. Joshua 12.3; 13.20; Ezek. 25.9. Beth-jesimoth: Num. 33.49.

Beth-lebaoth (bĕth-lĕb'āŏth), town of S Palestine. Joshua 19.6. Lebaoth: Joshua 15.32. BETH-BIREI corresponds with Beth-lebaoth in a parallel passage.

Bethlehem (bĕth'lĭhĕm,-lēəm) [Heb.,=house of bread or house of Lahm, a goddess], Arab. *Bayt Lahm,* town (1967 est. pop. 16,000), W Jordan. It is traditionally considered the birthplace of Jesus and is one of the world's great shrines. Situated on a hill in green, fertile country, Bethlehem looks across to the Dead Sea and beyond. Its inhabitants, who are mostly Christians, depend largely on pilgrims and tourists for their livelihood. Handicrafts, fashioned from olive wood and mother-of-pearl, and embroidered goods are made in the town. Bethlehem is also the trade center for surrounding farming villages and for the pastoral nomads who inhabit the area. In the Old Testament Bethlehem was the scene of the book of RUTH and the home of David. The tomb of RACHEL is nearby. Benjamin was born near Ephratah (or Ephrath), which was either an earlier name for Bethlehem or a nearby town. (Gen. 35.16–20, 48.7; 1 Sam. 16, 17; 2 Sam. 23.13-17; 1 Chron. 15-19). David and his family neglected their city, which became obscure, forgotten by all except those who looked to Bethlehem for the MESSIAH, the second David (Micah 5.2). The city later became important as the birthplace of Jesus. HADRIAN desecrated (A.D.135) the traditional place of the nativity with a grove sacred to ADONIS. In 315, Constantine destroyed the heathen grove and constructed instead the Church of the Nativity (completed 333). The church, rebuilt and enlarged by Justinian I in the 6th cent., is now shared by monks of Greek, Latin, and Armenian orders. The manger where Jesus was born is said to have been in the grotto under the church. Saint Jerome lived (386–420?) in the court of the church and produced there the Vulgate text of the Bible. From 1099 to 1187, Crusaders controlled Bethlehem, and in 1571 the city was annexed by the Ottoman Empire. It was part of the British-administered Palestine mandate from 1922 until 1948, when it joined Jordan. In the Arab-Israeli War of 1967, Bethlehem surrendered to Israeli troops without a battle.

Bethlehem, town (1970 pop. 29,460), Orange Free State, E central South Africa. It is situated in a farming and livestock area and has industries producing furniture and food products. Bethlehem was founded in 1860, and its main growth began after the railroad from Natal reached there in 1905.

Bethlehem, city (1970 pop. 72,686), Northampton and Lehigh counties, E Pa., on the Lehigh River; inc. as a city 1917. It is one of the most important centers of steel production in the United States and is the site of the Bethlehem Steel Corp. Much cement is also produced there. Bethlehem was settled in 1740–41 by Moravians and was incorporated as a borough in 1845. Threatened with destruction in 1757 by hostile Delaware and Shawnee Indians, it was saved by Paxinosa, a Shawnee chief. During the Revolutionary War one of the community buildings was used as a hospital for Continental soldiers. Points of interest in Bethlehem are the Central Moravian Church (c.1803), the Schnitz House (1749), and other early Moravian buildings. An internationally famous music festival performed by the Bach Choir is held in the city. Bethlehem is the seat of Lehigh Univ. and Moravian College.

Bethlem Royal Hospital, popularly known as Bedlam, oldest institution for the care and confinement of the mentally ill in England and one of the oldest in Europe. A priory in 1247, the building was converted to its later usage c.1400. Its administration, staff, and patients were moved in 1675, in 1815, and to its present location near Croydon in 1930. The word *bedlam* has long been applied to any place or scene of wild turmoil and confusion.

Bethlen, Gabriel (bĕth'lən), 1580–1629, prince of Transylvania (1613–29). He was chief adviser of Stephen BOCSKAY and was elected prince after the assassination of Gabriel BÁTHORY. A Protestant, though tolerant toward all religions, he allied himself (1619) with the Protestant FREDERICK THE WINTER KING and overran Hungary, of which he was elected king (1620). After Frederick's defeat at the White Mt. (1620), Bethlen signed with Holy Roman Emperor FERDINAND II the Treaty of Nikolsburg (1621), by which he renounced the royal title but retained control of seven Hungarian counties and received the rank of prince of the empire. He continued his relations with the Protestant powers opposing the emperor in the Thirty Years War and married the sister of the elector of Brandenburg; however, he kept the interests of Transylvania paramount. He was a wise administrator and encouraged the development of law and learning.

Bethlen, Count Stephen, 1874–1947?, Hungarian premier (1921–31). A Transylvanian, he entered the Hungarian parliament in 1901, and in 1919 he was a delegate to the Paris Peace Conference. Called to the premiership by Admiral Horthy, he prevented (1921), despite his monarchist leanings, the return of King Charles (Austrian Emperor Charles I) to avoid military intervention by the LITTLE ENTENTE. The chief aim of his foreign policy was the revision of the post-World-War-I Treaty of Trianon (see TRIANON, TREATY OF); a treaty of friendship (1927) with Italy advanced this cause. Bethlen survived a scandal over the forgery of francs in 1926, but his revisionism aroused the increasing suspicion of the Little Entente powers. In 1931, French bankers offered a loan to the hard-pressed government on condition that there be an end to revisionism, and Count Bethlen resigned. He was succeeded as premier by Count Julius Károlyi. Drawn at first toward collaboration with Nazi Germany, Bethlen grew increasingly opposed to Adolf Hitler and in 1940 opposed Hungary's alliance with Germany. In 1945 he was taken by the Russians to the USSR, apparently because of his efforts at concluding a separate peace with the Western powers. He was unofficially reported to have died there in prison.

Beth-maachah: see ABEL-BETH-MAACHAH.

Bethmann-Hollweg, Theobald von (tā'ōbält fən bät'män-hôl'vāk), 1856–1921, German chancellor. A career civil servant, he became minister of the interior (1905) and secretary of state (1907), and in 1909 succeeded Bernhard von BÜLOW as chancellor. He favored some reform and worked for a comprehensive insurance law, extension of the franchise, and greater autonomy for Alsace-Lorraine; his legislative efforts were supported in the Reichstag by a coalition of conservatives and centrists. Even though he greatly increased the German peacetime army, he did not desire World War I. When it began, however, he tried to justify the German stand. He denigrated the treaty guaranteeing Belgian neutrality as "a scrap of paper." Bethmann-Hollweg tried to restrict submarine warfare and to end the war (1916) by conciliation—an attempt that led to his overthrow (1917) by Ludendorff and Hindenburg. See biography by K. H. Jarausch (1973).

Beth-marcaboth (bĕth-mär'kəbŏth), town in Palestine, perhaps the same as MADMANNAH. Joshua 19.5; 1 Chron. 4.31.

Beth-meon (bĕth-mē'ən): see BETH-BAAL-MEON.

Beth-millo: see MILLO.

Bethnal Green: see TOWER HAMLETS.

Beth-nimrah (bĕth-nĭm'rə), town of Palestine. Num. 32.36; Joshua 13.27. Nimrah: Num. 32.3.

Bethpage, uninc. village (1970 pop. 18,555, including Old Bethpage), Nassau co., SE N.Y., on W Long Island. Grumman Aircraft Engineering Corp. has a large plant there. A village restoration in Old Bethpage features 20 pre-Civil War buildings. A state park is to the east.

Beth-palet (bĕth-pā'lət), unidentified town of S Palestine. Joshua 15.27. Beth-phelet: Neh. 11.26. Its adjective is Paltite. 2 Sam. 23.26. See PELONITE.

Beth-pazzez (bĕth-păz'ĕz), unidentified town. Joshua 19.21.

Beth-peor (bĕth-pē'ôr), town of Palestine where Baal-peor was worshiped. Num. 25.3; Deut. 3.29; 4.46; 34.6; Joshua 13.20.

Bethphage (bĕthfā'jē, -fāj), unidentified place, near Jerusalem, traditionally between Bethany and the Mount of Olives. Mat. 21.1; Mark 11.1; Luke 19.29.

Beth-phelet: see BETH-PALET.

Beth-rapha (bĕth-rā'fə), unidentified person or place. 1 Chron. 4.12.

Beth-rehob (bĕth-rē'hŏb), Aramaean principality or town of N Palestine. Judges 18.28; 2 Sam. 10.6. Rehob: Num. 13.21; 2 Sam. 10.8.

Bethsaida (bĕth-sā'ĭdə), birthplace of saints Peter, Andrew, and Philip. It was renamed Julias later. John 1.44; 12.21; Mark 6.45; 8.22; Mat. 11.21; Luke 10.13. Some identify Bethsaida with the Julias just E of the Jordan and N of the Sea of Galilee; others would place it on the eastern shore of the lake; still others suppose two Bethsaidas, one on the eastern and another on the northwestern shore.

Beth-shan (bĕth-shăn') or **Beth-shean** (bĕth-shē'ən), ancient town, at the meeting of the Vale of Jezreel with the Jordan valley. It was the most strategic point of E Palestine, with the crossing of four roads. Judges 1.27; 1 Sam. 31.10,12; 2 Sam. 21.12; 1 Kings 4.12; 1 Chron. 7.29. Bethsan: 1 Mac. 5.52; 12.40,41. Excavations (1921–33) revealed settlements of the 4th millennium B.C. From the 15th cent. B.C. to the 12th cent. B.C. it was a fortified Egyptian outpost, and later it was a Philistine town until it fell to the Israelites at the time of David. In Hellenistic times it was called Scythopolis, apparently because it fell to the Scyths in the 7th cent. B.C. It was a principal city of the Decapolis and a major trade center. The Arabs who took it (638 B.C.) named it Beisan. The present-day Israeli settlement called Bet Shean is nearby. See Alan Rowe, *A Topography and History of Beth-shan* (1930); G. M. FitzGerald, *Beth-shan* (1931).

Beth-shemesh (bĕth-shē'mĕsh). **1** The Egyptian Heliopolis. Jer. 43.13. **2** Town of Palestine, the modern Tel Bet Shemesh (Israel), W of Jerusalem. Excavations there have revealed traces of the Egyptian occupation in the 2d millennium B. C. Joshua 15.10; 21.16; 1 Sam. 6.9; 1 Kings 4.9; 2 Kings 14.11, 13; 1 Chron. 6.59; 2 Chron. 28.18. Ir-shemesh: Joshua 19.41. **3** Town of Issachar. Joshua 19.23. **4** Unidentified town of Naphtali. Joshua 19.38.

Beth-shittah (bĕth-shĭt'ə), town of Palestine, mentioned in connection with Gideon's battle against the Midianites. Judges 7.22.

Bethsura (bĕthsyo͞o'rə), the same as BETH-ZUR.

Beth-tappuah (bĕth-tăpyo͞o'ə), town, c.4 mi W of Hebron, of which it was perhaps a colony; now called Taffuh (Jordan). Joshua 15.53.

Bethuel (bĕthyo͞o'əl). **1** Father of Laban and Rebecca. Gen. 22.23; 28.5. **2** The same as BETHEL **2**.

Bethul (bĕth'əl), the same as BETHEL **2**.

Bethulia (bĕthyo͞o'lēə), city, Palestine, apparently located somewhere NE of Samaria, c.10 mi (16.1 km) from that city. It was the scene of the principal events of the book of Judith. It has been variously identified, by some even with Jerusalem.

Bethune, David: see BEATON, DAVID.

Bethune, Mary McLeod (bəthyo͞on'), 1875-1955, American Negro educator, b. Mayesville, S.C., grad. Moody Bible Institute, Chicago, 1895. The 17th child of former slaves, she taught (1895-1903) in a series of southern mission schools before settling in Florida to found (1904) the Daytona Normal and Industrial Institute for Negro Girls. From 1904 to 1942 and again from 1946 to 1947, she served as president of the institute, which, after merging with Cookman Institute (1923), became Bethune-Cookman College. A leader in the American Negro community, she founded the National Council of Negro Women (1935) and was director (1936-44) of Negro Affairs of the National Youth Administration. In addition, she served as special adviser on minority affairs to President Franklin Delano Roosevelt. At the 1945 conference that organized the United Nations, she was a consultant on interracial understanding. See biography by Rackham Holt (1964).

Bethune-Cookman College, at Daytona Beach, Fla.; United Methodist; coeducational. The school was formed as a result of a merger (1923) of the Daytona Normal and Industrial Institute for Girls (founded 1904) and the Cookman Institute (founded 1872). It became a four-year college in 1941. Founded primarily for blacks, it is open to all qualified students.

Beth-zur (bĕth-zûr'), town, Palestine, N of Hebron, on the Jerusalem road. It is the modern Khirbat Tubaygah (Jordan). Excavations (1924, 1931, 1957) have revealed settlements from the 19th cent. B.C. During the Hellenistic period it was important in the Maccabean campaigns. Joshua 15.58; 1 Chron. 2.45; Neh. 3.16. Bethsura: 1 Mac. 4.29; 6.31; 11.65.

Betjeman, John (bĕt'jəmən), 1906-, English poet, b. London. His verse combines a witty appraisal of the present with nostalgia for the past, especially the Victorian past. His published collections include *Mt. Zion* (1933), *Continental Dew* (1937), *Old Lights for New Chancels* (1940), *A Few Late Chrysanthemums* (1954), *High and Low* (1966), and *Collected Poems* (1971). He has also published several delightful architectural studies including *Ghastly Good Taste or a Depressing Story of the Rise and Fall of English Architecture* (1933, rev. ed. 1971) and *A Pictorial History of English Architecture* (1972). In 1972 he was named poet laureate of England. See *Summoned by Bells* (1960), his autobiography, which is written in verse.

Betonim (bĕt'ōnĭm), unidentified town, E of the Jordan. Joshua 13.26.

Bet Shean (bāt shĭän'), town (1972 pop. 11,300), NE Israel, in the Jordan River valley, c.300 ft (90 m) below sea level. Situated in a fertile farming region, it is a center for agricultural experiments. Textiles are manufactured. Archaeological excavations have traced settlements on the site back to the Bronze Age: Bet Shean was the site of an Egyptian administrative center during the XVIII and XIX dynasties (see EGYPT), a Scythian city from c.625 to 300 B.C., and the biblical city Beth-shan. In 64 B.C. it was taken by the Romans, rebuilt, and made the center of the DECAPOLIS. The modern Bet Shean was established in 1949 by Israeli settlers. Archaeological finds include temples of the Canaanite Bronze Age, a Hellenistic-Roman temple, and a Byzantine monastery. The town is also known as Beisan.

Betsiamites or **Bersimis,** river, c.240 mi (390 km) long, rising in the highlands of E Que., Canada, and flowing SE into the St. Lawrence River at Betsiamites. Two hydroelectric plants provide power; Bersimis Dam (1,050,000-kw capacity; completed 1956) impounds Lake Pipmuacan.

betta (bĕt'ə) or **fighting fish,** small, freshwater fish of the genus *Betta,* found in Thailand and the Malay Peninsula. Best known is the Siamese fighting fish, *Betta splendens.* Mature males of this species are about 2 in. (5 cm) long. In its native waters *B. splendens* is drab with small fins, but several centuries of breeding have produced multicolored varieties with extremely enlarged decorative fins, highly prized as aquarium fishes. Males of this species are extremely aggressive, and in Thailand they are used in fighting contests lasting as long as six hours, with spectators betting on the outcome. Bettas thrive in shallow, sunlit areas with soft or sandy bottoms. Males secrete a mucous, with which they build bubble nests. After the female of a pair lays her eggs, both members transfer them to the nest, which is then guarded by the male. Several hundred young hatch out in 24 to 30 days. Like its relatives the GOURAMI and the CLIMBING PERCH, the betta is equipped to breathe air as well as water and must surface from time to time. It is classified in the phylum CHORDATA, subphylum Vertebrata, class Osteichthyes, order Perciformes, family Anabantidae.

Bettendorf, city (1970 pop. 22,126), Scott co., E Iowa, on the Mississippi River; settled c.1840, inc. 1903. Its manufactures include aluminum products and farm equipment.

Betterton, Thomas, 1635?-1710, English actor and manager. He joined Sir William D'Avenant's company at Lincoln's Inn Fields theater in 1661 and became the leading actor of the Restoration stage, the theatrical leader of his time. In the role of Hamlet he was acknowledged as the greatest since Burbage. After D'Avenant's death (1668), he became the head of the company and moved to the Dorset Garden theater (1671), which he partially managed, and where he was especially successful in adaptations of Shakespeare by Dryden, Shadwell, Tate, and himself. Betterton managed the Drury Lane theater from 1682 until 1695, at which time he reopened a theater in Lincoln's Inn Fields, with Congreve's *Love for Love* as his first production. In 1705 he moved his company to the new Haymarket theater, built for them by Sir John Vanbrugh, where he made his last appearance in 1710. Sent to Paris by James II to study French technique, Betterton adopted new ideas in his theaters, especially in regard to scene design. See R. W. Lowe, *Thomas Betterton* (1891, repr. 1972). His wife, **Mary Saunderson Betterton,** d. 1711, was the first woman to act Shakespeare's great female characters, most notably Lady Macbeth. Both are buried in Westminster Abbey. See Rosamond Gilder, *Enter the Actress* (1931); Barbara Marinacci, *Leading Ladies* (1961).

Betti, Ugo (o͞o'gō bət'tē), 1892-1953, Italian dramatist and poet. A judge of the Roman high court by profession, he wrote poetry and plays in his spare time and became recognized as a major literary figure only late in life. Although his earliest published works were two volumes of poetry (1922 and 1932), he is remembered for his dramas. He wrote 27 plays and saw 24 of them produced. Among the most notable were *La padrona* [the mistress] (1927), *Frano allo scalo nord* [landslide at the north station] (1936), *Il cacciatore di anitre* [the duck hunter] (1940), *Il diluvio* [the flood] (1943), and *Delitto all'isola delle capre* [crime on goat island] (1950). Betti's outlook was predominantly pessimistic, concerned with man's moral responsibility, guilt, and forgiveness. Despite his frequently moralizing tone, he is ranked second only to Pirandello among 20th-century Italian dramatists. See translations of his most important plays by Henry Reed (1958), G. H. McWilliam (1964), and Gino Rizzo (1966).

Betto, Bernardino di: see PINTURICCHIO.

Beuckelszoon, Beuckelzoon, or **Beukels, Jan:** see JOHN OF LEIDEN.

Beulah [Heb.,=married, used of a woman], allegorical name for Israel. Isa. 62.4,5.

Beust, Friedrich Ferdinand (frē'drĭkh fĕr'dĭnänt boist), 1809-86, Saxon and Austrian politician. He held various portfolios in the Saxon ministry and served as premier (1853-66), but his opposition to Bismarck forced his resignation after Saxony's defeat in the Austro-Prussian War. He entered the service of Austria, becoming foreign minister (1866), prime minister (Feb., 1867), and chancellor (June, 1867). With the Hungarians Julius Andrássy and Francis Deak he negotiated the *Ausgleich* [compromise] of 1867, which resulted in the establishment of the AUSTRO-HUNGARIAN MONARCHY. Created a count in 1868, Beust was dismissed in 1871, but later served as ambassador to London (1871-78) and Paris (1878-82). See his memoirs (tr. 1887).

Beuthen: see BYTOM, Poland.

Bevan, Aneurin (ənī'rĭn bĕ'vən), 1897-1960, British political leader. A coal miner and trade unionist, he served (1929-60) in Parliament as a member of the Labour party. As minister of health (1945-51) he administered and developed the National Health Service instituted by the Labour government. A leader of the party's left wing, he resigned from the government in protest against the decisions to rearm Germany and cut social services. Briefly expelled from the party for insubordination in 1955, and unsuccessful in his contest with Hugh GAITSKELL for the party leadership, he was reconciled to the party and became its spokesman for colonial and foreign affairs. In ensuing years he favored British diplomatic neutralism and nuclear disarmament. See his autobiography (1952); biographies by M. M. Krug (1961) and Michael Foot (2 vol., 1962 and 1974).

bevatron: see PARTICLE ACCELERATOR.

Beveland, North, and **South Beveland** (bā'vəlänt), two former islands, Zeeland prov., SW Netherlands, in the Scheldt estuary. As a result of Dutch plans for a delta to shut off most of Zeeland from the North Sea, South Beveland became a peninsula of the mainland; North Beveland was linked to the peninsula by way of Walcheren island. A shipping canal connecting the Belgian port of Antwerp with the Rhine River traverses South Beveland. Agriculture and livestock breeding are the mainstays of the islands' economy. Dairying and the cultivation of sugar beets are the principal activities on North Beveland, which also has factories for sugar extraction. South Beveland specializes in the growing of wheat, potatoes, sugar beets and fruits and is also known for its fisheries and oyster culture. Wissenkerke, whose name derives from a beautiful 17th-century church, is the chief town of North Beveland; Goes, which has a 15th-century Gothic church, is South Beveland's main urban center. Heavy fighting occurred on both islands during World War II.

Beveridge, Albert Jeremiah, 1862-1927, U.S. Senator from Indiana (1899-1911) and historian, b. Highland co., Ohio. He was admitted to the bar (1887) and practiced law (1887-99) in Indianapolis. As a Republican Senator, he supported the policies of Theodore Roosevelt. With other INSURGENTS he opposed the PAYNE-ALDRICH TARIFF ACT (1909) and was defeated for reelection (1910). He became (1912) an organizer of the PROGRESSIVE PARTY, ran (1912) for governor of Indiana on the party's ticket, and lost. Thereafter he devoted himself principally to writing history. His thorough, sober lives of John Marshall (4 vol., 1916-19) and Abraham Lincoln (unfinished; 2 vol., 1928) are outstanding. See his *Russian Advance* (1903, repr. 1970); biography by John Braeman (1971); Claude Bowers, *Beveridge and the Progressive Era* (1932).

Beveridge, William Henry, 1879-1963, British economist, b. India, grad. Oxford, 1902. His fame as an authority on social problems was gained through investigations and writings in government service (1908-19), especially as director of labor exchanges, set up largely through his efforts, and in the food ministry, where he devised rationing during World War I. Knighted in 1919, he was director of the London School of Economics from that year until 1937, when he became master of University College, Oxford. *Social Insurance and Allied Services* (1942), a report prepared for the British government, proposed a social security system "from the cradle to the grave" for all British citizens. In 1944 his *Full Employment in a Free Society* advocated planned public spending, control of private investment, and other measures to assure full employment. He served (1944-45) as a Liberal member of Parliament and was in 1946 made 1st Baron Beveridge of Tuggal. Beveridge advocated state management to complement, not replace, individual initiative. This was a theme of such later writings as *Voluntary Action* (1948) and *A Defence of Free Learning* (1959).

Beverley, Robert, 1673-1722, Virginia colonial historian, author of *The History and Present State of Virginia* (1705). A substantial planter and colonial official, he wrote his book after finding numerous errors in the manuscript of a book on Virginia written by an Englishman. Vigorous, honest, and not without humor, his history was an immediate success; reprinted a number of times, it served to attract immigrants to Virginia. See edition by Louis B. Wright (1947, repr. 1968).

Beverley, municipal borough (1971 pop. 17,124), administrative center of the former county of East Riding of Yorkshire, NE England; since 1974 a part of the new nonmetropolitan county of Humberside. It is primarily a market town with some shipbuilding and such light industries as the manufacture of railroad and automobile accessories and leather. The famous large minster, or monastery church (13th cent.), was attached to a monastery founded by St. John of Beverley (d. 721) and transformed by ATHELSTAN into a college of canons. It contains the tomb of the Percy family and the ancient "chair of peace," which gave sanctuary from the laws of man. (The sanctuary, a privilege granted by Athelstan, applied in a 1-mi (1.6-km) radius around the minster; it was ended at the time of the Reformation.) The town gate is of the early 15th cent., and St. Mary's Church dates from the 14th cent.

Beverloo, Cornelis van: see CORNEILLE.

Beverly, city (1970 pop. 38,348), Essex co., NE Mass., on Massachusetts Bay; inc. as a city 1894. Its chief manufactures are shoe machinery and electronic equipment. Beverly was settled in 1626 by Roger Conant, one of the founders of Massachusetts. In 1775 the schooner *Hannah*, the first ship of the U.S. navy, was outfitted and commissioned by Gen. George Washington at Glover's Wharf in Beverly. In 1787, Beverly became the site of the first cotton mill in the United States. Points of interest include Balch house (1636), believed to be the oldest house in the United States; the John Cabot house (1781), which is preserved as a museum; and several other Colonial buildings. Beverly Farms, a residential and resort section of the city, was the summer home of Oliver Wendell Holmes. Endicott Junior College and North Shore Community College are in Beverly.

Beverly Hills. 1 City (1970 pop. 33,416), Los Angeles co., S Calif., completely surrounded by the city of Los Angeles; inc. 1914. Mainly residential, it is the home of many film and television personalities. 2 Village (1970 pop. 13,598), Oakland co., SE Mich., a residential suburb of Detroit, on the Rouge River; inc. 1958.

Bevin, Ernest (bĕv'ən), 1881–1951, British labor leader and statesman. An orphan who earned his own living from childhood, he began a long career as a trade union official when he became secretary of the dock workers' union in 1911. In 1921, Bevin merged his own union with many others to form the powerful Transport and General Workers' Union, of which he became general secretary. From 1925 to 1940 he sat on the general council of the Trade Union Congress, serving as chairman in 1937. Bevin played a leading organizing role in the general strike of 1926, but after the failure of that strike he worked to achieve greater cooperation between labor and the employers. He was enormously influential in Labour party politics in the 1930s but did not enter Parliament until invited to join Winston Churchill's coalition government in 1940. In that government he was minister of labor and national service and thus was responsible for mobilizing manpower for war uses. As foreign minister in the Labour government of 1945 to 1951, Bevin devoted himself to building up the strength of Western Europe in close cooperation with the United States and helped lay the groundwork for the North Atlantic Treaty Organization. He favored the establishment of a federated Arab-Israeli state in Palestine, but that proved impossible to achieve. See biographies by Trevor Evans (1946), Francis Williams (1952), and Alan Bullock (2 vol., 1960–1967).

Bevis of Hampton (bē'vĭs), English metrical romance of the early 14th cent. that also appears in Anglo-Norman, French, Italian, Scandinavian, Celtic, and Slavonic versions. Although its adventures are made up of such stock motifs as murder, mistaken identity, and revenge, the tale is nevertheless notable for its broad humor.

Bewick, Thomas (byo͞o'ĭk), 1753–1828, English wood engraver. Bewick pioneered in the revival of original wood engraving. Among his famous early works are his illustrations for Gay's *Fables* (1779) and *Select Fables* (1784) and for Ralph Beilby's *General History of Quadrupeds* (1790). In 1789 he engraved the Chillingham Bull, considered one of his finest blocks. He is best known for his classic illustrations of Beilby's *History of British Birds* (2 vol., 1797–1804). See his memoirs (1862); studies by Austin Dobson (1884, repr. 1969), Rudolph Ruzicka (1943), and Graham Reynolds (1949).

Bexhill (bĕks'hĭl'), municipal borough (1971 pop. 32,849), East Sussex, SE England. It is a summer resort and has a 14th-century manor house and an 11th-century church.

Bexley, borough (1971 pop. 216,172) of Greater London, SE England. It was created in 1965 by the merger of the municipal boroughs of Bexley and Erith, the urban district of Crayford, and part of the urban district of Chislehurst and Sidcup. The borough has many parks and open areas. Erith and Crayford are industrial centers. There are engineering and chemical works, oil and resin refineries, flour and seed-crushing mills, cloth printshops, and factories that produce electrical equipment, building materials, cable, paper products, plywood, and plastics. Erith is also a yachting resort. Parts of the borough have histories of more than 1,000 years, and there are several old churches. Viscount Castlereagh (1769–1822) lived at Crayford.

Bexley, city (1970 pop. 14,888), Franklin co., central Ohio; inc. 1908. It is a residential community completely within the confines of Columbus.

bey (bā), general title of respect used by Turkish peoples since ancient times. Originally given to tribal leaders, it was later used by the Ottomans to denote a provincial ruler. At first the Ottoman beys were appointed, but by the 18th cent. the title had become hereditary. In Ottoman Egypt, the beys were descendants of the former Mameluke rulers.

Beyazid I (bāyäzĭd'), 1347–1403, Ottoman sultan (1389–1402), son and successor of Murad I. He besieged Byzantine Emperor MANUEL II at Constantinople, then overcame the Turkish rulers in E Anatolia and defeated the army of Sigismund of Hungary (see SIGISMUND, Holy Roman emperor) at NIKOPOL. Ottoman expansion led to conflict with the conqueror TAMERLANE, and the two armies met at Ankara in 1402. Beyazid's troops consisted only of Serbs and the Janissaries, since the Tatars and most of his Turkish vassals had deserted him. His army was routed, and he died as Tamerlane's prisoner. His sons fought (1402–13) each other for the succession, and MUHAMMAD I emerged victorious. The name appears in other forms, e.g., Bajazet, Bayazid, and Bayazit.

Beyazid II, 1447–1513, Ottoman sultan (1481–1512), son and successor of Muhammad II to the throne of the Ottoman Empire (Turkey). With the help of the corps of Janissaries he put down the revolt of his brother Jem, who fled to Rhodes and then was held captive, as a threat to Beyazid, first by Pierre d'AUBUSSON, then by popes INNOCENT VIII and ALEXANDER VI. Transferred to the custody of Charles VIII of France, Jem died (1495) near Naples. A peace-loving monarch, Beyazid did little to advance Ottoman power but much to further Ottoman culture. He warred (1485–91) with the Mamelukes of Egypt, to whom he lost Cilicia, and allowed Cyprus to be seized (1489) by Venice. A war (1499–1503) with Venice ended to the sultan's disadvantage, and he then renovated his army and navy. Beyazid speedily rebuilt Constantinople after it was devastated (1509) by an earthquake. In 1510 civil war broke out between Beyazid's sons SELIM I and AHMED. In 1512, Beyazid was forced to abdicate by Selim's supporters, who included the Janissaries, and Selim became sultan.

Beyazid, 1612–1638?, Ottoman prince; brother of Sultan Murad IV. Considering Beyazid a dangerous rival, Murad ordered his execution. Beyazid's death is treated in Racine's tragedy, *Bajazet* (1672).

Beyle, Marie Henri: see STENDHAL.

Beyrouth: see BEIRUT, Lebanon.

Beza, Theodore (bē'zə) (Théodore de Bèze), 1519–1605, French Calvinist theologian. In 1548 he joined John Calvin at Geneva and soon became his intimate friend and chief aid. From 1549 to 1558, Beza was professor of Greek at Lausanne, where he wrote *De haereticis a civili magistratu puniendis* (1554), a defense of the conduct of Calvin and the Genevan magistrates in the notorious trial and burning of Servetus. In 1558 he became professor of Greek at Geneva, and in 1564 he succeeded Calvin in the chair of theology at Geneva. Beza came to be regarded as the chief advocate of all reformed congregations in France, serving with distinction at the Colloquy of Poissy (see POISSY, COLLOQUY OF). He was of great importance in aiding the edition of the Greek and Latin versions of the New Testament, and he gave Codex D, or Codex Bezae, one of the most important manuscripts of the Bible, to Cambridge Univ. He wrote various theological tracts and a biography of Calvin.

Bezai (bē'zā), family in the return from captivity. Ezra 2.17; Neh. 7.23; 10.18.

Bezaleel (bēzăl'ēĕl, bĕz'ələl). 1 The artist of the Tabernacle in the wilderness. Ex. 31.2–11; 35.30; 38.22; 1 Chron. 2.20; 2 Chron. 1.5. 2 Jew who had married a foreign wife. Ezra 10.30.

Bezborodko, Aleksandr Andreevich, Prince (əlyĭksän'dər əndrā'əvĭch bĕzbôrôd'kô), 1747–99, Russian statesman. He became secretary of petitions under Catherine II in 1775 and from 1780 served as head of the department of foreign affairs. During Catherine's reign foreign policy was determined largely by the empress, and Bezborodko generally went along with her schemes. He devised an imaginative plan for the partition of Turkey between Russia and Austria that fitted well with Catherine's unfulfilled dream of a new Byzantine Empire. He encouraged Catherine to participate with Austria and Prussia in the last two partitions of Poland (1793, 1795), by which Russia obtained Lithuania, Courland, and the W Ukraine. After Catherine's death (1796) her son, Paul I, made him grand chancellor, with virtual control of Russian foreign affairs. He held this post until his death.

Bezek (bē'zĕk). 1 Country or city of Adoni-bezek. Judges 1.5. 2 Bivouac of Israel. 1 Sam. 11.8.

Bezer (bē'zər). 1 Asherite. 1 Chron. 7.37. 2 Reubenite town, E of the Jordan. Deut. 4.43; Joshua 20.8; 21.36; 1 Chron. 6.78. Bezer is mentioned in the Moabite stone and may be identical with BOZRAH **2**.

Bezhitsa: see BRYANSK, USSR.

Béziers (bāzyā'), city (1968 pop. 82,271), Hérault dept., S France, in Languedoc. A communications and industrial center with an important trade in wines and liqueurs, it has ironworks, breweries, and factories making a great variety of products. An episcopal see from the 4th cent. to 1802, Béziers was involved in numerous religious wars. During the ALBIGENSIAN CRUSADE it was taken (1209) by Simon de Montfort; a horrible massacre followed. Béziers has a noted cathedral (13th–14th cent.) and some old churches.

bezique (bəzēk'), card game usually played with 128 cards by two players. Bezique developed in France and England in the 1860s and originally required only 64 cards; later there were variations for three players with a 96-card pack and for four players with 128 cards. PINOCHLE is similar and is probably derived from bezique. In the United States the most popular form is the two-handed game, known as rubicon bezique, in which four 32-card packs are shuffled together. The cards in each suit rank ace, ten, king, queen, jack, nine, eight, seven. Each player receives nine cards, and the remaining cards, face down, become the stock. Trump suit is determined by the first marriage (king and queen of the same suit) declared. The nondealer leads, and his opponent follows, playing any card he desires. Highest card of the suit led or highest trump wins the trick. The winner of a trick leads to the next trick after first drawing the top card of the stock, with his opponent then drawing the next card from the stock. Play continues with nine cards to a hand until the stock is exhausted. Certain combinations of cards score various points. The player with the most points wins and receives a bonus of 500. If the loser is rubiconed (has a total of less than 1,000 points), the winner's score includes the sum of his and the loser's final totals and a bonus of 1,000.

Bezruč, Petr (pĕt'ər bĕz'ro͝och), pseud. of **Vladimir Vašek,** 1867–1958, Czech poet, called the bard of Silesia. Bezruč's fame rests solely on the *Silesian Songs* (1903, enlarged ed. 1909). In these 88 stark, moving verses the poet protests the suppression by the Austrians of the Slavic peoples living between Silesia and Moravia. Bezruč was an admirer of Whitman, but his work belongs to no school. After World War II the Czech government granted him a pension.

Bezwada, India: see VIJAYAWADA.

Bhabha, Homi Jehangir (jəhän"gēr' bä'bä), 1909–66, Indian physicist, b. Bombay. He was educated at the Royal Institute of Science, Bombay, and at Cambridge, England, where he studied cosmic rays and atomic physics. He was the leading Indian atomic physicist of his time. In 1945 he became professor of theoretical physics and director of the Tata Institute of Fundamental Research, Bombay. He was named the first chairman (1948) of India's Atomic Energy Commission and became secretary (1954) of its atomic energy department. He was president of the UN Atoms for Peace conference in 1955.

Bhadravati (bədrä'vətē), city (1971 metropolitan area pop. 101,315), Karnataka state, S India, on the Bhadra River. The city contains iron and steel plants and paper mills.

Bhagalpur (bä'gəlpo͝or'), city (1971 pop. 172,700), Bihar state, NE India, on the Ganges River. It is a district administrative center and the market for an agricultural region. Bhagalpur Univ. and the remains of Buddhist monasteries are in the city.

Bhagavad-Gita (bŭg'əvəd-gē'tə) [Skt.,=song of the Lord], Sanskrit poem incorporated into the MAHAB-

HARATA, one of the greatest religious classics of Hinduism. The Gita (as it is often called) consists of a dialogue between Lord KRISHNA and Prince Arjuna on the eve of the great battle of Kurukshetra. Arjuna is overcome with anguish when he sees in the opposing army many of his kinsmen, teachers, and friends. Krishna persuades him to fight by instructing him in spiritual wisdom and the means of attaining union with God (see YOGA). The main doctrines of the Gita are karma-yoga, the yoga of selfless action performed with inner detachment from its results; jnana-yoga, the yoga of knowledge and discrimination between the lower nature of man and his soul, which is identical with the supreme self; and bhakti yoga, the yoga of devotion to a particular god—in this case, Krishna, who reveals himself to Arjuna as the avatara (incarnation) of Vishnu through his teaching and the manifestation of his cosmic form. The *Bhagavad-Gita* is essentially Upanishadic in content, but it differs significantly from the brahman-atman doctrine of the UPANISHADS in teaching that the highest God is personal and that love and surrender to God's grace is a better and easier spiritual path than that of pure knowledge. The *Gita* has been the subject of many commentaries and has been much translated. Its translators include Annie Besant, Sir Edwin Arnold, Sarvepalli Radhakrishnan, and Mohandas Gandhi. See Franklin Edgerton, *The Bhagavad Gita* (1944); Swami Nikhilananda, *The Bhagavad Gita* (1944); Vinoba Bhave, *Talks on the Gita* (1960); Eliot Deutsch, ed., *Bhagavad Gita* (1968).

Bhaktapur: see BHATGAON, Nepal.

bhakti (bŭk'tē) [Skt., =devotion], theistic devotion in Hinduism. Bhakti cults seem to have existed from the earliest times, but they gained strength in the first millennium A.D. The first full statement of liberation and spiritual fulfillment through devotion to a personal god is found in the BHAGAVAD-GITA. The Puranas (from the 1st cent. A.D.) further elaborated theistic ideas. Devotion to SHIVA and VISHNU and to the latter's avatara (incarnations), Rama and KRISHNA, continues to be practiced throughout India. Intense love for God and surrender to Him, reliance on His grace rather than on rituals, learning, or austerities, and the continuous repetition of His name are the means to the goal of His constant presence. The devotee may worship the chosen deity as child, parent, friend, master, or beloved. The bhakti tradition has tended to stress authentic inner feelings as opposed to institutional forms of religion and to disregard caste distinctions. Great devotees and saints such as the Alvars of S India (a Vaishnavite group of wandering singers), Mirabai, Tukaram, Tulsidasa, KABIR, and CHAITANYA have continuously inspired the cults, founded their own sects, and produced a great literature of songs and poems in their vernaculars.

Bhamo (bä'mō, bəmō'), town (1960 est. pop. 16,000), NE Burma, on the upper Irrawaddy River. Located c.900 mi (1,450 km) from the sea, it is the head of navigation on the Irrawaddy. Bhamo is the market town for the surrounding hill region and is also important for its ruby mines. Formerly significant as a center of overland trade with China, it was linked in World War II by the building of the Stilwell Road to Ledo in Assam, India. Although most of the population is now Kachin, in 1884 the Burmese authorities used Chinese freebooters to repel a Kachin attack on the town.

Bharat (bərŭt'), a name for the Republic of India. It is derived from Bharata, a tribe famous in Vedic tradition. Some Hindus prefer this name to that of *India*, a name they believe to be of foreign origin.

Bharatpur (bərŭt'pŏŏr), city (1971 pop. 69,442), Rajasthan state, N central India. It is a district administrative center and has railroad-car and glass factories. Fans and fly whisks are fashioned from ivory and sandalwood. The city is thought to have been founded in 1733 and named after Bharat, a figure in Hindu mythology. The British captured Bharatpur in 1826. The city is well known for its bird sanctuary.

Bhaskara (bŭs'kərə), called **Acarya** (əchär'yə) [Skt., =learned], b. 1114, Hindu mathematician and astronomer. According to the custom, he put his learned treatises into verse, adding, however, explanations in prose. His work *Siddhantasiromani* includes chapters on arithmetic, algebra, and astronomy that have been translated into English. He gives the first systematic exposition of the decimal system. By mentioning such items as rates of interest and the prices of slaves, he gives some indication of economic conditions in his day. He was at the head of the observatory at Ujjain.

Bhatgaon (bät'goun) or **Bhadgaon** (bäd'-), city (1971 pop. 104,703), E Nepal, in a valley c.4,000 ft (1,220 m) above sea level, surrounded by high Himalayan peaks. It is a processing center for the grains, vegetables, and other crops of the surrounding area. Grazing is also important. A religious center, Bhatgaon was founded in 865 by Raja Ananda Malla. When the Gurkhas conquered the Nepal valley in 1768, Bhatgaon surrendered peacefully, thereby escaping the plunder that befell Katmandu and Patan. Landmarks include many ornate temples and the well-preserved palace (c.1700) built by King Bhupatindra Malla. The city is also called Bhaktapur.

Bhatpara (bətpä'rə), city (1970 est. pop. 160,000), West Bengal state, NE India, on the Hooghly River. Once a center of Sanskrit learning, it is now part of the vast Hooghlyside industrial complex. Jute products are the chief manufactures.

Bhattacharya, Bhabhani (bəbä'nē bätəchär'yə), 1906–, Indian novelist, journalist, and translator. Bhattacharya was educated in India and England and has taught and traveled in many parts of the world. The themes of his novels, written in English, are drawn from the history and modern social problems of India. Sharp with social criticism, they deal with poverty and famine, caste and intolerance, and political inequality and injustice. His first work, *So Many Hungers!* (1948), describes in shocking terms a Bengal famine and the black-market corruption it produces. In *Music for Mohini* (1952) a modern city girl is forced by means of an arranged marriage into a repressive, traditional way of life. Bhattacharya attacks the caste system in *He Who Rides a Tiger* (1954), in which an untouchable masquerades successfully as a Brahmin priest. His other major works include the novels *A Goddess Named Gold* (1960) and *Shadow from Ladakh* (1966) and translations from the Bengali of some of Rabindranath Tagore's work. Bhattacharya's novels are internationally acclaimed for their irony and perceptive social commentary.

Bhave, Vinoba (vīnōbə bä'vä), 1895–, Indian religious figure, founder of the Bhoodan Movement. Born to a Brahman family in Maharashtra, Bhave left home while quite young to study Sanskrit in Benares (Varanasi). There he became inspired by the teachings of Mohandas K. Gandhi and soon joined him as a disciple. Far more austere and disciplined than Gandhi, Bhave was acknowledged by Gandhi as a spiritual superior. At Gandhi's request Bhave resisted British wartime regulations in 1940 and spent nearly five years in prison. After Gandhi died (1948), Bhave was widely accepted as his successor. More interested in land reform, accomplished voluntarily, than in politics, he founded in 1951 the Bhoodan Movement, or land-gift movement, and subsequently traveled thousands of miles by foot, accepting donations of land for redistribution to the landless. By 1969 the Bhoodan had collected over 4 million acres (1.6 million hectares) of land for redistribution. His writings include *The Principles and Philosophy of Bhoodan Yajna* (1955), *Talks on the Gita* (1960, 3d ed. 1964), and *The Steadfast Wisdom* (1966). See biography by Shriman Narayan (1970); T. K. Oommen, *Charisma, Stability and Change* (1972).

Bhavnagar (bounŭ'gər), city (1971 pop. 226,072), Gujarat state, W India, on the Gulf of Cambay; the chief port on the Kathiawar peninsula. Cotton is exported. The city manufactures bricks, tiles, and metal products.

Bhilainagar (bē'līnəgər) or **Bhilai** (bē'lī), city, (1971 pop. 174,557), Madhya Pradesh state, central India. It is the site of a large state-owned steel industry, built with Soviet assistance.

Bhils (bēlz), people, numbering more than 2 million, who inhabit portions of Pakistan and of W central India, especially S Rajasthan and Gujarat states. They speak an Indo-European language, Bhili, and retain a distinctive culture, much affected by, but not absorbed into, Hinduism. They were traditional enemies of the Rajputs and allies of the Moguls. See S. M. Doshi, *Bhils* (1971).

Bhilwara (bēlvä'rə), town (1971 pop. 82,101), Rajasthan state, NW India. The town is a district administrative center and a market for mica, wheat, maize, cotton, and wool. Stone dressing is an important occupation. Coins called *Bhilari* were formerly minted in the town.

Bholan Pass, Pakistan: see BOLAN PASS.

Bhopal (bō'päl), former principality, Madhya Pradesh state, central India. A region of rolling downs and thickly forested hills, it is predominantly agricultural. Its Buddhist monuments include the famous stupa (3d cent. B.C.) at Sanchi. Bhopal was founded in the early 18th cent. and was ruled from 1844 to 1926 by the begums of Bhopal, famous women leaders. Although the population was mainly Hindu, the princely family was Muslim. Bhopal became part of the state of Madhya Pradesh in 1956. The city of **Bhopal** (1971 pop. 309,285), the former capital of the principality and now the capital of Madhya Pradesh, was founded in 1728. It is a trade center with manufactures of cotton cloth, jewelry, and electrical goods.

Bhubaneswar (bŏŏbänĕ'swär), city (1971 pop. 105,514), capital of Orissa state, E central India, on a tributary of the Mahanadi River. A small village before it became the capital in 1947, it is now a model administrative center and the seat of Orissa Univ. of Agriculture and Technology. There are rolling mills and wire-cable works. Settlements on this site date back to the reign of ASOKA (3d cent. B.C.). The capital of the Kesaris dynasty of Orissa (5th–10th cent.) was here. Bhubaneswar, a religious center, once had c.7,000 shrines around its sacred lake; the remains of c.500 still stand, displaying many styles of Hindu and Buddhist art and architecture. The Lingaraja temple, with an elaborately carved tower, is the most famous.

Bhumibol Adulyadej (pŏŏ'mēpôl" ädŏŏl'yädĕt"), 1927–, king of Thailand (1946–), b. Cambridge, Mass. A member of the Chakri dynasty, he was at school in Switzerland when his brother, King Ananda, was killed (1946) under mysterious circumstances. Bhumibol ruled with a regent until 1950, when he was crowned and took power in his own right as Rama IX. His power is largely ceremonial. His name also appears as Phumiphon.

Bhusawal (bŏŏsä'vəl), town (1971 pop. 96,236), Maharashtra state, W central India. The town is on the Bombay-Delhi railroad. It has large railroad workshops and several cotton factories.

Bhutan (bŏŏtän'), kingdom (1974 est. pop. 1,300,000), 18,147 sq mi (47,000 sq km), in the E Himalayas, bordered on the S and E by India, on the N by the Tibet region of China, and on the W by Sikkim. PUNAKA is the traditional capital; Thimbu is the official capital. Great mountain ranges, rising in the N to Kula Kangri (24,784 ft/7,554 m), Bhutan's tallest peak, run north and south, dividing the country into forested valleys with some pastureland. The perpetually snow-covered Great Himalayas are uninhabited, except for some Buddhists in scattered monasteries. Bhutan is drained by several rivers rising in the Himalayas and flowing into India. Thunderstorms and torrential rains are common; rainfall averages from 200 to 250 in. (508–635 cm) on the southern plains. The valleys, especially the Paro, are intensively cultivated. The chief occupations are small-scale subsistence farming (with rice the chief crop) and the raising of yaks, cattle, sheep, pigs, and tanguns, a sturdy breed of pony valued in mountain transportation. Metal, wood, and leather working; papermaking; and the weaving of cloth, baskets, and mats are also important activities. Bhutan's people are mostly Bhotias, who call themselves Drukpas (dragon people). They are ethnically related to the Tibetans and practice a form of Buddhism closely related to the Lamaism (see TIBETAN BUDDHISM) of Tibet; many Bhutanese live in monasteries. Dzongka, the official language, is also basically Tibetan. In W Bhutan there is a sizable minority of Nepalese. Although its early history is vague, Bhutan seems to have existed as a political entity for many centuries. In the 16th cent. the Tibetans conquered and assimilated Bhutan's native tribes, and around 1630 a refugee lama from Tibet made himself the first Dharma Raja, or spiritual ruler, of Bhutan. He named a Deb

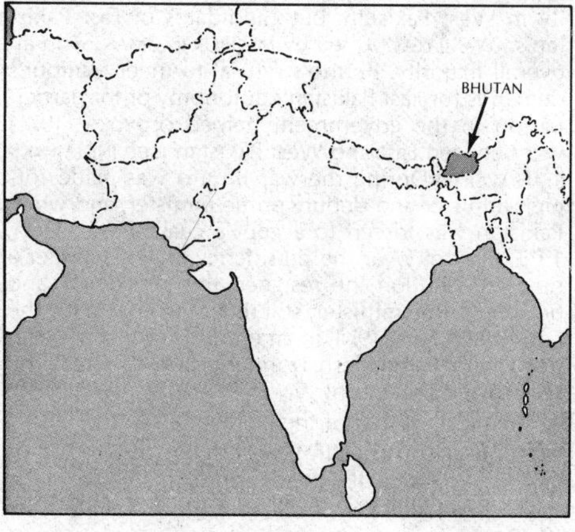

Raja, or temporal ruler, but real administrative power was soon wielded by provincial governors (*ponlops*), who reduced the Deb Raja to a figurehead. In 1720 the Chinese invaded Tibet and established suzerainty over Bhutan. Friction between Bhutan and Indian Bengal culminated in a Bhutanese invasion of Cooch-Behar in 1772, followed by a British incursion into Bhutan; but the Tibetan lama's intercession with the governor-general of British India improved relations. In 1774 a British mission arrived in Bhutan to promote trade with India. British occupation of Assam in 1826, however, led to renewed border raids from Bhutan. In 1864 the British occupied part of S Bhutan, which was formally annexed after a war in 1865; the Treaty of Sinchula provided for an annual subsidy to Bhutan as compensation. In 1907 the most powerful of Bhutan's provincial governors, Sir Ugyen Wangchuk, supported by the British, became the monarch of Bhutan, the first of a hereditary line. A treaty signed in 1910 doubled the annual British subsidy to Bhutan in return for an agreement to let Britain direct the country's foreign affairs. After India won independence, a treaty (1949) returned the part of Bhutan annexed by the British and allowed India to assume the former British role of subsidizing Bhutan and directing its defense and foreign relations; the Indians, like the British before them, promised not to interfere in Bhutan's internal affairs. After Chinese Communist forces occupied Tibet in 1950, Bhutan, because of its strategic location, became a point of contest between China and India. The Chinese claim to Bhutan (as part of a greater Tibet) and the persecution of Tibetan Buddhists led India to close the Bhutanese-Tibetan border and to build roads in Bhutan capable of carrying Indian military vehicles. In the 1960s, Bhutan also formed a small army, trained and equipped by India. The kingdom's admission to the United Nations in 1971 was seen as strengthening its sovereignty. Bhutan's monarch, the Druk Gyalpo (Dragon King), is assisted by a small advisory council. In 1954 a 130-member national assemby was created; about one fourth of its members are appointed by the king, and the rest are village headmen elected to the assembly for five-year terms. Political parties are banned; the Bhutan state congress, led by Nepalese, must operate from India. Bhutan's third hereditary ruler, King Jigme Dorji Wangchuk (reigned 1953–72), modernized Bhutanese society by abolishing slavery and the caste system, emancipating women, dividing large estates into small individual plots, and starting a secular educational system. Although Bhutan no longer has a Dharma Raja, Buddhist priests retain political influence. In 1969 the absolute monarchy gave way to a "democratic monarchy," in which the national assembly was empowered to select and remove the king and to veto his legislation. The assembly must also give the king a periodic vote of confidence. In 1972 the crown prince Jigme Singhi Wangchuk became the fourth hereditary king of Bhutan upon his father's death. He was crowned in June, 1974. See studies by Ram Rahul (1872) and Nagendra Singh (1972).

Bhutto, Zulfikar Ali (zo͝ol'fĭkär älē' bo͞ot'tō), 1928–, Pakistani political leader. A member of a rich and powerful family, he took a law degree in England and then returned (1953) to Pakistan, where he soon entered politics as the protégé of General Ayub Khan. Bhutto became minister of commerce in 1958 and held several other cabinet posts before becoming foreign minister in 1963. After criticizing Pakistan's agreement with India ending the 1965 war between the two countries, he left the government and formed (1967) an opposition party, the Pakistan People's party, which quickly gained great popular support. In the 1970 elections his party won a majority in West Pakistan, but candidates of East Pakistan's AWAMI LEAGUE, led by MUJIBUR RAHMAN, won an overall majority. Bhutto's refusal to meet Mujibur's demands for East Pakistan's autonomy or for participation in the government helped provoke (1971) war between East and West Pakistan (see INDIA-PAKISTAN WARS). During the war Bhutto was made foreign minister and deputy prime minister, and when Pakistan was forced to accept a cease-fire in Dec., 1971, he took over the presidency. In 1973, under a new constitution, he resigned the presidency and became prime minister, still retaining control of the country. In Feb., 1974, in an effort to normalize relations with Bangladesh (formerly East Pakistan), he recognized that country.

Bi, chemical symbol of the element BISMUTH.

Biafra, Bight of (bēä'frə), eastern bay of the Gulf of Guinea, W Africa. It extends approximately from the Niger River delta, in S Nigeria, to N Gabon. The bight gave its name to the secessionist Eastern Region of Nigeria (1967–70).

Biafra, Republic of, secessionist state of W Africa, in existence from May 30, 1967, to Jan. 15, 1970. At the outset Biafra comprised, roughly, the East-Central, South-Eastern, and Rivers states of the Federation of Nigeria, states inhabited mainly by the IBO people. The country, which took its name from the Bight of Biafra (an arm of the Atlantic Ocean), was established by Ibos who felt they could not develop—or even survive—within Nigeria. In Sept., 1966, numerous Ibos had been massacred in N Nigeria, where they had migrated in order to engage in commerce. The secessionist state was led by Lt. Col. Chukumeka Odumegwu OJUKWU and included some non-Ibo persons. Biafra's original capital was Enugu; Aba, Umuahia, and Owerri served successively as provisional capitals after Enugu was captured (Oct., 1967) by Nigerian forces. Seeking to maintain national unity, Nigeria imposed economic sanctions on Biafra from the start of the secession, and fighting between Nigeria and Biafra broke out in July, 1967. After initial Biafran advances, Nigeria attacked Biafra by air, land, and sea and gradually reduced the territory under its control. The breakaway state had insufficient resources at the start of the war—it was a net importer of food and had little industry—and depended heavily on its control of petroleum fields for funds to make purchases abroad. It lost the oil fields in the war, and more than one million of its civilian population are thought to have died as a result of severe malnutrition. At the time of its surrender on Jan. 15, 1970, Biafra was greatly reduced in size, its inhabitants were starving, and its leader, Ojukwu, had fled the country. During its existence Biafra was recognized by only five nations, although other countries gave moral or material support. Civilian groups were organized in a number of countries to publicize the case for Biafra and to raise funds for the secessionist state. See A. H. Kirk-Greene, ed., *Crisis and Conflict in Nigeria: a Documentary Sourcebook* (2 vol., 1971); Joseph Okpaku, ed., *Nigeria, Dilemma of Nationhood: An African Analysis of the Biafran Conflict* (1972).

Bialik, Hayyim Nahman (hī'yəm nä'mən byä'lĕk), 1873–1934, Hebrew poet, publisher in Odessa, Berlin, and Tel-Aviv, b. Volhynia, Russia. As an editor and publisher Bialik spread the ideas of the enlightenment (Haskalah). His fame began with the publication (1903) of his poem "In the City of Slaughter," inspired by a pogrom in Kishinev. Bialik's style is sometimes biblical, prophetic, and majestic, sometimes simple and lyrical; he had a great effect upon modern Hebrew literature. He wrote novels, humorous songs, and sketches; some of his work is in Yiddish, but his most important writings are in Hebrew. They have been widely translated (English translations of his poems were published in 1924, 1926, and 1948). Bialik translated into Hebrew Shakespeare's *Julius Caesar*, Cervantes's *Don Quixote*, Schiller's *Wilhelm Tell* and Heine's poems.

Białowieza (byälôvyĕ'zhä), Rus. *Byelovezhskaya Pushcha,* large forest, c.450 sq mi (1,170 sq km), E Poland and W USSR. Its varied trees (predominantly pines) shelter many animals, including boar, deer, European bison, and tarpan horse, and it was a favorite hunting ground of Polish kings. It passed to Prussia in 1795, was annexed by Russia in 1807, but was restored to Poland in 1921. In 1939, however, the forest was incorporated into the USSR. After World War II nearly half of the region was returned to Poland. Today both sections of the forest have animal preserves. The first Polish national park was established in the center of the forest in 1921.

Białystok (byälĭs'tôk), city (1970 pop. 166,619), capital of Białystok prov., NE Poland. It is a leading regional manufacturing center and a railway transportation point. Noted especially for its textile industry, the city also has factories producing machinery, metal goods, ceramics, food products, and precision instruments. Founded in 1310, Białystok was taken by Prussia in 1795 and by Russia in 1807; it was returned to Poland in 1921. About half of the city's population were killed by German occupation forces during World War II. Białystok has an academy of medicine and a technical college. Historical landmarks include a 16th-century church and an 18th-century palace.

Biard, Pierre (pyĕr byär), c.1567–1622, French Jesuit missionary in North America. He left a professorship of theology in Lyons to head the first Jesuit mission to Canada, coming to Port Royal (later Annapolis Royal) in Acadia in 1611. He was one of the founders (1613) of the French settlement at Bar Harbor on MOUNT DESERT ISLAND, in what is now Maine. He and all the colonists were soon taken prisoners by Samuel ARGALL. After a long captivity and a stormy return voyage Biard finally reached France, where he was accused of being in league with his English captors. His *Relation de la Nouvelle France* (1616), which has been of much value to later historians, embodied his reply to these charges.

Biarritz (byärēts'), town (1968 pop. 26,985), Pyrénées-Atlantiques dept., SW France, on the Bay of Biscay near the Spanish border. An ancient fishing village, it was a favorite vacation spot of Napoleon III and Empress Eugénie, whose visits sparked the growth of Biarritz into one of the world's most fashionable sea resorts.

Bias (bī'əs), fl. 6th cent. B.C., Greek sage, b. Priene. He is at best semilegendary but was called one of the SEVEN WISE MEN OF GREECE. Many epigrams were attributed to him by ancient writers.

bias, a voltage, current, or other input applied to a device or system as a reference or to set its conditions of operation. A bias is usually steady but may vary with time, usually within a fixed and known range and with a fixed and known frequency. In electronics, the most common forms of bias are the voltage applied to the grid of an ELECTRON TUBE to set its operating conditions and the current applied to the base of a TRANSISTOR to perform the same function. In tape recording, a bias current, usually alternating with a frequency in the ultrasonic range, is mixed with the signal to be recorded to minimize distortion produced by the tape itself.

biathlon (bīăth'lŏn), athletic competition in which cross-country skiers race across hilly terrain, occasionally stopping to shoot with rifles at fixed targets. The regulation course is about 12½ mi (20 km) long, and the four targets are placed at a range of 164 yd (150 m) from the athlete. Competitors are penalized for missing targets by having a standard length added to the course distance that they must complete. Originally a Swedish hunting competition, the biathlon first became an event of the Winter Olympics in 1960.

Bibai (bī'bī), city (1970 pop. 47,369), Hokkaido prefecture, central Hokkaido, Japan. It is a mining city located on the Ishikari coal field.

Bibb, William Wyatt, 1781–1820, first governor of Alabama (1817–20), b. Amelia co., Va. Graduated in medicine from the Univ. of Pennsylvania (1801), he began practice in Petersburg, Ga. He was a state legislator, U.S. Representative (1807–13), and U.S. Senator (1813–16). In April, 1817, President Monroe appointed him governor of the newly created territory of Alabama, and Bibb continued in office when the new state government was organized (1819). On his death, Thomas Bibb, a brother, succeeded him in office.

Bibbiena, Galli da: see BIBIENA, GALLI DA.

Biber, Heinrich Ignaz Franz von (hīn'rĭkh ĭg'näts fränts fən bē'bər), 1644–1704, Austrian musician. Biber was one of the first notable Central European violinists and may have been the first to employ *scordatura*, an unusual tuning of the violin to obtain special effects. He composed much violin music, some of it programmatic, that requires great virtuosity, and also various dramatic works.

Bibescu (bĭbĕs'ko͞o) or **Bibesco** (-kô), Rumanian noble family. A prominent member was **George Bibescu,** 1804–73, prince of Walachia (1842–48). The first to be elected to his post, he effected important financial reforms but was driven from the county in the Revolution of 1848. His brother **Barbu Bibescu,** 1799–1869, was adopted by Prince Stirbei, a Rumanian magnate, whose name he later assumed. He served as minister of the interior and subsequently was appointed hospodar [governor] of Walachia for a seven-year term (1849–56). In Feb., 1856, he decreed the abolition of slavery in Walachia.

Bibiena or **Bibbiena, Galli da** (gäl'lē dä bĕbyā'nä), family of Italian artists of the 17th and 18th cent. **Giovanni Maria Galli da Bibiena**, 1625–65, studied with Francesco Albani and painted chiefly altarpieces, examples of which are to be seen in the churches of Bologna. His son, **Ferdinando Galli Bibiena,** 1657–1743, the most renowned of the group, became celebrated throughout Europe for his architectural views and theatrical designs and for his magnificent decorations for public and court festivities. He wrote several treatises on architecture. A master of baroque illusionism, he created an effect of depth by extending the set pieces of his scene designs beyond the proscenium arch. **Francesco Galli Bibiena**, 1659–1739, brother of Ferdinando, is celebrated chiefly as the designer of great European theaters. Other members of the family include **Ales-**

sandro **Galli Bibiena,** 1687–c.1769, son of Ferdinando, a fresco painter and architect; **Giuseppe Galli Bibiena**, 1696–1756, second son and pupil of Ferdinando and, like him, renowned for his sumptuous decorations, designed principally for the courts and theaters of Vienna, Munich, Dresden, Bayreuth, and Prague; **Antonio Galli Bibiena**, 1700–1774, third son of Ferdinando, an architect and designer; and **Carlo Galli Bibiena**, 1728–1787, the son of Giuseppe, a painter and architect employed at many of the European courts. See A. H. Mayor, *The Bibiena Family* (1940).

Bible [Gr.,=the books], name used by Christians for their Scriptures. For the composition and the canon of the Bible, see OLD TESTAMENT; NEW TESTAMENT; APOCRYPHA; PSEUDEPIGRAPHA; articles on the several books. The traditional Christian view of the Bible is that it was all written under the guidance of God and that it is, therefore, all true, literally or under the veil of allegory. In recent times, however, the view of many Protestants has been influenced by the pronouncements of critics (see HIGHER CRITICISM); this has produced a counterreaction in the form of FUNDAMENTALISM, whose chief emphasis has been on the inerrancy of the Bible. The interpretation of the Bible is one of the principal points of difference between Protestants, who believe that individuals have the right to interpret the Bible as they read it, and the Roman Catholic Church, which teaches that it alone may interpret Scripture and that the individual may read the Bible only according to the interpretation of the church; such an interpretation is provided in the notes to the text that appear in Roman Catholic Bibles. These notes vary from edition to edition. Celebrated extant manuscripts of the Bible include Codex Vaticanus (Greek, 4th cent.), at the Vatican; Codex Sinaiticus (Greek, 4th cent.), in the British Museum, discovered by Lobegott Friedrich Konstantin von TISCHENDORF on Mt. Sinai; Codex Alexandrinus (Greek, 5th cent.), in the British Museum, given to King Charles I by Cyril Lucaris; and Codex Bezae (Greek and Latin, 6th cent.), at Cambridge, England, given by Theodore Beza. The most ancient fragments of the Hebrew text are the 2d cent. B.C. papyrus of Nash, discovered in 1902 in Al Fayyum, Egypt, and the DEAD SEA SCROLLS, containing several books and fragments of the Old Testament. The first great translation of the whole Bible was the VULGATE of St. JEROME, the Latin version still used by the Roman Catholic Church. The Greek text generally received in the East is, for the Old Testament, that of the SEPTUAGINT; the first translation of the Old Testament was the Aramaic TARGUM. The New Testament has come down to us in Greek. In England there were current from early times vernacular versions of parts of the Bible, especially of the Gospels, since the Gospel was often read at Mass in the vernacular after its recitation in Latin. John WYCLIF was one of the first to project the publication and distribution of the Bible in the vernacular among the English people, and two translated versions go by his name. In the 15th cent. the Lollards did much to extend the use of the Wyclifite translation. The next name in the history of the English Bible is that of William TYNDALE, whose translation was not from Latin, like Wyclif's, but from Hebrew and Greek. Its excellence is made evident in its use as a basis of the Authorized Version. Tyndale's New Testament (1525–26) was the first English translation to be printed. Contemporary with Tyndale was Miles COVERDALE. The second version of Coverdale and the translation of Thomas Matthew closely followed Tyndale. In 1539 the crown issued its first Bible, in the name of Henry VIII. This, the Great Bible, was done principally by Coverdale. The Geneva Bible, or Breeches Bible (". . . made themselves breeches," Gen. 3.7), was a revision of the Great Bible, financed and annotated by the Calvinists of Geneva. The Bishops' Bible (1568) was a recasting of Tyndale. The greatest of all English translations was the Authorized Version (AV), or King James Version (KJV), of 1611, made by a great committee of churchmen led by Lancelot ANDREWES and composed of many of the finest scholars in England. The beautiful English of this version has had great influence and is generally ranked in English literature with the work of Shakespeare. The phraseology of much of it is that of Tyndale. The Douay, or Rheims-Douay, Version was published by Roman Catholic scholars at Rheims (New Testament, 1582) and Douai, France (Old Testament, 1610); it was extensively revised by Richard CHALLONER. In the 19th cent. the project of revising the Authorized Version from the original tongues was undertaken by the Church of England with the cooperation of nonconformist churches. The results of this revision were the English Revised Version and the American Revised Version (pub. 1880–90). Many scholars, either cooperatively or independently, have translated the Bible into English. In other literatures also the translation of the Bible has had formative effect on the literary language, notably the case with Martin Luther's standard German translation. Occasionally translation of the Bible has been the first or the only notable work in a language—as for instance, the translation by ULFILAS into Gothic. In the 20th cent. American biblical scholars combined to produce the notable Revised Standard Version (RSV), published in 1952 and immediately adopted by many churches. A completely new translation, the work of a joint committee of representatives of all Protestant denominations in Great Britain, aided by Roman Catholic consultants, was begun in 1946. The New Testament was first published in 1961, and the entire Bible, called The New English Bible, appeared in 1970. New Roman Catholic translations were also undertaken, the Westminster Version in England, and a complete revision of the Rheims-Douay edition sponsored by the Confraternity of Christian Doctrine in the United States. The latter, after undergoing several major revisions and retranslations, was finally published as the New American Bible (1970). In addition, an English translation of the French Catholic Bible de Jerusalem (1961) appeared as the Jerusalem Bible (1966). See F. G. Bratton, *A History of the Bible* (1959); *The Cambridge History of the Bible* (3 vol., 1963–70); J. H. P. Reumann, *The Romance of Bible Scripts and Scholars* (1965); H. J. Frank, *The Bible through the Ages* (1967).

Bible Christians, denomination of Methodists in England founded by William O'Bryan. They seceded from the Wesleyan Methodist Church (1815–19) and in 1907 were merged with two other branches in the UNITED METHODIST CHURCH.

Bible societies, an essentially Protestant movement, formed for the translation, printing, and dissemination of the Holy Scriptures. An early important organization of this kind was the Canstein Bible Society established in 1710 by Baron von Canstein at Halle, Germany. In 1780 the Bible Society was formed in England to distribute Bibles among soldiers and sailors; the name was later changed to the Naval and Military Bible Society. A pioneer and leader is the British and Foreign Bible Society founded (1804) in London, which began its work with Welsh Bibles for Thomas CHARLES. With branches throughout the world, it has distributed Bibles in hundreds of languages. In the United States the formation of Bible societies began early in the 19th cent. Delegates from these associations founded (1816) the American Bible Society, which has many affiliates. Through its work, the Bible has been translated into many languages and has been widely distributed. In 1898 in Boscobel, Wis., a meeting occurred that led to the founding of the Christian Commercial Men's Association of America, more usually known as the Gideons, International. Its program of placing Bibles in hotel rooms for use by commercial travelers and others has been widely realized and has made the organization internationally known. In 1946 more than 20 national Bible societies formed an international association known as the United Bible Societies, with headquarters in London and in Geneva, Switzerland.

Biblical Antiquities, Book of: see PSEUDEPIGRAPHA.

biblical archaeology, term applied to the ARCHAEOLOGY of the biblical lands, especially those of the ancient Middle East. While the thousands of written texts found in the languages of the ancient Middle East illuminate the Bible itself, the artifacts uncovered by archaeologists help recreate the cultural setting of its time. Biblical archaeology developed in earnest in the early part of the 19th cent. when the British biblical scholar Edward Robinson traveled across Palestine and opened the way for study of the area. The founding (1865) of the Palestine Exploration Fund in Great Britain further encouraged research; by 1900 biblical archaeological societies had been formed in Germany, France, and the United States. The system developed by Flinders PETRIE at Tel-el-Hesy (see EGLON **2**) to date pottery is of the greatest importance for the archaeology of Palestine, where spectacular monuments and written material are rarely found. Other important excavations in Palestine were undertaken at JERICHO by John GARSTANG and others, MEGIDDO, SAMARIA, GIBEAH **1**, BETH-SHAN, LACHISH, EZION-GEBER, and HAZOR **1**. Outside of Palestine the important archaeological discoveries in the old lands of EGYPT, SUMER (see also UR), Babylonia (see also GILGAMESH and HAMMURABI), ASSYRIA, BYBLOS, Nuzi, UGARIT, and JORDAN (see also MOABITE STONE) have done much to increase knowledge of the Bible. The Palestine Dept. of Antiquities, founded 1918, encouraged research until the turbulent years preceding the establishment of the State of Israel in 1948; since that time some of the most important archaeological work has been conducted by Israeli archaeologists, e.g., the excavation of the ancient tel (an artificial mound formed by the debris of settlements of ancient cities) of Joppa in 1948 and 1955, and the work at Arad from 1962 to 1967. After more than 100 years of biblical archaeology, it is possible to read the Bible in a new light. It has become clear that ancient Palestine was an integral part of the whole cultural area of the ancient Middle East. Many obscurities have been cleared up, and the historical data of the Old Testament have been proved more accurate than suspected. Archaeology is less important for the New Testament because of the brevity of the period and the relative abundance of material available on it. However, the discovery of several manuscripts of the Greek New Testament of the 2d and 3d cent. and especially the DEAD SEA SCROLLS have added new evidence that the Gospels are of greater antiquity than had been thought. See Michael Du Buit, *Biblical Archaeology* (1960); G. E. Wright, *Biblical Archaeology* (1962); W. G. Williams, *Archaeology in Biblical Research* (1965); Paul Lapp, *Biblical Archaeology and History* (1969); Avraham Negev, ed., *Archaeological Encyclopedia of the Holy Land* (1972); E. M. Yamauchi, *The Stones and the Scriptures* (1972).

bibliography. The listing of books is of ancient origin. Lists of clay tablets have been found at Nineveh and elsewhere; the library at Alexandria had subject lists of its books. Modern bibliography began with the invention of printing and at first consisted of "trade" bibliographies, i.e., lists of the publications of important publishing houses, comparable to those in the present-day *Trade List Annual, Reference Catalogue of Current Literature* (British), and *Books in Print*. There have been efforts at universal bibliography; in 1545 at Zürich, Konrad von Gesner published his *Bibliotheca universalis;* in 1895 the International Institute of Bibliography was established at Brussels. There are also national bibliographies, such as the *Library of Congress Catalog* and the *British Museum Catalogue;* subject bibliographies, such as Sabin's *Dictionary of Books Relating to America;* and lists of the works of individual authors. Bibliographies of rare and old books include that of J. C. Brunet and *Book Prices Current. The Cumulative Book Index* is a monthly bibliography of books in the English language that cumulates annually. *The Cambridge Bibliography of English Literature* is useful for English publications, and the *Bibliographic Guide to the Study of the Literature of the U.S.A.*, by C. L. Gohdes, for American works. The *Bibliographical Index,* which is cumulative, and *World Bibliography of Bibliographies* are useful compilations. The term *bibliography* is also used to describe books as physical objects and their production history, and has been expanded to include nonprint media such as microfilm. Computers are currently used in the compilation of some bibliographies. See A. J. K. Esdaile, *Manual of Bibliography* (4th ed. 1967); Robert Downs, *Bibliography* (1967); E. W. Padwick, *Bibliographical Method* (1969); A. M. Robinson, *Systematic Bibliography* (3d ed. 1971); Philip Gaskell, *A New Introduction to Bibliography* (1972); Pearce Grove and Evelyn Clement, *Bibliographic Control of Nonprint Media* (1972).

Bibliothèque nationale (bēblēōtĕk' näsyônäl'), the great national library of France, in Paris, and one of the foremost libraries in Europe. It originated with the collections of writings made by early French kings, including Charlemagne. The collection of Charles V, placed in the tower of the old Louvre in the 14th cent., and a library belonging to the house of Orléans at Blois were brought together at Fontainebleau in the 16th cent. under Francis I. The collection was later transferred to Paris by Charles IX, and was expanded greatly under the supervision of Jean-Baptiste Colbert (17th cent.). Since 1537 the library has been the legal depository for all books published in France. It now has more than 7 million books and manuscripts, and an extensive accumulation of medals and coins, and maps and prints. The library is housed in a building erected from 1854 to 1875 in the Rue de Richelieu under the direction of Henri Labrouste; it was remodeled in 1932–39. There is also a branch at Versailles. The Bibliothèque nationale is a governmental archive, not a public library.

Bibracte (bĭbrăk'tē), former capital of the AEDUI, site atop Mont Beuvray, central France. There Caesar defeated (58 B.C.) the Helvetii (see GALLIC WARS). Excavations on the site have revealed a Gallic town.

Bibulus (Marcus Calpurnius Bibulus) (bĭb'yo͝oləs), d. 48 B.C., Roman statesman. The colleague in the consulship with Julius CAESAR in 59 B.C., he did everything in his power to block each move made by Caesar. A conservative republican, he was a strong partisan of Pompey. In 51 B.C. he was governor of Syria, and in 48 B.C. he died trying to halt Caesar in the Adriatic. His wife was Portia, daughter of Cato the Younger; she later married Brutus.

bicameral system, governmental system dividing the legislative function between two chambers, an "upper," such as the U.S. Senate and the British House of Lords, and a "lower," such as the U.S. House of Representatives and the British House of Commons. Although the term *bicameral* was coined by Jeremy Bentham as recently as 1832, division of the legislative branch of government according to function and composition is of long standing. The division of the English PARLIAMENT into separate houses of Lords and Commons in the 14th cent. may have arisen simply for the sake of convenience in transacting business; however, this division came to represent the historic cleavage of interest between nobles and commoners, with the balance of power, especially after the Glorious Revolution of 1688 and the gradual development of cabinet government in the 18th cent., shifting more and more to the commoners. The powers of the House of Lords were drastically reduced by the Parliament acts of 1911 and 1949, and though the house continues to debate and vote on bills, its function has become essentially advisory. The British colonies in North America gradually adopted the bicameral system; the upper chamber, whether elective or appointive, came to represent the colony as a whole, while delegates to the lower house were attached to particular constituencies. According to modern scholars, the adoption of the same system for the CONGRESS OF THE UNITED STATES reflected colonial practice, British example, and the widespread differences in property qualification for suffrage and office-holding purposes current at the time rather than the French philosophical influences once considered primary. In France some 18th-century theorists, such as Montesquieu, favored a bicameral legislature based on the British example, but the "natural rights" philosophers, such as Rousseau, opposed such a system. France experimented with various forms of legislature during the Revolutionary and Napoleonic periods but thereafter, despite numerous constitutional changes, retained a bicameral system. Where bicameral legislatures exist, the two chambers are based on different principles of representation in addition to possessing separate functions. After World War I the unicameral legislative system made headway in Eastern Europe, Latin America, and parts of the British dominions. See D. Schaffter, *The Bicameral System in Practice* (1929); J. A. Corry, *Elements of Democratic Government* (4th ed. rev. 1964); S. H. Beer, *Patterns of Government* (3d ed. 1973).

bicarbonate or **hydrogen carbonate,** chemical compound containing the bicarbonate radical, $-HCO_3$. The most familiar of such compounds is SODIUM BICARBONATE (baking soda). See CARBONATE.

bicarbonate of soda: see SODIUM BICARBONATE.

biceps, any muscle having two heads, or fixed ends of attachment, notably the biceps brachii at the front of the upper arm. Originating in the shoulder area, the heads of the biceps merge partway down the arm to form a rounded mass of tissue linked by a tendon to the radius, the smaller of the two forearm bones. When the biceps contracts, the tendon is pulled toward the heads, thus bending the arm at the elbow. For this reason the biceps is called a flexor. It works in coordination with the TRICEPS brachii, an extensor. The biceps also controls rotation of the forearm to a palm-up position, as in turning a doorknob. The size and solidity of the contracted biceps are a traditional measure of physical strength.

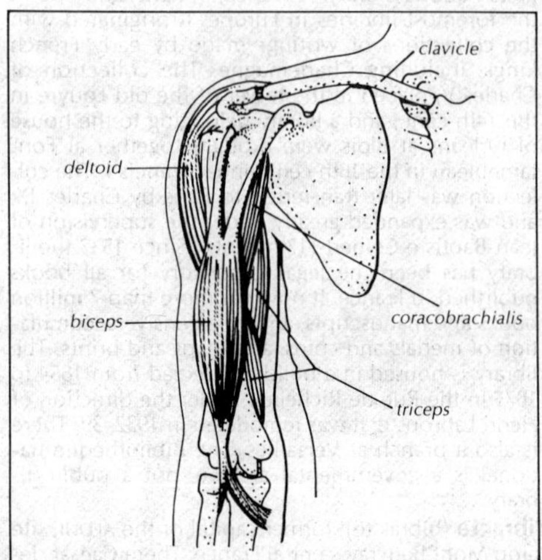

Biceps of arm

Bichat, Marie François Xavier (märē' fräNswä' zävyā' bēshä'), 1771–1802, French anatomist and physiologist. He studied the tissues, giving them that name and classifying them into 21 types; this work was the basis of modern histology. He wrote *Traité des membranes* (1800), *Recherches physiologiques sur la vie et sur la mort* (1800), *Traité d'anatomie descriptive* (1801–3, in 5 vol.), and *Anatomie générale* (1801).

bichir (bĭch'ər), common name for African freshwater fishes as of the family Polypteridae, and particularly for those of the genus *Polypterus.* Bichirs are among the most primitive of the ray-finned fishes, or Actinopterygii, the dominant group of modern fishes. The long, narrow body of *Polypterus* is 2 to 3 ft (60–90 cm) long and is covered by thick, rhombic scales made of an enamellike substance called ganoine. Such scales were also present in the earliest ray-finned fishes, now extinct, and are quite different from those of other living fishes. The dorsal fin of the bichir is split into a row of small, saillike finlets that are erected when the animal is agitated. Like the sharks and the rays, it has a pair of spiracles. The bichir seems especially adapted to life in dry environments. Instead of the SWIM BLADDER of most ray-finned fishes, it has a pair of lungs, somewhat like those of the LUNGFISHES, which enables it to survive out of water for several hours. It also resembles the lungfishes in having a pair of external gills when newly hatched. The bichir is a bottom-dwelling fish, found in the Nile and in the rivers of W Africa. When these rivers overflow in late summer, it moves out to spawn in the flood marshes. It is sometimes caught as a food fish. In addition to the ten species of *Polypterus,* the bichir family includes the reedfish, *Erpetoichthys calabaricus,* similar in character and distribution, but with a longer, more eellike form. Bichirs are classified in the phylum CHORDATA, subphylum Vertebrata, class Osteichthyes, order Polypteriformes, family Polypteridae.

Bichon Frise (bēshôN' frēs), breed of small dog developed in France after World War I. It stands from 8 to 12 in. (20–30 cm) high at the shoulder and has a profuse, silky coat that is loosely curled. It is solid white or white with apricot, cream, or gray markings. A relative of the Maltese, the Bichon was first bred in the United States in the 1950s. It is exhibited in the miscellaneous class at dog shows sanctioned by the American Kennel Club. See DOG.

Bichri (bĭk'rī), father of SHEBA **3**; but "son of Bichri" may stand for "descendants of BECHER **1**." The "Berites," supporters of Sheba, are apparently to be understood as "Bichrites." 2 Sam. 20.

Bickerdyke, Mary Ann, 1817–1901, Union nurse in the American Civil War, b. Mary Ann Ball in Knox co., Ohio. Generally called Mother Bickerdyke, she served throughout the war in the West and was beloved by the enlisted men, whose rights she championed; she was also a favorite with generals Grant and Sherman. After the war she lobbied in Washington to secure pensions for Civil War nurses and veterans. See biographies by N. B. Baker (1952) and A. L. DeLeeuw (1973).

Bickerstaff, Isaac, pseudonym used by Jonathan Swift and later by Richard Steele in the *Tatler.*

Bickerstaffe, Isaac, c.1735–c.1812, English dramatist, b. Ireland. Included among his comedies and ballad operas are *The Maid of the Mill* (produced in 1765) and *The Padlock* (produced in 1768).

Bicocca, La (lä bēkôk'kä), former village, Lombardy, N Italy, now part of Milan. There, in 1522, the vicomte de Lautrec, commanding a French army and Swiss mercenaries, was defeated by a combined Milanese, Spanish, and German force in the ITALIAN WARS.

bicycle, light, two-wheeled vehicle driven by pedals. The name *velocipede* is often given to early forms of the bicycle and to its predecessor, the dandy horse, a two-wheeled vehicle moved by the thrust of the rider's feet upon the ground. Probably the first practical dandy horse was the draisine, originated c.1816 by Baron Karl Drais von Sauerbronn, chief forester of the duchy of Baden, to facilitate his inspection tours. Introduced into England in 1818, it was slowly improved, and c.1839 Kirkpatrick MacMillan, a Scottish blacksmith, developed a machine mechanically propelled by foot treadles and incorporating cranks, driving rods, and handle bars. The French inventor Ernest Michaux introduced in 1855 a heavy crank-driven bicycle. This was perfected c.1865 by Pierre Lallement, whose velocipede, known as a "boneshaker," ran on iron-tired wooden rims, the front wheel larger than the rear. Major improvements followed rapidly and included a light, hollow steel frame, ball bearings, tangential metal spokes, and solid rubber tires. By the 1880s the front wheel attained a diameter up to 64 in. (163 cm). Although the larger the wheel, the greater the potential speed, the size was limited by the length of the rider's legs, and the speed by their strength. The safer tricycle, a three-wheeled vehicle similar in design to the bicycle, also attained a vogue in the 1880s, especially among women and short men. The safety bicycle, with wheels of approximately equal diameter and a sprocket-chain drive connecting the pedals with the rear wheels, was first manufactured at Coventry, England, c.1885 by the English machinist James Starley; following the invention of the pneumatic tire in 1888 by the Scotsman John Dunlop, the safety bicycle superseded the high-wheel form. Additions to safety or comfort include the freewheel (rear wheel that turns freely when the pedals are stopped or rotated backward), the coaster brake, the hand brake, variable drive gear, and adjustable handle bars. In the 1880s and 90s cycling became a fad of major proportions in the United States and Europe. Bicycle clubs were formed; both sexes participated in rides into the country, often on tandem bicycles. The League of American Wheelmen, organized in 1880, was a leader in the agitation for good roads. Although cycling declined in the United States with the introduction of automobiles, it has recently become very popular again. In most of the world the bicycle is still a more important means of transportation than the automobile. The worldwide production of bicycles is between 35 million and 40 million yearly. See MOTORCYCLE. See Frederick Alderson, *Bicycling* (1972); E. A. Sloane, *The Complete Book of Bicycling* (1972); R. A. Smith, *A Social History of the Bicycle* (1972). The sport of **bicycle racing** is widely popular, and several international competitions are held annually. In Olympic competition, medals are awarded in seven cycling events. Internationally famed is the annual Tour de France (originated in 1903) with the world's best cyclists competing over a road course more than 2,500 mi (4,000 km) long. Before World War II the six-day race, a professional event, was popular in the United States. Since World War II amateur events have become more common.

Bida (bēdä'), town (1969 est. pop. 64,000), W central Nigeria. It is the trade center for a rice-growing region and is noted for its fiber, glass, and metal handicrafts. In the 19th cent. Bida was the capital of an emirate of the Muslim FULANI empire centered in SOKOTO. The town was captured in 1897 by forces under Sir George GOLDIE, head of the British-chartered Royal Niger Company.

Bidault, Georges (zhôrzh bēdō'), 1899–, French political leader. An influential columnist (1932–39), he was imprisoned (1940–41) in World War II and then joined the French underground, becoming its leader. A founder of the Mouvement Républicain Populaire (MRP), one of France's leading postwar parties, he was president of the provisional government (1946), premier (1949–50), and several times foreign minister. Although a strong supporter of Charles De Gaulle in 1958, Bidault opposed the Gaullist policy of Algerian independence and broke with the MRP. In 1962, announcing that he was going underground, he formed the National Council of Resistance within the terrorist Secret Army Organization (OAS); the French government accused Bidault of having become head of the OAS. In exile from 1962, Bidault lived in Brazil and then in Belgium before returning (1968) to France. See his autobiography (tr. 1967).

Biddeford (bĭd'ĭfərd), city (1970 pop. 19,983), York co., SW Maine, on the Saco River; inc. as a town 1718, as a city 1855. Samuel de Champlain, a French explorer, visited the area in 1605. The first permanent settlement was established in 1630. During the 17th cent. the town exported lumber and fish, and in 1840 the first cotton mill was built. Biddeford, which has an industrial park, manufactures blankets, linens, shoes, boys' clothing, and electrical appliances. Biddeford Pool is a resort at the mouth of the Saco River. St. Francis College is in the city.

Biddle, Clement, 1740-1814, American Revolutionary soldier, b. Philadelphia. Early in the war, he helped organize the "Quaker Blues," a company of volunteers. He later served as deputy quartermaster general of the Pennsylvania and New Jersey militia, commissary general of forage under Nathanael Greene in the Carolina campaign, and quartermaster general of the Pennsylvania militia. After the war he was (1787-93) U.S. marshal in Pennsylvania, but he gained more note as an importing merchant of Philadelphia.

Biddle, Francis Beverley, 1886-1968, U.S. Attorney General (1941-45), b. Paris, France, of American parents. Secretary to Associate Justice O. W. Holmes (1912), he became a successful corporation lawyer. He served as National Labor Relations Board chairman (1934-35) and as appellate judge (1939-40) before succeeding Robert H. JACKSON as Solicitor General (1940) and as Attorney General. Biddle was (1945-46) a U.S. judge for the trial of war criminals at Nuremberg. See his autobiographical *A Casual Past* (1961) and *In Brief Authority* (1962).

Biddle, George, 1885-1973, American painter and writer on art, b. Philadelphia. After studying abroad Biddle settled in the 1930s in Croton-on-Hudson, N.Y., where he devoted himself to paintings of social import. During World War II he served as chairman of the War Dept. Art Commission and later held important offices in several national artists' organizations. Biddle painted the frescoes for the Dept. of Justice Building, Washington, D.C.; his major works include *Mother and Child* (Denver Art Mus.) and *Winter in Tortilla Flat* (Whitney Mus., New York City). He is the author of the autobiographical *An American Artist's Story* (1939), *Artist at War* (1944), *Yes and No of Contemporary Art* (1957), and *Tahitian Journals* (1968). See Massey Trotter, *Catalogue of the Lithographs of George Biddle* (1950).

Biddle, James, 1783-1848, U.S. naval officer and diplomat, b. Philadelphia. He became a midshipman in 1800. At the beginning of the War of 1812 he was first lieutenant on the *Wasp*; he later commanded the sloop *Hornet*. Sent out in the *Ontario* in 1817, he took formal possession of the Oregon country for the United States in 1818, helping to establish a claim that later was extremely important. Afterward he spent much time protecting U.S. shipping in South American waters when the difficult times of the new Latin American republics made the rights of neutrals hard to maintain. In 1846, James Biddle negotiated the first treaty between the United States and China.

Biddle, John, 1615-62, founder of English Unitarianism. From his examination of the Scriptures he lost belief in the doctrine of the Trinity and stated his conclusions in *Twelve Arguments Drawn Out of Scripture*. When the existence of this paper was made known to the magistrates in 1645, Biddle was imprisoned, as he was frequently thereafter. His *Twelve Arguments* was suppressed and burned publicly in 1647. Upon the publication of his *Two-fold Catechism* in 1654, he was tried for his life but received from Oliver Cromwell a sentence of banishment to the Scilly Islands. Returning in 1658, Biddle taught and preached until in 1662 he was again thrown into prison, where he died. His followers were called Biddelians, Socinians, or Unitarians. See biography by Joshua Toulmin (1789).

Biddle, Nicholas, 1750-78, American naval officer, b. Philadelphia. Biddle left the British navy in 1773. In the American Revolution he became captain in the patriot navy and daringly raided British shipping off the American coast. After receiving command (1777) of the ship *Randolph*, Biddle was killed and his ship destroyed in an encounter (1778) with the British warship *Yarmouth* off the coast of Barbados. See W. B. Clark, *Captain Dauntless* (1949).

Biddle, Nicholas, 1786-1844, American financier, b. Philadelphia. After holding important posts in the American legations in France and England, he returned to the United States in 1807 and became one of the leading lights of *Port-Folio*, a literary magazine, which he edited after 1812. He was also commissioned to write the history of the Lewis and Clark expedition, but turned over the job to Paul Allen, a Philadelphia journalist, when he was elected (1810) to the state house of representatives, where he served a single term. In 1819, President Monroe appointed him one of the government directors of the BANK OF THE UNITED STATES. He became its president in 1823, and his administration illustrated his belief in the necessity of a central banking institution to stabilize the currency and curb the inflationary tendencies of the era. He became the leading target of the Jacksonians in their war against the bank. After the bank failed of recharter, Biddle operated it as a private bank until it collapsed (1841) as an aftermath of the Panic of 1837. He was charged with fraud but was subsequently acquitted. Biddle's public correspondence dealing with national affairs (1817-44) was edited by Reginald McGrane (1919). See biography by T. P. Govan (1959); study by G. R. Taylor (1949); Bray Hammond, *Banks and Politics in America* (1957, repr. 1967); R. V. Remini, *Andrew Jackson and the Bank War* (1967).

Bideford (bĭd'əfərd), municipal borough (1971 pop. 11,766), Devonshire, SW England, on the Torridge estuary. Formerly a major seaport, it still maintains some foreign trade (timber is imported) and has a boatbuilding industry. Tourism and the manufacture of gloves and concrete products are other important industries. Bideford supplied ships used in the defeat of the Spanish Armada (1588) and was a port of embarkation for colonists going to America. It also participated in the colonial tobacco and saltfish trade. A 24-arch stone bridge dating from the 15th cent. spans the Torridge estuary. Sir Richard Grenville, the naval commander, was born in Bideford.

Bidermann, Jakob (yä'kôp bē'dərmän), 1578-1639, German Jesuit dramatist and poet. Based on saint and martyr legends, Bidermann's plays were among the finest artistic expressions of the Catholic Reformation in Germany. His chief work, *Cenodoxus* (1602), was a Faustian drama about mortality. Professor of rhetoric in Munich, later assistant to the Jesuit general in Rome, he also wrote *Belisar* (1607), *Marcarius* (1613), and *Himmelsglöcklein* [heavenly bells] (1620), a collection of songs.

Bidkar, captain under Ahab and Jehu. 2 Kings 9.25.

Bidpai or **Bidpay** (both: bĭd'pī), supposed name of the author of the fables of the PANCHATANTRA. The name first appears in an Arabic version of these fables—hence they are called the fables of Bidpai. The word is probably Sanskrit, meaning "wise man" or "court scholar."

Biedermeier (bē'dərmīər), name applied, at first in a joking spirit, to a period of culture and a style of furniture and decoration originating in Germany early in the 19th cent. It is believed to have been named for the worthy, bourgeois-minded "Papa Biedermeier," a humorous character featured in a series of verses by Ludwig Eichrodt, published in *Fliegende Blätter*. The Biedermeier period found expression in comfortable, homelike furnishings, simple in design and inexpensive in material, fitting the requirements of the German people in a time of little wealth following the Napoleonic Wars. Although the best Biedermeier furniture was produced between 1820 and 1830, the period is regarded as extending from 1816 to 1848. Later pieces were usually clumsy and tasteless. The designs were simplified forms of the French Empire and Directoire styles and of some 18th-century styles of England. Cabinets and other large pieces were severe in line and surface. Chairs and sofas show curved lines, frequently graceful, but sometimes exaggerated into swellings and contortions. Black lacquer was effectively substituted for the costly ebony of Empire pieces. Painted decorations reminiscent of peasant types were common.

Biel (bēl) or **Bienne** (byĕn), city (1970 pop. 64,333), Bern canton, NW Switzerland, at the northeast end of the Lake of Biel. A watchmaking center, Biel also has manufactures of machinery, automobiles, and pianos. There is a 16th-century Gothic town hall and a late Gothic church. Both French and German are spoken. The Schwab museum has archaeological relics of lake dwellings found in the **Lake of Biel,** or **Lake of Bienne** (15 sq mi/39 sq km), at the foot of the Jura mts. The lake is connected with the Lake of Neuchâtel by the Zihl Canal. It contains the Isle of Saint-Pierre (now a peninsula), made famous by J. J. Rousseau.

Biel-. For some Russian names beginning thus, see BEL-.

Bielefeld (bē'ləfĕlt), city (1970 pop. 168,937), North Rhine-Westphalia, N central West Germany. It has been noted since the 13th cent. for its handmade linens. Other manufactures include silks, sewing machines, bicycles, machinery, starch, clothing, and pharmaceuticals. Chartered in 1214, Bielefeld became a member of the Hanseatic League in 1270. In 1647 it passed to Brandenburg. It is the seat of a university founded in 1966.

Bieler, Manfred (män'frĕt bē'lər), 1934-, East German dramatist and novelist. Among Bieler's plays, written for radio, are *Die achte Trübsal* [the eighth misery] (1960), attacking anti-Semitism; *Die linke Wand* [the left wall] (1962), concerning the Mexican painter David Siqueiros; and *Nachtwache* [night watch] (1963), a portrait of contemporary times. The picaresque novel *Bonifaz oder der Matrose in der Flasche* (1963; tr. *The Sailor in the Bottle,* 1965) brought him international fame. His collection of stories, *Märchen und Zeitungen* [fairy tales and newspapers], appeared in 1966.

Bielitz: see BIELSKO-BIAŁA, Poland.

Biella (byĕl'lä), city (1971 pop. 54,065), Piedmont, NW Italy. It is a major cotton and wool textile manufacturing center. Biella came under the Visconti of Milan in 1353 and under the house of Savoy in 1379. Of note are several palaces (15th-16th cent.), an early Romanesque baptistery (10th cent.), and a Renaissance cathedral.

Bielski, Martin, Pol. *Marcin Bielski* (mär'tsēn byĕl'skē), c.1495-1575, Polish historian and poet. His history of Poland, the first historical work written in Polish, was completed by his son, Joachim Bielski.

Bielsko-Biała (byĕl'skô byä'lä), Ger. *Bielitz*, city (1970 pop. 105,601), S Poland, on the Biała River, a tributary of the Vistula. The city is a railway junction and has a noted woolen textile industry. Other manufactures include textile machinery, electrical equipment, and machine tools. It is also a tourist and winter sports center. Founded in the 13th cent., the city passed to Austria in 1772 and was returned to Poland in 1919. It was called Bielsko until 1950, when it joined the town of Biała, across the river, to form a single city.

Bienewitz, Peter: see APIANUS, PETRUS.

Bien Hoa (bēēn' wä), city (1968 est. pop. 83,000), S South Vietnam, c.20 mi (30 km) NE of Saigon. It is famous for its handmade pottery. In the city are saw mills and a rice-bag factory. There is a commercial airport. A large U.S. air base was established there during the Vietnam War.

Bienne, Switzerland: see BIEL.

biennial, plant requiring two years to complete its life cycle, as distinguished from an annual or a perennial. In the first year a biennial usually produces a rosette of leaves (e.g., the cabbage) and a fleshy root, which acts as a food reserve over the winter. During the second year the plant produces flowers and seeds and, having exhausted its food reserve, then dies. Short-lived perennials (e.g., the hollyhock) are often treated as biennials. Some biennials will, like annuals, bloom in the same season if sown early; others reseed themselves or produce offsets, thus perpetuating the plant indefinitely so that it becomes essentially a perennial. There are very few true biennials. Most are crop plants, such as carrots and parsnips, which are harvested for their succulent roots at the end of their first growing season.

Bienville, Jean Baptiste le Moyne, sieur de (zhäN bätēst' lə mwän syör də byăNvēl'), 1680-1768, colonizer and governor of Louisiana, b. Ville Marie (on the site of Montreal), Canada; son of Charles le Moyne, sieur de LONGUEUIL, and brother of Pierre le Moyne, sieur d'IBERVILLE. A midshipman in the royal navy, he served gallantly in Iberville's last expedition into the Hudson Bay region in 1697 and the next year accompanied Iberville's colonizing expedition to the mouth of the Mississippi. He was prominent in the preliminary explorations. Iberville, upon his departure, left Bienville at the Biloxi settlement as second in command to the sieur de Sauvole, and in 1701, when Sauvole died, Bienville became the leader of the settlement. He transferred the colony to Mobile Bay in 1702 and founded Mobile in 1710. After Iberville's death in 1706, only Bienville's heroic efforts kept the settlement alive in the face of famine, Indian hostility, the jealousy of Spain and Canada, and the neglect of France. In 1712, when Louisiana became a monopoly of the French merchant Antoine Crozat, Bienville was superseded as governor by Cadillac, but he regained his position in 1717. The colony grew rapidly in the next few years. New Orleans, which Bienville founded in 1718, succeeded Biloxi as Louisiana's capital in 1722. In 1719 he twice captured Pensacola from the Spanish. Fearing insurrections of Negro slaves, first brought to the colony under his direction, Bienville promulgated (1724) the Code Noir. Its provisions, completely regulating slave life, were humane for the times, and the code remained in force until Louisiana became part of the United States. An unsuccessful campaign in 1723 against the Natchez, whom he had previously defeated (1716), led to his recall (1725). Unsuccessful in defending his administration, he was relieved of the governorship. Upon Louisiana's subsequent decline, he was begged to return and was warmly received on his arrival in 1733. He led strenuous but indecisive expeditions (1736, 1739–40) against the Natchez and the Chickasaw. Worn out by his exertions, Bienville retired in 1743 and spent his remaining days in Paris. See biography by Grace King (1892).

Bié Plateau or **Bihé Plateau** (both: byĕ), highland region, western section of the central plateau of Angola, SW Africa; alt. 5,000 to 6,000 ft (1,520–1,830 m). Its cool climate and ample rainfall made it a favored area for European settlement. Corn, sisal, peanuts, and coffee are raised there. It is linked to the sea by the Benguela Railway. Nova Lisboa and Silva Porto are the chief towns.

Bierce, Ambrose Gwinett, 1842–1914?, American satirist, journalist, and short-story writer, b. Meigs co., Ohio. After distinguished Civil War service, he turned to journalism. In San Francisco he wrote for the *News-Letter*, of which he became editor in 1868. He soon established a reputation as a satirical wit, and his squibs and epigrams were much quoted. In London, from 1872 to 1875, he wrote for the magazine *Fun* and finished three books, including *Cobwebs from an Empty Skull* (1874). After his return to San Francisco, he wrote for the *Argonaut*, edited the *Wasp* (1881–86), and was a columnist for Hearst's *Sunday Examiner* (1887–96); his writings in the *Examiner* made him the literary arbiter of the West Coast. Later he was Washington correspondent for the *American* and a contributor to *Cosmopolitan*. His collection of sardonic definitions, *The Cynic's Word Book* (1906), was retitled *The Devil's Dictionary* in 1911. The short stories of Bierce were collected in such volumes as *Tales of Soldiers and Civilians* (1891) and *Can Such Things Be?* (1893). He was highly praised for *The Monk and the Hangman's Daughter* (1892), which he adapted from a translation of a German story. Bierce's distinction lies in his distilled satire, in the crisp precision of his language, and in his realistically developed horror stories. Disillusionment and sadness pervaded the latter part of his life. In 1913 he went to Mexico, where all trace of him was lost. See his *Collected Works* (12 vol., 1909–12; repr. 1966); *Collected Writings* (selected by Clifton Fadiman, 1946); biography by R. O'Connor (1967); study by M. E. Grenander (1971).

Bierstadt, Albert (bēr'stät), 1830–1902, American painter of Western scenery, b. Germany. After traveling and sketching throughout the mountains of Europe, he returned to the United States. He then journeyed (1859) to the West with a trail-making expedition. His immense canvases of the Rocky Mts. and the Yosemite emphasized grandeur and drama, sometimes at the expense of clarity. His works were popular and commanded great prices during his lifetime. They include *The Rocky Mountains* (Metropolitan Mus.); *Indian Encampment, Shoshone Village* (N.Y. Public Lib.); *The Last of the Buffalo* (Corcoran Gall.); and *Discovery of the Hudson River* and *The Settlement of California* (Capitol, Washington, D.C.).

Bifrost: see ASGARD.

bigamy (bĭ'gəmē), crime of marrying during the continuance of a lawful marriage. Bigamy is not committed if a prior marriage has been terminated by a DIVORCE or a decree of NULLITY OF MARRIAGE. In the United States if a husband or wife is absent and unheard of for seven (or in some states five) years and not known to be alive, he is presumed dead, and remarriage by the other spouse is not bigamous. It is not necessarily a defense to a charge of bigamy that the offending party believed in good faith that he was divorced or that his previous marriage was not lawful. The U.S. Supreme Court ruled in 1878 that plurality of wives (polygamy), as originally permitted by the Mormon religion, violated criminal law and was not defensible as an exercise of religious liberty.

big bang theory: see COSMOLOGY.

Big Ben, the bell in the Parliament tower (Westminster Palace), London, England. It was named for Sir Benjamin Hall, commissioner of works when the bell was installed in 1856. The name is often used to refer to the huge clock in the tower.

Big Bend National Park, 708,221 acres (286,627 hectares), W Texas; est. 1944. It is a triangle formed by the Rio Grande, which runs south, then north in a big bend and flows through deep canyons, notably the Santa Elena Canyon. The river, the desert plain, and the Chisos Mts. offer sharp contrasts in wilderness scenery, and the park has archaeological treasures, some petrified trees, vestiges of prehistoric Indian cultures, and rare forms of animal and plant life.

Big Black Mountain, peak, 4,145 ft (1,263 m) high, E Ky., in the Cumberland Mts.; highest point in Kentucky.

Big Dipper, familiar configuration of stars visible in the constellation Ursa Major (see URSA MAJOR AND URSA MINOR).

Bigelow, John, 1817–1911, American editor, author, and diplomat, b. Malden, N.Y. In 1838 he was admitted to the New York bar. From 1848 to 1861 he shared with William Cullen BRYANT the ownership and editing of the New York *Evening Post*. His antislavery and free trade editorials were especially vigorous. In 1861 he was appointed consul general at Paris, and later (1865–66) he served as U.S. minister to France. He is given much credit for preventing French recognition of the Confederacy; he also treated with great skill the problems arising from Napoleon III's attempts to establish an independent state in Mexico. His *France and the Confederate Navy* (1888) is a valuable historical work. Bigelow found in Paris the original manuscript of Benjamin Franklin's *Autobiography*, which he edited and published in 1868. His other works include a life of Franklin (1874) and an edition of Franklin's complete works (10 vol., 1887–88). See his *Retrospections of an Active Life* (5 vol., 1909–13).

Biggs, E. Power (Edward George Power Biggs), 1906–, Anglo-American organist. Biggs studied at the Royal Academy of Music, London. He emigrated to the United States in 1930. Through many recitals, radio broadcasts, and recordings, he helped to make the best organ music, particularly that of the baroque period and of the 20th cent., familiar to the American public.

Big Hole National Battlefield: see NATIONAL PARKS AND MONUMENTS (table).

Bighorn, river, 461 mi (741 km) long, formed in W central Wyo. by the confluence of the Wind and Pop Agie rivers and flowing north to join the Yellowstone River in S Mont. The Bighorn basin, part of the Missouri River basin project, has several dams that provide for flood control, irrigation, hydroelectricity, and recreation. Boysen and Yellowstone are the principal dams; the lake behind Yellowstone dam is the nucleus of Bighorn Canyon National Recreation Area (see NATIONAL PARKS AND MONUMENTS, table). In 1807 a U.S. trading post was established at the mouth of the Bighorn. The battle between the forces of Col. George Custer and the Sioux Indians took place (1876) near the junction of the Bighorn and the Little Bighorn rivers.

bighorn or **Rocky Mountain sheep,** wild sheep of W North America, formerly plentiful in mountains from Canada to Mexico. Indiscriminate hunting, disease, and scarcity of food have reduced its numbers, and in some areas it has been exterminated. It is a heavy, grayish brown animal, with a conspicuous whitish patch on its hindquarters; the male has heavy, curling horns, while the female has short, straight spikes. One type of bighorn lives at high altitudes in the W United States and another in desert regions. Alaskan types are the Dall's, or white, sheep and the Stone's, or black, sheep. Bighorn sheep are classified in the phylum CHORDATA, subphylum Vertebrata, class Mammalia, order Artiodactyla, family Bovidae.

Bighorn Mountains, range of the Rocky Mts., N central Wyo., extending c.120 mi (190 km) N into S Montana, E of the Bighorn River. Cloud Peak, 13,165 ft (4,013 m), is the highest point. The glaciated mountain range contains Bighorn National Forest.

bight, broad bend or curve in a coastline, forming a large open bay. The New York bight, for example, is the curve in the coast described by the southern shore of Long Island and the eastern shore of New Jersey. The term *bight* may also refer to the bay so formed.

Bignon, Louis Pierre Édouard (lwē pyĕr ādwär' bēnyôN'), 1771–1841, French diplomat and historian. He held diplomatic posts under Napoleon, was acting minister of foreign affairs during the Hundred Days, and signed the surrender of Paris after Waterloo. A member of the chamber of deputies in the Restoration, he was (1830) foreign minister under Louis Philippe, who raised him to the peerage. His major historical work, *Histoire de France sous Napoléon* (14 vol., 1829–50; completed posthumously by A. A. Ernouf), was commissioned by Napoleon.

bignonia (bĭgnō'nēə), common name for the family Bignoniaceae, a family of chiefly woody vines of the American tropics and also a few shrubs and trees. The trumpet creeper (of the genus *Bignonia*) and the trumpet flower, or trumpet vine (of the genus *Campsis*), both found wild in the SE United States, are sometimes cultivated for their orange-red trumpet-shaped flowers. The calabash tree of the tropics bears large fruits from which carrying gourds (called calabashes) are made and used locally; its wood is used for making pipes. The *Catalpa* genus of trees with showy flowers is valued in the United States for ornament and shade. The highly durable wood is used for lumber, as is that of the South American genus *Jacaranda* and of the West Indian boxwood (of the genus *Tabebuia*). The bignonias are classified in the division MAGNOLIOPHYTA, class Magnoliopsida, order Scrophulariales.

Bigod, Hugh, 1st **earl of Norfolk** (bĭ'gŏd, nôr'fək), d. 1177, English nobleman. He was instrumental in securing the throne for STEPHEN in 1135, but he subsequently switched his allegiance back and forth between Stephen and MATILDA, and it is not known for sure which one of them created him earl of Norfolk. He finally cast his lot with the future Henry II in 1153. In 1173 he joined the revolt of Henry's sons against their father. His lands were seized, his castle was burned, and a heavy fine was exacted.

Bigordi, Domenico: see GHIRLANDAIO, DOMENICO.

Bigot, François (fräNswä' bēgō'), 1703–77?, intendant of New France (1748–59), b. Bordeaux, France. At Louisburg, where he served (1739–45) as commissary, it has been said that he indulged in fraudulent practices that contributed to the downfall of that fort. Powerful friends in France secured for him the office of intendant of New France. Bigot arrived at Quebec in 1748 and immediately instituted a system of official theft by which every branch of the public service was laid under tribute to enrich himself and his friends. His corrupt administration reduced the colony to bankruptcy and helped bring on the fall of New France to the British. After the capture of Quebec in 1759 he returned to France, where he was arrested, imprisoned for nearly a year, compelled to make restitution, and then banished. The date of his death in Switzerland is uncertain.

Big Rapids, city (1970 pop. 11,995), seat of Mecosta co., W central Mich., at the falls of the Muskegon River; inc. 1869. The region has extensive natural gas wells. The city's major manufactures include shoes, machine tools, and wood products. Ferris State College, part of the Univ. of Michigan system, is in Big Rapids.

Big River: see FORT GEORGE, river.

Big Sioux (so͞o), river, 420 mi (676 km) long, rising in NE S. Dak. and flowing S into the Missouri River. It passes through an agricultural region that produces corn, oats, hogs, and beef cattle. The Big Sioux forms part of the border between Iowa and South Dakota.

Big Spring, city (1970 pop. 28,735), seat of Howard co., W central Texas; inc. 1907. The spring for which it was named once fed a branch of the Colorado River but is now dry. The city is the trade center for a farm and livestock region. A variety of oil-related industries have been developed since the discovery of oil in 1928. Points of interest in Big Springs include a historical museum and the Comanche Trail Park. A junior college is in the city; Webb Air Force Base is nearby.

Big Stone Lake, narrow lake, c.25 mi (40 km) long, on the Minn.-S. Dak. line. Located in the outlet channel of glacial Lake AGASSIZ, it is the source of the Minnesota River.

Bigtha, chamberlain of Ahasuerus. Esther 1.10.

Bigthan (bĭg'thən), chamberlain who conspired with Teresh against King Ahasuerus. Esther 2.21. He is called **Bigthana** in Esther 6.2.

big tree: see SEQUOIA.

Bigvai (bĭg'vāī, bĭgvā'ī). **1** Signer of the covenant. Ezra 2.2.; Neh. 7.7; 10.16. **2** Name of a family in the return. Ezra 2.14.; Neh. 7.19.

Bihar or **Behar** (bēhär'), state (1971 pop. 56,387,296), 67,198 sq mi (174,042 sq km), E central India. PATNA is the capital; RANCHI is an important administrative center. Bihar is bounded on the N by Nepal; on the E by West Bengal state; on the S by Orissa state; and on the W by Uttar Pradesh and Madhya Pradesh states. The predominantly agricultural northern area, crossed by the Ganges River, supports the bulk of the population. Rainfall, frequently inadequate, is supplemented by extensive irrigation. Rice is grown where possible; maize, wheat, barley, sugarcane, tobacco, and oilseed are also important crops. Jute is the main cash crop of the extreme northeast. The central and southern areas are hilly. The southeastern section is one of the greatest sources of India's mineral wealth; mica and copper are abundant, and iron ore, found in association with coal, is processed at the great Jamshedpur steelworks. The chief transportation lines run east and west, thus linking central India with the Bengal ports. Bihar's population, almost entirely Hindu, is unusually homogenous for India. The people speak Bihari, an Indo-European language. Bihar was the scene of Buddha's early life, and BODH GAYA is an ancient Buddhist center. Bihar was part of the ancient kingdom of Magadha. Muslims occupied it in 1193 and the Delhi sultans in 1497. In 1765 the British took over Bihar and merged it with Bengal. The province of Bihar and Orissa was formed in 1912, and Bihar became a separate province in 1936. About 3,150 sq mi (8,160 sq km) situated along Bihar's eastern boundary were transferred to West Bengal state in 1956. Bihar is governed by a chief minister and a cabinet responsible to a bicameral legislature with one elected house and by a governor appointed by the president of India. **Bihar** city (1971 pop. 100,052), on a tributary of the Ganges River, is an agricultural market.

Biisk: see BIYSK, USSR.

Bijapur (bĭjä'po͝or), town (1971 pop. 103,308), Karnataka state, SE India. It is a trade and district administrative center. Cotton ginning is an important activity. Bijapur is famous as the capital (15th-17th cent.) of the Deccan kingdom of Bijapur, under the Adil Shahi sultans. Among the town's many notable remains is the Gol Gumbaz, the tomb of Mahmud Shah.

Bijns, Anna (ä'nä bīns), c.1494-1575?, Flemish poet of Antwerp. Her three volumes (1528, 1548, 1567) of lyric verse place her among the foremost Dutch poets of her age. She excelled in robust satires passionately inveighing against the social evils of the day and deploring the Reformation. Bijns's religious poetry is sincere and moving.

Bika, El: see BIQA, AL.

Bikaner (bĭkənēr'), former native state, NW India. The state is now part of Rajasthan state. The region, almost entirely in the Thar desert, chiefly supports the raising of sheep and camels. Wool is spun and woven, and coal is mined. The city of **Bikaner** (1971 pop. 188,598), the capital of the former state, was founded in 1488. There are several beautiful 16th-century Rajput palaces. The city has five colleges that are affiliated with the Univ. of Rajasthan.

Bikini (bēkē'nē), atoll, c.2 sq mi (5.2 sq km), W central Pacific, one of the Ralik Chain, MARSHALL ISLANDS. It comprises 36 islets on a reef 25 mi (40 km) long. After its inhabitants were removed (1946) to Rongerik, Bikini was the scene of 23 U.S. atomic and hydrogen bomb tests between 1946 and 1958. The Bikini natives were transferred from Rongerik to Ujelang in 1947 and in 1949 were resettled on Kili. The atoll was declared safe for habitation in 1969. Bikini was formerly called Escholtz Island.

Bilac, Olavo (o͞olä'vo͞o bĕläk'), 1865-1918, Brazilian poet, journalist, and critic. He was the chief poet of the Brazilian group related to the French PARNASSIANS. His writings have an enameled elegance as well as sensual richness that gained them enduring acclaim. Some of them are gathered in *Poesias* (1888) and *Tarde* [afternoon] (1919).

Bilaspur (bēläs'po͝or'). **1** Former principality, Himachal Pradesh state, NW India, in the W Himalayas. It is the site of the Bhakra dam, a massive project on the Sulej River. The town of Bilaspur (1971 pop. 7,024), formerly the capital, trades in agricultural products. **2** Town (1971 pop. 130,804), Madhya Pradesh state, central India. Founded in the 17th cent., the city is a district administrative center and an agricultural market.

Bila Tserkva: see BELAYA TSERKOV, USSR.

Bilauktaung (bēlouk'toun), mountain range, extending c.250 mi (400 km) along the Thailand-Burma border from the Dawna Range SE to the Isthmus of Kra. The western slopes of the range, which receive the heavy rains of the monsoon, have a dense covering of tropical rain forest.

Bilbao (bĕlbä'ō), city (1971 pop. 410,490), capital of Vizcaya prov., N Spain, in the Basque Provinces, on both banks of the Nervión River, near the Bay of Biscay. A leading Spanish port and commercial center since the 19th cent., it is the center of an important industrial area, with rich iron mines nearby. The production of steel and chemicals and shipbuilding are the chief industries. Founded c.1300 on the site of an ancient settlement, Bilbao flourished from a wool export trade in the 15th and 16th cent. In the 19th cent. it was three times unsuccessfully besieged by the Carlists. In the Spanish civil war, Bilbao was the seat of the short-lived Basque autonomous government from 1936 until its capture (1937) by the Insurgents.

Bilbilis: see CALATAYUD, Spain.

Bilbo, Theodore Gilmore, 1877-1947, U.S. Senator (1935-47), b. near Poplarville, Pearl River co., Miss. After study at the Univ. of Nashville (1897-1900) and Vanderbilt Univ. law school (1905-7), he was admitted (1908) to the Tennessee bar. An ultraconservative Southern Democrat, he won political success by demagogic insistence on white supremacy. He was twice governor of Mississippi (1916-20, 1928-32) before his election to the U.S Senate. He died while Congress was investigating charges that he had disqualified himself for the Senate by using intimidation to keep Negroes from voting and by accepting bribes. See biography by A. W. Green (1963).

Bildad, the second, and perhaps the least consoling, of Job's comforters. Job 8; 18; 25; 42.9.

Bilderdijk, Willem (wĭl'əm bĭl'dərdīk), 1756-1831, Dutch poet. His work influenced Dutch literature throughout the 19th cent. He tutored Louis Bonaparte in Dutch and later conducted a small private college at Leiden, where he greatly influenced his pupils, notably Isaäc da Costa and Jacob van Lennep. Bilderdijk's work is of prodigious quantity and includes passionate love poetry as well as the religious verse for which he is best known. At its best, the poetry is so splendid that Bilderdijk is ranked among the great Dutch poets. His most ambitious effort is an unfinished epic, *De Ondergang der eerste Wareld* [the destruction of the first creation] (1820). His Dutch translation of the romanticists catalyzed that movement in Dutch literature, and a number of his own works were modeled after those of the British romantics.

bile, bitter alkaline fluid of a yellow, brown, or green color, secreted, in man, by the liver. Bile, or gall, is composed of water, bile acids and their salts, bile pigments, cholesterol, fatty acids, and inorganic salts. In man it is stored in the GALL BLADDER and, in response to the action of the hormone cholecystokinen (whose secretion by the intestine is stimulated by the presence of food), is secreted via the cystic and common ducts into the duodenum. The bile salts aid in digestion by emulsifying fats, enabling the absorption of fats and of the fat-soluble vitamins (A, D, E, and K) through the intestinal wall. Since unabsorbed fats tend to coat other foods and prevent the action of digestive enzymes, adequate fat absorption mediated by bile salts is necessary for the complete digestion of food and the prevention of decomposition of partially digested foods by intestinal bacteria. The alkaline bile acts to neutralize the stomach acid in the small intestine, providing a more optimum environment for the pancreatic enzymes. The bile is a route of excretion for many drugs and metabolites; cholesterol is excreted almost entirely in the bile, as are breakdown products of heme, such as bilirubin, that color the bile and are known as the bile pigments. If the flow of bile is impeded by inflammation, gall stones, or other abnormality, digestive disturbances and frequently JAUNDICE result.

Bileam (bĭl'ēəm), the same as IBLEAM.

Bilgah (bĭl'gə). **1** Priest. 1 Chron. 24.14. **2** Priest in the return. Neh. 12.5,18. He is called **Bilgai** at Neh. 10.8.

Bilhah (bĭl'hə). **1** Rachel's maid and Jacob's concubine. Gen. 29.29; 30.1-8; 35.22,25; 46.25; 1 Chron. 7.13. **2** City of Simeon, of unknown location. 1 Chron. 4.29. Baalah: Joshua 15.29. Balah: Joshua 19.3.

Bilhan (bĭl'hăn). **1** Horite. Gen. 36.27; 1 Chron. 1.42. **2** Benjamite. 1 Chron. 7.10.

Billaud-Varenne, Jacques Nicolas (zhäk nēkōlä' bēyō'-värĕn'), 1756-1819, French revolutionary. A violent antimonarchist in the Convention, the revolutionary national assembly, he became a member of the Committee of Public Safety. He proposed a centralization of power from which no one would be exempt; this proposal, passed as law, became the basis for the dictatorship of the REIGN OF TERROR. He plotted first against Georges DANTON and then against Maximilien ROBESPIERRE. After Robespierre's fall, however, he was deported to French Guiana for his role in the Terror. He refused an amnesty offered by Napoleon Bonaparte (later Emperor Napoleon I). Ultimately he went to Haiti, where he died.

Billerica (bĭlrĭ'kə), town (1970 pop. 31,648), Middlesex co., NE Mass., on the Concord River; settled 1637, inc. 1655. It is mainly residential. Billerica was one of the "praying Indian" towns of John Eliot. The town's historical attractions include several 17th-, 18th-, and 19th-century homes and an Indian site and burial ground dating back to 1,000 B.C.

billiards, any one of a number of games played with a tapered, leather-tipped stick called a cue and various numbers of balls on a rectangular, cloth-covered slate table with raised and cushioned edges. Games similar to billiards were popular in England and France in the 16th cent., and there is even evidence that a billiardslike game was played in the 14th cent. The country of origin is a matter of dispute—England, France, Italy, Spain, and China have been credited by various historians with its invention. The game in its present form was probably fully developed by 1800. There are three main types of billiards: carom billiards, pocket billiards (also known as pool), and snooker. Carom billiards is played with three balls, a cue ball and two object balls, on a pocketless table; scoring is by caroms only, i.e., by causing the cue ball to strike the object balls in specified ways. Pocket billiards is played with 15 object balls and a cue ball on a table with six pockets; the essential object of the game is to cause the object balls to enter the pockets. Snooker is similar to pocket billiards, except that it uses 21 object balls and smaller pockets. There are many additional variations of the basic games, depending on the number of balls used, the positioning of the balls, the boundaries on the table, and the scoring. Among the variations are Chicago, golf, rotation, balk-line, and bumpers. William Frederick HOPPE is generally considered the foremost billiards player of all time. See Clive Cottingham, *The Game of Billiards* (1964).

Billings, John Shaw, 1838-1913, American surgeon and librarian, b. Indiana. In the Civil War he was medical inspector of the Army of the Potomac. After the war he was given charge of the Surgeon General's Library in Washington. The catalog entries greatly increased under his supervision by 1873, and soon after he began work on the great *Index Catalogue*. Sixteen volumes appeared before his military retirement. In 1879 he initiated the *Index Medicus*, a monthly guide to current medical literature. Billings designed plans for the construction of Johns Hopkins Hospital. His essays on hospital administration and training remain classics. Under his librarianship (1864-95) the National Library of Medicine became one of the greatest medical library systems in the world. In 1889 he compiled the *National Medical Dictionary*. As director of the combined Astor, Lenox, and Tilden foundations in New York City, which were to become the NEW YORK PUBLIC LIBRARY, he consolidated the collections, planned and supervised the erection of the central library building, united the various free circulating libraries of the city, secured $5 million from Andrew Carnegie for branch buildings, and in general created the New York Public Library as it now stands. It was at Billings' suggestion that punched card machinery was developed, forming the beginnings of computer technology. He also supervised compilation of U.S. census information in 1880 and 1890. See his *Selected Papers* (comp. with a biography by F. B. Rogers, 1965); biographies by F. H. Garrison (1915) and H. M. Lydenberg (1924).

Billings, Josh, pseud. of **Henry Wheeler Shaw,** 1818-85, American humorist and lecturer, b. Lanesboro, Mass. After a roving life as farmer, explorer, and coal miner, he settled in Poughkeepsie, N.Y., as an auctioneer and real estate dealer. In 1860 he began to write humorous sketches and homespun philosophies in rural dialect and soon became a popular lecturer. His first collection was *Josh Billings: His Sayings* (1869), but his best humor was published in his annual *Farmer's Allminax* (1869-80). See study by D. B. Kesterson (1974).

Billings, William, 1746-1800, American hymn composer, b. Boston. A tanner by trade, he was one of the earliest American-born composers. He wrote popular hymns and sacred choruses of great vitality, using simple imitative counterpoint—hence their designation as "fuguing tunes." He often wrote his own texts, breaking with the colonial New England tradition of using psalm verses as texts for hymns. His self-reliance and lack of musical training made him relatively independent of European musical fashions. As a singing master, he introduced the use of both pitch pipe and violincello to improve the intonation of church choirs. A singing class he organized in 1774 became in 1786 the Stoughton Musical Society. During the American Revolution he wrote patriotic words to his best-known hymn, "Chester," beginning: "Let tyrants shake their iron rods,/And Slav'ry clank her galling chains." His songbooks include *The New England Psalm Singer* (1770), *The Singing Master's Assistant* (1778), and *The Continental Harmony* (1794). See biography by David McKay and Richard Crawford (1974); Murray Barbour, *The Church Music of William Billings* (1960, repr. 1972).

Billings, city (1970 pop. 61,581), seat of Yellowstone co., S Mont., on the Yellowstone River, in a valley surrounded by seven mountain ranges; inc. as a city 1885. Founded in 1882 by the Northern Pacific RR, Billings quickly became an important shipping point and fur-trading center. It is now a trade and manufacturing center for the S Montana and N Wyoming region. Oil refining, sugar refining, meat packing, and flour milling are the city's major industries. Wheat, sugar, beets, livestock, and wool are traded. Billings, the center of a recreational area, is near Custer National Forest and Yellowstone National Park. Rocky Mountain College and Eastern Montana College are in Billings.

Billingsgate (bĭl'ĭngzgĭt, -gāt), wharf and fish market in the City of London, Greater London, England, on the north bank of the Thames River. The market is named after a river gate in the old city wall. The word *Billingsgate*, a synonym for coarse language, arose from references to the speech of the district's fish porters.

Billiton: see BELITUNG.

bill of exchange: see DRAFT.

Bill of Rights, 1689, in British history, one of the fundamental instruments of constitutional law. It registered in statutory form the outcome of the long 17th-century struggle between the Stuart kings and the English Parliament. Its principles were accepted by William III and Mary II in the Declaration of Rights as a condition for ascending the throne after the revolution in which James II was dethroned (1688). The Bill of Rights stated that certain acts of James II were illegal and henceforth prohibited; that Englishmen possessed certain inviolable civil and political rights; that James had forfeited the throne by abdication and that William and Mary were lawful sovereigns; that the succession should pass to the heirs of Mary, then to Princess Anne (later queen) and her heirs; and that no Roman Catholic could ever be sovereign of England. By its provisions and implications it gave political supremacy to Parliament and was supplemented (1701) by the Act of SETTLEMENT.

Bill of Rights, in U.S. history: see CONSTITUTION OF THE UNITED STATES.

Billy the Kid, 1859–81, American outlaw, b. New York City. His real name was William H. Bonney. His family moved to Kansas and then to New Mexico when he was a child. He frequented saloons and gambling halls, and before he was 16 years old he had killed several men. In 1878 he led a gang in the Lincoln co. cattle war, killed a sheriff, and engaged in large-scale cattle rustling. John S. Chisum and other cattlemen secured (1880) the election of a new sheriff sworn to rid the country of the cattle thieves. Billy the Kid was captured, tried, and sentenced to death. He escaped but was again trapped and was shot by Sheriff Pat F. Garrett. See biographies by Pat F. Garrett (1882, repr. 1967), R. N. Mullin (1967), C. A. Siringo (1967), and C. W. Breihan (1970).

Biloxi (bĭlŭk'sē), city (1970 pop. 48,486), Harrison co., SE Miss., on a small peninsula between Biloxi Bay and Mississippi Sound, on the Gulf of Mexico; inc. as a town 1838, as a city 1896. The warm, almost tropical climate has made Biloxi a popular resort. In addition to tourism, major industries include fishing and boatbuilding, the packing and shipping of shrimps and oysters, and the manufacture of small appliances and fishing nets. The first white settlement in the lower Mississippi valley was established in 1699 across the bay at Old Biloxi (now Ocean Springs) by the French under Pierre Iberville. New Biloxi was founded in 1719 and was the capital of the French colony of Louisiana until 1722, when New Orleans replaced it. In the city are Keesler Air Force Base, a U.S. coast guard air station, and a U.S. veterans hospital. Nearby are "Beauvoir" (built 1852–54), the last home of Jefferson Davis; the Biloxi Light House (built 1848); and, off the coast, Ship Island, a Union fort in the Civil War. The city has a junior college, a symphony, and a theater group.

Bilshan, one who returned with Zerubbabel. Ezra 2.2; Neh. 7.7.

Bimeler, Joseph Michael (bī'mələr), 1778–1853, German religious leader, originally called Bäumler. A teacher of the separatists in Württemberg, in 1817 he led a group of them to America. In Ohio they founded the community of ZOAR.

bimetallism, in economic history, monetary system in which two commodities, usually gold and silver, were used as a standard and coined without limit at a ratio fixed by legislation that also designated both of them as legally acceptable for all payments. The term was first used in 1869 by Enrico Cernuschi (1821–96), an Italian-French economist and a vigorous advocate of the system. In a bimetallic system, the ratio is expressed in terms of weight, e.g., 16 oz of silver equal 1 oz of gold, which is described as a ratio of 16 to 1. As the ratio is determined by law, it has no relation to the commercial value of the metals, which fluctuates constantly. Gresham's law, therefore, applies; i.e., the metal that is commercially valued at less than its face value tends to be used as money, and the metal commercially valued at more than its face value tends to be used as metal, valued by weight, and hence is withdrawn from circulation as money. Working against that is the fact that the debtor tends to pay in the commercially cheaper metal, thus creating a market demand likely to bring its commercial value up to its face value. In practice, the instability predicted by Gresham's law overpowered the cushioning effect of debtors' payments, thereby making bimetallism far too unstable a monetary system for most modern nations. Aside from England, which in acts of 1798 and 1816 made gold the standard currency, all countries practiced bimetallism during the late 18th cent. and most of the 19th cent. See J. L. Laughlin, *The History of Bimetallism in the United States* (1897, repr. 1968).

Bimhal (bĭm'hăl), Asherite. 1 Chron. 7.33.

Biminis (bĭ'mĭnēz, bəmē'nēz), island group in the Straits of Florida, forming the northwest section of the Bahamas. The group includes North Bimini, South Bimini, and surrounding cays. Exceptionally good fishing attracts many tourists. According to legend, the Biminis are the location of the fountain of youth for which Juan Ponce de León searched.

binary star or **binary system,** pair of stars that are held together by their mutual gravitational attraction and revolve about their common center of mass. True binary stars are distinct from optical doubles—pairs of stars that lie nearly along the same line of sight from the earth but are not physically associated. Binary stars are grouped into three classes. A visual binary is a pair of stars that can be seen by direct telescopic observation to be a distinct pair with shared motion. A spectroscopic binary cannot be seen as two separate stars, even with the most powerful telescopes, but spectral lines from the pair show a periodic Doppler effect that indicates mutual revolution. Some lines indicate motion toward the earth while others indicate motion away; later, as the stars revolve around in their orbit, this pattern reverses. An eclipsing binary has the plane of its orbit lying in the line of sight, and shows a periodic fluctuation in brightness as one star passes in front of the other. The brighter star (A) of a binary is called the primary, and the less bright (B) is called the secondary; e.g., Sirius A and Sirius B are the primary and secondary components of the Sirius system. It seems likely that about half the stars in our galaxy are binary or multiple (a system of more than two stars moving around their mutual center of mass), since half the known stars within 30 light-years of the sun are binary or multiple. The masses of the components of a visual binary can be deduced from the observed motions and Newton's law of gravitation; these are the only stars, other than the sun, for which masses have been directly determined. Measurements of the masses of some of the visual binary stars have been used to verify the MASS-LUMINOSITY RELATION.

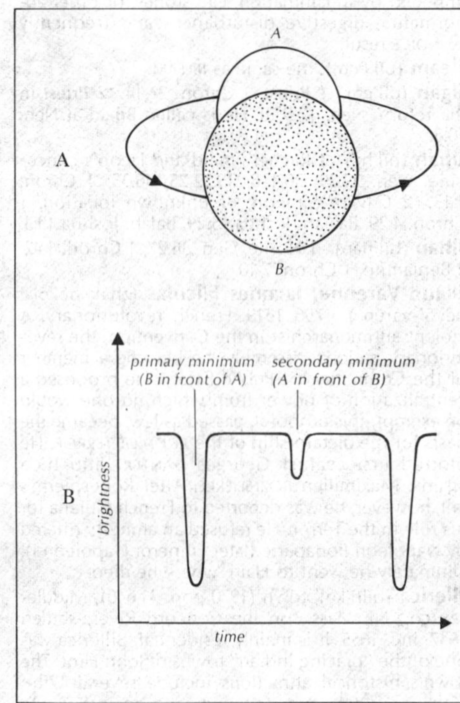

A. *Eclipsing binary: Primary component passing behind secondary (dimmer) component*

B. *Light curve for eclipsing binary*

binary system, NUMERATION system based on powers of 2, in contrast to the familiar DECIMAL SYSTEM, which is based on powers of 10. In the binary system, only the digits 0 and 1 are used. Thus, the first ten numbers in binary notation, corresponding to the numbers 0, 1, 2, 3, 4, 5, 6, 7, 8, and 9 in decimal notation, are 0, 1, 10, 11, 100, 101, 110, 111, 1000, and 1001. Since each position indicates a specific power of 2, just as the number 342 means $(3 \times 10^2) + (4 \times 10^1) + (2 \times 10^0)$, the decimal equivalent of a binary number can be calculated by adding together each digit multiplied by its power of 2; for example, the binary number 1011010 corresponds to $(1 \times 2^6) + (0 \times 2^5) + (1 \times 2^4) + (1 \times 2^3) + (0 \times 2^2) + (1 \times 2^1) + (0 \times 2^0) = 64 + 0 + 16 + 8 + 0 + 2 + 0 = 90$ in the decimal system. Binary numbers are sometimes written with a subscript "b" to distinguish them from decimal numbers having the same digits. As with the decimal system, fractions can be represented by digits to the right of the binary point (analogous to the decimal point). A binary number is generally much longer than the decimal equivalent; e.g., the number above, 1011010_b, contains seven digits while its decimal counterpart, 90, contains only two. This is a disadvantage for most ordinary applications but is offset by the greater simplicity of the binary system in COMPUTER applications. Since only two digits are used, any binary digit, or bit, can be transmitted and recorded electronically simply by the presence or absence of an electrical pulse or current. The great speed of such devices more than compensates for the fact that a given number may contain a large number of digits.

Binchois, Gilles (zhēl băNshwä'), c.1400–1460, Flemish composer. From about 1430 until his death Binchois served Philip the Good of Burgundy. His secular chansons are considered his best work. The 15th-century theorist Tinctoris ranked him with Dufay and Dunstable.

binder: see COMBINE.

bindweed: see MORNING GLORY.

Binea (bĭn'ēə), descendant of Saul. 1 Chron. 8.37; 9.43.

Binet, Alfred (älfrĕd' bĕnā'), 1857–1911, French psychologist. From 1894 he was director of the psychology laboratory at the Sorbonne. He is known for his research and innovation in testing human intelligence. With Théodore Simon he devised (1905–11) a series of tests that, with revisions, came into wide use in schools, industries, and the army. The Stanford, the Herring, and the Kuhlmann are important revisions. Binet and Simon wrote *Les Enfants anormaux* (1907, tr. *Mentally Defective Children*, 1914). Most of his writings were published in *Année psychologique*, a journal that he founded in 1895. See study by T. H. Wolf (1973).

Bing, Rudolf (ro͞o'dŏlf bĭng), 1902–, Austrian operatic manager. Naturalized a British subject in 1946, he was general manager of the Glyndebourne operatic festivals (1934–49) and artistic manager of the Edinburgh International Festival (1947–49). He became general manager of the Metropolitan Opera in New York in 1950. Bing was knighted in 1971 and retired the following year. See his *5000 Nights at the Opera* (1972).

Bingen (bĭng'ən), city (1970 pop. 23,724), Rhineland-Palatinate, W West Germany, where the Nahe River enters the Rhine. A busy river port, railroad junction, and tourist center, Bingen is also noted for its wine and tobacco manufactures. Dating from pre-Roman times, Bingen was fortified (1st cent. B.C.) by Drusus. In 983 it came under the rule of the archbishops of Mainz. Near Bingen, on a rock in the Rhine, is the famous Mäuseturm [Ger.,=mice tower], where, according to legend, Archbishop Hatto I of Mainz was devoured (913) by mice for wronging his subjects.

Bingham, Caleb, 1757–1817, American textbook writer, b. Salisbury, Conn. He taught until 1796, then became a bookseller and publisher in Boston. He wrote and published some of the earliest grammars, spelling books, and geographies. He was best known for his readers *The American Preceptor* (1794) and *The Columbian Orator* (1797), both widely used in New England schools for the next quarter century.

Bingham, George Caleb, 1811–79, American genre painter and politician, b. Augusta co., Va. His family moved (1819) to Missouri which was the site of most of Bingham's activities. In 1837 he studied for a short time at the Pennsylvania Academy of the Fine Arts. From 1856 to 1859 he traveled in Europe, studying at Düsseldorf for a time. Journeys on the Mississippi and through the South resulted in such paintings as *Fur Traders Descending the Missouri* (Metropolitan Mus.); *Daniel Boone Coming Through the Cumberland Gap* (1851; Washington Univ., St. Louis); and *Raftsmen Playing Cards* (City Art Mus., St. Louis). Bingham entered Missouri politics with his election to the legislature in 1848 (he had been defeated in 1846); he served as state treasurer (1862–65), after a year in the Union army, and became state adjutant general in 1875. Such pictures as *The Verdict of the People* and *Stump Speaking* (Mercantile Library Association, St. Louis) reflect his interest in politics. His scenes—vigorous, interesting in composition, humorous, and faithfully representing their time and locale—were very popular in his day, and engravings from them sold widely. See catalog and study by E. M. Bloch (2 vol., 1967); studies by A. W. Christ-Janer (1940) and J. F. McDermott (1959).

Bingham, Hiram, 1789–1869, American Congregationalist missionary, b. Bennington, Vt. In 1819 the American Board of Missions sent him, with others, to found the first Protestant mission in the Hawaiian Islands. Bingham adapted the Hawaiian language to writing, published *Elementary Lessons in Hawaiian* (1822), and, with his associates, translated the Bible into Hawaiian. See his *A Residence of Twenty-one Years in the Sandwich Islands* (1847, 3d ed. rev. 1969).

Bingham, Hiram, 1831–1908, American Congregationalist missionary, b. Honolulu; son of Hiram Bingham (1789–1869). In 1857 he founded a mission on Abaiang in the Gilbert Islands. Bingham adapted the language of the Gilbert Islands to writing. He translated the Bible and also prepared in Gilbertese a Bible dictionary, a hymnbook, and a commentary on the Gospels.

Bingham, Hiram, 1875–1956, American archaeologist, historian, and statesman, b. Honolulu; son of Hiram Bingham (1831–1908). He was educated at Yale (B.A., 1898), the Univ. of California (M.A., 1900), and Harvard (M.A., 1901; Ph.D., 1905) and later taught (1907–23) at Yale. Bingham headed expeditions sent from Yale in 1911, 1912, and 1914–15 to South America to study Inca ruins and was the discoverer of the Inca cities of Vitcos and Machu Picchu in 1911 and 1912; the road opened to Machu Picchu in 1948 was named the Hiram Bingham Highway. His well-known books deal with these expeditions and with Machu Picchu—*Journal of an Expedition across Venezuela and Colombia* (1909), *Across South America* (1911), *Inca Land* (1922), *Machu Picchu, a Citadel of the Incas* (1930), and *Lost City of the Incas* (1948). In World War I he was notable as an aviator, heading an Allied flying school in France. After leaving Yale, he served as lieutenant governor (1923–24) and governor (1925) of Connecticut and as U.S. Senator (1925–33). He also wrote on the Monroe Doctrine and other policies of state.

Bingham, Joseph, 1668–1723, English theologian. He is known for his learned work on Christian antiquities (10 vol., 1708–22).

Bingham Canyon or **Bingham,** town (1970 pop. 31), N central Utah, near Tooele, in a canyon of the Oquirrh Mts. SW of Salt Lake City. At first (1848) a farm of the Mormons Thomas and Sanford Bingham, it became in the 1860s a roaring mining town, dealing in gold, then silver and lead, and in the 20th cent. copper. One of the world's largest open-pit mines is located nearby. The town's single street, squeezed into a mountain gulch, is 6 mi (9.7 km) long.

Binghamton (bĭng'əmtən), industrial city (1970 pop. 64,123), seat of Broome co., S central N.Y., at the confluence of the Chenango and the Susquehanna rivers; settled 1787, inc. as a city 1867. It is the largest of the Triple Cities (Binghamton, Endicott, and Johnson City), which are famous for shoes. Many electronic products are also manufactured in the city. Binghamton grew mainly after the Chenango Canal connected it with Utica in 1837. The first railroad service began in 1869. The State Univ. of New York at Binghamton includes Harpur College. The city also has a junior college and a symphony orchestra. A state mental hospital is there. A state park is to the north.

Binh, Nguyen Thi (nəwĭn tē bĕn), 1927–, Vietnamese political leader, b. Saigon. She was a militant student leader in Saigon and was imprisoned (1951–54) by the French. She later joined the National Liberation Front (NLF), the Communist-supported antigovernment guerrilla organization in South Vietnam, and became a member of its central committee. She represented the NLF at the Vietnam peace talks in Paris, which began in 1968, and in 1969 she was named the foreign minister of the NFL-sponsored Provisional Revolutionary Government of South Vietnam. In 1973 she was a signer of the Vietnam peace accords.

Binh Dinh: see QUI NHON, South Vietnam.

Binney, Horace, 1780–1875, American lawyer, b. Philadelphia. A leading lawyer in Pennsylvania, Binney was appointed in 1808 a director of the First Bank of the United States. He served in Congress from 1833 to 1835 as an anti-Jacksonian. In 1844, opposing Daniel Webster, Binney argued successfully before the U.S. Supreme Court that a bequest of Stephen Girard to Philadelphia for philanthropic purposes was lawful. His argument had an important influence on the American law relating to charitable bequests. He wrote several biographies, as well as *Leaders of the Old Bar of Philadelphia* (1859). See biographies by C. C. Binney (1903, repr. 1972) and H. L. Carson (1907).

Binns, John Alexander, c.1761–1813, American agriculturist, b. Loudoun co., Va. He was one of the first to experiment with gypsum as a fertilizer and to convince others of its efficacy. Partly through example and partly through his pamphlet, *Treatise on Practical Farming* (1903), what came to be known as the Loudoun system of soil treatment spread rapidly throughout Virginia and Maryland and ultimately into other states.

Binnui (bĭn'yo͞oī), Levitical name common in Ezra and Nehemiah. The following can probably be distinguished. **1** Levite with Zerubbabel. Ezra 8.33; Neh. 3.24; 10.9; 12.8. Bavai: Neh. 3.18. Bani: Neh. 8.7. Bunni: Neh. 9.4. **2, 3** Men married to foreign wives. Ezra 10.30, 38. See also BANI **4.**

binocular, small optical instrument consisting of two similar TELESCOPES mounted on a single frame so that separate images enter each of the viewer's eyes. As with a single telescope, distant objects appear magnified, but the binocular has the additional advantage that it substantially increases the range of depth perception of the viewer because the magnified images are seen with both eyes. The frame of a binocular is usually hinged to permit adjustment of the distance between the telescopes. Focusing can be done by means of a wheel on the central axis between the telescopes; turning the wheel changes the distance from the objective lenses of the telescopes to the eyepieces. Separate focusing of each telescope from the eyepiece may be provided in some types of binocular. The term *binocular* now usually refers to the prism binocular, in which light entering each telescope through its objective lens is bent first one way and then the other by a pair of prisms before passing through one or more additional lenses in the eyepiece. The prisms aid in reducing the length of the instrument and in enhancing the viewer's depth perception by increasing the distance between the objective lenses. Other types of binocular include the opera glass and the field glass; both use Galilean telescopes, which do not employ prisms and which usually have less magnifying power than the telescopes in prism binoculars. A binocular is often specified by an expression such as "7×35" or "8×50"—the first number indicates how many times the binocular magnifies an object and the second number is the diameter of either objective lens in millimeters. The size of an objective lens is a measure of how much light it can gather for effective viewing.

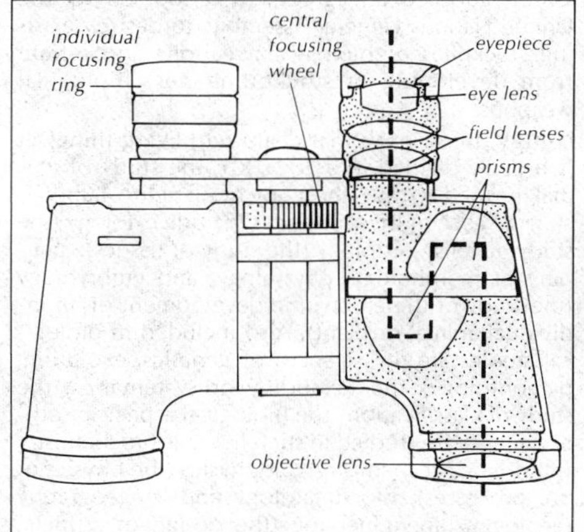

Binocular

binomial (bī''nō'mēəl), mathematical expression (see POLYNOMIAL) containing two terms, for example, $(x+y)$. Binomials occur widely in mathematics and physics and are often raised to a power. The binomial theorem, or binomial formula, gives the expansion of the *n*th power of a binomial $(x+y)$ for $n=1, 2, 3, \ldots$, as follows:

$$(x+y)^n = x^n + \frac{n}{1}x^{n-1}y + \frac{n(n-1)}{1\cdot 2}x^{n-2}y^2 + \frac{n(n-1)(n-2)}{1\cdot 2\cdot 3}x^{n-3}y^3 + \cdots + nxy^{n-1} + y^n,$$

where the ellipsis (. . .) indicates a continuation of terms following the same pattern. For example, using the formula and reducing fractions, one obtains $(x+y)^5 = x^5 + 5x^4y + 10x^3y^2 + 10x^2y^3 + 5xy^4 + y^5$. The coefficients 1, n, $n(n-1)/1\cdot 2$, etc., of x and y may also be found from an array known as Pascal's triangle (for Blaise Pascal), formed by adding adjacent numbers to find the number below them as follows:

1
1 1
1 2 1
1 3 3 1
1 4 6 4 1
1 5 10 10 5 1
. . . .

Bío-Bío (bē'ō-bē'ō), river, c.240 mi (390 km) long, rising in the Andes of central Chile and flowing NW to the Pacific Ocean near Concepción. It forms a natural divide between middle and southern Chile. It is navigable for much of its length by flat-bottomed boats. In colonial times bitter fighting took place along its banks between Spanish forces under Pedro de Valdivia and the Araucanian Indians. In 1612 the Bío-Bío was fixed as the boundary to Indian territory.

biochemical oxygen demand: see SEWERAGE.

biochemistry, science concerned chiefly with the chemistry of biological processes; it attempts to utilize the tools and concepts of chemistry, particularly organic and physical chemistry, for elucidation of the living system. The science has been variously referred to as physiological chemistry and as biological chemistry. "Molecular biology" is a term recently coined and used to describe the area of research, closely related to and often overlapping biochemistry, conducted by biologists whose approach to and interest in biology are principally at the molecular level of organization. The related field of biophysics brings to biology the techniques and attitudes of the physicist. The domain of the biological chemist is broad and encompasses any biological problem that is amenable to the investigative techniques of both chemistry and physics. Some examples which demonstrate the diversity of the subject matter of biochemistry include: the structures and physical properties of biological molecules, including the proteins, the carbohydrates, the lipids, and the nucleic acids; the mechanisms of enzyme action; the chemical regulation of metabolism; the molecular basis of genetic expression; the chemistry of vitamins; the electrochemical properties of cell membranes; chemo-luminescence; biological oxidation; energy utilization in the cell; and the chemistry of the immune response. Biochemistry has seen a great expansion of knowledge in areas bearing upon or related to chemical genetics since the report, made in 1953, of the structure of the genetic material, deoxyribonucleic acid, or DNA (see NUCLEIC ACID). That dramatic achievement in the history of biology was acknowledged by the award of the Nobel Prize in 1962 to three biochemists, James Watson, Francis Crick, and Maurice Wilkins. Much is now known about the way in which the DNA molecule is passed from one generation of cells to the next with maximal integrity of the code. At least as well studied is the chemical process by which the genetic information is translated into cellular protein. Closely related is the field of protein chemistry, which has also expanded rapidly in recent years, especially in the understanding of the mechanism of enzyme action. The field of membrane structure and function is one today commanding the attention of a great number of biochemical research scientists; the problems posed in attempting to delve into the complexities of biological membranes are thought by many to provide the current great challenge in biology.

biocide (bī'əsīd"), synonym for PESTICIDE.

biogenetic law, in biology, a law stating that the earlier stages of embryos of species advanced in the evolutionary process, such as humans, resemble the embryos of ancestral species, such as fish. The law refers only to embryonic development and not to adult stages; as development proceeds, the embryos of different species become more and more dissimilar. An early form of the law was devised by the 19th-century Russian zoologist K. E. von Baer, who observed that embryos resemble the embryos, but not the adults, of other species. A later, but incorrect, theory of the 19th-century German zoologist Ernst Heinrich Haeckel states that the embryonic development (ontogeny) of an animal recapitulates the evolutionary development of the animal's ancestors (phylogeny).

biography, reconstruction in print or on film, of the lives of real men and women. Together with autobiography—an individual's interpretation of his own life—it shares a venerable tradition, meeting the demands of different audiences through the ages. Among the most ancient biographies are the narrative carvings and hieroglyphic inscriptions on Egyptian tombs and temples (c.1300 B.C.), and the cuneiform inscriptions on Assyrian palace walls (c.720 B.C.) or Persian rock faces (c.520 B.C.). All these records proclaimed the deeds of kings, although accuracy often gave way to glorification. Among the first biographies of ordinary men, the Dialogues of Plato (4th cent. B.C.) and the Gospels of the New Testament (1st and 2d cent. A.D.) reveal their respective subjects by letting each speak for himself. Even these early achievements of biography, however, lack critical balance. Equilibrium was established by Plutarch in *The Parallel Lives* (2d cent. A.D.). His method was comparative, e.g., Theseus is matched with Romulus; Demosthenes with Cicero. In his conclusions, he evaluates the connection between the moral standards and worldly achievements of each. St. Augustine turned the same critical judgment on himself in his *Confessions* (4th cent.), comparing his character and conduct before and after his conversion to Christianity. During the Middle Ages credibility continued to be sacrificed to credulity. In the hagiographies, or lives of the saints, human flaws and actual events were bypassed in favor of saintly traits and miracles. Yet the few secular biographies produced in that era, Einhard's *Life of Charlemagne* (9th cent.), Eadmer's *Life of St. Anselm* (12th cent.), Jean de Joinville's *Memoirs of St. Louis IX* (13th cent.), and Jean Froissart's *Chroniques* (15th cent.), redeem the genre with their lively depiction of personalities and events. With the Renaissance came rekindled interest in worldly power and self-assertion. Benvenuto Cellini's *Autobiography* (16th cent.), recounting his escapades and artistic achievements, is a monument to the ego. St. Simon's *Memoirs* (late 17th cent.) describe Louis XIV and his court at Versailles and record the effect of the monarch's absolute power on the daily lives of others. In England, Samuel Pepys's *Diary*, John Evelyn's *Diary*, Izaak Walton's *Lives* and John Aubrey's *Lives of Eminent Men* (all mid-17th cent.) introduced informality and intimacy to their treatments. Each wrote about contemporaries who were their friends or acquaintances. By the 18th cent. literary biography (works about poets and men of letters) had become an important extension of the genre. Dr. Johnson's *Lives of the Poets* (1779–81) set the example for James Boswell's *Life of Samuel Johnson* (1791), the first definitive biography. This monumental work was drawn not only from Boswell's exact recollections of conversations with Johnson, but from letters, memoirs, and interviews with others in Johnson's circle as well. Two equally celebrated autobiographies, Benjamin Franklin's, noted for its practicality, and Jean-Jacques Rousseau's, noted for its candor, also mark this age. Among the avalanche of biographies and autobiographies published in the 19th cent. Goethe's *Dichtung und Wahrheit* (1808–31), Thomas Carlyle's *Sartor Resartus* (1833–34) and *Frederick the Great* (1858–65), and Ernest Renan's *Life of Jesus* (1863) are important. Also noteworthy was the publication of the *Dictionary of National Biography* (1882), edited by Leslie Stephen. As a result of Freud's discovery of the unconscious, the 20th cent. produced a new sort of biography—one that used the technique of psychoanalysis on the subject. Examples of such works are Freud's own *Leonardo Da Vinci* (1910) and Anaïs Nin's *Diaries* (1931–44). As antidotes to the tradition of the official biography Lytton Strachey wrote *Eminent Victorians* (1918) and *Queen Victoria* (1921), works that deflate and debunk. Twentieth-century biographers often sought to make structure a reflection of theme. Henry Adams's *Education of Henry Adams* (1918) explores the metaphor of the title; Thomas Merton's *Seven Story Mountain* (1948) follows the analogue of Dante's Inferno; and Lillian Hellman's *Pentimento* (1973), taking its title from an art historian's term, presents portrait sketches of the people in her life as seen from the vantage point of her maturity. Notable literary and scholarly biographers of the 20th cent. include Harold Nicolson, Allan Nevins, D. S. Freeman, André Maurois, J. H. Plumb, Carl Sandburg, Dumas Malone, Elizabeth Longford, and Leon Edel. Motion pictures and television have adapted the form of biography to their own needs. With Paul Muni as Louis Pasteur, Charles Laughton as Rembrandt, or Spencer Tracy as Thomas Edison, films have retraced for new audiences, although sometimes in a romanticized fashion, the paths to success taken by men of intelligence and character: the old Plutarchian formula. Documentary biographies, composed of newsreel clips and photographs, have been made about public figures such as Eleanor Roosevelt, the Duke of Windsor, and Martin Luther King, Jr. Two innovations of television are the dramatic documentary and the interview. Ken Russell's film essays, commissioned by the British Broadcasting Company (1965–70), on Elgar, Rossetti, Delius, Richard Strauss, and Isadora Duncan attempt to convey the essence of a person's character and work rather than just the facts of his life. Homage to Plutarch was evident again in the format of Edward R. Murrow's interview program, *Person to Person* (1953–59), where guests like Marilyn Monroe and Sir Thomas Beecham were deliberately paired. The television interview was expanded by such talk show hosts as Dick Cavett, who has led his guests, including Sir Noel Coward and Katharine Hepburn, to talk about their lives for an hour or longer. See H. G. Nicolson, *The Development of English Biography* (1928); E. H. O'Neill, *A History of American Biography* (1961); J. L. Clifford, ed., *Biography as an Art* (1962); R. D. Altick, *Lines and Letters* (1965); André Maurois, *Aspects of Biography* (tr. 1966).

biological clock: see RHYTHM, BIOLOGICAL.

biological warfare, employment in war of micoorganisms to injure or destroy men, animals, or crops; also called germ or bacteriological warfare. Limited attempts have been made in the past to spread disease among the enemy; e.g., military leaders in the French and Indian Wars tried to spread smallpox among the Indians. Biological warfare has scarcely been used in modern times and was prohibited by the 1925 Geneva Convention. However, many nations in the 20th cent. have conducted research to develop suitable military microorganisms, including strains of smallpox and plague and certain nonlethal agents. Such microorganisms can be delivered by animals (especially rodents or insects) or by aerosol packages, built into artillery shells or missile warheads and released into the atmosphere to infect by inhalation. In 1971 the United States and the Soviet Union adopted an agreement, endorsed by the United Nations General Assembly, to destroy existing stockpiles of biological weapons and refrain from developing or stockpiling new biological weapons.

biology, the science that deals with living things. It is broadly divided into ZOOLOGY, the study of animal life, and BOTANY, the study of plant life. Subdivisions of each of these sciences include cytology (the study of cells), histology (the study of tissues), anatomy or morphology, physiology, and embryology (the study of the embryonic development of an individual animal or plant). Also included in biological studies are the sciences of genetics, evolution, paleontology, and taxonomy or systematics, the study of classification. The biological aspects of other sciences are studied in such fields as biochemistry (physiological chemistry), biophysics (the physics of life processes), bioclimatology and biogeography (ecology), bioengineering (the design of artificial organs), biometry or biostatistics, bioenergetics, and biomathematics. Evidences of early man's observations of nature are seen in prehistoric cave art. Biological concepts began to develop among the early Greeks. The biological works of Aristotle include his observations and classification of his large collections of animals. The invention of the microscope in the 16th cent. gave a great stimulus to biology, broadening and deepening its scope and creating the sciences of microbiology, the study of microscopic forms of life, and biomicroscopy, the microscopic study of living cells. Among the many who contributed to the science are Claude Bernard, Cuvier, Darwin, T. H. Huxley, Lamarck, Linnaeus, Mendel, and Pasteur. See MARINE BIOLOGY. See H. G. Wells et al., *The Science of Life* (1934); Karl von Frisch, *Biology: The Science of Life* (tr. 1964); G. G. Simpson and W. S. Berk, *Life: An Introduction to Biology* (2d ed. 1965); Isaac Asimov, *The Intelligent Man's Guide to the Biological Sciences* (1968); U. N. Lanham, *Origins of Modern Biology* (1968); J. H. Painter, *Biology Today* (1972); Ernest Borek, *The Sculpture of Life* (1973); P. R. Ehrlich et al., *Introductory Biology* (1973); J. D. Ebert et al., *Biology* (1973); P. C. Hanawalt and R. H. Haynes, ed., *The Chemical Basis of Life: An Introduction to Molecular and Cell Biology, Readings from Scientific American* (1973).

bioluminescence, production of light by living organisms. Plants that are bioluminescent include certain mushrooms and bacteria that emit light continuously. The dinoflagellates, a group of marine algae, produce light only when disturbed. Bioluminescent animals include such organisms as ctenophores, annelid worms, mollusks, insects such as fireflies, and fish. The production of light in bioluminescent organisms results from the conversion of chemical energy to light energy. In fireflies, one type of a group of substances known collectively as luciferin combines with ADENOSINE TRIPHOSPHATE (ATP); the compound then reacts with oxygen to create an excited state that emits yellow light. The reaction is mediated by an enzyme, luciferase. The active substance in bacterial bioluminescence is riboflavin-5'-phosphate (see COENZYME). Different organisms produce different bioluminescent substances. Bioluminescent fish are common in ocean depths; the light probably aids in species recognition in the darkness. Other animals seem to use luminescence in courtship and mating and to divert predators or attract prey.

Bion (bī'ən), fl. 2d cent.? B.C., Greek bucolic poet, an imitator of Theocritus, b. Phlossa, near Smyrna. Only fragments of his work survive. The *Lament for Adonis*, attributed to him, was the model for Shelley's *Adonais* and was translated by Elizabeth Barrett Browning.

biophysics, application of various methods and principles of physical science to the study of biological problems. In physiological biophysics physical mechanisms have been used to explain such biological processes as the transmission of nerve impulses, the muscle contraction mechanism, and the visual mechanism. Theoretical biophysics tries to use mathematical and physical models to explain life processes. Radiation biophysics studies the response of organisms to various kinds of radiations. Biophysics has contributed important tools for the study of organic molecules, and especially of large molecules, which play an important part in biological processes. Paper chromatography, a direct development of adsorption techniques, is widely used to analyze tissues for chemical components. X-ray crystallography is used to determine molecular structures and has been particularly useful in studying the structure of NUCLEIC ACIDS. Among the optical methods used in the study of biological problems are photochemistry, light scattering, absorption spectroscopy (including the use of visible, ultraviolet, and infrared radiation), LASER beams, and double refraction birefringence. The recently developed scanning electron microscope gives a three-dimensional quality to pictures of specimens. Other methods in use are tracer techniques with isotopes, ionizing radiation, sedimentation, diffusion, viscosity, electrophoresis (or migration in an electric field), electrical potential differences, magnetic methods, and ultrasonics.

biopsy, examination of cells or tissues removed from a living organism. Excised material may be studied in order to diagnose disease or to confirm findings of normalcy. Preparatory techniques depend on the nature of the tissue and the kind of study intended. Incisions may be made and total or partial lesions removed in the form of wedges or cylindrical pieces, or scrapings of the surface membranes of internal organs may be collected. Needlelike instruments may be used to pierce the tissues and remove soft inner material. Once the tissue specimen has been obtained it is fixed, i.e., killed and coagulated, and chemical and histologic analyses are carried out. Tumors are routinely biopsied in order to determine whether they are malignant.

biosphere, irregularly shaped envelope of the earth's air, water, and land encompassing the heights and depths at which living things exist. The biosphere is a closed and self-regulating system (see ECOLOGY), sustained by grand-scale cycles of energy and of materials—in particular, carbon, oxygen, nitrogen, certain minerals, and water. The fundamental recycling processes are PHOTOSYNTHESIS, respiration, and the fixing of nitrogen by certain bacteria. Disruption of basic ecological activities in the biosphere can result from POLLUTION.

Biot, Jean Baptiste (zhäN bätĕst' byō), 1774-1862, French physicist, grad. École polytechnique (1797). He was professor of mathematics at Beauvais before becoming professor of mathematical physics at the Collège de France in 1800. From 1809 to 1849 he taught astronomy at the Sorbonne. With French physicist François Arago, Biot measured properties of gases, and with French physicist Felix Savart, he formulated a law for the magnetic force near a wire, the force being generated when the wire carries an electric current. He discovered that when light passes through some substances, including sugar solutions, the plane of polarization of the light is rotated by an amount that depends on the color of the light.

biotin: see VITAMIN; COENZYME.

biotite, iron-rich variety of phlogopite, one of the MICA minerals.

biplane, aircraft, typically of early design, having two sets of wings fixed at different levels, especially in a vertical stack with the fuselage included between them. See AIRPLANE.

Biqa, Al (äl bēkä') or **El Bika** (ĕl bēkä'), upland valley of Lebanon and Syria, 75 mi (121 km) long and 5 to 9 mi (8-14.5 km) wide, between the Lebanon and Anti-Lebanon ranges; highest part of the Rift Valley complex. The village of Baalbek, site of one of the largest temples of the Roman Empire, is located on the divide between the headwaters of the Orontes and Litani rivers in the northern part of the valley. In the area N of Baalbek, located in the rain shadow of the Lebanon mts., nomadic pastoralism is dominant. South of Baalbek, the Litani River (90 mi/145 km long) flows south through the most fertile part of the valley before turning west and cutting through the Lebanon mts. to the Mediterranean Sea. This section of Al Biqa, called the granary of Lebanon, is very flat, and farming is highly mechanized; vegetables, cereals, fruits, grapes, and cotton are the chief crops. A dam and irrigation project on the lower Litani supplies water to the dry, extreme southern part of Al Biqa, where cereals and grazing are important. The Biqa valley, once the heart of ancient Coele-Syria, has been the scene of warfare since the dawn of history. Al Biqa was included in a province of the Persian Empire and was later bitterly contested by the Seleucids and the Ptolemaic kings of Egypt. The city of Antioch, Turkey, was founded by Seleucus I, king of Syria, to dominate the region. The name also appears as El Beqa, El Bukaa, and El Bekaa.

Birch, Samuel, 1813-85, English Egyptologist. He wrote a dictionary of hieroglyphics and translated the Book of the Dead.

Birch, Thomas, 1779-1851, American artist, b. London. Birch settled in Philadelphia in 1793. Famous for his paintings of landscapes and historical scenes, he is also noted for a series of engravings of views of Philadelphia, which he executed with his father. During the War of 1812, Birch painted a series of scenes of naval engagements that include *The Macedonian* (1813).

birch, common name for some members of the Betulaceae, a family of deciduous trees or shrubs bearing male and female flowers on separate plants, widely distributed in the Northern Hemisphere. They are valued for their hardwood lumber and edible fruits and as ornamental trees. The species of Betulaceae native to the United States represent five genera—*Alnus* (ALDER), *Betula* (the birches), *Corylus* (HAZEL), and *Carpinus* (HORNBEAM) and *Ostrya* (hop hornbeam), both called ironwood. The sixth genus, *Ostryopsis*, is restricted to Mongolia. The birches, beautiful bushes or trees of temperate and arctic regions, are often found mingled with evergreens in northern coniferous forests. Most American species are trees of the Northeast; a few smaller and scrub species grow in the West. The close-grained hardwood of several of the trees is valued for furniture,

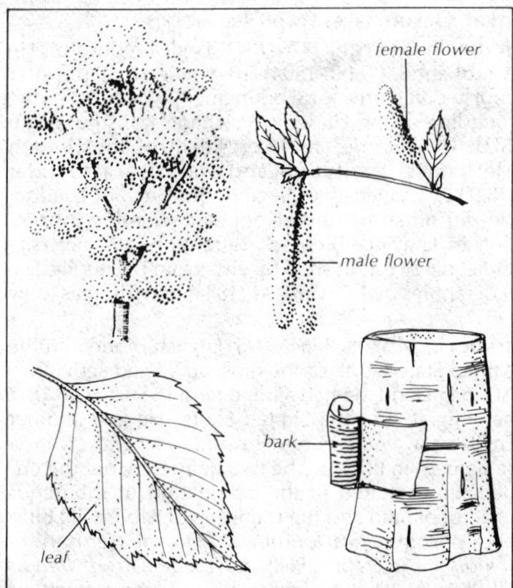

White birch, Betula papyrifera

flooring, and similar uses (in America, particularly that of the yellow birch, *B. lutea*); stained birch provides much of the so-called mahogany of lower-priced furniture. White-barked birches are often used as ornamental trees, e.g., the famous paper, or canoe, birch (*B. papyrifera*) of the N United States and Canada. Its bark, which separates in layers, was used by the Indians for canoes and baskets. Another familiar American species is the smaller gray birch (*B. populifolia*), also white-barked. It is often found on poor and rocky soil, especially in New England. Various birches have yielded sugar, vinegar, a tea from the leaves, and a birch beer from the sap. The sweet, or black, birch (*B. lenta*) is now the chief source of oil of WINTERGREEN. The Betulaceae is classified in the division MAGNOLIOPHYTA, class Magnoliopsida, order Fagales.

Bird, Isabella: see BISHOP, ISABELLA LUCY (BIRD).

Bird, Robert Montgomery, 1806-54, American playwright and novelist, b. New Castle, Del., M.D. Univ. of Pennsylvania, 1827. He wrote several prize-winning verse plays for the actor Edwin Forrest, notably *The Gladiator* (1831) and *The Broker of Bogota* (1834). A financial misunderstanding led to a break between the two friends, and Forrest, throughout his life, refused to release the copyrights he claimed to hold for the plays. Bird then began writing prose fiction and published the first of his popular romances, *Calavar* (1834), followed by a sequel, *The Infidel* (1835). Both works used Mexico as a background. *Nick of the Woods* (1837), his most popular novel, drew on his travels through America. In contrast to James Fenimore Cooper, Bird depicted the Indian as violent and debased. His romances, although complicated in plot, are dramatic and contain vivid character portrayal. See biography by his wife, M. M. Bird (1945); study by Dahl Curtis (1963).

bird, warm-blooded, egg-laying, vertebrate animal having its body covered with FEATHERS and its forelimbs modified into WINGS. Birds compose the class Aves (see CHORDATA). Like mammals, they have a four-chambered heart, and there is a complete separation of oxygenated and deoxygenated blood. The body temperature is from 2° to 14° higher than that of mammals. Birds have a relatively large brain, keen sight, and acute hearing, but little sense of smell. They are believed to have evolved from reptiles. The fossil remains of the archaeopteryx and of the archaeornis of the Jurassic period, found in S Germany, show reptilian tails, jaws with teeth, and clawed wings; but feathers were well developed. It is thought that the estimated 8,650 living species existed in their present form by the Pleistocene epoch. Birds are highly adapted for FLIGHT. Their structure combines lightness and strength. Body weight is reduced by the presence of a horny bill instead of heavy jaws and teeth and by the air sacs in the hollow bones as well as in other parts of the body. Compactness and firmness are achieved by the fusion of bones in the pelvic region and in other parts of the skeleton. The heavier parts of the body—the gizzard, intestines, flight muscles, and thigh muscles—are all strategically located for maintaining balance in flight. Feathers, despite their lightness, are highly protective against cold and wet. The flight feathers, especially, have great strength. Feathers are renewed in the process of MOLTING. Some birds, such as the ostrich, the penguin, and the kiwi, lack the power of flight and have a flat sternum, or breastbone, without the prominent keel to which the well-developed flight muscles of other birds are attached. In the majority of species there are differences between male and female in plumage coloring. In these birds the male (except in the phalarope) is usually the more brilliant or the more distinctly marked and is the aggressor in courtship. Unusual courtship displays are performed by several species, particularly by the ruffed grouse, the bird of paradise, the crane, the pheasant, and the peacock. BIRDSONG reaches its highest development during the breeding season, and singing ability is usually either restricted to or superior in the male. In spring and fall many birds migrate. Not all of the factors motivating this behavior are fully understood. These trips often involve flights of hundreds and even thousands of miles over mountains and oceans. Most birds build a NEST in which to lay their eggs. Some birds, such as the oriole, weave an intricate structure, while others lay their eggs directly on the ground or among a few seemingly carelessly assembled twigs. Eggs vary in size, number, color, and shape. Birds are of enormous value to man because of their destruction of insect pests and weed seeds. Many are useful as scavengers. The bills of birds are well adapted to their food habits. Specialized bills are found in the crossbill, hummingbird, spoonbill, pelican, and woodpecker. The game birds hunted by man for food and sport include grouse, pheasant, quail, duck, and plover. The chief domestic birds are the chicken, duck, goose, turkey, and guinea fowl. Parrots and many members of the finch family are kept as pets. See also MIGRATION OF ANIMALS. Among the periodicals devoted to the study of bird life are the *Auk*, the *Condor*, and the *Wilson Bulletin*. See

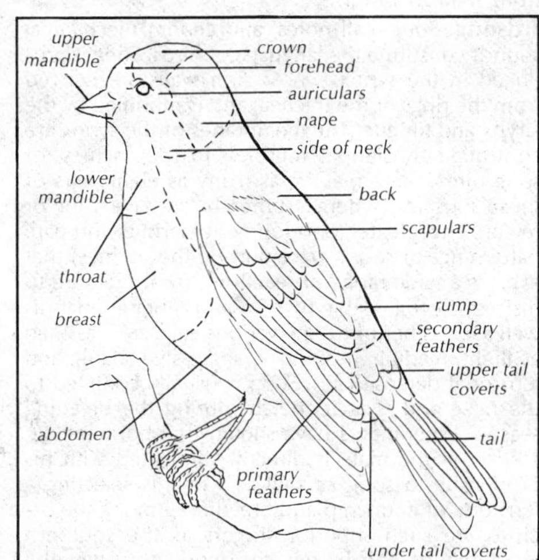

General anatomy of a bird

the series of books on life histories of North American birds by A. C. Bent; R. M. De Schauensee, *A Guide to the Birds of South America* (1970); Abram Rutgers and K. A. Norris, ed., *Encyclopaedia of Aviculture* (Vol. I, 1971 and Vol. II, 1972); U.S. Bureau of Sports Fisheries and Wildlife, *Birds in Our Lives* (1970); *Avian Biology*, ed. by D. S. Farmer and J. R. King (1971-); R. K. Murton, *Man and Birds* (1971); Josselyn Van Tyne and A. J. Berger, *Fundamentals of Ornithology* (1971); Hermann Heinzel, *The Birds of Britain and Europe with North Africa and the Middle East* (1972); Eliot Porter, *Birds of North America* (1972); Peter Matthiesen, *The Wind Birds* (1973).

bird of paradise, common name for any of 43 species of medium- to crow-sized passerine birds of New Guinea and the adjacent islands, known for the bright plumage, elongated tail feathers called wires, and brilliant ruffs of the males. Their common name is derived from 16th-century Spanish explorers, who believed them to be visitors from paradise. The standard-winged bird of paradise, *Semioptera wallaceii*, is brownish with a glimmering green gorget at the throat. At the end of the 19th cent. over 50,000 bird of paradise skins per year were exported; many species were almost wiped out. It is now illegal to import skins into the United States. The 13-in.

(32.5-cm) twelve-wired bird of paradise, *Seleucidis ignotus,* is found in mangrove swamps, and has brilliant yellow plumes and an iridescent green and black throat, which are displayed to the female during courtship. The smallest member of the family is the scarlet king bird of paradise. It is only 6 in. (15 cm) long and has green plumes and blue legs. Many species are polygamous, and the drab-colored female assumes all the nesting duties. The biological basis for the elaborate coloration and displays seems to be the need for an accurate means of distinction and recognition between species, since hybridization is disadvantageous. Birds of paradise are classified in the phylum CHORDATA, subphylum Vertebrata, class Aves, order Passeriformes, family Paradisaeidae.

bird-of-paradise flower, large tropical herb (*Strelitzia reginae*) of the family Musaceae (BANANA family), native to S Africa. Its large blue and orange blossom resembles an exotic bird; it is cultivated as an ornamental in warmer regions, as a greenhouse plant, and as a florists' cut flower. It is grown commercially chiefly in California and Hawaii. The bird-of-paradise is classified in the division MAGNOLIOPHYTA, class Liliatae, order Zingiberales, family Musaceae.

bird sanctuary: see WILDLIFE REFUGE.

Birdseye, Clarence, 1886–1956, American inventor and founder of the frozen food industry, b. Brooklyn, N. Y., studied at Amherst College. In 1912 he went to Labrador on a fur-trading expedition and when he returned to the United States in 1916 began experimenting with freezing foods, aiming at commercial application. He developed a method for freezing fish and in 1924 he was one of the founders of the General Foods Company, which began manufacturing various frozen food products. In 1929 the company was bought by the Postum Company (later the General Foods Corp.) for $22 million. By 1949, Birdseye had perfected the anhydrous freezing process, reducing the time needed for the operation from 18 hr to 1½ hr.

birdsong. Song, call notes, and certain mechanical sounds constitute the language of birds. Song is produced in the syrinx, whose firm walls are derived from the rings of the trachea, and is modified by the larynx and tongue. The membranes of the syrinx are controlled by slender muscles; in the oscines, or song birds, there may be as many as eight pairs of these muscles, whereas other birds have four or fewer. The greater development permits intricate patternings of sound (rare outside the oscines) that express a wide range of reactions, from pleasure to distress. Recognizable by man and other animals as well as by other birds, the various calls are classified as flight, feeding, nest, flock, aggressive, alarm, and territorial-defense calls. Song is usually confined to the male and is at its height during the breeding season. Experiments have shown that hormone secretion in the male is directly connected with his propensity to song as well as with his selecting a territory for courtship and breeding. Among the oscines are such superior singers as the southern mockingbird, the hermit and wood thrushes, the purple and house finches, the canyon wren, and the European skylark and nightingale. Natural mimicry is characteristic of the mimic thrushes, the jays and crows, and the starlings, while birds with imitative faculties developed in captivity are canaries, finches, parrots, ravens, crows, and mynas. There is evidence that songs are learned and that certain calls are inherited. Most birds have preferences regarding the place from which they sing, e.g., fence posts, treetops, thickets, the forest floor, or on the wing. Mechanical sounds include the drumming of the grouse, the tattooing of the woodpecker, and the clattering of the stork. See E. A. Armstrong, *A Study of Bird Song* (2d. enl. ed. 1973); Charles Hartshorne, *Born to Sing* (1973).

Bird Woman: see SACAJAWEA.

Biren, Ernst Johann von: see BIRON.

Birganj (bĕr'gänch), town (1961 pop. 10,769), S Nepal, near the Indian border. It is a market town for agricultural products.

Birgitta, Saint: see BRIDGET OF SWEDEN, SAINT.

Biringuccio, Vannocio (vän-nô'chō bērēn-gōōt'chō), 1480–c.1539, Italian metallurgist. He is best known for his practical manual of metallurgy, *De la pirotechnia* (1540, tr. 1942). As a young man Biringuccio learned about metallurgy through visits to forges and foundries. He directed an iron mine and forge near Siena and was master of its arsenal and mint. Exiled twice because of changing regimes, he served in Venice and Florence as a caster of cannon and as a fortifications engineer. He was later called to Rome to head the papal foundry.

Birkat Qarun, lake, Egypt: see MOERIS.

Birkbeck, George, 1776–1841, English educator. He established (1800–1804) in Glasgow a popular course of lectures for workingmen, which led to the founding of the Glasgow Mechanics' Institution in 1823. He became (1824) president of the London Mechanics' Institution and was also a founder (1827) of University College of the Univ. of London. He did much to further popular scientific instruction in England. Birkbeck Laboratory at University College was established by gifts from his pupils. See biographies by J. S. Godard (1884) and Thomas Kelly (1957).

Birkbeck, Morris, 1764–1825, English pioneer in the United States. One of the most advanced agriculturists in England, he had a huge farm in Surrey. In 1817 he emigrated to the United States. He and another English traveler, George Flower, sought to create a settlement in Illinois. The two quarreled, but the undertaking resulted in the occupation of thousands of acres of land and the founding of Albion, Ill. Birkbeck's *Notes on a Journey . . . to the Territory of Illinois* (1818, repr. 1968) and *Letters from Illinois* (1818, repr. 1968) helped to bring European settlers to the fertile prairies of the Middle West and are invaluable historical sources.

Birkenhead, Frederick Edwin Smith, 1st **earl of,** 1872–1930, British statesman and jurist. He was called to the bar in 1899 and entered the House of Commons as a Conservative in 1906. A brilliant orator, he soon gained prominence as a Conservative spokesman, particularly in the fight against Irish Home Rule. He was solicitor general (1915), attorney general (1915–19), in which capacity he prosecuted Sir Roger CASEMENT, and lord chancellor (1919–22). Created earl in 1922, he was (1924–28) secretary of state for India. His books include *International Law* (4th ed. 1911), *Famous Trials of History* (1927), *Law, Life, and Letters* (1927). See biography by his son, Frederick, 2d earl of Birkenhead (1933–35, rev. ed. 1959).

Birkenhead (bûr'kənhĕd), county borough (1971 pop. 137,738), Cheshire, W central England, at the mouth of the Mersey River; connected with Liverpool by the Mersey tunnel. Flour milling, shipbuilding, and commerce are the key industries. There are also engineering, food-processing, and clothing plants and a cattle market. There are extensive docks. The chief imports are grain and cattle; coal, flour, the byproducts of milling, and machinery are exported. Milling and shipbuilding were responsible for Birkenhead's rapid growth in the 19th cent. The borough has a technical and a theological college. In 1974, Birkenhead became part of the new metropolitan county of Merseyside.

Birkhoff, George David (bûr'kôf), 1884–1944, American mathematician. The son of a physician, he was educated at Harvard (B.A., 1905; Ph.D., 1907). He is known for his work on linear differential equations and difference equations. He was also deeply interested in the analysis of dynamical systems, celestial mechanics, number theory, and function spaces. In addition he wrote on the foundations of relativity and quantum mechanics and on art and music, e.g., *Aesthetic Measure* (1933). See his *Collected Mathematical Papers* (3 vol., 1950). His son, **Garrett Birkhoff,** 1911–, is also a mathematician, who has made several important contributions to abstract mathematics and to the teaching of mathematics. From 1934 on he developed the concept of a lattice, or abstract structure, and showed how a number of subjects, e.g., Boolean algebra, projective geometry, and affine geometry, could be treated as special types of lattices. His text *A Survey of Modern Algebra* (with Saunders MacLane, 1941) became a standard undergraduate textbook. See his *Lattice Theory* (1940, 3d ed. 1967).

birling (bûr'lĭng), sport performed on floating logs. It became popular with American lumberjacks after the middle of the 19th cent. In the main event of a birling tournament a contestant tries to spill his rival into the water by superior logrolling. Log-poling races and individual acrobatic performances on logs are also held. National birling contests in the United States have been held occasionally since 1898.

Birmingham, city (1971 pop. 1,013,366), central England, since 1974, part of the new metropolitan county of West Midlands. The city is equidistant from Bristol, Liverpool, Manchester, and London, England's main ports, and near the BLACK COUNTRY iron and coal deposits; it is connected to the Staffordshire mines by the Birmingham Canal, built in the 18th cent. Birmingham is Britain's second-largest city (in both area and population) and is the center of water, road, and rail transportation in the MIDLANDS. The chief industries are the manufacture of automobiles, motorcycles, and bicycles and their components and accessories. Other products include electrical equipment, paint, guns, and a wide variety of metal products. By the 15th cent., Birmingham was a market town with a large leather and wool trade; by the 16th cent. it was also known for its many metalworks. In the English Civil War the town was captured by the royalists. Birmingham's industrial development and population growth accelerated in the 17th and 18th cent. In 1762, Mathew Boulton and James Watt founded the Soho metalworks, where they designed and built steam engines. Joseph Priestley, the discoverer of oxygen, lived for a time in Birmingham. In 1791 a mob, incensed at his radical religious and political views, burned his home. The town was enfranchised by the 1832 REFORM BILL and was incorporated in 1838. John Bright represented it in Parliament from 1857 to 1889. During the 1870s, while Joseph Chamberlain was mayor, Birmingham underwent a large program of municipal improvements, including slum clearance and the development of gas and water works. Birmingham was among the first English localities to have a municipal bank, a comprehensive water-supply system, and development planning. The area of the city was enlarged in 1891 and again in 1911 under the Greater Birmingham scheme. Notable buildings include the town hall, built in 1834, modeled after the temple of Castor and Pollux in Rome; the 18th-century baroque-style Cathedral of St. Philip; and the 19th-century Cathedral of St. Chad, the first Roman Catholic cathedral to be built in England after the Reformation. Bull Ring, in the center of Birmingham, is the site of the city's oldest market. The city library includes an excellent Shakespeare collection. There is a museum and art gallery (noted for its pre-Raphaelite collection) and a museum of science and industry. Annual music festivals date from 1768. In the suburb of Edgesbaston are the Univ. of Birmingham and the Oratory of St. Philip Neri, a Roman Catholic shrine that was formerly the parish house of John Henry Cardinal Newman. In the center of the city is the Univ. of Aston. Birmingham was severely damaged in World War II and has been considerably rebuilt since then.

Birmingham (bûr'mĭnghăm'') **1** City (1970 pop. 300,910), seat of Jefferson co., N central Ala., in the Jones Valley near the southern end of the Appalachian system; inc. 1871. It is the largest city in the state and the leading iron and steel center in the South. Iron, coal, limestone, and other natural resources from the area supply the city's great iron and steel plants and its metalworking factories. By the middle of the 20th cent. the city's economy had become more diversified, and in addition to iron and steel, transportation equipment, construction materials, chemicals, and fabricated metals are produced. Commerce, banking, insurance, research, and government are also economically important. Founded and incorporated in 1871, Birmingham developed rapidly with the expansion of the railroads. An important trade and communications center, the city is connected with the Gulf of Mexico by canal and is a port of entry. Educational institutions in the city include Birmingham-Southern College, Miles College, Daniel Payne College, Samford Univ., the Univ. of Alabama in Birmingham, and two junior colleges. Birmingham supports a football and track stadium, botanical and Japanese gardens, a symphony, a ballet group, a theater, and an art museum; a Festival of Arts is held annually. Overlooking the city, on nearby Red Mt., is a huge iron statue of Vulcan, the mythical god of the forge. **2** City (1970 pop. 26,170), Oakland co., SE Mich., on the River Rouge; settled 1819, inc. as a village 1864, as a city 1933. The city is largely residential.

Birmingham-Southern College, at Birmingham, Ala.; United Methodist; coeducational; formed 1918 by the merger of Southern Univ. (chartered 1856; opened 1859 at Greensboro, Ala.) and Birmingham College (opened 1898). The Birmingham Conservatory of Music became a part of the college in 1953.

Birmingham University, at Birmingham, England; founded 1900. It has faculties of science and engineering, arts, medicine and dentistry, commerce and social science, and law, as well as a school of education. Associated with the university are the

Barber Institute of Fine Arts and the Shakespeare Institute.

Birney, James Gillespie, 1792–1857, American abolitionist, b. Danville, Ky. He practiced law at Danville from 1814 to 1818, before he moved to Alabama, where he served one term in the state legislature. Briefly (1832–34) an agent of the American Colonization Society before becoming an abolitionist, he returned (1833) to Kentucky, freed (1834) his inherited slaves, and helped organize (1835) the Kentucky Anti-Slavery Society. In 1837 he became executive secretary of the American Anti-Slavery Society, and he was a vice president of the World's Anti-Slavery Convention at London in 1840. In contrast to William Lloyd Garrison, Birney constantly advocated political action. He became the acknowledged leader of like-minded abolitionists who, forming the LIBERTY PARTY, nominated him for the presidency in 1840 and 1844. An injury sustained in 1845 took him out of public life. See his letters (ed. by D. L. Dumond, 1938); biographies by W. Birney (1969) and B. Fladeland (1955, repr. 1969).

Birobidzhan: see JEWISH AUTONOMOUS OBLAST, USSR.

Biron or **Biren, Ernst Johann von** (ĕrnst yōhän' fən bē'rôn, bē'rən), 1690–1772, duke of Courland (1737–43, 1763–69), favorite of Czarina Anna of Russia. A Baltic nobleman, he rose to an all-powerful position under Anna, through whose influence he was elected duke of Courland. After Anna's death (1740) he was made regent for her grandnephew Ivan VI. Biron's unscrupulousness had earned him general hatred, and shortly after he became regent a coup d'etat ousted and banished him (1741). In 1743, Augustus III of Poland deprived him of his duchy. Czar Peter III later recalled him and Catherine II secured the restoration of his title, but Biron never regained his former influence.

Birrell, Augustine (bĭr'əl), 1850–1933, English essayist and public official. As chief secretary for Ireland (1907–16) his failure to end the plotting that resulted in the Easter Rebellion of 1916 led to his retirement from politics. His works include the pleasant and urbane critical essays *Obiter Dicta* (3 vol.; 1884, 1887, 1924) and biographies of Charlotte Brontë (1887), William Hazlitt (1902), and Andrew Marvell (1905).

Birsha (bûr'shə), king of Gomorrah. Gen. 14.2.

birth or **labor,** delivery of the fetus by the viviparous mammal. Birth is also known as parturition. Human birth normally occurs about 280 days after onset of the last menstrual period before conception. Onset of labor, the first stage, is heralded by contractions of the uterus felt as cramplike pains in the abdomen or lower back that recur at intervals of 10 to 30 min and last about 40 sec; they increase in frequency until they occur at about 2-min intervals. With each contraction the cervix, or neck of the uterus, dilates until it becomes wide enough, about 4 in. (10 cm), to permit emergence of the baby. In the second stage of labor, the baby passes through the birth canal, most commonly head first, and is born. The effectiveness of uterine contractions in this stage are enhanced by the bearing-down abdominal contractions of the mother. The third stage of labor, which occurs about 15 to 30 min after the child is born, is characterized by the separation of the placenta from the uterine wall and its expulsion. The total time of labor averages 13 to 14 hr in women pregnant for the first time and 8 to 9 hr in women who have previously borne children. The pain of childbirth can be relieved with a variety of analgesic and sedative drugs, including morphine, barbiturates, and chloroform. However, many drugs that relieve pain also slow the uterine contractions or dangerously depress the baby's respiratory system. Spinal anesthetics, injected directly into the spinal cord, while not dangerous to the child, are difficult to administer accurately and are therefore potentially dangerous to the mother. In recent years so-called natural childbirth has come into wide use; the advantages are that the child is born undrugged and the mother can be conscious at the moment of birth. Natural childbirth emphasizes the ability of many women to give birth with a minimal amount of pain-killing drugs or none at all. The Dick-Read method, formulated by the British obstetrician of that name, emphasizes maternal understanding of the birth process as an aid to relaxation and exercises to strengthen muscles and encourage proper breathing. The Lamaze method, or psychoprophylaxis, is of Russian origin; it uses breathing exercises as a conditioned response to uterine contractions. Hypnosis has also been used experimentally. Birth often cannot proceed normally because of a defect of the cervix or weak uterine contractions; breech births, in which the feet or buttocks emerge first, and transverse births, in which the child is positioned across the uterus, usually require obstetrical intervention, such as forceps delivery, manually turning the baby, or performing a CESAREAN SECTION. About 10% of pregnancies terminate in deliveries that are too early, producing (after at least 200 days of gestation) premature infants requiring special care. Birth of a fetus prior to about 200 days of gestation is termed a miscarriage; birth within the first three months, an abortion. Stillbirth is the delivery of a dead child. Complications of childbirth affecting the newborn include infant blindness attributable to gonorrhea infection, now largely eliminated by routine administration of silver nitrate to the eyes; retrolental fibroplasia, a type of blindness common for some years in premature infants that was found to result from administration of high concentrations of oxygen and is now largely avoided; and ERYTHROBLASTOSIS FETALIS, or Rh disease, which can often be prevented. Puerperal fever, an infection of the mother's genital tract once common following labor and delivery, has now also been largely eliminated by preventive hygiene, especially in labor, and by antibiotic therapy. See PREGNANCY; OBSTETRICS.

birth control, practice of contraception for the purpose of limiting reproduction. Although contraceptive techniques had been known in ancient Egypt, Greece, and Rome, the modern movement for birth control began in Great Britain, where the writings of Thomas Robert MALTHUS stirred interest in the problem of overpopulation. In 1877, Annie BESANT and Charles BRADLAUGH were tried for selling *The Fruits of Philosophy,* a pamphlet on contraceptive methods, written in 1832 by an American, Charles Knowlton. After their famous trial, the Malthusian League was founded. In 1878 the first birth control clinic was founded in Amsterdam by Aletta Jacobs. In 1921, aided by Marie STOPES, the Malthusian League established a birth control clinic in London. The first U.S. birth control clinic, opened (1916) by Margaret SANGER in Brooklyn, N.Y., was closed by the police; she received a 30-day jail sentence. She helped organize (1917) the National Birth Control League; it became in 1921 the American Birth Control League, in 1942 the Planned Parenthood Federation of America, and in 1961 the Planned Parenthood-World Population. In 1936, the Federal law prohibiting dissemination of contraceptive information through the mails was modified. Throughout the 1940s and 50s, birth control advocates were engaged in numerous legal suits. In 1965, the U.S. Supreme Court struck down the one remaining state law (Connecticut) prohibiting the use of contraceptives. The Federal government began to take a more active part in the birth control movement in 1967, when 6% of the funds allotted to the Child Health Act was set aside for family planning; in 1970, the Family Planning Services and Population Act established separate funds for birth control. Sweden was one of the first countries to provide government assistance for birth control, which it did as early as the 1930s. Although the issue of birth control has been a controversial one in Marxist theory, the governments of the Soviet Union and of the People's Republic of China now supply birth control aid to their people. One of the most successful birth control programs is in Japan, where the birthrate has been dramatically reduced. Birth control on the international level is led by the International Planned Parenthood Federation, founded in 1952 and having members in 79 countries by 1973. Among religious bodies, the Roman Catholic Church has provided the main opposition to the birth control movement; Pope Paul VI reaffirmed this stance in a 1968 encyclical. The birth control movement gained new life in the 1960s and 70s as people became increasingly concerned about world POPULATION growth. Several of the underpopulated nations, however, have a stated policy of encouraging an increased birthrate, e.g., Argentina. Male birth control methods include withdrawal of the male before ejaculation (the oldest contraceptive technique) and use of the condom, a rubber sheath covering the penis. Contraceptive methods for women include the rhythm method—abstinence around the most likely time of ovulation—and precoital insertion into the vagina of substances (creams, foams, jellies, or suppositories) containing spermatocidal chemicals. The use of a diaphragm, a rubber cup-shaped device inserted before intercourse, prevents sperm from reaching the uterine cervix; it is usually used with spermatocidal substances. Intrauterine devices, or IUDs, are variously shaped small objects inserted by a doctor into the uterus; they apparently act by creating a uterine environment hostile either to sperm or to the fertilized egg. The so-called Pill, an oral contraceptive, involves a hormonal method in which estrogen and progestins (progesterone-like substances) are taken cyclically for 21 days a month. The elevated levels of hormones in the blood suppress production of the pituitary hormones (luteinizing hormone and follicle-stimulating hormone) that would ordinarily cause ovulation. Sterilization of the female, often but not always performed during a Cesarean section or shortly after childbirth, consists of cutting or tying both Fallopian tubes, the vessels that carry the egg cells from the ovaries to the uterus. In male sterilization (vasectomy) the vas deferens, the tubes that carry sperm from the testes to the penis, are interrupted. Sterilization, in most cases irreversible, involves no loss of libido or capacity for sex. No contraceptive yet devised is at once simple, acceptable, safe, effective, and reversible. Some, such as the diaphragm, condom, and chemical and rhythm methods, require high motivation by users; the Pill, which must be taken daily, often induces undesirable side effects, such as nausea, headache, weight gain, and increased tendency to develop blood clots. The IUDs, although requiring no personal effort or motivation, are often not tolerated or are expelled, and they sometimes cause uterine infection, septic abortion, and other problems. New birth control techniques, many still experimental, include the use of progestins that could be given by injection every three months; progestins embedded in inert carriers and implanted under the skin to release the hormones slowly and continuously; progestins incorporated into a plastic ring that a woman could insert in the vagina, needing to be changed only periodically; and IUDs carrying some antifertility agent. The use of any of various hormones that induce menstruation, and the use of a safe "morning after" or "minutes after" hormone, could eliminate some of the problems associated with continuous dosage hormones. Another experimental technique is immunization against human chorionic gonadotropin (HCG), a hormone secreted by a developing fertilized egg that stimulates production of progesterone by the ovary; the effect of the anti-HCG antibody would be to inactivate HCG and thereby induce menstruation even if fertilization occurred. See REPRODUCTIVE SYSTEM; MENSTRUATION; STERILIZATION. See Elizabeth Draper, *Birth Control in the Modern World* (1965); B. R. Berelson, *Family Planning Programs* (1969); G. J. Hardin, *Birth Control* (1970); Lawrence Lader, *The Margaret Sanger Story* (1955) and *Breeding Ourselves to Death* (1971).

birthmark, pigmented maldevelopment of the skin that varies in size, either present at birth or developing later. Birthmarks may appear as moles, varying in color from light brown to blue, and are either flat or raised above the surface of the skin. They are usually benign, unless they are situated in areas where constant irritation may cause them to become malignant (cancerous), in which case they should be removed surgically. The so-called port-wine stains and strawberry marks involve vascular tissue. The flat port-wine stains are not amenable to treatment. The strawberry marks generally disappear a few years after birth or may be treated by a physician, usually with caustic applications.

birth rate: see VITAL STATISTICS.

birthstone: see MONTH.

birthwort, common name for the Aristolochiaceae, a family of shrubs and woody climbing vines found in the tropics and other warm regions. The largest genus, *Aristolochia,* includes several plants cultivated in the United States as medicinals (e.g., the Virginia snakeroot and the birthwort) or as ornamentals for their curious flowers (e.g., the pelican flower and the Dutchman's-pipe, or pipe vine). The family also includes the North American wild ginger (*Asarum canadense*), unrelated to the true gingers of Asia. The Aristolochiaceae are classified in the division MAGNOLIOPHYTA, class Magnoliopsida.

Birzavith (bĭrzā'vĭth), Asherite. 1 Chron. 7.31.

Bisanthe: see TEKIRDAĞ.

Bisbee (bĭz'bē), city (1970 pop. 8,328), seat of Cochise co., SE Ariz., near the Mexican border; inc. 1900. It is the center of one of the greatest copper-producing areas in the country. Gold, silver, and lead are also mined. After the rich copper deposits were discovered (c.1876), the city was built in two steep-sided canyons, Mule Pass Gulch and Brewery Gulch. Nearby is Coronado National Memorial (see NATIONAL PARKS AND MONUMENTS, table), which commemorates Coronado's entry (1540) into the United States.

Biscay, Bay of, arm of the Atlantic Ocean, indenting the coast of W Europe from Ushant island (Île d'Ouessant) off Brittany, NW France, to Cape Ortegal, NW Spain. The bay is noted for its sudden, severe storms and its strong currents. The rocky northeastern and southern coasts of Biscay are irregular with many good harbors; numerous offshore islands are there. The southeastern shore is straight and sandy. The chief ports are Brest, Saint-Nazaire, La Rochelle, and Bayonne in France and San Sebastián, Bilbao, and Santander in Spain. Nantes and Bordeaux, at the head of the Loire and Garonne estuaries, respectively, in France, are also reached by oceangoing ships. There are several resorts along the French coast, notably Biarritz. The bay has important sardine-fishing grounds.

Biscayne Bay, shallow, narrow inlet of the Atlantic Ocean, c.40 mi (60 km) long, SE Fla. Famous resort areas, including Miami and Miami Beach, are on the northern shore. The house used as a retreat by President Richard Nixon is on Key Biscayne. Biscayne National Monument is at the southern end of the bay (see NATIONAL PARKS AND MONUMENTS, table).

Bisceglie (bĕshĕl'yā), city (1971 pop. 45,497), Apulia, S Italy, on the Adriatic Sea. It is a seaport and commercial center. Conquered by the Normans in the late 11th cent., the city later developed a prosperous merchant and military fleet. The duchy of Bisceglie was (16th cent.) a fief of Alfonso of Aragon, 2d husband of Lucrezia Borgia, and of their son Rodrigo. There are several churches of the 11th–12th cent., a fine Apulian Romanesque cathedral (11th–13th cent.), and ruins of an 11th-century Norman castle.

Biscoe, John, d. 1848, British navigator. Commanding a British sealer of the Enderby firm of London, he discovered (1831–32) ENDERBY LAND on the coast of Antarctica. His voyage gave Great Britain the chief basis for British claims to Antarctica. He also discovered Alexander Land.

Bishlam, deputy of Artaxerxes. Ezra 4.7.

Bishop, Elizabeth, 1911–, American poet, b. Worcester, Mass. Since her graduation from Vassar in 1934, she has lived in several places including Brazil. Her first volume of poetry, *North and South* (1946), was reprinted with additions as *North and South—A Gold Spring* (1955; Pulitzer Prize). Her poetic vision is penetrating and detached. Without straining for novelty, she finds symbolic significance in objects and events quietly observed. Among her works are her *Complete Poems* (1969) and several travel books, notably *Questions of Travel* (1965) and *Brazil* (1967). With Emanuel Brasil she edited *An Anthology of 20th Century Brazilian Poetry* (1972).

Bishop, Sir Henry Rowley, 1786–1855, English operatic conductor, composer or arranger of 120 dramatic works. He is known today for a setting of Shakespeare's "Lo, here the gentle lark" and the melody of *Home, Sweet Home* from J. H. Payne's comic opera, *Clari; or, The Maid of Milan* (1823).

Bishop, Isabel, 1902–, American painter, b. Cincinnati, Ohio. Influenced by the New York City painters of the 1930s, Bishop produced numerous paintings of working women. Her pensive nude studies, such as *Nude—1934,* demonstrate her understanding of delicate effects of light and shade.

Bishop, Isabella Lucy (Bird), 1831–1904, English traveler and writer, first woman member of the Royal Geographical Society. She traveled extensively and wrote a number of books, including *The English Woman in America* (1856), *The Hawaiian Archipelago* (1875), *A Lady's Life in the Rocky Mountains* (1879), *Unbeaten Tracks in Japan* (1880), *Journeys in Persia and Kurdistan* (1891), and *Korea and Her Neighbors* (1898). She founded several hospitals in China and Korea. See biography by Pat Barr (1970).

bishop: see ORDERS, HOLY.

Bishop Auckland (ôk'lənd), urban district (1971 pop. 33,292), Durham, NE England, on the Wear River. It is a busy market area, as well as a mining town producing coal that is highly suitable for coking. Located near the site of a Roman fort, Auckland has been a seat of the bishops of Durham since the 12th cent. The present palace was largely constructed in the 16th cent.

Bishop's University, at Lennoxville, Que., Canada; founded 1843 by the Anglican bishop of Quebec as a liberal arts college. In 1853 it gained university status. The university has faculties of arts, science, and theology, and a school of education.

Bishops' Wars, two brief campaigns (1639 and 1640) of the Scots against Charles I of England. When Charles attempted to strengthen episcopacy in Scotland by imposing (1637) the English Book of Common Prayer, the Scots countered by pledging themselves in the National Covenant (1638) to restore Presbyterianism. A general assembly of the Scottish church abolished episcopacy. The first war was ended without fighting by the Pacification of Berwick, in which Charles conceded the Scottish right to a free church assembly and a free parliament. However, the assembly that met promptly reaffirmed the covenant. In spite of the refusal of his Short Parliament to vote him money, Charles managed to raise another army, but it was unable to stop the Scots from invading England and occupying Northumberland and Durham. Charles made peace at Ripon (Oct., 1640), and his promise there to pay an indemnity to the Scots necessitated his calling the Long Parliament. See ENGLISH CIVIL WAR.

Bisk: see BIYSK, USSR.

Biskra (bēskrä'), city (1966 pop. 59,275), NE Algeria, at the foot of the Aures Mts. It is a commercial center for the nomads of the surrounding region. It was the Roman military base of Vescera; later it was an important Muslim town. After 1844 it served as a French base for operations in S Algeria. The surrounding oasis produces dates.

Bismarck, Otto von (bĭz'märk, Ger. ô'tō fən bĭs'märk), 1815–98, German statesman, known as the Iron Chancellor. Born of an old Brandenburg Junker family, he studied at Göttingen and Berlin, and after holding minor judicial and administrative offices he was elected (1847) to the Prussian Landtag [parliament]. There he opposed the liberal movement, advocated unification of Germany under the aegis of Prussia, and defended the privileges of his social class, the Junkers. As Prussian minister to the German diet at Frankfurt (1851–59) and as ambassador to St. Petersburg (1859–62) and to Paris (1862), he gained the insight and the experience that determined his subsequent policy. In 1862, WILLIAM I, to secure adoption of his army program then being strenuously opposed in parliament, appointed Bismarck premier. Bismarck, in direct violation of the constitution, dissolved parliament and collected taxes for the army without parliamentary approval. To expel Austria from the GERMAN CONFEDERATION now became Bismarck's chief aim. The disposition of SCHLESWIG-HOLSTEIN, former Danish territory annexed by Austria and Prussia after their defeat of the Danes in 1864, provided the necessary pretext. By the Gastein Convention of 1865 the two countries agreed to rule jointly—Austria was to administer Holstein and Prussia was to administer Schleswig; but friction soon developed. Bismarck accused Austria of violating the Gastein treaty and thus precipitated the AUSTRO-PRUSSIAN WAR (1866), which ended after seven weeks with the defeat of Austria. By the treaty signed at the end of the war, Germany was reorganized under Prussian leadership in the NORTH GERMAN CONFEDERATION, from which Austria was excluded. Fear of France, skillfully propagated by Bismarck, was to bring the remaining German states into the Prussian orbit when the candidature of a Hohenzollern prince to the throne of Spain caused friction with the French Emperor Napoleon III. To make sure that this friction would provoke war, Bismarck published the famous EMS DISPATCH. In the FRANCO-PRUSSIAN WAR (1870–71) that ensued the states of S Germany rallied to the Prussian cause as Bismarck had anticipated, and in Jan., 1871, William I of Prussia was proclaimed German emperor. Bismarck, the creator of the empire, became its first chancellor. When added to his Prussian positions (premier, foreign minister, and minister of commerce) the imperial chancellorship gave him almost complete control of foreign and domestic affairs. To maintain the peace necessary for the consolidation of the empire, he proposed to advance a strong military program, to gain the friendship of Austria, to preserve British friendship by avoiding naval or colonial rivalry, and to isolate France in diplomacy so that revanche would be impossible. Therefore, in 1872, he formed the THREE EMPERORS' LEAGUE (Germany, Austria-Hungary, and Russia) and also maintained friendly relations with Italy. The Balkan rivalries of Austria and Russia and the subsequent triumph of Austria at the Congress of Berlin (see BERLIN, CONGRESS OF), over which Bismarck presided, caused a rift in Russo-German relations. A defensive alliance with Austria was now concluded (1879), and this Dual Alliance became a Triple Alliance when Italy adhered in 1882 (see TRIPLE ALLIANCE AND TRIPLE ENTENTE). Friendship with Russia was revived in the Reinsurance Treaty of 1887. Bismarck, with his system of alignments and alliances, became the virtual arbiter of Europe and was acknowledged as its leading statesman. Bismarck's influence upon German domestic affairs was no less apparent. The empire, soon after its establishment, was disturbed by the KULTURKAMPF, a fierce struggle between the state on the one hand and the Roman Catholic Church and Catholic Center party on the other. The conflict initiated a period of cooperation between Bismarck and the liberals, who were violently anticlerical. However, the struggle lost intensity after Bismarck failed to break the power of the Center party, which made large gains in the Reichstag in 1878. The detente with the liberals foundered in the late 1870s after Bismarck's refusal to appoint three liberals to his ministry and his adoption of protective tariffs in place of the liberals' free trade position. Relations between Bismarck and the Center party continued to improve, and the chancellor turned his attention toward the socialists, who had increased their strength in the Reichstag particularly after the fusion of the Lassalle and Marxian socialists (1875). Bismarck at first met the socialist opposition with extremely repressive measures. The antisocialist law passed in 1878 prohibited the circulation of socialist literature, empowered the police to break up socialist meetings, and put the trial and punishment of socialists under the jurisdiction of police courts. Although the socialists were initially weakened, they again began to increase their number in parliament. Now, partly to weaken the socialists and partly as a result of his policy of economic nationalism, Bismarck instituted a program of sweeping social reform. Between 1883 and 1887, despite violent opposition, laws were passed providing for sickness, accident, and old age insurance; limiting woman and child labor; and establishing maximum working hours. Bismarck's new economic policy also resulted in the rapid expansion of German commerce and industry and the acquisition of overseas colonies and spheres of influence (see GERMANY). The Bismarckian era closed with the death of Emperor Frederick III. A struggle for supremacy between Bismarck and WILLIAM II developed immediately upon that emperor's accession in 1888 and ended with Bismarck's dismissal in 1890. Bismarck, created prince (*Fürst*) after the Franco-Prussian War, was now made duke (*Herzog*) of Lauenburg. He retired and spent the remainder of his life in verbal and written criticism of the emperor and his ministers and in defense of his own policies. See *Bismarck, the Man and the Statesman* (his reminiscences, tr. by A. J. Butler, 1898, repr. 1966); Erich Eyck, *Bismarck and the German Empire* (3d ed. 1968); A. J. P. Taylor, *Bismarck, the Man and the Statesman* (1955, repr. 1968); Otto Pflanze, *Bismarck and the Development of Germany* (2d ed. 1971).

Bismarck, city (1970 pop. 34,703), state capital and seat of Burleigh co., S central N. Dak., on hills overlooking the Missouri River; inc. 1873. A trade and distributing point for a large spring wheat, livestock, and dairy region, it is also the center for development of the rich oil reserves in nearby Williston Basin. Food items, farm machinery, woodwork, and concrete products are made. Lewis and Clark camped nearby in 1804–5. With the beginning of the river traffic in the 1830s, a steamboat port called the "Crossing on the Missouri" emerged there. In 1872, Camp Greeley (later Camp Hancock) was erected to protect the men who were building the Northern Pacific RR. When the railroad reached the fort the next year, a town was laid out; it was subsequently named Bismarck (for Germany's chancellor) in the hope of attracting German investment in the railroad. Bismarck boomed as a river port and railroad center and as a supply point for the Black Hills gold mines (1874). It became the territorial capital in 1883. Of interest are the state capitol (1932), a skyscraper; the state historical museum; and Camp Hancock museum. Mary College and a junior college are there. The state penitentiary is nearby.

Bismarck Archipelago, volcanic group (1969 est. pop. 213,000), 19,200 sq mi (49,730 sq km), SW Pacific, a part of Papua New Guinea. The group includes NEW BRITAIN (the largest island), NEW IRELAND, the ADMIRALTY ISLANDS, the Mussau Islands, LAVONGAI, the VITU ISLANDS, and the DUKE OF YORK ISLANDS. The islands are generally mountainous and have several active volcanoes. The chief agricultural products are copra, cacao, coffee, tea, and rubber. Some copper and gold are mined. The inhabitants are mainly Melanesians. Discovered in 1616 by the Dutch explorer Willem SCHOUTEN, the group became a German protectorate in 1884. Seized by Australian forces in World War I, the islands were mandated to Australia by the League of Nations in 1920. Japan operated several naval and air bases in the islands during World War II. In 1947, Australia received trusteeship over the group from the United Nations. The archipelago was included in Papua New Guinea when it became self-governing in 1973.

bismuth (bĭz'məth) [Ger. *Weisse Masse*=white mass], metallic chemical element; symbol Bi; at. no. 83; at. wt. 208.98; m.p. 271.3°C; b.p. about 1560°C; sp. gr. 9.75 at 20°C; valence +3 or +5. Bismuth is a silver-white, reddish-tinged, brittle metallic element with a rhombohedral crystalline structure. It exhibits more metallic properties than the other members of group Va of the PERIODIC TABLE. It occurs free in nature to a small extent. Bismuth does not tarnish in air, but when heated it burns to form yellow fumes of the trioxide. It reacts with the halogens and with sulfur and is dissolved in nitric acid and hot sulfuric acid. Its soluble compounds are poisonous, but some of its insoluble compounds are used in medicine to treat certain gastric disorders and skin injuries. Bismuth is the poorest heat conductor of all the metals except mercury; it is the most diamagnetic of all metals. The major ores of bismuth, bismuthinite (the sulfide), also called bismuth glance, and bismite (the oxide), are found extensively in South America but are rare in the United States, where bismuth is obtained as a by-product of lead and copper refining. Bismuth expands upon solidification; this unusual property makes it useful in type-metal alloys and for castings. The most important use of bismuth is in the manufacture of low-melting alloys, such as Wood's metal, used in electrical fuses and in automatic fire alarm and sprinkler systems. Bismuth was recognized as a metal by early observers, including Georg Agricola, in the 16th cent., but was believed to be a kind of lead or tin until Claud J. Geoffroy established it as a separate element in 1753.

bison, large hoofed mammal, genus *Bison,* of the cattle family. Bison have short horns and humped, heavily mantled shoulders that slope downward to the hindquarters. The European bison, or WISENT, *Bison bonasus,* is larger and has a less luxuriant mane and beard than the American species, *B. bison.* The American bison is commonly called BUFFALO, although true buffalo are African and Asian animals of the same family. *B. bison* is characterized by a huge, low-slung head and massive hump; its legs are shorter than those of the wisent. Males may reach a shoulder height of over 5 ft (1.5 m), a body length of 9 ft (2.7 m), and a weight of 2,500 lb (1,130 kg). The winter coat of the American bison is dark brown and shaggy; it is shed in spring and replaced by a coat of short, light-brown fur. Bison graze on prairie grasses, migrating south in search of food in the winter. They formerly roamed in vast herds over much of North America, especially on the Great Plains, and were hunted by the American Indians for their flesh and hides. With the arrival of European settlers they were subjected to a wholesale slaughter that resulted in their near extinction. They were killed for their tongues, regarded as a delicacy, and shot for sport from trains. At the beginning of the 19th cent. there were over 60 million bison in North America. By the middle of the century the bison was extinct E of the Mississippi, and by 1900 there remained only two wild herds in North America, one of plains bison in Yellowstone Park, and one of the larger variety, called wood bison, in Canada. Protective laws were passed beginning at the end of the last century, and the bison population has since risen from a few hundred to over 20,000. The wood bison may have vanished as a distinct race through hybridization with the plains bison. Bison are classified in the phylum CHORDATA, subphylum Vertebrata, class Mammalia, order Artiodactyla, family Bovidae. See F. G. Roe, *The North American Buffalo* (2d ed. 1970); Tom McHugh and Victoria Hobson, *The Time of the Buffalo* (1972).

Bispham, David Scull (bĭs'pəm), 1857–1921, American baritone, b. Philadelphia. He made his operatic debut in London in 1891 and was leading Wagnerian baritone of the Metropolitan Opera Company, New York City, from 1896 to 1903. He advocated English translation of foreign operas and supported native opera in English. In 1921 the Opera Society of America established the Bispham Memorial Medal Award for American composers of such operas. See his *Quaker Singer's Recollections* (1920).

Bissagos Islands: see GUINEA-BISSAU.

Bissau (bĭsou'), town (1970 pop. 62,101), former capital of Guinea-Bissau (Portuguese Guinea), a port in the Geba estuary, off the Atlantic Ocean. It is the country's largest city, major port, and administrative and military center. Bissau has been a free port since 1869 and handles some transit trade. Peanuts, hardwoods, copra, palm oil, and rubber are the chief items shipped. Bissau has little industry, except for food and beverage processing. The city was founded in 1687 by the Portuguese as a fortified port and trading center. In 1942 it became the capital of Portuguese Guinea but was replaced by Madina do Boe in 1974.

Bisschop, Simon: see EPISCOPIUS, SIMON.

Bisutun Inscription: see BEHISTUN INSCRIPTION.

bit: see DRILL.

bites and stings: see FIRST AID.

Bithiah (bĭthī'ə), a Pharaoh's daughter, wife of a Judahite. 1 Chron. 4.18.

Bithron (bĭth'rŏn), unidentified place, E of the Jordan, probably a wadi. 2 Sam. 2.29.

Bithynia (bĭthĭn'ēə), ancient country of NW Asia Minor, in present-day Turkey. The original inhabitants were Thracians who established themselves as independent and were given some autonomy after Cyrus the Great incorporated Bithynia into the Persian Empire. After the death of Alexander the Great, the Bithynians took advantage of the wars of the Diadochi to secure freedom from the Seleucids (297 B.C.). They established a dynasty under the leadership of Zipoetes who was succeeded (c.280 B.C.) by Nicomedes I, who founded Nicomedia as the capital of his flourishing state. During his time and the following reigns of Prusias I, Prusias II, and Nicomedes II, wars continued with the Seleucids and with Pergamum. In the 1st cent. B.C., Mithradates V of Pontus had designs on Bithynia, which was ruled by Nicomedes IV (sometimes confused with Nicomedes III), a client of Rome. When Nicomedes died (74 B.C.) he willed Bithynia to Rome. The last of the wars with Mithradates resulted. Bithynia was an important province of Rome. For some time after Pompey's rearrangement of the empire it was combined with western Pontus as a single colony. Pliny the Younger (see under PLINY THE ELDER) was governor of the province (A.D. c.110) under the emperor Trajan. The reign of Hadrian soon after seems to have marked the end of Bithynian prosperity. It was invaded briefly by the Goths (A.D. 298).

Bitlis (bĭtlĭs'), town (1970 pop. 20,556), capital of Bitlis prov., E Turkey, on a tributary of the Tigris River, at c.4,500 ft (1,370 m). Grains, fruit, and tobacco are grown nearby. Located on a passage through the Taurus mts., it was an important caravan center for centuries and was captured by Persians, Arabs, Seljuk Turks, Byzantines, and Ottoman Turks. In the 19th cent. the town had a large Armenian population.

Bitola (bē'tôlə), Serbo-Croatian *Bitolj,* formerly *Monastir,* city (1971 pop. 124,648), extreme S Yugoslavia, in Macedonia. It is a commercial and industrial center for the surrounding agricultural area. Bitola was a major agricultural center in Roman times. Later settled by Slavs, it became a bishopric in the 11th cent. In 1395 the Turks conquered Bitola, which became an important military and commercial center in the 15th and 16th cent. and a Balkan administrative center in the 19th cent. The city suffered much damage during the Balkan Wars (during which the Serbs took it from the Turks) and in World War I. Bitola is noted for its numerous mosques, churches, and a former Turkish market.

Bitolj: see BITOLA, Yugoslavia.

Biton (bī'tŏn) and **Cleobis** (klēō'bĭs), in Greek mythology, sons of the priestess Cydippe. When their mother wanted to see a famous temple of Hera, which was many miles away, the brothers dragged her chariot there. At the end of the long journey Cydippe prayed to Hera that her sons might receive the greatest of blessings. Their reward was instant and painless death.

Bitonto (bētôn'tō), city (1971 pop. 41,560), Apulia, S Italy. It is an agricultural market and is noted for its olive oil. The Spanish under Charles Bourbon defeated the Austrians there in 1734 during the War of the Polish Succession. The Apulian Romanesque cathedral (12th–13th cent.) is especially remarkable for its fine sculptures.

Bitterfeld (bĭ'tərfĕlt), city (1970 pop. 28,964), Halle district, central East Germany, on the Mulde River. It is an industrial center and rail junction. Manufactures include chemicals, aluminum, machinery, and plastics. Lignite is mined in the region. Bitterfeld was founded in the mid-12th cent. and passed to Prussia in 1815.

bittern, common name for migratory marsh birds of the family Ardeidae (HERON family). The American bittern (*Botaurus lentiginosus*), often called "stake driver" because of the male's booming call in the spring, is widely distributed in E North America. It is mostly nocturnal and feeds on frogs, fish, and insects. When pursued, the bittern escapes detection by standing motionless with bill uplifted, its brown and yellow markings and striped foreneck blending with the marsh grasses. It is about 2 to 3 ft (61–91 cm) tall; the western and eastern least bitterns, genus *Ixobrychus,* are about half this size. Of the 12 species of bitterns, 8 constitute the smaller birds. The female bittern builds the nest, which consists of an unkempt arrangement of sedge grass and reeds. The nests are built on the ground along rivers or lakeshores and house the clutch of 3 to 6 eggs. Both male and female share the incubation duties. Bitterns are classified in the phylum CHORDATA, subphylum Vertebrata, class Aves, order Ciconiiformes, family Ardeidae.

Bitterroot, river, c.120 mi (190 km) long, rising in SW Mont. and flowing north to join the Clark Fork River near Missoula. A Roman Catholic mission was built in the river valley in 1841, and the missionaries are credited with establishing farming in the area. The **Bitter Root project** irrigates c.17,000 acres (6,880 hectares).

bitterroot: see PURSLANE.

Bitterroot Range, part of the Rocky Mts., on the Idaho-Mont. line. The main range, running northwest-southeast, includes Trapper Peak (10,175 ft/3,101 m high); Mt. Garfield (10,961 ft/3,341 m), in an east-running spur to the south, is the highest peak. Discovered in the 1804–5 expedition of Lewis and Clark, this rugged mountain range has long been one of the most impenetrable in the United States; except for its foothills, it remains almost completely unexploited today.

bitters, various alcoholic beverages containing bitter principles, such as angostura bark, cascarilla, quassia, gentian, orange, quinine, and other flavoring agents, and prepared by infusion or distillation. They are used as appetizers, digestives, and flavoring for mixed drinks and frequently attain an alcoholic strength of 40%.

bittersweet, name for two unrelated plants, belonging to different families, both fall-fruiting woody vines sometimes cultivated for their decorative scarlet berries. One, called also woody NIGHTSHADE (*Solanum dulcamara*), is an Old World plant now naturalized in North America, belonging to the family Solanaceae (NIGHTSHADE family). The twigs and stems are occasionally used medicinally for a narcotic poison similar to belladonna. The more popular bittersweet (*Celastrus scandens*), a plant of the family Celastraceae (STAFF TREE family), grows in thickets from Maine to North Carolina and W to Nebraska. Its berry is surrounded by an orange-yellow capsule. Both bittersweets are classified in the division MAGNOLIOPHYTA, class Magnoliopsida. *S. dulcamara* belongs to the order Polemoniales, family Solanaceae. *C. scandens* belongs to the order Celastrales, family Celastraceae.

bitumen (bĭtyōō'mən), any of several mixtures of hydrocarbons, including asphalt, tar, and crude petroleum. Substances containing bitumens are called bituminous (e.g., bituminous coal).

bituminous coal: see COAL.

Bitzius, Albert: see GOTTHELF, JEREMIAS.

bivalve, aquatic mollusk of the class Pelecypoda ("hatchet-foot"), with a laterally compressed body and a shell consisting of two valves, or movable pieces, hinged by an elastic ligament. The valves cover the right and left sides of the animal; they are hinged dorsally (above the body) and open ventrally (below the body). Usually the two valves are similar and equal in size, but in some forms, such as the OYSTER, that attach to the substratum by one valve (i.e., lying on their sides), the left-hand (or upper) valve is larger than the right-hand (or lower) one. Two muscles, called adductors, run between the inner surfaces of the two valves; acting antagonistically to the hinge ligament, they enable the shell to close rapidly and tightly. Within the shell is a fleshy layer of tissue called the mantle; there is a cavity (the mantle cavity) between the mantle and the body wall proper. The mantle secretes the layers of the shell, including the inner nacreous, or pearly, layer. Sometimes a pearl is formed as a reaction to irritation, by the depositing of nacreous layers around a foreign particle. The head is much reduced, without eyes or tentacles, and a muscular hatchet-shaped foot projects from the front end of the animal, between the valves. The foot is used for burrowing, and, in some bivalves (e.g., razor clams), to swim. Many bivalves have two tubes, or siphons, extending from the rear end: one (the incurrent siphon) for the intake of oxygenated water and food, and one (the excurrent siphon) for the outflow of waste products. The two tubes may be joined in a single siphon, or "neck." The gills, suspended within a mantle cavity, are usually very large and

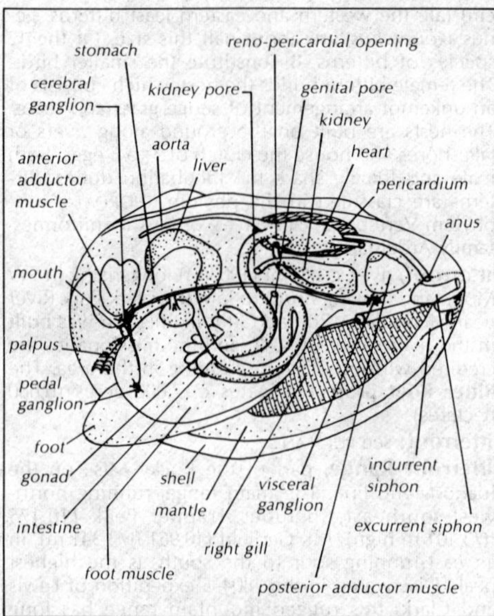

Internal anatomy of a clam, Anodonta, *representative mollusk of the class Pelecypoda (the bivalves)*

function in food gathering (filter feeding) as well as in respiration. As water passes over the gills, tiny organic particles are strained out and are carried to the mouth. Members of the order Septibranchia, however, lack gills and feed on small crustaceans and worms. Bivalves have a complete digestive tract; a reduced nervous system; a complete, open circulatory system with a chambered heart, arteries, veins, and blood sinuses; and excretory and reproductive organs. In most species the sexes are separate, and the eggs and sperm are shed into the water, where fertilization occurs. The larval stage is free-swimming and lacks a shell. Bivalves differ in their habits: some, such as the oysters and marine MUSSELS, have a reduced foot and are permanently attached to a substratum; some, such as the CLAMS and freshwater mussels, burrow rather slowly through the sand or mud using the foot; some, such as the COCKLE shells, live on or near the surface of the ocean floor; still others, such as the SHIPWORM, burrow through rocks or wood seeking protected dwellings and do damage to rock pilings and other marine installations. The SCALLOPS swim with great speed by suddenly clapping the shell valves together and ejecting water from the mantle cavity. Bivalves that are exposed at low tide, such as the marine mussels, keep their gills wet with water retained in the mantle cavity. Because of the enormous variety of sizes, shapes, surface sculpturing, and colors, shell characteristics are of great importance in the identification and classification of bivalves. Shells range in size from the tiny (1/16-in./2-mm) seed shells characteristic of members of the freshwater family Sphaeriidae to the GIANT CLAM, *Tridacna*, of the South Pacific, which attains a length of over 4 ft (120 cm) and may weigh over 500 lb (225 kg). Bivalves are an important food source for humans, as well as for gastropods, fish, and shore birds. They are classified in the phylum MOLLUSCA, class Pelecypoda.

Biwa (bē'wä), lake, c.40 mi (60 km) long and from 2 to 12 mi (3.2–19 km) wide, Shiga prefecture, S Honshu, Japan. The lake, shaped like the biwa, a musical instrument, is the largest in Japan and is a popular scenic resort. It abounds in fish; textile industries flank its shores. Canals from the lake to Kyoto provide water supply and a transportation route.

Biysk (bēsk), city (1970 pop. 186,000), S central Siberian USSR, on the Biya River. A port and the terminus of a branch of the Turkistan-Siberia RR, Biysk manufactures food-processing equipment. The city was founded as a fortress in 1709; its name is sometimes spelled Bisk or Biisk.

Bizerte (bēzĕrt'), Arab. *Banzart,* city (1966 pop. 51,708), N Tunisia, on the Mediterranean Sea. It is an important port, strategically situated near the narrowest part of the Mediterranean. The city also has processing industries. Bizerte was founded by Phoenicians. While the French ruled Tunisia, they improved and fortified the outer harbor and deepened the channel to the Lake of Bizerte, where there are naval works and the town of Menzel Bourgiba. The White Russian fleet (1920) and the Spanish republican fleet (1939) were interned at Bizerte. It was a German base in World War II and was heavily bombed (1943) by the Allies. Tunisian insistence that France evacuate its naval installations at Bizerte led to violent confrontations in 1961; the base was turned over to Tunisia in 1963.

Bizet, Georges (zhôrzh bēzā'), 1838–75, French operatic composer. The son of professional musicians, he entered the Paris Conservatory at the age of nine and won the Prix de Rome in 1857. He was a gifted pianist and composed instrumental music in his teens. Bizet is celebrated for his opera *Carmen* (1875), based on a story by Mérimée. One of the most popular operas ever written, *Carmen* has music that is lush, melodic, and brilliantly orchestrated. It unfolds a story of love, hate, jealousy, and murder, set in the exotic world of Spanish gypsies and bullfighters. Bizet's other works include the operas *The Pearlfishers* (1863), *The Fair Maid of Perth* (1867), and *Djamileh* (1872); Symphony in C Major (1855); and incidental music to Daudet's *L'Arlésienne*, in the form of two orchestral suites. See biographies by Winton Dean (1965) and Mina Curtiss (1958, repr. 1974).

Bizjothjah (bĭzjŏth'jə), name in a geographical list marred by copyists. Joshua 15.28.

Biztha, chamberlain of Ahasuerus. Esther 1.10.

Bjerknes, Vilhelm Frimann Koren (vĭl'hĕlm frē'män kô'rən byĕrk'nĕs), 1862–1951, Norwegian physicist and pioneer in modern meteorology. He worked on applying hydrodynamic and thermodynamic theories to atmospheric and hydrospheric conditions in order to predict future weather conditions. Bjerknes was professor at the universities of Oslo (1907–12, 1926–32); Leipzig (1912–17); and Bergen (1917–26), where he set up a geophysical institute. His work in meteorology and on electric waves was important in the early development of wireless telegraphy. His publications include *Fields of Force* (1906) and the classic book *On the Dynamics of the Circular Vortex with Applications to the Atmosphere and to Atmospheric Vortex and Wave Motion* (1921); he is also coauthor with J. W. Sandström (on Vol. I) and with T. Hesselberg and O. Devik (on Vol. II) of *Dynamic Meteorology and Hydrography* (Vol. I and II, 1910–11; Vol. III, 1951). He evolved a theory of cyclones known as the polar front theory with his son **Jakob Aall Bonnevie Bjerknes,** 1897–, who became a U.S. citizen in 1946. Jakob Bjerknes served as professor of meteorology at the Univ. of Bergen (1931–40) and at the Univ. of California (from 1940).

Björling, Jussi (yo͞os'sĭ byör'lĭng), 1907–60, Swedish tenor. He studied at the Royal Opera School in Stockholm, making his debut there in 1930 as Don Ottavio in Mozart's *Don Giovanni.* He made guest appearances in leading roles with opera companies in Copenhagen, Dresden, Prague, Vienna, Paris, and Buenos Aires. In the United States he was acclaimed at a recital in 1937 in Springfield, Mass. He appeared that year with the Chicago Civic Opera Company and was engaged for the 1938–39 season at the Metropolitan Opera House. During World War II Björling remained in Sweden, returning to the United States to rejoin the Metropolitan Opera Company in 1945. Because his voice was both lyric and dramatic, he had an extensive repertory, including leading roles in *La Bohème, Rigoletto, Il Trovatore,* and *Faust.*

Bjorneborg, Finland: see PORI.

Bjørnøya (byörn'öyä), island, 69 sq mi (179 sq km), in the Barents Sea, c.275 mi (440 km) N of Norway; southernmost island of Svalbard. It rises to 1,759 ft (536 m). There are polar fox and polar bear on the island. Probably known to Norsemen in the 12th cent., it was rediscovered by Willem Barentz, the Dutch navigator, in 1596, and was formally annexed by Norway in 1915. It is also known as Bear Island.

Bjørnson, Bjørnstjerne (byörn'styĕrnə byörn'sŏn), 1832–1910, Norwegian writer and political leader, one of the major figures of Norwegian literature. A brilliant journalist, he long had great influence in Norway. As a dramatist, he sought to break the Danish yoke on the Norwegian theater; as an orator, to revive Norwegian as a literary language; and as a reformer, to champion the rights of the oppressed. His celebrated *Synnøve Solbakken* (1857; first tr. 1881; *Sunny Hill,* 1932), was perhaps the first Norwegian major novel. Bjørnson succeeded his friend Ibsen as director of the Ole Bull Theater in Bergen (1857–59) and then became involved in politics, fighting against Norwegian amalgamation with Sweden and championing parliamentary democracy. To link the resurgent nation with its epic past he created sagalike dramas, the finest of which is the trilogy *Sigurd Slembe* (1862, tr. 1888). Bjørnson became national poet of Norway—one of his poems became the national anthem—and reached his pinnacle as a lyric poet while abroad in Europe (1860–63). Returning to Oslo in 1863, he was granted an annuity and directed the Oslo Theater until 1867. In the next years he wrote his finest works: the novel *The Fisher Girl* (1868, tr. 1871); the epic poem *Arnljot Gelline* (1870, tr. 1917); and *The Bankrupt* (1875, tr. 1914). After enduring a religious crisis (1878–79) Bjørnson accepted Darwinian evolution in a religious context, rejecting traditional religion. From this time his writings urged the liberation of the human spirit from dogma and prejudice. The story *Dust* (1882, tr. 1884) supported secular education; the play *A Gauntlet* (1883, tr. 1890) attacked the double standard; and the drama *Beyond Our Power* (2 parts, 1883–95; tr. of 1st part, *Pastor Sang,* 1893; tr. of 2d part, *Beyond Human Might,* 1914) treated basic social and philosophic conflicts in modern society. Bjørnson received the 1903 Nobel Prize in Literature. See biography by Harold Larson (1944); separate study in G. M. C. Brandes, *Henrik Ibsen* (1964).

Björnsson, Sveinn (svān byörn'sôn), 1881–1952, Icelandic diplomat and political leader, first president of Iceland (1944–52). A distinguished lawyer, he was elected to the Althing (Icelandic parliament) for the first time in 1914. From 1912 to 1920 he was president of the Reykjavík city council. During World War I, Björnsson undertook numerous diplomatic missions to Great Britain and the United States and afterward served as minister to Denmark (1920–41). He was regent of Iceland from 1941 to 1944, when, on Iceland's independence from Denmark, he became president. He was reelected in 1945 and 1949.

Bk, chemical symbol of the element BERKELIUM.

Blacher, Boris (blä'khər), 1903–, Estonian-German composer, b. Ying-k'ou, China. Blacher lived for six years in Siberia. He studied in Berlin and in 1953 became the director of the West Berlin Conservatory of Music. Blacher has written concertos for various instruments, numerous operas, including *200,000 Taler* (1969; after Sholem Aleichem), ballets, chamber music, and song cycles. He has experimented with variable meters or rhythmic rows, as in *Ornaments* (1953) for orchestra, and with abstract operas concerned with human situations but without plot.

Black, Greene Vardiman, 1836–1915, American dentist, b. Scott co., Ill. Professor at Chicago College of Dental Surgery (now part of Loyola Univ.) from 1883 to 1889 and professor (from 1891) and dean (from 1897) at the Northwestern Univ. dental school, he made large contributions to dentistry as teacher, as originator of methods and instruments, and as author. His works include *Formation of Poisons by Microörganisms* (1884), *Dental Anatomy* (1891), and *Operative Dentistry* (1908). The Black method of preparing amalgam alloys for fillings is still in use.

Black, Hugh, 1868–1953, Scottish-American theologian and author. After serving as a pastor in Paisley and Edinburgh, he emigrated to the United States in 1906 to begin a professorship of practical theology in Union Theological Seminary, New York City. His books include *Culture and Restraint* (1900), *Christ's Service of Love* (1907), *The New World* (1915), *The Adventure of Being Man* (1929), and *Christ or Caesar* (1938).

Black, Hugo LaFayette, 1886–1971, Associate Justice of the U.S. Supreme Court (1937–71), b. Harlan, Clay co., Ala. He received his law degree from the Univ. of Alabama in 1906. He practiced law and held local offices before serving (1927–37) in the U.S. Senate. As Senator he ardently supported New Deal measures, conducted Senate investigations of merchant-marine subsidies (1933) and lobbying (1935), and sponsored (1937) the Wages and Hours bill. His appointment to the Supreme Court by President Franklin Delano Roosevelt met strong opposition from the public and in the Senate because of his earlier membership in the Ku Klux Klan. Black was, however, a staunch defender of civil liberties, and he became the leader of the activists on the Supreme Court, consistently opposing congressional and state violations of free speech and due process. See study by Virginia Hamilton (1972).

Black, James, 1823–93, American temperance leader. A Pennsylvania lawyer, he was active in state and national temperance work. His plan for a National

Publication House was adopted by the National Temperance Convention (1865). In 1872, as presidential nominee of the Prohibition party, he gained some 5,000 votes.

Black, Jeremiah Sullivan, 1810–83, American cabinet officer, b. Somerset co., Pa. Admitted to the Pennsylvania bar in 1830, Black became a successful lawyer. As U.S. Attorney General (1857–60) under President Buchanan he hired Edwin M. Stanton, later his successor, to clear up the involved land-title cases in California. Black was less successful, however, in enforcing unpopular legislation concerning slavery. It was his opinion that although the seceding Southern states could not be coerced, Federal property in the South should be protected, and measures taken to resist armed rebellion. He replaced (Dec., 1860) Lewis Cass as Secretary of State and succeeded in persuading Buchanan to send supplies to Fort Sumter. Buchanan appointed him to the Supreme Court in Feb., 1861, but the Senate, with both Democrats and Republicans hostile to Black, refused to confirm him. See P. G. Auchampaugh, *James Buchanan and His Cabinet on the Eve of Secession* (1926); biography by W. N. Brigance (1934, repr. 1971).

Black, Joseph, 1728–99, Scottish chemist and physician, b. France. He was professor of chemistry at Glasgow (1756–66) and from 1766 at Edinburgh. He is best known for his theories of latent heat and specific heat. He also laid the foundations of chemistry as an exact science in his investigations on magnesium carbonate, during which he discovered carbon dioxide, which he called "fixed air."

Black, Max, 1909–, American analytical philosopher, b. Baku, Russia, grad. Cambridge Univ., Ph.D. Univ. of London, 1939. He taught at the Univ. of Ill. (1940–46) before going to Cornell Univ. (1946). Influenced by Ludwig Wittgenstein, he wrote *A Companion to Wittgenstein's Tractatus* (1964). His concern with clear language was expressed in *Language and Philosophy* (1949), *Models and Metaphors* (1962), *The Labyrinth of Language* (1968), and *Margins of Precision: Essays in Logic and Language* (1970).

black-and-tan coonhound: see COONHOUND, BLACK-AND-TAN.

Black Angus cattle: see ANGUS CATTLE.

Blackbeard, d. 1718, English pirate. His name was probably Edward Teach, Thatch, or Thach. It is supposed that he began as a privateer in the War of the Spanish Succession (1701–14) and at its end turned pirate. Between 1716 and 1718 he preyed on the shipping and coastal settlements of the West Indies and the Atlantic coast of North America, becoming notorious for his cruelty. His headquarters were in the Bahamas and the Carolinas. The compliant governor of North Carolina shared some of the booty, but despite such protection Blackbeard was killed by a British force sent from Virginia. Legend has romanticized Blackbeard's history.

Black Belt, term loosely applied to several areas of the U.S. South that are characterized by black soil and excellent cotton-growing conditions. The Black Belt of NE Mississippi and S central Alabama, in the heart of the Old South and generally associated with the term, was historically important as the nation's main cotton producer in the mid-1800s. Soil depletion, erosion, the boll weevil, and economic conditions combined to drive cotton from the region. Livestock, peanuts, and truck crops are now the chief crops. The Coastal Cuesta of central South Carolina and Georgia is one of the original cotton-producing areas in the United States. It remains an important cotton producer because of the extensive use of fertilizers and its proximity to textile mills. The Black Prairie of E Texas, extending north from the Gulf coastal plain to the Red River, has the state's richest farmland and is one the best cotton-growing areas in the United States.

blackberry, name for several species of thorny plants of the genus *Rubus* of the family Rosaceae (ROSE family). See BRAMBLE.

blackbird, common name in North America of a perching bird allied to the bobolink, the meadow lark, the oriole, and the grackle and belonging to the family Icteridae. The European blackbird, *Turdus merula*, is a thrush. The red-winged blackbird of E North America is a familiar sight, its scarlet shoulder patches conspicuous among the tall grasses of the marshes and wet meadows where it nests. It eats grain, insects, and weed seeds. Another common species is the yellow-headed blackbird, *Xanthocephalus xanthocephalus.* Except during the breeding season blackbirds usually travel in flocks. The yellow-headed, the tricolored red-winged, and brewer blackbirds are found in the West. The rusty blackbird, glossy blue-black in summer when the brown edging of its winter feathers has worn off, winters in the United States. Many members of the family are polygamous, although the incidence of polygamous behavior varies from population to population. For example, in the brewer blackbird, the male becomes polygamous only when there are more females than males; when the balance is even, monogamy is the rule. The female blackbird usually builds the nest, which consists of a cup-shaped structure made of grasses. Flocks of blackbirds may be as large as 5 million birds, and they often do serious crop damage when foraging for food. However, the birds are invaluable because of the insects they consume. Blackbirds are classified in the phylum CHORDATA, subphylum Vertebrata, class Aves, order Passeriformes, family Icteridae.

black body, in physics, an ideal black substance that absorbs all and reflects none of the radiant energy falling on it. Lampblack, or powdered carbon, which reflects almost 2% of the radiation falling on it, approximates an ideal black body. Since a black body is a perfect absorber of radiant energy, by the laws of thermodynamics it must also be a perfect emitter of radiation. The distribution according to wavelength of the radiant energy of a black body radiator depends on the absolute temperature of the black body and not on its internal nature or structure. As the temperature increases, the wavelength at which the energy emitted per second is a maximum decreases. This phenomenon can be seen in the behavior of an ordinary incandescent object, which gives off its maximum radiation at shorter and shorter wavelengths as it becomes hotter and hotter. First it glows in long red wavelengths, then in yellow wavelengths, and finally in short blue wavelengths. In order to explain the spectral distribution of black body radiation, Max Planck developed the QUANTUM THEORY in 1901. In thermodynamics the principle of the black body is used to determine the nature and amount of the energy emitted by a heated object.

blackbuck, small antelope, *Antilope cervicapra*, found in plains and open forest throughout India. Males are dark brown above and white below, with white rings around the eyes; they stand about 32 in. (81 cm) at the shoulder and weigh about 90 lb (41 kg). Their heavily ridged, corkscrew-shaped horns are about 18 in. (45 cm) long. The smaller, hornless females are fawn-colored above and white below. Blackbucks graze in herds of 10 to 100 individuals and, unlike most antelopes, graze mostly by day, even in intense heat. They are extremely swift animals; a cheetah can run down a blackbuck, but only if it overtakes it in the first few hundred yards. Although they have been hunted intensively by man, sometimes with the aid of cheetahs, blackbucks have survived in large numbers. They are classified in the phylum CHORDATA, subphylum Vertebrata, class Mammalia, order Artiodactyla, family Bovidae.

Blackburn, Joseph, b. c.1700, d. after 1765, American portrait painter. Little is known concerning him except that from 1750 to 1765 he painted portraits (usually signed J.B.), chiefly of members of distinguished families in Boston and Portsmouth, N.H. Imitating the English rococo style, he painted portraits of Col. Theodore Atkinson (Worcester Art Mus.); three members of the Greenleaf family (Metropolitan Mus.); and the Isaac Winslow Family (Mus. of Fine Arts, Boston).

Blackburn, county borough (1971 pop. 101,672), Lancashire, NW England. It was formerly a great cotton-weaving center, noted especially for calicoes. Textiles are still important, but now there are other large industries that make engineering equipment, radio parts, beer, felt, and carpets. Blackburn is also an agricultural market. The textile industry started very early—Blackburn checks (a linen product made of Irish flax) were well known about the middle of the 17th cent. When James Hargreaves invented (c.1765) the spinning jenny nearby, the manufacture of cotton goods received a new impetus. The completion of the Leeds-Blackburn-Liverpool Canal in 1816 substantially aided Blackburn's 19th-century economic growth. John Morley, the statesman, was born in Blackburn. There is a technical college in the borough. In 1974, Blackburn became part of the new nonmetropolitan county of Lancashire.

Black Canyon of the Gunnison National Monument: see NATIONAL PARKS AND MONUMENTS (table); GUNNISON, river.

black codes, in U.S. history, series of statutes passed by the ex-Confederate states, 1865–66, dealing with the status of the newly freed Negroes. They varied greatly from state to state as to their harshness and restrictiveness. Although the codes granted certain basic civil rights to Negroes (the right to marry, to own personal property, and to sue in court), they also provided for the segregation of public facilities and placed severe restrictions on the freedman's status as a free laborer, his right to own real estate, and his right to testify in court. The North interpreted the codes as an attempt by the South to reenslave the Negro. The FREEDMEN'S BUREAU prevented their enforcement, and the codes were later repealed by the radical Republican state governments.

Black Country, highly industrialized region, mostly in Staffordshire but partly in Worcestershire and Warwickshire, W central England. It includes the cities of Dudley, Rowley Regis (see WARLEY), Tipton, Walsall, Wednesbury, West Bromwich, and Wolverhampton. From the mid-18th to the mid-19th cent. the area's resources—coal, iron, clay, and limestone—made iron smelting and the manufacture of iron products the main industries. The black smoke from the factories gave the region its name. Today the iron and coal mines are depleted, and the manufacturing industries utilize iron, steel, brass, and copper from outside the region to make metal products. These include hardware, tubes, boilers, machinery and machine tools, home appliances, and road and rail vehicles. There are also chemical and constructional-engineering industries.

Black Death: see PLAGUE.

Black Douglas: see DOUGLAS, SIR JAMES DE, LORD OF DOUGLAS.

black earth: see CHERNOZEM.

Blackett, Patrick Maynard Stuart (blăk'ĭt), 1897–1974, English physicist. He was professor of physics at the Univ. of Manchester (1937–53) and in 1953 became professor at the Univ. of London. For his work in improving and extending the use of the Wilson cloud chamber and for his discoveries concerning cosmic rays he received the 1948 Nobel Prize in Physics. He is the author of *Military and Political Consequences of Atomic Energy* (1948, rev. ed. 1949; American ed. *Fear, War and the Bomb*, 1949) and *Atomic Weapons and East-West Relations* (1956). In 1965 he was elected president of the Royal Society, London.

black-eyed bean or **black-eyed pea:** see COWPEA.

black-eyed Susan or **yellow daisy,** North American daisylike wild flower (*Rudbeckia hirta*) of the family Compositae (COMPOSITE family) with yellow rays and a dark brown center. It is a weedy biennial or annual and grows in dry places. The black-eyed Susan and the other rudbeckias are called yellow coneflowers. The most widely cultivated is the golden glow (*R. laciniata hortensia*), a tall double-blossomed perennial. Black-eyed Susans are classified in the division MAGNOLIOPHYTA, class Magnoliopsida, order Asterales, family Compositae.

Blackfeet Indians: see BLACKFOOT INDIANS.

black fly, name for any of the FLIES of the family Simuliidae. The black fly is about ⅛ in. (32 cm) long and has large eyes, short legs, a stout, humped back, broad gauzy wings, and piercing-sucking mouthparts. Species of black flies occur worldwide. The female inflicts a painful bite, sucking the blood of birds and mammals, including humans. Livestock and other large mammals may be bitten to death by swarms of black flies; the black fly problem of some subarctic regions is so severe as to make human settlement impossible. Some tropical African and American species carry the larvae of roundworms that in human hosts cause swellings of the skin and eyes and sometimes blindness. The eggs of black flies are commonly laid in masses on wet rocks, logs, and plants; the larvae live in fast flowing water, clinging to rocks by means of anal sucking disks and straining out organic matter by fanlike head organs. Pupation occurs underwater; the pupa accumulates a bubble of air in its case, enabling it to rise to the surface and emerge when mature. The Adirondack black fly, *Simulium hirtipes*, the white stockinged black fly, *S. venustum*, the buffalo gnat, *S. pecuarum*, and the turkey gnat, *S. meridionale*, are common species. Black flies are classified in the phylum ARTHROPODA, class Insecta, order Diptera, family Simuliidae. See INSECT.

Blackfoot Indians, North American Indians of the Algonquian branch of the Algonquian-Wakashan linguistic stock (see AMERICAN INDIAN LANGUAGES). They occupied in the early 19th cent. a large range of territory around the Upper Missouri (above the Yellowstone) and North Saskatchewan rivers W to the Rockies. Their name derives from the fact that they dyed their moccasins black. There were three main tribes—the Siksika, or Blackfoot proper; the

Piegan; and the Kainah, or Blood. Although they did not form a unified political entity, they were united in defending their lands and in warfare. The Atsina Indians (related to the Arapaho) and the Athapascan-speaking Sarsi Indians were allied with the Blackfoot group. The Blackfoot were unremittingly hostile toward neighboring tribes and usually toward white men; intrusions upon Blackfoot lands were efficiently repelled. Prior to the mid-18th cent. they had moved into the N Great Plains area, acquired horses from southern tribes, and developed a nomadic Plains culture, largely dependent on the buffalo. Their only cultivated crop was tobacco, grown for ceremonial purposes. With the early coming of the white man, the Blackfoot gained wealth from the sale of beaver pelts, but the killing off of the buffalo and the near exhaustion of fur stocks brought them to near starvation. Presently there are some 6,200 Blackfeet on a reservation in Montana and another 2,600 on a reservation in Alberta. They continue to a small degree the rich ceremonialism that earlier marked their religion; important rituals include the sun dance and the vision quest. See J. C. Ewers, *The Blackfeet: Raiders on the Northwestern Plains* (1958, repr. 1967); H. A. Dempsey, *Crowfoot, Chief of the Blackfeet* (1972); Malcolm McFee, *Modern Blackfeet* (1972).

Black Forest, Ger. *Schwarzwald,* mountain range, SW West Germany, extending 90 mi (145 km) between the Rhine and Neckar rivers. Feldberg is the highest (4,898 ft/1,493 m) peak. The range is covered by dark pine forests and cut by deep valleys and small lakes. The Danube and Neckar rivers rise there. Lumbering is an important economic activity. Orchards and cattle are found in the valleys; grains are grown in the highlands. The Black Forest is famous for its clock and toy industries (cuckoo clocks, music boxes). It is a year-round resort area; Baden-Baden and Freiburg are the chief cities.

Black Friday, Sept. 24, 1869, in U.S. history, day of financial panic. In 1869 a small group of American financial speculators, including Jay GOULD and James FISK, sought the support of Federal officials of the Grant administration in a drive to corner the gold market. The attempt failed when government gold was released for sale. The drive culminated on a Friday, when thousands were ruined—the day is popularly called Black Friday. There was great indignation against the perpetrators. Several other days of financial panic have also been occasionally referred to as Black Friday.

black gum, ornamental deciduous tree (*Nyssa sylvatica*) native to E North America. The leaves turn bright scarlet in the fall. The very tough wood has been used for wheel hubs and other purposes. It is sometimes called sour gum, tupelo, and pepperidge, names also given other species of the genus, some native to Asia. The genus *Nyssa* is probably derived from an ancestral dogwood and is included by some botanists in the family Cornaceae (dogwood family) of the division MAGNOLIOPHYTA, class Magnoliopsida, order Cornales.

Black Hand, symbol and name for a criminal and terroristic secret society, and especially associated with the MAFIA and the CAMORRA. The Black Hand flourished in Sicily in the late 19th cent., and in the United States it was especially active in New York City at the beginning of the 20th cent. It is estimated that at one time 90% of New York City's Italian population was blackmailed by letters threatening death and marked with a black hand. Famous incidents associated with the Black Hand include the murder (1890) in New Orleans of chief of police Daniel Hennessy and the shooting (1909), in Palermo, Italy, of Lt. Joseph Petrosino of the New York City police.

black haw: see HONEYSUCKLE.

Black Hawk War, conflict between the Sac and Fox Indians and the United States in 1832. After the War of 1812, whites settling the Illinois country exerted pressure on the Indians. A treaty of 1804, which had no real claim to validity, provided for removal of the Sac and Fox Indians W of the Mississippi. An Indian leader, Black Hawk (1767–1838), who was born in the Sac village near the site of present Rock Island, Ill., and who had fought for the British in the War of 1812, denounced the treaty and resisted removal. Years of intermittent skirmishing followed. In 1831 the whites used force to impose a new treaty that compelled the Indians to retire from their lands. In April, 1832, Black Hawk, with some 400 braves and their families, returned to Illinois. Not receiving the support he expected, he admitted defeat, but when one of the peaceful emissaries he sent was shot down in cold blood, the outraged Black Hawk successfully attacked a larger white force, then retired into what is now Wisconsin. A large force of volunteers was gathered under Gen. Henry ATKINSON. The last battle of the war took place on the Bad Axe River, where Black Hawk was attacked by these troops and a Sioux war party. Trapped, he displayed a white flag, but this was ignored and almost all of his band, including women and children, were wiped out. Black Hawk himself escaped, surrendered to the Winnebago, was turned over for imprisonment, and was released in 1833 to return to the pitiful remnant of his tribe and his family in Iowa. Lorado Taft's colossal statue (1911) near Oregon, Ill., has come to be known as the Black Hawk Monument. See his autobiography (1833; ed. by Donald Jackson, 1955); Cyrenus Cole, *I Am a Man: The Indian Black Hawk* (1938).

blackhead, yellowish or blackish plug of material accumulated in the duct of a sebaceous gland. The material consists of keratin (horny cells of the epidermis) and modified sebum (oily secretions of the sebaceous gland). Blackheads are the primary lesions in ACNE. Treatment is the same as for acne, with frequent cleansing of the skin followed by the application of astringent solutions. Plugs should be extracted only by a physician, since damage to the surrounding tissues occasioned by squeezing often leads to scarring.

Blackheath, common, 267 acres (108 hectares) in Lewisham and Greenwich boroughs, London, England. It was the gathering place of highwaymen and of several martial groups, including the followers of Wat Tyler in 1381 and of Jack Cade in 1450, who made Blackheath the headquarters for their attacks on London.

Black Hills, rugged mountains, c.6,000 sq mi (15,540 sq km), enclosed by the Belle Fourche and Cheyenne rivers, SW S. Dak. and NE Wyo., and rising c.2,500 ft (760 m) above the surrounding Great Plains; Harney Peak, 7,242 ft (2,207 m) above sea level, is the highest point in the Black Hills and in South Dakota. The mountains received their name from the heavily forested slopes that appear black from afar. Indians, settlers, and railroad companies depended on wood from the Black Hills for fuel and building material. Gold was discovered in the hills in 1874 by an expedition led by Gen. George Custer, and the resulting gold rush drove out the Indians. White settlements grew rapidly after 1876, chiefly in such mining towns in South Dakota as Custer, Deadwood, Lead, Spearfish, and Rapid City, the largest city in the Black Hills. Gold is still mined in the area; Homestake Mine is the largest gold mine in the United States. Other important minerals found in the hills are uranium, feldspar, mica, and silver. The Black Hills are a major recreational area of the northern plains. Most of the slopes are in two national forests. Wind Cave National Park, Jewel Cave National Monument, Mt. Rushmore National Memorial, and Custer State Park are tourist spots.

black hole, in astronomy: see GRAVITATIONAL COLLAPSE.

Black Hole of Calcutta: see CALCUTTA.

black humor, in literature, drama, and film, grotesque or morbid humor used to express the absurdity, insensitivity, paradox, and cruelty of the modern world. Ordinary characters or situations are usually exaggerated far beyond the limits of normal satire or irony. For example, Stanley Kubrick's film *Dr. Strangelove; or, How I Learned to Stop Worrying and Love the Bomb* (1963) is a terrifying comic treatment of the circumstances surrounding an accidental dropping of an atom bomb, while Jules Feiffer's comedy *Little Murders* (1965) is a delineation of the horrors of modern urban life, focusing particularly on random assassinations. The novels of such writers as Kurt Vonnegut, Thomas Pynchon, John Barth, Joseph Heller, and Philip Roth contain elements of black humor.

Black Isle, peninsula, 18 mi (29 km) long and up to 9 mi (14.5 km) wide, Ross and Cromarty co., N Scotland, extending into Moray Firth. It has the best farmland in the county, producing grain and potatoes. Cattle are raised there.

blackjack, one of the world's principal gambling card games; also known as twenty-one or vingt-et-un. Each player receives one card face down and bets that this card plus one or more cards dealt face up will beat the dealer's hand without exceeding 21. An ace counts 1 or 11, a face card 10, and all other cards according to their face value. A score of 21 on the first two cards is the perfect hand, called blackjack.

Black Kettle, d. 1868, chief of the southern CHEYENNE INDIANS in Colorado. His attempt to make peace (1864) with the white men ended in the massacre of about half his people at SAND CREEK. Despite this treachery on the part of the whites, he continued to seek peace with them, and in 1865 he signed the Treaty of the Little Arkansas. The government ignored its guarantees, and Black Kettle tried again to negotiate, signing the Medicine Lodge Treaty of 1867. The Cheyenne might have retired to the reservation provided for them, had it not been for Gen. George Armstrong Custer. On Nov. 27, 1868, Custer and his 7th Cavalry attacked Black Kettle's camp on the Washita River without warning and killed the chief and hundreds of the Indians.

black lead: see GRAPHITE.

blackleg or **black quarter,** acute infectious disease of cattle, less often of sheep, caused by an organism of the genus *Clostridium.* It is characterized by inflammation of muscles with swelling and pain in the affected areas. Toxins formed by the organism produce severe muscle damage, and mortality is high. Animals between the ages of six months and two years are most commonly affected. Treatment with large doses of antibiotics is only partially successful; in endemic areas, young animals can be vaccinated for prevention.

black letter: see TYPE.

black light: see ULTRAVIOLET RADIATION.

black locust: see LOCUST.

black lung: see PNEUMOCONIOSIS.

blackmail, in law, exaction of money from another by THREAT of exposure of criminal action or of disreputable conduct. The term was originally used for the tribute levied until the 18th cent. upon the inhabitants of the Scottish border to provide immunity from raids by Scottish bands. Statutes often treat blackmail as a form of EXTORTION.

black market, term for the selling or buying of commodities at prices above the legal ceiling or beyond the amount allotted to a customer in countries that have placed restrictions on sales and prices. Such trading was common during World War II wherever the demand and the means of payment exceeded the available supply. Most of the warring countries attempted to equalize distribution of scarce commodities by rationing and price fixing. In the United States black-market transactions were carried on extensively in meat, sugar, tires, and gasoline. In Great Britain, where clothing and liquor were rationed, these were popular black-market commodities. In the United States, rationing terminated at the end of the war, but a black market in automobiles and building materials continued while the scarcity lasted. In the decades following World War II, as the countries of Eastern Europe were trying to industrialize their economies, extensive black-market operations developed because of a scarcity of consumer goods. During the prohibition era BOOTLEGGING was a black-market operation under a different name. Black marketing is also common in exchange of foreign for domestic currency, typically in those countries that have set the official exchange value of domestic currency too high in terms of the purchasing power of foreign money. Black-market money activities also grow when holders of domestic currency are anxious to convert it into foreign currency through a fear that the former is losing its purchasing power as a result of inflation. See Walter Rundell, *Black Market Money* (1964).

Blackmore, Sir Richard, c.1650–1729, English poet. He was physician to William III and to Queen Anne. Of Blackmore's copious writings, his best-known work is "The Creation" (1712), a poem meant to prove the existence of God. A mediocre poet, he was praised by Dr. Johnson and satirized by Pope in *The Dunciad.*

Blackmore, Richard Doddridge, 1825–1900, English novelist. Although trained as a lawyer and called to the bar, he abandoned his legal career because of ill health. His reputation rests chiefly on his romantic novel about the 17th-century outlaws of Exmoor, *Lorna Doone* (1869), but he wrote also 13 other novels—including *The Maid of Sker* (1872) and *Springhaven* (1887)—and several volumes of poetry. See biography by W. H. Dunn (1956, repr. 1974); study by K. G. Budd (1960).

Black Mountains: see APPALACHIAN MOUNTAINS; MITCHELL, MOUNT.

Blackmun, Harry Andrew, 1908–, Associate Justice of the U.S. Supreme Court (1970–), b. Nashville, Ill. Admitted to the bar in 1932, he practiced law until he became (1959) a Federal circuit court judge. He was appointed to the Supreme Court by President Richard M. Nixon. Widely praised for his scholarly and carefully drafted opinions, Blackmun tended toward a liberal view in civil rights cases, while remaining essentially conservative in other areas.

Blackmur, Richard P., 1904–65, American poet and critic, b. Springfield, Mass. Although he had no formal education after high school, he was a resident fellow (1940–48) and professor (1948–65) at Princeton. His volumes of literary essays include *The Double Agent* (1935), *Lion and the Honeycomb* (1955), and *Primer of Ignorance* (1967). He also wrote such volumes of poetry as *From Jordan's Delight* (1937) and *Second World* (1942).

Black Muslims, black nationalist religious movement in the United States, also called the Nation of Islam. It was founded (1930) in Detroit by Wali Farad (or W. D. Fard), whom his followers believed to be "Allah in person." When Farad disappeared mysteriously in 1934, Elijah MUHAMMAD assumed leadership of the group, first in Detroit and then in Chicago. Under his leadership the black separatist sect expanded, mainly among poor blacks and in prisons. Although the group numbered only about 8,000 when Muhammad took over, it grew rapidly in the 1950s and 60s particularly as a result of the preaching of one of its ministers, MALCOLM X. Tension between Muhammad and Malcolm developed, however, and Malcolm's subsequent suspension (1963) and assassination (1965), possibly by Muhammad's followers, caused great dissension in the movement, although this later abated. The Black Muslims are an extremely moralistic group and pray five times daily; they are forbidden to smoke, drink, gamble, or take narcotics. Shunning contact with whites as much as possible, they maintain a number of their own businesses, farms, stores, and schools. Black Muslims renounce their legal surnames (which they consider slave names) and adopt the letter X instead.

Black Panthers, U.S. black militant party, founded (1966) in Oakland, Calif., by Huey P. Newton and Bobby Seale. Originally espousing violent revolution as the only means of achieving black liberation, the Black Panthers called on all blacks to arm themselves for the liberation struggle. In the late 1960s party members became involved in a series of violent confrontations with the police (resulting in deaths on both sides) and in a series of court cases, some resulting from direct shoot-outs with the police and some from independent charges. Most notable among the trials were those of Huey Newton for killing a policeman in 1967 (three mistrials, the last in 1971); of Bobby Seale, as one of the "Chicago Seven" charged and convicted of conspiracy to violently disrupt the Democratic National Convention of 1968 (conviction later overturned), and as a codefendant in a Connecticut case charging murder of an alleged informer on the party (acquittal, 1971); and of 13 Panthers in New York City accused of conspiring to bomb public places (acquittal, 1971). The results of these trials were taken by many observers as confirmation of their suspicions that the Black Panthers were being subjected to extreme police harassment. Another incident that supported this view was the killing in a raid by Chicago police of Illinois party leader Fred Hampton and another Panther in 1969; review of this incident revealed that the two Panthers had been shot in their beds without any provocation. While controversy raged over the civil liberties issue, the Panthers themselves were riven with internal disputes. A major split took place, with Newton and Seale (who in 1972 announced their intention of abandoning violent methods) on the one side and Eldridge Cleaver (formerly the chief publicist for the party, who continued to preach violent revolution) on the other. Cleaver headed the so-called international headquarters of the party (until 1973) in Algeria.

Blackpool, county borough (1971 pop. 151,311), Lancashire, NW England, on the Irish Sea. One of England's most popular seaside resorts, Blackpool has 7 mi (11.3 km) of beaches and promenades, many sport and amusement facilities, and a tower 520 ft (158 m) high, modeled on the Eiffel Tower in Paris. Blackpool's manufactures include aircraft, biscuits, candy, and joinery. In 1974, Blackpool became part of the new nonmetropolitan county of Lancashire.

Black Prince: see EDWARD THE BLACK PRINCE.

black quarter: see BLACKLEG.

Black River. 1 River rising in SE Mo. and flowing c.300 mi (480 km) SE, then SW to the White River near Newport, Ark. It is partly navigable. Clearwater Dam is on the river near Piedmont, Mo. **2** River of N N.Y., c.120 mi (190 km) long, rising in the Adirondack Mts. and flowing mainly N and W to Black River Bay, an inlet of Lake Ontario. Its falls provide power for many factories, especially paper mills. **3** River, c.160 mi (260 km) long, rising in central Wis. and winding SW to the Mississippi River at La Crosse, Wis. It was important in the lumbering industry and is now used to transport coal and petroleum products. Big Manitou Falls, the highest falls in Wisconsin (165 ft/50 m), are in the river.

Black Sea, inland sea, c.159,600 sq mi (413,360 sq km), between Europe and Asia, connected with the Mediterranean Sea by the Bosporus, the Sea of Marmara, and the Dardanelles. It is c.750 mi (1,210 km) long, from 75 to 350 mi (120–560 km) wide, and has a maximum depth of 7,364 ft (2,245 m). The largest arm of the Black Sea is the Sea of Azov, which joins it through the Kerch Strait. The Black Sea is enclosed by the USSR on the north and east, by Turkey on the south, and by Bulgaria and Rumania on the west. The Black Sea was once part of a large body of water that included the Caspian and Aral seas. In the Tertiary period, it was separated from the Caspian Sea and was linked to the Mediterranean Sea. The Dnepr, Southern Bug, Dnestr, and Danube rivers are its principal feeders; the Don and Kuban rivers flow into the Sea of Azov. The rivers flowing into the northern part of the Black Sea carry much silt and form deltas, sandbars and lagoons along the generally low and sandy northern coast. The southern coast is steep and rocky. The Black Sea has two layers of water of different densities. The heavily saline bottom layer has little movement and contains hydrogen sulfide; it has no marine life. The top layer has low salinity and flows in a counterclockwise direction around the sea. It has many varieties of fish. There is little tidal action. The Black Sea is subject to severe winter storms, and waterspouts are common in summer. The Black Sea is an important navigation route and remains ice-free in winter. It is the chief sea outlet of the USSR; Odessa, Novorossiysk, and Sevastopol are the main Soviet ports. Other important ports are Constanța in Rumania; Varna and Burgas in Bulgaria; and Trabzon, Samsun and Zonguldak in Turkey. The Black Sea region, especially in the S Crimea and W Caucasus, is a popular resort area. The Pontus Euxinus [hospitable sea] of the ancients, the Black Sea has been navigated since prehistoric times. Its shores were colonized by the Greeks (8th–6th cent. B.C.) and later by the Romans (3d–1st cent. B.C.). Its importance increased with the founding of Constantinople (330 A.D.). In the 13th cent. the Genoese established their colonies on the Black Sea, and from the 15th to the 18th cent. it was a Turkish lake. The rise and expansion of Russia and its ambition to gain control of the Bosporus and the Dardanelles led it into protracted dispute with the Ottoman empire. In 1783, Russia annexed the Tatar Khanate of CRIMEA, which blocked its access to the sea, but suffered a setback as a Black Sea power as a result of the Treaty of Paris, which ended the Crimean War of 1856.

Black Shirts, colloquial term originally used to refer to the members of the *Fasci di combattimento,* units of the Fascist organization founded in Italy in March, 1919 by Benito MUSSOLINI. A black shirt was the most distinctive part of their uniform. The Black Shirts were mainly discontented ex-soldiers. Ultranationalist, they posed as champions of law and order and violently attacked Communists, socialists, and other radical and progressive groups. They broke up strikes, destroyed trade union headquarters, and drove socialist and Communist officials from office. In Oct., 1922, their activities culminated in the famous march on Rome, which brought Mussolini to power. Afterward, while the term "Black Shirts" continued to be used to refer to party militants in general, the name *Fasci di combattimento* designated the local party units.

black snake, name for several snakes, not all closely related, that are black in color. In the United States the name is applied chiefly to the black RACER and to the black rat snake (*Elaphe obsoleta*), both partly arboreal in their habits. The black rat snake, also called pilot black snake and mountain black snake, is found in the NE United States. Like other rat snakes, (*Elaphe* species), it is a constrictor and a valuable destroyer of rats and mice. It has shiny, slightly keeled scales and reaches a length of 8 ft (2.4 m). The poisonous Australian black snake belongs to the cobra family and has a hood. The North American black snakes are classified in the phylum CHORDATA, subphylum Vertebrata, class Reptilia, order Squamata, family Colubridae.

Blackstone, Sir William, 1723–80, English jurist. At first unsuccessful in legal practice, he turned to scholarship and teaching. He became (1758) the first Vinerian professor of law at Oxford, where he inaugurated courses in English law. British universities had previously confined themselves to the study of Roman law. Blackstone published his lectures as *Commentaries on the Laws of England* (4 vol., 1765–69), a work that reduced to order and lucidity the formless bulk of English law. It ranks with the achievements of Sir Edward Coke and Sir Matthew Hale, Blackstone's great predecessors. Blackstone's *Commentaries,* written in an urbane, dignified, and clear style, is regarded as the most thorough treatment of the whole of English law ever produced by one man. It demonstrated that English law as a system of justice was comparable to Roman law and the civil law of the Continent. Blackstone has been criticized, notably by Jeremy Bentham, for a complacent belief that, in the main, English law was beyond improvement and for his failure to analyze exactly the social and historical factors underlying legal systems. Blackstone's book exerted tremendous influence on the legal profession and on the teaching of law in England and in the United States. In his later life Blackstone resumed practice, served in Parliament, was solicitor general to the queen, and was a judge of the Court of Common Pleas. See *The Sovereignty of the Law,* selections from Blackstone's *Commentaries,* ed. and with an introd. by Gareth Jones (1973); biography by O. A. Lockmiller (1938); Jeremy Bentham, *A Comment on the Commentaries* (ed. by C. W. Everett, 1928); Paul Lucas, *Essays in the Margin of Blackstone's Commentaries* (1962).

Blackstone, river, c.50 mi (80 km) long, rising near Worcester, Mass., and flowing SE to Narragansett Bay at Providence, R.I. The river's clean water was a major factor in the early development of the area's textile industry.

black studies: see ETHNIC STUDIES.

blackthorn or **sloe,** low, spreading, thorny bush or small tree (*Prunus spinosa*) of the plum genus of the family Rosaceae (ROSE family), having black bark, white flowers, and deep blue fruits, usually rather acrid and not much larger than peas. Native to the Mediterranean area, the blackthorn is cultivated for hedges, its limbs are used in Ireland for canes and cudgels, and the juice of the berries is used in making brandy, sloe gin, and preserves and as a diluent of port. One of the hawthorns is sometimes called blackthorn. Blackthorn is classified in the division MAGNOLIOPHYTA, class Magnoliopsida, order Rosales, family Rosaceae.

Black Tom, part of Jersey City, N.J., also called Black Tom Island. In July, 1916, German saboteurs demolished U.S. munitions stores there; in Jan., 1917, they destroyed the Kingsland, N.J., munitions plant. Sued by the U.S. government in 1922 but vindicated in 1930 by an international claims commission, the German government, upon new hearings in 1939, was ultimately ordered to pay $50 million in damages.

Blacktown, city (1971 pop. 156,619), New South Wales, SE Australia. It is a suburb of Sydney.

Black Warrior, navigable river, 178 mi (286 km) long, rising in N central Ala. and flowing generally SW to the Tombigbee River. The Black Warrior drains a rich coal- and cotton-producing area and is an important outlet for the manufactured products of Birmingham, Ala.

Black Warrior, merchant steamer that plied between New York City and Mobile, usually stopping at Havana, Cuba. Her seizure on Feb. 28, 1854, by Spanish authorities at Havana and the imposition of a $6,000 fine on the grounds that she had violated customs regulations nearly caused war between the United States and Spain. The South, anxious to secure Cuba, was ready for war, but the North refused to support the idea, and after the *Black Warrior* was released the excitement subsided.

Black Watch or **Royal Highland Regiment,** Scottish infantry regiment. The first companies were raised in 1725 to watch the rebellious Scottish highlands and keep the peace, and the regiment was formed 1739–40. It became known as the Black Watch because of the dark colors of the regimental tartan. It was for a time the 43d, but since 1749 it has been the 42d regiment.

Blackwater, river, c.100 mi (161 km) long, rising in Co. Kerry, SW Republic of Ireland. It flows east through the dairy region of Co. Cork and Co. Waterford before turning abruptly south and entering the Atlantic Ocean at Youghal Bay. Salmon and trout are caught in the river.

Blackwell, Alice Stone, 1857–1950, American feminist, b. East Orange, N.J., grad. Boston Univ., 1881; daughter of Henry Brown Blackwell and Lucy Stone. She was an editor (1881–1917) of the *Woman's Jour-*

nal, first as assistant to her parents and after their death as editor in chief. Among her works are a biography of her mother (1930) and anthologies of poetry translated from several languages.

Blackwell, Antoinette Louisa (Brown), 1825–1921, American Unitarian minister, b. Henrietta, N.Y., grad. Oberlin College, 1847, and Oberlin Theological Seminary, 1850. One of the first women to receive a college education in the United States, she was ordained a Congregational minister in 1853, thus becoming the first ordained woman minister in the country. She later became a Unitarian. She was an active feminist, an abolitionist, and a temperance advocate. She was the sister-in-law of Henry B. Blackwell and Elizabeth Blackwell. Her books include *The Sexes throughout Nature* (1875) and *The Making of the Universe* (1914).

Blackwell, Elizabeth, 1821–1910, American physician, b. England; sister of Henry Brown Blackwell. She was the first woman in the United States to receive a medical degree, which was granted (1849) to her by Geneva Medical College (then part of Geneva College, early name of Hobart). With her sister, Emily Blackwell (1826–1910) who was also a doctor, and Marie Zackrzewska, she founded (1857) the New York Infirmary for Women and Children, which was expanded in 1868 to include a Women's College for the training of doctors, the first of its kind. In 1869, Dr. Blackwell settled in England, where she became (1875) professor of gynecology at the London School of Medicine for Women, which she had helped to establish. She wrote *Pioneer Work in Opening the Medical Profession to Women* (1895) and many other books and papers on health and education. See biographies by Ann McFerran (1966) and D. C. Wilson (1970).

Blackwell, Henry Brown, 1825–1909, American reformer, b. Bristol, England; brother of Elizabeth Blackwell. He was an abolitionist and later, with his wife, Lucy STONE, a worker for woman suffrage.

black whale, name for the black RIGHT WHALE and for the SPERM WHALE.

black widow, poisonous spider of the genus *Latrodectus,* found throughout North and South America and common in the SW United States. The name derives from the fact that the female, like those of many other spider species, may eat the male after mating. The adult is black with a red or reddish-orange hourglass-shaped marking on the lower abdominal surface. The female is somewhat less than ½ in. (1.3 cm) long, and the male is much smaller. The bite venom is a neurotoxin and may cause a severe reaction with intense local pain that spreads to other parts of the body. Occasional fatal cases, which result from respiratory paralysis, are usually limited to children. The most effective treatment is an antivenom. Black widow spiders are classified in the phylum ARTHROPODA, class Arachnida, order Araneae, family Theridiidae.

blackwood, name for several trees, especially an ACACIA.

bladder, urinary, muscular sac located in the pelvis that stores URINE and contracts to expel it from the body. Urine enters the bladder from the kidneys through the URETERS and is discharged from the body via the URETHRA. The bladder of the adult human can hold over a pint (0.6 liters) of urine. When the level of urine reaches about half this amount, pressure of the accumulating fluid stimulates nervous impulses that relax the external sphincter, a muscle that forms a dense band around the urethra at the base of the bladder. This muscle can be controlled voluntarily in most mammals. The muscles in the wall of the bladder also contract, forcing urine out through the urethra. The bladder is subject to infection (commonly called CYSTITIS) and the formation of stones. Its normal function may also be affected by nervous disorders or by external pressure, as from prostatic enlargement or pregnancy. See URINARY SYSTEM.

bladderwort, any plant of the genus *Utricularia,* insectivorous or carnivorous aquatic plants, many native to North America. Small animals are caught and digested in bladderlike organs of the finely divided submerged leaves. Bladderworts and similar related genera are an important element of aquatic and marsh flora on all continents. They are sometimes grown in aquariums as curiosities. Bladderworts are classified in the division MAGNOLIOPHYTA, class Magnoliopsida, order Scrophulariales, family Lentibulariaceae.

Bladensburg (blā'dənzbûrg), town (1970 pop. 7,488), Prince Georges co., S central Md., a residential suburb of Washington, D.C.; chartered 1742, inc. 1854. The defeat (Aug. 24, 1814) at Bladensburg of American troops under Gen. W. H. Winder permitted the British under Gen. Robert Ross to march on Washington, D.C., and burn many of the public buildings. The town was also the scene of a historic duel in which Stephen Decatur was mortally wounded (1820) by James Barron.

Blaeu, Willem Janszoon (vĭ'ləm yän'sōn blou), 1571–1638, Dutch cartographer and printer. He studied astronomy and instrument making under the Danish astronomer Tycho Brahe. The printing establishment he founded in Amsterdam was famed for its fine instruments, marine publications, globes and atlases, especially the great folio atlas compiled by Blaeu himself. He designed new presses incorporating important innovations and his shop had some claim to being the best of its time. The sons and grandsons of Blaeu continued his work.

Blagoveshchensk (bləgəvyĕsh'chĭnsk), city (1970 pop. 128,000), capital of Amur oblast, Far Eastern USSR, at the confluence of the Amur and Zeya rivers. A river port and railroad hub, Blagoveshchensk is also an agricultural center and a supply point for the Zeya gold-mining basin. Shipbuilding is carried on in the town. Russian pioneers settled Blagoveshchensk in 1644, but the area was returned to China in 1689. The city became a Russian army post in 1856.

Blagoyevgrad (blägô'yĕvgrät), city (1968 est. pop. 35,000), SW Bulgaria, is a farming region known especially for its tobacco. The city has one of the largest tobacco-fermentation factories in the Balkans. In Thracian times a settlement was established around the warm mineral springs that still attract visitors to Blagoyevgrad. The city is named for Dimiter Blagoev, founder of the Bulgarian Communist party.

Blaine, James Gillespie, 1830–93, American politician, b. West Brownsville, Pa. He taught school and studied law before moving (1854) to Maine, where he became an influential newspaper editor. A leader in the formation of the Republican party in Maine, Blaine was state chairman (1859–81) and was elected to three terms in the legislature. In 1863 he entered Congress, serving in the House of Representatives until 1876 and holding the speakership from 1869 to 1875. His friendship with James A. GARFIELD of Ohio and William B. Allison of Iowa brought him support in the West, but a slighting personal remark he made in 1866 about Roscoe CONKLING won him the lifelong enmity of that leader of the "Stalwart" Republicans. Blaine, leader of the "Half-Breed" Republicans, who were against the corrupt patronage practices of the "Stalwarts," was widely considered the logical Republican choice for President in 1876. Shortly before the party convention, however, a Democratic House investigating committee charged him with using his influence as speaker to secure a land grant for a railroad in Arkansas and with selling the railroad's bonds at a liberal commission. Blaine privately secured possession of the famous "Mulligan letters," which had been named as proof, before they could be placed on record, and he never surrendered them. He read portions of them, out of chronological order, before the House in an attempt to defend himself, but the episode was an important factor in his defeat for the presidential nomination at the 1876 Republican convention. Blaine, as U.S. Senator (1876–81), loyally supported President Rutherford B. Hayes. In 1880, Blaine was again a candidate for the presidential nomination, but the Conkling faction successfully prevented his nomination. The deadlock was broken by the choice of Blaine's friend, Garfield, with Chester A. Arthur, a Conkling man, nominated for Vice President. Blaine became Garfield's Secretary of State, but upon the President's assassination resigned. Retiring to private life, he wrote *Twenty Years of Congress* (2 vol., 1884–86). He was finally nominated for President in 1884 and ran against the Democratic candidate Grover CLEVELAND. Allusions to the "Mulligan letters" and to Cleveland's admitted paternity of an illegitimate child enlivened the bitter campaign. However, reform Republicans (MUGWUMPS) such as Carl SCHURZ preferred Cleveland's untainted public record to Blaine's private virtue. Their defection was made the more important when a tactless New York Presbyterian clergyman, the Rev. Samuel D. Buchard, spoke, in Blaine's presence, of the Democrats as "the party whose antecedents are rum, Romanism, and rebellion." Blaine's failure to disavow the remark offended the large Irish Catholic vote in New York; he lost that state by a scant thousand votes and thereby lost the election. In 1888, Blaine unexpectedly declined to run for President, supporting Benjamin Harrison, who, upon becoming President, made him Secretary of State again. Three days before the Republican convention of 1892, Blaine resigned to seek the nomination for President, but Harrison was renominated. Thereafter Blaine's health failed rapidly, and he died the next year. As Secretary of State, Blaine was particularly energetic in fostering closer relations with the Latin American nations. During his second term in office he was able to bring about and preside over the first Pan-American Congress (see PAN-AMERICANISM), thus laying the foundation for subsequent meetings, and the Pan American Union was established. Blaine hoped to increase commercial relations among American nations by reciprocal tariff treaties, and although the McKinley Tariff Act prevented this, his idea of tariff "reciprocity" gained some credence. He also concluded a treaty with Great Britain to submit the fur-seal controversy to arbitration (see under BERING SEA). See biographies by Edward Stanwood (1908) and D. S. Muzzey (1934, repr. 1963); A. F. Tyler, *The Foreign Policy of James G. Blaine* (1927, repr. 1965).

Blaine, city (1970 pop. 20,640), Anoka co., SE Minn., a suburb N of Minneapolis; settled 1862, inc. 1964. Construction is the major industry. The area was organized as a township in 1877 and was named in honor of James G. Blaine, then Senator from Maine.

Blair, Francis Preston, 1791–1876, American journalist and politician, b. Abingdon, Va. Through the Frankfort, Ky., journal *Argus of Western America,* which he edited with Amos KENDALL, Blair was an ardent supporter of Andrew Jackson. At William T. Barry's suggestion, he traveled to Washington and established the Washington (D.C.) *Globe* in Dec., 1830, which exerted great political influence as the Jacksonian "court journal" until 1841. Along with Kendall, Blair also was one of the leading members of the KITCHEN CABINET. In Washington he also founded the *Congressional Globe* (now the *Congressional Record*), in which the daily proceedings of Congress were recorded. When James K. Polk became President, Blair, a Van Buren Democrat, was forced to sell his interest in the Washington *Globe* to Thomas Ritchie. Later, because of his antislavery views, Blair was one of the founders of the Republican party, and he presided over its first national convention in 1856. In 1865 he engineered the futile HAMPTON ROADS PEACE CONFERENCE. An influential adviser to President Lincoln during the early years of the Civil War, he eventually returned to the Democratic party because he was opposed to radical Republicanism. See W. E. Smith, *The Francis Preston Blair Family in Politics* (1933); A. M. Schlesinger, Jr., *The Age of Jackson* (1945); B. J. Hendrick, *Lincoln's War Cabinet* (1946).

Blair, Francis Preston, 1821–75, American political leader and Union general in the Civil War, b. Lexington, Ky., son of Francis Preston Blair (1791–1876). A St. Louis lawyer, Blair led the Free-Soil party in Missouri in 1848, served as state legislator (1852–56), and as Congressman (1857–59; June, 1860; 1861–62). In Congress he attacked slavery as harmful to the interests of poor whites and became an energetic Lincoln supporter in 1860. Instrumental in keeping Missouri loyal to the Union by seizing, with Nathaniel LYON, secessionist Camp Jackson and the U.S. arsenal early in 1861, he was appointed major general of volunteers (Nov., 1862) and served in the Vicksburg, Chattanooga, and Atlanta campaigns. After the Civil War, Blair was denied political preferment by the radical Republicans and in 1868 ran for Vice President on the unsuccessful Democratic ticket with Horatio Seymour. He helped overthrow the radicals in Missouri in 1870 and was elected to the state legislature, which, in turn, sent him to the U.S. Senate (1871–73). See W. E. Smith, *The Francis Preston Blair Family in Politics* (1933); B. J. Hendrick, *Lincoln's War Cabinet* (1946).

Blair, James, 1656–1743, Church of England clergyman, missionary to colonial Virginia, and founder of the College of William and Mary, b. Scotland. At the request of the bishop of London, Blair traveled to Virginia in 1685 to revive and reform the church in the colony. He returned to England (1691) to petition for a college, which when chartered in 1693 was named William and Mary after the monarchs. Blair was made president for life. In 1694 he was appointed by the king to the Virginia council, of which he was a lifelong member (except for a brief period) and in 1740–41 president. With Henry Hartwell and Edward Chilton, Blair wrote *The Present State of Virginia and the College* (1727, ed. by H. D. Farish, 1940). See biography by Parke Rouse (1971).

Blair, Montgomery, 1813–83, U.S. Postmaster General (1861–64), b. Franklin co., Ky., son of Francis P. Blair (1791–1876). He resigned from the army in 1836 after serving against the Seminole Indians and settled in St. Louis as the legal and political protégé of Senator Thomas H. BENTON. A successful lawyer and mayor of St. Louis (1842-43), he moved to Washington, D.C., where he was the first U.S. solicitor in the Court of Claims and made many appearances before the U.S. Supreme Court, including one as counsel for Scott in the famous DRED SCOTT CASE. His antislavery views brought him to the Republican party, and he became Postmaster General in the Lincoln cabinet. To appease the radicals in the cabinet, the President forced his resignation before the election of 1864. Opposed to radical Republicanism, he returned to the Democratic party and was one of Samuel J. Tilden's counsel in the disputed election of 1876. See W. E. Smith, *The Francis Preston Blair Family in Politics* (1933); B. J. Hendrick, *Lincoln's War Cabinet* (1946).

Blair, Robert, 1699-1746, English poet and clergyman. His literary reputation rests solely on his didactic, blank-verse poem on death, *The Grave* (1743).

Blair Atholl (ăth'əl), parish, Perthshire, central Scotland, at the confluence of the Garry and the Tilt rivers. Blair Castle, begun c.1269, is the seat of the duke of Atholl and his Atholl Highlanders, Great Britain's only private army. The castle was an important fortress in Scotland's civil wars. In 1975, Blair Atholl became part of the Tayside region.

Blake, Edward, 1833-1912, Canadian Liberal party leader, b. Upper Canada (Ontario). A prominent constitutional lawyer, he was elected to the House of Commons in 1867. In 1871 he became prime minister of Ontario, and he later served as minister of justice (1875-77) in Alexander Mackenzie's government and as leader of the Liberal party (1880-87). After withdrawing from Canadian politics (1890), he sat in the British House of Commons (1892-1907) as an Irish nationalist. See biography by M. A. Banks (1957).

Blake, Nicholas: see DAY LEWIS, CECIL.

Blake, Robert, 1599-1657, English admiral. A merchant, he sat in the Short Parliament (1640) and joined the parliamentary side in the civil war. He defended Bristol, Lyme, and Taunton against royalist attacks (1643-45). Appointed a "general at sea" (1649), he embarked on a brilliant naval career in his middle age. In 1650 he pursued the royalist fleet under Prince Rupert to Portugal, where he intercepted a large Portuguese treasure fleet at the mouth of the Tagus River. He caught up with Rupert in the Mediterranean and virtually destroyed his fleet. In 1651 he captured the Scilly Islands from royalist privateers and helped to reduce Jersey. In the first of the DUTCH WARS he won several major victories against the Dutch and suffered one serious defeat. In 1655 he attacked and destroyed a Barbary pirate fleet at Porto Farino. In the winter of 1656-57 he blockaded the Spanish coast and sank the Spanish fleet at Santa Cruz. Made a member of the council of state in 1651, he helped to develop the effective Commonwealth navy. See Maurice Ashley, *Cromwell's Generals* (1954).

Blake, William, 1757-1827, English poet and artist, b. London. Although he exerted a great influence on English ROMANTICISM, Blake defies characterization by school, movement, or even period. At the same time, no poet has been more sensitive or responsive to the realities of the human condition and of his time. His father, a prosperous hosier, encouraged young Blake's artistic tastes and sent him to drawing school. At 14 he was apprenticed to James Basire, an engraver, with whom he stayed until 1778. After attending the Royal Academy, where he rebelled against the school's stifling atmosphere, he set up as an engraver. In 1782 he married Catherine Boucher, whom he taught to read and write and draw. She became his inseparable companion, assisting him in nearly all his work. Blake's life, except for three years at Felpham where he prepared illustrations for an edition of Cowper, was spent in London. *Poetical Sketches* (1783), his first book, was the only one published conventionally during his lifetime. He engraved and published all his other major poetry himself (the rest remained in manuscript), for which he originated a method of engraving text and illustration on the same plate. But like his artwork, his poetry enjoyed neither commercial nor critical success until long after his death. In *Songs of Innocence* (1789) and *Songs of Experience* (1794) the world is seen from a child's point of view, directly and simply but without sentimentality. In the first group, which includes such poems as "The Lamb," "Infant Joy," and "Laughing Songs," both the beauty and the pain of life are captured. The latter group, which includes "The Tyger," "Infant Sorrow," "The Sick Rose," and "London," reveal a consciousness of cruelty and injustice in the world, for which people, not fate, are responsible. As parables of adult life, the *Songs* are rich in meaning and implication. Blake's Prophetic Books combine, in poetry, vision, prophecy, and exhortation. They include *The Book of Thel* (1789), *The Marriage of Heaven and Hell* (c.1790), *The French Revolution* (1791), *America* (1793), *Europe* (1794), *The Book of Urizon* (1794), *The Book of Los* (1795), *Milton* (1804-8), and *Jerusalem* (1804-20). These comprise no less than a vision of the whole of human life, in which energy and imagination struggle with the forces of oppression both physical and mental. Blake exalted love and pure liberty, and abhorred the reductive, rationalist philosophy that served to justify the political and economic inequities attendant upon the Industrial Revolution. The Prophetic Books are founded in the real world, as are Blake's passions and anger, but they appear abstruse because they are ordered by a mythology devised by the poet, which draw from Swedenborg, Jacob Boehme, and other mystical sources. Despite this, and despite the fact that from childhood on Blake was a mystic who thought it quite natural to see and converse with angels and Old Testament prophets, he by no means forsook concrete reality for a mystical life of the spirit. On the contrary, reality, whose center was human life, was for Blake inseparable from imagination. The spiritual, indeed God himself, was an expression of the human. Blake's paintings and engravings, notably his illustrations of his own works, works by Milton, and of the Book of Job, are painstakingly realistic in their representation of human anatomy and other natural forms. But they are also radiantly imaginative, often depicting fanciful creatures in exacting detail. Nearly unknown during his life, Blake was generally dismissed as an eccentric or worse long thereafter. His following has gradually increased, and today he is widely appreciated. See his complete writings, ed. by Geoffrey Keynes (rev. ed. 1966); his letters, ed. by Geoffrey Keynes (2d ed. 1968); his notebook, ed. by D. V. Erdman (1973); biography by Mona Wilson, ed. by Geoffrey Keynes (3d ed. 1971); studies by K. J. Raine (2 vol., 1968), D. V. Erdman (2d ed. 1969), Geoffrey Keynes (2d ed. 1971), D. G. Gillham (1973), David Wagenknecht (1973), and A. K. Mellor (1974); Anthony Blunt, *The Art of William Blake* (1959); D. V. Erdman and J. E. Grant, ed., *Blake's Visionary Forms Dramatic* (1970).

Blakelock, Ralph Albert, 1847-1919, American landscape painter, b. New York City; son of a doctor. Educated for a medical career, he abandoned it for painting, in which he was largely self-taught. His life was one of hardship. At first his work was flatly rejected; later, those who purchased his paintings took gross advantage of him. Unable to support his family of ten, he went mad. Committed to an asylum in 1899, he was released in 1916, and did not paint again. By this time his paintings had been accorded recognition and brought great prices to dealers, but nothing to him. Blakelock's landscapes are painted in great detail with strong lights and silhouetted dark masses, expressing a melancholy and romantic temperament. The subjects, including landscapes with small Indian figures, are often drawn from his early journey to the West (1896). He is particularly noted for his moonlight effects. Among his well-known works are *Brook by Moonlight* (Toledo Mus. of Art); *Indian Encampment* and *Pipe Dance* (Metropolitan Mus.); and *Sunset* and *Moonrise* (National Gall. of Art, Washington, D.C.). Blakelock's work was among the most often forged of any American painter. See study by Lloyd Goodrich (1947).

Blakeslee, Albert Francis, 1874-1954, American botanist, b. Geneseo, New York. He received his Ph.D. at Harvard (1904) and was a member of the faculty until 1907. After several years as professor at Connecticut Agricultural College (now the Univ. of Connecticut), he joined the staff of the Carnegie Institution of Washington at Cold Spring Harbor, N.Y., and later served as its director (1936-41). In 1943 he became director of the Smith College Genetics Experiment Station. From his earliest research, the discovery of sexual reproduction in bread molds, his contributions to botany and genetics were of far-reaching significance. His study of the inheritance and geographical distribution of the jimson weed, *Datura,* has provided important information concerning chromosome behavior, genic balance, and species evolution. He introduced the use of the alkaloid colchicine to increase the number of chromosomes in the plant cell.

Blanc, Louis (lwē bläN), 1811-82, French socialist politician and journalist, b. Spain. In his noted *Organisation du travail* (1840, tr. *Organization of Work,* 1911), he outlined his ideal of a new social order based on the principle "From each according to his abilities, to each according to his needs." He advocated, as a first stage in the achievement of this goal, a system of social workshops (*ateliers sociaux*) controlled by workingmen with the support of the state. His attacks on the Louis Philippe government in *Histoire de dix ans* (5 vol., 1841-44, tr. *The History of Ten Years, 1830-1840,* 1844-45) stirred up agitation among the workers. As a member of the provisional government of 1848 he insisted on the establishment of the social workshops, but the plan was sabotaged under the leadership of Alexandre Thomas MARIE. Implicated in the subsequent insurrection of the workers, Blanc fled to England, where he remained until 1871. While in exile, he produced the 12-volume *Histoire de la Révolution française* (1847-64). After his return to France, he became (1871) a member of the national assembly and was later a leader of the left in the chamber of deputies. Blanc's ideas, representing a link between utopian and Marxist socialism, had great influence on the thought of later men, especially Ferdinand Lassalle and the German socialists. See biographies by Eduard Renard (1921) and L. A. Loubère (1961); D. C. McKay, *The National Workshops* (1933); Carl Landaur, *European Socialism* (1959).

Blanc, Mont: see MONT BLANC.

Blanchard, Jean Pierre (zhäN pyĕr bläNshär'), or **François Blanchard** (fräNswä'), 1753-1809, French balloonist. In 1785 he made with Dr. John Jeffries of Boston, Mass., the first crossing by air of the English Channel. His ascents at Philadelphia (1793) and New York City (1796) are thought to be the first in America.

Blanche of Castile (kăstēl'), 1185?-1252, queen of Louis VIII of France and regent during the minority (1226-34) of their son LOUIS IX. A forceful and capable ruler, she checked the coalitions of the great lords and frustrated the attempt (1230) of HENRY III of England to regain his father's lands in France. She remained a lifelong adviser to Louis IX, was again regent on his departure (1248) for the Holy Land, and was coregent with her son Alphonse from 1250 until her death.

Blanchot, Maurice (mōrēs' bläNshō'), 1907-, French novelist and literary critic. In his critical works, notably *L'Espace littéraire* (1955), Blanchot propounds the theory that literary compositions are organic entities separate from the external world. Such novels as *Thomas l'obscure* (1941; tr. 1973) and *Le Très-Haut* (1948) exemplify his theoretical ideas in their complex language and imaginary settings. Blanchot's later fiction has dispensed with plot, character, and other elements of representation.

Blanco, Antonio Guzmán: see GUZMÁN BLANCO.

Blanco Fombona, Rufino (ro͞ofē'nō bläng'kō fōmbō'nä), 1874-1944, Venezuelan poet, essayist, and novelist, one of the leaders of MODERNISMO. Active in Venezuelan political affairs, he was several times imprisoned. He lived in exile in France and Spain for a quarter of a century and contributed much toward spreading the knowledge of Spanish American literature abroad. A prolific writer, Blanco Fombona satirized politicians, the clergy, and Yankee imperialism. His poems, such as the collection *Cantos de la prisión y del destierro* [songs of prison and exile] (1911), are superior to his novels. The novels include *El hombre de hierro* [the man of iron] (1905) and *El hombre de oro* (1916, tr., *Man of Gold,* 1920). Blanco Fombona was most distinguished in the field of the essay. Well known are "La evolución política y social de Hispanomérica" (1911) and "El modernismo y los poetas modernistas" (1929).

Bland, Richard Parks, 1835-99, American statesman, b. near Hartford, Ky. He taught in rural schools in Kentucky and Missouri before he went to the gold fields of California in 1855. He was a prospector, miner, lawyer, and local official in mining towns of California, Colorado, and Nevada, and after 10 years he returned to Missouri and small-town law practice. In 1872 he was elected to the House of Representatives, where he served (except for 1895-97) until his death. A champion of Western interests and particularly of the free coinage of silver, he was the author of the original bill that, after major modifications by William B. Allison, became the Bland-Allison Act of 1878. Bland was not satisfied with this or the succeeding compromise, the SHERMAN SILVER PURCHASE ACT of 1890. He was a leader of the Western radicals who took over the Democratic national convention at Chicago in 1896, and was a leading candidate for the presidential nomination on the first three ballots. In the election he worked hard but futilely for the victory of William Jennings

Bryan. See W. V. Byars, *An American Commoner* (1900).

Bland-Allison Act, 1878, passed by the U.S. Congress to provide for freer coinage of silver. The original bill offered by Representative Richard P. Bland incorporated the demands of the Western radicals for free and unlimited coinage of silver. This was passed by the House but was unacceptable to the conservative Senate. Senator William B. Allison then offered an amended version. The act as adopted required the U.S. Treasury to purchase between $2 million and $4 million worth of silver bullion each month at market prices; this was to be coined into silver dollars, which were made legal tender for all debts. Attempts of the free-silver forces to replace the act with provision for unlimited coinage were defeated, as were attempts of the gold-standard forces to repeal it altogether. President Hayes and his successors weakened the act's effect by purchasing only the minimum amount of bullion. It remained law until replaced by the SHERMAN SILVER PURCHASE ACT of 1890.

Blankenburg (blăng'kənbo͝ork), **Blankenburg am Harz** (-äm härts), or **Bad Blankenburg** (bät'-), city (1970 pop. 10,628), Magdeburg district, W East Germany. It is a spa located at the northern foot of the Harz mts. and also has industries that manufacture woolens and paper. During his residence in Blankenburg (1837–45), the educator Friedrich Froebel founded the first kindergarten.

blanket, sheet, usually of heavy woolen, or partly woolen, cloth, for use as a shawl, bed covering, or horse covering. The blanketmaking of primitive people is one of the finest remaining examples of early domestic artwork. The blankets of Mysore, India, are famous for their fine, soft texture, so delicate that it is said their 18 ft (5.5 m) of length can be rolled inside a hollow bamboo rod. The loom of the American Indian, though simple in construction, can produce blankets so closely woven as to be waterproof. The Navaho, Zuñi, Hopi, and other Southwestern Indians are noted for their distinctive, firmly woven blankets. The Navahos were especially adept in producing beautifully designed blankets that were characterized by geometrical designs woven with yarns colored with vegetable dyes. During the mid-19th cent. the Navahos began to use yarns imported from Europe, because of their brighter colors. The ceremonial Chilcat blanket of the Tlingit Indians of the Northwest, generally woven with a warp of cedar bark and wool and a weft of goats' hair, was curved and fringed at the lower end. In the 20th cent., the electric blanket, with electric wiring between layers of fabric, gained wide popularity.

blanketflower: see GAILLARDIA.

blank verse: see PENTAMETER.

Blanqui, Jérôme Adolphe (zhärōm' ädôlf' bläNkē'), 1798–1854, French economist. Among his works are *Résumé de l'histoire du commerce et de l'industrie* (1826) and *Histoire de l'économie politique en Europe, depuis les anciens jusqu'à nos jours* (tr. 1880, repr. 1968).

Blanqui, Louis Auguste (lwē ôgüst'), 1805–81, French revolutionary and radical thinker. While a student in Paris, he joined (1824) a branch of the Carbonari, a revolutionary secret society; thenceforth he was prominent in every revolutionary upheaval in France until his death. More than half his life was spent in prison. In 1847 he set up the Central Republican Society, which was powerful in the February Revolution of 1848. An exile in Brussels (1865–70), Blanqui organized the extremist opposition against Napoleon III, in whose deposition (Sept. 4, 1870) he was instrumental. The crucial role played by Blanqui and his followers in the expulsion (Oct., 1870) of the moderate government of Paris led his opponents to compromise on a government headed by Adolphe Thiers, and shortly before the proclamation of the COMMUNE OF PARIS, Thiers had Blanqui arrested. The commune, whose temporary success was largely Blanqui's work, vainly offered its hostages in exchange for Blanqui. He was released in 1879 and was elected a deputy from Bordeaux, although the government did not allow him to serve. His followers, the Blanquists, were eventually absorbed into the unified socialist party. Advocating direct revolutionary action, Blanqui was among the first to conceive of the professional revolutionary. His social theories, stressing the class struggle and the dictatorship of the proletariat, profoundly influenced Karl Marx. See Blanqui's *Critique Sociale* (1885); R. W. Postgate, *Revolution from 1789–1906* (1920); studies by Neil Stewart (1939) and Alan Spitzer (1957, repr. 1970).

Blantyre (blăntī'ər), city (1971 est. pop. 169,000), S Malawi, in the Shire Highlands. It is the chief commercial and industrial center of Malawi with cement, food processing, and textile industries. Blantyre was founded in 1876 as a Church of Scotland mission station and was named for the birthplace of David Livingstone. In 1956, Blantyre was combined with Limbe to form one city.

Blarney, village, Co. Cork, SE Republic of Ireland. He who kisses the Blarney Stone, placed in an almost inaccessible position near the top of the thick stone wall of the 15th-century castle, is supposed to gain marvelous powers of persuasion. The castle was militarily important in the 17th-century wars of Oliver Cromwell and William III. Tweed is manufactured in the village.

Blasco Ibáñez, Vicente (vĕthän'tā blä'skō ēbä'nyāth) 1867–1928, Spanish novelist and politician, b. Valencia. Outspoken against the monarchy, Blasco Ibáñez published a radical republican journal, *El pueblo,* and was imprisoned 30 times for political activism. His novels are primarily realistic in conception. The early ones, set in Valencia, include *Flor de mayo* (1895, tr. *The Mayflower,* 1921), *La barraca* [the cabin] (1898), *Cañas y barro* (1902, tr. *Reeds and Mud,* 1928), and *La catedral* (1903, tr. *The Shadow of the Cathedral,* 1909). He traveled in South America, returning to Spain at the outbreak of World War I. He became a propagandist for the Allies, and his war novel, *Los cuatro jinetes del Apocalipsis* (1916, tr. *The Four Horsemen of the Apocalypse,* 1918), made him world famous. He died a voluntary political exile. See study by A. G. Day and E. C. Knowlton (1972).

Blashfield, Edwin Howland, 1848–1936, American mural painter and mosaic designer, b. New York City, studied with Bonnat in Paris. From the 1890s on he worked chiefly as a muralist, creating large works of a historical or allegorical nature, including *The Evolution of Civilization* (Library of Congress dome), decorations for the Wisconsin, Minnesota, and Iowa state capitols, and a large mosaic for the Church of St. Matthew, Washington, D.C. He also wrote *Mural Painting in America* (1913) and, with his wife, *Italian Cities* (1900, new ed. 1913).

Blasket Islands, group of rock islets, Co. Kerry, SW Republic of Ireland; a lighthouse is on one of the islets. Most of the inhabitants of the islands were moved to the mainland in 1953. Great Blasket, largest of the islands, was the stronghold of Piaras Ferriter, the last Irish chieftain to surrender to Oliver Cromwell.

blast cleaning: see SANDBLAST.

blast furnace, structure used chiefly in smelting, i.e., for the extraction of metals, mainly iron and copper, from their ores. The principle involved is that of the reduction of the ores by the action of carbon monoxide, i.e., the removal of oxygen from the metal oxide in order to obtain the metal. Blast furnaces differ in construction. The one used in the production of iron consists of a chimneylike structure (usually 80–100 ft/24–30 m high) made of iron or steel and lined with firebrick. It is narrow at the top, increasing in diameter downward, but narrowing again suddenly almost at the bottom, to form the hearth or crucible. There the fine molten products are caught. The furnace is fed from the top with a charge of definite quantities of ore, coke, and a flux, mostly limestone. Preheated compressed air is introduced at the bottom through pipes (tuyeres) entering just above the hearth. The air passes upward through the charge. The coke is oxidized to carbon dioxide, which changes to carbon monoxide at the high temperature. The carbon monoxide then reduces the ores and, taking on oxygen, reverts to carbon dioxide. This gas, together with unused carbon monoxide, nitrogen, and other constituents of the air originally introduced, is led off through a pipe from the top of the furnace and, being still at a high temperature, is employed to heat the stoves into which fresh air for the process is brought. As the operation proceeds, the mass in the furnace becomes molten and descends into the crucible. The iron sinks to the bottom; impurities, called the slag, being lighter, float on top. The slag is drained through a pipe in the upper portion of the crucible. The iron is tapped from below and run into sand molds to harden. The product is known as pig iron or cast iron (see IRON). Efforts to increase production rates have led to the addition of pure oxygen and steam and the sizing of ore to obtain better gas-solid contact. Flux and ore are sometimes combined into pellets. Pig iron prepared in the blast furnace is converted into steel by the BESSEMER PROCESS. Copper ore treated in a blast furnace yields a copper matte, from which only a part of the impurities are removed. It is usually further refined by electrolytic methods (see COPPER).

blasting, shattering, breaking, or splitting of rock or other material by the discharge of an EXPLOSIVE placed within or in contact with it. It is a necessary part of many engineering operations. An ancient method of breaking rock consisted of heating the rock by fire and then pouring water on it, the sudden contraction resulting in shattering or cleavage. Modern methods of blasting involve four operations: drilling the holes to receive the charge, placing it, stemming the hole (i.e., filling the hole above the charge with earth or clay), and igniting or detonating the charge. The location, size, and number of holes drilled depend upon local conditions and the nature of the work. The holes vary from 1 to 3 in. (2.5–7.6 cm) in diameter and from a few inches up to 20 ft (6.1 m) or more in depth. The charge is made up of some explosive, such as dynamite or ammonium nitrate; black powder, the oldest known explosive, is rarely used today. Multiple charges are sometimes set off, either simultaneously or in sequence.

blastomycosis: see FUNGUS INFECTION.

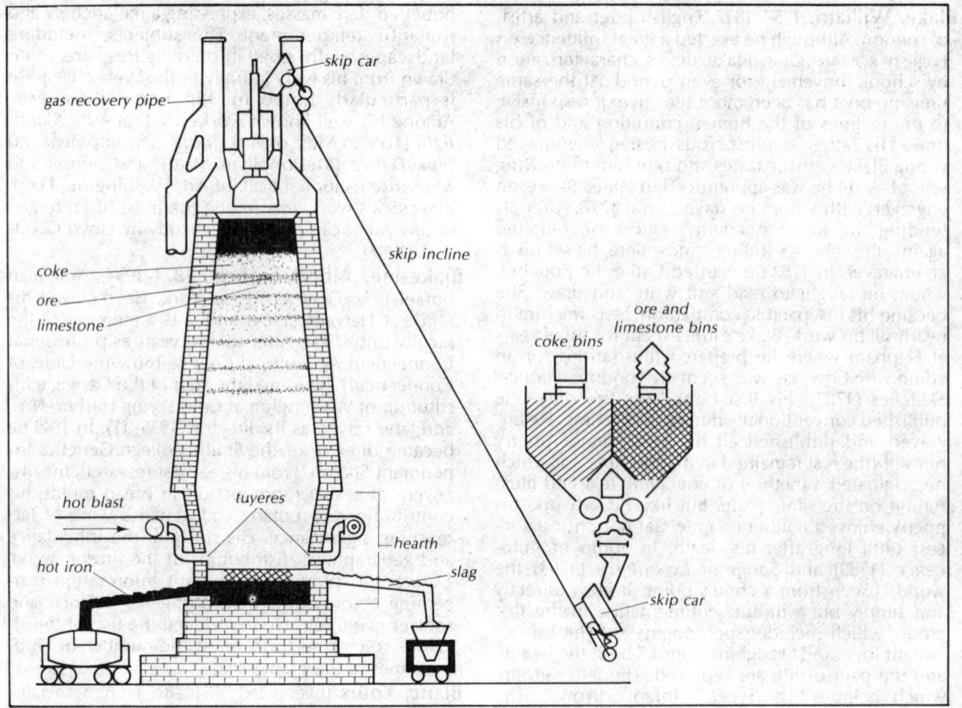

Blast furnace for production of iron

Blastus, Herod's chamberlain, mediator for the Tyrians and Sidonians. Acts 12.20.

Blau, Joseph Leon (blou), 1909–, American Jewish scholar and educator, b. Brooklyn, N.Y., grad. Columbia (A.B., 1931; M.A., 1933; Ph.D., 1945). He taught at Columbia from 1944, becoming professor of religion in 1962. Like his teacher Salo Wittmayer Baron, he stressed the effect of cross-cultural influences upon the development of Judaism in a number of works, among them *The Story of Jewish Philosophy* (1962), *The Jews of the United States, 1790–1840: A Documentary History* (ed. with S. W. Baron, 3 vol., 1963), and *Modern Varieties of Judaism* (1966). His *Christian Interpretation of the Cabala in the Renaissance* (1944) studied this process at work in the opposite direction. Also a student of John Dewey, Blau published a number of studies in American philosophy, among them *Men and Movements in American Philosophy* (1952).

Blaue Reiter, der (dĕr blou'ə rī'tər) (Ger.,=the blue rider), German expressionist art movement, lasting from 1911 to 1914. It took its name from a painting by Kandinsky, *Le cavalier bleu.* Following the BRÜCKE artists of the previous decade, this second wave of expressionism was led by Kandinsky, Klee, Marc, and Macke, in Munich. They sought to discover spiritual truths that they felt the impressionists had overlooked. Less united stylistically and as a group than the *Brücke,* their art ranged from the pure abstractions of Kandinsky to the romantic imagery of Marc. In 1911, Kandinsky and Marc prepared a significant collection of articles and illustrations published as the *Blaue Reiter* Album. Common to the artists in the group was a philosophical spirit, an intellectual approach to technique, and great lyrical spontaneity. The group disbanded at the outbreak of World War I. Marc and Macke were killed in battle. See study by H. K. Roethel (tr. 1972).

Blavatsky, Helena Petrovna (blətvăt'skē), 1831–91, Russian theosophist and occultist. She was the daughter of a German named Hahn who had settled in Russia and who was distantly connected with the Russian aristocracy. At the age of 16 she married an elderly man, Nicephore Blavatsky, whom she soon left. She traveled extensively in Asia, the United States, and Europe. An imposing and persuasive woman, she claimed to have spent seven years in Tibet, where she was supposedly initiated into mysteries of the occult. In 1873 she went to New York City, and in collaboration with prominent persons interested in spiritism she founded (1875) the Theosophical Society. The society soon experienced serious schisms, and in 1878 Madame Blavatsky, as she was known, left for India, where she established headquarters at Adyar near Madras. There she devoted herself, with some success, to theosophical organization and propaganda. She demonstrated many supernormal phenomena, which were accepted as miracles by her followers, but published claims of fraud in the 1880s and 90s seriously damaged her reputation. Her major works were *Isis Unveiled* (1877) and *The Secret Doctrine* (1888), which became the textbooks of her disciples. The day of her death (May 8) is celebrated by her followers as White Lotus Day. See bibliography under THEOSOPHY. See her memoirs (comp. by M. K. Neff, 2d ed. 1967); biography by John Symonds (1959, repr. 1960); a harshly critical work is G. M. Williams, *Priestess of the Occult* (1946).

Blaydon, urban district (1971 pop. 32,018), Durham, NE England, on the Tyne River. It manufactures iron and steel goods, bricks, and the by-products of coal from nearby mines. There are also engineering works. In 1974, Blaydon became part of the new metropolitan county of Tyne and Wear.

blazing star or **button snakeroot,** any plant of the genus *Liatris,* showy North American perennials of the family Compositae (COMPOSITE family). The blossoms, rosy purple or white, are in somewhat feathery heads along a usually wandlike stalk. Medicinal use has been made of a few species by both Indians and white men. Some are called gayfeather. Blazing star is classified in the division MAGNOLIOPHYTA, class Magnoliopsida, order Asterales, family Compositae.

blazonry (blā'zənrē), science of describing or depicting armorial bearings. The introduction, since the Middle Ages, of artificial rules and fanciful medieval terms has complicated the science, particularly in England. The chief part of blazonry is the description of the escutcheon, or shield, the essential part of the coat of arms. This involves the description of the color of the field on which devices are displayed. Arms are identified by their charges; the most common of these, the ordinaries, include lines of division, e.g., a cross, a chief (a band occupying the top third of the shield), a fess (a band across the shield in the middle), and a bend (a diagonal band). Other characteristic charges are heraldic animals or flowers, e.g., the lion, the fleur-de-lis, and the trefoil. The arms of younger sons should, in theory, show differences; thus a second son should display a crescent in his field. The bend sinister (a band from the upper right to the lower left of the shield) is not a difference and does not necessarily (as is popularly believed) indicate illegitimacy, which is usually blazoned by a wavy border around the shield. Blazonry also involves the description of the CREST above the shield and of the motto. The tinctures, or colors, used in blazonry are gold (or), white or silver (argent), red (gules), blue (azure), green (vert), purple, and black (sable). In England, blazonry is regulated by the HERALDS' COLLEGE. See also HERALDRY.

bleaching, process of whitening by chemicals or by exposure to sun and air, commonly applied to textiles, paper pulp, wheat flour, petroleum products, oils and fats, straw, hair, feathers, and wood. Chemical methods include oxidation, as by hypochlorites, ozone, and the per-compounds; reduction, as with sulphur dioxide; and adsorption, as by bone charcoal used to decolorize sugar solutions. Textiles have long been whitened by grass bleaching, a method virtually monopolized by the Dutch from the time of the Crusades to the 18th cent. They developed a technique in which goods were alternately soaked in alkaline solutions and grassed, or crofted, a procedure in which they are exposed to air and sunlight; the goods were then treated with sour milk to remove excess alkali. Later they substituted dilute sulfuric acid for the milk. In 1785 the French chemist Claude Berthollet suggested the commercial application of chlorine for bleaching, and in 1799 the Scottish chemist Charles Macintosh invented bleaching powder, or chloride of lime, the first of the modern chemical bleaches. Bleaching processes vary for different fibers. Cotton, naturally a grayish yellow, contains waxy and oily impurities that interfere with the action of dyes. It must be scoured and boiled in huge kettles (kiers) before bleaching. Grass bleaching has been combined with or superseded by chemical methods, which are deleterious unless rigidly controlled. Four degrees, ranging from quarter to full bleach, are recognized in the industry. Full bleach is reputed to weaken the fiber as much as 20 percent. Since chlorine bleaches react with the protein of animal fibers, silk and wool are commonly bleached with hydrogen peroxide. Although sulfurous acid or sulfur dioxide are also used for wool, they do not permanently whiten it. For effective bleaching, wool must first be scoured and silk must be degummed. Common bleaching agents used domestically are Javelle water, which is sodium hypochlorite in water, and other chlorine-based mixtures.

bleaching powder, white or nearly white powder that is usually a mixture of calcium chloride hypochlorite, $CaCl(OCl)$; calcium hypochlorite, $Ca(OCl)_2$; and calcium chloride, $CaCl_2$. Sometimes called chloride of lime, it can be prepared by reacting calcium hydroxide or slaked lime, $Ca(OH)_2$, with chlorine gas, Cl_2. It is used as a strong bleaching agent, as a disinfectant, and in making JAVELLE WATER. Bleaching powder was first produced in 1799 by Charles Tennant in Glasgow, Scotland.

Bled (blĕt), town, NW Yugoslavia, in Slovenia. Situated in the Julian Alps and on the small Lake of Bled, it is one of the most popular resorts in Yugoslavia. In the vicinity are a medieval castle, a former royal villa, and a church on an islet.

bleeding heart: see FUMITORY.

Bleimor: see CALLOC'H, JEAN PIERRE.

blende: see SPHALERITE.

Blenheim (blĕn'əm), Ger. *Blindheim,* village, Bavaria, S West Germany, on the Danube River. Between Blenheim and nearby Höchstädt, John Churchill, 1st duke of Marlborough, and Prince Eugene of Savoy defeated (Aug. 13, 1704) the French and Bavarians under marshals C. Tallard and F. Marsin in one of the most important battles of the War of the Spanish Succession. In gratitude for this and other military successes by the duke of Marlborough the English Parliament had an immense mansion, Blenheim palace, constructed near Woodstock, Oxfordshire, central England.

Blenheim, battle of, major engagement of the War of the Spanish Succession (see SPANISH SUCCESSION, WAR OF THE), fought on Aug. 13, 1704, at the village of Blenheim, near Höchstädt, Bavaria. Responding to appeals from Vienna, which was threatened by French and Bavarian forces, the English commander, John Churchill, duke of Marlborough, marched his army from the Netherlands to Bavaria and joined forces with the Austrian general, Prince Eugene of Savoy. At Blenheim their combined army overwhelmed a Franco-Bavarian force under Marshall Tallard and the elector of Bavaria. For the first time in two generations the French suffered a crushing defeat, and the results were immediate and far-reaching. Bavaria was conquered and Vienna saved. The territorial ambitions of Louis XIV beyond the Rhine were checked, and France was placed on the defensive.

Blenheim Park, estate, Oxfordshire, central England, near Woodstock. The stately palace was designed by Sir John VANBRUGH and stands on spacious grounds. Seat of the dukes of Marlborough, the palace was the gift of Queen Anne to the first duke in honor of his victories in the War of the Spanish Succession. Its construction lasted from 1705 to 1724.

Blennerhassett, Harman, 1765–1831, Anglo-Irish pioneer in America, an associate of Aaron Burr. Wealthy and gifted, he fell in love with and married his beautiful niece, Margaret Agnew. The couple was ostracized, and in 1796 Blennerhassett sold his estates and emigrated to the United States, where he bought (1798) part of what came to be called Blennerhassett Island. There he lived as a gentleman scholar interested in experiments in physics until Aaron BURR won (1805) his interest in Burr's plan of Western colonization. Blennerhassett advanced money to Burr. When President Jefferson proclaimed Burr's intentions traitorous, the local militia was mustered. Blennerhassett fled (Dec., 1806) down the river and was taken into custody. He was released after the government failed to convict Burr, but his fortunes were ruined. After a disastrous failure to recoup his losses on a Mississippi plantation, he attempted to practice law in Montreal, returned to England in 1822, and died on the island of Guernsey.

Blennerhassett Island, in the Ohio River, near Parkersburg, W.Va. On it Harman Blennerhassett built a mansion and a laboratory for his study. The island was ransacked by the local militia when Aaron Burr's schemes, with which Blennerhassett was connected, were declared traitorous by President Thomas Jefferson. See N. F. Schneider, *Blennerhassett Island and the Burr Conspiracy* (1938).

blenny, common name of various species of extremely numerous small fishes belonging to the families Blenniidae (combtooth blennies) and Notothеniidae (Antarctic blennies). They are characterized by elongated, tapering bodies and a continuous long dorsal fin. Blennies live among eelgrass in shallow brackish or fresh water and feed on small invertebrates. Some blennies have scales and some do not; certain species have fleshy filaments on the head. Tropical Atlantic species include the striped blenny (found as far north as New York) and the more southerly freckled blenny. The kelpfishes are a closely allied Pacific family. Those that live in kelp beds are mottled in coloration and those found in eelgrass are silver and green, matching their environment. The closely related wolffishes of the family Anarhichadidae, with large, tusklike teeth, are found in arctic Atlantic waters. They average 3 ft (90 cm) in length and are good food fishes, sold commercially as "ocean catfish". Blennies are classified in the phylum CHORDATA, subphylum Vertebrata, class Osteichthyes, order Perciformes, families Blenniidae and Nototheniidae.

Blériot, Louis (lwē blārēō'), 1872–1936, French aviator and inventor. He devoted the fortune acquired by his invention of an automobile searchlight to the invention and construction of monoplanes. After making several short-distance records, he was the first to cross (July 25, 1909) the English Channel in a heavier-than-air machine.

blesbok: see DAMALISK.

Blessington, Marguerite, countess of, 1789–1849, English author and famous beauty, b. Ireland. At the age of 14 she was forced by her father into marriage with Capt. Maurice St. Leger Farmer, a sadist who abused her. She soon left him and after his death married (1818) the earl of Blessington. In 1822 she began a liaison with Count D'Orsay (husband of her stepdaughter), and with him, after Blessington's death, set up a brilliant salon at Gore House, Kensington. To meet expenses she wrote a number of popular novels. Her most successful work, however, is her graphic journal of her *Conversations with Lord Byron* (1834). See biography by Michael Sadleir (rev. ed. 1947).

Blest Gana, Alberto (älbār'tō blĕst gä'nä), 1830–1920, Chilean novelist. He is considered the principal 19th-century Spanish American realist. Although as a diplomat he spent much of his life abroad, his novels, both social and historical, depict Chilean scenes. In both *Aritmética en el amor* (1860) and *Martín Rivas* (1862, tr. 1918), his masterpiece, he attacked the mores of the aristocracy and the upper middle class. His novel *Durante la reconquista* (1897) concerns the Chilean revolt against Spain.

Bleuler, Paul Eugen (poul oi'gən bloi' lər), 1857–1939, Swiss psychiatrist and neurologist. He served (1898–1927) as professor at the Univ. of Zürich. In 1911 he made an important contribution to the study of dementia praecox by introducing the term *schizophrenia*. He concluded that the disease was not one of dementia, a condition of diminished mentality, but a disharmonious state of mind in which contradictory tendencies exist together, splitting the harmony of the mind. He postulated a dichotomy of primary and secondary symptoms, the former caused by morbid somatic processes and the latter by psychogenic factors. See his *Dementia Praecox* (1911, tr. 1950).

Blida (blē'dä), town (1966 pop. 99,238), N Algeria, at the foot of the Atlas Mts. It is an administrative center and an agricultural trading town. Blida is surrounded by gardens and by orange, olive, and almond tree plantations. The city is noted for its fruit and flower essences. Built on the site of a Roman military base, Blida was founded in 1553 by Andalusians, who developed irrigation works and orange cultivation. Most of the old town was destroyed by earthquakes in 1825 and 1867.

Bligh, William (blī), 1754–1817, British admiral. He is chiefly remembered for the mutiny (1789) on his ship, the BOUNTY, but he had a long and notable career. He was sailing master on Capt. James Cook's last voyage (1776–79). Later he was a commander in the French wars, then (1805–8) governor of New South Wales, where he was briefly imprisoned (1808) by army mutineers in the so-called Rum Rebellion. Bligh was made a rear admiral in 1811 and a vice admiral in 1814. A brave and able officer, he was handicapped in dealing with men by his difficult temper. See biographies by Geoffrey Rawson (1930) and George Mackaness (rev. ed. 1951); H. V. Evatt, *The Rum Rebellion* (1938).

blight, general term for any sudden and severe plant disease or for the agent that causes it. Blights are characterized by withering and resultant death, without rotting, of the plant or its parts. The term is now applied chiefly to diseases caused by bacteria (e.g., bean blights and fire blight of fruit trees), viruses (e.g., soybean bud blight), and fungi (e.g., potato blights and chestnut blight). Other plant afflictions (caused by insects or unfavorable climatic conditions) that display similar symptoms are also called blights. See DISEASES OF PLANTS.

blimp: see AIRSHIP.

Blind, Karl (blĭnt), 1826–1907, German revolutionary and German-English writer. Arrested for his part in the German uprisings of 1848–49, he was later freed and from 1852 lived in England. There he became a distinguished writer on politics, history, literature, and especially German folklore and ethnology. He was the stepfather of the poet Mathilde Blind.

blindfish: see CAVE FISH.

Blind Harry or **Henry the Minstrel,** fl. late 15th cent., supposed Scottish poet. He is considered the author of the patriotic epic, *The Wallace,* which celebrates the life of Sir William Wallace. Violently anti-English, the poem was popular in Scotland down to the 18th cent. Since the skillful literary technique of *The Wallace* makes its composition by the traditionally blind and humble Harry unlikely, it is felt that the poem owes much to another hand. See edition by W. A. Craigie (1940).

blindness, partial or complete loss of sight. Blindness may be caused by injury, by lesions of the brain or optic nerve, by disease of the cornea or retina, by pathological changes originating in systemic disorders (e.g., DIABETES) and by CATARACT, GLAUCOMA, or retinal detachment. Blindness caused by infectious diseases, such as TRACHOMA, and by dietary deficiencies is common in underdeveloped countries where medical care is inadequate. Most infectious diseases of the eye can be prevented or cured. Blindness may also be congenital. A major cause of congenital blindness in the United States, ophthalmia neonatorum (caused by gonorrhea organisms in the maternal birth canal), is now prevented by placing silver nitrate solution in all newborn infants' eyes. COLOR BLINDNESS is an inability to distinguish colors, most commonly red and green. Snow blindness is a temporary condition resulting from a burn of the cornea caused by the reflection of sunlight on snow. Night blindness results from a deficiency of vitamin A. See EYE.

Blind River, town (1971 pop. 3,450), S Ont., Canada, on North Channel of Lake Huron. It is the center of the Algoma uranium fields. Just to the east of the town is Ontario's first uranium mine (1955).

blink microscope, in astronomy, device for determining a change in position or magnitude (brightness) of a star relative to other stars in the background. Two photographs of the same field or area of the sky are projected so that they precisely coincide. The combined image is viewed through a magnifying eyepiece while light from first one photograph and then the other is interrupted mechanically. A change in position or magnitude of a star can usually be detected since the star will seem to flicker or jump to and fro while the background stars remain steady in both position and brightness.

Bliss, Sir Arthur, 1891–, English composer. Bliss's teachers included Charles Stanford, Ralph Vaughan Williams, and Gustav Holst. He was made Master of the Queen's Musick in 1953. His early works, including pieces for wordless voices, were considered avant-garde. Bliss's works include ballets, cantatas, operas such as *The Olympians* (1949) and *Tobias and the Angel* (1958), the Colour Symphony (1932), a piano concerto (1938), quintets for oboe (1927) and clarinet (1931) with strings, and a concertina for cello and orchestra (1969). His autobiography was published in 1970.

Bliss, Daniel, 1823–1916, American missionary, b. Franklin co., Vt., founder of Syrian Protestant College (now the American Univ. of Beirut) in Lebanon. He went to Syria in 1855, returning in 1862 to secure funds and a charter for the college, which was opened in 1866; he was its president until 1902. See his *Reminiscences* (ed. by his son, 1920). His son, **Howard Sweetser Bliss,** 1860–1920, b. Syria, grad. Amherst, 1882, and Union Theological Seminary, 1887, succeeded him as president and enlarged and liberalized the college.

Bliss, Howard Sweetser: see BLISS, DANIEL.

Bliss, Philip Paul, 1838–76, American evangelist and writer of gospel songs, b. Clearfield co., Pa. A fine baritone voice and a handsome presence aided him in his work, and his songs became tremendously popular. After the publication of his *Gospel Songs* (1874) he became associated with Dwight L. Moody and joined Ira D. Sankey in producing a series of songbooks called *Gospel Hymns,* the first of which appeared in 1875. Among his songs are "Hold the Fort," "Let the Lower Lights Be Burning," and "Jesus Loves Me."

Bliss, Tasker Howard, 1853–1930, American army officer and statesman, b. Lewisburg, Pa., grad. West Point, 1875. He was (1898) chief of staff to Gen. James H. Wilson in the Puerto Rico campaign of the Spanish-American War, served (1898–1902) as collector of customs in Cuba, and in 1902 negotiated the treaty of reciprocity between Cuba and the United States. Several important administration appointments followed in the United States and in the Philippines, and he was appointed (1917) chief of staff of the U.S. army. He helped work out the mobilization plans followed by the United States in World War I. President Wilson promoted (1917) him to the rank of general and appointed him to the Allied Supreme War Council. As a delegate at the Paris Peace Conference, Bliss urged the admission of Germany and the USSR to the League of Nations and advocated postwar disarmament. See biography by Frederick Palmer (1934); study by D. F. Trask (1966).

blister, puffy swelling of the outer skin (epidermis) caused by burn, friction, or irritants like poison ivy. A response of the body to protect deeper tissue, blisters generally contain serum, the liquid component of blood. The so-called blood blister, however, forms over ruptured capillaries and therefore contains whole blood.

blister beetle, common name for certain soft-bodied, usually black or brown, mostly elongate and cylindrical beetles belonging to the family Meloidae. Blister beetles are common insects found feeding on the flowers and foliage of various plants. Occasionally some, e.g., POTATO BEETLES, become serious defoliating pests of potatoes, tomatoes, beets, asters, and other crops and flowers. The larvae are predacious or parasitic, feeding on the eggs of grasshoppers and of bees. Blister beetles undergo hypermetamorphosis, a complex life cycle with several different larval forms. The first of the six larval stages, called a triungulin, is a minute, active, and long-legged form that seeks out the host's nest; the following stages are grublike. Adults emerge in midsummer. One group of blister beetles has body fluids that contain cantharadin, a substance that can cause the skin to blister, from which the family gets its name. The Spanish fly (*Lytta vesicatoria*), a bright green or bluish blister beetle, is a common S European species from which cantharides are extracted and commercially prepared by crushing the wing covers (elytra) of the adults. This quite poisonous chemical is used medicinally as a skin irritant (in plasters), a diuretic, and an aphrodisiac. The lethal dosage for man is about .03 grams. Another group of meloid beetles has no cantharadin and is sometimes called the oil beetles because of the oily substance they secrete as protection against predators. Blister and oil beetles may be brushed into pans of kerosine or killed with systemic poisons or contact insecticides (except arsenic compounds). Blister beetles are classified in the phylum ARTHROPODA, class Insecta, order Coleoptera, family Meloidae.

blister gas: see POISON GAS.

blister rust: see RUST.

Blixen, Karen: see DINESEN, ISAK.

blizzard, winter storm characterized by high winds, low temperatures, and driving snow; according to the official definition given in 1958 by the U.S. Weather Bureau, the winds must be 35 mi (56 km) per hr or more and the temperature 20°F (−7°C) or lower. Blizzards are most common in the N Great Plains states—South Dakota is sometimes called "the Blizzard State"—but they also occur as far south as Texas and as far east as Maine.

bloat, excessive accumulation of gases in the rumen, the first stomach of a cud-chewing animal. Bloat is probably formed to a large extent by bacterial action. It occurs in all ruminants, but is most common in cattle; it appears typically in animals that graze on newly developed, highly productive, lush green pastures, especially during a wet summer on clover-dominant pastures. Bloat can result from excess frothiness of the ruminal ingesta or loss of tone and motility of the rumen. Both of these conditions will prevent the normal eructation process. Treatment consists of passing a tube to the stomach or of reducing the foam formation by oral administration of mineral or vegetable oils. Prevention is attempted by carefully controlled management practices, administration of antibiotics, and the use of nontoxic oils.

bloc, parliamentary [Fr.,=block], group of legislators formed to support special interests. A bloc may form because of a specific issue and dissolve when that issue has been resolved, or it may have a more permanent character, based on a more general interest. It is usually more tightly knit and aggressive than a coalition. The bloc has been a common device in legislatures made up of many parties, where it has tended to create two loose groups of "left" and "right." In nominally bipartisan legislatures, such as those of the United States, blocs are smaller groups and are usually organized to promote a specific economic or social interest or policy as, for example, the farm bloc. Recent years have seen the emergence of bloc voting by groups of states in the General Assembly of the United Nations.

Bloch, Ernest (blŏk), 1880–1959, Swiss-American composer. Among his teachers were Jaques-Dalcroze and Ysaÿe. He taught at the Geneva Conservatory, 1911–15, and at the Mannes School, New York, 1917–19; he was director of the Cleveland Institute of Music, 1920–25, and of the San Francisco Conservatory, 1925–30. His music is based in the classical tradition, but it has a peculiarly personal intensity of expression and often a distinct Hebraic quality, as in the Hebrew rhapsody *Schelomo* and the symphonic poem *Israel* (both 1916). Other outstanding works are an opera, *Macbeth* (1909); a concerto grosso, for string orchestra and piano (1925); the symphonic poems *America* (1926) and *Helvetia* (1929); a modern setting of the Jewish *Sacred Service* (1933); and *A Voice in the Wilderness,* for cello and orchestra (1937).

Bloch, Konrad E., 1912–, American biochemist, b. Neisse, Germany. He was educated at Munich and at Columbia (Ph.D., 1938). He taught at Columbia and at the Univ. of Chicago before going to Harvard in 1954. He became a U.S. citizen in 1944. He shared the 1964 Nobel Prize in Physiology and Medicine with Feodor Lynen for discoveries concerning the mechanism and regulation of cholesterol and fatty-acid metabolism.

Bloch, Marc (blôk), 1886–1944, French historian and an authority on medieval feudalism. He taught at the Univ. of Strasbourg from 1919, became professor at the Sorbonne in 1936, and was cofounder of the journal *Annales.* Bloch did much to promote the study of economic history. As a Jew, he was subject to German restrictions during World War II. He joined the French Resistance in Lyon in 1942, helping to publish the newspaper *Franc-Tireur,* a name adopted by the Resistance forces in the region. His activities led to his execution by the Germans in 1944. His *Strange Defeat* (tr. 1949) describes wartime France. Among Bloch's major works are *The Historian's Craft* (tr. 1953) and *French Rural History* (tr. 1966). His *Feudal Society* (tr. 1961) is a brilliant modern synthesis of the subject. In it Bloch stressed feudalism's rise from a mixed society and concluded that German elements reinforced feudal tendencies already present in the late Roman Empire. He described the feudal system as primarily a system of human relationships.

Block, Adriaen, fl. 1610-24, Dutch navigator. Eager to establish an Indian fur trade, Amsterdam merchants sent (1613) Block and another Dutch navigator to explore the region discovered by Henry Hudson. After wintering near Albany, Block sailed from the Hudson into Long Island Sound (1614), which he may have been the first European to enter, coming in through the East River passage that he named Hellegat (Hell Gate). He discovered the Connecticut River, sailed past and named Block Island, and explored Narragansett Bay. Block made the Figurative Map of 1614, showing details of the southern coast of New England and showing (the first to do so) Long Island and Manhattan as separate.

Block, Herbert Lawrence (Herblock), 1909-, American editorial cartoonist, b. Chicago. Herblock began drawing cartoons (1929-33) for the Chicago *Daily News,* later moving to the Newspaper Enterprise Association (1933-43) and to the Washington *Post* (1946-). His work has been syndicated widely and was awarded the Pulitzer Prize in 1942 and 1954. Collections of his cartoons include *The Herblock Book* (1952), *Herblock's Here and Now* (1955), *Straight Herblock* (1964), *Herblock's State of the Union* (1972), and *Herblock's Special Report* (1974).

blockade, use of naval forces to cut off maritime communication and supply. Blockades may be used to prevent shipping from reaching enemy ports, or they may serve purposes of coercion. The term is rarely applied to land sieges. During the Napoleonic wars, both France and Great Britain attempted to control neutral commerce through blockades and embargoes which neither could enforce with sufficient rigor. The Declaration of Paris (see PARIS, DECLARATION OF) proclaimed (1856) that blockades were henceforth to be announced to all affected parties and would be legal only if effectively enforced against all neutrals. In both World Wars blockades were made more effective by the employment, in addition to naval vessels, of mines and aircraft. North Vietnamese ports were mined and blockaded by the United States during later stages of the Vietnam War. Blockades have also occasionally been employed in times of peace as threats to implement diplomacy, as in the blockade of Cuba by the United States in 1962.

block and tackle: see PULLEY.

block book. Before and after the invention of printing from movable types in the mid-15th cent., some books were printed in Europe from engraved wooden blocks, with one block for each page. This method was developed by the 9th cent. A.D. in China. The practice has a richer history in the Orient than in the Occident since the number of characters used in Chinese writing made printing from movable type exceedingly difficult. Chinese and Japanese illustrated block books are often beautifully printed in colors. European block books, on the contrary, were crude and inexpensive. They were, however, the first examples of printed book illustration in the West. The best-known block book is the *Biblia pauperum* [poor man's Bible].

blockhouse, small FORTIFICATION, usually temporary, serving as a post for a small garrison. Blockhouses seem to have come into use in the 15th cent. to prevent access to a strategically important objective such as a bridge, a ford, or a pass. Later the term was broadened to include all detached and isolated small forts, especially those in country just captured from an enemy. The typical blockhouse was of two stories, with an overhanging second story and loopholes on all sides for gunfire. In the North American colonies, blockhouses were used in frontier communities as protection against Indian attacks; they were built of timber or stone (in New England) or of logs banked with earth (in the South and West). The frontier blockhouses were frequently surrounded by palisades and thus were technically stockaded forts. The principal use of blockhouses in present-day military fortification is in defending isolated units against small-arms fire. See PILLBOX.

Block Island, 7 mi (11.2 km) long and 3.5 mi (5.6 km) wide, off S R.I. at the eastern entrance to Long Island Sound. Visited by the Dutch navigator Adriaen Block in 1614, it was settled in 1661. The murder (1637) there of John Oldham, an English trader, was the direct cause of the Pequot War (see PEQUOT INDIANS). Characterized by numerous small ponds, low hills, and a mild climate, the island has long been a favorite fishing and resort area. Possessing two harbors, it accommodates both local fishing boats and summer pleasure craft. There are two lighthouses. The town of New Shoreham (1970 pop. 489; inc. 1672) is coextensive with the island.

block printing: see textile printing under TEXTILES.

block-signal system: see SIGNALING.

Blodgett, Katharine Burr, 1898-, American physicist and chemist, b. Schenectady, N.Y., B.A. Bryn Mawr, 1917, Ph.D. Cambridge, 1926. In 1918 she became research physicist for the General Electric Company, where she worked with Irving Langmuir on tungsten filaments and later on monomolecular layers. Further research produced the method of preparing nonreflecting glass and of measuring the thickness of monomolecular films within one microinch.

Bloemfontein (blo͝om'fŏntăn"), city (1970 pop. 148,282), capital of the Orange Free State and the judicial center of the Republic of South Africa. It is a transportation hub and industrial center, containing railroad workshops, food-processing plants, and factories that produce furniture, plastics, and glassware. Bloemfontein was founded in 1846 and served as the capital of the ORANGE FREE STATE Republic until its capture (1900) by British forces during the South African War. Afterward, it was the site of the final negotiations (1909) that led to the establishment (1910) of the Union of South Africa. Among the city's educational institutions are the Univ. of the Orange Free State (founded 1855; university status 1950) and a technical college.

Blois (blwä), town (1968 pop. 44,762), capital of Loir-et-Cher dept., central France, in Orléanais, on the Loire River. A commercial and industrial center with an outstanding trade in wines and brandies, it is also one of the most historic towns of France. The counts of Blois emerged in the 10th cent. as the most powerful feudal lords of France. Their line began with Thibaut the Cheat, who by various means acquired Touraine and Chartres; his successors added (11th-12th cent.) Champagne, Brie, and other lands, although in the west they were checked by the counts of Anjou. The last count of Blois, childless and heavily in debt, sold his fief to Louis, duc d'Orléans, who took possession in 1397. With the accession (1498) of Louis' grandson, Louis XII, as king of France, the countship passed to the crown as part of Orléanais. The town was a favorite royal residence. Louis XII was born in the Renaissance château there. Several States-General of France were held in the château, notably in 1576-77 and in 1588; Henri, duc de Guise, was assassinated there in 1588. The Treaties of Blois, signed in 1504-5, were a temporary settlement of the Italian Wars.

Blok, Aleksandr Aleksandrovich (əlyĭksän'dər əlyĭksän'drəvĭch blôk), 1880-1921, Russian poet, considered the greatest of the Russian SYMBOLISTS. As the leading disciple of Vladimir Soloviev, he voiced both mysticism and idealistic passion in an early cycle of love poems, *Verses about the Lady Beautiful* (1904). In 1905 he turned to themes of despair, degradation, and the attraction of evil. *The Unknown Woman* (1906) is his best-known poem of this period. Later he found hope in the idealization of Russia, welcoming the Revolution of 1917 in his epic poem *The Twelve* (1918, tr. 1920). This work celebrates the passion, violence, and exhilaration of the revolution, with which Blok later became disenchanted. *The Scythians* (1920) is directed against the Western forces fighting the Bolsheviks. See his selected poems, ed. by Avril Pyman (1972); his account of his journey to Italy, ed. by L. E. Vogel (1973); studies by F. D. Reeve (1962) and Robin Kemball (1965).

Blondel, François (fräNswä' blôNdĕl'), 1617-86, French architect. Blondel's best-known work is the triumphal arch called the Porte St.-Denis (1672), in Paris. In 1672 he became director of the Academy of Architecture. Blondel's writings, which exerted great influence, include *Cours d'architecture enseigné dans l'Académie royale d'architecture* (2 vol., 1675-83) and *Nouvelle Manière de fortifier les places* (1684). He advocated a strict adherence to a classical and rationalist doctrine of architecture. His nephew, **Jacques François Blondel,** 1705-74, opened the first French private school of architecture in 1739. As architect to the king he devised plans for the civic beautification of Metz and Strasbourg. He designed the town hall and Place d'Armes at Strasbourg and the west portal of the cathedral at Metz. His published works include *L'Architecture française* (1752), valuable for its engraved views of buildings that no longer exist, and *Cours d'architecture; ou, Traité de la décoration* (6 vol., 1771-77).

Blondel, Maurice, 1861-1949, French Catholic philosopher, b. Dijon. He was a professor at the universities of Montauban, Lille, and Aix-Marseille during his influential career. Like his contemporary Henri Bergson he was anti-rationalist and scorned science. In his first work, *L'Action* (1893, rev. ed. 1950), he laid the groundwork for his later thought. Blondel held that action could never be satisfied by any finite good and could only be fulfilled in God, whom he described as the "first principle and last term." In his positive affirmation of God he was close to St. Augustine, Plato, and Leibniz; he later also accorded legitimacy to the rational proofs of God's existence. His other chief works were *La Pensée* (2 vol., 1934-35) and *Le Problème de la philosophie catholique* (1932). See study by Henri Bouillard (1969).

Blondel de Nesle (blŭn'dəl də nĕl, Fr. blôNdĕl' də nĕl), fl. late 12th cent., French troubadour, a favorite of RICHARD I of England. Legend relates that after Richard was captured and imprisoned by Leopold V of Austria in 1193, Blondel wandered through Germany, singing a song known only to him and his lost master, until Richard answered from his prison. Blondel was then able to tell the English where Richard was held captive.

blood, fluid that is pumped by the heart and circulates throughout the body via the arteries, veins, and capillaries. An adult male of average size normally has about 6 qt (5.6 liters) of blood. The blood carries oxygen and nutrients to the body tissues and carries away carbon dioxide and other wastes. The colorless fluid of the blood, or plasma, contains a variety of cells and substances. Most numerous are the erythrocytes, or red blood cells, which number from 4.5 million to 6 million per cubic millimeter of blood. They carry out the exchange of oxygen and carbon dioxide between the lungs and the body tissues. In order to combine effectively with oxygen, the erythrocytes must contain a normal amount of the red protein pigment hemoglobin, which in turn is dependent on the amount of iron in the body. A deficiency of iron and therefore of hemoglobin leads to ANEMIA and poor oxygenation of the body tissues. Nucleated immature erythrocytes develop in the BONE MARROW. As they mature, the erythrocytes also lose their nuclei, become disk-shaped, and begin to produce hemoglobin. After circulating for about 120 days the erythrocytes wear out and are destroyed by the spleen. Although all red blood cells are essentially similar, certain structures on their surfaces vary from person to person; on the basis of these structures blood is classified into BLOOD GROUPS. The leukocytes, or white blood cells, defend the body against infecting organisms and foreign agents both in the tissues and in the bloodstream itself. Human blood contains about 5,000 to 10,000 leukocytes per cubic millimeter; the number increases in the presence of infection. An extraordinary and prolonged proliferation of leukocytes is known as LEUKEMIA, and is usually fatal. Conversely, a sharp decrease in the number of leukocytes (leukopenia), usually the result of drug toxicity, strips the blood of its defense against infection and is an equally serious condition. Leukocytes have nuclei and are classified into three groups. The granulocytes form in the bone marrow and account for about 70% of all white blood cells. There are three subdivisions of granulocytes: neutrophils, eosinophils, and basophils. Neutrophils constitute the vast majority of granulocytes. They are capable of amoeboid movement and can surround and destroy bacteria and other microorganisms. The eosinophils, ordinarily about 2% of the granulocyte count, increase in number in the presence of allergic disorders and parasitic infestations. The basophils account for about 1% of the granulocytes, and they may be the source of heparin, which delays blood clotting. The second group of white blood cells, the lymphocytes, are formed in the lymphoid tissue; under normal conditions they make up about 20% to 35% of all white cells. Lymphocytes tend to migrate into the connective tissue, where they develop into plasma cells that produce antibodies against foreign microorganisms. The third group, the monocytes, are derived from the phagocytic cells that line many vascular and lymph channels, called the reticuloendothelial system; monocytes, which are also produced from lymphocytes, ordinarily number 4% to 8% of the white cells. They attack and destroy organisms left behind by the granulocytes and lymphocytes. In certain diseases of long duration (tuberculosis, malaria, typhoid) the monocytes are thought to be the main instrument of defense. The blood also contains platelets, or thrombocytes, and other substances active in BLOOD CLOTTING. Also circulating in the plasma are the hormones that the endocrine glands secrete directly into the bloodstream. In addition, essential salts (like those of sodium and potassium), essential proteins (albumin, globulins, and fibrinogen), and metabolic wastes (such as urea) circulate in the plasma. Serum, a straw-colored liquid, is essentially plasma without fibrinogen. It is the liquid component of blood that separates from the clot. Serum is removed from whole blood by centrifuging and is put to various medical uses. Normal human serum is sometimes introduced into a patient to counteract surgical or traumatic shock or the loss of fluid resulting from severe burns. Human blood is classified into four major groups, an important distinction in successful BLOOD TRANSFUSION.

blood bank, site for collecting, processing, typing, and storing whole BLOOD and blood plasma. Whole blood may be preserved up to 21 days without losing its usefulness in BLOOD TRANSFUSIONS; an anticoagulant is added to it to prevent clotting. Blood plasma, the fluid portion of the blood, may be frozen and stored indefinitely. The earliest whole blood transfusions were performed during World War I, but the first blood bank was not established until 1937 at Cook County Hospital in Chicago. Today most hospitals maintain their own blood reserves and the U.S. Red Cross provides a nationwide distribution service.

blood clotting, process by which the blood coagulates to form solid masses, or clots. In minor injuries, small oval bodies called platelets, or thrombocytes, tend to collect and form plugs in blood vessel openings. To control bleeding from vessels larger than capillaries a clot must form at the point of injury. The coagulation of the blood is also initiated by the blood platelets. The platelets produce a substance that combines with calcium ions in the blood to form thromboplastin, which in turn converts the protein prothrombin into thrombin in a complex series of reactions. Thrombin, a proteolytic enzyme, converts fibrinogen, a protein substance, into fibrin, an insoluble protein that forms an intricate network of minute threadlike structures called fibrils and causes the blood plasma to gel. The blood cells and plasma are enmeshed in the network of fibrils to form the clot. Blood clotting can be initiated by the extrinsic mechanism, in which substances from damaged tissues are mixed with the blood, or by the intrinsic mechanism, in which the blood itself is traumatized. More than 30 substances in blood have been found to affect clotting; whether or not blood will coagulate depends on a balance between those substances that promote coagulation (procoagulants) and those that inhibit it (ANTICOAGULANTS). Prothrombin, a substance essential to the clotting mechanism, is produced by the liver in the presence of vitamin K. When the body is deficient in this vitamin, bleeding is more difficult to control. In hemophiliacs, or "bleeders," the blood's coagulation time is greatly prolonged (see HEMOPHILIA). The coagulation of blood within blood vessels in the absence of injury can cause serious illness or death, especially when a clot forms in the coronary arteries (THROMBOSIS) or cerebral arteries (APOPLEXY). To prevent coagulation of the blood in persons with known tendency to clot formation, and also as prophylaxis before performing surgery or blood transfusion, the blood's natural anticlotting substance, heparin, is reinforced by an additional amount of an anticoagulant such as Dicumarol injected into the body.

blood feud: see VENDETTA.

blood groups, substances in red blood cells, classified according to their immunological (antigenic) properties. Blood groups are genetically determined. Each has a specific chemical structure that is part of the surface structure of red blood cells. About 200 different blood group substances have been identified and placed within 19 known blood group systems. Like many other chemical substances, blood group substances act antigenically, i.e., when injected into a recipient they will elicit the formation of specific ANTIBODIES. Antigen-antibody reactions are studied in IMMUNOLOGY. The most commonly encountered blood group system is the OAB, or LANDSTEINER, system. Individuals may contain the A, B, or AB antigenic substances, or else lack these substances (type O). In the OAB system an individual who lacks one or more of these antigens will spontaneously develop the corresponding antibodies (agglutinins) shortly after birth. Thus a person with A type blood will naturally produce anti-B agglutinins, a person with B blood will produce anti-A agglutinins, and a person with O blood will produce anti-A and anti-B agglutinins; but a person with AB blood will not produce any agglutinins in this blood group system. In the special case of the OAB system, agglutinins are always present in the blood, and in BLOOD TRANSFUSION the donor blood must be compatible with the recipient's blood, i.e., the donor's blood must not contain antigen corresponding to the recipient's antibody. Other blood group systems, such as the MNSs, Lutheran, and P systems, are not as important in transfusion because they act like true antigen-antibody systems, i.e., antibodies do not appear in blood plasma until the individual has been immunized by exposure to the other blood group antigens as in previous transfusions. In general, blood group substances are weak antigens, and antibody formation after transfusion occurs less than 3% of the time. Immunization can occur by pregnancy as well as by transfusion. Thus, in the RH FACTOR blood group system, an Rh-negative mother carrying an Rh-positive fetus produces anti-Rh antibodies against fetal red blood cells that cross the placenta. These maternal anti-Rh antibodies move back across the placenta and cause hemolysis of the red blood cells in the fetal bloodstream. Blood group typing is used legally to establish paternity. Any blood factor that occurs in a child must be present in at least one of the child's biological parents; where a child lacks a blood antigen (as when his blood type is O) both biological parents must also lack that factor. Anthropologists use the frequency of occurrence of various blood groups as tools to study racial or tribal origins.

bloodhound, breed of large HOUND whose ancestors were known in the Mediterranean region before the Christian era. It stands about 25 in. (63.5 cm) high at the shoulder and weighs between 80 and 110 lb (36.3–49.9 kg). Its short, smooth coat may be black and tan, red and tan, or tawny. The skin is very loose and hangs in deep folds over the forehead and at the sides of the face, giving the dog its characteristically mournful expression. The oldest hound breed and probable progenitor of all the hounds, it was introduced into Europe long before the Crusades and became popular with the aristocracy and clergy. The latter, especially, were responsible for the dog's careful breeding and purity of strain, which led it to be called the "blooded hound," i.e., hound of noble ancestry. It was imported into the United States in the early 19th cent. Its sense of smell is second to no other breed and has earned it a singular reputation as a tracker of criminals and missing persons. Unlike the police or war dog, it does not attack the man or animal it is tracking. See DOG.

Blood Indians: see BLACKFOOT INDIANS.

bloodletting, also called bleeding, practice of drawing blood from the body in the treatment of disease. General bloodletting consists of the abstraction of blood by incision into an artery (arteriotomy) or vein (venesection, or phlebotomy). Local bloodletting is the abstraction of blood from smaller vessels by watercupping or by leeching. From antiquity through the 18th cent. bloodletting was widely practiced in western medicine. A broad assortment of ailments were believed to result from the impurity or superabundance of blood in the system; periodic bloodletting was felt to assure the patient of good health. In modern times the medicinal leech (*Hirudo medicinalis*) is still used in some areas of the world for the removal of blood from bruises and black eyes. Venesection is employed to treat erythremia, an abnormal condition characterized by the overproduction of red blood cells, and to relieve the congestion of blood resulting from acute heart failure.

blood poisoning: see SEPTICEMIA.

blood pressure, force exerted by the blood upon the walls of the arteries. The pressure in the arteries is initiated by the pumping action of the heart, and pressure waves can be felt at the wrist and at other points where arteries lie near the surface of the body (see PULSE). Blood pressure is strongest in the aorta, where the blood leaves the heart. It diminishes progressively in the smaller blood vessels and reaches its lowest point in the veins (see CIRCULATORY SYSTEM). Blood pressure is dramatically manifested when an artery is severed or pierced, and the blood (under pressure) ejects in spurts. Since the heart can pump blood into the large arteries more quickly than it can be absorbed and released by the tiny arterioles and capillaries, there is always considerable inner pressure in the arteries. The contraction of the heart (systole) causes the blood pressure to rise to its highest point, and relaxation of the heart (diastole) brings the pressure down to its lowest point. Since blood pressure varies in different arteries, the pressure in the brachial artery of the forearm is used as a standard. It is measured in millimeters of mercury by means of an instrument known as a sphygmomanometer. The normal readings in young people are about 120 mm for systolic pressure and about 80 mm for diastolic pressure, commonly written as 120/80 and read as "one-twenty over eighty." With age, and the constriction of the small arteries and then the larger ones, blood pressure increases, so that at 50 years it is considered normal to have a systolic pressure between 140 and 150, and a diastolic pressure of about 90. Factors other than heart action and the condition of the arteries also influence blood pressure. Temporary high blood pressure usually occurs during or following physical activity, nervous strain, and periods of rage or fear. Therapy for persistent high blood pressure consists of sufficient rest, mild sedation (especially with pressure-reducing drugs), a diet low in salt and protein, and reduction in weight where there is obesity. Low blood pressure (hypotension) is considered to be advantageous if it is not caused by disease or injury.

bloodroot: see POPPY.

bloodstone or **heliotrope,** green CHALCEDONY spotted with red, used as a gem stone. It is obtained from India, the United States, Brazil, and Australia.

blood test, examination of BLOOD routinely or as an aid in diagnosing a suspected disease. Tests may be performed on whole blood or on the plasma portion only. Blood volume tends to fluctuate with various disorders; it decreases after severe hemorrhage and increases with heart disease. Blood typing identifies the proteins at specific sites on the red blood cells, a necessity in determining compatibility for BLOOD TRANSFUSION. Microscopic counts of red blood cells are used in the diagnosis of ANEMIA and POLYCYTHEMIA, while white cell counts are vital in detecting infections or in confirming LEUKEMIA. Plasma may be collected, cultured, and inoculated with bacteria or other pathogens for the purpose of detecting the presence of antibodies, defending substances found in the blood; if the foreign body, or antigen, thrives in the culture there is an antibody deficiency. Plasma may also be examined for evidence of functional disorders, e.g., for blood sugar in testing for diabetes mellitus and for fat and cholesterol content in detecting susceptibility to heart and systemic disease.

blood transfusion, transfer of blood from the venous system of one person to that of another, or from one animal to another of the same species. Transfusions are performed to replace a large loss of blood and as supportive treatment in certain diseases and blood disorders. When whole blood is not needed, or when it is not available, plasma, the fluid of the blood without the blood cells, can be given. In giving a successful whole blood transfusion from one person to another it is necessary for the blood of the donor to be compatible with that of the recipient. Blood is incompatible when certain factors in red blood cells and plasma differ in donor and recipient; when that occurs, agglutinins (i.e., antibodies) in the recipient's blood will clump with the red blood cells of the donor's blood. The most frequent blood transfusion reactions are caused by substances of the Landsteiner, or OAB, BLOOD GROUP system and the Rh factor system. In the OAB system, group AB individuals are known as universal recipients because they can accept A, B, AB, or O donor blood. Persons with O blood are sometimes called universal donors because the red cells of this group are less likely to be agglutinated by the blood of any other group, but even O donor blood, if it has a high concentration of agglutinins, may initiate a transfusion reaction when large quantities are mixed with blood of another type. In the Rh factor system, agglutinins are not produced spontaneously in an individual but only in response to previous exposure to Rh antigens, as in some earlier transfusion. Transfusion reactions involving incompatibility eventually cause hemolysis, or disruption of donor cells. The resulting liberation of hemoglobin into the circulatory system, causing jaundice and kidney damage, can be lethal. In addition to providing for the compatibility of blood groups in transfusion, it is necessary to determine that the donor's blood is free of organisms that might cause SYPHILIS, MALARIA, or serum HEPATITIS. Sometimes there is a purely allergic reaction because allergic antibodies have been transmitted from the donor's blood, possibly because of some type of food recently ingested by the donor.

bloodworm, name for the larva of the MIDGE and for a red-blooded marine annelid worm.

Bloody Assizes: see JEFFREYS OF WEM, GEORGE JEFFREYS, 1ST BARON.

Bloom, Hyman, 1913–, American painter, b. Latvia. Bloom was brought to the United States and settled with his family in Boston in 1920. Primarily a philosophic painter of expressionistic style, Bloom reveals in his works the influence of Rouault and Soutine. His canvases are often thickly encrusted with flamboyant color. Many, such as *Slaughtered Animal* (1953; Univ. of California, Los Angeles), are concerned with death.

Bloomer, Amelia Jenks, 1818–94, American reformer, b. Homer, N.Y. She was editor (1848–54) of the *Lily,* first published in Seneca Falls, N.Y., and devoted to woman's rights and to temperance. In 1851 she recommended and adopted the reformed dress of short skirt and full trousers introduced by Elizabeth Smith Miller. Because she advertised it in the *Lily* and wore it in her lecture work, it became universally known as the Bloomer costume, or bloomers. See biography by her husband, D. C. Bloomer (1895); C. N. Gattey, *The Bloomer Girls* (1968).

Bloomfield, Leonard, 1887–1949, American linguist, b. Chicago. Bloomfield was professor at Ohio State Univ. (1921–27), at the Univ. of Chicago (1927–40), and at Yale (from 1940). His specialty for years was Germanic languages, especially in their comparative aspects. He became interested, however, in languages from a scientific, descriptive viewpoint. His masterpiece, *Language* (1933) is a standard text. It had a profound influence on linguistics, for it was a clear statement of principles that became axiomatic, notably that language study must always be centered in the spoken language, as against documents; that the definitions used in grammar should be based on the forms of the language, not on the meanings of the forms; and that a given language at a given time is a complete system of sounds and forms that exist independently of the past—so that the history of a form does not explain its actual meaning. His other works include *Tagalog Texts with Grammatical Analysis* (1917), *Linguistic Aspects of Science* (1939), *Spoken Dutch* (1945), and *Spoken Russian* (1945).

Bloomfield. 1 Town (1970 pop. 18,301), Hartford co., N Conn., a suburb of Hartford, in a tobacco and dairy region; settled c.1642, inc. 1835. Aircraft parts are manufactured, and the home office of a large insurance company is there. **2** Town (1970 pop. 52,029), Essex co., NE N.J., an industrial and residential suburb of Newark; settled c.1660, inc. as a town 1812, as a city 1900. Electrical equipment and pharmaceuticals are made in the town, which is also the seat of Bloomfield College. Named for the Revolutionary War general Joseph Bloomfield, who later became governor of New Jersey, Bloomfield was a supply point for both sides during the war. In the 19th cent. it was a trade and transportation hub. The Presbyterian church there dates from 1796. The author Randolph Bourne was born in Bloomfield.

Bloomgarden or **Blumengarten, Solomon,** pseud. **Yehoash** (yĕhō'ăsh), 1870–1927, American writer in Yiddish, b. Lithuania. He emigrated to America in 1891 and, except for 10 years in Colorado (1900–1910), lived chiefly in New York City. His poetry, which holds a high place in Jewish-American literature, includes the collections *Through Mist and Sunshine* (1913) and *In the Weaving* (2 vol., 1919–21). *The Feet of the Messenger* (1921) was translated into English (1923). Considered to be his greatest work was the translation of the entire Old Testament from Hebrew into Yiddish. With Charles D. Spivak he compiled a Hebrew-Yiddish dictionary (1911). A translation of his poems appeared in 1952.

Bloomington. 1 City (1970 pop. 39,992), seat of McLean co., central Ill.; inc. 1839. It is an important rail, commercial, and industrial center in a rich farm and coal area. In 1856 the state Republican party was organized in Bloomington, at which time Lincoln delivered his famous "lost speech" (no copy of which is known to exist). The city is the seat of Illinois Wesleyan Univ. and the Illinois Soldiers and Sailors Children's Home. Illinois State Univ. is in adjacent Normal (formerly North Bloomington). Of interest are the burial place of Adlai E. Stevenson and the David Davis Mansion, a state historic shrine. **2** City (1970 pop. 42,890), seat of Monroe co., S central Ind., in a densely forested region; settled 1816, inc. 1878. Electronic machinery, electrical appliances, and elevators are manufactured. Quarrying and marketing of the limestone abundant in the area has sustained the city's economy for many years. It is the seat of Indiana Univ., and its growth is closely related to the development of that institution. In the area are three state parks, a state forest, Hoosier National Forest, and lakes Monroe (Indiana's largest) and Lemon. **3** City (1970 pop. 81,970), Hennepin co., SE Minn., a suburb adjacent to Minneapolis; inc. 1953. Its many manufactures include lawn mowers, electronic equipment, and metal products.

Bloomsburg, industrial town (1970 pop. 11,652), seat of Columbia co., E Pa., on the Susquehanna River; settled 1772, inc. 1870. Carpets, aluminum products, and silk are among its manufactures. It is the only incorporated town in the state. Bloomsburg State College and a transportation museum are there.

Bloomsbury group, name given to the literary group that made Bloomsbury Square in London the center of its activities from 1904 to c.1939. It included Lytton Strachey, Virginia Woolf, Leonard Woolf, E. M. Forster, V. Sackville-West, Roger Fry, Clive Bell, and John Maynard Keynes. Not to be confused with a literary school, it was primarily a social clique that assembled on Thursday nights for conversation and became prominent as the fame of its members grew. By the 1920s its reputation as a cultural circle was fully established to the extent that its mannerisms were parodied and *Bloomsbury* became a widely used term connoting an insular, snobbish aestheticism. See J. K. Johnstone, *The Bloomsbury Group* (1954); Leonard Woolf, *Beginning Again* (1964); Quentin Bell, *Bloomsbury* (1969).

Bloor, Ella Reeve, 1862–1951, American radical, popularly known as Mother Bloor, b. Staten Island, N.Y. After an early career in the woman-suffrage and temperance movements she joined the Socialist party in 1902 and was an organizer until 1919 when she broke with the Socialists to help organize the Communist party. She served as chairman of the party's women's commission and was (1932–1948) a member of the national committee. She wrote *Women of the Soviet Union* (1930) and the autobiographical *We Are Many* (1940).

Blount, James Henderson (blŭnt), 1837–1903, American public official, b. Jones co., Ga. U.S. Representative from Georgia (1873–93), he was chosen by President Cleveland as a special commissioner to the Hawaiian Islands in 1893. There the creation of an American-fostered provisional government, under Sanford B. DOLE, in opposition to Queen LILIUOKALANI had caused a crisis. After investigation Blount declared against the provisional government, and in consequence Cleveland withdrew the treaty of annexation concluded with that government. He recalled the American minister and appointed Blount U.S. minister instead.

Blount, William, 1749–1800, American political leader, b. near Windsor, N.C. He served in the American Revolution and later became a legislator in North Carolina, a member of the Continental Congress (1782–83, 1786–87), and a delegate to the Federal Constitutional Convention (1787). Washington appointed (1790) him governor of the Territory South of the River Ohio (present-day Tennessee), and there he also had charge (1790–96) of Indian affairs. Blount handled this dual position successfully until financial difficulties forced him into a plan whereby frontiersmen and Indians were to help the British conquer Spanish Florida and Louisiana. Before the plan was discovered he presided over the Tennessee constitutional convention (1796) and became one of the state's first U.S. Senators. When the Florida plot was discovered he was expelled (1797) from the Senate. While impeachment proceedings (later dropped) were being instituted, Blount was elected (1798) to the Tennessee senate and was chosen its speaker. See biography by W. H. Masterson (1954, repr. 1969).

Blount, Winton Malcolm, 1921–, U.S. Postmaster General (1969–71), b. Union Springs, Ala. A successful building contractor, he was (1946–68) president and chairman of the board of Blount Brothers Corp. After serving (1968) as president of the U.S. Chamber of Commerce, Blount became (1969) Postmaster General in President Richard M. Nixon's cabinet. He ended the patronage filling of postmaster vacancies and presided over (1971) the shift of the U.S. Post Office from a cabinet department to a nonprofit government-owned corporation. In 1972 he ran unsuccessfully as the Republican candidate for the U.S. Senate from Alabama.

Blow, John, 1649–1708, English composer. He was organist and choirmaster at Westminster Abbey and the Chapel Royal and the teacher of Henry Purcell. He wrote more than 100 anthems and 10 sacred services, mostly unpublished, and a masque, *Venus and Adonis.*

Blow, Susan Elizabeth, 1843–1916, American educator, b. St. Louis. After study in New York City under a disciple of FROEBEL, she opened in Carondelet (now in St. Louis) the first successful public kindergarten (1873) and a training school for kindergarten teachers (1874). Among her books are *Symbolic Education* (1894), *Educational Issues in the Kindergarten* (1908), and a translation of Froebel's *Mutter- und Kose-Lieder* (called *Mother Play*) in two volumes (1895).

blowfly, name for FLIES of the family Calliphoridae. Blowflies are about the same size as, and resemble, the housefly; because they are usually metallic blue or green they are also called bluebottle or greenbottle flies. The eggs are laid on the material that serves as food for the larvae, e.g., decaying flesh and other organic matter. Blowflies are often carriers of disease, such as dysentery. The larvae of certain species of blowfly, raised under germ-free conditions and known as surgical maggots, were formerly used to consume dead tissue and thus promote healing. The screwworm fly, common in the S United States, may invade wounds or orifices in wild and domestic animals and sometimes in humans. In recent years the screwworm population has been reduced by releasing large numbers of sterilized male flies into the environment; the females, which mate only once, then lay eggs that fail to hatch. Blowflies are classified in the phylum ARTHROPODA, class Insecta, order Diptera, family Calliphoridae. See INSECT.

blowgun, hollow tube from which a dart or an arrow is blown by a man's breath. Blowguns were widely used by prehistoric peoples. In modern times they are still employed in SE Asia and by some Indian tribes of the Amazon and Guiana regions of N South America.

blowpipe. 1 In its simplest form in the laboratory, a hollow, tapering tube, through the wide end of which air is blown by the operator while the other end is introduced into the FLAME of a gas burner. The jet of flame that results is directed toward a material under study. The reaction caused by the flame can be used to identify the material. A bellows or other apparatus is often employed to produce a steady, continuous stream of air. Blowpipe analysis has been largely replaced by more accurate testing methods, such as the examination of an X-ray powder diffraction spectrum of the material. **2** In glassmaking, a long, straight hollow tube used to shape glass. Part of the shaping process involves blowing through the tube. See GLASS.

Bloy, Léon (lāôN' blwä), 1846–1917, French writer. A Roman Catholic and a social reformer, Bloy wrote violent and vituperative attacks on religious conformism and bitter portraits of his life and friends. His works decry cruelty and injustice, and their fervor made them influential in Europe. They include the autobiographical novels *Le Désespéré* [the hopeless one] (1886) and *La Femme pauvre* (1897, tr. *The Woman Who Was Poor,* 1939); *Salut par les Juifs* (1892), a tribute to the Jews; and a vast body of correspondence. See studies by Albert Béguin (tr. 1947), M. R. Brady (1969), and Rayner Heppenstall (1969).

Blücher, Gebhard Leberecht von (gĕp'härt lā'bərĕkht fən blü'khər), 1742–1819, Prussian field marshal, an outstanding military opponent of Napoleon I. An officer in the army of King Frederick II from 1760, he incurred royal displeasure when, believing himself passed over for promotion, he abruptly resigned in the early 1770s. He returned to service only in 1787 after Frederick's death. He fought well in the disastrous campaign of 1806 against the French and surrendered with honor near Lübeck. In the dark days that followed he helped Karl vom und zum STEIN, K. A. von HARDENBERG, and General SCHARNHORST recreate the Prussian opposition to Napoleon. He was a leader in the War of Liberation (1813–14). Although ill and subject to delusions, he won brilliant victories at Wahlstatt and Möckern and played a part in the defeat of the French at Leipzig. Crossing the Rhine, he led his army to Paris. In the Waterloo campaign of 1815, he was defeated at Ligny but arrived at the battle of Waterloo in time to make it a victory. In 1814 he was made prince of Wahlstatt. See study by E. F. Henderson (1911).

Blücher, Vasily Konstantinovich (vəsyē'lyē kənstäntyē'nəvĭch), 1889-1937?, Russian general. An enlisted man in the czarist army, Blücher joined the Bolshevik party in 1916. He rose to high command in the civil war that followed the Bolshevik revolution. Appointed commander in the Russian Far East, he drove the Japanese interventionists from Vladivostok (1922). He was sent (1924) to China as military adviser to the Kuomintang-Communist alliance. The Chinese knew him as "Galen." He later returned to Moscow and was assigned to command Soviet forces in the Far East. He was created marshal in 1936 but was a victim soon afterward of Joseph Stalin's purge of the military hierarchy. He was posthumously rehabilitated in 1956.

blue baby, infant born with a congenital heart defect that causes a bluish coloration of the skin. The color is most noticeable around the lips and at the tips of the fingers and toes; it is caused by cyanosis, or the presence of deoxygenated blood in the arteries. The cyanotic condition occurs when a large portion of the venous blood bypasses the lungs. Normally, deoxygenated blood from the veins is pumped from the right side of the heart to the lungs, where it is oxygenated (see CIRCULATORY SYSTEM). In some blue babies there is a hole in the atrial or ventricular septum between the left and right side of the heart allowing deoxygenated blood to pass directly into the aorta and thereby into the arteries. In other cases the pulmonary artery is too narrow to allow sufficient blood to pass into the lungs for oxygenation. Surgical correction of the defect is usually required and is usually quite successful. An incompatibility of fetal and maternal blood types may also cause a bluish coloration in newborn infants, a condition that results when red blood cells in the infant's blood are destroyed by antibodies in the mother's blood (see RH FACTOR). Sophisticated knowledge of blood types has made this condition increasingly rare.

Bluebeard, nickname of the chevalier Raoul in a story by Charles Perrault. In the story Bluebeard's seventh wife, Fatima, yielding to curiosity, opens a locked door and discovers the slain bodies of her predecessors. She is saved from death by the timely arrival of her brothers, for whose coming her sister Anne has been watching from a tower. Breton tradition links Bluebeard with the seigneur de Retz, but the story occurs in the folklore of several countries.

bluebell, common name for several plants belonging to completely different classes, particularly the BELLFLOWER and the Virginia cowslip, or Virginia bluebell, of the family Boraginaceae (BORAGE family) and the wood hyacinth, a squill of the family Liliaceae (LILY family). Bluebells of the former family are classified in the division MAGNOLIOPHYTA, class Magnoliopsida, order Lamiales, while those of the latter are in the same division but in the class Liliatae, order Liliales.

blueberry, plant of the large genus *Vaccinium,* widely distributed shrubs (occasionally small trees) of the family Ericaceae (HEATH family), usually found on acid soil. They are often confused with the related HUCKLEBERRY. Blueberries were a favorite food of the American Indians, who ate them fresh or dried them for winter use. The berries have been an article of commerce since early days. The high-bush blueberry (*V. corymbosum)* and the low-bush blueberry (*V. augustifolium* or *pennsylvanicum*), native to North America from Minnesota eastward, are the species most often cultivated, and greatly improved varieties are now grown in the East and West. Various species are sometimes called bilberry or whortleberry. The "huckleberry" of florists, sold for greenery, is a West Coast evergreen species, *V. ovatum,* called box blueberry and kinnikinick. The related cranberry is considered by some botanists to be of the same genus as the blueberries. Blueberries are classified in the division MAGNOLIOPHYTA, class Magnoliopsida, order Ericales, family Ericaceae.

bluebird, common name for a North American migratory bird of the family Turdidae (thrush family). The eastern bluebird, *Sialia sialis,* is among the first spring arrivals in the North. It is about 7 in. (17.8 cm) long. The plumage of the male appears vivid blue in bright light and black at a distance; the breast is cinnamon-red, the under parts white. The female's coloring is duller. The bluebird usually nests in orchards or on the edges of woodlands but will also use nesting boxes. As a destroyer of insects it is of great value; it also eats wild fruits. Related birds are the mountain, the western (genus *Sialia*) or chestnut-backed, and the Florida bluebirds. Bluebirds have a cheerful call and a sweet, warbling song. They raise several broods during a single mating season. The female is responsible for the incubation duties. Bluebirds are classified in the phylum CHORDATA, subphylum Vertebrata, class Aves, order Passeriformes, family Turdidae.

bluebonnet: see LUPINE.

bluebottle: see CORNFLOWER.

bluebottle fly: see BLOWFLY.

blue crab, common name for a CRUSTACEAN, *Callinectes sapidus,* found on the S Atlantic and Gulf coasts of North America. The blue crab is a member of the family of swimming crabs known as the Portunidae and is characterized by a broad, semitriangular carapace (shell) covering the thorax, by a narrow abdomen tucked under its body, and by five pairs of appendages called pereiopods, of which the first two bear large claws (chelae) and the last two are flattened paddles modified for swimming. It is the most common edible crab of the Atlantic coast, and several million pounds are fished commercially by trapping or trawling each year. It is sold both as the hard-shell variety and as the familiar delicacy known as the soft-shelled crab. In the hard-shell form, the crab is in an intermolt phase (between molts) and the exoskeleton is fully hardened (sclerotized). In its soft-shell stage, the crab is in the phase just after the molt but before the exoskeleton has hardened. Since, in nature, the crab retires to secluded areas at the time of the molt and is thus difficult to collect, commercial fishermen collect the crabs at the so-called "peeler" stage, which occurs two to three days before the molt. The crabs are then held in pens, on floats in the water, until just after the molt, when they are marketable. The ovaries of the female begin to develop only after mating has taken place. The female carries the young under her abdomen until they hatch as tiny larvae, which are only 1/25 in. (0.1 cm) long. The crabs molt many times and grow to 7 in. (17.8 cm) in about 200 days. Blue crabs are classified in the phylum ARTHROPODA, class Crustacea, order Decapoda, family Portunidae.

Blue Cross plans: see HEALTH INSURANCE.

blue-eyed grass: see IRIS.

Bluefield, city (1970 pop. 15,921), Mercer co., extreme SW W. Va., in the Allegheny Mts. adjacent to Bluefield, Va.; settled 1777, inc. 1889. It is a trade center and a shipping point for the Pocahontas coal field. Lumber and electrical equipment are produced. Bluefield State College is there, and nearby are two state parks.

Bluefields, town (1970 est. pop. 22,910), capital of Zelaya dept., SE Nicaragua, on Bluefields Bay at the mouth of the Escondido River. It is Nicaragua's chief Caribbean port. Bananas, hardwoods, and coconuts are exported. Bluefields was a rendezvous for English and Dutch buccaneers in the 16th and 17th cent. and became (1678) capital of the British protectorate over the MOSQUITO COAST. During the U.S. interventions (1912-15, 1926-33) in Nicaragua, marines were stationed at Bluefields.

bluefish, voracious marine fish of the family Pomatomidae, resembling the pompano but more closely related to the sea basses. Bluefish are found in the warm waters of the Indian Ocean, the Mediterranean Sea, and the Atlantic. They average 30 in. (75 cm) in length and 10 to 12 lb (4.5-5.5 kg) in weight. Their sweet and pleasant-tasting flesh and their streamlined agility make them excellent food and game fish. Bluefish wander erratically in dense schools, feeding on menhaden and mullet and leaving a trail of carnage, for they destroy much more than they consume; they are even known to regurgitate in order to gorge themselves more. Bluefish are classified in the phylum CHORDATA, subphylum Vertebrata, class Osteichthyes, order Perciformes, family Pomatomidae.

bluegill: see SUNFISH.

bluegrass, any species of the large and widely distributed genus *Poa,* chiefly range and pasture grasses of economic importance in temperate and cool regions. In general, bluegrasses are perennial with fine-leaved foliage that is bluish green in some species. One of the best known and most important is the sod-forming Kentucky bluegrass, or June grass (*P. pratensis*), believed to have been introduced from the Old World and now widely naturalized in the United States; Kentucky is known as the Bluegrass State because this species is so prevalent there. Others are rough bluegrass (*P. trivialis*), used for shady lawns; Sandberg bluegrass (*P. secunda*), the most common native species; and big bluegrass (*P. ampla*), an important range grass. Bluegrass is classified in the division MAGNOLIOPHYTA, class Liliatae, order Cyperales, family Gramineae.

bluegrass music: see COUNTRY AND WESTERN MUSIC.

blue-green algae: see SCHIZOPHYTA.

Blue Island, city (1970 pop. 22,958), Cook co., NE Ill., a residential and industrial suburb of Chicago, on the Little Calumet River; inc. 1843. It has oil refineries, railroad yards and shops, canneries, and plants manufacturing electric signals, plastic products, steel forgings, glass, chemicals, and medical and dental supplies.

blue jay, common name for a familiar bird (*Cyanocitta cristata*) of central and E North America, allied to the crow, the raven, and the magpie, belonging to the family Corvidae. Almost a foot (30 cm) long, it is handsome and conspicuous. Its upper parts, including the crest, are grayish violet blue. The wings and tail are bright blue with black and white markings, the neck is collared with black, and the under parts are gray and white. Except during the nesting season it has a raucous cry with hawklike and other imitative sounds. Some winter in their northern range, but many travel south. They feed chiefly on large insects, seeds, and nuts (especially acorns and beechnuts); they also eat eggs and nestlings. Blue jays are classified in the phylum CHORDATA, subphylum Vertebrata, class Aves, order Passeriformes, family Corvidae.

blue laws, legislation regulating public and private conduct, especially laws relating to Sabbath observance. The term was originally applied to the 17th-century laws of the theocratic New Haven colony; they were called "blue laws" after the blue paper on which they were printed. New Haven and other Puritan colonies of New England had rigid laws prohibiting Sabbath breaking, breaches in family discipline, drunkenness, and excesses in dress. Although such legislation had its origins in European SABBATARIAN and SUMPTUARY LAWS, the term "blue laws" is usually applied only to American legislation. With the dissolution of the Puritan theocracies after the American Revolution, blue laws declined; many of them lay forgotten in state statute books only to be revived much later. The growth of the PROHIBITION movement in the 19th cent. and early 20th cent. brought with it other laws regulating private conduct. Many states forbade the sale of cigarettes, and laws prohibited secular amusements as well as all unnecessary work on Sunday; provision was made for strict local censorship of books, plays, films and other means of instruction and entertainment. Although much of this legislation has been softened if not repealed, there are still many areas and communities in the United States, especially those where religious fundamentalism is strong, that retain blue laws. The Supreme Court has upheld Sunday closing laws ruling that such laws do not interfere with the free exercise of religion and do not constitute the establishment of a state religion.

Blue Mountains, uplifted, eroded part of the Columbia Plateau, c.6,500 ft (1,980 m) high, NE Oregon and SE Wash. Lava flows cover much of the surface. The upper, wooded slopes are used for lumbering. Irrigated farming (especially of peas and green beans) and cattle raising are carried on in the surrounding lowlands. Rock Creek Butte, 9,105 ft (2,775 m) high, is the highest point in the Blue Mts.

Blue Nile, Arab. *Al Bahr al Azraq,* river, c.1,000 mi (1,600 km) long, the chief headstream of the Nile, rising in Lake Tana, NW Ethiopia, at an altitude of c.6,000 ft (1,800 m). It flows generally S from the Lake Tana region, then W across Ethiopia, and finally NW into the Sudan. At Khartoum the Blue Nile merges with the White Nile to form the Nile proper. The flow of the Blue Nile reaches maximum volume in the rainy season (from June to September), when it supplies about two thirds of the water of the Nile proper. The Blue Nile used to cause the annual Nile flood before the completion in 1970 of the ASWAN HIGH DAM in Egypt. In Ethiopia the Blue Nile, also known there as the Abbai, flows in a deep gorge and receives many tributaries. There are dams on the Blue Nile at Roseires and Sennar in the Sudan; the latter is used to irrigate the AL JAZIRAH region. See Alan Moorehead, *The Blue Nile* (1962).

blueprint, white-on-blue photographic print, commonly of a working drawing used during building or manufacturing; also called a cyanotype. The plan is first drawn to scale on a special paper or tracing cloth through which light can penetrate. The drawing is then placed over so-called blueprint paper, prepared by treatment with a mixture of potassium ferricyanide and ammonium ferric citrate. When the drawing and the blueprint paper thus attached are exposed to a strong light, the ferric salt not lying beneath the lines of the drawing, and hence unprotected, is changed to a ferrous salt that reacts with the ferricyanide to form Turnbull's blue. This blue is the background of the finished print. The ferric salt under the lines of the drawing, hence protected from the light, remains unchanged and is dissolved away during the washing in water that must follow exposure. As a result, the lines of the original drawing appear white in the finished blueprint.

Blue Rider: see BLAUE REITER, DER.

Blue Ridge, eastern range of the Appalachian Mts., extending south from S Pa. to N Ga.; highest mountains in the E United States. Mt. Mitchell, 6,684 ft (2,037 m) high, is the tallest peak. Beginning with a narrow ridge in the north, c.10 mi (16 km) wide, the range broadens toward the south, reaching a maximum width of 70 mi (113 km) in North Carolina. Receiving much rain, the region is heavily forested; wood is the area's chief resource. The Blue Ridge was a barrier to the pioneers' westward movement. Numerous gaps cross the ridge; the gap at Harpers Ferry, W. Va., is an important railroad traverse. Most of the people of the Blue Ridge live on small farms in sheltered valleys and retain traditional lifestyles and speech. Subsistence agriculture is the main activity; corn is used to make whiskey. Commercial apple orchards are found in Virginia, Maryland, and Pennsylvania. The Blue Ridge is a major East Coast recreation area noted for its resorts and scenery. The APPALACHIAN TRAIL winds atop the range. Skyline Drive, Va., following the crest of the Blue Ridge in Shenandoah National Park, has many roadside lookouts. The **Blue Ridge Parkway** (see NATIONAL PARKS AND MONUMENTS, table), designed especially for motor recreation, links the Shenandoah and Great Smoky Mts. national parks.

blues: see JAZZ.

Blues and Greens, political factions in the Byzantine Empire in the 6th cent. They took their names from two of the four colors worn by the circus charioteers. Their clashes were intensified by religious differences. The Greens represented MONOPHYSITISM and the lower classes; the Blues, orthodoxy and the upper classes. In 532 the two factions joined in the Nika revolt against Emperor JUSTINIAN I and Empress THEODORA. However, Theodora's resolute stand and the aid of Belisarius and Narses ended the revolt. The factions continued to oppose each other into the 7th cent., but by the 9th cent. they had become mostly ceremonial.

bluestocking, derisive term originally applied to certain 18th-century women with pronounced literary interests. During the 1750s, Elizabeth Vesey held evening parties, at which the entertainment consisted of conversation on literary subjects. Eminent men of the day were invited to contribute to these conversations. Hannah MORE, Elizabeth MONTAGU, and Elizabeth CARTER, among others, continued this tradition. Boswell, in his *Life of Dr. Johnson,* states that these "bluestocking clubs" were so named because of Benjamin Stillingfleet, who attended in unconventional blue worsted stockings rather than the customary black silk stockings. In time the name *bluestocking* was applied solely to women of pedantic literary tastes.

bluestone, common name for the blue, crystalline heptahydrate of CUPRIC SULFATE. It also refers to a blue-gray sandstone that occurs in New York state.

bluet: see MADDER.

blue vitriol, the pentahydrate of CUPRIC SULFATE.

blue whale, a baleen WHALE, *Balenoptera muscula.* Also called the sulfur-bottom whale and Sibbald's rorqual, it is the largest animal that has ever lived. Blue whales have been known to reach a length of 100 ft (30.5 m) and to weigh as much as 120 tons; however, specimens even 80 ft (24.4 m) long are now very rare because of extensive WHALING. *B. muscula* is slate blue in color and has a dorsal fin. It is toothless, and has fringed baleen, or whalebone, plates in its mouth, which act as a food strainer. As water is expelled from the whale's mouth, plankton is trapped behind the strainer. The neck of the blue whale has 80 to 100 conspicuous furrows called ventral grooves, which alternately expand and contract as the animal takes in and expels water. The blue whale is cosmopolitan in distribution. In summer it inhabits polar seas, feeding in the water of melting icepacks; in winter it migrates to warmer latitudes, occasionally reaching the equator. Mating occurs at the end of winter, with a single calf born every second or third year, after a gestation period of 10 to 11 months. The calf is nursed for 6 months, and reaches puberty in about 3 yr. Blue whales may live as long as 50 yr. They are classified in the phylum CHORDATA, subphylum Vertebrata, class Mammalia, order Cetacea, family Balaenopteridae. See G. C. Small, *The Blue Whale* (1971).

Blum, Léon (lāôN' blo͞om), 1872–1950, French Socialist leader and writer. Well established in literary circles, he entered politics during the DREYFUS AFFAIR and rose to party leadership. In 1936 he brought about the coalition of Radical Socialists, Socialists, and Communists in the Popular Front, which won an overwhelming electoral victory. This first Popular Front government, which he headed, inaugurated the 40-hour week, collective bargaining, and compulsory arbitration; it also reorganized and nationalized the Bank of France; and nationalized the munitions industry. Conservative opposition to Blum's fiscal measures forced his resignation (1937). Blum served as vice premier (1937–38) under Camille CHAUTEMPS, was briefly premier in 1938, and opposed the Munich Pact. Arrested (1940) by the Vichy government, he was among the defendants in the abortive war-guilt trial at RIOM in 1942. Blum was imprisoned until the end of the war. After negotiating (1946) a credit agreement with the United States, he was again premier for a little more than a month in 1946–47, heading an active Socialist cabinet. The elder statesman of French Socialists, Blum gradually came to represent the moderate wing. His writings include *Marriage* (tr. 1937) and *For All Mankind* (tr. 1946, repr. 1969). See biographies by L. E. Dalby (1963) and Joel Colton (1966, repr. 1974).

Blume, Peter (blo͞om), 1906–, American painter, b. Russia. Blume emigrated to the United States in 1911. In his early work, such as *The Parade* (1930; Mus. of Modern Art, New York City), he sought to depict through symbolism the smooth, hard contours of the industrial world. His paintings, which gained recognition in the 1930s, are precise, linear, and fantastic treatments of modern social themes, painted in microscopic detail. Major works include the powerful antifascist *Eternal City* (1934–37; Mus. of Modern Art) and *The Rock* (1945–48; Art Inst., Chicago). See exhibition catalog by Frank Getlein (1968).

Blumenbach, Johann Friedrich (yōhän' frē'drĭkh blo͞o'mənbäkh), 1752–1840, German naturalist and anthropologist. He introduced and developed the science of comparative anatomy in Germany. His *De generis humani varietate nativa* (1775; tr. *On the Natural Varieties of Mankind,* 1865, repr. 1969) marked the beginnings of physical anthropology and described the five divisions of mankind which have been the basis of all subsequent racial classifications. Blumenbach's analysis of an extensive skull collection, published as *Collectio craniorum diversarum gentium* (1790–1828), established craniometric study. English translations of his works include *The Anthropological Treatises of Johann Friedrich Blumenbach* (1865, repr. 1969).

Blumengarten, Solomon: see BLOOMGARDEN, SOLOMON.

Blunden, Edmund Charles, 1896–1974, English author. Besides being a poet of rural England, he was an editor, biographer, and critic. His prose works include *Undertones of War* (1928), an account of his experiences in World War I; *Life of Leigh Hunt* (1930); *Charles Lamb and His Contemporaries* (1933); *Shelley* (1946); and *War Poets, 1914–1918* (1962). In 1966 he was named to the poetry chair at Oxford.

Blunt, Sir Anthony Frederick, 1907–, English art historian. Director of the Courtauld Institute of Art since 1947 and professor of the history of art at the Univ. of London, Blunt has also served since 1952 as Surveyor of the Queen's Pictures. His numerous writings include *Artistic Theory in Italy, 1450–1600* (1940); *François Mansart and the Origins of French Classical Architecture* (1941); *The Drawings of Poussin* (with Walter Friedlaender, 3 vol., 1939–53); *Art and Architecture in France, 1500–1700* (1953); *The Art of William Blake* (1959); *The Paintings of Nicolas Poussin* (1968); *Picasso's Guernica* (1968); and *Sicilian Baroque* (1968). He also wrote several catalogs of the drawings at Windsor Castle. See his bibliography, ed. by Elsa Scheerer, in *Studies in Renaissance and Baroque Art,* presented on his 60th birthday (1967).

Blunt, George William, 1802–78, American hydrographer; son of Edmund March Blunt, a pioneer publisher of nautical books and charts in Newburyport, Mass. He established (1821) himself in a similar business in New York and published the numerous editions of *Bowditch's Navigator, Blunt's Coast Pilot,* and nautical charts of the entire world. The copperplates of these maps and the copyrights to the *Navigator* and *Coast Pilot* were later purchased by the U.S. Hydrographic Office when that bureau began its publication work. From 1833 until his death, Blunt was first assistant in the U.S. Coast Survey. He served also for 32 years on the Board of Pilot Commissioners and did much to put through needed reforms in the U.S. Lighthouse Service.

Blunt, James Gilpatrick, 1826–81, American physician and Union general in the Civil War, b. Hancock co., Maine. He practiced medicine in Ohio and later in Kansas, where he became associated with John Brown in antislavery activity. Blunt served in the Union forces throughout the war and was made a brigadier general in 1862. The border region of Kansas, Missouri, and Arkansas was the principal scene of his activity. He was victorious at Old Fort Wayne (Oct., 1862) and at Cane Hill (Nov., 1862). With Gen. F. J. Herron, he drove back T. C. Hindman at Prairie Grove (Dec., 1862). In 1864, Blunt was instrumental in repulsing Sterling Price's raid in Missouri.

Blunt, Wilfrid Scawen (skō'ĭn), 1840–1922, English poet and political writer. After retiring c.1872 from the diplomatic service, he began a career of travel and political crusading. He wrote several works championing Indian, Egyptian, and Irish independence. His poetry, noted for its emotional force, includes *The Love Sonnets of Proteus* (1880) and *The Wind and the Whirlwind* (1883). See his diaries (1919–20); study by Thomas J. Assad (1964).

Bluntschli, Johann Kaspar (yō'hän käs'pär blo͞onch'lē), 1808–81, Swiss jurist and political scientist. Trained at the Univ. of Berlin, he taught law at Zürich and later at Munich and Heidelberg. He expounded the organic theory of the state in *Allgemeines Staatsrecht* (2 vol., 1851–52; partial tr. 1892), carrying the theory to a complete equation of the life of a state and the life of a person. In *Deutsches Privatrecht* [German private law] (2 vol., 1853–54), he attempted to contrast the indigenous elements in German law with those derived from Roman law. Bluntschli was of some political importance in Baden as a spokesman of the liberal Protestant middle class favoring unification of Germany under Prussia, and he was a founder of the Institute of International Law at Ghent.

Bly, Robert, 1926–, American poet, translator, editor, and publisher, b. Madison, Minn., grad. Harvard, 1950. His poems, personal and precisely observant, are informed by the American landscape. Among his volumes of poetry are *The Light Around the Body* (1967) and *Sleepers Joining Hands* (1972). As head of the Sixties Press he has influenced modern writing by printing unconventional poetry and translations from lesser-known foreign poets. His translations include Selma Lagerlof's *The Story of Gosta Berling* (1962) and *Neruda and Vallejo: Selected Poems* (1973).

Blyth (blīth), municipal borough (1971 pop. 34,617), Northumberland, NE England, at the mouth of the Blyth River. It is an industrial center and seaport, with shipbuilding and ship repair and a large trade in coal and timber. Ropes and sails, confectionery, textiles, and clothing are manufactured. The area south of the harbor is a seaside resort.

Blythe, David Gilmour, 1815–65, American artist, b. East Liverpool, Ohio. Working in Pennsylvania, Blythe produced GENRE scenes that depict the rough existence of the early frontier. Many of his paintings are satirical portrayals of the everyday world of early 19th-century America.

Blytheville (blīth'vĭl), city (1970 pop. 24,752), seat of Mississippi co., NE Ark., near the Mississippi River; inc. 1891. It is the trading center of the state's richest cotton area; soybeans and feed crops are also grown in the region. The city is an industrial center as well, manufacturing food products, office supplies, and chrome trim. Blytheville Air Force Base is there, and a game refuge is nearby.

B'nai B'rith (bənā' brĭth) [Heb.,= Sons of the Covenant], oldest and largest Jewish service organization in the United States. It was founded (1843) by American Jews "to provide service to their own people and to humanity at large." Its broad-based program allows B'nai B'rith to embrace a wide cross-section of American Jewry. Its subdivisions include the Hillel Foundation (for Jewish college students), the Anti-Defamation League (a civil rights organization), and B'nai B'rith Women. B'nai B'rith has about 500,000 members in 75 state and regional groups. The national office, located in Washington, D.C., publishes the *National Jewish Monthly* and other periodicals.

boa, name for live-bearing constrictor SNAKES of the family Boidae, found mostly in the Americas. This family, which also comprises the egg-laying PYTHONS of the Old World, includes the largest of all snakes, as well as many smaller ones. Members of the boa family have two functional lungs instead of one, as is found in other snakes, and vestiges of hind limbs; these primitive characteristics are indicative of their relationship to lizards. Each of the two tiny, internal leg bones ends in an external horny claw; the claws are much more prominent in males than in females. Boas capture their prey by striking with their teeth and simultaneously throwing their bodies in a coil around the victim. They then squeeze the animal so that, unable to expand its rib cage, it suffocates. Like other snakes, boas swallow the prey whole. Over 30 boa species are found from Mexico to South America, with the greatest variey in the tropics, and two in the United States. Boas may be terrestrial, arboreal, or burrowing. Some are brightly colored, like the green and white emerald tree boa of the tropics *(Boa canina),* or iridescent, like the wide-ranging rainbow boa *(Epicrates cenchris).* Best known is the boa constrictor *(Constrictor constrictor),* which lives in a variety of terrestrial habitats from S Mexico to central Argentina. It averages 6 to 9 ft (1.8–2.7 m) in length, occasionally reaching 14 ft (4.3 m), and has dark brown diamond markings on a lighter background. The South American anaconda *(Eunectes murinus)* is a semiaquatic boa that inhabits swamps and river shallows, catching animals that come to drink. The longest member of the boa family and the thickest of all snakes, it may reach 25 ft (7.9 m) in length and 3 ft (90 cm) in girth. The rubber boa *(Charina bottae)* is found in moist regions of the far W United States and extreme SW Canada. It is a burrower, about 18 in. (46 cm) long, with a narrow, blunt head, broad, blunt tail, and silver-green skin. It feeds chiefly on lizards and rodents. The rosy boa *(Lichanura roseofusca)* is found in chaparral in the SW United States and N Mexico; it grows about 3 ft (90 cm) long. It has large, dark brown spots on a lighter background. Several species of sand boa *(Eryx)* are distributed from India and central Asia to N Africa and SE Europe; all are burrowers in sand. There are also several boa species on Madagascar and several on Pacific islands. Boas are classified in the phylum CHORDATA, subphylum Vertebrata, class Reptilia, order Squamata, family Boidae.

Boabdil (bōəbdēl'), d. 1538, last Moorish king of GRANADA in Spain (1482–92). He seized the throne from his father and thus plunged Granada into civil war at the time the Castilians were beginning their attack on the kingdom. As the Christians overran western Granada, Boabdil secretly promised (1487) them that he would surrender the city of Granada in return for some cities held by the rival Granadian party. However, he repudiated the agreement, and in April, 1491, the Castilians laid siege to Granada. After valiant resistance, Boabdil surrendered in Jan., 1492, and fled to Morocco. His surrender marked the end of Moorish rule in Spain, and he is the subject of a number of romantic legends.

Boadicea (bō"ədĭsē'ə), d. A.D. 61, British queen of the Iceni (of Norfolk), properly called Boudicca. Her husband, King Prasutagus, died in A.D. 59 or 60, leaving half his property to the Roman emperor and half to his daughters. The Romans, however, seized the kingdom and began to despoil it, thus provoking the Iceni to revolt. Boadicea led them in sacking Colchester, London, and Verulamium (St. Albans). Her army was eventually crushed by the Roman governor Caius Suetonius Paulinus, and Boadicea took poison.

Boanerges (bō"ənûr'jēz), sons of Zebedee: see JAMES, SAINT (St. James the Greater), and JOHN, SAINT.

boar: see SWINE.

Boas, Franz (bō'ăs), 1858–1942, German-American anthropologist, b. Minden, Germany; Ph.D. Univ. of Kiel, 1881. He joined an expedition to Baffin Island in 1883 and initiated his fieldwork with observations of the Central Eskimos. In 1886 he began his investigations of the Indian tribes of British Columbia. After securing (1889) at Clark Univ. his first position in the United States, he was associated with the American Museum of Natural History from 1895 to 1905. Boas began to lecture at Columbia in 1896 and in 1899 became its first professor of anthropology, a position he held for 37 years. No one has more greatly influenced American anthropology. Boas reexamined the premises of physical anthropology and pioneered in applying statistical methods to biometric study. He was an early contributor to stratigraphic archaeology in Mexico. As a student of American Indian languages, Boas emphasized the importance of linguistic analysis from internal linguistic structure. His insistence on a rigorous methodology served to establish the scientific value of his contributions, and his methods and conclusions are still influential. Boas taught and inspired a generation of anthropologists, and wrote hundreds of scientific monographs and articles. His best-known works include *The Mind of Primitive Man* (1911, rev. ed. 1938); *Primitive Art* (1927, repr. 1955); *Anthropology and Modern Life* (1928, rev. ed. 1932); and two volumes of collected writings, *Race, Language and Culture* (1940) and *Race and Democratic Society* (1945). He edited *General Anthropology* (1938). See studies by A. L. Kroeber et al. (1943), W. R. Goldschmidt, ed. (1959), and M. J. Herskovits (1953, repr. 1973).

boat, small, open nautical vessel propelled by sail, oar, pole, paddle, or motor. The use of the term *boat* for larger vessels, although common, is somewhat improper, but the line between boats and ships is not easy to draw. A number of special types of boat are generally referred to by their individual names rather than by the generic term, e.g., the CANOE, the KAYAK (Eskimo decked canoe), and the UMIAK (Eskimo open boat). Simple dugouts, made from hollowed-out logs, have been known since prehistoric times to all peoples dwelling on waterways. The ancient Egyptians used boats made of acacia wood and held together with pegs. Modern wooden boats are built in four ways: with fore-and-aft planks laid with their edges flush (carvel-built); with fore-and-aft planks laid with overlapping edges (clinker-built); with inner and outer layers of planks running diagonally in opposite directions; and with planking consisting of large sheets of plywood. Many boats, however, are now made of molded fiber glass or of aluminum. Primitive boats in many parts of the world are stabilized by an outrigger—a parallel float attached by projecting arms. The varieties of boats in modern use are almost infinite. The Chinese junk, with high poop and overhanging bow, is large enough to be classified as a ship; the junk, together with the sampan (a wide, flat-bottomed skiff, often having a mat-covered cabin with living quarters), is a familiar sight in the rivers and coastal waters of the Far East. The lateen-rigged dhow, in which energetic Arab merchants of the Middle Ages plied their trade along all the shores of S Asia and E Africa, is still in use today. A familiar local craft on the Mediterranean is the flat-bottomed, canoelike, pole-driven gondola of the Venetian canals. A typical Mediterranean vessel of ancient times was the GALLEY, usually propelled by oars. Because the northern seas were stormier, the Viking boats, which the Norsemen were building by the 5th cent. A.D., were more seaworthy; they were believed to be the first clinker-built boats. Deckless or half-decked, with elevated bow and stern, these early boats took the Norsemen to all the coasts of Europe and across the Atlantic. The later rugged whaleboat was developed from the Viking type of construction and came to be used for numerous purposes. The fishing boats of the North and Baltic seas, also built on Viking principles, are roughly similar to whaleboats. Another important fishing boat is the dory, a small, versatile, flat-bottomed craft easily transported on shipboard and used in the entire N Atlantic. For bibliography, see separate articles on various types of boats.

boat-billed heron or **boatbill,** a tropical New World HERON, *Chochlearius chochlearius.* With shorter legs and a squatter appearance than most herons, this bird is remarkable chiefly for its broad bill, which is shaped like an overturned boat. Its coloring is dull brown, gray, and black and is similar in both the male and female. It is a nocturnal, shallow-water feeder, living on a diet of fishes and insects; it roosts and nests in trees. The boat-billed heron inhabits mangrove swamps from Mexico to S Brazil. It is classified in the phylum CHORDATA, subphylum Vertebrata, class Aves, order Ciconiiformes, family Ardeidae.

boating: see CANOEING; ICEBOATING; MOTORBOATING; ROWING; and SAILING.

Boa Vista (bō'ə vĕsh'tə), city (1970 pop. 36,491), capital of Roraima Federal Dist., NW Brazil, on the Rio Branco. Its economy is based on the processing and shipment of minerals (gold, bauxite, quartz, and oil) found in the surrounding region. Boa Vista became the capital when the district was created in 1943.

Boaz (bō'ăz). **1** Ruth's husband, ancestor of David. Ruth 2; 3; 4. Booz: Mat. 1.5; Luke 3.32. **2** Pillar of Solomon's Temple. See JACHIN AND BOAZ.

bobac (bō'băk): see MARMOT.

Bobadilla, Francisco de (frănthēs'kō dā bōbädē'-lyä), d. 1502, Spanish colonial governor. He superseded Columbus in the West Indies (1500) and sent him home as a prisoner. Recalled in 1502, he was drowned on the voyage to Europe.

bobbin, implement on which thread is wound, used in sewing, spinning, weaving, and lace making. Sometimes the wooden spools of sewing thread are called bobbins. The bobbin of a sewing machine is a metal cylinder, with a flange at each end, on which the lower thread is wound to be carried through the shuttle to the seam. In some primitive handweaving the weft, or woof, was wound on a bobbin flanged at one end and passed or carried by it through the warp. In tapestry weaving, bobbin looms are essential, as weft strands of different colors must go back and forth for the distance required by the design, somewhat in the manner of an embroidery needle darning in a pattern. In making pillow lace, bobbins form an important part of the equipment, as each thread of the pattern requires a different bobbin; intricate patterns call for hundreds of bobbins to hold the fine thread in order. Bobbins for lace making are made in various shapes and sizes, from a variety of materials, as walnut, rosewood, boxwood, and olive wood, glass, metal, ivory, coral, malachite, and bamboo, and are ornamented with carving, painting, or engraving.

Bobbio (bôb'byō), town, in Emilia-Romagna, N central Italy. It is a commercial center and a summer resort. St. COLUMBAN founded a monastery there in 612, and during the 9th–12th cent. it was a center of European cultural life. The monastery later declined, and the invaluable manuscripts of its great library were dispersed in the 15th and 16th cent. The monastery itself was dissolved in the early 19th cent.

bobcat: see LYNX.

Bobigny (bôbēnyē'), city (1968 pop. 39,453), capital of Seine-Saint Denis dept., N central France, an industrial suburb of Paris. Metals, food products, and toys are among the major manufactures.

bobolink (bŏb'əlĭngk"), common name in the N United States and Canada for an American songbird, *Dolichonyx oryzivorus,* related to the blackbird and the oriole, belonging to the family Icteridae. In spring the plumage of the male is black except for the white shoulders and lower back and the buff nape. After the breeding season the male assumes yellowish, brown-streaked plumage like that of the female, and his former voluble singing is reduced to a single call note. Bobolinks winter in South America; in Jamaica they are called butter birds. In the north they are insectivorous, but they may feed on rice crops during migration in the south. They have been known to gorge themselves in the eastern wild rice marshes and in cultivated fields in South Carolina and Georgia, becoming so fat that they used to be hunted as game birds. Because of these feeding habits they did serious damage to crops as they migrated, and they were called rice birds or reed birds. Bobolinks are now a protected species and are no longer hunted. Cup-shaped nests are built by the female in grassy fields. Polygamy occurs, but monogamy is more common. Bobolinks are classified in the phylum CHORDATA, subphylum Vertebrata, class Aves, order Passeriformes, family Icteridae.

Bobruisk: see BOBRUYSK, USSR.

Bobruysk (bəbro͞o'ĕsk), city (1970 pop. 138,000), Belorussia, W central European USSR, a port on the Berezina River. It is also a railway junction and tire-manufacturing center. Bobruysk has been known since the 15th cent.

bobsledding, winter sport in which a bobsled—an open, steel-bodied vehicle, with sledlike runners, that accommodates two or four persons—hurtles down a course of icy, snow-surfaced, steeply banked, twisting inclines. The crew of a four-man bobsled is composed of a driver and three bobbers, the last one being the brakeman. A two-man sled consists of a driver and his brakeman. An offspring of tobogganing, bobsledding was developed by a group of American and English vacationers at St. Moritz, Switzerland, in the late 19th cent. The sport was included in the first Winter Olympic games (1924) and has been an Olympic event since then. The Mt. Van Hoevenberg run at Lake Placid, N.Y., is the only course in the United States. On the straightaways of a course, sleds sometimes reach the exhilarating but dangerous speed of 90 mi (145 km) per hr.

bobwhite, common name for an American henlike bird of the family Phasianidae, which also includes the pheasant and the partridge. The eastern bobwhite quail (*Colinus virginianus*) is about 10 in. (25 cm) long. Its plumage is mixed brown, black, and white in the male and brown and buff in the female, making it almost invisible against the vegetation of weedy fields and edges of woodland. Bobwhites feed on insects and weed seeds. During much of the year they travel in coveys, sleeping at night in a compact circle, tails to the center. Thus they can fly out in all directions if alarmed. In spring when the coveys disperse, each male selects a territory in which to nest; the characteristic call of "bob-white" functions to attract a mate and to warn off other males. The female is responsible for nest building, and builds a nest on the ground in which she lays 12 to 15 eggs per clutch. Like most quails, bobwhites are monogamous. The large brood follows the hen; when danger threatens, the hen feigns injury until the young have scattered and hidden. Bobwhites are hunted as game birds and are often called quail or partridge; they can be raised on farms and multiply rapidly under protection. Bobwhites are classified in the phylum CHORDATA, subphylum Vertebrata, class Aves, order Galliformes, family Phasianidae.

Boca Raton (bō'kə rətōn'), city (1970 pop. 28,506), Palm Beach co., SE Fla., on the Atlantic; inc. 1925. Boca Raton is a resort city and manufactures computers, plastic products, electrical equipment, furniture, jewelry, paint and varnish, hovercraft, and many other products. Florida Atlantic Univ. and Marymount College are in the city.

Boca Tigris, China: see CANTON, river.

Boccaccino, Boccaccio (bōk-kät'chō bōk-kätchē'nō), c.1465–1525. Italian artist, b. Cremona. He probably made several trips to Venice, for his numerous paintings of the half-length *Madonna and Child with Saints* derive from Venetian models, particularly from those of Giovanni Bellini. His most impressive work is the fresco cycle of the *Life of the Virgin* along the nave in the cathedral at Cremona.

Boccaccio, Giovanni (jōvän'nē), 1313–75, Italian poet and storyteller, author of the *Decameron.* Born in Paris, the illegitimate son of a Tuscan merchant by a French woman, he was educated at Certaldo and Naples by his father, who wanted him to take up commerce and law. In Naples he met (1336) the woman (dubiously identified as Maria d'Aquino, illegitimate daughter of King Robert) whom he was to immortalize in prose and verse as Fiammetta. She is reputed to have introduced him at court and to have urged him to write (c.1340) his early *Filocolo,* a long vernacular prose romance. Other early works include the poem *Filostrato,* which infused the legendary story of Troilus and Cressida with the atmosphere of Neapolitan court life; the *Teseide,* a poem in the style of the *Aeneid;* the psychological romance *La Fiammetta* (written c.1344); the pastoral *Ninfale d'Ameto;* and the allegorical *Amorosa visione,* imitative of Dante. Boccaccio had been recalled to Florence in 1341, and there he met (1350) the great poet Petrarch, who became a lifelong friend. Emulating Petrarch, he became a Greek scholar and worked vigorously to reintroduce Greek works. In his middle years Boccaccio wrote (1348–53) his great secular classic, the *Decameron,* a collection of 100 witty and occasionally licentious tales set against the somber background of the Black Death. The tales treat a wide variety of characters and events and brilliantly reveal man as sensual, tender, cruel, weak, self-seeking, and ludicrous. With the *Decameron* the courtly themes of medieval literature began to give way to the voice and mores of early modern society. Boccaccio achieved stylistic mastery in the *Decameron,* which became a model for later efforts toward an endemically Italian style. After completing the tales, Boccaccio experienced a severe emotional crisis, during which he wrote the satire *Corbaccio,* a savage attack on the female sex. In the next years there followed *Bucolicum carmen* [pastoral songs], the huge *De casibus illustrem virorem* and *De claris mulieribus* (biographies of famous men and women), the mythological treatise *De genealogiis,* and the geographical dictionary *De montibus.* Boccaccio's old age was troubled by poverty and ill health, but his activity continued. He was commissioned (1371) by the commune of Certaldo to read daily from his beloved Dante, and in 1373 in Florence he began the lectures which became his famous *Commento* on the *Inferno.* There are several translations of the *Decameron* and also many anthologies and collections of particular stories in translation. See biographies by J. A. Symonds (1895, repr. 1968) and T. C. Chubb (1969); studies by N. E. Griffin and A. B. Myrick (1929), C. G. Osgood (1930), and H. G. Wright (1957).

Boccherini, Luigi (lōōē'jē bôk-kĕrē'nē), 1743–1805, Italian composer and cellist. Together with the violinist Filippo Manfredi he made a highly successful concert tour of Italy and France. After 1769 he was a composer and cellist in Spanish courts. He also served as composer to Frederick William II of Prussia (1787–97) and then returned to Madrid. Boccherini wrote more than 400 works, including 4 cello concertos, about 90 string quartets and about 125 string quintets. His chamber music, displaying complete mastery of the classical style, is remarkable for natural, expressive melodies and fluent instrumental writing. His famous minuet is from the String Quintet Op. 13, No. 4. Boccherini's style is often compared to that of Haydn, and the two composers admired each other's work.

Boccioni, Umberto (ōōmbĕr'tō bōt-chō'nē), 1882–1916, Italian futurist painter and sculptor. He played a primary role in the drafting of the manifesto of FUTURISM in 1910 and was the major figure in the movement until 1914. In his famous, characteristic painting, *The City Rises* (1910; Mus. of Modern Art, New York City), he interpreted powerfully the technological turbulence of modern civilization. Influenced by Medardo Rosso, Boccioni turned to sculpture in 1912 and sought to translate light and motion into mass. His sculpture *Unique Forms of Continuity in Space* (1913; Mus. of Modern Art) embodies his concept of "lines of force" to replace the use of straight lines.

Bocheru (bŏk'ərōō), descendant of Saul. 1 Chron. 8.38; 9.44. Perhaps the name should be translated "first-born"; see BECHER **1.**

Bochim (bō'kĭm), unknown place. Judges 2.1, 5.

Bochum (bō'khōōm), city (1970 pop. 343,968), North Rhine-Westphalia, W West Germany. Mentioned in the 9th cent. and chartered in 1321, it remained a small farming community until the development of nearby coal mines in the mid-19th cent. By the late 19th cent. it was a leading center of the Ruhr iron and steel industry; since the early 1960s its importance in coal and steel production has declined. Bochum today is an industrial and commercial center, a rail and road junction, and a growing vacation spot. Its manufactures include textiles, chemicals, machinery, and tobacco products. It is the seat of Ruhr Univ. (opened 1965) and museums of mining and geology.

Bock, Fedor von (fā'dôr fən bôk), 1880–1945, German field marshal. During World War II he led German armies in Poland, the Low Countries, France, and Russia. In 1941 he failed to take Moscow and was relieved of his command. In 1942 he commanded the army against Stalingrad (now Volgograd) but was removed by Adolf Hitler when he did not capture that city. Bock's bullet-ridden body was found by Allied soldiers near Hamburg in May, 1945. See Alfred W. Turney, *Disaster at Moscow* (1970).

Bockelszoon or **Bockelson, Jan:** see JOHN OF LEIDEN.

Böcklin or **Boecklin, Arnold** (both: är'nôlt bök'lēn), 1827–1901, Swiss painter. Most of his life was spent in Italy. With Feuerbach he led the group of painters known as "German Romans," who attempted to express an idealistic philosophy through art. His carefully constructed works are largely classical in theme and often theatrical in sentiment. Among his paintings are *Island of the Dead* (Metropolitan Mus.) and mythological frescoes (Basel).

Bocskay, Stephen (bôch'kī), 1557–1606, Hungarian noble, voivode [governor] (1604–6) and prince (1605–6) of Transylvania. Seeking to secure the independence of Transylvania, he supported his nephew, Prince Sigismund BÁTHORY of Transylvania, first against the pro-Turkish, then against the pro-Hapsburg, faction of nobles. Sigismund having abdicated (1602) in favor of the king of Hungary (Holy Roman Emperor Rudolf II), Stephen Bocskay in 1604 led a revolt with Turkish support against Rudolf's attempt to impose Roman Catholicism on Hungary. Stephen then acknowledged Sultan AHMED I as his suzerain, but refused his offer of recognition as king of Hungary. In 1606 he negotiated with Archduke (later Holy Roman Emperor) MATTHIAS a treaty at Vienna legalizing the partition of Hungary among the Hapsburgs (as kings), the sultan, and the prince of Transylvania. The old and sacred Hungarian crown of St. Stephen was returned from Vienna to Pressburg (now Bratislava), the capital of Hapsburg-held Hungary. The importance of the treaty, which was soon afterward supplemented by a peace between Austria and Sultan Ahmed, lay in the guarantee of constitutional and religious freedom for Hungary. Stephen was recognized as prince of Transylvania but died soon afterward, perhaps by poisoning.

BOD: see SEWERAGE.

Bode, Boyd Henry, 1873–1953, American educator, b. Ridott, Ill., grad. Pennsylvania College (Iowa), 1896, Univ. of Michigan, 1897, Ph.D. Cornell Univ., 1900. He taught philosophy at the Univ. of Wisconsin from 1900 to 1909 and at the Univ. of Illinois from 1909 to 1921, at which time he became professor of education at Ohio State Univ. He retired in 1944, having made the university an important center of graduate studies in the philosophy of education. His theories of education are revealed in *Fundamentals of Education* (1921), *Modern Educational Theories* (1927), and *Conflicting Psychologies of Learning* (1929). His *Progressive Education at the Crossroads* (1938) constitutes an incisive criticism of the progressive education movement.

Bode, Johann Elert (yō'hän ā'lĕrt bō'də), 1747–1826, German astronomer. From 1772 to 1825 he was astronomer of the Academy of Science, Berlin, and from 1786, director of the Berlin Observatory. He is celebrated as the founder (1774) of the *Berliner Astronomisches Jahrbuch,* but his most noted contribution to astronomy is the *Uranographia* (1801), a collection of star maps and a catalog of 17,240 stars and nebulae, 12,000 more than had appeared in earlier charts. In 1772 he devised a formula to express the relative distances of the planets from the sun. The same device had been thought out earlier by J. D. Titius of Wittenberg, but it is known as BODE'S LAW.

Bode, Wilhelm von (vĭl'hĕlm fən), 1845–1929, German art critic and writer. He abandoned law for art and archaeology in 1869. In 1872 he was made assistant in the Berlin Museum; in 1883, director of the department of Christian sculpture; and in 1890, director of the gallery of paintings. Under his supervision the museum grew into one of the world's greatest collections. From 1905 to 1920 he was director general of the royal museums of Prussia. His books include *Rembrandt* (with Hofstede de Groot, 8 vol., 1897–1905; tr. 1906), *Great Masters of Dutch and Flemish Painting* (tr. 1909), and *Florentine Sculptors of the Renaissance* (1902, tr. 1909).

Bodel, Jehan (zhäN bōdĕl'), b. c.1165, French trouvère of Arras. He is the author of one of the earliest dramas entirely in French, a mystery play entitled *Le Jeu de Saint Nicolas* (c.1200). See Grace Frank, *The Medieval French Drama* (1954).

Boden (bōō'dən), city (1970 pop. 19,982), Norrbotten co., NE Sweden, on the Luleålv River; chartered 1919. It is an important rail junction and a winter sports center. Forest products are manufactured, and there is good salmon fishing. Boden has a garrison and is the site of a strategic modern fortress.

Bodenbach: see DĚČÍN, Czechoslovakia.

Bodenheim, Maxwell (bō'dənhīm), 1893–1954, American novelist and poet, b. Hermanville, Miss. His poetry, which incorporates many techniques of the IMAGISTS, is cynical and often dwells on the grotesque. Important volumes of his verse are *Minna and Myself* (1918), *Against This Age* (1925), and *Selected Poems 1914–1944* (1946). Bodenheim's novels, although savagely realistic and often brutal, contain great energy, humor, and an occasional streak of evangelism. They include *Blackguard* (1923), *Replenishing Jessica* (1925), and *Georgia Man* (1927). For many years a fixture of the bohemian scene in New York City's Greenwich Village, Bodenheim slipped into alcoholism and poverty in the 1940s. In February, 1954, he and his third wife were found murdered in a furnished room belonging to Harold Weinburg, who confessed to killing them and was found insane.

Bodensee: see CONSTANCE, LAKE OF.

Bodenstein, Andreas Rudolf: see CARLSTADT.

Bode's law [for J. E. Bode], empirical relationship between the mean distances of the planets from the sun. If each number in the series 0, 3, 6, 12, 24, . . . (where a new number is twice the previous number) is increased by 4 and divided by 10 to form the series 0.4, 0.7, 1.0, 1.6, 2.8, 5.2, 10.0, 19.6, 38.8, 77.2, . . . , Bode's law holds that this series gives the mean distances of the planets from the sun, expressed in ASTRONOMICAL UNITS. When this relationship was discovered by Titius of Wittenberg in 1766 and published by Bode six years later, it gave good agreement with the actual mean distances of the planets that were then known—Mercury (0.39), Venus (0.72), Earth (1.0), Mars (1.52), Jupiter (5.2), and Saturn (9.55). Uranus, discovered in 1781, has mean orbital distance 19.2, which also agrees. The asteroid Ceres, discovered 1801, has mean orbital distance 2.77, which fills the apparent gap between Mars and Jupiter. However, Neptune, discovered 1846, has mean orbital distance 30.1, and Pluto, discovered 1930, has mean orbital distance 39.5; these are large discrepancies from the positions 38.8 and 77.2, respectively, predicted by Bode's law. Some theories of the origin of the solar system have tried to explain the apparent regularity in the mean orbital distances of the planets, arguing that it could not arise by chance, but must be a manifestation of the laws of physics. Some astronomers hold that the deviation of Neptune and Pluto from their predicted positions signifies that they are no longer at their original positions in the solar system. However, since Bode's law is not a law in the usual scientific sense, i.e., it is not universal and invariant, it alone should not be taken as evidence for such a conclusion.

Bodh Gaya or **Buddh Gaya** (both: bo͝od gä'yä), village (1971 pop. 6,993), Bihar state, E central India. According to tradition, BUDDHA received enlightenment under a pipal tree (bo tree) in Bodh Gaya. There are extensive relics of Buddhist sculpture, dating from the 8th to the 12th cent. A.D.

Bodhidharma: see ZEN BUDDHISM.

bodhisattva (bō"dĭsät'wə) [Sanskrit,=enlightenment-being], in early BUDDHISM the term used to refer to the Buddha before he attained supreme enlightenment; more generally, any being destined for enlightenment or intent on enlightenment. The spiritual path of the bodhisattva is the central teaching of Mahayana Buddhism. One becomes a bodhisattva by arousing the "mind of enlightenment," taking a vow to attain supreme enlightenment for the sake of all beings. The bodhisattva does not aspire to leave the round of birth-and-death (samsara) before all beings are saved; he is thus distinguished from the arahant of earlier Buddhism, who allegedly seeks NIRVANA only for himself and is regarded by Mahayanists as having an inferior spiritual attainment. The practice of a bodhisattva consists of the six "perfections" or paramitas: charity (*dana*), morality (*sila*), forbearance (*ksanti*), diligence (*virya*), meditation (*dhyana*), and wisdom (*prajna*). There are in Buddhism an actual congregation of bodhisattvas, both laymen and monks, and also many celestial bodhisattvas, who are worshiped along with the Gautama Buddha and the buddhas of other worlds. The most important celestial bodhisattvas are Avalokitesvara, the bodhisattva of compassion; Manjusri, the bodhisattva of wisdom, and Maitreya, who in heaven awaits birth as the next buddha. See also SUNYATA.

Bodin, Jean (zhäN bôdăN'), 1530?–1596, French social and political philosopher. He studied and taught at Toulouse and enjoyed a successful legal career. His most notable book, *Six livres de la republique* (1576, tr. *Six Bookes of the Commonweale,* 1606) ranks as a major work of political theory. During the last half of the 16th cent., France was experiencing severe disorders caused by religious disagreements between Roman Catholics and Huguenots (see RELIGION, WARS OF). Dismayed by this chaos, Bodin believed that a restoration of order could only be accomplished by religious toleration and the establishment of a fully sovereign monarch. These suggestions aroused a great deal of opposition in his time, but they now establish Bodin as a major theoretical contributor toward the development of the modern nation-state. His assertion that an absolutely sovereign monarch was necessary for a well-ordered state prefigured Hobbes and was an attack on remnants of feudal society. His economic policies concerning taxation and government involvement in trade were also influential. See studies by J. H. Franklin (1963 and 1973), and Beatrice Reynolds (1931, repr. 1969); J. W. Allen, *A History of Political Thought in the Sixteenth Century* (1961).

Bodinayakanur (bō"dĭnäyək"ənōōr'), town (1971 pop. 54,118), Tamil Nadu state, at the foot of the Western Ghats, SE India. A Bodinayakanur state is said to have been established in 1336. The area was seized by Hyder Ali in 1776 and ceded to the British in 1793. The town is surrounded by hills. It is a market for cardamom, coffee, tea, silk, and cotton, and it has cotton mills.

Bodleian Library (bŏd'lēən, bŏdlē'ən), at Oxford Univ. The original library, destroyed in the reign of Edward VI, was replaced in 1602, chiefly through the efforts of Sir Thomas BODLEY, who gave it valuable collections of books and manuscripts and in his will left a fund for maintenance. The library has one of the great collections of English books, including a major Shakespearean section; its extensive manuscript collection is especially rich in biblical and Arabic material. A new building for the library was opened in 1946. See H. H. E. Craster, *History of the Bodleian Library, 1845–1945* (1952); M. B. Bennett, *Bodleian Library* (1958).

Bodley, George Frederick (bŏd'lē), 1827–1907, English architect. One of the most prominent and prolific ecclesiastical architects of his time, Bodley was a pupil of Sir George Gilbert Scott, an adherent of the Victorian Gothic revival. A friend of William Morris and the other Pre-Raphaelites, he did much to foster good taste in the applied arts. Among his many works is Queens' College Chapel at Cambridge. His secular buildings include additions to Magdalen and other colleges at Oxford and the London school board offices. Besides his English work, he designed cathedrals in Tasmania, in San Francisco, and, with his pupil James Vaughan, the Cathedral of St. Peter and St. Paul in Washington, D.C. See B. F. L. Clarke, *Church Builders of the Nineteenth Century* (1938).

Bodley, Sir Thomas, 1545–1613, English scholar and diplomat, organizer of the BODLEIAN LIBRARY at Oxford Univ. He was a Greek scholar and teacher at Oxford, and in 1584 he was elected to Parliament. He spent 11 years (1585–96) abroad on diplomatic missions for Queen Elizabeth I. In 1598 his offer to restore Duke Humphrey's library was accepted by Oxford, and he spent the rest of his life and most of his fortune on it. See his *Letters to Thomas James, First Keeper of the Bodleian Library,* ed. by G. W. Wheeler (1926).

Bodmer, Johann Jakob (yō'hän yä'kôp bōd'mər), 1698–1783, Swiss critic, poet, and editor. He translated Milton's *Paradise Lost* and Middle High German poetry. Inspired by the *Spectator,* Bodmer published, with J. J. Breitinger, the critical journal *Discourse der Mahlern* (1721–23), which greatly influenced 18th-century German poetry. Bodmer, who championed Klopstock, Wieland, and Herder, is famous for his argument with Gottsched, whose rationalism he countered with an essay (1740) on fancy in poetry.

Bodmin, municipal borough (1971 pop. 9,204), county town of Cornwall, SW England. The county offices are now in Truro. Bodmin was formerly a busy market for tin and wool. The borough has a psychiatric hospital and a 15th-century church.

Bodo (bō'dö), city (1970 pop. 29,123), capital of Nordland co., W Norway, at the mouth of the Saltfjord, N of the Arctic Circle. It is a center for coastal shipping, tourism, and fishing and serves as the port of the SULITJELMA copper and pyrite mines. The city was heavily damaged in World War II. Of note is a modern cathedral (1956). Nearby is Bodin Church, a medieval stone structure.

Bodoni, Giambattista (jämbät-tē'stä bōdō'nē), 1740–1813, Italian printer b. Piedmont. He was the son of a printer and worked for a time at the press of the Vatican. Under the patronage of the duke of Parma, he produced stately quartos and folios with impressive title pages and luxurious margins. With BASKERVILLE in England and the DIDOT family in France, Bodoni was a leader in originating pseudo-classical typefaces. These were distinguished from the "old style" of CASLON by emphasizing the contrast of light and heavy lines and by long, level serifs. Bodoni's most notable publications include folio editions of Horace (1791), Vergil (1793), *The Divine Comedy* (1795), and Homer (1808). His coldly elegant books were frankly made to be admired for typeface and layout, not to be studied or read. He was apparently indifferent to the quality of the text he printed and to editing and proofreading. William Morris considered Bodoni's mechanical perfection in typography the ultimate example of modern ugliness.

body-marking, painting, tattooing, or scarification (cutting or burning) of the body for ritual, esthetic, medicinal, magic, or religious purposes. Evidence from prehistoric burials, rock carvings, and paintings indicates that body-marking existed in ancient times; ethnographic studies show that it is still practiced today. Markings may indicate religious dedication or alliance with a particular god; they may also serve as protection against some evil such as a disease, as identification with a certain group, such as the tribe, or as evidence of personal rank or status within the group. Among examples of the widespread custom of painting the body are the red ocher found in prehistoric burial sites, the blue woad of the ancient Britons, kohl used in Asia to enhance the beauty of the eyes, the use of henna on the fingernails in the Middle East, and the war paint of some American Indian tribes. The TATTOO is an extension of the practice. Scarification was used in ancient times as a property mark for slaves and more recently in Europe and elsewhere, until the latter part of the 19th cent., for the identification of criminals. Besides being employed for magical or ritual purposes, scarification has also been used for its supposed curative powers. The forms used in Africa include stretched lips and earlobes, filed teeth, and flattened skulls. See W. D. Hambly, *The History of Tattooing and its Significance* (1925); Henry Field, *Body-Marking in Southwestern Asia* (1958); W. C. Handy, *Forever the Land of Men* (1965).

body snatching, the stealing of corpses from graves and morgues. Before cadavers were legally available for dissection and study by medical students, traffic in stolen bodies was profitable. Those who engaged in the illicit practice were sometimes called resurrectionists; they were active from about the early 18th cent. to the middle 19th cent. Public opposition to any dissection of bodies was further aroused by discovery of the resurrectionists' activities; outbursts of violence occurred in Europe as well as in America. Robert Knox, an eminent British anatomist, became a victim of public attack because a body he had purchased for dissection proved to be that of one of a number of victims murdered by William Hare and an accomplice named William Burke for the purpose of selling the bodies; the murderers were brought to trial (1828) and convicted. This and other similar cases led to the passage (1832) in Great Britain of the Anatomy Act, which permitted the legal acquisition by medical schools of unclaimed bodies. In the United States dissection of the human body was practiced from the middle of the 18th cent.; riots and acts of violence frequently occurred in protest against lecturers on anatomy and medical students, who reputedly dug up bodies for study. In 1788 outraged citizens of New York City precipitated a riot while ransacking the rooms of anatomy students and professors at Columbia College Medical School in search of bodies. The following year body snatching was prohibited by law, thus creating a climate for the growth of an illegal group of professional body snatchers. It was not until 1854 that anatomy students were allowed access to unclaimed bodies from public institutions. See *The Diary of a Resurrectionist* (ed. by J. B. Bailey, 1896); Thomas Gallagher, *The Doctors' Story* (1967).

body temperature, internal temperature of a living organism. Mammals and birds are termed warm-blooded, or homeothermic, i.e., they are able to maintain a relatively constant inner body temperature, whereas other animals are cold-blooded, or poikilothermic, i.e., their body temperature varies according to the temperature of the environment. In man and other mammals, temperature regulation represents the balance between heat production from metabolic sources and heat loss from evaporation (perspiration) and the processes of radiation, convection, and conduction. In a cold environment, body heat is conserved first by constriction of blood vessels near the body surface and later by waves of muscle contractions, or shivering, which serve to increase metabolism. Shivering can result in a maximum fivefold increase in metabolism. Below about 40°F (4°C) the nude human cannot sufficiently increase the metabolic rate to replace heat lost to the environment. Another heat-conserving mechanism, goose bumps, or piloerection, raises the body hairs; although not especially effective in man, in animals it increases the thickness of the insulating fur or feather layer. In a warm environment, heat must be dissipated to maintain body temperature. In man, increased surface blood flow, especially to the limbs, acts to dissipate heat at the surface. At environmental temperatures above 93°F (34°C), or at lower temperatures when metabolism has been increased by work, heat must be lost by evaporation of the water in sweat. Men in active work may lose as much as 4 quarts per hour for short periods. However, when the temperature and humidity are both high, evaporation is slowed, and sweating is not effective. Most mammals do not have sweat glands but keep cool by panting (evaporation through the respiratory tract) and by increased salivation and skin and fur licking. Temperature regulatory mechanisms act through the autonomic nervous system and are largely controlled by the hypothalamus of the brain, which responds to stimuli from nerve receptors in the skin. Continued exposure to heat or cold results in some slow acclimatization, e.g., more active sweating in response to continued heat, and an increase in subcutaneous fat deposits in response to continued cold. Environmental extremes may result in failure to maintain normal body temperature. In both increased body temperature, or hyperthermia, and decreased body temperature, or hypothermia, death may result (see HEAT EXHAUSTION). Controlled hypothermia is used in some types of surgery to temporarily decrease the metabolic rate. FEVER, caused by a resetting of the temperature regulatory mechanism, is a response to fever-causing, or pyrogenic, substances, such as bacterial endotoxins or leucocyte extracts. The upper limit of body temperature compatible with survival is about 107°F (42°C), while the lower limit varies. In man the inner body temperature alternates in daily activity cycles; it is usually lowest in early morning and is slightly higher at the late afternoon peak. In human females there is also a monthly temperature variation related to the ovulatory cycle. In many mammals and birds the body temperature shows more pronounced cyclic variations than in man. For example, in hibernators, the body temperature may lower to only a few degrees above the environmental temperature during the dormant periods; mammalian hibernators reawake spontaneously and in their active period are homeothermic. Reptiles and other poikilothermic animals bask in warm weather and must hibernate in winter. The body temperature of fishes must remain close to that of the surrounding water, because heat is lost directly into the water during respiration; however, in some fishes, such as the bluefin tuna, a special network of fine veins and arteries called the rete mirabile provides a thermal barrier against loss of metabolic heat. The mechanism of temperature regulation in homeotherms is considered an important evolutionary advance, in that physical activity in such animals can be relatively independent of the environment.

Boece, Roman philosopher: see BOETHIUS.

Boece or **Boethius, Hector** (bōēs', bois, bōē'thēəs), 1465?–1536?, Scottish historian. He studied at the Univ. of Paris, where he knew Erasmus, and in 1498 he went to Aberdeen as the first principal of the new university. The most important of his works is a Latin history of Scotland (1527); it is a vast collection of historical fables from medieval chronicles, generously sprinkled with myths and miracles. Despite its shortcomings it was held in high repute until the 18th cent. It supplied Holinshed with the Duncan-Macbeth tale from which Shakespeare took his plot. In the 16th cent. it was translated into a metrical Scottish version by William Stewart and a better-known prose Scottish version by John Bellenden. See J. B. Black and W. D. Simpson, *Quatercentenary of the Death of Hector Boece* (1937).

Boecklin, Arnold: see BÖCKLIN, ARNOLD.

Boeheim, Martin: see BEHAIM, MARTIN.

Boehler, Peter (bö'lər), 1712–75, missionary and bishop of the MORAVIAN CHURCH, b. Germany. He went (1738) to Savannah, Ga., to minister to the Moravians. In 1740 he migrated with a group to Pennsylvania and there founded Nazareth and Bethlehem. He went to England and organized a new company of emigrants, the "Sea Congregation," which settled in Bethlehem in 1742. He was superintendent (1747–53) of the Moravian Church in England and was made a bishop in 1748. Boehler returned to America and directed the founding of new Moravian settlements from 1753 to 1764.

Boehm, Martin (bām), 1725–1812, American evangelical preacher, b. Conestoga, Pa. He was the son of a Palatinate Mennonite who settled in Lancaster co., Pa. Boehm became a Mennonite preacher c.1756 and a bishop in 1759. A personal conversion resulted in dissatisfaction with the formalism of his denomination and his adoption of a more evangelistic type of preaching. He was excluded from the Mennonite Church. In association with Philip William OTTERBEIN, whom he met c.1768, he traveled as an evangelist through Pennsylvania and Maryland and into Virginia, attracting large audiences, especially in the German settlements. Boehm was allied with the Methodists for a time, but finally became one of the founders of the United Brethren in Christ (see EVANGELICAL UNITED BRETHREN CHURCH), of which he was elected bishop at the first annual conference in 1800.

Boehme or **Böhme, Jakob** (bē'mə, Ger. yä'kôp bö'mə), 1575–1624, German religious mystic, a cobbler of Görlitz, in England also called Behmen. He was a student of the Bible and was influenced by Paracelsus. In his major works, *De signatura rerum* (tr. *The Signature of all Things,* 1912) and *Mysterium magnum,* Boehme describes God as the abyss, the nothing and the all, the primordial depths from which the creative will struggles forth to find manifestation and self-consciousness. Evil is a result of the striving of single elements of Deity to become the whole; conflict ensues as man and nature strive to achieve God who, in himself, contains all antithetical principles. Boehme exerted a profound influence on the philosophies of Baader, Schelling, Hegel, and Schopenhauer. Boehme claimed divine revelation and had many followers in Germany and Holland. Societies of Behmenites were formed in England; many of them were later absorbed by the Quakers. See *The Confessions of Jacob Boehme,* ed. by W. S. Palmer (1954); study by J. J. Stoudt (1957).

Boeotia (bēō'shə), region of ancient Greece. It lay N of Attica, Megaris, and the Gulf of Corinth. The early inhabitants were from Thessaly. A number of small cities scattered over the rough country—mountainous in the south, hilly in the north—may have had a sort of confederacy before the Boeotian League was formed (c.7th cent. B.C.). Thebes dominated the region and the league. The rival cities were Orchomenus, Plataea, and Thespiae. The history of Boeotia is largely a record of the vain attempts of these cities to escape the domination of Thebes and the attempts of Thebes to prevent encroachment on the region by others of the great city-states. Boeotia, therefore, was the scene of various important battles—PLATAEA, LEUCTRA, Coronea, and Chaeronea. After the defeat of the Persians at Plataea (479), the Greeks besieged Thebes for aiding the Persians, and the Boeotian League was disbanded. The league was temporarily revived in 457 B.C. before being defeated in the same year by Athens, which briefly attached the Boeotian cities to the Athenian empire. Thebes returned to power at the head of the league in 446. Later, after the victory of EPAMINONDAS over the Spartans, the history of Boeotia was completely absorbed into that of Thebes. Boeotia was the home of the poets Hesiod and Pindar.

Boer (bo͝or, bôr) [Du.,=farmer], inhabitant of South Africa of Dutch or French Huguenot descent. Boers are also known as Afrikaners. They first settled (1652) in what is now CAPE PROVINCE. After Great Britain annexed (1806) this territory, many of the Boers departed (1835–40) on the Great Trek (see TREK) and created republics in NATAL, the ORANGE FREE STATE, and the TRANSVAAL. Hostility between the Boers and the British resulted in the SOUTH AFRICAN WAR (1899–1902), after which the Boer territories were annexed and the Union of South Africa formed. There has been some tension between South Africans of British descent and the Boers. South Africa withdrew (1961) from the British Commonwealth and became a republic, an event that was strongly supported by Afrikaner nationalists. AFRIKAANS, the local form of Dutch, is an official language of the republic, along with English. Boer politicians were largely responsible for the inauguration of the policy of APARTHEID, which is applied to the non-white population of South Africa. See Sheila Patterson, *The Last Trek* (1957); John Fisher, *The Afrikaners* (1969).

Boerhaave, Hermann (hĕr'män bo͝or'hävə), 1668–1738, Dutch physician and humanist. One of the most influential clinicians and teachers of the 18th cent., Boerhaave spent almost his entire life in Leiden, which became a leading medical center of Europe. Like Thomas Sydenham he helped to revive the Hippocratic method of bedside instruction; he further insisted on post-mortem examination of patients whereby he demonstrated the relation of symptoms to lesions. He thus instituted the clinicopathological conference still in use today. Boerhaave's fame was enormous, extending far beyond Europe to China. Skilled as chemist, botanist, and anatomist, he adhered to no single tradition but combined the best features of the mechanistic and chemical schools in his own brand of eclecticism. His methods of instruction were spread throughout Europe by a host of students. The two works by which he is best remembered, the *Institutiones Medicinae* (1708) and the *Elementa Chemiae* (1732), remained standard textbooks for many decades.

Boeroe: see BURU, Indonesia.

Boer War: see SOUTH AFRICAN WAR.

Boethius (bōē'thēəs), **Boetius** (bōē'shəs), or **Boece** (bōēs') (Anicius Manlius Severinus Boethius), c.475–525, Roman philosopher and statesman. An honored figure in the public life of Rome, where he was consul in 510, he became the able minister of the Emperor Theodoric. Late in Theodoric's reign false charges of treason were brought against Boethius; after imprisonment in Pavia, he was sentenced without trial and put to death. While in prison he wrote his greatest work, *De consolatione philosophiae* (tr. *The Consolation of Philosophy,* 1943). His treatise on ancient music, *De musica,* was for a thousand years the unquestioned authority on music in the West. One of the last ancient Neoplatonists, Boethius translated some of the writings of Aristotle and made commentaries on them. His works served to transmit Greek philosophy to the early centuries of the Middle Ages. See H. F. Stewart, *Boethius* (1891); H. R. Patch, *The Traditions of Boethius* (1935, repr. 1970).

Boethius, Hector: see BOECE, HECTOR.

Boethus (bōē'thəs), fl. 1st half of 2d cent. B.C., Greek sculptor of genre subjects and worker in silver. He was born in Chalcedon and seems to have worked mainly at Rhodes. In the writings of Pliny and Pausanias he is mentioned as having made a bronze figure of a boy struggling with a goose and a statue of a seated boy. The figure of a boy with a goose in the Louvre may be one of many copies of this work. A second authenticated work, a bronze representing Agon, god of contests, as a winged boy (Tunis) was found in the remains of a ship of the 1st cent. B.C. wrecked off Tunis.

Boetius, Roman philosopher: see BOETHIUS.

bog, very old lake without inlet or outlet that becomes acid and is gradually overgrown with a characteristic vegetation (see SWAMP). Peat moss, or SPHAGNUM, grows around the edge of the open water of a bog (PEAT is obtained from old bogs) and out on the surface. With its continued growth, the moss forms a mat on the water in which other bog plants find a foothold, and humus and soil are slowly built up on the body of the water. Because of this formation bogs are sometimes treacherous (quaking bogs shake under the weight of a man) and have occasionally resulted in fatalities when a man or animal breaks through the vegetative crust. Because of their extreme acidity, bogs form a natural preservative and have been found to be a valuable repository of animals and plants of earlier times. Typical bog plants of today include, besides sphagnum, many orchids, the pitcher plant, the sundew, and the cranberry (old bogs are utilized for cranberry cultivation). Because of the reclamation of old bog lands by drainage and by their natural filling in, bogs in America are becoming rare, and with them their unique flora and fauna. One example of the latter is the bog turtle, *Clemmys muhlenbergi,* a tiny animal with a black, sculptured shell and orange head markings. The bog turtle has disappeared from most of its original habitat in the middle Atlantic states. Another consequence of the drainage and filling of bogs is the decreased water-holding capacity of the land, resulting in rapid run-off during rains and the increased siltation of rivers and streams.

Bogalusa (bōgəlo͞o'sə), city (1970 pop. 18,412), Washington parish, SE La.; inc. 1914. It is a manufacturing and trading center of the Pearl river valley. Its name derives from the Indian-named creek, Bogue Lusa ("smoky or dark waters"), that flows through the city. Bogalusa was founded in 1906 when the lumber industry established operations in this extensive pine area. The city still has pine nurseries. Its manufactures include paper and paper products, furniture, tung oil, machine parts, and food products.

Bogan, Louise, 1897–1970, American poet and critic, b. Livermore, Maine. She spent much of her life in New York City and was for many years poetry editor for the *New Yorker* magazine. Her verse is intense, personal, and yet restrained, revealing a metaphysical awareness of the tragedy of life. Among her volumes of poetry are *Body of This Death* (1923), *Poems and New Poems* (1941), *Collected Poems* (1954), and *The Blue Estuaries: Poems 1923–1968* (1968). Her other works include a literary history, *Achievement in American Poetry, 1900–1950* (1950); and collections of criticism, *Selected Criticism* (1958) and *A Poet's Alphabet* (1970). See her collected letters, ed. by Ruth Limmer (1973).

Boganda, Barthélémy (bärtālmē' bōgän'də), 1910–59, premier of the Central African Republic (1958–59). He was a Roman Catholic priest for a decade (1938–48) before turning exclusively to politics. Founder of the nationalist movement in the French territory of Ubangi-Shari, he became (1957) president of the federal grand council of French Equatorial Africa. When Ubangi-Shari joined the French Community as the Central African Republic in 1958, Boganda was the first premier. He died in an air crash and was succeeded by his cousin, David DACKO.

Bogarde, Dirk (dûrk bō'gärd), 1920–, English film actor, b. Hampstead; his original name was Derek Van den Bogaerde. In his early career Bogarde played romantic leads in such films as *So Long at the Fair* (1950) and *A Tale of Two Cities* (1958). He later showed great versatility playing character parts—the sinister valet in *The Servant* (1963), the dying, obsessed composer in *Death in Venice* (1971). His other films include *Esther Waters* (1948), *Doctor in the House* (1954), *Darling* (1965), *Accident* (1967), *The Damned* (1969), and *The Night Porter* (1974).

Bogardus, James, 1800–1874, American architect, b. Catskill, N.Y. Among the first to use cast iron in the construction of building facades, Bogardus was noted for his commercial building designs. His best-known works include the Iron Building at Centre and Duane streets in New York City. Bogardus's success with cast-iron exteriors led eventually to the adoption of steel-frame construction for entire buildings.

Bogart, Humphrey DeForest, 1899–1957, American film actor, b. New York City. After a succession of stage roles he achieved note with his portrayal of the tough gangster Duke Mantee in *The Petrified Forest* (1934). He was in films after 1930 but it was the re-creation (1936) of that role that brought him fame, and thereafter followed a succession of notable performances in *The Maltese Falcon* (1941), *Casablanca* (1942), *To Have and Have Not* (1944), *The Big Sleep* (1946), *Treasure of the Sierra Madre* and *Key Largo* (1948), and *The Caine Mutiny* (1954). He became famous for his portrayals of tough, cynical heroes. In 1952 he won an Academy Award for his performance in *The African Queen.* His work has had an enormous following since his death.

Boğazköy or **Boghazkeui** (bōäz'köy), village, N central Turkey. Boğazköy (or Hattusas as it was called) was the chief center of the Hittite empire (1400–1200 B.C.), which was consolidated by Shubbiluliuma (fl. 1380 B.C.). Hugo Winckler found there (1906–7) the principal Hittite inscriptions on 10,000 tablets; this discovery greatly added to the knowledge of Hittite civilization. Among the impressive remains are huge fortifications, gates, and temples. Below this level, archaeologists have found levels of an earlier period. Nearby is the Hittite carved sanctuary of Yazilikaya. Boğazköy is by tradition the site of Pteria, where Croesus and Cyrus the Great fought an indecisive battle (546 B.C.). The name of the village is also written Boghazkoy.

Boghazkeui: see BOĞAZKÖY.

bog iron ore: see LIMONITE.

bog lime: see MARL.

Bognor Regis (bŏg'nər rē'jĭs), urban district (1971 pop. 34,389), West Sussex, S central England. It is a seaside resort. At nearby Felpham is the cottage where the poet William Blake lived from 1801 to 1804. The title Regis was granted to the town after George V convalesced there in 1929.

Bogomils (bō'gōmĭlz), members of a religious group that flourished in Bulgaria and the Balkans from the 10th to the 15th cent. Their creed, a dualism adapted from the PAULICIANS and modified by other Gnostic and Manichaean sources, is attributed to Theophilus or Bogomil, a Bulgarian priest of the 10th cent. The movement was intensely nationalistic and political as well as religious and reflected resentment of Byzantine culture, Slavic serfdom, and imperial authority. Similar groups were known in other countries as CATHARI, Euchites, and Patarines. In the 12th cent. the Patarines were dominant in Bosnia and neighboring lands and began to proselytize in Italy. From there, the Cathari converted the ALBIGENSES of France. Through the combined efforts of the Western and Eastern churches and of the Holy Roman and Byzantine empires, the Bogomils were weakened and suppressed. They vanished in the expansion of Islam, but bits of their ideas and folklore persisted for centuries in Slavic lands. See Dmitri Obolensky, *Bogomiles* (1948).

Bogor (bō'gôr), formerly **Buitenzorg** (boi'tənzôrkh) [Dutch,=free from care], city (1961 pop. 154,092), W Java, Indonesia. At the foot of two volcanoes, it is a highland resort and an agricultural research center, known chiefly for its magnificent botanical gardens (laid out 1817). Adjacent to the gardens is the presidential country palace, formerly used by the Dutch governors. Rainfall is heavy in the area; tea is grown on the surrounding highlands, and coffee, rice, and rubber are also important crops. Automobile tires are among the manufactures. The site was selected as the resort residence of the Dutch governor-general in 1745, and the town grew around the palace. Bogor is the seat of the Indonesian general agricultural research station, a state agricultural university, two private universities, an army intelligence school, and forestry and rubber research institutes.

Bogorodsk: see NOGINSK, USSR.

Bogotá (bōgōtä'), city (1968 est. pop. 1,966,341; pop. of Bogotá Special District 2,148,387), central Colombia, capital and largest city of Colombia, and capital of Cundinamarca dept. A picturesque, spacious city, Bogotá is on a high, fertile plateau (c.8,560 ft/2,610 m) in the E Andes and has a cool, moist climate. Several rivers join at the site to form the Bogotá, a tributary of the Río Magdalena, the chief means of transportation in colonial times. Today Bogotá is the political, social, and financial center of the republic, although Medellín and Barranquilla enjoy economic supremacy. It is the marketing and processing center for a region of coffee, cocoa, and tobacco. The city is rich in splendid colonial architecture, notably the cathedral and the churches of San Ignacio and San Francisco. It has several universities and a museum with an internationally famous collection of pre-Columbian gold art. The region was a Chibcha Indian center before the city was founded in 1538 by Jiménez de Quesada and named Santa Fé de Bogotá (in memory of the Chibcha chief Bacatá). As capital and archiepiscopal see of the colonial viceroyalty of NEW GRANADA, the city became an early religious and intellectual center. Alexander von Humboldt called it (c.1800) the Athens of America in honor of its cultural and scientific institutions. Among them were the first astronomical observatory in South America, founded by José Celestino Mutis. The intellectual impact of the French Revolution inspired Antonio Nariño and others to agitate against Spanish rule. José Acevedo y Gómez led the first successful revolt in the city against Spain in 1810. Later Santander and Bolívar were prominent in Bogotá. After Bolívar's decisive victory at Boyacá (1819), Bogotá became the capital of Greater Colombia; when the country was divided in 1830, Bogotá became the capital of what was later called Colombia. Much of the city was damaged during rioting in 1948 following the assassination of the radical leader, Jorge Eliécer Gaitán. In 1955, Bogotá and the surrounding area were organized as a Special District of 613 sq mi (1,588 sq km). A short distance from the city is the Salto de Tequendama waterfall and the underground cathedral at the salt mines of Zipaquirá.

Bogra (bŏg'rə), town (1961 pop. 33,800), N Bangladesh, on the Karatoya River, a tributary of the Jamuna. It is a road junction and commercial center, with soap, match, and metalware industries. Bogra also contains a nursery for sericultural development. It has a college affiliated with Rajshahi Univ.

Bohan (bō'hăn), son of Reuben. Joshua 15.6; 18.17.

Bohemia, Czech *Cechy,* historic region (20,368 sq mi/52,753 sq km) and former kingdom, W Czechoslovakia. Bohemia is bounded by Austria in the southeast, by West and East Germany in the west and northwest, by Poland in the north and northeast, and by Moravia in the east. Its natural boundaries are the BOHEMIAN FOREST, the ERZGEBIRGE ("ore mountains") chain, the SUDETES, and the Bohemian-Moravian heights. With MORAVIA and Czech Silesia, Bohemia constitutes the traditional Czech lands of Czechoslovakia, and in its broader meaning Bohemia is often understood to include this entire area, which until 1918 was a Hapsburg crown land. Prague is the traditional Bohemian capital. Although Bohemia, with about 40% of Czechoslovakia's area and 45% of its people, is the country's most urbanized and densely inhabited region, agriculture and rural life and customs retain their importance. Central Bohemia consists of fertile lowlands and plateaus, drained by the Elbe and Vltava (Moldau) rivers. Grain, sugar beets, grapes and other fruit, flax, and the famous hops used in the breweries of PLZEŇ (Pilsen) are the principal crops. Mining (coal, silver, copper, lead, iron, and, at JÁCHYMOV, radium and uranium) and textile and glass manufactures are important in the mountain districts. Prague is the center of a heavy industrial region, and Plzeň is also known for the huge Skoda works, producing machinery and munitions. Bohemia is celebrated for its spas and beautiful resorts, notably KARLOVY VARY (Ger. *Karlsbad)* and MARIÁNSKÉ LÁZNĚ (Ger. *Marienbad*). The overwhelming majority of the population is Czech, but there are some Slovak, German, and other minorities. The Romans called the area Boiohaemia after the Boii tribe, probably Celtic, which was displaced (1st–5th cent. A.D.) by Slavic settlers, the Czechs. Subjugated by the Avars, the Czechs freed themselves under the leadership of Samo (d. c.658). The legendary Queen Libussa and her husband, the peasant PŘEMYSL, founded the first Bohemian dynasty in the 9th cent. Christianity was introduced by saints CYRIL AND METHODIUS while Bohemia was part of the great Moravian empire, from which it withdrew at the end of the century to become an independent principality. St. WENCESLAUS, the first great Bohemian ruler (920–29), successfully defended his land from Germanic invasion; but his brother, Boleslav I (929–67), was forced to acknowledge (950) the rule of Otto I, and Bohemia became a part of the Holy Roman Empire. The Bohemian principality retained autonomy in internal affairs, however. Later Přemyslide rulers acquired Moravia and most of SILESIA. German influence in Bohemia increased with the growth of the towns and the rise of trade between East and West. Silver, mined chiefly at KUTNÁ HORA, greatly added to the wealth and prestige of the dukes, who by the 12th cent. began to take part in the imperial elections. In 1198, OTTOCAR I was crowned king of Bohemia, which became an independent kingdom within the empire. The conquests and acquisitions of OTTOCAR II (1253–78) brought Bohemia to the height of its power and its greatest extent (from the Oder to the Adriatic), but his defeat by RUDOLF I of Hapsburg cost Bohemia all his conquests. After the Přemyslide line became extinct (1306), JOHN OF LUXEMBURG was elected king in 1310. The reign of his son, CHARLES IV (1346–78), who was crowned Holy Roman Emperor in 1355, was the golden age of Bohemia, and Prague became the seat of the empire. His Golden Bull (1356) permanently established the kings of Bohemia as ELECTORS. In the reigns of his successors, emperors WENCESLAUS and SIGISMUND, religious, political, and social tensions exploded in the movement, both religious and nationalist, of the HUSSITES against the Holy Roman Empire. THE HUSSITE WARS led to the defeat (1434) of the radical Taborites at the hands of the moderate Utraquists, who were supported by the great nobles. In 1436, by the so-called Compactata, the Utraquists returned to communion with the Roman Catholic Church and established Utraquism as the national religion. Meanwhile the crown had passed to ALBERT II, a Hapsburg, and then to LADISLAUS V of Hungary (in Bohemia, Ladislaus I). GEORGE OF PODEBRAD actually ruled for Ladislaus and was elected to succeed him as king in 1458. On his death (1471) the crown reverted to the kings of Hungary—ULADISLAUS II (Ladislaus II), MATTHIAS CORVINUS, and LOUIS II. The nobles profited from the disorders of the period and in 1487 secured vast privileges, reducing the peasantry to virtual serfdom. The accession (1526) of Archduke Ferdinand (later Emperor FERDINAND I) began the long Hapsburg domination of Bohemia. Ferdinand began the gradual process by which Bohemia was deprived of self-rule. He also introduced the Jesuits in order to secure the return of Bohemia to Roman Catholicism. The religious situation remained explosive. The conservative wing of the Utraquists had become almost indistinguishable from the Roman Church, and there had arisen a frankly Protestant movement, the Bohemian Brethren (see MORAVIAN CHURCH). The Brethren and their close allies, the Lutherans, won equality with the Utraquists by inducing Emperor Maximilian II to declare (1567) that the Compactata no longer were the law of the land. RUDOLF II was forced to grant freedom of religion by the so-called Letter of Majesty (*Majestätsbrief*) of 1609. When, in 1618, Emperor Matthias disregarded the *Majestätsbrief,* members of the Bohemian diet revolted and dramatized their position by throwing two imperial councillors out of the windows of Hradcin Castle on May 23, 1618. The so-called Defenestration of Prague precipitated the THIRTY YEARS WAR, which came to involve most of Europe. Matthias's son (later Emperor FERDINAND II) was declared deposed, and FREDERICK THE WINTER KING was elected king of Bohemia. Frederick and the Protestants were crushed in the battle of the WHITE MOUNTAIN (1620) by Ferdinand II. The Protestants were suppressed, and in 1627 Bohemia was demoted from a constituent Hapsburg kingdom to an imperial crown land; its diet was reduced to a consultative body. The Thirty Years War laid Bohemia waste; after the Peace of Westphalia (1648), forcible Germanization, oppressive taxation, and absentee landownership reduced the Czechs, except a few favored magnates, to misery. The suppression (1749) of the separate chancellery at Prague by MARIA THERESA and the introduction of German as the sole official language completed the process. JOSEPH II freed the serfs and permitted freedom of worship, but he incurred the hatred of the Czechs by his rigorous policy of Germanization. LEOPOLD II tried to conciliate the Czechs; he was the last ruler to be crowned king of Bohemia (1791). During the later 18th cent. the foundations of industrialization were laid in Bohemia; but the German population fared better than the mostly peasant Czechs. The 19th cent. brought a rebirth of Czech nationalism. Under the leadership of PALACKÝ a Slavic congress assembled at Prague in the Revolution of 1848, but by 1849, although the Czech peasantry had been emancipated, absolute Austrian domination had been forcibly restored. The establishment (1867) of the AUSTRO-HUNGARIAN MONARCHY thoroughly disappointed the Czech aspirations for wide political autonomy within a federalized Austria. Instead, the Czech lands were relegated to a mere province of the empire.

Concessions were made (1879) by the Austrian minister TAAFFE; Czechs entered the imperial bureaucracy and parliament at Vienna. However, many Czechs continued to advocate complete separation from the Hapsburg empire. Full independence was reached only at the end of World War I under the guidance of T. G. MASARYK. In 1918, Bohemia became the core of the new state of Czechoslovakia. After the Munich Pact of 1938, Czechoslovakia was stripped of the so-called Sudeten area, which was annexed to Germany. In 1939, Bohemia was invaded by German troops and proclaimed part of the German protectorate of Bohemia and Moravia. After World War II the pre-1938 boundaries were restored, and most of the German-speaking population was expelled. In 1948, Bohemia's status as a province was abolished, and it was divided into nine administrative regions. The administrative reorganization of 1960 redivided it into five regions and the city of Prague. See C. E. Maurice, *Bohemia from the Earliest Times to the Foundation of the Czecho-Slovak Republic in 1918* (2d ed. 1922); Josef Macek, *The Hussite Movement in Bohemia* (tr. 1965); R. J. Kerner, *Bohemia in the Eighteenth Century* (1932, repr. 1969); S. Z. Pech, *The Czech Revolution of 1848* (1969); Eduard Beneš, *Bohemia's Case for Independence* (1917, repr. 1971); R. J. Evans, *Rudolf II and his World* (1973).

Bohemian Forest, Czech *Český Les,* Ger. *Böhmerwald,* mountain range, extending c.150 mi (240 km) along the N Czechoslovakian-West German border and extending into Austria. The Czech name for its southern section is *Sumava.* A thickly wooded area, it rises to 4,780 ft (1,457 m) in the Grosser Arber (Czech *Javor*). There are many marshes, swamps, and peat bogs in the Bohemian Forest. Agriculture is limited because of the harsh climate; grazing is common. Coal, lignite, graphite, kaolin, and granite are extracted. The region is known for its glassmaking and woodworking.

Bohemian literature: see CZECH LITERATURE.

bohemium (bōhē'mēəm), former name of the chemical element RHENIUM.

Bohemond I (bŏ'həmŏnd), c.1056–1111, prince of Antioch (1099–1111), a leader in the First Crusade (see CRUSADES); elder son of ROBERT GUISCARD. With his father he fought (1081–85) against the Byzantine emperor ALEXIUS I. When his father's duchy of Apulia passed to his younger brother Roger, Bohemond made war against him and obtained S Apulia as a fief. In 1096 he joined the Crusaders. He swore the oath of fealty to Alexius at Constantinople (1097) and in 1098 at the siege of ANTIOCH devised the stratagem by which the city was captured. He subsequently made himself prince of Antioch, in defiance of his oath to Alexius, and over the opposition of Raymond IV of Toulouse, leader of the crusade. Captured by Muslims (1100), he was released in 1103. Returning to Europe, he married the daughter of Philip I of France and secured support for a crusade against Alexius, by whom he was defeated (1108) and as a result was forced to reaffirm his vassalage. In 1109 he was defeated by the Muslims at Harran. He did not return to Antioch, and his relative Tancred was regent for him. See biography by R. B. Yewdale (1924, repr. 1971).

Böhl de Faber, Cecilia: see CABALLERO, FERNÁN.

Bohlen, Charles Eustis, 1904–74, American diplomat, born Clayton, N.Y. He entered (1929) the U.S. Foreign Service and undertook consular assignments in Prague (1929–31), Paris (1931–34), Moscow (1934–35, 1937–40), and Tokyo (1940–41). A specialist in Russian affairs, Bohlen served as Russian interpreter for President Franklin Delano Roosevelt at the Teheran and Yalta conferences and for President Harry S. Truman at the Potsdam Conference. During the Truman administration he played a major role in formulating policy toward the USSR. Appointed ambassador to Russia in 1953, he was confirmed despite the opposition of a group of ultraconservative Senators. Serious differences with Secretary of State John F. Dulles led to his transfer (1957) to the Philippines. In 1959, Dulles's successor, Christian A. Herter, returned Bohlen to his primary field as special assistant for Soviet affairs. Bohlen later served (1962–68) as ambassador to France. He wrote *The Transformation of American Foreign Policy* (1969). See his autobiography, *Witness to History* (1973).

Böhm, Dominikus (dômē'nĕko͝os böm), 1880–1955, German architect. The widely varied styles of Catholic churches designed by Böhm have strongly influenced 20th-century ecclesiastical architecture in Europe and America. The Gothic fantasia of the Suabian War Memorial Church in Neu-Ulm (1923) and the simple parabolic vaulting of the church at Bischofsheim (1925) are examples of his expressionist period. By 1929, Böhm had achieved a rectangular simplicity in design as, e.g., in the church of Maria Königin at Marienburg outside Cologne (1954). Sankt Engelbert, Cologne-Riehl (1931–33), with its circular plan and paraboloid vaulting, is perhaps Böhm's finest work.

Böhm, Karl, 1894–, Austrian conductor. He studied with the musicologist Eusebius Mandyczewski and took a law degree before turning to conducting. After successful appearances with leading German orchestras, he was appointed director of the Vienna State Opera, a position he held from 1943 to 1945 and from 1954 to 1956. In 1956, Böhm gave his first American performance, conducting the Chicago Symphony Orchestra. He subsequently appeared with many European and American orchestras, including the Metropolitan Opera Orchestra and the New York Philharmonic-Symphony Orchestra. He shows a particular preference for the works of Mozart and Richard Strauss.

Böhm-Bawerk, Eugen (oigän' böm'-bä'vĕrk), 1851–1914, Austrian economist. Three times minister of finance (1895, 1897, and 1900), he initiated important tax reforms and farsighted financial policies. Rejecting the standard theory of value, Böhm-Bawerk posited a theory of interest and of capital that was based on psychological factors and on the nature of production. His theories marked an early point of departure from classical economics. Among his works are *Capital and Interest* (2 parts, 1884–89; tr. 1890, repr. 1970) and *Positive Theory of Capital* (1889, tr. 1923).

Böhme, Jakob: see BOEHME, JAKOB.

Böhmerwald: see BOHEMIAN FOREST.

Böhmisch-Leipa: see ČESKÁ LÍPA, Czechoslovakia.

Bohol (bôhôl'), island (1970 pop. 674,806), 1,491 sq mi (3,862 sq km), the Philippines, one of the Visayan Islands, SW of Leyte. It is a major corn-producing area. Rice, cacao, and hemp are also grown, and manganese and copper are mined. Bohol prov. comprises the main island and several offshore islands; its capital is at Tagbilaran.

Bohr, Niels Henrik David (nēls hăn' rēk dä'vēth bōr), 1885–1962, Danish physicist, one of the foremost scientists of modern physics. He studied at the Univ. of Copenhagen (Ph.D. 1911) and carried on research on the structure of the ATOM at Cambridge under Sir James J. Thomson and at Manchester under Lord Ernest Rutherford. In 1916, Bohr became professor of theoretical physics at the Univ. of Copenhagen, and in 1920 he was made director of the Institute of Theoretical Physics, which he was instrumental in founding. Rutherford had discovered the nucleus of the atom in 1911, but classical theory was unable to explain the stability of the nuclear model of the atom. Bohr provided the solution to this problem in 1913, when he postulated that electrons move around the nucleus of the atom in restricted orbits and explained the manner in which the atom absorbs and emits energy. He thus combined the QUANTUM THEORY with this concept of atomic structure. Much of the knowledge of modern physics was made possible by Bohr's initial revolutionary assumption that atomic processes cannot be explained by classical laws alone. Bohr was a leading figure in the continuing development of the quantum theory over the next twenty years. He received the 1922 Nobel Prize in Physics. When he visited the United States in 1938 and 1939, Bohr told American scientists of his belief, based on experiments reported by German scientists, that the uranium atom could be split into approximately equal halves. This was verified by scientists at Columbia. Bohr returned to Denmark but fled from the Nazi-occupied country in 1943. He gave valuable assistance in the atomic bomb research at Los Alamos, N.Mex., and in 1945 again returned to Denmark. His writings include *The Theory of Spectra and Atomic Constitution* (1922) and *Atomic Theory and the Description of Nature* (1934). See his collected works, ed. by León Rosenfeld (Vol. I, 1972); biography by R. E. Moore (1966). His brother, **Harald August Bohr,** 1887–1951, a mathematician, taught (1915–30) at the College of Technology in Copenhagen and in 1930 became professor at the Univ. of Copenhagen. His most noted contribution to mathematics was his formulation of the theory of almost periodic functions. See his collected mathematical works, ed. by Erling Følner and Børge Jessen, (3 vol., 1952).

Bohun, Henry de, 1st **earl of Hereford** (bo͞on, hĕ'rəfərd), 1176–1220, English nobleman. Although King John granted him the marcher lordship of Hereford in 1199, Henry was one of the barons who forced the king to accept the Magna Carta in 1215 and one of those appointed to oversee its observance. He fought against the king in the ensuing civil war. He died on a pilgrimage to the Holy Land.

Bohun, Humphrey V de, 2d **earl of Hereford** and 1st **earl of Essex,** d. 1275, English nobleman; son of Henry de Bohun, 1st earl of Hereford. A member of the household of Henry III, he inherited the earldom of Essex from a maternal uncle and in 1242 went with the king on his French campaign. In 1258 he joined the baronial opposition to Henry and was one of 24 men who drew up the PROVISIONS OF OXFORD. In the BARONS' WAR, however, he returned (1263) to the side of the king and was captured (1264) by Simon de Montfort at Lewes.

Bohun, Humphrey VII de, 3d **earl of Hereford** and 2d **earl of Essex,** d. 1298, English nobleman. He was constable of England and with Roger Bigod, earl of Norfolk, led the baronial opposition to EDWARD I that forced the king to sign the important confirmation of the charters (1297).

Bohun, Humphrey VIII de, 4th **earl of Hereford** and 3d **earl of Essex,** 1276–1322, English nobleman; son of Humphrey VII de Bohun. One of the lords ordainers who attempted to curb the powers of EDWARD II in 1310, he took part in the execution (1312) of the hated Piers GAVESTON. He fought for Edward at Bannockburn (1314), was captured by the Scots, and was exchanged. He was killed at Boroughbridge fighting on the baronial side against the king and the Despensers.

Boiardo or **Bojardo, Matteo Maria** (mät-tĕ'ō märē'ä bōyär'dō), 1441?–1494, Italian poet, count of Scandiano. A favorite at the Este court in Ferrara, he served on diplomatic missions and became ducal captain of Modena and later of Reggio. He wrote Latin eclogues and songs and lyric love poems, and he translated Herodotus, Xenophon, Lucian, and Apuleius. His great unfinished *Orlando Innamorato* (1st complete ed., 1506) is a transformation of the Roland epic, recounting the love of ROLAND for the pagan Angelica and her love for his cousin Rinaldo. In this work Boiardo fused elements of Arthurian and Carolingian poetic cycles with material from classical antiquity. The vigorous beauty of Boiardo's epic was lost in the revision by Francesco Berni, which supplanted it until the 20th cent. ARIOSTO continued the tale in *Orlando Furioso.* See study by Giacomo Grillo (1942).

Boieldieu, François Adrien (fräNswä' ädrēăN' bwäldyö'), 1775–1834, French composer. He studied with the organist of the cathedral in Rouen and composed one successful opera, *Le Calife de Bagdad* (1800), before he went to St. Petersburg. There he conducted (1803–11) the Imperial Opera. After his return to Paris his graceful *opéras comiques,* such as *Jean de Paris* (1812) and *La Dame blanche* (1825), were popular. He taught piano and composition at the Paris Conservatory.

boil or **furuncle,** tender, painful inflammatory nodule in the skin, which becomes pustular but with a hard center (see ABSCESS). It may be caused by any of various microbes, the most usual being *Staphylococcus aureus.* If proper care and precautions are not taken it may spread to many sites (a condition called furunculosis). Several adjoining furuncles that coalesce are known as a CARBUNCLE. The point of entry is usually a hair follicle or a sebaceous gland duct. Boils may occur anywhere in the skin but are most common at places where the skin is constantly exposed or chafed—neck, face, ear, armpit, breast, and extremities. The treatment of small boils consists of scrupulous cleanliness, protection from irritation, and applications of antibiotic ointments and moist heat. Large boils, especially those on the nose, upper lip, or near the eyes (where there is the greatest danger of their causing meningitis or blood poisoning), must be treated professionally with antibiotics. Such lesions should be incised and drained by a physician rather than allowed to discharge spontaneously.

Boileau-Despréaux, Nicolas (nēkôlä' bwälō'-dāprāō'), 1636–1711, French literary critic and poet. He was the spokesman of CLASSICISM, drawing his principles from his contemporaries, among them his friends Racine, Molière, and La Fontaine. His critical precepts are embodied in *L'Art poétique* (1674), a verse treatise; *Le Lutrin* (1683), a mock epic; 12 *Satires* (1st collected ed., 1716) and 12 *Épîtres* (1st collected ed., 1701), after Horace; and *Les Héros de roman* (1688), a dialogue in literary criticism. Revered in the 18th cent. as a literary lawgiver, he was later detested by the romantics. Boileau's poetic reputation rests on his satires, especially *Le Lutrin,* on the clerical world; *Satires III* and *VI,* on life in Paris; and

Satire X, on women. He was a zealous polemicist, notably in quarrels with Desmarets de Saint-Sorlin and Perrault. See edition of *Les Héros de roman* by T. F. Crane (1902); studies by Sister Marie Philip Haley (1938) and A. F. Clark (1925, repr. 1971).

boiler, device for generating steam. It consists of two principal parts: the furnace, which provides heat, usually by burning a fuel, and the boiler proper, a device in which the heat changes water into steam. A steam engine is driven by steam generated under pressure in a boiler. The amount of steam that can be generated per hour depends upon the rate of combustion of the fuel in the furnace and upon the efficiency of heat transfer to the boiler proper. Since the rate of combustion of the fuel in a furnace is largely dependent upon the quantity of air available, i.e., upon the draft, a sufficient supply of air is an important consideration in boiler construction. In some large installations the incoming air is preheated by the waste heat of the flue gases, and in order to increase the speed of combustion a forced draft (air at higher than atmospheric pressure) is often used. Two types of boilers are most common—fire-tube boilers, containing long steel tubes through which the hot gases from the furnace pass and around which the water to be changed to steam circulates, and water-tube boilers, in which the conditions are reversed. Water is changed to steam in these continuous circuits and also is superheated in transit. This additional heating of the steam increases the efficiency of the power-generating cycle. The SAFETY VALVE is used to prevent explosions by releasing steam if the pressure becomes too great. The construction of boilers in the United States is governed by the American Society of Mechanical Engineers' Boiler Construction Code. Progress in boiler design and performance have been governed by the continuous development of improved materials.

boiling point, temperature at which a substance changes its state from liquid to gas. A stricter definition of boiling point is the temperature at which the liquid and vapor (gas) phases of a substance can exist in equilibrium. When heat is applied to a liquid, the temperature of the liquid rises until the VAPOR PRESSURE of the liquid equals the pressure of the surrounding gases. At this point there is no further rise in temperature, and the additional heat energy supplied is absorbed as LATENT HEAT of vaporization to transform the liquid into gas. This transformation occurs not only at the surface of the liquid (as in the case of EVAPORATION) but also throughout the volume of the liquid, where bubbles of gas are formed. The boiling point of a liquid is lowered if the pressure of the surrounding gases is decreased. For example, water will boil at a lower temperature at the top of a mountain, where the atmospheric pressure on the water is less, than it will at sea level, where the pressure is greater. In the laboratory, liquids can be made to boil at temperatures far below their normal boiling points by heating them in vacuum flasks under greatly reduced pressure. On the other hand, if the pressure is increased, the boiling point is raised. For this reason, it is customary when the boiling point of a substance is given to include the pressure at which it is observed, if that pressure is other than standard, i.e., 760 mm of mercury or 1 atmosphere (see STP). The boiling point of a SOLUTION is always higher than that of the pure solvent; this boiling-point elevation is one of the COLLIGATIVE PROPERTIES common to all solutions.

Boisbaudran, Paul Émile Lecoq de (pôl āmĕl' ləkôk' də bwäbōdrăN'), 1838–1912, French discoverer of the elements gallium, samarium, and dysprosium. He also made contributions in the field of spectroscopy, including his experimentation with the rare-earth metals.

Boisbrûlés (bwäbrülā') [Fr.,=burnt wood], name given the descendants of the fur traders and Indians in W Canada, because of their dark complexion. The boisbrûlés, or brûlés, were in the early 19th cent. an important social group in the west and were particularly notable in the Red River Settlement and in Riel's Rebellion. In the later 19th cent. they were absorbed into the general population.

Bois de Boulogne (bwä də bo͞olō'nyə), park in Paris, France, bordering on the western suburb of NEUILLY-SUR-SEINE. A favorite pleasure ground since the 17th cent., the park contains the race courses of Auteuil and Longchamps and many delightful promenades and bridle paths.

Boise (boi'sē, -zē), city (1970 pop. 74,990), state capital and seat of Ada co., SW Idaho, on the Boise River; inc. 1864. The largest city in Idaho, Boise is an important trade and transportation center. Food processing and light manufacturing are the major activities, and there are many state and Federal government offices. A gold rush in the Boise valley and the establishment of a military post in 1863 led to the founding of Boise City, which grew as a distributing center for miners and became the capital of Idaho Territory in 1864. Later, particularly with the building of Arrowrock Dam (1911–15), the region was developed for farming, and Boise drew wealth from orchards and fields rather than mines. The BOISE PROJECT has increased the area's agricultural yield. In the city are Boise State College, a veterans hospital, and a state penitentiary.

Boise, river, c.160 mi (260 km) long, rising in SW Idaho and flowing west to join the Snake River at the Oregon line. In 1811 the Boise River, originally called Reed's River, was explored by an expedition financed by John Jacob Astor (1763–1848), an American merchant. Irrigation, hydroelectric power, and flood control are part of the Boise project.

Boise, Fort: see FORT BOISE.

Boise project, in the Boise, Payette, and Snake river valleys, SW Idaho and E Oregon; developed in 1905 by the U.S. Bureau of RECLAMATION for irrigation (360,000 acres/145,690 hectares), hydroelectricity (360,000 kw total capacity), flood control, and recreation. The project has turned the area into a major seed-producing area and one of the best dairy regions in the United States. Anderson Ranch, Arrowrock, and Boise dams are the principal facilities of the project's Arrowrock division, located between the Snake and Boise rivers; the Payette division, between the Payette and Boise rivers, includes Black Canyon, Cascade, and Deadwood dams.

Boisguilbert, Pierre le Pesant, sieur de (pyĕr lə pəzäN' syör də bwägēlbĕr'), 1646–1714, French economist. A local official of Rouen after 1689, he proposed a radical alteration of the French fiscal system in order to revive the finances of the nearly bankrupt state. Seeing the results of King Louis XIV's military expenditures in heavy taxation and oppression of the poor, Boisguilbert urged an income tax of 10 percent, particularly in *Le Détail de la France* (1695) and *Factum de la France* (1707). He insistently forced his advice on Michel Chamillart, controller general to Louis XIV. Chamillart had him exiled for six months in 1707. His name also appears as Boisguillebert. See biography by H. V. Roberts (1935).

Bois-le-Duc, Netherlands: see 'S HERTOGENBOSCH.

Boito, Arrigo (ärrē'go bô'ētō), 1842–1918, Italian composer and librettist. His opera *Mefistofele* (1868, rev. 1875), influenced by Wagner's music-drama, helped to bring about a new dramatic style in Italian opera. Its first performance at La Scala, Milan, caused a riot, but it subsequently became very popular. Another opera, *Nerone,* was posthumously finished and produced by Toscanini in 1924. Many consider Boito's masterpieces to be the librettos for Verdi's *Otello* and *Falstaff.* He also was librettist for Ponchielli's *La Gioconda* and wrote novels and poems.

Bojardo, Matteo Maria: see BOIARDO.

Bojer, Johan (yō'hän boi'ər), 1872–1959, Norwegian writer. Bojer's novels of contemporary Norwegian life treat social issues from a classical liberal viewpoint. *The Power of a Lie* (1903, tr. 1908) and *The Great Hunger* (1916, tr. 1918) illustrate his humanistic philosophy. The greater depth of *The Last of the Vikings* (1921, tr. 1923) and *Folk by the Sea* (1929, tr. 1931) won critical acclaim in Norway. Bojer's later novels include *The King's Men* (1938, tr. 1940) and *Skyld* (1948).

Bok, Derek Curtis, 1930–, American educator and university president, b. Bryn Mawr, Pa., grad. Stanford (B.A., 1951) and Harvard (LL.B., 1954). He became a professor of law at Harvard in 1958. From 1968 to 1971 he served as Dean of the Law School. In 1971 he was appointed president of Harvard University. He is coauthor of *Labor Law* (1962) and author of *Labor and the American Community* (1970).

Bok, Edward William, 1863–1930, American editor, b. Helder, Netherlands. His family emigrated to the United States in 1870. He founded the *Brooklyn Magazine* (later *Cosmopolitan*) in 1883. As editor (1889–1919), he made the *Ladies' Home Journal* a leading American magazine for women, introducing serious articles and crusades to a medium previously restricted to light entertainment. Bok published fiction by Howells, Twain, Bret Harte, and Kipling and articles by several American Presidents. Of the books he wrote, his autobiographical *Americanization of Edward Bok* (1920) was the most popular and won a Pulitzer Prize. He engaged in various philanthropic activities including the erection of the Bok Singing Tower, a carillon in Iron Mountain, Fla., and the endowment of the Woodrow Wilson professorship of literature at Princeton.

Bokassa, Jean Bedel (zhäN bĕdĕl' bōkäs'sä), 1921–, president of Central African Republic. He served (1939–61) in the French army and then organized his country's army, becoming commander in chief in 1963. In 1966 he led an army coup and became president and prime minister of the republic, holding several other cabinet posts in addition. He was appointed life president in 1972.

Boker, George Henry (bō'kər), 1823–90, American poet and playwright, b. Philadelphia, grad. Princeton, 1842. He is best remembered for his romantic and heroic tragedies, written in the manner of Elizabethan drama. The best of these were *Leonor de Guzman* (1853) and *Francesca da Rimini* (1855), based on the story of Francesca and Paolo. He also wrote a series of love sonnets. See biography by E. S. Bradley (1927, repr. 1972).

Bokhara: see BUKHARA, USSR.

Bokher, Elya: see LEVITA, ELIJAH.

Boksburg (bŏks'bûrg''), city (1970 pop. 104,745), Transvaal prov., NE South Africa. It is an important gold- and coal-mining center. Manufactures include railroad equipment, electrical and metal goods, clay products, canned foods, and refined petroleum. Boksburg, founded in 1887 as the administrative center of the East Rand, is the second oldest town on the WITWATERSRAND.

Bol, Ferdinand (fĕr'dĭnänt bôl), 1616–80, Dutch painter. He studied with Rembrandt in Amsterdam, and his early work (e.g., *Elizabeth Bas,* Amsterdam) has sometimes been confused with that of his master. His style was modified after 1650 through contact with van der Helst. Thereafter he moved away from a preoccupation with psychological probing and developed lighter tonalities and elegant forms. He is noted mainly for his portraits, a large collection of which is in the Rijks Museum and the Hermitage. Bol also executed a number of engravings.

Bolan Pass or **Bholan Pass** (both: bōlän'), gap in the central Brahui Range, W Pakistan; c.60 mi (100 km) long, alt. 5,880 ft (1,792 m). A railroad and highway cross the pass en route to the Afghanistan frontier. The pass, which is strategically located, was long used by traders, invaders, and nomadic tribes as a gateway to India.

Boldini, Giovanni (jōvän'nē bōldē'nē), 1842–1931, Italian portrait painter. Having worked in Florence and London, he reached his peak of creativity and success in Paris, painting romantic vignettes and portraits. His works are distinguished by the bravura of the brushwork. A portrait of Consuelo, Duchess of Marlborough, with Lord Ivor Spencer-Churchill is in the Metropolitan Museum.

Boldrewood, Rolf: see BROWNE, THOMAS ALEXANDER.

bolero (bəlâr'ō), national dance of Spain, introduced c.1780 by Sebastian Zerezo, or Cerezo. Of Moroccan origin, it resembles the FANDANGO. It is in 2-4 or 3-4 time for solo or duo dancing and is performed to the accompaniment of castanets, guitar, and the voices of the dancers. Ravel's *Bolero* is in this rhythm.

Boleslaus I (bō'ləslôs), c.966–1025, Polish ruler (992–1025), the first to call himself king; also called Boleslaus the Brave. He succeeded his father, MIESZKO I, as duke of Poland, seized the territories left to his two brothers under their father's will, and set about increasing his holdings. With the sanction of Holy Roman Emperor Otto III, he obtained (1000) the elevation of GNIEZNO into a metropolitan see, thus emancipating the Polish church from German control. Otto also supported plans for Polish political autonomy. Otto's successor, Holy Roman Emperor HENRY II, opposed Boleslaus's ambition; when Boleslaus overran Meissen and the East Mark, Henry refused to confirm his control of these territories. Boleslaus took advantage of dynastic troubles to occupy Bohemia in 1003; expelled in 1004, he still retained Moravia. He repelled a series of invasions of Poland by Henry. In 1018, in the Peace of Bautzen, Boleslaus received Lusatia as a fief of the Holy Roman Empire. Subsequently he campaigned successfully against Kiev. Boleslaus ranks among Poland's foremost rulers; he reorganized the administration, systematized taxation, and created a large standing army. Shortly before his death he was crowned king with the approval of the Holy See. He was succeeded by his son, MIESZKO II.

Boleslaus II, c.1039–1081, duke (1058–76), and later king (1076–79) of Poland; son and successor of Casimir I. Throughout his reign he opposed the influence of the Holy Roman Empire. He asserted Polish power in Bohemia, Hungary, and S Russia by interfering in their civil wars. As a reward for submitting his foreign policy to papal control he was crowned king in 1076. He became involved in a sharp conflict with the Polish clergy and nobility, and in 1079 he killed (or procured the death of) Stanislaus, bishop of Kraków. The death provoked immediate reaction; the king's younger brother, Ladislaus Herman, joined in league with the powerful nobles and seized the royal power. Excommunicated and deprived of his title by Pope Gregory VII, Boleslaus died in exile in Hungary.

Boleslaus III, 1085-1138, duke of Poland (1102-38). The kingdom had been divided by his father, Ladislaus Herman, between Boleslaus and his elder brother Zbigniew, whose legitimacy was disputed. Zbigniew was supported by the Holy Roman emperor and other powers; however, Boleslaus defeated Zbigniew and reunited the kingdom. He routed (1109) Holy Roman Emperor Henry V at Hundsfeld and warred against Bohemia, Hungary, and Kiev. Having also regained Pomerania, which Mieszko II had lost to Denmark, Boleslaus entrusted the Christianization of its inhabitants to the bishop of Bamberg. In 1135 at Merseburg he signed a treaty with Holy Roman Emperor Lothair II, by which he received Pomerania and Rügen as fiefs of the empire. Vainly seeking to prevent the disintegration of his kingdom, Boleslaus altered the law of succession of his dynasty (see PIAST). Among his sons, CASIMIR II was the most notable.

Boleslav I, d. 967, duke of Bohemia (929-67). He became duke by assassinating his elder brother, Duke Wenceslaus (see WENCESLAUS, SAINT). Although Boleslav was involved in constant warfare against the encroaching Germans, he was able to create a Bohemian state. He built fortresses to control restless tribes, conquered Moravia and part of Silesia, and encouraged the spread of Christianity. In 950 he was forced to recognize German suzerainty, although Bohemia remained largely autonomous.

Boleslav II, d. 999, duke of Bohemia (967-99), son and successor of BOLESLAV I. Continuing his father's policies, he largely completed the Christianization of Bohemia. In 973 he agreed to the establishment of the bishopric of Prague under the archbishop of Mainz, and in 993 he founded the first monastery in Bohemia. He supported his German overlords against Poland but also clashed with them in two wars. Boleslav strengthened his internal rule by eliminating princely rivals to his own Premyslide dynasty.

Boleyn, Anne (bŏŏl'ĭn, bŏŏlĭn'), 1507?-1536, second queen consort of HENRY VIII and mother of Elizabeth I. She was the daughter of Sir Thomas Boleyn, later earl of Wiltshire and Ormonde, and on her mother's side she was related to the Howard family. After spending some years in France, she was introduced to the English court in 1522. Soon Henry, who had already enjoyed the favors of her older sister, fell deeply in love with Anne. Unlike her sister, however, Anne refused to become his mistress, and this fact, coupled with Henry's desire for a male heir, led the king to begin divorce proceedings against KATHARINE OF ARAGÓN in 1527. In 1532, Anne finally yielded to the king, and the resulting pregnancy hastened a secret marriage (Jan., 1533) and the final annulment (May) by Archbishop CRANMER of Henry's previous marriage. Anne was crowned queen on June 1. Her delivery of a daughter (Elizabeth) in Sept., 1533, bitterly disappointed Henry, who soon took up with Jane SEYMOUR. In 1536, after the miscarriage of a son, Anne was brought to trial for adultery and incest. Whether she was guilty has never been determined, but a court, headed by her uncle Thomas Howard, duke of Norfolk, condemned her, and she was beheaded. Two days before her death her marriage was declared void by the Church of England. See the often published love letters of Henry VIII; biography by M. L. Bruce (1972); W. S. Pakenham-Walsh, *A Tudor Story: The Return of Anne Boleyn* (1963); M. H. Albert, *The Divorce* (1965).

Bolgari: see BULGARS, EASTERN.

bolide (bō'līd): see FIREBALL.

Bolingbroke, Henry of: see HENRY IV (England).

Bolingbroke, Henry St. John, Viscount: see ST. JOHN, HENRY, VISCOUNT BOLINGBROKE.

Bolívar, Simón (sēmōn' bōlē'vär), 1783-1830, South American revolutionary, called the Liberator, b. Caracas, Venezuela, of a wealthy creole family. Educated by tutors such as Andrés BELLO and Simón Rodríguez, he was deeply influenced by the teachings of Jean Jacques Rousseau. When the revolution against Spain broke out in 1810, he became an enthusiastic patriot, but in 1812 his forces were defeated at Puerto Cabello. This ill fortune increased dissension among the revolutionaries, and Bolívar was one of the men who seized and imprisoned the patriot leader, Francisco de MIRANDA. Bolívar went to Cartagena, where he cooperated with the forces of Antonio NARIÑO and won notable victories. In 1815, however, the patriots were again scattered and crushed by a royalist army under Pablo MORILLO. Bolívar escaped to the island of Jamaica and from there fled to Haiti. In the spring of 1816 he led an invasion of Venezuela, which proved a disastrous failure. He was forced to return to Haiti. However, in 1817, when the patriot army had proven unsuccessful against royalist forces, he was recalled as supreme commander. He reinforced the ranks of the rebel army by enlisting the support of José Antonio PÁEZ, leader of the llaneros (plainsmen), and of European volunteers, who were veterans of the Napoleonic wars. With a band of guerrilla fighters he resumed the war, occupied part of the lower Orinoco basin, and at Angostura (now CIUDAD BOLÍVAR) a congress elected him president of Venezuela. There in 1819 he conceived a bold plan of splitting the royalist forces. With a large force—made up largely of llaneros under Francisco de Paula SANTANDER and Páez—he crossed the flooded Apure valley, climbed to the bitterly cold Andean passes, and defeated the surprised Spanish forces at BOYACÁ (Aug. 7, 1819). The same year he was elected president of Greater Colombia (present-day Colombia, Venezuela, Ecuador, and Panama). In June, 1821, his victory at Carabobo sealed the freedom of the north, and Bolívar entered Caracas in triumph. Ecuador, however, was not taken from the Spanish until he and Antonio José de SUCRE won the battle of Pichincha in May, 1822. Bolívar then undertook to free Peru and the present Bolivia, where the forces of the great Argentine liberator José de SAN MARTÍN were already operating. At Guayaquil in July, 1822, Bolívar and San Martín joined in secret meetings. The events that occurred there are unknown, although speculation still continues after a century and a half. The outcome, in any case, was the withdrawal of San Martín. Bolívar was the commander in chief of the patriot forces that won at Junín in 1824. A little later the battle of Ayacucho marked the final triumph of the revolution in South America. Bolívar was unrivaled as the most powerful man of the continent. The president of Greater Colombia, he also organized the government of Peru and created Bolivia. In 1826 he expanded his vision of a united Spanish America by calling a conference of all the new republics at Panama; although little was actually accomplished, the meeting was the beginning of Pan-Americanism. There was much murmuring against his power and his somewhat high-handed methods; he was widely accused of imperial designs, and revolts and separatist movements shook the union. Bolívar declared himself dictator in 1828, and the next night, Sept. 24, 1828 ("the September night"), he barely escaped assassination by jumping from a high window and hiding. He was successful in a campaign against Peru to prevent Peruvian interference in Bolivia and Colombia, but he could not halt the crumbling of Greater Colombia. Venezuela and Ecuador seceded, and Bolívar, in poor health and disillusioned ("We have ploughed the sea," he said), resigned the presidency in 1830. Soon afterward he died of tuberculosis near Santa Marta. At the time of his death Bolívar was poor and bitterly hated, but it was not long before South Americans began to pay tribute to this passionate, headstrong idealist, who is today revered as the greatest Latin American hero. Monumental statues of Bolívar may be seen in the major cities of the Andean region. See biographies by Hildegarde Angell (1930), Salvador de Madariaga (1952, repr. 1969), and Gerhard Masur (rev. ed. 1969).

Bolivia (bōlĭv'ēə, Span. bōlē'vyä), republic (1973 est. pop. 5,250,000), 424,162 sq mi (1,098,581 sq km), W South America. SUCRE is the legal capital and seat of the judiciary, but LA PAZ is the political and commercial focus of the nation. One of the two inland countries of South America, Bolivia is shut in from the Pacific in the W by Chile and Peru; in the east and north it borders on Brazil, in the SE on Paraguay, and in the S on Argentina. Bolivia presents a sharp contrast between high, bleak mountains and plateaus in the west and lush, tropical rain forests in the east. In the southeast it merges into the semiarid plains of the CHACO. The Andes mountain system reaches its greatest width in Bolivia. Two cordilleras, the western one tracing the border with Chile and the eastern running north and south across the center of the country, are divided by a high plateau (altiplano), most of it 12,000 ft (3,660 m) above sea

level—barren, windswept, and segmented by mountain spurs. Despite the harsh conditions the altiplano is the population center of Bolivia. Many sections for want of drainage have brackish lakes and salt beds, notably the extensive Salar de Uyuni in the south. In the north are Lake Titicaca, which Bolivia shares with Peru, and Lake Poopó. This region, world famous for its breathtaking scenery, was the home of one of the great pre-Columbian civilizations. Well known are the ruins of TIAHUANACO. The eastern mountains, consisting of three major ranges, rise to the cold, forbidding heights of the Puna plateau (as high as 16,000 ft/4,880 m) and in the north to the snow-capped peaks of Illimani (21,184 ft/6,457 m) and Illampú (21,276 ft/6,485 m). In these mountains lies the source of the exploited wealth of Bolivia—its minerals. Tin is by far the most important product, but silver was once the chief metal, and copper, wolframite, bismuth, antimony, zinc, lead, and gold are also mined. The names of some mining towns, notably POTOSÍ and Oruro, are world famous. From the mountains, headstreams cut their way eastward carving deep gorges and fingerlike valleys. In these deep-cut valleys are some of the garden spots of Bolivia—Sucre, Cochabamba, and TARIJA. SANTA CRUZ, just east of the high mountains, is the only major city in tropical Bolivia. In the eastern foothills the headstreams gather to form the Beni, the Guaporé, and the Mamoré (tributaries of the Madeira, in Brazil), which flow through the torrid, humid YUNGAS, covered with dense rain forests, not yet adequately exploited, and inhabited mainly by Indians. The region is the most fertile in the country, yielding cacao, coffee, and tropical fruits, and in the early 20th cent. was a major source of wild rubber and quinine. Some of the more accessible valleys, with luxuriant scenery and a pleasantly warm climate, have become popular Bolivian resort areas. To the south, in the Chaco, are major petroleum deposits. Despite the importance of its mines, Bolivia still lives by a subsistence economy. More than half the people eke out a bare living from agriculture. Sugarcane, potatoes, corn, wheat, and rice are the leading crops. Industry is limited to processing and small-scale manufacturing. Bolivia's mineral wealth furnishes the bulk of its exports; foodstuffs, manufactured goods, and chemicals are imported. The United States and Great Britain are the chief trading partners. In 1969, Bolivia's per capita gross national product was $190. More than half the population of Bolivia is pure Indian, although the whites and the cholos (those of mixed Indian and white blood, or Indians assimilated to white culture) maintain economic, political, and social hegemony. The predominant Indian languages are Aymará and Quechua. Many tribes are untouched by the white culture. Most of the population is Roman Catholic, although many Indians retain the substance of their pre-Christian beliefs. There are eight universities in the country. The rate of illiteracy is about 70%. Bolivia has had more than 185 revolutions since it became independent in 1825. The latest constitution was adopted in 1967. It provides for a president elected for a four-year term and a bicameral congress. However, the congress has been suspended since Sept., 1969, and no presidential election has been held since 1966. The altiplano was a center of Indian life even before the days of the Inca, but the AYMARÁ had been absorbed into the Inca empire long before Gonzalo and Hernando PIZARRO began the Spanish conquest of the Inca in 1532. In 1538 the Indians in Bolivia were defeated. Uninviting though the high, cold country was, it attracted the Spanish because of its rich silver mines, discovered as early as 1545. Exploiters poured in, bent on quick wealth. Forcing the Indians to work the mines and the *obrajes* [textile mills] under duress, they remained indifferent to all development other than the construction of transportation facilities to remove the unearthed riches. Indian laborers were also used on great landholdings. Thus began the system of plunder economy and social inequality that persisted in Bolivia until recent years. Economic development was further retarded by the rugged terrain, and conditions did not change when the region was made (1559) into the audiencia of CHARCAS, which was attached until 1776 to the viceroyalty of Peru and later to the viceroyalty of La Plata. The revolution against Spanish control came early, with an uprising in Chuquisaca in 1809, but Bolivia remained Spanish until the campaigns of José de SAN MARTIN and Simón BOLÍVAR; independence was won only with the victory (1824) at AYACUCHO of Antonio José de SUCRE. After the formal proclamation of independence in 1825, Bolívar drew up (1826) a constitution for the new republic. The nation was named Bolivia, and Chuquisaca was renamed Sucre, after the revolutionary hero. Bolivia inherited ambitions and extensive territorial claims that proved disastrous, leading to warfare and defeat. At the time of independence it had a seacoast, a portion of the Amazon basin, and claims to most of the Chaco; in little more than a century all these were lost. The strife-ridden internal history of Bolivia began when the first president, Sucre, was forced to resign in 1828. A steady stream of egocentric, frequently barbarous caudillos plagued Bolivia thereafter. Andrés SANTA CRUZ, desiring to reunite Bolivia and Peru, invaded Peru in 1836 and established a confederation, which three years later was dissolved in blood on the battlefield of Yungay. Although a few presidents, notably José BALLIVIÁN, made efforts to reform the administration and improve the economy, the temptation to wholesale corruption was always strong, and honest reform was hard to achieve. The nitrate deposits of ATACAMA proved valuable, but the mining concessions were given to Chileans. Trouble over them led (1879), during the administration of Hilarión DAZA, to the War of the Pacific (see PACIFIC, WAR OF THE). As a result Bolivia lost Atacama to Chile. The next serious loss was the little-known region of the Acre River, which had become valuable because of its wild rubber. After a bitter conflict, Bolivia, under President José Manuel PANDO, yielded the area to Brazil in 1903 for an indemnity. Attempts at reorganization and reform, especially by Ismael MONTES, were overshadowed in the 20th cent. by military coups, rule of dictators, and bankruptcy. This repeated sequence led to foreign loans, such as the Nicolaus loan from North American bankers, sometimes at exorbitant rates. This led in turn to an increase of foreign influence, strengthened by foreign interests in mines and oil fields. Attempts to raise Bolivia from its status as an underdeveloped country met with little success, although great personal fortunes were amassed from tin mining by tycoons such as Simón I. PATIÑO. Conflicting claims to the Chaco, which was thought to be oil-rich, brought on yet another disastrous territorial war, this time with Paraguay (1932–35). The fighting ended in 1935 with both nations exhausted and Bolivia defeated and stripped of most of its claims in that area. The war and the defeat aggravated internal discontent, and programs, radical, conservative, and moderate, for curing the ills of the nation were hampered by military coups and countercoups. World War II proved a boon to the Bolivian economy by increasing demands for tin and wolframite. International pressure over pro-German elements in the government eventually forced Bolivia to break relations with the Axis and declare war (1943). Meanwhile, rising prices had aggravated the restiveness of the miners over miserable working conditions; strikes were brutally suppressed. The crisis reached a peak in Dec., 1943, when the nationalistic, pro-miner MNR (*Movimiento Nacional Revolucionario*) engineered a successful revolt. The regime, however, was not recognized by other American nations (except Argentina) until 1944, when pro-Axis elements in the MNR were officially removed. Bolivia then became a member of the United Nations. In 1946 the leader of the MNR-backed government, Major Gualberto Villaroel, was lynched. The conservative government installed in 1947 was soon threatened by opposition from the MNR and the extreme left; two serious MNR-led revolts broke out in 1949. In the 1951 presidential elections Victor Paz Estenssoro, the MNR candidate, won a majority of the votes, but was prevented from taking office by a military junta. The MNR, with the aid of the national police (the carabineros) and of a militia recruited from miners and peasants, then rebelled and took power. The revolutionary government proceeded to expropriate and nationalize the tin holdings of the huge Patiño, Hochschild, and Aramayo interests and inaugurated a program of agrarian reform. Civil rights and suffrage were extended to the Indians. Education, health, and construction projects were begun. In 1956 the MNR candidate, Hernán SILES ZUASO won the presidential election, and in 1960 the MNR further consolidated its power with the reelection of Victor Paz Estenssoro. The United States, in spite of losses incurred by American investors, stepped up its program of technical and financial assistance, and Siles Zuaso temporarily succeeded in stemming inflation. But economic and political factors weakened the government. Income from tin exports sank to a postwar low, thus crippling attempts at industrial diversification; technical and administrative incompetence was rife; the fiscal system, never sound, became chaotic, and, worst of all, an incredible eruption of dissident splinter groups, some fostering acts of political terror, brought all attempts at further reform to a virtual halt. In 1964 the government was overthrown by the military. A junta dominated by Gen. René BARRIENTOS ORTUÑO assumed power. The regime used troops to occupy the mines but did not rescind the important reforms of the MNR. Barrientos was elected president in 1966. A radical guerrilla movement, led by the Cuban Ernesto "Che" Guevara, was set back seriously when government troops killed Guevara in Oct., 1967. Barrientos died in a helicopter crash in 1969. His successor, Luis Adolfo Siles Salinas, was overthrown by Gen. Alfredo OVANDO CANDIA. Ovando nationalized, with compensation, the Gulf Oil Company facilities in Bolivia. A rightist military junta overthrew Ovando in Oct., 1970, but lasted only one day, succumbing to a leftist coup led by Gen. Juan José TORRES. Under Torres relations with the Soviet Union, which had been established by Ovando, became closer, to the detriment of ties with the United States. Torres was overthrown in Aug., 1971, by Col. Hugo Banzer Suárez, who was supported by both the MNR and its traditional rightist opponent, the Bolivian Socialist Falange. Banzer closed the universities and returned Bolivia to a pro-U.S. foreign policy. With his power insecure, Banzer frequently arrested politicians, alleging anti-government plots. Churchmen were accused of aiding the guerrilla National Liberation Army. In June, 1974, following months of protests from peasants, miners, students, and opposition politicians, there was an unsuccessful attempt to depose Banzer. The government was reorganized and an all-military cabinet was installed in July. See Harold Osborne, *Bolivia: A Land Divided* (3d ed. 1964); Robert Barton, *A Short History of the Republic of Bolivia* (2d ed. 1968); H. S. Klein, *Parties and Political Change in Bolivia, 1880–1952* (1969); D. B. Heath et al., *Land Reform and Social Revolution in Bolivia* (1969); W. E. Carter, *Bolivia: A Profile* (1971); J. M. Malloy and R. S. Thorn, ed., *Beyond the Revolution: Bolivia Since 1952* (1971); J. V. Fifer, *Bolivia: Land, Location, and Politics Since 1825* (1972); D. B. Heat, *Historical Dictionary of Bolivia* (1972).

Böll, Heinrich (hīn'rĭkh böl), 1917–, German novelist, short-story writer, and playwright. Böll presents a critical, antimilitarist view of modern society in a collection of masterful short stories, *Wanderer, kommst du nach Spa . . .* (1950; tr. *Traveller, If You Come to Spa . . .*, 1956), and the novels *Wo warst du, Adam?* (1951; tr. *Adam, Where Art Thou?*, 1955) and *Billard um halb zehn* (1959; tr. *Billiards at Half Past Nine*, 1961). Man's excesses and his inability to alter his destiny are among Böll's principal concerns in the narratives *Und sagte kein einziges Wort* (1953; tr. *Acquainted with the Night*, 1954), *Haus ohne Hüter* (1954; tr. *Tomorrow and Yesterday*, 1957), *Ansichten eines Clowns* (1963; tr. *The Clown*, 1965), and *Entfernung von den Truppen* (1964; tr. *Absent without Leave*, 1965). Many of Böll's works present his critical reflections on Catholicism and the church and his view of contemporary German society. Among his other notable works are a collection of travel essays, *Irish Journal* (tr. 1967); the novel *Gruppenbild mit Dame* (1971; tr. *Group Portrait with Lady*, 1973); and two anthologies in English, *Eighteen Stories* (1966) and *Children Are Civilians Too* (1970). Böll won the Nobel Prize in Literature in 1972. See study by W. J. Schwarz (tr. 1969).

Bollandists (bŏl'əndĭsts), group of Jesuits in Belgium, named for their early leader, Jean Bolland, a Flemish Jesuit of the 17th cent. They were charged by the Holy See with compiling an authoritative edition of the lives of the saints, the monumental *Acta sanctorum*, which is still being constantly brought up to date.

Bolley, Henry Luke, 1865–1956, American plant pathologist, b. Dearborn co., Ind. He is noted for his work on organisms causing diseases of crop plants (including the discovery of the cause of potato scab), for his methods of preventing oat smut, wheat bunt, and other diseases, and for developing varieties of wilt-resistant flax and rust-resistant wheat.

Bollingen (bôl'ĭgən), town (1970 pop. 26,121), Bern canton, W central Switzerland. It is a dairy and industrial center. There is a 16th-century church in the town.

Bollnäs (bôl'nĕs"), city (1970 pop. 13,498), E Sweden, on the Ljusnan River. It is an important trade center and has railroad workshops. A 15th-century church is there.

boll weevil or **cotton boll weevil,** cotton-eating WEEVIL, or snout beetle, *Anthonomus grandis*. Probably of Mexican or Central American origin, it appeared in S Texas in 1892 and has since spread to most of the cotton-growing regions of the United States, causing losses as great as $200 million a year to the cotton crop. The adult is grayish when young and black when older. It is about 1/4 in. (6 mm) long, with a snout, about half as long as the body, that is used to bore into the cotton boll, or seed pod. Both adults and larvae feed on the developing cotton fibers within the boll; females lay their eggs in holes made by eating, and the developing larvae eventually eat the entire contents of the boll. Earlier in the season some of the flower buds are destroyed in a similar manner; buds infested with larvae do not mature into bolls. Pupation (see INSECT) occurs within the bud or the boll. The entire metamorphosis from egg to adult takes about three weeks; from 2 to 10 generations occur each season. Adults can be destroyed by insecticides, but the larvae are protected within the boll. Another control measure aimed at the adults is elimination of the rubbish piles in which they take shelter during the winter. Fast-developing strains of cotton have been bred to minimize the amount of damage the larvae can do before harvesting. Devastation caused by the boll weevil has been a major reason for the change from a one-crop economy to more diversified agriculture in the South. The boll weevil is classified in the phylum ARTHROPODA, class Insecta, order Coleoptera, family Curculionidae. See U.S. Agricultural Research Service, Entomology Research Div., *The Boll Weevil* (rev. ed. 1969); bibliographies by H. A. Dunn (1964) and L. L Mitlin and Norman Mitlin (1968).

bollworm, name for the larvae of two different moths. The PINK BOLLWORM is a serious pest of cotton, and the CORN EARWORM, or cotton bollworm, attacks cotton, corn, and other crops.

Bologna, Giovanni, or **Giambologna** (jōvän'nē bōlō'nyä, jäm"bōlō'nyä), 1524–1608, Flemish sculptor, whose real name was Jean Bologne or Boulogne. Though born in Douai, France, he is identified chiefly with the Italian Renaissance as one of its greatest sculptors. His masterpiece, *Flying Mercury*, is in the Bargello, Florence. *The Rape of the Sabines* (Florence), with its spiraling forms and multiple viewpoints, is one of the finest examples of mannerist sculpture. This work exerted a profound influence on later art. Among his other works are the equestrian statues in Florence of the Medicis, one of Ferdinand I (see Browning's poem "The Statue and the Bust") and another of Cosimo I; two fountains in the Boboli Gardens, Florence; the bronze doors of the cathedral in Pisa; a Neptune fountain in Bologna; and the colossal statue *Apennines* at Pratolino. There are two of Giambologna's elegant statuettes of the Evangelists in the Metropolitan Museum and one at the museum of the Univ. of Kansas.

Bologna (bōlô'nyä), city (1971 pop. 490,036), capital of Emilia-Romagna and of Bologna prov., N central Italy, at the foot of the Apennines and on the Aemilian Way. It is a commercial and industrial center and a railroad junction. Manufactures include farm machinery, motor vehicles, metal goods, processed food, and chemicals. Originally an Etruscan town called Felsina, it became a Roman colony in 189 B.C. The city came under Byzantine rule in the 6th cent. A.D. and later passed to the papacy. In the early 12th cent. a strong free commune was established. The victory of Bologna over Emperor Frederick II at Fossalta (1249) added political power to the city, then known chiefly as an intellectual center. Bologna's famous university originated (c.1088) with its Roman law school (founded A.D. 425), where IRNERIUS and Accursius taught; medical and theological faculties and courses in the liberal arts were added in the 14th cent. In later years those active at the university included Malpighi, Galvani, and Marconi. Bologna has long been a center of printing, and its observatory (founded 1712) is the oldest in Italy. In politics the rivalry between the Guelphs and the Ghibellines enabled several ambitious families to seize power (13th-15th cent.). The Pepoli were succeeded by the Visconti of Milan and, after a short period of papal rule, by the BENTIVOGLIO (1446). In 1506, Pope Julius II reestablished papal rule, which was interrupted in 1797, when Bologna was made the capital of the Cispadane Republic, but resumed in 1815 after the Congress of Vienna. The coronation of Charles V at Bologna (1530) was the last imperial crowning by a pope. The Council of Trent met at Bologna in 1547-48. There were unsuccessful revolts against papal rule in 1831, 1843, and 1848, and in 1860 Bologna voted to unite with the kingdom of Sardinia. The city was heavily bombed by the Allies in World War II. It has retained a marked medieval aspect; many streets are arcaded. Noteworthy structures include the Palazzo Comunale (13th and 15th-16th cent.); the Renaissance-style Palazzo del Podesta; the palace of King Enzio (13th cent.); the Basilica of San Petronio (begun in 1390), with a 15th-century doorway by Jacopo della Quercia; the Church of Santo Stefano; the Church of San Giacomo Maggiore (founded 1267, major alterations in the 15th cent.); the Church of San Domenico (early 13th cent.); and the Archiginnasio (once the seat of the university and now a library). Bologna has an archaeological museum; an art gallery, with works by Bolognese artists, including FRANCIA, the CARRACCI, and Guido RENI; and a nuclear research institute. On hills near the city are the Renaissance Church of San Michele (in Bosco) and a former Carthusian monastery.

Bologna, University of, at Bologna, Italy; founded in the 11th cent. It originated as a school where law books brought from Ravenna were interpreted. It has faculties of law, political science, economics and commerce, letters and philosophy, teacher training, medicine, industrial chemistry, pharmacy, veterinary medicine, agriculture, engineering, and mathematics, physics, and natural sciences.

Bologne, Jean: see BOLOGNA, GIOVANNI.

bolometer (bōlŏm'ətər, bə-), instrument for detecting and measuring RADIATION, e.g., visible LIGHT, INFRARED RADIATION, and ULTRAVIOLET RADIATION, in amounts as small as one millionth of an ERG. The bolometer was invented in 1880 by Samuel P. Langley. Basically it consists of a radiation-sensitive resistance element in one branch of a Wheatstone bridge; changes in radiation cause changes in the electrical resistance of the element. The radiation-sensitive element may be a platinum strip, a semiconductor film, or any other substance whose resistance is altered by slight changes in the amount of radiant energy falling on it.

Bolsena (bōlsĕ'nä), town (1971 pop. 3,953), Latium, central Italy, on picturesque Lake Bolsena, near the site of the second VOLSINII. It is an agricultural and tourist center. Of note are an imposing castle (12th cent.) and the Church of Santa Cristina (11th-16th cent.).

Bolshevism and Menshevism (bōl'shəvĭzəm, bŏl'-, mĕn'shəvĭzəm), the two main branches of Russian SOCIALISM from 1903 until the consolidation of the Bolshevik dictatorship under LENIN in the civil war of 1918-20. The Russian Social Democratic Labor party, secretly formed at a congress at Minsk in 1898, was based on the doctrines of MARXISM. At the second party congress, held at Brussels and then London in 1903, Lenin's faction gained a majority. His group was thereafter known as the *Bolsheviki* [members of the majority], and his opponents as the *Mensheviki* [members of the minority], although the Bolsheviks promptly lost their numerical superiority. Lenin favored a small, disciplined party of professional revolutionaries; the Mensheviks wanted a loosely organized mass party. In a pamphlet published in 1905, Lenin outlined his concept of revolution in Russia: since the Russian bourgeoisie was too weak to lead its own revolution, the proletarians and peasants must unite to overthrow the czarist regime and establish a dictatorship of the proletariat and peasantry. The Mensheviks, led by PLEKHANOV, believed that Russia could not pass directly from its backward state to a rule by the proletariat and that first an intermediary bourgeois regime must be developed. These differences were not always clear-cut, and many Socialist leaders, such as TROTSKY, passed from one group to the other and back again. The RUSSIAN REVOLUTION of 1905 was a common effort of all revolutionary and reformist movements. In the first Duma of 1906, which was boycotted by the Social Democrats, the liberal Constitutional Democrats were the strongest party, but in 1907 the Social Democrats took part in the elections. In 1912 the Bolsheviks and Mensheviks formally became separate parties. In World War I, the Bolsheviks hoped for the defeat of czarist Russia and sought to transform the conflict into an international civil war that would bring the proletariat to power. The right wing of the Mensheviks supported Russia's war effort; the left wing called for pacifism. In the Russian Revolution of 1917 the Mensheviks participated in the Kerensky provisional government. Lenin, returning from exile in April, declared that Russia was ripe for an immediate socialist revolution. The Bolsheviks gained majorities in the important SOVIETS and overthrew the government in the October Revolution. The Mensheviks opposed this coup d'etat and participated in the short-lived Constituent Assembly (Jan., 1918), but they generally refused to side with the anti-Bolshevik forces during the civil war. The Mensheviks were suppressed by 1921. Meanwhile, in 1918, the Bolsheviks became the Russian Communist party. See Adam B. Ulam, *The Bolsheviks: The Intellectual and Political History of the Triumph of Communism in Russia* (1965, repr. 1968); Leonard Schapiro, *The Communist Party of the Soviet Union* (2d ed., rev. 1970).

Bolshoi Ballet, the principal ballet company of the Soviet Union. It began as a dancing school for the Moscow Orphanage in 1773. Opened in 1856, the Bolshoi Theatre in its early decades competed for preeminence with the Maryinsky Theatre of St. Petersburg. Alexander Gorsky revitalized it in the early 20th cent. and introduced a new dramatic realism to the classical ballets. Igor Moiseyev experimented with folk-dance ballets at the Bolshoi in the 1930s. The company is internationally acclaimed for its superb ensemble skills and for the spectacular realism of its scenery and costumes. Since the mid-1960s Maya PLIESETSKAYA has been the company's prima ballerina. The Bolshoi has toured both Europe and the United States with celebrated productions of such classics as *Giselle* and *Swan Lake*.

Bolton, Herbert Eugene, 1870-1953, American historian and teacher, b. Wilton, Monroe co., Wis. He taught history at the Univ. of Texas (1901-9), Stanford (1909-11), and the Univ. of California (1911-44) and became an outstanding authority on Spanish colonial days in the West. He edited and translated numerous important journals of Spanish soldiers and priests, widening the printed sources immeasurably, but he is perhaps better known for such works as *Texas in the Middle Eighteenth Century* (1921, repr. 1970), *The Spanish Borderlands* (1921), *Outpost of Empire* (1931, repr. 1966; the story of the founding of San Francisco), and the biographies *Rim of Christendom* (1936, repr. 1960; on Father Eusebio Francisco Kino) and *Coronado* (1949). For these sound studies of a colorful period Bolton employed a prose that reflected his own vigorous and colorful personality. He also promoted the study of the history of the Americas as a unit of human development; for this purpose he wrote a syllabus, *History of the Americas* (1928), and a survey of the colonial period, *Wider Horizons of American History* (1939, repr. 1967). He was also director from 1916 to 1940 of the Bancroft Library at the Univ. of California. See studies by Lewis Hanke, ed. (1964), and W. R. Jacobs et al. (1965).

Bolton or **Bolton-le-Moors** (bōl'tən-lə-mŏŏrz), county borough (1971 pop. 153,977), Lancashire, NW England. Since the late 18th cent., when spinning factories were built and a canal (1791) was constructed to Manchester, Bolton has been a cotton-textile center. Prior to that time, woolen weaving, which was stimulated by the immigration of Flemings in the 14th cent., was important. Besides the great textile plants (sheets, quilts, towels, bedcovers, and dress materials), there are factories that pack poultry and produce textile and other machinery, chemicals, leather goods, furniture, carpets, and paper. Samuel Crompton, inventor of the spinning mule (1779), was born nearby and is buried in Bolton. Sir Richard Arkwright invented the "water frame" there c.1768. In 1974, Bolton became part of the new metropolitan county of Greater Manchester.

Boltraffio or **Beltraffio, Giovanni Antonio** (jōvän'nē äntô'nyō bōlträf'fyō, bäl-), 1467-1516, Italian painter, b. Milan. He was a pupil of Leonardo da Vinci, whose style he adhered to faithfully. There are examples of Boltraffio's work in Milan; the National Gallery, London; and the Louvre.

Boltwood, Bertram Borden, 1870-1927, American chemist and physicist, b. Amherst, Mass., grad. Sheffield Scientific School, Yale, 1892. After graduate study at Leipzig and Yale (Ph.D., 1897), he taught at Yale until his death, serving from 1910 to 1927 as professor of radiochemistry. An expert in laboratory technique and apparatus, he gave much of his energy to planning and supervising the building of the Sloane Physics Laboratory and the Sterling Chemistry Laboratory, both at Yale. He did important research on radioactive elements (he discovered ionium, an isotope of thorium, but believed it to be a new element) and pioneered in the radioactive dating of geological strata.

Boltzmann, Ludwig (lo͝ot'vĭkh bôlts'män), 1844-1906, Austrian physicist, b. Vienna, educated at Univ. of Vienna. He began teaching (1869) at Graz Univ. In 1873 he became mathematics professor at Vienna and then physics professor at Graz (1876), Munich (1890), Vienna (1895), and Leipzig (1900). Boltzmann made important contributions to the kinetic theory of gases and to statistical mechanics—the Boltzmann constant, the ratio of the mean total energy of a molecule to its absolute temperature, is used widely in statistics and is named for him. Working independently, he demonstrated a law on radiation from a BLACK BODY that had been stated by the Austrian physicist Josef Stefan; hence the law is sometimes known as the Stefan-Boltzmann law.

Bolyai (bō'lyoi), family of Hungarian mathematicians. The father, **Farkas,** or **Wolfgang, Bolyai,** 1775-1856, b. Bolya, Transylvania, was educated in Nagyszeben from 1781 to 1796 and studied in Germany during the next three years at Jena and Göttingen, where he began a lifelong friendship with Carl F. Gauss. From 1804 to 1853 he was professor of mathematics at Maros Vásárhely. His primary interest was in the Euclidean parallel postulate. His principal work, the *Tentamen* (1832-33), inspired by his mathematically gifted son János, is an attempt at a rigorous and systematic foundation of geometry (Vol. I) and of arithmetic, algebra, and analysis (Vol. II). **János,** or **Johann, Bolyai,** 1802-60, b. Kolozsvár, Transylvania, was educated by his father in Maros Vásárhely and from 1818 to 1822 in Vienna, where he received military training at the imperial engineering academy. In 1820 he began to work in a direction that ultimately led him to a non-Euclidean geometry. In 1823, after vain attempts to prove the Euclidean parallel postulate, he developed his system by assuming that a geometry could be constructed without the parallel postulate. His theory of absolute space was published as an appendix to his father's *Tentamen* and constituted the sole work published in his lifetime.

Bolzano, Bernard (bōltsä'nō), 1781-1848, Czech philosopher, mathematician, and theologian. Though as a Catholic priest he himself was primarily concerned with religious and ethical questions, he is known today for his work in philosophy, methodology of science, mathematics, and logic. Among his important works are *Wissenschaftslehre* (1837), an attempt at a complete theory of science and knowledge; *Rein analytischer Beweis* (1817), which contains an early successful attempt to free differential calculus from the concept of infinitesimals; and *Theorie der reelen Zahlen,* which laid the cornerstone of the theory of real numbers. He tried to devise a geometry without the use of Euclid's parallel postulate, developed a fairly complete theory of real functions, and worked at an ideal language. However, his work did not attract the attention of his contemporaries and thus did not influence the development of mathematics.

Bolzano (bōltsä'nō), Ger. *Bozen* (bō'tsən), city (1971 pop. 103,267), capital of Bolzano prov., in Trentino-Alto Adige, N Italy, on the Isarco River near its confluence with the Adige. It is the center of the German-speaking part of S Tyrol and is a tourist and health resort noted for its Alpine scenery and mild climate. Its position on the Brenner road has made it the chief commercial center of the area since the Middle Ages, when important fairs were held there. The city's manufactures today include steel, plastics, aluminum products, and woolen goods. Bolzano was part of the bishopric of Trent from the 11th cent. until the 16th cent., when it was ceded to the Hapsburgs. It then followed the fortunes of TYROL and was awarded to Italy in 1919. The city was severely damaged in World War II. Noteworthy buildings include the Romanesque-Gothic cathedral (13th-16th cent.) and several houses of the 15th to 17th cent.

Boma (bō'mə), city (1967 est. pop. 79,000), Bas-Zaïre region, W Zaïre, on the Congo estuary. A port and railhead, it exports tropical timber, bananas, cacao, and palm products. Boma was the capital of the Congo Free State (after 1908 the Belgian Congo) from 1887 to 1929.

bombax, common name for the Bombacaceae, a family of deciduous trees, often tall and with unusually thick trunks, found chiefly in the American tropics. The family includes many commercially important members, e.g., the BAOBAB; the balsa, or corkwood (*Ochroma lagopus*), which yields the lightest lumber in the world; and the KAPOK and several species of the genera *Bombax* and *Cerba* whose seed fibers are used as filling material. The Bombacaceae are classified in the division MAGNOLIOPHYTA, class Magnoliopsida, order Malvales.

Bombay (bŏmbā'), former state, W central India, on the Arabian Sea. The state contained within its borders the former Portuguese colonies of Goa, Daman, and Diu. The region of Bombay has a rich history, and remains exist from the period (320-184 B.C.) when much of Bombay belonged to the Buddhist Maurya empire. Buddhism was supplanted (c.5th cent. A.D.) by Hinduism, which has been the major religion except during Muslim control (13th-18th cent.). In the 16th cent., Portugal was the leading foreign power in Bombay, but Great Britain predominated in the 17th cent. and by the early 19th cent. had formed the Bombay presidency, which included Sind. In 1937, Bombay was made a province. After India gained its independence in 1947, all former native states within the provincial boundary joined Bombay; Baroda and Kolhapur were the largest. In 1956, Bombay was reorganized as a state and absorbed parts of Hyderabad and Madhya Pradesh and the princely states of Kutch and Saurashtra. In 1960, however, Bombay state was divided into the new states of Gujarat and Maharashtra. The city of **Bombay** (1971 pop. 5,968,546), now the capital of Maharashtra state, occupies about 25 sq mi (65 sq km) on Bombay and Salsette islands just off the coast. Bombay Island was created in the 19th cent. by reclamation projects that combined seven basaltic islets. Today it is a peninsula of the larger Salsette Island to the north. Salsette Island itself is connected to the mainland by causeways and railroad embankments. The city of Bombay has the only natural deepwater harbor in W India. It is a transportation hub and industrial center. Industries include cotton-textile and chemical manufacturing and petroleum refining. There is an extensive system of hydroelectric stations, and nearby at Trombay is a nuclear reactor. Bombay University (founded 1857) is in the city. Bombay has many large suburbs. Among the largest are Andheri, Santa Cruz, Thana, and Ulhasnagar, all having populations of more than 100,000. The area of the city was ceded (1534) to Portugal by the sultan of Gujarat. Bombay, after it passed to Great Britain in 1661, was the headquarters (1668-1858) of the East India Company in India, and during the American Civil War it expanded to meet the world demand for cotton and became a leading cotton-spinning and weaving center. On Salsette Island are Buddhist caves. The nearby small island of Elephanta is noted for its antiquities. Bombay has the largest community of PARSIS in India.

Bomberg, David, 1890-1957, English artist. Bomberg was apprenticed to a lithographer in 1905 and studied under Walter SICKERT at the Westminster School of Art. His abstract works are filled with angular forms and painted in a hard-edge style.

Bomoseen, Lake (bōməsēn'), 7.5 mi (12 km) long, 1.5 mi (2.4 km) wide, W Vt., largest lake wholly within Vermont. Surrounded by wooded hills, it is a popular summer resort. Bomoseen State Park is on the west shore.

Bomu (bō'mōō), river, c.500 mi (800 km) long, rising in NE Zaïre and flowing generally westward. It forms part of the Zaïre-Central African Republic border. The Bomu merges with the Uele to form the Ubangi, a tributary of the Congo.

Bon, Cape (bŏn), **Ras at Tib** (räs ät tĭb), or **Ras Addar** (ädär'), peninsula, NE Tunisia, projecting c.50 mi (80 km) into the Mediterranean Sea toward Sicily. Cape Bon, the eastern terminus of the Saharan Atlas Mts., is a hilly, fertile region that supports citrus groves, vineyards, and tobacco plantations. During World War II the last German forces in North Africa surrendered to the Allies on Cape Bon in May, 1943.

Bona Dea (bō'nə dē'ə), in Roman religion, ancient fertility goddess worshiped only by women; also called Fauna. She was said to be the daughter, sister, or wife of Faunus. No man could be present at her annual festival in May.

Bonaire (bônĕr'), island (1970 pop. 8,191), 112 sq mi (290 sq km), in the Leeward Islands group of the Netherlands Antilles. Kralendijk is the chief town. Its good harbor has made Bonaire an export point. Sisal and salt are produced on the island, and goats and sheep are raised. Tourism is increasingly important.

Bonampak (bōnämpäk'), ruined city of the Late Classic period of the MAYA, close to TUXTLA, in Chiapas, S Mexico. Discovered in 1946, it consists of a group of temples, one of which is remarkable for a number of very well preserved frescoes, painted in bright, flat colors, depicting in considerable detail scenes of Maya life.

Bonanza Creek, stream, c.20 mi (30 km) long, W Yukon Territory, Canada. It flows NW to the Klondike River near Dawson. The first gold strike in the Yukon occurred there in 1896.

Bonaparte (bō'nəpärt), Ital. *Buonaparte* (bwōnäpär'-tā), family name of NAPOLEON I, emperor of the French. His father, **Carlo Buonaparte,** 1746-85, a petty Corsican nobleman, was a lawyer in Ajaccio. He supported (1768-69) Pasquale PAOLI, then changed sides and became one of the staunchest leaders of the pro-French party in Corsica. He sent his sons to be educated in France. Napoleon's mother, **Letizia,** or **Laetitia, Ramolino Bonaparte,** c.1750-1836, had simple virtues much admired by her son's followers. At Napoleon's court she was given the title Madame Mère. After the final downfall of Napoleon she found refuge in Rome. The eldest of the children of Carlo and Letizia to survive infancy was **Joseph Bonaparte,** 1768-1844. Having gained some note as French minister to Parma and to Rome and as a member of the Council of Five Hundred, Joseph negotiated a treaty (1800) with the United States and represented France in the peace negotiations at Lunéville (1801) and Amiens (1802). When Napoleon became emperor, Joseph bitterly protested being left out of the line of succession. In 1806, Napoleon made him king of Naples, which Joseph administered very inefficiently, and in 1808 he was made king of Spain instead. Thoroughly unsuccessful in defending his throne during the PENINSULAR WAR, he reluctantly abdicated in 1813. From 1815 to 1841 he lived mainly in the United States—at Bordentown, N.J. He died in Italy. Napoleon I himself was born in 1769. His brother **Lucien Bonaparte,** 1775-1840, first became prominent as president of the Council of Five Hundred. He took an important part in the coup d'etat of 18 Brumaire (1799); by boldly haranguing the troops while the council was about to outlaw Napoleon, who had lost his nerve, Lucien succeeded in dispersing the Five Hundred. The Directory was overthrown, and Napoleon became First Consul. However, Lucien was critical of his brother's policies and married a commoner against Napoleon's wishes. He went to live in Italy under the protection of Pope Pius VII, who made him prince of Canino. When Napoleon made the pope a prisoner, Lucien attempted to flee (1810) to the United States but was captured at sea by the British and interned in England. He returned to Italy in 1814 and became reconciled with Napoleon, who was then in Elba. Lucien returned to France in the Hundred Days, and after Waterloo he tried to secure the throne for Napoleon II. He died in exile in Italy. His sister **Elisa Bonaparte,** 1777-1820, married Felix Pasquale Bacciochi, an insignificant captain of infantry. Napoleon made her princess of Piombino and Lucca (1805) and grand duchess of Tuscany (1809). She was a competent administrator and was admired for her intelligence. After Waterloo she lived in retirement. Another brother, **Louis Bonaparte,** 1778-1846, was king of Holland (1806-10). He reluctantly married (1802) Hortense de BEAUHARNAIS. Napoleon forced him to abdicate because Louis, more concerned for the interests of the Dutch people than for those of France, defied the ruinous Continental System. He died in Italy. **Pauline Bonaparte,** 1780-1825, was Napoleon's favorite sister. A woman of remarkable beauty but of a vain, frivolous character, she was the subject of considerable scandal. She accompanied her husband, General LECLERC, on the expedition to Haiti. After Leclerc's death Napoleon arranged her marriage (1803) to Camillo Borghese, a member of the Roman nobility. They soon separated, however. Pauline, made princess of Guastalla in 1806, fell into temporary disfavor with her brother because of her hostility to Empress Marie Louise, but when Napoleon's fortune failed, Pauline showed herself more loyal than any of his other sisters and brothers. Another sister, **Caroline Bonaparte,** 1782-1839, went to France with the family in 1793 and married (1800) General MURAT. Her ambition, joined with that of her husband, made her grand duchess of Cleves and Berg and later (1808-15) queen of Naples. There she did much to stimulate art and letters and encouraged the recovery of the classical treasures of Pompeii and Naples. Her restless ambition was still unsatisfied; the birth of Napoleon's son destroyed her hope of succession for her own son. She and Murat entered upon intrigues with Napoleon's enemies, but with no positive result. After the fall of Napoleon, Clemens von METTERNICH tried to save Murat's throne. Murat's rashness, however, led to his execution, and Caroline fled to Austria. **Jérôme Bonaparte,** 1784-1860, Napoleon's youngest brother, served in the navy and was sent to the West Indies. On a visit to the United States he met Elizabeth PATTERSON, whom he married in 1803, although, as a minor, he lacked the necessary consent. Napoleon refused to recognize the marriage and had little difficulty in changing the mind of the flighty Jérôme, for whom he made (1807) a new match with Catherine of Württemberg. Jérôme became king of Westphalia (1807-13), fought in the Russian campaign, and led a division at Waterloo. He was more remarkable for his extravagant irresponsibility than for administrative or military skill. Leaving France after Waterloo, he returned in 1847 and later received honors at the court of his nephew, Napoleon III. There he was known as Prince Jérôme. Of the second generation of the family the most important was Louis Bonaparte's son, Louis Napoleon, who became emperor as NAPOLEON III (See separate article for NAPOLEON II, son of Napoleon I and Marie Louise). Other members of the family also became prominent. **Charles Lucien Jules Laurent Bonaparte,** 1803-57, prince of Canino, son of Lucien, lived in the United States from 1824 to 1833 and was important as a naturalist, particularly as author of *American Ornithology* (4 vol., 1825-33, in English). He took part in the Roman insurrection of 1848. **Pierre Napoléon Bonaparte,** 1815-81, another son of Lucien, after an adventurous career as soldier of fortune, became a French politician. Although a Republican, he accepted the empire of Napoleon III. In 1870 he killed the journalist Victor Noir in the heat of a quarrel but was acquitted of murder. He was notoriously immoral, as was his cousin **Napoléon Joseph Charles Paul Bonaparte,** 1822-91, commonly called Prince Napoleon or, more familiarly, Plon-Plon. The son of Jérôme and Catherine of Württemberg, he was named as successor to his cousin Napoleon III, in case the emperor should die childless. He was, however, a liberal and on occasion opposed the emperor's measures. His marriage (1859) to Princess Clotilde, the daughter of King Victor Emmanuel II, was a move in Napoleon III's Italian policy. Prince Napoleon became a pretender to the throne after the death of the only son of Napoleon III, **Napoléon Eugène Louis Jean Joseph Bonaparte,** 1856-79, the Prince Imperial, who was killed while fighting the Zulus as a member of the British army. **Napoléon Victor Jérôme Frédéric Bonaparte** (Victor Bonaparte), 1862-1926, inherited the claims of Prince Napoleon, his father. The daughter of Jérôme and Catherine of Württemberg, the princess **Mathilde Bonaparte,** 1820-1904, was prominent during and after the second empire as hostess to men of arts and letters. **Marie Bonaparte,** 1882-1962, granddaughter of Pierre Napoléon, was a disciple and friend of Sigmund Freud. She helped Freud escape from Vienna after the German invasion in 1938. By his American wife, Elizabeth Patterson, Jérôme had a son, **Jerome Napoleon Bonaparte,** 1805-70, from whom the American line is descended. The most prominent of this line was Charles Joseph BONAPARTE. See Walter Geer, *Napoleon and His Family* (3 vol., 1927-29); F. M. Kircheisen, *The Jovial King* (1928, tr. 1932); R. McNair Wilson, *Napoleon's Mother* (1933); C. E. Macartney and J. G. Dorrance, *The Bonapartes in America* (1939); Sidney Mitchell, *A Family Lawsuit: The Story of Elisabeth Patterson and Jérôme Bonaparte* (1958); Monica Stirling, *Madame Letizia* (1961); David Stacton, *The Bonapartes* (1966).

Bonaparte, Charles Joseph, 1851–1921, U.S. cabinet official, b. Baltimore; grandson of Jérôme Bonaparte and Elizabeth Patterson. A lawyer and political leader in Baltimore, he identified himself with reform causes. President Theodore Roosevelt appointed him one of the commissioners to investigate conditions in the Indian Territory and in 1905 appointed him Secretary of the Navy. In Dec., 1906, he shifted from this office to that of Attorney General, which he retained until the end of Roosevelt's administration. He was active in suits brought against the trusts and was largely responsible for breaking up the tobacco monopoly. He was one of the founders, and for a time the president, of the National Municipal League. See biography by J. B. Bishop (1922).

Bonar, Horatius (bŏn'ər), 1808–89, Scottish clergyman and hymn writer. In 1837 he became minister to the North Parish in Kelso; in 1843, Bonar, with his congregation, seceded in the movement leading to the formation of the Free Church. He wrote religious tracts and edited religious periodicals and collections of hymns, including *Hymns of Faith and Hope* (3 series, 1857–66). He is best remembered, however, for his fine hymn texts, such as *I Heard the Voice of Jesus Say.*

Bonar Law, Andrew: see LAW, ANDREW BONAR.

Bonaventure or **Bonaventura, Saint** (bŏnəvĕn'chər, bō"nävāntōō'rä), 1221–74, Italian scholastic theologian, cardinal, Doctor of the Church, called the Seraphic Doctor, b. near Viterbo, Italy. His original name was Giovanni di Fidanza. He entered (1238 or 1243) the Franciscan order, studied at the Univ. of Paris under Alexander of Hales, then taught there with St. Thomas Aquinas until 1255. He was made (1257) general of his order and (1273) cardinal bishop of Albano. He died while attending the Second Council of Lyons, at which he was a papal legate. Among his philosophic and theological works are commentaries on the *Sentences* of Peter Lombard and the "three little works"—*Breviloquium* (tr. 1947), *Itinerarium mentis in Deum* (tr. *The Mind's Road to God,* 1953), and *De reductione artium ad theologiam* (tr. 1939). He succeeded in reconciling Aristotle's learning to orthodox Augustinianism, and he was a proponent of moderate realism (see REALISM, in philosophy, **1**). His later mystical works bring the teachings of St. Bernard of Clairvaux and Hugh of Saint Victor to full flower. He emphasized the total dependence of all things upon God, and he wrote guides to mystic contemplation. He also wrote the official and much-translated life of St. Francis. Feast: July 14. See J. G. Bougerol, *Introduction to the Works of Bonaventure* (Am. ed. 1964); Étienne Gilson, *The Philosophy of St. Bonaventure* (new ed. 1965).

Bonaventure Island, 2½ mi (4 km) long and ¾ mi (1.2 km) wide, off E Que., Canada, in the Gulf of St. Lawrence, c.3 mi (5 km) N of Perce Rock. It has the largest bird sanctuary on the N Atlantic coast.

Bonavista Bay, arm of the Atlantic Ocean, c.40 mi (60 km) long and 40 mi (60 km) wide, E N.F., Canada. The bay is irregular and filled with islands. Cape Bonavista, the headland of the Bonavista Peninsula, marks the southern entrance to the bay and is the reputed landfall (1497) of John Cabot, the discoverer of Newfoundland. Bonavista is the chief fishing town.

Bond, Carrie Jacobs, 1862–1946, American song writer, b. Janesville, Wis. A self-taught musician, she composed about 175 songs, both words and music, gave concerts of them, and even published them herself. Eventually the popularity of such songs as *I Love You Truly, Just a-Wearyin' for You,* and *A Perfect Day* earned her a fortune. See her autobiography, *The Roads of Melody* (1927).

Bond, George Phillips, 1825–65, American astronomer, b. near Boston, grad. Harvard, 1845. He became the assistant of his father, William Cranch Bond, and in 1859 succeeded him as director of the Harvard College Observatory. Much of his work was done in cooperation with his father. While they were studying Saturn together, George in 1848 discovered its eighth satellite, Hyperion. His observations led him to reject the previously held theory that the rings of Saturn were of solid structure, though his hypothesis of their being in fluid state was in turn soon discarded. His memoir on the Donati comet of 1858 in the *Annals of the Harvard College Observatory,* Vol. III, remains the most complete description of a great comet that has been written. His revision of his father's work on the Orion nebula was published posthumously. His photographs of the moon created a sensation among astronomers in Europe when taken there in 1851. He was a pioneer in the use of photography in mapping the sky, determining stellar parallax, and measuring double stars. He also used photographs for determining the comparative brightness of the planets. See E. S. Holden, *Memorials of William Cranch Bond and of His Son George Phillips Bond* (1897).

Bond, Julian, 1940–, U.S. civil rights leader, b. Nashville, Tenn. As a student at Morehouse College, he participated (1960) in the sit-ins at segregated restaurants in Atlanta. He was a founder (1960) of the Student Nonviolent Coordinating Committee and served (1961–65) as its communications director. Elected (1965) to the Georgia state assembly, Bond was denied his seat because of his statements opposing the war in Vietnam. Reelected in 1966, he began serving after the U.S. Supreme Court unanimously upheld (Dec., 1966) his right to hold office. Bond led a group of black delegates to the 1968 Democratic Convention where he successfully challenged the party's unit rule and won representation at the expense of the regular Georgia delegation. He is the author of *A Time to Speak, a Time to Act* (1972). See biographies by John Neary (1971) and R. M. Williams (1971).

Bond, Sir Robert, 1857–1927, Newfoundland political leader. He was educated in England and later entered Newfoundland politics. In 1890, he negotiated a reciprocity agreement between Newfoundland and the United States, but protests from the rest of Canada prevented its ratification. After he became prime minister in 1900, he repurchased the railways and docks from private interests. His ministry was marked by attempts to diversify Newfoundland's economy away from fishing and by disputes over U.S. fishing in provincial waters. Bond's government fell in 1909, and his influence quickly declined. He was knighted in 1901.

Bond, William Cranch, 1789–1859, American astronomer, b. Portland, Maine. He early aided his father in the trades of silversmith and clockmaker in Boston. He soon became an expert in the making of chronometers and by 1812 was fashioning most of the superior ones used by ships sailing out of Boston. He developed a passion for astronomy, and, turning part of his home into an amateur observatory, he devoted all his free time to it. In 1815 he was sent by Harvard College to Europe to visit existing observatories and gather data preliminary to the building of an observatory at Harvard. In 1839 the observatory was founded; Bond supervised its construction and became its first director. In 1847 a 15-in. (37.5 cm) telescope, then matched in size by only one other in the world, was installed. With it, Bond made elaborate studies of sunspots, of the Orion nebula, and of the planet Saturn, publishing his results chiefly in the *Annals of the Harvard College Observatory.* Together with his son he developed the chronograph for automatically recording the position of stars, and he was a pioneer in the use of the chronometer and the telegraph for determining longitude. He and his son George Phillips Bond made the first practical use in America of Daguerre's photographic process applied to astronomy. See E. S. Holden, *Memorials of William Cranch Bond and of His Son George Phillips Bond* (1897).

bond, in finance, usually a formal certificate of indebtedness issued in writing by governments or business corporations in return for loans. It bears interest and promises to pay a certain sum of money to the holder after a definite period, usually 10 to 20 years. Security is usually pledged against a bond; unsecured bonds are regarded as a long-term obligation on the capital of the issuing body. Some bonds are convertible upon maturity into the stock of the issuing company. One method used to retire bonds is the sinking fund; in such a case the issuing body buys back some of its bonds each year and holds them itself, applying the interest to the fund. The entire bond issue, most of which the firm has already acquired, is then retired on maturity. In the case of serial bonds, part of the issue is called in and paid for in full each year. Bonds were sold by the U.S. government to finance both World Wars and are still an important money-raising device. U.S. government savings bonds are available in either the *H* series, which pay interest semiannually and mature in 10 years, or the *E* series, which are sold at discount and mature in 7 to 10 years. Government bonds are backed by the full faith and credit of the government issuing them, including its taxing power, and sometimes also by specifically designated security. Bonds are usually bought by those wishing conservative investment. A fidelity bond is a type of insurance agreement whereby one party guarantees to protect a second party against losses caused by the dishonesty of a third party who holds a position of trust. See Leonard A. Jones, *Bonds and Bond Securities* (4th ed., 4 vol., 1935–50); T. R. Atkinson, *Trends in Corporate Bond Quality* (1967); Alan Rabinowitz, *Municipal Bond Finance and Administration* (1969).

bond, chemical: see CHEMICAL BOND.

Bondfield, Margaret Grace, 1873–1953, British political and trade union leader. A Labour member of Parliament (1923–24, 1926–31), she served as secretary to the minister of labor (1924) and, under Ramsay MacDonald, as minister of labor (1929–31). She wrote and lectured extensively on labor and socialist movements.

bonding: see INSURANCE.

Bond Street, in Westminster, London, England, famous for its fashionable shops. Among the noted residents of Bond St. have been the authors Laurence Sterne, James Boswell, and Jonathan Swift; Admiral Horatio Nelson; and Lady Emma Hamilton.

Bône: see ANNABA, Algeria.

bone, hard substance that forms the SKELETON of the body in vertebrate animals. In the very young the skeleton is composed largely of cartilage and is therefore pliable, reducing the incidence of fracture and breakage in childhood. The inorganic, or mineral, content of bone is mainly calcium and phosphorus salts. The organic content is a gelatinous material called collagen. As the body grows older, the mineral content of the bones increases. In the elderly the extreme brittleness of bones increases the danger of fracture. Bones assume a variety of sizes and shapes; however, all bone tissue has a three-layered structure. A spongy layer forms the interior. Long bones (such as those in the arms and legs) are hollow, the inner spaces being filled with MARROW, important in the formation of blood cells. Surrounding the spongy, inner layer is a hard, compact layer that functions as the basic supportive tissue of the body. The outer layer is a tough membrane called the periosteum, which sheaths most bones. Although bone appears solid, it contains numerous microscopic canals permitting the passage of blood vessels and nerve fibers.

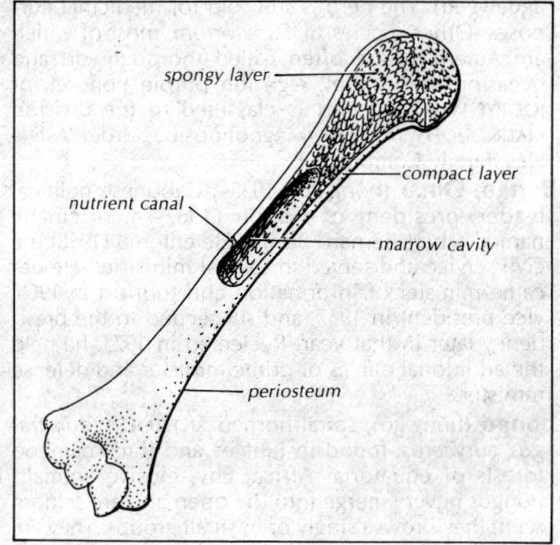

Bone

bone black, solid black material, largely carbon, produced by heating animal bones to high temperatures in the absence of air so as to drive off volatile substances. Finely divided bone black is useful as a pigment; bone char, a similar material, is an important source of activated charcoal for use in refining and decolorizing sugar.

bone china, variety of PORCELAIN developed by English potters in the last half of the 18th and early 19th cent. The clay is tempered with phosphate of lime or bone ash. This innovation greatly increased the strength of the porcelain during and after firing. See Bernard and Therle Hughes, *English Porcelain and Bone China, 1743–1850* (1955).

bonefish, common name for a fish belonging to either of two species of the family Albulidae. *Albula vulpes* is widespread in warm, shallow marine waters, and *Dixonina nemoptera* is found only in the West Indies. The bonefish is silvery in color, with a long, deeply forked tail and a single dorsal fin; it has a pointed head covered by a thick, transparent cartilage and a receding mouth filled with numerous small rounded teeth. *D. nemoptera* is distinguished by two long trailing filaments, one extending from its dorsal fin and one from its anal fin. Also known as ladyfish and banana fish, the bonefish may reach 3.5 ft (107 cm) in length, and 18 lb (8 kg) in weight. It is a bottom dweller of shallow, sandy areas where it feeds on crabs, shrimp, and worms. It is much prized as a game fish, despite the numerous tiny bones that limit its appeal as food. It is classified in the phylum CHORDATA, subphylum Vertebrata, class Osteichthyes, order Clupeiformes, family Albulidae.

bone meal, finely ground bone used as a fertilizer for its content of phosphate and nitrogen (about 23%–30% available phosphate and 2%–4% nitrogen); it is an expensive form of phosphoric acid when compared with SUPERPHOSPHATES. Bone meal is also fed to farm animals to supply needed mineral food constituents, e.g., calcium and phosphorus.

Boner or **Bonerius, Ulrich** (o͞ol'rĭkh bō'nər, bōnēr'-ēəs), fl. 14th cent., Swiss fabulist, a Dominican monk. His *Edelstein* (c.1345), a collection of 100 moralizing beast fables, was one of the first German books to be printed (1461).

boneset or **thoroughwort,** perennial North American herb (*Eupatorium perfoliatum*) of the family Compositae (COMPOSITE family), having terminal clusters of small, chiefly white blossoms. Indian and white man alike valued the plant for the bitter tea made from its leaves and flowers, for which it was often cultivated in gardens. The tea was used for treating colds, fever, and ague (whence the name agueweed). The herb is still sold for medicinal purposes. Other species of *Eupatorium,* most of which are American, are often called thoroughwort and occasionally boneset, e.g., the purple boneset, or JOE-PYE WEED. Boneset is classified in the division MAGNOLIOPHYTA, class Magnoliopsida, order Asterales, family Compositae.

Bongo, Omar (bông'gō), 1935–, Gabonese political leader, president of Gabon (1967–), originally named Albert-Bernard Bongo. He entered (1958) the civil service and served in several ministries. He became minister of information and tourism in 1966, vice president in 1967, and succeeded to the presidency later in that year. Reelected in 1973, he held the additional offices of prime minister and defense minister.

bongo (bŏng'gō), spiral-horned ANTELOPE, *Taurotragus eurycerus,* found in jungles and thick bamboo forests of equatorial Africa. Shy, elusive animals, bongos never emerge into the open and are seldom seen; they browse singly or in small groups. They are fairly large, heavy-bodied antelopes, with males standing 4 ft (120 cm) at the shoulder. Both sexes have horns; in the male these are up to 3 ft (90 cm) long. The body is rich chestnut brown with narrow white stripes running across the back and down the sides, a pattern that provides excellent camouflage in dense thickets. Bongos have been much prized as trophies by big-game hunters. They are classified in the phylum CHORDATA, subphylum Vertebrata, class Mammalia, order Artiodactyla, family Bovidae.

Bonheur, Rosa (bənör'), 1822–99, French painter of animals. She was a pupil of her father, Raymond Bonheur. Her paintings were regularly exhibited in the Salon from 1841. Bonheur's informed and sympathetic pictures of animal life were remarkably enlightened in approach. They gained her wide popularity, particularly in England and America, where much of her work is to be seen. Her most famous painting, *The Horse Fair* (1853–55) is in the Metropolitan Museum.

Bonhoeffer, Dietrich (dē'trĭkh bôn'hôfər), 1906–45, German Protestant theologian, imprisoned for two years and hanged for his role in the plot to overthrow Adolf Hitler. Bonhoeffer, who was influenced very early by the thinking of Karl Barth, urged a conformation to the form of Christ as the suffering servant in a total commitment of the self to the lives of others. His writings, many of them fragmentary, were collected and published posthumously. They include *The Cost of Discipleship* (tr. 1948), *Prisoner for God: Letters and Papers from Prison* (tr. 1953), *No Rusty Swords* (tr. 1965), and *Ethics* (tr. 1965). See biographies by Eberhard Bethge (1967), Mary Bosanquet (1968), André Dumas (1971), and Larry Rasmussen (1972).

Bon Homme Richard: see JONES, JOHN PAUL.

Bonichi, Gino: see SCIPIONE.

Boniface, Saint (bŏn'ĭfəs, -fās), c.675–754?, English missionary monk and martyr, called the Apostle of Germany, b. Devonshire, England. His English name was Winfrid. He was educated in the Benedictine monastery of Nursling, near Winchester. In 716 he made his first trip to Friesland to aid the mission of St. Willibrord, but unsettled conditions forced his return to England. In 718 he left England for Rome where Pope Gregory II encouraged his missionary zeal and gave him the name Boniface. Under the protection of the Frankish ruler Charles Martel, Boniface and his companions made many converts in Thuringia, Hesse, Franconia, and Bavaria. His chopping down of Donar's famed sacred oak at Fritzlar symbolized the advance of Christianity in pagan Germany. He established an orderly Christianity there closely tied to the papacy. He became regionary bishop (722) and metropolitan of Germany (731), creating new bishoprics under the supervision of his English disciples. He founded monasteries at Reichenau (724), Murbach (728), and FULDA (744), which became important centers of learning. As papal legate he reformed (c.745) the decaying Frankish Church. He was consecrated (745) archbishop of MAINZ. He was martyred by pagans in Friesland. Feast: June 5. See his correspondence tr. by E. Kylie (1966); biography by G. F. Muller (1964).

Boniface, Saint, d. 1009, German missionary, known also by his lay name, Bruno of Querfurt. He evangelized the Balts and died a martyr. He is known as the Apostle of the Prussians. Feast: June 19.

Boniface VIII, 1235–1303, pope (1294–1303), an Italian (b. Anagni) named Benedetto Caetani; successor of St. Celestine V. As a cardinal he was independent of the factions in the papal court, and he opposed the election of Celestine. Boniface was elected on Celestine's abdication, and during his first years he was opposed by those who had suffered from Celestine's retirement—the Neapolitans, the Colonna family, and the extreme Franciscans, among them Jacopone da Todi. To preclude schism, Boniface kept Celestine imprisoned for the rest of his life. Boniface reigned in a time of crisis in Europe. He wished to emulate St. Gregory VII and Innocent III, but he was no such statesman, and the times had changed. He interfered in Sicily, but he was openly flouted when Frederick II and the Sicilians forced Boniface to recognize Frederick as king. He brought CHARLES OF VALOIS into Italy to pacify Florence and succeeded only in stirring up more trouble. Dante was exiled in this struggle of Guelphs and Ghibellines. Boniface's contest with PHILIP IV of France was the principal feature of his career. The pope tried to stop Philip from his illegal levies on the clergy by the bull *Clericis laicos* (1296), enunciating the principle that laymen could not tax clerics without the consent of the Holy See. Philip retaliated by cutting off the contributions of the French church to Rome. In England the Pope faced an equally resistant EDWARD I, and in a subsequent bull (1297) Boniface relaxed the ruling. The dispute began again in earnest in 1301 with the trial of Bernard SAISSET, and Boniface never again yielded. Two of his statements in the controversy are famous—the bull *Ausculta fili* (1301), which summoned a synod of French to meet at Rome to discuss the reformation of French affairs, and the bull *Unam sanctam* (1302), an extreme statement (not naming Philip) of the principle that Catholic princes as well as others are subject to the pope in temporal (moral) and religious matters. Philip paid no attention, and in 1303 he sent Nogaret to Italy, soon proclaiming his intention of deposing the pope. Nogaret found the pope at Anagni and harassed him; the pope stood firm and according to tradition was slapped by Nogaret's companion, Sciarra Colonna. The outraged people of Anagni thereupon drove out the soldiery; Boniface was rescued and escorted to Rome. He died in a month. Philip pursued Boniface dead as he had alive. In 1310 he forced CLEMENT V to begin a process to determine that Boniface was heretical; that accusation was abandoned, but Clement consented to repudiate such of Boniface's acts as had hurt Philip. Boniface, an excellent canon lawyer, planned and promulgated a new revision of the code called the *Sext* (1298). He was the first to establish (1300) a holy year. He was succeeded by Benedict XI. See biography by T. S. Boase (1933); C. T. Wood, *Philip the Fair and Boniface VIII: State vs. Papacy* (1967).

Boniface IX, c.1345–1404, pope (1389–1404), a Neapolitan named Pietro Tomacelli; successor of Urban VI. The Avignon antipopes Clement VII and Benedict XIII were his contemporaries during the Great SCHISM. He succeeded in imposing his rule on the Papal States. He fortified Rome and brought Naples under the Roman obedience. His attempt to replenish the papal treasury proved unpopular, and he was accused of nepotism and simony. Boniface decreed the feast of the Visitation. He was succeeded by Innocent VII.

Boniface (bŏn'əfās), d. 432, Roman general. He defended (413) Marseilles against the Visigoths under Ataulf. Having supported GALLA PLACIDIA in her struggle with her brother, Emperor Honorius, Boniface fled to Africa in 422. There, as semi-independent governor, he supported (424) VALENTINIAN III against the usurper John and was rewarded with the title count of Africa. Recalled in 427, he rebelled; a civil war between Africa and the imperial government began. This struggle prepared the way for the invasion (429) of Africa by the Vandals under Gaiseric. A truce was arranged between Africa and Rome, and Boniface attacked the Vandals. He was defeated and besieged (430) at Hippo; during the siege his good friend St. Augustine died. Beaten again in 431, Boniface was recalled to Italy by Placidia to assist her against the general AETIUS. He defeated (432) Aetius but died of a wound received in the battle. The historian Procopius, without convincing evidence, held Boniface responsible for inviting the Vandals into Africa.

Bonifácio, José (zho͞ozā' bônēfä'sēō), 1763–1838, Brazilian statesman and scientist. He studied in Europe and gained international fame as a geologist before returning (1819) to Brazil. Seeking a peaceful solution to Brazilian unrest against Portuguese rule, he urged the establishment of a constitutional monarchy and influenced the prince regent to declare (1822) Brazilian independence and proclaim himself Emperor PEDRO I. Bonifácio served as first minister in the new empire, but his insistence upon a liberal constitution led to his banishment from Brazil (1823–29). Many of his ideas were included in the 1824 constitution, however, and he later (1831–33) served as tutor to Pedro II. He is regarded as the architect of Brazilian independence. His full name was José Bonifácio de Andrada e Silva.

Bonifacio (bōnēfä'chō), town (1968 pop. 2,433), S Corsica, France. A picturesque port with trade in olive oil and fish, Bonifacio faces Sardinia across the Strait of Bonifacio (7 mi/11.3 km wide). The oldest town of Corsica, it was founded (c.828) on the site of a citadel built by Boniface I, count of Tuscany. It later passed to Pisa and to Genoa. There is a Pisan-style church (12th–13th cent.). The town, surrounded by a rampart, is medieval in character.

Bonington, Richard Parkes, 1802–28, English painter. Moving to Calais at the age of 15, his first art study was with Louis Francia, who taught him watercolor and lithography. Bonington studied in Paris at the École des Beaux-Arts and in 1820 entered the studio of Gros. At that time he formed a close friendship with Delacroix, with whom he traveled to England. Bonington was the embodiment of the close link between the English landscape painters Constable and Turner and the budding school of French romanticists. He won early recognition from the Salon, but died of tuberculosis at the age of 26. Best known for his sparkling watercolors painted rapidly, directly from nature, Bonington also brought to his oil painting an immediacy and dexterity unusual in his day. He was a masterly lithographer as well. Represented in the Louvre and in most important British galleries, Bonington's work is best seen in the Wallace Collection, London. The Metropolitan Museum has two marines and a landscape. See study by R. P. Dubuisson (tr. 1924).

Bonin Islands (bō'nĭn), Jap. *Ogasawara-gunto,* volcanic island group (1967 est. pop. 200), c.40 sq mi (100 sq km), in the W Pacific Ocean, c.500 mi (800 km) S of Tokyo; part of Tokyo prefecture, Japan. The largest and principal island is Chichi (formerly Peel Island), c.10 sq mi (30 sq km), the site of Omura, the capital of the group, and Futami-ko (Port Lloyd), the chief harbor. The principal products are sugarcane, cocoa, bananas, and pineapples. The majority of the inhabitants are Japanese; there are some Koreans and Formosans. Discovered by the Japanese in the 16th cent. and later by the Spanish, the islands were claimed by the British in 1827. The islands were claimed by Japan in 1875 and placed under the Tokyo prefecture in 1880. In World War II the islands formed a major Japanese military stronghold and were the scene of land, sea, and air battles. The U.S. navy occupied the islands in 1945. Japan regained technical sovereignty over them in 1951, but they continued to be under U.S. military administration until 1968, when they were returned to Japan.

bonito: see MACKEREL.

Bonivard, François de: see BONNIVARD, FRANÇOIS DE.

Bonn (bŏn, Ger. bôn), city (1970 pop. 274,518), capital of the Federal Republic of Germany, North Rhine-Westphalia, W West Germany, on the Rhine River. It is the administrative center of West Germany and the site of foreign embassies. Villa Hammerschmidt there is the residence of the federal president, and Palais Schaumburg is the home of the federal chancellor. The parliament house (Ger.

Bundeshaus; built in the early 1950s) is located near the Rhine. Manufactures of the city include light-metal products, ceramics, office equipment, chemicals, and pharmaceuticals. Bonn was founded in the 1st cent. A.D. as the Roman garrison of *Castra Bonnensia.* It was devastated by the Normans in the 9th cent. and later became the residence (1238–1794) of the electors of Cologne and the scene of the coronations of Frederick the Handsome (1314) and Charles IV (1346) as kings of the Romans. During the Palatinate Succession War (1689), Bonn was destroyed by Elector Frederick III of Brandenburg. The city was rebuilt thereafter, largely in the baroque style. Bonn was occupied (1794) and later annexed (1798–1814) by France. In 1815 it passed to Prussia. In 1948–49 delegates from the parts of Germany occupied by France, Great Britain, and the United States met in Bonn and drafted a constitution for the Federal Republic of Germany. In 1949, Bonn was also made the capital of West Germany. In 1969 a number of nearby towns, including Bad Godesberg, were incorporated into Bonn. The house where Ludwig van Beethoven was born (1770) has been preserved and is a museum. Bonn is the seat of a famous university (founded 1784), whose main building formerly was the electoral palace (built 1697–1725). The city has a noteworthy church (11th–13th cent.) and museums of zoology and Rhenish culture.

Bonnard, Pierre (pyĕr bônärd'), 1867–1947, French painter, lithographer, and illustrator. In the 1890s he was associated with the NABIS. His delight in familiar views of everyday life was transmitted to canvas with joy and gentle fantasy. Sometimes called an intimist, he explored the play of sunlight in domestic interiors in an exuberant style close to impressionism (e.g., *Bowl of Fruit,* 1933; Philadelphia Mus. of Art). His later works exhibit more vivacious color and dynamic brushwork. Bonnard also designed sets for the stage. See studies by J. Elliott et al. (1964) and André Fermigier (1970).

Bonnat, Léon Joseph Florentin (lāôN' zhôzĕf' flôräNtăN' bônä'), 1833–c.1922, French portrait and historical painter. He received many academic honors and is best known for his portraits of famous men, including Thiers, Victor Hugo, and Dumas fils. Bonnat is represented in the Metropolitan Museum.

Bonnet, Charles (shärl bônā'), 1720–93, Swiss naturalist and philosopher. He drew attention to parthenogenesis in aphids, but his theories to explain his findings were highly fanciful and unscientific. His books include *Traité d'insectologie* (1745) and *Contemplation de la nature* (1764–65).

Bonnet, Georges (zhôrzh), 1889–1973, French politician. He entered politics as a Radical Socialist. A financial expert, he was prominent at international conferences on reparations and other economic questions. He was ambassador (1937) to the United States and several times finance minister, notably in the Camille Chautemps cabinet (1937–38). His stringent fiscal policy was partially responsible for the fall of the Chautemps government. As foreign minister (1938–39) in Édouard Daladier's cabinet, Bonnet helped to draft the Munich Pact, and as a member of the Vichy National Council (1941), he supported collaboration with Germany. Excluded from the Radical party, Bonnet entered the French national assembly in 1956 as a dissident radical, serving until May 1968.

bonnet shark: see HAMMERHEAD SHARK.

Bonneville, Lake (bŏn'əvĭl, bŏ'nĕvĭl, bŏn'vĭl), ancient lake, once covering c.19,500 sq mi (50,500 sq km), NW Utah. The lake expanded during the period of heavy precipitation brought on by the advancing glaciers of the Pleistocene epoch. At the end of the Pleistocene epoch the lake's area rapidly shrank. Its six terraces still exist and locate the different lake levels. Great Salt Lake, Lake Sevier, and Utah Lake are remnants of Lake Bonneville, which was named for U.S. explorer Benjamin de Bonneville.

Bonneville Dam, one of the major dams on the Columbia River, between Oregon and Wash. The dam, 2,690 ft (820 m) long and 197 ft (60 m) high, was built between 1933 and 1943 by the U.S. Corps of Engineers and was one of the largest hydroelectric projects undertaken under the NEW DEAL. It is used for navigation, flood control, and power production (518,400 kw annually). Locks permit ships to pass around the dam, and fish ladders allow salmon to spawn upriver.

Bonnie Prince Charlie: see STUART, CHARLES EDWARD.

Bonnivard or **Bonivard, François de** (both: fräNswä' də bônēvär'), c.1493–1570, Swiss patriot and historian. The prior of St. Victor, near Geneva, he supported the revolt of GENEVA against Charles III of Savoy, who imprisoned him from 1519 to 1521. He was again imprisoned from 1530 to 1536 in the castle of Chillon, romanticized in Lord Byron's poem "Prisoner of Chillon." Released by the Bernese, he later became a Protestant. Geneva honored him with a pension. His chronicle of Geneva was first published in 1831.

Bonny (bŏn'ē), town, SE Nigeria, in the Niger River delta, on the Bight of Biafra. In the 18th and 19th cent., Bonny was the center of a powerful trading state, and in the 19th cent. it became a leading exporter of palm oil. From 1885 to 1894 it was the administrative center of the British Oil Rivers Protectorate. Bonny declined in the 20th cent. but revived after 1961, when its port was modernized as the export point for petroleum refined at PORT HARCOURT.

Bononcini (bōnōnchē'nē) or **Buononcini** (bwō-), musical family of Modena, Italy. **Giovanni Maria Bononcini,** 1642–78, choirmaster and organist at Bologna and Modena, was a composer and the author of a treatise entitled *Musico prattico* (1673). His son **Giovanni Battista Bononcini,** 1670–c.1750, was a composer, chiefly of operas. In London he was the associate and later the rival of Handel. The opera *Muzio Scevola* (London, 1721) was a *pasticcio* by Bononcini, Filippo Mattei, and Handel. After failing in his operatic ventures Bononcini, charged with plagiarism, left England and spent the rest of his life in obscure wanderings. He composed operas, produced in Venice, from 1748. Another son, **Marc Antonio Bononcini,** 1677–1726, became musical director to the duke of Modena in 1721. He wrote many operas, most of which were produced in Venice. His opera *Camilla* (London, 1706) was one of those that helped begin the English fashion for Italian opera.

bonsai (bōn'sī), art of cultivating DWARF TREES. Bonsai, developed by the Japanese more than a thousand years ago, is derived from the Chinese practice of growing miniature plants. In bonsai cultivation, woody plants are kept small and in true proportion to their natural models by growing them in small containers, feeding and watering them only enough for healthy growth, pruning, and training branches in the desired shape by the application of wire coils; the term *bonsai* also refers to the plants dwarfed by this method. Weathered trees in harsh climates serve as natural models for aged-looking, gnarled, bent, and overhanging miniature trees. The selection of containers, the position of the plant in the container, and the choice of single plants or plant groupings are important aesthetic considerations. In Japan, various native evergreens, i.e., junipers, spruces, and pines, as well as many flowering deciduous trees are cultivated; in America many native species have been found suitable. The Brooklyn Botanic Garden in New York City houses an extensive bonsai collection. See Brooklyn Botanic Garden: *Handbook on Dwarfed Potted Trees: The Bonsai of Japan* (1974).

bontebok: see DAMALISK.

Bontecou, Lee (bŏn'təko͞o), 1931–, American artist, b. Providence, R.I. Bontecou is best known for her wall reliefs, constructions made of canvas stretched over wire armatures. Their large, bulging, roughly concentric shapes converging in a black, seemingly endless hole in the center give them a menacing quality. Examples of her work are in the Jewish Museum, New York City.

bontequagga (bŏn"tĕkwăg'ə): see ZEBRA.

bonus, extra amount in money, bonds, or goods over what is normally due. The term is applied especially to payments to employees either for production in excess of the normal (wage incentive) or as a share of surplus profits. The wage incentive was designed during the late 19th cent. not only to increase production but to reward the more skillful and more energetic workers. The hourly or weekly wage was to be figured as payment for a standard rate of work, and the workers who exceeded that standard were to receive a bonus. However, the system fell into disfavor with labor unions because rate cutting was often resorted to when bonuses became too high. Industrial engineers of the 1930s realized that definite standards of accomplishment and quality must be set to make wage incentives workable. Many firms have used an annual bonus plan for distributing abnormal profits to employees. The term is also applied to payments to former servicemen in addition to regular pensions and insurance. Veterans of World War I lobbied to obtain a bonus for their military service. In 1924 each veteran received an adjusted compensation certificate entitling him to a payment averaging $1,000 to be made in 1945. In 1932 about 15,000 unemployed veterans formed the "Bonus Expeditionary Force," or BONUS MARCHERS, and marched to Washington to demand immediate payment of the certificates. President Hoover ordered troops to oust them from Federal property. In 1936 Congress passed a law permitting the veterans to exchange their certificates for cashable bonds. A number of states voted veterans' bonuses after World War II and the Korean War. See W. W. Waters, *B.E.F.: The Whole Story of the Bonus Army* (1933, repr. 1969); V. D. Kennedy, *Union Policy and Incentive Wage Methods* (1945, repr. 1969); J. K. Louden, *Wage Incentives* (2d ed. 1959); Reginald Marriott, *Incentive Payment Systems* (3d rev. ed. 1968).

Bonus Marchers, in U.S. history, more than 20,000 veterans, most of them unemployed and in desperate financial straits, who, in the spring of 1932, spontaneously made their way to Washington, D.C. They demanded passage of a bill introduced by Representative Wright Patman providing for immediate payment of their World War I bonus. Calling themselves the Bonus Expeditionary Force, they camped in vacant government buildings and in open fields made available by police superintendent Pelham D. Glassford. The veterans conducted themselves in a peaceful and orderly way, but when the Senate defeated the Patman bill (June 17, 1932) the marchers refused to return home. On July 28, President Herbert Hoover ordered the army, under the command of Douglas MacArthur, to evict them forcibly. MacArthur had their camps set on fire, and the army drove the veterans from the city. Hoover was much criticized by the press and the general public for the severity of his response.

Bonvalot, Pierre Gabriel Édouard (pyĕr găbrēĕl' ādwär' bôNvälō'), 1853–1933, French explorer and author. In 1880–82 he visited central Asia, explored Kohistan, and returned to France by way of Bukhara, the Caspian sea, and the Caucasus. In 1886 he made the first crossing of the Pamirs, from Ferghana to Chitral, India. He crossed Tibet from Lob Nor to Tengri Nor (1889), traversed Asia from Siberia to Tonkin (1889–90), and led an official mission to Entotto, Ethiopia. His works include *De Moscou en Bactriane* (1884), *De Paris au Tonkin à travers Tibet inconnu* (1892), *L' Asie inconnue* (1896), and *Marco Polo* (1925).

booby, common name for some members of the family Sulidae, large, streamlined sea birds. Tropical and subtropical members of the family are called boobies; those of northern waters are called gannets. These birds have heavy bodies; long, pointed wings; long, wedge-shaped tails; and short, stout legs. They fish by diving on their prey from great heights and pursuing it underwater; air sacs under their skin cushion the impact with the water and provide buoyancy, as with pelicans. The masked, red-footed (*Sula sula*), and brown (*S. leucogaster*) boobies are found the world over; the Peruvian and blue-footed (*S. nebouxii*) boobies, on the west coasts of the Americas; and the Abbott's booby, in the Indian Ocean. The common gannet of the North Atlantic, *Morus bassanus,* breeds in the British Isles, in the Gaspé region of Canada, and on Bird Island in the Gulf of St. Lawrence. A Pacific gannet is one of the chief guano producers of the offshore islands of Peru. Gannets build crude nests of debris on narrow cliff ledges. The female lays a single egg, which she and the male incubate by covering it with their feet. Gannets have strong migration tendencies, while the boobies do not. The name booby is descriptive not only of the rather stupid facial expression of these birds, but also of their unwary, gullible behavior when hunted by man—a factor that accounts for their diminishing numbers. Boobies and gannets are classified in the phylum CHORDATA, subphylum Vertebrata, class Aves, order Pelecaniformes, family Sulidae.

book. The word *book* has come to have many meanings, e.g., any collection of sheets of paper, wood, or other material sewn or bound together (such as a bankbook), a division of a written work (books of the Bible, books of Caesar's *Gallic War*), and statements of financial accounting (bookkeeping). The primary meaning today is, however, a written work either in manuscript or in printed form that is of substantial length. A printed book is distinguished from a PAMPHLET in that it is larger (some publishers limit the term *book* to works of more than 64 or more than 96 pages). It is distinguished from a periodical in that it is a unit and issued as such. Early in the history of bookmaking the printed book was distinguished in size by the number of times the original large sheet of paper on which the type was printed had been folded, i.e., folio, quarto, octavo, and duodecimo. With the advent of machine-made paper, these sizes were standardized to measurements; the standard octavo is, according to the American Library Association, between 20 cm and 25 cm in height. Books apparently did not come into existence until long after writing, e.g., INSCRIPTION, was widespread. Fragmentary early papyri represented literature in ancient Egypt and may possibly be considered as books, although it is customary to speak of the BOOK OF THE DEAD as the first of the Egyptian papyrus books. The CUNEIFORM tablets gathered into the great Assyrian library of Assurbanipal represented an enormous collection of works, but the book as we know it may be said to be derived from the Egyptian writings on papyrus. The vast literature of the Greeks, collected in the greatest library of the ancient world, in Alexandria, was generally written on large sheets of papyrus, which were glued together and rolled up. The rolls varied greatly in size; many of them were about 1 ft (30 cm) wide and about 30 ft (9 m) long when unrolled. In the Hellenistic era large works were divided into tomes [from Gr., = cutting] that were stored together in cylinders and labeled. The method of having the leaves held together in quires (24 or 25 sheets) in the fashion of the modern book seems not to have originated until about the 2d cent. A.D. The manuscripts in leaves are commonly called codices (although the term *codex* may also be loosely used for any ancient manuscript). Most Roman production of books, therefore, was also in rolls. From at least the early part of the 2d cent. B.C. the more permanent vellum (a type of fine PARCHMENT first used in the Middle East) was also used for writing books, and this grew to be very popular in the Middle Ages when books were copied by monks in the scriptoria of monasteries. The codices were the first books to receive the protection of BOOKBINDING, an art that was highly developed before the advent of printing. In the scriptoria the art of ILLUMINATION flourished, making artistic masterpieces of many medieval liturgical volumes. An astonishing number of copies of books were made by hand copying. In ancient Rome hundreds of copies of a popular book were made in a fairly short time. The production of books in great quantity had to await the mechanical processes of printing from movable type. Printing was invented in China, where the first printed book is thought to date from the 9th cent. In the West movable metal type was developed by Johann GUTENBURG of Mainz, and to a very large extent the history of the book was henceforth the history of PRINTING. Book production developed very rapidly, the craft becoming enormously sophisticated by the 16th cent. Italian printers set the standards of format and quality retained in Europe until the 19th cent. Great printing houses arose in France and the Netherlands and, after a general decline in the 17th cent., in England and the United States. The 19th cent. witnessed machine replacement of all the old manual processes. By the end of the century printing quality had been so debased that a revolution, led by William MORRIS during the ARTS AND CRAFTS movement in England, was necessary to restore the concept of beauty to bookmaking. The bookselling business increased over the centuries with widespread education and improvement of transportation. In recent years the printing and distribution of comparatively inexpensive softcover books, or paperbacks, is responsible for a vastly expanded publishing industry. The standing of the book as an information source has been threatened since World War II by other media including television and computer systems. See BLOCK BOOK; BOOK CLUBS; BOOK COLLECTING; BOOK PUBLISHING; INCUNABULA; LIBRARY; MANUSCRIPT; TYPE; WRITING. For a brief and excellent bibliography, see Hellmut Lehmann-Haupt, *One Hundred Books about Bookmaking* (1949). See F. G. Kenyon, *Books and Readers in Ancient Greece and Rome* (2d ed. 1951); Edward Chiera, *They Wrote on Clay* (1958); F. L. Schick, *The Paperbound Book in America: The History of Paperbacks and Their European Background* (1959); R. B. McKerrow, *An Introduction to Bibliography for Literary Students* (1965); H. D. Vervliet, ed., *The Book through Five Thousand Years* (1972).

bookbinding. The art and business of bookbinding began with the protection of parchment manuscripts with boards. Papyrus had originally been produced in rolls, but sheets of parchment came to be folded and fastened together with sewing by the 2nd cent. A.D. In the Middle Ages the practice of making fine bindings for these sewn volumes rose to great heights; books were rare and precious articles, and many were treated with exquisite bindings: they were gilded, jeweled, fashioned of ivory, wood, leather, or brass. The techniques of folding and sewing together sheets in small lots, combining those lots with tapes, and sewing and fastening boards on the outside as protection changed but little from the medieval monastery to the modern book bindery. The invention of PRINTING greatly increased the demand for the bookbinder's work, establishing it as a business. The finest binding is still done by hand. In machine binding (called casing), the cover, or case, is made separate from the book and then glued to it. The covering of the boards, usually called the binding, is most frequently of cloth, heavy paper, vellum, leather, or imitations of leather. The preferred leathers are oasis goat and levant. Leather bindings are sometimes decorated by MARBLING, tooling, or EMBOSSING. See Hellmut Lehmann-Haupt, ed., *Bookbinding in America* (1941, repr. 1967); Ivor Robinson, *Introducing Bookbinding* (1968); F. E. Comparato, *Books for the Millions* (1971).

book clubs. As a phenomenon in American cultural life, book clubs have made an impact in two widely separated periods of history. During the 18th and 19th cent. book clubs were formed for the purposes of discussion and debate. Foremost among these was the Junto, a literary society formed by Benjamin Franklin in 1726; more representative was the Cadmus Club of Galesburg, Ill., founded in 1895, whose aims were the promotion of good fellowship, good reading, and literary works of local interest. What most people in the 20th cent. understand by the term "book club" is not a club at all but an organization that promotes the mail-order sale of books. Among the best known are the Book-of-the-Month Club, the Literary Guild, and the Book Find Club. There are also clubs to match more specialized interests, such as the Antiques Book Society, the Cook Book Club, and the Gamblers' Book Club. The workings of mail-order clubs—set up as they are to ensure that the tastes and choices of their readership will be met—are models of mass production and distribution methods aimed to supply individual selection. The Book Find Club buys publishers' printing plates in order to print its selections cheaply and bind them sturdily for mailing. In exchange, it offers the publisher a 10% royalty on sales. Club members must select a minimum number of books from a monthly list. They order negatively; that is, they let the club know which books they do not want by returning an order card. Although mail-order book clubs enjoy large memberships, they have lost ground to the paperback book industry since the 1950s.

book collecting, or bibliophily, is the acquiring of printed books that are, or are expected to become, rare and that possess permanent interest in addition to their text. Collecting has traditionally concentrated on first editions in the field of pure literature. Contemporary accounts mention personal manuscript collections in ancient Egypt, Greece, and Rome; but because manuscript media—scrolls and papyri—were scarce and expensive (and illiteracy general), collecting was done only by religious leaders and heads of state. During the Middle Ages monastic institutions were the main accumulators of valuable manuscripts. Book collecting proper began after the invention of movable type in the West (c.1437), which produced widespread literacy and a proliferation of inexpensive books. The aim of early collectors, such as Willibald Pirkheimer (1470–1530) and Jean GROLIER DE SERVIÈRES, was to assemble personal working libraries. Many early collections became the cornerstones of public libraries. The BODLEIAN LIBRARY at Oxford and the HARLEIAN LIBRARY of the British Museum were founded respectively on the private collections of Sir Thomas Bodley and Robert Harley, 1st earl of Oxford. By the end of the 17th cent., book auctioning was common throughout Europe. In the 18th cent. collectors shifted their focus from building up libraries to seeking original editions, including INCUNABULA, of earlier works. At first, criteria were more visual than literary: early printing, fancy binding, and colorful illumination. Richard Heber (1773–1833), whose collection of first editions of literature and history filled several houses, was one of the first collectors to consider contextual factors primary. During the 19th cent. first editions of native contemporary literature began to attract book collectors. The two most notable collectors of the second half of the century were Henry Huth (1815–78), an Englishman, and Robert Hoe, the first important American collector. In 1884, Hoe became the first president of the newly founded Grolier Club, a New York-based society dedicated to the appreciation of fine book production. The three greatest American book collectors were Henry Clay FOLGER, John Pierpont MORGAN, and Henry E. HUNTINGTON. During the 20th cent. book collecting on the massive scale practiced by Huntington has declined. The incursion into the field by institutional libraries has limited the circulation of rare books formerly dispersed by auction and through antiquarian bookshops. The three traditional approaches to collecting first editions are the author collection, the subject collection, and the cabinet collection. The latter is a collection of deliberately small size (originally a single bookcase) designed to represent the epitome of one bibliophilic category, such as 15th-century French illumination. The desirability of the first edition is based not only on speculative but also on historical considerations; a first edition is one step from a manuscript. Dealers and collectors usually define a first edition as the first appearance of a written work in book form, although some collectors have shown an interest in periodical serializations of works later published integrally. The most valuable first editions are of literary classics and early or obscure works of famous authors. Original editions of Shakespeare, Poe, and books issued by William Caxton have traditionally been the most sought-after items. Modern collectors who cannot afford the very few incunabula offered to the public—a Caxton printing of *The Canterbury Tales* was sold at a 1965 London auction for $84,000—collect in peripheral fields. Such fields include AMERICANA; books illustrated by famous artists; early books on natural history (especially those with colored plates); books printed by such noted private presses as the KELMSCOTT PRESS, the CUALA PRESS, and the NONESUCH PRESS; early books recounting travel and exploration; ancient manuscripts; and letters. But even books in these fields, sold at places of auction like Christie's in London and the Sotheby Parke-Bernet Gallery in New York City, bring substantial prices. For example, the following sales were reported in *American Book Prices Current* for the year 1969–70: first edition, first issue, of Walt Whitman's *Leaves of Grass* (1855)—$9,000; Kelmscott Press edition of Chaucer's works (1896)—$3,250; letter written by George Washington while at Valley Forge—$2,600. Individual pages of incunabula are also popular with collectors; single leaves of the Gutenberg Bible sold for $2,200 in 1969–70. During the 1960s and 70s works by 20th-century writers have brought substantial fees; e.g., in 1974 a first edition of W. H. Auden's *Poems,* privately published in 1928 and later autographed by the author with marginal notes by Auden and Stephen Spender, sold for $8,500. Book collectors use points, such as broken type and text excisions, to distinguish between different issues of first editions. Information on the existence, location, and prices of collector's items can be found in author bibliographies, dealer and auction catalogs, and book-collecting periodicals such as *The Colophon* (1930–1950), *The Book Collecting World,* and the *Antiquarian Bookman. American Book Prices Current* (published annually since 1895) lists titles and prices of books sold at important auctions in the United States, England, and Canada. See John T. and David A. Randall, *A Primer of Book Collecting* (rev. ed. 1966); John Carter, *Books and Book Collecting* (1957) and *Taste and Technique in Book Collecting* (1948, repr. 1970).

Booker T. Washington National Monument: see NATIONAL PARKS AND MONUMENTS (table).

book gill: see HORSESHOE CRAB.

bookkeeping, maintenance of systematic and convenient records of money transactions in order to show the condition of a business enterprise. The essential purpose of bookkeeping is to reveal the amounts and sources of the losses and profits for any given period. Proper bookkeeping should also reveal the nature and value of the assets and liabilities of a firm, as well as its net worth at the close of that period. Such records are kept in columnar form, using separate columns for the date of transaction, an explanation of the nature of the transaction, and its value. Other columns may be added. In general, two sets of columns are used, the assets being placed in one set of columns and the liabilities in another set (a money value having been assigned to all assets and all liabilities of the business). Such an arrangement is called double entry. A balance sheet may be compiled at any time by totaling each column and subtracting the smaller total from the greater to give either a surplus or a deficit. The result is called the net worth, and it gives an indication of the financial state of a firm. A detailed balance for a period between two balance sheets is called a profit and loss statement. The process of deciding whether to enter items into one set of columns or the other, i.e., into the debit side or the credit side, is called journalizing, since the analyzed items are placed in a journal, or daybook, soon after the transactions occur. Separate accounts of persons or sections are kept in a book called a ledger. The transfer of items from the journal to the ledger is called posting. In large businesses, the journal is broken into many sections, each concerning a separate function of the business, such as sales, purchases, accounts receivable, accounts payable, sales return, purchases return, and cash. Books from which or to which postings are made are known as principal books. Another class, called auxiliary books, includes invoice, inventory, order, cash, sales, bill, and checkbooks. Single-entry bookkeeping enters all debits and credits in a single set of columns in a journal and labels each entry *Dr.* (debit) or *Cr.* (credit). Thus in a single entry only one element of a transaction is entered. Single-entry bookkeeping fails to give detailed information as to the sources of gain or loss. The slip system uses carbon copies of original invoices, or slips, to be arranged as convenient, or the slips themselves constitute the original entries and are kept in filing cabinets. Card ledgers have each account on a separate card in a file case. The slip system, card ledgers, and loose-leaf ledgers are adapted to the use of bookkeeping machines. Such equipment ranges from the simple adding machine to the high-speed electronic computer, the use of which has revolutionized bookkeeping. All of the routine operations and most of the more complicated procedures, except overall organization of the accounts, can be performed by computers. The Babylonians, Egyptians, Greeks, and Romans kept business records. Double entry seems to have been first developed by the people of N Italy during the great commercial expansion of the 14th and 15th cent. and has consequently been called the Italian method. The system then spread to the Netherlands, England, and elsewhere. Single entry developed later. See also ACCOUNTING; AUDITING. A standard work is A. G. Hall, *Introduction to Modern Bookkeeping* (2d ed. 1970).

book lung, terrestrial respiratory organ characteristic of arachnids such as scorpions and primitive spiders. Each book lung consists of hollow flat plates. Air bathes the outer surface of the plates and blood circulates within them, facilitating the exchange of gases. In most species, adequate gas exchange occurs without any muscular movement to ventilate the lung.

Book of Changes (I Ching), classic ancient Chinese book of prophecy and wisdom. The oldest parts of its text are thought to have attained their present form in the century before Confucius. Its images and concepts were taken from mythology, history, and poetry of earlier ages and from the individual insights of the book's original authors. The *I Ching* consists of eight trigrams, corresponding to the powers of nature, which according to legend were copied by an emperor from the back of a river creature. The trigrams are used to interpret the future with the textual help of supplementary definitions, intuitions, and Confucian commentary. The best-known English edition is that by Cary F. Baynes (3d ed. 1970); it is a translation of the German version by Richard Wilhelm.

Book of Common Prayer, title given to the service book used in the Church of England and in other churches of the Anglican Communion. The first complete English Book of Common Prayer was produced, mainly by Thomas Cranmer, in 1549 under Edward VI. Essentially it was a selection and translation from the breviary and the missal, with some additions from other sources. It was made compulsory by the Act of Uniformity (1549). Revision, undertaken by Cranmer, resulted in the Prayer Book of 1552, which showed the influence of foreign reformers then resident in England, for it made possible a wide diversity of views regarding the Eucharist, all justified by this official service book. The prayer book was in use only about eight months before Queen Mary's repeal legislation restored Roman Catholicism in England. In 1559, under Elizabeth I, the Prayer Book of 1552 was restored in a slightly altered version. From 1645 to 1660, under the Commonwealth and Protectorate, the prayer book was suppressed. In a new revision after the Restoration, it was again declared the only legal service book for use in England by an Act of Uniformity (1662). Alterations in the 1662 revision were largely those making for liturgical improvement. In 1927 a revised form was submitted to Parliament, whose approval was (and is) still required, and passed by the House of Lords but rejected by the Commons; it was resubmitted (with certain modifications) in 1928 and again rejected. Nonetheless, the revised prayer book was quite widely adopted in the Church of England with episcopal approval. This situation was finally legalized by the Prayer Book Measure, passed by Parliament in 1965. In addition to authorizing revisions already in use, the act approved the experimental use of new forms of worship drawn up by a liturgical commission. In 1789, when the first General Convention of the Protestant Episcopal Church in the United States met, a revised version of the Book of Common Prayer was adopted; it embodied such changes as were required by the new conditions. In the U.S. Episcopal Church, as in other churches of the Anglican Communion over which the British Parliament has no control, there has been greater freedom in liturgical revision. See histories of the prayer book by J. H. Blunt (1868), F. E. Brightman (2d ed. 1921, repr. 1970), W. K. Lowther Clarke (1932, repr. 1959), and Verney Johnstone, Ernest Evans, and L. C. Lewis (1949); J. W. Suter and G. J. Cleaveland, *The American Book of Common Prayer* (1949); M. H. Shepherd, *The Oxford American Prayer Book Commentary* (1950); for a comparison of revisions, see J. H. Arnold, ed., *Anglican Liturgies* (1939).

Book of Concord, name under which the collected documents of the authoritative confessions of faith of the Lutheran Church were published in 1580, the 50th anniversary of the Augsburg Confession. The Apostles', Nicene, and Athanasian creeds were included with the particular Lutheran confessions that had appeared from 1530 to 1580. These were the Augsburg Confession, Apology of the Augsburg Confession, Schmalkald Articles, Luther's Larger and Smaller Catechisms, and the Formula of Concord.

book of hours, form of prayer book developed in the 14th cent. from the prayers of clerics appended to the main service. The subjects of the miniature illustrations (see MINIATURE PAINTING) were frequently derived from the appendix of the Psalter. The book of hours served as a devotional work containing various prayers and meditations appropriate to seasons, months, days of the week, and hours of the day. Many such books are masterpieces of ILLUMINATION and were symbols of refinement and wealth in fashionable houses of the 15th cent. Jean, duc de Berry, was among the most renowned collectors of books of hours, and his *Très Riches Heures* (Musée Condé, Chantilly), illustrated in part by the LIMBOURG BROTHERS (c.1415), is among the greatest achievements in this genre.

Book of Kells: see CEANANNUS MOR.

Book of the Dead, term used to describe Egyptian funerary literature. The texts consist of charms, spells, and formulas for use by the deceased in the afterworld and contain many of the basic ideas of EGYPTIAN RELIGION. At first inscribed on the stone sarcophagi, the texts were later written on papyrus and placed inside the mummy case. The earliest collection, known as the Heliopolitan Recension, dates from the XVIII dynasty (1580–1350 B.C.). It also contains selections from the two previous collections of Egyptian religious literature—the Coffin Texts of the Middle Kingdom (c.2000 B.C.) and the Pyramid Texts of the Old Kingdom (c.2600–2300 B.C.). The Theban Recension, a text that may be contemporary or slightly later, is distinguished by its distinctive format. There are several noteworthy papyruses, valuable for their art. Among them are the *Papyrus of Ani* and *The Book of the Dead of Hunefer.* The two most celebrated English translations were made by Sir Peter le Page Renouf (1892–97) and Sir E. Wallis Budge (1895, repr. 1967).

bookplate, label pasted in a book to indicate ownership, also called ex libris [Lat.,=from the books of]. The bookplate is usually of paper on which heraldic or other designs are engraved or printed. The earliest printed bookplates date from c.1480 in Germany. Dürer and Holbein designed and engraved a number of bookplates. A Stephen Daye bookplate of 1642 may have been among the first printed in the United States; the John Cotton plate of 1674 certainly was. Paul Revere was well known for his bookplate engravings, as was Nathaniel Hurd. The practice of designing bookplates flourished throughout the 18th and 19th cent. Fine examples are still being produced mainly for collectors and connoisseurs by a number of graphic artists including Leonard Baskin and Peter Lippman. See J. B. L. Warren (Lord De Tabley), *Guide to the Study of Bookplates* (1880); Walter Hamilton, *Dated Book-Plates* (1895); E. J. Kavanagh, ed., *Bookplates* (1966); C. D. Allen, *American Bookplates* (1895, repr. 1968).

book publishing. The term *publishing* means, in the broadest sense, making something publicly known. Usually it refers to the issuing of printed materials, such as books, magazines, periodicals, and the like. There is, however, great latitude of meaning, because publishing has never emerged, and cannot emerge, as a profession completely separate from printing on the one hand and the retailing of printed matter on the other. In the ancient world the making of extra copies of manuscripts for sale or distribution was widely practiced. There is some evidence of such treatment of manuscripts in Athens in the 5th cent. B.C., and the great libraries of the Hellenistic world encouraged the making of copies of manuscripts. In Rome there were booksellers—Horace mentions the Sosii, who were apparently brothers—and the copying of books by trained slaves reached considerable proportions. During imperial times there seems to have been an organized business of making and selling books. After the decline of Rome, the church was the sole preserver of learning, and the copying of manuscripts was limited to the monastic *scriptoria.* The humanists of the early Renaissance revived manuscript publication somewhat, but the immense labor required always kept reproduction at a minimum. With the introduction of printing to Europe in the middle of the 15th cent. (see TYPE), publishing at once sprang into lively existence. The author, the printer, and the publisher of a work were sometimes all the same man, as in the case of members of the Estienne family. The differentiation of printer, publisher, and bookseller appeared astonishingly early, however, as patrons of literature had books printed for distribution and booksellers had their printing done by others to meet the growing demand. The first important publishing house was that of the Elzevir family (see ELZEVIR, LOUIS), which first issued a book in 1583. The Elzevirs were businessmen rather than scholars like the Estiennes, and the business of bookselling grew as literacy spread. Conversely, printing, publishing, and bookselling spread learning across the West. Religious controversy bred polemics, and arguments committed to broadsides, pamphlets, and books were handed out zealously and bought eagerly by partisans. Not long after the appearance of printing came censorship, one of the bugaboos of publishing ever since. The opponents of censorship today are taking a short view when they say that censorship is increasing; it was not so long ago, in the days of the Puritan Revolution in England, that a man could have his ears cropped for injudiciously publishing works critical of the authorities. An interest in knowing the future also increased the amount of literature issued by bookseller-publishers, and almanacs and the like were issued for the wider public. With the steadily broadening mass of readers, great publishing houses slowly came into being; many were well established by the late 18th cent. Leipzig had become a printing center in the 15th cent. and retained its eminence, along with Munich; most of the larger German cities had flourishing publishing concerns by the end of the 19th cent. Modern cities with long traditions of publishing are Vienna, Florence, Milan, Zurich, Paris, London, and Edinburgh. The rate of literacy is very high in the Scandinavian countries, and publishing occupies a relatively larger place in the economy than in most Western countries. In the United States, Boston, Philadelphia, and New York City early took the lead in publishing, with the weight ultimately swinging to New York; in the 20th cent. this lead has been challenged somewhat by Western cities. During the 19th cent. specialization became increasingly evident. Music publishing became almost a completely separate business, as did map publishing. Somewhat less rigidly divorced from general publishing are the houses specializing in religious books, in textbooks, in art books, in technical books, and in reprints. Frequently a house issuing works for the general trade may also have a strong textbook department, a strong juvenile department, or a good list of sports books. Some houses founded for more or less special purposes may broaden their scope, as is sometimes the case with the UNIVERSITY PRESS. In the late 19th and 20th cent. specialization has also grown within many of the houses themselves. Thus, editorial departments become distinct from production, and both may be quite separate from sales, promotion, and distribution. The multiplication of technical specialties often goes much farther. For example, the copy editor who prepares a book for printing may have nothing to do with the policy-setting editor who chooses or helps to choose books for publication. This splintering of functions varies from one publishing firm to another. The necessity for numerous skills and specialties, however, creates a financial problem, particularly in the United States, where the extent of the country and the generally high standard of living tend to have a bearing on publishing and restrict much of the book trade to titles aimed at a large mass market. Also, since books are a luxury item, a purchaser can dispense with them when hard times cut down his spending money. One partial solution of the problem in the United States has been the issuance of paperback books, long a standard form of book publication in Europe. During the 1930s and 1940s the paperbound, pocket-size book rose meteorically in popularity in English-speaking countries, and in the 1950s the "quality" paperback appeared, presenting durable yet inexpensive editions of well-known writers. Indeed, it seemed probable that by 1980 the majority of books published would be paperbacks. Publishing has traditionally been an industry of numerous, small, family-owned firms. During the great publishing boom of the 1960s, however, American publishing houses were continually being bought by and consolidated with other companies. For example, Rinehart & Company and the John C. Winston Company were purchased by Henry Holt to form Holt, Rinehart & Winston, Inc. In addition, publishing firms were being taken over by conglomerate companies, e.g., Holt, Rinehart & Winston, Inc., was purchased by the Columbia Broadcasting System. During the 1960s the publishing industry expanded considerably: in 1963 total book sales were $1.5 billion, and in 1972, despite a cutback in federal school library funds, sales totaled $3.2 billion (some of the increase due to inflation) with a total of 37,000 titles sold. By the mid-1970s, however, it was evident that the effects of inflation and recession were causing the industry to contract. Companies were cutting their publication lists drastically, and many announced that they would no longer publish first novels by unknown authors. Historically, publishers cooperated in having copy-right laws passed to halt pirating of books and succeeded in establishing considerable regulation of book sales to enforce fixed prices. There are today active associations among publishers, the most notable in the United States being the American Book Publishers Council. In addition certain associations present awards for books of unusual merit, e.g., the National Book Committee presented the National Book Awards in five categories: fiction; poetry; arts and letters; history and biography; and science, philosophy, and religion. For material on magazine and newspaper publishing see JOURNALISM; NEWSPAPER; PERIODICAL; see also BOOK; BOOK COLLECTING; CHILDREN'S LITERATURE. See Chandler Grannis, ed., *What Happens in Book Publishing* (2d ed. 1967); H. S. Bailey, Jr., *The Art and Science of Book Publishing* (1970); A. P. Wales, ed., *Classified World Directory of Publishing* (1971); J. W. Tebbel, *A History of Book Publishing in the United States* (1972).

bookworm, popular name for the larvae of several beetles that bore through books, e.g., the drugstore, spider, and deathwatch beetles. Almost any insect that feeds on dry, starchy material (e.g., the book louse and the silverfish) may damage books.

Boole, George, 1815–64, English mathematician and logician. He became professor at Queen's College, Cork, in 1849. Boole wrote *An Investigation of the Laws of Thought* (1854) and works on calculus and differential equations. He developed a form of SYMBOLIC LOGIC, called Boolean algebra, that is of fundamental importance in the study of the foundations of pure mathematics and is also at the basis of computer technology.

boomerang (bo͞o'mərăng"), special form of throwing stick, used mainly by the aborigines of Australia. Other forms of throwing sticks were used by the peoples of ancient Egypt, Ethiopia, and India and by the Indians of the SW United States. The boomerang is sickle-shaped with arms slightly curved in opposite directions as in a propeller. The trajectory of a boomerang is usually an arc, but in some cases it is a full circle. The boomerang of the Australian aborigines (from whom the name is derived) is made in two types. The smaller boomerang, 12 to 30 in. (30.5 to 76.2 cm) long, is used only for sport and is thrown so that it returns to the thrower. The larger war boomerang is 24 to 36 in. (61 to 91.4 cm) long and does not return; it is used for hunting and warfare.

Boone, Daniel, 1734–1820, American frontiersman, b. Oley (now Exeter) township, near Reading, Pa. The Boones, English Quakers, left Pennsylvania in 1750 and settled (1751 or 1752) in the Yadkin valley of North Carolina. Daniel served as a wagoner in Braddock's ill-fated expedition (1755) against Fort Duquesne (Pittsburgh) and almost certainly took part in Gen. John Forbes's successful march on the same place in 1758. He became interested in Florida, but his wife, the former Rebecca Bryan, whom he married in 1756, refused to accompany him. He explored (1769–71) the Kentucky region thoroughly, and its prospects delighted him. Indian attacks turned back his first colonizing attempt (1773), but in March, 1775, as advance agent for Richard HENDERSON and the TRANSYLVANIA COMPANY and with an armed band of 30 men, he blazed the famous WILDERNESS ROAD and founded Boonesboro (or Boonesborough) on the Kentucky River. Henderson arrived in a few weeks with additional settlers, and later in the same season Boone guided a second party, including his family. When Kentucky was made a county of Virginia in 1776, he was elected a captain of militia. In the American Revolution, while on an expedition to find salt in the Blue Licks on the Licking River, Boone and his party were captured (Feb., 1778) by Shawnee Indians and taken to British headquarters at Detroit. Highly regarded by the Indians, he was adopted as a member of the tribe. He led his captors to think that he would prevail on the other settlers to surrender, but, after four months of captivity, he escaped in time to prepare Boonesboro for an attack by the Indians, which failed. A disgruntled element charged Boone with disloyalty, and although he was promptly acquitted and elected major, he left Boonesboro and, after collecting his family, which had returned to North Carolina after his capture, founded (1779) a new settlement, Boone's Station, near what is now Athens, Ky. He served several terms as representative in the Virginia legislature. His titles to large tracts of land were adjudged imperfect, and despite his services to Kentucky he lost his best holdings through ejectment suits. Disgusted, he and Rebecca followed (1799) a son to Missouri, where the Spanish government granted him a large tract in the Femme Osage valley and made him district magistrate. When the United States assumed jurisdiction over this territory after the Louisiana Purchase (1803), his land titles were again found to be defective, but the direct intercession of Congress (1814) restored part of his acreage. His adventures became well known through the so-called autobiographical account that appeared in the widely read *Discovery, Settlement, and Present State of Kentucke* (1784), by John Filson, and Lord Byron's verses on him in *Don Juan* gave his name international prominence. Historical scholarship has disproved many of the legends about him; nevertheless these still attest to those qualities of courage and determination that earned him enduring popularity. See biographies by John Bakeless (1965), R. G. Thwaites (1963, repr. 1971), and R. E. McDowell (1972).

Boone, city (1970 pop. 12,468), seat of Boone co., central Iowa, on the Des Moines River; inc. 1865. It is a railroad and industrial center with plants making machinery, steel fabrications, and plastic signs. It was laid out (1865) by the railroad, which built a long, high double-track bridge there. In 1887 it annexed the nearby rival town of Boonesboro (founded 1851). A junior college is in Boone, and a state park is nearby.

Boonesboro, former settlement, central Ky., on the Kentucky River. It was named for Daniel BOONE, who in 1775 built a small fort there under orders from the TRANSYLVANIA COMPANY, organized by the American colonizer Richard HENDERSON. The seat of the government of Transylvania for several years, Boonesboro was later abandoned because of repeated Indian attacks.

boot: see SHOE.

Boötes (bō-ō'tēz) [Gr.,=the herdsman], northern CONSTELLATION located to the SE of the Big Dipper in Ursa Major and W of Corona Borealis, the Northern Crown. It contains the brilliant orange star ARCTURUS. The figure traditionally associated with Boötes shows a man holding a staff in one hand and two leashed dogs in the other (the Hunting Dogs of the constellation Canes Venatici). Boötes is also known as the Keeper of the Bear because it follows Ursa Major, the Large Bear. It reaches its highest point in the evening sky in June.

Booth, family prominent in the SALVATION ARMY, founded by William BOOTH. His wife, Catherine Mumford Booth (1829–90), whom he married in 1855, played a leading part in the foundation and development of the Salvation Army, devoting herself particularly to the work among women and children. Their eldest son, Bramwell Booth (1856–1929), succeeded his father in 1912 as general of the Salvation Army. Another son, Ballington Booth (1859–1940), was commander (1885–87) of the Army in Australia and then commander (1887–96) in the United States, where his wife, Maud Charlesworth Ballington Booth (1865–1948), shared his labors; in 1896 they withdrew from the Salvation Army and founded the VOLUNTEERS OF AMERICA. A daughter of William Booth, Emma Moss Booth-Tucker (1860–1903), was in charge (1880–88) of the international training homes of the Salvation Army. She and her husband, Frederick St. George de Latour Booth-Tucker (1853–1929), who had resigned from the India civil service to join the Salvation Army, jointly commanded the Army in the United States from 1896 until her death in 1903. See BOOTH, EVANGELINE CORY.

Booth, Charles, 1840–1916, English social investigator, pioneer in developing the social survey method. Aided by the notable social scientist Beatrice Potter WEBB, he made an exhaustive statistical study of poverty in London, showing its extent, causes, and location. This was published as *Life and Labour of the People in London* (17 vol., 1891–1903). Booth was also active in reform groups interested in the poor and aged. His other writings include *Old Age Pensions and the Aged Poor* (1899) and *Industrial Unrest and Trade Union Policy* (1914). See his selected writings (1967); study by Thomas Simey and Margaret Simey (1960).

Booth, Edwin, 1833–93, one of the first great American actors, b. "Tudor Hall," near Bel Air, Md. The second son of Junius Brutus BOOTH, he made his debut at the Boston Museum (1849) as Tressel to his father's Richard III. After years of touring with his father in California, Hawaii, and Australia, in 1857 he appeared in New York City, being particularly successful as Richard III. His style was gentle and restrained, a far cry from the bombast of Edwin Forrest, and his portrayals were exquisitely detailed. He toured (1861–63) England and on the death of his first wife returned to New York and leased the Winter Garden Theatre, where in 1864 he presented his famous 100-night run of *Hamlet* (a record which was not broken until John Barrymore's 101-night run in 1922). His magnificent Shakespearean productions at the Winter Garden terminated in 1865, when his brother John Wilkes BOOTH assassinated President Lincoln. Because of the scandal that followed, Edwin Booth was forced to retire, but he returned to the Winter Garden in 1866. When it burned down, he built Booth's Theatre, New York (1869), where he acted with his second wife, Mary McVicker, and presented such stars as Salvini and Ristori in Shakespeare until his bankruptcy in 1873. He again toured (1880–82) England, at one time alternating with Henry Irving in the roles of Iago and Othello. Associated with Lawrence Barrett, he later appeared (1889–90) with Helena Modjeska. In 1891 he made his last appearance at the Brooklyn Academy of Music as Hamlet. The founder (1888) and first president of the Players' Club, he bequeathed his New York house to the organization. See his letters, ed. by D. J. Watermeier (1971); recollections by his daughter Edwina Booth Grossman (1894, repr. 1969); biographies by Eleanor Ruggles (1953), William Winter (1893, repr. 1968), and Richard Lockridge (1932, repr. 1971); C. H. Shattuck, *The Hamlet of Edwin Booth* (1969).

Booth, Evangeline Cory, 1865–1950, general of the SALVATION ARMY, b. England; daughter of William Booth. At the age of 17, she began evangelistic preaching. She was field commissioner of the Salvation Army in London for five years, commander of the Army in Canada from 1895 to 1904, and commander in the United States from 1904 to 1934. Booth was general of the international Salvation Army from 1934 to 1939. Her works include *Love is All* (1925), *Songs of the Evangel* (1927), and *Woman* (1930). See BOOTH, family. See biography by P. W. Wilson (1948).

Booth, John Wilkes (wĭlks), 1838–65, American actor, the assassin of Abraham LINCOLN, b. near Bel Air, Md.; son of Junius Brutus Booth and brother of Edwin Booth. He made his debut at the age of 17 in Baltimore, toured widely, and soon became a star, winning acclaim for his Shakespearean roles. Unlike the rest of his family, Booth was an ardent Confederate sympathizer. He had joined (1859) the Virginia militia company that assisted in the capture of John Brown, but he did not enter Confederate service in the Civil War. Instead, he continued with his theatrical career in the North. For some six months in 1864–65 Booth, an egomaniac, laid plans to abduct Lincoln and carry him to Richmond, a scheme that was frustrated when Lincoln failed to appear (March 20, 1865) at the spot where Booth and his six fellow conspirators lay in wait. On Good Friday, April 14, 1865, Booth, having learned that Lincoln planned to attend Laura Keene's performance of *Our American Cousin* at Ford's Theater in Washington on that evening, plotted the assassination of the President, Vice President Andrew Johnson, and Secretary of State William H. Seward. Lewis Thornton Powell, who called himself Payne, guided by David E. Herold, seriously wounded Seward and three others at Seward's house. George A. Atzerodt, assigned to Johnson, lost his nerve. The main act Booth naturally reserved for himself. His crime was committed shortly after 10 P.M., when he entered the presidential box unobserved, suddenly shot Lincoln, and vaulted to the stage (breaking his left leg in the process) shouting "*Sic semper tyrannis!* The South is avenged!" He then went behind the scenes and down the back stairs to a waiting horse upon which he made his escape. Not until April 26, after a hysterical two-week search by the army and secret service forces, was he discovered, hiding in a barn on Garrett's farm near Bowling Green, Caroline co., Va. The barn was set afire and Booth was either shot by his pursuers or shot himself rather than surrender. Although it has been said that no dead body was ever more definitely identified, the myth—completely unsupported by evidence—that Booth escaped has persisted. For the fate of others involved, see SURRATT, MARY EUGENIA. See memoir by his sister, Asia Booth Clarke; biographies by Philip Van Doren Stern (rev. ed. 1955) and Francis Wilson (1929, repr. 1972).

Booth, Junius Brutus, 1796–1852, Anglo-American actor. After experience in the provinces, he appeared at Covent Garden. In 1817, with his portrayal of Richard III, he established himself as a rival of Edmund Kean. In 1821 he emigrated to the United States, where he spent most of his remaining life. An imposing tragic actor with a full, rich voice and a rugged grandeur, Booth had an erratic personal life complicated by intemperate habits. He had three sons of whom two were in the theater: Junius Brutus Booth, Jr., who excelled as a manager and Edwin BOOTH, who surpassed his father as an actor. His third son was the assassin of President Lincoln, John Wilkes BOOTH. See Stanley Kimmel, *The Mad Booths of Maryland* (2d ed., 1969).

Booth, William, 1829–1912, English religious leader, founder and first general of the SALVATION ARMY, b. Nottingham. Originally a local preacher for the Wesleyan Methodists, he went (1849) to London and entered (1852) the ministry of the Methodist New Connexion Church, but in 1861 he began independent evangelistic work. In 1865, with the able help of his wife, Catherine Booth, he started the East London Revival Society (soon known as the Christian Mission) in Whitechapel, London. The Christian Mission developed in 1878 into the Salvation Army. General Booth, a remarkable organizer, traveled widely, extending the field of labor to other parts of the world and winning recognition wherever he went. In 1890 he published *In Darkest England and the Way Out* in collaboration with W. T. Stead. See BOOTH, family; BOOTH, EVANGELINE CORY. See biographies by G. S. Railton (2d ed. 1912), Harold Begbie (1920), St. John Ervine (2 vol., 1934), Harold C. Steele (1954), Edward Bishop (1964), and Richard Collier (1965).

Boothia Peninsula (bo͞o'thēə), 12,483 sq mi (32,331 sq km), S central Franklin dist., Northwest Territories, Canada; the northernmost (71°58'N) tip of the North American mainland. It is almost an island, being connected with the mainland only by the narrow Isthmus of Boothia. Topographically and in climate it is like the islands of the Arctic Archipelago. A narrow strait separates it in the north from Somerset Island. To the east the Gulf of Boothia separates it from Baffin Island. It is virtually uninhabited except for a few hundred settlers at Spence Bay and Thom Bay. The peninsula was discovered and explored (1829–33) by John Ross, the British explorer, and named for a patron of the expedition, Sir Felix Booth. Near the southwest end the expedition of Sir John Franklin, the British explorer, ended in tragedy. Roald Amundsen, a Norwegian, explored the peninsula in 1903–5.

Bootle, county borough (1971 pop. 74,208), Lancashire, NW England, at the mouth of the Mersey River. It has extensive docks adjacent to those of Liverpool. Besides shipping, Bootle's industries include tanning, tin smelting, engineering, and flour milling. In 1974, the borough became part of the new metropolitan county of Merseyside.

bootlegging, in the United States, the illegal distribution or production of liquor and other highly taxed goods. First practiced when liquor taxes were high, bootlegging was instrumental in defeating early attempts to regulate the liquor business by taxation. After the appearance of local and state option, those areas that voted to prohibit liquor were supplied with bootlegged liquor. There was also considerable smuggling from foreign countries in order to evade customs duties. In the period of PROHIBITION (1920–33) these activities increased greatly, and by 1930 they were well organized as a large illegitimate industry. Certain areas were dominated by gangs that fought to defend or extend their territory. Infamous gangsters such as Al CAPONE in Chicago and Legs Diamond in New York City were heavily involved in bootlegging. The retail outlet in the prohibition period was the speakeasy, though a house-to-house delivery system to established customers was also well developed. A high degree of organization also prevailed in international liquor SMUGGLING. The combination of graft and violence accompanying this industry became so intolerable that it was an important factor in the final repeal of prohibition. Bootlegging remains a practice in many areas where prohibition is still in practice. Other highly taxed products may also become a target for bootleggers; e.g., a system of bootlegging untaxed cigarettes into New York City existed in the early 1970s. See Kenneth Allsop, *The Bootleggers* (1961, repr. 1970); Andrew Sinclair, *Prohibition: The Era of Excess* (1962, repr. 1964); Harold Waters, *Smugglers of Spirits* (1971).

Booz (bō'ŏz), the same as BOAZ **1.**

Bopp, Franz (fränts bôp), 1791–1867, German philologist. A professor at the Univ. of Berlin from 1821 to 1864, he did research in many languages and earned a great reputation as a scholar by demonstrating the relationship of the Indo-European languages in his *Vergleichende Grammatik* [comparative grammar] (1833–52).

Bora, Katharina von: see LUTHER, MARTIN.

Bora-Bora (bō'rä bō'rä), volcanic island, 15 sq mi (39 sq km), South Pacific, in the Leeward group of the SOCIETY ISLANDS, FRENCH POLYNESIA. It is a mountainous island, with Mt. Taimanu (2,379 ft/725 m) the highest peak. Bora-Bora has a good harbor, which is a large lagoon surrounded by coral islets. Copra, oranges, and vanilla are produced on the island.

boracic acid: see BORIC ACID.

borage (bŏr'əj, bŭr'-), common name for the Boraginaceae, a family of widely distributed herbs and some tropical shrubs or trees characterized by rough or hairy stems, four-part fruits, and usually fragrant blossoms. Its species are most abundant in the Mediterranean area, but many are native to North America and are cultivated, e.g., the Virginia cowslip, or Virginia bluebell (*Mertensia virginica*), species of forget-me-not (genus *Myosotis*), and species of HELIOTROPE (genus *Heliotropium*). The family is classified in the division MAGNOLIOPHYTA, class Magnoliopsida, order Lamiales.

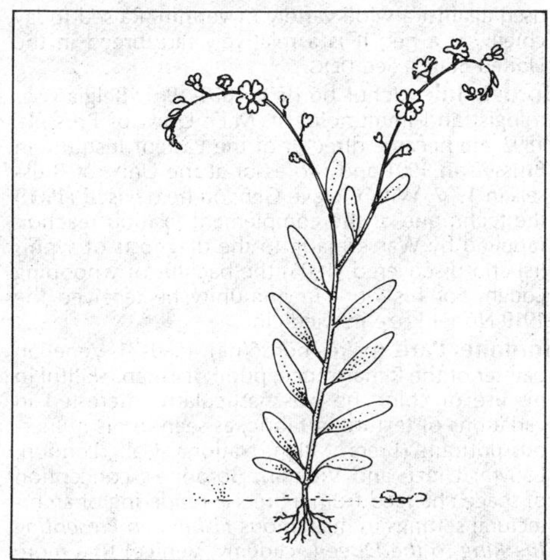

Forget-me-not, Myosotis virginica, *a member of the borage family*

Borah, William Edgar, 1865–1940, U.S. Senator (1907–40), b. near Fairfield, Ill. Admitted to the bar in Kansas in 1887, after 1890 he became prominent in law and politics at Boise, Idaho. Shortly after election to the Senate, he gained (1907) national attention by his prosecution of William HAYWOOD and two other leaders of the Western Federation of Miners, who were accused of conspiring to murder (1905) ex-Governor Frank Steurenberg. In the Senate he was outstanding as an orator, as an expounder of the Constitution, and as a Republican notable for his independent stands (he was sometimes called "the great opposer"). Borah was one of the Senate leaders in defeating the Versailles Treaty and the League of Nations after World War I. From 1924 to 1933 he was chairman of the Senate Committee on Foreign Affairs, and his major interest was in foreign policy. He early asked for recognition of the USSR, favored the collection of war debts, and opposed intervention in Latin American countries to protect U.S. investments. An advocate of disarmament and the outlawing of war, he suggested the Washington Conference of 1921–22 and promoted the Kellogg-Briand Pact; in 1939 he fought revision of the Neutrality Act. In domestic affairs, Borah staunchly favored prohibition. He spoke against economic monopoly and for enforcement of the antitrust laws, but he was opposed to extension of governmental powers and disapproved of the National Recovery Administration and many other New Deal measures. See biographies by C. O. Johnson (1936, new ed. 1967, repr. 1969) and M. C. McKenna (1961); studies by J. C. Vinson (1957), R. J. Maddox (1969), and LeRoy Ashby (1972).

Borah, Mount [for William E. Borah], peak, 12,662 ft (3,859 m) high, central Idaho, in the Lost River Mts.; highest point in the state.

Borås (bo͝orōs'), city (1970 pop. 73,475), Älvsborg co., SW Sweden, on the Viskan River. It is a transportation and commercial center and has numerous cotton and woolen textile factories. Borås was founded in 1632 by Gustavus II.

borax or **sodium tetraborate decahydrate** (sō'dēəm tĕ"trəbôr'āt dĕk"əhī'drāt), chemical compound, $Na_2B_4O_7 \cdot 10H_2O$; sp. gr. 1.73; slightly soluble in cold water; very soluble in hot water; insoluble in acids. Borax is a colorless, monoclinic crystalline salt; it also occurs as a white powder. It readily effloresces, especially on heating. It loses all water of hydration when heated above 320°C and fuses when heated above 740°C; a "borax bead" so formed is used in chemical analysis (see BEAD TEST). Borax is widely and diversely used, e.g., as a mild antiseptic, a cleansing agent, a water softener, a corrosion inhibitor for antifreeze, a flux for silver soldering, and in the manufacture of enamels, shellacs, heat-resistant glass (e.g., Pyrex), fertilizers, pharmaceuticals, and other chemicals. It is sometimes used as a preservative but is toxic if consumed in large doses. Naturally occurring borax (sometimes called tincal) is found in large deposits in the W United States (Borax Lake in Death Valley, Calif.; Nevada; and Oregon) and in Tibet. Borax can also be obtained from borate minerals such as kernite, colemanite, or ulexite. California is the chief source of borate minerals in the United States.

borax bead test: see BEAD TEST.

Borchgrevink, Carsten Egeberg (kär'stən ā'gəbĕr' bôrk'grā"vĭngk), 1864–1934, Norwegian-Australian antarctic explorer. He emigrated to Australia in 1888, and in 1894 he went south in a whaling vessel and at Cape Adare took part in the first landing on the continent of Antarctica. In 1898 he left England in command of a British-sponsored expedition on the *Southern Cross.* He disembarked at Cape Adare and sent the ship back to New Zealand. To prove that man could withstand the harsh climate of Antarctica, he and his companions spent the winter on the continent, the first to do so. In the spring he explored the Ross Sea, did extensive mapping of the Ross Barrier, and described its flora and fauna. See his *First on the Antarctic Continent* (1901).

Bordeaux (bôrdō'), city (1968 pop. 270,996), capital of Gironde dept., SW France, on the Garonne River. Bordeaux is a major economic and cultural center, and a busy port accessible to oceangoing ships from the Atlantic through the Gironde River. Although Bordeaux has important shipyards and industries (machines, chemicals, and airplanes), its principal source of wealth is the wine trade. Bordeaux wine is the generic name of the wine produced in the Bordelais region, which is dotted with châteaux that give their names to many vineyards. Known as Burdigala by the Romans, Bordeaux was the capital of the province of Aquitania and a prosperous commercial city. It became an archiepiscopal see in the 4th cent. Bordeaux's importance declined under Visigothic and Frankish rule (c.5th cent.), but was revived when the city became (11th cent.) the seat of the dukes of AQUITAINE. Eleanor of Aquitaine, who was born there, precipitated through her successive marriages to Louis VII of France and Henry II of England the long struggle between the two nations. As a result of these wars Bordeaux came under English rule, which lasted from 1154 to 1453. The city's commercial importance dates from this period. Reconquered by France, Bordeaux became capital of the province of Guienne. Louis XI established the powerful PARLEMENT of Bordeaux and granted great privileges to the university founded (1441) by Pope Eugene IV. The intellectual reputation of Bordeaux was made by Montaigne and Montesquieu, who were born nearby and who were both magistrates in the city. Bordeaux reached the height of its prosperity in the 18th cent. Its relations with England were always close; many English firms exporting wine and spirits established themselves in the city. Bordeaux was the center of the GIRONDISTS in the French Revolution and the site of the National Assembly of 1871 that established the Third Republic. In 1914 and again in 1940, at the onset of the World Wars, the city was the temporary seat of the French government. The Place des Quinconces, with its statues of Montaigne and Montesquieu, dominates the center of the city. Other points of interest are the Gothic Cathedral of St. André, several art museums, and some elegant 18th-century buildings designed by Victor Louis and Jacques Gabriel. An engineering school and a research center studying mass-media communications are also in Bordeaux.

Bordeaux mixture (bôrdō'), fungicide consisting of CUPRIC SULFATE and lime in water. Its fungicidal activity is associated with the slow formation of copper compounds, the ultimate toxicant being the cupric ion. It originated in France in 1885 and was widely used for spraying orchards, dusting crops, and treating seeds until c.1930. Since it was found that Bordeaux mixture frequently caused russeting of fruit, injured the leaves, and led to premature defoliation, it has been generally replaced by solutions made with powdered fixed copper. Sal soda Bordeaux, or Burgundy mixture, containing cupric sulfate and sodium carbonate (sal soda), was formerly used to spray small fruits but has been replaced by more convenient preparations. See PESTICIDE.

Borden, Sir Frederick William, 1847–1917, Canadian statesman, b. Cornwallis, N.S. He entered (1874) the Canadian House of Commons as a Liberal and served (1896–1911) as Wilfrid Laurier's minister of militia and defense. During his ministry, the last British troops were withdrawn from Canada (1901), the practice of appointing a British general to command the Canadian militia was ended, and Canada took control from Great Britain of the naval bases of Halifax and Esquimalt.

Borden, Gail, 1801–74, American dairyman, surveyor, and inventor, b. Norwich, N.Y. He was for several years a deputy surveyor in Mississippi; afterward he joined the colony of Stephen F. AUSTIN in Texas. There, besides farming, stock-raising, and newspaper activities, he superintended the surveying of lands for Austin. He laid out the city of Galveston, where he became collector of customs. After returning (1851) to New York, he worked on a process of evaporating milk, which he patented in 1856. Jeremiah Milbank backed him financially, and the Borden Milk Company (now Borden, Inc.) opened its first evaporating plant in 1858. During the Civil War his product was found to be of the greatest value for the army, and its use spread rapidly afterward. Borden subsequently also patented processes for concentrating fruit juices and other beverages. See biography by J. B. Frantz (1951).

Borden, Lizzie Andrew, 1860–1927, American woman accused of killing her father and her stepmother, b. Fall River, Mass. The elder Bordens were hacked to death with an ax on Aug. 4, 1892. Although Lizzie Borden claimed that she was out in the barn at the time, she was accused of the murders and tried. The trial, which aroused great public interest, ended with a verdict of not guilty. The case was never solved. See E. D. Radin, *Lizzie Borden: The Untold Story* (1961); Victoria Lincoln, *Private Disgrace* (1967); Robert Sullivan, *Goodbye Lizzie Borden* (1974).

Borden, Sir Robert Laird, 1854–1937, Canadian political leader, prime minister during World War I, b. Grand Pré, N.S. Called to the bar in 1878, he won a reputation as a constitutional lawyer. He was elected to the House of Commons in 1896 and in 1901 succeeded Sir Charles Tupper as leader of the Conservative party. He led the opposition until 1911, when Sir Wilfrid Laurier's Liberal government fell. During the election campaign Borden had opposed the creation of a separate Canadian navy and had criticized Laurier's reciprocity agreement with the United States. The agreement, which would have lowered tariffs between the two countries, was opposed by powerful economic interests in Canada. As prime minister, Borden headed a Conservative government until 1917 and a Union (coalition) government until his resignation in 1920. He is remembered for his leadership in carrying Canada through World War I and, subsequently, in defining the new status of the self-governing dominions in the British Empire. Largely through his efforts the dominions were given separate representation in the League of Nations, and the Canadian Parliament ratified the treaties that resulted from the peace conference of 1919. Borden later represented Canada at the naval armament conference in Washington (1921–22) and in the League of Nations. He was also chancellor of Queen's Univ. (1924–30). His *Canadian Constitutional Studies* (1922) and *Canada in the Commonwealth* (1929) are significant works. See his memoirs, ed. by Henry Borden (1938); H. A. Wilson, *Imperial Policy of Sir Robert Borden* (1966).

Border, the, region surrounding the boundary between England and Scotland. From the coast near Berwick along the Tweed River through the Cheviot Hills and on to Solway Firth, the narrow, rugged country is dotted with sites of battles between the Scots and the English. The wild country figures much in literature—in legend, in folklore, and particularly in the Border ballads.

border collie, breed of medium-sized, sheepherding dog developed in the British Isles. It stands about 18 in. (45.7 cm) high at the shoulder and weighs from 30 to 45 lb (13.6–20.4 kg). Its double coat consists of a soft, fuzzy underlayer and a harsh, very dense, wavy or slightly curly topcoat of varying lengths. Its color is black with white around the neck and on the chest, face, feet, and tip of tail. Bred for many years exclusively to develop its herding instinct, the border collie is unsurpassed as a sheep dog and has been used with equal success for herding cattle, swine, and poultry. It is exhibited in the miscellaneous class at dog shows sanctioned by the American Kennel Club. See DOG.

border terrier, breed of hardy, medium-sized TERRIER developed in the Border districts of N England in the 18th and 19th cent. It stands about 12 in. (30 cm) high at the shoulder and weighs from 13½ to 15½ lb (6.1–6.9 kg). Its weather-resistant double coat is composed of a short, dense underlayer and a close-lying, very wiry topcoat. It may be red, grizzle and tan, blue and tan, or wheaten in color, occasionally with a small amount of white on the chest. The border terrier was bred to hunt and kill the large hill fox of its native Border districts and came to be used against a wide variety of vermin. Raised today chiefly as a pet, it is a relatively rare breed in the United States. See DOG.

Bordet, Jules (zhül bôrdā'), 1870–1961, Belgian serologist and immunologist, M.D. Univ. of Brussels, 1892. He became director of the Pasteur Institute in Brussels in 1901 and professor at the Univ. of Brussels in 1907. With Octave Gengou he devised (1900) the technique of the complement-fixation reaction (applied by Wassermann to the diagnosis of syphilis) and discovered (1906) the bacillus of whooping cough. For his work in immunity he received the 1919 Nobel Prize in Medicine.

Bordone, Paris (pä'rēs bōrdô'nā), 1500–71, Venetian painter of the Renaissance; pupil of Titian. Skillful in his use of color, he was particularly interested in variations of texture in fabric, as seen in his numerous portraits (Brera, Milan; National Gall., London; Louvre; Uffizi; and Vienna). Bordone's conception of space changed from a precise rendering of architectural settings in his famous *Fisherman Presenting the Ring to the Doge* (Academy, Venice) to a more contorted mannerist treatment in *Christ and the Doctors* (Gardner Mus., Boston) and the *Gloria* (Academy, Venice). He created many sensual mythological paintings, including *Diana* and *Minerva at the Forge of Vulcan* (National Gall. of Art, Washington, D.C.).

bore, inrush of water that advances upstream with a wavelike front caused by the progress of incoming tide from a wide-mouthed bay into its narrower portion. The tidal movement tends to be retarded by friction as it reaches the shallower water and meets the river current; it therefore piles up and forms a low wall of water that moves upstream with considerable force and velocity as the tide continues to rise. In the mouth of the Amazon River a tidal bore known locally as the pororoca occurs every spring tide. It has a wall of water from 5 to 15 ft (1.5–4.6 m) high and advances at a speed of from 10 to 15 mi (16–24 km) per hr. The highest recorded bore (15 ft/4.6 m) is found in the Ch'ien-tang River near Hangchow, China. Bores are found also in the Bay of Fundy, in Solway Firth, in the Severn, Seine, and Hooghly rivers, and in Hangchow Bay.

Boreas (bōr'ēəs): see EOS.

borecole: see KALE.

Borel, Félix Édouard Émile (fālēks' ādwär' āmēl' bôrĕl'), 1871–1956, French mathematician. He is noted for his work in infinitesimal calculus and the calculus of probabilities. He was professor at the Univ. of Paris (1904–41), director of the Henri Poincaré Institute (from 1927), and a representative in the French chamber of deputies (1924–36).

Borel, Petrus, pseud. of **Joseph-Pierre Borel D'Hauterive,** 1809–59, French novelist, poet, and translator. Although trained as an architect, he soon turned to writing. Borel was the most extreme of the *bousingos*, a group of extravagant young romantic artists and writers. He loathed the bourgeoisie and believed in the hatred of men for each other. Among his works, whose aim was to shock, are *Rhapsodies* (1832) and *Madame Putip-her* (1839), both of which are horrifying and melodramic.

Borelli, Giovanni Alfonso (jōvän'nē älfôn'sō bôrĕl'lē), 1608–79, Italian physiologist, physicist, astronomer, and mathematician; son of a Spanish infantryman. His wide interests led to original contributions in many fields, including anatomy, epidemiology, the study of fermentation, volcanology, magnetism, fluid dynamics, and the observation of comets. In his study of disease he concluded, against most contemporaries, that meteorological and astrological causes were not at work, but that something entered the body and could be remedied chemically. In *Euclides restitutus* he reworked Euclid's *Elements* into a more concise form. He is perhaps best known for his *De motu animalium* (1679), a study of the mechanical basis of respiration, circulation, and muscular contraction in animals.

Boreman, Arthur Ingram, 1823–96, first governor of West Virginia (1863–69), b. Waynesburg, Pa. A member (1855–61) of the Virginia house of delegates, Boreman opposed secession and presided over the Wheeling Convention of June, 1861, which set up the loyal government of Virginia with Francis H. PIERPONT as governor. It was this government that consented to the partition of Virginia, and on June 20, 1863, Boreman was inaugurated as governor of the new state of West Virginia. Reelected governor in 1864 and 1866, he was elected in 1869 to the U.S. Senate, where he served until 1875.

Borenius, Tancred, 1885–1948, art historian and teacher, b. Finland. He became professor of the history of art at University College, London, in 1922. In 1933 he became director of the excavations of Clarendon Palace near Salisbury, England. Borenius was managing editor of the *Burlington Magazine* from 1940 to 1945. Among his many publications are *The Painters of Vicenza* (1909), *The Iconography of St. Thomas of Canterbury* (1929), and *Rembrandt: Selected Paintings* (1942).

borer, name applied to various animals that are injurious because of their ability to penetrate plant or animal tissues. Among insects, some borers are beetles, e.g., the flatheaded apple-tree borer, a serious pest of many shade and fruit trees; the roundheaded apple-tree borer; and the bronze birch, locust, elm, shot-hole, and poplar borers. Other boring insects are moths that are harmful in the larval stage, e.g., the peach, currant, squash, lilac, and southern cornstalk borers and the European CORN BORER. Marine borers include the boring sponge, certain marine worms, and some bivalve mollusks, e.g., the rock borer, the SHIPWORM, and the piddock, which are thought to secrete acids that dissolve rock and other substances. The HAGFISH, or borer, is a marine pest that burrows into the bodies of other fish.

Borgå (bôr'gō) or **Porvoo** (pôr'vō), city (1970 pop. 16,684), Uusimaa prov., S central Finland, on the Gulf of Finland at the mouth of the Porvoonjoki River. It is an export center for forest products and has plywood and cellulose mills, breweries, and a publishing industry. A trade center in the early Middle Ages, it was chartered in 1350. In 1809, Alexander I of Russia granted Finland a constitution at Borgå. Most of the population is Swedish-speaking. The home and grave of the Finnish national poet J. L. Runeberg is in Borgå.

Borger (bôr'gər), city (1970 pop. 14,195), Hutchinson co., extreme N Texas, in the Panhandle; inc. 1930. After the discovery of oil in 1925, Borger grew as the industrial center of a vast natural-gas and oil field. In the area are refineries, carbon-black plants, synthetic-rubber factories, and related enterprises. A junior college is in Borger.

Borgerhout (bôr'khərhout), city (1970 pop. 49,002), Antwerp prov., N Belgium, on the Albert Canal, an industrial suburb of Antwerp.

Borges, Jorge Luis (hôr'hā lōōēs' bôr'hās), 1899–, Argentine poet, critic and short-story writer, b. Buenos Aires. Borges has been widely hailed as the foremost contemporary Spanish American writer. He was educated in Switzerland and afterwards lived in Spain, where he became an exponent of *ultraísmo,* a poetic movement that followed the decline of MODERNISMO after World War I. *Ultraísmo* advocated the use of bold images and daring metaphors in an attempt to create pure poetry, divorced not only from the past but from reality. Borges, who brought the movement to Argentina, never adhered strictly to its tenets. He helped to found three avant-garde journals and served as director of the National Library and professor of English at the Univ. of Buenos Aires. His poems, collected in *Fervor de Buenos Aires* (1923), *Luna de enfrente* (1925), *Cuaderno San Martín* (1954), *Dreamtigers* (tr. 1964), *A Personal Anthology* (tr. 1967), *Selected Poems: 1923-1967* (1972), and *In Praise of Darkness* (tr. 1974), are often inspired by events of daily life or episodes of Argentine history. Characterized by lyricism, imagination, and boldness, they are, in his own words, "spiritual adventures." His essays, collected in *Inquisiciones* (1925) and *Otras inquisiciones* (1960, tr. 1964), deal with philosophical problems and questions of literary criticism. His tales, ranging from metaphysical allegories and fantasies (e.g., *The Book of Imaginary Beings,* 1967; tr. 1969) to sophisticated detective yarns, reveal a wide variety of influences (Kafka, Chesterton, Virginia Woolf) but are nevertheless strikingly original. Major collections of his short stories include *Historia universal de la infamia* (1935, tr. 1972), *Ficciones* (1944, tr. 1962), *El Aleph* (1949, tr. 1970), *Extraordinary Tales* (1955, tr. 1971), and *Dr. Brodie's Report* (tr. 1972). *Labyrinths* (tr. 1962) is a collection of stories and selected writings in translation. See studies by A. M. Barrenechea (tr. 1965), R. J. Christ (1969), Carter Wheelock (1969), Jaime Alazraki (1971); L. Dunham and Ivar Ivask, ed., *The Cardinal Points of Borges* (1971). See also Richard Burgin, *Conversations with Jorge Luis Borges* (1969).

Borgese, Giuseppe Antonio (jōōzĕp'pā äntō'nyō bōrjā'zā), 1882–1952, Italian-American author, b. near Palermo, Ph.D. Univ. of Florence, 1903. From 1910 to 1931 he taught at the universities of Rome and Milan. An anti-Fascist, he emigrated to the United States in 1931 and was naturalized in 1938. He taught at Smith (1932–35) and the Univ. of Chicago (from 1936). Secretary of the Committee to Frame a World Constitution, he was the chief author of its Chicago draft (1947). All his activities—philosophic, poetic, political—were colored by his concept of spiritual unity or, in his word, *syntax.* His works of criticism, fiction, and poetry include the novel *Rubè* (1921, tr. 1923) and, written in English, *Goliath: the March of Fascism* (1937) and *Common Cause* (1943).

Borghese (bōrgā'zā), Roman noble family, originally of Siena. It produced one pope, PAUL V, several cardinals, and many prominent citizens. The Borghese were noted patrons of arts and letters. Scipione Cardinal Borghese built the fine Villa Borghese in Rome. Camillo Borghese, a general under Napoleon I, married his sister Pauline BONAPARTE.

Borghese Villa or **Villa Umberto I** (vēl'lä ōōmbĕr'tō prē'mō), summer palace built by Scipione Cardinal Borghese outside the Porta del Popolo, Rome. Begun in 1605, the villa was transformed in the 18th cent. into a more elaborate edifice. In 1806 it yielded much of its priceless art to Paris. It is now government owned and has become the repository for many of the paintings from the Borghese Palace.

Borgholm (bôr'yəhôlm"), town (1970 pop. 2,409), Kalmar co., SE Sweden, on Öland Island and on the Kalmarsund, an arm of the Baltic Sea. It is a seaside resort. Of note are the ruins of Borgholm castle (13th cent.; rebuilt 16th–17th cent.), destroyed by fire in the early 19th cent.

Borgia (bōr'jä), Span. *Borja* (bôr'hä), Spanish-Italian noble family, originally from Aragón. When Alfonso de Borja, cardinal-archbishop of Valencia, was pope as Calixtus III (1455–58), several relatives followed him to Rome. His nephew Rodrigo became pope as ALEXANDER VI, and Rodrigo's illegitimate children were Cesare and Lucrezia Borgia; the later reputations of these Borgias made the family name a synonym for avarice and treachery. To the Spanish branch of the family belonged St. FRANCIS BORGIA and Francisco Borja (1581–1658), a Spanish general and viceroy of Peru. The direct line of the family, whose senior members bore the title duke of Gandia, died out in the 18th cent. See study by E. R. Chamberlin (1974).

Borgia, Cesare or **Caesar** (chā'zärā), 1476–1507, Italian soldier and politician, younger son of Pope ALEXANDER VI and an outstanding figure of the Italian Renaissance. Throughout his pontificate Alexander VI used his position to aggrandize his son and establish a papal empire in N and central Italy. Archbishop of Valencia and a cardinal by 1493, Cesare resigned the dignity after the death (1498) of his elder brother, the duke of Gandia, in whose murder he was probably involved. He now began his political career as papal legate to France. He struck an alliance with King Louis XII who made him duke of Valentinois (Valence), and married (1499) Charlotte d'Albret, a sister of the king of Navarre. The French having overrun Italy (see ITALIAN WARS), Cesare, with his father's encouragement, subdued (1499–1500) the cities of the ROMAGNA one by one. Made duke of Romagna (1501) by the pope, Cesare also seized (1502) Piombino, Elba, Camerino, and the duchy of Urbino, and he crowned his achievements by artfully luring his chief enemies to the castle of Senigallia, where he had some of them strangled. By killing his enemies, packing the college of cardinals, pushing his conquests as fast as possible, and buying the loyalty of the Roman gentry, he had hoped to make his position independent of the papacy or at least to insure that the election of any future pope would be to his liking. But before his schemes could be realized, Cesare was struck in 1503 by the same poison (or illness) that suddenly killed his father. Cesare recovered; however, his political power had suffered a fatal blow. Pius III, after a short reign, was succeeded by JULIUS II, an implacable enemy of Cesare Borgia. Louis XII then turned against him. Julius demanded the immediate return of what territory remained to Cesare and had him temporarily arrested. Returning to Naples, Cesare was soon arrested by the Spanish governor there as the result of collusion between Julius II and the Spanish rulers, Ferdinand and Isabella. Sent to prison in Spain, he escaped and finally found refuge (1506) at the court of the king of Navarre. He died fighting for him at Viana. His former possessions had passed under direct papal rule; thus, Cesare must be regarded as instrumental in the consolidation of the Papal States, even if that was not his purpose. Cesare has long been considered the model of the Renaissance prince, the prototype of Niccolò Machiavelli's *Prince*—intelligent, cruel, treacherous, and ruthlessly opportunistic. See biographies by W. H. Woodward (1913) and Rafael Sabatini (1923); Michael Mallett, *The Borgias* (1969).

Borgia, Francis: see FRANCIS BORGIA, SAINT.

Borgia, Lucrezia (lōōkrā'tsyä), 1480–1519, Italian noblewoman, famous figure of the Italian Renaissance; daughter of Pope ALEXANDER VI. Her first marriage (1492) to Giovanni Sforza of Pesaro was annulled in 1497, and she was married to Alfonso of Aragón, illegitimate son of Alfonso II of Naples. Her brother, Cesare Borgia, had her second husband murdered in 1500, and, in 1501, Lucrezia was married to Alfonso d'Este, who became duke of Ferrara in 1505. As duchess of Ferrara, Lucrezia at last escaped the vicious atmosphere of her family. Her brilliant court attracted many artists and poets, notably Ariosto, and her beauty and kindness won esteem for her. Rumors of her participation in her family's poison plots, of incestuous relations with her father and brother, and of her supposed extravagant vices have not been proved. Nevertheless, Lucrezia Borgia remains best known as portrayed in Victor Hugo's drama and Donizetti's opera, both based on these legends. See biographies by Maria Bellonci (tr. 1953) and Ferdinand Gregorovius (rev. ed. 1875, in German; tr. 1949, repr. 1968).

Borgia, Rodrigo: see ALEXANDER VI.

Borglum, Gutzon (John Gutzon de la Mothe Borglum), 1867–1941, American sculptor, b. Idaho; son of a Danish physician and rancher. He studied at the San Francisco Art Academy and in Paris at Julian's academy and the École des Beaux-Arts. His first commission after his return to New York in 1901 was the statue of Lincoln which stands in the rotunda of the Capitol, Washington, D.C. Other works of his earlier period were a statue of Henry Ward Beecher (Brooklyn), *Mares of Diomedes* (Metropolitan Mus.), and figures of the apostles for the Cathedral of St. John the Divine, New York City. He designed and began carving (1916) a Confederate memorial on Stone Mt., Ga. The work was interrupted by World War I but was resumed in 1924. As the result of a controversy with the Stone Mountain Memorial Association, Borglum ceased working and destroyed his models. His supervision of the gigantic MOUNT RUSHMORE NATIONAL MEMORIAL in South Dakota was begun in 1927. One of the largest sculptural projects in existence, with heads 60 ft (18.3 m) high, the Memorial was also a great engineering feat. Borglum had finished the heads of the four Presidents (Washington, Jefferson, Lincoln, and Theodore Roosevelt) when he died. The work was finished by his son Lincoln Borglum. Borglum was a man of tremendous vitality and decided opinions which led him into frequent controversies. His brother **Solon Hannibal Borglum,** 1868–1922, was also a sculptor, noted especially for his portrayal of horses, cattle, Indians, and cowboys. See R. J. Casey and Mary Borglum, *Give the Man Room: the Story of Gutzon Borglum* (1952); Willadene Price, *Gutzon Borglum, Artist and Patriot* (1961).

Borgognone: see BERGOGNONE.

Bori, Lucrezia (bô'rē), 1887–1960, Spanish soprano, whose real name was Borja (Ital. *Borgia*). She made her debut (1908) in Rome as Micaela in *Carmen,* later sang *Manon Lescaut* opposite Caruso in Paris (1910), and was long a leading performer at the Metropolitan Opera in New York City (1912–15; and, after a throat operation, 1920–36). After 1935 she was a director of the Metropolitan Opera Association. She was notable for her beauty and her stage presence as well as her lyric voice.

boric acid, any one of the three chemical compounds, orthoboric (or boracic) acid, metaboric acid, and tetraboric (or pyroboric) acid; the term often refers simply to orthoboric acid. The acids may be thought of as hydrates of boric oxide, B_2O_3. Orthoboric acid, H_3BO_3 or $B_2O_3 \cdot 3H_2O$, is colorless, weakly acidic, and forms triclinic crystals. It is fairly soluble in boiling water (about 27% by weight) but less so in cool water (about 6% by weight at room temperature). When orthoboric acid is heated above 170°C it dehydrates, forming metaboric acid, HBO_2 or $B_2O_3 \cdot H_2O$. Metaboric acid is a white, cubic crystalline solid and is only slightly soluble in water. It melts at about 236°C, and when heated above about 300°C further dehydrates, forming tetraboric acid, $H_2B_4O_7$ or $2B_2O_3 \cdot H_2O$. Tetraboric acid is either a vitreous solid or a white powder and is water soluble. When tetraboric or metaboric acid is dissolved it reverts largely to orthoboric acid. The major uses of the boric acids are in forming other boron compounds and in borate salts, e.g., BORAX. A dilute water solution of boric acid is commonly used as a mild antiseptic and eyewash. Boric acid is also used in leather manufacture, electroplating, and cosmetics. Boric acid can be crystallized from an acidified borax solution. It occurs as the mineral sassolite in the Tuscan region of Italy, where it is also recovered from hot springs and vapors. In the United States boric acid is recovered from brines from Searles Lake in California.

Borinage (bôrĕnäzh'), region, Hainaut prov., S Belgium, surrounding Mons and extending to the French border. A coal-mining district, it was formerly known for the miserable conditions of its miners.

boring mill, machine tool used to increase the size of a hole previously made in a workpiece, usually with the purpose of obtaining a required degree of finish and accuracy in the final hole. In a horizontal boring mill the workpiece is held stationary on a vertical table whose position can be adjusted. A spindle attached to a vertically adjustable head holds the cutting tool, which is fed horizontally into the work. In a vertical boring mill the workpiece is made to revolve on a horizontal circular table as the tool is fed in.

Boris I, d. 907, khan [ruler] of Bulgaria (852–89). Baptized in 864, he introduced Christianity of the Byzantine rite among the Bulgarians. There followed a rivalry between Rome and Constantinople for the loyalty of the Bulgarian church. In 889, Boris abdicated and retired to a monastery. His son was Czar Simeon I.

Boris III, 1894–1943, czar of Bulgaria (1918–43), son of Czar FERDINAND, on whose abdication he succeeded to the throne. He ruled constitutionally until 1934, then set up a military dictatorship under his premier, Kimon Georgiev, and in 1935 began his personal dictatorship. He turned toward the Axis Powers and in 1940 forced Rumania to restore S DOBRUJA to Bulgaria. While visiting Hitler in Berlin, he agreed to declare war on Great Britain and the United States, but not on Russia. His mysterious death soon followed. His son, SIMEON II, succeeded under a regency.

Boris Godunov: see GODUNOV, BORIS.

Borlänge (bôr'lĕng"ə), city (1970 pop. 29,652), Kopparberg co., S central Sweden, on the Dalälven

River; chartered 1944. It has major factories manufacturing iron and steel and paper and also sawmills, machine shops, and a school of engineering.

Borlaug, Norman Ernest (bôr'lôg), 1914–, U.S. agronomist, b. Cresco, Iowa, grad. Univ. of Minn. (Ph.D., 1941). He worked as researcher with the E. I. du Pont Company until 1944, when he joined the Rockefeller Foundation in Mexico. He became a director at the Foundation and headed a team of scientists from 17 nations experimenting with improvement of grains. In 1970 he was awarded the Nobel Peace Prize for his efforts to eradicate hunger and build international prosperity. His "green revolution," which involves the use of improved wheat seed, new types of higher-yield rice, and more efficient use of fertilizer and water, has provided larger food crops in many of the less-developed countries of the Middle East and Latin America. Borlaug is credited with Mexico's self-sufficiency in wheat production.

Bormann, Martin (bôr'män), 1900–1945, German National Socialist (Nazi) leader. He met Adolf Hitler in 1924 and soon became an important figure in the Nazi party hierarchy. He succeeded Rudolf Hess in Hitler's inner circle in 1941 after Hess's flight to Scotland. In 1942 he became Hitler's personal secretary. After Hitler's suicide in 1945, Bormann disappeared and was assumed dead. He was tried in absentia at Nuremberg and sentenced to death. Rumors persisted, however, that Bormann had escaped to Argentina. In 1973, after identification of a skeleton unearthed in West Berlin, the West German government declared him dead, a suicide on May 2, 1945.

Born, Bertrand de: see BERTRAND DE BORN.

Born, Max, 1882–1970, British physicist, b. Germany, Ph.D. Univ. of Göttingen, 1907. He was head of the physics department at the Univ.of Göttingen from 1921 to 1933. When Nazi policies forced him to leave Germany, he went to England; he was a lecturer at Cambridge Univ., then became (1936) a professor of natural philosophy at the Univ. of Edinburgh. Born was made a British citizen in 1939. In 1953 he retired to West Germany. Known for his research in quantum mechanics, he shared the 1954 Nobel Prize in Physics with Walter Bothe. Born's writings include *Problems of Atomic Dynamics* (1926, tr. 1960). See his autobiography, *My Life and My Views* (1968).

Börne, Karl Ludwig (lo͞ot'vĭkh bör'nə), 1786–1837, German journalist, of Jewish origin. His original name was Löb Baruch. He studied medicine and political science and held office in Frankfurt until, after the fall of Napoleon, a policy of racial discrimination was restored. His lucid and incisive writings, notably his *Briefe aus Paris* (1830–33), bitterly attacked German despotism and upheld the rights of the individual. With Heine, Börne was an initiator and leader of the revolutionary Young Germany movement in German literature.

Borneo, island (1970 est. pop. 6,800,000), c.287,000 sq mi (743,330 sq km), largest of the Malay Archipelago and third largest island in the world, SW of the Philippines and N of Java. Indonesian Borneo (called Kalimantan by the Indonesians) covers over 70% of the total area, and the Malaysian states of SABAH and SARAWAK and the British-protected sultanate of BRUNEI stretch across the north coast. The island largely consists of dense jungle and mountains, reaching its highest point at Mt. Kinabalu (13,455 ft/4,101 m) in Sabah. Much of the terrain is virtually impassable, and large areas are unexplored. Many of the rivers are navigable to small craft, however, and provide access into the interior. The largest rivers are the Kapuas in the west and the Barito in the south. The coastal area is generally swampy and fringed with mangrove forests. Banjarmasin, Pontianak, Balikpapan, Tarakan, Kuching, Brunei, and Sandakan are leading ports. The climate is tropical, i.e., hot and humid; annual rainfall averages more than 100 in. (254 cm), and there is a prolonged monsoon (generally from November to May). The fauna is roughly similar to that of Sumatra and includes the elephant, deer, orangutan, gibbon, Malay bear, and crocodile, and many varieties of snakes. Rhinoceroses, once numerous, have been extensively hunted and are now almost extinct. The island is one of the most sparsely populated regions in the world. The two major ethnic groups are the primitive DYAKS and the coastal Malays; Kalimantan was also a center for Chinese settlement. Kalimantan contains Indonesia's greatest expanse of tropical rain forests, including valuable stands of camphor, sandalwood, and ironwood, and many palms. The thick jungle and myriad insects discourage large-scale agriculture, but rice, sago, tobacco, millet, coconuts, pepper, sweet potatoes, sugarcane, coffee, and rubber are grown. Kalimantan contains some of Indonesia's most productive oilfields (discovered in 1888). Coal has been mined there for more than a century, and gold since earliest times. Other mineral resources include industrial diamonds, bauxite, and extensive reserves of low-grade iron ore, which are, however, little exploited. Borneo was visited by the Portuguese in 1521, and shortly thereafter by the Spanish, who established trade relations with the island. The Dutch arrived in the early 1600s, and the English c.1665. Dutch influence was established on the west coast in the early 1800s and was gradually extended to the south and east. The British adventurer James Brook took the north edge of the island in the 1840s, and present-day Sabah, Sarawak, and Brunei were declared British protectorates in 1880. The final boundaries were defined in 1905. In World War II the island was held by the Japanese from 1942 to 1945. Dutch Borneo became part of the republic of Indonesia in 1950. The union of Sabah and Sarawak with the federation of Malaysia in 1963 was resented by Indonesians; Indonesian guerrilla raids against both areas, begun in 1964, continued sporadically until Aug., 1966.

Bornholm (bôrn'hôlm), island group (1971 pop. 47,241), 227 sq mi (588 sq km), extreme E Denmark, in the Baltic Sea, near Sweden. Bornholm, the main island, constitutes almost all of the land area and population of the group; Christiansholm, Frederiksholm, and Graesholm are also part of the group. Bornholm is a low tableland, rocky and steep on its northern and western coasts. Farming, fishing, handicrafts, and tourism are the chief occupations; granite and kaolin are the main exports. Rønne is the principal town. Bornholm was divided (1149) between Denmark and Sweden, ruled (1327–1522) by the Danish archbishops, governed (1525–76) by Lübeck merchants, and ceded (1658) to Denmark. After Germany's surrender (May, 1945) in World War II, German forces made a desperate stand on Bornholm before Soviet troops forced them to surrender.

Bornu (bôr'no͞o), former Muslim state, mostly in NE Nigeria, extending S and W of Lake Chad. It began its existence as a separate state in the late 14th cent. From the 14th to the 18th cent. Bornu exported slaves, eunuchs, fabrics dyed with saffron, and other goods to N Africa. Bornu reached its peak under the *mai* (ruler) Idris Alawma (ruled 1570–1610), when it was the leading state in the central Sudan region. Bornu declined from the 17th cent. In the early 19th cent. it was severely threatened by the FULANI but maintained its independence when Muhammad al-Kanemi (ruled 1814–35), who established a new dynasty, revived the state. However, Bornu began to decline again after c.1850 because of weak rulers, and was conquered (1893–96) by the forces of Rabih, a Sudanese slave trader. In 1898, Bornu was divided among Great Britain, France, and Germany. In 1922 the German portion became part of the British Cameroons mandate of the League of Nations.

Borobudur or **Boroboeder** (both: bō"rōbo͝odo͝or'), ruins of one of the finest Buddhist monuments, in central Java, Indonesia. Built by the Sailendras of Sumatra, this magnificent shrine dates from about the 9th cent. It is a huge, truncated pyramid, covered with intricately carved blocks of stone that illustrate episodes in the life of the Buddha. A seated Buddha within may be seen from three platforms above the seven stone terraces that encircle the pyramid.

Borodin, Aleksandr Porfirevich (əlyĭksän'dər pərfē'rĭvĭch bôrôdyēn'), 1833–87, Russian composer, chemist, and physician. He studied at the academy of medicine in St. Petersburg, where he later taught chemistry. He also helped found a school of medicine for women. An amateur musician, he had little musical training, consisting mainly of study with Balakirev. His principal works are two symphonies; several fine songs; an orchestral tone poem, *In the Steppes of Central Asia* (1880); and an opera, *Prince Igor,* left unfinished, which Rimsky-Korsakov and Glazunov completed. It was first performed in St. Petersburg in 1890. He was one of a group of Russian nationalist composers known as The FIVE. See biography by Gerald Abraham; V. I. Seroff, *The Mighty Five* (1948); M. O. Zetlin, *The Five* (tr. 1959).

Borodino (bərədyĭnô'), village, central European USSR, c.70 mi (110 km) W of Moscow. It was the site, on Sept. 7, 1812, of a battle between Napoleon's Grande Armée and Gen. Mikhail Kutuzov's Russian forces defending Moscow. The battle, which cost some 108,000 casualties, is described in Tolstoy's *War and Peace.* Napoleon entered Moscow on Sept. 14 after severely battering but not totally defeating the Russians.

Boroimhe, Brian: see BRIAN BORU.

boron (bōr'ŏn) [New Gr. from *borax*], chemical element; symbol B; at. no. 5; at. wt. 10.811; m.p. about 2100°C; b.p. about 2500°C; sp. gr. 2.3 at 25°C; valence +3. Boron is a nonmetallic element existing as a dark brown to black amorphous powder or as an extremely hard, usually jet-black to silver-gray, brittle, lustrous, metallike crystalline solid (see ALLOTROPY). One tetragonal and two rhombohedral forms of crystalline boron are known. The chemistry of boron more closely resembles the chemistry of SILICON than that of the other elements in group IIIa of the PERIODIC TABLE, of which it is a member. The chemical reactivity of boron depends on its form; generally, the crystalline form is far less reactive than the amorphous form. For example, the amorphous powder is oxidized slowly in air at room temperature and ignites spontaneously at high temperatures to form an oxide; the crystalline form is oxidized only very slowly, even at higher temperatures. Boron forms compounds with oxgen, hydrogen, the halogens, nitrogen, phosphorus, and carbon (only diamond is harder than boron carbide). It also forms organic compounds. It is most commonly used in its compounds, especially BORAX and BORIC ACID. Boron is used as a deoxidizer and degasifier in metallurgy. Because it absorbs neutrons, it is used in the shielding material and in some control rods of nuclear reactors. Boron fibers, which have a very high tensile strength, can be added to plastics to make a material that is stronger than steel yet lighter than aluminum. Boron does not occur free in nature. Large deposits of borax, kermite, colemanite, and other boron minerals are found in the arid regions of the W United States. It occurs also in the mineral TOURMALINE. The simplest method of preparing boron is the reduction of boron trioxide by heating with magnesium; this yields the amorphous powder. Boron was first isolated in England in 1807 by Sir Humphry Davy and then in France in 1808 by Joseph Louis Gay-Lussac and Louis Jacques Thénard.

Borough, Stephen, 1525–84, English navigator. Under the direction of Richard CHANCELLOR he was master of the *Edward Bonaventure,* the first ship to round (1553) North Cape and reach Russia by the arctic route, and the only ship to return safely from the expedition. Thereupon, Sebastian Cabot and others who had fostered the plan formed the MUSCOVY COMPANY, establishing a profitable trade with Russia. Sailing again for that company, Borough in a voyage of 1556–57 reached Novaya Zemlya and discovered the strait south of it leading to the Kara Sea.

Borough, William, 1536–99, British naval officer. A younger brother of Stephen Borough, William accompanied him on early voyages and was himself a captain for the Muscovy Company. As a naval officer he took part in Sir Francis Drake's attack on Cádiz (1587) and also fought against the Spanish Armada (1588). He wrote accounts of his voyages and a treatise on the variation of the compass and compiled several charts.

borough: see CITY GOVERNMENT.

borough-English, a custom of inheritance in parts of England whereby land passed typically to the youngest son in preference to his older brothers. Of Anglo-Saxon origin, the custom was abolished by law in 1925. For alternative systems of inheritance in England see GAVELKIND and PRIMOGENITURE.

Borromean Islands: see MAGGIORE, LAGO, Italy.

Borromeo, Charles: see CHARLES BORROMEO, SAINT.

Borromini, Francesco (fränchä'skō bōr-rōmē'nē), 1599–1677, major Italian baroque architect. His first independent commission (begun 1634) was San Carlo alle Quattro Fontane, Rome. The church is noted for its undulating rhythm of architectural elements within a basically geometric plan. In 1642 he began the designs for Sant' Ivo della Sapienza, Rome, a dynamic hexagonal structure. He was also entrusted with the reconstruction of St. John the Lateran, as well as the completion of Sant' Agnese in the Piazza Navona and Sant' Andrea della Fratte. Borromini's innovations in palace as well as church design had a tremendous influence in Italy and northern Europe.

Borrow, George Henry, 1803–81, English writer and traveler. He led a nomadic life in England and on the Continent, where he was a translator and agent for the British and Foreign Bible Society. His friendship with the gypsies, whose language he learned, resulted in *The Zincali; or . . . the Gypsies of Spain* (1841). Although his most famous book is *The Bible in Spain* (1843), his best is probably the autobiographical *Lavengro* (1851), with its sequel, *Romany Rye* (1857). All Borrow's works are based on his wanderings. See Norwich edition of his works (16 vol., 1923–24); biography by C. K. Shorter (1920); study by R. R. Meyers (1966).

Borstal system, rehabilitation method in Great Britain for delinquent boys aged 16 to 21. The idea originated (1895) with the Gladstone Committee as an attempt to reform young offenders. The first institution was established (1902) at Borstal Prison, Kent, England. Main elements in the Borstal programs include education, regular work, vocational training, and group counseling. Those showing sufficient improvement are paroled to the Central After-Care Association, which supervises them during the period after release. Some Borstals, such as Lowdham Grange, are open, having no walls or gates. See Brendan Behan, *Borstal Boy* (1958); Roger Hood, *Borstal Re-Assessed* (1965).

bort: see DIAMOND.

Borten, Per (pĕr bôr'tôn), 1913–, Norwegian political leader and agronomist. Active in the agricultural administration and provincial government of Sør-Trøndelag (1946–65), he served as head of the region's Agrarian Youth Movement. He became a member of the Storting (parliament) in 1950 and in 1955 was made chairman of the Agrarian party. In 1965 he became prime minister. His coalition government of four non-Socialist parties resigned in 1971 after Borten had revealed confidential information about Norway's negotiations for Common Market membership.

Bortniansky, Dmitri Stepanovich (dəmē'trē styĭpä'nəvĭch bûrtnyän'skē), 1751–1825, Russian composer, studied with Galuppi in St. Petersburg and Venice. After producing two operas in Italy, in 1779 he returned to St. Petersburg. There, in 1796, he became director of the Imperial Chapel Choir, for which he set a high standard. He wrote mainly church music, combining Russian church style and Italian style. In 1882, Tchaikovsky completed an edition of his works, published in 10 volumes.

Boru, Brian: see BRIAN BORU.

Borysthenes, USSR: see DNEPR.

borzoi (bôr'zoi), breed of tall, swift HOUND developed in Russia in the early 17th cent., also called Russian wolfhound. It stands from 26 to 31 in. (66–81.2 cm) high at the shoulder and weighs about 85 lb (38.6 kg). Its long, silky coat may be flat, wavy or curly, and forms fringes of longer hair, or feathers, on the chest, back of legs, and tail. The coat may be any color but is usually white with lemon, brindle, tan, gray, or black markings. Originally bred for hunting wolves and coursing hares, it is now most popular as a show competitor and pet. See DOG.

Bos, Jerom: see BOSCH, HIERONYMUS.

Bosanquet, Bernard (bō'zənkĭt), 1848–1923, English philosopher, educated at Oxford. He lectured there (1871–81) and at St. Andrews (1903–8). His major works include *A History of Aesthetic* (1892), *The Philosophical Theory of the State* (1899), and *The Value and Destiny of the Individual* (1913). They exemplify the idealists' discontent with British empiricism at the end of the 19th cent. See biography by Helen Bosanquet (1924); J. H. Muirhead, ed., *Bernard Bosanquet and His Friends* (1935).

Bosboom-Toussaint, Anna Louisa Geertruida (ä'nä lo͞oē'zä härtroi'dä bôs'bōm-to͞osăN'), 1812–86, Dutch novelist. She published her first novel, *Almagro,* in 1837. Her perceptive historical fiction was written in ornate and purposely archaic style. One of her chief works treated modern life; this epistolary novel, *Majoor Frans* (1874, tr. *Major Frank,* 1886), exhibits a real appreciation of the problems of women.

Boscán Almogáver, Juan (hwän bōskän' älmôgä'vĕr), c.1495–1542, Spanish poet. A Catalan aristocrat, Boscán was a literary figure at the court of Ferdinand V. He introduced Italian poetic forms into Spanish poetry, thus revolutionizing its traditional system of metrics. Among his compositions, written in different combinations of the 11-syllable line, are sonnets and canciones. He also translated Castiglione's *Courtier.* His works were first printed in 1543 together with those of his collaborator and friend GARCILASO DE LA VEGA.

Boscath, the same as BOZKATH.

Boscawen, Edward (bŏskō'ən), 1711–61, British admiral. He was a popular naval hero, famous for his decisive courage displayed against France and Spain at Portobelo (1739), Cape Finisterre (1747), and Lagos Bay (1759). He is noted also for attempts to improve health conditions in the fleet.

Bosch, Hieronymus, or **Jerom Bos** (hērôn'ĭməs, yä'rôm bôs), c.1450–1516, Flemish painter. His surname was van Aeken; Bosch refers to Hertogenbosch, where he was born and worked. Little is known of his life and training. His paintings, executed in brilliant colors and with an uncanny mastery of detail, are filled with animated objects, bizarre plants and animals, and monstrous, amusing, or diabolical figures believed to have been suggested by folk legends, allegorical poems, moralizing religious literature, and aspects of late Gothic art. Some of his works appear to be intricate allegories; their symbolism, however, is obscure and has consistently defied satisfactory interpretation. Feverishly imaginative, Bosch had a passion for the grotesque, the exuberant, and the macabre. King Philip II of Spain collected some of his finest creations, such as the *Garden of Earthly Delights* (Prado). The *Temptation of St. Anthony* (Lisbon) and *The Last Judgment* were favorite themes. Other examples of his art may be seen in the Escorial and in Brussels. Examples of the *Adoration of the Magi* are in the Metropolitan Museum and in the Philadelphia Museum, which also has the *Mocking of Christ.* Bosch, who deeply influenced the work of Peter Bruegel the Elder, was hailed in the 20th cent. as a forerunner of the surrealists. See his paintings, ed. by G. Martin (1966, repr. 1971); studies by Charles de Tolnay (tr. 1966) and James Snyder, ed. (1973).

Bosch, Juan (hwän bōsh), 1909–, president of the Dominican Republic (Feb.–Sept., 1963). A teacher and writer, he spent 25 years in exile during the dictatorship of Rafael Trujillo and helped found the Dominican Revolutionary party. He returned (1961) to the Dominican Republic after the assassination of Trujillo and was elected president in the first free elections (Dec., 1962) held in 38 years. He introduced sweeping social and economic reforms but was ousted after seven months by military leaders who viewed him as too leftist. An attempt by his supporters to restore him to power in April, 1965, brought civil war and provoked armed intervention by U.S. troops. In 1966, Bosch was overwhelmingly defeated for the presidency by Joaquín BALAGUER. After a voluntary exile in Europe, Bosch returned (1970) and joined the opposition to President Balaguer. In 1973 he founded the Dominican Liberation party.

Boscobel (bŏs'kəbĕl), parish, Shropshire, W central England. The oak in which Charles II supposedly hid after his defeat by Oliver Cromwell in the battle of Worcester (1651) was near Boscobel House, which is still standing.

Boscoreale (bôs"kōrā-ä'lā), town (1971 pop. 18,674), in Campania, S Italy, at the foot of Vesuvius. Roman villas have been excavated in the town. Also, a celebrated collection of gold coins, jewelry, and silverwork (consisting mostly of plates and cups with relief ornamentation) dating from the 1st and 2d cent. A.D. was unearthed there in the late 1800s.

Boscovich, Ruggiero Giuseppe (ro͞od-jä'rō jo͞ozĕp'pā bôs'kōvĕch), 1711–87, Italian mathematician, astronomer, and physicist. He became a Jesuit and taught at Rome, Pavia, and Milan. Later he was director of optics for the French navy. An early advocate of Newton's theories, he wrote many works including one in which he introduced his molecular theory.

Bose, Sir Jagadis Chandra, or **Sir Jagadis Chunder Bose** (jəgä'dēs chŭn'drə bōs, chŭn'dər), 1858–1937, Indian physicist and plant physiologist, educated in Calcutta and at Christ's College, Cambridge. He was professor of physical science (1885–1915) at Presidency College, Calcutta, and founded the Bose Research Institute in Calcutta. He is noted for his researches in plant life, especially his comparison of the responses of plant and animal tissue to various stimuli. One of his inventions is the crescograph, a device for measuring plant growth. Among his publications are *Comparative Electro-Physiology* (1907), *Researches on Irritability of Plants* (1913), *The Physiology of Photosynthesis* (1924), *The Nervous Mechanism of Plants* (1926), and *Growth and Tropic Movements of Plants* (1929).

Bose, Subhas Chandra (sho͞obhäsh' chŭn'drə bōs), 1897–1945, Indian nationalist. He began his political career in Calcutta and soon became the leader of the left wing of the Indian National Congress party. He was president of the party in 1938–39 but was forced to resign after a dispute with Mohandas K. Gandhi; he advocated militancy to achieve independence for India and believed in dictatorship to unify the country. Jailed by the British for his Axis sympathies in World War II, he escaped (1941) and fled to Germany. In 1943 he headed in Singapore a Japanese-sponsored "provisional government of India" and organized an "Indian national army." Although sympathetic to totalitarianism, his collaboration was principally directed toward freeing India from British rule and the establishment of an independent regime. He was killed in an airplane crash. See his collected writings and letters, ed. by J. S. Bright (2d ed. 1947); biography by D. K. Roy (1966); study by Hugh Toye (1959).

Bosio, François Joseph, Baron (fräNswä' zhôzĕf' bärôN' bôsyō'), 1769–1845, French sculptor. He was employed by Napoleon I to make the bas-reliefs for the column of the Place Vendôme and also as portraitist to the imperial family. At that time he produced one of his best portrait busts—that of Empress Josephine (Dijon). Louis XVIII made him court sculptor, and Charles X conferred the title baron on him. Of his larger works the most important are the equestrian statue of Louis XVI (Place de Victoires); the quadriga (four-horse chariot) of the Arc de Triomphe du Carrousel; and *Hercules Struggling with a Serpent* (garden of the Tuileries).

Bosnia and Hercegovina (bŏz'nēə, hĕrtsəgōvē'nə), Serbo-Croatian *Bosna i Hercegovina,* constituent republic of Yugoslavia (1971 pop. 3,742,852), 19,741 sq mi (51,129 sq km), W central Yugoslavia. It consists of two regions—Bosnia in the north, and Hercegovina in the south. SARAJEVO, in Bosnia, is the capital. The chief city of Hercegovina is MOSTAR. The republic lies mostly in the Dinaric Alps and has one narrow outlet to the Adriatic Sea, but no port facilities. The Sava and its tributaries are the chief rivers. Half of the area is forested, and timber is an important product of Bosnia. Much of Hercegovina's terrain is denuded. About one fourth of the republic's land is cultivated; corn, wheat, and flax are the principal products of Bosnia and tobacco, cotton, fruits, and grapes of Hercegovina. Mining is important, and there are large deposits of lignite, iron ore, and bauxite, as well as smaller quantities of such minerals as copper and manganese. Despite some industrialization and development of the republic's extensive hydroelectric resources, it remains one of the poorer areas of Yugoslavia. The population speaks Serbo-Croatian and is divided among the Muslim, Roman Catholic, and Eastern Orthodox religions. The area was part of the Roman province of Illyricum. Bosnia was settled by Serbs in the 7th cent.; it appeared as an independent country by the 12th cent. but later at times acknowledged the kings of Hungary as suzerains. Medieval Bosnia reached the height of its power in the second half of the 14th cent., when it controlled many surrounding territories. Bosnia also annexed the duchy of Hum, which, however, regained autonomy in 1448 and became known as Hercegovina. During this period the region was weakened by religious strife among Roman Catholics, Orthodox, and Bogomils. Thus disunited, Bosnia fell to the Turks in 1463. Hercegovina held out until 1482, when it too was occupied and joined administratively to Bosnia. The nobility and a large part of the peasantry accepted Islam. Under Turkish rule, Bosnia and Hercegovina's economy declined. Physical remoteness facilitated the retention of medieval social structure, including serfdom (remnants of which lasted until the 20th cent.). Refusal by the Turkish to institute reforms led to a peasant uprising (1875) that soon came to involve outside powers and led to the Russo-Turkish War of 1877–78. After the war, the Congress of Berlin (1878) placed Bosnia and Hercegovina under Austro-Hungarian administration and occupation, while recognizing the sovereignty of the Turkish sultan. Austria-Hungary improved economic conditions in the area but sought unsuccessfully to combat rising Serbian nationalism, which mounted further when Bosnia and Hercegovina were completely annexed in 1908. The assassination (1914), by a Serbian nationalist, of Archduke Francis Ferdinand in Sarajevo precipitated World War I. In 1918 Bosnia and Hercegovina were annexed to Serbia. The dismemberment of Yugoslavia during World War II led to Bosnia and Hercegovina's incorporation into the German puppet state of Croatia. Much partisan guerrilla warfare raged in the mountains of Bosnia during the war. In 1946, Bosnia and Hercegovina became one of the six constituent republics of Yugoslavia. See B. E. Schmitt, *The Annexation of Bosnia, 1908–1909* (1937, repr. 1971); J. G. Wilkinson, *Dalmatia and Montenegro* (2 vol., 1848; repr. 1971).

Bosor (bō'sôr), the same as BEOR **1.**

Bosporus (bŏs'pərəs) [Gr., = ox ford, in reference to the story of Io], Turk. *Boğaziçi,* strait, c.20 mi (30 km) long and c.2,100 ft (640 m) wide at its narrowest, separating European from Asian Turkey and joining the Black Sea with the Sea of Marmara. İstanbul is situated on the Bosporus, which is lined with many historic remains and modern villas. At its narrowest point are two famous castles: Anadolu Hisar, built in 1390, on the Asian side and Rumeli Hisar, completed in 1452, on the European side. The strait was refortified by Turkey after the Montreux Convention of 1936 (see DARDANELLES). The Bosporus Bridge, one of the world's longest suspension bridges (3,524 ft/1,074 m long; opened 1973) spans the strait at İstanbul.

Bosporus, University of the, at İstanbul, Turkey; opened 1863 as Robert College, with funds contributed by Christopher R. Robert and other Americans for the higher education of Turkish men. Its name was changed in 1971. It has schools of engineering, arts and sciences, and administrative sciences. Instruction is in Turkish and English.

Bosse, Abraham (äbrä-äm' bôs), 1602–76, French engraver and painter. He studied art in Paris and became a teacher of perspective in the Académie royale. A prolific and skillful worker, he engraved more than 1,400 pieces. He is best known for his faithful representation of French civil life and costumes during the period of Louis XIII. Bosse wrote several valued treatises on art and perspective. One of his rare paintings, *The Foolish Virgins,* is in the Cluny Museum, Paris.

Bossier City (bō'zhər), city (1970 pop. 41,598), Bossier parish, NW La., on the Red River, across from Shreveport, with which it is connected by several bridges; inc. 1907. Barksdale Air Force Base, home of the Second U.S. Air Force, is the major employer.

bossism, in U.S. history, system of political control centering about a single powerful figure (the boss) and a complex organization of lesser figures (the machine) bound together by reciprocity in promoting financial and social self-interest. Bossism depends upon manipulation of the voters and thus always has some aspects of corruption and fraud, even though particular bosses and particular machines may do much good service for the community, the state, or the nation. Control of blocks of votes enables boss and machine to secure the nomination and election or appointment of candidates for public office; the officers thus chosen respond by advancing the interests of the machine. The boss became important in U.S. political life in the mid-19th cent., when many poor immigrants crowded into the cities. In return for their votes the boss offered them protection; he saw that the newcomers got financial and other help. The contact was direct and personal; the boss and his cohorts gave away coal and food, got the sick into hospitals, obtained leniency for the wayward through the courts, and secured government jobs and other work for the unemployed. Bossism was primarily on the local level, but the machines in very large cities soon exerted state and national influence, sometimes very powerful. The highly invidious implications of the term date from the exposure of the Tweed Ring (see under TWEED, WILLIAM MARCY) in New York City in 1872 (see also TAMMANY). Some of the men who came to nationwide notice as connected with bossism and machines in the late 19th and 20th cent. were Richard CROKER and Charles MURPHY of New York, Frank HAGUE of New Jersey, Thomas J. PENDERGAST of Kansas City, James M. CURLEY of Boston, William Hale THOMPSON of Chicago, William VARE of Philadelphia and Abraham RUEF of San Francisco. The original sort of bossism gradually declined with the assimilation of older immigrant stocks and reduction of new immigration, growing literacy, extension of government into the social-welfare area previously cared for by the machine, and increase in the number of jobs falling under civil-service requirements. In contemporary politics a new and more sophisticated type of boss has come into being; he uses techniques of public relations rather than personal contacts to build up his power and that of the machine. See H. F. Gosnell, *Machine Politics* (1937, repr. 1968); Samuel Lubell, *The Future of American Politics* (3d ed. 1965); E. C. Banfield and J. Q. Wilson, *City Politics* (1963, repr. 1966).

Bossuet, Jacques Bénigne (zhäk bānē'nyə bôsüā'), 1627–1704, French prelate, one of the greatest orators in French history. At an early age he was made a canon at Metz; he became bishop of Condom and was (1670–81) tutor to the dauphin (father of Louis XV), for whom he wrote his great *Discourse on Universal History* (1681, tr. 1778, 1821), *Politics Derived from Holy Writ* (1709), and *Treatise of the Knowledge of God and One's Self* (1722). In 1681 he became bishop of Meaux. Unrivaled for his eloquence, he is celebrated for his *Funeral Orations* (1689), particularly those on Henrietta of England, on her daughter, and on Condé, which are masterpieces of their kind. He was also a great moralist, a magnificent stylist, and a powerful controversialist, brilliantly attacking Fénelon and the quietists, the Jesuits, and the Protestants. See biographies by E. K. Sanders (1921) and E. E. Reynolds (1963); studies by Pierre Floquet (1864), G. Lanson (1895), Alfred Rebelliau (5th ed. 1900), and M. C. Gotaas (1953, repr. 1970).

Bostanai ben Chaninai (bôs'tänī bĕn khänēnī'), c.618–670, first Jewish exilarch (i.e., ruler of the Jewish exiles in Babylonia) under Arab rule. He is the subject of many legends. His name is also spelled Bustanai ben Haninai. ANAN BEN DAVID is said to have been among his descendants.

Boston, municipal borough (1971 pop. 25,995), administrative center of the Parts of Holland, Lincolnshire, E central England, on the Witham River. Boston's fame as a port dates from the 13th cent., when it was a Hanseatic port trading wool and wine. Having recovered from a decline in the 18th and 19th cent. caused by silting, Boston now exports coal, grain, agricultural machinery, potatoes, and cattle; it imports timber, grain, fruit, vegetables, and fertilizers. It is also a shellfishery center and a market for a rich lowland farm area. There are food-processing plants and other light industries. Puritans under John COTTON sailed in 1633 from Boston to Massachusetts Bay (renamed Boston). St. Botolph's Church is on the site of a 7th-century monastery, founded by St. Botolph, for whom the town is named (Botolph's tun, or town). The 288-ft (88-m) tower (called the Stump, because it does not come to a point) is a landmark. The guildhall, begun in 1545, was restored in 1911 and is now a museum.

Boston, city (1970 pop. 641,071), state capital and seat of Suffolk co., E Mass., at the head of Boston Bay; inc. 1822. The largest city in New England, Boston is a major financial center, a leading port, and an important market for fish and wool. Its industries include publishing, food processing, and the manufacture of shoes, textiles, machinery, and electronic equipment. Established by the elder John Winthrop in 1630 as the main colony of the MASSACHUSETTS BAY COMPANY, Boston was an early center of American Puritanism, with notable ministers and theocratic-minded statesmen contributing to the vigorous intellectual life. The Boston Public Latin School was opened in 1635; Harvard University was founded at nearby Cambridge in 1636; a public library was started in 1653; and the first newspaper in the Thirteen Colonies, the *Newsletter,* appeared in 1704. With its excellent port, Boston soon gained commercial ascendancy over the other towns of colonial Massachusetts. As the American Revolution approached, it became a center of opposition to the British. The Battle of Bunker Hill, fought there on June 17, 1775, was one of the first battles of the Revolution, and Boston was under siege until the British withdrew in March, 1776. After a short postwar depression, Boston entered a period of prosperity that lasted until the middle of the 19th cent. Ships built there made Boston known around the world. Prominent Boston families—the Cabots, the Lowells, the Lodges, and others—made fortunes from shipping and from mills and factories built on New England rivers to produce textiles and shoes. These prominent families built substantial houses on Beacon Hill and in the Back Bay sections and patronized the arts and letters, making Boston "the Athens of America." Despite the generally conservative tone of their culture, they backed reformers, notably the ABOLITIONISTS. Their influence persisted long after the growth of industry brought many immigrants (at first mostly Irish), and Boston changed from a commercial city surrounded by farms to an industrial metropolis. The city limits were expanded to include nearby cities and towns, some with traditions as old as Boston's own—Roxbury and West Roxbury (with the Roxbury Latin School, Forest Hills Cemetery, and BROOK FARM), Dorchester (where Richard Mather had been the minister), Charlestown, Brighton, and Hyde Park. The city of today, with its broad avenues running into the crooked narrow streets of colonial Boston, cherishes the landmarks of the past: the 17th-century house in which Paul Revere lived; Old North Church, famous for its part in Revere's story; Old South Meetinghouse, a rallying place for patriots during the Revolution; the old statehouse (1713), now a museum; the Boston Common, one of the oldest public parks in the country; Faneuil Hall; the golden-domed statehouse, with its facade designed by Charles Bulfinch; and the red-brick houses of Louisburg Square. Among notable Boston churches are King's Chapel, the birthplace of American Unitarianism (1785); the Mother Church of Christian Science; and Trinity Church (1872–77), designed by H. H. Richardson and decorated by John LaFarge. Boston Light (1716), at the entrance to Boston Harbor, is the oldest lighthouse in the United States. Boston is one of the great cultural centers of the nation. In the city are the Massachusetts Historical Society (founded 1791); the Boston Athenaeum (1807); the Boston Public Library; the New England Conservatory of Music; the Boston Symphony Orchestra; the Museum of Fine Arts; the Isabella Stewart Gardner Museum; and the offices of the *Christian Science Monitor.* Harvard Medical School is in Boston proper, as are the New England Medical Center and Massachusetts General Hospital. Other educational institutions include Boston Univ., Simmons College, Emerson College, Emmanuel College, and Northeastern Univ. The Boston Naval Shipyard (est. 1800, closed 1973) was the berth of the restored U.S.S. *Constitution,* which was originally launched (1797) a short distance away. The city has an international airport and a War Memorial Auditorium. It fields professional teams in the big leagues of all major sports. See H. and J. Kirker, *Bulfinch's Boston, 1787–1817* (1964); A. Taylor, *A Book of Boston* (3 vol., 1960–1964); W. M. Whitehill, *Boston in the Age of John Fitzgerald Kennedy* (1966) and *Boston: A Topographical History* (2d ed. 1968); G. B. Warden, *Boston, 1689–1776* (1970); P. R. Knights, *The Plain People of Boston: A Study in City Growth, 1830–1860* (1973); G. J. Lankevich, *Boston* (1974).

Boston College, mainly at Chestnut Hill, Mass.; coeducational; Jesuit; est. and opened 1863. The liberal arts school is at Lenox, and the schools of philosophy, theology, and geophysics are at Weston.

Boston ivy or **Japanese ivy,** tall-climbing woody vine (*Parthenocissus tricuspidata*) from the Orient, one of the most popular of city wall coverings. Of the same genus as the Virginia creeper and sometimes called AMPELOPSIS, it climbs by disk-tipped tendrils and has three-lobed, or three-parted, leaves, which develop vivid colors in the fall. Boston ivy is classified in the division MAGNOLIOPHYTA, class Magnoliopsida, order Rhaminales, family Vitaceae.

Boston Latin School, at Boston; opened 1635 as a school for boys; one of the oldest free public schools in the United States. Many famous men attended the school, including five signers of the Declaration of Independence and four presidents of Harvard Univ. In 1972 it became coeducational. See Philip Marson, *Breeder of Democracy* (1963).

Boston Massacre, 1770, pre-Revolutionary incident growing out of the resentment against the British troops sent to Boston to maintain order and to enforce the TOWNSHEND ACTS. The troops, constantly tormented by irresponsible gangs, finally (March 5, 1770) fired into a rioting crowd and killed five men—three on the spot, two of wounds later. The funeral of the victims was the occasion for a great patriot demonstration. The British captain, Thomas Preston, and his men were tried for murder, with Robert Treat Paine as prosecutor, John Adams and Josiah Quincy as lawyers for the defense. Preston and six of his men were acquitted; two others were found guilty of manslaughter, punished, and discharged from the army. See study by H. B. Zobel (1970).

Boston Mountains, most rugged part of the Ozarks, NW Ark. and E Okla., rising to 2,700 ft (823 m). Isolated because of its physical makeup, the region developed its own life-style; mountain people occupy small farms, cultivating the narrow valleys and living on the ridges. The Boston Mts., along with the rest of the highlands, have become a popular recreation center; Ozark National Forest is there.

Boston Museum of Fine Arts: see MUSEUM OF FINE ARTS, at Boston, Mass.

Boston Port Bill: see INTOLERABLE ACTS.

Boston Public Library, founded in 1852, chiefly through the gift of Joshua Bates. It is the oldest free public city library supported by taxation in the world. Its present building on Copley Square, designed by McKim, Mead, and White, was completed in 1895. The main hall is decorated with murals by Puvis de Chavannes. Other rooms have murals by Edwin Abbey and John S. Sargent. The library holds about 2.5 million volumes; its special collections include Spanish and Portuguese literature; histories of printing, the theater, and the woman's rights movement; the libraries of John Adams and Nathaniel Bowditch; and the Albert H. Wiggin collection of paintings and etchings. The library opened a new wing designed by Philip Johnson and John Burgee in 1973. See W. M. Whitehill, *Boston Public Library: A Centennial History* (1956).

Boston Symphony Orchestra, founded in 1881 by Henry Lee Higginson, who was its director and financial backer until 1918. Its outstanding conductors have been Sir George Henschel (1881–84), Arthur Nikisch (1889–93), Pierre Monteux (1919–24), Serge Koussevitzky (1924–49), Charles Munch (1949–62), Erich Leinsdorf (1962–69), William Steinberg (1969–73), and Seiji Ozawa (1973–). Symphony Hall, built for concerts of the orchestra, was opened in 1900. One of America's oldest orchestras, it has summer activities which include the Berkshire Festival and the Boston Pops Concerts. See M. A. De Wolfe Howe, *The Boston Symphony Orchestra* (1931); H. E. Dickson, *Gentlemen, More Dolce, Please* (1969).

Boston Tea Party, 1773. In the contest between British Parliament and the American colonists before the Revolution, Parliament, when repealing the TOWNSHEND ACTS, had retained the tea tax, partly as a symbol of its right to tax the colonies, partly to aid the financially embarrassed East India Company. The colonists tried to prevent the consignees from accepting taxed tea and were successful in New York and Philadelphia. At Charleston the tea was landed but was held in government warehouses. At Boston, three tea ships arrived and remained unloaded but Gov. Thomas Hutchinson refused to let the ships leave without first paying the duties. A group of indignant colonists, led by Samuel Adams, Paul Revere, and others, disguised themselves as Indians, boarded the ships on the night of Dec. 16, 1773, and threw the tea into the harbor. In reply Parliament passed the Boston Port Bill (see INTOLERABLE ACTS). See study by B. W. Labaree (1964).

Boston terrier, breed of small, lively NONSPORTING DOG developed in the United States in the second half of the 19th cent. It stands between 14 and 17 in. (35.6–43.2 cm) high at the shoulder and weighs from 13 to 25 lb (5.9–11.3 kg). Its short, smooth, glossy coat may be brindle or black, both with white markings. One of the few breeds native to the United States, it was developed in Boston from a cross between the bulldog and a now extinct white English terrier. Since its perfection in the 1880s, the Boston terrier has steadily increased in popularity as a companion and house pet. See DOG.

Boston University, at Boston, Mass.; coeducational; founded 1839, chartered 1869, first baccalaureate granted 1871. It is composed of 16 schools and colleges. Among its notable research facilities are a medical center (including the school of medicine, school of graduate dentistry, and university hospital), an urban institute, and an African studies center. See E. R. Speare, *Interesting Happenings in Boston University's History* (1957); W. O. Ault, *Boston University: The College of Liberal Arts, 1873–1973* (1973).

Boswell, James, 1740–95, Scottish author, b. Edinburgh; son of a distinguished judge. At his father's insistence young Boswell reluctantly studied law. Admitted to the bar in 1766, he practiced throughout his life, but his true interest was in a literary career and in associating with the great men of his day. Boswell first met Samuel Johnson on a trip to London in 1763. The same year he traveled about the Continent, where he made the acquaintance of Rousseau and Voltaire. He achieved literary fame with his *Account of Corsica* (1768), based on his visit to that island and on his acquaintance with the Corsican patriot Pasquale Paoli. Boswell married his cousin Margaret Montgomerie in 1769. In 1773 he became a member of Johnson's club, to which Burke, Garrick, Reynolds, and Goldsmith belonged. Later that year he and Johnson toured Scotland, a visit Boswell described in *The Journal of a Tour of the Hebrides with Samuel Johnson, LL.D.* (1785; complete edition from manuscript, 1936). His great work, *The Life of Samuel Johnson, LL.D.*, appeared in 1791. In it Boswell recorded Johnson's conversation minutely, but with a fine sense of critical judgment. So skillful was his work that Johnson is perhaps better remembered today for his sayings in the biography than for his own works. The curious combination of Boswell's own character (he was vainglorious, a heavy drinker, and a libertine) and his genius at biography have intrigued later critics, who conclude that he is probably the greatest biographer in Western literature. Misconduct led to poverty and ill health in his final years. In the 20th cent. great masses of Boswell manuscripts—journals, letters, and other papers—were discovered, most of them at Malahide Castle, Ireland. Lt. Col. Ralph H. Isham purchased the first in 1927 and sold these and later finds to Yale Univ. Publication of these "Yale Editions of the Private Papers," under the general editorship of Frederick A. Pottle, had reached many volumes by 1970. The recent findings, most particularly his voluminous journals, have enhanced Boswell's literary reputation. Always lively and, at times, even exciting, the journals portray Boswell's daily life in extraordinary detail. They are written in an easy, colloquial style, which resembles the style of many 20th-century authors. See Frederick A. Pottle, *James Boswell* (1966), the first volume of a definitive biography; studies by James L. Clifford, ed. (1970), David L. Passler (1971), Hesketh Pearson (1958, repr. 1972), and W. R. Siebenschuh (1972).

Bosworth Field, Leicestershire, central England. It was the scene of the battle (1485) at which Richard III was killed and the crown was passed to his opponent the earl of Richmond (Henry VII), first of the Tudors.

botanical garden, public place in which plants are grown both for display and for scientific study. An arboretum is a botanical garden devoted chiefly to the growing of woody plants. The plants in botanical gardens are labeled, usually with both the common and the scientific names, and they are often arranged in cultural or habitat groups, such as rock gardens, aquatic gardens, desert gardens, and tropical gardens. Botanical gardens perform diversified functions, e.g., the collection and cultivation of plants from all parts of the world, experimentation in plant breeding and hybridization, the maintenance of botanical libraries and herbariums, and the administration of educational programs for adults and children. The two most important gardens in the United States are the New York Botanical Garden, Bronx Park, New York City (est. 1891) and the Missouri Botanical Garden, St. Louis, Mo. (the earliest in the United States, founded c.1860 and affiliated with Washington Univ.). The Santa Barbara Botanic Garden, formerly Blaksley Botanic Garden, Santa Barbara, Calif. (est. 1926), is noted for its collection of desert and subtropical ornamental plants. Other well-known botanical gardens are the Arnold Arboretum, near Boston, Mass. (est. 1872 as part of Harvard Univ.); Brooklyn Botanic Garden, Brooklyn, N.Y. (est. 1910); Highland and Durand-Eastman parks, Rochester, N.Y.; Bartram's Gardens, Philadelphia (founded 1728); Fairchild Tropical Garden, Coconut Grove, Fla. (est. 1938); Fort Worth Botanic Garden, Fort Worth, Texas (est. 1933); Rancho Santa Ana Botanical Garden, Anaheim, Calif. (est. 1927); Huntington Botanical Garden, San Marino, Calif; the botanical gardens at Ottawa, Montreal, and Toronto, Canada; and the innumerable major botanical gardens of Europe, including the Royal Botanic Gardens, known as Kew Gardens, London; and the Jardin des Plantes, Paris. See Donald Wyman, *The Arboretums and Botanical Gardens of North America* (rev. ed. 1959); H. R. Fletcher et al., ed., *International Directory of Botanical Gardens* (2d ed. 1969).

botany, science devoted to the study of plants. Botany, microbiology, and zoology together compose the science of BIOLOGY. Man's earliest concern with plants was with their practical uses, i.e., for fuel, clothing, shelter, and, particularly, food and drugs. The Assyrians and Egyptians were experienced cultivators more than 8,000 years ago, and at approximately the same period the pre-Incas in Peru developed the techniques of maize cultivation that later dominated the Americas. The establishment of botany as an intellectual science came in classical times. In the 4th cent. B.C., Aristotle and his pupil Theophrastus worked out descriptions and principles of plant types and functions that remained the prototype for botanical observation for 1,000 years. During the stagnant period of the Middle Ages the knowledge of the classical scholars was preserved in the European monasteries and by the Arabs in the Middle East. In the 16th and 17th cent. an interest in botany revived in Europe and spread to America by way of European conquest and colonization. At that time the art of gardening (see GARDEN) stressed the utility of plants for man; the popular HERBAL, describing the medical uses of plants, mingled current superstition with fact. In the late 17th and the 18th cent. the influence of the ancient scholars was modified by the growth of scientific botany. Through careful and accurate observation the sciences of taxonomy and morphology (see BIOLOGY) were developed, providing the basis for the first systematic CLASSIFICATION of organisms, chiefly in the work of LINNAEUS. With the microscope came the development of plant anatomy and researches on the cell. New knowledge of the principles of chemistry and physics spurred experimentation in plant physiology, notably the early work of Stephen HALES on the sources and manufacture of plant food, which led to studies of such basic processes as PHOTOSYNTHESIS. Modern botany has expanded into all areas of biology. Perhaps most significant was the work of MENDEL in plant BREEDING at the middle (1859) of the 19th cent., from which grew the science of GENETICS. Allied with experimental botany are the various practical aspects that have developed into specific scientific disciplines (e.g., AGRICULTURE, AGRONOMY, HORTICULTURE, and FORESTRY). See Julius von Sachs, *History of Botany* (tr. 1890, repr. 1967); C. L. Wilson and W. E. Loomis, *Botany* (4th ed. 1967); C. B. Lees, *Gardens, Plants and Man* (1970).

Botany Bay, inlet, New South Wales, SE Australia, just S of Sydney. It was visited in 1770 by James Cook, who proclaimed British sovereignty over the east coast of Australia. The site of the landing is marked by a monument on Inscription Point. The bay was named by Cook and Sir Joseph Banks because of the interesting flora on its shores. Although Australia's first penal colony was often called Botany Bay, its actual site was at Sydney on Port Jackson.

Botev, Khristo (khrĭs'tō bô'tĕf), 1848–76, Bulgarian poet and patriot. At 17, Botev was sent to Russia, where he became enamored of socialist doctrine. He sought to promote revolution against the Ottoman domination and was killed in action leading a band of his own organizing. His few lyrics and ballads are filled with patriotic fervor. English translations of his work appear as *Khristo Botev Selections* (1948) and *Poems* (1955).

botfly, common name for several families of hairy FLIES whose larvae live as parasites within the bodies of mammals. The horse botfly secretes an irritating substance that is used to attach its eggs to the body hairs of a horse, mule, or donkey. When the animal licks off the irritant, the larvae are carried into the host's mouth and later migrate to the stomach. They attach themselves to the lining, where they feed until ready to pupate, and then drop to the ground with the feces. The larvae, which may cause serious damage to the digestive tract and weaken the animal, can be eliminated by a veterinarian. Sheep botflies lay their eggs in the nostrils of the host without alighting. The larvae work their way up into the head cavities causing fits of vertigo known as blind staggers; failure to eat because of irritability may result in death. Old World species of this family attack camels, elephants, horses, mules, donkeys, and deer. The warble flies, also called heel flies, or bomb flies, parasitize cattle and other animals. The larvae, called cattle grubs or cattle maggots, penetrate the skin of the host immediately after hatching; they migrate through the flesh, causing irritability, loss of weight, and decreased milk production, and then settle under the skin of the back, producing cysts, or warbles. Breathing holes made in the warbles by the larvae damage the hide. A species of human botfly found in Central and South America attaches its eggs to a bloodsucking mosquito that it captures and then releases. When the mosquito comes in contact with humans or other warm-blooded animals, the fly eggs hatch and the larvae fasten to the mammal's skin. The larvae bore into muscle tissue; infestation is called myiasis. For control methods, see bulletins of the U.S. Dept. of Agriculture. The botflies are classified in the phylum ARTHROPODA, class Insecta, order Diptera. Horse botflies are classified in the family Gasterophilidae; sheep botflies and warble flies are classified in the family Oestridae; the human botfly is classified in the family Cuterebridae. See INSECT.

Botha, Louis (bō'tə), 1862–1919, South African soldier and statesman. A Boer, he participated in the founding (1884) of the New Republic, which joined (1888) the Transvaal. Although Botha had little previous military experience, he brilliantly commanded Boer troops in the South African War. He besieged the British at Ladysmith and defeated their forces at Colenso. In 1900 he succeeded General Joubert as commander of the Transvaal army and led its remnants in guerrilla fighting. After the war (1902) he favored cooperation with the British. Botha was (1907–10) premier of the Transvaal. As the leader of the United South African, or Unionist, party he was prime minister of the Union of South Africa from its organization (1910) until his death, and he was ably assisted by Jan Christiaan SMUTS. In World War I, Botha declared South Africa a belligerent on the side of the Allies. He suppressed a Boer revolt and in 1915 led the forces that conquered the German colony of South West Africa. See biography by Earl Buxton (1924); Basil Williams, *Botha, Smuts, and South Africa* (1946); N. G. Garson, *Louis Botha or John X. Merriman* (1969).

Bothnia, Gulf of: see BALTIC SEA.

Bothwell, James Hepburn, 4th **earl of** (hĕ'bərn, bŏth'wəl), 1536?–1578, Scottish nobleman; third husband of MARY QUEEN OF SCOTS. Though a Protestant, he was a strong partisan of the Catholic regent, Mary of Guise, mother of Mary Queen of Scots. In 1562, Bothwell's old enemy, James Hamilton, earl of Arran, accused Bothwell of proposing to kidnap the queen, and Bothwell was imprisoned. He escaped and started for France, but was imprisoned for a year by the English before he reached it. Mary recalled him in 1565 to help her put down the rebellion by the earl of Murray, her half brother. In 1566, Mary's secretary, David Rizzio, was murdered by conspirators, among them her husband, Lord DARNLEY. Thereafter she trusted only Bothwell and was with him constantly. In Feb., 1567, Darnley was murdered. Bothwell was undoubtedly responsible, but he was acquitted in a trial that was a judicial mockery. Shortly after the trial, Bothwell abducted Mary and, having divorced his wife, married the queen. The Scottish nobles now rose against Bothwell and forced Mary to give him up (June, 1567). He fled to Denmark, where he was imprisoned and died insane.

bo tree or **pipal** (pē'pəl), fig tree (*Ficus religiosa*) of India held sacred by the Buddhists, who believe that Gautama received enlightenment under a bo tree at Bodh Gaya. A slip of this tree was planted at Anuradhapura to become one of the oldest known trees. The bo tree attains great size and age; the leaves, which hang from long, flexible petioles, rustle in the slightest breeze. Pipal is also spelled peepul or pipul. The bo tree is classified in the division MAGNOLIOPHYTA, class Magnoliopsida, order Urticales, family Moraceae.

Botsford, George Willis, 1862–1917, American historian, b. West Union, Iowa. After some years (1895–1901) at Harvard, he taught (1901–17) ancient history at Columbia. An outstanding authority on ancient history, he wrote numerous monographs and scholarly works but is best remembered for his high school and college textbooks. His *Hellenic History* (1922) was especially well received. He collaborated with E. G. Sihler on a source book, *Hellenic Civilization* (1915, repr. 1965).

Botswana (bŏtswä'nə), formerly **Bechuanaland** (bĕchōōä'nəlănd"), republic (1971 pop. 630,379), 231,804 sq mi (600,372 sq km), S central Africa. GABORONE is the capital. Botswana is bordered by South West Africa on the west and north, by Zambia at a

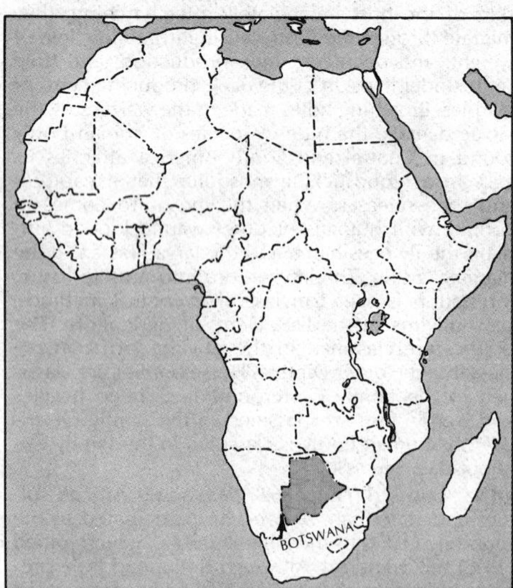

narrow strip in the north, by Rhodesia on the east, and by the Republic of South Africa on the east and south. The terrain is mostly an arid plateau (c.3,000 ft/910 m high) of rolling land. In the east are hills. The Kalahari Desert lies in the south and west. In the northwest the Okavango River drains into the vast region of the Okavango swamp and Lake Ngami, thus forming a huge marshland. Rainfall varies from less than 9 in. (23 cm) per year in the southwest to about 25 in. (64 cm) in the north. The climate ranges from subtropical to temperate. Most of Botswana's people are pastoralists, and cattle raising and the export of beef and other cattle products are the chief economic activities. The country's water shortage and consequent lack of sufficient irrigation facilities have hampered agriculture; only a small percentage of the potentially arable land is under cultivation. Sorghum, maize, millet, and beans are the principal subsistence crops, and cotton, peanuts, and sunflowers are the main cash crops. Many citizens of Botswana work in the mines of South Africa, and lesser numbers are employed in Rhodesia. Botswana's bleak economic outlook was dramatically brightened during the 1960s with the discovery of significant quantities of several minerals. The only known minerals in the country at the time of independence were manganese and some gold and asbestos. Large nickel, copper, and diamond deposits have since been found, as well as salt and soda ash; antimony and sulfur are known to exist, and the discovery of oil is a serious possibility. Vast coal deposits are also being worked. Development of a tourist industry has been based partly on the attraction of one of Africa's few remaining large natural game reserves. Despite the promise of growing wealth and economic diversification, Botswana is likely, because of its landlocked position, to remain heavily dependent on its white-ruled neighbors. South Africa provides port facilities, and Rhodesia controls and operates the railroad from Cape Town that passes through Botswana. There are also road links with South Africa and Rhodesia. South Africa has a customs union with Botswana, whose currency is the South African rand and whose chief trading partners are South Africa and Rhodesia. The country's population consists mainly of the Tswana, who are divided into eight major groups, all speaking Bantu languages. English and Tswana are the country's offical tongues. The great majority of the people practice traditional religions, but there is a small Christian minority. San (Bushmen) were the original inhabitants of what is now Botswana. In the 18th cent. the Tswana supplanted the San, who remained as serfs. David Livingstone and other European missionaries visited the area in the mid-19th cent. Beginning in the 1820s, the region was disrupted by the expansion of the Zulu and their offshoot, the Ndebele. However, Khama, chief of the Ngwato (the largest Tswana tribe), curbed the depredations of the Ndebele and established a fairly unified state. A new threat arose in the late 19th cent. with the incursion of Boers from neighboring Transvaal. After gold was discovered in the region in 1867, the Transvaal government sought to annex parts of Botswana. Although the British forbade annexation, the Boers continued to encroach on tribal lands during the 1870s and 80s. German colonial expansion in South West Africa caused the British to reexamine their policies, and, urged on by Khama, they established (1884–85) a protectorate called Bechuanaland. The southern part of the area was incorporated into Cape Colony in 1895. Until 1961, Bechuanaland was administered by a resident commissioner at Mafeking, in South Africa, who was responsible to the British high commissioner for South Africa. Britain provided for the eventual transfer of Bechuanaland to the Union of South Africa, which was established in 1910; in succeeding years, however, South Africa's attempts at annexation were countered by British insistence that Bechuanaland's inhabitants first be consulted. The rise of the National party in South Africa in 1948 and its pursuit of apartheid turned British opinion against the incorporation of Bechuanaland into South Africa. Although Bechuanaland spawned no nationalist movement, Britain granted internal self-government in 1965 and full independence on Sept. 30, 1966. Seretse Khama, grandson of Khama, was elected the first president. Botswana remained in the Commonwealth of Nations. The country has maintained close ties with its white-ruled neighbors and has refused to let its territory harbor guerrilla operations against them. Botswana's 1966 constitution provides for a parliament composed of the president and the national assembly. There is an advisory house of chiefs. See Isaac Schapera, *The Tswana* (1953); Anthony Sillery, *Founding a Protectorate* (1965); Zdenck Cervenka, *Republic of Botswana* (1970); Philippus Smit, *Botswana: Resources and Development* (1970); Anthony Sillery, *Botswana: a Short Political History* (1974).

Botta, Paul Émile (pôl āmēl' bôtä'), 1805–70, French archaeologist and government official. While consular agent at Mosul (1843) he made his renowned discoveries of Assyrian inscriptions at Khorsabad. Botta wrote *Monument de Ninive* (5 vol., 1849–50).

Böttger, Johann Friedrich (yō'hän frē'drĭkh bŏt'gər), 1682–1719, German chemist and originator of Dresden china. When the Swedish invasion of Saxony occurred (1706), Böttger and his aides were removed from Dresden to protect the secret of the process. He developed a variety of glazes, including black and a delicate violet, later much used. He made use of silver and gold in the decoration. His potteries were under royal patronage, and he was made director of the extensive works in 1708. He perfected white porcelain in 1715. The following year he was imprisoned because of an attempt to sell his secret.

Botticelli, Sandro (sän'drō bôt"tĭchĕl'lē), c.1444–1510, Florentine painter of the Renaissance, whose real name was Alessandro di Mariano Filipepi (älĕssän'drō dē märēä'nō fēlēpā'pē). He was apprenticed to Fra Filippo Lippi, whose delicate coloring can be seen in such early works as the *Adoration of the Kings* (National Gall., London) and *Chigi Madonna* (Gardner Mus., Boston). Elements of the more vigorous style of Pollaiuolo and Verrocchio soon entered his paintings, e.g., *Fortitude* (Uffizi), *St. Augustine* (Ognissanti), and *Portrait of a Young Man* (Uffizi). He became a favorite painter of the Medici, whose portraits he included, in addition to a self-portrait, among the splendid figures in the *Adoration of the Magi* (Uffizi). In 1481 Pope Sixtus IV asked him to help decorate the Sistine Chapel. After painting three biblical frescoes he returned to Florence, where he reached the height of his popularity. Through the Medici he came into contact with the Neoplatonic circle and was influenced by the ideas of Ficino and Poliziano. His enchanting mythological scenes, *Spring, Birth of Venus, Mars and Venus,* and *Pallas Subduing a Centaur,* have allegorical implications. In general they allude to the triumph of love and reason over brutal instinct. Probably in the 1490s he drew the visionary illustrations for the *Divine Comedy.* He painted a set of frescoes for the Villa Tornabuoni (Louvre) and created a series of radiant Madonnas, including the *Magnificat* and the *Madonna of the Pomegranate* (Uffizi). From Alberti's description, he re-created the famous lost work of antiquity, *The Calumny* of Apelles. The religious passion of Savonarola's sermons was reflected in Botticelli's work. His piety is evident in the *Nativity* (National Gall., London), *Last Communion of St. Jerome* (Metropolitan Mus.) and *Pietà* (Fogg Mus., Cambridge). His reputation probably declined, as he received fewer commissions. In the 19th cent. the Pre-Raphaelites rediscovered him. Supported by Ruskin, they admired the extreme refinement and poignancy of his conceptions. He is undoubtedly one of the greatest colorists of Florence and a master of rhythmic line. See studies by H. P. Horne (1908), Lionello Venturi (1949, repr. 1961), and G. C. Argan (tr. by J. Emmons, 1957).

Bottomley, Gordon, 1874–1948, English poet and dramatist, b. Yorkshire. His major artistic efforts were directed at reviving verse drama in English. Among his plays are *The Crier by Night* (1902), *The Riding To Lithend* (1909), *King Lear's Wife* (1915), and *Gruach* (1921); the latter two are "prefaces" to the action of *Lear* and *Macbeth* respectively. His volumes of poetry include *A Vision of Giorgione* (1910).

Bottrop (bôt'rôp), city (1970 pop. 106,657), North Rhine-Westphalia, W West Germany, in the RUHR district. It was a small town until 1863, when it began to develop as a coal-mining center. The city is today also an industrial center; its manufactures include chemicals, electrical equipment, and textiles. There are large carbonization plants there. Bottrop was known around the 11th cent. as Borgthorpe.

botulism (bŏch'əlĭz"əm), acute poisoning resulting from ingestion of food containing toxins produced by the bacillus *Clostridium botulinum.* The bacterium can grow only in an anaerobic atmosphere, particularly in canned foods. Consequently, botulism is almost always caused by preserved foods which have been improperly processed, usually a product canned imperfectly at home. The toxins are destroyed by boiling canned food for 30 min at 176°F (80°C). Once the toxins (which are impervious to destruction by the enzymes of the gastrointestinal tract) have entered the body, they interfere with the transmission of nerve impulses, causing disturbances in vision, speech, and swallowing, and ultimately paralysis of the respiratory muscles, leading to suffocation. Symptoms of the disease appear about 18 to 36 hr after ingestion of toxins. Botulinus antiserum is given to persons who have been exposed to contaminated food before they develop symptoms of the disease and is given to diagnosed cases of the disease as soon as possible. Botulism has a high mortality rate (about 65%) and requires expert nursing and medical care. See FOOD POISONING.

Botvinnik, Mikhail (mēkhəyĕl' bôt'vēnyĭk), 1911–, Russian chess player, b. St. Petersburg (now Leningrad). He ranked as a master at the age of 16 and won the USSR championship at 20. An electrical engineer by profession, he won the world championship after a round-robin tournament in Moscow in 1948. Botvinnik lost the title to Vassily Smyslov in 1957 but regained it in 1958. He lost again, to Mikhail Tal, in 1960, regained the title for two years, but was defeated by Tigran PETROSIAN in 1963.

Bouaké (bwä'kā, bwäkā'), town (1963 est. pop. 53,000), central Ivory Coast. It is a transportation hub and a commercial center and was once the crossroads for the caravan trade. Tobacco products are produced in the town, and gold and manganese are found nearby. A variant spelling is Bwake.

Bouchardon, Edme (ĕdmā' bōōshärdôN'), 1698–1762, French sculptor; pupil of Guillaume Coustou. He is known for his fountain in the Rue de Grenelle, Paris, and for numerous works at Versailles, in the Louvre, and in Saint-Sulpice, Paris. Bouchardon was famous for the classical purity of his style.

Boucher, François (fräNswä' bōōshā'), 1703–70, French painter. Boucher's art embodied the spirit of his time; it was elegant, frivolous, and artificial. He studied briefly with François Le Moyne but was also influenced by Watteau, many of whose works he engraved. At the age of 20 he won the Grand Prix, and from 1727 to 1731 he studied in Italy, being particularly attentive to works by Tiepolo and Albani. On his return he rapidly became the most fashionable painter of his day and a teacher and favorite of Mme de Pompadour. He produced a vast number of pictures, decorations, tapestry designs, stage settings for ballet and opera, and fine etchings. As a result, Boucher enjoyed many academic and official honors including that of director of the Gobelins tapestry works. He is best known, however, as a decorator and above all for his brilliant, voluptuous decorations of boudoirs. Fragonard was his pupil for a time. The Louvre and the Wallace Collection, London, excel in selections of Boucher's work. He is well represented in the United States by his *Peace and War* in the Museum of Fine Arts, Boston; his *Toilet of Venus* and *Birth and Triumph of Venus* in the Metropolitan Museum; and his *Voluptuary and Winter Scene* in the New-York Historical Society. Fine examples of his work are in the Frick Collection, New York City.

Boucher de Crèvecœur de Perthes, Jacques (zhäk, də krĕvkör' də pĕrt), 1788–1868, French writer and archaeologist. He was the first to show that man had existed in the Pleistocene epoch, thereby disputing the theory of diluvial CATASTROPHISM. He collected roughly chipped flint artifacts near Abbeville, France, and demonstrated that these man-made objects came from the same period as Ice Age fauna. See PALEOLITHIC PERIOD.

Bouches-du-Rhône (bōōsh-dü-rōn), department (1968 pop. 1,470,271), in Provence, SE France. It includes the island of Camargue in the Rhône delta. MARSEILLES is the capital.

Boucicault, Dion (bōō'sĭkō), 1822?–1890, Anglo-Irish dramatist and actor. At 19 he had success with his play *London Assurance* at Covent Garden, London. In 1853 he went to the United States with his wife, Agnes Robertson, an actress who was the adopted daughter of Charles Kean. Boucicault became known for his work there as well as in London. A prolific writer who successfully employed theatrical tricks, he wrote or adapted over 300 farces, comedies, and melodramas, in which he often acted. The most notable of these were *Grimaldi* (1855), *The Sidewalks of New York* (1857), *The Octoroon* (1859), *The Colleen Bawn* (1860), *Arrah-na-Pogue* (1864), *Rip Van Winkle* (1865, with Joseph Jefferson), *The O'Dowd* (1873), and *The Shaughraun* (1874). The growth of the road company that performs one play owes much to Boucicault's influence. See his *Art of Acting* (1916); study by R. G. Hogan (1969).

Boucicaut (bōōsēkō'), c.1366–1421, marshal of France and crusader against the Ottoman Turks, whose real name was Jean le Meingre. Captured by Ottoman Sultan Beyazid I at NIKOPOL (1396), he was ransomed. In 1399 the French sent him to defend Constantinople against Beyazid I. He was governor (1401–7) of Genoa, then under French protection, was captured by the English at Agincourt (1415), and died in England. He wrote several ballads and other poems.

Boucicaut Master (bōōsēkō'), active c.1375–1400, Franco-Flemish manuscript illuminator. The master was named for his greatest work, *The Hours of the Maréchal de Boucicaut* (Musée Jacquemart-André, Paris). In this work were combined the Italian advances in painting techniques, such as perspective, and the French style of ILLUMINATION.

Boudin, Eugène Louis (özhĕn' lwē bōōdăN'), 1824–98, French painter. He began painting at 25 in Paris. His best-known paintings are little beach scenes of Brittany, Normandy, and the Netherlands. Noted for the pervasive clarity and directness of his outdoor scenes, Boudin excelled in depicting nuances of light and atmosphere. He painted from nature, influencing the impressionists, notably Monet, to use this working method. Boudin is represented in the Louvre by several works and in the Metropolitan Museum by *Baie de Fourmis, Beaulieu* and *On the Beach at Trouville.* See study by G. J. Aubry (tr. 1969).

Boudinot, Elias (bōō'dĭnŏt), 1740–1821, political leader in the American Revolution, b. Philadelphia. A lawyer of Elizabethtown (now Elizabeth), N.J., he took an active part in anti-British activities and was a member of the Continental Congress both before and after the adoption of the Articles of Confederation (1777–78, 1781–84), serving as its president from 1782 to 1783. He ardently supported the U.S. Constitution and helped secure its ratification by New Jersey. He served in Congress (1789–95) and was director of the U.S. mint (1795–1805). He was an ardent philanthropist, notably for the Indians, and he was first president (1816–21) of the American Bible Society. See his *Journal of Events in the Revolution* (1894, repr. 1968); biography by G. A. Boyd (1956).

Boufflers, Louis François, duc de (lwē fräNswä' dük də bōōflĕr'), 1644–1711, marshal and peer of France. He served under the French commanders François de Créquy and the vicomte de Turenne. King Louis XIV created him a duke in 1694. His best-known exploits are his defense of Namur (1695) in the War of the Grand Alliance; and in the War of the Spanish Succession his defense of Lille against the duke of Marlborough and Prince Eugene (1708), and his skillful retreat from the field of Malplaquet (1709).

Bougainville, Louis Antoine de (lwē äNtwän' də bōōgăNvēl'), 1729–1811, French navigator. He accompanied Montcalm to Canada as aide-de-camp, and he later (c.1764) established a colony on the Falkland Islands but had to surrender the settlement to Spain (1766). Accompanied by naturalists and astronomers, he made a voyage around the world (1767–69), visiting Tahiti in the Society Islands, the Samoan group, and the New Hebrides, and rediscovering the Solomon Islands, the largest of which is named for him. In the American Revolution he fought Admiral Hood at Martinique. His name is also given to the strait between Bougainville and Choiseul Island, to a strait in the New Hebrides, and to the bougainvillaea vine. Bougainville's *Description d'un voyage autour du monde* (2 vol., 1771–72; tr. 1772) helped to popularize Rousseau's theories on the morality of man in his natural state and inspired Diderot to write (1772) his *Supplément au voyage de Bougainville,* a defense of sexual freedom.

Bougainville (bōō'gənvĭl, Fr. bōōgăNvĕl'), volcanic island (1964 pop. 64,100), c.3,880 sq mi (10,050 sq km), SW Pacific, largest of the SOLOMON ISLANDS. With the neighboring island of Buka, it forms a part of Papua New Guinea. Bougainville is rugged and densely forested. There are several good harbors, with the main port at Kieta. The economy is mainly agricultural; major exports are copra, ivory nuts, green snails, cocoa, tortoise shells, and trepang. Copper and gold are mined. The center of administration is at Sohano, a coral island in the Buka Passage. The island was discovered in 1768 by the French navigator Louis de Bougainville. Unlike the rest of the Solomon Islands, which became a British territory, Bougainville and Buka became part of German New Guinea in 1884. Occupied by Australian forces during World War I, Bougainville was mandated to Australia by the League of Nations in 1920. During World War II the island was the last Japanese stronghold in the Solomons.

bougainvillea or **bougainvillaea** (both: bōō"-gənvĭl'ēə) [for L. A. de Bougainville], any plant of the genus *Bougainvillaea* of the family Nyctaginaceae (FOUR-O'CLOCK family); chiefly tropical American woody vines with showy petallike bracts, usually in shades of brilliant red or purple. Bougainvillea are classified in the division MAGNOLIOPHYTA, class Magnoliopsida, order Caryophyllales, family Nyctaginaceae.

Bougie: see BEJAÏA, Algeria.

Bouguer, Pierre (pyĕr bōōgĕr'), 1698–1758, French mathematician and hydrographer. He made some of the first photometric measurements, calculating the intensity of the light of the sun as compared with that of the moon, and invented (1748) the heliometer. His works include *Essai d'optique sur la gradation de la lumière* (1729) and *La Figure de la terre* (1749).

Bouguereau, Adolphe William (ädôlf', bōōgrō'), 1825–1905, French academic painter. Best known for his glossy nudes, he was also highly popular in the 19th cent. as a painter of historical and religious subjects. His *La Jeunesse et l'Amour* is in the Louvre.

Bouillon, Frédéric Maurice de La Tour d'Auvergne, duc de (frādārēk' mōrēs' də lä tōōr dōvĕr'-nyə dük də bōōyôN'), c.1605–1652, French general; son of Henri de Bouillon. Brought up a Protestant, he campaigned in Holland under his uncle MAURICE OF NASSAU. In 1635 he entered the service of France. He rebelled against Cardinal RICHELIEU in 1641, but after a reconciliation he was given command (1642) of the French forces in Italy. Soon afterward he was arrested in the CINQ MARS conspiracy and, in return for pardon, ceded to France the sovereign principality of Sedan, which his family had held. He embraced Roman Catholicism, went to Rome, and commanded the papal troops. In 1649 he returned to France and took part in the FRONDE on the side of the princes. In 1651, however, he submitted and exchanged Sedan and Rocourt, which he then held as fiefs, for other territories.

Bouillon, Godfrey of: see GODFREY OF BOUILLON.

Bouillon, Henri de La Tour d'Auvergne, vicomte de Turenne, duc de (äNrē', vēkôNt' də türĕn'), 1555–1623, marshal of France, diplomat, and Protestant leader. He served with Henry IV against the Catholic LEAGUE but fled (1603) to Geneva when he was ordered arrested for his part in a conspiracy against the king. Under Marie de' Medici he returned and entered the council of regency, from which he withdrew after a quarrel with the queen. He participated in a series of pro-Calvinist intrigues but later retired to his independent duchy, which he had acquired through marriage in 1591. He founded a library and a Protestant college at Sedan. Bouillon was the grandson of Anne de Montmorency and the father of TURENNE.

Bouillon, town (1970 pop. 2,944), Luxembourg prov., SE Belgium, in the Ardennes on the Semois River, near the French border. It is a small manufacturing and tourist center. Its old castle belonged to Godfrey of Bouillon, one of the leaders of the First Crusade, who pledged (1095) the town and the surrounding duchy to the bishop of Liège to raise funds for the Crusade. Bouillon was nominally under the suzerainty of the prince-bishops of Liège until it passed (15th cent.) to William de la Marck, the "Boar of the Ardennes," whose descendants assumed the titles duke of Bouillon and prince of Sedan. The duchy was taken (1676) by Louis XIV of France and given to the La Tour d'Auvergne family. It was under direct French rule from 1794 to 1815, when it passed to the Netherlands. It became part of Belgium in 1830.

Boulanger, Georges Ernest (zhôrzh ĕrnĕst' bōōläNzhā'), 1837–91, French general and reactionary politician. He served in North Africa and Indochina, and in the Franco-Prussian War. Later, he was briefly commander of French troops in Tunisia. A protégé of Georges Clemenceau, the radical republican leader, he was appointed minister of war in 1886. Appealing to the French desire for revenge against Germany, he attracted the disparate elements hostile to the Third Republic. Boulanger's personal ambition soon alienated his republican supporters, who recognized in him a potential military dictator. Although he was forced from his ministry in 1887 and later deprived of his army command, Boulanger's ardent nationalism increased his mass appeal. Numerous royalists gave him financial aid, although Boulanger saw himself as a future dictator rather than a restorer of kings. Many times elected a parliamentary deputy, he was ineligible for the post until the government retired him from the army (1888); nevertheless, he built up wide electoral support and was overwhelmingly elected in Paris in Jan., 1889. A coup d'etat seemed probable, but Boulanger failed to act. Shortly afterwards the French government issued a warrant for his arrest for treasonable activity. Boulanger fled to Belgium. After his flight support for him dwindled, and the Boulangists, as his followers were called, were defeated in the general elections of July, 1889. Two years later, while still in exile, he committed suicide. See studies by F. H. Seager (1969) and James Harding (1971).

Boulanger, Nadia (nädyä'), 1887–, French conductor and musician, b. Paris. Boulanger is considered the outstanding contemporary teacher of composition. She studied at the Paris Conservatory, where in 1945 she was appointed professor. Boulanger taught at the École normale de Musique, Paris, and (since 1921) at the American Conservatory, Fontainebleau, becoming its director in 1950. As the teacher of such American composers as Walter Piston, Aaron Copland, Virgil Thomson, Roy Harris, and Marc Blitzstein, she has profoundly influenced contemporary American music. She has often visited the United States, as teacher, lecturer, organist, and guest conductor of the Boston Symphony (1938) and the New York Philharmonic (1939). She is noted for her conducting of choral works. Boulanger's sister Lily (1893–1918) was a distinguished composer.

Boulder, city (1970 pop. 66,870), seat of Boulder co., N central Colo.; inc. 1871. Situated c.5,350 ft (1,630 m) above sea level, it is a major resort of the Rocky Mts. and has mineral springs. Its manufactures include aircraft, computers, electronic equipment, chemicals, and sporting goods. The Univ. of Colorado, the National Center for Atmospheric Research, and many other scientific and research facilities are in the city. A U.S. atomic energy plant is nearby.

boulder, large stone formed and detached from its parent consolidated rock by weathering and erosion. In engineering and geology, especially in the United States, the term is applied to loose rocks having specific sizes according to various systems of classification. For example, in the Wentworth scale (for C. K. Wentworth, American geologist), a boulder has one linear dimension of at least 10.1 in. (25.4 cm). Boulders usually can be transported only by glacial ice. Hence, the occurrence of large boulders in abundance in a region is taken as evidence that the region has been subjected to glacial action in the past. See DRIFT; MORAINE; BOULDER CLAY.

Boulder City, residential city (1970 pop. 5,223), S Nev., just W of HOOVER DAM near Lake Mead; inc. 1959. Built (1932) by the Federal government as headquarters during the dam's construction, it became a self-governing municipality by act of Congress in 1958. It is a year-round tourist center and the headquarters of Lake Mead National Recreation Area.

boulder clay: see DRIFT.

Boulder Dam: see HOOVER DAM.

Boulez, Pierre (pyĕr bo͝olĕz'), 1925–, French composer and conductor. He studied at the Paris Conservatoire with Olivier Messiaen (1944–45) and studied 12-tone technique with René Liebowitz (1946). A radical leader of the avant-garde in music, Boulez produces compositions in which the techniques of SERIAL MUSIC are applied not only to melody and counterpoint but also to melody and rhythm. Because of its complexity, Boulez's work is difficult to perform and has elicited violent reactions from audiences. Among his compositions are *Le Soleil des eaux* (1948), for voice and orchestra; *Symphonie concertante* (1950), for piano and orchestra; *Pli selon pli* (1960); and *Éclat* (1965), for 15-piece chamber orchestra. Boulez was director of music for Jean-Louis Barrault's theater in Paris, and there he founded the Concerts Marigny and the Domaigne Musical to present avant-garde works. He has conducted major orchestras throughout the world and has published several works in French. In 1971 he became music director and conductor of the New York Philharmonic-Symphony Orchestra.

Boulle or **Buhl, André Charles** (both: äNdrā' shärl bo͝ol), 1642–1732, French cabinetmaker, the master of a distinctive style of furniture, much imitated, for which his name has become a synonym. In 1672 he was admitted to a group of skilled artists maintained by Louis XIV in the Louvre palace, and thereafter he devoted himself to creating costly furniture and objects of art for the king and court. Boulle's pieces, having in general the character of Louis XIV and RÉGENCE design, were built for the immense formal rooms of the period. Boulle, a master of MARQUETRY, specialized in the inlaying of ebony with precious woods and mother-of-pearl. Large areas were covered with tortoise shell, inlaid with arabesques of gilded brass. He added splendid bas-relief compositions, as well as sculptured rosettes, masks, and acanthus scrolls, all in gilded bronze. Superb examples of his art exist at Versailles, Fontainebleau, and the Louvre and in England at Windsor Castle and in the Wallace Collection, London. The title cabinetmaker to the king passed to his four sons, Jean Philippe, Pierre Benoît, André Charles, and Charles Joseph.

Boulogne, Jean: see BOLOGNA, GIOVANNI.

Boulogne-Billancourt (bo͝olô'nyə-bēyäNko͞or'), city (1968 pop. 109,380), Hauts-de-Seine dept., N central France, a suburb SW of Paris. One of the largest automobile factories in France is in the city. Other manufactures include airplanes, electrical goods, chemicals, bicycles, and processed foods. Part of the city is residential, with elegant homes bordering on the BOIS DE BOULOGNE. There is a 14th-century Gothic cathedral.

Boulogne-sur-Mer (bo͝olô'nyə-sür-mĕr'), city (1968 pop. 50,138), Pas-de-Calais dept., N France, in Picardy, on the English Channel. It is a great commercial seaport and the leading fishing port of France. It has canning and shipbuilding industries. From there the Romans sailed (A.D. 43) to conquer Britain, and there again Napoleon assembled an invasion fleet (which never sailed) in 1803–5. The port was a main base for British armies in World War I and a German submarine base in World War II. Most of the city was destroyed during the latter conflict. The Cathedral of Notre Dame (built 19th cent.; damaged 1941; since restored) is a great shrine of pilgrimage; it stands on a site where miracles were believed to have occurred in the 7th cent.

Boult, Sir Adrian, 1889–, English conductor. Boult studied conducting in Leipzig with Arthur Nikisch (1912–13). In 1930 he became conductor of the newly formed BBC Symphony Orchestra, and he was conductor of the London Philharmonic from 1950 to 1957. Boult led the premieres of many works by British composers and is considered an authoritative interpreter of Elgar and Vaughan Williams. He wrote *A Handbook on the Technique of Conducting* (1968). Boult was knighted in 1937. See his autobiography, *My Own Trumpet* (1973).

Boumedienne, Houari (ho͞oär'ē bo͞omĕdēĕn'), 1932?–, president and prime minister of Algeria. While studying in Cairo during the early 1950s he joined a group of expatriate Algerian nationalists that included Ahmed Ben Bella. Boumedienne secretly reentered Algeria (1955) to join a group of guerrillas operating in the province of Oran. He was (1960–62) chief of staff of the exiled National Liberation Army in Tunisia and served as Algeria's minister of defense from the time of its independence. After a series of disputes with Ben Bella, Boumedienne led a coup d'etat that overthrew his former ally's government. After the coup, Boumedienne assumed the posts of president, prime minister, and chairman of the revolutionary council. His government assumed a rigorous anti-Israeli stand.

bouncing Bet: see PINK.

Boundary Peak, 13,140 ft (4,005 m) high, SW Nev., in the White Mts. near the Calif. line. It is the highest point in Nevada.

Bound Brook, borough (1970 pop. 10,450), Somerset co., N central N.J., on the Raritan River; settled 1681, inc. 1891. It has large orchid and gardenia nurseries and chemical manufactures. The city's land was purchased from the Raritan Indians. In the Revolution, George Washington maintained an outpost there, and American forces were defeated (April, 1777) by Cornwallis. Local attractions include Washington's camp grounds and several 18th-century houses.

Bountiful, city (1970 pop. 27,853), Davis co., N central Utah; inc. 1892. It is a residential suburb N of Salt Lake City. Bountiful was settled by Mormons in 1847.

Bounty, British naval vessel commanded by William BLIGH. She set sail for the Pacific in Dec., 1787, to transport breadfruit trees from the Society Islands to the West Indies. In April, 1789, the ship's mate, Fletcher Christian, led a successful mutiny against Bligh. The captain and 18 of his crew were set adrift in a small open boat. By remarkable seamanship they went 3,618 mi (5,822 km), reached Timor in June, and proceeded to England. Some of the mutineers were later captured and court-martialed in England; three were executed. Other mutineers under Christian landed at PITCAIRN ISLAND, burned the Bounty, and founded a colony where their descendants continue to live. See George MacKaness, ed., *A Book of the Bounty* (1938); Alexander McKee, *H.M.S. Bounty* (1961).

bounty, amount paid by a government for the achievement of certain economic goals considered to be desirable. It is usually a premium paid for the increased production or export of certain goods. The bounty was an important technique of mercantilist economic policy. Whereas a SUBSIDY is a lump sum given in exchange for the meeting of some previously established condition, a bounty is given as a gratuity per unit of production. Bounties are usually in the form of direct cash payments. However, bounties can be in a concealed form such as exports relieved from payment of a tax or excise duty, special railway rates, rebates on taxes and import duties, credit facilities, and export credits guaranteed by the government. Effects of an export bounty can be destroyed by a countervailing duty imposed by an importing country. The compensatory export bounty is aimed at compensating producers for duties paid on imported raw materials used in making the particular commodity. Bounties have been also granted by states for roads, canals, railroads, and other public works. Bounties were frequently used by nations as an inducement to army enlistment. State governments in the United States give bounties for the killing of destructive animals.

Bouquet, Henry (bo͞okā'), 1719–65, British army officer in the French and Indian Wars. A French Swiss, he came to America in 1756 and distinguished himself as second in command to Gen. John FORBES in the successful expedition (1758) against Fort Duquesne (Pittsburgh). In PONTIAC'S REBELLION he decisively defeated the Indians in a hotly contested battle at Bushy Run (Aug., 1763) near Pittsburgh. In 1764, Bouquet, on an expedition into the Ohio country, forced the Shawnee and other Indians to lay down their arms. He was brigadier general commanding the Southern Dist. at his death. See his papers, ed. by S. K. Stevens et al. (2 vol., 1951–72); M. C. Darlington, *History of Colonel Henry Bouquet and the Western Frontiers of Pennsylvania* (1920, repr. 1971).

Bourassa, Henri (äNrē' bo͞oräsä'), 1868–1952, Canadian political leader and publisher, b. Montreal; grandson of Louis Joseph Papineau. He was elected as an Independent Liberal to the Canadian House of Commons in 1896 but resigned in 1899 in protest against sending Canadian troops to the South African War; he was almost immediately reelected. A man of oratorical and literary gifts, he rallied around him various groups discontented with the regime of Sir Wilfrid Laurier and welded them into a powerful opposition party in Quebec that became known as the Nationalist party; it took the stand that Canada should hold aloof from diplomatic entanglements with Great Britain and the United States. Opposing (1909–11) the bill to construct a Canadian navy, Bourassa withdrew enough support from Laurier to cause the fall of the government. In 1910 he founded, as the Nationalist journal, *Le Devoir,* a Montreal daily, and was its editor for many years. He led French Canadian opposition to participation in World War I, denouncing in violent terms the conscription act of 1917. See studies by Casey Murrow (1968) and Joseph Levitt (1969).

Bourbaki, Charles Denis Sauter (shärl dənē' sōtā' bo͞orbäkē'), 1816–97, French general of Greek ancestry. In the Algerian campaigns and the Crimean War he gained one of the highest military reputations in Europe. Offered the Greek throne (1862), he declined. In the Franco-Prussian War, put in command of the Army of the East by the provisional government, he failed to raise the siege of Belfort and was pursued to Switzerland, where his troops were disarmed and interned (Feb. 2, 1871).

Bourbon (bo͞orbôN'), royal family, orginally of France; a cadet branch of the Capetian dynasty. Its branches ruled Spain, the Two Sicilies, and Parma. It takes its name from the now ruined castle of Bourbon, at Bourbon-l'Archambault, Allier dept., which was the seat of a powerful family descended from Adhémar, a noble of the 9th cent. Robert of Clermont, sixth son of Louis IX of France, married (1272) Beatrice, heiress of Bourbon, and thus is considered the founder of the royal line. Robert's son, Louis, was created (1327) 1st duc de Bourbon. The ducal title remained with the descendants of his eldest son until 1527, when Charles, duc de Bourbon, died without issue. Because of his treason, his extensive fiefs (Bourbonnais, Marche, Auvergne, Forez) were seized by the crown and the ducal title was discontinued. A younger son of Louis, 1st duc de Bourbon, gave issue to the line of Bourbon-Vendôme. The marriage (1548) of Antoine de Bourbon, duc de Vendôme, with Jeanne d'Albret added vast territories in S France (see ALBRET) and the title king of Navarre to his other fiefs (Vendôme, Périgord, Rouergue). From Antoine's brother, Louis I de Condé, the houses of CONDÉ and CONTI were issued. Antoine's son became (1589) the first Bourbon king of France as HENRY IV, the older branches of Louis IX's issue having become extinct (see VALOIS). Henry IV was succeeded by his son, Louis XIII, and his grandson, Louis XIV. Louis XIV's descendants ruled France (except during the French Revolution and the Napoleonic era, 1792–1814) until the deposition (1830) of Charles X (see FRANCE); with the death (1883) of Henri, comte de CHAMBORD, grandson of Charles X, the senior French branch of Bourbon came to an end. From Louis XIV's brother Philip the cadet branch of Bourbon-Orléans (see ORLÉANS, family) is issued; it furnished one king, Louis Philippe (1830–48), and inherited the claim to the French crown in 1883. The line of **Bourbon-Spain** began with the accession (1700) of PHILIP V, a grandson of Louis XIV, to the Spanish throne. He was succeeded by Ferdinand VI, Charles III, Charles IV, and FERDINAND VII. Ferdinand VII set aside the Salic law of succession, introduced into Spain by Philip V, in favor of his daughter, ISABELLA II. Her succession was contested by the partisans of Don Carlos, second son of Charles IV, and of his descendants (see CARLISTS). Relative order was reestablished after Isabella's son was proclaimed (1874) king as Alfonso XII. His son, Alfonso XIII, was deposed in 1931 and died in exile in 1941. His marriage (1906) with Victoria of BATTENBERG introduced HEMOPHILIA into his family. His first and fourth sons died of minor accidents in 1938 and 1934, respectively. His second son, Jaime, early renounced his right of succession, which fell to Alfonso's third son, Don Juan, who was free from the disease. His son Juan Carlos, who married Princess Sophia of Greece, was chosen by the Spanish dictator Francisco FRANCO as his successor and future king of Spain. The line of **Bourbon-Sicily** came out of the Spanish line; it was founded by Ferdinand I of the TWO SICILIES, who succeeded (1759) his father as king of Naples and of Sicily when the latter became king of Spain as CHARLES III. His great-grandson, Francis II, was deposed in 1860; he had issue. The house of **Bourbon-Parma** was established (1748) in the duchy of PARMA and Piacenza by Philip, a younger son of Philip V of Spain and ELIZABETH FARNESE of Parma. Robert, fifth duke of the line, was deposed in 1859. Among his numerous children were Empress ZITA of Austria, SIXTUS OF BOURBON-PARMA, and Prince René, who married Princess Margaret of Denmark. René's and Margaret's daughter, Anne, married (1948) MICHAEL of Rumania.

Bourbon, Antoine de (äNtwän' də), 1518–62, duc de Vendôme, king of Navarre through his marriage to JEANNE D'ALBRET; father of Henry IV of France. He converted to Protestantism after his marriage (1548), becoming one of the most influential Huguenot leaders. Although he did not take part in the conspiracy of Amboise (March, 1560), which was masterminded by his brother Louis I de Condé (see under CONDÉ, family), he supported Condé in another plot later that year. It miscarried, and Antoine was forced to hand Condé over to Catherine de' Medici. Upon the death of Francis II in Dec., 1560, Antoine renounced his right to the regency for the minor Charles IX in return for Condé's release; he was awarded the prestigious but powerless position of royal lieutenant general. In 1561 he reembraced Roman Catholicism, joining the Guise-Montmorency alliance, which hoped to replace Catherine's regency with his own. He was killed the next year fighting the Protestants at Rouen.

Bourbon, Charles, duc de (shärl, dük də), 1490–1527, constable of France and governor of Milan. He distinguished himself at the battle of Marignano (1515) in the Italian Wars between King Francis I and Holy Roman Emperor Charles V. Enmity, encouraged by the queen mother, LOUISE OF SAVOY, arose between King Francis I and the duke, who went over to the emperor, after long negotiations, in 1523. His estates were confiscated. He fought against the French in Italy, notably at the battle of Pavia (1525), and was killed in an attack on Rome, which was sacked by his unpaid, mutinous troops. See biography by Charles Hare (1911).

Bourbonnais (bo͝orbônā'), former province, central France, in the northern part of the Massif Central. It was approximately the same area as today's Allier dept. The chief cities are Moulins, Montluçon, and Vichy. It is a largely arid plateau (except for the fertile Limagne area in the west), used for grazing and cattle raising. There are coal mines near Commentry and a large steel industry at Montluçon. Moulins, the ancient capital, has many historical monuments. The counts (later dukes) of Bourbon held the Bourbonnais as an appanage until 1527, when Francis I of France confiscated it upon the death of the constable Charles of Bourbon.

Bourbon-Parma, Bourbon-Sicily, and **Bourbon-Spain:** see BOURBON, royal family.

bourbot (bûr'bət): see COD.

Bourdelle, Émile Antoine (āmēl' äNtwän' bo͝ordĕl'), 1861–1929, French sculptor; son of a cabinetmaker of Montauban. He went to Paris in 1884, where he studied successively under Falguière, Dalou, and Rodin. Bourdelle differed sharply from Rodin in his preoccupation with the relation of sculpture to architecture. Seeking his inspiration in archaic Greece and the Gothic, he achieved his greatest success in heroic and monumental works such as *Hercules,* of which there is a cast in the Metropolitan Museum; his colossal *Virgin of Alsace;* his bas-reliefs for the Théâtre des Champs Élysées; and his monument to Americans who died in World War I (Pointe de Grave). He is also noted for his numerous portrait heads. See study by I. Jianu (1966).

Bourdon, Sébastien (sābästyăN' bo͝ordôN'), 1616–71, French painter. He imitated the styles of several painters including Claude Lorrain, Le Nain, and Poussin. Bourdon was active in Rome (1634–37), in Sweden (1652–54) as Queen Christina's court portrait painter, and in Paris; he also worked in his native Montpellier, where he painted *The Fall of Simon Magus* for the cathedral. The *Finding of Moses* is in the National Gallery of Art, Washington, D.C.

Bourdon gauge: see PRESSURE.

Bourg-en-Bresse or **Bourg** (bo͝ork-äN-brĕs'), town (1968 pop. 40,407), capital of Ain dept., in Burgundy, E central France. A major transportation hub, farm market, and gastronomic center, it is the chief city of Bresse. Machinery, morocco leather, furniture, shoes, and ceramics are also made. The church (late 15th cent.) of nearby Brou is one of the finest in France.

Bourgeois, Léon (lāôN' bo͝orzhwä'), 1851–1925, French statesman and social philosopher. He held cabinet posts, notably the premiership (1895–96) and was a delegate to the first and second Hague peace conferences and a member of the Permanent Court of Arbitration at The Hague. One of the earliest proponents of the League of Nations, he headed the French delegation in the League. In 1920 he was awarded the Nobel Peace Prize. His influential book, *Solidarité* (1896), advocated the use of public authority to achieve the solidarity increasingly necessary within and among nations.

bourgeoisie (bo͝orzhwäzē'), originally the name for the inhabitants of French medieval towns who worked as artisans and craftsmen and who occupied a socio-economic position between the peasants and the landlords in the countryside. The term was extended to include the middle class of France and subsequently of other nations. The bourgeoisie as a historical phenomenon did not begin to emerge until the development of medieval cities as centers for trade and commerce in Central and Western Europe, beginning in the 11th cent. The bourgeoisie, or merchants and craftsmen, began to organize themselves into corporations as a result of their conflict with the landed proprietors. Although trade and commerce existed in the ancient city-states of Greece and in the Roman Empire, it was primarily in the hands of those who were prevented from acquiring land. Thus, the bourgeoisie as a separate class preoccupied with material gain did not exist prior to the rise of the medieval cities. At the end of the Middle Ages, under the early national monarchies in Western Europe, the bourgeoisie found it in their interests to support the throne against the feudal disorder of competing local authorities. In England and the Netherlands, the bourgeoisie was the driving force in uprooting feudalism in the late 16th and early 17th cent. In the 17th and 18th cent., the bourgeoisie supported principles of constitutionality and natural right, against the claims of divine right and against the privileges held by nobles and prelates. The English, American, and French revolutions derived partly from the desire of the bourgeoisie to rid itself of feudal trammels and royal encroachments on personal liberty and on the rights of trade and property. In the 19th cent., the bourgeoisie, triumphantly propounding liberalism, gained political rights as well as religious and civil liberties. Thus modern Western society, in its political and also in its cultural aspects, owes much to bourgeois activities and philosophy. Subsequent to the Industrial Revolution, the class greatly expanded, and differences within it became more distinct, notably between the high bourgeois—industrialists and bankers—and the petty bourgeois—tradesmen and white-collar workers. By the end of the 19th cent., the capitalists (the original bourgeois) tended to be associated with a widened upper class, while the spread of technology and technical occupations was opening the bourgeoisie to entry from below. The term *bourgeois* has also long been used to imply an outlook associated with materialism, narrowness, and lack of culture—these characteristics were early satirized by Molière and have continued to be a subject of literary analysis. Within Karl Marx's theory of class struggle, the bourgeoisie plays a significant role. By overthrowing the feudal system it is seen as an originally progressive force that later becomes a reactionary force as it tries to prevent the ascendency of the proletariat (wage earners) in order to maintain its own position of predominance. Some writers argue that Marx's theory fails because he did not foresee the rise of a new, expanded middle class of professionals and managers, which, although wage earners, would not fit easily into his definition of the proletariat. See Nicholas Berdyaev, *The Bourgeois Mind and Other Essays* (1934, repr. 1966); Charles Morazé, *The Triumph of the Middle Classes* (1966); A. G. Frank, *Lumpenbourgeoisie* (1972).

Bourges (bo͝orzh), city (1968 pop. 73,998), capital of Cher dept., central France. It is a transportation center with foundries, arsenals, breweries, printing plants, and aeronautical and food industries. Known as Avaricum, Bourges was the Roman capital of Aquitania N of the Garonne River (see GAUL). It early became an archiepiscopal see and the capital of BERRY. Charles VII resided there while most of France was in English hands. In 1438 he promulgated the PRAGMATIC SANCTION OF BOURGES, which was revoked in 1461 by his son Louis XI, who was born in Bourges. Louis XI founded (1463) the Univ. of Bourges, where Jacques Cujas later taught; it was abolished in the French Revolution. The Cathedral of St. Etienne (13th cent.), one of the glories of French Gothic, is remarkable in that it has no transept. Jacques Cœur, whose splendid house still stands, and Louis Bourdaloue were born in Bourges.

Bourget, Paul (pôl bo͝orzhā'), 1852–1935, French novelist. His early novels were naturalistic, but *Le Disciple* (1889, tr. 1901) marked a change. This work recounts the destruction of a pupil who applies his master's naturalistic literary theories to life. Bourget thereafter wrote in a Catholic and strongly moralistic tone. His psychological analysis and classic style won admiration, but the conservatism of his views restricted his popularity. Representative of his more than 60 novels are *Cruelle Énigme* (1885, tr. *Love's Cruel Enigma,* 1891), *Cosmopolis* (1893, tr. 1893), *Le Démon de midi* (1914), and *Le Sens de la mort* (1915, tr. *The Night Cometh,* 1916). He also wrote verse, plays, and critical essays.

Bourget, Le, town (1968 pop. 49,302), Seine-Saint-Denis dept., N central France. One of the major airports of Paris is there. Charles Lindbergh landed at Le Bourget after his transatlantic flight of 1927.

Bourget, lake, 16 sq mi (41 sq km), c.11 mi (18 km) long and 2 mi (3.2 km) wide, NE Savoie dept., E France. It is famous for its scenic beauty. Aix-les-Bains and other resorts are located on its shores. The celebrated abbey of Haute-Combe (founded 12th cent.; restored 19th cent.) is situated on the western shore.

Bourgmont, Étienne Venyard, sieur de (ātyĕN' väNyär' syör də bo͝ormôN'), fl. 1706–25, French explorer in what is now the United States. He came to America c.1685. While he was acting commander of Detroit, he deserted his post in 1706 in the face of an Indian uprising caused by his intemperate actions in dealing with them. He fled to the wilderness and traveled over the region of the lower Missouri River. In 1719 the governor of New France sent Bourgmont back to France to report his discoveries, and in 1720 Bourgmont was made "commandant on the River Missouri" to block Spanish intrusion from the Southwest. In 1724 he went westward and made a treaty with the Comanche somewhere in present-day W Kansas. In 1725 he returned to France.

Bourgogne, Hôtel de: see HÔTEL DE BOURGOGNE.

Bourguiba, Habib (hä'bēb bo͝orgē'bə), 1903–, Tunisian statesman. Early active in the Destour party, he was an advocate of close cooperation with France. Later, however, he became a staunch nationalist and in 1934 formed the Neo-Destour party. Because of its anti-French agitation, the Neo-Destour was several times outlawed and Bourguiba was often imprisoned. In 1946 he escaped to Cairo and later went to the United States to promote Tunisian nationalism. He was imprisoned again from 1949 until he was released (1954) to negotiate an agreement that led to Tunisian autonomy (1954) and to independence in 1956. That year, he was elected premier. In 1957 he deposed the bey and was chosen president of the republic by the constituent assembly. A moderate, Bourguiba maintained close ties with the United States and favored negotiation with Israel. In Jan., 1974, he tentatively agreed to a plan for the eventual merger of Tunisia and Libya.

Bourignon, Antoinette (äNtwänĕt' bo͝orēnyôN'), 1616–80, Flemish Christian mystic, adherent of QUI-

ETISM. In 1636 she fled from home to avoid a marriage urged by her father, spent a short time in a convent, and was in charge (1653-62) of an orphanage. Believing herself divinely directed to restore the pure spirit of the Gospel, she gathered (1667) at Amsterdam a fanatical following. Moving from place to place, she took her printing press with her and disseminated her quietistic teachings. According to her alleged revelations, religion was a matter of internal emotion, not of faith and practice. Her mystical ideas found particular favor in Scotland, where Bourignianism was declared a heresy (1711) and candidates for the ministry were required to renounce it before ordination. Her autobiography was translated into English as *The Light of the World* (1696). See A. R. Macewen, *Antoinette Bourignon, Quietist* (1910).

Bourinot, Sir John George (bo͝or'ĭnō"), 1837-1902, Canadian historian and political scientist, b. Sydney, N.S. He is remembered as an authority on the Canadian constitution and government. His *Local Government in Canada* (1887), *Manual of the Constitutional History of Canada* (1888, rev. ed. 1901), *How Canada Is Governed* (1895, rev. ed. 1918), and other books are still authoritative.

Bourke-White, Margaret, 1904-71, American photo-journalist, b. New York City. One of the original staff photographers at *Fortune, Life,* and *Time* magazines, Bourke-White was noted for her coverage of World War II, particularly of the invasion of Russia and the liberation of Italy and of German concentration camps. Her series on the rural South during the depression, mining in South Africa, Korean guerrilla warfare, and American industry, and her portraits of world leaders are especially celebrated. Bourke-White's books include *Purple Heart Valley* (1944), *You Have Seen Their Faces* (1937; with her husband, Erskine CALDWELL), and *Portrait of Myself* (1963). She died after a 14-year battle with Parkinson's disease.

Bourmont, Louis Auguste, comte de Ghaisnes de (lwē ōgüst' kôNt də gân də bo͞ormôN'), 1773-1846, marshal of France. An émigré, he fought against the French Revolution under the prince de Condé, in the VENDÉE, and as a leader of the CHOUANS. Imprisoned in 1800, he escaped (1804) to Portugal, but in 1807 he was reconciled to Napoleon, whom he served in several campaigns. In the Hundred Days he deserted to the Prussians on the eve of Waterloo and joined the Bourbon standard. King Charles X made him minister of war (1829) and marshal (1830). He was successfully leading an army to Algeria when the revolution of 1830 made him an exile. In 1832 he aided Caroline de BERRY in her feeble insurrection; in 1840 he returned to France under an amnesty.

Bourne, Francis (bôrn), 1861-1935, English prelate, cardinal of the Roman Catholic Church. He entered the priesthood in 1884 and later was made bishop coadjutor of Southwark (1896), bishop of Southwark (1897), archbishop of Westminster (1903), and cardinal (1911). He accomplished a great deal by his moderate policies in avoiding difficulties between the Catholic Church and the state in England.

Bourne, Hugh (bo͝orn), 1772-1852, English founder of the sect of Primitive Methodists. In 1799 he joined the Wesleyan Methodists and became a preacher. In 1807 he began holding outdoor revival services, despite prohibitions by the Wesleyan Methodist Conference. His adherents gathered around him to establish a new community, whose first class was organized in 1810. In 1812 the name Primitive Methodists was adopted. Within the lifetime of the founder the sect gained over 110,000 members. From 1844 to 1846, Bourne visited the United States, where he gathered large congregations. See biography by J. T. Wilkinson (1952).

Bourne, Randolph Silliman (bôrn), 1886-1918, American author, b. Bloomfield, N.J., grad. Columbia, 1912. His critical examination of the American way of life established him as a spokesman for his generation. The books he wrote on progressive education, *The Gary Schools* (1916) and *Education and Living* (1917), reflect the influence of John Dewey. Bourne opposed U.S. entry into World War I and wrote pacifist and nonintervention articles, which were collected posthumously in *Untimely Papers* (1919). See his *History of a Literary Radical* (ed. by Van Wyck Brooks, 1920); biography by J. A. Moreau (1966).

Bourne, summer resort town (1970 pop. 12,637), Barnstable co., SE Mass., crossed by Cape Cod Canal; settled 1627, inc. 1884. The canal was bridged in 1935. Tourism is the chief industry, followed closely by fishing. Points of interest in the town include the Massachusetts Maritime Academy, a replica (built 1926) of the Aptucxet Trading Post (1627), Indian Burial Hill, Sacrifice Rock, and Wishing Rock.

Bournemouth (bôrn'məth), county borough (1971 pop. 153,425), Hampshire, S central England, on Poole Bay. It has grown since the middle of the 19th cent. from a small fishing village in the sheltered, pine-wooded valley of the Bourne to a popular resort and fine-arts center. It has an excellent sandy beach, a fine climate, and numerous parks. There is a municipal college. Mary Shelley, writer and wife of the poet, is buried in the parish churchyard. In 1974, Bournemouth became part of the new nonmetropolitan county of Dorset.

Bournonville, Auguste (ōgüst' bo͞ornôNvēl'), 1805-79, Danish dancer, choreographer, and teacher. Bournonville studied in Copenhagen and in Paris with Auguste Vestris. He joined the Royal Danish Ballet in 1830. As soloist and, after 1848, as choreographer of more than 50 works, he developed a distinctive romantic style and precision of technique which made the company internationally famous. Bournonville fought with extraordinary energy for the recognition in Denmark of ballet as an art form. His surviving dance works include a version of *La Sylphide* and *The Dancing School.*

Bourrienne, Louis Antoine Fauvelet de (lwē äNtwän' fōvəlā' də bo͞orēĕn'), 1769-1834, French political figure. He was a friend and for a time (1797-1802) private secretary to Napoleon, who made him a councillor of state. Bourrienne later supported the Bourbon restoration and was elected to the chamber of deputies, where he was a spokesman for the ultraroyalist followers of King Charles X. His memoirs (10 vol., 1829-31) are vivid but untrustworthy.

bourse (bo͞ors), term applied to a European STOCK EXCHANGE. The first international bourse was established in Antwerp in the 16th cent. The Paris bourse, dating from 1720, includes both the parquet, equivalent to the New York State Exchange and consisting of 70 members (who must be French citizens) ruled by a committee, and the coulisse, comparable to the lesser American exchanges and dealing in securities excluded from the parquet.

Boussingault, Jean Baptiste Joseph Dieudonné (zhäN bätēst' zhôzĕf' dyödônā' bo͞osăNgō'), 1802-87), French agricultural chemist. He was professor of chemistry at Lyons and later professor of agriculture and analytical chemistry at the Paris Conservatoire des Arts et Métiers. He is known especially for his research on the nitrogen cycle. He also worked on the composition of plant tissues and on the nutritive value of forages. He is credited with the idea of agricultural field experiments. In about 1834 he laid out a series of trials on his farm in which he weighed and analyzed both the materials applied to the soil as well as the crops produced. His *Économie rurale* (1844) was later republished as *Agronomie, chimie agricole, et physiologie* (1887-91) and translated into English and German. Boussingault's experiments, however, were not limited to agriculture; his research also included work on atomic weights and the properties of steel alloys.

Bouteflika, Abdelaziz (äbdĕl'äzēz" bo͞otĕflēkä'), 1937-, Algerian political leader. He fought against the French in the National Liberation Army and was appointed minister of sports shortly after independence (1962). As Algeria's foreign minister (1963), Bouteflika became a major spokesman of the nonaligned nations. In 1974 he served as president of the 29th UN General Assembly.

Boutens, Pieter Cornelis (pē'tər kôrnā'lĭs bou'təns), 1870-1943, Dutch poet. His *Verzen* (1898) won him early praise. His impressionistic and mystical lyric verse was marked by rhythmic freedom. Boutens made extensive translations, particularly from Greek.

Boutet de Monvel, Louis Maurice (lwē mōrēs' bo͞otā' də mônvĕl'), 1851-1913, French painter and illustrator. His fame rests chiefly on his decorative illustrations for children's books and his charming watercolors, e.g., *Chansons et rondes pour les enfants, Chansons de France, La Vie de Jeanne d'Arc,* and *Nos Enfants.*

Bouts, Dierick, Dirk, or **Thierry** (dē'rĭk, dĭrk, tyĕ'rē bouts), c.1420-1475, early Netherlandish painter, b. Haarlem, active in Louvain. Bouts was influenced by Roger van der Weyden, the van Eycks, and Petrus Christus. His elongated, often stiffly posed figures occupy landscapes that reveal a loving care for detail. His luminous panels have a calm beauty, particularly in the landscape backgrounds, where his sensitive treatment of changing color and light is demonstrated. The *Last Supper* altarpiece (St. Peter's, Louvain) is his major work. Two paintings of the Madonna and a portrait are in the Metropolitan Museum.

Boutwell, George Sewall, 1818-1905, American politician, b. Brookline, Mass. He served seven terms in the Massachusetts legislature between 1842 and 1851, was elected governor for the years 1851-52 by a coalition of Free-Soilers and Democrats, and was an organizer (1855) of the Republican party in Massachusetts. As U.S. Representative (1863-69), Boutwell, a leading radical Republican, was for a time chairman of the Committee on Reconstruction. He was one of the managers who handled the impeachment case against President Andrew Johnson, and he delivered one of the final arguments before the Senate. Although he had been (1862-63) the first commissioner of internal revenue, Boutwell knew little about finance. His selection as Secretary of the Treasury (1869-73) was representative of President Grant's many poor appointments. His one absorbing interest was the reduction of the national debt, and he neglected more important problems. His release of government gold defeated the famous attempt to corner the gold market on BLACK FRIDAY, Sept. 24, 1869, but the conspiracy need never have proceeded so far had he acted more promptly. He was a U.S. Senator from 1873 to 1877. See his *Reminiscences of Sixty Years in Public Affairs* (1902); Allan Nevins, *Hamilton Fish* (1936).

Bouvier, John (bo͞ovēr'), 1787-1851, American writer on law, b. France. He emigrated to Philadelphia in 1802 with his parents and later was a lawyer and journalist in Pennsylvania. His *Law Dictionary* (1839), compiled especially for American lawyers, a reference work for both the student and the practitioner, was revised and reprinted in the 19th and 20th cent.

Bouvier des Flandres (bo͞ovyā' dā fläN'drə), breed of powerful WORKING DOG perfected in Belgium around the beginning of the 20th cent. It stands from 23 to 28 in. (58-71 cm) high at the shoulder and weighs from 60 to 70 lb (27-32 kg). It has a fine, soft undercoat and a harsh, wiry outercoat ranging in color from fawn to black. Its ears are cropped and stand erect, and its tail is docked to approximately 4 in. (10 cm). The Bouvier is primarily a herder of cattle, but it has also been trained successfully as a police and war dog. See DOG.

Bouvines (bo͞ovēn'), village (1968 pop. 560), Nord dept., N France, in Flanders. In an epochal battle there in 1214, Philip II of France defeated the joint forces of King John of England, Emperor Otto IV, and the count of Flanders, establishing the power of the French monarchy.

Bovet, Daniele (bōvā'), 1907-, Italian pharmacologist, b. Switzerland, D.Sc. Univ. of Geneva, 1929. From 1929 to 1947 he was a researcher and then head of the laboratory of therapeutic chemistry at the Institut Pasteur in Paris. From 1947 he was associated with the Instituto Superiore de Sanità in Rome. He won the 1957 Nobel Prize in Physiology and Medicine for work in developing antihistamines, sulfa drugs, and curare derivatives and other muscle relaxants for use in surgery. He also became known for studies of the effects of mental illness on the chemistry of the brain. His writings include numerous works on microbiology, toxicology, and endocrinology.

Bow (bō), river, 315 mi (507 km) long, rising in the Rocky Mts., S Alta., Canada, and flowing SE through Banff National Park. It emerges from the mountains in the Bow River Pass and continues past Calgary southeastward across the plains to its junction with the Belly River to form the South Saskatchewan River. On the Bow is the Bassano or Horseshoe Bend Dam (built 1912).

bow (bō), implement used in playing stringed instruments. Its name originated from the fact that in its early form it resembled an archer's bow, but by the

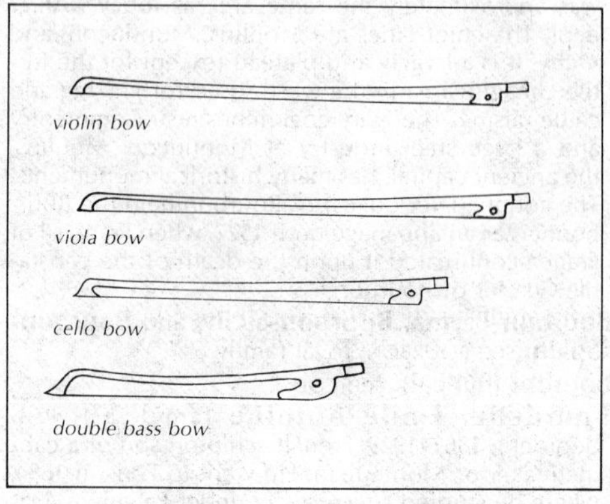

Bows

17th cent. the European bow had gradually become flat. The violin bow received its definitive form during the period from 1775 to 1781 at the hands of François Tourte (1747-1835). He made the bow of Pernambuco wood, gave it a slightly concave curvature, and invented the device by which the horsehairs are held in place and tightened. The violoncello and the double bass are played with a bow that is shorter and heavier than the violin bow.

bow and arrow, weapon consisting of two parts; the bow is made of a strip of flexible material, such as wood, with a cord linking the two ends of the strip to form a tension from which is propelled the arrow; the arrow is a straight shaft with a sharp point on one end and usually with feathers attached to the other end. The use of the bow and arrow for hunting and for war dates back to the Paleolithic period in Africa, Asia, and Europe. It was widely used in ancient Egypt, Mesopotamia, Persia, the Americas, and Europe until the introduction of gunpowder. Arrowheads were first made of burnt wood, then of flint and bone, later of bronze, and ultimately of steel. Greek and Roman armies employed heavy infantry rather than light infantry armed with bows and arrows, but the Romans made extensive use of mounted archers. With the rise of the armored knight in the Middle Ages, infantry was armed with bows and arrows. Archery continued to develop in the 14th cent. with the rise of the foot soldier. The crossbow, although known in Roman times, was not widely used until the Middle Ages. It consisted of a bow set on a stock, and was more powerful than the ordinary bow; it could fire arrows, darts, or stones. It was, however, slower than the longbow and more difficult to wield; even the arbalest, a later crossbow, was clumsy and slow. By the end of the 13th cent. use of the crossbow had declined, and at the battle of Crécy (1346) English longbowmen, firing from fixed positions, so thoroughly outclassed Genoese crossbowmen fighting for the French that the longbow replaced the crossbow as the dominant European projectile weapon. The longbow had originated in Wales, probably in the 12th cent., and became prominent in the Welsh Wars of Edward I in the late 13th cent. Also significant in the history of the bow and arrow is the Asiatic bow. It was made shorter and lighter for use on horseback, and though not so strong as the longbow it was more maneuverable and could be more rapidly fired. The Chinese also developed a longbow, which proved much less effective than the English variety. The rapid rate of fire attained by archers kept the bow and arrow in use in warfare long after gunpowder was introduced, for primitive firearms required much time to load. The North American Indians and the English were particularly noted as archers. See ARCHERY. See S. T. Pope, *Bows and Arrows* (2d ed. 1930, repr. 1962); D. F. Featherstone, *The Bowmen of England* (1967).

Bow Bells (bō), in the church of St. Mary-le-Bow (Bow Church), Cheapside, London, England. The church is located in mid-London, and tradition says that only one who is born within sound of the Bow Bells is a true Londoner, or Cockney. According to legend the Bow Bells called Dick Whittington (see WHITTINGTON, RICHARD) back to London. The fine steeple, which is over 222 ft (68 m) high, was constructed by Christopher Wren when he rebuilt the church after the great fire of 1666; the crypt of the original Norman church, with the arches (bows) for which the church is named, still stands.

Bowditch, Nathaniel, 1773-1838, American navigator and mathematician, b. Salem, Mass. He had no formal schooling after the age of 10. In 1795 he went to sea, and on five long voyages he carried out his studies in navigation and as a result corrected some 8,000 errors in Moore's *Practical Navigator,* first published in America in 1799. A new edition appeared under Bowditch's name as *The American Practical Navigator* (1802-19); it has been published by the U.S. Hydrographic Office since 1867. Bowditch made a translation (4 vol., 1829-39) of Laplace's *Mécanique céleste.* See biographies by his son N. I. Bowditch (3d ed. 1884) and Paul Rink (1969).

Bowdler, Thomas (boud'lər, bōd'-), 1754-1825, English editor. He is best known for his *Family Shakespeare* (10 vol., 1818), an expurgated edition for family reading that, although attacked for its prudery, was reprinted many times. Bowdler also edited (omitting passages of an irreligious or immoral tendency) selections from the Old Testament (1822) and Gibbon's *History of the Decline and Fall of the Roman Empire* (6 vol., 1826). His editorial activities gave rise to the term *bowdlerize,* which means to expurgate a book by deleting sections considered indelicate.

Bowdoin, James (bō'dən), 1726-90, American political leader, b. Boston. He was elected to the Massachusetts General Court in 1753 and served until 1774. Illness prevented him (1774) from taking his place as a delegate to the Continental Congress. Bowdoin was (1775-77) a leading figure in the council that governed Massachusetts during the Revolution, presided over the state constitutional convention in 1779, and served (1785-87) as governor of the state. A conservative, as governor he played an active role in suppressing SHAYS'S REBELLION and also forwarded the movement toward a centralized national government. Bowdoin College, in Maine, was named for him.

Bowdoin College, at Brunswick, Maine; coeducational; chartered 1794, opened 1802, named for James Bowdoin. One of the nation's older colleges, its alumni include Nathaniel Hawthorne, Henry Wadsworth Longfellow, and Franklin Pierce.

bowel: see INTESTINE.

Bowell, Sir Mackenzie (bō'əl), 1823-1917, Canadian prime minister, b. England. A leader of the Protestant and English interests in Canada, he served as a Conservative in the Canadian House of Commons (1867-92) and in the Senate (1892-1906). After the Conservative party took office in 1878, he held a number of cabinet posts. For two years (1894-96) he was prime minister, but in 1896 his cabinet was split by the resignation of half of the ministers, and he himself was obliged to resign. He was then chosen opposition leader in the Senate but did not play an active role in politics. He was knighted in 1895.

Bowen, Elizabeth (bō'ĭn), 1899-1973, Anglo-Irish novelist, b. Dublin. In impeccable prose she treated love and frustration through studies of complex psychological relationships. Her novels include *The Hotel* (1927), *To the North* (1932), *The House in Paris* (1936), *The Death of the Heart* (1938), and *The Heat of the Day* (1949). In her last three novels—*A World of Love* (1955), *Two Little Girls* (1964), and *Eva Trout; or, Changing Scenes* (1968)—Bowen was less concerned with rendering reality than with exploring truths best expressed in myth or parable. *Look at All Those Roses* (1941), *Ivy Gripped the Steps* (1946), and *A Day in the Dark and Other Stories* (1965) are volumes of short stories. Nonfiction works include *Bowen's Court* (1942), on her ancestral home; *The Shelbourne Hotel* (1951); and *Seven Winters; and Afterthoughts* (1962), a collection of childhood memories and literary studies. *Pictures and Conversations* (1975) is a collection of miscellaneous writings, including portions of a novel and autobiography left unfinished at Bowen's death. See study by A. E. Austin (1971).

bowerbird, common name for any of several species of birds of the family Ptilonorhynchidae, native to Australia and New Guinea, which build, for courtship display, a bower of sticks or grasses. Usually the males construct the bowers, some of which are large (up to 9 ft/275 cm high), while others are like small cabins or runways. The crestless gardener bowerbird, *Amblyornis inornatus,* makes a lawn around its bower. Colored stones, shells, feathers, flowers, and other bright objects, which are replaced when they become withered or worn, are used to decorate the lawns and the bowers. The satin bowerbird, *Ptilonorhyncus violaceus,* prefers blue decorative articles. The bower is constructed by the male in his effort to attract a female and has no other function than for the courtship performance. After mating has taken place in the bower, a nest is built by the female away from the bower, and there the clutch of two eggs is laid. The birds are crowlike and lack the showy plumage of the related bird of paradise. The bowers may be high pyramids, such as those built by the five species of maypole builder bowerbirds, or lower, more intricate, and painted with blue and green paints made of saliva and pigments, such as those built by the satin bowerbird and regent bowerbird *(Sericulus chrysocephalus).* The great gray bowerbird (genus *Chlamydera)* of Australia is the largest member of the family, being 15 in. (37.5 cm) long. Bowerbirds do not have very pleasant calls, but they are good mimics; sometimes other species' songs are included in their repertoires. Bowerbirds are classified in the phylum CHORDATA, subphylum Vertebrata, class Aves, order Passeriformes, family Ptilonorhynchidae.

Bowers, Claude Gernade (zhərnäd' bou'ərz), 1878-1958, American journalist, historian, and diplomat, b. Hamilton co., Ind. After serving as editor of the Fort Wayne *Journal Gazette* (1917-23), Bowers, as editorial writer on the New York *World* (1923-31) and political columnist on the New York *Journal* (1931-33), was an influential spokesman for the Democratic party. Ambassador to Spain (1933-39), Bowers remained in Madrid throughout the Spanish civil war. He then served (1939-53) as ambassador to Chile. Though much of his historical writing is vigorous, well written, and deservedly popular, it is frankly partisan, further praising or reappraising favorably the characters and accomplishments of Democratic leaders in the past, e.g., *The Party Battles of the Jackson Period* (1922, repr. 1965), *Jefferson and Hamilton* (1925), *The Tragic Era* (1929), *Jefferson in Power* (1936), and *The Young Jefferson, 1743-1789* (1945, repr. 1969). See his autobiographical *My Mission to Spain* (1954) and *Chile through Embassy Windows* (1958) and his memoirs, *My Life* (1962).

Bowers, Eilley, c.1827-1903, American frontier figure, b. Eilley Orrum in Scotland. She became a Mormon and moved (1855) to Nevada with her second husband. He returned (1857) to Salt Lake City, but she remained, earning her living by running a boarding house for miners. Her claim in the Comstock Lode was next to that of Lemuel Sanford Bowers, whom she later married. They were among the first to derive great wealth from the lode, and they erected a great mansion near Virginia City, Nev. Their mine soon gave out, and she died in poverty. See biography by Swift Paine (1929).

Bowery, the (bou'ərē, -'rē) [Dutch *Bouwerie*= farm], section of lower Manhattan, New York City. The Bowery, the street that gives the area its name, was once a road to the farm of New Amsterdam Governor Peter Stuyvesant, who is buried at St. Mark's-in-the-Bouwerie, an Episcopal church. The mail route (est. 1673) to Boston traveled this road. By the 1860s and 70s it had many fine theaters. Later the section became notorious for its saloons, dance halls, swindlers, petty criminals, and derelicts. In the 1960s a portion of the area was rehabilitated and several middle-income housing projects were built.

bowfin, primitive freshwater fish found in the Mississippi basin, the Great Lakes, and E to Vermont. The bowfin has a light covering of rounded, overlapping scales, a large mouth, and sharp teeth. Its swim bladder is capable of functioning as a lung, and the bowfin can survive out of water for a day. It prefers sluggish water and surfaces occasionally to gulp air. The female, up to 2 ft (60 cm) long, lays eggs. The smaller male builds the nest and guards the young after they hatch. Bowfins are also called freshwater dogfish; they are voracious and destructive feeders on fish and invertebrates and are sometimes cannibalistic. As game fish they are good fighters, but they are not regarded as food fish in most parts of the United States. Bowfins are classified in the phylum CHORDATA, subphylum Vertebrata, class Osteichthyes, order Amiiformes, family Amiidae.

bowhead whale: see RIGHT WHALE.

Bowie, James (bo͞o'ē, bō'ē), c.1796-1836, hero of the Texas Revolution, b. Logan co., Ky. Before arriving in Texas in 1828, he and his brother, Rezin Bowie, were noted frontiersmen in the backwoods of Catahoula parish, La. In Texas, James became a leader of the American settlers who opposed the Mexican government and joined in the Nacogdoches disturbances of 1832. When the revolution began in 1835, he was appointed colonel; he died at the ALAMO. Legend attributes the bowie knife to his invention, but there are many different accounts of its origin. See C. L. Douglas, *James Bowie* (1944); R. W. Thorp, *Bowie Knife* (1948).

Bowie (bo͞o'ē), city (1970 pop. 35,028), Prince Georges co., W central Md.; inc. 1916. It is mainly a residential community. Points of interest include the Woodward Mansion (c.1743), which now serves as the city hall, and Belair Stables, now a historical museum. Bowie State College is in the city, and a racetrack is nearby.

bowlegs (genu varum), outward curvature of the leg bone (tibia) or thighbone (femur) causing the knees to separate when the feet are placed together. When the condition is severe enough to be considered a deformity, the cause is usually a disorder that occurs early in life such as RICKETS, flat feet, a congenital disease, or an injury. Bowlegs can be corrected mechanically by braces, shoe wedges, or other orthopedic devices. In some cases the bone is straightened surgically.

Bowles, Chester Bliss (bōlz), 1901-, U.S. public official, b. Springfield, Mass.; grandson of Samuel Bowles (1851-1915). At first a journalist and an advertising man, Bowles was later (1942-43) head of the Connecticut Office of Price Administration (OPA) and then national OPA director (1943-46). He then served as director of the Office of Economic Stabilization. In 1948 he was elected governor of

Connecticut as a Democrat. Defeated for reelection in 1950, he was appointed (1951) ambassador to India, where he served until 1953. From 1959-61 he sat in the U.S. House of Representatives. Chosen chairman of the Democratic platform committee for the 1960 national elections, he led the fight for a strong civil rights plank and for a vigorous policy of foreign economic and technical aid. In 1961, he was Under Secretary of State. Again appointed (1963) ambassador to India, he served until 1969. Among his writings are *The Coming Political Breakthrough* (1959), *The Conscience of a Liberal* (1962), and *Promises to Keep: My Years in Public Life, 1941-1969* (1971).

Bowles, Paul, 1910-, American writer and composer, b. New York City. He studied in Paris with Virgil Thompson and Aaron Copeland and has composed many operas, ballets, and orchestral and chamber pieces. Since 1952 he has lived in Tangier, Morocco. His fiction often traces the psychic disintegration of civilized men when faced with a primitive environment. His works include the short-story collections *The Delicate Prey* (1950) and *The Time of Friendship* (1967); and the novels *The Sheltering Sky* (1949) and *Up Above the World* (1966). See his autobiography (1972). His wife was **Jane Auer Bowles,** 1917-73, American writer, b. New York City. Original and idiosyncratic, her works often treat the conflict between the weak and the strong. They include *Two Serious Ladies* (1943), a novel; and *In the Summer House* (1954), a play. See her *Collected Works* (1964).

Bowles, Samuel, 1797-1851, American newspaper editor, b. Hartford, Conn. He founded (1824) the Springfield (Mass.) *Republican,* a weekly. In 1844 it became a daily under the influence of his son, **Samuel Bowles,** 1826-78, b. Springfield, Mass., who had joined the *Republican* at 17. At 25, when his father died, he took control. His vigor, discipline, practical policies, and general editorial competence, together with the aid of an exceptional but small staff, made the Springfield *Republican* one of the half-dozen most influential newspapers in the United States. Bowles, by urging the union of all antislavery groups into a single national party, opened the way for the establishment of the Republican party in New England and became one of its most ardent members. He gave complete support to Lincoln and in the Reconstruction period opposed the legislation of the radicals and the carpetbaggers, in favor of milder measures. His condemnation of the political and financial corruption of the period resembled that of the MUCKRAKERS, and he was once sued by James Fisk for libel. In later life he traveled a great deal and sent letters about his travels back to his paper. Those of his Western trip of 1865 were collected in *Across the Continent* (1865), and those of his sojourn in Colorado, 1868, in *The Switzerland of America* (1869). See G. S. Merriam, *Life and Times of Samuel Bowles* (1885). His son, **Samuel Bowles,** 1851-1915, b. Springfield, Mass., was the third of the family to edit the *Republican.* He maintained its high quality by close editorial direction, but did little writing himself.

Bowles, William Lisle, 1762-1850, English poet, cleric, and literary critic. In 1804 he became vicar of Bremhill, Wiltshire, in 1818 chaplain to the prince regent, and in 1828 canon residentiary of Salisbury Cathedral. He won the admiration of Coleridge with the melancholy, rather emotional verse included in *Fourteen Sonnets* (1789). Bowles's other poetry includes *The Battle of the Nile* (1799), *The Sorrows of Switzerland* (1801), and *The Spirit of Discovery* (1804). In 1806 Bowles published an edition of Pope that was highly critical of the poet and his work; this led to an acrimonious controversy in which Bowles was vigorously assailed by Byron.

bowling, indoor sport, also called tenpins, played on an alley by rolling a ball at 10 maple pins. It is the most popular indoor participation sport in the United States, with over 20 million active players. A regulation bowling alley is constructed of polished wood and measures 41 to 42 in. (104.1 to 106.7 cm) wide and 60 ft (18.3 m) from the foul line to the center of the head pin (63 ft or 19.2 m to the end of the alley). A ball with three or four finger holes, weighing from 10 to 16 lb (4.5 to 7.26 kg) is thrown by a bowler at the pins, each of which is 15 in. (38.1 cm) high, set up in a triangular array in rows of increasing length (one through four) at the opposite end of the alley. A bowling contest is divided into 10 frames, with two throws allowed a bowler in each frame, if necessary. Each pin knocked down counts one point. Toppling all pins with the first ball is a strike and scores 10 points plus the total of the next two throws. Clearing the alley with two balls is a spare and scores 10 points plus the next throw. A perfect game, 300 points, requires 12 consecutive strikes. Bowling originated in ancient Germany, but the Dutch introduced the game in America, where it became popular in the 19th cent. Bowling, which was played with varying numbers of pins (e.g., in ninepins) throughout the ages, was standardized as a 10-pin game in the mid-19th cent. The popularity of bowling has been spurred by the invention of automatic pin-setting machines and the televising of contests. The American Bowling Congress (founded 1895) and the Women's International Bowling Congress (founded 1916) hold yearly championships. The Fédération Internationale des Quilleurs serves as the world governing body for the bowling committees of some 40 nations, including the United States and Canada. The games of duck pins, candle pins, and barrel pins are similar to bowling but are played with much smaller balls and pins. See J. L. Martin, *Bowling* (2d ed. 1971).

Bowling Green. 1 City (1970 pop. 36,253), seat of Warren co., S Ky., on the Barren River; inc. 1812. It is a shipping and marketing center for an area producing tobacco, corn, livestock, and dairy items. Textiles, apparel, automobile parts, woodwork, and heavy equipment are manufactured in the city. Bowling Green was occupied by the Confederates at the beginning of the Civil War until the Federal advance forced them to retreat in 1862. The city is the seat of Western Kentucky Univ. Nearby is Lost River Cave, said to have been a hideaway for the James brothers and for Gen. John Hunt Morgan. To the southwest lie the ruins of a Shaker settlement established in 1800. **2** City (1970 pop. 21,760), seat of Wood co., NW Ohio, in a farm area; inc. 1855. Tomato products, hydraulic hoists, and plastics are the chief manufactures. Bowling Green State Univ. is there.

Bowling Green State University, at Bowling Green, Ohio; coeducational; chartered 1910 as a normal school, opened 1914. It became a college in 1929, a university in 1935. The school maintains two-year centers in Bryan, Fostoria, and Fremont as well as a branch near Sandusky.

bowls, ancient sport (the bocce of Caesar's Rome is still played by Italians), especially popular in Great Britain and Australia, known as lawn bowls or bowling on the green in the United States. It was played in America before the American Revolution (hence Bowling Green in numerous place names), but later declined in popularity. Christian Schepflin revived the game in 1879 by forming the Dunellen (N.J.) Bowling Club. The usual "bowling green" is about 120 ft (36.58 m) square and is divided into six alleys, or rinks, each of which is 20 ft (6.1 m) wide and 120 ft long. A small white ball, called a jack, is thrown on the alley by one of the players at some spot not less than 25 yd (22.86 m) from the bowling mat. The object of the game is to roll a ball—weighing 3.5 lb (1.6 kg) and made biased so as to swerve while rolling—as close to the jack as possible, and, if necessary, to dislodge balls previously thrown by opponents. The American Lawn Bowls Association (founded 1915) standardizes rules in the United States; it is one of 10 national groups affiliated with the International Bowling Board (founded 1905). The sport called CURLING, played on ice, is related to bowls.

Bowman, Isaiah, 1878-1950, American geographer, b. Waterloo, Ont., B.S. Harvard, 1905, Ph.D. Yale, 1909. He taught geography at Yale (1905-15) and then became director (1915-35) of the American Geographical Society. He led the first Yale South American expedition (1907), served as geographer-geologist on the Yale Peruvian expedition (1911), and led the American Geographical Society Expedition to the Central Andes (1913). He was chief territorial adviser to President Wilson at the Versailles conference and served the Dept. of State as territorial adviser in World War II. He was a member of the executive committee of the National Research Council from 1919 to 1929 and was its chairman from 1933 to 1935. He was president of Johns Hopkins Univ. from 1935 until his retirement in 1948. His work on many commissions and boards includes contributions as an active officer of the Explorers Club, the Association of American Geographers, and the Council of Foreign Relations and as president (1931-34) of the International Geographical Union, and as vice president (1940-45) of the National Academy of Sciences. He was considered one of the greatest modern authorities on political geography. His books include *The Andes of Southern Peru* (1916) and *Desert Trails of Atacama* (1924); a standard work, *Forest Physiography* (1911); *The Pioneer Fringe* (1931), first of a series on world frontier areas; *The New World: Problems in Political Geography* (1922); and *Design for Scholarship* (1936).

Bowne, Borden Parker (boun), 1847-1910, American philosopher, b. Monmouth co., N.J. In 1876 he became head of the department of philosophy at Boston Univ. and later served as dean of the graduate school. In his philosophy, which he called personalism, he stressed the reality and freedom of the self and insisted on the central importance of personality. His masterpiece, *Metaphysics,* appeared in 1882. Other works include *Principles of Ethics* (1892), *The Immanence of God* (1905), *Personalism* (1908), and *The Essence of Religion* (1910). See J. R. Shive, *The Meaning of Individuality: A Comparative Study of Alfred North Whitehead, Borden Parker Bowne, and Edgar Sheffield Brightman* (1961); F. K. Lazarus, *Rāmānuja and Bowne* (1962).

Bowra, C. M. (Sir Cecil Maurice Bowra), 1898-1971, English classical scholar, b. China. Associated with Oxford Univ. throughout his adult life, he was warden of Wadham College (1922-71) and also served as professor of poetry (1946-51) and vice chancellor (1951-54). He was knighted in 1951. Although he wrote and edited books in many areas of literature, Bowra is particularly known for his studies of ancient Greek poetry and culture, notably *Tradition and Design in the Iliad* (1930), *Greek Lyric Poetry* (1936), *The Greek Experience* (1957), *Pindar* (1964), and *Homer* (1972). He also edited *The Oxford Book of Greek Verse in Translation* (1937).

Bowring, Sir John (bou'rĭng), 1792-1872, British diplomat, linguist, and writer. An extraordinarily versatile linguist, he is remembered for his anthologies and translations of poetry from many European and Oriental languages. He was a friend of Jeremy BENTHAM, whose works he later collected and edited, and became (1824) the first editor of Bentham's *Westminster Review.* He was a member of Parliament (1835-37, 1841-49) and went on numerous financial and commercial missions to Europe and the Middle and Far East. He served as consul at Canton and in 1854 was knighted and sent as governor to Hong Kong. There he precipitated a war with China by ordering (1856) the bombardment of Canton in a dispute over the right of the Chinese to remove a Chinese pirate from a Chinese ship when that ship was registered by the British (although, in this case, the registration had expired). His *Kingdom and People of Siam* (1857) was the result of a diplomatic mission in that country. See his *Autobiographical Recollections* (1877); G. L. Nesbitt, *Benthamite Reviewing* (1934).

Bow ware (bō), English porcelain, similar to CHELSEA WARE. It was made at Stratford-le-Bow from 1730 to 1776, when its factory was absorbed by the DERBY WARE pottery.

bowwood: see MULBERRY.

box, common name for the Buxaceae, a family of trees and shrubs with leathery evergreen leaves, native to the tropics and subtropics of the Old World and to Central America. The boxes (genus *Buxus*) have been widely introduced to other regions for use as hedge plants and for their wood. Boxwood is close-grained, strong and hard, and polishes well; it is valued for wood engraving, carving, and turning, and for making musical instruments. *Pachysandra procumbens,* a native American species of an otherwise Asiatic genus, is a low, creeping herb found in the S Appalachians and cultivated elsewhere as a ground cover. The box family is classified in the division MAGNOLIOPHYTA, class Magnoliopsida, order Euphorbiales.

box elder: see MAPLE.

boxer, breed of medium-sized, muscular WORKING DOG perfected in Germany in the 19th cent. but whose origins may be traced back in Europe to the 16th cent. It stands from 21 to 25 in. (53.3-63.5 cm) high at the shoulder and weighs from 60 to 75 lb (27.2-34 kg). It has a short, smooth, shiny coat of fawn or brindle, often with white markings on the head, chest, and feet, and a black muzzle. The ears are cropped to stand erect, and the tail is docked. A relative of numerous breeds of the bulldog type, the boxer was originally used in dogfighting and bull-baiting. Today it is trained as a police dog and as a guide dog for the blind. The boxer is also kept as a pet. See DOG.

Boxer Uprising, 1898-1900, antiforeign movement in China, culminating in a desperate uprising against Westerners and Western influence. By the end of the 19th cent. the Western powers and Japan had established wide interests in China. The Opium War (1839-42), which Great Britain had provoked, forced China to grant commercial concessions (see

TREATY PORT) and to recognize the principle of EXTRATERRITORIALITY. The concessions to Great Britain were soon followed by similar ones to France, Germany, and Russia. The CH'ING regime, already weakened by European encroachments, was more enfeebled by Japan's success in the First Sino-Japanese War (1894-95) and the subsequent further partitioning of China into foreign spheres of influence. The Ch'ing emperor, KUANG HSU, attempted to meet the imperialist threat by adopting modern educational and administrative reforms, but he stirred conservative opposition and was frustrated (1898) by the dowager empress, TZ'U HSI, who, favoring a last effort to expel foreign influence, supported armed resistance. She tacitly encouraged an antiforeign secret society called I Ho Ch'uan [Chinese,=righteous, harmonious fists] or, in English, the Boxers. The Boxers soon grew powerful, and late in 1899 the movement began to assume menacing proportions. Violent attacks on foreigners and on Chinese Christians occurred, particularly in the provinces of Chihli, Shansi, and Shantung; in Manchuria; and in Inner Mongolia. In those regions, railway building, a visible symbol of the foreigner, was most active; and Chinese Christians, especially Roman Catholics, adherents to the foreigners' religion, were most numerous. Also located there were the majority of territorial leaseholds acquired by the European powers. In June, 1900, the Boxers (some 140,000 strong and now led by the war party at court), occupied Peking and for eight weeks besieged the foreigners and the Chinese Christians there. Provincial governors in SE China suppressed the court's declaration of war and assured the powers of protection for foreign interests, thus limiting the area of conflict to N China. The siege was lifted in August by an international force of British, French, Russian, American, German, and Japanese troops, which had fought its way through from Tientsin. The Boxer Uprising thus ended. The Western powers and Japan agreed—mainly because of U.S. pressure to "preserve Chinese territorial and administrative entity" and because of mutual jealousies among the powers—not to carry further the partition of China. Nevertheless China was compelled (1901) to pay an indemnity of $333 million, to amend commercial treaties to the advantage of the foreign nations, and to permit the stationing of foreign troops in Peking. The United States later (1908) used some of its share of the indemnity for scholarships for Chinese students. China emerged from the Boxer Uprising with a greatly increased debt and was, in effect, a subject nation. See A. H. Smith, *China in Convulsion* (1901); G. N. Steiger, *China and the Occident* (1927); C. C. Tan, *The Boxer Catastrophe* (1955); Peter Fleming, *The Siege at Peking* (1959); V. W. W. S. Purcell, *The Boxer Uprising* (1963); Richard O'Connor, *The Spirit Soldiers* (1973).

boxfish: see TRUNKFISH.

boxing, sport of fighting with fists, also called pugilism and prizefighting. Mentioned by Homer and included in the ancient Olympian games, boxing is one of the oldest forms of competition known to man. It was popular with the Romans, who bound the fists with a knotted, and often metal-weighted, leather band, or cestus. The sport died out after the fall of Rome. It was revived in England in the early 18th cent., helped by royal patronage in the form of betting on or offering prizes to the contestants, as well as by the ring prowess of James Figg, the first British champion (1719-30), and the first set of rules, drawn up by Jack Broughton (1743). Its popularity soon spread to other countries. The use of bare fists declined after the marquess of QUEENSBERRY introduced (1865) his celebrated code of boxing rules, which became standard by 1889. The code called for boxing gloves, a limited number of 3-min rounds, the forbidding of gouging and wrestling, a count of 10 sec before a floored man is called the loser, and various other features of modern boxing. In the United States boxing was illegal for many years. New York was the first state to legalize it (1896), and others soon followed suit. Today, professional boxing is regulated in each state by athletic or boxing commissions, most of which are members of the World Boxing Association (WBA), founded in 1921. However, several states do not accept WBA rulings, and on occasion more than one champion reigns. Professional boxers, wearing gloves weighing at least 5 oz (141.75 grams) each, fight in a roped-off area, or ring, about 20 ft (6.1 m) square. Competitors are divided into classes according to maximum weight—flyweight (112 lb/50.81 kg), bantamweight (118 lb/53.53 kg), featherweight (126 lb/57.15 kg), lightweight (135 lb/61.24 kg), welterweight (147 lb/66.68 kg), middleweight (160 lb/72.58 kg), light heavyweight (175 lb/79.38 kg), and heavyweight (over 175 lb). John L. Sullivan was the bareknuckle champion from 1882 to 1892. After the Queensberry rules were generally accepted, the recognized world's heavyweight champions were: James J. Corbett (1892-97), Robert L. Fitzsimmons (1897-99), James J. Jefferies (1899-1905) [disputed 1905-10], Jack Johnson (1910-15), Jess Willard (1915-19), William H. (Jack) Dempsey (1919-26), Gene Tunney (1926-28) [disputed 1928-30], Max Schmeling (1930-32), Jack Sharkey (1932-33), Primo Carnera (1933-34), Max Baer (1934-35), James J. Braddock (1935-37), Joe Louis (Joseph Louis Barrow; 1937-49), Ezzard Charles (1949-51), Jersey Joe Walcott (Arnold Cream; 1951-52), Rocky Marciano (Rocco Marchegiano; 1952-56), Floyd Patterson (1956-59; 1960-62), Ingemar Johansson (1959-60), Charles (Sonny) Liston (1962-64), Muhammad Ali (Cassius Clay; 1964-67; 1974-) [disputed 1967-70 after Muhammad Ali's title was declared forfeit as a result of his refusal to enter the army], Joe Frazier (1970-73), George Foreman (1973-74). Other famous boxers include Henry Armstrong, Tony Canzoneri, Georges Carpentier, George Dixon, Johnny Dundee, Joe Gans, Harry Greb, Stanley Ketchel, Benny Leonard, Tommy Loughran, Kid McCoy, Jimmy McLarnin, Terry McGovern, Archie Moore, Battling Nelson, "Philadelphia" Jack O'Brien, "Sugar" Ray Robinson, Barney Ross, Mickey Walker, and Jimmy Wilde. Boxing reached its peak of popularity in the 1920s and 30s. Since World War II boxing has declined in popularity; rising admission prices and the influence of television have been the main factors in the decline. Most major championship fights are now telecast only on closed-circuit networks in theaters. Other injurious influences have been scandals, ring injuries and deaths, and monopolistic practices by promoters. The largest purse in boxing history was the $10 million split by George Foreman and Muhammad Ali in their 1974 bout in Zaïre, in which Ali regained the championship. Largely drawn by Ali, one of boxing's most colorful and controversial figures, many millions of people throughout the world watched his victory on either satellite or cable television. Amateur boxing in the United States is regulated by the Amateur Athletic Union. The National Collegiate Athletic Association championships and the Golden Gloves competition are other important amateur bouts. Boxing became part of the modern Olympic games in 1904. Olympic weight divisions correspond closely to those used in professional boxing. See Pierce Egan, *Boxiana* (1812, repr. 1971); N. S. Fleischer, *50 Years at Ringside* (1940, repr. 1969); John Durant, *The Heavyweight Champions* (4th ed., rev. and enl. 1971); Art Fischer et al., *Garden of Innocents* (1972); Rex Lardner, *The Legendary Champions* (1972).

box turtle, hard-shelled land TURTLE of the genus *Terrapene,* native to North America. Its lower shell, or plastron, has a hinge dividing it into front and rear sections; the animal can raise these sections to meet the upper shell, or CARAPACE, forming a secure box around its body. It is primarily a vegetarian, although it also eats insects, earthworms, and slugs. The box turtle hibernates during cold winters and mates in the spring. In summer the female buries from two to seven eggs, which hatch out in the early fall. The young often remain in the nest until the following spring. The Eastern box turtle, *Terrapene carolina,* is a woodland species found in the eastern and central United States. The Western species, *T. ornata,* is found in the grasslands of the central United States and northern Mexico. There are also several rare Mexican species. Box turtles are classified in the phylum CHORDATA, subphylum Vertebrata, class Reptilia, order Chelonia, family Emydidae.

Boyacá (bōyäkä'), town (1968 est. pop. 7,700), N central Colombia, near Tunja. At Boyacá on Aug. 7, 1819, revolutionary forces under Simón BOLÍVAR won the decisive engagement that assured the independence of present-day Colombia and Venezuela from Spain.

boyars (bōyärz'), upper nobility in Russia from the 10th through the 17th cent. The boyars originally obtained influence and government posts through their military support of the Kievan princes. Their power and prestige, however, soon came to depend almost completely on landownership. The boyars occupied the highest state offices and through a council advised the prince. When political power shifted to Moscow in the 14th and 15th cent., the boyars retained their influence. However, as the Moscow grand princes consolidated their power, the influence of the boyars was gradually eroded, particularly under Ivan III and Ivan IV. Their ancient right to leave the service of one prince for another was curtailed, as was their right to hold land without giving obligatory service to the czar. The political turmoil of the so-called time of troubles further weakened the boyars, and in the 17th cent. the rank and title of boyar was abolished by Peter I.

Boyce, William, c.1710-1779, English composer. After studying in London, he became a composer (1736) and later an organist (1758) of the Chapel Royal and Master of the King's Music in 1755. Although overshadowed by Handel, he was the foremost English-born composer of his day. He wrote symphonies, stage works, and much vocal music. His most important work is *Cathedral Music* (3 vol., 1760-78), a compilation of church music by many English composers.

boycott, concerted economic or social ostracism of an individual, group, or nation to express disapproval or coerce change. The practice was named (1880) after Capt. Charles Cunningham Boycott, an English land agent in Ireland whose ruthlessness in evicting tenants led his employees to refuse all cooperation with him and his family. In the United States the boycott is used chiefly in labor disputes; consumers' and businessmen's groups also resort to the method. Boycotts may be either primary or secondary. A typical example of a primary boycott is the refusal of aggrieved employees and their supporters to purchase the goods or services of an employer. A secondary boycott occurs when the aggrieved party attempts either to boycott a third party or to coerce it into joining an ongoing boycott. Thus, workers instituting a boycott may refuse to patronize firms that continue to deal with the initially boycotted party. Similarly, a secondary boycott would occur if workers struck an employer in order to force him to join the boycott of another firm. In the United States, such secondary actions are prohibited by both the Taft-Hartley Act (1947) and the Landrum-Griffin Act (1959), although little has been done to enforce the ban. During the late 1960s and early 70s the United Farm Workers union employed a series of boycotts in an attempt to gain recognition as the sole bargaining agent for grape and lettuce fieldworkers. The boycott has been used as a weapon in political and racial issues. Outstanding examples are the refusal of American colonials to buy British goods after the passage of the Stamp Act (1765), the Chinese boycott of U.S. goods (1905) because of the poor treatment of Chinese in America, the refusal of Gandhi's followers to buy British-made goods in India, and the Arab League boycott (1948) of all companies dealing with the state of Israel. The legal status of the boycott differs with various governments. See H. W. Laidler, *Boycotts and the Labor Struggle* (1914, repr. 1968).

Boyd, Alan Stephenson, 1922-, U.S. Secretary of Transportation (1967-69), b. Macclenny, Fla. A lawyer in Florida, he served as general counsel to the Florida Turnpike Authority (1955) and as a member (1955-59) and chairman (1957-58) of the Florida Railroad and Public Utilities Commission. He was named to membership on the Civil Aeronautics Board by President Eisenhower in 1959, becoming its chairman in 1961. In 1965, President Lyndon B. Johnson appointed him Undersecretary of Commerce for transportation, and in 1967 he became head of the newly created Dept. of Transportation.

Boyd, Belle, 1844-1900, Confederate spy in the Civil War, b. Martinsburg, Va. (now W.Va.). Operating (probably unofficially) in Martinsburg and Front Royal, she provided Gen. T. J. (Stonewall) Jackson with valuable information on Union activities in the Shenandoah Valley in 1862. In 1864, after being twice imprisoned and released, she went to England, supposedly with secret dispatches from Jefferson Davis to Confederate agents there. The first of her three husbands, a Union officer who had been her captor, followed her to England to marry her. After his death she began a career on the English stage (1866) and on her subsequent return to the United States toured widely, especially in the Middle West, giving dramatic talks about herself and sundry episodes of the Civil War. She wrote *Belle Boyd in Camp and Prison* (1865). See biography by L. A. Sigaud (1945).

Boyd, Ernest, 1887-1946, American critic and author, b. Dubin, Ireland. In the British consular service, he resigned in 1920 and settled in New York City, where he became an important literary figure. He contributed editorials to periodicals, wrote criticism on European literature, and translated modern French and German authors. His works include

Contemporary Drama of Ireland (1917), *Portraits, Real and Imaginary* (1924), *H. L. Mencken* (1925), *Guy de Maupassant* (1926), and *Literary Blasphemies* (1927). He was editor and translator of the complete works of Guy de Maupassant.

Boyd, Louise Arner, 1887–1972, American arctic explorer, b. San Rafael, Calif. She led a series of scientific explorations on the east coast of Greenland. The expedition of 1933, sponsored by the American Geographical Society, was described in her *The Fiord Region of East Greenland* (1935); on those of 1937 and 1938 a submarine ridge between Bear Island and Jan Mayen was made known; that of 1941 was undertaken for the National Bureau of Standards. In World War II she was (1942–43) a technical expert in the War Dept. In 1955, Boyd flew over the North Pole, the first woman to do so successfully; she photographed the area around the North Pole and the Arctic Sea. She wrote *The Coast of Northeast Greenland* (1948).

Boydell, John (boi'dəl), 1719–1804, English engraver and print publisher, originator and builder of the Boydell Shakespeare Gallery. He studied engraving in London and early began to amass his fortune with the publication of his engravings of views of England and Wales. It is as the publisher of works by other engravers, however, that he is better known. In 1786 he began the publication, by subscription, of prints illustrating Shakespeare's works. The leading English artists were commissioned and a gallery was built by Boydell to house the works. Because of financial reverses, the collection was sold by lottery in 1804.

Boyd Orr, John Boyd Orr, 1st **Baron,** 1880–1971, British nutritionist and agricultural scientist, b. Scotland, grad. Univ. of Glasgow. He served as professor of agriculture at the Univ. of Aberdeen (1942–45), as government consultant on nutrition and health, and as director general (1946–47) of the United Nations Food and Agriculture Organization. He made notable contributions to the science of nutrition and to the solution of world food problems, and he worked toward the establishment of a world government. Knighted in 1935, he was created baron in 1949. He was awarded the 1949 Nobel Peace Prize for advocating a world food policy based on human needs rather than trade interests. His writings include *The National Food Supply and Its Influence on Public Health* (1934), *Food and the People* (1943), *Food—The Foundation of World Unity* (1948), and *The White Man's Dilemma* (1953).

Boye, Karin (kä'rĕn bô'yĕ), 1900–1941, Swedish novelist, poet, and short-story writer. Boye's volumes of poetry, including *Moln* [clouds] (1922) and *Glömda land* [forgotten land] (1924), reveal an austere and ardent idealism as well as a seriousness and social awareness equal to that of her prose fiction. Her early novels, e.g., *Astarte* (1931) and *Kris* [crisis] (1934), are stylized and expressionist in style. *Kallocain* (1941), her last novel, is a fierce protest against totalitarianism. Boye died an apparent suicide at 40.

Boyen, Hermann von (boi'ən), 1771–1848, Prussian field marshal. After the Prussian defeat by Emperor NAPOLEON I and the disastrous treaties of Tilsit in 1807 (see TILSIT, TREATIES OF), he assisted SCHARNHORST in the reorganization of the Prussian army. As chief of staff to F. W. von BÜLOW, he fought (1813–14) against the French in the War of Liberation, and as minister of war (1814–19) he completed the reforms that were initiated earlier. His measures, including the introduction of general conscription and the development of a national guard, formed the basis of Prussian military strength. He was again minister of war from 1841 to 1847.

Boyer, Jean Pierre (zhäN pyĕr bwäyā'), 1776–1850, president of Haiti (1818–43). A free mulatto, he fought under TOUSSAINT L'OUVERTURE and then joined André RIGAUD, also a mulatto, in the latter's abortive insurrection against Toussaint. He returned in 1802 with the French army of Charles LECLERC but later joined the patriots under Alexandre PÉTION, who chose him as his successor. He united N and S Haiti after the suicide of Henri CHRISTOPHE (1820), and in 1822, taking advantage of the weakness of Spanish Santo Domingo, he took control of the whole island. Compulsory labor was instituted. In 1825 a French fleet forced Boyer to pay an exorbitant indemnity in return for French losses; France then recognized Haitian independence. Financial embarrassment, combined with the labor policy and the devastation of an earthquake in 1843, brought about Boyer's overthrow and permanent exile.

Boyesen, Hjalmar Hjorth (hyäl'mär hyôrt boi'ĕsĕn), 1848–95, American writer, b. Norway, educated at the universities of Leipzig and Christiania (Ph.D., 1868). He came to the United States in 1869 and became editor of *Fremad,* a Norwegian weekly published in Chicago. Later he was a professor at Cornell and Columbia universities; his scholarly works include *Goethe and Schiller* (1879) and *Essays on Scandinavian Literature* (1895). Boyesen is best remembered for his fiction, including *Gunnar* (1874), a romance of Norwegian life; and realistic urban novels, such as *The Mammon of Unrighteousness* (1891) and *The Social Strugglers* (1893). See biography by C. A. Glasrud (1963).

Boyle, Charles, 4th **earl of Orrery:** see ORRERY, CHARLES BOYLE, 4TH EARL OF.

Boyle, Kay, 1903–, American writer, b. St. Paul, Minn. She lived in Europe for 30 years and has taught English at San Francisco State College since 1963. Her novels and stories often illuminate a desperate moment when courageous action is demanded although tragedy will probably result. Among her works are the novel *Plagued by Nightingales* (1931); a short-story collection, *Nothing Ever Breaks Except the Heart* (1966); and an essay collection, *The Long Walk at San Francisco State and Other Essays* (1970).

Boyle, Richard, 1st **earl of Cork,** 1566–1643, English settler in Ireland. He first went to Ireland in 1588 and in 1602 purchased for a small sum Sir Walter Raleigh's large landholdings in Cork, Waterford, and Tipperary. His energy and success in improving the lands, building mills, establishing ironworks and other industries, founding towns, and creating trade were remarkable and won him rapid advancement. Created earl of Cork in 1620, he was appointed (1629) one of the lord justices of Ireland and in 1631 became lord high treasurer of the kingdom. In this position he came into conflict with Thomas Wentworth (later 1st earl of STRAFFORD), who arrived in Ireland as lord deputy in 1633. In their long struggle Strafford at first was successful in depriving Boyle of a large part of his privileges and income, but Boyle's patient marshaling of the forces of opposition to Strafford's Irish program was an important factor in the latter's downfall. He remained loyal to the crown, however, and helped put down the sudden Irish rebellion of 1641. Two of his seven sons became well known—Roger Boyle, 1st earl of Orrery, and Robert Boyle, the scientist. See Dorothea Townshend, *The Life and Letters of the Great Earl of Cork* (1904).

Boyle, Robert, 1627–91, Anglo-Irish physicist and chemist. The seventh son of the 1st earl of Cork, he was educated at Eton and on the Continent and conducted most of his researches at his own laboratories at Oxford (1654–68) and London (1668–91). He invented a vacuum pump and used it in the discovery (1662) of what is now known as Boyle's law (see GAS LAWS). Boyle is often referred to as the father of modern chemistry; he separated chemistry from alchemy and gave the first precise definitions of a chemical element, a chemical reaction, and chemical analysis. He also made studies of the calcination of metals, combustion, acids and bases, the nature of colors, and the propagation of sound. Although he was especially noted for his experimental work, Boyle also contributed to physical theory, supporting an early form of the atomic theory of matter, which he called the corpuscular philosophy, and using it to explain many of his experimental results. His extensive writings established him as the leading scientist of his time and contributed greatly to the dominance of the mechanistic theory following Newton's work. Boyle was one of the group at Oxford that later became the Royal Society, but he refused the presidency of the society in 1680, as well as many other honors. See his works, ed. by Thomas Birch (6 vol., 1772; repr. 1965–66); biography by R. E. W. Maddison (1969); study by Marie Boas Hall (1958, repr. 1968).

Boyle, Roger, Baron Broghill and 1st **earl of Orrery:** see ORRERY, ROGER BOYLE, 1ST EARL OF.

Boyle's law: see GAS LAWS.

Boylston, Zabdiel, 1679–1766, American physician, b. Brookline, Mass. He was privately educated in medicine and settled in Boston. In an epidemic of smallpox in 1721 he was persuaded by Cotton Mather to inoculate, thus introducing the practice to the United States. Beginning with his son and two slaves, he inoculated over 240 persons, all but six of whom survived. Public sentiment, however, was against the experiment, and the lives of both Boylston and Mather were threatened. In 1724, Boylston visited England, and his *Historical Account of the Small-Pox Inoculated in New England* was published there in 1726.

Boyne, river, c.70 mi (110 km) long, rising in the Bog of Allen, Co. Kildare, E Republic of Ireland, and flowing NE through Co. Meath, past Trim, to the Irish Sea near Drogheda. Salmon is caught in the river. In the battle of the Boyne (July, 1690) near Drogheda, the armies of King William III defeated the Catholic James II, who fled to France. The victory is commemorated annually by Irish Protestants.

Boynton Beach, city (1970 pop. 18,115), Palm Beach co., SE Fla., on the Atlantic coast; inc. 1920. It is a beach resort.

Boyron, Michel: see BARON, MICHEL.

Boys' Clubs of America, federation of more than 900 clubs organized (1906) in Boston as the Federated Boys' Clubs. Its purpose is to fight delinquency by providing leisure-time activities.

Boy Scouts, organization of boys over 12 years old, founded (1908) in Great Britain by Sir Robert BADEN-POWELL. It was incorporated in 1910 in the United States, where its appearance was connected with earlier organizations—the Sons of Daniel Boone, organized by Daniel Carter BEARD, and the Woodcraft Indians, organized by Ernest Thompson SETON. In the United States, James E. West was chief scout from 1911 to 1943. From those beginnings the movement spread throughout most of the world, with the organization and program basically the same in every country. It is intended to be nonmilitary and without racial, religious, political, or class distinctions. The community-level unit is the troop, which is subdivided into patrols of about 10 boys each. An adult scoutmaster administers the troop's program. Scouts are divided into classes—tenderfoot and second-class and first-class scouts. The program of activities aims at a threefold development, mental, moral, and physical; it stresses outdoor knowledge and skills and embraces training in citizenship, nature lore, wood and camp craft, manual arts, lifesaving, and sports. Boy Scouts have performed useful service in many civic projects, sharing in nationwide safety-first and city-improvement campaigns, acting as assistant traffic patrols, and aiding in the prevention of forest fires. The first of several international gatherings of Boy Scouts, called jamborees, was held in London in 1920. See Edwin Nicholson, *Education and the Boy Scout Movement in America* (1941, repr. 1973). Two related organizations, the Cub Scouts and the Explorer Scouts, offer similar programs to 8- to 10-year-olds and older teenagers, respectively. See GIRL SCOUTS.

boysenberry: see BRAMBLE.

Boys Town, village, Douglas co., E Nebr.; inc. 1936. The noted community was founded in 1917 by Father Edward J. Flanagan (1886–1948) for homeless or abandoned boys. The village is governed by the boys themselves and maintained by voluntary contributions.

Bozcaada (bōzjä"ä'dä) or **Tenedos** (tĕn'ədŏs), island (1970 pop. 2,030), 15 sq mi (39 sq km), NW Turkey, in the Aegean Sea. The strategically located island was a station of the Greek fleet during the Trojan War. Xerxes used it (5th cent. B.C.) as a base for the Persian fleet. The Ottoman Turks captured it in 1657.

Bozeman, John M. (bōz'mən), 1835–67, American pioneer. A Georgian, he went to the gold fields of Colorado (1861) and Montana (1862). In the winter of 1862–63 he traveled with a companion from Bannack, Mont., to Colorado by a route lying E of the Bighorn Mts. through lands reserved by treaty to the Indians. Since the only other approaches to Montana from the east were the long, circuitous Missouri River or a trail leading N from the Overland Trail in Idaho (which necessitated a double crossing of the Continental Divide), he was enthusiastic about his short cut, which became known as the **Bozeman Trail.** Several parties, including one guided by Bozeman himself, used the trail in 1864, and in 1865–66 the Federal government built forts Reno, Phil Kearney, and C. F. Smith to guard it. However, after the Fetterman Massacre, Dec., 1866, (see under FETTERMAN, WILLIAM JUDD), the trail S and E of Fort C. F. Smith was abandoned. In April, 1867, Bozeman was killed by Indians. Bozeman Pass, where the trail crossed the Belt Mts., and Bozeman, Mont., were named for him. See study by D. M Johnson (1971).

Bozeman, city (1970 pop. 18,670), seat of Gallatin co., SW Mont.; inc. 1883. The city is named after John M. Bozeman, a pioneer who led the first settlers there in 1864. Bozeman is the center of a farming and stock-raising area. Tourism is an important source of revenue; the city is the headquarters of Gallatin National Forest, and Yellowstone National Park is nearby. Montana State Univ. is in Bozeman.

Bozeman Trail: see under BOZEMAN, JOHN M.

Bozen: see BOLZANO, Italy.

Bozez (bŏ'zĕz) and **Seneh** (sē'nē), two cliffs, at the entrance to the ravine of Michmash (now the Wadi Suweinet). 1 Sam. 14.4,5.

Bozkath (bŏz'kăth), unidentified place, SW Palestine. Joshua 15.39. Boscath: 2 Kings 22.1.

Bozrah (bŏz'rə). **1** Important city of Edom, probably the modern Busayra (Jordan), SE of the Dead Sea. The prophets often linked the name Bozrah with that of Edom. Gen. 36.33; 1 Chron. 1.44; Isa. 34.6; Jer. 49.13,22; Amos 1.12; Micah 2.12. **2** City of Moab, perhaps identical with Bezer. Jer. 48.24.

Bozzaris, Marco or **Markos** (bōzăr'ĭs, -ză'rĭs, Gr. bôt'sărēs), c.1788–1823, Greek patriot. Exiled from his native Epirus in 1803, he joined ALI PASHA in 1820 and later was prominent in the Greek War of Independence, notably in the defense of Mesolóngion (1822–23) and at Karpenísion, where he defeated the Turks with a handful of men but died in battle.

Br, chemical symbol of the element BROMINE.

Brabant (Fr. brăbäN', Flemish brăbänt'), province (1970 pop. 2,176,373), 1,268 sq mi (3,284 sq km), central Belgium. BRUSSELS (the capital) and LOUVAIN are the chief cities. The densely populated province is drained by the Dijle, Senne, and Demer rivers. Much of its soil is fertile and is under cultivation, and there is much industry. Except in Brussels, the population is mostly Flemish-speaking. The province occupies the southern part of the former duchy of Brabant.

Brabant, duchy of, former duchy, now divided between Belgium (Brabant and Antwerp provs.) and the Netherlands (NORTH BRABANT prov.). Louvain, Brussels, and Antwerp were its chief cities. The duchy of Brabant emerged (1190) from the duchy of Lower Lorraine. In 1430 it passed to Philip the Good of Burgundy, and in 1477 it was taken by the Hapsburgs. (For the history of Brabant from 1477 to 1794 see NETHERLANDS, AUSTRIAN AND SPANISH.) Like the rest of the S Low Countries, Brabant owed its extraordinary prosperity during the Middle Ages to its wool and other textile industries and to the commercial enterprise of the inhabitants of its cities and towns. ANTWERP, its greatest city, was for a time the financial capital of Europe. The dukes of Brabant, who relied on the towns for money to finance their wars and their luxurious life styles, granted the towns virtual self-government and an ever-increasing share in the management of the duchy. In 1356 this trend culminated in the granting of a charter of liberties known as the *Joyeuse Entrée,* so called because each subsequent duke had to swear to it when entering Louvain after acceding. According to the charter, the dukes could not declare war, conclude alliances, or coin money without the consent of delegates of the clergy, nobility, and towns, who together formed an assembly later known as the Estates of Brabant. The charter was abolished (1789) by Emperor Joseph II. In 1830, S Brabant led the revolt against Dutch rule that resulted in independence for Belgium. Since 1840 the eldest son of the king of the Belgians has held the title duke of Brabant.

Brač (brăch), Ital. *Brazza,* island (1971 pop. 12,831), 152 sq mi (394 sq km), off the Dalmatian coast in the Adriatic Sea, W Yugoslavia. It is a popular summer resort and tourist spot. Supetar (Ital. *San Pietro*), a small port, is the island's chief town.

Bracara Augusta: see BRAGA, Portugal.

Brace, Charles Loring, 1826–90, American social reformer, b. Litchfield, Conn. He founded (1853) the Children's Aid Society of New York, a pioneer organization that established modern methods in child welfare. Among his books are *Short Sermons to Newsboys* (1866) and *Gesta Christi* (1882). See biography by Emma Brace (1894); Gordon Trasler, *In Place of Parents* (1960).

brace: see DRILL.

Bracegirdle, Anne, 1663?–1748, English actress. A pupil of Betterton, she was the delight of Colley Cibber and the favorite of Congreve, achieving her greatest successes as the heroines of Congreve's comedies, which were written for her. Eclipsed by Anne Oldfield, she retired in 1707, but in 1710 made a reappearance as Angelica in *Love for Love* together with Betterton and Mrs. Barry.

Brachiopoda (brākēŏp'ədə), phylum of shelled sessile or sedentary marine animals, commonly known as lamp shells, and characterized by a peculiar feeding organ, the lophophore. The shell consists of two parts, called valves, that completely enclose the body; the external appearance of the animal is much like that of a bivalve mollusk, or pelecypod, such as a clam. However, the valves of a lamp shell cover the top and bottom of the animal, while those of a clam cover the right and left sides. Furthermore,

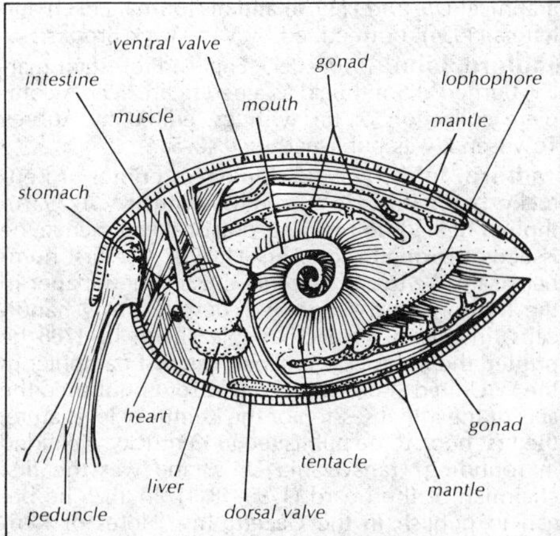

Internal anatomy of a lamp shell, Magellania, *representative of the phylum Brachiopoda*

the internal anatomy of brachiopods does not resemble that of pelecypods; the two groups are not related. There are two classes in the phylum: the Inarticulata, members of which have the valves held together by muscles alone, and the Articulata, members of which have interlocking processes that form a hinge. A complex set of muscles opens the shell for feeding and closes it for protection. In most brachiopods a short stalk called a pedicel, or peduncle, emerges between the valves or through an opening in the lower valve. Most sessile brachiopods attach to objects by means of the pedicel, but a few lack pedicels and attach directly by the ventral valve. Burrowing lamp shells have long pedicels, which they contract to retreat into the burrow. The lophophore consists of two tentacle-bearing arms, often spirally coiled, one on either side of the mouth. The tentacles have cilia that create currents, drawing water-bearing food particles and oxygen into the shell. Food particles are trapped in mucus on the tentacles and moved by the cilia to the mouth. Oxygen is absorbed through the body wall. Brachiopods have a simple digestive and nervous system, and are equipped with excretory organs called nephridia. The open circulatory system includes a contractile vessel, or heart, and sinuses for the flow of the colorless circulatory fluid to various parts of the body. Reproduction is sexual and the sexes are usually separate. In most species the eggs and sperm are shed into the sea, where fertilization results in the development of free-living, ciliated larvae. The larvae settle to the bottom after developing rudiments of the adult structures. A few species brood their young. Brachiopods are believed to be related to the shell-less bryozoans, or moss animals (phylum ECTOPROCTA), which also have a lophophore. Abundant at the start of the Cambrian period, brachiopods were widespread and numerous in ancient seas. About 30,000 extinct species are known, and members of the largest species were almost 1 ft (30 cm) in diameter. Fewer than 300 species are extant today, and these are relatively small, usually 1 to 2 in. (2.5–5 cm) across. All are marine and most prefer shallow water; they are sporadically distributed, although some are very abundant locally. Among the better known lamp shells are the burrowing *Lingula* (class Inarticulata) and the stalkless, sessile *Crania* (class Articulata).

Bracken, John, 1883–1969, Canadian political leader, b. Ontario. A noted agricultural expert, he was premier of Manitoba for 20 years (1922–42). In 1942 he was chosen to lead Canada's Conservative party, which he renamed Progressive Conservative. Elected in 1945 to the Canadian House of Commons, he served as leader of the opposition until 1948, when he resigned.

bracken or **brake,** common name for a tall fern (*Pteridium aquilinum*) with large triangular fronds, widespread throughout the world, often as a weed. It is considered poisonous to livestock when eaten in quantity, but the rootstocks and the young shoots, cooked, have been used for food. Bracken is also a source of tannin and is used for thatching and as bedding for livestock. A beverage is made from the roots. The names *bracken* and *brake* are sometimes also applied to other large, coarse ferns and, as general terms, to a thicket of such plants. Bracken is classified in the division POLYPODIOPHYTA, class Polypodiopsida, order Filicales, family Polypodiaceae.

Brackenridge, Henry Marie, 1786–1871, American writer, b. Pittsburgh; son of Hugh Henry Brackenridge. Admitted to the Pennsylvania bar in 1806, he moved to St. Louis, where he was a lawyer and journalist. Among his writings are *Views of Louisiana* (1814), part of which was one of the sources of Washington Irving's *Astoria,* and a pamphlet *South America* (1817), which puts forth a policy similar to the Monroe Doctrine. Sent to South America to study political conditions, he recounted his experiences in *Voyage to South America* (1819). His *Recollections of Persons and Places in the West* (1834) is a valuable historical source. See biography by W. F. Keller (1956).

Brackenridge, Hugh Henry, 1748–1816, American author and jurist, b. Scotland, grad. Princeton, 1771. He studied theology and served in the American Revolution as chaplain, but later turned to law. His early writings include two patriotic plays and some verse. In 1781 he moved to Pittsburgh, where he founded (1786) the Pittsburgh *Gazette,* the city's first newspaper, and helped to establish the Pittsburgh Academy (now the Univ. of Pittsburgh). A leading Pennsylvania supporter of the Federal Constitution, Brackenridge later acted (1794) as a peacemaker in the Whiskey Rebellion. He was also a justice of the Pennsylvania supreme court from 1799 to his death. He is, however, best known as an author. His satirical and picaresque novel, *Modern Chivalry* (6 vol., 1792–1805; rev. ed., 4 vol., 1804–7), written in a vigorous style, pictures backwoods life in America. In it, the moderate democrat Brackenridge ridicules the excesses of a raw democracy. He also wrote an account of the Whiskey Rebellion and several political tracts. See C. M. Newlin, *Life and Writings of Hugh Henry Brackenridge* (1932, repr. 1971); biography by Daniel Marder (1967).

bracket fungi: see FUNGI.

brackets: see PUNCTUATION.

Brackley, Thomas Egerton, Viscount: see ELLESMERE, THOMAS EGERTON, BARON.

Bracknell, new town and civil parish (1971 pop. 37,279), Easthampstead rural district, Berkshire, S England. Bracknell was designated one of the NEW TOWNS in 1949 to alleviate overpopulation in London. Its current population target is 60,000. In 1949, Bracknell was a market town of some 5,000 persons, with timber yards and a brickmaking industry. Its new industries include the manufacture of boilers, gasoline pumps, tools, clothing, and sealing compounds. There is a college of further education.

Bracquemond, Félix (fālĕks' bräkmôN'), 1833–1914, French engraver, painter, and decorator of ceramics. He is best known for his many etchings, both original and reproductions of famous paintings. Bracquemond was a chief founder of the influential Society of Painter-Engravers, established in France in 1889.

Bracton, Henry de, d. 1268, English writer on law. He was the author of *De legibus et consuetudinibus Angliae* [on the laws and customs of England], a broad, philosophic treatise that is often called the most important work on English law before that of Sir William BLACKSTONE. Sir Edward COKE and others used the work in their legal arguments against the king in the English civil war. See edition of *De legibus* by G. E. Woodbine (4 vol., 1915–42); edition of Bracton's notebook by F. W. Maitland (3 vol., 1887).

Bradbury, Ray, 1920–, American writer, b. Waukegan, Ill. A popular writer of SCIENCE FICTION, Bradbury skillfully combines social and technological criticism with delightful fantasy. His best-known works include the short-story collections *The Martian Chronicles* (1950) and *Dandelion Wine* (1957); the novels *Fahrenheit 451* (1953), *Something Wicked This Way Comes* (1962), and *The Halloween Tree* (1972); and a volume of poetry, *When Elephants Last in the Dooryard Bloomed* (1972).

Bradbury, William Batchelder, 1816–68, American hymn composer and music editor, b. York, Maine; pupil of Lowell Mason. He organized the Juvenile Music Festivals in New York, and later, after studying in Germany, he started music conventions in New Jersey. He compiled over 50 collections of Sunday-school songs, and his own tunes, such as those for *He Leadeth Me,* for *Just as I Am, without One Plea,* and for *Savior, like a Shepherd Lead Us,* are still popular.

Braddock, Edward, 1695–1755, British general in the French and Indian Wars. Although he had seen little active campaigning before 1754, Braddock was reputed to have a good knowledge of European military tactics and was noted as a stern disciplinarian. He was promoted to major general in 1754 and early in 1755 arrived in Virginia as commander in chief of the British forces in North America against the French. His immediate objective was the French stronghold at the forks of the Ohio (see FORT DUQUESNE). With some 700 colonial militiamen, whom he regarded disdainfully, and over 1,400 British regulars, he moved across the Alleghenies from Fort Cumberland (now Cumberland, Md.), building a road (the foundation of the National Road) as he went. The march was so slow, however, that he feared the French would reinforce Duquesne before he could reach there. Adopting the suggestion of one of his aides-de-camp, George Washington, he left the wagons behind him with one of the two British regiments and pushed ahead with about two thirds of his total force. While crossing the Monongahela River, Braddock was met (July 9, 1775) by a force of not more than 900 men (a few French, some Canadians, and many Indians) under Daniel Beaujeu, who had already learned of the advance. The British regulars, as unfamiliar with Indian-style fighting as their commander (although both had been given fair warning by the colonials), bolted from their column formation under the steady fire from a ubiquitous enemy safely concealed in ravines and behind trees. The affair turned into a bloody rout. Since the Indians paused to collect scalps and other trophies of war, the demoralized troops were able to rejoin the rear guard and both retreated safely to Fort Cumberland. Of the 1,459 actively engaged, 977 were killed or wounded, including 63 of the 89 officers, who—unlike the soldiers—fought bravely. Braddock himself had four horses shot from under him before he was mortally wounded. He died four days later at Great Meadows and was buried there, near the site of Uniontown, Pa. See D. S. Freeman, *George Washington*, Vol. II (1948); biography by Lee McCardell (1958).

Braddock, borough (1970 pop. 8,795), Allegheny co., W Pa., an industrial suburb of Pittsburgh, on the Monongahela River; settled 1742, inc. 1867. It is a steel-manufacturing center. On that site, in 1755, Gen. Edward Braddock was defeated by the French and the Indians.

Bradenton (brā'dəntən), city (1970 pop. 21,040), seat of Manatee co., SW Fla., on Tampa Bay at the mouths of the Braden and the Manatee rivers; inc. 1903. A popular winter resort with excellent fishing in the rivers, bay, and Gulf, it is also a shipping center for the citrus fruit and truck crops of the area. Travertine is quarried and refined there. Hernando DeSoto is believed to have landed near that site in 1539; the DeSoto National Memorial is to the west (see NATIONAL PARKS AND MONUMENTS, table). The area was settled (1850s) by Joseph Braden, whose castlelike home is a local landmark. An annual event (March) is the reenactment of the DeSoto landing.

Bradford, Andrew, 1686-1742, colonial printer of Pennsylvania, b. Philadelphia; son of William BRADFORD (1663-1752). Andrew learned the trade in his father's shop in New York City and in 1712 went to Philadelphia, where he established his own press and became a bookseller. In 1719 he began publication of the *American Weekly Mercury,* the first newspaper in Pennsylvania and the third in the colonies. He was imprisoned for publishing political criticism but defended his own case for freedom of the press, establishing a precedent for the defense of John Peter ZENGER. In 1741 he began publication of the short-lived (three issues) *American Magazine,* the first colonial magazine.

Bradford, Augustus Williamson, 1806-81, Civil War governor of Maryland (1862-66), b. Bel Air, Md. As a delegate to the 1861 peace conference in Washington, he strongly pleaded for the Union and became the Union party candidate for governor of Maryland. Elected by a large majority, partially as a result of intimidation at the polls by Union soldiers, Bradford served from 1862 to 1866, assuring Federal control of the state. In 1862 and 1863 he appealed for volunteers in a state-equipped local militia that helped turn back Confederate invasions of state territory. Denying that the Federal government had the power to free the slaves in Maryland, he called a state convention in 1864 that framed a new constitution abolishing slavery. See W. B. Hesseltine, *Lincoln and the War Governors* (1948).

Bradford, Gamaliel, 1863-1932, American biographer, b. Boston. After many unsuccessful years as a writer, he achieved literary fame as a biographer with his *Lee, the American* (1912). He perfected the method of writing "psychographs," or short portraits of historical figures. His works in this area include *Confederate Portraits* (1914), *Union Portraits* (1916), and *Damaged Souls* (1923). See his autobiographical *Life and I* (1928) and his journal (1933) and letters (1934), both edited by Van Wyck Brooks.

Bradford, John, 1510?-1555, English Protestant martyr, burned at Smithfield as a heretic in 1555. A complete collection of his writings, edited by Aubrey Townsend, was published in 1848-53.

Bradford, John, 1749-1830, pioneer printer of Kentucky, b. Virginia. He moved to Kentucky c.1779. Although he had no previous practical experience, he issued at Lexington on Aug. 11, 1787, the first number of the *Kentucky Gazette,* the first newspaper in the territory, and succeeded, despite many handicaps, in making it a creditable sheet. In 1788 he printed the *Kentucke Almanac,* the first pamphlet in the W United States. In 1792, Bradford published the acts of the initial session of the Kentucky legislature, the first book to be published in Kentucky. He aided in founding Transylvania Univ. and was the first chairman of the board (1799-1811). In 1826 he began to publish in the *Gazette* his "Notes of Kentucky," a valuable historical source, which continued until 1829.

Bradford, William, 1590-1657, governor of Plymouth Colony, b. Austerfield, Yorkshire, England. As a young man he joined the separatist congregation at Scrooby and in 1609 emigrated with others to Holland, where, at Leiden, he acquired a wide acquaintance with theological literature. Bradford came to New England on the *Mayflower* in 1620 and in 1621, on the death of John CARVER, was chosen leader of the Pilgrims. He remained governor for most of his life, being reelected 30 times; during the five years in which he chose not to serve, he was elected assistant. Bradford, though firm, used his large powers with discretion, and there were few complaints about his leadership. He maintained friendly relations with the Indians and struggled hard to establish fishing, trade, and agriculture. He stressed the obligations of the colonists to their London backers and was one of the eight colonial "undertakers" who in 1627 assumed Plymouth Colony's debt to the merchants adventurers. Given a monopoly of fishing and trading privileges, they finally discharged the debt in 1648. Bradford was more tolerant of other religious beliefs than were the Puritan leaders of Boston (although he was by no means consistent in this respect), and he was largely responsible for keeping Plymouth independent of the Massachusetts Bay colony. His famous *History of Plimoth Plantation,* not published in full until 1856, forms the basis for all accounts of the Plymouth Colony. The editions of W. T. Davis (1908), W. C. Ford (1912), and Samuel Eliot Morison (1952) are the best. See also G. F. Willison, *Saints and Strangers* (1945); biography by Bradford Smith (1951).

Bradford, William, 1663-1752, British pioneer printer in the American colonies. Born in Leicestershire, England, he served an apprenticeship under a London printer before emigrating in 1685 to Philadelphia, where he set up the first press. He added a bookstore in 1688 and was in 1690 one of the founders of the first paper mill in the colonies. He was arrested for printing a pamphlet critical of the Quaker government; his trial, at which no verdict was reached, was probably the first in the United States involving freedom of the press. Bradford moved (c.1693) to New York City where he became royal printer and issued some 400 items in the next 50 years, including the first American Book of Common Prayer (1710), some of the earliest of American almanacs and many pamphlets and political writings. In 1725 he began publication of the royalist New York *Gazette,* the first New York newspaper. Many of his descendants, including Andrew BRADFORD and William BRADFORD, became printers.

Bradford, William, 1722-91, American Revolutionary printer and patriot; grandson of William Bradford (1663-1752). He learned printing from his uncle, Andrew Bradford, in Philadelphia, and in 1742 he set up his own shop. He established the successful anti-British *Weekly Advertiser,* which competed for many years with Benjamin Franklin's newspaper, the *Pennsylvania Gazette.* He also printed a number of books and published (1757-58) the *American Magazine and Monthly Chronicle.* In 1754 he established the London Coffee House in Philadelphia; this became the seat of the merchants' exchange. Bradford opposed the Stamp Act and took an active part in opposition to British measures, becoming a leader of the Sons of Liberty. He advocated and became official printer to the First Continental Congress. Sacrificing his business, he became a major in the Continental Army and took part in the campaign in New Jersey. At Princeton he was badly wounded and his health shattered. His son, Thomas Bradford (1745-1838), carried on the business and published the *Merchants' Daily Advertiser.* See J. W. Wallace, *An Old Philadelphian* (1884).

Bradford, county borough (1971 pop. 293,756), West Riding of Yorkshire, N central England, on a small tributary of the Aire River. It is a center of the worsted industry, which dates from the Middle Ages. There is an important wool exchange. Besides woolens, other fabrics (including synthetics) are made. Electroplating, electrical engineering, and the manufacture of machinery and automobiles are also important industries. There are stone quarries nearby. Bradford's landmarks include the memorial hall, dedicated to Edmund Cartwright, inventor of the power loom; St. Peter's Church (1458), now the cathedral of the diocese of Bradford; and the Conditioning House, a unique textile-testing establishment. The Univ. of Bradford, Bradford Technical College, Bradford Regional College of Art, and Margaret McMillan Memorial College of Education are in the borough. In 1974, Bradford became part of the new metropolitan county of West Yorkshire.

Bradford, city (1970 pop. 12,672), McKean co., NW Pa., in the Alleghenies, near the N.Y. line; settled c.1823, inc. as a city 1879. The growth of the city was initiated by the discovery of oil (c.1871), and oil refining is still a major industry. Other products include electronic components, steel couplings, cutlery, chemicals, and explosives. A two-year branch of the Univ. of Pittsburgh is in the city. Nearby are Allegheny National Forest (with its dam and reservoir) and Allegany State Park (N.Y.); the area is popular for hunting and fishing.

Bradlaugh, Charles (brăd'lô), 1833-91, British social reformer, a secularist. Editor of the free-thinking weekly *National Reformer* from 1860 and later associated with Annie BESANT, he was an early advocate of woman's suffrage, birth control, free speech, national education, trade unionism, and other controversial causes. In 1880, Bradlaugh was elected to Parliament after several unsuccessful attempts. Rather than take a Bible oath to be sworn in as a member of Parliament, Bradlaugh, an atheist, demanded the right to take an affirmation. This action provoked a great deal of controversy, and it was not until 1886 that the matter was settled in his favor. His numerous works include *Land for the People* (1877), *The True Story of My Parliamentary Struggle* (1882), and *Speeches* (1890). See H. Bradlaugh Bonner, *Charles Bradlaugh* (7th ed. 1908); J. P. Gilmour, ed., *Champion of Liberty* (1933); Walter L. Arnstein, *The Bradlaugh Case* (1965); David Tribe, *President Charles Bradlaugh, M. P.* (1971).

Bradley, Andrew Cecil, 1851-1935, English scholar and critic, b. Cheltenham; brother of Francis Herbert Bradley. He taught at Oxford for many years and was professor of poetry there (1901-6). Bradley is noted for his *Shakespearean Tragedy* (1904), a classic work of criticism noted for its exposition of Hamlet, Othello, and Macbeth as psychological beings and of Shakespeare as a consummate interpreter of the human soul. Bradley's other works include *Oxford Lectures on Poetry* (1909) and *Ideals of Religion* (1940).

Bradley, Francis Herbert, 1846-1924, English philosopher. He was educated at Oxford, where he became a fellow of Merton College in 1876. His works include *Ethical Studies* (1876), *Principles of Logic* (1883), and *Appearance and Reality* (1893). In logic Bradley attacked the psychological tendencies of empiricism by differentiating sharply between the mental act as a psychological event and its universal meaning; to him only the latter was the concern of logic. In metaphysics Bradley held that absolute idealism, in which the world of appearance is characterized by contradiction, is opposed to the absolute, in which all contradiction, including the gulf between subject and object, is transcended. Although greatly influenced by Hegel, Bradley's metaphysics is generally considered a highly original contribution to philosophical thought. See his collection of essays (2 vol., 1935); studies by Richard Wollheim (1959), A. K. Ganguly (1964), and G. L. Vander Veer (1970).

Bradley, James, 1693-1762, English astronomer, educated at Oxford. His discovery of the aberration of light, announced in 1729, placed him among the foremost contemporary astronomers. His second important discovery, the nutation, or "nodding," of the earth's axis, was not made known until 1748, when it had stood the test of careful observations over a period of nearly 19 years. In 1742, Bradley became astronomer royal. Under his direction the observatory at Greenwich was supplied with new instruments.

Bradley, Omar Nelson, 1893–, U.S. general, b. Clark, Mo. A graduate of West Point, he served in World War I and filled various army administrative and academic posts before assuming (1943) command of the 2d Corps in World War II. Bradley was active (1943) in the N African and Sicilian campaigns and led (1944) the U.S. 1st Army in the invasion of Normandy. Later he commanded the U.S. 12th Army Group in the battle for Germany. Bradley acted (1945–47) as administrator of veterans' affairs, was appointed (1948) chief of staff of the U.S. army, and served (1949–53) as first permanent chairman of the joint chiefs of staff. Promoted to general of the army in 1950, he retired in 1953 to become a business executive. See his *Soldier's Story* (1951) and *Collected Writings* (4 vol., 1967).

Bradshaw, George, 1801–53, English map engraver and the originator of railway guides. *Bradshaw's Railway Time-Tables,* first published in 1839, became *Bradshaw's Monthly Railway Guide* (first issued 1841). He afterwards published *The Continental Railway Guide* and others.

Bradshaw, Henry, 1831–86, English librarian and antiquarian at Cambridge Univ. He discovered, organized, and made known the university's treasures of manuscripts and incunabula, especially those in Gaelic—the Book of Deer and old Celtic glossaries—and the early Waldensian records in the Piedmont MSS. He was dean of King's College from 1857 to 1865.

Bradshaw, John, 1602–59, English regicide judge. In 1649 he was made president of the parliamentary commission to try Charles I, other lawyers of greater prominence having refused the position. His conduct of the trial was arbitrary; he even refused the king the right to speak in his own defense. For a short time he was rewarded with honors and offices and acted (1649–53) as president of the council of state. He was forced to retire when Oliver Cromwell dissolved the council, and he became an opponent of the Protectorate.

Bradstreet, Anne (Dudley), c.1612–1672, early American poet, b. Northampton, England, considered the first significant woman author in the American colonies. She came to Massachusetts in the Winthrop Puritan group in 1630 with her father, Thomas Dudley, and her husband, Simon Bradstreet, both later governors of the state. A dutiful Puritan wife who raised a large family, she nevertheless found time to write poetry. In 1650 her first volume of verse appeared in London as *The Tenth Muse Lately Sprung Up in America.* It was followed by *Several Poems* (Boston, 1678), which contains "Contemplations," probably her best work. Her verses are often derivative and formal, but some are graced by realistic simplicity and genuine feeling. See her works ed. by J. Hensley (1967); biography by E. W. White (1971).

Bradstreet, John, c.1711–1774, British officer in the French and Indian Wars. A Nova Scotian, he was captured (1744) by the French and confined at LOUISBURG. After his exchange he described the weaknesses of the fortress, and in 1745 Sir William Pepperell captured the stronghold. For his services in the expedition, Bradstreet was promoted to the rank of captain and made lieutenant governor of St. John's, N.F., a post he held permanently. He led (1758) the successful expedition against Fort Frontenac, thereby cutting communications between the French forces in Canada and those on the Ohio River. Later he served (1759) under Lord AMHERST at Ticonderoga and Crown Point. In PONTIAC'S REBELLION, Bradstreet commanded the forces that garrisoned (1764) Detroit and other Western posts.

Bradstreet, Simon, 1603–97, colonial governor of Massachusetts, b. Lincolnshire, England. He emigrated to New England in 1630 and was assistant in the Massachusetts Bay Company for 49 years (1630–79) and for part of that time served as secretary (1630–36). In 1634, Bradstreet was sent with four others to the Plymouth, New Haven, and Connecticut colonies to negotiate concerning the formation of the New England Confederation, and on its organization became one of two Massachusetts representatives, a post he retained for 33 years. After the Restoration, John Norton and he went to England and succeeded in persuading Charles II to confirm the colony's charter. His first period as governor (1679–86) was followed by the unsuccessful royal administration of Sir Edmund ANDROS. He served as governor again, from 1689 to 1692. Anne BRADSTREET was his wife.

Bradwardine, Thomas (brăd'wərdēn), c.1295–1349, English mathematician, natural philosopher, and theologian. He was chaplain to Edward III (c.1338) and later Archbishop of Canterbury. As a mathematician he is known for his *Tractatus de proportionibus velocitatum* (1328), which goes beyond the usual scholastic approach in attempting to derive novel quantitative relations between speed and force; as a natural philosopher he defended Aristotle's concept of the plenum against atomistic views, e.g., in his *Tractatus de continuo.* His major theological work, *De causa Dei contra Pelagium,* takes a determinist position on the problem of free will.

Brady, Diamond Jim (James Buchanan Brady), 1856–1917, American financier and philanthropist, b. New York City. He was a bellboy and messenger and then worked for the New York Central RR in various capacities. He later was employed by a railroad supply company, and his selling ability rapidly brought him a fortune. He began collecting diamonds and other jewels and amassed 30 complete sets of jewelry estimated as worth well over $1 million. He was famous for his appetite and elaborate meals and was one of the best-known men in New York's Broadway night life. In 1912 he gave funds to Johns Hopkins Hospital, Baltimore (where he had received treatment) to found the James Buchanan Brady Urological Institute. See biography by Parker Morrell (1934, repr. 1970).

Brady, Mathew B., c.1823–96, American pioneer photographer, b. Warren co., N.Y. Brady learned the daguerreotype process from S. F. B. Morse and in 1844 opened his own photographic studio in New York City, which brought him widespread fame. He published *Gallery of Illustrious Americans* in 1850 and five years later experimented successfully with the wet-plate process. He began photographing President Lincoln in 1860. When the Civil War began Brady was authorized to accompany and photograph the armies; through his efforts a vast visual record of the war was preserved. In 1875 the government purchased part of Brady's collection, but the rest passed into private hands after the photographer's financial failure. In 1954 the Library of Congress acquired the enormous Handy collection of Brady's work. See Roy Meredith, *Mr. Lincoln's Camera Man* (1946, repr. 1974); J. D. Horan, *Mathew Brady, Historian with a Camera* (1955); H. D. Milhollen and D. H. Mugridge, comp., *Civil War Photographs* (1961).

Brady, Samuel, 1758–95, American frontiersman. He fought in several battles of the American Revolution but earned his name as a scout in the Ohio country under Daniel Brodhead and Anthony Wayne. His exploits were the subject of much frontier legend.

bradycardia: see ARRHYTHMIA.

Braga, Teófilo (təô'fəlo͞o brä'gä), 1843–1924, Portuguese intellectual and political leader, b. Ponta Delgada in the Azores. At the Univ. of Coimbra he was a member of the positivist circle of Quental. In 1871 he began to teach at the Univ. of Lisbon, writing voluminously on many subjects. He tried to apply the positivist principles of Comte in his general history of Portuguese Literature (10 vol., 1870–81). A republican and an anticlerical in politics, he was chosen as first president of the new republic of Portugal (1910–11) and served again briefly in 1915. His teaching had a great effect on Portuguese intellectual life, and his writing stimulated interest in Portuguese history and literature. Several collections of his poetry were published during his lifetime.

Braga, city (1970 municipal pop. 101,877), capital of Braga dist., NW Portugal, in Minho. It is an agricultural trade center with minor industry. The ancient Bracara Augusta, it had considerable importance in Roman days, but was of much more importance in the Middle Ages as the see of the bishop of Braga, who rivaled the bishop of Toledo in power. As the seat of Portugal's titular primate, the city is still a religious center. In the old cathedral is the tomb of Henry of Burgundy. Nearby is a summer resort with the well-known Church of Bom Jesus do Monte.

Bragança (brəgän'sə) or **Braganza** (-zə), town (1970 municipal pop. 33,928), capital of Bragança dist., NE Portugal, in Trás-os-Montes. It is of interest because of its castle, seat of the Braganza family, long the royal family of Portugal.

Braganza (brəgän'zä), royal house that ruled Portugal from 1640 to 1910 and Brazil from 1822 to 1889. It took its name from the castle of Braganza or Bragança. The line was descended from Alfonso, the natural son of John I of Portugal, who married the daughter of Nun'Alvares Pereira, the duke of Braganza. Although Alfonso's grandson, Ferdinand, was executed for alleged treason by John II, the family steadily increased its possessions. John, 6th duke of Braganza, married a niece of King John III, and when the Portuguese threw off Spanish rule in 1640, their grandson became king as John IV. The house of Braganza ruled Portugal until the establishment of a republic in 1910. After Brazil declared (1822) its independence, it was ruled as an empire under Pedro I, son of John VI of Portugal, and Pedro II until a revolution made it a republic in 1889.

Bragg, Braxton, 1817–76, Confederate general in the U.S. Civil War, b. Warrenton, N.C. A graduate of West Point, he fought the Seminole and in the Mexican War was promoted to lieutenant colonel for distinguished service at Buena Vista. He resigned from the army in 1856 and lived on his Louisiana plantation until the outbreak of the Civil War, when he was appointed a Confederate brigadier general and assigned to command the coast from Pensacola, Fla., to Mobile, Ala. Shortly after being promoted to major general (Jan., 1862), he assumed command of Gen. A. S. Johnston's 2d Corps, leading it in the battle of Shiloh (April). With Johnston's death, Bragg was made a general, and he succeeded (June) General Beauregard in command of the Army of Tennessee. His invasion of Kentucky (Aug.–Oct., 1862) was unsuccessful, ending in retreat to Tennessee after Gen. D. C. BUELL caught up with him at PERRYVILLE. A reorganized Union army under Gen. W. S. ROSECRANS was then sent against him and at MURFREESBORO (Dec. 31, 1862–Jan. 2, 1863) forced him to withdraw again. In the CHATTANOOGA CAMPAIGN, Bragg, victorious in the battle of Chickamauga, laid siege to the Union army in Chattanooga, but in Nov., 1863, Gen. U. S. Grant thoroughly defeated him and forced him to retire into Georgia. Gen. J. E. JOHNSTON took over his command (December) and Bragg went to Richmond, where he became military adviser to Jefferson Davis, with nominal rank as commander in chief of Confederate armies. After the war he was chief engineer of Alabama and later lived in Texas, where he died. See biography by D. C. Seitz (1924, repr. 1971); study by Grady McWhiney (Vol. I, 1969).

Bragg, Sir William Henry, 1862–1942, English physicist, educated at King William's College, Isle of Man, and Trinity College, Cambridge. He served on the faculties of the Univ. of Adelaide in Australia (1886–1908), the Univ. of Leeds (1909–15), and the Univ. of London (1915–23). From 1923 he was Fullerian professor of chemistry in the Royal Institution and director of the Davy-Faraday research laboratory. He shared with his son W. L. Bragg the 1915 Nobel Prize in Physics for their studies, using the X-ray spectrometer, of X-ray spectra and of crystal structure. He became a Fellow of the Royal Society in 1906 and served as president of the society from 1935 to 1940. In 1920 he was knighted. Among his works are *The World of Sound* (1920), *Concerning the Nature of Things* (1925), *An Introduction to Crystal Analysis* (1929), and *The Universe of Light* (1933). With W. L. Bragg he wrote *X Rays and Crystal Structure* (1915, 5th ed. 1925). See biography by Sir Kerr Grant (1952).

Bragg, Sir William Lawrence, 1890–1971, English physicist, b. Adelaide, Australia, educated in Australia and at Trinity College, Cambridge; son of W. H. Bragg. He was professor of physics at Victoria Univ., Manchester, from 1919 to 1937. From 1938 to 1953 he was professor of experimental physics at Cambridge and director of the Cavendish Laboratory. In 1954 he was made head of the Royal Institution. He shared with his father the 1915 Nobel Prize in Physics for their studies, with the X-ray spectrometer, of X-ray spectra and of crystal structure. In 1941 he was knighted. Among his works are *The Structure of Silicates* (1930, 2d enl. ed. 1932) and *Atomic Structure of Minerals* (1937). With his father he wrote *X Rays and Crystal Structure* (1915, 5th ed. 1925).

Brahe, Tycho (tī'kō brä), 1546–1601, Danish astronomer. The most prominent astronomer of the late 16th cent., he paved the way for future discoveries by improving instruments and by his precision in fixing the position of planets and stars. From Brahe's exact observations of the planets, Kepler devised his laws of planetary motions (see KEPLER'S LAWS). Brahe's achievements included the study of a supernova (first observed in 1572 and now known as Tycho's star) in the constellation Cassiopeia and the discoveries of a variation in the inclination of the lunar orbit and of the fourth inequality of the moon's motion. He never fully accepted the Copernican system but made a compromise between that and the Ptolemaic system. In the Tychonic system, the earth was the immobile body around which the sun revolved, and the five planets then known revolved around the sun. Given funds by the Danish king Frederick II, Brahe built on the island of Ven a castle, Uranienborg, and an observatory, Stjarneborg. He was deprived of his revenues by Christian IV in 1596 and left Ven (1597) and in 1599 settled near Prague under the patronage of the German emperor Rudolf II. He published (1588) *De mundi aetherii recentioribus phaenomenis*, the second volume of a projected three-volume work on his astronomical observations; from an incomplete manuscript and notes Kepler edited Volume I, *Astronomiae instauratae progymnasmata* (1602). Brahe's *Astronomiae instauratae mechanica* (1598) contained his autobiography and a description of his instruments. See biographies by J. L. Dreyer (1890, repr. 1963) and J. A. Gade (1947).

Brahm, Otto (ô'tō bräm), 1856–1912, German theatrical director, manager and critic. Inspired by the work of Antoine in Paris, he founded a theater, the Freie Bühne, in Berlin in 1889. There he devoted his efforts to eliminating from the German stage old-fashioned techniques by employing the theories and methods of the naturalists. In 1894 he became director of the larger DEUTSCHES THEATER and the acknowledged leader of the modern German theater movement.

Brahma (brä'mə), one of the three supreme gods of HINDUISM, the others being VISHNU and SHIVA. In the late Vedic period he was called Prajapati, the primeval man, whose sacrifice permitted the original act of creation. Although worshiped until Gupta times, his popularity declined, and today only a single temple near modern Ajmer is devoted to him. He is regarded as the creator and is reborn periodically in a lotus that grows from the navel of the sleeping Vishnu. His consort is Sarasvati, patroness of art, music, and letters, and the traditional inventor of the Sanskrit language. A basic unit in the Hindu chronology is the *kalpa*, or "day of Brahma," which is equal to 4,320,000,000 earthly years. The neuter form of the masculine name Brahma is Brahman.

Brahmagupta (brä"məgo͝op'tə), c.598–c.660, Hindu mathematician and astronomer. He wrote in verse the *Brahma-sphuta-siddhanta* [improved system of Brahma], a standard work on astronomy containing two chapters on mathematics that were translated into English by H. T. Colebrooke in *Algebra . . . from the Sanskrit of Brahmagupta* (1817). A shorter treatise, *The Khandakhadyaka* (tr. 1934), expounded the astronomical system of Aryabhata.

Brahman: see VEDANTA.

Brahman or **Brahmin** (both: brä'mən), member of the highest, or priestly, caste of the Hindus. The Brahmans alone may interpret the VEDAS and perform the Vedic sacrifice. The vast majority of Brahmans today are in occupations unrelated to religion, but they retain their social prestige and many caste conventions. The Brahmans of India are divided into 10 territorial subcastes, 5 in the north and 5 in the south.

Brahman cattle, breed of beef cattle developed in the S United States in the early 1900s by combining several breeds or strains of ZEBU cattle of India. Brahman cattle have a very distinctive appearance with a hump over the shoulders, loose skin under the throat, and large drooping ears; they are generally light to medium gray in color. Much of the contribution of this breed to beef production has been through crossing with European cattle, e.g., Hereford and Angus. These hybrid cattle exhibit hybrid vigor, i.e., they generally exhibit growth and reproductive rates greater than either of the parental types. Several new breeds of cattle have been developed in the United States based on Brahman-European crosses, some important ones being the Beefmaster (Brahman combined with SHORTHORN CATTLE and HEREFORD CATTLE), Brangus (Brahman combined with ANGUS CATTLE), Charbray (Brahman combined with CHAROLAIS CATTLE), and Santa Gertrudis (Brahman combined with Shorthorn). Brahman cattle have been extensively exported.

Brahmanism: see HINDUISM.

Brahmaputra (brämәpo͞o'trә) [Sanskrit,=son of Brahma], river, c.1,800 mi (2,900 km) long, rising in the Kailas range of the Himalayas, SW Tibet (China), and flowing through NE India to join with the Ganges River in central Bangladesh to form a vast delta; navigable for large craft c.800 mi (1,290 km) upstream. In Tibet, where it is called the Tsangpo, the river flows c.700 mi (1,130 km) east in a wide navigable channel and forms an important east-west transport route. In SE Tibet the river turns south and flows swiftly through deep, narrow gorges into India. In Assam state it takes the name Brahmaputra and flows c.450 mi (725 km) through the broad, fertile Assam valley. Entering Bangladesh, where it is called the Jamuna, the river continues south to the Bay of Bengal via the Ganges-Brahmaputra delta. The river's lower course is sacred to Hindus. Tea, rice, and sugarcane are the main crops of its fertile valley.

Brahmin: see BRAHMAN.

Brahmo Samaj (brä'mō səmäj') [Hindi,=society of God], Indian religious movement, founded in Calcutta in 1828 by Rammohun ROY. It promoted a monotheistic, reformed Hinduism with strong Islamic and Christian overtones, support for the rights of women, and opposition to such aspects of Hinduism as idolatry and animal sacrifice. Under Roy the organization attained considerable importance in E India until his death in 1833. After a decade of decline, it was revived by Debendranath Tagore in 1843. A schism divided the organization in 1865, when Keshub Chunder Sen split with Tagore and formed the Adi Brahmo Samaj, and in 1878 Sen's group itself divided. Sen's followers formed a new church, the Nava-Vidhana, while the dissidents founded the Sadharan Brahmo Samaj, which became dominant. The Brahmo Samaj movement had great influence in the 19th cent., but, although it still exists, it has had little impact on 20th-century Hinduism. See P. K. Sen, *Biography of a New Faith* (2 vol., 1950–54); K. C. Sen, *The Voice of Keshub* (1963); P. V. Kanal, *An Introduction to Dev-Samaj* (1965).

Brahms, Johannes (brämz, Ger. yōhän'nĕs bräms), 1833–97, German composer, b. Hamburg. Brahms ranks among the greatest masters of the romantic period. The son of a musician, he early showed astonishing talent in many directions; he chose as a boy to become a pianist. As accompanist to the violinist Eduard Reményi he attracted the notice of Johann Joachim, who introduced him to leading musical circles. Brahms became the devoted friend of Robert and Clara Schumann, both of whom admired his compositions. His later activities as pianist and as choral conductor were not very successful, but after he settled in Vienna his compositions brought him enough money to support himself in simple comfort. Brahms never married, although he had several love affairs and remained deeply attached to Clara Schumann for many years after her husband's death. His extreme self-criticism led him to destroy much of what he composed, thus limiting the number of his existing works but ensuring a uniformly high quality. In his music the romantic impulse is restrained by a reverence for the forms of the past. This blend of romantic feeling and classical spirit is exemplified in such works as his *Variations on a Theme by Handel* (1861), for piano, and the orchestral composition *Variations on a Theme by Haydn* (1873). In his day, Brahms's conservative romanticism was contrasted with Richard Wagner's dramatic romantic style, and a controversy raged between supporters of Brahms and the followers of the "neo-German" school led by Liszt and Wagner. Brahms wrote four symphonies, which are considered among the greatest in symphonic music. Major choral works include *Ein deutsches Requiem* [a German requiem] (1866) and *Schicksalslied* [song of destiny] (1868), both for chorus and orchestra. The Violin Concerto in D (1878), the Piano Concerto in B Flat (1878–81), and the Piano Quintet in F Minor (1864) are staples of the concert repertory. Brahms also composed sonatas, capriccios, intermezzos—works in almost every genre except opera. Throughout his life he devoted attention to chamber music and to songs, which vary from simple accompaniments for folk songs to solemn compositions such as *Vier ernste Gesange* [four serious songs] (1896). Many of his exquisite romantic lieder, in which the words, melody, and piano accompaniment are inseparably blended, are favorites among professional and amateur singers alike, and his lullaby has long been a familiar melody throughout the world. See his letters, ed. by Max Kalbeck (1909); biographies by Karl Geiringer (rev. ed. 1947) and Hans Gal (tr. 1963); study by Burnett James (1972).

Brahui (brähoo͞'ē), Dravidian language of Baluchistan. See DRAVIDIAN LANGUAGES.

Braid, James, 1795?–1860, English surgeon and writer on hypnotism and magic. The first to use the term *hypnotism* instead of *mesmerism* or *animal magnetism*, he also demonstrated that it was achieved by suggestion. His writings prepared the way for investigations into what was later called the unconscious mind.

Braidwood, Thomas, 1715–1806, English educator, grad. Univ. of Edinburgh. He established (1760) at Edinburgh the first school in Great Britain for deaf-mutes, moving it to London in 1783.

Brăila (braē'lä), city (1969 est. pop. 122,000), SE Rumania, in Walachia, on the Danube River. The chief grain-shipping port of Rumania, it is also a major industrial and commercial city. Machinery, metals, foodstuffs, and textiles are the principal products. Brăila probably dates from Greek times. It was burned by the Turks in 1462 and by Stephen the Great of Moldavia in 1470. Taken by the Turks c.1550, it played an important role in the Russo-Turkish Wars (18th cent.) and was captured several times by Russian forces. The Treaty of Adrianople (1829) awarded the city to the Rumanian principality of Walachia. The Cathedral of St. Michael, a state theater, and an art museum are in Brăila.

Braille, Louis (brāl, Fr. lwē brī'yə), 1809?–1852, French inventor of the Braille system of printing and writing for the blind. Having become blind from an accident at the age of 3, he was admitted at 10 to the Institution nationale des Jeunes Aveugles in Paris. Later he taught there. In order to make his instruction easier, he chose Charles Barbier's system of writing with points, evolving a much simpler one from that system. He was interested in music as well and for a time played the organ in a church in Paris. The **Braille system** consists of six raised points or dots used in 63 possible combinations. It is in use, in modified form, for printing, writing, and musical notation for the blind. See also BLINDNESS.

Brain, Dennis, 1921–57, British horn player. Brain studied with his father, Aubrey, at the Royal Academy of Music in London. He played principal horn with first the Royal Philharmonic and then the Philharmonia orchestras. He was killed in an automobile accident. Brain's extraordinary artistry has been preserved on many orchestral and solo recordings. Works were written for him by Hindemith, Britten, and other composers.

brain, the supervisory center of the NERVOUS SYSTEM in all vertebrates. It is also the site of emotions, memory, self-awareness, and thought. Occupying the SKULL cavity (cranium), the adult human brain normally weighs from 2¼ to 3¼ lb (1–1.5 kg). Differences in weight and size do not signify corresponding differences in mental ability. An elephant's brain weighs more than four times that of a human and a whale's brain, seven times; however, neither animal has the intelligence of the orangutan, whose brain weighs one third as much as man's. Sensory nerve cells feed information to the brain from every part of the body, external and internal. The brain evaluates the data, then sends directives through the motor nerve cells to muscles and glands, causing them to take suitable action. Alternatively, the brain may inhibit action, as when a person forces himself not to flinch from a blow, or it may simply store the

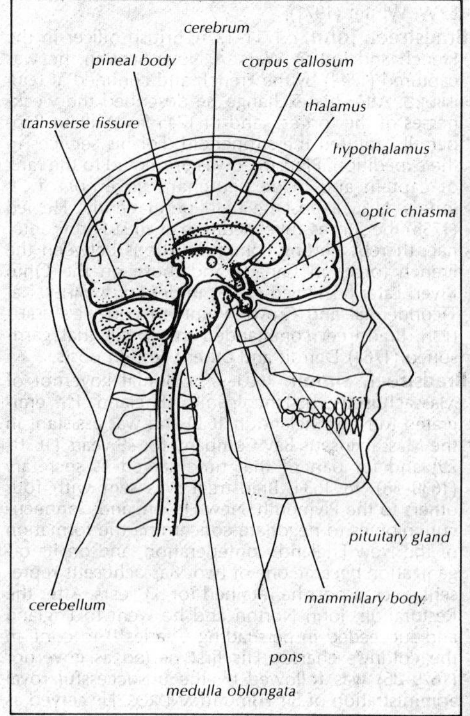

Brain

information for later use. Both incoming information and outgoing commands traverse the brain and the rest of the nervous system in the form of electrochemical impulses. By means of these impulses, the brain directly controls conscious or voluntary behavior, such as walking and thinking. It also controls, through feedback circuitry, most involuntary behavior, i.e., connections with the autonomic nervous system enable the brain to adjust heartbeat, blood pressure, fluid balance, and similar functions. The brain even influences apparently fully automatic activities such as those of the internal organs. Essentially the human brain consists of some 10 billion interconnected nerve cells with innumerable extensions. This interlacing of nerve fibers and their junctions allows a nerve impulse to follow any of a virtually unlimited number of pathways. The effect is to give man his seemingly infinite variety of responses to sensory input. What pathway a brain actually chooses for an impulse depends on many factors. Among them are: (1) the particular brain's physical characteristics; (2) temporary physical conditions, such as fatigue or malnourishment; (3) information previously implanted by experience and learning; (4) intensity of the stimulus producing the impulse; and (5) emotional states such as anger or melancholy. The billions of nerve cells in the brain are structurally supported by the hairlike filaments of glial cells. Smaller than nerve cells and ten times as numerous, the glia account for an estimated half of the brain's weight. They are thought to constitute the blood-brain barrier, stopping waste products and other poisons from reaching nerve cells through the network of cranial blood vessels. Nerve fibers in the brain are sheathed in a near-white substance called myelin and form the white matter of the brain. Nerve cell bodies, which are not covered by myelin sheaths, form the gray matter. Anatomically the brain has three major parts, the hindbrain (including the CEREBELLUM and the BRAINSTEM), the midbrain, and the forebrain (including the diencephalon and the cerebrum). Every brain area has an associated function, although no one area is completely responsible for any single function. The cerebellum coordinates muscular movements and, along with the midbrain, monitors posture. The brainstem, which incorporates the medulla and the pons, monitors involuntary activities such as breathing and vomiting. The THALAMUS, which forms the major part of the diencephalon, receives incoming sensory impulses and routes them to the appropriate higher centers. The HYPOTHALAMUS, occupying the rest of the diencephalon, regulates heartbeat, body temperature, and fluid balance. Above the thalamus extends the corpus callosum, a neuron-rich membrane underlying the cerebrum. The cerebrum, occupying the topmost portion of the skull, is by far the largest sector of the brain. Split vertically into left and right hemispheres, it is deeply fissured and grooved. Its upper surface, the cerebral cortex, contains most of the master controls of the body. In the cortex ultimate analysis of sensory data occurs, and motor impulses originate that initiate, reinforce, or inhibit the entire spectrum of muscle and gland activity. The parts of the cerebrum intercommunicate through association tracts consisting of connector neurons. Found profusely in the corpus callosum, these tracts account for approximately half of the total number of nerve cells in the brain. The tracts are believed to be the seats of reasoning, learning, and perhaps memory. The left half of the cerebrum controls the right side of the body; the right half controls the left side. Other important parts of the brain are the PITUITARY gland, the basal ganglia, and the reticular activating system (RAS). The pituitary is involved in growth regulation. The basal ganglia, located just above the diencephalon in each cerebral hemisphere, are thought to handle coordination and habitual but acquired skills like chewing and playing the piano. The RAS is a special system of nerve cells linking the medulla, pons, midbrain, and cerebral cortex. There is evidence that the RAS functions as a sentry. In a noisy crowd, for example, the RAS alerts a person when a friend speaks and enables that person to ignore other sounds. During both sleep and consciousness, the ceaseless electrochemical activity in the brain generates brain waves that can be electronically detected and recorded (see ELECTROENCEPHALOGRAPHY). The entire brain is enveloped in three protective sheets known as the MENINGES, continuations of the membranes that wrap the SPINAL CORD. The two inner sheets enclose a shock-absorbing cushion of cerebrospinal fluid. Few if any pain receptors exist in brain tissue. A headache is felt because of sensory impulses coming chiefly from the meninges or scalp. In invertebrates a group of ganglia or even a single ganglion may serve as a rudimentary brain. See Edwin Clarke and Kenneth Dewhurst, *An Illustrated History of Brain Function* (1973).

Braine, John, 1922–, English novelist, b. Bedford, Yorkshire. He was able to leave his job as a librarian after the success of his first novel, *Room at the Top* (1957). Ranked as one of the major works of England's ANGRY YOUNG MEN, this novel bitterly chronicles the rise of a young working-class man into the upper middle class of an English factory town. In its penetrating analysis of the English class structure and of psychological relationships, *Room at the Top* is representative of all Braine's novels. His other works include *Life at the Top* (1962), *The Jealous God* (1964), and *Writing A Novel* (1974).

Brainerd, David, 1718–47, missionary to the American Indians, b. Haddam, Conn. Licensed to preach in 1742, he spent his brief years among the Indians, first in New York and later in New Jersey and Pennsylvania. His diary was widely read and influenced many to enter the mission field. Parts of the diary were published during Brainerd's lifetime, and in 1749, Jonathan Edwards published the hitherto unprinted portion.

Brainerd, city (1970 pop. 11,667), seat of Crow Wing co., central Minn., on the Mississippi River, in a pine-forested and lake region; inc. 1881. Founded (1870) by the Northern Pacific RR, it is still a railroad center with repair shops. Lumbering and related enterprises (such as paper manufacturing) are its economic mainstays. A junior college is in the city.

brainstem, lower part of the BRAIN, adjoining and structurally continuous with the spinal cord. The upper segment of the human brainstem, the pons, contains nerve fibers that connect the two halves of the CEREBELLUM. It is vital in coordinating movements involving right and left sides of the body. Below the pons and continuous with the spinal cord is the medulla, which transmits ascending and descending nerve fibers between the spinal cord and the brain. The medulla also directly controls many involuntary muscular and glandular activities, including breathing, heart contraction, artery dilation, salivation, vomiting, and probably laughing. The nuclei of some of the nerves that originate in the brain are also located in the brainstem. Nerve fibers in the brainstem do not readily regenerate, hence injury may result in permanent loss of function. See also NERVOUS SYSTEM.

Braintree, town (1970 pop. 35,050), E Mass., a suburb of Boston; inc. 1640. Abrasives and rubber goods are among its manufactures. Braintree included Quincy (birthplace of John Adams and John Quincy Adams) until 1792 and Randolph until 1793. John Hancock and Gen. Sylvanus Thayer, superintendent of West Point from 1817 to 1833, were born in Braintree. The Thayer Academy, founded by the general, is in the town.

Braintree and Bocking, urban district (1971 pop. 24,839), Essex, E England, between the Pant (Blackwater) and Brain river valleys. There are textile, plastic, and metal-product industries. Bricks from ancient Roman roads (the district is on the line of the Roman Stone Street) were used in the church in Braintree.

Brain Trust, the group of close advisers to Franklin Delano Roosevelt when he was governor of New York state and during his first years as President. The name was applied to them because the members of the group were drawn from academic life. This informal advisory group on the New Deal included Columbia University professors Raymond MOLEY, Adolf A. BERLE, Jr., and Rexford G. TUGWELL and expanded to include many more academicians. It soon disintegrated, but the term has remained in common usage for similar groups. See study by Rexford G. Tugwell (1968).

brain wave: see ELECTROENCEPHALOGRAPHY.

brake, in botany: see BRACKEN.

brake, in technology, device to slow or stop the motion of a mechanism or vehicle. Friction brakes, the most common kind, operate on the principle that friction can be used to convert the mechanical energy of a moving object into heat energy, which is absorbed by the brake. The essential components of a friction brake are a rotating part, such as a wheel, axle, disk, or brake drum, and a stationary part that is pressed against the rotating part to slow or stop it. The stationary part usually has a lining, called a brake lining, that can generate a great amount of friction yet give long wear; it most often contains asbestos. The principal types of friction brake are the block brake, the band brake, the internal-shoe brake, and the disk brake. The block brake consists of a block, the stationary part, that is shaped to fit the contour of a wheel or drum. For example, a

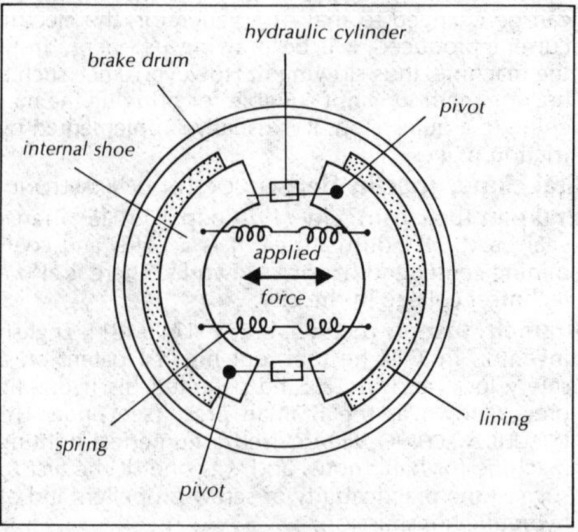

Shoe brake

wooden block applied to the rim of a wheel has long been used to slow or stop horse-drawn vehicles. A simple band brake consists of a metal band, the stationary part, that can be tightened around a drum by means of a lever. It is found on hoists and excavating machinery. The internal-shoe brake has a drum that contains two stationary semicircular pieces, or shoes, which slow or stop the motion of the drum by pressing against its inner surface. This is the type of brake most often found on automobiles, with an internal-shoe brake drum located on the central part of each wheel. A disk brake of the type used on automobiles has a metal disk and pistons with friction pads that can close on the disk and slow it. A manually operated brake pedal or handle is used to activate a brake. With low-power machinery or vehicles the operator can usually apply sufficient force through a simple mechanical linkage from the pedal or handle to the stationary part of the brake. In many cases, however, this force must

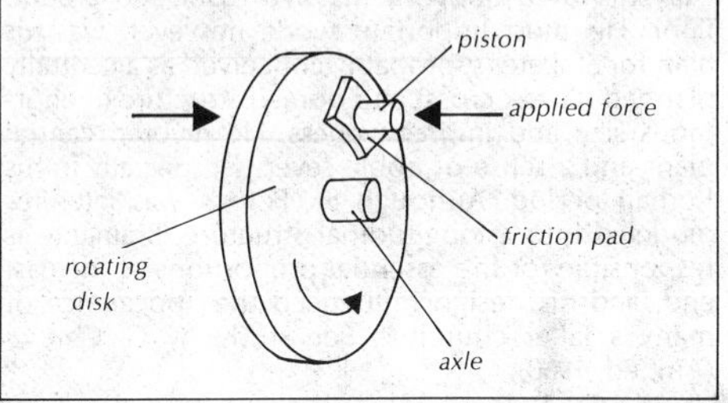

Disk brake

be multiplied by using an elaborate braking system. One such system, called the air brake system, or air brake, was invented by American manufacturer George Westinghouse and was first used on passenger trains in 1868. It is now widely used on railroad trains. The fundamental principle involved is the use of compressed air acting through a piston in a cylinder to set block brakes on the wheels. The action is simultaneous on the wheels of all the cars in the train. The compressed air is carried through a strong hose from car to car with couplings between cars; its release to all the separate block brake units at the same time is controlled by the engineer. An automatic feature provides for the setting of all the block brakes in the event of damage to the brake hose, leakage, or damage to individual brake units. The air brake is used also on subway trains, trolley cars, buses, and trucks. The hydraulic brake system, or hydraulic brake, is used on almost all automobiles (see HYDRAULIC MACHINE). When the brake pedal of an automobile is depressed, a force is applied to a piston in a master cylinder. The piston forces hydraulic fluid through metal tubing into a cylinder in each wheel where the fluid's pressure moves two pistons that press the brake shoes against the drum. The vacuum brake system, or vacuum brake, depends upon the use of a vacuum to force a piston in a cylinder to hold a brake shoe off a drum; when the vacuum is destroyed, the shoe is released and presses on the drum. In an automotive power brake system, extra pressure can be exerted on the hydraulic master cylinder piston by a vacuum brake's piston. A machine that is driven by an electric motor can sometimes use its motor as a brake.

Because inertia keeps the machine's shafts moving after the current to the electric motor has been shut off, the machine keeps the motor's armature turning. While this is happening, if the motor's action can be changed to that of a generator, the electric current produced will be drawing its energy from the machine, thus slowing it. However, since such a braking method is not suitable for bringing the machine to a quick stop, it is usually supplemented by friction brakes.

Brakelond, Jocelin de: see JOCELIN DE BRAKELOND.

Brakpan (brăk'păn), city (1970 pop. 113,115), Transvaal prov., NE South Africa. It is a gold- and coal-mining center and has an ironworks. There is also a technical college in the city.

Bramah, Joseph (brăm'ə, brä'-), 1748–1814, English inventor. In 1784 he took out his first patent on a safety lock, and in 1795 he patented his hydraulic press, known as the Bramah press (see under HYDRAULIC MACHINE). He devised a numerical printing machine for bank notes and was one of the first to suggest the practicability of screw propellers and of hydraulic transmission.

Bramante, Donato (dōnä'tō brämän'tā), 1444–1514, Italian Renaissance architect and painter, b. near Urbino. His buildings in Rome are considered the most characteristic examples of High Renaissance style. In 1477 he painted frescoes in the municipal palace at Bergamo. In Milan and neighboring cities including Pavia and Vigevano, he executed paintings that recall works by Piero della Francesca and Mantegna. Bramante designed much of the Church of Santa Maria presso San Satiro in Milan; its famous choir, painted in perspective, gives an illusion of great depth, although it is extremely shallow. He may also have planned the east end of Santa Maria delle Grazie, a spacious domed appendage to an older Gothic church. After 1499 he left for Rome, where he designed the simple but graceful cloister for Santa Maria delle Pace and the exquisitely proportioned circular Tempietto in the courtyard of San Pietro in Montorio. His other works in Rome include the Belvedere courtyard at the Vatican, designs for a massive Palace of the Tribunals, the choir of Santa Maria del Popolo and other churches, and his own large house with Doric columns rhythmically disposed above a massive rusticated ground floor. His most important work, however, was his plan for St. Peter's, probably conceived as a centrally planned (Greek cross) and domed structure of enormous size and impressiveness. He favored central plans and a sense of noble severity especially in his Roman period. Although St. Peter's was later remodeled into a longitudinal structure, Bramante is responsible for the essential proportions of the east end, and his design influenced the appearance of many smaller churches. See study by G. Chierci (Am. ed. 1960).

Bramantino (brämäntē'nō), c.1465–c.1535, Lombard painter and architect. His real name was Bartolomeo Suardi. He took the name of his master Bramante, whose style he followed closely. He became court painter to Francesco Maria Sforza. His works are noted for their fine architectural background. Examples of his art are the *Madonna and Angels* and *St. Martin* (both: Brera, Milan); and several paintings in the Metropolitan Museum and the National Gallery of Art, Washington, D.C. As an architect, Bramantino designed the Trivulzio Chapel (San Nazzaro, Milan). He also wrote a treatise on perspective, parts of which have been preserved.

bramble, name for plants of the genus *Rubus* [Lat.,=red, for the color of the juice]. This vast genus of the family Rosaceae (ROSE family), with representatives in many parts of the world, includes the blackberries, raspberries, loganberries, boysenberries, and dewberries. The plants are typically shrubs with prickly stems (called "canes") and edible fruits that botanically are not berries but aggregates of drupelets (see FRUIT). The underground parts of brambles are perennial and the canes biennial; only second-year canes bear flowers and fruits. Innumerable horticultural varieties have been bred. The native American black raspberry, or blackcap (*R. occidentalis*), and red raspberry (*R. strigosus*) as well as the European red raspberry (*R. idaeus*) are all cultivated in North America, chiefly in the Northeast. Numerous blackberry species and varieties are cultivated in many regions, particularly in the south central states. Closely resembling the blackberries, except for a more trailing or prostrate habit and a larger fruit, are the dewberries; the most common North American species (*R. procumbens*) is sometimes called running blackberry. The loganberries and boysenberries, with tart purplish fruits, are thought to be strains of either a variety of the Pacific dewberry (*R. ursinus*) or a hybrid between it and the red raspberry; the original plant appeared in the California orchard of Judge J. H. Logan in 1881. Bramble berries were eaten by the Indians. Berries are grown commercially in Europe and North America for sale as fresh, canned, and frozen fruit and for use in numerous types of preserves and fruit-flavored beverages and liqueurs. In England the name bramble is applied chiefly to the common wild blackberry. Other thorny shrubs are sometimes also called brambles. Brambles are classified in the division MAGNOLIOPHYTA, class Magnoliopsida, order Rosales, family Rosaceae.

Brameld, Theodore, 1904–, American educator, b. Neillsville, Wis., grad. Ripon College, 1926; Ph.D. Univ. of Chicago, 1931. After teaching philosophy at Long Island Univ. and Adelphi College, he was professor of the philosophy of education at the Univ. of Minnesota (1939–47), New York Univ. (1947–58), and Boston Univ. (1958–69). Brameld's theory of reconstructionism has received widespread attention in educational circles. This philosophy holds that a system of public education that is aware of the findings of the behavioral sciences can bring about fundamental changes in the social and economic structure of society. His writings include *Ends and Means in Education* (1950), *Philosophies of Education in Cultural Perspective* (1955), *Toward a Reconstructed Philosophy of Education* (1956), and *The Climactic Decades* (1970).

Brampton, town (1971 pop. 41,211), S Ont., Canada, NW of Toronto. It is noted for its greenhouses. Automobiles, optical goods, and other products are made.

bran, outer coat of a cereal grain—e.g., wheat, rye, and corn—mechanically removed from commercial flour and meal by bolting or sifting. Wheat bran is extensively used as feed for farm animals. Bran is used as food for humans (in cereals or mixed with flour in bread) to add roughage (i.e., cellulose) to the diet. It is also used in dyeing and calico printing.

Brancovan, Constantine (brän-kōvän'), 1654–1714, prince of Walachia (1688–1714). A skillful politician who secured domestic peace, he furthered Walachia's economic and cultural development. Under his rule, the "Brancovan" artistic style was created, an example of which can be seen in the palace at Mogoşoaia, near Bucharest. In 1709 he negotiated with Czar Peter I of Russia an alliance against his suzerain, Sultan Ahmad III, but he later withdrew. Accused of treason, he was deposed and, with his four sons, was beheaded at Constantinople.

Brancusi, Constantin (brănkyo͞o'zē, Rum. brän'ko͞osh), 1876–1957, Rumanian sculptor. Brancusi is considered one of the foremost of modern artists. In 1904 he went to Paris, where he worked under Mercié. He declined Rodin's invitation to work in his studio. Because of his radical, economic style, his abstract sculptures, *The Kiss* (1908), *Sleeping Muse* (1910), and the portrait of Mlle Pogany (1923; Musée d'Art moderne, Paris) have been the subjects of much controversy. He altered his technique from modeling to carving c.1910. In 1927 Brancusi won a lawsuit against the U.S. customs authorities who attempted to value his sculpture as raw metal. The suit led to legal changes permitting the importation of abstract art free of duty. Brancusi's work is notable for its extreme simplification of form, its organic and frequently symbolic character, and its consummate craftsmanship. He had a profound understanding of materials, working primarily in metal, stone, and wood. *Bird in Space* (1919; Mus. of Modern Art, New York City) is a characteristic work. Others are in the Solomon R. Guggenheim Museum, New York City, and in the museums of Chicago, Cleveland, and Philadelphia. See catalog by Sidney Geist (1969); biography by Ionel Jianu (1963); studies by Sidney Geist (1967) and A. T. Spear (1969).

Brand, Sir John Henry, or **Jan Hendrik Brand** (yän hĕn' drək bränt), 1823–88, South African politician, president of the Orange Free State, b. Capetown. He was called to the English bar in 1849 and practiced law in South Africa. In 1863 he was elected president of the struggling Orange Free State and immediately made war (1864–69) on the Basutos. Reelected in 1869 (and at each election until his death), Brand refused (1871) to become president of both the Orange Free State and the Transvaal because of the Transvaal's anti-British policy. He was knighted for his mediation services in the British-Transvaal disputes.

Brandeis, Louis Dembitz (brăn'dīs), 1856–1941, Associate Justice of the U.S. Supreme Court (1916–39), b. Louisville, Ky., grad. Harvard law school, 1877. A successful Boston lawyer (1879–1916), Brandeis distinguished himself by investigating insurance practices and by establishing (1907) Massachusetts savings-bank insurance. After defending (1900–1907) the public interest in Boston utility cases, he served (1907–14) as counsel for the people in proceedings involving the constitutionality of wages and hours laws in Oregon, Illinois, Ohio, and California. In *Muller* vs. *Oregon* (1908) he persuaded the U.S. Supreme Court that minimum-hours legislation for women was reasonable—and not unconstitutional—with a brief primarily consisting of statistical, sociological, economic, and physiological information. This "Brandeis brief," as it came to be called, revolutionized the practice of law. He opposed (1907–13) the monopoly of transportation in New England and successfully argued (1910–14) before the Interstate Commerce Commission against railroad-rate increases. In 1910 as one of the counsel in the congressional investigation of Richard A. BALLINGER, he exposed the anticonservationist views of President Taft's Secretary of the Interior. As an arbitrator (1910) of a strike of New York garment workers, (mostly Jewish), he became acutely aware of Jewish problems and afterward was a leader of the Zionist movement. An enemy of industrial and financial monopoly, he formulated the economic doctrine of the New Freedom that Woodrow Wilson adopted in his 1912 presidential campaign. Over the protests of the vested interests that Brandeis had alienated as "people's attorney," Wilson appointed (1916) him to the U.S. Supreme Court. Long an advocate of social and economic reforms, he maintained a position of judicial liberalism on the bench. With Oliver Wendell Holmes, he often dissented from the majority. After Franklin Delano Roosevelt became (1933) President, Brandeis was one of the few justices who voted to uphold most of Roosevelt's New Deal legislation. He retired from the bench in 1939. Brandeis Univ. is named after him. He wrote *Other People's Money* (1914) and *Business, a Profession* (1914). For selections of his writings, see Alfred Lief, ed., *The Social and Economic Views of Mr. Justice Brandeis* (1930); O. K. Fraenkel, ed., *The Curse of Bigness* (1935); Solomon Goldman, ed., *The Words of Justice Brandeis* (1953). See his letters, ed. by M. I. Urofsky and D. W. Levy (1971); biography by A. T. Mason (1946, repr. 1956); studies by S. J. Konefsky (1956, repr. 1974) and M. I. Urofsky (1971); A. M. Bickel, *The Unpublished Opinions of Mr. Justice Brandeis* (1957).

Brandeis University, at Waltham, Mass.; coeducational; chartered and opened 1948. Although Brandeis was founded by members of the American Jewish community, the university operates as an independent, nonsectarian institution. Its graduate school of arts and sciences was established in 1953. The university's Florence Heller Graduate School for Advanced Studies in Social Welfare is well known, as is its Wien International Scholarship Program. Adjoining the campus is the American Jewish Historical Society.

Brandenburg (brän'dənbo͝ork), former state, c.10,400 sq mi (26,940 sq km), central East Germany. Potsdam was the capital; other leading cities included Cottbus, Frankfurt-an-der-Oder, and Brandenburg. As constituted in 1947 under Soviet military occupation, Brandenburg consisted of the former Prussian province of Brandenburg minus those parts of the province lying E of the Oder and Neisse rivers (see GERMANY). It became (1949) one of the states of the German Democratic Republic, but it finally was abolished as an administrative unit in 1952. BERLIN was situated in, but was administratively separate from, Brandenburg. Drained by the Havel, Spree, and Oder rivers, the region encompassed by the former state has many lakes and pine forests. The Spree Forest, in Lower LUSATIA, is inhabited by Slavic-speaking WENDS, remnants of the population that inhabited Brandenburg at the time of its acquisition (12th cent.) by ALBERT THE BEAR. The Slavic principalities had been previously subdued by Charlemagne but had regained their independence. In the 10th cent. the German kings organized the North March, a small area on the Elbe, which was bestowed on Albert the Bear in 1134. Albert expanded his territory, and in 1150 he inherited the principality of Brandenburg from its last Wendish prince. The March of Brandenburg, as Albert's lands were called, were colonized by Germans and became Christianized. Albert's descendants, the Ascanians, ruled Brandenburg until their extinction in 1320. Emperor Louis IV, a Wittelsbach, gave (1323) the vacant fief to members of his own house, but Emperor CHARLES IV (who confirmed the margraves of Brandenburg as

ELECTORS of the Holy Roman Empire) forced the Wittelsbachs to surrender it and conferred (1373) it on his son Wenceslaus. When Wenceslaus became (1378) German king, Brandenburg went to his brother, later Emperor SIGISMUND, who in 1417 formally transferred it to FREDERICK I of the house of HOHENZOLLERN. Among Frederick's early successors were ALBERT ACHILLES (reigned 1470-86), who introduced primogeniture as the law of inheritance of the Hohenzollern family, and Joachim II (reigned 1535-71), who accepted the Reformation in 1539. In the 17th cent. the electors of Brandenburg acquired (1614) the duchy of CLEVES and other W German territories and (1618) the duchy of Prussia (roughly, the later EAST PRUSSIA). Although it suffered heavily in the Thirty Years War (1618-48), Brandenburg emerged as a military power under FREDERICK WILLIAM, the Great Elector (reigned 1640-88), who acquired E Pomerania and freed Prussia from Polish suzerainty. His son, Elector Frederick III, in 1701 took the title "king in Prussia" as FREDERICK I. The later history of Brandenburg is that of PRUSSIA.

Brandenburg, city (1970 pop. 93,660), Potsdam district, central East Germany, a port on the Havel River. It is an industrial center and rail junction. Manufactures include steel, textiles, machinery, and motor vehicles. Brandenburg was founded as a Slavic settlement called Brennabor or Brennaburg. It was conquered (12th cent.) by Albert the Bear and gave its name to the margraviate (later the province) of Brandenburg. Noteworthy buildings of the city include a 12th-century Romanesque church and the city hall (13th-14th cent.).

Brandes, Georg Morris Cohen (brän' dəs), 1842-1927, Danish literary critic. His invigorating influence brought the wide currents of contemporary European thought to Danish, Icelandic, and other Scandinavian literatures. He wrote and lectured in many languages and was conceded to be the greatest critic since Taine. Yet he was refused the chair in aesthetics at the University of Copenhagen in 1870 because he was a Jew, an atheist, and a radical. He was granted the same chair in 1902. After finishing *Critiques and Portraits* (1870), he traveled on the Continent, meeting, among others, Taine and Renan, who influenced his ideas and work. On his return he wrote *Main Currents in Nineteenth-Century Literature* (6 vol., 1872-90, tr. 1901-5), an attack on provincialism and reaction. An opponent of romanticism, Brandes helped direct the Scandinavian literatures toward realism and concern with social issues. He introduced feminism to Denmark. His review, the *Nittende Aarhundrede*, was discontinued after three years. Brandes spent some time in Berlin, where he came under the influence of Nietzsche. He was attacked during the war for maintaining total neutrality. Among his later works are *William Shakespeare* (1895-96, tr. 1898), *Goethe* (1915, tr. 1924), *Voltaire* (1916, tr. 1930), and *Jesus, a Myth* (1925, tr. 1926), a work which gained him many enemies.

Brando, Marlon, 1924-, American film actor, b. Omaha, Nebr. Noted for his mumbling delivery and understated naturalism, Brando has been acclaimed as both a great actor and an exciting Hollywood sex symbol. He starred on Broadway as the primitive, brutal Stanley Kowalski in Tennessee Williams's *A Streetcar Named Desire* (1947) and in the filmed version of the play (1952). His movies include *Viva Zapata!* (1952), *Julius Caesar* (1953), *On the Waterfront* (1954), *One-Eyed Jacks* (1960; also directed), *The Godfather* (1971), and *Last Tango in Paris* (1972). See Tony Thomas, *The Films of Marlon Brando* (1973).

Brandon, Saint: see BRENDAN, SAINT.

Brandon, Charles: see SUFFOLK, CHARLES BRANDON, 1ST DUKE OF.

Brandon, city (1971 pop. 31,150), SW Man., Canada, on the Assiniboine River. The business center of the wheat-raising area of SW Manitoba, Brandon has an extensive trade in farm products and machinery. It is the seat of the annual provincial exhibition and of the Manitoba Winter Fair. A dominion experimental farm adjoins the city. Brandon Univ. is in the city. Brandon is named for the old Hudson's Bay Company post, Brandon House, built in 1793.

Brandon, uninc. village (1970 pop. 12,749), Hillsborough co., W Fla., a suburb just E of Tampa. Chiefly residential, it is also a retail and service center. Citrus fruits and vegetables are grown in the area, and there are many cattle and dairy farms.

Brandon University, at Brandon, Manitoba, Canada; nondenominational; coeducational; founded 1899 as Brandon College. The school gained university status in 1967. It has faculties of arts, science, and education.

Brandt, Willy (vĭl'ē bränt), 1913-, German political leader. His name originally was Herbert Ernst Karl Frahm. He early became active in the Social Democratic party. Soon after Adolf Hitler came to power (1933), Brandt fled to Norway and began a journalistic career. He continued political activities there and became a Norwegian citizen. When Norway was invaded (1940), he was imprisoned briefly by the Germans but escaped to Sweden. Returning to Germany after World War II, he resumed (1947) German citizenship and served (1949-57) in the Bundestag. In 1957 he was elected mayor of West Berlin. In 1961 and 1965, he was the unsuccessful Social Democratic candidate for chancellor of the German Federal Republic. As chairman of the Social Democratic party, he was named (Dec., 1966) foreign minister in the Christian Democratic-Social Democratic coalition government headed by Kurt Kiesinger. After Brandt's party won the federal elections in Sept., 1969, he became (Oct.) chancellor with the support of the Free Democratic party. His government initiated peace talks with Eastern European countries and with East Germany. Nonaggression treaties were signed (1971) with the USSR and Poland, and a treaty with East Germany was signed in Dec., 1972. Brandt was awarded the 1971 Nobel Peace Prize for his efforts toward peace. He resigned on May 6, 1974, following the revelation that one of his close aides was an East German spy.

brandy [for brandywine, from Du.,=burnt, i.e., distilled, wine], strong alcoholic spirit distilled from wine or from marc, the residue of the wine press. The most noted brandy is cognac, made from white grapes in the Charente district of France. The label *Cognac, fine champagne* denotes the finest type of cognac, which comes from a small area around Cognac. Brandy is manufactured commercially in other districts of France, notably Armagnac, and in Spain, Portugal, Australia, Italy, South Africa, and the United States. Most fine brandies are distilled in pot stills constructed to retain the volatile ingredients. The product is blended and flavored, then stored in casks (preferably oak), where it mellows and takes on a yellow color; it acquires a deeper tint from long storage or the addition of caramel syrup. Brandy marketed in the United States must be matured in cask for at least four years. Brandy made from marc is very potent and is inferior to wine brandy. Liquor distilled from fermented beets, grains, or sugarcane is sometimes called brandy. The term, qualified by the name of a fruit, is applied to spirits distilled from the fermented juice of fruits other than the grape, e.g., peach brandy, cherry brandy, and plum brandy (slivovitz), which is extensively manufactured in the Balkans.

Brandy Station, small trading center, Culpeper co., Va. It was the scene of the greatest cavalry engagement of the Civil War (also called the battle of Fleetwood Hill), fought June 9, 1863. Gen. Alfred Pleasonton's Union cavalry surprised Confederate Gen. Jeb Stuart's cavalry and fought a hard battle before the approach of Confederate infantry forced a withdrawal across the Rappahannock. This engagement was followed by the GETTYSBURG CAMPAIGN.

Brandywine, battle of, in the American Revolution, fought Sept. 11, 1777, along Brandywine Creek. The creek, formed by two small branches in SE Pennsylvania, flows southeast to join, near Wilmington, Del., the Christina River, which empties into the Delaware. The British under Sir William Howe were advancing on Philadelphia from Elkton, Md., and General Washington, realizing that they would cross the stream, placed most of his army at Chadds Ford. Howe sent General Knyphausen to feint an attack at Chadds Ford, while he himself, with General Cornwallis, struck the American right flank, where Gen. John Sullivan could not check the attack. Washington ordered a retreat to Chester, Pa. The British continued their advance and took Philadelphia (Sept. 27, 1777). See H. S. Canby, *The Brandywine* (1941).

Branford, town (1970 pop. 20,444), New Haven co., S Conn., on Long Island Sound; settled 1644, inc. as a town 1930. Formerly a shipping and fishing center, the town is now mainly residential and manufactures prestressed concrete forms, automotive parts, wire, and other products.

Brangus cattle: see BRAHMAN CATTLE.

Brannan, Samuel, 1819-89, California pioneer, b. Saco, Maine. Converted to Mormonism, he edited a Mormon paper in New York City before leading a party of Mormons by sea from New York to California. In 1847 he founded the first newspaper in San Francisco, the *California Star.* Later he began a merchandising business at Sutter's Fort and soon gained extensive landholdings. Returning to San Francisco, he was active in the move to bring order to the lawless city and was an organizer and the first president (1851) of the Committee of Vigilance. See biographies by P. D. Bailey (1943, rev. ed. 1953, repr. 1959) and L. J. Stellman (1953).

Branner, Hans Christian, 1903-66, Danish writer. Branner's early novels, often concerned with the irrational fears of childhood, include *The Child Playing on the Shore* (1937). With *The Riding Master* (1949; tr. 1951) he turned to more complex Freudian themes, expressed in an increasingly symbolic vein. Later works include the plays *Siblings* (1952; tr. *The Judge*, 1955) and *Nobody Knows the Night* (1955), and a volume of poems, *Ariel* (1963). See study by T. L. Markey (1973).

Brant, Joseph, 1742-1807, chief of the Mohawk Indians. His Indian name is usually rendered as Thayendanegea. He served under Sir William Johnson in the French and Indian War, and Johnson sent him (1761) to Eleazar Wheelock's Indian school in Lebanon, Conn. Brant served (1763) under Johnson again in Pontiac's Rebellion. In the American Revolution he did much to bind the Indians to the British and Loyalist side. He fought (1777) at Oriskany in the Saratoga campaign. In 1778, leading the Indian forces, he joined Walter BUTLER, and together they raided Cherry Valley, where they massacred the defenseless inhabitants. He was an able leader in other raids. After the Revolution, failing to get a settlement of the Indian land question in the United States, he got lands and subsidies for his people in Canada around the present Brantford, Ont. A zealous Christian, he preached Christianity, translating the Book of Common Prayer and the Gospel of Mark into the Mohawk language. See biographies by J. W. Jakes (1969) and H. C. Robinson (1971).

Brant, Sebastian (säbäs'tyän bränt), 1457-1521, German humanist and moralist. He taught law at the Univ. of Basel and in 1503 became town clerk of Strasbourg. His verse allegory *Das Narrenschiff* [ship of fools] (1494) became world famous. Illustrated with woodcuts, it went through six editions in Brant's lifetime alone. The story tells of 112 fools—each representing a fashionable foible—who sail out to sea and die because of their folly. An English translation by Alexander Barclay appeared in 1509. See verse translation (with the woodcuts) by E. H. Zeydel (1944). The poem inspired the novel *Ship of Fools* (1962) by Katherine Anne Porter.

brant or **brant goose,** common name for a species of wild sea goose. The American brant, *Branta barnicla,* breeds in arctic regions and winters along the Atlantic coast. The head, neck, and tail are black, the back brownish gray, and the under parts grayish white. Hunters find the birds easy prey and their flesh palatable. Eelgrass (*zostera marina*) is their staple food, although of necessity they may seek other nourishment. The Old World barnacle goose, *B. leucopsis,* so named because it was thought to grow out of barnacles attached to driftwood, is very similar to the brant and is an occasional visitor to North America. The black brant migrates from its arctic breeding grounds to the Pacific coast. White brant is an alternate name for the snow goose, which belongs to the same family, and gray, or prairie, brant refers to the American white-fronted goose. Brants are classified in the phylum CHORDATA, subphylum Vertebrata, class Aves, order Anseriformes, family Anatidae.

Brantford, city (1971 pop. 64,421), S Ont., Canada, on the Grand River. It is a leading manufacturing city, noted particularly for its large farm implement factories. The city was named for the Mohawk chieftain Joseph BRANT, who led the Six Nations of the Iroquois to the region after the American Revolution and who is buried in the old Mohawk Church near the city. The Mohawk Institute, an Indian residential school, is nearby. Alexander Graham Bell was living in Brantford in 1876 when he made his first successful experiment in the transmission of sound by electric wire. A museum, formerly his home, exhibits the first telephone.

Branting, Hjalmar (yäl'mär brän'tĭng), 1860-1925, Swedish premier. A leader of the Social Democratic party, he was finance minister in 1917. As premier (1920, 1921-23, 1924-25) he was responsible for social reforms and for welfare legislation. Branting supported the League of Nations and shared the 1921 Nobel Peace Prize with Christian Louis Lange.

Brantôme, Pierre de Bourdeille, seigneur de (pyĕr də bo͝ordā'yə sänyör' də bräNtōm'), 1540?-1614, French courtier, soldier, and author of memoirs. He accompanied Mary Stuart to Scotland, served in the Spanish army in Africa, and joined the expedition of the Knights of St. John against the sultan. His *Vies des hommes illustres et des grands capitaines* and his *Livre des dames* (tr., *Lives of Fair and Gallant Ladies,* 1933) give a racy and vivid account of his time.

Braque, Georges (zhôrzh bräk), 1882-1963, French painter. He joined the artists involved in developing FAUVISM in 1905, and at l'Estaque c.1909 he was profoundly influenced by Cézanne. He met Picasso, and the two simultaneously explored form and structure with results that led to the development of CUBISM. In works such as the monumental *Nude* (1907-8; Cuttoli Coll., Paris) Braque exemplified the analytical phase of the movement with his keen sense of structure and orderly method of decomposing an object. In 1911 he introduced typographical letters into his canvases, thus leading the way to COLLAGE. After World War I, in which he was badly wounded, Braque veered away from the angularity of early cubism and developed a more graceful, curvilinear style, predominantly painting still life. His works showed restraint and subtlety both in design and color (e.g., *The Table,* Pulitzer Coll., St. Louis). Braque is represented in leading galleries in Europe and the United States. See his notebooks (tr. 1971); studies by Werner Hofmann (1961), E. B. Mullins (1969), and Francis Ponge et al. (tr. 1971).

Bras d'Or Lake (brä dôr), arm of the Atlantic Ocean, c.360 sq mi (930 sq km), indenting deeply into Cape Breton Island, N.S., SE Canada, and occupying much of the interior. A narrow channel links it with the sea. The region was the scene of important experiments in the early history of aviation. In 1907, Alexander Graham Bell founded at Baddeck the Aerial Experiment Association, and on Feb. 23, 1909, J. A. D. McCurdy piloted his airplane, the *Silver Dart,* a distance of half a mile.

Brasília (bräzēl'yä), capital city and federal district (1970 pop. 538,351) of Brazil, 2,264 sq mi (5,864 sq km), an enclave in the southwestern portion of Goiás state. One of the newest cities of the world, it was inaugurated in 1960. It is situated in the highlands of central Brazil, and its ultramodern public buildings (designed by Oscar NIEMEYER) dominate the sparsely settled countryside. The removal of the capital from Rio de Janeiro to the interior, to encourage the development of central Brazil, was long advocated, but not until President Juscelino Kubitschek instituted such legislation (1956) was the project activated. The city was laid out (1957) in the unconventional shape of an airplane by the Brazilian architect Lúcio Costa. Highways connecting the new capital with Belém, Belo Horizonte, Fortaleza, Pôrto Alegre, Rio de Janeiro, and São Paulo are completed or under construction.

Braşov (bräshôv'), Hung. *Brassó,* Ger. *Kronstadt,* city (1969 est. pop. 175,000), central Rumania, in Transylvania, at the foot of the Transylvanian Alps. The administrative center of the Braşov region, the city is a road and rail junction and a major industrial center. Tractors, trucks, machinery, chemicals, and textiles are among the chief manufactures. The city is also a noted resort and winter sports center. Founded in the 13th cent. by the Teutonic Knights, Braşov was a major center of trade and industry in the Middle Ages. It enjoyed considerable autonomy under the Hapsburg empire. After World War I the city, along with Transylvania, was ceded by Hungary to Rumania. There are sizable German and Hungarian minorities. From 1950 to 1960, Braşov was called Stalin or Oraşul-Stalin (city of Stalin). It has a large 14th-century church (called the Black Church because of fire damage in 1689), the 13th-century St. Bartholomew Church, and the 14th-century St. Nicholas Church (rebuilt 1751). Parts of the medieval town wall and the 17th-century citadel remain intact. There is also a polytechnic institute.

brass, ALLOY having copper (55%-90%) and zinc (10%-45%) as its essential components. The properties of brass vary with the proportion of copper and zinc and with the addition of small amounts of other elements. In general brass can be forged or hammered into various shapes, rolled into thin sheets, drawn into wires, and machined and cast. Its ductility reaches a maximum with about 30% zinc and its tensile strength with 45%—although this property varies greatly with the mechanical and heat treatment of the alloy. Cartridge brass (70% copper, 30% zinc) is used for cartridge cases, plumbing and lighting fixtures, rivets, screws, and springs. Aluminum brass (not exceeding 3% aluminum) has greater resistance to corrosion than ordinary brass. Brass containing tin (not exceeding 2%) is less liable to corrosion in sea water; it is sometimes called naval brass and is used in naval construction. Dutch metal (80%-85% copper, 15%-20% zinc) is used as a substitute for gold leaf. When iron is added to brass it produces hard, tough alloys. One of these is delta metal (55% copper, 41% zinc, 1%-3% iron, and fractional percentages of tin and manganese), which can be forged, rolled, or cast and is used for bearings, valves, and ship propellers.

brasses, monumental, or **sepulchral brasses,** memorials to the dead, in use in churches on the Continent and in England in the 13th cent. and for several centuries following. They are usually set in the pavement but occasionally are placed upright against a wall or stand free upon a plinth. Some, called palimpsests, are incised on brasses that have been used before on the opposite face. The engraving usually presents a figure of the deceased. Historical interest centers around the contemporary costumes, armor, heraldic designs, genealogy, and paleography revealed. Such brasses still exist in Belgium, especially in Bruges; in the Netherlands; and in Germany, where there are some exceptional 13th-century examples. In England the churches of Ipswich, Norwich, London, Bristol, and elsewhere disclose more than 7,000 examples covering the different periods of their use. Tens of thousands of brasses were destroyed during the Tudor dissolution of the monasteries. The majority of those that remain are of native design and craftsmanship and of the inset type; incised examples usually indicate Flemish origin. A few brasses are in Glasgow and Edinburgh churches. The image of the brass can be transferred to paper by rubbing with a black gum called cobbler's heel-ball or with crayon. Rubbing brasses has been a popular activity in England for many decades. See James Mann's *Monumental Brasses* (1957); A. C. Bouquet, *European Brasses* (1968); H. W. Macklin, *Monumental Brasses,* ed. John P. Phillips (repr. 1969).

brasses, ornamental. Brass, a copper-zinc alloy produced since imperial Roman times, is closely associated in art with bronze, a copper-tin alloy (see BRONZE SCULPTURE). Brass was generally fashioned into utilitarian objects such as bowls, pots, and jugs. In the Middle East, China, and Japan, brass was beaten and hollow-cast, and in India an excellent decorated brass known as Benares ware is still produced. In Europe, the Meuse valley became the center of ornamental work in copper and its alloys during the 11th cent. Although production spread to most of Western Europe, the work was known well into the 16th cent. as dinanderie, after Dinant, a Belgian town long the leader in this work. Early dinanderie included ecclesiastical objects such as fonts, tabernacles, and lecterns, and domestic articles such as the distinctive aquamanile, a vessel, often in the form of an animal, used for pouring water. The brass chandeliers of Norway, Sweden, and Holland were widely exported. In the 17th and 18th cent. small objects for domestic use, such as candlesticks, utensils, and hearth equipment were produced. Ormolu, a gilded or varnished brass or bronze, was often used in the fashioning of these objects and later for covering the wooden parts of furniture. Machine production killed the brass and bronze art industries in the late 19th cent.

Brassó, Rumania: see BRAŞOV.

Brasstown Bald, peak, 4,784 ft (1,458 m) high, N Ga., in the Blue Ridge of the Appalachian Mts., near the N.C. line; highest point in Georgia.

brass wind instrument: see WIND INSTRUMENT.

Brathwaite, Richard, 1588?-1673, English poet. His *Barnabae Itinerarium,* a doggerel travelogue of provincial England, was written first in Latin (1636) and later published with an English translation (*Barnabee's Journal,* 1638). Because the book was published under the pseudonym Corymbaeus, its true authorship was not discovered until 1818. His other works include *The English Gentleman* (1630) and *The English Gentlewoman* (1631), books that emphasized the honorable and generous behavior of the landed gentry.

Bratianu (brətĭä'nōō) or **Bratiano** (-nô), Rumanian family. **Ion Bratianu,** 1821-91, was prominent in the Revolution of 1848 and helped to secure (1866) the election of Prince Carol of Hohenzollern-Sigmaringen (Carol I of Rumania) to the throne. Bratianu headed (1876-88, except for April-June, 1881) a ministry that declared (1878) the full independence of Rumania from Turkey, which was secured in the treaty of San Stefano. His son, **Ion Bratianu,** 1864-1927, succeeded him as leader of the Liberals and was premier (1909-11, 1914-18). He resigned early in 1918 rather than accept the humiliating peace terms offered by the Central Powers but regained his position in Dec., 1918, and represented Rumania at the Paris Peace Conference (1919). In 1920 he resigned in protest against the minority clauses of the Treaty of Trianon with Hungary and the division of the Banat with Yugoslavia. From 1922 until his death (except for an interlude in 1926-27) Bratianu was premier, ruling Rumania as a virtual dictator; he prevented the accession of Carol II in 1927. He was succeeded briefly as premier by his brother, Vintila Bratianu. **Constantin Bratianu,** also called **Dinu Bratianu,** 1889-1950?, another member of the family, led the National Liberal party from 1934 and opposed both the dictatorship of Ion Antonescu and the Communist regime. He was reported to have died in prison.

Bratislava (brä'tĕslä'vä''), Ger. *Pressburg,* Hung. *Pozsony,* city (1970 pop. 283,539), S Czechoslovakia, on the Danube River and near the Austrian and Hungarian borders. It is Czechoslovakia's third largest city and the traditional capital of Slovakia. Bratislava is also an important road and rail center and a leading Danubian port. Industries include mechanical engineering, machine building, oil refining, food processing, and the manufacture of chemicals, textiles, electrical equipment, paper, wood products, and beer. Forests, vineyards, and large farms surround the city, which has an active trade in agricultural products. It is also a popular tourist center. A Roman outpost called Posonium by the 1st cent. A.D., Bratislava became a stronghold of the Great Moravian Empire in the 9th cent. After the death of Ottocar II (1278), Bratislava and much of S and E Slovakia fell under Hungarian rule. From 1541, when the Turks captured Buda, until 1784, Bratislava served as Hungary's capital and the residence of Hungarian kings and archbishops. The kings continued to be crowned there until 1835, and Bratislava was the meeting place of the Hungarian diet until 1848. Inhabited largely by German traders before the 19th cent., the city then became predominantly Magyar. In the 19th cent. it was the center of the emerging Slovak national revival, and after the union of the Czech and Slovak territories in 1918 it was incorporated into Czechoslovakia. From 1939 until 1945, Bratislava was the capital of a nominally independent Slovak republic that was governed by a pro-German regime. The Univ. of Jan Comenius (1919), the Slovak Academy of Sciences, a polytechnic university, a national theater, and several museums are in the city. The 9th-century castle, above the Danube, was rebuilt in the 13th cent. St. Martin's Cathedral, the Franciscan convent and church, and the old town hall are also 13th-century buildings. The new town hall occupies an 18th-century palace, formerly the residence of the primates of Hungary; the Treaty of PRESSBURG was signed there in 1805.

Brattleboro, town (1970 pop. 12,239), Windham co., SE Vt., on the Connecticut River; chartered 1753. The town grew near Fort Dummer, which was established in 1724 to protect the settlers from Indians. Once an artists' colony, Brattleboro is now a center for winter sports. Its manufactures include optical goods, paper and wood products, books, and purses. Rudyard Kipling married a native of Brattleboro, and they lived nearby. John Humphrey Noyes was born in Brattleboro. Mark Hopkins College is in the town.

Braun, Eva (ā'vä), 1912-45, mistress and later wife of the German dictator Adolf Hitler. She was a shop assistant to a Nazi photographer, through whom she met Hitler. She entered his household in 1936, although their relationship was kept secret. She had no influence on the government. Hitler married her in the last days of his life, and she joined him in suicide.

Braunschweig: see BRUNSWICK, Germany.

Brauwer, Adriaen: see BROUWER, ADRIAEN.

Brawley, city (1970 pop. 13,746), Imperial co., SE Calif.; inc. 1908. It is situated in an agricultural area of the Imperial Valley, SE of the Salton Sea. Cattle feeding and the production of beet sugar are the major industries. Nearly half the population is Mexican-American. The Imperial Valley Rodeo and Brawley Cattle Call is an important event in the city.

Braxton, Carter, 1736-97, political leader in the American Revolution, signer of the Declaration of Independence, b. King and Queen co., Va. He lived (1757-60) in England, returned to America, and served in the house of burgesses (1761-71, 1775) and in the Continental Congress (1775-76, 1777-83, 1785).

Bray, Thomas, 1656-1730, English clergyman and philanthropist. In 1696 he was selected by the bishop of London as his commissary to establish the Anglican church in Maryland. Bray recruited missionaries and assembled parochial libraries for North America. He sent out more than 30 parish libraries, which also served in many cases as circulating libraries. He established similar libraries in England and Wales. He founded (1699) the Society for Promoting Christian Knowledge to carry on his work. Bray visited Maryland in 1700 and was instrumental in the passage of a revised provincial Church Act (1702). He secured the charter (1701) for the noted Society for the Propagation of the Gospel in Foreign Parts. Rector of St. Botolph Without, Aldgate, London, from 1706 until his death, he was interested in many religious and charitable enterprises, among them the relief of prisoners in England, with which James Oglethorpe was also concerned. In 1723 a charity society, "Dr. Bray's Associates," was founded, which in 1730 was concerned in a petition for the charter of Georgia. His major written work was *A Course of Lectures Upon the Church Catechism* (9 vol., 1696). See biography by E. L. Pennington (1934); C. T. Laugher, *Thomas Bray's Grand Design* (1974).

Brazil (brəzĭl'), Port. *Brasil,* republic (1973 est. pop. 99,000,000), 3,286,470 sq mi (8,511,965 sq km), E South America. It is a federation of 22 states, four territories, and BRASÍLIA, the federal district and site of the capital city of the same name. By far the largest of the Latin American countries, Brazil occupies nearly half the continent of South America, stretching from the Guiana Highlands in the north to the plains of Uruguay and Paraguay in the south. In the west it spreads to the equatorial rain forest, bordering on Bolivia, Peru, and Colombia; in the east it juts far out into the Atlantic toward Africa. Its vast extent covers a great variety of land and climate, for although Brazil is mainly in the tropics (the equator crosses it in the north and the Tropic of Capricorn crosses it in the south), the southern part of the great central upland is cool and yields the produce of temperate lands. The people are also diverse in origin, and Brazil boasts that the new "race" of Brazilians is a successful amalgam of Indian, Negro, and European strains. Portuguese is the official language, and a large part of the population is at least nominally Roman Catholic. Most of the estimated 150,000 Indians (chiefly of Tupí or GUARANÍ linguistic stock) are found in the rain forests of the Amazon River basin, which occupies all the north and north central portions of Brazil. Most of Brazil's great cities are on the Atlantic coast or the banks of the great rivers. The chief city within the Amazon region is MANAUS. Wild rubber, once of great economic importance, and other forest products are gathered in the region, but the states of AMAZONAS, PARA, and ACRE, and the territories of AMAPÁ, RORAIMA, and RONDÔNIA are still largely of potential rather than actual economic value. At the mouth of the Amazon is the city of BELÉM, chief port of N Brazil. Southeast of the Amazon mouth is the great seaward outthrust of Brazil, the region known as the Northeast. The states of MARANHÃO and PIAUÍ form a transitional zone noted for its many babassu and carnauba palms. The Northeast proper—including the states of CEARÁ, RIO GRANDE DO NORTE, PARAÍBA, PERNAMBUCO, ALAGOAS, SERGIPE, and the northern part of BAHIA—was the center of the great sugar culture that for centuries dominated Brazil. The Northeast has also contributed much to the literature and culture of Brazil. In these states the general pattern is a narrow coastal plain (formerly supporting the sugarcane plantations and now given over to diversified subtropical crops) and a semiarid interior, or SERTÃO, subject to recurrent droughts. This region has been the object of vigorous reclamation efforts by the government in recent years. The "bulge" of Brazil reaches its turning point at the Cape of São Roque. To the northeast lie the islands of FERNANDO DE NORONHA territory, and to the south is the important port and airport of NATAL. South of the "corner" of Brazil, the characteristic pattern of Brazilian geography becomes notable: the narrow and interrupted coastal lowlands are bordered on the west by an escarpment; in some places, however, the escarpment actually reaches the sea. Above the escarpment is the great Brazilian plateau, which tapers off in the southernmost state, Rio Grande do Sul, where it is succeeded by the plains of the Rio de la Plata country. The escarpment itself appears from the sea as a mountain range, generally called the Serra do Mar [coast range], and the plateau is interrupted by mountainous regions, such as that in Bahia, which separates E Bahia from the valley of the São Francisco River. The chief cities of the Northeast are the ports of RECIFE in Pernambuco and SALVADOR in Bahia. There are a number of excellent harbors farther south: VITÓRIA in Espírito Santo; RIO DE JANEIRO, the

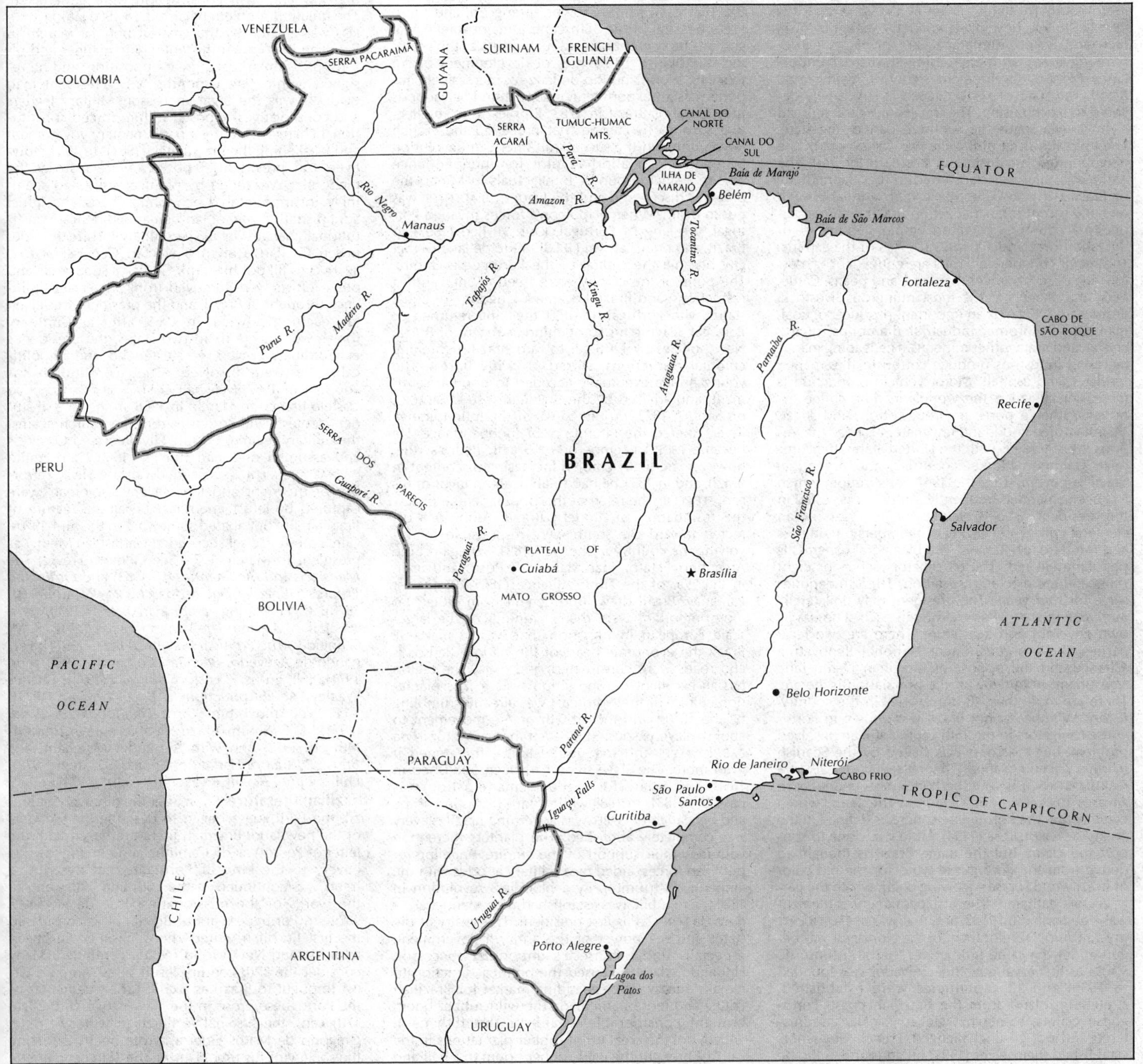

former capital, one of the most beautiful and most capacious harbors in the world; SANTOS, the port of São Paulo and the greatest coffee port in the world; and PÔRTO ALEGRE in Rio Grande do Sul. In the east and southeast is the heavily populated region of Brazil—the states that in the 19th and 20th cent. received the bulk of European immigrants and took hegemony away from the old Northeast. The states of GUANABARA and RIO DE JANEIRO, with the great steel center of VOLTA REDONDA, are heavily industrialized. Neighboring SÃO PAULO state has even more industry (50% of all of Brazil's industry) and a well-developed agriculture. The city of SÃO PAULO on the plateau has continued the vigorous and aggressive development that marked the region in the 17th and 18th cent., when the *paulistas* went out in the famed *bandeiras* (raids), searching for Indian slaves and gold and opening the rugged interior. They were largely responsible for the development of the gold and diamond mines of MINAS GERAIS state, the second most populous state in Brazil, and for the building of its old mining center of Vila Rica (OURO PRÊTO), now succeeded by BELO HORIZONTE as capital. Minas has some of the finest iron reserves in the world, as well as other mineral wealth, and is becoming industrialized. Settlement also spread from São Paulo southward, particularly in the 19th and early 20th cent. when coffee from São Paulo's *terra roxa* [purple soil] had become the basis of Brazilian wealth, and coffee growing spread to PARANÁ. That state, in the west, runs out to the "corner" where Brazil, Argentina, and Paraguay meet at the natural marvel of the Iguaçu Falls in the Paraná River. The more southern states of SANTA CATARINA and RIO GRANDE DO SUL, developed to a large extent by German and Slavic immigrants, are primarily cattle-growing areas with increasing industrial importance. Frontier development is continuing in central Brazil. The state of MATO GROSSO is still largely devoted to stock raising. The transcontinental railroad from Bolivia spans the southern part of the state. The federal district of Brasília was carved out of the neighboring plateau state of GOIÁS, to the east. The national capital was transferred to the planned city of Brasília in 1960. Despite a high annual growth rate and recent industrialization Brazil is still an agricultural country. Agriculture employs about 60% of the labor force and accounts for 70% of the exports. The major commercial crops are coffee, cocoa, cotton, sugarcane, oranges, bananas, and beans. Cattle, pigs, and sheep are the most numerous livestock. Besides iron, Brazil is an important producer of coal, manganese, chrome, industrial diamonds, quartz crystal, and many other minerals. The leading manufacturing industries produce cotton textiles, paper, fertilizer, and asphalt. Motor vehicle production is increasing. Brazil is the world's leading coffee exporter. Other exports are iron, cotton, and sugar. Manufactured goods and raw materials head the imports. Most trade is with the United States, the European Common Market countries, and Argentina. Brazil is governed by the 1967 constitution, which has been amended frequently. Authority is vested in the president, who is elected for five years by an electoral college consisting of members of congress and the state legislatures. The bicameral congress is popularly elected. The 66 senators serve for eight years and are elected in rotation. The 310 deputies serve for four years. The president may unilaterally intervene in state affairs, although each state has its own governor and legislature. There are two legal parties, the pro-government National Renovating Alliance and the opposition Brazilian Democratic Movement. About 70% of the population is literate. There are more than 40 universities in the country.

History. Whether or not Brazil was known to Portuguese navigators in the 15th cent. is still an unsolved problem, but the coast was visited by the Spanish mariner Vicente Yáñez Pinzón (see under PINZÓN, MARTÍN ALONSO) before the Portuguese under Pedro Alvares CABRAL in 1500 claimed the land, which came within the Portuguese sphere as defined in the Treaty of TORDESILLAS (1494). Little was done to support the claim, but the name Brazil is thought to derive from the Portuguese word for the red color of brazilwood [*brasa*=glowing coal], which the early visitors gathered. The first permanent settlement was not made until 1532, and that was at SÃO VICENTE in São Paulo. Development of the Northeast was begun about the same time under Martím Afonso de SOUSA as first royal governor. Salvador was founded in 1539, and 12 captaincies were established, stretching inland from the Brazilian coast. Portuguese claims, somewhat lackadaisically administered, did not go unchallenged. French Huguenots established themselves (1555) on an island in Rio de Janeiro harbor and were routed in 1567 by a force under Mem de SÁ, who then founded the city of Rio de Janeiro. The Dutch made their first attack on Salvador (Bahia) in 1624, and in 1633 the vigorous Dutch West India Company was able to capture and hold not only Salvador and Recife but the whole of the Northeast; the region was ably ruled by JOHN MAURICE OF NASSAU. No aid was forthcoming from Portugal, which had been united with Spain in 1580 and did not regain its independence until 1640. It was a naval expedition from Rio itself that drove out the Dutch in 1654. The success of the colonists helped to build up self-confidence among the settlers. Farther south, the *bandeirantes* from São Paulo had been trekking westward since the beginning of the 17th cent., thrusting far into Spanish territory and extending the western boundaries of Brazil, which were not delimited until the negotiations of the Brazilian diplomat RIO BRANCO in the late 19th and early 20th cent. The Portuguese also had ambitions to control the Banda Oriental (present Uruguay) and in the 18th cent. came into conflict with the Spanish there; the matter was not completely settled even by the independence of Uruguay in 1828. Meanwhile the sugar culture had come to full flower in the Northeast, where the plantations were furnishing most of the sugar demanded by Europe. The native Indians were not adaptable to the backbreaking labor of the cane fields, and Negro slaves were imported in large numbers. Dependence on a one-crop economy was lessened by the development of the mines in the interior, particularly those of Minas Gerais, where gold was discovered late in the 17th cent. Mining towns sprang up, and Ouro Prêto became in the 18th cent. a major intellectual and artistic center boasting such artists as the sculptor ALEIJADINHO. The center of development began to swing south, and Rio de Janeiro, increasingly important as an export center, supplanted Salvador as the capital of Brazil in 1763. Ripples from intellectual stirrings in Europe that preceded the French Revolution and the successful American Revolution brought on an abortive plot for independence among a small group of intellectuals in Minas; the plot was discovered and the leader, TIRADENTES, was put to death. When Napoleon's forces invaded Portugal, the king of Portugal, JOHN VI, fled (1807) to Brazil, and on his arrival (1808) in Rio de Janeiro that city became the capital of the Portuguese Empire. The ports of the colony were freed of mercantilist restrictions, and Brazil became a kingdom, of equal status with Portugal. In 1821 the king returned to Portugal, leaving his son behind as regent of Brazil. New policies by Portugal toward Brazil, tightening colonial restrictions, stirred up wide unrest. The young prince eventually acceded to popular sentiment, and advised by the Brazilian José BONIFÁCIO, on Sept. 7, 1822, on the banks of the little Ipiranga River, uttered the fateful cry of independence. He became PEDRO I, emperor of Brazil. Pedro's rule, however, gradually kindled increasing discontent in Brazil, and in 1831 he had to abdicate in favor of his son, PEDRO II. The reign of this popular emperor saw the foundation of modern Brazil. Ambitions directed toward the south were responsible for involving the country in the war (1851–52) against the Argentine dictator, Juan Manuel de Rosas, and again in the War of the Triple Alliance (1865–70) against Paraguay. Brazil drew little benefit from either; far more important were the beginnings of the large-scale European immigration that was to make SE Brazil the economic heart of the nation. Railroads and roads were constructed, and today the region has an excellent transportation system. The plantation culture of the Northeast was already crumbling by the 1870s, and the growth of the movement to abolish slavery, spurred by such men as Antônio de CASTRO ALVES and Joaquim NABUCO, threatened it even more. The slave trade had been abolished in 1850, and a law for gradual emancipation was passed in 1871. In 1888 while Pedro II was in Europe and his daughter ISABEL was governing Brazil, slavery was completely abolished. The planters thereupon withdrew their support of the empire, enabling republican forces, aided by a military at odds with the emperor, to triumph. By a bloodless revolution in 1889 the republic was established with Manuel Deodoro da FONSECA as first president. The rivalry of the states and the power of the army in government, especially under Fonseca's unpopular successor, Floriando PEIXOTO, caused the political situation to remain uneasy. The expanding market for Brazilian coffee and more particularly the wild-rubber boom brought considerable wealth as the 19th cent. ended, but the creation of rubber plantations in the Far East brought the wild-rubber boom to a halt and hurt the economy of the Amazon region after 1912. Brazil sided with the Allies in World War I, declaring war in Oct., 1917, and shared in the peace settlement, but later (1926) it withdrew from the League of Nations. Measures to reverse the country's growing economic dependence on coffee were taken by Getúlio VARGAS, who came into power through a revolution in 1930. By changing the constitution (notably in 1937) and establishing a type of corporative state he centralized government (the *Estada Novo*—new state) and began the forced development of basic industries and diversification of agriculture. His dictatorial rule, although it aroused much opposition, reflected a new consciousness of nationality. The Brazilian spirit, which had been unconsciously represented in folk art and folk music, now was consciously expressed, particularly in the paintings of Cândido PORTINARI and the music of Heitor VILLA-LOBOS. World War II brought a new boom (chiefly in rubber and minerals) to Brazil, which joined the Allies on Aug. 22, 1942, and under foreign minister Oswaldo Aranha took a large part in inter-American affairs. In 1945 the army forced Vargas to resign, and Gen. Eurico Gaspar Dutra was elected president. Brazil's economic growth was plagued by inflation, and this issue enabled Vargas to be elected in 1950. His second administration was marred by economic problems and corruption, and in 1954 he resigned and committed suicide. He was succeeded by João Café Filho. Juscelino KUBITSCHEK was elected president in 1955. Under Kubitschek the building of Brasília and an ambitious program of highway and dam construction were undertaken. The inflation problem persisted. In 1960 Jânio QUADROS was elected by the greatest popular margin in Brazilian history. But his autocratic manner and reform program aroused great opposition, and he resigned within seven months. Vice President João GOULART was the legal successor. Military leaders and conservatives opposed to him forced constitutional changes creating a parliamentary government and weakening the presidency (1961). In 1963, however, full presidential powers were restored by plebiscite. Weakened by political strife and seemingly insurmountable economic chaos, the leftist administration of Goulart demanded radical constitutional changes. In 1964 a military insurrection deposed Goulart. Congress elected General CASTELO BRANCO to fill out his term. Goulart's supporters and other leftists were removed from power and influence throughout Brazil, and the president was given far-reaching powers. In 1965, after anti-military forces won elections in two states, the president's extraordinary powers were extended, and all political parties were dissolved. A new constitution was adopted in 1967. Marshall COSTA E SILVA succeeded Castelo Branco in March. In 1968, in the face of student protests and criticism from the church against the military regime, Costa e Silva recessed Congress and assumed one-man rule. In 1969 Gen. Emílio GARRASTAZÚ MÉDICI succeeded Costa e Silva. Terrorism of the right and left (several diplomats were captured by leftist guerrillas) became a feature of Brazilian life but abated somewhat in the mid-1970s. Gen. Ernesto Geisel succeeded Garrastazú Médici as president in March, 1974. See Gilberto Freyre, *The Mansions and the Shanties* (tr. 1963) and *Order and Progress; Brazil from Monarchy to Republic* (tr. 1970); C. H. Haring, *Empire in Brazil* (1958, repr. 1968); R. M. Levine, *The Vargas Regime* (1970); R. M. Schneider, *The Political System of Brazil* (1971); Fernando de Azevedo, *Brazilian Culture* (tr. 1950, repr. 1971); E. B. Burns, *A History of Brazil* (1971); Charles Wagley, *An Introduction to Brazil* (rev. ed. 1971); T. E. Weil and others, *Area Handbook for Brazil* (1971); T. L. Smith, *Brazil: People and Institutions* (4th ed. 1972) and with Alexander Marchant, ed., *Brazil, Portrait of Half a Continent* (1951, repr. 1972); Philip Raine, *Brazil, Awakening Giant* (1974).

Brazilian literature. Soon after the discovery of Brazil, the Portuguese began to describe the wonders of the new land. Brazilian literature began with the letter of Pedro Vaz de Caminha announcing the discovery to the king of Portugal. That descriptive trend was continued in the 16th and 17th cent. in the works of the missionaries. José de ANCHIETA wrote in Portuguese about Brazil and is considered the first Brazilian writer. The dualism of European tradition and New World feeling continued. Many consider the 17th-century Jesuit priest Antônio VIEIRA (brought to Brazil as a child) the true master of the Portuguese prose in the classic style. In the late 17th cent. the first native Brazilian writer of note, Gregório de Matos Guerra, wrote poetry satirizing the society of his time. During the 18th cent. poetic "academies" sprang up in various parts of Brazil. The most famous was in Minas Gerais; it included José Basílio da Gama, author of the epic poem *Uruguai*, and Tomás Antônio Gonzaga, best known for his pastoral love poem *Marília de Dirceu* (1792). This group had helped introduce revolutionary ideas from France into Brazil. Independence from Portugal in 1822 fostered national feeling and ushered in the romantic era, which is generally dated from the appearance in 1836 of volumes of poetry by Domingos José Gonçalves de Magalhães, visconde de Araguaia, and by Manuel de Araújo Pôrto-Alegre. The two major Brazilian romantic poets were Antônio GONÇALVES DIAS, who glorified the Indian and the native soil, and Antônio de CASTRO ALVES, a leader in the fight for the abolition of slavery. His social awareness introduced a new dimension into the nascent "Brazilianism." A more introspective mood was created by Álvares de Azevedo. The romantic era also witnessed the birth of the novel in Brazil, notably *O Guarani* (1857) by José de ALENCAR and the later *Iracema.* A realist note was sounded by Alfredo d'Escragnolle Taunay in his novel *Inocência* (1872) and in *Memórias de um sargento de milícias* (2 vol., 1854–55) by Manuel Antônio de Almeida. The works of the man generally considered the greatest of Brazilian writers, Joaquim Maria MACHADO DE ASSIS, were in the same realist vein. His novels and short stories are noted for their psychological depth and classic purity of style. Contemporary with Machado de Assis were the Parnassian poets, headed by Olavo Bilac, but theirs was an isolated trend. Seven years before the appearance of Bilac's *Poesias,* Aluízio de Azevedo had published *O Mulato* (1881), a novel that dealt in naturalistic fashion with the Brazilian scene and characters. In 1902, Euclides da CUNHA wrote his masterly description of an uprising in the Brazilian northeast, *Os sertões* (tr. *Rebellion in the Backlands,* 1944). Concern with the native soil and with social problems was henceforth to predominate in Brazilian literature. *Canaan,* a pessimistic novel of ideas by José Pereira da Graça Aranha, appeared in the same year, and the stories of José Bento Monteiro Lobato also became popular. Even the Paris-born "art for art's sake" movement, called modernism, had a strong nativist and sociological bias. It began in Brazil as a poetic movement led by Mário de Andrade (whose prose work, *Macunaíma,* made pioneer use of the vernacular in 1928), and it was soon joined by other poets of stature, including Manuel Bandeira. The naturalistic novel came into its own in the 1930s with the works of Graciliano Ramos, José LINS DO RÊGO, and Jorge AMADO. Their concern with the Brazilian northeast has been continued by writers such as João Guimarães Rosa, whose poetic novel *Grande sertão: veredas* appeared in 1958. The chief trend of the 20th cent., inspired by the writings of the great jurist Ruy BARBOSA at the turn of the century and by the sociological works of Gilberto FREYRE (begun in the 1930s), is toward critical and scholarly works. At the same time, the more subjective trend continues with, among others, novelists Rachel de Queiroz, José Americo de Almeida, and Érico Lopes VERÍSSIMO, poets Jorge de Lima, Guilherme de Almeida, Vinícius de Morais, Augusto Frederico Schmidt, and Cecília Meireles, dramatists Nelson Rodrigues and Ariano Suassuna, and short-story writer Clarice Lispector. See Samuel Putnam, *Marvelous Journey* (1948); D. S. Loos, *The Naturalistic Novel of Brazil* (1963); Alfrânio Coutinho, *An Introduction to Literature in Brazil* (tr. 1969); Elizabeth Bishop, ed., *An Anthology of Twentieth-Century Brazilian Poetry* (1972).

Brazil nut, common name for the Lecythidaceae, a family of tropical trees. It includes the anchovy pear (*Grias cauliflora*), a West Indian species with edible fruit used for pickles, and several lumber trees of South America, e.g., the cannon-ball tree, some species of *Barringtonia,* and the Brazil nut trees (genus *Bertholletia*). The latter are found chiefly in Brazil along the Amazon and Orinoco rivers. The edible Brazil nuts grow clumped together in large, round, woody and extremely hard seed pods the size of a large apple. The meat of the seed (the "nut") is very rich in oil. The Brazil nut family is classified in the division MAGNOLIOPHYTA, class Magnoliopsida, order Lecythidales.

brazilwood, common name for several trees of the family Leguminosae (PULSE family) whose wood yields a red dye. The dye has largely been replaced by synthetic dyes for fabrics, but it is still used in high-quality red inks. The bright red wood, which takes a high polish, is used in cabinetwork and for making violin bows. The East Indian redwood, or sapanwood (*Caesalpinia sappan*), was called "bresel wood" when it was first imported to Europe in the Middle Ages; Portuguese explorers used this name for a similar South American tree (*C. brasiliensis*), from which the name Brazil for its native country purportedly derives. Brazilwoods are classified in the division MAGNOLIOPHYTA, class Magnoliopsida, order Rosales, family Leguminosae.

brazing, method of joining metal parts. The parts are cleaned and then heated above the melting point of the brazing metal, which is then applied; on cooling, it solidifies and serves to bond the parts together. Brazing metal is generally harder and has a higher melting point than common SOLDER.

Brazos (brăz'əs), river, 870 mi (1,410 km) long (1,210 mi/1,947 km long with its main tributary), rising in E N. Mex. From its source it flows SE across Texas to enter the Gulf of Mexico at Freeport. The Brazos flows through the fertile farming area of N Texas, where it is used for irrigation. The river supplies water to nearby cities; several dams provide flood control and hydroelectric power. The river is navigable upstream.

Brazza, Pierre Paul François Camille Savorgnan de (pyĕr pōl fräNswä' kämē'yə sävôrnyäN' də bräzä'), 1852–1905, Franco-Italian empire builder. He was born Pietro Paolo Savorgnan di Brazza but adopted the French form of his name in 1874, when he became a French citizen. After visiting (1874) Gabon he returned (1875) on the orders of the French government to explore West Africa. In 1879, in an attempt to forestall the efforts of Henry M. Stanley to annex the Congo basin for Belgium, Brazza explored the upper Congo. He founded (1880) Franceville (now in Gabon) and Brazzaville (now in the Congo Republic) and established a protectorate over the kingdom of Makoko. Although he failed to deter Stanley, he added c.193,000 sq mi (499,900 sq km) to the French empire in central Africa. He served as a French colonial official from 1883 and was commissioner general of the French Congo (1886–98). See Richard West, *Brazza of the Congo* (1972).

Brazza: see BRAČ, Yugoslavia.

Brazzaville (brăz'əvĭl, Fr. bräzävēl'), city (1972 est. pop. 184,000), capital of the People's Republic of the Congo, on Stanley (Malebo) Pool of the Congo River. It is the nation's largest city and its administrative, communications, and economic center. The chief industries are beverage processing, tanning, and the manufacture of construction materials, matches, and textiles. There are also machine shops. An important port on the Congo River, Brazzaville receives wood, rubber, agricultural products, and other items and sends them by railroad to POINTE NOIRE, a port on the Atlantic Ocean. Motorboats connect Brazzaville with KINSHASA, Zaïre, across Stanley Pool. The city was founded in 1880 by Savorgnan de BRAZZA, the French explorer. It was the capital of FRENCH EQUATORIAL AFRICA from 1910 to 1958 and was the center of Free French forces in Africa during World War II. The city's main growth began after 1945. It houses a Center for Higher Studies (1961), a teachers college, and an art school. At a conference in Brazzaville in 1944, African leaders from French West and Equatorial Africa for the first time publicly called for reforms in French colonial rule, thus starting the colonies on the road to independence. In late 1960 leaders of newly independent French-speaking African nations met in the city; the "Brazzaville group" of states, which adopted a moderate political stance on most African and international issues of the time, took its name from this meeting.

Brea (brā'ə), city (1970 pop. 18,447), Orange co., S Calif.; inc. 1917. It is an industrial, commercial, and residential community in an oil and citrus-fruit area. Most industries are related to the production and processing of oil. Other manufactures include rubber products, tools, and chemicals. The city developed during an oil boom in the early 1900s. Points of interest include the campsite of the Spanish explorer Don Gaspar de Portolá, the first European to visit the area.

Breadalbane, John Campbell, 1st **earl of** (brədôl'bĭn, brĕd-), 1635?–1717, Scottish nobleman. He took part in the royalist rising of 1654 and helped George Monck to further the restoration (1660) of Charles II. In 1688 he privately supported James II, but he did not commit himself openly and took advantage of the Act of Indemnity to swear allegiance to William III (1689). His strong position among the highland clans made him a useful intermediary in negotiating the submission of the chiefs in 1691. He has been blamed for instigating the massacre of the MacDonalds of Glencoe (1692), allegedly using their failure to submit on time as a pretext for settling old scores with that clan. However, there is no evidence that he was personally involved in that episode. He took no active part in negotiating the Act of Union (1707), but he was a representative peer in the united Parliament (1713–15). He gave nominal support only to the Jacobite rebellion of 1715.

Breadalbane (brĕdôl'bĭn), mountainous district, Perthshire, central Scotland. The district, picturesque and little cultivated, is the site of Breadalbane power scheme (118,000-kw capacity).

breadfruit: see MULBERRY.

breadroot or **Indian breadroot,** perennial plant (*Psoralea esculenta*) of the family Leguminosae (PULSE family), native to the American prairies and valued by the Indians for the starchy tuberous root that was much used for food, eaten raw or roasted or dried for winter use. The breadroot has bluish pealike blossoms and in general resembles the lupine. The plant was the prairie turnip or *pomme de prairie* of Western pioneers. Other species of *Psoralea* have also supplied food. Breadroot is classified in the division MAGNOLIOPHYTA, class Magnoliopsida, order Rosales, family Leguminosae.

breaker: see WAVE, in oceanography.

Breakspear, Nicholas: see ADRIAN IV.

breakwater, offshore structure to protect a harbor from waves. When it also serves as a pier, it is called a quay; when covered by a roadway it is called a mole. In the United States a breakwater commonly consists of a long mound of stone rubble. The flow of waves up its slope and the formation of swirls by its rough surface dissipate wave energy. In Europe the typical breakwater is a vertical wall, usually of concrete, built on a rock base; it reflects the waves without dissipating their energy. A pneumatic breakwater consists of perforated pipes discharging air bubbles. A similar hydraulic breakwater has underwater pipes that direct streams of water against approaching waves. Under the right conditions both types cause waves to break. The Chesapeake breakwater was the first built in the United States. See COAST PROTECTION.

Bréal, Michel Jules Alfred (mĕshĕl' zhül älfrĕd' brāäl'), 1832–1915, French philologist. He is best known for his *Essai de semantique* (1897), which gave great impetus to scientific interest in the field of semantics.

Bream, Julian (Alexander), 1933–, English guitarist and lutenist. Bream was first taught guitar by his father and studied piano and cello at the Royal College of Music. He made his debut at the age of 12. An outstanding performer, Bream has a repertory ranging from Dowland to Henze. Many compositions have been written for him.

bream: see SUNFISH.

breast: see MAMMARY GLAND.

Breasted, James Henry (brĕs'tĭd), 1865–1935, American Egyptologist, b. Rockford, Ill., grad. North Central College, 1888, M.A. Yale, 1891, Ph.D. Univ. of Berlin, 1894. He began teaching at the Univ. of Chicago in 1894 and was (1905–33) professor of Egyptology and Oriental history there. Breasted was also director of the Haskell Oriental Museum (1895–1901) and after 1919 director of the Oriental Institute of the Univ. of Chicago. He made archaeological discoveries of great importance in Egypt and directed researches in Mesopotamia. Besides many reports and monographs, he wrote some general works, including *The Development of Religion and Thought in Ancient Egypt* (1912) and *The Dawn of Conscience* (1933). Two of his textbooks were *History of Egypt from the Earliest Times to the Persian Conquest* (rev. ed. 1928) and *Ancient Times* (rev. ed. 1944). Breasted translated and edited Egyptian historical sources in *Ancient Records of Egypt* (5 vol., 1906–27). His son, Charles Breasted, wrote a memoir of him, *Pioneer to the Past* (1943).

breathing: see RESPIRATION.

Brébeuf, Jean de (zhäN də brāböf'), 1593–1649, French Roman Catholic missionary, one of the Jesuit Martyrs of North America. A Norman, he was sent (1625) to Quebec and did missionary work among the Huron Indians. The warfare of the Huron and Iroquois caused the abandonment of his mission in 1628, and in 1629 on the surrender of Quebec to the English he went back to France. In 1633 he returned to Canada and carried on his work among the Indians, enduring great hardships. In 1649 the Iroquois took the Huron village and the mission. Father Brébeuf and his colleague, Gabriel LALEMANT, were tortured to death. He was canonized in 1930. Feast: Sept. 26 or (among the Jesuits) March 16. See his

Travels and Sufferings of Father Jean de Brébeuf among the Hurons of Canada, ed. by Théodore Besterman (tr. 1938); biography by F. X. Talbot (1949).

breccia: see CONGLOMERATE.

Brèche de Roland (brĕsh də rôlăN'), narrow gorge (alt. 9,200 ft/2,804 m), Hautes-Pyrénées dept., SW France, in the Pyrenees. It leads into the Cirque de Gavarnie, a natural amphitheater. According to legend Roland, one of Charlemagne's knights, created the breach with his sword.

Brecht, Bertolt (originally Berthold) (both: bĕr'tôlt brĕkht), 1898–1956, German dramatist and poet. His brilliant wit, his outspoken Marxism, and his revolutionary experiments in the theater have made Brecht a vital and controversial force in modern drama. His early plays were realistic; in them the downtrodden struggled for survival in a disorganized world, and violence and disaster were recurrent. In the later 1920s Brecht turned to expressionism, as in *Mann ist Mann* [man is man] (1926), and began to develop his so-called epic theater, in which narrative, montage, self-contained scenes, and rational argument were used to create a shock of realization in the spectator. Sets and lighting were designed to prevent the illusion of the theater from gaining sway, and Brecht revealed elements of the staging process itself. Songs played an important part—for these Brecht wrote the lyrics for music by Hindemith, Kurt Weill, Hanns Eisler, and others. *Die Dreigroschenoper* [the threepenny opera] (1928), with music by Kurt Weill, is based on John Gay's *Beggar's Opera*; it reveals Brecht's continued hostility toward the capitalist social structure as well as his bittersweet compassion for humanity. Under National Socialism Brecht went into exile (1933), settling in Denmark and later in the United States. Works written in his most mature phase include *Mutter Courage und ihre Kinder* [Mother Courage and her children] (1941) and *Der gute Mensch von Sezuan* (tr. *The Good Woman of Setzuan,* 1943), both concerned with ethical conduct. An outstanding example of epic theater is *Der Kaukasische Kreidekreis* [the Caucasian chalk circle] (1955). From 1948, Brecht lived in East Berlin, where he directed the state-supported Berliner Ensemble. Notable English translations of Brecht's plays are those by Eric Bentley, which include *Seven Plays by Bertolt Brecht* (1961). See his collected plays ed. by Ralph Manheim and John Willett (tr. 1970); biographies by F. Ewen (1967) and M. Esslin (rev. ed. 1971); studies by J. Willett (rev. ed. 1968), W. Haas (tr. 1970), and John Fuegi (1972).

Breck, James Lloyd, 1818–76, American Episcopal clergyman and missionary, b. Philadelphia. In 1841 he established a seminary at Nashotah, Wis., with which he was connected until 1850, when he turned to missionary work among the Ojibwa Indians in Minnesota. In 1858, with Bishop Henry B. Whipple, he founded at Faribault, Minn., the Seabury Divinity School and church schools for boys and girls. See T. I. Holcombe, *An Apostle of the Wilderness* (1903).

Breckinridge, John, 1760–1806, American statesman, b. Augusta co., Va; grandfather of John Cabell Breckinridge. After he was admitted (1785) to the bar, he practiced law in Charlottesville, Va. Elected (1792) to the U.S. Congress, he soon resigned and moved to Lexington, Ky. He was (1795–97) attorney general of the new state, and as a member (1798–1801) of the state legislature he secured (1798) the enactment of the Kentucky Resolutions (see KENTUCKY AND VIRGINIA RESOLUTIONS). Breckinridge also prepared the stronger resolutions passed in the Kentucky legislature the next year in answer to criticisms of the earlier resolutions. In the U.S. Senate (1801–5) he was a leading spokesman of Western interests and played an important role in the passage of legislation bringing about the Louisiana Purchase. He was appointed U.S. Attorney General by President Jefferson in 1805 and died in office.

Breckinridge, John Cabell, 1821–75, Vice President of the United States (1857–61) and Confederate general, b. Lexington, Ky. A lawyer, Breckinridge served in the Kentucky legislature (1849–51) and in the House of Representatives (1851–55). He was chosen by the Democrats in 1856 as a Southern running mate for Buchanan. As Vice President in a difficult period he distinguished himself by dignified and impartial presiding over the Senate. When a division within the Democratic ranks occurred in 1860, he became the presidential candidate of the Southern faction. Breckinridge claimed that no power existed in the Federal or local government to restrict slavery in any area while it was in territorial status. Believing in secession as a right, he nevertheless disapproved of such a course at that time. He received 72 electoral votes in the November election. During the remainder of his term as Vice President, he attempted to secure the adoption of some compromise. As Senator (elected 1859) in the special session that began in July, 1861, he consistently opposed the administration's war measures. He failed in efforts to have Kentucky call a convention to act on secession. When the state declared for the Union in Sept., 1861, Breckinridge offered his services to the Confederacy. Appointed brigadier general in Oct., 1861, he served with distinction throughout the war, mostly in the West. On Feb. 4, 1865, he was made secretary of war for the Confederacy. When the South surrendered, Breckinridge fled to Europe via Cuba but was permitted to return (1869) by an amnesty proclamation issued in 1868. See biography by Lucille Stillwell (1936).

Breckinridge, Sophonisba Preston, 1866–1948, American pioneer social worker, educator, and author, b. Lexington, Ky., grad. Wellesley, 1888, Ph.D. Univ. of Chicago, 1901. She was the first woman to be admitted (1897) to the bar in Kentucky, but abandoned the practice of law to enter social work at Hull House, Chicago. After 1902 she taught at the Univ. of Chicago, where later she was professor of social economy (1925–29) and then professor of public welfare (1929–33). In 1934 she was president of the American Association of Schools of Social Work. As a delegate to the Pan-American Conference at Montevideo, Uruguay, in 1933, she was the first woman to represent the United States at an international conference. Her published works include *The Delinquent Child and the Home* (with Edith Abbott, 1912), *Family Welfare in a Metropolitan Community* (1924), *Public Welfare Administration in a Metropolitan Community* (1927), and *Women in the Twentieth Century* (1933).

Brecknock (brĕk'nŏk, -nək) or **Brecon** (brĕk'ən), municipal borough (1971 pop. 6,283), county town of Breconshire, S Wales, at the junction of the Honddu and Usk rivers. It is a market for the surrounding agricultural and cattle-raising area. Brecknock was founded by the Normans c.1091. In the town are fragments of an 11th-century castle; Christ College, founded by Henry VIII in 1542; and the 11th-century priory church of St. John, which became a cathedral in 1923. In 1974, Brecknock became part of the new nonmetropolitan county of Powys.

Brecknockshire, Wales: see BRECONSHIRE.

Brecon: see BRECONSHIRE; BRECKNOK.

Breconshire (brĕk'ənshĭr), or **Brecon,** county (1971 pop. 53,234), S Wales. The region is mountainous, rising to its greatest height in the Brecon Beacons (2,907 ft/886 m). In the Usk and Wye river valleys sheep (for mutton and wool) and beef cattle are grazed. Oats, barley, and wheat are Breconshire's major crops. Forestry is also important. Some coal is mined in the south, and limestone is quarried. Brecon Beacons National Park, in the southern part of the county, consists of 519 sq mi (1,344 sq km) of scenic land. Breconshire, in a region that may have been inhabited during the Stone and Bronze ages, gets its name from Brychan, a native prince who ruled after the Romans left c.400 A.D. The county was seized from the Welsh princes by the Normans in 1092. In 1974, Breconshire became part of the new nonmetropolitan counties of Gwent, Mid Glamorgan, and Powys.

Breda (brădä'), city (1971 pop. 122,068), North Brabant prov., S Netherlands, at the confluence of the Mark and Aa rivers. It is an industrial and transportation center; its manufactures include machinery, textiles, and canned foods. Breda was founded by the 11th cent. The city was successfully besieged (1624–25) by the Spaniards under Ambrogio Spinola; the surrender of its heroic garrison is the subject of a famous painting by Velázquez. Points of interest in the city include a 13th-century Gothic church (Groote Kerk) and a castle (now a military academy).

Breda, Compromise of, 1566: see GUEUX.

Breda, Declaration of, 1660: see RESTORATION, in English history.

Breda, Treaty of, 1667: see DUTCH WARS.

Bredero, Gerbrand Adriaenszoon (hĕr'bränt ädrēän'zōn brā'dĕrō), 1585–1618, Dutch dramatist and poet. He is considered the major Dutch poet of his generation, particularly for his spontaneous love sonnets. The first Dutch master of comedy, Bredero was an important innovator; he drew upon classical elements as well as Renaissance models. His masterpiece, *De Spaansche Brabander* [the Spaniard from Brabant] (1617), is a realistic comedy of Amsterdam life and reveals the influence of Spanish romanticism. Bredero's work was collected in three volumes in 1890.

breeder reactor: see NUCLEAR REACTOR.

breeding of plants and animals refers to the purposeful selection of certain parent organisms for propagation in order to improve the breed, variety, or strain. Selective breeding has been carried on by man to some extent since the domestication of plants and animals in the Neolithic period. In early Chinese civilizations rice crops were improved by selection, and in the early Indian civilizations of North and South America corn was thus improved. Cattle, horses, dogs, and other useful animals were long bred by selection. Breeding began to be established on a more scientific basis after the rediscovery of the laws of inheritance of Gregor Mendel. Among plants, pure lines are established by self-pollinating a plant and planting the seed it produces. The choice plants are then self-pollinated, and the process is repeated through a number of generations until a strain is developed that shows little variation. In recent years it has been found that by making crosses between such established pure lines, pure-line hybrids can be developed that have greater vigor than the pure lines and still retain uniformity of characteristics. In the United States much of the corn is produced from pure-line hybrid seed. Animals are said to be pure bred if in the breeding strain desirable characteristics are transmitted through generations with a uniformity approaching that shown by pure-line plants. The strains result from a series of crosses that involve considerable inbreeding. To prevent loss of vigor and reproductivity it is necessary to avoid too many crosses between very closely related animals. Crosses are therefore made between strains within a breed and sometimes between certain breeds. New breeds and varieties of established breeds are developed chiefly by hybridization and by breeding individuals in which mutations occur by chance. ARTIFICIAL INSEMINATION also plays an important role in the breeding of livestock. See GENETICS; HEREDITY; HYBRID.

Breed's Hill: see BUNKER HILL, BATTLE OF.

Bregenz (brā'gĕnts), city (1971 pop. 22,800), capital of Vorarlberg province, extreme W Austria, on the Lake of Constance (Bodensee). It is a lake port and a winter sports center and has industries that manufacture cotton and silk textiles, food products, and machinery. There is a large hydroelectric plant. Located on a site settled in the Bronze Age, Bregenz was chartered c.1200 and in 1726 became the administrative center of Vorarlberg. Nearby is the Bregenz Forest, a densely wooded highland noted for its scenic beauty.

Breiđafjörđur (brā'thäfyör"thür), large inlet of the Denmark Strait, c.75 mi (120 km) long and 45 mi (70 km) wide, W Iceland, between the Vestfjarđa and Snaefellsnes peninsulas. Hvammsfjörđur and Gilsfjörđur are eastern arms.

Breisach (brī'zäkh), town (1970 est. pop. 5,000), Baden-Württemberg, SW West Germany, on the Rhine River. Its manufactures include wine and paper. An old town, it has long been coveted because of its strategic location. It was fortified by the Romans, who called it *Mons Brisiacus*. It became an imperial town in 1275. BERNHARD OF SAXE-WEIMAR took the town in 1638. Louis XIV secured it for France in the Peace of Westphalia (1648) and ceded it back to the emperor in the Treaty of Ryswick (1697), but built a new fort, Neuf-Brisach (Ger. *Neu Breisach*), on the opposite side of the Rhine. The French repeatedly captured Breisach during the 18th cent. but gave it to Baden in 1805.

Breisgau (brīs'gou), region, Baden-Württemburg, SW West Germany, including the Rhine plain and the western slopes of the Black Forest. Freiburg is the chief city. Fruit and wine are the main products. After the extinction (1218) of the first house of ZÄHRINGEN, it was divided among various heirs. Most of it passed to the Hapsburgs in 1368. France held the region at various times in the 17th–18th cent. In 1805 the Breisgau was divided between Baden and Württemburg; the latter gave its share to Baden in 1810.

Breitenfeld (brī'tənfĕlt"), village, Leipzig dist., S central East Germany. It gave its name to two battles of the Thirty Years War. Gustavus Adolphus of Sweden there defeated the imperial forces under Count Johannes Tilly and Marshal Gottfried Pappenheim in 1631, and the Swedes under General Lennart Torstensson there routed the imperial troops under Archduke Leopold William in 1642.

Bremen (brā'mən), city (1970 pop. 582,277), capital of the state of Bremen, N West Germany, on the Weser River. Known as the Free Hanse City of Bremen (Ger. *Freie Hansestadt Bremen*), it is West Germany's largest port after Hamburg and is a commercial and industrial center trading in cotton, wool, tobacco, and copper. Manufactures include ships, steel, machinery, electrical equipment, textiles, beer, and foodstuffs, including roasted coffee. Bremen is Germany's oldest port city. It was made an archbishopric in 845, and under Archbishop Adalbert (1043–72) it included all of Scandinavia, Iceland, and Greenland. The archbishops held temporal sway over a large area between the Weser and Elber rivers, but the city of Bremen itself remained virtually independent as its importance grew. In 1358 it became one of the leading members of the HANSEATIC LEAGUE. It accepted the Reformation in 1522, and in 1646 it was made a free imperial city. It stubbornly fought to preserve this status after the archbishopric had been assigned to Sweden by the Peace of Westphalia and later was ceded (1719) by Sweden to the elector of Hanover (George I of England). Bremen was occupied by France from 1810 to 1813. The city's overseas trade—from the late 18th cent. particularly with the United States—grew in the 19th cent., partly because of the founding (1827) of nearby Bremerhaven and the establishment (1857) of Norddeutscher Lloyd (North German Lloyd), a large shipping company. The city joined the German Empire in 1871. After World War I there was a short-lived (1918–19) socialist republic of Bremen. The city was badly damaged by bombs during World War II, but numerous historic monuments remain, including the Gothic city hall (1405–9); the statue of Roland, the medieval hero, which was erected in 1404 as a symbol of the city's freedom; the cathedral (begun 1043), a blend of Romanesque and Gothic styles; and two noted churches—the Liebfrauenkirche (13th cent.) and the Johanneskirche (14th cent.). The city has a major art museum and a museum of overseas ethnology. The state of **Bremen** (1970 pop. 723,000), 156 sq mi (404 sq km), was formed in 1947 by combining Bremen and Bremerhaven.

Bremer, Fredrika (frĕdrē'kə brā'mər), 1801–65, Swedish writer and feminist, b. Finland. Her novels of everyday life include *The H Family* (1829), *The President's Daughters* (1834), and *The Home* (1839). She recorded impressions of travel in America (1849–51) in *Homes in the New World* (1853); letters from this book were translated as *America of the Fifties* (1924). Her later novels advocate the emancipation of woman. See study by S. A. Rooth (1955).

Bremerhaven (brā'mərhä"fən), city (1970 pop. 140,455), in the state of Bremen, N West Germany, at the mouth of the Weser River, near the North Sea. It is one of the largest fishing ports in Europe and is a major passenger and freight port. Founded in 1827, Bremerhaven in 1939 was absorbed by Wesermünde, which had been formed in 1924 as the result of the merger of the cities of Geestemünde and Lehe. In 1947 the combined municipality was renamed Bremerhaven and returned to the state of Bremen. The first regular ship service between continental Europe and the United States was started in Bremerhaven in 1847.

Bremersdorp, Swaziland: see MANZINI.

Bremerton (brĕm'ərtən), city (1970 pop. 35,307), Kitsap co., NW Wash., an excellent harbor on an arm of Puget Sound; inc. 1901. The city was platted (1891) when the area was selected as the site for the U.S. Puget Sound Naval Shipyard, and today Bremerton's economy is centered around that great installation. All types of U.S. naval vessels (including Polaris submarines) are built and repaired in the six drydocks there. Auxiliary facilities include a naval torpedo station and a naval ammunition depot. Although the great majority of residents are employed by the U.S. government, there are some logging and wood-product enterprises, and tourism is important. Bremerton is the gateway to the Olympic peninsula, with easy access to the Cascade and Olympic mts. It is surrounded on three sides by water, and numerous ferries ply the inland seas of Puget Sound, linking the city to nearby resort islands. The U.S.S. *Missouri*, docked there, is a national shrine; it was the scene of the official Japanese surrender at the end of World War II. Bremerton has a junior college. Three state parks are nearby.

bremsstrahlung (brĕm'shträ"ləng): see X RAY.

Brendan, Saint, d. 577?, Irish abbot of Clonfert, Co. Galway. A popular medieval story told how he traveled westward to wonderful islands—an Irish version of a widespread legend. His feast is May 16. A perhaps different St. Brendan (d. 573) was a friend of Columba and founder of the monastery at Birr. The name is often written Brandon.

Brennan, William Joseph, Jr., 1906–, Associate Justice of the U.S. Supreme Court (1956–), b. Newark, N.J. After receiving his law degree from Harvard, he was admitted (1931) to the bar and practiced law in Newark. During World War II he did legal work in the U.S. army. In New Jersey after the war he served as a superior court judge (1949–50), appellate division judge (1950–52), and justice of the state supreme court (1952–56). President Eisenhower appointed him to succeed Sherman Minton on the Supreme Court. A liberal on the bench, he supported individual liberties and a greater guarantee of justice to the poor.

Brenner Pass (brĕ'nər), Ital. *Brennero,* Alpine pass, 4,495 ft (1,370 m) high, connecting Innsbruck, Austria, with Bolzano, Italy. The lowest of the principal Alpine passes, it was an important Roman route through which many invasions of Italy were made. A long carriage road was built c.1772, and the railroad was completed in 1867. The pass became the border between Italy and Austria after World War I. During World War II, Hitler and Mussolini held meetings there.

Brennus, fl. c.389 B.C., legendary Gallic leader. He occupied Rome but failed to take the Capitol from MANLIUS (Marcus Manlius Capitolinus). According to legend, when the tribute that the Romans had agreed to pay was being weighed, a Roman complained, whereupon Brennus threw his sword on the scale, crying,"Vae victis!" [woe to the vanquished]. His historical existence is dubious.

Brennus, d. 279 B.C., Gallic leader. He was in command of the band of Gauls (or Galatians) who invaded Greece in 279 B.C. At first halted at Thermopylae, he later turned and took the pass into Doris. He was wounded in an unsuccessful attack on Delphi and is supposed to have committed suicide on the northward retreat after the Gauls were attacked by the Thessalians.

Brent, Margaret, 1600?–1671?, early American feminist, b. Gloucester, England. With her two brothers and a sister, she left England to settle (1638) in St. Marys City, Md., where she acquired an extensive estate; she was the first woman in Maryland to hold land in her own right. Under the will of Gov. Leonard Calvert, Margaret Brent was made executor of his estates. She also acted as attorney (i.e., agent) for Lord Baltimore. As an important woman of affairs in the colony, she demanded (1648) a place in the colonial assembly. Her claim was refused while the heirs contested her handling of the Calvert estates. Shortly thereafter she moved to Virginia but kept her Maryland property. See M. E. W. Ramey, *Chronicles of Mistress Margaret Brent* (1915); E. A. Dexter, *Colonial Women of Affairs* (1924, repr. 1972).

Brent, borough (1971 pop. 278,541) of Greater London, SE England. Brent was created in 1965 by the merger of the municipal boroughs of Wembly and Willesden. The area is a rail and industrial center. Its manufactures include automobile parts, clocks and watches, and electrical equipment. At Wembly is a large sports stadium that was originally built for the British Empire Exposition of 1924–25.

Brentano, Clemens (brĕntä'nō), 1778–1842, German poet of the romantic school; brother of Bettina von Arnim. While studying at Halle and Jena he met Wieland, Herder, and Goethe, but his sympathies were with the younger German romantics. With Achim von Arnim he collaborated on *Des Knaben Wunderhorn* [the boy's magic horn] (1806–8), a folk-song collection that influenced Eichendorff, Heine, and the brothers Grimm. Brentano wrote plays, lyric poems, fairy tales, and such *Novellen* as *Geschichte vom braven Kasperl und dem schönen Annerl* (1817, tr. *Honor,* 1847). See study by J. F. Fetzer (1974).

Brentano, Franz (frānts), 1838–1917, German philosopher and psychologist. He was a teacher (1866–73) at Würzburg, and in 1874 he became professor of philosophy at Vienna. In 1880 he retired to write and study. His best-known book, *Psychologie vom empirischen Standpunkte* (1874), attempts to establish psychology as an independent science. Brentano believed that mental processes were the data of psychology and were to be regarded as acts rather than as passive processes. He influenced Edmund HUSSERL and Alexius MEINONG. See studies by Gustav Bergmann (1967) and A. C. Rancurello (1968).

Brentwood, urban district (1971 pop. 57,976), Essex, SE England. It is mainly residential but produces some agricultural equipment, film, and prefabricated concrete. Brentwood was on an important coach road from London to Colchester; the 15th-century White Hart Inn remains standing.

Brentwood. **1** City (1970 pop. 11,248), St. Louis co., E Mo., a residential suburb W of St. Louis; inc. 1919. Its manufactures include pencils, leather goods, women's apparel, hospital and pharmaceutical supplies, and plastic products. **2** Uninc. town (1970 pop. 27,868), Suffolk co., SE N.Y., on central Long Island, in the town of Islip. It is mainly residential, with some light industry. Josiah Warren led (1851) an experiment in communal living in Brentwood. **3** Borough (1970 pop. 13,732), Allegheny co., W Pa., a residential suburb of Pittsburgh; inc. 1915. There is some light industry.

Brescia (brā'shä), city (1971 pop. 210,067), capital of Brescia prov., Lombardy, N Italy. It is a commercial and industrial center and a railroad junction. Manufactures include machinery, firearms, textiles, and processed food. A Gallic town, it later became a Roman stronghold (1st cent. B.C.) and then the seat of a Lombard duchy. In the 12th cent. it was made an independent commune. It subsequently fell under the domination of a long series of outside powers (including Verona, Milan, Venice, and Austria), until it united with Italy in 1860. In the 18th and 19th cent. Brescia was a revolutionary center, and in 1849 the city heroically resisted the Austrians for 10 days before it capitulated. Of note in Brescia are Roman remains; the Romanesque Old Cathedral (11th cent.); the baroque New Cathedral (17th cent.); the Lombard-Romanesque Church of San Francesco; and a Renaissance-style city hall. In the 16th cent. Brescia was the seat of a flourishing school of painting headed by G. B. Moroni and his pupil Moretto.

Breshkovsky, Catherine (brĕshkôf'skē), 1844–1934, Russian revolutionary, called "the little grandmother (*babushka*) of the Russian Revolution." Of a noble family, she began on her father's estates the education of the peasants and other social reforms. These, carried into a larger field, brought her over 30 years of imprisonment and exile in Siberia. Released from exile by Kerensky after the Revolution of 1917, she returned to Russia, but found herself out of sympathy with the Bolshevik regime and left the country. Her letters and memoirs were edited by Alice Stone Blackwell with the title *Little Grandmother* (1917). See her autobiographical *Hidden Springs of the Russian Revolution* (1931).

Breslau: see WROCŁAW, Poland.

Bressanone (brās-sänô'nā), Ger. *Brixen,* town (1971 pop. 16,025), Trentino-Alto Adige, N Italy, on the Brenner Road, and at the confluence of the Isarco and Rienza rivers. Bressanone and its surrounding territory were ruled by prince-bishops from the 11th cent. In 1803 the bishopric was secularized and passed to Austria as a part of the TYROL. The town passed to Italy with the S Tyrol in 1919; it retains a mixed German and Italian population. Of note are the cathedral (13th cent., with a baroque interior) and the Palazzo Vescovile (17th cent.).

Bresse (brĕs), region, in Burgundy, E France, between the Ain and Saône rivers. Bourg-en-Bresse is the historic capital. A fertile farm area, it is famous for its chickens and wines. To the south is the Dombes, a region dotted with thousands of ponds, partially drained and reclaimed. Bresse was part of the duchy of SAVOY until 1601, when it was ceded to France along with Bugey (a district between the Ain and the Rhône) and the Territory of Gex. All three were added to Burgundy prov.

Bresson, Robert (rôbĕr' brĕsôN'), 1907–, French film director and scriptwriter, b. Bromont-Lamottie, France. Bresson's films tend to be austere and unadorned, concerned more with intellectual and spiritual values than plot or character. He prefers to use nonprofessional actors. His works include *Les Dames du Bois de Bologne* (1944), *Le Journal d'un curé de campagne* (1950), *Un condamné à mort s'est échappé* (1956), *Pickpocket* (1959), *Procès de Jeanne d'Arc* (1961), *Au Hazard, Balthazar* (1966), *Mouchette* (1966), *Une Femme douce* (1969), and *Lancelot of the Lake* (1974). See *The Films of Robert Bresson* (ed. by Ian Cameron, 1970).

Brest (brĕst), city (1968 pop. 159,857), Finistère dept., NW France, on an inlet of the Atlantic Ocean. It is a commercial port and an important naval station. There is a national engineering school in Brest. Electronics equipment and clothing are the chief manufactures. The city dates from Gallo-Roman times. The spacious, landlocked harbor was created in 1631 by Cardinal Richelieu as a military base and arsenal. In 1683, during the reign of Louis XIV, Marshal Vauban built the ramparts and a castle. The French repulsed the English in 1694 off Brest; in 1794 the English, under Lord Howe, defeated the French fleet. During World War II the Germans had a huge submarine base at Brest. Their heavily fortified submarine pens showed few cracks under Allied air raids; but the city itself was almost completely destroyed. The German garrison capitulated to U.S. troops in 1944.

Brest (brĕst), formerly **Brest-Litovsk** (-lĭtôfsk'), Pol. *Brześć nad Bugiem,* city (1970 pop. 122,000), capital of Brest oblast, W European USSR, in Belorussia, at the confluence of the Western Bug and Mukhavets rivers near the Polish border. It is a major industrial, commercial, and transportation center. Industries include shipbuilding, food processing, and the production of metals, textiles, and electrical machinery. Founded by Slavs in 1017 as Bereste, the city was conquered by the Mongols in 1241 and by Lithuania in 1319. During the 14th cent. it was renamed Brest-Litovsk. In 1569 it became capital of the newly merged Polish and Lithuanian state. Brest passed to Russia in the third partition of Poland (1795). German forces took the city in 1915 and three years later signed the Treaty of Brest-Litovsk with Soviet Russia there. Held by Poland between the world wars, Brest was regained by the USSR in 1939, occupied by Germany from 1941–44, and finally liberated by the Soviet army.

Brest-Litovsk, Treaty of (brĕst-lĭtôfsk'), separate peace treaty in World War I, signed by Soviet Russia and the Central Powers, March 3, 1918, at Brest-Litovsk (now BREST, Belorussia). After the separate armistice of Dec. 5, 1917, long, bitter negotiations were conducted by Leon Trotsky for Russia, Richard von Kühlmann for Germany, and Count Ottokar Czernin for Austria-Hungary (Turkey and Bulgaria were also represented). Trotsky at one point suspended negotiations, but Germany resumed warfare and the Soviets—on the insistence of Lenin—accepted the German ultimatum, which set conditions even harsher than at first. Russia recognized the independence of Ukraine and Georgia; confirmed the independence of Finland; gave up Poland, the Baltic states, and part of Belorussia to Germany and Austria-Hungary; and ceded Kars, Ardahan, and Batum to Turkey. Later, Germany demanded a large indemnity. The general armistice of Nov. 11, 1918, forced Germany to renounce the treaty, and Russia also declared it null and void. The western frontiers of Russia were later agreed upon by a series of separate treaties. See J. W. Wheeler-Bennett, *The Forgotten Peace* (1938, repr. 1966).

Brethren, German Baptist sect. They are popularly known as Dunkards, Dunkers, or Tunkers, from the German for "to dip," referring to their method of baptizing. The Brethren evolved from the Pietist movement in Germany. The first congregation was organized there in 1708 by Alexander Mack. Persecution drove them to America where, under Peter Becker, they settled (1719) in Germantown, Pa. From that and other settlements in Pennsylvania they spread westward and into Canada. The Brethren oppose war and advocate temperance, the simple life, plain dress, and "obedience to Christ rather than obedience to creeds and cults." The original group, at present the largest in the United States, is the Church of the Brethren (Conservative Dunkers); the local churches are united by an annual conference that elects a general board to supervise the national church program. From the Church of the Brethren there have been separations into the Seventh-Day Baptists, German (1728; see BEISSEL, JOHANN CONRAD); Church of God (New Dunkards, 1848); Old German Baptist Brethren (1881); and the Brethren Church (Progressive Dunkers, 1882). The Brethren baptize by trine immersion, the candidate being immersed once for each member of the Trinity. They practice foot washing and the love feast. See M. G. Brumbaugh, *A History of the German Baptist Brethren in Europe and America* (1899, repr. 1961); V. S. Fisher, *The Story of the Brethren* (1957). See RIVER BRETHREN (for Brethren in Christ, River Brethren, and Yorker Brethren); CHRISTADELPHIANS (for Brethren of Christ); HUTTERIAN BRETHREN; MORAVIAN CHURCH.

Brethren in Christ: see RIVER BRETHREN.

Brétigny, Treaty of (brātēnyē'), 1360, concluded by England and France at Brétigny, a village near Chartres, France. It marked a low point in French fortunes in the HUNDRED YEARS WAR. After John II of France, who had been captured (1356), was set free by the English at the price of 3 million gold crowns, he ceded to Edward III (without exacting feudal homage) Poitou, Aunis, Saintonge, Angoumois, Guienne, Gascony, Calais, and other territories. Edward then abandoned his claim to the French throne. The peace did not last, however, and by 1373 all but the Bordeaux district had been reconquered by Bertrand DU GUESCLIN.

Breton, André (äNdrā' brətôN'), 1896–1966, French writer, founder and theorist of the surrealist movement. He studied neuropsychology and was one of the first in France to publicize the work of Freud. At first a Dadaist, he collaborated with Philippe Soupault in automatic writing in *Les Champs magnétiques* (1921). He then turned to SURREALISM, writing three manifestos (1924, 1930, 1934) and opening a studio for "surrealist research." Breton helped to found several reviews: *Littérature* (1919), *Minotaure* (1933), and *VVV* (1944). His other works include *Nadja* (1928, tr. 1960), a semiautobiographical novel; *What is Surrealism?* (1934, tr. 1936); *Ode à Charles Fourier* (1946); and *L' Art Magique* (1957). See study by A. E. Balakian (1971).

Breton, Jules Adolphe Aimé Louis (zhül ädôlf' āmā' lwē), 1827–1906, French painter of rustic scenes and peasant life. Breton's *Peasant Girl Knitting* (Metropolitan Mus.) is well known. His works frequently reflect a social and humanitarian concern. Breton was the author of two autobiographies.

Breton, Nicholas (brĕt'ən), 1551?–c.1623, English author, a prolific and versatile writer of verse and prose. His best work, written in a lyrical and pastoral vein, appeared in *The Arbor of Amorous Devices* (1597), *England's Helicon* (1600), and *The Passionate Shepherd* (1604). See his poems (ed. with biography by Jane Robertson, 1952); *A Mad World My Masters and Other Prose Works* (ed. by Ursula Kentish-Wright, 1929).

Breton literature (brĕt'ən), in the Celtic language of Brittany. Although there are numerous allusions in other literatures of the 12th to 14th cent. to the "matter of Brittany," which includes the stories of Tristan and King Arthur, no Breton texts remain from this period. The earliest ones date from the 15th cent. Until the 19th cent., texts included songs, stories, and plays, all popular and mostly of unknown authorship. The plays were imitations of late medieval French miracles. As elsewhere in Europe, serious collecting of Breton folk literature began in the 19th cent. Jean François Le Gonidec (1775–1838) pioneered with a dictionary of the language in 1821. Théodore Hersart de La Villemarqué assembled an anthology of folk poems but was attacked for his dubious scholarship. A more sophisticated collector was François Marie Luzel (1821–95). The mid-19th cent. saw the birth of a cultivated literature, mainly in stories and verse. Auguste Brizeux (1803–58) was the best known of the poets who wrote in their native Breton. Others were J. Guillome and Prosper Proux (1811–73). In the late 19th cent. an intensification of the campaign to revive local literary traditions resulted in the establishment of several folk theaters and in the expansion and modification of the vocabulary by writers. Among the leading writers of the late 19th and the 20th cent. are the poets Emil Ernault (b. 1852), Jean Pierre CALLOC'H, and Robert Le Masson; the storytellers Louis and Louise Herrieu, Louis Héno, and Jakez Riou; and the playwright Tanguy Malemanche. During the 19th and 20th cent. a large number of Breton folk tales and songs have been collected. The diversity and richness of this collection make it unique in world literature.

Bretonneau, Pierre (pyĕr brətônō'), 1778–1862, French physician. He performed (1825) the first successful tracheotomy for laryngeal diphtheria, wrote a treatise (1826) distinguishing between scarlet fever and diphtheria (which he named), described typhoid fever, and stated (1855) the germ theory of disease (which later became established largely through Pasteur's work).

Breton Succession, War of the, 1341–65, an important episode of the HUNDRED YEARS WAR. Duke John III of Brittany died in 1341 without heirs. The succession was contested by his half brother, John de Montfort, who was backed by Edward III of England, and by CHARLES OF BLOIS, who had married Jeanne de Penthièvre, a niece of the late duke. Charles and Jeanne were supported by Philip VI, John II, and Charles V of France. The resulting war continued through several truces. In the battle of Auray (1364), Charles of Blois was defeated and killed, despite the support of his faithful follower, Bertrand DU GUESCLIN. The issue was settled by the Treaty of Guérande in 1365, when the Montfort heir was recognized by France as ruler of Brittany. An attempt (1378–79) by Charles V to confiscate Brittany for the French crown met the resistance of the Bretons and of Jeanne de Penthièvre. Du Guesclin, who commanded the royal army, made no serious effort to subdue the Bretons, and the attempt failed.

Brett, Reginald Baliol, 2d **Viscount Esher:** see ESHER, REGINALD BALIOL BRETT, 2D VISCOUNT.

Bretton Woods Conference, name commonly given to the United Nations Monetary and Financial Conference, held (July 1–22, 1944) at Bretton Woods, N.H. The conference resulted in the creation of the International Monetary Fund, to promote international monetary cooperation, and of the International Bank for Reconstruction and Development. By Dec., 1945, the required number of governments had ratified the treaties creating the two organizations, and by the summer of 1946 they had begun operation.

Breuer, Josef (yō'zĕf broi'ər), 1842–1925, Austrian physician. He was the first to use (1880–82) the cathartic method to cure hysteria. His therapy and theory, when developed by FREUD, became psychoanalysis. Together they wrote *Studies in Hysteria* (1895).

Breuer, Marcel Lajos (broi'ər), 1902–, American architect and furniture designer, b. Hungary. During the 1920s he was associated, both as student and as teacher, with the BAUHAUS in Germany. In 1925, Breuer won renown with his design of the first tubular steel and laminated plywood chair. He built only one private house (Wiesbaden, 1932) before leaving Germany to work in Switzerland and England. Breuer became associate professor of architecture at Harvard Univ. in 1937 and from 1937 to 1941 was a partner of Walter GROPIUS, with whom he designed several outstanding houses. He developed exterior sun shielding and made bold sculptural use of poured concrete. With Nervi and B. H. Zehrfuss he planned the Paris headquarters of the UN Educational, Scientific, and Cultural Organization (1958). Among Breuer's major later designs are St. John's Abbey, Collegeville, Minn. (1953–61); the U. S. embassy at The Hague; the Whitney Museum of American Art, New York City (1966); and the New York Univ. Technology I and II buildings (1969), New York City. See his *Sun and Shadow*, ed. by Peter Blake (1955), *Buildings and Projects*, ed. by Cranston Jones (1962), and *New Buildings and Projects*, ed. by Tician Papachristou (1970).

Breughel, family of painters: see BRUEGEL.

Breuil, Henri (äNrē' brö'yə), known as **Abbé Breuil,** 1877–1961, French archaeologist, paleontologist, and cleric. He taught at the Institut de Paléontologie Humaine, Paris, after 1910. He was one of the first to record and interpret Paleolithic art and the rock carvings and paintings in Europe and Africa. His principal work is *Four Hundred Centuries of Cave Art* (tr. 1952). See biography by A. H. Brodrick (1963).

Breviary of Alaric (ă'lərĭk), Visigothic code of Roman law issued (506) by King Alaric II for his Roman subjects in Spain and S Gaul. It is also known as the *Lex Romana Visigothorum.* Based largely on the THEODOSIAN CODE and accompanied by valuable commentaries, it was a compilation of contemporary Roman law for the Roman element of the population; the Germanic element was under the authority of the earlier code issued by EURIC. Although both codes were later superseded by the *Forum judicum* of King RECCESWINTH, the Breviary remained influential in preserving Roman law in the S and E of France. See GERMANIC LAWS.

brevium: see PROTACTINIUM.

brewer's yeast: see YEAST.

brewing: see BEER.

Brewster, Sir David, 1781–1868, Scottish physicist and natural philosopher. He is noted especially for his research into the polarization of light (the invention of the kaleidoscope was one result of his studies). He improved the spectroscope and persuaded the British government to adopt his dioptric system of lighthouse illumination. For 21 years Brewster was principal of the United College of St. Salvator and St. Leonard, in St. Andrews, Scotland, and in 1859 he became principal of the Univ. of Edinburgh. He was a steady contributor to scientific publications. Included in his numerous writings are *A Treatise on Optics* (1831) and *Memoirs of the Life, Writings, and Discoveries of Sir Isaac Newton* (1855).

Brewster, Kingman, Jr., 1919–, American educator, b. Longmeadow, Mass., grad. Yale (A.B., 1941) and Harvard (LL.B., 1948). He was a professor of law at Harvard from 1950 to 1960. From 1961 to 1963 he was provost of Yale. In 1963 he became president of Yale. Among his writings are *Antitrust and American Business Abroad* (with M. Katz, 1959) and *Law of International Transactions and Relations* (1960).

Brewster, William, 1567–1644, English separatist and Plymouth colonist. After studying briefly at Cambridge he became the chief member of the congregation at Scrooby that broke away, or separated, from the Anglican Church in 1606; the members, after their migration to Holland in 1608, were known as Pilgrims. On his press at Leiden, Brewster printed a number of religious books and tracts that were distributed throughout England. Returning to England in 1617, he helped make arrangements for the Pilgrim migration to America and in 1620 embarked on the *Mayflower* with his wife, two sons, and two indentured boys. Brewster, an elder of the church from the time he lived in Leiden, was the sole religious leader of the Plymouth Colony until 1629, but because he was not ordained, he confined his ministry to services of prayer and praise only. Although he held no lay offices, he was very influential, being one of the eight who undertook (1627) to discharge the debt to the colony's backers. See biographies by Ashbel Steele (1857, repr. 1970) and Dorothy Brewster (1970).

Brezhnev, Leonid Ilyich (lāyō'nĕd ĭlyēch' brĕzh'nĕf), 1906–, Soviet leader. He joined the Communist party in 1931 and rose steadily in the party hierarchy. In 1952 he became a secretary of the Communist party central committee. After suffering a slight political setback following Joseph Stalin's death in 1953, Brezhnev filled a number of party posts. In 1957, as protégé of Nikita Khrushchev, he became a member of the presidium (later politburo) of the central committee. From 1960 to 1964, he was chairman of the presidium of the Supreme Soviet, or titular head of state. Following Nikita Khrushchev's fall from power in Oct., 1964, which Brezhnev helped to engineer, he was named first secretary (later general secretary) of the Communist party. Although sharing power with Alexei KOSYGIN, Brezhnev emerged as the chief figure in Soviet politics. In 1968, in support of the Soviet invasion of Czechoslovakia, he enunciated the "Brezhnev doctrine," which asserted that the USSR could intervene in the domestic affairs of any Soviet bloc nation if Communist rule were threatened. While maintaining a tight rein in Eastern Europe, he favored closer relations with the Western powers, and he helped (1972–74) bring about a détente with the United States.

Březina, Otokar (ô'tôkär brzhĕ'zĭnä), 1868–1929, Czech lyric poet, leader of the Czech SYMBOLISTS, whose original name was Václav Jebavý. The first collection of his poetry, *Tajemné dálky* [mysterious distances], appeared in 1895. It was followed by four more volumes of mystic, highly imaginative verse, and by one of essays, *Hudba pramenů* [the music of the springs] (1903). Březina is considered one of the greatest of Czech poets.

Brian Boru or **Brian Boroimhe** (both: brī'ən, brēn; bərōō', bərō'), 940?–1014, king of Ireland. A clan prince, he succeeded his brother Mathghamhain, who had seized the throne of Munster from the Eogharacht rulers (963). Brian subjugated all Munster, then extended his power over all S Ireland, and in 1002 became high king of Ireland by right of conquest. As his power increased, relations with the Norse rulers on the Irish coast grew steadily worse. Sitric, king of the Dublin Norse, formed against Brian a coalition of Norse of Ireland, the Hebrides, the Orkneys, and Iceland as well as Brian's Irish enemies. On Good Friday (April 23), 1014, Brian's forces met and annihilated the allies at Clontarf, near Dublin. Soon afterward he was murdered in his tent. Brian's victory broke the Norse power in Ireland forever, but Ireland fell into anarchy.

Briand, Aristide (ärēstēd' brēäN'), 1862–1932, French statesman. A lawyer and a Socialist, he entered (1902) the chamber of deputies and helped to draft and pass the law (1905) for separation of church and state. Made (1906) minister of education and minister of religion to execute the law, he was ejected from the Socialist party for participating in the bourgeois cabinet of premier Jean Sarrien. In 1909 he became premier for the first of 10 times. In World War I, Briand headed (1915–17) two successive coalition cabinets and made the decision to hold VERDUN at any cost. His government fell in March, 1917; attacked by Georges Clemenceau for attempting to negotiate a peace with Germany in 1917, Briand retired. After the war he emerged as a leading advocate of international peace and cooperation, and he is best remembered for his devotion to this cause. The cabinet he headed in 1921 fell because of his unpopular criticism of the Treaty of Versailles and his moderate demands at international conferences, where he worked for a reconciliation with Germany without the sacrifice of French security. As foreign minister from 1925 to 1932 he was the chief architect of the LOCARNO PACT (1925) and the KELLOGG-BRIAND PACT (1928), and he shared the 1926 Nobel Peace Prize with Gustav Stresemann. An impressive orator, Briand was a prominent figure in the League of Nations. He advocated a plan for a United States of Europe.

briar: see BRIER.

Briard (brēärd'), breed of muscular, wiry WORKING DOG whose origins may be traced back to 12th-century France. It stands from 22 to 27 in. (55.9–68.6 cm) high at the shoulder and weighs between 70 and 80 lb (31.8–36.3 kg). Its moderately long, stiff, slightly wavy coat is usually black, tawny, or gray, although any solid color except white is acceptable. Raised for centuries to herd and protect sheep, the Briard has more recently been trained as a police and war dog. It is also kept as a pet. See DOG.

Brice, Fanny, 1891–1951, American comedienne, b. New York City as Fanny Borach. Brice appeared in burlesque and vaudeville from 1906. She starred in the Ziegfeld "Follies" from 1910 onward, and in Broadway shows, emphasizing her plainness by means of a comic awkwardness. In 1937 she created for radio the popular role of Baby Snooks. She appeared in the films *My Man* (1928), *The Great Ziegfeld* (1936), and *Ziegfeld Follies* (1944). Three films have been based on her life, including *Funny Girl* (1968). See biography by Norman Katkov (1953).

Brices Cross Roads National Battlefield Site: see NATIONAL PARKS AND MONUMENTS, table.

brick, ceramic structural material that, in modern times, is made by pressing clay into blocks and firing them to the requisite hardness in a kiln. Bricks in their most primitive form were not fired but were hardened by being dried in the sun. Sun-dried bricks were utilized for many centuries and are used even today in regions with the proper climate. Examples from approximately 5,000 years ago have been discovered in the Tigris-Euphrates basin, and the ancient races occupying this region may have been the first users of brick. In Babylonia there was a lack of both timber and stone, and the thick clay deposited by the overflowing rivers was the only material adaptable to building. The Persians and the Assyrians used sun-dried blocks of clay for walls of great thickness, facing them with a protective coating of fired bricks. The Egyptians and the Greeks used bricks only to a limited extent, as they had access to plentiful supplies of stone and marble. The Romans manufactured fired bricks in enormous quantities and gave them an important role as a basic structural material in buildings throughout the Roman Empire. Bricks played an important part in early Christian architecture until the decline of the empire. Whereas the Romans had usually concealed their brickwork beneath a decorative facing of stone or marble, the Byzantines devised a technique for exposing the bricks and giving them a full decorative expression. This technique influenced the Romanesque style and brought especially good results in Lombardy and in Germany, where bricks came to be arranged in immensely varied patterns. Since the Middle Ages, brickwork has been in constant use everywhere, adapting itself to every sort of construction and to every change of architectural style. At the beginning of the 19th cent. mechanical brick-making processes began to be patented and by the latter half of the century had almost entirely replaced the ancient hand-fashioning methods. Contemporary American building bricks are rectangular blocks with the standard dimensions of about 2¼ by 3¾ by 8 in. (5.7 by 9.5 by 20.3 cm). Good bricks are resistant to atmospheric action and high temperatures and are more durable than stone. Where heat resistance is especially important, fire bricks are used; these are made of special refractory clays called fire clays and are fired at very high temperatures.

bridal wreath: see SPIRAEA.

Bride, Saint: see BRIDGET, SAINT.

bride price: see MARRIAGE.

Bridewell (brīd'wəl), district in London, England, between Fleet St. and the Thames River. The Bridewell house of correction, demolished in 1863, was on the site of a palace built by Henry VIII and given by Edward VI to the City of London in 1553 for use as a training school for homeless apprentices. The building later became a prison as well. *Bridewell* thus came to be used as a general term for a prison or house of correction.

bridge, structure built over water or any obstacle or depression to allow the passage of pedestrians or vehicles. In ancient times and among primitive peoples a log was thrown across a stream, or two vines or woven fibrous ropes (the upper for a handhold and the lower for a footwalk) were thrown across, to serve as a bridge. Later, arched structures of stone or brick were used; traces of these, built from 4000 to 2000 B.C., have been found in Palestine. The Romans built long, arched spans, many of which are still standing. In England the rather crude arched stone bridges had heavy piers (intermediate supports) that were a great obstruction to river traffic, and the roadway was often lined with small shops. In the early days in the United States, since wood

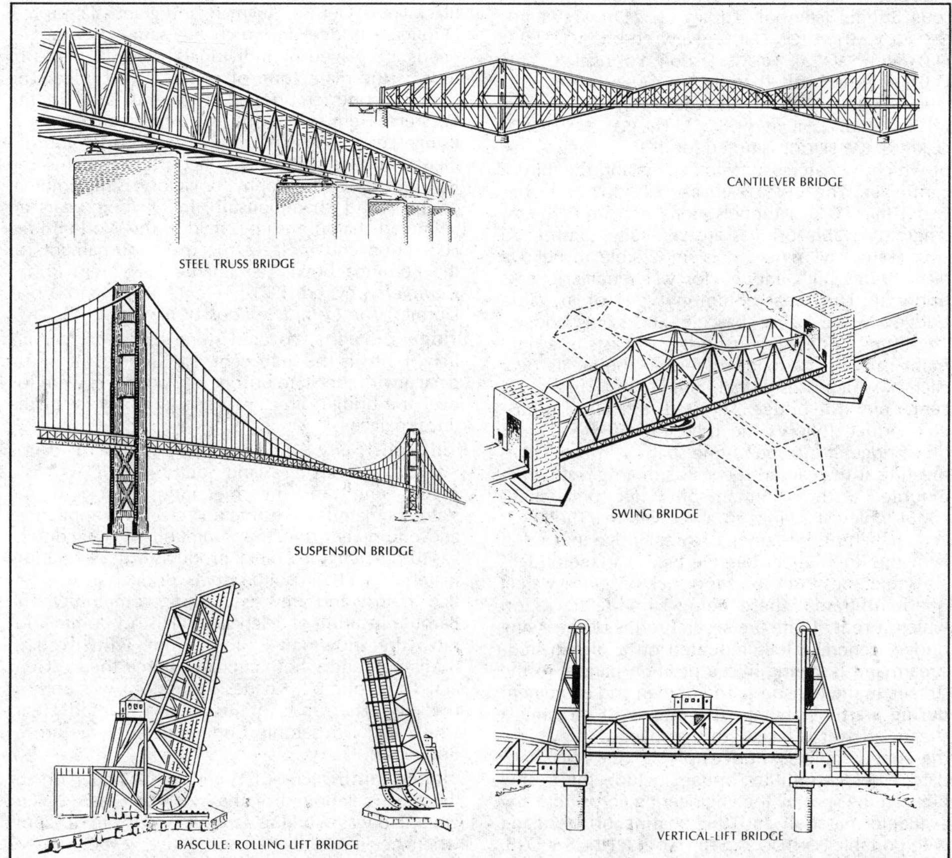

Bridges

was abundant and cheap, the arched type of bridge did not develop. Wood is now seldom used, since a wooden bridge may be destroyed by rot or fire. In the middle part of the 19th cent. many bridges were built of cast and wrought iron. Robert Stephenson, an English engineer, designed and built a bridge of this type across Menai Strait in North Wales (1850). Another is Victoria Bridge across the St. Lawrence at Montreal. The disadvantage of cast iron for bridges is its low tensile strength. The development of the Bessemer process for converting cast iron into steel revolutionized bridgebuilding. It became possible to design framed structures with greater ease and flexibility. Single-piece, rolled steel beams can support spans of 50 to 100 ft (15.2–30.5 m), depending on the load. Larger, built-up beams are made for longer spans. The truss can span even greater distances and carry heavy loads; it is therefore commonly used for railroad bridges. A large truss span may have a length of about 300 ft (90 m). Longer spans are those of arch bridges; the Bayonne Bridge between New York and New Jersey and the Sydney Harbor Bridge in Australia are the longest, at 1,652 ft (504 m) and 1,650 ft (503 m), respectively. The CANTILEVER, however, is more common for spans of such lengths. The cantilevered Forth Bridge (1890) in Scotland was the first major structure built entirely of steel, the material that made possible its two record-setting spans of 1,710 ft (521 m) each. They remained the longest in existence until 1917, when the Quebec Bridge was built; it has an 1,800-ft (549-m) span. Today, however, the suspension bridge is used for the longest spans. It has a roadway suspended by vertical cables that are attached to two or more main cables. The main cables are hung on two towers and have their ends anchored in bedrock or concrete. The earliest suspension bridges built in America were those constructed by the American builder James Finley. The design of suspension bridges advanced when J. A. Roebling, a German-born engineer who emigrated to the United States, developed the use of wire cables and stiffening trusses. He completed a suspension bridge over the Niagara River in 1854. He also designed the Brooklyn Bridge across the East River (completed 1883), which was the world's longest suspension bridge at the time of its construction, having a main span of 1,595.5 ft (487 m). Today the 20 longest spans in the world are suspended. Eleven of them are in the United States. Ten of the 20 have been built since 1960. The eight longest main spans are the VERRAZANO-NARROWS BRIDGE, New York City, 4,260 ft (1,298 m); GOLDEN GATE BRIDGE, San Francisco, 4,200 ft (1,280 m); Mackinac Straits Bridge, Mich., 3,800 ft (1,158 m); Bosporous Bridge, İstanbul, Turkey, 3,524 ft (1,074 m); GEORGE WASHINGTON BRIDGE, New York City, 3,500 ft (1,067 m); SALAZAR BRIDGE, Lisbon, Portugal, 3,323 ft (1,013 m); the Forth Road Bridge, Queensferry, Scotland, 3,300 ft (1,006 m); and the Severn Bridge, Bristol, England, 3,240 ft (988 m). The SAN FRANCISCO-OAKLAND BAY BRIDGE is noted for its three long spans, of which two are suspension spans and the third a cantilever. The CHESAPEAKE BAY BRIDGE-TUNNEL has two 1-mi (1.6-km) tunnels along its 18-mi (28-km) length. Movable bridges are generally constructed over waterways where it is impossible to build a fixed bridge high enough for water traffic to pass under it. The most common types of movable bridge are the lifting, bascule, and swing bridges. The lifting bridge, or lift bridge, consists of a rigid frame carrying the road and resting abutments, over each of which rises a steel frame tower. There is no center pier. The bridge is hoisted vertically. The bascule bridge follows the principle of the ancient drawbridge. It may be in one span or in two halves meeting at the center. It consists of a rigid structure mounted at the abutment on a horizontal shaft, about which it swings in a vertical arc. The lower center span of the famous Tower Bridge in London is of the double-leaf bascule type. Bascule bridges are sometimes built to swing back on a heavy steel quadrant frame, there being suitable tracks on which it rolls. There are several forms of the swing bridge; generally it is mounted on a pier in midstream and is swung into a position parallel to the stream. In the transportation of men and equipment during wartime, where the means of crossing a stream or river is lacking or has been destroyed by the enemy, military bridges play a vital role. Standard types of military bridge include the trestle, built on the spot by the engineering corps from any available material, and the floating bridge made with portable PONTOONS. See VIADUCT; PIER. See D. B. Steinman and S. R. Watson, *Bridges and Their Builders* (rev. ed. 1957); D. B. Steinman, *Famous Bridges of the World* (rev. ed. 1961); H. Shirley-Smith, *The World's Great Bridges* (rev. ed. 1965); Robert Silverberg, *Bridges* (1966); H. J. Hopkins, *A Span of Bridges: An Illustrated History* (1970).

bridge, card game derived from WHIST, played with 52 cards by four players in two partnerships. The game probably originated in the Middle East in the 19th cent. Auction bridge, one form of the game, was developed by the British in India and later was popular in England and the United States. It is still played but has largely been supplanted by contract bridge, which achieved popularity after important innovations were made in 1925 by Harold S. Vanderbilt. Its phenomenal popularity owed much to the activities of Ely CULBERTSON. The craze subsided but was later revived; books, tournaments, and newspaper columns on bridge abound. The cards in contract bridge rank from ace down to two; in bidding, suits rank spades, hearts, diamonds, and clubs. After all cards are dealt, so that each player holds 13 cards, the dealer begins the auction, which proceeds in rotation to the left. Each player must bid, pass, double (increase the value of the previously stated contract), or redouble (only after a double, further increasing the point value of the contract). A bid is an offer to win a stated number of tricks over six with a named suit as trump or with no-trump. The lowest bid is one, the highest seven. Each bid, i.e., "one diamond," "one no-trump," "four hearts," must be higher than the preceding bid, with no-trump ranking above spades. Artificial bids are those that convey certain information to a partner and are not meant to be taken literally. The highest bid of the auction becomes the contract after three consecutive passes end the bidding. The player who first named the suit (or no-trump) specified in the winning bid becomes the declarer. The player to the left of the declarer leads any card face up, and the next hand, that of the declarer's partner, is placed face up on the table, grouped in suits. This is known as the dummy, and the declarer selects the cards to be played from this hand. The object of the game for both partnerships is to win as many tricks as possible, a trick being the three cards played in rotation after the lead. Suits must be followed; if a player has no cards in the suit led, he may play any card. Highest trump or, if no trump card is played, highest card of the suit led wins. Points are awarded for the number of tricks won. Culbertson devised the honor count system to evaluate a hand for bidding. The point count (or standard American) system introduced by Charles H. Goren in the 1940s has generally replaced honor count. Numerous conventions are used in bridge, but the four standard ones are Blackwood, Gerber, Stayman, and grand-slam force. Duplicate bridge, in which the same prearranged hands are played by individuals, pairs, or teams of four, is the main form of competitive bridge. The laws of contract bridge are promulgated in the Western Hemisphere by the American Contract Bridge League, which holds various bridge tournaments. In international contract bridge matches the Bermuda bowl, the trophy for victory, is the emblem of the world championship. In Olympic years an olympiad championship is held by the World Bridge Federation and replaces the team tournament for the Bermuda bowl. See Charles H. Goren, *Bridge Complete* (rev. ed. 1971); Terence Reese and Albert Dormer, *The Complete Book of Bridge* (1974).

Bridge of Sighs, covered stone bridge in Venice, Italy, built in the 16th cent. to connect the ducal palace with the state prison. The prisoners were led over the bridge directly to prison after trial in the ducal palace.

Bridgeport, city (1970 pop. 156,542), Fairfield co., SW Conn., on Long Island Sound; inc. 1836. It is a port of entry and the chief industrial city in the state. Its manufactures include electrical appliances and equipment, firearms, ammunition, helicopters, gas turbine engines, metal products, trucks, building materials, and aerosol products. Bridgeport was settled in 1639 and grew as a fishing community. The Barnum Institute of Science and History commemorates the showman P. T. Barnum, who lived in Bridgeport and whose circus wintered there. "General Tom Thumb" (Charles S. Stratton) was born in the city. The Univ. of Bridgeport, Sacred Heart Univ., and Housatonic Community College are in Bridgeport.

Bridger, James, 1804–81, American fur trader, one of the most celebrated of the MOUNTAIN MEN, b. Virginia. He was working as a blacksmith in St. Louis when he joined the Missouri River expedition of William H. ASHLEY in 1822. From that time until the fur trade declined in the 1840s he was a trader and trapper in the mountains, becoming familiar with most of the country N of Spanish New Mexico and E of California. He was associated with Thomas Fitzpatrick and Jedediah Smith in many of their journeys, and he is generally credited with being the first white man to see (1825) Great Salt Lake. He was the guide for the party of Marcus Whitman, and in 1843 he and a partner, Louis Vasquez, opened Fort Bridger on the OREGON TRAIL. They later were forced by the Mormons to give up the post. Bridger was a guide, notably to Gen. A. S. Johnston on the Mormon campaign in 1857, to an expedition to the present Yellowstone Park (a region he did much to publicize), and to the surveying party of Gen. G. M. Dodge for the Union Pacific RR. He came to be famous for his talk, was a fine spinner of "tall tales," and was one of the most picturesque figures of the frontier. See biographies by J. C. Alter (1925; rev. ed. 1962, repr.1967), Stanley Vestal (pseud. of W. S. Campbell; 1946, repr. 1970), and Gene Caesar (1961); Bernard De Voto, *Across the Wide Missouri* (1947).

Bridger, Fort: see FORT BRIDGER STATE PARK.

Bridges, Calvin Blackman, 1889–1938, American geneticist, b. Schuyler Falls, N.Y., grad. Columbia (B.S., 1912; Ph.D., 1916). In his research he collaborated with T. H. Morgan, A. H. Sturtevant, and H. J. Muller, the group that developed many of the concepts of modern genetics through their study of the fruit fly, *Drosophila*. He continued with the Morgan group as a research associate of the Carnegie Institution in Washington from 1919. His contributions to modern genetics include the proof of the chromosome theory of heredity, formulation of the theory of genic balance, and the detailed study of giant salivary chromosomes in relation to the positions of genes. He was co-author of *The Mechanism of Mendelian Heredity* (1915).

Bridges, Charles, fl. 1683–1740, English portrait painter, active (c.1735–c.1740) in Virginia. He was the most skillful practitioner of aristocratic portrait painting in the South at that time. Among the works attributed to him are *Mann Page the Second* (College of William and Mary) and *Maria Taylor Byrd* (Metropolitan Mus.).

Bridges, Harry (Alfred Renton Bridges), 1901–, American labor leader, b. Melbourne, Australia. Arriving (1920) as an immigrant seaman in San Francisco, he became a longshoreman and militant labor organizer. Bridges led (1934) the West Coast maritime workers' strike, which expanded into an abortive general strike, and in 1937 he set up the International Longshoremen's and Warehousemen's Union (ILWU), and became West Coast director of the Congress of Industrial Organizations (CIO). Proceedings in 1939 to deport him as a Communist alien ended when he was officially absolved of Communist affiliation. The U.S. House of Representatives passed (1940) a bill to deport him, but it was ruled (1945) illegal by the Supreme Court. He became a citizen in 1945. His support of Henry A. Wallace for President in 1948 resulted in his ouster as CIO regional head. He was convicted and sentenced (1950) to a five-year prison term for swearing falsely at his 1945 naturalization hearing that he had never been a member of the Communist party. In 1953, the U.S. Supreme Court dismissed the indictment for perjury against Bridges, thus voiding his prison sentence. He was reindicted on similar charges, but in 1955, a Federal district judge ruled that the government had failed to prove that he was a Communist or that he had concealed that fact when he was naturalized. Shortly thereafter the U.S. Justice Dept. announced it had given up its long fight to deport Bridges. In 1958 he was granted a U.S. passport. In 1971 and 1972 Bridges led the ILWU in a strike that tied up the West Coast waterfront for several weeks. See study by C. P. Larrowe (1972).

Bridges, Robert Seymour, 1844–1930, English poet. In 1882 he abandoned medical practice to devote himself to writing. An excellent metrist, he wrote many beautiful lyrics and longer poems, noted for their refined simplicity and perfection of form. Although not a well-known poet, in 1913 he was made poet laureate. In 1929, when Bridges was 85, he published *The Testament of Beauty,* a philosophical poem on the evolution of the human soul. It achieved immediate popularity and is considered his greatest work. Long interested in prosody, Bridges published two important works on the subject, *Milton's Prosody* (1893) and *John Keats* (1895). He also published the poems of his friend Gerard Manley Hopkins. See studies by Albert Guérard, Jr. (1942) and E. C. Wright (1951).

Bridget, Saint, 453?–523?, Irish holy woman. She is often called St. Brigid, St. Bride, or St. Bridget of

Kildare. Little is known of her, but she did found a great monastery at Kildare. She is buried at Downpatrick with St. Patrick and St. Columba, and with them she is patron of Ireland; hence her nickname Mary of the Gael. St. Bridget is associated notably with charity and justice. Devotion to her was widespread in Great Britain before the Reformation, as witness many names, e.g., Bridewell, Kilbride, Kirkbride, and McBride. Feast: Feb. 1. See study by Alice Curtayne (1954).

Bridget of Sweden, Saint, c.1300–1373, Swedish nun, one of the great saints of Scandinavia. She was a noblewoman at court and the mother of eight children. After her husband's death she founded the Order of the Most Holy Savior (the Bridgettines). In 1349 she went to Rome and became famous for her holy life. She labored for the reform of religious life in Italy and for the return of the pope from Avignon to Rome. Her account of her numerous visions was widely read during the Middle Ages. St. Bridget is patron of Sweden. She is also called Birgitta. Feast: Oct. 8. See biography by Johannes Jorgensen (2 vol., tr. 1954).

Bridgeton. **1** City (1970 pop. 19,992), St. Louis co., E Mo., on the Missouri River; settled c.1765, inc. 1843. Refrigerators are among its manufactures. **2** City (1970 pop. 20,435), seat of Cumberland co., S N.J., on the Cohansey River; settled 1686, inc. 1865. Once a rural farm center, it is now highly industrialized, with glassworks, fertilizer plants, and food-processing, textile, and garment industries. Bridgeton's downtown is highly Victorian in appearance, but the city has several 18th-century buildings, including Potter's Tavern (recently restored), a revolutionary center in colonial days; and a Presbyterian church (1792). The city's liberty bell, now in the county courthouse lobby, rang on July 7, 1776, for the reading of the Declaration of Independence. Bridgeton's zoo, the largest municipal zoo in the state, draws many visitors.

Bridgetown, city (1970 pop. 8,868), capital, commercial center, and chief port of BARBADOS, West Indies. It is, in addition, a tourist and health resort. Sugar, rum, and molasses are the leading exports, and Bridgetown also serves as an important transshipment point. The city, which was founded by the British in 1628, is the site of a college of the Univ. of the West Indies.

Bridge View, village (1970 pop. 12,522), Cook co., NE Ill., a residential suburb of Chicago; inc. 1947.

Bridgewater, town (1970 pop. 11,829), Plymouth co., E Mass.; inc. 1656. Its iron foundry industry dates from colonial times. Bridgewater State College and a state prison are there.

Bridgman, Elijah Coleman, 1801–61, first American Protestant missionary to China, b. Belchertown, Mass. He served as a missionary in China from 1830 until his death. His *Chinese Chrestomathy* appeared in 1841; his Chinese translation of the Bible (in collaboration with M. S. Culbertson) was published posthumously in 1862.

Bridgman, Frederic Arthur, 1847–1927, American painter of genre and of scenes of Near Eastern antiquity, b. Tuskegee, Ala. He studied under Gérôme in Paris, where he remained as an important figure in the large American colony. Among his romantic, academic paintings are *The Procession of the Bull Apis* (Corcoran Gall.) and *Awaiting his Master* (Art Inst., Chicago). He also wrote several books, including *Winters in Algeria* (1890).

Bridgman, Laura, 1829–89, first blind deaf-mute to be successfully educated, b. Hanover, N.H. Under the guidance of Dr. S. G. HOWE, of the Perkins Institution (now in Watertown, Mass.), she learned to read and write and to sew so well that she eventually became a sewing teacher at the school, where she remained until her death. See biography by L. E. Richards (1928).

Bridgman, Percy Williams, 1882–1961, American physicist, b. Cambridge, Mass., grad. Harvard (B.A., 1904; Ph.D., 1908). From 1910 he taught at Harvard, as professor from 1919. He won the 1946 Nobel Prize in Physics for his work in high pressures. He is known also for his studies of electrical conduction in metals and properties of crystals and for his writings on the philosophy of modern science. His works include *The Logic of Modern Physics* (1927), *The Nature of Physical Theory* (1936), and *Nature of Thermodynamics* (1941).

Bridgwater, municipal borough (1971 pop. 26,598), Somerset, SW England, on the Parrett River estuary. It is a port for seaborne traffic and a market town. Bridgwater is the only place in England that produces bathbricks, which are made from clay and sand deposited by the river and are used for scouring metals. Other manufactures are bricks, tiles, furniture, and preserves. Admiral Robert Blake was born in Bridgwater.

Bridlington (brĭd'lĭngtən, bûr'-), municipal borough (1971 pop. 26,729), East Riding of Yorkshire, NE England. It has a well-protected harbor on Bridlington Bay, and its beaches and pavilions make it a popular holiday resort. The Royal Yorkshire Yacht Club has its headquarters there. The borough administers Flamborough Head and most of the intervening coast line. Bridlington is an ancient market town and port. An Augustinian priory founded during the reign of Henry I has been restored. Of interest are Roman and early British remains and Bayle Gate (14th cent.). In 1974, Bridlington became part of the new nonmetropolitan county of Humberside.

Brie (brē), region, Marne and Seine-et-Marne depts., N France, E of Paris. Rich in wheat and cattle, it is famous for Brie cheese. The smaller section of the region (*Brie française*) forms part of the Île-de-France and is very fertile. There, many of the huge farms are fortresslike in their imposing architecture. Meaux, the former capital and major commercial center; Melun; and Château-Thierry are the chief towns. The former county of Meaux (E Brie) was combined (11th cent.) with that of the Troyes to form the county (later province) of Champagne and Brie.

Brienne, Étienne Charles Loménie de: see LOMÉNIE DE BRIENNE, ÉTIENNE CHARLES.

Brienz (brēĕnts'), town (1970 pop. 2,796), Bern canton, central Switzerland, on the northeast shore of the Lake of Brienz. A center of the Swiss woodcarving industry, it is also a resort. The **Lake of Brienz** (11 sq mi/28 sq km), traversed by the Aare River, is highly scenic.

brier or **briar,** name sometimes given any thorny plant, more specifically the SWEETBRIER, and the greenbrier. French brier, or brierroot, is a name for the root of the European white HEATH so widely used in the manufacture of smoking pipes.

Briey (brēā'), town (1968 pop. 5,012), Meurthe-et-Moselle dept., in Lorraine, NE France. It is at the center of the huge Briey iron-ore basin (see LORRAINE) and has a chemical industry.

Brig (brĕk), Fr. *Brigue,* town (1970 pop. 5,191), Valais canton, S Switzerland, on the Rhône River, at the north entrance of the Simplon Tunnel. Although it has a noted 17th-century palace, Brig is primarily known as the junction of the Simplon, Lötschberg, and Furka rail lines.

brig, two-masted sailing vessel, square-rigged on both masts. Brigs have been used as cargo ships and also, in the past, as small warships carrying about 10 guns. They vary in length between 75 and 130 ft (23–40 m), with tonnages up to 350. A brigantine is a somewhat smaller two-masted vessel, square-rigged on the foremast but with a fore-and-aft mainsail. In earlier times it carried a square topsail on the mainmast. A hermaphrodite brig is identical with the brigantine except that it carries no topsail on its mainmast; most U.S. brigs since 1860 have actually been of this type.

Briga: see BRIGUE AND TENDE.

brigandage (brĭg'əndĭj), robbery, blackmail, kidnapping, and plundering committed by armed bands. Laxity in administration, social and political demoralization, economic or political oppression, and racial or religious antagonisms may give rise to brigandage, especially if the terrain of the area provides suitable hiding places for the brigands. Inhabitants of an invaded state sometimes resort to brigandage, and those held under intolerable economic subjection adopt it as a means of retaliation. In such conditions, the bandit is often protected by a sympathetic public opinion, and, like the legendary Robin Hood, may become a popular hero, the symbol of resistance to tyranny. Brigandage then becomes a mixture of violent spoliation and patriotism or altruism. Brigandage more frequently flourishes during the disintegration of a state (as the decline of the Roman Empire), at a time of major economic and social change (as among the robber barons at the end of the feudal ages), after a great war, in the early stages of frontier settlement (as in early California and in the Australian bush), or in national borderlands (as on the Scottish border). When a strong centralized authority develops, when a disciplined constabulary is organized, or when public disapproval of brigandage becomes manifest, it disappears. The brigand leader, in a chaotic society, may extend his jurisdiction over a wide area, and although his ends may be selfish, he can contribute to the social order by establishing a recognized authority. The lawless lives of brigands and highwaymen have often become legends. Stories of gallantry and heroism have gathered about many brigands, especially those who were the victims of social or political oppression, who were rebels rather than bandits. Ballads and folk tales have grown about many leaders, and the names of brigands are known to all: Dick Turpin, the highwayman; Hereward the Wake; Robin Hood; Stenka Razin, the Cossack; Fra Diavolo of Italy; and Jesse James of the United States. See C. J. Finger, *Highwaymen* (1925, rep. 1970); Danilo Dolci, *Outlaws* (1961); Christopher Hibbert, *Highwaymen* (1968); Eric Hobsbawm, *Bandits* (1969).

Briggs, Charles Augustus, 1841–1913, American clergyman, theologian, and educator, b. New York City, studied at the Univ. of Virginia, Union Theological Seminary, and the Univ. of Berlin. From 1875 until his death he was a member of the faculty of Union Theological Seminary, serving as professor of Hebrew and the cognate languages. In 1890 he was appointed to the chair of biblical theology. The address on the authority of Holy Scripture that he gave at that time caused his trial for heresy (1892) before the New York presbytery. Although acquitted, Dr. Briggs was suspended (1893) from the Presbyterian ministry by the General Assembly; thereupon Union Theological Seminary severed its relations with the Assembly. He later (1900) entered the Episcopal ministry. Among his many books are *A Critical and Exegetical Commentary on the Book of Psalms* (2 vol., 1906) and *Hebrew and English Lexicon of the Old Testament* (with Francis Brown and S. R. Driver, completed 1906). See his *Inaugural Address and Defense* (first printed in 1891 and 1893, repr. 1972); C. E. Hatch, *The Charles A. Briggs Heresy Trial* (1969).

Briggs, Clare A., 1875–1930, American cartoonist, b. Reedsburg, Wis. He won a national reputation with the contributions he made to the Chicago *Tribune* from 1907 to 1914. From 1914 until his death his cartoons appeared in the New York *Tribune* syndicate. Among his best-known creations are "Mr. and Mrs." and "In the Days of Real Sport." The droll simplicity of his drawings was characteristic of American graphic humor of the 1920s.

Briggs, Henry, 1561–1630, English mathematician. He was the first professor of geometry at Gresham College, London (1596–1619), and Savilian professor of astronomy at Oxford (from 1619). After publication of Napier's work on logarithms in 1614, Briggs suggested that the logarithms be tabulated to the base 10, and Napier agreed to the alteration. Briggs wrote *Arithmetica logarithmica* (1624), a work containing logarithmic tables for 30,000 natural numbers to 14 places. His logarithms are known today as common logarithms.

Briggs, Le Baron Russell, 1855–1934, American educator, b. Salem, Mass., grad. Harvard (B.A., 1875; M.A., 1882). As a teacher at Harvard he developed, with Barrett Wendell, a prescribed and widely imitated freshman English course. A number of able contemporary writers were influenced by his graduate course in creative writing. He became professor of English in 1890 and of rhetoric and oratory in 1904. In 1891 he was appointed dean of the college and from 1903 to 1923 served as president of Radcliffe. His works include *School, College, and Character* (1901), *Routine and Ideals* (1904), *Girls and Education* (1911), and *Men, Women, and Colleges* (1925). See R. W. Brown, *Dean Briggs* (1926).

Brigham, Albert Perry, 1855–1932, American geographer, b. Perry, N.Y., grad. Colgate Univ., 1879, M. A. Harvard, 1892. After nine years in the Baptist ministry (1882–91) he became professor of geology at Colgate, where he taught for 30 years. A founder of human geography, Brigham helped to shape the development of geographic thought in the United States by recognizing and expounding upon the influence of the earth on man. He published many articles and textbooks including *Geographic Influences in American History* (1903), a book that widely influenced history students and scholars.

Brigham City, city (1970 pop. 14,007), seat of Box Elder co., N Utah; inc. 1869. It is the center of a large farm area served by the Ogden River project. Sheep, cattle, wheat, sugar beets, garden crops, and orchard fruit are raised. The city has woolen mills, granaries, and food-processing plants, and a sugar refinery is nearby. It was founded as Box Elder in 1851, and its name was changed to honor Brigham Young in 1856. A U.S. Indian school is in the city, and just west is the Golden Spike National Historic Site, which marks the spot in which the last railroad spike was driven in 1869. A bird refuge is nearby.

Brigham Young University, at Provo, Utah; Latter-Day Saints; coeducational; opened as an academy in 1875 and became a university in 1903.

Brighouse, municipal borough (1971 pop. 34,111), West Riding of Yorkshire, N central England, on the Calder River. It is a center of woolen, cotton, and silk milling and produces carpets, leather goods, machinery, radio and television equipment, dyes, and soap. Stone quarries are nearby. Also in the vicinity is the traditional grave of Robin Hood. In 1974, Brighouse became part of the new metropolitan county of West Yorkshire.

Bright, John, 1811–89, British statesman and orator. He was the son of a Quaker cotton manufacturer in Lancashire. A founder (1839) of the Anti-Corn Law League, he rose to prominence on the strength of his formidable oratory against the CORN LAWS. A staunch laissez-faire capitalist, and, with RICHARD COBDEN, a bastion of the MANCHESTER SCHOOL of economics, he resented the protection given to landholders by these laws at the expense of manufacturing interests. After the repeal (1846) of the corn laws, Bright's principal concern was parliamentary reform, which he pursued relentlessly until passage of the third Reform Bill in 1884. A member of Parliament for Manchester (1847–57), he lost his seat because of his opposition to British involvement in the Crimean War, which he considered un-Christian and against Britain's economic interests. He represented Birmingham (1858–89) and served in William Gladstone's cabinets as president of the Board of Trade (1868–70) and chancellor of the duchy of Lancaster (1873–74, 1880–82). He supported Gladstone on the issues of disestablishment of the Church of Ireland (1869) and Irish land reforms, but he opposed Home Rule for Ireland. His laissez-faire views also made him oppose direct government intervention to improve the conditions of the poor. He resigned (1882) in protest against intervention in Egypt for the same reasons that had led him to oppose the Crimean War. See his speeches (ed. by J. E. T. Rogers, 1868) and public addresses (also ed. by J. E. T. Rogers, 1879); biographies by G. M. Trevelyan (2d ed. 1925) and A. S. Turberville (1945).

Bright, Richard, 1789–1858, English physician. In London he was the leading consultant of his time, and he contributed many important clinical observations. He was the author of the significant *Reports of Medical Cases* (Vol. I, 1827). This contained his description of certain forms of NEPHRITIS, or kidney disease, known generally as Bright's disease and of dropsy resulting from kidney disease, as distinct from cardiac dropsy. Bright was a physician at Guy's Hospital.

bright-line spectrum: see SPECTRUM.

Brighton, county borough (1971 pop. 166,081), East Sussex, SE England. The largest and most popular resort in S England, Brighton also has engineering works and factories that manufacture office machinery, machine tools, electrical apparatus, vacuum cleaners, shoes, and paint. Formerly a small fishing village, it became a fashionable resort and was patronized, starting in 1783, by the Prince of Wales (later George IV), who built the Royal Pavilion. Entertainment is provided on the West Pier and the Palace Pier and in the Dome, formerly the royal stables and now a hall; these, together with the seaside promenade and the aquarium, are notable features. The Univ. of Sussex is in Brighton. In 1974 the borough became part of the new nonmetropolitan county of East Sussex.

Brighton, city (1971 pop. 39,103), Victoria, SE Australia, part of the Melbourne urban agglomeration, on Port Phillip Bay. It is a residential area and resort.

Bright's disease: see NEPHRITIS.

Brigid, Saint: see BRIDGET, SAINT.

Brigue and Tende (brĕg, täNd), Ital. *Briga* and *Tenda,* two small districts (1968 pop. 2,726), Alpes-Maritimes dept., SE France, on the French-Italian border. With several smaller frontier areas in the Mont Cenis and Mont Blanc regions, they were ceded to France by Italy in 1947 after a referendum. Brigue and Tende are largely French-speaking. Before 1947 the strategic Col de Tende, a pass now situated on the border, was entirely within Italy.

Brill or **Bril,** Flemish painters, brothers. **Mattys Brill** (mä'tĭs), 1550–83, went to Rome early in his career and executed frescoes for Gregory XIII in the Vatican. **Paul Brill,** 1554–1626, probably studied in Rome with his brother and succeeded him at the Vatican. His calm, well-observed landscapes exercised a great influence on Italian art. His works after 1600 show his mature style; the landscape elements are arranged like stage-set wings receding diagonally into depth, his brushwork is broader, and his atmospheric effects refined. His frescoes and oils are found in many Roman churches. *Martyrdom of St. Clement* (Vatican), against a seascape, is perhaps his best-known work. He often painted small landscapes on copper.

Brill, Abraham Arden, 1874–1948, American psychiatrist, b. Austria, grad. New York Univ., 1901, M.D. Columbia, 1903. He came to the United States alone at the age of 13. After studies with C. G. Jung in Switzerland, he returned to the United States in 1908 to become one of the earliest and most active exponents of psychoanalysis, being the first to translate into English most of the major works of Freud as well as books by Jung. He taught at New York Univ. and Columbia, was a practicing psychoanalyst, and wrote *Psychoanalysis: Its Theories and Practical Application* (1912) and *Fundamental Conceptions of Psychoanalysis* (1921).

Brillat-Savarin, Anthelme (äNtĕlm' brēyä'-sävärăN'), 1755–1826, French lawyer, economist, and gastronomist, famous for his witty treatise on the art of dining, *La Physiologie du goût* (1825). It has been frequently republished and was translated into English as *The Physiology of Taste* (1925, rev. ed. 1971). An émigré during the Reign of Terror, Brillat-Savarin spent some time in the United States.

Brill's disease: see TYPHUS.

brimstone: see SULFUR.

Brindaban, India: see VRINDABAN.

Brindisi (brēn'dēzē), Latin *Brundisium,* city (1971 pop. 79,784), capital of Brindisi prov., in Apulia, S Italy. A modern port on the Adriatic Sea, it has been noted since ancient times for its traffic with the E Mediterranean. Manufactures include petrochemicals, plastics, and food products. Its excellent harbor was a Roman naval station, a chief embarkation point for the Crusaders (12th–13th cent.), and an important Italian naval base in World War I. One of the two columns marking the terminus of the Appian Way still stands; Brindisi also has Romanesque churches, a fine cloister, and a castle built (13th cent.) by Emperor Frederick II.

brine shrimp, common name for a primitive CRUSTACEAN that seldom reaches more than ½ in. (1.3 cm) in length and is commonly used for fish food in aquariums. Brine shrimp, which are not closely related to true shrimp, can be found almost everywhere in the world in inland salt waters, although they are completely absent from oceans. They can live in water having several times the salinity of sea water, but they can also tolerate water having only one tenth the marine salt concentration. Brine shrimp usually occur in huge numbers and can be seen in vast windblown lines in the Great Salt Lake. Their absence from the sea has been explained by their vulnerability to attack by predators and the absence of the latter in their inland saline habitat. Although brine shrimp are considered to be members of a single genus, *Artemis,* and possibly a single species, there are several varieties. Generally, they have stalked, compound eyes and tapered bodies with a trunk that bears 11 pairs of leaflike legs. Females have a brood pouch from which active young are liberated under favorable conditions. Otherwise eggs are laid parthenogenetically (unfertilized by sperm) or fertilized and can either hatch immediately or be dried and remain viable for many years. These eggs are remarkably resistant to adverse environmental conditions, which is why they can be hatched so easily in salt water and used for fish food; adult brine shrimp are also used as food in aquariums and are generally sold frozen. Brine shrimp are classified in the phylum ARTHROPODA, class Crustacea, subclass Branchiopoda, order Anostraca.

Brinker, Maureen Connolly: see CONNOLLY, MAUREEN.

Brinkley, David, 1920–, American news broadcaster, b. Wilmington, N.C. He joined the National Broadcasting Company in 1943. Brinkley and Chet HUNTLEY developed documentary techniques for televised analyses of public affairs. Their *Huntley-Brinkley Report* series (1956–71) won several awards, including the Peabody, Sylvania, and "Emmy" awards. As a news analyst Brinkley is noted for his terse, biting comments and his dry wit.

Brinton, Crane (Clarence Crane Brinton), 1898–1968, American historian, b. Winsted, Conn. He received his Ph.D. from Oxford in 1923 and began teaching at Harvard the same year, becoming full professor in 1942. He wrote extensively on the history of Western political and moral philosophy and is considered an expert on the dynamics of revolutionary movements. His many books include *A Decade of Revolution* (1934), *The Anatomy of Revolution* (1938, rev. ed. 1965), *Ideas and Men* (1950, 2d ed. 1963), *A History of Western Morals* (1959), *The Shaping of Modern Thought* (1963), and *The Americans and the French* (1968).

Brinvilliers, Marie Madeleine d'Aubray, marquise de: see POISON AFFAIR.

Brion, Amiral de: see CHABOT, PHILIPPE DE.

Briosco, Andrea (ändrĕ'ä brēôs'kō), 1470?–1532, Italian architect and sculptor, known also as Andrea Riccio [curly-headed], b. Padua. As an architect, he created models for the church of Santa Giustina and for a chapel in Sant' Antonio in Padua. His fame rests chiefly on his bronze sculpture. In close contact with Paduan humanists, he carried out involved allegorical programs in his Paschal candlestick (Sant' Antonio) and the Della Torre monument (Verona). Drawing upon mythological themes, he combined delightful fantasy with a first-rate knowledge of antiquity.

briquette (brĭkĕt'), a block of compressed coal dust, peat, or charcoal used for FUEL.

Brisbane, Albert (brĭz'băn), 1809–90, American social theorist, b. Batavia, N.Y. After studying with Charles FOURIER in Paris, he returned to the United States as an enthusiastic advocate of Fourierism. His *Social Destiny of Man* (1840) aroused widespread interest, especially that of Horace Greeley, who gave him a column in the *Tribune.* Brisbane was instrumental in the founding of the phalanxes at BROOK FARM and Red Bank, N.J. The failure of most of the other communal experiments was disastrous for the Fourierist cause, but Brisbane reaffirmed his convictions in his *General Introduction to Social Science* (1876). His wife, Redelia Brisbane, edited and wrote an introduction to his autobiography, published posthumously as *Albert Brisbane: A Mental Biography* (1893, repr. 1969). His son, Arthur Brisbane (1864–1936), was editor of the New York *Evening Journal* and other Hearst papers. See biography by O. Carlson (1937).

Brisbane, Sir Thomas Makdougall (brĭz'bən, -băn), 1773–1860, British soldier, astronomer, and colonial administrator in Australia, b. Scotland. From 1793 to 1814 he served in the army in Flanders, in the West Indies, in Spain, and in Canada, rising to the rank of brigadier general. In 1821 he was appointed governor of New South Wales, where he encouraged agriculture, land reclamation, exploration, and, most important, immigration, thus stimulating the transformation of New South Wales from a dependent convict outpost into a free, self-supporting colony. He had poor financial sense, however, and was recalled in 1825. Brisbane had an observatory built (1822) at Paramatta, near Sydney, where work was done (1822–26) resulting in the "Brisbane Catalogue" of 7,385 stars. After his return to Scotland, he founded an observatory at Makerstoun, where valuable observations on magnetism were started (1841); these were incorporated into three volumes in the transactions of the Royal Society of Edinburgh. He was made president of the society in 1833. The city of Brisbane and the Brisbane River in Australia were named for him.

Brisbane (brĭz'bən), city (1971 pop. 699,371; urban agglomeration pop. 816,987), capital of Queensland, E Australia, on the Brisbane River above its mouth on Moreton Bay. It has shipyards, oil refineries, food-processing plants, textile mills, automobile plants, and railroad workshops. Principal exports are wool, meat, fruit, sugar, and coal and other minerals. The area was settled in 1824 as a penal colony, and the city was named in 1834 for Sir Thomas Brisbane, governor of New South Wales. In 1925 the Greater Brisbane Act unified the administration of 19 formerly separate localities. Brisbane is the seat of the Univ. of Queensland (1909), a national art gallery (1895), and a museum (1871). There are Anglican and Roman Catholic cathedrals.

Briseis: see ACHILLES; AGAMEMNON.

Brissot de Warville, Jacques Pierre (zhäk pyĕr brēsō' də värvēl'), 1754–93, French revolutionary and journalist. A lawyer of humble origin, he began his career by writing numerous pamphlets and books. His *Théorie des lois criminelles* (1781) was a plea for penal reform. He was imprisoned briefly in the Bastille for writing a seditious pamphlet. Brissot visited the Netherlands, Switzerland, England, and the United States. He was interested in humanitarian schemes and founded the abolitionist Société des Amis des Noirs. After his return to France in 1789 he began to edit the *Patriote français,* which later became the organ of the GIRONDISTS (at first called Brissotins). Brissot, feeling that war would spread the principles of the French Revolution, did much to foment it with his violent diatribes against monarchs. In the Legislative Assembly his great influence on the conduct of foreign affairs was largely responsible for the French declaration of war on Austria in 1792. On this issue the Girondists broke with the JACOBINS. A power struggle between the two groups ensued, and the Girondists were defeated. The Jacobin victory over the Girondists resulted in his execution. He left memoirs. See biography by Eloise Ellery (1915, repr. 1970).

bristlecone pine, common name for the PINE species *Pinus longaeva,* found in the White Mountains of California. Specimens are known that are nearly 5,000 years old.

Bristol, George Digby, 2d earl of, 1612-77, English courtier; son of John Digby, 1st earl of Bristol. At first a member of the parliamentary opposition to Charles I, he later fought for the king in the English civil war. Afterward he served Louis XIV of France. On his return to England after the Restoration (1660), he was ineligible for office because he had been converted to Roman Catholicism. Having served Charles II in exile as secretary of state, he exerted some influence at court until his attempt to impeach the earl of Clarendon for treason failed in 1663. See biography by Dorothea Townshend (1924).

Bristol, John Digby, 1st earl of, 1580-1653, English diplomat. He spent most of the years 1611-24 at the Spanish court, where as ambassador he conducted the prolonged negotiations for the marriage of Prince Charles (later CHARLES I) to the Spanish infanta. Digby was made earl of Bristol in 1622, but the next year the visit of Charles and the duke of Buckingham to Madrid brought to an end the already deadlocked marriage negotiations, and the new earl fell into disfavor. He was recalled and confined to his house until he protested before Parliament. He was then accused of treason by Charles (then king) and imprisoned (1626) without trial in the Tower of London until Parliament released him in 1628. Bristol was for a time a supporter of parliamentary opposition to the crown, but as Parliament became more extreme, he joined the king's group of advisers. In 1642 he was committed to the Tower briefly by Parliament but rejoined Charles at Oxford after the outbreak of the civil war. Later he opposed continuing the war. He died in exile in Paris.

Bristol, county borough (1971 pop. 45,203), Gloucestershire, SW England, at the confluence of the Avon and Frome rivers. Bristol, a leading international port, has extensive facilities, including docks at Avonmouth and Portishead. Automobiles, tractors, machinery, clay, chemicals, coke, and tea are exported from Bristol; wine, grain, petroleum, tobacco, dairy products, fruit, and lumber are imported. General and nuclear engineering and the design and manufacture of aircraft are the largest industries; others are flour milling, printing, and the manufacture of paper, footwear, and tobacco products. Bristol has been a trading center since the 12th cent. First chartered as a city in 1155, it became a separate county by order of Edward III in 1373, the first provincial town to receive this honor. During the reign of Edward III the manufacture of woolen cloth was developed. The cloth was exported chiefly to Ireland, Spain, and Portugal. From Bristol the explorers John and Sebastian Cabot (to whom there is a monument on Brandon Hill) sailed to Newfoundland and America. In the 18th cent. Bristol was active in the colonial triangular trade: English goods went to Africa; African slaves to the West Indies; and West Indian sugar, rum, and tobacco to Bristol. The slave trade was opposed by John Wesley and by Quakers, who were influential in Bristol. In 1838 the *Great Western,* one of the first transatlantic steamships, was launched from Bristol. The port declined during the late 18th and early 19th cent. because of competition from Liverpool, the end of slave trading, and the decline of the West Indian trade. It revived in the mid-19th cent. Points of interest in Bristol include the 14th-century church of St. Mary Redcliffe, known for its fine architecture; a 14th-century cathedral (rebuilt 1868-88) with a Norman chapter house and gateway; the Merchant Venturers' Almshouses; University Tower; and some notable examples of Regency architecture. The Clifton suspension bridge, spanning the Avon and the scenic Avon Gorge, connects Bristol with Clifton. Bristol has a famous university. The city was heavily damaged during World War II. The poets Thomas Chatterton and Robert Southey were born there. In 1974, Bristol became part of the new nonmetropolitan county of Avon.

Bristol. 1 Industrial city (1970 pop. 55,487), Hartford co., central Conn., on the Pequabuck River; settled 1727, inc. 1785. Its clockmaking industry dates from 1790. It also has a steel mill and plants that make ball bearings, mechanical springs, electric and electronic equipment, paper boxes, and a great variety of metal parts. The American Clock and Watch Museum is in the city. A chrysanthemum festival is held yearly. **2** Industrial borough (1970 pop. 12,085), Bucks co., SE Pa., on the Delaware River opposite Burlington, N.J.; settled 1697, inc. 1720. Its many manufactures include paper, chemicals, textiles, aircraft parts, and metal products. The third oldest borough in the state, it was once a busy river port with important shipbuilding activities. Among its historic structures is the Friends Meetinghouse, built c.1710. A restoration of 17th- and 18th-century buildings is to the north, and a replica of William Penn's country manor is to the northeast. **3** Town (1970 pop. 17,860), seat of Bristol co., E R.I., a port of entry on Narragansett Bay; inc. as a Plymouth Colony town 1681, ceded to Rhode Island 1746. An early center of commercial trade, the port was (18th-19th cent.) a base for slave trading, privateering, whaling, and shipbuilding. The Herreshoff boat yard, where many winners of the America's Cup were built, was in operation there until 1945, and present-day Bristol is still a yachting and yacht-building center. It has a large rubber industry. King Philip's War (1675-76) began and ended on the site of the town, and a monument on Mt. Hope marks the spot where King Philip fell. The Haffenreffer Museum of Anthropology has notable collections of Indian relics. On Hope St. is a row of preserved colonial homes. The town is the seat of Roger Williams College and the Rhode Island Soldiers' Home. Mt. Hope Bridge connects Bristol with Portsmouth. The 1938 and 1954 hurricanes caused heavy damage to the shore and harbor. **4** Industrial city on the Tenn.-Va. line, Sullivan co., Tenn. (1970 pop. 20,064), independent and in no county in Virginia (1970 pop. 14,857); settled 1749 as Sapling Grove, inc. as separate towns 1856, as Bristol city 1890. The two cities, although separate municipalities, are economically a unit that is the transportation and processing center of a mountainous region producing tobacco, coal, and livestock. Shelby's Fort, built there in 1771, was frequented by Daniel Boone and other early pioneers; the King's Mountain campaign in the Revolutionary War was mounted there. Two hundred years of controversy preceded the location of the state line down the middle of State Street. King College is in the Tennessee section of the city, and Virginia Intermont College and a junior college are on the Virginia side. In the area are Bristol Caverns, largest in the Smoky Mts., and an international car-racing speedway.

Bristol, University of, at Bristol, England; established 1876 as University College, Bristol. In 1909 it gained university status. It has faculties of arts, science, medicine, engineering, law, social sciences, and education. The Race Relations Research Unit (founded 1970) is affiliated with the university.

Bristol Avon: see AVON **1,** England.

Bristol Channel, inlet of the Atlantic Ocean, c.85 mi (140 km) long and from 5 to 50 mi (8.1-80 km) wide, stretching westward from the mouth of the River Severn and separating Wales from SW England. Its chief bays are Milford Haven, Carmarthen, and Swansea (Wales), and Barnstaple and Bridgwater (England). There are many cities on or near the channel; among the largest are Bristol, Newport, Cardiff, and Swansea. Along the coast of S Wales there is a great concentration of economic activity, and Bristol Channel serves as a major shipping corridor. Milford Haven, a major oil-importing center, has a harbor that can accommodate large modern tankers. Coal is exported from Barry and from Port Talbot, also an important steel-producing center.

Bristow, Benjamin Helm (brĭs'tō), 1832-96, American cabinet officer, b. Elkton, Ky. He was admitted to the Kentucky bar in 1853. Bristow, a Union officer in the Civil War, was a state senator (1863-65), U.S. attorney for the Kentucky district (1866-70), and the first U.S. Solicitor General (1870-72). In June, 1874, President Grant appointed him Secretary of the Treasury. He thoroughly reorganized the department after the scandalous administration of William A. RICHARDSON, and he strengthened his growing reputation by a courageous and successful prosecution of the powerful WHISKEY RING. However, he incurred Grant's hostility and was virtually forced to resign in June, 1876. There was a strong movement in the Republican party to run Bristow for President in 1876, but the nomination ultimately went to Rutherford B. Hayes. Moving to New York City in 1878, he spent the remainder of his life as a distinguished and successful lawyer. See biography by Ross A. Webb (1969).

Britain, alternate name for the United Kingdom of Great Britain and Northern Ireland. It is derived from *Britannia,* the name given by the Romans to the portion of the island of Great Britain that they occupied. It has sometimes been used to refer to Great Britain in the period before the Germanic invasions of the 5th cent. A.D. After the union (1707) of England and Scotland, parliamentary legislation for a time used "South Britain" and "North Britain" to refer to the two parts.

Britain, Battle of: see BATTLE OF BRITAIN.

britannia metal, silvery-white ALLOY of tin with antimony, copper, and sometimes bismuth and zinc. It is very similar in appearance to pewter, but is harder. It is used widely for the manufacture of tableware.

Britannicus (Claudius Tiberius Germanicus Britannicus), A.D. 41?-A.D. 55, Roman prince, son of CLAUDIUS I and MESSALINA, so called in honor of Claudius' conquests in Britain. After Claudius' marriage to AGRIPPINA II, mother of NERO, Britannicus was passed over as heir in favor of Nero. He was poisoned after Nero's accession. His death is the subject of Racine's drama *Britannicus.*

British Cameroons: see NIGERIA, FEDERATION OF; CAMEROON, UNITED REPUBLIC OF.

British Columbia, province (1971 pop. 2,184,621), 366,255 sq mi (948,600 sq km), including 6,976 sq mi (18,068 sq km) of water surface, W Canada. VICTORIA is the capital and the second largest city. The largest city, and chief port, is VANCOUVER; other centers include NEW WESTMINSTER, NORTH VANCOUVER, NANAIMO, and PRINCE RUPERT. British Columbia, the westernmost province of Canada, is bounded on the E by Alberta, on the S by Montana, Idaho, and Washington, on the W by the Pacific Ocean, on the NW by Alaska, and on the N by the Yukon and by the Mackenzie dist. of the Northwest Territories. Off its deeply indented Pacific coast lie many islands, notably Vancouver Island (c.280 mi/450 km long) and the sparsely inhabited Queen Charlotte Islands. The province is almost wholly mountainous, with the Rocky Mts. in the southeast, the Coast Mts. along the Pacific, and the Stikine Mts. in the northwest. Chief of the many rivers is the Fraser, which, with its tributaries, drains much of central and S British Columbia as it flows to the Pacific. Other rivers in that region include the upper Columbia and the Kootenay. In the north are the Peace, the Stikine, the Nass, and the Skeena. Hydroelectric power in British Columbia is highly developed; gigantic plants along the rivers operate huge pulp and paper mills. The largest station, at Kemano on the Nechako River, serves one of the biggest aluminum plants in the world, at Kitimat. Innumerable long, narrow lakes are found throughout the interior, supplying vast backwaters for dams. Large areas of central and N British Columbia are sparsely settled, almost three fourths of the population crowding the southwest coastal tip. Less than 10% of the province can be used for grazing or cultivation, since nearly three fourths of the land is covered with forests. British Columbia's evergreens make up about half of all of Canada's timber. Lumbering and related enterprises (such as pulp and paper manufacturing) are the province's major industries. Next in importance is mining; British Columbia is rich in mineral resources, and geologists, technicians, and adventurers are continually searching for new deposits. The

silver mine at Kimberley is the largest in the world; copper is mined principally at Princeton and Britania; gold chiefly along the Bridge River and in Cariboo and Osoyoos dists.; iron ore primarily on Vancouver and Texada islands. Lead and zinc are mined in many places, the world's largest deposits being at Kimberley. Other minerals found in the province include coal, crude petroleum, asbestos, natural gas, and sand and gravel. British Columbia ranks first among the provinces in fishing; the most important catches are salmon, halibut, and herring. Beef is also an important product. Cattle are raised along the Fraser River; the Texas longhorn, introduced there c.1870, is still thriving, and the area is known for its sprawling ranches. Other industries include food processing and the manufacture of chemicals, furniture, transportation equipment, and electrical items. British Columbia attracts millions of visitors annually, and the land is a hunting and fishing paradise. There are four national parks—Glacier, Mt. Revelstoke, Yoho, and Kootenay—and hundreds of provincial parks and camping grounds. The climate along the west coast, tempered by the warm Japan Current, has made that area, especially Vancouver and Victoria, very attractive to tourists. The area was originally inhabited by Indians of the Pacific Northwest (known especially for their totem poles and POTLATCHES). Juan Peréz was probably the first white man to sail (1774) along the coast, but he did not make a landing. In 1778, Capt. James Cook, on his last voyage, explored the coast in his search for the Pacific entrance to the elusive Northwest Passage and claimed the area for Great Britain. John Meeres established (1788) a fur-trading post on Nootka Sound and built a schooner, but he was driven out (1789) by a Spaniard, Estevan José Martinez. Rival British and Spanish claims for the area were resolved by the Nootka Convention in 1790 (see NOOTKA SOUND). The British sent George Vancouver to take possession of the land, and from 1792 to 1794 he explored and mapped the coast. In 1793, Sir Alexander Mackenzie reached the Pacific overland; he was followed early in the 19th cent. by fur traders and explorers of the NORTH WEST COMPANY who crossed the mountains to establish posts in New Caledonia, as the region was then called. After the HUDSON'S BAY COMPANY absorbed the North West Company in 1821, the region became a preserve of the new company. In 1843, Fort Victoria was established by James Douglas as a trading post for the company. Three years later rival British and American claims to the area were settled when the boundary was set at the 49th parallel (see OREGON, state). Further controversy resulted in the SAN JUAN BOUNDARY DISPUTE. Partly as protection against further American expansion, Vancouver Island was ceded (1849) by the Hudson's Bay Company and became a crown colony, of which Sir James Douglas was made governor in 1851. In 1858 gold was discovered in the sand bars of the Fraser River and additional deposits were found on many of its tributaries. The great gold rushes that resulted brought profound changes. Fort Victoria boomed as a supply base for the miners, and a town quickly sprang up around it. Officials of the crown came to keep order, and to supervise government projects and the building of roads. Some 30,000 miners moved into what was then unorganized territory; this led to the creation (1858) of a new colony on the mainland, called British Columbia, and the end of the Hudson's Bay Company's supremacy. In 1863 the newly settled territory about the Stikine River was added to British Columbia. In 1866, Vancouver Island and British Columbia were combined, and in 1871 this united British Columbia, lured by the promise of financial aid and a transcontinental railroad that would link it to the rest of Canada, voted to join the new Canadian confederation. The Canadian Pacific Railway finally reached Vancouver in 1885, and a new era began. By providing access to new markets, the railroads furthered agriculture, mining, and lumbering; steamship service with the Orient was inaugurated, and Vancouver grew as a busy port, serving many provinces. The opening (1914) of the Panama Canal was a further boost to trade and commerce. A long dispute with the United States over the Alaska boundary was finally settled by the Alaska Boundary Commission in 1903. Politically, the Conservatives and Liberals alternated in power from 1903 (when the national parties were first introduced into British Columbian politics) until 1941, when a wartime coalition was formed. The SOCIAL CREDIT party came into power in 1952, under the leadership of W. A. C. Bennett, and retained control until 1972, when the New Democratic party, led by David Barrett, won a majority. British Columbia sends 6 senators (appointed) and 23 representatives (elected) to the national Parliament. The Univ. of British Columbia is at Vancouver. See F. H. Goodchild, *British Columbia* (1951); J. H. S. Reid, *Mountains, Men, and Rivers* (1954); R. E. Watters, ed., *British Columbia* (1958); M. A. Ormsby, *British Columbia* (1958, repr. 1971); J. L. Robinson, ed., *British Columbia* (1972).

British Columbia, University of, at Vancouver, British Columbia, Canada; provincially supported; coeducational; chartered 1908, opened 1915. It has faculties of arts, science, graduate studies, applied science, agricultural sciences, dentistry, commerce and business administration, education, law, forestry, medicine, and pharmaceutical sciences, as well as schools of architecture, home economics, librarianship, nursing, physical education and recreation, rehabilitation medicine, social work, and community and regional planning.

British Commonwealth of Nations: see COMMONWEALTH OF NATIONS.

British East Africa, inclusive term for several former British dependencies, especially Kenya, Uganda, Tanganyika, and Zanzibar.

British East India Company: see EAST INDIA COMPANY, BRITISH.

British Empire, overseas territories linked to Great Britain in a variety of constitutional relationships, established over a period of three centuries. The establishment of the empire resulted primarily from commercial and political motives and emigration movements; its long endurance resulted from British command of the seas and preeminence in international commerce, and from the flexibility of British rule. At its height in the late 19th and early 20th cent., the empire included territories on all continents, comprising about one quarter of the world's population and area. The origins of the empire date from the late 16th cent. with the private commercial ventures, chartered and encouraged by the crown, of CHARTERED COMPANIES. These companies sometimes had certain powers of political control as well as commercial monopolies over designated geographical areas. Usually they began by setting up fortified trading posts, but where no strong indigenous government existed the English gradually extended their powers over the surrounding area. In this way scattered posts were established in India and the East Indies (for spices, coffee, and tea), defying Portuguese and later Dutch hegemony, and in Newfoundland (for fish) and Hudson Bay (for furs), where the main adversaries were the French.

The First Empire. In the 17th cent. European demand for sugar and tobacco led to the growth of plantations on the islands of the Caribbean and in SE North America. These colonies, together with those established by Roman Catholics and Protestant dissenters in NE North America, attracted a considerable and diversified influx of European settlers. Organized by chartered companies, the colonies soon developed representative institutions, evolving from the company governing body and modeled on English lines. The need for cheap labor to work the plantations fostered the growth of the African slave trade. New chartered companies secured posts on the African coasts as markets for captured slaves from the interior. An integrated imperial trade arose, involving the exchange of African slaves for West Indian molasses and sugar, English cloth and manufactured goods, and American fish and timber. To achieve the imperial self-sufficiency required by prevailing theories of MERCANTILISM, and, more immediately, to increase British wealth and naval strength, the NAVIGATION ACTS were passed, restricting colonial trade exclusively to British ships and making England the sole market for important colonial products. Developments in the late 17th and early 18th cent. were characterized by a weakening of the Spanish and Dutch empires, exposing their territories to British encroachment, and by growing Anglo-French rivalry in India, Canada, and Africa. At this time the British government attempted to assert greater direct control over the expanding empire. In the 1680s the revision of certain colonial charters to bring the North American and West Indian colonies under the supervision of royal governors resulted in chronic friction between the governors and elected colonial assemblies. The early 18th cent. saw a reorganization and revitalization of many of the old chartered companies. In India, from the 1740s to 1763, the British EAST INDIA COMPANY and its French counterpart were engaged in a military and commercial rivalry in which the British were ultimately victorious. The political fragmentation of the Mogul empire permitted the absorption of one area after another by the British. The Treaty of Paris (1763; see under PARIS, TREATY OF) firmly established the British in India and Canada, but the financial burdens of war involved the government in difficulties with the American colonies. The success of the AMERICAN REVOLUTION marked the end of the first British Empire.

The Second Empire. The voyages of Capt. James Cook to Australia and New Zealand in the 1770s and new conquests in India after 1763 opened a second phase of territorial expansion. The victories of the Napoleonic Wars added further possessions to the empire, among them Cape Colony, Mauritius, Ceylon, Trinidad and Tobago, St. Lucia, British Guiana, and Malta. During the second empire mercantilist ideals and regulations were gradually abandoned in response to economic and political developments in Great Britain early in the 19th cent. Britain's new industrial supremacy lent greater force to doctrines of FREE TRADE, which, as part of their critique of mercantilism, questioned the economic value of political ties between the colonies and the mother country. The plight of large nonwhite populations within the empire became a matter of concern to humanitarians. Abolition of the slave trade (1807) and of slavery (1833) was accompanied in the colonies by efforts to improve the lot of indigenous groups. Better communications and the establishment of a regular civil service facilitated the development of a more efficient colonial administration. But the growth, notably in the English-speaking colonies, of national identity and of relative national self-sufficiency, as well as a trend of opinion in Britain favoring colonial self-government, made the British, now engaged in liberalizing their own governing institutions, willing to concede certain powers of self-government to the white colonies. In 1839, Lord Durham, in response to unrest in Canada, issued his "Report on the Affairs of British North America." Durham stated that to retain its colonies Britain should grant them a large measure of internal self-government. The BRITISH NORTH AMERICA ACT of 1867 inaugurated a pattern of devolution followed in most of the European-settled colonies by which Parliament gradually surrendered its direct governing powers; thus Australia and New Zealand followed Canada in becoming self-governing dominions. On the other hand, the British assumed greater responsibility in Africa and in India, where the INDIAN MUTINY had resulted (1858) in the final transfer of power from the East India Company to the British government. To govern territories with large indigenous populations, the crown colony system had been developed. Such colonies, of which one of the most enduring has been Hong Kong, were ruled by a British governor and consultative councils composed primarily of his nominees; these, in turn, often delegated considerable powers of local government to local rulers. In the later decades of the 19th cent. there occurred a revival of European competition for empire in which the British acquired or consolidated vast holdings in Africa—such as Nigeria, the Gold Coast (later Ghana), Rhodesia, South Africa, and Egypt—and in Asia—such as Burma and Malaya. The size and wealth of the empire and the anxieties produced by European colonial competition stimulated a desire for imperial solidarity. The IMPERIAL CONFERENCE, begun in 1887, represented an attempt to strengthen Britain's ties with those colonies that had become self-governing territories.

From Empire to Commonwealth. World War I brought the British Empire to the peak of its expansion, but in the years that followed came its decline. Victory added, under the system of MANDATES, new territories, including Palestine, Trans-Jordan, Iraq, and several former German territories in Africa and Asia. Imperial contributions had considerably strengthened the British war effort (more than 200,000 men from the overseas empire died in the war; the dominions and India signed the Versailles Treaty and joined the League of Nations), but at the same time expectations were raised among advanced colonial populations that an increased measure of self-government would be granted. Nationalist agitation against economic disparities, often stimulated by acts of racial discrimination by British settlers, was particularly strong in India (see INDIAN NATIONAL CONGRESS) and in parts of Africa. Although loath to lessen its hold over countries it had done much to develop, and thereby to incur great economic and political loss, Britain gradually capitulated to the pressures of nationalist sentiment. Iraq gained full sovereignty in 1932; British privileges in Egypt were modified by treaty in 1936; and concessions were made toward self-government in India and later in the African colonies. In 1931 the Statute of Westminister (see WESTMINISTER, STATUTE OF) officially recognized the independent and equal status under the crown of the former dominions within a British COMMONWEALTH OF NATIONS, thus marking the advent of free cooperation among equal partners. After World War II self-government advanced rapidly in all parts of the empire. In 1947, India was partitioned and independence granted to the new states of India and Pakistan. In 1948 the mandate over Palestine was relinquished, and Burma gained independence as a republic. Other parts of the empire, notably in Africa, gained independence and subsequently joined the British Commonwealth. Probably the outstanding impact of the British Empire has been the dissemination of European ideas, and particularly of British political institutions and of English as a lingua franca throughout a large part of the world. At the start of 1975 Great Britain still administered, as colonies, protectorates, or trust territories, many dependencies throughout the world. They included Brunei and Hong Kong in E Asia; the Seychelles in the Indian Ocean; Gibraltar in the Mediterranean; the Falkland Islands, Bermuda, and St. Helena in the Atlantic; the Cayman Islands, British Virgin Islands, Turks and Caicos Islands, and several of the Leeward and Windward Islands in the West Indies; British Honduras (Belize) in Central America; and Pitcairn Island, the Solomon Islands, the New Hebrides Islands (jointly with France), and the Gilbert and Ellice Islands in the Pacific. These dependencies have varying degrees of self-government. Great Britain claims authority over the state of Rhodesia, which, however, unilaterally declared its independence in 1965. See IMPERIALISM. See Paul Knaplund, *The British Empire, 1815–1939* (1941, repr. 1969) and *Britain, Commonwealth and Empire, 1901–1955* (1956); A. L. Burt, *The Evolution of the British Empire and Commonwealth from the American Revolution* (1956); *The Cambridge History of the British Empire* (8 vol., 1929–59; 2d ed. 1963–); R. A. Huttenback, *The British Imperial Experience* (1966); J. A. Williamson, *A Short History of British Expansion* (2 vol., 6th ed. 1967); C. E. Carrington, *The British Overseas* (2d ed. 1968); Colin Cross, *The Fall of the British Empire* (1968, repr. 1970); Max Beloff, *Imperial Sunset* (1969); Nicholas Mansergh, *The Commonwealth Experience* (1969); G. S. Graham, *A Concise History of the British Empire* (1970) and *Tides of Empire* (1972).

British Guiana: see GUYANA.

British Honduras (hŏndo͞or'əs,-dyo͞o'-), British crown colony (1970 pop. 119,645), 8,867 sq mi (22,965 sq km), Central America, on the Caribbean Sea. It is also known as Belize. The capital is Belmopan; BELIZE, the capital until 1970, is the main port.

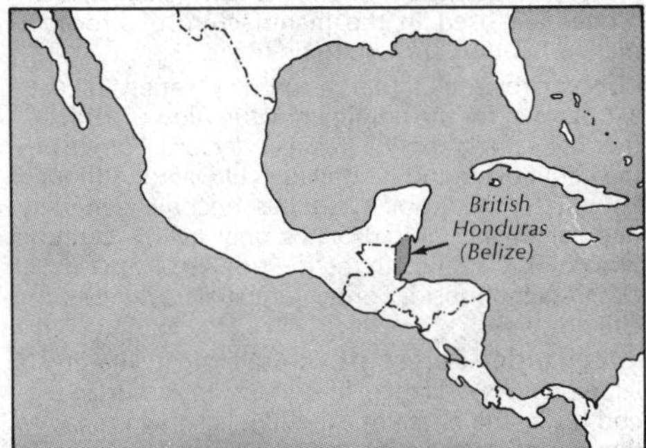

British Honduras is bounded on the N by Mexico, on the S and W by Guatemala, and on the E by the Caribbean. The land is generally low, with mangrove swamps and cays along the coast, but in the south rises to Victoria Peak (c.3,700 ft/1,128 m high). The climate is subtropical. Although most of the area is heavily forested, yielding mahogany, cedar, and logwood, there are regions of fertile savannas and barren pine ridges. Only a small fraction of the land is cultivated. In addition to woods, the chief products are sugarcane, chicle, citrus fruits, and timber. The people are predominantly of black African ancestry, but there are large minorities of Mayan Indian descendants (in the interior) and Spanish-Americans. English is the official language, but Spanish is widely spoken. Once part of the Mayan civilization, the region was probably traversed by Cortés on his way to Honduras, but the Spanish made no attempt at colonization. British buccaneers, who used the cays to prey on Spanish shipping, founded Belize (early 17th cent.). British settlers from Jamaica began the exploitation of timber. Spain contested British possession several times until defeated at the last battle of St. George's Cay (1798). From 1862 to 1884 the colony was administered by the governor of Jamaica. Since 1821, Guatemala has claimed the territory as part of its inheritance from Spain. As British Honduras has progressed toward independence, the tension between Britain and Guatemala over the issue has increased. In 1964 the colony gained complete internal self-government. It has a bicameral legislature; the main political organization is the People's United party. The capital was moved to the new city of Belmopan in 1970 after a hurricane devastated Belize. See S. L. Caiger, *British Honduras, Past and Present* (1952); D. A. G. Wadell, *British Honduras* (1961); Norman Ashcraft, *Colonialism and Underdevelopment: Process of Political Economic Change in British Honduras* (1973).

British Imperial System of weights and measures: see ENGLISH UNITS OF MEASUREMENT.

British Isles: see GREAT BRITAIN; IRELAND.

British Museum, the national repository in London for treasures in literature, science, and art. It has departments of manuscripts, of printed books, of antiquities, of prints and drawings, of coins and medals, and of ethnography. The museum was established by act of Parliament in 1753 when the collection of Sir Hans Sloane, begun in the previous century and called the Cabinet of Curiosities, was purchased by the government and was joined with the Cotton collection (see COTTON, SIR ROBERT BRUCE) and the Harleian Library (see HARLEY, ROBERT). In 1757 the royal library was given to the museum by George II. The institution was opened in 1759 under its present name in Montague House, but the acquisition of the library of George III in 1823 necessitated larger quarters. The first wing of the new building was completed in 1829, the quadrangle in 1852, and the great domed reading room in 1857. Later other additions were built. Sir Anthony PANIZZI began the printing of the library's catalog. The library is vast and splendid; among its rarest manuscripts are included *Beowulf, Magna Carta*, the 4th-century Greek bible known as the Codex Sinaiticus, Froissart's *Chronicles*, and a unique papyrus of Aristotle. The library is increased partly by the copyright law requiring the deposit of each book printed in the United Kingdom. The museum's collection of prints and drawings is one of the finest in the world. The natural history collection was transferred (1881–83) to buildings in South Kensington and called the Natural History Museum. One of the major exhibits of the Egyptian department is the basalt slab known as the Rosetta Stone (see under ROSETTA). The Greek treasures include the ELGIN MARBLES and the Caryatid from the Erectheum. The museum's special collections include a vast number of clocks and timepieces, ivories, and the SUTTON HOO treasure. See J. M. Crook, *The British Museum* (1972); *Treasures of the British Museum* (1972); Edward Miller, *That Noble Cabinet* (1974).

British North America Act, law passed by the British Parliament in 1867 that provided for the unification of the Canadian provinces into the dominion of Canada. The act also functions as the constitution of Canada, providing for a government similar to that of the United Kingdom. The act enumerates the powers of the provincial legislatures and gives the residual powers to the dominion; its interpretation by the privy council has somewhat nullified this design by giving a very extended scope to the provincial power of "property and civil rights," and a doctrine of "emergency powers" has been developed in order to give the dominion the authority needed by a national government in time of war. The power of amendment is still nominally vested in the British Parliament, which in practice, however, acts only on the request of the Canadian Parliament. Numerous attempts to make wide-ranging changes in the act have failed because of a lack of unanimity among Canada's provinces. See Edward Porritt, *Evolution of the Dominion of Canada* (1918, repr. 1972).

British North Borneo: see SABAH, Malaysia.

British Somaliland: see SOMALI DEMOCRATIC REPUBLIC.

British South Africa Company: see RHODESIA.

British thermal unit, abbr. Btu., unit for measuring heat quantity in the customary system of ENGLISH UNITS OF MEASUREMENT, equal to the amount of heat required to raise the temperature of one pound of water at its maximum density [which occurs at a temperature of 39.1 degrees Fahrenheit (°F)] by 1°F. The Btu may also be defined for the temperature difference between 59°F and 60°F. One Btu is approximately equivalent to the following: 251.9 calories; 778.26 foot-pounds; 1055 joules; 107.5 kilogram-meters; 0.0002928 kilowatt-hours. A pound (0.454 kilogram) of good coal when burned should yield 14,000 to 15,000 Btu; a pound of gasoline or other fuel oil, approximately 19,000 Btu.

British Togoland: see TOGOLAND.

British West Africa, former inclusive term for the British colonies of Cameroons, Gambia, Gold Coast, Nigeria, Sierra Leone, and Togoland.

British West Indies: see WEST INDIES.

Britomartis (brĭt'ōmär'tĭs), in ancient mythology, Cretan goddess, sometimes identified with Artemis. To escape the amorous pursuit of Minos, she jumped into the sea, but fishermen caught her in their nets and transported her to Aegina, where she was worshiped as Aphaea. According to another legend, she vanished in a grove sacred to Artemis and was deified as Dictynna.

Brittany (brĭt'ənē), Breton *Breiz*, Fr. *Bretagne*, region and former province, NW France. It is a peninsula between the English Channel on the north and the Bay of Biscay on the south and comprises five departments, Ille-et-Vilaine, Côtes-du-Nord, Finistère, Morbihan, and Loire-Maritime. The economy of the region is based on agriculture, fishing, and tourism. Apples, from which the distinctive Breton cider is made, are grown extensively inland. Industry includes shipbuilding at ST. NAZAIRE and NANTES, food processing, and automobile manufacturing. There is a nuclear power plant in the Arrée Mts. The coast, particularly at the western tip, is irregular and rocky, with natural harbors (particularly at BREST, LORIENT, and SAINT-MALO) and numerous islands. Important rivers include the Loire, the Odet, the Vilaine, and the Sèvre Nantaise. A part of ancient Armorica, the area was conquered by Julius Caesar in the GALLIC WARS and became part of the province of Lugdunensis (see GAUL). It received its modern name when it was settled (c.500) by Britons whom the Anglo-Saxons had driven from Britain. Breton history is a long struggle for independence—first from the Franks (5th–9th cent.), then from the dukes of Normandy and the counts of Anjou (10th–12th cent.), and finally from England and France. In 1196, Arthur I, an ANGEVIN, was acknowledged as duke. King John of England, who presumably murdered him (1203), failed to obtain the duchy, which passed to Arthur's brother-in-law, Peter I (Peter Mauclerc). The extinction of his direct line led to the War of the BRETON SUCCESSION (1341–65), a part of the HUNDRED YEARS WAR (1337–1453). With the end of the Breton war, the dukedom was won by the house of Montfort. The dukes of Montfort tried to secure Brittany's neutrality between France and Britain during the remainder of the Hundred Years War. The unsuccessful rebellion of Duke Francis II against the French crown led to the absorption of Brittany into France after the accession of his daughter, Anne of Brittany, in 1488. King Francis I formally incorporated the duchy into France in 1532. Brittany's provincial PARLEMENT met at Rennes, and its provincial assembly remained powerful until the French Revolution. The 16th and 17th cent. were generally peaceful in Brittany, but the region, never reconciled to centralized rule, became one of the early centers of revolt in 1789. However, its staunch Catholicism and conservatism soon transformed it into an anti-Revolutionary stronghold; the CHOUANS (anti-Revolutionary peasants) were never fully subdued, and in S Brittany and the neighboring VENDÉE the Revolutionary government resorted to ruthless reprisals. Breton nationalism grew in the 19th cent. and was fueled by the anticlericalism of the Third Republic. The Breton autonomists, long successfully repressed by the French government, nevertheless resisted German bids for collaboration in World War II. In more recent years the emigration of the young has resulted in a serious decline in the region's population. Brittany and the Breton people have retained many old customs and traditions. Breton, their Celtic language (akin to Welsh), is spoken in traditionalist Lower (i.e., western) Brittany outside the cities (see BRETON LITERATURE). Costumes featuring high lace headdresses are distinctive in every community and are worn widely on Sundays and holidays. Religious festivals, at which ships, birds, and houses are blessed, are characteristic of Breton fetes, and there are formal religious processions and pilgrimages. Brittany has remarkable stone calvaries, some built at the close of the 16th cent. to ward off the plague. Many megalithic monuments, formerly ascribed to the DRUIDS, dot the Breton landscape, notably at CARNAC. See P. R. Giot et al., *Brittany* (1960); Nora K. Chadwick, *Early Brittany* (1969).

Brittany spaniel, breed of medium-sized SPORTING DOG whose origins may be traced back hundreds of years to France and Spain. It stands about 19 in. (48.3 cm) high at the shoulder and weighs between 30 and 40 lb (13.6–18.1 kg). Its dense, flat or wavy coat is dark orange and white or liver and white. Many Brittany spaniels are born tailless or very short-tailed, and a tail that is more than 4 in. (10.2 cm) long is docked to that length. Although it is a "leggy" spaniel, it has a compact body—its height at its shoulder often equals its body length. The Brittany is a first-rate hunter and may easily be trained to retrieve, both on land and water. It is the only spaniel that points its quarry. See DOG.

Britten, Benjamin, 1913–, English composer. Britten is considered the most significant British composer since Purcell. As a youth he showed facility in the composition of instrumental works, displaying technical brilliance and colorful orchestration. One example, *A Young Person's Guide to the Orchestra* (1945), written for a film, is based on a theme by Purcell. His most characteristic expression is achieved in vocal music. His many song cycles and choral works include *A Boy Was Born* (1933) and *A Ceremony of Carols* (1942). Britten's great *War Requiem* (1962), based on the bitter war poems of Wilfred Owen, was sung at the dedication in England of the reconstructed Coventry Cathedral, destroyed during World War II. In his operas, which include *Paul Bunyan* (1941), *Peter Grimes* (1945), *The Rape of Lucretia* (1946), *The Turn of the Screw* (1954), *A Midsummer Night's Dream* (1960), and *Death in Venice* (1973), he evinced a sensitivity to text and a fondness for variation technique, dynamic dissonance, and the use of ground basses. See biographies by P. M. Young (1968), Imogen Holst (2d ed. 1970), and E. W. White (new ed. 1970).

brittle star, common name for echinoderms belonging to the class Ophiuroidea. The name is derived from their habit of breaking off arms as a means of defense. New arms are easily regenerated. They are also called serpent stars because of the snakelike movements of the five mobile, slender arms. Brittle stars can be distinguished from SEA STARS, or starfish, by their rounded central disk, sharply set off from the arms. They have the water-vascular system and tube feet common to all echinoderms; unlike sea stars, brittle stars lack open grooves (ambulacral grooves) on the lower surface of the arms, and the tube feet serve as tactile organs. Also unlike sea stars, brittle stars walk with their arms; only some species use the tube feet for locomotion. Each arm contains a series of jointed bonelike plates, or ossicles, which determine the freedom of arm movements. Brittle stars can move quickly and in any direction. They are relatively small, usually less than 1 in. (2.5 cm) across the central disk, although the arms may be quite long. They are inconspicuous and often nocturnal, living under rocks, among seaweed, or buried in the sand. All are marine species, feeding on detritus and small living or dead animals. The arms move the larger food masses to the mouth, where they are fragmented by a complex jaw apparatus. Tube feet move smaller particles to the mouth, and some species, like *Ophiocomina nigris* of the Pacific coast, can take tiny food particles like a filter-feeder, trapping them in mucus and using ciliary currents to deliver them to the mouth. As a rule, sexes are separate, and fertilization occurs in the open sea after gametes have been discharged. A characteristic armed larval stage, the ophiopluteus, undergoes a profound metamorphosis to produce the rayed adult form. About 2,000 species of ophiuroids are known, and a number are common along American coasts. Brittle stars are classified in the phylum ECHINODERMATA, class Ophiuroidea.

Britton, John, 1771–1857, English antiquary and topographer. The long list of his writings includes biographies, critical works on art and literature, and the descriptions of landscapes and buildings for which he is famous. *The Beauties of Wiltshire* (3 vol., 1801–25) was written with E. W. Brayley. The two friends wrote part of *Beauties of England and Wales* (18 vol., in 25, 1801–15), but because of difficulties with the publishers, they did not complete the series. Britton was influential in the movement to preserve ancient monuments. See his autobiography (3 parts, 1849–50).

Britton, Nathaniel Lord, 1859–1934, American botanist, grad. Columbia School of Mines, 1879. He taught geology and botany at Columbia, 1879–96. He was the New York Botanical Garden's first director and until his retirement in 1929 had a major part in its growth. His own contributions, chiefly in the field of tropical botany, include hundreds of thousands of specimens, many of great rarity, gathered on his trips to the tropics. His chief works include *An Illustrated Flora of the Northern United States, Canada, and the British Possessions* (with Addison Brown, 1896–98); *The Bahama Flora* (with C. F. Millspaugh, 1920); and four volumes on cacti (with J. N. Rose, 1919–23).

Brixen: see BRESSANONE, Italy.

Brixham: see TORBAY.

Brno (bûr'nô), Ger. *Brünn,* city (1970 pop. 335,918), central Czechoslovakia, at the confluence of the Svratka and Svitava rivers. It is the second largest city of Czechoslovakia and the chief city of Moravia. Brno is an industrial center, known particularly for its woolen industry and for its manufacture of textiles, machinery (notably tractors), machine tools, and armaments. The famous Bren gun, later made in Enfield, England, was developed in Brno. Tourism is also economically important, and the city holds a large annual international trade fair. Originally the site of a Celtic settlement, Brno grew between two hills, one of which, the Spielberg (Czech *Špilberk*), had a castle known in the 11th cent. The city became part of the kingdom of Bohemia, whose king, Ottocar I, confirmed Brno's ancient charter, a model of liberal town government, in 1229. King Wenceslaus I made it a free city by royal decree in 1243, and Brno flourished in the 13th and 14th cent. In the Hussite Wars it sided with the Roman Catholic Church. The city was besieged in 1645 by the Swedes and served as headquarters for Napoleon I during the battle of Austerlitz in 1805. The Spielberg castle, which was captured by Hapsburg forces during the Thirty Years War, became (1740–1855) their most notorious political prison. Franz von der Trenck and Silvio Pellico (who described it in *Le mie prigioni*) were its most celebrated inmates. In the 19th cent. Brno became one of the foremost manufacturing towns of the Austrian empire. Most Germans were expelled from the city after World War II. Brno's landmarks include the cathedral (15th cent.), the old and new town halls, and several fine Gothic and baroque churches. Masaryk Univ. (founded 1919), Beneš Technical College, a music conservatory, and several fine museums are also located in the city.

Broach (brōch) or **Baroach** (bərōch'), town (1971 pop. 92,263), Gujarat state, W India, on the Gulf of Cambay. A port at the mouth of the Namada River, Broach ships cotton and timber. Textiles are manufactured there. Broach was an important Buddhist center in the 7th cent. Under the Rajput dynasty (750–1300), it was the chief port of W India.

broaching: see QUARRYING.

broadcasting, transmission of sound or images to a large number of receivers by radio or television. In the United States the first regularly scheduled radio broadcasts began in 1920 with the transmission of the Harding-Cox election returns by Frank Conrad over 8XK (later KDKA) in Pittsburgh. The sale of ADVERTISING was started in 1922, establishing commercial broadcasting as an industry. Radio became increasingly attractive as an advertising medium with the coming of network operation. A coast-to-coast hookup was tentatively effected early in 1924, and expansion of both audience and transmission facilities continued rapidly. By 1927 there were two major networks, and the number of stations had so increased that it caused serious overlapping in transmission channels. Legislation (see FEDERAL COMMUNICATIONS COMMISSION) designed to meet this problem was enacted, and the government has since maintained some control over the technical and business activities of the industry. By 1970 over 4,200 commercial radio stations were operating in the standard broadcasting (amplitude modulation, or AM) band. There were also over 2,000 frequency modulation (FM) stations on the air. Experiments in broadcasting television began in the 1920s, but were interrupted by World War II. After the war the number of commercial TV stations grew from 9 in 1947 to 672 by 1970. To offset the dominance of commercial broadcasting, the Corporation for Public Broadcasting was established in 1968 as a non-profit, nongovernmental agency to finance the growth of noncommercial radio and television; by 1972 the network served over 200 stations. See RADIO; TELEVISION. See Eric Barnouw, *A History of Broadcasting in the United States* (3 vol., 1966, 1968, and 1971).

Broad Church: see ENGLAND, CHURCH OF.

Broads, the, region, c.5,000 acres (2,020 hectares), mainly in Norfolk, E England, extending inland to Norwich from the coast. It is composed of wide, interlocking shallow lakes, connected by the Waveney, Yare, and Bure rivers; there are more than 200 mi (320 km) of navigable waterways. The Broads is a vacation center and wildlife sanctuary.

Broadstairs and Saint Peter's, urban district (1971 pop. 19,996), Kent, SE England. The district is in the region known as the Isle of Thanet. It is a residential area and resort and was once a retreat of Charles Dickens, whose residence there is now called Bleak House.

Broadview Heights, village (1970 pop. 11,463), Cuyahoga co., NE Ohio, a suburb of Cleveland; inc. 1926.

Broadway, famous thoroughfare of New York City. The longest street in the world, it extends 150 mi (241 km), from Bowling Green near the foot of Manhattan island N to Albany. Throughout its length within New York City, Broadway is chiefly a commercial street. At WALL ST. it runs through the financial center of the country; N of Union Square (14th St.) it passes a clothing and merchandising section with large department stores, entering the theater district at TIMES SQUARE (42d St.). There it becomes the noted "Great White Way," illuminated at night by a profusion of electric signs and lights. Points of interest along Broadway include Trinity Church (Wall St.); St. Paul's Chapel, built 1766 (near City Hall); the Woolworth Building (at Barclay St.); the Lincoln Center for the Performing Arts (64th–67th streets); COLUMBIA UNIV. (113th–121st streets); the Columbia-Presbyterian Medical Center (168th St.); and Van Cortlandt Park (at the north end of the city). Broadway was laid out by the Dutch and was the principal street of NEW AMSTERDAM; it was extended north as the colony grew.

Broca, Paul (pōl brôkä'), 1824–80, French pathologist, anthropologist, and pioneer in neurosurgery. A professor in Paris at the Faculty of Medicine and at the Anthropological Institute, he was a founder of the Anthropological Society of Paris (1859) and of the *Revue d'anthropologie* (1872). An authority on aphasia, he localized the brain center for articulate speech in the convolution of Broca, or Broca's area (the third convolution of the left frontal lobe). He originated methods of classifying hair and skin color and of establishing brain and skull ratios.

brocade, fabric, originally silk, generally reputed to have been developed to a high state of perfection in the 16th and 17th cent. in France, Italy, and Spain. The fabric is characterized by a compact warp-effect background with one or more fillings used in the construction to make the motif or figure. The filling threads, often of gold or silver in the original fabrics of this name, float in embossed or embroidered effects in the figures. Motifs may be of flowers, foliage, scrollwork, pastoral scenes, or other design. Its uses include curtaining, hangings, pillows, portieres, evening wraps, and church vestments. Similar techniques are used in the manufacture of brocades made of cotton and synthetic fibers.

broccoli (brŏk'əlē) [Ital.,=sprouts], variety of CABBAGE grown for the edible immature flower panicles. It is the same variety (*Brassica oleracea botrytis*) as the cauliflower and is similarly cultivated. Although known to the Romans, it has become generally popular in the United States only in this century. Broccoli is classified in the division MAGNOLIOPHYTA, class Magnoliopsida, order Capparales, family Cruciferae.

Brocéliande, Forest of (brōsālēäNd'), Ille-et-Vilaine dept., NW France, in Brittany. In Arthurian legend it was the home of Merlin. It is known today as the Forest of Paimpont.

Broch, Hermann (hĕr'män brôkh), 1886–1951, Austrian novelist. His powerful trilogy *Die Schlafwandler* (1931–32, tr. *The Sleepwalkers,* 1932) is written in a complex style reminiscent of James Joyce. Dealing with three different classes and periods, it describes the disintegration of social values and of organic coherence in the modern world. Broch, also a successful mathematician and businessman, lived in the United States after 1938. See his *The Guiltless* (1950, tr. 1973).

Brock, Sir Isaac, 1769–1812, British general, Canadian hero of the War of 1812. A British army officer, he was sent to Canada in 1802 and was given command (1806) of Upper and Lower Canada. He strengthened defenses and made plans for a navy. In 1811 he was made major general and was appointed administrator of Upper Canada. At the outbreak of war, Brock joined forces with Tecumseh on the Western frontier and moved against Detroit. He captured Gen. William Hull's army (1812) and gained control of the upper lakes. For this he received a knighthood and the title "hero of Upper

Canada." After Detroit he successfully defended Queenston Heights on the Niagara frontier, but was killed while leading a charge. See study by S. H. Adams (1957).

Brock, Sir Thomas, 1847–1922, English sculptor. One of the leading sculptors under the reign of Victoria, he enjoyed a long and successful career. He became an Academician in 1891 and was knighted in 1911. His work shows dignity and restraint. His bust of Longfellow (Westminster Abbey), his colossal Victoria Memorial, in front of Buckingham Palace, and his equestrian statue, *Black Prince* (Leeds) are notable examples of his work.

Brocken (brôk'ən), granite peak, 3,747 ft (1,142 m) high, W East Germany; highest peak of the Harz mts. Popular legend makes it the meeting place of the Walpurgis Night or Witches' Sabbath. The "Brocken scene" in Goethe's *Faust* is set there.

Brockton, industrial city (1970 pop. 89,040), Plymouth co., E Mass.; settled c.1700, set off from Bridgewater 1821, inc. as a city 1881. It has a large shoe and leather products industry. Textiles and clothing, machinery and machine tools, plastics, and electrical and electronic equipment are also produced. A junior college, an art center, and a historic museum are in the city. Brockton has an annual fair, which has been held since 1874. A state park is nearby.

Brock University, at St. Catharines, Ont., Canada; coeducational; founded 1964. It has a faculty of arts and science and a college of education. The university has developed a special interest in administration and in urban and Asian studies.

Brockville, city (1971 pop. 19,765), SE Ont., Canada, on the St. Lawrence River. It is in a rich dairy region. The city's manufactures include telecommunications equipment, power tools, and baby foods. In summer it is a tourist resort.

Brockway, Zebulon Reed, 1827–1920, American penologist, b. Lyme, Conn. As superintendent of the House of Correction in Detroit, he tried to introduce in 1869 the indeterminate sentence for first offenders. His ideas were incorporated in a Michigan statute but were nullified by the courts. He aided New York state legislation by organizing the first state reformatory for adult males, built at Elmira, and was its first superintendent (1876–1900). He introduced a system of military training, physical training, education, and trade instruction, with merits as incentives to good behavior. The success of his Elmira experiments led to the introduction of the indeterminate sentence in other states. He wrote *Fifty Years of Prison Service* (1912).

Brod, Max (mäx brōd), 1884–1968, Israeli writer and composer, b. Prague. Brod is best known for his historical novels, notably *The Redemption of Tycho Brahe* (1916, tr. 1928) and *Reubeni, Prince of the Jews* (1925, tr. 1928). A lifelong friend of Franz Kafka, he wrote an excellent biography of Kafka (1937, tr. 1947) and also edited Kafka's writings. Brod's numerous other works include a biography of Heine (1934, tr. 1956), an autobiography (1960), and plays, poems, novels, and essays. His musical compositions include works for orchestra, notably Requiem Hebraicum, and for voice and piano. Long an active Zionist, Brod left Prague for Palestine in 1939 where he directed the Habima Theater.

Broderick, David Colbreth (brō'dərĭk), 1820–59, American politician, b. Washington, D.C. Brought up in New York City, he was active in Tammany Hall before moving to California in 1849. He became equally active in politics there, being a member of the state constitutional convention of 1849. He was elected to the state senate in 1850 and was chosen to preside over it in 1851. Broderick, who drew his support chiefly from Northerners, fought bitterly for control of the Democratic party in the state against U.S. Senator William M. GWIN, leader of the proslavery element. Both were sent to the U.S. Senate in 1857 under a compromise by which Broderick was to have control of the Federal patronage. However, President Buchanan and Gwin ignored the understanding, and Broderick fiercely attacked them both. He was killed by Chief Justice David S. Terry of the California supreme court, a supporter of Gwin, in a famous duel near San Francisco. An eloquent eulogy at his elaborate funeral and editorial reverberations throughout the land made him the martyr of the Union cause in California. See biographies by Jeremiah Lynch (1911) and D. A. Williams (1969).

Brodhead, Daniel, 1736–1809, American Revolutionary officer and Indian fighter, b. probably near Albany, N.Y. He was taken as an infant to Pennsylvania, where he later served as deputy surveyor general (1773–75). In the Revolution he commanded a detachment of militia in the battle of Long Island, was sent (1778) to Pittsburgh, and became commandant there in 1779. In that year he led an expedition up the Allegheny River against the Indians; this was linked with the expedition of John Sullivan in New York. When in 1781, the Delawares broke their treaty, he invaded their territory. He was removed from his command but later was brevetted brigadier general. For 11 years (1798–1809) he was surveyor general of Pennsylvania.

Brodie, Steve, 1863–1901, Brooklyn bookmaker who gained immediate fame and a measure of immortality by allegedly jumping off the Brooklyn Bridge and surviving the fall, on July 23, 1886. It was claimed that Brodie had not, in fact, jumped from the bridge but that a dummy was used as he hid under a pier. In any case he gained the publicity he was seeking, and a tavern he opened shortly after in the Bowery became a mecca for sightseers.

brodiea or **brodiaea** (both: brədē'ə), any plant of the genus *Brodiaea*, herbs of the family Liliaceae (LILY family) with narrow leaves and blue or purple star-shaped flowers. The many North American species include the golden brodiea (*B. ixioides*) and the common, or white, brodiea (*B. hyacinthina*), called also wild hyacinth. Both are found in hilly regions of the Pacific states. Temperate South American species include the spring starflower (*B. uniflora*), which is commonly cultivated. The small onionlike bulbs of brodieas were eaten by American Indians and called "grass nuts." Brodiea is classified in the division MAGNOLIOPHYTA, class Liliatae, order Liliales, family Liliaceae.

Broederlam, Melchior (mĕl'khēôr brō'dərläm), active c.1381–1409, Franco-Flemish painter. Broederlam was among the first practitioners of the International Gothic style (see GOTHIC ARCHITECTURE AND ART). He was court painter after 1387 to Philip the Bold, duke of Burgundy. Influenced by Italian painting, Broederlam attempted to place figures in perspective, as in his panels for *Baerze's Retable* (Musée de la Ville, Dijon).

Brogan, Denis William, 1900–1974, British historian and political scientist, b. Glasgow, Scotland. He was educated at the Univ. of Glasgow, Oxford, and Harvard and was professor of political science at Cambridge from 1939 to 1968; in addition, he lectured at various American universities. Brogan was best known as an interpreter of American history and politics for British readers; he also wrote widely on modern France. His writings include *The American Political System* (1933), *France under the Republic* (1940), *Politics and Law in the United States* (1941), *The American Character* (1944), *The Era of Franklin D. Roosevelt* (1950), *Politics in America* (1954), *America in the Modern World* (1960), *American Aspects* (1964), and *Worlds in Conflict* (1967). He was knighted in 1963.

Broglie (brôglē'), French noble family of Piedmontese origin, who settled in France in the 17th cent. **Victor Maurice, comte de Broglie,** 1647–1727, was marshal of France and fought in the wars of King Louis XIV. His son **François Marie, duc de Broglie,** 1671–1745, marshal of France, fought at Malplaquet (1709), in the War of the Polish Succession, and in the War of the Austrian Succession. King Louis XV conferred on him the ducal title inherited by his son **Victor François, duc de Broglie,** 1718–1804, marshal of France, who distinguished himself in the War of the Austrian Succession and the Seven Years War. Holy Roman Emperor Francis I made him prince of the Holy Roman Empire (1757), a title that remained in the family. In the French Revolution he emigrated and commanded (1792) the army of the princes against the revolutionary forces. **Charles François, comte de Broglie,** 1719–81, brother of Victor François, was ambassador to Poland (1752) and later headed the so-called "secret cabinet" of Louis XV, the king's secret organization of political advisers and spies. **Achille Charles Léon Victor, duc de Broglie,** 1785–1870, grandson of Victor François, was a statesman and diplomat under Emperor Napoleon I and a leader of the moderate liberals after the Restoration. He occupied several cabinet posts, including that of premier (1835–36), under King Louis Philippe, and was (1847–48) ambassador to London. After the February Revolution (1848) he was elected (1849) to the assembly. He opposed Emperor Napoleon III. He married a daughter of Mme de Staël. His son, **Jacques Victor Albert, duc de Broglie,** 1821–1901, was a historian and politician. He was a member of the national assembly (1871), ambassador to London (1871–72), premier (1873–74; 1877), and a liberal monarchist leader in the senate. He wrote *Histoire de l'église et de l'empire romain au IVe siècle* (6 vol., 1856–66), an apologia for the Church as preserver of civilization in the late Roman period; *The King's Secret* (tr. 1879), based on the career of his great-granduncle, Charles François de Broglie; *An Ambassador of the Vanquished* (tr. 1896); and *Frederick the Great and Maria Theresa* (tr. 1883). He also edited the memoirs of his father (tr. 1887). He was the grandfather of the scientists Maurice, duc de Broglie, and Louis Victor, prince de Broglie (see separate articles).

Broglie, Louis Victor, prince de, 1892–, French physicist. In 1932 he became professor in the faculty of sciences, Univ. of Paris. It was known from the earlier QUANTUM THEORY that waves sometimes exhibited a particlelike behavior. De Broglie hypothesized (1924) that particles should also exhibit certain wavelike properties, a prediction that led to the development of wave mechanics, a form of quantum mechanics. The existence of these matter waves was confirmed experimentally in 1927, and de Broglie received the 1929 Nobel Prize in Physics for his theory. He was elected permanent secretary of the Academy of Sciences in 1942 and has been a member of the French Academy since 1944. His many works on physics and the philosophy of science include *An Introduction to the Study of Wave Mechanics* (1930, tr. 1930), *Revolution in Physics* (tr. 1953), and *Non-Linear Wave Mechanics* (1956, tr. 1960).

Broglie, Maurice, duc de, 1875–1960, French physicist; brother of Louis Victor, prince de Broglie. His contributions include notable work on X rays and in atomic physics, radioactivity, and electricity. He became a member of the Academy of Sciences in 1924 and of the French Academy in 1934.

Broken Arrow, city (1970 pop. 11,787), Tulsa co., NE Okla., a suburb of Tulsa.

Broken Hill, city (1971 pop. 29,743), New South Wales, SE Australia, near the South Australia border. Since 1884 it has been a principal center of zinc and silver mining in Australia.

broker, one who acts as an intermediary in a sale or other business transaction between two parties. Such a person conducts individual transactions only, is given no general authority by his employers, discloses the names of the principals in the transaction to each other, and leaves to them the conclusion of the deal. He neither possesses the goods sold nor receives the goods procured; he takes no market risks and transfers no title to goods or to anything else. He earns his commission, or brokerage, when the contract of sale has been made, regardless of whether the contract is satisfactorily executed. He is paid by the party with whom he first negotiates. In practice, merchants and other salesmen act as brokers at times. Brokers are most useful in establishing trade connections in those large industries where a great many relatively small producers (e.g., farmers) compete for a wide market. They operate in strategic cities and keep in active touch with the trade needs of their localities and with one another. They are important in determining prices, routing goods, and guiding production, and in those functions play a part similar to the highly organized exchanges. Brokers also negotiate trades in property not directly affecting production. Such are stockbrokers and real estate brokers. Employment agents are really brokers, as they bring together the buyers and sellers of labor. Merchandise brokers arrange sales between manufacturers and wholesalers or retailers, between producers and users of raw materials, and sometimes between two manufacturers. Small concerns use retail brokers instead of maintaining their own sales forces. Insurance brokers bring together insurance companies and those who want insurance. They are most useful to those needing several types of insurance protection and to those whose large risks must be divided among many companies. Real estate brokers negotiate sales and leases of farms, dwellings, and business property and are often also insurance brokers. Ship brokers keep informed of the movement of vessels, of cargo space available, and of rates for shipment and sell this information to shippers. They serve tramp carriers in the main, inasmuch as the larger ship lines have their own agents. Such brokers also serve as post agents, in which capacity they settle bills for stores and supplies, pay the wages of the crew, and negotiate insurance for the vessel and cargo. They also arrange the sale of ships. In the organized markets, such as grain and stock exchanges, commission merchants and straight selling displace brokerage in large part, but between cities and where there is no active exchange, brokers in grain and other commodities are active. Members of organized exchanges usually act as commission merchants or trade on their own account. However, in the New York Stock Exchange a group of members called "floor brokers" perform the actual trading on the exchange floor for representatives of commission houses, taking no responsibility and receiving a small fee. In the United States, note brokers buy promissory notes from businessmen and sell them to banks. Traders in acceptances and foreign bills of exchange are known in the United States as acceptance dealers. Customs brokers are not actually brokers; they act as agents for importers in estimating duties and clearing goods. The PAWNBROKER is a private money lender. See Margaret Hall, *Distributive Trading* (1950); R. L. Kohls, *Marketing of Agricultural Products* (1961).

Bromberg: see BYDGOSZCZ, Poland.

Brome, Richard (bro͞om, brōm), c.1590–1652, English dramatist. He was the friend, servant, and disciple of Ben Jonson. Primarily a writer of realistic satiric comedy, picturing the life and manners of Caroline bourgeois London, he also produced several tragicomedies, but with much less success. The main features of his plays are the humour characters (see HUMOR), complicated comic intrigue, and an abundance of action. The majority of his comedies were performed between 1629 and 1642, the most noteworthy being *The Northern Lass, The City Wit,* and *The Jovial Crew.* See study by R. J. Kaufmann (1961).

brome grass, common name for any plant of the genus *Bromus,* chiefly large, coarse grasses of a weedy nature; some, however, are useful as forage, and others are cultivated for decoration. Some of the better-known bromes are the smooth brome (*B. inermis,* sometimes called awnless, or Hungarian, brome), often cultivated for pasture or for holding banks; rescue grass (*B. catharticus*), a forage in the Southern states; and chess, or cheat (*B. secalinus*), a pest of grainfields, formerly believed by some to be degenerate wheat. Many species of brome grasses develop sharp-barbed fruits at maturity that are injurious to stock (whence the name ripgut grass for some); before maturity these are often used for forage. Brome grasses are classified in the division MAGNOLIOPHYTA, class Liliatae, order Cyperales, family Gramineae.

bromeliad, common name for plants of the family Bromeliaceae (PINEAPPLE family).

bromide, any of a group of compounds that contain BROMINE and a more electropositive element or radical. Bromides are formed by the reaction of bromine or a bromide with another substance; they are widely distributed in nature. Most metal bromides are water soluble; exceptions are bromides of copper, lead, mercury, and silver that are very slightly soluble in water. Potassium bromide, KBr, and sodium bromide, NaBr, are the familiar bromides used in medicine as sedatives; they should be used under a doctor's direction since they are habit-forming. Magnesium bromide, found in seawater, is a source of pure bromine. Silver bromide is one of the light-sensitive silver salts used in films, plates, and printing papers for photography. Hydrobromic acid is a water solution of hydrogen bromide, a gas. The presence of a bromide in a water solution can be detected by adding chlorine and carbon disulfide, CS_2; the bromine is displaced from its compound and dissolves in the CS_2, giving it a characteristic orange color.

bromine (brō'mēn,-ĭn) [Gr.,=stench], volatile, liquid chemical element; symbol Br; at. no. 35; at. wt. 79.904; m. p. -7.2°C; b. p. 58.78°C; sp. gr. of liquid 3.12 at 20°C; density of vapor 7.14 grams per liter at STP (see separate article); valence −1, +1, +3, +5, or +7. At ordinary temperatures bromine is a brownish-red liquid that gives off a similarly colored vapor with an offensive, suffocating odor. It is a member of the HALOGEN family in group VIIa of the PERIODIC TABLE. It is the only nonmetallic element that is liquid under ordinary conditions. It is soluble in water to some extent; the aqueous solution, called bromine water, acts as an oxidizing agent. It is also soluble in alcohol, ether, and carbon disulfide. Bromine is less active chemically than CHLORINE or FLUORINE but is more active than IODINE. It forms compounds similar to those of the other halogens (see BROMIDE). Oxides of bromine are unstable, but two acids, hypobromous acid, HBrO, and bromic acid, $HBrO_3$, are known with their salts. Hydrobromic acid is the aqueous solution of hydrogen bromide, HBr. Bromine does not occur uncombined in nature but is found in combination with other elements, notably sodium, potassium, magnesium, and silver. In compounds it is present in seawater, in mineral springs, and in common salt deposits, e.g., those at Stassfurt, Germany. It occurs in the United States, principally in Michigan, Ohio, and West Virginia. Bromine for commercial purposes is obtained by treating brines (from salt wells or seawater) with chlorine, which displaces the bromine. It is important in the preparation of organic compounds, such as ethylene dibromide, which is used in conjunction with an antiknock compound in gasoline. Bromine has a powerful corrosive action on the skin, destroying the tissue, and the vapor is strongly irritating to the eyes and the membranes of the nose and throat. The element was discovered in seawater by Antoine Jérôme Balard in 1826.

Bromley, borough (1971 pop. 304,357) of Greater London, SE England. The borough was created in 1965 by the merger of the former municipal boroughs of Bromley and Beckenham, the urban districts of Orpington and Penge, and part of the urban district of Chislehurst and Sidcup. It is the largest of the 32 Greater London boroughs. Bromley is mainly residential. The Crystal Palace, site of the 1851 Great Exhibition, was within the borough until fire destroyed it in 1936. William Pitt the younger, the statesman, and H. G. Wells, the writer, were born in what is now Bromley.

Bromsgrove, urban district (1971 pop. 40,669), Worcestershire, central England. Bromsgrove is an ancient market town and road junction. It is predominantly residential but has some industry, including a large forging works. In 1974, Bromsgrove became part of the new nonmetropolitan county of Hereford and Worcester.

bronchitis, inflammation of the mucous membrane of the bronchial tubes. It can be caused by viral or bacterial infections or by allergic reactions to irritants such as tobacco smoke. The disease is characterized by low-grade fever, chest pains, hoarseness, and productive cough. Acute bronchitis is rarely serious in otherwise healthy adults, but it can be dangerous in infants, children, or adults who suffer from underlying respiratory disease, especially emphysema. It may subside or, particularly with continued exposure to irritants, may persist and progress to chronic bronchitis or pneumonia. The more prolonged chronic bronchitis is frequently secondary to a serious underlying disorder. Bronchial inflammation can be severe; cough and bronchial spasms are treated with antihistamines, cough suppressants, and bronchodilators. Antibiotics are used if there is evidence of bacterial invasion.

bronchopneumonia: see PNEUMONIA.

bronchoscope, long, tubular instrument with a light at the tip that is inserted through the windpipe and bronchial tubes to examine these structures. By passing other instruments through it, foreign bodies and obstructions can be removed and tissue or secretions may be removed for microscopic observation. Gustav Killian, German laryngologist, in Freiburg, Germany, was the first to experiment with such a device in 1895. Chevalier Jackson adapted the bronchoscope to serve as an aid to the breathing of a patient during surgery in 1903, and he improved the system of illumination in the instrument; he is regarded as the father of bronchoscopy.

bronchus: see LUNGS.

bronco: see MUSTANG.

Brongniart, Adolphe Théodore (ädôlf' tāōdôr' brôNyär'), 1801–76, French botanist; son of Alexandre Brongniart. He was a pioneer in the study of vegetable physiology and was author of an important work on vegetable fossils (1828–37) and of a valuable first account of pollen. His classification of plants in the natural history museum at Paris was the basis of the system now used in Germany. He helped establish the *Annales des sciences naturelles* and founded the Société botanique de France.

Brongniart, Alexandre (äläksäN'drə), 1770–1847, French geologist, mineralogist, and chemist. As director of the Sèvres porcelain factory from 1800, he was responsible for its international fame. Brongniart established basic principles of ceramic chemistry that are incorporated in his *Traité des arts céramiques et des poteries* (1844). With Georges Cuvier he wrote *Essai sur la geographie mineralogique des environs de Paris* (1811), in which a system of stratigraphy was developed that relied on the use of fossils for the precise dating of strata. He also devised a system for the classification of reptiles.

Bronk, Detlev Wulf, 1897–, American biologist and administrator, b. New York City, grad. Swarthmore College (B.A., 1920), Ph.D. Univ. of Michigan, 1926. He was professor of medical physics at the Univ. of Pennsylvania from 1929 to 1949 and also director of the Institute of Neurology (1936–40, 1942–49). From 1949 to 1953 he was president of Johns Hopkins. In 1953 he became president of the Rockefeller Institute for Medical Research (now Rockefeller Univ.), New York City. Bronk has also served as president and chairman of many important scientific societies. In his lectures he has asked for an understanding of science in terms of human values.

Brontë, Charlotte (brŏn'tē), 1816–55, English novelist, **Emily Jane Brontë,** 1818–48, English novelist and poet, and **Anne Brontë,** 1820–49, English novelist. They were daughters of Patrick Brontë (1777–1861), an Anglican clergyman of Irish birth, educated at Cambridge. In 1820 he became incumbent of Haworth, West Riding of Yorkshire. The next year his wife died, and her sister, Elizabeth Branwell, came to the parsonage to care for the six Brontë children, five girls and one boy, Branwell. Maria and Elizabeth, the two oldest girls, were sent to the Cowan Bridge school for the daughters of poor clergymen. In spite of the harsh conditions there, Charlotte and Emily were also sent in 1824, but were brought home after Maria and Elizabeth contracted tuberculosis and died. At home for the next five years, the children were left much to themselves, and they began to write about an imaginary world they had created. This escapist writing, transcribed in tiny script on small pieces of paper, continued into adulthood and is a remarkable key to the development of genius in Charlotte and Emily. In 1831, Charlotte was sent to Miss Wooler's school at Roe Head. She became a teacher there in 1835, but in 1838 she returned to Haworth. At home she found the family finances in wretched condition. Branwell—talented as a writer and painter, on whom his sisters' hopes for money and success rested—had lost three jobs and was declining into alcoholism and opium addiction. To increase their income Charlotte and her sisters laid ill-considered plans to establish a school. In order to study languages Emily and Charlotte spent 1842 at the Pensionnat Héger in Brussels, but returned home at the death of their aunt, who had willed them her small fortune. Both girls were offered positions at the *pensionnat,* but only Charlotte returned in 1843. She went home the following year, because, it is thought, she was in love with M. Héger and had aroused the jealousy of Mme Héger. Mr. Brontë's failing eyesight and the rapid degeneration of Branwell made this an unhappy period at home. When Charlotte discovered Emily's poetry in 1845, Anne revealed hers, and the next year the collected poems of the three sisters, published at their own expense, appeared under the pseudonyms Currer, Ellis, and Acton Bell. In 1847, Emily's novel *Wuthering Heights* and Anne's *Agnes Grey* were published as a set, and although *The Professor* by Charlotte was rejected, her *Jane Eyre* (1847) was accepted and published with great success. The identity of the sisters as authors was at first unknown even to their publishers. It was not until after the publication of Charlotte's *Shirley* in 1849 that the truth was made public. By then tragedy had all but destroyed the Brontë family. In September, 1848, Branwell died; Emily caught cold at his funeral and, refusing all medical aid, died of tuberculosis the following December. Anne, whose *Tenant of Wildfell Hall* appeared in 1848, also died of tuberculosis in May, 1849. Now that the people who had occupied most of her life were gone, Charlotte began to make trips to London where she was lionized. Her *Villette* appeared in 1853. In 1854 she married her father's curate, Arthur Bell Nichols, with whom she seems to have been happy. She died, however, of pregnancy toxemia complicated by the Brontë susceptibility to tuberculosis, after only a year of marriage. *The Professor* was published posthumously in 1857. Of the three Brontë sisters Anne was the least talented. Still her novels have been praised for their realism, integrity, and moral force. *Agnes Grey* is the unadorned story of a governess's life and *The Tenant of Wildfell Hall* tells of a young girl's marriage to a rake. Charlotte Brontë was the most professional of the sisters, consciously trying to achieve financial success from the family's literary efforts. Her novel *Jane Eyre,* the story of a governess and her passionate love for her Byronic employer, Mr. Rochester, is ranked among the great English novels. Strong, violently emotional, somewhat melodramatic, *Jane Eyre* brilliantly articulates the theme found in all Charlotte's work—the need of women for both love and independence. The undisputed genius of the family was Emily Brontë. An unyielding and enigmatic personality, she produced only one novel and a few poems, yet she is ranked among the giants of English literature. Her masterpiece, *Wuthering Heights,* is the wild, passionate story of the intense, almost demonic, love between Catherine Earnshaw and the gypsy foundling Heathcliff. The action of the story is chaotic and unremittingly violent; its characters are less people than forces. Indeed, the novel would be extraordinarily difficult to read were it not for the power of Emily Brontë's vision and the beauty and energy of her prose. Some of her powerful lyrics are counted with the best of English poetry. The early (1857) biography of Charlotte by Mrs. Gaskell is still valuable, as are the books on the Brontës by Clement K. Shorter. The poems of Emily have been edited by C. W. Hatfield (1941), the Brontë letters by Muriel Spark (1954). See the reconsideration of Mrs. Gaskell's *Life* by Margaret Lane (1953, repr. 1973); biographies of each of the Brontës by Winifred Gérin: Anne (1959), Charlotte (1967), Branwell (1961, repr. 1972), and Emily (1972); biographies of the family by Lawrence and Elizabeth Hanson (4th ed. 1967) and Phyllis Bentley (1947, repr. 1973). See also F. E. Ratchford, *The Brontës' Web of Childhood* (1941, repr. 1964); *Emily Brontë: Her Life and Work,* Part 1 (biographical) by Muriel Spark, Part 2 (critical) by Derek Sanford; *Charlotte Brontë: Style in the Novel,* by Margot Peters (1973); *The Brontës and Their Background,* by Tom Winnifrith (1973).

Brontosaurus (brŏntəsôr'əs) [Gr.,=thunder lizard], formerly the genus name of a quadruped herbivorous DINOSAUR, probably over 70 ft (21 m) long and over 30 tons in weight, with a long neck and tail and a brain weighing about one pound. The genus name of this semiaquatic group has been officially changed to *Apatosaurus.* The eyes and nostrils of these amphibious dinosaurs were located toward the top of the skull, permitting them to see and breathe with only the top of the head above water. Bones of the brontosaur and other sauropods have been found in the Morrison formation of the late Jurassic and early Cretaceous strata in Colorado, Wyoming, and other Western states. The brontosaur is classified in the phylum CHORDATA, subphylum Vertebrata, class Reptilia, order Saurischia.

Bronx, the, borough of New York City, coextensive with Bronx co. (1970 pop. 1,472,216), land area 41 sq mi (106 sq km), SE N.Y.; settled 1641 by Jonas Bronck (a Dane acting for the Dutch West India Company), chartered as a part of Greater New York City 1898. The only mainland borough of New York City, it comprises the southern part of a peninsula bordered on the W by the Hudson River, on the SW by the Harlem River (which separates it from Manhattan), on the S by the East River, and on the E by Long Island Sound. To the north is Westchester co., of which the Bronx was a part until its southern portion was annexed by New York City in 1875 and the remainder in 1898. Among the many bridges linking the borough to Manhattan and Queens are the Henry Hudson across Spuyten Duyvil (where the Harlem River joins the Hudson) to Manhattan, the Triborough to Manhattan and Queens, and the Bronx-Whitestone and the Throgs Neck to Queens. It is also connected to Manhattan by subway lines. Although chiefly a crowded, residential borough, some of the more than 80 mi (129 km) of waterfront is given over to shipping, warehouses, factories, and an enormous wholesale produce market. Large areas of the borough are set aside for parks, notably Bronx Park, with the outstanding New York Zoological Park (Bronx Zoo) and the New York Botanical Garden; Van Cortlandt Park, containing the Van Cortlandt House (1748); and Pelham Bay Park, with Orchard Beach on Long Island Sound. Among the institutions of higher learning in the Bronx are Fordham Univ., Manhattan College, Albert Einstein College of Medicine (of Yeshiva Univ.), the New York State Maritime College, Herbert H. Lehman College, and Bronx Community College. Other points of interest are Yankee Stadium and the Edgar Allan Poe cottage (1812). City Island, in Long Island Sound, is a boating center.

Bronx, river, c.20 mi (30 km) long, issuing from Kensico Reservoir, SE N.Y., and flowing SW through the Bronx into the East River. The Bronx River Parkway, one of the first landscaped superhighways in the New York City area, parallels a portion of the river.

bronze, in art: see BRONZE SCULPTURE.

bronze, in metallurgy, alloy of copper, tin, zinc, phosphorus, and sometimes small amounts of other elements. Bronzes are harder than brasses. Most are produced by melting the copper and adding the desired amounts of tin, zinc, and other substances. The properties of the alloy depend on the proportions of its components. Bronzes with different properties have different uses. Aluminum bronze has high strength and resists corrosion; it is used for bearings, valve seats, and machine parts. Leaded bronze, containing from 10% to 29% lead, is cast into heavy duty bushings and bearings. Silicon bronze is used for telegraph wires and chemical containers. Phosphor bronze is used for springs. Bronze is used for coins, medals, steam fittings, and GUNMETAL and was formerly employed for cannon. Because of its particularly sonorous quality, bell metal, containing from 20% to 24% tin, is used for casting bells. Bronze has long been used in art, e.g., for castings, engravings, and forgings.

Bronze Age, period in the development of technology when metals were first used regularly in the manufacture of tools and weapons. Pure copper and bronze, an alloy of copper and tin, were used indiscriminately at first; this early period is sometimes called the Copper Age. The earliest use of cast metal can be deduced from clay models of weapons; CASTING was certainly established in the Middle East by 3500 B.C. Following the NEOLITHIC PERIOD, the development of a metallurgical industry coincided with the rise of urbanization. The organized operations of mining, smelting, and casting undoubtedly required the specialization of labor and the production of surplus food to support a class of artisans, while the search for raw materials stimulated the exploration and colonization of new territories. This process culminated in the civilizations of MESOPOTAMIA and SUMER. Later, the MINOAN CIVILIZATION and the MYCENAEAN CIVILIZATION opened extensive trade routes in central Europe, where tin and copper were mined. This activity fostered native industries and political unification, especially in Hungary, Austria, and the Alpine region. It laid the foundations of the IRON AGE civilization, which was to follow under Greek, Etruscan, and Scythian influences. In the New World the earliest bronze was cast in Bolivia A.D. c.1100. The INCA civilization used bronze tools and weapons but never mastered iron. See V. G. Childe, *The Prehistory of European Society* (1958, repr. 1962); J. W. Alsop, *From the Silent Earth* (1964); Grahame Clark, *World Prehistory: An Outline* (2d ed. 1969).

bronze sculpture. Bronze is ideal for casting art works; it flows into all crevices of a mold, thus perfectly reproducing every detail of the most delicately modeled sculpture. It is most susceptible to the graver's tool and admirable for REPOUSSÉ work. Bronze, used in early times for objects later made of other materials, constitutes a record of ancient arts and life. The Egyptians used bronze, cast and hammered, for utensils, armor, and statuary far in advance of the BRONZE AGE in Europe. The Greeks were unexcelled in bronze sculpture. Among the few surviving examples of their work are two masterpieces: *The Zeus of Artemisium* (National Mus., Athens) and *The Delphic Charioteer* (Delphi Mus.). Examples of Etruscan artisans' work include a bronze chariot found at Monteleone (Metropolitan Mus.) and the celebrated Capitoline Wolf (Palazzo dei Conservatori, Rome). The Romans took quantities of bronze statues from Greece and made thousands themselves. They employed bronze for doors and for furniture, utensils, and candelabra, of which some were recovered at Pompeii and Herculaneum. Early medieval bronzes consisted mainly of utensils and domestic and ecclesiastical ornaments. During the Renaissance, Italian sculptors wrought magnificent bronzes of many sorts, outstanding among which are Ghiberti's doors to the baptistry of Florence and the sculptures of Donatello, Verrocchio, Giovanni Bologna, Pollaiuolo, and Cellini. The work of Peter Vischer was influential in Germany. A series of monumental effigies of the monarchs are among the finest English bronzes. France was known in the 18th cent. for gilded bronze furniture mounts. In the Orient bronzes of superb quality have been produced since ancient times. Major modern sculptors who have worked in bronze include Rodin, Epstein, Brancusi, and Lipchitz. The classic description of Renaissance bronze casting is given in Cellini's *Autobiography* (1558-62). See D. G. Mitten and S. F. Doeringer, *Master Bronzes from the Classical World* (1968); George Savage, *A Concise History of Bronzes* (1968).

Bronzino, Il (ēl brōntsē'nō), 1503-72, Florentine painter, an important mannerist, whose real name was Agnolo di Cosimo di Mariano. Bronzino was a pupil and adopted son of Jacopo da Pontormo. Continuing the tradition of his master, he specialized and excelled in portraiture. He depicted many elegant and celebrated men and women of the time; his portraits included *Cosimo I de' Medici* and his wife *Eleanor of Toledo* (both: Uffizi); *Lodovico Capponi* (Frick Coll., New York City); and *Portrait of a Boy* (Metropolitan Mus.). In 1540 he became court painter to Cosimo I. Bronzino's sophisticated portraits are cold, unemotionally analytical and painted in a superbly controlled technique. The long, chilly faces and postures of his aristocratic subjects express an undisguised arrogance popular in the mannerist period. Bronzino's work had an influence on court portraiture throughout Europe and extended even to Elizabethan England. His *Venus, Cupid, Folly, and Time* (Uffizi) conveys a covert eroticism beneath a moralizing allegory. Of his religious works, *The Descent of Christ into Limbo* (Uffizi) is the most famous. See study by C. H. Smyth (1972).

Brook, Alexander, 1898–, American painter, b. Brooklyn, N.Y. Brook's paintings, which are consistently realistic, include portraits, still-life subjects, landscapes, and figures. His color is subtle and reserved. A deep respect for human personality characterizes much of his work, often with overtones of wry humor or irony. Among his major works are *Amalia* (Toledo Mus. of Art), *Peggy Bacon and Metaphysics* (Univ. of Nebraska), and *The Sentinels* (Whitney Mus., New York City). Brook was married (1920-40) to the artist Peggy BACON and later to the painter Gina Knee.

Brook, Peter, 1925–, English theatrical director. An innovative and controversial figure, Brook mounts energetic productions in which the stage is utilized totally; he often has his actors singing, playing musical instruments, and performing acrobatics. His first production was *Dr. Faustus* in 1943, which was followed by such productions as *The Infernal Machine, The Respectful Prostitute, The Beggar's Opera, Marat/Sade, A Midsummer Night's Dream,* and *King Lear.* He has also directed films, such as *Moderato Cantabile* (1960) and *Lord of the Flies* (1963); and operas, including *Faust* and *Eugene Onegin.* See his *The Empty Space* (1969); biography by J. C. Trewin (1971).

Brooke, Alan Francis: see ALANBROOKE, ALAN FRANCIS BROOKE, 1ST VISCOUNT.

Brooke, Sir Charles Anthony Johnson: see BROOKE, SIR JAMES.

Brooke, Sir Charles Vyner: see BROOKE, SIR JAMES.

Brooke, Edward William, 1919–, U.S. Senator (1967–), b. Washington, D.C. Admitted to the bar in 1948, he served (1963-66) as attorney general of Massachusetts, where he gained a reputation as a vigorous prosecutor of organized crime. Elected (1966) as a Republican to the U.S. Senate, he became the first black Senator since Reconstruction. Brooke served (1967) on the President's Commission on Civil Disorders, which investigated the causes of race riots in American cities, and played (1970) a major role in the successful fight against confirmation of the nomination of G. Harrold Carswell to the U.S. Supreme Court. He is the author of *The Challenge of Change* (1966). See biography by J. H. Cutler (1972).

Brooke, Fulke Greville, 1st Baron, 1554-1628, English author and statesman. A favorite of Queen Elizabeth I, he held many official positions during his lifetime. His *Life of Sir Philip Sidney* (1652) was more a historical and personal commentary than a biography. The bulk of his work (published posthumously) reflects his concern with the degeneration of the monarchy, foreshadowed by the death of Elizabeth. Many young poets of the time were indebted to him for his patronage. See his *Poems and Dramas* ed. by Geoffrey Bullough (1939) and selected writings ed. by Joan Rees (1973); biographies by Joan Rees (1971) and R. A. Rebholz (1971).

Brooke, Henry, c.1703-1783, Irish author. Educated at Trinity College, Dublin, he studied law in London before returning to Ireland permanently. In 1735 he published his long philosophical poem, *Universal Beauty.* His discursive novel, *The Fool of Quality* (5 vol., 1767-70), which was inspired by the theories of Rousseau, reveals Brooke's acute awareness of the political and social situation of his day.

Brooke, Sir James, 1803-68, rajah of Sarawak on Borneo, b. India, of English parents. After active service in Burma (1825-26), he retired (1830) from the army of the East India Company and, during a voyage to the East Indies, conceived a plan to suppress piracy. He sailed (1838) for Borneo, and on the west coast there he assisted (1840) Muda Hassim, uncle of the reigning sultan, to suppress rebel Dyak tribes. For his services he was made (1841) rajah by the sultan of Brunei and proceeded to create a government and to put down head-hunting and piracy. He revised the tax system and administered justice personally. He was given a baronetcy by the British government and entrusted with the governorship (1847-57) of Labuan. Chinese traders in opium precipitated an uprising (1867), in which Kuching, the capital of Sarawak, was burned. Brooke was engaged sporadically in suppressing many tribal rebellions. He was succeeded by his nephew, **Sir Charles Anthony Johnson Brooke,** 1829–1917. Sir Charles extended the authority of the government to all parts of the country, and by the abolition of slavery and other reforms he made the country productive and the people prosperous. He was succeeded by his son, **Sir Charles Vyner Brooke,** 1874–1963. Sir Charles was forced out of Sarawak in 1942 by the Japanese invasion. In spite of the fact that his nephew, Anthony W. D. Brooke, acted as his heir apparent and head of the provisional government during the war, Sir Charles ceded Sarawak to the British government as a crown colony in 1946. See Sir Steven Runciman, *The White Rajahs* (1960); Robert Pringle, *Rajahs and Rebels* (1970); Nicholas Tarling, *Britain, the Brookes and Brunei* (1972).

Brooke, Rupert, 1887–1915, English poet. At the outbreak of World War I he joined the Royal Naval Division, served at Antwerp, and was in the Dardanelles expedition when he died of blood poisoning at the island of Skíros. Handsome and athletic, Brooke was also charming, intellectual, and witty, and was universally sought in society. His early fame and tragic death have made him an almost legendary figure. He wrote two small volumes of poetry, *Poems* (1911) and *1914 and Other Poems* (1915). His verse is exuberant and charming, the romantic patriotism of his war sonnets contrasting sharply with the bitter, disillusioned poetry of Owen and Sassoon. See his letters, ed. by Geoffrey Keynes (1968); biographies by Arthur Stringer (1948, repr. 1972) and Christopher Hassall (1964, repr. 1972); bibliography by Geoffrey Keynes (1954).

Brookeborough, Basil Stanlake Brooke, 1st Viscount, 1888–1973, Northern Irish politician. After serving in the cavalry in World War I he was elected to the Senate of the first Northern Ireland Parliament (1921). He resigned the following year to lead the Ulster special constabulary against the Irish Republican Army's border raids in Fermanagh. Reelected (1929) as a Unionist member of Stormont, he served as minister of agriculture (1933–41), minister of commerce (1941–45), and prime minister (1943–63). A staunch advocate of Protestant dominance in Ulster, he remained opposed to any reconciliation with the Republic of Ireland. Created Viscount Brookeborough in 1952, he continued to sit at Stormont until 1968.

Brook Farm, 1841–47, an experimental farm at West Roxbury, Mass., based on cooperative living. Founded by George Ripley, a Unitarian minister, the farm was initially financed by a joint-stock company with 24 shares of stock at $500 per share. Each member was to take part in the manual labor in an attempt to make the group self-sufficient. Intellectual life was stimulating, with such members as Nathaniel Hawthorne, John S. Dwight, Charles A. Dana, and Isaac Hecker, and such visitors as Ralph Waldo Emerson, W. H. Channing, Margaret Fuller, Horace Greeley, and Orestes Brownson. Brook Farm was mainly an outgrowth of UNITARIANISM, although most of the members had left that church and were advocates of the literary and philosophical movement known as TRANSCENDENTALISM. Economically, the community's excellent school was the most successful part of the venture (anticipating John Dewey's progressive-education ideas of learning from experience); agriculture showed little profit because of the sandy soil and the inexperience of the farmers. The popularity of the doctrines of Charles FOURIER led, especially through the efforts of Albert Brisbane, to Brook Farm's conversion to a phalanx in 1844. The group, however, did not long survive the financial disaster of the burning (1846) of the uncompleted central building. The *Harbinger* (1845–49), printed at Brook Farm and edited by Ripley, was rather a Fourierist weekly newspaper than the organ of Brook Farm and was continued in New York City with Parke Godwin as editor after 1847. See E. R. Curtis, *A Season in Utopia* (1961, repr. 1971).

Brookfield. 1 Village (1970 pop. 20,284), Cook co., NE Ill., a residential suburb of Chicago; inc. 1893. The noted Chicago Zoological Park (Brookfield Zoo) is there. **2** City (1970 pop. 32,140), Waukesha co., SE Wis., a suburb of Milwaukee; inc. 1954. It has iron foundries and light manufacturing.

Brookhaven, city (1970 pop. 10,700), seat of Lincoln co., SW Miss.; inc. 1859. It is situated in a dairy, timber, and farm area; nearby are oil and gas fields. The city's manufactures include textiles, mobile homes, electronic equipment, lawnmowers, and thermometers.

Brookhaven National Laboratory, scientific research center, Upton, Long Island, N.Y. It was founded in 1947 by Associated Universities Inc., which is a management corporation sponsored by nine eastern U.S. universities. This corporation runs the laboratory under a contract with the U.S. Atomic Energy Commission. At Brookhaven an international staff conducts multidisciplinary scientific work, e.g., fundamental studies of atomic nuclei, investigations of the effects and uses of nuclear radiation, and research and development in nuclear technology. Among the laboratory's equipment are a number of highly sophisticated nuclear reactors, particle accelerators, and electronic computers. The facilities also include a medical research center for work in nuclear medicine. Science students are drawn from universities throughout the world to work at the laboratory as part of their training.

Brookings, Robert Somers, 1850–1932, American businessman and philanthropist, b. Cecil co., Md. He earned a fortune in business in St. Louis, Mo., and retired in 1897 to devote himself to philanthropy. As chairman of the corporation of Washington Univ. from 1897 to 1914 he was primarily responsible for the rebuilding of that institution. He founded the Brookings Institution in Washington, D.C. See biography by Hermann Hagedorn (1936).

Brookings, city (1970 pop. 13,717), seat of Brookings co., E S. Dak., on the Big Sioux River; inc. 1883. A trade center in a livestock and grain region, the city is an important seed-processing point. Other industries produce medical and dental equipment; aluminum windows, doors, and awnings; concrete products; and fabricated structural steel. In the city is South Dakota State Univ., whose campus houses an agricultural experiment station. The South Dakota Memorial Art Center is in Brookings.

Brookings Institution, at Washington, D.C.; chartered 1927 as a consolidation of the Institute for Government Research (est. 1916), the Institute of Economics (est. 1922), and the Robert S. Brookings Graduate School of Economics and Government (est. 1924). It provides statistics, general information, and personnel for research to the U.S. government. The institution also helps trained scholars to study contemporary economic, governmental, and international problems by financing research projects and publishing their findings.

Brookline (bro͝ok'līn), town (1970 pop. 58,886), Norfolk co., E Mass., a residential suburb adjacent to Boston; settled 1630s, set off from Boston and inc. 1705. It was known as "Muddy River" when part of Boston. The birthplace of President John F. Kennedy in Brookline is a national historic site. Other points of interest are Amy Lowell's home and an antique auto museum. Brookline is the site of Hebrew College.

Brooklyn. 1 Uninc. city (1970 pop. 13,896), Anne Arundel co., central Md. **2** Borough of New York City (1970 pop. 2,601,852), 71 sq mi (184 sq km), coextensive with Kings co., SE N.Y., at the southwestern extremity of Long Island; settled 1636, chartered as a part of Greater New York 1898. Brooklyn is a residential and industrial region, with the largest population of the city's five boroughs; among its manufactures are machinery, textiles, paper products, and chemicals. The borough is the center of an important foreign and domestic commerce and has extensive waterfront facilities. The Brooklyn, Manhattan, and Williamsburg bridges span the East River, connecting Brooklyn with Manhattan; beneath the river are the Brooklyn-Battery Tunnel (for vehicular traffic) and subway tunnels. The Verrazano-Narrows Bridge (completed 1964) connects the borough with Staten Island. Hollanders and Walloons settled about Gowanus and Wallabout bays in 1636 and 1637; about nine years later Dutch farmers established the hamlet of Breuckelen, near the present borough hall. Becoming Brooklyn under the English, it was incorporated as a village (Brooklyn Ferry) in 1816 and was chartered as a city in 1834. As it grew, Brooklyn absorbed many settlements and villages, such as Flatbush, New Utrecht, and Gravesend (all settled in the 17th cent.). Williamsburg was absorbed in 1855, and Brooklyn became the third largest city in the United States. In 1898, when it became a borough of New York City, its population was about one million. Among the numerous educational institutions in the borough are Brooklyn College, Polytechnic Institute of New York, Pratt Institute, St. Joseph's College, Packer Collegiate Institute, and Long Island Univ. The New York Naval Shipyard (popularly known as the Brooklyn Navy Yard) was located on the East River from 1801 until its closing in the late 1960s, at which time the installation was turned over to private enterprise. Fort Hamilton (built 1831 as a harbor defense) overlooks the Narrows of New York Bay. Near beautiful Prospect Park, the scene of fierce fighting in the Revolution (see LONG ISLAND, BATTLE OF) is the main building of the Brooklyn Public Library. Also in that area are the Brooklyn Museum, with noted collections of Egyptian, Oriental, and primitive art; the Brooklyn Botanic Garden; and the Brooklyn Children's Museum—these, along with the Brooklyn Academy of Music, are under the direction of the Brooklyn Institute of Arts and Sciences. Among the many structures that give the borough its appellation "City of Churches" are the Reformed Protestant Dutch Church of Flatbush (first built 1654; rebuilt 1796), St. Ann's Episcopal Church (est. 1784), and Plymouth Church of the Pilgrims, where Henry Ward Beecher preached. Other points of interest in the borough include CONEY ISLAND, with its beach and amusement park; Sheepshead Bay, a fishing and boating center; the invaluable historical library of the Long Island Historical Society; the New York Aquarium (at Coney Island); Brooklyn Heights Historic District; and the Lefferts Homestead (1777). Marine Park and parts of Jamaica Bay are included in Gateway National Recreation Area. The *Daily Eagle*, a noted newspaper published in Brooklyn from 1841 until 1959, had Walt Whitman as one of its editors. See H. C. Syrett, *The City of Brooklyn, 1865–1898* (1944, repr. 1968); R. F. Weld, *Brooklyn is America* (1950, repr. 1967) and *Brooklyn Village, 1816–1834* (1932, repr. 1970); Walt Whitman, *Walt Whitman's New York* (1861, repr. 1972). **3** City (1970 pop. 13,142), Cuyahoga co., NE Ohio, a residential suburb of Cleveland; inc. 1867.

Brooklyn Bridge, vehicular suspension bridge, New York City, southernmost of the bridges across the East River, between lower Manhattan and Brooklyn; built 1869–83. The achievement of J. A. Roebling and his son W. A. Roebling, it has a span of 1,595 ft (486 m). It was the first steel-wire suspension bridge in the world and was the world's longest suspension bridge at the time of its completion. See David McCullough, *The Great Bridge* (1972).

Brooklyn Center, city (1970 pop. 35,173), Hennepin co., SE Minn., a residential suburb of Minneapolis; inc. 1911. It has some light industry.

Brooklyn College of the City University of New York; coeducational; opened 1930 by merging the Brooklyn branches of City and Hunter colleges. The baccalaureate program is tuition-free to New York City residents. See NEW YORK, CITY UNIVERSITY OF.

Brooklyn Institute of Arts and Sciences, cultural institution founded in 1823 as the Brooklyn Apprentices Library Association. The scope was broadened in 1843 and the name changed to The Brooklyn Institute. In 1890 the institution was reorganized and reincorporated under its present name. It includes the Brooklyn Museum (designed by McKim, Mead, and White and begun in 1895), a Children's Museum, the Brooklyn Academy of Music, and a botanical garden, opened in 1911. The Brooklyn Museum is famous for its large collection of Egyptian art and its Egyptological library. Other important features are the collections of primitive arts; Oriental art; American and European costumes; American decorative arts, including 25 completely furnished rooms; a comprehensive collection of American painting and sculpture of the 18th to 20th cent.; and the print collection. The Children's Museum, opened in 1899, was the first in the country; it contains natural history and ethnological collections. The Brooklyn Academy of Music, in operation since 1859, presents concerts, plays, ballets, and lectures.

Brooklyn Park, city (1970 pop. 26,230), Hennepin co., SE Minn., a suburb of Minneapolis; chartered as a city 1969. Potatoes are grown and wood products are made in Brooklyn Park. North Hennepin State Junior College is there.

Brook Park, city (1970 pop. 30,774), Cuyahoga co., NE Ohio, a suburb of Cleveland; inc. 1914. The Cleveland municipal airport is there.

Brooks, Gwendolyn, 1917–, American poet, b. Topeka, Kansas. She grew up in the slums of Chicago. Brooks's poems deal with the experience of being black in America. She won the 1950 Pulitzer Prize for poetry for *Annie Allen* (1949), becoming the first black woman to win this award. Her verse was collected in *The World of Gwendolyn Brooks* (1970), which also includes an earlier novelette, *Maud Martha* (1953). The poems in *Riot* (1970) are written in street dialects. See her autobiography (1972).

Brooks, Maria Gowen, 1795?–1845, American poet, b. Medford, Mass. Her first collection of verse, *Judith, Esther, and Other Poems* (1820), was praised by Southey, who named her "Maria del Occidente," which she later used as a pseudonym. While living in Cuba she wrote the epic *Zophiel; or, The Bride of Seven* (1833) and *Idomen; or, The Vale of Yumuri* (1843). Her poetry, especially the *Ode to the Departed* (1843), was esteemed both in America and abroad.

Brooks, Phillips, 1835-93, American Episcopal bishop, b. Boston. After rectorships (1859-69) in Philadelphia, he began (1869) his memorable ministry at Trinity Church, Boston, where he became one of the most influential ministers of his time. In 1891 he was consecrated bishop of Massachusetts. His lectures at Yale were published as *Lectures on Preaching* (1877), and his Bohlen lectures in Philadelphia as *The Influence of Jesus* (1879). The Christmas hymn "O Little Town of Bethlehem" was included in his *Christmas Songs and Easter Carols* (1903). See *Life and Letters* (ed. by A. V. Allen, 2 vol., 1900); biographies by William Lawrence (1930) and R. W. Albright (1961).

Brooks, Preston Smith, 1819-57, U.S. Congressman (1852-57), b. Edgefield District, S.C. A lawyer and the nephew of Senator Andrew Pickens Butler, he is remembered as the man who in 1856 caned Charles SUMNER after Sumner had bitterly criticized Senator Butler. The slander in Sumner's speech and the brutality in Brooks's action showed how the rift was widening between North and South. Resigning, Brooks was promptly reelected.

Brooks, Van Wyck, 1886-1963, American critic, b. Plainfield, N. J., grad. Harvard, 1908. His first book, *The Wine of the Puritans* (1909), presented the thesis that American culture has been so pervaded by puritanism with its materialistic emphasis that the artistic side of the nation's life has been profoundly neglected. Although this theme was developed in such subsequent books as *America's Coming-of-Age* (1915), *The Ordeal of Mark Twain* (1920), and *The Pilgrimage of Henry James* (1925), later works, including *Emerson and Others* (1927), indicate his growing respect for American literature. In 1937 he won the Pulitzer Prize in history for *The Flowering of New England* (1936). Other volumes followed in the series he called *Makers and Finders: New England: Indian Summer* (1940), *The World of Washington Irving* (1944), and *The Times of Melville and Whitman* (1947). In this series, his masterwork, Brooks interprets American literary history; it is a vivid, varied chronicle, rich in anecdote and infused with the author's humanism. Among Brooks's innumerable other books are such autobiographical works as *Days of Phoenix* (1957), *From a Writer's Notebook* (1958) and *An Autobiography* (1965). See *The Van Wyck Brooks-Lewis Mumford Letters,* ed. by R. E. Spiller (1970).

Brooks Range, mountain chain, northernmost part of the Rocky Mts., extending about 600 mi (970 km) from east to west across N Alaska. Mt. Chamberlin 9,020 ft (2,749 m) high, near the Canadian border, is the highest peak. Rugged, barren, snow-covered, and uninhabited, Brooks Range separates the oil-rich Arctic Ocean coastal plain from the Yukon River basin.

broom, common name for plants of two closely related and similar Old World genera, *Cytisus* and *Genista,* of the family Leguminosae (PULSE family). They are mostly twiggy leguminous shrubs with abundant yellow or white (in *Cytisus,* purple also) pealike blossoms. The common, or Scotch, broom (*Cytisus scoparius*) is naturalized in parts of North America; the tops have been much used as a diuretic. The Canary broom, or so-called genista of florists, is *Cytisus canariensis,* a yellow-flowered evergreen shrub. Species of the genus *Genista* include *Genista tinctoria,* called also dyer's-greenweed, which yields yellow-to-green dyes. Other plants are also called broom. Broom is classified in the division MAGNOLIOPHYTA, class Magnoliopsida, order Rosales, family Leguminosae.

broomcorn: see SORGHUM.

broom rape, common name for plants of the Orobanchaceae, the broom rape family. The broom rapes are parasitic on the roots of other plants; they have small leaves and little or no green color. In some species the leaves are absent entirely. Most species are found in dry sandy areas of the Old World. Broom rapes are classified in the division MAGNOLIOPHYTA, class Magnoliopsida, order Scrophulariales.

Brosamer, Hans (häns brō'zämər), c.1500-1554, German painter and engraver. His work shows the influence of Cranach, Dürer, and Holbein. Recent scholarship has attempted to reattribute a large body of works bearing the signature *HB* which are no longer thought to be by Brosamer. Among works accepted as his are many portraits.

Broschi, Carlo: see FARINELLI, CARLO BROSCHI.

Brosse, Salomon de (sälōmôN' də brôs), 1571-1626, French architect, trained by his grandfather, Jacques du Cerceau, the elder. Designing in terms of mass, rather than surface decoration, he paved the way for the next generation in the use of classicism as the style which denoted royalty. In Paris his works include the Luxembourg Palace (1615-20) built for Marie de' Medici and the facade of Saint-Gervais (1616). At Rennes he built the Parliament House (1618), now the Palais de Justice. Also attributed to him are the château of Blerancourt and the hunting château erected for Louis XIII at Versailles.

Brotherhood of the New Life: see HARRIS, THOMAS LAKE.

Brothers, Richard, 1757-1824, English religious fanatic, b. Newfoundland. A naval officer, he traveled widely and moved to London in 1787. Shortly afterward he proclaimed himself a descendant of David, prince of the Hebrews, and ruler of the world. He gained a small following. After demanding that King George III turn over his crown to him, Brothers was confined as a criminal lunatic. Later moved to a private asylum, he was released in 1806. He wrote *A Revealed Knowledge of the Prophecies and Times* (2 vol., 1794).

Brothers of the Sword: see LIVONIAN BROTHERS OF THE SWORD.

Brough, John (brŭf), 1811-65, Civil War governor of Ohio (1864-65), b. Marietta, Ohio. In 1844, after publishing newspapers in Marietta and Lancaster, he became owner and editor of the Cincinnati *Enquirer,* which he made one of the leading Democratic organs in the West. Brough served in the state legislature, and as state auditor (1839-45) he thoroughly reorganized Ohio's financial system. Although a Democrat, Brough so vigorously supported the Union during the Civil War that the Republicans nominated him for governor in 1863, and he soundly defeated the Copperhead leader, Clement L. VALLANDIGHAM. He was one of the most effective state leaders of the period. See W. B. Hesseltine, *Lincoln and the War Governors* (1948).

Brougham, Henry Peter, 1st **Baron Brougham and Vaux** (bro͞om, vôz, vôks), 1778-1868, British statesman, b. Edinburgh. As a young lawyer in Scotland he helped to found (1802) the *Edinburgh Review* and contributed many articles to it. He went to London, was called (1808) to the English bar, and entered (1810) Parliament as a Whig. Brougham took up the fight against the slave trade and opposed the restrictions on trade with the Continent. In 1820 he won popular renown as chief attorney to Queen Caroline (see CAROLINE OF BRUNSWICK), and in the next decade he became a liberal leader in the House of Commons. He not only proposed educational reforms in Parliament, but also was one of the founders of the Society for the Diffusion of Useful Knowledge (1825) and of the Univ. of London (1828). As lord chancellor (1830-34) he effected many legal reforms to speed procedure and established the central criminal court. In later years he spent much of his time in Cannes, which he established as a popular resort. See Arthur Aspinall, *Lord Brougham and the Whig Party* (1927, repr. 1972); biography by F. R. Hawes (1957).

Broun, Heywood Campbell (bro͞on), 1888-1939, American newspaper columnist and critic, b. Brooklyn, N.Y. He worked on the New York *Tribune* (1912-21) and the New York *World* (1921-28), where his syndicated column, "It Seems to Me," began. In 1928 he transferred it to the Scripps-Howard newspapers, including the New York *World-Telegram,* where it appeared until he moved it to the New York *Post* just before his death. In his column Broun constantly championed the underdog, criticized social injustice, and backed emerging labor unions. A founder of the American Newspaper Guild, he was its first president from 1933 until his death. In 1930, Broun ran unsuccessfully for congress as a Socialist. His books include *The A. E. F.* (1918); *The Boy Grew Older* (1922) and *Gandle Follows His Nose* (1926), novels; and a biography of Anthony Comstock (with Margaret Leech, 1927). *It Seems to Me* (1935) and *Collected Edition* (ed. by H. H. Broun, 1941) give the best of his column.

Broussel, Pierre (pyĕr bro͞osĕl'), c.1575-1654, councillor of the Parlement of Paris under Louis XIII and Louis XIV. His opposition to the tax program proposed by Cardinal MAZARIN made him popular. The uprising after his arrest in 1648 caused his early release and was the start of the first FRONDE. In July, 1652, the Parisians chose him provost of the merchants, i.e., virtual mayor. He resigned in September in order to facilitate the reconciliation between the rebels and the court, and he died in obscurity.

Brouwer or **Brauwer, Adriaen** (both: ädrēän' brou'wər), c.1606-1638, Flemish painter who worked in Haarlem. He studied with Hals at the same time as did the young Ostade, and the influence of their two styles, as well as that of Rubens, is apparent in his paintings. Brouwer is noted for his depictions of peasant life, particularly of drinking scenes and humorously treated single figures sleeping or smoking. Brouwer's early canvases were richly colored, in the Flemish style, while his later works (1631-38) were often monochromatic, a characteristic of the contemporary Dutch fashion. His lively canvases were popular in his own time. Brouwer was also an important master of landscape and a superb draftsman. His *Drinkers at a Table* (Brussels) and *The Smokers* (Metropolitan Mus.) are characteristic. See study by G. Knuttel (tr. 1962).

Browder, Earl Russell, 1891-1973, American Communist, b. Wichita, Kansas. He became converted to socialism as a boy, and after imprisonment (1917-18, 1919-20) for opposing the draft he joined the Communist party. Following his return from a trip to China for the party, he was secretary-general of the party (1930-44) and president of the Communist political association (1944-45), which briefly replaced the party. He was the Communist party's candidate for President (1936,1940) and editor in chief of the *Daily Worker* (1944-45). In 1940 he was convicted of passport fraud, and he was imprisoned in 1941, but he was freed by President Franklin D. Roosevelt in 1942. During World War II he advocated greater cooperation between the Soviet Union and the West. When the war ended, this policy was repudiated by the leaders of the USSR and resulted in his removal from all party offices (1945) and from the party (1946). Among his works are *Communism in the United States* (1935), *What Is Communism?* (1936), *The People's Front* (1938), *War or Peace with Russia?* (1947), and *Marx and America* (1958).

Browere, John Henri Isaac, 1792-1834, American sculptor, b. New York City, studied painting in New York under Archibald Robertson and sculpture in Europe. He is known for his life masks, many of famous Americans, which he produced in hopes of establishing a national gallery of bronze busts. Among his subjects were John Adams, John Quincy Adams, Thomas Jefferson, De Witt Clinton, and James and Dolley Madison (N.Y. State Historical Assoc., Cooperstown). The artistry of Browere's work lies in the choice of expression and the manipulation of facial details and hair; all his portraits are singularly strong in effect. See C. H. Hart, *Browere's Life Masks of Great Americans* (1899).

Brown, Benjamin Gratz, 1826-85, U.S. Senator (1863-67) and governor of Missouri (1871-73), b. Lexington, Ky. An able lawyer in St. Louis, Brown was a leader in the Free-Soil movement in Missouri and later helped form the Republican party there. In the memorable Missouri election of 1870, Brown and his supporters defeated the radical Republicans, and he thus became prominent in the rise of the national LIBERAL REPUBLICAN PARTY. He was the party's candidate for Vice President on the unsuccessful ticket headed by Horace GREELEY in 1872. He later became a Democrat. See biography by Norma L. Peterson (1965).

Brown, Charles Brockden, 1771-1810, American novelist and editor, b. Philadelphia, considered the first professional American novelist. After the publication of *Alcuin: A Dialogue* (1798), he wrote such novels as *Edgar Huntly* (1799), *Arthur Mervyn* (2 vol., 1799-1800), and *Ormond* (1799), in which he presented arguments for social reform. *Wieland* (1799) was by far his most popular work and foreshadowed the psychological novel. To support himself after 1800 he became a merchant but also edited successively three periodicals, wrote political pamphlets, and projected a compendium on geography. See critical biographies by L. R. Wiley (1950) and D. L. Clark (1952); study by D. A. Ringe (1966).

Brown, Elmer Ellsworth, 1861-1934, American educator, b. Chautauqua co., N.Y., grad. Illinois State Normal Univ., 1881, and studied at the Univ. of Michigan and in Germany. He taught education at the Univ. of Michigan (1891-93) and at the Univ. of California (1893-1906). After directing the reorganization of the Bureau of Education as U.S. commissioner of education (1906-11), he became chancellor of New York Univ., retiring in 1933. He wrote *The Making of Our Middle Schools* (1903) and *A Few Remarks* (1933).

Brown, Ford Madox, 1821-93, English historical painter, b. Calais, France. Although closely affiliated with the Pre-Raphaelites in London, he never joined the brotherhood. Examples of his paintings are *Work* (1852-63; Manchester Art Gall.); *The Last of England* (1855; Birmingham Gall.); and his series of 12 frescoes in the town hall of Manchester, depicting the history of that city. He was the grandfather of Ford Madox Ford.

Brown, George, 1818-80, Canadian statesman and journalist, b. Scotland. In 1837 he emigrated to the United States, but after five years in New York City, he settled in Toronto, Ont. There he founded (1844) the Toronto *Globe,* which under his editorship became the most powerful political journal in Upper Canada. He wholeheartedly supported Robert Baldwin and the movement for responsible government. Elected in 1851 as a Reform member of the Canadian legislative assembly, Brown in time became leader of the "Clear Grits" faction, which opposed the influence of the French Canadians in the assembly. He urged the secularization of the Clergy Reserves (lands reserved for the Protestant churches), a national school system, the purchase of the Northwest Territories, and representation by population instead of the equal representation for Quebec and Ontario as established by the Act of Union (1840). Brown played an important role in the movement for confederation. Despite his personal and political hatred for Sir John A. MACDONALD, he joined (1864) "the great coalition" ministry and with Macdonald and others went to England in 1865 to urge Canadian confederation. He resigned that year from the government because of his inability to work with Macdonald and left Parliament in 1867. He later (1873) accepted appointment to the Canadian Senate, serving until he was shot to death by an insane employee. See biography by J. M. S. Careless (2 vol., 1959-1963).

Brown, George Alfred, 1914-, British politician. The son of a prominent trade union official, he worked as a salesman (1931-36) and an organizer for the Transport and General Workers Union (1936-42). The union sponsored his parliamentary candidacy for Belper, Derbyshire, which he represented from 1945 to 1970. A member of the right wing of the Labour party and a supporter of Hugh Gaitskell, Brown succeeded (1960) Aneurin Bevan as deputy leader of the party. Harold Wilson defeated him in the 1963 election for Gaitskell's successor as party leader, but Brown remained deputy leader until 1970. In Wilson's Labour government he was secretary of state for economic affairs (1964-66) and foreign secretary (1966-68). He was not reelected in 1970 and was made a life peer taking the title Baron George-Brown. See his memoirs, *In My Way* (1971); biography by W. N. Connor (1964).

Brown, George Douglas: see DOUGLAS, GEORGE.

Brown, Helen Gurley, 1922-, American writer and editor, b. Green Forest, Ark. The Depression taught her to develop competitive attributes, and she rose from secretarial jobs to advertising copywriter and account executive. In 1962 she published the bestselling *Sex and the Single Girl*—sequel *Sex and the New Single Girl* (1970)—which advised unmarried women on ways to maximize their potential. In 1966 she became editor of *Cosmopolitan,* reviving the faltering magazine by directing it toward single young career women.

Brown, Henry Kirke, 1814-86, American sculptor, b. Leyden, Mass. He studied portrait painting with Chester Harding and later turned to sculpture, which he studied in Italy. Returning to America in 1846, he settled in New York City. His early sculptures show the influence of Italian neoclassicism. Several works reflect his interest in American Indians. His finest achievement is the bronze equestrian statue of Washington in Union Square, New York City (1856). Among his later works are four statues in the Capitol, Washington, D.C.

Brown, Jacob Jennings, 1775-1828, American general, b. Bucks co., Pa. In the War of 1812 he defeated (May, 1813) a British attempt to take Sackets Harbor, N.Y., and the next year became commander of the Niagara frontier. Brown crossed the Niagara, took Fort Erie, and drove the British back toward York (now Toronto). On July 25, 1814, he fought the battle of LUNDY'S LANE, in which he was wounded. From 1821 to 1828 he was general-in-chief of the U.S. army.

Brown, Jimmy, 1936-, American football player, b. St. Simon Island, Ga. A high school and college star in all sports, but particularly in football, he joined the Cleveland Browns of the National Football League in 1957. Considered one of the greatest fullbacks in the history of the sport, Brown, who retired from the game in 1965 to pursue a career as a film actor, holds the lifetime records for most touchdowns (126), most yards gained rushing (12,312), and highest rushing average (5.22). He was elected to the Professional Football Hall of Fame in 1971.

Brown, John, 1800-1859, American abolitionist, b. Torrington, Conn. He spent his boyhood in Ohio. His life was a succession of business failures, in Ohio, Pennsylvania, Massachusetts, and New York, before he became prominent in the 1850s. An ardent abolitionist (he once kept a station on the UNDERGROUND RAILROAD at Richmond, Pa.), Brown in 1855 settled with five of his sons in Kansas to help win the state for freedom. He became "captain" of the colony on the Osawatomie River. The success of the proslavery forces, particularly their sack of LAWRENCE, aroused Brown, and in order "to cause a restraining fear" he, with four of his sons and two other men, deliberately murdered five proslavery men living on the banks of the Pottawatamie River. In this he asserted he was an instrument in the hand of God. His exploits as a leader of an antislavery band received wide publicity, especially in abolitionist journals, and as Old Brown of Osawatomie he became nationally known. Late in 1857 he began to enlist men for a project that he apparently had had in mind for some time and that took definite form at a convention of his followers held at Chatham, Ont., the next spring. He planned to liberate the slaves through armed intervention by establishing a stronghold in the Southern mountains to which the slaves and free Negroes could flee and from where further insurrections could be stirred up. Early in 1859, Brown rented a farm near Harpers Ferry, Va. (now W.Va.), and there collected his followers and arms. On the night of Oct. 16, with 21 followers, he crossed the Potomac and without much resistance captured the U.S. arsenal at Harpers Ferry, made the inhabitants prisoners, and took general possession of the town. Strangely enough, he then merely settled down, while the aroused local militia blocked his escape. That night a company of U.S. marines, commanded by Col. Robert E. Lee, arrived, and in the morning they assaulted the engine house of the armory into which Brown's force had retired. In the resulting battle, 10 of Brown's men were killed, and Brown himself was wounded. News of the raid aroused wild fears in the South, and to the North it came as a great shock. On Dec. 2, 1859, Brown was hanged at Charles Town. His dignified conduct and the sincerity of his calm defense during the trial won him sympathy in the North and led him to be regarded as a martyr. The standard contemporary account is contained in *The Life, Trial and Execution of Captain John Brown* (1859, repr. 1969). See biographies by O. G. Villard (rev. ed. 1965), S. B. Oakes (1970); and J. Abels (1971); Allan Keller, *Thunder at Harper's Ferry* (1958); J. C. Malin, *John Brown and the Legend of Fifty-Six* (1942, repr. 1970); R. O. Boyer, *The Legend of John Brown* (1973).

Brown, John, 1810-82, Scottish essayist. He was a physician. His writing was collected in *Horae Subsecivae* (3 vol., 1858-82), which included his unique picture of a dog, *Rab and His Friends* (1859), and a memoir of that gifted child known to Walter Scott's circle as "Pet Marjorie," *Marjorie Fleming* (1863). See his letters (ed. by his son and D. W. Forrest, 1907).

Brown, John Carter, 1797-1874, American book collector and philanthropist, b. Providence, R.I.; son of Nicholas Brown. In about 1840 he began collecting books printed before 1800 relating to America, and the result was a remarkable library of 5,600 volumes. These were catalogued by John BARTLETT (4 vol., 1865-71). Several thousand volumes were added to the library before Brown's death. After his son, John N. Brown, died, the library was donated to Brown Univ. (named for Nicholas Brown) with funds and endowment for a special building on the campus to house it. It is known as the John Carter Brown Library.

Brown, Joseph Emerson, 1821-94, U.S. public official, b. Pickens District, S.C. As governor of Georgia during the Civil War, Brown quarreled with Jefferson Davis over conscription and the suspension of the writ of habeas corpus despite their common secessionist stand. After the war Brown briefly became a Republican but returned to the Democratic fold, and in 1880 he was appointed to the U.S. Senate seat of John B. GORDON, which he retained until his retirement in 1891. Along with Gordon and Alfred H. Colquitt, Brown controlled Georgia politics for many years. See studies by L. B. Hill (1939, repr. 1972) and D. C. Roberts (1973).

Brown, Moses, 1738-1836, American manufacturer and philanthropist, b. Providence, R.I. He was associated with his brothers John, Joseph, and Nicholas in the family's mercantile activities before establishing (1790), with Samuel SLATER, the first water-powered cotton mill in the United States. Largely because of Brown's influence, Rhode Island College (later renamed Brown Univ. in honor of his brother Nicholas) was moved in 1770 from Warren to Providence. Brown contributed generously to the college. Moses Brown School in Providence, a leading preparatory institution for boys, was established (1819) by Quakers on land donated by him. See biography by Mack Thompson (1962).

Brown, Nicholas, 1769-1841, American manufacturer and philanthropist, b. Providence, R.I., grad. Rhode Island College (renamed Brown Univ. in 1804 for him), 1786. He extended the internationally known mercantile business of his father, Nicholas Brown. Later his own firm, Brown and Ives, came to control most of the waterpower on the Blackstone River, where his uncle, Moses Brown, and Samuel Slater had pioneered in the cotton textile industry. He was the treasurer (1796-1825) and, for a long period of time, the benefactor of his alma mater. Butler Hospital was founded (1847), in Providence, by his bequest for the care of the mentally ill. See J. B. Hedges, *Browns of Providence Plantations* (2 vol., 1952; repr. 1968).

Brown, Norman O., 1913-, American scholar and social critic, b. El Oro, Mexico; grad. Oxford, 1936. A classicist influenced by Freud, Brown thinks that the degree to which sexuality has been inhibited in America has led, not only to the stifling of instincts, but also to a perversion of human drives from life and art to money and death. His works include *Life Against Death: The Psychoanalytical Meaning of History* (1959), *Love's Body* (1966), *Hermes the Thief* (1969), and *Closing Time* (1973).

Brown, Olympia, 1835-1926, American Universalist minister and woman-suffrage leader, b. Prairie Ronde, Mich.; grad. Antioch College, 1860, and the theological school of St. Lawrence Univ., 1863. She was one of the first women in America to be ordained (1863) to the ministry. For 30 years she was president of the Wisconsin Woman's Suffrage Association. In 1873 she married Henry Willis, but retained her own name.

Brown, Robert, 1773-1858, Scottish botanist and botanical explorer. In 1801 he went as naturalist on one of Matthew Flinders's expeditions to Australia, returning (1805) to England with valuable collections. In his *Prodromus florae Novae Hollandiae et Insulae Van Diemen* (1810) he described Australian flora. A leading botanist of his day, he served as librarian to the Linnaean Society and to Sir Joseph Banks and later as curator at the British Museum. He observed BROWNIAN MOVEMENT in 1827 and discovered the cell nucleus in 1831. His studies of several plant families and of pollen were also notable.

Brown, Samuel Robbins, 1810-80, American missionary and educator, b. East Windsor, Conn. As missionary (1839-47) to China, he took charge of a school founded by the Morrison Educational Association. When he returned (1847) to the United States, three students accompanied him, the first Chinese to come to America to be educated. Brown had an important part in the founding of Elmira College. From 1859 to 1879 he worked as a missionary in Japan.

Brown, Walter Folger, 1869-1961, American cabinet officer, b. Massillon, Ohio. A lawyer of Toledo, Ohio, he became prominent in Republican politics and was (1927-29) Assistant Secretary of Commerce. As Postmaster General (1929-33) under President Hoover, Brown secured a reduction of air mail rates and a consolidation of air mail routes—policies that aided the development of commercial aviation.

brown algae: see PHAEOPHYTA.

brown coal: see LIGNITE.

Brown Deer, village (1970 pop. 12,582), Milwaukee co., SE Wis., on the Milwaukee River; inc. 1955. It is a residential suburb N of Milwaukee. The major industry is the manufacture of meters.

Browne, Charles Farrar: see WARD, ARTEMUS.

Browne, Hablot Knight, pseud. **Phiz,** 1815-82, English illustrator. At 21 he was chosen by Charles Dickens to illustrate *Pickwick Papers.* His success was immediate, and in due course he illustrated many of Dickens's novels as well as works of Harrison Ainsworth and Charles Lever. Browne also contributed popular cartoons to *Punch* and painted numerous watercolors and several oils.

Browne, Robert, c.1550-1633, English clergyman and leader of a group of early separatists popularly known as Brownists. Browne conceived of the church as a self-governing local body of experiential believers in Christ. Preaching without a license, Browne attacked the forms of government and the discipline of the Established Church; he gathered a congregation at Norwich c.1580. In 1581 he and his followers sought refuge in Holland. There he published (1582) several treatises that are generally regarded as the first expression of the principles of CONGREGATIONALISM. Circulation in England of these tracts was punishable by death. Upon his return to England in 1584, Browne was imprisoned and later excommunicated. But by 1586 he was sufficiently reconciled with the Church of England to be made master of the Stamford grammar school, and in 1591 he submitted to episcopal ordination and became rector of Adchurch, Northamptonshire. See biographies by Champlin Burrage (1906) and F. J. Powicke (1910).

Browne, Sir Thomas, 1605–82, English author and physician, b. London, educated at Oxford and abroad, knighted (1671) by Charles II. His *Religio Medici,* in which Browne attempted to reconcile science and religion, was written about 1635. After circulating in manuscript, it was first published in a pirated edition (1642); an authorized edition followed (1643). Inspired by the discovery of funeral urns near Norwich, he wrote *Hydriotaphia: Urn Burial* (1658), a solemn reflection on death and immortality, in which he expressed a belief in the futility of things here on earth. Published with *Urn Burial* was the more optimistic *The Garden of Cyrus,* a work devoted to the mystic symbolism of the number five. Browne's philosophy is now primarily of historical interest. It is the quality of his faith and, particularly, his mode of expression that make him one of the outstanding figures in the history of English literature. His other notable works are *Pseudodoxia Epidemica* (1646), commonly known as *Vulgar Errors,* and *Christian Morals* (1716). See edition of his works (ed. by Geoffrey Keynes, 6 vol., 1928–31); biographies by Edmund Gosse (1905) and J. S. Finch (1950); studies by W. P. Dunn (1950), Joan Bennett (1962), and Leonard Nathanson (1967).

Browne, Thomas, d. 1825, Loyalist commander in the American Revolution. A resident of Augusta, Ga., he was the victim of colonist violence in 1775, when he was tarred and feathered for ridiculing the Continental Congress. Later he organized (1778) a Loyalist troop in Florida and raided settlements in S Georgia. In 1780 he captured Augusta; in 1781 he was forced to surrender to Andrew Pickens and Henry Lee. After his exchange he was a colonel in the Queen's Rangers in South Carolina and was defeated (May, 1782) by Anthony Wayne. Browne, who was fiercely hated by the colonists, escaped and lived out his life in the British West Indies.

Browne, Thomas Alexander, pseud. **Rolf Boldrewood,** 1826–1915, Australian author. A squatter, a magistrate, and a commissioner in the gold fields, he wrote many books of life in Australia, such as *Robbery under Arms* (1888) and *Ghost Camp* (1902).

Browne, William (William Browne of Tavistock) (tăv'ĭstŏk), 1591?–1645?, English poet. An imitator of Spenser, he did his finest work in pastoral poetry, of which *Britannia's Pastorals* (1613, 1616, 1825) and *The Shepherd's Pipe* (with George Wither and others, 1614) are the best examples.

Brownell, Herbert, Jr., 1904–, U.S. Attorney General (1953–57), b. Peru, Nebr. Admitted to the bar in 1927, he practiced law in New York City and served in the New York state legislature (1933–37). He managed Thomas E. Dewey's campaigns for the governorship of New York in 1942 and for the presidency in 1944 and 1948. From 1944 to 1946 he was chairman of the Republican national committee. In 1952, Brownell helped bring about the nomination and election of Dwight D. Eisenhower as President. As Eisenhower's Attorney General, Brownell figured prominently in the administration's controversial loyalty-security program.

brown hematite: see LIMONITE.

Brownian movement or **motion,** zigzag, irregular motion exhibited by minute particles of matter when suspended in a fluid. The effect has been observed in all types of colloidal suspensions (see COLLOID)—solid-in-liquid, liquid-in-liquid, gas-in-liquid, solid-in-gas, and liquid-in-gas. It is named for the botanist Robert Brown who observed (1827) the movement of plant spores floating in water. The effect, being independent of all external factors, is ascribed to the thermal motion of the molecules of the fluid. These molecules are in constant irregular motion with a velocity proportional to the temperature. Small particles of matter suspended in the fluid are buffeted about by the molecules of the fluid. Brownian motion occurs for particles about 0.001 mm in diameter; these are small enough to share in the thermal motion, yet large enough to be seen with a microscope or ultramicroscope. The first satisfactory theoretical treatment of Brownian motion was made by Albert Einstein in 1905. Jean Perrin made a quantitative experimental study of the dependence of Brownian motion on temperature and particle size that provided verification for Einstein's mathematical formulation. Perrin's work is regarded as one of the most direct verifications of the KINETIC-MOLECULAR THEORY OF GASES.

brownie, in Celtic folklore, household spirit associated with farmsteads. Brownies help with chores, but, if criticized, they will make mischief, such as spoiling crops. If payment other than food is offered a brownie, he vanishes from a farm forever.

Browning, Elizabeth Barrett, 1806–61, English poet, b. Durham. A delicate and precocious child, she spent a great part of her early life in a state of semi-invalidism. She read voraciously—philosophy, history, literature—and she wrote verse. In 1838 the Barrett family moved to 50 Wimpole St., London. Six years later Elizabeth published *Poems,* which brought her immediate fame. The volume was a favorite of the poet Robert Browning, and he began to correspond with her. The two fell in love, but their courtship was secret because of the opposition of Elizabeth's tyrannical father. They married in 1846 and traveled to Italy, where most of their married life was spent and where their one son was born. Mrs. Browning threw herself into the cause of Italian liberation from Austria. "Casa Guidi," their home in Florence, is preserved as a memorial. Happy in her marriage, Mrs. Browning recovered her health in Italy, and her work as a poet gained in strength and significance. Her greatest poetry, *Sonnets from the Portuguese* (1850), was inspired by her own love story. *Casa Guidi Windows* (1851), on Italian liberty, and *Aurora Leigh* (1857), a novel in verse, followed. During her lifetime Mrs. Browning was considered a better poet than her husband. Today her life and personality excite more interest than her work. Although as a poet she has been criticized for diffuseness, pedantry, and sentimentality, she reveals in such poems as "The Cry of the Children" and some of the *Sonnets from the Portuguese* a highly individual gift for lyric poetry. See *The Letters of Robert Browning and Elizabeth Barrett Browning, 1845–46* (1899, new ed. 1930); Rudolph Besier, *The Barretts of Wimpole Street* (1930), the most popular dramatization of the Brownings's love story; biographies by F. Winwar (1950), G. B. Taplin (1957), and Isabel C. Clarke (1929, repr. 1970); study by Alethea Hayter (1963); bibliography by Warner Barnes (1967).

Browning, Orville Hickman, 1806–81, U.S. Secretary of the Interior (1866–69), b. Harrison co., Ky. One of the organizers of the Republican party in Illinois, Browning helped secure his friend Lincoln's nomination (1860) for President, but later, as U.S. Senator from Illinois (1861–63), he opposed Lincoln on the emancipation question. After Lincoln's death Browning supported Andrew Johnson's Reconstruction policy in opposition to the radical Republicans. He joined Johnson's cabinet in Sept., 1866, and was one of the President's closest friends and advisers during the impeachment struggle. His diary, edited by T. C. Pease and J. G. Randall (2 vol., 1927–33), is an important and detailed source for the Lincoln and Johnson administrations. See biography by M. G. Baxter (1957).

Browning, Robert, 1812–89, English poet. His remarkably broad and sound education was primarily the work of his artistic and scholarly parents—in particular his father, a London bank clerk of independent means. *Pauline,* his first poem, was published anonymously in 1833. In 1834 he visited Italy, which eventually became his second homeland. He won some recognition with *Paracelsus* (1835) and *Sordello* (1840). In 1837, urged by William Macready, the Shakespearean actor, Browning began writing for the stage. Although not especially successful, he wrote eight verse plays during the next nine years, two of which were produced—*Strafford* in 1837 and *A Blot in the 'Scutcheon* in 1843. The narrative poem *Pippa Passes* appeared in 1841; it and subsequent poems were later published collectively as *Bells and Pomegranates* (1846). Included were "My Last Duchess" and "Soliloquy of the Spanish Cloister," both dramatic monologues; this form proved to be the ideal medium for Browning's poetic genius. Other notable poems of this kind are "Fra Lippo Lippi," "Andrea del Sarto," and "The Bishop Orders His Tomb." In 1846, after a romantic courtship, Browning secretly married the poet Elizabeth Barrett and took her to Italy, where they lived for 15 happy years. There he wrote *Christmas Eve and Easter Day* (1850) and *Men and Women* (1855). In 1861, after the death of his wife, he returned to England, where he wrote *Dramatis Personae* (1864). This was followed by what is considered his masterpiece, the murder story *The Ring and the Book* (4 vol., 1868–69). Set in 17th-century Italy, the poem reveals, through a series of dramatic dialogues, how a single event—a murder—is perceived by different people. Browning gained recognition slowly, but after the publication of this work he was acclaimed a great poet. Societies were instituted for the study of his work in England and America. His later works include *Dramatic Idyls* (2 vol., 1879–80) and *Asolando* (1889). Browning's thought is persistently optimistic. He believed in commitment to life. His psychological portraits in verse, ironic and indirect in presentation, and his experiments in diction and rhythm have made him an important influence on 20th-century poetry. He was buried in Westminster Abbey. See variously published volumes of his letters; biographies by Maisie Ward (vol. I, 1967; vol. II, 1969), Betty Miller (1952, repr. 1973), and William Irvine and Park Honan (1974); studies by Robert Langbaum (1963), Philip Drew (1966 and 1970), R. E. Gridley (1972), and Thomas Blackburn (1967, repr. 1973); W. C. DeVane, *A Browning Handbook* (2d ed. 1955).

Brownists: see BROWNE, ROBERT.

Brownlow, William Gannaway (broun'lō), 1805–77, U.S. politician, governor of Tennessee (1865–69), known as the "Fighting Parson," b. Wythe co., Va. Brownlow won a large following in E Tennessee as an itinerant preacher, editor of the Jonesboro *Whig,* and, after 1849, editor of the influential Knoxville *Whig.* Along with Andrew Johnson, whom Brownlow despised, he shared the Unionist leadership in E Tennessee, although he did not oppose slavery. In Oct., 1861, his paper was suppressed by the Confederates, and Brownlow was imprisoned until March, 1862. Early in 1865 he became governor of Tennessee and instituted a destructive Reconstruction regime that proclaimed martial law and persecuted Confederate elements in the state. He was reelected in 1867 and served as U.S. Senator from 1869 to 1873. See the narrative of his experiences during the Civil War, *Rise, Progress, and Decline of Secession* (1862); biography by E. M. Coulter (1937, repr. 1971).

Brown-Séquard, Charles Édouard (broun-sākär', -sākwär'), 1817–94, physiologist, b. Mauritius, of French and American parents. He taught at Harvard (1864–68), practiced medicine in New York City (1873–78), and succeeded (1878) Claude Bernard at the Collège de France. He was known for his research on the functions of the sympathetic nervous system and the spinal cord; he also studied the physiological effects of the injection of genital gland extracts and of the application of heat to the cortex. His most important work was on internal secretions. He is considered a founder of endocrinology, especially organotherapy.

Brownson, Orestes Augustus, 1803–76, American author and clergyman, b. Stockbridge, Vt. Largely self-taught, he became a vigorous and influential writer on social and religious questions. He was a Presbyterian, but left that church to become first a Universalist and then a sort of free-lance minister, working for such socialistic schemes as the short-lived Workingmen's party. Later he was a Unitarian minister until in 1836 he started his own church, the Society for Christian Union and Progress. As founder and editor of the *Boston Quarterly Review* (1838–42) and as editor of the *Democratic Review* (1842–44), he condemned social inequalities. At this time he was one of the transcendentalists and was so interested in BROOK FARM as to send his son there. He entered the Roman Catholic Church in 1844, and later, as editor of the new *Brownson's Quarterly Review,* he attacked non-Catholic beliefs. Among his books are *New Views of Christianity, Society, and the Church* (1836); two autobiographical novels, *Charles Elwood; or, The Infidel Converted* (1840) and *The Convert* (1857); and *The American Republic* (1865). See biography by his son, Henry F. Brownson (3 vol., 1898–1900), who also edited his works (20 vol., 1882–87, repr. 1966), biographies by Arthur Schlesinger, Jr. (1939, repr. 1966), Theodore Maynard (1943, repr. 1971), and A. D. Lapati (1965); studies by Lawrence Roemer (1953) and Leonard Gilhooley (1972).

brownstone, red to brown variety of SANDSTONE. Its unusual color is caused in some instances by the presence of red iron oxide which acts as a cement, binding the sand grains together. Vast thicknesses (up to 20,000 ft/6,096 m) of brownstone were deposited in the present-day Connecticut River valley region of Massachusetts and Connecticut and in central New Jersey during the latter part of the TRIASSIC PERIOD. Quarries in these regions were the source for much of the building stone used in the late 19th and early 20th cent. in the construction of the many brownstone houses in New York City. Similar, but more brightly colored, sandstones also were deposited in the Rocky Mt. region during the Triassic period and JURASSIC PERIOD. These deposits are called "redbeds" and make up the colorful landscapes of the Painted Desert of Arizona.

Brownsville, city (1970 pop. 52,522), seat of Cameron co., extreme S Texas, on the Rio Grande c.17 mi (30 km) from its mouth at the Gulf of Mexico; inc. 1850. It is an important port of entry across the river from Matamoros, Mexico; a deepwater channel (completed 1936) accommodates ocean vessels. Brownsville is a trade, processing, and distributing point for the rich, irrigated lower Rio Grande valley, and has many industries, especially those connected with oil and natural gas. Other products include shrimp, electronic equipment, and aircraft parts. The establishment of Fort Texas there by Gen. Zachary Taylor in 1846 invited a Mexican attack that precipitated the Mexican War. Taylor later fought the battles of Palo Alto and Resaca de la Palma in coming to the fort's relief. The fort was renamed (1846) for Major Jacob Brown, killed while commanding its defense. Active until 1944, Fort Brown was held briefly by Union forces in the Civil War; the last battle of that war was fought 14 mi (23 km) east of the fort at Palmito Hill on May 13, 1865. The town of Brownsville grew around the fort and was a cattle-shipping point in the late 19th cent. In 1906 a group of black soldiers stationed at Fort Brown were blamed for a night gun raid on the town that resulted in the death of an innocent citizen; although interrogations of the soldiers produced no evidence, President Theodore Roosevelt, in a highly controversial directive, ordered the dishonorable discharge of 167 of the black soldiers. In 1972 the Secretary of the Army reversed the order, changing the discharges to honorable. Brownsville has a junior college, an international airport, and a notable zoo. Nearby recreational areas include Padre Island National Seashore.

Brown Swiss cattle, one of the oldest breeds of cattle, originating in Switzerland where the cows were used as triple-purpose animals (dairy, beef, and draft). They are large, fleshy, and slow-maturing, with body color ranging from gray or light brown to dark brown. Introduced in the United States in 1869, they have been used mainly as a dairy breed.

browntail moth, common name for a moth, *Nygmia phaeorrhoea,* of the tussock moth family. It is a serious pest of forest and shade trees, especially oak. It was introduced from Europe about the same time as the related gypsy moth in the late 19th cent. Browntail moth adults are white, with a tuft of brownish hairs at the tip of the abdomen; the abdomen of the male is rust colored. The female, with a wingspread of 1½ in. (3.8 cm) is slightly larger than the male. The dark, red- and white-mottled larvae, or caterpillars, may completely defoliate trees. They have nettling hairs that cause a skin rash if touched. Young larvae overwinter in small clumps of leaves fastened together with silk, emerging in early spring. In early summer they pupate in a cocoon in the soil, and the nocturnal adult emerges in about three weeks. An introduced fungus has helped keep this pest in check, and it has not spread in North America beyond New England. However, it is still a serious pest in parts of Eurasia. Good pruning of overwintering leaf nests and spraying are important control measures. The browntail moth is classified in the phylum ARTHROPODA, class Insecta, order Lepidoptera, family Liparidae.

brown thrush: see MIMIC THRUSH.

Brown University, at Providence, R.I.; for men; chartered 1764 as Rhode Island College at Warren, opened 1765. It moved to Providence in 1770 and was renamed for Nicholas BROWN in 1804. Pembroke College, a separate though affiliated college for women, was established in 1891. The John Carter Brown Library (see BROWN, JOHN CARTER) is especially significant for its early Americana.

Brown vs. Board of Education of Topeka, Kansas, case decided by the U.S. Supreme Court in 1954. Linda Brown was denied admission to her local elementary school in Topeka, Kansas, because she was black. When the case came before the Supreme Court, the court, in an opinion by Chief Justice Earl Warren, unanimously overruled the separate but equal doctrine of PLESSY VS. FERGUSON and held that de jure segregation in the public schools was unconstitutional. The court stressed that the badge of inferiority stamped on minority children by segregation hindered their full development no matter how equal the physical facilities. The unequal treatment of children violated the equal protection clause of the Fourteenth Amendment to the U.S. Constitution. After hearing arguments on implementation, the court declared in 1955 that schools must be integrated "with all deliberate speed." Restricted in application to de jure segregation, the decision was applied mainly to Southern systems. After strong resistance, Southern states slowly began integration under Federal court orders and the threat of loss of Federal funds. The decision provided a tremendous impetus to the civil rights movement of the 1950s and 60s and immeasurably hastened the end of segregation in all public facilities and accommodations. In 1973 the doctrine was applied to the school system of Denver, Colo., where segregation had until then been achieved through the gerrymandering of school districts.

Brownwood, city (1970 pop. 17,368), seat of Brown co., central Texas; inc. 1876. It is an industrial community; its products include brick, clothing, glass, furniture, feather products, mobile homes, plastic pipe, food products, beverage cartons, concrete mixers, reflective products, sportswear, cable, and wire. Brownwood processes and ships pecans, peanuts, cattle, wool, poultry, and meat from the surrounding agricultural area. Nearby Lake Brownwood is a large reservoir used for irrigation as well as for fishing and boating. In the city is Howard Payne College. The Douglas MacArthur Academy of Freedom is on its campus.

Bruay-en-Artois (brüä'-äN-ärtwä'), town (1968 pop. 28,628), Pas-de-Calais dept., NE France, on the Loire River. Primarily a coal-mining center, the town also produces fuels, boilers, clothing, beer, and candy.

Brubeck, Dave, 1920–, American pianist and composer, b. Concord, Calif. Brubeck began studying piano at the age of four and later studied composition with Milhaud and Schoenberg. In 1951 he organized a modern jazz quartet. His music, influenced by modern classical composers, is distinguished by complex harmony and the use of meters not typical in jazz. He has made numerous recordings and foreign tours.

Bruce, Scottish royal family descended from an 11th-century Norman duke, Robert de Brus. He aided William I in his conquest of England (1066) and was given lands in England. His son was granted fiefs in Scotland, and the family therefore rendered homage in both kingdoms. The 5th Robert the Bruce was married to Isobel, second daughter of David, earl of Huntingdon, brother of the Scottish kings Malcolm IV and William the Lion. The son of that marriage, the 6th Robert the Bruce, was a claimant to the Scottish throne after the death of Margaret Maid of Norway in 1290. The crown, however, was awarded by EDWARD I to John de BALIOL, grandson of the eldest daughter of David of Huntingdon. A grandson of this Robert was the famous Robert Bruce or Robert the Bruce who became king of Scotland as ROBERT I. The brother of Robert I, Edward BRUCE, was crowned king of Ireland in 1316. The young son of Robert I succeeded his father as David II and was in turn succeeded by his nephew, ROBERT II, son of Robert I's daughter Marjory and the first king of Scotland of the STUART family.

Bruce, Sir David, 1855–1931, British bacteriologist, b. Melbourne, Australia. He isolated (1887) the bacterium of Malta fever; the disease was renamed brucellosis after him, and the genus of bacteria causing it, *Brucella.* Bruce also discovered the cause and mode of transmission of nagana (a disease of horses and cattle) and (with David N. Nabarro and Sir Aldo Castellani) of African sleeping sickness. He was head of the Royal Society's commission to study sleeping sickness in Uganda (1903, 1908–10) and Malta fever in Malta (1904–6).

Bruce, Edward, d. 1318, Scottish king of Ireland, brother of ROBERT I of Scotland. He aided his brother in the war for independence from England and in 1315 was declared heir to Robert's throne. With Robert's approval he then invaded Ulster, to which he had some hereditary claim. He was crowned king of Ireland in 1316 and found many Irish allies against the Anglo-Irish rulers. However, he failed to consolidate his gains and was killed in battle in 1318.

Bruce, James, 1730–94, Scottish explorer in Africa. He explored Roman ruins in N Africa (1755) from Tunis to Tripoli and visited Crete, Rhodes, and Asia Minor. In 1768 he traveled down the Red Sea as far as the straits of Bab el Mandeb. From Massawa he struck inland for Gondar, then the capital of Ethiopia. He rediscovered (1770) the source of the Blue Nile, which he followed (1771) to its confluence with the White Nile. He wrote *Travels to Discover the Source of the Nile, 1768–73* (3d ed. 1813). For his travels in Barbary, see R. L. Playfair, *Travels in the Footsteps of Bruce* (1877). See biography by J. M. Reid (1968).

Bruce, James, 8th **earl of Elgin:** see ELGIN, JAMES BRUCE, 8TH EARL OF.

Bruce, Lenny, 1925–66, American comedian, b. Long Island, N.Y., as Leonard Alfred Schneider. Possessed of a cynical, surreal, and intensely comic view of the world, Bruce brutally satirized such sensitive areas of American life as sex, religion, and race relations. His comedy left no group unscathed, and his routines were replete with four-letter words. Consequently Bruce was continually being arrested and tried for obscenity and forbidden to perform. He was also arrested for narcotics violations. In Aug., 1966, he died of an overdose of narcotics at the age of 41. After his death Bruce became a cult figure, considered by many to be a martyr to the cause of free speech. His autobiography, *How to Talk Dirty and Influence People* (1965), sold well, and his nightclub routines were collected and published as *The Essential Lenny Bruce* (1966). *Lenny,* a musical based on his life and including much of his comic material, was a hit on Broadway in 1971. After his cult popularity had diminished, he was still regarded as a seminal figure in American culture, whose influence could be seen in the work of important novelists, playwrights, and filmmakers of the 1970s. See biography by Albert Goldman (with Lawrence Schiller), *Ladies and Gentlemen, Lenny Bruce!!* (1974).

Bruce, Stanley Melbourne (mĕl'bərn), 1883–1967, Australian political leader. Educated at Cambridge, he was called to the bar (1906) in England. After service in World War I, he entered the commonwealth legislature in 1918, was treasurer (1921–23) in the cabinet of W. M. Hughes, and served (1923–29) as prime minister. He was notable for promoting the closest relations of Australia with the empire compatible with Australian self-government, and he also advocated international cooperation. Bruce served as Australian delegate to the League of Nations and in 1936 was president of the council. From 1933 to 1945 he was high commissioner for Australia in London. In 1947 he was made Viscount Bruce of Melbourne.

Bruce, Thomas, 7th **earl of Elgin:** see ELGIN, THOMAS BRUCE, 7TH EARL OF.

Bruce, Victor Alexander, 9th **earl of Elgin:** see under ELGIN, JAMES BRUCE, 8TH EARL OF.

Bruce, William Speirs, 1867–1921, Scottish explorer and authority on the polar regions. He first went to the Antarctic as ship's surgeon in 1892 and later did survey work in Franz Josef Land and oceanographic work in the Arctic Ocean. He led (1902–4) the Scottish National Antarctic Expedition in the *Scotia,* performing much valuable scientific research in the Weddell Sea and discovering Coats Land. Bruce established a meteorological station on Laurie Island (in the South Orkney group). He edited the reports of the expedition (6 vol.) and wrote *Polar Exploration* (1911). Bruce made a number of voyages to Spitsbergen and became an authority on the islands. See R. N. Rudmose Brown, *A Naturalist at the Poles* (1923).

brucellosis (brōō"səlō'sĭs) or **Bang's disease,** infectious disease of farm animals that is sometimes transmitted to humans. In humans the disease is also known as undulant fever, Mediterranean fever, or Malta fever. In susceptible animals, primarily cattle, swine, and goats, brucellosis causes sterility and death. The symptoms are spontaneous abortion and inability to conceive in females and inflammation of sex organs in male animals. Animal brucellosis is transmitted by contact or by such mechanical vectors as contaminated food, water, and excrement. The disease is caused by three species of *Brucella* bacteria, and the causative organism is present in aborted fetuses and uterine secretions; antibodies to the bacteria are present in the blood or milk, an important diagnostic factor. Measures for prevention and control of brucellosis include vaccination of calves, blood tests of adults, and slaughtering of infected animals. Human brucellosis is an occupational disease among farmers, slaughterhouse workers, and others who come in direct contact with infected animals or their products (raw meat or unpasteurized dairy products). The most prominent symptoms are weakness and intermittent fever. The disease persists for months if left untreated but is seldom fatal in humans. There is no effective vaccine for human brucellosis, and antibiotics are the usual treatment.

Bruce of Melbourne, Stanley Melbourne Bruce, Viscount: see BRUCE, STANLEY MELBOURNE.

Bruch, Max (mäks bro͝okh), 1838–1920, German composer. He conducted the Liverpool Philharmonic Orchestra (1880–83) and taught at the Berlin Hochschule (1892–1910). His Violin Concerto in G Minor (1868) and his variations on the *Kol Nidre* (1881) for cello and orchestra are his best-known compositions.

brucine (bro͞o'sēn), alkaloid similar to STRYCHNINE. See NUX VOMICA.

Bruck an der Mur (bro͝ok än dĕr mo͞or), city (1971 pop. 16,400), in Styria prov., E central Austria, at the confluence of the Mur and the Mürz rivers. Manufactures include metal products and paper. Bruck was founded in 1263 by King Ottocar II of Bohemia. There is a 15th-century Gothic church in the city.

Brücke, Die [Ger.,=the bridge], German expressionist art movement, lasting from 1905 to 1913. Influenced by the art of *Jugendstil* (the German equivalent of art nouveau), Van Gogh, and the primitive sculpture of Africa and the South Seas, the *Brücke* group developed an art of fervent emotionalism. Founded in Dresden by Kirchner, Schmidt-Rottluff, and Heckel, the group invited Nolde and Pechstein to join in 1906 and Otto Mueller in 1910. They lived and worked communally, periodically issuing portfolios of their graphic art, which at first bore a rather communal style. By 1911 most of them had gone to Berlin. In their exhibitions they displayed brutally deformed, boldly colored portraits, landscapes, and city themes. Like their French contemporaries developing FAUVISM, the art of the *Brücke* expressionists was intense and violent but more inclined toward primitivistic and demonic qualities, symbolism, and introspection. Their uncomfortable art was essentially a reaction against impressionism and realism but lacked a coherent definition. The members fell out in 1913 over a statement of their aims formulated by Kirchner.

Bruckner, Anton (än'tōn bro͝ok'nər), 1824–96, Austrian composer. He taught himself to play the organ, and in 1856 he was appointed organist at the Linz cathedral. He became court organist in Vienna in 1867, and later he taught at the Vienna Conservatory and at the university there. He established a reputation as a virtuoso organist on trips to France in 1869 and to England in 1871, but as a composer he gained recognition slowly. In his composition he was influenced by the chromatic harmony and orchestral grandeur of Wagner's music. At the same time, Bruckner's work is marked by contrapuntal complexity and extended melodies, in the formal tradition of Beethoven and Schubert. His outstanding works are the Masses in D Minor (1864), in E Minor (1866), and F Minor (1867–71); a *Te Deum* (1881–84); and nine symphonies, of which the Fourth or *Romantic* (1874), the Eighth, or *Apocalyptic* (1884–87), and the Ninth (1895–96) are best known. He also wrote motets, cantatas, chamber music, piano and organ pieces, and pieces for male chorus. See studies by H. F. Redlich (1955), Erwin Doernberg (1960, repr. 1968), and R. Simpson (Am. ed., 1968).

Brudenell, James Thomas: see CARDIGAN, JAMES THOMAS BRUDENELL, 7TH EARL OF.

Bruegel, Brueghel, or **Breughel** (all: brö'gəl), outstanding family of Flemish genre and landscape painters. The foremost, **Pieter Bruegel,** the Elder, c.1525–1569, called Peasant Bruegel, studied in Antwerp with his future father-in-law, Pieter Coeck van Aelst, but was influenced primarily by Bosch. In 1551 he became a member of the Antwerp Guild. Bruegel visited Italy in the early 1550s. However, he remained close to the Flemish tradition and employed his native powers of minute observation in depicting the whole living world of field and forest and of sturdy peasants at work and play. He was, himself, a learned city-dweller and friend of humanists. His paintings of genre subjects have allegorical or moralizing significance. In his tremendous range of invention, Bruegel approached Bosch in creating nightmarish fantasies in such works as *The Fall of the Rebel Angels* (Brussels). He also painted cheerful, acutely perceived scenes of daily life, e.g., *Peasant Wedding* (Vienna), for which he is best known. The *Fall of Icarus* (versions in Brussels and New York) is his only mythological subject. He painted religious histories—*Numbering at Bethlehem* (Brussels), *Way to Calvary* (Vienna), with figures clothed in contemporary Flemish dress; parables—*The Sower* (Antwerp), *The Blind Leading the Blind* (Naples); genre scenes—*Children's Games, Peasant Dance* (both: Vienna); and landscapes showing the activities of the months—(several in Vienna, *Harvesters* in the Metropolitan Mus.); and other works. A skilled draftsman and etcher, Bruegel uses a delicate line to define his figures. His people are stubby in proportion, but lively and solid. His color is remarkably sensitive, as is his feeling for landscape. His compositions are often based on diagonal lines, creating gentle rhythms and allowing planes of landscape to unfold into the distance. See studies by Ludwig Münz (1961), Wolfgang Stechow (1971), and Fritz Grossmann (3d ed. 1973). His son, **Pieter Bruegel,** the Younger, 1564–1637, often copied his father's works. Two of his paintings are in the Metropolitan Museum. His brother, **Jan Bruegel,** 1568–1625, called Velvet Bruegel, specialized in still life, rendered with extreme smoothness and finesse. He was a friend of Rubens, and occasionally supplied floral ornament for works from Rubens's shop. He was also adept at landscape. Representative works are in Brussels and Berlin.

Bruges (bro͞ozh, Fr. brüzh), Flemish *Brugge,* city (1970 pop. 51,300), capital of West Flanders prov., NW Belgium, connected by canal with Zeebrugge (on the North Sea), its outer port. It is a commercial, industrial, and tourist center and a rail junction. Manufactures include lace, textiles, ships, railroad cars, communications equipment, chemicals, and processed food. Bruges was founded on an inlet of the North Sea in the 9th cent. and became (11th cent.) a center of trade with England. In the 13th cent. it flourished as the major entrepôt port of the HANSEATIC LEAGUE and as one of the chief wool-processing centers of Flanders. New ports (notably SLUIS) were founded to help accommodate its increasing trade. At its zenith (14th cent.), Bruges was one of the great commercial hubs of Europe. An early COMMUNE of the Low Countries, the city held extensive political privileges and often played a part in the chronic struggle between England, France, and the counts of Flanders. Its government, at first in patrician hands, gradually passed to the trade guilds of the wool industry. When Philip IV of France annexed Flanders in 1301, Bruges led the rebellion against him. The French garrison was massacred (1302), and shortly afterward the citizen-army of Bruges was led to victory in the BATTLE OF THE SPURS. Despite frequent political disturbances, Bruges continued to prosper until the Flemish wool industry declined (early 15th cent.) as a result of foreign competition. In addition, the North Sea inlet on which Bruges was located silted up completely by 1490, and the city lost its access to the sea and to its outer ports. By c.1500, Antwerp had replaced Bruges as the major entrepôt of N Europe. The commercial and industrial revival of Bruges began only in 1895, with the start of extensive repairs to its port; in 1907 the Zeebrugge canal was opened. The city was occupied by the Germans in World Wars I and II. Bruges was the cradle of FLEMISH ART during the rule (14th–15th cent.) of the Burgundian dukes in Flanders. Jan van Eyck, Gerard David, and many other masters are richly represented in the churches, public buildings, and museums of the city. Among its noted structures are the Hospital of St. John (12th cent.), containing several masterpieces by Hans Memling; the 13th-century market hall or clothworkers hall, with its famous carillon; the city hall (14th cent.); the Church of Notre Dame (13th–15th cent.), with the tombs of Charles the Bold and Mary of Burgundy and with Michelangelo's *Virgin*; the Cathedral of Saint-Sauveur (begun 10th cent.); and the Chapel of the Precious Blood (begun 12th cent.), a major place of pilgrimage.

Brugmann, Karl (kärl bro͝ok'män), 1849–1919, German philologist. A professor at Leipzig, Brugmann believed that scientific rules of linguistics do not admit of exceptions. With the help of others, notably Hermann Osthoff, Wilhelm Scherer, and Berthold Delbrück, he did much work in Indo-European linguistics and issued a large comparative grammar of Indo-European languages that is still a standard reference.

Brühl, Heinrich, Graf von (hīn'rĭkh gräf' fən brül), 1700–1763, Saxon statesman. He was adviser to Augustus II, king of Poland and elector of Saxony, and gained control of both governments after the accession (1733) of AUGUSTUS III. Brühl advanced the economic and cultural development of Saxony but did not succeed in making the Polish crown hereditary with the Saxon rulers. An able diplomat, he neglected Saxon military preparation and sought powerful allies. When King Frederick II of Prussia made (1756) a surprise attack on Saxony, initiating the SEVEN YEARS WAR in Europe, Brühl fled with his king to Poland. There he remained throughout the war, while Frederick exploited Saxony. Charges that Brühl amassed his fortune through fraud have not been proved.

Bruhn, Erik (ĕr'ĭk bro͞on), 1929–, Danish ballet dancer, b. Copenhagen. Bruhn joined the Royal Danish Ballet in 1947 and became a soloist there in 1949. He is widely regarded as one of the world's foremost dancers, combining dramatic flair with a subtle precision of style. Best-known for his roles in *La Sylphide, Giselle,* and *Swan Lake,* he has appeared throughout the world as guest artist and director with many companies, including the American Ballet Theatre.

Brulé, Étienne (ātyĕn' brülā'), c.1592–1632, French explorer in North America. He arrived (1608) in the New World with Samuel de Champlain, who sent him (1610) into the wilderness to learn about the Indians and the land. He lived with the Huron Indians and accompanied (c.1612) a group of them to Georgian Bay of Lake Huron. In 1612 he guided Champlain to that lake, and on the return journey they were, so far as is known, the first white men to see Lake Ontario. Brulé was then sent to the headwaters of the Susquehanna River and followed it to Chesapeake Bay. On his way back he was captured by the Iroquois and tortured, but he escaped (1618). He lived with the Huron once again, making many explorations of which no definite record remains. He probably visited Lake Superior and thus saw all the Great Lakes except Lake Michigan, being the first white man to do so. In 1629 he piloted the English vessels that captured Quebec and his old commander, Champlain. Then he retired to live an increasingly dissolute life among the Huron. He was killed in an Indian quarrel, and his remains were eaten. See C. W. Butterfield, *History of Brulé's Discoveries and Explorations, 1610–1626* (1898).

Brumaire (brümâr'), second month of the FRENCH REVOLUTIONARY CALENDAR. The coup d'etat of 18 (actually 18–19) Brumaire (Nov. 9–10, 1799), engineered chiefly by Sieyès, overthrew the DIRECTORY and established the CONSULATE under Napoleon. It nearly failed because of Napoleon's inept conduct at the Council of Five Hundred, but the situation was saved by his brother Lucien BONAPARTE.

Brummell, Beau (George Bryan Brummell) (brŭm'əl), 1778–1840, English dandy and wit. Brummell was greatly admired for his fastidious appearance and confident manner. He was an intimate of the prince regent (later George IV), and as such influenced men of society to wear dark, simply cut clothes and elaborate neckwear. He is also credited with having set the fashion for trousers rather than breeches. Having quarreled with the prince, and deeply in debt from gambling, Brummell fled to France, where, ironically, he lived for 14 years in poverty and squalor. He died insane in a hospital at Caen. See biographies by C. M. Franzero (1958) and Samuel Tenenbaum (1967).

Brunanburh, battle of (bro͞o'nənbûrg), A.D. 937, a victory won by ATHELSTAN, king of the English, over a coalition of Irish, Scots, and Britons (or Welsh) of Strathclyde. The site of the battle is not known. The battle is celebrated in a poem in the *Anglo-Saxon Chronicle.* See translation by Dorothy Whitelock and others (1962).

Brundisium: see BRINDISI, Italy.

Brunehaut: see BRUNHILDA.

Brunei (bro͞onī'), sultanate (1971 pop. 135,665), 2,226 sq mi (5,765 sq km), NW Borneo, on the South China Sea; a British protectorate since 1888. Its two sections are surrounded by SARAWAK, Malaysia. Oil is Brunei's main export. Rubber is also produced, and cassava, pineapples, bananas, rice, and other crops are raised. A majority of the population are Malays, but the small Chinese community (c.35,000) dominates the economy. Islam is the predominant religion. A native sultanate was established on Brunei in the 15th cent. At one time the sultan controlled nearly all of Borneo, but by the 19th cent. his power had declined and Brunei had become a haven for pirates. In 1888 the British established a protectorate over Brunei, administered by a British resident, although the sultan retained formal authority. The Japanese overran the area during World War II. In 1959 a written constitution went into effect. Under it, as amended in 1965, the sultanate remains and the protectorate is governed by a chief minister, council of ministers, and elected legislative council. There was a leftist revolt in 1962. The Federation of Malaysia was planned to include Brunei, but at the last moment the sultan refused to join. The capital and major port of Brunei is **Bandar Seri Begawan** (formerly Brunei; 1971 pop. 36,574).

Brunel, Sir Marc Isambard (bro͞onĕl'), 1769–1849, British engineer and inventor. Born in France, he came to the United States in 1793 as a royalist refugee. He became chief engineer of New York City, and his projects included building the old Bowery theater (burned in 1821) and constructing a canal between Lake Champlain and the Hudson. In 1799 he went to England, where he patented machinery for making ships' blocks and later invented many other mechanical labor-saving devices. In 1825, Brunel began the construction of the Thames Tunnel (the first in which a shield was used; see TUNNEL). In 1841 he was knighted. See biography by Paul Clements (1970); study by Peter Hay (1973). In the work on the tunnel Sir Marc was assisted by his son, **Isambard Kingdom Brunel,** 1806–59, British civil engineer and an authority on railway traction and steam navigation. He was engineer of the Great Western Railway, building bridges and docks. Later he constructed railways in Italy and was a consulting engineer in Australia and India. He is best known, however, for his designing and construction of the three ocean steamships the *Great Western* (1838), which was the first transatlantic steam vessel, the *Great Britain* (1845), the first ocean screw steamship, and the *Great Eastern* (1858), the largest steam vessel of its time. See biographies by his son, Isambard Brunel (1870; repr. 1972), and L. T. Rolt (1959); Celia Brunel Noble, *The Brunels: Father and Son* (1938).

Brunelleschi, Filippo (fēlĕp'pō bro͞onĕl-lĕs'kē), 1377–1446, first great architect of the Italian Renaissance, a Florentine by birth. Trained as sculptor and goldsmith, he designed a trial panel, *The Sacrifice of Isaac* (1401; Bargello, Florence) for the bronze doors of the Florence baptistery. The commission, however, was won by Lorenzo GHIBERTI. Thereafter, Brunelleschi became more interested in architectural planning. He made several trips to Rome, where he devoted himself to the study of classical buildings. About 1420 he drew two panels in perspective (now lost) that had important consequences for both architectural and art theory. The Church of San Lorenzo, Florence, reveals his systematic use of perspective in the careful proportioning of the interior structure and in the articulation of spatial volumes. In the Ospedale degli Innocenti (foundling hospital; 1419–45), Brunelleschi introduced a motif that was widely imitated during the Renaissance—a series of arches supported on columns. In 1420 he began to build the dome for the cathedral in Florence. This octagonal ribbed dome is one of the most celebrated and original domical constructions in architectural history. Brunelleschi's other works include the churches of Santa Maria degli Angeli and Santo Spirito and the Pazzi Chapel, all in Florence. His designs exhibit beauty of detail and elegance, as well as mastery of construction. See studies by A. Mantonio (1970), F. D. Prager (1970), and Isabelle Hyman, ed. (1973).

Brunetière, Ferdinand (fĕrdēnäN' brünətyĕr'), 1849–1906, French literary critic. An opponent of naturalism, he believed that literature should reflect a moral order. His vast learning is evident in the masterly *Manuel de l'histoire de la littérature française* (1897) and in the history of French literature from 1515, most of which was published (1904–17) posthumously from his notes. See study by Elton Hocking (1936).

Brunhild (bro͞on'hĭld), **Brünnehilde** (brün"əhĭld'ə), or **Brynhild** (brĭn'hĭld), mighty female warrior of Germanic mythology and literature. In the Nibelungenlied, a medieval German epic poem (see under NIBELUNGEN), she is the warlike queen of Iceland, whom Siegfried defeats in combat and wins for his brother-in-law, Gunther. Hating Siegfried, Brunhild contrives his death at the hands of Gunther's henchman, Hagen. In the Icelandic version of the story, the VOLSUNGASAGA, as Brynhild, she is the chief of the Valkyries. Sigurd (Siegfried) saves her from an enchanted stronghold, and the two fall in love. Later, Gudrun makes him forget Brynhild by means of a magic potion and takes him as her husband; Sigurd then wins Brynhild for Gunnar (Gunther). After bringing about Sigurd's death, Brynhild destroys herself on his funeral pyre. Wagner in his opera cycle *The Ring of the Nibelungs,* in which she is Brünnehilde, makes her a Valkyrie who defies her father, the god Wotan (see WODEN), to help the lovers Siegmund and Sieglinde. Wotan places her sleeping on a mountaintop surrounded by fire, from which she is rescued by Siegfried. He is made by magic to forget her, and for his unfaithfulness she brings about his death, her own death on his pyre, and the burning of Valhalla.

Brunhilda (brənhĭl'də) or **Brunehaut** (brünō'), d. 613, Frankish queen, wife of SIGEBERT I of the East Frankish kingdom of Austrasia; daughter of Athanagild, the Visigothic king of Spain. After the murder (567) of her sister Galswintha, who was the wife of Sigebert's brother Chilperic I of the West Frankish kingdom of Neustria, and Chilperic's marriage to his mistress FREDEGUNDE, Brunhilda was the major instigator in the war against Neustria. The struggle continued between Brunhilda and Fredegunde after the death (575) of Sigebert and the murder (584) of Chilperic. Throughout the reigns of her son, Childebert II, and of two grandsons, Brunhilda was the actual ruler of Austrasia and of Burgundy, when by her design that country was united with Austrasia after the death (592) of King GUNTRAM. She was endowed with the gifts of a great statesman, but her unscrupulousness in the execution of her plans earned her the fierce hatred of the nobles, whom she nonetheless controlled. She was finally betrayed by them to Fredegunde's son, CLOTAIRE II of Neustria. He put her to a horrible death.

Brünig Pass (brü'nĭkh), 3,396 ft (1,035 m) high, ancient route between the Forest Cantons and the Bernese Alps, central Switzerland. It is crossed by a highway and a railroad.

Brüning, Heinrich (hīn'rĭkh brün'ĭng), 1885–1970, German chancellor. Elected to the Reichstag in 1924, he was a leader of the Catholic Center party and a fiscal expert. In 1930 he was appointed chancellor of the Reich to put German finances in order. The Reichstag, which failed to support him, was dissolved (1930), and new elections were ordered. The new Reichstag was equally unable to produce a working majority, but Brüning continued to govern by decree. His drastic deflationary measures were very unpopular. In foreign policy he attempted to gain equality for Germany among the great powers and to persuade the former Allied powers to rescind German arms limitation. Brüning was forced to resign in 1932 by President Hindenburg, who appointed Franz von Papen as the new chancellor. Brüning left Germany in 1934 and from 1937 to 1952 was a member of the faculty at Harvard. In 1951 he resumed residence in Germany and became a professor of political science at the Univ. of Cologne. From 1955 until his death he was professor emeritus there.

Brünn: see BRNO, Czechoslovakia.

Brünnehilde: see BRUNHILD.

Brunner, Emil (ā'mēl bro͞on'ər), 1889–1966, Swiss Protestant theologian. The clearest and most systematic thinker of the school of dialectical theology, he was a professor of theology at the Univ. of Zürich (1924–53) and Christian Univ., Tokyo (1953–55). He several times visited and lectured in the United States. Like Karl BARTH he challenged the leaders of modern rational and liberal Christian theology and proclaimed a theology of revelation. The Christian faith, he maintained, arises from the encounter between man and God as He is revealed in the Bible. Brunner, in attempting later to leave a place for natural theology in his system, came into conflict with Barth over the question of natural revelation—Brunner refusing to separate theology completely from the general consciousness of man. His more important works include *Die Mystik und das Wort* (1924), *Der Mittler* (1927, tr. *The Mediator,* 1934), *Das Gebot und die Ordnungen* (1932, tr. *The Divine Imperative,* 1937), *Der Mensch in Widerspruch* (1937, tr. *Man in Revolt,* 1939), *Wahrheit als Begegung* (1938, tr. *The Divine-Human Encounter,* 1943), and *Christianity and Civilization* (2 vol., 1948–49). See studies by P. K. Jewett (1954) and C. W. Kegley, ed. (1962); Cornelius Van Til, *The New Modernism* (1946).

Brunnich's murre: see MURRE.

Bruno, Saint, 925–965, German churchman and statesman; brother and chief adviser of the first Holy Roman emperor, Otto I, whose chancellor he was from c.950. He was made (953) archbishop of Cologne and in the same year became duke of LOTHARINGIA. He organized the civil service, led the revival of learning, and reformed the monasteries according to the pattern laid down by the Cluniac reform. He is also known as St. Bruno the Great. Feast: Oct. 11.

Bruno, Saint, c.1030–1101, German monk, founder of the CARTHUSIANS, b. Cologne. He studied and taught at Rheims. In 1084 he took six companions and founded a little monastery in the Alps, which became the mother house of the Carthusian order (see CHARTREUSE, GRANDE). In 1090, Pope Urban II, whom Bruno had taught, called him to Rome as a counselor. He died in Italy in retirement at a monastery he had founded. Feast: Oct. 6.

Bruno, Giordano (jōrdä'nō bro͞o'nō), 1548–1600, Italian philosopher, b. Nola. He entered the Dominican order early in his youth but was accused of heresy and fled (c.1576) to take up a career of study and travel. He taught briefly at Toulouse, Paris, Oxford, and Wittenberg, but, personally restless and in constant opposition to the traditional schools, he found no permanent post. His major metaphysical works, *De la causa, principio, et uno* (1584, tr. *The Infinite in Giordano Bruno,* 1950) and *De l'infinito, universo et mondi* (1584), were published in France. Further works appeared in England and Germany. Bruno also wrote satire and poetry. In 1591 he returned to Venice, where he was tried for heresy by the Inquisition. After imprisonment at Rome, he was burned to death. Bruno challenged all dogmatism, including that of the Copernican cosmology, the main tenets of which, however, he upheld. He believed that our perception of the world is relative to the position in space and time from which we view it and that there are as many possible modes of viewing the world as there are possible positions. Therefore we cannot postulate absolute truth or any limit to the progress of knowledge. He pictured the world as composed of individual elements of being, governed by fixed laws of relationship. These elements, called monads, were ultimate and irreducible and were based on a pantheistic infinite principle, or cause, or Deity, manifest in us and in all the world. He was the first to state what has now become the cosmic theory. Bruno's influence on later philosophy, especially that of Spinoza and Leibniz, was profound. See D. W. Singer, *Giordano Bruno: His Life and Thought, with annotated trans. of his . . . "On the Infinite Universe and Worlds"* (1950, repr. 1968); I. L. Horowitz, *The Renaissance Philosophy of Giordano Bruno* (1952); Ksenija Atanasijevic, *The Metaphysical and Geometrical Doctrine of Bruno* (tr. 1972); P. H. Michel, *The Cosmology of Giordano Bruno* (tr. 1973).

Bruno of Querfurt: see BONIFACE, SAINT (d. 1009).

Bruno the Great, Saint: see BRUNO, SAINT (d. 965).

Brunschvicg, Léon (lāōN' brün'shvĕk), 1869–1944, French philosopher, b. Paris. From 1909 until his death he taught at the Sorbonne. Brunschvicg's philosophy, which has had considerable influence on modern European thought, is usually called critical idealism. He extended the teachings of Kant and Hegel and also drew upon Plato, Descartes, Spinoza, and Pascal. He regarded mathematics as the highest level yet reached by human thought, and maintained that judgment preceded all other activities of the mind. For Brunschvicg, God was whatever enables us to live the life of the spirit. His principal works are *La Modalité du jugement* (1897); *Les Étapes de la philosophie mathématique* (1912); *Le Progrès de la conscience dans la philosophie occidentale* (2 vol., 1927); and *La Raison et la religion* (1939).

Brunswick, dukes of: see CHARLES WILLIAM FERDINAND; FERDINAND; FREDERICK WILLIAM.

Brunswick, Ger. *Braunschweig,* former state, E West Germany–W East Germany, surrounded by the former Prussian provinces of Saxony, Hanover, and Westphalia. In 1946 it was included (except for several small territories placed in East Germany) in the West German state of Lower Saxony. Braunschweig (the former capital), Goslar, Helmstedt, and Wolfenbüttel were the chief towns. The region of Braunschweig is situated on the North German plain and in the northern foothills of the Harz mts. The land is drained by the Leine and Oker rivers. The duchy of Braunschweig emerged (13th cent.) from the remnants of the domains of Henry the Lion, the duke of Saxony, to whom Emperor Frederick I had left only the territories of Braunschweig and Lüneburg (roughly modern Braunschweig and Hanover). The Guelphic house repeatedly divided into several branches, the main ones being Braunschweig-Wolfenbüttel and Braunschweig-Lüneburg. In 1692 the duke of Braunschweig-Lüneburg became elector of Hanover. The Braunschweig-Wolfenbüttel line (itself a cadet branch of the Lüneburg line since 1634) ruled over Braunschweig and had, among its dukes, the famous generals Charles William Ferdinand (1735–1806) and Frederick William (1771–1815). Frederick William recovered (1813) the duchy, which Napoleon I had incorporated (1807) in the kingdom of Westphalia. The line became extinct in 1884, and Braunschweig was ruled by regents until 1913, when Ernest Augustus of Cumberland, grandson of King George V of Hanover, was made duke. A member of the North German Confederation from 1866 and of the German Empire from 1871, Braunschweig became a republic in 1918 and then joined the Weimar Republic.

Brunswick or **Braunschweig** (broun'shvīk), city (1970 pop. 223,700), Lower Saxony, E West Germany, on the Oker River. It is an industrial and commercial center; its manufactures include pianos, optical equipment, food products, and printed materials. Motor vehicles are assembled there. Reputedly founded c.861 and chartered in the 12th cent., Braunschweig became (13th cent.) a prominent member of the Hanseatic League. In 1753 the residence of the dukes of Braunschweig was shifted there from Wolfenbüttel. In 1830 the duke was deposed and the city became a self-governing municipality. The city has a 12th-century Romanesque cathedral, which contains the tombs of Henry the Lion (d. 1195) and Emperor Otto IV (d. 1218); several Gothic churches; and a famous fountain representing Till Eulenspiegel, the legendary prankster. The city is the site of a technical university and an art museum. The philosopher and dramatist Gotthold Lessing (1729–81) is buried in Brunswick.

Brunswick. **1** City (1970 pop. 19,585), seat of Glynn co., SE Ga., on St. Simon's Sound near the Atlantic coast; laid out 1771–72, inc. 1856. It is a port of entry, and its sheltered harbor is used by coastal freighters and fishing and shrimping fleets. The gateway to offshore resort islands (see SEA ISLANDS), Brunswick has a large seafood-processing industry and a great variety of manufactures, based principally upon forest products (e.g., naval stores, turpentine, pine oil, pulp, paper, lumber). The city was named for George III of the house of Brunswick (Hanover). It has a junior college, and a large U.S. naval training station for radar operators is nearby. **2** Town (1970 pop. 16,195), Cumberland co., S Maine, on the Androscoggin River and Casco Bay, in a resort area; settled as a trading post in 1628, inc. 1738. It is a growing commercial center for S Maine, with plants that make footwear, clothing, and paint brushes. Bowdoin College (1794) and a U.S. naval air station are in Brunswick. Nathaniel Hawthorne and Henry Wadsworth Longfellow were students at Bowdoin College during the 1820s, and Longfellow later taught there. A house dating from 1808 was once his home. Hawthorne's first novel, *Fanshawe* (1828) was printed in the town. In 1851, Harriet Beecher Stowe, then a Bowdoin faculty wife, wrote *Uncle Tom's Cabin* there; her house is a national landmark. In the first half of the 19th cent. Brunswick enjoyed prosperity based on shipbuilding. After the Civil War, textiles became the chief industry. The town's textile mill closed in 1955. **3** City (1970 pop. 15,852), Medina co., N Ohio, a suburb of Cleveland; settled 1815 as part of the Connecticut Western Reserve, inc. 1960. A small farm community for many years, its population burgeoned with the housing boom after World War II. It has a tire retread plant and a factory that makes powdered metals for roof coatings.

Brusa, Turkey: see BURSA.

Brush, George de Forest, 1855–1941, American painter, b. Shelbyville, Tenn., studied in New York City at the National Academy of Design and with Gérôme in Paris. His early, scrupulously realistic paintings of Indians gave way, in later work, to Italianate figure compositions. Examples of his work are *Mother and Child* (Mus. of Fine Arts, Boston) and *Mother and Child* (Corcoran Gall.).

brush turkey: see MEGAPODE.

brush wolf: see COYOTE.

Brusilov, Aleksey Alekseyevich (əlyĭksyā' əlyĭksyā'əvĭch broōsē'ləf), 1853–1926, Russian general. As a commander in World War I, he won victories in Galicia. In 1916 he organized the Russian offensive against Austria, which relieved the pressure on the Allies. The offensive, successful at first, cost Russia at least a million lives. Brusilov was briefly commander in chief under the Kerensky provisional government set up after the Russian Revolution (1917), and in 1920 he joined the Soviet army's staff in directing the war against Poland.

Brussels (brŭ'səlz), Fr. *Bruxelles,* Flemish *Brussel,* city (1970 pop. 161,080), capital of Belgium and of Brabant prov., central Belgium, on the Senne River and at the junction of the Charleroi-Brussels and Willebroek canals. The city is officially bilingual (French and Flemish). Brussels is an important commercial, financial, industrial, administrative, and cultural center and a major rail junction. Among its varied manufactures are pharmaceuticals, electronics equipment, machine tools, rubber, processed food, and lace. It is the seat of the Council of Ministers and of the Commission of the European Communities; of the Economic and Social Committee of the European Economic Community; and of the North Atlantic Treaty Organization. Brussels was inhabited by the Romans and later (7th cent. A.D.) by the Franks; an oratory was founded there (c.600) by the bishop of Cambrai on an island in the Senne. The city was fortified (c.1100) and became (late 12th cent.) a commercial center on the trade route from Bruges and Ghent to the Rhineland. It developed into a center of the wool industry in the 13th cent. In the 15th cent. the arts flourished there and many stately mansions (some still standing) were built. Brussels became (1430) the seat of the dukes of Burgundy and later (1477) of the governors of the Spanish (after 1714, Austrian) Netherlands. In 1561 the Willebroek Canal, connecting Brussels with the Scheldt River, was completed. Renowned for the luxury and gaiety of its life, the city became (late 16th cent.) the center of the duque de Alba's grim reign of terror. The city suffered heavily in the wars fought in the Low Countries in the 16th to 18th cent. Brussels changed hands several times in the French Revolutionary Wars; later, during the Waterloo campaign (1815), it was Wellington's headquarters. From 1815 to 1830 it was, with The Hague, the alternate meeting place of the Netherlands parliament; in 1830 it became the capital of independent Belgium. Brussels was occupied by the Germans in World Wars I and II. The historical nucleus of the city, the medieval and Renaissance Grand' Place, a large square, is the site of the Gothic city hall (15th cent.); the Renaissance-style Maison du Roi or Broodhuis (13th cent.), meeting place of the old States-General of the Netherlands; and a number of rebuilt Gothic guildhalls. Near the Grand' Place is the famous fountain of a small boy urinating, *Mannekin-Pis* (1619). The rest of Brussels is mostly modern, with contemporary style office buildings and broad boulevards that circle the city along its former ramparts. Other noteworthy buildings include the Collegiate Church of St. Michael and St. Gudule (founded in the 11th cent. and rebuilt in the 13th–15th cent.), which contains many noted Flemish paintings; the late-18th-century Palais de la Nation (parliament building); the Palais de Justice (late 19th cent.); and the Palais du Roi (royal palace). Brussels is the seat of a university (founded 1834), a noted conservatory, and academies of art, science, and medicine. There are also excellent art museums and a botanical garden. In 1958 Brussels was the site of a world's fair.

Brussels carpet: see CARPET.

Brussels griffon, breed of sturdy TOY DOG developed in Belgium in the 18th and 19th cent. It stands about 8 in. (20.3 cm) high at the shoulder and weighs from 6 to 12 lb (2.7–5.5 kg). There are two varieties, the wirehaired and the smooth. The coat of the former is dense and wiry with a fringe of hair around the eyes, nose, cheeks, and chin. Its color is reddish brown, black, or a combination of these two. The smooth variety, called Brabançon, has a short, finely textured coat and may be reddish brown or black marked with reddish brown, but not solid black. Believed to have been produced by crossing affenpinschers with the pug, and possibly the toy spaniels, the Brussels griffon is popular as a companion and house pet. See DOG.

Brussels sprouts, variety (*gemmifera*) of CABBAGE producing small edible heads (sprouts) along the stem. It is cultivated like cabbage and was first developed in Belgium and France in the 18th cent. Brussels sprouts are classified in the division MAGNOLIOPHYTA, class Magnoliopsida, order Capparales, family Cruciferae.

Brustein, Robert, 1927–, American educator and drama critic, b. New York City, grad. Columbia (Ph.D., 1957). Since 1966 he has been Dean of the Yale Drama School. An exacting critic of American theater, he brings great knowledge of the medium and moral vision to his work. He has written drama criticism for such periodicals as the *New Republic* and the *New York Review of Books.* His books include *The Theatre of Revolt* (1964), *Seasons of Discontent* (1965), and *Revolution as Theatre* (1971).

Brut, Brute (both: broōt), or **Brutus** (broō'təs), a Trojan, legendary founder of the British race, descendant of Aeneas. His story appears in Nennius and in Geoffrey of Monmouth, and his name gives the titles to long poems by Wace and Layamon.

Bruttium (brŭ'tēəm), ancient region, S Italy, roughly occupying the present CALABRIA, the "toe" of the Italian peninsula. Bruttium faced Sicily across the Strait of Messina. Inhabited in the interior by the Brutii (whose chief town was Cosenza) and by the Lucani, it was settled (8th cent. B.C.) along the coast by Greek colonists. SYBARIS and CROTONA were among the most prosperous towns of the colonies of MAGNA GRAECIA. The Romans conquered Bruttium in the 3d cent. B.C. RHEGIUM and VIBO VALENTIA were important Roman cities of Bruttium. The region passed to Byzantium after the fall of Rome and became known as Calabria.

Brutus (broō'təs), in ancient Rome, a surname of the Junian gens. **Lucius Junius Brutus,** fl. 510 B.C., was the founder of the Roman republic. He feigned idiocy to escape death at the hands of Lucius Tarquinius Superbus (see under TARQUIN). Roman historians tell how he led the Romans in expelling the Tarquins after the rape of Lucrece, how he became one of the first praetors (there were no consuls), and how he executed his sons for plotting a Tarquinian restoration. **Decimus Junius Brutus Gallaecus,** fl. 138 B.C., consul, consolidated the province of Farther Spain and stopped the encroaching Lusitanian tribesmen. **Marcus Junius Brutus,** d. c.77 B.C., was a partisan of LEPIDUS (d. 77 B.C.) in the struggle with CATULUS (d. 60 B.C.); POMPEY had him murdered. His wife Servilia was the half sister of Cato the Younger. Their son was **Marcus Junius Brutus,** 85? B.C.–42 B.C. He and Caius Cassius Longinus (see under CASSIUS) were the principal assassins of Julius CAESAR. He had sided with Pompey, but after the battle of PHARSALA, Caesar pardoned him, made him governor of Cisalpine Gaul (46 B.C.), and, in 44 B.C., urban praetor. Nevertheless, he joined Cassius in the plot against Caesar. After the murder of Caesar, Brutus went east and, in the republican cause, joined Cassius and held Macedonia with him. Late in 42 B.C., Octavian (later AUGUSTUS) and Antony arrived, and a battle was fought at Philippi. When it went against the republicans, Brutus committed suicide. Brutus' wife Portia was the daughter of Cato the Younger. Brutus had a contemporary reputation as a Stoic philosopher, and his admirers have regarded him as a second Cato, driven reluctantly to commit murder in order to save the republic. His detractors, on the other hand, have considered his friendship with the self-seeking Cassius as indicative of his true character. A lesser member of the conspiracy was **Decimus Junius Brutus,** d. 43 B.C., a partisan of Caesar against Pompey and a favorite of the dictator. Caesar gave him command in Gaul and appointed him to be his heir in case of Octavian's death. After Caesar's death, Brutus refused to surrender Cisalpine Gaul. In 43 B.C., Antony, to whom the senate had assigned the province, besieged Brutus at Mutina (modern Modena). He tried to escape and was killed.

Brüx: see MOST, Czechoslovakia.

Bruyn, Barthel Bartholomaeus (bär'təl bärtōlōmā'oōs broin), 1493–1555, German Renaissance painter, active in Cologne from 1515. Known especially for his portraits, which combine Northern realism with Italian-inspired monumentality and breadth, Bruyn also painted religious works such as the high altar at Essen Cathedral (1522). A portrait of a man and three religious works are in the Philadelphia Museum; many of his works are in Germany.

Bruyn, Cornelis de (kôrnā'lĭs də), 1652–c.1726, Dutch portrait painter and traveler. He painted for some years in Italy, where he was known, in Rome, as Adonis. Bruyn is remembered chiefly for the records of his extensive travels in Egypt, Persia, India, and other countries, illustrated with his own designs.

Bry, Théodore de (tēōdôr' də brē, brī), 1528–98, Flemish engraver and publisher, b. Liège. He spent most of his life in Frankfurt-am-Main. He visited London, where he executed a series of 12 plates, *The Procession of the Knights of the Garter,* and another of 34 plates, *The Funeral of Sir Philip Sidney.* The British geographer Hakluyt assisted him in obtaining materials for an illustrated collection of voyages and travels, *Collectiones peregrinationum* (1590–1634). Bry also published a series of portraits of famous men and illustrated the works of Thomas Hariot and J. J. Boissard. His son **John Théodore de Bry,** 1561–1623, assisted him and continued or completed several of his works.

Bryan, William Jennings, 1860–1925, American political leader, b. Salem, Ill. He practiced law at Jacksonville, Ill., and in 1887 he moved to Lincoln, Nebr. Bryan was a U.S. Representative from 1891 to 1895 but was defeated for the U.S. Senate in 1894. The next two years he spent as editor in chief of the Omaha *World-Herald.* Having ardently identified himself with the FREE SILVER forces in Congress, he became their most popular speaker in a preconvention drive to control the Democratic national convention at Chicago in 1896. At the convention his famous "Cross of Gold" speech so swayed the delegates that his nomination for President was assured, even though he was only 36 years old. The POPULIST PARTY also nominated him, but the conservative, gold Democrats ran John M. Palmer. The chief issue of the campaign was Bryan's proposal for free and unlimited coinage of silver, which he thought would remedy the economic ills then plaguing farmers and industrial workers. He lost the bitterly fought contest to Republican William MCKINLEY, whose campaign was skillfully managed by Marcus A. HANNA. Bryan controlled the Democratic convention in 1900 and saved the silver plank from removal by Eastern gold factions, but he agreed to put the campaign emphasis on anti-imperialism. Defeated again by McKinley, Bryan in 1901 started the *Commoner,* a widely read weekly that kept him in the public eye. His reduced party power in 1904 resulted in the compromise nomination of Alton B. PARKER, a conservative New Yorker, upon a platform dictated by Bryan. Parker, however, disavowed the silver plank, and Bryan unwillingly acquiesced. Parker's overwhelming defeat by Theodore Roosevelt turned the Democrats again to Bryan, who in 1908 was nominated a third time. Roosevelt's candidate, William H. TAFT, defeated him. The last Democratic convention in which Bryan played an important role was that of 1912, where his switch to Woodrow WILSON helped gain Wilson the nomination. Upon his election Wilson named Bryan Secretary of State. Bryan was influential in holding the Democrats together during the first 18 months of Wilson's administration, when unity was essential to the enactment of the President's reform legislation. He had little previous experience in foreign affairs but studied international questions conscientiously. With some 30 nations he negotiated treaties providing for investigation of all disputes. Antiwar leanings made Bryan more conciliatory than Wilson toward Germany. His Latin American policies, particularly those involving Nicaragua, caused a good deal of friction. Disliking the strong language of the second *Lusitania* note drafted by Wilson, he resigned on June 9, 1915, rather than sign it. However, he supported Wilson in the 1916 election and after war was declared. In the 1920 Democratic convention at San Francisco he fought in vain for a prohibition plank, and in 1924 at New York City he supported William G. McAdoo against Alfred E. Smith, but he was no longer the party's leader. In his later years Bryan, a Presbyterian, devoted himself to the defense of fundamentalism. He addressed legislatures urging measures against teaching evolution and appeared for the prosecution in the famous SCOPES TRIAL in Tennessee. Although he won the case in the trial court, Bryan's beliefs were subjected to severe ridicule in a searching examination by opposing counsel, Clarence DARROW. Five days after the trial, Bryan died in his sleep. Although the nation consistently rejected him for the presidency, it eventually adopted many of the reforms he urged—the income tax, popular election of Senators, woman suffrage, public knowledge of newspaper ownership, and prohibition. See the memoirs (1925, repr. 1971), begun by Bryan and finished by his widow; biographies by W. C. Williams (1936), P. W. Glad (1960), P. E. Coletta (3 vol., 1964–69), and L. W. Koenig (1971); studies by L. W. Levine (1965) and P. W. Glad, ed. (1968). His brother, **Charles Wayland Bryan,** 1867–1945, b. Salem, Ill., was for many years W. J. Bryan's political secretary and business agent. He was publisher and associate editor of the *Commoner*, mayor of Lincoln, Nebr., and governor of Nebraska.

Bryan, city (1970 pop. 33,719), seat of Brazos co., E central Texas; inc. 1872. Settled in the early 19th cent. in an area of large plantations, Bryan was long a cotton center. Farms producing alfalfa, truck crops, dairy goods, and poultry now occupy much of the land. Bryan's manufactures include aluminum products, furniture, building materials, agricultural chemicals, business forms, loose-leaf binders, shoe soles, electronic components, gravel extractions, and laboratory research equipment. The Research and Development Center of Texas A & M Univ. is in Bryan.

Bryansk (brēänsk'), city (1970 pop. 1,582,000), capital of Bryansk oblast, central European USSR, on the Desna River. The city is a transportation hub, and it forms an important industrial district with nearby Bezhitsa, with which it was incorporated in 1956. There are ironworks and locomotive, machine, and cement plants. Bryansk is also a major distributing center for natural gas. Originally called Brinyu and later Debryansk, the city was first known in 1146. For a time it was the capital of a principality. Bryansk later passed to Lithuania and in the 16th cent. was annexed by Muscovy. It served as a fortress until the 19th cent.

Bryant, William Cullen, 1794–1878, American poet and newspaper editor, b. Cummington, Mass. The son of a learned and highly respected physician, Bryant was exposed to English poetry in his father's vast library. As a boy he became devoted to the New England countryside and was a keen observer of nature. In his early poems such as "Thanatopsis," "To a Waterfowl," "Inscription for the Entrance to a Wood," and "The Yellow Violet," all written before he was 21, he celebrated the majesty of nature in a style that was influenced by the English romantics but also reflected a personal simplicity and dignity. Admitted to the bar in 1815 after a year at Williams and private study, Bryant practiced law in Great Barrington, Mass., until 1825, when he went to New York City. By that time he was already known as a poet and critic. He became associate editor of the New York *Evening Post* in 1826, and from 1829 to his death he was part owner and editor in chief. An industrious and forthright editor of a highly literate paper, he was a defender of human rights and an advocate of free trade, abolition of slavery, and other reforms. He also holds an important place in literature as the earliest American theorist of poetry. In his *Lectures on Poetry* (delivered 1825; published 1884) and other critical essays he stressed the values of simplicity, original imagination, and morality. During his later career Bryant traveled widely, made many public speeches, and continued to write a few poems (e.g., "The Death of the Flowers," "To the Fringed Gentian," and "The Battle-Field"). His blank verse translation of the *Iliad* appeared in 1870, that of the *Odyssey* in 1872. See biographies by Parke Godwin (2 vol., 1883; repr. 1967), John Bigelow (1890, repr. 1970), H. H. Peckham (1950, repr. 1971), and C. H. Brown (1971).

Bryaxis (brĭăk'sĭs), 4th cent. B.C., Greek sculptor. With Scopas, Leochares, and Timotheus, he worked on the sculptures of the Mausoleum at Halicarnassus (c.350 B.C.). Among other works attributed to him were several statues, including one of Apollo in the grove of Daphne, near Antioch. In 1891 at Athens his signature was discovered on a base for a tripod. The base is sculptured in relief with figures of horsemen.

Bryce, James Bryce, Viscount, 1838–1922, British historian, statesman, and diplomat, b. Belfast. After his education at the Univ. of Glasgow and at Oxford, he practiced law in London for a short time before becoming professor of civil law at Oxford. He wrote monumental works in several fields; the first of these was his *History of the Holy Roman Empire* (1864), a book still widely used. He entered politics and became a leader of the Liberal party, occupying a variety of posts, including the presidency of the Board of Trade and the chief secretaryship of Ireland. His interest in sociology and philosophy is evident in the second of his great treatises, *The American Commonwealth* (1888), a classic that is still read and used. Bryce was ambassador to the United States from 1907 to 1913; he was one of the most popular ever to be in Washington, since his knowledge of Americans, as revealed in his writings, was profound. He was created a peer in 1914. His other major works were *Studies in History and Jurisprudence* (1901) and *Modern Democracies* (1921). See biography by H. A. L. Fisher (2 vol., 1927, repr. 1973); *Bryce's American Commonwealth* (1939, abr. ed. 1959); E. S. Ions, *James Bryce and American Democracy 1870–1922* (1968, repr. 1970).

Bryce Canyon National Park, 36,010 acres (14,573 hectares), SW Utah; est. 1924. The Pink Cliffs of the Paunsaugunt Plateau, c.2,000 ft (610 m) high, were formed by water, frost, and wind action on alternate strata of softer and harder limestone; the result is colorful and unique erosional forms, including miniature cities, cathedrals, and spires. The BASKET MAKERS were probably the first Indians to inhabit the area; many of their artifacts are exhibited.

Bryhtnoth: see BYRHTNOTH.

Brynhild: see BRUNHILD.

Bryn Mawr (brĭn mär), uninc. village (1970 pop. 5,737), Montgomery co., SE Pa., a suburb of Philadelphia. It is the seat of Bryn Mawr College (for women), opened in 1885 by the Society of Friends. A junior college is also in Bryn Mawr.

Bryn Mawr College, at Bryn Mawr, Pa; undergraduate for women, graduate coeducational; opened 1885 by the Society of Friends, with a bequest from Joseph W. Taylor of Burlington, N.J. Modeled on a group curriculum plan at Johns Hopkins Univ., Bryn Mawr was one of the first women's colleges in the United States to offer graduate degrees. The library is especially noted for its collection of rare books and medieval incunabula. The school maintains a cooperative program with Haverford College and Swarthmore College.

bryony: see GOURD.

Bryophyta, division of green land plants that includes the MOSSES (class Bryopsida), the LIVERWORTS (Marchantiopsida), and the hornworts (Anthocerotopsida). Bryophytes differ from ferns, cone-bearing plants, and flowering plants in that they lack a vascular system for the transportation of water. Since their cells must absorb water directly from the air or the ground, nearly all bryophytes grow in moist places. The conspicuous green plant body of a bryophyte is the haploid, or GAMETOPHYTE, generation of the plant life cycle. It consists of a small stem with leaflike projections, as in all mosses and most liverworts, or a leafless, flattened body (thallus), as in some liverworts and all hornworts. The plant is anchored by means of threadlike structures called rhizoids. The leaflike structures and the rhizoids lack the complex internal anatomy found in the leaves and roots of plants with vascular systems. The gametophyte reproduces sexually, giving rise to a diploid, or sporophyte, generation; the sporophyte is a structure that grows directly out of the gametophyte and is at least partly dependent on the gametophyte for nourishment (see ALTERNATION OF GENERATIONS). In mosses, germinating spores (haploid) produce a green filamentous structure on the surface, called a protonema, the first stage of the gametophyte. Erect branches arise out of the protonema. After the branches produce rhizoids, the protonema dies. Antheridia (or sperm-producing structures) and archegonia (egg-producing structures) are borne in clusters on the tips of the branches of the gametophytes; these structures are usually microscopic. The different sex organs may be in a single cluster, in separate clusters on the same branch, or on separate branches, depending on the species. In the hornworts, antheridia and archegonia are borne either on the same thallus or, in some species, on separate thalli; the antheridia are borne either singly or in small groups, and the archegonia are borne singly. In the liverworts, the gametophyte may be a thallus or may be leafy; the antheridia and archegonia are borne on special branches that arise from the leafy stem. In all bryophytes fertilization is dependent on water—usually a film of water or the splashing of raindrops—for the transfer of sperm to the egg. Chemical stimuli direct the motile flagellate sperm to the archegonium. The fertilized egg (zygote) grows out of the gametophyte, which is also the source of its nourishment. Typically the sporophyte is a slender stalk from 1 to 2 in. (2.5–5 cm) long, with a capsule at the tip; in some species it may be green and manufacture some of its own food. Cells within the capsule undergo meiosis (reduction division) to produce haploid spores. In many mosses the capsule has a lid, the operculum, which is shed, releasing spores. In other bryophytes the mature capsule ruptures in other ways to release spores. The liverworts and hornworts are generally inconspicuous plants; common liverworts include species of the genera *Porella* and *Marchantia. Anthoceros* is the most familiar temperate-zone hornwort genus. The mosses are generally divided into three orders, with the order Bryales most prominent. The bryophytes are important because they are pioneer plants and soil builders on surfaces lacking other vegetation. SPHAGNUM moss (order Sphagnales) has been economically important as packing material and as PEAT. It is now believed that the bryophytes descended from green algae by way of now extinct ancestors (the RHYNIOPHYTA).

Bryozoa (brī"əzō'ə), name of a phylum, in older systems of classification, that included the invertebrate animals now classified in the phyla ENTOPROCTA and ECTOPROCTA. The term bryozoan (or moss animal) is still commonly used for members of the Ectoprocta.

Bryson, Lyman, 1888–1959, American educator, b. Valentine, Nebr., grad. Univ. of Michigan (B.A., 1910; M.A., 1915). He taught there from 1913 to 1917. From 1918 to 1924 he was active in Red Cross work. He was appointed professor at Teachers College, Columbia, in 1935, and during World War II he worked in the Office of War Information. Consultant on public affairs for the Columbia Broadcasting System, he was instrumental in popularizing such forms of adult education as the public forum. Among his books are *Adult Education* (1936), *Which Way America?* (1939), *The New Prometheus* (1941), *Science and Freedom* (1946), and *The Next America* (1952).

Brythonic (brĭthŏn'ĭk), group of languages belonging to the Celtic subfamily of the Indo-European family of languages. See CELTIC LANGUAGES.

Bryusov, Valery Yakovlevich (vəlyĕ'rē yä'kəvlyĭvĭch brēōō'səf), 1873–1924, Russian poet, novelist, and critic. He was the spearhead of the SYMBOLIST movement and wrote highly polished and esoteric verse celebrating sensual pleasures. Of his poetry, *Stephanos* (1906) is perhaps the best known. His two novels are *The Fiery Angel* (1903), concerning 16th-century German mystics, and *Altar of Victory* (1913). Bryusov was revered for his scholarly criticism. He also translated a number of works by French, American, and Armenian poets.

Brześć nad Bugiem: see BREST, USSR.

Btu: see BRITISH THERMAL UNIT.

Bubastis (byōōbăs'tĭs), ancient city, NE Egypt, in the Nile delta, near the modern Az Zagaziq. Capital of Egypt in the XXII and XXIII dynasties, it began to decline after the second Persian conquest (343 B.C.). Bubastis was the center of the worship of the lion-headed (or cat-headed) goddess Bast. In the time of Herodotus it had an annual Saturnalia, an orgiastic festival honoring the god SATURN. As Pi-beseth, Bubastis is mentioned in Ezek. 30.17. Excavations were made in 1886, 1887, and 1906. Among the finds were a chapel of the VI dynasty (proving that the site dates back to the Old Kingdom) and a great temple built in the 8th cent. B.C.

bubble chamber, device for detecting charged particles and other radiation by means of tracks of bubbles left in a chamber filled with liquid hydrogen or other liquefied gas. It was invented in 1952 by Donald Glaser. The bubble chamber consists essentially of a sealed chamber to be filled with a liquefied gas and constructed so that the pressure inside can be reduced quickly. The liquid is originally at a temperature just below its BOILING POINT. When the pressure is reduced, the boiling point becomes lowered so that it is less than the temperature of the liquid, leaving the liquid superheated. When a charged particle passes through this superheated liquid, it leaves a trail of tiny gas bubbles that can be illuminated and photographed. The track of a charged particle can be used to identify the particle and to analyze complex events in which it may be involved. If a magnetic field is present, the tracks of the particles will be curved, positively charged particles curving in one direction and negatively charged particles curving in the opposite direction. The degree of curvature depends on the mass, speed, and charge of the particle. Neutral particles can be detected indirectly by applying various CONSERVATION LAWS to the events recorded in the bubble chamber or by observing their decay into pairs of oppositely charged particles. The bubble chamber is particularly useful for studying high-energy particles that would pass through a CLOUD CHAMBER too quickly to leave a detailed enough track but which pass more slowly through the bubble chamber because of the greater density of the liquid. Liquid hydrogen and helium are commonly used in bubble chambers, with special equipment needed to maintain these gases in their liquid state (see LOW-TEMPERATURE PHYSICS). For experiments requiring very dense liquids, a variety of organic compounds may be used. See ELEMENTARY PARTICLES; PARTICLE ACCELERATOR; SPARK CHAMBER.

Buber, Martin (bōō'bĕr), 1878–1965, Jewish philosopher, b. Vienna. Educated at German universities, he was active in Zionist affairs, and he taught philosophy and religion at the University of Frankfurt-am-Main (1924–33). From 1938 to 1951 he held a professorship in the sociology of religion at the Hebrew University in Jerusalem. Greatly influenced by the mysticism of the HASIDIM, which he interpreted in many of his works, and by the Christian existentialism of Søren Kierkegaard, Buber evolved his own philosophy of religion, especially in his book *I and Thou* (1923, 2d ed. 1958). Conceiving the relations between God and man not as abstract and impersonal, but as an inspired and direct dialogue, Buber has also had a great impact on contemporary Christian thinkers. He worked to permeate political Zionism with ethical and spiritual values and strongly advocated Arab-Israeli understanding. Among his writings are *Jewish Mysticism and the Legends of Baalshem* (1931), *Mamre* (tr. 1946, repr. 1970), *Moses* (1946), and *The Origin and Meaning of Hasidism* (2 vol., tr. 1960). See his *A Believing Humanism: My Testament, 1902–1965* (tr. 1967) and his *Meetings*, ed. by Maurice Friedman (1973); Aubrey Hodes, *Martin Buber: An Intimate Portrait* (1971).

bubonic plague: see PLAGUE.

Buçaco: see BUSSACO, Portugal.

Bucaramanga (bōō"kärämäng'gä), city (1968 est. pop. 250,000), capital of Santander dept., N central Colombia, in the eastern highlands of the Andes. A leading commercial city, Bucaramanga is in the center of Colombia's rich coffee and tobacco area. Founded in 1622, the city still preserves many monuments from the colonial period. Bucaramanga also has a huge sports arena.

Bucareli y Ursúa, Antonio María (äntō'nyō märē'ä bōōkärā'lē ē ōōrsōō'ä), 1717–79, Spanish colonial administrator. He served in the Spanish army and as governor of Cuba before succeeding (1771) the marqués de Croix as viceroy of New Spain (Mexico). His administration, which lasted until his death, brought peace and prosperity, and Bucareli was widely popular. See B. E. Bobb, *The Viceregency of Antonio María Bucareli in New Spain, 1771–1779* (1962).

buccaneer: see PIRACY.

Bucephalus (byōōsĕ'fələs), favorite horse of Alexander the Great. There are legends of his speed and the wondrous deeds that Alexander performed while riding him. He died in 326 B.C. after the battle on the Hydaspes River. The city Bucephala was founded there by Alexander in his honor.

Bucer or **Butzer, Martin** (byōō'sər, bōōt'sər), 1491–1551, German Protestant reformer. His original name was Kuhhorn [cow's horn], of which Bucer is a Greek translation. At 14 years of age he joined the Dominican order, and he studied at Heidelberg, where he heard (1518) Luther in his public disputation on the doctrine of free will. Influenced by the reformist thought, Bucer left the order and accepted a pastorate at Landstuhl. In 1523 he entered upon the work of the Reformation in Strasbourg—preaching, writing, and helping to lay the foundations of the Protestant educational system. Many of his activities were devoted to attempts to reconcile the differences in regard to the Eucharist (see LORD'S SUPPER) which divided the Lutherans from the Swiss and S German reformers. Bucer's position was closer to that of the Swiss leader, Zwingli, and in this as in other doctrinal matters he is credited with a spiritual kinship to Calvin. In spite of his desire for unity, Bucer rejected the Augsburg Confession (see CREED), drawn up in 1530 in the hope of achieving religious peace. It was not until a personal meeting with Luther in 1536 that, in the Wittenberg Concord, Bucer was successful in securing agreement on the Eucharist among himself, Luther, and the reformers of S Germany. When Bucer failed to subscribe to the Augsburg Interim (1548)—a compromise between Roman Catholics and Protestants proposed by Holy Roman Emperor Charles V—he found it expedient to accept the invitation of Cranmer and moved to England. There, highly honored, he taught at Cambridge and tutored Edward VI, at whose request he wrote *De regno Christi*. See Hastings Eells, *Martin Bucer* (1931); Constantin Hopf, *Martin Bucer and the English Reformation* (1946).

Buch, Christian Leopold, Freiherr von (krĭs'tyän lā'ōpôlt frī'hĕr fən bōōkh), 1774–1853, German geologist and paleontologist, graduate of the mining academy, Freiberg, Germany. One of the most influential geologists of his age, he is noted especially for his study of volcanism. In addition to a valuable geological map of Germany, his works include geological and paleontological studies of several areas in Europe.

Buchan, John, 1st **Baron Tweedsmuir** (bŭk'ən, twēdz'myōōr), 1875–1940, Scottish author and statesman. Included among his works are a four-volume history (1921–22) of World War I; biographies of Julius Caesar (1932), Scott (1932), and Cromwell (1934); and adventure novels, including *The Thirty-nine Steps* (1915), *The Path of the King* (1921), and *Mountain Meadow* (1941). Elected to Parliament in 1927, he was appointed governor general of Canada in 1935 and was raised to the peerage. His administration of Canada was popular, and he promoted good relations with the United States. See his autobiography, *Pilgrim's Way* (1940); biography by Janet Smith (1965).

Buchanan, Franklin (byōōkă'nən), 1800–1874, American naval officer, b. Baltimore. Appointed a midshipman in 1815, Buchanan rose to be a commander in 1841. He was chief adviser to Secretary of the Navy George BANCROFT in planning the U.S. Naval Academy at Annapolis and was its first superintendent (1845–47). In Sept., 1861, he took the rank of captain in the Confederate navy, commanding the *Virginia* (formerly the *Merrimack*) against the Union blockading squadron in Hampton Roads (March 8, 1863). Wounded in that engagement, he took no part in the battle of the MONITOR AND MERRIMACK the next day. Promoted to ranking officer in the Confederate navy, he was forced to surrender to David G. FARRAGUT in the battle of Mobile Bay (Aug. 5, 1864). See biography by C. L. Lewis (1929).

Buchanan, George, 1506–82, Scottish humanist. Educated at St. Andrews and Paris, he became (1536) tutor to James V's illegitimate son James Stuart (later earl of Murray). He was imprisoned (1539) for satirizing the Franciscans but escaped to the Continent. He taught at Bordeaux, where Montaigne was among his pupils, and at Coimbra and became highly regarded as a Latin poet. Returning to Scotland in 1560, Buchanan declared himself a Protestant. He became an opponent of Mary Queen of Scots after the murder (1567) of Lord Darnley and in 1571 published the *Detectio Mariae Reginae*, a bitter attack on the queen. From 1570 to 1578 he was tutor of the young king James VI (later James I of England). Buchanan's *Rerum Scoticarum historia* (1582) is a useful source for his time, but his most influential work was the *De jure regni apud Scotos* (1579), which argued that the king rules by popular will and for the general good. See biographies by P. Hulme Brown (1890) and Donald Macmillan (1906).

Buchanan, James, 1791–1868, 15th President of the United States (1857–61), b. near Mercersburg, Pa., grad. Dickinson College, 1809. He studied law at Lancaster, Pa., and in practice there gained a considerable reputation for his wide learning and brilliant oratory. Thus prepared, he went into state politics, then entered the national scene as Congressman (1821–31), and was later minister to Russia (1832–33) and Senator (1834–45). A Federalist early in his career, he was later a conservative mainstay of the Democratic party. He served (1845–49) as Secretary of State under President Polk and although Polk exercised a strong personal hand in foreign affairs, Buchanan ably seconded his efforts. The quarrel with Great Britain over Oregon was settled peacefully. That with Mexico, which followed the annexation of Texas and the failure of the mission of John SLIDELL, led to the Mexican War and the Treaty of Guadalupe Hidalgo (1848). Under President Pierce, Buchanan served (1853–56) as minister to Great Britain. He collaborated with Pierre SOULÉ, minister to Spain, and John Y. MASON, minister to France, in drawing up the OSTEND MANIFESTO (1854), which was promptly repudiated by the U.S. Dept. of State. His open advocacy of purchasing Cuba (which would presumably have come into the Union as a slave-holding state) won him the hatred of the abolitionists, whom he in turn despised as impractical troublemakers. He was nominated as a Democratic candidate for the presidency in 1856, with John C. BRECKINRIDGE as his running mate, and he won the election over John C. Frémont, the candidate of the newly formed Republican party, and Millard Fillmore, candidate of the Whig and Know-Nothing parties. Buchanan did not have the majority of the popular vote, and his moderate views were disliked and mistrusted by extremists both in the North and in the South. Although he attempted to keep the "sacred balance" between proslavery and antislavery factions, in his administration the United States plunged toward the armed strife of the Civil War. Buchanan, who disapproved of slavery as morally wrong, felt that under the Constitution slavery had to be protected where it was established and that the inhabitants of a new territory should decide whether that territory should be free or slave. He angered many in the North by renewing efforts to purchase Cuba and by favoring the proslavery Lecompton Constitution in KANSAS. As his administration drew to a close, after the election (1860) of Abraham Lincoln to succeed him as President, Buchanan was faced with the secession of the Southern states. Very learned in constitutional law, he maintained that no state had the right to secede, but he held, on the other hand, that he had no power to coerce the erring states. He believed that the Federal government was authorized to use force only in protecting Federal property and in collecting customs. Therefore the question of the Federal forts in

Southern states became of great importance, particularly in South Carolina. Buchanan tried desperately to keep peace and promised South Carolina Congressmen that no hostile moves would be made as long as negotiations were in progress. When Major Robert Anderson moved U.S. troops from Fort Moultrie to FORT SUMTER, there was an outcry from South Carolina that the President's promise had been broken. Buchanan defended Anderson but, reluctant to act, sent supplies to Fort Sumter only belatedly. He was battered with criticism from North and South, and shortly after his administration ended, gunfire at Fort Sumter precipitated the war. John Bassett Moore edited his works (12 vol., 1909–11). See biographies by G. T. Curtis (1883, repr. 1969) and P. S. Klein (1962).

Buchans, town (1971 pop. 2,338), central N.F., Canada, on Red Indian Lake. It has a large mine that yields lead, silver, zinc, and copper.

Bucharest (bo͞o'kərĕst, byo͞o'-), Rum. *Bucureşti,* city (1969 est. pop. 1,526,000), capital and largest city of Rumania, SE Rumania, in Walachia, on the Dîmboviţa River, a tributary of the Danube. It is Rumania's chief industrial and communications center. Machine-building, metalworking, engineering, oil refining, food processing, and the manufacture of textiles, chemicals, automobiles, and footwear are the chief industries. The city, probably founded in the late 14th cent., was first known as *Cetatea Dambovitei* [Dambovita citadel] and was a military fortress and commercial center astride the trade routes to Constantinople. It became (1459) a residence of the Walachian princes and changed its name (15th cent.) to Bucharest. In 1698 the city became the capital of Walachia under Constantine Brancovan; after the union (1859) of Walachia and Moldavia it was made (1861) the capital of Rumania. The Treaty of Bucharest (1913) stripped Bulgaria of its conquests in the Second Balkan War (see BALKAN WARS). During World War I, Bucharest was occupied (1916–18) by the Central Powers. After Rumania's surrender to the Allies (Aug., 1944) in World War II, German planes severely bombed the city; Soviet troops entered on Aug. 31, by which time a coalition of leftist parties had seized power. Bucharest served as headquarters of the Cominform from 1948 to 1956. Today it is a modern city, with fine parks, libraries, museums, and theaters, and is the seat of the patriarch of the Rumanian Orthodox Church. Landmarks include the Metropolitan Church (1649), the 17th-century St. George Church, the Radu Voda (1649) and Stavropoleos (1724–30) churches, and the Athenaeum, devoted to art and music. Among the city's educational institutions are the old university (founded 1864), the new university (1935), an engineering college, and several academies and scientific institutes.

Buchenwald (bo͞o'khənvält''), village, Erfurt dist., SW East Germany, in the Buchenwald forest, near Weimar. It was the site of a CONCENTRATION CAMP established by the National Socialist (Nazi) regime.

Buchman, Frank Nathan Daniel (bo͝ok'mən), 1878–1961, American evangelist, b. Pennsburg, Pa. The international movement he founded has been variously called First Century Christian Fellowship, the Oxford Group, Moral Re-Armament (often known as MRA), and Buchmanism. Buchman was ordained in the Lutheran ministry in 1902. He was head (1905–15) of religious work at Pennsylvania State College. In 1921, Buchman, after five years of extension lecturing for the Hartford Theological Foundation, visited England. There he preached "world-changing through life-changing" among the students at Oxford, hence the name Oxford Group. In 1938 he instituted a campaign known as Moral Re-Armament. The work of evangelism for personal and national spiritual reconstruction is conducted informally and intimately in groups gathered in educational institutions, in church congregations, or in homes. "House parties" take the place of conferences, and religious experiences are shared in personal confessions. The evangelists stress absolute honesty, purity, love, and unselfishness. Moral Re-Armament has always been a controversial organization, resulting from its strident anti-Communist positions as well as from Buchman's open admiration of Adolf Hitler. See his speeches, *Remaking the World* (new and rev. ed. 1961); Peter Howard, *Frank Buchman's Secret* (1962); Gösta Ekman, *Experiment with God: Frank Buchman Reconsidered* (tr. 1972).

Buchner, Eduard (ā'do͞oärt bo͞okh'nər), 1860–1917, German chemist. He taught at Berlin, Breslau, and, from 1911, at Würzburg. He discovered (1896) that alcoholic fermentation of sugars is caused by yeast enzymes and not by the yeast cells themselves. Zymase, part of the enzyme system causing fermentation, was discovered by him in 1903. For this work he received the 1907 Nobel Prize in Chemistry.

Büchner, Georg (gā'ôrk bükh'nər), 1813–37, German dramatist. He was a student of medicine and a political agitator. He died at the age of 24, leaving a powerful drama, *Danton's Death* (1835, tr. 1928); a fragmentary tragedy, *Wozzeck* (1850, tr. 1928), which Alban Berg adapted for his opera; and a comedy, *Leonce and Lena* (1850, tr. 1928). Büchner greatly admired the poet J. M. R. Lenz, whom he made the hero of a novella, *Lenz* (1838, tr. 1955), which he never completed. See collections of his plays ed. by Victor Price (tr. 1971) and Michael Hamburger (tr. 1972); studies by A. H. J. Knight (1951) and Ronald Hauser (1974).

Buck, Carl Darling, 1866–1955, American philologist, b. Orlando, Maine. Buck taught at the Univ. of Chicago from 1892 to 1933. His *Grammar of Oscan and Umbrian* (1904) is still authoritative.

Buck, Pearl (Sydenstricker), 1892–1973, American author, b. Hillsboro, W.Va., grad. Randolph-Macon Women's College, 1914. Pearl Buck was awarded the 1938 Nobel Prize in Literature. Until 1924 she lived principally in China, where she, her parents, and her first husband, John Lossing Buck, were missionaries. She is famous for her vivid, compassionate novels about life in China. *The Good Earth* (1931; Pulitzer Prize), considered her finest work, describes a Chinese peasant's rise to wealth and brilliantly conveys a sense of the daily life of ordinary Chinese people. Among her other novels of China are *East Wind: West Wind* (1930), *Dragon Seed* (1942), *Peony* (1948), *Imperial Woman* (1956), and *Mandala* (1971). In 1935, Pearl Buck married her publisher Richard J. Walsh, president of the John Day Company. In 1949 she founded Welcome House, which provided care for the children of Asian women and American soldiers; the Pearl Buck Foundation of Philadelphia, to which she consigned most of her royalties, aids in the adoption of Amerasian children. During her lifetime Buck produced more than 85 books, including works for children, plays, biographies—such as those of her parents, *The Exile* (1936) and *Fighting Angel* (1936)—and many works of nonfiction, such as *China As I See It* (1970) and *The Kennedy Women* (1972). See her autobiography, *My Several Worlds* (1954); biography by T. F. Harris (2 vol., 1969–71).

buckeye: see HORSE CHESTNUT.

Buckhaven and Methil (mĕth'ĭl), burgh (1971 pop. 21,318), Fife, E Scotland, on the Firth of Forth. Methil is a leading port; coal mined in the area is among the exports. In the burgh is Wemyss Castle (13th cent.), where Mary Queen of Scots met Lord Darnley in 1565. In 1975, Buckhaven and Methil became part of the Fife region.

Buckholdt, Johann: see JOHN OF LEIDEN.

Buckhurst, Lord: see SACKVILLE, CHARLES, and SACKVILLE, THOMAS.

Buckingham, dukes of (Stafford line): see STAFFORD, EDWARD; STAFFORD, HENRY; STAFFORD, HUMPHREY.

Buckingham, George Nugent Temple Grenville, 1st **marquess of:** see GRENVILLE, GEORGE NUGENT TEMPLE, 1ST MARQUESS OF BUCKINGHAM.

Buckingham, George Villiers, 1st **duke of** (vĭl'yərz, bŭk'ĭng-əm), 1592–1628, English courtier and royal favorite. He arrived (1614) at the English court as JAMES I was tiring of his favorite, Robert Carr, earl of Somerset. Villiers was made a gentleman of the bedchamber (1615) and, after Somerset's disgrace, rose rapidly, becoming earl of Buckingham (1617), marquess, (1618), and lord high admiral (1619). In 1620 he married Lady Katherine Manners, daughter of the Roman Catholic earl of Rutland. By this time Buckingham controlled dispensation of the king's patronage, which enabled him to grant lucrative monopolies to his relatives. In 1621, Parliament began to investigate abuses of these monopolies, but Buckingham prevented action against himself (though not against his friend Sir Francis BACON) by joining in the condemnation of his relatives. Buckingham favored the proposed marriage of Prince Charles (later CHARLES I) with the Infanta Maria of Spain and in 1623 went with Charles to Madrid. There his arrogance contributed to the final breakdown of the long deadlocked marriage negotiations. Buckingham, now a duke, returned to England, advocating war with Spain, which made him the hero of Parliament. He lost that popularity rapidly by negotiating (1624) the marriage of Charles with another Catholic princess, Henrietta Maria, sister of Louis XIII of France. He was also blamed for the disastrous failure (Feb.–March, 1625) of an English expedition, under Graf von Mansfeld, to recover the Palatinate for FREDERICK THE WINTER KING; Buckingham failed to supply it adequately. By this time Charles had become king, and Buckingham was more powerful than ever, a fact that enraged Parliament. After the complete failure (Oct., 1625) of an expedition against Cádiz, Buckingham was impeached (1626), and Charles dissolved Parliament to prevent his trial. The following year Buckingham himself led an expedition (another failure) to relieve the HUGUENOTS of La Rochelle, and Parliament delivered another remonstrance against him. The duke was at Portsmouth preparing another expedition for La Rochelle when he was killed by John Felton, a discontented naval officer. The romantic aspects of the duke's career figure largely in Alexander Dumas's historical novel, *The Three Musketeers.* See biographies by C. R. Cammell (1939) and Hugh Ross Williamson (1940).

Buckingham, George Villiers, 2d **duke of,** 1628–87, English courtier; son of the 1st duke. Brought up with the royal family and educated at Cambridge, he was a strong royalist in the English civil war. In 1648 he escaped to the Continent, where he became a privy councillor of the exiled CHARLES II. He accompanied Charles to Scotland in 1650 and fought at Worcester (1651), but later intrigues with Oliver Cromwell's government estranged him from Charles. In 1657, Buckingham returned to England and married Mary, the daughter of the Puritan general Thomas Fairfax of Cameron. He hoped thereby to recover his estates, which had been confiscated in 1651, but instead he was imprisoned until 1659. After the Restoration (1660) he regained the favor of Charles II and was one of the most powerful courtiers of the reign. Vain and ambitious, he was known for his recklessness, quarrelsome temper, and lack of principle. He was a member of the CABAL and a bitter rival of his fellow minister, the earl of ARLINGTON. He was furious when he was kept in ignorance of the provisions of the secret Treaty of Dover (1670) with Louis XIV. Attacked by the House of Commons for misusing public funds and conducting secret negotiations with France and by the House of Lords for his open liaison with the countess of Shrewsbury (whose husband he had killed in a duel in 1668), he was dismissed from office in 1674. He joined the enemies of the duke of York (later James II) and participated vigorously in the outcry against Roman Catholics in the furor over Titus Oates's Popish Plot (1678), although he had earlier been much in favor of religious tolerance. He did not vote for exclusion of the duke of York from succession to the throne, however, and in 1684 was restored to favor and retired from politics. Buckingham showed the good as well as the bad aspects of the Restoration courtier: he patronized science and literature, had refined tastes, wrote poetry, religious tracts, and plays, and dabbled in chemistry. He was producer and partial author of a celebrated satire on heroic drama, *The Rehearsal* (1671; ed. by Montague Summers, 1914). See biographies by R. P. T. Coffin (1931), H. W. Chapman (1949), and J. H. Wilson (1954).

Buckingham Palace (bŭk'ĭng-əm), residence of British sovereigns from 1837, Westminster metropolitan borough, London, England, adjacent to St. James's Park. Built (1703) by the duke of Buckingham on the site of a mulberry grove, it was purchased (1761) by George III and was remodeled (1825) by John Nash; the eastern facade was added in 1847. The great ballroom was added in 1856, and in 1913 Sir Aston Webb designed a new front. The palace has nearly 600 rooms and contains a collection of paintings, including many royal portraits, by noted artists.

Buckinghamshire (bŭk'ĭng-əmshĭr), **Buckingham,** or **Bucks,** county (1971 pop. 586,211), central England. The county town is AYLESBURY. The Thames River forms the southern boundary of the county. In S Buckinghamshire are the chalky Chiltern Hills with their beech forests; furniture made from beechwood is the county's most notable manufacture. The area is mostly agricultural; barley, wheat, oats, and beans are the chief crops of the fertile Vale of Aylesbury in N Buckinghamshire. Cattle, pigs, sheep, and poultry are raised farther south. In ancient times Icknield Street and Watling Street crossed the county, which has extensive Roman and pre-Roman remains. Thomas Gray is buried at Stoke Poges, in the country churchyard that inspired his "Elegy." The poet John Milton had a cottage for a time at Chalfont St. Giles, and William Cowper spent many years at Olney. Also in Buckinghamshire are Hughenden Manor, home of the statesman Benjamin Disraeli; Chequers, a historic Tudor mansion and residence of British prime ministers since 1921; and Eton College, England's most famous public school. In 1974, Buckinghamshire was reorganized as a nonmetropolitan county.

Buck Island Reef National Monument: see NATIONAL PARKS AND MONUMENTS (table).

Buckland, William, 1784–1856, English geologist. He was dean of Westminster from 1845. First to note in England the action of glacial ice on rocks, he did much to bring physical and natural science into high repute and was responsible for giving Oxford (where he was a student and later a fellow) an international name in science. He wrote *Reliquiae Diluvianae* (1823) and *Geology and Mineralogy Considered with Reference to Natural Theology* (1836). Francis T. Buckland, English surgeon and naturalist, was his son.

Buckle, Henry Thomas, 1821–62, English historian. Contemptuous of the historical writing of his day with its intense concern with politics, wars, and heroes, Buckle undertook the ambitious plan of writing a history of civilization, treating all men in their relation with each other and with the natural world around them. At the time of his early death he had completed only two volumes of his panoramic *History of Civilization in England* (1857–61; new ed. in 1 vol., 1904). Attempting to make history a genuine science, Buckle arrived at various "laws" of history by an inductive process. It is easy to point out that these "laws"—e.g., the law of climate, by which he demonstrated that only in Europe could men reach high levels of civilization—were to a large extent only rationalizations of his own progressive and liberal views. Yet the effect that the book had in shaping English liberal thought was immediate and huge. It profoundly influenced later scientific historians, and it helped to fasten attention on masses rather than individuals, on the wide levels of all life rather than politics, and on the interrelations of man and nature rather than man and morals. See G. R. St. Aubyn, *A Victorian Eminence: Life and Works of Henry Thomas Buckle* (1964).

Buckley, William F., Jr., 1925–, American editor, author, and lecturer, b. New York City, grad. Yale, 1946. Buckley is a popular, eloquent, and witty spokesman for the conservative point of view. Editor of *American Mercury* (1951–52), he founded the *National Review* in 1955. In 1965 he was an unsuccessful candidate for mayor of New York City. He has hosted the weekly television show "Firing Line" since 1966 and writes a syndicated newspaper column. His books include *God and Man at Yale* (1951), *The Unmaking of a Mayor* (1966), and *Four Reformists–A Guide for the Seventies* (1973). His experience as a delegate to the 29th session of the UN General Assembly is recounted in *United Nations Journal: A Delegate's Odyssey* (1974).

Bucknell University, at Lewisburg, Pa.; coeducational; founded 1846 as the Univ. of Lewisburg. Its present name was adopted in 1886.

Buckner, Simon Bolivar, 1823–1914, Confederate general, b. Hart co., Ky., grad. West Point, 1844. In 1860, Buckner, a Louisville businessman, secured passage of a bill creating a large Kentucky militia and as inspector general trained it. Although he attempted to keep Kentucky neutral during the Civil War, when the legislature became strongly Unionist he took a commission as Confederate brigadier general (Sept., 1861). At FORT DONELSON (Feb., 1862) he surrendered to Grant and was taken prisoner but was soon exchanged and promoted to major general. He fought in Bragg's invasion of Kentucky (Oct., 1862), Mobile (Dec., 1862–63), and Chattanooga (Sept., 1863), and commanded the Dept. of East Tennessee (May–Aug., 1863) and Louisiana from 1864 to the end of the war. Later he was editor of the Louisville *Courier* and governor of Kentucky (1887–91). See biography by A. M. Stickles (1940).

Bucks: see BUCKINGHAMSHIRE.

buckthorn, common name for some members of the Rhamnaceae, a family of woody shrubs, small trees, and climbing vines widely distributed throughout the world. The buckthorns (several species of the genus *Rhamnus*) and the jujube (*Zizyphus jujuba*) are cultivated for their ornamental foliage. The jujube was also used locally and exported for use in confectionery and as a flavoring, now largely replaced by artificial flavorings. The lotus of Tennyson's "Lotus-Eaters" is thought to have been the jujube. Other members of the family yield dyes and a limited amount of lumber, e.g., cogwood, a hardwood. Other American species of *Rhamnus* are the redberry, the Indian cherry, and, in California, *Rhamnus purshiana,* which yields the purgative cascara sagrada. Buckthorn is classified in the division MAGNOLIOPHYTA, class Magnoliopsida, order Rhamnales.

buckwheat, common name for certain members of the Polygonaceae, a family of herbs and shrubs found chiefly in north temperate areas and having a characteristic pungent juice containing oxalic acid. Species native to the United States are most common in the West. The largest genus of the family, *Polygonum* (or *Persicaria*), contains the knotweeds and the smartweeds, found in many parts of the world. The common smartweed (*P. hydropiper*) is an annual sometimes called water pepper for its acrid quality. Several species of the dock genus (*Rumex*) are sorrels (the common name used also for the similarly acrid but unrelated OXALIS). The garden, or green, sorrel (*R. acetosa*) and the sheep, red, or field sorrel (*R. acetosella*) have long been used in Europe for salads and greens. Among the plants used as potherbs are the patience or spinach dock (*R. patientia*) and the tanner's dock (*R. hymenosepalus*); the latter is the source of canaigre, a substance used for tanning. Economically the important members of the family are of the rhubarb genus (*Rheum*) and the buckwheat genus (*Fagopyrum*), both native to Asia. Most of the rhubarb cultivated for the edible thick, fleshy leafstalks is *R. rhaponticum,* called also pieplant and wine plant. Medicinal rhubarb is obtained from this and other species of the genus. The cultivated buckwheat (*F. esculentum*) has been grown in the Old World since the Middle Ages as a honey plant and for its characteristic three-cornered grain, which is utilized for poultry and stock feed. Buckwheat flour is used in the United States, Japan, and eastern Europe; the plant is sown as a cover crop and is a food staple. The genus *Eriogonum* includes the wild, or yellow, buckwheat (*E. alleni*), restricted to the Appalachian shale barrens, and many Western species, e.g., the desert trumpet (*E. inflatum*), a desert flower of arid plains and plateaus. The interesting genus *Koenigia* has only one species, but it is found in arctic regions, in the Himalayas, and in Tierra del Fuego. Buckwheat is classified in the division MAGNOLIOPHYTA, class Magnoliopsida, order Polygonales, family Polygonaceae.

bucolics: see PASTORAL.

Bucureşti: see BUCHAREST.

Bucyrus (byo͞osī'rəs), city (1970 pop. 13,111), seat of Crawford co., N central Ohio, on the Sandusky River, in a farm area; settled 1818, inc. 1886. It is a trade and industrial center and has varied manufactures.

bud, in lower plants and animals, a protuberance from which a new organism or limb develops; in seed plants, a miniaturized twig bearing compressed rudimentary lateral stems (branches), leaves, or flowers, or all three, and protected in cold climates by overlapping bud scales. In warm climates buds grow all year; in temperate climates they grow in summer and remain dormant in the winter. The winter buds (particularly the larger terminal buds on twigs) of trees and shrubs are almost always so characteristic that they serve to identify the species. The "eyes" of a potato are undeveloped buds. See BUDDING; STEM.

Budaeus: see BUDÉ, GUILLAUME.

Budapest (bo͞o'dəpĕst"), city (1970 pop. 1,940,212), capital of Hungary, N central Hungary, on both banks of the Danube. The largest city of Hungary and its industrial, cultural, and transportation center, Budapest has varied manufactures, notably machinery, iron and steel, chemicals, pharmaceuticals, and textiles. Together with its industrial suburbs (particularly Csepel, Kispest, Pestszenterzsébet, Pestszentlőrinc, and Újpest, all joined to Budapest in 1949), the city accounts for about half of Hungary's total industrial production. Budapest was formed in 1873 by the union of Buda (Ger. *Ofen*) and Óbuda (Ger. *Alt-Ofen*) on the right bank of the Danube River with Pest on the left bank. Buda, situated among a series of hills, was traditionally the center of government buildings, palaces, and villas belonging to the landed gentry. Pest, a flat area, has long been a commercial and industrial center. The area around Budapest may have been settled as early as the Neolithic era. Aquincum, the Roman capital of Lower Pannonia, was near the modern Óbuda, and Pest developed around another Roman town. Both cities were destroyed by Mongols in 1241, but in the 13th cent. King Béla IV built a fortress (Buda) on a hill around there, and in the 14th cent. Emperor Sigismund built a palace for the Hungarian rulers. Buda became the capital of Hungary in 1361, reaching its height as a cultural center under Matthias Corvinus. Pest fell to the Turks in 1526, Buda in 1541. When Charles V of Lorraine conquered them for the Hapsburgs in 1686, both Buda and Pest were in ruins. They were resettled, Buda with Germans, Pest with Serbs and Hungarians. Buda, a free royal town after 1703, had a renaissance under Maria Theresa, who built a royal palace and in 1777 transferred to Buda the university founded in 1635 by Peter Pazmany at Nagyzombat. The university was later moved (1784) to Pest. In the 19th cent. Pest flourished as an intellectual and commercial center; after the flood of 1838, it was rebuilt on modern lines. Buda became largely a residential sector. After the union of Buda and Pest in 1873, the united city grew rapidly as one of the two capitals of the Austro-Hungarian monarchy. The city was by 1917 Hungary's leading commercial center and was already ringed by industrial suburbs. Also a beautiful city, Budapest became famed for its literary, theatrical, and musical life and attracted tourists with its mineral springs, its historic buildings, and its parks. Especially notable is the large municipal park and the showplace of Margaret Island (Hung. *Margit Sziget*), in the Danube, where St. Margaret, daughter of Béla IV, had lived in a convent. With the collapse of the Austro-Hungarian monarchy (Oct., 1918), Hungary, under Count Michael Karolyi, was proclaimed an independent republic. Budapest became its capital. When Karolyi resigned (March, 1919) the Communists, led by Béla Kun, gained temporary control of the city and established a Soviet republic in Hungary; but his troops were defeated in July, and Budapest was occupied and looted by Rumanian forces. In Nov., 1919, Budapest was seized by forces of Admiral Horthy, who in March, 1920, was proclaimed a regent of Hungary. In Oct., 1944, Horthy announced Hungary's withdrawal, as Germany's ally, from World War II, and that same month German troops occupied Budapest. After a 14-week siege the city fell (Feb., 1945) to Soviet troops. Almost 70% of Buda was destroyed or heavily damaged, including the royal palace and the Romanesque Coronation Church. When Hungary was proclaimed a republic (Jan., 1946), Budapest became its capital. In 1948 the Hungarian Communists, backed by Soviet troops, seized control of Hungary and proclaimed it (Aug., 1949) a people's republic. Budapest was the center of a popular uprising against the Hungarian Communist regime in Oct.–Nov., 1956 (see HUNGARY). Educational and cultural institutions in the city include Roland Eötvös Univ. (1635), the Hungarian Academy of Sciences, the National Széchenyi Library, the National Museum, the National Theater, and the State Opera House.

Budaun (bədoun'), town (1971 pop. 72,109), Uttar Pradesh state, N India, on the Sot River. An administrative center, it trades in grain, cotton, sugarcane, and oilseed. It was an important military outpost under the Mogul empire. The Great Mosque (the Jama Masjid), which dates from 1223, is in Budaun.

Buddha (bo͞o'də, bo͞o-) [Skt.,=the enlightened One], usual title given to the founder of BUDDHISM. He is also called the Tathagata [he who has come thus], Bhagavat [the Lord], and Sugata [well-gone]. He probably lived from 563 to 483 B.C. The story of his life is overlaid with legend, the earliest written accounts dating 200 years after his death (see BUDDHIST LITERATURE). His given name was Siddhartha and his family name Gautama (or Gotama). He was born the son of a king of the Sakya clan of the Kshatriya, or warrior, caste (hence his later epithet Sakyamuni, "the sage of the Sakyas"), in the Himalayan foothills in what is now S Nepal. It was predicted at his birth that he would become either a world ruler or a world teacher; therefore his father, King Suddhodana, who wished Siddhartha to succeed him as ruler, took great pains to shelter him from all misery and anything that might influence him toward the religious life. Siddhartha spent his youth in great luxury, married, and fathered a son. The scriptures relate that at the age of 29, wishing to see more of the world, he left the palace grounds in his chariot. He saw on successive excursions an old man, a sick man, a corpse, and a mendicant monk. From the first three of these sights he learned the inescapability of suffering and death, and in the serenity of the monk he saw his destiny. Forsaking his wife, Yashodhara, and his son, Rahula, he secretly left the palace and became a wandering ascetic. He first studied yogic meditation under the teachers Alara Kalama and Udraka Ramaputra, and after mastering their techniques, decided that these did not lead to the highest realization. He then undertook fasting and extreme austerities, but after six years gave these up fearing that they might cause his death before he attained illumination. Taking moderate food, he seated himself under a pipal tree at Bodh Gaya and swore not to stir until he had attained the supreme enlightenment. On the night of the full moon, after overcoming the attacks and temptations of Mara, "the evil one," he reached enlightenment, becoming a Buddha at the age of 35. Leaving what was now the Bodhi Tree, or Tree of Enlightenment, he proceeded to the Deer Park at Sarnath, N of Benares (Varanasi), where he preached his first sermon to five ascetics who had been with him when he practiced austerities. They became his first disciples. The first sermon, known as "the setting into motion of the wheel of the dharma," contained the basic doctrines of the "four noble truths" and the "eightfold path." For the remainder of his life he traveled and taught in the Gangetic plain, instructing disciples and giving his teaching to all who came to him, regardless of caste or religion. He spent much of his time in monasteries donated to the sangha, or community of monks, by wealthy lay devotees. Tradition says that he died at the age of 80. He appointed no successor but on his deathbed told his disciples to maintain the *sangha* and achieve their own liberation by relying on his teaching. He was cremated and his relics divided among eight groups, who deposited them in shrines called *stupas.* See E. J. Thomas, *The Life of Buddha as Legend and History* (3d ed. 1952, repr. 1960); A. C. A. Foucher, *The Life of the Buddha* (1963, repr. 1972); Trevor Ling, *The Buddha* (1973).

Buddh Gaya, India: see BODH GAYA.

Buddhism (bŏŏd'ĭzəm), religion and philosophy founded in India in the 6th to 5th cent. B.C. by Siddhartha Gautama, called the BUDDHA. One of the great Asian religions, it is divided into two main schools: the Theravada, or Hinayana, which predominates in Sri Lanka (formerly Ceylon), Burma, and SE Asia; and the Mahayana, found in China, Korea, and Japan. A third school, the Vajrayana, is confined largely to Tibet (see TIBETAN BUDDHISM). Buddhism has largely died out in the country of its origin, India, except for the presence there of many refugees from the Communist Chinese regime in Tibet.

Early Buddhism. India during the lifetime of the Buddha was in a state of religious and cultural ferment. Sects, teachers, and wandering ascetics abounded, espousing many different philosophical views and religious practices. Some of these sects derived from the Brahmanical tradition (see HINDUISM), while others opposed the Vedic and Upanishadic ideas of that tradition. Buddhism, which did not recognize the efficacy of Vedic ritual and did not accept the caste system, and which spread its teachings in the dialects of the people, was by far the most successful of the heterodox or non-Vedic systems. Buddhist tradition tells how Siddhartha Gautama, born a prince and raised in luxury, renounced the world at the age of 29 to search for an ultimate solution to the problem of the suffering innate in the human condition. After six years of spiritual discipline he achieved the supreme enlightment and spent the remaining 45 years of his life teaching and establishing a community of monks, the sangha, to continue his work. The basic doctrines of early Buddhism, which remain common to all Buddhism, include the "four noble truths": Existence is suffering (*dukhka*); suffering has a cause, namely craving and attachment (*trishna*); there is a cessation of suffering, which is NIRVANA; and there is a path to the cessation of suffering, the "eightfold path" of right views, right resolve, right speech, right action, right livelihood, right effort, right mindfulness, and right concentration. Buddhism characteristically describes reality in terms of process and relation rather than entity or substance. Experience is analyzed into five aggregates (*skandhas*). The first, form (*rupa*), refers to material existence; the following four, feelings (*vedana*), ideas (*samjna*), volitions (*samskara*), and consciousness (*vijnana*), refer to psychological processes. The central Buddhist teaching of non-self (*anatman*) asserts that in the five aggregates no independently existent, immutable self, or soul, can be found. All phenomena arise in interrelation and in dependence on causes and conditions and thus are subject to inevitable decay and perishing. The casual conditions are defined as a 12-membered chain called dependent origination (*pratityasamutpada*); its links are: ignorance, predisposition, consciousness, name-form, the senses, contact, craving, grasping, becoming, birth, old age and death, whence again ignorance. With this distinctive view of cause and effect, Buddhism accepts the doctrine common to other Indian religions of samsara, or bondage in the repeating cycles of birth-and-death, the momentum to rebirth being afforded by one's actions, both physical and mental (see KARMA). The release from this cycle of rebirth and suffering is the total transcendence called nirvana. The ideal of early Buddhism was the perfected saint, arahant or arhat, who had attained liberation by purifying himself of all defilements and desires. From the beginning, meditation and observance of moral precepts were the foundation of Buddhist practice. There are 10 major precepts for monks, of which laymen keep the first five. The ten are: no taking of life, no stealing, no unchaste acts, no false speaking, no drinking of intoxicants, no eating at improper times, no seeing of secular entertainments, no use of garlands, perfumes, and other adornments, no high and wide beds, and no receiving of money. The monastic order (sangha) is venerated along with the dharma, or religious teaching, and the Buddha as one of the "three jewels." Lay practices such as the worship of stupas (burial mounds containing relics) were probably present from earliest times, giving rise to later ritualistic and devotional practices. After the Buddha's death his teachings were transmitted at first by oral tradition and later written down in the 2d and 1st cent. B.C. (see BUDDHIST LITERATURE; PALI LITERATURE). Different sects arose probably very quickly, with varying views on a number of religious and philosophical issues, the latter concerning primarily the analyses of experience elaborated as the systems of ABHIDHARMA. Knowledge of early differences is limited, however, because the earliest extant written version of the scriptures is the Pali canon (1st cent. A.D.) of the Theravada school of Ceylon. Although Theravada [doctrine of the elders] is known to be only one of many early schools of Buddhism (traditionally numbered at 18), its beliefs are generally accepted as representative of early Buddhist doctrine as described above.

Mahayana Buddhism. From other of the early schools of Buddhism developed the lines of thought that led toward the positions advocated by Mahayana [great vehicle] Buddhism; it gave itself this name in polemical writings to distinguish itself from what it called the Hinayana [lesser vehicle], Theravada, and related schools. Mahayana is identifiable as a definable movement through the appearance, beginning in the 1st cent. B.C., of a new class of literature, the Mahayana sutras. The main philosophical tenet of the Mahayana is that all things are empty, or devoid of self-nature (see SUNYATA). Its chief religious concept was that of the BODHISATTVA, who replaced the arahant as the ideal and was distinguished from him by his vow to postpone entry into nirvana (although meriting it) until all others may be similarly enlightened and saved. The state of bodhisattva was an actual goal of both lay and monastic Buddhists; it was also the name of a class of celestial beings who were worshiped along with the Buddha. The Mahayana developed doctrines of the eternal and absolute nature of the Buddha, of which the historical Buddha was regarded as a temporary manifestation. Teachings that consciousness is intrinsically pure developed into ideas of potential Buddhahood innate in all beings. The chief philosophical schools of Indian Mahayana were the MADHYAMIKA, founded by Nagarjuna (2d cent. A.D.), and the YOGACARA, founded by the brothers Asanga and Vasubandhu (4th cent. A.D.). In this later Indian period, authors in different schools wrote specialized treatises, Buddhist logic was systematized, and the practices of TANTRA came into prominence.

The Spread of Buddhism. In the 3d cent. B.C. the Indian emperor ASOKA greatly strengthened Buddhism by his support and sent Buddhist missionaries as far afield as Syria. In the succeeding centuries, however, Buddhism began to decline in India itself, losing adherents to Hinduism. The destruction of Buddhist centers by the invasions of the White Huns (6th cent.) and the Muslims (11th cent.) were other major factors leading to the virtual extinction of Buddhism in India by the 13th cent. In the meantime, however, its beliefs had spread widely. Ceylon was converted to Buddhism in the 3d cent., and Buddhism has remained its national religion up to the present. The Indian Buddhist scholar Buddhaghosa (5th cent. A.D.) produced some of Theravada Buddhism's most important scholastic writings after taking up residence in Ceylon. Buddhism entered Tibet in the 7th cent. A.D. and flourished there, its main philosophy being that of the Madhyamika and its practices those of the Tantra. The religion reached SE Asia in the first five centuries A.D. Both Mahayana and Hinayana were established, but today the surviving forms are mostly Hinayana. About the 1st cent. A.D. Buddhism entered China along trade routes from central Asia. There followed a four-century period of assimilation. In the 3d and 4th cent. Buddhist concepts were interpreted by analogy with native philosophy, mostly Taoism, but the work of the great translators KUMARAJIVA and HSUAN-TSANG established a basis for better understanding of Buddhist concepts. The 6th cent. saw the development of the great philosophical schools, each centering on a certain scripture and having a lineage of teachers. Two such schools, the T'ien-t'ai and the HUA-YEN, made a synthesis of the widely varying scriptures and doctrines that had come to China from India and arranged them in hierarchical order. Branches of Madhyamika and Yogacara were also founded. The two great nonacademic sects were Ch'an Buddhism, or ZEN BUDDHISM, whose chief practice was sitting in meditation to achieve "sudden enlightenment," and PURE LAND BUDDHISM, which advocated repetition of the name of the Buddha Amitabha to attain rebirth in his paradise. Buddhism in China encountered opposition from Confucianism and Taoism and resistance from government threatened by the growing power of the sangha, which was tax-exempt. The great persecution by the emperor Wu-tsung in 845 dealt Chinese Buddhism a blow from which it never fully recovered. The only schools that retained vitality were Zen and Pure Land. These increasingly fused with one another and with the native religion, and after the decline of Buddhism in India, neo-Confucianism rose to intellectual and cultural dominance. From China and Korea, Buddhism was imported into Japan. Its schools, with the exception of the nationalistic Nichiren sect, established by Nichiren (1222–82), were those of Chinese Buddhism. The philosophical schools were transmitted first, and Buddhism until the 12th cent. was centered in the life of the nobility. Zen and Pure Land grew to become popular movements after the 13th cent. After World War II new sects arose in Japan such as the Soka Gakkai, a branch of Nichiren, and the Rissho-koseikai. They have attracted a large following. See T. W. Rhys Davids, *Buddhism, Its History and Literature* (1896, 5th ed. 1962); H. C. Warren, *Buddhism in Translations* (1896, repr. 1963); C. N. E. Eliot, *Japanese Buddhism* (1935, repr. 1969); K. P. Landon, *Southeast Asia, Crossroads of Religion* (1949, repr. 1969); E. A. Burtt, ed., *The Teachings of the Compassionate Buddha* (1955, repr. 1963); Christmas Humphreys, *A Popular Dictionary of Buddhism* (1962); Edward Conze, *Buddhism: Its Essence and Development* (1953, repr. 1959) and *Buddhist Thought in India* (1962, repr. 1967); Erik Zürcher, *Buddhism* (1962); K. S. S. Ch'en, *Buddhism in China* (1964, repr. 1972), and *Buddhism: The Light of Asia* (1968); R. H. Robinson, *The Buddhist Religion* (1970); M. E. Spiro, *Buddhism and Society* (1970); D. A. Fox, *The Vagrant Lotus* (1973); Trevor Ling, *The Buddha* (1973).

Buddhist literature. During his lifetime the Buddha taught not in Vedic Sanskrit, which had become unintelligible to the people, but in his own NE Indian dialect; he also encouraged his monks to propagate his teachings in the vernacular. After his death, the Buddhist canon was formulated and transmitted by oral tradition, and it was written down in several versions in the 2d and 1st cent. B.C. Its main divisions, called *pitakas* [baskets], are the Vinaya or monastic rules, the Sutra (Pali *Sutta*) or discourses of the Buddha, and the ABHIDHARMA (Pali *Abhidhamma*) or scholastic metaphysics. Also included are the Jataka, stories about the previous births of the Buddha, many of which are non-Buddhist in origin. The only complete Indian version of the canon now extant is that of the Ceylonese Theravada school, in the Pali language, written 29–17 B.C. (see PALI LITERATURE). North Indian Buddhist texts were written in a type of Sanskrit influenced by the vernaculars. Mahayana Buddhism produced its own class of sutras, and all schools of Buddhism generated a considerable body of commentary and philosophy. The entire corpus of Buddhist writings was translated into Chinese over a period of a thousand years, beginning in the 1st cent. A.D. This was a collaborative effort of foreign and Chinese monks. Its most recent edition, the *Taisho Daizokyo* (1922–33), is in 45 volumes of some 1,000 pages of Chinese characters each. Translation of Buddhist texts into Tibetan was begun in the 7th cent. The final redaction of the canon was by the Buddhist historian Bu-ston (1290–1364) and is in two sections, the *Kanjur* (translation of the Buddha's word) and the *Tanjur* (translation of treatises), consisting altogether of about 320 volumes of Tibetan script. The Tibetan translation is extremely literal, following the Sanskrit almost word for word and based on standardized Sanskrit-Tibetan equivalences for Buddhist terms; thus it is particularly useful for scholars. See Lucien Stryk, ed., *World of the Buddha* (1968).

budding, type of GRAFTING in which a plant bud is inserted under the bark of the stock (usually not more than a year old). It is best done when the bark will peel easily and the buds are mature, as in spring, late summer, or early autumn. Budding is a standard means of propagating roses and most fruit trees in nurseries.

buddleja or **buddleia:** see LOGANIA.

Budé, Guillaume (gēyōm' büdā'), 1467–1540, French humanist, b. Paris. Budé, known also by the Latinized form of his name, Budaeus, was a towering figure of the Renaissance. He was secretary to Louis XII, coming to power and prestige under Francis I. With the latter's patronage he established the study of classical works. Budé persuaded Francis to found the COLLÈGE DE FRANCE and to amass a library at Fontainebleau, which became the nucleus of the BIBLIOTHÈQUE NATIONALE. Acquainted with nearly all the great minds of his age, Budé carried on a voluminous correspondence in several languages. His treatises on language helped to establish the discipline of philology. He translated and commented on Greek literature.

Budenny, Semyon Mikhailovich (sĭmyôn mēkhī'ləvĭch bŏŏdyô'nē), 1883–1973, Russian marshal. A sergeant major in the czarist cavalry, he joined the Communist party in 1919, helped to organize the Soviet cavalry, and served in the Russian civil war (1918–20). He was made marshal in 1935. He commanded in the war against Finland (1940) and was made deputy commissar for defense. In World War II, he was placed in command of the southwest Soviet forces. His gross incompetence was a major cause of the severe defeat inflicted by the Germans on the Russian forces at Kiev in 1941. Budenny was shifted to the rear.

Budge, John Donald (Don Budge), 1915–, American tennis player, b. Oakland, Calif. He won the U.S. and British (Wimbledon) singles titles in 1937 and 1938. Budge also was a member of the 1937 U.S. team that won the Davis Cup from Great Britain. In 1938 he scored the grand slam of tennis by winning the U.S., Australian, French, and British singles championships (the first person to do so); in the same year Budge and Gene Mako won the U.S. doubles crown. He turned professional in 1939. He wrote *How Lawn Tennis is Played* (1937) and *On Tennis* (1939).

Budgell, Eustace (bŭj'əl), 1686–1737, English essayist. He was a cousin of Addison, through whose aid he obtained several public offices. Budgell contributed to the *Tatler,* the *Spectator,* and the *Guardian,* and wrote pamphlets against the ministry in the *Craftsman.* He lost a fortune in the collapse of the South Sea Bubble and later became involved in the losing end of a controversy over a sum of money left him by Matthew Tindal. He ended his life by committing suicide.

budgerigar (bŭj'ərēgär"): see PARAKEET.

budget, inclusive list of proposed expenditures and expected receipts of any person, enterprise, or government for a definite period, usually one year. Budget estimates are based on the expenditures and receipts of a similar previous period, modified by any expected changes. The governmental budget originated during the late 18th cent. in England. In the United States an annual Federal budget was not required until the passage (1921) of the Budget and Accounting Act. According to the act, the President must annually submit to Congress a budget that shows the condition of the Treasury at the end of the last completed fiscal year, its estimated condition at the end of the current fiscal year, and its estimated condition at the end of the ensuing year if the budget proposals are carried out; the revenues and expenditures during the last completed year and the estimates thereof for the current year; recommendations of provisions for meeting the revenues and expenditures for the ensuing year; and any other data considered helpful to Congress in its determination of the government's financial policy. No other administrative officer is allowed to make revenue recommendations unless asked to do so by Congress. To help the President, the Budget and Accounting Act also created the Bureau of the Budget, under the Treasury Dept., to receive, compile, and criticize estimates of expenditure needs submitted by the various governmental services and to study in detail all government services and recommend to the President any changes that will increase their economy and efficiency. The bureau was transferred (1939) to the executive office of the President. The national budget is often regarded as one of the major policy statements of a presidential administration. Since the beginning of World War II the national budget has grown immensely, mainly because of increased defense expenditures. Revenues, however, have not always kept pace with expenditures, often leading to annual budget deficits. Thus, the 1972 Federal budget, with a deficit of some $22 billion, was about 25 times as large as the $9.1 billion budget of 1940. Every state in the United States has some form of budget system. See B. F. Davie, *Modern Political Arithmetic* (1970); R. D. Lee, *Public Budgeting Systems* (1973).

Budweis: see ČESKÉ BUDĚJOVICE, Czechoslovakia.

Buell, Abel (byŏŏ'əl), 1742–1822, American silversmith, engraver, and type founder, b. Killingworth, Conn. He engraved a number of maps, including maps of the Florida coast and a large wall map of the United States, the first produced in America after the Treaty of Paris in 1783. He experimented in type founding, cast the first font of native-made American type (1769), and later supplied type to Connecticut printers. He invented machinery for cutting and polishing precious stones, for coining money, and for a period produced copper coins for the state. He also established in 1795, at New Haven, one of the first cotton mills in the country (which soon failed), and was involved in many other projects. See biography by L. C. Wroth (rev. ed. 1958).

Buell, Don Carlos, 1818–98, Union general in the Civil War, b. near Marietta, Ohio, grad. West Point, 1841. Buell was appointed brigadier general of volunteers in the Civil War (May, 1861), helped organize the Army of the Potomac, and took command of the Dept. of Ohio (Nov., 1861). He supported Grant's move up the Tennessee and Cumberland rivers by marching on Bowling Green, and after the fall of Fort Donelson he pursued the retreating Confederates to Nashville. In March, 1862, he was placed under Gen. H. W. Halleck and made major general of the Army of the Ohio, in which service he played a decisive role at Shiloh (see SHILOH, BATTLE OF). He forced the Confederates to retreat from Kentucky at Perryville (Oct. 8, 1962) but was dilatory in his pursuit. He was replaced by Gen. W. S. ROSECRANS; subsequently he was investigated by the military and discharged. See B. J. Fry, *The Army under Buell* (1886).

Buena Park (bwā'nə), city (1970 pop. 63,646), Orange co., S Calif.; inc. 1953. Food is processed, and tourism is an important industry. Knott's Berry Farm, a re-created gold rush town with many additional features and activities; a movieland wax museum; and a Japanese village surrounding a deer compound are there.

Buenaventura (bwā"nävăntŏŏ'rä), city (1968 est. pop. 78,700), W Colombia, a port on the Pacific Ocean. The city, located on Cascajal Island in Buenaventura Bay, is the shipping point for the tobacco and sugar of the Cauca valley. Coffee, platinum, gold, and hides are also exported. The original settlement was founded in 1545 and was burned by Indians at the end of the 16th cent. Buenaventura's importance as a port came with the opening of the Panama Canal and with the improvement of communications inland in the 1930s.

Buena Vista, battle of, military engagement in the Mexican War, fought Feb. 22–23, 1847. The battle site was just S of Saltillo, Coahuila, in Mexico. Gen. Zachary TAYLOR, disobeying orders from the U.S. government, had advanced here. Gen. Santa Anna, having gathered a Mexican army, made a long march north and, attacking Taylor's forces furiously, outflanked them. The fighting was hard and at the end of the second day seemed a drawn battle, but on the night of Feb. 23 the Mexican army withdrew, leaving Taylor in control of the north of Mexico.

Buenos Aires (bwā'nəs ī'rēz, –âr'ēz, Span. bwā'nōs ī'rās), city and federal district (1970 pop. 2,972,453; metropolitan area 8,352,900), the capital of Argentina, E Argentina, on the Río de la Plata. One of the largest cities of Latin America, Buenos Aires is Argentina's chief port and its financial, industrial, commercial, and social center. Located on the eastern edge of the Pampa, Argentina's most productive agricultural region, and linked with Uruguay, Paraguay, and Brazil by a great inland river system, the city is the distribution hub and trade outlet for a vast area. The historical importance of its port, one of the world's busiest, has led the citizens of Buenos Aires to call themselves *porteños* [people of the port]. Meat, meat products, grain, dairy products, hides, wool, flax, and linseed oil are the chief exports. Buenos Aires, the most heavily industrialized city of Argentina, is a major food-processing center, with huge meat-packing and refrigeration plants and flour mills. Other leading industries are metalworking, automobile manufacturing, oil refining, printing and publishing, machine building, and the production of textiles, chemicals, paper, clothing, beverages, and tobacco products. Buenos Aires is a modern city of great wealth. In its center are the Plaza de Mayo, a square whose buildings include the Casa Rosada [pink house], office of the national president, and the cabildo, former meeting place of the colonial town council and now the home of a national museum. The Avenida de Mayo extends from the square to the Palace of the National Congress, c.1 mi (1.6 km) away. Other famous streets are the Avenido 9 de Julio (commemorating the date of Argentina's independence from Spain, July 9, 1816), said to be the world's widest boulevard; Calle Florida, the main shopping thoroughfare; and the Avenida de Corientes, which is the nucleus of the theater and nightclub district, often called the Broadway of Argentina. Buenos Aires also has many beautiful parks, including Palmero Park. The cathedral (completed 1804) is a well-known landmark containing the tomb of José de San Martín. Among the numerous educational, scientific, and cultural institutions are the Univ. of Buenos Aires (est. 1821), several private universities, the National Library, and the Teatro Colon, one of the world's most famous opera houses. *La Prensa* and *La Nacion* are daily newspapers famous throughout the Spanish-speaking world. The city has a modern subway system and is a railroad hub, as well as a center of inland seaborne traffic. Nearby, at Ezeiza, is a large international airport. Buenos Aires is inhabited mostly by people of Spanish and Italian extraction, but there are many residents of French, British, German, and Syrian background and some communities of Paraguayans and other Latin Americans. The city was first founded in 1536 by a Spanish royal gold-seeking expedition under Pedro de Mendoza. However, Indian attacks forced the settlers in 1539 to move Asunción (now the capital of Paraguay), and in 1541 the old site was burned by Indians. A second and permanent settlement was planted in 1580 by Juan de Garay, who set out from Asunción. Although Spain long neglected Buenos Aires in favor of the riches of Mexico and Peru, the settlement's growth was enhanced by the development of trade, much of it contraband. In 1617 the province of Buenos Aires, or Río de la Plata, was separated from the administration of Asunción and was given its own governor; a bishopric was established there in 1620. During the 17th cent. the city ceased to be endangered by Indians, but French, Portuguese, and Danish raids were frequent. Buenos Aires remained subordinate to the Spanish viceroy in Peru until 1776, when it became the capital of a newly created viceroyalty of the Río de la Plata, including much of present-day Argentina, Uruguay, Paraguay, and Bolivia. Prosperity increased with the gradual removal of restrictions on trade, which formerly had to pass through Lima, Peru. The creation of an open port at Buenos Aires by Charles III of Spain, however, only made the *porteños* more desirous of separation from the Spanish Empire. In 1806, when Spain was allied with France during the Napoleonic Wars, British troops invaded Buenos Aires; their expulsion by the colonial militia without Spanish help further stimulated the drive for independence from Spain. Another British attack was repelled the following year. On May 25, 1810 (now celebrated as a national holiday), armed citizens of the cabildo, or town council, successfully demanded the resignation of the Spanish viceroy and established a provisional representative government. This action inaugurated the Latin American revolt against Spanish rule. Argentina's official independence (July 9, 1816) was followed by a long conflict between the unitarians, strongest in Buenos Aires prov., who advocated a centralized government dominated by the city of Buenos Aires, and the federalists, mostly from the interior provinces, who supported provincial autonomy and equality. In 1853 the city and province of Buenos Aires refused to participate in a constituent congress and seceded from Argentina. National political unity was finally achieved when Bartolomé Mitre became Argentina's president in 1862 and made Buenos Aires his capital. Bitterness between Buenos Aires and the province continued, however, until 1880, when the city was detached from the province and federalized. A new city, La Plata, was built as the provincial capital. Argentine railroad construction in the second half of the 19th cent. stimulated settlement and cultivation of the pampas, whose products Buenos Aires marketed and exported. The city's spectacular economic development attracted immigration from all over the world.

Buero Vallejo, Antonio (äntō'nyō bwä'rō välyä'-hō), 1916–, Spanish playwright, b. Guadalajara. His plays are highly serious with a strong moral vein, and they often depict characters consumed by despair and frustration. His best-known works, of paramount importance to the revitalization of the contemporary Spanish theater, include *Historia de una escalera* [the story of a staircase] (1949), *La tejedora de sueños* [the weaver of dreams] (1952), and *El tragaluz* [the skylight] (1967). See study by M. T. Halsey (1973).

Buffalo, city (1970 pop. 462,768), seat of Erie co., W N.Y., on Lake Erie and the Niagara and Buffalo rivers; inc. 1832. With more than 37 mi (60 km) of waterfront, it is an important port of entry and one of the largest grain-distributing ports in the United States. It is also a major railroad hub. Buffalo is a great flour-milling center and has an enormous steel mill, many automobile plants, some of the world's largest electrochemical and electrometallurgical industries, and numerous other diversified manufactures. In 1803 a village was laid out on the site of modern Buffalo by Joseph Ellicott for the Holland Land Company. The village was almost destroyed by fire (1813) in the War of 1812 and recovered slowly until the opening of the Erie Canal in 1825. Transportation was a primary factor in the city's growth, and Buffalo became a major Great Lakes port. Its educational institutions today include the State Univ. of New York at Buffalo, State Univ. College of Arts and Science at Buffalo, Canisius College, D'Youville College, and Rosary Hill College. Of interest are the Albright-Knox Art Gallery, the Buffalo Museum of Science, the county historical museum, and the Buffalo Zoological Gardens. Notable buildings include the city hall (1932); the Prudential Building (1895–96), designed by Louis Sullivan; and the Larkin office building, designed by Frank Lloyd Wright. Buffalo has a music hall and a philharmonic orchestra. A state mental hospital and a state institute for the study of malignant diseases are also located there. The Peace Bridge (1927) connects Buffalo with Fort Erie, Canada. The city also has an international airport. Grover Cleveland became mayor of Buffalo in 1882. There in 1901, at the Pan-American Exposition, President McKinley was assassinated; Theodore Roosevelt took the presidential oath in Buffalo. The McKinley monument and the Theodore Roosevelt Inaugural National Historic Site (see NATIONAL PARKS AND MONUMENTS, table) commemorate the two events. Millard Fillmore's home was in Buffalo.

buffalo, name commonly applied to the American BISON but correctly restricted to certain related African and Asian mammals of the cattle family. The water buffalo, or Indian buffalo, *Bubalus bubalis,* is found in S Asia. It is a large, extremely strong, dark gray animal, standing nearly 6 ft (180 cm) at the shoulder and weighing up to 2,000 lb (900 kg). Its widely spread horns curve out and back in a semicircle and may reach a length of 6 ft (180 cm). For many centuries it has been domesticated as a draft animal, but wild forms still exist in Borneo and herds descended from domesticated animals live in a wild state elsewhere. Water buffalo live in swampy areas and near rivers, where they wallow in the mud. Wild water buffalo are extremely fierce and have been known to kill fully grown tigers. The domestic forms are somewhat more docile. They are used throughout S Asia to pull plows and carts; they are of little importance as dairy animals, as their milk is scant. Their diet consists chiefly of grass. The anoa, *Anoa depressicornus,* also called dwarf buffalo or wood buffalo, is the smallest of the buffalo, standing only 40 in. (100 cm) high at the shoulder; it is found in the Celebes. Its slightly larger relative, the tamarou, *Anoa mindorensis,* is found in the Mindoro region of the Philippines. Both are forest dwellers. The large, fierce CAPE BUFFALO is found in Africa. Buffalo are classified in the phylum CHORDATA, subphylum Vertebrata, class Mammalia, order Artiodactyla, family Bovidae. See D. A. Dary, *The Buffalo Book* (1974).

Buffalo, University of: see NEW YORK, STATE UNIV. OF.

buffalo berry: see OLEASTER.

Buffalo Bill, 1846–1917, American plainsman, scout, and showman, b. near Davenport, Iowa. His real name was William Frederick Cody. His family moved (1854) to Kansas, and after the death of his father (1857) he set out to earn the family living, working for supply trains and a freighting company. In 1859 he went to the Colorado gold fields, and in 1860 he rode briefly for the Pony Express. His adventures on the Western frontier as an army scout and later as a buffalo hunter for railroad construction camps on the Great Plains were the basis for the stories later told about him. Ned BUNTLINE in 1872 persuaded him to appear on the stage, and, except for a brief period of scouting against the Sioux in 1876, he was from that time connected with show business. In 1883 he organized Buffalo Bill's Wild West Show, and he toured with it throughout the United States and Europe for many years. Wyoming granted him a stock ranch, on which the town of Cody was laid out. He died in Denver and was buried on Lookout Mt. near Golden, Colo. The exploits attributed to him in the dime novels of Buntline and Prentice Ingraham are only slightly more imaginative than his own autobiography (1920). See R. J. Walsh and M. S. Salsbury, *The Making of Buffalo Bill* (1928); biographies by D. B. Russell (1960, repr. 1969) and John Burke (1973).

buffalo bur: see NIGHTSHADE.

buffalo clover: see LUPINE.

buffalo fish: see SUCKER.

buffalo grass, low perennial grass (*Buchloë dactyloides*) of the plains regions, one of the most important range grasses. Its dense matted growth is valuable also in erosion control. Buffalo grass usually grows together with the grama, or mesquite, grasses (genus *Bouteloua*), especially blue grama and sideoats grama. These taller grasses have the same distribution as buffalo grass, but none of them produce a continuous sod, as prairie grasses do. Buffalo grass is classified in the division MAGNOLIOPHYTA, class Liliatae, order Cyperales, family Gramineae.

Buffalo Grove, village (1970 pop. 11,799), Cook and Lake counties, NE Ill.; inc. 1958.

Buffalo National River, Ark.: see NATIONAL PARKS AND MONUMENTS, table.

buffer, solution that can keep its relative acidity or alkalinity constant, i.e., keep its *p*H constant, despite the addition of strong acids or strong bases. Buffer solutions are frequently solutions that contain either a weak acid and one of its salts or a weak base and one of its salts. Many acid-base reactions take place in living organisms. However, for organisms to perform certain vital functions, the body fluids associated with these functions must maintain a constant *p*H. For example, blood must maintain a *p*H of close to 7.4 in order to carry oxygen from the lungs to cells; blood is therefore a powerful buffer.

Buffet, Bernard (bĕrnär' büfā'), 1928–, French painter. Buffet's melancholy paintings are characterized by a prominent black line and grayed, muddied colors. His subjects include still life, city scenes, and figures. Buffet illustrated Jean Cocteau's *La Voix Humaine* (1957).

Buffon, Georges Louis Leclerc, comte de (zhôrzh lwē ləklĕrk' kôNt də büfôN'), 1707–88, French naturalist and author. From 1739 he was keeper of the Jardin du Roi (later the Jardin des Plantes) in Paris and made it a center of research during the Enlightenment. He devoted his life to his monumental *Histoire naturelle* (44 vol., 1749–1804), a popular and brilliantly written compendium of data on natural history interspersed with Buffon's own speculations and theories. Of this work, the volumes *Histoire naturelle des animaux* and *Époques de la nature* are of special interest. His famous *Discours sur le style* was delivered (1753) on his reception into the French Academy. See study by O. E. Fellows and S. F. Milliken (1972).

Bug (bo͞og, bŭg, Rus. bo͞ok), Ukr. *Buh,* river, c.480 mi (770 km) long, rising in the Volhynian-Podolian hills, the Ukraine, W European USSR. It flows N along the Polish-Ukrainian and Polish-Belorussian borders past Brest and then NW through Poland to join the Vistula River near Warsaw. It is linked with the Dnepr by the Dnepr-Bug Canal via the Pina River and with the Niemen by the Augustov Canal via the Narva River. The Bug is also known as the Western Bug.

Bug or **Southern Bug,** Rus. *Yuzhny Bug,* Ukr. *Pivdynnyy Buh,* river, c.490 mi (790 km) long, rising in the Volhynian-Podolian hills, the Ukraine, W European USSR. The Bug, flowing generally SE into the Black Sea, is navigable for c.100 mi (160 km) from Voznesensk to its mouth.

bug, common name correctly applied to insects belonging to the order Hemiptera (suborder Heteroptera), although members of the order Homoptera (e.g., MEALYBUG) are sometimes referred to as bugs, as are other insects in general. The true bugs (Hemipterans) have a characteristic pair of front wings that are partially thickened and darkened at the base and partially membranous at the apex. Development is gradual through an incomplete METAMORPHOSIS with a number of nymphal stages before the reproductively mature adult stage is reached. Most bugs are terrestrial, but many are aquatic (e.g., various WATER BUGS). Although bugs vary greatly in size, color, and physical appearance, they all have piercing-sucking mouthparts in the form of a jointed beak. Most species suck plant juices (e.g., the SQUASH BUG and CHINCH BUG); however, some suck the blood of other insects and spiders (e.g., the ASSASSIN BUG and BACKSWIMMER). Others, such as the BEDBUG, feed on man and other animals. Many of these insects characteristically secrete defensive substances (e.g., the STINK BUG). The true bugs are classified in the phylum ARTHROPODA, class Insecta, order Hemiptera.

Buganda, kingdom, E Africa: see UGANDA.

Bugayev, Boris Nikolayevich: see BELY, ANDREI.

bugbane, any plant of the genus *Cimicifuga,* tall north-temperate perennials of the family Ranunculaceae (BUTTERCUP family). The white spirelike bloom has a rank odor that attracts flies, which pollinate the plant. Common in woodlands of E North America is *C. racemosa,* black snakeroot, or black cohosh, sometimes gathered for its medicinal root. Other plants are also called bugbane and snakeroot; most plants called cohosh belong to the related BANEBERRY genus. Bugbane is classified in the division MAGNOLIOPHYTA, class Magnoliopsida, order Ranunculales, family Ranunculaceae.

Bugeaud de la Piconnerie, Thomas Robert (tōmä' rōbĕr' büzhō' də lä pēkōnərē'), 1784–1849, marshal of France, duc d'Isly, general and administrator in Algeria. He served in the army of the French emperor Napoleon I until forced into retirement in 1815. Returning to public life after the July Revolution of 1830, he became a deputy. Sent twice (1836, 1837) to Algeria on special missions, he returned again in 1841 to undertake the pacification of Algeria as governor general. His celebrated victory at Isly (1844) finally broke the power of ABD AL-KADIR. Bugeaud attempted to cooperate with the Arabs, to promote military colonization, and to encourage French settlers, but the unpopularity of his policies forced his resignation in 1847. He was named commander of the troops in Paris by Louis Philippe during the February Revolution of 1848. A strong general, he was feared in France as a potential dictator. He wrote on colonial, military, and economic subjects.

Bugenhagen, Johann (yō'hän bo͞o'gənhä''gən), 1485–1558, German Protestant reformer. Born in Pomerania, he is sometimes called Dr. Pomeranus. Bugenhagen, an ordained priest, was attracted to the reform movement by Martin Luther's writings. In 1521 he went to Wittenberg and entered upon a lasting friendship with Luther and Melanchthon. He was a lecturer in the university and pastor of the principal church in Wittenberg. Much of Bugenhagen's attention was devoted to ecclesiastical and educational organization in Brunswick, Hamburg, Lübeck, Pomerania, and Denmark. Bugenhagen helped Luther in his translation of the Bible. Of his own literary works the most important is *Interpretatio in librum Psalmorum* (1523). See biography by W. M. Ruccius (1924).

Bugge, Sophus (sō'fo͞os bo͞o'gə), 1833–1907, Norwegian philologist. He made a notable edition of the Old Norse runes, and his was the first critical edition (1881–89; 2d series 1896) of the poems of the *Eddas.*

bugle, brass wind musical instrument consisting of a conical tube coiled once upon itself, capable of producing five or six harmonics. It is usually in G or B flat. Its principal use is for military and naval bugle calls, such as taps and reveille, and, in earlier times, for hunting calls. In the early 19th cent., keyed bugles were made in order to obtain a complete scale.

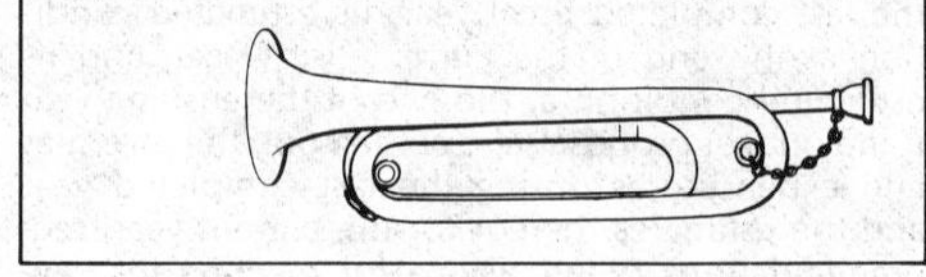

Bugle

Buhl, André Charles: see BOULLE, ANDRÉ CHARLES.

building and loan association: see SAVINGS AND LOAN ASSOCIATION.

Buisson, Ferdinand Édouard (fĕrdēnäN' ädwär' büēsôN'), 1841–1932, French educator and Nobel Peace Prize winner. He studied at the Sorbonne and later taught (1866–70) in Switzerland. After 1870 he served in the French department of education, first as an inspector of schools and later as a director of primary education, resigning in 1886 to become professor of pedagogy at the Sorbonne. He produced the *Dictionnaire de pédagogie* (1882–93). From 1902 to 1914 and again from 1919 to 1924, he was a member of the chamber of deputies and was also active in working for civil rights. An ardent pacifist, he attended (1867) the first congress of the International Peace League; with Ludwig Quidde of Germany he received the 1927 Nobel Peace Prize.

Buitenzorg: see BOGOR, Indonesia.

Bujumbura (bo͞o″jəm'bo͝or'ə), city (1971 est. pop. 57,200), capital of Burundi and of Bujumbura prov., W Burundi, a port on Lake Tanganyika. Formerly known as Usumbura, it is Burundi's largest city and its administrative, communications, and economic center. Manufactures include food products, cement and other building materials, textiles, soap, shoes, and metal goods. Livestock and agricultural produce from the surrounding region are traded in the city. Bujumbura is Burundi's main port and ships most of the country's chief export, coffee, as well as cotton, skins, and tin ore, via Lake Tanganyika to Tanzania and Zaïre. The city attracts many tourists. A small village in the 19th cent., Bujumbura grew after it became (1899) a military post in German East Africa. After World War I it was made the administrative center of the Belgian Ruanda-Urundi League of Nations mandate. Its name was changed from Usumbura to Bujumbura when Burundi became independent in 1962. The Univ. of Bujumbura (1960) is there. The city has an international airport.

Bukavu (bo͞okä'vo͞o), city (1970 pop. 135,000), capital of Kivu region, E Zaïre, a port on Lake Kivu. It is an administrative, commercial, and transportation center. Hides and coffee are processed. The city was founded in 1901 and was formerly known as Costermansville. In 1967, Bukavu was briefly held by rebel Katangan and mercenary forces. A school of mines is there.

Bukhara (bəkä'rə), city (1970 pop. 112,000), capital of Bukhara oblast, S Central Asian USSR, in Uzbekistan, in the Zeravshan River valley. The name is also spelled Bokhara. On the Shkhrud irrigation canal system, it is the center of a large cotton district and has textile mills as well as cotton-ginning industries and the largest karakul skin processing plant in the USSR. First mentioned in Chinese chronicles in the 5th cent. A.D., Bukhara is one of the oldest trade and cultural centers in central Asia. It came under the Arab caliphate in the 8th cent. and became a major center of Islamic learning. During the 9th and 10th cent. it was the capital of the Samanid state. From the 16th cent. to 1920 it was the capital of the khanate of Bukhara, which was ceded to Russia in 1868. From 1920 to 1924 it was the capital of the Bukhara People's Republic. There are many monuments, including the mausoleum of Ismail Samanid (892–907), the minaret of Kalyan (1127), the mosque of Magoki-Attari (12th cent.), the Ulugbek (1417–18) and Mir-Arab (1535–36) medressehs (schools), and the medresseh of Abdylazizkhana (1651–52). The population is mainly Uzbek, with Arab, Afghan, and Jewish minorities.

Bukhara, emirate of, former state, central Asia, in TURKISTAN, in the Amu Darya River basin. Part of ancient Sogdiana, it was ruled (A.D. 709–874) by the Umayyad Arabs and played an important role under the Samanid dynasties (875–1000). It was a trade, transport, and cultural center of the Islamic world. The Seljuk Turks ruled from 1004 to 1133; later, the realm was conquered by Jenghiz Khan (1220) and in the 14th cent. by Tamerlane. The Timurid dynasties ruled until the invasion of Uzbek tribes early in the 16th cent. The Bukhara emirate was founded by the Uzbek Khan Sheybani, who between 1500 and 1507 conquered the Timurid domains in Transoxania. In 1555, Abdullah Khan transferred the capital from Samarkand to Bukhara, from which the state then took its name. Internal feuds weakened Bukhara, it split into a number of principalities, and in 1740 it was conquered by Nadir Shah of Persia. In 1753, Bukhara again became an independent emirate but did not recover its supremacy over Khorezm, Merv, Badakhshan, Tashkent, and the Fergana Valley. Bukhara's population consisted principally of Uzbeks (who remained politically dominant), Sarts, and Tadzhiks. Defeated by Russia in 1866, the emirate became a Russian protectorate in 1868. In 1920, after a prolonged battle with Bolshevik forces, the last emir was driven into Afghanistan. The Bukhara People's Soviet Republic was established (1920) and lasted until 1924. In the same year it was proclaimed a socialist republic and was included in the USSR; a few months later, however, it was dismembered and divided between Uzbekistan, Tadzhikistan, and Turkmenistan.

Bukhari, al- (bo͝ok-härē'), d. 870, Arabic scholar and Muslim saint, b. Bukhara. He traveled widely over Muslim regions and made a tremendous collection of the traditional sayings of the Prophet. It is regarded in ISLAM as the commentary par excellence and the law book second only to the Koran. The tomb of al-Bukhari, near Samarkand, is a noted place of pilgrimage.

Bukharin, Nikolai Ivanovich (nyĭkəlī' ēvä'nəvĭch bo͝okhä'rēn), 1888–1938, Russian Communist leader and theoretician. A member of the Bolshevik wing of the Social Democratic party, he spent the years 1911–17 abroad and edited (1916) the revolutionary paper *Novy Mir* [new world] in New York City. He took part in the Bolshevik Revolution in Nov., 1917 (Oct., 1917, O.S.) in Russia and became a leader in the COMINTERN and editor of the Soviet newspaper *Pravda* [truth]. In 1924 he was made a full member of the politburo. As STALIN rose to power in the 1920s, Bukharin first allied with him against KAMENEV and Zinoviev. An advocate of slow agricultural collectivization and industrialization (the position of the so-called right opposition), Bukharin lost (1929) his major posts after that position was defeated by the Stalinist majority in the party. He edited *Izvestia* [news] briefly in 1934 but was dismissed. In 1938 he was tried publicly for treason and was executed. He wrote and translated many works on economics and political science. See study by S. F. Cohen (1973).

Bukidnon (bo͝okĭd'nōn, Sp. bo͝okēdh'nōn), province (1970 pop. 400,307), N central Mindanao, the Philippines. Malaybalay is the provincial capital. Much of the area is on a high plateau (alt. c.2,000 ft/610 m). With very fertile soil and a heavy, evenly distributed annual rainfall, Bukidnon is of great importance agriculturally. Intensely cultivated, it is the nation's major pineapple-producing region and a center of coffee production. A great variety of fruits is also grown, primarily for canning and export. The province has a high percentage of owner-operated farms. Central Mindanao Univ. is at Musuan.

Bukki (bŭk'ī). **1** Descendant of Aaron. 1 Chron. 6.5,51; Ezra 7.4. **2** Danite. Num. 34.22.

Bukkiah (bəkī'ə), Levite. 1 Chron. 25.4,13.

Bukovina (bo͞okəvē'nə), Rum. *Bucovina,* Ukr. *Bukovyna,* historic region of E Europe, in W Ukraine and NE Rumania. Traversed by the Carpathian Mts. and the upper Prut and Siretul rivers, it is heavily forested [*Bukovina* means "beechwood" in Rumanian] and produces timber, textiles, grain, and livestock. Petroleum and salt are produced in quantity; other mineral resources include manganese, iron, and copper. CHERNOVTSY, in the Ukraine, is the chief city. The population is largely Rumanian in S Bukovina and Ukrainian in the north. Most of the region's Jews were exterminated during World War II. A part of the Roman province of Dacia, Bukovina was overrun after the 3d cent. A.D. by the Huns and other nomads. It later (10th–13th cent.) belonged to the Kievan state (see KIEV) and the Galich and Volhyna principalities. After the Mongols withdrew from Moldavia, Bukovina became (14th cent.) the nucleus of the Moldavian principality. The term *Bukovina* was first mentioned in an agreement concluded in 1412 between King Ladislaus II of Poland and Sigismund of Hungary. In 1514, Bukovina, then part of Moldavia, became tributary to the Turkish sultans. Ceded by the Ottoman Empire to Austria in 1775, it was at first a district of Galicia but in 1848 was made, as a titular duchy, a separate Austrian crownland. The region won limited autonomy from Austria, and in 1861 Chernovtsy was made the seat of a provincial diet. Bukovina became an object of irredentism when Rumania achieved full independence in 1878. The country's boundaries encompassed SUCEAVA, the ancient capital of Moldavia, but Chernovtsy was incorporated into Austria. With the dissolution of the Austrian empire in 1918, the Ukrainian national council at Chernovtsy voted the incorporation of N Bukovina into the West Ukrainian Democratic Republic. The Treaty of Saint-Germain (1919) gave only the southern part of Bukovina to Rumania, but the subsequent Treaty of Sèvres awarded Rumania the entire region. Self-government was suppressed in N Bukovina. In a treaty of June, 1940, Rumania ceded the northern part of Bukovina (c.2,140 sq mi/5,540 sq km) to the USSR, which incorporated it into the Ukrainian SSR. Although Rumanian troops reoccupied N Bukovina during World War II, the Rumanian peace treaty of 1947 confirmed Soviet possession of the area. N Bukovina now forms part of the Chernovtsy oblast in the Ukraine. The remainder of the area (c.1,890 sq mi/4,895 sq km) forms one of the historical provinces of Rumania and is part of the administrative region of Suceava.

Bulawayo (bo͝oləwä'yō), city (1970 est. pop. 70,000), SW Rhodesia. It is the second largest city of Rhodesia and an important industrial, commercial, and railroad center. Among its manufactures are textiles, motor vehicles, metal products, and cement. Founded by the British in 1893, it was the scene (1896) of a Matabele revolt. Nearby are the 18th-century African ruins of Khami.

bulb, thickened, fleshy plant bud, usually formed under the surface of the soil, which carries the plant over from one blooming season to another. It may have layers (as in the onion and hyacinth) or scales (as in some lilies)—both of which are highly modified leaves. Many popular outdoor and house plants, such as the tulip and the narcissus, are grown from bulbs, some of them out of their usual flowering season by forcing. Not true bulbs, but often so called, are the CORM of the crocus and the gladiolus, the TUBER of the dahlia and the potato, and the RHIZOME of certain irises. All such organs are specialized subterranean stems serving for food storage and asexual reproduction. See Marc Reynolds and W. L. Meachem, *The Complete Book of Garden Bulbs* (1972).

bulbul, antelope: see HARTEBEEST.

bulbul (bo͝ol'bo͝ol), bird, common name for members of the family Pycnonotidae, comprising 119 species of medium-sized, dull-colored passerine birds with short necks and wings, native to Africa and S Asia. Bulbuls are famed as songsters and are popular as cage birds in the Orient; frequently mentioned in Persian poetry, the word *bulbul* is often mistranslated "nightingale." Bulbuls range in size from 6 in. (15 cm) to about 12 in. (30.5 cm). They inhabit grasslands and shrubby countrysides, from sea level to 10,000 ft (3,050 m) in the Himalayas. A common Asian species, the red-whiskered bulbul, *Pycnonotus jocosus,* is easily tamed and is popular as a cage bird. Bulbuls feed mainly on fruits and berries and sometimes do crop damage. They build cleverly concealed cup-shaped grass nests, in which the female lays from three to five eggs per clutch. Both parents brood the nestlings. Bulbuls are classified in the phylum CHORDATA, subphylum Vertebrata, class Aves, order Passeriformes, family Pycnonotidae.

Bulfinch, Charles, 1763–1844, American architect, b. Boston. A member of the Boston board of selectmen in 1791, he was chosen chairman in 1799—an office equivalent to mayor and held by Bulfinch for 19 years. Of the numerous structures that he designed in Boston, most have long been demolished, including the Federal Street Theater (1794), the first theater in New England. His chief monumental works remain—the statehouse in Boston (1799), University Hall at Harvard (1815), and the Massachusetts General Hospital (1820). From 1818 to 1830 Bulfinch carried to completion the CAPITOL at Washington; of his own contributions there remains the west portico, with the terraces and steps forming the approach to it. In this work and in the Massachusetts statehouse he evolved an architectural composition that has been used for state capitols throughout the country. He designed a memorial column on Beacon Hill (1789), Massachusetts State Prison (1803), a number of Massachusetts courthouses, and Franklin Crescent in Boston (1793). The last was a long curved row of 16 residences, inspired by the continuous block of houses that had been erected by Robert Adam and others in England. The First Church of Christ in Lancaster, Mass. (1816–17), one of the few remaining churches of the many that he designed, is one of his finest works. While Bulfinch's works fall into the general category of "early American" architecture, they bear a distinctive stamp of his own. Their elegance, repose, and refinement of detail rank them among the best products of the nation's early years. See H. Kirker, *The Architecture of Charles Bulfinch* (1969).

Bulfinch, Thomas, 1796–1867, American author, b. Newton, Mass., grad. Harvard, 1814. He wrote a series of works popularizing fable and legend, including *The Age of Fables* (1855), *The Age of Chivalry* (1858), *Legends of Charlemagne* (1863), and *Oregon and Eldorado* (1866).

Bulgakov, Mikhail Afanasyevich (mēkhəyēl' əfənä'syəvĭch bo͞olgä'kəf), 1891–1940, Russian novelist and playwright. He wrote satirical stories (*The Deviliad,* 1925, tr. 1972) and comedies (*Zoe's Apartment,* 1926)and the long novel *The White Guard* (1925, tr. 1971), in which a Kievan family hostile to the revolution is sympathetically and realistically portrayed. He condensed and dramatized this as *The Days of the Turbines* (1926, tr. 1934). The novel *The Master* *and Margarita* (tr. 1967), which he worked on intermittently from 1928 until his death, is considered his most important work. His other novels include *The Heart of a Dog* (1925, tr. 1968). Bulgakov was officially criticized for several of his works. See *The Early Plays of Mikhail Bulgakov: 1926–1936* (tr. 1972).

Bulganin, Nikolai Aleksandrovich (nyĭkəlī' əlyĭksän'drəvĭch bo͝olgä'nyĭn), 1895–, Soviet military and political leader. He held posts in industrial management, was mayor of Moscow (1931–37) and chairman of the state bank (1937–41), and served on a military council in World War II. Made a marshal and a deputy premier in 1947, and a full member of the politburo in 1948, he was also defense minister under Joseph Stalin and later under Georgi Malenkov. With the support of Nikita KHRUSHCHEV, who was then head of the Communist party, Bulganin succeeded Malenkov as premier (Feb., 1955). In 1958, however, he was forced from office by Khrushchev, who took over the post of premier. Bulganin was accused of having sided with the "antiparty faction" that opposed Khrushchev in 1957; he was expelled from the central committee of the Communist party in Sept., 1958.

Bulgari: see BULGARS, EASTERN.

Bulgaria (bŭlgâr'ēə), republic (1973 est. pop. 8,620,000), 42,823 sq mi (110,912 sq km), SE Europe, on the E Balkan Peninsula. It is bounded by the Black Sea on the east, by Rumania on the north, by Yugoslavia on the west, by Greece on the south, and by European Turkey on the southeast. SOFIA is the capital. Other important cities are VARNA and BURGAS (the main Black Sea ports of Bulgaria), PLOVDIV and RUSE. Central Bulgaria is traversed from east to west by ranges of the Balkan Mts. A fertile plateau runs north of the Balkans to the Danube River, which forms most of the northern border. In the southwest is the Rhodope range, which includes Bulgaria's highest point, Musala mt. (9,592 ft/2,923 m). The Thracian plain lies south of the Balkans and east of the Rhodope. The Danube, the Iskŭr, the Maritsa, and the Struma are the principal rivers. Bulgaria's mineral resources include brown coal (lignite), bauxite, iron ore, lead, zinc, and oil and natural gas. There are many mineral springs. Traditionally an agricultural country, Bulgaria has been considerably industrialized since World War II. The leading industries are engineering, metallurgy, and the production of chemicals and fertilizers. Agriculture, however, remains the chief occupation; the principal crops are wheat, corn, barley, and sugar beets. Grapes and other fruit, as well as roses, are grown, and much stock is raised. Most of the land was collectivized by 1958. The chief exports are foodstuffs and attar of roses; manufactured goods and fuels are the leading imports. The population consists chiefly of Bulgars (85.5%) and Turks (8.6%), with small minorities of Macedonians and Gypsies. About 27% belong to the Orthodox Eastern Church, and 7% are Muslims. In 1953 the Bulgarian patriarchate was reestablished; it had been disestablished in 1946. Institutions of higher education include the universities of Sofia, Plovdiv, and Varna. Ancient Thrace and Moesia, which modern Bulgaria occupies, were settled (6th cent. A.D.) by Slavic tribes. In 679–80, Bulgar tribes from the banks of the Volga (see BULGARS, EASTERN) crossed the Danube, subjugated the Slavs, and settled permanently in the territory of Bulgaria. The language and culture remained Slavic, and by the 9th cent. the Bulgars had fully merged with the Slavs. The first Bulgarian empire (681–1018), established by Khan Asparuhk, or Isperikh (ruled 680–701), and his successor, Terrel (ruled 701–718), soon emerged as a significant Balkan power and a threat to Byzantium. In 809 the khan Krum (ruled 803–814) captured Sofia from the Byzantines, defeated (811) Emperor Nicephorus I, besieged Constantinople, and withdrew only after obtaining yearly tribute. In the 9th cent. Bulgaria became the arena of political and cultural rivalry between Constantinople and Rome. In 865, BORIS I adopted Christianity, and in 870 Constantinople recognized the independence of the Bulgarian church. Bulgaria received Byzantine culture through the Slavic literary language developed by St. Cyril and St. Methodius in Moravia and brought to the Balkans by their disciples. The first Bulgarian empire reached its height under SIMEON I (893–927), who took the title of czar. After his death the country was rent by the heresy of the BOGOMILS. In the 10th cent. Bulgaria crumbled under the attacks of a reinvigorated Byzantium, and in 1018 it was annexed by Emperor BASIL II. Byzantine domination was weakened by the invasions of the PECHENEGS and CUMANS and by internal disorders at Constantinople. The second Bulgarian empire (1186–1396) rose in 1186 when Ivan Asen (Ivan I) was crowned czar at TRNOVO. His son, Kaloyan, crowned in 1204 with the approval of the pope, defeated (1205) Emperor Baldwin I of Constantinople. The height of Bulgar power was reached under Ivan II (Ivan Asen), whose rule (1218–1241) extended over nearly the whole Balkan Peninsula except Greece. His successors could not maintain his empire. In 1330, Macedonian Bulgaria was conquered by Serbia. After the battles of Kossovo (1389) and NIKOPOL (1396) Bulgaria was absorbed into the Ottoman Empire. Turkish rule was often oppressive, and rebellions were frequent. By recognizing the authority of the Orthodox Eastern Church in Constantinople over all Christians in their empire, the Turks undermined the basis of Bulgarian culture. A determined effort was made to destroy Bulgarian Christianity and the Bulgarian language. The role of the Phanariots (see PHANAR) was particularly resented. Although the administration (1864–69) of MIDHAT PASHA made Bulgaria briefly a model province, by then Bulgarian nationalism was strong. The Mount Athos monastery had continued to use Bulgarian; there, in 1762, a monk had written a history, the first modern literary work in Bulgarian. Bulgarian schools were allowed to open in 1835. In 1870 the Bulgarian Church was reestablished. In 1876 a rebellion, led by Stefan STAMBULOV, broke out. The subsequent Turkish reprisals (famous as the "Bulgarian atrocities") provided a reason for the Russians to liberate (1877–78) their neighbors (see RUSSO-TURKISH WARS). The Treaty of San Stefano created a large autonomous Bulgaria within the Ottoman Empire—a Bulgaria that Russia expected to dominate. In order to avert the expansion of Russian influence in the Balkans, a European congress was called to revise the treaty (see BERLIN, CONGRESS OF). By the new terms Bulgaria was reduced to the territory between the Danube and the Balkans, while present-day S Bulgaria—then called Eastern RUMELIA—became a separate autonomous province, and Macedonia remained under direct Turkish rule. ALEXANDER (Alexander of Battenberg), first prince of Bulgaria, annexed (1885) Eastern Rumelia and repulsed a consequent Serbian attack. His successor, Prince FERDINAND of Saxe-Coburg-Gotha, profiting from the revolution of the Young Turks in the Ottoman Empire in 1908, proclaimed Bulgaria independent with himself as czar. Bulgaria was victorious against Turkey in the first (1911–12) of the BALKAN WARS, but claims to Macedonia involved it in the Second Balkan War with its former allies Greece and Serbia, and it was soon defeated. By the Treaty of Bucharest (1913), Bulgaria lost S DOBRUJA and a large part of Macedonia. The Macedonian issue was largely responsible for the entry in 1915 of Bulgaria into World War I on the side of Germany and Austria-Hungary. There was much domestic opposition to the war, and when Bulgaria's military position crumbled, Ferdinand fled and BORIS III succeeded (1918). In the peace (see NEUILLY, TREATY OF) Bulgaria was forced to pay reparations and lost its outlet to the Aegean Sea to Greece and some territory to Yugoslavia; S Dobruja was confirmed in Rumanian possession. The Agrarian party cabinet established (1919) by STAMBULISKI held power until overthrown (1923) in a bloody coup. An era of political confusion ensued, dominated by the violent activities of an irredentist Macedonian terrorist group. The world economic crisis of 1929 had a disastrous impact on impoverished Bulgaria as markets for agricultural exports shrunk. In 1934, Kimon Georgiev became premier with the help of the army and ended constitutional government, but he was ousted in 1935 by Boris III, who established his personal dictatorship. Bulgaria saw in an alliance with Germany in World War II an opportunity to satisfy its territorial claims. In 1940, Germany forced Rumania to restore to Bulgaria S Dobruja. In 1941, Bulgaria occupied parts of Yugoslavia and Greece (including Macedonia), and declared war on Great Britain and the United States—but not the Soviet Union, because the populace was pro-Russian. The child SIMEON II succeeded when Boris died mysteriously (1943). In 1944 the Soviet Union declared war on Bulgaria, and Soviet troops entered the country (September). Pro-Allied political forces (Communists, Agrarians, and the pro-Soviet army officers), headed by Georgiev, seized power immediately. Bulgaria declared war on Germany, and an armistice with the USSR followed (October). After a short period of coalition rule, the Communists succeeded in taking over the government. The monarchy was abolished, and in 1946 Bulgaria was proclaimed a republic with Georgi DIMITROV as premier. The peace treaty with the Allies (1947) allowed Bulgaria to keep S Dobruja, but no gains were made in Macedonia. Dimitrov proceeded to eliminate possible opponents. The Agrarian leader Nikola Petrov was executed (1947). A new constitution was enacted, and Bulgaria became a one-party state. Industry was nationalized and farms collectivized. Bulgaria closely followed the Soviet Union in its domestic and foreign policies; after the expulsion of Yugoslavia from the Cominform in 1948, Bulgaria sided with the USSR. Dimitrov's successor, Vulko Chervenko, massively purged the Communist party (1950). In 1951–52, Bulgaria deported to Turkey some 160,000 citizens of Turkish origin. Relations with Greece and Turkey improved somewhat after 1954. Bulgaria joined (1949) the Council for Economic Mutual Assistance and in 1955 became a member of the Warsaw Treaty Organization and the United Nations. In the mid-1950s the government loosened its grip somewhat. Stalinists fell from power and purge victims were rehabilitated (posthumously in some cases). In 1965 army officers and party officials unsuccessfully attempted a coup. Bulgaria aided the USSR in the invasion of Czechoslovakia in 1968. A new constitution was adopted in 1971. It provided for a unicameral national assembly to be elected every five years. The assembly elects a council of state and the cabinet of ministers. But actual power resides in the Communist party, which heads the Fatherland Front, a grouping of organizations that support the regime. See W. S. Monroe, *Bulgaria and Her People* (1914); Steven Runciman, *A History of the First Bulgarian Empire* (1930); L. A. D. Dellin, ed., *Bulgaria* (1957); Mercia MacDermott, *A History of Bulgaria, 1393–1885* (1962); J. F. Brown, *Bulgaria under Communist Rule* (1970); Ferdinand Schevill, *A History of the Balkan Peninsula* (1922, repr. 1971).

Bulgarian languages, member of the South Slavic group of the Slavic subfamily of the Indo-European family of languages (see SLAVIC LANGUAGES). Bulgarian is the native tongue of more than eight million people, most of whom live in Bulgaria, where it is the official language. It is also spoken to some extent in bordering and nearby countries. Although the Bulgars were originally a Turkic-speaking people from Asia, they merged with the Slavic tribes whom they conquered in the 7th cent. A.D. in the territory of present-day Bulgaria and took over their Slavic language. Old Bulgarian is an alternate name for the literary and liturgical language of the 9th to 11th cent. A.D. that is usually called Old Church Slavonic (see CHURCH SLAVONIC). From Old Church Slavonic, in Bulgaria, a later local form known as Bulgarian Church Slavonic evolved, which was current from the 12th to 15th cent. The Turkish conquest of Bulgaria in 1396 seriously hampered the development of the Bulgarian language for several centuries. After the Bulgarians threw off the Turkish yoke in 1878, a modern literary language based on the vernacular came into its own. Modern Bulgarian, which is generally said to date from the 16th cent., borrowed many words from Greek and Turkish during the period of Turkish domination; more recently it has borrowed words from Russian, French, and German. The Bulgarian language lacks definite rules for stress; therefore, the accent of every word must be learned individually. Unlike most other Slavic tongues, Bulgarian has a definite article. This is in the form of a suffix joined to the noun. Another difference between Bulgarian and most other Slavic languages is that Bulgarian has almost completely dropped the numerous case forms of the noun. It uses position and prepositions (like English) to indicate grammatical relationships in a sentence instead of cases (like Russian). Despite these differences, Bulgarian closely resembles the other Slavic languages, especially with regard to grammar. A modified form of the Cyrillic alphabet is used for writing Bulgarian. See S. B. Bernshtein, *Short Grammatical Sketch of the Bulgarian Language* (tr. 1952); H. I. Aronson, *Bulgarian Inflectional Morphophonology* (1968).

Bulgarian literature. For early ecclesiastical writings, see OLD CHURCH SLAVONIC. Modern Bulgarian literature stems from the work of Father Paisi, who in 1762 began his history of the Slav Bulgarians, in an effort to inspire national feeling and to stimulate the use of the Bulgarian language. There was not at that time even a single printing press in Bulgaria. His imitators continued the effort to make Bulgarian a literary language, but the period of struggle for political and ecclesiastical independence (1840–75) saw the real beginnings of a national literature in the work of the poets Sava Rakovski (1821–67) and Petko Rachev Slaveykov (1827–95), the story writer Lyuben Karavelov (1837–79), the dramatist Vasil Drumev (1841–1901), and the great national poet Khristo BOTEV, who died fighting the Turks. Ivan VAZOV was the first professional man of letters, writing plays, novels, poetry, and short stories. After Bulgaria's liberation from Turkish rule (1876), the literature of the country became less revolutionary. A group of regional writers of the late 19th cent. included Todor Genchov Vlaykov (1865–1943), Georgi P. Stamatov (1869–1942), Anton Strashimirov (1872–1937), the satirist Stoyan Mikhaylovski (1856–1927), and Aleko Konstantinov (1863–97), whose humorous *Bay-Ganyu* is one of the most popular of Bulgarian novels. The poet Pencho Slaveykov (1866–1912), a son of P. R. Slaveykov, led in introducing other European literatures and literary trends into Bulgaria; his *Song of Blood* (1911–13) is an epic of the struggle against the Turks. Others of his period were the symbolist poet Peyo K. Yavorov (1878–1914), the poet and dramatist Petko Y. Todorov (1879–1916), and the story writer Elin Pelin (1878–1949). Bulgaria's losses in the Balkan Wars and World War I gave rise to a poetry whose chief quality was mysticism. Among the poets of this period are the symbolist Nikolay Liliyev, Dora Gabe and Elisaveta Bagryans, and Dimcho Debelyanov (1887–1916). The prose writers of the early 20th cent. include the novelists of peasant life Iordan Iovkov (1884–1938) and Dobri Nemirov (1882–1945), and the psychological novelist Georgi Raichev. After 1945, the writers most admired include the poets Khristo Smyrnenski (1898–1923), Khristo Radevski, and Nikola Vaptsarov (1909–42), and the prose writers Lyudmil Stoyanov, Georgi Karaslavov, and Dimiter Dimov, author of the popular novel *Tobacco.* Recent Bulgarian literature has undergone Soviet influence. Although there was a relaxation of the pressure to conform to SOCIALIST REALISM after Stalin's death (1953), controls were reintroduced in 1957. See Vivian Pinto, *Bulgarian Prose and Poetry* (1957); Clarence Manning and Roman Smal-Stocki, *The History of Modern Bulgarian Literature* (1960); C. A. Moser, *A History of Bulgarian Literature* (1972).

Bulgarin, Faddey Venediktovich (fədyä' vĭnyədyĕk'təvĭch bo͝olgä'rĕn), 1789–1859, Russian journalist and novelist, b. Poland. Bulgarin's original name was Tadeusz Bulharyn. In 1825 he and Nicholas Grech founded the influential conservative daily *Northern Bee,* in which he inveighed against liberal writers, notably Pushkin. He wrote several historical novels, including *Ivan Vyzhigin* (1830, tr. 1831).

Bulgars, Eastern, Turkic-speaking people, who possessed a powerful state (10th–14th cent.) at the confluence of the Volga and the Kama, E European Russia. The Bulgars appeared on the Middle Volga by the 8th cent. and became known as the Eastern, Volga, or Kama Bulgars. Another branch of the same people moved west into present Bulgaria and merged with the Slavs. The Eastern Bulgars accepted Islam in the 10th cent. From the 10th to the 12th cent. the Bulgar state was at the height of its power. Its chief city, the Great Bulgar, was a prosperous trade center. Destroyed by the Mongols in 1237, the state flourished again until it was conquered by Tamerlane in 1361. It finally disappeared after its capture by the grand duke of Moscow in 1431. The modern Tatars and Chuvash may be descended from the Eastern Bulgars. The Great Bulgar and the Bulgars themselves are sometimes called Bulgari or Bolgari.

Bulge, Battle of the: see BATTLE OF THE BULGE.

Bull, Olaf (ō'läf bo͝ol), 1883–1933, Norwegian lyric poet. The son of a successful writer, Bull began his career as a journalist. His poetic brilliance was revealed by the publication of his collection *Digte* [poems] (1909). He is noted for a style characterized by flawlessness of form and the use of daring imagery. Among his other major collections is *Metope* (1927).

Bull, Ole Bornemann (ō'lə bŏr'nəmän), 1810–80, Norwegian violinist. After his debut in Paris (1832) he toured in Europe and in the United States, playing mainly his own compositions and Norwegian folk music. He founded a theater for national drama at Bergen (1849), and in 1852 he attempted to found a Norwegian settlement in Pennsylvania. See biography by Mortimer Smith (1943, repr. 1973).

bull [Lat. *bulla*=leaden seal], apostolic letter containing some important pronouncement of the pope. The papal bull is more solemn than the papal brief or ENCYCLICAL. The letter, traditionally sealed with lead, but in special circumstances with silver or gold, begins with the name of the pope and his title as *servus servorum Dei* [servant of the servants of God]. Today only the consistorial bull, the most solemn of all papal pronouncements, carries the leaden seal; all other bulls and lesser documents have a red ink seal. Famous bulls include *Clericis laicos* (1296) and *Unam sanctam* (1302) issued by Boniface VIII in his struggle with Philip IV of France; the Bull of Demarcation (1493) by Alexander VI; *Exsurge Domine* (1520) by Leo X against Martin Luther; *Unigenitus* (1713) by Clement XI, against Jansenism; *Dominus ac Redemptor* (1773) by Clement XIV, suppressing the Jesuits; *Quanta cura* (1864) by Pius IX, introducing the *Syllabus errorum; Pastor aeternus* (1871) by Pius IX, on papal infallibility; and *Munificentissimus Deus* (1950) by Pius XII, defining the dogma of the Assumption of the Virgin Mary. Pope John XXIII issued a consistorial bull, *Humanae Salutis* in 1961 to convoke the 21st ecumenical council. The papal bull is used to proclaim the canonization of a saint. A bullarium is a collection of papal bulls; the most famous bullaria are the Roman Bullarium (1733–62) and the Turin Bullarium (1857–85).

Bull, The, English name for TAURUS, a CONSTELLATION.

bullbaiting, 17th-century amusement, particularly popular in England, in which trained dogs (bulldogs) attacked a tethered bull. Bullbaiting, along with bullrunning (in which the bull was run down and killed by humans), bearbaiting, cockfighting, and dogfighting, was prohibited in Great Britain by an act of Parliament in 1835.

bull bat: see GOATSUCKER.

bulldog, breed of thick-set NONSPORTING DOG developed in the British Isles many centuries ago. It stands from 13 to 15 in. (33–38.1 cm) high at the shoulder and weighs from 40 to 50 lb (18.1–22.7 kg). Its short, straight, flat-lying coat is a glossy brindle, white, red, or fawn in color. The low-slung body, broad chest, large skull, and undershot jaw of the bulldog give it an appearance of stubbornness and defiance, two qualities necessary to its original role as a bullbaiter and pit fighter. These "sports" also required a high degree of ferocity, but after 1835, when such contests were made illegal, viciousness and intractability were progressively eliminated from the breed. Today the bulldog makes a gentle, devoted companion and pet. See DOG.

Buller, Sir Redvers Henry, 1839–1908, British general. His military career began in China, and he later took part in the suppression of the Red River Rebellion (1870) in Canada. In Africa he fought in the Kafir and Zulu wars (1878–79), against the Boers in the Transvaal (1881), and against the Mahdists in the Sudan (1884–85). As adjutant general (1890–97), Buller reorganized the army's supply and transport services. He was made commander in chief of troops in the South African War in 1899, but his initial failure to relieve the besieged town of Ladysmith led to his supersession (1899) by Lord Roberts of Kandahar. See memoir by Lewis Butler (1907); biography by C. H. Melville (1923); study by Julian Symons (1963).

bullfighting, national sport and spectacle of Spain. Called *corrida de toros* in Spanish, the bullfight takes place in a large outdoor arena known as the *plaza de toros.* The object is for one of the bullfighters, the matador, to kill a wild bull, or toro, with a sword. The matador is assisted by five other toreros: two picadors, mounted on armored horses, and three *peones,* or capemen on foot, also called *banderilleros* because they plant in the bull the short barbed sticks known as *banderillas.* An early type of bullfighting was practiced by the Minoans, Greeks, and Romans. The Moors probably introduced the sport to Spain (c.11th cent.), whence it spread to S France and Morocco. Originally the central figure in the Spanish bullfight was the mounted torero; Francisco Romero is generally credited with being the first (c.1726) torero to fight on foot. A modern bullfight consists of three stylized parts, sometimes likened to the three acts of a drama, preceded by the color and pageantry of a grand ceremonial parade (*paseíllo*) in which the matadors and other toreros take part. After the parade, the president, the official who supervises the proceedings, signals for the first bull to be sent out. The toreros then wave capes (*capas*) at the bull, forcing the animal to make a charge; this is known as "running" the bull. In this first part the picadors administer four *pic* (lance) thrusts; there may be more or fewer thrusts depending on the condition of the animal. In the second part, which is brief, the *banderilleros* come out and, while on the run, plant the *banderillas* on the withers of the bull behind the neck muscle; these sting the bull and often spur him into making a livelier charge in the third part. Then comes the matador. He holds the *muleta,* a small cloth cape, in one hand, and his sword in the other. Using the *muleta,* he makes daring passes at the bull that are often of great grace and beauty. He thus works at dominating the animal until the latter stands with his four feet square on the ground and his head hung low; according to ritual and law, the matador must then kill the bull by thrusting his sword between the animal's shoulder blades and into the heart. If the matador has performed well he may be awarded an ear or the tail of the bull as a token of his craftsmanship. In the typical bullfight program there are six bulls and three matadors. Each matador contests two bulls, chosen by lot on the morning of the fight. A matador's performance requires great skill and courage, and successful matadors such as Pedro ROMERO (grandson of Francisco Romero), Juan BELMONTE, JOSELITO, MANOLETE, Carlos Arruza, and Manuel Benitez (El Cordobes) reaped immense awards of praise and money. The fighting bulls are bred and selected for spirit and strength. They must weigh not less than 542 kg (1,194 lb) and are usually from four to five years old. Bullfighting is also popular in the Latin American countries of Mexico, Peru, Colombia, Venezuela, and Ecuador, and in S France. Critics contend that it is an inhumane spectacle of animal torture. Aficionados say it is an important part of Spanish culture and ritual. The Portuguese practice a style of bullfighting from horseback (*rejoneo*) in which the bull is not killed. See Ernest Hemingway, *Death in the Afternoon* (1932, repr. 1971); Kenneth Tynan, *Bull Fever* (1955, rev. ed. 1966); Rex Smith, ed., *Biography of the Bulls* (1957); Angus MacNab, *Fighting Bulls* (1959); Barnaby Conrad, *La Fiesta Brava* (1953) and *Barnaby Conrad's Encyclopedia of Bullfighting* (1961); Larry Collins and Dominique Lapierre, *Or I'll Dress You in Mourning* (1968); Adolfo Bollain et al., *Bulls and Bullfighting* (1970); John Fulton, *Bullfighting* (1971).

bullfinch: see FINCH.

bullfrog, common name of the largest North American frog, *Rana catesbeiana.* Native to the E United States, this species has been successfully introduced in the West and in other parts of the world. The body length is 4 to 8 in. (10–20 cm), and the legs may be up to 10 in. (25 cm) long. An aquatic form with fully webbed toes, the bullfrog can close its nostrils and lie at the bottom of a pond for some time. Males have a loud, booming call. Bullfrog tadpoles require two or three years to become adults. The bullfrog is the only frog whose legs are marketed in quantity for food in the United States. Several other large frogs of the genus *Rana* are called bullfrogs in other regions. Bullfrogs are classified in the phylum CHORDATA, subphylum Vertebrata, class Amphibia, order Anura, family Ranidae.

bullhead, common name for several species of fish. See CATFISH; SCULPIN.

Bullinger, Heinrich (hīn'rĭkh bo͞o'lĭng-ər), 1504–75, Swiss Protestant reformer. After the death of Zwingli in 1531, Bullinger became pastor of the principal church in Zurich and a leader of the reformed party in Switzerland. He played an important part in compiling the first Helvetic Confession (1536), a creed based largely on Zwingli's theological views as distinct from Lutheran doctrine. In 1549 the Consensus Tigurinus, drawn up by Bullinger and Calvin, marked the departure of Swiss theology from Zwinglian to Calvinist theory. His later views were embodied in the second Helvetic Confession (1566), which was accepted in Switzerland, France, Scotland, and Hungary and became one of the most generally accepted creeds of the reformed churches. He wrote a life of Zwingli and edited his complete works.

Bullitt, William Christian (bo͝ol'ĭt), 1891–1967, American diplomat, b. Philadelphia. A member of the American delegation to the Paris Peace Conference following World War I, he was sent by President Wilson on a secret mission to Russia. When his report favoring recognition of the Communist government was rejected, he resigned and later bitterly attacked the Versailles Treaty before the Senate. After 12 years of private life, he was made special assistant to Cordell Hull and served (1933-36) as first U.S. ambassador to the USSR. Later he was ambassador to France (1936-40), ambassador at large in the Middle East (1941-42), and special assistant to the Secretary of the Navy (1942-43). He served (1944-45) as a major in the Free French army under Charles De Gaulle. See his *The Great Globe Itself* (1946); *For the President*, selections from his diplomatic correspondence with President Franklin Delano Roosevelt, ed. by O. H. Bullitt (1972); biography by Beatrice Farnsworth (1967).

bull mastiff (măst'ĭf), breed of powerful WORKING DOG developed in England in the second half of the 19th cent. It stands from 24 to 27 in. (61-68.6 cm) high at the shoulder and weighs from 100 to 130 lb (45.4-59 kg). Its dense, short coat may be fawn, red, or brindle, with a darker shading on the ears and muzzle. Because of the increasing need to protect game preserves and large estates from poachers, English gamekeepers began to cross existing breeds in an attempt to produce a dog that would possess the required speed, strength, aggressiveness, good night vision, and the capacity to remain silent at the approach of the poacher. It would be the task of the desired dog to knock down the intruder and keep him down until he was captured, rather than simply alarming him into running away. After many breeds were tried, mastiff and bulldog stock were crossed, producing a dog with all the necessary qualities, the bull mastiff. Today it is raised as a guard and show dog and as a pet. See DOG.

Bull Moose party: see PROGRESSIVE PARTY.

bull nettle: see NIGHTSHADE.

Bull Run, small stream, NE Va., c.30 mi (50 km) SW of Washington, D.C. Two important battles of the Civil War were fought there on July 21, 1861, and Aug. 29-30, 1862. The **first battle of Bull Run** (or first battle of Manassas) was the first major engagement of the war. On July 16, 1861, the Union army under Gen. Irvin MCDOWELL began to move on the Confederate force under Gen. P. G. T. BEAUREGARD at Manassas Junction. Gen. Robert Patterson's force at Martinsburg, which was to prevent the Confederate army under Gen. Joseph E. JOHNSTON at Winchester from uniting with Beauregard, failed, and by July 20 part of Johnston's army had reached Manassas. On July 21, McDowell, turning Beauregard's left, attacked the Confederates near the stone bridge over Bull Run and drove them back to the Henry House Hill. There Confederate resistance, with Gen. Thomas J. JACKSON standing like a "stone wall," checked the Union advance, and the arrival of Gen. E. Kirby Smith's brigade turned the tide against the Union forces. The unseasoned Union volunteers retreated, fleeing along roads jammed by panicked civilians who had turned out in their Sunday finery to watch the battle. The retreat became a rout as the soldiers made for the defenses of Washington, but the equally inexperienced Confederates were in no condition to make an effective pursuit. The South rejoiced at the result, while the North was spurred to greater efforts to win the war. See R. H. Beatie, *Road to Manassas.* The **second battle of Bull Run** (or second battle of Manassas) was also a victory for the Confederates. In July, 1862, the Union Army of Virginia under Gen. John POPE threatened the town of Gordonsville, a railroad junction between Richmond and the Shenandoah valley. Gen. Robert E. LEE sent Stonewall Jackson to protect the town, and on Aug. 9, 1862, Jackson defeated Nathaniel Banks's corps, the vanguard of Pope's army, in the battle of Cedar Mt. (or Cedar Run). When George McClellan's army was gradually withdrawn from Harrison's Landing on the James River (where it had remained after the SEVEN DAYS BATTLES) to reinforce Pope, Lee concentrated his whole army at Gordonsville. He planned to strike before Pope could be reinforced. Pope withdrew to the north side of the Rappahannock River. Lee followed to the south side and on Aug. 25 boldly divided his army. By Aug. 28, Jackson had marched to the Union right and rear, destroyed Union communications and supplies, and stationed his troops just west of the first Bull Run battlefield, where he awaited the arrival of James Longstreet with the rest of Lee's army. Pope was attacking Jackson when Longstreet came up on Aug. 29. The attack was repulsed, but Pope, mistaking a re-formation of Jackson's lines for a retreat, renewed it the next day. After the Union troops were again driven back, Lee ordered Longstreet to counterattack. Longstreet, supported by Jackson, swept Pope from the field. The Union forces retreated across Bull Run, badly defeated. Lee's pursuit ended at Chantilly, where the Union forces stopped Jackson on Sept. 1, 1862. Pope then withdrew to Washington. Both battlefields are included in Manassas National Battlefield Park (est. 1940). See E. J. Stackpole, *From Cedar Mountain to Antietam* (1959); Allan Nevins, *The War for the Union* (Vol. II, 1960).

bull terrier, breed of large, muscular TERRIER originating in England around 1835. It stands from 19 to 22 in. (48.3-55.9 cm) high at the shoulder and weighs from 30 to 36 lb (13.6-16.3 kg). Its short, flat-lying, harsh coat is glossy white or, in the colored variety, most popularly brindle with white markings. Developed for dogfighting from a cross of bulldog and a now extinct English terrier, the bull terrier was renowned for its courage, strength, and intelligence. However, down through the years English breeders placed increasing emphasis on the breed's overall disposition and less on its aggressiveness. As a result, the bull terrier of today is a friendly, gentle dog that makes a responsible and devoted companion. See DOG.

Bulnes, Manuel (mänwĕl' bo͞ol'nās), 1799-1866, president of Chile (1841-51). He served in the revolt against Spain and commanded the victorious Chilean forces at the battle of Yungay (1839), where the Peru-Bolivia confederation of Andrés SANTA CRUZ was destroyed. Bulnes, a conservative, was elected president and, through stern and repressive measures, fostered economic and educational progress.

Bülow, Bernhard Heinrich Martin, Fürst von (bĕrn'härt hīn'rĭkh mär'tĭn fürst fən bü'lō), 1849-1929, German chancellor. He held many diplomatic posts before he became, through the influence of Friedrich von HOLSTEIN, foreign secretary in 1897 and succeeded Hohenlohe-Schillingsfürst as chancellor in 1900. He inadvertently increased German isolation by his failure to gain the friendship of England and by his aggressive foreign policy. He antagonized France by his actions in the Moroccan crisis of 1905 (see MOROCCO). Bülow later alienated Russia in the Bosnian crisis of 1908 by thwarting Russian goals for the opening of the Dardanelles and supporting Austria-Hungary's annexation of Bosnia and Hercegovina. As a result he strengthened the Triple Entente between Great Britain, France, and Russia (see TRIPLE ALLIANCE AND TRIPLE ENTENTE). Bülow lost the confidence of Emperor William II in the *Daily Telegraph* affair (Oct., 1908) in which William indiscreetly revealed his foreign policy toward Britain in an interview with the London newspaper; the interview caused a national uproar. Bülow had approved the text of William's remarks, but had not read them. Bülow subsequently lost support in the Reichstag over a proposed tax and was forced to resign in 1909. He later (1914-15) was ambassador to Italy. See his memoirs (tr. 4 vol., 1931-32).

Bülow, Friedrich Wilhelm, Freiherr von (frē'drĭkh vĭl'hĕlm frī'hĕr), 1755-1816, Prussian general in the Napoleonic Wars. After his victories (1813) over the French at Gross Beeren and at Dennewitz he was created count of Dennewitz. In 1815 he played a conspicuous part in the Waterloo campaign.

Bülow, Hans Guido, Freiherr von (häns gē'dō), 1830-94, German pianist and conductor. After hearing Wagner's *Lohengrin* in 1850 at Weimar under Liszt's direction, he studied piano with Liszt and later conducted the premieres of several of Wagner's operas. In 1857 he married Liszt's daughter Cosima, who left him in 1869 and later became the wife of Wagner. While retaining his admiration of Wagner's music, Bülow became the most ardent champion of Brahms. He framed the aphorism that Bach, Beethoven, and Brahms are the three B's of music. One of the first pianists to be concerned with stylistically proper performances, Bülow made critical editions of the works of many composers. The first of the modern virtuoso conductors, he achieved his greatest distinction as conductor (1880-85) of the ducal orchestra at Meiningen.

bulrush: see SEDGE.

Bultmann, Rudolf Karl (bo͝olt'män), 1884-, German existentialist theologian, educated at the universities of Tübingen, Berlin, and Marburg. He taught at the universities of Breslau and Giessen and from 1921 to 1950 was professor at the Univ. of Marburg. Strongly influenced by the existentialist philosophy of Martin Heidegger, Bultmann is best known for his work on the New Testament, which he reduced—with the exception of the Passion—to basic elements of myth, which then have application to contemporary concerns. His approach is termed "demythologization." His classic work is *Theology of the New Testament* (tr. 1951). Other writings in English translation include *Essays, Philosophical and Theological* (1952, tr. 1955), *Primitive Christianity in its Contemporary Setting* (1949, tr. 1963), *Jesus and the World* (1951, tr. 1958), *The Gospel of John* (1953, tr. 1971), *The History of the Synoptic Tradition* (1957, 2d ed. tr. 1968); see also his selected shorter writings, *Existence and Faith* (tr. 1960); studies by E. T. Lang (1968), Walter Schmithals (tr. 1968), and André Malet (tr. 1969).

Bulwer, William Henry Lytton Earle, Baron Dalling and Bulwer (bo͝ol'wər; lĭt'ən), 1801-72, English diplomat and author; brother of the novelist Edward Bulwer-Lytton. He was known most of his life as Sir Henry Bulwer. Although he sat in Parliament for some years (1830-37, 1868-71), he was most prominent as a diplomat. As secretary of the embassy in Constantinople (1837-38) he secured a commercial treaty with Turkey. He was ambassador to Spain (1843-48) during the affair of the Spanish Marriages (see ISABELLA II) but was ordered to leave by the dictator Ramón Narváez, whom he offended. As minister to Washington (1849-52), he concluded the important CLAYTON-BULWER TREATY of 1850. Among his later diplomatic posts were Florence, Bucharest, and, again, Constantinople (1858-65). He was created a baron in 1871. His writings include *An Autumn in Greece* (1826), *France: Social, Literary, and Political* (1834-36), *Historical Characters* (1867), and biographies of Lord Byron (1835) and Viscount Palmerston (1870-74, unfinished).

Bulwer-Lytton, Edward George Earle Lytton, 1st **Baron Lytton,** 1803-73, English novelist. The son of Gen. William Bulwer and Elizabeth Lytton, he assumed the name Bulwer-Lytton in 1843 when he inherited the Lytton estate "Knebworth." He was created Baron Lytton of Knebworth in 1866. His varied and highly derivative novels won wide popularity. Many of his early novels of manners—*Falkland* (1827), *Paul Clifford* (1830), and *Eugene Aram* (1832)—reflect the influence of his friend William GODWIN. Bulwer-Lytton, however, is best remembered for his extremely well-researched historical novels, particularly *The Last Days of Pompeii* (1834) and *Rienzi* (1835). In 1849, with *The Caxtons*, he began a series of humorous domestic novels, which had recently become the vogue. His utopian novel, *The Coming Race*, prefigured the works of Wells and Huxley. A member of Parliament from 1831 to 1841, Bulwer-Lytton was a reformer, but in 1852 he returned to Parliament as a Conservative. In 1858 he was appointed colonial secretary. He was also a successful dramatist. His plays include *The Lady of Lyons* (1838), *Richelieu* (1839), and *Money* (1840). See study by S. B. Liljegren (1957); Charles Shattuck, ed., *Bulwer and Macready* (1958).

Bulwer-Lytton, Edward Robert, 1st **earl of Lytton,** pseud. **Owen Meredith,** 1831-91, English diplomat and poet; son of the novelist, Bulwer-Lytton. He was in the diplomatic service from 1850 to 1875, when Disraeli appointed him viceroy of India; for his services in the Afghan wars he was created (1880) an earl. He was ambassador to France from 1887 until his death. His poems, written at first under his pseudonym, include *The Wanderer* (1858), a collection of lyrics; *Lucile* (1860) and *Glenaveril* (1885), long narrative poems; and *King Poppy* (1892), an epic fantasy. His verse has been criticized for its affectation and prolixity. He also wrote a biography of his father, which appeared in 1883. See his letters (1937); studies by Lady Betty Balfour (1899) and A. B. Harlan (1946).

bumblebee: see BEE.

Bunah (byo͞o'nə), Judahite. 1 Chron. 2.25.

Buna rubber (bo͞o'nə, byo͞o'-): see RUBBER.

Bunau-Varilla, Philippe Jean (fēlēp' zhäN bünō'-värēyä'), 1859-1940, French engineer, prominent in the PANAMA CANAL controversy. An engineer after 1884 in the original French company for building the canal, he was chief engineer before the company went bankrupt in 1889 and was the organizer (1894) of the new company that took over the rights of the old one. Unable to develop his plans in France, he undertook to sell the company to the United States, converting (1901) Mark Hanna and President McKinley, who had been interested in the Nicaragua route, to the Panama project. After new opposition developed, he persuaded the French directors to reduce the price of the company, and President Theodore Roosevelt was won over to the Panama plan. When difficulties arose with the Colombian government, Bunau-Varilla conspired with insurrectionists in Panama and touched off (1903) a successful revolution. As minister from the new Panamanian republic to the United States, he negotiated the Hay-Bunau-Varilla Treaty, which gave the United States control of the Panama Canal. In World War I a water chlorination process that he had developed was used at the battle of Verdun. See his *Panama* (tr. 1913) and *From Panama to Verdun* (tr. 1940).

bunchberry: see DOGWOOD.

Bunche, Ralph Johnson, 1904–71, U.S. government official and United Nations diplomat, b. Detroit. He taught political science at Howard Univ. from 1928, becoming a full professor in 1938. He also did worldwide research in colonial administration and race relations. In government service after 1941, he worked under the joint chiefs of staff and was a chief research analyst in the Office of Strategic Services. The first Negro to be a division head in the Dept. of State (July–Oct., 1945), he entered the United Nations in 1946 as director of the Trusteeship Division. He became (Dec., 1947) principal secretary of the UN Palestine Commission and helped to bring peace to the Holy Land. For his work there he was awarded the 1950 Nobel Peace Prize. He served as undersecretary general for special political affairs from 1958 until his retirement due to poor health shortly before his death.

Bundaberg, city (1971 pop. 27,394), Queensland, E Australia, on the Burnett River. It is a sugar-refining center and a port.

Bundestag (bo͝on'dĕstäkh") [Ger.,=federal parliament], lower house of the parliament of the Federal Republic of Germany (West Germany). It succeeded the REICHSTAG. It is a popularly elected body that elects the chancellor, passes all legislation and ratifies the most important treaties. It can remove the chancellor by a vote of no confidence, but only if it simultaneously elects a new chancellor. In the German Democratic Republic (East Germany), the Volkskammer [people's chamber] according to the constitution exercises similar powers. The upper house of the West German parliament, the Bundesrat [federal council], represents the states. It must approve certain laws.

bundling, courtship custom, thought to have originated in Holland and the British Isles. It was extended to America, particularly to New England, and most widely practiced in the years prior to the Revolution of 1776. Engaged or courting couples, dressed or partially dressed, traditionally lay together on a bed pursuing their romance. They were sometimes separated by a board, or the girl's legs were tied together, or the couple was in some other way constrained from completing the sexual act. As a formal custom the practice was abandoned in the early 19th cent. because of widespread social disapproval.

Bundy, McGeorge, 1919–, U.S. educator and government official, b. Boston. An intelligence officer in the U.S. army during World War II, he joined (1949), the Harvard faculty and later became (1953) the youngest dean of the faculty of arts and sciences there, serving until 1961. As the special assistant to Presidents Kennedy and Lyndon B. Johnson for national security affairs (1961–66), Bundy supervised the staff of the National Security Council and played a major role in making foreign policy. He supported (1961) the Bay of Pigs invasion, helped determine (1962) strategy during the Cuban missile crisis, and strongly advocated the increasing U.S. military involvement in Vietnam. He resigned from government service to become (1966) president of the Ford Foundation. Bundy is the author of *The Strength of Government* (1968).

bungalow [from Indian *bangla,*=house], dwelling built in a style developed from that of a form of rural house in India. The original bungalow typically has one story, few rooms, and a maximum of cross drafts, with high ceilings, unusually large window and door openings, and verandas on all sides to shade the rooms from the intense light and tropical heat. Dwellings of this general type became popular in S California, with numerous differences in plan and materials, and were termed bungalows. The word thus came to be used for a cottage or for any small house with verandas covered by low, wide eaves.

Bunin, Ivan Alekseyevich (bo͞o'nĭn, Rus. ēvän' əlyĭksyā'yəvĭch bo͞o'nyĭn), 1870–1953, Russian writer. Born of a poor aristocratic family, he was encouraged in his literary precocity. His first volume of verse was published in 1891. He traveled extensively, writing while working as a librarian and statistician. Bunin won the Pushkin Prize in 1903 for his own verse and for his translations of works by Byron and Longfellow. *The Village* (1910, tr. 1923), a novel in the Turgenev tradition, won him international fame. It depicts the ugliness of peasant life before the Revolution of 1905. The story "Dry Valley" describes the decline of the country gentry. Bunin is best known for his short stories, particularly for the title story of the collection *The Gentleman from San Francisco* (1916, tr. 1923), which treats powerfully the themes of vanity and death. His autobiographical novel *The Well of Days* (1930, tr. 1933) is equally celebrated. Bunin's *Memories and Portraits* (1950, tr. 1951) contains reminiscences of famous contemporaries. His elegant style, descriptive genius, and choice of themes place Bunin among the classic Russian authors. A nostalgia for the aristocracy contributed to his reactionary political stance, which compelled him to leave Russia in 1919. His last years were spent in France. Bunin was awarded the 1933 Nobel Prize in Literature. See study by Serge Kryzytski (1971).

bunion, swelling or thickening around the first joint of the big toe. The toe is forced inward and compresses the other toes. The fluid-filled sac, or BURSA, in the toe joint becomes inflamed (a condition called bursitis), which may lead to pain, deformity, and an inability to wear ordinary shoes. Bunions may arise from years of wearing ill-fitting shoes. However, congenital bone deformities are usually indicated when they occur on both feet. Proper foot care, especially in selecting shoes, is the most important aspect of treatment and prevention. The toes can often be straightened by pads or splints, and orthopedic shoes are generally prescribed. Serious cases may require surgery.

Bunker Hill, battle of, in the American Revolution, June 17, 1775. Detachments of colonial militia under Artemas WARD, Nathanael Greene, John STARK, and Israel PUTNAM laid siege to Boston shortly after the battles of Lexington and Concord. However, Thomas Gage, British commander in the city, made no attempt to break the siege until he was reinforced (in May) by troops led by William HOWE, Sir Henry Clinton, and John Burgoyne. The Continental forces learned of the British plan to take the heights of Dorchester and Charlestown, and William PRESCOTT was sent to occupy Bunker Hill outside Charlestown. Prescott instead chose the neighboring Breed's Hill to the southeast, but the engagement that ensued has become known as the battle of Bunker Hill. Howe was ordered to attack the American position, and after two slaughterous failures a third charge dislodged the Americans, who had run out of powder. The British victory failed to break the siege, and the gallant American defense heightened colonial morale and resistance. See T. J. Fleming, *Now We Are Enemies: The Story of Bunker Hill* (1960); R. M. Ketchum, *The Battle for Bunker Hill* (1962).

Bunni (bŭn'ī), Levitical name mentioned in confusing passages. Neh. 10.15; 11.15. In one case the name seems to be an alternative of BINNUI **1.**

Bunsen, Christian Karl Josias, Freiherr von (krĭs'tyän kärl yōzē'äs frī'hĕr fən bo͝on'zən), 1791–1860, Prussian diplomat and scholar. He studied theology at the Univ. of Göttingen. He was a friend of King Frederick William IV and urged him to accept liberal ideas. Bunsen was minister to the papal court at Rome (1824–38) and ambassador to Bern (1839–41) and to London (1842–54), but he was recalled from London because he supported alliance with the Western powers in the Crimean War. A scholar of note, Bunsen wrote on religion, language, literature, history, and law.

Bunsen, Robert Wilhelm (bŭn'sən, Ger. rō'bĕrt vĭl'hĕlm bo͝on'zən), 1811–99, German scientist, educated at the Univ. of Göttingen, where he received his doctorate in 1830. He served on the faculties of several universities and was at Heidelberg from 1852 to 1889. His first important contribution to chemistry came with his investigation of certain organic compounds of arsenic, in the process of which he discovered that ferric oxide could be used as an antidote to arsenic poisoning. From his studies of the gaseous products of blast furnaces he evolved a method of gas analysis, presented in his book *Gasometrische Methoden* (1857). With Kirchhoff at Heidelberg he discovered by spectroscopy the elements cesium and rubidium. Bunsen wrote many articles and collaborated with Kirchhoff on *Chemische Analyse durch Spektralbeobachtungen* (1860). His important contributions to petrology and chemicogeology include the explanation of GEYSER action. He invented and improved various kinds of laboratory equipment, including the Bunsen cell (see CELL, in electricity), the Bunsen photometer (see PHOTOMETRY), and the BUNSEN BURNER.

Bunsen burner, gas burner, commonly used in scientific laboratories, consisting essentially of a hollow tube which is fitted vertically around the flame and which has an opening at the base to admit air. A smokeless, nonluminous flame of high temperature is produced. The underlying principle of the Bunsen burner is basic to common gas stoves and lamps.

Bunshaft, Gordon, 1909–, American architect, b. Buffalo, N.Y. As chief designer for the architectural firm of SKIDMORE, OWINGS, AND MERRILL, Bunshaft was responsible for Lever House, New York City's first glass curtain-wall skyscraper (1952), which has been widely imitated. Among his other works are the Manufacturers Trust Company building on Fifth Ave. at 43d St. in Manhattan, New York City; a complex of buildings near Hartford for the Connecticut General Life Insurance Company; the Albright-Knox Art Gallery, Buffalo; and the Banque Lambert, Brussels (1965).

bunt: see SMUT.

bunting, common name for small, plump birds of the family Fringillidae (FINCH family). Among the American buntings are the indigo bunting, in which the summer plumage of the male reflects sunlight as a rich, metallic blue; the painted bunting, or nonpareil (*Passerina ciris*), with showy red, blue, and green plumage; the hardy snow bunting (*Plectrophenax nivalis*), whose winter plumage is white marked with light brown on the head and sides; and the lazuli bunting of the West, turquoise above with a chestnut breast and white wing bars. European buntings include the corn, snow, and cirl buntings, the yellowhammer, and the ortolan (*Emberiza hortulana*), which is caught and fattened as a table delicacy. Buntings are also called sparrows in the United States. They are classified in the phylum CHORDATA, subphylum Vertebrata, class Aves, order Passeriformes, family Fringillidae.

Buntline, Ned, pseud. of Edward Zane Carroll Judson, 1823–86, American adventurer and writer. In 1845 he founded in Nashville *Ned Buntline's Own,* a sensational magazine. After being lynched (1846) for a murder, but secretly cut down alive and released, he went to New York City, where he resumed the magazine. He led a mob in the Astor Place riot of 1849 against the English actor Macready. In the '50s he turned up in St. Louis as an organizer of the Know-Nothing movement. After 1846 Buntline wrote more than 400 action novels, forerunners of the DIME NOVELS. Typical are *The Mysteries and Miseries of New York* (1848) and *Stella Delorme; or, The Comanche's Dream* (1860). In 1872 he persuaded W. F. Cody (Buffalo Bill) to act in his play, *The Scouts of the Plains,* which started Cody on his stage career. See biography by James Monaghan (1952).

Buñuel, Luis (lo͞oēs' bo͝onyo͞oĕl'), 1900–, Spanish film director working in France, Mexico, and Spain. He joined Dali to make some early surrealistic films, notably *Un Chien andalou* (1928). His powerful and realistic *Las hurdes* (1932) is a documentary about Spanish agrarian poverty. *Los olvidados* (1949), made in Mexico, brutally portrays his view of human corruption and cruelty. Harshly critical of the church and of crusading morality, Buñuel continued to examine social hypocrisy and turpitude in *Viridiana* (1961), *Diary of a Chambermaid* (1964), *Belle de Jour* (1966), *Tristana* (1970), *The Discreet Charm of the Bourgeoisie* (1972), and *The Phantom of Liberty* (1974).

bunya-bunya (bŭn'yə-bŭn'yə): see MONKEY-PUZZLE TREE.

Bunyan, John, 1628–88, English author, b. Elstow, Bedfordshire. After a brief period at the village free school, Bunyan learned the tinker's trade, which he followed intermittently throughout his life. Joining the parliamentary army in 1644, he served until 1647. The reading of several pious books and a constant study of the Bible intensified Bunyan's religious beliefs, and in 1653 he began acting as lay preacher for a congregation of Baptists in Bedford. In this capacity he came into conflict with the Quakers led by George FOX and turned to writing in defense of his beliefs. In 1660 agents of the restored monarchy arrested him for unlicensed preaching, and he remained in prison for the next 12 years. During this period Bunyan wrote nine books, the most famous of which is *Grace Abounding to the Chief of Sinners* (1666), a fervent spiritual autobiography. Soon after his release in 1672 he was reimprisoned briefly and wrote the first part of his masterpiece *The Pilgrim's Progress from This World to That Which Is to Come,* published in 1678. A second part appeared in 1684. By the time Bunyan was released from his second imprisonment, he had become a hero to the members of his sect, and he continued preaching and writing until his death. The principal works of these later years are *The Life and Death of Mr. Badman* (1680) and *The Holy War* (1682). *Pilgrim's Progress* is an allegory recounting Christian's journey from the City of Destruction to the Celestial City; the second part describes the manner in which Christian's wife, Christiana, makes the same pilgrimage. Remarkable for its simple, biblical style and its vivid presentation of character and incident, *Pilgrim's Progress* is considered one of the world's great works of literature. Bunyan's continued popularity rests on the spiritual fervor that permeates his works and on the compelling style in which they are written. His prose unites the eloquence of the Bible with the vigorous realism of common speech. See biography by O. E. Winslow (1961); studies by H. A. Talon (1951), W. Y. Tindall (1934, repr. 1964), David E. Smith (1966), and Roger Sharrock (rev. ed. 1968).

Bunyan, Paul, legendary American lumberjack. He was the hero of a series of "tall tales" popular through the timber country from Michigan westward. Bunyan was known for his fantastic strength and gigantic size. He is said to have ruled his gargantuan lumber camp between the winter of the blue snow and the spring that came up from China. His prized possession was Babe the Blue Ox, the distance between whose horns measured 42 ax handles and a plug of tobacco. In Southern lumber camps a similar legendary figure is known as Tony Beaver. See collections of legends by Louis Untermeyer (1945) and H. W. Felton (1947); study of the legend by D. G. Hoffman (1952, repr. 1966).

Buonaparte: see BONAPARTE and NAPOLEON I.

Buonarroti, Michelangelo: see MICHELANGELO BUONARROTI.

Buoninsegna, Duccio di: see DUCCIO DI BUONINSEGNA.

Buononcini, Italian musicians: see BONONCINI.

buoy (boi, bo͞o'ē), float anchored in navigable waters to mark channels and indicate dangers to navigation (isolated rocks, mine fields, cables, and the like). The shape, color, number, and marking of the buoy are significant, but unfortunately the significance varies in different countries, and the color-code system devised by the International Maritime Conference at Washington, D.C., in 1889 was not adopted. Although the spar buoys (upright posts) used in northern latitudes are usually wooden, large buoys are generally made of steel or iron. Nun buoys have conical tops; can buoys, flat tops. Buoys may be fitted with bells or whistles (usually operated by motion of the waves), and battery-powered light buoys are much used; radio buoys came into use in 1939. There are also mooring buoys, used for the anchoring of ships. In 1972 the United States launched the first of a series of 100-ton data buoys, which, it was planned, would encircle the globe transmitting oceanographic and meteorological data via satellite.

buoyancy, upward force exerted by a fluid on any body immersed in it. Buoyant force can be explained in terms of ARCHIMEDES' PRINCIPLE.

bur or **burr,** popular name for fruits that have barbed, pointed, or rough outgrowths. By clinging to the fur or hair of animals and the clothing of man they are transported from the parent plant, often great distances. Some common burs include those of the chestnut, burdock, bur marigold, and cocklebur. Burs are particularly obnoxious to sheep growers because of the difficulty of removing them from wool.

Buraimi (bo͞orī'mē), group of small oases, SE Arabia, on the border between Abu Dhabi and Oman. In the 1950s the area, rich in oil, was claimed by Saudi Arabia, causing a dispute with Great Britain, which at the time was the protector of Oman and Abu Dhabi.

Burano (bo͞orä'nō), former town, now part of Venice, in Venetia, NE Italy, built on four islets in the Lagoon of Venice. It is a fishing center and has been famous for its lace since the 15th cent.

Burbage, Richard, 1567?–1619, first great English actor. The leading tragedian of the CHAMBERLAIN'S MEN, he originated the title roles in Shakespeare's *Hamlet, Lear, Othello,* and *Richard III.* He also appeared in many of the first productions of plays by Thomas Kyd, Beaumont and Fletcher, Ben Jonson, and John Webster. His name came to symbolize acting of the highest quality. Burbage's father, James Burbage, had built the first permanent theater in London in 1576, called the Theatre. In 1598 the building was removed to Bankside and set up as the GLOBE THEATRE by Richard's brother, Cuthbert, on the death of their father. The brothers also inherited shares in the Blackfriars Theatre, built by their father in 1596, which became the winter home of the company.

Burbank, Luther, 1849–1926, American plant breeder, b. Lancaster, Mass. He experimented with thousands of plant varieties and developed many new ones, including new varieties of prunes, plums, raspberries, blackberries, apples, peaches, and nectarines. Besides the Burbank potato, he produced new tomato, corn, squash, pea, and asparagus forms; a spineless cactus useful in cattle feeding; and many new flowers, especially lilies and the famous Shasta daisy. His methods and results are described in his books—*How Plants Are Trained to Work for Man* (8 vol., 1921) and, with Wilbur Hall, *Harvest of the Years* (1927) and *Partner of Nature* (1939)—and in his descriptive catalogs, *New Creations.* After 1875 his work was done at Santa Rosa, Calif. See D. S. Jordan and Vernon Kellogg, *The Scientific Aspects of Luther Burbank's Work* (1909); E. B. Beeson, *The Early Life and Letters of Luther Burbank* (1927); W. L. Howard, *Luther Burbank* (1945); Ken Kraft, *Luther Burbank* (1967).

Burbank, city (1970 pop. 88,871), Los Angeles co., S Calif.; inc. 1911. Aircraft manufacturing is the major industry. Several motion-picture and television studios are in Burbank.

burbot (bûr'bət): see COD.

Burchfield, Charles, 1893–1967, American painter, b. Ashtabula, Ohio, studied at the Cleveland School of Art. From 1921 to 1929 he worked as a wallpaper designer. His paintings, predominantly in watercolor, fall into three periods: from 1916 to the early 1920s, poetic evocations of nature; from the early 1920s to the early 1940s, bold, somber landscapes and urban scenes; and after 1943, a return to lyric expressions of nature. Burchfield is widely known for his depiction of crumbling Victorian mansions, false-front stores, and other relics of the late 19th cent. Weather and sunlight effects are important in all his work. Among his many works in museums are *Setting Sun through the Catalpas* (Cleveland Mus. of Art), *October* (Columbus Gall. of Fine Art, Ohio), *Freight Cars Under a Bridge* (Detroit Inst. of Arts), and *An April Mood* (Whitney Mus., New York City). See *The Drawings of Charles Burchfield* with text by the artist (1968); study by John Baur (1956).

Burckhardt, Jacob Christoph (yä'kôp krĭs'tôf bo͝ork'härt), 1818–97, Swiss historian, one of the founders of the cultural interpretation of history. Of patrician background, he studied under Ranke at the Univ. of Berlin and taught (1844–53, 1858–93) art history and history at the Univ. of Basel. His best-known work is *Die Kultur der Renaissance in Italien* (1860, *The Civilization of the Renaissance in Italy,* available in many English editions). It remains the great classic on the subject, although its primarily political and cultural interpretation of the Renaissance period is a controversial issue among historians. Believing in a pattern of culture peculiar to each age, Burckhardt found the shift from corporate medieval society to the modern spirit in the history of Italy in the 14th and 15th cent. The strife between empire and papacy had created a political and moral vacuum, which resulted in the birth of the modern self-conscious state and in the liberation of the creative individual. Burckhardt saw Renaissance humanism as the revival of classical antiquity, and he conceived the era as one of man's joyous new discovery of himself and the world about him. He profoundly influenced his friend Nietzsche, and the work of J. A. Symonds is based largely on Burckhardt's synthesis. In *The Age of Constantine the Great* (1852, tr. 1949), Burckhardt analyzed the transition from classical times to the Middle Ages. Among his other works on history and art is *Cicerone* (1855), a guide to Italian art. Burckhardt feared that the spiritual and aesthetic human values were doomed to submersion by the rise of industrial democracy.

Burckhardt, John Lewis, 1784–1817, explorer, b. Switzerland, educated in Germany. Supported by an English association for promoting African discovery, he visited Egypt and Syria (1809–13), rediscovered PETRA (1812), then, posing as a learned Muslim, he became the first Christian to reach Medina. He died while preparing to set out from Upper Egypt for his original goal, the Niger River. Included in his *Travels in Arabia* (1829) is a notable account of Mecca. His journals, published by the African Association, include *Travels in Nubia* (1819), *Travels in Syria and the Holy Land* (1822), *Notes on the Bedouin and Wahábys* (1830), and *Arabic Proverbs* (1830). See biography by Katharine Sim (1969).

Burckmair, Hans: see BURGKMAIR, HANS.

burdock, common name of any plant of the genus *Arctium* of the family Compositae (COMPOSITE family), coarse biennials indigenous to temperate Eurasia and mostly weedy in North America. The flowers, usually purple, are followed by roundish many-seeded burs. The great burdock (*A. lappa*) has been used medicinally and (in Japan) cultivated as a vegetable called gobo. The common burdock is *A. minus.* The cocklebur is sometimes confused with burdock. Burdock is classified in the division MAGNOLIOPHYTA, class Magnoliopsida, order Asterales, family Compositae.

Burdwan (bərdwän'), town (1971 pop. 144,970), West Bengal state, E central India. It has cutlery and tool industries but is chiefly known for its 108 linga temples dedicated to Siva. Rice is the chief product of the surrounding area. Burdwan is a district administrative center and the seat of Burdwan Univ. A hydroelectric project on the nearby Damodar River has aided the town's growth.

bureaucracy, the administrative structure of any large organization, public or private. Ideally bureaucracy is characterized by hierarchical authority relations, defined spheres of competence subject to impersonal rules, recruitment by competence, and fixed salaries. Its goal is to be rational, efficient, and professional. Max WEBER, the most important student of bureaucracy, described it as technically superior to all other forms of organization and hence indispensable to large, complex enterprises. However, because of the shortcomings that have in practice afflicted such large administrative structures, the terms *bureaucracy* and *bureaucrat* in popular usage usually carry a suggestion of reprobation and imply incompetence, a narrow outlook, duplication of effort, and application of a rigid rule without due consideration of specific cases. Bureaucracy existed in imperial Rome and China and in the national monarchies, but in modern states complex industrial and social legislation has called for a vast growth of administrative functions of government. The power of permanent and nonelective officials to apply and even initiate measures of control over the national administration and economy has raised the bureaucracy to critical importance in the life of the state, and critics object that it is largely unresponsive to control by the people or their elected representatives. The institution of the OMBUDSMAN has been one means adopted in an attempt to remedy this situation. Administrative bureaucracies in private organizations have also grown rapidly, especially since the development of the corporation. See CIVIL SERVICE. See H. H. Gerth and C. Wright Mills, *From Max Weber: Essays in Sociology* (1946, repr. 1958); Marshall Dimock, *Administrative Vitality: The Conflict with Bureaucracy* (1959); M. Crozier, *The Bureaucratic Phenomenon* (1964); Martin Albrow, *Bureaucracy* (1970); P. M. Blau, *Bureaucracy in Modern Society* (2d ed. 1971).

Bureya (bo͞orā'ä), mountain range, Khabarovsk Kray, SE Far Eastern USSR, extending into NE China as the Lesser Khingan range. The site of the Bureya coal basin, it rises to c.7,150 ft (2,180 m) and yields iron and coal. The Bureya River, c.445 mi (720 km) long, rises in the N Bureya range and flows southwest to join the Amur River.

Burgas (bo͝orgäs'), city (1968 est. pop. 126,500), SE Bulgaria, on the Black Sea. It rivals Varna as the chief export port of Bulgaria and is an important commercial center. Fishing and fish canning, flour milling, sugar refining, copper mining, and soap making are carried on in Burgas, which also has engineering works and an oil refinery. The city was founded (18th cent.) on the site of a 14th-century fortified town.

Burgdorf (bo͝ork'dôrf), Fr. *Berthoud,* town (1970 pop. 15,888), NW Switzerland, on the Emme River. It is a manufacturing and cheese-trading town. There is a 12th-century castle in which J. H. Pestalozzi, the educational reformer, held (1799–1804) his first school.

Burgenland (bo͝or'gənlänt), province (1971 pop. 272,000), 1,530 sq mi (3,963 sq km), E Austria. The capital is EISENSTADT. It is a narrow, hilly region bordering Czechoslovakia in the northeast and Hungary in the east, and it is indented by Neusiedler Lake. It is primarily agricultural, but industry and tourism are being developed. A battleground for nearly 1,000 years, Burgenland has many castles, fortified churches, and walled villages. It is the newest of the Austrian provinces; its territory was transferred from Hungary by the treaties of Saint-Germain (1919) and Trianon (1920). SOPRON, the region's leading town, was returned (1921) to Hungary after a plebiscite.

Bürger, Gottfried August (gôt'frēt ou'go͞ost bür'gər), 1747–94, German poet. He is best known for his ballads in folk-song style; the famous *Lenore* (1773) was widely translated and had far-reaching influence. Bürger edited and wrote for the Göttingen *Musenalmanach* and taught aesthetics at the Univ. of Göttingen. He translated many works of Homer, Shakespeare, and others, as well as the famous stories of Baron Munchausen. His unconventional approach to poetry was severely criticized by Schiller. See study by W. A. Little (1974).

Burger, Warren Earl, 1907–, American jurist, fourteenth Chief Justice of the United States (1969–), b. St. Paul, Minn. After receiving his law degree in 1931 from St. Paul College of Law (now Mitchell College of Law), he was admitted to the Minnesota bar and taught and practiced law in St. Paul. He was (1953–56) assistant attorney general in charge of the civil division of the Department of Justice before becoming judge of the U.S. Court of Appeals for the District of Columbia. He was appointed to the Supreme Court by President Nixon. A conservative and an advocate of judicial restraint, Burger led the court in halting and sometimes reversing the liberal decisions of the court headed by his predecessor Earl Warren, particularly in criminal cases.

Burges, William (bûr'jĭz), 1827–81, English architect. An ardent proponent of medievalism, he was prominent in the GOTHIC REVIVAL. Burges is known for his designs for Cork Cathedral (1862) and Trinity College, Hartford, Conn., and for the rebuilding of Cardiff Castle (1865).

Burgess, Anthony (bûr'jĭs), 1917–, English novelist, b. Manchester, grad. Manchester Univ., 1940. He taught school in England and in the Far East and pursued an early interest in music. His many novels are marked by an adroit use of language and a surreal, darkly comic imagination. Burgess's best-known work is *A Clockwork Orange* (1962), a thriller set in a classless, futuristic society, in which an intelligent young hoodlum asserts his individuality by deliberately choosing to do evil. His other works include the novels *Inside Mr. Enderby* (1961), *MF* (1971), and *Napoleon Symphony: A Novel in Four Movements* (1974); and *Here Comes Everybody* (1965), a study of James Joyce.

Burgess, Gelett (Frank Gelett Burgess), 1866–1951, American humorist, b. Boston. His ability as an illustrator led him into magazine work, and he was soon writing humorous articles and stories to accompany his illustrations. His best-known poem, "The Purple Cow," first appeared in the San Francisco periodical the *Lark* (1895–97), of which he was an editor and steady contributor. Among his books are *Goops and How to Be Them* (1900) and *Are You a Bromide?* (1907).

Burgess, John William, 1844–1931, American educator and political scientist, b. Tennessee. He served in the Union army in the Civil War and after the war graduated from Amherst (1867). He was admitted to the Massachusetts bar in 1869, but did not practice. That same year he joined the faculty of Knox College. In 1871 he went to Germany, where he studied at the universities of Göttingen, Leipzig, and Berlin. He returned in 1873 to teach history and political science at Amherst. In 1876 he began his long association with Columbia; he was professor of political science and constitutional law until 1912. Burgess, with Nicholas Murray BUTLER, was a major influence in the creation (1880) of a faculty and school of political science, the first such faculty organized for graduate work in the country and the chief step in changing Columbia College into a university. He was dean of the Faculty of Political Science from 1890 until his retirement. In 1906–7 he served as first Roosevelt professor at the Univ. of Berlin. Burgess's fundamental political philosophy was expressed in *Political Science and Comparative Constitutional Law* (1890–91), the more permanently valuable portions of which were republished as *The Foundations of Political Science* (1933). He interpreted American history in *The Middle Period, 1817–1858, The Civil War and the Constitution, 1859–1865,* and *Reconstruction and the Constitution, 1866–1876;* a trilogy published between 1897 and 1902, to which was added *The Administration of Rutherford B. Hayes* (1915). In *Recent Changes in American Constitutional Theory* (1923) he protested against the encroachment of the Federal government upon state and individual rights and immunities. He founded the *Political Science Quarterly.* See his autobiography, *The Reminiscences of an American Scholar* (1934); R. G. Hoxie, *A History of the Faculty of Political Science, Columbia University* (1955).

Burgh, Hubert de, d. 1243, chief justiciar of England under kings John and HENRY III. Having served as a royal minister and commander in France, he was appointed justiciar by John in 1215. He continued in this position after John's death (1216) and in 1217 took part in the defeat of the French fleet at Sandwich that led to the withdrawal of Prince Louis (later LOUIS VII of France) from England. Thereafter the justiciar rapidly became the most powerful man in the government of the young Henry III. His administration temporarily strengthened the position of the crown against the unruly barons, but his own territorial acquisitions made him many enemies. After 1227, when Henry was declared of age, relations between Hubert and the king deteriorated. Hubert tried to prevent the king's disastrous expedition to France (1230); he also apparently approved the widespread English movement to resist the drain of money to the papacy. In the meantime the justiciar's longtime rival Peter des ROCHES intrigued against him, and finally in 1232 Hubert was deprived of office on charges of disloyalty to the crown. He was imprisoned but eventually became reconciled with Henry and successfully withstood a revival of the old charges in 1239. See biography by Clarence Ellis (1952).

Burgh, Ulick de, earl of Clanricarde: see CLANRICARDE, ULICK DE BURGH, 5TH EARL OF.

Burghers, in the 18th cent., a party of the Secession Church of Scotland, resulting from one of the "breaches" in the history of Presbyterianism. To qualify as a burgess in certain burghs one was required to take an oath accepting the "true religion presently professed within this realm." Opinion differed as to whether this referred to the Protestant religion in general or to the Established Church. Those in the Secession Church who understood the oath in the former sense were the "Burghers," or the Associate Synod. Opposed to them were the Anti-Burghers, or the General Associate Synod, who refused to take the oath. The two bodies mutually excluded each other in 1747. By the end of the century both divisions were further split apart into "Old Light Anti-Burghers" and "Old Light Burghers" and "New Lights" in each division, over questions of civil magistracy. In 1820 Old Lights and New Lights were brought together again in the United Secession Church.

Burghley or **Burleigh, William Cecil,** Ist **Baron** (both: bûr'lē), 1520–98, English statesman. He first rose to prominence during the protectorate of Edward Seymour, duke of Somerset, and he served as secretary of state (1550–53) during the ascendancy of John Dudley, duke of Northumberland. He avoided direct involvement in Northumberland's seizure (1553) of the throne for Lady Jane Grey and thus did not lose favor when Mary I succeeded. Although he held no office during her reign, he was sent on several diplomatic missions and sat in Parliament. He was reappointed to office by ELIZABETH I, whom he served faithfully for 40 years—as secretary (1558–72) and as lord treasurer (1572–98). He continued to sit in Parliament, as a commoner until 1571 and as Lord Burghley thereafter, and was Elizabeth's chief spokesman there, as well as administrative head of her government. One of his greatest skills was his ability to function as a liaison, representing royal policy to Parliament and keeping Elizabeth in touch with its feelings. His personal religious sympathies were with the Puritans, but politically he considered the interests of the country best served by a middle-of-the-road Anglican church, which he supported against both Protestant and Roman Catholic extremes. He urged Elizabeth to marry and perpetuate a Protestant Tudor house, and he supported the cause of the Scottish Protestants against the Roman Catholic Mary Queen of Scots. He was not able to maintain a policy of moderation, however. A succession of Catholic plots against Elizabeth led to increasing harshness toward Catholics generally and finally the execution of Mary Queen of Scots. In the privy council Burghley took a decisive role in the suppression of the Catholic revolts, but he was opposed to the entrance of England into European wars on behalf of the Protestants. This policy was defeated (1585) by the Puritan wing of the council under Robert Dudley, earl of Leicester, and Sir Francis Walsingham. Although Elizabeth's favorites often opposed Burghley's influence, his role as chief adviser was never seriously challenged. See biography by B. W. Beckingsale (1967); Conyers Read, *Secretary Cecil and Queen Elizabeth* (1955) and *Lord Burghley and Queen Elizabeth* (1960).

Burgis, William (bûr'jĭs), fl. 1717–31, American engraver and publisher of maps and views, b. London. His name appears as publisher on the views *South Prospect of ye Flourishing City of New York* (1717; copy, N.Y. Historical Society); *The New Dutch Church in New York City; A Prospect of the Colledges in Cambridge in New England* (only known copy, Massachusetts Historical Society, Boston); *A South East View of the Great Town of Boston;* and *Plan of Boston in New England* (copy, Lib. of Congress, Washington, D.C.). The mezzotint *The Boston Light House* is the only plate which contains Burgis's name as engraver (copy, U.S. Lighthouse Board, Washington, D.C.).

Burgkmair or **Burckmair, Hans** (both: häns bo͝ork'mīər), 1473–1531, German engraver, woodcut designer, and painter. Having learned woodcutting from Schongauer, he settled in 1498 in his native Augsburg. His work shows the influence of his friend Dürer, whose enthusiasm for the Italian Renaissance he shared. Among his well-known paintings are the *Rosary Altar* (Augsburg) and *Holy Family* (1511; Berlin). After c.1508 he executed designs for woodcuts for Emperor Maximilian I; among these prints a series of episodes in the emperor's life is notable. Among his other works of graphic art are *Death as Destroyer* (1520) and *Virtues and Vices.*

burglary, at COMMON LAW, the breaking and entering of a dwelling house of another at night with the intent to commit a FELONY, whether the intent is carried out or not. This definition has been generally adopted with some modifications in the criminal law of the various states of the United States. At common law burglary is primarily an offense against the security of habitation, not against the property as such, but today by statute burglary usually includes breaking into places other than dwellings. Breaking as well as entering is essential to commission of the crime; to constitute a breaking, the use of physical force is necessary and sufficient, even though the amount of force may be slight, e.g., turning a key, opening a partly closed window, pushing out a windowpane. Entry through FRAUD (as by posing as a guest), through THREAT, or through CONSPIRACY with servants is deemed by the law equivalent to breaking and is called "constructive breaking." By statute most states do not restrict burglary to action at night, as the common law does. Burglary under common law requires that the intent be to commit a felony, but some statutes declare that the intent need only be "to commit some crime." See ROBBERY.

Bürglen (bürk'lən), town (1970 pop. 3,401), Uri canton, central Switzerland. It is the legendary birthplace of William TELL. A 16th-century chapel stands on the supposed site of Tell's house.

Burgos (bo͝or'gōs), city (1970 pop. 119,915), capital of Burgos prov., N Spain, in Old Castile, on a mountainous plateau c.2,800 ft (850 m) above sea level, near the Arlanzón River. It is an important trade center with a large tourist industry. It was one of the ancient capitals of Castile but is chiefly known for its outstanding architecture and great historic tradition. Founded c.855, it was the seat of the county of Castile under the kings of León and became the capital of the kingdom of Castile under Ferdinand I (1035). The royal residence was moved (1087) to Toledo, and Burgos lost some of its cultural importance. In the civil war of 1936–39, Burgos was the capital of Franco's regime. Its most notable building is the cathedral of white limestone, begun in 1221, one of the finest examples of Gothic architecture in Europe; its lofty, filigree spires dominate the city. The CID, a native of Burgos, is buried in the cathedral. Among the many other landmarks are the castle, atop a hill overlooking the city; the Gothic Church of San Esteban, and the Arco de Santa María, a 16th-century gateway leading to the cathedral.

Burgoyne, John (bərgoin'), 1722–92, British general and playwright. In the Seven Years War, his victory over the Spanish in storming (1762) Valencia de Alcántara in Portugal made him the toast of London. He was elected to Parliament in 1761 and took his seat in 1763. In 1772 his attack on the East India Company helped bring about some reform of the company in the Regulating Act of that year. As the American Revolution was beginning, he was sent (1775) with reinforcements to support General Gage at Boston. Burgoyne witnessed the battle of Bunker Hill and returned home in disgust (Dec., 1775). He joined (1776) Sir Guy Carleton in Canada and served at Crown Point; but, critical of Sir Guy's inaction, Burgoyne returned to England to join Lord George Germain in laying the plans that resulted in the SARATOGA CAMPAIGN. In the summer of 1777, Burgoyne began the ill-fated expedition with an army poorly equipped, untrained for frontier fighting, and numbering far less than he had requested. After minor initial success, stiffened American resistance coupled with the failure of Barry ST. LEGER and Sir William HOWE to reach Albany led to his surrender at Saratoga (Oct. 17, 1777). He returned to England, was given (1782) a command in Ireland, and managed the impeachment of Warren HASTINGS. Burgoyne wrote several plays, of which *The Heiress* (1786) is best known. See biographies by Showell Styles (1962) and N. B. Gerson (1973). His illegitimate son **Sir John Fox Burgoyne** (1782–1871) served with distinction in the Peninsular War. In the Crimean War his advice was followed in attacking Sevastopol from the south—an action that led to a long and hard siege. He was created field marshal in 1868.

bur grass: see SANDBUR.

Burgundians, medieval French political faction: see ARMAGNACS AND BURGUNDIANS.

Burgundy (bûr'gəndē), Fr. *Bourgogne* (bo͝orgô'nyə), historic region, E France. The name once applied to a large area embracing several kingdoms, a free county (see FRANCHE-COMTÉ), and a duchy. The present region is identical with the province of Burgundy of the 17th and 18th cent. It is now administratively divided into the departments of Yonne, Côte-d'Or, Saône-et-Loire, Ain, and Nièvre. Burgundy west of the Saône River is generally hilly; the southeast includes the southern spurs of the Jura mts.; the center is a lowland, extending south almost to the junction of the Saône and Rhône rivers (see BRESSE). A rich agricultural country, Burgundy is especially famous for the wine produced in the Chablis region, the mountains of the Côte d'Or, and the Saône and Rhône valleys. Dijon is the historic capital; other cities are Autun, Auxerre, Beaune, Bourg-en-Bresse, Chalon-sur-Saône, and Mâcon. The territory, conquered by Caesar in the GALLIC WARS, was divided first into the Roman provinces of Lugdunensis and Belgic Gaul, then into Lugdunensis and Upper Germany (see GAUL). It prospered, and Autun became a major intellectual center. In the 4th cent. Roman power dissolved, and the country was invaded by Germanic tribes. It was finally conquered (c.480) by the Burgundii, a tribe from Savoy. The Burgundii accepted Christianity, established their *Lex Burgundionum,* and formed the First Kingdom of Burgundy, which at its height covered SE France and reached as far south as Arles and W Switzerland. Conquered (534) by the FRANKS, it was throughout the Merovingian period subjected to numerous partitions. Burgundy nevertheless survived as a political concept, and after the partitions of the Carolingian empire two new Burgundian kingdoms were founded, Cisjurane Burgundy, or PROVENCE, in the south (879) and Transjurane Burgundy in the north (888). These two were united (933) in the Second Kingdom of Burgundy (see ARLES, KINGDOM OF). A smaller area, corresponding roughly to present Burgundy, was created as the duchy of Burgundy by Emperor Charles II in 877. In 1002, King Robert II of France made good his claim to the duchy, but his son, Henry I, gave it in 1031 as a fief to his brother Robert, whose line died out in 1361. The golden age of Burgundy began (1364) when John II of France bestowed the fief on his son, PHILIP THE BOLD, thus founding the line of Valois-Bourgogne. Philip and his successors, JOHN THE FEARLESS, PHILIP THE GOOD, and CHARLES THE BOLD, acquired—by conquest, treaty, and marriage—vast territories, including most of the present Netherlands and Belgium, the then extensive duchy of Luxembourg, Picardy, Artois, Lorraine, S Baden, Alsace, the Franche-Comté, Nivernais, and Charolais. In the early 15th cent. the dukes of Burgundy, through their partisans in France, dominated French politics (see ARMAGNACS AND BURGUNDIANS). England, at first supported by Burgundy in the HUNDRED YEARS WAR, suffered a crucial setback when Philip the Good withdrew that support in the Treaty of Arras (1435). A great power, Burgundy at that time had the most important trade, industry, and agriculture of Europe. Its court, a center of the arts, was second to none. The wars of ambitious Charles the Bold, however, proved ruinous. Charles, opposed by the determined and resourceful Louis XI of France, was defeated by the Swiss at Grandson, Morat (1476), and Nancy (1477), where he lost his life. His daughter, MARY OF BURGUNDY, by marrying Emperor Maximilian I, brought most of the Burgundian possessions (but not the original French duchy) to the house of Hapsburg. The duchy itself was seized by Louis XI, who incorporated it into the French crownlands as a province, to which Gex, Bresse, and Charolais were added later by Henry IV and Louis XIV. See studies by Richard Vaughan (1962, 1966, and 1970); Otto Cartellieri, *The Court of Burgundy* (1929, repr. 1972).

Burgundy mixture: see BORDEAUX MIXTURE.

Burhanpur (bûr'hänpo͝or"), town (1971 pop. 105,349), Madhya Pradesh state, W central India, on the Tapti River. It trades in cotton and oilseed, and is known for its gold and silver embroidery. Founded c.1400, Burhanpur has a partially ruined palace (c.1610) of Akbar.

burial, disposal of a corpse in a GRAVE or TOMB. The first evidence of deliberate burial was found in European caves of the Paleolithic period. Prehistoric discoveries include both individual and communal burials, the latter indicating that pits or ossuaries were unsealed for later use or that servants or members of the family were slain to accompany the deceased. Both practices have been followed by various peoples into modern times. The ancient Egyptians developed the coffin to keep bodies from touching the earth; this burial practice was continued by the Greeks and Romans when they used the burial form of disposal. The word *burial* has been applied to funerary practices other than interment, such as sea burial, or tree burial (which usually precedes later interment). Secondary burial frequently occurs to terminate a period of mourning (see FUNERAL CUSTOMS). See also CEMETERY.

Buriat-Mongolia: see BURYAT AUTONOMOUS SOVIET SOCIALIST REPUBLIC.

Buridan, Jean (byo͝or'ĭdən, Fr. zhäN bürēdäN'), d. c.1358, French scholastic philosopher. Rector of the Univ. of Paris, he was a follower of William of Occam and a nominalist. His theory of the will was that choice is determined by the greater good and that the freedom man possesses is the power to suspend choice and reconsider motives for action. Traditionally but almost certainly erroneously he is supposed to have used the simile of "Buridan's ass"—an unfortunate animal midway between two identical bundles of hay and starving to death because it cannot choose between them.

Burkburnett (bûrkbərnĕt'), city (1970 pop. 9,230), Wichita co., N Texas, near the Okla. line; inc. 1913. A shipping center for livestock, cotton, and wheat, it also has many oil wells and refineries. The area's first big gusher (1918) brought a boom that transformed the quiet little community into one of the wildest and roughest of all the oil towns; at one time its population approached 30,000.

Burke, Edmund, 1729–97, British political writer and statesman, b. Dublin, Ireland. The son of a Protestant father and a Roman Catholic mother and himself a Protestant, he never ceased to criticize the stupidity of the English administration in Ireland and the galling discrimination against Catholics. After graduating (1748) from Trinity College, Dublin, he began the study of law in London but abandoned it to devote himself to writing. His satirical *Vindication of Natural Society* (1756) attacked the political rationalism and religious skepticism of Henry St. John, Viscount Bolingbroke, and his *Philosophical Enquiry into the Origin of Our Ideas of the Sublime and Beautiful* (1757) was a study in aesthetics. In 1759 he founded the *Annual Register,* a periodical to which he contributed until 1788. Burke was a member of Samuel Johnson's intimate circle. His political career began in 1765 when he became private secretary to the marquess of ROCKINGHAM, then prime minister, and formed a lifelong friendship with that leader. He also entered Parliament in 1765 and there strove for a wiser treatment of the American colonies. In 1766 he spoke in favor of the repeal of the Stamp Act, although he also supported the Declaratory Act, asserting Britain's constitutional right to tax the colonists. In his famous later speeches on American taxation (1774) and on conciliation with the colonies (1775), he did not abandon that position; rather he urged the imprudence of exercising such theoretical rights. At a time when political allegiances were based largely on family connections and patronage and political opposition was generally regarded as factionalism, Burke, in his *Thoughts on the Cause of the Present Discontents* (1770), became the first political philosopher to argue the value of political parties. He called for a limitation of crown patronage (so-called "economical reform") and as postmaster general (1782–83) in the second Rockingham ministry was able to enact some of his proposals. He was also interested in reform of the East India Company and drafted the East India Bill presented (1783) by Charles James FOX. Influenced by Sir Philip FRANCIS, he also instigated the impeachment and long trial of Warren HASTINGS. Hastings was acquitted, but Burke's speeches created some new awareness of the responsibilities of empire and of the injustices perpetrated in India and previously unpublicized in England. Although he championed many liberal and reform causes, Burke believed that political, social, and religious institutions represented the wisdom of the ages; he feared political reform beyond limitations on the power of the crown. Consequently, his *Reflections on the Revolution in France* (1790) made him the spokesman of European conservatives. His stand against the French Revolution—and, by implication, against parliamentary reform—caused him to break with Fox and his Whigs in 1791. Burke's *Appeal from the New to the Old Whigs* (1791) shows how closely he approached the Tory position of the younger William PITT. Burke left, in his many and diverse writings a monumental construction of British political thought that had far-reaching influence among conservatives in England, America, and France for many years. He held unrestricted rationalism in human affairs to be destructive and affirmed the utility of habit and prejudice and the importance of continuity in political experience. He withdrew from political life in 1795. See his correspondence (9 vol., 1958–70); selections ed. by W. J. Bate (1960); biography by P. M. Magnus (1939, repr. 1973); studies by T. W. Copeland (1949, repr. 1970), Charles Parkin (1956, repr. 1968), C. B. Cone (2 vol., 1957–64), P. J. Stanlis (1958, repr. 1965); G. W. Chapman (1967), Russell Kirk (1967), and B. T. Wilkins (1967).

Burke, John, 1787–1848, Irish genealogist. He issued (1826) *A Genealogical and Heraldic Dictionary of the Peerage and Baronetage of the United Kingdom.* He published the guide irregularly until 1847, after which it became an annual, commonly called *Burke's Peerage.* It was edited from 1847 to 1892 by his son, **Sir John Bernard Burke,** 1814–92, who was knighted (1854) and appointed (1855) keeper of the state papers in Ireland. As a companion to *Burke's Peerage,* he established the regular publication of another work begun by his father, commonly called *Burke's Landed Gentry.* His other works include *The Romance of the Aristocracy* (1855) and *Vicissitudes of Families* (1859–63).

Burke, Kenneth, 1897–, American critic, b. Pittsburgh, Pa. He was music critic for *The Dial* (1927–29) and *The Nation* (1934–36). A profound thinker whose writings have influenced other critics, Burke sees literature as "symbolic action"—man must view everything through a haze of symbols (language). Among his works are *Counter-Statement* (1931); *Attitudes Towards History* (1937); *A Grammar of Motives* (1962); *Collected Poems* (1968); and *The Complete White Oxen* (1968), short fiction.

Burke, Robert O'Hara, 1820–61, Irish explorer of Australia. After service in the Belgian and Austrian armies he went (1853) as inspector of police to Melbourne. In 1860, with W. J. Wills and eight other whites, he left Menindee, on the Darling River, to cross the continent. Dissensions broke up the party, but the leaders reached the estuary of the Flinders River, in the Gulf of Carpentaria. On the return journey both Burke and Wills died from famine and exposure. Although the geographical achievements of the expedition itself were few, rescue parties seeking it added much to the knowledge of central Australia. See C. G. D. Roberts, *Discoveries and Explorations in the Century* (1906); Max Colwell, *The Journey of Burke and Wills* (1971).

Burlamaqui, Jean Jacques (zhäN zhäk bo͝orlämäkē'), 1694–1748, Swiss jurist. His chief works are *Principes du droit naturel* [principles of natural law] (1747) and *Principes du droit politique* [principles of political law] (1751). He attempted to demonstrate the reality of natural law by tracing its origin in God's rule and in human reason and moral instinct. He believed that both international and domestic law were based on natural law.

Burleigh, Henry Thacker (bûr'lē), 1866–1949, American baritone and composer, b. Erie, Pa.; pupil of Dvořák at the National Conservatory, New York, where he later taught. He was soloist at St. George's Church, New York City, from 1892 to 1946 and also at Temple Emanu-El for 25 years. His concert arrangements of Negro spirituals such as *Deep River,* employing chromatic harmonies in the style of art songs, are widely used.

Burleigh, William Cecil, 1st **Baron:** see BURGHLEY.

Burleson, Albert Sidney (bûr'ləsən), 1863–1937, U.S. Postmaster General (1913–21), b. San Marcos, Texas; grandson of Edward Burleson. He was a lawyer of Austin, Texas, and a member of the U.S. House of Representatives (1899–1913) before resigning to take a cabinet post under President Wilson. His methods of administering communications in World War I angered many: businessmen, who charged him with inefficiency and interference with private business; labor unions, because he forbade strikes of postal employees; and liberals, whose antiwar periodicals he banned from the mails. Burleson continued to exercise strict control and to advocate government ownership of communications. In 1918 he established airmail service.

Burleson, Edward, 1798–1851, pioneer of Texas, b. Buncombe co., N.C. After living in Tennessee and serving under Andrew Jackson in the war against the Creek Indians (1813–14), he moved to Texas. He distinguished himself in the Texas Revolution and was later (1840) successful in the warfare against the Cherokee in East Texas. Burleson was a senator, then vice president of the Republic of Texas, but was defeated for the presidency in 1844. He also served in the Mexican War.

burlesque (bûrlĕsk′) [Ital.,=mockery], form of entertainment differing from comedy or farce in that it achieves its effects through caricature, ridicule, and distortion. It differs from satire in that it is devoid of any ethical element. The word first came into use in the 16th cent. in an opera of the Italian Francesco Berni, who called his works *burleschi.* Early English burlesque often ridiculed celebrated literary works, especially sentimental drama. Beaumont and Fletcher's *Knight of the Burning Pestle* (1613), Buckingham's *The Rehearsal* (1671), Gay's *Beggar's Opera* (1728), Fielding's *Tom Thumb* (1730), and Sheridan's *Critic* (1779) may be classed as dramatic burlesque. In the 19th cent. English burlesque depended less on parody of literary styles and models. H. J. Bryon was a major writer of the new, pun-filled burlesque. The extravaganza and burletta were forms of amusement similar to burlesque, the latter being primarily a musical production. They were performed in small theaters in an effort to evade the strict licensing laws that forbade major dramatic productions to these theaters. American stage burlesque (from 1865), often referred to as "burleycue" or "leg show," began as a variety show, characterized by vulgar dialogue and broad comedy, and uninhibited behavior by performers and audience. Such stars as Al Jolson, W. C. Fields, Mae West, Fannie Brice, Sophie Tucker, Bert Lahr, and Joe Weber and Lew Fields began their careers in burlesque. About 1920 the term began to refer to the "strip-tease" show, which created its own stars, such as Gypsy Rose Lee; in c.1937 burlesque performances in New York City were banned. With the increase in popularity of nightclubs and movies, the burlesque entertainment died. See studies by C. V. Clinton-Baddeley (1952, repr. 1974); R. P. Bond (1932, repr. 1964), and J. D. Jump (1972).

Burlin, Natalie Curtis, 1875–1921, American writer and musician, b. New York City, studied music in France and Germany. She was one of the leading transcribers of the primitive music of America and Africa, and it was through her efforts that Indian music was encouraged, rather than forbidden by law, in government schools. She visited the Navaho, Zuñi, Hopi, and other Indian tribes, recording words and music with fidelity. Songs of African tribes and American Negroes are also included in her works—*Songs of Ancient America* (1905), *The Indians' Book* (1907), *Hampton Series Negro Folk-Songs* (4 vol., 1918–19), and *Songs and Tales from the Dark Continent* (1920).

Burlingame, Anson (bûr′lĭng-gām), 1820–70, American diplomat, b. New Berlin, N.Y. He became a lawyer in Boston and later (1855–61) a Congressman. Defeated for reelection, he was made (1861) minister to China. By his tact and understanding of Chinese opposition to the autocratic methods of foreigners in the treaty ports, he won a place as adviser to the Chinese government. In 1867, China sent him as head of a mission to visit foreign lands in order to secure information and sign treaties of amity. He visited Washington, London, and capitals on the Continent. One result was a treaty between China and the United States, supplementary to the 1858 treaty. This, usually called the **Burlingame Treaty,** was signed in 1868. It was a treaty of friendship based on Western principles of international law. One clause encouraged Chinese immigration—laborers were then much in demand in the West; later the heavy influx of Chinese under its provisions caused friction on the West Coast and led to the exclusion of Chinese immigrants (see CHINESE EXCLUSION). See biography by F. W. Williams (1912, repr. 1972).

Burlingame, city (1970 pop. 27,320), San Mateo co., W Calif., on San Francisco Bay; founded 1868, inc. 1908. Burlingame is mainly residential, with some commercial and light industries. The city is named for U.S. diplomat Anson Burlingame.

Burlingame Treaty: see under BURLINGAME, ANSON.

Burlington, Richard Boyle, 3d earl of, 1694–1753, English patron and architect of the Neo-Palladian movement. Even before age 21, when he became a member of the Privy Council and Lord High Treasurer of Ireland, he showed an interest in architecture. In 1714, Burlington made a tour of Italy and also subscribed to the *Vitruvius Britannicus* of Colin CAMPBELL. He employed Campbell to remodel the Burlington House in London (c.1717). In 1719, Burlington was again in Italy, specifically to study the architecture of Palladio. Through his patronage of other artists, notably William Kent, and in his own buildings, he furthered the revival of an architecture based on the styles of Palladio and Inigo Jones. The most important of Burlington's own works are the villa for his estate at Chiswick (begun 1725) and the Assembly Room, York (1730).

Burlington, town (1971 pop. 87,023), SE Ont., Canada, on Lake Ontario. It is a suburb of Hamilton.

Burlington. 1 City (1970 pop. 32,366), seat of Des Moines co., SE Iowa, on four hills overlooking the Mississippi (spanned there by rail and highway bridges); inc. 1836. It is a farm, shipping, and manufacturing center with railroad shops and docks. Zebulon Pike selected this spot for a fort in 1805. An Indian village, Sho-quo-quon ("Flint Hills") was there. White settlement began in 1833. Burlington was the temporary capital of Wisconsin Territory (1837) and of Iowa Territory (1838–40). One of the oldest newspapers in the state, the Burlington *Hawk-Eye,* is still published. The city has a junior college and several parks along the Mississippi. **2** Town (1970 pop. 21,980), Middlesex co., E Mass., a residential suburb of Boston, in a farm area; settled 1641, inc. 1799. Its pre-Revolutionary meetinghouse, remodeled, still stands. **3** City (1970 pop. 11,991), Burlington co., W N.J., on the Delaware (bridged there to Bristol, Pa.) between Trenton and Camden, in a rich farm area; settled 1677 by Friends, inc. 1733. A shipping point for farm and dairy products, it also has varied manufactures. Burlington grew mainly as a port; it was capital of West Jersey from 1681 until the union of East and West Jersey (1702), and thereafter until 1790 was alternate capital with Perth Amboy. It was on a Philadelphia–New York coach line, and railroad tracks were laid down Broad St. in 1834. The first colonial money was printed there by Benjamin Franklin in 1726, and the first newspaper in New Jersey appeared in 1777. G. W. Doane, for many years rector of old St. Mary's (built 1703), founded St. Mary's Hall for girls there (1837). The newer St. Mary's church was designed by Richard Upjohn. The Friends' school (1792; now the Y.W.C.A.) and meetinghouse (1784) still stand. The birthplaces of James Fenimore Cooper and of James Lawrence are preserved. **4** City (1970 pop. 35,930), Alamance co., N N.C., on the Haw River; settled c.1700, inc. 1866. It is a great textile center in a heavily industrialized area, with plants manufacturing textiles, hosiery, and yarn. In May, 1771, 2,000 colonial "Regulators" clashed with British troops c.5 mi (8 km) south of Burlington; the site is in Alamance Battleground State Park. In the city are a notable wildlife museum and the Technical Institute of Alamance. Elon College is to the west. **5** City (1970 pop. 38,633), seat of Chittenden co., NW Vt., on Lake Champlain; settled 1773, inc. 1865. The largest city in the state, it is a port of entry and a major industrial center. Missile and ordnance parts, data-processing machinery, textiles, canned goods, and wood and steel products are its chief manufactures. Battery Park, famous for sunset views, was the scene of an abortive British naval attack (Aug. 3, 1813) during the War of 1812. The city is the seat of the Univ. of Vermont, Trinity College, and Champlain College (a junior college). American Revolutionary hero Ethan Allen spent his last years near Burlington village (part of his farm is included in Ethan Allen Park) and is buried nearby. The Burlington *Free Press* (founded 1827) became Vermont's first daily newspaper in 1848. The philosopher John Dewey was born in the city.

Burma, Union of, republic (1969 est. pop. 26,980,000), 261,789 sq mi (678,033 sq km), SE Asia. The capital is RANGOON. Burma is bounded on the W by Bangladesh, India, and the Bay of Bengal, on the N and NE by China, on the E by Laos and Thailand, and on the S by the Andaman Sea. The most densely populated part of the country is the valley of the Irrawaddy River, which, with its vast delta, is one of the main rice-growing regions of the world. MANDALAY, the country's second largest city, is on the Irrawaddy in central Burma. The Irrawaddy basin is inhabited by the Burmans proper, a Mongoloid race who came down from Tibet by the 9th cent. The valley is surrounded by a chain of mountains that stem from the E Himalayas and spread out roughly in the shape of a giant horseshoe; the ranges and river valleys of the Chindwin (a tributary of the Irrawaddy) and of the Sittang and the Salween (both to

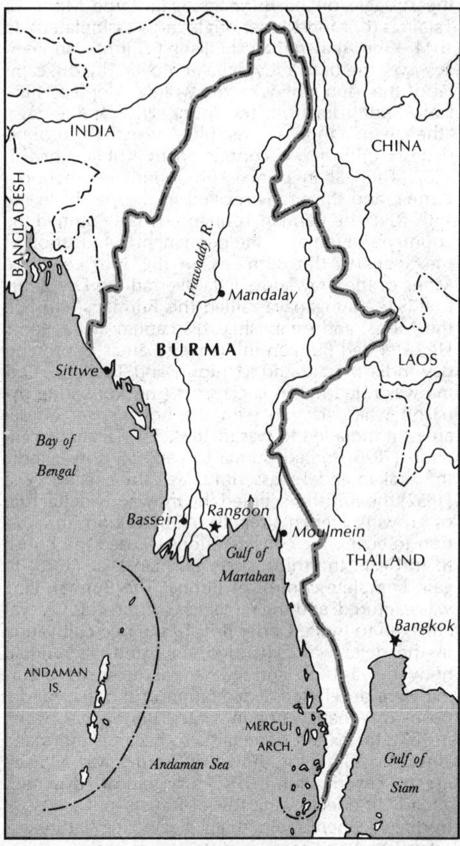

the E of the Irrawaddy) trend from north to south. In the mountains of N Burma (rising to more than 19,000 ft/5,791 m) and along the India-Burma frontier live various Mongoloid peoples; the most important are the Kachins (in the Kachin State in the north) and the Chins (in the Chin Special Division in the west). These peoples practice shifting cultivation (*taungya*) and cut teak in the forests. Between the Bay of Bengal and the hills of the Arakan Yoma is the ARAKAN, a narrow coastal plain with the port of SITTWE. In E Burma on the Shan Plateau is the SHAN STATE, home of the Shans, a Tai race closely related to the Siamese. South of the Shan State are the mountainous Kayah State and the Kawthule State; the Karens, who inhabit this region, are of Tai-Chinese origin, and many are Christians. South of the Kawthule State is the TENASSERIM region, a long, narrow strip of coast extending to the Isthmus of Kra. At its northern end is the port of MOULMEIN, Burma's third largest city. Most of Burma has a tropical, monsoon climate; however, N of the Pegu Hills around Mandalay is the so-called Dry Zone with a rainfall of 20 to 40 in. (51–102 cm). On the Shan Plateau temperatures are moderate. Burma suffered extensive damage in World War II, and some sectors of its economy have not yet fully recovered. Most of the population work in agriculture and forestry, and rice accounts for about half of the agricultural output. (Until 1964, Burma was the world's largest rice exporter.) Other important crops are sugarcane, groundnuts, and pulses. Burma's forests, which are government-owned, are the source of teak and other hardwoods. The country is rich in minerals. Petroleum is found E of the Irrawaddy in the Dry Zone. Tin and tungsten are mined in E Burma; the Mawchi mines in Kayah State are also rich in tungsten. In the Shan State, NW of Lashio, are the Bawdwin mines, the source of lead, silver, and zinc. Coal and iron deposits have also been found in Burma. Gems (notably rubies and sapphires) are found near MOGOK. Since the 13th cent., Burma has exported to China jade from the Hunkawng valley in the north. Aside from food-processing establishments, there are few manufacturing industries in Burma. The country's chief trade partners are Japan, Great Britain, West Germany, and India. Rice and teak are the leading exports, and machinery, transportation equipment, and textiles are the chief imports. Hinayana Buddhism is the religion of about 85% of the population. Burmese (the tongue of the Burmans) is the official language, but the Shans, Kachins, and Karens speak their own languages; in all, over 100 languages are spoken in Burma. There are colleges and universities in Rangoon and Mandalay.

History. Burma's early history is mainly the story of the struggle of the Burmans against the Mons, or Talaings (of Mon-Khmer origin, now assimilated). In 1044, King Anawratha established Burman supremacy over the Irrawaddy delta and over Thaton, capital of the Mon kingdom. Anawratha adopted Hinayana Buddhism from the Mons. His capital, Paga, "the city of a thousand temples," was the seat of his dynasty until it was conquered by Kublai Khan in 1287. Then Shan princes predominated in upper Burma, and the Mons revived in the south. In the 16th cent. the Burman Toungoo dynasty unified the country and initiated the permanent subjugation of the Shans to the Burmans. In the 18th cent. the Mons of the Irrawaddy delta overran the Dry Zone. In 1758, Alaungapaya rallied the Burmans, crushed the Mons, and established his capital at Rangoon. He extended Burman influence to areas in present-day India (Assam and Manipur) and Thailand. Burma was ruled by his successors (the Konbaung dynasty) when friction with the British over border areas in India led to war in 1824. The Treaty of Yandabo (1826) forced Burma to cede to British India the Arakan and Tenasserim coasts. In a second war (1852) the British occupied the Irrawaddy delta. Fear of growing French strength in the region, in addition to economic considerations, caused the British to instigate the third Anglo-Burman War (1885) to gain complete control of Burma. The Burman king was captured, and the remainder of the country was annexed to India. Under British rule rice cultivation in the delta was expanded, an extensive railroad network was built, and the natural resources of Burma were developed. Exploitation of the rich oil deposits of Yenangyaung in central Burma was begun in 1871; the export of metals also became important. Until the 20th cent., however, Burma was allowed no self-government. In 1923 a system of "dyarchy," already in effect in the rest of British India, was introduced, whereby a partially elected legislature was established and some ministers were made responsible to it. In 1935 the British gave Burma a new constitution (effective 1937), which separated the country from British India and provided for a fully elected assembly and a responsible cabinet. During World War II, Burma was invaded and quickly occupied by the Japanese, who set up a nominally independent Burman regime under Dr. Ba Maw. Disillusioned members of the Burmese Independent Army (which the Japanese had formed secretly before the war to assist in expelling the British) under Aung San formed an anti-Japanese resistance movement, the Anti-Fascist People's Freedom League (AFPFL). Allied forces drove the Japanese out of Burma in April, 1945. In 1947 the British and Aung San reached agreement on full independence for Burma. Most of the non-Burman peoples supported the agreement, although the acquiescence of many proved short-lived. Despite the assassination of Aung San in July, 1947, the agreement went into effect in Jan., 1948. Burma became an independent republic outside the British Commonwealth of Nations. The new constitution provided for a bicameral legislature with a responsible prime minister and cabinet. Non-Burman areas were organized as the Shan, Kachin, Kawthule, and Kayah states and the Chin Special Division; each possessed a degree of autonomy. The government, controlled by the socialist AFPFL, was soon faced with armed risings of Communist rebels and of Karen tribesmen, who wanted a separate Karen nation. International tension grew over the presence in Burma of Chinese Nationalist troops who had been forced across the border by the Chinese Communists in 1950 and who were making forays into China. Burma took the matter to the United Nations, which in 1953 ordered the Nationalists to leave Burma. In foreign affairs Burma has followed a generally neutralist course. It refused to join the Southeast Asia Treaty Organization and was one of the first countries to recognize the Communist government in China. In the elections of 1951–52 the AFPFL triumphed. The AFPFL leaders intended to socialize the country rapidly, but lower rice prices after the Korean War and a shortage of trained personnel forced the abandonment of most of the plans. In 1958 the AFPFL split into two factions; with a breakdown of order threatening, Premier U Nu invited General Ne Win, head of the army, to take over the government (Oct., 1958). After the 1960 elections, which were won by U Nu's faction, civilian government was restored. However, as rebellions among the minorities flared and opposition to U Nu's plan to make Buddhism the state religion mounted, conditions deteriorated rapidly. In March, 1962, Ne Win staged a military coup, discarded the constitution, and established a Revolutionary Council, made up of military leaders who ruled by decree. While the federal structure was retained, a hierarchy of workers' and peasants' councils was created. A new party, the Burma Socialist Program party, was made the only legal political organization. The Revolutionary Council fully nationalized the industrial and commercial sectors of the economy. Discussions were entered into with the minority peoples in 1963, but no agreement was reached. Insurgency became a major problem of the Ne Win regime. Pro-Chinese Communist rebels—the "White Flag" Communists—were active in the northern part of the country, where, from 1967 on, they received aid from Communist China; the Chinese established links with the Shan and Kachin insurgents as well. The deposed U Nu, who managed to leave Burma in 1969, also used minority rebels to organize an anti-Ne Win movement, the National Liberation Council, among the Shans, Karens, and others in the east. However, in 1972, U Nu split with minority leaders over their assertion of the right to secede from Burma. By the early 1970s the various insurgent groups controlled about one third of Burma. Ne Win and other top leaders resigned from the military in 1972 but continued to retain power. A new constitution, providing for a unicameral legislature and one legal political party, took effect in Mar., 1974, and the Revolutionary Council was disbanded. Ne Win continued as prime minister. See J. F. Cady, *A History of Modern Burma* (1958); F. N. Trager, *Burma: From Kingdom to Republic* (1966); M. Htin Aung, *A History of Burma* (1967); Hugh Tinker, *The Union of Burma* (4th ed. 1967); F. S. Donnison, *Burma* (1970); Norma Bixler, *Burma: A Profile* (1971); J. W. Henderson et al., *Area Handbook for Burma* (1971).

bur marigold or **sticktight,** common name for any species of *Bidens,* a genus of chiefly weedy North American plants of the Compositae (COMPOSITE family) with two-pronged burlike fruits (achenes) that have gained various species such additional names as beggar-ticks, Spanish needles, tickseed, and bootjacks. A few showy yellow-flowered species are occasionally cultivated. Many of the common names are also used for other weeds with burs. Bur marigold is classified in the division MAGNOLIOPHYTA, class Magnoliopsida, order Asterales, family Compositae.

Burma Road, in China and Burma, extending from the Burmese railhead of Lashio to K'un-ming, Yünnan prov., China. About 700 mi (1,130 km) long and constructed through rough mountain country, it was a remarkable engineering achievement. Undertaken by the Chinese after the start of the Sino-Japanese war in 1937 and completed in 1938, it was used to transport war supplies landed at Rangoon and shipped by railroad to Lashio. This traffic increased in importance to China after the Japanese took effective control of the Chinese coast and of Indochina. The Ledo Road (later called the Stilwell Road) from Ledo, India, into Burma was begun in Dec., 1942. In 1944 the Ledo Road reached Myitkyina and was joined to the Burma Road. Both roads have lost their former importance and are in a state of disrepair. See study by Leslie Anders (1965).

Burmese, language belonging to the Tibeto-Burman subfamily of the Sino-Tibetan family of languages (see SINO-TIBETAN LANGUAGES). It is spoken by about 18 million people in the Union of Burma, where it is both the principal and the official language. Burmese can be described as monosyllabic because root words generally consist of a single syllable. Context, word order, and the use of musical pitch or tones, of which Burmese has three, help to differentiate the meanings of the many homonyms. Syllables are often used in combination, thereby increasing the number of ideas that can be expressed. Burmese has its own alphabet, which is ultimately descended from an old script from S India. There is a great difference between the spoken and written forms of the language. See John Okell, *Reference Grammar of Colloquial Burmese* (1969); William S. Cornyn, *Spoken Burmese* (1971).

Burmese cat: see CAT.

burn, injury resulting from exposure to heat, electricity, radiation, or caustic chemicals. Three degrees of burn are commonly recognized. In first-degree burns the outer layer of SKIN, called epidermis, becomes red, sensitive to the touch, and often swollen. Medical attention is not required but application of an ointment may relieve the pain. Second-degree burns are characterized by the variable destruction of epidermis and the formation of blisters; nerve endings may be exposed. The more serious cases should be seen by a physician and care should be taken to avoid infection. Local therapy includes application of a chemical such as silver nitrate to produce a soft crust, reduce the threat of infection, and relieve the pain. Third-degree burns involve destruction of the entire thickness of skin and the underlying connective tissue. In the more severe cases underlying bones are also charred. The surface area involved is more significant than the depth of the burn. SHOCK must be prevented or counteracted; blood transfusion may be required to replace lost body fluids. Invasion of various bacteria must be prevented or cured by administering antibiotics and other drugs. Morphine may be employed to ease pain. Long-term treatment may include TRANSPLANTATION of skin tissue from other parts of the body.

Burne-Jones, Sir Edward, 1833–98. English painter and decorator, b. Birmingham. Expected to enter the Church, he went to Exeter College, Oxford, where he met William MORRIS, who became his lifelong friend. He left Oxford to study painting with Rossetti in London and joined the PRE-RAPHAELITES. Burne-Jones's early work shows Rossetti's strong influence, which was later replaced by his emulation of Botticelli and Mantegna. Burne-Jones rose to success in 1877 with the opening of the Grosvenor Gallery. Among his well-known paintings are *King Cophetua and the Beggar Maid* (1884; Tate Gall., London); *Depths of the Sea;* and *Star of Bethlehem* (Birmingham Gall.). His works described a dreamlike, medieval world, a vision popular with his contemporaries. His designs for stained glass, executed by Morris and Company, may be seen in churches throughout England. Burne-Jones also created the woodcut illustrations for the Kelmscott Press edition of the works of Chaucer. In his day he received many honors, and his delicate, though mannered, work continues to be admired. See his drawings, studies, and paintings, ed. by Piccadilly Gallery (1971); studies by L. D. Cecil (1960) and Martin Harrison and Bill Waters (1973).

Burnes, Sir Alexander, 1805–41, British traveler in India. As an army officer in India, he studied Oriental languages. In 1832 he left Lahore in Afghan dress and traveled by way of Peshawar and Kabul across the Hindu Kush to Balkh and from there by Bukhara, Asterabad, and Teheran to Bushire. On his return to England (1883) he was honored. In 1839 he was appointed political resident at Kabul, where he was assassinated two years later. See his *Narrative of a Visit to the Court of Scinde* (1830), *Travels into Bokhara* (1834), and *Cabool* (1842). See also biography by J. D. Lunt (1969).

Burnet, David Gouverneur, 1788–1870, provisional president of Texas (1836), b. Newark, N.J.; son of William Burnet (1730–91). He went to Texas c.1817, and his legal training enabled him to become a spokesman for the American settlers there as dissension with the Mexican government grew. Appointed (1834) a district judge, he opposed the measures of the Mexican government and was gradually led to favor the independence of Texas from Mexico. In 1836 he drew up the declaration of independence at the convention at Washington-on-the-Brazos, where he was made president ad interim of Texas. His eight-month administration in the chaotic times during and after the revolution (see TEXAS) was not effective. He quarreled bitterly with Sam Houston and thereafter opposed him in politics. Burnet was vice president under Mirabeau B. Lamar, was defeated by Houston for the presidency in 1841, and was chosen in 1866 (because he had opposed secession) U.S. Senator from Texas in the Reconstruction era, but was denied his seat. See biography by Mary Clarke (1969).

Burnet, Gilbert (bûr'nĭt), 1643–1715, British bishop and writer. He studied abroad, held (1665–69) the living of Saltoun in Scotland, and was appointed (1669) professor of divinity at Glasgow Univ. He went to London in 1673 and was lecturer at St. Clements until his defense of his friend Lord William Russell made it unsafe for him in England after the Rye House Plot executions. During James II's reign Burnet's anti-Catholic writing and preaching barred him from court, and he found favor and friendship with William of Orange at The Hague. Accompanying William to England, he was a trusted adviser to William III and Mary and was made bishop of Salisbury. His celebrated *History of My Own Times* (published only 1723–24; ed. by M. J. Routh, 6 vol., 1833) is fiercely biased against James

II, but it is also an informative contemporary source for the period. Burnet made a translation of Sir Thomas More's *Utopia*. He also wrote *History of the Reformation in England* (3 vol., 1679–1714; abridged ed. 1719), notable for its understanding of the economic, social, and cultural causes and effects of the Reformation, and many lesser works on history and theology. See biography by T. E. S. Clarke and H. C. Foxcroft (1907).

Burnet, Sir Macfarlane, 1899–, Australian virologist and physician. He was resident pathologist (1923–24) at the Royal Melbourne Hospital and a Beit fellow (1926–27) at the Lister Institute, London. He became assistant director (1928) and director (1944) of the Walter and Eliza Hall Institute at the Royal Melbourne Hospital. From 1944 he was professor of experimental medicine at the Univ. of Melbourne. He lectured at several universities in the United States, including Harvard (1944), Johns Hopkins (1950), and Vanderbilt (1958). An expert on viruses and virus diseases, Burnet made important contributions to the understanding of influenza and the development of immunity against it. He shared the 1960 Nobel Prize in Medicine and Physiology with P. B. Medawar for their work in immunological tolerances, specifically the reactions of the body to the transplantation of foreign living tissues. His writings include *Natural History of Infectious Disease* (3d ed. 1962) and *Viruses and Man* (2d ed. 1955). See his autobiography (1969).

Burnet, Thomas, c.1635–1715, English cleric and scientist, b. Croft, in Yorkshire, England. He was educated at Northallerton and Cambridge. Following travels in Europe, Burnet published in 1681 the first two parts of his theory of the formation of the earth under the title *Telluris theoria sacra* (English version *Sacred Theory of the Earth,* 1684), in which he held that at the time of the Deluge the earth was crushed like an egg, the fragments of the shell becoming mountains. Burnet's book attracted much attention, and his description of the creation of mountains and his stress on the account of creation in Genesis influenced the new science of geology for a hundred years. In his *Archaeologiae philosophicae* (1692) he treated the account of the fall of man as an allegory. See M. H. Nicolson, *Mountain Gloom and Mountain Glory* (1963).

Burnet, William, 1688–1729, English colonial governor in America; son of Gilbert Burnet. As governor of New York and New Jersey (1720–28), he advocated extending the trade with the Indians, thereby seeking to bind the Iroquois to the British and keep them from French influence—a move that was to be of great significance in the French and Indian Wars. He had the first English fort on the Great Lakes built at Oswego. His efforts to regulate trade were opposed by Albany merchants who made great profit in selling English goods to French traders. Burnet was embroiled in arguments with the assembly over policies and finance. After he dissolved the assembly in 1727, he was transferred to govern Massachusetts and New Hampshire.

Burnet, William, 1730–91, political leader in the American Revolution, b. near the present Elizabeth, N.J.; father of David G. Burnet. A physician practicing in Newark, Burnet was chairman of the Revolutionary committee of safety there. He set up (1775) a military hospital and helped to furnish troops and supplies for the Continental army. He became surgeon general of the army for the eastern district and was also a member of the Continental Congress in 1776 and in 1780.

burnet, hardy perennial herb of the family Rosaceae (ROSE family) found in temperate regions, usually with white or greenish flowers. The European species are sometimes cultivated for the leaves, which are used in salads, for flavoring, and formerly as a poultice to stop bleeding—hence the botanical name *Sanguisorba* [from Lat.,=absorbing blood]. Burnet is classified in the division MAGNOLIOPHYTA, class Magnoliopsida, order Rosales, family Rosaceae.

Burnett, Frances Eliza Hodgson, 1849–1924, American author, b. Manchester, England. In 1865 she went to Knoxville, Tenn. with her family. She is famous for her children's books, particularly *Little Lord Fauntleroy* (1886; successfully dramatized by the author in 1888), *Sara Crewe* (1888), and *The Secret Garden* (1911). See biography by Ann Thwaite (1974).

Burnett, James: see MONBODDO, JAMES BURNETT, LORD.

Burney, Charles, 1726–1814, English music historian, composer, and organist. His *General History of Music* (1776–89; 2d ed., 1935) was one of the first important music histories in English. He wrote *The Present State of Music in France and Italy* (1771) and *The Present State of Music in Germany* (1773). They were published together as *Dr. Burney's Musical Tours in Europe* (1959). The work describes European society, life, and customs as well as music and important musicians. His daughter, the novelist Fanny Burney, compiled his memoirs (1832). See biographies by P. A. Scholes (1848) and R. H. Lonsdale (1965).

Burney, Fanny, later **Madame D'Arblay** (därblā'), 1752–1840, English novelist; daughter of Charles Burney, the composer and organist. Although she received no formal education, she read prodigiously and had the benefit of conversation with her father's famous friends, including David Garrick and Samuel Crisp. Her first novel, *Evelina* (1778), was published anonymously, but Miss Burney soon acknowledged its authorship and achieved literary prominence. She became an intimate friend of Samuel Johnson and his circle. Her second novel, *Cecilia,* appeared in 1782, *Camilla* in 1796, and *The Wanderer* in 1814. The theme of her books is the entry into society of a virtuous, but inexperienced young girl, her mistakes and her gradual coming of age. Miss Burney spent five unhappy years (1786–91) as a member of Queen Charlotte's household. In 1793 she married General D'Arblay, a French émigré. Her diary and letters give an excellent account of English culture and society from 1768 to 1840. See biography by Emily Hahn (1950); studies by Joyce Hemlow (1958) and M. E. Adelstein (1969).

Burnham, Daniel Hudson, 1846–1912, American architect and city planner b. Henderson, N.Y., d. Heidelberg, Germany. He was trained in architects' offices in Chicago. With John W. Root he established in Chicago a partnership (1873) which gained many of the most important architectural commissions of the day. Their Chicago works included the Monadnock Building; the 20-story Masonic Temple Building (1892), the first important skeleton skyscraper; the Reliance Building, and the "Rookery" offices, the first suitably planned modern office building. Other works were the Flatiron Building and the Wanamaker store in New York City, the Union Passenger Station in Washington, and buildings in Cleveland, Buffalo, and San Francisco. Burnham and Root designed the general plan for the Columbian Exposition at Chicago (1893), exerting through it an enormous influence upon contemporaneous civic design. In 1901, Burnham served with C. F. McKim, F. L. Olmsted, Jr., and Augustus Saint-Gaudens on the Senate Park Commission in planning for the future beautification of Washington, D.C. With E. H. Bennett he created a civic improvement plan of great importance for Chicago (1907), much of which has since been put into execution. He also prepared plans for Baltimore, Duluth, and San Francisco and was commissioned by the U.S. government to design plans for Manila and other cities in the Philippines, including Baguio, the summer capital.

Burnham, Forbes, 1923–, prime minister of Guyana (1964–), formerly British Guiana. His full name is Linden Forbes Sampson Burnham. Of black African descent, he received a law degree (1947) from the Univ. of London. Returning to his homeland, he founded (1950), with Cheddi JAGAN, a political party devoted to gaining independence from Great Britain. He broke with Jagan in 1955 to form a more moderate party. In the 1964 elections his party trailed Jagan's, but Burnham, overcoming Jagan's plurality by uniting with a small third party, was named prime minister. He led his country to independence within the British Commonwealth (1966), and, despite vigorous opposition from Jagan, was reaffirmed in his position as prime minister in elections in 1968 and 1973. With enormous U.S. aid, he furthered public works and decreased the country's high unemployment rate. He promoted the nationalization of natural resources and attempted to ease racial tensions between Negroes and East Indians by opening government positions to the East Indians.

Burnham, Sherburne Wesley, 1838–1921, American astronomer, b. Thetford, Vt. After serving as observer at Dearborn Observatory, Chicago (1877–81, 1882–84), and as astronomer at Lick Observatory (1888–92), he was from 1893 astronomer at Yerkes Observatory and professor of astronomy at the Univ. of Chicago. Although his interest in astronomy had begun with amateur observations, he became outstanding in the field, especially through his discoveries of double stars. He wrote *General Catalogue of Double Stars* (1906) and *Measures of Proper Motion Stars* (1913).

burning bush, name for a North American plant of the family Celastraceae (STAFF-TREE family). The scriptural burning bush not consumed by fire (Ex. 3.2) is sometimes associated with a bramble or thorn and was adopted by the Presbyterian Church as an emblem of its early persecution. Burning bush is classified in the division MAGNOLIOPHYTA, class Magnoliopsida, order Celastrales, family Celastraceae.

Burnley, county borough (1971 pop. 76,483), Lancashire, NW England. Coal mining and cotton weaving, the keys to Burnley's growth, are still important industries. Associated with cotton-cloth production are calico printing and the manufacture of textile machinery. Other products of Burnley are electrical heating appliances, kitchen equipment, and gas turbines.

Burns, Arthur F., 1904–, American economist, b. Austria, grad. Columbia Univ. (A.B., 1925; A.M., 1925; Ph.D., 1934). He taught economics at Rutgers Univ. (1927–44), and then joined (1944) the faculty of Columbia, where he became John Bates Clark professor of economics in 1959. A member of the National Bureau of Economic Research from 1933, he was director of research (1945–53) and president (1957–67) of that organization. Under President Eisenhower, Burns was chairman (1953–56) of the Council of Economic Advisers. He returned to government service as economic counselor (1969–70) to President Nixon and as chairman (1970–) of the board of governors of the Federal Reserve System.

Burns, John, 1858–1943, British union leader and politician. A factory worker as a child, he was largely self-educated and was led by his reading to radical socialism. Burns became an outstanding orator, and in 1889 he was one of the leaders of the London dock strike, an attempt to organize the ill-paid unskilled laborers. Burns was elected (1892) to Parliament among the first labor representatives, but he quarreled with James Kier HARDIE and soon abandoned both socialism and the trade union movement. Henceforth associated with the Liberals, he was president of the local government board (1905–14), but resigned from the cabinet in protest against Britain's entry into World War I. He retired from Parliament in 1918. See biographies by G. D. H. Cole (1943) and William Kent (1950).

Burns, Otway, c.1775–1850, American privateer, b. Onslow co., N.C. At the outbreak of the War of 1812, he outfitted the Baltimore clipper *Snap-Dragon* as a privateer and began one of the most spectacular privateering careers in American history. He destroyed and captured millions of dollars worth of British shipping and had a $50,000 price set on his head by the British. After the war Burns turned to shipbuilding and later served (1821–35) in the North Carolina legislature. See biography by W. F. Burns (1905).

Burns, Robert, 1759–96, Scottish poet. The son of a hard-working and intelligent farmer, Burns was the oldest of seven children, all of whom had to help in the work on the farm. Although always hard pressed financially, the elder Burns, until his death in 1784, encouraged his sons with their education. As a result, Burns as a boy not only read the Scottish poetry of Ramsay and the collections compiled by Hailes and Herd, but also the works of Pope, Locke, and Shakespeare. By 1781, Burns had tried his hand at several agricultural jobs without success. Although he had begun writing, and his poems were circulated widely in manuscript, none were published until 1786. At this time he had already begun a life of dissipation, and he was not only discouraged but poor and was involved simultaneously with several women. He decided to marry Mary Campbell and migrate to Jamaica. To help finance the journey, he published at Kilmarnock *Poems, Chiefly in the Scottish Dialect* (1786), which was an immediate success. Mary Campbell died before she and Burns could marry, and Burns changed his mind about migration. He toured the Highlands, brought out a second edition of his poems at Edinburgh in 1787, and for two winters was socially prominent in the Scottish city. In 1788 he married Jean Armour, who had borne him four children, and retired to a farm at Ellisland. By 1791 Burns had failed as a farmer, and he moved to nearby Dumfries, where he held a position as an exciseman. He died at 37 after a severe attack of rheumatic fever. Burns's art is at its best in songs such as "Flow Gently, Sweet Afton," "My Heart's in the Highlands," and "John Anderson My Jo." Two collections contain 268 of his songs—George Thomson's *Select Collection of Original Scottish Airs for the Voice* (6 vol., 1793–1811) and

James Johnson's *Scots Musical Museum* (5 vol., 1787-1803). Some of these, such as "Auld Lang Syne" and "Comin' thro' the Rye," are among the most familiar and best-loved poems in the English language. But his talent was not confined to song; two descriptive pieces, "Tam o' Shanter" and "The Jolly Beggars," are among his masterpieces. Burns had a fine sense of humor, which was reflected in his satirical, descriptive, and playful verse. His great popularity with the Scots lies in his ability to depict with loving accuracy the life of his fellow rural Scots, as he did in "The Cotter's Saturday Night." His use of dialect brought a stimulating, much-needed freshness and raciness into English poetry, but Burns's greatness extends beyond the limits of dialect. His poems are written about Scots, but, in tune with the rising humanitarianism of his day, they apply to man's universal problems. See his poems (ed. by J. L. Robertson, 1953); biographies by Maurice Lindsay (2d ed., 1968) and R. T. Fitzhugh (1970); studies by David Daiches (rev. ed. 1967, and 1971).

Burnside, Ambrose Everett, 1824-81, Union general in the U.S. Civil War, b. Liberty, Ind. He saw brief service in the Mexican War and remained in the army until 1853, when he entered business in Rhode Island. In the Civil War, Burnside commanded a brigade at the first battle of Bull Run and was made (Aug., 1861) a brigadier general of volunteers. His expedition to the North Carolina coast (1862), resulting in the capture of Roanoke Island, New Bern, Beaufort, and Fort Macon, won him a major generalcy and much prestige. He commanded under G. B. McClellan in the ANTIETAM CAMPAIGN and shortly afterward succeeded that general in command of the Army of the Potomac. After a costly defeat at the battle of Fredericksburg (see FREDERICKSBURG, BATTLE OF) in Dec., 1862, Burnside asked President Lincoln either to sustain him in dismissing Joseph HOOKER and several other generals who opposed his plans, or to remove Burnside himself. Lincoln relieved him in favor of Joseph Hooker. As commander of the Dept. of the Ohio (March-Dec., 1863), he occupied E Tennessee, took Knoxville, and repulsed James Longstreet's attempt to recapture the town. In 1864 he commanded under generals Meade and Grant in Virginia. Held partially responsible for the fiasco at PETERSBURG, he was relieved. Burnside was elected governor of Rhode Island in 1866 and was reelected in 1867 and 1868. From 1875 to his death he was a U.S. Senator. He originated the fashion of wearing long side whiskers, thus the term *burnsides* or *sideburns.* See biography by B. P. Poore (1882); K. P. Williams, *Lincoln Finds a General* (Vol. II, 1950).

Burr, Aaron, 1756-1836, American political leader, b. Newark, N.J. A brilliant law student, he interrupted his study to serve in the American Revolution and proved himself a valiant soldier in the early campaigns of the war for independence. In 1779 ill health forced him to leave the army. Upon admission (1782) to the bar, he plunged with characteristic energy into the practice of law and of politics. He served as member (1784-85; 1797-99) of the New York assembly, as state attorney general (1789-91), and as U.S. Senator (1791-97). Defeated for reelection to the assembly in 1799, he set about organizing the Republican (see DEMOCRATIC PARTY) element in New York City for the election of 1800, for the first time making use of the Tammany Society for political purposes. The result was an unexpected victory for the Republicans, who gained control of the state legislature. Since the legislature named the presidential electors and New York was the pivotal state, Burr's victory insured the election of a Republican President. The intention of the party was to make Thomas JEFFERSON President and Burr Vice President, but confusion in the ELECTORAL COLLEGE resulted in a tie vote. This threw the election into the House of Representatives, dominated by the Federalist Alexander HAMILTON. Hamilton, who regarded Jefferson as the lesser evil of the two Republicans, helped to secure Jefferson the presidency, and on the 36th ballot Burr became Vice President. Burr presided over the Senate with a dignity and impartiality that commanded respect from both sides, and in 1804 his friends nominated him for the governorship of New York. Hamilton again contributed to his defeat, in part by statements reflecting on Burr's character. Burr challenged Hamilton to a duel and mortally wounded him. The circumstances of Hamilton's death brought Burr's political career to an end. Soon after, he left Washington on a journey to New Orleans, at that time a center of Spanish conspirings for possession of the lower Mississippi valley. Burr, unaware that Gen. James Wilkinson was in the pay of the Spanish, laid plans with him; what exactly Burr's plans were has never been made clear. Speculation ranges from the establishment of an independent republic in the American Southwest to seizure of territory in Spanish America. With money secured from Harman BLENNERHASSETT, Burr acquired the Bastrop grant on Washita River to serve as a base of operations. In the autumn of 1806, he and his party of 60-odd colonists, well-armed and supplied, began the journey downstream from Blennerhassett Island. Burr's earlier trip to New Orleans had brought him under suspicion; now distrust became widespread. Wilkinson, in an effort to save himself, turned against Burr, fanned the distrust, and in dispatches to Washington accused Burr of treason. Burr was arrested. He was tried for treason in the U.S. Circuit Court at Richmond, Va., Chief Justice John MARSHALL presiding, and found not guilty. Popular opinion nonetheless condemned him, and his remaining years were spent out of public life. He was married in 1833 to the famous Madame Jumel; they were divorced in 1834. See his correspondence with his daughter, Theodosia (ed. by Mark Van Doren, 1929); biographies by Nathan Schachner (1937, repr. 1961), S. H. Wandell and Meade Minnegerode (1925, repr. 1971), H. M. Alexander (1937, repr. 1973) and Philip Vail (1974); H. C. Syrett and J. G. Cooke, ed., *Interview in Weehawken* (1960); Jonathan Daniels, *Ordeal of Ambition* (1970).

Burrillville, town (1970 pop. 10,087), Providence co., NW R.I.; inc. 1806. Its manufactures include textiles and plastics.

Burritt, Elihu, 1810-79, American reformer, b. New Britain, Conn. A blacksmith, he studied mathematics, languages, and geography and became known as "the learned blacksmith." Profoundly idealistic, he supported many reform causes—antislavery, temperance, and self-education—and he pleaded for them when he edited (1844-51) the weekly *Christian Citizen* at Worcester, Mass. Most of all, however, he worked to promote world peace, organizing world peace congresses. Burritt argued for cheaper international postal rates and greater intellectual exchange among nations. Among his much-read books were *Sparks from the Anvil* (1846) and *Ten Minute Talks* (1873). See Merle Curti, ed., *The Learned Blacksmith* (his letters and journals, 1937, repr. 1973); biography by Peter Tolis (1968).

burro: see ASS.

Burroughs, Edgar Rice, 1875-1950, American novelist, creator of the character Tarzan. He is the author of *Tarzan of the Apes* (1914) and numerous other jungle and science fiction thrillers.

Burroughs, John, 1837-1921, American naturalist and author, b. Roxbury, N.Y.; son of a farmer. He became in turn a journalist, a treasury clerk in Washington, and a bank examiner and in 1874 settled on a farm near Esopus, N.Y., where he devoted his time to fruit culture and literature. In his first book, *Walt Whitman, Poet and Person* (1867), he was the first to give adequate recognition to the genius of his poet friend. In the bulk of his prose he made widely popular the type of nature essay that Thoreau had written. His best-known books are *Wake Robin* (1871); *Locusts and Wild Honey* (1879); *Fresh Fields,* a travel book (1884); *Signs and Seasons* (1886); and his one volume of poems, *Bird and Bough* (1906). A growing interest in philosophy and in science is evident in *Time and Change* (1912), *The Summit of the Years* (1913), *The Breath of Life* (1915), and *Accepting the Universe* (1922). "The Sage of Slabsides" became the friend of John Muir, Theodore Roosevelt, Edison, Ford, and other important men of his day. Although attached to his farm home, he traveled to the Pacific coast, the South, the West Indies, Europe, and (with the Harriman expedition) Alaska, observing natural phenomena everywhere and recording them in simple, expressive prose. See his autobiography, *My Boyhood* (1922); biographies by Elizabeth Burroughs Kelley (1959) and P. G. Westbrook (1974).

Burroughs, William S., 1914- American novelist, b. St. Louis, Mo., grad. Harvard, 1936. A narcotics addict from age 30 to age 45, Burroughs has lived most of his life abroad. *Junkie* (1953), published under the pseudonym William Lee, is an autobiographical account of his experiences as a drug addict. Burroughs's best-known work is the novel *Naked Lunch* (1959), a grim and horrifying depiction of the addict's existence with surrealistic portrayals of the drug experience. His other works include *Nova Express* (1964), *The Soft Machine* (1966), *The Ticket That Exploded* (1967), and *Exterminator!* (1973).

Bursa (bo͝orsä'), city (1970 pop. 275,917), capital of Bursa prov., NW Turkey. The market center of a rich agricultural region, Bursa is a commercial and industrial center, noted for its silk textiles. Founded at the end of the 3d cent. B.C. by the king of Bithynia, Prusias I, it was called Prusia ad Olympium. It was captured by the Seljuk Turks in 1075, taken by the Crusaders in 1096, and in 1204 passed to the Byzantines. Captured in 1326 by the Ottoman Turks under Sultan Orkhan, it became the Ottoman capital and was embellished with mosques, baths, and a caravansary. It was sacked by Tamerlane in 1402, and Adrianople (now Edirne) became (1413) the new capital of the Ottomans. There are many fine old mosques, notably the Green Mosque (1421) and the mosque of Beyazid I (1399). The town is sometimes called Brusa.

bursa (bûr'sə), closed fibrous sac lined with a smooth membrane that produces a viscous lubricant called synovial fluid. Bursas are found wherever muscles or tendons rub against other muscles, tendons, or bones. The bursas function in two ways: they lubricate points of friction, and they dissipate force by distributing it through a fluid medium. Normally the bursas produce just enough synovial fluid to reduce friction, but constant irritation may lead to an oversecretion and consequent enlargement of the bursa, a condition known as BURSITIS. In the hand and foot the bursa assumes a tubular form, called the synovial sheath, and encloses the tendons along their entire length.

bursitis (bərsī'təs), acute or chronic inflammation of a BURSA, or fluid sac, located close to a joint. Sacs of fluid may develop about a joint in response to irritation or injury, as in a bunion, and may become inflamed, causing pain, restricting motion, and producing more fluid than can be absorbed readily. An attack of bursitis usually causes great pain and tenderness in the affected area. It is treated with rest, antibiotics, X-ray therapy, diathermy, or cortisone, depending upon the cause and the degree of involvement. Superficial bursas, not necessary to the function of a joint, or bursas that have become calcified, may be excised.

Burton, Ernest De Witt, 1856-1925, American biblical scholar, b. Granville, Ohio. From 1882 to 1923 he served as professor of New Testament literature and interpretation at the Univ. of Chicago, of which he became president in 1923. He wrote *A Short Introduction to the Gospels* (rev. by H. R. Willoughby, 1926); with E. J. Goodspeed, *Harmony of the Synoptic Gospels* (1917) and *Harmony of the Synoptic Gospels in Greek* (1920); and, with Shailer Mathews, *The Life of Christ* (rev. ed. 1927). See biography by T. W. Goodspeed (1926).

Burton, Harold Hitz, 1888-1964, Associate Justice of the U.S. Supreme Court (1945-58), b. Jamaica Plain (now part of Boston), Mass. Admitted to the bar in 1912, he built a prosperous law practice in Cleveland and taught law (1923-25) at Western Reserve Univ. (now Case Western Reserve Univ.). He later served as a representative (1929-31) in the Ohio state assembly and as a reform mayor (1935-40) of Cleveland. As U.S. Senator (1941-45), Burton vigorously pressed for U.S. participation in the United Nations. Appointed by President Harry S. Truman to the Supreme Court, he firmly supported the decisions overturning racial segregation in schools and public transportation.

Burton, Richard, 1925-, British actor, b. Pontrhydfen, Wales; his original name was Richard Jenkins. A dark, somber actor with a splendid speaking voice, Burton specializes in heavily dramatic roles. He appeared with the Old Vic in *Henry V* and *Othello* and on Broadway in *Camelot* (1961) and *Hamlet* (1964). His films include *The Robe* (1953), *Cleopatra* (1962), *Becket* (1964), *The Spy Who Came In from the Cold* (1965), *Who's Afraid of Virginia Woolf?* (1966), and *The Klansman* (1974). His second wife was the actress Elizabeth TAYLOR.

Burton, Sir Richard Francis, 1821-90, English explorer, writer, and linguist. He joined (1842) the service of the East India Company and, while stationed in India, acquired a thorough knowledge of the Persian, Afghan, Hindustani, and Arabic languages. In 1853, in various disguises, he made a famous journey to Mecca and Medina, about which he wrote the vivid *Personal Narrative of a Pilgrimage to El-Medinah and Meccah* (3 vol., 1855-56). With John Speke he took a party to Somaliland; he alone, disguised as an Arab merchant, made the journey to Harar, Ethiopia, where he met with the local ruler. He went with Speke to uncharted E central Africa to discover the source of the Nile; he found Lake Tanganyika (1858) but abandoned the attempt to reach Lake Nyasa. After a visit to the United States, Burton published an account of the Mormon settlement at

Utah in his *City of the Saints* (1861). While consul (1861–65) at Fernando Po, off W Africa, he explored the Bight of Biafra and conducted a mission to Dahomey, Benin, and the Gold Coast. He explored Santos, in Brazil, while consul (1865) there, and after crossing the continent wrote *Explorations of the Highlands of Brazil* (1869). After a short period (1869–71) as consul at Damascus he was consul (1872–90) at Trieste, where he died. His last years were devoted chiefly to literature. He published remarkable literal translations of Camões and of the *Arabian Nights* (16 vol., 1885–88). See annotated bibliography by N. M. Penzer (1923); biographies by Lady Burton (2 vol., 1893, repr. 1973), G. M. Stisted (1893, repr. 1970), Seton Dearden (rev. ed. 1953), Alfred Bercovici (1962), and F. M. Brodie (1966).

Burton, Robert, 1577–1640, English clergyman and scholar, b. Leicestershire, educated at Oxford. He served as librarian at Christ Church, Oxford, all his life; in addition he was vicar of St. Thomas, Oxford, and later was rector of Seagrave, Leicestershire. A bachelor, he led an uneventful, scholarly life. His famous work, *The Anatomy of Melancholy,* appeared in 1621 under the pen name Democritus Junior. Enlarged and revised several times before his death, this treatise originally set out to explore the causes and effects of melancholy, but it eventually covered many areas in the life of man, including science, history, and political and social reform. The work is divided into three main portions: The first defines and describes various kinds of melancholy; the second puts forward various cures; and the third analyzes love melancholy and religious melancholy. Burton's prose style is informal, anecdotal, and thoroughly idiosyncratic, and he includes quotations from a wide range of literature—the Bible, the classics, the Elizabethan authors. See studies by W. R. Mueller (1952) and Lawrence Babb (1959).

Burton upon Trent, county borough (1971 pop. 50,175), Staffordshire, W central England, on the Trent River and the Grand Trunk Canal. Brewing, begun there by Benedictine monks, is the most famous industry. From the 11th cent. to the Reformation, the area's history was closely connected with the Benedictine abbey (founded 1002), of which there are remains. Other industries in the borough manufacture foundry products, tires, footwear, chemicals, and locomotives.

Buru or **Boeroe** (both: bo͞o'ro͞o), island (c.3,500 sq mi/9,065 sq km), E Indonesia, in the Moluccas, W of Ceram. Namlea is the chief town and port. Forest products, including cajeput oil, gums and resins, and timber, are exported.

Burundi (bərŭn'dē), republic (1973 est. pop. 3,725,000), 10,747 sq mi (27,834 sq km), E central Africa, bordering on Rwanda in the north, on Tanzania in the east, on Lake Tanganyika in the southwest, and on Zaïre in the west. BUJUMBURA is the capital and Gitega is the only other major town. The country falls into three main geographic regions. The narrow area in the west, which includes the Ruzizi River and Lake Tanganyika, is part of the western branch of the Great Rift Valley and includes some lowland. To the east of this region are mountains, which run north-south and reach an altitude of c.8,800 ft (2,680 m). Further east is a region of broken plateaus with somewhat lower elevations (c.4,500–6,000 ft/1,370–1,830 m), where most of the population lives. The inhabitants of Burundi are divided among three ethnic groups: the Hutu (about 85% of the population), who are mostly agriculturalists; the Tutsi (about 14%), who dominate the government of the country; and the Twa (about 1%), who are Pygmies. For the most part the Tutsi and the Hutu have a lord-serf relationship, with the Hutu tending the farmlands and cattle owned by the Tutsi. French and Kirundi (a Bantu language) are both official languages. About half the people are Christian, mostly Roman Catholic; the rest follow traditional beliefs. Burundi's poor transportation system and its distance from the sea have tended to limit economic growth. The economy is almost entirely agricultural. Most persons are engaged in subsistence farming, growing beans, cassava, maize, and plantains. Coffee (Burundi's chief export), cotton, and tea are also cultivated. Large numbers of cattle, goats, and sheep are raised. Especially among the Tutsi, a person's status is determined by the number of cattle he owns; however, the animals play a small role in the economy. The country's few manufactures include basic consumer goods, such as processed food, beverages, clothing, and footwear. Bastnaesite, cassiterite, kaolin, and gold are mined in small quantities. Burundi's imports usually considerably exceed the value of its exports. The United States, Belgium, Luxembourg, and Great Britain are the chief trade partners. Most exports are sent by ship to Kigoma in Tanzania and then by railroad to Dar es Salaam on the Indian Ocean. There is a university in Bujumbura.

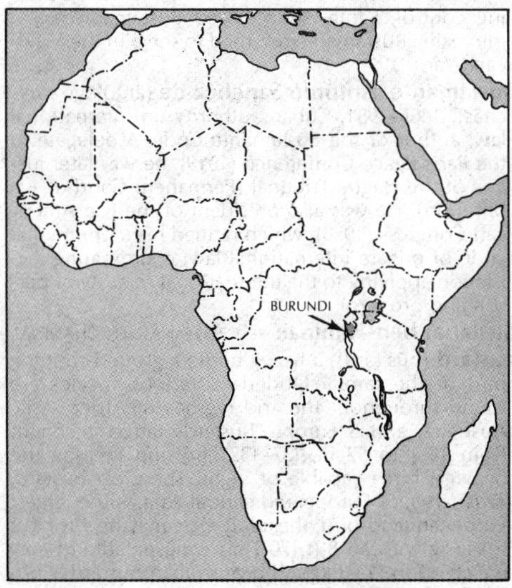

History. The Twa were the original inhabitants of Burundi and were followed (c.1200), and then outnumbered, by the Hutu. Probably in the 15th cent., the Tutsi migrated into the area from the northeast, gained dominance over the Hutu, and established several states. By the 19th cent., the country was ruled by the mwami (king)—a Tutsi who controlled the other Tutsi of the region in a vassal relationship. In 1890, Burundi (along with Rwanda) became part of GERMAN EAST AFRICA, but the Germans began to govern the area only in 1897. During World War I, Belgian forces occupied (1916) Burundi, and in 1919 it became part of the Belgian League of Nations mandate of RUANDA-URUNDI (which in 1946 became a UN trust territory). Under the German and Belgian administrations Christianity was spread, but the traditional social structure of Burundi was not altered, and there was little economic development. On July 1, 1962, the country became an independent kingdom ruled by the mwami of Burundi. The mid-1960s were marked by fighting between the Tutsi and Hutu and by struggles for power among the Tutsi. In 1965 a coup attempted by the Hutu failed, and the Tutsi retaliated by executing most Hutu political leaders and many other Hutu. In July, 1966, Mwambutsa IV was deposed by his son, who became Ntare V in Oct., 1966. The new ruler was deposed by a military coup in Nov., 1966. A republic was established and Michel Micombero, a Tutsi, became president. Following an attempted coup in 1969, Micombero concentrated power in his hands and headed the country's only legal political party, the Unity and National Progress party; a new constitution was adopted in 1970. Renewed fighting between the Tutsi and Hutu in the early 1970s resulted in the death of many thousands of Hutu. In 1972 a rebellion attempting to return Ntare V to power was crushed by the government; Ntare was executed and the Hutu were further repressed. See J. B. Webster, *The Political Development of Rwanda and Burundi* (1966); J. A. Nenguin, *Contributions to the Study of the Prehistoric Cultures of Rwanda and Burundi* (1967); G. C. McDonald et al., *Area Handbook for Burundi* (1969); René Lemarchand, *Rwanda and Burundi* (1970).

Bury, John Bagnell (băg'nəl byo͞o'rē), 1861–1927, Irish historian, an authority on the East Roman Empire. He was professor at the Univ. of Dublin from 1893 to 1902 and at Cambridge from 1902. Bury considered history a science—"not less, and not more." He stressed historical continuity, and he thought that accident was a frequent determinant in the history of premodern societies. His breadth of viewpoint is reflected in his attention to administration, institutions, topography, and the arts, which contributed to his unrivaled knowledge of late Roman and Byzantine times. *History of the Eastern Empire from the Fall of Irene to the Accession of Basil I, A.D. 802–867* (1912) is but one of his many outstanding studies. Bury also wrote authoritatively on ancient Greece, and his works include as well *History of Freedom of Thought* (1913), *The Idea of Progress* (1920), and a scholarly *Life of St. Patrick* ((1905). His edition (7 vol., 1896–1900) of Gibbon's *Decline and Fall* was masterful. Bury edited Pindar's Nemean and Isthmian odes and was an editor of and contributor to *The Cambridge Ancient History.*

Bury, Richard de: see RICHARD DE BURY.

Bury (bĕ'rē), county borough (1971 pop. 67,776), Lancashire, NE England, on the Irwell River and linked by canal with Bolton and Manchester. A textile city since the time of Edward III, when wool weaving was introduced by the Flemings, Bury has factories for the spinning, weaving, and bleaching of cotton. Hats, paper, machines, and boilers are among its other manufactures. Sir Robert Peel, the statesman, and John Kay, inventor of the "flying shuttle," were born in Bury. In 1974, Bury became part of the new metropolitan county of Greater Manchester.

Buryat Autonomous Soviet Socialist Republic (bo͝oryät'), autonomous republic (1970 pop. 812,000), c.135,600 sq mi (351,200 sq km), SE Siberian USSR, N of Mongolia, extending between Lake Baykal and the Yablonovy mts. ULAN-UDE is the capital. The republic is mountainous and heavily forested and has rivers and lakes that are rich in fish and that provide hydroelectric power. In the mountains are valuable deposits of coal, iron ore, tungsten, molybdenum, gold, wolfram, nickel, bauxite, and manganese. The Buryat ASSR is one of Siberia's most prosperous areas. The chief sectors of the economy are mining, lumbering, and livestock raising. Agriculture, found mainly in the Selenga River valley, is based on spring wheat and fodder crops. There are fisheries and fish-canning plants on Lake Baykal. Fur breeding and trading are important in the north, where nomads also keep reindeer herds. Major manufactures of the Buryat ASSR include machinery (notably locomotives for the Trans-Siberian RR, which traverses the republic), metal products, pulp, paper, and textiles. The Buryats, former nomads who have largely adopted a sedentary existence, are descended from the Huns, Mongols, Evenki, and Turks. They speak a Mongolian language and generally adhere to Lamaist Buddhism or to Russian Orthodoxy. Buryats constitute about 35% of the republic's population and engage mostly in stock raising. Russians make up a majority of the population, and there are Evenki, Tuvinian, Tatar, and Ukrainian minorities. Russian penetration of the region began in the 1620s and advanced for a century in the face of Buryat resistance until annexation occurred in 1727, followed by intensive Russian colonization. The Buryat-Mongol ASSR was formed in 1923 and retained that name until 1958.

Bury St. Edmunds, municipal borough (1971 pop. 25,629), administrative center of West Suffolk, E central England. It is the market and processing center for the surrounding rich farm region. The borough also has engineering works, a brewery, timber yards, and a beet-sugar factory. In 903 the remains of King Edmund were interred here in a monastery, founded c.630, which later became a famous shrine and Benedictine abbey founded by Canute. In 1214, English barons struggling against King John took an oath in the abbey to compel him to accept their demands. The result was the MAGNA CARTA (1215). Among the buildings of historical interest in the borough are a Norman gate, ruins of St. James Cathedral, and a 15th-century church. Moyses Hall, a Norman residence, is now a museum. In 1974, Bury St. Edmunds became part of the new nonmetropolitan county of Suffolk.

bus [from Lat. *omnibus*=for all), large public conveyance. A horse-drawn urban omnibus was introduced in Paris in 1662 by Blaise Pascal and his associates, but it remained in operation for only a few years. The omnibus reappeared c.1812 in Bordeaux, France, and afterward in Paris (c.1827), London (1829), and New York City (1830). It often carried passengers both inside and on the roof. Buses were motorized early in the 20th cent.; motorbus transportation increased rapidly and is now used in most countries. A number of railroad companies operate subsidiary lines. A network of bus lines links all parts of the United States. Bus lines have grown at the expense of railroads in intercity travel and of street railways in local travel. Buses are powered usually by gasoline or diesel engines, but in a few cities electric motors fed from overhead wires are used. The construction of small buses is similar to that of heavy automobiles, while the construction of large buses is similar to that of heavy trucks. Some large buses can seat more than 60 passengers.

Busaco: see BUSSACO, Portugal.

Busch, Adolf (ä'dôlf bo͝osh), 1891–1952, German-Swiss violinist. He studied at the Cologne Conservatory. From 1919 to 1935 he headed outstanding chamber music groups, and with his brother Hermann Busch, cellist, and his son-in-law Rudolf Serkin, pianist, he played many trio recitals. In his early compositions he was influenced by his friend Max Reger. Another brother, **Fritz Busch,** 1890-1951, was musical director of the opera in Stuttgart (1919-22) and in Dresden (1922-33), afterward conducting in Europe, particularly at the Glyndebourne Festivals in England, and later at the Metropolitan Opera in New York City (1945-50).

Busch, Wilhelm, 1832-1908, German cartoonist, painter, and poet. After studying at the academies of Antwerp, Düsseldorf, and Munich, he joined the staff of the *Fliegende Blätter,* to which he contributed highly popular humorous drawings from 1859 to 1871. His humorous, illustrated poems for children, such as *Max and Moritz* (1865; tr. by Christopher Morley, 1932), are simply drawn, yet highly spirited. Busch's delightful series of wordless pictures were highly influential in the development of the comic strip.

Büsching, Anton Friedrich (än'tōn frē'drĭkh büsh'ĭng), 1724-93, German geographer and educator. He was professor of philosophy in Göttingen, was a Protestant minister, and was director of a Gymnasium in Berlin. He advocated the collection of data similar to the kind of data now used in political and economic geography. The most important of his many works is *Neue Erdbeschreibung* (10 vol., 1754-92; Vol. XI was written after his death), six volumes of which, describing the geography of Europe, were translated into English as *A New System of Geography* (1762).

Bush, Vannevar, 1890-1974, American electrical engineer and physicist, b. Everett, Mass., grad. Tufts College (B.S., 1913). He went to Massachusetts Institute of Technology (MIT) in 1919; there he was professor (1923-32) and vice president and dean of engineering (1932-38). During this period at MIT he designed the differential analyzer, one of the earliest computers. From 1939 until 1955 he was president of the Carnegie Institution, and from 1941 to 1945 he was also the director of the U.S. Office of Scientific Research and Development. In this later position he administered the U.S. war effort to utilize and advance military technology. He directed such programs as the development of the first atomic bomb, the perfection of radar, and the mass production of sulfa drugs and penicillin. In 1955 he returned to MIT, retiring in 1971.

bush baby, name for several small, active nocturnal primates of the LORIS family, found in forested parts of Africa. Bush babies, also called galagos, form the subfamily Galaginae. The smallest are about 1 ft (30 cm) long, including the long, furry tail. All have fluffy fur, small pointed faces with large eyes, and naked, highly mobile ears. Their pupils contract so as to be almost invisible. The long hind legs are specialized for jumping; the fingers and toes are long and slender, with fleshy terminal pads; and the thumb and big toe are opposable. Extremely swift and agile, bush babies leap like squirrels from branch to branch and hop on their hind legs on the ground. They feed on insects and vegetable matter. Senegal bush babies (*Galago senegalensis*) are familiar as pets. They are gregarious and spend much time grooming each other with their front teeth. Bush babies are classified in the phylum CHORDATA, subphylum Vertebrata, class Mammalia, order Primates, family Lorisidae.

bushbuck, small, delicate, spiral-horned ANTELOPE, *Tragelaphus scriptus,* of tropical Africa. Bushbucks live in pairs in thick forest, browsing on leaves and shrubs by night and resting during the day. Their chief predator is the leopard. Adult males stand less than 3 ft (90 cm) high at the shoulder and weigh about 100 lb (45 kg). The horns, borne only by the male, are about 16 in. (40 cm) long. The coat is reddish brown with scattered white markings. Other species of the genus *Tragelaphus* are known as nyalas and sitatungas, although animals of this genus are sometimes referred to collectively as bushbucks. All are retiring, largely nocturnal antelopes, and in all the female is hornless. The nyala, *T. angasi,* is a medium-sized antelope that inhabits the bush country and thickets of central Africa. The mountain nyala, *T. buxtoni,* is a very large antelope of the highlands of Ethiopia; the male may stand 4½ ft (135 cm) high. The sitatunga, or marsh buck, *T. spekei,* is a large antelope found in swampy forests in central Africa; it is a good swimmer, but it is awkward on land. Bushbucks are classified in the phylum CHORDATA, subphylum Vertebrata, class Mammalia, order Artiodactyla, family Bovidae.

Bushehr (bo͞oshĕr') or **Bushire** (-shĭr'), city (1971 est. pop. 40,000), SW Iran, on the Persian Gulf. It is one of the chief ports of Iran and is the terminus of a trade route from Shiraz, Esfahan, and Tehran. Its harbor provides good protective anchorage, but it is too shallow to allow oceangoing vessels to approach the shoreline. Carpets, agricultural products, cotton, and wool are exported. Bushehr was founded in 1736 by Nadir Shah. It was used by the British as a base for their Persian Gulf fleet in the 18th cent. and became a major commercial port in the 19th cent.

bushel: see ENGLISH UNITS OF MEASUREMENT.

Bushey, urban district (1971 pop. 23,729), Hertfordshire, SE England. Bushey is a residential district just N of Greater London. The local church contains windows by William Morris.

bushido (bo͞o'shēdō, bo͞oshēdō') [Jap., = way of the warrior], code of honor and conduct of the Japanese nobility. Of ancient origin, it grew out of the old feudal bond that required unwavering loyalty on the part of the vassal. It borrowed heavily from Zen Buddhism and Confucianism. In its fullest expression the code emphasized loyalty to one's superior personal honor, and the virtues of austerity, self-sacrifice, and indifference to pain. For the warrior, commerce and the profit motive were to be scorned. The code was first formulated in the Kamakura period (1185-1333) and put into writing in the 16th cent.; the term itself, however, did not come into use until the 17th cent. It became the standard of conduct for the DAIMYO and SAMURAI under the Tokugawa shoguns and was taught in state schools as a prerequisite for government service. After the Meiji restoration (1868), it was the basis for the cult of emperor worship taught until 1945.

Bushire: see BUSHEHR, city, Iran.

bushmaster, large venomous snake, *Lachesis muta,* of Central America and N South America. It is a member of the PIT VIPER family, which also includes the rattlesnake. The largest New World snake, it reaches a length of 8 to 12 ft (2.5-5.5 m). It is gray and brown, with a diamond pattern. Unlike most pit vipers, which bear live young, the bushmaster lays eggs. It is classified in the phylum CHORDATA, subphylum Vertebrata, class Reptilia, order Squamata, family Crotalidae.

Bushmen: see SAN.

Bushnell, Horace (bo͝osh'nəl), 1802-76, American Congregational minister, b. Bantam, Conn. Bushnell became (1833) pastor of the North Church, Hartford, Conn. He wrote *Christian Nurture* (1847) and *God in Christ* (1849). Because of certain views of the Trinity allegedly expressed in the latter, unsuccessful attempts were made to bring him to trial for heresy. Bushnell's dignified reply was made in *Christ in Theology* (1851). His repudiation of the austerity of Calvinism and his stress on the presence of the divine in humanity and nature had profound influence in shaping liberal Protestant thought. Ill health obliged him to retire from the active ministry in 1859, but he continued to write. His works include *The Vicarious Sacrifice* (1866), in which he developed the well-known "moral influence theory" of the atonement; *Sermons on Living Subjects* (1872); and *Forgiveness and Law* (1874). See the *Life and Letters,* ed. by his daughter, Mrs. M. B. Cheney (1880, 1903; repr. 1969); biographies by T. T. Munger (1899) and William R. Adamson (1966); studies by A. J. W. Myers (1937), B. M. Cross (1938), and William A. Johnson (1963).

bushrangers, bandits who terrorized the bush country of Australia in the 19th cent. The first bushrangers (c.1806-44) were mainly escaped convicts who fled to the bush and soon organized gangs. Their crimes were checked effectively by various Bushranging Acts passed after 1830. With the discovery of gold, however, bushrangers of a new type appeared and flourished from 1850 to 1870, largely brigand-adventurers who attacked gold convoys. The last of the bushrangers were the men of the Kelly gang. This band of desperadoes was exterminated in 1880 when three members were trapped and killed at a hotel in Glenrowan, Victoria, and Edward (Ned) Kelly was hanged at Melbourne. See studies by W. F. Wannan (1963) and T. A. Prior (1966).

Busia, Kofi Abrefa (kō'fē äbrā'fä bo͞osē'ä), 1913-, political leader in Ghana. He was educated in Africa and in England and taught sociology in African, American, and European universities in the 1950s and 60s. He served (1951-59) in Ghana's national assembly, where he was opposition leader. In 1969 he became prime minister when his Progress party triumphed in the elections. Busia was overthrown in 1972 and went into exile in Great Britain.

Buskerud (bo͞os'kəro͞od), county (1972 est. pop. 201,000), c.5,725 sq mi (14,830 sq km), SE Norway. Drammen (the capital) and Ringerike are the chief towns. The county extends from the Oslofjord in the southeast to the Hardangervidda plateau in the northwest and includes the Hallingdal and Numedal valleys. Farming and the manufacturing of forest products and textiles are the main occupations.

Busoni, Ferruccio Benvenuto (fār-ro͞ot'chō bānvāno͞o'tō bo͞ozō'nē), 1866-1924, Italian pianist and composer. A child prodigy, he gave a concert in Trieste at the age of eight, which was followed by many appearances conducting and performing his own compositions. His style of piano playing was similar to that of Liszt, whom he greatly admired. He later taught at the conservatories in Helsinki and Moscow and from 1891 to 1894 at the New England Conservatory of Music, Boston. He transcribed for piano many of the organ works of J. S. Bach and edited his *Well-tempered Clavier.* Busoni's own compositions include piano pieces, a piano concerto, a violin concerto, and operas. His writings on musical and aesthetic subjects include his *Sketch of a New Esthetic* (tr. 1911). See his letters to his wife (tr. 1938); biography by H. H. Stuckenschmidt (tr. 1971).

Busra: see BASRA, Iraq.

Bussaco or **Busaco,** Port. *Buçaco* (all: bo͞osä'kō), locality, W central Portugal, in Beira, near Coimbra and around Mt. Bussaco. Now a summer resort, it was formerly a place of seclusion and penitence for monks. At Bussaco in 1810, British and Portuguese troops under Wellington decisively defeated the French in the Peninsular War.

Bussora: see BASRA, Iraq.

Bustamante, Alexander (bŭs"təmăn'tē), 1884-, prime minister of Jamaica (1962-67). The son of an Irish father and a Jamaican mother, he was adopted and taken to Spain as a child. He joined the Spanish army, then traveled extensively, working at a wide variety of jobs. Returning to Jamaica in 1932, he became active in the labor movement, gaining prominence with his flaming oratory, and founded the country's largest trade union. After being jailed (1941-42) as a rabble-rouser, he formed (1943) the Jamaica Labour party, a relatively conservative group that attracted right-wing support. He was chief minister (1953-55) and became prime minister in April, 1962; independence within the British Commonwealth was achieved that August. A flamboyant, demagogic leader, he maintained close relations with the United States and launched an ambitious five-year program of public works and land reform. Illness caused him to retire from politics in 1967. He was knighted by Queen Elizabeth II in 1955.

Bustamante, Anastasio (änästä'syō bo͞ostämän'tā), 1780-1853, Mexican general and president (1830-32, 1837-41). He served in the royalist army against Hidalgo y Costilla and Morelos y Pavón, but his adherence to the Plan of Iguala in support of Agustín de Iturbide was a decisive factor in the latter's success. Vice president under Guerrero, he engineered a successful revolution (1829-30) with the aid of SANTA ANNA. At Bustamante's order Guerrero was captured and shot, but Bustamante in turn fell from power when Santa Anna seized the government (1832). When Santa Anna's failure to crush the Texas revolution temporarily weakened his political hold, Bustamante returned from exile in France and was again president. His regime was reactionary and was plagued by revolution, by trouble with the French, by the blockade of Veracruz (1838), and especially by Santa Anna, who had recovered popularity. Seizing control, Santa Anna forced Bustamante again into exile. Bustamante returned to serve in the Mexican War.

Bustamante, Antonio Sánchez de (äntō'nyō sän'chās), 1865-1951, Cuban authority on international law, author of the Bustamante Code. A delegate to the Paris Peace Conference (1919), he was later justice of the Hague Tribunal (Permanent Court of Arbitration). He was also president of the Pan American Congress (1928), which ratified his monumental code of private international law, coordinating legislation applying to the international security of person and property.

Bustanai ben Haninai: see BOSTANAI BEN CHANINAI.

bustard (bŭs'tərd), a heavy-bodied, ground-running bird of the family Otididae. Various species are found throughout the arid regions of Africa, Asia, Australia, and S Europe. Bustards range in length from 14½ to 52 in. (37-132 cm) and include the heaviest birds capable of flight. The great bustard, *Otis tarda,* of Europe and central Asia, is the largest European land-bird; the adult male may be 4 ft (10.2 m) long with an 8-ft (20.3-m) wingspread and may weigh 30 lb (13.6 kg). The Australian bustard, *Cho-*

rictis australis, is of similar size. Bustards are stocky birds with long necks and strong legs; their feet are built for running, with flat toes, broad soles, and no hind toe. The species vary in color from gray to brown, and many are spotted or barred above and white, buff, or black below. Bustards live mainly on grassy plains or in brushlands. Although they are strong fliers, they seldom leave the ground. They wander about in flocks of a dozen or more birds, feeding on leaves, seeds, and insects, especially beetles. The males are polygamous and fight fiercely during the breeding season. The female lays and incubates from one to five eggs, according to the species; the chicks are able to fly at the age of six weeks. Bustards have been extensively hunted for food; they are extinct in Britain and are becoming scarce in the northern part of their range. They are classified in 16 genera and 23 species of the phylum CHORDATA, subphylum Vertebrata, class Aves, order Gruiformes, family Otidedae.

bustard quail or **button quail,** any of the small ground-running Old World birds of the family Turnicidae. Also called a hemipode, it resembles a true quail in appearance and way of life but is more closely related to sandgrouse and pigeons. Bustard quails have short tails and rounded wings and lack a hind toe. They are secretive birds, inhabiting grass and brush country and open woodlands, and are found throughout Australia, S Asia, and Africa, with one species extending into S Spain. They travel singly, in pairs, in small family groups, or, in some species, in coveys of 15 to 30 birds. Their diet consists of seeds, shoots, and small insects. The bustard quail female is larger and more colorful than the male, and takes the lead in courtship; she has a specialized vocal organ for giving the booming mating call. The nest is on the ground and is constructed by both sexes. After the female has laid her clutch, typically of four eggs, the male incubates the eggs and rears the young. There are 15 species of bustard quail, classified in two genera of the phylum CHORDATA, subphylum Vertebrata, class Aves, order Gruiformes, family Turnicidae.

Busto Arsizio (bo͞o'stō ärsē'tsyō), city (1971 pop. 78,632), Lombardy, N Italy. It is a leading center of the Italian cotton industry; metal goods and shoes are also manufactured. The Church of Santa Maria di Piazza was designed (1515) by Bramante.

Butades of Sicyon (bū'tədēz, sĭ'shēŏn), fl. c.600 B.C., semilegendary Greek sculptor. He worked at Corinth and was supposed to have been the first to model in clay.

butadiene (byo͞ot"ədī'ēn), colorless, gaseous hydrocarbon. There are two structural isomers of butadiene; they differ in the location of the two carbon-carbon double bonds in the butadiene molecule. One (1,2-butadiene) has the formula $CH_2{:}C{:}CHCH_3$. The other (1,3-butadiene), often called simply butadiene, has the formula $CH_2{:}CHCH{:}CH_2$; it is used in the manufacture of synthetic rubber, latex paints, and nylon and is obtained chiefly by dehydrogenation of butane and butene obtained by cracking petroleum. CHLOROPRENE and ISOPRENE are the 2-chloro- and 2-methyl- derivatives of 1,3-butadiene; they also are used in the synthesis of rubber.

butane (byo͞o'tān), C_4H_{10}, gaseous ALKANE, a hydrocarbon that is obtained from natural gas or by refining petroleum. It can be liquefied at room temperature by compression. There are two structural ISOMERS of butane. In normal butane, or *n*-butane, the four carbon atoms are joined in a continuous, unbranched chain; in isobutane, or 2-methylpropane, three of the carbon atoms are joined to the fourth by single bonds, resulting in a branched structure. The two isomers differ in certain of their chemical and physical properties, e.g., liquid *n*-butane has a higher boiling point (-0.6°C) at atmospheric pressure than that of liquid isobutane (-10.2°C).

butanoic acid, IUPAC name for BUTYRIC ACID.

Butaritari (bətärē'tärē), also known as Makin (mä'kĭn, mŭg'ĭn), triangular atoll, (4.5 sq mi/11.7 sq km), central Pacific, in the GILBERT ISLANDS. The town of Butaritari on the southernmost islet is a port of entry and the headquarters of a copra company. Butaritari became a part of the British colony of the GILBERT AND ELLICE ISLANDS in 1915. During World War II it was the first central Pacific island to be regained by the Allies (Nov., 1943). Butaritari was formerly called Pitt Island.

butcher bird: see SHRIKE.

Bute, John Stuart, 3d **earl of** (byo͞ot), 1713–92, British politician. He was prominent as a friend of Frederick Louis, prince of Wales, as early as 1747 and became the tutor of Frederick's impressionable son, the future GEORGE III. When George became king in 1760, Bute was appointed a privy councilor, first gentleman of the bedchamber, and (March, 1761) a secretary of state. George III's policies of destroying the Whig monopoly of political power, of making the monarch supreme over Parliament, and of ending the war with France were pursued largely under Bute's influence. After the resignation (Oct., 1761) of William Pitt (later earl of Chatham) from office, Bute became chief minister. Although he concluded the Treaty of Paris (1763), ending the increasingly unpopular war, he lacked parliamentary support and resigned shortly thereafter. George III rapidly outgrew his youthful dependence on his friend. See biography by J. A. Lovat Fraser (1912); Romney Sedgewick, ed., *Letters from George III to Lord Bute, 1756–1766* (1936); R. Pares, *George III and the Politicians* (1953).

Bute, island and county, Scotland: see BUTESHIRE.

Buteshire (byo͞ot'shĭr) or **Bute** (byo͞ot), county (1971 pop. 13,237), W Scotland. The county consists primarily of the islands of Bute (the most important island and seat of Rothesay, the county town), ARAN, and the Cumbraes. Agriculture (potatoes, oats, hay, and turnips), the main occupation of the county, is chiefly concentrated in the less hilly central and southern parts of Bute. Cattle and sheep raising and fishing (herring and whitefish) are also important. The scenery and bracing climate of the islands make them popular with tourists. In 1975, Buteshire became part of the Strathclyde region.

Butler, Alban, 1710–73, English Roman Catholic priest, compiler of lives of the saints. He was educated at Douai and was president of the English seminary at Saint-Omer. His monumental work, *The Lives of the Fathers, Martyrs, and Principal Saints* (4 vol. in 7, 1756–59), was the basis for the enlarged edition, *The Lives of the Saints* (12 vol., 1926–38), and for the completely revised work, *Butler's Lives of the Saints* (ed. by Herbert Thurston, S.J., and Donald Attwater, 4 vol., 1956), which is a standard, popular reference book.

Butler, Benjamin Franklin, 1795–1858, American political leader and cabinet officer, b. Columbia co., N.Y. Butler, like his former law associate, Martin Van Buren, was a member of the ALBANY REGENCY, and he devoted himself and his considerable power to reform politics. He was Attorney General (1833–37) under President Jackson and for a time held (1836–37) that post and the office of Secretary of War concurrently. He also served (1837–38) as Attorney General under President Van Buren, but he refused later cabinet appointments. He helped to revise (1825) the New York state statutes and organized what is today the law school of New York Univ.

Butler, Benjamin Franklin, 1818–93, American politician and Union general in the Civil War, b. Deerfield, N.H. He moved to Lowell, Mass., as a youth and later practiced law there and in Boston. He was elected to the state legislature in 1852 and 1858 and ran unsuccessfully for governor in 1859 and 1860. Butler was a Democrat but a strong Unionist. At the beginning of the Civil War his contingent of Massachusetts militia was one of the first to reach Washington. He restored order (May, 1861) in secessionist Baltimore and was given command at Fort Monroe. He commanded the troops that accompanied Admiral Farragut in taking New Orleans and was made military governor of the city. There his highhanded rule (May–Dec., 1862) infuriated the people of New Orleans and the South and earned him the name "Beast." The government, severely criticized both at home and abroad for his actions, finally removed him. In May, 1864, as commander of the Army of the James, Butler was defeated by Beauregard at DREWRYS BLUFF and was bottled up at Bermuda Hundred until Grant crossed the James in June. After he failed to take FORT FISHER in Dec., 1864, he was removed from active command. From 1867 to 1875 Butler, by then a rabid radical Republican, was in Congress. He was one of the House managers who conducted the impeachment proceedings against President Andrew Johnson, and he ardently advocated the party's Reconstruction policy. He was said to have great influence with President Grant. Butler was (1877–79) an independent Greenbacker in Congress. After several unsuccessful attempts to secure the governorship of Massachusetts, he was elected by the Greenbackers and Democrats in 1882. In 1884 he received the nominations of the Anti-Monopoly and Greenback parties for President. Regarded by many as an unprincipled demagogue of great ability, Butler aroused intense antagonisms and was nearly always in controversy. See his autobiography (1892); biographies by R. S. Holzman (1954), H. L. Trefousse (1957), R. S. West, Jr. (1965), and H. P. Wash, Jr. (1969).

Butler, James: see ORMONDE, JAMES BUTLER, 12TH EARL AND 1ST DUKE OF.

Butler, John, 1728–96, Loyalist commander in the American Revolution, b. New London, Conn. He served in the French and Indian Wars and distinguished himself especially by leading the Indians in the successful British attack (1759) under Sir William Johnson against Niagara. Electing the British side after the Revolution broke out, he became a deputy to Guy Johnson at Niagara and worked to keep the Indians friendly to the British. In the Saratoga campaign (1777) he and Indian troops accompanied Gen. Barry St. Leger in the unsuccessful expedition down the Mohawk valley. Later he organized a Loyalist troop called Butler's Rangers, and with them he and his son, Walter BUTLER, attacked the frontier settlements. John Butler in 1778 raided the Wyoming Valley, defeated Zebulon BUTLER, took Forty Fort, and then was unable to keep his Indian allies from perpetrating the Wyoming Valley massacre. Later that year Walter Butler and Joseph Brant led a similar raid on Cherry Valley, and this also ended in a massacre. The name of Butler was thereafter anathema to the patriots. John Butler was defeated (1779) by the expedition of Gen. John SULLIVAN at Newtown near the present Elmira, N.Y.; later in the war Butler joined with Sir John JOHNSON in frontier raids. See Howard Swiggett, *War out of Niagara* (1933, repr. 1963).

Butler, Joseph, 1692–1752, English bishop, theologian, and moral philosopher. He was preacher (1718–26) at the Rolls Chapel, London; his tenure there produced the noted *Fifteen Sermons* (1726), in which he set forth his moral philosophy. While rector of Stanhope (1725–40), he was also prebendary of Salisbury and, later, of Rochester. In 1738 he was made bishop of Bristol and in 1740 became dean of St. Paul's, London. In 1750 he was appointed to the see of Durham, one of the richest in England. He also served as clerk of the closet to Queen Caroline and later to King George II. It is as a writer that he is chiefly remembered. His great book, *The Analogy of Religion, Natural and Revealed, to the Constitution and Course of Nature* (1736) was aimed at combating the influence of deism in England by demonstrating the reasonableness of Christianity. See biographies by E. C. Mossner (1936, repr. 1971) and W. J. Norton (1940); study by A. E. Duncan-Jones (1952)

Butler, Nicholas Murray, 1862–1947, American educator, president of COLUMBIA UNIV. (1902–45), b. Elizabeth, N.J., grad. Columbia (B.A., 1882; Ph.D., 1884). Holding a Columbia fellowship, he studied at Paris and Berlin, specializing in philosophy. Beginning in 1885 he was made successively assistant, tutor, and adjunct professor of philosophy at Columbia. He became (1886) president of the Industrial Education Association, reshaped it into what is today Teachers College, Columbia, and was (1889–91) the institution's first president. He was intimately associated with John W. BURGESS in the struggle to create a university organization and was largely responsible for the expansion of Columbia College into Columbia Univ. In 1890 he became professor of philosophy and education and dean of the Faculty of Philosophy and in 1901 acting president of Columbia. The next year he formally succeeded Seth Low as president. He instituted the Summer Session, University Extension (now the School of General Studies), the School of Journalism, the Medical Center, and other units which have contributed to the magnitude of present-day Columbia. An advocate of peace through education, Butler helped to establish the Carnegie Endowment for International Peace, of which he was a trustee and later president (1925–45). His efforts in behalf of disarmament and international peace won him international prestige, and he shared with Jane Addams the 1931 Nobel Peace Prize. Prominent in national, state, and New York City politics, he remained a regular Republican party member despite differences with its platforms. Though a close friend of Theodore Roosevelt, he refused to join the Progressive movement of 1912, and that year Butler received the Republican electoral votes for Vice President after the death of Vice President James S. Sherman, the regularly nominated candidate. He later was the leading Republican advocate of the repeal of the Eighteenth Amendment, urged economy in government, and supported local reform movements. He was (1928–41) president of the American Academy of Arts and Letters. His books include *Education in the United States* (1910), *The International Mind* (1913), *The Meaning of Education* (rev. ed. 1915), *Scholarship and Service* (1921), *The Faith of a Liberal* (1924), *The Path to*

Peace (1930), *Looking Forward* (1932), *Between Two Worlds* (1934), and *The World Today* (1946). See his autobiography, *Across the Busy Years* (2 vol., 1939–40); Richard Whittemore, *Nicholas Murray Butler and Public Education* (1970); *Bibliography of Nicholas Murray Butler, 1872-1932* (1934).

Butler, Pierce, 1866–1939, Associate Justice of the U.S. Supreme Court (1923–39), b. Dakota co., Minn. Admitted (1888) to the bar, he practiced in St. Paul, specialized in railroad law, and became an expert in railroad-valuation cases, serving (1913–22) both the U.S. and Canadian governments. In the Supreme Court, to which he was appointed by President Harding, he was generally considered a conservative. See D. J. Danelski, *A Supreme Court Justice Is Appointed* (1964).

Butler, Richard Austen, 1902–, British statesman. Educated at Cambridge, he entered Parliament in 1929 as a Conservative. After holding various minor government offices, he became (1941) minister of education and piloted through Parliament the Education Act of 1944, which provided free primary and secondary education for all. He was briefly minister of labor in 1945 before the Conservatives lost power. As chancellor of the exchequer from 1951 to 1955, he led the country out of wartime austerity but opposed major reduction in social services. Leader of the House of Commons from 1955 to 1961, Butler also served as lord privy seal (1955–59), home secretary (1957–62), deputy prime minister and first secretary of state (1962–63), and foreign secretary (1963–64). Retiring from political life, he was given a life peerage as Baron Butler of Saffron Walden and became (1965) master of Trinity College, Cambridge.

Butler, Samuel, 1612–80, English poet and satirist. During the Puritan Revolution he served Sir Samuel Luke, a noted officer of Cromwell. After the restoration of Charles II, he wrote his famous mock-heroic poem *Hudibras* (pub. in 3 parts, 1663, 1664, 1678), an envenomed satire against the Puritans in which Luke was the model for the butt Sir Hudibras. He was also the author of other verse satires, some of them not published until the 20th cent. See the John Wilders edition of his *Hudibras* (1967).

Butler, Samuel, 1835–1902, English author. He was the son and grandson of eminent clergymen. In 1859, refusing to be ordained, he went to New Zealand, where he established a sheep farm and in a few years made a modest fortune. He returned to England in 1864 and devoted himself to a variety of interests, including art, music, biology, and literature. Besides exhibiting some of his paintings (1868–76) at the Royal Academy, he composed several works in collaboration with Henry Festings Jones, among them the Handelian *Narcissus: A Dramatic Cantata* (1888). His *Erewhon*, in which he satirized English social and economic injustices by describing a country in which manners and laws were the reverse of those in England, appeared in 1872. It brought Butler immediate literary fame. *Erewhon Revisited* was published in 1901. Butler opposed Darwin's explanation of evolution, finding it too mechanistic, and he expounded his own theories in *Evolution Old and New* (1879), *Unconscious Memory* (1880), and *Luck or Cunning as the Main Means of Organic Modification?* (1887). In his single novel, the autobiographical *The Way of All Flesh* (1903), he attacked the Victorian pattern of life, in particular the ecclesiastical environment in which he was reared. Brilliantly ironic and witty, *The Way of All Flesh* is ranked among the great English novels. Butler's notebooks were published in 1912. See selections from the notebooks ed. by Geoffrey Keynes and Brian Hill (1951). See also Arnold Silver, ed., *The Family Letters of Samuel Butler, 1841-1886* (1962); biographies by H. F. Jones (1921, repr. 1973), L. E. Holt (1964), and Philip Henderson (1953, repr. 1967); study by W. G. Becker (1925, repr. 1964).

Butler, Thomas: see OSSORY, THOMAS BUTLER, EARL OF.

Butler, Walter, 1752?–1781, Loyalist officer in the American Revolution, b. New York state; son of John BUTLER. He was an officer in his father's Loyalist troop, Butler's Rangers. He was captured (1777) by the patriots and sentenced to death, but the sentence was commuted. He escaped and in 1778 led the Rangers in a raid. This ended with the Cherry Valley massacre, for which his Indian commander, Joseph BRANT, blamed Butler. Walter Butler was killed in a skirmish with patriot troops under Marinus WILLETT in the Mohawk valley. See Howard Swiggett, *War out of Niagara* (1933, repr. 1963).

Butler, William Orlando, 1791–1880, American general and political leader, b. Carrollton, Ky. He served in the War of 1812 and distinguished himself in the battle of New Orleans. He was a Congressman from 1839 to 1843. In the Mexican War he was a major general of volunteers and was second in command to Zachary Taylor at Monterrey, where Butler was wounded. After the fighting ended he succeeded Winfield Scott as commander in chief and superintended the evacuation of the U.S. soldiers from Mexico. In 1848 he was vice presidential candidate on the unsuccessful Democratic ticket headed by Lewis Cass. Although a slaveholder, he opposed secession and supported the Union cause in the Civil War.

Butler, Zebulon, 1731–95, American colonial leader, b. Ipswich, Mass. After serving in the French and Indian Wars, Butler led a group of Connecticut settlers to the WYOMING VALLEY in N Pennsylvania. He was military leader of the Connecticut settlers in the Pennamite Wars and served as director of the SUSQUEHANNA COMPANY. Butler represented (1774–76) the Wyoming Valley in the Connecticut assembly. A colonel in the Revolution, he was defeated (1778) by Loyalists under John BUTLER and fled to Forty Fort; the Wyoming Valley massacre followed. Butler escaped and later was military commandant of the region.

Butler, city (1970 pop. 18,691), seat of Butler co., W Pa.; inc. as a borough 1817, as a city 1917. It is located in an area rich in coal, natural gas, oil, and limestone. Among its manufactures are steel, railroad-car parts, copper tubing, machinery, and petroleum products. Moraine State Park and a community college are there.

Butlerov, Aleksandr Mikhailovich (əlyĭksän'dər mēkhīl'əvĭch bo͞ot'lyərôf), 1825–1886, Russian chemist. As professor at the Univ. of Kazan he founded the first school of Russian chemists and directed research designed to confirm the classical theory of chemical structure, which he helped to create. His later work included investigations of polymerization reactions and applications of the theory of chemical structure to organic chemistry.

Butler University, at Indianapolis, Ind.; coeducational; chartered 1850 as North Western Christian Univ. Its present name was adopted in 1877.

Buto (byo͞o'tō), ancient city, N Egypt, in the Nile delta. The precise location is uncertain. Capital of Lower Egypt in prehistoric times (before 3100 B.C.), it had a temple dedicated to the serpent goddess Buto. During the Saïte period (663–525 B.C.) it was revived as an important religious center.

Butor, Michel (mēshĕl' bütôr'), 1926–, French novelist and critic. As one of the chief exponents of the new novel, or antinovel, Butor is less interested in the outcome of action in his novels than he is in the action itself. His technique involves the use of shifting time sequences, strong visual images, and the interior monologue. He often focuses on one small area of experience to reveal the larger complexity of life. His novels include *Passage de Milan* (1954), *L'Emploi du Temps* (1956; tr. *Passing Time*, 1960), *La Modification* (1957; tr. *Second Thoughts*, 1958), *Degrès* (1960, tr. 1962), *Mobile* (1962; tr. *Mobile: Study for a Representation of the U.S.*, 1963), and *Niagara: A Stereophonic Novel* (tr. 1969). He has also written numerous critical pieces. See study by Michael Spencer (1973).

Bütschli, Otto (ô'tō büch'lē), 1848–1920, German zoologist. He was professor of zoology at the Univ. of Heidelberg. His researches on invertebrate animals advanced knowledge of the development of gastropods, insects, and other forms; the structure of nematode worms; and processes of division of the nucleus and cell. A significant contribution was his theory (1878) of the structure of protoplasm, which suggested that it is alveolar or foamlike; he helped to establish that it is fluid in nature.

Butt, Isaac, 1813–79, Irish politician and nationalist leader. A member of both the Irish and the English bar, he was a noted conservative lawyer and scholar and an opponent of Daniel O'CONNELL. After the Irish famine experience of the 1840s, however, he became increasingly liberal, defended participants in the abortive Young Ireland revolt (1848), and entered (1852) Parliament as a Liberal-Conservative. He continually urged land tenure reform, defended the Fenian leaders, and founded (1870) the Home Rule Society. By 1874 the parliamentary group, the Home Rule League, comprised 56 members under his leadership. He remained nominal leader of the HOME RULE movement until his death, although effective leadership gradually passed to Charles Stewart PARNELL. See L. J. McCaffrey, *Irish Federalism in the 1870's* (1962); David Thornley, *Isaac Butt and Home Rule* (1964).

Butte (byo͞ot), city (1970 pop. 23,368), seat of Silver Bow co., SW Mont.; inc. 1879. It is a trade, distribution, and industrial center. The mining industry has dominated the city's economy since its establishment in 1862. Copper is the major product, and zinc, silver, manganese, gold, lead, and arsenic are also extracted from the numerous mines in the region. First a gold-mining camp, then a silver center, Butte gained importance when copper was discovered (c.1880) and Marcus Daly with his Anaconda Copper Mining Company began to exploit the "richest hill on earth." The expansion of the open-pit copper mine within the city limits is forcing sections of the city to relocate. Butte's reputation as a "wide-open" town reached its height during the "War of the Copper Kings." The Montana College of Mineral Science and Technology is in the city. Local attractions include tours of the mines, a mining museum, and the Columbia Gardens recreational area, maintained for the public by the Anaconda Company. Butte is the headquarters of Deerlodge National Forest.

butte, an isolated hill with steep sides and a flat top, resulting from the more rapid erosion of the surrounding areas. Buttes are characteristic of the plains of the W United States. See MESA.

butter, dairy product obtained by churning the fat from milk until it reaches a solidified form. In most areas the milk of cows is the basis, but elsewhere that of goats, sheep, and mares has been used. Butter was known by 2000 B.C., although in ancient times it was used less as a food than as an ointment, a medicine, or an illuminating oil. At first it was rudely churned in skin pouches thrown back and forth or swung over the back of trotting horses. As butter became a staple food, various sorts of hand churns were devised, including rotating, swinging, and rocking containers operated by plungers. Butter-making on the farm consists of allowing the milk to cool in pans, letting the cream rise to the top, skimming the cream off, and letting it ripen by natural fermentation; it is then churned. Exclusively farm-made until about 1850, butter has become increasingly a factory product. The centrifugal cream SEPARATOR, introduced into the United States c.1880, and a method devised in 1890 by Stephen Moulton BABCOCK to determine the butterfat content of milk and cream gave impetus to large-scale production. The application of principles of chemistry and bacteriology facilitates the making of butter of uniform quality. The percentage of fat extraction and the time required for churning depend on the composition of the butterfat (see FATS AND OILS); the temperature, acidity, richness, and viscosity of the cream; the speed and motion of the churn; and the size of the fat globules. Commercial butter usually contains from 80% to 85% milk fat, from 12% to 16% water, and about 2% salt. Sweet, or unsalted, butter is favored in Europe, but other markets prefer at least 2% salt. Renovated or process butter is made from rancid or inferior butter, melted and refined, then rechurned. Whey butter, made from cream separated from whey, is usually oily and of inferior quality. The natural color of butter, derived from the carotene of green plant fodder, ranges from pale yellow to deep gold. Australia, France, West Germany, New Zealand, the Soviet Union, and the United States are the leading producers; Denmark, New Zealand, and Australia, the chief exporters; and Great Britain, a heavy importer. The major production centers in the United States are in the N Middle West, especially Minnesota, Iowa, and Wisconsin. Clarified butter, butterfat with the milk solids removed, is useful in cooking and has good keeping qualities. It is made in quantity in Egypt and in India, where it is known as GHEE. The high dietary value of butter is due to its large proportion of easily digested fat and to its vitamin A and vitamin D content.

butter-and-eggs, common name for a plant of the family Scrophulariaceae (FIGWORT family) and sometimes for other yellow-and-orange flowers. Butter-and-eggs plants are classified in the division MAGNOLIOPHYTA, class Magnoliopsida, order Scrophulariales, family Scrophulariaceae.

buttercup or **crowfoot,** common name for the Ranunculaceae, a family of chiefly annual or perennial herbs of cool regions of the Northern Hemisphere. Thought to be one of the most primitive families of dicotyledenous PLANTS, the Ranunculaceae typically have a simple flower structure in which each flower part may be separate rather than fused into a single organ (see FLOWER). Some botanists believe that the preference of this family for swamps and wet places also indicates its low evolutionary position. The family includes numerous familiar wild flowers and many cultivated ornamentals. Well-known representatives are the ACONITE, ANEMONE, BANEBERRY, BUGBANE, CLEMATIS (one of the few vine species), COLUMBINE, GLOBEFLOWER, HELLEBORE, HEPATICA, LARKSPUR, LOVE-IN-A-MIST, MARSH MARIGOLD (the American cowslip), MEADOW RUE, and PEONY. The largest genus, *Ranunculus*, comprises the buttercups and crowfoots, names often used interchangeably. Found throughout arctic, north temperate, and alpine regions, with species in the Andes and in subantarctic areas, this genus is characterized by glossy yellow flowers (hence the name buttercup) and deeply cut leaves (supposedly resembling crows' feet). Like some other members of the family, species of this genus contain an acrid juice that makes them unpalatable for livestock and in some species poisonous. A dozen or more species are common in every part of the United States. Among those cultivated for garden and cut flowers are some double-blossomed Old World species, e.g., the turban, or Persian, buttercup (*R. asiaticus*), valued for the variety of its colors (all but blue), and the creeping buttercup (*R. repens*), native to both North America and Europe. *R. ficaria*, of Eurasia, is the lesser celandine—a name more commonly applied to some plants of the poppy family, which it resembles. Many buttercups are aquatic plants, hence the Latin name for the genus *Ranunculus* [little frog]. The buttercup family is classified in the division MAGNOLIOPHYTA, class Magnoliopsida, order Ranunculales.

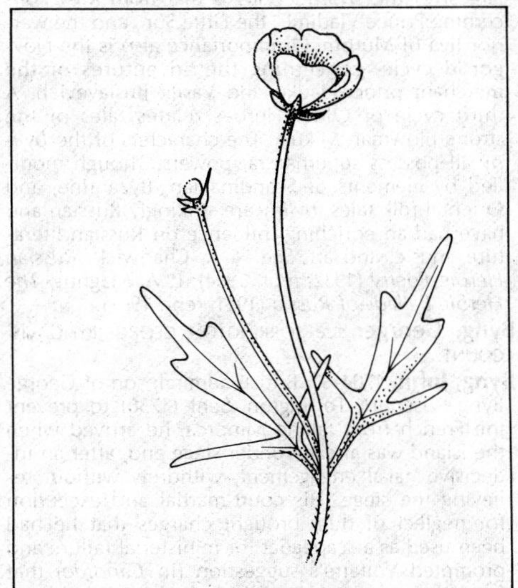

Common buttercup, Ranunculus acris

Butterfield, Herbert, 1900–, English historian. He was educated at Cambridge and became professor of modern history there in 1944. His works cover a variety of topics in modern European history; outstanding are his volumes on 18th-century English history and historiography and his *Origins of Modern Science* (1949). *The Whig Interpretation of History* (1931) showed that many accepted views of English history had grown from the bias of such Whig historians as T. B. Macaulay. In *George III, Lord North, and the People* (1948), Butterfield traced political reform ideas in England in the era of the American Revolution. A critic of the historical method of L. B. Namier, Butterfield emphasizes great ideas as being central to man's development. Other works include *The Englishman and His History* (1944), *Christianity and History* (1950), and *History and Human Relations* (1951). He was knighted in 1968.

Butterfield, John, 1801–69, American stagecoach proprietor and expressman, b. near Albany, N.Y. Beginning as a stage driver out of Albany, he rose to ownership of a large network of stage lines. He helped to merge his express company with others to form (1850) the American Express Company. In 1857, when Congress established the overland mail route to Los Angeles, Butterfield was awarded the mail contract. He organized the service on the 2,800-mi (4,500-km) southern route efficiently and continued it until 1861, when the stages were moved to the central route. He also promoted the development of telegraph lines and railroads, and in 1865 he was elected mayor of Utica, N.Y.

Butterfield, William, 1814–1900, English Gothic-revival architect. Favored by the Ecclesiological Society for his Pugin-like correctness in recalling Gothic forms, Butterfield rose to prominence in the middle of the 19th cent. The brilliant polychromy that he created through his combinations of brick, stone, and tile (e.g., All Saints' Church, London; 1849–59) introduced the High Victorian Gothic manner. The softer hues of the interior and the variously textured stone of the church at Baldersby St. James near Beverley in Yorkshire (1856) mark what is perhaps Butterfield's finest church. General interest in polychromy soon waned, but Butterfield continued in this mode with Keble College, Oxford (1868–70), and several buildings at Rugby School (1868–72).

butterfish: see HARVEST FISH.

butterfly, any of a large group of INSECTS found throughout most of the world; with the MOTHS, they comprise the order Lepidoptera. There are about 12 families of butterflies. Like moths, butterflies have coiled, sucking mouthparts and two pairs of wings that function as a single pair; the wings are covered with scales that come off as dust when the insect is handled. Butterflies can be distinguished from moths in several ways: The antennae of butterflies are knobbed at the tips, while those of moths almost never have terminal knobs and are often feathery; the body of a butterfly is more slender and usually smoother than that of a moth; butterflies are active by day, while most moths are nocturnal; when at rest most butterflies hold the wings vertically, while most moths flatten them against the surface on which they are resting. The skippers are intermediate in characteristics, but they are usually called butterflies. The Lepidoptera, especially the butterflies, are known for the beautiful colors and patterns of their wings. Red, yellow, black, and white pigments are found in the scales; the blues and greens, and the metallic, iridescent hues found especially in tropical species, are caused chiefly by refraction. Some butterflies are protectively colored to match the environment. Many conspicuously colored species are distasteful to birds, which learn to avoid them, and others are protected by their resemblance to the distasteful species (see MIMICRY). Most adult moths and butterflies feed on nectar sucked from flowers. In the process they may transfer pollen from one flower to another, and many plants depend on moths or butterflies for pollination. Metamorphosis is complete, that is, the insect goes through four stages: egg, LARVA, PUPA, and adult. The eggs, which hatch in 2 to 30 days, are usually laid on a plant that the larva (called a CATERPILLAR) uses for food. Most caterpillars eat leaves. After the last of several molts the larva is transformed into a pupa with a hard, often sculptured outer integument, within which it changes to the adult form. The butterfly pupa is called a chrysalis, or chrysalid. Most chrysalids (unlike the pupae of most moths) are not enclosed in a cocoon; however, they are usually suspended from some object by a silken thread and may have a partial covering. Except in those species which winter in the pupa stage, the adult usually emerges from the integument in two or three weeks. Members of some species winter in the egg stage, others as larvae or adults. The adults of most species, however, live only about a month. Some butterflies migrate, usually traveling toward the equator in the fall and away from it in the spring. The North American monarch butterfly makes mass migrations of several thousand miles. Among the most beautiful butterflies are the swallowtails, found all over the world, the monarchs, and the peacock and tortoiseshell butterflies. Butterflies are classified in the phylum Arthropoda, class Insecta, order Lepidoptera. The true butterflies form the superfamily Papilionoidea, and the skippers form the superfamily Hesperoidae. See L. G. Higgins and N. D. Riley, *A Field Guide to the Butterflies of Britain and Europe* (1970); Michael Dickens, *The World of Butterflies* (1973); H. L. Lewis, *Butterflies of the World* (1973).

butterfly fish, common name for certain members of the Chaetodontidae, a family of reef-dwelling tropical fishes that also includes the angelfishes and is closely allied to the spadefishes and the tangs. All have compressed bodies and small mouths and teeth. Butterfly fish are carnivorous, feeding on crabs, barnacles, and other invertebrates. The fast and aggressive common butterfly fish, 5 to 8 in. (12.5–20 cm) long, is marked by dark lines through the eyes and near the tail. The angelfishes have spines on their gill covers and long filaments on their dorsal fins. The queen angelfish, a good food fish that reaches 2 ft (60 cm) in length, is colored in blues and yellows; the smaller, more numerous common angelfish is similar. The French angelfish is black with yellow scale edgings; the black angelfish is solid black; and the bizarre rock beauty has a black body with yellow head, fins, and tail. The spadefishes are larger (up to 3 ft/90 cm) and faster than the angelfishes and are valued both as food and as game fishes. They are barred in black and white. The tangs have variable coloration. They include the violet-brown doctorfish or surgeonfish, the 8-in. (20-cm) blue tang, and the larger and more abundant ocean tang of deep waters. The butterfly fishes are classified in the phylum CHORDATA, subphylum Vertebrata, class Osteichthyes, order Perciformes, family Chaetodontidae.

butterfly flower, fringeflower, or **poor-man's-orchid,** any of the showy plants of the genus *Schizanthus* of the family Solanaceae (NIGHTSHADE family), native to Chile but grown elsewhere as garden or greenhouse annuals. The flowers resemble butterflies and are found in a variety of colors, usually mottled. Butterfly flowers are classified in the division MAGNOLIOPHYTA, class Magnoliopsida, order Polemoniales, family Solanaceae.

butterfly weed: see MILKWEED.

butternut: see WALNUT.

butterwort, common name for several species of the plant genus *Pinguicula* of the north temperate zone and the mountains of tropical America. It is a member of the family Lentibulariaceae (BLADDERWORT family).

Buttle Lake, 11 sq mi (28 sq km), central Vancouver Island, SW British Columbia, Canada. It is the site of major zinc and copper deposits.

button quail: see BUSTARD QUAIL.

buttons, knoblike appendages used on wearing apparel either for ornament or for fastening. Although buttons were sometimes used as fasteners by Greeks and Romans, they were more often merely ornamental disks. They first became widely used when fitted garments came into use in the 13th cent., and their popularity has varied with the changes in fashion. In the 16th cent. they were magnificent and were classed among the vanities; made of silver or gold and jeweled, they were often set in a long row touching one another. In the 17th cent. cloth-covered buttons with embroidered decoration were popular; buttons appeared on everything, even handkerchiefs. The Puritans, considering buttons a vanity, used hooks and eyes. Early settlers in North America often used buttons in trading with the Indians. The manufacture of buttons began in the United States c.1826. Buttons, originally made of bronze or bone, have also been made of materials such as metal, porcelain, paste, wood, ivory, horn, pearl, glass, and plastic. There are two main types, those made with holes and those with shanks. The latter have a loop of metal let in through a hole or soldered into place. See S. C. Luscombe, *The Collector's Encyclopedia of Buttons* (1967).

buttonwood: see PLANE TREE.

buttress, mass of masonry built against a wall to strengthen it. It is especially necessary when a vault or an arch places a heavy load or thrust on one part of a wall. In the case of a wall carrying the uniform load of a floor or roof, it is more economical to buttress it at certain intervals than to make the entire wall thicker. Even when a wall carries no load, it is usually buttressed rather than uniformly thickened. For a load-bearing brick wall more than 8 ft (2 m) high a buttress is used every 20 ft (6 m). The decorative possibilities of the buttress were discovered in the ancient temples at Abu Shahrein in Mesopotamia (3500–3000 B.C.), where they were used both as utilitarian and decorative forms. The Romans employed buttresses, which sometimes projected from the exteriors of the walls and were then left as mere piles of masonry, without architec-

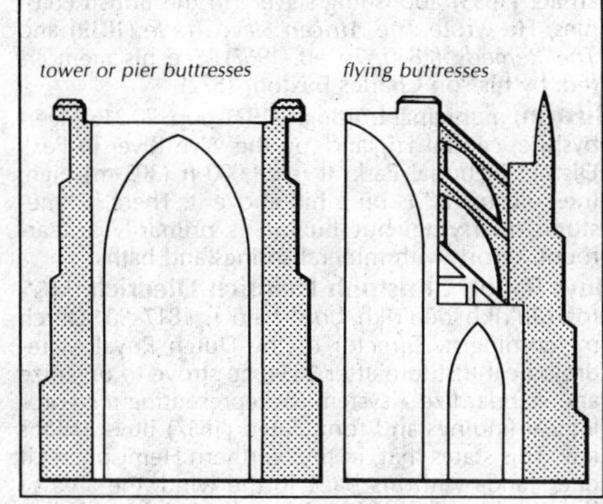

Types of buttresses

tural treatment. But in the large structures, such as basilicas and baths, the buttresses that received the thrusts from the main vaulting were confined to the interior of the building, where they served also as partition walls. The basilica of Constantine in Rome (A.D. 312) exemplifies this arrangement. In the medieval church, the groined vaults, concentrating their great lateral thrusts at points along the exterior walls, required buttresses as an essential element to achieve stability. Beginning with Romanesque architecture about A.D. 1000, a steady evolution of buttresses can be traced, from the simple, slightly projecting piers of the 11th cent. to the bold and complex Gothic examples of the 13th, 14th, and 15th cent. Builders in England, Germany, and N France achieved striking architectural effects. They devised the flying buttress, an arch of masonry abutting against the wall of the nave; the thrust of the nave vault could thus be received and transferred to the vertical buttress built against the outside walls of the side aisles. These flying arches, at first concealed beneath the roofs, began to be exposed outside the roofs in the mid-12th cent. Later they were enriched with gables, stone tracery, and sculpture and were topped with pinnacles to give them extra weight. They constitute, especially in such French cathedrals as Amiens, Beauvais, and Notre-Dame de Paris, the true expression of the elasticity and equilibrium which were the basic principles of the Gothic structural system.

Butuan (bo͞oto͞o'än), city (1970 est. pop. 116,900), capital of Agusan del Norte prov., NE Mindanao, the Philippines. It is a port on the Agusan River near its mouth at Butuan Bay. An outlet for the fertile Agusan River valley, it is one of the fastest growing cities in the Philippines.

butyl rubber (byo͞o'tĭl): see RUBBER.

butyric acid (byo͞otĭr'ĭk) or **butanoic acid** (byo͞otənō'ĭk), $CH_3CH_2CH_2CO_2H$, viscous, foul-smelling, liquid carboxylic acid; m.p. about −5°C; b.p. 163.5°C. It is miscible with water, ethanol, and ether. It is a low molecular weight FATTY ACID that is present in butter as an ester of glycerol; the odor of rancid butter is due largely to the presence of free butyric acid. Butyric acid is used in the manufacture of plastics. Isobutyric acid, or 2-methylpropanoic acid, $(CH_3)_2CHCO_2H$, is a geometric ISOMER of the butyric acid described above; it has different physical properties but similar chemical properties.

Butzer, Martin: see BUCER, MARTIN.

Buxar or **Baxar** (both: bəksär'), village (1971 pop. 31,694), West Bengal state, E central India. A British victory over the Nawab of Oudh at Buxar in 1764 assured British control of the Bengal area.

Buxtehude, Dietrich (dē'trĭkh bo͝oks"təho͞o'də), 1637-1707, Swedish composer and organist. From 1668 until his death he was organist at Lübeck, where he established a famous series of evening concerts that attracted musicians from all over northern Germany. On one occasion J. S. Bach walked about 200 miles (320 km) to hear these concerts, and his own style was much influenced by Buxtehude's choral, orchestral, and organ music. His best-known works are freely developed organ fugues and concerted choral music.

Buxton, Sir Thomas Fowell, 1786-1845, British social reformer. As a member of Parliament (1818-37) he began his reform activities immediately with the publication of *An Inquiry Whether Crime and Misery Are Produced or Prevented by Our Present System of Prison Discipline;* this work led to the establishment of the Society for the Reformation of Prison Discipline. An abolitionist, Buxton succeeded William Wilberforce as leader of the antislavery group. His efforts resulted in the passage of an act (1833) abolishing slavery in the British colonies. He wrote *The African Slave Trade* (1839) and *The Remedy* (1840, 2d ed. 1967). See his memoirs (ed. by his son Charles Buxton, 1872).

Buxton, municipal borough (1971 pop. 20,316), Derbyshire, central England, on the Wye River in Peak District National Park. It is c.1,000 ft (305 m) high; the "old town" is on a hill above it. There is limestone quarrying, but Buxton is primarily a year-round resort, with mineral springs and baths.

Buys Ballot, Christoph Heinrich Diedrich (krĭs'tôf hīn'rĭkh dēd'rĭkh bois'-bälō'), 1817-90, Dutch meteorologist. Director of the Dutch Royal Meteorological Institute after 1854, he strove to organize and standardize a system for representing meteorological findings and formulated (1857) Buys Ballot's law. This states that, in the Northern Hemisphere, if one stands with his back to the wind, the area of low pressure is to his left. In the Southern Hemisphere the reverse is true. The explanation lies in the deflection, caused by the earth's rotation, in the movement of air from areas of high pressure to areas of lower pressure. A related law had been deduced earlier by the U.S. meteorologist William Ferrel.

Büyük Menderes, river, Turkey: see MAEANDER.

Buz (bŭz). **1** Son of Nahor and Milcah. Gen. 22.21. He was apparently the eponym of an Arabian tribe. Jer. 25.23. The term Buzite is probably derived from his name. Job 32.2. **2** Gadite. 1 Chron. 5.14.

Buzău (bo͞ozû'o͞o), city (1968 est. pop. 55,000), SE Rumania, in Walachia, on the Buzău River. It is a district administrative center, an important railroad junction, and a market for petroleum, timber, and grain. Buzău is also an active industrial city, with oil refineries, foundries, distilleries, and a textile industry. Long the residence of an Orthodox bishop, it has an episcopal palace and a 16th-century cathedral, restored in 1740.

Buzi (byo͞o'zī), father of Ezekiel. Ezek. 1.3.

buzzard, common name for hawks of the genus *Buteo* and the genus *Pernis,* or honey buzzard, of the Old World family Accipitridae. Honey buzzards feed on insects, wasp and bumblebee larvae, and small reptiles. The name buzzard is also incorrectly applied to various hawks and New World vultures, such as the turkey vulture (*Cathartes aura*) and the black vulture (*Coragyps atratus*) of the family Cathartidae. Buzzards are classified in the phylum CHORDATA, subphylum Vertebrata, class Aves, order Falconiformes, family Accipitridae.

Buzzards Bay, inlet of the Atlantic Ocean, 30 mi (48 km) long, from 5 to 10 mi (8-16 m) wide, SE Mass., connected with Cape Cod Bay by the Cape Cod Canal and bounded on the SE by the Elizabeth Islands. Its shores are very irregular. The village of Buzzards Bay (1970 pop. 2,422), seat of Cape Cod Canal administration, is in the town of Bourne on the shore of the bay.

Byblos (bĭb'ləs), ancient city, Phoenicia, a port 17 mi (27 km) NNE of modern Beirut, Lebanon. The principal city of Phoenicia during the 2d millennium B.C., it long retained importance as an active port under the Persians. Byblos was the chief center of the worship of Adonis. Because of its papyruses, it was also the source of the Greek word for *book* and, hence, of the name of the Bible. Excavations of Byblos, especially since 1922, have shown that trade existed between Byblos and Egypt as early as c.2800 B.C. A syllabic script found at Byblos dates from the 18th to the 15th cent. B.C. The name of the modern town on the site, Jebail, preserves the form Gebal, the name given the city in the Old Testament (Ezek. 27.9). The inhabitants are called Giblites (Joshua 13.5). The Gebal of Psalms 83.7 is almost certainly not the same city; it is otherwise unknown.

Bydgoszcz (bĭd'gôshch), Ger. *Bromberg,* city (1970 pop. 280,460), capital of Bydgoszcz prov., N central Poland, on the Brda River, a tributary of the Vistula. One of Poland's major inland ports, it stands on the Bydgoszcz Canal (built 1773-74), which links the Brda and Noteć rivers and is part of the Vistula-Oder waterway. The city is also an important railway junction. Its chief industries produce machinery and machine tools, electrical equipment, metal goods, precision instruments, and chemicals. Chartered in 1346, the city developed during the Middle Ages around the site of a prehistoric fort. In the 15th and 16th cent. it became an important commercial center. It passed to Prussia in 1772 and was returned to Poland in 1919. Occupied by German forces from 1939 to 1945, the city suffered heavy damage in World War II. The most notable surviving building is a 15th-century Gothic church.

Byelo-. For some names beginning thus, see BELO-; e.g., for Byelorussia, see BELORUSSIA.

Byles, Mather, 1707-88, American clergyman and poet, b. Boston. Famous minister of the Hollis St. Congregational Church, Boston, from 1732, he was dismissed for his Tory sympathies after the British evacuation of Boston. From his uncle, Cotton Mather, he inherited a valuable library, to which he added his own unique collection. His poetry, imitative but witty, appeared in *Poems on Several Occasions* (1744) and other volumes; his prose includes sermons and *The Flourish of Annual Spring* (1741). See A. W. H. Eaton, *The Famous Mather Byles* (1914, repr. 1972).

byliny (bĭlē'nē) [Rus.,=what has happened], Russian scholarly term first applied in the 1840s to a great body of narrative and heroic poems. They are called by the folk *stariny* [Rus.,=what is old]. Most *byliny* are loosely connected with historical events dating from the 11th to the 16th cent., particularly the siege of Kazan (1552), and have been handed down by word of mouth by professional reciters. The poems were first collected and studied in the 18th cent. The largest of the *byliny* cycles is that from Kiev concerning Prince Vladimir, the Little Sun, and the warrior Ilya of Murom. Of importance also is the Novgorod cycle, concerning the adventures of the merchant prince Sadko and Vasily Buslayevich. A third cycle of Older Heroes relates tales of the strong plowman Mikula. The characters of the *byliny* all possess supernatural powers. Though modified by elements of Scandinavian, Byzantine, and Oriental folk tales, *byliny* are strikingly Russian and have had an enriching influence on Russian literature, music, and art. See N. K. Chadwick, *Russian Heroic Poetry* (1932, repr. 1964); L. A. Magnus, *The Heroic Ballads of Russia* (1921, repr. 1967).

Byng, George: see TORRINGTON, GEORGE BYNG, VISCOUNT.

Byng, John, 1704-57, British admiral; son of George Byng, Viscount Torrington. Sent (1756) to prevent the French from taking Minorca, he arrived when the island was already under siege and, after an indecisive naval engagement, withdrew without relieving the siege. His court-martial and execution for neglect of duty brought charges that he had been used as a scapegoat for ministerial failure and prompted Voltaire's suggestion (in *Candide*) that from time to time the British find it desirable to shoot an admiral "pour encourager les autres" [to encourage the others]. See study by D. B. E. Pope (1962).

Byng, Julian Hedworth George, 1st **Viscount Byng of Vimy,** 1862-1935, British general. He served in India and South Africa and had several commands in World War I. In April, 1917, Canadian troops under his command took Vimy Ridge, in N France. For his distinguished services he was made a baron and, in 1926, a viscount. He was governor general of Canada from 1921 to 1926.

Bynkershoek, Cornelius van (kôrnā'lĭs vän bĭng'kərs-ho͝ok), 1673-1743, Dutch writer on international law. His *De dominio maris* [on the rule of the seas] (1702, tr. 1923) is a classic on maritime law, and he also wrote on diplomatic rights and, in *Quaestiones juris publici* [questions of public law] (1737), on public law. It was Bynkershoek who first proposed the "three-mile limit" rule, which states that a nation may claim sovereignty over territorial waters to a distance of 3 mi (4.8 km) from shore.

Bynner, Witter (bĭn'ər), 1881-1968, American poet, b. Brooklyn, N.Y., grad. Harvard, 1902. As a poet Bynner had a remarkable facility for catching the cadences of other writers and cultures. Under the pseudonym Emanuel Morgan he collaborated with Arthur Davidson Ficke in writing *Spectra* (1917), a book parodying contemporary poetic vogues such as imagism; *Spectra* was for a time considered a serious work (see LITERARY FRAUDS). With Dr. Kaing Kung-Ho, Bynner translated 300 Chinese poems published in *The Jade Mountain* (1929). His other works include several plays and essays; a reminiscence of D. H. Lawrence, *Journey with Genius* (1951); and such volumes of poetry as *Grenstone Poems* (1917), *Indian Earth* (1929), *Selected Poems* (1943), *Take Away the Darkness* (1947), and *New Poems* (1960).

Byrd, Harry Flood (bûrd), 1887-1966, U. S. Senator from Virginia (1933-65), b. Martinsburg, W.Va.; brother of Richard E. Byrd. Educated at Shenandoah Academy in Winchester, Va., he became publisher of the Winchester *Star* and an important figure in state Democratic politics. His administration as governor (1926-30) was marked by the development of the state highway system. Appointed Senator in 1933, he was continually reelected until his retirement in 1965. He was a leading conservative Democrat and opposed the New Deal and later progressive measures. For many years he was chairman of the Senate Finance Committee, and he advocated government economy.

Byrd, Richard Evelyn, 1888-1957, American aviator and polar explorer, b. Winchester, Va. He took up aviation in 1917, and after World War I he gained great fame in the air. He commanded the naval air unit with the Arctic expedition of D. B. MacMillan in 1925; he and Floyd Bennett flew from Spitsbergen to the North Pole and back in 1926 (the first men to fly over the pole); and in 1927 he and three companions made one of the spectacular flights across the Atlantic. A record of his flights was presented in *Skyward* (1928). Two years later he led a well-equipped and efficiently organized expedition to Antarctica. Establishing a base at LITTLE AMERICA, he discovered the Rockefeller Range and Marie Byrd

Land, and late in 1929 he and Bernt BALCHEN flew to the South Pole and back. The large party gathered much scientific information. In 1930, Byrd was promoted to rear admiral, and his *Little America* was published. His second large expedition was organized in 1933, and headquarters were established once again at Little America. As winter approached, he set up an advance base 123 mi (198 km) closer to the South Pole and stayed there alone for several months making observations. *Discovery* (1935) and *Alone* (1938) were records of this fruitful expedition. In 1939-40 he was again in the Antarctic commanding a government expedition, and in 1946-47 he headed the U.S. navy expedition, the largest yet sent to the region (see ANTARCTICA). In 1955, Byrd was placed in command of all U.S. Antarctic activities, and in 1955-56 he led his fifth expedition to the region. Due mainly to his efforts, the U.S navy organized (1955-59) Operation Deep Freeze. Byrd's explorations form much of the basis for U.S. claims in Antarctica. See Martin Gladych, *Admiral Byrd of Antarctica* (1960); E. P. Hoyt, *The Last Explorer* (1968).

Byrd, William, 1543-1623, English composer, organist at Lincoln Cathedral and, jointly with Tallis, at the Chapel Royal. Although Roman Catholic, he composed anthems and services for the English Church in addition to his great Roman masses and Latin motets. He was highly esteemed by his contemporaries and was favored by Queen Elizabeth I, who, in 1575, granted to Byrd and Tallis a patent for the exclusive printing and selling of music. Byrd also composed music for the virginal and other instruments. See studies by E. H. Fellowes (2d ed. 1948), and Imogen Holst (1972).

Byrd, William, 1652-1704, English planter in early Virginia. He came to America as a youth and took up lands he had inherited on both sides of the James River, including the site that would later be Richmond. In 1691 he moved to "Westover," long famous as the Byrd family home. His landed fortune was increased by his interest in trade, and he served (1703) as president of the Virginia council. Byrd's wealth, culture, and character made him the ideal tidewater aristocrat. He was the father of William Byrd (1674-1744).

Byrd, William, 1674-1744, American colonial writer, planter, and government official; son of William Byrd (1652-1704). After being educated in England, he became active in the politics of colonial America. He served as member of the house of burgesses, as receiver-general of Virginia, as Virginia council member, and as colonial agent in England. Byrd inherited a great estate from his father and ultimately owned over 179,000 acres (72,000 hectares). In 1737 he had the city that was to be Richmond laid out on one of his estates. His service in 1728 as one of the commissioners to survey the North Carolina-Virginia boundary and his many trips into the backwoods provided the material for much of his writings; *A History of the Dividing Line, A Journey to the Land of Eden,* and *A Progress to the Mines* were all based on his diaries. Byrd's polished style and crisp wit, in addition to his valuable record of Southern life, have won him a reputation as one of the foremost colonial authors. At his death he left a library of some 4,000 volumes at his Westover estate. See his diaries and other writings (1941, 1942, 1970); biography by Pierre Marambaud (1971).

Byrde, William: see BYRD, WILLIAM.

Byrhtnoth (bĭrkht'nōth) or **Bryhtnoth** (brĭkht'nōth), d. 991, alderman of the East Saxons. Leader of the English forces in the battle of MALDON, he was killed in the battle and was buried at Ely.

Byrnes, James Francis, 1879-1972, American public official, Secretary of State (1945-47), governor of South Carolina (1951-55), b. Charleston, S.C. He studied law while working (1900-1908) as a court reporter, owned and edited a newspaper in Aiken, S. C., and represented (1911-25) South Carolina in the House. As Senator (1931-41), Byrnes, a Southern Democrat, became budgetary expert for the New Deal. He served as an Associate Justice of the Supreme Court (1941-42), but resigned and became director of economic stabilization (1942) and later (1943) director of war mobilization. As Secretary of State he tried to mend postwar differences with the USSR. He later became extremely anti-Soviet. An opponent of racial integration, he was elected governor of South Carolina, and opposed further Federal centralization. See his *Speaking Frankly* (1947) and *All in One Lifetime* (1958).

Byrom, John (bī'rəm), 1692-1763, English shorthand expert and poet, educated at Trinity College, Cambridge. He devised an early shorthand system, which he taught in Manchester. Although he copyrighted his system in 1742, his book, *The Universal English Shorthand*, was not published until after his death. He was a great admirer of William Law, and much information about Law is found in Byrom's *Private Journal and Literary Remains* (1854-57). He wrote *Seasonably Alarming and Humiliating Truths in a Metrical Version of Certain Select Passages Taken from the Works of William Law* (1774) and other facilely rhyming, rather eccentric religious verse.

Byron, George Gordon Noel Byron, 6th **Baron** (bī'rən), 1788-1824, English poet and satirist, son of Capt. John ("Mad Jack") Byron and his second wife, Catherine Gordon of Gight. His father died in 1791, and Byron, born with a clubfoot, was subjected alternately to the excessive tenderness and violent temper of his mother. In 1798, after years of poverty, Byron succeeded to the title and took up residence at the family seat, "Newstead Abbey." He subsequently attended Dulwich school and Harrow (1801-5) and then matriculated at Trinity College, Cambridge. Although the academic atmosphere did nothing to lessen Byron's sensitivity about his lameness, he made several close friends while at school. His first volume, *Fugitive Pieces* (1806), was suppressed; revised and expanded, it appeared in 1807 as *Poems on Various Occasions.* This was followed by *Hours of Idleness* (1807), which provoked such severe criticism from the *Edinburgh Review* that Byron replied with *English Bards and Scotch Reviewers* (1809), a satire in heroic couplets reminiscent of Pope, which brought him immediate fame. He left England the same year for a grand tour through Spain, Portugal, Italy, and the Balkans. He returned in 1811 with Cantos I and II of *Childe Harold* (1812), a melancholy, philosophic poem in Spenserian stanzas, which made him the social lion of London. It was followed by the verse tales *The Giaour* (1813), *The Bride of Abydos* (1813), *The Corsair* (1814), *Lara* (1814), *The Siege of Corinth* (1816), and *Parisina* (1816). Byron's name at this time was linked with those of several women, notably Viscount Melbourne's wife, Lady Caroline Lamb. In Jan., 1815, he married Anne Isabella Milbanke, a serious, rather cold, young woman with whom he had little in common. She gave birth to a daughter, Augusta Ada, the following December. In 1816 she secured a separation. Although her reasons for such an action remain obscure, evidence indicates that she discovered the existence of an incestuous relationship between Byron and his half-sister, Mrs. Augusta Leigh. Although his many attachments to women are notorious, Byron was actually ambivalent toward women. There is some evidence that he had several homosexual relationships. In April, 1816, a social outcast, Byron left England, never to return. He passed some time with Shelley in Switzerland, writing Canto III of *Childe Harold* (1816) and *The Prisoner of Chillon* (1816). With the party was Shelley's sister-in-law, Claire Clairmont, who had practically forced Byron into a liason before he left England, and who, in Jan., 1817, bore him a daughter, Allegra. Settling in Venice (1817), he led for a time a life of dissipation, but produced Canto IV of *Childe Harold* (1818), *Beppo* (1818), and *Mazeppa* (1819) and began *Don Juan.* In 1819 he formed a liaison with the Countess Teresa Guiccioli, who remained his acknowledged mistress for the rest of his life. Byron was induced to interest himself in the cause of Greek independence from the Turks and sailed for Missolonghi, where he arrived in 1824. He worked unsparingly with Prince Alexander Mavrocordatos to unify the divergent Greek forces, but caught a fever and died the same year. Ranked with Shelley and Keats as one of the great Romantic poets, Byron became famous throughout Europe as the embodiment of romanticism. His good looks, his lameness, his flamboyant life style all contributed to the formation of the Byronic legend. By the mid-20th cent. his reputation as a poet had been eclipsed by growing critical recognition of his talents as a wit and satirist. Byron's poetry covers a wide range. In *English Bards and Scotch Reviewers* and in *The Vision of Judgment* (1822), he wrote 18th-century satire. He created the "Byronic hero," who appears consummately in the Faustian tragedy *Manfred* (1817)—a mysterious, lonely, defiant figure whose past hides some great crime. *Cain* (1821) raised a storm of abuse for its skeptical attitute toward religion. The verse tale *Beppo* is in the *ottava rima* (eight-line stanzas in iambic pentameter) that Byron later used for his acknowledged masterpiece *Don Juan* (1819-24), an epic-satire combining Byron's art as a storyteller, his lyricism, his cynicism, and his detestation of convention. See his letters and diaries, ed. by Leslie Marchand (2 vol., 1973; others planned); biographies by André Maurois (1930, repr. 1964), Leslie Marchand (3 vol., 1957; and 1 vol., 1970); studies by Peter Quennell (rev. ed. 1967; and 1941, repr. 1957), G. Wilson Knight (1952 and 1957), L. A. Marchand (1965), and Michael G. Cooke (1969).

Byron, John, 1723-86, British vice admiral and explorer. Sailing in 1740 with Admiral George Anson on a voyage around the world, he was shipwrecked off Chile. His *Narrative of Great Distresses on the Shores of Patagonia* (1768) is said to have been used by his grandson, the poet George Gordon, Lord Byron, in writing *Don Juan.*

Byström, John Niklas (bü'ström), 1783-1848, Swedish sculptor. He spent part of his life in Rome. Byström made colossal statues of kings of Sweden for Stockholm, but he was most successful in portraying women and children.

Bytom (bĭ'tôm), Ger. *Beuthen,* city (1970 pop. 186,993), SW Poland, in the Katowice mining region. An important industrial center, it has factories producing metal products and furniture. A Polish king built a fortress on the site in the 11th cent., and by the 12th cent. the lead and zinc mines of the region were being exploited. The city was chartered in 1254, and in the late 13th cent. served briefly as the capital of an independent principality that passed under the rule of Bohemia. The Hapsburgs held the city from 1526 until 1742, when it passed to Prussia. In a plebescite after World War I a majority of the population voted to join Poland, but Germany held onto the city. It was finally incorporated into Poland in 1945. Bytom has an opera house and museum.

Bytown: see OTTAWA, Canada.

Byzantine art and architecture include not only works produced in the city of Byzantium after Constantine made it the capital of the Roman Empire (A.D. 330) but also the work done under Byzantine influence, as in Venice, Ravenna, Norman Sicily, and in Syria, Greece, Russia, and other Eastern countries. For more than a thousand years, until the conquest of Constantinople by the Turks in 1453, Byzantine art retained a remarkably conservative orientation; the major phases of its development emerge from a background marked by adherence to classical principles. Artistic activity was temporarily disrupted by the Iconoclastic controversy (726-843), which resulted in the wholesale destruction of figurative works of art and the restriction of permissible content to ornamental forms or to symbols like the cross. The pillaging of Constantinople by the Frankish Crusaders in 1204 was perhaps a more serious blow; but it was followed by an impressive late flowering of Byzantine art under the Paleologus dynasty. Byzantine achievements in mosaic decoration brought this art to an unprecedented level of monumentality and expressive power. Mosaics were applied to the domes, half-domes, and other available surfaces of Byzantine churches in an established hierarchical order. The center of the dome was reserved for the representation of the Pantocrator, or Christ as the ruler of the universe, whereas other sacred personages occupied lower spaces in descending order of importance. The entire church thus served as a tangible evocation of the celestial order; this conception was further enhanced by the stylized poses and gestures of the figures, their hieratic gaze, and the luminous shimmer of the gold backgrounds. Because of the destruction of many major monuments in Constantinople proper, large ensembles of mosaic decoration have survived chiefly outside the capital, in such places as Salonica, Nicaea, and Daphni in Greece and Ravenna in Italy. An important aspect of Byzantine artistic activity was the painting of devotional panels, since the cult of ICONS played a leading part in both religious and secular life. Icon painting usually employed the ENCAUSTIC technique. Little scope was afforded individuality; the effectiveness of the religious image as a vehicle of divine presence was held to depend on its fidelity to an established prototype. A large group of devotional images has been preserved in the monastery of St. Catherine on Mt. Sinai. The development of Byzantine painting may be seen also in manuscript illumination. Among notable examples of Byzantine illumination are a lavishly illustrated 9th-century copy of the Homilies of Gregory Nazianzus and two works believed to date from a 10th-century revival of classicism, the Joshua Rotulus (or Roll) and the Paris Psalter. Enamel, ivory, and metalwork objects of Byzantine workmanship were highly prized throughout the Middle Ages; many such works are found in the treasuries of Western churches. Most of these objects were reliquaries or devotional panels, although an important series of ivory caskets with pagan subjects has also been preserved. Byzantine silks, the manufacture of which was a state monopoly, were also eagerly sought and treasured as goods of utmost luxury. The architecture of the Byzantine Empire was based on the great legacy of Roman formal and technical achievements. Constantinople had been purposely founded as the Christian counterpart and successor to the leadership of the old pagan city of Rome. The new capital was in close contact with the Hellenized East, and the contribution of Eastern culture, though sometimes overstressed, was an important element in the development of its architectural style. The 5th-century basilica of St. John of the Studion, the oldest surviving church in Constantinople, is an early example of Byzantine reliance upon traditional Roman models. The most imposing achievement of Byzantine architecture is the Church of Holy Wisdom (see HAGIA SOPHIA). It was constructed in a short span of five years (532–37) during the reign of Justinian. Hagia Sophia is without a clear antecedent in the architecture of late antiquity, yet it must be accounted as culminating several centuries of experimentation toward the realization of a unified space of monumental dimensions. Throughout the history of Byzantine religious architecture, the centrally planned structure continued in favor. Such structures, which may show considerable variation in plan, have in common the predominance of a central domed space, flanked and partly sustained by smaller domes and half-domes spanning peripheral spaces. Although many of the important buildings of Constantinople have been destroyed, impressive examples are still extant throughout the provinces and on the outer fringes of the empire, notably in Bulgaria, Russia, Armenia, and Sicily. A great Byzantine architectural achievement is the octagonal church of San Vitale (consecrated 547) in Ravenna. The church of St. Mark's in Venice was based on a Byzantine prototype, and Byzantine workmen were employed by Arab rulers in the Holy Land and in Ottonian Germany during the 11th cent. Secular architecture in the Byzantine Empire has left fewer traces. Foremost among these are the ruins of the 5th-century walls of the city of Constantinople, consisting of an outer and an inner wall, each originally studded with 96 towers. Some of these can still be seen. See Alexander van Millingen, *Byzantine Churches in Constantinople* (1912); André Grabar, *Byzantine Painting* (tr. 1953); D. Talbot Rice, *Art of Byzantium* (1959) and *Art of the Byzantine Era* (1963); William MacDonald, *Early Christian and Byzantine Architecture* (1963).

Byzantine Empire, successor state to the Roman Empire (see under ROME), also called Eastern Empire and East Roman Empire. It was named after Byzantium, which Emperor Constantine I rebuilt (A.D. 330) as CONSTANTINOPLE and made the capital of the entire Roman Empire. Although not foreseen at the time, a division into Eastern and Western empires became permanent after the accession (395) of HONORIUS in the West and ARCADIUS in the East. Throughout its existence the Byzantine Empire was subject to important changes in its boundaries. The core of the empire consisted of the Balkan Peninsula (i.e., Thrace, Macedonia, Epirus, Greece proper, the Greek isles, and Illyria) and of Asia Minor (present-day Turkey). The empire combined Roman political tradition, Hellenic culture, and Christian beliefs. Greek was the prevalent language, but Latin long continued in official use. The characteristic Oriental influence began with Constantine I, who also introduced Christianity. Orthodoxy triumphed over ARIANISM under Arcadius' predecessor, Theodosius I, but violent religious controversy was chronic. The reigns (395–527) of Arcadius, Theodosius II, Marcian, Leo I, Leo II, Zeno, Anastasius I, and Justin I were marked by the invasions of the Visigoths under ALARIC I, of the Huns of ATTILA, and of the AVARS, the SLAVS, the Bulgars (see BULGARIA), and the Persians. After the Western Empire fell (476) to ODOACER, Italy, Gaul, and Spain were theoretically united under Zeno but were actually dominated by, respectively, the Ostrogoths, the Franks, and the Visigoths, while Africa was under the Vandals. During this period arose the heresies of NESTORIANISM and MONOPHYSITISM and the political parties of BLUES AND GREENS to divide the Byzantines.

An Age of Revival. Under the rule (527–65) of JUSTINIAN I and THEODORA, Byzantine power grew. Their great generals, BELISARIUS and NARSES, checked the Persians, repressed political factions, and recovered Italy and Africa, while TRIBONIAN helped the emperor to codify ROMAN LAW. During Justinian's reign a great revival of Hellenism took place in literature, and Byzantine art and architecture entered their most glorious period. Much was lost again under his successors. The LOMBARDS conquered most of Italy; however, the Pentapolis, Rome, Sardinia, Corsica, Liguria, and the coasts of S Italy and Sicily long remained under Byzantine rule, and at RAVENNA the exarchs governed until 751. The Persians, under KHOSRU I, made great gains against the empire, though Emperor Maurice temporarily checked them in 591. The emperor Heraclius (610–41) defeated the Persians but was barely able to save Constantinople from the Avars. Muslim conquests soon afterward wrested Syria, Palestine, Egypt, Africa, and Sicily from the empire. Heraclius' attempt to reconcile Monophysitism and orthodoxy merely led to the new heresy of MONOTHELETISM. His military reorganization of the provinces into *themes* proved effective and was continued by Constans II (641–48). Constantine IV (668–85) saved Constantinople from Arab attack. The 7th cent. was marked by increasing Hellenization of the empire, outwardly symbolized by the adoption of the Greek title Basileus by the emperors. The church, under the patriarch of Constantinople, became increasingly important in public affairs. Theology, cultivated by emperors and monks alike, was pushed to extremes of subtlety. Literature and art became chiefly religious. Under Justinian II and his successors the empire was again

RULERS OF THE BYZANTINE EMPIRE *(including dates of reign)*

Constantine I (the Great), 330–37	Romanus I Lecapenus, 919–44
Constantius, 337–61	Constantine VII (restored), 944–59
Julian (the Apostate), 361–63	Romanus II, 959–63
Jovian, 363–64	Basil II Bulgaroktonos, 963
Valens, 364–78	Nicephorus II Phocas, 963–69
Theodosius I (the Great), 379–95	John I Tzimisces, 969–76
Arcadius, 395–408	Basil II (restored), 976–1025
Theodosius II, 408–50	Constantine VIII, 1025–28
Marcian, 450–57	Zoë and Romanus III Argyrus, 1028–34
Leo I (the Great or the Thracian), 457–74	Zoë and Michael IV (the Paphlagonian), 1034–41
Leo II, 474	Zoë and Michael V Calaphates, 1041–42
Zeno, 474–75	Zoë and Theodora, 1042
Basiliscus, 475–76	Zoë, Theodora, and Constantine IX Monomachus, 1042–50
Zeno (restored), 476–91	Theodora and Constantine IX, 1050–55
Anastasius I, 491–518	Theodora, 1055–56
Justin I, 518–27	Michael VI Stratioticus, 1056–57
Justinian I (the Great), 527–65	Isaac I Comnenus, 1057–59
Justin II, 565–78	Constantine X Ducas, 1059–67
Tiberius II Constantinus, 578–82	Michael VII Ducas (Parapinaces), 1067–68
Maurice, 582–602	Romanus IV Diogenes, 1068–71
Phocas, 602–10	Michael VII Ducas (restored), 1071–78
Heraclius, 610–41	Nicephorus III Botaniates, 1078–81
Constantine III and Heracleonas, 641	Alexius I Comnenus, 1081–1118
Heracleonas, 641	John II Comnenus, 1118–43
Constans II Pogonatus, 641–68	Manuel I Comnenus, 1143–80
Constantine IV, 668–85	Alexius II Comnenus, 1180–83
Justinian II Rhinotmetus, 685–95	Andronicus I Comnenus, 1183–85
Leontius, 695–98	Isaac II Angelus, 1185–95
Tiberius III, 698–705	Alexius III Angelus, 1195–1203
Justinian II (restored), 705–11	Isaac II (restored) and Alexius IV Angelus, 1203–4
Philippicus Bardanes, 711–13	Alexius V Ducas, 1204
Anastasius II, 713–15	Theodore I Lascaris, 1204–22
Theodosius III, 716–17	John III Vatatzes or Ducas, 1222–54
Leo III (the Isaurian or the Syrian), 717–41	Theodore II Lascaris, 1254–58
Constantine V Copronymus, 741–75	John IV Lascaris, 1258–61
Leo IV (the Khazar), 775–80	Michael VIII Palaeologus, 1259–82
Constantine VI, 780–97	Andronicus II Palaeologus, 1282–1328
Irene, 797–802	Andronicus III Palaeologus, 1328–41
Nicephorus I, 802–11	John V Palaeologus, 1341–76
Stauracius, 811	John VI Cantacuzenus (usurper), 1347–55
Michael I, 811–13	Andronicus IV Palaeologus, 1376–79
Leo V (the Armenian), 813–20	John V Palaeologus (restored), 1379–91
Michael II (the Stammerer), 820–29	John VII Palaeologus (usurper), 1390
Theophilus, 829–42	Manuel II Palaeologus, 1391–1425
Michael III (the Drunkard), 842–67	John VII Palaeologus (restored as coemperor), 1399–1412
Basil I (the Macedonian), 867–86	John VIII Palaeologus, 1425–48
Leo VI (the Wise or the Philosopher), 886–912	Constantine XI Palaeologus, 1449–53
Alexander, 912–13	
Constantine VII Porphyrogenitus, 913–19	

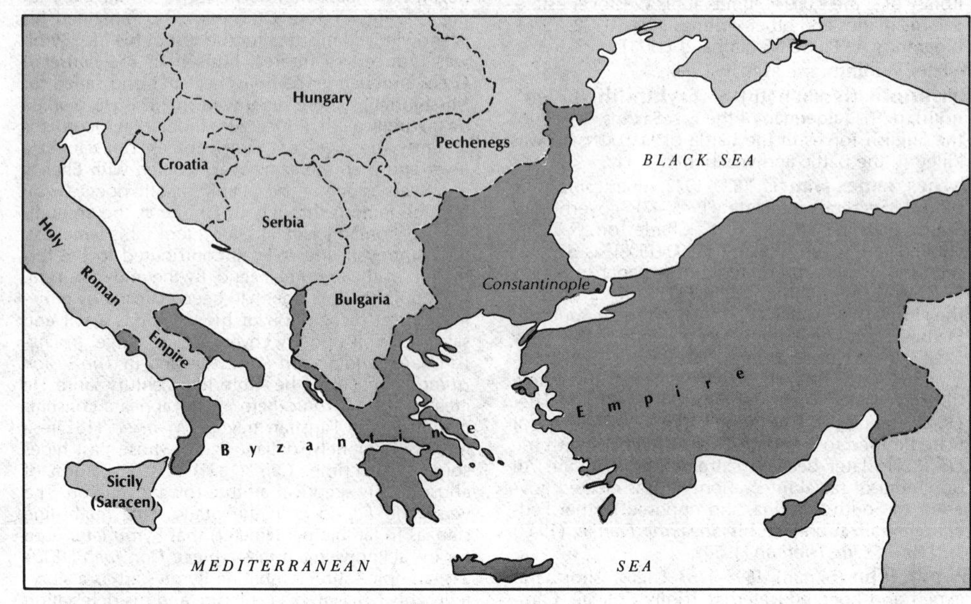

Byzantine Empire (c.1000)

menaced by Arabs and Bulgars, but the Isaurian emperors Leo III (717–41) and Constantine V stopped the Arab advance and recovered Asia Minor. The grave issue of ICONOCLASM, which they precipitated, led to the loss of Rome. In 800, during the reign of Irene, the Frank CHARLEMAGNE was crowned emperor of the West at Rome. Thus ended even the theoretical primacy of Byzantium over Europe.

The Oriental State. The political division of East and West was paralleled by a religious schism, intensified by the patriarch PHOTIUS, between the Roman and the ORTHODOX EASTERN CHURCH, later culminating in a complete break (1054). In all aspects the Byzantine Empire, having lost its claim to universality, became a Greek monarchy, though Constantinople still remained the center of both Greek and Roman civilization. Compared with its intellectuals, artists, writers, and artisans, those of Western Europe were crude and barbarous, though sometimes more vigorous and original. In the empire the administrative machinery was huge, and competition among the courtiers was intense. Complex diplomacy, intrigue, and gross violence marked the course of events; yet moral decay did not prevent such emperors as Basil I, founder of the Macedonian dynasty, and his successors (notably Leo VI, Romanus I, Constantine VII, Nicephorus II, John I, and Basil II) from giving the empire a period of splendor and power (867–1025). The eastern frontier was pushed to the Euphrates River, the Bulgars were subjugated, and the Balkan Peninsula was recovered. Russia, converted to Christianity, became an outpost of Byzantine culture. In the unceasing struggle between the great landowners and the small peasantry, most of the emperors favored the peasants. Economic prosperity was paralleled by a new golden age in science, philosophy, and architecture.

The Ebb of Power. With the rule of Zoë (1028–50) anarchy and decline set in. The Seljuk TURKS increased their attacks, and with the defeat (1071) of Romanus IV at Manzikert most of Asia Minor was permanently lost. The Normans under Robert GUISCARD and BOHEMOND I seized S Italy and attacked the Balkans. Venice ruled the Adriatic and challenged Byzantine commercial dominance in the East, and the Bulgars and Serbs reasserted their independence. Alexius I (1081–1118) took advantage of the First Crusade (see CRUSADES) to recover some territory in Asia Minor and to restore Byzantine prestige, but his successors of the COMNENUS dynasty were at best able to postpone the disintegration of the empire. After the death (1180) of Manuel I the Angelus dynasty unwittingly precipitated the cataclysm of the Fourth Crusade. In 1204 the Crusaders and the Venetians sacked Constantinople and set up a new empire (see CONSTANTINOPLE, LATIN EMPIRE OF) in Thrace, Macedonia, and Greece. The remainder of the empire broke into independent states, notably the empires of NICAEA and of TREBIZOND and the despotate of EPIRUS. In 1261 the Nicaean emperor Michael VIII conquered most of the tottering Latin empire and reestablished the Byzantine Empire under the PALAEOLOGUS family (1261–1453). The reconstructed empire was soon attacked from all sides, notably by CHARLES I of Naples, by Venice, by the Ottoman Turks, by the new kingdoms of Serbia and Bulgaria, and by Catalonian adventurers under Roger de FLOR. At the same time, the empire began to break down from within—the capital was at odds with the provinces; ambitious magnates were greedy for land and privileges; religious orders fought each other vigorously; and church and state were rivals for power. Eventually the Turks encircled the empire and reduced it to Constantinople and its environs. Manual II and John VIII vainly asked the West for aid, and, in 1453, Constantinople fell to Sultan MUHAMMAD II after a final desperate defense under Constantine XI. This is one of the dates conventionally accepted as the beginning of the modern age. The collapse of the empire opened the way for the vast expansion of the Ottoman Empire to Vienna itself and also enabled IVAN III of Russia, son-in-law of Constantine XI, to claim a theoretical succession to the imperial title. The classic, though biased, work on Byzantine history is Gibbon's *Decline and Fall of the Roman Empire.* More recent standard works are those of J. B. Bury, Charles Diehl, A. A. Vasil'ev, George Ostrogorsky, and N. H. Baynes. See Steven Runciman, *Byzantine Civilization* (1933, repr. 1959); J. M. Hussey, *The Byzantine World* (3d rev. ed. 1967); R. J. H. Jenkins, *Byzantium* (1967); Dimitri Obolensky, *The Byzantine Commonwealth* (1971).

Byzantine music, the music of the Byzantine Empire composed to Greek texts as ceremonial festival or church music. Long thought to be only a further development of ancient Greek music, Byzantine music is now regarded as an independent musical culture, with elements derived from Syrian and Hebrew as well as Greek sources. Its beginnings are dated by some scholars as in the 4th cent., after the founding of the Eastern Empire by Constantine I. Although two Greek instruments, the kithara and the aulos, were used, the principal instrument of Byzantium was the organ. No purely instrumental music is extant, however, and the exact nature of the instrumental accompaniment of vocal music is not certain. The eight Byzantine *echoi* (singular *echos*) correspond roughly to the eight MODES of plainsong, but they were groups of melodies made of certain definite formulas. The Byzantine music that survives is all sacred, with the exception of some acclamations for the emperor. Byzantine chant was monodic, in free rhythm, and often attempted to depict melodically the meaning of the words. The language was Greek. The Byzantine hymn, of which there were three types, was the greatest contribution of this culture. The *troparion,* a hymn, was inserted between the verses of the Psalms, and eventually the *troparia* overshadowed the Psalms. The origin of the *kontakion,* a hymn important in the 6th and 9th cent., is ascribed to Romanus, active during the reign of Anastasius I; it consisted of 18 or 24 strophes all in similar meter, with a contrasting introductory strophe. The subject matter was usually biblical. Often an acrostic is formed by the first letter of each stanza. The time of Romanus and of Sergius (fl. early 7th cent.) is called the golden age of Byzantine music. In the 8th cent. the outstanding hymn writers were St. John of Damascus and Cosmas of Jerusalem. The chief type of hymn was the *kanon,* a series of odes, theoretically nine but often only eight in number, referring to the nine canticles of the Old and New Testaments. Until the 9th cent., poet and composer were always one; later, hymns were set to already existing melodies. With the codification of the Greek liturgy in the 11th cent. there was a general decline in hymnody. Musical activity ceased with the fall of Constantinople (1453). Russian chant, the chant of the modern Greek Orthodox Church, and to a small extent Gregorian chant all owe something to Byzantine chant. Byzantine notation was originally only a system of *ekphonetic* symbols serving to remind a singer of a melody he already knew. Neumes derived from the *ekphonetic* notation were in use from c.950 until 1200. From 1110 to 1450 a staffless notation indicating the *echos,* starting note, and subsequent intervals of a melody was in use. It is largely decipherable today. Signs were added to it in the centuries that followed; the notation used in the Greek Church today was devised in the 19th cent. by Chrysanthus, a Greek archimandrite, because of the confusion in deciphering the manuscripts of early Byzantine music. See Gustave Reese, *Music in the Middle Ages* (1940); studies of Byzantine music and hymnography by S. I. Savas (1965) and A. L. Burkhalter (1968).

Byzantine rite: see ORTHODOX EASTERN CHURCH.

Byzantium (bĭzăn'shēəm, -shəm, -tēəm), ancient city of Thrace, on the site of the present-day İstanbul, Turkey. Founded by Greeks from Megara in 667 B.C., it early rose to importance because of its position on the Bosporus. In the Peloponnesian War it was captured and recaptured by the contending forces. It was taken (A.D. 196) by Roman Emperor Septimius Severus. Constantine I ordered (A.D. 330) a new city built there; this was CONSTANTINOPLE, later the capital of the Byzantine Empire. See Charles Diehl, *Byzantium: Greatness and Decline* (tr. 1957); Michael Maclagan, *The City of Constantinople* (1968).

C

C, third letter of the ALPHABET. In position and form, but not in meaning, it corresponds to Greek gamma (see G). In English it is pronounced variously, e.g., in *can, cent, church,* and *loch.* In MUSICAL NOTATION it symbolizes a note in the scale. In chemistry it is the symbol of the element CARBON. The capital letter is the Roman numeral for 100.

Ca, chemical symbol of the element CALCIUM.

Caaba: see KAABA.

Cabal (kəbăl'), inner group of advisers to Charles II of England. Their initials form the word (which is, however, of older origin)—Clifford of Chudleigh, Ashley (Lord Shaftesbury), Buckingham (George Villiers), Arlington (Henry Bennet), and Lauderdale (John Maitland). Although they were never a working ministry, one or more of this group dominated court policy from 1667 through 1673. See study by Maurice Lee (1965).

cabala or **cabbala** (both: kăb'ələ) [Heb.,=tradition], esoteric system of interpretation of the Scriptures based upon a tradition claimed to have been handed down orally from Abraham. Despite that claimed antiquity, the system appears to have been given its earliest formulation in the 11th cent. in France, and from there spread most notably to Spain. There were undoubtedly precedents, however; cabalistic elements are discernible in Jewish Gnosticism, which has its roots in the early Christian era. Beyond the specifically Jewish notions contained within the cabala, some scholars believe that it reflects a strong Neoplatonic influence, especially in its doctrines of emanation and the transmigration of souls. In the late 15th and 16th cent., Christian thinkers found support in the cabala for their own doctrines, out of which they developed a Christian cabala. Cabalistic interpretation of Scripture was based on the belief that every word, letter, number, and even accent contained mysteries interpretable by those who knew the secret. The names for God were believed to contain miraculous power and each letter of the divine name was considered potent; cabalistic signs and writings were used as amulets and in magical practices. The two principal sources of the cabalists are the *Sefer Yezirah* (tr. *Book of Creation,* 1894) and the *Zohar* (tr. 1949). The first develops, in a series of monologues supposedly delivered by Abraham, the doctrine of the *Sefirot* (the powers emanating from God, through which the world is created and its order sustained), using the primordial numbers of the later Pythagoreans in a system of numerical interpretation. It was probably written in the 3d cent. The *Zohar* is a mystical commentary on the Pentateuch. It was written by Moses de León (13th cent.) but attributed by him to Simon ben Yohai, the great scholar of the 2d cent. Following the expulsion (1492) of the Jews from Spain, cabala became more messianic in its emphasis, as developed by the Lurianic school of mystics at Safed, Palestine. Cabala in this form was widely adopted and created fertile gound for the movement of the pseudo-Messiah SABBATAI ZEVI. It was also a major influence in the development of HASIDISM. Cabala still has adherents, especially among Hasidic Jews. See J. F. C. Fuller, *The Secret Wisdom of the Qabalah* (1937); J. L. Blau, *The Christian Interpretation of the Cabala in the Renaissance* (1944, repr. 1965); A. E. Waite, *The Holy Kabbalah* (1960); Gershom Scholem, *Major Trends in Jewish Mysticism* (3d ed. 1954, repr. 1965) and *On the Kabbalah and Its Symbolism* (1965); Herbert Weiner, *Nine and One Half Mystics: the Kabbalah Today* (1969).

Caballé, Montserrat (mōnsĕrät' käbälyā'), 1933–, Spanish soprano. After voice study with Eugenia Kemeny and Conchita Badia in Barcelona, she made her operatic debut in Basel, Switzerland, singing Mimi in Puccini's *La Bohème.* She became an overnight success with American audiences in 1965 after singing in Donizetti's *Lucrezia Borgia* at Carnegie Hall in New York City. That same year she made her debut at the Metropolitan Opera as Marguerite in Gounod's *Faust.* Her voice is noted for its purity and precise control. Caballé has sung over 40 operatic roles, including the Marschallin in Richard Strauss's *Der Rosenkavalier* and the title role in *Salomé.*

Caballero, Fernán (fārnän' käbälyā'rō), pseud. of **Cecilia Böhl de Faber** (thāthē'lyä böl dā fäbär'), 1796–1877, Spanish novelist and folklorist. Born in Switzerland, she spent most of her adult life in Andalusia, where her novels are set. Although their tone is didactic and their plots sentimental, they successfully reflect contemporary regional life. The first, *La Gaviota* (1849, tr. *The Sea Gull,* 1864), effected the creation of the modern Spanish novel of customs. Others are *Lágrimas* [tears] (1858) and *Clemencia* (1862). Some of her folk tales were translated as *Spanish Fairy Tales* (1920). See biography by P. H. Klibbe (1973).

cabbage, leafy garden vegetable of many widely dissimilar varieties, all probably descended from the wild, or sea, cabbage (*Brassica oleracea*) of the family Cruciferae (MUSTARD family), found on the coasts of Europe. It is used for food for man and stock, mostly in Europe and North America. Well-known varieties of the species include the cabbages, BROCCOLI, BRUSSELS SPROUTS, CAULIFLOWER, collards, KALE, and KOHLRABI. All grow best in cool, moist climates. They are attacked mostly by insect pests. The true cabbages (var. *capitata*) include the white and red types and the Savoy type (grown mostly in Europe), with curly, loose leaves. Inexpensive and easily stored, cabbage is important in the diet of many poorer peoples. Popular cabbage dishes include sauerkraut and slaw (raw cabbage). Chinese cabbage, or petsai, chiefly a salad plant, is a separate species (*B. pekinensis*) grown in many varieties, especially in the Far East. Cabbages with multicolored leaves are becoming popular as ornamental border plants for flower gardens. Cabbages are classified in the division MAGNOLIOPHYTA, class Magnoliopsida, order Capparales, family Cruciferae.

cabbage looper, moth larva, *Trichoplusia ni,* that feeds by night on the leaves of cabbage and related plants and is a serious agricultural pest. Like the inchworms (of another moth family), cabbage loopers lack walking appendages in the middle of the body and progress by drawing the rear end up to the front end and then straightening. A cabbage looper has a smooth green body with a white stripe along each side and reaches a length of 1¼ in. (3.2 cm). It pupates in a cocoon on the underside of a leaf. The adult moth is brown with a white spot on each wing. Cabbage loopers are classified in the phylum ARTHROPODA, class Insecta, order Lepidoptera, family Noctuidae.

cabbala: see CABALA.

Cabbon (kăb'ŏn), town, SW Palestine. Joshua 15.40.

Cabell, Branch (James Branch Cabell) (kă'bəl), 1879–1958, American novelist, b. Richmond, Va., grad. William and Mary, 1898. After various experiences as a journalist and a coal miner he began writing fiction. His early works, which are sophisticated novels deriding conventional history, include *Gallantry* (1907), *Chivalry* (1909), and *The Rivet in Grandfather's Neck* (1915). Many of Cabell's most popular novels are set in the imaginary medieval kingdom of Poictesme; among these are *The Cream of the Jest* (1917), *Jurgen* (1919)—Cabell's most famous work because of its attempted suppression on charges of obscenity—and *The Silver Stallion* (1926). Cabell's novels are usually pointedly anti-realistic, and many of them can be considered moral allegories. Although he was enormously popular in the 1920s, his highly artifical prose style and subject matter lost favor with critics and public alike by the 1930s. His nonfictional writing includes *Beyond Life* (1919), *The St. Johns* (with A. J. Hanna, 1943), and *Here Let Me Lie* (1947). See studies by Joe L. Davis (1962), Desmond Tarrant (1967), Hugh Walpole (1920, repr. 1973), and L. D. Rubin (1959, repr. 1973).

Cabet, Etienne (ātyĕn' käbā'), 1788–1856, French utopian socialist. He was elected to the chamber of deputies in 1831, but his bitter attacks on the government resulted in his conviction for treason. He escaped prison by exiling himself to Great Britain (1834–39), where he developed a theory of communism influenced by Robert Owen. Cabet's *Voyage en Icarie* (1840) depicted an ideal society in which an elected government controlled all economic activity and supervised social affairs, the family remaining the only other independent unit. The book was extremely popular, and Cabet gained many followers. A group of them attempted unsuccessfully (1848) to found an Icarian community on the Red River in Texas. The next year Cabet established a temporary colony at the old Mormon town of Nauvoo, Ill., but serious dissension arose in 1856, and he was not reelected president. He died soon after in St. Louis. Most of the Icarians moved to lands they had purchased near Corning, Iowa, where branch communities survived until 1898. Other works by Cabet include *Histoire populaire de la Révolution française* (4 vol., 1839–40), *Colonie icarienne aux États-Unis d' Amerique* (1856), and *Le vrai Christianisme suivant Jésus Christ* (1846). See Albert Shaw, *Icaria: A Chapter in the History of Communism* (1884); S. A. Piotrowski, *Etienne Cabet and the Voyage en Icarie* (1935).

Cabeza de Vaca, Álvar Núñez (äl'vär nōō'nyāth käbā'thä dā vä'kä), c.1490–c.1557, Spanish explorer in the American Southwest. Cabeza de Vaca [cow's head] was not actually a surname but a hereditary title in his mother's family; he is frequently called simply Álvar Núñez. He came to the New World as treasurer in the expedition of Pánfilo de NARVÁEZ that left Spain in 1527 and reached Florida (probably Tampa Bay) in 1528. When hardship and Indian hostility caused the end of the expedition, Cabeza de Vaca was one of the survivors whose barges were shipwrecked on an island on the Texas coast. Later scholars have argued extensively over the identification of that island, but Galveston Island and Mustang Island are popular as possibilities. The story is one of the most remarkable in the annals of exploration. After much suffering as slaves of the Indians inhabiting the island, Cabeza de Vaca and three other survivors escaped and started a long journey overland. His companions were Alonso del Castillo Maldonado, Andrés Dorantes, and Estevanico (an Arab or possibly a Negro). They gained great repute among the Indians as healers since remarkable cures were attributed to their Christian prayers. Their route westward is disputed as much as the island of the shipwreck, but after much wandering they did reach W Texas, and then probably New Mexico and Arizona, and possibly (some argue) even California before, turning south in 1536, they arrived in Culiacán in Mexico and told their story to Spaniards there. They were almost certainly the first white men to see the buffalo, and their stories about the Pueblo Indians gave rise to the legend of the Seven Cities of Cibola, later magnified by Fray MARCOS DE NIZA, and brought explorers in search of El Dorado. Cabeza de Vaca's own account, *Los naufragios* [the shipwrecked men] (1542) is the chief document of the startling adventures of his party. An English translation (1851) by Thomas Buckingham Smith was reprinted in F. W. Hodges's *Spanish Explorers in the Southwestern United States* (1907) and in I. R. Blacker and H. M. Rosen's *The Golden Conquistadores* (1960). After returning to Spain, Cabeza de Vaca was appointed governor of the Río de la Plata region and reached Asunción after an overland journey from the Brazilian coast in 1542. His South American career was sadly different from that in North America. He got into much trouble with the popular Domingo Martínez de IRALA. After he returned from a journey up the Paraná River to Bolivia, he was arrested, accused of high-handed practices, imprisoned for two years, and sent back to Spain. There he was found guilty but was pardoned by the king. Cabeza de Vaca wrote his own account of South American events in his *Comentarios* (1555). See Morris Bishop, *The Odyssey of Cabeza de Vaca* (1933); Cleve Hallenbeck, *Álvar Núñez Cabeza de Vaca: The Journal and Route of the First European to Cross the Continent of North America, 1534–1536* (1940); J. U. Terrell, *Journey into Darkness* (1962); M. W. Rodman, *Odyssey of Courage* (1967); Haniel Long, *The Marvelous Adventures of Cabeza de Vaca* (1973).

cabildo (käbēl'dō), autonomous municipal council, the lowest administrative unit in the Spanish government. The institution was especially influential in Spanish America, where it was set up in the early 16th cent. in imitation of the Castilian *ayuntamiento*, the name it was at first briefly called. Composed originally of elected administrative officials, usually local landowners, it was the only institution in which creoles could participate. It was presided over by the *alcalde mayor*, the administrator of a provincial division, who was assisted in judicial matters by *alcaldes ordinarios* (see ALCALDE). The cabildo exercised considerable executive, legislative, and judicial powers; it distributed lands, imposed taxes, provided for police service, and supervised trade and public facilities such as hospitals and jails. In case of emergency the council could choose a governor, lieutenant governor, or captain general. The cabildo steadily evolved in the course of the 16th and 17th cent. into an appointive, proprietary, and hereditary body of generally 4 to 12 councilors. Corruption and inefficiency became common. The degree of local autonomy at first granted by the crown was soon hedged in by the increasing centralization of power in higher authorities, such as the AUDIENCIA and viceroyalty. The cabildo regained importance during the independence movement of the early 19th cent. As the only self-perpetuating organ of local self-government with an ancient tradition of civil autonomy, it served as a convenient rallying place for voicing nationalistic ideas.

Cabinda (kəbĭn'də), Portuguese exclave (1960 pop. 58,547), c.2,800 sq mi (7,300 sq km), W Africa; administered from Angola. The town of Cabinda is the chief population center. The territory is bounded on the N by the Congo Republic, on the E and S by Zaïre, and on the W by the Atlantic Ocean. Cabinda was once geographically part of Angola but was separated from it in 1885 when the Belgian Congo (now Zaïre) acquired a corridor to the sea along the lower Congo River. Largely tropical forest, the region produces hardwoods, coffee, cacao, crude rubber, and palm oil products. Petroleum production began in 1968 and increased dramatically in the early 1970s. In late 1974, Portugal planned to grant Cabinda independence within 2 years at most, but it was not decided whether the territory would become a separate state or remain attached to Angola.

cabinet, group of advisers to the head of the state who themselves are usually the heads of the administrative government departments. The nature of the cabinet differs widely in various countries. In Great Britain, where the cabinet system originated, it was at first a committee of the privy council and rose to its modern status only after the sovereignty of PARLIAMENT had been established by the Glorious Revolution of 1688 and the gradual emergence of party government in the 18th cent. The British cabinet is a body of ministers drawn from the party that possesses a majority in the House of Commons; it is responsible to the Commons for the conduct of the administration. The cabinet is chosen by the PRIME MINISTER, who is guided by the necessity of choosing a group that will represent the disparate elements in his party. The defeat in the Commons of an important ministerial measure or a general election adverse to the government results in the fall of the cabinet. In continental European countries, where the two-party system is not the rule, the coalition cabinet is more common. Cabinet members need not be selected from the majority party nor necessarily from the legislature, and they may speak in either house of the legislature. The U.S. cabinet was not specifically established by the Constitution; it evolved through custom and is now defined by statute law. The members of the cabinet are not members of either house of Congress and are responsible, individually and not as a body, to the President, who appoints them with the approval of the Senate and may remove them at will. The cabinet member may not speak in Congress, though he is often called before congressional committees. As an advisory body, the U.S. cabinet is generally a weak institution and is often overshadowed by a strong President and his staff. The first cabinet appointments (1789) were the secretaries of State, the Treasury, and War. Since then the size and composition of the cabinet has varied considerably. Presently the 11 executive departments whose heads sit in the cabinet are the departments of State; the Treasury; Defense; Justice; the Interior; Agriculture; Commerce; Labor; Health, Education, and Welfare; Housing and Urban Development; and Transportation. See Richard Fenno, Jr., *The President's Cabinet* (1959); Ivor Jennings, *Cabinet Government* (3d ed. 1969).

Cabira: see SIVAS.

Cabiri: see KABEIROI.

Cable, George Washington, 1844–1925, American author, b. New Orleans. He is remembered primarily for his early sketches and novels of Creole life, which established his reputation as an important local-color writer. Cable served as a Confederate soldier in the Civil War and afterwards was a writer and reporter for the New Orleans *Picayune*. His short stories of New Orleans culture began to appear in *Scribner's Monthly* in 1873; they were collected and published as *Old Creole Days* (1879). Among his novels are *The Grandissimes* (1880), *Madame Delphine* (1881), *Dr. Sevier* (1884), and *Gideon's Band* (1914). Cable's works depict the picturesque life of Creoles in antebellum Louisiana with charm and freshness. Discernable in some of them is the author's moral opposition to slavery and class distinction. After 1884, Cable lived in Northampton, Mass. His later works, notably the essays collected in *The Silent South* (1885) and *The Negro Question* (1890), reveal his concern with social evils, particularly with the betrayal of the freed Negro. See his letters, ed. by L. L. Leffingwell (1928, repr. 1967); biographies by Arlin Turner (1956) and L. D. Rubin (1969); study by P. C. Butcher (1959).

cable, usually wire cordage of great strength or heavy metal chain used for hauling, towing, supporting the roadway of a suspension bridge, or securing a large ship to its anchor or mooring. A cable may also be a line used for the transmission of electrical signals. One type of electric cable consists of a core protected by twisted wire strands and suitably insulated, especially when it is used to cross oceans undersea; a message transmitted thus by cable is a cablegram or cable. The insulated wire that conducts electricity from generator to consumer is also called a cable; it often contains multiple conductors and must be of sufficient gauge to carry large currents. Its insulation must withstand high voltages. France and England were first successfully connected by submarine telegraphic cable in 1845. The first permanent transatlantic cable was laid in 1866 by Cyrus West Field, although demonstrations of its possibility had been made in 1858. A coaxial cable was first installed between New York City and Philadelphia in 1935, and in 1936 the first telephone message was transmitted over it. The coaxial cable, which is virtually immune to external electromagnetic noise, consists of a tube made of copper or other conducting material through the center of which extends a wire conductor separated from the outer conductor by an insulator. A number of such conducting units are held together by a covering of insulating material. By means of the coaxial cable a large number of telegraph and telephone messages and also television images can be transmitted simultaneously.

Cabochiens (käbōshyăN'), popular faction in Paris in the early 15th cent. Composed largely of small tradespeople and members of the butchers' and skinners' guilds, it was named after one of the leaders, Simon Lecoustellier, called Caboche, a skinner. Opposed to the ruinous and corrupt fiscal practices of the government and the extravagance of the court, the Cabochiens espoused the cause of JOHN THE FEARLESS of Burgundy in the civil war (1411–13) between ARMAGNACS AND BURGUNDIANS. In 1413 they rebelled, violently seized the government of Paris, and promulgated the so-called *ordonnance cabochienne*, containing radical reforms. The Cabochiens were soon suppressed by the victorious Armagnacs.

Cabot, George, 1752–1823, American merchant and politician, b. Salem, Mass. He went to sea and became captain of one of the ships owned by his brothers John and Andrew Cabot of Beverly, who in 1777 took him into their firm. Cabot also helped develop the family's cotton mills in Beverly. A Federalist, he was (1791–96) one of Alexander Hamilton's most trusted followers in the U.S. Senate. Made a director of the Bank of the United States in 1793, he became president of its Boston branch in 1803. In the Federalist discontent at the beginning of the 19th cent., Cabot was a leader of the ESSEX JUNTO and presided over the HARTFORD CONVENTION. See biography by his grandson, Henry Cabot Lodge (1877).

Cabot, John, fl. 1461–98, English explorer, probably b. Genoa, Italy. He became a citizen of Venice in 1476 and engaged in the Eastern trade of that city. This experience, it is assumed, was the stimulus of his later explorations. Like Columbus (though there is no evidence that either influenced the other), he apparently believed that the riches of the Far East might be more easily reached by sailing west. He went to England, probably in the 1480s, and resided chiefly at Bristol, a port then promising as a base for discovery. Under a patent granted by Henry VII (March 5, 1496), Cabot sailed from Bristol in 1497 and discovered the North American coast touching at Cape Breton Island or Newfoundland. In 1498 he again sailed for America to explore the coast. The fate of the expedition is unknown, although there is presumptive evidence that it reached America and that some of its members returned. The English claims in North America were based on his discovery. His son was Sebastian Cabot. See H. P. Biggar, *The Precursors of Jacques Cartier* (1911); J. A. Williamson, *Voyages of the Cabots* (1929); C. R. Beazley, *John and Sebastian Cabot: The Discovery of North America* (1964); Richard C. Howard, *Bristol and the Cabots* (1967).

Cabot, Sebastian, b. 1483–86?, d. 1557, explorer in English and Spanish service; son of John Cabot. He may well have accompanied his father on the 1497 and 1498 voyages, and he was for many years given the credit for his father's achievements. In the 19th cent., scholars, finding discrepancies in the Sebastian stories, branded him an impostor and applied his accounts to the 1498 voyage of John Cabot. However, recent research indicates that the Sebastian narratives relate to a later voyage (1509) made in search of the Northwest Passage. He may have reached Hudson Bay. In 1512 he entered Spanish service and in 1518 became chief pilot. After the return of Magellan's ship *Victoria*, he sailed (1526) from Sanlúcar de Barrameda with the ostensible purpose of loading spices in the Moluccas. Instead he explored the Río de la Plata country, spending several years along the Paraguay, Plata, and Paraná rivers, but the hostility of the Indians and the scarcity of food forced him to leave the country. He returned to Spain in 1530, a distrusted and discredited man. In 1548 he reentered English service, and in 1553 he became governor of a joint-stock company (later the MUSCOVY COMPANY) organized to seek a Northeast Passage and open trade with China. Under his instructions an expedition sailed the same year under Sir Hugh Willoughby, who was lost in midvoyage and was replaced by Richard CHANCELLOR. The expedition reached the White Sea, and a commercial treaty was negotiated with Russia, breaking the monopoly of the Hanseatic League. See J. A. Williamson, *The Voyages of the Cabots* (1929); C. R. Beazley, *John and Sebastian Cabot: The Discovery of North America* (1964); Richard C. Howard, *Bristol and the Cabots* (1967); Richard Biddle, *A Memoir of Sebastian Cabot* (repr. 1970).

Cabral, Pedro Alvares (pĕ'dro͞o əlvä'rəsh kəbräl'), c.1467–c.1520, Portuguese navigator. A friend of Vasco da Gama, in 1500 he was sent out by Manuel I as head of a fleet destined for India. Bartolomeu DIAS was one of his officers. Cabral went far west of his course and reached the coast of Brazil, which he claimed for Portugal. Proceeding onward, he reached Madagascar, Mozambique, and the Indian coast. At Calicut, trouble arose over establishing a post for trade and for converting the Muslims. He bombarded the city but had to retreat in order to save his East Indian cargo. The ships returned to Portugal with rich cargoes, but his methods of diplomacy were severely criticized. The old story was that Cabral discovered Brazil because he had been driven off his course by storms. This has been questioned, and it has been urged that even before the Spaniard Vicente Yáñez Pinzón saw the Brazilian coast (Jan., 1500), Portuguese navigators had been there and that Portugal, wishing to obtain the land, had managed to secure a revision of the pope's original demarcation of the world into Spanish and Portuguese zones of exploration. Certainly the Treaty of Tordesillas (1494) adjusted the former line and put Brazil in the Portuguese zone, but the issue is still a subject of debate. See W. B. Greenlee, comp., *The Voyage of Pedro Alvares Cabral to Brazil and India: From Contemporary Documents and Narratives* (tr. 1938, repr. 1972).

Cabrera, Manuel Estrada: see ESTRADA CABRERA.

Cabrera, Ramón, conde de Morella (rämōn' käbrā'rä kōn'dā dā mō"rā'lyä), 1806–77, Spanish Carlist general. Noted for his valor and cruelty during the first Carlist war, he refused to accept the Carlist defeat in 1839 and continued the war in Valencia and Catalonia until driven into France in 1840. After a brief reappearance (1848–49) as the leader of Carlist guerrillas in Catalonia, he returned to France and then went to England. In 1875 he recognized Alfonso XII as king.

Cabrillo, Juan Rodríguez (hwän rôthrē'gāth käbrē'-lyō), d. 1543, Spanish conquistador and discoverer of California, b. Portugal. In 1520 he landed

C

in Mexico with Pánfilo de Narváez and joined in the conquests of Mexico and Guatemala. Accompanying Pedro de ALVARADO up the west coast of Mexico, he assumed command of the expedition and continued the voyage after Alvarado's death. He discovered San Diego Bay on Sept. 28, 1542, landing at Point Loma Head, now in Cabrillo National Monument. He then sailed on to Northwest Cape beyond San Francisco Bay, which he did not find. Returning to winter on San Miguel Island off the Santa Barbara coast, he died Jan. 3, 1543.

Cabrillo National Monument: see NATIONAL PARKS AND MONUMENTS (table).

Cabrini, Saint Frances Xavier (zä'vyər kəbrē'nē), 1850-1917, American nun, founder of the Missionary Sisters of the Sacred Heart of Jesus, b. near Lodi, Italy. Founded in Italy in 1880, her order was expressly for charitable and religious work among the very poor. She was sent by Pope Leo XIII to the United States (1889) to aid Italian immigrants arriving there. She lived mainly in New York City and Chicago, directing the establishment of hospitals, orphanages, nurseries, and schools in the United States and in Latin America. Her sanctity, highly regarded in her lifetime, became famous after her death. She was beatified by Pope Pius XI in 1938 and canonized in 1946 by Pius XII. Mother Cabrini was the first U.S. citizen to be canonized. Her principal shrine is the Mother Cabrini High School in New York City, where she is buried. Feast: Dec. 22. See Pietro Di Donato, *Immigrant Saint: The Life of Mother Cabrini* (1960).

Cabul (kā'bəl), town, NW Palestine, the modern Kabul (Israel). Joshua 19.27; 1 Kings 9.13.

cacao (kəkā'ō, -kā'-), tropical tree (*Theobroma cacao*) of the family Sterculiaceae (STERCULIA family), native to South America, where it was first domesticated and was highly prized by the Aztec Indians. It has been extensively cultivated in the Old World since the Spanish conquest. The fruit is a pod containing a sweetish pulp in which are embedded rows of seeds, the cocoa "beans" of commerce. To obtain cocoa, the harvested pods are fermented by naturally occurring bacteria and yeasts to eliminate their bitter, astringent quality. The seeds are then cured and roasted. The clean kernels, called cocoa nibs, are manufactured into various products. Their large percentage of fat, removed by pressure, is the so-called cocoa butter used in fine soaps and cosmetics and in medicine for emollients and suppositories; the residue is ground to a powder (cocoa) and used for beverages and flavoring. CHOCOLATE is a product in which the cocoa butter has been retained. Cacao products have a high food value because of the large proportion of fat, carbohydrates, and protein. Cacao is classified in the division MAGNOLIOPHYTA, class Magnoliopsida, order Malvales, family Sterculiaceae.

Caccini, Giulio (jōō'lyō kät-chē'nē), c.1546-1618, Italian composer and singer. Some of his songs were included in Peri's *Dafne* (c.1597), the first known opera. Both he and Peri composed settings of Ottavio Rinuccini's *Euridice* (1600), the earliest operas of which the music is extant. *Nuove musiche* (1601), a collection of his madrigals and arias, is the most important collection among the early examples of monodic style.

Cáceres, Andrés Avelino (ändrās' ävälē'nō kä'-sārās), 1836?-1923, president of Peru (1886-90, 1894). He was a commander in the war with Chile (see PACIFIC, WAR OF THE) and continued to wage guerrilla warfare long after Peru had been conquered. Bitterly opposed to the peace made by the government of Miguel IGLESIAS, Cáceres attempted to seize control in 1884, but failed. Gathering more troops, he entered Lima in 1885 and forced Iglesias to hold an election. Cáceres was chosen president. In 1894 his party forced congress to elect him president, but Nicolás de PIÉROLA soon overthrew the new government. Cáceres later held important diplomatic posts.

Cáceres (kä'thārās), city (1970 pop. 56,064), capital of Cáceres prov., W central Spain, in Estremadura. Products of cork, leather, pottery, and cloth are made there. Cáceres was an important Roman colony. It fell to the Moors in the 8th cent. but was recaptured (1229) by Alfonso IX. The old town, on top of a hill and encircled by turreted walls, has many notable structures.

cachalot: see SPERM WHALE.

Cachin, Marcel (märsĕl' käshăN'), 1869-1958, French Communist leader. An early leader of the Socialist party, he was instrumental in bringing many Socialists into the first French Communist party in 1920. Long the leader of the Communists in the chamber of deputies and editor of the Communist daily *Humanité,* he became the first Communist senator in 1935. He was expelled from his seat after the German-Soviet nonaggression pact in Aug., 1939, and was subsequently arrested. In 1945 he was elected to the national assembly, where he sat until his death.

cacomistle (kăk'əmĭs"əl), small New World mammal, genus *Bassaricus,* related to the RACCOON. There are two species, one found in Mexico and the SW United States, the other in Central America. The North American cacomistle, *B. astutus,* also known as ringtail, ring-tailed cat, and coon cat, ranges north to N Colorado and S Oregon and west to E Texas. Its body is slender and squirrellike, its face pointed and foxlike. The head and body are about 15 in. (38 cm) long; the bushy tail is of equal length. The body fur is yellowish gray, the tail ringed with dark brown and white. The face is marked with dark brown and white, but there is no mask like that of the raccoon. Swift, agile, and able climbers, cacomistles prefer regions with trees, but they live in a variety of habitats. They are nocturnally active and are seldom seen. They are usually found in pairs and make dens in hollow trees, caves, rock crevices, or abandoned buildings. Cacomistles feed primarily on small animals but also eat some vegetable matter. They are classified in the phylum CHORDATA, subphylum Vertebrata, class Mammalia, order Carnivora, family Procyonidae.

cactus, any plant of the family Cactaceae, a large group of succulents found almost entirely in the New World. A cactus plant is conspicuous for its fleshy green stem, which performs the functions of leaves (commonly insignificant or absent), and for the spines (not always present) of various colors, shapes, and arrangements. Cactus flowers are notably delicate in appearance although usually large and showy; they are commonly yellow, white, or shades of red and purple. Cactus fruits are berries and the larger ones are sometimes edible. Cacti are sometimes used as a substitute for wood, as stock feed, and for hedges. The plants vary from small round globes to epiphytes, vines, and large treelike forms. The reduced leaf surface, the enlarged fleshy stem, which is well fitted to store water and to retain it, and the ramified and extensive root system (much reduced in cultivated cacti) make the plant particularly adapted to regions of high temperature and long dry periods. Cacti are not restricted to desert regions, however, for in America they range from the tropics into Canada. A cactus plant appears on the coat of arms of Mexico, and the blossom of the giant cactus, or saguaro (*Cereus giganteus*), is the state flower of Arizona. Most cacti bloom in the spring for a very short period, sometimes for only a few hours. The blossoms are noticeably sensitive to light, and often different species blossom only at specific times of the day. One of the most famous of the cacti is the night-blooming cereus usually classified as *Selenicereus* or *C. grandiflora* (several other night-blooming cactus species bear the same common name). Its fragrant blossoms unfold at a visible rate after sunset and last only a single night. In many of its native habitats the flowering of this cactus is celebrated with festivals. The largest cactus genus is *Opuntia,* jointed-stemmed species recognizable by the fleshy stems made up of either cylindrical (in the cane cacti and the chollas) or flattened (in the prickly pears) joints called pads. The large pear-shaped berries of several of these species are edible, e.g., the cultivated varieties of the Indian fig and the tuna. This fruit is common in Mexican markets; the plants have been widely naturalized in the Mediterranean countries, Australia, and elsewhere as a source of food. Most opuntias grow so rapidly to a large and ungainly size that they are unsuitable for cultivation as ornamentals, and in the wild often become weeds. However, the major economic importance of the cactus family is in the florists' trade. Among those cultivated for their showy blossoms are the Christmas cactus (*Zygocactus*) and species of *Echinocereus* and of *Epiphyllum,* the orchid cactus. The pincushion cacti (*Mammillaria*), the golden ball cactus (*Echinocactus*), and the hedgehog cactus (*Echinopsis*) are among the many grown as oddities for their curious appearance. The nopal (*Nopalea coccinellifera*) is the cactus traditionally cultivated as a host for the COCHINEAL insect. The hallucinatory drug PEYOTE comes from a cactus of the same aboriginal name. Cactus is classified in the division MAGNOLIOPHYTA, class Magnoliopsida, order Caryophyllales, family Cactaceae.

Cadalso Vázquez, José de (hōsā' dä kät͟häl'sō väth'käth), 1741-82, Spanish poet, critic, and satirist. Cadalso Vázquez's rhapsodic prose autobiography, *Noches lúgubres* (1798), probably suggested by Edward Young's *Night Thoughts,* heralded the Spanish romantic movement. However, he is best known for *Los eruditos a la violeta* (1772), a satire on contemporary pedantry, and *Cartas marruecas* [Moroccan letters] (1793), an analysis of Spanish social decadence.

Cadamosto, Luigi da (lōōē'jē dä kädämô'stō), 1432?-1488, Venetian navigator in the service of Prince Henry the Navigator of Portugal. He seems to have entered Portuguese service in 1454, and he left a record of a voyage in 1455 that is valuable for the information it gives concerning Portuguese activity in the Canary Islands. He and a Genoese, Antonio de Nola, also in Prince Henry's service, went down the African coast to the Gambia River. In 1456 or 1457, Cadamosto reached the Cape Verde Islands, but the question of discovery of the islands is not settled. They may have been sighted by the Portuguese years before; they may have been discovered just a year before; they may have been first visited by Cadamosto. His name also appears as Alvise da Cadamosto.

cadaverine: see DECAY OF ORGANIC MATTER.

Cadbury, Dame Elizabeth, 1858-1935, English social worker and philanthropist, b. Elizabeth Mary Taylor, studied in France and Germany; wife of George Cadbury. She became interested in social service and was active in many organizations working for improvement in education, housing, and peace. She was a member of the Birmingham Education Committee after 1911 and of the International Council of Women and was city councilor of Birmingham (1919-25), president (1925) of the National Council of Evangelical Free Churches, and a justice of the peace (1926). In 1934 she was made Dame Commander of the British Empire.

Cadbury, George, 1839-1922, English manufacturer and social reformer; husband of Elizabeth Mary Cadbury. In 1861, Cadbury and his brother Richard assumed control of their father's Birmingham cocoa and chocolate factory. Interested in housing problems, the brothers moved (1880) the plant to Bournville and laid out a garden village. The successful venture influenced European model housing and GARDEN CITY projects. Agitation for national old-age pensions and insurance was financed by Cadbury, who also worked to eliminate harsh labor conditions. See biography by A. G. Gardiner (1923).

caddis fly, any of various insects of the order Trichoptera, with four hairy wings usually held back rooflike over the abdomen, long antennae, and chewing mouthparts. The aquatic larvae, or caddis worms, which somewhat resemble caterpillars, are food for many freshwater fishes; they are called creepers when used as bait. The larvae build and inhabit underwater cases or nets made from a silken threadlike material they produce, or from materials such as twigs, sand, and leaves. Most larvae feed on plants and debris caught in the cases; among the net-building species some are predacious. Many seal their cases, and spin cocoons and pupate within. Caddis flies are classified in the phylum ARTHROPODA, class Insecta, order Trichoptera.

Caddo (kăd'ō), North American Indians whose language belongs to the Caddoan branch of the Hokan-Siouan linguistic stock (see AMERICAN INDIAN LANGUAGES). These people gave their name not only to the linguistic branch but also to the Caddo confederacy, a loose federation of tribes that in prehistoric times occupied lands from the Red River valley in Louisiana to the Brazos River valley in Texas and N into Arkansas and Kansas. Members, besides the Caddo, included the Arikara, the Pawnee, the Wichita, and others. The culture of these loosely knit peoples was similar. Generally they were sedentary, living in villages of conical huts, although they did raise horses. The culture of the Caddo proper was marked by a clearly defined system of social stratification and by a religion that closely regulated daily life. Some 1,000 now reside on a reservation in Oklahoma. See J. T. Hughes, *Prehistory of the Caddoan-Speaking Tribes* (1968).

Cade, Jack, d. 1450, English rebel. Of his life very little is known. He may have been of Irish birth; some of his followers called him John Mortimer and claimed he was a cousin of Richard, duke of York. In 1450 he appeared as the leader of a well-organized uprising in the S of England, principally in Kent, usually known as Jack Cade's Rebellion. The protests were mainly political, not social, although the 14th cent. Statute of Labourers (which attempted to freeze wages and prices) was among the grievances. Others were the loss of royal lands in France, the extravagance of the court, the corruption of the royal favorites, and the breakdown of the administration of justice. The rebels defeated the royal army at Sevenoaks, entered London, executed Lord Saye and Sele (who was blamed for the losses in France), and sacked several houses. The government then offered pardon to Cade's men and so dispersed them. Cade himself was mortally wounded while resisting arrest. See E. N. Simons, *Lord of London* (1963).

cadence, in music, the ending of a phrase or composition. In singing the voice may be raised or may be lowered, or the singer may execute elaborate variations within the key. In instrumental music, with development of the theory of harmony, the cadence was made completely dependent on the change of chord. If the dominant chord comes before the tonic, the cadence is authentic; if the subdominant chord comes before the tonic, the cadence is plagal. If the dominant chord leads into another harmony, the cadence is called deceptive. The reverse order of tonic to dominant is a half cadence. See Walter Piston, *Harmony* (3d ed. 1962).

Cadillac, Antoine de la Mothe (Fr. äNtwän' də lä môt kädēyäk'), c.1658–1730, French colonial governor in North America, founder of Detroit. Of the minor Gascon nobility, he came to America in 1683 to seek his fortune and lived for a time at Port Royal (now Annapolis Royal, N.S.) and then on a grant of land in present-day Maine. He became a favorite of Frontenac, the governor of New France, and in 1694 he was placed in charge of the frontier post at MACKINAC. In 1699, Cadillac went to France to urge establishment of a post on the Detroit River, which he believed would offer a better strategic position against the English than Mackinac. Receiving a grant of land, trade privileges, and command of the new post, he set out with a band of colonists. Detroit was founded in 1701. Cadillac persuaded many of the Indian tribes to settle near the new colony. In 1711 he was appointed to the governorship of the vast territory of Louisiana. He reached his new post in 1713 to begin an administration that was remarkable only for the frequency and fierceness of internal quarrels. He was recalled in 1716 and spent his last years in Gascony. See biography by A. C. Laut (1931).

Cádiz (kä'dēth), city (1970 pop. 135,743), capital of Cádiz prov., SW Spain, in Andalusia, on the Bay of Cádiz. Picturesquely situated on a promontory (joined to the Isla de León, just off the mainland), it is today chiefly a port exporting wines and other agricultural items and importing coal, iron, and foodstuffs. Shipbuilding and fishing are other industries. There is a Spanish naval base in Cádiz and a U.S. naval base at nearby Rota. The Phoenicians founded (c.1100 B.C.) on the site the port of Gadir, which became a market for tin and the silver of Tarshish. It was taken (c.500 B.C.) by the Carthaginians and passed late in the 3d cent. B.C. to the Romans, who called it Gades. It flourished until the fall of Rome, but suffered from the barbarian invasions and declined further under the Moors. After its reconquest (1262) by Alfonso X of Castile, its fortifications were rebuilt. The discovery of America revived its prosperity, as many ships from America unloaded their cargoes there. Columbus sailed from Cádiz on his second voyage (1495). In 1587, Sir Francis Drake burned a Spanish fleet in its harbor, and in 1596 the earl of Essex attacked and partly destroyed the city. But it continued to flourish and in 1718, after Seville's port had become partially blocked by a sandbar, Cádiz became the official center for New World trade. After Spain lost its American colonies, the city declined. During the siege by the French—which Cádiz resisted for two years (1810–12) until relieved by Wellington—the Cortes assembled in the city and issued the famous liberal constitution for Spain (March, 1812). The clean, white city has palm-lined promenades and parks. Its 13th-century cathedral, originally Gothic, was rebuilt in Renaissance style; the new cathedral was begun in 1722. Cádiz has several museums and an art gallery with works by Murillo, Alonso Cano, and Zurbarán. In the church of the former Capuchin convent hangs the *Marriage of St. Catherine* by Murillo, who was at work on this painting when he fell from a scaffold to his death. Manuel de Falla is buried in Cádiz.

Cadman, Charles Wakefield, 1881–1946, American composer, b. Johnstown, Pa. Although he is known to the public principally for two songs—*From the Land of the Sky-blue Water,* based on an Indian theme, and *At Dawning*—he composed operas, such as *Shanewis* (1918), *The Sunset Trail* (1925), and, the most successful of these, *A Witch of Salem* (1926). He also wrote orchestral music, including *Hollywood Suite* (1932) and *Dark Dancers of the Mardi Gras* (1933), and piano music.

cadmium (kăd'mēəm) [from *cadmia,* Lat. for *calamine,* with which cadmium is found associated], metallic chemical element; symbol Cd; at. no. 48; at. wt. 112.4; m.p. 321°C; b.p. 765°C; sp. gr. 8.65 at 20°C; valence +2. Cadmium is a lustrous, silver-white, ductile, very malleable metal. It belongs to group IIb of the PERIODIC TABLE, and resembles ZINC in its chemical properties. Like zinc, it tarnishes in moist air. Cadmium oxide, a brown powder formed by burning the metal in air, is used in electroplating; it is also made by heating cadmium hydroxide. Cadmium forms a carbonate, a chloride, and several complex ions. Cadmium yellow (the sulfide) is a very durable yellow pigment used in paints. The major use of cadmium is as a coating that is electroplated on iron and steel to prevent corrosion; it is preferable to zinc for protection from alkalies. Cadmium is also used in so-called fusible metals, which are low-melting alloys such as Wood's metal, used in automatic fire sprinklers and alarm systems. Cadmium is used in alkaline nickel-cadmium electric storage cells, which have a greater storage capacity than an equal weight of lead-acid storage cells. It has also found some use in the control of nuclear reactions, since it absorbs neutrons. Cadmium does not occur uncombined in nature; greenochite, a cadmium sulfide mineral found near Greenoch, Scotland, is the only commercial ore. Cadmium is obtained principally as a by-product of the smelting and refining of ores of zinc, especially zinc sulfides, and of lead and copper. The element was discovered in 1817 by Friedrich Stromeyer.

Cadmus, in Greek legend, son of Agenor and founder of Thebes. Misfortune followed his family because he killed the sacred dragon that guarded the spring of Ares. Athena told him to sow the dragon's teeth, and from these sprang the Sparti [sown men], ancestors of the noble families of Thebes. Cadmus married Harmonia, daughter of Ares and Aphrodite. At their wedding he presented her with a sacred robe and necklace, made by Hephaestus, which later brought misfortune to their possessors (see AMPHIARAUS; ALCMAEON). They had four daughters—Ino, Semele, Autonoe, and Agave. In their old age Cadmus and Harmonia were turned into serpents by Zeus and sent to live in the Elysian fields.

Cadogan, William Cadogan, 1st **Earl** (kədŭ'gən), 1675–1726, British general and diplomat. He is remembered chiefly as the faithful friend and brilliant subordinate of the 1st duke of MARLBOROUGH. In addition to serving (1702–11) as the latter's quartermaster general, he was the able commander of a dragoon regiment known as Cadogan's Horse and played a distinguished part in Marlborough's many victories in the War of the Spanish Succession. When the duke fell from power in 1711, Cadogan went into exile in the Netherlands. He conducted dealings with Hanover for the English Whigs, and after the Hanoverian George I ascended (1714) the British throne, he received new commands and honors. Cadogan helped to suppress the Jacobite uprising of 1715, was created earl in 1718, and was made commander in chief of the army after Marlborough's death in 1722. He also had high diplomatic duties in the resettlements among Great Britain, France, the Netherlands, the Holy Roman Empire, and Spain in the years 1714–20.

Cadorna, Luigi (lo͞oē'jē kädôr'nä), 1850–1928, Italian field marshal. His father, Raffaele Cadorna, was a general in the wars of the Risorgimento and took Rome in 1870. Luigi Cadorna, a count, became the head of the army general staff and reorganized the Italian army before World War I. Until the Italian defeat at Caporetto in 1917 he was in fact commander of military operations, while King Victor Emmanuel III was nominally commander in chief. Cadorna wrote two military works on World War I and a biography of his father.

Cadoudal, Georges (zhôrzh kädo͞odäl'), 1771–1804, French royalist conspirator. A commander of the CHOUANS, he led the counterrevolutionists in the VENDÉE. He fled to England in 1801 after the failure of an attempted assassination of Napoleon Bonaparte. In 1803 he returned as the leader of another conspiracy against Napoleon. Generals Charles PICHEGRU and Jean Victor MOREAU were implicated in the plot. Insurrections were planned in Paris and in the provinces, but the conspiracy was uncovered by Joseph FOUCHÉ, the minister of police. Cadoudal was executed, and the duc d'ENGHIEN, unjustifiably linked with the plot, was kidnaped and summarily shot. The conspiracy, exaggerated in report, was used as a pretext to transform the Consulate into Napoleon's empire.

caduceus (kədyo͞o'sēəs), wing-topped staff, with two snakes winding about it, carried by Hermes, given to him (according to one legend) by Apollo. The symbol of two intertwined snakes appeared early in Babylonia and is related to other serpent symbols of fertility, wisdom, healing, and of sun gods. This staff of Hermes was carried by Greek heralds and ambassadors and became a Roman symbol for truce, neutrality, and noncombatant status. By regulation, it has since 1902 been the insignia of the medical branch of the U.S. army. The caduceus is much used as a symbol of commerce, postal service, and ambassadorial positions and since the 16th cent. has largely replaced the one-snake symbol of Asclepius as a symbol of medicine.

Cadwaladr or **Cadwallader** (both: kădwäl'ədər), d. 664?, semilegendary Welsh king, leader of the Celtic resistance against the Anglo-Saxons. Later bards made him a national hero, and Welsh tradition deems him the last Welsh king to wear the crown of Britain.

caecilian (sēsĭl'ēən), any of the legless, tailless tropical amphibians of the family Caecilidae. Most adult caecilians resemble earthworms superficially but have vertebrate characteristics such as jaws and teeth. They range in size from 7 in. to 4.5 ft (18 cm–140 cm); most are about 1 ft (30 cm) long. Their bodies are ringed with grooves, which in some species contain small scales imbedded in the skin; possession of scales is a primitive amphibian trait. There is a groove on either side of the head, each containing a retractable sensory tentacle. The eyes of caecilians are nearly functionless, and some species are eyeless. Caecilians are found in swampy places in most tropical parts of the world, but are seldom seen because of their burrowing behavior. They eat small invertebrates such as termites and earthworms. A few species remain aquatic as adults and resemble eels. There are about 50 species of caecilians, divided into 16 genera. They are classified in the phylum CHORDATA, subphylum Vertebrata, class Amphibia, order Gymnophiona (or Apoda), family Caecilidae.

Cædmon (kăd'mən), fl. 670, English poet. He was reputed by Bede to be the author of early English versions of various Old Testament stories. According to Bede, Cædmon was an ignorant herdsman who received his poetic powers through a vision. During his later years he became a lay brother in the abbey of Whitby. In 1655, Franciscus Junius, a Dutch scholar, published the text of several Old English poems, including "Exodus" and "Daniel," and ascribed them to Cædmon; modern scholars dispute this conclusion. See E. V. K. Dobbie, *Cædmon's Hymn and Bede's Death Song* (1937); study by S. H. Gurteen (1896, repr. 1969).

Caelian, hill: see *Rome before Augustus* under ROME.

Caen (käN), city (1968 pop. 114,398), capital of Calvados dept., N France, in Normandy, on the Orne River. It is a busy port, canalized (by Napoleon I) directly to the sea. The commercial center of the rich CALVADOS region, it is highly industrialized, with a thermal power station and extensive steel works along the Orne; the nearby iron-ore mines are the second largest in France. The city's manufactures include automobiles, heavy equipment, electronic gear, and textiles (especially lace). Caen's importance dates from the 11th cent., when it was a favorite residence of William I of England (William the Conqueror). During the French Revolution it was a rallying place for the federalists; Charlotte Corday lived there. The town, an architectural gem, was largely destroyed in the fighting which raged there during the NORMANDY CAMPAIGN of World War II; the 14th-century Church of St. Peter's lost its famous spire, while the castle of William the Conqueror and the town hall (17th cent.) were destroyed beyond repair. However, three outstanding examples of 11th-century NORMAN ARCHITECTURE were preserved: the Abbaye aux Hommes [men's abbey], founded by William the Conqueror, who is buried there; the Abbaye aux Dames [women's abbey], founded by Queen Matilda; and the Church of St. Nicholas. The university (founded 1432 and also destroyed) has been rebuilt; in 1964 its technical institute became the National School of Advanced Electronics and Electromechanic Studies. A school of hydrography is also in Caen.

Caere (sē'rē), ancient city of Etruria, c.30 mi (50 km) N of Rome, Italy, at the site of the modern Cervetri. Although a few miles from the sea, it had ports at Alsium (near modern Palo) and Pyrgi (modern Santa Severa). During the 7th and 6th cent. B.C., Caere reached the period of its greatest prosperity. In recent times the cemeteries have been excavated, and the monumental tumuli have yielded vases, pottery, and other art objects, revealing much about ETRUSCAN CIVILIZATION.

Caerleon (kärlē'ən), urban district (1971 pop. 6,235), Monmouthshire, SE Wales, on the Usk River. Militarily important during the Roman period, Caerleon has extensive remains of Isca, a Roman fortress, including an amphitheater, soldiers' quarters, walls, and baths. Stones, bronzes, pottery, and coins are exhibited in the Legionary Museum. Caerleon is also famous for its connection with Arthurian legend; it is often identified with CAMELOT. In 1974, Caerleon became part of the new nonmetropolitan county of Gwent.

Caernarvon (kərnär'vən, kär-), municipal borough (1971 pop. 9,253), county town of Caernarvonshire, NW Wales, on Menai Strait. Petroleum is imported and slate exported. Tourism is important. The castle, begun by Edward I c.1284, is a fine example of a medieval fortress. The Prince of Wales is invested at Caernarvon. In 1974, the borough became part of the new nonmetropolitan county of Gwynedd.

Caernarvonshire, county (1971 pop. 122,852), NW Wales. The county town is Caernarvon. The region is largely mountainous except for the Lleyn peninsula, which forms the northern boundary of Cardigan Bay, and a coastal section along Menai Strait in the northwest. Snowdon (3,560 ft/1,085 m) is the highest mountain in England and Wales. The Conway, chief river of the county, flows along Caernarvonshire's eastern boundary, separating it from Denbighshire. Sheep and cattle are raised, and slate quarrying and tourism are significant. There is an aluminum plant at Dolgarrog. Historical remains include evidence of considerable Roman settlement. In 1974, Caernarvonshire became part of the new nonmetropolitan county of Gwynedd.

Caerphilly (kärfĭl'ē), urban district (1971 pop. 40,689), Mid Glamorgan, S Wales. In a coal area, it is also a market center and is noted for its cheese. Its 13th-century castle is the largest in Wales.

Caesalpinus, Andreas (ăn'drēəs sĕsălpī'nəs), Latinized from **Andrea Cesalpino** (ändrĕ'ä chāzälpē'nō), 1519–1603, Italian botanist and physiologist. He was physician to Pope Clement VIII. He described, in part and as a theory only, the circulation of blood. His chief work, *De plantis* (1583), contains the first classification of plants according to their fruits, based on a comparative study of his large collection. Linnaeus considered him the first true systematist.

Caesar (sē'zər), ancient Roman patrician family of the Julian gens. There are separate articles on its two most distinguished members, Julius Caesar and Augustus. Another distinguished member of the family was **Lucius Julius Caesar,** d. 87 B.C., consul (90 B.C.). He proposed a law extending Roman citizenship to Roman allies that had not joined in the Social War against Rome (90 B.C.). He was killed in the beginning of the civil war by partisans of MARIUS. His brother **Caius Julius Caesar Strabo Vopiscus,** d. 87 B.C., is mentioned as an orator in Cicero's *De oratore.* He was killed with his brother. His name also appears as Vopisius. The son of Lucius Julius Caesar, also named **Lucius Julius Caesar,** d. after 43 B.C., was one of Julius Caesar's legates in Gaul (52 B.C.). He accompanied the dictator into Italy during the civil war. After the assassination of Julius Caesar he was allied with Marc ANTONY, whose mother, Julia, was his sister. In 43 B.C. he and Antony fell out, and only the pleas of Julia to her son saved her brother in the proscription. When Octavius (later AUGUSTUS) was adopted (44 B.C.) into the Julian gens, he took the name Caesar. His successors as emperors took the name Caesar until HADRIAN, who kept the title Augustus for the emperor and allowed the heir apparent to be called Caesar. This became the custom afterward. The imperial use of the name Caesar was perpetuated in the German *kaiser* and the Russian *czar.*

Caesar, Julius (Caius Julius Caesar), 102? B.C.–44 B.C., Roman statesman and general. Although he was born into the Julian gens, one of the oldest patrician families in Rome, Caesar was always a member of the democratic or popular party, probably as a result of the example and patronage of his uncle by marriage, Caius MARIUS. In 87 B.C., Marius appointed him flamen Dialis [priest of Jove]. Caesar made the most of their relationship, strengthening its political implications when he married (83 B.C.) Cornelia, the wealthy daughter of Lucius Cornelius CINNA, colleague of Marius and enemy of SULLA. In 82 B.C., Sulla ordered Caesar to divorce Cornelia. When he refused, he was proscribed, his property was confiscated, Cornelia's dowry was taken, and he was shorn of his priesthood. He fled from Rome (81 B.C.) and went to Asia to serve in the army. On Sulla's death, Caesar returned (78 B.C.) to Rome and began his political career as a member of the popular party. One of his first acts was to prosecute Cneius Cornelius Dolabella, a senatorial governor, for extortion in Macedonia. The case was unsuccessful, but it gained Caesar popularity with his party and repute for oratory. In 74 B.C. he went into Asia to repulse a Cappadocian army. After his return his role was that of the rising young statesman, agitating for the reform of the government on popular lines and helping to advance the position of POMPEY, who had become virtual head of the popular party. Caesar was made military tribune before 70 B.C. As quaestor in Farther Spain in 69 B.C. he helped Pompey to obtain the supreme command for the war in the East. He returned to Rome in 68 B.C. and continued to support the enactment of popular measures and to prosecute senatorial extortionists. In Pompey's absence he was becoming the recognized head of the popular party. At the funerals of his wife, Cornelia, and his aunt (68 B.C.), he extolled Marius, the Julian gens, and Cinna. In 65 B.C. or 64 B.C., when he was curule aedile [superintendent of public works], Caesar had the trophies and statue of Marius set up secretly one night in the Capitol. These two incidents made him popular with the people but earned him the hatred of the senate. In 63 B.C. he was elected pontifex maximus, allegedly by heavy bribes. He then undertook the reform of the CALENDAR with the help of Sosigenes. The result was one of his greatest contributions to history, the Julian calendar. In Dec., 63 B.C., Caesar advocated mercy for CATILINE and the conspirators and thus increased the enmity of the senatorial party and its leaders, CATO THE YOUNGER and Quintus Lutatius Catulus (see CATULUS, family). In 62 B.C., CLODIUS and Caesar's second wife, Pompeia, were involved in a scandal concerning the violation of the secret rites of Bona Dea, and Caesar obtained a divorce, saying, "Caesar's wife must be above suspicion." Having served in Farther Spain as proconsul in 61 B.C., he returned to Rome in 60 B.C., ambitious for the consulate. Against senatorial opposition he achieved a brilliant stroke—he organized a coalition, known as the First Triumvirate, made up of Pompey, commander in chief of the army; Marcus Licinius Crassus, the wealthiest man in Rome (see CRASSUS, family); and Caesar himself. Pompey and Crassus were jealous of each other, but Caesar by force of personality kept the arrangement going. In 59 B.C. he married CALPURNIA. In the same year, as consul, he secured the passage of an agrarian law providing Campanian lands for 20,000 poor citizens and veterans, in spite of the opposition of his senatorial colleague, Marcus Calpurnius BIBULUS. Caesar also won the support of the wealthy equites by getting a reduction for them in their tax contracts in Asia. This made him the guiding power in a coalition between people and plutocrats. He was assigned the rule of Cisalpine and Transalpine Gaul and Illyricum with four legions for five years (58 B.C.–54 B.C.). The differences between Pompey and Crassus grew, and Caesar again moved (56 B.C.) to patch up matters, arriving at an agreement that both Pompey and Crassus should be consuls in 55 B.C. and that their proconsular provinces should be Spain and Syria respectively. From this arrangement he drew an extension of his command in Gaul to 49 B.C. In the years 58 B.C. to 49 B.C. he firmly established his reputation in the GALLIC WARS. In 55 B.C., Caesar made explorations into Britain, and in 54 B.C. he defeated the Britons, led by Cassivellaunus. Caesar met his most serious opposition in Gaul from VERCINGETORIX, whom he defeated in Alesia in 52 B.C. By the end of the wars Caesar had reduced all Gaul to Roman control. These campaigns proved him one of the greatest commanders of all time. In them he revealed his consummate military genius, characterized by quick, sure judgment and indomitable energy. The campaigns also developed the personal devotion of the legions to Caesar. His personal interest in the men (he is reputed to have known them all by name) and his willingness to undergo every hardship made him the idol of the army—a significant element in his later career. In 54 B.C. occurred the death of Caesar's daughter Julia, Pompey's wife since 59 B.C. She had been the principal personal tie between the two men. During the years that Caesar was in Gaul, Pompey had been gradually leaning more and more toward the senatorial party. The tribunate of Clodius (58 B.C.) had aggravated conditions in Rome, and Caesar's military successes could hardly have failed to arouse Pompey's jealousy. Crassus' death (53 B.C.) in Parthia ended the First Triumvirate and set Pompey and Caesar face to face. The senate began to support Pompey, and in 52 B.C. he was made sole consul. Meanwhile, Caesar had become a military hero as well as a champion of the people. The senate feared him and wanted him to give up his army, knowing that he hoped to be consul when his term in Gaul expired. In Dec., 50 B.C., Caesar, who was in quarters in Ravenna, wrote the senate that he would give up his army if Pompey would give up his. The senate heard the letter with fury and, at the insistence of Quintus Caecilius Metellus Pius Scipio (see SCIPIO, family), demanded that Caesar disband his army at once or be declared an enemy of the people—an illegal bill, for Caesar was entitled to keep his army until his term was up. Two tribunes faithful to Caesar, Marc ANTONY and CASSIUS (Quintus Cassius Longinus), vetoed the bill and were quickly expelled from the senate. They fled to Caesar, who assembled his army and asked for the support of the soldiers against the senate. The army called for action, and on Jan. 19, 49 B.C., Caesar with the words "Iacta alea est" [the die is cast] crossed the Rubicon, the stream bounding his province, to enter Italy. Civil war had begun. His march to Rome was a triumphal progress. The senate fled to Capua. Caesar proceeded to Brundisium, where he besieged Pompey until Pompey fled (March, 49 B.C.) with his fleet to Greece. Caesar set out at once for Spain, which Pompey's legates were holding, and pacified that province. Returning to Rome, Caesar held the dictatorship for 11 days in early December, long enough to get himself elected consul, and then set out for Greece in pursuit of Pompey. Caesar collected at Brundisium a small army and fleet—so small, in fact, that Bibulus, waiting with a much larger fleet to prevent his crossing to Epirus, did not yet bother to watch him—and slipped across the strait. He met Pompey at Dyrrhachium but was forced to fall back and begin a long retreat southward, with Pompey in pursuit. Near PHARSALA, Caesar camped in a very strategic location. Pompey, who had a far larger army, attacked Caesar but was routed (48 B.C.) and fled to Egypt, where he was killed. Caesar, having pursued Pompey to Egypt, remained there for some time, living with CLEOPATRA, taking her part against her brother and husband Ptolemy XII, and establishing her firmly on the throne. From Egypt he went to Syria and Pontus, where he defeated (47 B.C.) Pharnaces II with such ease that he reported his victory in the words "Veni, vidi, vici" [I came, I saw, I conquered]. In the same year he personally put down a mutiny of his army and then set out for Africa, where the followers of Pompey had fled, to end their opposition led by Cato. On his return to Rome, where he was now tribune of the people and dictator, he had four great triumphs and pardoned all his enemies. He set about reforming the living conditions of the people by passing agrarian laws and by improving housing accommodations. He also drew up the elaborate plans (which Augustus later used) for consolidating the empire and establishing it securely. In the winter of 46 B.C.–45 B.C. he was in Spain putting down the last of the senatorial party under Gaius Pompeius, the son of Pompey. He returned to Rome in Sept., 45 B.C., and was elected to his fifth consulship in 44 B.C. In the same year he became dictator for life and set about planning a campaign against Parthia, the only real menace to Rome's borders. His dictatorial powers had, however, aroused great resentment, and he was bitterly criticized by his enemies, who accused him of all manner of vices. When a conspiracy was formed against him, however, it was made up of his friends and protégés, among them Cimber, Casca, Cassius, and Marcus Junius BRUTUS. On March 15 (the Ides of March), 44 B.C., he was stabbed to death in the senate house. His will left everything to his 18-year-old grandnephew Octavian (later AUGUSTUS). It is curious that Caesar probably knew of the conspiracy but made no attempt to defend himself. Caesar made the Roman Empire possible by uniting the state after a century of disorder, by establishing an autocracy in place of the oligarchy, and by pacifying Italy and the provinces. It should be noted that he had destroyed an oligarchy, not a democracy, to establish his dictatorship. His success in his dealings with other persons is a testimony to his social grace, and even Cicero (who hated him) said that he would rather spend an evening in conversation with Caesar than in any other way. Caesar has always been one of the most controversial characters of history. His admirers have seen in him the defender of the rights of the people against an oligarchy. His detractors have seen him as an ambitious demagogue, who forced his way to dictatorial power and destroyed the republic. That he was gifted and versatile there can be little doubt.

He excelled in war, in statesmanship, and in oratory. His literary works are highly esteemed. Of them his commentaries on the Gallic Wars (seven books) and on the civil war (three books) survive. They are masterpieces of clear, beautiful, concise Latin, and they are among the most reliable histories of antiquity as well as being classic military documents. Caesar wrote poetry, but the only surviving piece is a poem on Terence. A literary classic on Caesar is Shakespeare's tragedy *Julius Caesar.* Plutarch is the most famous ancient source. See biographies by Guglielmo Ferrero (tr. 1933, repr. 1962), A. L. Duggan (new ed. 1966), J. P. V. D. Balsdon (1967), and Michael Grant (1969); T. R. Holmes, *The Roman Republic* (3 vol., 1923, repr. 1967); L. R. Taylor, *Party Politics in the Age of Caesar* (1949, repr. 1961).

Caesar, Lucius Julius: see under CAESAR, family.

Caesarea: see CHERCHEL.

Caesarea Libani, ancient city of Lebanon: see ARKITE.

Caesarea Mazaca (mă'zəkə), ancient city of Asia Minor, also called Caesarea of Cappadocia. As Mazaca it was the residence of the Cappadocian kings. The city was renamed (c.10 B.C.) Caesarea by Archelaus, king of Cappadocia. It continued down the ages as a trade center and is the modern KAYSERI, Turkey.

Caesarean section: see CESAREAN SECTION.

Caesarea Palestinae (sĕsərē'ə pălĭstī'nē, sĕzə-, sēzə-), old city, NW Palestine, c.20 mi (32 km) S of Mt. Carmel. It was taken (104 B.C.) by Alexander Jannaeus, leader of the Maccabees, and was made (30 B.C.) the capital of Herod the Great. The Jewish citizens were massacred by the Romans in A.D. 66. There have been excavations since 1958.

Caesarea Philippi (fĭlĭp'ī), ancient city, N Palestine, at the foot of Mt. Hermon. It was built by Philip the Tetrarch in the 1st cent. A.D. Its site (Paneas) had long been a center for the worship of Pan. Jesus was in the vicinity (Mat. 16.13), but there is no proof that he entered the city. The modern name is Baniyas.

Caesarion: see PTOLEMY XIV.

Caetano, Marcello (mərsĕ'lo͞o kăätă'no͞o), 1906–, Portuguese lawyer and statesman. He received a doctorate in law (1931) from the Univ. of Lisbon, where he taught after 1932, serving as professor (1940–68) and as rector (1959–62). A close associate of António de Oliveira Salazar, he was instrumental in planning the dictator's corporate form of government, the *Estado Novo,* and from the 1930s held various positions in the regime. He served as minister for the colonies (1944–47) and deputy prime minister (1955–58). He became prime minister of Portugal in 1968 after Salazar had been incapacitated by a stroke. While adhering to the basic conservative policies of his predecessor, including retention of the Portuguese overseas colonies, suppression of dissent, and staunch anti-Communism, he initiated modest political and economic reforms. Caetano's government was overthrown by a military coup in April, 1974, and he was exiled to Madeira and later to Brazil, where he settled in a monastery.

cafeteria: see RESTAURANT.

Caffa: see FEODOSIYA, USSR.

caffeine, odorless, slightly bitter alkaloid found in COFFEE, TEA, kola nuts, ilex plants (the source of the Latin American drink yerba MATÉ), and, in small amounts, in cocoa (see COLA; CACAO). It can also be prepared synthetically from URIC ACID. When used in moderation, caffeine acts as a mild STIMULANT to the nervous system and is harmless to most persons. Caffeine increases the heart rate and rhythm, affects the circulatory system, and increases urination. It also stimulates secretion of stomach acids and is therefore harmful to individuals with ulcers; it may also contribute to formation of ulcers. Excessive intake of caffeine can result in restlessness, insomnia, heart irregularities, and delirium.

Caffieri (Fr. kăfyārē', Ital. käf-fyä'rē), French family of artists. **Philippe Caffieri** (1634–1716) left Italy to enter the service of Louis XIV at the Gobelin factory. He and a son, **Jacques Caffieri** (1678–1755), were employed by the architect Le Brun to make adornments for the palace and gardens at Versailles. Philippe is recorded as having made carved wood decorations for the ambassadors' staircase in the palace. Jacques's superb creations were chiefly in the rococo style. He made bronzes for the king's chamber (1738) and for the council room. His son, **Philippe Caffieri II** (1714–74), worked with him, and together they produced an immense volume of metalwork, including sumptuous ormolu (imitation gold made of brass) mountings for furniture, adornments for several of the royal palaces, e.g., Fontainebleau and Choisy, and casings for clocks—notably a celebrated astronomical clock presented to Louis XV. Another son of Jacques, **Jean Jacques Caffieri** (1725–92), was a sculptor especially noted for statues and portrait busts. His *Père Pingré* is in the Louvre.

Cagayan (kăgī'ən, kăgäyän'), river, c.220 mi (350 km) long, rising in the mountains of central Luzon, Philippines, and flowing N to the Pacific Ocean at Aparri. It is navigable to small oceangoing vessels for c.15 mi (20 km) upstream. Tobacco is the chief crop of the basin.

Cage, John, 1912–, American composer, b. Los Angeles, Calif. A controversial figure, Cage is famous for his unorthodox musical theories and experimental compositions. He attended Pomona College and later studied with Arnold Schoenberg, Adolph Weiss, and Henry Cowell. In 1943 he moved to New York City, where his concerts featuring percussion instruments attracted attention. For these performances he invented the "prepared piano," in which objects of such materials as metal, wood, and rubber were attached to a piano's strings, thus altering pitch and tone and producing sounds resembling those of a minuscule percussion group. Cage's *Bacchanale* (1938) and *Sonatas and Interludes* (1946–48) were composed for the "prepared piano." One of Cage's most innovative ideas is his theory of "total soundspace"—the concept that all sound, including nonmusical sound and the absence of sound, can be used in musical composition. *4'3"* (1952), probably his most famous piece, consists of 4 minutes and 33 seconds of silence punctuated only by whatever random environmental sounds happen to occur. Another of Cage's influential ideas is his concept of composition by chance, in which the notes and sounds of a musical composition are determined by such methods as the roll of dice or a consultation of the *I Ching* (see ALEATORY MUSIC). For example, his famous *Imaginary Landscape No. 4* (1953) is scored for 12 radios tuned at random, whereas *Reunion* (1968) consists of the sounds made by the movement of pieces in a chess game played on an electrified board. For some years associated with Merce Cunningham, Cage has also written music for the dance, to be played independent of the choreography. He has also written several books, among them *Silence* (1961) and *A Year From Monday* (1968).

Cagliari (kä'lyärē), city (1971 pop. 224,449), capital of Sardinia and of Cagliari prov., S Sardinia, Italy, on the Gulf of Cagliari (an arm of the Mediterranean Sea) and at the mouth of the Mannu River. It is the largest city in Sardinia and is a modern port and an industrial center. A flourishing Carthaginian city, it was taken by Rome in 238 B.C. Cagliari endured Arab invasions in the 8th and 9th cent. A.D. The city was a Pisan stronghold during the wars with Genoa (11th–14th cent.); its subsequent history is largely that of SARDINIA. Cagliari was the site of a submarine base in World War II and was heavily bombed by the Allies. Noteworthy structures include the Romanesque-Gothic cathedral (13th cent.), the Basilica of San Saturnino (5th cent.), a large Roman amphitheater, and the massive tower of St. Pancras (built by Pisans in 1304).

Cagliostro, Alessandro, Conte (älĕs-sän'drō kōn'tā kälyō'strō), 1743–95, Italian adventurer, magician, and alchemist, whose real name was Giuseppe Balsamo. After early misadventures in Italy he traveled in Greece, Arabia, Persia, and Egypt. While in Italy, he married Lorenza Feliciani, who became his assistant on his trips to the cities of Europe, where he posed as a physician, alchemist, mesmerist, necromancer, and Freemason. He claimed the secret of the philosopher's stone and of miraculous philters and potions. As the Grand Copt of the order of Egyptian Masonry he organized many lodges. His reputation was amazing, particularly at the court of Louis XVI. Implicated in the Affair of the DIAMOND NECKLACE, he was imprisoned, acquitted, and banished. Cagliostro returned to Rome in 1789, where the Inquisition charged him with heresy and sorcery and condemned him to die. The sentence was commuted to life imprisonment, and he died in a dungeon. Cagliostro has fascinated later generations as well as his contemporaries, and he appears often in literary works. See biographies by Frank King (1929), W. R. H. Trowbridge (new ed. 1961), and François Rebadeau Dumas (tr. 1968); H. C. Schnur, *Mystic Rebels* (1949, repr. 1971).

Cagney, James, 1904–, American movie actor, b. New York City. He worked on Broadway as an actor and dancer before appearing in films. He is best remembered as the brash, sadistic tough guy in such movies as *Public Enemy* (1930) and *The Roaring Twenties* (1939). His many other films include *Angels With Dirty Faces* (1936), *The Fighting Sixty-Ninth* (1940), *Yankee Doodle Dandy* (1942), *White Heat* (1949), *Come Fill The Cup* (1951), *Love Me or Leave Me* (1955), *Man of a Thousand Faces* (1957), and *One Two Three* (1961).

Caguas (kä'gwäs, kä'wäs), city (1970 pop. 63,215), E central Puerto Rico. Largest of Puerto Rico's inland cities, Caguas is an industrial center. Sugar refining and varied manufacturing are carried on.

Cahan, Abraham (kän), 1860–1951, Russian-American journalist, Socialist leader, and author, b. Vilnius, Lithuania. He emigrated to New York City in 1882, entered journalism, and helped found the *Jewish Daily Forward* (1897); as editor in chief after 1902, he made it the most influential Jewish daily in America. He was a founder of the Social Democratic party in 1897 and after 1902 supported the Socialist party. Active in spreading socialist teachings among Jewish workers, he encouraged the unionization of East Side garment workers and supported them in their strikes. Cahan's writings in English, particularly *Yekl: a Tale of the New York Ghetto* (1896), *The Imported Bridegroom and Other Stories* (1898), and *The Rise of David Levinsky* (1917), have a high place in immigrant literature. He also wrote, in Yiddish, *Blätter von mein Leben* (5 vol., 1926–31), an autobiography.

Cahokia (kəhō'kēə), village (1970 pop. 20,649), St. Clair co., SW Ill., a residential suburb of East St. Louis, on the Mississippi River; inc. 1927. The first permanent settlement in Illinois, it was named for a tribe of the Illinois Indians. The French established a mission in 1699 and a fur-trading post later. With Kaskaskia, it became a leading center of French influence in the upper Mississippi valley. Cahokia was occupied by the British in 1765 and captured by the Americans under George Rogers Clark in 1778. The town has several buildings dating from the 18th cent. Parks College of Aeronautical Technology, a part of St. Louis Univ., is in the village. Nearby is Cahokia Mounds State Park.

Cahokia Mounds, approximately 85 Indian earthworks in Cahokia State Park, SW Ill., near East St. Louis; largest group of mounds N of Mexico. Monks' Mound, a rectangular, flat-topped earthwork, 100 ft (30.5 m) high with a 17-acre (6.9-hectare) base, is the largest mound; it is named for Trappist monks who settled on top of it in the early 19th cent. Excavation has not answered all the questions concerning the people who constructed the mounds. They were village dwellers living in a fertile river-bottom area; their culture flourished from c.1300 to c.1700. The mounds, which were probably bases for temples and houses of the chiefs, constitute a national historic landmark.

Cahors (käôr'), town (1968 pop. 17,775), capital of Lot dept., S central France, in Quercy, on the Lot River. A commercial center, it has canneries, distilleries, and factories making a great variety of products. It was an important Roman town, an early episcopal see, and the capital of Quercy. It was ruled by its bishops until the 14th cent. and was one of the major banking centers of medieval Europe; the Cahorsin money lenders were among the most famous. The Univ. of Cahors, founded in 1322 by Pope John XXII (who was born there), was united in 1751 with that of Toulouse. The old part of Cahors is of great architectural interest. Part of the medieval fortifications, including a fortified bridge, still stand. The Cathedral of St. Étienne (12th–15th cent.), with Byzantine cupolas, and the palace of John XXII (begun 14th cent.; never completed) are among its many edifices.

Caiaphas (Joseph Caiaphas) (kā'yəfəs), high priest of the Jews, a Sadducee, son-in-law of Annas. He presided at the council that condemned Jesus to death. Later, he joined in the examination of Peter and John. Mat. 26.57–68; John 11.47–54; 18.24; Acts 4.6.

Caicos Islands: see TURKS AND CAICOS ISLANDS.

Caillaux, Joseph (zhōzĕf' käyō'), 1863–1944, French statesman. Son of a former cabinet minister, he entered the French civil service as inspector of finance. He later became finance minister in the cabinet of René Waldeck-Rousseau (1899–1902) and in the cabinet of Georges Clemenceau (1906–9), winning considerable unpopularity by introducing the income tax. As premier in 1911, he reached a peaceful settlement of the crisis over MOROCCO with Germany. However, he was severely attacked by the nationalists, and his cabinet fell in 1912. In 1913 he again became minister of finance. He resigned in 1914 to defend his wife, who had shot and killed Gaston Calmette, editor of *Le Figaro,* for attacking Caillaux's private life. Mme Caillaux was acquitted. Caillaux expressed pacifist sentiments during World War I and allegedly made contact with the Germans to discuss a negotiated peace. He was arrested (1917) and sentenced (1920) to three years imprisonment for involvement with the enemy. After his civil rights were restored under a general amnesty, Caillaux served as finance minister in the cabinets of Paul Painlevé (1925) and Aristide Briand (1926), but after each appointment a hostile chamber of deputies forced his resignation. He was subsequently elected to the senate. See Rudolph Binion, *Defeated Leaders: The Political Fate of Caillaux, Jouvenel, and Tardieu* (1960).

Caillié, René (rənā' kāyā'), 1799–1838, French explorer in Africa. He was the first European to visit Timbuktu and return. The son of poor French peasants, he was obsessed with the idea of seeing Timbuktu. After 11 years of preparation, he reached the desert city, disguised as a Muslim trader, and remained there two weeks. See Galbraith Welch, *The Unveiling of Timbuctoo: The Astounding Adventures of Caillié* (1938).

caiman: see ALLIGATOR.

Cain (kān). **1** Eldest son of Adam and Eve, a tiller of the soil. In jealousy he killed his brother Abel and became a fugitive. Gen. 4. **2** City, W Palestine. Joshua 15.57.

Cain, James M., 1892–, American novelist, b. Annapolis, Md., grad. Washington College, 1910. He taught journalism at St. John's College (1924–25) and wrote political commentaries for the New York *World* (1924–31). His "hard-boiled" novels usually concern middle-class lovers who are driven to crime and violence. His novels include *The Postman Always Rings Twice* (1934), *Double Indemnity* (1936), *Mildred Pierce* (1941), *The Magician's Wife* (1966), and *Rainbow's End* (1974). Several of his novels have been made into successful movies.

Cainan (kā'năn), in the Gospel genealogy. **1** The same as KENAN. **2** Son of Arphaxad. Luke 3.36.

Caine, Hall (Sir Thomas Henry Hall Caine), 1853–1931, English novelist. Secretary to Dante Gabriel Rossetti, he lived with him from 1881 until the poet's death and wrote *Recollections of Rossetti* (1882). His enormously popular novels, some of Manx life, others on biblical themes, include *The Shadow of a Crime* (1885), *The Deemster* (1887), *The Manxman* (1894), *The Christian* (1897), *The Prodigal Son* (1904), and *The Master of Man* (1921). See his autobiography, *My Story* (1908); study by C. F. Kenyon (1901, repr. 1974).

cairn, pile of stones, usually conical in shape, raised as a landmark or a memorial. In prehistoric times it was usually erected over a burial. A BARROW is sometimes called a cairn.

Cairnes, John Elliot (kârnz), 1823–75, Irish economist, a follower of John Stuart Mill. His *Slave Power* (1862), a defense of the North in the American Civil War, made a great impression in England. Among his works are *The Character and Logical Method of Political Economy* (1857) and *Some Leading Principles of Political Economy Newly Expounded* (1874). See Adelaide Weinberg, *John Elliot Cairnes and the American Civil War* (1970).

Cairngorms, group of mountains forming part of the Grampian system, central Scotland, between the Dee and the upper Spey rivers; they rise to c.4,300 ft (1,310 m). The name cairngorm is given to an ornamental yellow or brown quartz found in the mountains. The group includes the peaks Ben Macdhui, Braeriach, and Cairngorm. The region is being developed for winter sports.

Cairns, city (1971 pop. 30,059), Queensland, NE Australia, on Trinity Bay. It is a principal sugar port of Australia; lumber and other agricultural products are also exported. The city's proximity to the Great Barrier Reef has made it a tourist center.

cairn terrier, breed of small working TERRIER developed on the Isle of Skye in the 19th cent. It stands about 10 in. (25 cm) high at the shoulder and weighs about 14 lb (6.4 kg). The weather-resistant double coat consists of a soft, furry underlayer and a profuse, hard outercoat about 2 in. (5 cm) long. It may be any color except white, often with dark ears, muzzle, and tip of tail. Originally bred to rout furbearing vermin from the rocky crags and cliffs of its native island, the cairn was also bred as a water dog to hunt otters. At an early stage in its history it was accepted into the household as a companion and watchdog, the roles for which it is principally raised today. See DOG.

Cairo (kī'rō), Arab. *Al Qahirah,* city (1970 est. pop. 4,961,000), capital of Egypt and its Cairo governorate, N Egypt, a port on the Nile River near the head of its delta. The city includes two islands in the Nile, Zamalik (Gezira) and Rawdah (Roda), which are linked to the mainland by bridges. Cairo has the largest population of any city in the Middle East and Africa. It is Egypt's administrative center and, along with Alexandria, the heart of its economy. Cairo's manufactures include textiles, food products, pharmaceuticals, chemicals, plastics, and metals. The first railroad in Africa (built 1855) linked Cairo with Alexandria, and today Cairo has extensive rail facilities and is also a road hub. Almost directly across the Nile from Cairo was MEMPHIS, an ancient Egyptian capital. Babylon, a Roman fortress city, occupied a part of SE Cairo now known as Old Cairo. Cairo was founded in 969 by the Fatimid general Jauhar Al Rumi to replace nearby Al Qatai (established in the 9th cent. by an Abbasid governor of Egypt) as the capital of Egypt. In the 12th cent. Saladin ended Fatimid rule and established the Ayyubite dynasty (1171–1250). To defend the city against an attack by Crusaders, Saladin erected (c.1179) the citadel, which still stands, and extended the walls of the city (originally built by Jauhar), parts of which remain. Cairo prospered under the rule of the Mamelukes, who added many buildings of high artistic merit, but the city declined after it was conquered (1517) by the Ottoman Empire. At the time of its capture (1798) by French forces led by Napoleon I, the city had about 250,000 inhabitants. British and Turkish forces ousted the French in 1801, and Cairo was returned to Ottoman control. Under Muhammad Ali (ruled 1805–49), Cairo became the capital of a virtually independent country and increased in commercial importance. Many Europeans settled in the city. During World War II, Cairo was the Allied headquarters and supply center for the Middle East and was the site (1943) of the CAIRO CONFERENCE. From 1958 to 1961 the city was the capital of the United Arab Republic, which joined Egypt and Syria. Today much of Cairo is modern, with wide streets; its famed mosques, palaces, and city gates are found mostly in the older sections. The mosques of Amur (7th cent.), Ibn Tulun (876–79), Hasan (c.1356), and Qait Bay (1475) are especially noted for their bold design. Khedive Ismail's palace on Zamalik island is a notable 19th-century structure. The Mosque of Al Azhar (970) and adjoining buildings house Al Azhar Univ., considered the world's leading center of Koranic studies. Cairo is also the seat of the American Univ. in Cairo, Cairo Polytechnic Institute, the Higher Institute of Finance and Commerce, the College of Fine Arts, and the Higher Institute of Theatrical Arts. The Univ. of Cairo is nearby, in Al Jizah. Cairo has many museums; the Egyptian National Museum is especially noted for its holdings of ancient Egyptian art. The Nilometer, a graduated column first built in 716 and used to measure the Nile water level, is on Rawdah island, where the infant Moses is believed to have been found in the bulrushes. Cairo is the center of Coptic Christianity in Egypt.

Cairo (kā'rō, kâ'rō), city (1970 pop. 6,277), seat of Alexander co., extreme S Ill., on a levee-protected tongue of land between the Mississippi and Ohio rivers (spanned there by several bridges); inc. 1857. A port of entry, it is a center for shipping by river, rail, and highway and the processing and distributing point for a large and fertile farm area. Manufactures include flour, lumber, cottonseed oil, textiles, woodwork, and silica. The city and surrounding area are popularly called "Egypt" because of the deltalike geographical similarity. Settlement was attempted there in 1818, but permanent settlement did not begin until 1837. Cairo was a strategic point in the Civil War; it was a crowded military camp, a depot for Union supplies, and General Grant's headquarters during much of his Western campaign. The city has often been endangered by floods, but Federal flood control projects have decreased the danger. Fort Defiance State Park, the site of a Civil War fort, on the southern edge of town, offers a magnificent view of the convergence of the Ohio and Mississippi rivers.

Cairo Conference, Nov. 22–26, 1943, World War II meeting of U.S. President Franklin Delano Roosevelt, British Prime Minister Winston Churchill, and Generalissimo Chiang Kai-shek of China at Cairo, Egypt. A joint declaration pledged continuation of the war against Japan until unconditional Japanese surrender, forswore territorial ambitions, and promised to strip Japan of all territory acquired since 1895. Korea was to receive independence "in due course." The TEHERAN CONFERENCE was held immediately afterward.

Cairoli, Benedetto (bānādĕt'tō kīrô'lē), 1825–89, Italian patriot and premier. One of five brothers all noted as heroes of the Risorgimento, he was the only brother to survive the wars leading to Italian unification. Benedetto took part in the expedition of Giuseppe GARIBALDI to Sicily in 1860 and later became a leftist member of parliament, advocating, with Giuseppe MAZZINI, the occupation of Rome. Premier in 1878 and from 1879 to 1881, he resigned his office after failing to prevent the establishment of a French protectorate over TUNISIA, which was a blow to Italian colonial policy.

caisson (kā'sən, -sŏn) [Fr.,=big box], in engineering, a chamber, usually of steel but sometimes of wood or reinforced concrete, used in the construction of foundations or piers in or near a body of water. There are several types. The open caisson is a cylinder or box, open at the top and bottom, of size and shape to suit the projected foundation and with a cutting edge around the bottom. It is sunk by its own weight and by excavation, then filled with concrete. Pneumatic caissons are usually employed in riverbed work or where quicksand is present. In this type the cylinder or box has an airtight bulkhead high enough above the cutting edge to permit men to work underneath it. The air in the chamber beneath the bulkhead is kept under pressure great enough to prevent the entrance of water, while shafts through the bulkhead permit the passage of men, equipment, and excavated material between the bottom and the surface. At the top of each shaft is an AIR LOCK to permit communication with the outside without altering the air pressure in the working chamber. As the working chamber moves down, the caisson above the bulkhead and about the shafts is filled with concrete, and when a sufficient depth or bedrock is reached, the working chamber itself is filled, so that there is a solid block of concrete from base to top. Workers leaving a pneumatic caisson after hours of labor under high pressure are given special decompression treatment to accustom them to the lower atmospheric pressure and thus to prevent caisson disease (see DECOMPRESSION SICKNESS). A type of caisson often called a camel is used to raise sunken vessels. It consists of a cylinder filled with water, which is sunk, attached to the vessel, and emptied by pump or compressed air, so that its buoyancy can assist in raising the vessel. Caissons are also sometimes used for closing the entrance to dry docks or as a substitute for gates in canal locks.

caisson disease: see DECOMPRESSION SICKNESS.

caisson sinking: see SHAFT SINKING.

Caithness (kāth'nĕs, kāthnĕs'), county (1971 pop. 27,754), 686 sq mi (1,777 sq km), NE Scotland, northernmost county of the Scottish mainland. WICK is the county town. The Thurso is the chief river. The northeastern section of Caithness, flat and treeless, contains most of the county's small percentage of arable land. The southwest is barren, with peat moors and sheep runs. Agriculture and fishing are the main occupations; there are growing dairy and glassmaking industries. Britain's first large nuclear breeder reactor was opened at DOUNREAY in 1959. Originally part of the Pictish nation, Caithness was absorbed into the Viking earldom in the 9th cent. and reverted to Scottish rule only in 1202. It was the scene of frequent clan warfare until the end of the 17th cent. In 1975, Caithness became part of the Highland region.

Cajal, Santiago Ramón y: see RAMÓN Y CAJAL.

Cajamarca (kähämär'kä), city (1969 est. pop. 28,000), N Peru. An important commercial center, Cajamarca is situated at an altitude of c.9,000 ft (2,740 m) and has a cool, dry climate. Most of the population is Indian. Grains and alfalfa are raised in the region, and gold, silver, and copper come from nearby mines. Francisco PIZARRO captured the Inca ruler ATAHUALPA in 1532 at Cajamarca. Inca ruins and nearby thermal springs attract many tourists.

Cajetan, Saint (kăj'ətăn, kä"yātän'), 1480–1547, Italian churchman and reformer. Son of the count of Thiene, he studied civil and canon law, but abandoned work as a jurist at the papal court to become a priest. He advocated communities of priests who lived in poverty and worked among the people. He was the leader in founding the congregation of the Theatines, formally begun in 1524 and named for a cofounder and first superior, the bishop of Chieti [Lat.= *Theate*], who was later PAUL IV. Cajetan's vigor in reform made him a notable figure, and the Theatines were very active in the Catholic Reformation. Cajetan was canonized in 1671. Feast: Aug. 7.

Cajetan [Lat.,=from Gaeta], 1469?–1534, Italian prelate, cardinal of the Roman Catholic Church, b. Gaeta. His original name was Giacomo de Vio. He joined the Dominicans (c.1484), became general of his order (1508), and was made a cardinal (1517). He played a leading role at the Fifth Lateran Council as an advocate of reform. As papal legate in Germany in 1518 and 1519 he attempted to reconcile the differences of Martin Luther with the church. He strongly opposed the divorce of Henry VIII of England from Katharine of Aragón. Cajetan's political skills helped secure the elections of Holy Roman Emperor Charles V and Pope Adrian VI. Always a student, he translated parts of the Bible, and his commentaries are published with the *Summa* of St. Thomas Aquinas in the pontifical edition of that work.

Cakchiquel: see QUICHÉ.

cake, originally a small mass of dough baked by turning on a spit; in present usage a dessert made of flour, sugar, eggs, seasonings, usually some leavening and liquid besides the eggs, and shortening. This last ingredient is not always used; unshortened cakes depend mainly on beaten eggs for leavening (e.g., spongecake and angel food cake). The early method of making sweet cake was by adding other ingredients to a portion of bread dough. Some cakes, such as fruitcake or poundcake, called for many eggs and for wine, brandy, or sack (an Elizabethan wine), these ingredients supplying the leavening agent. Modern cakes are generally raised with baking powder, baking soda, or beaten eggs.

Calabar (kăləbär', kăl'əbär), city (1969 est. pop. 89,000), SE Nigeria, a port on an estuary of the Gulf of Guinea. Rubber is processed, and palm oil, cacao, rubber, and timber are exported. Calabar, an important Niger delta trading state in the 19th cent., grew as a center of the palm oil trade.

calabash: see GOURD.

Calabrese, Il: see PRETI, MATTIA.

Calabria (kälä'brēä), region (1971 pop. 1,962,899), 5,822 sq mi (15,079 sq km), S Italy, a peninsula projecting between the Tyrrhenian Sea and the Ionian Sea, separated from Sicily by the narrow Strait of Messina. It forms the toe of the Italian "boot." CATANZARO is the capital of Calabria, which is divided into Catanzaro, Cosenza, and Reggio di Calabria provs. (named after their capitals). The region is generally mountainous, with narrow coastal strips. Farming is the main occupation; olives, plums, grapes, citrus fruit, and wheat are grown, and sheep and goats are raised. Fishing is well developed along the Strait of Messina. The region's few manufactures include processed food, wine, forest products, chemicals, and metal goods. There are several large hydroelectric plants. The ancient BRUTTIUM, the region was named Calabria in the 8th cent.; before then Calabria referred to the present S APULIA. Taken in the 11th cent. by ROBERT GUISCARD, Calabria was first part of the Norman kingdom of Sicily and after 1822 became part of the kingdom of Naples (see NAPLES, KINGDOM OF). The region was conquered by Garibaldi in 1860. Feudal landholding patterns prevailed in Calabria until the 20th cent. These, along with malaria, destructive earthquakes (particularly in 1905 and 1908), droughts, and poor transportation facilities, have hindered the economic development of the region and resulted in large-scale emigration (late 19th cent.–20th cent.) to foreign countries and to the industrial cities of N Italy. There is a polytechnic institute at Reggio di Calabria.

caladium (kəlā'dēəm): see ARUM.

Calah (kā'lə) or **Kalakh** (kä'läkh), ancient city of Assyria, S of Nineveh and therefore S of present Mosul, Iraq. Known as Calah in the Bible, it is the same as the ancient Nimrud, named after a legendary Assyrian hunting hero. Calah emerged as a famous city when Ashurnasirpal II chose (c.880 B.C.) the site for his capital. Excavations carried on since the mid-19th cent. have revealed remarkable bas-reliefs, ivories, and sculptures. Also discovered were the palaces of Ashurnasirpal II, Shalmaneser III, and Tiglathpileser III. Calah continued to be a royal residence even after Nineveh became the political capital. The famous black obelisk of Shalmaneser III was discovered in Calah by A. H. Layard in 1846. Calah is mentioned in Gen. 10.11,12.

Calahorra (käläôr'rä), town (1970 pop. 16,340), Logroño prov., NE Spain, in Old Castile, on the Cidacos River near its confluence with the Ebro. Calahorra is a farm (cereals and grapes) and manufacturing center. Known in ancient times as Calagurris, it is the place where Pompey unsuccessfully besieged (76–72 B.C.) the rebel Sertorius. An old cathedral (c.5th cent.; restored 15th cent.) and some Roman ruins survive today, and the Casa Santa, where the martyrs Emeterius and Celedonius are said to be buried, is the site of an annual pilgrimage. Quintilian was born in the town.

Calais (kălā'), city (1968 pop. 74,908), Pas-de-Calais dept., N France, in Picardy, on the Strait of Dover. An industrial center with a great variety of manufactures, it has been a major commercial seaport and a communications center with England since the Middle Ages. It was fortified (13th cent.) by the counts of Boulogne. In 1347, after a siege of 11 months, Calais fell to Edward III of England. A bronze monument by Rodin commemorates the famous episode of the six burghers who offered their lives to save the town; they were spared when Edward's queen, Philippa, interceded. The city remained in English hands until it was recovered (1558) by the French under François de Lorraine, the duke of Guise. It was the scene of much fighting (1940, 1944) in World War II. A Gothic church survived.

calamander wood: see EBONY.

Calamity Jane, c.1852–1903, American frontier character, b. Princeton, Mo. Her real name was Martha Jane Canary, and the origin of her nickname is obscure. Little is known of her early life beyond the fact that she moved with her parents to Virginia City, Mont., in 1865 and that she grew up in mining camps and rough frontier communities. In 1876 she appeared in Deadwood, S.Dak., dressed in men's clothes and boasting of her marksmanship and her exploits as a pony-express rider and as a scout with Custer's forces. In her later years she toured the West in a burlesque show and appeared at the Pan-American Exposition in Buffalo, N.Y. She died in poverty and obscurity in Deadwood, where she is buried beside Wild Bill Hickock. See biographies by Duncan Aikman (1927) and Mrs. Glenn Clairmonte (1959); R. J. Casey, *The Black Hills and Their Incredible Characters* (1949).

calamus (kăl'əməs): see ARUM.

Calamy, Edmund (kăl'əmē), 1600–1666, English Presbyterian preacher. For 10 years he was lecturer at Bury St. Edmunds until in 1636 his opposition to the observance of certain church ceremonies forced him to withdraw and so identify himself with the Puritan party. He was pastor (1639–62) of the Church of St. Mary Aldermanbury in London. A leader among the Presbyterians, Calamy was a member of the Westminster Assembly (1643). He was one of the five authors of the composite work *Smectymnuus,* directed against Bishop Joseph Hall's apology for a moderate episcopacy. Opposed to the execution of Charles I, Calamy was among those sent to meet Charles II in Holland. At the Restoration, he was made a chaplain to the king, but declined a bishopric. Ejected under the Act of Uniformity (1662), he was imprisoned for a short time for having preached after ejection. A number of his sermons were published. His grandson, **Edmund Calamy,** 1671–1732, nonconformist minister in London, also published many sermons, but he is particularly remembered for his *Account of the Ministers . . . Ejected by the Act for Uniformity* (1702), edited by A. G. Matthews as *Calamy Revised* (1934). His autobiography appeared in 1829.

Calan, Abraham: see CALOVIUS, ABRAHAM.

Calatayud (kälätäyōōth'), town (1970 pop. 17,217), Zaragoza prov., NE Spain, in Aragón, on the Jalón River. It is in an agricultural area and has sugar refineries. Founded (8th cent.) by the Moors and conquered (1120) by Alfonso I of Aragón, it retains a Moorish castle and the collegiate Church of Santo Sepulcro, once the main church of the Knights Templars in Spain. Near Calatayud stood ancient Bilbilis, birthplace of Martial.

Calatrava, Campo de (kämpō' thā kälāträ'vä), region in Ciudad Real prov., central Spain, in New Castile. It gave its name to the **Knights of Calatrava,** Spain's oldest military order, whose original seat was the fortress of Calatrava la Vieja, now in ruins. Founded (1158) by the Cistercians as a defense against the Moors, the order was very powerful, holding large possessions until the 13th cent.; later it declined. In 1499 the title of grand master passed to the Castilian crown and thence to the Spanish crown.

calcareous rock: see LIMESTONE; MARBLE.

calcareous soil (kălkâr'ēəs), soil formed largely by the weathering of calcareous rocks and fossil shell beds. Different varieties usually contain chalk, marl, and limestone and frequently a large amount of phosphates. They are often very fertile, as in the case of the buckshot soils of the S United States. Sometimes calcareous soils are flinty, thin, and dry. They often form a large part of the soil of deserts, which may prove very fertile when sufficient moisture for crops is applied.

Calcasieu (kăl'kəsōō), river c. 200 mi (320 km) long, rising in W central La. and flowing S through Lake Charles and Calcasieu Lake to the Gulf of Mexico. The river, which is partly navigable, connects the port of Lake Charles city with the Intracoastal Waterway and the Gulf of Mexico.

calceolaria (kăl"sēəlâr'ēə): see FIGWORT.

Calchas (kăl'kəs), in Greek legend, priest whose prophecies aided the Greeks in the TROJAN WAR. In medieval romances, he is the father of Cressida.

calcia: see CALCIUM OXIDE.

calciferol: see VITAMIN.

calcination (kăl"sənā'shən), in metallurgy, process of heating solid material to drive off volatile chemically combined components, e.g., carbon dioxide. It is sometimes a step in the extraction of metals from ores. Calcination is distinguished from drying, in which mechanically held water is driven off by heating, and from roasting, in which a material is heated in the presence of air to oxidize impurities. Originally calcination meant the method of obtaining lime (calcium oxide) from limestone by heating it to drive off carbon dioxide.

calcite (kăl'sīt), very widely distributed mineral, commonly white or colorless, but appearing in a great variety of colors owing to impurities. Chemically it is calcium carbonate, $CaCO_3$, but it frequently contains manganese, iron, or magnesium in place of the calcium. It crystallizes in the hexagonal system, its crystals being characterized by highly perfect cleavage. Calcite also occurs in a number of massive forms, in which it may be coarsely to finely granular (as in marble), compact (as in limestone), powdery (as in chalk), or fibrous. One crystalline form, called dogtooth spar because of its dogtooth appearance, exhibits faces of perfect scalene triangles. Another form, satin spar, is finely fibrous and has a satin luster. ICELAND SPAR is clear, transparent calcite. Other important forms of the mineral are LIMESTONE, MARBLE, CHALK, MARL, STALACTITE AND STALAGMITE formations, TRAVERTINE, and Oriental ALABASTER. Millions of tons of calcite, in the form of limestone and marble, are mined annually. Besides its use as a building stone, it is the raw material for quicklime and cement, and is used extensively as a flux in smelting and as a soil conditioner.

calcium (kăl'sēəm) [Lat.,=lime], metallic chemical element; symbol Ca; at. no. 20; at. wt. 40.08; m.p. about 845°C; b.p. 1487°C; sp. gr. 1.55 at 20°C; valence +2. Calcium is a malleable, ductile, silver-white, relatively soft metal with face-centered, cubic crystalline structure. Chemically it resembles strontium and barium; it is classed with them as an ALKALINE-EARTH METAL in group IIa of the PERIODIC TABLE. Calcium is chemically active; it tarnishes rapidly when exposed to air and burns with a bright yellow-red flame when heated, mainly forming the nitride. It reacts directly with water, forming the hydroxide. It combines with other elements, e.g., with oxygen, carbon, hydrogen, chlorine, fluorine, arsenic, phosphorus, and sulfur, forming many compounds. Calcium metal is usually prepared by electrolysis of fused calcium chloride to which a little calcium fluoride has been added. It is used in alloys with other metals, such as aluminum, lead, or copper; in preparation of other metals, such as thorium and uranium, by reduction; and (like barium) in the manufacture of vacuum tubes to remove residual gases. The metal is of little commercial importance compared to its compounds, which are widely and diversely used. The element is a constituent of LIME, chloride of lime (bleaching powder), MORTAR, plaster, cement (see CEMENT, HYDRAULIC), CONCRETE, WHITING, putty, precipitated CHALK, GYPSUM, and plaster of Paris. Tremolite, a form of asbestos, is a naturally occurring compound of calcium, magnesium, silicon, and oxygen. Calcium carbide reacts with water to form acetylene gas; it is also used to prepare calcium cyanamide, which is used as a fertilizer. The phosphate is a major constituent of bone ash. The arsenate and the cyanide are used as insecticides. Generally, calcium compounds show an orange or yellow-red color when held in the Bunsen burner flame. Although calcium is the fifth most abundant element in the earth's crust, of which it constitutes about 3.6%, it is not found uncombined. It is found widely distributed in its compounds, e.g., ICELAND SPAR, MARBLE, LIMESTONE, FELDSPAR, APATITE, CALCITE, DOLOMITE, FLUORITE, GARNET, and LABRADORITE. It is a constituent of most plant and animal matter. Calcium is essential to the formation and maintenance of strong bones and teeth. In the human adult the bone calcium is chiefly in the form of the phosphate and carbonate salts. A sufficient store of vitamin D in the body is necessary for the proper utilization of calcium. Calcium also functions in the regulation of the heart beat and in the conversion of prothrombin to thrombin, a necessary step in the clotting of blood. Calcium bicarbonate causes temporary hardness in water; calcium sulfate causes permanent hardness. Although LIME (calcium oxide) has been known since ancient times, elemental calcium was first isolated by Sir Humphry Davy in 1808.

calcium carbonate, $CaCO_3$, white chemical compound that is the most common nonsiliceous mineral. It occurs in two crystal forms, calcite, which is hexagonal, and aragonite, which is rhombohedral. Calcium carbonate is largely insoluble in water but is quite soluble in water containing dissolved carbon dioxide, combining with it to form the bicarbonate $Ca(HCO_3)_2$. Such reactions on LIMESTONE (which is mainly composed of calcite) account for the formation of stalactites and stalagmites in caves. Iceland spar is a pure form of calcium carbonate and exhibits birefringence, or double REFRACTION.

calcium chloride, $CaCl_2$, chemical compound that is crystalline, lumpy, or flaky, is usually white, and is very soluble in water. The anhydrous compound is hygroscopic; it rapidly absorbs water and is used to dry gases by passing them through it. Calcium chloride is commercially available usually as the dihydrate, $CaCl_2 \cdot 2H_2O$; it is used to melt ice on roads, to control dust, in brines for refrigeration, and as a preservative in foods. It is also used in the monohydrate and hexahydrate forms. Calcium chloride is a by-product of the SOLVAY PROCESS (a major source of the compound) and is present in natural brines.

calcium hydroxide, $Ca(OH)_2$, colorless crystal or white powder. It is prepared by reacting CALCIUM OXIDE (lime) with water, a process called slaking, and is also known as hydrated lime or slaked lime. When heated above 580°C it dehydrates, forming the oxide. Like the oxide, it has many uses, e.g., in LIMING soil, in sugar refining, and in preparing other compounds. It is a strong base and is widely used as an inexpensive alkali, often as a suspension in water (milk of lime); it is used in leather tanning to remove hair from hides. It is used in WHITEWASH, MORTAR, and plaster. It is only slightly soluble in water, about 0.2 grams per 100 cubic centimeters, so its solutions are weakly basic. Limewater is a clear, saturated water solution of calcium hydroxide. It is used in medicine to treat acid burns and as an antacid. Because calcium hydroxide readily reacts with carbon dioxide, CO_2, to form calcium carbonate, a mixture of gases can be tested for the presence of CO_2 by shaking it with limewater in a clear container; if CO_2 is present, a cloudy calcium carbonate precipitate will form.

calcium oxide or **calcia,** chemical compound, CaO, a colorless, cubic crystalline or white amorphous substance. It is also called lime, quicklime, or caustic lime, but commercial lime often contains impurities, e.g., silica, iron, alumina, and magnesia. It is prepared by heating CALCIUM CARBONATE (e.g., LIMESTONE) in a special lime kiln to about 500°C to 600°C, decomposing it into the oxide and carbon dioxide. Calcium oxide is widely used in industry, e.g., in making porcelain and glass; in purifying sugar; in preparing BLEACHING POWDER, calcium carbide, and calcium cyanamide; in water softeners; and in mortars and cements. In agriculture it is used for treating acidic soils (LIMING). It is incandescent when heated to high temperatures; the Drummond light, or limelight, provides a brilliant white light by heating a cylinder of lime with the flame of an oxyhydrogen torch. Calcium oxide is a basic anhydride, reacting with water to form CALCIUM HYDROXIDE; during the reaction (slaking) much heat is given off and the solid nearly doubles its volume.

Calcol (kăl'kŏl), Judahite. 1 Chron. 2.6. Chalcol: 1 Kings 4.31.

calculating machine, device for performing numerical computations; it may be mechanical, electromechanical, or electronic. The electronic COMPUTER is also a calculating machine but performs other functions as well. Early devices used to aid in calculation include the ABACUS (still common in the Orient) and the counting rods, or "bones," of the Scottish mathematician John Napier. The SLIDE RULE, invented in 1622 by William Oughtred, an English mathematician, is still widely used to make approximate calculations. In 1642, Pascal devised what was probably the first simple adding machine using geared wheels. In 1671 an improved mechanism for performing multiplication by the process of repeated addition was designed by Gottfried W. von Leibniz. A machine using the Leibniz mechanism was the first to be produced successfully on a commercial scale; devised in 1820 by the Frenchman Charles X. Thomas, it could be used for adding, subtracting, multiplying, or dividing. A mechanism permitting the construction of a more compact machine than the Leibniz mechanism was incorporated into a machine devised late in the 19th cent. by the American inventor Frank S. Baldwin. Later the machine was redesigned by Baldwin and another American inventor, Jay R. Monroe. At about the same time, W. T. Odhner of Russia constructed a machine using the same device as Baldwin's. Charles Babbage, an English mathematician, and William S. Burroughs, an American inventor, also made important contributions to the development of the calculating machine. The simple modern adding machine is equipped with a keyboard on which numbers to be added are entered, a lever to actuate the addition process, and an accumulator to display the results. A full keyboard may consist of 10 columns of keys with 9 keys in each column, numbered 1 through 9. Each column can be used to enter a figure in a particular decimal place so that a number up to 10 digits long can be entered; if no key is pressed in a given column, a zero is entered in that decimal place. The lever is pulled in one direction when a number is to be added and in the opposite direction when it is to be subtracted. The accumulator is a set of geared wheels, each corresponding to a decimal place and having the digits 0 through 9 printed on its circumference. When a given wheel makes a complete rotation, the next wheel is advanced by one digit. There are many variations on this basic setup. Some machines provide only 10 keys, numbered 0 through 9, on which to enter numbers. Most modern machines have an electric motor that actuates the addition process when a special key on the machine is depressed; some have a mechanism that prints on a paper tape the individual entries and the totals. With some modifications, printing adding machines can be used as calculators, i.e., machines that can also multiply and divide. Mechanical rotary calculators are more sophisticated devices, designed to provide rapid answers to involved calculations. They normally do not provide printed results. Electronic calculators became available in the early 1960s, and in the early 1970s miniature types, some of them pocket size, were marketed as consumer items. Electronic calculators have 10 keys that can be used to enter numbers into the machine; additional keys are provided to enable the user to perform a range of operations, from basic arithmetic in simple devices to the generation of complex mathematical functions in more advanced types. The results of an operation are either shown on an electronic display or are printed. Some of these machines are actually small computers with limited memory and programming capabilities. Electronic calculators are considered to be superior to mechanical machines because they are generally faster, smaller, quieter, more reliable, and more versatile. See G. R. Brookspear, *The Fundamental Operations of Calculating and Adding Machines* (1962); A. L. Walker et al., *How to Use Adding and Calculating Machines* (3d ed. 1967).

calculus, branch of MATHEMATICS that studies continuously changing quantities. The calculus is characterized by the use of infinite processes, involving passage to a LIMIT. Two kinds of limit are of particular interest in the calculus. The differential calculus arises from the study of the limit of a quotient, $\Delta y/\Delta x$, as the denominator Δx approaches zero, where x and y are variables, y may be expressed as some FUNCTION of x, or $f(x)$, and Δy and Δx represent corresponding increments, or changes, in y and x. The limit of $\Delta y/\Delta x$ is called the derivative of y with respect to x and is indicated by dy/dx or D_xy:

$$\lim_{\Delta x \to 0} \Delta y/\Delta x = dy/dx = D_xy.$$

The symbols dy and dx are called differentials (they are single symbols, not products), and the process of finding the derivative of $y=f(x)$ is called differentiation. The derivative $dy/dx=df(x)/dx$ is also denoted by y', or $f'(x)$. The derivative $f'(x)$ is itself a function of x and may be differentiated, the result being termed the second derivative of y with respect to x and denoted by y'', $f''(x)$, or d^2y/dx^2. This process can be continued to yield a third derivative, a fourth derivative, and so on. Although the method of increments used to find the limit of $\Delta y/\Delta x$ can be applied to all differentiation, in practice formulas have been developed for finding the derivatives of all commonly encountered functions. For example, if $y=x^n$, then $y'=nx^{n-1}$, and if $y=\sin x$, then $y'=\cos x$. In general, the derivative of y with respect to x expresses the rate of change in y for a change in x. In physical applications, the independent variable (here x) is frequently time; e.g., if $s=f(t)$ expresses the relationship between distance traveled, s, and time elapsed, t, then $s'=f'(t)$ represents the rate of change of distance with time, i.e., the speed, or velocity. Everyday calculations of velocity usually involve dividing the distance traveled, Δs, by the time elapsed, Δt, during the period in question; this ratio, $\Delta s/\Delta t$, is the average velocity for the time period Δt. The derivative $f'(t)=ds/dt$, however, gives the velocity for any particular value of t, i.e., the instantaneous velocity. Geometrically, the derivative is interpreted as the slope of the line tangent to a curve at a point. If $y=f(x)$ is a real-valued function of a real variable, the ratio $\Delta y/\Delta x=(y_2-y_1)/(x_2-x_1)$ represents the slope of a straight line through the two points $P(x_1,y_1)$ and $Q(x_2,y_2)$ on the graph of the function. If P is taken closer to Q, then x_1 will approach x_2 and Δx will approach zero. In the limit where Δx approaches zero, the ratio becomes the derivative $dy/dx=f'(x)$ and represents the slope of a line that touches the curve at the single point Q, i.e., the tangent line. This property of the derivative yields many applications for the calculus, e.g., in the design of optical mirrors and lenses and the determination of projectile paths. The second important kind of limit encountered in the calculus is the limit of a sum of elements when the number of such elements increases without bound while the size of the elements diminishes. For example, consider the problem of determining the area under a given curve $y=f(x)$ between two values of x, say a and b. Let the interval between a and b be divided into n subintervals, from $a=x_0$ through $x_1, x_2, x_3, \ldots, x_{i-1}, x_i, \ldots$, up to $x_n=b$. The width of a given subinterval is equal to the difference between the adjacent values of x, or $\Delta x_i=x_i-x_{i-1}$, where i designates the typical, or ith, subinterval. On each Δx_i a rectangle can be formed of width Δx_i, height $y_i=f(x_i)$ (the value of the function corresponding to the value of x on the right-hand side of the subinterval), and area $\Delta A_i=f(x_i)\Delta x_i$. In some cases, the rectangle may extend above the curve, while in other cases it may fail to include some of the area under the curve; however, if the areas of all these rectangles are added together, the sum will be an approximation of the area under the curve. This approximation can be improved by increasing n, the number of subintervals, thus decreasing the widths of the Δx's and the amounts by which the ΔA's exceed or fall short of the actual area under the curve. In the limit where n approaches infinity (and the largest Δx approaches zero), the sum is equal to the area under the curve:

$$A=\lim_{n\to\infty}\sum_{i=1}^{n}\Delta A_i=\lim_{n\to\infty}\sum_{i=1}^{n}f(x_i)\Delta x_i=\int_a^b f(x)dx.$$

The last expression on the right is called the integral of $f(x)$, and $f(x)$ itself is called the integrand. This method of finding the limit of a sum can be used to determine the lengths of curves, the areas bounded by curves, and the volumes of solids bounded by curved surfaces, and to solve other similar problems. An entirely different consideration of the problem of finding the area under a curve leads to a means of evaluating the integral. It can be shown that if $F(x)$ is a function whose derivative is $f(x)$, then the area under $f(x)$ between a and b is equal to $F(b)-F(a)$. This connection between the integral and the derivative is known as the Fundamental Theorem of the Calculus. Stated in symbols:

$$\int_a^b f(x)dx=F(b)-F(a), \text{ where } F'(x)=f(x).$$

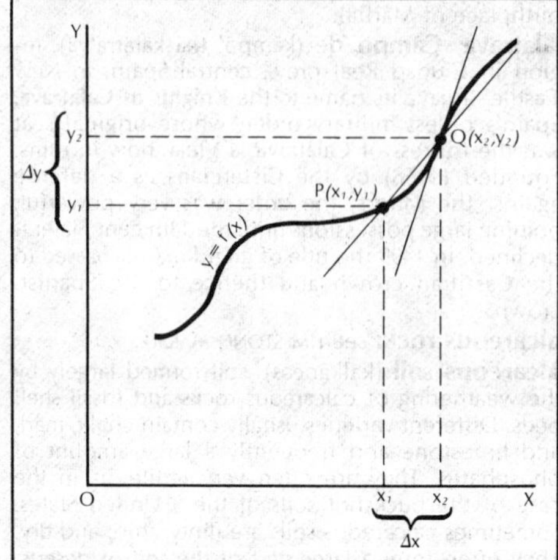

The derivative f′(x) *of the function* f(x) *at the point* Q *represents the slope of the tangent line at that point.*

The function $F(x)$, which is equal to the integral of $f(x)$, is sometimes called the antiderivative of $f(x)$, while the process of finding $F(x)$ from $f(x)$ is called

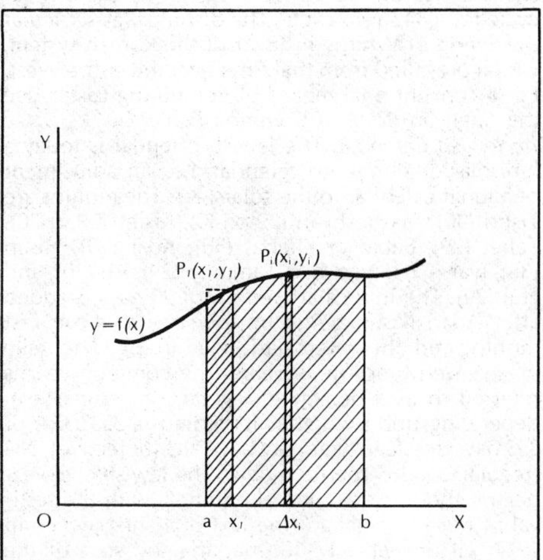

The area under the curve y = f(x) *may be found by calculating the sum of the elements of area* ΔA, *whose width is* Δx *and whose height is* f(x).

integration or antidifferentiation. The branch of calculus concerned with both the integral as the limit of a sum and the integral as the antiderivative of a function is known as the integral calculus. The type of integral just discussed, in which the limits of integration, *a* and *b*, are specified, is called a definite integral. If no limits are specified, the expression is an indefinite integral. In such a case, an arbitrary constant *C* must be added to the function $F(x)$ resulting from integration, since in computing the derivative any constant terms having derivatives equal to zero are lost; the expression for the indefinite integral of $f(x)$ is

$$\int f(x)\,dx = F(x) + C.$$

The value of the constant *C* must be determined from various boundary conditions surrounding the particular problem in which the integral occurs. The calculus has been developed to treat not only functions of a single variable, e.g., *x* or *t*, but also functions of several variables. For example, if $z = f(x,y)$ is a function of two independent variables, *x* and *y*, then two different derivatives can be determined, one with respect to each of the independent variables. These are denoted by $\partial z/\partial x$ and $\partial z/\partial y$ or by $D_x z$ and $D_y z$. Three different second derivatives are possible, $\partial^2 z/\partial x^2$, $\partial^2 z/\partial y^2$, and $\partial^2 z/\partial x \partial y = \partial^2 z/\partial y \partial x$. Such derivatives are called partial derivatives. In any partial differentiation all independent variables other than the one being considered are treated as constants. The calculus and its basic tools of differentiation and integration serve as the foundation for the larger branch of mathematics known as ANALYSIS. The English physicist Isaac Newton and the German mathematician G. W. Leibniz, working independently, developed the calculus during the 17th cent. See Richard Courant and Fritz John, *Introduction to Calculus and Analysis*, Vol. I (1965); Morris Kline, *Calculus: An Intuitive and Physical Approach* (2 vol., 1967); A. W. Goodman, *Modern Calculus with Analytic Geometry* (2 vol., 1967–1968).

calculus of variations, branch of MATHEMATICS concerned with finding maximum or minimum conditions for a relationship between two or more variables that depends not only on the variables themselves, as in the ordinary CALCULUS, but also on an additional arbitrary relation, or constraint, between them. For example, the problem of finding the closed plane curve of given length that will enclose the greatest area is a type of isoperimetric (equal-perimeter) problem that can be treated by the methods of the variational calculus; the solution to this special case is the circle. Another famous problem is the brachistochrone problem, that of finding the curve along which an object will slide to a point not directly below it in the shortest time; the solution is a cycloid curve (a curve traced out by a fixed point on the circumference of a circle as the circle rolls along a straight line). In general, problems in the calculus of variations involve solving the definite integral (single or multiple) of a function of one or more independent variables, $x_1, x_2, \ldots$, one or more dependent variables, $y_1, y_2, \ldots$, and derivatives of these, the object being to determine the dependent variables as functions of the independent variables such that the integral will be a maximum or minimum. The calculus of variations was founded at the end of the 17th cent. and was developed by Jakob and Johann Bernoulli, Isaac Newton, G. W. Leibniz, Leonhard Euler, J. L. Lagrange, and others.

Calcutta (kălkŭt'ə), city (1971 pop. 3,141,180), capital of West Bengal state, E India, on the Hooghly River. It is the second-largest city in India and one of the largest in the world. Ten of Calcutta's suburbs—Howrah, South Suburban, Bhatpara, South Dum Dum, Kamarhati, Garden Reach, Panihati, Baranagar, Hooghly-Chinsura, and Serampore—have well over 100,000 people. The population of Greater Calcutta in 1971 was 7,005,362. Its area is 228.5 sq mi (591 sq km). Calcutta is the chief port and major industrial center of E India; jute is milled, and textiles, chemicals, paper, and metal products are manufactured. Calcutta's airport is the busiest in India. Nearly 60 languages are spoken in the city, which suffers from terrible poverty, chronic unemployment, overcrowding, inadequate transportation, and the resultant social unrest. Calcutta was founded c.1690 by the British East India Company. In 1756 the nawab of Bengal, Siraj-ud-daula, captured Calcutta and killed most of its garrison by imprisoning it overnight in a small, stifling room, known as the notorious "black hole." Robert Clive retook the city in 1757. From 1833 to 1912, Calcutta was the capital of India. The Univ. of Calcutta (founded 1857), several unaffiliated colleges, and the Indian Museum, which houses one of the world's outstanding natural history collections, are in the city. The Maidan, a large river-front park surrounded by government buildings, is Calcutta's most attractive section.

Caldara, Antonio (äntô'nyō käldä'rä), 1670–1736, Italian composer. In 1714, Caldara obtained a position at the imperial court in Vienna, where he remained until his death. He composed a large amount of sacred and secular vocal music, as well as chamber works. His canons were especially popular. Franz Joseph Haydn was influenced by Caldara.

Caldecott, Randolph (kôl'dəkət), 1846–86, English artist and illustrator. He is famous for his drawings of contemporary English country life and for his charming and humorous illustrations, including those for Washington Irving's *Old Christmas* and *Bracebridge Hall* and Blackburn's *Breton Folk*. Perhaps his best are the colored illustrations for a series of 16 children's picture books, including *The House that Jack Built* and *The Grand Panjandrum Himself*. The Caldecott Medal for excellence in children's-book illustration is named for him. See memoir by Henry Blackburn (1886, repr. 1969).

Calder, Alexander (kôl'dər), 1898–, American sculptor, b. Philadelphia; son of a prominent sculptor, Alexander Stirling Calder. Among the most innovative modern sculptors, Calder was trained as a mechanical engineer. In 1930 he went to Paris and was influenced by the art of Mondrian and Miró. In 1932 he exhibited his first brightly colored constellations, called MOBILES, consisting of painted cut-out shapes connected by wires and set in motion by wind currents. The Museum of Modern Art, New York City, has several examples. These buoyant inventions and his witty wire portraits, his colorful and complex miniature zoo (1925; Whitney Mus., New York City), and his immobile sculptures known as STABILES, have brought Calder world renown. Many of his recent works are huge, heavy, and delicately balanced mobiles produced for public buildings throughout the world. Calder is also noted for his book illustrations and stage sets. He has studios in Roxbury, Conn., and Paris. See his autobiography (1966) and *Mobiles and Stabiles* (1968); study by J. J. Sweeney (1951); Jean Lipman, ed., *Calder's Circus* (1972).

Caldera, Rafael (räfäĕl' käldä'rä), 1916–, president of Venezuela (1969–74). A lawyer and professor of sociology, he was first elected to the chamber of deputies in 1941 and was a founder of the center-right Christian Social party in 1946. He was imprisoned several times during the dictatorial regime of Marcos Pérez Jiménez, which he opposed. After the dictator's overthrow Caldera in 1958 ran unsuccessfully for the presidency; he served instead as president of the chamber of deputies. In the elections of Dec., 1969, he won the presidency with barely 30% of the vote. Faced with an uncooperative congress, he had difficulty in getting legislation passed. He was awarded a life seat in the senate at the end of his term.

caldera: see CRATER.

Calderón Bridge (käldārōn'), site of a decisive battle in the Mexican revolution against Spain, fought on the Lerma River E of Guadalajara, Jalisco, Mexico. On Jan. 17, 1811, insurgents commanded by HIDALGO Y COSTILLA met the royalists under CALLEJA DEL REY. On the point of victory, Hildalgo's men were panicked by the explosion of an ammunition wagon. Their flight led to the collapse of the independence movement under Hidalgo.

Calderón de la Barca, Pedro (pā'thrō käldārōn' dā lä bär'kä), 1600–1681, Spanish dramatist, last important figure of the Spanish Golden Age, b. Madrid. Educated at a Jesuit school and the Univ. of Salamanca, he turned from theology to poetry and became a court poet in 1622. His more than 100 plays were carefully contrived, subtle, and rhetorical. The earlier plays, of the cloak-and-dagger school, include *La dama duende* [the lady fairy] and *Casa con dos puertas mala es de guardar* [the house with two doors is difficult to guard]. His finest work is in his more than 70 *autos sacramentales* (one-act religious plays), among them *El divino Orfeo* and *A Dios por razón de estado* [to God for reasons of state]. Of his philosophical dramas the best known are *El mágico prodigioso* [the wonderful magician] and *La vida es sueño* [life is a dream], one of the masterpieces of the Spanish theater. Calderón took holy orders in 1651 and thereafter wrote few plays except the *autos*, of which he supplied two a year for the Corpus Christi festival. See studies by Salvador Madariaga (1920, repr. 1965), J. H. Parker and A. M. Fox (1971), Edwin Honig (1972), and Heinz Gerstinger (tr. 1973).

Calderón Guardia, Rafael Ángel (räfäĕl' äng'hĕl käldārōn' gwär'dēä), 1900–1970, president of Costa Rica (1940–44). A practicing physician, he entered politics in 1934, serving successively as vice president and president of congress (1935–39). He was leader of the Republican, or Calderista, party. As president, he brought Costa Rica into World War II on the Allied side and cooperated closely with the United States. He later served (1966–70) as ambassador to Mexico.

Caldwell, Erskine (kôld'wəl), 1903–, American author, b. White Oak, Ga. His realistic and extremely earthy novels of the rural South include *Tobacco Road* (1933), *God's Little Acre* (1933), *This Very Earth* (1948), and *Summertime Island* (1969). Among his volumes of short stories are *Jackpot* (1940) and *Gulf Coast Stories* (1956). With his first wife, Margaret BOURKE-WHITE, he published *You Have Seen Their Faces* (1937), about Southern sharecroppers.

Caldwell, Taylor (Janet Taylor Caldwell), 1900–, American novelist, b. London, England. Her best-selling works range from romance to satire to fictionalized biography and often reflect her Christian heritage. They include *Dynasty of Death* (1938), *The Devil's Advocate* (1952), *Dear and Glorious Physician* (1959), *The Captain and the Kings* (1972), and *Glory and the Lightning* (1974).

Caldwell, Zoë (zō'ē), 1934?–, Australian actress. Caldwell joined the Shakespeare Memorial Theatre Company at Stratford-on-Avon in 1958. Her Broadway debut in *Slapstick* earned her the Antoinette Perry Award, as did her playing of the lead in *The Prime of Miss Jean Brodie* (1963). Her other theatrical performances include *Colette* (1970) and *A Gift to the Nation* (1971).

Caldwell, city (1970 pop. 14,219), seat of Canyon co., SW Idaho, on the Boise River; inc. 1890. On the site of an Oregon Trail camping ground, the city is now a major processing and distribution center for an agricultural and livestock area. Mobile homes and recreational vehicles are manufactured. It is the seat of an agricultural-experiment station and The College of Idaho.

Caleb (kā'lĕb), principal spy sent into Canaan, noted for his faithfulness to God. Num. 13.6; 14; 32.12; Joshua 14.6–14. The name is mentioned elsewhere, apparently in connection with a clan inhabiting S Palestine. 1 Sam. 30.14; 1 Chron. 2.18,19,42,46,48,49. Chelubai: 1 Chron. 2.9. The name **Caleb-ephratah** (-ĕf'rətə) at 1 Chron. 2.24 is a textual error.

Caledonia (kă"līdō'nēə), Roman name for that part of the island of Great Britain that lies N of the firths of Clyde and Forth. The name first occurs in the works of Lucan (1st cent. A.D.) and has been used in modern times rhetorically and poetically to mean all of Scotland or the Scottish Highlands.

Caledonian Canal, waterway, c.60 mi (100 km) long, cutting across Highland region (Inverness-shire), N Scotland, from Moray Firth to Loch Linnhe by way of the Great Glen. Built in two phases (1803–22 and 1843–47; opened 1822) to save shallow-draft vessels the circuitous route around N Scotland, it is of little use today except for pleasure craft. Of the waterway, 38 mi (61 km) consists of the natural waters of Lochs Ness, Oich, and Lochy. The canal has 29 locks.

Calef, Robert (kā'ləf), 1648–1719, known primarily as author of *More Wonders of the Invisible World* (1700). A Boston cloth merchant, probably born in England, he bitterly attacked Cotton MATHER for his part in the Salem, Mass., WITCHCRAFT trials. The book, published in London because Boston printers would not accept it, generally condemned the view of witchcraft then prevailing and had a salutary effect throughout New England. It is reprinted in S. G. Drake, comp., *The Witchcraft Delusion in New England,* (3 vol., 1866, repr. 1970).

calendar [Lat., from Kalends], system of reckoning time for the practical purpose of recording past events and calculating dates for future plans. The calendar is based on noting ordinary and easily observable natural events, the cycle of the sun through the seasons with EQUINOX and SOLSTICE, and the recurrent phases of the moon. The earth completes its orbit about the sun in 365 days 5 hr 48 min 46 sec—the length of the solar year. The moon passes through its phases in about 29½ days; therefore, 12 lunar months (called a lunar year) amount to more than 354 days 8 hr 48 min. The discrepancy between the years is inescapable, and one of the major problems for man since his early days has been to reconcile and harmonize solar and lunar reckonings. Some peoples have simply recorded time by the lunar cycle, but, as skill in calculation developed, the prevailing calculations generally came to depend upon a combination. The fact that months and years cannot be divided exactly by days and that the years cannot be easily divided into months has led to the device of intercalation. The simplest form of this is shown in ancient calendars which have series of months alternating between 30 and 29 days, thus arriving at two mean months of 29½ days each. Similarly four years of about 365¼ days each can be approximated by taking three years of 365 days and a fourth year of 366. This fourth year with its intercalary day is the leap year. If calculations are by the lunar cycle, the surplus of the solar over the lunar year (365 over 354) can be somewhat rectified in three years by adding an extra (intercalary) month of 33 days. Reckoning of day and year was considered necessary by practical peoples to determine sacred days, to arrange plans for the future, and to keep some intelligible record of the past. There were, therefore, various efforts to reconcile the count in solar, lunar, and semilunar calendars, from the Egyptians and the Greeks to the Chinese and the MAYA. The problem was fundamental. So for chroniclers was the establishment of a fixed point in time for calculating years in an ERA.

The Roman Calendar. The prevailing modern method of constructing a calendar in the Christian West came originally from the Egyptians, who worked out a formula for the solar year (12 months of 30 days each, five extra days a year, and an extra day every four years). This was to be adopted later by the Romans. In its most primitive form the Roman calendar had no such refinement. It apparently had 10 months, which were (to use corresponding English terms whenever possible): March (31 days), April (29 days), May (31 days), June (29 days), Quintilis (31 days), Sextilis (29 days), September (29 days), October (31 days), November (29 days), and December (29 days). To fill out the 365 days a number of blank days or occasional intercalary months were used. Later, January (29 days) and February (28 days) were added at the end of the year. In the time of the early republic the so-called year of Numa was added. The Romans thus arrived at a cycle of four years: the first year had four months of 31 days, seven of 29, and one, February, of 28; the second year had a February of 23 days and an intercalary month of 27 days; the third year was like the first; the fourth year had a February of 24 days and an intercalary month. The chief trouble with this system was that in a four-year cycle there were four days too many. What was worse, the PONTIFEX MAXIMUS was given the power soon after 200 B.C. to regulate the calendar (which for ordinary civil purposes was expressed in terms of the consulates of whatever men held it). The practice grew up of using the intercalations for the promotion of political ends to lengthen or to shorten an official's term. When Julius Caesar was pontifex maximus, the calendar had been so much abused that January was falling in autumn.

The Julian Calendar. At this point the methods of the Egyptian calendar were borrowed for the Roman. Julius Caesar on the advice of the astronomer Sosigenes added 90 days to the year 46 B.C. (67 days between November and December, 23 at the end of February). This caused the spring of 45 B.C. to begin in March. To retain this position of the seasons, he changed the length of most of the months: March, May, Quintilis (subsequently named August to honor Augustus), and October he left as they were; he added 2 days each to January and Sextilis (subsequently named July after Julius Caesar himself); February was 28 days long except that in every fourth year a day was inserted between the 23d and the 24th of the month. In Roman computation three days in the month were used for counting the date. These three were the Kalends (1st day of the month), the Nones (the 7th day in March, May, July, and October, the 5th in the other months), and the Ides (the 15th day in March, May, July, and October, the 13th in the other months). The days were counted before, not after, the Kalends, Nones, and Ides. Thus, Jan. 10 was the fourth day before the Ides of January or the fourth day of the Ides of January, because the Romans counted inclusively. Jan. 25 was the eighth of the Kalends of February, Feb. 3 was the third of the Nones of February. Feb. 23 was the seventh of the Kalends of March and remained so when an intercalary day was inserted every fourth year between it and Feb. 24; hence in a leap year there were two days counted as the sixth of the Kalends of March. The leap year was therefore called bissextile [Lat.,=sixth twice]. There is a legend that alterations in the length of the months were made later by Augustus to flatter his own vanity, but there seems to be no foundation for this story.

The Gregorian Calendar. The Julian year is 365 days 6 hr, hence a little too long. Therefore, by the 16th cent. the accumulation of surplus time had displaced the vernal equinox to March 11 from March 21, the date set in the 4th cent. In 1582 Pope Gregory XIII rectified this error. He suppressed 10 days in the year 1582 and ordained that thereafter the years ending in hundreds should not be leap years unless they are divisible by 400. The year 1600 was a leap year under both systems, but 1700, 1800, and 1900 were leap years only in the unreformed calendar. The reform was accepted, immediately in most Roman Catholic countries, more gradually in Protestant countries, and in the Eastern Church the Julian calendar was retained until the 20th cent. The present generally accepted calendar is therefore called Gregorian, though it is only a slight modification of the Julian.

Old Style and New Style. The reform was not accepted in England and the British colonies in America until 1752. By that date the English calendar was 11 days different from that of the Continent. For the period before the reform was introduced, the Gregorian style is called the New Style (N.S.), and the Julian the Old Style (O.S.). New Style years begin Jan. 1, but Old Style years began usually March 25. Thus Washington's birthday, which is Feb 22, 1732 (N.S.) was Feb. 11, 1731 (O.S.). To avoid confusion sometimes both styles are given; thus 1731/32 or 1731/2 or 11 Feb. 1731/22 Feb. 1732.

The Christian Ecclesiastical Calendar. The church calendar with its movable feasts shows an interesting example of a harmony of several different systems. The key to it is the reconciliation of the seven-day week with the Roman calendar (see WEEK). The resurrection of Jesus has always been traditionally reckoned as having taken place on a Sunday (first day of the week); hence the annual feast celebrating the event, EASTER, should fall on a Sunday. The Bible places the Passion with relation to the Passover. Since the Jewish Passover is on the evening of the 14th (eve of the 15th) Nisan (see below), it may fall on any day of the week; hence Easter must fall on a Sunday near the 14th Nisan. In ancient times some Eastern Christians celebrated Easter on the 14th Nisan itself; these were called *Quartodecimans* [Lat.,=fourteenth]. In 325 the First Council of Nicaea determined that Easter should fall on the Sunday following the full moon next after the vernal equinox, the full moon being theoretically the 14th day, and Nisan beginning with a new moon in March. The vernal equinox was considered by the church to fall on March 21. The paschal, or Easter, moon is the moon the 14th day of which falls next after (not on) March 21. Today Easter is calculated mathematically according to a system not taking all factors of the lunar period into consideration, hence it nearly always varies somewhat from what it should be according to true astronomical calculation. Several different systems have been used for determining Easter; today some Eastern churches use a different one from that of the West. In the 6th and 7th cent. in England, there was a great dispute between Christians who derived their rite from the Celts and Christians who had been converted as a result of the mission of St. Augustine. The dispute over Easter arose because the Celts retained a computation for Easter based on a lunar cycle of 84 years, while the Romans had, in the 5th cent., given up the 84-year cycle for a 532-year cycle. The dispute was settled at the Synod of Whitby in favor of the Roman system, which prevailed from that time over the entire West. For a conventional means of computing Easter, see the Anglican *Book of Common Prayer.*

The Jewish Calendar. The Jewish calendar is today a lunisolar or semilunar calendar, i.e., an adjustment of a lunar calendar to the solar year. The months are Tishri (30), Marheshvan (29 or 30), Kislev (29 or 30), Tebet (29), Sebat or Shebat (30), Adar (29), Nisan (30), Iyar (29), Sivan (30), Tammuz (29), Ab (30), and Elul (29). The intercalary month of 30 days is added after Adar, Nisan being in ancient times the first month, and the intercalation is arranged to take place seven times in 19 years. The common year is referred to as a defective, regular, or perfect year, depending upon whether its length is 353, 354, or 355 days; the leap year may have 383 (defective), 384 (regular), or 385 (perfect) days. The Jewish civil year begins about the autumnal equinox, with the festival of Rosh ha-Shanah (the first of Tishri), which in 1974 fell on Sept. 17–18, marking the start of the Jewish year 5735.

The Muslim Calendar. The Muslim calendar is the only widely used purely lunar calendar, its year varying from 354 to 355 days. Hence the seasons and months have no connection, and there are about 33 Muslim years to every 32 Gregorian years. The months are Muharram (30), Safar (29), 1st Rabia (30), 2d Rabia (29), 1st Jumada (30), 2d Jumada (29), Rajab (30), Shaban (29), Ramadan (the fast, 30), Shawwal (29), Dhu-l-Kada (30), and Dhu-l-Hijja (month of the pilgrimage, 29 or 30).

Other Calendars. The old Chinese calendar was devised to have six 60-day cycles, each cycle having 10-day periods and three such periods going to make up a month. By the 5th cent. B.C. the solar year was calculated at 365.2444 solar days and the solar month at 29.53059 days. The difference between solar time and the cycles was adjusted by intercalary months and shorter intercalary periods. The years were arranged in major cycles of 60 years with minor cycles of 5 years each. An interesting calendar is that of the MAYA, who used a year of 365 days divided into 18 20-day periods, with a 5-day period at the end. A recurrent series of 20 days was used also, like our week. A remarkable feature was that the year was never readjusted to the error in its length; instead, the feasts and dates were adjusted to the calendar. The AZTEC calendar was very similar. Many attempts have been made to devise new calendars, adjusting the months more regularly to the solar year, discarding the week, making the months equal in length, and the like, but they have never been widely adopted. The most celebrated is the FRENCH REVOLUTIONARY CALENDAR. In the 20th cent. the movement toward calendar reform has been strong, the aim being not to abandon but to refine the intercalary system of the Julian-Gregorian calendar. For the method of computing years from a fixed point (e.g., the birth of Christ and the HEGIRA), see ERA. The adoption of such era systems has made computation of time much easier. The Athenian system of identifying years by archons, the Roman system of identifying them by consuls, and the system used both earlier and later of reckoning by the year of the reign of certain kings offers enormous difficulties, and the establishment of chronology is one of the major problems in ancient and medieval history. The classic work on chronology is that of the Benedictines, first published in 1750, *L'Art de vérifier les dates des faits historiques* [the art of verifying the dates of historical acts]. See P. W. Wilson, *The Romance of the Calendar* (1937); Harold Watkins, *Time Counts: The Story of the Calendar* (1954); K. G. Irwin, *The Three Hundred Sixty-Five Days* (1963).

calendering, a finishing process by which paper, plastics, rubber, or textiles are pressed into sheets and smoothed, glazed, polished, or given a moiré or embossed surface. The material is passed through a series of rollers; the resulting surface depends on the pressure exerted by the rollers, on their temperature, composition, and surface designs, and on the type of coating or glaze previously applied to the material to be calendered.

calendula (kəlĕn'jələ), any species of the genus *Calendula,* Old World plants of the family Compositae (COMPOSITE family). The common calendula (*C. officinalis*), an annual with yellow to deep orange flower heads produced through a long blooming season, was a popular garden flower in Shakespeare's time—his "marigold." Its dried florets have been used as a food coloring and for flavoring stews and soups (whence the name pot marigold) and have also long been used medicinally. Calendula is classified in the division MAGNOLIOPHYTA, class Magnoliopsida, order Asterales, family Compositae.

Calexico (kəlĕk'sĭkō), city (1970 pop. 10,625), Imperial co., S Calif., at the Mexican border; inc. 1908. A port of entry from its adjacent sister city of Mexicali, Mexico, it is also a trade center in the southern part of the fertile Imperial Valley.

calf, golden, idol erected by the Israelites on several occasions. Aaron made one while Moses was on Mt. Sinai. Ex. 32. Jeroboam placed one at Bethel and another at Dan (1 Kings 12.26-32). Hosea denounced one in Samaria (Hosea 8.5,6). A bull cult was widespread in Canaan at the time of the invasion of the Israelites. The use of such a cult recalls Apis in Egypt and the Minotaur in Crete.

Calgary (kăl'gərē), city (1971 pop. 403,319), S Alta., Canada, at the confluence of the Bow and Elbow rivers. Calgary is a wholesale and processing center for a large agricultural and stock-raising area. It is also the headquarters of many oil and natural gas firms. The city began (1875) as a fort of the Northwest Mounted Police. It is the site of the Univ. of Calgary. The Calgary Stampede, inaugurated 1912, is an annual rodeo.

Calgary, University of, at Calgary, Alta., Canada; coeducational; provincially supported; founded 1945 as a branch of the Univ. of Alberta. It gained full autonomy in 1966. It has faculties of arts and science, fine arts, business, education, engineering, environmental design, medicine, and graduate studies, as well as schools of nursing, physical education, and social welfare. The Banff School of Fine Arts is affiliated with the university.

Calhoun, John Caldwell (kăl″ho͞on'), 1782-1850, American statesman and political philosopher, b. near Abbeville, S.C., grad. Yale, 1804. He studied law under Tapping Reeve at Litchfield, Conn., and began (1808) his public career in the South Carolina legislature. Frontier born, he acquired a large plantation by marrying (1811) his cousin, Floride Calhoun. Later he came to represent the interests of the Southern planter aristocracy. A Congressman (1811-17) and acting chairman of the House Committee on Foreign Affairs, Calhoun was one of the leading "war hawks," who whipped up enthusiasm for the War of 1812. He remained a nationalist for some time after the war, speaking for a strong army and navy, for encouragement of manufacturing, for internal improvements, and for a national bank; many of these causes he later opposed. Calhoun was an efficient Secretary of War (1817-25) under President Monroe and was Vice President (1825-29) under John Quincy Adams. Throughout Adams's administration he opposed the President and aligned himself with the supporters of Andrew JACKSON. An able constitutional lawyer, he made an imposing figure skillfully presiding over the Senate. When the Jacksonians finally triumphed in 1828, Calhoun was again elected Vice President, and it was widely assumed that he would succeed Jackson in office. But relations between the two men soon cooled. Calhoun, prodded by his wife and his supporters, offended the President in the Eaton affair (see O'NEILL, MARGARET). Jackson finally became furious when he discovered that years before Calhoun had privately denounced Jackson's conduct in Florida while publicly giving the impression that he had supported the general. Primarily, however, Jackson and Calhoun had come to disagree on the nature of the Union. As the preeminent spokesman for the South, Calhoun tried to reconcile the preservation of the Union with the fact that under the Union the South's dominant agricultural economy was being neglected and even injured at the expense of the ever-increasing commercial and industrial power of the North. When a still higher tariff replaced (1832) the Tariff of Abominations of 1828, Calhoun maintained that the Constitution, rightly interpreted, gave a state the power to nullify Federal legislation inimical to its interests. He returned to South Carolina, had a state convention called, and directed the passage of the famous ordinance of NULLIFICATION. In Dec., 1832, he quit the vice presidency after being elected to the Senate, where he eloquently defended his STATES' RIGHTS principles in dramatic debates with Daniel Webster. The firmness of Andrew Jackson and the compromise tariff proposed by Henry CLAY resolved the nullification crisis in 1833, but the larger issue of states' rights persisted, leading ultimately to SECESSION and the Civil War. Meanwhile, Martin VAN BUREN, Calhoun's bitter political enemy, held the vice presidency in Jackson's second term and went on to succeed Jackson in the office Calhoun had coveted for many years. As the abolitionists grew stronger in the North, Calhoun became an outspoken apologist for slavery and bent every effort to maintain the delicate balance between North and South in the Senate by opposing the prohibition of slavery in newly admitted states. Thus, while serving briefly (1844-45) as Secretary of State under John Tyler, he completed negotiations for the admission of Texas as a slave state, but later tried to avert war with Mexico. Again (1845-50) in the Senate, he advocated compromise in the Oregon boundary dispute but opposed the admission of California as a free state in the debates over the COMPROMISE OF 1850. In rejecting the Wilmot Proviso, Calhoun set forth the theory that all territories were held in common by the states and that the Federal government merely served as a trustee of the lands. His *Disquisition on Government* and *Discourse on the Constitution and Government of the United States*, both published posthumously, crystallized his political philosophy. The Constitution, he stated, established a government of concurrent majorities composed of two elements—the state governments and the Federal government. Hence the states enjoy the power of veto, or nullification, and the right of secession results necessarily from the origin of the Union as a compact among the sovereign parties. His theories attempted to formulate democracy in terms of protection for a minority, specifically, the South, and they were later embodied in the Confederate constitution. Because his ideas are associated with an institution—slavery—offensive to the idealism of most Americans, Calhoun has never been a popular figure in U.S. history. He was, however, the intellectual giant of political life in his day. Calhoun's plantation, with his house, Fort Hill, is now the campus of Clemson Univ. See his works (ed. by R. K. Crallé, 6 vol., 1851-55); his papers (ed. by R. L. Meriwether and W. E. Hemphill, Vol. I-VII, 1959-1973); biographies by C. M. Wiltse (3 vol., 1944-51), M. L. Coit (1950), and G. M. Capers (1968).

Cali (kä'lē), city (1971 est. pop. 950,500), capital of Valle del Cauca dept., W Colombia, on the Cali River. It is an industrial and commercial center of the upper Cauca valley. Livestock, minerals, lumber, and farm products are shipped through the city; and tires, tobacco products, textiles, paper, chemicals, and building materials are manufactured. Cali is also a tourist center. The city was founded in 1536, but its growth is relatively recent, with the population more than doubling in the 1950s. In the city are two universities and the headquarters of the Cauca valley development project, which is modeled after the Tennessee Valley Authority. Cali's landmarks include an aqueduct and a cathedral.

Caliari, Paolo: see VERONESE, PAOLO.

calico, plain weave cotton fabric in one or more colors. Calico, named for Calicut, India, where the fabric originated, was mentioned by historians before the Christian era and praised by early travelers for its fine texture and beautiful colors. Block-printed cottons from Calicut imported into England c.1630 were called calicuts. The name calico was soon applied to all Oriental cottons having an equal number of warp and weft threads, then to all plain weave cottons. In the latter part of the 18th cent. calico became an important item in England's growing textile industry.

calico cat: see CAT.

Calicut (kă'lĭkət) or **Kozhikode** (kō'zhəkōd″), city (1971 pop. 333,980), Kerala state, SW India, on the Malabar coast of the Arabian Sea. Once the leading port of S India, it declined in the 19th cent. but remains the center of India's timber trade. Cashew nuts, spices, tea, and coffee are exported. Calicut was (1498) Vasco da Gama's first Indian port of call, and the city soon became a center for European traders. The term *calico* was first applied to Calicut cotton cloth, which was then an important manufacture. Calicut passed to British rule in 1792.

California, state (1970 pop. 19,953,134), 158,693 sq mi (411,014 sq km), W United States, admitted as the 31st state of the Union in 1850. The capital is SACRAMENTO. The largest cities and major seaports are LOS ANGELES, SAN FRANCISCO, OAKLAND, and SAN DIEGO. California is bounded on the N by Oregon, on the E by Nevada and Arizona (from which it is separated by the Colorado River), on the S by Mexico, and on the W by the Pacific Ocean. Ranking first among the U.S. states in population and third in area, California has a diverse topography and climate. A series of low mountains known as the Coast Ranges extends along the 1,200-mi (1,930-km) coast. The region from Point Arena, N of San Francisco, to the southern part of the state is subject to tremors and sometimes to severe earthquakes caused by the San Andreas fault. The Coast Ranges receive heavy rainfall

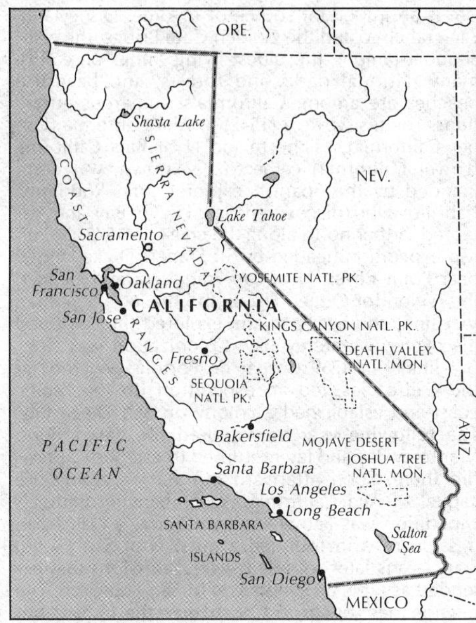

in the north, where the giant cathedral-like redwood forests prevail, but the climate of these mountains is considerably drier in S California, and S of the Golden Gate no major rivers reach the ocean. Behind the coastal ranges in central California lies the great Central Valley, a long alluvial valley drained by the Sacramento and San Joaquin rivers. In the southeast lie vast wastelands, notably the Mojave Desert, site of Joshua Tree National Monument. Rising as an almost impenetrable granite barrier E of the Central Valley is the Sierra Nevada range, which includes Mt. Whitney, Kings Canyon National Park, Sequoia National Park, and Yosemite National Park. The Cascade Range, the northern continuation of the Sierra Nevada, includes Lassen Volcanic National Park. Death Valley National Monument is E of the S Sierra Nevada. Although agriculture is second to industry as the basis of the state's economy, California is a leading state in the production of fruits and vegetables and is the largest producer in the United States of many crops, including tomatoes, carrots, lettuce, asparagus, broccoli, spinach, and strawberries. The state's most valuable crops are hay, grapes, tomatoes, and cotton. Cattle and dairy products also contribute a major share of farm income. The state produces the major share of U.S. domestically produced wine. California's farms are highly productive as a result of good soil, a long growing season, and the use of modern agricultural methods. Irrigation is widely used. The gathering and packing of crops is done largely by seasonal migrant labor (including thousands of Mexicans), and one of California's major social problems is the improvement of the farm workers' condition. Fishing is another important industry; California leads the nation in commercial fishing. Much of the state's manufacturing depends on the processing of farm produce and upon such local natural resources as mineral deposits and forests. Petroleum is the state's most valuable mineral, and in the late 1960s California ranked third in the country in oil production. Other important products are natural gas, cement, and sand and gravel. Since World War II heavy industry in the state has increased enormously, notably in the manufacture of transportation equipment, electronic equipment, machinery, and metal products. Defense-contract industries, particularly in S California, represent a major base of the region's economy and have contributed to the growing wealth and population of the area. California has long been a major U.S. center for motion-picture and television film production, but in the late 1960s its position became threatened by a trend toward on-location filming. One of the state's most acute problems is the need for an adequate water supply. The once fertile Owens valley is now arid, its waters tapped by Los Angeles 175 mi (282 km) away, and water is piped to the coast across the Mojave Desert from the Colorado River 200 mi (322 km) away. In the lush, fruit-growing Imperial Valley, irrigation is controlled by the All-American Canal, which also draws from the Colorado. To the N in the Central Valley the water problem is one of bad distribution, an imbalance lessened by the vast CENTRAL VALLEY PROJECT. California's pleasant climate and natural beauty have attracted many retired persons, and senior-citizen communities have sprung up in the state. Tourism is an important source of income. Disneyland, San Francisco and the Golden Gate Bridge, the giant Sequoia (among the oldest living things on earth), many national parks and forests, and beautiful beaches are among California's numerous attractions. The first voyage (1542) to Alta California (Upper California), as the region N of Baja California (Lower California) came to be known, was commanded by the Spanish explorer Juan Rodríguez Cabrillo, who discovered San Diego Bay and explored farther north along the coast. In 1579 an English expedition headed by Sir Francis Drake landed near Point Reyes, N of San Francisco, and claimed the region for Queen Elizabeth I. In 1602, Sebastián Vizcaíno, another Spaniard, explored the coast and discovered Monterey Bay. Colonization was slow, but finally in 1769 Gaspar de Portolá, governor of the Californias, led an expedition up the Pacific coast and established a colony on San Diego Bay. The following year he explored the area around Monterey Bay and later returned to establish a presidio there. Soon afterward Monterey became the capital of Alta California. Accompanying Portolá's expedition was Father Junipero Serra, a Franciscan missionary who founded a mission at San Diego. Franciscans later founded several missions that extended as far N as Sonoma, N of San Francisco. The missionaries sought to Christianize the Indians but also forced them to work as manual laborers, helping to build the missions into vital agricultural communities. Cattle raising was of primary importance, and hides and tallow were exported. The missions have been preserved and are now open to visitors. In 1776, Juan Bautista de Anza founded San Francisco, where he established a military outpost. The early colonists, called the Californios, lived a pastoral life and for the most part were not interfered with by the central government of New Spain (as the Spanish empire in the Americas was called) or later (1820s) by that of Mexico. The Californios did, however, become involved in local politics, as when Juan Bautista Alvarado led a revolt (1836) and made himself governor of Alta California, a position he later persuaded the Mexicans to let him keep. Under Mexican rule the missions were secularized (1833–34) and the Indians released from their servitude. The degradation of the Indian, which continued under Mexican rule and culminated after U.S. settlers came to the area, was described by Helen Hunt Jackson in her novel *Ramona* (1884). Many mission lands were subsequently given to Californios, who established the great ranchos, vast cattle-raising estates. Colonization of California remained largely Mexican until the 1840s. Russian fur traders had penetrated S to the California coast and established Fort Ross, N of San Francisco, in 1812. Jedediah Strong Smith and other trappers made the first U.S. overland trip to the area in 1826, but U.S. settlement did not become significant until the 1840s. In 1839, Swiss-born John Augustus Sutter arrived and established his "kingdom" of New Helvetia on a vast tract in the Sacramento valley. He did much for the overland American immigrants, who began to arrive in large numbers in 1841. Some newcomers met with tragedy, including the DONNER PARTY, which was stranded in the Sierra Nevada after a heavy snowstorm. Political events in the territory moved swiftly in the next few years. After having briefly asserted the independence of California in 1836, the Californios drove out the last Mexican governor in 1845. Under the influence of the American explorer John C. Frémont, U.S. settlers set up (1846) a republic at Sonoma under their home-styled Bear Flag. The news of war between the United States and Mexico (1846–48) reached California soon afterward. On July 7, 1846, Commodore John D. Sloat captured Monterey, the capital, and claimed California for the United States. The Californios in the north worked with U.S. soldiers, but those in the south resisted U.S. martial law. In 1847, however, U.S. Gen. Stephen W. Kearny defeated the southern Californios. By the Treaty of Guadalupe Hidalgo (1848), Mexico formally ceded the territory to the United States. In the same year a major event in California's history occurred: while establishing a sawmill for John Sutter near Coloma, James W. Marshall discovered gold and touched off the California gold rush. The forty-niners, as the gold-rush miners were called, came in droves, spurred by the promise of fabulous riches from the MOTHER LODE. San Francisco rapidly became a boom city, and its bawdy, lawless coastal area, which became known as the Barbary Coast, gave rise to the vigilantes, extralegal community groups formed to suppress civil disorder. American writers such as Bret Harte and Mark Twain have recorded the local color as well as the violence and human tragedies of the roaring mining camps. With the gold rush came a huge increase in population and a pressing need for civil government. In 1849, Californians sought statehood and, after heated debate in the U.S. Congress arising out of the slavery issue, California entered the Union as a free, nonslavery state by the Compromise of 1850. San Jose became the capital. Monterey, Vallejo, and Benicia each served as the capital before it was finally moved to Sacramento in 1854. In 1853, Congress authorized the survey of a railroad route to link California with the eastern seaboard, but the transcontinental railroad was not completed until 1869. In the meantime communication and transportation depended upon ships, the stage coach, the pony express, and the telegraph. Chinese laborers were imported in great numbers to work on railroad construction. The Burlingame Treaty of 1868 (see BURLINGAME, ANSON) provided, among other things, for unrestricted Chinese immigration. That was at first enthusiastically endorsed by Californians; but after a slump in the state's shaky economy, the white settlers viewed the influx of the lower-paid Chinese laborers as an economic threat. Ensuing bitterness and friction led to the Chinese Exclusion Act of 1882 (see CHINESE EXCLUSION). A railroad-rate war (1884) and a boom in real estate (1885) fostered a new wave of overland immigration. Cattle raising on the ranchos gave way to increased grain production. Vineyards were planted by 1861, and the first trainload of oranges was shipped from Los Angeles in 1886. By the turn of the century the discovery of oil, industrialization resulting from the increase of hydroelectric power, and expanding agricultural development attracted more settlers. Los Angeles grew rapidly in this period and, in population, soon surpassed San Francisco, which suffered greatly after the great earthquake and fire of 1906. Improvements in urban transportation stimulated the growth of both Los Angeles and San Francisco; the advent of the cable car and the electric railway made possible the development of previously inaccessible areas. As industrious Japanese farmers acquired valuable land and a virtual monopoly of California's truck-farming operations, the issue of Oriental immigration again arose. The bitter struggle for the exclusion of Orientals plagued international relations, and in 1913 the California Alien Land Act was passed despite President Woodrow Wilson's attempts to block it. The act provided that persons ineligible for U.S. citizenship could not own agricultural land in California. Successive waves of settlers arrived in California, attracted by a new real-estate boom in the 1920s and by the promise of work in the 1930s. The influx during the 1930s of displaced farm workers, depicted by John Steinbeck in his novel *The Grapes of Wrath*, caused profound dislocation in the state's economy. During World War II the Japanese in California were removed from their homes and placed in relocation centers. Industry in California expanded rapidly during the war; the production of ships and aircraft attracted many workers who later settled in the state. Prosperity and rapid population growth continued after the war. Many Negroes who came during World War II to work in the war industries settled in California. By the 1960s they constituted a sizable minority in the state, and racial tensions reached a climax. In 1964, California voters approved an initiative measure, Proposition 14, allowing racial discrimination in the sale or rental of housing in the state, a measure later declared unconstitutional by the U.S. Supreme Court; and in 1965 riots broke out in Watts, a predominantly black section of Los Angeles. Also in the 1960s migrant farm workers in California formed a union and struck many growers to obtain better pay and working conditions. Unrest also occurred in the state's universities, where student demonstrations and protests in 1964 provoked disorders. In 1970, S California was struck by the worst brush fire in state history, and in 1971 a severe earthquake hit S California along the San Andreas fault. The state's first constitution was adopted in 1849. The present constitution dates from 1879 and provides for initiative, referendum, and recall of public officials. The state's executive branch is headed by a governor elected for a four-year term. California's bicameral legislature has a senate with 40 members elected for four-year terms and an assembly with 80 members elected for two years. Local government is carried out on the county and city level. The state elects 2 Senators and 43 Representatives to the U.S. Congress and has 45 electoral votes. Republicans have played a more dominant role than Democrats in California politics during the 20th cent. Ronald Reagan, a former movie actor and leading conservative Republican, was elected governor in 1966 and reelected in 1970. In 1974, Edmund G. Brown, Jr., a Democrat and the son of a former governor (1959–67), was elected governor. Among the state's more prominent institutions of higher learning are the Univ. of California, with eight campuses; Occidental College and the Univ. of Southern California, at Los Angeles; Stanford Univ., at Stanford; the California Institute of Technology, at Pasadena; Mills College, at Oakland; and the Claremont Colleges, at Claremont. See R. G. Cleland, *From Wilderness to Empire* (rev. ed. by G. S. Dumke, 1959); D. E. Fehrenbacher, *A Basic History of California* (1964); Federal Writers' Project, *California, A Guide to the Golden State* (rev. ed. 1967); L. Pitt, *The Decline of the Californios: A Social History of the Spanish Speaking Californians, 1846–1890* (1967); R. Kirsch, *West of the West: Witnesses to the California Experience, 1542–1906* (1968); R. J. Roske, *Everyman's Eden: A History of California* (1968); C. A. Hutchinson, *Frontier Settlement in Mexican California* (1969); A. F. Rolle, *California: A History* (2d ed. 1969); J. W. Caughey, *California* (3d ed. 1970); Walton Bean, *California: An Interpretive History* (2d. ed. 1973).

California, Gulf of, arm of the Pacific Ocean, c.700 mi (1,130 km) long and 50 to 130 mi (80–209 km) wide, NW Mexico; separates Baja California from the Mexican mainland. The gulf is part of a depression in the earth's surface that extends inland to the Coachella Valley, S Calif. The Imperial Valley and the Salton Sea, once part of the gulf, have been cut off from it by the growth of the Colorado River delta. The gulf deepens from north to south; its greatest depth is c.8,500 ft (2,590 m). The coastline is irregular, with numerous islands; Tiburon, inhabited by aboriginal tribes, is the largest. Storms and tidal currents hinder navigation in the gulf. Commercial and sport fishing thrive; pearl, sponge, and oyster beds are harvested. The region is a developing tourist center; La Paz, Guaymas, and Mazatlán are major cities. The area was first explored in 1538 by the Spaniard Francisco de Ulloa.

California, Lower: see BAJA CALIFORNIA.

California, University of, at nine campuses, main campus at Berkeley; land-grant and state supported; coeducational; the largest state university system in the United States; chartered 1868, opened 1869 when it took over the College of California (est. 1853 at Oakland as Contra Costa Academy). In 1873 it moved to the present Berkeley campus. At Berkeley are the Lawrence Radiation Laboratory; the main library, which houses over 4 million manuscripts and a large number of collections relating to many fields; and an extensive museum system including museums of paleontology, zoology, and anthropology. The Los Angeles campus (est. 1881 as Los Angeles State Normal School, transferred to the university 1919) is known for its theater department. The brain and nuclear medicine institutes are among the several research programs there. At La Jolla is the Scripps Institution of Oceanography (est. 1901, transferred to the university 1912), whose research facilities include several ships and marine laboratories. In the 1950s the institution became the nucleus of the San Diego campus, which added an undergraduate program in 1964. The San Francisco campus (est. 1864 as Toland Medical College, transferred to the university 1934) is employed exclusively by the medical sciences. Other campuses are at Riverside (est. 1907 as the Citrus Experiment Station), Santa Barbara (est. 1891 as a private school, transferred to the university 1944), Davis (opened 1909), Irvine (est. 1960, opened 1965), and Santa Cruz (est. 1965). The university also operates the Los Alamos Scientific Laboratory, the Lick Observatory, numerous agricultural experiment stations, and a statewide extension service.

California Institute of Technology, at Pasadena, Calif.; originally for men, became coeducational in 1970; founded 1891 as Throop Polytechnic Institute; called Throop College of Technology, 1913–20. The institute's research facilities, principally in science and engineering, include the Jet Propulsion Laboratory (operated in conjunction with the National Aeronautics and Space Administration), the Hale Observatories (originally the Mount Wilson and Palomar observatories), the Guggenheim Aeronautical Laboratory, and a cosmic ray laboratory.

California Joe, 1829–76, American frontiersman and scout, whose real name was Moses Embree Milner, b. Stanford, Ky. He went to California in the gold rush, later moving into the Oregon country. He was a sharpshooter for the Union army during the Civil War, after which he became a scout in the Indian campaigns, serving under George A. Custer and Philip H. Sheridan; both commended him in reports. Custer once appointed him chief of scouts, but California Joe got so drunk within a few hours that he had to be demoted. In 1875 he guided the government expedition led by W. P. Jenny to investigate the mineral resources of the Black Hills. He was shot in a private quarrel. See biography by his grandson, J. E. Milner, and E. R. Forrest (1935).

California poppy: see POPPY.

California State College System, coordinating agency established 1960 by the merging of individual California state colleges, consisting of 19 campuses, 14 of which have university status. It is one of the three California public systems of higher education, the other two being the Univ. of California system (see CALIFORNIA, UNIV. OF) and the California junior college system. The oldest school in the system (founded 1857) at San Jose was the first institution of public higher education in California. The newest campus was opened at Bakersfield in 1970. The other branches are at Dominguez Hills, Fullerton, Hayward, Long Beach, Los Angeles, San Bernardino, Pomona, San Luis Obispo, Chico, Fresno, Arcata (Humboldt campus), Sacramento, San Diego, Northridge, San Francisco, and Turlock (Stanislaus campus). The university's special programs include an off-campus degree program and weekend colleges. In 1972 the system's official title became the California State University and Colleges.

californium (kăl'ĭfôr"nēəm), artificially produced, radioactive metallic chemical element; symbol Cf; at. no. 98; mass number of most stable isotope 251; m.p., b.p., and density unknown; valence +3. Californium is a member of the ACTINIDE SERIES of chemical elements, found in group IIIb of the PERIODIC TABLE. Its chemical properties are similar to those of LANTHANUM. Twelve isotopes of californium are known, with half-lives ranging from about 4 min for californium-242 to about 800 years for californium-251, the most stable isotope. Californium-249 (half-life 323 years) is most useful for chemical investigations; it is obtained by the decay of berkelium-249. Four solid compounds of californium have been prepared; they are the trichloride, oxychloride, oxyfluoride, and oxide. Californium-252 (half-life 2.6 years) is produced in nuclear reactors for use as a source of neutrons. Californium was first produced in 1950 by Glenn T. SEABORG, S. G. Thompson, A. Ghiorso, and K. Street in a cyclotron at the Univ. of California at Berkeley by bombarding curium-242 with alpha particles, resulting in californium-245 (half-life 45 min).

Caligula (kəlĭg'yo͝olə), A.D. 12–A.D. 41, Roman emperor (A.D. 37–A.D. 41); son of GERMANICUS CAESAR and AGRIPPINA I. His real name was Caius Caesar Germanicus. As a small child, he wore military boots, whence his nickname [*caligula*=little boots]. After the death (A.D. 33) of his brother, Drusus, Caligula and Tiberius' grandson, Tiberius Gemellus, were the heirs apparent. On the death of TIBERIUS the army helped make Caligula emperor. Shortly afterward he became severely ill; it is widely believed that he was thereafter insane. He earned a reputation for ruthless and cruel autocracy, and torture and execution became the order of the day. He was responsible for serious disturbances among the Jews, and he nearly caused a rebellion in Palestine by attempting to erect a statue of himself in their temple. He is reported to have made his horse a consul and a member of a priestly college. His reign ended when Chaerea, a tribune of the Praetorian Guard, assassinated him. CLAUDIUS I succeeded to the throne. See J. P. V. D. Balsdon, *The Emperor Gaius* (1934).

caliphate (kăl'ĭfāt", -fĭt), the rulership of ISLAM. Islam is, theoretically, a theocracy, and its caliph the vicegerent of God. When Muhammad the Prophet died, a caliph [Arabic,=successor] was chosen to rule in his place. The caliph had temporal and spiritual authority but was not permitted prophetic power; this was reserved for Muhammad. The first caliph was ABU BAKR. He was succeeded by UMAR, UTHMAN, and ALI. These are the Orthodox caliphs. After Ali's death there was a division in Islam. MUAWIYA became caliph and founded the UMAYYAD dynasty, chiefly by force of arms. Its capital was Damascus. The SHIITES, however, continued to recognize the descendants of Ali and in 750 won the caliphate for them, massacring the members of the Umayyad family. These Shiite caliphs were of the ABBASID family. Their caliphate is sometimes called the caliphate of Baghdad. One Umayyad, ABD AR-RAHMAN I, escaped the general massacre of his family and fled to Spain; there the emirate of Córdoba was set up in 780. This later became the caliphate of Córdoba, or the Western caliphate, and persisted until 1031. A third contemporaneous caliphate was established by the FATIMIDS in Africa and lasted from 909 to 1171. After the fall of Baghdad to the Mongols under Hulagu Khan in 1258, the Abbasids fled to Egypt. After this date the caliphate was virtually nonexistent, since the Abbasids in Egypt had not the slightest power. The Ottomans captured Egypt in 1517; Selim I assumed the title of caliph (by questionable right). The Ottoman sultans, however, kept the title until the last sultan, Muhammad VI, was deposed. He was succeeded briefly by a cousin, but in 1924 the caliphate was abolished altogether. A year later Husayn ibn Ali, king of Arabia, proclaimed himself caliph, but he was forced to abdicate by Ibn Saud. Since then several pan-Islamic congresses have attempted to establish a rightful caliph. See William Muir, *The Caliphate* (1898, repr.1964); Alfred von Kremer, *Orient under the Caliphs* (tr. 1920); T. W. Arnold, *The Caliphate* (1924, repr. 1966); A. S. Tritton, *The Caliphs and their Non-Muslim Subjects* (1930, repr. 1970); Muhammad Ali, *Early Caliphate* (tr. 1947); S. Khuda Bakhsh, *The Caliphate* (1954); P. K. Hitti, *History of the Arabs* (10th ed. 1970).

Calisher, Hortense (kăl'ĭshər), 1911–, American author, b. New York City, grad. Barnard, 1932. Her novels are difficult to categorize, blending character analysis with complex story lines. Written in careful yet constantly fresh prose, they have been compared to works by Dickens and James. Among her works are *Extreme Magic* (1964), a short-story collection, and the novels *False Entry* (1961), *Textures of Life* (1963), *The New Yorkers* (1969), *Queenie* (1971), and *Standard Dreaming* (1972). See Calisher's *Herself* (1972).

calisthenics: see GYMNASTICS.

Calixtines: see HUSSITES.

Calixtus I, Callixtus I (both: kəlĭk'stəs), or **Callistus I, Saint** (kəlĭs'təs), c.160–c.222, pope (217–222), a Roman; successor of St. Zephyrinus. As archdeacon to Zephyrinus he established the famous Calixtus Cemetery, where all the popes of the 3d cent. except Calixtus himself are buried. His election to the papacy was opposed by HIPPOLYTUS (later antipope), who accused him of monarchianism and of laxness in disciplining repentant sinners. Calixtus in fact excommunicated the chief monarchianist, SABELLIUS. His other important action, to grant absolution under conditions of true contrition to certain classes of sinners (apostates, murderers, adulterers), considered by many as unforgivable, was important in the development of the church's doctrine of penance. Calixtus died in the reign of Alexander Severus and may have been a martyr. He was succeeded by St. Urban I. Feast: Oct. 14.

Calixtus II, Callixtus II, or **Callistus II,** d. 1124, pope (1119–24), a Burgundian named Guy; successor of Gelasius II. He was archbishop of Vienne during the INVESTITURE controversy with Holy Roman Emperor HENRY V. When Gelasius died while in exile in France, Calixtus was consecrated pope at Vienne. He immediately summoned a large council at Rheims (1119) that proceeded to anathematize the emperor and the antipope that Henry had installed (1118), Gregory VIII. Public reaction sided with the pope and the antipope was imprisoned. Henry, confronted by a church united against him, submitted. He signed (1122) the famous Concordat (see WORMS, CONCORDAT OF) guaranteeing the freedom of the church in its elections. Thus was the investiture controversy ended and the reform program of Gregory VII realized. Calixtus then called to Rome (1123) the first great ecumenical council of the West (see LATERAN COUNCIL, FIRST) to ratify the achievements of the Hildebrandine reform. He was succeeded by Honorius II.

Calixtus III, Callixtus III, or **Callistus III,** 1378–1458, pope (1455–58), a Spaniard (b. Játiva) named Alonso de Borja or, in Italian, Alfonso Borgia; successor of Nicholas V. He acted as arbitrator between his friend Alfonso V of Aragón and the papacy, and for this he was made a cardinal (1444). Calixtus was elected soon after the fall of Constantinople, and he promptly proclaimed a crusade against the Turks. He spared nothing to aid John HUNYADI, who won a victory with St. John Capistran at Belgrade (1456). In 1457, Calixtus turned to SCANDERBEG, in Albania, sent him money, and named him captain general of the crusade. Calixtus' reign was embittered by a quarrel with Alfonso, who expected returns, notably the march of Ancona, for his friendship. The pope would not give away church lands and resented Alfonso's failure to help the crusade. Calixtus' nepotism gave the Borgia family its position in Italy. Calixtus was, like other Borgias, an able administrator. He was succeeded by Pius II.

Calixtus, Georgius (jôr'jēəs), 1586–1656, German theologian, whose original name was Georg Callisen. He extended the influence of MELANCHTHON, advocating syncretism, and sought a basis, such as the Apostles' Creed, for uniting Christian churches. Because he tended to minimize the differences in doctrine and to emphasize the importance of Christian living, he was charged by some of the Lutherans with favoring Roman Catholic dogmas and by others with pro-Calvinism. He failed to win the Lutherans to his support at the Conference of Thorn (1645).

call, in securities trading, contract allowing the holder to purchase a given stock at a specific price within a designated period of time. It is the opposite of a put, which is a contract allowing the holder to sell a given stock at a specific price within a designated period of time. Puts and calls are both types of privileges, or options, that add flexibility to the securities market. In return for his use of a put or call, the investor must pay a fee to the securities seller (the maker), who, in turn, pays a commission to the broker who brought the two parties together. Calls are generally used by investors who want to profit from a rise in stock prices but, at the same time, want to avoid sharp losses. Thus, an investor holding a call chooses one of two options. If the market advances he can buy the designated security at the lower price quoted in the call, and then sell the stock at a profit. If the market declines, he can simply exercise his option not to buy the stock, thereby avoiding a major loss, the only expense being the cost of the option. Unlike a call, a put is used by investors seeking to profit from a fall in stock prices. For example, an investor holding a put for a stock that declines in price is able to sell the stock at the higher price quoted in the put, thereby profiting by the amount the stock declines from the put price; if the stock price rises the investor can lose only the money used to purchase the put option. Puts and calls are generally written for one, two, three, or six months, although any period over 21 days is accepted by the New York Stock Exchange. A straddle and a spread are combinations of puts and calls occasionally used by sophisticated investors. In a more generalized sense, the term *call* may refer to any demand for payment. See L. T. Alverson, *How to Write Puts and Calls* (1968); Paul Sarnoff, *Puts and Calls: The Complete Guide* (1970); Louis Engel, *How to Buy Stocks* (5th rev. ed. 1971).

calla or **calla lily:** see ARUM.

Callaghan, Morley (Morley Edward Callaghan), 1903–, Canadian novelist. During the 1920s he spent time in Paris, where he became friends with Ernest Hemingway, whose influence can be detected in Callaghan's spare literary style. Callaghan's novels and short stories are marked by a Christian view of life. They often concern individuals whose essential characteristic is a strong, and often unintentional, sense of self. Among his best-known novels are *Such Is My Beloved* (1934) and *The Many Colored Coat* (1960). Callaghan's other works include the novels *Strange Fugitive* (1928) and *A Passion in Rome* (1961) and such story collections as *Native Argosy* (1929) and *Stories* (1967). His years in Paris are recalled in *That Summer in Paris: Memories of Tangled Friendships with Hemingway, Fitzgerald and Some Others* (1963).

Callao (käyou'), city (1970 est. pop. 335,400), capital of Lima dept., W Peru, on Callao Bay of the Pacific Ocean. It is Peru's major seaport. The harbor, which is sheltered by an island and a small peninsula, handles more than three fifths of the nation's imports and exports. Callao was founded in 1537, at the same time that Francisco PIZZARO founded Lima. As the gateway to Lima it was frequently attacked. The English navigator Sir Francis Drake sacked the city in 1578. It was held by Spanish loyalists until 1826, even though Peru achieved independence in 1821. Later, during the War of the Pacific (see PACIFIC, WAR OF THE), Callao was occupied (1881–83) by Chile. Subjected to earthquakes and tidal waves, the city was completely destroyed in 1746 and was severely damaged in 1940. Several landmarks from the colonial period survive.

Callas, Maria Meneghini (mărē'ä mĕnĕgē'nē kä'läs), 1923–, Greek-American soprano, b. New York City. At 13, Callas moved to Greece, where she studied at the Royal Conservatory in Athens. Her professional debut took place in 1947 at Verona. In 1949, Callas married the Italian industrialist Giovanni Battide Meneghini; they separated in 1959. She first appeared at La Scala (Milan) in 1950, at Covent Garden

(London) in 1952, and at the Metropolitan Opera in 1956. Callas is celebrated for her dramatic intensity and versatility. Her acting in Pasolini's film *Medea* (1970) was widely acclaimed.

Calleja del Rey, Félix María (fäˈlĕks märēˈä kälyäˈhä dĕl rā), 1750–1826, Spanish general, viceroy of New Spain (1813–16), conde de Calderón. In command of the post of San Luis Potosí when the revolution under HIDALGO Y COSTILLA broke out, he led a large force into the field and defeated Hidalgo at Aculco and at Calderón Bridge and besieged MORELOS Y PAVÓN in Cuautla (1812). As viceroy, Calleja continued to repress revolution, and by the time he left Mexico most of the insurrectionists were defeated. After his return to Spain, he held several high posts.

Calles, Plutarco Elías (plōōtärˈkō ālēˈäs käˈyās), 1877–1945, Mexican statesman, president (1924–28). In 1913 he left schoolteaching to fight with Álvaro OBREGÓN and Venustiano CARRANZA against Victoriano HUERTA. In 1920 he joined Obregón and Adolfo de la HUERTA in the rebellion against Carranza. After Obregón's term as president, Calles, who had been a cabinet member, became the presidential nominee. Adolfo de la Huerta, claiming election fraud, revolted (Dec., 1923), but Obregón and Calles established their supremacy by force (1924); Calles became president. His administration was noted for its revolutionary zeal, which often precipitated violence. At the outset agrarian reform was pursued vigorously but recklessly. Many rural schools were built, although teachers were still scarce and underpaid. Material improvements were given special attention; vast road-building and irrigation projects were undertaken. The struggle between church and state reached a new level of bitterness. In 1926 the enforcement of anticlerical legislation provoked violence; in 1926–27 the *cristeros*, terrorists whose slogan was "Viva Cristo Rey" [long live Christ the King] took up arms in the states of Colima, Jalisco, and Michoacán. Military chieftains reciprocated by victimizing innocent Roman Catholics, and government officials used the strife to political advantage. At the same time legislation over land and petroleum rights brought about a serious dispute with the United States; relations between the two countries improved when Dwight W. MORROW was appointed (1927) ambassador, and the oil question was temporarily settled. Calles created and directed a powerful national army and dissolved the private militia that threatened internal peace. He unified the government and molded the National Revolutionary party into the dominant force in Mexican politics. Calles rapidly lost his radicalism when he gained power and became a landowner and financier; he moved toward dictatorship. Already in control of the labor movement, he made himself the force behind the Callistas, a circle of financiers and industrialists who dominated the country's economy and politics. Thus he became undisputed *Jefe Máximo*, or political chieftain, of Mexico. When Obregón was assassinated (1928) after his reelection to the presidency, Callas appointed Emilio Portes Gil. In 1930 he declared the agrarian reform program a failure. In the same year he engineered the election of Pascual Ortiz Rubio. Two years later he removed him to appoint Gen. Abelardo Luján Rodríguez. The mighty labor union, CROM (see LOMBARDO TOLEDANO, VICENTE), was smashed. The conflict with the church, temporarily subdued (1929) by Morrow, was resumed; priests were openly persecuted. Communist unions, previously used by Calles in his campaign against the CROM, were ruthlessly suppressed, and a Callista-backed fascist organization, the Gold Shirts, harassed minority groups. As the new champion of conservatism, Calles in 1935 openly opposed the policies of his former protegé, Lázaro CÁRDENAS, but was defeated in the contest; in 1936 he was exiled. He was allowed to return under an amnesty in 1941. See study by R. H. Murray (1927); biography (in Spanish) by R. J. Zevada (1971).

Calley, William L.: see MY LAI INCIDENT.

Callias (kălˈēəs), fl. 449 B.C., Athenian statesman; he was related to Cimon and also to Aristides. He distinguished himself at the battle of Marathon (490 B.C.) and was a three-time winner of the Olympic chariot races. Callias was sent to Susa to negotiate for peace c.449 B.C. The result of his work was an agreement usually called the Peace of Callias (or Treaty of Callias); by it ARTAXERXES I agreed to respect the independence of the Delian League and its members and to send no warships into Greek waters; in return Athens agreed not to interfere with Persian "influence" in Asia Minor, Cyprus, and Egypt. There is doubt that such a treaty was actually ever drawn up; however, peace did exist between Persia and the cities of Greece until the end of the century. According to ancient historians, when Callias returned to Athens he was fined 50 talents for betraying the city. Callias was also supposed to have been one of the negotiators of a treaty between Athens and Sparta (446–445 B.C.) that resulted in 30 years of peace.

Callias, d. c.370 B.C., Athenian leader, one of the generals of the Peloponnesian War. In his old age Callias was one of the ambassadors sent to Sparta with Callistratus to negotiate a peace treaty in 371 B.C. The treaty was ineffective, and friction between EPAMINONDAS of Thebes and AGESILAUS II of Sparta became acute. Callias was a rich man and his wealth was ridiculed by his contemporaries, including Aristophanes. His house is the scene of Xenophon's *Symposium* and Plato's *Protagoras*.

Callicrates (kəlĭkˈrətēz), 5th cent. B.C., Greek architect. In association with Ictinus he built (447–432 B.C.) the Parthenon at Athens. At Athens also he designed (c.427) the Temple of Nike.

calligraphy (kəlĭgˈrəfē) [Gr.,=beautiful writing], skilled penmanship practiced as a fine art. In Europe two sorts of handwriting came into being very early. Cursive script was used for letters and records, while far more polished writing styles, called uncials, were used for literary works. Both styles can be seen in PAPYRUS fragments from the 4th cent. B.C. After the first cent. A.D., the development of the half uncial or minuscule letter from the Roman capital gave rise to an extraordinarily beautiful and long-lasting calligraphy. As tools and materials of high quality came into use, masterpieces of calligraphic art were produced, e.g., the Irish *Book of Kells* (8th cent.; Trinity College, Dublin; see under KELLS) and the English *Lindisfarne Gospels* (8th cent.; British Mus.; see HOLY ISLAND). Carolingian minuscule script and its spendid and complex derivative, known as Gothic, were the principal calligraphic styles from the 9th to the 14th cent. The humanistic handwriting style of the Renaissance, a deliberate imitation of Carolingian minuscule, was both aesthetically pleasing and extremely legible. The Italian manuscript copyists of the middle to late 15th cent. produced many glorious calligraphic works. Among the best known of these masters were Matteo Contugi, Gianrinaldo Mennio, and Pierantonio Sallando. Alphabet design became a subject of study, and several technical treatises were published on writing styles. By the late 16th cent., with the secure establishment of the printing press, the art of calligraphy declined generally throughout Europe. Penmanship of a relatively inferior sort was taught in elementary schools in England and in the United States until the late 19th cent. The 20th cent. has experienced a revival of interest in the art, influenced by the work of Owen Jones and William MORRIS. Fine calligraphy is currently taught in art and craft schools and is exhibited in museums. In the East calligraphy has been consistently practiced as a major aesthetic expression. In China, from the 5th cent. B.C., when it was first used, calligraphy has always been considered equal, or even superior, to painting. Chinese calligraphy began with a simplified seal script, known as "chancery script," in which the width of the strokes varies and the edges and ends are sharp. The perfection of the brush in the 1st cent. A.D. made possible the stylization of chancery script into "regular script," distinguished by its straight strokes of varying width, and clear, sharp corners, and a cursive "running hand." The Japanese value calligraphy as highly as do the Chinese. They began to practice it only in the 7th cent. A.D., with the introduction of Buddhist manuscripts from China. KUKAI, c.800, invented the syllabic script which was based on Chinese characters. This art is also practiced with the limited letter alphabet of Arabic. Because the Muslim faith discourages pictorial representation and reveres the Koran, the Islamic peoples esteem calligraphy as highly as do those of the Far East. The earliest Islamic calligraphy is found in the beautiful Korans, written with black ink or gold leaf on parchment or paper in formal, angular script. Begun by the 8th cent., this script was fully developed by the 10th. Elaborations, such as foliation, interfacing, and other complexities were invented later, but they are used only for decorative work. Korans continued to be copied in austere and monumental letters. In the 12th cent., rounded cursive style was invented and spread throughout Islam. Many different cursive scripts developed thereafter. In Islam calligraphy decorates mosques, pottery, metalwork, and textiles, as well as books. See INSCRIPTION; PALEOGRAPHY. See Georg Schwarder, *Calligraphy* (1959); Heather Child, *Calligraphy Today* (1964); Dorothy Miner, ed., *2,000 Years of Calligraphy* (1965, repr. 1972); Arthur Baker, *Calligraphy* (1973).

Callimachus (kəlĭmˈəkəs), fl. 2d half of 5th cent. B.C., Greek sculptor from Athens. He was famous as the maker of the gold lamp in the Erechtheum and a seated image of Hera for a temple at Plataea. There are several Roman copies of his works; one is *Pan and the Three Graces* (Capitoline Mus., Rome). He reputedly originated the Corinthian capital and invented the running drill used for simulating the folds of drapery in marble.

Callimachus, fl. c.265 B.C., Hellenistic Greek poet and critic, b. Cyrene. Educated at Athens, he taught school at Eleusis, a suburb of Alexandria, before obtaining work in the Alexandrian library. There he drew up a catalogue, with such copious notes that it constituted a full literary history. He also wrote criticism and other works in prose, but is most notable as a poet. His works were extraordinarily numerous; it is said that he wrote more than 800 different pieces. Of these, six hymns (meant only for reading, with no religious use), a number of epigrams, and fragments of other poems survive. His greatest work was the *Aetia*, a collection of legends strung together. Other longer poems of which fragments survive are *The Lock of Berenice, Hecale*, and *Iambi*. Callimachus' poetry is notable for brevity, polish, wit, learning, and inventiveness in form. His literary quarrel with Apollonius of Rhodes over whether well-crafted short poems were superior to long poems is well known.

Callinus (kəlīˈnəs), fl. 7th cent. B.C., Greek poet. He is the earliest of the known elegiac poets. An excerpt from a patriotic exhortation to his fellow Ephesians is the longest of the few fragments of his poetry that survive.

Calliope (kəlīˈəpē): see MUSES; ORPHEUS.

calliope, in music, an instrument also called steam organ or steam piano in which steam is forced through a series of whistles controlled by a keyboard. It is usually played mechanically, and its shrill music is a familiar accompaniment of circus parades. It is named for the Muse of Eloquence.

calliopsis (kălˈˈēŏpˈsĭs): see COREOPSIS.

Callirrhoë (kəlĭrˈōē): see ALCMAEON.

Callisthenes (kəlĭsˈthənēz), c.360–c.327 B.C., Greek historian of Olynthus; nephew of Aristotle. He accompanied Alexander the Great into Asia as the historian of the expedition. At first he compared Alexander to a god, but later he became one of the principal critics of the orientalizing manners of the court. He was suspected of complicity in a conspiracy against Alexander and put to death; and this turned the Peripatetics, Aristotle's followers, against Alexander. Callisthenes' histories of contemporary affairs in Greece are lost. In medieval times he was believed to be the author of the standard biography of Alexander, a work that actually was written much later than Callisthenes' lifetime.

Callisto (kəlĭsˈtō), in Greek mythology, an attendant of Artemis. Because she forsook her chastity and bore a son, Arcas, to Zeus, she was transformed into a bear by Artemis. According to another legend she was changed into a bear by the jealous Hera. Arcas, while out hunting, was about to kill her when Zeus intervened and transferred them both to the heavens, Callisto becoming the constellation Ursa Major [great bear] and Arcas becoming Arcturus.

Callisto, in astronomy, one of the 12 known moons, or natural satellites, of JUPITER.

Callistratus (kəlĭsˈtrətəs), d. c.360 B.C., Athenian statesman and orator. Believing Thebes to be more dangerous to Athens than Sparta, he favored a peace with Sparta. He and CALLIAS in 371 B.C. were the delegates to negotiations on an ineffective peace treaty. His failure to check Thebes led to his impeachment in 366 B.C., but he saved himself with his brilliant defense—an oration that is supposed to have inspired Demosthenes to study rhetoric. After new failure he fled Athens and was condemned in absentia for having urged Athens to allow Thebes to occupy Oropus in Boetia. When he returned he was put to death.

Callistus: see CALIXTUS.

Callixtus: see CALIXTUS.

Calloc'h, Jean Pierre (zhäN pyĕr kälôkh'), 1888–1917, Breton poet. Important in the revival of Breton literature, he wrote in the Vannes dialect of Brittany. His lyrical verse displays a love for the sea and a fascination with death; his chief work, *Ar en deulin* [on both knees] (1925), celebrates the life of Breton fishermen. Calloc'h, who died in World War I, is often regarded as Britanny's finest poet. He sometimes wrote under the pseudonym Bleimor.

Callot, Jacques (zhäk kälō'), c.1592–1635, French etcher and engraver, b. Nancy. Callot was an influential innovator and a brilliant observer of his time. In 1612 he went to Florence where he learned to etch and where he developed and introduced the use of a hard varnish ground that allowed both greater flexibility and finesse. In the service of Cosimo II de' Medici, he created many works: the *Capricci,* small, vivacious figure groups; gay scenes of Medici court life; the vast *Fair at Impruneta* (1620); and sparkling illustrations of the theater, among them his *Commedia dell' arte* group, which was reproduced in his *Balli* (1621). On Cosimo's death in 1621, Callot returned to Nancy and, under the patronage of the ducal court, gained a considerable reputation. He became known for his fantasies, grotesques, beggars, and caricatures, then much in vogue. He was commissioned in 1627 by the Infanta Isabella of Brussels to engrave the siege of Breda, and by Louis XIII to etch the sieges of Rochelle and the island of Ré and a series, *Views of Paris.* Too independent for court favor and deeply affected by the scenes of carnage he had witnessed, he retired to Nancy, where he executed in 1633 his masterwork, the two series entitled *Miseries of War.* These studies of human brutality and suffering were the first dispassionate, unromanticized treatment of the horror of war; they were used as source material by Goya for his war etchings. Callot produced nearly 1,500 plates and 2,000 drawings in a wide variety of styles and subjects. The grandeur and brilliance of his work profoundly influenced many major masters, including Rembrandt and Watteau. His technical innovations established important procedures for subsequent etchers. See the complete illustrated catalog with the definitive study by J. Lieure (5 vol., 1924–29, in French); studies by Edwin Bechtel (1955) and Brown Univ. Art Dept. (1970).

callus: see CORNS AND CALLUSES.

Calmar: see KALMAR, Sweden.

Calmet, Augustin (ōgüstăN' kälmā'), 1672–1757, French biblical scholar, a Benedictine abbot at Nancy and Sens. His critical commentaries were widely studied until the 19th cent. when the higher criticism changed the technique of biblical criticism. He also wrote a valuable history of Lorraine.

Calmette, Léon Charles Albert (lāôN' shärl älbĕr' kälmĕt'), 1863–1933, French physician and bacteriologist. He was founder and director of the Pasteur institutes at Saigon and at Lille. From 1917 he was affiliated with the Pasteur Institute in Paris. He discovered a serum for snake bite, studied bubonic plague at Oporto, and with Alphonse Guérin introduced BCG, a tuberculosis vaccine. He wrote *Recherches expérimentales sur la tuberculose* (1907–14), *Tuberculose chez l'homme et chez les animaux* (1920; tr. 1923), and *La Vaccination préventive . . . par le BCG* (1927).

Calneh (kăl'nē). **1** Place, in S Babylonia, founded by Nimrod with other cities; the word may mean "all of them." Gen. 10.10. **2** Unidentified city, possibly in N Syria. Amos 6.2. It is perhaps the same as **Calno,** named with Carchemish. Isa. 10.9. Some identify it with Canneh.

Calonne, Charles Alexandre de (shärl älĕksäN'drə də kälôn'), 1734–1802, French statesman, controller general of finances (1783–87). Faced with a huge public debt and a steadily deteriorating financial situation, Calonne adopted a spending policy to inspire confidence in the nation's financial position. Brief prosperity was followed by a ruinous collapse. He then proposed a direct land tax and the calling of provincial assemblies to apportion it, a stamp tax, and the reduction of some privileges of the nobles and clergy. To gain support, Calonne had King Louis XVI call an Assembly of Notables, but the Assembly (1787) refused to consider Calonne's proposals and criticized him bitterly. Dismissed and replaced by Étienne Charles LOMÉNIE DE BRIENNE, Calonne fled (1787) to England, where he stayed until 1802. Many of Calonne's official papers have been published and two general works on politics have been translated into English, *Considerations on the Present and Future State of France* (1791) and *The Political State of Europe* (1796).

calorie, abbr. cal, unit of HEAT energy in the metric system. The measurement of heat is called CALORIMETRY. The calorie, or gram calorie, is the quantity of heat required to raise the temperature of 1 gram of pure water 1°C. The kilocalorie, or kilogram calorie, is the quantity of heat required to raise the temperature of 1 kg of pure water 1°C; it is equal to 1,000 cal. The kilocalorie is used in dietetics for stating the heat content of a food, i.e., the amount of heat energy that the food can yield as it passes through the body; in this context, the kilocalorie is usually called simply the calorie. The amount of heat energy needed to effect a 1°C temperature increase in 1 gram of water varies with temperature (see HEAT CAPACITY); thus the temperature range over which the heating takes place must be stated to define the calorie precisely. The 15° calorie, or normal calorie, is widely used in chemistry and physics; it is measured by heating a 1-gram water sample from 14.5°C to 15.5°C at 1 atmosphere pressure. The 4° calorie, also called the small calorie or therm, is measured from 3.5°C to 4.5°C (water is most dense at 3.98°C); the large calorie, or Calorie, is equivalent to 1,000 small calories. The average value of the calorie in the range 0°C to 100°C is called the mean calorie; it is $\frac{1}{100}$ of the energy needed to heat 1 gram of water from its melting point to its boiling point. The calorie may also be defined by expressing its value in some other energy units. The 15° calorie is equivalent to 4.185 JOULES (J), 1.162×10^{-6} kilowatt-hours, 3.968×10^{-3} British thermal units, and 3.087 foot-pounds; the 4° calorie equals 4.204 J; and the mean calorie equals 4.190 J. Two other calories sometimes used are the International Steam Table calorie, equal to 4.187 J, and the thermochemical calorie, equal to 4.184 J. When the calorie is used for precision measurement of heat energy, the particular calorie being used must be specified.

calorimeter: see CALORIMETRY.

calorimetry, measurement of HEAT and the determination of HEAT CAPACITY. Heat is evolved in exothermic processes and absorbed in endothermic processes; such processes include chemical reactions, transitions between the states of matter, and the mixing of two substances to form a solution (see THERMODYNAMICS). A number of different units are used in heat measurement, e.g., the CALORIE, the BRITISH THERMAL UNIT (Btu), and the JOULE. The apparatus used in heat measurement is called a calorimeter. The measurement given by the most common type of calorimeter depends upon the temperature change in a fixed quantity of water (or some other liquid whose heat capacity is known) when heat is transferred between the water and an exothermic or endothermic process. If the temperature change is not too large, then the heat transferred is equal to the heat capacity of the water times the mass of the water times the change in temperature. The accuracy of this method of heat measurement depends on the assumption that all the heat transferred in the process passes into or out of the water in which the temperature change is measured, no heat being lost to the environment and none being absorbed by the walls of the container. The amount of heat given off by the combustion of a fuel can be determined very accurately in the so-called bomb calorimeter, which consists of a combustion chamber (the "bomb") set in another chamber filled with water. Heat generated by combustion of the fuel is transmitted to the water, raising its temperature. The calorie content of food is tested this way.

Calovius, Abraham (kəlō'vēəs), 1612–86, German Lutheran theologian, whose original name was Kalan or Calan. He was (1637–43) a professor of theology at Königsberg, then pastor at Danzig, and after 1650 teacher, general superintendent, and finally dean of the theological faculty at Wittenberg. In his many tracts he defended the strict orthodox party against Catholic, Socinian, Arminian, and other views. He particularly attacked the syncretistic doctrines of Georgius CALIXTUS.

Calpe (kăl'pē), ancient name, possibly Phoenician in origin, of GIBRALTAR. It is one of the PILLARS OF HERCULES, at the eastern end of the Strait of Gibraltar.

Calpurnia (kălpûr'nēə), d. after 44 B.C., Roman matron. The daughter of Lucius Calpurnicus Piso Caesoninus (see under PISO, family), she was married to Julius Caesar in 59 B.C. She was loyal to him despite his many infidelities and his neglect. The picture of her in Shakespeare's *Julius Caesar* is drawn mainly from Plutarch.

Calpurnius (Titus Calpurnius Siculus) (kălpûr'nēəs), fl. 1st cent. A.D., Roman poet. His *Eclogues* (seven pastorals) imitate Vergil with grace and charm.

Caltagirone (käl"täjērô'nä), city (1971 pop. 37,458), SE Sicily, Italy. An agricultural and sulfur-mining center, it has been famous for its majolica ware since the Arab occupation (9th cent.).

Caltanissetta (käl"tänēs-sĕt'tä), city (1971 pop. 60,072), capital of Caltanissetta prov., central Sicily, Italy. It is an agricultural center and an important sulfur-producing center. Of note are the Church of Santa Maria degli Angeli (14th cent.) and a 16th-century cathedral.

Calumet (kăl'yo͞omĕt"), industrial region of NW Ind. and NE Ill., along the south shore of Lake Michigan. It has one of the world's greatest concentrations of heavy industry, especially steel manufacturing. The chief cities of the region are Gary, East Chicago, and Hammond (all in Indiana).

calumet [Fr.,=reed], name given by the French in Canada to the peace pipe of the North American Indians; it consisted of a long, feathered stem, with or without pipe bowl. Such pipes were considered sacred, offering communion with the animate powers of the universe and embodying the honor and the source of power of the Indians who possessed them. Every aspect of their fashioning and decoration was symbolic and varied from tribe to tribe. Calumets were particularly used at the conclusion of peace treaties and in ceremonies of adoption. They served as ambassadors' credentials and were passports of safe-conduct wherever recognized. To refuse to smoke the calumet when invited was considered an extreme insult. The pipes were principally used by the Siouan and Algonquian peoples of the Great Plains and in the SE United States. However, pipes were used throughout most of North America, and communal smoking, wherever found, usually carried the guarantees of amity, granted with food sharing. In the Middle West PIPESTONE was much used in making them.

Calumet City, city (1970 pop. 32,956), Cook co., NE Ill., an industrial suburb in the greater Chicago metropolitan area, near the Ind. line; settled 1868, inc. 1911. It has steelworks and chemical and meat-packing industries. Formerly called West Hammond, it grew as a suburb of Hammond, Ind.

Calumet Harbor, artificial harbor on Lake Michigan, at the mouth of the Calumet River, NE Ill., in S Chicago. The harbor, dredged to 27 ft (8 m), is formed behind a breakwater extending c.2 mi (3.2 km) into Lake Michigan. It is the fastest developing unit of the Port of Chicago and the principal terminal for shipping on the Great Lakes and the St. Lawrence Seaway. The chief products handled there are the raw materials for steelmaking, finished iron and steel products, and grain. The dredged and dock-lined Calumet River (c.8 mi/13 km long) connects the harbor with **Lake Calumet** (c.2 sq mi/5 sq km) in S Chicago. Once a shallow body of water with marshy shores, the lake has been transformed into a modern deepwater port. Heavy industries, huge grain storage bins, and warehouses surround it. Canals connect the lake with the Calumet region of Indiana and with the Illinois Waterway.

Calumet Park, village (1970 pop. 10,069), Cook co., NE Ill., a residential suburb of Chicago; inc. 1912.

Calvados (kälvädôs'), department (1968 pop. 519,695), in Normandy, N France, on the English Channel. CAEN is the capital.

Calvaert, Denis or **Denys** (both: dənē' käl'värt), 1540–1619, Flemish mannerist painter in Italy, where he was known as Il Fiammingo. He studied in Antwerp and later in Bologna under Prospero Fontana. While a student he assisted in the execution of frescoes in the Vatican. On returning to Bologna he established a school, where he taught Guido Reni and Domenichino. Most of Calvaert's carefully drawn works, painted in smooth enamellike colors, are in the churches and national museum of Bologna.

Calvary (kăl'vərē) [Lat.,=a skull] or **Golgotha** (gŏl'gəthə) [Heb.,=a skull], place, where Jesus was crucified, outside the wall of Jerusalem. Its location is not certainly known. Mat. 27.33; Mark 15.22; Luke 23.33; John 19.17–20. The traditional identification of the site of Calvary was made by St. Helena, when she found (327) what was believed to be a relic of the Cross (see CROSS). The spot is within the Church of the HOLY SEPULCHER. In the 19th cent. Charles G. Gordon proposed a site near the Damascus Gate; this is called the Garden Tomb or Gordon's Calvary.

Calvé, Emma (kälvā'), 1858–1942, French operatic soprano; pupil of Mme Marchesi. She sang in the principal opera houses of Europe and between 1893 and 1904 sang often at the Metropolitan Opera, New York City, where her portrayal of Carmen was especially acclaimed. See her autobiography (1922).

Calverley, Charles Stuart, 1831–84, English poet and translator. Expelled from Oxford for a youthful prank, he earned academic honors at Cambridge. He became famous for the wit and erudition of his light verse, particularly his parodies (published under the initials C. S. C.). A barrister, he suffered an injury in 1867 that resulted in a brain concussion and curtailed his legal career. His published works include *Translations into English and Latin* (1866) and *Fly Leaves* (1872).

Calvert, Cecilius, 2d **Baron Baltimore,** c.1605–1675, first proprietor of the colony of MARYLAND. He received the province in 1632 as a grant from the king, in place of his father, George Calvert, who died as the charter was being issued. Cecilius Calvert never visited the province himself, but governed it by deputies until his death, his last deputy being his only son, Charles Calvert, who succeeded to his title. See W. H. Browne, *George Calvert and Cecilius Calvert* (1890); C. C. Hall, *The Lords Baltimore and the Maryland Palatinate* (1902).

Calvert, Charles, 3d **Baron Baltimore,** 1637–1715, second proprietor of Maryland. He was sent over as deputy governor of that province in 1661 by his father, Cecilius Calvert, 2d Baron Baltimore, and at his father's death in 1675 succeeded to the proprietorship. A Roman Catholic faced by an overwhelming Protestant population, he ruled arbitrarily, restricting the suffrage, and filling the offices with his partisans. He became involved in a bitter dispute with William PENN over the northern boundary of his grant and in 1684 went to England to defend himself in this dispute and to answer charges of favoring Catholics and obstructing customs collection. He never returned. His charter was overthrown by a Protestant revolt in 1689, and in 1692 a royal government was established. See C. C. Hall, *The Lords Baltimore and the Maryland Palatinate* (1902).

Calvert, Edward, 1799–1883, English painter and engraver. A great admirer of William Blake, Calvert, along with several of his contemporaries, formed a group around Blake called the Brotherhood of the Ancients. Calvert's art celebrated the life of primitive society. In his later work he was deeply influenced by a visit in 1844 to Greece. See Laurence Binyon, *The Followers of William Blake* (1925).

Calvert, George, 1st **Baron Baltimore,** c.1580–1632, colonizer. In 1606 he became private secretary to Sir Robert Cecil, then a secretary of state. His advance was rapid. In 1609 he became a member of Parliament, in 1613 clerk of the privy council, and in 1619 secretary of state and a member of the privy council. He defended the measures of James I in the House until his resignation in 1625, when he declared himself a Roman Catholic. The king then created him Baron Baltimore. Calvert had been a member of the Virginia Company and a member of the council of the New England Company, but, wishing to found his own colony, he was granted in 1623 the peninsula of Avalon in Newfoundland. He spent much money on a colony that was established there, but it did not prosper, and in 1629 Baltimore petitioned for a grant farther south where the weather was less severe. In 1632 the king granted him the territory N of the Potomac River that became the province of Maryland. Baltimore prepared the charter of his proposed colony but died before it could be accepted. The grant passed to his son, Cecilius Calvert. See C. C. Hall, *The Lords Baltimore and the Maryland Palatinate* (1902).

Calvin, John, 1509–64, French Protestant theologian of the Reformation, b. Noyon, Picardy. Calvin early prepared for an ecclesiastical career; from 1523 to 1528 he studied in Paris. His opinions gradually turned to disagreement with the Roman position, and a demonstrated ability at disputation led him in 1528, at his father's instance, to study law at Orléans and Bourges. After his father's death in 1531 he returned to Paris, where he pursued his own predilection—the study of the classics and Hebrew. He came under the humanist influence and became interested in the growing rebellion against conservative theology. He experienced c.1533 what he later described as a "sudden conversion," and he turned all his attention to the cause of the Reformation. As a persecuted Protestant, Calvin found it necessary to travel from place to place, and at Angoulême in 1534 he began the work of systematizing Protestant thought in his *Institutes of the Christian Religion,* considered one of the most influential theological works of all time. Completed at Basel in 1536 and later frequently revised and supplemented, the original work contained the basic Calvinist theology. In the *Institutes* Calvin diverged from Catholic doctrine in the rejection of papal authority and in acceptance of justification by faith alone, but many of his other positions, including the fundamental doctrine of predestination, had been foreshadowed by Catholic reformers and by the Protestant thought of Martin Luther and Martin Bucer. In 1536, Calvin was persuaded by Guillaume Farel to devote himself to the work of the Reformation at Geneva, and there Calvin instituted the most thoroughgoing development of his doctrine. At first the Genevans were unable to accept the austere reforms and departures from established church customs, and in 1538 the opposition succeeded in banishing Farel and Calvin from the city. Calvin went to Basel and then to Strasbourg, where he spent three fruitful years preaching and writing. By 1541 the Genevans welcomed Calvin, and he immediately set himself to the task of constructing a government based on the subordination of the state to the church. Once the Bible is accepted as the sole source of God's law, the duty of man is to interpret it and preserve the orderly world that God has ordained. This goal Calvin set out to achieve through the establishment of ecclesiastical discipline, in which the magistrates had the task of enforcing the religious teachings of the church as set forth by the synod. The Genevan laws and constitution were recodified; regulation of conduct was extended to all areas of life. Ecclesiastical discipline was supplemented by a systematized theology, with the sacraments of baptism and the Lord's Supper given to unite man into the fellowship of Christ. Calvin wrote extensively on all theological and practical matters. He was involved in many controversies. Among them were his violent opposition to the Anabaptists; his disagreement with the Lutherans over the LORD'S SUPPER, which resulted in the separation of the Evangelical Church into Lutheran and Reformed; and his condemnation of the anti-Trinitarian views of Michael SERVETUS, which ended in the notorious trial and burning of Servetus in 1553. The extension of Calvinism to all spheres of human activity was extremely important to a world emerging from an agrarian, medieval economy into a commercial, industrial era. Unlike Luther, who desired a return to primitive simplicity, Calvin accepted the newborn capitalism and encouraged trade and production, at the same time opposing the abuses of exploitation and self-indulgence. Industrialization was stimulated by the concepts of thrift, industry, sobriety, and responsibility that Calvin preached as essential to the achievement of the reign of God on earth. The influence of Calvinism spread throughout the entire Western world, realizing its purest forms through the work of John KNOX in Scotland and through the clergymen and laymen of the civil war period in England and the Puritan moralists in New England. See selections from his writings, ed. by John Dillenberger (1971); Quirinus Breen, *John Calvin* (1931, repr. 1968); Georgia Harkness, *John Calvin: The Man and His Ethics* (1931); W. C. Northcott, *John Calvin* (1946); A. T. Davies, *John Calvin and the Influence of Protestantism on National Life and Character* (1946); A. M. Schmidt, *John Calvin and the Calvinist Tradition* (tr. 1960); Kilian McDonnell, *John Calvin, the Church, and the Eucharist* (1967).

Calvin, Melvin, 1911–, American organic chemist and educator, b. St. Paul, Minn., grad. Michigan College of Mining and Technology, 1931, Ph.D. Univ. of Minnesota, 1935. In 1937 he joined the faculty at the Univ. of California, where he became director (1946) of the bioorganic division of the Lawrence Radiation Laboratory (which became the Laboratory of Chemical Biodynamics in 1960) and professor (1947) of chemistry. For his work in determining the chemical reactions that occur when a plant assimilates carbon dioxide, Calvin was awarded the 1961 Nobel Prize in Chemistry. His writings include *The Photosynthesis of Carbon Compounds* (with J. A. Bassham, 1962) and *Chemical Evolution* (1969).

Calvinism, term used in several different senses. It may indicate the teachings expressed by John CALVIN himself; it may be extended to include all that developed from his doctrine and practice in Protestant countries in social, political, and ethical, as well as theological, aspects of life and thought; or it may be employed as the name of that system of doctrine accepted by the Reformed churches (see PRESBYTERIANISM), i.e., the Protestant churches called Reformed in distinction from those professing Lutheran doctrines (see also REFORMED CHURCHES). Early Calvinism differed from Lutheranism in its rejection of consubstantiation regarding the sacrament of the Lord's Supper, in its rigid doctrine of predestination, in its notion of grace as irresistible, and in its theocratic view of the state. Luther believed in the political subordination of the church to the state; Calvinism produced the church-dominated societies of Geneva and Puritan New England. Calvinism, stressing the absolute sovereignty of God's will, held that only those whom God specifically elects are saved, that this election is irresistible, and that man can do nothing to effect this salvation. This strict Calvinism was challenged by Jacobus ARMINIUS, whose more moderate views were adopted by the Methodists and the BAPTISTS. Calvinism challenged Lutheranism throughout Europe, spread to Scotland, influenced the Puritans of England, and received its expression in the United States in the modified New England theology of the elder Jonathan EDWARDS. The doctrinal aspects of Calvinism receded under the rationalism of the 18th and 19th cent. In more recent times, however, in the Reformed theology of Karl BARTH the Calvinist stress on the sovereignty of God has found new and vital expression. See J. T. McNeill, *The History and Character of Calvinism* (1954, repr. 1967); B. G. Armstrong, *Calvinism and the Amyraut Heresy* (1969).

Calvinistic Methodist Church, Protestant Christian denomination, closely allied to PRESBYTERIANISM. It originated in Wales (1735–36) with the evangelistic preaching of Howell Harris, Daniel Rowlands, and others. In Wales it is considered to be the only denomination distinctly Welsh in origin, and it has developed into the most important of the Welsh nonconformist churches. The Methodist societies that evolved under the Welsh revivalists were so organized as to prevent any break with the Established (i.e., Anglican) Church. They were for a time associated with the Methodists of England; for some six years, from c.1742, George WHITEFIELD was the leader of the Welsh Calvinists. Those in England who accepted his views, as opposed to the Arminian doctrines taught by John WESLEY, either remained within the Church of England, joined the Connexion of the countess of HUNTINGDON, or in time became affiliated with the Congregationalists or Independents. The Welsh Calvinistic Methodists, however, held their own vigorously and grew in numbers. Thomas CHARLES of Bala, who joined them in 1784, was a leader of wide influence in religious and educational work. In 1811 they separated from the Established Church and set up a new church, Presbyterian in polity. In 1823 a confession of faith was adopted. Later, theological schools were founded at Bala and at Trevecca. The church was formally guaranteed autonomy in 1933. The Calvinistic Methodist Church was introduced (c.1826) into the United States by Welsh settlers in central New York state. In 1920 it united with the Presbyterian Church in the United States.

Calvo, Carlos (kär'lōs käl'vō), 1824–1906, Argentine diplomat and historian. He spent much of his life in diplomatic service abroad. He edited a collection of Latin American treaties and did other historical work but was most important as a writer on international law. Although he was influenced by Henry Wheaton, his development of international doctrines broke new paths. His best-known work is *Derecho internacional teórico y práctico de Europa y América* (Paris, 1868; greatly expanded in subsequent editions, which were published in French). In this book he expressed the principle known as the **Calvo Doctrine,** which would prohibit the use of diplomatic intervention as a method of enforcing private claims before local remedies have been exhausted. It is wider in scope than the DRAGO DOCTRINE, which grew out of it. The **Calvo Clause,** found in constitutions, treaties, statutes, and contracts, is the concrete application of the doctrine. Used chiefly in concession contracts, the clause attempts to give local courts final jurisdiction and to obviate any appeal to diplomatic intervention.

Calvus: see under LICINIUS, Roman gens.

calycanthus, any plant of the genus *Calycanthus,* aromatic shrubs of N North America, Asia, and Australia. An American type, the Carolina allspice, is cultivated for the aromatic fragrance of its flowers. Calycanthus is classified in the division MAGNOLIOPHYTA, class Magnoliopsida, order Magnoliales, family Calycanthaceae.

Calypso (kəlĭp'sō), nymph, daughter of Atlas, in Homer's *Odyssey.* She lived on the island of Ogygia and there entertained Odysseus for seven years. Although she offered to make him immortal if he would remain, Odysseus spurned the offer and continued his journey.

calyx (kā'lĭks): see SEPAL.

cam, mechanical device for converting a rotating motion into a reciprocating, or back-and-forth, motion, or for changing a simple motion into a complex one. A simple form of cam is a circular disk set eccentrically on a shaft in order to induce (when the shaft rotates) a rising and falling motion in a rod or some other moving part held against its edge. There are cams of many diverse shapes, e.g., oval, elliptical, and scalloped-edged, each shape being designed to induce the particular kind of motion required in a moving part. Cams are widely used in many different kinds of machines.

Camacho, Manuel Ávila: see ÁVILA CAMACHO, MANUEL.

Camagüey (kämägwä', kämäwä'), province (1970 pop. 813,204), E Cuba. CAMAGÜEY is the capital. The area is a vast prairie, surrounded on three sides by extensive coastal plains. The major economic activities are cattle raising (practiced there since the early colonial period) and the cultivation of sugarcane. Meat-packing, pineapple canning, and other agricultural processing industries are carried on.

Camagüey, city (1970 pop. 196,854), capital of Camagüey prov., E Cuba. The island's third most populous city, Camagüey, is a leading hub of rail, road, and air transport as well as an important commercial center. The economy is based on agriculture and cattle raising. Industries (mainly meat-packing and dairy processing) are mostly related to agriculture. Founded in 1514 as Santa Maria del Puerto Principe, the city was moved to its present site in 1528 and renamed for the Indian village that previously occupied that site. During the colonial period Camagüey produced salted beef for the Spanish fleets and was often sacked by English, French, and Dutch pirates. The city, which has retained much of its Spanish colonial atmosphere, is noted for its churches, mansions, and narrow twisting streets.

Camargue (kämärg'), island, c.215 sq mi (560 sq km), Bouches-du-Rhône dept., SE France, in the Rhône delta. Formed by sedimentation, the marshy island has numerous shallow lagoons cut off from the sea by sandbars. The northern part of the island has been partially reclaimed and is used for cattle raising (the cowboys are called *gardiens*). There are reed-covered swamps in the south.

Camarillo (kă"mərē'yō), city (1970 pop. 19,219), Ventura co., S Calif.; inc. 1964. It is the center of a fertile farm area where citrus fruits and flowers are grown. Camarillo also has electronic and aerospace industries and plants that manufacture magnetic tape and containers. St. John's College and a state mental hospital are located there.

camass or **camas** (both: kăm'əs), any species of the genus *Camassia* (or *Quamasia*), hardy North American plants of the family Liliaceae (LILY family), chiefly of moist places in the far West, where their abundance has given rise to various place names. The bulbs of the common camass (*C. quamash*) were a staple food of Northwestern Indians; it is now cultivated as an ornamental for its showy blue to white blossoms. Camass, or quamash, was the Indian name. An eastern camass is called wild hyacinth. The death camass (*Zygadenus venenosus*), with leaves poisonous to sheep, is similar in appearance but distinguishable by having three styles instead of six. Camass is classified in the division MAGNOLIOPHYTA, class Liliatae, order Liliales, family Liliaceae.

Cambacérès, Jean Jacques Régis de (zhäN zhäk rāzhēs' də käNbäsärĕs'), 1753-1824, French revolutionary and legislator. He was deputy to the National Convention, member of the Committee of Public Safety and of the Council of Five Hundred, second consul under Napoleon (1799-1804), and archchancellor of the empire. Throughout his career, his chief interest was in developing the principles of revolutionary jurisprudence. He played a major part in the preparation of the CODE NAPOLÉON. In 1808, Cambacérès was made duke of Parma. Minister of justice in the HUNDRED DAYS (1815), he was exiled after the restoration of the monarchy until 1818.

Cambay (kămbā'), town (1971 pop. 62,133), Gujarat state, W India, on the Mahi River estuary. The industries of Cambay include textile weaving and carpet making. Oil and natural gas are found nearby at Lunej. Once a great port under the Muslim rulers of Gujarat (14th-15th cent.), Cambay lost its importance when the harbor silted up. Until 1948 the town was the capital of the former princely state of Cambay. The **Gulf of Cambay,** a shallow arm of the Arabian Sea, lies between Kathiawar peninsula and Gujarat.

Cambert, Robert (rōbĕr' käNbĕr'), c.1628-1677, French composer; pupil of Chambonnières. His *Pastorale d'Issy* (1659) and other works are among the first real French operas. With the librettist Pierre Perrin (1625-75) he created French RECITATIVE in operas, including *Pomone* (1671), which contains all the elements of later French opera such as short symphonies, airs, and dialogues. Both men founded the first French opera company in 1669, but after losing control of this venture to Jean Baptiste Lully, Cambert settled in London where he was murdered.

Cambiaso, Luca (lo͞o'kä kämbyä'zō), 1527-85, leading Italian painter and sculptor of the Genoese school, known also as Luchetto da Genova; son and pupil of Giovanni Cambiaso, a fresco painter. His inventiveness and facile execution in both oil and fresco won him early recognition. His best works are in churches and palaces of Genoa and vicinity. In 1583 he went to Spain, where he worked on the decoration of the Escorial.

Cambio, Arnolfo di: see ARNOLFO DI CAMBIO.

cambium (kăm'bēəm), thin layer of reproductive tissue lying between the bark and the wood of a stem, most active in woody plants. The cambium produces new layers of phloem on the outside and of xylem (WOOD) on the inside, thus increasing the diameter of the STEM. In herbaceous plants the cambium is almost inactive; in monocotyledonous plants it is usually absent. In regions where there are alternating seasons, each year's growth laid down by the cambium is discernible because of the contrast between the large wood elements produced in the spring and the smaller ones produced in the summer. These are the annual rings, by which the age of a tree can be established. A tree dies when it is "ringed," or girdled, i.e., cut through the cambium layer. The cork cambium, which lies outside the phloem layer, produces the cork cells of BARK.

Cambodia (kămbō'dēə), officially Khmer Republic, republic (1973 est. pop. 7,200,000), 69,898 sq mi (181,035 sq km), SE Asia. PHNOM PENH is the capital. Cambodia is bordered by Laos on the north, by South Vietnam on the east, by the Gulf of Siam on the south, and by Thailand on the west and north. The heart of the country is a saucer-shaped, gently rolling alluvial plain drained by the Mekong River and shut off by mountain ranges; the Dangrek Mts. form the frontier with Thailand in the northwest and the Cardamom Mts. are in the southwest. About half the land is tropical forest. In general, Cambodia has a tropical monsoon climate, with the wet southwest monsoon occurring between November and April and the dry northeast monsoon the remainder of the year. During the rainy season the Mekong swells and backs into the Tônlé Sap (Great Lake), increasing the size of the lake almost threefold. The seasonal rise of the Mekong floods almost 400,000 acres (162,000 hectares) around the lake, leaving rich silt when the waters recede. Conditions are ideal for the cultivation of rice, by far the country's chief crop. Livestock raising (cattle, buffalo, poultry, and hogs) and extensive fishing supplement the diet. Corn, vegetables, fruits, peanuts, tobacco, cotton, and sugar palms are also raised. Pepper is grown in the south, and great amounts of rubber are produced on large plantations. In the early 1970s, however, heavy fighting in the countryside put almost all of the rubber plantations out of operation. Rice and rubber are traditionally the principal exports of Cambodia, but exports have fallen sharply since the onset (1970) of the civil war. Inadequate transportation hampers exploitation of the country's vast forests. Mineral resources are limited; phosphate rock, limestone, semiprecious stones, and salt are extracted. The country's industries are based primarily on the processing of agricultural, fish, and timber products. Cambodian industry has relied on considerable foreign capital; the People's Republic of China financed the construction of textile, plywood, paper, glass, and cement factories, and Czechoslovakia supplied a sugar refinery and tire and tractor-assembly plants. In the early 1970s, Cambodia accepted foreign aid from the United States as well as from Japan, Australia, New Zealand, Great Britain, Thailand, and Malaysia. Enormous amounts of U.S. military and economic aid financed the government's fight against insurgency. A major U.S. peacetime project was the construction of a four-lane highway linking Phnom Penh with the new seaport (completed 1960) of Kompong Som (formerly Sihanoukville) on the Gulf of Siam. Cambodia is connected by road systems with Thailand, Laos, and South Vietnam; waterways are an important supplement to the roads. The country has two rail lines, one extending from Phnom Penh to the Thai border and the other from Phnom Penh to Kompong Som. One of the few underpopulated countries of SE Asia, Cambodia is inhabited by Cambodians (or Khmers), who comprise about 85% of the population. There are large minorities of Vietnamese and Chinese; other ethnic groups include the Cham-Malays and the hill tribesmen. Hinayana Buddhism is the state religion and about 90% of the people are Buddhists; the Cham-Malays are Muslims. Khmer is the national language, but French is widely used.

History. The Funan empire was established in what is now Cambodia in the 1st cent. A.D. By the 3d cent. the Funanese, under the leadership of Fan Shih-man (reigned 205-25), had conquered their neighbors and extended their sway to the lower Mekong River. In the 4th cent., according to Chinese records, an Indian Brahman extended his rule over Funan, introducing Hindu customs, the Indian legal code, and

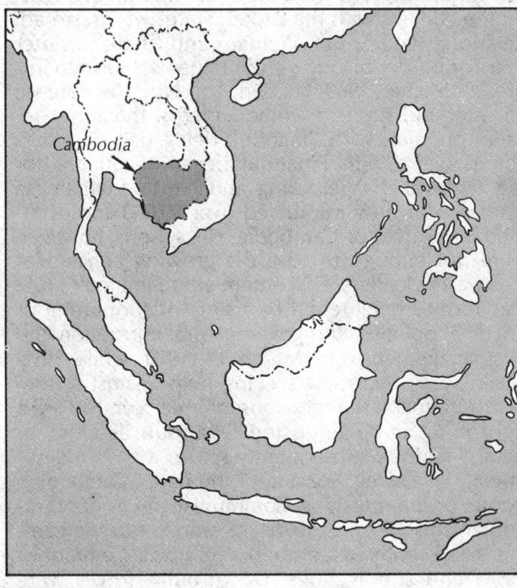

the alphabet of central India. In the 6th cent. Khmers from the rival Chen-la state to the north overran Funan. With the rise of the KHMER EMPIRE, Cambodia became dominant in SE Asia. After the fall of the empire (15th cent.), however, Cambodia was the prey of stronger neighbors. To pressure from Siam on the western frontier was added in the 17th cent. pressure from ANNAM on the east; the kings of Siam and the lords of Hue alike asserted overlordship and claims to tribute. In the 18th cent. Cambodia lost three western provinces to Siam and the region of COCHIN CHINA to the Annamese. Intrigue and wars on Cambodian soil continued into the 19th cent., and in 1854 the king of Cambodia appealed for French intervention. A French protectorate was formally established in 1863, and French influence was consolidated by a treaty in 1884. Cambodia became part of the Union of INDOCHINA in 1887. In 1907 a French-Siamese treaty restored Cambodia's western provinces. In World War II, under Japanese occupation, Cambodia again briefly lost those provinces to Siam. In Jan., 1946, France granted Cambodia self-government within the French Union; a constitution was promulgated in May, 1947. A treaty signed in 1949 raised the country's status to that of an associated state in the French Union, but limitations on the country's sovereignty persisted. King Norodom Sihanouk campaigned for complete independence, which was finally granted in 1953. Early in 1954, Communist VIET MINH troops from Vietnam invaded Cambodia. The GENEVA CONFERENCE of 1954 led to an armistice providing for the withdrawal of all foreign forces from Cambodia. An agreement between France and Cambodia (Dec., 1954) severed the last vestige of French control over Cambodian policy. Cambodia withdrew from the French Union in 1955 and was admitted into the United Nations later that year. King Norodom Sihanouk abdicated in March, 1955, in order to enter politics; his father, Norodom Suramarit, succeeded him as monarch. Sihanouk subsequently formed the Popular Socialist party and served as premier. After Suramarit's death in 1960, the monarchy was represented by Sihanouk's mother, Queen Kossamak Nearireak. Sihanouk was installed in the new office of chief of state. Throughout the 1960s, Sihanouk struggled to keep Cambodia neutral as the neighboring countries of Laos and South Vietnam came under increasing Communist attack (see VIETNAM WAR). Sihanouk permitted the use of Cambodian territory as a supply base and refuge by North Vietnamese and VIET CONG troops while accepting military aid from the United States to strengthen his forces against Communist infiltration. In 1963, Sihanouk accused the United States of supporting antigovernment activities and renounced all U.S. aid. Following a series of border incidents involving South Vietnamese troops, Cambodia in 1965 severed diplomatic relations with the United States. Sihanouk remained on friendly terms with the Communist countries, especially Communist China, and established close relations with France. Economic conditions deteriorated after the renunciation of U.S. aid, and North Vietnamese and Viet Cong troops continued to infiltrate. In the spring of 1969 the United States instituted aerial attacks against Communist strongholds in Cambodia; these bombings, carefully kept secret from the American people, later became an important issue in U.S. politics. As Communist infiltration increased, Sihanouk began to turn more toward the West, and in July, 1969, diplomatic ties with the United States were restored. Relations with South Vietnam and Thailand, after years of border disputes and incidents, began to improve. In Aug., 1969, Lt. Gen. Lon Nol, the defense minister and supreme commander of the army, became premier, with Sihanouk delegating considerable power to him. Sihanouk began negotiating for the removal of Viet Cong and North Vietnamese troops, who now numbered over 50,000 and occupied large areas of Cambodia. His actions, however, were not enough to ease the growing concern of many army leaders. Discontent with Sihanouk's rule was further heightened by rising inflation, ruinous financial policies, and governmental corruption and mismanagement. On March 18, 1970, while Sihanouk was in Moscow seeking help against further North Vietnamese incursions, premier Lon Nol led a right-wing coup deposing Sihanouk as chief of state. Sihanouk subsequently set up a government-in-exile in Peking. Soon after the coup, Cambodian troops began engaging Communist forces on Cambodian soil. In April, 1970, U.S. and South Vietnamese troops entered Cambodia to attack Communist bases and supply lines. U.S. ground forces were withdrawn by June 30, but South Vietnamese troops remained, occupying heavily populated areas. The actions of the South Vietnamese troops in Cambodia and the resumption of heavy U.S. air bombings in their support, with the inevitable destruction of villages and killing of civilians, alienated many Cambodians and may have created considerable sympathy for the Communists. The number of Cambodian Communists (known as the Khmer Rouge) increased from about 3,000 in March, 1970, to over 30,000 within a few years. Most of the North Vietnamese and Viet Cong troops were able to withdraw, leaving in progress a raging civil war fought by Cambodians but financed by the United States, North Vietnam, and Communist China. On Oct. 9, 1970, the national assembly declared Cambodia a republic and changed the country's name to the Khmer Republic. By that time, however, the national government controlled less than one third of Cambodia's total land area: Phnom Penh, most of the provincial capitals, and the central plain S of Tônlé Sap. Despite extensive U.S. military aid, the insurgents retained firm control of the northeast provinces and most of the countryside. In Feb., 1971, Lon Nol suffered a paralytic stroke and vice premier Sisowath Sirik Matak assumed power (although Lon Nol technically remained premier). Fighting between government and insurgent forces became increasingly savage and bitter, culminating in a major government defeat (Dec., 1971) on a highway N of Phnom Penh, after which most of Cambodian territory E of the Mekong River fell to the insurgents. In 1972 student agitation in Phnom Penh for the removal of Sisowath Sirik Matak from power led to the resignation (March 10) of chief of state Cheng Heng, who transferred his post to the ailing Lon Nol. Two days later Lon Nol dissolved the government and declared himself president as well as chief of state and commander in chief. A new constitution providing for a presidency was approved by popular referendum in April, and Lon Nol was formally elected president in June, 1972; the defeated candidates charged irregularities in the election. Meanwhile, more and more territory fell into Communist hands, despite intensive U.S. bombing attacks which persisted until the halt imposed by the U.S. Congress in Aug., 1973. The government's military position became desperate, with government forces concentrating primarily on keeping communications open with an increasingly beleaguered Phnom Penh. In Sept., 1972, severe food shortages in Phnom Penh sparked two days of rioting and large-scale looting, in which government troops participated. Lon Nol, aided by his brother Lon Non, exerted an increasingly oppressive rule, with massive political arrests and newspaper seizures. U.S. pressure for a more representative government finally resulted (April, 1973) in the appointment of a member of the opposition party, In Tam, to the premiership, but the experiment was short-lived; In Tam resigned in Dec., 1973 and was succeeded by Long Boret of the ruling party. The Khmer Rouge insurgents launched a large-scale attack against Cambodia's third largest city, Kompong Cham, in Sept., 1973, and shelled Phnom Penh in 1974 and early 1975, inflicting heavy civilian casualties. Before the country was torn by civil war the government had made great strides in expanding educational facilities. Cambodia has about ten institutions of higher learning, including the National Univ. of Phnom Penh, the Univ. of Fine Arts, and the Technical Univ., all in Phnom Penh, and technical universities in Battambang, Kompong Cham, and Takeo. See M. F. Herz, *A Short History of Cambodia* (1958); D. J. Steinberg et al., *Cambodia* (1959); R. M. Smith, *Cambodia's Foreign Policy* (1965); Michael Leifer, *Cambodia, The Search for Security* (1967); F. P. Munson et al., *Area Handbook for Cambodia* (1968); Milton Osborne, *The French Presence in Cochinchina and Cambodia* (1969); Maslyn Williams, *The Land in Between: The Cambodian Dilemma* (1970).

Cambodian art and architecture: see ANGKOR and KHMER EMPIRE.

Cambon, Jules Martin (zhül märtăN' käNbôN'), 1845–1935, French diplomat; brother of Pierre Paul Cambon. He served (1891–96) as governor general of Algeria, where he pursued a conciliatory policy and was largely responsible for the decree (1896) establishing administrative autonomy for Algeria. In 1897 he was made ambassador to the United States, and he mediated the peace preliminaries of the Spanish-American War. He was ambassador at Madrid (1902–7) and at Berlin (1907–14), and from 1920 to 1922 he was chairman of the Council of Ambassadors, the group charged with overseeing the enforcement of the Treaty of Versailles (1919). His political works include *The Diplomatist* (tr. 1931). See biography by Geneviève Tabouis (tr. 1938).

Cambon, Pierre Joseph (pyĕr zhôzĕf'), b. 1754 or 1756, d. 1820, French financier and revolutionary. A merchant of Montpellier, he became a member of the Legislative Assembly and the Convention, and he guided the financial policy of the Revolution from Oct., 1791, to April, 1795. He refunded the debt, calling in all old government bonds (both royal and revolutionary), and issuing new certificates at 5%; that put a halt to wild speculation in bonds. His measure also freed the government temporarily from repaying the principal on the debt. Advocating war to "free" Europe, he advanced the policy of exploiting conquered territory. His fiscal program, which failed to halt inflation, was attacked by Maximilien ROBESPIERRE, whose fall was partly caused by Cambon's countercharges. Cambon was distrusted by the Thermidorians, and his career ended after his brief triumph. He was exiled after the Bourbon restoration.

Cambon, Pierre Paul (pōl), 1843–1924, French diplomat; brother of Jules Martin Cambon. Named resident minister to Tunis in 1882, he conceived and organized the new Tunisian protectorate under the bey. As ambassador to Great Britain (1898–1920), he helped to create the Entente Cordiale (1904) and the Anglo-Russian agreement of 1907, and he encouraged Great Britain to enter World War I (see TRIPLE ALLIANCE AND TRIPLE ENTENTE). He was one of the most able diplomats in French history.

Camborne-Redruth (kăm'bôrn, -bûrn, rĕd'rōōth), urban district (1971 pop. 42,029), Cornwall, SW England. The neighboring urban districts of Camborne and Redruth were combined in 1934. Tin and copper mines in the area have been greatly depleted, but rock drills and mining machinery are made in the district, and the School of Metalliferrous Mining is in Camborne. John Wesley preached to outdoor gatherings near the present mines. At the summit of Carn Brea hill are prehistoric remains.

Cambrai (käNbrā'), city (1968 pop. 39,922), Nord dept., N France, a port on the Escaut (Scheldt) River. It has long been known for its fine textiles and gave its name to cambric, first manufactured there. Clay, metal, and wood products are also manufactured in Cambrai. An episcopal see since the 4th cent., and seat of an archdiocese since the 16th cent., Cambrai and the surrounding county of Cambrésis were ruled by the bishops under the Holy Roman Empire until they were seized by Spain (1595) and by France (1677). Fénelon was archbishop from 1695 to 1715. The original cathedral was destroyed in 1793. Cambrai suffered devastation in both world wars; it was occupied by the Germans from 1914 to 1918 and from 1940 to 1944.

Cambrai, League of, 1508–10, alliance formed by Holy Roman Emperor Maximilian I, King Louis XII of France, Pope Julius II, King Ferdinand V of Aragón, and several Italian city-states against the republic of Venice to check its territorial expansion. The republic was soon on the verge of ruin. Its army was defeated by the French at Agnadello (1509); most of the territories it had occupied were lost; and Maximilian entered Venetia. The republic had to make concessions to the pope and to Ferdinand. In 1510 the pope became reconciled to Venice and began forming the HOLY LEAGUE against France. The republic emerged from the war having suffered serious losses but by no means crushed.

Cambrai, Treaty of, called the **Ladies' Peace,** treaty negotiated and signed in 1529 by Louise of Savoy, representing her son Francis I of France, and Margaret of Austria, representing her nephew Holy Roman Emperor Charles V. The treaty renewed the Treaty of Madrid (see FRANCIS I), except that it did not exact the surrender of Burgundy to Charles.

Cambria (kăm'brēə) [Latinized form of Welsh *Cymry*=Welshmen], ancient name of Wales.

Cambrian Mountains (kăm'brēən), rugged upland plateau occupying most of Wales; Aran Fawddwy (2,970 ft/905 m) is the highest point in the mountains. The area has deep lakes and is cut by numerous river valleys; the Wye and Severn rivers rise there. Sheep grazing is the principal economic activity.

Cambrian period [Lat. *Cambria*=Wales], first period of the Paleozoic geologic era (see GEOLOGIC ERAS, table). It was named by the English geologist Adam Sedgwick, who first studied (1831–35) in NW Wales the great sequence of rocks characteristic of the period. Comprising mainly sedimentary ROCK, i.e., conglomerate, sandstone, shale, and limestone, they were formed in shallow seas that covered large areas of North America, Europe, and Asia. In the United States, Lower Cambrian, or Waucobian, formations are found chiefly in the Appalachian and Cordilleran geosynclines, or downward thrusts of the earth's crust, which were then arms of a sea; the most notable deposits are the sandstone near Waucoba Springs, S Calif., and the thick strata, or layers, of conglomerate and sandstone in Georgia, Tennessee, and North Carolina. Middle Cambrian, or Albertan, formations are rare in the Appalachian region, which was above water in the Middle Cambrian, but they are found in New Brunswick, near Braintree, Mass., and throughout the Cordilleran region. In the Upper Cambrian, or Croixian, epoch, the shallow seas spread over a great part of the continent, depositing, among other formations, the St. Croix sandstone of Wisconsin and the upper Mississippi valley, some of the Arbuckle limestone of Oklahoma, and the Potsdam sandstone on the northern slope of the Adirondacks and elsewhere. In the USSR the Cambrian beds are remarkable in that they comprise mostly undisturbed and unconsolidated sand and clay despite their great age. The Cambrian rocks are notable as the first to contain many easily recognizable fossils. The known Cambrian fauna—all marine—includes every phylum of invertebrates; the possibility that vertebrate fossils may be found cannot be excluded. The dominant animal was the trilobite, and the various rock series are distinguished according to the different genera of trilobites they contain. Brachiopods, snails, and sponges were also common. The seemingly abrupt appearance of such a highly developed and diversified fauna is best explained by the assumption that more primitive forms flourished during the interval between the close of the Precambrian era and the beginning of the Cambrian, of which all geologic record has been destroyed by erosion.

Cambridge (kām'brĭj), municipal borough (1971 pop. 98,519), county town of Cambridgeshire and Isle of Ely, E central England, on the Cam River. It is an ancient market town, and although light industries such as the manufacture of agricultural tools, precision instruments, radios, and cement have developed on the outskirts, the town is most famous as the site of CAMBRIDGE UNIV. Originally the site of a Roman fort, the town was an administrative and trading center in Anglo-Saxon times. William I built a fort and mint there. Two monastic establishments were built in early medieval times. The university was founded in the 13th cent. The present town still maintains much of its medieval atmosphere and appearance. There are many old inns, hostels, houses, winding streets, and narrow passages that have not altered greatly with time. Cambridge abounds in medieval churches, the most important of which are St. Benet's or Bene't's, the oldest, dating back to the late Saxon period; St. Edward's (begun 12th cent.), where Hugh Latimer preached; St. Mary the Great (1478), the university church; and the Church of the Holy Sepulchre, one of the four Norman round churches in England. In 1974, the borough became part of the newly reorganized nonmetropolitan county of Cambridgeshire.

Cambridge. 1 City (1970 pop. 11,595), seat of Dorchester co., E Md., Eastern Shore, a port of entry on the Choptank River at its mouth on Chesapeake Bay; founded 1684, inc. as a city 1884. The state's second largest deepwater port (after Baltimore), it is a fishing and yachting center. The city has shipyards, seafood and vegetable canneries, and electronic, clothing, and printing industries. The Meredith house (1760) there is headquarters for the county historical society. Nearby Old Trinity Church (c.1675; restored 1960) is said to be the oldest church in the United States still in use. **2** City (1970 pop. 100,361), seat of Middlesex co., E Mass., across the Charles River from Boston; settled 1630 as New Towne, inc. as a city 1846. A famous educational and research center, it is the seat of Harvard Univ. (founded 1636), Radcliffe College, Massachusetts Institute of Technology, Lesley College, and several theological seminaries. It is also an industrial city; its manufactures include electrical machinery, scientific instruments, rubber goods, glass, wire cables, and machine shop products. Its printing and publishing industry dates from about 1639, when Stephen Daye established the first printing press in America. Cambridge was a gathering place for colonial troops; there, on July 3, 1775, Washington took command. It was the first seat of the Massachusetts constitutional convention of 1780. Craigie House (1759), which served as Washington's headquarters (1775-76), was the home of Longfellow from 1837 until his death in 1882. Other historic structures are Elmwood (1767), the birthplace and home of James Russell Lowell; the Cooper-Frost-Austin house (c.1657); and the Episcopal church (1761). Lowell, Longfellow, Mary Baker Eddy, and many other notable people are buried in Mt. Auburn Cemetery. **3** Industrial city (1970 pop. 13,656), seat of Guernsey co., E central Ohio, in a farm, coal, natural gas, and clay area; settled 1798 by immigrants from the isle of Guernsey, inc. 1837. It is the trade and manufacturing center for a dairy and livestock area. Lakes and parks surround the city, and the large Salt Fork State Park is nearby. Muskingum College is to the west, in New Concord.

Cambridge Bay, Canadian government post and weather station, on the southeast shore of Victoria Island, Franklin district, Northwest Territories.

Cambridge Platform, declaration of principles of church government and discipline, forming in fact a constitution of the Congregational churches. It was adopted (1648) by a church synod at Cambridge, Mass., and remains the basis of the temporal government of the churches. It had little to do with matters of doctrine and belief. The Congregationalists of Connecticut later subscribed (1708), in the Saybrook Platform, to a more centralized church government, resembling Presbyterianism. See also CONGREGATIONALISM.

Cambridge Platonists, group of English philosophers, centered at Cambridge Univ. in the latter half of the 17th cent. In reaction to the mechanical philosophy of Thomas Hobbes this school revived certain Platonic and Neoplatonic ideas. Chief among these was a mystical conception of the soul's relation to God and the belief that moral ideas are innate in man. Although tending toward mysticism, the school also stressed the importance of reason, maintaining that faith and reason differ only in degree. The assertion of the founder of the school, Benjamin Whichcote, that "the spirit in man is the cradle of the Lord" became the motto for the entire movement. Other leading members were Ralph CUDWORTH, Henry MORE, and John Smith. See G. R. Cragg, ed., *The Cambridge Platonists* (1968); Ernst Cassirer, *The Platonic Renaissance in England* (tr. 1953, repr. 1970).

Cambridgeshire and Isle of Ely, county (1971 pop. 302,507), E central England. The county town is CAMBRIDGE. Most of the area is alluvial fenland, rising to the low, chalky East Anglian Hills in the south, with the Gogmagog Hills near Cambridge the most conspicuous feature. The main rivers are the Ouse, with its tributaries, and the Nene. Efforts to reclaim the fens date back to the days of Roman occupation, but in the subsequent periods of invasion by Danes, Saxons, and Normans they were abandoned. The fens were finally drained in the 17th cent. Cornelius Vermuyden, a Dutchman, completed a vast drainage project in 1653. Agriculture predominates in the county. Wheat, barley, potatoes, sugar beets, and fruits are raised, and there is market gardening. Food processing is an important industry. Among other industries are radio engineering and the manufacture of cement, bricks, and scientific instruments. The urban district of Ely has been an ecclesiastical center for centuries. Cambridge Univ. dates from the early 13th cent. In 1974, Cambridgeshire and Isle of Ely became part of the new nonmetropolitan county of Cambridgeshire.

Cambridge University, at Cambridge, England. Originating in the early 12th cent. (legend places its origin even earlier than that of OXFORD UNIV.), Cambridge was organized into residential colleges, like those of Oxford, by the end of the 13th cent. Its colleges, with their dates of founding, are Peterhouse, or St. Peter's (1284), Clare (1326), Pembroke (1347), Gonville (1348; refounded as Gonville and Caius, 1558), Trinity Hall (1350), Corpus Christi (1352), King's (1441), Queens' (1448), St. Catharine's (1473), Jesus (1496), Christ's (1505), St. John's (1511), Magdalene (1542; pronounced môd'lĭn), Trinity (1546), Emmanuel (1584), Sidney Sussex (1596), Downing (1800), Selwyn (1882), Churchill (1960), and Fitzwilliam College (founded 1887 as a noncollegiate society, became a college 1968). The women's colleges are Girton (1869), Newnham (1873), and New Hall (1954). Girton and Newnham were pioneers in university education for women. Although women took university examinations in the 1880s and after 1921 were awarded degrees, their colleges were not admitted to full university status until 1948. Hughes Hall (1885) and St. Edmund's Hall (1896) are noncollegiate institutions for undergraduates. Darwin College (1964), Wolfson College (1965; founded as University College, renamed 1973), Lucy Cavendish Collegiate Society (1965), and Clare Hall (1966) are graduate institutions. Cambridge was a center of the new learning of the Renaissance and of the theology of the Reformation; in modern times it has excelled in science. Its faculties include classics, divinity, English, architecture and history of art, modern and medieval languages, Oriental studies, music, economics and politics, history, law, philosophy, engineering, geography and geology, mathematics, biology, archaeology and anthropology, and medicine. Its famous Cavendish Laboratory of experimental physics was opened in 1873; the Cavendish professors have been outstanding names in physics. The chapel of King's College (1446), the Fitzwilliam Museum, and the botanic gardens are notable features of the university. Instruction at Cambridge is similar to the system at Oxford, except that tutors are called supervisors and the degree examination is known as the tripos. Until 1948, Cambridge Univ. sent two representatives to Parliament. The Cambridge Univ. Press dates from the 16th cent. See Edmund Vale, *Cambridge and Its Colleges* (1959); F. A. Reeve, *Cambridge* (1964); C. R. Benstead, *Portrait of Cambridge* (1968).

Cambuluc: see PEKING, China.

Cambyses (kămbī'sēz), two kings of the Achaeminid dynasty of Persia. **Cambyses I** was king (c.600 B.C.) of Ansham, ruling as a vassal of Media. According to Herodotus he married the daughter of the Median king Astyages; some scholars dispute this. Cambyses' son was CYRUS THE GREAT. **Cambyses II,** d. 521 B.C., was the son and successor of Cyrus the Great and ruled as king of ancient Persia (529–521 B.C.). He disposed of his brother SMERDIS in order to gain unchallenged rule. He invaded Egypt, defeating (525 B.C.) Psamtik at Pelusium and sacking Memphis. His further plans of conquest in Africa were frustrated, and at home an impostor claiming to be Smerdis raised a revolt. Cambyses died, possibly by suicide, when he was putting down the insurrection. Darius I succeeded him.

Camden, Charles Pratt, 1st **Earl:** see PRATT, CHARLES, 1ST EARL CAMDEN.

Camden, John Jeffreys Pratt, 2d **Earl** and 1st **Marquess:** see under PRATT, CHARLES, 1ST EARL CAMDEN.

Camden, William, 1551–1623, English scholar, chief historian and antiquary of Elizabethan times. His two chief works are *Britannia* (1586) and *Annales rerum Anglicarum et Hibernicarum regnante Elizabetha* [annals of affairs in England and Ireland in the reign of Elizabeth]. He was a conscientious scholar in editing old manuscripts and in collecting materials of antiquarian interest. He was also a teacher (1575–97) and headmaster (1593–97) at Westminster School and helped to revive the study of Anglo-Saxon. He wrote a Greek grammar long popular in English secondary schools and aided Sir Robert COTTON in collecting materials.

Camden, borough (1971 pop. 200,784) of Greater London, SE England. Camden was created in 1965 by the merger of the metropolitan London boroughs of Hampstead, Holborn, and St. Pancras. Hampstead is a residential district popular with writers and artists. John Keats, John Constable, George Du Maurier, and Kate Greenaway, as well as Karl Marx, lived there. It is also known as a piano-making center. Highgate Cemetery in Hampstead contains the graves of George Eliot, Michael Faraday, Herbert Spencer, Christina Rosetti, and Karl Marx. Within Holborn is part of Bloomsbury, another artists and writers area. Holborn also houses the BRITISH MUSEUM, the Univ. of London, Gray's Inn and Lincoln's Inn (see INNS OF COURT), law courts, the Royal College of Surgeons, and Hatton Garden, known for its trade. Benjamin Disraeli was born in Holborn, which is also the site of London's tallest building, the Post Office Tower. St. Pancras has three famous railroad stations: Euston, King's Cross, and St. Pancras.

Camden. 1 City (1970 pop. 15,147), seat of Ouachita co., S Ark., on the Ouachita River; inc. 1847. It is a railroad and river shipping point. Its manufactures include paper, pottery, furniture, air conditioners, and house trailers. **2** Industrial city (1970 pop. 102,551), seat of Camden co., W N.J., a port of entry on the Delaware River opposite Philadelphia, settled 1681, inc. 1828. The arrival of the Camden and Amboy RR in 1834 spurred the city's growth as a commercial, shipbuilding, and manufacturing center. Some of its present large industries had their beginnings in the 19th cent.: Richard Esterbrook in 1858 opened a steel-pen factory, and the Campbell canned-foods company originated in 1869. Other manufactures are electric and electronic goods, and paper and wood products. Walt Whitman's home is preserved, and the poet is buried in the city, where he lived from 1873. Of interest are the Campbell Museum and the county historical society's museum in Charles S. Boyer Memorial Hall (formerly the Joseph Cooper house; built 1726). Access to Philadelphia is via the Walt Whitman Bridge (1957) and the Benjamin Franklin Bridge (1926). Rutgers Univ. at Camden is there.

camel, hoofed ruminant of the family Camelidae. The family consists of three genera, the true camels of Asia (genus *Camelus*); the wild GUANACO and the domesticated ALPACA and llama, all of South America (genus *Lama*); and the VICUÑA, also of South America (genus *Vicugna*). The two species of true camel are the single-humped Arabian camel, or dromedary, *Camelus dromedarius,* a domesticated animal used in Arabia and North Africa, and the two-humped Bactrian camel (*C. bactrianus*) of central Asia. Some wild Bactrian camels exist in Turkistan and Mongolia. The humps are storage places for fat. Camels range in color from dirty white to dark brown and have long necks, small ears, tough-skinned lips, and powerful teeth, some of which are sharply pointed. The camel uses the mouth in fighting. Adapfations to desert life include broad, flat, thick-soled cloven hoofs that do not sink into the sand; the ability to go without drinking for several days—or longer if juicy plants are available; and valvular nostrils lined with hairs for protection against flying sand. Horny pads help to protect the chest, knees, and thigh joints against injury from the hard surfaces on which the camel sleeps. Strong camels usually carry from 500 to 600 lb (230 to 270 kg) and cover about 30 mi (48 km) a day. Some Bactrian camels can transport 1,000 lb (450 kg). A light, fleet breed of dromedary is used for riding and not for bearing heavy loads. The name dromedary was formerly applied to any swift riding camel. Geologic findings indicate that the camel originated in North America, that one group migrated to Asia and the other to South America, and that both became extinct in North America probably after the glacial period. Camels are classified in the phylum CHORDATA, subphylum Vertebrata, class Mammalia, order Artiodactyla, family Camelidae.

camellia (kəmēl'yə) [for G. J. Kamel], any plant of the genus *Camellia,* evergreen shrubs or small trees native to Asia but now cultivated extensively in warm climates and in greenhouses for their showy white, red, or variegated blossoms and glossy, dark-green foliage. Camellias are closely related to the tea plant, both being members of the family Theaceae (TEA family). Several species yield oil from the seeds, e.g., the widely cultivated *C. japonica* (commonly called japonica) and, especially, the Asiatic *C. sasanqua,* the source of tea-seed oil used in textile and soap manufacture and, when suitably refined, for cooking. Camellias are classified in the division MAGNOLIOPHYTA, class Magnoliopsida, order Theales, family Theaceae.

Camelot (kăm'əlŏt), in ARTHURIAN LEGEND, the seat of King Arthur's court. The origin of the name is unknown. It has been variously located at Cadbury Camp, Somerset; Winchester; Camelford; and Caerleon.

Camembert cheese (kăm'əmbâr, Fr. kämäNbĕr'), unpressed rennet cheese, drained on straw mats and ripened with a penicillium mold to a creamy consistency. Made since the late 18th cent. near Camembert village, NW France, it is exported in considerable quantity.

Camenae (kəmē'nē), in Roman mythology, water nymphs gifted in prophecy. At Rome they had a sacred spring from which the vestals drew water for their rites. In later myth they were identified with the Greek Muses.

cameo (kăm'ēō), small relief carving, usually on striated precious or semiprecious stones or on shell. The design, often a portrait head, is commonly cut in the light-colored vein, and the dark one is left as the background. Glass of two colors in layers may be cameo-cut; a famous Roman example is the PORTLAND VASE. The art originated in Asia as a decoration on the reverse side of seals. The Greeks were noted for their exquisite designs and cutting on jewelry and on decorations for jewel caskets, vases, cups, and candelabra. The Romans were adept cutters, and Rome remains a center of experts in this art. The art was revived during the Renaissance, and cameo jewelry was a vogue of the Victorian era.

cameo cat: see CAT.

camera, lightproof box or container, usually fitted with a lens, through which an image of the scene being viewed is focused and recorded on film or some other light-sensitive material contained within. The original concept of the camera dates from Grecian times, when Aristotle referred to the principle of the **camera obscura** [Lat.,=dark chamber] which was literally a dark box—sometimes large enough for the viewer to stand inside—with a small hole, or aperture, in one side. (A lens was not employed for focusing until the Middle Ages.) An inverted image of a scene was formed on an interior screen; it could then be traced by an artist. The first diagram of a camera obscura appeared in a manuscript by Leonardo da Vinci in 1519, but he did not claim its invention. The recording of a negative image on a light-sensitive material was first achieved by the Frenchman Joseph Nicéphore Niépce in

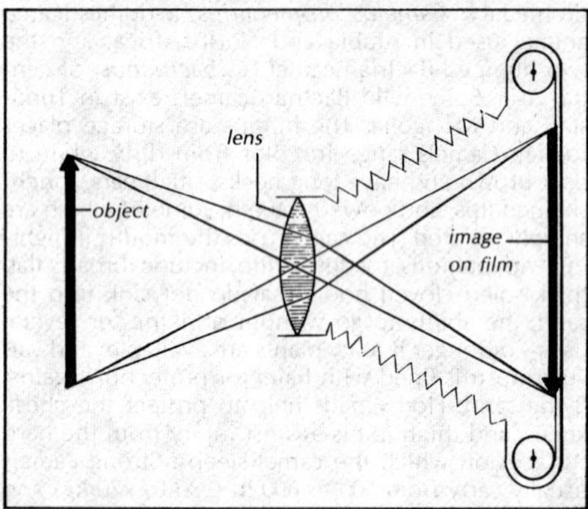

Image formed by a camera

1826; he coated a piece of paper with asphalt and exposed it inside the camera obscura for eight hours. Today there are many different types of camera in use, all of them more or less sophisticated versions of the ancient camera obscura. Nearly all of them are made up of the same basic parts: body, lens, shutter, viewfinder, and focusing mechanism. Except for pinhole cameras, which focus the image on the film through a tiny hole, all other cameras use a lens for focusing. The focal length of a lens, i.e., the distance between the rear of the lens (when focused on infinity) and the film, determines the angle of view and the size of objects as they appear on the film. The speed of a lens is indicated by reference to its maximum opening, or aperture, through which light enters the camera. This aperture, or *f*-stop, is controlled by an iris diaphragm (a series of overlapping metal blades that form a circle with a hole in the center whose diameter can be increased or decreased as desired) inside the lens. The higher the *f*-stop number, the smaller the aperture, and vice versa. A shutter controls the time during which light is permitted to enter the camera. There are two basic types of shutter,—leaf-type and focal-plane. The leaf-type shutter employs a ring of overlapping metal blades similar to those of the iris diaphragm, that may be closed or opened to the desired degree. It is normally located between the lens elements but occasionally is placed behind or in front of the lens. The focal-plane shutter is located just in front of the film plane, and has one or two cloth or metal curtains that travel vertically or horizontally across the film frame. By adjusting the shutter speed in conjunction with the width of aperture, the proper amount of light (determined by using a light meter and influenced by the relative sensitivity of the film being used) for a good exposure can be obtained. The image is focused on the film by adjusting the distance between the lens and the film. In most 35-mm cameras (among the most widely used of modern cameras) this is done by rotating the lens, thus moving it closer to or farther from the film. With twin-lens reflex and larger view cameras, the whole lens and the panel to which it is attached is moved toward or away from the film. To view the subject for composing (and, usually, to help bring it into focus) nearly every camera has some kind of viewfinder. One of the simplest types, employed in most view cameras, is a screen that is placed on the back of the camera and replaced by the film in making the exposure. This time-consuming procedure is avoided in the modern 35-mm single-lens (and other) reflex cameras by placing the screen in a special housing on top of the camera. Inside the camera, in front of the film plane, there is a movable mirror that bounces the image from the lens to the screen for viewing and focusing, and then flips out of the way when the shutter is tripped, so that the image hits the film instead of the mirror. The mirror returns automatically to place after the exposure has been made. In rangefinder cameras the subject is generally viewed by means of two separate windows, one of which views the scene directly and the other of which contains an adjustable optical mirror device. When this device is adjusted by rotating the lens, the image entering through the lens can be brought into register, at the eyepiece, with the image from the direct view, thereby focusing the subject on the film. Most of today's 35-mm cameras, both rangefinder and reflex models, incorporate a rapid film-transport mechanism, lens interchangeability (whereby lenses of many focal lengths, such as wide-angle and telephoto, may be used with the same camera body), and a built-in light meter. Many also have an automatic exposure device whereby either the shutter speed or the aperture is regulated automatically (by means of a very sophisticated solid-state electronics system) to produce the "correct" exposure. Simple box cameras, which are no longer manufactured, and most of the cameras of the Eastman Kodak Instamatic type are fixed-focus cameras with limited or no control over exposure. Twin-lens reflex cameras use one lens solely for viewing, while the other focuses the image on the film. Also very popular today are the new, compact, 35-mm rangefinder cameras; 126 cartridge cameras; and the subminiature cameras, including the new 110 "pocket" variation of the Instamatic type and the sophisticated Minox, which uses 9.5-mm film. Other categories in use include roll- and sheet-film single-lens reflex (SLR) cameras that use 120 and larger size films; self-processing Polaroid cameras (see LAND, EDWIN H.); press cameras and view cameras that use 2¼ × 3¼ in., 4 × 5 in., 5 × 7 in., 8 × 10 in., and 11 × 14 in. film sizes; stereo cameras, the double slides from which require a special viewer; and various special types such as the super wide-angle and the panoramic cameras. (The numbers 110, 120, and 126 are film-size designations from the manufacturer and do not refer to actual measurements.) See PHOTOGRAPHY, STILL. The **motion picture camera** comes in a variety of sizes, from 8 mm to 35 mm, but all operate on the same basic principles. Exposures are usually made at a rate of 18 or 24 frames per second (fps), which means that as the film goes through the camera it stops for a very brief moment to expose each frame. This is accomplished in nearly all movie cameras by a device called a rotary shutter—basically a half-circle of metal that spins, alternately opening and closing an aperture, behind which is located the film. To make the film travel along its path and hold still for the exposure of each frame, a device called the claw is required. This is another small piece of metal that alternately pops into the sprocket holes or perforations in the film, pulls the film down, then retracts to release the film while the frame is being exposed, and finally returns to the top of the channel in which it moves to grasp the next frame. The movement of the shutter and claw are synchronized, so that the shutter is closed while the claw is pulling the frame downward and open for the instant that the frame is motionless in its own channel or gate. Motion picture film comes in spools or cartridges. The spool type, employed mostly in 16- and 35-mm camera systems, must be threaded through the camera and attached to the take-up spool by hand, whereas a film cartridge—available for most of today's popular super-8-mm systems—avoids this procedure. In all modern movie cameras the film is driven by a tiny electric motor that is powered by batteries. Lenses for movie cameras also come in "normal," wide-angle, and long focal lengths. Some older cameras had a turret on which were mounted all three lens types. The desired lens could be fixed into position by simply rotating the turret. Many modern super-8 cameras come with a single zoom lens, incorporating many focal lengths that are controlled by moving a certain group of lens elements toward or away from the film. Most of these cameras have an automatic exposure device that regulates the *f*-stop according to the reading made by a built-in electric eye. Movie camera lenses are focused in the same way as are still cameras lenses. For viewing purposes, most of today's super-8's use a beam splitter—a partially silvered reflector that diverts a small percentage of the light to a ground-glass viewfinder, while allowing most of the light to reach the film. Other cameras have a mirror-shutter system which transmits all the light, at intervals, alternately to film and viewfinder. Many of the super-8 cameras also contain some kind of rangefinder, built into the focusing screen, for precise focusing. Although various kinds of devices for making pictures in rapid succession had been employed as early as the 1860s, the first practical motion picture camera—made feasible by the invention of the first flexible (paper base) films—was built in 1887 by E. J. Marey, a Frenchman. Two years later Thomas Edison invented the first commercially successful camera. However, cinematography was not accessible to amateurs until 1923, when Eastman Kodak produced the first 16-mm reversal safety film, and Bell & Howell introduced cameras and projectors with which to use it. Systems using 8-mm film were introduced in 1923; super-8, with its smaller sprocket holes and larger frame size, appeared in 1965. See MOTION PICTURE PHOTOGRAPHY. See *The Encyclopedia of Photography* (1971); *The Focal Encyclopedia of Photography* (rev. ed. 1972); David MacLoud, *Peterson's Guide to Movie Making* (1973).

Camerarius, Rudolph Jacob (kămərâr'ēəs, Ger. rōō'dôlf yä'kôp kämərä'rēōōs), 1665–1721, German botanist and physician. The first to present a clear and definite picture of sex in plants, Camerarius based his conclusions on careful experiments and observations. He described the stamen as the male organ and the ovary as the female organ and emphasized their relationship to the formation of seeds. He became a professor at the Univ. of Tübingen in 1688.

Cameron, Andrew Carr, 1834–90, American labor leader, b. Berwick-on-Tweed, England. He worked as a printer in Chicago, where he became interested in the labor movement. In the *Workingmen's Advocate*, which he edited from 1864 to 1877, he strongly advocated independent political action by labor. Cameron helped found the National Labor Union in 1866 and was its delegate to the convention of the International Workingmen's Association in Basel in 1869. He was president of the Chicago Trades Assembly, the Grand Eight Hour League, and the Illinois State Labor Association.

Cameron, John, c.1579–1625, Scottish scholar and theologian. As teacher, lecturer, and preacher at Bordeaux, Saumur, and other cities on the Continent, he came to be celebrated for his learning and ability. He was appointed (1622) principal of the Univ. of Glasgow by James I of England, but his belief in the divine right of kings and his stand for passive obedience made it impossible for him to remain in this post long. Returning to France after less than a year, he became (1624) professor of divinity at Montauban. Not long afterward he was attacked by an enemy of the doctrine of passive obedience and died. His writings, in Latin and French, were largely concerned with his views on man's free will and the grace of God. Those who held the same opinions were sometimes known as Cameronites and practiced a moderate form of Calvinism. His collected works were published in 1642, with a memoir by Louis Cappel.

Cameron, Julia Margaret, 1815–79, English pioneer photographer, b. Calcutta. Born and married into the high ranks of the British Civil Service, Cameron became an intimate of many of the most famous people of her day. In 1864 she became an ardent amateur photographer, demanding long, arduous sittings from her illustrious friends. She sought to illuminate the inner person of her subject, and her celebrated portraits, including those of Tennyson, Carlyle, Ellen Terry, and Longfellow, are remarkably spontaneous. Some of her works were published as *Victorian Photographs of Famous Men and Fair Women* (rev. ed. 1973). See biographies by Helmut Gernsheim (2d ed. 1969) and Brian Hill (1973).

Cameron, Richard, 1648-1680, Scottish leader of the Cameronians, an extreme group of COVENANTERS. In 1672, under the influence of the open-air preacher John Welch, he became a Covenanter preacher and was known for his eloquence. Strongly opposing the measures aimed at reestablishing the Episcopal Church in Scotland, and objecting to any state control of the church, he led a small company who, in the Sanquhar Declaration (1680), disowned the royal authority of Charles II. A price was set on Cameron's head and within a short time he and a little band of supporters were overtaken by royal troops. Cameron and many of his group were killed. Later (1743) the Cameronians, growing in numbers, formed a presbytery, taking the name Reformed Presbyterians. This denomination is still represented by congregations in Scotland, the north of Ireland, and North America, but the greater number united (1876) with the Free Church of Scotland, which, in 1929, incorporated them in the reunited Church of Scotland. A body of Cameronians formed the nucleus (1689) of the celebrated Cameronian regiment of the British army. See biography by John Herkless (1896).

Cameron, Simon, 1799-1889, American politician and financier, b. Lancaster co., Pa. From humble beginnings he rose to be a newspaper publisher and with considerable success branched out into canal and road construction, railroad promotion, banking, and iron and steel manufacturing. His private wealth brought him influence in the Democratic party; he played a major role in winning the vice presidential nomination for Martin Van Buren in 1832 and in James Buchanan's election to the Senate the following year. Cameron was elected (1845) to Buchanan's vacated seat in the U.S. Senate but, defeated for reelection, served only until 1849. Having joined the new Republican party in 1856, he was returned (1857) to the Senate when three Democratic legislators also voted for him. In the Senate, Cameron bitterly attacked the pro-Southern policies of his former friend President Buchanan. At the Republican national convention in Chicago in 1860 he was a candidate for the presidential nomination but after the first ballot supported Abraham Lincoln, first exacting from Lincoln's managers, however, the promise of a cabinet post. Lincoln reluctantly recognized the bargain, made without his knowledge, and Cameron resigned from the Senate to serve (March, 1861-Jan., 1862) as Secretary of War. The President's worst fears were realized as notorious corruption in army contracts and appointments aroused the nation. Lincoln eased him out gracefully by appointing him minister to Russia, but Cameron resigned that post in Nov., 1862. The House of Representatives passed (April, 1862) a resolution of censure against him, but Cameron bounded back in 1867, when, in defeating Andrew H. Curtin for the Senate, he became absolute Republican boss of Pennsylvania. He retired from the Senate and from active participation in politics in 1877 but only after making sure that his son, James Donald Cameron, succeeded him in the Senate. The machine he created, later run by his son, Matthew S. QUAY, Boies PENROSE, William S. VARE, and Joseph R. Grundy successively, so dominated Pennsylvania that it was not until Franklin Delano Roosevelt's victory in 1936 that the Democrats carried the state in a national election. See biography by E. S. Bradley (1966); L. F. Crippen, *Simon Cameron: Ante-Bellum Years* (1942, repr. 1972).

Cameron, Thomas Fairfax, 3d **Baron Fairfax of:** see FAIRFAX OF CAMERON, THOMAS FAIRFAX, 3d BARON.

Cameron, Verney Lovett, 1844-94, English traveler in Africa. A naval officer, he served (1868) in the British expedition against Ethiopia and assisted in the suppression of the East African slave trade. He was sent (1873) by the Royal Geographical Society to relieve Livingstone but, finding him dead, recovered his papers, explored and mapped Lake Tanganyika, and proceeded to the Atlantic, the first European to cross equatorial Africa. His expedition was recorded in *Across Africa* (1877). In 1882 he explored the Gold Coast with Sir Richard Burton and was coauthor with him of *To the Gold Coast for Gold* (1883).

Cameron of Lochiel, Donald (lŏkh-ēl'), 1695?-1748, Scottish clan chieftain, known as the Gentle Lochiel; grandson of Sir Ewen Cameron. He was the first of the major chieftains to join Charles Edward Stuart, the Young Pretender, in the unsuccessful Jacobite uprising in 1745. He was wounded in the battles of Falkirk and Culloden (1746) and escaped to France with the pretender.

Cameron of Lochiel, Sir Ewen or **Evan,** 1629-1719, chief of the Scottish highland clan of Cameron after 1647. On behalf of Charles II he led his clan in an uprising against the Commonwealth in 1653, and only in 1658 did he submit to the Puritan general George MONCK. He accompanied Monck to London in 1660 and was received at the court of the restored Charles II. He was knighted in 1681. A supporter of James II, he took part in the Jacobite victory over the forces of William III at Killiecrankie in 1689 and sent his clan to aid the Jacobite rebellion of 1715. Lochiel was a romantic warrior of great strength, and from one of his feats Sir Walter Scott drew his description of the fight between Roderick Dhu and Fitz James in *The Lady of the Lake*.

Cameroon, United Republic of, republic (1973 est. pop. 6,100,000), 183,568 sq mi (475,442 sq km), W central Africa. It is bordered on the W by the Gulf of Guinea, on the NW by Nigeria, on the NE by Chad, on the E by the Central African Republic, on the S by the Congo Republic, Gabon, and Equatorial Guinea, and on the SW by the Bight of Biafra. YAOUNDÉ is the capital, and DOUALA is the largest city and main port. Cameroon is triangular in shape. A coastal strip 10 to 50 mi (16-80 km) wide in the southwest is covered with swamps and dense, tropical rain forests; it has one of the wettest climates in the world, with an average annual rainfall of 152 in. (386 cm). Near the coast are volcanic peaks, dominated by Cameroon Mt. (13,354 ft/4,070 m), the highest point in the country. Beyond the coastal marshes and plains, the land rises to a densely forested plateau c.1,000 ft (300 m) above sea level. The

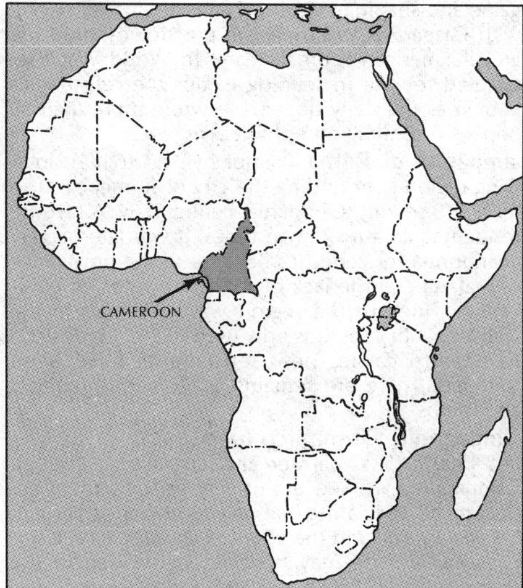

interior of the country is a plateau c.2,500 to 4,000 ft (760-1,220 m) high, where forests give way to savanna. This plateau forms a barrier between the agricultural south and the pastoral north. The extreme northern regions, near Lake Chad, are dry, thornbush lands. Among the many rivers that drain Cameroon are the Benue, the Wuori, the Sanaga, and the Nyong. The country consists of the former French Cameroons and the southern portion of the former British Cameroons. The French, or eastern, section constitutes four fifths of the country and supports the bulk of the population. With more than 150 ethnic groups, Cameroon has one of the most diverse populations in Africa. Bantu-speaking peoples, such as the Douala, predominate along the southern coast and in the forested areas. In the highlands are the Bamiléké. Important northern groups include the Fulani and the Kirdi. Islam is the dominant religion of the northern, Arabic-influenced regions; most of the southerners are animists, although Christianity has made some converts. The north, where cattle raising is the chief occupation, is the least economically developed part of Cameroon, whose regional disparities pose a major problem for the government. Agriculture is the mainstay of the country's economy. Cameroon is one of the world's leading cocoa producers; coffee, bananas, palm products, tobacco, peanuts, and rubber, all grown mainly on plantations, are also important. Cotton production is centered in the Benue River valley. Only about 10% of the country's land is cultivated. The principal subsistence crops are bananas, cassava, plantains, peanuts, millet, sorghum, and manioc. Fishing and forestry follow agriculture as leading occupations, but the vast timber reserves remain largely untapped. Cameroon's mineral resources include gold, diamonds, bauxite, tin, and mica. Prospecting for oil and natural gas is under way. The Edéa Dam on the Sanaga River provides the bulk of the country's electricity and powers a large aluminum smelter; all the finished aluminum is exported. The country's other industries are focused around agricultural processing and the manufacture of light consumer goods; an inadequate transportation system has hampered further industrialization. Cameroon's exports consist mainly of agricultural products, France being the major trading partner, followed by other members of the European Common Market. The official languages of Cameroon are French and English. Throughout history the region witnessed numerous invasions and migrations, especially by the Fulani, Hausa, Fang, and Kanuri. Contact with Europeans began in 1472, when the Portuguese reached the Wuori River estuary, and a large-scale slave trade ensued, carried on by Portuguese, Spanish, Dutch, French, and English traders. In the 19th cent., palm oil and ivory became the main items of commerce. The British established commercial hegemony over the coast in the early 19th cent., and British trading and missionary outposts appeared in the 1850s; but the English were supplanted by the Germans, who in 1884 signed a treaty with the Douala people along the Wuori estuary and proclaimed the area a protectorate. The Germans began constructing the port of Douala and then advanced into the interior, where they developed plantations and built roads and bridges. An additional area was acquired from France in 1911 as compensation for the surrender of German rights in Morocco. Two years later, German control over the Muslim north was consolidated. French and British troops occupied the region during World War I. After the war the area ceded in 1911 was rejoined to French Equatorial Africa, and in 1919 the remainder of Cameroon was divided into French and British zones, which became League of Nations mandates. Little social or political progress was made in either area, and French labor practices were severely criticized. Both mandates, however, remained loyal to the Allies in World War II. In 1946 they became United Nations trust territories. In the 1950s guerrilla warfare raged in the French Cameroons instigated by the radical nationalist Union of the Peoples of the Cameroons, which demanded immediate independence and union with the British Cameroons. France granted self-government to the French Cameroons in 1957 and internal autonomy in 1959. On Jan. 1, 1960, the territory became independent, with Ahmadou Ahidjo as its first president. The British-administered territory was divided into two zones, both administratively linked with Nigeria. In a UN-sponsored plebiscite in early 1961, the northern zone voted for union with Nigeria, and the southern for incorporation into Cameroon, which was subsequently reconstituted as a federal republic with two prime ministers and legislatures but a single president. National integration proceeded gradually. In 1966 the dominant political parties in the east and west merged into the Cameroon National Union (CNU). In 1972 the population voted favorably on a national referendum to adopt a new constitution setting up a unitary state to replace the federation. A presidential form of government was retained. Cameroon is a one-party state, with the CNU in control. There is a 120-member national assembly. See W. R. Johnson, *The Cameroon Federation* (1970); V. T. Levine, *The Cameroon Federal Republic* (1971); N. N. Rubin, *Cameroun* (1972).

Cameroon Mountain (kăm'ərōōn), active volcano, 13,354 ft (4,070 m) high, in the Cameroon Highlands, W Cameroon; highest point in W Africa. The western side of the mountain receives an average annual rainfall of more than 400 in. (1,016 cm) and is covered with tropical rain forest. Cocoa, banana, rubber, and tea plantations are found on the lower slopes.

Cameroons, Fr. *Cameroun,* Ger. *Kamerun,* former German colony, W Africa, on the Gulf of Guinea and extending N to Lake Chad. Germany's penetration of the area began in 1884 and by 1902 its possession was recognized. A portion of French Equatorial Africa was added in 1911 in return for the surrender of German rights in Morocco. In World War I, French and British troops occupied the Cameroons. After the war the territory ceded in 1911 was rejoined to French Equatorial Africa, and in 1919 the remainder of the Cameroons was divided into French and British zones, which became mandates under the League of Nations. In 1946 the mandates were made trust territories of the United Nations. **British Cameroons** consisted of two noncontiguous sections lying on the eastern border of Nigeria; the more southerly extended to the coast. **French Cameroons** was administered as a separate territory with the capital at Yaoundé. In 1960, French Cameroons became the Cameroon Republic; in 1961 the southern section of British Cameroons was joined to the Cameroon Republic to form the Federal Republic of Cameroon (United Republic of Cameroon after 1972), while the northern section passed to Nigeria.

Camillus (Marcus Furius Camillus) (kəmĭl'əs), d. 365? B.C., Roman hero. He was a patrician who, the Roman historians say, was elected dictator five times (396, 390, 386, 368, 367 B.C.) and on each occasion won a signal victory. He captured Veii, saved Rome from the Gauls, defeated the Aequi and Volscians, took Praeneste (the modern Palestrina), and defeated the Gauls at Alba Longa. Modern historians do not accept in full the traditional account of Camillus' victories.

Camisards (kăm'ĭsärdz, Fr. kämēsär'), Protestant peasants of the Cévennes region of France who in 1702 rebelled against the persecutions that followed the revocation (1685) of the Edict of Nantes (see NANTES, EDICT OF). The name was probably given them because of the shirts they wore in night raids. Led by the young Jean CAVALIER and Roland LAPORTE, the Camisards met the ravages of the royal army with guerrilla methods and withstood superior forces in several battles. In 1704, Marshal Villars, the royal commander, offered Cavalier vague concessions to the Protestants and the promise of a command in the royal army. Cavalier's acceptance broke the revolt, although others, including Laporte, refused to submit unless the Edict of Nantes was restored; scattered fighting went on until 1710. See A. E. Bray, *The Revolt of the Protestants of the Cévennes* (1870); H. M. Baird, *Huguenots and the Revocation of the Edict of Nantes* (1895).

Cammaerts, Émile (āmēl' kä'märts), 1878–1953, Belgian poet. In 1908 he settled in England, becoming a professor at the Univ. of London in 1933. His poetry of World War I, which appeared in French, was translated and collected in *Belgian Poems* (1915) and *New Belgian Poems* (1916). Later works, in English, include *Upon This Rock* (1943), a poignant character sketch of a son killed in the war, and volumes on Belgian history and culture.

Camões or **Camoens, Luís de** (both: lōōēsh' dĭ kəmoiNsh'), 1524?–1580, Portuguese poet, the greatest figure in Portuguese literature. Born of a poor family, Camões gained wide familiarity with classic literature at the Univ. of Coimbra. It is thought that he fell in love with a lady of the Lisbon court, Dona Caterina de Ataíde, who became the inspiration for his fiery love poems. Banished from court in 1546 because of this romance, he served as a soldier in a Moroccan campaign, where he lost an eye. After his return from Africa he was imprisoned in 1552 for wounding a minor court aide in a street fight. He was released the next year after consenting to serve in India. Apparently he had already begun his most celebrated work, *The Lusiads* [Port. *Os Lusíadas*= sons of Lusus, i.e., the Portuguese] (1572), but this journey may have caused him to make Vasco da Gama's voyage over the same route the central theme of his epic. After fighting in India, Camões was given an official post at Macao in China. In 1558 charges were brought against him for maladministration at Macao, and he was put aboard a ship for Goa in India. The ship was wrecked, but he managed to save his manuscript for *The Lusiads,* and he returned to Portugal in 1570 by way of Mozambique. The publication of his epic won him a meager royal pension. Camões's last years were spent in poverty, and in 1580 he died in obscurity, although his work had begun to enjoy world fame. By 1655 it had appeared in English in a version by Sir Richard Fanshawe. Although modeled on Vergil and showing the influence of Ariosto, it is imitative of neither and is a great epic in its own right. The beauty of its poetry is enlivened by a vigorous and realistic narrative that embraces not only the voyage of Vasco da Gama but also much of Portuguese history. Apart from *The Lusiads,* however, Camões's flawlessly crafted sonnets and lyrics would have won him lasting fame. See J. D. M. Ford's edition of *The Lusiads* with English notes to accompany the Portuguese text (1946); study by H. H. Hart (1962).

camomile: see CHAMOMILE.

Camon (kā'mŏn), unidentified place. Judges 10.5.

Camorra (kəmôr'ə), Italian secret criminal association in Naples. Of controversial origin, it first came to light in 1830. Its activities spread by intimidation, blackmail, and bribery until Naples was controlled by the hierarchical organization, which even sold its electoral backing and had its own parliamentary deputies. The Camorra appears to have been used by the Bourbon rulers of Naples as a quasi-police network to crush opposition. Efforts to break the power of the Camorra, begun in the 1880s, culminated in the 1911 murder trial at which numerous members were convicted. The Camorra was suppressed after Benito Mussolini's takeover in 1922.

camouflage (kăm'əfläzh), in warfare, the disguising of objects with artificial aids, especially for the purpose of making them blend into their surroundings or of deceiving the observer as to the location of strategic points. The principle, of course, is observed in the world of nature (see PROTECTIVE COLORATION) and has long been used by man. Scientific camouflage was greatly developed in World War I, when the French, in particular, used elaborate devices to conceal military objectives and industrial plants. False landscapes were created, using wire screens as a foundation for foliage, and ships were dazzle-painted to conceal their course by distortion of perspective. In World War II camouflage was further developed and was used on a large scale by all belligerents. With the development of RADAR and AERIAL PHOTOGRAPHY during that war, camouflage diminished greatly in utility; however, camouflage again became important, particularly in the guerrilla campaigns of the Vietnam War.

Camp, Walter Chauncey, 1859–1925, American football expert, b. New Britain, Conn., grad. Yale, 1880. He was a prominent athlete at Yale, where he was football coach after 1888; later, Camp became athletic director. Often called the father of American football, he had a leading role in developing the game and shaping its rules. Camp originated (1889), with Caspar W. Whitney, the practice of choosing an All-American football team. In World War I he adapted for use in training camps the calisthenics known as the daily dozen. He wrote more than 30 books on football and physical fitness.

Campagna di Roma (kämpä'nyä dē rô'mä), low-lying region surrounding the city of Rome, c.800 sq mi (2,070 sq km), Campania, central Italy. A favorite residential area in Roman times, it was later largely abandoned for centuries because of the prevalence of malaria and the lack of sufficient water for cultivation. Much of the region was reclaimed in the 19th and 20th cent. It is now used to grow crops and to pasture cattle; new settlements have been founded. There are remains of Roman aqueducts and tombs.

Campagnola, Domenico (dōmĕ'nēkō kämpänyô'lä), 1500–c.1564, painter and engraver. Although Campagnola worked exclusively in Italy, there are documents indicating that he was of German origin. He was a pupil and the adopted son of Giulio Campagnola, and he may have assisted Titian in the decorating of the Scuola del Santo. He painted chiefly in the churches of Padua. His best-known works are three frescoes in the Scuola del Carmine, Padua; *Four Prophets* (Academy, Venice); and *Holy Family* (Pitti Palace, Florence). His composition and warmth of color indicate his debt to Titian. Campagnola is celebrated also for his engravings, woodcuts, and masterly pen-and-ink drawings, which resemble Titian's closely in their clear linear quality and deep shading. Examples are in the Uffizi and in the British Museum.

Campagnola, Giulio (jōō'lyō), b. c.1482, d. after 1513, Italian painter and engraver. He painted miniatures and altarpieces but is best known for his finely executed engravings, many of them after the works of Giovanni Bellini and Giorgione.

campaign, political, organized effort to secure nomination and election of candidates for government offices. In the United States, the most important political campaigns are those for the nomination and election of candidates for the offices of President and Vice President. In each political party such nominations are made at a national CONVENTION preceding the presidential election. The contending parties are organized with a national chairman at the head of an elaborate system of national, state, and local committees. The committees have campaigns to run at all levels, but nothing else approaches the effort made in presidential campaigns. The costs have become enormous, political advertising, especially television, being the greatest expense. As a result, parties and candidates need to raise many millions of dollars. Financial contributions by corporations, individuals, and Federal employees, as well as expenditures by the parties' national committees have been restricted by law. Closer regulation of contributions was established by Congress in 1972 and again in 1974, when a measure of public financing was allowed for. In Great Britain the system of parliamentary government permits the overthrow of the cabinet by a vote of no confidence at any time, and, compared with U.S. congressional elections, this results in a more unified party campaign. British parliamentary and local elections are never held concurrently; campaigns are short and intensive, and party expenditures are comparatively very moderate and are fixed by law. See V. O. Key, *Politics, Parties and Pressure Groups* (5th ed. 1964); N. W. Polsby, *Presidential Elections* (3d ed. 1971); D. D. Dunn, *Financing Presidential Elections* (1972); H. E. Alexander, *Money in Politics* (1972).

Campan, Jeanne Louise Henriette (zhän lwēz äNrēĕt' känpäN'), 1752–1822, French educator and author. She served as a reader to Louis XV's daughters and as lady-in-waiting to Marie Antoinette. In 1792 she founded a school for girls at Saint-Germain, which Hortense de Beauharnais attended, and directed it until her appointment (1806) as principal of the academy established by Napoleon at Écouen. She retired in 1814. Among her works, published posthumously, are *Mémoires sur la vie privée de Marie Antoinette* (1823), *Journal anecdotique* (1824), and *Correspondance inédite avec la reine Hortense* (1835).

Campaña, Pedro: see KEMPENER, PIETER DE.

Campanella, Tommaso (tōm-mä'zō kämpänĕl'lä), 1568–1639, Italian Renaissance philosopher and writer. He entered the Dominican order at the age of 15, and although he was frequently in trouble with the authorities, he never left the church. Imprisoned in 1599 on the grounds that he was plotting against the Spanish rule of Naples, he was released in 1626 on the representation of Pope Urban VIII. His best-known work is *Civitas solis* (1623, tr. *The City of the Sun*), an account of a utopian society that closely follows the pattern of Plato's *Republic.* Although he retained much of scholasticism and insisted on the preeminence of faith in matters of theology, he emphasized perception and experiment as the media of science. His importance, like that of Francis Bacon and Bruno, depends largely on his anticipation of what came to be the scientific attitude of empiricism. For his *Civitas solis,* see Henry Morley, ed., *Ideal Commonwealths* (1890). See biography by B. M. Bonansea (1969).

Campania (kämpä'nyä), region (1971 pop. 5,054,822), 5,249 sq mi (13,595 sq km), central Italy, extending from the Apennines W to the Tyrrhenian Sea and from the Garigliano River S to the Gulf of Policastro. It includes the islands of Capri, Ischia, and Procida. NAPLES is the capital of Campania, which is divided into Benevento, Caserta, Naples, and Salerno provs. (named for their capitals). The central coast of the region is mostly high and rocky, with volcanic ridges and the crater of Vesuvius. However, the northern and southern coastal areas are fertile plains, famous since ancient times for their agricultural output. The interior of Campania is mountainous. Farm products of the region include grapes, citrus fruit, olives, apricots, grain, and vegetables. Industry is mostly clustered along the shore of the Bay of Naples; manufactures include textiles, shoes, chemicals, pharmaceuticals, refined petroleum, metal goods, wine, and motor vehicles. There is also a thriving tourist industry. Various Italic tribes, Greek colonists, Etruscans, and Samnites lived in the region before it was conquered (4th–2d cent. B.C.) by Rome. In Roman times the term *Campania* referred mainly to Naples and its surrounding area. After the fall of Rome the Goths and the Byzantines occupied the region; it later became part of the Lombard duchy of Benevento (except Naples and Amalfi, which were independent republics). In the 11th cent. the Normans conquered Campania, and in the 12th cent. it became part of the kingdom of Sicily. Naples soon rose to prominence, and after the SICILIAN VESPERS revolt (1282) it was made the capital of a separate kingdom. For the later history of Campania, see NAPLES, KINGDOM OF and TWO SICILIES, KINGDOM OF THE. In World War II there was heavy fighting around Naples after the Allied landing (Sept., 1943) at SALERNO. There is a university at Naples.

campanile (kămpənē'lē, Ital. kämpänē'lä), Italian form of bell tower, constructed chiefly during the Middle Ages. Built in connection with a church or a town hall, it served as a belfry and watch tower and often functioned as a civic or commemorative monument. The campanile generally stands as a detached unit. At the top is the bell platform, where the main architectural emphasis, generally a group of arched openings, is concentrated. Originating in the 6th cent., the campaniles were the earliest church towers in Europe and were generally circular in shape; examples of this type remain at Ravenna. Beginning with the 8th cent., the square plan became most common, being constructed in all parts of Italy. The Lombardy section produced the richest development of the campanile. Brick is the material most used, often combined with stone for the cornices and string courses, the latter surrounding the tower at each story level in the Roman examples. The celebrated campanile of Florence, known as Giotto's campanile (1334), is entirely faced in marble and ornamented with sculptures. Also of marble is the leaning tower at PISA.

campanula (kămpăn'yələ): see BELLFLOWER.

Campbell, Scottish noble family, the head of which is the duke of Argyll. The Campbells of Lochow (Lochawe) rose to power in W Scotland in the later Middle Ages. In 1445, Sir Duncan Campbell of Lochow (d. 1453) received the title of Baron Campbell, and his grandson Colin Campbell (d. 1493), 2d Baron Campbell, was created 1st earl of Argyll in 1457. In the succeeding century the earls of Argyll played an ever more prominent role in Scottish affairs. Archibald Campbell (d. 1558), 4th earl of Argyll, became one of the leading Protestant lords of the congregation. Even more important, however, was his son Archibald Campbell, 5th earl of ARGYLL, also a lord of the congregation, who was deeply involved in the upheavals of the reign of Mary Queen of Scots. He was succeeded by his half-brother, Colin Campbell (d. 1584), 6th earl of Argyll, who was in turn succeeded by his son Archibald Campbell (1575–1638), 7th earl of Argyll. The 7th earl became a Roman Catholic and in 1619 surrendered management of his estates to his son Archibald Campbell, 8th earl and 1st marquess of ARGYLL. The 8th earl and his son Archibald Campbell, 9th earl of ARGYLL, were the most powerful Presbyterian nobles in Scotland during the tumultuous events of the 17th cent.; both were executed for treason. Archibald Campbell, the 10th earl, finally managed to regain the family estates and was created (1701) 1st duke of ARGYLL. He and, more especially, his kinsman John Campbell, 1st earl of BREADALBANE, have been blamed (possibly unjustly) for the massacre (1692) of the MacDonalds of Glencoe by Campbell soldiers. John Campbell, 2d duke of ARGYLL, and his brother Archibald Campbell, 3d duke of ARGYLL, kept the family in the forefront of Scottish affairs. The 3d duke, however, died without legitimate issue, and the succession passed to a cadet branch of the family, the Campbells of Mamore. Of subsequent holders of the title the most prominent were George Douglas Campbell (1823–1900), 8th duke of Argyll, who held a series of cabinet positions, the most important as secretary of state for India in William Gladstone's first ministry (1868–74); and John Douglas Sutherland Campbell (1845–1914), 9th duke of Argyll, who married Princess Louise, daughter of Queen Victoria, and was governor general of Canada (1878–83).

Campbell, Alexander, 1788–1866, clergyman, cofounder with his father, Thomas Campbell (1763–1854), of the DISCIPLES OF CHRIST. Of Scottish lineage, both were born in Ireland and educated at the Univ. of Glasgow. Both were Anti-Burgher Presbyterians, a division opposed to the discipline of the main church. In 1807 the father went to America, where he was welcomed among the Scotch-Irish in SW Pennsylvania. His habit of asking all Presbyterians to join his church members in the communion service was contrary to a ruling of the Anti-Burgher synod in which he was preaching, and his action was condemned by his presbytery. Although his synod upheld him, the atmosphere remained so hostile that he and his followers, who were popularly called Campbellites, withdrew. In 1809 they formed the Christian Association of Washington, Pa., setting forth its purposes in a "Declaration and Address" that is considered the most important document of the Disciples body. In that year Campbell was joined in America by his son, Alexander, and the other members of his family. In c.1812, having accepted the doctrine of immersion, the Campbells and their followers were invited to join the Baptists. Until c.1827 they were nominally Baptists, but there were differences which caused trouble. Alexander Campbell, who had by this time assumed the leadership, advocated a return to scriptural simplicity in organization and doctrine; his followers became known as Reformers. He founded (1823) the *Christian Baptist* to promote his views and traveled throughout the new Western states, addressing large audiences. He edited (from 1830) the *Millennial Harbinger,* wrote *The Christian System* (1839), and in 1840 founded Bethany College in West Virginia and became its president. Meanwhile, the Reformers had seceded from or been forced out of many Baptist churches, and Campbell suggested that they form congregations and call themselves Disciples of Christ. Many of the "Christians," led chiefly by Barton Warren STONE, joined congregations of the Disciples; in 1832 the two leaders agreed to unite their efforts. See Robert Richardson, *Memoirs of Alexander Campbell* (2 vol., 1868–70); D. R. Lindley, *Apostle of Freedom* (1957); S. M. Eames, *The Philosophy of Alexander Campbell* (1966); E. J. Wrather, *Creative Freedom in Action* (1968).

Campbell, Colin, d. 1729, Scottish architect, who, in England, became one of the initiators of the Neo-Palladian movement. Campbell's most important contribution to this revival of classicizing architecture was his publication of *Vitruvius Britannicus* (3 vol., 1715, 1717, 1725). These volumes consisted of engravings of classical buildings in England—at first mainly those of Inigo Jones, but the later volumes presented designs by Campbell and other contemporary architects. Campbell's major buildings were Wanstead House, Essex (1715–20, destroyed), which incorporated what Campbell claimed to be England's first classical portico; the remodeling of Burlington House, London (c.1717); and Mereworth Castle, Kent (1723). They derive from obvious Palladian precedents. Through his writings and his executed buildings, Campbell's influence on English architecture was great.

Campbell, Colin, Baron Clyde, 1792–1863, British general. He commanded troops in China (1842–46) and India (1847–54) and in the famous victory at BALAKLAVA (1854) in the Crimean War. For his services in India in suppressing the Indian Mutiny (1857) he was created baron in 1858. He was made a field marshal in 1862. See biography by Lawrence Shadwell (1881).

Campbell, Donald Malcolm, 1921–67, British automobile and boat racer. The son of Sir Malcolm Campbell, from whom he inherited his passion for assaulting speed records and his mechanical inclinations, he helped to design a hull that would not disintegrate at speeds over 200 mi (322 km) per hr on water. His work attracted the attention of numerous British engineering firms and government departments. Campbell was killed in his jet-powered boat *Bluebird* as he tried to reach a speed of 300 mi (483 km) per hr. At the time of his death he held the world's speed record on water, 276.33 mi (444.89 km) per hr and had driven at an average speed of 403.1 mi (648.9 km) per hr on land. See biography by Douglas Young-James (1968).

Campbell, John, 1653–1728, American editor, b. Scotland. After emigrating to Boston, he was postmaster of the city from 1702 to 1718 and wrote newsletters for regular patrons. In 1704 he started printing these newsletters as a weekly half sheet, devoted mostly to foreign news, entitled the *Boston News-Letter.* Sold to Bartholomew Green in 1722, it was the first successfully established paper to appear in colonial America.

Campbell, John Francis, 1822–85, Scottish Gaelic scholar. He is known for *Popular Tales of the West Highlands* (4 vol., 1860–62) and *Leabhar na Feinne* (1872), a collection of Gaelic folk ballads. A meteorologist also, he invented an instrument to record the intensity of the sun's rays.

Campbell, John, 1st **Baron Campbell,** 1779–1861, British jurist. He was a member of the Whig party in the House of Commons from 1830 and in the Lords from 1841. Ambitious legally rather than politically, he became attorney general (1834–41), lord chief justice (1850), and lord chancellor (1859). Campbell was associated with legal reforms in the areas of real estate and local government, but his role was that of organizing the investigating commissions and guiding the bills through Parliament. He was more directly responsible for the Libel Act (1843), the Copyright Act (1846), and the Obscene Publications Act (1857). He wrote *Lives of the Lord Chancellors* (1845–47) and *Lives of the Chief Justices* (1849–57).

Campbell, Sir Malcolm, 1885–1949, English automobile and speedboat racer. A racing enthusiast from boyhood, Campbell set many speed records for motorcycles, airplanes, automobiles, and motorboats and in 1931 was knighted for his accomplishments. Driving his famed automobile *Bluebird* at Bonneville Flats, Utah, in 1935, Sir Malcolm was the first to reach the 300 mi (483 km) per hr mark. He then turned to speedboat racing and in 1939 set a new record of 141 mi per hr. His son Donald Campbell (1921–67) raised the water speed record to more than 300 mi per hr before his boat, also known as *Bluebird,* exploded in the water, killing him.

Campbell, Mrs. Patrick, 1865–1940, English actress, whose maiden name was Beatrice Stella Tanner. Remembered today for her association with G. B. Shaw, she was an actress of great beauty and wit. She made her debut in 1888 but achieved her first London success in 1893 in the title role of Pinero's *Second Mrs. Tanqueray.* In 1901 she made the first of her numerous tours to the United States; in 1912 she met Shaw at whose request she created the role of Eliza Doolittle in *Pygmalion.* See her *My Life and Some Letters* (1922, repr. 1969) and her correspondence with Shaw (ed. by Alan Dent, 1952). Jerome Kilty's play *Dear Liar* (1960) is based on the Campbell-Shaw correspondence.

Campbell, Robert: see ROB ROY.

Campbell, Robert, 1804–79, American fur trader and merchant, one of the mountain men, b. Ireland. He came to the United States c.1824. Having been advised to lead an outdoor life because of a lung ailment, he joined (1825) a fur trapping expedition. He trapped and traded in the Rocky Mts. until 1832, when he and William Sublette formed a partnership, which offered competition to the American Fur Company. Suffering reverses, they confined their activities to the mountain territory. The partnership was dissolved in 1842, and Campbell returned to St. Louis, where he amassed a fortune in merchandising, real estate, and banking. In 1851 and again in 1869 he served as Indian commissioner.

Campbell, Robert, 1808–94, Canadian fur trader and explorer, b. Scotland. Employed as a young man by the Hudson's Bay Company, he was sent in 1834 to the Mackenzie River region, where he remained until 1852. He discovered the Pelly River in 1840, descending it in 1843 to its confluence with the Lewes River to form the Yukon. Here he established Fort Selkirk in 1848. Later (1850–51) he followed the Yukon to its junction with the Porcupine River at Fort Yukon. He worked as a trader for Hudson's Bay until 1871, when he was discharged, and spent his last years as a rancher in Manitoba. He wrote *The Discovery and Exploration of the Pelly River* (1883). See Clifford Wilson, *Campbell of the Yukon* (1970).

Campbell, Roy, 1901–57, South African poet. His persuasive and robust poetry, reminiscent of the 19th-century English romantics, includes *The Flaming Terrapin* (1924), *Mithraic Emblems* (1936), and *Flowering Rifle* (1939). A fascist, Campbell fought with Franco's army in the Spanish civil war. During World War II, Campbell served with the British army in Africa. His collected poems were published in 1957. See his autobiography (1952).

Campbell, Thomas, 1763–1854, American clergyman, a founder of the DISCIPLES OF CHRIST. See CAMPBELL, ALEXANDER, his more famous son.

Campbell, Thomas, 1777–1844, Scottish poet. He is best known for his war poems "Hohenlinden," "The Battle of the Baltic," and "Ye Mariners of England." Among his other volumes of poetry are *The Pleasure of Hope* (1799), *Gertrude of Wyoming* (1809), and *Theodoric* (1824).

Campbell, William, 1745–81, American Revolutionary soldier, b. Augusta co., Va.; brother-in-law of Patrick Henry. He fought in Lord Dunmore's War (1774) and helped expel the royal governor from Williamsburg in 1776. Campbell and his group of Virginia riflemen in 1780 joined Sevier and Shelby at Kings Mt. (see CAROLINA CAMPAIGN), where he was in command. Later Campbell saw action at Guilford Courthouse, at Eutaw Springs, and in the Yorktown campaign.

Campbell, (William) Wilfred, 1861–1918, Canadian poet, b. Kitchener, Ont. Although ordained an Episcopal minister, he spent most of his life as a civil servant. His fame rests mainly on *Lake Lyrics* (1889), a volume of nature poetry. He also wrote historical novels and poetic dramas, and he edited the *Oxford Book of Canadian Verse* (1913). See his *Poetical Works* (1923).

Campbell. 1 City (1970 pop. 24,770), Santa Clara co., W Calif., in the fertile Santa Clara valley; founded 1885, inc. 1952. A processing center for fruits and vegetables, it has a huge fruit-drying facility. **2** City (1970 pop. 12,577), Mahoning co., NE Ohio, on the Mahoning River, adjacent to Youngstown; inc. 1908. It has extensive ironworks and steelworks.

Campbell-Bannerman, Sir Henry, 1836–1908, British statesman. Entering Parliament (1868) as a Liberal, he served as secretary to the admiralty (1882–84), secretary of state for Ireland (1884), and secretary of state for war (1886, 1892–95). He was knighted in 1895. In 1899 he was elected leader of the Liberal party (succeeding Sir William Harcourt) and led opposition to British policy in the South African War (1899–1902). When the Conservative government resigned in 1905, Campbell-Bannerman became prime minister. Before ill-health caused his retirement in 1908 he had furthered many Liberal measures, including that of self-government for the Transvaal and the Orange Free State. See biographies by J. A. Spender (1923) and John Wilson (1974).

Campbellites: see CAMPBELL, ALEXANDER; DISCIPLES OF CHRIST.

Campbellton (kăm'bəltən), city (1971 pop. 10,335), N N.B., Canada, on the Restigouche River near the head of Chaleur Bay. The city has large sawmills and is a shipping port for pulpwood. It is a starting point for canoe, fishing (salmon and trout), and hunting trips into the forested interior.

Camp Borden, large military training establishment, S Ont., Canada, NW of Toronto. It covers an area of 20,000 acres (8,094 hectares) and also includes an armored-vehicle range at Meaford, to the northwest.

Camp David, U.S. presidential retreat, Md.: see Catoctin Mountain Park under NATIONAL PARKS AND MONUMENTS (table).

Campeche (kämpä'chā), state (1970 pop. 250,391), 19,672 sq mi (50,950 sq km), SE Mexico, on the Gulf of Campeche. The city of Campeche is the capital. Comprising most of the western half of the YUCATÁN peninsula, the state lies in hot, humid, and unhealthy lowlands. Rainfall in the southwestern sector is heavy. Much of the state is extensively forested, and logwood (called *campeche* in Spanish) is one of the chief exports. Agriculture (especially the growing of sisal hemp) and stock raising are important, and some minerals are exploited. Using Campeche as a base, the Spanish explorer Francisco de Montejo led (1531–35) expeditions against the Maya Indians. The coast was a haunt of pirates from the 17th cent. to the 19th cent. The principal ports are Campeche and Carmen, a small town on an island at the entrance to the Laguna de Términos.

Campeche (kämpä'chā), city (1970 est. pop. 70,000), capital of Campeche state, SE Mexico, on the Yucatán peninsula. It is fortified and surrounded by 18th-century walls. Fish canning is the chief industry. The harbor is shallow, and vessels must anchor far from shore. Campeche, once the site of the pre-Columbian town called Kimpech (whose remains are still observable), was founded in 1540 by the son of the Spanish conquistador Francisco de Montejo. It was sacked frequently by English buccaneers. From 1862 to 1864, French forces blockaded the city. The city has a 16th-century cathedral.

Campeggio, Lorenzo (lōrĕnt'sō kämpĕd'jō), 1472?–1539, Italian churchman and diplomat, cardinal of the Roman Catholic Church. He was well known as a jurist before turning to the church (c.1510) upon the death of his wife. He was made bishop in 1512 and cardinal the following year. He was chosen as legate for the most delicate missions. In 1518 he went to England to secure the adherence of HENRY VIII to an alliance against Turkey. He did not succeed, but he received (1524) the bishopric of Salisbury from Henry, which he held *in absentia* until 1534. In 1528, Cardinal Campeggio went again to England to act with Cardinal WOLSEY as judge in the divorce of KATHARINE OF ARAGÓN. He followed his instructions to temporize and adjourned the hearing. Cardinal Campeggio was sent to Germany in 1524 to attempt a pacification of the Lutherans, but except for a promise from Holy Roman Emperor Charles V to enforce the Edict of Worms he obtained nothing. He ardently supported the reformation of the church, especially of the papal court and of the administration of the Holy See.

Camperdown (kăm'pərdoun"), Du. *Kamperduin* [the dune of Kamp], locality near the village of Kamp, North Holland prov., NW Netherlands, on the North Sea. In 1797 the British defeated the Dutch in a naval battle off Camperdown.

Camp Fire Girls, American organization for girls from 6 to 18 years old. It was founded (1910) by Luther Halsey GULICK (1865–1918) and other educators "to perpetuate the spiritual ideals of the home" and "to stimulate and aid in the formation of habits making for health and character." The seven crafts of its program are the home, the creative arts, the outdoors, frontiers (of science), business, sports and games, and citizenship. The Camp Fire members are divided into four age groups—Blue Birds (6 to 8), Camp Fire Girls (9 to 11), Junior Hi Camp Fire Girls (12 to 13), and Horizon Clubs (14 to 18). The official organ of the organization is the *Camp Fire Girl.*

Camp Gagetown, military camp, S central N.B., Canada. It was established in 1952 and is the largest (436 sq mi/1,129 sq km) military camp in Canada.

Camphausen, Ludolf (lo͞o'dôlf kämp'houzən), 1803–90, Prussian statesman and businessman. A leading merchant in Cologne, he headed the liberal ministry appointed by King Frederick William IV of Prussia after the revolutionary outburst of March, 1848. He was forced to resign in June when the Prussian assembly became more liberal and the king more conservative. He was an important figure at the FRANKFURT PARLIAMENT.

camphor, $C_{10}H_{16}O$, white, crystalline solid KETONE with a characteristic pungent odor and taste. It melts at 176°C and boils at 204°C. The natural variety, Japan camphor, is obtained by steam distillation of the wood of the camphor tree (*Cinnamomum camphora*) native to China, Japan, and Formosa (its chief natural source). Since this source is inadequate, camphor is widely synthesized from α-pinene, which is obtained from oil of turpentine. Camphor is widely used as a plasticizer in the manufacture of celluloid and some lacquers. It is used in medicine as a stimulant, a diaphoretic, and an inhalant. Camphor ice is a mixture, containing principally camphor and wax, used for external application. Camphor is practically insoluble in water but soluble in alcohol, ether, chloroform, and other solvents. The alcoholic solution is known as spirits of camphor.

Campi, Giulio (jo͞o'lyō käm'pē), c.1500–c.1572, Italian painter and architect, founder of a school of painters at Cremona. He was a pupil of his father, Galeazzo Campi (c.1475–1536), a well-known painter, and of Giulio Romano, and he studied the works of Correggio and Raphael. Giulio produced many excellent altarpieces and frescoes in Milan, Mantua, and Cremona; the frescoes in the Church of Santa Margherita, Cremona, are entirely his work. Among his pupils were his two brothers, Cavaliere **Antonio Campi,** b. before 1536, d. 1591, painter, architect, and historian of Cremona, and **Vincenzo Campi,** 1532–91, whose works consist principally of portraits and still-life pieces. Another brother was **Bernardino Campi,** 1522–c.1590, a painter of great skill with a vigorous and original style, excelling in fresco painting and portraiture. Bernardino's most important work is the series of biblical frescoes in the cupola of San Sigismondo, Cremona, a work of colossal dimensions admirably executed.

Campian, Thomas: see CAMPION, THOMAS.

Campin, Robert (käm'pĭn), 1378–1444, Flemish painter who with the van Eycks ranks as a founder of the Netherlandish school. This artist has been identified as the Master of Flémalle on the basis of three panels in Frankfurt-am-Main said to have come from the abbey of Flémalle near Liège. Campin was active in Tournai, having become a citizen of that city in 1410 and the dean of the painters' guild in 1423. To him have been attributed the *Mérode Altarpiece* in the Cloisters, New York City, a *Nativity* in Dijon, the *Annunciation* and *Marriage of the Virgin* in Madrid, the *Madonna of Humility* in London, and a number of other panels in various collections. Campin's style matured in the fresh climate of one of the mercantile urban centers of Northern Europe, where artistic taste came increasingly to reflect the values of the rising middle class. His works are characterized by a robust and highly developed realism and concern for the details of daily life, which constituted an important stage in the stylistic evolution leading to the art of Jan van Eyck. It is believed that Roger Van der Weyden was apprenticed in Campin's workshop. See Erwin Panofsky, *Early Netherlandish Painting* (1953); M. S. Frinta, *The Genius of Robert Campin* (1966).

Campina Grande (kəmpē'nä grän'dĭ), city (1970 pop. 195,794), Paraíba state, NE Brazil, on the Borborema plateau. It is an important commercial and financial center and a shipping point for products from the Brazilian interior (hides and skins, cotton, and agave). Industries in the city are linked to agriculture and cattle raising. Textiles, leather goods, cheese, and butter are the principal products. The city was founded in the late 17th cent. and developed rapidly as an important point on the route from the coast to the interior.

Campinas (kəmpē'nəs), city (1970 pop. 376,497), São Paulo state, S Brazil. It is a growing industrial and financial city, the processing and distributing center for a diversified agricultural region, and a major transportation hub. Consumer products, agricultural tools, and railroad equipment are among its manufactures. The city was founded in the 18th cent. Coffee cultivation in the region and the city's location as the main railroad junction in the state accounted for its prosperity by the late 19th cent. As coffee production moved westward, the economy diversified. Campinas has a famed agronomical-research institute and a state university.

Campion, Saint Edmund (kăm'pēən), c.1540–1581, English Jesuit martyr, educated at St. Paul's School and St. John's College, Oxford. As a fellow at Oxford he earned the admiration of his colleagues and his students and the favor of Queen Elizabeth by his brilliance and oratorical ability. He went (1569) to Dublin to help in the proposed restoration of the university there. Although he had reluctantly taken orders as a Protestant, he had open Roman Catholic leanings and fled in disguise (1571) to England and then to the Continent, where he studied at Douai, joined (1573) the Society of Jesus, and was ordained (1578). In 1580 he and another Jesuit, Robert PERSONS, were sent as Jesuit missionaries to England. Campion's travels were marked by many conversions and did much to guarantee the survival of Roman Catholicism in England. Copies of his secretly printed pamphlet, *Decem rationes* [10 reasons], against the Protestants, appeared at Oxford in 1581. The long pursuit by the government ended (July, 1581) with the taking of Campion. He was racked three times, but though his body was broken he conducted debates with Protestant theologians brilliantly and won more converts. He defended himself ably against trumped-up charges of sedition but was nevertheless condemned and hanged, drawn, and quartered. He was beatified in 1886. In 1970, Campion and the other English and Welsh martyrs of the Reformation were canonized. See biography by Evelyn Waugh (3d ed. 1961).

Campion or **Campian, Thomas,** 1567–1620, English poet, composer, and lutenist, a physician by profession. Campion wrote lyric poems that he and other composers set to music. His graceful, simple lute songs were published in five *Books of Airs* (1601–1617). He wrote a treatise on English poetry, condemning the use of rhyme, but he used rhyme freely in his own poems. His treatise *A New Way of Making Fowre Parts in Counterpoint* (1613) has often been republished. See study by Edward Lowbury et al. (1970).

campion: see PINK.

Camp LeJeune, U.S. marine corps base, 82,969 acres (33,576 hectares), SE N.C., SE of Jacksonville; est. 1941. It is the major East Coast training center and support base for the Atlantic Fleet Marine Force.

camp meeting, outdoor religious meeting, held usually in the summer and lasting for several days. The camp meeting was a prominent institution of the American frontier. It originated under the preaching of James MCGREADY in Kentucky early in the course of a religious revival (c.1800) and spread throughout the United States. Immense crowds flocked to hear the noted revivalist preachers, bringing bedding and provisions in order to camp on the grounds. The meetings were directed by a number of preachers who relieved each other in carrying on the services, sometimes preaching simultaneously in different parts of the camp grounds. Shouting, shaking, and rolling on the ground often accompanied the tremendous emotional release that followed upon "conversion," although these extravagances were opposed and discouraged by conservative ministers. Camp meetings were usually held by evangelical sects, such as the Methodists and Baptists, and by the Cumberland Presbyterians and other newer denominations that developed out of the religious revival. In modified form they continued to be a feature of social and religious life in the region between the Alleghenies and the Mississippi River until comparatively recent times; in a sense, they survive in summer conferences and assemblies, such as the Chautauqua Institution and the Ocean Grove Camp Meeting Association. See C. A. Johnson, *The Frontier Camp Meeting* (1955).

Campoamor, Ramón de (rämōn' dā kämpōämōr'), 1817–1901, Spanish poet, the first to break with the romantic tradition of long, tragic, and emotional poetry. One of the most popular Spanish poets of his time, he was noted for his humorous short poems collected in *Doloras* (1846), *Pequeños poemas* (1872–74), and *Humoradas* (1886–88). Less well known are the two long narrative poems, *Colón* [Columbus] (1853) and *El drama universal* (1869). Campoamor's works are no longer generally popular.

Campobasso (käm"pōbäs'sō), city (1971 pop. 41,807), capital of Molise and of Campobasso prov., S central Italy. It is an agricultural and industrial center. Manufactures include cement, soap, textiles, and cutlery. In the city are a 15th-century castle and a museum of archaeology.

Campobello (kăm″pōbĕl′ō), island, 9 mi (14.5 km) long and 3 mi (4.8 km) wide, in Passamaquoddy Bay, N.B., Canada, just off the coast of Maine. The island passed to Canada by the Convention of 1817. President Franklin Delano Roosevelt had a summer home in Welchport, the main settlement, for many years. It is now preserved in Roosevelt-Campobello International Park (see NATIONAL PARKS AND MONUMENTS, table).

Campo Formio, Treaty of (käm′pō fôr′myō), Oct., 1797, peace treaty between France and Austria, signed near Campo Formio, a village near Udine, NE Italy, then in Venetia. It marked the end of the early phases of the FRENCH REVOLUTIONARY WARS. The treaty generally ratified the preliminary Peace of Leoben, signed at the conclusion of Napoleon Bonaparte's Italian campaign (see NAPOLEON I). Bonaparte signed for France, Count Cobenzl for Austria. Austria ceded its possessions in the Low Countries (the present-day Belgium) to France and secretly promised France the left bank of the Rhine. The republic of Venice, invaded despite its attempts to maintain neutrality, was dissolved and partitioned: all Venetia E of the Adige, as well as Istria and Dalmatia, passed to Austria; the present provinces of Bergamo and Brescia went to the newly founded CISALPINE REPUBLIC; the IONIAN ISLANDS went to France.

Campomanes, Pedro Rodríguez de, conde de Campomanes (pā′thrō rôthrē′gāth kōn′dā dā kämpōmä′nās), b. 1723, d. 1802 or 1803, Spanish statesman, economist, and author. As minister under Charles III and briefly under Charles IV, he introduced administrative, social, and economic reforms. He wrote on the revival of industry and on the professional education of the working classes.

Campos, Arsenio Martínez de: see MARTINEZ DE CAMPOS, ARSENIO.

Campos (käm′po͞os), city (1970 pop. 319,112), Rio de Janeiro state, SE Brazil, on the Paraíba River near its mouth. It is the commercial hub of a rich agricultural region and a transportation center. More than half of the state's sugar output is produced in Campos. There are also distilleries in the city. Campos was founded in the early 17th cent. and under the empire was an important slave center.

Campus Martius: under ROME see *Rome before Augustus; Roman Empire; Renaissance and Modern Rome.*

Cam Ranh Bay (käm rän), inlet of the South China Sea, 10 mi (16 km) long and 20 mi (32 km) wide, S central South Vietnam. It is an excellent harbor linked to the sea by a strait (1 mi/1.6 km wide). The bay was the site of one of the largest U.S. military facilities (est. 1965) in South Vietnam during the Vietnam War.

Camrose, city (1971 pop. 8,673), central Alta., Canada. It is in a mixed farming area and is a railroad center. Camrose Lutheran College is there.

Camulodunum, England: see COLCHESTER.

Camus, Albert (älbĕr′ kämü′), 1913–60, French writer, b. Algiers. Camus was one of the most important authors and thinkers of the 20th cent. While a student at the Univ. of Algiers, he formed a theater group and adapted, directed, and acted in plays. He became active in social reform and was briefly a member of the Communist party. Shortly after his essay *Noces* [weddings] appeared (1939), he went to Paris as a journalist. In World War II he joined the French resistance and was principal editor of the underground paper *Combat.* Noted for his vigorous, concise, and lucid style, Camus soon gained recognition as a major literary figure. His belief that man's condition is absurd identified him with the existentialists, but he denied allegiance to that group; his works express rather a courageous humanism. The characters in his novels and plays, although keenly aware of the meaninglessness of the human condition, assert their humanity by rebelling against their circumstances. His essay *Le Mythe de Sisyphe* (1942, tr. *The Myth of Sisyphus,* 1955) formulates his theory of the absurd and is the philosophical basis of his novel *L'Étranger* (1942, tr. *The Stranger,* 1946) and of his plays *Le Malentendu* (1944, tr. *Cross Purpose,* 1948) and *Caligula* (1944, tr. 1948). The essay *L'Homme révolté* (1951, tr. *The Rebel,* 1954), dealing with historical, spiritual, and political rebellion, treats themes found in the novels *La Peste* (1947, tr. *The Plague,* 1948) and *La Chute* (1956, tr. *The Fall,* 1957). Other works include the plays *L'État de siège* (1948, tr. *State of Siege,* 1958); and *Les Justes* (1950, tr. *The Just Assassins,* 1958); journalistic essays; and stories. Camus was awarded the 1957 Nobel Prize in Literature. See his *Notebooks* ed. by Philip Thody (2 vol., 1963, 1965); studies by John Cruikshank (1960), Germaine Brée (4th ed. 1972), Donald Lazere (1973), and Lev Braun (1974).

Cana (kā′nə), ancient town of Galilee. Here Jesus performed his first miracle by turning water into wine at a wedding. John 2.1,11; 4.46,54; 21.2.

Canaan (kā′nən). **1** Son of Ham and the ancestor for whom the Canaanites were named. Gen. 9.20–27; 10.6,15,19. **2** Territory, the same as ancient Palestine, lying between the Jordan, the Dead Sea, and the Mediterranean and sometimes including Transjordan. It was the Promised Land of the Israelites, and after their delivery from Egypt they subjugated it. Gen. 12.5; Ex. 3.8; Num. 13.17,29; 14.45; 21.3; Joshua 22.11,32; Judges 1. The Canaanites are the inhabitants of Canaan and are probably related to the Amorites. In Mark 3.18 the name signifies one of the Zealots. Chanaan is a variant of Canaan. See UGARIT; ASHERAH; BAAL; PHILISTIA; PHOENICIA.

Canada, country (1971 pop. 21,568,311), 3,851,787 sq mi (9,976,128 sq km), N North America. The capital is OTTAWA. It is a federation of 10 provinces—NEWFOUNDLAND, NOVA SCOTIA, NEW BRUNSWICK, PRINCE EDWARD ISLAND, QUEBEC, ONTARIO, MANITOBA, SASKATCHEWAN, ALBERTA, and BRITISH COLUMBIA—and the YUKON TERRITORY and the NORTHWEST TERRITORIES. Canada occupies all of North America N of the United States (and E of Alaska) except for the French islands of St. Pierre and Miquelon. It is bounded on the E by the Atlantic Ocean, on the N by the Arctic Ocean, and on the W by the Pacific Ocean and Alaska. A transcontinental border, formed in part by the Great Lakes, divides Canada from the United States; Nares and Davis straits separate Canada from Greenland. The ARCTIC ARCHIPELAGO extends far into the Arctic Ocean. Canada has a very long and irregular coastline; Hudson Bay and the Gulf of St. Lawrence indent the east coast and the Inside Passage extends along the west coast. The ice-clogged straits between the islands of N Canada form the Northwest Passage. During the Ice Age all of Canada was covered by a continental ice sheet that scoured and depressed the land surface, leaving a covering of glacial drift, depositional landforms, and innumerable lakes and rivers. Aside from the Great Lakes, which are only partly in the country, the largest lakes of North America—Great Bear, Great Slave, and Winnipeg—are entirely in Canada. The St. Lawrence is the chief river of E Canada. The Saskatchewan, Nelson, Churchill, and Mackenzie river systems drain central Canada, and the Columbia, Fraser, and Yukon rivers drain the western part of the country. Canada has a bowl-shaped geologic structure rimmed by highlands, with Hudson Bay at the lowest point. The country has eight major physiographic regions—the Canadian Shield, the Hudson Bay Lowlands, the Western Cordillera, the Interior Lowlands, the Great Lakes-St. Lawrence Lowlands, the Appalachians, the Arctic Lowlands, and the Innuitians. The exposed portions of the Canadian Shield cover more than half of Canada. This once-mountainous region, which contains the continent's oldest rocks, has been worn low by erosion over the millennia. Its upturned eastern edge is indented by fjords. The Shield is rich in minerals, especially iron and nickel, and in potential sources of hydroelectric power. In the center of the Shield are the Hudson Bay Lowlands, encompassing Hudson Bay and the surrounding marshy land. The Western Cordillera, a geologically young mountain system parallel to the Pacific coast, is composed of a series of north-south trending ranges and valleys that form the highest and most rugged section of the country; Mt. Logan (19,850 ft/6,050 m) is the highest point in Canada. Part of this region is made up of the Rocky Mts. and the Coast Mts., which are separated by plateaus and basins. The islands off W Canada are partially submerged portions of the Coast Mts. The Western Cordillera is also rich in minerals and timber and potential sources of hydroelectric power. Between the Rocky Mts. and the Canadian Shield are the Interior Lowlands, a vast region filled with sediment from the flanking higher lands. The Lowlands are divided into the prairies, the plains, and the Mackenzie Lowlands. The prairies are Canada's granary, while grazing is important on the plains. The smallest and southernmost region is the Great Lakes-St. Lawrence Lowlands, Canada's heartland. Dominated by the St. Lawrence River and the Great Lakes, the region provides a natural corridor into central Canada, and the St. Lawrence Seaway gives the interior cities access to the Atlantic. This section, which is composed of gently rolling surface on sedimentary rocks, is the location of extensive farmlands, large industrial centers, and most of Canada's population. In SE Canada and on Newfoundland is the northern end of the Appalachian Mt. system, an old and geologically complex region with a generally low and rounded relief. The Arctic Lowlands and the Innuitians are the most isolated areas of Canada and are barren and snow covered for most of the year. The Arctic Lowlands comprise much of the Arctic Archipelago and contain sedimentary rocks that may have oil-bearing strata. In the extreme north, mainly on Ellesmere Island, is the Innuitian Mt. system, which rises to c.10,000 ft (3,050 m). Canada's climate is influenced by latitude and topography. The Interior Lowlands make it possible for polar air masses to move south and for subtropical air masses to move north into Canada. Hudson Bay and the Great Lakes act to modify the climate locally. The Western Cordillera serves as a climatic barrier that prevents polar air masses from reaching the Pacific coast and blocks the moist Pacific winds from reaching into the interior. The Cordillera has a typical highland climate that varies with altitude; the western slopes receive abundant rainfall, and the whole region is forested. The Interior Lowlands are in the rain shadow of the Cordillera; the southern portion has a steppe climate in which grasses predominate. S Canada has a temperate climate, with snow in the winter (especially in the east) and cool summers. Farther to the north, extending to the timberline, is the humid subarctic climate characterized by short summers and a snow cover for about half the year. On the Arctic Archipelago and the northern mainland is the tundra, with its mosses and lichen, permafrost, near year-round snow cover, and ice fields. A noted phenomenon off the coast of E Canada is the persistence of dense fog, which is formed when the warm air over the Gulf Stream passes over the cold Labrador Current as the two currents meet off Newfoundland.

Economy. Manufacturing is Canada's most important economic activity, engaging 22% of the work force. The remainder are employed in service industries (27%), trade (17%), construction (6%), transportation (6%), finance, real estate, and insurance (6%), government (6%), and agriculture (5%). Manufacturing accounts for more than half the value of all Canadian production. The leading products are motor vehicles, pulp and paper, processed meat, petroleum, iron and steel, dairy products, and processed metals. Industries are centered in Ontario, Quebec, and, to a lesser extent, British Columbia. Agriculture contributes about one tenth of the value of production. The sources of the greatest farm income are livestock and dairy products. Among the biggest income-earning crops are wheat, oats, barley, and corn. Canada is one of the world's leading agricultural exporters, especially of wheat. Manitoba, Saskatchewan, and Alberta are the great grain-growing provinces, and, with Ontario, are also the leading sources of beef cattle. The main fruit-growing regions are found in Ontario, British Columbia, Quebec, and Nova Scotia. Apples and peaches are the principal fruits grown in Canada. The fur industry, once so important, but no longer dominant in the nation's economy, is centered in Ontario. Canada is a leading mineral producer. It is the world's largest source of asbestos, nickel, zinc, and silver, and the second largest source of potash, molybdenum, gypsum, uranium, and sulfur. The mineral wealth is located in many areas; some of the most productive regions are Sudbury, Ont. (copper and nickel); Timmins, Ont. (lead, zinc, and silver); and Kimberley, British Columbia (lead, zinc, and silver). Petroleum is found in Alberta and Saskatchewan. Fishing is an important economic activity in Canada. Cod and lobster from the Atlantic and salmon from the Pacific are the principal catches. About two thirds of the take is exported. The United States is Canada's leading trading partner, followed by Great Britain and Japan. Manufactured goods comprise the bulk of the imports; motor vehicles and parts are both the largest import and export. Other important exports are newsprint, wheat, and minerals. A major problem for Canada is that large segments of its economy—notably in manufacturing, petroleum, and mining—are controlled by foreign, especially U.S. interests. This deprives the nation of much of the profits of its industries and makes the economy vulnerable to developments outside Canada.

People. More than 40% of the Canadian population are of British descent, and some 30% are of French origin. Nearly 75% of the total population live in cities, the largest of which are MONTREAL, TORONTO, EDMONTON, VANCOUVER, CALGARY, HAMILTON, and Ottawa. Canada has complete religious liberty. The country is about equally divided between Roman Catholics and Protestants. The largest Protestant denominations are United Church of Canada, Anglican Church of Canada, and Presbyterian. English and French are the official languages, and federal documents are published in both languages.

Government. Canada is an independent constitutional monarchy and a member of the Commonwealth of Nations. The monarch of Great Britain and Northern Ireland is also the monarch of Canada and is represented in the country by the office of governor general. The basic constitutional document is the British North America Act of 1867. The Canadian federal government has authority in all matters not specifically reserved to the provincial governments. The provincial governments have power in the fields of property, civil rights, education, and local government. They may levy only direct taxes. The federal government may veto any provincial law. Power on the federal level is exercised by the Canadian Parliament and the cabinet of ministers, headed by the prime minister. The Parliament has two houses: the Senate and the House of Commons. There are a maximum of 110 senators, apportioned among the provinces and appointed by the governor general upon the advice of the prime minister. Senators may serve until age 75. Members of the House of Commons are elected, largely from single-member constituencies. After the 1971 census there were 264 members. Elections must be held at least every five years. The Commons may be dissolved and new elections held at the request of the prime minister. There are two main political parties; the Liberal party and the Progressive Conservative (or Conservative) party. Other important parties are the right-wing SOCIAL CREDIT party, the socialist New Democratic party, formerly the CO-OPERATIVE COMMONWEALTH FEDERATION, and the French Canadian nationalist Union Nationale. Canada has an independent judiciary; the highest court is the Supreme Court, with nine members.

Early History and French-British Rivalry. An unknown number of Indians and Eskimos inhabited Canada before the white man arrived. The Vikings landed in Canada A.D. c.1000. John CABOT, sailing under English auspices, touched the east coast in 1497. In 1534, the Frenchman Jacques CARTIER planted a cross on the Gaspé Peninsula. These and many other voyages to the Canadian coast were in search of a northwest passage to Asia. Subsequently, French-English rivalry dominated Canadian history until 1763. The first permanent white settlement in Canada was founded in 1605 by the sieur de MONTS and Samuel de CHAMPLAIN at Port Royal (now ANNAPOLIS ROYAL, N.S.) in ACADIA. A trading post was established in Quebec in 1608. Meanwhile the English, moving to support their claims under Cabot's discoveries, attacked Port Royal (1614) and captured Quebec (1629). However, the French regained Quebec (1632), and through the Company of New France (Company of One Hundred Associates), began to exploit the fur trade and establish new settlements. The French were primarily interested in fur trading. Between 1608 and 1640, fewer than 300 settlers arrived. The sparse French settlements sharply contrasted with the relatively dense English settlements along the Atlantic coast to the south. Under a policy initiated by Champlain, the French supported the Huron Indians in their warfare against the Iroquois; later in the 17th cent., when the Iroquois crushed the Huron, the French colony came near extinction. Exploration, however, continued. The Company of New France was disbanded (1663) by the French government, and the colony was placed under the rule of a royal governor, an intendant, and a bishop. The power exercised by these authorities may be seen in the careers of Louis de Buade, comte de FRONTENAC, the greatest of the colonial governors, Jean TALON, the first and greatest of the intendants, and François Xavier de LAVAL, the first bishop of Quebec. There was, however, conflict between the rulers, especially over the treatment of the Indians—the bishop regarding them as potential converts, the governor as means of trade. Meanwhile, both missionaries, such as Jacques MARQUETTE, and traders, such as RADISSON and Groseilliers, were extending French knowledge and influence. The greatest of all the empire builders in the west was Robert Cavelier, sieur de LA SALLE, who descended the Mississippi to its mouth and who envisioned the vast colony in the west that was made a reality by men like Duluth, Bienville, Iberville, and Cadillac. The French, however, did not go unchallenged. The English had claims on Acadia, and the Hudson's Bay Company in 1670 began to vie for the lucrative fur trade of the West. When the long series of wars between Britain and France broke out in Europe, they were paralleled in North America by the FRENCH AND INDIAN WARS. The Peace of Utrecht (1713) gave Britain Acadia, the Hudson Bay area, and Newfoundland. To strengthen their position the French built additional forts in the west (among them Detroit and Niagara). The decisive battle of the entire struggle took place in 1759, when Wolfe defeated Montcalm on the Plains of ABRAHAM, bringing about the fall of Quebec to the British. Montreal fell in 1760. By the Treaty of Paris in 1763, France ceded all its North American possessions to Britain (except Louisiana, which went to Spain).

British North America. The French residents of Quebec strongly resented the Royal Proclamation of 1763, which imposed British institutions on them. Many of its provisions, however, were reversed by the QUEBEC ACT (1774), which granted important concessions to the French and extended Quebec's borders westward and southward. This act infuriated the residents of the Thirteen Colonies (the fu-

Cross-references are indicated by SMALL CAPITALS.

ture United States). In the American Revolution the Canadians remained passively loyal to the British crown, and the effort of the Americans to take Canada failed dismally (see QUEBEC CAMPAIGN). Loyalists from the colonies in revolt (see UNITED EMPIRE LOYALISTS) fled to Canada and settled in large numbers in the Maritime Provinces and Quebec. The result, in Quebec, was sharp antagonism between the deeply rooted, Catholic French Canadians and the newly arrived, Protestant British. To deal with the problem the British passed the Constitutional Act (1791). It divided Quebec into Upper Canada (present-day Ontario), predominantly British and Protestant, and Lower Canada (present-day Quebec), predominantly French and Catholic. Each new province had its own legislature and institutions. This period was one of further exploration. Alexander MACKENZIE made voyages in 1789 to the Arctic Ocean and in 1793 to the Pacific. Mariners also reached the Pacific Northwest, and such men as Capt. James COOK, John Meares, and George VANCOUVER secured for Britain a firm hold on what is now British Columbia. During the War of 1812, Canadian and British soldiers repulsed several American invasions. The New Brunswick boundary (see AROOSTOOK WAR) and the boundary W of the Great Lakes was disputed with the United States for a time, but since the War of 1812 the long border has generally been peaceful. Rivalry between the NORTH WEST COMPANY and the Hudson's Bay Company erupted into bloodshed in the RED RIVER SETTLEMENT and was resolved by amalgamation of the companies in 1821. The new Hudson's Bay Company then held undisputed sway over RUPERT'S LAND and the Pacific West until U.S. immigrants challenged British possession of Oregon and obtained the present boundary (1846). After 1815 thousands of immigrants came to Canada from Scotland and Ireland. Movements for political reform arose. In Upper Canada, William Lyon MACKENZIE struggled against the FAMILY COMPACT. In Lower Canada, Louis J. Papineau led the French Canadian Reform party. There were rebellions in both provinces. The British sent Lord Durham to study the situation, and his famous report (1839) recommended the union of Upper and Lower Canada under responsible government. The two Canadas were made one province by the Act of Union (1841) and became known as Canada West and Canada East. Responsible government was achieved in 1849 (it had been granted to the MARITIME PROVINCES in 1847), largely as a result of the efforts of Robert BALDWIN and Louis H. LAFONTAINE. The movement for federation of all the Canadian provinces was given impetus in 1860s by the need for common defense, the desire for some central authority to press railroad construction, and the necessity for a solution to the problem posed by Canada West and Canada East, where the British majority and French minority were in conflict. When the Maritime Provinces, which sought union among themselves, met at the Charlottetown Conference of 1864, delegates from the other provinces of Canada attended. Two more conferences were held—the Quebec Conference later in 1864 and the London Conference in 1866 in England—before the British North America Act in 1867 made federation a fact. The four original provinces were Ontario (Canada West), Quebec (Canada East), Nova Scotia, and New Brunswick.

The New Nation. The new federation acquired the vast possessions of the Hudson's Bay Company in 1869. The Red River Settlement became the province of Manitoba in 1870. In 1873, Prince Edward Island joined the federation, and Alberta and Saskatchewan were admitted in 1905. Newfoundland joined in 1949. Canada's first prime minister was John A. MACDONALD (served 1867–73 and 1878–91), who sponsored the CANADIAN PACIFIC RAILWAY. In the West, religious tension and objections to lack of political representation and unfair land-grant and survey laws produced rebellions of métis, led by Louis RIEL in 1869–70 and 1884–85. Under the long administration (1896–1911) of Sir Wilfrid LAURIER, rising wheat prices attracted vast numbers of immigrants to the Prairie Provinces. Between 1891 and 1914, more than three million people came to Canada, largely from continental Europe. In the same period, mining operations were begun in the Klondike and the Canadian Shield. Large-scale development of hydroelectric resources helped foster industrialization and urbanization. Under the premiership of Robert L. BORDEN, Canada followed Britain and entered World War I. The struggle over military conscription, however, deepened the cleavage between French Canadians and their fellow citizens. During the depression that began in 1929, the Prairie Provinces were hard hit by droughts that shriveled the wheat fields. Farmers, who had earlier formed huge cooperatives, sought to press their interests through political movements such as Social Credit and the Co-Operative Commonwealth Federation. Under the premiership of W. L. Mackenzie KING, Canada played a vital role on the Allied side in World War II. Despite economic strain Canada emerged from the war with enhanced prestige and took an active role in the United Nations. Canada joined the North Atlantic Treaty Organization in 1949. Since the war, uranium, iron, and petroleum resources have been exploited; uses of atomic energy have been developed; and hydroelectric and thermal plants have been built to produce electricity for new and expanded industries. King was succeeded by Louis ST. LAURENT, the first French-speaking prime minister. John G. DIEFENBAKER, a Conservative, came to power in 1957. A major problem for Canada in recent decades has been to prevent economic domination by the United States. The St. Lawrence Seaway was opened in 1959. The Liberals returned to office in 1963 under Lester B. PEARSON. After much bitter debate, the Canadian Parliament in 1964 approved a new national flag, with a design of a red maple leaf on a white ground, bordered by two vertical red panels. The new flag symbolized a growing Canadian feeling against emphasizing Canada's ties with Great Britain. The Pearson government enacted a comprehensive social security program. The Montreal international exposition, Expo '67, opened in 1967 and was applauded for displaying a degree of taste and interest far superior to that of most such exhibitions. Pearson was succeeded by Pierre Elliot TRUDEAU, a Liberal, in 1968. The Trudeau government was faced with the increasingly violent separatist movement active in Quebec in the late 1960s and early 70s. In elections in Oct., 1972, Trudeau's Liberal party failed to win a majority, but he continued as prime minister, dependent on the small New Democratic party for votes to pass legislation; in July, 1974, the Liberals reestablished a majority, winning 141 of 264 seats in the House of Commons, and Trudeau remained prime minister.

CANADIAN PRIME MINISTERS SINCE CONFEDERATION *(including party and dates in office)*

Sir John A. Macdonald [Conservative] 1867–73
Alexander Mackenzie [Liberal] 1873–78
Sir John A. Macdonald [Conservative] 1878–91
Sir John J. C. Abbott [Conservative] 1891–92
Sir John S. D. Thompson [Conservative] 1892–94
Sir Mackenzie Bowell [Conservative] 1894–96
Sir Charles Tupper [Conservative] 1896
Sir Wilfred Laurier [Liberal] 1896–1911
Sir Robert L. Borden [Conservative/Unionist] 1911–20
Arthur Meighen [Conservative] 1920–21
W. L. M. King [Liberal] 1921–26
Arthur Meighen [Conservative] 1926
W. L. M. King [Liberal] 1926–30
Richard B. Bennett [Conservative] 1930–35
W. L. M. King [Liberal] 1935–48
Louis St. Laurent [Liberal] 1948–57
John G. Diefenbaker [Progressive/Conservative] 1957–63
Lester B. Pearson [Liberal] 1963–68
Pierre Elliott Trudeau [Liberal] 1968–

Bibliography. Classic works on early Canada are those of Francis Parkman. See also Edgar McInnis, *Canada, a Political and Social History* (3d ed. 1969); R. R. Kruegel and R. G. Corder, *Canada, a New Geography* (1970); G. M. Wrong, *The Rise and Fall of New France* (2 vol., 1928; repr. 1970); D. G. Creighton, *The Story of Canada* (rev. ed. 1971); National Geographic Society, Washington, D.C., *Exploring Canada from Sea to Sea* (3d ed. 1971); Wilfrid Eggleston, *The Road to Nationhood* (1946, repr. 1972); John MacDougall, *Rural Life in Canada* (1913, repr. 1973); R. C. Brown and Ramsay Cook, *Canada, 1896–1921: A Nation Transformed* (1974). See also the multivolume history *Canadian Centenary Series* (1963–).

Canada balsam, yellow, oily, resinous exudation obtained from the BALSAM FIR. It is an oleoresin (see RESIN) with a pleasant odor but a biting taste. It is a TURPENTINE rather than a true balsam. On standing, the essential oil in Canada balsam evaporates, leaving behind the resin as a hard, transparent varnish. Canada balsam is valued as an optical mounting cement, e.g., for lenses and microscope slides, since it yields, when dissolved in an equal volume of xylene, a noncrystallizing cement with a refractive index nearly equal to that of ordinary glass. It is used also in paints and polishes.

Canada Company, land settlement company chartered in England in 1826. It was initiated by the Scottish novelist John Galt, who proposed that Upper Canada (Ontario) sell government lands in order to raise money to compensate settlers who had suffered losses from the War of 1812. Galt became (1827) the company's representative in Canada. The Canada Company acquired lands along the Lake Huron side of the S Ontario peninsula and founded Guelph and Goderich. In general the company was one of the most successful colonizing schemes, meeting its charter requirements by 1843. It remained in operation until the 1950s.

Canada First movement, party that appeared in Canada soon after confederation (1867). Its purpose was to encourage the growth of nonpartisan loyalty to the new dominion of Canada. In Toronto, in 1874, it founded the *Nation* and the National Club and entered the political field as the Canadian National Association, which encouraged immigration and native industry, and a more independent stance for Canada. Although its official career was shortlived, the party's ideals were expressed by Canadian writers and were absorbed by the older political parties. In this way the movement had an effect on the development of Canadian nationalism. See W. S. Wallace, *The Growth of Canadian National Feeling* (1927).

Canada jay: see JAY.

Canada rice: see WILD RICE.

Canada thistle: see THISTLE.

Canaday, John, 1907–, American art critic, b. Fort Scott, Kansas. Canaday is noted for his conservative position in the art world. It is expressed in his column for the New York *Times,* which covers a wide range of art subjects. He is an authority on 19th-century art. His works include *Mainstreams of Modern Art* (1961), *Culture Gulch* (1969), and *Lives of the Painters* (4 vol., 1969). Early in 1974, Canaday began a weekly column of restaurant reviews for the *Times.* He also writes mysteries under the pseudonym Mathew Head.

Canadian, river, 906 mi (1,458 km) long, rising in NE N.Mex. and flowing E across N Texas and central Okla. into the Arkansas River in E Okla. In the mid-1800s, the Canadian River valley was followed by pioneers going West along the Fort Smith–Santa Fe Trail. Eufaula Reservoir stores the water of the Canadian and North Canadian rivers; its dam generates electricity. Sanford Dam impounds Lake Meredith, which lies over one of the world's largest natural gas fields. The lake is part of Lake Meredith National Recreation Area (see NATIONAL PARKS AND MONUMENTS, table).

Canadian art and architecture. Among the outstanding art forms of early colonial Canada was French-Canadian wood carving, chiefly sculptured figures of saints and retables for the churches. This art flourished from 1675 (when Bishop Laval established a school of arts and crafts near Quebec) until c.1850. The art reached its height after the separation from France when, freed from the French Renaissance tradition, it developed a local character beautifully exemplified in such work as that in the Church of the Holy Family on Orléans Island and in the Provincial Museum at Quebec. The two great Quebec families of carvers were the Levasseurs (18th cent.) and the Baillairgés (19th cent.). The colonial period also produced fine embroidery (examples are kept at the Ursuline convent, Quebec) and several outstanding portraits executed in a naive folk-art style. Before 1880 almost the only other paintings and drawings produced in Canada were those by the colonial topographers, many of them English army officers. Most of this work is purely documentary. Paul KANE, who painted Indians, and Cornelius KRIEGHOFF, who depicted the life of the settlers, were the earliest GENRE painters. Thomas Davies produced vibrant landscapes in watercolor in the second half of the 18th cent. J. A. Fraser, known for his scenes of the Rockies, was instrumental in founding the Ontario College of Art at Toronto in 1875. Five years later the Royal Canadian Academy of Arts (at Montreal) and the National Gallery of Canada (at Ottawa) were founded. Since 1910 the National Gallery has played an active part in Canadian life through its traveling exhibits. Its collection is the finest in Canada. Today there are art schools and galleries in all the major Canadian cities. In the late 19th cent. the outstanding artists were the landscapists Daniel Fowler, F. M. Bell-Smith, and Robert Gagen; the portrait painters Robert Harris, Antoine Palamondon, and Théophile Hamel; and two great cartoonists, J. W. Bengough and Henri Julien. They were followed by a number of celebrated painters, including George A. Reid, Franklin Brownell, Florence Carlyle, F. McG. Knowles, Horatio WALKER, M. A. de Foy SUZOR-CÔTÉ, William Brymner, Maurice Cullen, Tom THOMSON, and J. W. MORRICE, who worked chiefly outside Canada and is perhaps the most celebrated of Canadian landscapists. In 1920, Franklin Carmichael, Lawren Harris, A. Y. Jackson, Franz H. Johnston, Arthur Lismer, J. E. H. MacDonald, and F. Horsman Varley formed the Group of Seven, dedicated to painting the Canadian landscape. Traveling and working all over the dominion, they did much to awaken the interest of the country at large. Their approach, which emphasized flat, strongly colored design, tended toward a poster style. The cultural center of the Seven was Toronto; in Montreal toward the end of World War II a new, radical group was formed, including Alfred PELLAN, John Lyman, P. E. Borduas, and J. P. RIOPELLE. They evolved the *automatiste* movement, influenced by Matisse, Picasso, and SURREALISM. Other major painters, working in a wide variety of styles, include David MILNE, Emily CARR, Pegi Nicol MacLeod, B. C. Binning, J. L. Shadbolt, and Harold Town. In the late 1960s the OP ART movement flourished in Montreal. Canadian painters currently at work employ a variety of styles and cannot be grouped as a school. After the decline of wood carving, little sculpture was produced until 1900. Philippe HÉBERT, Suzor-Côté, Alfred Laliberté, Tait McKenzie, and Walter Allward became well-established sculptors. Among the later sculptors, Emanuel Hahn, Louis Archambault, Elizabeth Wyn Wood, and Henri Hébert are notable. The French Canadians have an important tradition in such decorative arts and crafts as metalworking and rug hooking. In the graphic arts Clarence Gagnon, W. J. Phillips, and Albert Dumouchel are considered among the foremost Canadian print makers of the 20th cent. Canadian architecture adheres in the main to foreign trends, especially in the planning of public buildings. From the 18th to the 20th cent., French Renaissance, English Georgian, regency, and Gothic revival designs were successively dominant. A notable example of Gothic revival is found in the buildings of Parliament Hall, Ottawa (begun 1859), by Thomas Fuller and others. Based on the ideas of H. H. Richardson, well-known structures in the château style are the Château Frontenac (1890), Quebec City, and the Banff Springs Hotel (1913), Banff, Alberta. Major modern buildings include the Electrical Building and Civic Auditorium, Vancouver, British Columbia, and the Shakespearean Festival Theatre, Stratford, Ont. Church and domestic architecture in Canada have consistently shown originality. Particularly in Quebec during the colonial period, charming rural stone houses and churches were developed—typically low and rectangular, with steep pitched roofs and uptilting eaves. Safdie's remarkable "Habitat," a dynamic and original approach to housing, was erected in Montreal for Expo '67. For a discussion of Canadian Indian art see NORTH AMERICAN INDIAN ART. See studies on Canadian art by Graham McInnes (rev. ed. 1950), J. R. Harper (1966 and 1972), and William Townsend, ed. (1970); on architecture by Alan Gowans (1958) and Pierre Mayrand and John Bland (1971); Dennis Reid, *A Concise History of Canadian Painting* (1974).

Canadian football: see under FOOTBALL.

Canadian literature, English. Although Canadian writing began as an imitative colonial literature, it has steadily developed its own national characteristics. Because of the huge immigrations, first of New England Puritans from 1760 on and later of American Loyalists during the Revolution, Canadian literature followed U.S. models almost until the confederation in 1867. Before 1800 the rigors of pioneering left little time for the writing or the appreciation of literature. The only notable works were journals, such as that of Jacob Bailey, and the recorded travels of explorers, such as Henry Kelsey, Samuel Hearne, and Sir Alexander Mackenzie. The first Canadian novelist of note was John Richardson, whose *Wacousta* (1832) popularized the genre of the national historical novel. With *The Clockmaker* (1836) T. C. Haliburton began his humorous series on Sam Slick, the Yankee peddler. Historical novelists writing c.1900 included William Kirby, author of *The Golden Dog* (1877), and Sir Gilbert Parker, author of *The Seats of the Mighty* (1896). The novels of Sara Jeannette Duncan, such as *A Social Departure* (1890), were noted for their satire and humor. The Rev. C. W. Gordon (Ralph Connor) produced *Black Rock* (1898), a series of novels on pioneer life in W Canada. Animal stories became popular in the works of Ernest Thompson Seton, Sir C. G. D. Roberts, and Margaret Marshall Saunders. Since 1900, Canadian novels have tended toward stricter realism, but have remained predominantly regional. Among the most prominent authors have been Lucy M. Montgomery, author of *Anne of Green Gables* (1908); Mazo de la Roche, well known for her series on the Whiteoaks family of Jalna; Frederick P. Grove, author of *Settlers of the Marsh* (1925), a novel of farm life; and Laura Salverson and Nellie McClung, novelists of immigrant and rural life in W Canada. Important novelists during and after World War II include Morley Callaghan, Gwethalyn Graham, John Buell, Hugh MacLennan, Mordecai Richler, Malcolm Lowry, Ethel Wilson, Robertson Davies, Brian Moore, Margaret Laurence, and Margaret Atwood. Their novels have focused attention on Canadian city life, social problems, and the large problem of Canadian cultural division. Stephen Leacock is well known for his humorous essays as well as for his scholarship. Other notable essayists include Sir Andrew Macphail, Archibald MacMechan, and Lorne Pierce. Genuinely Canadian poetry was late in developing. In the 18th cent. Puritan hymnists, such as Henry Alline, and refugee Tory satirists, such as Jonathan Odell, took their models from American colonial or English neoclassical literature. Before the confederation of 1867 the only poets of note were Charles Sangster, the first to make use of native material, and Charles Heavysege, whose long poetic drama *Saul* brought him widespread acclaim. Starting c.1880, the "confederation school"—C. G. D. Roberts, Archibald Lampman, Bliss Carman, and Duncan Campbell Scott—began producing a large body of romantic poetry, describing nature and Canadian rural life. In 1905, long after her death in 1887, Isabella V. Crawford was recognized as an important poet; she was followed by Emily Pauline Johnson and Marjorie Pickthall. Other poets of the early part of the century included Wilfred Campbell, W. H. Drummond, Francis Sherman, John McCrae, and the greatly popular Robert W. Service. In 1926 the prolific E. J. Pratt broke away from the romantic tradition with *The Titans*; his highly original and powerful epics place him among the foremost Canadian poets. Notable contemporary poets in the Pratt tradition include Kenneth Leslie, Earle Birney, W. W. E. Ross, Dorothy Livesay, and Anne Marriott. Other poets sharing the modern cosmopolitan tradition of the United States and W Europe are F. R. Scott, L. A. Mackay, A. M. Klein, P. K. Page, Irving Layton, Raymond Souster, James Reaney, Margaret Avison, Phyllis Webb, Leonard Cohen, and Margaret Atwood. See bibliography by R. E. Watters (2d ed. 1972); C. F. Klinck, ed., *A Literary History of Canada* (1965); Edmund Wilson, *O Canada* (1965); Norah Story, *The Oxford Companion to Canadian History and Literature* (1967); A. J. M. Smith, ed., *Modern Canadian Verse in English and French* (1967); R. P. Baker, *A History of English Canadian Literature to the Confederation* (1920, repr. 1968).

Canadian literature, French. Except for the narratives of French explorers (such as Samuel de Champlain and Pierre Esprit Radisson) and missionaries, no notable writing was produced before the British conquest of New France in 1759. Since that time the inspiration of most Canadian writing in French has been the passionate concern of French Canadians to preserve their identity in a country dominated by the English language and cultural tradition and by the Protestant religion. There has been little contact between the two literatures. Until the 20th cent. French Canadian literature found its models mainly in writers of France and its themes in nationalism, the simple lives and folkways of the habitants, and the devotion to the Roman Catholic Church. The first artistic expression of this spirit was F. X. Garneau's *Histoire du Canada* (1845–48), still the classic of French Canadian nationalism. Other historians, including Benjamin Sulte, Thomas Chapais, and L. A. Groulx, also placed their emphasis on pride in and protection of their French heritage. This school of thought inspired the first nationalist poet, Octave Crémazie, and the Quebec school of poets, novelists, and historians who began a deliberate effort in 1861 to create a national literature, with such French authors as Hugo and Lamartine as their chief models. The group included Philippe Aubert de Gaspé, J. B. A. Ferland, Louis-Honoré Fréchette, Pamphile LeMay, Abbé H. R. Casgrain, Antoine Gérin-Lajoie, and Nérée Beauchemin. There developed c.1900 a new group of writers, chiefly in Montreal, who tried to achieve the stricter technique and keener artistic perceptions of the PARNASSIANS of France. These more sophisticated poets included Charles Gill, René Chopin, and Louis Dantin. Some writers of the new group, such as Émile Nelligan, considered French Canada's first native poetic genius, and Paul Morin, abandoned the national note for exotic subjects; others, such as Albert Lozeau and Albert Ferland, found inspiration in Canadian nature. About this time men of letters, notably Adjutor Rivard, began a movement to preserve the purity of the French language in Canada. Influential critics included Camille Roy, Henri d'Arles, and the poet Louis Dantin. In the novel, a rural romanticism was expressed in the works of Félicité Angers (Laure Conan). A more realistic fiction took impetus from Louis Hémon's *Maria Chapdelaine* (1913), a novel of the peasants of the Lake St. John country. There followed a stream of fiction on habitant life in the backwoods, on the farms, and in the villages, by such native Canadians as Robert Choquette, F. A. Savard, Claude Henri Grignon, Roger Lemelin, and Ringuet. Although some novels were set in cities and the notable author Robert Charbonneau explored the psychological defeatism of his characters, the realistic regional novel about the simple Catholic community remained dominant until the 1950s. Important poets since 1914 include Clément Marchand, whose inspiration is often religious; Alfred DesRochers, who writes of the life of the soil; and Robert Choquette and Roger Brien, whose romantic lyrics are eloquently individualistic. Following World War II there was evidence of a new, less self-conscious spirit. Poets and novelists, trying to settle the vexing problem of language, declared that pure French should be standard, with the use of Canadianisms accepted wherever these served a purpose. Although it was still possible to detect the influence of France (often with a lag of 30 years), at midcentury much creative writing in Canada, as elsewhere, was characterized by experiment with subject matter and technique. Among the poets of the new trend were Anne Hébert, Alain Grandbois, Saint-Denys-Garneau, Gatien Lapointe, Pierre Trottier, Rina Lasnier, Fernand Oellette, and Jacques Godbout and Jean Guy Pilon, the last two forming the nucleus of a group in Montreal which started the literary magazine *Liberté* in 1959. In fiction of the 1950s and 60s urban problems replaced rural concerns, and irony and skepticism national pride. Foremost among contemporary novelists are Gabrielle Roy, Yves Thériault, Robert Elie, Roger Lemelin, André Langevin, Jean Simard, Claire Martin, Marie-Claire Blais, and Girard Bessette. See Ian F. Fraser, *The Spirit of French Canada* (1939); Edmund Wilson, *O Canada* (1964); A. J. M. Smith, ed., *Modern Canadian Verse in English and French* (1967); Norah Story, *The Oxford Companion to Canadian History and Literature* (1967).

Canadian Mounted Police: see ROYAL CANADIAN MOUNTED POLICE.

Canadian National Railways, government owned but corporately operated transportation system in Canada, extending from coast to coast with many branch lines in each province and in the United States. The system is an amalgamation of five separate railroad enterprises that were unified in 1922. The system also operates telegraph, steamship, and air services.

Canadian Pacific Railway, transcontinental transportation system in Canada and extending into the United States, privately owned and operated. The construction of a railroad crossing the continent in Canadian territory was one of the conditions on which British Columbia entered the confederation in 1871. After many difficulties and a political scandal, intensive work began in 1880. The main line from Montreal to the Pacific coast was completed in 1885.

Canadian Shield or **Laurentian Plateau,** U-shaped region of ancient rock, the nucleus of North America, stretching N from the Great Lakes to the Arctic Ocean. Covering more than half of Canada, it also includes most of Greenland and extends into the United States as the Adirondack Mts. and the Superior Highlands. The first part of North America to be permanently elevated above sea level, it has remained almost wholly untouched by successive encroachments of the sea upon the continent. It is the earth's greatest area of exposed Archaean-age rock; the metamorphic rocks of which it is largely composed were probably formed in the Precambrian era. Repeatedly uplifted and eroded, it is today an area of low relief (c.1,000–2,000 ft/305–610 m above sea level) with a few monadnocks and low mountain ranges (including the Torngat and Laurentian Mts.) probably eroded from the plateau during the Cenozoic era. During the Pleistocene epoch, continental ice sheets depressed the land surface (see HUDSON BAY), scooped out thousands of lake basins, and carried away much of the region's soil. Drainage is generally very poor on the shield. The southern part of the shield has thick forests while the north is covered with tundra. The region is largely undeveloped but has great water-power potential and is a source of minerals, timber, and fur-bearing animals.

canafistula (kän″yəfĭs′chələ): see SENNA.

canaigre (kənĭ′grē): see BUCKWHEAT.

Çanakkale (chänäk′kälĕ) or **Chanakkale** (-kälä), city (1970 pop. 27,074), capital of Çanakkale prov., NW Turkey, on the Asian shore of the Dardanelles. It is famous for its fine pottery and has an important fish-canning industry. The city has long been fortified and has a 15th-century fort, which is still used by the Turkish army. In World War I the city and fort were bombarded (1915) during the Gallipoli campaign. Near Çanakkale are the mouth of the historic Aegospotamos River and the ruins of the ancient towns of Abydos and Sestos.

Çanakkale Boğazı, Turkey: see DARDANELLES.

Canal, Antonio: see CANALETTO.

canal, an artificial waterway constructed for navigation or for the movement of water. The digging of canals for irrigation probably dates back to the beginnings of agriculture, and traces of canals have been found in the regions of ancient civilizations. Canals are also used to provide municipal and industrial water supplies. The drainage of wet lands may be accomplished by means of a canal; by this method the Fens of England and the Zuider Zee in the Netherlands were drained. Canals can be used for flood control by diverting water from threatened areas into storage basins or to other outlets. In some cases canals are used to generate electricity; the Moscow-Volga Canal is used for such a purpose. Navigation canals developed after irrigation canals and for a long time were level, shallow cuts, or had inclined planes up which vessels were hauled from one level to the next; locks (see LOCK, CANAL) developed separately in China (10th cent.) and Europe (Holland; 13th cent.). Over the years canals have been expanded in width and depth in order to accommodate larger craft, and they have, in some cases, been constructed to form bridges or to pass through tunnels to overcome topographic difficulties. Movement on canals was long accomplished by animal tows or by poling; in the 20th cent. mechanized tows and self-propelled barges appeared. The GRAND CANAL of China (the longest in the world) was completed in the 13th cent. and is the most notable of the early canals. France, Belgium, Holland, and Germany were the first in Europe to develop inland waterway systems by using canals to connect rivers; these countries now have a dense network of waterways (see RHINE CANALS; MIDLAND CANAL). Canal building was widespread in the 18th and 19th cent. During that period England developed an elaborate canal network, and there was also a canal-building boom in the United States in the 19th cent., especially after the completion of the ERIE CANAL. However, the rise of railroads brought a decline in the building and use of canals as inland waterways. Canals have been built to shorten sea voyages or to make them less hazardous, e.g., the SUEZ CANAL, the PANAMA CANAL, and the KIEL CANAL. Canals improve conditions on natural waterways by bypassing falls (the WELLAND SHIP CANAL), shallows, or swift currents (the Sip Canal in the Danube River's Iron Gate gorge). Canals may provide inland cities with direct access to the sea (the MANCHESTER SHIP CANAL), or shorten the distance between cities (the ALBERT CANAL). In the 20th cent. canals regained importance, as modern technology provided the means to overcome greater topographic obstacles and facilitated the construction of larger canals and the expansion of existing ones. See T. C. Bridges, *Great Canals* (1936); P. S. Payne, *The Canal Builders* (1959); H. S. Drago, *Canal Days in America* (1972).

Canal du Midi (känäl′ dü mēdē′), canal, c.150 mi (240 km) long, linking Sète and Toulouse, S France. It was built to carry oceangoing ships between the Atlantic Ocean and the Mediterranean Sea, but because of its size it now carries only barge traffic.

Canalejas y Méndez, José (hōsā′ känälā′häs ē män′dāth), 1854–1912, Spanish politician. After holding several cabinet posts, he became premier in 1910. A democratic radical who hoped to reform the Liberal party, Canalejas advocated curbing the power of the religious orders and breaking up the large estates, but made little progress. His firm measures against labor unrest alienated many of his left-wing supporters, and he was assassinated by an anarchist.

Canaletto (känälĕt′tō), 1697–1768, Venetian painter, whose original name was Antonio Canal. He studied with his father, Bernardo Canal, a theatrical scene painter, and spent several years in Rome. Returning to Venice, he devoted himself to painting the linear, dramatic, and topographically accurate Venetian scenes upon which his fame chiefly rests. From 1746 to 1755 he lived in England and produced many fine landscapes, notably those of Eton College. He painted series of picturesque views for English collectors, one of which is in the collection of the Duke of Bedford. Canaletto is unsurpassed as an architectural painter. His works are finely detailed yet delicate and airy. Among his notable works are *View on the Grand Canal* and *Regatta on the Grand Canal* (National Gall., London); *Church of Santa Maria Della Salute* (Louvre); *View of Venice* (Uffizi); and *The Piazzetta, Venice* (Metropolitan Mus.). He was a master draftsman and produced many superb drawings and etchings that were not preparatory but complete in themselves. Toward the end of his life his painting became increasingly mechanical and mannered but in no way less skillful. Examples of Canaletto's works are in the major European and American collections. His nephew and pupil, Bernardo Bellotto, was also called Canaletto. See studies by Vittorio Moschini (tr. 1956) and W. G. Constable (1961).

Canal Zone: see PANAMA CANAL ZONE.

Cananaean (kānənē′ən), epithet of St. SIMON.

Canandaigua (kănəndā′gwə), city (1970 pop. 10,488), seat of Ontario co., W central N.Y., in the Finger Lakes region, at the northern end of Canandaigua Lake; settled 1789, inc. 1913. It is a resort and farm-trade center, with various industries. The county historical-society museum contains a copy of the treaty with the Iroquois Confederacy, signed there in 1794 by Timothy Pickering. The courthouse was the scene of Susan B. Anthony's trial (1873) for voting. A U.S. veterans' hospital is in Canandaigua.

Canandaigua Lake: see FINGER LAKES.

Canaris, Constantine: see KANARIS, CONSTANTINE.

Canaris, Wilhelm (vĭl′hĕlm känä′rĭs), 1887–1945, German admiral. He occupied various positions in the German navy during and after World War I. In 1935 he was made chief of the *Abwehr* [military intelligence]. A conservative, Canaris at first welcomed Hitler, but Hitler's methods and the fear that a new war would destroy Germany drove him into the opposition. The *Abwehr* became a center of conspiracy against the regime. Under Canaris's protection, one of his subordinates, Hans Oster, helped organize opposition to the Nazi regime. In April, 1943, many of Oster's co-conspirators were arrested and the *Abwehr* was put under constant surveillance, but Canaris was not dismissed until Feb., 1944. He was arrested shortly after the attempt (July, 1944) on Hitler's life, though he was not directly involved in the plot. He was executed by the Gestapo in April, 1945.

Canarsee Indians (kənär′sē), North American Indians whose language belongs to the Algonquian-Wakashan linguistic stock (see AMERICAN INDIAN LANGUAGES). They occupied the western part of Long Island, N.Y., and sold the site of Brooklyn to the Dutch. They paid tribute to the Mohawk, and when they stopped paying and defied the Mohawk, they were almost destroyed.

canary, common name for a familiar cage bird of the family Ploceidae (Old World FINCH family), descended from either the wild serin finch or from the very similar wild canary, *Serinus canarius,* of the Canary Islands, Madeira, and the Azores and introduced into Europe in the late 15th or early 16th cent. The wild birds are usually gray or green; selective breeding has produced both plain and variegated birds, mostly yellow and buff but sometimes greenish. Germany is traditionally the center for training and breeding canaries; the Harz mt. and the St. Andreasberg canaries originated there. The birds are trained to sing by exposure to other birds of superior ability or to musical instruments. The song of roller canaries is a series of "tours," a complex set of rolling trills delivered with the bill almost closed; choppers sing with the bill open. Canaries breed rapidly in captivity and with proper care may live to 15 years or more. Canaries are classified in the phylum CHORDATA, subphylum Vertebrata, class Aves, order Passeriformes, family Ploceidae.

Canary Islands, Span. *Islas Canarias,* group of seven islands (1970 pop. 1,170,224), 2,808 sq mi (7,273 sq km), off Spanish Sahara, in the Atlantic Ocean. They constitute two provinces of Spain. Santa Cruz de Tenerife (1970 pop. 590,514), 1,239 sq mi (3,209 sq km), includes Tenerife, Palma, Gomera, and Hierro. Las Palmas (1970 pop. 579,710), 1,569 sq mi (4,064 sq km), includes Grand Canary, Lanzarote, and Fuerteventura. Fuerteventura is 67 mi (108 km) from the African coast. The islands, of volcanic origin, are rugged; Mt. Teide (12,162 ft/3,707 m) is the highest point in Spain. Pliny mentions an expedition to the Canaries c.40 B.C., and they may have been the Fortunate Islands of later classical writers. They were occasionally visited by Arabs and by European travelers in the Middle Ages. Jean de Béthencourt, a Norman, settled at Lanzarote in 1402 and, with the support of the kingdom of Castile, became its king in 1404. The Treaty of Alcácovas (1479) between Portugal and Spain recognized Spanish sovereignty over the Canaries; conquest of the Guanches, the indigenous inhabitants of the islands, was completed in 1496. The islands became an important base for voyages to the Americas. The Canaries were frequently raided by pirates and privateers; Las Palmas beat off Francis Drake in 1595 but was ravaged by the Dutch in 1599. In the French Revolutionary Wars, Horatio Nelson was repulsed (1797) at Santa Cruz. Wine was the main export of the Canaries until the grape blight of 1853; its place was taken by cochineal until aniline dyes came into general use; sugarcane then became the chief commercial crop. Today the leading exports are bananas, tomatoes, potatoes, and tobacco, which are grown where irrigation is possible. There is fishing on the open seas, and the Canaries, with their warm climate and fine beaches, have become a major tourist center.

canary wood or **canary whitewood,** name applied to the timber of the tulip tree (see MAGNOLIA) in some parts of the United States and to an Australian eucalyptus, the Indian mulberry, and to two species of the genus *Persea* of the laurel family.

canasta: see RUMMY.

Canberra (kăn′bərə), city (1971 pop. 141,575), capital of Australia, in the Australian Capital Territory, SE Australia. The Canberra urban agglomeration (1971 pop. 156,334) includes a small area in New South Wales. The federal government is the largest employer in Canberra; there are also printing and service industries. The site chosen (1908) for the capital city was first settled in 1824. In 1913, Canberra officially became the second capital of the commonwealth (succeeding Melbourne); however, although the Parliament first met there in 1927, the transfer of federal functions was not completed until after World War II. The city was planned by the American architect Walter Burley Griffin. Canberra is the seat of the Royal Military College, Australian National Univ., Mount Stromlo Observatory, and other research and scientific institutions.

Canby, Edward Richard Sprigg, 1817–73, Union general in the Civil War, b. Kentucky, grad. West Point, 1839. He fought in the Seminole War and in the Mexican War. In the Civil War, Canby commanded the Dept. of New Mexico, where he thoroughly repelled the Confederate invasion (1862). He was made a brigadier general of volunteers in March, 1862, and was on special duty in the War Dept. in Washington from Jan., 1863, to March, 1864, except for four months as the commander of New York City during the DRAFT RIOTS of 1863. Canby was promoted to major general in May, 1864, and assigned to command the Military Division of West Mississippi. He captured Mobile in April, 1865, and in May received the surrender of the last Confederate armies. After the war Canby held various commands in the South until 1870, when he was sent to the Dept. of the Columbia on the Pacific coast. He was killed during a peace conference with the MODOC INDIANS. See biography by M. L. Heyman, Jr. (1959).

Canby, Henry Seidel, 1878–1961, American editor and critic, b. Wilmington, Del., grad. Yale, 1899. He taught at Yale for over 20 years, achieving professorial rank in 1922. He established and edited (1920–24) the *Literary Review* of the New York *Evening Post,* afterwards joining with others to found and edit (1924–36) the *Saturday Review of Literature; Seven Years' Harvest* (1936) is his intellectual diary culled from its files. His critical and literary works include *Classic Americans* (1931), *Thoreau* (1939), *Whitman* (1943), *The Brandywine* (1941), *The Gothic Age of the American College* (1936), and *Turn West, Turn East: Mark Twain and Henry James* (1951).

cancan (kăn′kăn), a lively French dance marked chiefly by high kicking. It was developed in Paris in the 1830s and became a popular social dance there. By the mid-19th cent. it was incorporated into dance revues and stage productions. Jacques Offenbach wrote the best-known cancan music. Henri de

Toulouse-Lautrec made celebrated paintings and lithographs of famous cancan dancers.

Cancer [Lat.,=the crab], in astronomy, CONSTELLATION lying on the ECLIPTIC (the sun's apparent path through the heavens) between Gemini and Leo; it is a constellation of the ZODIAC. It contains the star cluster PRAESEPE, but no bright stars. The tropic of Cancer takes its name from this constellation, in which the summer solstice was located about 2,000 years ago. Now, because of the PRECESSION OF THE EQUINOXES, the summer solstice has moved westward into the constellation Gemini. Cancer reaches its highest point in the evening sky in March.

cancer, common term for NEOPLASMS, or tumors, that are malignant. Like benign tumors, malignant tumors do not respond to body mechanisms that limit growth. Unlike benign growths, malignant tumors show an atypical cell structure, with undifferentiated, rather than functional, specialized cells. Also unlike normal cells, cancer cells growing in laboratory tissue culture do not stop growing when they touch each other on a glass or other solid surface but grow in masses several layers deep; they are said to lack contact inhibition. Loss of contact inhibition accounts for two other characteristics of cancer cells: invasiveness of surrounding tissues, and metastasis, or spreading via the lymph system or blood to other tissues and organs. Cancers are graded as to degree of malignancy on a scale of one through four; often, however, the distinction between even benign and malignant neoplasms is obscure. Virtually all organs and tissues are susceptible to cancer. Cancer tissue, growing without limits, competes with normal tissue for nutrients, eventually killing normal cells by nutritional deprivation. Cancerous tissue also causes secondary effects, with the symptoms of a malignant growth caused by the pressure of the growing tumor against surrounding tissue, or the metastasis of cancer cells and their invasion of other organs. Symptoms are often nonspecific, e.g., weakness, loss of appetite, and weight loss. Sometimes side effects of tumor growth are more severe than the actual effects of the malignancy; for example, some tumors secrete materials such as serotonin and histamine that can cause drastic vascular changes. A tumor of an endocrine gland, such as an adrenal carcinoma, may be responsible for producing enormously increased numbers of hormone-secreting cells. Conversely, cancers that destroy tissue may also have serious effects, e.g., malignant destruction of bone tissue may raise the blood level of calcium. A large proportion of human cancers may be caused, or at least triggered, by various chemical agents. Alkylating agents such as NITROGEN MUSTARD are thought to have a carcinogenic effect because they chemically alter the cell's nucleic acids. Nitrites, common additives in processed meat, react with amines in the stomach to form nitrosoamines, which some authorities believe may be carcinogenic to humans. Other commonly occurring carcinogens are azo dyes, polycyclic hydrocarbons, and urethane. Certain carcinogens present occupational hazards. Asbestos particles, once inhaled, remain in the lung and act as an irritant. In the asbestos and construction industries, workers have a high probability of developing a fatal cancer of the chest lining or abdominal lining 25 to 30 years after the initial inhalation of ASBESTOS. Oral cancer, common in India, is commonly attributed to the chewing of betel nuts. Although the apparently increasing incidence of some types of highly malignant cancers, e.g., certain lung cancers and LEUKEMIAS, may be a result of improvements in disease detection and diagnosis, an increase in cigarette smoking and an increase of atmospheric pollutants are also thought to play a part. Other cancers may be triggered by such changes in the body's internal environment as hormone imbalances. For example, as first reported in 1970, some daughters of mothers who had been given diethylstilbestrol (DES) during pregnancy to prevent miscarriage, developed vaginal adenocarcinomas as young women. There are genetic tendencies for certain types of cancer, e.g., breast or stomach cancer, and certain benign tumors, e.g., certain tumors of the eye, cartilage, and skin, some of which may later become malignant. Physical agents such as X rays and radioactive elements are also carcinogenic; the high incidence of leukemia and other cancers in Japanese survivors of the atomic bombing of Hiroshima and Nagasaki is evidence of this carcinogenic effect. In light-skinned people who spend much time outdoors, sunlight may be carcinogenic. Sometimes irritations and diseases may predispose an individual to cancer, as in the occurrence of cancer of the esophagus associated with frequently swallowing very hot liquids. Increasing evidence implicates viruses in induction of cancer. In the early 20th cent., Peyton Rous, an American virologist, showed that certain fowl sarcomas could be transmitted by injection of an agent invisible under the microscope and later shown to be an RNA-containing virus. Since then other oncogenic, or tumor-causing, viruses have been identified in experimental animals. Viruses of the herpes group, some of which cause cold sores and chicken pox, have been shown to cause cancer in experimental animals. Recent evidence indicates that other members of the herpes group, such as the virus causing infectious mononucleosis, may cause human cancer. Cancers can often be detected by visual observation, palpation, X-ray study, inspection by various optical probing instruments (endoscopy), and BIOPSY. Cancers caught early, before metastasis, have the best cure rates. Once found, cancers are treated by surgery, chemotherapy, and radiation. Surgery is most effective if the cancer is caught early, while still localized. Some cancers that spread to the lymph system have frequently prompted extensive surgical removal of tissue (see MASTECTOMY). Many cancers formerly treated surgically are now being attacked by other means, e.g., radiation therapy. Use of radioactive elements specific for particular target organs, such as radioactive iodine specific for the thyroid gland, is effective in treating malignancies of those organs. Laser beams are used to treat certain cancers, and certain subatomic particles, i.e., pions, are being used experimentally. Chemotherapeutic agents that are IMMUNOSUPPRESSIVE DRUGS are used to selectively destroy cancer cells. In general they interfere with nucleic acid and protein synthesis; rapidly proliferating cells like cancer cells are most susceptible. Hormones such as ESTROGEN and TESTOSTERONE, which may be carcinogenic under some conditions, are also used in cancer chemotherapy. Unfortunately, currently available chemotherapeutic agents are not usually curative but merely ameliorate the severity of the disease; in addition, they are often toxic to normal rapidly proliferating cells such as bone marrow cells. A chemotherapeutic technique known as isolated perfusion can be used to minimize exposure to many toxic drugs. In this method a pump and two tubes are attached to two places in a network of blood vessels so that the drug only circulates through the part of the system that is malignant. New approaches to cancer therapy, still largely in the experimental stage, include immunological methods such as vaccinating against cancer-causing viruses or injecting sensitized lymphocytes, i.e., antibody-forming cells (see IMMUNITY). Recent research is also directed toward elucidating the cellular events that are manifested as uncontrolled growth and cancer. The fact that there are many ways to interfere with the controls on genes may help to explain why cancer is apparently caused by a diversity of agents, and why agents that interfere with the expression of genetic information, e.g., nitrogen mustard, radiation, and some hormones, are sometimes carcinogenic and sometimes therapeutic. See A. C. Braun, *The Cancer Problem* (1969); Victor Richards, *Cancer: The Wayward Cell* (1972); B. N. Brooke, *Understanding Cancer* (1973); D. M. Prescott, *Cancer: the Misguided Cell* (1973).

Candace (kăn'dəsē, kăndā'sē), title for queens in ancient Ethiopia. One of them made war (c.22 B.C.) on the Roman governor of Egypt, who defeated her and destroyed Napata, her capital. Another Candace is mentioned in the Bible as the queen of the eunuch converted by Philip (Acts 8.27-39).

Candela, Felix (fā'lēks kändā'lä), 1910–, Mexican architect, b. Madrid. Candela studied in Madrid but was forced to flee Spain after his participation in the Spanish civil war. He went to Mexico in 1939 and set up his own construction firm, gaining renown for his design of thin-shelled concrete domes. Among his best-known works are the Cosmic Ray Pavilion (1950–51) for Mexico's University City; the Church of La Virgen Milagrosa (1953), Mexico City; and Los Manantiales restaurant (1958), Xochimilco. See study by Colin Faber (1963).

candela (kăndĕ'lə), abbr. cd, official name for the CANDLE, the unit of luminous intensity in the INTERNATIONAL SYSTEM OF UNITS. See PHOTOMETRY.

candelabrum (kăn"dəlā'brəm), primarily a support for candles, designed in the form of a turned baluster or a tapered column, also a branched candlestick or a lampstand. Though most used and developed during the Renaissance, the candelabrum originated in Etruria and Rome. Candelabra found in Etruscan and Pompeiian ruins are usually of bronze. From ancient Rome come the tall and monumental candelabra used in temples and public buildings. Of bronze or marble, they had triangular pedestals from which rose columnar shafts, finely sculptured and terminating at the top in a bowl used for holding illuminating oil and incense. With these as inspiration, Italian Renaissance artists produced superb candelabra in rich materials for altars, chapels, and processions. In that period the distinctive form of the candelabrum came also to be a ubiquitous decorative motive, used freely in architectural ornament, tapestry borders, stained-glass windows, and furniture. It was even converted (especially in Lombardy) into a definite architectural element, taking the place of a column or colonnette, as in windows of the Certosa at Pavia. See F. W. Robins, *The Story of the Lamp (and the Candle)* (1939).

Candia, Crete: see IRÁKLION.

candle, cylinder of wax or tallow containing a wick, used for illumination or for ceremonial purposes. The evidence of ancient writings is not conclusive as to the history of the candle; words translated "candle" may have meant "torch" or "lamp," and the "candlestick" was probably a stand for one of these lights. The candle probably evolved from wood, rushes, or cords dipped in fat or pitch. Candles as well as lamps were used in Roman times; by the Middle Ages candles (tallow for the poor and wax for the wealthier) were quite common in Europe. Tallow, beeswax, and vegetable wax such as bayberry in the American colonies, candleberry in the East, and waxberry in South America were supplemented by spermaceti in the late 18th cent., by stearine c.1825, and by paraffin c.1850. Twisted strands for wicks were replaced (c.1825) by the plaited wick. Candles were commonly made by repeated dipping in melted tallow, by pouring tallow or wax into molds, or by pouring beeswax over the wicks. Most modern candles are machine-made by a molding process, although candle making as an art survives in industrialized countries. In literature, art, and religion the candle has had a wide range of symbolism; it commonly represents joy, reverence for the divine, and sacrifice (since the candle spends itself). Candles have been especially important in Jewish religious services. In the Roman Catholic Church candles are blessed on Candlemas Day. The very large paschal candle stands at the Gospel side of the altar; it is blessed and lighted during the Exsultet on the vigil of Easter and is relighted at important ceremonies until Ascension Day.

candle, in weights and measures, unit of luminous intensity; it is defined as 1/60 of the intensity of a BLACK BODY, or ideal radiator, at the temperature at which platinum solidifies (2046°K). The candle is one of the fundamental units of the INTERNATIONAL SYSTEM OF UNITS; its official name is the candela. See PHOTOMETRY.

candleberry: see BAYBERRY.

candlefish: see SMELT.

Candlemas, Feb. 2, Christian festival commemorating the Purification of the Blessed Virgin and the Presentation of Christ in the Temple. The name Candlemas is derived from the procession of candles, inspired by the words of Simeon "a light to lighten the Gentiles" (Luke 2.32). In the Roman Catholic Church the candles for use in the ensuing year are blessed on this day. An old superstition claims that the weather is foretold by the ground hog (see WOODCHUCK) on Candlemas.

candlepower: see PHOTOMETRY.

Candlewood Lake, 8.4 sq mi (21.8 sq km), W Conn. It is formed behind a power dam S of the Rocky River's junction with the Housatonic River. Along its 65-mi (105-km) shoreline are summer resorts and recreational facilities.

candy: see CONFECTIONERY.

candytuft, any plant of the genus *Iberis* of the family Cruciferae (MUSTARD family), low-growing plants of the Old World. A number of half-hardy annuals and evergreen perennials are cultivated—chiefly in borders and rock gardens—for the flat-topped or elongated clusters of flowers of various colors. Candytufts are classified in the division MAGNOLIOPHYTA, class Magnoliopsida, order Capparales, family Cruciferae.

cane, in botany, name for the hollow or woody, usually slender and jointed stems of plants (particularly RATTAN and other bamboos) and for various tall grasses, e.g., SUGARCANE, sorghum, and also other grasses used in the S United States for fodder. The large, or giant, cane (*Arundinaria macrosperma or gigantea*), a BAMBOO grass native to the United States, often forms impenetrable thickets 15 to 25 ft (3.6–7.6 m) high—the canebrakes of the South. The stalks are used locally for fishing poles and other purposes, and the young shoots are sometimes eaten as a potherb.

cane, walking stick. Probably used first as a weapon, it gradually took on the symbolism of strength and power and eventually authority and social prestige. Ancient Egyptian rulers carried the symbolic staff, and in ancient Greece, some gods were represented with a staff in hand. In the Middle Ages, the long staff or walking stick was carried by pilgrims and shepherds. A scepter carried in the right hand symbolized royal power; carried in the left hand of a king the staff represented justice. The church, too, adopted the staff for its officials; the pastoral staff (crosier), which is long and has a crooked handle, symbolizes the bishop's office. The word *cane* was first applied to the walking stick after 1500, when bamboo was first used. After 1600 canes became highly fashionable for men. Made of ivory, ebony, and whalebone, as well as of wood, they had highly decorated and jeweled knob handles. They were often made hollow in order to carry possessions or supplies or, in some cases, to conceal a weapon. In the late 17th cent. oak sticks were extensively used, especially by the Puritans. The cane continued in men's fashions throughout the 18th cent.; as with the women's fan certain rules became standard for its use. From time to time women adopted the cane, particularly for a short time when Marie Antoinette carried the shepherd's crook. In the 19th cent. the cane became a mark of the professional man; the gold-headed cane was especially favored. See Kurt Stein, *Canes and Walking Sticks* (1973).

Canea, Crete: see KHANIÁ.

Canellopoulos, Panayotis: see KANELLOPPULOS, PANAYOTIS.

cane sugar: see SUCROSE.

Caney Fork, river, 144 mi (232 km) long, rising in central Tenn. and flowing NW to the Cumberland River. On Caney Fork are Great Falls Dam and Center Hill Dam, which provide flood control and power for the surrounding area and impounds a 36-sq mi (93-sq km) lake. Caney Fork is part of the Tennessee Valley Authority.

Canfield, Dorothy: see FISHER, DOROTHY CANFIELD.

Canfield, Richard Albert, 1855–1914, American gambler, b. New Bedford, Mass. A well-known gambling operator in Providence, R.I., Canfield went in the 1880s to New York, where his gambling establishment became famous. It was closed in 1904 largely through the efforts of W. T. JEROME, district attorney. Canfield was a noted art collector. The solitaire game Canfield was named for him. See biography by Alexander Gardiner (1930).

Can Grande della Scala: see SCALA, CAN FRANCESCO DELLA.

Caniapiscau: see KANIAPISKAU, river, Canada.

Canisius, Peter: see PETER CANISIUS, SAINT.

Canis Major [Lat.,=greater dog], CONSTELLATION lying near the celestial equator, SE of Orion. Known as the Large Dog (CANIS MINOR is the Small Dog), it was associated with the figure of a dog by many cultures; the ancient Greeks identified it as one of Orion's hunting dogs, while the Scandinavians called it Sigurd's dog. It contains SIRIUS, the brightest star in the heavens, also known as the Dog Star. Other bright stars in Canis Major are ADHARA (Epsilon Canis Majoris), Mirzam (Beta Canis Majoris), and Wezen (Delta Canis Majoris). The constellation reaches its highest point in the evening sky in February.

Canis Minor [Lat.,=lesser dog], small CONSTELLATION lying near the celestial equator, E of Orion and NE of Canis Major, the Large Dog. Known as the Small Dog, Canis Minor is traditionally identified as one of Orion's hunting dogs. It contains the bright star PROCYON. The constellation reaches its highest point in the evening sky in late February.

Cankar, Ivan (ĕ'vŏn tsän'kär), 1876–1918, Slovenian poet. Considered one of the great Slovenian literary figures, he was influential in the development of modern satire, symbolic drama, and the psychological novel. The struggle of the outcast poor is a theme of his satirical novel *Yerney's Justice* (1907, tr. 1926) and many other works. Cankar also wrote satires on politics and culture.

canker, small sore on the inside of the mouth. A canker appears as a shallow, whitish ulcer surrounded by a thin, red area. It is tender, sometimes painful, and may occur singly or as one of a group of sores. Cankers develop on the inner surfaces of the lips or cheeks, on the gums, under the tongue, or on the roof of the mouth. The cause is unknown, but cankers have been associated with friction, injury, allergy, and viral infection. They generally heal by themselves in a few days but can be recurrent.

cankerworm, name for two destructive INCHWORMS, or larvae of geometrid moths. The spring cankerworm *(Paleacrita vernata)* and the fall cankerworm *(Alsophila pometaria)* are named for the seasons at which the adults emerge from underground pupation. The spring cankerworm larva overwinters as a pupa, the fall cankerworm as an egg. The larvae, dark green to brown and about 1 in. (2.5 cm) long, feed on the leaves of orchard and shade trees. The spring cankerworm has two pairs of posterior appendages (prolegs); the fall cankerworm has three. The wingless female lays her eggs on the bark, and one control method is the placing of bands of sticky paper around the tree trunks to trap the females before laying. When alarmed, cankerworms drop and hang suspended in mid-air at the end of a long silken thread secreted from their mouths; they ascend this thread after the danger has passed. The English sparrow was originally introduced in the United States to combat the spring cankerworm. Cankerworms are classified in the phylum ARTHROPODA, class Insecta, order Lepidoptera, family Geometridae. For control methods see bulletins of the U.S. Dept. of Agriculture.

canna [Lat.,=cane], any plant of the genus *Canna,* tropical and subtropical perennials, grown in temperate regions in parks and gardens for the large foliage and spikelike, usually red or yellow blossoms. Today, most cultivated cannas are hybrids, but two species are found wild in the S United States, one called Indian shot because of the hard shotlike seeds. *C. edulis,* Queensland arrowroot, is cultivated in the tropics for its rootstock, a commercial ARROWROOT starch. Canna is classified in the division MAGNOLIOPHYTA, class Liliatae, order Zingiberales, family Cannaceae.

cannabis: see HEMP; MARIJUANA.

Cannae (kăn'ē), ancient village, Apulia, SE Italy, scene in 216 B.C. of Hannibal's crushing defeat of the Romans. Hannibal's troops assumed a crescent-shaped formation to meet the Roman troops, which were especially concentrated in the center. As the Romans advanced, Hannibal by brilliant strategy managed to encircle the entire Roman force and cut it to pieces.

Cannanore (kăn'ənōr", -nôr"), town (1971 pop. 55,111), Kerala state, SE India. Formerly the capital of the Kolattiri Raja, it traded with Arabia and Persia in the 12th and 13th cent. Vasco da Gama visited Cannanore in 1498 at the invitation of the Kolattiri Raja, and it became a Portuguese settlement. Control passed to the Dutch in the mid-17th cent., and the British captured Cannanore in 1783. Today it is a military station and a district administrative center. Coconut products, rice, pepper, timber products, dried fish, cotton fabrics, and tobacco are traded.

Canneh (kăn'ē), unidentified city, apparently in N Syria. Ezek. 27.23. See CALNEH **2.**

cannel coal: see COAL.

Cannes (kăn), town (1968 pop. 68,021), Alpes-Maritimes dept., SE France. An important and fashionable resort on the French Riviera, Cannes also has shipbuilding and textile industries. Napoleon I landed nearby on his return (1815) from Elba. Churches from the 16th and 17th cent. are in the old part of town. An international film festival is held in Cannes each spring.

cannibalism (kăn'ĭbəlĭzəm) [from Span. *caníbal,* referring to the Carib Indians], practice of certain peoples of eating human flesh. The practice of cannibalism has been noted in such widely divergent places as Africa, South America, the South Pacific islands, and the West Indies. According to available anthropological evidence, the partaking of human flesh was almost always a ritual practice. Only very rarely, under the pressure of such calamities as famine or isolation by a snowstorm, an airplane crash, or a shipwreck, have human beings resorted to eating other human beings in order to survive. Various skeletal prehistoric finds suggest that ancient man practiced HEAD-HUNTING and cannibalism, but associated evidence strongly supports the magico-religious theory that victims for these rites were always sought among alien groups. Various peoples, however, have been known to eat part of their kinsmen's corpses out of respect for the deceased and in order to absorb some magic powers. This aim of life transfer seems to lie behind all cannibalism and head-hunting. The two practices rarely occur together, and some anthropologists believe that the latter may have evolved from the former. Among a few peoples, which may represent a connecting link, the head of the enemy is preserved and the rest of his body or selected parts of it are eaten. See Garry Hogg, *Cannibalism and Human Sacrifice* (1958, repr. 1966).

Canning, Charles John Canning, Earl, 1812–62, British statesman; third son of George Canning. Succeeding to the peerage conferred on his mother, he took his seat as Viscount Canning in the House of Lords (1837) and served as Sir Robert Peel's undersecretary for foreign affairs (1841–46) and Lord Aberdeen's postmaster general (1853–55). Appointed (1856) governor general of India, he became known as "Clemency Canning" for his efforts to restrain revenge against the Indians during the INDIAN MUTINY. In 1858, when the power of government was transferred from the East India Company to the British crown, Canning became the first viceroy of India. He was created earl in 1859 and retired in 1862. See H. S. Cunningham, *Earl Canning and the Transfer of India* (1892).

Canning, George, 1770–1827, British statesman. Canning was converted to Toryism by the French Revolution, became a disciple of William Pitt, and was his undersecretary for foreign affairs (1796–99). To bring ridicule upon English radicals and Whigs who favored the Revolution, he contributed numerous articles to the *Anti-Jacobin* (1797–98). During the war against Napoleon I, he served as treasurer of the navy (1804–6) and was foreign minister (1807–9). He exerted great influence in military affairs, planning the seizure of the Danish fleet at Copenhagen (1807) and supporting British intervention in Spain and Portugal (see PENINSULAR WAR). However, he quarreled with Lord CASTLEREAGH, and after a duel, in which Canning was wounded, both resigned from the ministry. He later served (1816–20) as president of the board of control for India, resigning in protest against the government's prosecution of Queen Caroline. Recalled to the foreign office after Castlereagh's suicide (1822), he reversed previous policy toward the HOLY ALLIANCE, refusing to cooperate in the suppression of European revolutions. He protested the decisions of the Congress of VERONA (1822) and, although unable to prevent French intervention in Spain, later sent an army to Portugal to foil absolutist intervention there. His policies toward the Spanish colonies in America, whose independence he recognized, led to the promulgation of the MONROE DOCTRINE. He arranged the French-Russian-British agreement, which, after his death, resulted in Greek independence. After the death of Lord Liverpool, Canning became (April, 1827) prime minister, but he died four months later. See biography by Wendy Hinde (1973); studies by D. Marshall (1938), C. A. Petrie (2d ed., 1946), H. W. V. Temperley (1925, repr. 1966, and 1905, repr. 1968).

Canning, Stratford: see STRATFORD DE REDCLIFFE, STRATFORD CANNING, VISCOUNT.

canning, process of hermetically sealing cooked food for future use. It was discovered in the early part of the 19th cent. by a Frenchman, Nicolas APPERT. The process proved moderately successful and was put into practice in other European countries and in the United States. A patent was taken out (c.1815) in New England by Ezra Daggett for the canning of seafood, pickles, jams, and sauces. In 1820, William Underwood in Boston and Thomas Kensett in New York City began to produce canned foods commercially. Because of the food requirements of soldiers during the American Civil War, considerable amounts of canned meats and vegetables were produced. The canning of seafood at Eastport, Maine, began in 1843. Salmon from the Columbia River was canned in 1866 and in Alaska in 1872. Glass containers were used at first but proved bulky, costly, and brittle. Peter Durand, an Englishman, patented the first tin canister in 1810, and in 1825 the first U.S. patent was obtained. Early canmaking was slow and expensive; sheets of tin were cut with shears, bent around a block, and the seams heavily soldered. A good tinsmith could make only about 60 cans a day. The industry began to assume importance with the invention in 1847 of the stamp can. A machine for shaping and soldering was exhibited in 1876 at the Centennial Exposition at Philadelphia. The open-top can of the 20th cent., with a soldered lock seam and double-seamed ends, permits easy cleaning and filling. Cans used for foods that react with metals, causing discoloration (usually harmless), may be coated with a lacquer film. Highly specialized machinery, knowledge of bacteriology and food chemistry, and more efficient processes of cooking have combined to make the commercial canning of food an important feature of modern life. The range of products now canned has increased enormously and may be grouped as meat and poultry; fruits and vegetables; seafood; milk; and preserves, jams, jellies, pickles, and sauces. The general principles of commercial and home canning are the same, but in the factory more accurate control of procedures is practiced and highly specialized machinery is available. The canning process begins with cleaning or washing the product. During the next steps the edible parts are separated from the inedible parts (just as in ordinary food preparation, e.g., by peeling, trimming, and so forth). Certain foods, especially vegetables, need to be blanched (scalded), to arrest enzyme action that may cause color, flavor, or texture deterioration, or to reduce the size of the product. After the food is put into cans, the can is thermally exhausted in order to release undesirable gases. Once the can is sealed, it is subjected to heat so that any microorganisms inside the can will be destroyed. The canned product is then cooled and labeled.

Cannizzaro, Stanislao (stänēslä'ō kän-nēt-tsä'rō), 1826–1910, Italian chemist. From 1861 he was professor at Palermo and from 1871 at Rome, where he was also a member of the senate and of the council of public instruction. He is known for his discovery of cyanamide, for obtaining alcohols from aldehydes by Cannizzaro's reaction (in which benzaldehyde is converted to benzoic acid and benzyl alcohol, in the presence of a strong alkali), and for distinguishing between molecular and atomic weights. Of fundamental importance was his explanation of how atomic weights may be determined systematically on the basis of Avogadro's law regarding the volumes of gases and vapors; hydrogen is used as a reference standard and, for elements whose compounds are not volatile (do not form vapors by evaporation), the SPECIFIC HEAT is used in the determination of the atomic weight.

Cannock, urban district (1971 pop. 55,873), Staffordshire, W central England. It is a mining town dependent upon the rich coal deposits of Cannock Chase, a nearby moorland. Cannock's other industries are metalworking and brick making.

Cannon, Annie Jump, 1863–1941, American astronomer, b. Dover, Del., grad. Wellesley (B.S., 1884; M.A., 1907). In 1897 she became an assistant in the Harvard College Observatory, where from 1911 to 1938 she was astronomer and curator of astronomical photographs. In the course of her photographic work she discovered 300 variable stars, 5 new stars, 1 spectroscopic binary, and many stars with bright lines or variable spectra. She made a bibliography of variable stars that includes about 200,000 references and completed a catalog of some 300,000 stellar spectra, besides preparing many papers on the subject.

Cannon, George Quayle, 1827–1901, Mormon apostle, b. Liverpool, England. He and his parents were converted to Mormonism in 1840; from the Isle of Man they emigrated to Nauvoo, Ill., in 1842, moving to Utah in 1847. In 1850, Cannon founded a Mormon mission in Hawaii. He became an apostle in 1859 and was assigned to England, where for four years he edited the *Millennial Star* and supervised missionary work. He served as a member of the Utah territorial council and as private secretary to Brigham Young, of whose will he was an executor. In 1867 he became editor of the influential *Deseret News*. Cannon was elected (1872) territorial delegate from Utah to Congress, but in 1882 he was refused his seat, under the Edmunds antipolygamy law. In 1888 he suffered imprisonment for practicing polygamy.

Cannon, Joseph Gurney, 1836–1926, speaker of the U.S. House of Representatives (1903–11), b. Guilford co., N.C. A lawyer in Illinois, Cannon served as a Republican in Congress from 1873 to 1923, except for the years 1891–93 and 1913–15, when first the Populists and then the Progressives were able to defeat him. As speaker he carried the traditional power of his office to appoint all legislative committees to its ultimate arbitrary extremes, dictatorially ruling the House in the interest of his fellow "Old Guard" Republicans and suppressing minority groups. In March, 1910, insurgent Republicans, led by George W. Norris and supported by all the Democrats, passed a resolution that, by providing that the House itself should appoint the important Committee on Rules with the speaker ineligible for membership, broke Cannon's power. See C. R. Atkinson, *The Committee on Rules and the Overthrow of Speaker Cannon* (1911); L. W. Busbey, *Uncle Joe Cannon* (1927, repr. 1971); Blair Bolles, *Tyrant from Illinois* (1951, repr. 1974); W. R. Gwinn, *Uncle Joe Cannon, Archfoe of Insurgency* (1957).

Cannon, Walter Bradford, 1871–1945, American physiologist. While still a medical student at Harvard, Cannon was the first to demonstrate (1897) that bismuth could be utilized as a contrast medium in the roentgenologic examination of the gastrointestinal tract. His interest in the physiological effects of emotional stimuli, especially on digestion, led to the publication in 1919 of *Bodily Changes in Pain, Hunger, Fear and Rage*. He later concentrated his attention on the adrenal glands and by 1929 was emphasizing the emergency function of these glands in meeting vital threats to the body and in maintaining the equilibrium of the many processes of the organism. In 1932, while professor of physiology at Harvard, he introduced the important concept of homeostasis.

Cano, Alonso (älōn'sō kä'nō), 1601–67, Spanish baroque painter, sculptor, and architect. Cano was the outstanding draftsman of the Spanish baroque. He studied under Pacheco and received painting and architecture commissions from King Philip IV. He was named chief architect of the cathedral at Granada. His architectural masterpiece is the design for the cathedral facade (1667), erected after his death. Cano executed both the sculpture and paintings for his monumental altarpieces and did independent religious pictures and portraits for the cathedral. Examples of his paintings are *Descent into Limbo* (Los Angeles County Mus.); *Way to Calvary* (Worcester Art Mus., Mass.); and portrait of an ecclesiastic (Hispanic Society of America, New York City). His sculptures, including statues of saints in Granada Cathedral, are executed with vigor and sensitivity. See study by H. E. Wethey (1955).

Cano, Juan Sebastián del (hwän säbästyän' dĕl), c.1476–1526, Spanish navigator, the first to circumnavigate the globe. Under Magellan he commanded the *Concepción* and after Magellan's death in the Philippines took command of the expedition. From the Philippines to the Molucca islands Cano sailed new waters, arriving in Spain with the *Victoria* and 18 men on Sept. 6, 1522. He set out in 1525 on a second voyage to the Moluccas by Magellan's route but died while crossing the Pacific.

canoe, long, narrow watercraft with sharp ends originally used by most primitive peoples. It is usually propelled by means of paddles, although sails and, more recently, outboard motors are also used. The canoe varies in material according to locality and in design according to the use made of it. In North America, where horses were not generally used and where the interlocking river systems were unusually favorable, the canoe in its various types was highly developed. Where large logs were available, it took the form of the hollowed-out log, or dugout, especially on the N Pacific coast, where immense trees grew at the water's edge, where an intricate archipelago invited navigation in ocean waters, and where the tribes came to depend to a large extent upon sea life for their food supply. A semiseafaring culture developed there, and the great canoes of the Haida and Tlingit tribes, with high, decorated prows, capable of carrying 30 to 50 people, began to resemble the boats of Viking culture. On the northern fringe of the American forest where smaller tree trunks were found and rapid rivers and many portages favored a lighter craft, the bark canoe dominated, reaching its highest development in the birchbark canoe. At portages this light canoe could be lifted on one's shoulders and easily transported. A third type of primitive canoe is that made from skins, found where trees are lacking. The bullboat of the Plains Indian, little more than a round tub made of buffalo hides stretched over a circular frame, was its crudest form. A much finer form is the kayak of the Eskimo, made of sealskin stretched over a frame constructed of driftwood or whalebone. In the South Seas, canoes were developed for use on long voyages from island to island, and ingenious outriggers were developed to give stabilization to the canoe under sail. It was the birchbark canoe that carried such explorers as Jacques Marquette, Sir Alexander Mackenzie, and David Thompson on their journeys. It was the canoe that carried fur traders out to trade with the Indians; thus it played an important part in early American history. The double-bladed paddle—used in North America only by the Eskimo—is almost always in use on wide bodies of water affected by wind and tidal currents. The substitution of canvas for birch bark in making canoes is credited to the Oldtown or Penobscot Indians in Maine; the canvas-covered wooden canoe is sometimes called the Oldtown canoe. All-wood canoes made of basswood or cedar, very popular in Canada, are sometimes called Peterborough canoes after a canoe-making center. Plywood canoes made in Canada and elsewhere have also been popular. The majority of canoes made today, however, are manufactured of a tough but light aluminum alloy. This type of canoe contains an air pocket in either end to ensure flotation. Modern canoes are also made of fiber glass, plastic, and even a hard-rubber nonsinkable compound. The sail used on the modern canoe is usually the triangular lug sail known as the lateen. The decked sailing canoe used for racing carries two and sometimes three sails; its navigator uses a sliding seat (sometimes called the monkey seat) on which he balances, frequently out over the water on either side, to prevent his craft from heeling over too far. This canoe, clocked at 16 knots or more, and the Samoan canoe (with an outrigger), exceeding 20 knots, were the fastest watercraft under sail until the advent of the CATAMARAN. See Terence T. Quirke, *Canoes the World Over* (1952).

canoeing, sport of propelling a canoe through water. John MacGregor, an English barrister and founder of the Royal Canoe Club (est. 1865), is generally credited with being the initiator of modern sport canoeing. Between 1849 and 1869, MacGregor wrote a number of highly popular books in which he described his experiences on long canoe trips throughout Europe. Sport canoeing today may either involve recreational journeys or fixed-distance racing. Racing canoes are propelled by either sails or paddles. The International Challenge Cup, one of the oldest existing canoeing trophies, was originally offered by the New York Canoe Club (1885) as a perpetual challenge sailing prize. Canoe racing with paddles first became an official Olympic event at the Berlin games in 1936. The two types of Olympic canoe races are those among kayaks and Canadian canoes. The kayak, a buoyant arctic canoe that is completely covered except for its cockpit(s), is raced by both men and women. The Canadian, the typical North American canoe, is raced only by men. Hunters, fishermen, and outdoorsmen use canoes as combination recreation-transportation vehicles. This type of canoeing is especially popular in the N United States. White-water canoeing, in which the vessel is navigated through rapids, is quite popular in the W United States, especially along the Colorado River. See studies by John Malo (1969 and 1971).

canon, in Christendom, term of several meanings. Decrees of church councils are usually called canons; since the Council of Trent the expression has been especially reserved to dogmatic pronouncements of ecumenical councils. The body of ratified conciliar canons is a large part of the legislation of CANON LAW. A canon is also an official list, as in canonization, i.e., enrollment among the saints, and of the names of books of the Bible accepted by the church (see OLD TESTAMENT; NEW TESTAMENT; APOCRYPHA; PSEUDEPIGRAPHA). The central, mainly invariable part of the Mass is the canon. The term is also applied in the Western Church to certain types of priests. There are canons regular, priests living in community under a rule but not cloistered like monks; the Augustinian, or Austin, canons and the Premonstratensians are the best known of these. The priests attached to a cathedral or large church are sometimes organized into a group, or college, and called canons secular; a church having such a group is a collegiate church. Cathedral canons often have diocesan charges or pastoral duties apart from the cathedral. Canons of the Church of England are mostly cathedral canons.

canon, in music, a type of counterpoint employing the strictest form of IMITATION. All the voices of a canon have the same melody, beginning at different times. Successive entrances may be all at the same pitch or at different pitches. Another form of canon is the circle canon, or ROUND, e.g., SUMER IS ICUMEN IN. In the 14th and 15th cent. retrograde motion was employed to form what is known as crab canon, or canon cancrizans, wherein the original melody is turned backward to become the second voice. In the 15th and 16th cent. mensuration canons were frequently written, in which the voices sing the same melodic pattern written in different note values, i.e., to be sung at different speeds. Bach made noteworthy use of canon, particularly in the *Goldberg Variations*. Beethoven, Mozart, Haydn, Schumann, and Brahms wrote canons, and Franck used the device in the last movement of his violin sonata. It is an essential device of SERIAL MUSIC.

Canonchet: see KING PHILIP'S WAR.

Canon City (kăn'yən), city (1970 pop. 9,206), seat of Fremont co., S central Colo., at the mouth of the Grand Canyon of the Arkansas River (see ROYAL GORGE); laid out 1859 on the site of a blockhouse built (1807) by Zebulon M. Pike, inc. 1872. It is a health and tourist resort in a spectacularly scenic area with mineral springs. Marble and limestone are quarried, and a great variety of minerals are found in the region. A restored mining town is nearby.

Canonicus (kənŏn'ĭkəs), c.1565–1647, North American Indian chief, who ruled the Narragansett Indians when the Pilgrims landed in New England. He granted (1636) Rhode Island to Roger WILLIAMS and because of William's influence remained friendly to the settlers, despite their aggressive ways. See H. M. Chapin, *Sachems of the Narragansetts* (1931).

canonization (kăn"ənĭzā'shən), in the Roman Catholic Church, process by which a person is classified as a SAINT. It is now performed at Rome alone, although in the Middle Ages and earlier bishops everywhere used to canonize. Canonization is not necessary for martyrs, who are considered to be enrolled among the saints on their death, but in recent years the church has approved the cult of canonized persons only. The process of canonization is a trial (or cause), at which the saint is said to be defended by the church; a prosecutor is appointed to attack all evidence alleged in favor of canonization. The prosecutor is popularly called *advocatus diaboli* [devil's advocate], his opponent the *advocatus Dei* [God's advocate]. This evidence consists primarily of the proof of four miracles attributable to the saint and proof that the saint's life was exemplary. Beatification, by which a person is called blessed and his cult is approved for localities and orders, requires two miracles. Miracles attributed to saints are considered probable or pious opinions, and Catholics are not required to believe in them. The first solemn canonization seems to have been that of St. Ulrich late in the 10th cent. The method of formal canonization was set by the enactments of Urban VIII that came into force in 1634.

canon law, in the Roman Catholic Church, the body of law based on the legislation of the councils (both ecumenical and local) and the popes, as well as the bishops (for diocesan matters). It is the law of the church courts and is to be distinguished from other parts of ecclesiastical law, such as liturgical law. However, when liturgical law overlaps with canon law, the great body of canon law, promulgated in the *Codex juris canonici* [code of canon law] in 1917 (and effective since 1918), prevails, although exceptions to this rule are noted in the code. The code itself, the culmination of centuries of legal growth, consists of 2,414 canons, with an analytical index (at the beginning) and nine appended documents; it superseded all previous compilations. It does not contain all of canon law, which continues to grow, but it is the base of the present-day law, and the study of canon law consists mainly in mastering the code and its application. It lays down rules for the governance and regulation of the clergy and the church, including such matters as the qualifications, duties, and discipline of the clergy and the administration of the sacraments (more particularly the laws regarding holy orders and the sacrament of marriage). Canon law embraces both general laws applicable in the church universal, such as those on requirements for the priesthood and those on marriage, and local laws applicable only in certain dioceses. The early law grew particularly from the letters of the bishops of Rome that settled matters of ecclesiastical government and discipline from the end of the 1st cent. A.D. Such papal letters and pronouncements are called decretals. Joined to them are the canons of the councils of the church regarding church discipline and governance. From the 4th cent. this legislation grew profuse, and attempts to collect and correlate the laws began early (see CONSTITUTIONS, APOSTOLIC). These collections were not always authorized and were sometimes not genuine, as in the case of the FALSE DECRETALS. It was not until the middle of the 12th cent. that the great genius of the canon law, GRATIAN, following after IVO OF CHARTRES, applied the methods of Roman law in bringing order out of the chaos of conflicting and uncoordinated legislation. His *Concordantia discordantanium canonum* (c.1140) or *Decretum Gratiani,* called in English *Gratian's Decree,* became the basis for future compilations of the law. Important among the later additional works were the collections of decretals under Gregory IX, called the *Extravagantes* or *Extra* because they were outside *Gratian's Decree;* the collection issued (1298) by Boniface VIII and called *Liber sextus* [the sixth book] because it added to the five books of decretals promulgated by Gregory; the collection promulgated (1317) by John XXII, drawn mostly from the constitutions of Clement V at the Council of Vienne and called the *Clementinae;* the work commonly called *Corpus juris canonici,* which in 1500 combined all the preceding with the *Extravagantes* of John XXII and the *Extravagantes communes* (decretals from Boniface VIII through Sixtus IV) and was to be the fundamental work in canon law for centuries. The Council of Trent (1545–63, with interruptions) by its decrees concerning the church and church discipline was a landmark in canon law. Legislation in the church continued and had reached considerable confusion by the time that, in 1904, St. Pius X announced the undertaking of the *Codex juris canonici.* This was drafted by a commission of cardinals headed by Cardinal Gasparri; all the resources of the church were used to produce this code. In 1917, when the code was finished, a permanent commission of cardinals was set up to interpret it. In 1959, Pope John XXIII convoked the Second Vatican Council and announced a revision of the code of 1917; in 1963 he appointed a pontifical commission for the revision of the code, which replaced the 1917 commission. Canon law has had a profound influence on the law of countries where the Roman Catholic Church has been the state church. In the Middle Ages the church courts had very wide jurisdiction—e.g., in England, control of the law of personal property—and because they were well regulated, they tended to attract many borderline cases that might have been the business of the developing royal courts (see BENEFIT OF CLERGY). Catholics of Eastern rites have their own separate codes of canon law, approved by the Roman Catholic Church. The term "canon law" is also used for ecclesiastical law in churches of the Anglican Communion. The Anglican *Constitutions and Canons Ecclesiastical* (1603) was a collection of rulings, not based on the old canon law, but given equal force with the canon law. See A. G. Cicognani, *Canon Law* (rev. ed. 1949); Stanislaus Woywod, *Practical Commentary on the Code of Canon Law* (rev. ed. 1949); J. A. Abbo and J. D. Hannan, *The Sacred Canons* (2d rev. ed. 1960); René Metz, *What is Canon Law?* (1960); T. L. Bouscaren and A. C. Ellis, *Canon Law* (4th rev. ed. 1966); J. E.Biechler, ed., *Law for Liberty* (1967).

Canonsburg, borough (1970 pop. 11,439), Washington co., SW Pa.; inc. 1802. It is an industrial center in a coal-mining area. Its varied manufactures include steel and metal products and pottery. A gram of radium produced there was presented to Mme Curie in 1921 when she visited the town. The Log Cabin School (est. 1777; the first school west of the Alleghenies) is preserved; it was the precursor of Washington and Jefferson College, now in Washington, Pennsylvania. The Black Horse Tavern in Canonsburg was a famous gathering place for leaders of the Whisky Rebellion (1794). Roberts House (1804) is an example of W Pennsylvania manor architecture. A state school and hospital for the mentally retarded is nearby.

Canopus (kənō'pəs), ancient city of N Egypt, 12 mi (19 km) E of Alexandria. Canopus, the pilot of Menelaus' ship, died there. In Hellenistic times Canopus was known as a pleasure city for the rich. Vases capped with the figure of a human head, called Canopic vases, were used to hold the viscera of embalmed bodies. The Decree of Canopus, issued there in 238 B.C. and found at Tanis, has been of value in studying the ancient Egyptian language. The modern village of ABU QIR is near the ancient ruins.

Canopus, in astronomy, 2d brightest star in the sky, located in the constellation Carina, which is part of the ancient constellation Argo Navis; Bayer designation α Carinae; 1970 position R.A. $6^h23.3^m$, Dec. $-52°41'$. It has an apparent MAGNITUDE of -0.72, second only to Sirius among the bright stars. Canopus is a yellowish-white giant star of SPECTRAL CLASS F0 I-II. Its distance is about 100 light-years. It is probably named after the ancient Egyptian city of Canopus.

Canosa di Puglia (känô'zä dē pōō'lyä), Lat. *Canusium,* city (1971 pop. 30,059), Apulia, S Italy, on the Ofanto River. It is a commercial and agricultural center. The city flourished under the Romans and was noted for its wool and its fine vases, many of which have been unearthed in nearby tombs (3d and 4th cent. B.C.). The Romans fled to Canusium after their disasterous defeat by Hannibal at nearby Cannae (216 B.C.). The city was destroyed by the Arabs in the 9th cent. but was resettled by the Normans in the 11th cent. There are other Roman remains, including walls, an amphitheater, and a gate. The city also has an 11th-century Romanesque cathedral and the mausoleum of the Norman leader Bohemond I (d. 1111), which has fine sculptured bronze doors.

Canossa (kănôs'sä), village, in Emilia-Romagna, N central Italy, in the Apennines. There are ruins of the 10th-century castle of the powerful feudal family that took its name from the place. In the 10th and 11th cent. they ruled over much of Tuscany and Emilia. MATILDA, countess of Tuscany, was the last of the family. In Jan., 1077, the castle was the scene of penance done by Emperor HENRY IV to obtain from Pope Gregory VII the withdrawal of the excommunication against him. The pope was Matilda's guest at the castle, and Henry is said to have stood three days barefoot in the snow before being admitted to the pope's presence. Henry was absolved, but the peace between him and the pope was short-lived. The political implications of this episode inspired Bismarck to coin the phrase "to go to Canossa" (i.e., to submit to the demands of the Roman Catholic Church) in the Kulturkampf.

Canova, Antonio (äntô'nyō känô'vä), 1757–1822, Italian sculptor. He was a leading exponent of the neoclassical school whose influence on the art of his time was enormous. Canova's monumental statues and bas-reliefs are executed with extreme grace, polish, and purity of contour. His first important commission was the monument (1782–87) to Clement XIV in the Church of the Apostles, Rome, followed by that to Clement XIII (completed 1792) in St. Peter's. He then received numerous major commissions from many countries. An admirer of Napoleon, Canova executed a bust of the emperor from life and several other portraits, including two where Napoleon is represented nude in the guise of a Roman emperor. His statue (1820) of George Washington for the statehouse at Raleigh, N.C. (destroyed), was dressed in Roman armor. Canova's memorabilia, consisting of sketches, casts, a few oil paintings, and a voluminous correspondence, are divided between the Gipsoteca in Possagno, his birthplace, and the Civic Museum in Bassano.

Cánovas del Castillo, Antonio (äntô'nyō kä'nōväs dĕl kästē'lyō), 1828–97, Spanish conservative politician, historian, and man of letters. He was instrumental in securing the restoration (1875) of Alfonso XII and was premier for six years (with short interruptions in 1875 and 1879) thereafter. To stabilize the monarchy, he worked out a political arrangement that rotated power within a narrow group, and after 1881 he alternated as premier with the Liberal party leader, Sagasta. He was assassinated by an anarchist. The editor of *Historia general de España* (18 vol., 1891–97), he also wrote several historical and critical works.

Canrobert, François Certain (fräNswä' sĕrtăN' känrôbĕr'), 1809–95, marshal of France. After brilliant service in Africa, he returned to Paris and aided Louis Napoleon (later NAPOLEON III) in the coup d'etat of 1851. He served in the Crimean War and was for a time commander in chief. Later, he distinguished himself in the Italian War of 1859 and in the Franco-Prussian War (1870–71). He became a senator under the Third Republic.

Canso, town (1971 pop. 1,209), S central N.S., Canada, on the Atlantic Ocean, near Cape Canso, the easternmost point of Nova Scotia peninsula proper. The harbor was much used by fishing fleets in colonial times and was fortified by the British in 1720. The Gut, or Strait, of Canso, scarcely 1 mi (1.6 km) wide in places, separates Nova Scotia peninsula from Cape Breton Island.

Cantabrian Mountains (kăntā'brēən), N Spain, extending c.300 mi (480 km) along the Bay of Biscay from the Pyrenees to Cape Finisterre. Torre de Cerredo (8,687 ft/2,648 m) in the Europa group in the central section is the highest peak. The mountains are rich in minerals, especially coal and iron; the slopes are farmed. The streams on the northern slope are used to generate hydroelectricity. The Ebro River rises on the southeast slope.

Cantacuzene (kăn"təkyōōzēn') or **Cantacuzino** (kän'täkōōzē'nô), noble Rumanian family of Greek origin, tracing its descent from the Byzantine emperor JOHN VI (John Cantacuzene). Under Ottoman rule members of the family were among the Phanariots (see under PHANAR) who governed Walachia and Moldavia. By the mid-17th cent., part of the family had settled in Walachia. A Russian branch of the family held high positions in the army and as governors of Bessarabia. **Serban Cantacuzene,** 1640–88, hospodar [governor] of Walachia (1678–88), took part in the Turkish siege of Vienna (1683), outwardly on the side of the Turks but in reality supplying intelligence information to the Austrians and conducting secret negotiations with them. He was poisoned, probably because of his pro-Austrian feelings. During his rule Rumanian was substituted for Slavonic as the liturgical language, and the first Rumanian Bible was printed (1688) under his auspices. **George Cantacuzene,** 1837–1913, the head of the Rumanian Conservative party, held several important government posts, most notably the premiership (1905-7).

Cantacuzene, John: see JOHN VI, Byzantine emperor.

Cantal (käNtäl'), department (1968 pop. 169,330), S central France, in Auvergne. AURILLAC is the capital.

cantaloupe: see GOURD; MELON.

cantata (kəntä'tə) [Ital.,=sung], composite musical form similar to a short unacted opera or brief ORATORIO, developed in Italy in the baroque period. The term was first used in 1620 to refer to strophic variations in the voice part over a recurrent melody in the bass accompaniment. Gradually the cantata came to contain contrasting sections of recitative and aria separated by instrumental passages, often in the current operatic style. In the second half of the 17th cent. the secular cantata was standardized by Stradella, Alessandro Scarlatti, and other members of the Neapolitan school into two arias with recitatives. This form was very popular through the 18th cent. as a vehicle for virtuoso singing. In France the cantata was adapted by Rameau to contain three arias with recitatives. In Germany the sacred cantata was more popular than the secular. It incorporated extensive choral and instrumental sections. A particular variety, the chorale cantata, utilized the verses of hymns and frequently the hymn tunes in various parts of the cantata. This type, as written by J. S. Bach, opens with a chorus, which is followed by recitatives and arias for each soloist, and then closes with a harmonized chorale. After Bach the cantata became, in general, a diminutive form of the oratorio.

Canterbury, city (1971 pop. 130,334), New South Wales, SE Australia. It is a suburb of Sydney.

Canterbury, county borough (1971 pop. 33,157), Kent, SE England, on the Stour River. Economically unimportant except for its tourism, Canterbury is famous as the long-time spiritual center of England. In 597, St. Augustine went to England from Rome to convert the island peoples to Christianity. He founded an abbey at Canterbury and became the first archbishop of Canterbury and primate of all England. The early cathedral was burned and rebuilt several times. After the murder (1170) of Thomas à Becket and the penance of Henry II, Canterbury became famous throughout Europe as the object of pilgrimage, and the *Canterbury Tales* of Chaucer relate the stories told by a fictional group of pilgrims. The present cathedral was begun under Archbishop Lanfranc, the first Norman archbishop. Constructed from 1070 to 1180 and from 1379 to 1503, it is a magnificent structure, its architecture embodying the styles of several periods and various architects. Noteworthy are the great 15th-century tower (235 ft/72 m high); the long transepts; the screen separating the raised choir from the Perpendicular nave; the east chapel (called the Corona or Becket's Crown), which contains the marble chair in which the archbishops are enthroned; Trinity Chapel, which held the shrine of St. Thomas until 1538, when Henry VIII ordered it destroyed and the accumulated wealth confiscated; the chapel in which French Protestants worshiped in the 16th cent. and where services are still held in French; the northwestern transept (where a stone slab commemorates the exact site of Thomas a Becket's murder); and the tombs of Henry IV and Edward the Black Prince. During World War II the cathedral was the object of severe German reprisal raids (June, 1942), which destroyed the library and many other surrounding buildings, but the cathedral itself received no direct hits. The city of Canterbury is also of great historical interest, with a 14th-century gate and remains of the old city walls; St. Martin's Church (established before St. Augustine's arrival and known as the Mother Church of England); the old pilgrims' hostel called the Hospital of St. Thomas; and several fine old inns. Christopher Marlowe was born at Canterbury and educated at King's School (of very ancient origin) there before going to Cambridge. Other schools are the Univ. of Kent at Canterbury, and theological, art, and teacher-training colleges. In 1974, the borough became part of the new nonmetropolitan county of Kent.

Canterbury bells: see BELLFLOWER.

Canterbury Tales: see CHAUCER, GEOFFREY.

cantharides: see BLISTER BEETLE.

Can Tho (kăn tō, kəntô'), city (1968 est. pop. 88,000), S South Vietnam, a port on the Mekong River delta. Rice and fish are traded. It is the seat of the Univ. of Can Tho. The city has a commercial airport.

Canticles, another name for the SONG OF SOLOMON.

cantilever (kăn'təlēvər), beam supported rigidly at one end to carry a load along the free arm or at the free end. A slanting beam fixed at the base is often used to support the free end, as in a common bracket. The springboard is a simple cantilever beam, and the cantilever design is often used for canopies, balconies, sidewalks outside the trusses of bridges, and large cranes such as those used in shipyards. By the use of cantilever trusses, obstructing columns are eliminated in theaters. The cantilever principle is one of the methods that may be used in constructing a BRIDGE.

Canton, John, 1718-72, English physicist. He is known for his research in magnetism and in electricity, especially his experiments in electrostatic induction. Canton was the first in England to verify Benjamin Franklin's conclusions about lightning. He invented an electroscope and an electrometer and demonstrated the compressibility of water.

Canton (kăn"tŏn', kăn'tŏn"), Mandarin *Kuangchou,* city (1970 est. pop. of 2,300,000), capital of Kwangtung prov., S China, a major deepwater port on the Pearl River delta. Among the largest cities in the country, Canton is the transportation, industrial, financial, and trade center of S China. It has shipyards, an integrated steel complex, paper mills, a long-established textile industry (silk, cotton, jute, and more recently synthetic fibers), and factories producing tractors, machinery, machine tools, boilers, tires, bicycles, sports equipment, porcelain, cement, and chemicals. The hub of water transportation along the Pearl River, it is the southern terminus of the Canton-Han-k'ou RR. It has a large international airport and is linked with Hong Kong by the Canton-Kowloon RR. Canton is the marketplace for China's world trade; great national trade expositions, held there every spring and fall (since 1957), attract thousands of businessmen from all over the world. Canton became a part of China in the 3d cent. B.C. Hindu and Arab merchants reached Canton in the 10th cent., and the city became the first Chinese port regularly visited by European traders. In 1511, Portugal secured a trade monopoly, but it was broken by the British in the late 17th cent.; in the 18th cent. the French and Dutch were also admitted. Trading, however, was restricted until the Treaty of Nanking (1842) following the Opium War, which opened the city to foreign trade. Following a disturbance, French and British forces occupied Canton in 1856. Later the island of Shameen was ceded to them for business and residential purposes, and this reclaimed sandbank with its broad avenues, gardens, and fine buildings was known for its beauty; it was restored to China in 1946. Canton was the seat of the revolutionary movement under Sun Yat-sen in 1911; the Republic of China was proclaimed there. From Canton the Nationalist armies of Chiang Kai-shek marched northward in the 1920s to establish a government in Nanking. In 1927, Canton was briefly the seat of one of the earliest Communist communes in China. The fall of Canton to the Communist armies in late Oct., 1949, signalled the Communist takeover of all China. Under the Communist government, Canton was developed as an industrial center and a modern port, with a great trade to and from Hong Kong. The city is also a cultural and educational center with several institutions of higher learning, notably Sun Yat-sen Univ. and Chinan Univ. Tourist attractions include a large pagoda overlooking the river, now a museum of ceramics; the huge Temple of the Six Banyan Trees; and a park, with pavilions, commemorating the 1927 conflict between the Communists and the KUOMINTANG. Nearby are Ts'ung Hua hot springs and an important army base.

Canton. 1 City (1970 pop. 14,217), Fulton co., W central Ill., in the corn belt; inc. 1849. It is a trade and industrial center for a coal and farm area. Its industries include coal mining and the manufacture of farm equipment and clothing. A junior college is there. **2** Town (1970 pop. 17,100), Norfolk co., E Mass., a residential and industrial suburb of Boston; settled 1630, inc. 1797. Rubber goods, textiles, plastics, and paper products are manufactured. Paul Revere operated a copper-rolling mill there. The town has a state hospital for the physically handicapped. **3** City (1970 pop. 10,503), seat of Madison co., W central Miss.; inc. 1836. It is a trade and processing center in a cotton, truck farm, and timber area. There are a number of fine old antebellum houses. **4** City (1970 pop. 110,053), seat of Stark co., NE Ohio, at the junction of three branches of Nimishillen Creek; inc. 1822. It is a steel-processing center in a great iron and steel area. Other manufactures include roller bearings, heavy office equipment, water softeners, and forgings. In Canton are Malone College and a football hall of fame. Walsh College is in suburban North Canton. William McKinley lived in Canton; his grave and monument are in the McKinley State Memorial. The Stark County Historical Center, adjacent to the memorial, contains a McKinley museum.

Canton or **Pearl,** Chin. *Chu-chiang,* river, 110 mi (177 km) long, S Kwangtung prov., S China. Formed at Canton by the confluence of the Si and Pei rivers, it flows E then S past Canton and Huang-pu island to form a large estuary between Hong Kong and Macao. The river links Canton to Hong Kong and the South China Sea and is one of China's most important waterways. The estuary, called Boca Tigris, is kept open for ocean vessels by dredging.

Canton Island, coral atoll (1967 est. pop. 130), 3.5 sq mi (9 sq km), central Pacific, largest of the PHOENIX ISLANDS, c.2,000 mi (3,220 km) SE of Honolulu, Hawaii. Annexed by the British at the end of the 19th cent., the island was also claimed by American guano companies. In 1937 the British built a radio station on Canton, but in 1938 the United States formally claimed the island and placed it under the Dept. of the Interior. British and American colonists were brought to Canton in 1938 but were evacuated during World War II. In 1939 both Great Britain and the United States agreed on joint control of Canton and nearby Enderbury Island for 50 years.

Cantor, Eddie, 1892-1964, American entertainer, b. New York City, originally named Edward Israel Iskowitz. Cantor became one of the best-known theatrical figures of his day. His style was typified by lively footwork, rolling eyes, and an utterly individual singing voice. On stage from 1907 and a Ziegfeld star from 1916, Cantor had numerous movie successes and a series of his own radio and television shows. See his autobiographical *As I Remember Them* (1963).

Cantor, Georg (gä'ôrkh kän'tôr), 1845-1918, German mathematician, b. St. Petersburg. He studied under Karl Weierstrass and taught (1869-1913) at the Univ. of Halle. He is known for his work on transfinite numbers and on the development of set theory, which is the basis of modern analysis, as well as for his definition of irrational numbers. His approach to the concept of the infinite revolutionized mathematics by challenging the processes of deductive reasoning and led to a critical investigation of the foundations of mathematics.

cantor [Lat.,=singer], a singer or chanter, especially one who performs the solo chants of a church service. The office of cantor, at first an honorary one, originated in the Jewish synagogues, in which from early times it was the custom to appoint a lay member to represent the congregation in prayer. The cantillation of prayers, and later of parts of the Scriptures, was transmitted by oral tradition. The notation of the chants was forbidden. In the 6th cent. poetic prayer forms were developed, and with them more complicated modes, or music, thus necessitating professional cantors. In the early Christian church, cantors known as *precentors* had charge of the musical part of the service. In modern Roman Catholic and Anglican services cantors sing the opening words of hymns and psalms.

Canusium: see CANOSA DI PUGLIA, Italy.

Canute (kənōōt', kənyōōt'), 995?-1035, king of England, Norway, and Denmark. The younger son of Sweyn of Denmark, Canute accompanied his father on the expedition of 1013 that invaded England and forced ÆTHELRED to flee to Normandy. When Sweyn died (1014), the Danes in England swore fealty to Canute, but on Æthelred's return from Normandy, Canute withdrew to Denmark, where his older brother, Harold, had become king. In 1015, Canute reinvaded England with a powerful army that conquered most of Wessex, harried the Danelaw, and conquered Northumbria. After the Danish victory in the battle of ASSANDUN, Canute divided England with EDMUND IRONSIDE, Æthelred's son. When Edmund died, late in 1016, Canute was accepted as sole king. He gave England peace and strove to continue English traditions by restoring the church to high place and codifying English law. To forestall dynastic quarrels he banished his wife (and their son Sweyn) and married Emma, the widow of Æthelred. His son by Emma was Harthacanute. In 1018 or 1019 he succeeded to the throne of Denmark and was forced to lead several expeditions to assert his rights there and in the Danish provinces in Norway. In 1028, after an uprising had expelled Olaf II of Norway, Canute was recognized as ruler of that kingdom. He made his son Harthacanute king of Denmark, and in 1029 he made his son Sweyn king of Norway, with Sweyn's mother as regent. She and Sweyn were driven out by 1035, and Norway was ruled by Olaf's son Magnus. Canute established friendly relations with the Holy Roman Empire and attended the coronation of Conrad II in Rome in 1027. At the end of his reign Canute led an army into Scotland to stop Scottish invasions under Malcolm II. Canute was succeeded by his illegitimate son, Harold Harefoot, then by Harthacanute. The name also appears as Cnut or Knut. See biography by L. M. Larson (1912, repr. 1970); F. M. Stenton, *Anglo-Saxon England* (3d ed., 1971).

Canute the Saint, d. 1086, king (1080–86) and patron saint of Denmark. He built churches and cathedrals and raised the bishops to the rank of prince. In 1085 he made an unsuccessful attempt to invade England. He was killed by a mob enraged by the imposition of heavy fines and a tithe. Feast: Jan. 19.

canvas, strong, coarse cloth of cotton, flax, hemp, or other fibers, early used as sailcloth. Left in its natural color, bleached, or dyed, it has a wide variety of uses, as for game, duffel, sport, mail and nose bags, tennis shoes, covers, tents, and awnings. Waterproofed with tar, paint, or the like, it is called tarpaulin and used to protect boats, hatches, and machinery. Duck is a fine light quality used for summer clothing, awnings, and sails. Artists' canvas is a light, smooth, single-warp texture, specially treated to receive paint. Art or embroidery canvas is an open-mesh type, usually linen, for working in crewels and for needlepoint.

canvasback: see DUCK.

Canyon de Chelly National Monument [De Chelly, Sp. corruption of Navaho *Tsegi* = rock canyon], 83,840 acres (33,930 hectares), NE Ariz.; est. 1931. The area contains the ruins of several hundred prehistoric Indian villages, most of them built A.D. 350–1300. The spectacular cliff dwellings include Mummy Cave, with a three-story tower house. Artifacts have been found, and there are numerous pictographs in rock shelters and on cliff faces. The earliest people living in the region were the BASKET MAKERS, predecessors of the PUEBLO INDIANS. The NAVAHO came to the canyon c.1700, and it became their chief stronghold. In 1805 a Spanish expedition fought the Navaho in a rock shelter, now called Massacre Cave, in Canyon del Muerto (site of a prehistoric Indian burial ground). In 1864 a U.S. cavalry force under Kit Carson engaged the Navaho in Canyon de Chelly.

Canyonlands National Park, 257,640 acres (104,267 hectares), SE Utah; est. 1964. Located in a desert region, the park contains a maze of deep canyons and many unusual features carved by wind and water, including spires, pinnacles, and arches; surrounding mesas rise more than 7,800 ft (2,377 m). Cataract Canyon, through which the raging waters of the Colorado and Green rivers flow, contains one of the world's largest exposures of red sandstone. Island in the Sky, a plateau overlooking the junction of the Green and Colorado rivers, has walls that drop in giant steps 2,200 ft (671 m) to the canyon floor. Upheaval Dome, pushed upward by the pressure of surrounding rock on underground salt deposits, contains a crater 1 mi (1.6 km) wide and 1,500 ft (457 m) deep. Also found in the park are many Indian petroglyphs drawn on rocks c.1,000 years ago. Bighorn sheep, mule deer, and beaver live in the park.

canzone (käntsô'nā) or **canzona** (–nä), in literature, Italian term meaning lyric or song. It is used to designate such various literary forms as Provençal troubadour poems and the lyrics of Dante, Petrarch, and other Italian poets of the 13th and 14th cent. The term was revived in the 19th cent. by Italian lyric poets, among them Giosuè Carducci.

canzone or **canzona,** in music, a type of instrumental music in Italy in the 16th and 17th cent. The term had previously been given to strophic songs for five or six voices; usually the canzone had three sections. The instrumental canzone was written in imitation of lute or keyboard transcriptions of French chansons. Frescobaldi used it in a series of fugal sections, each a rhythmic variation of the same theme. The thematic unity of his example was adopted by Froberger and other German composers, and this development led to the fugue. The canzone for instrumental ensemble became, in the hands of Giovanni Gabrieli and his followers, a structure consisting of sections of imitation in duple meter alternating with passages in triple meter.

caoutchouc (kou'cho͝ok), natural RUBBER obtained as a LATEX from various tropical plants, e.g., the PARÁ RUBBER TREE. It is much more elastic than BALATA or GUTTA-PERCHA. It is the most familiar and widely used of the natural rubbers. It is usually processed by coagulating the latex and by milling or smoking the solid rubber. It is then further treated, e.g., by VULCANIZATION, to produce useful articles.

cap: see HAT.

Capa, Robert, 1913–54, American photographer of war, b. Hungary. From the early 1930s, Capa recorded with profound concern the spectacle of humanity caught in war. In 1936 he covered the Spanish civil war, making the photograph of a Loyalist at the instant of death that has become a classic. In 18 years he covered five wars; the result is a powerful and very personal indictment. In 1946, Capa helped found Magnum, a select agency for photojournalists. His books include *Death in the Making* (1938) and *Images of War* (1964). Capa was killed at 41 by a North Vietnamese land mine while photographing French combat troops.

Capablanca, José Raúl (hōsā' räo͞ol' käpäbläng'kä), 1888–1942, Cuban chess player, b. Havana. Champion of Cuba at the age of 12, he won the world's championship from Emanuel LASKER in 1921, retaining the title until he was defeated by Alexander ALEKHINE in 1927. His game was almost free from false interpretations of position, and his technique, although facile, was highly refined. See his *My Chess Career* (1920, rev. ed. 1966), *Chess Fundamentals* (1921, repr. 1967), *A Primer of Chess* (1935), and *Capablanca's Last Chess Lectures* (1967); Harry Golombek, ed., *Capablanca's Hundred Best Games of Chess* (1947, repr. 1965).

capacitance, in electricity, capability of a body, system, circuit, or device for storing electric charge. Capacitance is expressed as the ratio of stored charge in coulombs to the impressed potential difference in volts. The resulting unit of capacitance is the FARAD [for Michael Faraday]. In an electric circuit the device designed to store charge is called a CAPACITOR. An ideal capacitor, i.e., one having no resistance or inductance, may be spoken of as a capacitance. When an alternating current flows through a capacitor, the capacitor produces a reactance that resists the current (see IMPEDANCE).

capacitor or **condenser,** device for the storage of electric charge. Simple capacitors usually consist of two plates made of an electrically conducting material (e.g., a metal) and separated by a nonconducting material (e.g., glass, paraffin, mica, oil, or air). The LEYDEN JAR is a simple capacitor. If an electrical potential (voltage) is applied to the plates of a capacitor (e.g., by connecting one plate to the positive and the other to the negative terminal of a storage battery), the plates will become charged, one positively and one negatively. If the externally applied voltage is then removed, the plates of the capacitor remain charged, and the presence of the electric charge induces an electrical potential between the plates. This phenomenon is called electrostatic induction. The capacity of the device for storing electric charge (i.e., its capacitance) can be increased by increasing the area of the plates, by decreasing their separation, or by varying the substance used as an insulator. The property of this insulator (or dielectric) that affects the capacitance of the device is its acceptance of an induced electric field; the dielectric constant is a measure of the increase in capacitance due to a particular substance. Capacitors are used in many electrical and electronic devices. One type of variable capacitor, commonly used in the tuning circuits of radio sets, consists of two sets of semicircular plates, one set fixed and the other mounted on a movable shaft. By rotating the shaft the plates can be moved, increasing or decreasing the overlap of area of the plates, and thus increasing or decreasing the capacitance. For each different value of the capacitance the tuning circuit responds to a different particular frequency, and thus the circuit is able to select stations broadcasting on different frequencies.

Capaneus: see SEVEN AGAINST THEBES.

Cap de la Madeleine (kăp də lä mädlĕn'), city (1971 pop. 31,463), S Que., Canada, at the confluence of the St. Maurice and St. Lawrence rivers. Newsprint and paper products, plywood, aluminum products, and clothing are manufactured there. The shrine and sanctuary of Nôtre Dame du Cap is in the city.

Cape Breton Highlands National Park (brĕt'ən), 367 sq mi (951 sq km), N Cape Breton Island, N. S., Canada; est. 1936. It covers a large tableland and includes sections of the rugged Atlantic coastline.

Cape Breton Island, island (1971 pop. 170,007), 3,970 sq mi (10,282 sq km), forming the northeastern part of N.S., Canada, and separated from the mainland by the narrow Gut, or Strait, of Canso. The easternmost point is called Cape Breton. The center of the island is occupied by the Bras d'Or salt lakes. Gently sloping in the south, the island rises to rugged hills in the wilder northern part. The inhabitants are mainly of Scottish Highlander descent. There are many summer resorts on the lakes and fishing villages on the coast. In the northeast are steelworks dependent on the extensive Sydney coal fields. The Cabot Trail, a scenic road through Cape Breton Highlands National Park, commemorates the discovery of Cape Breton Island in 1497 by John Cabot. The island was a French possession from 1632 to 1763. After the Peace of Utrecht (1713) many Acadians migrated there from mainland Nova Scotia, which was ceded to the English. They renamed the island Île Royale and established the fortress at LOUISBURG. With the final cession of Canada to the British (1763), Cape Breton was attached to Nova Scotia. It was made a separate colony in 1784, with Sydney as its capital, but was rejoined to Nova Scotia in 1820.

cape buffalo, species of short-haired African ungulate, or hoofed mammal, *Syncerus caffer.* The cape, or African, buffalo may reach 7 ft (2.1 m) in length, weigh more than 1,500 lb (670 kg), and reach a height of 5 ft (1.5 m) at the shoulder. Coat color and horn shape seem to vary with the animal's habitat, which ranges from high grass savanna to equatorial forest and extends from Lake Chad south to the Cape of Good Hope and from Senegal, on the Atlantic coast, to Ethiopia, on the Indian Ocean. Cape buffalo gather in herds of up to a thousand animals; they graze and drink in the early morning and evening and rest during the heat of midday and at night. They are aggressive and powerfully built, and can easily fend off the attack of a lion. They mate in January or February; after a gestation period of 11 months the cow gives birth to a single calf. Its life span is about 16 years. Cape buffalo are classified in the phylum CHORDATA, subphylum Vertebrata, class Mammalia, order Artiodactyla, family Bovidae.

Cape Canaveral, low, sandy promontory extending E into the Atlantic Ocean from a barrier island, E Fla., separated from Merritt Island by the Banana River, a lagoon; named (1963) Cape Kennedy in memory of President John F. Kennedy, it reverted to its original name in 1973. The John F. Kennedy Manned Space Flight Center of the National Aeronautics and Space Administration is located at Cape Canaveral. Since 1947 the cape has been the principal U.S. launching site for long-range missiles, earth satellites, and manned space flights. The first U.S. space satellite (Explorer I; 1958); John Glenn, the first American to orbit the earth (1962); and Neil Armstrong (see ASTRONAUTS), the first man on the moon (1969); were launched into space from the cape. The region around Cape Canaveral has attracted many rocket and guided-missile-related industries. Patrick Air Force Base is nearby.

Cape Coast, town (1970 pop. 51,764), capital of Central Region, S Ghana, on the Gulf of Guinea. The town is an export port and fishing center. It grew up around European forts built in the 17th cent. The British made it their headquarters in 1664. It was capital of the Gold Coast until superseded by ACCRA in 1877. Cape Coast is also an educational center.

Cape Cod, narrow peninsula of glacial origin, 399 sq mi (1,033 sq km), SE Mass., extending 65 mi (105 km) E and N into the Atlantic Ocean. It is generally flat, with sand dunes, low hills, and numerous lakes. The cape's familiar hook-shape is a result of the action of winds and ocean currents on the sand and gravel. Bartholomew Gosnold, an English explorer, visited the cape in 1602 and named it for the abundant codfish found in surrounding waters. Fishing, whaling, shipping, and salt making were important until the late 1800s; tourism and cranberry growing (Cape Cod is the nation's largest producer of cranberries) are now the main industries. Candle making and boatbuilding are also carried on. Towns on Cape Cod include Provincetown, site of the Pilgrim's first landing (1620); Barnstable, where the Hyannis home of the Kennedy family is located; Falmouth, location of Woods Hole, an oceanographic center; and Bourne, through which the **Cape Cod Canal** passes. This lockless canal, 17.5 mi (28.2 km) long, 32 ft (10 m) deep, was built (1910–14) from private funds. It was purchased by the U.S. government in 1927. The canal accommodates oceangoing vessels and cuts the distance between New York City and Boston by 75 mi (121 km). Parts of Cape Cod constitute **Cape Cod National Seashore** (44,600 acres/18,050 hectares; est. 1961). It contains beaches, sand dunes, heathlands, marshes, fresh-water ponds, and historic sites including the first Marconi Wireless Station in the United States.

Cape Colony: see CAPE PROVINCE.

Cape Dezhnev (dĕzh'nəf, Russ. dyăsh'nyəf) or **East Cape,** northeasternmost point of Asia, Far Eastern

USSR, on Chukchi Peninsula and on the Bering Strait. It is named after the Russian navigator who discovered it in 1648. It was first called East Cape by Capt. James Cook.

Cape Fear River, 202 mi (325 km) long, formed in E central N.C. by the junction of the Deep and Haw rivers, and flowing southeast to enter the Atlantic Ocean N of Cape Fear; longest river entirely within North Carolina. Dams and locks make the river navigable to Fayetteville, N.C.; its estuary forms part of the Intracoastal Waterway. During the colonial period the river was a main route to the interior.

Cape Girardeau (jĭrär'dō, jērərdō'), city (1970 pop. 31,282), Cape Girardeau co., SE Mo., overlooking the Mississippi River; founded 1793, inc. as a city 1843. It is a transportation, trade, and distribution center with factories that manufacture a variety of products. Its position on the river, near the confluence with the Ohio River, spurred its early growth. During the Civil War it was occupied by Union forces, and four forts were built there. A minor battle occurred on April 26, 1863. Fort D (1861) and other old buildings are among today's points of interest. The city is known for its roses; one display garden has numerous varieties. Southeast Missouri State Univ. is there. The city is connected with Illinois by a highway bridge.

Cape jasmine: see MADDER.

Čapek, Josef (chä'pĕk), 1887–1945, Czech writer and painter. He collaborated with his brother Karel on a number of plays and short stories. On his own he wrote the utopian play *Land of Many Names* (1923, tr. 1926) and several novels. *Poems from a Concentration Camp* (1946) were written in Belsen, where he died. As a painter, Josef Čapek developed an original primitivist style. His works of art criticism include *The Humblest Art* (1920).

Čapek, Karel, 1890–1938, Czech playwright, novelist, and essayist. He is best known as the author of two brilliant satirical plays—*R. U. R. (Rossum's Universal Robots;* 1921, tr. 1923), which introduced the word *robot* into the English language, and *The Insect Play,* written with his brother Josef (1921, tr., 1923). These plays embody Čapek's attacks on technological and materialistic excesses. Of his other plays *The Makropoulos Secret* (1923, tr. 1925) satirizes man's search for immortality. Janáček used it as the basis for his opera *The Makropoulos Affair* (1925). Čapek's *Power and Glory* (1937, tr. 1938), condemns totalitarianism. He also wrote travel sketches, romances (e.g., *Krakatit,* 1924, tr. 1925), and essays. His three volumes of conversations with Thomas G. Masaryk (1928–35, tr. 1934, 1938) form a political biography. Čapek's three philosophical novels, *Hordubal* (1934, tr. 1934), *Meteor* (1934, tr. 1935), and *An Ordinary Life* (1935, tr. 1936) are mystical in tone and are not closely related to his other works. See study by W. E. Harkins (1962).

Cape Kennedy: see CAPE CANAVERAL, Fla.

Capell, Edward (kā'pəl), 1731–81, English Shakespearean scholar. His 10-volume edition of Shakespeare (1768) was the first to incorporate exact collations of all available old texts. He followed this with a commentary, *Notes and Various Readings to Shakespeare* (3 vol., 1783).

Capella, Martianus (märshēā'nəs kəpĕl'ə), fl. 5th cent.?, Latin writer, b. Carthage. His one famous work, *The Marriage of Mercury and Philology,* also called the *Satyricon* and *Disciplinae,* is a long allegory about the liberal arts. Its popularity in medieval schools was universal. The author is also known as Felix Capella and may have lived in the 4th cent.

Capella, brightest star in the constellation AURIGA; Bayer designation α Aurigae; 1970 position R.A. $5^h14.5^m$, Dec. +45°58'. Capella is a yellow giant star of SPECTRAL CLASS G8 III and is also a spectroscopic BINARY STAR with a component of spectral class F. Its apparent MAGNITUDE of 0.06 makes it the 6th-brightest star in the sky. Capella is about 45 light-years from the earth. Its name is from the Latin for "little she-goat."

Capelle, Eduard von (ā'do͝oärt fən käpĕl'ə), 1855–1931, German admiral. As secretary for the navy (1916–18) he reinstituted (1917) unrestricted submarine warfare in World War I.

Capello, Bianca (byäng'kä käpĕl'lō), 1548–87, grand duchess of Tuscany (1579–87). Of a noble Venetian family, she eloped (1563) with a Florentine, Pietro Bonaventuri, who was later killed (1569). She was the mistress, then (1579) the wife, of Francesco de' MEDICI. After a banquet the grand duke and his duchess died suddenly, but rumors that they had been poisoned were never substantiated.

Cape Lookout National Seashore: see NATIONAL PARKS AND MONUMENTS (table).

Cape May, city (1970 pop. 4,392), Cape May co., S N.J., at the end of Cape May peninsula, on the Atlantic Ocean; settled in the 1600s, inc. 1857. One of the nation's oldest beach resorts, it became popular in the mid-19th cent., when it was known as the "President's Playground"; Lincoln, Grant, Arthur, Buchanan, Hayes, and Benjamin Harrison vacationed there. The city's various mansions and Victorian hotels comprise a high concentration of notable 19th-century architecture. **Cape May,** the southern extremity of New Jersey, has a lighthouse on Cape May Point at the entrance to Delaware Bay. The cape is bisected by a canal, c.3 mi (4.8 km) above the point, which was constructed by the Federal government in 1942–43 as a war emergency measure to provide an alternative to the longer, more hazardous route around the cape. The canal is part of the New Jersey Intracoastal Waterway. In the past few decades erosion has washed away nearly .2 mi (.3 km) of the cape in the area of Cape May Point.

Cape Province, formerly **Cape of Good Hope Colony,** province (1970 pop. 4,991,224), 278,465 sq mi (721,224 sq km), S Republic of South Africa. The capital and largest city is CAPE TOWN, which is also the country's legislative capital. Other cities include EAST LONDON, KIMBERLEY, PORT ELIZABETH, and UITENHAGE. Cape Province has a diversified economy. Grain, fruit, tobacco, and chicory are cultivated, chiefly in the fertile coastal regions; cattle, sheep, and goats are raised in the interior. Marine fishing is pursued, especially in the southwest, and diamonds, iron ore, manganese, asbestos, and copper are mined. Industry is centered in Cape Town, Port Elizabeth, Uitenhage, and East London. Manufactures include textiles, clothing, processed foods, wine and liquor, motor vehicles, refined petroleum, and footwear. The province has an excellent road and rail system. Cape Town, Port Elizabeth, and East London are major seaports. Institutions of higher education include the Univ. of Cape Town, Rhodes Univ. (Grahamstown), and the Univ. of Stellenbosch. Although the Cape of Good Hope was first circumnavigated in 1488 by Bartolomeu Dias and later (1497) by Vasco da Gama, the first European settlement of the region was only in 1652, when Jan van Riebeeck founded a resupply station for the Dutch East India Company on TABLE BAY; the station subsequently became Cape Town. At the time of Van Riebeeck's landing, Cape Province was inhabited by San (Bushmen) and Khoikhoi (Hottentots) in the southern and central areas, and by Bantu-speaking black Africans on the northern and eastern fringes (see BANTU LANGUAGES). The Dutch East India Company brought Dutch settlers to Cape Town, who farmed and raised livestock and were called BOERS [Du.,=farmers]. In 1689, French HUGUENOTS began to arrive; they developed the wine industry. The company ruled the Cape until 1795, except for a brief period (1781–84) of French occupation. In 1779 the first of numerous frontier wars (continuing until 1877) between Europeans and the Xhosa (a Bantu-speaking people) erupted. These so-called Kaffir Wars were mainly over land and cattle. During the French Revolutionary and Napoleonic Wars (1792–1815), Britain occupied the Cape from 1795 to 1803, when the Dutch regained control; Holland formally ceded it to Great Britain in 1806. The British named the territory Cape of Good Hope Colony and encouraged immigration from England. The new British settlers soon conflicted with the Boers over anglicization of the courts, control of farm- and pastureland, and slaveholding. Beginning in 1835 many Boers left Cape Colony (see TREK), seeking more land and escape from British rule. The Boers founded a temporary republic in NATAL and longer lasting republics in the TRANSVAAL and ORANGE FREE STATE. In 1850, Cape Colony had about 140,000 residents of European descent. In 1853 the colony was allowed to elect a legislature to advise the governor, and in 1872 it received internal self-government. In 1867 diamonds were discovered in the Kimberley region, which in 1880 was annexed by the Cape. The British and the remaining Boers generally cooperated until the 1890s, when the British, and especially Cecil RHODES (then prime minister of Cape Colony), sought to unite the Transvaal and the Orange Free State with the Cape and Natal. In 1895–96, L. S. JAMESON staged an unsuccessful raid from Cape Colony into the Transvaal, which greatly increased tension between Britons and Boers. The South African War (1899–1902) followed soon thereafter. In 1910 the Cape Colony joined with Natal, the Transvaal, and the Orange Free State to become a founding province of the Union of South Africa.

caper, common name for members of the Capparidaceae, a family of tropical plants found chiefly in the Old World and closely related to the family Cruciferae (MUSTARD family). *Capparis spinosa* is cultivated in the Mediterranean area for its flower buds—capers—which are pickled and used as a condiment. The spiderflower (*Cleome spinosa*) is a common garden annual. The family also includes a few species indigenous to the United States, e.g., the burro-fat (*Isomeris*), a common desert shrub of the Southwest. The caper family is classified in the division MAGNOLIOPHYTA, class Magnoliopsida, order Capparales.

Capernaum or **Capharnaum** (kəpûr'nāəm; kəfär'nāəm), town, NE Palestine, on the northwestern shore of the Sea of Galilee, closely associated with Jesus' ministry. John 2.12; 6.59; Mat. 11.23; 8; 9; Mark 1; 2; Luke 4; 5. A synagogue of the 3d cent. was excavated on the site (Kefar Nahum, Israel) and partially restored.

Cape Sable Island, 7 mi (11.2 km) long and 3 mi (4.8 km) wide, SW N.S., Canada. It is connected to the mainland by a causeway over Barrington Passage. Clark's Harbour (1971 pop. 1,082), a fishing port, is on the west coast.

Capetians (kəpē'shənz), royal house of France that ruled continuously from 987 to 1328; it takes its name from HUGH CAPET. Related branches of the family (see VALOIS; BOURBON) ruled France until the final deposition of the monarchy in the 19th cent. The first historical ancestor was ROBERT THE STRONG, count of Anjou and of Blois. His son, EUDES, count of Paris, was elected (888) king after the deposition of the Carolingian king Charles III (Charles the Fat). From 893 to 987 the crown passed back and forth between CAROLINGIANS and descendants of Robert the Strong. Eudes's brother, ROBERT I, was chosen king in 922 but died in 923. The title, waived by his son, HUGH THE GREAT, passed to Robert's son-in-law, RAOUL, duke of Burgundy. In 987, Hugh's son, Hugh Capet, became king. His direct descendants remained on the throne until the death (1328) of Charles IV, when it passed to the related house of Valois. The successors of Hugh Capet were Robert II, Henry I, Philip I, Louis VI, Louis VII, Philip II, Louis VIII, Louis IX, Philip III, Philip IV, Louis X, John I, Philip V, and Charles IV. Their reign marked the expansion of royal authority, the revival of towns and commerce, and the beginning of the modern French state. See Robert Fawtier, *The Capetian Kings of France* (1941, tr. 1960).

Cape Town or **Capetown,** city (1970 pop. 691,296), legislative capital of the Republic of South Africa and capital of its CAPE PROVINCE, a port on the Atlantic Ocean. The city lies at the foot of Table Mt. (c.3,570 ft/1,090 m) and on the shore of Table Bay. Cape Town is a commercial and industrial center; food processing, wine-making, printing, and the manufacture of clothing and plastic and leather goods are the chief industries. An important port, Cape Town exports mainly gold, diamonds, and fruits. Tourism is of growing economic importance for the city, with its beaches and pleasant climate. The city is linked by road and rail with the rest of South Africa. Cape Town was founded in 1652 by Governor Jan van Riebeeck as a supply station on the Dutch East India Company's sea route to the East. In 1795 the British occupied the city. It was returned to the Dutch in 1803 but recaptured in 1806 by the British, who established Cape of Good Hope Colony with Cape Town as capital. When the Union of South Africa was formed in 1910, Cape Town became its legislative capital and Pretoria its administrative capital. Cape Town's attractions include the Castle, a fortress dating from 1666; the Dutch Reformed church (begun 1699); Old Town House (1755), which contains a museum of 17th-century Flemish and Dutch paintings; and botanical gardens. The Cape Malay section of the city is noted for its old Dutch-style houses and its mosques. Cape College for Advanced Technical Education is in Cape Town; nearby is the Groote Schuur estate, which includes the prime minister's residence and the Univ. of Cape Town.

Cape Verde Islands, Port. *Ilhas do Cabo Verde,* overseas province of Portugal (1970 pop. 272,017), c.1,560 sq mi (4,040 sq km), W Africa, in the Atlantic Ocean about 300 mi (480 km) W of Dakar, Senegal. It is an archipelago made up of 10 islands and 5 islets, which fall into two main groups—the Barlavento, or Windward, in the north, which include Santo Antão, São Vicente, Santa Luzia, São Nicolau, Boa Vista, and Sal, and the Sotavento, or Leeward, in the south, which include SÃO TIAGO (c.600 sq mi/1,550 sq km, the largest island), Fogo, Maio, and Brava. Praia, located on São Tiago, is the capital; other towns include Mindêlo on São Vicente, Ribeira on Santo Antão, Sal Rei on Boa Vista, and Santa Maria on Sal. The islands are mountainous and of volcanic origin; the only active volcano is at the archipelago's highest point, Cano (c.9,300 ft/2,830 m), which is located on Fogo. About 60% of the population is of mixed black African and European descent, and most of the rest are black Africans; there are also a few Portuguese settlers. Most persons are Roman Catholic. Farming, the main economic activity, is severely limited by the small annual rainfall. Occasionally, as in the early 1970s, there are severe droughts. The main crops are maize, bananas, potatoes, tomatoes, pulses, arabica coffee, groundnuts, physic nuts, and sugarcane. Goats, hogs, cattle, and sheep are raised. Tuna and lobster are the main catches of a small, but growing, fishing industry. Puzzolana and salt are the only minerals extracted. The islands' manufactures are limited to processed food, beverages, and tobacco products. Mindêlo is an important coaling station for ships, and transatlantic flights are serviced at an airport on Sal. The islands carry on a small foreign trade, mostly with Portugal; the annual cost of imports is usually much higher than the earnings from exports. The main imports are foodstuffs, textiles, and machinery; the leading exports are salt, coffee, and foodstuffs. Many of the islanders work in Portugal, in other Portuguese holdings in Africa, and in the United States, and the money they send home constitutes an important contribution to the islands' economy. The Cape Verde Islands probably were discovered (1456) by Luigi da Cadamosto, a navigator in the service of Prince Henry of Portugal; at that time they were uninhabited. Diogo Gomes, a Portuguese explorer, visited the islands in 1460, and colonists from Portugal began to settle there in 1462. Soon thereafter, black Africans from W Africa were brought to the islands as slaves. Later a Portuguese penal colony was established, and some of the convicts remained after their terms had been completed. Slavery was abolished on the islands in 1876. Portuguese Guinea (now Guinea-Bissau) was administered as part of the Cape Verde Islands until 1879. In 1951 the status of the islands was changed from colony to overseas province. In contrast to Portugal's other African holdings, there was little agitation for independence in the 1960s and early 70s. Although some persons belonged to the outlawed African Party for Independence in Guinea-Bissau and Cape Verde (PAIGC), which advocated the union of the two areas into one nation, the movement was never strong in the islands. Because of important military bases there, Portugal dealt separately with the islands during the negotiations with the PAIGC that led to the independence (Sept., 1974) of Guinea-Bissau; it was decided to let the political future of the Cape Verde Islands be determined by a referendum. See James Duffy, *Portuguese Africa* (1959); T. B. Duncan, *Atlantic Islands: Madeira, the Azores, and the Cape Verdes in Seventeenth-century Commerce and Navigation* (1972).

Cape York Peninsula, 280 mi (451 km) long, N Queensland, Australia, between the Gulf of Carpentaria and the Coral Sea. It is largely tropical jungle and sparsely populated. Weipa is the largest town.

Capgrave, John, 1393–1464, English author and Augustinian friar. One of the most learned men of his day, he was a distinguished theologian, philosopher, and historian. His writings, many of which have been lost, include a chronicle of England up to 1417 and the Latin works *De illustribus Henricis* [on illustrious men named Henry] and *Nova legenda Angliae* [new legends of England], a rewriting of a collection of lives of English saints by a monk of Tynemouth.

Cap-Haïtien (kăp-āēsyăN'), city (1971 pop. 46,217), N Haiti, on the Atlantic Ocean. Haiti's second largest city, it is a major seaport, commercial center, and tourist attraction. Coffee, cacao, and sugar are exported. Founded by the French c.1670, the city was the capital of colonial Haiti for a century. In 1791, Cap-Haïtien was captured by Toussaint L'Ouverture, leader of a slave rebellion. From 1811 to 1820 it served as capital of the kingdom of Henri Christophe, whose Sans Souci Palace and famous citadel, La Ferrière, still stand. Despite earthquakes (notably in 1842), bombings, and civil strife, Cap-Haïtien retains some picturesque colonial charm. It is also known as Le Cap.

Capharnaum (kəfär'nāəm), the same as CAPERNAUM.

Caphtor (kăf'tôr), home of the Philistines before they went to Canaan. Its inhabitants are called Caphtorim. Gen. 2.23; 10.14; Deut. 2.23; 1 Chron. 1.12; Jer. 47.4; Amos 9.7. Caphtor is now generally identified with Crete.

capillarity or **capillary action,** phenomenon in which the surface of a liquid is observed to be elevated or depressed where it comes into contact with a solid. For example, the surface of water in a clean drinking glass is seen to be slightly higher at the edges, where it contacts the glass, than in the middle. Capillarity can be explained by considering the effects of two opposing forces: adhesion, the attractive (or repulsive) force between the molecules of the liquid and those of the container, and cohesion, the attractive force between the molecules of the liquid (see ADHESION AND COHESION). Adhesion causes water to wet a glass container and thus causes the water's surface to rise near the container's walls. If there were no forces acting in opposition, the water would creep higher and higher on the walls and eventually overflow the container. The forces of cohesion act to minimize the surface area of the liquid (see SURFACE TENSION); when the cohesive force acting to reduce the surface area becomes equal to the adhesive force acting to increase it (e.g., by pulling water up the walls of a glass), equilibrium is reached and the liquid stops rising where it contacts the solid. In some liquid-solid systems, e.g., mercury and glass or water and polyethylene plastic, the liquid does not wet the solid, and its surface is depressed where it contacts the solid. Capillarity is one of the causes of the upward flow of water in the soil and in plants.

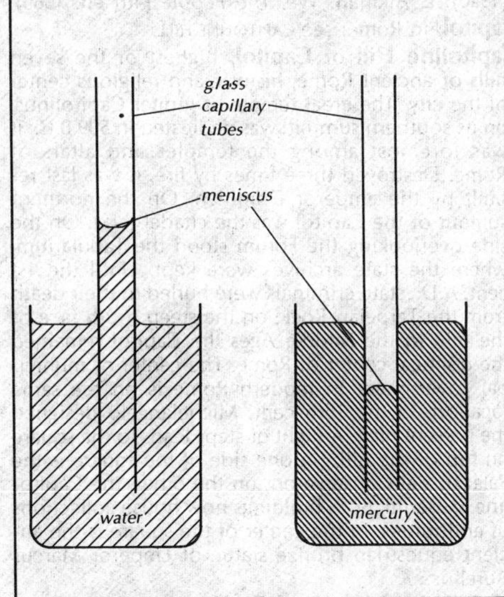

Capillarity: Water wets the walls of a capillary tube and thus rises, causing the upper surface, or meniscus, of the liquid to be concave; mercury does not wet the walls of a capillary tube and thus sinks, producing a convex meniscus.

capillary, microscopic blood vessel, smallest unit of the CIRCULATORY SYSTEM. Capillaries form a network of tiny tubes throughout the body, connecting arterioles (smallest ARTERIES) and venules (smallest VEINS). Through the thin capillary walls, which are composed of a single layer of cells, the nutritive material and oxygen in the blood pass into the body tissues, and waste matter and carbon dioxide in turn are absorbed from the tissues into the bloodstream.

capital, in architecture, the crowning member of a column, pilaster, or pier. It acts as the bearing member beneath the lintel or arch supported by the shaft and has a spreading contour appropriate to its function. The most primitive type, of which examples were found in the Beni Hassan tombs, Egypt, consisted of a square block. In later forms the capital had three well-defined parts: the neck, or necking, where it joins the shaft; the echinus, or spreading member above it; and the abacus, or block at the top. In Egypt such types were developed as early as 1500 B.C.; papyrus buds, the lotus, and the palm leaf were used as motifs of ornamentation. The Greeks perfected three types belonging to three separate orders of architecture—the DORIC ORDER, the IONIC ORDER, and the CORINTHIAN ORDER—which were also used in slightly modified forms by the Romans. The classic forms of capitals continued in use after the fall of Rome, but the Romanesque and Gothic designers introduced new forms rich in variety: grotesque heads, birds, and animals. In the 15th cent., with the Renaissance, came a return to the classical orders that continued in use until the late 19th and early 20th cent. when the modernists cast out classical decoration.

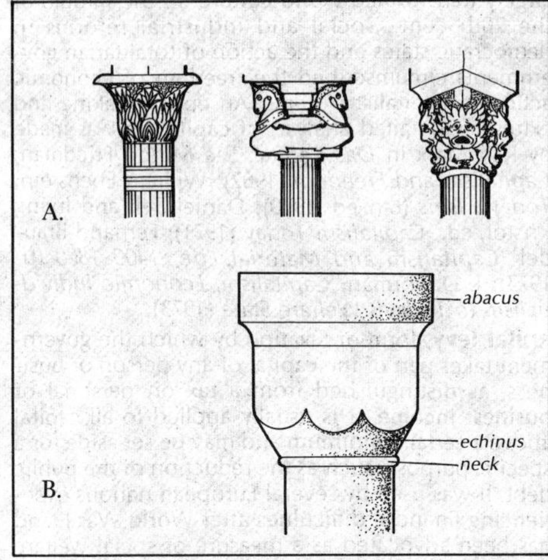

A. *Types of capitals*

B. *Parts of a capital*

capital, in economics, the entire stock of goods from which an income is derived. As originally used in business, capital denoted interest-bearing money. In classical economic theory it was one of the three major factors of production, along with land and labor. In the broad sense, all tools, machines, stores of merchandise, houses, means of transportation, lands, and such paper as stocks and bonds—any materials used to extract, transport, create, or alter goods—can be called capital. Marketable intangibles, such as credits, good will, promises, patents, and franchises, are also included by some economists. Capital goods (e.g., tractors) are distinguished from consumer goods (e.g., passenger cars) in that the former provide for future wants, while the latter provide only for the present. Distinction is also made between capital stocks, or circulating capital (e.g., raw materials, goods in process, finished goods, and sometimes wages), and capital instruments, or fixed capital (e.g., machines, tools, railways, and factories). Capital may be classed as specialized, such as railway equipment, or unspecialized, such as lumber or other raw materials having many uses. Economic theorists believe that capital arose out of the need to use the world's limited natural materials efficiently. The scarcity of the earth's resources necessitates the creation of materials (capital) that can act on the resources in such a way as to make more goods available to society than would normally exist. For example, a tractor enables man to coax more corn out of his limited supply of land. Capital is thought to accumulate from savings derived from incomes, presence of monopolies, previous profits, speculation, and recapitalization. See Irving Fisher, *The Nature of Capital and Income* (1906); F. A. von Hayek, *The Pure Theory of Capital* (1941, repr. 1962); B. S. Keirstead, *Capital, Interest, and Profits* (6th ed. 1959); S. S. Kuznets, *Capital in the American Economy* (1961); Donald Dewey, *Modern Capital Theory* (1965); J. F. Childs, *Profit Goals and Capital Management* (1968).

capital gains: see CAPITAL LEVY.

capitalism, economic system characterized by private ownership of property and of the means of production and by well-developed financial institutions. Generally the capitalist system is also thought of as embodying the concepts of freedom of individual initiative, competition, inheritance, and the profit motive. Along with SOCIALISM, it is one of the two major economic systems of the modern world. Capitalism has existed in at least partial form in the economies of all civilizations, but its modern importance dates from the INDUSTRIAL REVOLUTION that began in the 18th cent., when bankers, merchants, and industrialists—the bourgeoisie—began to displace landowners in political, economic, and social importance, particularly in Great Britain. Capitalism stresses freedom of individual economic enterprise, but even when, as in the early 19th cent., the economy was least restricted, the ultimate right of the state to supervise and regulate industry and trade was questioned by few. In the 19th and the early

20th cent., the profit motive called into being vast credit, manufacturing, and distributing institutions, and the social and economic effects of capitalism largely transformed world culture. In the middle of the 20th cent., social and industrial reforms in democratic states and the action of totalitarian governments circumscribed the freedom of economic action in capitalist systems. An epoch-making and extremely detailed analysis of capitalism was made by Karl Marx in *Das Kapital.* See Milton Friedman, *Capitalism and Freedom* (1962); William Ebenstein, *Today's Isms* (6th ed. 1970); Daniel Bell and Irving Kristol, ed., *Capitalism Today* (1971); Fernand Braudel, *Capitalism and Material Life, 1400-1800* (tr. 1973); J. D. Forman, *Capitalism, Economic Individualism to Today's Welfare State* (1973).

capital levy, form of taxation by which the government takes part of the capital of any person or business, as distinguished from a tax on personal or business income. It is usually applied to all capital above a certain minimum and may be set aside for a specific purpose, such as the reduction of the public debt. It was used by several European nations experiencing financial difficulties after World War I, and has been advocated as a measure of social welfare and a deterrent to war profits. Opponents of the capital levy stress its implied penalty on saving. In World War II, Great Britain and the United States resorted to tremendous direct taxation in order to accomplish many of the aims of the capital levy. A special tax on capital gains, at a rate more favorable than the tax rate on earned income, has been a part of the U.S. system since the New Deal. The U.S. capital-gains tax is levied on profits earned by the sale of capital assets, such as stocks. Many other nations also impose taxes on capital gains. See M. J. Bailey, et al., ed., *Taxation of Income From Capital* (1969).

capital punishment, imposition of the death penalty by the state. Capital punishment was widely applied in ancient times; it is found (c.1750 B.C.) in the Code of Hammurabi. Methods included beheading, stoning, impaling, drowning, and burning. From the fall of Rome to the beginnings of the modern era, capital punishment was practiced throughout Western Europe. Death by burning was carried out in Europe as late as the 18th cent., and in England at the beginning of the 19th cent. over 200 crimes still carried the death penalty. The modern movement for the abolition of capital punishment began in the 18th cent. with the writings of Montesquieu and Voltaire; another strong influence was Cesare BECCARIA, especially his *Essay on Crimes and Punishments* (1764). In Great Britain, Jeremy Bentham was influential in having the number of capital crimes reduced in the 18th and 19th cent. Since then, the movement has continued to gain strength worldwide. By the 1970s only France and Spain in Western Europe still retained the death penalty for crimes. Capital punishment was also practiced in Australia, in Africa, and in most of Asia. On June 29, 1972, the U.S. Supreme Court ruled that capital punishment, because it was being arbitrarily, or inconsistently, imposed, was no longer legal. Although this ruling voided the Federal and state death penalty laws then in effect, it left the way open for Congress or state legislatures to enact new capital punishment laws in the future. A number of states enacted such laws soon after the ruling. See John Laurence, *A History of Capital Punishment* (1960); J. A. Joyce, *Capital Punishment: A World View* (1961); H. A. Bedau, ed., *The Death Penalty in America* (2d ed. 1967); J. A. McCafferty, ed., *Capital Punishment* (1972); Michael Meltsner, *Cruel and Unusual* (1973).

Capito, Wolfgang Fabricius (kăp'ĭtō, Ger. vôlf'găng fäbrē'tsyo͝os kä'pētō), 1478-1541, German Protestant reformer, whose original family name was Köpfel. As a well-known humanist, he brought about communication between Erasmus and Luther. Capito worked with Martin BUCER in an attempt to unify the Evangelical churches of Germany, France, and Switzerland.

Capitol, seat of the U.S. government at Washington, D.C. It is the city's dominating monument, built on an elevated site that was chosen by George Washington in consultation with Major Pierre L'ENFANT. The building as it now stands took many years to build and is the result of the work of several architects. In 1792 a competition was held to select an architect, but William THORNTON gained the President's approval with a plan separately submitted and was appointed. In 1793 the President set the cornerstone, with Masonic rites, and the building was begun. Later three additional architects were employed—E. S. HALLET, George Hadfield (d.1826), and James HOBAN. In 1814 the uncompleted building was burned by the British, and B. H. LATROBE, who had been appointed (1803) surveyor of public buildings, undertook its restoration. He was succeeded in 1818 by Charles BULFINCH, who brought the design to completion in 1830. The building proved inadequate and was greatly enlarged (1851-65) by T. U. WALTER, who added the extensive House and Senate wings at either end and the imposing dome, c.288 ft (90 m) in height, which dominates the composition. The building proper is over 750 ft (229 m) long, including approaches c.350 ft (110 m) wide. In 1960 the east front of the Capitol was extended 32 ft (9.8 m) and the original sandstone facade was replaced by marble. See I. T. Frary, *They Built the Capitol* (1940); L. Aikman, *We, The People* (4th ed. 1966).

Capitol, in Rome: see CAPITOLINE HILL.

Capitoline Hill or **Capitol,** highest of the seven hills of ancient Rome, historic and religious center of the city. The great temple of Jupiter Capitolinus, on its southern summit, was dedicated in 509 B.C.; it was foremost among the temples and altars of Rome. Destroyed three times by fire, it was last rebuilt by the emperor Domitian. On the northern summit of the Capitol was the citadel (arx). On the side overlooking the Forum stood the Tabularium, where the state archives were kept. Until the 1st cent. A.D., state criminals were hurled to their death from the Tarpeian Rock, on the steep south face of the hill. In the Middle Ages the Capitol remained the political center of Rome. The center of municipal government in modern Rome is on the same location. In the 16th cent. Michelangelo designed the present plan. A flight of steps leads to the square on top of the hill; on one side of the square is the Palazzo dei Conservatori, on the other, the Capitoline Museum. Both buildings now house collections of antiquities. In the center of the square is the ancient equestrian bronze statue of Emperor Marcus Aurelius.

Capitol Reef National Park: see NATIONAL PARKS AND MONUMENTS (table).

capitularies (kəpĭch'o͞olĕr"ēz), decrees and written commands of the Carolingian kings of the Franks, so called because they were divided into *capitula,* or chapters. Both legislative and administrative, they were the chief written instrument of royal authority. The ordinances were issued either by the king alone or by the king and his counselors. They also served to amend or extend the GERMANIC LAWS as they applied to the entire Carolingian empire. Several capitularies—such as the exemplary *De villis*—dealt with the administration of the royal domains; others dealt with the church. Most important were the *missi dominici,* addressed by Charlemagne to his envoys. These contained instructions for the administration of the empire and instituted farreaching reforms. Capitularies issued in the late Carolingian period foreshadowed the feudal system and are collected in the MONUMENTA GERMANIAE HISTORICA. The term *capitularies* is applied also to similar documents in other fields.

Capo d'Istria, Giovanni Antonio, Count (kä'pō dē'strēä), Gr. *Joannes Antonios Capodistrias* or *Kapodistrias,* 1776-1831, Greek and Russian statesman, b. Corfu. After administrative work in the Ionian Islands he entered (1809) Russian service and was until 1822 a close adviser in foreign affairs to Czar Alexander I; he represented Russia at the Congress of Vienna. After his resignation and retirement to Switzerland in 1822, he actively elicited support for Greek independence. In 1827 the Greek national assembly elected him president of Greece. He was a dedicated reformer, but his autocratic methods, nepotism, factionalism, and Russian affiliations aroused opposition and led to his assassination. See studies by W. P. Kaldis (1963) and C. M. Woodhouse (1973).

Capodistria: see KOPER, Yugoslavia.

Capone, Al (Alfonso or Alphonse Capone) (kəpōn'), 1899-1947, American gangster, b. Naples, Italy. Brought up in New York City, he became connected with organized crime and was involved in murder investigations. In 1920 he moved to Chicago and became a lieutenant to John Torrio, a notorious gang leader. They established numerous speakeasies in Chicago in the prohibition era. After eliminating his opponents "Scarface" Capone took over control from Torrio. He was implicated in brutal murders and received tribute from businessmen and politicians. His crime syndicate—which terrorized Chicago in the 1920s and controlled gambling and prostitution there—was estimated by the Federal Bureau of Internal Revenue to have taken in $105 million in 1927 alone. Capone was indicted (1931) by a Federal grand jury for evasion of income tax payments and was sentenced to an 11-year prison term. In 1939, physically and mentally shattered by syphilis, Capone was released. See biographies by F. D. Pasley (1930, repr. 1971) and John Kobler (1971); Kenneth Allsop, *The Bootleggers and Their Era* (1970).

Capote, Truman (kăpō'tē), 1924–, American author, b. New Orleans. His fictional writings reflect a private but highly imaginative world of grotesque, narcissistic, and strangely innocent people. *Other Voices, Other Rooms* (1948), his first novel, is the story of a young boy's painful search for identity. He has published another novel, *The Grass Harp* (1951); two collections of short stories, *Tree of Night* (1949) and *Breakfast at Tiffany's* (1958); a report of his trip to Russia, *The Muses Are Heard* (1956); *A Christmas Memory* (1966); and a collection of nonfiction pieces, *The Dogs Bark: Public People and Private Places* (1973). He also collaborated on the screenplay for the film *Beat the Devil* (1953). In 1966, Capote published *In Cold Blood,* a chilling, semidocumentary study of a senseless, brutal murder in Kansas, which he called a "nonfiction novel."

Cappadocia (kăpədō'shə), ancient region of Asia Minor, watered by the Halys River (the modern Kızıl Irmak), in present E central Turkey. The name was applied at different times to territories of varying size. At its greatest extent Cappadocia stretched from the Halys valley E to the Euphrates River, from the Black Sea S to the heights of the Taurus and Anti-Taurus ranges. Mostly a high plateau, it was famous for its mineral resources, particularly its copper and iron. Cappadocia maintained its local Asian traditions in contrast to the Mediterranean seacoast of Asia Minor, which was dominated by the Aegean culture. Several thousand tablets, written in cuneiform by Assyrian colonists in Cappadocia, have been found at Kültepe (Kanish); they show that a highly developed trade existed between Assyria and Asia Minor before 1800 B.C. At that time Cappadocia was the heart of an old Hittite state. Later the Persians controlled Cappadocia. It did not yield fully to the conquest of Alexander the Great, and during the 3d cent. B.C. it gradually developed as an independent kingdom. PONTUS now became completely separated from Cappadocia. The kings had their capital at Mazaca (later CAESAREA MAZACA); the only other important cities were Tyana and Melitene, though Iconium was at times in Cappadocia. In the 2d and 1st cent. B.C. the Cappadocian dynasty maintained itself largely by siding with Rome. Invaded in 104 B.C. by Mithridates VI and c.90 B.C. by his son-in-law, Tigranes of Armenia, Cappadocia was restored by Pompey. Antony replaced the king, who had been disloyal to Rome in the Parthian invasion at the time of Julius Caesar, and in A.D. 17 Rome annexed the region as a province. Cappadocia became prosperous. Christianity was introduced early (1st cent. A.D.). The name appears in the Bible, though its importance as a separate region was already declining and later disappeared.

Capponi, Gino, Marchese (jē'nō käp-pō'nē), 1792-1876, Italian politician, historian, and educator. He played an important part in the Risorgimento. His theory of education anticipated the thought of John Dewey. In 1848 he was president of the constitutional government in Tuscany, and he became a senator after the annexation (1860) of Tuscany to the kingdom of Sardinia. Of his historical writings, the history of the Florentine republic (3 vol., 1875) is best known.

Caprera (käprā'rä), island, 6 sq mi (15.5 sq km), NE Sardinia, Italy, in the Strait of Bonifacio. It was the residence (1856-82) of Garibaldi, who is buried there.

Capri (kä'prē), Lat. *Capreae,* island (1971 pop. 7,725), 4 sq mi (10.4 sq km), Campania, S Italy, in the Bay of Naples off the tip of the Sorrento Peninsula. It is an international tourist center, celebrated for its striking scenery, delightful climate, and luxurious vegetation. There are two small towns on the island, Capri and Anacapri. The Blue Grotto is the most famous of the many caves along the island's high, precipitous coast. Monte Solaro, the highest point (1,932 ft/589 m), commands a magnificent view. On the island are remains of the 12 fine villas built there by the Roman emperors Augustus and Tiberius. The local architecture has Roman, Norman, and Arabic features.

Capricornus (kăprĭkôr'nəs) [Lat.,=the goat horn], inconspicuous southern CONSTELLATION lying on the ECLIPTIC (the sun's apparent path through the heavens) between Sagittarius and Aquarius; it is one of the constellations of the ZODIAC. Known as the Sea

Goat, it has been depicted from earliest times either as a goat or as a figure with its forepart like that of a goat and its hind part like the tail of a fish. The tropic of Capricorn takes its name from this constellation, in which the winter solstice was located about 2,000 years ago. Now, because of the PRECESSION OF THE EQUINOXES, the winter solstice has moved westward into Sagittarius. Capricornus contains a globular STAR CLUSTER that can be seen on a very clear night. The constellation reaches its highest point in the evening sky in late September.

caprifig (kăp′rəfĭg″): see FIG.

Caprivi, Leo, Graf von (lā′ō gräf fən käprē′vē), 1831–99, German chancellor, whose full name was Georg Leo, Graf von Caprivi de Caprara de Montecuculi. A former army officer and head of the admiralty, he succeeded (1890) Bismarck as chancellor. Under him the antisocialist law was abrogated and military service was shortened from three to two years. Favoring industrial over agrarian interests, he negotiated (1892–94) a series of reciprocal trade agreements to stimulate industrial exports. The agreements reduced duties on agricultural products and aroused agrarian opposition to Caprivi, which contributed to his dismissal (1894). Prince Hohenlohe-Schillingsfürst succeeded him as chancellor.

Caprivi Strip (käprē′vē) or **Caprivi Zipfel** (tsĭp′fəl) [Ger. *Zipfel*=tip, point], region, c.300 mi (480 km) long and 50 mi (80 km) wide, NE South West Africa, bordered on the N by Angola and Zambia and on the S by Botswana. It is named for the German chancellor Leo, Graf von Caprivi, who obtained it from Great Britain as part of a general settlement (1890) between the two countries. It gave the former German colony of South West Africa access to the Zambezi River.

Capsian culture: see QAFSAH, Tunisia.

Captain Jack (d. 1873), subchief of the MODOC INDIANS and leader of the hostile group in the MODOC WAR (1872–73). Jack, whose Indian name was Kintpuash, had agreed (1864) to leave his ancestral home and live on a reservation with the Klamath Indians. He found it impossible to live on friendly terms with his former enemies, and after killing a Klamath medicine man, Jack and a group of followers left the reservation. They resisted arrest (Nov., 1872) and fled into the lava beds in California. Their strong defensive position frustrated numerous attempts by U.S. troops to dislodge them. In April, 1873, a peace commission headed by Gen. Edward Richard Sprigg CANBY met with Jack and several of his men. At a prearranged signal, Jack shot Canby dead. The army renewed its efforts to capture them and forced the Modocs to take refuge elsewhere. The Indians, who were tired of fighting, began to give themselves up, and on June 1, Captain Jack was captured. He was taken to Fort Klamath, where on Oct. 3, 1873, he and three of his warriors were hanged for the murder of Canby. See biography by D. P. Payne (1938).

Capua (kä′pwä), town (1971 pop. 17,581), Campania, S Italy, on the Volturno River. It is an agricultural center and occupies the site of ancient CASILINUM. Ancient Capua, situated 3 mi (4.8 km) to the southeast, where Santa Maria Capua Vetere (1968 est. pop. 31,500) now lies, was a Roman town strategically located on the Appian Way. During the second of the PUNIC WARS it went over (216 B.C.) to the side of Hannibal, but was retaken by Rome in 211 B.C. Later it was an important colony under the Roman Empire. After Capua was destroyed (A.D. 841) by the Arabs, its inhabitants moved to Casilinum and founded modern Capua. Strongly fortified to defend nearby Naples, Capua suffered several sieges, including ones by Cesare Borgia (1501) and the Piedmontes (1860). Of note are a Roman bridge, a 9th-century cathedral (frequently restored), an 11th-century castle, and a museum of archaeology and sculpture.

Capuana, Luigi (lo͞oē′jē käpwä′nä), 1839–1915, Italian critic and novelist. His activities included teaching, scientific study, and politics. He wrote in almost every genre, but his reputation rests upon his naturalistic novels and criticism. Among his best works are the short stories in *Paesane* [peasant women] (1894), the novel *Il marchese di Roccaverdina* (1901), and his *Studi della letteratura contemporanea* (1879–82). His stories for children include *Nimble Legs* (1903, tr. 1927) and *Once upon a Time* (1882, tr. 1892). See study by S. E. Scaglia (1952).

capuchin (kăp′yo͞ochĭn), name for New World MONKEYS of the genus *Cebus,* widely distributed in tropical forests of Central and South America. Medium-sized monkeys, they have a body length of 14 to 24 in. (36–61 cm), with a tail up to 20 in. (50 cm) long, and weigh 2 to 4 lb (0.9–1.8 kg). The coat is black or brown, with lighter markings on the chest in some species. The flattened face is naked and pink. Members of some species have manes resembling the cowls of capuchin monks. The tail is partially prehensile, that is, it can be used for grasping but not with the dexterity displayed by most New World monkeys. It is usually carried with the end curled in a spiral, hence the alternate name, ringtail monkey. Capuchins travel in groups through the trees, making loud sounds, and rarely descend to the ground. They feed on leaves, fruit, insects, small animals, and bird eggs. Intelligent and friendly, they are easily trained and are well known from circuses and as the classic organ-grinder's monkey. In the wild they use simple tools, such as rocks, for such tasks as cracking the hard shells of fruits. They are classified in the phylum CHORDATA, subphylum Vertebrata, class Mammalia, order Primates, family Cebidae.

Capuchins (kăp′yo͞ochĭnz) [Ital.,=hooded ones], Roman Catholic religious order of friars, one of the independent orders of FRANCISCANS, officially the Friars Minor Capuchin [Lat. abbr., O.M.Cap.]. The order was founded (1525–28) in central Italy as a reform within the Observants, led by Matteo di Bascio. It is one of the largest orders. Born, like the Jesuits, at the beginning of the Catholic Reformation, the Capuchins became a major force in church activity, especially in preaching and in missions. With the Jesuits they did much to revive Catholicism in the parts of Europe where Protestantism had prevailed. The Capuchins have been very important in foreign missions; they were early arrivals in French Canada. See study by Father Cuthbert (1928, repr. 1971).

Capulin Mountain National Monument: see NATIONAL PARKS AND MONUMENTS (table).

capybara (kăpĭbâr′ə), mammal of Central and much of South America. It is the largest living member of the order Rodentia (the rodents) reaching a length of 4 ft (120 cm) and a weight of 75 to 100 lb (34–45 kg). Its brownish hair flecked with yellow is coarse and scanty, and its tail rudimentary. The feet are partially webbed, and there are four thick-nailed toes on the front feet and three on the hind feet. The capybara is an expert swimmer and diver. It eats vegetation and sometimes damages crops. It is hunted for food, its hide is made into gloves, and its bristles are used in brushes. It is also called water hog and carpincho. Capybaras are classified in the phylum CHORDATA, subphylum Vertebrata, class Mammalia, order Rodentia, family Hydrochoeridae.

Caquetá, river, Colombia: see JAPURÁ.

caracal (kăr′əkəl) or **Persian lynx,** mammal of the family Felidae (cat family), native to Asia and Africa. It is considered by some to be a link between the true cats and the true LYNXES. It is reddish brown with black-tufted ears. Its total length is about 3¼ ft (105 cm). It preys on small deer, hares, birds, and other animals; in some regions it is trained to catch such game for man. Caracals are classified in the phylum CHORDATA, subphylum Vertebrata, class Mammalia, order Carnivora, family Felidae.

Caracalla (kărəkăl′ə), 188–217, Roman emperor (211–17); son of Septimius SEVERUS. His real name was Marcus Aurelius Antoninus, and he received his nickname from the caracalla, a Gallic tunic he regularly wore. He was made caesar in 196 and augustus in 198, but he resented having to share these honors with his brother Geta. Early in his career he revealed his ruthless character by bringing about the downfall of his father-in-law, the political leader Plautianus, through false reports. After Septimius Severus died, leaving the empire to his two sons, Caracalla murdered (212) the more popular Geta and ordered a general massacre of Geta's followers and sympathizers (including the jurist Papinian). He thus ushered in a reign infamous for cruelty and bloodshed. Caracalla did, however, pacify the German frontier. He also extended Roman citizenship to all free inhabitants of the empire, presumably not out of generosity but to increase his income from taxes in order to meet staggering expenses. He tried to buy popularity with his soldiers and planned an ambitious campaign to extend his father's conquests into old Persia. When leading an expedition in Asia, Caracalla was murdered by MACRINUS, who succeeded him. The famous Baths of Caracalla were erected in his reign.

caracara (kär″əkär′ə): see FALCON.

Caracas (kərä′kəs, kərä′-, Span. kärä′käs), city (1970 est. metropolitan area pop. 2,175,438), N Venezuela, the capital and largest city of the country, near the Caribbean Sea. Its port is La Guaira. With an elevation of c.3,100 ft (945 m), Caracas has a pleasant climate, which contributed to making it rather than Valencia the economic and political center of Spanish colonization in Venezuela. Caracas is the commercial, industrial, and cultural hub of the nation. As a result of the oil boom of the 1950s the city expanded prodigiously. Enormous sums were spent on public works, notably the futuristic University City, school construction, slum clearance projects, a new aqueduct, and an impressive highway cloverleaf, known to Caracans as "the octopus." The symbol of the new Caracas is the twin-towered complex housing government offices known as Centro Bolívar. A colossal shopping center, the Helicoid, was built on a hill outside the city. In addition to oil refining, industries include textile milling, sugar refining, and meat-packing. Caracas was founded in 1567 as Santiago de León de Caracas by Diego de Losada. The city was sacked by the English in 1595 and by the French in 1766. Two of South America's great revolutionary leaders, Francisco de Miranda (1750) and Simón Bolívar (1783) were born in the city. Independence from Spain was declared in Caracas in July, 1811. However, the city was almost completely destroyed by an earthquake on March 26, 1812, negating the revolution led by Miranda. Bolívar captured the city in Aug., 1813, but abandoned it after a crushing defeat in June, 1814. Finally, after his victory at Carabobo, he made a triumphal entry in June, 1821.

Caractacus (kərăk′təkəs) or **Caradoc** (kərăd′ək), fl. A.D. 50, British king; son of Cymbeline. After the Roman invasion of A.D. 43, he led British resistance until defeated in A.D. 50. He was captured and taken to Rome. Emperor Claudius, admiring his courage, spared his life.

Caragiali, Ion Luca (yōn lo͞o′kä käräjä′lĭ), 1853–1912, Rumanian author and theatrical manager. In 1888 he became director of the Bucharest National Theater. Among his comedies satirizing the modernization of Rumanian society are *The Lost Letter* (1884) and *Carnival Adventures* (1885). His *False Accusation* (1889) is a tragedy. Caragiali also wrote short stories and novels.

Caraglio, Giovanni Jacopo (jōvän′nē yä′kōpō kärä′lyō), c.1500–1565, Italian engraver and designer, known also as Jacobus Parmensis and Jacobus Veronensis. He was a pupil of Raimondi and achieved distinction as an engraver on copper and, later, as a designer of medals and engraver of gems. His plates, about 70 in number, are chiefly reproductions of works of the Italian masters—Raphael, Titian, Michelangelo, and others.

Caraites: see KARAITES.

carapace (kâr′əpās), shield, or shell covering, found over all or part of the dorsal portion of an animal. In lobsters, shrimps, crayfish, and crabs the carapace is the part of the exoskeleton that covers the head and thorax and protects the dorsal and lateral surfaces. The term *carapace* is also used to describe the hard, protective covering of the cephalothorax of the horseshoe crab. The carapace of a turtle's shell is composed of expanded ribs and vertebrae overlain by dermal plates and horny scales.

Carausius (kərô′shēəs), d. 293, Gallo-Roman military commander. He was stationed in Gaul, but Emperor MAXIMIAN suspected him of conspiring with the Germans and condemned him to death. Carausius fled to Britain and established his rule there, defying attempts to conquer him. Diocletian and Maximian finally recognized (c.289) him as coemperor, and he established his rule in NE Gaul as well as in Britain. In 293, however, Constantius (later Constantius I) defeated him, and he was murdered by one of his own men.

Caravaca (käräva′kä), town (1970 pop. 18,415), Murcia prov., SE Spain, in Murcia, on the Caravaca River. It is a farm center for an area producing cereals, potatoes, fruits, and grapes. It has textile and brandy manufactures. The miraculous Cross of Caravaca was formerly kept in the Church of the Most Holy Cross (1617). Many ancient remains have been found in the area.

Caravaggio, Michelangelo Merisi da (mēkālän′jālō mārē′zē dä kärävăd′jō) or **Amerigi da Caravaggio** (ä″mārē′jē), 1573–1610, Italian painter. His surname Caravaggio came from his birthplace. After an apprenticeship with a mediocre painter in Milan, he arrived in Rome where he eventually became a pensioner of Cardinal Francesco del Monte for whom he produced several paintings, among them the *Concert of Youths* (Metropolitan Mus.). Most of Caravaggio's genre pieces such as the *Fortune Teller* (Louvre) are products of his early Roman years, but after completing the *Calling of St. Matthew* and the *Martyrdom of St. Matthew* (c.1598–99; San Luigi de'

Francesi), he devoted himself almost exclusively to religious compositions and portraiture. His violent temper and erratic disposition involved him in several brawls, and in 1606 he fled Rome after killing a young man in a duel. He spent the last four years of his life in Naples, Malta, Syracuse, and Messina. A revolutionary in art, Caravaggio was accused of imitating nature at the expense of ideal beauty. In religious scenes his use of models from the lower walks of life was considered irreverent. He generally worked directly on the canvas, a violation of current artistic procedure. His strong chiaroscuro technique of partially illuminating figures against a dark background was immediately adopted by his contemporaries, and although he had no pupils, the influence of his art was enormous. Its effect can be seen throughout Europe, from Ribera in Spain to Rembrandt in Holland. See study by Bernard Berenson (1954); Walter Friedlaender, *Caravaggio Studies* (1955, repr., 1970).

Caravaggio, Polidoro Caldara da (pōlēdô'rō kāldä'rä), c.1496–1543, Italian painter. His surname Caravaggio came from his birthplace. A student of Raphael, he was responsible for some of the monochrome decorations in the Vatican Stanze as well as for a few of the scenes in the Loggia. After Raphael's death (1520) Polidoro entered upon a career as a decorator of house facades. These chiaroscuro decorations, based on scenes taken from ancient history, survive now mainly through engravings and drawings. Greatly admired in his own time, Polidoro exercised considerable influence on later generations. In 1527 he left Rome, traveling to Naples and Messina. Of his paintings from this period the *Christ on the Way to Calvary* (Naples) is perhaps the most impressive.

caravan, group of travelers or merchants banded together and organized for mutual assistance and defense while traveling through unsettled or hostile country. Caravan trade is associated with the history of the Middle East as far back as the records of ancient civilizations extend and seems to have been well developed before sea commerce began. It is evident that all trade from one fertile area to another in this region had to be organized from the first, since long distances of desert trail separated settled parts and since local governments could not guarantee protection against tribes eager for loot and pillage. Such wares as jewels, spices, perfumes, dyes, metals, rare woods, ivory, oils, and textiles (chiefly silk) are associated with the trade. Camels were the main carriers from Egypt to Mesopotamia and throughout the Arabian peninsula. They were introduced into N Africa and the Sahara region in the 3d cent. A.D. Donkeys were used in Asia Minor. Trade naturally prospered in the period of the great empires, when the caravan routes could be controlled and protected; and it was to secure control of such routes that many wars were fought and conquests made in ancient times. An empire provided for the establishment of inns, or caravansaries, for the accommodation of travelers along the way. Such improvements facilitated the movement of troops to protect the routes. Cities rose and fell in ancient times in proportion to the rise and fall in the trade of the caravan routes upon which they were located. Basically the caravan system underwent little change until challenged in modern times by the motor truck and the airplane. Travelers having occasion to cross desert spaces usually joined merchant caravans. Since the advent of Islam, the pilgrimage of the devout to Mecca has given rise to the long pilgrim caravans that are a feature of the pilgrimage season each year. The closest approach to caravan trade in the New World was the wagon train commerce that developed over the Sante Fe Trail. See Mikhail Rostovtzev, *Caravan Cities* (1932, repr. 1971); E. W. Bovill, *The Golden Trade of the Moors* (1958).

caravel (kăr'əvĕl") or **carvel** (kär'vəl), three-masted sailing vessel, generally square-rigged with the aftermast lateen-rigged. It had a roundish hull with a high bow and stern. The term "carvel-built" (see BOAT) was derived from its method of construction. A change from bulkier ships to caravels, with their small displacement, enabled the Portuguese in the 15th cent. to take the lead among Western nations in exploring the African coast; the caravel thereafter was of primary importance in the era of expansion and exploration. Columbus's flagship, the *Santa Maria*, was a typical caravel.

Caraway, Hattie Wyatt, 1878–1950, U.S. Senator (1932–45), b. near Bakerville, Tenn. In 1932 she was appointed to fill the unexpired Senate term from Arkansas of her late husband, Thaddeus H. Caraway. With the support of Huey Long, she was elected for a full term later that year, becoming the first woman to be elected to the U.S. Senate. After failing to win renomination in 1944, she was appointed (1945) by President Franklin Delano Roosevelt to the Federal Employees Compensation Commission.

caraway (kăr'əwā), biennial Old World plant (*Carum carvi*) of the family Umbelliferae (CARROT family), cultivated in Europe and North America for its aromatic seeds. They are small and ovate, with a pleasant spicy flavor, and are used as a condiment; as seasoning of pastry and bread doughs, cabbage, sausage, and some kinds of cheese; and as flavoring for certain liqueurs (as kümmel). The volatile oil expressed from the seeds is a stimulant and a carminative. Caraway is classified in the division MAGNOLIOPHYTA, class Magnoliopsida, order Umbellales, family Umbelliferae.

carbaryl (kär'bärəl): see INSECTICIDE.

carbide, any one of a group of compounds that contain carbon and one other element that is either a metal, boron, or silicon. Generally, a carbide is prepared by heating a metal, metal oxide, or metal hydride with carbon or a carbon compound. Calcium carbide, CaC_2, can be made by heating calcium oxide and coke in an electric furnace; it reacts with water to yield acetylene and is an important source of the gas. Barium carbide reacts similarly. Aluminum carbide reacts with water to yield methane. Some carbides are unaffected by water, e.g., chromium carbide and silicon carbide. SILICON CARBIDE, almost as hard as diamond, is used as an abrasive. Tungsten carbide, also very hard, is used for cutting edges of machine tools. Iron carbides are present in steel, cast iron, and some other iron alloys.

Carbo, Cneius Papirius (nē'əs pəpĕr'ēəs kär'bō), d. 82 B.C., Roman political leader. He was consul three times (85 B.C., 84 B.C., 82 B.C.) and one of the leaders of the party of MARIUS. After the death of Marius he and his colleague, CINNA, gathered (84 B.C.) an army to oppose SULLA in Italy. When Cinna was murdered in a mutiny, Carbo became chief commander. Sulla gathered strength as he moved slowly N through Italy, and much of Carbo's force deserted. He was defeated at Faventia (present-day Faenza) by Quintus Caecilius Metellus Pius (see under METELLUS) and fled to Africa. He later crossed to Sicily, where he was captured, condemned, and executed by Pompey.

carbohydrate, any member of a large class of chemical compounds that includes sugars, starches, cellulose, and related compounds. These compounds are produced naturally by green plants from carbon dioxide and water (see PHOTOSYNTHESIS). Carbohydrates are important as foods; they supply energy and are used in the production of fats. They are also used in various forms in industry and commerce. There are three main classes of carbohydrates. Monosaccharides are the simple sugars, e.g., FRUCTOSE and GLUCOSE; they have the general formula $(CH_2O)_n$, in which n is an integer larger than 2. Disaccharides include LACTOSE, MALTOSE, and SUCROSE. Upon hydrolysis, a disaccharide molecule yields two monosaccharide molecules. Most disaccharides have the general formula $C_n(H_2O)_{n-1}$, with n larger than 5. Polysaccharides include such substances as CELLULOSE, DEXTRIN, GLYCOGEN, and STARCH; they are polymeric compounds made up of the simple sugars and can be hydrolyzed to yield simple sugars. The disaccharides are sometimes grouped with the simpler polysaccharides (usually those made up of three or four simple sugar units) to form a class of carbohydrates called the oligosaccharides.

carbolic acid: see PHENOL.

carboloy (kär'bəloi) [portmanteau word from carbon and alloy], an alloy containing cobalt, tungsten, and carbon. This alloy is extremely hard, harder than steel; it is used to cut steel, porcelain, quartz, and other materials. Its hardness is little affected by heat, and it retains a sharp cutting edge even at red heat.

carbon [Lat.,=charcoal], nonmetallic chemical element; symbol C; at. no. 6; at. wt. 12.011; m.p. about 3550°C; graphite sublimes about 3375°C; b.p. 4827°C; sp. gr. 1.8–2.1 (amorphous), 1.9–2.3 (graphite), 3.15–3.53 (diamond); valence +2, +3, +4, or −4. Although carbon makes up only .032% of the earth's crust, it is very widely distributed and forms a vast number of compounds. There are more carbon compounds than there are compounds of all other elements combined. Carbon exists in the stars; a series of thermonuclear reactions called the carbon cycle (see NUCLEOSYNTHESIS) is a source of energy for some stars. Carbon in the form of diamonds has been found in meteorites. It is found free in nature in at least three distinct forms (see ALLOTROPY). One form, GRAPHITE, is a very soft, dark gray or black, lustrous material with either a hexagonal or rhombohedral crystalline structure. DIAMOND, a second crystalline form, is the hardest substance known. In a third form, the so-called amorphous carbon, the element occurs partly free and partly combined with other elements; CHARCOAL, COAL, COKE, lampblack, PEAT, and LIGNITE are some sources of amorphous carbon. A fourth form, "white" carbon, is believed to exist. Carbon has the capacity to act chemically both as a metal and as a nonmetal. It is a constituent of all organic matter. The study of carbon compounds, both natural and synthetic, is called organic chemistry. PLASTICS, foods, TEXTILES, and many other common substances contain carbon. HYDROCARBON fuels (e.g., natural gas), marsh gas, and the gases resulting from the combustion of fuels (e.g., carbon monoxide and carbon dioxide) are compounds of carbon. With oxygen and a metallic element, carbon forms many important carbonates, such as calcium carbonate (limestone) and sodium carbonate (soda). Certain active metals react with it to make industrially important carbides, such as silicon carbide (known as carborundum), calcium carbide, used for producing acetylene gas, and tungsten carbide, an extremely hard substance used for rock drills and metalworking tools. Coke is used as a fuel in the production of iron. Carbon electrodes are widely used in electrical apparatus. The "lead" of the ordinary pencil is graphite mixed with clay. The successful linking in the 1940s of carbon with silicon has led to the development of a vast number of new substances known collectively as the SILICONES. All living organisms contain carbon; the human body is about 18% carbon by weight. In green plants carbon dioxide and water are combined to form simple sugars (CARBOHYDRATES); light from the sun provides the energy for this process (PHOTOSYNTHESIS). The energy from the sun is stored in the chemical bonds of the sugar molecule. Anabolism, the synthesis of complex compounds (such as FATS, PROTEINS, and NUCLEIC ACIDS) from simpler substances, involves the utilization of energy stored by photosynthesis. Catabolism is the release of stored energy by the oxi-

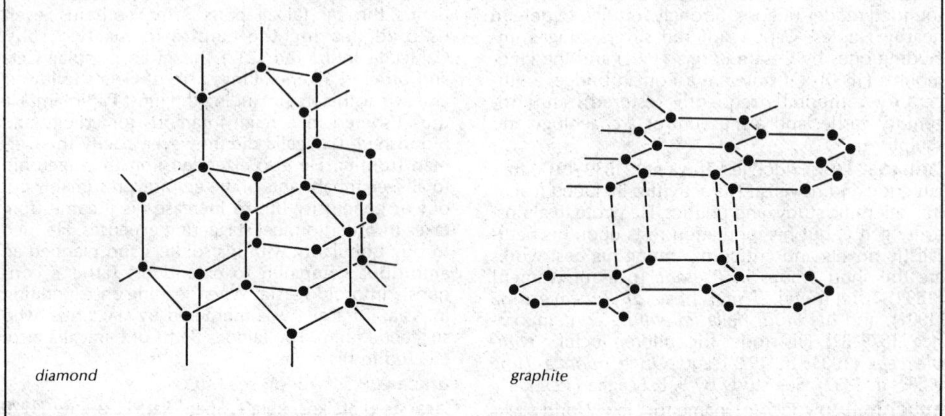

The two solid forms of carbon: In the diamond crystal each carbon atom is surrounded symmetrically by four other carbons (at each of the corners of a tetrahedron). In the graphite crystal the atoms bond to three other carbons to form flat sheets.

dative destruction of organic compounds; water and carbon dioxide are two by-products of catabolism. This continuing synthesis and degradation involving carbon dioxide is known as the biological carbon cycle. Seven isotopes of carbon are known. Carbon-12 was chosen by the IUPAC in 1961 as the basis for ATOMIC WEIGHTS; it is assigned an atomic mass of exactly 12 atomic mass units. Carbon-13 is used as a radioactive tracer. Carbon-14, which has a half-life of 5,730 years, is a naturally occurring isotope that can also be produced in a nuclear reactor. It is used extensively as a research tool in tracer studies; a compound synthesized with carbon-14 is said to be "tagged" and can be traced through a chemical or biochemical reaction. Carbon-14 has been used in the study of such problems as utilization of foods in animal nutrition, catalytic petroleum processes, photosynthesis, and the mechanism of aging in steel. It is also used for determining the age of archaeological specimens (see DATING, GEOLOGIC). Carbon has been known to man in its various forms since ancient times. See Isaac Asimov, *The World of Carbon* (rev. ed. 1966); P. L. Walker, Jr., and P. A. Thrower, ed., *Chemistry and Physics of Carbon* (11 vol., 1966–74).

carbonado: see DIAMOND.

Carbonari (kärbōnä'rē) [Ital.,=charcoal burners], members of a secret society that flourished in Italy, Spain, and France early in the 19th cent. Possibly derived from Freemasonry, the society originated in the kingdom of Naples in the reign of Murat (1808–15) and drew its members from all stations of life, particularly from the army. It was closely organized, with a ritual, a symbolic language, and a hierarchy. Beyond advocacy of political freedom its aims were vague. The Carbonari were partially responsible for uprisings in Spain (1820), Naples (1820), and Piedmont (1821). After 1830 the Italian Carbonari gradually were absorbed by the RISORGIMENTO movement; elsewhere they disappeared.

carbonate, chemical compound containing the carbonate RADICAL or ION, CO_3^{-2}. Most familiar carbonates are SALTS that are formed by reacting an inorganic BASE (e.g., a metal HYDROXIDE) with CARBONIC ACID. Normal carbonates are formed when equivalent amounts of acid and base react; bicarbonates, also called acid carbonates or hydrogen carbonates, are formed when the acid is present in excess. SODIUM CARBONATE, Na_2CO_3, SODIUM BICARBONATE, $NaHCO_3$, and POTASSIUM CARBONATE, K_2CO_3, are widely used. Smelling salts is ammonium carbonate. Calcium carbonate is found in shells of animals and in ICELAND SPAR, LIMESTONE, and MARBLE; it is used in the production of lime (CALCIUM OXIDE). Barium carbonate occurs as the mineral witherite. Magnesium carbonate occurs as MAGNESITE and in DOLOMITE (with calcium carbonate). Iron carbonate is a ferrous compound that occurs in nature as SIDERITE. WHITE LEAD used as a pigment in paints is basic lead carbonate. Only ammonium, potassium, and sodium carbonates are readily soluble in water. Alkali metal carbonates are stable when heated, but other carbonates decompose, releasing CARBON DIOXIDE. Carbonates also give off carbon dioxide when treated with dilute acids, e.g., hydrochloric acid.

carbon black, mixture of partially burned hydrocarbons. Carbon black is produced by partial combustion of NATURAL GAS. It is used as a black pigment for inks and paints, and is used in large amounts by the tire industry in the production of vulcanized rubber. Lampblack resembles carbon black, but is produced by burning liquid hydrocarbons, e.g., kerosene; it is often somewhat oily, is duller than carbon black, and may have a bluish undertone. It is sometimes used in making contact brushes for electrical apparatus.

carbon cycle, in biology, the exchange of carbon between living organisms and the nonliving environment. Living organisms are composed of matter derived from the environment and engage in a continual exchange of matter with their surroundings; as old cells die and their materials return to the environment, new cells are formed of newly incorporated substances. Carbon is the central element in most compounds of which organisms are composed, and it is derived from free carbon dioxide, that found in air (or, in an aquatic environment, in water). The process of incorporating inorganic molecules into the more complex molecules of living matter is called fixation. Nearly all carbon dioxide fixation is accomplished by means of PHOTOSYNTHESIS, in which green plants form carbohydrates from carbon dioxide and water, using the energy of sunlight to drive the chemical reactions involved. A few microorganisms fix insignificant amounts of carbon dioxide by using other energy sources, such as oxidation of iron. Green plants use carbohydrates to build the other organic molecules that make up

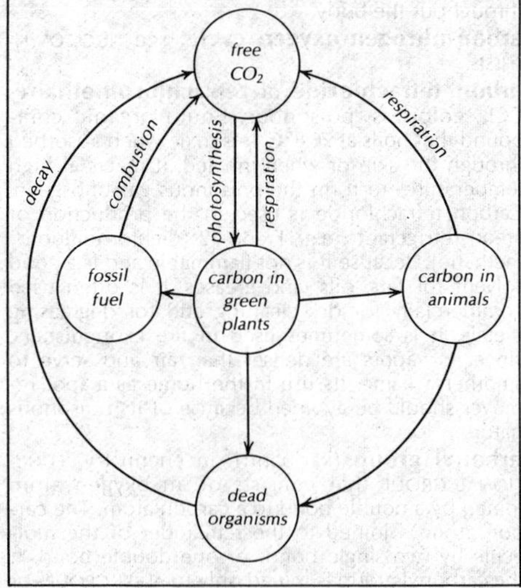

Carbon cycle

their cells, such as cellulose, fats, proteins, and nucleic acids. Some of these compounds require the incorporation of nitrogen (see NITROGEN CYCLE). When carbohydrates are oxidized in cells they release the energy stored in their chemical bonds, and some of that energy is also used by the cell to drive other reactions. In the process of oxidation, or respiration, oxygen from the atmosphere (or from water) is combined with portions of the carbohydrate molecule, producing carbon dioxide and water, the compounds from which the carbohydrates were originally formed. However, not all of the carbon atoms incorporated by the plant can be returned to the atmosphere by its own respiration; some remain fixed in the organic materials that make up its cells. When the plant dies, its tissues are consumed by bacteria and other microorganisms, a process called decay. These microorganisms, which cannot make carbohydrates from carbon dioxide and water, break down the organic molecules of the plant and use them for their own cell-building and energy needs; by their respiration more of the carbon is returned to the atmosphere. Animals, which likewise cannot make their own carbohydrates, feed on plants or on other animals; ultimately their matter and energy are derived from plants. The carbon-containing molecules that an animal derives from other organisms are reorganized to build its own cells or oxidized for energy by respiration, releasing carbon dioxide and water. When the animal dies it too is decayed by microorganisms, resulting in the return of more carbon to the atmosphere. Carbon-containing molecules in wood (or other dry, slow-decaying organic materials) may be oxidized by burning, or combustion, also producing carbon dioxide and water. Under conditions prevailing on earth at certain times, green plants have decayed only partially and have been transformed into fossil fuels—coal, peat, and oil. These materials are made of organic compounds formed by the plants; when burned, they too restore carbon dioxide to the atmosphere.

Carbondale. 1 City (1970 pop. 22,816), Jackson co., S Ill.; inc. 1869. It is a railroad division point and the retail center of a coal-mining and farming area. Southern Illinois Univ. is the major employer. Memorial Day was inaugurated (1868) in Carbondale by Gen. John A. Logan. Giant City State Park and a wildlife refuge are nearby. **2** Industrial city (1970 pop. 12,808), Lackawanna co., NE Pa., on the Lackawanna River; inc. 1851. Its important activities are anthracite coal mining and the manufacture of mining machinery, machine shop products, chemicals, and clothing. It is also a vacation center in a lake and mountain region. Terence Powderly, the labor leader, was born there.

carbon dioxide, chemical compound, CO_2, a colorless, odorless, tasteless gas that is about one and one-half times as dense as air under ordinary conditions of temperature and pressure. It does not burn and will not support combustion of ordinary materials. Although it is not a poison, it can cause death by suffocation if inhaled in large amounts. It is a fairly stable compound but decomposes at very high temperatures into carbon and oxygen. It is fairly soluble in water, one volume of it dissolving in an equal volume of water at room temperature and pressure; the resultant weakly acidic aqueous solution is called CARBONIC ACID. The gas is easily liquefied by compression and cooling. If liquid carbon dioxide is quickly decompressed it rapidly expands and some of it evaporates, removing enough heat so that the rest of it cools into solid carbon dioxide "snow." Carbon dioxide has familiar uses. Formed by the action of yeast or baking powder, it causes the rising of bread dough. It provides the sparkle in carbonated beverages such as soda water. In some fire extinguishers it is expelled through a nozzle and settles on the flame, smothering it. It is a raw material for PHOTOSYNTHESIS in green plants and is a product of animal RESPIRATION. It is also a product of the decay of organic matter. It occurs in nature both free and in combination (e.g., in CARBONATES). It is part of the ATMOSPHERE, making up about 1% of the volume of dry air. Because it is a product of combustion of carbonaceous fuels (e.g., coal, coke, fuel oil, gasoline, and cooking gas), there is usually more of it in city air than in country air. In various parts of the world—notably in Italy, Java, and Yellowstone National Park in the United States—it is formed underground and issues from fissures in the earth. Natural mineral waters such as Vichy water sparkle (effervesce) because excess carbon dioxide that dissolved in them under pressure collects in bubbles and escapes when the pressure is released. The chokedamp (see DAMP) of mines, pits, and old, unused wells is largely carbon dioxide. Carbon dioxide has varied commercial uses. Its greatest use as a chemical is in the production of carbonated beverages; it is also used in water softening, in the manufacture of aspirin and lead paint pigments, and in the SOLVAY PROCESS for the preparation of sodium carbonate. It also has numerous nonchemical uses. It is used as a pressurizing medium and propellant, e.g., in aerosol cans of food, in fire extinguishers, in target pistols, and for inflating life rafts. Because it is relatively inert, it is used to provide a nonreactive atmosphere, e.g., for electric arc welding of steel and for packaging foods, such as coffee, that can be spoiled by oxidation during storage. Solid carbon dioxide, known as dry ice, is used as a refrigerating agent. There are three principal commercial sources for carbon dioxide. High-purity carbon dioxide is produced from some wells. The gas is obtained as a by-product of chemical manufacture, as in the fermentation of grain to make alcohol and the burning of limestone to make lime. It is also manufactured directly by burning carbonaceous fuels. For commercial use it is available as a liquid under high pressure in steel cylinders, as a low-temperature liquid at lower pressures, and as the solid dry ice. A standard test for the presence of carbon dioxide is its reaction with limewater (a saturated water solution of CALCIUM HYDROXIDE) to form a milky-white precipitate of calcium hydroxide.

carbon disulfide, CS_2, liquid organic compound; it is colorless, foul-smelling, flammable, and poisonous. It can be prepared by direct reaction of carbon, e.g., as charcoal, with sulfur. It is widely used as a solvent, e.g., for rubber, and is used to treat alkali cellulose in the viscose process (a source of rayon and cellophane). Carbon disulfide reacts with chlorine in the presence of a catalyst to form carbon tetrachloride.

carbonic acid, H_2CO_3, a weak dibasic acid (see ACIDS AND BASES) formed when CARBON DIOXIDE dissolves in water; it exists only in solution. Carbonic acid forms carbonate and bicarbonate (or acid carbonate) salts (see CARBONATE) by reaction with bases. It contributes to the sharp taste of carbonated beverages.

Carboniferous period (kärbənĭf'ərəs), fifth period of the PALEOZOIC ERA of geologic time (see GEOLOGIC ERAS, table). The Carboniferous period was marked by vast, coal-forming swamps and a succession of changes in the earth's surface that, continuing into the PERMIAN PERIOD, ended the Paleozoic era. The events of the Carboniferous fall naturally into two divisions, the Mississippian and the Pennsylvanian; in America the break in sequence is so sharp that each division is commonly considered an independent period. In the Lower Carboniferous, or Mississippian, period, the interior of North America was submerged several times by shallow seas in which were formed limestone, shale, and sandstone. In the Appalachian region, especially in Pennsylvania, great deposits of sandstone and shale were laid down by the erosion products from the eastern coastal highlands. In the Far West the Rocky Mt. region was covered by shallow seas which deposited the Madison limestone and the Redwall limestone of the Grand Canyon. The Lower Carboniferous in Europe, as in America, was a period of submergence and was also one of great volcanic activity. In the British Isles and adjacent areas the mountain limestone was formed; E of the Rhine, the culm shale, sandstone, and conglomerate; and in the USSR, the Coal Measures. The close of the Lower Carboniferous was marked by mountain building in New Brunswick, Nova Scotia, the S Appalachian region, the SW United States, and Europe. In the Upper Carboniferous, or Pennsylvanian, period, there was at least one great submergence; however, the sea level oscillated and caused the formation of great marshes with extensive vegetation that was later transformed into coal. In the E United States great deltas of sediments, now represented by the Pottsville conglomerate, were formed during the early Pennsylvanian. In Kansas, Nebraska, Arkansas, and Texas, the Pennsylvanian beds are chiefly shale, sandstone, and coal; over the Cordilleran region, marine limestone, with little coal; on the Pacific coast from California to Alaska, limestone and shale. The Carboniferous coal fields of North America include the anthracite field of E Pennsylvania; the Appalachian field, from Pennsylvania to Alabama; the Michigan field; the eastern interior field, in Indiana, Illinois, and Kentucky; the western interior and southwestern field, stretching from Iowa to Texas; the Rhode Island field; and the Acadian field of SE Canada. In the Upper Carboniferous of Western Europe, the Millstone Grit, equivalent to the Pottsville conglomerate, is followed by the Coal Measures, which include the Welsh, English, Belgian, Westphalian, and Saar Basin fields. In the Mediterranean region and in the USSR, the Upper Carboniferous resembles that of W North America. The Upper Carboniferous was a period of marked crustal disturbances. In Europe the Paleozoic Alps were thrust up; in Asia, the Altai and the Tien Shan; in North America, the Arbuckle and Wichita mts. and the ancestral S Rockies. The Indian peninsula became an active site of deposition; in the Himalayan geosyncline and much of China, mountain building was dominant. Crustal movements in the Andean geosyncline of South America affected the pattern of sedimentation over much of the continent. The plant life of the Carboniferous period was extensive and luxuriant, especially in the Pennsylvanian. It included ferns and fernlike trees; giant horesetails, called calamites; club mosses, or lycopods, such as Lepidodendron and Sigillaria; seed ferns; and cordaites, or primitive conifers. Land animals included primitive amphibians, reptiles (which first appeared in the Upper Carboniferous), spiders, millipedes, land snails, scorpions, enormous dragonflies, and more than 800 kinds of cockroaches. The inland waters were inhabited by fishes, clams, and various crustaceans; the oceans by mollusks, crinoids, sea urchins, and one-celled lime-making foraminifers.

carbonite: see COKE.

carbon monoxide, chemical compound, CO, a colorless, odorless, tasteless, extremely poisonous gas that is less dense than air under ordinary conditions. It is very slightly soluble in water and burns in air with a characteristic blue flame, producing carbon dioxide; it is a component of PRODUCER GAS and WATER GAS, which are widely used artificial fuels. It is a reducing agent, removing oxygen from many compounds and is used in the reduction of metals, e.g., IRON (see BLAST FURNACE), from their ores. At high pressures and elevated temperatures it reacts with hydrogen in the presence of a catalyst to form METHANOL. Carbon monoxide is formed by combustion of carbon in oxygen at high temperatures when there is an excess of carbon. It is also formed (with oxygen) by decomposition of carbon dioxide at very high temperatures (above 2000°C). It is present in the exhaust of internal combustion engines (e.g., in automobiles) and is generated in coal stoves, furnaces, and gas appliances that do not get enough air (because of a faulty draft or for other reasons). Carbon monoxide is an extremely poisonous gas. Breathing air that contains as little as 0.1% carbon monoxide by volume can be fatal; a concentration of about 1% can cause death within a few minutes. The gas is especially dangerous because it is not easily detected. Early symptoms of carbon monoxide poisoning include drowsiness and headache, followed by unconsciousness, respiratory failure, and death. First aid for a victim of carbon monoxide poisoning requires getting him to fresh air; administering ARTIFICIAL RESPIRATION and, if available, oxygen; and, as soon as possible, summoning a doctor. When carbon monoxide is inhaled it reacts with hemoglobin, the red blood pigment that normally carries oxygen to all parts of the body. Because carbon monoxide is attracted to the hemoglobin about 210 times as strongly as is oxygen, it takes the place of oxygen in the blood, causing oxygen starvation throughout the body.

carbon-nitrogen-oxygen cycle: see NUCLEOSYNTHESIS.

carbon tetrachloride or **tetrachloromethane,** CCl_4, colorless, poisonous, liquid organic compound that boils at 76.8°C. It is toxic when absorbed through the skin or when inhaled. It reacts at high temperatures to form the poisonous gas phosgene. Carbon tetrachloride is used in the production of Freon refrigerants, e.g., Freon-12 (dichlorodifluoromethane). Because it is not flammable and is a good solvent for fats, oils, and greases, it is often used commercially for dry cleaning and for degreasing metals. It is sometimes used in fire extinguishers, since its vapors are denser than air and serve to smother a flame. Its use in the home as a spot remover should be avoided because of its poisonous nature.

carbonyl group (kär'bənĭl), in chemistry, FUNCTIONAL GROUP that consists of an oxygen atom joined by a double bond to a carbon atom. The carbon atom is joined to the remainder of the molecule by two single bonds or one double bond. If the carbonyl group is joined only to ALKYL GROUPS or ARYL GROUPS, the compound is a KETONE; if it is joined to at least one hydrogen atom, the compound is an ALDEHYDE. The chemical reactivity of aldehydes and ketones is primarily due to the difference in ELECTRONEGATIVITY between carbon and oxygen. Because oxygen has the greater affinity for electrons, it acquires a partial negative charge, becoming electron-rich; the carbon atom of the carbonyl group thus becomes electron-deficient, acquiring a partial positive charge. One major type of reaction of aldehydes and ketones involves the addition of an electron-rich chemical species to the electron-deficient carbon atom of the carbonyl group. Another type of reaction is due to the tendency of the electron-deficient carbon atom of the carbonyl group to partially attract electrons from carbon atoms adjacent to it in the molecule, thus increasing the acidity of hydrogen atoms that are bonded to the adjacent carbon.

Carborundum: see SILICON CARBIDE.

carboxyl group (kärbŏk'sĭl), in chemistry, FUNCTIONAL GROUP that consists of a carbon atom joined to an oxygen atom by a double bond and to a HYDROXYL GROUP, OH, by a single bond. Carboxylic acids are compounds whose molecules contain a carboxyl group that is joined to a hydrogen atom, an ALKYL GROUP, or an ARYL GROUP by a single bond to its carbon atom. Dicarboxylic acids, compounds that contain two carboxyl groups, are important in a number of industrial processes. The four main types of reactions of carboxylic acids are chiefly due to either the weak acidity of the hydroxyl hydrogen or to the difference in ELECTRONEGATIVITY between carbon and oxygen. One type involves cleavage of the hydroxyl oxygen-hydrogen bond, e.g., reaction with an alcohol to form an ESTER or reaction with an alkali to form a water-soluble salt. A second type involves addition of an electron-rich species to the electron-deficient carbon atom of the carboxyl group. A third type is characterized by the joining of a carbon atom directly to the carboxyl group. A fourth type involves the loss of carbon dioxide (decarboxylation). The second and third types are similar to reactions of the CARBONYL GROUP; the carboxyl group may be thought of as a carbonyl group joined to a hydroxyl group.

carboxylic acid: see CARBOXYL GROUP.

carbuncle, acute inflammatory nodule of the skin caused by bacterial invasion into the hair follicles or sebaceous gland ducts. It is actually a BOIL, but one that has more than one focus of infection, i.e., involves several follicles or ducts. Carbuncles occur more often in men because of their more extensive body hair growth. The infection is treated by applying antibiotics systemically and directly to the lesion and by incision and drainage at the proper time.

carburetor, part of a gasoline engine in which liquid fuel is converted into a vapor and mixed with a regulated amount of air for combustion in the cylinders. Land vehicles, boats, and light aircraft have a float carburetor, in which a float regulates the fuel level in a reservoir from which the fuel is sucked into the intake manifold at a restriction called a venturi. This venturi metering system controls the flow of a continuous pumped spray into the intake manifold downstream from the carburetor. When there is an individual spray for each cylinder and the injection is an intermittent, timed spurt, or is metered differently, the device is usually called a fuel injector, not a carburetor.

Carcas (kär'kəs), king's chamberlain. Esther 1.10.

Carcassonne (kärkäsôn'), city (1968 pop. 46,329), capital of Aude dept., S France, in Languedoc. The old city, a medieval fortress atop a hill, is one of the architectural marvels of Europe. The new city, across the Aude River, is a farm trade center with rubber, shoe, and textile manufactures. The Romans fortified the hilltop site in the 1st cent. B.C.; towers built (c.6th cent.) by the Visigoths are still intact; and the viscounts of Carcassonne added to the fortifications in the 12th cent. A stronghold of the ALBIGENSES, the fortess was taken by Simon de Montfort in 1209. It yielded to the king in 1247, at which time Louis IX (St. Louis) founded the new city across the river. The outer ramparts of the fortress were constructed during St. Louis's reign, and the work was continued, with intricate defense devices, under Philip III. When completed, the fortress was widely considered impregnable; Edward the Black Prince was stopped at its walls in 1355. However, its usefulness ended in 1659, with the annexation to France of the province of Roussilon. The ramparts were gradually abandoned and fell into disrepair; they were restored by Viollet-le-Duc in the 19th cent.

Carchemish (kär'kĭmĭsh, kärkē'mĭsh), ancient city, Turkey, on the Euphrates River, at the Syrian border, c.35 mi (56 km) SE of Gaziantep. It was an important Neo-Hittite city and was prosperous in the 9th cent. B.C. before it was destroyed by the Assyrians. Even then it continued as an important trade center. There, in 605 B.C., Nebuchadnezzar defeated Necho (2 Chron. 35.20; Jer. 46.2; Isa. 10.9). Among the excavated remains are sculptured neo-Hittite reliefs with hieroglyphic Hittite inscriptions. See British Museum, *Carchemish* (3 vol. in 2, 1914–52).

carcinogen: see CANCER.

carcinoma: see NEOPLASM.

Carco, Francis (fräNsēs' kärkō'), 1886–1958, French poet and novelist, b. New Caledonia of Corsican parents. His real name was François Carcopino. The bohemian Parisian life he cherished is portrayed in several of his novels, including *Jesus-la-caille* (1914). Among his verses are *La Bohème et mon cœur* (1912) and *Poèmes en prose* (1948).

cardamom (kär'dəməm): see GINGER.

Cardamom Hills, range, c.4,000 ft (1,220 m) high, c.1,000 sq mi (2,590 sq km), Kerala state, southern tip of India. Tea, coffee, teak, bamboo, turmeric, and cardamom, which gives the area its name, are grown in the hills.

Cardamom Mountains, Thai *Banthat,* Khmer *Kravanh,* mountain group extending c.100 mi (160 km) along the Thai-Cambodian border, E of Chanthaburi, SE Thailand. Ta Det (3,667 ft/1,118 m) is the highest peak. The mountains receive monsoon rains and have a dense vegetation cover.

Cardano, Geronimo (jārō'nēmō kärdä'nō), 1501–76, Italian physician and mathematician. His works on arithmetic and algebra established his reputation. Barred from official status as a physician because of his illegitimate birth, he practiced as a medical astrologer. His major work, *De subtilitate rerum* (1550), on natural history, is perceptive and implies a grasp of evolutionary principles. His book on games of chance represents the first organized theory of probability. Cardano described a tactile system similar to Braille for teaching the blind and thought it possible to teach the deaf by signs. See his *The Book of my Life* (1643, tr. 1930); studies by Oystein Ore (with a tr. of Cardano's *Book of Games of Chance,* 1965) and Alan Wykes (1969).

Cárdenas, García López de (gärthē'ä lō'pĕth dā kär'dānäs), fl. 1540, Spanish explorer in the Southwest. A member of the 1540 expedition of Francisco Vásquez de CORONADO, he was selected to lead a party from Cibola (the Zuñi country of New Mexico) to find a river of which the Hopi Indians had spoken. After 20 days' march he became the first white man to see the GRAND CANYON of the Colorado River. He was not, however, the discoverer of the Colorado itself, for Hernando de ALARCÓN had explored its lower waters a month earlier.

Cárdenas, Lázaro (lä'särō), 1895–1970, president of Mexico (1934–40). He joined the revolutionary forces in 1913 and rose to become a general. He was governor (1928–32) of his native state, Michoacán, and held other political posts before he was, with the support of Plutarco E. CALLES, elected president. After a bitter conflict Cárdenas sent (1936) Calles into exile and organized a vigorous campaign of socialization of industry and agriculture based on the constitution of 1917. Large land holdings were broken up and distributed to small farmers on the EJIDO system, and many foreign-owned properties, especially oil fields, were expropriated. His policy, founded on his determination to make Mexico a modern democracy, became anathema to large landowners, industrialists, and foreign investors, but—himself a mestizo—he won the support of the Indians and of the Mexican working classes. Cárdenas relinquished his office at the end of his term, thus acting in accord with his desire for democratic and orderly constitutional processes. Cárdenas was recalled to public service as minister of national defense (1942-45). His political influence as the leader of the Mexican left wing continued in the years after World War II. See study by J. C. Ashby (1967).

Cárdenas, city (1970 pop. 55,209), N central Cuba, a port on Cárdenas Bay. It processes and exports sugar and sisal and has industries producing tobacco, beer, and soap. A fishing fleet is based at Cárdenas, which is also an important commercial center. The city was founded in 1828 as a shipping point for the sugar industry of the surrounding area.

cardiac failure: see CONGESTIVE HEART FAILURE.

Cardiff (kär'dĭf), county borough (1971 pop. 278,221), county town of Glamorganshire, S Wales, on the Taff River near its mouth on the Bristol Channel. Until the early 20th cent. Cardiff was one of the greatest coal-shipping ports in the world. Present industries include shipbuilding and repairing, metal casting, engineering, oil and gasoline distribution, and food processing. There are British Broadcasting Corp. studios in Cardiff. The construction of docks by the 5th marquess of Bute in 1839 stimulated the growth of Cardiff. The Port of Cardiff includes the docks at Penarth and Barry. There is a canal to Merthyr Tydfil (opened 1794), with a branch to Aberdare. Cardiff Castle, the residence of the marquess of Bute until 1947, was first built in 1090 on the site of a Roman fort. Robert, duke of Normandy, was imprisoned (1126-34) in the castle. Owen Glendower partly destroyed it in 1404. In Cathays Park the group of public buildings includes the National Museum of Wales, the law courts, the city hall, Glamorgan county hall, and the University College of South Wales and Monmouthshire (one of the four constituent colleges of the Univ. of Wales). Other schools are City of Cardiff College (teacher training) and Welsh College of Advanced Technology. Llandaff, which has a notable medieval cathedral, has been part of Cardiff county borough since 1922. The parish church of St. John dates partly from the 13th and partly from the 15th cent. In 1974, Cardiff became part of the new nonmetropolitan county of South Glamorgan.

Cardigan, James Thomas Brudenell, 7th **earl of,** 1797-1868, British general. In the Crimean War he led the disastrous cavalry charge at BALAKLAVA (1854) that Tennyson immortalized in *The Charge of the Light Brigade.* The charge was made on a misunderstood order, and the brigade was destroyed. Quarrels with his officers showed him a vain and contentious man. The cardigan sweater was named for him. See biography by Piers Compton (1972).

Cardiganshire, county (1971 pop. 54,844), W Wales, on Cardigan Bay. The county town is Cardigan, but ABERYSTWYTH is of greater importance. The region is largely one of pleasant, rolling hills, with fertile valleys and a narrow coastal plain. The chief river is the Teifi. Agriculture predominates but there is also some fishing and the manufacture of woolens. The county long resisted English influence, and the Welsh language and Welsh customs are well preserved. In 1974, Cardiganshire became part of the new nonmetropolitan county of Dyfed.

Cardigan Welsh corgi, breed of short, long-bodied WORKING DOG believed to have been introduced into Wales from Central Europe c.1200 B.C. It stands about 12 in. (30.5 cm) high at the shoulder and weighs from 15 to 25 lb (6.8-11.3 kg). Its dense, medium-length, straight coat is of harsh texture and may be red, brindle, sable, black and tan, black, or blue-merle in color, often with white markings on the face, chest, neck, feet, and tip of tail. Originally used as a guardian and hunter, the Cardigan later came to be raised as a drover of cattle. Working to the whistled commands of its master, it would nip at the heels of the livestock and then avoid their lethal kicks by dropping to the ground. With the sale and division of the common pastureland and the increasing use of fences, the usefulness of the Cardigans as drovers was eliminated and the breed became scarce. Revived by the diligence of modern breeders, the Cardigan today is raised for show competition and as a family companion. See DOG.

cardinal [Lat.,=belonging to the hinge], in the Roman Catholic Church, a member of the highest body of the church below the pope. This, the sacred college of cardinals of the Holy Roman Church, is the electoral college of the PAPACY. Its members are appointed by the pope. There are three classes. Cardinal bishops are the bishops of seven sees around Rome (Ostia, Velletri, Porto and Santa Rufina, Albano, Frascati, Palestrina, and Sabina and Poggio Mirteto) and Eastern rite patriarchs; the first of these in order of creation is dean of the college and ex officio bishop of Ostia in addition to his other see. Cardinal priests are mostly archbishops outside the Roman province; the title "cardinal archbishop"—often applied to these men—simply represents the union of the two dignities in one man. Cardinal deacons are priests with functions in the papal government. Cardinal priests and cardinal deacons have titles corresponding to churches of the Roman diocese. A cardinal's insignia resemble those of a bishop, except for the characteristic red, broad-brimmed, tasseled hat, which is conferred by the pope but not subsequently worn. Cardinals are styled "Eminence." Apart from papal elections, the cardinals have great importance as the privy council of the pope. Hence those who are not bishops away from Rome must live at Rome. They meet with the pope in consistories, public and secret, but most of the business they transact is done in their various jurisdictional capacities. Thus the cardinals in residence at Rome make up a cabinet for the pope, directing the work of the Curia Romana, as the papal administration is called. This is made up of standing committees and courts, the departments of administration divided among them. Since there is no division of powers in the headship of the church, most organs of the Curia have power to judge, to command, and to legislate. The acts of these bodies are validated by papal approbation, and they therefore bind Roman Catholics as direct pontifical acts. Only the pope himself can speak finally in matters of faith and morals (see INFALLIBILITY). The Curia may be divided into Roman congregations, Roman tribunals, curial offices, and secretariats. A Roman congregation consists of a group of cardinals, headed by a prefect, together with two staffs which transact most of the business—the *congresso* of major officials and a staff of minor officials chosen by competitive examination and assigned to less important affairs. The congregation proper, i.e., the cardinals, makes all major decisions. The following are the Roman congregations (founded by Sixtus V in 1588, reorganized by Pius X in 1908, and by Paul VI at the close of the Second Vatican Council): Congregation of the Doctrine of the Faith (formerly, of the Holy Office; see INQUISITION), of which the pope is prefect, concerned with doctrinal orthodoxy; Congregation of the Consistory, of which the pope is prefect, for the preparation of agenda for consistories and the regulation of dioceses of the Western Church not under the Propaganda (see below); Congregation of the Sacraments, for legislation on administration of the sacraments and for dispensations concerning them; Congregation of the Council, for the regulation of councils and of benefices, properties, and the like, for dispensations from the commandments of the church, and for the maintenance of the shrine of Loreto; Congregation of Religious, for all concerns of all seculars and regulars, of both sexes; Congregation for the Propagation of the Faith (the Propaganda), for all concerns of the MISSIONS of the Latin rite; Congregation of the Eastern Church, for all concerns of the Eastern rites in communion with the pope and of every person involved, except for the Russian Catholics, who are under a separate commission; Congregation of Sacred Rites, for all public worship of the Latin rite, for canonizations, liturgical books, and the like; Congregation of the Ceremonial, for liturgical ceremonies involving the pope and the sacred college; Congregation for Extraordinary Ecclesiastical Affairs, virtually a board of assistants to the secretariat of state; Congregation of Seminaries and Universities, for the administration of education, of seminaries, and of ecclesiastical research; Congregation of the Fabric, for the maintenance of St. Peter's Church. Of the Roman congregations, the two whose influence is felt most deeply throughout the church are probably the Congregation of the Faith and the Propaganda. The Roman tribunals are three secret courts, the highest of the church; each is headed by a cardinal, and its work is handled by trained canonists. They are the Apostolic Penitentiaria, for all cases of conscience appealed by any Catholic to the pope and for the regulation of indulgences; the Apostolic Signatura, the court of final appeal of the church, considering only cases involving the members of, or appealed from, the Rota; the Sacred Roman Rota, the court of appeal from diocesan courts and the lower court of Vatican City, hearing all cases requiring trial and evidence, except cases of conscience, cases of canonization, and cases involving sovereigns of states (reserved to the pope in person). The curial offices are now to a large extent unimportant and honorary. They are the Apostolic Chancery, to issue bulls of foundations and the like; the Apostolic Dataria, to handle matter concerning candidates for papal benefices, pensions, and the like; the Apostolic Camera, headed by the chamberlain of the Holy Roman Church, to administer the property (except revenue) of the Holy See, notably in the vacancy of the papal see. The secretariats are the secretariat of state, headed by the cardinal secretary of state, who has charge of all matters involving relations with political governments and has for his aid a large staff and the Congregation of Extraordinary Ecclesiastical Affairs, and the secretariat of briefs, in charge of the official Latin correspondence of the pope. A secretariat for promoting Christian unity and another for dealings with non-Christians were established by Paul VI. Besides these permanent departments there are always some special commissions of cardinals, e.g., for the Russian Church, for the revision of the Vulgate, for biblical study, and for sacred art. The term *cardinal* was formerly applied to important clergymen of all sorts and countries, but in the Middle Ages it was officially restricted to the Roman province. The college of cardinals is the modern derivative of the advisory board of clergymen of the ancient diocese of Rome, used by the pope for advice and transaction of business. Pope Sixtus V set the maximum number of cardinals at 70, a tradition maintained for centuries until the pontificate of Pope John XXIII. Following the lead of Pius XII, John XXIII and Paul VI have promoted the international character of the college. In 1973 the number of cardinals was increased to 145. See studies by T. B. Morgan (1946, repr. 1971), G. D. Kittler (1960), and F. B. Thornton (1963).

cardinal or **redbird,** common name for a North American songbird of the family Fringillidae (New World FINCH family). In the eastern cardinal, *Richmondena cardinalis,* the male is bright scarlet with black throat and face; the female is brown with patches of red. Both sexes have crests and red bills. The Arizona, gray-tailed, Louisiana, and San Lucas cardinals frequent the S United States and Mexico. The pyrrhuloxia of the SW United States, gray with red face, crest, breast, and tail, is called gray cardinal or parrotbill. Cup-shaped nests are built by male and female, and the male helps rear the young. Cardinals are essentially monogamous, and are not very gregarious. They are classified in the phylum CHORDATA, subphylum Vertebrata, class Aves, order Passeriformes, family Fringillidae.

cardinal flower: see LOBELIA.

carding, process by which fibers are opened, cleaned, and straightened in preparation for spinning. The fingers were first used, then a tool of wood or bone shaped like a hand, then two flat pieces of wood (cards) covered with skin set with thorns or teeth. Primitive cards, rubber-covered and toothed with bent wires, are still employed by Navaho women. Modern carding dates from the use of revolving cylinders patented in 1748 by Lewis Paul. A mechanical apron feed was devised in 1772, and Richard Arkwright added a funnel that contracted the carded fiber into a continuous sliver. See COMBING.

cardiovascular system: see CIRCULATORY SYSTEM.

Cardozo, Benjamin Nathan (kärdō'zō), 1870-1938, American jurist, Associate Justice of the U.S. Supreme Court (1932-38), b. New York City. He was admitted to the bar (1891) and practiced law until he was elected (1913) to the New York supreme court on a fusion ticket. Cardozo was appointed (1914) to the court of appeals, was elected (1917) for a 14-year term, and in 1927 was elected chief judge of the court, which, largely through his influence, gained international fame. He was prominent in the efforts of the American Law Institute to restate and simplify the law, and he advocated a permanent agency to function between the courts and legislatures to aid in framing effective legislation. He was active in a number of Jewish movements. He was appointed (1932) by President Herbert Hoover to the Supreme Court to succeed Oliver Wendell Holmes. Cardozo was one of the foremost spokesmen on sociological jurisprudence, and his views on the relation of law to social change made him one of the most influential of U.S. judges. With Justices Louis D. Brandeis and Harlan F. Stone, he upheld much New Deal legislation, dissenting from the majority opinion. His philosophy of law and the judicial process was developed in three classics of jurisprudence: *The Nature of the Judicial Process* (1921), *The Growth of the Law* (1924), and *The Paradoxes of Legal Science* (1928). He also wrote *Law and Literature and Other Essays and Addresses* (1931). See the selection of his writings edited by M. E. Hall (1947); biography by J. P. Pollard (1935, repr. 1970); studies by B. H. Levy (rev. ed. 1969) and W. C. Cunningham (1972).

cards, playing: see PLAYING CARDS.

Cardston, town (1971 pop. 4,130), SW Alta., Canada, near the U.S. boundary. It was founded in 1887 by Mormons from Utah under the leadership of Charles Ora Card, son-in-law of Brigham Young. The chief Mormon temple of Canada is in the town. Nearby is the Blood Indian Reserve, the largest in Canada.

Carducci or **Carducho, Bartolomeo** (bärtōlōmĕ'ō kärdōōt'chē, kärdōō'kō), 1560-1638, Italian painter, sculptor, and architect in Spain. He studied with Federigo Zuccaro, whom he accompanied (1585) to the court of Madrid. He assisted Tibaldi in decorating the library ceiling of the Escorial and executed some of the cloister frescoes. His masterpiece, *Descent from the Cross,* is in San Felipe el Real, Madrid. His brother **Vincenzo Carducci,** 1576-1638, succeeded him as court painter to Philip III. Vincenzo is the author of the *Diálogos de la pintura* (1633). The paintings of both brothers, though different in style, are marked by sobriety and an insistence upon moral tone.

Carducci, Giosuè (jōzōōā'), 1835-1907, Italian poet and teacher. He was professor of literature at the Univ. of Bologna from 1860 to 1904. He was a scholar, an editor, an orator, a critic, and a patriot, although his defection from republicanism and his anti-Catholicism brought him into disfavor even with his students. He was awarded the 1906 Nobel Prize in Literature. Carducci ranks with the greatest Italian poets; his verse is classic in design, with a deep and wide range of emotion. His chief works include *Rime* (1857), *Inno a Satana* [hymn to Satan] (1865), *Decennali* (1871), *Nuove poesie* (1873), *Odi barbari* (1877, 1882, 1889), *Rime nuove* (1889, tr. *New Rhymes,* 1916), and *Rime e ritme* (1898). See translations by G. L. Bickersteth (1913), Maud Holland (1927), William Fletcher Smith (1939), and Arthur Burkhard (1947); studies by John Bailey (1926) and S. E. Scaglia (1937).

Carducho, Bartolomeo: see CARDUCCI, BARTOLOMEO.

Cardwell, Edward Cardwell, Viscount, 1813-86, British statesman. He entered Parliament (1842) as a supporter of Sir Robert Peel, under whom he was secretary to the treasury (1845-46). He was president of the Board of Trade (1852-55) under Lord Aberdeen and secretary for Ireland (1859-61) and chancellor of the duchy of Lancaster (1861-64) under Lord Palmerston. While colonial secretary (1864-66) he worked toward federation in Canada. As war secretary (1868-74) under Gladstone, he reformed the British army, abolishing the purchase of commissions, shortening the term of enlistment, and creating a reserve.

CARE (Cooperative for American Relief Everywhere), nonprofit, nonsectarian federation of agencies devoted to channeling relief and self-help materials to needy people in foreign countries. Organized (1945) to help war-ravaged Europe, CARE soon expanded its program to include underdeveloped nations in Asia, Africa, and Latin America. Since its founding, CARE has distributed more than $200 million in supplies including foodstuffs, textiles, books, and agricultural and other tools. In 1962 the Medical International Cooperation Organization (MEDICO), a worldwide medical assistance program founded (1958) by Dr. Thomas Dooley and Dr. Peter Comanduras, became a part of CARE.

Careah (kārē'ə), variant of KAREAH.

Carême, Marie Antoine (märē' äNtwän' kärĕm'), 1784-1833, celebrated French cook and gastronomist. He was chef for Talleyrand, Czar Alexander I, George IV, and Baron Rothschild. His writings on the culinary art include *L'Art de la cuisine française* (5 vol., 1833-34).

Carew, George, Baron Carew of Clopton and **earl of Totnes,** 1555-1629, English soldier and statesman. He began his military career in Ireland in 1574 and served (1588-92) as master of the ordnance there. He took part in the naval expeditions to Cádiz (1596) and the Azores (1597) and in 1598 was an envoy to France. Appointed (1600) lord president of Munster, he aided the lord deputy, Lord Mountjoy, in defeating Hugh O'Neill, earl of TYRONE. Under James I, Carew was unable to save his friend Sir Walter Raleigh from execution, but he himself received honors, including his earldom in 1626. An antiquarian, he collected material on the history of Ireland, used later by his secretary, Sir Thomas Stafford, to prepare the important *Pacata Hibernia; or, An Historie of the Late Warres of Ireland* (1633).

Carew, Thomas, 1595?-1639?, English author, one of the CAVALIER POETS. Educated at Merton College, Oxford, he had a short diplomatic career on the Continent, then returned to England and became a favorite of Charles I and a court official. He is best known for his courtly, amorous lyrics, such as "Ask me no more where Jove bestows" and "He that loves a rosy cheek," but of equal importance are his "Elegy on the Death of Dr. Donne," and the highly erotic poem, "A Rapture." In his use of metaphysical and classical material, he shows the influence of both John Donne and Ben Jonson. See ed. of his works by Rhodes Dunlap (1949); study by E. I. Selig (1958, repr. 1970).

Carey, Henry, 1687-1743, English author. After the first collection of his poems appeared in 1713, he turned to writing for the stage. Primarily a writer of farce comedy, his greatest success was *Chrononhotonthologos* (1734), a burlesque on theatrical bombast. He is best remembered, however, for his songs, in particular the ballad "Sally in Our Alley."

Carey, Henry Charles, 1793-1879, American economist, b. Philadelphia; son of Mathew CAREY. In 1835 he retired from publishing, where he had done notable work, to devote himself to economics. His *Principles of Political Economy* (3 vol., 1837-40) and *Principles of Social Science* (3 vol., 1858-59) were among the first important American works in the field. Carey opposed the dominant British political economy of the day, particularly the "pessimism" of Ricardo and Malthus, and led in the theoretical development of American economic nationalism. He advocated the protective tariff but believed generally in laissez-faire. See studies by A. D. H. Kaplan (1931, repr. 1973) and A. W. Green (1951).

Carey, Mathew, 1760-1839, American publisher, bookseller, and economist, b. Dublin. In his Dublin journal he violently attacked English rule of Ireland, was imprisoned for a month, fled to France, where he worked in Benjamin Franklin's printing shop at Passy, returned to Ireland, and finally emigrated (1784) to Philadelphia. There a gift from Lafayette enabled him to establish (1785) the *Pennsylvania Herald.* From 1787 to 1792 he edited and published the *American Museum,* making it the leading American magazine of the period. In 1790, Carey began his career as bookseller and publisher on a large scale. In this double capacity he stimulated the growth of American letters. Although many of his own political pamphlets were controversial, the most famous, *The Olive Branch* (1814), was written during the War of 1812 in an effort to unite the Republican and Federalist parties in support of the war. His copious writings advocating the American protective system are interesting documents for the study of American economic history. The economist Henry Charles Carey was his son. See biography by E. L. Bradsher (1912, repr. 1968).

Carey, William, 1761-1834, English Baptist missionary and Orientalist, one of the first Protestant missionaries to India. He helped found the Baptist Missionary Society in 1792 and shortly thereafter went to India. Carey did most of the work in publishing the Bible in many Indian vernaculars. He wrote grammars of the vernaculars and several dictionaries. He became a professor of Sanskrit at Fort William College, Calcutta. See biographies by S. P. Carey (8th ed. rev. 1934) and W. B. Davis (1963).

Carey Land Act, sponsored by Sen. Joseph M. Carey and passed by the U.S. Congress in 1894. The act provided for the transfer to Western states of U.S.-owned desert lands on the condition that they be irrigated. Settlers were permitted to buy up to 160 acres (64.7 hectares) of the land at 50¢ per acre plus the cost of water rights. Hopes that the act would hasten reclamation and settlement were disappointed.

Cargill, Donald, 1619?-1681, Scottish COVENANTER. He was a minister in Glasgow from c.1655 until 1662, when he was expelled for denouncing the Restoration and resisting the establishment of the episcopacy in Scotland. After escaping wounded from the battle of Bothwell Bridge (1679), he joined Richard Cameron in the Sanquhar Declaration (1680) against Charles II. Cargill, having excommunicated the king, the duke of York, and others, was arrested and executed.

cargo cult, native religious movement found in Melanesia, holding that at the millennium the spirits of the dead will return and bring with them cargoes of modern goods for distribution among its adherents. The cult had its beginnings in the 19th cent. and received great impetus from World War II, when the Western armed forces littered the islands with surplus cargo. The cult aims to restore a past time and to regain the good will of ancestors who are being lured into giving cargo to the white foreigners, cargo originally intended for the native Melanesians. Cargo cults are revivalistic, in that the adherents expect the restoration of a golden age in which they will be reunited with their ancestors, and nativistic (see NATIVISM), in that the whites are to be driven away. However, as the cargo is composed principally of European goods, and native goods and rituals are abandoned, both the nativistic and revivalistic aspects of cargo cults are qualified by a strong motive toward ACCULTURATION.

Caria (kâ'rēə), ancient region of SW Asia Minor, S of the Maeander River, which separated it from Lydia. The territory is in present SW Asiatic Turkey. The Carians were probably a native people, but their region was settled by both Dorian and Ionian colonists. Caria was a center of the Ionian revolt (c.499 B.C.) that was a prelude to the Persian Wars. Some of the communities joined (c.468 B.C.) the Delian League. In the 4th cent. B.C. the region was united under a dynasty of princes, of whom the most celebrated was MAUSOLUS. Alexander the Great conquered Caria, and it changed hands often in the wars after his death. In 125 B.C. it was made a Roman province (part of the province of Asia). Cnidus, Halicarnassus, and Miletus were famous Carian cities.

Carías Andino, Tiburcio (tēbōōr'syō kärē'äs ändē'nō), 1876-1969, president of Honduras (1933-49). A strong-handed dictator, his term was twice extended by congress. Some improvements were made in communication and education. After Carías announced his retirement in 1948, presidential elections were held. Juan Manuel Gálvez, the government candidate, won easily.

Caribbean Sea (kâr''ĭbē'ən, kərĭb'ēən), tropical sea, c.750,000 sq mi (1,942,500 sq km), arm of the Atlantic Ocean, Central America. It is bordered on the N and E by the West Indies archipelago, on the S by South America, and on the W by the Central American isthmus. The Caribbean is linked to the Gulf of Mexico by the Yucatán Channel; to the Atlantic by many straits, of which the Windward Channel and Mona Passage are the most important; and to the Pacific Ocean by the Panama Canal. The Magdalena is the largest river entering the sea; Lake Maracaibo is its largest embayment. Geologically, the Caribbean Sea consists of two main basins separated by a broad, submarine plateau; Bartlett Deep, a trench between Cuba and Jamaica, contains the Caribbean's deepest point (22,788 ft/6,946 m below sea level). The Caribbean's water is clear, warm (75°F/24°C), and less salty than the Atlantic; the basin has a very low tidal range (c.1 ft/.3 m). The Caribbean Sea has a counterclockwise current; water enters through the Lesser Antilles, is warmed, and exits via the Yucatán Channel, where it forms the Gulf Stream. Volcanic activity and earthquakes are common in the Caribbean, as are destructive hurricanes that originate over the sea or in the Atlantic. The Caribbean was discovered by Christopher Columbus in 1493 and was named for the Carib Indians. Spain claimed the area, and its ships searched for treasure. With the discovery of the Pacific Ocean in 1513 the Caribbean became the main route of Spanish expeditions and, later, of convoys. Pirates and warships of rival powers preyed on Spanish ships in the Caribbean. Although Spain controlled most of the sea, Britain, France, Holland, and Denmark established colonies on the islands along the eastern fringe. The 1800s brought U.S. ships into the Caribbean, especially after 1848, when many gold-seekers crossed the sea to reach California via Panama. After unsuccessful French attempts in the late 1800s to build a canal across Panama, the United States, in 1903, assumed control of the project; the 1914 opening of the Panama Canal paved the way for increased U.S. interest and involvement in this strategic sea, sometimes called the "American Mediterranean." Several Caribbean islands have U.S. military bases, many of which were established during World War II as support bases to protect the Panama Canal. The naval base at Guantanamo Bay, Cuba (est. 1899) is the oldest U.S. Caribbean base. U.S. policy since the MONROE DOCTRINE of 1823 has been to exclude foreign powers from the Caribbean; however, in 1959, Cuba became the first country to come under strong foreign (Soviet) influence. U.S. intervention in the affairs of Caribbean countries, most recently in the Cuban missile crisis of 1962 and the landing of U.S. marines at Santo Domingo in 1965, reflects the region's importance in U.S. eyes. Petroleum, iron ore, bauxite, sugar, coffee, and bananas are the main local products moved on the sea. Economically, the region is dependent on U.S. patronage. The Caribbean Sea has also acted as a barrier, isolating the islands and preventing the mingling of peoples on the scale characteristic of Latin America.

Caribbees (kâr'ĭbēz), name sometimes applied to the islands of the Caribbean or even to all the West Indies. More specifically the Caribbees are the Lesser Antilles and include the Leeward Islands, the Windward Islands, and the Virgin Islands.

Carib Indians (kăr'ĭb), native people formerly inhabiting the Lesser Antilles, West Indies. They seem to have overrun the Lesser Antilles and to have driven out the ARAWAK about a century before the arrival of Christopher Columbus. The original name by which the Caribs were known, *Galibi*, was corrupted by the Spanish to Caníbal and is the origin of the English word *cannibal.* Extremely warlike and ferocious, they practiced cannibalism and took pride in scarification (ritual cutting of the skin) and fasting. Among these Indians the Carib language was spoken only by the men, while the women spoke Arawak. This was so because Arawak women, captured in raids, were taken as wives by the Carib men. Fishing, agriculture, and basketmaking were the chief domestic activities. The Caribs were expert navigators, crisscrossing a large portion of the Caribbean in their canoes. After European colonization began in the 17th cent., they were all but exterminated. A group remaining on St. Vincent mingled with Negro slaves who escaped from a shipwreck in 1675. This group was transferred (1795) by the British to Roatán island off the coast of Honduras. They have gradually migrated north along the coast into Guatemala. A few Caribs survive on a reservation on the island of Dominica. The Carib, or Cariban, languages are a separate family, believed to have originated in Brazil. Carib-speaking tribes are found in N Honduras, British Honduras, and N South America.

Cariboo Mountains (kăr'ĭbo͞o), range, c.200 mi (320 km) long, E British Columbia, Canada, rising to 11,750 ft (3,582 m) at Mt. Sir Wilfrid Laurier. It runs roughly parallel with the main Rocky Mt. range to the northeast, from which it is separated by the Rocky Mt. Trench, there occupied by the Fraser River. In the foothills to the west is the Cariboo dist., scene of the famous Cariboo gold rush of 1860. Many camps sprang up in the region, and much gold was taken out, but after 1866 the diggings declined. Many gold-seekers stayed on in the region, and today there are several thousand who make their living by a combination of mining, hunting, and farming. The Cariboo wagon road, built (1862–65) by the government, facilitated the settlement of the interior of the province. It started from Yale, at the head of navigation on the Fraser River, and ended in the Cariboo dist. nearly 400 mi (640 km) to the north. Bowron Lake and Wells Gray provincial parks are in the Cariboo Mts.

Caribou (kâr'ĭbo͞o), town (1970 pop. 10,419), Aroostook co., NE Maine, on the Aroostook River; inc. 1859. A processing and shipping hub for a great potato-growing region, it is also a winter sports center.

caribou, name in North America for the genus (*Rangifer*) of deer from which the Old World REINDEER was originally domesticated. Caribou are found in arctic and subarctic regions. They are the only deer in which both sexes have antlers. The broad hooves support the animal (males may weigh over 300 lb/90 kg) on boggy land or snow and have sharp edges that enable it to traverse rocky or frozen surfaces and to dig down to the grass and lichens on which it sometimes feeds. In North America there are two main types: the woodland caribou of the bogs and coniferous forests from Newfoundland to British Columbia, with palmate antlers up to 4 ft (120 cm) wide; and the barren-ground caribou of the tundra of Alaska and N Canada, which has many-branched, slender antlers and which may undertake mass migrations in search of food. Caribou are classified in the phylum CHORDATA, subphylum Vertebrata, class Mammalia, order Artiodactyla, family Cervidae.

caricature, a satirical drawing, plastic representation, or description which, through gross exaggeration of natural features, makes its subject appear ridiculous. Although 16th-century Northern painters, such as Holbein, Bruegel, and Bosch, employed certain elements of caricature, no comic tradition was established until the 17th cent. with the work of the Carracci. In the 18th cent. caricature flourished in England in the works of Hogarth, Rowlandson, and Gillray. The genre expanded to include political and social as well as personal satire, developing into the art of the CARTOON. Periodicals of caricature, such as the French *Charivari* (1832), followed by *Punch* in England, *Simplicissimus* in Germany, and *Puck, Life,* and *Judge* in the United States, were quite popular in the 19th cent. They featured work by Daumier, George Cruikshank, John Tenniel, Art Young, E. W. Kemble, and Daniel Fitzpatrick. Modern caricaturists of note include David Low, Ronald SEARLE, Max Beerbohm, Al Hirschfeld, David Levine, and H. L. Block. Sculpture generally lends itself less well to caricature, but an exception exists in the series of heads by Franz Xavier Messerschmidt (1736–83) which represent exaggerated states of emotion and character. In literature, caricature has been a popular form since the ancient Greeks. Through verbal exaggeration and distortion the writer achieves an immediate, comic, often satiric effect. No one has made wider use of the literary caricature than Dickens. See M. D. George, *Hogarth to Cruikshank: Social Change in Graphic Satire* (1967); R. E. Shikes, *The Indignant Eye: The Artist as Social Critic* (1969).

carillon, in music: see BELL.

Carina (kərē'nə) [Lat.,=the keel], southern CONSTELLATION, representing the keel of the ancient constellation Argo Navis, or Ship of the Argonauts. Carina contains CANOPUS, the second brightest star in the sky. It also contains the False Cross, a combination of four stars very similar to the Southern Cross (see CRUX); however, the long axis of the False Cross does not point toward the south celestial pole. In 1843 a nova was observed in Carina. Carina reaches its highest point in the evening sky in March.

Carinthia (kərĭn'thēə), Ger. *Kärnten*, province (1971 pop. 526,000), c.3,680 sq mi (9,531 sq km), S Austria. KLAGENFURT is the capital. Predominantly mountainous, it is the southernmost Austrian province, bordering on Italy and Yugoslavia in the south. The GROSSGLOCKNER, the highest point in Austria, rises in the northeast, at the Tyrol province border. Carinthia has mines (lead, zinc, iron, and lignite) and well-developed farms (especially in the fertile Drava, or Drau, plain). Manufactures of the province include forest products, construction materials, chemicals, and metal goods. There is also an active tourist trade, particularly along the Wörther See, a lake near Klagenfurt. In 976, Carinthia, which then included Istria, Carniola, and Styria, was detached from BAVARIA and made an independent duchy. Acquired by Ottocar II of Bohemia in 1269, it fell to RUDOLF I of Hapsburg in 1276 and in 1335 became an Austrian crown land. By the Treaty of Saint-Germain (1919) the province lost some minor territories to Italy and Yugoslavia. The only Austrian province with an appreciable ethnic minority, Carinthia has a Slovene population in the south.

Carinus (Marcus Aurelius Carinus) (kərī'nəs), d. 285, Roman emperor (283–85). He was the son of CARUS, who left Carinus as ruler in the West when he went to the East on a campaign against the Parthians. On the death of Carus, Carinus succeeded in the West, and his brother Numerianus succeeded in the East. After the murder of Numerianus, DIOCLETIAN was chosen (284) emperor in the East by the soldiers. Carinus set out to defeat the new claimant and met him in battle. At the moment of victory, however, Carinus was murdered by one of his own soldiers, and Diocletian became sole emperor.

Carissimi, Giacomo (jä'kōmō kärēs'sēmē), 1605–74, Italian composer. Most of his life was spent in Rome, where he wrote chamber cantatas in a style that lasted for over a century. His Latin oratorios, of which *Jephtha* is best known, are among the earliest extant examples of true oratorio. Famous as a teacher, he had among his pupils Alessandro Scarlatti.

Carlén, Emilie Smith Flygare-: see FLYGARE-CARLEN.

Carleton, Guy, 1st **Baron Dorchester,** 1724–1808, governor of Quebec and British commander during the American Revolution. He began his service in America in 1758 and distinguished himself in the French and Indian War. After 1766, as lieutenant governor, acting governor, and governor of Quebec, he proved to be a very able administrator. He fostered the QUEBEC ACT of 1774, which brought about better relations between the British and the French Canadians. The loyalty of the French Canadians to the British in the American Revolution was at least partly the result of the act. On the other hand, it infuriated the colonists in the present United States and helped bring on revolution. When Thomas Gage resigned as commander in chief of British forces in America, the command was divided—Sir Guy Carleton had command in Canada, and Sir William Howe had command farther south. When the American Revolutionaries launched their QUEBEC CAMPAIGN, Carleton had few men and was forced to abandon Montreal, which fell to the forces under Richard Montgomery. Withdrawing to Quebec, Carleton repelled (Dec. 31, 1775) an attack led by Montgomery and Benedict Arnold and withstood a long winter siege. British reinforcements in the spring enabled him to push the American forces out of Canada to Crown Point, which he took in the autumn of 1776. Disagreements with the British colonial secretary, Lord George Germain, led to his being replaced as commander by Gen. John Burgoyne in 1777. Carleton resigned as governor and left Canada in 1778, when he was succeeded by Sir Frederick Haldimand. In Feb., 1782, after the Yorktown campaign had already effectively ended the American Revolution, Carleton replaced Sir Henry Clinton as commander in chief of the British forces. His delicate task was to suspend hostilities, withdraw the forces from the New York and Vermont frontiers, and protect the Loyalists—both those who were emigrating to Canada and those who were attempting to reestablish themselves in their old homes. He was again governor of Quebec from 1786 to 1796. High-principled and able, Carleton was perhaps the most admirable British colonial commander in America in his time. See biography by A. G. Bradley (new ed. 1926, repr. 1966).

Carleton, Will, 1845–1912, American poet, b. Hudson, Mich. He is best known for his sentimental poems of rural life, the most famous being "Over the Hill to the Poorhouse." Among his works are *Farm Ballads* (1873), *Farm Legends* (1875), and *City Ballads* (1885).

Carleton, William, 1794–1869, Irish author. His *Traits and Stories of Irish Peasantry* (5 vol., 1830–33) realistically depicts his own rural youth. This was followed by *Tales of Ireland* (1834), *Fardorougha the Miser* (1839), and *The Black Prophet* (1847). See study by Benedict Kiely (1947).

Carleton College, at Northfield, Minn.; coeducational; chartered 1866 by Congregationalists, presently nonsectarian. It was called Northfield College until 1872, when it was renamed for William Carleton, a benefactor.

Carleton University, at Ottawa, Ont., Canada; nonsectarian; coeducational; founded 1942 as Carleton College. It achieved university status in 1957. It has faculties of arts, science, engineering, and graduate studies, and schools of architecture, commerce, journalism, public administration, social work, and international affairs.

Carl XVI Gustaf: see CHARLES XVI GUSTAVUS.

Carlile, Richard (kärlīl'), 1790–1843, English journalist, reformer, and freethinker. For his radical writings and efforts to secure the freedom of the press, he spent over nine years in prison. He republished suppressed works by Thomas Paine, William Hone, and others, brought out his own *Political Litany* (1817), and while he was imprisoned kept his weekly, the *Republican,* going (1819–26) with the help of his wife and sister. See biography by G. A. Aldred (1923).

Carlisle, Charles Howard, 1st **earl of** (kärlīl'), 1629–85, English statesman. A member of the prominent HOWARD family, he held various offices under Oliver Cromwell and remained in favor after the Restoration (1660) of Charles II. He was created earl in 1661 and served on several diplomatic missions. From 1677 to 1681 he was governor of Jamaica.

Carlisle, Frederick Howard, 5th **earl of,** 1748–1825, British statesman. A member of the distinguished Howard family, he went to the American colonies on an unsuccessful peace mission (1778) and served (1780–82) as lord lieutenant of Ireland. In 1798 he was made guardian of Lord Byron, who ridiculed him in the satirical poem *English Bards and Scotch Reviewers* (1809).

Carlisle, county borough (1971 pop. 71,497), county town of Cumberland, NW England, near the junction of the Caldew, Eden, and Petteril rivers. It is an important rail center and manufactures textiles, biscuits, and metal products. There is also an important livestock auction. Carlisle's location was formerly strategic. The Roman camp Luguvallium stood there, near Hadrian's Wall. The site figured prominently in the border warfare between the English and the

Scots during the Middle Ages. Mary Queen of Scots was imprisoned there in 1568. During the ENGLISH CIVIL WAR parliamentarians captured Carlisle. A technical college is in the borough. In 1974, Carlisle became part of the new nonmetropolitan county of Cumbria.

Carlisle (kärlīl', kär'līl), industrial borough (1970 pop. 18,079), seat of Cumberland co., S Pa.; inc. 1782. Its manufactures include shoes, rugs, and quartz crystals. In the French and Indian War the Forbes (1758) and the Bouquet (1763) expeditions were organized there. A munitions depot during the Revolution, Carlisle was a headquarters for Washington during the WHISKEY REBELLION in 1794. Molly Pitcher is buried in the Old Graveyard there. The borough was a stop on the Underground Railroad and was attacked during the Civil War by Gen. Fitzhugh Lee. Carlisle is the seat of a U.S. Army War College and Dickinson College. The Carlisle Indian School, founded in 1879 by R. H. Pratt, was there.

Carlisle Indian School, in Carlisle, Pa., the first Federally supported school for Indians to be established off a reservation; it was founded in 1879 by Richard Henry PRATT. Its football team, led by Jim THORPE and coached by Glenn WARNER, brought the school nationwide attention. Pratt, who strenuously opposed the Indian Bureau's efforts to establish schools closer to the reservations, was relieved of his superintendency in 1904. The school was closed in 1918.

Carlists, partisans of Don CARLOS (1788–1855) and his successors, who claimed the Spanish throne under the SALIC LAW of succession, introduced (1713) by Philip V. The law (forced on Philip by the War of the Spanish Succession to avoid a union of the French and Spanish crowns) was abrogated by Ferdinand VII in favor of his daughter, who succeeded him (1833) as ISABELLA II. Ferdinand's brother, Don Carlos, refused to recognize Isabella and claimed the throne. A civil war followed, and in the hope of autonomy, most of the Basque Provs. and much of Catalonia supported Carlos. The Carlists' conservative and clericalist tendencies gave the dynastic conflict a political character, since the upper middle classes profited from the sale of church lands and supported Isabella. In 1839 the Carlist commander Rafael Maroto yielded, but in Catalonia the Carlists under Ramón CABRERA continued the struggle until 1840. After the failure of a peace plan that proposed marriage between Isabella and Don Carlos's son, Don Carlos, conde de Montemolín (1818–61), the latter made an unsuccessful attempt at an uprising in 1860. Montemolín's claims were revived by his nephew, Don Carlos, duque de Madrid (1848–1909), after the deposition (1868) of Isabella. Two insurrections (1869, 1872) failed, but after the abdication (1873) of King AMADEUS and the proclamation of the first republic, the Carlists seized most of the Basque Provs. and parts of Catalonia, Aragón, and Valencia. The ensuing chaos and brutal warfare ended in 1876, over a year after ALFONSO XII, son of Isabella, was proclaimed king. Don Carlos escaped to France. In the next half century many defected from Carlist ranks, and several rival groups formed. Pressure against the church by the second republic (1931–39) helped revive Carlism, and the Carlists embraced the Nationalist cause in the Spanish civil war (1936–39). Under the Franco regime Carlism was for many years an obstacle to plans for restoring the main branch of the Bourbon dynasty, but in 1969, Franco overrode Carlist objections and named the Bourbon prince Juan Carlos as his successor. See Edgar Holt, *Carlist Wars in Spain* (1967).

Carloman, d. 880, king of Bavaria, Carinthia, Pannonia, and Moravia (876–80) and of Italy (877–80), son of LOUIS THE GERMAN and father of Arnulf, emperor of the West. He failed (875) to prevent the assumption of the imperial crown by his uncle, Charles II (Charles the Bald). In 879 he was incapacitated by a paralytic stroke and transferred to his brothers the authority to rule. He was the first German king to become king of Italy.

Carloman, 751–71, son of Pepin the Short. He and his brother, CHARLEMAGNE, shared the succession to their father's kingdom; Carloman ruled the southern portion. Attempts to end rivalry between the brothers failed, and when Carloman died Charlemagne seized his domain. Carloman's wife and children went to the court of DESIDERIUS, who, as an enemy of Charlemagne, supported their claims.

Carloman, d. 884, king of the West Franks (France), son of King LOUIS II (Louis the Stammerer). He became joint ruler with his brother LOUIS III in 879. His reign was disturbed by revolts in Burgundy, by the loss (879) of Provence to Boso, count of Arles, and by an invasion of the Normans. He became sole ruler at his brother's death (882). He was succeeded as French king by Emperor of the West Charles III (Charles the Fat).

Carloman, d. 754, mayor of the palace in the kingdom of AUSTRASIA after the death (741) of his father, Charles Martel. Ruling with his brother, PEPIN THE SHORT, he carried on successful wars against the dukes of Aquitaine, the Saxons, the Swabians, and the Bavarians. The brothers helped St. Boniface reform the Frankish Church, bringing church and state into closer relationship. In 747, Carloman retired to a monastery.

Carlos. For Spanish and Portuguese kings thus named, see CHARLES.

Carlos, 1545–68, prince of the Asturias, son of Philip II of Spain and Maria of Portugal. Don Carlos, who seems to have been mentally unbalanced and subject to fits of homicidal mania, was imprisoned by his father in 1568. When he died shortly afterward, it was rumored (falsely) that Philip had poisoned him. Friedrich von Schiller deliberately idealized his character in his tragedy *Don Carlos,* portraying him as a champion of liberalism, unhappily in love with his stepmother, ELIZABETH OF VALOIS.

Carlos (Carlos María Isidro de Borbón), 1788–1855, second son of Charles IV of Spain. He was the first Carlist pretender. After his father's abdication (1808) he was, with the rest of his family, held a prisoner in France until 1814. A conservative and a devout Catholic, he was supported by the clerical party when he refused to recognize Isabella, daughter of his brother, FERDINAND VII, as successor to the Spanish throne. When his niece became queen (1833) as ISABELLA II, Don Carlos took up arms. Defeated in 1839, he escaped to France and renounced his claim in favor of his son, Don Carlos, conde de Montemolín. See CARLISTS.

Carlotta, Span. *Carlota* (kärlō'tä), 1840–1927, empress of Mexico, daughter of Leopold I of Belgium, christened Marie Charlotte Amélie. She married MAXIMILIAN, archduke of Austria, on July 27, 1857, and accompanied him when he went to Mexico as emperor (1864). After Napoleon III decided to withdraw the French troops from Mexico and the fate of the empire became apparent, she went to Europe (1866) and sought the aid of Napoleon III and the pope. Her pleas were in vain, and her overwrought mind gave way under the strain. The Mexican empire ended with the execution of Maximilian in 1867, but the unhappy empress survived it by 60 years. See studies by Egon Corti (1928, repr. 1968), Richard O'Connor (1971), and Joan Haslip (1971).

Carlow (kär'lō), county (1971 pop. 34,025), 346 sq mi (896 sq km), SE Republic of Ireland. The chief towns are CARLOW, the county town; Bagenalstown, on the Barrow River, which forms much of the western boundary of the county; and Tullow, on the Slaney River which crosses the county from north to south. The granitic uplands of the Blackstairs Mts. in the southeast are a conspicuous feature in an otherwise fertile lowland region. Wheat, barley, and sugar-beet farming, cattle raising, and dairying are occupations of the region. There are also flour-milling, malting, and sugar-refining industries. Organized as a county in the early 13th cent., Carlow was strategically situated on the southern edge of the English PALE. In the 13th cent. it had palatinate privileges.

Carlow, urban district (1971 pop. 9,384), county town of Co. Carlow, SE Republic of Ireland, on the Barrow River. It is an agricultural market in a dairy region, with sugar refining, flour milling, brewing, and shoe manufacturing. There are ruins of a 12th-century castle. Carlow is the seat of the Roman Catholic diocese of Kildare and Leighlin. Of strategic importance, it was burned in 1405 and in 1577; in 1798 there was a fierce street battle fought by insurgent United Irishmen. St. Patrick's College for priests opened there in 1798.

Carl Sandburg Home National Historic Site: see NATIONAL PARKS AND MONUMENTS (table).

Carlsbad: see KARLOVY VARY, Czechoslovakia.

Carlsbad (kärlz'băd). **1** Resort city (1970 pop. 14,944), San Diego co., S Calif., on the Pacific coast; settled in the 1880s, inc. 1952. It has an electronic industry, machine shops, and a crystal silica quarry. Major agricultural products are tomatoes and flowers; the flower fields in bloom are a tourist attraction. The discovery there of mineral springs with waters identical to those at Carlsbad (Karlovy Vary), in Bohemia (now part of Czechoslovakia), led to the settlement and naming of the town. There are two lagoons, one freshwater and one tidewater, and many water sports facilities. La Costa resort spa is there. **2** City (1970 pop. 21,297), seat of Eddy co., SE N.Mex., on the Pecos River, in a grazing and irrigated farm area; settled 1888, inc. 1918. Great quantities of potash are mined and refined there. Other industries include agriculture, ranching, and tourism. The climate is mild, and two dammed lakes within the city provide water recreation. The Carlsbad reclamation project, begun in 1906, serves more than 20,000 acres (8,094 hectares). A two-year branch of New Mexico State Univ. is located in Carlsbad. There is a state zoological and botanical park on the city's outskirts, and Carlsbad Caverns National Park is nearby.

Carlsbad Caverns National Park, 46,753 acres (18,921 hectares), SE N.Mex., in the Guadalupe Mts.; est. as a national park 1930. These limestone caves, with remarkable stalactite and stalagmite formations and huge chambers, began forming 60 million years ago as groundwater started dissolving the rock. The caverns, among the largest in the world, were discovered c.1900 and still have not been completely explored. The temperature of the caves remains constant at 56°F (13.3°C). Seven miles (11.3 km) of trail are electrically lighted. The Big Room, 754 ft (230 m) below the surface, is the most majestic of the many chambers; its perimeter is c.1¼ mi (2 km) long. Each evening during the spring, summer and fall, the countless bats that inhabit the cave swarm out to feed on insects.

Carlsbad Decrees, 1819, resolutions adopted by the ministers of German states at a conference at Carlsbad that was convened and dominated by Prince METTERNICH following the murder of August von KOTZEBUE by a student. The decrees provided for uniform press censorship and close supervision of the universities, with the aim of suppressing all liberal agitation against the conservative governments of Germany, particularly by the student organizations (see BURSCHENSCHAFT). The resolutions, ratified by the diet of the German Confederation, remained in force until 1848.

Carlscrona: see KARLSKRONA, Sweden.

Carlson, Evans Fordyce, 1896–1947, U.S. marine officer, b. Delaware co., N.Y. Enlisting at 16 in the army, he served in the Philippines and Hawaii and in France during World War I. In the U.S. marine corps after 1922, he saw service in Cuba, Nicaragua, Japan, and especially China, where in 1937 he studied guerrilla warfare intensively. Angered by censorship of his reports, he resigned, but in 1941 he applied for recommissioning. During World War II he organized and commanded Carlson's Raiders, a guerrilla unit that achieved fame by its raids on Makin Island (Aug., 1942) and Guadalcanal (Nov., 1942). In 1946 he was promoted to brigadier general and retired from service. He wrote *The Chinese Army* (1940) and *Twin Stars of China* (1940). See biography by Michael Blankfort (1947).

Carlstadt, Karlstadt (both: kärl'shtät), or **Karolostadt** (kä'rôlōshtät''), c.1480–1541, German Protestant reformer, whose original name was Andreas Rudolph Bodenstein. As early as 1516, Carlstadt presented theses denying free will and asserting the doctrine of salvation by grace alone. In 1518 he supported Luther against the attacks of Johann Maier von Eck by maintaining the supremacy of Scripture and in 1519 he appeared with Luther against Eck in the public disputation at Leipzig. He soon became known as the most extreme of the Wittenberg reformers. During Luther's stay at the Wartburg (1521–22) he became the leader at Wittenberg and began to put his radical beliefs into effect. His extreme spiritualization of religion tended to undermine the importance of the church and the sacraments. Upon his return Luther accused Carlstadt of betrayal and restored the more orthodox practices. Accused of revolutionary political activity he fled to Switzerland where he was protected by the Zurich preachers and became professor of theology at Basel.

Carlton Club, British political and social club (founded 1832). Located in London, it was long the center of the Conservative party organization. Since World War II the club has been primarily social. See study by Sir C. A. Petrie (1955).

Carlyle, Jane Baillie Welsh, 1801–66, English woman of letters; wife of Thomas Carlyle, whom she married in 1826. She possessed a genius for letter writing, manifest in the volumes of her published correspondence (1883, 1924, 1931). See edition of her letters by Trudy Bliss (1950); biography by E. A. Drew (1928, repr. 1973); study by Lawrence Hanson (1952).

Carlyle, Thomas, 1795–1881, English author, b. Scotland. He studied (1809–14) at the Univ. of Edinburgh, intending to enter the ministry, but left when his doubts became too strong. He taught mathematics before returning to Edinburgh in 1818 to study law. However, law gave way to reading in German literature. He was strongly influenced by Goethe and the transcendental philosophers and wrote several works interpreting German romantic thought, including a *Life of Schiller* (1825) and a translation (1824) of Goethe's *Wilhelm Meister*. In 1826 he married Jane Baillie Welsh, a well-informed and ambitious woman who did much to further his career. They moved to Jane's farm at Craigenputtock in 1828. There he wrote *Sartor Resartus* (published 1833–34 in *Fraser's Magazine*), in which he told his spiritual autobiography. He saw the material world as mere clothing for the spiritual one. The God of his beliefs was an immanent and friendly ruler of an orderly universe. In denying corporeal reality, Carlyle reflected his revulsion from the materialism of the age. In 1832, Ralph Waldo Emerson went to Craigenputtock, and began a friendship with Carlyle that was continued in their famous correspondence. In 1834 the Carlyles moved to London to be near necessary works of reference for the projected *French Revolution*. Finally completed in 1837 (the first volume had been accidentally burned in 1835), the book was received with great acclaim. Although it vividly re-creates scenes of the Revolution, it is not a factual account but a poetic rendering of an event in history. Carlyle extended his view of the divinity of man, particularly in his portraits of the great leaders of the Revolution. In subsequent works he attacked laissez-faire theory and parliamentary government and affirmed his belief in the necessity for strong, paternalistic government. He was convinced that society does change, but that it must do so intelligently, directed by its best men, its "heroes." His lectures, published as *On Heroes, Hero-Worship, and The Heroic in History* (1841), express his view that the great men of the past have intuitively shaped destiny and have been the spiritual leaders of the world. His other works expanded his ideas—*Chartism* (1840); *Past and Present* (1843), contrasting the disorder of modern society with the feudal order of 12th-century England; *Oliver Cromwell's Letters and Speeches* (1845); *Latter-Day Pamphlets* (1850); *Life of John Sterling* (1851); and a massive biography of a hero-king, Frederick the Great, on which he spent the years 1852–65. In 1866 his wife died, and the loss saddened the rest of his life. One of the most important social critics of his day, Carlyle influenced many men of the younger generation, among them Matthew Arnold and Ruskin. His style, one of the most tortuous yet effective in English literature, was a compound of biblical phrases, colloquialisms, Teutonic twists, and his own coinings, arranged in unexpected sequences. See his *Reminiscences* (1881) and numerous collections of his letters and his wife's; biographies by J. A. Froude (4 vol., 1882–84, repr. 1971) and D. A. Wilson (6 vol., 1923–34, repr. 1971; Vol. VI finished by D. W. MacArthur); studies by Emery Neff (1932, repr. 1968), Eric Bentley (1944), Julian Symons (1952, repr. 1970), George B. Tennyson (1966), and A. J. LaValley (1968).

Carmagnola, Francesco Bussone da (fränchĕs′kō bo͞os-sô′nä dä kärmänyô′lä), c.1380?–1432, Italian condottiere. He fought for Filippo Maria Visconti, duke of Milan, in his wars against Florence and Venice but later fell out with Visconti and entered the service of Venice. After 1425 he commanded Florentine and Venetian forces against Milan. His irresolute conduct of the war led the Venetians to suspect treason, and he was tried and executed.

Carman, Bliss (kär′mən), 1861–1929, Canadian poet, b. Fredericton, N.B. He studied at the universities of New Brunswick and Edinburgh and at Harvard. While at Harvard (1886–88) he began a friendship with Richard Hovey that later resulted in their joint publication of the series *Songs from Vagabondia* (1894, 1896, 1901). Carman's poetry is emotional, optimistic, and impressionistic, filled with vivid, sensuous imagery. Among his numerous volumes of verse are *Behind the Arras* (1895), the series *Pipes of Pan* (1902–5), and *Echoes from Vagabondia* (1912). The best of these and other poems are collected in *Later Poems* (1921) and *Ballads and Lyrics* (1923). His *Talks on Poetry and Life*, lectures on Canadian literature, was published in 1926. See biography by Odell Shepard (1924); study by Donald Stephens (1966).

Carman, Harry James, 1884–1964, American historian and educator, b. Greenfield, Saratoga co., N.Y. He was a grade school teacher and a high school principal before becoming an instructor and then an assistant professor at Syracuse Univ. (1914–17). In 1918 he began teaching at Columbia, where he attained the rank of professor in 1931. From 1925 to 1931 he was assistant to the dean of Columbia College, and from 1943 to 1950 he was dean. He was appointed a member of the Board of Higher Education of New York City in 1938 and served on the New York State Board of Mediation from 1941 to 1955. Among his works are *Social and Economic History of the United States* (2 vol., 1930–34), *Lincoln and the Patronage* (with R. H. Luthin, 1943), *A History of the American People* (with H. C. Syrett, rev. ed. 1962), and *A Short History of New York State* (with others, 1957). He also edited several works concerning early American agriculture, on which he was a leading authority: Jared Eliot's *Essays upon Field Husbandry in New England* (with Rexford G. Tugwell, 1934), *American Husbandry* (1939), and *Jesse Buel, Agricultural Reformer: Selections from His Writings* (1947). Carman was also the editor of a valuable compilation, *A Guide to the Principal Sources for American Civilization, 1800–1900, in the City of New York* (with A. W. Thompson, 2 vol., "Manuscripts," 1960, and "Printed Sources," 1962).

Carmarthen (kərmär′thən), municipal borough (1971 pop. 13,072), county town of Carmarthenshire, S Wales, on the Towy River. It is a port for small vessels, a transportation hub, a cattle market, and a dairy center. In the Middle Ages Carmarthen was an important wool port. Its old castle (now in ruins) was the headquarters of Welsh chieftains. Carmarthen's parish church of St. Peter (14th cent.) is noteworthy. Trinity College is a teacher-training school. Merlin, the wizard of Arthurian legend, was reputedly born in Carmarthen. In 1974, Carmarthen became part of the new nonmetropolitan county of Dyfed.

Carmarthenshire, county (1971 pop. 162,313), 919 sq mi (2,380 sq km), S Wales. The county town is CARMARTHEN. Largest of the Welsh counties, it is hilly, with lower land along the coast of Carmarthen Bay (off the Bristol Channel) and in the fertile valley of the Towy River. The county is generally devoted to agriculture (dairy farming is most important), but part of the great S Wales coalfield extends into the southeast corner of the county around Llanelly. Metal products, textiles, and lenses are among the manufactured goods. There are remains of prehistoric and Roman settlements. In 1974, Carmarthenshire became part of the new nonmetropolitan county of Dyfed.

Carmathians: see KARMATHIANS.

Carmel, Mount [Heb.,=garden land], mountain ridge, NW Israel, extending 13 mi (21 km) NW from the plain of Esdraelon to the Mediterranean Sea, where it ends in a promontory marking the southern limit of the Bay of Haifa. Its highest point is 1,792 ft (546 m), and it is one of the most striking physical features of Israel. Long an object of veneration, it was associated in biblical times with the lives of the prophets Elijah and Elisha (Isa. 35.2; Amos 9.3; 1 Kings 18). From the mountainside vineyards comes the renowned Mt. Carmel wine; there are also olive groves. At the foot of Mt. Carmel is the port of Haifa. On its slopes are a Bahaist garden shrine, with the tombs of Bab-ed-din and of Abdul Baha (see BAHAISM), and a 19th-century Carmelite monastery.

Carmel-by-the-Sea or **Carmel** (kärmĕl′), village (1970 pop. 4,525), Monterey co., S Calif., at the neck of Monterey peninsula on Carmel Bay; inc. 1916. It is a tourist spot as well as an artists' and writers' community (Jack London and Robinson Jeffers both lived and worked there); art shows and an annual Bach festival are held in the village. The bay, named in 1602 by Carmelite friars in Vizcaíno's expedition, is famed for its beauty. Mission San Carlos Borromeo, the burial place of Father Junípero Serra, is nearby.

Carmelites (kär′məlīts), Roman Catholic order of mendicant friars. Originally a group of hermits, apparently European, living on Mt. Carmel, Palestine, their supervision was undertaken (c.1150) by St. Berthold. In 1238 they moved to Cyprus, and thence to Western Europe. St. Simon Stock (d. 1265), an Englishman, was their second founder. He transformed them into an order of friars resembling Dominicans and Franciscans and founded monasteries at Oxford, Cambridge, Paris, and Bologna. They rapidly became prominent in university life. An enclosed order of Carmelite nuns was established. The Carmelites, like other orders, declined in the 15th cent. They were revived by St. THERESA (of Ávila) and St. JOHN OF THE CROSS in 16th-century Spain. These great contemplatives gave the order a special orientation toward mysticism. Their reformed branch is the Discalced (or Barefoot) Carmelites; it is now more numerous than the Carmelites of the Old Observance. The Discalced Carmelites cultivate the contemplative life in all aspects, and they have produced many works on mystical theology. St. THERESA (of Lisieux) is a well-known Discalced Carmelite of the 19th cent. In 1790 the first community came to the United States and settled near Port Tobacco, Md. There are presently about 6,900 priests and brothers living in Carmelite communities, with 500 living in the United States. See E. Allison Peers, *Spirit of Flame* (1944, repr. 1961); Peter Rohrback, *Journey to the Carith* (1966).

Carmen Sylva: see ELIZABETH, queen of Rumania.

Carmi (kär′mī). **1** Father of Achan. Joshua 7.1,18; 1 Chron. 2.7. In spite of textual difficulties this can probably be identified as the Carmi of 1 Chron. 4.1. **2** Reuben's son. Gen. 46.9; Ex. 6.14; Num. 26.6; 1 Chron. 5.3.

Carmichael, uninc. residential city (1970 pop. 37,625), Sacramento co., N central Calif., on the American River.

carmina burana: see GOLIARDIC SONGS.

Carmona, António Oscar de Fragoso (əntô′nyō əshkär′ dĭ frəgô′so͞o kərmô′nə), 1869–1951, Portuguese general and political leader. When Gen. Manuel de Oliveira Gomes da Costa overthrew the democratic regime in 1926, Carmona was made foreign minister in the new government. Shortly afterward he deposed Gomes da Costa and served (1926–28) as head of the provisional government. Elected president in 1928, Carmona won (1935, 1942, 1949) each successive election. The regime he established was dictatorial, dominated after 1928 by António de Oliveira SALAZAR.

Carmona (kärmō′nä), town (1970 pop. 24,378), Sevilla prov., SW Spain, in Andalusia. It is a farm center for an area raising cattle, cereals, fruits, and olives. Ferdinand III of Castile took Carmona from the Moors in 1247 after a year-long siege. It has numerous examples of Gothic, Moorish, and baroque architecture, including the imposing ruins of an alcazar. A large Roman necropolis was discovered nearby in 1881.

Carnac (kärnăk′), town (1968 pop. 3,681), Morbihan dept., NW France, in Brittany, at the foot of the Quiberon peninsula. It is the site of remarkable MEGALITHIC MONUMENTS, particularly the MENHIR. The menhirs, formerly ascribed to the druids, extend along the coast in 11 parallel rows, 1,100 yd (1,006 m) long; some are 20 ft (6.1 m) high. The sea resort of Carnac-Plage is nearby.

Carnaim (kär′nāĭm): see ASHTEROTH KARNAIM.

Carnap, Rudolf, 1891–1970, German-American philosopher. He taught philosophy at the Univ. of Vienna (1926–31), where he became a member of the VIENNA CIRCLE, and at the German Univ. in Prague (1931–35). After going to the United States he taught at the Univ. of Chicago (1936–52) and at the Univ. of California at Los Angeles (1954–62). Carnap was one of the most influential of contemporary philosophers; he is known as a founder of LOGICAL POSITIVISM and made important contributions to logic, semantics, and the philosophy of science. In *Logische Syntax der Sprache* (1934; tr. *The Logical Syntax of Language*, 1937) he defined philosophy as "the logic of the sciences" and considered it a general language whose only legitimate concern could be to describe and criticize the language of the particular sciences. All propositions were held to be either tautological (embodying logical or mathematical systems), scientific (embodying philosophy properly understood), or nonsensical (embodying the nonverifiable propositions of traditional philosophy). Through an analysis of scientific, logical, and mathematical language he revealed the inadequacies of everyday speech. Carnap later modified this extreme view, which rejects almost all of traditional philosophy. His other works include *Introduction to Semantics* (1942), *Meaning and Necessity* (1947, 2d ed. 1956), *Logical Foundations of Probability* (1950), and *Einfuhrung in die symbolische Logik* (1954; tr. *Introduction to Symbolic Logic and its Applications*, 1958). See studies by P. A. Schilpp, ed. (1963) and Richard Butrick (1970).

Carnarvon, George Edward Stanhope Molyneux Herbert, 5th **earl of** (kärnär′vən), 1866–1923, English Egyptologist. With Howard Carter he excavated in the Valley of the Kings in Luxor, Egypt, from 1906 to 1922. The final and most famous of their discoveries was the tomb of Tutankhamen. Lord Carnarvon died before it was thoroughly explored. He collaborated with Howard Carter on the report *Five Years' Explorations at Thebes* (1912).

Carnarvon, Henry Howard Molyneux Herbert, 4th **earl of,** 1831–90, British statesman. As colonial secretary (1866–67) under the earl of Derby he introduced the British North America Act, which made Canada a confederation. In the same office (1874–78) under Disraeli he was unsuccessful in an attempt to create a federation in South Africa. His policy as lord lieutenant of Ireland (1885–86) was conciliatory but failed to stem Irish nationalism. See correspondence, 1874–1878, ed. by C. W. de Kiewiet (1955); biography by A. H. Hardinge (1925).

Carnatic (kärnăt'ĭk), region, SW India, on the Arabian Sea. The early European settlers sometimes applied the term Carnatic to all of S India. The region was the site of the earliest European settlements in India, those of Portugal. During the 18th cent. the Carnatic plains became the arena for the struggle between Great Britain and France for supremacy in India.

carnation: see PINK.

carnauba, WAX obtained from the wax palm, or carnauba (*Copernicia cerifera*), of Brazil. It is secreted by the leaves, apparently in defense against the hot winds and droughts of its native habitat, and the resultant coating is removed by drying and flailing. The hardest, highest-melting natural wax known, its many commercial uses include the production of polishes, lubricants, and floor waxes. A similar wax is obtained from the trunk of *Ceroxylon andicola*, the wax palm of the Andes.

Carneades (kärnē'ədēz), 213–129 B.C., Greek philosopher, b. Cyrene. He studied at Athens under Diogenes the Stoic, but reacted against Stoicism and joined the ACADEMY, where he taught a skepticism similar to that of Pyrrho. While denying the possibility of absolute certainty in knowledge, he held that probable knowledge was available to guide the actions of men. He recognized three degrees of probability, and his work anticipated modern discussions of the nature of empirical knowledge.

Carnegie, Andrew (kärnā'gē), 1835–1919, American industrialist and philanthropist, b. Dunfermline, Scotland. His father, a weaver, found it increasingly difficult to get work in Scottish factories and in 1848 brought his family to Allegheny (now Pittsburgh), Pa. Andrew first worked in a cotton mill as a bobbin boy, then advanced himself as a telegrapher, and became (1859) a superintendent for the Pennsylvania RR. He resigned (1865) his railroad position to give personal attention to the investments he had made (1864) in iron manufactures. By 1873 he had recognized America's need for steel and, concentrating on steel production, began his acquisition of firms which were later consolidated into the Carnegie Steel Company. Carnegie's success was due in part to efficient business methods, to his able lieutenants, and to close alliances with railroads. Another factor was his partnership with Henry C. FRICK. Carnegie, concentrating on production rather than stock-market manipulations, further expanded his plants and consolidated his hold in the depression of 1893–97. By 1900 the Carnegie Steel Company was producing one quarter of all the steel in the United States and controlled iron mines, coke ovens, ore ships, and railroads. It was in these circumstances that the U.S. Steel Corp. was formed to buy Carnegie out. He had long been willing to sell—at his own price—and in 1901 he transferred possession for $250 million in bonds and retired from business. He lived a large part of each year after 1887 in Scotland on his great estate on Dornoch Firth. His essay "The Gospel of Wealth" (1889) set forth his idea that rich men are "trustees" of their wealth and should administer it for the good of the public. Carnegie's benefactions (totaling about $350 million) included Carnegie Hall (1892) in New York City, the Carnegie Institution of Washington (1902), the Carnegie Hero Fund Commission (1904), the Carnegie Foundation for the Advancement of Teaching (1905), the Carnegie Endowment for International Peace (1910), and over 2,800 libraries. See his autobiography (1920, repr. 1963); biographies by B. J. Hendrick (1932, repr. 1969), A. F. Harlow (1953), and J. F. Wall (1970).

Carnegie, borough (1970 pop. 10,864), Allegheny co., SW Pa., an industrial suburb of Pittsburgh; inc. 1894. A steel town, it also has coal mines and plants making chemicals and electrical equipment. The Neville House was the home of Gen. John Neville, an officer in the French and Indian and Revolutionary Wars. The borough was named for Andrew Carnegie.

Carnegie Corporation of New York, foundation established (1911) to administer Andrew Carnegie's remaining personal fortune for philanthropic purposes. Initially endowed with $125 million, the foundation received another $10 million from the residual estate. By 1970 its assets exceeded $283 million. Carnegie directed the foundation's activities until his death in 1919; in accordance with his early interests he established the policy of grants for free public libraries and church organs. In the years following his death the trustees followed a more general policy leading to "the advancement and diffusion of knowledge and understanding." The foundation has financed many studies in its areas of main interest—U.S. education and underprivileged groups. Since 1917 a small portion of the foundation's income has been used for studies within the British Commonwealth. Andrew Carnegie also established the Carnegie Endowment for International Peace (1910), the Carnegie Foundation for the Advancement of Teaching (1905), and the Carnegie Hero Fund Commission (1904).

Carnegie Institute of Technology: see CARNEGIE-MELLON UNIV.

Carnegie-Mellon University, at Pittsburgh, Pa.; est. 1967 through the merger of the Carnegie Institute of Technology (founded 1900, opened 1905) and the Mellon Institute of Industrial Research (founded 1913). The university is made up of six divisions and includes additional facilities for nuclear, computer, and educational research. The university was the first in the United States to offer academic degrees in the field of drama.

carnelian (kärnēl'yən) or **cornelian** (kôr-, kər-), variety of red CHALCEDONY, used as a gem. It is distinguished from SARD by the shade of red, carnelian being bright red and sard brownish. The red coloring is apparently caused by iron oxide.

Carniola (kärnēō'lə), Croatian *Kranj*, historic region, NW Yugoslavia, in Slovenia. The history of this largely mountainous area is closely linked with that of SLOVENIA. The first known inhabitants, a Celtic tribe called the Carni, were displaced by the Romans, who made Carniola part of their province of Pannonia. Slovenes settled Carniola in the 6th cent. Charlemagne later incorporated it into his empire. The region became a march, or margraviate, under Bavarian suzerainty in the 10th cent. and in 1269 was acquired by Bohemia. It passed to the Austrian Hapsburgs in 1282 and was made (1364) a titular duchy. In 1849 its status was raised to a crown land. LJUBLJANA was its chief city. After World War I, Carniola was divided between Italy and Yugoslavia, but the Italian part passed to Yugoslavia in 1947.

Carnion (kär'nēŏn): see ASHTEROTH KARNAIM.

carnival, communal celebration, especially the religious celebration in Roman Catholic countries that takes place just before LENT. Since early times carnivals have been accompanied by parades, masquerades, pageants, and other forms of revelry that had their origins in pre-Christian pagan rites, particularly fertility rites that were connected with the coming of spring and the rebirth of vegetation. One of the first recorded instances of an annual spring festival is the festival of Osiris in Egypt; it commemorated the renewal of life brought about by the yearly flooding of the Nile. In Athens, during the 6th cent. B.C., a yearly celebration in honor of the god Dionysus featured a float dedicated to him that was wheeled through the city streets to the accompaniment of songs, dances, and ribald merrymaking. This is the first recorded instance of the traditional use of floats for spring festivals. It was during the Roman Empire that carnivals reached an unparalleled peak of civil disorder and licentiousness. Developing out of folk celebrations and the Greek mysteries of Dionysus, the major Roman carnivals were the Bacchanalia, the Saturnalia, and the Lupercalia. In Europe the tradition of spring fertility celebrations persisted well into Christian times, particularly in Teutonic regions, where carnivals reached their peak during the 14th and 15th cent. Because carnivals are deeply rooted in pagan superstitions and the folklore of Europe, the Catholic Church found it impossible to stamp them out and ultimately was driven to the position of having to accept many of them as part of church activity. The immediate consequence of church influence may be seen in the medieval Feast of Fools, which included a mock Mass and a blasphemous impersonation of church officials, and the Feast of the Ass, which retained many pagan rites and was at times very bawdy. Eventually, however, the power of the church made itself felt, and the carnival was stripped of its most offending elements. The church succeeded in dominating the activities of the carnivals, and eventually they became directly related to the coming of Lent. The major celebrations are generally on Shrove Tuesday (see MARDI GRAS); however, in Germany the carnival season, or *Fasching,* begins on the Epiphany (Jan. 6) in Bavaria and on Nov. 11 in the Rhineland. In recent times, the term *carnival* has also been loosely applied to include local festivals, traveling circuses, bazaars, and other celebrations of a joyous nature, regardless of their purpose or their season.

carnivore (kär'nəvôr''), term commonly applied to any animal whose diet consists wholly or largely of animal matter. In animal systematics it refers to members of the mammalian order Carnivora (see CHORDATA). This large order is divided into two suborders, the Fissipedia, or land carnivores, and the Pinnipedia, or fin-footed carnivores. The Fissipedia encompasses two superfamilies: one (Canoidea) includes the DOG, BEAR, RACCOON, and WEASEL families and the other (Feloidea) includes the CAT, CIVET, and HYENA families. The Pinnipedia, often classified as a separate order, includes the SEAL, SEA LION, and WALRUS families. The term *herbivore* refers to animals whose diets consist wholly or largely of plant matter; *omnivore* refers to animals that eat both animal and plant matter. Unlike the term *carnivore,* these terms do not refer to any one group in animal systematics.

carnivorous plants: see BLADDERWORT; PITCHER PLANT; VENUS'S-FLYTRAP.

Carnot, Hippolyte (ēpôlēt' kärnō'), 1801–88, French statesman; son of Lazare Carnot. He shared his father's exile after 1815 and returned to France in 1823. A follower of Claude Henri de SAINT-SIMON, he participated in the July Revolution of 1830. He came to oppose the July Monarchy and was elected three times as an opposition member of the chamber of deputies. He took part in the radical agitation that led to the February Revolution of 1848 and became minister of education in the provisional government. Entering (1864) the *corps législatif,* he joined the liberal opposition to Emperor Napoleon III, after whose downfall he became a member of the constituent assembly (1871) and then a senator for life (1875).

Carnot, Lazare Nicolas Marguerite (läzär' nēkôlä' märgərēt'), 1753–1823, French revolutionary, known as the organizer of victory for his role in the FRENCH REVOLUTIONARY WARS. A military engineer by training, Carnot became the military genius of the Revolution and was chiefly responsible for the success of the French in the wars. A member of the Legislative Assembly, the Convention, and the Committee of Public Safety, he made himself almost indispensable through his military knowledge. After the fall of Maximilien Robespierre, who was primarily responsible for the Reign of Terror, Carnot managed to avoid punishment for his own part in the Terror and became a member of the DIRECTORY. He was ousted from the Directory in the coup d'etat of 18 Fructidor (Sept., 1797) and fled abroad. He returned in 1799 and served as minister of war (1800) and in the tribunate under Napoleon Bonaparte (NAPOLEON I). In the next few years he wrote several works on mathematics and military engineering; in 1810 appeared his masterpiece, *De la défense des places fortes,* long considered the classic work on fortification. Carnot was the best-known advocate of the principle of active defense. In 1814 he returned to active service and conducted the defense of Antwerp. In the Hundred Days he served as minister of the interior. Exiled after the restoration of the monarchy, he died in Magdeburg, Prussia. See biographies by Huntley Dupre (1940) and Marcel Reinhard (2 vol., 1950–52, in French).

Carnot, Nicolas Léonard Sadi (nēkōlä' lāônär' sädē'), 1796–1832, French physicist, a founder of modern thermodynamics; son of Lazare N. M. Carnot. His famous work on the motive power of heat (*Réflexions sur la puissance motrice du feu,* 1824) is concerned with the relation between heat and mechanical energy. Carnot devised an ideal engine in which a gas is allowed to expand to do work, absorbing heat in the process, and is expanded again without transfer of heat but with a temperature drop. The gas is then compressed, heat being given off, and finally it is returned to its original condition by another compression, accompanied by a rise in temperature. This series of operations, known as Carnot's cycle, shows that even under ideal conditions a heat engine cannot convert into mechanical energy all the heat energy supplied to it; some of the heat energy must be rejected. This is an illustration of the second law of thermodynamics. Carnot's work anticipated that of Joule, Kelvin, and others.

Carnot, Sadi (sädē'), 1837–94, French statesman, president of the Third Republic (1887–94); son of Hippolyte Carnot. As minister of public works (1880–85) and of finance (1886), he remained untainted by the financial scandals of the time. He succeeded Jules Grévy in the presidency; his tenure was disturbed by the agitation for General BOULANGER and by the Panama Canal scandal, concerning bribery of public officials. He was assassinated by an Italian anarchist. Jean Paul Pierre Casimir-Perier succeeded him.

Carnovsky, Morris (kärnŏv'skē), 1897–, American actor, b. St. Louis, Mo. After his New York City debut in *The God of Vengenance* (1922), he joined the Theatre Guild and later performed with The Group Theatre, of which he was a founding member. He worked as an actor and director for the Actors Laboratory Theatre in Hollywood (1945-50). Carnovsky has concentrated on Shakespearean roles since his first appearance at Stratford, Conn., in 1956. His films include *Cyrano de Bergerac* (1951).

Caro, Annibale (än-nē'bälā kä'rō), 1507-66, Italian poet, friend of Cellini, Varchi, and Bembo. He is best known for his translation of the *Aeneid;* for his poems in praise of opposing royal houses; and for his letters, which were among the finest of his age.

Caro or **Karo, Joseph ben Ephraim** (kä'rō), 1488-1575, eminent Jewish codifier of law, b. Toledo, Spain. He left Spain as a child when the Jews were expelled (1492) and finally settled in Safed, Palestine. His literary works rank among the masterpieces of rabbinical literature. Chief among them are the *Bet Yosef* [house of Joseph] and *Shulhan Aruk* [the table set], parts of which are still used as the authoritative code for Orthodox religious and legal disputes. This code owes its fame and popularity as much to the opposition it aroused and the many commentaries it inspired as it does to its merits. Caro was also a noted cabalist (see CABALA) who claimed to have had heavenly visitations. He recorded much of this in a diary later edited to appear as a commentary on the Pentateuch (*Maggid Mesharim,* 1646). See study by R. J. Werblowsky (1962).

carob (kăr'əb), leguminous evergreen tree (*Ceratonia siliqua*) of the family Leguminosae (PULSE family), native to Mediterranean regions but cultivated in other warm climates, including Florida and California. The large red pods have been used for food for animal and man since prehistoric times. The pods and their extracted content have numerous common names, e.g., locust bean gum and St.-John's-bread—the latter from the belief that they may have been the "locust" eaten by John the Baptist in the wilderness (Mark 1.6). Carob is used also for curing tobacco, in papermaking, and as a stabilizer in food products. It has been claimed that the seeds were the original of the carat, the measure of weight for precious jewels and metals. Carob is classified in the division MAGNOLIOPHYTA, class Magnoliopsida, order Rosales, family Leguminosae.

Carol I, 1839-1914, prince (1866-81) and first king (1881-1914) of Rumania, of the house of Hohenzollern-Sigmaringen. He is also called Charles I. A Prussian officer, he was elected to succeed the deposed Alexander John Cuza as prince of Rumania. He reformed the Rumanian constitution and laid the groundwork for the country's monetary system, military organization, and railroad network. Exploitation of Rumanian oil fields began in his reign. Economic development, however, did not improve the lot of the peasants, and an uprising in 1907 was cruelly suppressed. Carol sided with Russia in the Russo-Turkish War of 1877-78 and obtained at the Congress of Berlin (see BERLIN, CONGRESS OF) full independence for Rumania, which he declared a kingdom in 1881. Carol's wife was Princess ELIZABETH of Wied. He was succeeded by his nephew Ferdinand.

Carol II, 1893-1953, king of Rumania, son of King Ferdinand and Queen Marie. While crown prince, he contracted a morganatic marriage with Zizi Labrino but divorced her to marry (1921) Princess Helen of Greece. He soon formed a liaison with Magda LUPESCU, with whom he lived in Paris after being forced (1925) to renounce his right of succession. On the death (1927) of King Ferdinand, Carol's son MICHAEL became king, but Carol, having divorced Queen Helen in 1928, returned to Rumania in 1930, supplanted his son, and had himself proclaimed king de jure since 1927. A turbulent period began (see RUMANIA). In 1938, Carol formed a royal dictatorship. A contest between the king and the fascist IRON GUARD ensued, with assassinations and massacres on both sides. Forced to call on Ion ANTONESCU to form a government (1940), Carol was deposed and fled abroad with Lupescu, whom he finally married in Brazil in 1947. Michael once more became king. Carol died in Portugal.

carol, popular hymn, of joyful nature, in celebration of an occasion such as May Day, Easter, or Christmas. The earliest English carols date from the 15th cent. The carol is characterized by simplicity of thought and expression. Many are thought to be adaptations of pagan songs. Despite the folk-song character of true carols, many Christmas hymns composed in the 19th cent. have been called carols. The oldest printed carol is the *Boar's Head Carol,* printed in 1521 by Wynkyn de Worde. Carols of French origin are called noels. See W. J. Phillips, *Carols, Their Origins, Music and Connection with Mystery-Plays* (1921); R. L. Greene, *The Early English Carols* (1935); Percy Dearmer et al., ed., *The Oxford Book of Carols* (1928, repr. 1964); Edmonstoune Duncan, *The Story of the Carol* (1911, repr. 1968).

Carol City, uninc. residential city (1970 pop. 27,361), Dade co., SE Fla., between Miami and Fort Lauderdale and near the Atlantic Ocean.

Carolina campaign, 1780-81, of the American Revolution. After Sir Henry Clinton had captured CHARLESTON, he returned to New York, leaving a British force under Cornwallis to subordinate the Carolinas to British control. Cornwallis swept north and capped his success in the battle of Camden on Aug. 16, 1780. The American force was completely routed, the gallant Baron de Kalb was mortally wounded, and the American commander, Horatio Gates, fled from the field, outdistancing officers and men in retreat. Patriot defense was broken in the Carolinas, where only the swift and secretly moving guerrilla bands of Francis Marion, Thomas Sumter, and Andrew Pickens harassed the invaders. The American cause spurted upward, however, with the remarkable battle of Kings Mt. (Oct. 7, 1780), where bands of frontier riflemen under Isaac Shelby, John Sevier, and William Campbell surrounded a British raiding party under Patrick Ferguson; the British commander fell, and his men surrendered. This victory prefaced the campaign fought in North Carolina by Gen. Nathanael Greene (who had been appointed to succeed Gates) and his lieutenants, notably Light-Horse Harry Lee and Daniel Morgan. It was Morgan who at the head of a raiding party met and all but annihilated Cornwallis's raiders under Banastre Tarleton at Cowpens (Jan. 17, 1781). Cornwallis pushed north and at Guilford Courthouse (March 15, 1781) won a Pyrrhic victory over Greene; the British had technically won but had to retreat to British-held Wilmington, N.C., and then to Virginia. Greene then joined the guerrilla leaders in freeing South Carolina. Again the Americans were defeated—by Lord Rawdon at Hobkirks Hill (April 25, 1781) and by Col. Alexander Stewart at Eutaw Springs (Sept. 8, 1781)—and again the British had to retreat, returning to Charleston. The campaign was a British failure and was, moreover, a triumph for the patriots because it set the stage for the YORKTOWN CAMPAIGN.

Carolina parakeet, small, long-tailed bird, *Canuropsis carolinensis,* now believed extinct. The Carolina parakeet was the northernmost representative of the parrot family. It had green plumage with a yellow head and orange cheek patches and forehead. The largest specimens were 13 in. (33 cm) in length, including the tail feathers. It was formerly distributed throughout the SE United States, as far north as Virginia and as far west as Texas; the last specimens were seen in S Florida early in the 20th cent. A fruit eater, the Carolina parakeet was an agricultural pest and was therefore exterminated by farmers. It is classified in the phylum CHORDATA, subphylum Vertebrata, class Aves, order Psittaciformes, family Psittacidae. See PARAKEET.

Caroline, Fort: see FORT CAROLINE.

Caroline Affair. In 1837 a group of men led by William Lyon MACKENZIE rebelled in Upper Canada (now Ontario), demanding a more democratic government. There was much sympathy for their cause in the United States, and a small steamer, the *Caroline,* owned by U.S. citizens, carried men and supplies from the U.S. side of the Niagara river to the Canadian rebels on Navy Island just above Niagara Falls. On the night of Dec. 29, 1837, a small group of British and Canadians loyal to the Upper Canadian government crossed the river to the U.S. side where the *Caroline* was moored, loosed her, set fire to her, and sent her over the falls. One American was killed in the incident. Americans on the border were aroused to intense anti-British feeling, and soldiers under Gen. Winfield Scott were rushed to the scene to prevent violent American action. The affair passed over, though it had an aftermath, when one of the men who had taken part in the attack boasted of that fact when he was in the United States and was arrested as a criminal. That matter, too, was smoothed over, but the Caroline Affair and the Aroostook War helped to make relations with Great Britain very tense in the years before the Webster-Ashburton Treaty.

Caroline Islands, archipelago (1969 est. pop. 66,900), c.830 sq mi (2,150 sq km), W Pacific, just north of the equator; included in 1947 in the U.S. Trust Territory of the Pacific Islands (see PACIFIC ISLANDS, TRUST TERRITORY OF THE) under United Nations trusteeship. The Caroline Islands include four of the Trust Territory's six administrative districts: PALAU, YAP, TRUK, and PONAPE. The islands are fertile and rich in minerals. There are deposits of phosphate, guano, bauxite, and iron; coconuts, sugarcane, and tapioca are produced. The chief exports are dried bonito, copra, and tapioca. Most of the inhabitants are Micronesian, but in the eastern islands there are some Polynesians. There is evidence of Chinese contact with the western islands in the 7th cent. A.D. The first Europeans to visit the Carolines were the Spanish in 1526, but the islands did not come under Spain's control until 1886. After the Spanish-American War the islands were sold (1899) to Germany. They were occupied in 1914 by the Japanese, who in 1920 were given a League of Nations mandate over them. Annexed to Japan in 1935, the islands were heavily bombed prior to American occupation during World War II.

Caroline of Ansbach (äns'bäkh), 1683-1737, queen consort of GEORGE II of England, daughter of the margrave of Brandenburg-Ansbach. She married George in 1705 while he was electoral prince of Hanover and bore him three sons and five daughters. After his accession (1727) she gave active support to Sir Robert WALPOLE. Her political influence over the king lasted until her death. See biographies by R. L. Arkell (1939) and Peter Quennell (1940).

Caroline of Brunswick, 1768-1821, consort of GEORGE IV of England. The daughter of Charles William Ferdinand, duke of Brunswick, she married George (then prince of Wales) in 1795. She bore him one daughter, but the couple separated in 1796 and Caroline, deprived of her child, lived in retirement. An accusation that she had borne an illegitimate child occasioned a commission of inquiry (1806), which found her innocent but imprudent. Caroline went abroad in 1814, but when George became king in 1820 she returned to claim her rights as queen. The government immediately instituted proceedings against her in the House of Lords for divorce on the grounds of adultery. Caroline was probably guilty of the charge, but her persecution by a profligate husband aroused popular sympathy for her and the bill was dropped. See biographies by Joanna Richardson (1960) and E. F. L. Russell (1967); Roger Fulford, *The Trial of Queen Caroline* (1967).

Carolingian architecture and art. In the 8th cent. a gradual change appeared in Western culture and art, reaching its apex under CHARLEMAGNE. The new architecture, inspired by the forms of antiquity, abandoned the small boxlike shapes of the Merovingian period and used instead spacious basilicas often intersected by vast transepts. In some churches, such as Fulda and Cologne, the central nave ended in semicircular apses. An innovation of Carolingian builders, which was to be of incalculable importance for the later Middle Ages, was the emphasis given to the western extremity of the church. The facade, flanked symmetrically by towers, or simply the exterior of a massive complex (westwork), became the focal point of the structure. The function of the westwork is still debated. It had an elevation of several stories, the lowest a vaulted vestibule to the church proper, and above, a room reached by spiral staircases, which may have served as a chapel reserved for high dignitaries. The outstanding structure of the Carolingian period still in existence is the palatine chapel at Aachen, dedicated by Pope Leo III in the year 805. It is centralized in plan and surmounted by an octagonal dome. The throne of the emperor stood overlooking the central space within an upper gallery, which could be reached directly from the imperial apartments. The design of the palatine chapel appears to have been based in part on the 5th-century Church of San Vitale in Ravenna. Other important structures still partly preserved, or known through documentary evidence, include the churches of Saint-Denis, Corbie, Centula (Saint-Riquier), and Reichenau. The best-preserved artistic achievements of the age are works of small dimensions—manuscript illumination, ivory carving, and metalwork. Besides the imperial court, at Aachen, the leading centers of art were the monasteries in Tours, Metz, Saint-Denis, and near Rheims. The earliest liturgical manuscripts of the Carolingian period, such as the Gospel book signed by the scribe Godescalc (written between 781 and 783), are characterized by a tentative and not always successful fusion of ornamental motifs of chiefly Anglo-Saxon and Irish origin and by figures derived from antiquity. Full-page portraits of the four evangelists were often designed. Later Carolingian miniatures show an increasing familiarity with the heritage of late antiquity and in some instances are perhaps influenced by Byzantine art. The manuscripts owe much of their beauty to the new minuscule form of writing, remarkable for its clarity and form. The most-influential work was the Utrecht Psalter, illustrated in a mode of nervous and flickering intensity quite unparalleled in earlier Western art. Closely allied in style to the miniatures were the ivory carvings, many of them originally part of book covers. Metalwork objects are rarer, although literary evidence shows that goldsmiths and enamel workers were active. The large golden altar of Sant' Ambrogio in Milan (executed in 835), the portable altar of Arnulf (now in Munich), several splendid book covers, and other sumptuously decorated objects provide insight into the artistic accomplishments of the period, which ended in the late 9th cent. See A. K. Porter, *Medieval Architecture: Its Origin and Development* (2 vol., 1909, 1912, repr. 1969); Adolph Goldschmidt, *German Illumination* (Vol. I: *Carolingian Period*, 1928, repr. 1969); Roger Hinks, *Carolingian Art* (1935, repr. 1962); Howard Saalman, *Medieval Architecture* (1962).

Carolingians (kărəlĭn'jēənz), dynasty of Frankish rulers, founded in the 7th cent. by PEPIN OF LANDEN, who, as mayor of the palace, ruled the East Frankish Kingdom of Austrasia for Dagobert I. His descendants, PEPIN OF HERISTAL, CHARLES MARTEL, CARLOMAN, and PEPIN THE SHORT, continued to govern the territories under the nominal kingship of the MEROVINGIANS. In 751, Pepin the Short deposed the last Merovingian king, Childeric III, and became sole Frankish king. The family was at its height under Pepin's son, CHARLEMAGNE, who was crowned emperor of the West in 800. His empire was divided by the Treaty of Verdun (843) after the death of his son, Emperor LOUIS I, among Louis's three sons. LOTHAIR I inherited the imperial title and the middle part of the empire. LOUIS THE GERMAN founded a dynasty that ruled in Germany (kingdom of the East Franks) until 911, his successors being CHARLES III (Charles the Fat), ARNULF, and LOUIS THE CHILD. The third son of Louis I, CHARLES II (Charles the Bald), founded the French Carolingian dynasty, which ruled, with interruptions, until 987. Its rulers were LOUIS II (Louis the Stammerer), LOUIS III, CARLOMAN, CHARLES III (Charles the Simple), LOUIS IV (Louis d'Outremer), LOTHAIR (941–86), and LOUIS V. In the Carolingian period feudal principles were formulated, and a landed economy was firmly established. The kings and emperors worked closely with church officials; Charlemagne became the pope's protector. See Heinrich Fichtenau, *The Carolingian Empire* (1949; tr. 1957, repr. 1965); E. S. Duckett, *Carolingian Portraits* (1962, repr. 1969); F. L. Ganshof, *The Carolingians and the Frankish Monarchy* (tr. 1971).

Carolus-Duran (kärôlüs'-düräN'), 1837–1917, French painter whose original name was Charles Auguste Émile Durand. He was influenced by Courbet and studied in Lille and Paris. In 1861 he won a pension and traveled in Italy and Spain. Best known as the teacher of many famous painters (including Sargent), he became the director of the Académie de France à Rome in 1905. The Louvre has many of his portraits. His study of Mrs. William Astor is in the Metropolitan Museum.

Carondelet, Francisco Luis Hector, baron de (frănthēs'kō lo͞oēs' ĕktôr' bärôn' dā kärôndălĕt'), c.1748–1807, governor of Louisiana (1791–97) and West Florida (1791–95), b. Noyelles, Flanders. He married into the Las Casas family, prominent in Spanish colonial affairs. He came to New Orleans from the governorship of Salvador and was unfortunately not well informed about Louisiana problems. Ignorant of the English language and local customs, and faced with conflicting rumors of American hostility, he became convinced in 1792 that the Americans were planning to invade Louisiana. With unwarranted aggressiveness, he stirred up the Indians of the Southwest, concluding an alliance with four great tribes and establishing Spanish posts in their territory. He revived intrigues with Kentucky frontiersmen looking toward the establishment of an independent state in the West. Relations between Spain and the United States were severely taxed. After Carondelet was replaced by Manuel Gayoso de Lemos, he was made president of the audiencia and governor general of Quito (1799–1807). See A. P. Whitaker, *The Spanish-American Frontier, 1783–1795* (1927, repr. 1969).

Carossa, Hans (häns kärôs'ä), 1878–1956, German poet and novelist. His autobiographical novel *Childhood* (1922, tr. 1930) and its sequels (1928, 1941) are noted for clear, graceful style. *Fuhrung und Geleit* [guidance and companionship] (1933) contains warm vignettes of his literary mentors and friends, among them Mann, Rilke, and Hesse. Other works are *A Roumanian Diary* (1924, tr. 1929), the novel *Doctor Gion* (1931, tr. 1933), and volumes of poems (1938, 1949).

carotene, organic compound composed of carbon and hydrogen and found as an accessory pigment in many higher plants, particularly carrots, sweet potatoes, and leafy vegetables. Carotene is thought to assist in trapping light energy for photosynthesis or to aid in chemical reduction. It is important in animal biology as the main dietary source of vitamin A (see VITAMIN), which is produced by splitting one molecule of carotene into two molecules of vitamin A. Carotene that is thus converted is called provitamin A. This reaction occurs in either the liver or intestinal wall. The absorption of dietary carotene is dependent on the action of bile and is greatly decreased by the presence of mineral oil. Its absorption is less efficient than that of vitamin A. Margarine is sometimes artificially colored by the addition of carotene.

Carothers, Wallace Hume, 1896–1937, American chemist, b. Burlington, Iowa. He received his doctorate at the Univ. of Illinois in 1924, teaching there for the next two years as instructor in organic chemistry. Carothers then took a similiar post at Harvard. In 1928 he was made head of the research group in organic chemistry of the E. I. du Pont de Nemours company in Wilmington, Delaware. His work there on compounds of high molecular weight led to the discovery of the first synthetic rubber, neoprene. While with du Pont, he also investigated the physical and chemical properties of polyamides, showing that these compounds could be melt-spun into fibers or made into transparent film. This work resulted in the discovery of nylon.

Carouge (kärо͞ozh'), city (1970 pop. 14,055), Geneva canton, SW Switzerland, on the Arve River. It is an industrial center. Carouge was chartered in 1786 by King Victor Amadeus III of Sardinia and was joined to Geneva canton in 1816.

carp, hardy freshwater fish, *Cyprinus carpio*, the largest member of the MINNOW family. A native of Asia, the carp was introduced into Europe and America and has become so well established that it is called the English sparrow of the fishes. Many variations in color and form have developed. Carp have four barbels ("whiskers") around the mouth and are usually dark greenish or brown (occasionally yellowish or silvery), with red on some of the fins. Most carp are scaled, although the mirror carp has only a few scattered scales and the leather carp has none. Carp may reach a length of 3 ft (91 cm) and a weight of 25 lbs (11.3 kg). They are bottom feeders, eating chiefly aquatic plants but also insects and small animals; their habit of rooting in the mud often makes the water unfit for the feeding and spawning of other fishes. However, they are valued commercially as food fish, especially in Europe, where they are sometimes bred and raised for this purpose. Ornamental varieties are bred in Japan. Carp are classified in the phylum CHORDATA, class Osteichthyes, order Cypriniformes, family Cyprinidae.

Carpaccio, Vittore (vēt-tô'rā kärpät'chō), c.1450–1522, Venetian painter, influenced by Gentile and Giovanni Bellini. His delightful narrative paintings reflect the pageantry of 15th-century Venice. They also offer a fanciful view of the Orient, gained through contemporary drawings. His style is notable for its rich color, luminosity, and wealth of detail. Among his best paintings are the cycle depicting the life of St. Ursula, the St. George series, the *Presentation in the Temple* (all: Academy, Venice); scenes from the life of St. Stephen (Louvre; Brera, Milan); *Meditation on the Passion* (Metropolitan Mus.); *Saint Reading* and other works (National Gall. of Art, Washington, D.C.). See T. Pignatti's *Carpaccio* (1958).

Carpathians (kärpā'thēənz) or **Carpathian Mountains,** Czech, Pol., and Ukr. *Karpaty*, Rum. *Carpaţii*, major mountain system of central and E Europe, extending c.930 mi (1,500 km) along the north and east sides of the Danubian plain. The geologically young mountains, part of the main European chain, link the Alps with the Balkans. The Carpathians begin in SE Czechoslovakia and extend NE to the Polish-Czechoslovak border. There the Northern Carpathians, comprising the Beskids and the Tatra, run east along the border, then SE through the W Ukraine, USSR; in Rumania they are continued by the Transylvanian Alps (or Southern Carpathians), which extend SW to the Danube River. The highest peaks are Gerlachovka (8,737 ft/2,663 m) in the Tatra and Moldoveanu in the Transylvanian Alps. The Carpathians are rich in minerals and timber. The region's cold winters and hot summers make it a year-round resort. Although the Carpathians are a barrier to the southward movement of cold air masses, numerous low passes facilitate overland travel between the densely populated areas that flank the system. The Carpathians themselves are sparsely populated, with the greatest number of people found in the larger agricultural valleys to the south.

Carpathian Ukraine: see ZAKARPATSKAYA OBLAST, USSR.

Carpathus, Greece: see KÁRPATHOS.

Carpaţii: see CARPATHIANS.

Carpeaux, Jean-Baptiste (zhäN-bätēst' kärpō'), 1827–75, French sculptor and painter. He studied with François Rude and won the Prix de Rome. Carpeaux rose to fame with his *Ugolino* (1860–62; Louvre) and became a favorite of the Second Empire, receiving many portrait commissions. Of his sculpture groups, the best known is *The Dance* on the facade of the Opéra, Paris. His *Neapolitan Shell-Fisher* and his portrait busts of Napoleon III, Dumas fils, Gérôme, and Empress Eugenie are in the Louvre, along with numerous paintings, including *Bal costumé aux Tuileries, Les Trois Souverains*, and several portraits. The works of Carpeaux exhibit a freedom and force which distinguish them from the banality of his period.

carpe diem (kär'pĕ dē'ĕm), a descriptive term for literature that urges readers to live for the moment [from the Latin phrase "seize the day," used by Horace]. The theme, which was widely used in 16th- and 17th-century love poetry, is best exemplified by a familiar stanza from Robert Herrick's "To the Virgins, to Make Much of Time":

Gather ye rosebuds while ye may,
Old time is still a-flying;
And this same flower that smiles today
Tomorrow will be dying.

Shakespeare's version of the theme takes the following form in *Twelfth Night*:

What is love? 'Tis not hereafter;
Present mirth hath present laughter
  What's to come is still unsure.
In delay there lies no plenty;
Then come and kiss me, sweet and twenty,
  Youth's a stuff will not endure.

Carpentaria, Gulf of (kärpəntâr'ēə), arm of the Arafura Sea, 305 mi (491 km) wide and 370 mi (595 km) long, indenting the northern coast of Australia. On its eastern shore, near Weipa, lies a vast bauxite deposit. Willem Jansz explored the gulf in 1606.

Carpenter, Edward, 1844–1929, English author. Although ordained a minister in 1869, he became a Fabian socialist in 1874 and renounced religion. Among his works on social reform are *Towards Democracy* (1883–1902), a long unrhymed poem revealing the influence of his friend Walt Whitman; *England's Ideal* (1887); *Civilization: Its Cause and Cure* (1889); and *Love's Coming of Age* (1896), which treats relations between the sexes. See the autobiographical *My Days and Dreams* (1916); Émile Delavenay, *D. H. Lawrence and Edward Carpenter* (1971).

Carpenter, George Rice, 1863–1909, American educator, b. Labrador, grad. Harvard, 1886. After study abroad, he returned to teach at Harvard (1888–90) and Massachusetts Institute of Technology (1890–93). From 1893 he was professor of rhetoric at Columbia. He wrote a number of textbooks on literature and rhetoric and biographies of Longfellow, Whittier, and Whitman.

Carpenter, John Alden, 1876–1951, American composer, b. Park Ridge, Ill.; pupil of J. K. Paine at Harvard and of Elgar. His music, refined and skillfully written, influenced by French impressionism, often conveys the spirit and the scenes of American life, in such works as the orchestral suite *Adventures in a Perambulator* (1914) and the ballets *Krazy Kat* (Chicago, 1921) and *Skyscrapers* (New York, 1926). A Spanish flavor and jazz, frequently elements in his music, are both found in *Patterns* (1932) for orchestra. Other important works are his ballet *The Birthday of the Infanta* (Chicago, 1919), a violin concerto (1937), a concertino for piano and orchestra (1915), songs, symphonies, and chamber music.

Carpenter, Malcolm Scott, 1925–, American astronaut, b. Boulder, Colo. The second American to go into orbital flight around the earth, he made his historic and suspenseful flight on May 24, 1962. In his three-orbit trip he repeated the earlier success of John GLENN. Carpenter's second orbit was under manual control, and during it he discovered that he could make small changes in the capsule's orientation in space by movements of his head and arms. On descending, his capsule, *Aurora 7,* overshot the pickup area by 250 mi (212 km) causing nationwide concern for his safety. A commander in the U.S. navy, Carpenter had served with an antisubmarine patrol during the Korean War. From 1965 to 1967 he was a member of the navy aquanaut project and in 1969 retired from the navy to go into private business.

Carpenter, Mary, 1807–77, English educator. She devoted her life to the establishment of schools and institutions and the promotion of educational reforms. In 1835 she organized the Working and Visiting Society, in 1846 opened a school for poor children, and in 1852 founded a juvenile reformatory (see her *Juvenile Delinquents: Their Condition and Treatment,* 1852). Her agitation for reformatory and industrial schools contributed to the passage of the Juvenile Offenders Act (1857) and furthered the movement for free day schools. She made four visits to India after 1866, interesting herself in Indian education, and also lectured in the United States. See biography by J. E. Carpenter (1879, 2d ed. 1881, repr. 1973).

Carpenter, Rhys, 1889–, American archaeologist and classicist, b. Cotuit, Mass.; grad. Columbia (B.A., 1908; Ph.D., 1916). He taught classical archaeology at Bryn Mawr (1913–55) and was director of the American School for Classical Studies at Athens (1927–32; 1946–48). His writings include *The Humanistic Value of Archaeology* (1933), *Folktale, Fiction and Saga in the Homeric Epics* (1946), and *Greek Sculpture* (1960).

Carpentersville, village (1970 pop. 24,059), Kane co., NE Ill., on the Fox River; inc. 1887. Pumps and valves are the chief manufactures.

Carpentier, Alejo (älä'hō kärpĕntyār'), 1904–, Cuban novelist and musicologist. Carpentier was a journalist and professor of music history at the National Conservatory. Regarded as one of the most powerful Spanish-American writers of recent decades, he wrote novels that emphasized the exotic in Caribbean life. Among his works are *Ecue-Yamba-O* (1933), *La música en Cuba* (1946), *The Lost Steps* (1953, tr. 1956), *El acoso* (1956), *The Kingdom of This World* (1949, tr. 1957), and *War of Time* (1963, tr. 1970).

Carpentras (kärpäNträs'), town (1968 pop. 22,130), Vaucluse dept., SE France, in Provence. It is an important farm market and a small industrial center. Of Gallo-Roman origin, it was an episcopal see from the 3d cent. and was ruled by its bishops until the French Revolution. The long conclave that elected Pope John XXII met in Carpentras. The town served as the capital of the Comtat Venaissin from 1229 to 1791. Of interest are St. Siffrein Church (15th cent.) and a Gallic arch with sculptures.

carpentry, trade concerned with constructing wood buildings, the wooden portions of buildings, or the temporary timberwork used during the construction of buildings. It comprises the larger and more structural aspects of woodwork, rather than the delicate assembling which is the province of cabinetmaking and JOINERY. The craft dates from the earliest use of tools. Though no actual examples of carpentry survive from antiquity, many remains of the earliest known stone architecture exhibit forms which are undoubtedly imitative of still earlier constructions in wood. This is especially apparent in most Asian architecture, and certain details of Greek temples are suggestive of carpentry prototypes. Some monumental wood buildings of the 7th cent. still stand in Japan, a country where intricate, beautiful carpentry has prevailed throughout its history. In the United States, expert carpentry has existed ever since the construction of dwellings by the colonists in the first half of the 17th cent. Rough carpentry refers to the "framing" of a wood building, namely, the erection of the structural frame or skeleton composed of the vertical members, or studs, the horizontal members of foundation sills, floor joists, and the like, the inclined members, or rafters, for the roof, and the diagonal members for bracing. Finished carpentry is the setting in place, over the rough frame, of all finishing members of both exterior and interior, such as sheathing, siding, stairs, the casings of doors and windows, flooring, wainscoting, and trim. The amount of permanent carpentry required in many modern buildings has been greatly reduced by the use of such substitute materials as concrete and steel. However, the large amount of concrete used has resulted in a great increase in the amount of carpentry performed to make temporary forms in which the concrete can be cast. See CENTERING. See F. M. Mix, ed., *Practical Carpentry* (1963); R. J. De Cristoforo, *The Practical Handbook of Carpentry* (1969).

carpet or **rug,** thick fabric, usually woolen (but often synthetic), commonly used today as a floor covering. Carpets were formerly woven to protect the body from cold, to be spread on a dais or before a seat of honor, to cover a table, couch, or wall, or to form the curtains of a tent. There is evidence of the existence of handwoven carpets in antiquity. On the rock tombs of Beni Hassan, Egypt, c.2500 B.C., men are depicted with the implements of rug weaving. Other evidence of the early use of rugs is seen in the drawings on the ancient palace walls of Nineveh. In the mountainous region of the East stretching from Turkey through Persia and central Asia into China, where the fleece of the sheep and the hair of the camel and goat grow long and fine, the art of carpet-weaving reached its height early in the 16th cent. The Oriental artist worked on a handloom consisting essentially of two horizontal beams on which the warp (the vertical threads) was stretched; on the lower one the finished carpet was rolled while the warp unrolled from the upper one. The yarn for the pile, spun and dyed by hand, was cut in lengths of about 2 in. (5.1 cm) and knotted about the warp threads, one tuft at a time, after one of the two established ways of tying—the Ghiordes, or Turkish, knot and the Senna, or Persian, knot. After a row of knots had been placed across the width of the loom, two or more weft, or horizontal, threads of cotton or flax were woven in and beaten into place with a heavy beater, or comb. The tufts, or pile, thus appeared only on the face of the fabric, which when completed was sheared to perfect smoothness. Although the hair of the camel and the goat was used in the weaving of Oriental rugs, the wool of the sheep was the essential component. Beautiful silk rugs interwoven with gold thread were made in the 16th and 17th cent. The quality of a carpet depends on the materials used and the number of knots per square inch of surface, which may vary from 40 to 1,000. In North America the Navahos and other Indian tribes have for generations produced substantial rugs without pile, woven somewhat in the manner of TAPESTRY on simple handlooms. In the palaces of Montezuma remarkable floor coverings were found that utilized the plumage of birds. The primitive use of rushes or straw has survived in the form of Chinese and Japanese mattings. In 1608, King Henry IV of France established weavers in the Louvre. About 20 years later an old soap works, the Savonnerie, near Paris, was converted to carpet weaving, and its name remains attached to one of the finest types of handmade carpet, now made at the Gobelin tapestry factory. Tapestries for walls and floors were made at Aubusson at an early date. In 1685 the revocation of the Edict of Nantes scattered skilled Protestant carpetmakers over Europe. Centers of weaving were established in England, first at Kidderminster (1735) and later at Wilton and Axminster. Cheaper, more easily manufactured floor covering soon came into demand, and the making of ingrain, or reversible, carpets began at Kidderminster. The weavers of Flanders had made a loom that produced a pile by looping the worsted warp threads, and this loom, although guarded, was copied by a Kidderminster weaver; soon many looms in England were making Brussels carpet. Axminster was England's headquarters for imitation Oriental or tufted-pile carpet. Until about 1840 all carpets were made on handlooms with such devices and improvements as could be operated by hand or foot power; then Erastus Bigelow's power loom (first used in 1841), which made it possible for carpets to be mass produced, revolutionized the industry. A few classifications—Oriental, European handwoven, Brussels, Wilton, velvet, Axminster, chenille, ingrain, rag, hooked, straw, and fiber—embrace the entire range of carpets, both antique and modern. To the first class belong not only the genuine antique Orientals, now rare, but also the modern reproductions. The materials are dyed with aniline dyes instead of vegetable dyes and then woven. Many are washed in chlorine solutions to give an effect of age or in glycerine to simulate the luster of fine wool. Commercial methods have somewhat standardized and debased the characteristic ancient patterns, but the modern Orientals are still commercially important. Some traditional Oriental rugs are still produced, incorporating the deep, rich color and intricate patterns of Persia, the brighter hues and conventionalized figures of Asian Turkey, the simpler designs and primitive colorings of Turkistan and the Caucasus, and the symbolic ornament of China. A limited number of European handwoven carpets, both Aubussons (tapestry) and Savonneries (pile), are now made in most Western countries. Modern commercial carpets are woven on complex and highly specialized machines, a development from Bigelow's power loom. Brussels carpet has a warp and weft of linen, with a pile of worsted yarn drawn into loops by means of wires. It is called three-, four-, or five-frame, depending on the number of bobbins carrying different colored warp threads, which make the pattern. Tapestry Brussels is an inexpensive single-frame sort, either yarn printed or piece printed. Wilton is made on the same principle, except that the loops that form the pile are cut as they are woven into place. Velvet is an equivalent of tapestry Brussels with the pile cut. Axminster, similar in effect to Oriental, uses unlimited colors in design made on machines that loop the tufts, one color at a time, and then interlock the weft about them. Chenille, or chenille Axminster, is made in two stages; first the chenille thread, or fur, as it is called, is made, then it is folded and ironed so that the woolen fibers are like a fringe along a cotton or linen chain. This fur is then woven into a strong backing of linen with the nap on the surface. Ingrain, no longer widely used, is a plain-weave fabric, of two- or three-ply woolen weft on a concealed cotton warp. Rag carpets, made of used rags sewn together for warp, were first woven on household looms; they became commercially important in the latter part of the 19th cent. Hooked rugs are made of narrow strips of woolen cloth drawn by a pointed hook through a canvas foundation on which a design is indicated. Although handmade rugs are still produced in some countries, e.g., Turkey, carpet manufacturing has become a highly mechanized industry, notably in the United States, Great Britain, Canada, Belgium, and Japan. See Wilhelm von Bode and Ernest Kühnel, *Antique Rugs from the Near East* (tr. of 4th rev. ed. 1970); George Robinson, *Carpets and Other Textile Floorcoverings* (2d rev. ed. 1972).

carpetbaggers, epithet used in the South after the Civil War to describe Northerners who went to the South during RECONSTRUCTION to make money. Although regarded as transients because of the carpetbags in which they carried their possessions (hence the name *carpetbaggers*), most intended to settle in the South and take advantage of speculative and commercial opportunities there. With the support of the Negro vote the carpetbaggers played an important role in the Republican state governments. The corrupt activities of some made the term *carpetbagger* synonymous with any outsider who meddles in an area's political affairs for his own benefit. See bibliography under RECONSTRUCTION.

carpet beetle, name for several BEETLES that are highly destructive to carpets and upholstery and are classified in the same family as the larder beetles. Adult beetles of this family are pollen eaters, but the larvae feed on a variety of animal matter. The reddish to yellow-brown carpet beetle larvae feed on wool, fur, leather, and on plant fibers that are soiled with grease, doing more damage to household goods than the clothes moth. The adults, 0.08 to 0.2 in. (3–5 mm) long, solid black or black-and-white patterned, leave the house after emerging from the pupal stage. The larvae of the species commonly called larder beetles feed on meats and cheese; the larvae of other species in the family are pests in museums, feeding on dried insect collections. Carpet beetles are classified in the phylum ARTHROPODA, class Insecta, family Dermestidae, genera *Attagenus* and *Anthrenus.*

carpincho (kärpĭn'chō): see CAPYBARA.

Carpini, Giovanni de Piano (jōvän'nē dā pyä'nō kärpē'nē), c.1180–1252, Italian traveler and Franciscan monk, b. Pian del Carpini (now Piano della Magione), Umbria. He was a companion of St. Francis of Assisi and spread Franciscan teachings in Germany and Spain. In 1245 he was sent by Pope Innocent IV to the court of the MONGOLS. With a Pole, Friar Benedict, he started from Lyons, went to Kiev, then across the Dnepr to the Don and the Volga, where he found the camp of a Mongol prince. He then traveled across central Asia to the imperial court at Karakorum in Mongolia. A journey of c.3,000 mi (4,830 km) was accomplished on horseback in 106 days. At Karakorum he witnessed the installation (1246) of Jenghiz Khan's grandson as the great khan of the Mongols. Carpini returned to Lyons in 1247, and his careful account of the journey, known as *Liber Tartarorum*, proved invaluable. It is a full record of Mongol manners, history, policy, and military tactics; it was the first of such works to appear in Europe.

Carpocrates (kärpŏk'rətēz), fl. c.130–c.150, Alexandrian philosopher, founder with his son Epiphanes of a Hellenistic sect, notoriously licentious, related to Gnosticism. Epiphanes wrote a treatise, *On Justice,* that advocated communal ownership of property, including women; he died, age 17, at Cephalonia and was long worshiped as a deity there. The Carpocratians believed that men had formerly been united with the Absolute, had been corrupted, and would, by despising creation, be saved in this life or else later through successive transmigrations. Jesus, they held, was but one of several wise men who had achieved deliverance.

car puller: see WINCH.

Carpus, man of Troas. 2 Tim. 4.13.

Carr, Edward Hallett, 1892–, English political scientist and historian. Educated at Cambridge, he was in the diplomatic service until 1936, professor of international relations (1936–47) at University College of Wales, Aberystwyth, and assistant editor for the London *Times* (1941–46). Carr's writings include biographies of Feodor Dostoyevsky (1931), Karl Marx (1934), and Mikhail Bakunin (1937), as well as important studies on international relations and on the Soviet Union. His major work is the *History of Soviet Russia* (Vol. I–IX, 1950–71), considered by many to be the definitive work in English on Soviet history.

Carr, Emily, 1871–1945, Canadian painter. She studied (1889–c.1895) at the San Francisco School of Art and later in London and in Paris. In Victoria, British Columbia, she taught painting and visited Indian villages. From her study of totem poles and other Indian art, she developed a powerful style marked by simplified forms and a fauvist intensity of color. She wrote *Klee Wyck* (1941) and *The House of All Sorts* (1944). See her autobiography, *Growing Pains* (1946).

Carr, Eugene Asa, 1830–1910, Union general in the U.S. Civil War, b. Concord, Erie co., N.Y., grad. West Point, 1850. In the Civil War he distinguished himself at Wilson's Creek (1861) and Pea Ridge (1862), was made (March, 1862) a brigadier general of volunteers, and fought in the campaigns at Vicksburg (1863) and Mobile (1865). After the war Carr was a well-known cavalry leader and Indian fighter in the West. Promoted to brigadier general in 1892, he was retired in 1893. See biography by J. T. King (1963).

Carr, Robert: see SOMERSET, ROBERT CARR, EARL OF.

Carrà, Carlo, 1881–1966, Italian painter. Trained as a decorator, he became associated with the artists involved in the development of FUTURISM. He then moved toward a more carefully structured art form, related to cubism but concerned with the dynamics of movement. After meeting CHIRICO in 1916, Carrà became a spokesman of the metaphysical school. A prolific writer on art, he also exerted considerable influence as a teacher.

Carracci (kärät'chē), family of Italian painters of the Bolognese school, founders of an important academy of painting. **Lodovico Carracci,** 1555–1619, a pupil of Tintoretto in Venice, was influenced by Correggio and Titian. He also studied in Bologna, Padua, and Parma. With his cousins, Agostino and Annibale, and with Anthony de la Tour, he established in Bologna an academy of painting that sought to unite in one system the preeminent characteristics of each of the great masters. The school rapidly became one of the outstanding schools in Italy, and Lodovico remained its head until his death. Its noted pupils include Guido Reni, Francesco Albani, and Domenichino. Excelling as a teacher, Lodovico was also a painter of talent and energy. Excellent examples of his art abound in the churches of Bologna and elsewhere in Italy. Among the best are *Sermon of John the Baptist* (Pinacoteca, Bologna) and *Vision of St. Hyacinth* (Louvre). His cousin **Agostino Carracci,** 1557–1602, left the goldsmith's trade and studied painting with Prospero Fontana. He excelled in engraving and devoted most of his time to it until he joined his cousin and his brother in the founding of their academy and in the execution of numerous joint painting commissions. In 1597 he went to Rome and collaborated with Annibale in the decorating of the Farnese Palace gallery; he executed the admirable frescoes *Triumph of Galatea* and *Rape of Cephalus* (cartoons in the National Gall., London). He died in Parma just after completing his great work, *Celestial, Terrestrial, and Venal Love,* in the Casino. Other notable examples of his art are *The Last Communion of St. Jerome* (Pinacoteca, Bologna), *Adulteress before Christ,* and the masterly engraving of Tintoretto's *Crucifixion.* His brother **Annibale Carracci,** 1560–1609, a pupil of Lodovico Carracci, was a painter of unusual skill and versatility. He spent seven years studying the works of the masters, particularly those of Correggio and Parmigiano, in Venice and Parma. Returning to Bologna, he aided in the conducting of the academy school until 1595, when he went to Rome to assist in the Farnese gallery. The ceiling, for which he made thousands of preliminary drawings according to an elaborate structural system, was rich in illusionistic elements. It included feigned architectural and sculptural forms which had great impact on later painters. Well known among his numerous works are *Christ and the Woman of Samaria* (Brera, Milan); *Flight into Egypt* (Doria Gall., Rome); *The Dead Christ* (Louvre); and *The Temptation of St. Anthony* (National Gall., London). See study by Donald Posner (2 vol. 1971).

carrageen: see SEAWEED.

Carrantuohill (kă"rəntōō'əl), mountain, 3,414 ft (1,041 m) high, Co. Kerry, SW Republic of Ireland, in Macgillicuddy's Reeks; highest peak in Ireland.

Carranza, Venustiano (vänōōstyä'nō kärän'sä), 1859–1920, Mexican political leader. While senator from Coahuila, he joined (1910) Francisco I. MADERO in the revolution against Porfirio Díaz. When President Madero was overthrown (1913) by Victoriano HUERTA, Carranza promptly took the field against Huerta. Fighting in the north, he was joined by other insurgents, notably Alvaro OBREGÓN and Francisco VILLA; Emiliano ZAPATA led a peon uprising in the south. Huerta was finally forced to resign and Carranza assumed (Aug., 1914) the executive powers. Villa and Zapata refused to recognize Carranza's authority, however, and plunged the country into another civil war. Carranza, aided by Obregón, emerged supreme by Aug., 1915, although Zapata and Villa continued their rebellions in the south and north. Carranza was pressed by Obregón to accept the Constitution of 1917, which contained potentially radical reform measures that Carranza opposed and subsequently failed to enforce. In 1920, Carranza attempted to prevent Obregón from succeeding him as president, and Obregón revolted. Carranza fled Mexico City, and was ambushed and murdered by a local chieftain in Tlaxcalantongo.

Carranza de Miranda, Bartolomé de (bärtōlōmā' dā kärän'thä dā mērän'dä), 1503–76, Spanish churchman. He joined the Dominicans (1520) and taught at Valladolid. He was active in the first part of the Council of Trent, where he distinguished himself for his vigorous support of the rule that bishops must reside in their sees. In 1554, Philip II of Spain sent him to England to aid in the restoration of Roman Catholicism. In 1558 he was made archbishop of Toledo (primate of Spain); the same year he attended Holy Roman Emperor Charles V in his last days. His commentary on the catechism appeared in 1558, and it was apparently from passages in this that he was accused of heresy. He was arrested in 1558 (with King Philip's permission); his case dragged on in Spain until 1564, when the archbishop appealed to Rome. At length, in 1576, he was found not guilty of heresy but was compelled to renounce certain propositions.

Carrara (kär-rä'rä), city (1971 pop. 67,736), Tuscany, N central Italy, near the Ligurian Sea. It is the most important center of the Italian MARBLE industry; the famous white Carrara marble is quarried in the nearby Alpi Apuane. Chemicals and metal goods are also manufactured in Carrara. With Massa, the city constituted the principality, later duchy, of Massa and Carrara (15th–19th cent.). Carrara has a fine 12th-century cathedral; the former ducal palace (16th cent.) now houses the Fine Arts Academy.

Carrel, Alexis, 1873–1944, American surgeon and experimental biologist, b. near Lyons, France, M.D. Univ. of Lyons, 1900. Coming to the United States in 1905, he joined the staff of the Rockefeller Institute in 1906 and served as a member from 1912 to 1939. For his work in suturing blood vessels, in transfusion, and in transplantation of organs, he received the 1912 Nobel Prize in Physiology and Medicine. In World War I he developed, with Henry D. Dakin, a method of treating wounds by irrigation with a sodium-hypochlorite solution. With Charles A. Lindbergh he invented an artificial, or mechanical, heart, by means of which he kept alive a number of different kinds of tissue and organs; he kept tissue from a chicken's heart alive for 32 years. In 1939 he returned to France. He wrote *Man the Unknown* (1935) and, with Lindbergh, *The Culture of Organs* (1938).

Carreño, Teresa (tārā'sä kärā'nyō), 1853–1917, Venezuelan pianist; pupil of L. M. Gottschalk and Anton Rubinstein. Her debut was made in New York in 1862. She appeared as an opera singer for a brief period but thereafter continued her piano career, becoming known as one of the foremost pianists of her time. She composed a festival hymn for the Bolívar centenary, 1883, and was a teacher of Edward MacDowell. See biography by Marta Milinowski (1940).

Carreño de Miranda, Juan (hwän kärā'nyō dā mērän'dä), 1614–85, Spanish baroque painter. A protégé of Velázquez, Carreño eventually succeeded his master as painter to the Spanish court. He is best known for his elegant portraits, such as that of the queen mother, Mariana (Prado). Carreño also painted numerous religious pictures and frescoes for the churches and palaces of Madrid, Segovia, and Toledo.

Carrera, José Miguel (hōsā' mēgĕl'), 1785–1821, Chilean revolutionist. With his brothers, Juan José and Luis, he overthrew the revolutionary junta headed by MARTÍNEZ DE ROZAS in 1813 and dominated Chile until replaced by Bernardo O'HIGGINS later that year. He again seized control in 1814, precipitating a civil war that facilitated Spanish reconquest of Chile. Later he was forbidden by José de San Martín to reenter Chile. San Martín and O'Higgins ordered the execution at Mendoza of his brothers. Involving Argentina in civil turmoil, Carrera was on the point of invading Chile when he too was captured and beheaded at Mendoza.

Carrera, Rafael (räfäĕl'), 1814–65, president of Guatemala, a caudillo. He led the revolution against the anticlerical liberal government of Guatemala, and his ultimate success in 1840 helped to destroy the Central American Federation. Illiterate and of mixed blood, he received unquestioned support from the Indian masses; a conservative devoted to the church, he recalled the Jesuits and restored the power of the church in the state. Until his death Carrera dominated Guatemala and was the most powerful figure in Central America, intervening to strengthen, restore, or install conservative governments in the other Central American countries.

Carrera Andrade, Jorge (hôr'hā kärā'rä ändrä'thä), 1903–, Ecuadorian poet. Carrera's early poems and some of his later work reveal his profound pro-Indian feeling and his interest in social revolution. As he matured his concern with the purely aesthetic aspects of poetry was intensified. His lyrics are graceful and charming and reveal a flair for original images. Among his works are the essay collections *Latitudes* (1934) and *La tierra siempre verde* (1955); the poetry volumes *Secret Country* (1922, tr. 1946), *Rol de la manzana* (1935), *Registro del mundo* (1940), and *Edades poéticas* (1958); and an autobiography (1970). See his *Selected Poems* (tr. 1972).

Carrère, John Merven (kərâr'), 1858–1911, American architect, b. Rio de Janeiro. After graduating from the École des Beaux-Arts, Paris, he worked under McKim, Mead, and White in New York City, and from 1886 until his death practiced in partnership with Thomas Hastings. The best-known works of Carrère and Hastings are the New York Public Library (commission awarded in competition; completed 1911), the office buildings of the Senate and the House, and the Carnegie Institution, Washington, D.C.

Carrero Blanco, Luis (lōōēs' kär-rā'rō blăng'kō), 1903–73, Spanish statesman and naval officer. After graduation (1922) from the Spanish naval academy, Carrero Blanco first gained distinction fighting the North African Berbers in the mid-1920s. Following the Spanish civil war, during which he served in the Nationalist navy, he became chief of naval operations on the admiralty staff and one of Francisco Franco's intimate collaborators. In 1951 he was appointed ministerial undersecretary in charge of coordinating the policies of the separate ministries. Made vice admiral (1963) and admiral (1966), Carrero Blanco increasingly controlled government affairs as vice premier (1967–73). In June, 1973, when Franco separated the duties of chief of state and head of government, Carrero Blanco became premier. Since he had been influential in developing contacts with monarchist groups, his appointment was generally regarded as a step toward Franco's planned restoration of the monarchy under Juan Carlos. In Dec., 1973, he was assassinated in Madrid, apparently by Basque nationalists, in retaliation for the government's execution of Basque militants.

Carrhae (kâr'ē), Roman name for the ancient Mesopotamian city of HARAN. The name Carrhae is best known because of the battle of Carrhae in 53 B.C. M. Licinius Crassus (see CRASSUS, family) was defeated by the Parthians, who by their archery routed the Roman force.

carriage, wheeled vehicle, in modern usage restricted to passenger vehicles that are drawn or pushed, especially by animals. Carriages date from the Bronze Age; early forms included the two-wheeled cart and four-wheeled wagon for transporting goods. An early passenger carriage was the CHARIOT, but Roman road-building activity encouraged the development of other forms. From the fall of Rome, horses and litters were used exclusively until the 12th cent., when goods carts and wagons were gradually reintroduced. The coach, a closed four-wheeled carriage with two inside seats and an elevated outside seat for the driver, is believed to have been developed in Hungary and to have spread among the royalty and nobility of Europe in the 16th cent. The hackney coach, which was any carriage for hire, was introduced in London c.1605. During the 17th cent. coaches became lighter and less ornate and in England the public STAGECOACH became common. France developed the gig, a light two-wheeled carriage, which was the forerunner of the chaise, the sulky, and the Cuban *volante*. The numerous forms developed in the 18th cent. include the chariot, a closed carriage with one seat; the landau, a coach whose top folded back from the center in two sections; the barouche coach, which had a folding hood fixed at the back; and the phaeton, any member of a family of four-wheeled carriages, usually with low sides. The hansom cab, patented by J. A. Hansom in 1834, was a closed carriage with an elevated driver's seat in back. Lord Brougham based the carriage known by his name on the hansom. The victoria, popular after 1850, was similar to the phaeton but had only one seat for passengers. The carriage-building trade became firmly established in the United States after the War of 1812; the most distinctive model was a light four-wheeled buggy with open sides and a folding top. The term *carriage* is sometimes used to refer to railroad passenger cars.

Carrickfergus (kărĭkfûr'gəs), municipal borough (1971 pop. 15,162), Co. Antrim, E Northern Ireland, on the shore of Belfast Lough. A minor fishing port, it has an important textile industry. There also are iron works, and rock salt is mined. A castle and church first built in the 12th cent. are still standing. John Paul Jones fought (1778) a victorious battle offshore from Carrickfergus.

Carrick-on-Shannon, county town (1971 pop. 6,411) of Co. Leitrim, N Republic of Ireland. It is a farm market and a center for trout fishing.

Carrier, Jean Baptiste (zhäN bätēst' kärēā'), 1756–94, French Revolutionary. An extreme Jacobin, he demanded the establishment of a revolutionary tribunal, and, as a revolutionary representative to Nantes in the Reign of Terror, he instituted noyades, or wholesale drownings, and committed other atrocities. Although he was denounced to the Convention, of which he was a member, and was recalled to Paris, he temporarily escaped punishment during the Thermidorian reaction (July, 1794; see THERMIDOR). In November, however, he was arrested and executed.

Carriera, Rosalba (rōzäl'bä kär-rēä'rä), 1675–1757, Italian portrait and miniature painter, one of the greatest of her day. At 24 she had achieved a reputation throughout Italy and abroad for her miniatures and crayon portraits. In 1705 she was elected to the Academy of St. Luke (Rome), the Academy of Bologna, and the Florence Academy. In 1720 she visited Paris, where she painted the portraits of the young Louis XV, the regent, and other court figures. Returning to Italy, she visited the courts of Modena, Parma, and Vienna, receiving honors and commissions wherever she went. Her portraits are delicate in color and vivacious. She is well represented in most of the European galleries. *Muse Crowned with Laurel* is in the Louvre.

Carrière, Eugène (özhĕn' käryĕr'), 1849–1906, French painter and lithographer. He is best known for his spiritual interpretations of maternity and family life. His figures and heads emerge from a brownish penumbra, usually with an expression of deep melancholy. Characteristic are his *Crucifixion* and *Maternity* (both: Louvre). He also painted some large canvases for the Sorbonne and the Hôtel de Ville, Paris. Among his works are many notable portraits, including those of Verlaine, Daudet, and Edmond de Goncourt (all: Louvre).

carrier wave: see MODULATION.

Carrington, Henry Beebee, 1824–1912, U.S. army officer and historian, b. Wallingford, Conn., grad. Yale, 1845, and afterwards studied at Yale Law School. Carrington ably reorganized the Ohio state militia and subsequently became adjutant general. In the Civil War he helped to save West Virginia for the Union by sending Ohio militia there. Later, as chief mustering officer of Indiana, he sent over 100,000 men to the war and was instrumental in quelling the operations of a secret society of Southern sympathizers. After the war, as commander of the Mountain Dist. of the Dept. of the Platte, he led the force that in 1866 attempted to open and guard the Bozeman Trail route to Montana. He planned and built forts C. F. Smith and Phil Kearney on this route. Blamed for the Fetterman massacre (see under FETTERMAN, WILLIAM JUDD), he was later exonerated. After his retirement from the army, Carrington was (1869–78) professor of military science at Wabash College. His *Battles of the American Revolution* (1876), supplemented by a volume of maps (1881), is a standard work. *Ab-sa-ra-ka* (1868), memoirs by his first wife, deals with his life on the plains.

Carroll, Anna Ella, 1815–93, alleged adviser to Abraham Lincoln in the Civil War. A member of the Protestant branch of the Carroll family of Maryland, she was a press agent for the Know-Nothing movement in the 1850s. It is claimed that Carroll was responsible for the successful Union strategy of the early Western campaigns and for numerous other decisions on high policy. See biography by Sydney Greenbie and Marjorie Greenbie (1952).

Carroll, Charles, 1737–1832, political leader in the American Revolution, signer of the Declaration of Independence, b. Annapolis, Md. After completing his education in France and England, he returned home (1765) and his father gave him a large estate near Frederick, Md., known as Carrollton Manor; he was afterwards styled Charles Carroll of Carrollton. As leader of the Roman Catholic element, he opposed support of the established Anglican Church, presenting his views in a series of articles written for the *Maryland Gazette.* He threw himself boldly into revolutionary activities, and in 1776 the Continental Congress appointed him, together with Benjamin Franklin and Samuel Chase, to seek Canadian support for the Continental cause. His journal is one of the chief sources for study of this unsuccessful mission. Carroll served (1776–78) in the Continental Congress; he refused to attend the Federal Constitutional Convention (1787), but he later supported the Constitution. He was U.S. Senator from Maryland, serving from 1789 until 1792. See biographies by K. M. Rowland (1898, repr. 1968), Joseph Gurn (1932), and E. H. Smith (1942, repr. 1971).

Carroll, James, 1854–1907, American bacteriologist and army surgeon, b. Woolwich, England, M.D. Univ. of Maryland, 1891. He went to Canada at 15 and later joined the U.S. army. A member of the Yellow Fever Commission under Walter Reed, he voluntarily submitted to the bite of an infected mosquito, contracted yellow fever, and recovered. This proved the mosquito to be the carrier of the disease. Carroll also proved that the infectious agent is a filterable virus.

Carroll, John, 1735–1815, American Roman Catholic churchman, b. Maryland. He studied as a child with Jesuits at Bohemia, Md., and later at Saint-Omer in Flanders, since Catholic secondary education was not allowed in Maryland. He joined the Jesuits in 1753, studied at Liège, and was ordained in 1769. After the suppression of the Jesuits he returned to America and traveled about, ministering to the scattered Catholics. He had a private chapel, for Catholic churches were forbidden by law. He ardently supported the American Revolution and accompanied Benjamin Franklin (who was his close friend) on the vain mission to Quebec (1776) to persuade the Canadians to join the Revolutionary cause. Seeing that American Roman Catholics should be free of supervision by the vicar apostolic of London, he led in petitioning Rome for the appointment of a priest in America with some episcopal powers. In 1784, Father Carroll was made superior of the missions in the United States. In the same year he published a controversial pamphlet, *An Address to the Roman Catholics of the United States of America*, to combat a paper impugning the loyalty of Catholics. In 1790 he was consecrated bishop of Baltimore. He invited the Sulpicians, who opened a seminary at Baltimore, and he founded GEORGETOWN UNIV. He encouraged many communities and founded schools throughout his diocese. In 1808 he became archbishop, with suffragans at Boston, New York City, Philadelphia, and Bardstown, Ky. His last years were somewhat clouded by misunderstandings with the Catholics in Philadelphia and New York. See biographies by J. G. Shea (1888), P. K. Guilday (1922), and A. M. Melville (1955).

Carroll, Lewis, pseud. of **Charles Lutwidge Dodgson,** 1832–98, English writer and mathematician, b. Daresbury, Cheshire. Educated at Christ Church College, Oxford, he was nominated to a studentship (life fellowship) in 1852, and he remained at Oxford for the rest of his life. Although his fellowship was clerical, Carroll never proceeded higher than his ordination as a deacon in 1861. Shy and afflicted with a stammer, he felt himself unsuited to the demanding life of a minister. He did lecture in mathematics at Christ Church from 1855 until 1881. Among his mathematical works, now almost forgotten, is *Euclid and His Modern Rivals* (1879). Carroll is chiefly remembered as the author of the famous children's books *Alice's Adventures in Wonderland* (1865) and its sequel *Through the Looking Glass* (1872), both published under his pseudonym and both illustrated by Sir John Tenniel. He developed these stories from tales he told to the children of Dean Liddell, one of whom was named Alice. Many of his characters—the Mad Hatter, the March Hare, the White Rabbit, the Red Queen, and the White Queen—have become familiar figures in literature and conversation. Although numerous satiric and symbolic meanings have been read into Alice's adventures, the works can be read and valued as simple exercises in fantasy. Carroll himself said that in the books he meant only nonsense. He also wrote humorous verses, the most popular of them being *The Hunting of the Snark* (1876). His later stories for children, *Sylvie and Bruno* (1889) and *Sylvie and Bruno Concluded* (1893), though containing interesting experiments in construction, are failures. Carroll remained a confirmed and hard-working bachelor all his life. Because of his stammer he found association with adults difficult and was at ease only in the company of children, especially little girls. Early in 1856 he took up photography as a hobby; his photographs of children are still considered remarkable. See his complete works (ed. by Alexander Woolcott, 1939) and many recent editions; Martin Gardner, ed., *The Annotated Alice* (1960, repr. 1970); biographies by Derek Hudson (1954, repr. 1958) and F. B. Lennon (3d ed., 1972); Stuart Collingwood, *Life and Letters* (1898, repr. 1968); Robert Phillips, ed., *Aspects of Alice* (1971).

Carroll, Paul Vincent, 1900–1968, Irish playwright. His plays, vigorous commentaries on the conflicts of village life in Ireland, include *Shadow and Substance* (1937), *The White Steed* (1939), *The Wise Have Not Spoken* (1946), and *The Wayward Saint* (1955). See his *Irish Stories and Plays* (1958).

Carrollton. **1** City (1970 pop. 13,520), seat of Carroll co., W Ga., on the Little Tallapoosa River; inc. 1897. A trade center for a fertile farm area, it has textile dyeing plants and factories making wires and chrome plating. West Georgia College is there. **2** City (1970 pop. 13,855), Dallas and Denton counties., N Texas, a suburb of Dallas, in a rapidly growing and industrializing area. Metal products, aircraft parts, and electronic equipment are the major products.

carrot, common name for some members of the Umbelliferae, a family (also called the parsley family) of chiefly biennial or perennial herbs of north temperate regions. Most are characterized by aromatic foliage, a dry fruit that splits when mature, and an umbellate inflorescence (a type of flattened flower cluster in which the stems of the small florets arise from the same point, like an umbrella). The seeds or leaves of many of these herbs have been used for centuries for seasoning or as greens (e.g., ANGELICA, ANISE, CARAWAY, CHERVIL, CORIANDER, CUMIN, DILL, FENNEL, LOVAGE, and PARSLEY). The carrot, CELERY, and PARSNIP are vegetables of commercial importance. The common garden carrot (*Daucus carota sativa*) is a ROOT CROP, probably derived from some variety of the wild carrot (or QUEEN ANNE'S LACE). In antiquity several types of carrot were grown as medicinals, and in Europe carrots have long been grown for use in soups and stews. The custom of eating carrots raw as a salad has become widespread in the 20th cent. Carrots are a rich source of carotene (vitamin A), especially when they are cooked. Several types of carrot have also been cultivated since ancient times as aromatic plants. Some are still

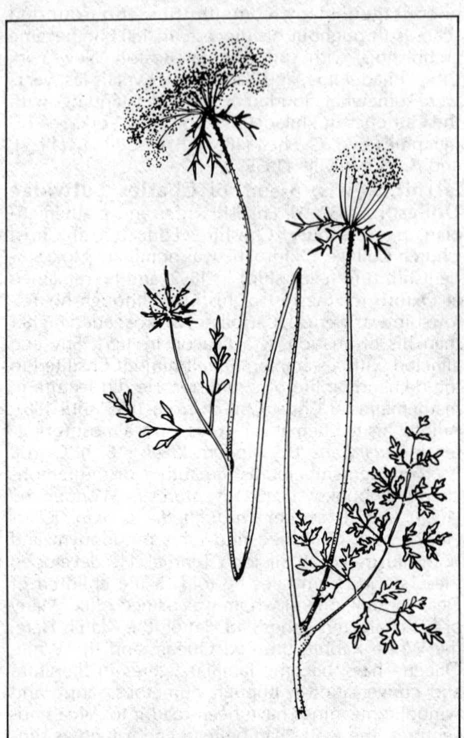

Carrot, Daucus carota

planted as fragrant garden ornamentals, such as the button snakeroot and sweet cicely. A few members of the Umbelliferae produce lethal poison; it was one of these, the poison hemlock, that Socrates was compelled to take. The water hemlock is also poisonous. Carrots are classified in the division MAGNOLIOPHYTA, class Magnoliopsida, order Umbellales, family Umbelliferae.

Carrucci, Jacopo: see PONTORMO, JACOPO DA.

Carshena (kärshē'nə), counselor of Ahasuerus. Esther 1.14.

car sickness: see MOTION SICKNESS.

Carso: see KARST, Yugoslavia.

Carson, Edward Henry Carson, Baron, 1854–1935, Irish politician. After a successful legal career in Dublin, he was elected to the British Parliament in 1892 and called to the English bar in 1893. He soon established himself as a prominent trial lawyer in London, especially after his brilliant and devastating cross-examination of Oscar Wilde in the Queensberry libel case (1895). Carson was solicitor general in the Conservative government from 1900 to 1905. He had long opposed Home Rule for Ireland, fearing dominance of Protestant Ulster by the Catholic South, and in 1912 he organized military resistance in Ulster against the attempt of the Liberal government to impose it. Faced with the threat of civil war, the government eventually conceded that Ulster should be excluded from the Home Rule settlement. During World War I, Carson served as attorney general (1915) in Herbert Asquith's coalition government and as first lord of the admiralty (1916–17) and member of the war cabinet (1917–18) under David Lloyd George. He resigned as leader of the Ulster Unionists in 1921, was made a baron in the same year, and served (1921–29) as lord of appeal in ordinary. See biographies by Edward Marjoribanks and Ian Colvin (3 vol., 1932–36) and H. M. Hyde (1953).

Carson, Kit (Christopher Carson), 1809–68, American frontiersman and guide, b. Madison co., Ky. In 1811 he moved with his family to the Missouri frontier. After his father's death, he was apprenticed to a saddler in Old Franklin, an outfitting point on the Santa Fe Trail, but in 1826 he ran away, joining a caravan for Santa Fe and continuing on to Taos, N.Mex., which became his home and his headquarters. For the next 14 years he made his living as a teamster, cook, guide, and hunter for exploring parties. In 1842, while returning from St. Louis by boat up the Missouri, he met J. C. FRÉMONT, who employed him as a guide for his Western expeditions of 1842, 1843–44, and 1845. He became famous as a result of Frémont's reports of his skill and courage. After Los Angeles was taken in 1846 by U.S. military forces, he was ordered to Washington with dispatches. In New Mexico he met Gen. Stephen Kearny's troops, and Kearny commanded him to guide his forces to California. When Kearny's men were surrounded in California, Carson, E. F. Beale, and an Indian made their way by night through enemy lines to secure aid from San Diego. In 1847 and again in 1848, Carson was sent east with dispatches. He determined to retire to a sheep ranch near Taos, but plundering by Indians compelled him to continue as an Indian fighter. In 1853 he was appointed U.S. Indian agent, with headquarters at Taos, a position he filled with notable success. At the outbreak of the Civil War he helped organize and commanded the 1st New Mexican Volunteers, who engaged in campaigns against the Apache, Navaho, and Comanche Indians in New Mexico and Texas. At the end of the war he was made a brigadier general, in command (1866–67) of Fort Garland, Colo. See his autobiography (ed. by Blanche C. Grant, 1926; ed. by M. M. Quaife, 1935); biographies by Stanley Vestal (1928) and M. M. Estergreen (1962, repr. 1967); E. L. Sabin, *Kit Carson Days* (rev. ed. 1935).

Carson, Rachel Louise, 1907–64, American writer and marine biologist, b. Springdale, Pa., M.A. Johns Hopkins, 1932. Her well-known books on sea life—*Under the Sea Wind* (1941), *The Sea Around Us* (1951), and *The Edge of the Sea* (1954)—combine keen scientific observation with rich poetic description. Her *Silent Spring* (1962) is a provocative study of the dangers involved in the use of insecticides. See Philip Sterling, *Sea and Earth* (1970); Paul Brooks, *The House of Life* (1972).

Carson, city (1970 pop. 71,150), Los Angeles co., S Calif., an industrial and residential suburb of Los Angeles; inc. 1968. Oil refining is the major industry, but fabricated metals, paper and many other products are manufactured. Carson is the site of the largest branch of California State College (Dominguez Hills) and a junior college.

Carson City, city (1970 pop. 15,468), state capital, W Nev., in the Carson valley; inc. 1875. The city is a trade center for a mining and agricultural area. The state government is a major employer, and tourism is important. The city was laid out in 1858 on the site of Eagle Station, a trading post established (1851) on the immigrant trail from Salt Lake City to California. It served as a supply station for miners in the valley, achieved importance with the discovery (1859) of the COMSTOCK LODE, and later became the terminus of the railroad carrying ore. In 1861, when the Territory of Nevada was created, the city was made the capital, and in 1864 it became the state capital—largely through the efforts of William Morris Stewart. A U.S. mint, which closed in 1893, is now occupied by the Nevada State Museum. By act of the legislature, following a statewide referendum, Carson City and Ormsby county were consolidated into one community in July, 1969.

Carson Sink, swampy area, c.100 sq mi (260 sq km), W Nev.; a remnant of ancient Lake Lahontan. Fallon National Wildlife Refuge is located there. The **Carson River** (c.125 mi/200 km long), fed by melted snow, flows into the sink. The river's course was followed by California-bound travelers in the 1850s and 1860s. Lahontan Dam, part of the Newlands project, impounds river water for irrigation and produces electricity.

Carstares or **Carstairs, William,** 1649–1715, Scottish statesman and Presbyterian divine. While studying theology at Utrecht, he became a friend of William of Orange (later William III of England). He was imprisoned in Edinburgh (1674–79) for alleged coauthorship of *An Account of Scotland's Grievances* and again imprisoned and tortured in Edinburgh (1683) as a suspect in the RYE HOUSE PLOT. He returned to Holland where he was made chaplain to William of Orange. He accompanied William to England in 1688 and became so powerful in his efforts to reconcile the new king and the Scottish church and to frustrate the Episcopalian Jacobites that he was nicknamed "the Cardinal." His influence continued under Queen Anne as he worked for the union of England and Scotland, served as principal of the Univ. of Edinburgh from 1703, and was four times moderator of the general assembly of the Church of Scotland. See biography by R. H. Story (1874).

Carstens, Asmus Jacob (äs'mo͝os yä'kôp kär'stəns), 1754–98, German historical painter and engraver, b. Schleswig. He studied in Copenhagen and in Italy. He was influenced by the work of Giulio Romano. Carstens was a popular professor at the Berlin Academy where, through such pupils as Peter von Cornelius, he had a great influence on German historical painting. *Homer Singing* is a characteristic work.

Carstensz, Mount, New Guinea: see DJAJA PEAK.

Cartagena (kärtähā'nä), city (1968 est. pop. 256,600), capital of Bolívar dept., NW Colombia, a port on the Bay of Cartagena in the Caribbean Sea. Oil refining and the manufacture of sugar, tobacco, hides, textiles, and cosmetics are the principal industries. Tourism is also important. Cartagena was founded in 1533 and became the treasure city of the Spanish Main, where precious stones and minerals from the New World awaited transshipment to Spain. Although the harbor was guarded by 29 stone forts and the city was encircled by a high wall of coral, Cartagena suffered sackings and invasions—in 1544, 1560, and in 1586 (by Sir Francis Drake). In 1741 it withstood a three-month British siege. The city was the first of those in Colombia and Venezuela to declare (1811) absolute independence from Spain. Known as the Republic of Cartagena, it was one of the bases used by Simón Bolívar to launch his campaign to liberate Venezuela. In 1815 the city was besieged and captured by the Spanish general Pablo MORILLO, who inflicted savage reprisals on the population. Captured by rebel forces in 1821, Cartagena was incorporated into Colombia. After the revolution the city lost its importance and did not regain it until the 20th cent., with the improvement of communications and the laying of a pipeline to the oil fields of the Magdalena basin. Shady plazas and narrow cobblestone streets make Cartagena one of the most picturesque cities in Latin America. Points of interest include walls and fortifications from colonial times, a 16th-century cathedral, and the Univ. of Cartagena.

Cartagena (kärtähā'nä), Lat. *Carthago Nova,* city (1970 pop. 146,904), Murcia prov., SE Spain, on the Mediterranean Sea. A major seaport and naval base, it has a fine natural harbor, protected by forts, with a naval arsenal and important shipbuilding and metallurgical industries. Lead, iron, and zinc are mined and processed nearby, but the rich silver mines exploited in ancient times by Carthaginians and Romans are now almost exhausted. The city is an episcopal see. It was founded by Hasdrubal c.225 B.C. and soon became a flourishing port, the chief Carthaginian base in Spain. Captured (209 B.C.) by Scipio Africanus Major, it continued to flourish under the Romans. The Moors, who took it in the 8th cent., later included it in Murcia. The Spaniards recovered it definitively in the 13th cent. Cartagena was sacked (1585) by Sir Francis Drake and figured later in the Peninsular and Carlist wars. It served as the Loyalist naval base during the civil war (1936–39). In the 20th cent. it has suffered from the competition of other Mediterranean ports (e.g., Barcelona, Málaga, and Valencia). The medieval Castillo de la Concepción, whose ruins are surrounded by fine gardens, commands a splendid view of the city and harbor. No traces of the ancient city remain.

Cartago (kärtä'gō), city (1968 est. pop. 22,000), central Costa Rica. The raising of livestock and the production of coffee are its main industries. Cartago was founded in 1563. It was the political center of Costa Rica until independence was won from Spain in 1821 and has remained a conservative stronghold. It was destroyed by an eruption (1723) of Irazú volcano and was severely damaged by earthquakes in 1822, 1841, and 1910. Cartago's principal church is the scene of annual pilgrimages.

Cartan, Élie Joseph (ālē' zhôzĕf' kärtäN'), 1869–1951, French mathematician. The son of a village blacksmith, he graduated from the École normale and taught at the universities of Montpellier, Lyons, Nancy, and finally Paris, where he was professor from 1912 to 1940. He developed powerful methods of attacking problems in fields related to modern topology, notably Lie groups, differential systems, and differential geometry; his discoveries are basic to mathematical formulations of quantum mechanics and general relativity. New applications are still found for his work, which is collected in *Oeuvres complètes* (1952–55). The importance of his contributions was recognized belatedly with his election to the French Academy of Sciences in 1931.

Carte, Richard D'Oyly (doi'lē kärt), 1844–1901, English impresario. His choice of presentations did much to raise the level of English musical theater. In 1875 he produced *Trial by Jury,* the first operetta of Sir William S. GILBERT and Sir Arthur SULLIVAN, and he subsequently produced all their other works. In 1881 he built the Savoy Theatre (the first to be lighted electrically), which the operettas made famous. The D'Oyly Carte company still performs Gilbert and Sullivan's works.

cartel, national or international organization of manufacturers or traders allied by agreement to fix prices, limit supply, divide markets, or to fix quotas for sales, manufacture, or division of profits among the member firms. In that it often has international scope the cartel is broader than the TRUST, and in that it carries on manufacture it differs from the speculative CORNER or ring. Of German origin, the cartel achieved prominence in the world depression of the 1870s, which coincided with the unification of Germany and the growth of its economy. The existence of cartels is in opposition to classic theories of economic competition and the free market, and they are forbidden by law in many nations. In Germany, however, by the outset of World War II, nearly all industry was controlled by cartels closely supervised by the government. Opponents of cartels have alleged that they have driven competing firms out of existence, reduced volume of trade, raised prices to consumers, and protected inefficient members from competition. Cartels were blamed for having benefited German aggression by furnishing markets, profits, and technical data to Germany before World War II. Supporters of cartels claim that they protect the weaker participating firms, do away to an extent with limitations on trade resulting from high tariffs, distribute risks and profits equitably, stabilize markets, reduce costs, and hence protect consumers. The U.S. government legalized export associations in 1918 and has itself participated in agreements regulating production and international trade in foodstuffs, rubber, and other commodities. Because they imply the agreement and supervision of several governments, cartels in international trade are usually felt to be less harmful than those which tend to create monopolies in the home market for participants. Formal international agreements, involving governments as well as private firms, still control price, output, and distribution in some industries, notably in diamonds and in oil. Although not referred to as cartels, these agreements have the same general effect on world trade. See also TARIFF. See G. W. Stocking and M. W. Watkins, *Cartels or Competition?* (1948, repr. 1968); K. L. Mayall, *International Cartels* (1951); J. P. Miller, *Competition: Cartels and Their Regulation* (1962); Estes Kefauver, *In a Few Hands* (1965); Heinrich Kronstein, *The Law of International Cartels* (1973).

Carter, Elizabeth, 1717-1806, English poet and translator. Under the pen name Eliza she contributed for years to the *Gentleman's Magazine.* One of the group of 18th-century women known as the bluestockings, she was a friend of Johnson, Burke, Reynolds, and Horace Walpole. Collections of her poems appeared in 1738 and 1762. Her translations of Epictetus were published in 1758. See her memoirs (1807); study by Alice C. C. Gaussen (1906); *Bluestocking Letters* (ed. by R. B. Johnson, 1926).

Carter, Elliott, 1908–, American composer, b. New York City. Carter is considered by many to be the most important contemporary American composer. He was a pupil of Walter Piston, E. B. Hill, and Gustav Holst at Harvard and studied with Nadia Boulanger in Paris (1932-35). Carter's mature music is organized into highly intellectualized contrapuntal patterns to which sympathetic listeners attribute great emotional power. He characteristically uses tempo as an element of form. Among his notable works are the ballet *Pocahontas* (1939), a cello and piano sonata (1948), three string quartets (1951, 1958-59, 1973), *Variations* (1953-55) for orchestra, a piano concerto (1966), and a concerto for orchestra (1969).

Carter, Hodding, 1907-72, American journalist and news publisher, b. Hammond, La. After teaching briefly at Tulane Univ., he worked as a newspaperman until starting (1932) his own paper, the Hammond (La.) *Daily Courier,* which was distinguished by its opposition to Huey Long's control of Louisiana. In 1936 he moved to Greenville, Miss., and started another paper, which became the *Delta Democrat-Times.* After service with the army bureau of public relations in World War II, he returned to his paper to write a series of articles on racial, religious, and economic intolerance that won him the 1945 Pulitzer Prize for distinguished reporting. Particularly cited was his plea for fairness for returning Nisei soldiers. Among his works—both fiction and nonfiction—are *Mississippi* (1942), *Where Main Street Meets the River* (1953), *The Angry Scar: The Story of Reconstruction* (1959), *First Person Rural* (1963), and *Doomed Road of Empire* (1971).

Carter, Howard, 1873-1939, English Egyptologist. He served (1891-99) with the Egyptian Exploration Fund and later helped to reorganize the antiquities administration for the Egyptian government. Carter's successful excavations (1906-22) with Lord Carnarvon in the Valley of the Kings in Luxor, Egypt, include the tombs of Amenophis I, Hatshepsut, and Thutmose IV. His greatest achievement was the discovery in 1922 of the tomb of Tutankhamen. With A. C. Mace he wrote *The Tomb of Tut.ankh.amen* (Vol. I-II, 1923; Vol. III, 1933, repr. 1963). See study by Barry Wynne (1972).

Carter, Mrs. Leslie, 1862-1937, American actress, b. Lexington, Ky., whose maiden name was Caroline Louise Dudley. She became a protégée of BELASCO and first appeared in 1890 in *The Ugly Duckling.* His *Heart of Maryland* (1895) brought her recognition, and her success continued in his productions of *Zaza* (1899), *Du Barry* (1901), and *Adrea* (1905). Their association ended with her second marriage in 1906, after which her stage popularity diminished.

Carter, Nick, fictional detective character in dime novels said to have been created by J. R. Coryell in the 1880s. The firm of Street & Smith, New York City, published over 1,000 stories about Nick Carter, written variously by F. V. R. Dey, E. T. Sawyer, G. C. Jenks, and others. The name Nicholas Carter was used as a pseudonym by many authors of dime novels.

Carter, Samuel Powhatan, 1819-91, American naval officer and Union general in the Civil War, b. Elizabethton, Tenn., grad. Annapolis, 1846. In the Civil War he was transferred from the navy to the War Dept., sent to organize Union troops in East Tennessee, made brigadier general of volunteers (May, 1862), and given command of a cavalry division in the Army of the Ohio. Discharged from service as brevet major general (1866), he returned to the navy. In 1882 he was made a rear admiral on the retired list. Carter is said to have been the only American who was both a major general and a rear admiral.

Carteret, Sir George (kär'tərĕt), c.1610-1680, proprietor of East Jersey (see NEW JERSEY). He served in the British navy, fought for the royalists, and became (1643) lieutenant governor of his native island of Jersey. In 1663, with several others, he was granted the proprietorship of Carolina and in 1664, in conjunction with Lord Berkeley, was granted part of New Jersey. His widow sold his claim to 12 purchasers who joined with 12 others as the 24 proprietors of East New Jersey.

Carteret, John: see GRANVILLE, JOHN CARTERET, 1ST EARL.

Carteret, Philip, 1639-82, first colonial governor of NEW JERSEY. Carteret, commissioned by the proprietor, Sir George Carteret, his fourth cousin, arrived in the province in 1665. He soon faced disputes over confused land titles and rebellion by tenant farmers against quitrents (fixed rents). After the division of New Jersey in 1676, he was made governor of East Jersey. Mounting difficulties with Sir Edmund ANDROS over the right to collect customs duties led to Carteret's imprisonment by Andros and his eventual restoration by the duke of York (later James II).

Carteret, borough (1970 pop. 23,137), Middlesex co., NE N.J., on Arthur Kill, opposite Staten Island; inc. 1906. It has oil and copper refineries and industries producing steel, chemicals, and cigars.

Cartesian coordinates (kärtē'zhən) [for René Descartes], system for representing the relative positions of points in a plane or in space. In a plane, the point *P* is specified by the pair of numbers (x,y) representing the distances of the point from two intersecting straight lines, referred to as the *x*-axis and the *y*-axis. The point of intersection of these axes, which are called the coordinate axes, is known as the origin. In rectangular coordinates, the type most often used, the axes are taken to be perpendicular, with the *x*-axis horizontal and the *y*-axis vertical, so that the *x*-coordinate, or abscissa, of *P* is measured along the horizontal perpendicular from *P* to the *y*-axis (i.e., parallel to the *x*-axis) and the *y*-coordinate, or ordinate, is measured along the vertical perpendicular from *P* to the *x*-axis (parallel to the *y*-axis). In oblique coordinates the axes are not perpendicular; the abscissa of *P* is measured along a parallel to the *x*-axis, and the ordinate is measured along a parallel to the *y*-axis, but neither of these parallels is perpendicular to the other coordinate axis as in rectangular coordinates. Similarly, a point in space may be specified by the triple of numbers (x,y,z) representing the distances from three planes determined by three intersecting straight lines not all in the same plane; i.e., the *x*-coordinate represents the distance from the *yz*-plane measured along a parallel to the *x*-axis, the *y*-coordinate represents the distance from the *xz*-plane measured along a parallel to the *y*-axis, and the *z*-coordinate represents the distance from the *xy*-plane measured along a parallel to the *z*-axis (the axes are usually taken to be mutually perpendicular). Analogous systems may be defined for describing points in abstract spaces of four or more dimensions. Many of the curves studied in classical geometry can be described as the set of points (x,y) that satisfy some equation $f(x,y)=0$. In this way certain questions in geometry can be transformed into questions about numbers and resolved by means of ANALYTIC GEOMETRY.

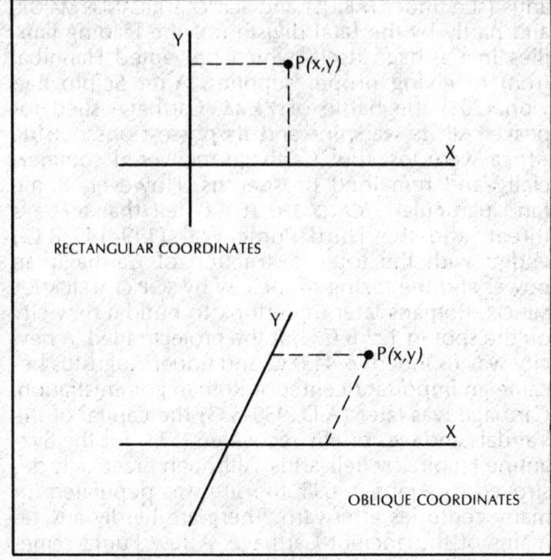

Cartesian coordinates

Cartesian philosophy: see DESCARTES, RENÉ.

Carthage (kär'thĭj), ancient city, on the northern shore of Africa, on a peninsula in the Bay of Tunis and near modern Tunis. The Latin name, Carthago or Cartago, was derived from the Phoenician name, which meant "new city" (the old city being Utica). It was founded (traditionally by DIDO) from Tyre in the 9th cent. B.C. The city-state built up trade and in the 6th and 5th cent. B.C. began to acquire dominance in the W Mediterranean. Merchants and explorers established a wide net of trade that brought great wealth to Carthage. The state was tightly controlled by an aristocracy of nobles and wealthy merchants. Although a council and a popular assembly existed, these soon lost power to oligarchical institutions, and actual power was in the hands of the judges and two elected magistrates (suffetes). There was also a small but powerful senate. The greatest weakness of Carthage lay in the rivalry of two blocs of leading families that traditionally backed opposing policies. The most important division was between those favoring land expansion and those favoring sea power. The maritime faction was generally in control, and about the end of the 6th cent. B.C. the Carthaginians established themselves on Sardinia, Malta, and the Balearic Islands. The navigator Hanno in the early 5th cent. is supposed to have sailed down the African coast as far as Sierra Leone. The statesman Mago arrived at treaties with the Etruscans, the Romans, and some of the Greeks. However, Sicily, which lay almost at the front door of Carthage, was never brought completely under Carthaginian control. The move against the island, begun by settlements in W Sicily, was brought to a halt when the Carthaginian general HAMILCAR (a name that recurred in the powerful Carthaginian family usually called the Barcas) was defeated (480 B.C.) by GELON, tyrant of Syracuse, in the battle of Himera. The Greek city-states of Sicily were thus preserved, but the Carthaginian threat continued and grew with the steadily increasing power of Carthage. Hamilcar's grandson, Hannibal (another name much used in the family), destroyed Himera (409 B.C.), and his colleague Himilco sacked Acragas (modern Agrigento) in 406 B.C. SYRACUSE resisted the conquerors, and a century later Carthage was threatened by the campaign (310-307?) of the tyrant Agathocles on the shores of Africa. After his death, however, Carthage had practically complete control over all the W Mediterranean. In the 3d cent. B.C., Rome challenged that control in the PUNIC WARS (so called after the Roman name for the Carthaginians, Poeni, i.e., Phoenicians). The first of these wars (264-241) cost Carthage all remaining hold on Sicily. Immediately after the First Punic War a great uprising of the mercenaries occurred (240-238). HAMILCAR BARCA put down the revolt and compensated for the loss of Sicilian possessions by undertaking conquest in Spain, a conquest continued by HASDRUBAL. This growth of power again activated trouble with Rome, and the Second Punic War took place (218-201). Although the Carthaginian general was the formidable HANNIBAL, Carthage was finally defeated, partly by the Roman generals Quintus Fabius Maximus Rullianus (see under FABIUS) and SCIPIO AFRICANUS MAJOR, and partly by the fatal division of the leading families in Carthage itself, which prevented Hannibal from receiving proper supplies. After Scipio had won (202) the battle of ZAMA, Carthage sued for peace. All its warships and its possessions outside Africa were lost, but Carthage recovered commercially and remained prosperous. However, Rome (and particularly CATO THE ELDER) felt that to be a threat, and the Third Punic War (149-146 B.C.) ended with the total destruction of Carthaginian power and the razing of the city by SCIPIO AFRICANUS MINOR. Romans later undertook to build a new city on the spot in 122 B.C., but the project failed. A new city was founded in 44 B.C. and under Augustus became an important center of Roman administration. Carthage was later (A.D. 439-533) the capital of the Vandals and was briefly recovered (533) for the Byzantine Empire by Belisarius. Although practically destroyed by Arabs in 698, the site was populated for many centuries afterward. There are hardly any remains of the ancient Carthage. A few Punic cemeteries, shrines, and fortifications have been discovered, and there are some Roman ruins including baths, an amphitheater, and other buildings. Louis IX of France (St. Louis) died there when on crusade. A chapel in his honor stands on the hill that is traditionally identified as Byrsa Hill, site of the ancient citadel. The Lavigérie Museum is also there. See B. H. Warmington, *Carthage* (2d ed. 1969); T. A. Dorey and D. R. Dudley, *Rome against Carthage* (1971).

Carthage, city (1970 pop. 11,035), seat of Jasper co., SW Mo., on the Spring River, in a rich farm area; inc. 1873. Its gray marble quarries are the largest of their kind in the world, and Carthage marble is a major product. Carthage became county seat in 1842. A Civil War battle was fought there July 5, 1861; the city was burned and was rebuilt after the war. Points of interest include the log cabin courthouse (1842) and the George Washington Carver National Monument, site of Carver's birthplace, at nearby Diamond.

Carthusians (kärthōō'zhənz), small order of monks of the Roman Catholic Church [Lat. abbr.,=O. Cart.]. It was established by St. BRUNO at La Grande Chartreuse (see CHARTREUSE, GRANDE) in France in 1084. The Carthusians are peculiar among orders of Western monasticism in cultivating a nearly eremitical life: each monk lives by himself with cell and garden and, except for communal worship, scarcely meets the others. No order is more austere. The Carthusian enclosure is called charterhouse in English, and its architecture differs necessarily from that of the Benedictine ABBEY. The CHARTERHOUSE of London was famous, and the CERTOSA DI PAVIA, Italy, is an architectural monument. The Carthusians are devoted mainly to contemplation. In 1973 they numbered 440 members throughout the world, of whom there were 10 in the United States, living at the Charterhouse of Arlington, Vt. They are unchanging in their rule, their independence, and their original way of life. There are a very few Carthusian nuns following a similar rule. CHARTREUSE is the well-known liqueur manufactured by Carthusians in France.

Cartier, Sir Georges Étienne (zhôrzh ātyĕn' kärtyā'), 1814-73, Canadian statesman, b. Quebec prov. He was called to the bar of Lower Canada (Quebec) in 1835. He took part in the rebellion of 1837 inspired by Louis Joseph PAPINEAU and was forced to flee to the United States, but he returned to Canada in 1838. In 1848 he was elected to the legislative assembly of Canada, where he became a leader of the French Canadians. With Sir John A. MACDONALD, his ally in Upper Canada, he formed the Macdonald-Cartier ministry (1857-62). He was the leading French Canadian advocate of confederation of British North America, played a prominent role in the Charlottetown and Quebec conferences of 1864, and was mainly influential in persuading his compatriots to accept the federation proposals. On the other hand, in order to protect the French Canadians, he insisted on a federal system rather than a more centralized form of government. As one of Macdonald's most trusted colleagues, Cartier became minister of militia in the first dominion government. In 1868 he went to England with William McDougall to arrange for the purchase of the Hudson's Bay Company territory. He also had an important part in the projection of the Grand Trunk and Canadian Pacific railroads. See biographies by John Boyd (1914, repr. 1971) and A. D. DeCelles (1926).

Cartier, Jacques (zhäk), 1491-1557, French navigator, first explorer of the Gulf of St. Lawrence and discoverer of the St. Lawrence River. He made three voyages to the region, the first two (1534, 1535-36) directly at the command of King Francis I and the third (1541-42) under the sieur de Roberval in a colonization scheme that failed. On the first voyage he entered by the Strait of Belle Isle, skirted its barren north coast for a distance and then coasted along the west shore of Newfoundland to Cape Anguille. From there he discovered the Magdalen Islands and Prince Edward Island and, sailing to the coast of New Brunswick, explored Chaleur Bay, continued around the Gaspé Peninsula, and landed at Gaspé to take possession for France. Continuing to Anticosti Island, he then returned to France. Hitherto the region had been considered cold and forbidding, interesting only because of the Labrador and Newfoundland fisheries, but Cartier's reports of a warmer, more fertile region in New Brunswick and on the Gaspé and of an inlet of unknown extent stimulated the king to dispatch him on a second expedition. On this voyage he ascended the St. Lawrence to the site of modern Quebec and, leaving some of his men to prepare winter quarters, continued to the Indian village of Hochelaga, on the site of the present-day city of Montreal, and there climbed Mt. Royal to survey the fertile valley and see the Lachine Rapids and Ottawa River. On his return he explored Cabot Strait, ascertaining Newfoundland to be an island. His *Brief Récit et succincte narration* (1545), a description of this voyage, was his only account to be published in France during his life. On his third trip he penetrated again to the Lachine Rapids and wintered in the same region, but gained little new geographical information. Roberval did not appear until Cartier was on his way home, and Cartier refused to join him. Although Cartier's discoveries were of major geographical importance and the claims of the French to the St. Lawrence valley were based on them, he failed in his primary object, the discovery of the Northwest Passage and natural resources. The region remained virtually untouched until the early 17th cent. The best edition of the voyages is H. P. Biggar, *The Voyages of Jacques Cartier* (1924).

Cartier-Bresson, Henri (äNrē' kärtēā'-brĕsôN'), 1908-, French photojournalist. Cartier-Bresson is renowned for his countless memorable images of 20th-century individuals and events. Achieved with the simplest of techniques, his works are remarkable for their flawless composition and for the sense they convey of the rush of time arrested. His photographs are uncropped and unmanipulated. In 1944, after escaping from a German prison camp, Cartier-Bresson organized underground photography units. He is the author of many photographic books including *The Decisive Moment* (1952), *People of Moscow* (1955), *China in Transition* (1956), *The World of Henri Cartier-Bresson* (1968), *The Face of Asia* (1972), and *About Russia* (1974). He was a founder of the Magnum photo agency. See François Nourissier, *Cartier-Bresson's France* (tr. 1971).

cartilage (kär'təlĭj), flexible semiopaque CONNECTIVE TISSUE without blood vessels or nerve cells that forms part of the skeletal system in man and other vertebrates, also called gristle. Temporary cartilage makes up the skeletal system of the fetus and the infant but is gradually replaced by bone as the body matures. Permanent cartilage remains throughout life, as in the external ear, nose, larynx, and windpipe. Cartilage is also present about the JOINTS, where it reduces friction and imparts flexibility.

Cartimandua, fl. 1st cent. A.D., British queen of the Brigantes. Ruler of the largest and most powerful tribe in Roman Britain (inhabiting the area that is now Yorkshire), she surrendered CARACTACUS to the Romans (A.D. 51). The Romans supported her rule as a client-queen in order to stabilize the region and quell dynastic conflicts. She was overthrown in A.D. 69 when she repudiated her husband, Venutius, for his armor-bearer. The Brigantes were then subjugated under direct Roman rule.

cartography: see MAP.

cartoon [Ital. *cartone*=paper]. In the fine arts, a full-sized preliminary drawing for a work to be afterwards executed in fresco, oil, mosaic, stained glass, or tapestry. Glass and mosaic are cut exactly according to the patterns taken from the cartoons while in tapestry the cartoon is inserted beneath the warp to serve as a guide. In FRESCO painting, the lines of the cartoon are perforated and transferred to the plaster surface by pouncing (dusting with powder through the perforations). The Italian Renaissance painters made very complete cartoons, and such works as Raphael's cartoons for the Sistine Chapel tapestries (Victoria and Albert Mus.) are considered masterpieces. In England in 1843 a series of drawings appeared in *Punch* magazine that parodied the fresco cartoons submitted in a competition for the decoration of the new Houses of Parliament. In this way *cartoon,* in journalistic parlance, came to mean any single humorous or satirical drawing employing distortion for emphasis, often accompanied by a caption or a legend. Cartoons, particularly editorial or political cartoons, make use of the elements of CARICATURE. The political cartoon first appeared in 16th-century Germany during the Reformation, the first time such art became an active propaganda weapon with social implications. While many of these cartoons were crudely executed and remarkably vulgar, some, such as Holbein's *German Hercules,* were excellent drawings produced by the best artists of the time. In England, in the 18th cent., the cartoon became an integral and effective part of journalism through the works of Hogarth, Rowlandson, and Gillray. Daumier, in France, became well known for his virulent satirical cartoons. By the mid-19th cent. editorial cartoons had become regular features in American newspapers and were soon followed by sports cartoons and humorous cartoons. The effect of political cartoons on public opinion was amply demonstrated in the elections of 1871 and 1873 when the power of Tammany Hall was broken and Boss Tweed imprisoned largely through the efforts of Thomas Nast and his cartoons for *Harper's Weekly.* In 1922 the first Pulitzer Prize for editorial cartooning was won by Rollin Kirby of the New York *World.* Other noted political cartoonists include John T. McCutcheon, C. D. Batchelor, Jacob Burck, Bill Mauldin, Rube Goldberg, Tom Little, Patrick Oliphant, and Herblock (Herbert Block). Humorous nonpolitical cartoons became popular with the development of the color press, and in 1893 the first color cartoon appeared in the New York *World.* In 1896, R. F. Outcault originated *The Yellow Kid,* a large single panel cartoon with some use of dialogue in balloons, and throughout the '90s humorous cartoons by such artists as T. S. Sullivant, James Swinnerton, Frederick B. Opper, and Edward W. Kemble began to appear regularly in major newspapers and journals. The *New Yorker* and the *Saturday Evening Post* were among the most notable American magazines to use outstanding single cartoon drawings. The single cartoons soon developed into the narrative newspaper COMIC STRIP, although the single panel episodic tradition has been retained, exemplified by the work of humorists such as Charles Addams, Peter Arno, Saul Steinberg, James Thurber, William Steig, Helen Hokinson, Mary Petty, Whitney Darrow, the Englishmen Rowland Emmett and Ronald Searle, and the French cartoonists André François and Bil. See studies by David Low (1953), Osbert Lancaster (1964); R. E. Shikes, *The Indignant Eye* (1969); John Geipel (1972).

Cartouche (kärtōōsh'), 1693-1721, nickname of Louis Dominique Bourguignon, French highwayman. His band terrorized the Paris area until his capture. He was broken on the wheel. Cartouche's daring exploits have been celebrated in stories, dramas, ballads, and popular prints.

Cartwright, Edmund, 1743-1823, English inventor and clergyman. He was the inventor of an imperfect power loom that, when finally patented (1785), became the parent of the modern loom. It was the first machine to make practical the weaving of wide cotton cloth. A few of Cartwright's many other inventions were a wool-combing machine (1789), a machine for ropemaking (1792), and an engine (1797) that used alcohol as fuel. He cooperated with Fulton on his experiments with steam navigation.

Cartwright, John, 1740-1824, English reformer and pamphleteer; brother of Edmund Cartwright. He had an early career in the navy. He declined to fight the American colonists and wrote *American Independence: the Interest and Glory of Great Britain* (1774). A major in the Nottinghamshire militia (1775-92), he was deprived of his commission in the hysteria at the time of the French Revolutionary Wars. He came to be called the "father of reform" for his advocacy of universal manhood suffrage, parliamentary and army reform, and abolition of slavery. See F. D. Cartwright, ed., *The Life and Correspondence of Major Cartwright* (2 vol., 1826; repr. 1969); biography by J. W. Osborne (1972).

Cartwright, Peter, 1785-1872, American Methodist preacher, b. Virginia. He was a circuit rider in Kentucky, Tennessee, Indiana, Ohio, and Illinois for nearly 50 years. In 1846 he was defeated as a candidate for Congress by Abraham Lincoln. An interest in education led Cartwright to aid in founding Illinois Wesleyan Univ. and Illinois Conference Female Academy (now MacMurray College). The methods and experiences of the pioneer preacher are vividly recorded in his autobiography (1857) and other books. See biographies by H. H. Grant (1931) and Sydney and Marjorie Greenbie (1955).

Cartwright, Sir Richard John, 1835–1912, Canadian politician, b. Kingston, Ont. He was elected as a Conservative to the legislative assembly of Canada (1863) and to the first dominion House of Commons (1867), but he later joined the Liberals. He was minister of finance (1873–78) in Alexander Mackenzie's administration. As minister of trade and finance (1896–1911) in Sir Wilfrid Laurier's government, Cartwright was acting prime minister on several occasions. He entered the Senate in 1904. A noted public speaker, he was the Liberal party's spokesman on financial matters and an earnest advocate of trade reciprocity with the United States. See his reminiscences (1912).

Cartwright, William, 1611–43, English author and divine. An ardent royalist and a disciple of Ben Jonson, he had a high reputation in his day both as a preacher and as an author. In addition to his poems, which are now almost entirely forgotten, Cartwright wrote plays, of which *The Ordinary* (1635?) and *The Royal Slave* (1636) were the most successful. See his works (ed. with an introduction by G. Blakemore Evans, 1951).

Caruaru (kərōōərōō'), city (1970 pop. 142,808), Pernambuco state, NE Brazil, on the Ipojuca River. It is a commercial center in an agricultural and cattle-raising area.

Carucci, Jacopo: see PONTORMO, JACOPO DA.

Carus (Marcus Aurelius Carus) (kâr'əs), d. 283, Roman emperor (282–83). Praetorian prefect under PROBUS, he was made emperor by the soldiers after the murder of Probus. Leaving his son CARINUS in command of the West, Carus and another son, Numerianus, went on a campaign in the East. He defeated the Sarmatians, successfully attacked the Parthians, and took Ctesiphon. Soon afterward he died mysteriously.

Carus, Paul, 1852–1919, American philosopher, born and educated in Germany. For many years he was editor of the *Open Court* and the *Monist,* periodicals devoted to philosophy and religion. His philosophy was monistic, seeking to establish religion on a scientific basis. Among his many works were *Fundamental Problems* (1889), *The Religion of Science* (1893), *The Gospel of Buddha* (1900), *The History of the Devil* (1900), and *The Principle of Relativity* (1913).

Caruso, Enrico (kərōō'sō, Ital. änrē'kō kärōō'zō), 1873–1921, Italian operatic tenor, b. Naples. The natural beauty, range, and power of his voice made him one of the greatest singers in the history of opera. He studied for three years with Guglielmo Vergine and made his operatic debut in Naples in 1894. His first major success came in London in 1902, and he achieved even greater triumph with his American debut in 1903 at the Metropolitan Opera as the duke in *Rigoletto.* He remained the reigning favorite at the Metropolitan until a short time before his death (from pleurisy). He also made guest appearances in Europe and Latin America, interrupting his busy career only for a throat operation in 1908–9. He sang more than 50 roles in Italian and French operas, such as *La Traviata, Aida, La Bohème, Tosca,* and *Carmen.* After his death his recordings perpetuated his fame. His highly emotional interpretation of Canio in *I Pagliacci* perhaps won the most rapturous public applause, but roles in Verdi and Puccini operas and his recitals showed his artistry to better advantage. See biographies by Dorothy Park Benjamin Caruso (new ed. 1963) and Stanley Jackson (1972).

Carvajal, Francisco de (fränthēs'kō dā kärvähäl'), 1464?–1548, Spanish conquistador. For 40 years he fought in European wars before going to Mexico and subsequently to Peru, where he aided Francisco Pizarro. He grew rich from the tributory labor of Indians, thousands of whom died in his mines at Potosí. He supported (1542) VACA DE CASTRO against the revolt of Diego de Almagro the younger, but when the New Laws to protect the Indians were put in force in Peru (1544), he joined the revolt of Gonzalo PIZARRO. He was captured with Gonzalo Pizarro and executed.

carvel: see CARAVEL.

Carver, George Washington, 1864?–1943, American agricultural chemist, b. Diamond, Mo., grad. Iowa State College (B.S., 1894; M.A. 1896). Born a slave, he later, as a free man, earned his college degree. In 1896 he joined the staff of Tuskegee Institute as director of the department of agricultural research, retaining that post the rest of his life. His work won him international repute. Carver's efforts to improve the economy of the South (he dedicated himself especially to bettering the position of Negroes) included the teaching of soil improvement and of diversification of crops. He discovered hundreds of uses for the peanut, the sweet potato, and the soybean and thus stimulated the culture of these crops. He devised many products from cotton waste and extracted blue, purple, and red pigments from local clay. From 1935 he was a collaborator of the Bureau of Plant Industry. Carver contributed his life savings to a foundation for research at Tuskegee. In 1953 his birthplace was made a national monument. See biographies by Rackham Holt (rev. ed. 1966) and Lawrence Elliott (1966).

Carver, John, c.1576–1621, first governor of Plymouth Colony. A wealthy London merchant, in 1609 he emigrated to Holland, where he soon joined the Pilgrims at Leiden. His excellent character and his fortune, of which he gave liberally to the congregation, served to make him a leader. Carver, the chief figure in arranging for the Pilgrim migration to America, secured the backing of merchant friends in London, enlisted a number of capable settlers who came directly from England, and hired and provisioned the *Mayflower* for the journey. After the signing of the Mayflower Compact he was elected (1620) governor for one year and was probably responsible for the choice of the site at Plymouth. On his death, William BRADFORD succeeded him. See G. F. Willison, *Saints and Strangers* (1945).

Carver, Jonathan, 1710–80, American explorer, b. Weymouth, Mass. He served in the French and Indian War and in 1766 was hired by Robert ROGERS to undertake a journey to some of the Western tribes. He journeyed to the Mississippi and up that river to a point several days' journey above the present site of Minneapolis. In the spring of 1767 he returned to Prairie du Chien, where by Rogers's orders he joined the expedition to search out the "Western Ocean." When their journey northwestward was prevented by war between the Sioux and Chippewa, they ascended the Chippewa River and crossed to Lake Superior, the coast of which they followed to Grand Portage. Carver went to London in 1769 with the intention of publishing a narrative of his travels and of pressing claims for compensation for his services, for Rogers, having exceeded his authority in employing Carver, could not pay him. After nine years of struggle and poverty, Carver published the first edition of his *Travels through the Interior Parts of North America in the Years 1766, 1767, and 1768* (1778). The popularity of this book, the first English account of the upper Great Lakes and Mississippi region, is attested by the 32 editions, or more, through which it passed.

Cary, Henry Francis, 1772–1844, English translator. A graduate of Christ Church College, Oxford, he was assistant librarian in the British Museum from 1826 to 1837. He translated several classical writers, including Aristophanes and Pindar. His blank-verse rendering (1814) of Dante's *Divine Comedy* is still a standard translation.

Cary, Joyce (Arthur Joyce Lunel Cary), 1888–1957, English author. From 1910 to 1920 he served as an administrator and soldier in Nigeria. Several of his early works, including *Mister Johnson* (1939), reflect his African experiences. Cary is perhaps best known for his two trilogies. Both these works, full of humor and compassion, convey a sense of the gradual change in the social and political structure of modern England. The first trilogy consists of *Herself Surprised* (1941), *To Be a Pilgrim* (1942), and *The Horse's Mouth* (1944), the last book featuring the visionary, iconoclastic painter Gully Jimson; the second trilogy consists of *Prisoner of Grace* (1952), *Except the Lord* (1953), and *Not Honour More* (1955). Cary wrote many other novels, in addition to political studies and poems. A collection of his short stories, *Spring Song,* was published posthumously in 1960. See biography by Malcolm Foster (1968); studies by Robert L. Bloom (1963), Jack S. Wolkenfeld (1968), and R. W. Noble (1973).

Cary, Lucius: see FALKLAND, LUCIUS CARY, 2D VISCOUNT.

caryatid (kărēăt'ĭd), a sculptured female figure serving as an ornamental support in place of a column or pilaster. It was a frequently used motif in architecture, furniture, and garden sculpture during the Renaissance, the 18th cent., and notably, the CLASSIC REVIVAL of the 19th cent., when caryatids were popular as mantelpiece supports. The motif appeared in Egyptian and Greek architecture; the most celebrated example extant is the Porch of the Caryatids, forming part of the ERECHTHEUM. Here six beautifully sculptured figures, acting as columns, support an entablature on their heads. They are considered the only faultless examples of a form that ranks as somewhat questionable architecturally. Caryatids were used also in two small treasuries (6th cent. B.C.) at Delphi.

Caryatid

Casa, Giovanni della (jōvän'nē dĕl'lä kä'zä), 1503–56, Italian cleric and poet. He was archbishop of Benevento and papal nuncio to Venice. He wrote lyric verse, a life of Bembo, and a treatise on etiquette, the *Galateo* (1560, tr. 1576). His verse is often of great dignity and formal beauty. See Lorna de' Lucchi, *An Anthology of Italian Poems* (1922).

casaba melon: see MELON.

Casablanca (kă"səblăng'kə, kä"zə–, Span. kä"säbläng'kä), Arab. *Dar-al-Baida,* city (1970 est. pop. 1,395,000), W Morocco, on the Atlantic Ocean. It is the largest city of Morocco and handles over two thirds of the country's commerce. Phosphates comprise 75% of the total export traffic, and petroleum products are the major imports. The city's leading industries produce textiles, glass, and bricks. Casablanca is on the site of Anfa, a prosperous town that the Portuguese destroyed in 1468; they resettled it briefly in 1515 under its present name. Almost destroyed by an earthquake in 1755, Casablanca was rebuilt (1757) by Muhammad XVI. It was occupied by the French in 1907. During World War II, Casablanca was the scene of one of the three major Allied landings in North Africa (Nov., 1942) and of a conference between Franklin Delano Roosevelt and Winston Churchill (Nov., 1943).

Casablanca Conference, Jan. 14–24, 1943, World War II meeting of U.S. President Franklin Delano Roosevelt and British Prime Minister Winston Churchill at Casablanca, French Morocco. A joint declaration pledged that the war would end only with the unconditional surrender of the Axis states. No agreement was reached on the claims for leadership of the rival French generals, Henri H. Giraud and Charles de Gaulle, who also attended the conference.

Casadesus, Robert (käsädäsüs'), 1899–1973, French pianist and composer, b. Paris. Casadesus was born into a family remarkable for its numerous celebrated musicians. After study at the Paris Conservatory, he embarked in 1922 on a long and distinguished concert career. After 1940, Casadesus lived in the United States, where he taught and composed. He became director of the American Conservatory at Fontainebleau in 1945. Noted as a pianist of lyric sensitivity, he often appeared in concert with his wife, the pianist Gaby Casadesus. Their son, **Jean Casadesus,** 1927–71, was also a well-known concert pianist.

Casa Fuerte, Juan de Acuña, marqués de: see ACUÑA, JUAN DE.

Casa Grande (kä'sä grän'dā), city (1970 pop. 10,536), Pinal co., S Ariz.; inc. 1915. It lies in an irrigated farm area near the Casa Grande Mts. The city was named after an excavated Indian pueblo that is now included in the nearby Casa Grande Ruins National Monument (see NATIONAL PARKS AND MONUMENTS, table). Casa Grande is a retail trade center of S central Arizona.

Casal, Julián del (ho͝olyän' dĕl käsäl'), 1863–93, Cuban poet, b. Havana. A friend of Rubén Darío, Casal became a leader in MODERNISMO. He was greatly influenced by the French PARNASSIANS. Afflicted with a painful form of tuberculosis, he wrote verse expressing deep pessimism. To escape his agony he often chose subjects from antiquity and far-off lands, especially Japan. His best-known collections are *Hojas al viento* [leaves in the wind] (1890) and *Bustos y rimas* [busts and rhymes] (1893).

Casale Monferrato (käsä'lā mōnfār-rä'tō) or **Casale,** city (1971 pop. 43,697), Piedmont, NW Italy, on the Po River. Manufactures include cement and electrical appliances, and much wine is produced in the region. It became the capital of the marquisate of MONTFERRAT in 1435 and was strongly fortified. In the mid-16th cent. the city came under Mantua, and in 1703 it passed to the house of Savoy. Of note are the Romanesque cathedral (12th cent.) and the citadel (15th cent., now a barracks).

Casals, Pablo (Pau) (pä'blō käsäls', pou), 1876–1973, Spanish virtuoso cellist and conductor. Casals is considered the greatest 20th-century master of the cello and a distinguished composer, conductor, and pianist. A prodigy, he began his concert career in 1891. In 1905 he formed a chamber trio with Jacques Thibaud (1880–1953) and Alfred Cortot. His career as a conductor began in 1919, when the Orquestra Pau Casals, Barcelona, gave its first concert. Casals gained an international reputation for brilliant expressive technique that remains unsurpassed. His superb interpretations of the Bach unaccompanied cello suites brought him worldwide adulation. In 1939, Casals settled at Prades in S France, a voluntary exile in protest against the Spanish government. In 1950 he began to conduct annual music festivals in Prades. In 1956 he moved to Puerto Rico, where the following year he inaugurated annual music festivals at San Juan. He married his third wife, his student Martita Montañes, in 1957. He performed at the United Nations (1958) and the White House (1961), and conducted a celebrated concert of some 80 cellists at Lincoln Center (1972). See his memoirs (1970); biography by H. L. Kirk (1974); Lillian Littlehales, *Pablo Casals* (rev. ed. 1948).

Casanova de Seingalt, Giovanni Giacomo (kăzənō'və, Ital. jōvän'nē jä'kōmō käzänō'vä dā sāngält'), 1725–98, Venetian adventurer and author. His first name also appears as Jacopo. He studied for the church but was expelled from school for immorality. A life of adventure took him all over Europe. He supported himself by gambling, spying, writing, and, especially, by his power to seduce women, and his personal charm affected the foremost persons of his time. Arrested (1755) in Venice, he accomplished the notable feat of escaping (1756) from the "leaden roofs" of the state prison. In Paris, where he enjoyed favor in court circles, he became director of the lottery and amassed a fortune. In 1785 Casanova retired to the castle of Dux, Bohemia, where his friend Count Waldstein employed him as librarian. A man of learning and taste, with interests ranging from mathematics, poetry, and literary and musical criticism to commercial and political projects, Casanova left many writings. His memoirs, written in French, became world-famous. Only abridged versions were published until 1960, when the complete memoirs began to appear in French and in German translation. Accurate as to history, the memoirs probably contain much invented personal matter. Other papers, in prose and verse, were released in 1930. See his autobiography tr. by W. R. Trask (12 vol. in 6, 1967–71); biographies by J. R. Childs (1961) and J. Masters (1969).

Casas, Bartolomé de las: see LAS CASAS.

Casaubon, Isaac (ēzäk' käzōbôN'), 1559–1614, English classical scholar and theologian, b. Geneva. He became professor of Greek at Geneva and at Montpellier and by his learning attracted the notice of Henry IV, who made him royal librarian. After Henry's death, he was invited to England by the archbishop of Canterbury. He joined the Church of England and in 1610 James I granted him a royal stipend. The next year Casaubon became an English subject, remaining in England the rest of his life. He was buried in Westminster Abbey. Casaubon's great works are his editions of the classics, particularly Athenaeus and the *Characters* of Theophrastus. His diary, *Ephemerides,* was edited by his son, **Florence Étienne Méric Casaubon,** 1599–1671, who was also a classical scholar.

Casca (Publius Servilius Casca Longus) (kăs'kə), d. c.42 B.C., Roman politician, one of the assassins of Julius CAESAR. Casca was the first to stab Caesar. He died (presumably by suicide) soon after the battle of Philippi.

Cascade Range, mountain chain, c.700 mi (1,130 km) long, extending S from British Columbia to N Calif., where it joins the Sierra Nevada; it parallels the Coast Ranges, 100–150 mi (161–241 km) inland from the Pacific Ocean. Many of the range's highest peaks are volcanic cones, covered with snowfields and glaciers; Lassen Peak, 10,457 ft (3,187 m) high, in Lassen Volcanic National Park, is still volcanically active. Mt. Rainier (14,410 ft/4,392 m), in Mount Rainier National Park, is the highest point in the Cascades; Mt. Shasta and Mt. Hood are other prominent peaks. The Klamath, Columbia, and Fraser rivers flow from east to west across the range. Of the many lakes in the Cascades, Crater Lake, in Crater Lake National Park, and Lake Chelan, in Lake Chelan National Recreation Area, are the most famous. Other Federal lands in this popular recreation area are North Cascades National Park, Ross Lake National Recreation Area, and Lava Beds National Monument; national forests cover an extensive area. Receiving more than 100 in. (254 cm) of precipitation annually, the Cascades are a major source of water in the U.S. Northwest. Hydroelectricity is generated on the western slope; irrigation is used in the fertile eastern side valleys. Timber is the region's chief resource. The **Cascade Tunnel,** 8 mi (12.9 km), is the longest railroad tunnel in North America.

Casco Bay (kăs'kō), deep inlet of the Atlantic Ocean, 200 sq mi (518 sq km), SW Maine. The bay, with its more than 200 wooded, hilly islands, has many summer estates and resorts. Portland, Maine, is the principal harbor.

case, in language, one of the several possible forms of a given noun, pronoun, or adjective that indicates its grammatical function (see INFLECTION); it is usually a series of suffixes attached to a stem, as in Latin *amicus,* "friend" (nominative); *amicum* (accusative); *amici* (genitive); and *amico* (ablative and dative). In English, nouns have two cases, e.g., *man* (common or nominative) and *man's* (possessive or genitive), and a few pronouns have three, e.g., *he* (nominative), *him* (objective), and *his* (possessive). The fact that there are only two cases represents a loss in the English case system as Old English also used accusative, dative, and sometimes instrumental, cases. Latin has six cases, nominative, genitive, dative, accusative, ablative, and vocative. The hypothetical ancestor of the Indo-European languages had eight cases, the above six plus the instrumental and locative cases. The Altaic and Finno-Ugric language families also use case systems. German has four cases, Russian six, Finnish sixteen. In Europe, the concept was first introduced by the Greeks, although Sanskrit grammarians established it independently. The names of the most common cases derive from Greek by way of Latin translation, as does the term *case* itself.

casehardening: see HARDENING.

casein (kā'sēn), well-defined group of proteins found in milk, constituting about 80% of the proteins in cow's milk, but only 40% in human milk. Casein is a remarkably efficient nutrient, supplying not only essential amino acids, but also some carbohydrates and the inorganic elements calcium and phosphorus. The calcium caseinates form an insoluble white curd when acidified by hydrochloric acid or sulfuric acid, or when milk is soured by bacterial contaminants. Acid casein is used widely in cheese, adhesives, water paints, for coating paper, and in printing textiles and wallpaper. In neutral solutions the enzyme rennin converts one of the caseins to an insoluble curd; most of the protein in cheese is RENNET casein curd. When treated with formaldehyde the curd forms casein plastic, used for manufacturing imitation tortoiseshell, jade, and lapis lazuli.

Case Institute of Technology: see CASE WESTERN RESERVE UNIV.

Casella, Alfredo (älfrā'dō käsĕl'lä), 1883–1947, Italian composer, pianist, conductor, and writer on music; pupil of Gabriel Fauré at the Paris Conservatory. He taught piano at the Paris Conservatory (1911–15) and at the St. Cecilia Conservatory, Rome (1915–23). In 1917 he organized a society, later known as Corporazione delle Nuove Musiche, to promote the recognition of contemporary music. He is the author of *The Evolution of Music throughout the History of the Perfect Cadence* (tr. 1924). His best-known compositions are the ballets *Il convento veneziano* (1912) and *La Giara* (Paris, 1924), the latter based on a novel by Pirandello. Other works are piano pieces, songs, chamber music, orchestral works, and concertos. See his memoirs, *Music in My Time* (tr. 1955).

Casement, Sir Roger David, 1864–1916, Irish revolutionary. While in British consular service, he exposed (1904) the atrocious exploitation of wild-rubber gatherers in the Congo (thus helping to bring about the extinction of the Congo Free State in 1908) and later exposed similar conditions in South America. He was knighted for these services. Although an Ulster Protestant, Casement became an ardent Irish nationalist. After the outbreak of World War I he went first to the United States and then to Germany to secure aid for an Irish uprising. The Germans promised help, but Casement considered it insufficient and returned to Ireland in April, 1916, hoping to secure a postponement of the Easter Rebellion (see IRELAND). Arrested immediately after his landing from a German submarine, he was tried, convicted, and hanged for treason. To further blacken his name, some British agents had circulated his diaries, which showed him to be a homosexual. The diaries were probably genuine, but the manner of their use helped to inspire controversy about the possibility of forgery. See biographies by Peter Singleton-Gates and Maurice Girodias (1959) and Brian Inglis (1974).

Caserta (käzĕr'tä), city (1971 pop. 62,928), capital of Caserta prov., Campania, S central Italy. It is an agricultural and commercial center and a transportation junction. The surrender of the German forces in Italy to the Allies took place there on April 29, 1945. Caserta is noted for its magnificent royal palace (built 1752–74) and gardens. There is an academy of aeronautics in the city.

Case Western Reserve University, at Cleveland; coeducational in most divisions; est. 1967 through the merger of the Case Institute of Technology (chartered 1880, opened 1881) and Western Reserve University (chartered and opened 1826). The university is made up of 13 schools and colleges, including three coordinate undergraduate resident colleges.

Casgrain, Henri Raymond (äNrē' rāmōN' käsgrăN'), 1831–1904, French Canadian historian. He traveled widely in Europe, collecting documents relevant to Canadian history, and wrote enthusiastic histories, such as *Légendes canadiennes* (1861), *Un Pélerinage au pays d'Évangéline* (1887), *Les Pionniers canadiens* (1876), and *Wolfe and Montcalm* ("Makers of Canada" series; rev. ed. 1926).

cash, popular term for ready MONEY. In commerce and banking the term is used in contradistinction to commercial paper. To "cash" such paper means to convert it into currency. In bookkeeping terms such as "petty cash" and "cashbook," the word has the same meaning. "Cash payment" is opposed to "credit," though cash payment may be made in coin, in notes, or by check.

Cashel (kă'shəl) [Irish,=castle], urban district (1971 pop. 2,693), Co. Tipperary, S central Republic of Ireland. Now an agricultural market, it was the ancient capital of the kings of Munster and was the stronghold of Brian Boru. On the Rock of Cashel, rising 300 ft (91 m) in the center of town, are the ruins of the 13th-century St. Patrick's Cathedral, a round tower (10th cent.), an ancient cross, and Cormac's Chapel (12th cent.). Below the Rock are the ruins of Hore Abbey (1272). Cashel is the seat of a Roman Catholic archbishop and of an Anglican bishop.

cashew (kăsh'o͞o, kəsho͞o'), tropical American tree (*Anacardium occidentale*) of the family Anacardiaceae (SUMAC family), valued chiefly for the cashew nut of commerce. The tree's acrid sap is used in making a varnish that protects woodwork and books from insects. The fruit is kidney-shaped, about an inch in length, and has a double shell. The kernel, which is sweet, oily, and nutritious, is much used for food in the tropics after being roasted to destroy the caustic juice. It yields a light-colored oil said to be the equal of olive oil and is utilized in various culinary ways. In the West Indies it is used to flavor wine, particularly Madeira, and is imported into Great Britain for this purpose. The nut grows on the end of a fleshy, pear-shaped stalk, called the cashew apple, which is white, yellow, or red, juicy and slightly acid, and is eaten or fermented to make wine. Cashews are classified in the division MAGNOLIOPHYTA, class Magnoliopsida, order Sapindales, family Anacardiaceae.

Casilinum (kăsĭlī'nəm), ancient town, Campania, S Italy, 18 mi (29 km) N of present-day Naples.

Founded (c.600 B.C.) probably by the Etruscans, it became (5th cent. B.C.) the capital of the Samnites. Under the Romans it was an important military station controlling the bridge of the Appian Way over the Volturno River. It was destroyed by the Saracens in the 9th cent. A.D.; the inhabitants of nearby CAPUA moved there soon after and changed its name from Casilinum to Capua.

Casimir I (kăs'əmēr), c.1015-1058, duke of Poland (c.1040-1058), son of MIESZKO II. He succeeded in reuniting the central Polish lands under the hegemony of the Holy Roman Empire, but he was never crowned king. He is also called Casimir the Restorer. His son and successor was Boleslaus II.

Casimir II, 1138-94, duke of Poland (1177-94), youngest son of Boleslaus III. A member of the PIAST dynasty, he drove his brother Mieszko III from power at Kraków in 1177 and became the principal duke of Poland. At the Congress of Leczyca (1180) the nobility and clergy, in return for privileges he had granted them, vested Casimir's descendants with hereditary rights to the crown. Casimir himself was never crowned king.

Casimir III, 1310-70, king of Poland (1333-70), son of Ladislaus I and last of the PIAST dynasty. Called Casimir the Great, he brought comparative peace to Poland. By the Congress of Visegrad (1335) he promised to recognize the suzerainty over Silesia of John of Luxemburg, king of Bohemia; in return John renounced all claim to the Polish throne. In 1339, Casimir officially acknowledged John's power. By the Treaty of Kalisz (1343) with the TEUTONIC KNIGHTS, Casimir consolidated his territories, and later he acquired much of the duchy of Galich-Vladmir. He strengthened the royal power at the expense of the nobility and clergy; codified Polish law in the Statute of Wislica, alleviating the lot of the peasants (hence he was "king of the peasants"); improved the condition of the Jews; encouraged industry, commerce, and agriculture; and founded (1364) the Univ. of Kraków. Casimir was succeeded by his Angevin nephew, King Louis I of Hungary.

Casimir IV, 1427-92, king of Poland (1447-92). He became (1440) ruler of Lithuania and in 1447 succeeded his brother Ladislaus III as king of Poland. He united the two nations more closely by placing them on an equal footing. With the Second Peace of Torun (1466) he ended a 13-year war against the Teutonic Knights in his favor; Poland gained territories and the Knights accepted Polish suzerainty over the area they retained. Calling (1467) the first Polish diet, he confirmed the privileges of the aristocracy. His marriage to an Austrian Hapsburg enabled his son Ladislaus to become king of Bohemia and later king of Hungary as Uladislaus II. Casimir was succeeded by his sons John I (1492-1501), Alexander I (1501-5), and Sigismund I (1506-48).

Casimir-Perier, Jean Paul Pierre (zhäN pōl pyĕr käzēmĕr'-pĕryā'), 1847-1907, French president (June, 1894-Jan., 1895). He held several cabinet posts before serving as premier in 1893. He created the ministry of colonies and acted to suppress anarchist activities. In 1894 he succeeded Sadi Carnot as president of the French republic. He was attacked by the increasingly important left-wing parties and resigned early in 1895. Félix Faure succeeded him.

casino or **cassino** (both: kəsē'nō), card game played with a full deck by two to four players. Four cards are dealt to each player, and four open cards are dealt to the table. Each player in turn must take in cards by matching his cards with cards of corresponding indices on the table (he may take two or more totaling his card's value); build, add to one or more table cards to total the index value of a card remaining in his hand (there are other building variations); or trail, lay a card face up on the table. The game ends after all the cards of the deck are dealt in successive hands of four cards each. The object is to take the greatest number of cards (counting 3 points); the greatest number of spades (counting 1 point); the ten of diamonds, or big casino (2 points); the two of spades, or little casino (1 point); and the aces (counting 1 point each). Casino probably originated in Italy.

Casiphia (kăsĭf'ēə, kăsĭfī'ə), place, on the way from Babylon to Jerusalem. Ezra 8.17.

Casiquiare (käsēkyä'rā), river, c.100 mi (160 km) long, S Venezuela. Also called the Canal Casiquiare, it is a branch of the Orinoco and flows SW to the Río Negro, thus linking the Orinoco and Amazon basins. The Casiquiare's flow was naturally diverted by the headward erosion of the Río Negro.

Casket Letters: see MARY QUEEN OF SCOTS.

Caslon, William (kăz'lən), 1692-1766, English type designer, b. Worcestershire. He worked first in London as an engraver of gunlocks, then set up his own found· · in 1716. The merits of Caslon's types were rediscovered after a brief eclipse in the popularity of John BASKERVILLE'S types. Caslon's individual letters are less impressive than those of Baskerville and Giambattista BODONI, but their regularity, legibility, and sensitive proportions constituted a remarkable achievement in design. His typefaces were used for most important printed works from c.1740 to c.1800. One such example is the first printed version of the United States Declaration of Independence. Some Caslon types are still in use. His business was carried on by his eldest son, William (1720-78). See biography by Johnson Ball (1974).

Casluhim (kăs'lyŏŏhĭm, kăslyōō'-), ancient unidentified tribe. Gen. 10.14; 1 Chron. 1.12.

Caso, Alfonso (älfōn'sō kä'sō), 1896-1970, Mexican archaeologist. An authority on the ancient high civilizations of Mexico, he directed explorations at MITLA and MONTE ALBÁN during the 1920s and 30s. Among his many books and articles are *The Religion of the Aztecs* (tr. 1937), *Thirteen Masterpieces of Mexican Archeology* (tr. 1938), and *The Aztecs: People of the Sun* (tr. 1958).

Casona, Alejandro (älähän'drō käsō'nä), 1903-, pseudonym of Alejandro Rodríguez Alvarez, Spanish poet and playwright, b. Besullo. Since 1937 he has lived in Latin America, spending much time writing and directing films in Argentina. Written with sensitivity and delicate irony, his plays combine poetic realism with philosophical ideas. They include *Nuestra Natacha* [our Natacha] (1936), *La barca sin pescador* [the boat without a fisherman] (1945), and *Carta a una desconocida* [letter to an unknown woman] (1957).

Casorati, Felice (fālē'chā käsōrä'tē), 1886-1963, Italian painter. Influenced by Beardsley and other English engravers, Casorati, together with CARRÀ, was involved in the symbolist movement. He was instrumental in the formation of the metaphysical school. An ironic tone and cool refinement are characteristic of his works (e.g., *Still Life,* c.1942-43; National Gall. of Modern Art, Rome).

Caspar: see WISE MEN OF THE EAST.

Casper, city (1970 pop. 39,361), alt. 5,123 ft (1,561 m), seat of Natrona co., E central Wyo., on the North Platte River; inc. 1889. It is a rail, distributing, processing, and trade center in a farming, ranching, and mineral-rich area. An oil boom town since the first well was tapped in 1890, it has large oil refineries and many oil-affiliated industries. Open-pit uranium mining nearby is important, and gas, coal, and bentonite deposits are also exploited. The city has wool and livestock markets, meat-packing plants, and a growing tourist industry. At this fording place on the Oregon Trail the Mormons in 1847 established a ferry, which was in the 1850s superseded by Platte Bridge. The city was founded (1888) with the coming of the railroad and burgeoned with the discovery of oil at Salt Creek, followed by the Teapot Dome and Big Muddy finds. In 1948 wells in the Lost Soldier field of Sweetwater co. brought another boom. Casper has a junior college. Nearby are the Central Wyoming Fairgrounds, with a county pioneer museum; Old Fort Caspar Museum (the fort has been restored; a clerk's error accounts for the later spelling of the name); and Casper Mt. (c.8,000 ft/2,440 m high), with a recreational area. Tourist attractions in the surrounding area include Hell's Half Acre, a spectacular eroded area; Independence Rock, a granite landmark on the Oregon Trail; and a petrified forest of subtropical trees.

Caspian Gates: see DERBENT, USSR.

Caspian Kara-Kum: see KARA-KUM, USSR.

Caspian Sea, Lat. *Mare Caspium* or *Mare Hyrcanium,* salt lake, c.144,000 sq mi (373,000 sq km), USSR and Iran, between Europe and Asia; the largest inland body of water in the world. The largest part lies in Soviet territory; only the extreme southern shore belongs to Iran. The Caspian is 92 ft (28 m) below sea level. It reaches its maximum depth, c.3,200 ft (980 m), in the south; the shallow northern half averages only about 17 ft (5 m). The Caucasus rise from the southwestern shore, and the Elburz Mts. parallel the southern coast. The Caspian receives the Volga (which supplies more than 75% of its inflow), Ural, Emba, Kura, and Terek rivers, but it has no outlet. The rate of evaporation is particularly high in the eastern inlet called KARA-BOGAZ-GOL, which is exploited for salt. Variations in evaporation account for the great changes in the size of the sea during the course of history. The construction of large dams and lakes on the Volga is the major reason for the recent lowering of the Caspian's water level, a problem that has reached serious proportions. The chief ports on the Caspian are Baku, a major oil center, and Astrakhan, at the mouth of the Volga. The sea is an important transportation artery; oil and oil products are shipped across it from Baku to Astrakhan and up the Volga. The Caspian is also of great importance for its fisheries and sealeries. The northern part of the sea is the chief source of beluga caviar.

Cass, Lewis, 1782-1866, American statesman, b. Exeter, N.H. He established (1802) himself as a lawyer in Zanesville, Ohio, became a member (1806) of the state legislature, and was U.S. marshal for Ohio from 1807 to 1812. In the War of 1812, Cass's command was included against his will in the forces that Gen. William Hull surrendered to the British at Detroit in Aug., 1812. Cass later fought with distinction at the battle of the Thames (Oct. 5, 1813). Left in command at Detroit, Cass was also appointed governor of Michigan Territory, a post he filled ably for 18 years (1813-31). As Secretary of War (1831-36), he favored removal of the Indians beyond the Mississippi and supported President Jackson in the nullification crisis. Minister to France (1836-42) and U.S. Senator from Michigan (1845-48, 1849-57), Cass was the Democratic candidate for President in 1848, but because of the defection of the antislavery Democrats led by Martin VAN BUREN, who became the candidate of the FREE-SOIL PARTY, he lost the election to the Whig candidate, Zachary Taylor. President Buchanan made (1857) Cass his Secretary of State, but he resigned in Dec., 1860, in protest against the decision not to reinforce the forts of Charleston, S.C. See biography by F. B. Woodford (1951).

Cassander (kəsăn'dər), 358-297 B.C., king of Macedon, one of the chief figures in the wars of the DIADOCHI. The son of Antipater, he was an officer under Alexander the Great, but there was ill feeling between them. After his father's death, Cassander engaged in vigorous warfare against Antipater's successor as regent, Polyperchon. He was successful, and by 318 he had a preponderant influence in Macedonia and Greece. Alexander's mother, Olympias, challenged this and put Philip III, Alexander's half brother, and many others to death. Cassander pursued her, crushed her army, and condemned her to death (316). Later, to strengthen his claim to the throne, he married Alexander's half sister, Thessalonica, and in 311 he murdered Alexander's widow, Roxana, and their son. He resisted the efforts of Antigonus I to rebuild the empire and was one of the coalition that defeated Antigonus and Demetrius at Ipsus in 301. Secure in his position, he founded the cities of Thessaloníki and Cassandreia (on the site of Potidaea) and rebuilt Thebes.

Cassandra (kəsăn'drə), in Greek legend, Trojan princess, daughter of Priam and Hecuba. She was given the power of prophecy by Apollo, but because she would not accept him as a lover, he changed her blessing to a curse, causing her prophecies never to be believed. While seeking refuge from the Greeks during the Trojan War, she was dragged from the temple of Athena and violated by the Locrian Ajax. After the war she was the slave of Agamemnon and was killed with him by his wife Clytemnestra.

Cassandre, Adolphe Mouron (ädôlf' mŏŏrôN' käsäN'drə), 1901-68, French poster artist, b. Russia. By 1923 he was celebrated as the artist of *Bûcheron* [woodcutter], a poster made for a cabinetmaker. Later works include posters for tennis matches, fairs, magazines, wines, shoes, horse races, steamships, and railways. Cassandre's originality made his designs classics of advertising.

Cassandreia, ancient Greece: see POTIDAEA.

Cassano d'Adda (käs-sä'nō däd'dä), town (1971 pop. 13,863), Lombardy, N Italy, on the Adda River. It is an agricultural and industrial center. At Cassano d'Adda the French under Vendôme defeated the imperial forces under Prince Eugene of Savoy in 1705 (see SPANISH SUCCESSION, WAR OF THE). The town is also the site of the victory (1799) of the Russians under Suvarov over the French under Moreau during the French Revolutionary Wars.

Cassatt, Mary (kəsăt'), 1845-1926, American figure painter and etcher, b. Pittsburgh. Most of her life was spent in France, where she was greatly influenced by her great French contemporaries, particularly Manet and Degas, whose friendship and esteem she enjoyed. She allied herself with the impressionists early in her career. Motherhood was Cassatt's most frequent subject. Her pictures are notable for their refreshing simplicity, vigorous treatment, and pleasing color. She excelled also as a pastelist and etcher, and her drypoints and color prints are greatly admired. She is well represented in public and private galleries in the United States. Her best-known pictures include several versions of *Mother and Child* (Metropolitan Mus.; Mus. of Fine Arts, Boston; Worcester, Mass., Art Mus.); *Lady at the Tea-Table* (Metropolitan Mus.); *Modern Women,* a mural painted for the Women's Building of the Chicago exposition; and a portrait of the artist's mother. See catalog by A. D. Breeskin (1970); biography by J. M. Carson (1966).

cassava (kəsä'və) or **manioc** (măn'ēŏk), any plant of the genus *Manihot* of the family Euphorbiaceae (SPURGE family). The roots, which resemble sweet potatoes and are eaten in much the same way, yield cassava starch, a staple food in the tropics. The cassava is native to Brazil and has long been cultivated there by the Indians as a major food source. Cassava roots are also fermented to make an alcoholic beverage, are the source of TAPIOCA, or Brazilian arrowroot, and are utilized in other ways, e.g., for cotton sizing and laundry starch. Most cassava flour is made from *M. esculenta,* sometimes called bitter cassava because of the presence in the raw roots of prussic acid in sufficient quantities to be deadly. This poison is dispelled by cooking. Some cultivated varieties with a lesser acid content, called sweet cassava, are edible raw and can be used for fodder. Cassava is classified in the division MAGNOLIOPHYTA, class Magnoliopsida, order Euphorbiales, family Euphorbiaceae.

Cassegrain focus: see TELESCOPE.

Cassel, Gustav (go͞os'täf kä'səl), 1866–1945, Swedish economist and authority on international monetary problems. He was a delegate to many world economic conferences and wrote valuable papers on foreign exchange. Among his books are *Money and Foreign Exchange after 1914* (1922), *Fundamental Thoughts on Economics* (1925), and *On Quantitative Thinking in Economics* (1935).

cassia (kăsh'ə): see CINNAMON; SENNA.

Cassian, John (kăsh'ən) (Johannes Cassianus), 360–435, Christian monk and theologian. He settled at Marseilles (415) and established religious houses for men and for women. He was attacked for Semi-Pelagianism (see PELAGIANISM), but he was trusted in Rome. His *Collations,* spiritual writings for monks, and his *Institutes,* on monasticism, had critical influence on the thought of St. Benedict, St. Gregory, and hence on all Benedictines, in matters touching ascetic and mystical life. He wrote against Nestorianism. See study by Owen Chadwick (2d ed. 1968).

Cassini (käs-sē'nē), name of a family of Italian-French astronomers, four generations of whom were directors of the Paris Observatory. **Gian Domenico Cassini,** 1625–1712, was born in Italy and distinguished himself while at Bologna by his studies of the sun and planets, particularly Jupiter; he determined rotational periods for Jupiter, Mars, and Venus. He was called to Paris in 1669 to supervise the building of the Royal Observatory and remained there to direct it. While at Paris he discovered four of Saturn's satellites, studied the division in the planet's ring system that now bears his name, and began the mapping of the meridian passing through Paris in order to verify the Cartesian hypothesis of the elongation of the earth. His son **Jacques Cassini,** 1677–1756, took over the observatory after 1700 and continued the mapping of the Paris meridian, adding to it a measurement of the perpendicular to the arc in 1733–34. The triumph of the opposing Newtonian hypothesis of the flattening of the earth caused him to retire in 1740, and he was replaced by his son, **Cesar-François Cassini de Thury,** 1714–84, who continued his father's geodesic work and planned the first modern map of France. On his death, his son **Jean-Dominique Cassini,** 1748–1845, undertook the reorganization and restoration of the observatory. He completed his father's map of France and participated in the geodesic operations joining the Paris and Greenwich meridians. He lost his post in 1793 because of his monarchial views and was briefly imprisoned by the revolutionary government in 1794. He abandoned scientific work in 1800, becoming president of the General Council of Oise. He was decorated by Napoleon I and Louis XVIII and retired in 1818.

Cassini's division: see SATURN.

Cassino (käs-sē'nō), town (1971 pop. 24,695), in Latium, central Italy, in the Apennines, on the Rapido River. It is a commercial and agricultural center. The peace between Emperor Frederick II and Pope Gregory IX was signed there in 1230. During World War II (late 1943) the town and the nearby Benedictine abbey of MONTE CASSINO were strongly defended by Germans blocking the Allied advance on Rome. After five months of concentrated ground attacks and attempts to divert German troops by landings at ANZIO and NETTUNO, the Allies finally captured the German positions in May, 1944. Cassino was reduced to rubble but was largely rebuilt. Of note is the cathedral (18th cent., rebuilt after 1944), which contains the alleged remains of St. Benedict and his sister St. Scholastica. Until 1871, Cassino was called San Germano.

cassino: see CASINO.

Cassiodorus (Flavius Magnus Aurelius Cassiodorus Senator) (kăshōdō'rəs), c.485–c.585, Roman statesman and author. He held high office under Theodoric the Great and the succeeding Gothic rulers of Italy, who gave him the task of putting into official Latin their state papers and correspondence. These he later collected as *Variae epistolae* (tr. by Thomas Hodgkin, 1886). After retiring to his estate he founded two monasteries; in one of these the monks devoted leisure time to copying old manuscripts, which were thus preserved. Among Cassiodorus' works were his *History of the Goths,* preserved in the abridgment by JORDANES, and a treatise on orthography.

Cassiopeia (kăs"ēəpē'ə), in Greek mythology: see ANDROMEDA.

Cassiopeia, in astronomy, prominent northern CONSTELLATION located almost directly opposite the Big Dipper across the north celestial pole. Five bright stars in the constellation form a rough *W* (or *M*) in the sky. Some see in this formation the shape of a chair known as Cassiopeia's Chair. Tycho's Star, a SUPERNOVA, appeared in the constellation in 1572 and disappeared in 1574. In this constellation is located Cassiopeia A, a discrete radio source emitting 21-cm radiation with great intensity. Cassiopeia reaches its highest point in the evening sky in November, but because of its location near the pole it is visible throughout the year to most northern observers.

Cassirer, Ernst (ĕrnst käsĕr'ər), 1874–1945, German philosopher. He was a professor at the Univ. of Hamburg from 1919 until 1933, when he went to Oxford; he later taught at Yale and Columbia. A leading representative of the Marburg Neo-Kantian school, Cassirer at first devoted himself to a critical-historical study of the problem of knowledge. This work bore fruit in the monumental *Das Erkenntnisproblem in der Philosophie und Wissenschaft der neueren Zeit* (3 vol., 1906–20) and *Substanzbegriff und Funktionsbegriff* (1910, tr. *Substance and Function,* 1923). In his chief work, *Philosophie der symbolischen Formen* (3 vol., 1923–29, tr. *Philosophy of Symbolic Forms,* 1953–57), he applied the principles of Kantian philosophy toward the formation of a critique of culture. His view that all cultural achievements (including language, myth, and science) are the results of man's symbolic activity led Cassirer to a new conception of man as the "symbolic animal." Cassirer wrote many other studies on science, myth, and various historical subjects. These include two written in English: *An Essay on Man* (1944) and *Myth of the State* (1946). See P. A. Schilpp, ed., *The Philosophy of Ernst Cassirer* (1949, repr. 1958); studies by C. H. Hamburg (1956) and S. W. Itzkoff (1971).

cassiterite (kəsĭt'ərīt), heavy, brown-to-black mineral, tin oxide, SnO_2, crystallizing in the tetragonal system. It is found as short prismatic crystals and as irregular masses, usually in veins and replacement deposits associated with granites. Since it is hard, heavy, and resistant to weathering, it often concentrates in alluvial deposits derived from cassiterite-bearing rocks. It is the principal ore of tin and is mined in many countries; the most important sources are Malaysia, Thailand, China, Indonesia, Bolivia, and the USSR. Except for Bolivia, nearly all of this production is from alluvial deposits.

Cassites: see KASSITES.

Cassius (kăsh'əs), ancient Roman family. There were a number of well-known members. **Spurius Cassius Viscellinus,** d. c.485 B.C., seems to have been consul several times. In 493 B.C. he negotiated a treaty establishing equal military assistance between Rome and the Latin cities. In 486 he proposed that land be distributed equally among the Roman and the Latin poor (see AGRARIAN LAWS). It is said that the patricians, outraged at the suggestion, accused Cassius of royal aspirations and had him executed. A descendant, **Quintus Cassius Longinus,** d. 45 B.C., won a reputation for greed and corruption when he was a quaestor in Spain (54 B.C.). He and ANTONY, as tribunes in 49 B.C., vetoed the attempts of the senate to deprive Julius CAESAR of his army. When the senate overrode the tribunes on Jan. 7, 49 B.C., Cassius and Antony fled to Caesar, who crossed the Rubicon and began the civil war. After Caesar's triumph, Cassius was given (47 B.C.) a post in Farther Spain. There was a rebellion against him, and Caesar had to come from Italy to put it down. Cassius died in a shipwreck. Best known of all was **Caius Cassius Longinus,** d. 42 B.C., leader in the successful conspiracy to assassinate Julius Caesar. He fought as a quaestor under Marcus Licinius Crassus (see under CRASSUS, family) at CARRHAE in 53 B.C. and saved what was left of the army after the battle. He supported Pompey against Caesar but was pardoned after the battle of PHARSALA. He was made (44 B.C.) peregrine praetor and Caesar promised to make him governor of Syria. Before the promise could be fulfilled, Cassius had become ringleader in the plot to kill Caesar. The plot involved more than 60 men (including Marcus Junius Brutus, Publius Servilius Casca, and Lucius Tillius Cimber) and was successfully accomplished in the senate on the Ides of March in 44 B.C. When the people were aroused by Antony against the conspirators, Cassius went to Syria. He managed to capture DOLABELLA at Laodicea and coordinated his own movements with those of Brutus. Antony and Octavian (later AUGUSTUS) met them in battle at Philippi. In the first engagement Cassius, thinking the battle lost, committed suicide. Another of the conspirators was **Caius Cassius Parmensis,** d. 30 B.C. He fought at Philippi and later with Sextus Pompeius. He later sided with Antony in the naval battle off Actium and was killed by order of Octavian.

Cassius Dio Cocceianus: see DION CASSIUS.

Cassivellaunus (kă"sĭvĭlô'nəs), fl. 54 B.C., British chieftain, a leader in the resistance against the invasion of Julius Caesar in 54 B.C. Caesar crossed the Thames River into Cassivellaunus' home country. Aided by discontented British tribes, he attacked Cassivellaunus in his strong fort in the marshes (probably at Wheathampstead, Hertfordshire) and drove the Britons out with heavy losses. Cassivellaunus sued for peace, which Caesar granted in return for hostages and annual tribute.

cassone (käs-sô'nā), the Italian term for chest or coffer, usually a bridal or dower chest, highly ornate and given prominence in the home. Major artists such as Uccello and Botticelli painted cassone panels, and prominent sculptors were also employed to carve elaborate chests. The cassone was usually decorated with mythological or historical episodes. It became one of the first means of bold secular expression in Renaissance art.

cassowary (kăs'əwâr"ē), common name for a flightless, swift-running, pugnacious forest bird of Australia and the Malay Archipelago, smaller than the ostrich and emu. The plumage is dark and glossy and the head and neck unfeathered, wattled, and brilliantly colored, with variations in the coloring in different species. The head bears a horny crest. The female is larger than the male, though both sexes are similar in color. They are monogamous and nest in shallow nests of leaves on the ground in forests. Only the male incubates the female's three to six dark-green eggs. Cassowaries are primarily nocturnal. Their diet consists mainly of fruits and berries, although some eat insects and small animals. Cassowaries are notoriously vicious and have attacked and killed men with their sharp, spikelike toenails. They are fast runners, attaining speeds up to 30 mi (48 km) per hr. Cassowaries are classified in the phylum CHORDATA, subphylum Vertebrata, class Aves, order Casuariiformes, family Casuariidae.

Castagno, Andrea del (ändrĕ'ä dĕl kästä'nyō), c.1423–1457, major Florentine painter of the early Renaissance. His first recorded painting (1440; now destroyed), effigies of hanged men, enemies to the Florentine regime, brought him fame in spite of its disconcerting subject. Two years later he was in Venice, frescoing the ceiling of the chapel in San Zaccaria. He returned to Florence and c.1445 began the cycle of the *Passion of Christ* for the church of Sant' Apollonia. Best known of these scenes is the *Last Supper.* Castagno combined a rigorous perspective with harsh, metallic lighting that greatly intensified the drama of the scene. He decorated the hall of the Villa Pandolfini with heroic figures, including Pippo Spano, Dante, Petrarch, and Boccaccio. Here the influence of Donatello can be felt, particularly in the vitality and plastic rendering of forms. In the Annunziata Church there is a powerful conception of the *Savior and St. Julian.* His last dated work is the equestrian statue of Niccolò da Tolentino in the cathedral. Other examples of his art are *David* (National Gall. of Art, Washington, D.C.) and the *Resurrection* (Frick Coll., New York City).

Castaldi, Pamfilo (päm'fēlō kästäl'dē), c.1398–c.1490, Italian humanist and printer. He was the first printer of the city of Milan. Some credit him with the invention of movable type. See GUTENBERG, JOHANN.

Castalia (kăstā'lyə), in Greek mythology, spring on Mt. Parnassus. Named for a nymph, it was sacred to the MUSES and was said to give poetic inspiration to those who bathed in it.

Castalion or **Castellio, Sébastien** (kăstăl'yən, kăstĕl'yō), 1515–63, French Protestant theologian. Castalion was with Calvin at Strasbourg and Geneva until he split with Calvin over doctrinal differences and moved to Basel. He obtained a chair of Greek literature in the university there. Castalion is known for his defense of religious toleration in the preface to his Latin translation of the Bible (1551). In 1554 he published, under the pseudonym Martinus Bellius, *Concerning Heretics* (tr. 1935), in which he protested the execution of Servetus. The name also appears as Castellion and Châtillon. See Stefan Zweig, *Right to Heresy* (1936).

castanets, percussion instruments known to the ancient Egyptians and Greeks, possibly of Oriental origin, now used primarily in Spanish dance music or

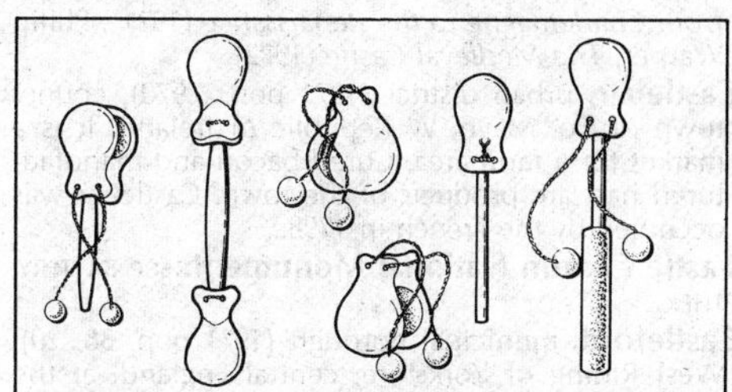

Castanets

imitations of it. There are many kinds, the most common consisting of two small matching pieces of hard wood or ivory, joined at the inner edge and used with a thin strap in the player's hand; they are snapped together between the palm and fingers. Castanets are also occasionally used in orchestral music.

caste [Port. *casta*=basket], ranked groups based on heredity within rigid systems of social stratification, especially those that constitute Hindu India. Some scholars, in fact, deny that true caste systems are found outside India. The caste is a closed group whose members are severely restricted in their choice of occupation and degree of social participation. Marriage outside the caste is prohibited. Social status is determined by the caste of one's birth and may only rarely be transcended. Certain religious minorities may voluntarily constitute a quasi-caste within a society, but they are less apt to be characterized by cultural distinctiveness than by their self-imposed social segregation. A specialized labor group may operate as a caste within a society otherwise free of such distinctions (e.g., the ironsmiths in parts of Africa). In general, caste functions to maintain the status quo in a society. Nowhere is caste better exemplified by degree of complexity and systematic operation than in India. The Indian term for caste is *jati,* which generally designates a group varying in size from a handful to many thousands. There are thousands of such *jatis,* and each has its distinctive rules, customs, and modes of government. The term *varna* (literally meaning "color") refers to the ancient and somewhat ideal fourfold division of Hindu society: (1) the Brahmans, the priestly and learned class; (2) the Kshatriyas, the warriors and rulers; (3) the Vaisyas, farmers and merchants; and (4) the Sudras, peasants and laborers. These divisions may have corresponded to what were formerly large, broad, undifferentiated social classes. Below the category of Sudras were the untouchables, or Panchamas (literally "fifth division"), who performed the most menial tasks. Although there has been much confusion between the two, *jati* and *varna* are different in origin as well as function. The various castes in any given region of India are hierarchically organized, with each caste corresponding roughly to one or the other of the *varna* categories. Traditionally, caste mobility has taken the form of movement up or down the *varna* scale. Indian castes are rigidly differentiated by rituals and beliefs that pervade all thought and conduct (see DHARMA). Extreme upper and lower castes differ so widely in habits of everyday life and worship that only the close intergrading of intervening castes and the intercaste language communities serve to hold them together within the single framework of Indian society. The explanation that Indian castes were originally based on color lines to preserve the racial and cultural purity of conquering groups is inadequate historically to account for the physical and cultural variety of such groups. Castes may reflect distinctiveness of religious practice, occupation, locale, culture status, or tribal affiliation, either exclusively or in part. Divergence within a caste on any of these lines will tend to produce fission that may, in time, result in the formation of new castes. Every type of social group as it appears may be fitted into this system of organizing society. The occupational barriers among Indian castes have been breaking down slowly under economic pressures since the 19th cent., but social distinctions have been more persistent. Attitudes toward the untouchables only began to change in the 1930s under the influence of Mohandas Gandhi's teachings. Although untouchability was declared illegal in 1949, resistance to change has remained strong. As increased industrialization produced new occupations and new social and political functions evolved, the caste system adapted and thus far has not been destroyed. See McKim Marriott, ed., *Village India* (1955); M. N. Srinivas, *Social Change in Modern India* (1966); Anthony de Reuck and Julie Knight, ed., *Caste and Race* (1967); Louis Dumont, *Homo Hierarchicus: The Caste System and Its Implications* (1970).

Castelar y Ripoll, Emilio (āmē'lyō kästälär' ē rēpō'lyə), 1832–99, Spanish statesman and author. A professor of history and philosophy at the Univ. of Madrid and a republican leader, he was foreign minister and then president (1873–74) of Spain's first republic. Ruling virtually as a dictator, he was partially successful in restoring order to the war-torn country, but he, and the republic, were overthrown by a military coup d'etat. After the restoration (1875) of Alfonso XII he was a member of the political opposition in the Cortes. He wrote historical, political, and literary works.

Castel Gandolfo (kästĕl' gändôl'fō), town (1971 pop. 4,694), in Latium, central Italy, in the Alban Hills, overlooking Lake Albano. Possibly occupying the site of ancient Alba Longa, it is the papal summer residence. The papal palace (17th cent.), its magnificent gardens, the Vatican observatory (founded 1936), and the Villa Barbarini enjoy extraterritorial rights. The Church of St. Thomas of Villanova was designed (17th cent.) by Bernini.

Castellammare di Stabia (kästĕl"läm-mä'rā dē stä'byä), city (1971 pop. 68,656), in Campania, S Italy, on the Bay of Naples. A summer resort and spa, it has thermal mineral springs that have been used since Roman times. It is also a commercial and industrial center, with navy yards founded in 1783. Manufactures include food products, paper, and cement. The city was built on the site of Stabiae, a favorite Roman resort, which was buried in the eruption of Mt. Vesuvius in A.D. 79. The royal villa, Quisisana (built 1310, rebuilt 1820), is now a hotel.

Castellani, Sir Aldo, 1877–1971, British-Italian bacteriologist, b. Florence, Italy. He demonstrated the cause and mode of transmission of sleeping sickness (with Sir David Bruce and David Nabarro, 1903), discovered the spirochete of yaws (1905), and did other original work in bacteriology and in parasitic diseases of the skin. He also lectured in tropical medicine in London and Ceylon, was professor of tropical medicine at Tulane Univ. and at Louisiana State Univ., and founded in Rome the Royal Institute for Tropical Diseases. With A. J. Chalmers he wrote *Manual of Tropical Medicine* (1910, 3d ed. 1919). He was knighted in 1928. See his autobiography (1960).

Castellio or **Castellion, Sébastien:** see CASTALION, SÉBASTIEN.

Castello or **Castelli, Bernardo** (bārnär'dō kästĕl'lō, -tĕl'lē), 1557–1629, Italian painter of the Genoese school; pupil of Cambiaso, whose style he imitated. He was a friend of Tasso and made the designs for *Jerusalem Delivered,* some of which were subsequently engraved by Agostino Carracci. Castello executed numerous works in the churches of Genoa. His son, **Valerio Castello,** 1625–59, a painter of historical scenes, was influenced by Procaccini and Correggio but created a fine style of his own. He executed many frescoes of high merit for the churches and monasteries of Genoa. His best-known painting is *The Rape of the Sabines* (Genoa).

Castello, Giovanni Battista (jōvän'nē bät-tēs'tä), c.1509–c.1569. Italian painter and architect; called Il Bergamasco to distinguish him from Bernardo Castello, who also worked in Genoa. Giovanni was born near Bergamo where many of his works still exist. After a trip to Rome he returned to Genoa, where he worked with Luca Cambiaso on the Palazzo Imperiale. Giovanni's propensity for grotesque decorations is best seen in the Palazzo Pallavicino (now the Palazzo Garega-Cataldi). In 1567 he went to Spain, where he became architect and painter to Philip II.

Castello, Valerio: see CASTELLO, BERNARDO.

Castellón de la Plana (kästĕlyōn' dā lä plä'nä), city (1970 pop. 93,968), capital of Castellón de la Plana prov., E Spain, in Valencia, 3 mi (4.8 km) from its Mediterranean port of Grao. It is a farm center with fishing, mining, and handcraft industries. The city was reconquered (1233) from the Moors by James I of Aragon. In 1251 it was moved 2 mi (3.2 km) from a hilltop to its present site on a plain (hence "de la Plana").

Castelnau, Michel de (mēshĕl' də kästĕlnō'), c.1520–1592, French diplomat and soldier. He early attracted the favorable notice of the cardinal of Lorraine (Charles de Guise) and performed important services for Anne, duc de Montmorency, and King Henry II. In the religious wars he went on missions to England, Scotland, the Netherlands, and Savoy and fought in the royal army; from 1575 to 1585 he served as ambassador to England. Upon his return he fell out with the Guises and rendered valuable services against the Catholic LEAGUE to kings Henry III and Henry IV. Although a Catholic, he favored a policy of moderation toward the Huguenots. He left valuable memoirs.

Castelo Branco, Humberto (o͞ombĕr'to͞o kəshtĕ'lo͞o brăng'ko͞o), 1900–1967, president of Brazil (1964–67). An army officer, he served as chief of staff of the Brazilian army before participating in the coup that ousted President João Goulart in April, 1964. Elected provisional president by Congress to succeed Goulart, he wielded enormous power, curtailing political freedoms and imposing sweeping economic reforms. The latter, while stringent and unpopular, helped spur the country's economic growth, curb inflation, and reestablish Brazil's credit rating abroad. He was succeeded in office by his war minister, Artur da Costa e Silva.

Castel Sant' Angelo (kästĕl' säntän'jälō), **Hadrian's Mausoleum,** or **Hadrian's Mole,** massive construction on the right bank of the Tiber in Rome. Originally built (A.D. 135–39) by Emperor Hadrian as a MAUSOLEUM for himself and his successors, it was later decorated and fortified as a place of refuge for the popes and was connected to the Vatican by a secret passage. It was used as a fortress and prison until 1870 and is now a museum.

Castiglione, Baldassare, Conte (bäldäs-sä'rā kōn'tā kästēlyō'nā), 1478–1529, Italian soldier, author, and statesman attached to the court of the duke of Milan and later in the service of the duke of Urbino. His famous *Libro del cortegiano* (1528, tr. *The Courtier,* 1561), a treatise on etiquette, social problems, and intellectual accomplishments, is one of the great books of its time. Written at a time when the author served as envoy to Pope Leo X, it gives a vivid and elegant picture of 15th- and 16th-century court life. His book had enormous influence on behavior at courts as far away as England, where it contributed to an ideal of aristocracy embodied in the person and accomplishments of Sir Philip Sidney. Castiglione's portrait was painted by Raphael (c.1515), his tomb designed by Giulio Romano, and his epitaph composed by Bembo.

Castiglione, Giovanni Benedetto (jōvän'nē bānādĕt'tō), 1610?–1670, Italian painter and engraver of the Genoese school, called Il Grechetto. In his later years Castiglione was court painter at Mantua. He is best known for his landscapes and rural scenes with animals, but he also painted portraits and religious works, such as the *Nativity* (Genoa). His pictures are full of life and movement, their colors rich and glowing. Castiglione's etchings, numbering about 70 and reflecting the influence of Rembrandt, are among the best produced in Italy during his century. His treatment of light and shade is particularly fine. A number of his oil-on-paper sketches are in the Royal Library at Windsor.

Castiglione delle Stiviere (kästēlyō'nā dĕl'lā stēvyĕ'rā), town (1971 pop. 13,328), Lombardy, N Italy. The French army under Napoleon I and Augereau defeated the Austrians there in 1796.

Castile (kăstēl'), Span. *Castilla* (kästē'lyä), region and former kingdom, central and N Spain, traditionally divided into Old Castile (Span. *Castilla la Vieja*) in the north and New Castile (Span. *Castilla la Nueva*) in the south. Old Castile (1970 pop. 2,135,788) comprises the provinces of Ávila, Burgos, Logroño, Santander, Segovia, Soria, Valladolid, and Palencia, named after their chief cities. New Castile (1970 pop. 5,164,026) comprises the provinces and cities of Ciudad Real, Cuenca, Guadalajara, Madrid, and

Toledo. Castile is generally a vast underdeveloped region surrounding the highly industrialized Madrid area. It includes most of the high plateau of central Spain, across which rise the rugged Sierra de Guadarrama and the Sierra de Gredos, forming a natural boundary between Old and New Castile. The upper Duero, the Tagus, and Guadiana rivers form the chief basins. The soil of Castile, ravaged by centuries of erosion, is poor, and the climate severe. Old Castile has grain growing and sheep raising; in more fertile areas, especially in New Castile, olive oil and grapes are produced. Scattered forests yield timber and naval stores. Agricultural methods are largely primitive, but irrigation, introduced by the Romans and the Moors, has progressed significantly in recent decades. Of the industries which flourished in the 14th and 15th cent. (particularly wool and silk textiles), few have survived. Mineral resources, except for the rich mercury mines of Almadén, are of minor economic importance. The name Castile derives from the many castles built there by the Christian nobles early in the reconquest from the Moors (8th-9th cent.). Old Castile at first was a county of the kingdom of León, with Burgos its capital. Its nobles (notably Fernán González) secured virtual autonomy by the 10th cent. Sancho III of Navarre, who briefly annexed the county, made it into a kingdom for his son, Ferdinand I, in 1035. León was first united with Castile in 1037, but complex dynastic rivalries delayed the permanent union of the two realms, which was achieved under Ferdinand III in 1230. The Castilian kings played a leading role in the fight against the Moors, from whom they wrested New Castile. They also had to struggle against the turbulent nobles and were involved in dynastic disputes which plunged the country into civil war (see ALFONSO X). PETER THE CRUEL limited the vast privileges of the nobles, but they were permanently curbed only late in the 15th cent. In 1479, after Isabella I had defeated the dynastic claims of Juana la Beltraneja, a personal union of Castile and Aragón was established under Isabella and her husband, FERDINAND II of Aragón. The union was confirmed with the accession (1516) of their grandson, Charles I (later Emperor CHARLES V), to the Spanish kingdoms. Charles suppressed the uprisings of the COMUNEROS in 1520-21. With the decline of Catalan and Valencia during that period, Castile became the dominant power in Spain. It was the core of the Spanish monarchy, centralized in Madrid (the capital after the 16th cent.). Its dialect became the standard literary language of Spain, and the character of its people—proud and austere—has become typical of the entire Spanish nation.

Castilla, Ramón (rämōn' kästē'yä), 1797-1867, president of Peru (1845-51, 1855-62). He fought under Antonio José de Sucre in the revolution against Spain (1821-24) in Peru and took part in the civil wars that followed. An army general, energetic and resolute, he twice eliminated his rivals by armed force to become president. He developed the guano, saltpeter, and nitrate industries, helped to reorganize finances, abolished slavery in Peru, and promulgated (1860) a new constitution that became the basis of future Peruvian government. Although he overlooked considerable administrative corruption, Castilla brought unwonted order and a measure of prosperity to the republic.

Castillejo, Cristóbal de (krēstō'bäl dā kästēlyā'hō), c.1490-1550, Spanish poet of the Renaissance. As secretary to the king of Bohemia, Castillejo visited Vienna and other European cities. His poems are grouped under the titles *Obras de amores* [works of love] and *Obras morales y de devoción* [moral and devotional works]. His *Diálogo de la vida de corte* is a clever and perceptive picture of life at court. He championed the traditional Spanish as against the Italian verse form.

Castillo de San Marcos National Monument: see SAINT AUGUSTINE, Fla.

Castillon-la-Bataille (kästēyôN"-lä-bätä'yə), town (1968 pop. 3,102), Gironde dept., SW France, in Guienne, on the Dordogne River. An ancient port, it has a wine and liqueur trade and a leather industry. There, in 1453, the French defeated the English in the final great battle of the Hundred Years War. It was formerly called Castillon or Castillon-et-Capitourlan.

casting or **founding,** shaping of metal by melting and pouring into a mold. Most castings, especially large ones, are made in sand molds. Sand, mixed with a binder to hold it together, is pressed around a wooden pattern that leaves a cavity in the sand. Molten metal is poured into the cavity and allowed to solidify. Permanent metal molds are used to make many small, simple parts; shell molding gives greater accuracy for a large volume of semiprecision parts. A two-step process, investment casting, produces small, complex shapes. Wax or plastic replicas of the parts are molded in accurate metal molds. These replicas are covered with sand in a box to make the final mold. When the whole mold is heated, the replica melts, leaving behind a cavity into which metal is poured. Large numbers of small, precise parts of metals that have a low melting point, such as zinc, are made by DIE-CASTING; in an automatic process, molten metal is forced under pressure into metal molds. Cast iron and cast steel are more brittle than forged iron and forged steel (see FORGING).

casting, plaster: see PLASTER CASTING.

cast iron: see IRON.

Castle, Barbara Anne, 1911–, British politician. She entered Parliament in 1945 as a Labour member and soon established herself as an influential member of the party's left wing. She served (1950) on the party's national executive committee and was (1958-59) party chairman. When the Labour party was returned to power in 1964, she became minister of overseas development. As minister of transport (1965-68), she instituted a breath-analyzer test for suspected drunken drivers. From 1968 to 1970 she served as minister for employment and productivity; in this capacity she administered the Labour government's wage-restraint policy in the face of trade-union opposition. While Labour was out of office (1970-74) she was opposition spokesman on social security, and she became minister for social security when the party returned to power in 1974.

Castle, Vernon, 1887-1918, English dancer, originally named Vernon Castle Blythe. He studied civil engineering, but turned to the stage and made his debut in 1907. In 1911 he married **Irene Foote** (1893-1969, b. New Rochelle, N.Y.), and in Paris in 1912 their versions of such dances as the "Texas Tommy" and the "Grizzly Bear" brought them fame. The team originated the "Castle walk," the one-step, and the "hesitation" waltz, and Mrs. Castle introduced bobbed hair and the slim, boyish figure to the ballroom and the world of fashion. Castle was a pilot during World War I and was killed during a training mission in Texas. See Irene Castle, *Castles in the Air* (1958).

castle, type of fortified dwelling characteristic of the Middle Ages. FORTIFICATION of towns had been devised since antiquity, but in the 9th cent. feudal lords began to develop the private fortress-residence known as the castle. It served the twofold function of residence and fortress because of the conditions of medieval life, in which war was endemic. The site of the castle was preferably on a defensible height. England and France, in general, did not afford such inaccessible locations as did the Rhine valley in Germany. The castle of W Europe was a Norman creation, an outgrowth of the 10th- and 11th-century mound castle, which consisted of a great artificial mound of earth, the motte, surrounded by a dry ditch, or fosse, and surmounted by a wooden blockhouse and its encircling palisade. Until well into the 12th cent., the only English development was the occasional substitution of a massive masonry keep inside the palisade—a form typified in the Tower of London. As siegecraft (see SIEGE) was evolved, provisions were made for an aggressive defense. A castle that became the model for many English and Norman castles was the formidable castle built at Arques in Normandy by Henry I of England. A square donjon, or keep, was set against the strong outer walls of masonry; the entrance was protected by a double gate, two flanking round towers, and advanced earthworks. The place enclosed by the outer circuit of walls was usually divided into two courts, or baileys, by a palisade. Subterranean passages made detection of underground forays easy. In the Near East the Crusaders developed great castles with double circuits of curving outer walls and towers or turrets to overlook all sections of the wall. The form of these castles had an influence throughout the Continent and the British Isles. Thus early in the 13th cent. the medieval castle, a mixture of Norman, English, and Byzantine elements, reached its full flower, as typified in the Château Gaillard on the Seine in France and in Alnwick and the Conisborough in England. In general, the castle was planned for security; the living quarters were rude, poorly lighted, and without provisions for comfort. Typically, the keep contained the living quarters of the lord and his family, the rooms of state, and the prison cells. Two independent systems of walls, each a fortress in itself, extended around the keep; the sections of the walls were flanked by towers, usually round, and the principal entrance was protected by strong gate towers, the massive gateway, with its PORTCULLIS and drawbridge, and the barbican, or advanced outwork. The defenders operated from galleries at the tops of walls and from the flat roofs of towers, whose battlements were provided with recesses with flaring sides, called embrasures, and openings, or machicolations, for shooting and dropping missiles on the attackers. The fully developed castle was thus marked by successive series of defenses; the fall of the outer works did not necessarily mean the loss of the entire castle. With the use of gunpowder and consequent perfection of ARTILLERY, the castle lost its military importance. The manor house replaced the castle as the residence of the wealthy landowner, but the architectural influence of the castle has persisted even to the present day, when crenelations and towers are still found in country houses. See CHÂTEAU. See S. Toy, *History of Fortification from 3000 B.C. to A.D. 1700* (1955); W. D. Simpson, *Castles in Britain* (1966); Alberto Weissmüller, *Castles from the Heart of Spain* (1967); William Anderson, *Castles of Europe from Charlemagne to the Renaissance* (1971); Philip Warner, *The Medieval Castle* (1972).

Castlebar, urban district (1971 pop. 5,970), county town of Co. Mayo, W Republic of Ireland. It is a market for a farm area. Cured bacon and manufactured hats are products of the town. Castlebar was occupied by the French in 1798.

Castle Clinton National Monument: see BATTERY, THE.

Castleford, municipal borough (1971 pop. 38,220), West Riding of Yorkshire, central England, at the junction of the Aire and Calder rivers. Chartered as a municipal borough in 1955, it has bottleworks, chemical works, and collieries. The site of an ancient Roman town lies within its borders. In 1974, Castleford became part of the new metropolitan county of West Yorkshire.

Castlemaine, Barbara, countess of: see CLEVELAND, BARBARA VILLIERS, DUCHESS OF.

Castle Pinckney, fortification at the harbor entrance of Charleston, S.C.; built in 1797, when war with France seemed imminent, and named for the American diplomat Charles Cotesworth Pinckney. It was a factor in the confrontation at FORT SUMTER (1860), the start of the Civil War.

Castlereagh, Robert Stewart, 2d **Viscount** (kă'sə-lrā), 1769-1822, British statesman, b. Ireland. Entering the Irish Parliament in 1790 and the British Parliament in 1794, he was acting chief secretary for Ireland at the time of the Irish rebellion of 1798. Having worked for the Act of Union of England and Ireland (1800), he resigned with William Pitt in 1801 when George III refused to allow CATHOLIC EMANCIPATION. President of the India board of control from 1802 to 1806, he also served (1805-6, 1807-9) as secretary of war. In the latter office, he planned the reorganization and expansion of the army and the effective coordination of British land and sea power. He dispatched a British expedition to Portugal, and after the early disasters in the Peninsular War he succeeded in putting Arthur Wellesley (later duke of Wellington) in command. The opposition of his colleague George CANNING to Castlereagh's policies flared into a serious quarrel. Castlereagh accused Canning of political betrayal, and they fought (1809) a duel. Canning was wounded, and both resigned. As foreign secretary (1812-22), Castlereagh helped to organize the successful final coalition against Napoleon I, partly by secret treaties promising territorial changes. In the Treaty of Chaumont (1814) he obtained that "concert of Europe" later confirmed by the QUADRUPLE ALLIANCE. He advocated a moderate peace settlement for France, including restoration of the Bourbon monarchy and the limitation of France to her prewar boundaries. A dominant figure at the Congress of Vienna (1814-15; see VIENNA, CONGRESS OF), Castlereagh worked for the establishment of the United Netherlands and the German Confederation. He favored an independent Poland but was compelled to accept a repartitioning of that country. Castlereagh placed great hope in the "congress system" agreed on at Vienna, by which the great powers would consult regularly for the maintenance of peace. However, he did not approve of outright intervention in the domestic affairs of other countries and protested, in increasingly explicit terms, the assumption of this right by the powers of the HOLY ALLIANCE. By the time of his death it is almost certain that he had decided to break with the wartime allies. In England, however, he was much criticized for his apparent cooperation with those same autocratic governments, and he was also blamed for repressive actions to curb unrest in England, though he was not directly responsible for them. He became (1821) the 2d marquess of Londonderry on his father's death, but committed suicide the next year. One of the foremost statesmen of his time, Castlereagh was cold in personality and lacked ability as an orator; he never gained an easy popularity. See biographies by J. A. R. Marriott (1936) and C. J. Bartlett (1966); H. A. Kissinger, *A World Restored* (1957, repr. 1964).

Castle Shannon, borough (1970 pop. 11,899), Allegheny co., SW Pa., a residential suburb S of Pittsburgh; inc. 1919.

castor: see BEAVER.

Castor (kăs'tər), bright star in the constellation GEMINI; Bayer designation α Geminorum; 1970 position R.A. 7ʰ32.7ᵐ, Dec. +31°57′. Slightly dimmer than POLLUX, with which it forms the Twins, Castor has an apparent MAGNITUDE of 1.58, which still makes it one of the 25 brightest stars in the sky. Castor is actually a six-star system, being a visual triple each component of which is a BINARY STAR; the three components are an eclipsing binary and a pair of spectroscopic binaries. The two brightest components are white, main-sequence stars of SPECTRAL CLASSES A1 and A5. The system is about 50 light-years distant.

Castor and Pollux (pŏl'əks), in classical mythology, twin heroes called the Dioscuri; Castor was the son of LEDA and Tyndareus, Pollux the son of Leda and Zeus. Pollux is the Latin name for the Greek Polydeuces. Castor excelled as a horseman and Pollux as a boxer. They were great warriors and were noted for their devotion to each other. In one version of the legend, after Castor was killed by Lynceus, Pollux, in accordance with the classical tradition that one of every set of twins is the son of a god and thus immortal, begged Zeus to allow his brother to share his immortality with him. Zeus arranged for the twins to divide their time evenly between Hades and Heaven, and in their honor he created the constellation Gemini. According to another legend, Castor was killed by Idas. The Dioscuri were widely regarded as patrons of mariners and were responsible for SAINT ELMO'S FIRE. They were especially honored by the Romans, on whose side they were said to have appeared miraculously during the battle of Lake Regillus.

castor bean, bean produced by *Ricinus communis,* a plant of the SPURGE family.

castoreum: see BEAVER.

castor oil, yellowish oil obtained from the seed of the castor bean. The oil content of the seeds varies from about 20% to 50%. After the hulls are removed the seeds are cold-pressed. Medicinal castor oil is prepared from the yield of the first pressing; this is used as a purgative and laxative. Oil from the second pressing is used as a lubricant for machinery, as a softening agent in making artificial leather, in the dressing of genuine leather, in brake fluids, and in paints and plastic materials. The residue can be used as fertilizer and (after the poisonous substance, ricin, is removed) as cattle feed. Other products having similar properties and uses have been gradually replacing castor oil.

Castracani, Castruccio (kästro͞ot'chō kästräkä'nē), 1281–1328, duke of Lucca. His early life was spent in exile. After his return he was made captain (1316), then lord of Lucca (1320) for life. In the political wars that plagued Italy in the 14th cent. he led the Ghibellines of all Tuscany (see GUELPHS AND GHIBELLINES), waged long wars against Florence, and conquered Volterra, Pistoia, and the Lunigiana. In 1327, Holy Roman Emperor Louis IV recognized him as duke of Lucca. After quelling a rebellion in Pistoia, he died. His principality disappeared with him.

castration, removal of the sex glands of an animal, i.e., testes in the male, or ovaries and often the uterus in the female. Castration of the female animal is commonly referred to as spaying. Castration results in sterility, decreased sexual desire, and inhibition of secondary sex characteristics. It is performed for the purpose of improving the quality of meat and decreasing the aggressiveness of farm animals; in pet animals it prevents unwanted mating behavior, reproduction, and wandering. Removal of the sex glands in humans is sometimes necessary to prevent the spread in the body of cancerous growths.

castrato (kăsträ'tō) [Ital.,=castrated], a male singer with an artificially created soprano or alto voice, the result of castration in boyhood. The combination of the larynx of a youth and the chest and lungs of a man produced a powerful voice of great range and unique sound. Castrati were especially popular in churches and opera in Europe during the 17th and 18th cent. The greatest castrato was Carlo Broschi FARINELLI.

Castrén, Matthias Alexander (mätē'äs älĕksän'dər kästrān'), 1813–52, Finnish philologist, one of the first scholars to study the Finno-Ugric languages. Castrén was long a professor at the Univ. of Helsingfors (now Helsinki).

Castres (käs'trə), city (1968 pop. 42,920), Tarn dept., SW France, on the Agout River. It has been a textile center since the 13th cent., and its machine tools are known worldwide. Wood products, especially furniture, are also manufactured. Once the site of a Roman encampment, Castres grew around a Benedictine monastery founded in 647 A.D. Protestantism took hold in the 16th cent. but was suppressed by Louis XIII. The revocation (1685) of the Edict of NANTES jeopardized the city's economy by expelling Protestants, but Castres prospered anew under Louis XIV. There are several 17th- and 18th-century churches.

Castries, town (1960 pop. 4,353), capital and commercial center of St. Lucia, British West Indies. Its excellent landlocked harbor is one of the best in the West Indies. Castries was founded by the French in 1650.

Castriota, George: see SCANDERBEG.

Castro, Américo (ämā'rēkō käs'trō), 1885–1972, Spanish philologist and literary critic, b. Brazil. His numerous works include *El pensamiento de Cervantes* [the ideas of Cervantes] (1925), *Iberoamérica: su presente y su pasado* [Iberoamerica: its present and past] (1941), and *España en su historia: cristianos, moros y judíos* (1948; tr. *The Structure of Spanish History,* 1954).

Castro, Cipriano (sēprēä'nō), 1858?–1924, president of Venezuela (1901–8). In 1899 he usurped the government, overthrowing Andrade. Called the Lion of the Andes by his followers, he was a stern and arbitrary caudillo, who nevertheless improved the country's economy. Castro's administration is notable because of the financial claims (see VENEZUELA CLAIMS) made by several foreign powers and his defiance of them. He retired briefly in 1906 and was succeeded by Juan Vicente GÓMEZ, but after having violent disagreements with Gómez, Castro again assumed power. In 1908 Castro went to Europe. Gómez immediately deposed him and took control. Castro died in exile.

Castro, Fidel (fēdĕl'), 1926–, Cuban revolutionary and political leader, premier of Cuba (1959–). A young lawyer, Castro openly criticized the dictatorship of Fulgencio BATISTA Y ZALDÍVAR in 1952. On July 26, 1953, he led an unsuccessful attack on an army post in Santiago de Cuba and was imprisoned. Released (1955) in a general amnesty, he went to Mexico where he organized the 26th of July movement. In Dec., 1956, he landed in SW Oriente prov. with a small group of rebels. Castro and 11 others, including his brother Raúl and Ernesto "Che" GUEVARA, survived the initial encounter and hid in the mountains of the SIERRA MAESTRA, where, despite severe hardships, they built up a following and led the increasingly effective guerrilla campaign that toppled the Batista regime on Jan. 1, 1959. Widely hailed as a liberator, Castro soon proved to be extraordinary as a demagogue; he was a brilliant propagandist and a powerful orator. He established a totalitarian regime, directing the wholesale arrests and execution of Batista supporters, and—in a remarkably short time—he destroyed the old army structure and replaced it with his own military forces under the command of his brother Raúl. He proceeded to collectivize agriculture, to expropriate all native and foreign industry, and to promote close ties with Communist countries. He instituted sweeping reforms, uprooting the Cuban social order to the advantage of the lower classes and the general disadvantage of the propertied classes, many of whom fled. In Dec., 1961, he openly declared himself to be a Marxist-Leninist. By constantly denouncing "Yankee imperialism," by aligning himself and the Cuban revolution with the underprivileged peoples of Latin America, Asia, and Africa, and by dramatizing the symbols of his struggles against Batista, he kept alive his image as a folk hero. He weathered his own disastrous economic experiments, the cancellation of the U.S. sugar quota, the rupture of diplomatic relations with the United States and almost all of the Latin American countries, the U.S. Bay of Pigs invasion (April, 1961), an economic blockade, an unexpected compromise by the USSR in the 1962 crisis over missile bases in Cuba, and a protracted shortage of food and consumer goods. His announced goal of extending the Cuban revolution to other countries suffered a severe setback with the capture and death (1967) of "Che" Guevara in Bolivia. Although relying on Soviet aid, Castro maintained a remarkable degree of independence. While his initial enormous prestige dwindled, he remained an important charismatic symbol of revolution and social change. He wrote *Ten Years of Revolution* (1964) and *History Will Absolve Me* (1968). See Theodore Draper, *Castro's Revolution: Myths and Realities* (1962) and *Castroism: Theory and Practice* (1965); Lee Lockwood, *Castro's Cuba, Cuba's Fidel* (1967, repr. 1969); Andrés Suárez, *Cuba: Castroism and Communism 1959–1966* (1967); Enrique Meneses, *Fidel Castro* (1968); H. L. Matthews, *Fidel Castro* (1969); P. W. Bonsal, *Cuba, Castro, and the United States* (1971); Maurice Halperin, *The Rise and Decline of Fidel Castro* (1972).

Castro, Inés de, or **Inez de Castro** (both: ī'nĕz də kăs'trō, Port. ĕnĕsh' dĭ kăsh'tro͞o), d. 1355, Spanish noblewoman, a celebrated beauty, and a tragic figure in Portuguese history. She went (1340) to Portugal as a lady in waiting to Constance of Castile, wife of the heir to the Portuguese throne, Dom Pedro (later PETER I). He fell in love with her. Although his father, Alfonso IV, banished her from court, the prince continued to see her. After Constance died (1345), he established a household with her at Coimbra, where she bore him four children. Her brothers, however, gained political influence and aroused the opposition of Alfonso's advisers. Three of those advisers persuaded the king that Inés must be removed to preserve the legitimate succession to the throne and with his permission murdered Inés. Dom Pedro, overcome with grief and anger, led a rebellion against his father; but peace was restored, and the prince promised to forgive the murderers. When he became (1357) king, however, he extradited two from Castile and executed them horribly; the third escaped. Peter announced that he had been secretly married to Inés and had two tombs erected at Alcobaça depicting the life story of Inés in marble. It is not true that he had her disinterred and crowned as queen, but that story was immortalized in a drama of Juan Ruiz de Alarcón y Mendoza. The romantic story of the love affair has been a favorite theme of Portuguese writers and has been much used by Spanish and other writers also. Inés's sons subsequently contested the claim of their half brother, John I, to the Portuguese throne.

Castro, Rosalía de (rōsälē'ä dā), 1837–85, Spanish poet and novelist. Castro's book of verse *Cantares gallegos* (1863) was the first important poetry in Galician since the 13th cent.; it reflected the lyrical appeal of Galician folk songs. The melancholy *Follas novas* (1880) was followed by the despairing verse, in Castilian, of *En las orillas del Sar* (1884, tr. *Beside the River Sar,* 1937), written while Castro was suffering with terminal cancer. Her sensitive and compassionate poetry with its metrical innovations has exerted considerable influence on modern poets. Castro's novels of Galician life, e.g., *La hija del mar* [the daughter of the sea] (1859), are less significant.

Castro, Vaca de: see VACA DE CASTRO, CRISTÓBAL.

Castro, Greece: see KÁSTRON.

Castro Alves, Antônio de (əntô'nyo͞o dĭ käs'tro͞o äl'vəs), 1847–71, Brazilian poet. A disciple of Victor Hugo, he came to fame with *Espumas flutuantes* [tossing spume] (1871). The poems of Castro Alves are nationalist and socially conscious. Best known is *O navio negreiro* [the slave ship], which was instrumental in the abolition of slavery in Brazil. His study of law was cut short by his death, of tuberculosis, at 24.

Castrogiovanni: see ENNA, Italy.

Castrop-Rauxel (käs'trôp-rouk'səl), city (1970 pop. 84,146), North Rhine-Westphalia, W West Germany, on the Rhine-Herne Canal, an industrial city of the RUHR district. Chemicals and other light industrial goods are produced there.

Castro Valley, uninc. city (1970 pop. 44,760), Alameda co., W Calif., near San Francisco Bay. It is chiefly residential, with some light industry.

Castro y Bellvís, Guillén de (gēlyān' dā käs'trō ē bĕlvēs'), 1569–1631, Spanish dramatist, best known of the Valencian group of playwrights of the Golden Age. Three of his plays dramatize episodes from *Don Quixote.* His masterpiece, *Las mocedades del Cid* [the youthful adventures of the Cid], is a historical drama that furnished Corneille with the material for his play *Le Cid.* Castro enjoyed considerable success during his lifetime.

casuistry (kăzh'yo͞oĭstrē) [Lat. *casus*=case], art of applying general moral law to particular cases. Although most often associated with theology (it has been utilized since the inception of Christianity), it is also used in law and psychology. The function of casuistry is to analyze motives so individual judgments can be made in accordance with an established moral code. The term is often used in a pejorative sense to indicate specious or equivocal reasoning.

cat, name applied broadly to the carnivorous mammals constituting the family Felidae, and specifically to the domestic cat, *Felis catus.* The great roaring cats, the LION, TIGER, JAGUAR, LEOPARD, and snow leopard are anatomically very similar to one another and constitute the genus *Panthera.* The clouded leopard, *Neofelis,* and the cheetah, *Acinonyx,* are big cats that do not roar. The medium-sized and small cats are classified by different zoologists in varying numbers of genera, but in the system most widely used at present they are all put in the single genus *Felis,* despite the great variation among them. Among these cats are the PUMA (or cougar), the LYNX (including the bobcat), the OCELOT, the JAGUARUNDI, the SERVAL, and many small species described by the name cat or wildcat, such as the golden cat and European wildcat, as well as the domestic cat. The small cats are generally ticked, striped, or spotted. Many of them can interbreed with the domestic cat, and some can be tamed if caught young. Of all the carnivores, cats are the most exclusive flesh-eaters and are the most highly adapted for hunting and devouring their prey. All cats have rounded heads, short muzzles, large eyes, sensitive whiskers about the mouth, and erect pointed ears. They have short, wide jaws equipped with long canine teeth and strong molars with sharp cutting edges. Their tongues are coated with sharp recurved projections called papillae that aid in drinking and grooming. Cats have five toes on the forefeet and four on the hind feet. The fifth toe is set high on the forefoot and does not touch the ground during walking, but it is used in grooming and capturing prey. The ends of the toes bear strong, sharp, curved claws. In all but the cheetah the claws are completely retractile, being withdrawn into protective sheaths when not in use. This mechanism is a distinguishing feature of the cat family, although it occurs in a less developed form in some civets. All cats, with the exception of the lynx and related species, have long tails which they use for balance. The musculo-skeletal system is extremely flexible, allowing cats to arch and twist their bodies in a variety of ways. Most cats have good vision and are able to see well in very dim light; their color vision is weak. Their sense of hearing is excellent and, at least in the small cats, can detect frequencies of up to 40,000 Hz or higher. The sense of smell is not as highly developed as in the dog; its keenness may vary from one species to another. Cats are extremely agile; they can run faster than any other mammal for short distances and are remarkable jumpers. They are also good swimmers and members of many species appear to enjoy bathing. All are able to climb trees, but they vary in their behavior from almost exclusively terrestrial (e.g., the lion) to largely arboreal (e.g., the clouded leopard). Most are more or less solitary, but cheetahs live in family groups and lions live in groups, called prides, of up to 30 individuals. Most cats stalk their victims with great stealth and silence; even the lion, which lives in open country, usually lies in concealment until it can pounce on its victim. Only the cheetah, the swiftest of all mammals, runs down its prey. Cats live in a wide variety of habitats, although they are most numerous in warm climates. Even a single species, such as the tiger, may range from cold northern regions to the tropics. All continents except Australia and Antarctica have native species.

Domestic cats. Cats have been domesticated since prehistoric times, perhaps for as long as 5,000 years. (Dogs are believed to have been domesticated for about 50,000 years.) They have been greatly valued as destroyers of vermin, as well as for their ornamental qualities. The ancient Egyptian domestic cat, which spread to Europe in historic times, was used as a retriever in hunting as well as for catching rats and mice. It was probably derived from *Felis lybica* or one of the other North African wildcats. The modern domestic cat, *F. catus,* is probably descended from this animal, perhaps with an admixture of other wildcat species, or of species domesticated at various times in other parts of the world. Cats were venerated in the ancient Egyptian and Norse religions; they have also been the object of superstitious fear, especially in the Middle Ages, when they were tortured and burned as witches. Cats vary considerably in size; males commonly weigh 9 to 14 lb (4.1–6.4 kg) and females 6 to 10 lb (2.2–4.5 kg). They have coats of varying length and a wide variety of colors: black, white, and many shades of red, yellow, brown, and gray. A cat may be solid-colored or have patches or shadings of a second color. An extremely common pattern, probably derived from wild ancestors, is tabby: a red, brown, or gray background, striped with a lighter shade of the same color. The tortoiseshell pattern is a mixture of red, yellow, and black patches. The calico pattern is similar, but with large patches of white. Besides the common house cat, with its natural variation, the species *F. catus* includes recognized breeds with characteristics maintained by breeders and fanciers through selective mating. Breeds are established when particular traits breed true for several generations. The short-haired breeds are in general more slender and active than the long-haired. The long-haired breeds are the Persian and Himalayan; *angora* is an old term denoting any long-haired cat. Persians may be black, white, or any of a great variety of colors, including calico, tortoiseshell, tabby, and cameo (cream with red shadings). The Himalayan breed resulted from the crossing of a Siamese with a Persian cat; Himalayans have the stocky bodies and long hair of Persians, with Siamese coloring. All other breeds are short-haired. Abyssinians have long bodies and ruddy brown coats with ticking (marking on each hair) of darker brown or black. They are thought to be the most unchanged descendants of the ancient Egyptian domestic cat. Siamese are slender cats with almond-shaped blue eyes, and white, cream, or fawn-colored coats with brown or gray areas, called points, on the feet, tail, ears, and face. Show Siamese are divided according to color of their coats and markings into seal-, chocolate-, blue-, lilac-, and red-point types. Burmese are small, muscular, roundheaded cats with medium to dark brown coats. Manx are tailless cats of various colors; their hind legs are longer than their forelegs, so that the rump is elevated. They probably arose by mutation on the Isle of Man in the Irish Sea, although tailless cats also occur in the Orient. The Russian Blue has bright green eyes and an evenly blue-gray coat, distinguished for having two layers of short, thick fur. The Rex is a recent breed resulting from mutation and is the only curly-haired cat. Its short, woolly coat may be any color. Domestic shorthair is also a recognized category in American cat shows; cats of this group differ from the common household cat only in having known parentage for at least two generations. The known lineage of an animal is called its pedigree. The Maine coon cat is a nonpedigreed strain of large domestic cats found in Maine and believed to be descended from Persians; coon cats weigh up to 25 lb (11.3 kg). Maltese does not connote a breed but is a name applied indiscriminately to gray cats. Cat fanciers' associations exist to set standards, establish pedigrees, and conduct cat shows. There are seven such associations in the United States, one in Canada, and one in Great Britain. Cats are classified in the phylum CHORDATA, subphylum Vertebrata, class Mammalia, order Carnivora, family Felidae. See Michael Boorer, *Wild Cats* (1970); Claire Necker, *The Natural History of Cats* (1970); A. M. Currah, ed., *The Cat Compendium* (1972); C. M. Ing and Grace Pond, *Champion Cats of the World* (1972); G. N. Henderson and D. J. Coffey, ed., *The International Encyclopedia of Cats* (1973); G. B. Schaller, *Golden Shadows, Flying Hooves* (1973).

catabolism, subdivision of METABOLISM involving all degradative chemical reactions in the living cell. Large polymeric molecules such as polysaccharides, nucleic acids, and proteins are first split into their constituent monomeric units, after which the monomers themselves can be broken down into such simple cellular metabolites as lactic acid, acetic acid, carbon dioxide, ammonia, and urea. The first set of reactions provides the necessary building blocks for the construction of new polymeric molecules. The second set of reactions usually involves the process of oxidation and is accompanied by a release of chemical free energy, not all of which is lost as heat, but is partially conserved through the coupled synthesis of ADENOSINE TRIPHOSPHATE. The hydrolysis of this compound is subsequently used to drive almost every energy-requiring reaction in the cell. Thus catabolism also provides the source of chemical energy necessary for the maintenance of the living cell.

catacombs (kat'əkōmz), cemeteries of the early Christians, arranged in extensive subterranean vaults and galleries. Besides serving as places of burial, the catacombs were used as hiding places from persecution, as shrines to saints and martyrs, and for funeral feasts; it is doubtful, despite a widespread belief, that they were ever regularly used for religious services. Catacombs exist mainly at Rome but also at Naples, Chiusi, and Syracuse and at Alexandria and Susa in N Africa as well as in Asia Minor and other areas inhabited by the early Christians. The cemeteries at Paris, once thought to be catacombs, are actually depleted stone quarries and were not used for burial until the late 18th cent. Although among Greeks and Romans cremation was the rule, there was no bar against burial for Christians or Jews (Jewish catacombs have also been found at Rome, although the term is most generally used for Christian burial places) and the catacombs were not constructed in secrecy. Ordinances forbade interment within the city limits. All the Roman catacombs consequently are outside the city gates. They lie from 22 to 65 ft (6.7–19.8 m) beneath ground level and occupy a space estimated at more than 600 acres (243 hectares), although much of this is in several levels, one above another. The oldest remains date from the 1st cent. A.D., and construction continued until the early 5th cent. Excavated in those places where the subsoil tufa or soft rock possessed the suitable granular structure, they consisted primarily of narrow passages, generally about 3 ft (91 cm) wide. Lining the walls of these passages, are the loculi, or recesses, for the bodies. These niches, arranged one above another in tiers, were sealed after the burials with slabs of marble or terra-cotta that bore painted or incised inscriptions. Some passages contained separate chambers or cubicula, usually about 12 ft (4 m) square but sometimes circular or polygonal, which were privately owned family vaults or contained the tomb of a martyr. In these the bodies were often in carved sarcophagi that stood within arched niches. The walls and ceilings were plastered, and sometimes open shafts for lighting extended to the ground above. In some catacombs rooms are arranged in groups; in the catacombs of Sant'Agnese such a group forms a miniature church. In addition, the intricate underground corridors undoubtedly served as possible refuges from anti-Christian violence. The spreading of the catacombs, the joining together of separate areas, and the cutting of passages, one above the other in as many as five successive levels, eventually produced burial places of labyrinthine character. The walls and ceilings of plaster were customarily painted with fresco decorations, and in these can be studied the beginnings of Christian art. Religious subjects started to appear in the 2d cent., the earlier frescoes being confined to the use of symbols. Even after official recognition of Christianity in 313, burials continued, through a desire for interment near the martyrs. The invasions of Goths, Vandals, Lombards, and Saracens brought about the plundering of the catacombs and the robbing of their graves for the bones of saints. Several popes worked at restoring these sacred places, but by the 8th cent. the bodies had been mainly transferred to churches; by the 10th cent. the catacombs, filled with debris, were forgotten. In 1578 they were rediscovered. Their preservation and maintenance have since been under control of the papacy. In the Roman liturgy the requirement that Mass be said in the presence of lighted candles and over martyrs' relics is in conscious reminiscence of the catacombs. Exhaustive publications based upon researches in the catacombs were produced by the archaeologist Battista de Rossi (1822–94). The catacombs discovered in the vicinity of Rome in 1956 and 1959 contained frescoes of notable historical interest. See W. H. Adams, *Famous Caves and Catacombs* (1886, repr. 1972); Stephen Benko and J. J. O'Rourke, ed., *The Catacombs and the Colosseum* (1971).

Catalan art. In Catalonia and the territories of the counts of Barcelona, art flowered in the early Middle Ages and continued to flourish through the Renaissance. Some of the finest surviving altar-panel paintings of the Romanesque period are Catalan. Many of these are preserved in the Museo del Parque, Barcelona, together with numerous frescoes transferred from the apses of Romanesque churches. The small churches, often bare of sculptural ornament, were elaborately painted throughout, although usually only the decoration of the apse has survived. A fine example from Santa María del Mar, Barcelona, is in the Museum of Fine Arts, Boston. Superb examples of architectural sculpture also exist in many Catalan churches of the period. Also Romanesque is the famous illuminated Bible from the abbey of Farfa, now in the Vatican. Catalan art shares most of the characteristics of the international Romanesque style. A more obviously regional character is found in the Catalan painting of the 14th cent. and in the work of Ferrer Bassa and Jaime Serra, although Sienese influence is noteworthy. With the 15th cent., particularly in the paintings of

Jaime Huguet, of Jaime, Rafael, and Pablo Vergós, and of other masters, the school reached its maturity in a profuse and highly decorative religious art of great beauty. Only with Luis Dalmáu in the middle of the century did direct Flemish influence appear, and it never gained ascendancy. The great period of Catalan painting as such ended with the 15th cent., although the province has never ceased to produce great individual artists. Several prominent artists of the 20th cent. were of Catalonian origin, notably Juan Gris, Joan Miró, and Salvador Dali. See Chandler R. Post, *A History of Spanish Painting* (9 vol., 1930-47), Vol. VII; George Kubler and Martin Soria, *Art and Architecture in Spain and Portugal* (1959).

Catalan language (kăt'əlăn,–lən), member of the Romance group of the Italic subfamily of the Indo-European family of languages. It is spoken by close to 6 million people in the regions of Catalonia and Valencia in Spain, the Balearic Islands, the region of Roussillon in SE France, the city of Alghero in Sardinia, and lastly in Andorra (where it is the official tongue). Like the other ROMANCE LANGUAGES, Catalan is descended from Latin. It is written in the Roman alphabet. It is also the medium of a noteworthy literature. See William J. Entwistle, *The Spanish Language, Together with Portuguese, Catalan and Basque* (2d ed. 1962); Joan Gili, *Introductory Catalan Grammar* (3d ed. 1967).

Catalan literature, like the Catalan language, developed in close connection with that of Provence. In both regions the rhymed songs of the troubadours flourished as an art form from the 11th to the 14th cent. In the 13th cent. court chroniclers gave a fixed form to Catalan prose, and the language became an expressive literary medium in the works of the great Ramon LULL. At the end of the 14th cent. the art of the troubadours began to wane, and in the 15th cent. the influence of Dante and Petrarch was strong, particularly on the work of the poet Auzìas MARCH. From the rise of Castile during the Renaissance, Catalan literature was eclipsed until the 19th cent., when it experienced a marked revival. The great writers of this period were the dramatist Angel GUIMERÀ and the poet Mosèn Jacinto VERDAGUER. In the 20th cent. Catalan literature flourished. The realistic regional novel had first-rate exponents in Narcis Oller (1846-1930), Joaquim Ruyra (1858-1939), and Prudenci Bertrana (1867-1941). Joan Maragall (1860-1911) was regarded by Miguel de Unamuno as the best lyric poet of the Iberian peninsula. A unique and exotic note was the aesthetic dilettantism advocated by Eugenio d'ORS. After the end of the Spanish civil war the regime of Francisco Franco persecuted Catalan authors and imposed a ban on Catalan books and publications. Although Catalan literary life proceeded underground, it was not until after World War II that normal activity was resumed. The postwar years saw the return of Catalan language and literature to the curriculum of Spanish universities and the establishment of numerous awards for achievement in Catalan literature, e.g., the City of Barcelona Prize for Catalan Poetry. Notable postwar poets include Joseph Foix, Marìa Manent, and Thomàs Garcés. See Arthur Terry, *Catalan Literature* (1972).

catalepsy (kăt'əlĕpsē), pathological condition characterized by a loss of consciousness accompanied by rigidity of muscles that keeps limbs in any position in which they are placed. Attacks vary from several minutes to days and occur in a variety of clinical syndromes, most frequently in schizophrenia, epilepsy, and hysteria.

Catalina Island: see SANTA CATALINA.

catalog, descriptive list, on cards or in a book, of the contents of a library. Assurbanipal's library at Nineveh was cataloged on shelves of slate. The first known subject catalog was compiled by Callimachus at the Alexandrian Library in the 3d cent. B.C. The library at Pergamum also had a catalog. Early in the 9th cent. A.D. the catalogs of the libraries of the monastery at Reichenau and of the abbey at Saint-Riquier, N France, included summaries of the works cataloged. In 1472 the monastic library at Clairvaux was recataloged and one of the earliest union catalogs was made—of the contents of 160 Franciscan monastery libraries in England. In 1475 the Vatican librarian, Platina, cataloged that library's 2,527 volumes. About 1660, Clement, librarian of the Bibliothèque du Roi under Louis XV, compiled a subject catalog and inventory of manuscripts. The printing of the British Museum catalog was begun by PANIZZI as keeper (1837-56) of printed books. Charles A. CUTTER devised the modern dictionary catalog (with author, title, and subject arranged in one alphabet) for the Boston Athenaeum library. Melvil DEWEY devised his decimal system in the 1870s; the system was widely applied in smaller libraries and many large ones. In 1901 the Library of Congress began the practice of printing their catalog entries on cards 3 by 5 in. (7.6 by 12.7 cm) and distributing them to other libraries for a small fee. The National Union Catalogue, begun in 1952 by the Library of Congress, collates the card catalog entries of most large American libraries and prints the results in book form. Cataloging processes are currently being mechanized with the aid of computer systems to provide more extensive and generally superior bibliographic services. See Archer Taylor, *Book Catalogues: Their Varieties and Uses* (1957); *Anglo American Cataloguing Rules*, prepared by the American Library Association et al. (1970); M. F. Tauber and Hilda Feinberg, comp., *Book Catalogs* (1971).

Catalonia (kătəlō'nēə), Span. *Cataluña*, region (1970 pop. 5,122,567), NE Spain, stretching from the Pyrenees at the French border southward along the Mediterranean Sea. It comprises four provinces, named after their capitals: BARCELONA, GERONA, LÉRIDA, and TARRAGONA. Barcelona is the historic capital. Mostly hilly, with pine-covered mountains, it also has some highly fertile plains. Cereals, olives, and grapes are grown, and one third of the wines of Spain are produced there. The beautiful 240-mi (386-km) seacoast has fine harbors and an active tourist trade. The Ebro, Segre, and Cinca rivers furnish hydroelectric power for the industries in Barcelona and Gerona provs.; chief products are textiles, automobiles, airplanes, locomotives, and foundry and other metal items. Trade has been active along the coast since Greek and Roman times. The history of medieval Catalonia (which, like Castile, took its name from its many castles) is that of the counts of Barcelona, who emerged (9th cent.) as the chief lords in the Spanish March founded by Charlemagne. United (1137) with Aragón through marriage (see RAYMOND BERENGAR IV), Catalonia nevertheless preserved its own laws, its cortes, and its own language (akin to Provençal). CATALAN ART and CATALAN LITERATURE flourished in the Middle Ages. In the cities, notably Barcelona, the burgher and merchant classes grew very powerful. Catalan traders rivaled those of Genoa and Venice, and their maritime code was widely used in the 14th cent. They, and adventurers like Roger de Flor, were largely responsible for the expansion in the Mediterranean of the house of Aragón (see ARAGÓN, HOUSE OF). Catalonia failed in its rebellion (1461-72) against John II of Aragón, and after the union (1479) of Aragón and Castile, Catalonia declined. The centralizing policy of the Spanish kings, the shifting of trade routes with the consequent loss of commercial income, pirate attacks, and recurring plagues and famines were all major factors. Agitation for autonomy was always strong. In the Thirty Years War (1618-48), Catalonia rose against Philip IV, and in the War of the Spanish Succession it sided with Archduke Charles against Philip V, who in reprisal deprived it of its privileges. In the late 19th and 20th cent. it was a center of socialist and anarchist strength. In 1932 the Catalans established a separate government, first under Francisco Macía, then under Luis Companys, which in 1932 won autonomy from the Spanish Cortes. A revolution (1934) for complete independence failed, but in 1936 autonomy was restored. In the civil war of 1936-39, Catalonia sided with the Loyalists and suffered heavily. Barcelona was the Loyalist capital from Oct., 1938, to Jan., 1939. Catalonia fell to Franco in Feb., 1939.

catalpa (kətăl'pə): see BIGNONIA.

catalyst, substance that can cause a change in the rate of a CHEMICAL REACTION without itself being consumed in the reaction; the changing of the reaction rate by use of a catalyst is called catalysis. Substances that increase the rate of reaction are called positive catalysts or, simply, catalysts, while substances that decrease the rate of reaction are called negative catalysts or inhibitors. Catalysts work by changing the ACTIVATION ENERGY for a reaction, i.e., the minimum energy needed for the reaction to occur. This is accomplished by providing a new mechanism or reaction path through which the reaction can proceed. When the new reaction path has a lower activation energy, the reaction is said to be catalyzed; the rate of reaction will be increased because there will be a higher proportion of interactions (i.e., collisions) between reactants with enough energy to cause a reaction. If the activation energy for the new path is higher, the reaction rate is decreased and the reaction is said to be inhibited. Enzymes are the commonest and most efficient of the catalysts found in nature. Most of the chemical reactions that occur in the human body and in other living things are high-energy reactions that would occur slowly, if at all, without the catalysis provided by enzymes. For example, in the absence of catalysis, it takes several weeks for starch to hydrolyze to glucose; a trace of the enzyme ptyalin, found in human saliva, accelerates the reaction so that starches can be digested. Some enzymes increase reaction rates by a factor of one billion or more. Enzymes are generally specific catalysts; that is, they catalyze only one reaction of one particular reactant or substrate. Usually the enzyme and its substrate have complementary structures and can bond together to form a complex that is more reactive due to the presence of FUNCTIONAL GROUPS in the enzyme, which stabilize the transition state of the reaction or lower the activation energy. Catalysis is also important in chemical laboratories and in industry. Some reactions occur faster in the presence of a small amount of an acid or base and are said to be acid catalyzed or base catalyzed. For example, the hydrolysis of esters is catalyzed by the presence of a small amount of base. In this reaction, it is the hydroxide ion, OH^-, that reacts with the ester, and the concentration of hydroxide ion is greatly increased over that of pure water by the presence of the base. Although some of the hydroxide ions provided by the base are used up in the first part of the reaction, they are regenerated in a later step from water molecules; the net amount of hydroxide ion present is the same at the beginning and end of the reaction, so the base is thought of as a catalyst and not as a reactant. Finely divided metals are often used as catalysts; they adsorb the reactants onto their surfaces (see ADSORPTION), where the reaction can occur more readily. For example, hydrogen and oxygen gases can be mixed without reacting to form water, but if a small amount of powdered platinum is added to the gas mixture, the gases react rapidly. Hydrogenation reactions, e.g., the formation of hard cooking fats from vegetable oils, are catalyzed by finely divided metals or metal oxides. The commercial preparation of sulfuric acid and nitric acid also depends on such surface catalysis. Other commonly used surface catalysts, in addition to platinum, are copper, iron, nickel, palladium, rhodium, silica gel (silicon dioxide), and vanadium oxide. Some substances that are not themselves catalysts increase the activity of a catalyst when added with it to some reaction; such substances are called promoters. Alumina is a promoter for iron when it is used to catalyze the reaction of hydrogen and nitrogen to form ammonia. In some reactions one of the reaction products is a catalyst for the reaction; this phenomenon is called self-catalysis or autocatalysis. An example is the reaction of permanganate ion with oxalic acid to form carbon dioxide and manganous ion, in which the manganous ion acts as an autocatalyst. Such reactions are potentially dangerous, since the reaction rate may increase to the point of explosion. Inhibitors are also of interest to the chemist. Because oxygen is an inhibitor of free-radical reactions, many of which are important in the synthesis of polymers, such reactions must be performed in an oxygen-free environment, e.g., under a blanket of nitrogen gas. The toxicity of certain poisons, e.g., carbon monoxide and the nerve gases, is due to their inhibition of life-sustaining catalytic reactions in the body. Substances that react with catalysts to reduce or eliminate their effect are called poisons; arsenic compounds are catalytic poisons for platinum.

catamaran (kăt"əmərăn'), watercraft made up of two connected hulls. Originally used by the natives of Polynesia, the catamaran design was adopted by Western boat builders in the 19th cent. Because the twin hulls of the Polynesian catamaran are actually logs or other pieces of wood, the vessel is more like a raft than a boat. An extremely stable craft, it can be paddled or sailed even in the heavy waves of the S Pacific. The American Nathanael Herreshoff first built Western-type catamarans in the 1870s. The twin-hulled sailing or motor boat has since become a popular pleasure craft, largely because of its speed and stability. Catamarans range from 12 ft (3.7 m) to over 100 ft (30.5 m) in length and are among the world's fastest sailing craft.

Catamarca (kätämär'kä), city (1970 pop. 58,186), capital of Catamarca prov., NW Argentina. It is an agricultural and mining center located in a valley that produces wine, cotton, alfalfa, and livestock. Founded in 1683, Catamarca has a 17th-century Franciscan monastery and a church that is a pilgrimage site and a national monument. Tourists are attracted by the area's mineral springs.

catamount: see PUMA.

Catania (kätä'nyä), city (1971 pop. 397,939), capital of Catania prov., E Sicily, Italy, on the Gulf of Catania, an arm of the Ionian Sea, and at the foot of Mt. Etna. It is a busy port and a major commercial and industrial center. Manufactures include chemicals, silk and cotton textiles, and asphalt. The city also has a fishing industry. Founded (late 8th cent. B.C.) by Chalcidian colonists, Catania was a flourishing Greek town and was later a Roman colony. It was rebuilt after earthquakes in 1169 and 1693 and after a severe volcanic eruption in 1669. In 1862, Garibaldi organized at Catania his expedition to Rome that was stopped at Aspromonte. The city was heavily damaged in World War II. Points of interest include the extensive Bellini Gardens (named for the 19th-century composer, who was born in Catania); the cathedral (originally built in the 11th cent.); and Ursino castle, built (13th cent.) by Emperor Frederick II. The city has a university (founded 1444) and an observatory.

Catanzaro (kätändzä'rō), city (1971 pop. 85,316), capital of Catanzaro prov. and of Calabria, S Italy, on a hill above the Ionian Sea. It is a commercial and industrial center, with flour mills and distilleries. Founded (10th cent.) by the Byzantines, Catanzaro was famous (11th–17th cent.) for its velvets and damasks.

catapult (kăt'əpŭlt"), mechanism used to throw missiles in ancient and medieval warfare. There were two major types in wide use. One, a large crossbow, shot spears at a low trajectory (see BOW AND ARROW). The other type threw large stones, pots of boiling oil, and Greek fire (a flammable mixture used by the Byzantine Greeks) at a high trajectory and was used for attacking or defending fortifications. Catapults were widely employed in SIEGE warfare, but with the introduction of artillery in the 14th cent. they passed from use. However, in the 20th cent. a form of catapult using hydraulic pressure was reintroduced as a means of launching aircraft from warships.

cataract, in medicine, opacity of the lens of the eye, which impairs vision. In the young, cataracts are generally congenital or hereditary; later they are usually the result of degenerative changes brought on by advanced age or systemic disease (diabetes). Cataracts brought on by aging are most common; most individuals over 60 exhibit some degree of lens opacity. Injury, extreme heat, X rays, nuclear radiation, inflammatory disease, and toxic substances also cause cataracts. Advanced cataracts are treated by surgical removal of the lens, and contact lenses are used to compensate for the missing lens.

Catargiu, Lascar (kätärjōō'), 1823–99, Rumanian statesman, of an ancient Walachian family. Unsuccessful as Conservative candidate (1859) against Alexander John Cuza for the rule of Moldavia, he became leader of the Conservative opposition. He served several times as premier of Rumania (May–July, 1866; 1871–76; 1889; 1891–95) and effected financial and agrarian reforms.

catastrophism (kətăs'trəfĭzəm), in geology, the doctrine that at intervals in the earth's history all living things have been destroyed by cataclysms, e.g., floods or earthquakes, and replaced by an entirely different population. During these cataclysms the features of the earth's surface, such as mountains and valleys, were formed. The theory, popularly accepted from the earliest times, was attacked in the late 18th cent., notably by James Hutton, who may be regarded as the precursor of the opposite doctrine of UNIFORMITARIANISM. Catastrophism, however, was more easily correlated with religious doctrines, e.g., the Mosaic account of the Flood, and remained for some time the interpretation of the earth's history accepted by the great majority of geologists. It was systematized and defended by the Frenchman Georges Cuvier, whose position as the greatest geologist of his day easily overbore all opposition. In the 19th cent. it was attacked by George Poulett Scrope and especially by Sir Charles Lyell, under whose influence the contrary doctrine gradually became more popular.

catatonia (kăt"ətō'nēə), mental state characterized by statuesque posturing and muscular immobility, mutism, apparent stupor, and paralysis of the will. The muscles are held in a pliant state of tonus called waxy flexibility, and the catatonic person obediently permits himself to be rearranged into awkward positions that he may subsequently hold for hours. In contrast to the above stuporous or withdrawn form of catatonia, catatonic excitements may occur in which continuous incoherent shouting, unstinting psychomotor agitation, and a violent destructiveness toward persons and objects alike can lead to collapse and death if untreated. First described by Karl Kahlbaum in 1874 as catatonia, or tension insanity, the entity was included with hebephrenia and paranoia in Emil Kraepelin's concept of dementia praecox. All of these were subsumed under Eugen Bleuler's concept of SCHIZOPHRENIA in 1911, when the important distinction was made that there was no dementia involved—no defect of memory or intellect. Indeed, the apparently stuporous and totally unresponsive catatonic will often later describe having been acutely sensitive to persons and events around him during the catatonic state.

Catawba Indians (kətô'bə), North American Indians whose language belongs to the Siouan branch of the Hokan-Siouan linguistic stock (see AMERICAN INDIAN LANGUAGES). They occupied a region in South Carolina. A large and powerful group, they waged incessant but unsuccessful war against the Cherokee and the Indians of the Ohio River valley, sending war parties to great distances. Fighting and epidemics of smallpox reduced them to a small group in the 18th cent. Until 1962 the Catawba lived on a small reservation in South Carolina; at that time they terminated their relationship with the Federal government and distributed the tribal estate among the remaining members. See D. S. Brown, *The Catawba Indians* (1966); C. M. Hudson, *The Catawba Nation* (1970).

cat bear: see PANDA.

catbird: see MIMIC THRUSH.

catch crop, any quick-growing crop sown between seasons of regular planting to make use of temporary idleness of the soil or to compensate for the failure of a main crop. It may be such rapid-maturing vegetables as radishes, onions grown from sets, or spinach (planted between rows of slower growing crops); quick-growing crops such as rye, millet, or buckwheat; or an annual legume, such as soybean, which is valuable as fodder or, when plowed under, increases the soil's fertility. See COVER CROP.

catchfly: see PINK.

catchment area or **drainage basin,** area drained by a stream or other body of water. The limits of a given catchment area are the heights of land—often called drainage divides, or watersheds—separating it from neighboring drainage systems. The amount of water reaching the river, reservoir, or lake from its catchment area depends on the size of the area, the amount of precipitation, and the loss through evaporation (determined by temperature, winds, and other factors and varying with the season) and through absorption by the earth or by vegetation; absorption is greater when the soil or rock is permeable than when it is impermeable. A permeable layer over an impermeable layer may act as a natural reservoir, supplying the river or lake in very dry seasons. The catchment area is one of the primary considerations in the planning of a reservoir for water-supply purposes.

Cateau, Le (lə kätō'), town (1968 pop. 9,314), Nord dept., N France, in French Flanders. It was formerly known as Le Cateau-Cambrésis. It has textile, metallurgical, and ceramic industries. In a treaty signed there in 1559, the last English foothold on the continent was returned to France. Le Cateau was the scene of much fighting in World War I. A museum contains much of the work of Matisse, who was born there.

Cateau-Cambrésis, Treaty of (kätō'-käNbrāzē'), 1559, concluded at Le Cateau, France, by representatives of HENRY II of France, PHILIP II of Spain, and ELIZABETH I of England. It put an end to the 60-year conflict between France and Spain, begun with the ITALIAN WARS, in which HENRY VIII and later MARY I of England had intermittently sided against France. The terms were a triumph for Spain. France restored Savoy, except Saluzzo, to Duke EMMANUEL PHILIBERT, acknowledged Spanish hegemony over Italy, and consented to a rectification of its border with the Spanish Netherlands. CALAIS, however, was confirmed in French possession by England. Henry II's sister, Margaret, was given in marriage to Emmanuel Philibert of Savoy; Henry's daughter, Elizabeth of Valois, was given to Philip II of Spain.

catechism (kăt'əkĭzəm) [Gr.,=oral instruction], originally oral instruction in religion, later written instruction. Catechisms are usually written in the form of questions and answers. Almost as old as Christianity, they were used especially for the instruction of converts and children. Catechisms were popular in the later Middle Ages and assumed even greater significance in the Reformation through Martin Luther's emphasis on the religious education of children. His Small Catechism (1529) is still the standard book of the Lutheran church. The greatest Calvinist catechism was the Heidelberg Catechism (1563). It was revised at Dort (1619) and was used in Dutch and German Reformed churches; other catechisms are the Longer and Shorter Catechisms of 1647 and 1648, drawn up to supplement the Westminster Confession; they are used in the Presbyterian churches. The catechism for the Anglican Communion is included in the Book of Common Prayer. A catechism long in use in the Roman Catholic Church was that prepared by the Jesuit Peter Canisius, which appeared in 1555. The catechism of the Council of Trent, a document of high authority issued in 1566, is not really a catechism but a manual of instruction for use by the clergy. The best-known Catholic catechism in England is the Penny Catechism, adopted by the bishops of England and Wales; that in the United States is the Baltimore Catechism.

catecholamine (kăt"əkôl'əmēn), any of several compounds occurring naturally in the body that help regulate the sympathetic NERVOUS SYSTEM. The catecholamines include such compounds as EPINEPHRINE, or adrenaline, isoproterenol, norepinephrine, and dopamine. They resemble one another chemically in having an aromatic portion (catechol) to which is attached an amine, or nitrogen-containing group. Epinephrine and norepinephrine are secreted by the adrenal medulla and norepinephrine is also secreted by some nerve fibers. These substances prepare the body to meet emergencies such as cold, fatigue, and shock, and norepinephrine is probably a chemical transmitter at nerve synapses. Dopamine is an intermediate in the synthesis of epinephrine; in addition, a deficiency of dopamine in the brain is responsible for the symptoms of the condition PARKINSONISM. Medical administration of the drug l-dopa, which is presumed to be converted to dopamine in the brain, relieves the symptoms. Epinephrine and isoproterenol are both used medically to stimulate heartbeat and to treat emphysema, bronchitis, and bronchial asthma and other allergic conditions. Epinephrine is also used in the treatment of the eye disease glaucoma.

catechu (kăt'əchōō) or **cutch,** extract from the heartwood of *Acacia catechu*, a leguminous tree of the PULSE family, native to India and Burma. Catechu is a fast brown dye used for various shades of brown and olive, including the familiar khaki, and also in tanning. White cutch is a synonym for gambier, a leaf extract of a shrub (*Uncaria gambir*) of the madder family, which is similarly used.

categorical imperative: see KANT, IMMANUEL.

category, philosophical term that literally means predication or assertion. It was first used by Aristotle, whose 10 categories formed a list of all the ways in which assertions can be made of a subject. Immanuel Kant's 12 categories constitute an exhaustive list of the a priori forms through which a person knows the phenomenal world. The term has also been used in many other senses by various philosophers.

category, in taxonomy: see CLASSIFICATION.

Catena, Vincenzo di Biagio (vēnchĕn'tsō dē byä'jō kätā'nä), c.1470–1531, Venetian painter. His early work, reflecting the influence of Giovanni Bellini, includes the two paintings of *Madonna and Child with Saints* in the Walters Art Gallery, Baltimore, and the Academy, Venice. In his later period Catena followed closely the style of Giorgione. The best works of this period are *The Doge Loredan Kneeling before the Madonna* (Correr Mus., Venice); *The Martyrdom of St. Christina* (Church of Santa Maria Mater Domini, Venice); and *Christ Giving the Keys to St. Peter* (Gardner Mus., Boston). See monograph by Giles Robertson (1954).

Caterham and Warlingham (kā'tərəm, wôr'lĭng-əm), urban district (1971 pop. 35,781), Surrey, SE England. A residential suburb of London, it has engineering, chemical, perfume, and printing industries.

caterpillar, common name for the LARVA of a MOTH or BUTTERFLY. Caterpillars have distinct heads and are segmented and wormlike. They have three pairs of short, jointed legs (retained in the adult) on the thorax; in addition, they have unjointed, fleshy appendages, called prolegs, on some abdominal segments. The prolegs end in clusters of tiny hooks. There is a row of simple eyes on either side of the body. Sawfly larvae are often mistaken for caterpillars, but their prolegs have no hooks and they have a single simple eye on each side. Almost all caterpillars are vegetarian and have strong jaws for chewing. The chewing mouth parts and the prolegs disappear during the PUPA stage, as the larva is transformed into an adult. Caterpillars have silk glands that open into a mouth part called the spinneret. The caterpillar exudes a silk strand continuously as it moves along; small caterpillars swing by the strand when dropping from a height. Many caterpillars use the thread to build a cocoon in which to pupate. Most molt their skin (to accommodate growth) five or six times before pupation. Some caterpillars have smooth skin; others are hairy, such as the woolly bear, or hedgehog, caterpillar of the Isabella tiger moth. The caterpillars of the larger night-flying moths (e.g., the luna moth and polyphemus moth) are smooth and green and may be over 3 in. (7.5 cm) long. Caterpillars are equipped with various protective devices. The io moth caterpillar has sharp spines connected with glands that secrete an irritating substance. Others have irritating bristles, and the SWALLOWTAIL BUTTERFLY larva emits a repellent odor when disturbed. Nevertheless, caterpillars form the major part of the diet of many birds and other animals. Caterpillars are voracious eaters and some cause considerable economic damage. Among these are the appleworm, the CUTWORM, and the larvae of the BEE MOTH, the CODLING MOTH, and the CLOTHES MOTH. Some moths and butterflies remain caterpillars for two or three months, others for about 10 months, hibernating through the winter in this stage. In the arctic regions are some forms that require two or three years to develop from egg to adult.

catfish, common name applied to members of the freshwater fish families constituting the suborder Nematognathi. The catfish is related to the SUCKER and the MINNOW and like them has a complex set of bones forming a sensitive hearing apparatus. Catfish are omnivorous feeders and are valuable scavengers. They are named for the barbels ("whiskers") around their mouths and have scaleless skins, fleshy, rayless posterior fins, and sharp defensive spines in the shoulder and dorsal fins. They are able to use the SWIM BLADDER to produce sounds. Some species, such as the stone and tadpole catfishes and the madtom, can inflict stings by means of poison glands in the pectoral spines. Catfish are usually dull-colored, though the madtoms of E North American streams are brightly patterned. Members of most madtom species are no more than 5 in. (12.7 cm) long; some are less than 2 in. (5 cm) long. Danube catfish called wels, or sheatfish, reach a length of 13 ft (4 m) and a weight of 400 lb (180 kg). The South American catfishes show great diversity: There are small, delicate species armored with bony plates; parasitic types that live in the gills of other fish; and one catfish of the E Andes in which the pelvic fins are modified into suckers that enable it to cling to rocks. African species include the ELECTRIC FISH and the Nile catfish, which swims upside down to feed at the water's surface and has a white back and a dark belly, the reverse of the normal coloration. Of the 30 American species the largest and most important is the blue, or Mississippi, catfish, an excellent food fish weighing up to 150 lb (70 kg). Best known is the smaller channel catfish, which reaches 20 lb (9 kg) and has a deeply forked tail and slender body. The stonecat, 10 in. (25.4 cm) long, is found in clear water under logs and stones. The bullheads, or horned pouts, are catfish of muddy ponds and streams, feeding on bottom plants and animals. Bullheads have square or slightly rounded tails and may reach 1 ft (30 cm) in length and 2 lb (0.9 kg) in weight. The black, yellow, and brown bullhead species are common in the waters of the central and eastern states. There are no catfish in the Pacific except the introduced white catfish. Marine catfish found during the summer in bays and harbors of the Atlantic and Gulf states include the 2-ft (61-cm) gaff-topsail catfish, named for its long, ribbonlike pectoral and dorsal fins, and the smaller sea catfish, a very common trash fish. The males of both these species carry the fertilized eggs in their mouths (and therefore do not eat) until well after the young hatch, a period of two months. In certain other species the eggs are embedded in the underside of the female. Some tropical catfish survive dry seasons by burrowing into the mud or by crawling overland in search of water. Catfishes are classified in the phylum CHORDATA, subphylum Vertebrata, class Osteichthyes, order Cypriniformes, suborder Nematognathi.

catgut or **gut,** cord made from the intestines of various animals (especially sheep and horses, but not cats). The membrane is chemically treated, and slender strands are woven together into cords of great strength, which are used for stringing musical instruments such as the violin and the harp. Roman strings, imported from Italy, are considered the best for musical instruments. Catgut is also used for stringing tennis rackets and for some surgical sutures.

Cathari (kăth'ərī) [Gr.,=pure], name for members of the widespread dualistic religious movement of the Middle Ages. Carried from the Balkans to Western Europe, Catharism flourished in the 11th and 12th cent. as far north as England. It was known by various names and in various forms (see BOGOMILS; ALBIGENSES). Catharism was descended from GNOSTICISM and MANICHAEISM and echoed many of the ideas of MARCION. The Cathari tended to reject not only the outward symbols of the Christian church, such as the sacraments and the hierarchy, but also the basic relationship between God and man as taught by Christianity. Instead, the Cathari believed in a dualistic universe, in which the God of the New Testament, who reigned over spiritual things, was in conflict with the evil god (or Satan), who ruled over matter. Asceticism, absolute surrender of the flesh to the spirit, was to be cultivated as the means to perfection. There were two classes of the Cathari, the believers and the Perfect. The believers passed to the ranks of the Perfect on acceptance of the *consolamentum*, a sort of sacrament that was a laying on of hands. The Catharist concept of Jesus resembled modalistic MONARCHIANISM in the West and ADOPTIONISM in the East. Persecution, such as that by the INQUISITION, and the efforts of popes like Innocent III wiped out Catharism by the 15th cent. See E. Holmes, *The Albigensian or Catharist Heresy* (1925); Jacques Madaule, *The Albigensian Crusade* (tr. 1967); J. R. Strayer, *The Albigensian Crusades* (1971).

cathartic (kəthär'tĭk): see LAXATIVE.

Cathay (kăthā'), medieval name for China, derived from the Khitai, a seminomadic people of S Manchuria whose rule under the Liao dynasty (937–1125) extended to N China. It was popularized by Marco Polo (c.1254–c.1324) and usually applied only to China N of the Yangtze River. S China was sometimes called Mangi.

cathedral, church in which a bishop presides. The designation is not dependent on the size or magnificence of a church edifice, but is entirely a matter of its assignment as the church in which the bishop shall officiate. Romanesque cathedrals (see ROMANESQUE ARCHITECTURE AND ART) were massive, blocklike, domed and heavily vaulted structures based on the traditional BASILICA form, reflecting the style dominant in Europe from c.1050 to c.1200. The tall, wide nave arcade or colonnade, flanked by shallower, shorter aisles, ran from decorative exterior portals to a large ambulatory and an apse with radiating chapels. The nave was crossed by a TRANSEPT and illuminated by a CLERESTORY pierced by small windows so as not to diminish the strength of the supporting walls. The Romanesque cathedral is a strong visual whole with interrelated parts that emphasize its basic structural clarity. The great cathedrals of the 13th and 14th cent. are the culminating expression of GOTHIC ARCHITECTURE. These buildings are distinctive in their consistent use of ribbed VAULTS, pointed ARCHES, ROSE WINDOWS, BUTTRESSES, geometric TRACERY, and variegated STAINED GLASS. All of these elements were combined into a design of infinite complexity and richness. Gothic interior structure, also based on basilica form, included a long central arcaded or colonnaded nave with flanking aisles, a transept, a choir, ambulatory, and apse with radiating chapels. Stained glass was used to create a light, lacy effect of spiderweb airyness, made possible by buttressing the comparatively thin walls. The exterior facade was ornamented with great portals covered with sculpture and surmounted by double towers. Further towers often rose above transepts and crossing, and the rear portion of the entire edifice was engulfed in a profusion of buttresses and pinnacles. The building's structure is entirely subordinated visually to the intricacy of its details. Among the most important medieval cathedrals are the following: *France*—Amiens, Beauvais, Bourges, Chartres, Le Mans, Notre-Dame de Paris, Rouen, Rheims, Strasbourg; *England*—Canterbury, Durham, Ely, Lincoln, Peterborough, Salisbury, Wells, Westminster Abbey, Winchester, York; *West Germany*—Bonn, Cologne, Mainz, Speyer, Ulm, Worms; *Belgium*—Antwerp, Brussels, Louvain, Ypres; *Italy*—Como, Florence, Milan, Monreale, Orvieto, Pisa, Siena, *Spain*—Ávila, Burgos, Barcelona, Salamanca, Seville, Toledo; *Sweden*—Lund, Uppsala. Among major cathedrals built in modern times and adhering to medieval styles of architecture are St. Patrick's Cathedral and the Cathedral of St. John the Divine (Episcopal) in New York City and the cathedrals of Washington, D.C., and Liverpool, England. See Auguste Rodin, *Cathedrals of France* (1960); G. H. Cook, *The English Cathedral through the Centuries* (1965); Wim Swaan, *The Gothic Cathedral* (1970).

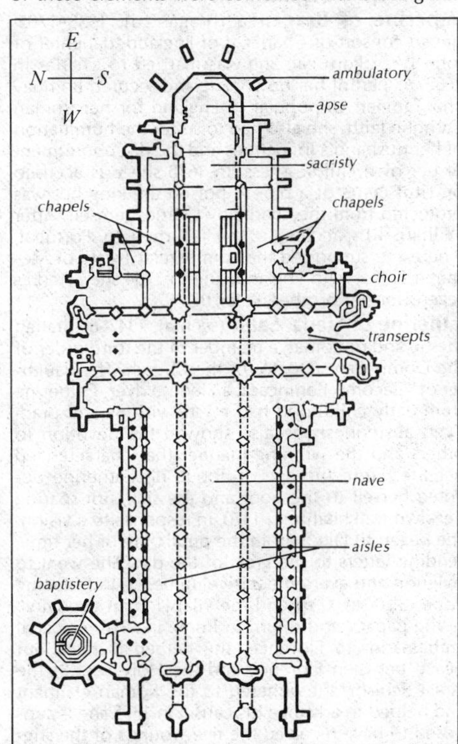

Floor plan of a cathedral

Cather, Willa Sibert, 1876–1947, American novelist and short-story writer, b. Winchester, Va., considered one of the great American writers of the 20th cent. When she was nine her family moved to the Nebraska prairie frontier. She graduated from the Univ. of Nebraska in 1895 and worked as a journalist and as a teacher in Pittsburgh. In 1904 she went to New York City. The publication of *The Troll Garden* (1905), her first collection of short stories, led to her appointment to the editorial staff of *McClure's Magazine*. She eventually became managing editor and saved the magazine from financial disaster. After the publication of *Alexander's Bridge* in 1912, she left *McClure's* and devoted herself to creative writing. For many years she lived quietly in New York City's Greenwich Village. The first of her novels to deal with her major theme is *O Pioneers!* (1913), a celebration of the strength and courage of the frontier settlers. Other novels with this theme are *My Ántonia* (1918), *One of Ours* (1922; Pulitzer Prize), and *A Lost Lady* (1923). *The Song of the Lark* (1915) focuses on another of Cather's major preoccupations—the need of the artist to free himself from inhibiting influences, particularly that of a rural or small-town background; the tales collected in *Youth and the Bright Medusa* (1920) and the novel *Lucy Gayheart* (1935) also treat this theme. With success and increasing age Cather became convinced that the beliefs and way of life she valued were disappearing. This disillusionment is poignantly evident in her novel *The Professor's House* (1925). She subsequently turned to North America's far past for her material: to colonial New Mexico in *Death Comes for the Archbishop* (1927), widely regarded as her masterpiece, and to 17th-century Quebec for *Shadows on the Rock* (1931), in both novels blending history with religious reverence and loving characterizations. The volumes *My Mortal Enemy* (1926) and *The Old Beauty and Others* (1948) present her highly skilled shorter fiction. Her intense interest in the craft of fiction is shown in the essays in *Not Under Forty* (1936) and *On Writing* (1949). Cather herself was a master of that craft, her novels and stories written in a pellucid style of great charm and stateliness. See biographies by E. K. Brown (completed by Leon Edel, 1953) and J. L. Woodress (1970); studies by D. Daiches (1951), E. A. Bloom and L. D. Bloom (1962), and J. M. Schroeter (1967).

Catherine, Saint, 4th cent.?, Alexandrian virgin martyr. Nothing certain is known of her life, and in 1969 her name was dropped from the liturgical calendar. According to tradition she was learned. She was condemned to die on the wheel and was saved by a miracle, but was later beheaded. Her principal shrine is the great monastery of Mt. Sinai. Attributes: sword, crown, palm, wheel, and book. The marriage of St. Catherine to Christ, a popular Renaissance subject, represents symbolically the dedication of her virginity. Feast: Nov. 25.

Catherine I, 1683?–1727, czarina of Russia (1725–27). Of Livonian peasant origin, Martha Skavronskaya was a domestic when she was captured (1702) by

Russian soldiers. As mistress of Aleksandr D. MENSHIKOV she met Czar Peter I (Peter the Great), who made her his mistress. After her conversion from the Lutheran to the Orthodox Church (when she changed her name from Martha to Catherine), Peter, who had divorced his first wife, married her (1712). In 1724 he had her crowned czarina and joint ruler. Her loyalty and devotion to her difficult husband were remarkable. When Peter died without naming a successor, Menshikov and the imperial guards raised Catherine to the throne. Her policy was dominated by Menshikov. Peter II succeeded her; her daughter Elizabeth became czarina in 1741.

Catherine II or **Catherine the Great,** 1729–96, czarina of Russia (1762–96). A German princess, she was the daughter of Christian Augustus, prince of Anhalt-Zerbst. She emerged from the obscurity of her relatively modest background when, in 1744, Czarina Elizabeth of Russia, partly on the recommendation of Frederick II of Prussia, chose her as the wife of the future Czar PETER III. Accepting the Orthodox faith, she changed her original name, Sophie, to Catherine. Her successful effort to become completely Russian made her popular with important political elements who opposed her eccentric husband. Neglected by the czarevich, Catherine read widely, especially Voltaire and Montesquieu, and informed herself of Russian conditions. In Jan., 1762, Peter succeeded to the throne, but he immediately alienated powerful groups with his program and personality. In June, 1762, a group of conspirators headed by Grigori ORLOV, Catherine's lover, proclaimed Catherine autocrat, and shortly afterward Peter was murdered. Catherine began her rule with great projects of reform. She drew up a document based largely on the writings of BECCARIA and Montesquieu to serve as a guide for an enlightened code of laws. She summoned a legislative commission (with representatives of all classes except the serfs) to put this guide into law, but she disbanded the commission before it could complete the code. Some have questioned the sincerity of Catherine's "enlightened" outlook, and there is no doubt that she became more conservative as a result of the peasant rising (1773–74) under PUGACHEV. As a result, the nobility's administrative power was strengthened when Catherine reorganized (1775) the provincial administration to increase the central government's control over rural areas. This reform established a system of provinces, subdivided into districts, which endured until 1917. In 1785, Catherine issued a charter that made the gentry of each district and province a legal body with the right to petition the throne, freed nobles from taxation and state service, made their status hereditary, and gave them absolute control over their lands and peasants. Another charter, issued to the towns, proved of little value to them. Catherine extended serfdom to parts of the Ukraine and transferred large tracts of state lands to favored noblemen. The serfs' remaining rights were strictly curtailed. She also encouraged colonization of ALASKA and of areas gained by conquest. She increased Russian control over the Baltic provinces and the Ukraine. Catherine attempted to increase Russia's power at the expense of its weaker neighbors, Poland and Turkey. In 1764 she established a virtual protectorate over Poland by placing her former lover Stanislaus Poniatowski on the Polish throne as STANISLAUS II. Catherine eventually secured the largest portion in successive partitions of Poland among Russia, Prussia, and Austria (see POLAND, PARTITIONS OF). Catherine's first war with Turkey (1768–74; see RUSSO-TURKISH WARS) ended with the Treaty of Kuchuk Kainarji, which made Russia the dominant power in the Middle East. Catherine and her advisers, particularly POTEMKIN, developed a program known as the Greek project, which aimed at a partition of Turkey's European holdings among Russia, Austria, and other countries. However, her attempts to break up the Ottoman Empire met with only partial success. In 1783 she annexed the Crimea, which had gained independence from Turkey by the Treaty of Kuchuk Kainarji. Her triumphal tour of S Russia, accompanied by Potemkin, provoked the Turks to renew warfare (1787–92). The Treaty of Jassy (1792) confirmed the annexation of the Crimea and cemented Russia's hold on the northern coast of the Black Sea. Catherine also extended Russian influence in European affairs. In 1778 she acted as mediator between Prussia and Austria in the War of the Bavarian Succession, and in 1780 she organized a league to defend neutral shipping against Great Britain, which was then engaged in the war of the American Revolution. Catherine increased the power and prestige of Russia by skillful diplomacy and by extending Russia's western boundary into the heart of central Europe. An enthusiastic patron of literature, art, and education, Catherine wrote memoirs, comedies, and stories, and corresponded with the French Encyclopedists, including Voltaire, Diderot, and d'Alembert (who were largely responsible for her glorious contemporary reputation). She encouraged some criticism and discussion of social and political problems until the French Revolution made her an outspoken conservative and turned her against all who dared criticize her regime. Although she had many lovers, only Orlov, Potemkin, and P. L. Zubov (1767–1822) were influential in government affairs. She was succeeded by her son Paul I. See biographies by Kazimierz Waliszewski (tr. 1894, repr. 1968), Katharine Anthony (1925), Zoe Oldenbourg (1965), and L. J. Oliva (1971); G. S. Thomson, *Catherine the Great and the Expansion of Russia* (1947, repr. 1962); M. E. von Almedingen, *Catherine, Empress of Russia* (1961); Marc Raeff, ed., *Catherine the Great: A Profile* (1972).

Catherine de' Medici (dĕ mĕd'ĭchē, Ital. dā mĕ'dēchē), 1519–89, queen of France, daughter of Lorenzo de' Medici, duke of Urbino. She was married (1533) to the duc d'Orléans, later King Henry II. Neglected during the reign of her husband and that of her eldest son, Francis II, she became (1560) regent for her son CHARLES IX, who succeeded Francis. She remained Charles's adviser until his death (1574). Concerned primarily with preserving the power of the king in the religious conflicts of the time, with the aid of her chancellor Michel de L'HÔPITAL, she at first adopted a conciliatory policy toward the Huguenots, or French Protestants. The outbreak (1562) of the Wars of Religion (see RELIGION, WARS OF), however, led her to an alliance with the Catholic party under François de GUISE. After the defeat of royal troops by the Huguenot leader Gaspard de COLIGNY, Catherine agreed (1570) to the peace of St. Germain. Subsequently Coligny gained considerable influence over Charles IX. Fearing for her own power, and opposed to Coligny's schemes for expansion in the Low Countries, which might lead to war with Spain, Catherine and Henri de Guise arranged Coligny's assassination. When the first attempt failed, she took part in planning the massacre of SAINT BARTHOLOMEW'S DAY (1572) in which Coligny and hundreds of other Protestants were murdered. After the accession of her third son, Henry III, she vainly tried to revive her old conciliatory policy. See Edith Sichel, *Catherine de' Medici and the French Reformation* (1905, repr. 1969) and *The Later Years of Catherine de' Medici* (1908, repr. 1969); Paul Van Dyke, *Catherine de Médicis* (1922); Ralph Roeder, *Catherine de' Medici and the Lost Revolution* (1937); Sir J. E. Neale, *The Age of Catherine de Medici* (1962); W. H. Ross, *Catherine de' Medici* (1973).

Catherine Howard, queen of England: see HOWARD, CATHERINE.

Catherine of Aragón: see KATHARINE OF ARAGÓN.

Catherine of Braganza (brəgăn'zə), 1638–1705, queen consort of Charles II of England, daughter of John IV of Portugal. She was married to Charles in 1662. As part of her dowry England secured Bombay and Tangier. Unpopular in England for her Roman Catholic faith, she also had to suffer the humiliation of her husband's infidelities and the disappointment of her own childlessness. In 1678 she was accused by Titus OATES of a plot to poison the king but was protected from the charge by Charles himself. After William III's accession she returned to Portugal, where she supported the commercial Treaty of Methuen (1703) with England, and in 1704 she acted as regent for her brother, Peter II.

Catherine of Siena, Saint (sēĕn'ə), 1347–80, Italian mystic and diplomat, a member of the third order of the Dominicans, Doctor of the Church. The daughter of Giacomo Benincasa, a Sienese dyer, Catherine from early childhood had mystic visions and practiced austerities; she also showed the devotion to others and the winning manner that characterized her life. From the age of about 19, Catherine devoted herself to the poor and the sick, not sparing her own frail health. In 1370, in response to a vision, she began to take part in the public life of her time, sending letters to the great of the day. She went to Avignon and exerted decisive influence in inducing Pope GREGORY XI to end the "Babylonian captivity" of the papacy and return to Rome in 1376. As papal ambassador to Florence, she helped bring about peace between Florence and the Holy See. In the Great Schism, she adhered to the Roman claimant and helped to advance his cause. In 1375 she is supposed to have received the five wounds of the stigmata, visible only to herself until after her death. She was the center of a spiritual revival almost everywhere she went. A formidable family of devoted followers gathered around her. Her mysticism contains overwhelming love for humanity as well as love for God. Though she never learned to write, she dictated hundreds of letters and a notable mystic work, commonly called in English *The Dialogue of Saint Catherine of Siena* or *A Treatise on Divine Providence* (or both as title and subtitle), which has been much used in devotional literature. She was one of the major religious figures of the Middle Ages. Feast: April 30. The accounts of her life collected by her followers were used in a biography by her confessor, Fra Raimondo da Capua (1398). See *Saint Catherine as Seen in Her Letters* (ed. by V. D. Scudder, 1905); biographies by Alice Curtayne (1929), Sigrid Undset (tr. 1954), and J. M. Perrin (tr. 1965); F. P. Keyes, *Three Ways of Love* (1963).

Catherine of Valois (văl'wä, Fr. välwä'), 1401–37, queen consort of Henry V of England, daughter of Charles VI of France. Married in 1420, she bore Henry the son who was to become Henry VI. Some years after Henry V's death (1522), Catherine married the Welshman Owen TUDOR; from them the Tudor kings of England were descended.

Catherine Parr, queen of England: see PARR, CATHERINE.

Catherine Tekakwitha (tĕk"äkwĭth'ə), 1656–80, American Indian holy woman, b. Auriesville, N.Y. Her name is sometimes given as Kateri Tegakouita. She was the daughter of a Mohawk chief and was baptized a Roman Catholic at the age of seven by a Jesuit missionary. Her tribesmen jeered and stoned her for her adopted faith, and she eventually went to a missionary settlement in Canada. Piety led her to the severest asceticism. The movement for her beatification began in the 1930s. See biography by M. C. Buehrle (1954).

Catherine the Great: see CATHERINE II.

cathode, ELECTRODE through which current leaves an electric device. In ELECTROLYSIS, it is the negative electrode in the electolytic cell.

cathode-ray tube, special-purpose electron tube in which electrons are accelerated by high-voltage anodes, formed into a beam by focusing electrodes, and projected toward a phosphorescent screen that forms one face of the tube. The beam of electrons leaves a bright spot wherever it strikes the phosphor

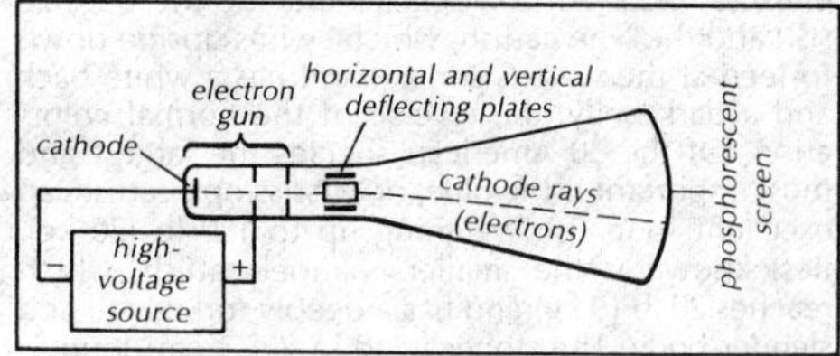

Cathode-ray tube

screen. To form a display, or image, on the screen, the electron beam is deflected in the vertical and horizontal directions either by the electrostatic effect of electrodes within the tube or by magnetic fields produced by coils located around the neck of the tube. Some cathode-ray tubes can produce multiple beams of electrons and have phosphor screens that are capable of displaying more than one color. Principally, these are made for color television receivers, but some are made for special-purpose OSCILLOSCOPES. Cathode-ray tubes are also used in radar and sonar displays.

Catholic Apostolic Church, religious community originating in England c.1831 and extending later to Germany and the United States (1848). It was founded under the influence of Edward IRVING; its members are sometimes called Irvingites. Because of their prophetic gifts, 12 apostles (including Henry DRUMMOND) were in 1835 set aside as officers. They were expected to survive until the Second Coming of Christ, but the last of them died in 1901. When the apostles began to die, a schism took place in Germany over the appointing of successors. This led to the formation (1863) of the New Apostolic Church, the formal name of the present-day sect. An angel, or bishop, presides over each congregation; he is assisted by pastors, teachers, and others. Symbolism and mystery of worship characterize the elaborate liturgy, which has borrowed much from the Roman Catholic Church, including devotion to the Blessed Virgin Mary. Much emphasis is given to the Second Coming of Christ. The membership is about 50,000, half of which is in Germany. See P. E. Shaw, *The Catholic Apostolic Church* (1946); R. A. Davenport, *Albury Apostles* (1970).

Catholic Church [Gr.,=universal], the body of Christians, living and dead, considered as an organization. It is common for Christian groups to identify their particular churches (exclusively or not) as the Catholic Church. The word *catholic* was first used c.110 to describe the Church by St. Ignatius of Antioch. In speaking of the time before the Reformation, Catholic is technically used to mean orthodox (i.e., those accepting the decrees of Leo I and the Council of Chalcedon). Today in English it usually means the Roman Catholic Church. Protestants use the words in their original sense to designate the Christian Church taken as a whole.

Catholic Emancipation, term applied to the process by which Roman Catholics in the British Isles were relieved in the late 18th and early 19th cent. of civil disabilities. They had been under oppressive regulations placed by various statutes dating as far back as the time of Henry VIII (see PENAL LAWS). This process of removing the disabilities culminated in the Catholic Emancipation Act of 1829 (and some subsequent provisions), but it had begun a number of years before. Priest hunting, in general, ended by the mid-18th cent. In 1778, English Catholics were relieved of the restrictions on land inheritance and purchase. A savage reaction to these concessions produced the Gordon Riots (see GORDON, LORD GEORGE) of 1780, and the whole history of Catholic Emancipation is one of struggle against great resistance. In 1791 the Roman Catholic Relief Act repealed most of the disabilities in Great Britain, provided Catholics took an oath of loyalty, and in 1793 the army, the navy, the universities, and the judiciary were opened to Catholics, although seats in Parliament and some offices were still denied. These reforms were sponsored by William PITT the Younger, who hoped thereby to split the alliance of Irish Catholics and Protestants. But Pitt's attempt to secure a general repeal of the Penal Laws was thwarted by George III. Pope Pius VII consented to a royal veto on episcopal nominations if the Penal Laws were repealed, but the move failed. In Ireland the repeal (1782) of Poynings' Law (see under POYNINGS, SIR EDWARD) was followed by an act (1792) of the Irish Parliament relaxing the marriage and education laws and an act (1793) allowing Catholics to vote and hold most offices. By the Act of Union (1800) the Irish Parliament ceased to exist, and Ireland was given representation in the British Parliament. Then, since the Irish were a minority group in the British legislature, many English ministers began to advocate Catholic Emancipation, influenced also by the decline of the papacy as a factor in secular politics. Irish agitation, headed by Daniel O'CONNELL and his Catholic Association, was successful in securing the admission of Catholics to Parliament. In 1828 the TEST ACT was repealed, and O'Connell, although still ineligible to sit, secured his election to Parliament from Co. Clare. Alarmed by the growing tension in Ireland, the duke of WELLINGTON, the prime minister, allowed the Catholic Emancipation Bill, sponsored by Sir Robert PEEL, to pass (1829). Catholics were now on the same footing as Protestants except for a few restrictions, most of which were later removed. The Act of SETTLEMENT is still in force, however, and Catholics are excluded from the throne and from the office of lord chancellor. See studies by Bernard Ward (1911), Denis Gwynn (1929), J. A. Reynolds (1954, repr. 1970), and G. I. T. Machin (1964); S. L. Gwynn, *Henry Grattan and His Times* (1939, repr. 1971).

Catholic League, in French history: see LEAGUE.

Catholic University of America, at Washington, D.C.; Roman Catholic; coeducational, the only university belonging to the U.S. hierarchy of the Roman Catholic Church; founded 1887 and opened 1889. It includes a college of arts and sciences as well as schools of canon law, sacred theology, and social service. The university has access to the facilities of the national laboratories at Oak Ridge, Tenn., and participates in a cooperative program with the Armed Forces Radiobiology Research Institute at Bethesda, Md.

Catiline (Lucius Sergius Catilina) (kăt'ĭlīn), c.108 B.C.–62 B.C., Roman politician and conspirator. At first a conservative and a partisan of Sulla, he was praetor in 68 B.C. and governor of Africa in 67 B.C. The next year he was barred from candidacy for the consulship by accusations of misconduct in office, charges that later proved false. Feeling with some justification that he had been cheated, he concocted a wild plot to murder the consuls. He and the other conspirators were acquitted (65 B.C.). Catiline became more bitter than ever against the conservatives and began to advocate popular demagogic proposals. When in 63 B.C. he ran again for consul, he found CICERO, the incumbent, and the conservative party anxious to stop his election at any cost. Catiline was defeated, prompting him to try for the consulship by force. He sent money for the troops in Etruria and spread lavish promises in Rome. Cicero became alarmed and on Nov. 8, with facts gained from Catiline's mistress, accused him in the senate (*First Oration against Catiline*). Catiline fled to Etruria. The conspirators remaining in the city did not cease activities but even approached some ambassadors of the Allobroges. The ambassadors reported the whole plot to Cicero, who arrested the conspirators and arraigned them in the senate on Dec. 3. On Dec. 5 they were condemned to death and executed, in spite of a most eloquent appeal from Julius CAESAR to use moderation. Cicero's haste and summary behavior were technically illegal, and it was on a charge (by CLODIUS) of executing these Roman citizens without due process of law that Cicero was exiled. Catiline did not surrender; he fell in battle at Pistoia a month later. The prime sources for Catiline's conspiracy are Cicero's four orations against him and Sallust's biography of him. Both of these are prejudiced and unreliable. Catiline's treason may be partly explained, although not condoned, by the ruthless and devious means used against him. The affair did little credit to any concerned, except for the honest and patriotic CATO THE YOUNGER and possibly for Julius Caesar, who made a daring plea to a vindictive and ruthless majority on behalf of the conspirators whom he scorned. See study by Lester Hutchinson (1967).

Catinat, Nicolas (nēkōlä' kätēnä'), 1637–1712, marshal of France. The son of a magistrate, he won promotion by merit rather than by wealth or descent. In the War of the Grand Alliance he commanded against Duke Victor Amadeus II of Savoy, whom he defeated in N Italy at Staffarda (1690) and at Marsaglia (1693). Early in the War of the Spanish Succession, he commanded the French army in Italy, against Prince Eugene of Savoy, but after suffering reverses he was replaced. He retired in 1705 and later wrote his memoirs.

cation (kăt'ī'ən), atom or group of atoms carrying a positive charge. The charge results because there are more protons than electrons in the cation. Cations can be formed from a metal by oxidation (see OXIDATION AND REDUCTION), from a neutral base (see ACIDS AND BASES) by protonation, or from a polar compound by ionization. Cationic species include Na^+, Mg^{++}, and NH_4^+. The cations of the TRANSITION ELEMENTS have characteristic colors in water solution. SALTS are made up of cations and ANIONS. See ION.

Cat Island: see SAN SALVADOR, island.

Catledge, Turner, 1901–, American newspaperman, b. Ackerman, Miss. He worked for several southern newspapers before being hired by the New York *Times* in 1929. He became a political reporter, eventually heading the *Times*'s Washington News Bureau. He was made managing editor, and later executive editor, and in 1968 became vice president of the New York Times Company. He has been semiretired since 1970, remaining a member of the board of directors of the *Times*. See his autobiography, *My Life and Times* (1971).

Catlin, George, 1796–1872, American traveler and artist, b. Wilkes-Barre, Pa. Educated as a lawyer, he practiced in Philadelphia for two years but turned to art study and became a portrait painter in New York City. He went west c.1832 to study and paint the Indians, and after executing numerous portraits and tribal scenes he took his collection to Europe in 1839. In 1841 he published *Manners, Customs, and Condition of the North American Indians*, in two volumes, with about 300 engravings. Three years later he published 25 plates, entitled *Catlin's North American Indian Portfolio*, and, in 1848, *Eight Years' Travels and Residence in Europe*. From 1852 to 1857 he traveled through South and Central America and later returned for further exploration in the Far West. The record of these later years is contained in *Last Rambles amongst the Indians of the Rocky Mountains and the Andes* (1868) and *My Life among the Indians* (ed. by N. G. Humphreys, 1909). Of his 470 full-length portraits of Indians and tribal scenes, the greater part constitutes the Catlin Gallery of the National Museum, Washington, D.C.; some 700 sketches are in the American Museum of Natural History, New York City. His observations of the Indians have been questioned as to accuracy. He was the first white man to see the Minnesota pipestone quarries, and pipestone is also called catlinite. See Harold McCracken, *George Catlin and the Old Frontier* (1959); Robert Plate, *Palette and Tomahawk: the Life of George Catlin* (1962); M. C. Roehmer, *The Catlin Family Papers* (1966).

catnip or **catmint,** strong-scented perennial herb (*Nepeta cataria*) of the family Labiatae (MINT family), native to Europe and Asia but naturalized in the United States. A tea of the leaves and flowing tops has long been used as a domestic remedy for various ailments. Catnip is best known for its stimulating effect on cats. Catnip is classified in the division MAGNOLIOPHYTA, class Magnoliopsida, order Lamiales, family Labiatae.

Catoche, Cape (kätō'chā), extremity of Yucatán peninsula, SE Mexico. It was the first Mexican land seen by the Spanish (1517).

Catoctin Mountain Park: see NATIONAL PARKS AND MONUMENTS (table).

Catonsville (kā'tənzvĭl), uninc. city (1970 pop. 54,812), Baltimore co., N Md., a suburb of Baltimore. A state hospital and park are nearby.

Cato Street Conspiracy: see THISTLEWOOD, ARTHUR.

Cato the Elder (kā'tō) or **Cato the Censor,** Lat. *Cato Major* or *Cato Censorius*, 234–149 B.C., Roman statesman and moralist, whose full name was Marcus Porcius Cato. He fought in the Second Punic War and later served as quaestor (204), aedile (199), praetor (198), consul (195), and censor (184). He was renowned for his devotion to the old Roman ideals—simplicity of life, honesty, and unflinching courage. He inveighed against extravagance and new customs, but his policy was not aimed at repression but rather at reform and the rebuilding of Roman life. He sought to restrict seats in the senate to the worthy and undertook much building, including the repair of the city sewers. He was sent on an official visit to Carthage in his old age. Upon his return he expressed stern disapproval of Carthaginian ways and told the senate to destroy Carthage. He thus helped to bring on the Third Punic War, in which Carthage was destroyed. Probably his detestation of luxury and cultivated ways inspired the deep hatred that he had for the Scipio family. He himself deliberately affected a rustic appearance and rustic manners. However, he complacently accepted class division and treated his servants harshly. He wrote many works, most of which are now lost. Probably the most influential was his history of early Rome. His *De agri cultura* or *De re rustica*, translated as *On Farming*, is a practical treatise that offers valuable information on agricultural methods and country life in his day.

Cato the Younger or **Cato of Utica,** 95 B.C.–46 B.C., Roman statesman, whose full name was Marcus Porcius Cato; great-grandson of Cato the Elder. Reared by his uncle Marcus Livius Drusus, he showed an intense devotion to the principles of the early republic. He had one of the greatest reputations for honesty and incorruptibility of any man in ancient times, and his Stoicism put him above the graft and bribery of his day. His politics were extremely conservative, and his refusal to compromise made him unpopular with certain of his colleagues. He was from the first a violent opponent of Julius CAESAR and, outdoing CICERO in vituperation of the conspiracy of CATILINE in 63 B.C., tried to implicate Caesar in that plot, although maintaining his fairness to all. As a result he was sent (59 B.C.) to Cyprus by CLODIUS in what amounted to exile. He and his party supported POMPEY after the break with Caesar. He accompanied Pompey across the Adriatic and held Dyrrhachium (modern Durazzo) for him until after the defeat at Pharsala. Then he and Quintus Caecilius Metellus Pius Scipio (see SCIPIO, family) went to Africa and continued the struggle against Caesar there. Cato was in command at Utica. After Caesar crushed (46 B.C.) Scipio at THAPSUS, Cato committed suicide, bidding his people make their peace with Caesar. Cicero and Marcus Junius BRUTUS (Cato's son-in-law) wrote eulogies of him while Caesar wrote his *Anticato* against him; the noble tragedy of his death has been the subject of many dramas. He became the symbol of probity in public life. See biography by J. M. Conant (1953).

cat's-eye, gemstone that displays a thin band of reflected light on its surface when cut as a cabochon. Its name is derived from its supposed resemblance to the eye of a cat. The optical effect, known as chatoyancy, is caused by the reflection of light from very thin, closely spaced filaments in parallel arrangement within the stone. True cat's-eye, a variety of CHRYSOBERYL from Ceylon (now Sri Lanka) and Brazil, is the most valuable, but some quartz, tourmaline, and a few other minerals that display chatoyancy are also used as gems. A golden-yellow species called tiger's-eye is a type of naturally altered crocidolite asbestos.

Catskill (kăt'skĭl), village (1970 pop. 5,317), seat of Greene co., SE N.Y., on the Hudson River; settled

17th cent. by Dutch, inc. 1806. Connected with the manufacturing town of Hudson, N.Y., by the Rip Van Winkle Bridge (completed 1935), it is a gateway to resorts in the Catskill Mts. The Catskill Game Farm is nearby. Thomas Cole lived and painted in the village.

Catskill Aqueduct: see ASHOKAN RESERVOIR, N.Y.

Catskill Mountains, dissected plateau of the Appalachian Mt. system, SE N.Y., just W of the Hudson River, to which it descends abruptly in places. This glaciated region, which is well wooded and rolling, with deep gorges and many beautiful waterfalls, is drained by the headstreams of the Delaware River and by Esopus, Schoharie, Rondout, and Catskill creeks. Most of the summits are c.3,000 ft (910 m) above sea level; Slide Mt. (4,180 ft/1,274 m) and Hunter Mt. (4,040 ft/1,231 m) are the highest. Close to New York City, the area is a popular summer and winter resort. Ashokan Reservoir is a source of the New York metropolitan area's water supply. Catskill Forest Preserve embraces some of the most impressive scenery of the Catskills, including the region of the Rip Van Winkle legend. See Alf Evers, *The Catskills,* (1972).

Catt, Carrie Chapman, 1859-1947, American suffragist and peace advocate, b. Carrie Lane, Ripon, Wis., grad. Iowa State College, 1880. She was superintendent of schools (1883-84) in Mason City, Iowa. In 1885 she married Lee Chapman, a journalist (d. 1886), and in 1890, George Catt, an engineer (d. 1905). From 1890 to 1900 an organizer for the National American Woman Suffrage Association, she became its president in 1900. She led the campaign to win suffrage through a Federal amendment to the Constitution. After the ratification of the Nineteenth Amendment (1920), she organized the League of Women Voters for the education of women in politics. At the Berlin convocation of the International Council of Women she helped organize the International Woman Suffrage Alliance, of which she was president from 1904 to 1923. After 1923 she devoted her efforts chiefly to the peace movement. With Nettie R. Shuler she wrote *Woman Suffrage and Politics* (1923). See biography by M. G. Peck (1944).

cattail or **reed mace,** any plant of the genus *Typha,* perennial herbs found in almost all open marshes. The cattail (also called club rush) has long narrow leaves, sometimes used for weaving chair seats, and a single tall stem bearing two sets of tiny flowers, the male flowers above the female. The pollinated female flowers form the familiar cylindrical spike of fuzzy brown fruits; the male flowers drop off and leave a naked stalk tip. The starchy rootstock can be used for food. Cattails are classified in the division MAGNOLIOPHYTA, class Liliatae, order Typhales, family Typhaceae.

Cattaneo, Carlo (kät-tänĕ'ō), 1810-69, Italian nationalist and philosopher, b. Milan. He edited (1839-44) the journal *Il Politecnico,* and in 1848 he led the nationalist revolt in Milan against Austria, which he related in *L'insurrezione di Milano nel 1848.* Forced into exile after the end of the first Italian war for independence, he eventually settled in Lugano, Switzerland, where he revived and edited (1860-63) *Il Politecnico.* An empiricist and a social positivist, Cattaneo saw philosophy as having primarily a social role: the philosopher's business is to deal with the problems of current history. History was not conceived by Cattaneo as following from any first principles; its phenomena were plural and subject to change, so its problems were also continually different. What is consistently true about the problems of history is that they are social, and the notion of a philosopher as a detached intelligence is both psychologically and practically untenable. See C. M. Lovett, *Carlo Cattaneo and the Politics of the Risorgimento* (1973).

Cattermole, George, 1800-1868, English watercolor painter and illustrator. His subject matter was varied, and his works were popular during his lifetime. He painted picturesque scenes of antique subjects in a romantic mode. He made illustrations for some of Dickens's works, including *Barnaby Rudge.* Cattermole is represented in most of the important British galleries.

cattle, name for the RUMINANT mammals of the genus *Bos,* and particularly those of the domesticated species, *Bos taurus* and *B. indica.* The term oxen is used more or less synonymously; it sometimes includes other closely related animals, such as the BUFFALO and the BISON. In more restricted usage, ox refers to a mature castrated male used for draft purposes. In the nomenclature of domestic cattle a grown male is a bull, a grown female a cow, an infant a calf, and an animal between one and two years old a yearling. A female that has not given birth is a heifer; a castrated male is a steer. Most cattle have unbranched horns consisting of a horny layer surrounding a bone extension of the skull; these horns, unlike those of deer, are not shed. Some domestic breeds are naturally hornless, and some customarily have their horns removed. Western, or European, domestic cattle (*Bos taurus*) are thought to be descended mainly from the AUROCHS, a large European wild ox domesticated during the Stone Age. A smaller species, the Celtic shorthorn, was the most important domestic ox of the Stone Age and may also be involved in the ancestry of *B. taurus.* The ZEBU, or Indian ox, *B. indica,* is the humped domestic species of Asia and Africa; in the United States this type of cattle is called Brahman. The YAK, *B. grunniens,* exists in Asia in both wild and domestic forms. There are also wild and semi-domesticated species in Asia. Domestic cattle were first brought to the Western Hemisphere by Columbus on his second voyage. Wealth has sometimes consisted chiefly of cattle and has been measured in terms of the number of cattle a person owns; the word *pecuniary* is derived from the Latin *pecus,* cattle, and the words *cattle, chattel,* and *capital* are related. Breeding for improvement of beef and dairy qualities was practiced by the Romans but was not established on scientific principles until the middle of the 18th cent. by English livestock breeder Robert Bakewell. The principal beef breeds include the ANGUS and HEREFORD. The principal dairy breeds include the AYRSHIRE, BROWN SWISS, GUERNSEY, HOLSTEIN-FRIESIAN, and JERSEY. The chief dual-purpose breeds include the DEVON, RED POLL, and SHORTHORN. Associations have been formed by breeders interested in improving the various breeds. Cattle are classified in the phylum CHORDATA, subphylum Vertebrata, class Mammalia, order Artiodactyla, family Bovidae. See also BEEF; DAIRYING. See publications of the U.S. Dept. of Agriculture; A. L. Neumann and R R. Snapp, *Beef Cattle* (6th ed. 1969); J. E. Rouse, *World Cattle* (2 vol., 1970).

cattleya (kăt'lēə): see ORCHID.

Catton, Bruce, 1899–, American historian, b. Petoskey, Mich. He studied at Oberlin College and then entered upon a varied career as a journalist (1926–42) and public official (1942-52). His service with the War Production Board during World War II led to his first major book, *The War Lords of Washington* (1948). After 1952 he devoted himself to full-time literary work, serving as an editor from 1954 (senior editor, 1959) of the *American Heritage* magazine. In 1954 he received the Pulitzer Prize for his historical work, *A Stillness at Appomattox* (1953). Catton has written extensively on the military history of the Civil War; his many works include *Mr. Lincoln's Army* (1951), *Glory Road* (1952), *This Hallowed Ground* (1956), *Grant Moves South* (1960), *Grant Takes Command* (1969), *The Centennial History of the Civil War* (3 vol., 1961-65), and *Prefaces to History* (1970).

Catullus (Caius Valerius Catullus) (kətŭl'əs), 84? B.C.-54? B.C., Roman poet, b. Verona. Of a well-to-do family, he went c.62 B.C. to Rome, where he and other young writers formed a cult of youth. He fell deeply in love, probably with Clodia, sister of the demagogue Publius Clodius. She was a beautiful, notorious woman, suspected of murdering her husband. Catullus wrote to his beloved, addressed as Lesbia (to recall Sappho of Lesbos), a series of superb little poems that run from early passion and tenderness to the hatred and disillusionment that overwhelmed him after his mistress was faithless. Of the 116 extant poems attributed to him, three (18-20) are almost certainly spurious. They include, besides the Lesbia poems, poems to his young friend Juventius; epigrams, ranging from the genial to the obscenely derisive; elegies; a few long poems, notably "Attis" and a nuptial poem honoring Thetis and Peleus; and various short pieces. His satire is vigorous and flexible, his light poems gay and full-bodied. He was influenced by the Alexandrians and drew much on the Greeks for form and meter, but his genius outran all models. Catullus is one of the greatest lyric poets of all time. Two of the most popular of his poems are the 10-line poem, touching and simple, which ends, "frater ave atque vale" [hail, brother, and farewell], and "On the Death of Lesbia's Sparrow." See translations by Peter Whigham (1966), James Michie (1969), Reney Myers and R. J. Ormsby (1970); studies by A. L. Wheeler (1934, repr. 1964), Tenney Frank (1928, repr. 1965), and Kenneth Quinn (1959, 1970, and 1972).

Catulus (kăch'ōōləs), family of ancient Rome, of the Lutatian gens. **Caius Lutatius Catulus** was consul in 242 B.C. He won the great Roman naval victory over Carthage off the Aegates (modern Aegadian Isles) that ended the First Punic War. **Quintus Lutatius Catulus,** d. 87 B.C., was consul in 102 B.C. His colleague in the consulship was MARIUS, with whom he went north to oppose a Germanic invasion. He had to retreat before the Cimbri until Marius returned from Gaul. The two then defeated the Cimbri near Vercelli in 101 B.C. He later opposed Marius in the Social War and favored Sulla. Proscribed by the Marians, he either committed suicide or was killed. He was the patron of a literary circle and was himself a writer and a philospher. Cicero praises his oratory. His son, also **Quintus Lutatius Catulus,** d. c.60 B.C., was consul in 78 B.C. He opposed the constitutional changes sought by Marcus Lepidus (d. 77 B.C.; see under LEPIDUS), and when Lepidus led a revolt, Catulus and Pompey defeated him. Catulus was censor in 65 B.C. He was the leader of the archconservative group. He led the minority opposing the conferring of unusual powers on Pompey by the Manilian Law in 66 B.C., and he was one of the bitterest opponents of Julius Caesar.

Cauca (kou'kä), river, c.600 mi (970 km) long, rising in the Cordillera Central, near Popayán, W Colombia. It flows north in a rift valley between the Cordillera Central and Cordillera Occidental to the Magdalena River. It is navigable in its lower course and drains a fertile valley; coffee is the chief crop. The valley has many minerals including gold. There is a river-control and utilization scheme on the upper Cauca.

Caucasia: see CAUCASUS.

Caucasian and **Caucasoid:** see RACE.

Caucasian Gates: see DARYAL.

Caucasian languages, family of languages spoken by about five million people in the CAUCASUS region of the USSR. The Caucasian languages take their name from the Caucasus Mountains, on the slopes of which their original homeland is believed to have been located. This linguistic family was once considerably more extensive; however, only about 25 of its tongues have survived into modern times. There are two major subdivisions of the Caucasian family of languages, northern and southern. Whether or not these two branches are related linguistically is still disputed, but Georgian scholars since the 1930s have regarded as proved the kinship of all the Caucasian tongues. The northern group consists of about 20 languages native to two million people. Its most important members are Chechen and Abkhaz, which are spoken in the Soviet Union, and Adyghe (with its two dialects of Kabardin and Circassian), which is spoken not only in the USSR, but also to some extent in Turkey and Syria. The southern group of Caucasian languages includes four tongues with some three million speakers. Georgian, the leading member of the northern group, is the mother tongue of well over two million people in the Georgian SSR of the USSR and in neighboring areas of Turkey and Azerbaijan in Iran. It is a modern representative of the language of the ancient Colchians, of whom the celebrated mythological figure Medea was one. A literature in Georgian goes back to the 5th cent. A.D., and the language has two alphabets of its own, one of which is still in use, although increasingly the Cyrillic alphabet is being adopted. In general, the Caucasian languages have inflection and tend to be agglutinative in that different linguistic elements, each of which exists separately and has a fixed meaning, are often joined to form one word. Phonetically, the Caucasian tongues are distinctive, combining simplicity of vowels with abundant richness of consonants. Many of the Caucasian languages are spoken by comparatively few people (that is, fewer than 100,000), and they are gradually giving ground to Russian. The chances for survival for many of the Caucasian tongues are not considered good. An exception is Georgian, which has a comparatively large number of speakers, whose cultural development is higher than that found among other Caucasian-speaking peoples. See Bernhard Geiger et al., *Peoples and Languages of the Caucasus* (1959).

Caucasus (kô'kəsəs), Rus. *Kavkaz,* region and mountain system, SE European USSR. The mountain system extends c.750 mi (1,210 km) from the mouth of the Kuban River on the Black Sea SE to the Apsheron peninsula on the Caspian Sea. As a divide between Europe and Asia, the Caucasus has two major regions—North Caucasia and Transcaucasia. North Caucasia, composed mainly of plain (steppe) areas, begins at the Manych Depression and rises to the south, where it runs into the main mountain range, the Caucasus mts. This is a series of chains running northwest-southeast, including Mt. Elbrus (18,481 ft/5,633 m), the Dykh-Tau (17,050 ft/5,197 m), the Koshtan-Tau (16,850 ft/5,134 m), and Mt. Kazbek (16,541 ft/5,042 m). The Caucasus mts. are crossed by several passes, notably the MAMISON and the DARYAL, and by the GEORGIAN MILITARY ROAD and the OSSETIAN MILITARY ROAD, which connect North Caucasia with the second major section, Transcaucasia. This region includes the southern slopes of the Caucasus mts. and the depressions that link them with the Armenian plateau. North Caucasia, part of the Russian Soviet Federated Socialist Republic, includes KRASNODAR KRAY (with ADYGE AUTONOMOUS OBLAST), STAVROPOL KRAY (with the Cherkess Autonomous Oblast), KABARDINO-BALKAR AUTONOMOUS SOVIET SOCIALIST REPUBLIC, North Ossetian Autonomous Soviet Socialist Republic, DAGESTAN AUTONOMOUS SOVIET SOCIALIST REPUBLIC, and parts of the Rostov and GROZNY oblasts. Transcaucasia includes the GEORGIAN SOVIET SOCIALIST REPUBLIC (including the ABKHAZ AUTONOMOUS SOVIET SOCIALIST REPUBLIC, the ADZHAR AUTONOMOUS SOVIET SOCIALIST REPUBLIC, and the South Ossetian Autonomous Oblast), the AZERBAIJAN SOVIET SOCIALIST REPUBLIC (including the NAKHICHEVAN AUTONOMOUS SOVIET SOCIALIST REPUBLIC and the NAGORNO-KARABAKH Autonomous Oblast), and the ARMENIAN SOVIET SOCIALIST REPUBLIC. Over 40 languages are spoken by the ethnic groups of the entire region. The Ossetians, Kabardinians, Circassians, and Dagestani are the major groups in North Caucasia. The Armenians, Georgians, and Azerbaijani are the largest groups in Transcaucasia. The Kura and Rion river valleys have traditionally been the main thoroughfares of the Caucasus. Now the Rostov-Makhachkala-Baku RR links North Caucasia with Transcaucasia, and there is a line connecting Rostov-na-Donu and Armavir with the port of Batumi, beyond the Caucasus. In Transcaucasia the main line cuts through the center of the region from Baku, Tbilisi, and Kutaisi, and there are lines along the Turkish border and the Caspian Sea. Oil is the major product in the Caucasus, with fields at Baku, Grozny, and Maikop. There is an oil pipeline from Baku, on the Caspian, through Tbilisi to Batumi, on the Black Sea, and pipelines from the fields at Grozny to the port of Makhachkala and to Rostov-na-Donu. Iron and steel are produced at Rustavi from the ores of Azerbaijan. Manganese is mined at Chiatura, and there are ferro-manganese plants at Zestafoni. Power for these industries is produced at several large hydroelectric stations, notably at Kura. On the mountain slopes, which are densely covered by pine and deciduous trees, there is stock raising. In the valleys, citrus fruits, tea, cotton, grain, and livestock are raised. Along the Black Sea coast between Anapa and Sochi there are many resorts and summer homes. PYATIGORSK and KISLOVODSK are notable among the health and mineral resorts in North Caucasia. Major cities in the Caucasus are BAKU, YEREVAN, GROZNY, ORDZHONIKIDZE (formerly Dzaudzhikau), TBILISI, Krasnodar, Novorossiysk, Batumi, Kirovabad, and Leninakan. The Caucasus figured greatly in the legends of ancient Greece; Prometheus was chained on a Caucasian mountain, and Jason and his Argonauts sought the Golden Fleece at Colchis. Persians, Khazars, Arabs, Huns, Turko-Mongols, and Russians have invaded and migrated into the Caucasus and have given the region its ethnic and linguistic complexity. The Russians assumed control in the 19th cent. after a series of wars with Persia and Turkey. The people of Georgia and Armenia, then predominantly Christian, accepted Russian hegemony as protection from Turkish persecution. In Azerbaijan, Dagestan, and the historic region of CIRCASSIA, the people were largely Muslim. They bitterly fought Russian penetration and were pacified only after the Shamyl uprising. In World War II the invading German forces launched (July, 1942) a major drive to seize or neutralize the vast oil resources of the Caucasus. They penetrated deeply, but in Jan., 1943, the Soviets launched a winter offensive and by October had driven the Germans from the region. The romantic beauty of the Caucasus is much celebrated in Russian literature, most notably in Pushkin's poem "Captive of the Caucasus," Lermontov's novel *A Hero of Our Time*, and Tolstoy's novels *The Cossacks* and *Hadji Murad*.

Caucasus Indicus: see HINDU KUSH.

Cauchon, Pierre (pyĕr kōshôN'), d. 1442, bishop of Beauvais, France, president of the ecclesiastic court that convicted (1431) JOAN OF ARC at Rouen. His violent partisanship for the English made a fair trial impossible. Cauchon's procedure was repudiated by the church in the rehabilitation trial (1456) of Joan. See W. P. Barrett, *The Trial of Jeanne d' Arc* (1931).

Cauchy, Augustin Louis, Baron (ōgüstăN' lwē bärôN' kōshē'), 1789–1857, French mathematician. He was professor simultaneously (1816–30) at the École polytechnique, the Sorbonne, and the Collège de France in Paris. While a political exile (1830–38) he taught at the Univ. of Turin. He returned to the Sorbonne in 1848. Besides his influential work in every branch of mathematics (especially the theory of functions, integral and differential calculus, and algebraic analysis) he contributed to astronomy, optics, hydrodynamics, and other fields. Among his nearly 800 publications are works on the theory of waves (1815), algebraic analysis (1821), elasticity (1822), infinitesimal calculus (1823, 1826–28), differential calculus (1827), and the dispersion of light (1836).

caucus: see CONVENTION.

Cauda, Greece: see GÁVDHOS.

caudillo (kôdēl'yō Span. kouthē'yō), [Span.,=army chieftain], type of Spanish-American political leader that arose with the wars for independence from Spain. Caudillos have varied greatly in character, methods, and aims, but they share certain characteristics. The caudillo is frequently a MESTIZO, whose political platform is of little consequence, but whose personal magnetism commands the blind allegiance of the masses. He is daring and skilled in military matters. Although he almost invariably becomes an oligarch, he often begins his career by opposing the white plutocracy and sometimes the power of the church. In the eyes of the peasants, he is often a messiah. Caudillo rule tends to be based upon rigid discipline, although it is often brutal and arbitrary. The power of the caudillo is unchecked, and those under his rule are unprotected by any system of constitutional rights. Some famous caudillos have been Juan Manuel de ROSAS and Juan Facundo QUIROGA of Argentina, Gabriel GARCÍA MORENO of Ecuador, Porfirio DÍAZ of Mexico, and Rafael Leonidas TRUJILLO MOLINA of the Dominican Republic. In Spain, where Gen. Francisco Franco adopted the title *el Caudillo*, the term is used literally and possesses no disparaging connotations.

Caudine Forks (kô'dīn), narrow passes in the Southern Apennines, S Italy, on the road from Capua to Benevento. There, in 321 B.C., the Samnites routed a Roman army.

Caughnawaga (kä'näwä"gə), community and Indian reserve, S Que., Canada, on the St. Lawrence River opposite Lachine. It was founded (1676) as a refuge for Iroquois converts to the Christian faith.

Caulaincourt, Armand Augustin Louis, marquis de (ärmäN' ōgüstăN' lwē märkē' də kōlăNko͞or'), b. 1772 or 1773, d. 1827, French diplomat and general, created duke of Vicenza by Napoleon I. He became (1802) Napoleon's aide-de-camp, and as ambassador to Russia (1807–11) he opposed the emperor's war policy. He accompanied Napoleon as aide-de-camp in the Russian campaign and on his two-week dash from Russia to Paris (1812). Caulaincourt was foreign minister when Napoleon abdicated in 1814 and again during the HUNDRED DAYS. His remarkable memoirs of the years 1812 to 1815 were first published in 1933 and appeared in English as *With Napoleon in Russia* (1935) and *No Peace with Napoleon!* (1936).

cauliflower (kô'lə-), variety of CABBAGE, with an edible head of condensed flowers and flower stems. Broccoli is the horticultural variety (*botrytis*); both were cultivated in Roman times. Cauliflower is classified in the division MAGNOLIOPHYTA, class Magnoliopsida, order Capparales, family Cruciferae.

Caupolicán (koupōlēkän'), d. 1558, leader of the Araucanian Indians who fiercely resisted the Spanish conquest of Chile. He attempted to carry on the reconquest begun by LAUTARO and won a victory over the Spanish conquistador Pedro de Valdivia. After a heroic but futile battle to keep the Spanish from recapturing Concepción, Caupolicán was forced to retreat into the forest. There he was surprised, captured, tortured, and killed. His fame rests partly on *La Araucana*, the epic poem of Alonso de Ercilla y Zúñiga.

Caus or **Caux, Salomon de** (both: sälōmôN' də kō) 1576–1626, French engineer and physicist, educated in England. From 1614 to 1620 he was engineer to the Elector Palatine, Frederick, at Heidelberg. Because of his *Les Raisons des forces mouvantes avec diverses machines* (1615), an early exposition of the principle of steam power, he has been considered the originator of the steam engine.

causality, relationship between the cause and its effect. The scientific conception that given stimuli under controlled conditions must inevitably produce standard results is generally accepted by philosophers. Systems vary, however, in the degree of emphasis that they place on the role of chance in changing a situation. David Hume felt that in causal relations we have no evidence of any power exerted by the cause on the effect. Immanuel Kant thought the notion of cause a fundamental category of understanding, while others argue a strictly mechanical theory of causality. The introduction of the principle of indeterminacy into modern physics has necessitated a modification of traditional concepts.

cause, in philosophy, that which produces, and therefore accounts for, some change. A distinction is often made between a cause that produces something new (e.g., a moth from a caterpillar) and one that produces a change in an existing substance (e.g., a statue from a piece of marble). The cause-and-effect relationship is known as CAUSALITY. Aristotle distinguished four causes (efficient, final, material, and formal), and later philosophers developed others, often duplicatory. Aristotle's causes may be illustrated by the following example: a statue is created by a sculptor (the efficient) who makes changes in marble (the material) in order to have a beautiful object (the final) with the characteristics of a statue (the formal).

caustic, any strongly corrosive chemical substance, especially one that attacks organic matter. A caustic alkali is a metal hydroxide, especially that of an alkali metal; caustic soda is sodium hydroxide, and caustic potash is potassium hydroxide. Silver nitrate is another caustic substance; it is sometimes called lunar caustic. Most inorganic acids, e.g., sulfuric acid, are caustic, especially when concentrated.

caustic lime: see CALCIUM OXIDE.

caustic potash: see POTASSIUM HYDROXIDE.

caustic soda: see SODIUM HYDROXIDE.

cautery, searing or destruction of living animal tissue by use of heat or caustic chemicals. In the past, cauterization of open wounds, even those following amputation of a limb, was performed with hot irons; this served to close off the bleeding vessels as well as to discourage infection. In modern times cautery is used only on small lesions, e.g., to close off a bleeding point in the nasal mucous membrane or to eradicate a wart or other benign lesion. This is accomplished either by the application of a caustic substance such as nitric acid, or by the use of an electrically charged platinum wire (electrocautery).

Cauto (kou'tō), longest river in Cuba, c.150 mi (240 km) long, rising in the Sierra Maestra. It flows NW and W to the Caribbean Sea just N of Manzanillo.

Cauvery (kô'vərē), river, c.475 mi (760 km) long, rising in the Western Ghats, Karnataka state, and flowing SE across a plateau, through Tamil Nadu state, to the Bay of Bengal, S India; the Bhavani and Noyil are its main tributaries. At its mouth is a great, fertile delta that is irrigated by an extensive canal system, one of the oldest in India; the Grand Anicut dam and canal were built in the 11th cent. by the CHOLA kings. Before entering the delta, the river is divided by Sivasamudram island and drops 320 ft (98 m), forming Cauvery Falls. On the left falls is India's first hydroelectric plant (built 1902), which supplies most of S India with power. The Cauvery, India's second most sacred river, is sometimes called the Ganges of the South. According to Hindu legend, Vishnumaya, daughter of the god Brahma, was born on earth as the child of a mortal, Kavera Muni. In order to bring beatitude for Kavera Muni, she became a river whose water would purify all sins.

Caux, Salomon de: see CAUS, SALOMON DE.

Cavaignac, Louis Eugène (lwē özhĕn' kävänyäk'), 1802–57, French general. He participated in the French conquest of Algeria and was promoted to general in 1844. After the outbreak of the February Revolution in 1848, he became governor general of Algeria. Elected to the national assembly, he returned to Paris and was appointed minister of war. He used his dictatorial powers to quell the threatened uprising of the working classes in the JUNE DAYS of 1848. In the presidential election he was badly defeated by Louis Napoleon (later NAPOLEON III). Arrested after Louis Napoleon's coup d'etat of 1851, he was soon released and elected to the national assembly, but he refused to swear allegiance to Napoleon III and could not serve.

Cavalcanti, Guido (gwē'dō kävälkän'tē), c.1255–1300, Italian poet; friend of Dante, whose work was greatly influenced by Cavalcanti's style. He belonged to the White faction in the struggle of the Guelphs in Florence and was exiled to Sarzana. There he fell ill with malaria and died soon after his recall. Much of his verse, very little of which remains, is in the *Canzone d'amore* [song of love]. For translations, see his *Sonnets and Ballate* (tr. by Ezra Pound, 1912) and Lorna de' Lucchi, *An Anthology of Italian Poems* (1922).

Cavalcaselle, Giovanni Battista (jōvän'nē bät-tēs'-tä kävälkäsĕl'lä), 1820–97, Italian art critic and writer. Cavalcaselle studied painting at the Academy of Venice and traveled extensively through Italy studying its art treasures. He participated in the Revolution of 1848 and escaped to England, where he remained for several years. While there he produced in collaboration with Joseph A. Crowe their first joint work, *Early Flemish Painters* (1856). Cavalcaselle returned to Italy in 1857. The writings of Crowe and Cavalcaselle include the still basic *History of Painting in Italy* (3 vol., 1864–66).

Cavalier, Jean (zhäN kävälyā'), 1681?–1740, French Protestant soldier, a leader of the CAMISARDS. From his home in the Cévennes region of France, he fled to Geneva (1701) when persecution of the Protestants became intolerable, but he returned when he knew that the Protestants were about to rebel. As chief leader of the Camisards, he showed remarkable military genius. In 1704 he made peace with Marshal Villars and received from King Louis XIV a commission as colonel and a pension. The peace was repudiated by his followers because it did not restore the Edict of Nantes (see NANTES, EDICT OF). Distrustful of the king, Cavalier fled from France. He fought for the duke of Savoy and later for England in Spain against the French. His later years were spent in Great Britain, where he was given a pension, made major general, and appointed governor of the isle of Jersey. The *Memoirs of the Wars of the Cévennes,* published in 1726 and dedicated to Lord Carteret, is attributed to Cavalier. See biography by A. P. Grubb (1931).

cavalier, in general, an armed horseman. In the English civil war the supporters of Charles I were called Cavaliers in contradistinction to the ROUNDHEADS, the followers of Parliament. The royalists used the designation until it was replaced by TORY.

Cavaliere d'Arpino: see CESARI, GIUSEPPE.

Cavalieri, Francesco Bonaventura (fränchās'kō bōnävāntōō'rä kävälyā'rē), 1598–1647, Italian mathematician, a Jesuit priest. Professor at Bologna from 1629, he invented the method of indivisibles (1635) that foreshadowed integral calculus.

Cavalieri, Lina (lē'nä kävälyĕ'rē), 1874–1944, Italian operatic soprano. After her debut in Lisbon in 1900 she achieved great success throughout Europe and in the United States in the lyric French and Italian roles. Renowned as much for her great beauty and fiery temperament as for her light, pleasant voice, she sang with the Metropolitan Opera Company, New York City, (1906–8) and with Oscar Hammerstein's Manhattan Opera Company (1909–10).

cavalier King Charles spaniel, breed of small dog developed in the early 20th cent. from the English toy spaniel. It stands about 12 in. (30 cm) high at the shoulder and weighs from 13 to 18 lb (6–8 kg). Its long, silky coat may be slightly wavy, but never curly, and forms a fringe of longer hair, or feathers, on the ears, legs, tail, and feet. Although it is usually white with chestnut markings, it may have any of the color patterns of the English toy spaniel. Around 1926 there began a revival of interest in the toy spaniel that had been popular in 17th cent. England. This dog, often depicted in the paintings of that period, was larger than the modern type and had a less domed skull and longer nose. By selective breeding of modern toy spaniels that resembled this older type, a new breed, the cavalier, was developed in the relatively short span of approximately 20 years. A widely popular dog in England that is also gaining recognition in the United States, the cavalier King Charles is exhibited in the miscellaneous class at dog shows sanctioned by the American Kennel Club. See DOG.

Cavalier poets, a group of English poets associated with Charles I and his exiled son. Most of their work was done between c.1637 and 1660. Their poetry embodied the life and culture of upper-class, pre-Commonwealth England, mixing sophistication with naïveté, elegance with raciness. Writing on the courtly themes of beauty, love, and loyalty, they produced finely finished verses, expressed with wit and directness. The poetry reveals their indebtedness to both Ben Jonson and John Donne. The leading Cavalier poets were Robert Herrick, Richard Lovelace, Sir John Suckling, and Thomas Carew.

cavalla (kəväl'ə): see POMPANO.

Cavalli, Pietro Francesco (pyĕ'trō fränchĕs'kō käväl'lē), 1602–76, Italian composer, whose real name was Caletti-Bruni; pupil of Monteverdi, whom he succeeded as choirmaster of St. Mark's, Venice. He wrote many operas, including *Didone* (1641), *Giasone* (1649), *Serse* (1654), and *Ercole Amante* (1662), all of which show the full development of the bel canto aria.

Cavallini, Pietro (pyĕ'trō käväl-lē'nē), c.1250–c.1330, Italian painter and mosaicist. Working in a classical style, he had an important influence on the art of Cimabue and Giotto. His surviving works are frescoes in Santa Cecilia, Rome, and in Santa Maria Donnaregina, Naples. He designed some beautiful mosaics in the Church of Santa Maria in Trastevere, Rome.

cavalry, part of a military force, consisting of mounted troops trained to fight from horseback. Cavalry was used by the ancient Egyptians, but it was more extensively employed by the ancient Hittites, Assyrians, Babylonians, and Persians. Some of the Greek city-states had mounted troops, but the typical Greek force was heavy infantry. The Romans also employed cavalry. Horsemen were particularly useful in scouting and in pursuit of a routed enemy but remained at a disadvantage against well-disciplined infantry until saddles were introduced (4th cent. A.D.) in the time of Constantine I. The wide and expert use of cavalry in Europe came with the invaders from the East, the Huns, Avars, Magyars, and Mongols. In medieval Europe the mounted knight became the typical warrior, and cavalry dominated in the incessant small wars. With the reintroduction of mass fighting at the end of the Middle Ages, infantry came to the fore again. The use of firearms did much to enhance the importance of infantry, but horsemen remained valuable for their rapid striking power and mobility. Cavalry was prominent in the armies of Louis XIV and Frederick II (Frederick the Great), and particularly under Napoleon the cavalryman became the elite of the fighting forces, although most of the actual fighting was done by the infantry. Gaily uniformed cuirassiers, dragoons, hussars, and lancers were prominent in European armies of the 19th cent., and most of these forces were recruited from the nobility and the landed gentry. Cavalry was of great value during the 19th cent. on the African, American, and British-Indian frontiers, where mobility was essential in fighting lightly armed natives. It was also much used in the U.S. Civil War. However, the value of cavalry, already diminished by the development of rifles, plummeted with the introduction of machine guns and other automatic weapons at the end of the 19th cent. In World War I, because of the trench warfare, horsemen were used only in small numbers on the plains of E Europe and the Middle East. Cavalry was employed against Germany at the beginning of World War II by the Polish and Soviet armies. However, it finally disappeared as a force in modern warfare when highly mobile tank units were introduced. In 1946 the U.S. army abolished the cavalry as a separate arm of the service, merging what remained of it with the armored forces. See J. D. Lunt, *Charge to Glory* (1960); G. C. Anglesey, *A History of the British Cavalry* (vol. 1, 1973).

Cavan (kăv'ən), county (1971 pop. 52,674), 730 sq mi (1,891 sq km), N Republic of Ireland. The county town is Cavan. It is a hilly region of lakes (Lough Oughter chief among them) and bogs, and the climate is extremely damp and cool. Most of the soil is clay. The Erne is the principal river, and the Shannon has its source in Cavan. Pastoral agriculture is the chief occupation; very little land is under cultivation, and that mostly in very small farms. Manufactures are negligible. Cavan was organized as a shire of Ulster prov. in 1584.

Cavan, urban district (1971 pop. 3,268), county town of Co. Cavan, N Republic of Ireland. It is a farm market and the seat of the Roman Catholic and Anglican dioceses.

Cave, Edward, 1691–1754, English publisher. He founded (1731) the *Gentleman's Magazine,* the first modern magazine in English. Cave gave Samuel Johnson his first regular literary employment when he printed (1741–44) Johnson's parliamentary reports, "Debates in the Senate of Magna Lilliputia," in his periodical. Later Cave published other works by Johnson.

cave, a hollow, either above or below ground. Caves may be formed by the chemical and mechanical action of a stream upon soluble or soft rock, of rainwater seeping through soluble rock to the groundwater level, or of waves dashed against a rocky shore. Volcanic action (accompanied by the formation of gas pockets in lava or the melting of ice under lava) and earthquakes or other earth movements are also sources of cave formation. Limestone regions almost invariably have caves; some of these are notable for their STALACTITE AND STALAGMITE formations or for their magnitude and unearthly beauty. Some caves were the means of preserving both the remains of prehistoric man and animals and indications of man's early culture. Speleology, the scientific study of caves and their plant and animal life, contributes to knowledge of biological adaptation and evolution. Some cave animals lack sight, and both plants and animals living where light is excluded show loss of pigment. Among famous caves in the United States are Carlsbad Caverns National Park (N.Mex.), Mammoth Cave National Park (Ky.), and Wind Cave National Park (Black Hills, S.Dak.); Luray Caverns (Va.); and Wyandotte Cave (Ind.). In Europe there are celebrated caves in Belgium, Dalmatia, Gibraltar, Capri, Sicily, Postojna, and England (Kent's Cavern and Kirkdale). The caves of the Pyrenees and the Dordogne are famed for their prehistoric paintings (see PALEOLITHIC ART), and those of Ajanta, India, and Tunhwang, China, for their Buddhist frescoes. Fingal's Cave in the basalt of the Hebrides off Scotland is one of the many caves about which there are legends. The caves of Iceland and Hawaii are volcanic. See CAVE DWELLER. See C. E. Mohr and T. L. Poulson, *The Life of the Cave* (1966); D. R. McClurg, *The Amateur's Guide to Caves and Caving* (1973).

cave art: see PALEOLITHIC ART; ROCK CARVINGS AND PAINTINGS.

Cavedone, Giacomo (jä'kōmō kävädô'nā), 1577–1660, Italian painter, of the Bolognese school. He assisted Guido Reni in Rome, but his reputation as a master of color and composition was won through his paintings in the churches of Bologna. His paintings were strong in naturalistic detail and reflected Venetian influence. *Virgin and Child with SS. Alò and Petronius* is in the Pinacoteca Nazionale in Bologna.

cave fish, common name for blind, cave-dwelling fishes of the family Amblyopsidae. The Amblyopsidae are whitish fish, up to 5 in. (13 cm) long. With the exception of a single species, all members of the family live in the limestone cave region of the Mississippi basin. The three species that live in caves have nonfunctioning rudimentary eyes. The other two species, the springfish and the ricefish (or riceditch killifish), have small, functional eyes. The ricefish, which superficially resembles the toothed minnows, is found in streams and swamps of the SE United States. The cave fish and their relatives are classified in the phylum CHORDATA, subphylum Vertebrata, class Osteichthyes, order Cyprinodontiformes, family Amblyopsidae.

Cavell, Edith (kăv'əl), 1865–1915, English nurse. When World War I broke out, she was head of the nursing staff of the Berkendael Medical Institute in Brussels. In 1915 she was arrested by the German occupation authorities and pleaded guilty to a charge of harboring and aiding Allied prisoners and assisting some 130 to cross the Dutch frontier. She was shot Oct. 11, 1915, despite the efforts of Brand Whitlock, U.S. minister to Belgium, to secure a reprieve. See biography by A. E. Clark-Kennedy (1965).

Cavendish (kăv'əndĭsh), pseud. of **Henry Jones,** 1831–99, English card game expert. Jones studied medicine, practiced in London, and retired in 1868. He became a leading authority on card games and was the first man to formulate a system of playing whist. He was the author of *Principles of Whist: Stated and Explained by "Cavendish"* (1862) and later wrote books on piquet, écarté, billiards, lawn tennis, and croquet.

Cavendish, Lord Frederick Charles: see PHOENIX PARK MURDERS.

Cavendish, George, 1500–1561?, English gentleman, usher to Cardinal Wolsey. His biography of Wolsey, written in 1557, remained in manuscript until 1641 and first appeared in entirety in Christopher Wordsworth's *Ecclesiastical Biography* (1810). One of the great books of the English Renaissance, the work imparts tragic stature to Wolsey's life by contrasting the splendor of his early career with the ignominy of his last days. The book was long attributed to Cavendish's brother William, but in 1814 Joseph Hunter clearly established its authorship. See S. W. Singer, ed., *The Life of Cardinal Wolsey* (1825).

Cavendish, Henry, 1731–1810, English physicist and chemist, b. Nice. He was the son of Lord Charles Cavendish and grandson of the 2d duke of Devonshire. He was a recluse, and most of his writings were published posthumously. His great contributions to science resulted from his many accurate experiments in various fields. His conclusions were remarkably original. His chief researches were on heat, in which he determined the specific heats for a number of substances (although these heat constants were not recognized or so called until later); on the composition of air; on the nature and properties of a gas that he isolated and described as "inflammable air" and that Lavoisier later named HYDROGEN; and on the composition of water, which he demonstrated to consist of oxygen and his "inflammable air." In his *Electrical Researches* (1879) he anticipated some of the discoveries of Coulomb and Faraday. His experiments to determine the density of the earth led him to state it as 5.48 times that of water. His *Scientific Papers* were collected in two volumes (*Electrical Researches* and *Chemical and Dynamical*) in 1921. See biography by A. J. Berry (1960); J. G. Crowther, *Scientists of the Industrial Revolution* (1963).

Cavendish, Thomas, 1560–92, English navigator. He commanded a ship in the flotilla under Sir Richard Grenville sent (1585) by Sir Walter Raleigh to establish the first colony in Virginia. In 1586, in command of three vessels, he sailed from England on a voyage round the world (the third to be made), crossing from the coast of W Africa to Patagonia, where he discovered a fine harbor that he named Port Desire. He ravaged Spanish towns and shipping on the west coast of South America and thence continued his journey by way of the Philippines, East Indies, and Cape of Good Hope, returning to England in 1588 after a voyage of more than two years. A second circumnavigation that commenced in 1591 ended disastrously; his fleet of five ships was dispersed, and he died at sea.

Cavendish, William: see NEWCASTLE, WILLIAM CAVENDISH, DUKE OF.

Cavendish Laboratory: see CAMBRIDGE UNIV.

Caventou, Joseph Bienaimé (zhôzĕf' byăNnāmā' kävăNtōō'), 1795–1877, French chemist. He was professor at the École de Pharmacie, Paris. With P. J. Pelletier he isolated quinine (from cinchona bark), strychnine, and brucine and studied the green pigment in plants (which they named chlorophyll).

Caves of the Thousand Buddhas: see TUN-HUANG.

caviar or **caviare** (kăv'ēär), the roe (eggs) of various species of sturgeon prepared as a piquant table delicacy, especially in the Soviet Union and Iran. The ovaries of the fish are beaten to loosen the eggs, which are then freed from fibers, fat, and membrane by being passed through a sieve. The liquid is pressed off, and the eggs are mildly salted and sealed in small tins or kegs. Fresh caviar (the unripe roe), made in winter from high-grade eggs, is scarce and consequently expensive, especially when imported. Less choice varieties are cured with 10% salt. The eggs, black, green, brown, and the rare yellow or gray, may be tiny grains or the size of peas. The caviar in the Soviet Union comes chiefly from the vicinity of the Black and Caspian seas and from the Danube provinces. In the United States an imitation of sturgeon caviar is produced from the roe of other fish, such as paddlefish, whitefish, cod, and salmon.

Cavite (kävē'tä), city (1970 est. pop. 77,100), Cavite prov., SW Luzon, the Philippines. The city, situated on a small peninsula in Manila Bay, has been important as a naval base and trade center since the days of the Spanish. In the Spanish-American War it was captured by Dewey on May 1, 1898. The United States established a major naval base at Sangley Point just opposite the city proper. In World War II this base was bombed (Dec. 10, 1941) by the Japanese and virtually destroyed—a major blow to the defense of the Philippines. After the Philippines acquired independence it was agreed (1947) that the United States would retain the base for a 99-year period; subsequent negotiations reduced the time to 25 years, beginning in 1967. The Philippine government also maintains a naval school center at Cavite.

Cavour, Camillo Benso, conte di (kämēl'lō bān'sō kôn'tā dē kävōōr'), 1810–61, Italian statesman, premier (1852–59, 1860–61) of Sardinia (see SARDINIA, KINGDOM OF). The active force behind King VICTOR EMMANUEL II, he was responsible more than any other man for the unification of Italy under the house of Savoy (see RISORGIMENTO). Of a noble Piedmontese family, he entered the army early but came under suspicion for his liberal ideas and was forced to resign in 1831. He then devoted himself to travel, agricultural experimentation, and the study of politics. In 1847 he founded the liberal daily, Il Risorgimento, through which he successfully pressed King Charles Albert of Sardinia to grant a constitution to his people and to make war on Austria in 1848–49. A member of parliament briefly in 1848 and again in July of the following year, he became minister of agriculture and commerce (1850), finance minister (1851), and premier (1852). As premier, he aimed at making the kingdom of Sardinia the leading Italian state by introducing progressive internal reforms. Having reorganized the administration, the financial and legal system, industry, and the army, he won for Sardinia prestige and a place among the powers through participation in the Crimean War (1855). Conscious of the failures of the 1848–49 revolution, Cavour probably did not believe that the creation of a unified Italy was feasible within his lifetime; until at least 1859 he strove rather for an aggrandized N Italian kingdom under the house of Savoy. To achieve this goal he wooed foreign support against Austrian domination. In 1858, by an agreement reached at Plombières, he won the backing of Emperor Napoleon III of France for a war against Austria, promising in exchange to cede Savoy and possibly Nice to France. Austria was maneuvered into declaring war (1859), but Cavour refused to accept the separate armistice of VILLAFRANCA DI VERONA between France and Austria. He resigned the premiership but returned to office in 1860. In that year Tuscany, Parma, Modena, and the Romagna voted for annexation to Sardinia, and Giuseppe GARIBALDI overran the Two Sicilies. Cavour, taking advantage of the auspicious circumstances for Italian unification, sent Sardinian troops into the Papal States, which, with the exception of Latium and Rome, were soon annexed to Sardinia. By his superior statesmanship Cavour convinced Garibaldi to relinquish his authority in the south and avoided foreign intervention in favor of the dispossessed rulers and of the pope, whose interests he professed to be safeguarding. The annexation (1860) of the kingdom of the Two Sicilies was consummated with the abdication (1861) of Francis II. Cavour's labors were crowned two months before his death, when the kingdom of Italy was proclaimed under Victor Emmanuel II. See studies by D. Mack Smith (1954 and 1971); Massimo Salvadori, *Cavour and the Unification of Italy* (1961).

cavy (kā'vē), name for several species of South American rodents of the family Caviidae, including the domestic GUINEA PIG. The wild cavies are usually small, rounded, and tailless, with fur of a uniform shade of brown. Nocturnal animals, they occupy a variety of habitats, especially dense vegetation. An unusual, large species is the Patagonian cavy, or mara (*Dolichotis patagonum*), a long-legged, harelike animal that reaches a length of about 2½ ft (76 cm) and lives in arid regions. The CAPYBARA belongs to a related family. Some cavies are hunted for food in South America. Cavies are classified in the phylum CHORDATA, subphylum Vertebrata, class Mammalia, order Rodentia, family Caviidae.

Cawdor (kô'dər), village, Nairnshire, NE Scotland, SW of Nairn. Cawdor Castle, whose earliest construction dates from 1454, was represented by Shakespeare, following tradition, as the scene of the slaying (1040) of Duncan by MACBETH. In 1975, Cawdor became part of the Highland region.

Cawnpore, India: see KANPUR.

Caxias do Sul (kəshē'əsh dōō sōōl), city (1970 pop. 144,284), Rio Grande do Sul state, S Brazil. It is an important metallurgical center and has the most extensive vineyards in Brazil. There is little agriculture because of the rough terrain. The city was founded in 1875.

Caxton, William, c.1421–1491, English printer, the first to print books in English. He served apprenticeship as a mercer, and from 1463 to 1469 was at Bruges as governor of the Merchants Adventurers in the Low Countries, serving as a diplomat for the English king. He learned printing in Cologne in 1471–72, and at Bruges in 1475 he and Colard Mansion printed *The Recuyell of the Historyes of Troye*, his own translation from the French, and the first book printed in English. In 1476 he returned to England, and at Westminster in 1477 he printed *Dictes or Sayengis of the Philosophres*, the first dated book printed in England. Caxton is known to have printed about 100 books, many dealing with themes of chivalry. He was the translator, from French, Latin, and Dutch, of about one third of the books that he printed, and for some he wrote original prologues, epilogues, and additions. His books are of superb craftsmanship and are carefully edited. One of the typefaces used by Caxton is the original Old English type. The size of this type of Caxton's (14 point) is known as English. WYNKYN DE WORDE, his successor as a printer, was his assistant at Westminster, and the printers Richard Pynson and Robert Copland refer to Caxton (possibly figuratively) as their master. See biographies by N. S. Aurer (1926, repr. 1965), H. R. Plomer (1925, repr. 1968), N. F. Blake (1969), and William Blades (1877, repr. 1971).

Cayenne (kīĕn', kāĕn'), city (1967 pop. 19,668), capital of FRENCH GUIANA, on Cayenne island at the mouth of the Cayenne River. The city has a shallow harbor, and deep-draft ships must anchor some distance out. Timber, rum, essence of rosewood, and gold are exported. Cayenne was founded by the French in 1643, but it was wiped out by an Indian massacre and was not resettled until 1664. Throughout the 17th cent. the city and its surrounding region were sharply contested by Great Britain, France, and the Netherlands. It was occupied (1808–16) by both the British and the Portuguese. From 1851 to 1946 the city was the center of French penal settlements in Guiana, and part of its population is made up of prisoners' descendants. Cayenne's development has long been hindered by internal strife, a hot, wet climate, and the prevalence of disease. In the city are the Pasteur Institute, which specializes in the study of tropical diseases, and several buildings from the colonial period. The city gives its name to cayenne pepper, a very sharp condiment found on the island in abundance.

Cayes, Haiti: see AUX CAYES.

Cayey (kīā'), town (1970 pop. 21,562), SE Puerto Rico, in the Sierra de Cayey Mts. It is a sugar, tobacco, and poultry center and a summer resort. Cigars and clothing are manufactured. Cayey was founded in 1774. Outside the town is a U.S. military reservation, Henry Barracks.

Cayley, Arthur (kā'lē), 1821–95, English mathematician. He was admitted to the bar in 1849. In 1863 he was appointed first Sadlerian professor of mathematics at Cambridge. His researches, which covered the field of pure mathematics, included especially the theory of matrices and the theory of invariants. The algebra of matrices was the tool Heisenberg used in 1925 for his revolutionary work in quantum mechanics. The concept of invariance is important in modern physics, particularly in the theory of relativity. Cayley's collected papers were published in 13 volumes (1889–98).

Cayley, Sir George, 1773–1857, British scientist. He is recognized as the founder of aerodynamics on the basis of his pioneering experiments and studies of the principles of flight. He experimented with wing design, distinguished between lift and drag, and formulated the concepts of vertical tail surfaces, steering rudders, rear elevators, and air screws. Although powered flight was impossible in his time because of the lack of an engine with a high enough power-to-weight ratio, he was able to calculate the power required for different speeds and loads. Cayley was also a founder of the Regent Street Polytechnic, London.

Caylus, Anne Claude Philippe de Tubières, comte de (än klōd fēlēp' də tübyĕr' kôN də kälüs'), 1692–1765, French archaeologist and antiquarian. Caylus learned drawing from Watteau. He traveled in Europe and Asia and became known as an etcher and as a patron of the arts. He was the champion of classical purity and influenced the development of the Louis XVI style. He is said to have initiated the scientific study of the antique. His collections are in the Louvre. Caylus's *Recueil d'antiquités égyptiennes, étrusques, grecques, romaines, et gauloises* (7 vol., 1752–67) is the major 18th-century work of antiquarian scholarship; it did much to encourage interest in and study of classical subjects.

Caylus, Marie Marguerite, comtesse de (märē märgərēt' kôNtĕs' də), 1673–1729, French writer and actress. A noted beauty and wit, she was lauded for her performance at Saint-Cyr in Racine's *Esther*. Her *Souvenirs* (1770), edited by Voltaire, describe the court of Louis XIV with vivacity and taste.

Cayman Islands (kā'mən), archipelago (1970 pop. 10,249), 100 sq mi (259 sq km), British West Indies. Georgetown, the capital and chief port, is on Grand Cayman; the other islands are Little Cayman and Cayman Brac. The inhabitants, who are of mixed European and black African descent, engage in shipbuilding, turtle and shark fishing, coconut raising, and lumbering; exports include green turtles, turtle shells, shark skins, coconuts, and dyewood. Tourism is also a major industry. The islands were discovered by Christopher Columbus in 1503.

Cayuga Indians: see IROQUOIS CONFEDERACY.

Cayuga Lake (kāyōō'gə, kī-, kə-), 38 mi (61 km) long and 1 to 3.5 mi (1.6–5.6 km) wide, W central N.Y.; longest of the Finger Lakes. It is connected by canal and by the Seneca River with the Barge Canal to the north. Cornell Univ. and Wells College overlook Cayuga's clifflike banks. Near the southern end of the lake are Taughannock Falls, 215 ft (66 m) high.

cayuse (kīyōōs'): see MUSTANG.

Cayuse Indians (kīyōōs'), North American Indians who formerly occupied parts of NE Oregon and SE Washington. They were closely associated with the Nez Percé. They spoke a language belonging to the Sahaptin-Chinook branch of the Penutian linguistic stock (see AMERICAN INDIAN LANGUAGES). A mission was established (1836) among them by Marcus WHITMAN called Waiilatpu. In 1847 the Cayuse, blaming the missionaries for an outbreak of smallpox, attacked the mission and killed the Whitmans and their helpers. The settlers then declared war and subdued the Cayuse. In 1855 they were placed on the Umatilla Reservation, which they continue to share with the Wallawalla and Umatilla Indians; by the 1970s they numbered about 650. A small horse bred by them gave the name cayuse to all Indian ponies. See R. H. Ruby and J. A. Brown, *The Cayuse Indians* (1972).

Cb, formerly chemical symbol of the element columbium, now called NIOBIUM.

Cd, chemical symbol of the element CADMIUM.

CDP (cytidine diphosphate): see CYTOSINE.

Ce, chemical symbol of the element CERIUM.

Ceanannus Mor or **Kells,** urban district (1971 pop. 2,395), Co. Meath, NE Republic of Ireland, on the Blackwater River. It is a market town and was once a royal residence for Irish kings. Noteworthy are the relic of an ancient monastery founded in the 6th cent. by St. Columba, the round tower, and several ancient crosses. The **Book of Kells,** now one of the treasures of the Trinity College library in Dublin, is a beautifully illuminated manuscript of the Latin Gospels, with notes on local history, found in the ancient monastery and believed to have been written in the 8th cent. The manuscript is generally regarded as the finest example of Celtic illumination.

Ceará (sēərä'), state (1970 pop. 4,366,970), 57,149 sq mi (148,015 sq km), NE Brazil, on the Atlantic Ocean. FORTALEZA (sometimes called Ceará) is the capital.

Ceauşescu, Nicolae (nēkōlī' choushĕs'kōō), 1918–, Rumanian statesman. The son of a peasant, he early became active in the Rumanian Communist movement and was arrested as a revolutionary; he spent the late 1930s and early 40s in prison, where he became acquainted with the future first secretary of the Rumanian Communist party, Gheorghe Gheorghiu-Dej. Escaping in 1944, Ceauşescu held a variety of posts within Communist party and government ranks after the Communist takeover in 1948. He soon became a member of the party's central committee and then, in 1955, a member of the politburo. Upon Gheorghiu-Dej's death in March, 1965, he was chosen first secretary of the central committee of the Communist party and continued his mentor's policy of nationalism and independence from the USSR within the context of Marxism-Leninism. He promoted closer relations with the People's Republic of China and with the West, as well as industrial and agricultural development. In Dec., 1967, he assumed the office of president of the state council, or head of state.

Cebu (sābōō'), island (1970 pop. 1,632,642), 1,702 sq mi (4,408 sq km), one of the Visayan Islands, the Philippines, between Leyte and Negros. The coastal plains are intensely cultivated and densely populated. The island is a leading peanut and corn producer; rice, sugarcane, coconuts, and hemp are also grown. There are major coal and copper deposits. Fertilizer is made from local pyrite. Magellan landed on the island in 1521; the wooden cross he planted is a major tourist attraction. The island, with several small adjacent islands, comprises Cebu province, the capital of which is the city of **Cebu** (1970 pop. 342,116), the second (after Manila) most important harbor and city in the Philippines. With its excellent port, which handles both interisland and overseas shipping, it is the trade and manufacturing center of the Visayan Islands. The city has sugar mills, cement factories, shipyards, metalworks, and automobile repair and assembly plants. The first permanent Spanish settlement in the Philippines, it was founded in 1565 as San Miguel by López de Legaspi; it was capital of the Spanish colony until 1571. As a major Japanese base in World War II, it was largely destroyed by U.S. bombs. It has been rebuilt and today is a charming mixture of old and new, East and West. A Roman Catholic archdiocese, it has a bishop's palace, a cathedral, and a church with a jewel-encrusted gold statue of the Holy Child, said to have been given by Magellan. Cebu is the seat of the Univ. of San Carlos (1595), the Univ. of the Southern Philippines, the Univ. of the Visayas, Southwestern Univ., an institute of technology, several colleges, and many private schools.

Cecco d'Ascoli (chĕk'kō däs'kōlē), 1269?–1327, Italian astrologer, mathematician, poet, and physician, whose real name was Francesco degli Stabili, b. Ascoli. A teacher of astrology at several institutions in Italy, he was professor of mathematics and astrology at the Univ. of Bologna (1322–24). He was denounced as heretical largely because, in defending astrology against Dante's attack on it in the *Divine Comedy,* Cecco himself had accused the great poet of heresy; he was burned at the stake. His chief work was *L'acerba,* an allegorical didactic poem of encyclopedic range.

Čech, Svatopluk (svä'tôplōōk chĕkh), 1846–1908, Czech poet and novelist. His strong Pan-Slavism and his love for democracy and freedom won him great popularity. His political enthusiasms animate many of his writings. Among Čech's major epics are *The Adamites* (1873), *Žižka* (1879), and *Václav of Michalovice* (1880). He also wrote idyllic verse on Czech country life, notably *In the Shade of the Linden Tree* (1879), and satirical novels, including the utopian *Excursion of Mr. Broucek to the Moon* (1886).

Cecil, Lord David (Lord Edward Christian David Gascoyne Cecil), 1902–, English biographer. He was professor of English literature at Oxford (1948–70). Cecil's works are all distinguished for their artistry as well as for their sound scholarship. His masterpiece is his life of Lord MELBOURNE, published in two volumes, *The Young Melbourne* (1939) and *Lord M.* (1954). His other works include *Sir Walter Scott* (1933), *Jane Austen* (1935), *Walter Pater: Scholar Artist* (1955), and *Max* (1964), a study of Max Beerbohm. *The Cecils of Hatfield House, an English Ruling Family* (1973) is about his own family.

Cecil, Edgar Algernon Robert, 1st **Viscount Cecil of Chelwood** (sĕs'əl), 1864–1958, British statesman, known in his earlier life as Lord Robert Cecil; 3d son of the 3d marquess of Salisbury. A Conservative who held several ministerial posts, Cecil gained fame largely through untiring advocacy of internationalism. In 1919 he collaborated with U.S. President Woodrow Wilson in drafting the Covenant of the League of Nations. He was created a viscount in 1923 and awarded the Nobel Peace Prize in 1937. See his autobiography, *A Great Experiment* (1941).

Cecil, Robert: see SALISBURY, ROBERT CECIL, 1ST EARL OF.

Cecil, Robert Arthur Talbot Gascoyne-: see SALISBURY, ROBERT ARTHUR TALBOT GASCOYNE-CECIL, 3D MARQUESS OF.

Cecil, William: see BURGHLEY, WILLIAM CECIL, 1ST BARON.

Cecilia, Saint, 2d or 3d cent., Roman virgin martyr. An ancient and famous account of her life is factually valueless. As patron of music, she is represented at the organ. St. Cecilia is the subject of one of the *Canterbury Tales,* of a song by Dryden, and an ode by Pope. Cecily is an English form of her name. Feast: Nov. 22.

Cecrops (sē'krŏps), in Greek mythology, founder and first king of Athens. A primeval being, he was half man and half serpent. As a maker of laws, he abolished human sacrifice, established monogamy, and initiated burial of the dead.

cecum (sē'kəm): see INTESTINE.

cedar, common name for a number of trees, mostly coniferous evergreens. The true cedars belong to the small genus *Cedrus* of the family Pinaceae (PINE family). All are native to the Old World from the Mediterranean to the Himalayas, although several are cultivated elsewhere as ornamentals, especially the cedar of Lebanon (*C. libani*). This tree, native to Asia Minor and North Africa, is famous for the historic groves of the Lebanon mts., frequently mentioned in the Bible. The wood used in building the Temple and the house of Solomon (1 Kings 5, 6, and 7) may, however, have been that of the deodar cedar (*C. deodara*), native to the Himalayas. It has fragrant wood, durable and fine grained, and is venerated by the Hindus, who call it Tree of God. The name cedar is used (particularly in North America, where no cedars are native) for other conifers, e.g., the JUNIPER (red cedar), ARBORVITAE (white cedar), and others of the family Cupressaceae (CYPRESS family). Several tropical American trees of the genus *Cedrela* of the mahogany family are also called cedars. True cedars are classified in the division PINOPHYTA, class Pinopsida, order Coniferales, family Pinaceae.

Cedar Breaks National Monument: see NATIONAL PARKS AND MONUMENTS (table).

Cedar Creek, small tributary of the North Fork of the Shenandoah River, N of Strasburg, N Va. It was the scene of a Civil War battle (Oct. 19, 1864) in which Union general P. H. Sheridan defeated J. A. Early.

Cedar Falls, city (1970 pop. 29,597), Black Hawk co., N Iowa, on the Cedar River; inc. 1854. It developed as a milling center in the late 19th-cent. after the coming of the railroad. Its manufactures include pumps, farm machinery, tools and dies, golfing equipment, and refuse disposal equipment. Cedar Falls is the seat of the Univ. of Northern Iowa and of the Evangelical Campgrounds, scene of the annual Interdenominational Bible Conference.

Cedar Mountain: see BULL RUN, SECOND BATTLE OF.

Cedar Rapids, city (1970 pop. 110,642), seat of Linn co., E central Iowa, on the Cedar River; inc. as a city 1856. It is named for the surging rapids in the river. One of Iowa's principal commercial and industrial cities, Cedar Rapids is a distribution and rail center for an extensive agricultural area. The city's major manufactures are cereals, communications equipment, farm and road machinery, syrup, plastic products, trampolines and other gymnastic equipment. Coe College, Mt. Mercy College, and Kirkwood Community College are there. Points of interest include a large Masonic library (1884); an art museum with a collection by the American artist Grant Wood; and the landscaped Municipal Island, a strip of land in the main channel of the Cedar River, on which the municipal building and a neoclassical war memorial are located. The Duane Arnold Energy Center, the first nuclear powered generator in Iowa, is in Cedar Rapids.

cedar waxwing: see WAXWING.

Cedron (sē'drən). **1** The same as KIDRON. **2** Place, near Jamnia, fortified against the Maccabees. 1 Mac. 15.39–41; 16.9.

Cefalù (chāfälōō'), town (1971 pop. 12,062), N Sicily, Italy, a port on the Tyrrhenian Sea. It is a commercial and fishing center and a seaside resort. Formerly known as Cephaloedium, it made an alliance with Carthage in 396 B.C. The town was later taken by the Arabs (mid-9th cent. A.D.) and the Normans (11th cent.). Its famous cathedral, started in 1131 by King Roger II, is one of the finest examples of Norman architecture in Sicily.

Cegléd (tsĕg'lād), city (1970 pop. 38,082), central Hungary. It is a road and rail hub and a trade center for agricultural products.

Ceiba, La (lä sā'bä), city (1961 pop. 24,863), N Honduras, capital of Atlántida dept., on the Caribbean Sea. It is the commercial and processing center of a rich agricultural region. Coconuts and citrus fruits are exported. The city was Honduras's main banana port until disease ruined the surrounding plantations in the 1930s. La Ceiba is located at the foot of Peak Bonito (5,000 ft/1,524 m), has fine beaches, and is a departure point for the Bay Islands. More than 1,000 people were killed when the city was struck (1974) by Hurricane Fifi.

ceiling balloon: see WEATHER BALLOON.

ceilometer (sēlŏm'ĭtər), in aviation and meteorology, automatic instrument used to record ceiling, i.e., the altitude of the lowest cloud layer covering more than half of the sky. The ceilometer consists essentially of a projector, a detector, and a recorder. The projector emits an intense beam of light into the sky. The detector, located at a fixed distance from the projector, uses a photoelectric cell to detect the projected light when it is reflected from clouds. In the fixed-beam ceilometer, the light is beamed vertically into the sky by the projector and the detector is aligned at various angles to intercept the reflected light; in the rotating-beam ceilometer, the detector is positioned vertically and the light projected at various angles. In either case, trigonometry is used to determine the altitude of the clouds reflecting the light from a knowledge of the angle at which the light is detected and the distance between the projector and detector. The recorder is calibrated to indicate cloud height directly. False readings from extraneous light sources are reduced by modulating the projected light beam so that it can be recognized when it is reflected.

Cela, Camilo José (kämē'lō hōsā' thā'lä), 1916–, Spanish novelist, short-story writer, and poet, b. Iria Flavia. Among the writers to emerge after the Spanish civil war, he won critical acclaim with the novel *La familia de Pascual Duarte* (1942; tr. *The Family of Pascual Duarte,* 1964). Its brutal realism and crudeness of language are characteristic of Cela's style. His other novels include *La colmena* (1951; tr. *The Hive,* 1953) and *Mrs. Caldwell habla a su hijo* (1953; tr. *Mrs. Caldwell Speaks to Her Son,* 1968). See studies by D. W. Foster (1967) and D. W. McPheeters (1969).

Celaenae (sīlē'nē), ancient city of Asia Minor, in Phrygia, near the source of the Maeander River, in present-day W central Turkey. In the days of the Persian Empire, Cyrus the Great had a palace there, and Xerxes I built a fort. Alexander the Great conquered the city in 333 B.C. Seleucus I moved the inhabitants to neighboring Apamea. Modern Dinar is on the site.

Čelakovsky, František (frän'tĭshĕk chĕ'läkôfskĭ), 1799–1852, Czech folklorist and poet. A disciple of Herder and a romantic Pan-Slavist, he collected Slavic folk songs from 1822 to 1827. These he later imitated in his own intricate free verses, *Echoes of Russian Song* (1829) and *Echoes of Czech Song* (1830). At Breslau he became (1841) the first professor of Slavic languages in a Central European university.

celandine: see POPPY.

Celano, Thomas of: see THOMAS OF CELANO.

Celaya (sälä'yä), city (1970 pop. 143,703), Guanajuato state, W central Mexico. In a region watered by the Lerma irrigation works, Celaya is the center of a prosperous bean, maize, and cereal growing area. Cattle raising and the associated dairy industry are also important. Founded in 1571, Celaya was frequently involved in Mexican wars. It was the first city to be captured (Sept. 28, 1810) by Hidalgo y Costilla. In 1915, Álvaro Obregón decisively defeated Francisco Villa at Celaya.

Celebes (sĕl'əbēz) or **Sulawesi** (so͞o"läwä'sē), island (1970 est. pop., including offshore islands, 8,925,000), c.73,000 sq mi (189,070 sq km), largest island in E Indonesia, E of Borneo, from which it is separated by the Makasar Strait. MAKASAR is its chief city and port; other important towns are Manado, Gorontalo, and Palopo. Extremely irregular in shape, it comprises four large peninsulas separated by three gulfs—Tomini on the northeast, Tolo on the southeast, and Boni on the south. The terrain is almost wholly mountainous, with many active volcanoes. Mt. Rantemario (11,286 ft/3,440 m) and Mt. Rantekombola (11,335 ft/3,455 m) are the highest peaks. There are numerous lakes, of which Towuti is the largest and Tondano, with its waterfall, is the most beautiful. Asian and Australian elements are comingled in the fauna, which includes the babirusa (resembling swine), the small wild ox called anoa (found only in the Celebes), the baboon, some rare species of parrot, and a large number of crocodiles. Valuable stands of timber cover much of the island; many forest products are exported. Mineral resources include nickel, gold, diamonds, sulfur, and low-grade iron ore. The mountainous terrain, with only a few narrow coastal plains, limits agriculture; many inhabitants seek their livelihood from the sea, and there are trepang and mother-of-pearl industries. Celebes is, however, a major source of copra for the country, and corn, rice, cassava, yams, tobacco, and spices are grown. The inhabitants are Malayan, except for some primitive tribes in the interior. The largest ethnic group are the Makasarese-Bugis, who are renowned as seafaring traders; they are Muslim. In the north are the Minahassa, who are Christian. The Portuguese first visited the Celebes in 1512. The Dutch expelled the Portuguese in the 1600s and conquered the natives in the Makasar War (1666–69). In 1950, Celebes became one of 10 provinces of the newly created republic of Indonesia; it has since been divided into 4 provinces. The Univ. of North and Central Sulawesi is in Manado, and private universities are in Manado, Gorontalo, and Makasar. The **Celebes Sea** is north of the island, between it and the Philippines.

Celebrezze, Anthony Joseph (sələbrē'zē), 1910–, U.S. Secretary of Health, Education, and Welfare (1962–65), b. Anzi, Italy. He was taken to the United States as a child. He later practiced law in Cleveland before being elected (1951) to the Ohio state senate. A Democrat, he was elected mayor of Cleveland in 1953 and was reelected four times. In the 1961 election he received almost three quarters of the total vote and carried every ward in the city. President John F. Kennedy appointed him to the cabinet in 1962 to succeed Abraham A. Ribicoff. He resigned in 1965 to become a U.S. circuit court judge.

celery, biennial plant (*Apium graveolens*) of the family Umbelliferae (CARROT family), of wide distribution in the wild state throughout the north temperate Old World and much cultivated also in America. It was first cultivated as a medicinal, then (during the Middle Ages) as a flavoring, and finally as a food, chiefly for soups and salads. The seeds are still used for seasoning. Celeriac is a variety cultivated chiefly in N Europe for the large edible turnip-like root. Celery is classified in the division MAGNOLIOPHYTA, class Magnoliopsida, order Umbellales, family Umbelliferae.

celesta (sĭlĕ'stə), keyboard musical instrument patented in 1886 by Auguste Mustel of Paris. It consists of a set of steel bars fastened over wood resonators and struck by hammers operated from the keyboard.

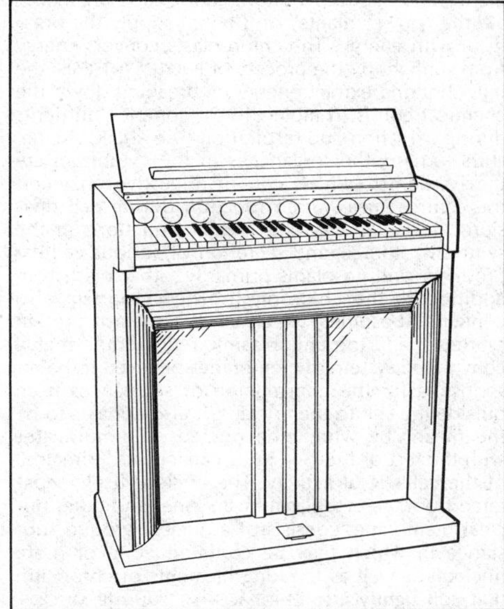

Celesta

The compass is four octaves upward from middle C. Its tone is delicate and ethereal. Tchaikovsky, in his *Nutcracker Suite,* was one of the first composers to write for it.

celestial coordinate system: see ECLIPTIC COORDINATE SYSTEM.

celestial equator: see EQUATORIAL COORDINATE SYSTEM.

celestial horizon, one axis of the HORIZON COORDINATE SYSTEM. It is the great circle on the celestial sphere midway between the observer's zenith and nadir; it divides the celestial sphere into two equal hemispheres. The observer may be unable to see all the stars that lie above his celestial horizon because of obstructions such as buildings, trees, or mountains; he may be able to see some stars that lie below his celestial horizon because of atmospheric refraction.

celestial mechanics, the study of the motions of astronomical bodies as they move under the influence of their mutual GRAVITATION. Celestial mechanics analyzes the orbital motions of planets, comets, asteroids, and natural and artificial satellites within the solar system as well as the motions of stars and galaxies. Newton's laws of motion and his theory of universal gravitation are the basis for celestial mechanics. Calculating the motions of astronomical bodies is a complicated procedure because many separate forces are acting at once, and all the bodies are simultaneously in motion. The only problem that can be solved exactly is that of two bodies moving under the influence of their mutual gravitational attraction. A special case of the problem involving three bodies has been solved, and each of the 12 asteroids called the Trojan Group represent examples of it; they are characterized by being equidistant from both Jupiter and the sun. Since the sun is the dominant influence in the solar system, an application of the two-body problem leads to the simple elliptical orbits as described by KEPLER'S LAWS; these laws give a close approximation of planetary motion. More exact solutions, which consider the effects of the planets on each other, cannot be found in a straightforward way. However, methods accounting for these other influences, or PERTURBATIONS, have been devised; they allow successive refinements of an approximate solution to be made to almost any degree of precision. In computing the motions of stars and the rotations of galaxies, statistical methods are often used.

celestial meridian, VERTICAL CIRCLE passing through the north celestial pole and an observer's ZENITH. It is an axis in the HORIZON COORDINATE SYSTEM.

celestial pole, one of the two points at which the earth's axis of rotation intersects the CELESTIAL SPHERE. The celestial pole is important as a reference point in the EQUATORIAL COORDINATE SYSTEM; the celestial meridian passes through it, as do the hour circles of the stars. The polestar (see POLARIS) lies within 0.5° of the north celestial pole. Although there is no bright star near the south celestial pole, the Southern Cross (see CRUX) points directly to it. The ALTITUDE of the celestial pole in an observer's hemisphere is equal to the observer's latitude on the earth.

celestial sphere, imaginary sphere of infinite radius with the earth at its center. It is used for describing the positions and motions of stars and other objects. For these purposes, any astronomical object can be thought of as being located at the point where the line of sight from the earth through the object intersects the surface of the celestial sphere. In ASTRONOMICAL COORDINATE SYSTEMS, the coordinate axes are great circles on the celestial sphere. In most systems of this type, the reference points are fixed on the sphere, so the two coordinates needed to locate a body are relatively constant.

Celestine I, Saint (sĕl'əstĭn), d. 432, pope (422–32), an Italian; successor of St. Boniface I. The opposition of St. Cyril of Alexandria to NESTORIANISM inspired both sides to appeal to the pope, who judged that Nestorius should be excommunicated if he refused to retract. Celestine sent legates to the Council of Ephesus with orders not to discuss, but to judge. Celestine also advanced orthodoxy in the West by suppressing Semi-Pelagianism in Gaul and by sending Germanus of Auxerre to Britain. He was succeeded by St. Sixtus III. Feast: July 27.

Celestine V, Saint, 1215–96, pope (elected July 5, resigned Dec. 13, 1294), an Italian (b. Isernia) named Pietro del Murrone; successor of Nicholas IV. Celestine's election ended a two-year deadlock among the cardinals over a successor to Nicholas IV. Although he was known for his austere life as a hermit and for his extremist followers, who called themselves Celestines, he proved a most ineffectual pope and an easy prey to opportunists. King Charles II of Naples quickly dominated him and kept the pope in Naples. Celestine granted privileges and offices to all who asked for them, turned the duties of his office over to a committee of three cardinals, and kept to his cell. His reign was so chaotic that he himself abdicated after only five months and ordered a new election. His successor, Boniface VIII, canceled his official acts and, to avert possible schism among Celestine's ardent followers, kept Celestine in confinement until his death. Celestine was canonized in 1313. Feast: May 19.

celestite (sĕl'əstīt) or **celestine** (sĕl'əstĭn, -tīn), mineral appearing in blue-tinged or white orthorhombic crystals or in fibrous masses. The natural sulfate of strontium, $SrSO_4$, it is important as a source of strontium and of certain of its compounds, e.g., strontium hydroxide, used in refining beet sugar, and strontium nitrate, used in red signal flares. It occurs in England, in Sicily, and in the United States on islands in Lake Erie and also in Pennsylvania, New York, and Ohio.

celiac disease: see SPRUE.

celiac plexus: see SOLAR PLEXUS.

celibacy, voluntary refusal to enter the married state, with abstinence from sexual activity. It is one of the typically Christian forms of ASCETICISM. In ancient Rome the VESTAL virgins were celibates, and successful MONASTICISM has everywhere been accompanied by celibacy as an ideal. Among ancient Jews the ESSENES were celibates. In the Judaism of postexilic times, sexual activity in the married state was considered lawful and good; otherwise it was unlawful. This rule remained in Christianity. But the mainstream of Christian tradition from the start has interpreted the Gospels and epistles as teaching that voluntary celibacy, especially virginity, is peculiarly meritorious. 1 Cor. 7. In the Orthodox Eastern churches, monks and nuns are celibates, but the ordinary parish clergy are married; generally they must be married before ordination and may not remarry. Eastern bishops are widowers or unmarried, hence they are usually from monasteries rather than parishes. In the West, celibacy has been common among the parish clergy since the 3d cent., and as time passed, the Holy See became adamant in opposing the marriage of the secular clergy. The chief problem of reformers in the early Middle Ages was to end concubinage among the clergy; marriage of the clergy having fallen into disrepute, the violations were of the laws of chastity rather than of marriage. In the 12th cent. the most stringent laws were enacted, and by the time of the Reformation popular opinion tolerated neither concubinage nor marriage in the clergy. The Roman Catholic Church in the Roman rite allows no sacerdotal marriage, but the clergy of Eastern rites united with the Holy See are often married before ordination. Protestants have rejected voluntary celibacy as an ideal. A standard apologetic explanation of the Western discipline of celibacy for parish priests is that marriage would prevent the priest from giving his complete attention to his parish. Since the Second Vatican Council, the Roman Catholic Church has restored the diaconate to a prominent place in the ministry and accepts married men into it. In the face of criticism, however, the council, Pope Paul VI, and various national groupings of bishops have insisted on the retention of celibacy for priests.

Céline, Louis Ferdinand (lwē fĕrdēnäN' sālēn'), 1894–1961, French author, whose real name was Louis Ferdinand Destouches. Céline wrote sensationally misanthropic novels, such as *Journey to the End of Night* (1932, tr. 1934) and *Death on the Installment Plan* (1936, tr. 1938). Based on his experiences as a doctor during World War I, these works portray the vileness of humanity through frank, often obscene, language. *Mea Culpa* (1937, tr. 1937) is a renunciation of Communism. His later works include the autobiographical novels *Castle to Castle* (1957, tr. 1968), *North* (tr. 1972), and *Rigadoon* (1961, tr. 1974), which form a trilogy recounting Céline's nightmarish journey through Germany to Denmark in the last days of the Third Reich. See study by Erika Ostrovsky (1967).

Celje (tsĕ'lyĕ), city (1971 pop. 157,515), NW Yugoslavia, in Slovenia. It is an industrial center where agricultural machinery, textiles, and chemicals are manufactured. Founded (1st cent. A.D.) by the Roman Emperor Claudius, it was the seat (1341–1456) of the powerful Slovenian counts of Celje (or Cilli). In the city are a 13th-century monastery and a 16th-century palace.

cell, in biology, the unit of structure and function of which all plants and animals are composed. The cell is the smallest unit in the living organism that is capable of carrying on the essential life processes: sustaining metabolism for the production of energy and reproducing for the self-perpetuation of the organism. There are many unicellular organisms (e.g., BACTERIA and PROTOZOA) in which the single cell performs all the life functions. In higher organisms, a division of labor has evolved in which groups of cells have differentiated into specialized TISSUES, which in turn are grouped into organs and organ systems. Because almost all cells are microscopic, knowledge of the component cell parts has increased proportionately to the development of the MICROSCOPE and other specialized instruments and of allied experimental techniques. In both plants and animals, the cell is differentiated into the CYTOPLASM; the cell membrane, which surrounds it; and the nucleus, which is contained in it. In plant cells there is, in addition to the membrane, a thickened cell wall, usually composed chiefly of CELLULOSE secreted by the cytoplasm. Included in the cytoplasm are many discrete bodies (called organelles), vacuoles containing cell sap, and inert granules and crystals. The most important of the organelles are the chloroplasts (occurring only in the cells of green plants) and the mitochondria. Both these organelles are the "power plants" of life that supply the organism with energy. The chloroplasts convert energy from sunlight by the process of PHOTOSYNTHESIS; the mitochondria extract energy by breaking down the chemical bonds in molecules of complex nutrients during oxidation and respiration (see ADENOSINE TRIPHOSPHATE). Other organelles in the cytoplasm are the lysosomes, which contain digestive enzymes; the centrosomes, which function during cell division; the Golgi apparatus, which functions in the synthesis, storage, and secretion of various cellular products; and, in plants primarily, other plastids in addition to the chloroplasts. The cytoplasm also contains ribosomes, which are the sites of protein synthesis, and the endoplasmic reticulum, a highly convoluted system of membranes believed to be responsible for the transmission of substances from outside the cell to the nucleus. It also appears to be the means by which the nucleus communicates with the rest of the cell, in its capacity as "director" of the cell's total activity. The nucleus itself, separated from the cytoplasm by an inner and outer nuclear membrane, consists of a nuclear ground substance in which may be contained one or more nucleoli as well as the long filaments of chromatin that coil tightly into CHROMOSOMES during MITOSIS. The chromatin directs the metabolic functions of the whole cell and, during cell division, passes on its "code" to the new cell by exactly replicating itself. Among those who contributed to early knowledge of cells through their use of the microscope were Antony van LEEUWENHOEK, Robert HOOKE, and Marcello MALPIGHI. In the 19th cent. Matthias J. SCHLEIDEN and Theodor SCHWANN developed what is now known as the cell theory. The very careful observations made by these and other men were primarily of the physical and mechanical attributes of the cell. Just as scientists now realize that atoms cannot be thought of only as physical units of matter but must also be described as manifestations of energy, so living cells too must be viewed as more than a complicated architecture of physical "building blocks" or components. It is now known that many processes, such as the passage of substances across the cell membrane, are a series of chemical and electrostatic phenomena rather than purely mechanical functions. The study of the cell is called cytology; the study of its chemical processes is cytochemistry. See A. G. Loewy and Philip Siekevitz, *Cell Structure and Function* (2d ed. 1969); C. P. Swanson, *The Cell* (3d ed. 1969); E. J. Ambrose and D. M. Easty, *Cell Biology* (1970); Ernest Borek, *The Sculpture of Life* (1973).

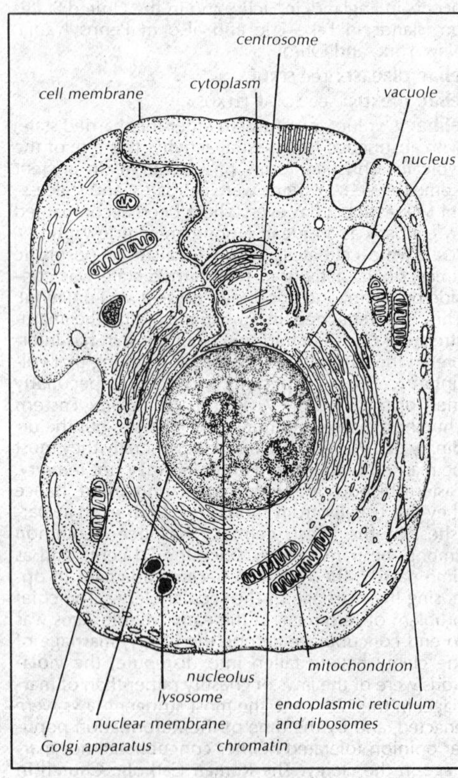

Animal cell

cell, in electricity, source of electric current that operates by chemical action, converting chemical energy into electrical energy. A cell consists essentially of two dissimilar substances, a positive ELECTRODE and a negative electrode, that conduct electricity, and a third substance, an ELECTROLYTE, that acts chemically on the electrodes. A group of several such cells connected together is called a battery. One simple form of cell consists of a glass jar containing a dilute solution of acid into which are introduced the electrodes of the cell, a strip of copper and a strip of zinc. When the two electrodes are connected externally by a conductor, such as a piece of copper wire, an electric current is produced in the wire. Electrons leave the zinc electrode and enter the wire. Upon reaching the copper electrode, they pass back into the solution. There they are captured by the hydrogen ions of the acid, forming hydrogen gas that evolves from the solution on and near the copper electrode. The zinc electrode diminishes in size as the action proceeds; the copper is unaffected, but the hydrogen bubbles, collecting rapidly in great numbers, form a covering over the copper electrode and interfere with the cell's action—a condition called polarization. There are several kinds of cells, differing in electrode material and electrolyte. The voltage, or electromotive force (abbreviated emf), depends upon the chemical properties of the substances used but is not affected by the size of the electrodes or the amount of electrolyte. The Leclanché cell is a single-fluid cell having a negative electrode of zinc, a positive electrode of carbon, and an electrolyte of ammonium chloride solution. It produces an emf of 1.46 volts. Similar to the Leclanché cell is the common dry cell, so called because the electrolyte is in the form of a paste instead of a pure liquid solution. The cell parts are contained in a zinc cylinder that acts as the negative electrode. The cylinder is closed at one end and is lined on its entire inside surface with a layer of absorbent material. A carbon rod surrounded by manganese dioxide is inserted into the cylinder, forming the positive electrode of the cell. The manganese dioxide is mixed with carbon granules to improve its conductivity and to absorb the electrolyte. The electrolyte consists of a solution composed mainly of water, zinc chloride, and ammonium chloride. The open end of the cylinder is sealed with pitch, and the entire cell is enclosed in a jacket with a tin-plated top and bottom that enables the cell to be electrically connected to a circuit. The principal parts of an alkaline dry cell are a manganese dioxide positive electrode, a zinc negative electrode, and an electrolyte of alkaline potassium hydroxide. Such a cell can operate up to 10 times as long as a common dry cell. The principal parts of a mercury dry cell are a positive electrode of mercuric oxide, a negative electrode of zinc, and an electrolyte of potassium hydroxide. This cell has a relatively constant output voltage during most of its operating life, and it maintains its ability to generate current even after several years of storage. See BATTERY, ELECTRIC; ELECTRIC CIRCUIT; FUEL CELL; SOLAR CELL.

cella (sĕl'ə), that portion of a Roman temple which was enclosed within walls, as distinct from the open colonnaded porticoes which formed the rest of it. It corresponds to the NAOS in Greek temples. The cella housed the statue of the deity to whom the temple was dedicated and was also used as a treasury. Sometimes it extended the whole width of the building, instead of being kept entirely within free-standing colonnades. The cella was generally a single chamber, but there were sometimes two chambers, or even three, as in the temple of Jupiter, on the Capitoline Hill.

cell division: see CELL; MITOSIS; MEIOSIS.

Celle (tsĕl'ə), city (1970 pop. 57,155), Lower Saxony, N West Germany, on the Aller River. Its manufactures include food products, machinery, chemicals, and textiles. Celle was chartered in 1294. Its castle was the residence of the dukes of Lüneburg-Celle, a branch of the house of Braunschweig, from 1378 to 1705. The castle still houses a famous 17th-century Baroque theater.

Cellini, Benvenuto (chĕlē'nē, Ital. bānvānōō'tō chāl-lē'nē), 1500–1571, Italian sculptor, metalsmith, and author. His remarkable autobiography, written between 1558 and 1562, reads like a picaresque novel. It is, in fact, one of the most important documents of the 16th cent. Cellini tells of his escapades with the frankness and consummate egoism characteristic of the Renaissance man. He was born in Florence, the son of a musician; he studied music until his 15th year, when he was apprenticed to a goldsmith. Banished from Florence after fighting a duel, he went from town to town working for local goldsmiths and in 1519 went to Rome. Under the patronage of Pope Clement VII he became known as the most skillful worker in metals of his day, producing medals, jewel settings, caskets, vases, candlesticks, metal plates, and ornaments. Imprisoned on false charges, he worked at the court of Francis I at Paris after his release. He returned to Florence in 1545 and remained until his death in 1571. The decorative quality of his work, its intricate and exquisite detail and workmanship, are typical of the best of the period. Unfortunately, most of his works have perished. The famous gold and enamel saltcellar of Francis I and the gold medallion of *Leda and the Swan* (both: Vienna Mus.) are perhaps the best examples of those remaining. His sculptures, most of them executed in the later Florentine period, include the colossal bronze bust of Cosimo I (Bargello); the bronze bust of Altoviti (Gardner Mus., Boston); the *Nymph of Fontainebleau* (Louvre); the life-size *Crucifixion*, a white marble Christ on a black cross (Escorial); and the renowned *Perseus with the Head of Medusa* (Loggia dei Lanzi, Florence), a beautifully wrought bronze statue surmounting a marble pedestal lavishly adorned with statuettes and carvings. See translation of his autobiography by J. A. Symonds (1888; many later editions).

cello or **'cello:** see VIOLIN.

cellophane, thin, transparent sheet or tube of regenerated CELLULOSE. Cellophane is used in packaging and as a membrane for DIALYSIS. It is sometimes dyed and can be moisture-proofed by a thin coating of PYROXYLIN. There are several steps in the preparation of cellophane from raw cellulose. The cellulose is first treated with an alkali, e.g., sodium hydroxide, and mixed with carbon disulfide to form viscose (see VISCOSE PROCESS). The viscose is aged for several days and then forced through a straight or circular slit into a dilute acid solution. The dissolved cellulose precipitates, and this regenerated cellulose has a lower molecular weight and a less orderly structure than the cellulose from which it is formed.

cellosolve: see GLYCOL.

celluloid [from *cellulose*], transparent, colorless synthetic PLASTIC made by treating cellulose nitrate with camphor and alcohol. Celluloid was the first important synthetic plastic and was widely used as a substitute for more expensive substances, such as ivory, amber, horn, and tortoise shell. It is highly flammable and has been largely superseded by newer plastics with more desirable properties. It has been used for combs, brush handles, billiard balls, knife handles, buttons, and other useful objects.

cellulose, chief constituent of the CELL walls of plants. Chemically, it is a carbohydrate that is a high molecular weight polysaccharide. Raw cotton is composed of 91% pure cellulose; other important natural sources are flax, hemp, jute, straw, and wood. Cellulose has been used for the manufacture of paper since the 2d cent. Insoluble in water and other ordinary solvents, it exhibits marked properties of absorption. Because cellulose contains a large number of HYDROXYL GROUPS, it reacts with acids to form ESTERS and with alcohols to form ETHERS. Cellulose derivatives include guncotton, fully nitrated cellulose, used for explosives; celluloid (the first plastic), the product of cellulose nitrates treated with camphor; collodion, a thickening agent; and cellulose acetate, used for plastics, lacquers, and fibers such as RAYON.

Celman, Miguel Juárez: see JUÁREZ CELMAN.

Céloron de Blainville, Pierre Joseph de (pyĕr zhôzĕf' sālərôN' də blăNvēl'), 1693–1759, French Canadian soldier, b. Montreal. He was commandant at Michilimackinac (1734–42), Detroit (1742–43, 1750–53), Niagara (1744–46), and Crown Point (1746–47). In 1739–40 he led a detachment south to what is now Tennessee to cooperate with the Sieur de Bienville in a campaign against the Chickasaw Indians and was decorated for his conduct. His most famous service was as leader of the expedition sent by the governor of New France in 1749 to take official possession of the Ohio valley and warn English traders to leave.

Celsius, Anders (ăn'dərs sĕl'sēŭs), 1701–44, Swedish astronomer. While professor of astronomy at the Univ. of Uppsala (1730–44), he traveled through Germany, France, and Italy, visiting great observatories. At Nuremberg in 1733 he published a collection of 316 observations of the aurora borealis made by himself and others. While in Paris he was instrumental in bringing about an expedition (of which he became a member) organized by the French Academy for the measurement of an arc of the meridian in Lapland (1736). He supervised the building of an observatory at Uppsala in 1740 and became its director; while there he pioneered in the measuring of the magnitude of stars, using photometric methods. In 1742 he invented the centigrade (or Celsius) thermometer. His works include *De observationibus pro figura telluris determinanda* (1738).

Celsius temperature scale (sĕl'sēəs), TEMPERATURE scale according to which the temperature difference between the reference temperatures of the freezing and boiling points of water is divided into 100 degrees. The freezing point is taken as 0 degrees Celsius and the boiling point as 100 degrees Celsius. The Celsius scale is widely known as the centigrade scale because it is divided into 100 degrees. It is named for the Swedish astronomer Anders Celsius, who established the scale in 1742. Temperatures on the Celsius scale can be converted to equivalent temperatures on the FAHRENHEIT TEMPERATURE SCALE by multiplying the Celsius temperature by 9/5 and adding 32° to the result, according to the formula $9/5C+32=F$.

Celsus (sĕl'səs), 2d cent., Roman philosopher, an aggressive antagonist of Christianity. His works have been lost, but the substance of his *True Discourse* is given by Origen in his *Against Celsus*, ed. and tr. by Henry Chadwick (1953, repr. 1965).

Celsus, Aulus Cornelius, fl. A.D. 14, Latin encyclopedist. His only extant work, *De re medicina,* consists of eight books on medicine believed to have been written A.D. c.30. He was not esteemed as a scientist in his time, but his was one of the first works to be rediscovered and printed (Florence, 1478) during the Renaissance and was very influential, largely because of its splendid Latin style. It was translated by James Grieve in 1756 and by W. G. Spencer in 1935. Celsus' first name is also written Aurelius.

Celt (sĕlt, kĕlt) or **Kelt** (kĕlt). **1** One who speaks a Celtic language or who derives ancestry from an area where a Celtic language was spoken; i.e., one from Ireland, the Scottish Hebrides and Highlands, the Isle of Man, Wales, Cornwall, or Brittany. **2** A member of a group of peoples first found early in the 2d millennium B.C. in SW Germany and E France. The Celts were a group of tribes speaking Indo-European dialects. Armed with iron weapons and mounted on horses, they spread rapidly over Europe, crossing into the British Isles, moving S over France, Italy, and Spain, fighting the Macedonians, and penetrating into Asia Minor, where they raided Hellenistic centers. The Celts introduced the newly developed iron industries. Their wealth from trade and from raiding helped to maintain their dominance over Central Europe during the Iron Age. The LA TÈNE culture developed among the Celts. Greek influences that stimulated Celtic culture included the introduction of the chariot and of writing. Art flourished in richly ornamented styles. The Celts lived in semifortified villages, with a tribal organization that became increasingly hierarchical as wealth was acquired. Priests, nobles, craftsmen, and peasants were clearly distinguished, and the powers of the chief became kinglike. The Celts believed in a demonic universe and relied on the ministry of the DRUIDS. Much Western European folklore is derived from the Celts. By the 4th cent. B.C. they could no longer withstand the encroaching Germanic tribes, and they lost most of their holdings in the north and in W Germany. From that time on, Celtic history becomes confused with that of the many unsettled tribes in Europe. Celtic language and culture were variously dispersed among peoples of little historical identity, and until the 20th cent. historians obscured the very important differences among these groups by naming them all Celts. Further confusion has resulted from the designation of the Celts as a racial group. To the Greeks and Romans, the Celts were tall, muscular, and light-skinned, but it is believed that these were qualities of the Celt warriors rather than Celts in general. The term *Celtic* is actually a cultural one, unrelated to physical heredity. It implies a cultural tradition maintained through many centuries of common history in the same general area. See also IRON AGE. See T. G. E. Powell, *The Celts* (1958, rev. ed. 1959); Henri Hubert, *The Rise of the Celts* (1966); Nora Chadwick, *The Celts* (1970).

Celtes, Conradus Protucius (kŏn'rädəs prō'-to͞otsēəs kĕl'təs), pseud. of **Konrad Pickel** (kôn'rät pĭk'əl), 1459–1508, German scholar and humanist. He traveled widely, lectured at several universities, became librarian to Maximilian I, and founded various societies dedicated to classical learning. He was made (1487) first German poet laureate. Of his works—didactic, lyric, and dramatic—his odes in the manner of Ovid and Horace are noteworthy. Celtes discovered the works of the nun HROTSWITH or Roswitha von Gandersheim.

Celtic art. The earliest clearly Celtic style in art was developed in S Germany and E France by tribal artisans of the mid- to late 5th cent. B.C. With the dispersal of Celtic tribes during the next five centuries, their characteristically sophisticated designs were spread throughout Europe and the British Isles. Although some classical influence was evident in Celtic work, most of the complex, linear, highly ornamented pieces that survive reveal an inspiration of great originality and power. Stylized and fantastic plant and animal forms, as well as strong, geometrical, intertwining patterns, decorated the surfaces of household and ritual vessels, weapons, and body ornaments. The principal materials used in the surviving pieces of metalwork, most numerous of the remains, are gold and bronze. Some painted ceramics and enamel work survive as well from the early period. Frequently, Greek-inspired arabesque motifs were modeled in low relief. Artisans of the British Isles adapted Celtic design in the 3d cent. B.C., producing distinctive, vigorous works that soon owed little to Continental originals. Asymmetrical line engraving gained ascendancy in the 1st cent. B.C. for decorated weaponry and utensils. Two hundred years later Roman influence had effectively overwhelmed Celtic styles, although typical motifs were retained well into the medieval period. Numerous first-rate examples of Celtic craftsmanship may be seen at the British Museum. See J. R. Allen, *Celtic Art in Pagan and Christian Times* (1912); Paul Jacobsthal, *Early Celtic Art* (2 vol., 1944); George Bain, *The Methods of Construction of Celtic Art* (1951); C. F. Fox, *Pattern and Purpose: A Survey of Early Celtic Art in Britain* (1958); Ian Finlay, *Celtic Art* (1973).

Celtic Church, name given to the Christian Church of the British Isles before the mission (597) of St. Augustine of Canterbury from Rome. Founded in the 2d or 3d cent. by missionaries from Rome or Gaul, the church was well established by the 4th cent. when it sent representatives to the Synod of Arles (314) and to the Council of Rimini (359). It continued to spread in the 5th cent. due to the work of St. Ninian in Scotland, St. Dyfrig in Wales, and St. Patrick in Ireland. The heresies of the 4th cent. that played a significant role in church affairs on the Continent seem to have had little influence in Britain, and although it was the home of Pelagius (see PELAGIANISM), his teachings did not gain followers there until 421 with an influx of refugees from the Continent. The missions of St. Germanus of Auxere (429 and 447) against the Pelagians in Britain and the spread of monasticism from Gaul attest to contacts with the church on the Continent. The Saxon invasions, beginning c.450, all but destroyed Celtic culture, dealing a deathblow to the Celtic Church in England through the destruction of the towns in which it had gained its greatest following. The few small Christian communities that survived were to be found in Wales and Ireland and in N and SW Britain. The period of peace that followed the British defeat of the Saxons at Mons Badonicus (c.500) once again allowed for growth of the Celtic Church (especially through the work of St. COLUMBA), although isolation from the Continent continued until the mission of St. Augustine. Having converted King Æthelbert of Kent to Christianity, St. Augustine attempted to convince the leaders of the Celtic Church to change those practices (such as the dating of Easter and the forms of baptism and tonsure) that were at variance with the Roman Church and to accept the imposition of a diocesan organization on the essentially monastic structure of their church. He failed, and it was not until the Synod of Whitby (664, see WHITBY, SYNOD OF) that such agreement was largely reached, although independent Celtic churches continued on for some time in Wales and Ireland. See N. K. Chadwick, *The Age of the Saints in the Early Celtic Church* (1961); James Bulloch, *The Life of the Celtic Church* (1963).

Celtic languages (sĕl'tĭk, kĕl'-), subfamily of the Indo-European family of languages. At one time, during the Hellenistic period, Celtic speech extended all the way from Britain and the Iberian Peninsula in the west across Europe to Asia Minor in the east, where a district still known as Galatia recalls the former presence there of Celtic-speaking Gauls. Later, however, in the course of the Roman conquest, Celtic speech tended to yield to Latin, and by the 5th cent. A.D. Celtic had virtually disappeared from continental Europe. Today the Celtic languages that have survived into the modern era are limited almost entirely to the British Isles and French Brittany, where these tongues are spoken by a total of about three million people. The Celtic subfamily is made up of three groups of languages: the Continental, the Brythonic (also called British), and the Goidelic (also called Gaelic). Continental Celtic, which includes all Celtic idioms on the Continent with the exception of Breton, died out following the fall of the Western Roman Empire in the late 5th cent. A.D. The principal example of this group is the now extinct language Gaulish, for little remains of any other Continental Celtic tongues. Gaulish was once the language of Gaul proper (now modern France). Evidence of Gaulish is found both in words and in personal and proper names referred to by ancient Greek and Latin writers as well as in more than a hundred Gaulish inscriptions from Gaul and N Italy (ranging in date from the 3d cent. B.C. to the 3d cent. A.D.). Coins and Greek and Latin inscriptions in Europe also preserve Celtic place-names and personal names. Yet the material as a whole is quite limited, furnishing only a number of proper names, a small vocabulary, and certain indications regarding the sounds and grammar of Gaulish and of Continental Celtic in general. The Brythonic group includes Breton, Cornish, and Welsh. They are all descendants of British, the Celtic language of the ancient Britons of Caesar's day. The emergence of Welsh, Cornish, and Breton from British as separate languages probably took place during the 5th and 6th cent. A.D. and was a result of the Germanic invasions of Britain. Breton today reaches more than one million people in Brittany, most of whom are bilingual, speaking also French. It is not surprising that Breton, unlike Welsh, has many loan words from French. Breton is by no means descended from ancient Gaulish, but rather from the Celtic dialects taken by Welsh and Cornish immigrants from the British Isles who were fleeing Germanic invasions and found refuge in Armorica (now French Brittany) in the 5th and 6th cent. A.D. Surviving literary documents in Breton go back only as far as the 15th cent., but the earlier stages of the language are known through glosses and proper names (see BRETON LITERATURE). Cornish, once the Celtic language of Cornwall, became extinct in the late 18th cent. Cornish proper names in manuscripts of the 10th cent. A.D. are the oldest recorded traces of the language. A number of Cornish place-names have survived, and some Cornish words appear in the English spoken in Cornwall today. The Cornish language was written in the Roman alphabet. It is not noted for an outstanding literature (see CORNISH LITERATURE). Modern efforts to revive Cornish have had little success. Welsh (called *Cymraeg* or *Cymric* by its speakers) is the language today of about one million people, chiefly in Wales (a western peninsula of Great Britain) but also in the United States, to which a number of Welsh people have migrated. Most speakers of Welsh in Great Britain also use English, with perhaps 50,000 limiting themselves to Welsh. The oldest extant Welsh texts are from the 8th cent. A.D. (see WELSH LITERATURE). Welsh and Breton have discarded the originally numerous Indo-European cases for the noun and use only one case. Both employ the Roman alphabet for writing. The accent in Welsh and Breton generally falls on the next-to-last syllable, with the exception of a single Breton dialect that has the accent on the last syllable. The third group of the Celtic subfamily is Goidelic, to which Irish (also called Irish Gaelic), Scottish Gaelic, and Manx belong. The term *Erse* is used as a synonym for Irish and sometimes even for Scottish Gaelic. All the modern Goidelic tongues are descendants of the ancient Celtic speech of Ireland. It is thought that the Celtic idiom first came to Ireland shortly before the Christian era. An official language of Ireland, Irish is spoken by approximately 900,000 people in that country and by 50,000 more in Northern Ireland, though most speakers of Irish also use English (see IRISH LANGUAGE). Scottish Gaelic is the tongue of about 100,000 persons in the Highlands of Scotland and an additional 30,000 in Canada. Most of these people also speak English. Gaelic speech began to reach Scotland in the late 5th cent. A.D., when it was brought by the Irish invaders of that country. However, a truly distinctive Scottish Gaelic did not appear before the 13th cent. The chief difference between Scottish Gaelic and Irish results from the substantial Norse influence on the former. There are four cases for the noun (nominative, genitive, dative, and vocative) in Scottish Gaelic, which uses the Roman alphabet (see GAELIC LITERATURE). Manx is a dialect of Scottish Gaelic that was once spoken on the Isle of Man, but it has almost entirely died out there. First recorded in writing in the early 17th cent., Manx does not have an important literature. It shows a strong Norse influence and is written in the Roman alphabet. The rules of pronunciation for all the Celtic languages are extremely complicated. For example, the final sound of a word frequently brings about a phonetically changed initial consonant of the next word, as in Irish *fuil,* "blood," but *ar bhfuil,* "our blood." Another example is Welsh *pen,* "head," but *fy mhen,* "my head." In order to look up a word in the dictionary, one has to be familiar with these rules of phonetic change, or mutation. There are only two genders in the Celtic languages, masculine and feminine. Words of Celtic origin that have been absorbed by English include *bard, blarney, colleen, crock, dolmen, druid, glen, slogan,* and *whiskey.* An interesting feature of Celtic languages is that in several characteristics they resemble some non-Indo-European languages. These characteristics include the absence of a present participle and the use instead of a verbal noun (found also in Egyptian and Berber), the frequent expression of agency by means of an impersonal passive construction instead of by a verbal subject in the nominative case (as in Egyptian, Berber, Basque, and some Caucasian and Eskimo languages), and the positioning of the verb at the beginning of a sentence (typical of Egyptian and Berber). See INDO-EUROPEAN. See Henry Lewis and Holger Pedersen, *A Concise Comparative Celtic Grammar* (1937); K. H. Jackson, *Language and History in Early Britain* (1953).

Celtic literature: see BRETON LITERATURE; CORNISH LITERATURE; GAELIC LITERATURE; WELSH LITERATURE.

Celtic religion: see DRUIDS.

cement, hydraulic, building material typically made by heating a mixture of limestone and clay until it almost fuses and then grinding it to a fine powder. Once it is mixed with water, cement will harden even if immersed in water. It may also be mixed with water and aggregates (crushed stone, sand, and gravel) to form CONCRETE. A cement made by grinding together lime and a volcanic product found at Pozzuoli on the Bay of Naples (hence called pozzuolana) was used in ancient Roman construction works, notably the Pantheon. During the Middle Ages the quality of cements declined. In the 18th cent. John Smeaton, an English engineer, was commissioned to rebuild the Eddystone lighthouse off the coast of Cornwall, England. In the course of the project he found that a natural cement made from clayey limestone was superior to other available cements for a building that must stand in water. The production of natural cement began in the United States c.1820. It was made by processing cement rock from various deposits, such as those found in Rosendale, N.Y. In 1824, Joseph Aspdin, an English bricklayer, patented a process for making what he called portland cement, a natural cement with properties superior to its predecessors. Modern portland cement is made by mixing substances containing lime, silica, alumina, and iron oxide and then heating the mixture until it almost fuses. During the heating process dicalcium and tricalcium silicate, tricalcium aluminate, and a solid solution containing iron are formed. Gypsum is later added to these products during a grinding process. Portland cement is by far the most widely used hydraulic cement. Natural cement, although slower-setting and weaker than portland cement, is still employed to some extent and is occasionally blended with portland cement. Aluminous, or aluminate, cement is used when a quick-setting cement is necessary. It is made from limestone and bauxite.

cemetery, name used by early Christians to designate a place for burying the dead. First applied in Christian burials in the Roman CATACOMBS, the word *cemetery* came into general usage in the 15th cent. Group burials have been found in Paleolithic caves, and fields of prehistoric grave mounds, or BARROWS, are located throughout Europe, Asia, and North America. In the ancient Middle East, graves were often grouped around temples and sanctuaries. In Greece the dead were buried outside the city walls along the roads leading into the city in a necropolis (city of the dead). Christian belief in resurrection made chapel crypts and churchyards desirable for burial, but overcrowding and the rise of urban centers made it necessary to establish cemetery plots outside the city limits. Graveyards of all periods tend to reflect the familial and class groupings of their living society. Among the many beautiful and historic cemeteries of Europe are the Père-Lachaise in Paris and the Campo Santo in Pisa. A noteworthy U.S. cemetery is the ARLINGTON NATIONAL CEMETERY. The National Park Service also maintains cemeteries (see NATIONAL PARKS AND MONUMENTS, table). See FUNERAL CUSTOMS; GRAVE; TOMB.

Cenchrea (sĕn'krēə) or **Cenchreae** (-krē-ē"), port of ancient Greece, on the Saronic Gulf, ESE of Corinth. Acts 18.18; Rom. 16.1.

Cenci, Beatrice (bāätrē'chā chān'chē), 1577–99, Italian noblewoman, tragic figure of the late Renaissance. Her father, Francesco Cenci (1549–98), was a Roman noble noted for his viciousness. In 1595 he imprisoned Beatrice and her stepmother Lucrezia in a lonely castle; his cruel treatment finally led Beatrice, with the complicity of her stepmother, her brothers, and perhaps her lover, to procure his murder. After a famous trial (1599) the conspirators were put to death. This tragedy, often cited as an example of the dissipation and cruelty of 16th-century Rome, is the subject of, among other works, Francesco D. Guerrazzi's novel *Beatrice Cenci,* Percy Bysshe Shelley's tragedy *The Cenci,* and Alberto Ginastera's opera *Beatrix Cenci.* A painting by Guido Reni in the Barberini Palace, Rome, is sometimes said to represent her. See Corrado Ricci, *Beatrice Cenci* (1923, tr. 1925).

Cendrars, Blaise (blĕz säNdrär'), 1887–1961, French writer. He was at various times an art critic, a journalist, and a film director, and he traveled widely, notably in China and Africa. For a while he was associated with *cubisme,* a movement that attempted to apply the principles of cubism to literature. He was particularly noted for his fast-paced adventure novels. His works include *Du Monde entier* (1919), poems; *Petits Contes nègres pour les enfants blancs* (1928; tr. *Little Black Stories for Little White Children,* 1929), stories; and the novel *L'Or* (1925; tr. *Sutter's Gold,* 1926).

Cenis, Mont (môN sənē'), Ital. *Moncenisio,* Alpine pass, 6,831 ft (2,082 m) high, on the French-Italian border. It is one of the great invasion routes in Italian history. Napoleon I built a new road there in 1810. The Mont Cenis railroad tunnel (c.8 mi/13 km long) was built in 1871 and connects Turin, Italy, with Chambéry, France, via Modane, France; it is one of the world's longest railroad tunnels.

Cennini, Cennino (chān-nē'nō chān-nē'nē), c.1370–1440, Florentine painter, follower of Agnolo Gaddi. None of his paintings is extant. He is most famous for having written the *Libro dell' arte* (written 1400?, tr., *The Craftsman's Handbook,* 1933). This treatise marks a transition between medieval and Renaissance concepts of art. Closely following the tradition of Giotto, he offers detailed advice about the established technique of painting. At the same time, Cennini was one of the first to call for imagination in art and to advocate the elevation of painting from artisanship to the fine arts.

Cenozoic era (sēnəzō'ĭk, sĕn-), fifth and last major division of geologic time (see GEOLOGIC ERAS, table). Following the disturbances of the late MESOZOIC ERA, the geography of North America at the beginning of the Cenozoic attained substantially its present form. The only areas subjected to inundation by shallow marine waters were the Atlantic and Gulf coasts and a small area on the Pacific coast. It is in the Cenozoic era that man appeared. The life of this era has been dominated by the mammals, which were most numerous in the TERTIARY PERIOD and have declined, with the exception of a few specialized types, in the QUATERNARY PERIOD. The elapsed portion of the Cenozoic is about 65,000,000 years, less than half the estimated duration of the Mesozoic. See also GEOLOGY.

censor (sĕn'sər), title of two magistrates of ancient Rome (from c.443 B.C. to the time of Domitian). They took the census (by which they assessed taxation, voting, and military service) and supervised public behavior. They also had charge of public works and filled vacancies among the senators and knights.

Censorinus (sĕnsōrī'nəs), fl. c.238, Roman grammarian. He wrote *De die natali* [on the day of birth], an essay partly astrological, partly chronological, which affords much information on ancient methods of computing time.

censorship, official prohibition or restriction of any type of expression believed to threaten the political, social, or moral order. It may be imposed by governmental authority, local or national, by a religious body, or occasionally by a powerful private group. It may be applied to the mails, speech, the press, the theater, dance, art, literature, photography, the cinema, radio, or television. Censorship may be either preventive or punitive, according to whether it is exercised before or after the expression has been made public. The practice has been in use since ancient times, and was particularly thoroughgoing under autocratic and heavily centralized governments, from the Roman Empire to the totalitarian states of the 20th cent., especially Fascist Italy, Nazi Germany, and the Communist states. In other countries, censorship is accepted as inevitable in times of war, but it has been imposed to varying degrees even in peacetime. In the Middle Ages the attempts to uproot heresy and the establishment of the Inquisition were examples of censorship, as are the modern instances of book burning. The absolute monarchs of the 17th and 18th cent. imposed strict controls, and because the Reformation had resulted in a reshuffling of the relations between CHURCH AND STATE, these controls were used to persecute opponents of the established religion of a particular state, Roman Catholic or Protestant. A form of book banning was adopted by the Roman Catholic Church in the INDEX, a list of publications that the faithful were forbidden to read. The last edition of the Index was published in 1948; Pope Paul VI, in 1966, decreed that it would be discontinued but that papal lists of prohibited books would continue to be issued. Paradoxically, in the lands under Calvinist domination (such as Geneva, Scotland, and England of the Puritan period), where the ideals of liberty and freedom first blossomed, regulation of private conduct and individual opinion was rigorous, and censorship was strong. In the Soviet Union, Boris Pasternak's *Doctor Zhivago,* which won the 1958 Nobel Prize in Literature, was not permitted publication, and the novels of Aleksandr Solzhenitsyn, considered by many as masterpieces, have been banned since 1966. In Britain during the 19th and 20th cent., the object of censorship has most often been literature regarded as obscene. With the passage of the

Obscene Publications Act in 1857, there followed many criminal prosecutions and seizures of so-called obscene books. This law remained in effect for over a century when a new one superseded it in 1959. The new law provided that the opinion of artistic or literary experts could be submitted as evidence in deciding obscenity cases and that an alleged obscene work had to be judged as a whole rather than in part. However, in 1971 the editors of an underground periodical, *Oz,* were convicted in a much publicized trial for violating postal laws. An appeal court held that a periodical need not be judged as a whole, an apparent reversal of the 1959 act, which had stated otherwise. Censorship has existed in the United States since colonial times, but its emphasis has gradually tended to shift from the political to the sexual. Attempts to suppress political freedom of the press in the American colonies were recurrent; a notable example was the trial of John Peter ZENGER. The Bill of Rights in the U.S. Constitution guarantees freedom of the press, of speech, and of religion. Nevertheless, there have been examples of official political censorship, notably in the actions taken under the Sedition Act of 1798 (see ALIEN AND SEDITION ACTS), suppression of abolitionist literature in the antebellum South, and local attempts to repress so-called radical publications in the 19th and 20th cent. Long before World War I there were vigilante attacks, such as those by Anthony COMSTOCK, on what was reckoned obscene literature, and the U.S. Post Office expanded (1873) its ban on the shipment of obscene literature and art; but it was after World War I that public controversy over censorship raged most fiercely. Until the Tariff Act was amended in 1930, many literary classics were not allowed entry into the United States on grounds of obscenity. Even subsequently, attempts persisted, and *Ulysses* by James Joyce was not allowed into the country until after a court fight in 1933. Other works of literature involved in obscenity cases included *Lady Chatterley's Lover* by D. H. Lawrence, *Tropic of Cancer* by Henry Miller, and *Fanny Hill* by John Cleland. Beginning in 1957, the Supreme Court began a series of decisions that tended to relax restrictions on so-called obscene materials. Although these decisions covered a 15-year period, not all obscenity cases during this time were dismissed. In a famous case in the 1960s, Ralph Ginzburg was convicted of advertising in an obscene manner. As the Supreme Court decisions struck down many state obscenity laws, the states responded by passing laws prohibiting the sale of obscene materials to minors, and these were upheld (1968) by the Supreme Court. The liberalizing trend, however, was reversed in 1973, when the Supreme Court ruled that the individual states could decide, according to local standards, what is obscene. Another variety of censorship that was much attacked and much defended was the effort to keep out of schools and colleges textbooks and teaching that might be deleterious to what was termed "the American form of government" (see ACADEMIC FREEDOM). In the 1960s, the issue of sex education in schools became highly controversial. Films have also been the target of censorship. The producers of motion pictures, dependent for success upon widespread public approval, somewhat reluctantly adopted a self-regulatory code of morals (see HAYS, WILL H.). Although the code has been relaxed and revised (1956, 1966, and 1970), the 1973 Supreme Court ruling on obscenity will certainly have an effect on the degree to which films will be censored at the local level. Another area of censorship involves radio and television broadcasting. Since 1934, local stations have operated under licenses granted by the Federal Communications Commission, which is expressly forbidden to exercise censorship. However, the required three-year review of a station's license invites indirect censorship. The issue of government secrecy was dealt with in the Freedom of Information Act of 1966, which stated that, with some exceptions, people have the right of access to government records. The issue was challenged in 1971, when a secret government study that came to be known as the PENTAGON PAPERS was published by major newspapers. The government sued to stop publication, but the Supreme Court ruled in favor of the newspapers (see PRESS, FREEDOM OF THE). See Robert Downs, *The First Freedom* (1960); P. S. Jennison, *Freedom to Read* (1963); M. L. Ernst, *Censorship* (1964); Paul Boyer, *Purity in Print* (1968); Edward De Grazia, *Censorship Landmarks* (1969); E. J. R. Widmer, *Freedom and Culture* (1970).

census, periodic official count of the number of persons and their condition and of the resources of a country. In ancient times, among the Jews and Romans, such enumeration was mainly for taxation and conscription purposes. The introduction of the modern census—a periodic and thorough statistical review—began in the 17th cent. The first efforts to count people in areas larger than cities at regular periods were in French Canada (1665), Sweden (1749), the Italian states (1770), and the United States (1790). The first British census was taken in 1801. The Belgian census of 1846, directed by Adolphe QUETELET, was the most influential in its time because it introduced a careful analysis and critical evaluation of the data compiled. Most industrialized countries now take a census every 5 to 10 years. Scientific census taking in the United States began with the decennial census of 1850, when the scope and methods were greatly improved by making the individual the unit of study. In 1902 the Bureau of the Census was established in the Dept. of Commerce, and in 1972 the Bureau was combined with the Office of Business Economics to form the Social and Economic Statistics Administration. The census is considered the most vital source of statistical information about a nation, providing invaluable data to social scientists and government planners. See A. H. Scott, *Census U.S.A.* (1968); W. S. Holt, *The Bureau of the Census* (1929, repr. 1973).

centaur (sĕn'tôr), in Greek mythology, creature, half man and half horse. The centaurs were fathered by IXION or by Centaurus, who was Ixion's son. Followers of Dionysus, they were uncouth and savage, but some, such as CHIRON, became friends and teachers of men.

Centaurus (sĕntôr'əs), southern CONSTELLATION located N and E of Crux, the Southern Cross. It is known especially for its bright stars ALPHA CENTAURI and HADAR. It also contains Centaurus A, a radio galaxy, as well as a globular STAR CLUSTER visible to the naked eye. Centaurus reaches its highest point in the evening sky in May.

Centennial Exposition, International, held in Philadelphia from May to Nov., 1876, to celebrate the 100th anniversary of the Declaration of Independence. The buildings, in Fairmount Park, included the Main Building, covering 20 acres (8 hectares), Machinery Hall, Agricultural Hall, Horticultural Hall, and Memorial Hall, many state buildings, and buildings of 37 foreign countries. The total number of persons attending in 159 days was almost 10 million. This was the first of a series of world's fairs that the United States was to hold, and it set a high standard, exhibiting in graphic manner the technical advances and industrial growth of the nation. Memorial Hall, a Renaissance structure of granite, became part of the Pennsylvania Museum of Art.

center, in politics, a party following a middle course. The term was first used in France in 1789, when the moderates of the National Assembly sat in the center of the hall. It can refer to a separate party in a political system, e.g., the Catholic Center party of imperial and Weimar Germany, or to the middle group of a party consisting of several ideological factions.

centering, the framework of wood or of wood and steel built to support a masonry arch or vault during its construction. The centering itself must be rigidly supported, either by posts from the ground or by trusses when piers are available to receive their ends. After the centering is built, the setting of the masonry proceeds equally from the ends or sides toward the central point, where the keystone of the arch or the crowning blocks of the vault are finally wedged into position. The centering is removed after setting in the case of arches where the shape is dependent on the cement or concrete, but in other instances, e.g., where dressed stone is used with a lime mortar joint, it is better to remove the centering before setting, so that gravity will control the disposition of the stones. Removal of the centering is a delicate operation, since undue stress on one part endangers the whole structure. The Romans built vast domes and vaults of concrete with the aid of wood centerings and of integral brick ribs within the vault itself. Arches of steep rise may sometimes be built without centering. Brunelleschi is said to have dispensed with it in constructing the steep dome of the cathedral of Florence. Today inflatable plastic balloons are often used instead of centering.

Center Line, city (1970 pop. 10,379), Macomb co., SE Mich., a suburb of Detroit; inc. 1925.

center of gravity: see CENTER OF MASS.

center of mass, the point at which all the MASS of a body may be considered to be concentrated in analyzing its behavior. Since mass is usually observed in a gravitational field, often the center of mass is also called the center of gravity. The center of mass of a sphere of uniform density coincides with the center of the sphere. The center of mass of a body need not be within the body itself; the center of mass of a ring or a hollow cylinder is located in the enclosed space, not in the object itself. A body suspended or balanced at its center of mass will be stable; there will be no net MOMENT acting on it. Sometimes a problem may be analyzed from the point of view of the center of mass of an entire system of objects, such as several colliding elementary particles or a multiple-star system. For example, the complex motions of the earth and moon about the sun become somewhat simpler when viewed from the common center of mass of the earth-moon system, located about 1,000 mi (1,600 km) below the earth's surface. It is this point that is moving in an elliptical orbit around the sun rather than the center of mass of the earth alone.

Center Point, uninc. town (1970 pop. 15,675), Jefferson co., N central Ala., a suburb of Birmingham.

Centerville, city (1970 pop. 10,333), Montgomery co., SW Ohio, a residential suburb of Dayton; inc. 1879. It has a small industrial park.

centigrade temperature scale: see CELSIUS TEMPERATURE SCALE.

centimeter, abbr. cm, unit of length equal to 0.01 METER, the basic unit of length in the METRIC SYSTEM. The centimeter is the unit of length in the CGS SYSTEM. It is approximately equal to 0.39 inch, or 1 inch equals about 2.54 centimeters.

centipede, common name for members of a single class, Chilopoda, of the phylum ARTHROPODA. Centipedes are widely distributed in temperate and tropical lands, living in the soil or surface litter, and under logs or rocks. The largest species, *Scolopendra gigantea,* may reach 12 in. (30 cm) in length; many other tropical species are over 6 in. (15 cm) long. Temperate species are usually only about 1 in. (2.5 cm) long. The flattened body is divided into a head and a trunk composed of segments, or somites. The head bears long antennae, jaws, and two pairs of maxillae used for food-handling. Although the name *centipede* means "hundred-legged," the average is actually about 35 pairs of legs, one pair on each body segment except for the last two, the pregenital and genital segments. The appendages of the trunk's first segment are modified into claws that are equipped with poison glands and are used to kill or stun prey. Larger centipedes can cause a painful bite, but the poison is not powerful enough to cause death in humans. Centipedes are chiefly nocturnal and predominantly carnivorous, feeding on insects or other small arthropods, though the largest species can kill small vertebrates. Sexes are separate, and some species have extensive courtship ceremonies. Members of the orders Lithobiomorpha and Scutigeromorpha have 15 pairs of legs as adults. These centipedes release eggs singly in the soil. Not all of the body segments are present at the time of hatching, and the young add somites and pairs of legs as they molt. Lithobiomorphs are widely distributed in temperate and subtropical regions. The swift scutigeromorphs have very long legs; the last pair is often extended to the rear, serving as posterior tactile appendages. Although especially abundant in the tropics, they include *Scutigera forceps,* the rather common house centipede of temperate climates. The house centipede has long, delicate legs and compound eyes. It feeds on roaches, clothes moths, and other insects. Members of the orders Geophilomorpha and Scolopendromorpha produce clusters of eggs, which are guarded while they develop. A full set of body segments and legs is present at hatching. Geophilomorphs have very long, slender bodies with from 31 to over 180 pairs of short legs. They are burrowing forms and are found

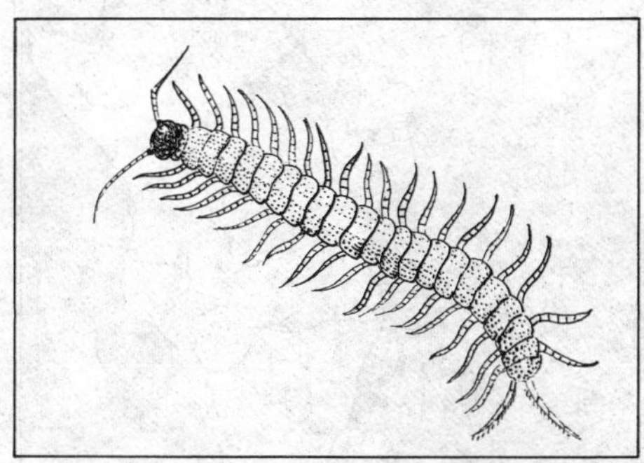

Centipede, representative of the class Chilopoda

in the soil from temperate to tropical regions. The scolopendromorphs are also widely distributed, but are more abundant in the tropics. They have from 21 to 23 pairs of legs and include the largest and most colorful centipede species. Centipedes belong to the phylum ARTHROPODA, subphylum Mandibulata, class Chilopoda.

Central African Republic, republic (1973 est. pop. 1,700,000), 240,534 sq mi (622,983 sq km), central Africa. BANGUI is the capital. The landlocked nation is bordered by Chad in the north, Sudan in the east, Zaïre and the Congo Republic in the south, and Cameroon in the west. The terrain consists of a 2,000–3,000 ft (610–910 m) undulating plateau, mainly covered by savanna; dense tropical forests in the south; and a semidesert area in the east. The Bongo Massif in the northeast reaches a height of c.4,500 ft (1,370 m). The country is drained by numerous rivers, but only the Ubangi is commercially navigable. Rainfall is heavy in the south. There are no railroads, and the network of all-weather roads is inadequate; rivers are the chief means of transportation. Population density is only about six persons per square mile. The chief ethnic groups are the Mandjia-Baya, the Banda, the Mbaka, and the Zandé. French is the official language, but Sangho is the lingua franca. More than half the population practices traditional animist religions; the remainder is predominantly Christian. The overwhelming majority of the people are engaged in agriculture, although only about 2% of the land is under cultivation. Cassava, millet, rice, and peanuts are grown for subsistence. The principal cash crops and exports are cotton and coffee; cocoa, rubber, and palm products are raised in the southwest. Timber is also an important product and export. There have been recent attempts to develop a livestock (mainly cattle) industry, despite unfavorable climate and the prevalence of the tsetse fly. Mining, formerly limited to diamonds (another leading export), has become increasingly important with extraction of uranium, begun in 1972. Industry is limited to food and mineral processing and to the production of light consumer goods. Inadequate transportation has been a major obstacle to the country's economic development. The Central African Republic belongs to the French franc zone and trades chiefly with France. Most exports are shipped via Pointe-Noire, in the Congo Republic, more than 1,100 mi (1,770 km) away. Among the country's educational institutions are a university at Bangui (founded 1970) and two agricultural colleges. Between the 16th and the 19th cent., much of the region was subject to devastating slave raids. The Baya people, seeking refuge from the Fulani of N Cameroon, arrived in what is now the Central African Republic in the early 19th cent.; the Banda, fleeing the Muslim Arab slave raiders of Sudan, came later in the century. French expeditions, pushing out from the Congo and making treaties with local tribal chiefs, occupied the area in 1887. It was organized in 1894 as the colony of Ubangi-Shari and was united administratively with Chad in 1906 and incorporated into French Equatorial Africa in 1910. Chad later became a separate French territory. Much of the region was leased to French concessionaires, whose fostering of forced labor and other abuses sparked rebellions in 1928, 1935, and 1946. The population of Ubangi-Shari actively supported the Free French forces during World War II. In 1946 the colony was given its own territorial assembly and representation in the French parliament. In the French constitutional referendum of 1958 the country opted for membership in the French Community. It received autonomy and took its present name. Full independence was attained on Aug. 13, 1960, under President David Dacko. (The nationalist leader Barthélémy Boganda, founder of the country's only political party, the Mouvement d'évolution sociale de l'Afrique noire [MESAN], had been killed in a plane crash in 1959.) The Central African Republic had a parliamentary government until Dec., 1965, when a military coup led by Col. Jean-Bédel Bokassa (Boganda's nephew) overthrew the Dacko regime, dissolved the national assembly, and abrogated the constitution. The military regime, with Bokassa as both president and head of MESAN, has dealt harshly with dissenters. There have been frequent cabinet changes and Bokassa has personally taken charge of various branches of the civil service. Close relations with France have been maintained. The Central African Republic is an associate member of the European Common Market and belongs to the French-oriented Afro-Malagasy Common Organization and the five-nation Central African Customs and Economic Union. It also holds membership in a monetary union with other equatorial African states and Cameroon, all of whom share a central bank and common currency. In 1968 the Central African Republic, Chad, and Zaïre formed a loose union of central African states. See Virginia Thompson and Richard Adloff, *The Emerging States of French Equatorial Africa* (1960); V. T. LeVine, *Political Leadership in Africa* (1967); Pierre Kalck, *Central African Republic* (tr. 1971).

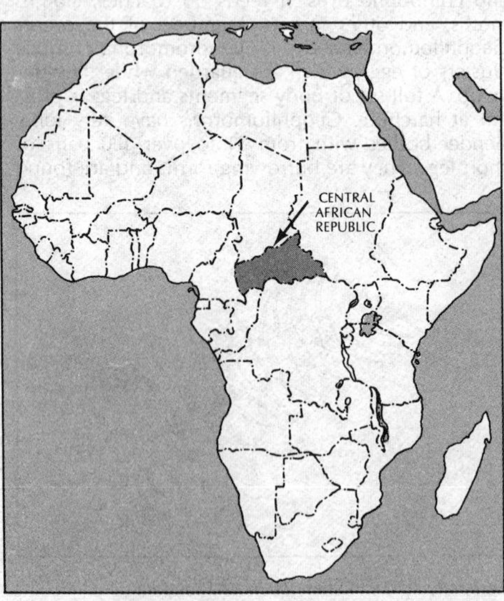

Central America, narrow, southernmost portion of the continent of North America, linked to South America by the Isthmus of Panama. It separates the Caribbean Sea from the Pacific Ocean. From a geological standpoint, Central America includes the land (c.276,400 sq mi/715,900 sq km) between the Isthmus of Tehuantepec, S Mexico, and the Isthmus of Panama; although it includes four states and one territory of Mexico and excludes the republic of Panama (which occupies an arm of South America), the term is generally applied to the colony of Belize (British Honduras) and the republics of Guatemala, Honduras, El Salvador, Nicaragua, Costa Rica, and Panama. The mountains of N Central America are an extension of the mountain system of W North America and are related to the islands of the West Indies. The middle portion of Central America is an active zone of volcanoes and earthquakes; it contains the Nicaragua Depression, which includes the huge lakes Nicaragua and Managua. The ranges of S Central America are outliers of the Andes Mts. of South America. Tajumulco (13,846 ft/4,210 m high), a volcano in Guatemala, is the region's highest peak. Central America's climate varies with altitude from tropical to cool. The eastern side of the region receives heavy rainfall. Bananas, coffee, and cacao are the chief crops of Central America, and gold and silver are mined there. The Inter-American Highway traverses W Central America. See R. C. West and J. P. Augelli, *Middle America: Its Lands and Peoples* (1966); E. G. Squier, *Notes on Central America* (1855, repr. 1969); H. C. Espy and Lex Creamer, *Another World: Central America* (1970).

Central American Common Market (CACM), trade organization formed in 1960 by a treaty on economic integration between Guatemala, Honduras, Nicaragua, and Salvador. Costa Rica later became a member. By the mid-1960s the group had made impressive advances toward economic integration, and by 1970 trade between member nations had risen more than tenfold over 1960 levels. During the same period, imports doubled and a common tariff was established for 98% of the trade with nonmember countries. In 1967, at the conference of American presidents at Punta del Este, Uruguay, it was decided that CACM, together with the LATIN AMERICAN FREE TRADE ASSOCIATION, would be made the basis for a comprehensive Latin American common market. However, by the middle of the 1970s little progress toward a Latin American common market had been made, and CACM, after a decade of economic gains, had been weakened by internal strife. After the Salvador-Honduras conflict of 1969, Honduras rescinded its CACM trade agreements—thus, in effect, withdrawing from CACM. In 1972 meetings were held to restructure the association.

Central American Federation or **Central American Union,** political confederation (1825–38) of the republics of Central America—Costa Rica, Guatemala, Honduras, Nicaragua, and Salvador. United under a captaincy general in Spanish colonial times, they gained independence in 1821 and were briefly annexed to the Mexican empire formed by Agustín de Iturbide. The nations joined in a loose federal state, appointing (1825–29) as first president Manuel José Arce, who was succeeded (1830–38) by the liberal leader, Francisco MORAZÁN. Political and personal rivalries between liberals and conservatives, poor communication, and the fear of the hegemony of one state over another led to dissolution (1838) of the congress and the defeat (1839) of Morazán's forces by Rafael CARRERA. In 1842, Morazán made an abortive attempt to reestablish the federation from Costa Rica. Later efforts by Nicaragua, Honduras, and Salvador failed. The attempts of Justo Rufino BARRIOS (1885) and José Santos ZELAYA (1895) only increased existing enmities. At the Central American conference of 1922–23 the U.S. recommendation of a union was not favorably received, partly because of earlier U.S. policies in Panama and Nicaragua. Nevertheless, geography, history, and practical expedience are factors that constantly encourage union. In 1951 the organization of Central American States was formed to help solve common problems, and in 1960 the five nations established the CENTRAL AMERICAN COMMON MARKET. See T. L. Karnes, *The Failure of Union: Central America, 1824–1960* (1961); Nino Maritano, *A Latin American Economic Community* (1970).

Central Asiatic Railroad: see TRANS-CASPIAN RAILROAD.

Central Australia: see NORTHERN TERRITORY, Australia.

central bank, financial institution designed to regulate and control the fiscal and monetary activities of a nation. Usually state owned, central banks turn all or most of their profits over to the government. They are responsible for issuing notes to be used as legal tender, maintaining adequate reserve backing for the nation's banks, and controlling the flow of money and precious metals. Such responsibilities are met by regulating the discount rate, making reserve advances to commercial banks, trading in government obligations, clearing checks, and acting as the government's fiduciary agent in its dealings with other governments and other central banks. In essence, the central bank acts as a banker's bank and as its government's bank. Although the term was hardly known before 1900, the concept of central banking dates back to at least 1694, when the Bank of England was founded. Another early central bank was the Swedish Riksbank. Today every economically developed nation possesses the equivalent of a central bank, most of which have been modeled after the Bank of England. Notable central banks include France's Banque de France, Germany's Deutsche Bundesbank, and the U.S. FEDERAL RESERVE SYSTEM (established 1913). Central banking in the United States developed as a result of the weakness of state banks following the lapse of the BANK OF THE UNITED STATES.

Central Falls, industrial city (1970 pop. 18,716), Providence co., N R.I., on the Blackstone River; set off from Lincoln and inc. 1895. Electric light bulbs are made there.

Centralia (sĕntrā'lēə). **1** City (1970 pop. 15,217), Clinton and Marion counties, S Ill., in an oil, coal, farm, and fruit region; inc. 1859. Founded in 1853 by the Illinois Central RR and named accordingly, it is the shipping center for the products of the area. Its railroad yards are still its major industry, but the city has varied manufactures, including clothing, candy, and stoves and heaters. A junior college is there. **2** City (1970 pop. 10,054), Lewis co., SW Wash., at the confluence of the Chehalis and Skookumchuck rivers; inc. 1889. It is a railroad junction and a farm trade center, with a great lumbering industry. A massive electric steam plant and two nearby dams make the city a major power center. A junior college and the county fairgrounds are there. A violent clash between townspeople and organized lumber workers occurred in Centralia on Nov. 11, 1919.

Central Intelligence Agency (CIA), independent executive bureau of the U.S. government established by the National Security Act of 1947. It replaced the wartime OFFICE OF STRATEGIC SERVICES (1942–45), the first U.S. intelligence agency. The CIA was established to gather intelligence information abroad and report to the President and to the National Security Council, his advisory body. For secrecy, it was given (1949) special powers under the Central Intelligence Act; its director may spend the agency's funds without accounting for them, and the size of its staff is never divulged. Employees, exempt from civil service procedures, may be hired, investigated, or dismissed as the CIA sees fit. To safeguard civil liberties in the United States, however, the CIA is denied domestic police powers; for operations in the United States it must enlist the services of the Federal Bureau of Investigation. Faulty intelligence reports prior to the Korean War led (1950) to the appointment of Gen. Walter Bedell Smith as director. Allen Welsh DULLES, a veteran intelligence agent who was director from 1953 to 1961, strengthened the agency and emboldened its tactics. The CIA has often been criticized for taking an active role in the internal affairs of foreign countries. The agency was heavily involved in the 1961 invasion of Cuba, the failure of which deeply embarrassed the United States. In 1971 the U.S. government acknowledged that the CIA had recruited and paid an army fighting in Laos. In 1973 the CIA came under Congressional investigation for its role in the PENTAGON PAPERS case: The agency had provided members of the White House staff, on request, with a personality profile of Daniel Ellsberg, defendant in the Pentagon Papers trial in 1973; and it had supplied materials that were used in the break-in at Ellsberg's psychiatrist's office in 1971 by members of a special unit established by the White House to investigate internal security leaks. The CIA's involvement in domestic affairs was a direct violation of the National Security Act of 1947, and efforts were begun in Congress to strengthen provisions barring the agency from domestic operations. Operations of the CIA again came under attack in 1974 when it was revealed that the agency had been involved in Chilean internal affairs during the administration of Salvador ALLENDE GOSSENS. Further revelations of CIA domestic surveillance prompted President Ford to establish a commission of inquiry in Jan., 1975; at the same time Congress set up its own investigations. After Dulles's retirement John Alex McCone was (1961-65) director of the agency. He was succeeded by William F. Raborn (1965-66), Richard M. HELMS (1966-72), James R. Schlesinger (1973), and William E. Colby (1973-). See Andrew Tully, *CIA: The Inside Story* (1962); L. B. Kirkpatrick, *The Real CIA* (1968); H. H. Ransom, *The Intelligence Establishment* (rev. ed. 1970); P. J. McGarvey, *CIA: The Myth and the Madness* (1972).

Central Michigan University, at Mount Pleasant, Mich.; coeducational; est. 1892 as a normal school, became Central State Teachers College in 1927, achieved university status in 1959. From 1938 to 1958 graduate courses were offered in association with the Univ. of Michigan. The university maintains a forest of over 200 acres (81 hectares) used for botanical and biological research. The Clarke Historical Library contains material on the Old Northwest Territory.

central nervous system: see NERVOUS SYSTEM.

Central Park, 840 acres (340 hectares) largest park in Manhattan, New York City; bordered by 59th St. on the south, Fifth Ave. on the east, 110th St. on the north, and Central Park West on the west. The land, acquired by the city in 1856, was improved according to the plans of U.S. landscape architects Frederick L. Olmsted and Calvert Vaux. The park has rolling terrain with lakes and ponds, greeneries, bridle paths, walks, and park drives. There are many playgrounds and other recreational facilities, including the Wollman Skating Rink. The Metropolitan Museum of Art stands in the park on Fifth Ave.; other points of interest include a formal garden, a zoo, an Egyptian obelisk called "Cleopatra's Needle," a New York City reservoir, and the Mall, where concerts are given. In the open-air Delacorte Theater, Shakespearean dramas and other plays are presented free of charge.

Central Powers, in WORLD WAR I, the coalition of Germany, Austria-Hungary, Bulgaria, and the Ottoman Empire.

Central Provinces and Berar: see MADHYA PRADESH.

Central Treaty Organization (CENTO), international governmental organization, formed in 1955 for the military defense of the Middle East. The initial pact was signed by Turkey and Iraq. Great Britain, Pakistan, and Iran joined later that year. In 1956, although it did not become a full member, the United States pledged to cooperate. Originally known as the Middle East Treaty Organization, the association was based on the Baghdad Pact of 1955. After Iraq left the organization in 1959, the name was changed to CENTO, and headquarters were moved from Baghdad to Ankara. The CENTO powers are also pledged to economic and social cooperation in the Middle East.

Central Utah Project, N central Utah; begun 1959 near Vernal, Utah, by the U.S. Bureau of Reclamation in conjunction with the COLORADO RIVER STORAGE PROJECT. Water, collected from streams in the Uinta Mts., is carried across the Wasatch Range to the densely populated Salt Lake City region by a system of dams, reservoirs, tunnels, aqueducts, and canals. Strawberry Dam and Reservoir, in which the water is stored, provides water for domestic and industrial use, irrigation, hydroelectricity, fish and wildlife preservation, and flood control.

Central Valley, great trough of central Calif., c.450 mi (720 km) long and c.50 mi (80 km) wide, between the Sierra Nevada and the Coast Ranges. The Sacramento and San Joaquin rivers drain most of the valley before converging in a huge delta and flowing into San Francisco Bay. The delta is California's leading truck-farming and horticultural area. The Central Valley is the largest agricultural belt in California. With its long growing season and rich soil, the valley has the largest single concentration of fruit farms and vineyards in the United States; cotton, grain, and vegetables are also grown. Precipitation ranges from 30 in. (76 cm) in the north to 6 in. (15.2 cm) in the south. Two thirds of the valley's agricultural land is located in the south, while two thirds of the water is in the north. The Central Valley project attempts to remedy this problem by bringing water from the Sacramento basin in the north into the San Joaquin Valley in the south. The Tulare Lake basin in the extreme southern part of the valley is very dry and has alkaline conditions that make it almost totally unsuitable for irrigation. The Central Valley was first seen by Spanish explorers in the 1500s but remained virtually uninhabited until 1848, when gold was discovered nearby. In the late 1800s the valley became a rich agricultural region, with wheat as the main crop. Irrigation was introduced in the 1880s.

Central Valley project, central Calif., long-term general scheme for the utilization of the water of the Sacramento River basin in the north for the benefit of the farmlands of the San Joaquin Valley in the south, undertaken by the U.S. Bureau of Reclamation in 1935. The aims of the program are flood control; improvement of navigation; the development of hydroelectric power, irrigation, and municipal and industrial water supply; protection of the Sacramento delta from seawater encroachment; and the propagation and preservation of fish and wildlife. The project irrigates c.300,000 new acres (121,410 hectares) and supplements c.938,000 acres (379,610 hectares) of cultivated land. Shasta and Keswick dams on the Sacramento River, and Friant Dam with its reservoir, Lake Millerton, on the San Joaquin River, were among the first units built. Canals transport water throughout the valley; among the most important are the Friant-Kern Canal, the Madera Canal, the Delta Cross Channel (which uses Sacramento water to fight soil salinity in the delta), and the Delta-Mendota Canal. The Central Valley project, which will include 48 dams and reservoirs, 20 large canals, and numerous power plants, is still in progress. Among the newer hydroelectric dams are San Luis (424,000-kw capacity), Spring Creek (150,000 kw), and Judge Francis Carr (134,000 kw); Auburn Dam (240,000-kw capacity) was scheduled for completion in the mid-1970s. Folsom Dam (162,000-kw capacity) is one of several units constructed in the valley by the U.S. Corps of Engineers.

Centreville, city (1970 pop. 11,378), St. Clair co., SW Ill., a suburb of East St. Louis.

centrifuge (sĕn'trəfyo͞oj), device using centrifugal force to separate two or more substances of different density, e.g., two liquids or a liquid and a solid. The centrifuge consists of a fixed base or frame and a rotating part in which the mixture is placed and then spun at high speed. One type is used for the separation of the solid and the liquid parts of blood. Test tubes containing blood specimens are set in the rotating part in holders so arranged that when the rotary motion begins the test tubes swing into a slanted or a horizontal position with the open ends toward the axis of rotation; the heavier, solid part of the blood is thrown outward into the bottom of the tube and the lighter liquid part comes to the top. Another common type of centrifuge called the cream separator is used to separate cream from whole milk. Uranium-235, which is found in nature mixed with uranium-238, must be separated to be used to produce nuclear energy. The separation can be done by a centrifuging process in which the uranium, contained in gas molecules, is rotated at high speed in a chamber so that the more massive molecules containing uranium-238 concentrate near the outer edge of the chamber and the lighter molecules containing uranium-235 concentrate near the axis. Several stages of centrifuging are needed to effect the required degree of separation. The first successful centrifuge was built in 1883 by Carl G. P. de Laval, a Swedish engineer, whose design was used chiefly for cream separators. The ultracentrifuge, devised in the 1920s by the Swedish chemist Theodor Svedberg, found wide application in scientific research. Using an optical system with it to observe sedimentation rates, Svedberg determined accurately the molecular weights of substances including proteins and viruses. Centrifuges are also used for such diverse purposes as simulating gravitational fields in space and for drying laundry.

centriole: see MITOSIS.

centripetal force and **centrifugal force,** action-reaction force pair associated with circular MOTION. According to Newton's first law of motion, a moving body travels along a straight path with constant speed (i.e., has constant VELOCITY) unless it is acted on by an outside FORCE. For circular motion to occur there must be a constant force acting on a body, pushing it toward the center of the circular path. This force is the centripetal ("center-seeking") force. For a planet orbiting the sun, the force is gravitational; for an object twirled on a string, the force is mechanical; for an electron orbiting an atom, it is electrical. The magnitude F of the centripetal force is equal to the mass m of the body times its velocity squared v^2 divided by the radius r of its path: $F=mv^2/r$. According to Newton's third law of motion, for every action there is an equal and opposite reaction. The centripetal force, the action, is balanced by a reaction force, the centrifugal ("center-fleeing") force. The two forces are equal in magnitude and opposite in direction. The centrifugal force does not act on the body in motion; the only force acting on the body in motion is the centripetal force. The centrifugal force acts on the source of the centripetal force to displace it radially from the center of the path. Thus, in twirling a mass on a string, the centripetal force transmitted by the string pulls in on the mass to keep it in its circular path, while the centrifugal force transmitted by the string pulls outward on its point of attachment at the center of the path. The centrifugal force is often mistakenly thought to cause a body to fly out of its circular path when it is released; rather, it is the removal of the centripetal force that allows the body to travel in a straight line as required by Newton's first law. If there were in fact a force acting to force the body out of its circular path, its path when released would not be the straight tangential course that is always observed.

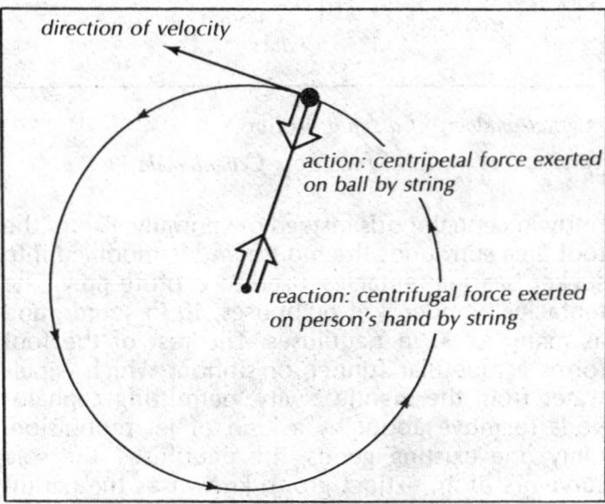

Centripetal and centrifugal forces: When a ball is swung in a circle at the end of a string, centripetal and centrifugal forces act as shown above.

centumviri (sĕntŭm'vĭrī) [Lat.,=a hundred men], in ancient Rome, law court of a varying number of members that heard civil cases having to do with land and property claims. Each Roman tribe was represented in it. Under the empire the centumviri had to deal chiefly with inheritance. The last mention of it is in A.D. 395.

century plant: see AMARYLLIS.

Ceos, Greece: see KÉA.

cephalic index (səfăl'ĭk) [Gr. *kephale*=head], ratio of the breadth of the head to its length. Expressed as a percental number, it provides the simplest description of the geometric relation of two dimensions. The index is obtained by dividing the maximum width of the cranium by its maximum length and multiplying by 100. In ANTHROPOMETRY, the cephalic index has been the favored measurement. A cephalic index of 80 or more is called brachycephalic or broad; a measurement between 75 and 80 is mesaticephalic; below 75 is considered dolicocephalic or long. The cranial index is the same ratio taken on a skull.

Cephalonia, Greece: see KEFALLINÍA.

cephalopod, member of the class Cephalopoda, the most highly organized group of mollusks (phylum MOLLUSCA), and including the SQUIDS, OCTOPUSES, CUTTLEFISH, and NAUTILUSES. The class as a whole has become adapted for a free-swimming existence. Cephalopods are able to move about rapidly, and most are aggressive carnivores. The part of the body that forms the foot in other mollusks is located anteriorly in cephalopods instead of ventrally. Part of the foot area surrounds the mouth and is modified into sucker-bearing tentacles, used to capture prey. The tentacles number 8 in octopuses, 10 in squids, and as many as 90 in nautiluses. The rest of the foot forms a muscular funnel, or siphon, which expels water from the mantle cavity, permitting cephalopods to move about by a kind of jet propulsion. Only one existing genus, the nautiluses, the sole survivors of an extinct group known as the nautiloids, possesses an external shell. In the squid and cuttlefish the shell has become internalized and reduced, and in the octopus it is completely absent. The cephalopod head is large and is equipped with prominent eyes that resemble those of vertebrate animals. The class Cephalopoda has a fossil record of 10,000 species, although only 400 exist today. The nautiloid group was dominant through Paleozoic times, and the AMMONITES flourished in the Mesozoic era.

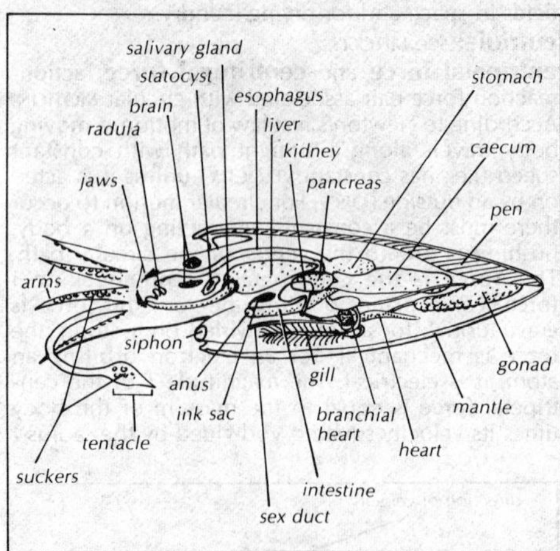

Internal anatomy of a squid, Loligo, *representative mollusk of the class Cephalopoda*

cephalosporin (sĕf″əlōspôr′ĭn), any of a group of ANTIBIOTICS derived from species of fungi of the genus *Cephalosporium* and closely related chemically to PENICILLIN. Cephalosporins act against both gram-positive and gram-negative bacteria (see GRAM'S STAIN) by inhibiting bacterial cell wall synthesis. They are used to treat urinary infections and infections of penicillin-resistant staphylococci, especially in patients sensitive to penicillin.

Cephalus (sĕ′făləs), in Greek mythology, husband of Procris. The two swore eternal fidelity, but Eos, who had fallen in love with Cephalus, persuaded him to test his wife. Cephalus disguised himself and offered to pay Procris to commit adultery. When she yielded, he angrily deserted her. Later they were reconciled; but eventually Procris became suspicious and followed Cephalus one night while he was hunting. Mistaking his wife for an animal, Cephalus killed her. He then wandered for many years but was unable to escape his grief and finally leaped to his death from a precipice.

Cephas (sē′fəs), Jesus' name for St. Peter. John 1.42.

cepheid variable (sē′fēĭd), rather small class of variable stars that brighten and dim in an extremely regular fashion. The periods of the fluctuations (the time to complete one cycle from bright to dim and back to bright) range from 1 to 50 days. These stars are important because the period of a cepheid depends on its intrinsic brightness, or absolute MAGNITUDE, in a known way: the brighter the star, the greater its period. All cepheid variables with the same period have nearly the same intrinsic brightness, but their apparent brightnesses differ because they are at different distances. By observing a cepheid's period, one can determine how bright it actually is. By comparing this intrinsic brightness to how bright it appears to be, one can determine its distance. This property makes the cepheids invaluable in estimating interstellar and intergalactic distances, and they are often called the "yardsticks of the universe." The cepheid class takes its name from the first one discovered (1784), which is located in the constellation Cepheus. Cepheids are yellow supergiant stars, and their fluctuations in luminosity result from an actual physical pulsation, with attendant changes in surface temperature and size. The stars are hottest and brightest when expanding at maximum rate midway between their largest and smallest size. The period-luminosity relation was discovered by studying the many cepheids in the Magellanic Clouds, the two closest galaxies; these stars are all almost equally distant. It was found that the brighter variables had the longer periods. The absolute magnitude of a few cepheids is required to infer absolute, rather than merely relative, distances. These absolute magnitudes were measured by a statistical study of the proper motions of cepheids within our own galaxy. Difficulties in this method caused an overestimation of the absolute magnitude of all cepheid variables. It was also found that there are two distinct classes of cepheids with different period-luminosity relations. The correction of these errors in the 1950s led to a dramatic doubling of estimated cosmological distances.

Cephisodotus (sĕfĭsŏ′dətəs), Gr. *Kephisodotos,* fl. 4th cent. B.C., two Greek sculptors. The elder, the master and probably the father or the brother of Praxiteles, is noted for the statue *Irene and Plutus (Peace and Wealth).* The original was erected on the Areopagus at Athens c.372 B.C. to celebrate the victory of Timotheus over the Spartans. The best copy is in Munich. Cephisodotus, the Younger, a son of Praxiteles, continued the Praxitelean tradition into the early 3d cent. B.C.

Ceram (sā′răm), island (1970 est. pop. including offshore islands, 100,000), c.6,600 sq mi (17,100 sq km), E Indonesia, W of New Guinea, second largest of the Moluccas. Its chief port and town is Wahai. Traversed by a central mountain range rising to more than 10,000 ft (3,050 m), the island is c.210 mi (340 km) long and c.40 mi (60 km) wide. The interior has dense rain forests and is largely unexplored. Copra, resin, sago, and fish are important commercial products. Oil is exploited in the northeast near Bula. Portuguese missionaries were active there in the 16th cent. Dutch trading posts were opened in the early 17th cent., and the island came under nominal Dutch control c.1650. Variants of the name are Seran and Serang.

Ceramic Gulf: see CERAMICUS SINUS.

ceramics (sərăm′ĭks) includes all forms of POTTERY, from crude EARTHENWARE to the finest PORCELAIN. The term is usually applied to handmade objects, such as figurines and fine dinnerware.

Ceramicus Sinus (sĕrəmī′kəs sī′nəs) or **Ceramic Gulf** (sərăm′ĭk), ancient name of the Gulf of Kos, or of Kerme, SW Turkey, an inlet of the Aegean Sea. The celebrated city of Halicarnassus, capital of Cappadocia, was on the gulf.

Cerano, Il: see CRESPI, GIOVANNI BATTISTA.

ceratotherium: see RHINOCEROS.

Ceraunian Mountains (sĭrôn′ēən), Albanian *Kanalit,* coastal range, S Albania, extending northwest c.70 mi (110 km) from the Greek border to the Strait of Otranto; Mt. Çikës (6,726 ft/2,050 m) is the highest peak. At the northern end the rugged range forks around Vlorë Bay; the west fork ends in Cape Linguetta (Albanian *Gjuhëzës*). The range is sometimes called the Acroceraunian Mts.

Cerberus (sûr′bərəs), in Greek mythology, many-headed dog with a mane and a tail of snakes; offspring of Typhon and Echidna. He guarded the entrance of Hades. One of the 12 labors of Hercules was to capture him.

Cerdic (kûr′dĭk, sûr′-), d. 534, traditional founder of the kingdom of Wessex. A Saxon, he and his son Cynric are said to have landed on the southern coast of England in 495. Little is certain about him except that later West Saxon kings traced their descent from him through his son Cynric and his grandson Ceawlin.

cerebellum (sĕr″əbĕl′əm), portion of the BRAIN that coordinates movements of voluntary (skeletal) muscles. In the cerebellum, motor impulses from the cerebrum are organized and modulated before being transmitted to muscle. As the muscle tissue responds, sensory nerve cells in the muscle return information to the cerebellum. Thus throughout a period of muscular activity, the cerebellum is able to adjust speed, force, and other factors involved in movement. The overall result is smooth and balanced muscular execution. If the cerebellum is injured, an activity like walking becomes a series of jerks: the muscles involved contract too much or too little and operate out of sequence. Maintaining muscle tone is also a function of the cerebellum. Filling most of the skull behind the brainstem and below the cerebrum, the human cerebellum approximates an orange in size and consists of two hemispherical lobes. The grooved surface of the cerebellum is gray matter, composed chiefly of nerve cells. The interior, dense with nerve fibers, is white matter. Three main nerve tracts link the cerebellum with other brain areas.

cerebral palsy (sərē′brəl pôl′zē), disability caused by brain damage before or during birth, resulting in a loss of muscular control and coordination. Most cases are thought to be caused by oxygen deficiency during the birth process. The severity of the affliction is dependent on the extent of the brain damage. Those with mild cases may have only a few affected muscles, while severe cases can result in total loss of coordination or paralysis. Nowadays it is believed that there are six different forms of the disability, each caused by damage to a different area of the brain. The spastic type, accounting for over half of the cases, results from damage to the motor areas of the cerebral cortex and causes the affected muscles to be contracted and overresponsive to stimuli. Athetosis, caused by damage to the basal ganglia, results in sudden, exaggerated movements. The two types of ataxia cause either an impaired sense of balance or a lack of coordinated movements. In flaccid paralysis, the muscles are flabby and unresponsive; patients with spastic rigidity are unable to contract their muscles, while those with tremor suffer from repeated muscular contractions. About 25% of those affected suffer some degree of mental retardation. There is no cure for the disorder and treatment usually includes physical, occupational, and speech therapy. Sometimes appliances such as braces are helpful, as well as certain surgical procedures.

cerebrospinal meningitis: see MENINGITIS.

cerebrum: see BRAIN.

ceremony, expression of shared feelings and attitudes through more or less formally ordered actions of an essentially symbolic nature performed on appropriate occasions. A ceremony involves stereotyped bodily movements, often in relation to objects possessing symbolic meaning. For example, people bow or genuflect, tip hats, present arms, slaughter cattle, salute flags, and perform a myriad of other actions. Ceremonies express, perpetuate, and transmit elements of the value and sentiment system and aim at preserving such values and sentiments from doubt and opposition; moreover, they intensify the solidarity of the participants. Ceremonies are found in all societies.

Cerenkov radiation: see CHERENKOV RADIATION.

Ceres, in astronomy, the first ASTEROID to be discovered. It was found on Jan. 1, 1801, by G. Piazzi. He took three distinct observations; on the basis of these the mathematician Gauss calculated Ceres' orbit with such accuracy that it was found one year later within 0.5° of the predicted position. Ceres is the largest and most massive of the asteroids; it has a diameter of c.470 mi (750 km) and a mass 1/100,000 that of the earth. Its ORBIT has a semimajor axis of 2.78 ASTRONOMICAL UNITS and a period of 1,681 days.

Ceres (sĕr′ēz), in Roman religion, goddess of grain; daughter of Saturn and Ops. She was identified by the Romans with the Greek Demeter. Her worship was connected with that of the earth goddess and involved not only fertility rites but also rites for the dead. Her chief festival was the Cerealia, celebrated on April 19, and her most famous cult was that of the temple on the Aventine Hill. There is much argument about the origins and nature of her cults.

cereus: see CACTUS.

Cerignola (chārēnyô′lä), city (1971 pop. 47,683), Apulia, S Italy. It is an agricultural center and a transportation junction. The city suffered a severe earthquake in 1731 and was largely rebuilt. Nearby, in 1503, the Spanish under Gonzalo Fernández de Córdoba defeated the French under Louis XII (see ITALIAN WARS).

Cerinthus (sĭrĭn′thəs), fl. A.D. c.100?, Jewish-Christian religious leader, b. Ephesus. He held tenets influenced by Gnosticism and similar to those of the Ebionites. He taught that the Christ descended into Jesus at his baptism and left him again before the Passion.

cerium (sĕr′ēəm) [from the asteroid Ceres], metallic chemical element; symbol Ce; at. no. 58; at. wt. 140.12; m.p. about 800°C; b.p. 3468°C; sp. gr. 6.77 at 25°C; valence +3 or +4. Cerium is a soft, malleable, ductile, iron-grey metal with hexagonal or cubic crystalline structure. It is slightly harder than lead. It is the most abundant of the RARE-EARTH METALS of group IIIb of the PERIODIC TABLE. It does not tarnish rapidly in dry air but quickly loses its luster in moist air. It oxidizes slowly in cold water and rapidly in hot water. It is attacked by solutions of alkalis and by concentrated or dilute acids. When heated it burns with a brilliant flame to form the oxide (ceria) that exhibits incandescence and is used in making lamp mantles (see WELSBACH MANTLE). The metal is used as a core for the carbon electrodes of arc lamps. The element forms alloys with other metals. An alloy of cerium and iron is used as the flint in cigarette and gas lighters. Minute particles of this alloy ignite in the air when scratched from the surface of the larger mass. Cerium is prepared by electrolysis of the chloride or by reduction of the fused fluoride with calcium. Cerium was recognized in 1803 in the oxide (ceria) as a new metal by M. H. Klaproth and by J. J. Berzelius and Wilhelm Hisinger; it was named for the asteroid Ceres, which had been discovered only two years earlier. The metal was obtained in a very impure state by C. G. Mosander and by Friedrich Wöhler some thirty years later; the nearly pure metal was not obtained until 1875 by W. F. Hillebrand and T. H. Norton.

CERN: see EUROPEAN ORGANIZATION FOR NUCLEAR RESEARCH.

Cernauti: see CHERNOVTSY, USSR.

Cernuda, Luis (lo͞oēs' thärno͞o'thä), 1904–, Spanish poet. Cernuda fled Spain after the Spanish civil war and taught abroad. His works include *La realidad y el deseo* [reality and desire] (1936), a collection of his delicate surrealist verse; and *Oknos el affarero* (1943), a prose lyric. He has also written about contemporary Spanish poetry (1957) and English lyric poetry (1958). See *The Poetry of Luis Cernuda* (bilingual ed. 1971); studies by John A. Coleman (1964) and Philip Silver (1965).

Cernuschi, Henri (chärno͞o'skē), 1821–96, Italian politician and economist. A strong republican, he was a leader in the Milan revolt of 1848 in support of Giuseppe Garibaldi. In 1850 he went to France, where he became a director of the Bank of France. Cernuschi vigorously advocated BIMETALLISM and is said to have coined the word. His writings include many pamphlets on the subject, notably *Silver Vindicated* (1876).

Cerré, Jean Gabriel (zhäN gäbrēĕl' sĕrā'), 1734–1805, frontiersman and trader in the American Midwest, b. Montreal, Canada. By 1755 he had established a fur-trading post at Kaskaskia, Ill., where for many years he was a prominent and powerful figure. He outfitted many traders and hunters for the Missouri region and maintained close relations with the Indians. The British made efforts to gain his support in the American Revolution, but he allied himself with the patriots and gave George Rogers Clark provisions and financial aid. Later he moved to St. Louis, where his influence was maintained until his death.

Cerro de Pasco (sĕr'rō thā päs'kō), city (1961 pop. 21,363), capital of Pasco dept., central Peru. At an altitude of 13,973 ft (4,259 m), it is one of the highest cities in the world. Cerro de Pasco is noted for its silver mines, which, according to tradition, were discovered in 1630. When silver deposits declined late in the 19th cent., the exploitation of other metals, chiefly copper, again made Cerro de Pasco Peru's leading mining center. From the nearby Minasraga mines comes about 80% of the world's supply of vanadium.

Cerro Gordo (sā'rō gōr'thō), mountain pass, E Mexico, on the road between Veracruz and Jalapa, site of a decisive battle (April 17–18, 1847) of the Mexican War. General Santa Anna, having established himself firmly at and behind the pass, attempted to halt the advance of Gen. Winfield SCOTT from Veracruz to Mexico City. Although the Mexicans thought their position impregnable, the Americans were able to rout the weak left flank and take the pass from the rear. Santa Anna was defeated, and Jalapa occupied. Capt. Robert E. Lee (who scouted out a route for the flanking movement) and Lt. U. S. Grant took part in the battle.

Cerro Tololo Inter-American Observatory (sā'rō tōlō'lō), astronomical OBSERVATORY located on Cerro Tololo peak, Chile, with offices in La Serena, about 40 mi (64 km) to the west. It is operated by the Association of Universities for Research in Astronomy (AURA), which also operates Kitt Peak National Observatory in Arizona. The principal instrument is a 158-in. (401-cm) reflecting telescope, the largest in the Southern Hemisphere and the twin of the 158-in. reflector at Kitt Peak. Other equipment of the observatory includes 60-in. (152-cm), 36-in. (91-cm), and twin 16-in. (41-cm) reflectors, the 24-in. (61-cm) Curtis-Schmidt telescope formerly at the Univ. of Michigan, and the Fabry-Perot interferometer. Also at Cerro Tololo, a half mile from the summit, is a 24-in. reflector belonging to the Lowell Observatory.

Certosa di Pavia (chārtô'zä dē pävē'ä), former Carthusian abbey of Pavia. One of the most magnificent of all monastic structures, it has been maintained as a national monument since 1866. The church, forming its nucleus, was begun in the style of the Italian Gothic in 1396 by Gian Galeazzo Visconti, duke of Milan. Little more than the nave was executed in this style, since the Renaissance, diffusing its new taste, quickly dominated the design of the edifice. The facade seems to have been begun in 1491 by a group of architects and sculptors under the leadership of Giovanni Antonio Amadeo; it was finished in the mid-16th cent. Built of rich marbles and profusely ornamented with fine sculptural decorations, it is one of the masterpieces of Renaissance decorative design. The two large arcaded cloisters are of richly ornamented terra-cotta. The main choir was badly damaged in World War II but was restored between 1953 and 1959.

cerussite (sēr'əsīt), colorless to white or gray mineral, sometimes yellowish or greenish, transparent to opaque, very brittle, crystallizing in the orthorhombic system and occurring also in granular and massive form. It is a carbonate of lead, $PbCO_3$, formed by the action of carbonate and bicarbonate solutions on galena. It is an important ore of lead widely distributed throughout the world and found associated with galena and other lead minerals.

Cervantes Saavedra, Miguel de (sərvăn'tēs, Span. mēgĕl' dā thĕrvän'tās sä"ävāthrä), 1547–1616, Spanish novelist, dramatist, and poet, author of *Don Quixote de la Mancha,* b. Alcalá de Henares. Little is known of Cervantes's youth. He went to Italy (1569), where, in the service of a cardinal, he studied Italian literature and philosophy, which were later to influence his work. In 1570 he enlisted in the army and fought in the naval battle of Lepanto (1571), receiving a wound that permanently crippled his left arm. While returning to Spain in 1575 he was captured by Barbary pirates and was sold as a slave; he eventually became the property of the viceroy of Algiers. After many attempted escapes, he was ransomed in 1580, at a cost that brought financial ruin to himself and to his family. As a government purchasing agent in Seville (1588–97), he proved less than successful; his unbusinesslike methods resulted in deficits, and he was imprisoned several times. His first published work was an effusive pastoral romance in prose and verse, *La Galatea* (1585). Between 1582 and 1587 he wrote more than 20 plays, only 2 of which survive. He was 58 when Part I of his masterpiece, *Don Quixote* (1605; Part II, 1615) was published. As a superb burlesque of the popular romances of chivalry, *Don Quixote* was an enormous and immediate success. A spurious Part II was published in 1614, probably spurring Cervantes to complete the work. *Don Quixote* is considered a profound delineation of man's two conflicting attitudes toward the world and his relationship to it: his idealism and his realism. The work has been appreciated as a satire on unrealistic extremism, an exposition of the tragedy of idealism in a corrupt world, or a plea for widespread reform. Whatever its intended emphasis, the work presented to the world an unforgettable description of the transforming power of illusion, and it had an indelible effect on the development of the European novel. Don Quixote is a country gentleman who has read too many chivalric romances. He and the peasant Sancho Panza, as his squire, set forth on a series of extravagant adventures. The whole fabric of 16th-century Spanish society is detailed with piercing yet sympathetic insight. The addled idealism of Don Quixote and the earthy acquisitiveness of Sancho serve as catalysts for numerous humorous and pathetic exploits and incidents. Its panorama of characters, the excellence of its tales, and its vivid portrayal of human nature contribute to the enduring influence of *Don Quixote.* In later years Cervantes wrote other works of fiction, including *Novelas ejemplares* (1613), 12 original tales of piracy, gypsies, and human passions, drawn from his own experience and molded by his mature craftsmanship. Some of these stories in themselves prove him one of the great literary masters. Among the most acclaimed translations of *Don Quixote* are those by Samuel Putman (1949) and J. M. Cohen (1950). See biographies by Luis Astrana Marín (in Spanish, 7 vol. 1948–58), Fernando Díaz Plaja (tr. 1970), Francisco Navarro y Ledesma (tr. 1973) and R. L. Predmore (1973); studies by Lowry Nelson (1969), Angel Flores and M. J. Benardete, ed. (1948, repr. 1969); bibliographies by D. B. Drake (vol I, 1968), R. L. Grismer (2 vol., 1942–43; repr. 1971).

Cervera y Topete, Pascual (päskwäl' thĕrvā'rä ē tōpā'tā), 1839–1909, Spanish admiral. During the SPANISH-AMERICAN WAR of 1898 he was given command of the Atlantic fleet and sent, against his own advice, to Cuba. He was blockaded by the American fleet in the harbor of Santiago de Cuba from May until July 3. Then, in an attempt to run the blockade, he lost his entire fleet and was captured. After his release he was tried and absolved from responsibility for the disaster.

Cervetri: see CAERE.

Cervin, Mont, or **Monte Cervino:** see MATTERHORN.

Cerynean hind (sĕrĭnē'ən), in Greek mythology, golden-horned hind sacred to Artemis. The fourth labor of Hercules was to capture the hind.

Césaire, Aimé (ĕmā' sāzĕr'), 1913–, West Indian poet and essayist who writes in French. After studying in Paris he became concerned with the plight of blacks in what he considers a decadent Western society. With Léopold SENGHOR and Léon DAMAS he formulated the concept of *négritude,* which urges blacks to reject assimilation and cultivate consciousness of their own racial qualities and heritage. Césaire voiced this idea through poetry, collected in such volumes as *Les armes miraculeuses* (1946) and *Ferrements* (1960) and in the essay *Discours sur le colonialism* (1950, tr. 1972). In addition to his literary output, which comprises poetry, plays, and historical essays on black leaders, Césaire has held a number of government positions in his native Martinique, including that of mayor of Fort-de-France. See study by Susan Frutkin (1973).

Cesalpino, Andrea: see CAESALPINUS, ANDREAS.

cesarean section, delivery of an infant by surgical removal from the uterus through an abdominal incision. The operation is of ancient origin; a Roman law permitted the fetus to be delivered in this manner if the mother died in the last four weeks of pregnancy. The name of the operation derives from the legend that Julius Caesar was born in this fashion. The possibility of saving the mother by such an operation was slight until an improved technique was evolved in the late 19th cent. The procedure was also aided by antisepsis and other developments that made surgery as a whole more successful. Cesarean section is performed nowadays when factors that make natural childbirth too hazardous are present, such as an abnormally narrow pelvis, pelvic tumors, hemorrhage due to accident, or an abnormal position of the fetus within the uterus. Since the wall of the uterus is weakened in the area where the incision is made, subsequent deliveries are usually also by cesarean section.

Cesari, Giuseppe, called **Cavaliere d'Arpino** (jo͞ozĕp'pā chā'zārē kävälyā'rā därpē'nō), 1568–1640, Italian late mannerist painter. Cesari's outstanding works are the frescoes in the Capitol and in the Borghese Chapel, Church of Santa Maria Maggiore, Rome. Other works are *Adam and Eve Expelled from Paradise* (Louvre); a self-portrait (Uffizi); and *Perseus and Andromeda* (Metropolitan Mus.). Several eminent baroque painters, including Caravaggio, were his pupils.

Cesena (chāzā'nä), city (1971 pop. 86,070), in Emilia-Romagna, N central Italy, on the Sávio River. It is an agricultural market and a food-processing center. Cesena flourished (1379–1465) under the MALATESTA family, who built (15th cent.) a castle on a hill overlooking the city. The castle includes the splendid Renaissance-style Malatestiana Library, which contains numerous valuable manuscripts.

Cesis (tsā'sēs, -zēz), Ger. *Wenden,* town (1967 est. pop. 17,000), W European USSR, in Latvia, on the Gauja River. It is a rail terminus, an agricultural market town, and a popular summer resort. Founded in 1209, Cesis was the seat of the Livonian Knights and became a member of the Hanseatic League. In 1561 it passed to Poland-Lithuania. Attacked by the forces of Ivan the Terrible in 1577, the fortress was blown up by its own garrison. Cesis was transferred to Sweden in 1629, to Russia in 1721, and to newly independent Latvia in 1918. It was the site in 1919 of a Latvian victory over a German free corps.

cesium (sē'zēəm) [Lat.,= bluish gray], a metallic chemical element; symbol Cs; at. no. 55; at. wt. 132.905; m.p. 28.5°C; b.p. about 700°C; sp. gr. 1.873 at 20°C; valence +1. Cesium is a ductile, soft-as-wax, silver-white metallic element. It is in group Ia of the PERIODIC TABLE. An ALKALI METAL, it is the most alkaline of all elements. Cesium liquefies in a warm room; mercury and gallium are the only other metals with this property. Chemically cesium resembles rubidium and potassium. It is the most reactive metal and is never found uncombined in nature. Pure cesium can be prepared by electrolysis of fused cesium cyanide in an inert atmosphere; the pure metal must be kept under an inert liquid or gas or in a vacuum to protect it from air and water. Cesium reacts readily with oxygen; it is sometimes used to remove traces of the gas from vacuum tubes and from light bulbs. It reacts with ice; it reacts explosively with water to form cesium hydroxide, the strongest BASE known. Cesium reacts with the halogens to form a fluoride, chloride, bromide, and iodide. It also forms a sulfate, carbonate, nitrate, and cyanide. The chloride is used in photoelectric cells, in optical instruments, and in increasing the sensitivity of electron tubes. Cesium compounds are used in the production of glass and ceramics and as antishock agents in conjunction with drugs containing arsenic. Cesium-137, a waste product of nuclear reactors, is a radioactive isotope used in the treatment of cancer. Cesium is found in the mineral pollux, or pollucite, which occurs on the island of Elba, in SW Africa, in the United States in Maine and South Dakota, and in Manitoba, Canada. Commercially useful quantities of inexpensive cesium are now available as a by-product of the production of lithium metal. Minute quantities of cesium chloride are found in mineral springs and in seawater. In 1860, R. W. Bunsen and G. R. Kirchoff discovered the element (the first to be discovered by the use of the SPECTROSCOPE) and named it for the two bright blue lines characteristic of its spectrum. It was first isolated by Carl Sefferburg in 1881 by electrolysis of its salts.

Česká Lípa (chĕ'skä lē'pä), Ger. *Böhmisch-Leipa,* city (1970 pop. 17,008), N Czechoslovakia, in Bohemia, near the East German and Polish borders. A railway junction, it manufactures railroad cars, mining equipment, and electrical instruments. The city has an old castle and an Augustinian monastery.

České Budějovice (chĕs'kā bo͝o'dyĕyôvĭtsĕ), Ger. *Budweis,* city (1970 pop. 78,037), SW Czechoslovakia, in Bohemia, on the Vltava (Moldau) River. An important road and rail hub and river port, České Budějovice is famous for its breweries. Other industries produce machinery, enamelware, food products, and pencils. The city was founded in the 13th cent. It is noted for its inner town, with an arcaded square, and for a nearby castle.

Český Les: see BOHEMIAN FOREST.

Český Těšín: see TESCHEN.

Céspedes, Carlos Manuel de (kär'lōs mänwĕl' dā sä'spāthās), 1819–74, Cuban revolutionist. He completed his education in Spain and there took part (1843) in a revolution led by Juan Prim. On returning (1868) to Cuba he began the revolt by proclaiming the demands of Cuban liberals. The TEN YEARS WAR followed. He was elected president by the revolutionists (1869), but other leaders, notably Ignacio Agramonte, disagreed with him; discontent increased, and he was deposed (1873). He was killed in 1874, probably by Spanish soldiers.

Céspedes, Carlos Manuel de, 1871–1939, president of Cuba (1933), b. New York City; son of Carlos Manuel de Céspedes (1819–74). He actively participated in the Revolution of 1895 and the Spanish-American War. When Gerardo MACHADO was overthrown in Aug., 1933, Céspedes became provisional president, but was forced to resign after a coup (Sept. 5) by a student junta supporting Ramón GRAU SAN MARTÍN.

Céspedes, Pablo de (pä'blō dā thās'pāthās), 1538–1608, Spanish artist, poet, and scholar. He studied for the priesthood and subsequently studied painting with Federigo Zuccaro in Rome. There he spent some 20 years and won a considerable reputation as painter, architect, and sculptor. On his return to Spain in 1577, he was appointed canon of the Córdoba Cathedral, where the best of his surviving works remain, including the well-known *Last Supper.* He was the author of a comparison of ancient and modern painting, of a work on the Córdoba Cathedral, and of treatises on architecture.

cesspool: see SEPTIC TANK.

cestode: see PLATYHELMINTHES; TAPEWORM.

cestus or **caestus:** see BOXING.

Cetewayo, Cetywayo (both: sĕtĭwā'ō, -wī'ō, kĕ-), or **Ketchwayo** (kĕchwī'ō), c.1836–1884, king of the Zulus. Cetewayo gained ascendancy in 1856, when he defeated in battle and killed his younger brother, who was the favorite of their father, Umpanda. On his father's death in 1872, Cetewayo took over. He was determined to resist European advances in his territory, and in Dec., 1878, he rejected British demands that he disband his troops. The British attacked in 1879, and after losing two engagements they utterly defeated Cetewayo at Ulundi. After a period of exile he was reinstated (1883) in rule over part of his former territory. Discredited by his defeats in the eyes of his subjects, Cetewayo was soon driven out of Zululand to die in exile.

Cetinje (tsĕ'tĭnyĕ), town (1971 pop. 22,032), SW Yugoslavia, in Montenegro. It grew around a monastery founded in 1485. The town became the residence of Montenegro's ruling prince-bishops and remained the capital of Montenegro until 1945. The monastery, the burial place of the Montenegrin princes, and the former royal palace (now a museum) remain.

Cetywayo: see CETEWAYO.

Ceuta (thāo͞o'tä), city (1970 est. pop. 67,000), c.7 sq mi (18 sq km), NW Africa, a possession of Spain, on the Strait of Gibraltar. An enclave in Morocco, Ceuta is administered as an integral part of Cádiz prov., Spain. It is located on a peninsula whose promontory forms one of the PILLARS OF HERCULES. The city, which has a European appearance, is a free port, with a large harbor and ample wharves; it is also a refueling and fishing port. Food processing is an important activity. Ceuta is connected with Tétouan, Morocco, by road and rail. Built on a Phoenician colony, the city was held by Carthaginians, Romans, Vandals, Byzantines, and Arabs (711). Taken by Portugal in 1415 (the first permanent European conquest in Africa), it then passed (1580) to Spain. It has remained Spanish despite several attacks, notably a prolonged siege (1694–1720) by the Sultan Moulay Ismail.

Cévennes (sāvĕn'), mountain range, S France, bordering the Massif Central on the southeast. The Cévennes proper occupy the central section of a mountainous arc (average height 3,000 ft/910 m), swinging generally NE from the Montagne Noire (NE of Toulouse) to Mont Pilat (SW of Lyons). Between the Cévennes proper and the Montagne Noire are the Causses—barren limestone plateaus intersected by deep chasms and ravines. The Loire, Allier, Lot, Tarn, Aveyron, Hérault, Gard, and Ardèche rivers all radiate from the Cévennes or the Causses. Mont Lozère (5,584 ft/1,702 m) is the highest peak of the Cévennes proper; Mont Mézenc rises to 5,753 ft (1,754 m). The cultivation of silkworms and the manufacture of silk were characteristic of the area, but the silk industry has greatly declined. Exploitation of coal in the Grand' Combe-Bessèges area has activated industry at Alès, making this area the most progressive in the Cévennes. Intensive sheep raising in the interior has worsened erosion.

Ceylon: see SRI LANKA.

Cézanne, Paul (pōl säzän'), 1839–1906, French painter, b. Aix-en-Provence. Cézanne was the leading figure in the revolution toward abstraction in modern painting. From early childhood he was a close friend of Émile Zola, who for a time encouraged the painter in his work. Cézanne went to Paris in 1861; there he met Pissarro, who was a continuing strong influence in his development. He divided his time between Provence and the environs of Paris until his retirement to Aix in 1899. Cézanne's early work is marked by a heavy use of the palette knife, from which he created thickly textured and violently deformed shapes and scenes of a fantastic, dreamlike quality. Although these impulsive paintings exhibit few of the features of his later style, they anticipate the expressionist idiom of the 20th cent. Through Pissarro, he came to know Manet and the impressionist painters. He was concerned, after 1870, with the use of color to create perspective, but the steady, diffused light in his works is utterly unrelated to the impressionist preoccupation with transitory light effects. *House of the Hanged Man* (1873–74; Louvre) is characteristic of his impressionist period. He exhibited at the group's show of 1874 but later diverged from the impressionist mode of expression and developed a firmer structure in his paintings. Cézanne sought to "re-create nature" by simplifying forms to their basic geometric equivalents, utilizing color and considerable distortion to express the essence of landscape (e.g., *Mont Sainte-Victoire,* 1885–87; Phillips Coll., Washington, D.C.), still life (e.g., *The Kitchen Table,* 1888–90; Louvre), and figural groups (e.g., *The Card Players,* 1890–92; one version, S. C. Clark Coll., New York City). Although his portraits are also geometric in approach, they remain vital studies of character, e.g., *Madame Cézanne* (c.1885; S. S. and V. White Coll., Ardmore, Pa.) and *Amboise Vollard* (Musée du Petit Palais, Paris). Cézanne developed a new type of spatial pattern. Instead of adhering to the traditional focalized system of perspective, he portrayed objects from shifting viewpoints. He created vibrating surface effects from the play of flat planes against one another and from the subtle transitions of tone and color. In all his work he revealed a reverence for the integrity and dignity of simple forms by rendering them with an almost classical structural stability. His *Bathers* (1898–1905; Philadelphia Mus. of Art) is the monumental embodiment of several of Cézanne's formal visual systems. Cézanne worked in oil, watercolor, and drawing media, often making several versions of his works. His influence upon the course of modern art, particularly upon CUBISM, is enormous and profound. His theories spawned a whole new school of aesthetic criticism, especially in England, that has ranked Cézanne among the foremost French masters. There are fine collections of his paintings in the Louvre; the Metropolitan Museum and the Museum of Modern Art, New York City; and the Barnes Foundation, Merion, Pa. See his letters, ed. by John Rewald (tr. 1941); his drawings, ed. by Adrien Chappuis (1973); his watercolors, ed. by Theodore Reff (1963); catalogue raisonné by Adrien Chappuis (2 vol., tr. 1973); biographies by John Rewald (new ed. 1967) and Jack Lindsay (1969); studies by Roger Fry (new ed. 1958), Meyer Schapiro (2d. ed. 1962), and Wayne Andersen (1970).

Cf, chemical symbol of the element CALIFORNIUM.

cgs system, system of units of measurement based on the METRIC SYSTEM and having the CENTIMETER of length, the GRAM of mass, and the SECOND of time as its fundamental units. Other cgs units are the DYNE of force and the ERG of work or energy. The units of the cgs system are generally much smaller than the comparable units of the MKS SYSTEM; the impracticality of their size has led most scientists to favor the mks system. The cgs system is still used for some calculations, however; for example, densities are often expressed in grams per cubic centimeter rather than the more complicated and less familiar mks equivalent.

Chaadayev, Piotr Yakovlevich (pyô'tər yä'kəvlyĭvĭch chädä'yĕv), 1794–1856, Russian philosopher. An aristocrat by birth, he was converted to Roman Catholicism. In 1836 the first of his *Philosophical Letters* appeared in a Moscow journal. Its devastating attack on Russian institutions, such as autocracy, the church, and serfdom, created a sensation. Chaadayev was declared insane and was confined to his home. His vigorous writings helped clarify the basic differences between the SLAVOPHILES AND WESTERNIZERS. See his major works, ed. by R. T. McNally (1969); study by R. T. McNally (1971).

Chaban-Delmas, Jacques (zhäk shäbäN'-dĕlmä'), 1915–, French political leader, whose name originally was Jacques Delmas. He joined the French resistance in 1940, using the nom de guerre "Chaban," which he later adopted legally. He entered the chamber of deputies as a Radical in 1946, but soon joined the party of General de Gaulle. From 1947 he was mayor of Bordeaux and also served in several cabinets. He was president of the national assembly from 1958 until his appointment in 1969 as premier by President Pompidou. His government faced several scandals, including charges that he had evaded personal income taxes. Although Chaban-Delmas won a vote of confidence in May, 1972, he was considered too liberal by many hard-line Gaullists, and Pompidou forced him to resign in July. In 1974 he ran unsuccessfully for the presidency.

Chabanel, Noël (St. Noël Chabanel) (nôĕl' shäbänĕl'), 1613–49, French missionary in North America, a Jesuit. He entered the Society of Jesus in 1630, came as a missionary to New France in 1643, and worked among the Huron Indians. He was captured by the Iroquois and put to death. Chabanel was canonized in 1930 with other missionaries (including Isaac Jogues and Jean de Brébeuf) and laymen. As a group they are known as the Martyrs of North America. Feast: Sept. 26 or (among the Jesuits) March 16.

Chabannes, Antoine de, comte de Dammartin (äNtwän' də shäbän' kôNt də dämmärtăN'), 1408?–1488, French soldier in the Hundred Years War. He served with Joan of Arc, distinguishing himself at the siege of Orléans in 1428–29, fought as a captain of *écorcheurs,* or armed bands, and took part in the PRAGUERIE revolt (1440). Pardoned by King Charles VII, he was appointed to various offices and presided over the committee that procured the conviction of the financier, Jacques CŒUR. After the accession (1461) of King Louis XI he was imprisoned. He escaped and joined (1465) the League of the Public Weal against LOUIS XI, but was pardoned once more and became one of the king's most trusted officers.

Chabas, Paul Émile (pōl āmēl' shäbäs'), 1869–1937, French academic painter. He is remembered chiefly for his nude, *September Morn,* which created a sensation when it was exhibited in 1912. It was sold to a Russian, hidden during the Russian Revolution, and in 1935 rediscovered in a private collection in Paris. It is now owned by the Metropolitan Museum.

Chablis (shäblē'), village (1968 pop. 1,982), Yonne dept., central France, in Burgundy. It is famous for the white wine named for it. There is a remarkable early Gothic church (12th cent.).

Chabot, Philippe de (fēlēp' də shäbō'), also known as **Amiral de Brion** (brēôN'), 1480–1543, count of Charny and of Buzançois, admiral of France. After a successful campaign (1536) in Savoy and Piedmont, he was, through the intrigues of Anne, duc de MONTMORENCY, accused and convicted (1541) of misconduct in office, but he was pardoned by King Francis I. Chabot was instrumental in arranging the voyages of Giovanni da VERRAZANO.

Chabrier, Alexis Emmanuel (ālěksē' ěmänüěl' shäbrēā'), 1841–94, French composer. His best-known works are an orchestral rhapsody, *España* (1883); an opera, *Le Roi malgré lui* (1887); and piano pieces, such as *Habanera* (1885) and *Bourrée fantasque* (1891). Chabrier's works display vivid harmonic and orchestral color and musical drollery. His music influenced such French composers as Ravel and Satie.

Chacabuco, battle of, Feb. 12, 1817, fought between Chilean independence forces and Spanish troops. It took place just N of Santiago, Chile. José de SAN MARTÍN, with Bernardo O'HIGGINS, assaulted and decisively defeated the Spanish forces, thus gaining entry into Santiago, where O'Higgins was then installed as supreme director of Chile. One year later, to the day, the independence of Chile was proclaimed. The battle climaxed a torturous three-week march across the Andes from Argentina, where San Martín had trained his army.

Chaco; Chaco Austral; Chaco Boreal; Chaco Central; and **Chaco War:** see GRAN CHACO.

Chaco Canyon National Monument: see NATIONAL PARKS AND MONUMENTS (table).

chaconne (shäkôn') and **passacaglia** (pä"səkäl'yə), two closely related musical forms popular during the baroque period. Both are in triple meter time and employ a recurring harmonic pattern of four or eight bars. Compositions labeled *passacaglia* often have, in addition, a recurring sequence of pitches, called ostinato, usually in the bass line. J. S. Bach's Chaconne from the D Minor Violin Suite and his Passacaglia in C Minor for organ are the most famous examples of these forms.

Chad (chăd, chäd), Fr. *Tchad,* republic (1973 est. pop. 3,800,000), 495,752 sq mi (1,284,000 sq km), N central Africa. NDJAMENA is the capital. Chad is bordered by the Central African Republic on the south, Sudan on the east, Libya on the north, and Cameroon, Niger, and Nigeria on the west. The terrain in the south is wooded savanna; it becomes brush country near Lake Chad. The only important rivers are the Chari and the Logone, both of which flow into Lake Chad and are used for irrigation and seasonal navigation. Northern Chad is a desert that merges with the S Sahara; areas of the mountainous Tibesti region there are 11,000 ft (3,353 m) high. The country has no railroads and few all-weather roads. Its landlocked position, great distance from the coast, poor transportation network, and inadequate natural resources have severely hampered economic development. The economy is based primarily on sedentary agriculture and nomadic pastoralism. The best farming zone is in the south, where rainfall is sufficient for the cultivation of cotton and peanuts (the country's leading cash crops) for export and some subsistence crops. Natron is the country's chief mineral; tungsten has been found in the arid Tibesti region. Industry is limited to food processing and the production of textiles and light consumer goods. Chad belongs to the French franc zone and is an associate member of the European Common Market; French is the official language. The country comprises two distinct, and often hostile, population groupings. In the politically dominant south, where the bulk of the population is concentrated, live sedentary agricultural black African peoples, including the Saras, Massa, and Moudang; they are mostly animists, but some are Christians. In the north are seminomadic and nomadic Muslim tribes, including Bedouin Arabs, Fulani, Tuareg, and Wadaians; herding is their main occupation. Traditionally, the region around Chad was a focal point for trans-Saharan trade routes. Arab traders penetrated the area in the 7th cent. Shortly thereafter, nomads from N Africa, probably related to the Berbers, entered the region; they eventually established the

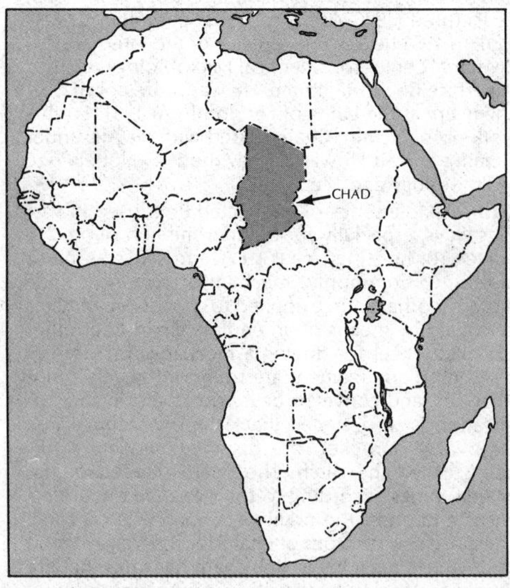

state of Kanem, which reached its zenith in the 13th cent. Its kings converted to Islam, the religion also practiced by the successor state of Bornu. The Wadai and Bagirmi empires arose in the 16th cent.; they warred with Bornu and in the 18th cent. surpassed it in power. By the early 1890s all of these states, weakened by internal dissension, fell under the control of the Sudanese conqueror Rabih. French expeditions advanced into the region in 1890, and French sovereignty over Chad was recognized by agreements among the European powers. In 1900, French forces defeated Rabih's army, and by 1913 the conquest of Chad was completed; it was organized as a French colony in French Equatorial Africa and remained under military rule. Chad was later linked administratively with Ubangi-Shari (now the Central African Republic), but in 1920 it again became a separate colony. It was granted its own territorial legislature in 1946. In the French constitutional referendum of 1958, Chad chose autonomy within the French Community. Full independence was attained on Aug. 11, 1960, with Ngarta Tombalbaye as the first president. Tombalbaye steadily strengthened his control over the country, and by 1965 it had become a one-party state. The president is chosen for a seven-year term by an electoral college composed of the national assembly, heads of urban and rural communities, and tribal chiefs. A council of ministers assists the president. The unicameral national assembly serves for five years. Chad is a member (with Cameroon, Niger, and Nigeria) of the Chad Basin Commission. Discontent among northern Muslim tribes with the increasing power of Tombalbaye's southern-dominated government evolved into a full-scale guerrilla war in 1966. Invoking its defense pact with France, the government of Chad requested French troops to help battle the guerrillas. These troops were withdrawn in 1971, and the revolt was over by 1973. Chad suffered severely from the W African drought that began in the late 1960s and continued unabated in 1974. See Virginia Thompson and Richard Adloff, *The Emerging States of French Equatorial Africa* (1960); G. M. Carter, ed., *National Unity and Regionalism in Eight African States* (1966); Guy de Lusignan, *French-Speaking Africa since Independence* (1969); H. D. Nelson, ed., *Area Handbook for Chad* (1972).

Chad, Lake (chăd, chäd), N central Africa. It lies mainly in the Republic of Chad and partly in Nigeria, Cameroon, and Niger. The size of the lake varies seasonally from c.4,000 to c.10,000 sq mi (10,360–25,900 sq km). It is divided into north and south basins, neither of which is generally more than 25 ft (7.6 m) deep, although the lake was formerly much larger and attained a depth of c.930 ft (285 m) in the 19th cent. The CHARI River is the chief tributary of Lake Chad, which has no outlets.

Chadderton, urban district (1971 pop. 32,406), Lancashire, NW England. Cottons and electrical and aircraft equipment are manufactured. In 1974, Chadderton became part of the new metropolitan county of Greater Manchester.

Chadds Ford: see BRANDYWINE, BATTLE OF.

Chadwick, Sir Edwin, 1800–1890, English social reformer. For many years an assistant to Jeremy Bentham, Chadwick applied Bentham's utilitarianism to the reform (1834) of the Poor Law and to the development of public health measures, particularly in his *The Sanitary Conditions of the Labouring Population* (1842). He was largely responsible for the passage of the Public Health Act of 1848, which established a board of health. Chadwick's chief writings were collected and edited by B. W. Richardson as *The Health of Nations* (1887). See biography by Samuel Finer (1952, repr. 1970).

Chadwick, Florence May, 1918–, American distance swimmer, b. San Diego, Calif. She began swimming at the age of six, and four years later she swam the San Diego Bay Channel, the first child to do so. On Aug. 8, 1950, she broke Gertrude Ederle's 24-year record for English Channel swims by women. Florence Chadwick covered the 20 mi (32 km) from France to England in 13 hr 20 min. She also swam (Sept., 1951) from England to France, the first woman to swim the channel in both directions. In 1952 she became the first woman to swim the 21-mi (34-km) Catalina Channel off Long Beach, Calif., breaking speed records for any swimmer (13 hr 47 min). She swam the Bosporus, the Dardanelles, and the strait of Gibraltar in 1953.

Chadwick, George Whitefield, 1854–1931, American composer, b. Lowell, Mass., studied in Germany. In 1882 he joined the faculty of the New England Conservatory of Music, of which he was director from 1897 until his death. His chief compositions are the overtures *The Miller's Daughter* (1884) and *Rip Van Winkle* (1879); the opera *Judith* (1901); and especially *Symphonic Sketches* (1908) and the song *A Ballad of Trees and the Master* (1899). Although much influenced by German music, Chadwick's best works have been described as having Yankee humor and impudence.

Chadwick, Sir James, 1891–1974, English physicist, grad. Manchester Univ., 1908. He worked at Manchester under Ernest Rutherford on radioactivity. He was assistant director of radioactive research in the Cavendish Laboratory, Cambridge (1923–35), professor at the Univ. of Liverpool (1935–48), and master of Gonville and Caius College, Cambridge (1948–58). For his discovery of the NEUTRON in 1932 he received the 1935 Nobel Prize in Physics. He was knighted in 1945.

Chadwick, Lynn, 1914–, English sculptor. After studying architecture, Chadwick began his career as a sculptor in 1945. He first produced wire MOBILES, and after 1955 he turned to triangular works of great mass that are largely abstract. Several of his works are in the Museum of Modern Art, New York City.

Chaeronea (kěrənē'ə), ancient town of Boeotia, Greece, in the Cephissus (now Kifisós) River valley and NW of Thebes. There the Athenians and Thebans were defeated (338 B.C.) by the Macedonians under Philip II, and in 86 B.C. Sulla defeated the army of Mithridates VI of Pontus under Archelaus. Chaeronea was the birthplace of Plutarch.

Chaetognatha (kētôgnăth'ə), phylum of predominantly pelagic marine animals commonly known as arrowworms. Arrowworms have slender, transparent bodies, usually under 1 in. (2.5 cm) long. Lateral and caudal fins propel the animal in sudden darting

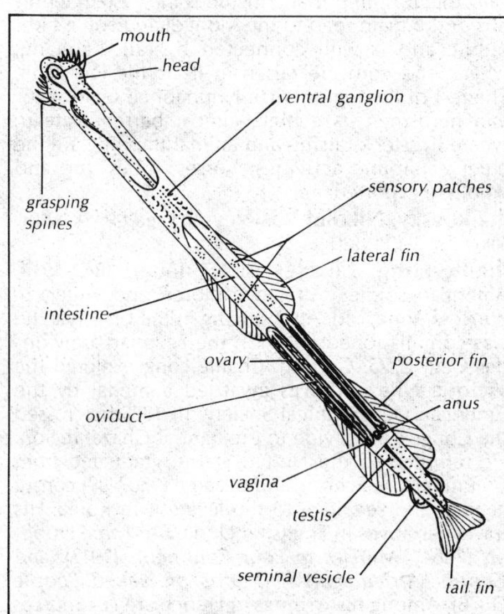

Anatomy of an arrow worm, Sagitta, *representative of the phylum Chaetognatha*

movements. The well-developed head bears eyes and other sense organs, grasping spines used in the capture of prey, and rows of teeth flanking the mouth. A protective hood can be folded down over the bristles and teeth. The digestive system includes a glandular pharynx, a straight intestine, and a short, muscular rectum. The nervous system centers in a bilobed, dorsal brain and several other nerve ganglia. Although widely distributed, arrowworms prefer warm, shallow seas and are particularly plentiful in the Indo-Pacific region. They are voracious predators; some feed on freshly hatched fish nearly as large as themselves. They are influential planktonic consumers when abundant.

chaffinch: see FINCH.

Chagai (chä'gī), town, W Pakistan, near the border with Afghanistan, on the trade route to Afghanistan and Iran. Pastoral Baluchi and Brahui tribes inhabit the region, which is noted for its oriental alabaster and other ornamental stones. British forces occupied Chagai in 1897.

Chagall, Marc (märk shəgäl'), 1889–, Russian painter. In 1907, Chagall left his native Vitebsk for St. Petersburg, where he studied under L. N. BAKST. In Paris (1910) he began to assimilate cubist characteristics into his expressionistic style. He is considered a forerunner of SURREALISM. After some years in Russia, Chagall returned to France in 1922, where he has spent most of his life. His frequently repeated subject matter is drawn from Jewish life and folklore; he is particularly fond of flower and animal symbols. His major early works include murals for the Jewish State Theater (now in the Tretyakov Mus., Moscow). Among his other well-known works are *I and the Village* (1911; Mus. of Modern Art, New York City) and *The Rabbi of Vitebsk* (Art Inst., Chicago). He designed the sets and costumes for Stravinsky's ballet *Firebird* (1945). Chagall's twelve stained-glass windows, symbolizing the tribes of Israel, were exhibited in Paris and New York City before being installed (1962) in the Hadassah-Hebrew Univ. Medical Center synagogue in Jerusalem. His two vast murals for New York's Metropolitan Opera House, treating symbolically the sources and the triumph of music, were installed in 1966. Much of Chagall's work is rendered with an extraordinary formal inventiveness and a deceptive fairy-tale naïveté. Chagall has illustrated numerous books, including Gogol's *Dead Souls*, La Fontaine's *Fables*, and *Illustrations for the Bible* (1956). A museum of his work opened in Nice in 1973. His name is also spelled Shagall. See his autobiography (1931, tr. 1960); biography by Jean-Paul Crespelle (1970); studies by Franz Meyer (tr. 1964), J. J. Sweeney (1946, repr. 1970), and Werner Haftmann (1974).

Chahar (chä-här), Mandarin *Ch'a-ha-erh*, former province (109,527 sq mi/283,675 sq km), N China. Chang-chia-k'ou (Kalgan) was the capital. It was abolished as a province in 1952; most of it was incorporated in the Inner Mongolian Autonomous Region, and the rest was divided between Shansi and Hopeh provs. The Chinese, who constitute a majority of the population of the Chahar region, are concentrated in the southern tip of the territory, which contains Chang-chia-k'ou and lies between two sections of the Great Wall. This area, economically the most important, includes the eastern terminus of the main road to the Mongolian People's Republic and is well connected by rail. Kaoliang, wheat, and corn are raised in its fertile loess soil. The rest of the region, mainly inhabited by Mongolian herdsmen, is a high, almost barren plateau, where livestock raising and animal trapping are the chief economic activities; horses, hides, fur, and wool are exported.

Chaikovsky, Nikolai Vasilyevich: see CHAYKOVSKY, NIKOLAI VASILYEVICH.

Chaillé-Long, Charles (shäyā'-lông), 1842–1917, American soldier, African explorer, and writer, b. Princess Anne, Md. After serving in the Civil War, he was commissioned (1869) in the Egyptian army under Gen. C. G. Gordon. Chaillé-Long explored the Victoria Nile and was awarded a medal by the American Geographical Society. In 1875 he crossed the Congo-Nile divide to the Bahr al Ghazal region. He returned to the United States, graduated from Columbia Law School, and became (1887–89) consul general and secretary to the legation in Korea. His travel narratives in English include *The Three Prophets* (1884), *My Life in Four Continents* (1912), and *Central Africa: Naked Truths of Naked People* (1876). Among his writings in French are *Les Sources du Nil* (1891), *L'Égypte et ses provinces perdues* (1892), and *La Corée ou Tschösen* (1894).

Chaillu, Paul Belloni du: see DU CHAILLU.

Chain, Ernst Boris, 1906–, English biochemist, b. Berlin, Germany. In 1933 he left Germany and went to England, where he conducted research at Cambridge from 1933 to 1935 and at Oxford from 1935; he lectured (1936–48) in chemical pathology at Oxford. In 1951 he became director of the International Research Center for Chemical Microbiology, Istituto Superiore de Sanità, Rome. He was professor of biochemistry at the Univ. of London from 1961. For his work on penicillin, Chain shared with Sir Alexander Fleming and Sir Howard Florey the 1945 Nobel Prize in Physiology and Medicine.

chain, flexible series of connected links used in various ways, especially for the transmission of motive power, for hoisting (see PULLEY), and for securing or fastening. Commonly, mechanical energy from a motor or other source applied to a sprocket wheel is conveyed by means of an endless chain to another sprocket wheel for driving a mechanism. Examples of such an arrangement are found in bicycles, motorcycles, and conveyor belts. The chain in this application is so designed that each consecutive link fits over a sprocket, the distance between links being called the pitch. The relative speed of the wheels varies according to their relative circumferences and, thus, the number of sprockets on each. There are several types of chain for the transmission of power. A detachable-link chain has links that are simple rectangles, each with a connecting hook at one end by which it is attached to the next link. A pintle chain has links that are approximately U-shaped. The closed end of each link fits into the open end of the next one; a pin holds the two links together. A block chain consists of metal blocks that are joined together by side plates and pins to form links. A roller chain has links consisting of side plates with hollow cylindrical rollers between them. Pins pass through the rollers and side plates to hold the links together. A silent, or inverted-tooth, chain has links made of toothed metal plates. A number of these links are placed side by side to form a group. Each group is joined to another one by meshing the ends of the links of both groups and inserting a pin there. By repeating the process a chain can be formed. Its width can be varied by varying the number of links in a group. Although not completely silent, this type of chain is quieter than other power transmission chains. The coil chains used in hoists and for locking or fastening purposes are of the open-link type, comprising solid interlocked rings, or of the stud-link type, in which a stud, or bar, across the link keeps the chain from kinking.

chain compound: see ALIPHATIC COMPOUND.

chain gang: see CONVICT LABOR.

chain reaction, self-sustaining reaction that, once started, continues without further outside influence. Proper conditions for a chain reaction depend not only on various external factors, such as temperature, but also on the quantity and shape of the substance undergoing the reaction. A chain reaction can be of various types, but nuclear chain reactions are the best known. A line of dominoes falling after the first one has been pushed is an example of a mechanical chain reaction; a pile of wood burning after it has been kindled is an example of a chemical chain reaction. In the latter case each piece of wood, as it burns, must release enough heat to raise nearby pieces to the kindling point. The wood, therefore, must be piled close enough together so that not too much heat is lost to the surrounding air. The conditions for a nuclear chain reaction can be understood by analogy. In the case of the fission of a nucleus, the reaction is begun by the absorption of a slow neutron. Each fission produces two or three fast neutrons. In order to sustain a chain reaction, a sample must be large enough to slow the neutrons so that one can be captured by another nucleus and produce a second fission. The sample must also be compact to prevent neutrons from escaping. The minimum quantity of a fissionable material necessary to sustain a nuclear chain reaction is called the critical mass. In a nuclear fission bomb, a chain reaction is started by forcing together two or more samples of fissionable material, each of less than critical mass, to form one sample of supercritical mass. The number of subsequent fissions produced by a single fission is always greater than one and increases rapidly (exponentially) with time. In a fission reactor, the number of subsequent fissions must be exactly one. If the rate is less, the chain reaction will stop; if greater, it will soon grow out of control. In one type of fission reactor, a combination of fuel rods and control rods are moved in or out of a solid block of moderating material to control the reaction rate. In another type of reactor, the temperature of a liquid moderator controls the reaction. See also NUCLEAR REACTOR. Nuclear-fusion chain reactions are initiated by very high temperatures. In a thermonuclear bomb, the necessary high temperatures are created by the explosion of a fission bomb within the fusion bomb. The principal problem in the development of controlled fusion reactors has been the containment and control of the fusion fuel at such temperatures, which are far above the melting point of any known solid. See also NUCLEAR ENERGY.

chain snake: see KING SNAKE.

chain store: see STORE.

chair, movable piece of furniture combining a seat with a supporting back, with or without arms, and usually designed to accommodate one person. Before the 17th cent. chairs were symbolic of wealth and authority; the ordinary person rested on a bench or stool or storage chest. The Egyptians created exquisite carved and painted chairs, the legs of which were fashioned to represent animal legs and feet, and the seats of which were adorned with valuable woven cloth or hide. The Greek *klysmos*, as depicted on classical pottery, was an elegant, armless chair with an S-shaped profile of the rear leg and back. It was the prototype for the many Greek revival furniture styles. The Romans designed the curule with an X-shaped frame, a style that has also been frequently revived. Characteristic chairs of the

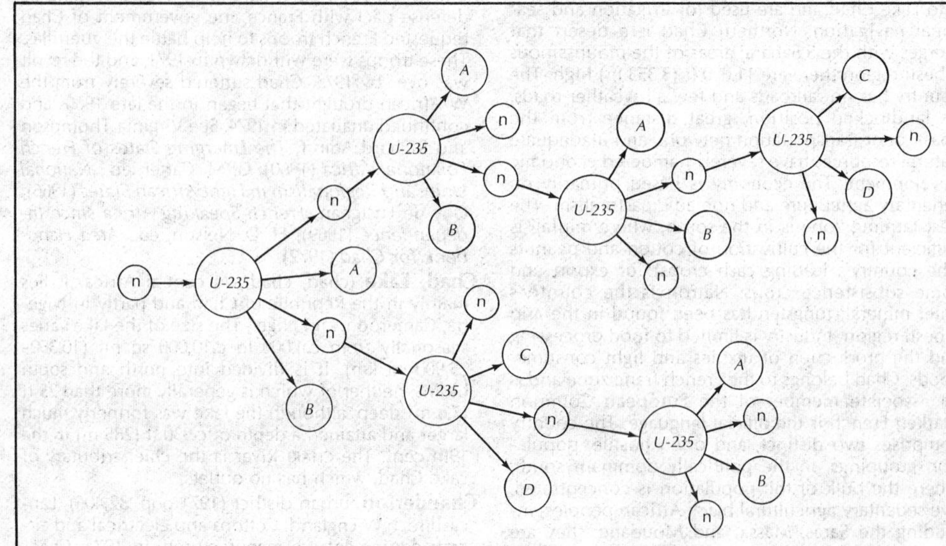

Chain reaction: A neutron (n) strikes the uranium nucleus (U-235), causing it to split into fission products A and B and release two neutrons. These neutrons can in turn cause further fissions. In some cases, a different pair of products, C and D, may be produced. The atomic numbers of the products always add up to 92, the atomic number of uranium.

Middle Ages had tall slab backs and sides and were often draped in velvet or canopied to provide warmth. Oriental influence, brought about by increased trade in the 17th cent., was reflected in curvilinear designs and the use of caning for back panels and seats. At the end of the century upholstery was introduced, and the "easy chair" became a popular item throughout the 18th cent. and later. Technological advances exerted a prodigious influence upon chair design of the 19th and 20th cent. Coiled springs, bent woods, papier-mâché, plastics, molded foam, prefabricated metal, and synthetic fabrics have all inspired furniture designers and architects (including Harry Bertoia, Eero Saarinen, Marcel Breuer, and Alvar Alto) to create bold new chair forms, many created in keeping with the aesthetic of FUNCTIONALISM.

Chaitanya (chītŭn'yə), 1485–1533, Indian mystic, also called Gauranga ("the Golden"). He was born of Brahman parents in Nabadwip, Bengal, a center of Sanskrit learning. As a young man he attained prominence as a scholar, but at 22 he underwent a profound religious conversion and became an ecstatic devotee of KRISHNA. At 24 he became a renunciant and left Nabadwip on pilgrimage, finally settling in Puri, Orissa, where he lived the rest of his life. His charisma made him the leader of an important sect of Vaishnavites that is still active. He emphasized the importance of nonritualistic worship in the form of *kirtan,* or religious song and dance, and devotion focusing on the love of Krishna and his consort Radha as the archetype of mystical union. Chaitanya is regarded by his followers as an avatar (incarnation) of Krishna and Radha in a single form. See BHAKTI.

Chaka (shä'kä), d. 1828, paramount chief (1818–28) of the Zulus. He organized an army of some 40,000 tribesmen, and after reducing many enemy tribes to vassalage, he subjugated all of what is now Natal. Chaka was murdered by his half brother, Dingaan. The name is also spelled Shaka.

chakra: see YOGA.

Chalcedon (kăl'sĭdŏn, -dən, kălsē'dən), ancient Greek city of Asia Minor, on the Bosporus. It was founded by Megara on the shore opposite Byzantium in 685 B.C. Taken by the Persians and recovered by the Greeks, it was later a possession of the kings of Bithynia, from whom it passed (A.D. 74) to Rome. The Council of Chalcedon was held there in A.D. 451. The site is in the suburbs of İstanbul.

Chalcedon, Council of, fourth ecumenical council, convened in 451 by Pulcheria and Marcian, empress and emperor of the East, to settle the scandal of the Robber Synod and to discuss Eutychianism (see EUTYCHES). It deposed the principals in the Robber Synod and destroyed the Eutychian party. Its great work, however, was its *Definition* regarding the nature and person of Jesus Christ. Based upon the formulation given by Pope St. Leo I in his famous *Tome* to Flavian, it declared (contrary to the view taken by Eutychianism) that the second Person of the Trinity has two distinct natures—one divine and one human. It was also proclaimed that these two natures exist inseparably in one person. This definition became the test of orthodoxy in the East and the West. The Roman Catholic Church has never admitted a decree of the council that made the patriarch of Constantinople single head of the Church in Eastern Europe.

chalcedony (kălsĕd'ənē) [from Chalcedon], form of quartz the crystals of which are so minute that its crystalline structure cannot be seen except with the aid of a microscope. Chalcedony has a waxy luster and is translucent to transparent. The name chalcedony is applied more specifically to white, gray, blue, and brown varieties. Some varieties differing in color because of the presence of impurities are AGATE, BLOODSTONE, CARNELIAN, CHRYSOPRASE, JASPER, ONYX, SARD, and SARDONYX.

Chalcidice, Greece: see KHALKIDIKÍ.

Chalcis, Greece: see KHALKÍS.

Chalcol (kăl'kŏl), the same as CALCOL.

chalcopyrite (kăl"kəpī'rīt, kăl'kōpī"rīt) or **copper pyrites** (pīrī'tēz, pə-), brass-yellow mineral, sometimes with an iridescent tarnish. It is a sulfide of copper and iron, $CuFeS_2$. It crystallizes in the tetragonal system but is usually found in the massive form. Chalcopyrite is of primary origin and occurs in igneous and metamorphic rocks and in metalliferous veins. It is an important ore of copper and is widely distributed throughout the world.

Chaldaea or **Chaldea** (both: kăldē'ə), properly the southernmost portion of the valley of the Tigris and the Euphrates rivers. Sometimes it is extended to include Babylonia and thus comprises all S Mesopotamia, as in the Bible (e.g., Gen. 11.28; Jer. 50.10). The Chaldaeans were a Semitic people who first came into S Babylonia c.1000 B.C. With the death of Assur-bani-pal (626 B.C.), Nabopolassar seized the throne and established a new Babylonian or Chaldaean empire. The empire flourished under Nabopolassar's son Nebuchadnezzar II, but it declined rapidly thereafter and came to an end when Babylon fell to Cyrus the Great in 539 B.C. The study of astronomy and astrology was developed in this period, and "Chaldean" came to mean simply "astrologer," as in Daniel 1.4 and among the Romans. The term is also understood in the Bible to mean Aramaean.

Chaldean rite: see NESTORIAN CHURCH.

Chaleur Bay (shəlo͝or'), inlet of the Gulf of St. Lawrence, c.85 mi (140 km) long and from 15 to 25 mi (24–40 km) wide, between N N.B. and the Gaspé Peninsula, E Que., Canada. It is the submerged valley of the Restigouche River, which enters at its head. Chaleur Bay is a famous fishing ground for cod, herring, mackerel, and salmon, and there are many Acadian fishing villages on both coasts. The bay was discovered and named by Jacques Cartier in 1534.

Chalgrin, Jean François (zhäN fräNswä' shälgrăN'), 1739–1811, French architect. He studied under Servandoni and in Italy as a winner of the Grand Prix de Rome (1758). He rebuilt (1777) part of the Church of St. Sulpice in Paris. His most influential work was the Church of St. Philippe-du-Roule, in which he reintroduced a basilica plan to French ecclesiastical architecture. He also enlarged the buildings of the Collège de France and, after the Revolution, altered the palace of the Luxembourg to serve as headquarters for the Directory. In 1806 he was commissioned by Napoleon to design a commemorative arch to the victorious armies of France, and the executed scheme for the ARC DE TRIOMPHE DE L'ÉTOILE was chiefly Chalgrin's, although he died shortly after commencement of the actual construction.

Chaliapin, Feodor Ivanovich (fyô'dər ĕvä'nəvĭch shəlyä'pyĭn), 1873–1938, Russian operatic bass. His powerful and supple voice, together with his tremendous physique, his gusto, and his superb ability as a naturalistic actor, made him one of the greatest performers in the history of opera. Taught by the singer Usatov, he first gained notice in 1894 in St. Petersburg; then he sang in Moscow and rapidly won an international reputation. After the Russian Revolution he was a lauded "artist of the people," but disagreement with the Soviet government caused him to remain outside Russia after 1921, although he maintained that he was not anti-Soviet. After an unspectacular American debut at the Metropolitan Opera in New York in 1907, he returned in 1921 and sang there with immense success for eight seasons. His most famous role was the lead in Moussorgsky's *Boris Godunov,* but he also won praise as Ivan the Terrible in Rimsky-Korsakov's *Maid of Pskov,* in the title role of Boito's *Mefistofele,* and as Mephistopheles in Gounod's *Faust.* His recitals, which included popular Russian music, were also highly successful wherever he performed. See his autobiography as told to Maxim Gorky, ed. by Nina Froud and James Hanley (1968).

chalice [Lat.,=cup], ancient name for a drinking cup, retained for the eucharistic or communion cup. Its use commemorates the cup used by Jesus Christ at the Last Supper. Celebrated examples are the Great Chalice of Antioch (Syriac), of embossed silver, excavated there in 1910 and attributed to the 1st cent., and an elaborately ornamented chalice found in 1868 at Ardagh, Ireland, and believed to be Celtic work of the 9th or 10th cent. See GRAIL, HOLY.

chalk, mineral of CALCIUM CARBONATE, similar in composition to limestone, but softer. It is characteristically a marine formation and sometimes occurs in great thickness; the chief constituents of these chalk deposits are the shells of minute animals called Foraminifera. Chalk has been laid down in all periods of geologic time, but most of the best-known deposits, e.g., the cliffs of the English Channel, date from the Cretaceous period. Chalk is used in the manufacture of putty, plaster, cement, quicklime, mortar, and rubber goods and also for blackboard chalk. Harder forms are used as building stones. Poor soils containing an excessive proportion of clay are frequently improved and sweetened by mixing chalk into them.

Chalkley, Thomas, 1675–1741, Quaker mariner and missionary preacher, b. England. He made his home after 1701 in Philadelphia, Pa. He traded chiefly with the West Indies, navigating his own ship, and made preaching tours up and down the colonies from New England to the Carolinas and also through England, Scotland, and Wales. Chalkley's journal (1747), simple in style and elevated in thought, was widely read by many generations of Quakers.

Chalk River Nuclear Laboratories, nuclear research center located on the Ottawa River in Ont., Canada, 125 miles (201 km) NW of Ottawa. Founded in 1944 by the Canadian government, it is now operated by a government corporation, Atomic Energy of Canada Limited. It is the largest nuclear research center in Canada and is devoted to exploring the peaceful uses of atomic energy.

Challenger expedition, British oceanographic expedition under the direction of the Scottish professor Charles Wyville Thompson and the British naturalist Sir John Murray. Taking place from 1872 to 1876, it opened the era of descriptive oceanography. The team sailed in the converted 18-gun corvette, *Challenger,* the first vessel specifically equipped for general oceanographic research. The expedition cruised almost 69,000 nautical mi (130,000 km) in the Atlantic, Pacific, and Antarctic oceans, gathering data on temperature, currents, water chemistry, marine organisms, and bottom deposits at 362 oceanographic stations scattered over 14 million sq mi (36 million sq km) of ocean floor. Its major contributions, covered in a 50-volume, 29,500-page report that took 23 years to compile, included the first systematic plot of currents and temperatures in the ocean; a map of bottom deposits that has not been changed much by more recent studies; an outline of the main contours of the ocean basins, incorporating the discovery of the mid-Atlantic Ridge and the then record 26,900-ft (8,200-m) Challenger Deep in the Mariana Trench; the discovery of 715 new genera and 4,717 new species of ocean life forms; and the discovery of prodigious life forms even at great depths in the ocean. See H. N. Mosely, *A Naturalist on the "Challenger"* (1879); Sir C. Wyville Thompson, *Voyage of the "Challenger"* (2 vol., 1877); Eric Linklater, *The Voyage of the Challenger* (1972).

Challoner, Richard (chăl'ənər), 1691–1781, English Roman Catholic prelate. Brought up a Protestant, he became a Roman Catholic in his teens and was ordained in 1716. In 1730 he returned from Douai to England, where he was widely known for the number of conversions he made. In 1738 he was forced to leave England because he published an open reply to an anti-Catholic pamphlet by an Anglican. In 1739, Challoner was appointed coadjutor of the vicar apostolic in London. He was consecrated titular bishop of Debra in 1741. The rest of his life he spent working among his people (after 1758 as vicar apostolic) in the face of great difficulties. From 1765 to 1780 a series of efforts were instigated to molest English Catholics, and Bishop Challoner was involved; in the Gordon riots (1780) he had to flee London for his life. He was an indefatigable writer. He revised the Douay version of the Bible, his revision becoming the standard one chiefly used by English-speaking Catholics. His chief learned works are on English Catholicism since the Reformation; they did much to preserve the memory of English Catholics. He wrote a number of devotional works; *The Garden of the Soul* (1740) was especially popular. Bishop Challoner's translations of the *Imitation of Christ* were standard. See biography by Michael Trappes-Lomax (1936).

Chalmers, Thomas (chä'mərz, chô'-), 1780–1847, Scottish preacher, theologian, and philanthropist, leader of the Free Church of Scotland. His preaching and his interest in philanthropic work during his ministry (1815–23) in Glasgow brought wide recognition. In 1823, Chalmers became professor of moral philosophy at St. Andrews Univ. and in 1828 was made professor of theology at the Univ. of Edinburgh. His Bridgewater treatise (1833) *On the Adaptation of External Nature to the Moral and Intellectual Constitution of Man* brought him a number of honors. Chalmers took a leading part (1843) in organizing the Free Church of Scotland, formed when, after much friction between church and state and trouble over patronage, 470 clergymen withdrew from the Established Church. His foresight had planned for the rapid organizing of the Free Church of Scotland, of which he was the first moderator. He was made principal (1843–47) of the New College (Free Church) at Edinburgh. His published works fill 34 volumes. See biographies by M. O. W. Oliphant (1893), Adam Philip (1929), and Hugh Watt (1943).

Chalmette National Historical Park: see NATIONAL PARKS AND MONUMENTS (table).

Châlons-sur-Marne (shälôN'-sür-märn), city (1968 pop. 54,075), capital of Marne dept., NE France, in Champagne, on the Marne River. It is a commercial and industrial center. Among its manufactures are electrodes, paper, hosiery, foundry products, and musical and precision instruments. There, in 451, the Huns under Attila were defeated by Actius. Although badly damaged in both World Wars, it still retains its cathedral (13th-17th cent.) and many remarkable Gothic churches. An arts and crafts school is there.

Chalon-sur-Saône (shälôN'-sür-sōn), town (1968 pop. 52,746), Saône-et-Loire dept., E central France, in Burgundy, on the Saône River and the Canal Central. It is an inland port with a large wine and grain trade. The town contains a thermal power station; its many manufactures include metal products, electrical equipment, barges, textiles, chemicals, and glass. Of pre-Roman origin, it was the capital of King Guntram of Burgundy (6th cent.) and the scene of 10 church councils, most notably the one convoked by Charlemagne in 813. Its cathedral, begun in the 12th cent., was completed in the 15th cent.

Chalukya (chä'lo͝okyə), S Indian dynasty that ruled in the Deccan. It was founded by Pulakesin I (reigned 543-566), who established himself at Badami (in Bijapur). His grandson Pulakesin II (c.608-c.642) expanded his domain while defending his northern frontier against HARSHA. He also captured (c.624) Vengi (in E Andhra Pradesh) and gave it to his brother Vishnuvardhana, founder of the Eastern Chalukya dynasty, which ruled Vengi until the 11th cent. The Chalukyas of Badami were in constant conflict with the Palavas. The dynasty lost power to another family in 757, but it recovered ascendancy in the Deccan c.973, its power now centered at Kalyani. The history of the Kalyani Chalukya kingdom was largely one of war with the Cholas and defense against the incursions of the Turks and Arabs who were plundering N India. The kingdom broke up in 1189, and the last Chalukya ruler died in 1200.

chalybite (kăl'əbīt"): see SIDERITE.

Cham (käm), pseud. of **Amédée de Noé** (ämādā' də nōā'), 1819-79, French caricaturist and lithographer. He abandoned a military career to produce over 4,000 designs, many of them caricatures and sketches of French and Algerian life.

Chamavi: see GERMANS.

Chamberlain, Sir Austen (Joseph Austen Chamberlain), 1863-1937, British statesman; son of Joseph Chamberlain and half brother of Neville Chamberlain. He entered Parliament as a Conservative in 1892. He was chancellor of the exchequer (1903-5), secretary of state for India (1915-17), a member of Lloyd George's war cabinet (1918), again (1919-21) chancellor of the exchequer, and lord privy seal (1921-22). Although he succeeded Bonar Law as Conservative leader in 1921, he opposed the Conservative withdrawal that brought down Lloyd George's government in 1922. From 1924 to 1929, Chamberlain was foreign secretary under Stanley Baldwin. The LOCARNO PACT of 1925 was largely his work, and in the same year he was awarded (with Charles C. Dawes) the Nobel Peace Prize. He last held a cabinet position in 1931, but he continued to be influential in Parliament until his death. See his *Down the Years* (1935), *Politics from Inside* (1936), and *Seen in Passing* (1937); Sir Charles Petrie, *Life and Letters of Sir Austen Chamberlain* (1939-40).

Chamberlain, Houston Stewart, 1855-1927, Anglo-German writer, b. England. The son of a British admiral, he was educated in France and in Germany, where he settled. He became an admirer of Richard Wagner; he eventually married Wagner's daughter and became a German citizen. His chief work, *Foundations of the Nineteenth Century* (1899, tr. 1910), is a major document of racist doctrine. Aristocratic and anti-Semitic, Chamberlain glorified the Teutons and credited them with all modern achievement. His ideas on "racial purity" were adopted and reshaped as the racist policies of Adolf Hitler. His other works include a biography of Wagner (1896, tr. 1897).

Chamberlain, John, 1927-, American sculptor, b. Rochester, Ind. In the late 1950s, Chamberlain became known for his welded assemblages of smashed automobile parts and colored scrap metal. His work is represented in the Los Angeles County Museum and the Museum of Modern Art, New York City.

Chamberlain, Joseph, 1836-1914, British statesman. After a successful business career, he entered local politics and won distinction as a reforming mayor of Birmingham (1873-76). Entering Parliament as a Liberal in 1876, Chamberlain advocated radical social reform and served under William Gladstone as president of the Board of Trade (1880-85). In 1886, however, he broke with Gladstone, leading the defection from the Liberal party of the Liberal Unionists (those Liberals who opposed Home Rule for Ireland). In 1887-88 he negotiated a treaty with the United States to settle the fisheries dispute between that country and Canada. Chamberlain became leader of the Liberal Unionists in the House of Commons in 1891, and in 1895 he joined the Conservative government as colonial secretary. While maintaining his interest in social reform at home, he pursued a vigorous colonial policy aimed at imperial expansion, cooperation, and consolidation. Although a parliamentary inquiry cleared him of complicity in the Jameson Raid (see JAMESON, SIR LEANDER STARR), there is some evidence that he was at least aware of the conspiracy. His subsequent attempts to reach a settlement with the Boers failed, resulting in the South African War (1899-1902). After the war he worked for a conciliatory peace. Chamberlain's belief in the need for closer imperial union led him to espouse the cause of imperial preference in tariffs. However, this proposed abandonment of Great Britain's traditional free trade policy provoked great controversy, and in 1903 he resigned from office to spend three years in an attempt, through the Tariff Reform League, to convert the country to his views. His campaign split the Liberal Unionist-Conservative bloc and contributed to its defeat in the election of 1906. Ill health ended Chamberlain's public life in 1906, but his tariff policy was adopted (1919, 1932) within the lifetime of his sons, Austen and Neville. See E. E. Gulley, *Joseph Chamberlain and English Social Politics* (1926); W. L. Strauss, *Joseph Chamberlain and the Theory of Imperialism* (1942, repr. 1971); biography (to 1903 only) by J. L. Garvin and Julian Amery (6 vol., 1932-51); studies by Peter Fraser (1966), Michael Hurst (1967), and R. V. Kubicek (1969).

Chamberlain, Joshua Lawrence, 1828-1914, Union general in the Civil War, b. Brewer, Maine, grad. Bowdoin, 1852, and Bangor Theological Seminary, 1855. He taught at Bowdoin from 1855 to 1862, when he became lieutenant colonel in the 20th Maine Infantry. Chamberlain was awarded the Congressional Medal of Honor for his defense of Little Round Top at Gettysburg (1863), and in June, 1864, Grant promoted him brigadier general of volunteers on the field for his gallantry before Petersburg. He was governor of Maine (1867-71) and president of Bowdoin (1871-83). He wrote *The Passing of the Armies* (1915), which deals with the final campaigns in the East. See biography by W. M. Wallace (1960).

Chamberlain, Neville (Arthur Neville Chamberlain), 1869-1940, British statesman; son of Joseph Chamberlain and half brother of Sir Austen Chamberlain. The first half of his career was spent in business and, after 1911, in the city government of Birmingham, of which he became lord mayor in 1915. In 1917 he served as director of national service, supervising conscription, and the following year, at the age of 50, he was elected to Parliament as a Conservative. During the 1920s he served both as chancellor of the exchequer (1923-24) and minister of health (1923, 1924-29). In the latter position, he enacted a series of important reforms that simplified the administration of Britain's social services and, simultaneously, systematized local government. In 1931 he again became chancellor of the exchequer and held that office until he succeeded Stanley Baldwin as prime minister in 1937. Chamberlain's belief that the German leader, Hitler, was a rational statesman like himself (and who, therefore, could not want another general war), resulted in the policy of "appeasement" that culminated in the MUNICH PACT. However, as German aggression continued, he changed his views and in March, 1939, pledged support to Poland in the event of German invasion. After the outbreak of World War II, Chamberlain remained as prime minister until, after the British debacle in Norway, he was forced to resign in May, 1940. He was lord president of the council under Winston Churchill until Oct., 1940, and died a few weeks later. See his *In Search of Peace* (1939); biographies by Keith Feiling (1946, repr. 1970), Iain Macleod (1961), and William R. Rock (1969).

Chamberlain, Wilton Norman (Wilt Chamberlain), 1936-, American basketball player, b. Philadelphia. At the Univ. of Kansas he was twice named to the All-America basketball team. He left (1958) college to join the Harlem Globetrotters. Beginning in 1959 he played a total of 14 seasons in the National Basketball Association (NBA) with the Philadelphia Warriors, San Francisco Warriors, Philadelphia 76ers, and Los Angeles Lakers. He broke almost every scoring record. With his great height (over 7 ft 1 in./216 cm) and unusual agility he was the top NBA scorer in 7 consecutive seasons (1959-65) and led the league in field goal percentage for 9 seasons and in rebounds for 11. He scored more points than any other player (31,419) and achieved the highest scoring average in the game's history. Among his records are the most points (100) scored in one game and the most free throws (28) in one game. In 1973 he became player-coach of the San Diego Conquistadors of the American Basketball Association but was prevented from playing because of a legal dispute. He announced his retirement in 1974. See his autobiography (1973); biography by George Sullivian (rev. ed. 1971).

Chamberlain's Men, Elizabethan theatrical company for which Shakespeare wrote his plays and served as actor. Organized in 1594, they performed at the Globe Theatre and at the Blackfriars Theatre. Under the patronage of James I they became c.1603 the King's Men. The members shared in the ownership of the theater and the profits, and usually all took part in the performances. Richard BURBAGE and Will Kemp were the most famous players. The most important rival company was the ADMIRAL'S MEN. See also QUEEN'S MEN.

Chamberlin, Thomas Chrowder, 1843-1928, American geologist, b. Mattoon, Ill., grad. Beloit College, 1866. He was professor of geology at Beloit (1873-82), president of the Univ. of Wisconsin (1887-92), and professor of geology and director of the Walker Museum at the Univ. of Chicago (1892-1919). Chamberlin was chief geologist of the geological survey of Wisconsin (1873-82) and the founder (1893) of the *Journal of Geology*. While studying glaciation and climates in past geologic times he noted defects in the nebular hypothesis of Laplace that led him to formulate, with the American astronomer F. R. Moulton, the planetesimal hypothesis of the origin of the SOLAR SYSTEM. Chamberlin wrote *The Geology of Wisconsin* (1873-82), *A Contribution to the Theory of Glacial Motion* (1904), *A General Treatise on Geology* (with Rollin D. Salisbury, 1906), *The Origin of the Earth* (1916), and *Two Solar Families* (1928).

chamber music, ensemble music for small groups of instruments, with only one player to each part. Its essence is individual treatment of parts and the exclusion of virtuosic elements. Originally played by amateurs in courts and aristocratic circles, it began to be performed by professionals only in the 19th cent. with the rise of the concert hall. In the broadest sense it existed as early as the Middle Ages. The *ricercare* and the concerted *canzone* of the 16th cent. are properly chamber music, although unlike later forms they were not for specific instruments but were usually performed by voices and whatever instruments were at hand. During the baroque period the chief type was the trio SONATA. About 1750 the string quartet with its related types—trio, quintet, sextet, septet, and octet—arose. As developed by Haydn and Mozart the quartet became the principal chamber-music form. It was used by Beethoven and Schubert, whose quartets are the last of the classical period, and by the chief composers of the romantic period—Mendelssohn, Schumann, Brahms, Dvořák, Franck, d'Indy, and Reger. In the early 20th cent. the coloristic possibilities of the quartet were exploited by Debussy and Ravel. More recently the different forms of chamber music have been used extensively for experiments in atonality, percussive rhythms, and serial techniques by such composers as Schoenberg, Bartók, Webern, Berg, Stravinsky, Sessions, and Piston. See D. F. Tovey, *Essays in Musical Analysis: Chamber Music* (1944, 4th impression 1956); W. W. Cobbett, ed., *Cyclopedic Survey of Chamber Music* (3 vol., 2d ed. 1963); H. E. Ulrich, *Chamber Music* (2d ed. 1966).

chamber of commerce, local association of businessmen organized to promote the welfare of their community, especially its commercial interests. Each chamber of commerce usually has a board of directors elected by the members, and work is done through committees. Among the activities frequently carried on by these committees are industrial surveys and efforts to attract new industries to the city, housing surveys, efforts to provide parking space and promote safety, and advertising the advantages of the city to tourists and to organizations as a convention site. The *chambre de commerce* of Marseilles (1599) was the first organization to use the name; the idea spread through France in the 17th and 18th cent. The first to be formed in Great

Britain was on the island of Jersey (1768). In America the first was the Chamber of Commerce of the State of New York, organized in 1768. By 1870 there were 40 throughout the United States. The local chambers are federated in the Chamber of Commerce of the United States (founded 1912), which maintains at its Washington, D.C., headquarters a technical staff and lobbies in the interests of its member organizations. Its organ is the *Nation's Business.* The International Chamber of Commerce (founded 1920) has its headquarters in Paris. See also TRADE ASSOCIATION.

Chambers, Sir Edmund Kerchever, 1866–1954, English literary critic and Shakespearean scholar. He wrote *The Mediaeval Stage* (1903), *The Elizabethan Stage* (1923), *Arthur of Britain* (1927), *William Shakespeare* (1930), and studies of S. T. Coleridge (1938) and Matthew Arnold (1947).

Chambers, Robert, 1802–71: see CHAMBERS, WILLIAM.

Chambers, Whittaker, 1901–61, U.S. journalist and spy, b. Philadelphia. He joined the U.S. Communist party in 1925 and wrote for its newspaper before engaging (1935–38) in espionage work for the USSR. He left the party in 1939 and began working for *Time* magazine. In 1948 he testified before the House Un-American Activities Committee (later House Committee on Internal Security) and accused Alger HISS, then president of the Carnegie Endowment for International Peace and a former State Dept. official, of being a Communist party member. Hiss sued for libel, and Chambers then accused him of having been part of an espionage ring. Chambers led investigators to his Maryland farm where he produced from a hollowed out pumpkin State Dept. documents that he alleged were given to him by Hiss. This led to an indictment against Hiss for perjury, and after two trials he was found guilty (1950) and imprisoned. The case was extremely controversial, and both men were vehemently attacked and defended. See Chambers's autobiography, *Witness* (1952, repr. 1968); Alistair Cooke, *A Generation on Trial* (1950, 2d ed. 1952); Ronald Seth, *The Sleeping Truth* (1968).

Chambers, Sir William, 1723–96, English architect, b. Gothenburg, Sweden. He traveled extensively in the East Indies and in China making drawings of gardens and buildings, many of which were later published. He studied architecture in France and Italy and established (1755) his practice in England where he designed decorative architecture for Kew Gardens. From the founding (1768) of the Royal Academy to the end of his life, Chambers was a dominant figure in its councils. His *Treatise on the Decorative Part of Civil Architecture* (1759) became a standard and influential work on classic design. The foremost official architect of his day in England, he continued the neo-Palladian tradition, which he adapted to the prevailing classical taste. His chief work, Somerset House, is an extensive block of government offices, begun in 1776. He also had charge of various alterations at Trinity College, Dublin, and designed additions to Blenheim Palace, the observatory in Richmond Park, and casinos in many parks of the nobility. He became private architect to King George III and was made (1782) surveyor general. Chambers was buried in Westminster Abbey.

Chambers, William, 1800–1883, and **Robert Chambers,** 1802–71, Scottish authors and publishers. Their firm of W. and R. Chambers is best known for *Chambers's Edinburgh Journal,* which William started in 1832 and for which both brothers wrote, and *Chambers's Encyclopaedia* (10 vol., 1859–68), which has gone through several editions. Robert published several books on history and in geology, including the anonymous *Vestiges . . . of Creation* (1844), a forerunner of Darwin's *Origin of Species.* William, always interested in public improvement, was lord provost of Edinburgh, 1865–69.

Chambersburg, borough (1970 pop. 17,315), seat of Franklin co., S Pa., in a fertile farm area; settled 1730, inc. 1803. Food products, steam and pneumatic hammers, sheet-metal goods, clothing, and concrete and lumber products are manufactured. Chambersburg was the headquarters of abolitionist John Brown in 1859 and of Confederate Gen. Robert E. Lee before the battle of Gettysburg. The town was raided by Confederate cavalry in 1862 and again in July, 1864, when it was burned after refusing to pay an indemnity of $100,000 in gold. It is the seat of Wilson College and of an adjoining junior college and girls' preparatory school. Caledonia State Park is to the east.

Chambéry (shäNbārē'), town (1968 pop. 58,813), capital of Savoie dept., E France, in the Alpine trough. It is a communications center with many manufactures. An archiepiscopal see from the 5th cent., it was the capital of Savoy from 1232 to 1562. Among its old edifices is a 16th-century cathedral.

Chambly (shäNblē'), city (1971 pop. 11,469), S Que., Canada, on the Richelieu River, E of Montreal. **Chambly Fort** was built in 1665 and was a strategic point in the defense of New France against the British and the Iroquois. The British captured it in 1760. It was seized by the invading Americans in 1775 and burned when they withdrew in 1776. The partially restored fort is a national historic site.

Chambord, Henri Charles Ferdinand Marie Dieudonné, comte de (äNrē' shärl fĕrdēnäN' märē' dyōdônā' kôNt də shäNbôr'), 1820–83, BOURBON claimant to the French throne, posthumous son of Charles Ferdinand, duc de BERRY. His original title was duke of Bordeaux. His grandfather, Charles X, abdicated in his favor during the Revolution of 1830, and he is known to the legitimists as Henry V, although he never held the throne. He accompanied Charles into exile and spent most of the rest of his life at Frohsdorf, Austria. In 1832 his mother, Caroline de BERRY, made an unsuccessful attempt to overthrow Louis Philippe. Efforts to reconcile his claims with those of the Orleanist pretender, Louis Philippe Albert d'ORLÉANS, after the February Revolution of 1848, met with little success. In 1871, after the fall of the Second Empire, Chambord's prospects improved, and in 1873 the Orleanist pretender relinquished his claims in Chambord's favor. However, his stubborn adherence to the Bourbon flag in preference to the national flag, the tricolor of the French Revolution, destroyed his chance of recognition. He died without issue, and his claims passed to the house of Bourbon-Orléans.

Chambord, château, park, and village (1968 pop. 267), all owned by the state, in Loir-et-Cher dept., N central France. The huge Renaissance château, built by Francis I and set in an immense park and forest (c.13,600 acres/5,500 hectares), was used chiefly by Louis XIV and by Stanislaus I of Poland. Louis XV gave Chambord to Maurice de Saxe, who died there in 1750. Napoleon I later presented it to Marshal Berthier, and in 1821 it went by national subscription to the duke of Bordeaux, who took the title count of Chambord. Repurchased by the state in 1932, Chambord is now open to the public.

chameleon (kəmē'lēən, -mēl'yən), small- to medium-sized lizard of the family Chamaeleonidae. About eighty species are found in sub-Saharan Africa, with a few in S Asia. The so-called common chameleon, *Chamaeleo chamaeleon,* is found around the Mediterranean. Chameleons have laterally flattened bodies and bulging, independently rotating eyes. They are variously ornamented with crests, horns, and spines. The toes are united into one bunch on either side of the foot, forming a pair of grasping tongs. Chameleons feed on small animals, chiefly insects, and they are unique among lizards in possessing very long, sticky tongues with which they capture their prey. Typical chameleons (members of the very large genus *Chamaeleo*) are arboreal and have long, prehensile tails. They move very slowly, with a rocking movement, grasping a branch with feet and tail. The changes in skin color, seen in certain other lizards as well, are under hormonal and nervous control. They are not affected by the color of the background but by stimuli such as light, temperature, and emotion. However, the shades of brown, gray, and green assumed by chameleons do generally blend with the forest surroundings. The American chameleon, or anole (*Anolis carolinensis*), is not a true chameleon, but a small lizard of the iguana family, found in the SE United States and noted for its color changes. True chameleons are classified in the phylum CHORDATA, subphylum Vertebrata, class Reptilia, order Squamata, family Chamaeleonidae.

Chamfort, Sébastien Roch Nicolas (säbästyăN' rōk nĕkōlä' shäNfôr'), 1740–94, French writer. He is remembered only for his maxims and epigrams. His acute observations on literature, morals, and politics made him popular at court, despite his republican beliefs. In the Reign of Terror Chamfort was denounced, and he committed suicide.

Chamillart or **Chamillard, Michel** (both: mēshĕl' shämēyär'), 1652–1721, French statesman. He was named controller general of finances (1699), minister of state (1700), and minister of war (1701). To raise funds Chamillart resorted to the sale of offices and titles, loans, lotteries, manipulation of the currency, and anticipation of revenues. To these means he added a wartime capitation tax, imposed from 1695 to 1698 and again after 1701, but he could not meet the mounting expenses of the government, especially after the outbreak (1701) of the War of the Spanish Succession. The deficit and the national debt grew huge, and the marquis de Vauban censured the disorder of the tax system. Chamillart resigned the finances to Nicolas DESMARETS in 1708 and gave up his other offices in 1709.

Chaminade, Cécile Louise Stéphanie (sāsĕl' lwēz stāfänē' shämēnäd'), 1857–1944, French composer and pianist; pupil of Benjamin Godard in composition. She was a popular concert pianist and wrote many graceful, romantic piano pieces and songs. Among her more ambitious compositions are a lyric symphony, *Les Amazones,* and a ballet, *Callirhoë* (both 1888), which includes *Scarf Dance.*

Chamisso, Adelbert von (Louis Charles Adelaide de Chamisso), (ä'dəlbĕrt fən shəmī'sō), 1781–1838, German poet and naturalist, b. France. He served as page at the court of William II and, after army service and travels, became keeper of the royal botanical gardens. He edited (1804–6) the *Musenalmanach* and was a member of Mme de Staël's circle. His sentimental poetic cycle *Frauenliebe und Leben* (1830) was set to music by Schumann. *Peter Schlemihls wundersame Geschicte* (1814), his tale of a man who sold his shadow to the devil, has become legend. He also wrote plays, an account of his travels in the Pacific (1836), and a work on linguistics (1837).

Chamizal National Memorial: see NATIONAL PARKS AND MONUMENTS (table).

chamois (shăm'ē), hollow-horned, hoofed mammal, *Rupicapra rupicapra,* found in the mountains of Europe and the E Mediterranean. It is about the size of a large goat and is light brown with a black tail, a black back stripe, and black markings on its face. In winter its coat is darker. Its uniquely shaped horns are erect, with terminal hooks pointed backward. The hooves can cling to rocky surfaces because of their elasticity, and the animal is able to leap with agility. It ranges to the snow line in summer, but in winter stays in lower areas. In autumn the adult males, which live apart from the herds of females and young, return for mating. The young are born in spring. The skin was the original chamois leather, but the name is now applied also to leather made from the skins of other animals. The chamois has been introduced into New Zealand. Chamois are classified in the phylum CHORDATA, subphylum Vertebrata, class Mammalia, order Artiodactyla, family Bovidae.

chamomile or **camomile** (both: kăm'əmīl) [Gr.,= ground apple], name for various related plants of the family Compositae (COMPOSITE family), especially the perennial *Anthemis nobilis,* the English, or Roman, chamomile, and the annual *Matricaria chamomilla,* the German, or wild, chamomile. Both are European herbs with similar uses. The former has an applelike aroma and is the chamomile most frequently grown for ornament (often as a ground cover) and for chamomile tea, made from the dried flower heads, which contain a volatile oil. The oil from the similar flowers of the wild chamomile was most often used medicinally, particularly as a tonic; today its chief use is as a hair rinse. Chamomile is classified in the division MAGNOLIOPHYTA, class Magnoliopsida, order Asterales, family Compositae.

Chamonix (shämônē'), town (1968 pop. 8,403), Haute-Savoie dept., E France, at the foot of Mont Blanc. The principal base for climbing Mont Blanc and for visiting the Mer de Glace, it is a popular summer and winter resort. It has the world's highest (12,605 ft/3,842 m) aerial cable car and is linked by tunnel with Courmayeur, Italy.

Chamorro, Emiliano (āmēlyä'nō chämō'rō), 1871–1966, president of Nicaragua (1917–20, 1926). A conservative army chief, Chamorro supported the revolt (1909) against José Santos Zelaya. Originally at odds with the United States, he was a signer of the Bryan-Chamorro Treaty, which granted the United States an option on the NICARAGUA CANAL. He opposed all liberal regimes, including that of Anastasio Somoza.

Chamoun, Camille (kämē'yə shāmōn'), 1900–, Lebanese political leader. First elected to parliament in 1934, Chamoun held a variety of governmental posts before serving as president of Lebanon (1952–58). A Maronite Christian, Chamoun was opposed by Muslim leaders who disliked his pro-Western policies. The Muslim groups openly rebelled against Chamoun's government in 1958, and, in response to Chamoun's request for help, U.S. marines were sent to support the government. After 1958, Chamoun served as leader of Lebanon's Liberal Nationalist party.

Champa, the kingdom of the Chams, which flourished in Vietnam from the 2d cent. A.D. until the

17th cent. It was probably of Indian cultural origin, and at its greatest extent occupied ANNAM as far north as S North Vietnam. In its early period, Champa mainly warred with China and was forced to change its capital several times; late in the 9th cent. its capital was established in the neighborhood of Hué, and the later capital was Vijaya, farther south. Champa repeatedly made war on its stronger neighbor, Annam; it was sometimes allied and sometimes opposed to the KHMER EMPIRE. In the 12th cent. the Chams invaded Cambodia and sacked Angkor; subsequently they fell for a time under Khmer rule. Decisively defeated by the Annamese in 1472, the Chams were forced to yield most of their territory N of Tourane (Da Nang). In the 17th cent. the rest of the Cham kingdom fell to the Annamese, and the remnants of the people were scattered. Chams still form small, impoverished minorities in South Vietnam, but in Cambodia a large colony prospers. Although most of those in Annam worship Hindu gods, those of Cambodia are Muslim. Ruins of Cham temples, adorned with bas-reliefs and with statues, are found in S Annam. See Georges Maspéro, *The Kingdom of Champa* (tr., 1949).

Champagne, Philippe de: see CHAMPAIGNE.

Champagne (shäNpä'nyə), region and former province, NE France, consisting mainly of Aube, Marne, Haute-Marne, and Ardennes depts. The region is almost, but not fully, coextensive with the former provinces of Champagne and Brie. Abutting in the west on the Paris basin, Champagne is a generally arid, chalky plateau, cut by the Aisne, Marne, Seine, Aube, and Yonne rivers. Agriculture, except in the Ardennes dept., is mostly confined to the valleys. Crests divide the plateau from northwest to southeast into several areas. In the east, bordering on Lorraine, is the so-called Champagne Humide [wet Champagne], largely agricultural, and the Langres Plateau. In the center is the Champagne Pouilleuse [Champagne badlands], a bleak and eroded plain, traditionally used for sheep grazing; however, Troyes and Châlons-sur-Marne, its principal towns, are located in fertile valleys and are centers of the wool industry. A narrow strip along the westernmost crest of Champagne is extremely fertile, and the small area around Rheims and Epernay furnishes virtually all of the champagne wine exported by France. Other fertile districts are around Rethel and Sens. Champagne's central and open location made it a major European battlefield from the invasion by Attila's Huns, whom Actius defeated at Châlons in 451, to World War I, which left vast areas scorched. Yet the same geographic position gave the towns of Champagne a commercial prosperity in direct contrast to the bleakness of the countryside. In the Middle Ages, Champagne was famous for its great fairs, held at Troyes (the capital), Provins, Lagny-sur-Marne, and Bar-sur-Aube. Merchants from all over western Europe met six times each year. Their laws regulating trade had a profound influence on later commercial customs; the troy weight for precious metals is still used. Prosperity was accompanied by cultural brilliance, culminating in the work of Chrétien de Troyes and in the Gothic cathedral at Rheims. The county of Champagne had passed to the counts of Blois in the 11th cent.; the main branch held Champagne after 1152. The domain was greatly extended; large parts of France, including Blois, Touraine, and Chartres, were dependent upon the Champagne counts. Most famous of the counts was Thibaut IV, who in 1234 inherited the crown of Navarre from his uncle Sancho VII. In 1286 the daughter and heir of Henry III, Count of Champagne and King of Navarre, married Philip IV of France. When their son ascended the French throne (as Louis X) in 1314, Champagne was incorporated into the royal domain. The bishoprics of Rheims and Langres were added later. Champagne declined in prosperity thereafter; however, the enduring popularity of its sparkling wine, which was developed at the end of the 17th cent., somewhat revitalized its economy. More recently, efforts have been made to reforest the area and reclaim it from erosion.

champagne (shămpān'), sparkling white wine made from grapes grown in the old French province of Champagne. The best champagne is from that part of the Marne valley whose apex is Rheims, the center of the industry. Champagne was reputedly developed by a monk, Dom Pérignon, in the 17th cent. It is a mixture of black Pinot Noir and white Chardonnay grapes and is named for the vintners and shippers responsible for each blend. The small, slightly acid grapes are laboriously cultivated. After the first fermentation the wine is blended; it undergoes a secondary fermentation, then is drawn off into bottles reinforced to withstand high internal pressure, and is sweetened to induce further fermentation. The carbonic acid retained in the bottle after the final fermentation renders champagne sparkling. The wine is matured in the labyrinthine tunnels of the old chalk quarries of Rheims. The sediment formed is collected on the cork by tilting the bottle neck downward and frequently rotating it by hand. After fermentation comes the *dégorgement* process, whereby the neck of the bottle is frozen and the cork is removed; the lump of frozen sediment shoots out, propelled by the pressure in the bottle. The space left is filled with the proper dosage of cane sugar dissolved in wine and usually fortified with cognac. *Brut* champagne is theoretically not sweetened; extra dry champagne, very lightly. An American sparkling wine called champagne is made in New York and California.

Champaign (shămpān'), city (1970 pop. 56,532), Champaign co., E central Ill.; inc. 1860. It adjoins the city of Urbana and is a commercial and industrial center in a fertile farm area. Its manufactures include metal products, academic apparel, and electrical equipment. The Univ. of Illinois at Urbana-Champaign and Parkland College are there. Champaign, founded in 1855 with the arrival of the Illinois Central RR, was first called West Urbana.

Champaigne or **Champagne, Philippe de** (both: fēlēp' də shäNpä'nyə), 1602–74, French painter, b. Brussels, of Flemish parents. In 1621 he went to Paris, where he worked with Poussin on the Luxembourg Palace. In 1628 he became painter to the queen, Marie de' Medici. For her and for Richelieu he executed many religious paintings, still to be seen in French churches, and numerous portraits. From 1640 on he became absorbed in the Jansenist movement and has been called the painter of Port-Royal. His later work is characterized by sober realism, simplicity, and austerity. His best-known paintings include his frescoes at Vincennes and in the Tuileries, his portrait of his daughter, a nun at Port-Royal (1662), and a penetrating study of Richelieu (both: Louvre). Basing his portrait style on patterns established by Rubens and Van Dyck, he rendered his subjects with an air of static majesty.

Champ-de-Mars (shäN-də-märs), former parade ground of Paris, France, between the École militaire and the Seine River. There, at the Fête de la Fédération (July 14, 1790), Louis XVI took an oath to uphold the new constitution. On its vast grounds several expositions were held, notably that of 1889, when the Eiffel Tower was erected there.

Champeaux, William of: see WILLIAM OF CHAMPEAUX.

Champfleury: see HUSSON, JULES.

Championnet, Jean Étienne (zhäN ātyĕn' shäNpyônĕ'), 1762–1800, French general in the FRENCH REVOLUTIONARY WARS. Placed in command of the Army of Rome in 1798, he captured (1799) Naples from the Second Coalition and set up the PARTHENOPEAN REPUBLIC. However, he got into trouble with the Directory by denouncing the malpractices of one of its agents in Naples; moreover, his harsh rule caused popular discontent, and he was recalled in disgrace. Later acquitted, he commanded the Army of the Alps, but was unable to win success with this badly organized unit and resigned. He died shortly after.

Champlain, Samuel de (shămplān', Fr. sämüĕl' də shäNplăN'), 1567–1635, French explorer, the chief founder of New France. After serving in France under Henry of Navarre (King Henry IV) in the religious wars of the period, he was given command of a Spanish fleet sailing to the West Indies, Mexico, and the Isthmus of Panama. He described this three-year tour to the French king in *Bref Discours* (1859). In 1603 he made his first voyage to New France as a member of a fur-trading expedition. He explored the St. Lawrence River as far as the rapids at Lachine and, after his return to France, described his voyage in *Des Sauvages* (1603). With the sieur de Monts, who had a monopoly of the trade of the region, Champlain returned in 1604 to found a colony, which was landed at the mouth of the St. Croix River. In 1605 the colony moved across the Bay of Fundy to Port Royal (now Annapolis Royal, N.S.), and in the next three years Champlain explored the New England coast S to Martha's Vineyard, discovering Mt. Desert Island and most of the larger rivers of Maine and making the first detailed charts of the coast. After the sieur de Monts's privileges had been revoked, the colony had to be abandoned, and through the efforts of Champlain a new one was established on the St. Lawrence River. In 1608, in the ship *Le Don de Dieu,* he brought his colonists to the site of Quebec, where they started what was to be the capital of a great colony. In the spring of 1609, accompanying a war party of Huron Indians against the Iroquois, Champlain discovered the lake that bears his name, and near Crown Point, N.Y., the Iroquois were met and routed by French troops. The incident is believed to be largely responsible for the later hatred of the French by the Iroquois. In 1612, Champlain returned to France, where he received a new grant of the fur-trade monopoly. Returning in 1613, he set off on a journey to the Western lakes. He reached only Allumette Island in the Ottawa River that year, but in 1615 he went with Étienne Brulé and a party of Huron Indians to Georgian Bay on Lake Huron, returning southeastward by way of Lake Ontario. Accompanying another Huron war party to an attack on an Onondaga village in present-day New York, Champlain was wounded and forced to spend the winter with the Indians. Thereafter he made no more explorations but devoted all his time to the welfare of the colony, of which he was the virtual governor. He helped to persuade Richelieu to found the Company of One Hundred Associates, which was to take over the interests of the colony. In 1629, Quebec was suddenly captured by the English, and Champlain was carried away to four years of exile in England; there he prepared the third edition of his *Voyages de la Nouvelle France* (1632). When New France was restored to France in 1632, Champlain returned. In 1634 he sent Jean NICOLET into the West, thus extending the French explorations and claims as far as Wisconsin. He died on Christmas Day, 1635, and was buried in Quebec. His works were issued by the Champlain Society (1922–36) with English and French texts. See C. W. Colby, *The Founder of New France* (1915); biographies by N. E. Dionne (1905, repr. 1963), Ralph Flenley (1924), L. H. Sharp (1944), Morris Bishop (1948), and S. E. Morison (1972).

Champlain, Lake, 125 mi (201 km) long and from 0.5 to 14 mi (0.8–23 km) wide, forming part of the N.Y.-Vt. border and extending into Quebec. It is the fourth-largest freshwater lake in the United States (490 sq mi/1,269 sq km). Lake Champlain lies in a broad valley between the Adirondacks and the Green Mts. A link in the Hudson-Saint Lawrence waterway, the lake is connected with the Hudson (at Fort Edward) by the Champlain division of the Barge Canal; the Richelieu River connects the lake with the St. Lawrence. Lake George drains into it through a narrow channel, and many islands dot its surface, including Grand Isle, Isle La Motte, and Valcour Island. The region is noted for its beautiful scenery and has many resorts. Plattsburgh, N.Y., and Burlington, Vt., are the largest cities on the lake's shores. The lake, discovered by Samuel de Champlain in 1609, was the scene of battles in the French and Indian War and the American Revolution at Crown Point and Ticonderoga, of a naval engagement in 1776, and of the important American victory of Thomas MACDONOUGH in the War of 1812.

champlevé (shäNləvā'), technique for the ENAMEL decoration of metal objects. It was used by the Celts and Romans and employed by medieval metalworkers for jewelry and RELIQUARIES until the 14th cent. Champlevé is produced by hollowing out parts of a design in metal and filling in the hollows with enamel. The technique has been revived by 20th-century craftsmen.

Champney, Benjamin (chămp'nē), 1817–1907, American painter, b. New Ipswich, N.H. Champney studied drawing and was apprenticed to a lithographer in Boston. He traveled to Europe in 1846, painting panoramic vistas of the Rhine and scenes of the Revolution of 1848.

Champollion, Jean François (zhäN fräNswä' shäNpôlyôN'), 1790–1832, French Egyptologist. He is considered the founder of the science of Egyptology. His first important accomplishment was his two-volume work on the geography of ancient Egypt, which appeared when he was 24. In 1821 by use of the Rosetta stone (see under ROSETTA) he established the principles for deciphering the Egyptian hieroglyphics. Champollion became director of the Egyptian museum at the Louvre and professor at the Collège de France. He is sometimes called Champollion le Jeune to distinguish him from his elder brother, who gave him his early training. **Jean Jacques Champollion-Figeac** (-fēzhäk'), 1778–1867, was an archaeologist, a professor at Grenoble, and a curator of manuscripts at the Bibliothèque nationale. He also served as a professor of paleography at the École des Chartes and librarian at the Palace of Fontainebleau.

Champs Élysées (shäN zālēzā'), avenue of Paris, France, leading from the Place de la Concorde to the

Arc de Triomphe. It is celebrated for its tree-lined beauty, its commodious breadth, the elegance of its cafés, theaters, and shops, and the fountain display at its center. Begun by Louis XIV and completed by Louis XV, it led through open country until the early 19th cent.

Chanaan (kā'nən), variant of CANAAN **2.**

Chanakkale, Turkey: see ÇANAKKALE.

Ch'an Buddhism: see ZEN BUDDHISM.

Chancay (chăng-kī'), archaeological site in central Peru, center of the ancient Cuismancu empire. Culturally influenced by the CHIMU, the Cuismancu dominated less territory and were not as powerful. Nonetheless they built sizable cities and were somewhat more materially advanced than their southern neighbors, the Chincha (see ICA). The Cuismancu were conquered by the Inca in the 15th cent.

chance, in mathematics: see PROBABILITY.

chancel, primarily that part of the church close to the altar and used by the officiating clergy. In the early churches it was separated from the nave by a low parapet or open railing (*cancellus*), its name being thus derived. San Clemente at Rome has one of the few preserved examples. With the development of the choir, additional space was taken, between the SANCTUARY and the nave, for the accommodation of the canons and singers. The chancel rail was moved forward, and the entire space became known as the choir, although it is also termed the chancel; there is no strict differentiation in the usage. In the Middle Ages the chancel rail was replaced by lofty choir screens (see ROOD), especially in English cathedrals and in monastic churches.

Chancellor, Richard, d. 1556, English navigator. When, largely under the inspiration of Sebastian Cabot, a group of men in England undertook to finance a search for the Northeast Passage to Asia, Chancellor was chosen as second in command under Sir Hugh Willoughby. They sailed in 1553, and Chancellor and Stephen Borough, in the *Edward Bonaventure,* managed to get through dangerous arctic waters to the White Sea. Chancellor then traveled overland across Russia to Moscow at the invitation of Ivan IV. His negotiations prepared the way for trade with Russia and the formation of the MUSCOVY COMPANY. Returning from a second voyage to Russia, he was shipwrecked and perished off the coast of Scotland. Since Willoughby had earlier come to grief, it was Stephen Borough who continued the work of opening the northern route to Russia for the Muscovy Company.

Chancellorsville, battle of, May 2–4, 1863, in the American Civil War. Late in April, 1863, Joseph Hooker, commanding the Union Army of the Potomac, moved against Robert E. Lee, whose Army of Northern Virginia (less than half the size of Hooker's) had remained entrenched on the south side of the Rappahannock River after the battle of FREDERICKSBURG. Hooker, with four corps, crossed the river above Fredericksburg and took up a strong position near Chancellorsville, located 10 mi (16 km) W of Fredericksburg; he sent John Sedgwick, with two corps, to cross below Chancellorsville. Although outflanked, Lee did not retreat but, leaving 10,000 men under Jubal A. Early to watch Sedgwick, moved on Hooker, who fell back to a defensive position in the wilderness around Chancellorsville. Lee attacked on May 2: T. J. (Stonewall) JACKSON led his 2d Corps on a brilliant 15-mi (24-km) flanking movement against the Union right, while Lee, with his small remaining force, feinted along the rest of the line. Jackson fell upon and routed the surprised Union troops but, unfortunately for the South, was mortally wounded by his own men. The next day the Confederate wings united (James Ewell Brown STUART succeeding Jackson) and drove Hooker back further. Hooker failed to use his superior forces, but called for Sedgwick, who drove Early from Marye's Heights (May 3) and reached Salem Church, 5 mi (8 km) W of Fredericksburg. There part of Lee's force joined Early and repulsed Sedgwick (May 4–5). Sedgwick and Hooker then withdrew across the river. Chancellorsville, Lee's last great victory, led to his invasion of the North in the GETTYSBURG CAMPAIGN. See John Bigelow, *The Campaign of Chancellorsville* (1910); E. J. Stackpole, *Chancellorsville: Lee's Greatest Battle* (1958).

chancery: see EQUITY.

Chan Chan (chän chän), ruins of an ancient Indian city near Trujillo, N Peru. The city was probably begun in the period from A.D. 800 to 1000, and it is estimated that it once contained 200,000 people. Chan Chan is generally accepted as the capital of the CHIMU, a pre-Inca civilization. It is on a large plain of the coastal desert, which was made arable by ambitious and extensive irrigation works. Covering c.11 sq mi (28 sq km), the city comprised at least 10 self-contained, walled-in units. The walls, built of adobe brick, are decorated with relief designs.

Chan-chiang or **Chankiang** (both: chän-jēäng), Cantonese *Tsamkong,* official Chinese name for the former French territory of Kwangchowan (325 sq mi/840 sq km) on Kuang-chou Bay, S Kwangtung prov., China. It was leased from China in 1898 for 99 years but was returned in 1945. Its chief city, Fort-Bayard, was renamed **Chan-chiang** (1970 est. pop. 220,000) and since 1955 has been developed as a major seaport, servicing ships up to 10,000 tons, and as a regional trade center. The city has textile, chemical, shipbuilding, and electric power industries, and is linked by rail to Kwangsi prov.

chancre: see SYPHILIS.

chancroid: see VENEREAL DISEASE.

Chanda (chän'də), town, Maharashtra state, central India, on the Irar River. It is a district administrative center. Chanda is near the Wardha valley coal fields. Its chief industries are rice milling and pig-iron casting. The town is surrounded by a wall that acts as a flood barrier. Chanda was the capital of the Gond kingdom from the 12th to the 18th cent. The tombs of the Gond kings and several temples are in the town.

Chandernagor (chŭn"dərnəgôr') or **Chandannagar** (shändĕrnägôr'), town (1971 pop. 75,960), West Bengal state, E India, on the Hooghly River, a suburb of Calcutta. Founded by the French in 1686, it was of great commercial importance until the 19th cent. It was ceded by France and became part of India in 1951.

Chandigarh (chŭn'dēgər), union territory (1971 pop. 256,972), 44 sq mi (114 sq km) and city (1971 pop. 218,807), NW India. The city is the capital of both Haryana and Punjab states. It was designed by the architect Le Corbusier and built largely in the 1950s on a site chosen for its healthy climate and plentiful water supply. The city was constructed because the capital of Punjab in British India, Lahore, was given to Pakistan when India was partitioned in 1947. Punjab Univ. is in Chandigarh. The union territory is administered by the central government of India.

Chandler, Albert Benjamin, 1898–, U.S. baseball commissioner (1945–51) and politician, b. Corydon, Henderson co., Ky. "Happy" Chandler was a lawyer in Versailles, Ky., when he went into politics. He served as lieutenant governor (1931–35), governor (1935–39), and U.S. Senator (1939–45), before becoming baseball commissioner. He retired after major league club owners refused to renew his contract. From 1955 to 1959, Chandler was again governor of Kentucky.

Chandler, Raymond Thornton, 1888–1959, American detective-story writer, b. Chicago, educated in England. After serving with the Canadian forces in World War I, he entered the oil business in California. Bankrupt during the depression, he began writing and published his first detective story, *The Big Sleep,* in 1939. Subsequent novels include *Farewell My Lovely* (1940), *The High Window* (1942), *The Lady in the Lake* (1943), *The Little Sister* (1949), *The Long Goodbye* (1953), and *Playback* (1958). Well plotted and brutally realistic, Chandler's novels convincingly depict California's seedy lowlife. They all feature Philip Marlowe, a tough yet honorable private detective with a brash sense of humor.

Chandler, Zachariah, 1813–79, U.S. Senator from Michigan (1857–75, 1879) and Secretary of the Interior (1875–77), b. Bedford, N.H. He moved to Detroit in 1833 and through merchandising, land speculation, and banking became a millionaire. Mayor of Detroit (1851–52), he helped organize and was long the boss of the Republican party in Michigan. Old Zack, as he was called, was an able and uncompromising abolitionist. A leading radical Republican, most closely associated with Benjamin F. WADE, he was a member of the congressional committee on the conduct of the war, and he violently opposed Lincoln's Reconstruction program. Chandler remained a powerful figure in the Senate until he was turned out by the Democratic landslide of 1874. He then entered the cabinet of President Grant and was also chairman of the Republican National Committee in the disputed election of 1876. See biographies by W. C. Harris (1917) and M. K. George (1969); T. H. Williams, *Lincoln and the Radicals* (1941).

Chandler, city (1970 pop. 13,763), Maricopa co., S central Ariz., in the Salt River valley; inc. 1920. It is a residential community in an area that produces cotton, alfalfa, and citrus fruit. Sugar is processed, and computer components, mobile homes, and containers are produced in Chandler. Williams Air Force Base is nearby and contributes to the city's economy, as do tourists, who are especially attracted by the San Marcos Golf Resort. Many of Chandler's citizens work in nearby Phoenix.

Chandos, Sir John, d. 1370, English soldier and administrator of English territories in France. A friend of Edward the Black Prince, he won distinction in the Hundred Years War by his bravery at Poitiers (1356) and by his capture (1364) of Bertrand DU GUESCLIN at Auray. He was made constable of Guienne in 1362 and senechal of Poitiers in 1365. In the Spanish campaign of the Black Prince he again defeated and captured (1367) Du Guesclin at Nájera. He was mortally wounded in a battle with Gascon nobles at Lussac, near Poitiers.

Chandragupta (Chandragupta Maurya)(chăndrəgoo͝p'tə), fl. c.321 B.C.–c.298 B.C., Indian emperor, founder of the MAURYA dynasty and grandfather of Asoka. The Greek form of his name is Sandracottus or Sandrocottus. It is possible that he expelled the last of the garrisons Alexander the Great had established in NW India. He conquered the Magadha kingdom (in modern Bihar) and eventually controlled all India N of the Vindhya Hills. In c.305, Chandragupta, with a huge army, defeated SELEUCUS I (Nicator) who had invaded NW India in an attempt to regain Alexander's Indian provinces. Seleucus had to yield parts of Afghanistan to Chandragupta, and some sort of marriage alliance followed. From Megasthenes, a Seleucid envoy at the court of Chandragupta, comes much of the information about the period. The emperor dwelt in an enormous, ornate palace at Pataliputra (Patna) and administered a highly bureaucratic government, which controlled the entire economic life of N India. He was advised by Kautilya (also called Chanakya), a very able but unscrupulous Brahman, who is known as the author of the *Arthasastra,* a Machiavellian political tract. Chandragupta established a vast secret service system and, fearing assassination, rarely left his palace. Jain tradition says that he abdicated his throne, became a Jain monk, and fasted to death.

Chandragupta I and **II,** two Indian emperors. See GUPTA.

Chanel, Gabrielle (Coco): see under FASHION.

Chaney, Lon (chā'nē), 1883–1930, American film actor, b. Colorado Springs, Colo. Chaney was the son of deaf-mute parents. He made more than 150 silent films. A master of the use of grotesque, distorting makeup, he is best remembered for his work in horror films such as *The Phantom of the Opera* (1925). His son, Lon Chaney, Jr. (1907–), made many horror films and westerns.

Changarnier, Nicolas (nēkôlä' shäNgärnyä'), 1793–1877, French general and politician. He served in Algeria and was briefly (1848) governor general of Algeria, succeeding Louis Cavaignac. Elected to the constituent assembly in 1848 after the FEBRUARY REVOLUTION, he resigned after the rising of the June Days to head the Paris national guard. Later the regular army troops in Paris were added to his command. A monarchist and Orleanist, Changarnier came to oppose the policies of Louis Napoleon and was exiled after the coup d'etat of 1851. He returned in 1859 and took part in the defense of Metz (1870) in the Franco-Prussian War. Again elected a deputy in 1871, he opposed a republic. He was made a life senator in 1875.

Chang-chia-k'ou or **Changkiakow** (both: chäng-jēä-kou), Mongolian *Kalgan,* city (1970 est. pop. 1,000,000), NW Hopeh prov., China, near a gateway of the Great Wall and on the Peking-USSR RR. A major trade center for N China and Mongolia, it has food-processing plants, machine shops, and tanneries. The meeting place of caravans traveling from Peking to Ulan Bator, it was an important military center under the Manchu dynasty but declined somewhat after the opening (1905) of the Trans-Siberian RR. In 1928 it became the capital of Chahar prov., which was abolished in 1952.

Chang Chih-tung (jäng jûr-doo͝ng), 1837–1909, Chinese Ch'ing dynasty statesman and educational reformer. He occupied the high post of governor-general for over two decades, first of Kwangtung and Kwangsi provs. (1884–89), and later of Hunan and Hupei provs. (1889–1907). In that position he vigorously pressed the late Ch'ing self-strengthening program, establishing an arsenal, iron- and steelworks, military and naval academies, and schools of mining, agriculture, commerce, and industry. Chang encouraged the early reform movement between 1895 and 1898 (see K'ANG YU-WEI), advocating a balance between study of the Chinese heritage and adoption of Western scientific and technical knowledge. In the end, however, he supported the coup of Empress Dowager T'ZU HSI against the Hundred Days' Reform (1898), convinced that K'ang was surrendering too much to Western culture. After the disastrous Boxer Uprising he urged radical educational change including a public school system from kindergarten to university and abolition of the traditional civil service CHINESE EXAMINATION SYSTEM. He was appointed (1907) head of the new ministry of education. See W. Ayers, *Chang Chih-tung and Educational Reform in China* (1971).

Ch'ang-chou or **Changchow** (both: jäng-jō), city, S Kiangsu prov., E central China, on the Grand Canal. It is a food and textile center. Other manufactures include fertilizer, machine tools, and motor vehicles. Ch'ang-chou became industrialized in the late 19th cent. It was called Wutsin prior to 1949.

Changchow: see CH'ANG-CHOU, China.

Ch'ang-ch'un or **Changchun** (both: chäng'-cho͞on), city (1970 est. pop. 1,500,000), capital of Kirin prov., China, on the railroad between Harbin and Lü-ta. An industrial city, it is the country's major center of motor vehicle production, with enormous truck and tractor works. Railroad cars, tires, pharmaceuticals, and textiles are also manufactured. An aluminum plant is west of the city. Ch'ang-ch'un is the "Hollywood" of China, with government-owned motion picture studios that produce propaganda films. As Hsinking [Chin.,=new capital], it was the capital of the former state of Manchukuo (1932-45). During this period the city was rebuilt along modern lines. Many of the large administrative buildings have been converted into universities; these include Kirin Univ., a polytechnical university, a medical college, and several technical institutes.

changeling, in popular superstition, a fairy child substituted for a human baby. It was believed that evil fairies stole healthy unbaptized infants and left in their place a fairy child. Hence, sickly and peevish babies were sometimes called changelings.

change ringing: see BELL.

Chang Hsueh-liang (chäng' shüĕ'-lyäng'), 1898-, Chinese war lord, son of CHANG TSO-LIN. On the death (1928) of his father, he succeeded as military governor of Manchuria. He was then known as Chang Hsiao-liang but later changed his name. He supported Chiang Kai-shek against a rebellious northern army in 1929-30 and was made vice commander in chief of all Chinese forces and a member of the central political council. Ousted (1931) by the Japanese from Manchuria, he suffered loss of prestige. In 1936, with the help of Chinese Communists, he had Chiang kidnapped at Sian, allegedly to compel cooperation between the Kuomintang and the Communists and to force a declaration of war against Japan. Chiang Kai-shek was released unconditionally a few weeks later. Chang, tried and sentenced for his part in the affair, was pardoned but kept in custody. He was taken to Taiwan when the Nationalist regime fled there in 1949.

Ch'ang-hua or **Changhwa** (both: chäng-hwä), city (1969 pop. 133,514), central Taiwan. It is a transportation center as well as a market for rice, oranges, and pineapples. The city's industries produce wood and paper products, textiles, canned food, refined sugar, and machinery. Settled in the 17th cent., Ch'ang-hua was once an important fort.

Changkiakow: see CHANG-CHIA-K'OU, China.

Ch'ang-pai (chäng'bī'), or **Changpai** mountain range, largely in NE China and partly in North Korea; Paitou Shan (9,003 ft/2,744 m) is the highest peak. The Ch'ang-pai range is economically important for timber and coal deposits. The Yalu, Tumen, and Sungari rivers rise there.

Ch'ang-sha or **Changsha** (both: chäng-shä), city (1970 est. pop. 850,000), capital of Hunan prov., S China, on the Hsiang River. The name, which means "long sandbank," is derived from an island in the river. Ch'ang-sha is an agricultural distribution and market center, an important stop on the Peking-Canton RR, and a river port. Rice is processed, meats are canned, and paper products, fertilizer, trucks, ceramics, and a wide variety of handicrafts are made. The city was founded in the early 3d cent. B.C. and has long been noted as a literary and educational center. As Tanchow it was the capital of the Chu kingdom (10th cent.). It became a treaty port in the early 1900s. Mao Tse-tung was educated in Ch'ang-sha, and in 1927 he led a Communist uprising there. The city is the birthplace of many notable Chinese literary figures and statesmen, including Chia Yi, a Han dynasty essayist, and Tseng Kuo-fan, a 19th-century diplomat and general. Ch'ang-sha is the seat of several institutions of higher learning, notably Hunan Univ. and a medical college. An important Chinese air force base is there.

Ch'ang-te or **Changteh** (both: chäng-dŭ), city (1970 est. pop. 225,000), N Hunan prov., China, on the Yüan River. Formerly a treaty port, it is now a storage and shipping point for tung oil, medicinal herbs, and wood. Manufactures include ceramics, machine tools, textiles, leather, and processed foods. The city was founded during the Han dynasty.

Chang Tso-lin (jäng dzō-lĭn), 1873-1928, Chinese general. Chang was of humble birth. As the leader of a unit of Manchurian militia he assisted (1904-5) the Japanese in the Russo-Japanese War. He held various military posts under the Chinese republic. From his appointment (1918) as inspector general of Manchuria until his death he controlled Manchuria, and from 1920 he constantly warred to extend his rule southward, joining in a three-way struggle with WU P'EI-FU and FENG YÜ-HSIANG for control of the Peking government. His Fengtien army occupied the Peking-Tientsin area (1926) until driven out by the NORTHERN EXPEDITION of CHIANG KAI-SHEK (1928). Chang died when the train in which he was retreating to Mukden before the Kuomintang army was bombed (for reasons still unclear) by officers of the Japanese army in Manchuria. His son, CHANG HSÜEH-LIANG, succeeded to control of Manchuria.

Chankiang: see CHAN-CHIANG, China.

channeling: see QUARRYING.

Channel Islands, archipelago (1971 pop. 125,243), 75 sq mi (194 sq km), 10 mi (16 km) off the coast of Normandy, France, in the English Channel. The main islands are JERSEY, GUERNSEY, ALDERNEY, and SARK, and there are several smaller islands, including Herm, Jethou, and Lithou; all the islands are dependencies of the British crown. The mild and sunny climate (35-40 in./89-102 cm rainfall a year) and the fertile soil have made the islands chiefly agricultural. Large quantities of vegetables, fruits, and flowers are shipped to English markets. Dairying is the chief occupation of the islanders. The famous Jersey and Guernsey breeds of cattle are kept pure by local laws. The islands are a favorite resort of tourists and vacationers. The chief ports are ST. HELIER (Jersey) and ST. PETER PORT (Guernsey). The islands are divided into two administrative bailiwicks, one of which, Jersey, has more than half the total population. The other, Guernsey, includes all the islands except Jersey. Each bailiwick has its own lieutenant governor appointed by the crown, its own chief magistrate and legislature, and its own judicature. The inhabitants are mostly of Norman descent, but on Alderney the stock is mainly English. The English language is spoken everywhere, although French is the official language of Jersey. A Norman patois and Norman customs are still maintained by the natives. Christianization took place in the 6th cent., largely through the efforts of St. Helier and St. Sampson. In the 10th cent. the isles became possessions of the duke of Normandy. At the Norman conquest they were joined to the English crown; they remained under the control of King John and England in 1204 when Philip II of France confiscated the duchy of Normandy. The French attempted unsuccessfully to reestablish control in the 14th cent. and later. In World War II, after the evacuation of some 10,000 military and civilian personnel, the islands were occupied (1940) by German forces. See study by John Uttley (1966).

Channel Islands National Monument: see NATIONAL PARKS AND MONUMENTS (table); SANTA BARBARA ISLANDS.

Channing, Edward, 1856-1931, American historian, b. Dorchester, Mass.; son of William Ellery Channing (1818-1901). He was a prominent teacher at Harvard from 1883 until his retirement in 1929, holding a professor's rank from 1897. Channing wrote *English History for American Readers* (with Thomas W. Higginson, 1893); *The United States of America, 1765-1865* (1896, 2d ed. 1930, repr. 1941); *Guide to the Study and Reading of American History* (with Albert B. Hart, 1896; rev. and augmented ed. by Channing, Hart, and Frederick J. Turner, 1912), an excellent brief bibliography of American history; *Students' History of the United States* (1898, 5th ed., rev. 1924); and *The Jeffersonian System, 1801-1811* ("American Nation" series, 1906, repr. 1968). Most of these books were, however, either incidental to, or preparation for, the great work to which Channing devoted most of his life—*A History of the United States* (6 vol., 1905-25), embracing the years from 1000 to 1865. Based throughout on the author's extensive knowledge of the sources, remarkably accurate in fact, and excellently written, it is generally considered one of the finest histories of the United States ever produced by one man. The final volume on the Civil War won a Pulitzer Prize in 1926.

Channing, William Ellery, 1780-1842, American Unitarian minister and author, b. Newport, R.I. At 23 he was ordained minister of the Federal St. Congregational Church in Boston, where he served until his death. He was a leader among those who were turning from Calvinism, and his sermon at Jared Sparks's ordination in Baltimore (1819) earned him the name "the apostle of Unitarianism." In 1820 he organized the Berry St. Conference of Ministers, which in 1825 formed the American Unitarian Association. Channing's plea was for humanitarianism and tolerance in religion rather than for a new creed. Not only a great preacher but a lucid writer, Channing influenced many American authors, including Emerson and other transcendentalists and Holmes and Bryant. Channing was not by nature a controversialist and never allied himself with the abolitionists, but his writings on slavery helped prepare for emancipation. In his denunciations of war, his discussion of labor problems, and his views on education, he was ahead of his time. His works (6 vol., 1841-43) passed through many editions. See his *Life . . . with Extracts from His Correspondence* (ed. by W. H. Channing, 3 vol., 1848); biographies by J. W. Chadwick (1903), M. H. Rice (1961), and Jack Mendelsohn (1971); R. L. Patterson, *The Philosophy of William Ellery Channing* (1952, repr. 1972).

chansons de geste (shäNsôN' də zhĕst) [Fr.,=songs of deeds], a group of epic poems of medieval France written from the 11th through the 13th cent. Varying in length from 1,000 to 20,000 lines, assonanced or (in the 13th cent.) rhymed, the poems were composed by trouvères and were grouped in cycles about some great central figure such as Charlemagne. The origin of the form is disputed, but probably the first chansons were composed after the year 1000 by the joint efforts of wandering clerks and jongleurs (itinerant minstrels) to attract pilgrims to shrines where heroes of the chansons were supposedly buried. Sung by jongleurs to the accompaniment of a primitive viol, they spread to England, Germany, Italy, and Iceland. The earlier chansons—epic, aristocratic, and militantly Christian—passed as real history to their medieval listeners, though much of the material was legendary. Some later chansons utilize fantastic adventure or reflect bourgeois elements. The oldest extant chanson, and also the best and most famous, is the *Chanson de Roland,* composed c.1098-1100 (see ROLAND); others are *Raoul de Cambrai, Huon de Bordeaux, Aliscans,* and *Renaud de Montauban.* See W. C. Calin, *The Epic Quest: Studies in Four Old French Chansons de Geste* (1966) and Jessie Crosland, *The Old French Epic* (1971).

chant, general name for one-voiced, unaccompanied, liturgical music. Usually it refers to the liturgical melodies of the Orthodox, Roman Catholic, and Anglican branches of Christianity. Roman Catholic chant, commonly called Gregorian or PLAINSONG, is diatonic, modally organized (see MODE), and has a free rhythm determined by the text. Anglican chant is a harmonized, metrical adaptation to English texts of the Gregorian method of psalm singing, in which a short melody is adjusted to the length of different psalm verses by repeating one tone, the recitation tone, for any number of words in the text. The texts of Anglican chant, used in many Protestant churches, are from the BOOK OF COMMON PRAYER.

Chantaburi: see CHANTHABURI, Thailand.

chanter: see BAGPIPE.

chantey or **shanty** (both: shăn'tē), work song with marked rhythm, particularly one sung by a group of sailors while hoisting sail or anchor or pushing the capstan. Often it has solo stanzas sung by a leader, the chanteyman, with a chorus repeated after each by the entire group. Similar songs are sung by shore gangs and lumbermen, and all are related to the work chanting of group labor throughout the world, such as the barcaroles of Italian boatmen, the songs of West Indian shoremen, or the Oriental rope chants. Many universally known chanteys, such as *Way, Haul Away* and *Wide Missouri,* are of American origin. See Robert Frothingham, ed., *Songs of the Sea and Sailor's Chanteys* (1924); Frank Shay, ed., *American Sea Songs and Chanteys* (1948); Stan Hugill, ed., *Shanties from the Seven Seas* (1961).

Chanthaburi (chäntä"bo͞orē'), town (1960 pop. 10,795), capital of Chanthaburi prov., SE Thailand, near the Gulf of Siam. It is an agricultural trade center in an area growing rice, pepper, and coffee. Precious gems (principally rubies and sapphires) are mined nearby. Originally part of the Khmer Empire, the town passed to Thailand in 1576. It was occupied by French forces from 1893 to 1905.

Chantrey, Sir Francis Legatt, 1781–1841, English sculptor, famous for his portrait busts and statues. Among his many well-known works are equestrian statues of Wellington and George IV (London); and a statue of George Washington (Statehouse, Boston).

Chanukah: see HANUKKAH.

Chanute, city (1970 pop. 10,341), Neosho co., SE Kansas, on the Neosho River; inc. 1873 following the consolidation of four contiguous towns. It is a processing and trade center for a rich agricultural region, with a great variety of manufactures. A junior college is there. Nearby is the site of a mission (1824–29), the first in Kansas.

Chany (chənē'), saltwater lake, 1,280 sq mi (3,315 sq km), S Siberian USSR, in the Baraba Steppe. The Chulym River flows into the lake.

Chanzy, Antoine Eugène Alfred (äNtwän' özhĕn' älfrĕd' shäNzē'), 1823–83, French general. After service in Algeria, Italy, and Syria, he was refused a major command in the FRANCO-PRUSSIAN WAR because he was distrusted by the emperor Napoleon III. After the fall of the empire he was put in command of the Army of the Loire and opposed the Prussians with great skill. Chanzy was elected to the national assembly. Captured by the Commune of Paris in 1871, he was detained for several days. Chanzy was later governor general of Algeria (1873–79) and ambassador to Russia (1879–81), and in 1875 he was made senator for life. Nominated for president without his approval in 1879, he received a large vote in the election.

Ch'ao-an or **Chaoan** (both: chou-än), city, E Kwangtung prov., China, on the Han River. It is also called Chaochow (Ch'ao-chou). It is a trade center with textile, machinery, porcelain, and sugar-refining industries.

Chaochow: see CH'AO-AN, China.

Chao K'uang-yin (jou kwäng-yĭn), Chinese emperor (960–79), founder of the SUNG dynasty. A leading general during the short-lived Later Chou dynasty (951–60), he usurped the throne, and by the time of his death he had reunited most of China proper. Chao's reign followed the FIVE DYNASTIES period (907–60), an era of frequent political change. His greatest accomplishment, and the reason for the longevity of the Sung, was his replacement of the system of autonomous local military commanders with large professional armies under the control of the central government.

Chao Phraya (chou präyä'), **Mae Nam Chao Phraya,** or **Menam Chao Phraya** (both: mä-näm'-), chief river of Thailand, c.140 mi (230 km) long, formed by the confluence of the Ping (c.300 mi/480 km long) and the Nan (c.500 mi/800 km) rivers at Nakhon Sawan, W central Thailand. It flows S past Bangkok to the Gulf of Siam and is navigable for its entire length. With its tributaries, the Chao Phraya drains most of W Thailand; its valley is the country's main rice-producing region. The many distributaries of the Chao Phraya delta are interconnected by canals that serve both for irrigation and for transportation.

Chaos (kā'ŏs), in Greek mythology, vacant, unfathomable space. From it arose all things, earthly and divine. There are various legends explaining it. In the Pelasgian creation myth, EURYNOME rose out of Chaos and created all things. In the Olympian myth, Gaea sprang from Chaos and was the mother of all things. Eventually the word chaos came to mean a great confusion of matter out of which a supreme being created all life.

Chapais, Sir Thomas (shäpā'), 1858–1946, Canadian politician and historian, b. Quebec prov.; son of Jean Charles Chapais (1811–85). Thomas Chapais became professor of history at Laval Univ. He was appointed to the legislative council of Quebec in 1892, became speaker in 1895, and president of the executive council in 1896. In 1919 he was appointed to the Canadian Senate, and in 1930 he represented Canada in the Assembly of the League of Nations. He served as a cabinet minister in 1897 and from 1936 to 1939. A noted French Canadian historian, his most important works were his biographies *Jean Talon* (1904), *The Great Intendant* (1914), and *Montcalm* (1911), and his *Cours d'histoire du Canada* (8 vol., 1919–34). He was knighted in 1935.

Chapala (chäpä'lä), lake, c.50 mi (80 km) long and 8 mi (12.8 km) wide, W Mexico, in Jalisco and Michoacán states. It is the largest lake in Mexico. Set in a depression on the central plateau, Lake Chapala is fed by the Lerma River, which flows into it from the east, and is drained by the Río Grande de Santiago, which flows out by the northeastern corner. It is a popular scenic resort. Fishing is an important native occupation. Since the early 1950s the waters have been receding at an alarming rate and the lake is rapidly becoming choked with water hyacinths; studies have been initiated to determine an effective conservation program. Towns along the shore range from Indian villages to American retirement colonies.

chaparral (chăpərăl'), type of plant community in which shrubs are dominant. It occurs usually in regions having from 10 to 20 in. (25–50 cm) of rainfall annually, which are thus more dry than forest regions and less dry than deserts. Where the rate of evaporation is high, chaparral may be found where the rainfall is well above 20 in. Generally chaparral country has most of its rainfall in the winter. The vegetation includes both evergreen and deciduous forms, the dominant species varying in different areas. Chaparral is well exemplified in parts of the W and SW United States, although similar growth is found in many parts of the world. Climax areas (see ECOLOGY) are well represented by the largely deciduous growths in Colorado, E Utah, and N New Mexico. A subclimax area extends from South Dakota to Texas and through part of the Great Basin. Among the chief species of plants in these regions are Gambel oak (*Quercus utahensis*), mountain mahogany (*Cercocarpus parvifolius*), squawbush (*Rhus trilobata*), western chokeberry (*Prunus demissa*), western serviceberry (*Amelanchier alnifolia*), and mesquite (*Prosopis glandulosa*). Evergreen shrubs are characteristic of the chaparral found in the southern half of California, especially near the coast, and extending into Nevada and Arizona. Among the dominant forms are several species of buckthorn (*Ceanothus*), manzanita (*Arctostaphylos tomentosa* and *A. pungens*), and the holly-leaved cherry (*Prunus ilicifolia*). A species of scrub oak (*Quercus dumosa*) is the chief deciduous form. Chaparral growth is sometimes so dense that it is almost impenetrable.

chapbook, one of the pamphlets formerly sold in Europe and America by itinerant agents, or "chapmen." Chapbooks were inexpensive—in England often costing only a penny—and, like the broadside, they were usually anonymous and undated. The texts were similar to those of current tabloid newspapers and therefore reveal much about the popular taste of the 16th, 17th, and 18th cent. The term is occasionally used to refer to old manuscripts showing national character through the use of vernacular expressions.

Chapei: see SHANGHAI, China.

chapel, subsidiary place of worship. It is either an alcove or chamber within a church, a separate building, or a room set apart for the purpose of worship in a secular building. A movable shrine containing the *cappa*, or cloak, of ST. MARTIN was first called a *cappella;* hence a sanctuary that is not called a church. Though the churches of the early Middle Ages possessed only the single altar of the apse, chapels became necessary with the increase of relics and of devotions at altars sacred to numerous saints. At first they appeared as minor apses, flanking the main apse. After the 10th cent., in order to accommodate the increasing number of pilgrims, a complex series of radiating chapels was developed behind the high altar. In the 13th cent. chapels were added to the side-aisle bays of choir and nave. In England the strongly projecting transepts provided the favored space for a relatively small number of chapels. In France the Lady Chapel (dedicated to the Virgin) is the central chapel of the *chevet* and is sometimes larger than the others, while in England it occurs directly behind the high altar. Peculiar to English cathedrals are the small chantry chapels, mostly of the 14th and 15th cent., either built and endowed by individuals for their private Masses or serving to enclose the tombs of bishops and other churchmen. From the early Middle Ages, members of royalty had the right to an independent private chapel. Such are the separate building of the Sainte-Chapelle, Paris; St. George's Chapel at Windsor; and Henry VII's magnificent chapel at Westminster, London. In addition, there were royal mortuary chapels, the most celebrated being that of Charlemagne (796–804), at Aachen, since converted into a cathedral. Numerous lords of medieval castles and manor houses established private chapels, over which episcopal jurisdiction was enforced as completely as possible. The two main chapels at the Vatican are the Pauline Chapel (1540), designed by Antonioda SANGALLO for Paul III, and the Sistine Chapel (1473), built by Sixtus IV and celebrated for its great fresco decorations by MICHELANGELO and other masters. Two of the most famous French modern chapels (built in the 1950s) are the chapel at Vence designed by Matisse and the one at Ronchamp by Le Corbusier; both are freestanding buildings.

Chapelain, Jean (zhäN shäplăN'), 1595–1674, French critic and poet. His works include *Pucelle* (1656), an epic poem about Joan of Arc. Chapelain was a founding member of the French Academy, for which he composed a celebrated attack upon Pierre Corneille's *Le Cid.*

Chapel Hill, town (1970 pop. 25,537), Orange co., central N.C., at the edge of the Piedmont; founded 1792, inc. 1851. It is the seat of the Univ. of North Carolina, which is the mainstay of the town's economy.

Chapin, Schuyler G., 1923–, American operatic manager, b. New York City. He studied music with Nadia Boulanger. In 1953 he joined Columbia Artists as tour manager; he also served with Columbia Records as director of artists and repertoire. From 1964 until 1969 he was vice president in charge of programming of Lincoln Center for the Performing Arts. Upon the death (1972) of Goeran Gentele (whose assistant he had been), Chapin succeeded him, first as acting general manager and then as general manager of the Metropolitan Opera.

Chaplin, Charlie (Sir Charles Spencer Chaplin), 1889–, English film actor, director, producer, writer, and composer, b. London. After appearing in London music halls, in 1910 Chaplin joined a pantomime troupe. While touring the United States, he was noticed by Mack SENNETT. For the Keystone Company (1914–15) he created the famous wistful tramp characterized by derby, moustache, baggy trousers, and awkward walk. In 1918 Chaplin became an independent producer, releasing his films through United Artists, which he founded in 1919 with D. W. GRIFFITH, Douglas FAIRBANKS, and Mary PICKFORD. Chaplin often composed his films' background music. His major films include *The Kid* (1920), *The Gold Rush* (1924), *The Circus* (1928), *City Lights* (1931), *Modern Times* (1936), *The Great Dictator* (1940; his first speaking part), *Monsieur Verdoux* (1947), and *Limelight* (1952). In 1966 he directed *A Countess from Hong Kong.* After much American press and government criticism of his politics and personal behavior, Chaplin settled in Switzerland in 1952. In 1975 he was knighted by Queen Elizabeth II. He is married to Oona O'Neill, daughter of Eugene O'Neill. See his *My Trip Abroad* (1922) and autobiography (1964); biographies by Charles Chaplin, Jr. (1960) and Parker Tyler (1947, repr. 1972); G. D. McDonald et al., *The Films of Charlie Chaplin* (1965).

Chapman, George, 1559?–1634, English dramatist, translator, and poet. His great contributions to English literature are his poetic translations of Homer's *Iliad* (1612) and *Odyssey* (1614–15). Chapman was a classical scholar, and his work shows the influence of the Stoic philosophers, Epictetus and Seneca. In his best-known tragedies, *Bussy D'Ambois* (1607) and *The Conspiracy and Tragedy of Byron* (1608), the hero is destroyed by his inability to control his inward passions and resist outward temptation. Chapman wrote and collaborated on nearly a dozen comedies, the most notable being *All Fools* (1605) and *Eastward Ho!* (1605), the latter written with Ben Jonson and John Marston. Included among his other works are several metaphysical poems, a completed version of Marlowe's *Hero and Leander* (1598), and translations of Petrarch and Hesiod. See studies by Millar MacLure (1966) and Charlotte Spivack (1967).

Chapman, John, 1774–1845, American pioneer, more familiarly known as Johnny Appleseed, b. Massachusetts. From Pennsylvania—where he had sold or given saplings and apple seeds to families migrating westward—he traveled c.1800 to present-day Ohio, sowing apple seeds as he went. For over 40 years Johnny Appleseed continued to wander up and down Ohio, Indiana, and W Pennsylvania, visiting his forest nurseries to prune and care for them and helping hundreds of settlers to establish orchards of their own. His ragged dress, eccentric ways, and religious turn of mind attracted attention, and he became a familiar figure to settlers. Scores of legends were told of him after he died. However, it was verified that in the War of 1812 he traveled 30 mi (48 km) to summon American troops to Mansfield, Ohio, thus forestalling a raid by Indian tribes who were allied with the British. He died near Fort Wayne, Ind. See biographies by H. A. Pershing (1930) and Robert Price (1954).

Chapman, John Gadsby, 1808–90, American painter, b. Alexandria, Va. Chapman is noted for his colored etchings of the Roman compagna and the American landscape. His historical painting *The Baptism of Pocahontas* is in the Capitol in Washington, D.C.

Chapman, John Jay, 1862–1933, American essayist and poet, b. New York City, grad. Harvard. He was admitted to the bar in 1888 but after 10 years abandoned law for literature. A friend of William James and other Boston intellectuals of the time, Chapman was a fiery and pertinent observer of his environment. Among his works are *Emerson and Other Essays* (1898), *Memories and Milestones* (1915), *Greek Genius and Other Essays* (1915), *Songs and Poems* (1919), and *New Horizons in American Life* (1932). He also wrote several plays, including *The Treason and Death of Benedict Arnold* (1910). See his selected writings ed. by J. Barzun (new ed. 1968); studies by R. B. Hovey (1959) and M. H. Bernstein (1964).

Chapman, Maria Weston, 1806–85, American abolitionist, b. Weymouth, Mass. In 1834 she became a close associate of William Lloyd Garrison, helped organize the Boston Female Anti-Slavery Society, and for several years was treasurer of the Massachusetts Anti-Slavery Society. She edited (1877) the autobiography of her friend Harriet Martineau.

Chapra (chä'prə), city (1971 pop. 83,166), Bihar state, NE India, on the Gogra River near its junction with the Ganges. It is a rail and road junction. In the 18th cent. the French, Dutch, Portuguese, and British had factories in the area that were destroyed by floods. In the early 20th cent. the city was ravaged by plague. Chapra has two colleges affiliated with Bihar Univ.

Chaptal, Jean Antoine (zhäN äNtwän' shäptäl'), 1756–1832, French chemist, industrialist, and statesman. He became (1781) professor of chemistry at Montpellier, and during the Revolution he was active in gunpowder production. Later, as minister of the interior (1801–9) and director general of commerce and manufactures (1815) under Napoleon I, he introduced far-reaching reforms in medicine, industry, and public works. Chaptal's writings pioneered in the application of chemical principles to industrial processes.

chapter house, a building in which the chapter of the clergy meets. Its plan varies, the simplest being a rectangle. At Worcester, England, the Norman builders created a circular chapter house (c.1100), with vaulting springing from a central pillar. Subsequent examples, adopting this central support for their vaulted roofs but frequently having a polygonal plan, are among the most distinctive achievements of the English Gothic builders. Those at Salisbury, Wells, and Westminster Abbey (1250) are octagonal, while that at Lincoln is decagonal. At York, the octagonal room (c.1300) exhibits a departure in that it dispenses with the central column and is covered with a vaulted wooden roof.

Chapultepec (chäpōōl"tāpĕk') [Aztec,=grasshopper hill], rocky hill S of Mexico City. It was originally developed as a playground for Aztec emperors. A castle built there in the late 18th cent. as a summer home for the Spanish viceroys later became the traditional home of the rulers of Mexico. Chapultepec, heavily fortified, was the scene of spectacular fighting during the MEXICAN WAR; U.S. Gen. Winfield SCOTT ordered the storming of Chapultepec on Sept. 12, 1847, and it fell the next day. Nevertheless, its heroic defenders, particularly the "boy heroes" from the adjoining military college who preferred death to surrender, became for Mexicans a symbol of glory. Both Emperor Maximilian and, later, Porfirio Díaz, beautified the grounds and embellished the castle. In 1937, Mexican President Lázaro Cárdenas declared the castle a museum of colonial history and ethnography. The Inter-American Conference on the Problems of War and Peace, which met in 1945, is commonly called the Chapultepec Conference (see PAN-AMERICANISM).

Chapultepec, Act of: see PAN-AMERICANISM.

char: see SALMON.

characin (kâr'əsĭn), common name for members of the Characidae, a large and diverse family comprising 700 species of freshwater fishes. The characins are related to the carp and the catfish. They are found in Africa and in tropical America, especially in the Amazon. Most species are active and predacious. Most notorious are the piranhas, or caribes (*Serrasalmus* species), with their powerful jaws and razor-sharp triangular teeth, capable of killing humans and cattle. Various small, colorful characin species, called tetras, are used in aquariums. A small characin found in Mexican streams is interesting for the stages of blindness it exhibits: those which live far back in caves are eyeless; those found near the entrance have imperfect eyes; and the specimens living in open water have normal eyes. A cross of a blind with a normal specimen produces offspring with varying degrees of eye degeneracy. Characins are classified in the phylum CHORDATA, class Osteichthyes, order Cypriniformes.

charade (shərād'), verbal, written, or acted representation of a word, its syllables, or a number of words. The object is to guess the idea being conveyed. Winthrop M. PRAED wrote many of the well-known charades, and a good description of the acted charade is found in Thackeray's *Vanity Fair*. In the United States a charade acted in pantomime and having a set time limit had considerable popularity in the 1930s and 40s and is still a popular form of home amusement.

Charashim (kăr'əshĭm) [Heb.,=craftsmen; cf. Neh. 11.35], unidentified valley, Palestine, probably near Lydda. 1 Chron. 4.14.

Charbray cattle (shär'brā"): see BRAHMAN CATTLE.

Charcas (chär'käs), Spanish colonial AUDIENCIA and presidency in South America, known also as Upper Peru and Chuquisaca. Charcas roughly corresponded to modern Bolivia but included parts of present Argentina, Chile, Peru, and Paraguay, encompassing a territorial expanse that led to disputes and wars after independence had been won. It was established in 1559 and was attached to the viceroyalty of Peru until joined (1776) to the newly created viceroyalty of La Plata. The prosecutor of Charcas, José de Antequera y Castro, led (1721) the first major creole uprising against viceregal authority. The city of SUCRE was sometimes called Charcas.

charcoal, substance obtained by partial burning or destructive distillation of organic material. It is largely pure CARBON. The most common variety, wood charcoal, was formerly prepared by piling wood into stacks, covering it with earth or turf, and setting it on fire. In this process volatile compounds in the wood (e.g., water) pass off as vapors into the air, some of the carbon is consumed as fuel, and the rest of the carbon is converted into charcoal. In the modern method, wood is raised to a high temperature in an iron retort, and industrially important by-products, e.g., methanol (wood alcohol), acetone, and acetic acid, are saved by condensing them to their liquid form. Charcoal, being almost pure carbon, yields a larger amount of heat in proportion to its volume than is obtained from a corresponding quantity of wood; as a fuel it has the further advantage of being smokeless. Charcoal is also obtained from substances other than wood; that obtained from bones is called bone black, animal black, or animal charcoal. Because of its porous structure, finely divided charcoal is a highly efficient agent for filtering the adsorption of gases and of solids from solution. It is used in sugar refining, in water purification, in the purification of factory air, and in gas masks. By special heating or chemical processes the adsorptive property can be greatly increased; charcoal so treated is known as activated charcoal.

Charcot, Jean Baptiste (zhäN bätēst' shärkō'), 1867–1936, French neurologist and explorer in the antarctic region; son of Jean Martin Charcot. He became (1896) director of clinics at the Univ. of Paris but soon gave up medicine for exploration. In two voyages (1903–7, 1908–10) he surveyed the coast of Antarctica from Palmer Peninsula to Charcot Land, obtaining valuable scientific data. After 1920, Charcot made seven scientific voyages to Greenland aboard his ship, the *Pourquoi Pas?*. In 1935 he came out of retirement for a final expedition to Greenland. Crashing into a reef, Charcot went down with his celebrated ship off the coast of Iceland. His antarctic voyages were recorded in his *Le Pourquoi Pas? dans l'antarctique* (1910, tr. *The Voyage of the Why Not? in the Antarctic*, 1911).

Charcot, Jean Martin (zhäN märtăN' shärkō'), 1825–93, French neurologist. He developed at the Salpêtrière in Paris the greatest clinic of his time for diseases of the nervous system. He made many important observations on these diseases, described the characteristics of tabes dorsalis, differentiated multiple sclerosis and paralysis agitans, and wrote on many neurological subjects. Charcot's insight into the nature of hysteria is credited by Sigmund Freud, his pupil, as having contributed to the early psychoanalytic formulations on the subject. See biography by Georges Guillain (1959); study by A. R. Owen (1971).

chard: see ARTICHOKE; BEET.

Chardin, Jean-Baptiste-Siméon (zhäN-bätēst'-sēmāōN' shärdăN'), 1699–1779, French painter. He was a major figure of 18th-century painting. While the Académie royale still advocated history painting as the noblest form of art, Chardin painted simple still lifes and domestic interiors. His ability to evoke textures was extraordinary, as were his muted tones, delicate touch, and unusually abstract compositional skill. His particular ability to render still-life forms naturalistically and simple genre scenes without sentimentality ensured his reputation. A number of modern schools of painting are indebted to the abstract nature of Chardin's compositions. The Louvre has many of his oils and pastel portraits, including *Benediction* and *Return from Market*. *Blowing Bubbles* and a portrait of *Mme Chardin* are at the Metropolitan Museum. Other paintings are in the National Gallery of Art, Washington, D.C., and in the Museum of Fine Arts, Boston. See studies by H. E. A. Furst (1907) and G. Wildenstein (1963, repr. 1969).

Chardzhou (chərjô'ōō), city (1970 pop. 96,000), capital of Chardzhou oblast, SW Central Asian USSR, in the Turkmen Republic, on the Amu Darya River. An inland port, it has shipyards and is a cotton and silk manufacturing center. Its superphosphate plant produces fertilizer for much of Central Asian USSR. Chardzhou was founded in the late 19th cent. as a fortress.

Charente (shäräNt'), department (1968 pop. 331,016), W France. The capital is Angoulême. The brandy distilled at COGNAC is world renowned.

Charente, river, 220 mi (354 km) long, rising near Limoges, W France, and flowing W to the Bay of Biscay. The river flows past Angoulême (the head of navigation), Cognac, Saintes, and Rochefort, and through an important cattle-raising region. Along its western course are the celebrated vineyards from which cognac brandy is made. The Charente carries little commercial traffic.

Charente-Maritime (shäräNt'-märētēm'), department (1968 pop. 483,622), W France, on the Atlantic coast, formerly Charente-Inférieure. La Rochelle is the capital.

Chares (kâr'ēz, kā'-), fl. 3d cent. B.C., Greek worker in bronze from Lindus, Rhodes; pupil of Lysippos. He was the sculptor of the COLOSSUS of Rhodes and is said to have founded the Rhodian school of sculpture. No known works have survived.

charge, property of matter that gives rise to all electrical phenomena (see ELECTRICITY). The basic unit of charge, usually denoted by e, is that on the PROTON or the ELECTRON; that on the proton is designated as positive ($+e$) and that on the electron is designated as negative ($-e$). All other charged ELEMENTARY PARTICLES have charges equal to $+e$, $-e$, or some whole number times one of these, with the possible exception of the quark, a hypothetical particle whose charge could be $\frac{1}{3}e$ or $\frac{2}{3}e$. Every charged particle is surrounded by an electric FIELD of FORCE such that it attracts any charge of opposite sign brought near it and repels any charge of like sign, the magnitude of this force being described by COULOMB'S LAW (see ELECTROSTATICS). This force is much stronger than the gravitational force between two particles and is responsible for holding protons and electrons together in atoms and for chemical bonding. When equal numbers of protons and electrons are present, the atom is electrically neutral, and more generally, any physical system containing equal numbers of positive and negative charges is neutral. Charge is a conserved quantity; the net electric charge in a closed physical system is constant (see CONSERVATION LAWS). Whenever charge is created, as in the decay of a neutron into a proton, an electron, and an antineutrino, equal numbers of positive and negative charges must be created. Although charge is conserved, it can be transferred from one body to another. Electric current, on which much of modern technology is dependent, is a flow of charge through a conductor (see CONDUCTION). Although current is usually treated as a continuous quantity, it actually consists of the transfer of millions of individual charges from atom to atom, typically by the transfer of electrons. A precise description of the behavior of electric charge in crystals and in systems of atomic and molecular dimensions requires the use of the QUANTUM THEORY.

chargé d'affaires: see DIPLOMATIC SERVICE.

Chari or **Shari** (both: shä'rē), longest river of interior drainage in Africa, c.650 mi (1,050 km) long, rising in the uplands of the Central African Republic, N central Africa. It flows NW across S Chad, past Sarh (Fort Archambault), Bousso, and Ndjamena (Fort-Lamy), and enters Lake Chad through a wide delta. The Logone River is its chief tributary. During the summer rainy season, the river floods much of the surrounding area.

Charikar (chä'rĭkär), city (1969 est. pop. 90,000), NE Afghanistan. It is noted for its pottery and high-quality grapes. During the 1960s Afghanistan's largest textile factory was built nearby, bringing a great increase in Charikar's population.

chariot, earliest and simplest type of carriage and the chief vehicle of many ancient peoples. The chariot was known among the Babylonians before the introduction of horses c.2000 B.C. and was first drawn by asses. The chariot and horse introduced into Egypt c.1700 B.C. by the Hyksos invaders undoubtedly contributed to their military success. Simultaneously the use of the chariot spread over the Middle East, chiefly as a war machine. The Assyrians are credited with introducing chariots with scythes mounted on the wheels as weapons, a type later adopted by the Persians. In Greece and Rome the chariot was never used to any extent in war, possibly because of generally unfavorable topography. It was, however, prominent in games and processions, becoming in Rome the inevitable carriage of the triumphal procession. Here also the chariot races of the circus were developed. The ancient chariot was a very light vehicle, drawn by two or more horses hitched side by side. The car was little else than a floor with a waist-high semicircular guard in front. British chariots were open in front, had a curved wall behind, often had seats, and sometimes had scythes on the wheels.

Charites: see GRACES.

Charlemagne (Charles the Great or Charles I) (shär'ləmān) [O.Fr.,=Charles the great], 742?–814, emperor of the West (800–814), Carolingian king of the Franks (768–814). Elder son of PEPIN THE SHORT and a grandson of CHARLES MARTEL, he shared with his brother CARLOMAN in the succession to his father's kingdom. At Carloman's death (771), young Charles annexed his brother's lands, disinheriting Carloman's two young sons, who fled with their mother to the court of DESIDERIUS, king of the Lombards. When Desiderius conquered part of the papal lands and attempted to force Pope ADRIAN I to recognize Carloman's sons, Charles intervened (773) on the side of the pope and defeated the Lombards. At Rome, Charles was received by Adrian as patrician of the Romans (a title he had received with his father in 754), and he confirmed his father's donation to the Holy See. Shortly afterward he took Pavia, the Lombard capital, and assumed the iron crown of the Lombard kings of Italy. In 778 he invaded Spain, hoping to take advantage of civil war among the Muslim rulers of that kingdom, but was repulsed at Saragossa. In later campaigns conducted by local counts, Barcelona was captured (801) and a frontier established beyond the Pyrenees. Charles's struggle with the pagan Saxons, whose greatest leader was WIDUKIND, lasted from 772 until 804. By dint of forced conversions, wholesale massacres, and the transportation of thousands of Saxons to the interior of the Frankish kingdom, Charles made his domination over Saxony complete. In 788 he annexed the semi-independent duchy of Bavaria, after deposing its duke, Tassilo. He also warred successfully against the Avars and the Slavs, establishing a frontier south of the Danube. Meanwhile the new pope, LEO III, was threatened with deposition by the Romans and in 799 appealed to Charles. Charles hastened to Rome to support Leo, and on Christmas Day, 800, was crowned emperor by the pope. His coronation legitimized Charles's rule over the former Roman empire in W Europe and finalized the split between the Byzantine and Roman empires. After years of negotiation and war, Charles received recognition from the Byzantine emperor Michael I in 812; in return Charles renounced his claims to Istria, Venice, and Dalmatia, which he had held briefly. The end of Charles's reign was troubled by the raids of Norse and Danish pirates (see NORSEMEN), and Charles took vigorous measures for the construction of a fleet, which his successors neglected. His land frontiers he had already protected by the creation of marches. In his government he continued and systematized the administrative machinery of his predecessors. He permitted conquered peoples to retain their own laws, which he codified when possible, and he issued many CAPITULARIES (gathered in the MONUMENTA GERMANIAE HISTORICA). A noteworthy achievement was the creation of a system by which he might personally supervise his administrators in even the most distant lands; his *missi dominici* were personal representatives with wide powers who regularly inspected their assigned districts. He maintained contact with the lesser magnates through annual consultative assemblies. He tried to help the poorer freemen by reducing their military obligations and by removing their obligation to attend county assemblies. He strove to educate the clergy and exercised more direct control over the appointment of bishops. Like the Byzantine emperors, he acted as arbiter in theological disputes by summoning councils, notably that at Frankfurt (794), where ADOPTIONISM was rejected and the decrees of the Second Council of Nicaea (see NICAEA, SECOND COUNCIL OF) were condemned. He stimulated foreign trade and entertained friendly relations with England and with HARUN AR-RASHID. In 813, Charlemagne designated his son LOUIS I as co-emperor and his successor and crowned him at AACHEN. Charlemagne's court at Aachen was the center of an intellectual renaissance. The palace school, under the leadership of ALCUIN, became particularly famous; numerous schools for children of all classes were also established throughout the empire during Charles's reign. The preservation of classical literature was due almost entirely to his initiative. Prominent figures of the Carolingian renaissance, other than Alcuin, included PAUL THE DEACON and EINHARD. Charlemagne himself, although scarcely to be considered educated by later standards, showed great taste for learning and strove for purity in his Latin. In his daily life he affected the simple manners of his Frankish forebears, wore Frankish clothes, and led a frugal existence, except for his habit of keeping several wives and concubines. He was beatified after his death and in some churches has been honored as a saint. His physical appearance probably differed vastly from the bearded and patriarchal figure of the legend. Indeed, Charlemagne's actual achievements and prestige were of such magnitude that later generations enlarged them to fantastic proportions. Surrounded by his legendary 12 peers, he became the central figure of a cycle of romance. At first, legend pictured him as the champion of Christendom; later he appeared as a vacillating old man, almost a comic figure. His characterization in the *Chanson de Roland* (see ROLAND) has impressed itself indelibly on the imagination of the Western world. The vogue of the Charlemagne epic ebbed somewhat after the Renaissance but was revived again in the 19th cent. by Victor Hugo and other members of the Romantic school. Charlemagne's creation (or re-creation) of an empire was the basis of the theory of the HOLY ROMAN EMPIRE; it was his example that Napoleon I had in mind when he tried to assume his succession in 1804. Einhard wrote a contemporary biography of Charlemagne. See Heinrich Fichtenau, *The Carolingian Empire* (1949, tr. 1957); Donald Bullough, *The Age of Charlemagne* (1966); Jacques Boussard, *The Civilization of Charlemagne* (tr. 1968). For the literary aspect, see Thomas Bulfinch, *Legends of Charlemagne* (1863), and J. L. Weston, *The Romance Cycle of Charlemagne and His Peers* (1901).

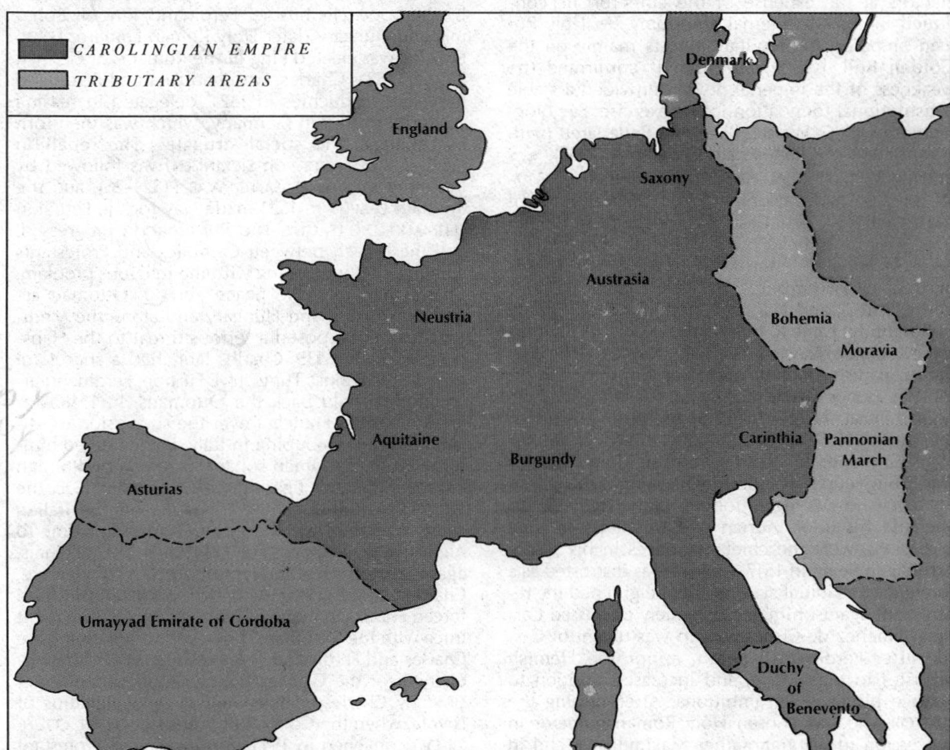

Carolingian Empire (814)

Charleroi (shärlərwä'), town (1970 pop. 23,689), Hainaut prov., S Belgium, on the Sambre River and on the Charleroi-Brussels Canal. It is a commercial and industrial center and a rail junction. Manufactures include steel, glass, machinery, processed food, and chemicals. Coal and iron are mined in the region. Charleroi was founded in 1666 and named for Charles II of Spain. It was of strategic importance in the wars of the 17th and 18th cent. The Germans won a battle there (1914) in World War I. It is noted for its modern public buildings, such as the town hall (1936), and is the seat of a technical university.

Charles I, emperor of the West and Frankish king: see CHARLEMAGNE.

Charles II or **Charles the Bald,** 823–77, emperor of the West (875–77) and king of the West Franks (843–77), son of Emperor LOUIS I by a second marriage. The efforts of Louis to create a kingdom for Charles were responsible for the repeated revolts of Louis's elder sons that disturbed the latter part of Louis's reign. When LOTHAIR I, the eldest and heir to the imperial title, attempted to reunite the empire after Louis's death (840), Charles and LOUIS THE GERMAN marched against their brother and defeated him at Fontenoy (841). Reaffirming their alliance in 842 (see STRASBOURG, OATH OF), they signed (843) with Lothair the Treaty of Verdun (see VERDUN, TREATY OF), which divided the empire into three parts. The part roughly corresponding to modern France fell to Charles. He was almost continuously at war with his brothers and their sons, with the Norsemen (or Normans, as they came to be known in France), and with rebellious subjects. When Charles's nephew LOTHAIR, son of Lothair I and king of Lotharingia, died in 869, Charles seized his kingdom but was forced by the Treaty of MERSEN (870) to divide it with Louis the German. In 875, at the death of his nephew Louis II, who had succeeded Lothair I as emperor, Charles secured the imperial crown. His reign witnessed the growth of the power of the nobles at the expense of the royal power and thus marked the rise of local feudalism. Charles's chief adviser was Archbishop HINCMAR.

Charles III or **Charles the Fat,** 839–88, emperor of the West (881–87), king of the East Franks (882–87), and king of the West Franks (884–87); son of LOUIS THE GERMAN, at whose death he inherited Swabia (876). He succeeded to the East Frankish or German kingship after the deaths of his brothers Carloman (880) and Louis the Younger (882), with whom he had shared the kingdom of Louis the German. He had also gained Italy from Carloman and was crowned emperor by Pope John VIII in 881. After the death of the heirs of CHARLES II in France, he became (884) West Frankish king, thus reuniting briefly the empire of Charlemagne. A weak ruler, he was unable to protect his lands from invasion and in 886, when he went to relieve Paris, which was besieged by the NORSEMEN, he ransomed the city instead of fighting and allowed the invaders to ravage Burgundy. He was deposed in 887 and was succeeded in Germany by ARNULF and briefly in France by EUDES.

Charles IV, 1316-78, Holy Roman emperor (1355-78), German king (1347-78), and king of Bohemia (1346-78). The son of JOHN OF LUXEMBOURG, Charles was educated at the French court and fought the English at CRÉCY, where his father's heroic death made him king of Bohemia. Pope CLEMENT VI, to whom he had promised far-reaching concessions, helped secure his election (1346) by the imperial electors as antiking to Holy Roman Emperor LOUIS IV. Louis's death (1347), the popular desire for peace, which was fostered by the ravages of the Black Death (bubonic plague), and the absence of a strong leader to unite the opposition enabled Charles to make good his claim to the crown by 1349. In 1355 he journeyed to Rome, where, on Easter Sunday, he was crowned emperor by the papal legate (the pope was then residing at Avignon). His coronation with papal approval ended years of conflict between popes and emperors, during which time the imperial rulers had tried to regain control of Italy and the papacy. Although the emperors continued to be crowned at Rome, they were excluded from Italian affairs. At the same time, Charles's Golden Bull of 1356 ended papal interference in the Holy Roman Empire by eliminating the need for papal approval and confirmation of emperors. Although he had virtually renounced imperial pretensions in Italy through his treaty with Clement VI, Charles supported the plans of Urban V to return the papacy from Avignon to Rome. Charles's major concern was to strengthen his dynasty. Through skillful diplomacy he acquired Brandenburg (1373) and added to his territories in Silesia and Lusatia. He ensured the succession of his son WENCESLAUS by bribing the electors to name him German king (1376). To raise the money for the bribes, he imposed even higher taxes on the cities. This led to a revolt by a league of Swabian cities. Charles obtained peace (1378) by granting concessions. During Charles's reign Bohemia flourished. His imperial capital was at Prague, where he founded (1348) CHARLES UNIVERSITY (the oldest in Central Europe) and rebuilt the Cathedral of St. Vitus. By introducing new agricultural methods and by expanding industries, he fostered economic life. He drew up a code of laws, the *Maiestas Carolina* (1350)—which, however, was rejected by the diet—and he protected the lower classes by giving them courts in which to sue their overlords. Through Charles's efforts as margrave of Moravia, Prague was elevated (1344) to an archbishopric, thus gaining ecclesiastic independence. By the Golden Bull, which strengthened the electors at the expense of the emperor, he confirmed Bohemia's internal autonomy. As Holy Roman emperor, his reputation rests mainly on the Golden Bull, which, although it confirmed the weakness of the imperial power, provided a stable constitutional foundation for its exercise. See biographies by G. G. Walsh (1924) and Bede Jarett (with a translation of Charles's autobiography, 1935).

Charles V, 1500-1558, Holy Roman emperor (1519-58) and, as Charles I, king of Spain (1516-56); son of PHILIP I and JOANNA of Castile, grandson of Ferdinand II of Aragón, Isabella of Castile, Holy Roman Emperor Maximilian I, and Mary of Burgundy. He inherited a vast empire. The Netherlands, Luxembourg, Artois, and Franche-Comté (or Free County of Burgundy) came to him on the death (1506) of his father. Aragón, Navarre, Granada, Naples, Sicily, Sardinia, Spanish America, and joint kingship with his mother (who was insane) over Castile devolved upon him at the death (1516) of Ferdinand II. On the death (1519) of Maximilian I he inherited the Hapsburg lands in Austria. Born at Ghent, Charles was brought up in Flanders by his aunt, MARGARET OF AUSTRIA, who was regent for him in the Netherlands. She and his tutor, Adrian of Utrecht (later Pope ADRIAN VI), were the chief influences in his youth. Arriving in Spain in 1517, Charles was distrusted as a foreigner. His initial actions only heightened the resentment against him. He brusquely dismissed Cardinal Jiménez de Cisneros, who was regent of Castile after Ferdinand's death, appointed Flemish favorites to high office, and increased taxation to finance his imperial ambitions. After bribing the ELECTORS, he was chosen Holy Roman emperor in succession to his grandfather Maximilian I, and in 1520 he departed for Germany. Charles sought to become leader of a universal empire. His imperial dreams were encouraged by M. A. di GATTINARA, whose influence replaced that of Charles's Flemish advisers.

Struggle for Empire. The chief problems Charles faced were the Protestant REFORMATION in Germany; the dynastic conflict with King FRANCIS I of France, particularly for supremacy in Italy; and the advance of the Ottoman Turks. Shortly after his election Charles began his lifelong struggle with France (see ITALIAN WARS), which required immense expenditures. In 1520 he signed the Treaty of Gravelines with King HENRY VIII of England, and in 1521 he invaded N Italy, then controlled by France. The fiscal onus for the war rested on Spain and provoked violent reaction, particularly in Castile, which resented Charles's high-handedness in obtaining funds from the Castilian Cortes. Toledo, Segovia, and other Castilian cities revolted in the brief war (1520-21) of the *comuneros.* Initially aimed at limiting the royal power, the uprising was later marked by violent class warfare. It was put down at the battle of Villalar; Juan de PADILLA and other leaders were executed. Charles later won the loyalty of his Spanish subjects. In Germany, at the fateful Diet of Worms (see WORMS, DIET OF) in 1521, Charles secured a satisfactory compromise regarding the REICHSREGIMENT but unyieldingly opposed the doctrines of Martin Luther. In his written opinion, Charles declared himself ready to stake his dominions, friends, blood, life, and soul on the extinction of heresy. Late in May, 1521, he signed the Edict of Worms, outlawing Luther and his followers. However, Charles's preoccupation with the war with France prevented him from checking the spread of Luther's doctrines. Also, Charles was not always supported by the popes, who were concerned with the threat to their temporal power and independence posed by imperial domination of Italy. After the French defeat at Pavia (1525) and the capture of Francis I, Charles seemed triumphant in Italy; Francis signed (1526) the humiliating Treaty of Madrid, by which he renounced his Italian claims and ceded Burgundy to Charles. On his release, however, Francis repudiated the treaty and organized the anti-imperial League of Cognac. The pope, Venice, Milan, and Florence joined the league. Charles sent an imperial army to Italy composed mostly of German Lutherans. Led first by Georg von FRUNDSBERG and then by Charles de BOURBON, the army defeated the league and then marched on Rome, where the force sacked (1527) the city and besieged Pope CLEMENT VII. Although the "German Fury" was disavowed by Charles, he profited from the outrage, extorting large sums of money from the pope. The Treaty of Cambrai (see CAMBRAI, TREATY OF) with France and the Peace of Barcelona with the pope (both 1529) confirmed Charles's position in Italy and secured his coronation as Holy Roman emperor at Bologna (1530). Charles was the last German emperor to be crowned by the pope. His brother Ferdinand, king of Bohemia and Hungary (later Holy Roman Emperor FERDINAND I), was elected king of the Romans, or German king, in 1531. Charles, who had awarded Ferdinand the Austrian duchies in 1521, delegated increasing authority to him in Germany, which was then torn by religious and social struggles. The rebellion (1522-23) of Franz von SICKINGEN was followed by the more serious PEASANTS' WAR (1524-26), and the Swabian League in 1531 made way for the Lutheran SCHMALKALDIC LEAGUE. The Reformation progressed, and the breach between Catholics and Protestants widened. Before dealing with the religious problem, Charles had to make peace abroad. Ottoman assaults in Austria and Hungary and along the Mediterranean coast posed a serious threat to the Hapsburg lands. In 1535, Charles launched a successful expedition against Tunis. In E Europe, Ferdinand attempted to hold back the Ottomans. In 1536, war broke out with Francis I over the succession to Milan. Intent on recouping in Italy, Francis allied himself with the Ottoman sultan, SULAYMAN I. Although a truce ended the fighting with Francis in 1538, the Ottomans continued their assaults on the Italian coast. A second expedition by Charles, this time to Algiers, was unsuccessful (1541). In 1542, Francis, again allied with Sulayman, renewed warfare. Charles joined (1543) with Henry VIII and in 1544 forced Francis to make peace at CRÉPY. A subsequent truce with the Ottomans, however humiliating, gave Charles and Ferdinand some respite. At last the way opened for the Catholic Reformation, ardently desired by Charles and forwarded by St. Ignatius of Loyola, when the Council of Trent (see TRENT, COUNCIL OF) convened in 1545. Turning on the Protestant princes of Germany, Charles split their ranks by winning over MAURICE of Saxony and others, attacked the Schmalkaldic League in 1546, defeated (1547) JOHN FREDERICK of Saxony at Mühlberg, and imprisoned PHILIP OF HESSE. At the Diet of Augsburg (1547) he secured the incorporation of the Netherlands into the Hapsburg hereditary possessions and forced through the Augsburg Interim (1548), a compromise profession of doctrine that he then tried to impose on the Protestants with the help of Spanish troops. In 1552, Maurice of Saxony changed sides again, called in Henry II of France, Francis's successor, and even attempted to capture Charles at Innsbruck.

Withdrawal from Power. Balked in his efforts to recapture Metz, which had been seized by Henry II, and realizing the necessity of compromising with Protestantism, Charles preferred to empower Ferdinand to treat, and he left Germany, never to return. Ferdinand negotiated the religious Peace of Augsburg (see AUGSBURG, PEACE OF), but war with France continued. It ended after Charles's death, with the Treaty of CATEAU-CAMBRESIS (1559), a triumph for Spain. In his remaining years Charles made a series of abdications that left the Hapsburg dominions divided between Austria and Spain. In 1554 he gave Naples and Milan to his son Philip, whom he married to Queen Mary I of England; in 1555 he turned over the Netherlands to Philip, and in 1556 he made him king of Spain and Sicily as Philip II. In 1556 also, he practically surrendered the empire to Ferdinand, and in 1558 he formally abdicated as emperor. Although he retired (1556) to the monastery of Yuste, he took an active interest in politics until his death. Two of his illegitimate children were Don JOHN OF AUSTRIA and MARGARET OF PARMA. During Charles's rule the Spanish Empire was tremendously expanded in the New World. In Italy, Spanish power had become paramount. Even England seemed about to fall to Spain through Philip's marriage, and Charles's own marriage with Isabella of Portugal brought the Portuguese crown to Philip in 1580. Yet Charles failed in his purpose to return the Protestants to the Roman Catholic Church, and the human and financial cost of constant warfare drained Spanish resources; moreover, Charles's hopes for a universal empire were thwarted by the political realities of Western Europe. His integrity, strength of will, and sense of duty were conspicuous. His appearance has been made familiar by two portraits by TITIAN. The classic works on Charles V are the biography by Karl Brandi (1937, tr. 1939, repr. 1968) and R. B. Merriman, *The Rise of the Spanish Empire in the Old World and the New,* Vol. III (1926, repr. 1972); see also biographies by Gertrude von Schwarzenfeld (tr. 1957) and Otto von Hapsburg (tr. 1970).

Charles VI, 1685-1740, Holy Roman emperor (1711-40), king of Bohemia (1711-40) and, as Charles III, king of Hungary (1712-40); brother and successor of Holy Roman Emperor Joseph I. Charles was the last Holy Roman emperor of the direct Hapsburg line. In 1700 he was designated successor in Spain to King Charles II, who was childless. On his deathbed, however, Charles II left his throne to Philip of Anjou (PHILIP V), grandson of King LOUIS XIV of France; Philip was proclaimed king in Nov., 1700. War broke out immediately against Louis XIV and Philip (see SPANISH SUCCESSION, WAR OF THE). Although Charles, with the aid of British troops, invaded Spain and proclaimed himself king as Charles III in 1704, he was able to maintain himself only in Catalonia, with his capital at Barcelona. When Charles's brother Joseph I died (1711), Charles succeeded him as Holy Roman emperor. His accession led to England's withdrawal from the war since the English did not wish to see the reunification of the empire of CHARLES V. A treaty (see UTRECHT, PEACE OF; 1713) was signed between France and Charles's former allies, Holland and England. Charles continued fighting. He finally concluded peace in 1714. By the terms of the peace Philip V remained king of Spain and Charles received most of the Spanish possessions in the Low Countries and in Italy. Philip's subsequent attempt to overthrow the settlement in Italy resulted (1718) in the formation of the QUADRUPLE ALLIANCE against him. The war was ended by the Treaty of The Hague (1720), which repeated the terms of 1713-14, except that Charles obtained Sicily from Savoy in exchange for Sardinia. In E Europe, Charles continued to defend his lands against Turkish invasions (1716-18). In a campaign against the Turks the imperial commander EUGENE OF SAVOY obtained for Hungary the Banat and N Serbia. Charles was later forced to return these lands to the Ottoman Empire (Turkey) after several defeats in the Turkish war of 1736-39. Near the end of his reign in the War of the

POLISH SUCCESSION (1733–35) Charles was again involved in a conflict with France and Spain. By the Treaty of Vienna (1738) he was forced to give up Sicily and Naples to Spain, but received Parma and Piacenza. Since Charles had no male heirs, one of his chief concerns was to secure the succession to the Hapsburg lands for his daughter, MARIA THERESA. His last years were spent in an effort to win European approval of the PRAGMATIC SANCTION of 1713, which made Maria Theresa his heir. Although the Pragmatic Sanction was guaranteed by the Treaty of Vienna, the succession was contested on his death (see AUSTRIAN SUCCESSION, WAR OF THE). Charles was a patron of learning and the arts, particularly of music. A mercantilist, he encouraged commerce and industry.

Charles VII, 1697–1745, Holy Roman emperor (1742–45) and, as Charles Albert, elector of Bavaria (1726–45). Having married a daughter of Holy Roman Emperor Joseph I, he refused to recognize the PRAGMATIC SANCTION of 1713 by which Holy Roman Emperor Charles VI (his wife's uncle) reserved the succession to the Hapsburg lands for his daughter, MARIA THERESA. On Charles VI's death (1740) he advanced his own claim and joined with Frederick II (of Prussia), France, Spain, and Saxony to attack Maria Theresa (see AUSTRIAN SUCCESSION, WAR OF THE). In 1742 he was elected Holy Roman emperor, but Bavaria was overrun by Austrian troops. Shortly before his death he regained his territories. Francis I, husband of Maria Theresa, was elected emperor to succeed him.

Charles I, 1887–1922, last emperor of Austria and, as Charles IV, king of Hungary (1916–18); son of Archduke Otto and grandnephew and successor of Emperor Francis Joseph. He married ZITA of Bourbon-Parma. The death (1914) of his uncle, FRANCIS FERDINAND, made Charles heir to the throne. He showed skill as a commander in World War I. After his accession he put out peace feelers. His correspondence with his brother-in-law, Prince SIXTUS OF BOURBON-PARMA, justified French claims to Alsace-Lorraine. The Allies published (April, 1918) the correspondence, thus causing friction between Austria and Germany and diminishing Charles's popularity. Charles vainly tried to save the Austro-Hungarian monarchy by proclaiming (Oct. 16, 1918) an Austrian federative state. Hungary and Czechoslovakia declared their independence, and on Nov. 3, Charles had to consent to unconditional surrender in the armistice concluded with General Armando Diaz. Charles abdicated as emperor of Austria on Nov. 11 and as king of Hungary on Nov. 13; early in 1919 he and his family went into exile in Switzerland. After the triumph of the monarchists in Hungary in 1920, he attempted unsuccessfully to regain the Hungarian throne in March, 1921, and again in October, when the regent, HORTHY, had him arrested. Charles was exiled to Madeira and there died of pneumonia. His son, Archduke Otto, inherited his claim to the throne. See biographies by Herbert Vivian (1932) and Gordon Shepherd (1968).

Charles I, 1600–1649, king of England, Scotland, and Ireland (1625–49), second son of James I and Anne of Denmark. He became heir to the throne on the death of his older brother Henry in 1612 and was made prince of Wales in 1616. The negotiations for his marriage to the Spanish infanta were unpopular in England, and Charles himself turned against Spain after his unhappy visit to Madrid (1623) in the company of George Villiers, 1st duke of BUCKINGHAM. Apart from these negotiations, he took little part in politics before he succeeded (Feb., 1625) his father as king. A shy and dignified figure, he was popular at that time, but he immediately offended his Protestant subjects by his marriage to the Catholic HENRIETTA MARIA, sister of Louis XIII of France. Charles's favorite, Buckingham, was unpopular, and the foreign ventures under Buckingham's guidance were unfortunate, particularly the unsuccessful expedition to Cádiz (1625) and the two disastrous attempts to relieve French Protestants in La Rochelle (1627 and 1628). Nor would Parliament willingly grant money to help Charles's sister, Elizabeth of Bohemia, and the Protestants in the Thirty Years War. The reign quickly resolved itself into the bitter struggle for supremacy between the king and Parliament that finally resulted in the ENGLISH CIVIL WAR.

The Struggle with Parliament. Parliament had the whip hand in its control of money grants to the king and adopted the tactic of withholding grants until its grievances were redressed. The Parliament of 1625 refused money, demanded ministers it could trust, and was soon dissolved by Charles. That of 1626 was dissolved when it started impeachment proceedings against Buckingham. Charles, to meet his needs for money, resorted to quartering troops upon the people and to a forced loan, which he attempted to collect by prosecutions and imprisonments. Forced to call Parliament again in 1628, he was compelled to agree to the PETITION OF RIGHT, in return for a badly needed subsidy. Charles prorogued Parliament when it declared that his continued collection of customs duties was a violation of the Petition. Although Buckingham was assassinated (1628), the parliamentary session of 1629 was bitter. It closed dramatically with a resolution condemning unauthorized taxation and attempts to change existing church practices. Charles then governed without Parliament for 11 years, which were marked by popular opposition to strict enforcement of the practices of the Established Church by Archbishop William LAUD and to the ingenious devices employed by the government to obtain funds. The royally controlled courts of high commission and Star Chamber waged a harsh campaign against nonconformists and recusants, and large emigrations to America, of both Puritans and Catholics, took place. The trial (1637–38) of John HAMPDEN for refusal to pay a tax of ship money, greatly increased public indignation. Meanwhile Charles's deputy in Ireland, Thomas Wentworth, earl of STRAFFORD, was carrying out a wide program of reforms through his oppressive policy of "Thorough."

The Supremacy of Parliament. Conditions in England reached a crisis when Charles attempted (1637) to force episcopacy upon the Scots, an attempt that was violently opposed by the Scottish COVENANTERS and that resulted in the BISHOPS' WARS. Unable to wage war effectively, Charles summoned (1640) the so-called Short Parliament, which demanded redress of grievances before granting funds and was dissolved. Another attempt to carry on the war without Parliament failed, and the famous Long Parliament was summoned (1640). Under the leadership of John PYM, John Hampden, and Sir Henry VANE (the younger), Parliament secured itself against dissolution without its own consent and brought about the death of Strafford, the abolition of the courts of high commission and Star Chamber, and the end of unparliamentary taxation. Charles professed to accept the revolutionary legislation, though he was known to hold strong views on the divine right of monarchy. Parliament's trust in the king was further undermined when his queen was implicated in the army plot to coerce Parliament, and Charles was, quite unjustly, suspected of complicity in the Irish massacre (1641) of Protestants in Ulster. In 1641, Parliament presented its Grand Remonstrance, calling for religious and administrative reforms and reciting in full its grievances against the king. Charles repudiated the charges, and his unsuccessful attempt to seize five opposition leaders of Commons in violation of traditional privilege was the fatal blunder that precipitated civil war.

Civil War and Defeat. There were no decisive victories in the war until Charles was defeated at Marston Moor (1644) and Naseby (1645). In 1646 he gave himself up to the Scottish army, which delivered him to Parliament. He was ultimately taken over by the English army leaders, who were now highly suspicious of Parliament. He escaped (Nov., 1647) to Carisbrooke, on the Isle of Wight, where he concluded an alliance with the discontented Scots, which led to the second civil war (1648) and another royalist defeat. Parliament, now reduced in number by Pride's Purge (see under PRIDE, THOMAS) and controlled by Charles's most powerful enemies, established a special high court of justice (see REGICIDES), which tried Charles and convicted him of treason for levying war against Parliament. He was beheaded on Jan. 30, 1649. To the royalists he became the martyred king who wrote the EIKON BASILIKE. By his opponents he was considered a double-dealing tyrant. He was in some ways a stupid and obstinate man, unable to understand, much less control, the intense religious passions and rapid political development of his age. He listened to the foolish advice first of Buckingham and then of his wife but never gave his full trust to his ablest servants, Laud and Wentworth; and he indulged in dangerous halfway measures that undermined confidence in him. His downfall was as much due to the weakness of his character as to his sincere religious and political beliefs. See biographies by E. J. Simpson (1952) and Christopher Hibbert (1968); H. Ross Williamson, *Charles and Cromwell* (1946); Godfrey Davies, *The Early Stuarts, 1603–1660* (2d ed. 1959); Christopher Hill, *The Century of Revolution, 1603–1714* (1961); C. V. Wedgwood, *The Great Rebellion: The King's Peace, 1637–1641* (1955) and *A Coffin for King Charles* (1964).

Charles II, 1630–85, king of England, Scotland, and Ireland (1660–85), eldest surviving son of CHARLES I and Henrietta Maria. Prince of Wales at the time of the English civil war, Charles was sent (1645) to the W of England with his council, which included Edward Hyde (later 1st earl of CLARENDON) and Thomas Wriothesley, 4th earl of SOUTHAMPTON. In 1646, Charles was forced to escape to France, where he stayed with his mother and was tutored by the philosopher Thomas Hobbes. In 1649, Charles vainly attempted to save his father's life by presenting to Parliament a signed blank sheet of paper, thereby granting whatever terms might be requested. After his father's execution (1649), Charles was proclaimed king in Scotland and in parts of Ireland and England. He accepted the terms of the Scottish COVENANTERS and went (1650) to Scotland, where he was crowned (1651), after agreeing to enforce Presbyterianism in England as well as Scotland. In 1651 he marched into England but was defeated by Oliver Cromwell at the battle of Worcester. Charles then escaped to France, where he lived in relative poverty. The Anglo-French negotiations of 1654 forced Charles into Germany, but he moved to the Spanish Netherlands after he had concluded (1656) a treaty with Spain. In 1660 Gen. George MONCK engineered Charles's RESTORATION to the throne, and the king returned to England. Charles had promised a general amnesty in his conciliatory Declaration of Breda, and he and Clarendon, who became first minister, acted immediately to secure passage of the Act of Indemnity, pardoning all except the REGICIDES. Charles also favored religious toleration (largely because of his own leanings toward Roman Catholicism), but the strongly Anglican Cavalier Parliament, which first convened in 1661, passed the series of statutes known as the CLARENDON CODE, which was designed to strike at religious nonconformity. The king attempted unsuccessfully to suspend these statutes by the declaration of indulgence of 1662, which he was forced (1663) to withdraw. Charles's government endorsed the foreign policy of the Commonwealth with its NAVIGATION ACTS, which contributed to the outbreak (1664) of the second of the DUTCH WARS. While the war was being waged, London suffered the great plague of 1665 and the fire of 1666. Clarendon fell from power in 1667, the year the war ended, to be replaced by the CABAL ministry. Charles then took England into the Triple Alliance (1668) with Holland and Sweden, but he simultaneously sought the support of Louis XIV of France, with whom he negotiated the secret Treaty of Dover (1670). By this treaty, designed to free the king from dependence on Parliament, Charles was to adopt Roman Catholicism, convert his subjects, and wage war against the Dutch, for which Louis was to advance him a large subsidy and 6,000 men. In 1672 the third Dutch War began. Many suspected it to be a cloak for the introduction of arbitrary government and Roman Catholicism. Charles was forced to rescind (1672) his second declaration of indulgence toward dissenters, to approve (1673) the TEST ACT, and to sign (1674) a peace with the Dutch. Thomas Osborne, earl of DANBY, became chief minister on the disintegration of the Cabal and inaugurated a foreign policy friendly to Holland. Charles, unable to secure money from an increasingly hostile Parliament, signed a series of secret agreements with Louis XIV, by which he received large French subsidies in return for a pro-French policy, although he feigned sympathy with the anti-French movement at home. His alliance with Louis, however, was broken (1677) by the marriage of his niece Mary to his nephew (and Louis's archenemy) William of Orange (later William III). Anti-Catholic feeling in England exploded (1678) in the affair of the Popish Plot (see OATES, TITUS), in which Charles did not intervene until his wife, CATHERINE OF BRAGANZA, was accused. However, the affair was made use of by the 1st earl of SHAFTESBURY, who led a movement to exclude Charles's brother, the Catholic duke of York (later JAMES II), from succession to the throne, promoting instead the claim of Charles's illegitimate son the duke of MONMOUTH. In 1681 the king dissolved Parliament to block passage of Shaftesbury's Exclusion Act, and thenceforth Charles ruled as an absolute monarch, without a Parliament. His personal popularity increased after the exclusion crisis and particularly after the unsuccessful RYE HOUSE PLOT. He took steps to root out the supporters of exclusion (now known as the Whigs) from positions of power, coercing municipal governments into obedience by the threat that he would rescind the city charters. Charles died a Roman Catholic and was succeeded by his brother James. He had no legitimate offspring but many children by his various mistresses, who included Lucy WALTER, Barbara Villiers (duchess of CLEVELAND), Louise Kéroualle (duchess of PORTSMOUTH), and Nell GWYN. Charles was a ruler of considerable political skill. His reign was marked by a gradual increase in the power of Parliament, which he learned to circumvent rather than manipulate. The period also saw the rise of the great political parties, WHIG and TORY; the advance of colonization and trade in India, America, and the East Indies; and the great progress of England as a sea power. The pleasure-loving character of the king set the tone of the brilliant Restoration period in art and literature. See contemporaneous accounts by Gilbert Burnet, John Evelyn, and Samual Pepys; letters ed. by Arthur Bryant (rev. ed. 1955) and Hesketh Pearson (1960); G. N. Clark, *The Later Stuarts* (2d ed. 1956); David Ogg, *England in the Reign of Charles II* (2 vol., 2d ed. 1962); studies by D. T. Witcombe (1966), M. P. Ashley (1971), and Christopher Falkus (1972).

Charles I, Frankish king: see CHARLEMAGNE.

Charles II, French King: see CHARLES II, emperor of the West.

Charles III or **Charles the Fat,** French king: see CHARLES III, emperor of the West.

Charles III (Charles the Simple), 879–929, French king (893–923), son of King Louis II (Louis the Stammerer). As a child he was excluded from the succession at the death (884) of his half brother Carloman and at the deposition (887) of King CHARLES III (Charles the Fat), who succeeded Carloman. Instead, EUDES, count of Paris, succeeded Charles the Fat. In 893, however, Charles was crowned by a party of nobles and prelates and became sole king at the death of Eudes in 898. He put an end to Norse raids by the Treaty of Saint-Clair-sur-Epte (911), ceding to the Norse leader Rollo part of the territory later known as Normandy, and in 911 Charles acquired Lorraine. In 922 some of the barons revolted and crowned Robert I, brother of Eudes, king. In 923, at the battle of Soissons, Robert was killed, but Charles was defeated. RAOUL of Burgundy was elected king, and Charles was imprisoned.

Charles IV (Charles the Fair), 1294–1328, king of France (1322–28), youngest son of Philip IV, brother and successor of Philip V. Charles continued his brother's work of strengthening the royal power. He also increased the royal revenues, notably by debasing the coinage. Pope John XXII, having declared Holy Roman Emperor Louis IV deposed, offered (1324) to support Charles for emperor, but the plan came to nothing. Charles invaded (1324) Guienne (Aquitaine), a possession of the English king, and in 1327 he compelled England to cede to France the Guienne districts around Agen and Bazas and to pay a large indemnity. The English, however, retained the rest of Guienne. Charles, the last king of the Capetian dynasty, was succeeded by Philip VI, of the Valois line.

Charles V (Charles the Wise), 1338–80, king of France (1364–80). Son of King JOHN II, Charles became the first French heir apparent to bear the title of dauphin after the addition of the region of Dauphiné to the royal domain in 1349. Regent during his father's captivity in England (1356–60, 1364), Charles dealt successfully with the JACQUERIE revolt, with the intrigues of King CHARLES II of Navarre, and with the popular movement headed by Etienne MARCEL, who had armed Paris against the dauphin. Becoming king in 1364, Charles stabilized the coinage and took steps to rid France of the companies of *écorcheurs,* marauding bands of discharged soldiers. Aided by his great general, Bertrand DU GUESCLIN, he almost succeeded in driving the English from France. Charles and his ministers, the MARMOUSETS, strengthened the royal authority, introduced a standing army, built a powerful navy, and instituted reforms that put fiscal authority more firmly in the hands of the crown. A patron of the arts and of learning, he established the royal library and interested himself in the embellishment of the Louvre and in the construction of the palace at Saint-Pol. However, his love of pomp and his lack of economy put a severe economic burden on the country. In the last year of his life he sided with Pope Clement VII against Pope Urban VI at the beginning of the Great Schism (see SCHISM, GREAT). His son, Charles VI, succeeded him.

Charles VI (Charles the Mad or Charles the Well Beloved), 1368–1422, king of France (1380–1422), son and successor of King Charles V. During his minority he was under the tutelage of his uncles (particularly PHILIP THE BOLD, duke of Burgundy), whose policies drained the royal treasury and provoked popular uprisings in France and in Flanders. Charles freed himself of this influence in 1388, took as his counselor his brother Louis, duc d'ORLÉANS, and recalled his father's ministers, the MARMOUSETS. After 1392, Charles suffered from recurrent insanity and was not active in the government. Philip of Burgundy returned to power. His rule was challenged by Louis d'Orléans and the conflict eventually resulted in war between Philip's successor, JOHN THE FEARLESS, and supporters of the Orleanists, known as Armagnacs (see ARMAGNACS AND BURGUNDIANS). The struggle was complicated by the invasion of France by King Henry V of England. In 1420, under the influence of the Burgundians, who were allied with Henry V and his wife ISABEL OF BAVARIA, Charles accepted the Treaty of TROYES, recognizing Henry V as his successor.

Charles VII (Charles the Well Served), 1403–61, king of France (1422–61), son and successor of Charles VI. His reign saw the end of the HUNDRED YEARS WAR. Although excluded from the throne by the Treaty of TROYES, Charles took the royal title after his father's death (1422) and ruled S of the Loire, while John of Lancaster, duke of BEDFORD, who was regent for King Henry VI of England, controlled the north and Guienne (Aquitaine). Vacillating and easily influenced by corrupt favorites, particularly Georges de LA TRÉMOILLE, Charles waged only perfunctory warfare against the English. He was prodded into action by the siege of Orléans (1429) in which JOAN OF ARC helped save the city from the English. After the capture of Orléans, Charles was crowned (1429) at Rheims. He reverted to his earlier inactivity until 1433, when La Trémoille was replaced by more scrupulous and energetic advisers, such as the comte de Richemont (later ARTHUR III, duke of Brittany) and the comte de DUNOIS. In 1435, Charles agreed to the Treaty of ARRAS, which reconciled him with the powerful duke, PHILIP THE GOOD of Burgundy, who had been an ally of the English. He recovered Paris the following year. In 1440, Charles suppressed the PRAGUERIE, and in 1444 a truce was signed with England, which lasted until 1449. By the battle of Formigny and the capture of Cherbourg (1450) the English were expelled from Normandy, and the battle of Castillon (1453) resulted in their withdrawal from Guienne. Charles, although dominated by his mistress, Agnès SOREL, proved an able administrator. He reorganized the army and remodeled French finances, established heavy taxation, particularly through the *taille,* a direct land tax. In 1438, Charles issued the PRAGMATIC SANCTION of Bourges, which established the liberty of the French Roman Catholic Church from Rome. In his reign commerce was expanded by the enterprise of Jacques CŒUR. The end of Charles's rule was disturbed by the intrigues of the dauphin, who succeeded him as LOUIS XI.

Charles VIII, 1470–98, king of France (1483–98), son and successor of Louis XI. He first reigned under the regency of his sister ANNE DE BEAUJEU. After his marriage (1491) to ANNE OF BRITTANY, he freed himself from the influence of the regency and prepared to conquer the kingdom of NAPLES, to which his father had acquired a claim through Charles, duke of Maine, from RENÉ of Naples. Urged by Ludovico SFORZA, he invaded (1494) Italy; after a triumphal march through Pavia, Florence, and Rome, he took (Feb., 1495) Naples. A league against him, formed by Milan, Venice, Spain, Holy Roman Emperor Maximilian I, and Pope Alexander VI, forced his hasty retreat, in which he distinguished himself against odds at the battle of Fornovo (July, 1495). His remaining troops in Naples were defeated, and at the time of his death he was forming new plans of conquest. He left no male heir and was succeeded by his cousin Louis XII. The conflict of France and Spain in Italy marked the beginning of the ITALIAN WARS. Charles's expedition fostered the introduction of the Italian Renaissance in France. The history of his reign was recorded by his contemporary, Philippe de COMINES. See J. S. C. Bridge, *A History of France from the Death of Louis XI,* Vol. I–II (1922–24).

Charles IX, 1550–74, king of France. He succeeded (1560) his brother Francis II under the regency of his mother, CATHERINE DE' MEDICI. She retained her influence throughout his reign. After 1570, however, Charles was temporarily under the sway of the French Huguenot leader Gaspard de COLIGNY. Catherine, fearing for her power, persuaded her weak son to approve the massacre of SAINT BARTHOLOMEW'S DAY in which Coligny and thousands of other Huguenots were murdered. Charles IX was succeeded by his brother Henry III.

Charles X, 1757–1836, king of France (1824–30); brother of King Louis XVI and of King Louis XVIII, whom he succeeded. As comte d'Artois he headed the reactionary faction at the court of Louis XVI. He left France (July, 1789) at the outbreak of the French Revolution and became a leading spirit of the ÉMIGRÉ party. After his failure to aid the VENDÉE insurrection, he stayed in England until the Bourbon restoration (1814). During the reign of LOUIS XVIII he headed the ultraroyalist opposition, which triumphed after the assassination (1820) of Charles's son the duc de BERRY. The event caused the fall of the ministry of Élie DECAZES and the advent of the comte de VILLELE, who continued as chief minister after Charles's accession. Among the many attempts of Charles and Villèle to reestablish the ancien régime, as the prerevolutionary order is called, the law (1825) indemnifying the émigrés for lands confiscated during the Revolution and measures increasing the power of the clergy met with particular disapproval. The bourgeoisie and the liberal press joined in attacking the Villèle cabinet, which resigned in 1827. Villèle's successor, the vicomte de MARTIGNAC, vainly tried to steer a middle course, and in 1829 Charles appointed an uncompromising reactionary, Jules Armand de POLIGNAC, as chief minister. To divert attention from internal affairs, Polignac initiated the French venture in ALGERIA. However, his dissolution (March, 1830) of the liberal chamber of deputies and his drastic July Ordinances, establishing rigid control of the press, dissolving the newly elected chamber, and restricting suffrage, resulted in the JULY REVOLUTION. Charles abdicated in favor of his grandson, the comte de CHAMBORD, and embarked for England. However, the duc d'Orléans, whom Charles had appointed lieutenant general of France, was chosen "king of the French" as LOUIS PHILIPPE. See studies by V. W. Beach (1967 and 1971).

Charles I, 1288–1342, king of Hungary (1308–42), founder of the ANGEVIN dynasty in Hungary; grandson of Charles II of Naples, who had married a daughter of Stephen V of Hungary. On the death (1301) of Andrew III, last of the Arpad dynasty, Charles was the candidate of Pope Boniface VIII for the crown of St. Stephen, but the Hungarians elected WENCESLAUS III of Bohemia; in 1308 the Hungarian diet at last chose Charles, who was crowned in 1310. He reorganized the army on a feudal basis, using the nobility for its personnel, and taxed the bourgeoisie. Silver and gold mines became state monopolies, and in 1338 gold became the accepted currency. He encouraged trade and increased the privileges of the cities. He married his second son to Joanna I of Naples and took as his second wife Elizabeth, daughter of King Ladislaus I of Poland. In 1339 he secured the succession to Casimir III of Poland for his eldest son, later Louis I of Hungary.

Charles II, king of Hungary: see CHARLES III, king of Naples.

Charles III, king of Hungary: see CHARLES VI, Holy Roman emperor.

Charles IV, king of Hungary: see CHARLES I, emperor of Austria.

Charles I (Charles of Anjou), 1227–85, king of Naples and Sicily (1266–85), count of Anjou and Provence, youngest brother of King Louis IX of France. He took part in Louis's crusades to Egypt (1248) and Tunisia (1270). After obtaining Provence by marriage (1246), he extended his influence into Piedmont. He became senator of Rome (1263, 1265–78) and undertook to champion the papal cause against MANFRED in the kingdom of Naples and Sicily. In reward, he was crowned king (1266) by Pope Clement IV. Charles defeated (1266) Manfred at Benevento and defeated and executed CONRADIN in 1268. As leader of the Guelphs, or papal faction, he gained political hegemony in Italy and won suzerainty over several cities in Tuscany, Piedmont, and Lombardy, but his overbearing policies led to a cooling of his relations with the papacy. Planning to establish his own empire, he allied himself with the deposed Byzantine emperor, BALDWIN II, against MICHAEL VIII and fought for years in the Balkans. Corfu, Epirus, and Albania were taken, but the crushing taxes necessitated by his wars and his appointment of oppressive French officials to exact them led to the SICILIAN VESPERS (1282). The ensuing war against the Sicilian rebels and PETER III of Aragón, chosen by the rebels as king of Sicily, continued under Charles's son and successor, Charles II. Charles I was the founder of the first ANGEVIN dynasty in Naples.

Charles II (Charles the Lame), 1248–1309, king of Naples (1285–1309), count of Anjou and Provence, son and successor of CHARLES I. In the war of the SICILIAN VESPERS between Charles I and Peter III of Aragón for possession of Sicily, Charles was captured (1284) in a naval battle by the Aragonese. His father died while he was in captivity and Charles succeeded to the Neapolitan throne, although he was not crowned until 1289, following his release. The war in Sicily against James (JAMES II of Aragón), son and successor of Peter III, continued until James's renunciation of Sicily and recognition of Charles II as king in 1295. The Sicilians, however, refused to accept the reestablishment of French rule and set up James's brother, FREDERICK II, as king; war was resumed. Finally, in 1302, after the failure of a French expedition to Sicily sponsored by Pope Boniface VIII, the Peace of Caltabellotta was signed; Charles II and Pope Boniface VIII agreed that Frederick II would remain king, but Sicily was to go to Charles or his heir on Frederick's death.

Charles III (Charles of Durazzo), 1345-86, king of Naples (1381-86) and, as Charles II, of Hungary (1385-86); great-grandson of Charles II of Naples. Adopted as a child by JOANNA I of Naples, he later lived at the court of Louis I of Hungary. In 1380, Pope Urban VI summoned Charles to dethrone Joanna because of her support of the antipope, Clement IV; Joanna repudiated Charles as her heir in favor of Louis of Anjou (see LOUIS I, king of Naples). Charles conquered Naples, imprisoned Joanna, and was crowned (1381) by the pope. Joanna died by his order. Charles repulsed attacks on Naples by Louis of Anjou. In 1385, elected king of Hungary over SIGISMUND, Charles was crowned but was soon assassinated. He was succeeded in Naples by his son, Lancelot, and in Hungary by Sigismund.

Charles II (Charles the Bad), 1332-87, king of Navarre (1349-87), count of Évreux; grandson of King Louis X of France. He carried on a long feud with his father-in-law, John II, king of France, procuring the assassination (1354) of John's favorite, Charles de La Cerda, and forming an alliance with King Edward III of England. In 1356 Charles was treacherously seized by John and imprisoned, but he was rescued after the capture of John at Poitiers. He helped to suppress (1358) the JACQUERIE revolt and was chosen by Étienne MARCEL to defend Paris against the dauphin (later King Charles V), but he betrayed this trust. Until his death he was involved in quarrels with Charles V and with Castile and in intrigues with England.

Charles III (Charles the Good), 1361-1425, king of Navarre (1387-1425), count of Évreux; son and successor of Charles II. He settled (1404) his inherited differences with France and later tried to negotiate between the Armagnacs and Burgundians. His reign was peaceful and beneficent. His daughter Blanche and her husband, John (later John II of Aragón), succeeded him.

Charles I, 1863-1908, king of Portugal (1889-1908), son and successor of Louis I. A cultured man, learned in language and oceanography, Charles had little opportunity to display his administrative talents in a reign beset by political stagnation and financial troubles. Portuguese and British ambitions clashed over Africa, and in 1890, Great Britain issued an ultimatum demanding that the Portuguese cease attempts to expand their African empire. The Portuguese complied, but the issue raised strong feeling against Charles's rule. Financial affairs grew worse, and Germany sought to obtain part of the Portuguese African empire. After a revolt in 1906, Charles empowered João Franco, head of the Regenerator (conservative) party, to establish a dictatorial government. This provoked another revolt in 1908, in the course of which Charles and his eldest son were assassinated in a public square in Lisbon. Charles's second son, MANUEL II, succeeded to the throne.

Charles I and **Charles II,** kings of Rumania: see CAROL I and CAROL II.

Charles I, king of Spain: see CHARLES V, Holy Roman emperor.

Charles II, 1661-1700, king of Spain, Naples, and Sicily (1665-1700), son and successor of Philip IV. The last of the Spanish Hapsburgs, he was physically crippled and mentally retarded. His mother, Mariana of Austria, was regent for him and continued to rule after his majority. Her bias in favor of Austria aroused opposition, and she was forced into exile (1677) by Charles's illegitimate brother, JOHN OF AUSTRIA. After John's death (1679) she again exercised power. Charles's reign saw the continued loss of Spanish foreign power, as was evident in the War of DEVOLUTION and the War of the GRAND ALLIANCE, and a severe decline in Spain's economy, society, and intellectual life. The indolent grandees and the clergy regained a political role. Tax exemptions for privileged groups brought high taxes on industry and agriculture, and emigration increased. Before his death the childless Charles named Philip of Anjou as his heir. Philip's succession (as Philip V) provoked the War of the SPANISH SUCCESSION.

Charles III, 1716-88, king of Spain (1759-88) and of Naples and Sicily (1735-59), son of Philip V and ELIZABETH FARNESE. Recognized as duke of Parma and Piacenza in 1731, he relinquished the duchies to Austria after conquering (1734) Naples and Sicily in the War of the POLISH SUCCESSION. His reign in Naples was beneficent. In 1759 he succeeded his half brother, Ferdinand VI, to the Spanish throne, Naples and Sicily passing to his third son, Ferdinand (later Ferdinand I of the Two Sicilies). Charles at first was neutral in the SEVEN YEARS WAR, but after concluding the FAMILY COMPACT of 1761 with France, he involved Spain in the war in time to share France's defeat. By the Treaty of Paris of 1763 he ceded Florida to England but received Louisiana from France. Territorial disputes with Portugal in the Río de la Plata region were settled by the Treaty of San Ildefonso (1777). In the American Revolution, Charles entered (1779) the war on the American side and by the Treaty of Paris of 1783 regained Florida and Minorca. Spain prospered under the rule of Charles, who is regarded as the greatest Bourbon king of Spain and one of the "enlightened despots." His reign is noted for economic and administrative reforms and for the expulsion of the Jesuits (1767). Charles was ably assisted by ARANDA, FLORIDABLANCA, Campomanes, and Jovellanos. He was succeeded by his son Charles IV. See biography by C. A. Petrie (1971).

Charles IV, 1748-1819, king of Spain (1788-1808), second son of Charles III, whom he succeeded in place of his imbecile older brother. Unlike his father, Charles IV was an ineffective ruler and in 1792 virtually surrendered the government to GODOY, his chief minister and the lover of his wife, María Luisa. Spain entered the French Revolutionary Wars in 1793, but in 1795 made peace with France in the second Treaty of Basel. By the Treaty of San Ildefonso (1796) Spain allied itself with France and became involved in the war with England. It suffered major naval defeats at Cape St. Vincent (1797) and Trafalgar (1805). The convention of Fontainebleau (1807) precipitated the events leading to the PENINSULAR WAR. As French troops marched on Madrid in March, 1808, a popular uprising led to a coup d'etat at Aranjuez; the king was forced to abdicate in favor of his son, FERDINAND VII. Napoleon I tricked both father and son into a meeting with him at Bayonne, France, and forced them to abdicate in turn. The royal family was held captive in France until 1814, while Joseph Bonaparte was king of Spain. Charles IV and his family have been frankly portrayed by Goya, who enjoyed their favor.

Charles IX, 1550-1611, king of Sweden (1604-11), youngest son of Gustavus I. He was duke of Södermanland, Närke, and Värmland before his accession. During the reign of his brother, John III (1568-92), he opposed John's leanings toward Catholicism. After John's death he acted as regent, summoned (1593) an assembly of clergy and nobles to Uppsala, and had it establish Lutheranism as the state religion. This measure was passed in anticipation of the arrival (1594) of John III's Catholic son and heir, King SIGISMUND III of Poland, who was obliged to pledge himself to uphold Protestantism in Sweden as a condition for his coronation. Sigismund left Sweden in the same year, and Charles summoned the Riksdag, was made regent against the king's wishes, and ousted all Catholic officials. The Swedish nobles were loyal to Sigismund, but the people supported Charles. Sigismund landed an army at Kalmar (1598), was defeated by Charles at Stangebro, and was deposed by the Riksdag in 1599. To consolidate his power Charles had most of his opponents executed, but he refused to accept the Swedish crown until Sigismund's brother, John, renounced it in 1604. In 1600 he invaded Livonia and thus began the long Polish-Swedish wars that ended only with the Peace of OLIVA in 1660. Charles's claim to Lapland involved him in the unsuccessful Kalmar War (1611-13) with CHRISTIAN IV of Denmark. He died before the conclusion of the war and was succeeded by his son, Gustavus II.

Charles X, 1622-60, king of Sweden (1654-60), nephew of Gustavus II. The son of John Casimir, count palatine of Zweibrücken, he brought the house of Wittelsbach to the Swedish throne when his cousin, Queen CHRISTINA, abdicated in his favor. Before his accession, Charles had gained both military and diplomatic experience, fighting under TORSTENSSON in the Thirty Years War and serving under Chancellor OXENSTIERNA. As king, Charles remedied Christina's loss of crown lands by securing their restitution at the Riksdag of 1655. He reopened hostilities with Poland and took Warsaw and Kraków in 1655, but Polish resistance became formidable after the heroic and successful defense of CZĘSTOCHOWA. Charles's position deteriorated quickly. Czar Alexis of Russia invaded Livonia, FREDERICK III of Denmark declared war (1657) on Sweden, and Frederick William of Brandenburg deserted his alliance with Sweden. Charles hastened to Denmark, crossed the frozen sea to threaten Copenhagen, and forced the Danes to make peace. By the Treaty of Roskilde (1658) Sweden's southern boundary was extended to the sea; Denmark ceded to Sweden the provinces of Skåne, Halland, Blekinge, and Bohuslan and also Bornholm and part of Norway. Denmark's refusal to renounce an alliance with the Netherlands caused Charles to resume the war in 1658. England, the Netherlands, and France intervened in favor of Denmark. Charles, after concluding a truce with Russia (1658), began to negotiate for a general peace. He died suddenly before the negotiations were ended and was succeeded by his son, Charles XI. His wars were settled to the advantage of Sweden. By the Treaty of Copenhagen (1660) Sweden regained its four southern provinces from Denmark and by the Treaty of Kardis (1661) with Russia the two countries returned to the prewar status quo. (For the settlement with Poland, see OLIVA, PEACE OF.) During Charles's reign Sweden lost NEW SWEDEN in America to the Dutch.

Charles XI, 1655-97, king of Sweden (1660-97), son and successor of Charles X. Charles ascended the throne at the age of five, so a council of regency ruled until 1672. The regency ended Swedish wars with favorable peace treaties (see CHARLES X), but mismanaged internal affairs. On reaching his majority Charles obtained from the Riksdag the restitution of the crown lands that had been given away. Sweden was involved in the third of the DUTCH WARS as an ally of Louis XIV. Charles was defeated (1675) at Fehrbellin by FREDERICK WILLIAM of Brandenburg, who overran Swedish Pomerania, known also as Hither Pomerania. Against Denmark Charles was more successful, particularly at Landskrona (1677). At the Treaty of Saint-Germain (1679) with Brandenburg, Charles, through the influence of Louis XIV, regained Hither Pomerania. The Peace of Lund (1679) with Denmark drew the Scandinavian nations closer together, and in 1680, Charles married Princess Ulrika of Denmark. In Sweden Charles set about increasing the royal power at the expense of the nobles. The Riksdag of 1682 gave him absolute power, which he used efficiently. His son succeeded him as Charles XII.

Charles XII, 1682-1718, king of Sweden (1697-1718), son and successor of Charles XI. The regency under which he succeeded was abolished in 1697 at the request of the Riksdag. At the coronation he omitted the usual oath and crowned himself. Charles's youth and inexperience invited the coalition (1699) of PETER I of Russia, AUGUSTUS II of Poland and Saxony, and FREDERICK IV of Denmark that challenged Swedish supremacy in the Baltics. The resulting NORTHERN WAR quickly revealed Charles's abilities. In one of the most brilliant campaigns in history, Charles forced Denmark to make peace (Aug., 1700), defeated Peter I at Narva (Nov., 1700), subjugated Courland (1701), invaded Poland and, declaring Augustus II dethroned, secured the election (1704) of STANISLAUS I as king of Poland. In 1706 he invaded Saxony and forced Augustus to recognize Stanislaus as king, end his alliance with Russia, and surrender his adviser, PATKUL, whom Charles then had broken on the wheel. Charles then concentrated on his chief enemy, Peter I. He secured the alliance of the Cossack leader MAZEPA and invaded Russia in 1708. The Swedish army was outnumbered, weakened by long marches and a cold winter, and without the active leadership of Charles, who was wounded; it suffered a disastrous defeat by the Russians at Poltava. Much of the army was captured, and Charles fled to Turkey, where he persuaded Sultan AHMAD III to declare war (1710) on Russia. After the Peace of the Pruth (1711) between Russia and Turkey, Charles, who had taken residence near Bender in Bessarabia, became an increasingly unwelcome guest. He was requested to leave Turkey but obstinately refused. A whole Turkish army was sent (1713) to dislodge him from his house; Charles defended it with a handful of men for several hours until he was forced by fire to make a sortie. Taken prisoner and detained near Adrianople, he feigned sickness for over a year. Late in 1714 he unexpectedly arrived at Swedish-occupied Stralsund and defended it against the Prussians and the Danes until Dec., 1715. When it fell he escaped to Sweden and proceeded to invade (1716) Norway. He was killed in the Swedish trenches while besieging the fortress of Fredriksten. He was succeeded by his sister, Ulrica Leonora, who was forced to recognize a new constitution that gave most of the power to the nobles and clergy. During her reign the Northern War ended (1721) with substantial Swedish losses. Charles's amazing military ability, his grandiose ambitions, and his perseverance through the greatest hardships have made him one of the heroes of modern times. His final failure cost Sweden its rank as a great power. The classic biography is Voltaire's *History of Charles XII.* See also biographies by R. N. Bain (1895, repr. 1969), J. A. Gade (1916), F. G. Bengtsson (tr. 1960), and R. M. Hatton (1968).

Charles XIII, 1748–1818, king of Sweden (1809–18) and Norway (1814–18). He became regent for his nephew, GUSTAVUS IV, after the assassination (1792) of his brother Gustavus III. He introduced some liberal policies, but these were abandoned at the end of his regency (1796). Called to the throne at the forced abdication (1809) of his nephew, Charles accepted a new constitution that limited the monarch's power, and he signed treaties with Denmark and France and a treaty ceding Finland to Russia. In 1810 he adopted the French marshal Bernadotte (later King Charles XIV) as his heir, and thereafter left all affairs in his hands.

Charles XIV (Charles John; Jean Baptiste Jules Bernadotte) (zhäN bäptēst' zhül bĕrnädôt'), 1763–1844, king of Sweden and Norway (1818–44), French Revolutionary general. Bernadotte rose from the ranks, served brilliantly under Napoleon Bonaparte in the Italian campaign (1796–97), was French ambassador at Vienna (1798), and was minister of war (1799). He had a prominent part in the victory of Austerlitz in 1805. Napoleon made him marshal of the empire (1804) and prince of Ponte Corvo (1806). However, his relations with the emperor were cool. While commanding in N Germany he negotiated with the Swedes, who were impressed by his generous conduct. In 1809, GUSTAVUS IV of Sweden abdicated and was succeeded by his aged and childless uncle, Charles XIII. In need of both a suitable successor to Charles and an alliance with Napoleon, Sweden turned to Bernadotte. After receiving the support of Napoleon and joining the Lutheran Church the marshal accepted. He was elected crown prince by the Riksdag and adopted (1810) by Charles XIII as Charles John. The infirmity of the old king and the dissensions in the council of state put the reins of government in the hands of the crown prince. He favored the acquisition of Norway from Denmark rather than the reconquest of Finland from Russia, and thus he threw in his lot with Russia and England against Napoleon and Denmark. His Swedish contingent played an important part in the defeat of Napoleon at the battle of Leipzig (1813), and in 1814, having marched his army into Denmark, he forced the Danes to cede Norway in the Treaty of Kiel. Norway, which had declared its independence, was subdued, and by a majority vote of the Norwegian Storting (1814) the country was united with Sweden under a single king. The Congress of Vienna confirmed the union but restored the town of Ponte Corvo to the pope. He succeeded to the throne in 1818 as Charles XIV. He maintained peace throughout his reign, which was marked by internal improvements, notably the completion of the Göta Canal and a reform of the school system. However, his increasing opposition to the liberals made him unpopular by the end of his reign. The founder of the present Swedish dynasty, he was succeeded by his son, Oscar I. See D. P. Barton, *Bernadotte: The First Phase* (1914), *Bernadotte and Napoleon* (1920), and *Bernadotte, Prince and King* (1925); F. D. Scott, *Bernadotte and the Fall of Napoleon* (1935).

Charles XV, 1826–72, king of Sweden and Norway (1859–72), son and successor of Oscar I. A liberal and popular ruler, he consented to many reforms, including the creation of a bicameral parliament. He was succeeded by his brother, Oscar II.

Charles XVI Gustavus (Carl Gustaf), 1946–, king of Sweden (1973–), grandson and successor of Gustavus VI; son of Prince Gustaf Adolf of Sweden and Princess Sibylla of Saxe-Coburg-Gotha. Brought up by his grandfather and mother after the death of his father in 1947, he attended a Swedish boarding school, served in the armed forces, and studied for a year at Uppsala Univ. A new constitution, passed shortly before his grandfather's death and effective in 1975, made the king a ceremonial figurehead, divesting him of traditional status as supreme commander of the armed forces and of the right to formally nominate new premiers and to open the Swedish parliament.

Charles (Charles Philip Arthur George), 1948–, prince of Wales, eldest son of Queen Elizabeth II of Great Britain and heir apparent to the British throne. He was created prince of Wales in 1958 and invested with that title in a colorful ceremony at Caernarvon Castle in 1969. A graduate of Cambridge Univ., Charles entered the Royal Navy in 1971.

Charles, 1771–1847, archduke of Austria; brother of Holy Roman Emperor Francis II. Despite his epilepsy, he was the ablest Austrian commander in the French Revolutionary and Napoleonic wars; however, he was handicapped by unwise decisions imposed on him from Vienna. After the disastrous campaign of 1805, Charles was appointed minister of war and chief commander of the Austrian forces. He reorganized the army and headed the patriotic faction at court. In 1809 he defeated Napoleon I at Aspern (May) but was beaten at Wagram (July). In both battles he exacted a heavy toll from the French. Shortly afterward he retired because of political differences with Francis. He was also called Charles Louis. See F. L. Petre, *Napoleon and the Archduke Charles* (1908).

Charles I, 953–992?, duke of Lower Lorraine (977–91); younger son of King Louis IV of France. He claimed the French throne when his nephew, Louis V of France, died (987) without issue, but he was set aside in favor of HUGH CAPET. Charles seized Laon (988) and Rheims (989), but was betrayed (991) by the bishop of Laon, who turned him over to Hugh. Charles died in prison. With the death of his sons the French Carolingian dynasty ended.

Charles IV, 1604–75, duke of Lorraine. He succeeded to the duchy in 1624 but was to lose it several times because of his anti-French policy. In 1633, French troops invaded Lorraine in retaliation for Charles's support of Gaston d'ORLÉANS. Forced to make humiliating concessions to France, he abdicated (1634) in favor of his brother and entered the imperial service in the Thirty Years War. He briefly recovered his lands in 1641 and 1644, but he was excluded from the Peace of Westphalia (1648) at the war's conclusion. Although he joined the Spanish during the FRONDE, he communicated with the French government and as a result was imprisoned by the Spanish (1654–59). In 1661, at the price of heavy concessions to King Louis XIV, Charles recovered Lorraine and the duchy of Bar. Expelled once more by the French in 1670, Charles later helped to instigate the alliance of Spain and the Holy Roman emperor with the Dutch in the third of the DUTCH WARS. In 1675 he defeated François de Créquy at Konzer Bruck.

Charles V (Charles Leopold), 1643–90, duke of Lorraine; nephew of Duke Charles IV. Deprived of the rights of succession to the duchy, he was forced to leave France and entered the service of the Holy Roman emperor. He was twice a candidate for the Polish crown (1669 and 1674). Although he took the ducal title on his uncle's death in 1675, France still held Lorraine. He was commander of the imperialist forces in the third of the Dutch Wars. At Nijmegen he refused (1678) to accept Lorraine on King Louis XIV's terms. He took part in the defense of Vienna (1683) and in expelling the Turks from Hungary. Charles V married (1678) Eleanora Maria, sister of Holy Roman Emperor Leopold I.

Charles, Jacques Alexandre César (zhäk älĕksäN'-drə säzär' shärl), 1746–1823, French physicist. He confirmed Benjamin Franklin's electrical experiments, became interested in aeronautics, and was the first to use hydrogen gas in balloons. In this type of balloon, known as the Charlière, he made an ascent in 1783 of almost 2 mi (3.2 km). He became professor of physics at the Conservatoire des Arts et Métiers, Paris. Inventor of a thermometric hydrometer, he also improved various devices, the Gravesande heliostat and Fahrenheit's aerometer among others, and anticipated Gay-Lussac's law of the expansion of gases. For Charles's law, see GAS LAWS.

Charles, Thomas, 1755–1814, Welsh nonconformist clergyman. He was brought up under Methodist influence, attended Oxford (1775–78), and was ordained in the Church of England. He held curacies in Somersetshire but resigned them and returned to Bala, Wales, where in 1784 he joined the CALVINISTIC METHODIST CHURCH. Gifted in working with children, he began (1785) to establish Welsh language schools. He secured and distributed thousands of Welsh Bibles and helped to found the British and Foreign Bible Society (see BIBLE SOCIETIES). At Bala in 1803, Charles established a printing press for Welsh textbooks. See William Hughes, ed., *Life and Letters of the Rev. Thomas Charles* (1881).

Charles, William, 1776–1820, American cartoonist, etcher, and engraver, b. Edinburgh, Scotland. He probably came to the United States to avoid prosecution for his satirical drawings. He is best known for his cartoons of the War of 1812, in which he mocked the English in the rough, biting style of Gillray. An example of his work is *Admiral Cockburn Burning and Plundering Havre-de-Grace* (Maryland Historical Society).

Charles, river, c.60 mi (97 km) long, rising in E Mass. and flowing generally NE to Boston Bay. Boat races are held on the river.

Charles Albert, 1798–1849, king of Sardinia (1831–49), first king of the Savoy-Carignano line (see SAVOY, HOUSE OF). Although not entirely unsympathetic to the revolutionary movement in Sardinia, Charles Albert nevertheless informed his relative, King VICTOR EMMANUEL I, of the impending uprising of 1821. Upon Victor Emmanuel's subsequent abdication in favor of his brother Charles Felix, Charles Albert was temporarily appointed regent pending the new ruler's arrival. He granted a constitution, which Charles Felix repudiated. Having fallen into royal disfavor for this liberalism, Charles Albert went into exile and in 1823 participated in crushing a liberal regime in Spain to regain Charles Felix's good graces. After Charles Felix died, Charles Albert acceded to the throne. He issued a new code of law, abolished internal tariffs, and, to forestall a revolution, granted (1848) a constitution. He twice declared war on Austria, fighting two campaigns (1848, 1849) during the RISORGIMENTO. Successful at first, he was routed at Custozza (1848) and again at Novara (1849). Charles Albert then abdicated in favor of his son, Victor Emmanuel II, and went into exile in Portugal, where he soon died.

Charles Augustus, 1757–1828, duke and, after 1815, grand duke of Saxe-Weimar-Eisenach; friend and patron of Goethe, Schiller, and Herder. Though his duchy was small, he was important in German politics. He helped FREDERICK II of Prussia form (1785) the *Fürstenbund* [league of princes] to check Austria's attempt under Holy Roman Emperor JOSEPH II to expand Austrian influence in the empire. He fought in the French Revolutionary Wars and against Napoleon I until 1806, when he was forced to join the CONFEDERATION OF THE RHINE. At the Congress of Vienna after Napoleon's defeat his duchy was enlarged and he was raised to a grand duke. Assisted by Goethe, he made WEIMAR a center of literature, science, art, and liberal political thought. In 1816 he introduced a constitution.

Charles Borromeo, Saint (bōrōmĕ'ō), 1538–84, Italian churchman, b. near Lago Maggiore. His uncle, PIUS IV, summoned Charles, a student at Pavia, to Rome in 1560. In rapid order he was made cardinal-deacon, administrator of the Papal States and of the archdiocese of Milan, and papal secretary of state. Despite a large personal fortune, St. Charles lived a simple, ascetic life. He was most zealous in encouraging reform in the church and was largely responsible for reopening (1560) the Council of Trent, of which he was the guiding spirit. In 1563 he was ordained priest, consecrated bishop, and then received the pallium for the see of Milan. He was 28 years old when, at Milan, he began introducing vigorous reforms, especially in the education of the clergy, enforcing the council's decrees for the institution of diocesan seminaries. He was exceedingly strict with the clergy, and he met much opposition. In 1569 some disaffected men tried to assassinate him. He worked untiringly to alleviate suffering in the pestilence of 1576. He was an exemplary pastor. There is a huge statue of him near Lago Maggiore and a monument to him in the cathedral at Milan, which he had completely redecorated. Feast: Nov. 4.

Charlesbourg (shärl'bŏŏrg), city (1971 pop. 33,443), S Que., Canada. It is a northern suburb of Quebec city. One of the oldest parishes in the province, it includes part of the seigniory first granted to the Jesuits in 1626 and was settled in 1659. Its earlier name was Bourg Royal.

Charles d'Orléans: see ORLÉANS, CHARLES, DUC D'.

Charles Edward Stuart: see STUART, CHARLES EDWARD.

Charles Emmanuel I, 1562–1630, duke of Savoy (1580–1630), son and successor of EMMANUEL PHILIBERT. He continued his father's efforts to recover territories lost to the duchy, but his reckless, although cunning, diplomacy undermined many of the sound economic and political achievements of the previous decades. His goal to incorporate Geneva, Saluzzo, and MONTFERRAT into Savoy caused him to oscillate in his alliances between France and Spain. In the long run he met with only limited success. In 1602 he tried unsuccessfully to reconquer Geneva by surprise attack. He recovered Saluzzo from the French by the Treaty of Lyons (1601), giving up, in exchange, Bresse, Bugey, Gex, and Pinerolo, but he lost Saluzzo just before his death. He waged war over the succession to Montferrat for much of the first quarter of the 16th cent. At the time of his death his duchy was overrun by the French. Charles Emmanuel, called the Great, was succeeded by his son, Victor Amadeus I.

Charles Martel (märtĕl') [O.Fr., = Charles the Hammer], 688?–741, Frankish ruler, illegitimate son of PEPIN OF HERISTAL and grandfather of Charlemagne. After the death of his father (714) he seized power in Austrasia from Pepin's widow, who was ruling as regent for her grandsons, and became mayor of the palace. He subsequently subdued the W Frankish kingdom of Neustria and began the reconquest of Burgundy, Aquitaine, and Provence. Having subjugated many of the German tribes across the Rhine, he encouraged the activities of St. BONIFACE and other missionaries among them; he did not, however, support the papacy against the LOMBARDS. Charles Martel halted the advance of the Muslims of Spain by his victory in the battle of Tours (732). Although he never assumed the title of king, he divided the Frankish lands, like a king, between his sons Pepin the Short and Carloman. See Ferdinand Lot, *The End of the Ancient World and the Beginnings of the Middle Ages* (1927 tr. 1961).

Charles Mound, hill, 1,241 ft (378 m) high, NW Ill., near the Wis. line; highest point in the state.

Charles of Blois (Charles of Châtillon) (blwä, shätēyôN'), c.1319–1364, duke of Brittany; nephew of Philip VI of France. He was one of the chief participants in the War of the BRETON SUCCESSION and was killed at the battle of Auray. An extremely pious man, he has been beatified.

Charles of Valois (välwä'), 1270–1325, French prince and military leader, third son of Philip III and father of Philip VI. He dominated the reign in France of his nephew Louis X. On the excommunication (1284) of PETER III of Aragón, Pope Martin IV made Charles of Valois king of Aragón and Sicily. Charles, however, was defeated and in 1290 renounced his claim. In return he received Anjou and Maine as part of the dowry of his first wife (the daughter of Charles II of Naples). Later he unsuccessfully sought to obtain the crowns of the Byzantine and Holy Roman empires, which he held claim to through his second wife. At different times he also tried to secure the crowns of Arles and France, where he hoped to be regent after the death of Louis X. He campaigned for Pope Boniface VIII in Italy and took Florence in 1301.

Charles of Viana (vēä'nä), 1421–61, Spanish prince, heir of Navarre; son of Blanche of Navarre and John (later JOHN II) of Aragón. After his mother's death (1441) he ruled Navarre for his father, but serious differences between the two soon plunged the country into civil war. He was twice imprisoned by his father and died shortly after an uprising in Catalonia had forced John to recognize him as his heir.

Charles River Bridge Case, decided in 1837 by the U.S. Supreme Court. The Charles River Bridge Company had been granted (1785) a charter by the state of Massachusetts to operate a toll bridge. The state later authorized (1828) a competing bridge that would eventually be free to the public. The Charles River Bridge Company brought suit against the competing company, claiming that the state charter had given it a monopoly. The court upheld the state's authorization to the other company, holding that since the original charter did not specifically grant a monopoly, the ambiguity in the contract would operate in favor of the public, thus allowing a competing bridge. The holding modified the DARTMOUTH COLLEGE CASE, which held that a state could not unilaterally amend a charter.

Charles's law: see GAS LAWS.

Charles the Bad: see CHARLES II, king of Navarre.

Charles the Bald, French king: see CHARLES II, emperor of the West.

Charles the Bold, 1433–77, last reigning duke of Burgundy (1467–77), son and successor of PHILIP THE GOOD. As the count of Charolais before his accession, he opposed the growing power of King LOUIS XI of France by joining (1465) the League of Public Weal. In 1468 he had Louis arrested during their interview at Péronne and compelled him to help in subduing Liège, where Louis had incited a revolt. Charles allied himself with England by his marriage (1468) to Margaret, the sister of King Edward IV. Master of the Low Countries, Charles ruled Burgundy, Flanders, Artois, Brabant, Luxembourg, Holland, Zeeland, Friesland, and Hainault; he dreamed of reestablishing the kingdom of LOTHARINGIA. He needed Alsace, Lorraine, and a royal title to achieve his goal. In 1473 he met Holy Roman Emperor Frederick III at Trier to arrange a marriage between his daughter Mary and Frederick's son, the future Maximilian I; Charles was to have been crowned king of Lotharingia. However, the emperor broke off negotiations; the marriage took place (1477) only after Charles's death. Meanwhile, Charles continued to conquer the lands that separated his possessions. His struggles with the Alsatian towns and his occupation (1473) of Lorraine alienated the Swiss cantons, which were allied with France. In 1474 war broke out between Charles and the Swiss. Charles's English ally, Edward IV, invaded France (1475), but accepted a bribe from Louis XI and ceased hostilities. Charles was routed (1476) by the Swiss at Grandson and Morat. Early in 1477, at Nancy, Charles was defeated utterly and killed by the Swiss and the Lorrainers. His heiress, MARY OF BURGUNDY, lost part of her possessions to France, the rest passing to the Hapsburgs through her marriage with Maximilian. Once powerful Burgundy ceased to exist as a state. Charles, who earned his surname by his impetuous gallantry, was a capable, though harsh, ruler; however, his achievements were short-lived. See the chronicles of Philippe de COMINES; biographies by J. F. Kirk (3 vol., 1863–68) and Richard Vaughan (1974); J. L. A. Calmette, *The Golden Age of Burgundy* (tr. 1962).

Charles the Fat, French king: see CHARLES III, emperor of the West.

Charles the Great, Frankish king, emperor of the West: see CHARLEMAGNE.

Charleston. 1 City (1970 pop. 16,421), seat of Coles co., E Ill.; inc. 1835. Shoes, electronic equipment, farm buildings, and tools are manufactured in this industrial, rail, and trade center located in an agricultural area, and Eastern Illinois Univ. is there. A Lincoln-Douglas debate was held in Charleston on Sept. 8, 1858. Local attractions include an enormous statue of Lincoln and nearby Lincoln Log Cabin State Park (the site of Thomas Lincoln's reconstructed farmhouse) and Fox Ridge State Park. **2** City (1970 pop. 66,945), seat of Charleston co., SE S.C.; founded 1680, inc. 1783. The oldest city in the state and one of the chief ports of entry in the SE United States, Charleston lies on a low, narrow peninsula between the Ashley and Cooper rivers at the head of the bay formed by their confluence. In the bay, or bordering on it, are Sullivans Island, site of Fort Moultrie; James Island; Morris Island, with a lighthouse; Fort Sumter; and Castle Pinckney. Many transportation routes converge at Charleston, and through its excellent, almost landlocked harbor an extensive coastal and foreign trade is carried on. Among the city's many and varied manufactures are fertilizers, chemicals, steel, asbestos, cigars, pulp and paper, and textiles and clothing. Charleston is the headquarters for the 6th U.S. naval district and for the U.S. air force defense command. The extensive military facilities include a Polaris submarine base and a huge navy yard (est. 1901). The English under William Sayle settled (1670) at Albemarle Point, on the western bank of the Ashley River, c.7 mi (11 km) from modern Charleston. They later moved (1680) to Oyster Point, where their capital, Charles Town (as it was first called) had been laid out. The city, surviving Spanish and Indian threats, became the most important seaport in the Southern colonies (exporting indigo, rice, and deerskins) and the leading center of wealth and culture in the South. Non-English immigrants, among whom the French Huguenots were most prominent, added a cosmopolitan touch. Charleston was an early theatrical center, and the Dock Street Theatre (opened 1736) was one of the first theaters to be established in the country. In the American Revolution, after being successfully defended (1776, 1779) by William Moultrie, Charleston was surrendered (May 12, 1780) by Benjamin Lincoln to the British under Sir Henry Clinton, who held it until Dec. 14, 1782. The capital was moved to Columbia in 1790, but Charleston remained the social and economic center of the region. The South Carolina ordinance of secession (Dec., 1860) was passed in Charleston, and the city was the scene of the precipitating act of the Civil War, the firing on Fort Sumter (April 12, 1861). With its harbor blockaded and the city itself under virtual siege by Union forces (1863–65), Charleston suffered partial destruction but did not fall until Feb., 1865, after it had been isolated by Sherman's army. A violent earthquake on Aug. 31, 1886, took many lives and made thousands homeless, and periodic hurricanes and tornadoes (one in 1938 was particularly severe) have also caused great damage. Despite these repeated devastations, many of the charming colonial buildings survive; outstanding among them are St. Michael's Episcopal Church (begun 1752), noted for its chimes, and the Miles Brewton house (1765–69). Among the many other points of interest are the Old Powder Magazine (1719); the Old Slave Mart Museum and Gallery; the Gibbes Art Gallery; the Charleston Museum (1773), one of the oldest museums in the country; and Fort Sumter National Monument (see NATIONAL PARKS AND MONUMENTS, table). The waterfront, called the Battery, and the Grace Memorial Bridge over the Cooper River are famous Charleston landmarks. Cabbage Row surrounds a court that was the original Catfish Row of DuBose Heyward's novel *Porgy*. The city's picturesque old homes and winding streets, historic attractions, and unique charm, together with its pleasant climate, nearby beaches, and beautiful gardens (especially the Middleton Place, Magnolia Gardens, and Cypress Gardens) attract thousands of visitors each year. The annual azalea festival is an important event. The city is the seat of the Citadel, the Medical Univ. of South Carolina, the Baptist College at Charleston, and the College of Charleston (1790), which in 1837 became the first municipal college in the United States. The Isle of Palms, a resort island E of Charleston, is noted for its fine ocean beaches. See R. G. Rhett, *Charleston: An Epic of Carolina* (1940); Robert Molloy, *Charleston: A Gracious Heritage* (1947); *This is Charleston* (rev. ed. by S. G. Stoney, 1970). **3** City (1970 pop. 71,505), state capital and seat of Kanawha co., W central W.Va., on the Kanawha River where it is joined by the Elk River; inc. 1794. The second largest city in the state, Charleston is an important transportation and trading center for the highly industrialized Kanawha valley and a major chemical, glass, and metal production area. Additional manufactures are based on the salt, coal, natural gas, clay, sand, timber, and oil of the region. The city grew around the site of Fort Lee (1788). Daniel Boone lived there from 1788 to 1795. The capital was transferred there from Wheeling in 1870, moved back to Wheeling in 1875, then returned to Charleston in 1885 after an election to determine the permanent site. The capitol building (completed 1932) was designed by Cass Gilbert. The city is the seat of Morris Harvey College. The Sunrise cultural center contains an art gallery, museum, planetarium, and notable gardens. West Virginia State College is nearby.

charleston, social dance of the United States popular in the mid-1920s. The charleston is characterized by outward heel kicks combined with an up-and-down movement achieved by bending and straightening the knees in time to the syncopated 4/4 rhythm of ragtime JAZZ. The steps are thought to have originated with the Negroes living on a small island near Charleston, S.C. Performed in Charleston as early as 1903, the dance made its way into Harlem stage shows by 1913. It gained popularity when it was performed in the Negro musical *Runnin' Wild* on Broadway in 1923. The show's male chorus line danced and sang James P. Johnson's "Charleston" to the accompaniment of Southern-style clapping and stomping. Both dance and song became the rage throughout the United States. The dance was thought to express the reckless daring, abandon, and restlessness of the jazz-age flappers. During the peak of the charleston craze a policeman in St. Louis performed the dance while directing traffic.

Charlestown, former city, now part of Boston, Middlesex co., E Mass., on Boston Harbor, between the Mystic and the Charles rivers; settled 1629, included in Boston 1874. The oldest part of Boston, it was the site of the U.S. navy yard (est. 1801, closed 1973) where the U.S.S. *Constitution* was moored. The battle of BUNKER HILL was fought at Charlestown on June 17, 1775. Samuel Morse was born in Charlestown.

Charlestown, town (1970 est. pop. 2,800) on the island of Nevis, British West Indies. It is a port that ships goods to St. Kitts. Cotton, sugarcane, livestock, and some food crops are raised. Alexander Hamilton was born in Charlestown.

Charles University, at Prague, Czechoslovakia; also called University of Prague. The oldest and one of the most important universities of central Europe, it was founded in 1348 by Holy Roman Emperor Charles IV, for whom it is named. The faculty was organized in four so-called nations, the Czech, Saxon, Bavarian, and Polish. The struggle between the German and Czech nationalities in Bohemia was reflected in the university when, in 1403, the Czech nation, including Jan HUSS, was outvoted by the three other nations in a controversy regarding John Wyclif's doctrines. When in 1409 the three foreign nations opposed the request of Holy Roman Emperor WENCESLAUS to take a neutral attitude between the two rival popes in the Great Schism, Wenceslaus changed the statutes of the university. By the Decree of Kutna Hora he gave three votes to the Czech nation and one vote to the other three nations. Shortly after that Czech victory, Huss himself became rector of the university. As a result of the Decree of Kutna Hora the Germans left the university and founded the Univ. of Leipzig. The Germanization of the university, which began after the battle of the White Mt. (1620), reached its peak in 1774 when German was made the language of instruction. In 1882 the university was divided into two branches—Charles Univ., which was Czech, and Ferdinand Univ., which was German. After the creation of independent Czechoslovakia in 1918 this division was maintained, although the Czech university received the greater facilities. The German university was abolished after World War II.

Charles William Ferdinand, 1735–1806, duke of Brunswick (1780–1806), Prussian field marshal. He had great success in the Seven Years War (1756–63) and was commander in chief (1792–94) of the Austro-Prussian armies in the FRENCH REVOLUTIONARY WARS. Although he sympathized with some of the goals of the Revolution, he led the German army in its ill-fated march into France in 1792 and issued a manifesto threatening severe reprisals against the revolutionaries. Defeated at Valmy (1792), in 1793 he routed the French at Kaiserslautern and Pirmasens. He again commanded the Prussian armies in 1806 and was defeated by the French marshal Davout at Auerstedt. He was blinded in the battle and died soon after. His son was FREDERICK WILLIAM, duke of Brunswick.

Charlet, Nicolas Toussaint (nēkôlä' to͞osăN' shärlā'), 1792–1845, French lithographer and painter. He was famous for his lithographs depicting political and social subjects. Those concerning the Napoleonic Wars are among his best known. Charlet was an influential teacher as well as one of the most popular printmakers of his day.

Charleville-Mézières (shärləvĕl'-māzyĕr'), town (1968 pop. 58,872), capital of Ardennes dept., NE France, on the Meuse River, in Champagne. It was formed in 1966 when the twin cities of Charleville and Mézières were merged, along with three small communities. It is a commercial and metalworking center. Mézières was an old fortified town, founded in the 9th cent.; Charleville was founded (1606) by, and named for, Charles de Gonzague, duke of Rethel. The area has often been captured by the Germans (1815, 1870, 1914, 1940), and Mézières in particular suffered heavy damage in both World Wars. Its recovery (1918) by the Allies marked the last major battle of World War I.

Charlevoix, Pierre François Xavier de (pyĕr fräNswä' zävyā' də shärləvwä'), 1682–1761, French Jesuit traveler and historian. He taught at the Jesuit college in Quebec and at the Collège Louis le Grand in Paris. In 1720 he journeyed to America to explore the West and visit the Jesuit missions. Voyaging up the St. Lawrence, through the Great Lakes, and along the Illinois River, he reached the Mississippi and descended it to New Orleans. After a shipwreck in the Gulf of Mexico he returned to France. In 1744 he issued his *Histoire de la Nouvelle France* (tr., 6 vol., 1900), which in a valuable appendix contains a detailed journal of his trip, the only full description of the interior of America in the first third of the 18th cent.

charlock: see MUSTARD.

Charlotte (Charlotte Sophia), 1744–1818, queen consort of George III of England. The niece of Frederick, duke of Mecklenburg-Strelitz, she was married to George in 1761 and bore him 15 children. When the king became permanently insane in 1810, she was given charge of his person and his household.

Charlotte, 1896–, grand duchess of Luxembourg (1919–64). The second daughter of Duke William of Nassau-Weilburg and a Portuguese princess, Marie Anne of Braganza, she succeeded her sister, Marie-Adelaide, who had abdicated in her favor. In Nov., 1919, Charlotte maried Prince Felix of Bourbon-Parma. During the German occupation in World War II, the grand duchess and her family went into exile, eventually settling in Montreal. They returned home in April, 1945. In Nov., 1964, Charlotte abdicated in favor of her son, Jean.

Charlotte (shär'lət), city (1970 pop. 241,178), seat of Mecklenburg co., S N.C.; inc. 1768. The largest city of the state and the foremost commercial and industrial center of the Piedmont region, Charlotte is a transportation hub and distribution point for the Carolina manufacturing belt, now the nation's leading textile area. The bountiful hydroelectric power from the Catawba River serves the city's industries. Its products include textiles, chemicals, apparel, machinery, food, and printed materials. Charlotte, named for Queen Charlotte, wife of King George III of England, was settled c.1750. The citizens of the county were among the most outspoken in their opposition to the British government, and it was at Charlotte that the MECKLENBURG DECLARATION OF INDEPENDENCE was signed in May, 1775. Hezekiah Alexander, a leading citizen of Charlotte, was the chief advocate of the declaration; his colonial home, the Rock House, is a historical museum. In his brief occupation of the city (Sept.–Oct., 1780), British Gen. Charles Cornwallis called it a "hornet's nest of rebellion." The Univ. of North Carolina at Charlotte, Queens College, Johnson C. Smith Univ., and a junior college are in the city. The Mint Museum of Art is a reproduction of the U.S. Mint, located there from 1837 until 1913. The Charlotte Coliseum has one of the largest steel, aluminum, and precast concrete domes in the world. President James K. Polk was born in Charlotte.

Charlotte Amalie (əmäl'ē), town (1970 pop. 12,372), capital of the VIRGIN ISLANDS of the United States, on St. Thomas Island. It is the commercial center of the islands, a free port, and a popular tourist resort. Founded in the late 17th cent., Charlotte Amalie was a center of Danish colonial life. It became important as a trading center during the American Civil War. It was renamed St. Thomas in 1921, but the former Danish name was restored in 1937. The town still retains a Danish flavor in its architecture and street names.

Charlotte Elizabeth: see ELIZABETH CHARLOTTE OF BAVARIA.

Charlottenburg: see BERLIN, Germany.

Charlottesville (shär'lətsvĭl), city (1970 pop. 38,880), seat of Albemarle co., central Va., on the Rivanna River, in a Piedmont farm region known for its apples; founded 1762, chartered as a city 1888. Textiles are made there. Charlottesville is the seat of the Univ. of Virginia. British Gen. John Burgoyne's captured army was quartered nearby in 1779–80, and in 1781 Sir Banastre Tarleton raided the city. Nearby are Monticello, home of Thomas Jefferson; Ash Lawn, home of James Monroe; the birthplaces of Meriwether Lewis and George Rogers Clark; and Michie Tavern Museum.

Charlottetown, city (1971 pop. 19,133), capital and chief port of Prince Edward Island, E Canada, on the southern coast. Food processing and tourism are the main industries. The French established (c.1720) a fort and settlement across the harbor, known as Port la Joie. Charlottetown was laid out by the British in 1768 and named for Queen Charlotte, consort of George III. Its growth was slow until the middle of the 19th cent., when it became noted for the sailing vessels it built for fishing and lumber transport. In the city is the Univ. of Prince Edward Island. The **Charlottetown Conference** of the Maritime Provs. (1864) was the first step toward Canadian confederation.

Charlton, Bobby (Robert Charlton), 1937–, English soccer (football) player. He joined the Manchester United team in 1954, playing inside forward and was a vital power behind the team's successes. Holder of numerous championship medals, he wrote several books about the sport including *My Soccer Life* (1965), *Forward for England* (1967), *This Game of Soccer* (1967), and *The Book of European Football* (1969).

charm, magical formula or INCANTATION, spoken or sung, for the purpose of securing blessing, good fortune, or immunity from evil. It presupposes a belief in demons or malignant spirits. The formula was frequently inscribed upon an AMULET, talisman, or trinket to be worn for protection.

Charolais (shärôlā'), small region, Saône-et-Loire dept., E central France, in Burgundy, in the Massif Central, named after the town of Charolles. Cattle breeding is the chief occupation. The countship of Charolais was acquired by Philip the Bold, Duke of Burgundy, in 1390. In 1477 the county passed to the Hapsburgs; from then on it shared the fortunes of FRANCHE-COMTÉ until it was acquired from Spain by Louis XIV and was definitively united with France and incorporated into Burgundy in 1761.

Charolais cattle (shâr'əlā"), breed of beef animal with a rugged, muscular appearance and solid creamy to wheat-colored coat. Originated in France, it was first imported to the United States in 1936 by way of Mexico.

Charon: see HADES.

Charondas (kərŏn'dəs), 6th cent. B.C., Sicilian lawgiver, a native of Catana. His laws, which were admired by Aristotle, were used by the cities of Chalcidian foundation in Sicily and Italy.

Charpentier, Gustave (güstäv' shärpäNtyā'), 1860–1956, French composer; pupil of Massenet. His best-known works are the opera *Louise* (1900), portraying bohemian Parisian life, and his orchestral suite *Impressions d'Italie* (1892).

Charran (kăr'ăn), variant of HARAN, the place. Acts 7.2,4.

Charron, Pierre (pyĕr shärôN'), 1541–1603, French Roman Catholic theologian and philosopher. He was an important contributor to 17th-century theological thought, combining an individual form of skepticism with a strict adherence to Catholicism based on the emphasis of the importance of faith over reason. After practicing law for several years, he took orders and soon gained a reputation as an eloquent preacher. He became chaplain to Margaret, wife of Henry IV. His *Traité des trois vérités* (1594) set forth proofs, first, that there is a God and that a true religion exists; second, that no other religion than that of the Christians is true; and, third, that in the Roman Catholic Church alone is salvation found. In 1600 he published a collection of 16 sermons. In his most famous work, the *Traité de la sagesse* (1601), the influence of Montaigne, with whom he had a close relationship, appears. The skepticism of that work awoke criticism and later a summary and apology, *Petit traité de la sagesse,* was published.

chart, term referring to MAPS prepared for marine navigation and for air navigation. All charts show, in some convenient SCALE, geographic features useful to the navigator, as well as indications of direction, e.g., true north (the direction of the geographic North Pole), magnetic north (the direction indicated by the north-seeking end of a magnetic compass needle), and magnetic declination (the difference between these two directions). Data shown on marine charts include the outline and nature of coasts, with landmarks; currents and undercurrents (both direction and force); winds; tides; location and type of lighthouses, buoys, beacons, and lightships; position of rocks, bars, reefs, shoals, wrecks, or other dangers; contour and nature of bottom (mud, sand, rock, or gravel); and depth. Depth is indicated in great detail in harbors and shallow and intricate waterways; the value indicated is usually that at mean low water. Most national governments publish charts of their coasts and harbors; the British admiralty has done the most work along these lines. In the United States the Coast and Geodetic Survey and the Hydrographic Office of the Dept. of the Navy issue charts; these are drawn using the gnomonic or Mercator MAP PROJECTIONS. Aeronautical charts show natural or man-made surface features by the use of various symbols. These charts give locations of radio-navigation stations and graphic representations of the directional information they broadcast; radio communication channels of airports and spacecraft centers; standard flight paths; and dangerous or forbidden areas (e.g., certain military installations). Elevations on the earth's surface are indicated by contour lines. The U.S. Coast and Geodetic Survey issues many kinds of aeronautical charts.

charter, document granting certain rights, powers, or functions. It may be issued by the sovereign body of a state to a local governing body, university, or other corporation or by the constituted authority of a society or order to a local unit. The term was widely applied to various royal grants of rights in the Middle Ages and in early modern times. The most famous political charter is the MAGNA CARTA of England. Chartered companies held broad powers of trade and government by royal charter. In colonial America, chartered colonies were in theory, and to an extent in fact, less subject to royal interference than were royal colonies.

chartered companies, associations for foreign trade, exploration, and colonization that came into existence with the formation of the European nation states and their overseas expansion. An association received its charter from the state and sometimes had state support. In the regulated company each member was an independent trader operating with his own capital and bound only by the general rules of the company charter. In the joint stock company the organization itself transacted the business, operating on the joint capital invested by members, each of whom shared proportionately in the profits and losses. The company received a monopoly of trade or colonization in a certain region and customarily exercised lawmaking, military, and treaty-making functions, subject to the approval of the home government, besides other privileges. The English Merchants Adventurers (1359) was more of a guild organization, but it foreshadowed such companies as England's Muscovy (1555), Levant (1581), East India (1600, perhaps the greatest of them all), and Hudson's Bay (1670) and Holland's Dutch East India (1602). Such colonizing companies as the Virginia Company (1606), the Massachusetts Bay Company (1629), the French Royal West Indian Company (1664–74), the Santo Domingo Company (1698), and the Dutch West India Company (1621) were more quickly taken over by their governments. Later 19th-century colonizing and trading companies, such as the British North Borneo (1881), Royal Niger (1886), British South Africa (1888), and German East Africa (1884), did not last long and had more restricted powers, but attested to the continuing significance of the chartered company. In a technical sense, the modern corporation is a chartered company. See George Cawston, *The Early Chartered Companies, 1296–1858* (1896, repr. 1968); Rudolph Robert, *Chartered Companies and their Role in the Development of Overseas Trade* (1969).

Charterhouse [Fr.,=Chartreuse], in London, England, once a Carthusian monastery (founded 1371), later a hospital for old men and then a school for boys, endowed in 1611. The school, which became a large public school, was removed (1872) to Godalming, Surrey. W. M. Thackeray, a pupil at the school, describes it in *The Newcomes*.

Charter Oak, white oak tree that until 1856 stood in Hartford, Conn., and was thought to be 1,000 years old. There is a tradition that when Sir Edmund Andros, as governor general of New England, demanded (1687) that the charter of Connecticut be surrendered by the colonists at Hartford, the document was hidden in a hollow of the tree.

Chartier, Alain (älăN' shärtyā'), b. c.1385, d. c.1433, French writer, secretary to Charles VII. His most popular work was the love poem *La Belle Dame sans mercy* (1424), which provided Keats with a title. *Le Quadrilogue invectif* (1422), a political pamphlet in vigorous prose, called for French solidarity to combat the turmoil of the Hundred Years War.

Chartier, Émile Auguste (āmēl ōgüst'), 1868–1951, French essayist and philosopher who wrote under the pseudonym Alain. He is best known for thousands of aphoristic essays, called *propos*, which he contributed to his own weekly *Libres Propos* and other journals. These essays cover a variety of literary and political topics, many of them expressing Chartier's commitment to pacifism and distrust of official power. His many other works include *Système des beaux arts* (1920) and *Histoire de mes pensées* (1936). See *Alain on Happiness* (1973).

Chartism, workingmen's political reform movement in Great Britain, 1838–48. It derived its name from the People's Charter, a document published in May, 1838, that called for voting by ballot, universal male suffrage, annual Parliaments, equal electoral districts, no property qualifications for members of Parliament, and payment of members. The charter was drafted by the London Working Men's Association, an organization founded (1836) by William Lovett and others, but the movement gathered momentum largely because of the fervor and rhetorical talents of Feargus O'CONNOR. He traveled widely, especially in the north, where recurrent economic depressions and the constraints of the new POOR LAW (1834) had bred especially deep discontent, and recruited support for the charter. In Aug., 1838, the charter was adopted at a national convention of workingmen's organizations in Birmingham. The following February another convention, calling itself the People's Parliament, met in London. A Chartist petition was presented to Parliament (and summarily rejected), but the convention rapidly lost support as the multiplicity of aims among its members and rivalries among its leaders became apparent. Riots in July and a confrontation between Chartist miners and the military at Newport, Wales, in November led to the arrest of most of the Chartist leaders by the end of 1839. In 1840, O'Connor founded the National Charter Association (NCA) in an attempt to centralize the organization of the movement, but most of the other leaders refused to support his efforts. It was the NCA that drafted and presented to Parliament the second Chartist petition in 1842. It too was overwhelmingly rejected. By this time the vitality of Chartism was being undermined by a revival of trade unionism, the growth of the Anti-Corn Law League, and a trend toward improvement in working-class economic conditions. O'Connor himself began to devote himself to a scheme for settling laborers on the land as small holders. The last burst of Chartism was sparked by an economic crisis in 1847–48. In April, 1848, a new convention was summoned to London to draft a petition and a mass demonstration and procession planned to present the petition to Parliament. The authorities took extensive precautions against trouble, but the demonstration was rained out and the procession, which had been forbidden, did not take place. This fiasco marked the end of Chartism in London, although the movement survived for a while in some other parts of the country. See G. D. H. Cole, *Chartist Portraits* (1941, repr. 1965); Asa Briggs, ed., *Chartist Studies* (1959); Mark Hovell, *The Chartist Movement* (3d ed. 1967); Dorothy Thompson, ed., *The Early Chartists* (1971); J. T. Ward, *Chartism* (1973).

Chartres, Robert d'Orléans, duc de: see ORLÉANS, family.

Chartres (shär'trə), city (1968 pop. 34,469), capital of Eure-et-Loir dept., NW France, in Orléanais, on the Eure River. Chartres is of great historic and artistic interest; it is also a regional market with many industries, including metallurgy, and the production of chemicals and electronic equipment. An ancient town, it was the probable site of the great assemblies of the DRUIDS. The Normans burned it in 858. During the Middle Ages Chartres was the seat of a countship; it became a possession of the French crown in 1286. Francis I made it a duchy in 1528. Chartres' fame today stems largely from its magnificent Gothic Cathedral of Notre Dame (12th to 13th cent.), remarkable for its two spires (375 ft/114 m and 350 ft/107 m), its stained glass windows, and its superb sculpture. Henry Adams in *Mont-Saint-Michel and Chartres* made it a symbol of the medieval spirit. Inside the cathedral St. Bernhard of Clairvaux preached the Second Crusade (1146) and Henry IV was crowned king of France (1594).

chartreuse (shärtrōōz'), LIQUEUR made exclusively by Carthusians at their monastery, La Grande Chartreuse, France, until their expulsion in 1903. The French distillery and trademark were sold, and the order set up a new plant in Tarragona, Spain. The monks' product is identified by the name *Liqueur des Pères Chartreux*. Readmitted to France in 1941, the Carthusians resumed manufacture there. Green chartreuse contains about 57% alcohol; the sweeter yellow variety, about 43%.

Chartreuse, Grande (gräNd shärtröz'), mountainous massif, Isère dept., SE France, in the Dauphiné Alps; Chamechaude Peak (6,847 ft/2,087 m) is the highest point. There in a high valley St. Bruno founded (1084) the famous monastery, La Grande Chartreuse, the principal seat of the Carthusians until 1903, when the order was expelled from France. The Carthusians returned to their monastery in 1941. The monastery was destroyed several times; the present buildings (now a museum) date mainly from the 17th cent. Chartreuse liqueur originated there.

Charvaka (chär'väkə): see INDIAN PHILOSOPHY.

Charybdis (kərĭb'dĭs), in Greek mythology, a female monster. Because she stole Hercules' cattle, Zeus hurled her into the sea. There she lay under rocks across from Scylla and sucked in and spewed out huge amounts of water, creating a whirlpool.

Chase, Mary Ellen, 1887–1973, American educator and writer, b. Blue Hill, Maine, grad. Univ. of Maine, 1909. She taught (1918–26) English at the Univ. of Minnesota, where she received her Ph.D. in 1922. Her works set in Maine, excellent in their regional fidelity, include a biography and the novels *Mary Peters* (1934), *Silas Crockett* (1935), and *Windswept* (1941). She also wrote biblical studies such as *Life and Language in the Old Testament* (1955) and children's books like *The Story of Lighthouses* (1965). Her autobiographical volumes are *A Goodly Heritage* (1932), *A Goodly Fellowship* (1939), and *The White Gate* (1954). See biography by P. D. Westbrook (1965).

Chase, Philander, 1775–1852, American Episcopal bishop, b. Cornish, N.H. After experience as a missionary in the West, he was elected (1818) first bishop of Ohio, where he founded Kenyon College in 1824 with funds that he secured largely in England. In 1835, Chase became bishop of Illinois; from 1843 he was presiding bishop of the church. See his *Reminiscences* (2 vol., 2d ed. 1848); biography by L. C. Smith (1903).

Chase, Salmon Portland, 1808–73, American public official and jurist, 6th Chief Justice of the United States (1864–73), b. Cornish, N.H. Admitted to the bar in 1829, he defended runaway Negroes so often that he became known as "attorney general for fugitive slaves." Chase became prominent in the Liberty party and later in the Free-Soil party, and was elected by a coalition of Free-Soilers and antislavery Democrats to the U.S. Senate, where (1849–55) he eloquently opposed such proslavery measures as the Compromise of 1850 and the Kansas-Nebraska Act. He was elected governor of Ohio in 1855 at the head of a Republican ticket that was dominated by Know-Nothings; by 1857, when he was reelected, he was a leading member of the new Republican party. Chase was a splendid figure of a man, a "sculptor's ideal of a President," and few Americans have ever gone after that high office with more determination—or less success. He sought the Republican nomination in 1860, but since he lacked the full support of even his own state's delegation and since many considered him an extreme abolitionist, his chance passed quickly. Again elected to the Senate, he served only two days in March, 1861, before resigning to become Lincoln's Secretary of the Treasury. In that difficult position he took part in framing for Congress the new fiscal legislation necessitated by the Civil War, collected new taxes, placed unprecedentedly large loans with reluctant investors, and directed vast expenditures. To assist in government financing and also to improve the status of the currency, he proposed the national bank system (established in Feb., 1863), which is generally considered his greatest achievement. Ambition and a high regard for his own worth made Chase a difficult man to work with; after refusing four previous attempts, Lincoln finally accepted Chase's resignation on June 29, 1864. Chase failed in his effort to secure the presidential nomination, but he remained an important national figure, and on Dec. 6, 1864, after the death of Roger B. Taney, Lincoln appointed him Chief Justice of the United States. He took a moderate stand in most of the important Reconstruction cases. His dissenting opinion in the SLAUGHTERHOUSE CASES subsequently became the accepted position of the courts as to the restrictive force of the Fourteenth Amendment. On the other hand, his decision (1870) in *Hepburn* vs. *Griswold* (see LEGAL TENDER CASES) was soon reversed. For his fairness in presiding over the Senate in the impeachment trial of President Andrew Johnson, he was furiously denounced by his old radical friends. Chase persisted in seeking the presidency, but neither the Democrats in 1868 nor the Liberal Republicans in 1872 were interested in him. See biography by A. B. Hart (1899, repr. 1969); David Donald, ed., *Inside Lincoln's Cabinet: The Civil War Diaries of Salmon P. Chase* (1954, repr. 1970); J. W. Schuckers, *Life and Public Services of Salmon P. Chase* (1874, repr. 1970).

Chase, Samuel, 1741–1811, political leader in the American Revolution, signer of the Declaration of Independence, Associate Justice of the U.S. Supreme Court (1796–1811), b. Somerset co., Md. A lawyer, he participated in pre-Revolutionary activities and was a delegate to the First and Second Continental Congresses. In 1776 he was appointed, together with Benjamin Franklin and Charles Carroll of Carrollton, to win Canada over to the Revolutionary cause, but the plan failed. Chase helped to influence Maryland opinion to support independence from Great Britain. Although he opposed adoption of the U.S. Constitution, he later became a strong Federalist and President Washington appointed him (1796) to the U.S. Supreme Court. A series of brilliant and influential decisions established his leadership in the court until he was eclipsed by the rising genius of John Marshall. Chase was impeached (1804) by the U.S. House of Representatives for discrimination on the bench against Jeffersonians. Tried before the Senate (1805), he was found not guilty. This verdict discouraged further attempts to impeach justices for purely political reasons.

Chase, Stuart, 1888–, American economist and author, b. Somersworth, N.H., studied (1907–8) at Massachusetts Institute of Technology, grad. Harvard, 1910. He worked (1910–17) as a certified public accountant and later investigated (1917–22) the meatpacking industry for the Federal Trade Commission. He served as a consultant with the National Resources Committee (1934), the Resettlement Administration (1935), the Securities Exchange Commission (1939), the Tennessee Valley Authority (1940–41), and the United Nations Educational, Scientific, and Cultural Organization (1949). He is the author of many articles and books on economics. Among his best-known works are *The Tragedy of Waste* (1925), *Your Money's Worth* (with F. J. Schlink, 1927), *Men and Machines* (1929), *The Economy of Abundance* (1934), *Rich Land, Poor Land* (1936), *Democracy under Pressure* (1945), *The Proper Study of Mankind* (1948), *Live and Let Live* (1960), *Money to Grow On* (1964), and *The Most Probable World* (1968).

Chase, William Merritt, 1849–1916, American painter, b. Williamsburg, Ind., studied in Indianapolis and in Munich under Piloty. In 1878 he began his long career as an influential teacher at the Art Students League of New York and later established his own summer school of landscape painting in the Shinnecock Hills on Long Island. Proficient in many media, Chase is best known for his spirited portraits and still lifes in oil. His *Carmencita, Lady in Black,* and portrait of Whistler (all: Metropolitan Mus.) and *My Daughter Alice* (Cleveland Mus.) are characteristic. He was president of the Society of American Artists for 10 years and a member of the National Academy of Design. See K. M. Roof, *Life and Art of William M. Chase* (1917).

Chassériau, Théodore (tāōdôr' shäsārēō'), 1819–56, French painter, b. Santo Domingo. He entered Ingres's studio at the age of 12; five years later he gained immediate recognition with the exhibition of his *Cain, Cursed* and *Return of the Prodigal.* Chassériau was the only artist of the age who successfully combined Ingres's sense of line and Delacroix's rich color and vitality and, at the same time, created his own personal style. After his visit to Algeria in the 1840s, he emphasized the exotic, romantic elements in his painting, while still adhering to classical techniques. Among his best-known works are the *Two Sisters, Arabian Challenge,* and *Tepidarium* (all: Louvre). His mural decorations for the Cour des Comptes of the Palais d'Orsay, Paris, were destroyed except for a few fragments preserved in the Louvre. His untimely death cut short a brilliant career.

Chassidim: see HASIDIM.

Chastelard, Pierre de Boscosel de (pyĕr də bôskôzĕl' də shätəlär'), c.1540–1563, French gallant. Madly in love with Mary Queen of Scots, who exchanged verses with him, he hid in her bedchamber and was discovered and forgiven. When he repeated the offense, he was executed. The story was dramatized by Swinburne.

Chastellain, Georges (zhôrzh shätəlăN'), c.1405–1475, French chronicler, historiographer to the dukes of Burgundy. The surviving fragments of his *Grande Chronique* are a valuable 15th-century source.

chat, name applied to several Old World perching birds, such as the wheatear (see THRUSH), the whinchat, and the stonechat, and to a common American WARBLER.

château (shătō', Fr. shätō'), royal or seigniorial residence and stronghold of medieval France—the counterpart of the English CASTLE of the period. In such a fortress, peasants of the surrounding country took refuge during time of war. The early fortified château, called a *château-fort,* reached its culmination in the late 15th cent., when the magnificent feudal Pierrefonds was built near Compiègne. The 16th-century château, with its gardens and outbuildings, was usually surrounded by a moat, but was only lightly fortified. Notable châteaux of the transition period between the military château and the later country estate with extensive landed property are those of the Loire, Indre, and Cher valleys, such as Chambord, Amboise, Blois, Chenonceaux, Azay-le-Rideau, and Chaumont. See study by François Gébelin (tr. 1964).

Chateaubriand, François René, vicomte de (fräNswä' rənā' vēkôNt' də shätōbrēäN'), 1768–1848, French writer. Chateaubriand was a founder of ROMANTICISM in French literature. Of noble birth, he grew up in his family's isolated castle of Combourg. In 1791 he visited the United States, supposedly to search for the Northwest Passage, although he apparently did not go beyond Niagara Falls. He returned to France but became an émigré and lived in England until 1800. There he published his first book, *Essai historique, politique, et moral sur les révolutions* (1797). *The Genius of Christianity* (1802, tr. 1856) made Chateaubriand the most important author of his time in France. Two tragic love stories included in this volume, "Atala" (1801) and "René" (1802), exemplify the melancholy, exotic description of nature and the evocative language that became a trademark of romantic fiction. His other works include *The Martyrs* (1809, tr. 1812, 1859), which celebrated the victory of Christianity over paganism, and *Les Aventures du dernier Abencérage* (1826), a narrative of romance set in Spain. In 1803, Napoleon appointed Chateaubriand secretary of the legation to Rome and then minister to Valaise, but in 1804, upon the execution of the duc d' Enghien, he resigned and became a bitter anti-Bonapartist. Later he supported the Bourbons and became a peer (1815), ambassador to London (1822), and minister of foreign affairs (1823–24). In 1830 he abandoned political affairs and spent his final years with Mme Récamier composing his *Memoires d'outre-tombe* [memoirs from beyond the tomb] (1849–50). Chateaubriand's musical prose enriched the French language. Although his accounts of travel were plagiaristic and partly imaginary, they were rich and moving. See his *Travels in America* tr. by R. Switzer (1968); his memoirs (ed. by Robert Baldick, 1961); biographies by André Maurois (1938) and Friedrich Sieburg (1961).

Château d'If (shätō"dēf'), castle built in 1524 on the small rocky isle of If, in the Mediterranean Sea off Marseilles, SE France. Long used as a state prison, it was made famous by Alexandre Dumas's *Count of Monte Cristo.*

Chateaugay, river, c.50 mi (80 km) long, rising in Chateaugay Lake in the Adirondacks, NE N.Y., and flowing through Quebec to empty into the St. Lawrence 10 mi (16 km) below Montreal, opposite the mouth of the Ottawa River. In the War of 1812 the battle of Chateaugay was fought (1813) on the banks of the river in Quebec between an American invading force of 7,000 under Gen. Wade Hampton and some 750 Canadians and Indians. The Americans were defeated and had to abandon their plan to attack Montreal.

Château-Renault, François Louis Rousselet, marquis de (fräNswä' lwē ro͞osəlā' märkē' də shätō'-rənō'), 1637–1716, French vice admiral and marshal. He escorted the deposed king of England, James II, to Ireland (1689), fought against the Anglo-Dutch fleet at Beachy Head (1690), and commanded the Franco-Spanish fleet that was destroyed (1702) at Vigo.

Châteauroux (shätōro͞o'), city (1968 pop. 51,201), capital of Indre dept., central France, on the Indre River. It has textile, metal, and food-processing industries. Châteauroux grew around a 10th-century castle built by the lords of Déols. Historic buildings in the city include the Église des Cordeliers (a former church that is now a jewelry museum) and the church of St. Martial (12th–16th cent.).

Château-Thierry (shätō'-tyĕrē'), town (1968 pop. 11,629), Aisne dept., N France, on the Marne River. The town was the focal point of the second battle of the Marne (1918), which ended the last German offensive of World War I. An imposing monument to the U.S. soldiers who fought in the battle is just outside the town. The birthplace of Jean de La Fontaine is preserved as a museum.

Châtellerault (shätĕlrō'), town (1968 pop. 36,642), Vienne dept., W central France. It is an industrial center where armaments, cutlery, camping equipment, plywood, and clothing are produced. There are many buildings dating from the 15th to the 17th cent. in the old part of town, including the house (now a museum) where René Descartes spent his childhood.

Chatham, William Pitt, 1st earl of (chăt'əm), 1708–78, British statesman, known as the Great Commoner. A member of a family whose wealth had been made in India, he entered Parliament in 1735. With his older brother he became a member of a group known as "Cobham's cubs" (after their leader Lord Cobham) or the "boy patriots," who opposed the ministry of Sir Robert WALPOLE, particularly its foreign policy, and supported Frederick Louis, prince of Wales, in his quarrel with King George II. After the fall (1742) of Walpole, Pitt was the leading critic of Lord Carteret (later earl of GRANVILLE) in his conduct of the War of the Austrian Succession. Although detested by the king, Pitt entered the government as postmaster general of the forces in 1746 and won great popularity by his unusual honesty in refusing the usual perquisites of that office. He was dismissed in 1755, but the early disasters in the SEVEN YEARS WAR gave him such an opportunity to denounce government policies in his eloquent speeches that in 1756 George II was forced to call on him to become a secretary of state. The next year he formed a coalition ministry with Thomas Pelham-Holles, duke of NEWCASTLE. Pitt wished to conduct the war primarily against the French to win imperial supremacy, a policy popular with the mercantile interests and with the generally anti-French public. His subsidies to Frederick II of Prussia, his efficient handling of military supplies, his shrewd choice of commanders, his insistence on naval expansion, and his ability to raise English morale resulted in the defeat of the French power in India and the capture of the French provinces in Canada. After the accession of GEORGE III, however, Pitt was forced to resign (1761), and he fiercely denounced the terms of the Treaty of Paris (1763), by which the war was concluded. He joined the opposition in protesting the prosecution (1763) of John WILKES and the imposition of the STAMP ACT (1765) on the American colonies. In 1766, Pitt was recalled to office as lord privy seal, accepted the title earl of Chatham, and formed such a broadly based ministry that it was soon impossibly divided. Troubled by increasing mental illness and gout, Chatham exercised little control over this administration, and his chancellor of the exchequer, Charles TOWNSHEND, not only sabotaged his plans to reorganize the East India Company but passed the ill-fated TOWNSHEND ACTS (1767). In virtual retirement from 1767, he resigned office in 1768. In his rare speeches in the House of Lords thereafter, he urged conciliation of the American colonies, and after the outbreak of the American Revolution he favored any peace settlement short of granting the colonies independence. On this issue he broke with the Whigs, and his last speech was a plea against the disruption of the empire he had done so much to build. At its conclusion he collapsed and was carried home to die. Proud, dramatic, and patriotic, Chatham excelled as a war minister and orator. He was the father of William Pitt. See biographies by Basil Williams (1913, repr. 1966), O. A. Sherrerd (1952), J. H. Plumb (1953, repr. 1965), and J. W. Derry (1962); D. A. Winstanley, *Lord Chatham and the Whig Opposition* (1912, repr. 1966).

Chatham, city (1971 pop. 35,317), S Ont., Canada, E of Detroit, Mich., on the Thames River. It is an industrial center in a rich mixed farming and fruit-raising region.

Chatham, municipal borough (1971 pop. 56,921), Kent, SE England, on the Medway River. Chatham, Rochester, and Gillingham form a contiguous urban area known as the Medway Towns. Chatham is a great naval station, with well-equipped dockyards, dry docks, and shipbuilding and repairing equipment. The Royal Naval Dockyard is the largest installation. The first dockyard was established by Elizabeth I in 1588. There are also flour mills and timber works. The Roman WATLING STREET ran through Chatham.

Chatham Island: see SAVAI'I.

Chatham Islands, island group (1968 est. pop. 500), 373 sq mi (966 sq km), South Pacific, c.425 mi (680 km) E of New Zealand, to which it belongs. The two largest islands are Chatham Island, which has a large central lagoon, and Pitt Island. The chief town is Waitangi, on Chatham Island. The inhabitants engage mainly in sheep raising, sealing, and fishing. The islands were discovered by Britons in 1791. The native Moriori population was nearly exterminated when Maoris from New Zealand invaded in 1830.

Châtillon, Sébastien: see CASTALION, SÉBASTIEN.

Châtillon-sur-Seine (shätēyôN'-sür-sĕn), town (1968 pop. 6,746), Côte d'Or dept., N central France, in Burgundy, on the Seine River. It was a residence of the early dukes of Burgundy and has a 10th-century church. The town was the site of unsuccessful peace negotiations (1814) between Napoleon I and his opponents.

Chatsworth, estate, Derbyshire, central England, near Chesterfield. It is the seat of the dukes of Devonshire. The present Chatsworth House was begun in 1687. Its gardens, libraries, picture galleries, and collections of sculpture are noted.

Chattahoochee, river, 436 mi (702 km) long, rising in N Ga., and flowing generally south to join the Flint River in Lake Seminole on the Ga.-Fla. line; the combined waters form the Apalachicola River, c.90 mi (140 km) long, which flows S to Apalachicola Bay, NW Fla. The Jim Woodruff Dam impounds Lake Seminole and has a capacity of 30,000 kw of electricity. The Columbia, Walter F. George, Bartletts Ferry, and Goat Rock dams produce power and regulate navigation on the Chattahoochee. Buford Dam forms Lake Sidney Lanier (used for recreation) and is the source of Atlanta's water supply. The Flint River, 330 mi (531 km) long, rising in W central Georgia, is navigable to Bainbridge, Ga., and is a valuable source of power in W Georgia.

Chattanooga (chătəno͞o gə), city (1970 pop. 119,082), seat of Hamilton co., E Tenn. on both sides of the Tennessee River near the Georgia line inc.

1839. It is a port of entry and an important manufacturing and marketing center for a widespread area. Foremost among its many manufactures are textile and metal products, chemicals, and primary metals. It is also a resort center, almost entirely surrounded by mountains, with many historical and tourist attractions on or near Lookout Mt., Missionary Ridge, and Signal Mt. West of the city, the Tennessee River cuts through the Cumberland Plateau in a magnificent gorge, c.1,000 ft (300 m) deep. The Cherokees were defeated on this site in 1794, and a trading post was established in 1810, followed by the Brainerd mission in 1817. Regular steamship service began in 1835. A center first of salt shipping and then of cotton shipping, the city expanded with the arrival of the railroads in the 1840s and 50s. It was of great strategic importance in the Civil War (see CHATTANOOGA CAMPAIGN). Northern industrialists developed the iron industry there during the 1870s. Electric power, augmented by the Tennessee Valley Authority project after 1933, has played an important role in the city's development. Chickamauga Dam is nearby. Southeast and southwest of the city lies Chickamauga and Chattanooga National Military Park (est. 1890), part of which lies in Georgia. Other points of interest include the Rock City Gardens, with unusual lichen-covered sandstone formations; a wildlife sanctuary; historic cemeteries; and numerous old buildings. A U.S. coast guard station is on Lake Chickamauga. The Univ. of Tennessee at Chattanooga is there. Adolph S. Ochs owned the Chattanooga *Times* from 1878 until his death.

Chattanooga campaign, Aug.-Nov., 1863, military encounter in the American Civil War. Chattanooga, Tenn., which commanded Confederate communications between the East and the Mississippi River and was also the key to loyal E Tennessee, had been an important Union objective as early as 1862 (see BUELL, DON CARLOS). In 1863, the Union general William ROSECRANS, commanding the Army of the Cumberland, forced Braxton BRAGG to withdraw his Confederate army from middle Tennessee (June-Aug.) and maneuvered him out of Chattanooga (Aug. 16-Sept. 8). Deceived into believing that Bragg was retreating upon Atlanta, Rosecrans pursued and was trapped by the Confederates at Chickamauga Creek, c.12 mi (20 km) S of Chattanooga. Strengthened by James Longstreet's corps, which had traveled some 650 mi (1,050 km) from Lee's army through Virginia and the Carolinas to join him, Bragg routed the Union right at the Battle of Chickamauga (Sept. 19-20). He could not crush the Union left under George H. THOMAS, however; Thomas held off the enemy until Rosecrans ordered him to withdraw to Chattanooga. Bragg then took up a position extending along Missionary Ridge across Chattanooga Valley to Lookout Mt. and laid siege to the town. In a historic movement, Joseph Hooker and two corps from the Army of the Potomac circled nearly 1,200 mi (1,900 km) via Indianapolis to bolster the Union forces. But Rosecrans had lost control of the situation, and an alarmed Federal administration at Washington called for U.S. GRANT, who arrived at Chattanooga on Oct. 23, 1863. Generals W. F. Smith and Joseph Hooker executed a coup (Oct. 26–29) that restored a sorely needed supply line on the Tennessee River, so Grant was ready to move by late November. Sherman, who had brought up reinforcements from Vicksburg, commanded the left; Thomas, the center; and Hooker, the right. Bragg's forces had been weakened by the departure of Longstreet on an unsuccessful expedition to Knoxville. On Nov. 24, Hooker drove the Confederates from Lookout Mt. in the Battle above the Clouds. On Nov. 25, Sherman could make no headway against Missionary Ridge from its northern end, so Grant ordered the center to advance. Thomas's men—Philip Sheridan conspicuous among them—displayed great courage and boldness, proceeding to carry Bragg's position at the top; there Hooker's forces joined them in routing the Confederates. By nightfall Bragg was in full retreat to Georgia. The victory left Chattanooga in Union hands for the rest of the war. See study by M. H. Fitch (1911); Fairfax Downey, *Storming of the Gateway* (1960, repr. 1969).

chattel (chăt'əl), in law, any property other than a freehold estate in land (see TENURE). A chattel is treated as personal property rather than real property regardless of whether it is movable or immovable (see PROPERTY). Certain uses of the term (e.g., chattel mortgage) refer only to movable property. Otherwise the term also includes chattels real, i.e., those estates in land that do not constitute a freehold.

Chatterjee, Bankim Chandra (bəng'kĭm chŭn'drə chä'tərjē), 1838–94, Indian nationalist writer, b. Bengal. He popularized a Bengali prose style that became the vehicle of the major nationalist literature of the region. Born a Brahman, he received an English education and his first novel was written in English. In 1872 he founded the *Bangadarshan,* a journal modeled on the *Spectator.* Chatterjee, who frequently used the pseudonym Ramchandra, wrote many novels that wedded political and philosophical commentary with historical romance. His favorite theme—India as a divine motherland—did much to reinforce Hindu orthodoxy and alienate the Indian Muslims. *Bandemataram* (Hail to the Mother), the title of a song in his novel *Anandamath* (1882), became a slogan of the Indian National Congress. The song was ultimately adopted as the Indian national anthem. Other writings include *The Poison Tree* (tr. 1884) and *Krishna Kanta's Will* (tr. 1895).

Chatterton, Thomas, 1752-70, English poet. The posthumous son of a poor Bristol schoolmaster, he was already composing the "Rowley Poems" at the age of 12, claiming they were copies of 15th-century manuscripts at the Church of St. Mary Redcliffe, Bristol. In 1769 he sent several of these poems to Horace Walpole, who was enthusiastic about them. When Walpole was advised that the poems were not genuine, he returned them and ended the correspondence. After this crushing defeat, Chatterton went to London in 1770, trying, with small success, to sell his poems to various magazines. On the point of starvation, too proud to borrow or beg, he poisoned himself and died at the age of 17. An original genius as well as an adept imitator, Chatterton used 15th-century vocabulary, but his rhythms and his approach to poetry were quite modern. The "Rowley Poems" were soon recognized as modern adaptations written in a 15th-century style, but the vigor and medieval beauty of such poems as "Mynstrelles Songe" and "Bristowe Tragedie" revealed Chatterton's poetic genius. This gifted, rebellious youth later became a hero to the romantic and Pre-Raphaelite poets, several of whom, notably Keats and Coleridge, wrote poems about him. See his complete works, ed. by D. S. Taylor with B. B. Hoover (2 vol., 1971); biographies by E. H. W. Meyerstein (1930, repr. 1972) and John C. Nevill (1948, repr. 1973).

Chaucer, Geoffrey (jĕf'rē chô'sər), c.1340–1400, English poet, one of the most important figures in English literature. The known facts of Chaucer's life are fragmentary and are based almost entirely on official records. He was born in London between 1340 and 1344, the son of John Chaucer, a vintner. In 1357 he was a page in the household of Prince Lionel, later duke of Clarence, whom he served for many years. In 1359–60 he was with the army of Edward III in France, where he was captured by the French but ransomed. By 1366 he had married Philippa Roet, who was probably the sister of John of Gaunt's third wife; she was a lady-in-waiting to Edward III's queen. During the years 1370 to 1378, Chaucer was frequently employed on diplomatic missions to the Continent, visiting Italy in 1372–73 and in 1378. From 1374 on he held a number of official positions, among them comptroller of customs on furs, skins, and hides for the port of London (1374–86) and clerk of the king's works (1389–91). The official date of Chaucer's death is Oct. 25, 1400. He was buried in Westminster Abbey. Chaucer's literary activity is often divided into three periods. The first period includes his early work (to 1370), which is based largely on French models, especially the ROMAN DE LA ROSE and the poems of Guillaume de Machaut. Chaucer's chief works during this time are the *Book of the Duchess,* an allegorical lament written in 1369 on the death of Blanche, wife of John of Gaunt, and a partial translation of the *Roman de la Rose.* Chaucer's second period (up to c.1387) is called his Italian period because his works then were modeled primarily on Dante and Boccaccio. His major works of the second period include *The House of Fame,* recounting the adventures of Aeneas after the fall of Troy; *The Parliament of Fowls,* which tells of the mating of fowls on St. Valentine's Day and is thought to celebrate the betrothal of Richard II to Anne of Bohemia; a prose translation of Boethius' *De consolatione philosophiae*; the unfinished *Legend of Good Women,* a poem telling of nine classical heroines, which introduced the heroic couplet (two rhyming lines of iambic pentameter) into English verse; the prose fragment, *The Treatise on the Astrolabe,* written for his son Lewis; and *Troilus and Criseyde,* based on Boccaccio's *Filostrato,* one of the great love poems in the English language (see TROILUS AND CRESSIDA). In *Troilus and Criseyde,* Chaucer perfected the seven-line stanza later called rhyme royal. To Chaucer's final period, in which he achieved his fullest artistic power, belongs his masterpiece, *The Canterbury Tales* (written mostly after 1387). This unfinished poem, about 17,000 lines, is one of the most brilliant works in all literature. The poem introduces a group of pilgrims journeying from London to the shrine of St. Thomas à Becket at Canterbury. To help pass the time they decide to tell stories. The pilgrims together represent a wide cross section of 14th-century English life. Their tales include a variety of medieval genres from the humorous fabliau to the serious homily, and they vividly indicate medieval attitudes and customs in such areas as love, marriage, and religion. Through Chaucer's superb powers of characterization the pilgrims—such as the earthy wife of Bath, the gentle knight, the worldly prioress, the evil summoner—come intensely alive. Chaucer was a master storyteller and craftsman, but because of a change in the language after 1400, his metrical technique was not fully appreciated until the 18th cent. Only in Scotland in the 15th and 16th cent. did his imitators understand his versification. The best editions of Chaucer's works are those of F. N. Robinson (1933) and W. W. Skeat (7 vol., 1894–97); of *The Canterbury Tales,* that of J. M. Manly and Edith Rickert (8 vol., 1940); of *Troilus and Criseyde,* that of R. K. Root (1926). See Charles Muscatine, *Chaucer and the French Tradition* (1960); G. G. Coulton, *Chaucer and his England* (1950, repr. 1963); M. A. Bowden, *A Reader's Guide to Geoffrey Chaucer* (1964); G. G. Williams, *A New View of Chaucer* (1965); Maurice Hussey et al., *Introduction to Chaucer* (1965); D. W. Robertson, Jr., *Chaucer's London* (1968); G. L. Kittredge, *Chaucer and His Poetry* (1915, repr. 1970); Ian Robinson, *Chaucer's Prosody* (1971) and *Chaucer and the English Tradition* (1972); P. M. Kean, *Chaucer and the Making of English Poetry* (2 vol., 1972). Bibliographies for 1908 to 1953 by D. D. Griffith (rev. ed. 1954) and for 1954 to 1963 by W. R. Crawford (1967).

Chaudière (shōdyĕr'), river, 115 mi (185 km) long, rising in Lac Mégantic, SE Que., Canada, near the Maine-Que. boundary and flowing generally N to the St. Lawrence River opposite the city of Quebec. A hydroelectric power plant at Chaudière Falls (130 ft/40 m high) supplies electricity to the Quebec city region.

Chaudière Falls, in the Ottawa River in the heart of the city of Ottawa, Ont., Canada. The river is narrowed by rocky cliffs to a width of c.200 ft (60 m) and drops 50 ft (15 m) in a series of cascades. Several bridges cross the river there, passing over the falls.

Chauliac, Guy de (gē də shōlyăk'), c.1300–1368, French surgeon. At Avignon he was physician to Pope Clement VI and to two of his successors. His *Chirurgia magna* (1363) was used as a manual by physicians for three centuries.

Chaumette, Pierre Gaspard (pyĕr gäspär' shōmĕt'), 1763–94, French Revolutionary. A member of the CORDELIERS, he collaborated with Jacques HÉBERT to eliminate the royalists and to introduce (1793) the cult of Reason. Chaumette was general prosecutor (1792–94) and a chief leader of the Commune of Paris. Although he instituted social and moral reforms, his private life is reputed to have been less than pure. When Maximilien Robespierre turned upon the Hébertists, Chaumette tried in vain to escape the guillotine by renouncing Hébert.

Chaumonot, Joseph Marie (zhôzĕf' märē' shōmōnō'), 1611–93, French Jesuit missionary to the New World. He arrived in 1639 in Quebec. He worked first with BRÉBEUF among the Huron Indians near Georgian Bay until the time of the massacres and destruction by the Iroquois (1649); he escaped and led 400 Huron to the reservation appointed for them on the Île d'Orléans at Quebec. He next went into central New York to preach to the Iroquois (1655–58) and then returned to Quebec, where he remained. His autobiography is important, and his Huron grammar is unique.

Chaumont (shōmōN'), town (1968 pop. 27,569), capital of Haute-Marne dept., NE France, in Champagne, at the confluence of the Marne and Saize rivers. It is a railroad and light industrial center. Iron is mined nearby. The Treaty of Chaumont, signed on March 1, 1814, by England, Russia, Prussia, and Austria, laid the foundation for the HOLY ALLIANCE.

Chauncy, Charles, 1705–87, American Congregational clergyman, b. Boston. He was ordained as a minister of the First Church, Boston, in 1727 and remained in that pulpit for 60 years. Next to Jonathan Edwards, his great opponent, Chauncy was probably the most influential clergyman of his time in New England. As an intellectual he distrusted emotionalism and opposed the revivalist preaching of the GREAT AWAKENING in his *Seasonable Thoughts on the State of Religion in New England* (1743) and other pamphlets. He became the leader of the "Old Lights" or liberals in theology in the doctrinal disputes following the Great Awakening. He was also the leader in the opposition to the establishment of an Anglican bishopric in the American colonies, writing his *Compleat View of Episcopacy* (1771) and other works on the subject. A firm believer in the colonial cause, he clearly set forth the political philosophy of the American Revolution in sermons and pamphlets during the period. After the war he defended the doctrine of Universalism in two anonymous tracts: *Salvation for All Men* (1782) and *The Mystery Hid from Ages and Generations* (1784). See Williston Walker, *Ten New England Leaders* (1901, repr. 1969).

Chausson, Ernest Amédée (ĕrnĕst' āmādā' shōsôN'), 1855–99, French composer. His various compositions reflect the influence of César Franck and also suggest Debussy. Of his songs, perhaps the best known are *Les Heures* (1896) and *Oraison* (1896). His Symphony in B Flat Major is popular, and his *Jardin aux lilas* has been used for a ballet. He also wrote chamber music, church music, and poetic pieces for violin and for piano. See biography by J. P. Barricelli (1955, repr. 1973).

Chautauqua Lake, 18 mi (29 km) long and from 1 to 3 mi (1.6–4.8 km) wide, W N.Y., near Lake Erie, in a resort area. Grapes and other fruits are grown in the region.

Chautauqua movement, development in adult education somewhat similar to the LYCEUM movement. It derived its name from the institution at Chautauqua, N.Y. There, in 1873, John Heyl VINCENT and Lewis Miller proposed to the Methodist Episcopal camp meeting they were attending that secular as well as religious instruction be included in the summer Sunday-school institute. Established on that basis in 1874, the institute developed into an eight-week summer program, offering courses to adults in the arts, sciences, and humanities. Thousands attended the institution each year. For those who could not attend, there were courses for home study groups, and lecturers were sent out to supplement the material furnished from the organization's publishing house. Other communities were inspired to form local Chautauquas, and possibly two or three hundred were organized, though few were so successful as the original. To lecture to their members these local groups brought authors, explorers, musicians, and political leaders, and a variety of entertainment was furnished. The Chautauquas had something of the spirit of the revival meeting and something of the county fair. In 1912 the movement was organized commercially, and lecturers and entertainers were furnished to local groups on a contract basis. This commercial endeavor was extremely successful, persisting until c.1924; soon after that the circuits ended, although the assembly at Chautauqua continued with a diminished membership. See J. H. Vincent, *The Chautauqua Movement* (1886, repr. 1971); A. E. Bestor, *Chautauqua Publications* (1934); Rebecca Richmond, *Chautauqua: an American Place* (1934); Gay MacLaren, *Morally We Roll Along* (1938); Victoria Case and R. O. Case, *We Called It Culture: The Story of Chautauqua* (1948, repr. 1970); J. E. Gould, *The Chautauqua Movement* (1961).

Chautemps, Camille (kämē'yə shōtäN'), 1885–1963, French politician. A Radical Socialist leader, he was premier in 1930 and in 1933–34, when the STAVISKY AFFAIR (in which he was not directly implicated) caused his resignation. A member of the first Popular Front cabinet of Socialists and Communists (1936–37) under Léon Blum, he headed the second, less radical, Popular Front cabinet (1937–38). Vice premier of the Vichy government, Chautemps came (1940) to the United States on a mission and did not return to France. He was subsequently expelled from the Radical party. In 1947 he was tried and convicted in absentia for collaborating with the Vichy regime. In 1954 his sentence was voided by the statute of limitations.

Chauveau, Pierre Joseph Olivier (pyĕr zhôzĕf' ôlēvyā' shōvō'), 1820–90, French Canadian educator and politician, prime minister of Quebec (1867–73), b. Quebec. He became superintendent of education (1855) in Lower Canada. During his tenure normal schools were established and separate schools were created for English-speaking and French-speaking students. With the achievement of confederation (1867), Chauveau became the first prime minister of the province of Quebec. He also held the portfolios of minister of education and provincial secretary. In 1873 he was appointed to the Canadian Senate, of which he was speaker (1873–74). In 1878 he became professor of Roman law at Laval Univ. Chauveau wrote the novel *Charles Guérin* (1852), several biographies, poetry, and essays, including *L'Instruction publique du Canada* (1876).

chauvinism (shō'vənĭzəm), word derived from the name of Nicolas Chauvin, a soldier of the First French Empire. Used first for a passionate admiration of Napoleon, it now expresses exaggerated and aggressive nationalism. As a social phenomenon, chauvinism is essentially modern, becoming marked in the era of acute national rivalries and imperialism beginning in the 19th cent. It has been encouraged by mass communication, originally by the cheap newspaper. Chauvinism exalts consciousness of nationality, spreads hatred of minorities and other nations, and is associated with militarism, imperialism, and racism. In the 1960s, the term "male chauvinist" appeared in the women's liberation movement; it is applied to males who refuse to regard females as equals.

Chaux-de-Fonds, La (lä shō-də-fôN'), city (1971 pop. 42,347), Neuchâtel canton, NW Switzerland, in the Jura mts., near the French border. It is one of the largest watch-manufacturing centers in Switzerland.

Chavannes, Puvis de: see PUVIS DE CHAVANNES.

Chávez, Carlos (kär'lōs shä'väs), 1899–, Mexican composer and conductor. In 1928, Chávez established the Symphony Orchestra of Mexico, which he conducted until 1949. He was also director (1928–34) of the National Conservatory of Music, where he radically reformed the curriculum. He used elements of Mexican Indian music and Indian instruments in his *Xochipilli Macuilxochitl* (1940). The influence of Stravinsky is evident in several of his strongly rhythmic works. His most important compositions include the ballet *El fuego nuevo* (1921); the ballet-symphony *H.P.* [horsepower] (1926–27); *Sinfonía Antigona* (1933); a piano concerto (1938–40); a violin concerto (1948–50); the Fourth and Fifth symphonies (both 1953); and *Invention,* for string trio (premiere, 1965). Chávez is the author of *Toward a New Music* (1937) and *Musical Thought* (1961).

Chavez, Cesar Estrada (sā'sär āsträ'thä shä'vās), 1927–, American agrarian labor leader, b. near Yuma, Ariz. A migrant worker, he became involved (1952) in the self-help Community Service Organization (CSO) in California, working among Mexicans and Mexican-Americans; from 1958 to 1962 he was its general director. In 1962, he left the CSO to organize wine grape pickers in California and formed the National Farm Workers Association. Using strikes, fasts, picketing, and marches, he was able to obtain contracts from a number of major growers. In 1966 his organization merged with the Agricultural Workers Organizing Committee of the AFL-CIO to form the United Farm Workers Organizing Committee of the AFL-CIO. Chavez also launched (1968) a boycott against the table grape growers, mobilizing consumer support throughout the United States. In 1972 the United Farm Workers (UFW), with Chavez as president, became a member union of the AFL-CIO. Chavez expanded its efforts to include all California vegetable pickers and launched a lettuce boycott, as well as extending his organizational efforts to Florida citrus workers. His successes in California were sharply diminished, however, as the result of a jurisdictional dispute with the International Brotherhood of Teamsters over the organization of field workers; in 1973 the Teamsters cut heavily into UFW membership by signing contracts with former UFW grape growers, but Chavez renewed the grape workers' strike.

Chavín de Huantar (chävēn' dā wän'tär), archaeological site in the northeastern highlands of Peru. It was probably the chief ceremonial and urban center of the earliest civilization (fl. c.700 B.C.–c.200 B.C.) of the Andes, now called the Chavín. Highly developed and sophisticated, the Chavín built large temples with painted relief sculpture of mythical beasts, and produced boldly designed ceramics, gold objects, and textiles. See J. Alden Mason, *Ancient Civilizations of Peru* (1961); J. H. Rowe, *Chavín Art: An Inquiry into Its Form and Meaning* (1962); E. P. Benson, ed., *Dumbarton Oaks Conference on Chavín, 1968* (1971).

Chaykovsky, Nikolai Vasilyevich (nyĭkəlī' vəsē'-lyəvĭch chĭkôf'skē), 1850–1926, Russian socialist. As a student in St. Petersburg he joined (1869) a utopian socialist student group (later known as the "Chaykovsky circle") that influenced the development of the Narodniki (populist) movement. He emigrated to the United States and established (1875) a utopian community in Kansas. It failed, and Chaykovsky moved (1880) to England, becoming active in radical émigré activities but also coming under the influence of western notions of liberal democracy. In 1905 he returned to Russia and devoted himself to promoting the cooperative movement, also becoming a leader of the People's Socialist party. After the Bolshevik revolution he headed (1918–19) the anti-Bolshevik government at Archangel under the auspices of the Allied expeditionary force. He died in exile in Paris. The name is variously spelled Chaikovsky, Tchaikovsky, and Tschaikovsky.

Chazars: see KHAZARS.

Cheadle and Gatley (chē'dəl, găt'lē), urban district (1971 pop. 60,648), Cheshire, NW England. The district is both residential and industrial. Industries include engineering works and the manufacture of chemicals, drugs, and bricks. It has a 17th-century hall and a church with a 16th-century nave and two chapels. In 1974, Cheadle and Gatley became part of the new metropolitan county of Greater Manchester.

Cheaha (chē'hô), peak, 2,407 ft (734 m) high, E Ala., in the Talladega Mts.; highest point in Alabama. It is included in Talladega National Forest.

Cheb (khĕp), Ger. *Eger,* city (1970 pop. 26,051), NW Czechoslovakia, in Bohemia, near the West and East German borders. A commercial and manufacturing center in a lignite-mining area, Cheb has industries producing woolen textiles, machinery, watches, and optical goods. The city is also an important railroad junction, serving Karlovy Vary and other famous spas nearby. Originally a Slavic village, Cheb was contested and alternately ruled (12th–14th cent.) by Bohemia and by the German emperors. It was finally incorporated into Bohemia in 1322 by John of Luxemburg. The city, which suffered greatly during the Hussite Wars, retained a privileged status until the 16th cent. Industrialization and the coming of the railroad stimulated rapid growth in the 19th cent. Present-day landmarks include the ruins of a 12th-century castle, two 13th-century monasteries, and the 17th-century castle in which Wallenstein was murdered in 1634.

Chebar (kē'bär), river of Mesopotamia, by which captive Jews were settled. Ezek. 1.1,3; 3.15.

Cheboksary (chĕbəksä'rē), city (1970 pop. 216,000), capital of Chuvash Autonomous SSR, NW European USSR, a port on the Volga River. It is the center of an agricultural region and the site of a hydroelectric station. Founded in the 14th cent. as a fortress, the city has a 17th-century cathedral.

Chechaouèn (shĭshô'wən) or **Xauen** (hou'än), town (1960 pop. 13,712), N Morocco, in the Rif Mts. Because Chechaouèn is a holy city of Islam, its people long discouraged Christian visitors. It was founded c.1471 as a bulwark against the Portuguese in Ceuta. Captured by the Spanish in 1920, the town fell (1924) to Abd el-Krim in the Rif War.

Chechen-Ingush Autonomous Soviet Socialist Republic (chĭchĕn'-ĭnggo͞osh'), autonomous republic (1970 pop. 1,065,000), 7,452 sq mi (19,301 sq km), SE European USSR, in the N Caucasus. GROZNY is the capital. The Grozny fields represent a major source of Soviet oil; the republic also has sizable deposits of natural gas, limestone, marl, gypsum, alabaster, and sulfur. Mineral waters make the region an important health center. Agriculture is concentrated mainly in the valleys of the Terek and the Sunzha, the republic's chief rivers. The republic's industries include oil refining, food processing, wine and cognac making, fruit canning, and the manufacture of chemicals and oil field equipment. The population, which is concentrated in the mountain foothills, consists of Russians, Chechen, and Ingush. More than 40% of the population is urban. Both the Chechen and Ingush are Sunni Muslims and speak a Caucasian language. Known since the 17th cent., the Chechen became the most active opponents of czarist Russia's conquest and occupation (1818–1917) of the Caucasus. They fought the Russians bitterly during the SHAMYL rebellion until its collapse in 1859. The Ingush, who first settled in the lowlands in the 17th cent., were for a long time not distinguished from the Chechen. The Bolsheviks seized the region in 1918 but were dislodged the following year by counterrevolutionary forces under Gen. A. I. Denikin. With Soviet power reestablished, the area was included in 1921 in the Mountain People's Republic. The Chechen Autonomous Oblast was created in 1922 and the Ingush Autonomous Oblast in

1924; the two were joined in 1934 to form the Chechen-Ingush Autonomous Oblast, which became an autonomous republic in 1936. As a result of collaboration by Chechen and Ingush units with the invading Germans during World War II, many Chechen and Ingush were deported (1944) to Central Asia after Soviet forces drove the Germans out of the Caucasus. The deportees were returned to the Caucasus in 1956, and the republic was reestablished in 1957.

Che-chiang: see CHEKIANG, province, China.

check or **cheque,** bill of exchange (see DRAFT) drawn upon a bank or trust company or broker connected with a clearinghouse (see CLEARING). Upon presentation of a check, the bank or other drawee pays cash to the bearer or to a specified person. Payment is made from those funds of the maker or drawer that are in a primary demand deposit account (checking account) with the drawee. The check is intended for prompt presentation, rather than for use as a continuing currency. When the check is presented, the drawee pays the designated sum to the holder and cancels the check, which is then returned to the drawer as his receipt. To prevent fraud, checks are usually of tinted paper and are filled in with ink; the figures may be punched out of the paper or embossed. Many checks also have identifying code numbers that have been printed with magnetically active ink. The numbers enable banks to clear checks mechanically and thereby speed up operations. Whether or not the check will be paid by the bank depends upon its recognition of the drawer's signature and upon the bank's confidence in the person presenting the check for payment. A bank becomes primarily liable for payment only when it "certifies" on a check that the necessary funds are in the bank to the credit of the drawer. However, a bank is usually responsible to its depositor for paying forged checks. All local checks accepted by a bank are turned over daily to a clearinghouse, which cancels checks due from and to all banks of a given neighborhood, the balances alone being paid in cash. Banks settle out-of-town checking claims by means of entries made in the books of the appropriate Federal Reserve banks. Checks were probably used in Italy in the 15th cent. and in Holland in the 16th, from where their use spread to England and the American colonies in the 17th cent. Their rise to first place as a medium of exchange in industrialized nations took place in the 19th cent., their importance varying with differences in banking facilities, the density of population, and commercial activity. About 90 percent of all transactions in the United States are said to be effected by checks.

checkerberry: see WINTERGREEN.

checkers, game for two players, known in England as draughts. It is played on a square board, divided into 64 alternately colored—usually red and black or white and black—square spaces, identical with a chessboard. Each player is provided with 12 pieces (in the form of disks) of his own color, and all play is conducted on the black squares. Players sit on opposite sides of the board and alternately move their pieces diagonally in a forward direction. Upon reaching the last rank of the board, pieces are "crowned," and the kings may move both backwards and forwards diagonally. The object is to eliminate from play the opponent's pieces by "jumping" them. The game has been played in Europe since the 16th cent., and the ancients played a similar game. See Edward Lasker, *Chess and Checkers: The Way to Mastership* (3d ed. 1960); Thomas Wiswell, *The Science of Checkers and Draughts* (1973).

Cheddar, village, Somerset, SW England. It is chiefly a tourist center. Limestone is quarried, and strawberries are grown. Nearby Cheddar Gorge towers c.400 ft (120 m) high, with imposing limestone cliffs and numerous caves from which relics of prehistoric man have been excavated. The town gives its name to the famous cheese, which has been made there since at least the 16th cent.

Cheddar cheese, hard rennet cheese. It has been a noted product of Cheddar, district of Somerset, England, for over three centuries and is now made in many other countries, especially Australia, Canada, New Zealand, and the United States.

Chedorlaomer (kĕd'ərlā'ōmər, -lāō'-), king of Elam. With him were allied Amraphel, king of Shinar; Arioch, king of Ellasar; and Tidal, "king of nations." They attacked the Cities of the Plain and were pursued and slain by Abraham. Gen. 14.1-16.

Cheektowaga (chēk"tōwä'gə), uninc. town (1970 pop. 113,844), Erie co., W. N.Y., E of Buffalo.

cheese, food known from ancient times and consisting of the curd of milk separated from the whey. The milk of various animals has been used in the making of cheese: the milk of mares and goats by the ancient Greeks, camel's milk by the early Egyptians, and reindeer's milk by the Laplanders. Sheep's milk and goat's milk are still widely used, but cow's milk is most common. The milk may be raw or pasteurized, sweet or sour, whole, skimmed, or with cream added. The chief milk protein, casein, is coagulated by the enzyme action of RENNET or pepsin, by lactic acid produced by bacterial action, or by a combination of the two. The draining off of the whey (milk serum) is facilitated by heating, cutting, and pressing the curd. The yield of cheese is usually about 10 lb per 100 lb of milk and is higher for the soft cheeses, which retain more moisture. The numerous cheeses (often named for their place of origin) depend for their distinctive qualities on the kind and condition of the milk used, the processes of making, and the method and extent of curing. They may be divided into two classes, hard cheeses, which improve with age under suitable conditions, and soft cheeses, intended for immediate consumption. Very hard cheeses include PARMESAN and Romano; among the hard cheeses are CHEDDAR, Edam, Emmental, Gouda, Gruyère, Provolone, and Swiss. The semisoft cheeses include brick, Gorgonzola, Limburger, ROQUEFORT, Muenster, and STILTON; some of the soft cheeses are Brie, CAMEMBERT, COTTAGE, Neufchâtel, and ricotta. Microorganisms introduced, or permitted to develop, in cheese during the ripening process impart distinctive flavors and textures. Roquefort, Stilton, and Gorgonzola owe their bluish marbling to molds; Emmental and brick are ripened by bacteria that produce gas, which is entrapped in the curd and thus forms holes; Limburger attains a creamy consistency through bacteria-ripening. During the curing period the casein is broken down into a more digestible form by enzyme action. Cheese is valuable in the diet as a source of protein, fat, insoluble minerals (calcium, phosphorus, sulfur, and iron), and, when made from whole milk, vitamin A. Process cheese is a blend of young and ripened cheeses or of different varieties, ground, heated with water and up to 3% of emulsifying salts, and poured into molds, usually loaf-shaped. It is often homogenized and pasteurized. Cheese, especially in the United States, is increasingly made in the factory by application of the principles of microbiology and chemistry. Wisconsin is the largest producer of cheese in the United States. Whey, a by-product of cheese making, consists of water, lactose, albumin, soluble minerals, fats, and proteins. Formerly wasted or used in livestock feeding, whey is now used for the preparation of milk sugar, lactic acid, glycerin, and alcohol, or is condensed and added to process cheese. It may be made into cheese such as the Scandinavian primost and mysost. See A. L. Simon, *Cheeses of the World* (2d ed. 1965); B. H. Axler, *The Cheese Handbook* (1968).

cheetah (chē'tə), carnivore of the CAT family, *Acinonyx jubatus,* found in Africa S of the Sahara and in SW Asia as far east as India. The cheetah's method of hunting deviates from that of most cats in that it runs down its prey, rather than stalking it and pouncing upon it for the kill. This doglike method of hunting is suited to its habitat, which is open grassland. The swiftest four-footed animal alive, it can achieve bursts of speed of over 60 mi (95 km) per hr and is the only animal capable of running down black bucks and gazelles. It is also unique among cats in having nonretractile claws. An average cheetah is about 2½ ft (75 cm) tall at the shoulder and weighs about 100 lb (45 kg). It has long legs and a tawny coat with closely spaced round black spots. Cheetahs are tamable and have been used for centuries in India for hunting game; they are sometimes called hunting leopards. Formerly numerous all over their range, they are now nearly extinct in India. Cheetahs are classified in the phylum CHORDATA, subphylum Vertebrata, class Mammalia, order Carnivora, family Felidae.

Cheever, John, 1912–, American author, b. Quincy, Mass. His expulsion from Thayer Academy was the subject of his first short story, published by the *New Republic* when he was 17. With meticulously rendered detail, Cheever writes about life in the affluent American suburbs. Although his works are usually comic, his view is that of a moralist, and he finds disintegration and evil in the world of plaid stamps and cocktail parties. There is often a surreal element in his stories. Among his works are the novels *The Wapshot Chronicle* (1957), *The Wapshot Scandal* (1964), and *Bullet Park* (1969); and the short-story collections *The Brigadier and the Golf Widow* (1964) and *The World of Apples* (1973).

Chefoo: see YEN-T'AI, China.

Cheju (chä'jo͞o), Jap. *Saishu,* island and province of South Korea (1970 pop. 365,522), c.700 sq mi (1,810 sq km), c.60 mi (100 km) SW of the Korean peninsula. Korea's largest island, Cheju is of volcanic origin and rises to c.6,400 ft (1,950 m) in Halla-san, an extinct volcano. Fishing, dairy farming, and livestock breeding are the chief occupations on the mountainous, heavily wooded island; agriculture is practiced on the slopes and in the valleys. The island was often used as a place of exile. After the Korean War it became a haven for refugees.

Cheka: see SECRET POLICE.

Cheke, Sir John, 1514–57, English scholar. As professor of Greek at Cambridge he taught Roger Ascham and later was tutor to Edward VI. A Protestant, he was imprisoned by Mary I. Although most of his works are Latin translations from the Greek, his works in English are noted for their simple, lucid prose.

Chekhov, Anton Pavlovich (chĕk'ôf, Rus. əntôn' päv'ləvĭch chĕ'khəv), 1860–1904, Russian short-story writer, dramatist, and physician, b. Taganrog. The son of a grocer and grandson of a serf, Chekhov earned enduring international acclaim for his stories and plays. His early works, broad humorous sketches and tales published under a pseudonym, were written to support himself and his family while he studied for his medical degree in Moscow. Under this strain he contracted tuberculosis, which ravaged him all his life. Chekhov's first large collection, *Motley Stories* (1886), brought him critical respect; it was followed by the collections *At Twilight* (1887) and *Stories* (1888), from which "The Steppe" won for him the Pushkin Prize. Chekhov's many hundreds of stories concern human folly, the tragedy of trivialities, and the oppression of banality. His characters are drawn with compassion and humor in a clear, simple style noted for realistic detail. In his plays as well as his stories Chekhov emphasizes character and mood; his plots describe the desolation of lonely men and the misunderstandings that accrue from self-absorption and desperation. His focus on internal drama was an innovation that had enormous influence on both Russian and foreign writing. Chekhov was an active humanitarian: In 1890 he wrote *The Island of Sakhalin,* a study of the lives of convicts that helped to effect social reform; as a physician he fought two cholera epidemics. Chekhov wrote several farces related to his early stories, but his first major drama to be produced was *Ivanov* (1887). His success as a dramatist was assured when the burgeoning Moscow Art Theatre took his works for their own and built superb productions of them, beginning with *The Seagull* in 1898. They followed this with his masterpieces *Uncle Vanya* (1899), *The Three Sisters* (1901), and *The Cherry Orchard* (1904), his last great work. Among the finest works of Chekhov's later years are his hundreds of letters to notable contemporaries. For the final three years of his life Chekhov was happily married to Olga Knipper, an actress with the Moscow Art company, and although they were often separated, they were together at a German health resort when he died, at 44. Most of Chekhov's works are available in English. Several lesser-known works appear in Avrahm Yarmolinsky, *The Unknown Chekhov* (1954). See his letters, ed. by Simon Karlinsky (1973) and Avrahm Yarmolinsky (1973); biographies by David Magarshack (1952, repr. 1960), E. J. Simmons (1962), and Daniel Gillès (tr. 1968); studies of his prose by T. G. Winner (1966) and V. L. Smith (1973); studies of his plays by Maurice Valency (1966), J. L. Styan (1971), and David Magarshack (1973); critical essays, ed. by R. L. Jackson (1967).

Chekiang (chĕ'kyăng', jŭ'jēăng'), Mandarin *Chechiang,* province (1968 est. pop. 31,000,000), c.40,000 sq mi (103,600 sq km), SE China, on the East China Sea. The capital is HANGCHOW. The province includes many islands, notably the CHOU-SHAN ARCHIPELAGO. Except for the level area in the north, which is part of the Yangtze deltaic region, Chekiang is mountainous, with only a few breaks to the heavily indented coast, chiefly at Ning-po and Wenchow. The province is drained by numerous rivers, including the Ch'ien-t'ang (the main river), the Wu, and the Ling. Over one third of the area is forested; pine and bamboo predominate. Most of Chekiang has a wet climate, with a long frost-free period and high summer temperatures. Rice is the leading food crop and tea the major industrial crop. The plains N of Hangchow receive less precipitation and have high cotton, wheat, and hemp production; most of the cotton is woven in Shanghai, although there are textile mills in Hangchow, the only population center in the province with any significant industry. Rapeseed, corn, and sweet potatoes are also grown. There are tung and mulberry trees, and silk is produced, although nowhere near prewar levels when Chekiang was the country's major silk-producing province. Fishing is extensive, with motorized junks now in use; the Chou-shan island area is one of the richest fishing grounds in China. Iron, aluminum, coal, and fluorspar are mined in the province. Chekiang is served by the Shanghai-Hangchow-Nanch'ang RR, which has a branch to Ning-po. Chekiang, part of the kingdom of Wu, passed into the Chinese orbit in the 3d cent. B.C. It flourished in the 12th and 13th cent. as the center of the Southern Sung dynasty. Originally called Yüeh for its local tribes, Chekiang received its present name (the ancient name of the Ch'ien-t'ang River) in the Ming dynasty (1368–1644). It passed to Manchu control in 1645. Chekiang was devastated in the Taiping Rebellion (1850–65), was partly occupied by the Japanese in the Second Sino-Japanese War, and fell to the Communists in 1949. T'ienmu Mt. is a tourist and pilgrimage center, with many temples. Chekiang Univ. is in Hangchow.

Chelal (kē'lăl), Israelite of the return who married a foreign wife. Ezra 10.30.

Chelan, Lake, 55 mi (89 km) long and from 1 to 2 mi (1.6–3.2 km) wide, located in a deep narrow gorge in the Cascade Range, NW Wash.; third-deepest freshwater lake in the United States. Fed by streams from the Cascade Range, the lake flows into the Columbia River via the Chelan River. Lake Chelan Dam, built at the lake's outlet, generates electricity. The northern part of the lake is part of the Lake Chelan National Recreation Area (see NATIONAL PARKS AND MONUMENTS, table).

chelating agents. Certain organic compounds are capable of forming coordinate bonds (see CHEMICAL BOND) with metals through two or more atoms of the organic compound; such organic compounds are called chelating agents. The compound formed by a chelating agent and a metal is called a chelate. A chelating agent that has two coordinating atoms is called bidentate; one that has three, tridentate; and so on. EDTA, or ethylenediaminetetraacetate, $(^{-}O_2CCH_2)_2NCH_2CH_2N(CH_2CO_2^{-})_2$, is a common hexadentate chelating agent. Chlorophyll is a chelate that consists of a magnesium ion joined with a complex chelating agent; heme, part of the hemoglobin in blood, is an iron chelate. Chelating agents are important in textile dyeing, water softening, and enzyme deactivation and as bacteriocides.

Chéliff (shālĕf'), river, c.420 mi (680 km) long, N Algeria. It rises in the Amour mts. of the Saharan Atlas and empties into the Mediterranean Sea near Mostaganem. The Chéliff, the longest river in Algeria, is not navigable, but its waters are used for irrigation and hydroelectric power.

Chellean-Abbevillian: see PALEOLITHIC PERIOD.

Chellean man: see HOMO ERECTUS.

Chelluh (kĕl'ə), Jew who married a foreign wife. Ezra 10.35.

Chełm (khĕlm), Rus. *Kholm,* city (1970 pop. 38,789), E Poland. It is a railway junction and has industries manufacturing metals, farm tools, machinery, furniture, and liquors. An old Slavic settlement, Chełm was chartered in 1233. It passed to Poland in 1377, to Austria in 1795, and to Russia in 1815. The Treaty of Brest-Litovsk (1918) transferred the city to Ukraine, but it passed to Poland in 1921. After Chełm was freed from German occupation in World War II, the new Polish republic was proclaimed there (July 22, 1944) by the Polish Committee of National Liberation. Chełm is noted for its cathedral.

Chełmno, (khĕlm'nô), Ger. *Kulm,* city (1970 pop. 38,800), N central Poland. Its industries manufacture metals, bricks, and farm tools. Chartered in 1223, it was transferred to the Teutonic Knights in 1228, passed to Poland in 1466, and was included in Prussia in 1772. It reverted to Poland in 1919. Among its historic buildings are two Gothic churches and a 16th-century town hall.

Chelmsford, Frederic John Napier Thesiger, 3d **Baron** and 1st **Viscount** (nā'pēər, thĕs'ĭjər, chĕlms'fərd), 1868–1933, British colonial administrator. After serving as governor of Queensland and New South Wales in Australia (1905–13), he went to India, becoming viceroy in 1916. His regime was noteworthy for the Montagu-Chelmsford Report (1918), produced in collaboration with Edwin Montagu, secretary of state for India, which recommended a large measure of self-government for the Indians. The ensuing reforms were limited, however, dividing responsibility so as to make government difficult, and were opposed by Mohandas Gandhi. Before the reforms were implemented, growing disorders led to the massacre at AMRITSAR (1919). Chelmsford returned to England in 1921 and was created a viscount. He served as first lord of the admiralty in the Labour government of 1924.

Chelmsford, municipal borough (1971 pop. 58,125), county town of Essex, SE England. It is a market center (especially for cattle) for the surrounding agricultural district. Manufactures include electrical equipment, radios, ball bearings, rope, and agricultural equipment. Other industries are milling and malting. A Roman town on this site was excavated in 1849.

Chelmsford (chĕmz'fərd, chĕlmz'-), town (1970 pop. 31,432), Middlesex co., NE Mass.; inc. 1655. It is chiefly a residential town with wool and nylon industries and granite quarries.

Chelsea, England: see KENSINGTON AND CHELSEA.

Chelsea, city (1970 pop. 30,625), Suffolk co., E Mass., a suburb of Boston; settled 1624, inc. as a town 1739, as a city 1857. Its industries include printing and the manufacture of rubber and plastic products, electrical machines, shoes and shoe accessories, and paint. Oil storage tanks line Chelsea's docks, which connect with the Atlantic by way of the Chelsea River. From 1624 to 1739, Chelsea was part of Boston and was called Winnisimmet. At the battle of Chelsea Creek (1775) Revolutionary forces made one of their first captures of a British ship. During the siege of Boston (1775–76), one wing of George Washington's army was stationed at Chelsea. George Washington slept at the Cary-Bellingham House, which was built in 1659 and remains standing.

Chelsea ware, chinaware made in the mid-18th cent. at a factory in Chelsea, London. The earliest specimens extant are dated 1745 and have the potter's mark of a triangle and the word *Chelsea.* Nicholas Sprimont in the late 1740s directed the factory's production. An extremely fine ware was developed, inspired perhaps by Sèvres porcelain. The mid-1750s, during which a red anchor mark was employed, saw the production of what are considered to be among the best of European porcelains. They are often based on designs of Meissen ware and have a soft, clear white body and clean soft colors. There was also a deep blue, gold-decorated type. Characteristic figure subjects were produced, as were miniatures for curtain tiebacks, scent bottles, dressing-table accessories, and toys. The soft paste of which the china was made lent itself to both modeling and painting. The plant was merged with the Derby factory in 1770. See study by William King (1922).

Cheltenham (chĕlt'nəm), municipal borough (1971 pop. 69,734), Gloucestershire, W central England. It has been a health and holiday resort since the discovery of mineral springs in 1716. Products include bricks, beer, rubber goods, and anesthetics. There are numerous Regency houses, Georgian squares, and parks and gardens. Cheltenham has three famous schools for boys and one for girls and two teacher training colleges. Cheltenham is the site of an annual Festival of British Contemporary Music, a Festival of Literature, and several other similar events.

Chelub (kē'ləb). **1** Judahite. 1 Chron. 4.11. **2** Father of David's officer Ezri. 1 Chron. 27.26.

Chelubai (kēlyōō'bī), the same as CALEB.

Chelyabinsk (chĭlyä'bĭnsk), city (1970 pop. 875,000), capital of Chelyabinsk oblast, W Siberian USSR, in the southern foothills of the Urals and on the Mias River. It also lies on the Trans-Siberian RR. One of the major metallurgical and industrial centers of the USSR, Chelyabinsk produces steel and agricultural machinery and processes ore. Founded in 1736 as a Russian frontier outpost, it was chartered in the 1740s and grew into an agricultural and coal-trading town. Its industrial growth began with the building of its first steel plant in 1930.

Chelyuskin, Cape (chĭlyōō'skĭn), northernmost point (lat. 77°43'N) of Asia, Krasnoyarsk Kray, N central Siberian USSR. It is named after the Russian navigator who discovered it in 1742.

Chemarims (kĕm'ərĭms), Gentile priests, a term left untranslated in Zeph. 1.4 only.

chemical analysis, the study of the chemical composition and structure of substances. More broadly, it may be considered the corpus of all techniques whereby any exact chemical information is obtained. There are two branches in analytical chemistry: qualitative analysis and quantitative analysis. Qualitative analysis is the determination of those elements and compounds that are present in a sample of unknown material. Quantitative analysis is the determination of the amount by weight of each element or compound present. The procedures by which these aims may be achieved include testing for the chemical reaction of a putative constituent with an admixed reagent or for some well-defined physical property of the putative constituent. Classical methods include use of the analytical balance, gas manometer, buret, and visual inspection of color change. Gas and paper chromatography are particularly important modern methods. Physical techniques such as use of the mass spectrometer are also employed. For samples in the gaseous state, optical spectroscopy provides the best technique for determining which atomic and molecular species are present.

chemical bond, mechanism whereby ATOMS combine to form MOLECULES. There is a chemical bond between two atoms or groups of atoms when the forces acting between them are strong enough to lead to the formation of an aggregate with sufficient stability to be regarded as an independent species. The number of bonds an atom forms corresponds to its VALENCE. The amount of energy required to break a bond and produce neutral atoms is called the bond energy. All bonds arise from the attraction of unlike charges according to Coulomb's law; however, depending on the atoms involved, this force manifests itself in quite different ways. The principal types of chemical bond are the ionic, covalent, metallic, and hydrogen bonds. The ionic bond results from the attraction of oppositely charged ions. The atoms of metallic elements, e.g., those of sodium, lose their outer electrons easily, while the atoms of nonmetals, e.g., those of chlorine, tend to gain electrons. The highly stable ions that result retain their individual structures as they approach one another to form a stable molecule or crystal. In an ionic crystal like sodium chloride, no discrete diatomic molecules exist; rather, the crystal is composed of independent Na^+ and Cl^- ions, each of which is attracted to neighboring ions of the opposite charge. Thus the entire crystal is a single giant molecule. A single covalent bond is created when two atoms share a pair of electrons. There is no net charge on either atom; the attractive force is produced as the electron pair shuttles back and forth between the two atoms. If the atoms share more than two electrons, double and triple bonds are formed, because each shared pair produces its own bond. By sharing their electrons, both atoms are able to achieve a highly stable electron configuration corresponding to that of an INERT GAS. For example, in methane (CH_4), carbon shares an electron pair with each hydrogen atom; the total number of electrons shared by carbon is eight, which corresponds to the number of electrons in the outer shell of neon; each hydrogen shares two electrons, which corresponds to the electron configuration of helium. In most covalent bonds, each atom contributes one electron to the shared pair. In certain cases, however, both electrons come from the same atom. As a result, the bond has a partly ionic character and is called a coordinate link. Actually, the only purely covalent bond is that between two identical atoms. The ionic and covalent bonds are idealized cases; most bonds are of an intermediate type. Covalent bonds are of particular importance in organic chemistry because of the ability of the carbon atom to form four covalent bonds. These bonds are oriented in definite directions in space, giving rise to the complex geometry of organic molecules. If all four bonds are single, as in methane, the shape of the molecule is that of a tetrahedron. The importance of shared electron pairs was first realized by the American chemist G. N. Lewis (1916), who pointed out that very few stable molecules exist in which the total number of electrons is odd. His octet rule allows chemists to predict the most probable bond structure and charge distribution for molecules and ions. With the advent of quantum mechanics, it was realized that the electrons in a shared pair must have opposite spin, as required by the Pauli EXCLUSION PRINCIPLE. The MOLECULAR ORBITAL THEORY was developed to predict the exact distribution of the electron density in various molecular structures. The American chemist Linus Pauling introduced the concept of resonance to explain how stability is achieved when more than one reasonable molecular structure is possible: The actual molecule is a coherent mixture of the two structures and oscillates rapidly between them. Unlike the ionic and covalent bonds, which are found in a great variety of molecules, the metallic and hydrogen bonds are highly specialized. The metallic bond is responsible for the crystalline structure of pure metals. This bond cannot be ionic because all the atoms are identical, nor can it be covalent, in the ordinary sense, because there are too few valence electrons to be shared in pairs among neighboring atoms. Instead, the valence electrons are shared collectively by all the atoms in the crystal. The electrons behave like a free gas moving within the lattice of fixed positive ionic cores. The extreme mobility of the electrons in a metal explains its high thermal and electrical conductivity. Hydrogen bonding is a strong electrostatic attraction between two independent polar molecules, i.e., molecules in which the charges are unevenly distributed, usually containing nitrogen, oxygen, or fluorine. These elements have strong electron-attracting power, and the hydrogen atom serves as a bridge between them. The hydrogen bond, which plays an important role in molecular biology, is much weaker than the ionic or covalent bonds. It is responsible for the structure of ice. See Linus Pauling, *The Nature of the Chemical Bond* (3d ed. 1960).

chemical engineering: see ENGINEERING.

chemical equation, group of symbols representing a CHEMICAL REACTION. The chemical equation $2H_2+O_2 \rightarrow 2H_2O$ represents the reaction of hydrogen and oxygen to form water. The arrow points in the direction of the reaction—from the reactants (substances that react) toward the product or products. In this case the reactants are hydrogen (written H_2 because each molecule consists of two atoms of hydrogen) and oxygen (written O_2 because each molecule consists of two atoms of oxygen) and the product is water. The coefficient 2 before the H_2 indicates that two molecules of hydrogen take part in the reaction, and the 2 before the H_2O indicates that two molecules of water are produced. When no number is written, as in front of the O_2, a one is assumed; one molecule of oxygen takes part in the reaction. The equation shows that two molecules of hydrogen react with one molecule of oxygen to form two molecules of water. Because of the relationship between molecules and the MOLE, the equation also shows that two moles of hydrogen react with one mole of oxygen to form two moles of water. The same sort of relationship holds with the gram-FORMULA WEIGHT. There are three steps involved in writing a chemical equation. The first step is to decide which substances are the reactants and which are the products. For example, natural gas (cooking gas) burns in air, providing heat and producing no visible products. The natural gas is principally methane, and the portion of the air that reacts (supports combustion) is oxygen. These are the reactants. Products of the reaction are heat and two invisible gases, carbon dioxide and water vapor. We can now write the word equation methane+oxygen→carbon dioxide+water vapor+heat. The next step is to determine the correct formula for each substance and substitute it for the name. The equation now becomes $CH_4+O_2 \rightarrow CO_2+H_2O$. (A notation for heat is often omitted.) The final step is to balance this equation. As the equation is now written, three oxygen atoms are produced from two, and four hydrogen atoms become only two. This cannot occur, since atoms are not created or destroyed in chemical reactions. The equation is already balanced for carbon, since there is one carbon atom on the reactant side and one carbon atom on the product side. There are four hydrogen atoms in the methane molecule on the reactant side, so there must be four hydrogen atoms in water molecules on the product side (since water is the only product containing hydrogen); thus there must be two water molecules, each containing two hydrogen atoms. The equation can now be written $CH_4+O_2 \rightarrow CO_2+2H_2O$. It is not yet balanced, since there are only two oxygen atoms shown as reactants and four as products. The equation is completely balanced by showing two oxygen molecules (four atoms) as reactants: $CH_4+2O_2 \rightarrow CO_2+2H_2O$. There are a number of other symbols used in chemical equations. A symbol written above or below the reaction arrow indicates special reaction conditions. For example, when mercuric oxide is heated it decomposes into mercury metal and oxygen gas; this reaction is shown by the equation $2HgO \xrightarrow[\Delta]{} 2Hg+O_2\uparrow$. The Greek letter delta under the arrow represents the heating. The upward-pointing arrow after the O_2 indicates that this product is gaseous and escapes. When a precipitate is formed by a reaction, the substance that precipitates is often followed by a downward-pointing arrow, e.g., $AgNO_3+NaCl \xrightarrow{H_2O} AgCl\downarrow+NaNO_3$. The H_2O above the arrow shows that the reaction takes place in the presence of water—in this case, in water solution. The formulas $AgNO_3$, NaCl, and $NaNO_3$ do not represent molecules, since these substances are almost completely ionized in water solution (See ION). When CHEMICAL EQUILIBRIUM occurs in a reaction, the double arrow ($\rightleftharpoons$) is used instead of the single arrow. For example, liquid water dissociates to form hydronium ions (H_3O^+) and hydroxide ions (OH^-). These ions exist in equilibrium with water molecules. The equation is $2H_2O \overset{H_2O}{\rightleftharpoons} H_3O^++OH^-$. The sign = is sometimes used in place of the double arrow.

chemical equilibrium, state of balance in which two opposing reversible CHEMICAL REACTIONS proceed at constant equal rates with no net change in the system. For example, when hydrogen gas, H_2, and iodine gas, I_2, are mixed, and gaseous hydrogen iodide, HI, is formed according to the equation $H_2+I_2 \rightarrow 2HI$, no matter how long the reaction is allowed to proceed some quantity of hydrogen and iodine will remain unreacted. The reason reactants in a reversible reaction are never completely converted to product is that an opposing reaction is taking place simultaneously, i.e., some of the newly formed HI is being converted back into hydrogen and iodine. For any particular temperature, a point of equilibrium is reached at which the rates of the two opposing reactions are equal and there is no further change in the system. This equilibrium point is characterized by specific relative concentrations of reactants and products and will also be reached from the opposite direction, i.e., if one starts with hydrogen iodide and allows it to decompose into hydrogen and iodine. The equilibrium point can be described by the mass action expression, which defines the equilibrium constant, K_{eq}, in terms of the ratio of the molar CONCENTRATIONS of the products to those of the reactants. For the reversible reaction used as an example, the equilibrium constant is $K_{eq}=[HI]^2/[H_2][I_2]$; for the general reversible reaction $nA+mB+\cdots \rightleftharpoons pC+qD+\cdots$, the equilibrium constant is:

$$K_{eq}=\frac{[C]^p\,[D]^q\cdots}{[A]^n\,[B]^m\cdots}$$

where [A], [B], [C], [D], . . . are the molar concentrations of the substances and $n, m, p, q, \cdots$ are the coefficients of the balanced chemical equation. The larger the equilibrium constant for a given reaction, the more the reaction is favored, since a larger value of K_{eq} means larger concentrations of the products relative to the reactants. The equilibrium constant is related to the change in the standard free energy, $G°$, of the system by the equation $\Delta G° = -RT \cdot \ln K_{eq}$, where R is a constant, T is the temperature in degrees Kelvin, and $\ln K_{eq}$ is the natural logarithm of the equilibrium constant. Chemical equilibrium can be defined for many types of chemical processes, such as DISSOCIATION of a weak acid in solution, solubility of slightly soluble salts, and oxidation-reduction reactions. In all of these cases, the equilibrium constant or its analogue is defined for certain conditions of temperature and other factors. If any of these factors change, the system will respond to establish a new equilibrium, in accordance with LE CHÂTELIER'S PRINCIPLE.

chemical kinetics: see CHEMICAL REACTION.

chemical reaction, process by which one or more substances may be transformed into one or more new substances. Energy is released or is absorbed, but no loss in total molecular weight occurs. When, for example, water is decomposed, its molecules, each of which consists of one atom of oxygen and two of hydrogen, are broken down; the hydrogen atoms then combine in pairs to form hydrogen molecules and the oxygen atoms to form oxygen molecules. In a chemical reaction, substances lose their characteristic properties. Water, for example, a liquid which neither burns nor supports combustion, is decomposed to yield flammable hydrogen and combustion-supporting oxygen. In some reactions heat is given off (exothermic reactions), and in others heat is absorbed (endothermic reactions). Furthermore, the new substances formed differ from the original substances in the energy they contain. Chemical reactions are classified according to the kind of change that takes place. When a compound, which consists of two or more elements or groups of elements, is broken down into its constituents, the reaction is called simple decomposition. When two compounds react with one another to form two new compounds, the reaction is called double decomposition. In so-called replacement reactions the place of one of the elements in a compound is taken by another element reacting with the compound. When elements combine to form a compound, the reaction is termed chemical combination. OXIDATION AND REDUCTION reactions are extremely important. Reversible reactions are those in which the chemical change taking place may be paralleled by another change back to the original substances. The rates at which chemical reactions proceed depend upon various factors, e.g., upon temperature, pressure, and the concentration of the substances involved and, sometimes, upon the use of a chemical called a CATALYST. In some chemical reactions, such as that of photographic film, light is an important factor. The changes taking place in a chemical reaction are represented by a CHEMICAL EQUATION. An element's activity, i.e., its tendency to enter into compounds, varies from one element to another.

chemical warfare, employment in war of flame, incendiaries, smoke, poison gases, and other toxic substances. In earliest recorded history, armies attacking or defending fortified cities threw burning oil and flaming fireballs upon each other. A primitive type of FLAMETHROWER was employed as early as the 5th cent. B.C.; modern types are still in use. In the Middle Ages before the introduction of gunpowder a flammable composition known as GREEK FIRE was widely used. Smoke from burning straw or other material was employed in early times, but its effectiveness is uncertain. By the middle of the 19th cent. the potentialities of POISON GAS were envisioned. It was effectively employed during World War I, when the Germans released (April, 1915) chlorine gas against the Allies. The Germans also introduced MUSTARD GAS later in the war. Afterward, the major powers continued to stockpile gases for possible future use. Lethal types were not employed during World War II. The Germans did, however, invent and stockpile a form of nerve gas during the war; it is odorless and colorless and attacks the body muscles, including the involuntary muscles. It is the most lethal and insidious weapon of chemical warfare. Besides potentially lethal gases, which attack the skin, blood, or nervous or respiratory system and require hospitalization of the victim, there are also nonlethal incapacitating agents, which, like TEAR GAS, cause temporary physical disability or, like LSD-25, produce temporary mental effects, such as confusion, fright, or stupor. Such agents may be employed in riot control as well as in warfare. Various forms of defoliants can also be used to destroy crops or clear away heavy vegetation; the latter operation was employed by the United States as an antiguerrilla tactic during the Vietnam War. The potential effectiveness of chemical warfare is increased by the development of modern methods of dissemination; e.g., chemical agents can be disseminated in artillery shells, grenades, or missiles, or by burning-type generators that use heat to vaporize and spread the chemical. See Stockholm International Peace Research Institute (SIPRI), *The Problems of Chemical and Biological Warfare* (Vols. I, IV, V, 1971–).

chemin de fer (shəmăn' də fûr, Fr. shəmăN' də fĕr) [Fr.,=railroad], gambling card game popular in France. It differs from BACCARAT, which it replaced in popularity, in that there are usually ten or more players and the bank moves from player to player in rotation.

Chemin des Dames (shəmăN' dā däm) [Fr.,=ladies' road], road running along a crest between the Aisne and Ailette rivers, N France. Built during Roman times, the road was the site of the battle (57 B.C.) in which Julius Caesar defeated the Gauls. Chemin des Dames received its name in the 18th cent. when Louis XV's daughters traveled along the road to Bove Castle with their ladies-in-waiting. During World War I the Germans held the road.

chemistry, branch of SCIENCE concerned with the properties, composition, and structure of substances and the changes they undergo when they combine or react under specified conditions. Chemistry can be divided into branches according to either the substances studied or the types of study conducted. The primary division of the first type is between inorganic and ORGANIC CHEMISTRY. Divisions of the second type are physical chemistry and analytical chemistry. The original distinction between organic and inorganic chemistry arose as chemists gradually realized that compounds of biological origin were quite different in their general properties from those of mineral origin; organic chemistry was defined as the study of substances produced by living organisms. However, when it was discovered in the 19th cent. that organic molecules can be produced artificially in the laboratory, this definition had to be abandoned. Organic chemistry is most simply defined as the study of the compounds of carbon.

Physical chemistry is concerned with the physical properties of materials, such as their electrical and magnetic behavior and their interaction with electromagnetic fields. Subcategories within physical chemistry are thermochemistry, ELECTROCHEMISTRY, and chemical kinetics. Thermochemistry is the investigation of the changes in ENERGY and ENTROPY that occur during chemical reactions and phase transformations (see STATES OF MATTER). Electrochemistry concerns the effects of electricity on chemical changes and interconversions of electric and chemical energy such as that in a voltaic cell. Chemical kinetics is concerned with the details of chemical reactions and of how equilibrium is reached between the products and reactants. Analytical chemistry is a collection of techniques that allows exact laboratory determination of the composition of a given sample of material. In qualitative analysis, all the atoms and molecules present are identified, with particular attention to trace elements. In quantitative analysis, the exact weight of each constituent is obtained as well. Stoichiometry is the branch of chemistry concerned with the weights of the chemicals participating in chemical reactions. The earliest practical knowledge of chemistry was concerned with METALLURGY, pottery, and dyes; these crafts were developed with considerable skill, but with no understanding of the principles involved, as early as 3500 B.C. in Egypt and Mesopotamia. The basic ideas of element and compound were first formulated by the Greek philosophers during the period from 500 to 300 B.C. Opinion varied, but it was generally believed that four elements (fire, air, water, and earth) combined to form all things. Aristotle's definition of a simple body as "one into which other bodies can be decomposed and which itself is not capable of being divided" is close to the modern definition of element. About the beginning of the Christian era in Alexandria, the ancient Egyptian industrial arts and Greek philosophical speculations were fused into a new science. The beginnings of chemistry, or ALCHEMY, as it was first known, are mingled with occultism and magic. Interests of the period were the transmutation of base metals into gold, the imitation of precious gems, and the search for the elixir of life, thought to grant immortality. Muslim conquests in the 7th cent. A.D. diffused the remains of Hellenistic civilization to the Arab world. The first chemical treatises to become well known in Europe were Latin translations of Arabic works, made in Spain A.D. c.1100; hence it is often erroneously supposed that chemistry originated among the Arabs. Alchemy developed extensively during the Middle Ages, cultivated largely by itinerant scholars who wandered over Europe looking for patrons. In the hands of the "Oxford Chemists" (Robert Boyle, Robert Hooke, and John Mayow) chemistry began to emerge as distinct from the pseudoscience of alchemy. Boyle (1627–91) is often called the founder of modern chemistry (an honor sometimes also given Antoine Lavoisier, 1743–94). He performed experiments under reduced pressure, using an air pump, and discovered that volume and pressure are inversely related in gases (see GAS LAWS). Hooke gave the first rational explanation of COMBUSTION—as combination with air—while Mayow studied animal respiration. Even as the English chemists were moving toward the correct theory of combustion, two Germans, J. J. Becher and G. E. Stahl, introduced the false phlogiston theory of combustion, which held that the substance phlogiston is contained in all combustible bodies and escapes when the bodies burn. The discovery of various gases and the analysis of air as a mixture of gases occurred during the phlogiston period. Carbon dioxide, first described by J. B. van Helmont and rediscovered by Joseph Black in 1754, was originally called fixed air. Hydrogen, discovered by Boyle and carefully studied by Henry Cavendish, was called inflammable air and was sometimes identified with phlogiston itself. Cavendish also showed that the explosion of hydrogen and oxygen produces water. C. W. Scheele found that air is composed of two fluids, only one of which supports combustion. He was the first to obtain pure oxygen (1771–73), although he did not recognize it as an element. Joseph Priestley independently discovered oxygen by heating the red oxide of mercury with a burning glass; he was the last great defender of the phlogiston theory. The work of Priestley, Black, and Cavendish was radically reinterpreted by Lavoisier, who did for chemistry what Newton had done for physics a century before. He made no important new discoveries of his own; rather, he was a theoretician. He recognized the true nature of combustion, introduced a new chemical nomenclature, and wrote the first modern chemistry textbook. He erroneously believed that all acids contain oxygen. The assumption that compounds were of definite composition was implicit in 18th century chemistry. J. L. Proust formally stated the law of constant proportions in 1797. C. L. Berthollet opposed this law, holding that composition depended on the method of preparation. The issue was resolved in favor of Proust by John Dalton's atomic theory (1808). The atomic theory goes back to the Greeks, but it did not prove fruitful in chemistry until Dalton ascribed relative weights to the atoms of chemical ELEMENTS. Electrochemical theories of chemical combinations were developed by Humphry Davy and J. J. Berzelius. Davy discovered the alkali metals by passing an electric current through their molten oxides. Michael Faraday discovered that a definite quantity of charge must flow in order to deposit a given weight of material in solution. Amedeo Avogadro introduced the hypothesis that equal volumes of gases at the same pressure and temperature contain the same number of molecules. William Prout suggested that all elements are composed of hydrogen atoms. Organic chemistry developed extensively in the 19th cent., prompted in part by Friedrich Wohler's synthesis of urea (1828), which disproved the belief that only living organisms could produce organic molecules. Other important organic chemists include Justus von Liebig, C. A. Wurtz, and J. B. Dumas. In 1852, Edward Frankland introduced the idea of valency (see VALENCE), and in 1858 F. A. Kekule showed that carbon atoms are tetravalent and are linked together in chains. Kekule's ring structure for benzene opened the way to modern theories of organic chemistry. Henri Louis Le Châtelier, J. H. van't Hoff, and Wilhelm Ostwald pioneered the application of thermodynamics to chemistry. Further contributions were the phase rule of J. W. Gibbs, the ionization equilibrium theory of S. A. Arrhenius, and the heat theorem of Walther Nernst. Ernst Fischer's work on the amino acids marks the beginning of molecular biology. The PERIODIC TABLE of the elements is the culmination of a long effort to find regular, systematic properties among the elements. PERIODIC LAWS were put forward almost simultaneously and independently by J. L. Meyer in Germany and D. I. Mendeleev in Russia (1869). An early triumph of the new theory was the discovery of new elements that fit the empty spaces in the table. William Ramsay's discovery, in collaboration with Lord Rayleigh, of argon and other inert gases in the atmosphere extended the periodic table. At the end of the 19th cent., the discovery of the ELECTRON by J. J. Thomson and of RADIOACTIVITY by A. E. Becquerel revealed the close connection between chemistry and PHYSICS. The work of Ernest Rutherford, H. G. J. Moseley, and Niels Bohr on atomic structure (see ATOM) was applied to molecular structures. G. N. Lewis, Irving Langmuir, and Linus Pauling developed the electronic theory of CHEMICAL BONDS, directed valency, and molecular orbitals (see MOLECULAR ORBITAL THEORY). Transmutation of the elements, first achieved by Rutherford, has led to the creation of elements not found in nature; in work led by Glenn Seaborg, elements heavier than uranium have been produced. See Linus Pauling, *College Chemistry* (3d ed. 1964); J. H. Hildebrand and R. E. Powell, *Principles of Chemistry* (7th ed. 1964); Isaac Asimov, *A Short History of Chemistry* (1965); J. R. Partington, *A Short History of Chemistry* (3d ed. 1960, repr. 1965); A. J. Berry, *From Classical to Modern Chemistry* (1954, repr. 1968); J. V. Quagliano and L. M. Vallarino, *Chemistry* (3d ed. 1969); L. P. Eblin, *The Elements of Chemistry* (2d ed. 1970); M. J. Sienko and R. A. Plane, *Chemistry* (4th ed., 1971).

Chemnitz or **Kemnitz, Martin** (both: kĕm'nĭts), 1522–86, German Lutheran theologian. Under the tutelage of Phillip MELANCHTHON, he accepted and defended Lutheran doctrine, both in lecturing and in writing. Largely through his endeavors the Formula of Concord, one of the nine creeds of the Book of Concord, was adopted by the Lutherans of Saxony and Swabia.

Chemnitz: see KARL-MARX-STADT, East Germany.

Chemosh (kē'mŏsh), god of the Moabites. Solomon erected an altar to him at Jerusalem; Josiah destroyed it. Num. 21.29; 1 Kings 11.7; 2 Kings 23.13; Jer. 48.7,13,46. See MILCOM.

chemosphere: see ATMOSPHERE.

chemosynthesis: see AUTOTROPH.

chemotaxis: see TAXIS.

chemotherapy, treatment of disease with chemicals or DRUGS. One chemotherapeutic approach is the development of selectively toxic substances, i.e., substances that can destroy or inhibit infecting organisms or, as in cancer, malignant tissue, but do not damage normal host tissue. In treating infection, selectively toxic agents may block a biochemical reaction necessary to the viability of the pathogen but not to that of the host; for example, PENICILLIN blocks synthesis of bacterial cell walls, a component animal cells lack. Other chemotherapeutic substances differentially affect biochemical reactions in different tissues; thus antimetabolites such as METHOTREXATE and CYTOXAN are more toxic to rapidly proliferating cells such as those associated with cancer than to normal cells. Other drugs act in various ways to produce effects that initiate or enhance some normal body function; for instance, neostigmine blocks the action of an enzyme limiting transmission of nerve impulses and thereby acts as a nervous system stimulant. The usefulness of chemotherapeutic agents also depends on their pharmacological action, e.g., their rate of absorption, rapidity of action and rate of excretion, degree of storage in the body, effects of products of their metabolic breakdown, and potential for causing HYPERSENSITIVITY reactions. Some drugs are given prophylactically, to prevent infection, e.g., penicillin is given to rheumatic fever patients to prevent reinfection by the causative organism, the streptococcal bacterium.

chemotroph: see AUTOTROPH.

Chemulpo: see INCHON, Korea.

Chemung (shĭmŭng'), river, c.45 mi (70 km) long, formed in S central N.Y. by the junction of the Cohocton and Tioga rivers near Corning, N.Y., and flowing SE past Elmira to the Susquehanna River near Sayre, Pa. The Chemung valley was the scene of fighting in the Revolutionary campaign of John Sullivan; the battle of Newtown occurred in 1779 near the site of Elmira.

chemurgy (kĕm'ərjē), branch of applied chemistry concerned with preparing industrial products from agricultural raw materials. Among such products are plastics manufactured from casein and soybean; soaps derived from animal and vegetable fats; cellulose fiber products made from, for example, straws, stubble, cobs, and hulls; and starches derived from surplus grains. Chemurgy is a wide-ranging discipline involving chemistry, genetics, bacteriology, and physics.

Chenaanah (kēnā'ănə, -nā-ā'-). **1** Benjamite. 1 Chron. 7.10. **2** Father of Zedekiah, Ahab's false prophet. 1 Kings 22.11,24; 2 Chron. 18.10,23.

Chenab (chēnäb'), one of the "five rivers" of the Punjab, 675 mi (1,086 km) long, rising in the Punjab Himalayas, W Kashmir, and flowing NW, then SW through Pakistani Punjab to join the Sutlej River. The Ravi and Jhelum rivers are the chief tributaries. The Chenab supplies water for an important irrigation system.

Chenani (kēnā'nī), Levite. Neh. 9.4.

Chenaniah (kĕnənī'ə), Levite. 1 Chron. 15.22; 26.29.

Chen-chiang (jŭn-jēäng) or **Chinkiang** (chĭn'-kyăng', jĭn'jēăng'), city (1970 est. pop. 250,000), S Kiangsu prov., China, a port at the junction of the Grand Canal with the Yangtze River. It is also on the Shanghai-Nanking RR. An important commercial and industrial center, it is known for its silk, vinegar, and pickled vegetables. Other processed foods, pharmaceuticals, machine tools, and paper products are also made. Chen-chiang was known in the Sung dynasty (12th cent.), flourished under the Ming and Manchu dynasties, was held by the Taipings and ravaged (1857), and was opened to foreign trade in 1859. It was a British concession until 1927 when it was returned to China. It declined in the late 19th cent. when the Grand Canal lost its importance, but flourished again as capital (1928–49) of Kiangsu. The Kiangsu medical college is there.

cheng, Chinese stringed instrument similar to the zither. It is also spelled *jeng* and *tseng.* See also SHENG, an altogether different instrument for which the spelling *cheng* is occasionally used.

Cheng, Chi (jē jŭng), 1943?–, Taiwanese track athlete. Considered the best woman athlete in Taiwan at age 18, she went to the United States to train and study. She was bronze medal winner in the 1968 Olympic games, and in 1970 she set the women's world record for the 100-meter hurdles (26.2 sec), the 100-yd/91-m dash (10 sec), and the 200-yd/183-m dash (22.6 sec).

Cheng-chou or **Chengchow** (both: jŭng-jō), city (1970 est. pop. 1,500,000), capital of Honan prov., E central China. An important railroad center, the city is at the junction of the Lung-hai (east-west) and the Peking-Canton (north-south) railroads. The textile center of Honan prov., and a flourishing industrial city, Cheng-chou has grown about sevenfold since 1949. In addition to textiles, manufactures include chemicals, aluminum, fertilizer, processed meats, agricultural machinery, and electrical equipment. An opencut coal mine is nearby. An agricultural institute and a medical college are in the city. Chengchou was formerly called Chenghsien.

Chengchow: see CHENG-CHOU, China.

Chenghsien: see CHENG-CHOU, China.

Ch'eng-te or **Chengteh** (both: chŭng-dŭ), city (1970 est. pop. 200,000), N Hopeh prov., China, near the Luan River. It is a distribution center for lumber products, fruits, and pharmaceuticals, and has an iron mine. The city is N of Peking, with which it is connected by rail. The former summer capital of the Ch'ing dynasty (1644-1911), Ch'eng-te is surrounded by large parks with lakes, palaces, and pavilions. The most notable building is a Lamaist temple duplicating the main shrine in Lhasa, Tibet. Until 1956 the capital of former Jehol prov., Ch'eng-te was formerly called Jehol.

Ch'eng-tu (chŭng-do͞o) or **Chengtu,** city (1970 est. pop. 2,000,000), capital of Szechwan prov., SW China, on the Min River. It is a port and the commercial center of the Ch'eng-tu plain, the main farming area of Szechwan. Products include textiles, processed foods, chemicals, machinery, and paper. High-grade iron ore is mined at nearby Lu-ku. Ch'eng-tu, an old walled city, was in existence during the Ch'un-ch'iu period (770-475 B.C.). It was the capital of the Shu Han dynasty (3d cent. A.D.) and one of the earliest (9th cent. A.D.) printing centers in China. A cultural seat since ancient times, it is commonly called "little Peking." Its numerous institutions of higher learning include Szechwan Univ., Ch'eng-tu Technical Univ., and two medical colleges. The cottage where Tu Fu wrote his poetry (8th cent.) was restored in 1955.

Chénier, André (äNdrā' shānyā'), 1762-94, French poet, by some critics considered the greatest in 18th-century France. He was born in Constantinople, where his father was consul general, and was educated in France. From 1787 to 1790 he was attached to the French embassy in London. Active in the early phase of the French Revolution, he was later horrified by Jacobin excesses. In 1792 he contributed denunciatory pamphlets to the *Journal de Paris,* organ of moderate royalism. He was arrested in March, 1794, by order of Robespierre, and was guillotined only three days before the end of the Terror. Chénier vivified the French classical tradition in his *Élégies* and *Bucoliques.* The *Iambes* are stirring political satires in verse. Most of his works were published after his death; *La Jeune Captive,* one of his most moving poems, appeared in 1795 and the first collected edition of his works in 1819. His life inspired the opera *Andrea Chénier* by Umberto Giordano. See biographies by V. Loggins (1965) and F. Scarfe (1965).

Chénier, Marie Joseph (märē' zhôzĕf'), 1764-1811, French poet and dramatist, b. Constantinople; brother of André Chénier. A member of the Convention, the Council of Five Hundred, and the Tribunate during the French Revolution, he wrote a number of political and historical plays, notably *Charles IX* (1789). Besides the comprehensive *Tableau historique de l'état et des progrès de la littérature française depuis 1789* (1816), he is famous for his songs of the Revolutionary period, particularly the *Chant du départ.*

Chennault, Claire Lee (shĕn'ôlt"), 1890-1958, American general, b. Commerce, Texas. In World War I he was a pioneer in air pursuit tactics. Retired (1937) from the army, he went to China and organized air defenses for Chiang Kai-shek. He formed there (1941) the American Volunteer Group (known as the Flying Tigers). Recalled (1942) to duty, he headed the U.S. air task force in China and retired (1945) as a major general. See biography by R. L. Scott (1959, repr. 1973); study by his wife Anna Chennault (1963).

Chenonceaux (shənôNsō'), village, Indre-et-Loire dept., W central France, in Touraine, on the Cher River. It is famous for its château (built 1515-22), the residence, successively in the 16th cent., of Diane de Poitiers and Catherine de' Medici. The wing of the château over the river was added by Catherine in 1560.

Ch'en Tu-hsiu (chŭn do͞o-shyo͞o), 1879-1942, Chinese educator and Communist party leader. He was active in the republican revolution of 1911 and was forced to flee to Japan after taking part in the abortive "second revolution" of 1913 against YUAN SHIH-K'AI. In 1915 he founded the journal *New Youth* in Shanghai. Articles by Ch'en, LI TA-CHAO, HU SHIH, and others encouraged Chinese youth to create a new culture free from Confucianism. He was dean of the school of arts and sciences of Peking Univ. from Jan., 1917, until forced to resign under conservative pressure in March, 1919. Ch'en was converted to Marxism in the period following the student-led intellectual revolution known as the MAY FOURTH MOVEMENT (1919). He founded (1920) two Marxist groups, and in 1921 representatives of these groups met with representatives of groups organized by Li Ta-chao (neither Ch'en nor Li were present) to found the Communist party. He was dismissed from party leadership and withdrew from the party in 1927 over his opposition to the COMINTERN-ordered policy of armed insurrection.

Ch'en Yi (chŭn yē), 1901-72, Chinese Communist general and statesman. Ch'en was a political instructor (1925) in the Kuomintang Whampoa Military Academy and participated in the NORTHERN EXPEDITION. After the Kuomintang-Communist alliance collapsed (1927), he joined the Fourth Red Army (1928) and was an early supporter of Mao Tse-tung. One of the outstanding Communist military commanders, Ch'en became acting commander (1941) and then commander (1946) of the New Fourth Army. After 1949 he was mayor of Shanghai and a dominant figure in E China. He succeeded CHOU EN-LAI as foreign minister (1958), serving during a period of intense rivalry between China and Russia for influence among the nations of the Middle East, Africa, and Latin America. Ch'en was severely criticized during the CULTURAL REVOLUTION. After 1967 his role was eclipsed by Chou, who resumed direction of foreign policy in his capacity as prime minister.

Cheops: see KHUFU.

Chephar-haammonai (kē'fär-hāăm'ōnā), town of Benjamin. Joshua 18.24.

Chephirah (kēfī'rə), town of Benjamin, NW of Jerusalem. Joshua 9.17; 18.26; Ezra 2.25; Neh. 7.29.

Chephren: see KHAFRE.

cheque: see CHECK.

Cher (shĕr), department (1968 pop. 304,601), central France, in BERRY. Chief cities are VIERZON and BOURGES, the capital.

Cher, river, c.200 mi (320 km) long, rising in the Massif Central and flowing generally NW across central France to join the Loire below Tours. The Berry Canal parallels part of the river.

Cheran (kĕr'ăn), Horite. Gen. 36.26; 1 Chron. 1.41.

Cherbourg (shĕrbo͝or'), city (1968 pop. 38,243), Manche dept., NW France, in Normandy, on the English Channel, at the tip of the Cotentin peninsula. It is a naval base and seaport with related industries. The site has been settled since ancient times and was frequently fought over by the French and English because of its strategic value. Fortifications were begun under Louis XIV.

Cherchel or **Cherchell** (both: shĕrshĕl'), town (1966 pop. 11,667), N Algeria, a port on the Mediterranean Sea. Settled by Carthaginians, it became the capital of Mauretania before and during Roman times and was named Caesarea in 25 B.C. It remained an important military and commercial port under the Romans. Taken by Barbarossa (1516), it became a corsair refuge. French forces occupied the town in 1832. Cherchel is rich in relics, especially of the Roman period.

Cheremiss: see MARI AUTONOMOUS SOVIET SOCIALIST REPUBLIC, USSR.

Cheremkhovo (chĕrĭmkô'və), city (1970 pop. 99,000), SE Siberian USSR, on the Trans-Siberian RR. The center of the Cheremkhovo coal basin, the city forms part of an industrial complex based mainly on coal, oil refining, and chemical production.

Cherenkov, Pavel Alekseyevich (pä'vĭl əlyĭksyā'-yəvĭch chərĕng'kəf), 1904–, Soviet physicist. He shared with the Soviet physicists I. M. Frank and I. Y. Tamm the 1958 Nobel Prize in Physics for his discovery (1934) of CHERENKOV RADIATION. His research opened the way to new studies of high-energy subatomic particles and of cosmic rays.

Cherenkov radiation or **Cerenkov radiation** [for P. A. Cherenkov], light emitted by a transparent medium when charged particles pass through it at a speed greater than the speed of light in the medium. The effect, discovered by Cherenkov in 1934 while he was studying the effects of gamma rays on liquids and explained in 1937 by I. E. Tamm and I. M. Frank, is analogous to the creation of a SONIC BOOM when an object exceeds the speed of sound in a medium, and the light is emitted only in directions inclined at a certain angle to the direction of the particles' motion, just as the sonic shock wave is restricted to certain angles. Cherenkov radiation is produced by electrons of the transparent medium that have been displaced by gamma rays rather than by the gamma rays themselves, and it is not dependent on temperature. It is used in the Cherenkov counter, a device for detecting fast particles and determining their speeds or distinguishing between particles of different speeds.

Cherepovets (chĕrĭpəvyĕts', chĕrĭpô'vyĭts), city (1970 pop. 188,000), NE European USSR, on the Rybinsk Reservoir. A rail and water transportation center of the Volga-Baltic Waterway, it has an iron and steel complex that supplies Leningrad's metallurgical industries. Chemical plants for the production of fertilizers are also there. Cherepovets arose (14th cent.) as a settlement around a monastery.

Chéret, Jules (zhül shārā'), 1836-1932, French painter and draftsman, originator of the modern POSTER. His colorful, sophisticated designs for the theater and opera influenced Toulouse-Lautrec. Chéret introduced color lithography into France in 1866.

Cherethims (kĕr'əthĭmz), the same as the Cherethites.

Cherethites and Pelethites (kĕr'əthīts, pĕl'əthīts), David's officers. 2 Sam. 8.18; 15.18; 20.7,23; 1 Kings 1.38,44; 1 Chron. 18.17. The Cherethites, or Cherethims, are mentioned alone in 1 Sam. 30.14, Ezek. 25.16, and Zeph. 2.5.

Cheribon: see TJIREBON, Indonesia.

Cherith (kēr'ĭth), brook flowing into the Jordan opposite Samaria. 1 Kings 17.3,5.

Cherkassy (chĭrkä'sē), city (1970 pop. 158,000), capital of Cherkassy oblast, in Ukraine, S European USSR, a port on the Dnepr River. Situated on the shore of the Kremenchug Reservoir, Cherkassy has important chemical-fiber and fertilizer industries. Founded at the end of the 13th cent., Cherkassy was a fortress in the 14th cent. and served as the seat of the Ukrainian hetmans of right-bank UKRAINE from 1386 to 1694. The city passed to Russia in 1793.

Cherkess Autonomous Oblast: see KARACHAY-CHERKESS AUTONOMOUS OBLAST.

Cherkessk (chĭrkĕsk'), city (1970 pop. 67,000), capital of Karachayevo-Cherkess Autonomous Oblast, Stavropol Kray, SE European USSR, on the Kuban River. Founded in 1825 as Batalpashinsk, it manufactures electrical equipment and shoes and has food-processing plants.

Chernigov (chĭrnyĕ'gəf), Ukr. *Chernihiw,* city (1970 pop. 159,000), capital of Chernigov oblast, W central European USSR, in the Ukraine, on the Desna River. It is a rail junction, a river port, and an air and highway transport hub. Industries include ship repairing, woodworking, food and wool processing, and the manufacture of metal goods and machinery. First mentioned in 907, Chernigov is one of the oldest cities of Kievan Russia. From the 11th to 13th cent., Chernigov was the capital of a principality of the same name, but the city declined after the Mongol invasion of 1239. It passed to Lithuania in the 14th cent. and to Russia in the 16th cent. It was under Polish control during part of the 17th cent. Chernigov's architectural monuments include the 11th-century Spasski Cathedral, the Church of the Assumption in the Yelets Monastery (11th cent.), and Ivan Mazeppa's baroque army building (17th-18th cent.).

Chernov, Viktor (vĕk'tər chĭrnôf'), 1876-1952, Russian revolutionary. One of the founders of the SOCIALIST REVOLUTIONARY PARTY, he served as minister of agriculture under Kerensky in the provisional government set up after the overthrow of the czar in Nov., 1917 (Oct., 1917, O.S.). He was president of the short-lived constituent assembly (Jan., 1918). After its dissolution, Chernov headed an anti-Bolshevik government in Samara (now Kuibyshev). Early in 1921 he fled abroad. He died in New York City. Chernov wrote *The Great Russian Revolution* (tr. 1936).

Chernovtsy (chĭrnôf'tsē), Ger. *Czernowitz,* Rumanian *Cernauti,* city (1970 pop. 187,000), capital of Chernovtsy oblast, SW European USSR, in the Ukraine, on the Prut River and in the Carpathian foothills. It is a rail junction and the economic, cultural, and scientific center of the region of Bukovina. Industries include woodworking, food processing, and the manufacture of machinery, textiles, chemicals, footwear, and hosiery. One of Russia's oldest towns, Chernovtsy was part of Kievan Russia. It passed to Austria in 1775 and in 1849 became the capital of Bukovina. During the 19th and early 20th cent., the city was a center of the Ukrainian national movement. With the dissolution of Austria-Hungary in 1918, Chernovtsy was transferred to Rumania, which held it until the USSR seized N Bukovina in 1940. The city has a university (est. 1875), a 13th-century fortified castle, a 17th-century wooden church, and a 19th-century Orthodox Eastern cathedral.

chernozem (chĕr'nəzĕm") or **black earth,** variety of soil rich in organic matter in the form of HUMUS. It is generally a modified type of LOESS. True chernozem is black in color, but there are various grades, shading off into gray and chestnut-brown soils. It forms in areas that have cold winters, hot summers, and rapid evaporation of precipitation; generally only tall grass is found native on chernozem. It has large quantities of nutrients, excellent structure, and good water-holding capacity, making it very suitable for agriculture. It is most widely distributed in Russia, where it forms a large part of the good agricultural soil, but soils similar to the Russian are also found in India and the central and N central United States.

Chernyaiev, Mikhail Grigoryevich: see TCHERNAIEV.

Chernyshevsky, Nikolai Gavrilovich (nyĭkəlī' gəvrē'ləvĭch chĕrnĭshĕf'skē), 1828–89, Russian socialist reformer. He was the leading disciple of Vissarion BELINSKY inside Russia; from 1853 to 1857 he wrote for the radical journal *Contemporary,* presenting and expanding the principles of Belinsky, who himself also wrote for the journal. Chernyshevsky advocated basic agrarian reform and emancipation of the serfs, and he envisioned the village commune as a transition to socialism. In 1862 he was arrested and was later sent to Siberia. In prison he formulated his ideas in the vastly influential novel *What Is to be Done?* (1863, rev. tr. 1961). His *Selected Philosophical Works* was published in English in Moscow in 1953. Chernyshevsky is looked upon as a forerunner of the Russian revolutionary movement. See biographies by F. B. Randall (1967) and W. F. Woehrlin (1971).

Cherokee (chĕr'əkē), language belonging to the Iroquoian branch of the Hokan-Siouan linguistic family. See AMERICAN INDIAN LANGUAGES.

Cherokee Indians, largest and most important single Indian group in the SE United States, formerly occupying the mountain areas of North and South Carolina, Georgia, Alabama, and Tennessee. The Cherokee language belongs to the Iroquoian branch of the Hokan-Siouan linguistic stock (see AMERICAN INDIAN LANGUAGES). By the 16th cent. they had a settled, advanced culture based on agriculture. Hernando de Soto visited them in 1540. They were frequently at war with the Iroquois tribes of New York, but generally sided with the British against the French and proved valuable allies. Soon after 1750 they suffered a severe smallpox epidemic that destroyed almost half the tribe. Formerly friendly with the Carolina settlers, the Cherokee were provoked into war with the colonists in 1760, and two years of warfare followed before the Cherokee sued for peace. In 1820 they adopted a republican form of government and in 1827 established themselves as the Cherokee Nation under a constitution. This instrument provided for an elective principal chief, a senate, and a house of representatives. Much of their progress was due to the invention of a Cherokee syllabary or syllabic alphabet by SEQUOYAH, also known as George Guess. Its 85 characters represented all the sounds in the Cherokee language and permitted the keeping of tribal records and, later, the publication of newspapers in Cherokee. The discovery of gold in Cherokee territory resulted in pressure by the whites to obtain their lands. A treaty was extracted from a small part of the tribe, which bound the whole tribe to move beyond the Mississippi River within three years. Although the Cherokees overwhelmingly repudiated this document and the U.S. Supreme Court upheld the nation's autonomy, the state of Georgia secured an order for their removal, which was accomplished by military force. President Andrew Jackson refused to intervene, and in 1838 the tribe was deported to the Indian Territory (later in Oklahoma). Their leader at this time and until 1866 was Chief John Ross. Thousands died on the march or from subsequent hardships. They made their capital at Tahlequah, instituted a public school system, published newspapers, and were the most important of the Five Civilized Tribes. In the U.S. Civil War their allegiance was divided between North and South, large contingents serving on each side. By a new treaty at the close of the war they freed their Negro slaves and admitted them to tribal citizenship. In 1892 they sold their western territorial extension, known as the Cherokee Strip, and in 1906 disbanded as a tribe, becoming then U.S. citizens. About 4,500 Cherokee are still in W North Carolina, the descendants of the few who successfully resisted removal or returned after the removal. See M. L. Starkey, *The Cherokee Nation* (1946, repr. 1972); H. T. Malone, *Cherokees of the Old South* (1956); John Gulick, *Cherokees at the Crossroads* (1960); D. H. Corkran, *The Cherokee Frontier: Conflict and Survival, 1740–1762* (1962); G. S. Woodward, *The Cherokee* (1963); Irvin Peithmann, *Red Men of Fire* (1964); Thurman Wilkins, *Cherokee Tragedy* (1970).

cheroot (shərōōt'): see CIGAR AND CIGARETTE.

cherry, name for several species of trees or shrubs of the genus *Prunus* (a few are sometimes classed as *Padus*) of the family Rosaceae (ROSE family) and for their fruits. The small round red to black fruits are botanically designated drupes, or stone fruits, as are those of the closely related peach, apricot, and plum. The cherry is one of the most commonly grown home-orchard fruits. About 600 varieties are cultivated, practically all derived from two species—*P. avium* (sweet cherries) and *P. cerasus* (sour cherries). Both are believed to be native to Asia Minor and have long been cultivated; they were mentioned in the writings of the ancients. Sour cherries are hardier and more easily grown than sweet cherries and are mostly self-fertile, while many sweet cherries must be cross-pollinated to bear well. The fruit is popular raw, in preserves, and in pies; cherry cider and liqueurs (see MARASCHINO) are also made. Europe is the largest producing area. Several species of the **flowering cherry,** many native to the Far East, are cultivated as weeping or erect trees for their beautiful, usually double flowers. The Japanese make a national festival of cherry-blossom time; the city of Tokyo presented a number of trees to Washington, D.C., where they have become a popular spring attraction. The species of American **wild cherry** include the chokecherry, pin cherry, and wild black cherry. These have smaller fruits than the cultivated cherries and are seldom used except for jelly. Wood of the wild black cherry, or rum cherry (*P. serotina*), usually reddish in color, is fine grained and of high quality. It takes a high polish and is prized for cabinetwork. The aromatic bark and leaves contain hydrocyanic acid, characteristic of many cherries. The **cherry laurel** (*P. laurocerasus* or *Laurocerasus officinalis*) is an Old World evergreen species cultivated elsewhere in many varieties as an ornamental. The leaves are sometimes used as a flavoring and in making cherry laurel water. The American cherry laurel (*P.* or *L. caroliniana*), called mock orange in the South, is similar but larger. For the cherry plum, or myrobalan, see PLUM. Cherries are classified in the division MAGNOLIOPHYTA, class Magnoliopsida, order Rosales, family Rosaceae.

Chersiphron (kûr'sĭfrən), fl. 6th cent. B.C., Cretan architect. According to tradition he was the builder of the original archaic Ionic temple of Artemis at EPHESUS in Asia Minor (550 B.C.). He and his son Metagenes were said to be coauthors of a treatise on architectural engineering.

Cherson: see SEVASTOPOL, USSR.

Chersonese (kûrsōnēs') or **Chersonesus** (–nē'səs) [Gr.,=peninsula], name applied in ancient geography to several regions. See CRIMEA (Chersonesus Taurica or Scythia); GALLIPOLI PENINSULA (Chersonesus Thracica); MALAY PENINSULA (Chersonesus Aurea); JUTLAND (Chersonesus Cimbrica).

chert: see FLINT.

Chertsey (chûrt'sē), urban district (1971 pop. 44,886), Surrey, SE England. Its market gardens serve London. There are varied engineering works.

cherub, plural **cherubim,** kind of ANGEL. Cherubim were probably thought of, anciently, as composite creatures like the winged creatures of Assyria. In Jewish tradition, they are described (Ezek. 10) as having four faces and four wings and also as beautiful young men; but late Christian art made plump children of them, as in Raphael's *Sistine Madonna.* With the seraphim (see SERAPH) they are said to be in the very presence of God. The color surrounding them is traditionally blue. See Gen. 3.24; Ex. 25.18–22; 37.6–9; 1 Kings 6.23–28; Pss. 18.10; 80.1.

Cherubini, Luigi (lwē'jē kärōōbē'nē), 1760–1842, Italian composer, who lived in Paris after 1788. Before he was 16 he wrote masses and other sacred works, and he later composed Italian opera. In Paris he assimilated French operatic tradition and wrote operas of broad dramatic scope with rich orchestration, such as *Médée* (1797) and *Les Deux Journées* (1800), which influenced Beethoven's vocal music. In 1816 he became professor of composition at the Paris Conservatory and in 1822 its director. Renowned for his contrapuntal skill, in his later years he wrote mostly sacred music, including his masses in F Major (1809) and A Major (1825) and his Requiem in D Minor (1836).

chervil, name for two similar edible Old World herbs of the family Umbelliferae (CARROT family). The salad chervil is *Anthriscus cerefolium.* Its leaves, like those of the related dill and parsley, are used for seasoning. The turnip-rooted chervil (*Chaerophyllum bulbosum*) is cultivated for its edible root. Other species of *Chaerophyllum* [Gr.,=gladdening leaf, for the fragrant foliage] are also called chervil, e.g., the native American *C. procumbens.* Chervil is classified in the division MAGNOLIOPHYTA, class Magnoliopsida, order Umbellales, family Umbelliferae.

Chesalon (kĕs'əlŏn), town of Judah, called also Mt. Jearim, W of Jerusalem. Joshua 15.10.

Chesapeake (chĕs'əpēk), city (1970 pop. 89,580), independent and in no county, SE Va.; inc. 1963. Chesapeake was created (1963) by merging the former city of South Norfolk with all of Norfolk co. Within its vast area are residential sections; much farmland, with related agricultural industries; and a large part of the Great Dismal Swamp. There are also industries manufacturing a great variety of products, including fertilizer, chemicals, lumber and wood items, steel equipment, and cement. The Battle of Great Bridge was fought (1775) in Chesapeake. The Dismal Swamp Canal was completed in 1822.

Chesapeake, U.S. frigate, famous for her role in the *Chesapeake* affair (June 22, 1807) and for her battle with the H.M.S. *Shannon* (June 1, 1813). The *Chesapeake* left Norfolk, Va., for the Mediterranean under the command of James BARRON in June, 1807. Just outside U.S. territorial waters the H.M.S. *Leopard* stopped her and demanded the right to search her for British deserters. Barron refused to allow this, and shortly afterwards the *Leopard* opened fire. Unprepared for action, Barron was forced to submit and allow the impressment of four of his crew (two of whom were American-born). The incident caused intense indignation, and war seemed imminent. In the War of 1812, the refitted *Chesapeake,* commanded by James LAWRENCE, engaged (June 1, 1813) the H.M.S. *Shannon* outside Boston harbor. Lawrence was mortally wounded, and his last command is reportedly the famous "Don't give up the ship!" The *Chesapeake* was, however, captured. See studies by Kenneth Poolman (1961), Peter Padfield (1968), and H. F. Pullen (1970).

Chesapeake and Delaware Canal, sea-level canal, 19 mi (31 km) long, 250 ft (76 m) wide, and 27 ft (8.2 m) deep, connecting the head of Chesapeake Bay with the Delaware River. Built in 1824–29, the canal was bought by the Federal government in 1919 and later was enlarged and modernized. It is part of the Intracoastal Waterway and can accommodate oceangoing vessels. See study by R. D. Gray (1967).

Chesapeake and Ohio Canal, former waterway, c.185 mi (300 km) long, from Washington, D.C., to Cumberland, Md., running along the north bank of the Potomac River. A successor to the Potomac Company's (1784–1828) navigation improvement project, the Chesapeake and Ohio Canal was planned to extend W to Pittsburgh. Work was begun in 1828, but financial and labor problems (leading in 1834 to the first use of Federal troops to settle a labor dispute), as well as opposition from the rival Baltimore and Ohio RR, delayed completion to Cumberland until 1850. Although extension to Pittsburgh proved impractical, the canal experienced a busy period in the 1870s carrying coal from the Cumberland mines. The canal was used until it was damaged by floods in 1924. It was sold in 1938 to the U.S. government. The canal, partially restored, was made a national monument in 1961. In 1971 it became a national historic park. See study by G. W. Ward (1899, repr. 1973).

Chesapeake & Ohio Railway (C&O), U.S. transportation company with railroad lines in eight states, Washington, D.C., and Ontario, Canada. Founded as the Louisa RR Company in Virginia in 1836, the railroad changed its name to the Virginia Central Company in 1850. It served the Confederate armies during the Civil War and was severely damaged by Union raids. In 1869 financier Collis P. Huntington purchased the line; it received its present name in 1878. The C&O, one of the most solvent railroads in the United States, receives nearly all of its net income from carrying freight and is the nation's largest carrier of bituminous coal. In 1963 the C&O acquired control of the BALTIMORE & OHIO RR.

Chesapeake Bay, inlet of the Atlantic Ocean, c.200 mi (320 km) long, from 3 to 30 mi (4.8–48 km) wide, and 3,237 sq mi (8, 384 sq km), separating the Delmarva Peninsula from the mainland, E Md. and E Va. The bay is the drowned mouth of the Susquehanna River and also is fed by many other rivers including the Potomac, Rappahannock, and James. Chesapeake Bay is entered from the Atlantic Ocean through a 12-mi-wide (19-km) gap between capes

Henry and Charles, Va. The CHESAPEAKE BAY BRIDGE-TUNNEL runs across the mouth of the bay. An important part of the Intracoastal Waterway, the bay is linked with the Delaware River by the Chesapeake and Delaware Canal. Baltimore, Md., is the largest city and main port on the bay; Norfolk, Va., is an important port and naval base. Commercial fishing (oysters and crabs) is important; the bay is also used for recreation. The English colonist John Smith explored and charted Chesapeake Bay in 1608, a year after the first white settlement at Jamestown, Va., was established.

Chesapeake Bay Bridge-Tunnel, 18 mi (29 km) long, across the mouth of Chesapeake Bay, E Va., connecting Cape Charles with Norfolk, Va. Opened in 1964, the complex consists of a chain of low trestle bridges, two high bridges, and two tunnels (each 1 mi/1.6 km long) under the shipping channels. The tunnels are anchored on four man-made islands.

Chesapeake Bay retriever, breed of large SPORTING DOG developed in the United States. It stands about 24 in. (61 cm) high at the shoulder and weighs about 65 lb (29.5 kg). Its thick, short double coat ranges in color from a very dark brown to the faded tan called deadgrass. Webbed feet, powerful shoulders and hindquarters, and an oily outercoat that tends to shed water, combine to make the Chesapeake a very efficient retriever in the iciest water. Although bred to retrieve ducks, it is also widely used to hunt on land and has been trained as a guide dog. See DOG.

Chesed (kē'sĕd), nephew of Abraham. Gen. 22.22.

Chesha Bay (chĕ'shə), Rus. *Cheshskaya Guba,* inlet of the Barents Sea, 84 mi (135 km) wide and 62 mi (100 km) long, Nenets National Okrug, N central European USSR. It receives the Chesha, Vizhas, Oma, and Pesha rivers.

Cheshire (chĕsh'ər) or **Chester,** county (1971 pop. 1,542,624) W central England. The county town is CHESTER. The terrain is generally low, flat, and fertile. Its chief rivers are the Mersey and the Dee, which separates Cheshire from Wales. The Wirral peninsula separates the estuaries of the two rivers. The county is important agriculturally and industrially. It engages extensively in dairy farming and grows potatoes and wheat. The chief industries are engineering, salt mining, shipbuilding, oil refining, and the manufacture of railroad cars, textiles, textile machinery, soap, paper, and chemicals. The principal industrial centers are NORTHWICH, BIRKENHEAD, STOCKPORT, CREWE, and MACCLESFIELD. Communication by road, rail, and canal (the MANCHESTER SHIP CANAL) is excellent. Cheshire was made a palatinate by William I and maintained some of its privileges as such until 1830. The numerous black-and-white-timbered manor houses attest to the county's prosperity in the 16th and 17th cent. In the last century the population of the county greatly increased with the industrialization and suburbanization of the Wirral peninsula and the part of Cheshire just S of Manchester. In 1974, most of Cheshire became part of the new nonmetropolitan county of Cheshire; NW Cheshire (including Birkenhead) became part of the new metropolitan county of Merseyside, and NE Cheshire (including Stockport) became part of the new metropolitan county of Greater Manchester.

Cheshire, town (1970 pop. 19,051), New Haven co., S central Conn., in a farm area; settled 1695, inc. 1780. It is chiefly residential, with some machine shop manufactures. The painter John Frederick Kensett was born in Cheshire.

Cheshunt (chĕs'ənt), urban district (1971 pop. 44,947), Hertfordshire, SE England. A suburb of London, it is a prominent market-gardening district. Theobalds Park, an 18th-century mansion, is noteworthy.

Chesil (kē'sĭl), the same as BETHEL **2**.

Chesney, Francis Rawdon, 1789–1872, British soldier and explorer in Asia. His examination of a route for the Suez Canal (1829) demonstrated the feasibility of building a canal and led the vicomte de LESSEPS to undertake the project. In 1835, Chesney commanded an expedition to survey N Syria. He proved the navigability of the Tigris and Euphrates and urged the adoption of a Euphrates route to India. In 1856 and 1862 he was associated with a Euphrates valley railroad project, but the scheme fell through. His works include *The Expedition for the Survey of the Rivers Euphrates and Tigris* (2 vol., 1850) and *Narrative of the Euphrates Expedition* (1868). See biography by his wife and his daughter (ed. by Stanley Lane-Poole, 1885).

Chesnutt, Charles Waddell, 1858–1932, American author, b. Cleveland, Ohio. In 1887 he was admitted to the Ohio bar. Chesnutt is considered the first American Negro novelist. He is best known for *The Conjure Woman* (1899), a series of dialect stories about Negro slave life. His other works include *The Wife of His Youth* (1899), a group of stories; a biography of Frederick Douglass (1899); and several novels.

chess, game for two players played on a square board composed of 64 square spaces, alternately dark (commonly designated as Black) and light (White) in color. The board is placed so that a light-colored square is in the corner to the right of each player, who is provided with 16 pieces, or chessmen, of his own color. At the outset of the game eight pieces are set down in the horizontal row of squares, or rank, nearest each player. The pieces (and their abbreviations) are: two rooks (R), or castles, in the corner squares; two knights (N, Kt, or S) in the adjoining squares; two bishops (B) next to the knights; the queen (Q) on the remaining square corresponding to her color; and the king (K) on the other remaining center square; one pawn (P) is placed immediately in front of each of these pieces. Each type of piece is moved according to specific rules and is removed from the board when it is displaced by the move of one of the opposing pieces into its square. The object in chess is to trap, or checkmate, the opponent's king. Several systems of notation are used to describe the moves of the pieces. The most popular one is the descriptive system, also called English notation. According to that system each vertical row of squares, or file, is named for the pieces on it at the beginning of the game. The ranks are numbered 1 through 8 away from the player, either White or Black, who is moving. A move is described by naming the piece that is moved and the square that it is moved to. The square is designated by the name of its file and the number of its rank, with each player counting from his side of the board. When only one piece of a kind can make a particular move, the piece's original position is not specified in the notation. The symbol - means "to" and the symbol x means "takes," indicating a capture. If, for example, White's first move were to advance the pawn in front of his king two squares, the notation would read P-K4. Various players are known for their openings, middle games, or end games, with many of the moves named for the great players who have originated them or for countries, as in the Ruy Lopez opening or the Sicilian defense. Chess has fascinated people for centuries, and there is evidence that a game similar to modern chess was played in the 6th and 7th cent. It probably originated in India, spreading to Persia and then to the Levant, and it may have been introduced into Europe by the Muslims. By the 13th cent., it was played all over Western Europe and had undergone little change from the game as played by the Persians. Outstanding players of their day who were considered world champions were: 1747–95, François Philidor of France; 1815–20, Alexandre Deschappelles of France; 1820–40, Louis de la Bourdonnais of France; and 1843–51, Howard Staunton of England. The first modern international chess tournament was held in London in 1851. Since then official world champions have been: 1851–58 and 1862–66, Adolph Anderssen of Germany; 1858–62, Paul C. Morphy of the United States; 1866–94, Wilhelm Steinitz of Austria; 1894–1921, Emanuel Lasker of Germany; 1921–27, José R. Capablanca of Cuba; 1927–35 and 1937–46, Alexander A. Alekhine of France; 1935–37, Max Euwe of the Netherlands; 1948–57, 1958–60, 1961–63, Mikhail Botvinnik of the USSR; 1957–58, Vassily Smyslov of the USSR; 1960–61, Mikhail Tal of the USSR; 1963–69, Tigran Petrosian of the USSR; 1969–72, Boris Spassky of the USSR; and 1972–74, Robert J. Fischer of the United States. The 1972 World Chess Championship match, held in Reykjavík, Iceland, received unprecedented worldwide coverage and brought Fischer, the winner, a purse of over $156,000. Fischer resigned the title in 1974, the first player ever to do so. Chess has an extensive literature. A good book for beginners is Capablanca's *A Primer of Chess* (1935, repr. 1963). See H. J. R. Murray, *A History of Chess* (1913, repr. 1962); H. A. Davidson, *A Short History of Chess* (1949, repr. 1968); Fred Reinfeld, *Complete Book of Chess Stratagems* (1958, repr. 1972); Israel A. Horowitz and P. L. Rothenberg, *Complete Book of Chess* (1969); Anne Sunnucks, ed., *Encyclopedia of Chess* (1970); Larry Evans, *Chess World Championships 1972: Fischer-Spassky* (1972); Edward Lasker, *The Game of Chess* (1972); H. C. Schonberg, *Grandmasters of Chess* (1973).

Chester, county borough (1971 pop. 62,696), county town of Cheshire, W central England, on a sandstone height above the Dee River. It is a railroad junction. Its manufactures include electrical switchgear, paint, and window panes. Tourism is also economically important. Formerly Chester had great military importance, and it was a significant port for centuries. Under the name Castra Devana or Deva it was the headquarters of the Roman 20th legion. It was ravaged by Æthelfrith of Northumbria in the 7th cent. and the Danes in the 9th cent. Æthelflaed of Mercia fortified Chester again in the 10th cent. William I took it in 1070 and the following year granted it to his nephew, Hugh Lupus, as a palatine earldom. Chester served the English crown as a defensive bastion and was used as a base for operations against Wales from 1275 to 1284. During the ENGLISH CIVIL WAR Parliamentarians took Chester by siege in 1646. Ireland was the town's primary trading partner. Its role as a port peaked from c.1350 to 1450; silting and the rise of Liverpool contributed to the end of this role by the late 18th cent. Modern Chester is medieval in appearance. It is the only city in England that still possesses its entire wall. Interesting features are the red sandstone wall with a walk along the top; Agricola's Tower; 15th- and 16th-century timbered houses; the cathedral, with architecture of styles from Norman to Late Perpendicular; the Roodee, on which races have been held since 1540; St. John's Church (formerly a cathedral); Grosvenor Museum; and "The King's School," a public school founded by Henry VIII in 1541. Characteristic of Chester are the Rows, a double tier of shops formed by recessing the second stories of the buildings along the main streets. This creates a sheltered walk upon the roofs of the street-level stores. The Chester Plays (see MIRACLE PLAY) originated in the town. In 1974, Chester became part of the new nonmetropolitan county of Cheshire.

Chester, city (1970 pop. 56,331), Delaware co., SE Pa., on the Delaware River, an industrial suburb of Philadelphia; settled c.1644 by Swedes, inc. as a city 1866. It is a port of entry and has an important shipbuilding industry that dates from before the Civil War. In addition to one of the largest shipyards and drydocks in the United States, there are steel mills, oil refineries, automobile assembly plants, and factories making a huge variety of products, including aircraft parts, chemicals, and electrical equipment. The oldest city in the state, Chester (established as Upland) was the site of William Penn's first landing (1682) in America. Penn renamed the settlement and convened (1682) the first assembly of the province there. Historic attractions include the foundations of the original settlement, in Governor Printz Park; the Morton Homestead (1654); the Caleb Pusey House, at Landingford Plantation (1683); the old courthouse (1724); and the Washington House (1747), where Washington wrote his report (1777) on the battle of Brandywine.

Chesterfield, Philip Dormer Stanhope, 4th **earl of,** 1694–1773, English statesman and author. A noted wit and orator, his long public career, begun in 1715, included an ambassadorship to The Hague (1728-32), a seat in Parliament, and a successful tenure as lord lieutenant of Ireland (1745-46). His literary fame rests upon his letters to his illegitimate son, Philip Stanhope (first pub. 1774), designed for the education of a young man, and upon his letters to his godson (pub. 1890). See edition of his letters by Bonamy Dobree (6 vol., 1932) and additional letters edited by S. L. Gulick, Jr. (1938); study by Samuel Shellabarger (rev. ed. 1951, repr. 1971).

Chesterfield, municipal borough (1971 pop. 70,153), Derbyshire, central England. An important industrial center, the borough produces mining equipment, railroad cars, metal products, and many other goods. Of interest are the Stephenson Memorial Hall (named in honor of the inventor George Stephenson, who lived and is buried in Chesterfield), the 16th-century grammar school, and the 14th-century church with a twisted spire.

Chesterfield Inlet, Canadian government post in the Keewatin dist., Northwest Territories, at the mouth of Chesterfield Inlet of Hudson Bay.

Chester Plays: see MIRACLE PLAY.

Chesterton, Gilbert Keith, 1874–1936, English author. Conservative, even reactionary, in his thinking, Chesterton was a convert (1922) to Roman Catholicism and its champion. He has been called the "prince of paradox" because his dogma is often hidden beneath a light, energetic, and whimsical style. A prolific writer, Chesterton wrote studies of Browning (1903) and Dickens (1906); several novels including *The Napoleon of Notting Hill* (1904) and *The Man Who Was Thursday* (1908); a noted series of crime stories featuring Father Brown as detective; many poems, collected in 1927; and his famous essays, collected in *Tremendous Trifles* (1909), *Come to Think of It* (1930), and other volumes. He was the editor of *G. K.'s Weekly,* an organ of the Distributist League, which advocated the small-holding system. An amusing artist, he illustrated books by Hilaire BELLOC, his friend and collaborator. See his autobiography (1936); biography by Dudley Barker (1973); studies by Christopher Hollis (1970), A. M. Bogaerts (1940, repr. 1972), and Julius West (1915, repr. 1973).

chestnut, name for any species of the genus *Castanea,* deciduous trees of the family Fagaceae (BEECH or oak family) widely distributed in the Northern Hemisphere. They are characterized by thin-shelled, sweet, edible nuts borne in a bristly bur. The common American chestnut, *C. dentata,* is native E of the Mississippi but is now nearly extinct because of the chestnut blight, a disease from Asia caused by the fungus *Endothia parasitica.* Efforts are being made to breed a type of American chestnut resistant to the disease, by crossing it with the blight-resistant Chinese and Japanese chestnuts, in order to replace the old chestnut forests, some of which are still standing as dead, or "ghost," forests. The dead and fallen logs are still the leading domestic source of tannin. Chestnut wood is porous, but it is very durable in soil and has been popular for fence posts, railway ties, and beams. Edible chestnuts are now mostly imported from Italy, where the Eurasian species (*C. sativa*) has not been destroyed. The CHINQUAPIN belongs to the same genus. Chestnuts are classified in the division MAGNOLIOPHYTA, class Magnoliopsida, order Fagales, family Fagaceae.

Chesulloth (kēsŭl'ŏth), town, N Palestine, the same as CHISLOTH-TABOR. Joshua 19.18.

Chesuncook Lake (chĭsŭn'ko͝ok), 22 mi (35 km) long and from 1 to 4 mi (1.6-6.4 km) wide, N central Maine. The western branch of the Penobscot River flows through the lake, which is in a noted hunting and fishing region. Baxter State Park is nearby.

Chevalier, Guillaume Sulpice: see GAVARNI.

Chevalier, Maurice (shəvăl'yā, Fr. mōrēs' shəvälyā'), 1888-1972, French singer and film actor. He made his debut in 1900 singing and dancing at the Casino de Tourelles, Paris. As the dancing partner of Mistinguett and as the star of several Paris music halls, he won his public by his charm and inimitable smile; by 1928 his reputation was international. Among his later films are *Love in the Afternoon* (1956), *Gigi* (1958), *Can-Can* (1959), and *Fanny* (1961). See his autobiographies *With Love* (1960) and *I Remember It Well* (1970); study by Gene Ringgold (1973).

Chevalier, Michel (mēshĕl'), 1806-79, French economist. An ardent Saint-Simonian as a youth, he later favored a form of welfare capitalism. He advocated industrial development as the key to social progress. Also a proponent of free trade, he negotiated with Richard Cobden the Anglo-French trade treaty of 1860. His *Lettres sur l'Amérique du Nord* (1836) extols the United States.

Cheverus, Jean Louis Anne Madeleine Lefebvre de (zhäN lwē än mädəlĕn' ləfĕ'vrə də shəvrüs'), 1768-1836, French churchman, first Roman Catholic bishop of Boston (1810-23). He was ordained in France and had to flee (1792) during the French Revolutionary Wars. In England he lived by teaching until 1796, when he went to Boston. He worked all over New England and was known for his work with the Indians in Maine. He was also highly esteemed as a physician. In 1810 he was consecrated bishop of Boston. At length his health began to fail, and he asked for transfer to France. Catholics and Protestants in the United States begged him to remain, but he accepted a transfer to the see of Montauban (1823). In 1826 he became archbishop of Bordeaux and in 1836 cardinal. He did much to extend the tolerance of Roman Catholicism in America. See biography by A. M. Melville (1958).

Cheves, Langdon (chĭ'vĭs), 1776-1857, American statesman, b. Abbeville District (now Abbeville co.), S.C. Admitted to the bar in 1797, he became one of the leading lawyers of Charleston. In the U.S. House of Representatives (1810-15) he was one of the "war hawks" who agitated for hostilities with Britain. He served as chairman of the Ways and Means Committee and in 1814 succeeded Henry Clay as speaker. In this capacity Cheves cast the deciding vote against Alexander J. Dallas's bill for establishing the Second Bank of the United States, but it was chartered anyway in 1816. The bank was badly mismanaged until Cheves, elected a director and president in 1819, restored its credit. On his resignation in 1822, Nicholas Biddle took over the bank.

Cheviot (shĭv'ēət, shĕv'-), city (1970 pop. 11,135), Hamilton co., extreme SW Ohio, a residential suburb of Cincinnati; settled early 1800s, inc. 1904. It has diverse light manufacturing industries.

Cheviot Hills (chĕv'ēət, chēv'-), range, c.35 mi (56 km) long, extending along part of the border between Scotland and England. The highest point is The Cheviot (2,676 ft/816 m). The North Tyne and branches of the River Tweed rise there. Since World War II the hills have been reforested. Northumberland National Park (398 sq mi/1,031 sq km; est. 1956) and Border National Forest Park occupy most of the hills. The Cheviots have been the scene of much border strife. They are celebrated in the ballad "Chevy Chase." A fine type of sheep, the cheviot, is bred there.

Chevreul, Michel Eugène (mēshĕl' özhĕn' shəvröl'), 1786-1889, French chemist. He studied under L. N. Vauquelin, was director of the Gobelin tapestry works, and from 1830 was professor, and from 1860 to 1879 director, at the natural history museum at Paris. Noted for his researches in the composition of animal fats (by which he contributed to the development of the soap and candle industry), he discovered and named olein and stearin and wrote *Recherches sur les corps gras d'origine animale* (1823). He also worked and wrote on color contrasts; the results of his studies influenced the neoimpressionist painters Seurat and Signac.

Chevreuse, Marie de Rohan-Montbazon, duchesse de (märē' də rōäN'-môNbäzôN' düshĕs' də shəvröz'), 1600-1679, French beauty and politician, an intimate of the French queen, Anne of Austria. Her continuous intrigues in opposition to King Louis XIII's minister, Cardinal Richelieu, caused her to be banished repeatedly from the court and to be exiled. She proved to be even more dangerous abroad because of her intrigues with France's enemies, notably Duke Charles IV of Lorraine. In the FRONDE she at first served as a link with Spain against Cardinal Mazarin, Richelieu's successor, but subsequently she became Mazarin's ally. See biography by Michael Charol (1971).

chevrotain, name for four species of small, ruminant mammals of Africa and SE Asia. Although they are also called mouse deer, chevrotains are not closely related to true deer, and are classified in a family of their own. The smallest of the hoofed mammals, they stand 8 to 14 in. (20-66 cm) high at the shoulder, depending on the species. The body is rabbitlike, with an arched back; the legs are very slender and end in small feet; the snout is tapered and somewhat piglike. The reddish-brown coat is spotted with white in most species. Chevrotains lack antlers but have tusklike upper canine teeth, used by the males for fighting. The upper incisors are lacking. Solitary, nocturnal animals of thick forests, chevrotains browse on leaves, twigs, and fruit. They sometimes rest in the branches of low trees. The water chevrotain *(Hyemoschus aquaticus)* of Africa is always found near water and takes to the water when pursued. The other chevrotains (*Tragulus* species) are found from India to Indonesia and the Philippines. Chevrotains are classified in the phylum CHORDATA, subphylum Vertebrata, class Mammalia, order Artiodactyla, family Tragulidae.

Chevy Chase (chĕv'ē), village (1970 pop. 16,424), Montgomery co., W central Md., a residential suburb of Washington, D.C.; inc. 1914.

Chew, Benjamin, 1722-1810, American public official and judge, b. Anne Arundel co., Md. He read law in Philadelphia under Andrew Hamilton and was admitted (1746) to the bar. After practicing law at New Castle and Dover, Del., Chew returned to Philadelphia, where he held several public offices and was attorney general (1755-69). He was chief justice of the Pennsylvania supreme court from 1774 until the outbreak of the American Revolution, when he was suspected of Loyalist sympathies. He was arrested but was discharged soon afterward. He later served (1791-1808) as president of the high court of errors and appeals of Pennsylvania. See biography by B. A. Konkle (1932).

chewing gum, confection consisting usually of CHICLE, flavorings, and corn syrup and sugar (although there are gums with artificial sweeteners on the market). Prehistoric people are believed to have chewed resins. Spruce resin was chewed as a thirst quencher by American Indians, from whom pioneers adopted the custom. Refined paraffin was later used and then chicle, which was probably first imported into the United States through Mexico. A chicle gum was patented in 1869 by William and Semple. In the present-day manufacture of chewing gum blocks of chicle are ground, melted, and cleared in a whirling vat, and then the flavorings (e.g., fruits, licorice, mints) and other ingredients are added. The gum is rolled through sheeting machinery and chopped into sticks or into candy-coated pellets. Insoluble plastics may be mixed with or substituted for the chicle. Although the United States is the major producer, exporter, and consumer, the industry has also been established in Canada, Japan, Egypt, West Germany, and especially the Latin American countries.

Cheyenne (shīăn', -ĕn'), city (1970 pop. 40,914), alt. 6,062 ft (1,848 m), state capital and seat of Laramie co., SE Wyo., near the Colo. and Nebr. lines; inc. 1867. It is a market for sheep and cattle ranches and a shipping center with good transportation facilities. The city sprang up after the Union Pacific RR selected this site for a division point in 1867. It was made territorial capital in 1869. In the 1870s the development of the area as a cattle-ranching section and the opening of the Black Hills gold fields stimulated the city's growth. Cheyenne revives its past annually with a Frontier Days celebration, first held in 1897. Landmarks include the state capitol and the supreme court building, housing the state historical museum and library. Nearby are Francis E. Warren Air Force Base, a veterans hospital, and a U.S. horticultural station.

Cheyenne, river, 527 mi (848 km) long, rising in E Wyo. and flowing NE to the Missouri River near Pierre, S.Dak. The Cheyenne basin is part of the Missouri River basin project. The U.S. Bureau of Reclamation has established a project on the Belle Fourche River, the Cheyenne's main tributary; the Rapid Valley irrigation project in the Cheyenne valley; and the Angostura Dam, for irrigation, hydroelectric power, and flood control, on the Cheyenne itself.

Cheyenne Indians, North American Indians whose language belongs to the Algonquian branch of the Algonquian-Wakashan linguistic stock (see AMERICAN INDIAN LANGUAGES). The Cheyenne abandoned their settlements in Minnesota in the 17th cent., leaving the region to the hostile Sioux and Ojibwa. Gradually migrating W along the Cheyenne River and then south, they established earth-lodge villages and raised crops. After the introduction of the horse (c.1760) they eventually became nomadic buffalo hunters. The tribe split (c.1830) when a large group decided to settle on the upper Arkansas River and take advantage of the trade facilities offered by Bent's Fort. This group became known as the Southern Cheyenne. The Northern Cheyenne continued to live about the headwaters of the Platte River. For the next few years the Southern Cheyenne, allied with the Arapaho, were engaged in constant warfare against the Kiowa, Comanche, and Apache. Peace was made c.1840, and the five tribes became allies. The Cheyenne were generally friendly toward white settlers, until the discovery of gold in Colorado (1858) brought a swarm of gold seekers into their lands. By a treaty signed in 1861 the Cheyenne agreed to live on a reservation in SE Colorado, but the U.S. government did not fulfill its obligations, and the Indians were reduced to near starvation. Cheyenne raids resulted in punitive expeditions by the U.S. army. The indiscriminate massacre (1864) of warriors, women, and children at SAND CREEK, Colo., was an unprovoked assault on a friendly group. The incident aroused the Indians to fury, and a bitter war followed. Gen. George CUSTER destroyed (1868) Black Kettle's camp on the Washita River, and fighting between the whites and the Southern Cheyenne ended, except for an outbreak in 1874-75. The Northern Cheyenne joined with the Sioux in massacring Custer and his 7th Cavalry at the Battle of the Little Bighorn in 1876. They finally surrendered in 1877 and were moved south and confined with the Southern Cheyenne in what is now Oklahoma. Plagued by disease and malnutrition, they made two desperate attempts to escape and return to the north. A separate reservation was eventually established for them in Montana. See G. B. Grinnell, *The Fighting Cheyennes* (1915, repr. 1956) and *The Cheyenne Indians* (2 vol., 1923, repr. 1972); E. A. Hoebel, *The Cheyennes* (1960); D. J. Berthrong, *The Southern Cheyennes* (1963); Joseph Millard, *The Cheyenne Wars* (1964); John Stands in Timber and Margot Liberty, *Cheyenne Memories* (1967); P. J. Powell, *Sweet Medicine* (2 vol., 1969).

Cheyne, Thomas Kelly (chā'nē), 1841-1915, English clergyman and biblical critic, educated at Oxford. While studying at Göttingen, he was influenced by Georg Ewald and gained a view of German biblical criticism little known at the time in England. From 1885 to 1908 he was Oriel professor of the interpretation of Scripture at Oxford as well as canon of Rochester. He was the author of many books of biblical criticism; his most celebrated work was on the Major Prophets and on the Psalms. He also wrote *Jewish Religious Life after the Exile* (1898) and *The Reconciliation of Races and Religions* (1914). With J. S. Black, Cheyne edited the *Encyclopaedia Biblica* (4 vol., 1899-1903).

Chezib (kē'zĭb), probably the same as ACHZIB **2**.

Chiabrera, Gabriello (gäbrē-ĕl'lō kyäbrĕ'rä), 1552-1638?, Italian poet. He adapted classical forms to Italian verse and wrote graceful lyrics in the manner of Anacreon. Wordsworth translated some of his verse.

Chia-hsing (jēä-shĭng) or **Kashing** (kä'shĭng'), town, N Chekiang prov., SE China, at the junction of the Grand Canal, the Whangpoo River, and the Hangchow-Shanghai RR. An important marketing center for rice and silk, it has textile mills, food-processing establishments, and cement plants.

Chia-i or **Chiayi** (both: jēä-ē), city (1969 pop. 234,359), S Taiwan. It is an agricultural market for rice, peanuts, vegetables, sugarcane, and timber from the surrounding area. The city is also the headquarters for the Chia-i irrigation system and is a transportation center.

Chia-ling (jēä-lĭng) or **Kialing** (kyä'lĭng), river, c.450 mi (720 km) long, rising in S Kansu prov., central China, and flowing S through Shensi and Szechwan provs. to join the Yangtze River at Chungking; it receives the Fou and Ch'u rivers. One of the Yangtze's chief tributaries, the Chia-ling is navigable up through the Szechwan basin, an important agricultural and industrial area.

Chia-mu-ssu (jēä-mōō-sōō) or **Kiamusze** (kyä'-mōō'sōō', jēä'-), city (1970 est. pop. 275,000), E Heilungkiang prov., China. It is the chief port on the lower reaches of the Sungari River; the city has coal, aluminum, lumber, paper, textile, farm machinery, and beet-sugar-processing industries. There are rail connections to Harbin, to North Korea, and to the Soviet Union. Nearby Santaokang is the site of a huge state farm that was equipped by the USSR. The city was formerly the capital of Hokiang prov.

Chi'an or **Kian** (both: jē-än), city (1970 est. pop. 100,000), central Kiangsi prov., China. It is a major commercial port on the Kan River and an important road hub. There are coal mines in the vicinity. Chi'an is known for its pagoda. The city was formerly called Luling.

Chiang Ching (jēäng jĭng), c.1913-, Chinese Communist political leader, wife of Mao Tse-tung. Born Li Yun-ho, she changed her name to Lan Ping when she began an acting career in the 1930s. She joined the Communist party in 1938, the same year that she adopted her present name. In 1939 she married Mao Tse-tung and thereafter remained in the background of Chinese Communist affairs until the outbreak of the Cultural Revolution (1966-69). Appointed deputy director (1966) of the Cultural Revolution, she established herself as a leading radical figure. She replaced practically all earlier works of drama, art, and music with works designed specifically to spread Maoist doctrine. She has been a member of the politburo since 1969, and is considered one of the most powerful political figures in China.

Chiang Ching-kuo (jēäng jĭng-gwô), 1909-, Chinese Nationalist leader, eldest son of CHIANG KAI-SHEK. After spending 12 years in the Soviet Union, he returned to China (1937) and served in minor government posts. Following the Nationalist retreat to Taiwan (1949), he rose to control the armed forces and intelligence agencies, and became a powerful figure within the Kuomintang party. He served as Nationalist China's defense minister from 1965 until his appointment as premier in 1972. He is considered Chiang Kai-shek's probable successor as leader of the Nationalist government on Taiwan.

Chiang Kai-shek (jēäng kī-shĕk, jyäng), 1887-, Chinese Nationalist leader. He is also called Chiang Chung-cheng. He was graduated (1909) from a military academy in Japan, and was then assigned for field training with a regiment of the Japanese army. He returned to China in 1911 and took part in the revolution against the Manchus. Chiang was active (1913-16) in attempts to overthrow the government of YÜAN SHIH-KAI. When SUN YAT-SEN established (1917) the Canton government, Chiang served as his military aide. In 1923 he was sent by Sun to the USSR to study military organization and to seek aid for the Canton regime. On his return he was appointed commandant of the newly established (1924) Whampoa Military Academy; he grew more prominent in the KUOMINTANG after the death (1925) of Sun Yat-sen. In 1926 he launched the NORTHERN EXPEDITION, leading the victorious Nationalist army into Hankow, Shanghai, and Nanking. Chiang, following the original policy of Sun Yat-sen, cooperated with the Chinese Communists and accepted Russian aid, but in 1927 he dramatically reversed himself, initiating the long civil war between the Kuomintang and the Communists. By the end of 1927, Chiang controlled the Kuomintang, and in 1928 he became head of the Nationalist government at Nanking and generalissimo of all Chinese Nationalist forces. Thereafter, under various titles and offices, he exercised virtually uninterrupted power as leader of the Nationalist government. In 1936, Gen. CHANG HSUEH-LIANG siezed him at Sian, supposedly to force him to terminate the civil war against the Communists and to establish a united front against the encroaching Japanese. A partial truce was concluded between Chiang and the Communists, and Chiang was released. Despite the outbreak of the Sino-Japanese War in 1937 the agreement soon broke down, and, by 1940, Chiang's best troops were being used against the Communists in the northwest. After the Japanese took Nanking and Hankow, Chiang moved his capital to Chungking. As the Sino-Japanese War merged with World War II, Chiang's international prestige increased. He attended the Cairo Conference (1943) with Franklin Delano Roosevelt and Winston Churchill. He and his wife, who had been Soong Mei-ling (see SOONG, family), were the international symbols of China at war, but Chiang was bitterly criticized by Allied officers, notably Joseph W. Stilwell, and argument raged over his internal policies and his conduct of the war. After the war ended Chiang failed to achieve a settlement with the Communists, and civil war continued. In 1948, Chiang became the first president elected under a new, liberalized constitution. He soon resigned, however, and his moderate vice president, Gen. LI TSUNG-JEN, attempted to negotiate a truce with the Communists. The talks failed, and, in 1949, Chiang resumed leadership of the Kuomintang to oppose the Communists, who were sweeping into S China in strong military force and reducing the territories held by the Nationalists. By 1950, Chiang and the Nationalist government had been driven from the mainland to the island of TAIWAN (Formosa). On Taiwan, Chiang took firm command and established a virtual dictatorship. He reorganized his military forces with U.S. aid and then instituted limited democratic political reforms. Chiang continued to promise reconquest of the Chinese mainland and at times landed Nationalist guerrillas on the China coast, often to the embarrassment of the United States. His international position was weakened considerably in 1972 when the United Nations, reversing its former policy, expelled his regime and accepted the Communists as the sole legitimate government of China. His writings have appeared in English as *China's Destiny* (1947) and *Soviet Russia in China* (1957). See biographies by Robert Berkov (1938), H. K. Tong (rev. ed. 1953), and Richard Curtis (1969); P. P. Y. Loh, *The Early Chiang Kai-Shek* (1971).

Chiangmai (jēäng'mī') or **Chiengmai** (jēĕng'-), city (1970 pop. 89,272), capital of Chiangmai prov., N Thailand, on the Ping River, near the Burmese border. It is Thailand's third largest city and the economic, cultural, and religious center of the northern provinces. The terminus of a railroad from Bangkok, Chiangmai is also linked to the capital by air and highway. The city is a shipping point for the agricultural products of the surrounding region. Long the center of Thailand's teak industry, Chiangmai also produces silver and wood articles, pottery, and silk and cotton goods. Chiangmai's population is mainly Lao. The city, a center of a Lao kingdom from the 11th cent., became after the 14th cent. a target of dispute between the Burmese and the Siamese. The Burmese invasions ceased in the 19th cent., and Chiangmai was fully incorporated into Thailand. The city consists of an 18th-century walled town on the right bank of the Ping and a new town on the left bank that developed around the railroad station. The Univ. of Chiangmai (1963), a teachers college, and a technical institute are in the city.

Chianti, Monti (mōn'tē kyän'tē), small range of the Apennines, c.15 mi (25 km) long, in Tuscany, central Italy, W of the Arno River; rises to c.3,000 ft (915 m). The celebrated Chianti wines are produced on its slopes.

Chiapas (chēä'päs), state, (1970 pop. 1,578,180), 28,732 sq mi (74,416 sq km), SE Mexico, on the Pacific Ocean between Guatemala and the Isthmus of Tehuantepec. TUXTLA is the capital. Chiapas is crossed by mountain ranges rising from the isthmus and extending SE into Guatemala. They are separated by low, subtropical valleys. Paralleling the coastal plain is the Sierra Madre de Chiapas, a range reaching its greatest height in Tacaná volcano. The state's principal river valley is the Grijalva, northeast of which are the central highlands, populated predominantly by Indians. Farther to the northeast, in the El Desierto region, are lower ranges, lakes, and valleys, falling away toward the Usumacinta River and the jungle plains of Tabasco. This sparsely inhabited region contains valuable forests of dyewoods and hardwoods and is also the site of several Mayan cities (notably PALENQUE). The area is also the retreat of the Lacandones, a gradually disappearing Indian group often thought to be related to the ancient Maya. The climate of Chiapas, except for the highlands, is excessively hot. Rainfall is heavy from June to November. Subsistence crops are grown; and coffee (of which Chiapas is a leading national producer), rubber, and cacao are economically important, as is livestock breeding. The state's rich mineral resources, especially silver, gold, and copper, remain mostly unexploited. In general, economic development has been hindered by remoteness and inadequate communication; but railroads, airlines, and the Inter-American Highway link Tuxtla with the highland towns and are opening up the interior. Conquered with difficulty by the Spanish, Chiapa, as it was then called, was attached to the captain generalcy of Guatemala. Never ethnologically, geographically, nor politically a part of colonial Mexico, Chiapas maintained a quasi independence during the political anarchy that followed the collapse in 1823 of the empire of Agustín de Iturbide. This status separated Chiapas from the Central American states and oriented it toward Mexico. Interesting archaeological sites have been discovered near the Indian village of Chiapa de Corzo. The state's Indians are known for their colorful dances and costumes.

chiaroscuro (kyärōskōō'rō) [Ital.,=light and dark], term once applied to an early method of printing woodcuts from several blocks and also to works in black and white or monotone. Today it is used loosely to refer to the distribution of light and dark in painting. The works of Caravaggio and Rembrandt exemplify the dramatic use of chiaroscuro effects.

chiasma (kīăz'mə): see CROSSING OVER.

Chiatura (chēətōō'rə), city (1970 pop. 25,000), SE European USSR, in Georgia, on the Kvirila River. One of the world's largest manganese producers, Chiatura alone accounted for half of the world's manganese trade before World War I. The ore is shipped to the Black Sea port of Poti for export to the Ukraine and abroad.

Chiavenna (kyävän'nä), town (1971 pop. 7,166), Lombardy, N Italy. It is a commercial center. Historically a strategic point, it commands both the Splügen and Maloja passes between Italy and Switzerland.

Chiba (chē'bä), city (1970 pop. 482,089), capital of Chiba prefecture, central Honshu, Japan, on Tokyo Bay. It is a manufacturing center noted for textiles and paper products. It was the residence of the Chiba daimyo from the 12th to the 16th cent. The city retains an 8th-century Buddhist temple. Chiba prefecture (1970 pop. 3,365,282), 1,954 sq mi (5,061 sq km), is a fertile agricultural region and a resort area. Chiba, the port of Choshi, and Funabashi are the major cities.

Chibcha (chĭb'chə), group of Indian tribes of the eastern cordillera of the Andes of Colombia. Although trade with neighboring tribes was common, the Chibcha seem to have evolved their culture in comparative isolation. They were the most highly developed of the Colombian Indians, practicing agriculture, melting and casting gold and copper ornaments, mining emeralds, weaving textiles, and making pottery. They evolved a stratified society of overlords and vassals, in which succession to office was matrilineal and inheritance of personal property was patrilineal. Among the commoners, or farmers, organization was patrilineal. The priesthood constituted a hereditary noble class. Religious ceremonies included human sacrifice. The source of the legend of *El Dorado* is attributed to them, probably because of a Chibcha ceremony, also partly legendary, in which a new ruler was covered with gold dust each year, and then washed in a sacred lake. The Chibcha were conquered by the Spanish conquistador Gonzalo JIMÉNEZ DE QUESADA between 1536 and 1541. The Chibcha languages, a separate language family, are spoken in Colombia and spread northward to other areas. Surviving Chibcha-speaking tribes, such as the Cuna and Lenca of Central America, have experienced much culture change since the Spanish conquest.

Chicago (shĭkä'gō, shĭkô'gō), city (1970 pop. 3,369,359), seat of Cook co., NE Ill., on Lake Michigan; inc. 1837. The second largest city in the country and the heart of a metropolitan area of almost 7 million people, it is the commercial, financial, industrial, and cultural center for a vast region and a great midcontinental shipping point. It is a port of entry; a major Great Lakes port, located at the junction of the St. Lawrence Seaway with the Mississippi River system; the busiest air center in the country; and an important rail and highway hub. An enormous variety of goods are manufactured there and shipped all over the world. Chicago has large grain mills and elevators, iron- and steel-works, steel-fabrication plants, stockyards, meat-packing establishments, and printing and publishing houses. Among its many other products are machinery, musical instruments, electronic equipment, furniture, chemicals, household appliances, foods, and clothing. Chicago covers over 200 sq mi (520 sq km); it extends more than 20 mi (32 km) along the lakefront, then sprawls inland to the west. Its metropolitan area stretches in the north to Evanston and other residential cities and in the south to industrial suburbs on the border of Indiana and beyond. The city's arteries are its boulevards, expressways, and a system of elevated railways (part of it a subway). The elevated lines extend into the heart of the city, making a huge rectangle for passenger convenience in transferring from one to another. This is the celebrated Loop, which gives its name to the downtown section. In or near the center of the city are the Merchandise Mart, the world's largest commercial building; the Chicago Public Library, which has neighborhood and traveling branches; the John Crerar Library of scientific books; the Chicago Board of Trade building; and the Chicago Civic Opera. La Salle St. is the financial center; State St. is known for its shops, and Randolph St. for its theaters. On the lakefront, which has many beaches, are Grant Park, with the Art Institute of Chicago, the Chicago Natural History Museum, the Adler Planetarium, the Buckingham Memorial Fountain, and the John G. Shedd Aquarium. Nearby is the huge stadium of Soldier Field, home of the Chicago Bears, the city's major-league professional football team. To the north along the lakefront is Michigan Boulevard, which, leaving the towering skyscrapers behind, proceeds past the rich hotels of the "gold coast" and enters the residential district of the north. In this section lies Lincoln Park, with the Chicago Historical Society building, the Chicago Academy of Sciences, a zoological garden, and a conservatory; sculpture in the park includes the noted standing figure of Abraham Lincoln (1887) by Augustus Saint-Gaudens and the John P. Altgeld memorial monument (1915) by Gutzon Borglum. The south side of Chicago is the seat of the Univ. of Chicago, with its imposing Gothic buildings and attractive spaciousness. Nearby is Jackson Park, with the Museum of Science and Industry. Much of the south side is, however, given over to industry and to poor residential areas, including the homes of most of Chicago's large black population. There, also, are the Union Stock Yards (founded 1865) and, at the southern edge of the city, enormous iron- and steelworks. The west side extends over a vast area and is usually spoken of as a region of nationalities because the many groups living there, though crowded next to each other physically, are more or less separate culturally. These neighborhoods grew up rapidly in the late 19th and early 20th cent. In the west, too, are large industrial areas and two well-known parks—Garfield Park, with its noted conservatory, and Humboldt Park. The west is famous for Hull House, the settlement house founded (1889) by Jane Addams. In 1961 the Hull House location, part of an urban renewal project, was selected as the site of a branch of the Univ. of Illinois in Chicago. The west stretches out in a series of suburbs, both poor and well-to-do. Other points of interest in Chicago are O'Hare International Airport, busiest in the nation; McCormick Place, the mammoth convention and exhibition center on the lakefront; the Auditorium, designed by Louis H. Sullivan; St. Patrick's Church (dedicated 1856); and the ugly but beloved water tower that survived the great fire. Notable as dividing lines in the city are the two branches of the Chicago River. In early days the river was of great value because the narrow watershed between it and the Des Plaines River (draining into the Mississippi through the Illinois River) offered an easy portage that led explorers, fur traders, and missionaries to the great central plains. Father Marquette and Louis Jolliet arrived there in 1673, and the spot was well known for a century before Jean Baptiste Point Sable (or Point du Sable) set up a trading post at the mouth of the river. John Kinzie, who succeeded him as a trader, is usually called the father of Chicago. The military post, FORT DEARBORN, was established in 1803. In the War of 1812 its garrison perished in one of the most famous tragedies of Western history. Fort Dearborn was rebuilt in 1816, and the construction of the Erie Canal in the next decade speeded the settling of the Middle West and the growth of Chicago. Harbor improvements, lake traffic, and the peopling of the prairie farmlands brought prosperity to the city. The Illinois and Michigan Canal, authorized by Congress in 1827 and completed in 1848, was soon rendered virtually obsolete by the railroads. By 1860 a number of lines connected Chicago with the rest of the nation, and the city was launched on its career as the great midcontinental shipping center. Gurdon S. Hubbard had already contributed to the establishment of the meat-packing industry, with its large stockyards. In 1871 the shambling city built of wood was almost entirely destroyed by a great fire (which legend says was started when Mrs. O'Leary's cow kicked over a lantern). The fire, one of the most famous disasters of U.S. history, killed several hundred people, rendered 90,000 homeless, and destroyed some $200 million worth of property. Chicago was rebuilt as a city of stone and steel. Industries sprang up, attracting thousands of immigrants. Many peoples have contributed to the modern city, including Germans, Scandinavians, Irish, Jews, Italians, Poles, Czechs, Lithuanians, Croats, Greeks, Chinese, and American Negroes. With industry came labor troubles, highlighted by the HAYMARKET SQUARE RIOT of 1886 and the great strikes at Pullman in 1894 (see DEBS, EUGENE V., and ALTGELD, JOHN P.). Upton Sinclair's novel of the Chicago stockyards, *The Jungle*, aroused public indignation and led to investigations and subsequent improvements. The city, although proud of its reputation for brawling lustiness, was also the center of Middle Western culture. Theodore Thomas and the Chicago Symphony Orchestra founded a great musical tradition. Chicago's literary reputation was established in the early 20th cent. by such men as Carl Sandburg, Theodore Dreiser, Eugene Field, Edgar Lee Masters, and James T. Farrell. Most notable in the development of American thought and taste in art was the WORLD'S COLUMBIAN EXPOSITION of 1893. One of the architects at the fair was Louis H. Sullivan who, together with D. H. Burnham, John W. Root, Frank Lloyd Wright, and others, made Chicago a leading architectural center; it was there that one of the distinctive U.S. contributions to architecture, the skyscraper, came into being. Chicago's continuing interest in this type of structure is seen in the John Hancock Center (1968), the Standard Oil building (1973), and the Sears Tower (1974). The city has long been an important printing center, and the circulation of the Chicago *Tribune* is now among the largest in the country. The city has many colleges and universities, including, besides the Univ. of Chicago, De Paul Univ., Northeastern Illinois Univ., Illinois Institute of Technology, Loyola Univ. of Chicago, Mundelein College, Roosevelt Univ., St. Xavier College, Chicago State Univ., Columbia College, North Park College, parts of Northwestern Univ., and several branches of the Univ. of Illinois. There are a number of theological seminaries, schools of music, art, and law, and numerous junior colleges. The noted Newberry Library and the Library of International Relations are in Chicago. The first decade of the 20th cent. saw the development of many agencies concerned with civic improvement, among them the City Club (1903), the Chicago Association of Commerce (1908), and the City Plan Commission (1909), which directs the development of the city. However, between World War I and 1933, Chicago earned unenviable renown as the home ground of gangsters—Al Capone being perhaps the most notorious—and its reputation for gangster warfare persisted long after that violent era had passed. Despite the worldwide depression of the 1930s, Chicago's world's fair, the Century of Progress Exposition (1933–34), proved how greatly the city had prospered and advanced. Perhaps the single most significant event in World War II occurred (Dec. 2, 1942) under the west stand of the Univ. of Chicago's Stagg Field, when a group of scientists working on the government's atomic bomb project achieved the world's first nuclear chain reaction. With the war came a considerable growth of the Chicago metropolitan area. In 1954 the Lyric Opera of Chicago was established, reviving the city's tradition of having its own opera company. Chicago's many cultural attractions and points of interest help make it a popular convention city. Among the many political conventions held there were the Republican national conventions of 1952 and 1960, and the Democratic national conventions of 1952, 1956, and 1968. See Lloyd Lewis and H. J. Smith, *Chicago: The History of Its Reputation* (1929); M. M. Quaife, *Checagou: From Indian Wigwam to Modern City, 1673–1835* (1933); Ernest Poole, *Giants Gone: Men Who Made Chicago* (1942); Alson J. Smith, *Chicago's Left Bank* (1953); B. L. Pierce, *A History of Chicago* (3 vol., 1937–57); H. M. Mayer, *The Port of Chicago and the St. Lawrence Seaway* (1957); R. A. Cromie, *The Great Chicago Fire* (1958); H. M. Karlen, *The Governments of Chicago* (1958); T. A. Herr, *Seventy Years in the Chicago Stockyards* (1968); H. M. Mayer, *Chicago: Growth of a Metropolis* (1969).

Chicago, river, formed in Chicago by the junction of its North Branch (24 mi/39 km long) and South Branch (10 mi/16 km long), and flowing southeast via a canal into the Des Plaines River at Lockport, Ill. The river formerly flowed east, then northeast via a channel, into Lake Michigan. Its course was reversed by the **Chicago Sanitary and Ship Canal,** built (1892–1900) on the South Branch to prevent the pollution of Lake Michigan by Chicago's sewage; locks prevent the river from entering the lake. The use of Lake Michigan's water to flush the canal was a heated political and interstate issue in the 1920s. The controversy was settled in 1930 when the U.S. Supreme Court ordered a reduction in the amount of water being diverted from the lake; this decision forced Chicago to build sewage treatment plants. The canal, 30 mi (48 km) long, 22 ft (6.7 m) deep, and from 162 to 290 ft (49–88 m) wide, is an important part of the Illinois Waterway. The channels of the Chicago River and the North Branch have been improved to aid deep-draft vessels and barges. The old Illinois and Michigan Canal, opened in 1848, was the earlier shipping link and ran parallel to the present waterway.

Chicago, Art Institute of: see ART INSTITUTE OF CHICAGO.

Chicago, University of, at Chicago; coeducational; inc. 1890, opened 1892 primarily through the gifts of John D. Rockefeller. Because of the progressive programs and distinguished faculty established under its first president, William R. HARPER (1891–1906), the Univ. of Chicago immediately achieved prominence in American education. Under Robert M. HUTCHINS (1929–51) it established a unique program of admitting students to the undergraduate division after only two years of high school and granting B.A. degrees at the age of 18 or 19. Survey courses were developed and comprehensive examinations were substituted for regular course requirements. However, under Lawrence Kimpton (1951–60), this program was largely abandoned. Significant among the university's graduate and research facilities are the Pritzker School of Medicine; the Enrico Fermi Institute for Nuclear Studies; the McDonald Observatory, at Fort Davis, Texas; the Yerkes Observatory, at Williams Bay, Wis.; and the school of education.

Chicago Heights, city (1970 pop. 40,900), Cook co., NE Ill., S of Chicago; settled in the 1830s, inc. as a city 1901. It is an industrial community where steel, automobile bodies, castings, railroad cars, and chemicals are manufactured. Prairie State College is in Chicago Heights.

Chicago Natural History Museum: see FIELD MUSEUM OF NATURAL HISTORY.

Chicago Portage Railroad National Historic Site: see NATIONAL PARKS AND MONUMENTS (table).

Chicago Sanitary and Ship Canal: see CHICAGO, river.

Chicago Symphony Orchestra, founded in 1891 by Theodore Thomas, who conducted it until 1905. Orchestra Hall was built for it in 1904 with funds raised by public subscription. Frederick Stock, Thomas's assistant, succeeded him and conducted the orchestra until 1942. Rafael Kubelik, its conductor from 1950 to 1953, was followed by Fritz Reiner, who conducted until his death in 1963. In 1968, Georg Solti was named conductor. The orchestra plays a summer season at Ravinia, a suburb of Chicago.

chicha (chē'chä), term applied to various alcoholic beverages in use among the Indians of Bolivia, Colombia, and Peru. It is made by fermenting a mixture of water, sugar, and masticated grains or berries. In pre-Colombian times it was used in religious ceremonies. The ancient Incas strictly controlled its use, but later consumption was unregulated.

Chichén Itzá (chēchän' ētsä'), city of the ancient MAYA, central Yucatán, Mexico. It was founded around two large cenotes, or natural wells. According to one system of dating, it was founded c.514, probably by the ITZÁ and after being abandoned (692) and reoccupied (c.928) was chosen by Kulkulcán (see QUETZALCOATL) as his capital sometime between 968 and 987. After being defeated by Mayapán in 1194, the Itzá abandoned the city for the last time. Spanning two great periods of Maya civilization, Chichén Itzá shows both Classic and Post-Classic architectural styles. The Classic style is massive, with heavy decorative sculpture and cramped interiors. The later buildings have plainer, more austere lines, with the sculpture based on the Mexican feathered-serpent motif and columns. TOLTEC influence is strong. The Castillo, or principal temple of Kulkulcán, is representative of the period. Rare among Maya buildings is the round tower called the Caracol [snail shell], built in the Post-Classic period; it was probably an astronomical observatory. Into Chichén Itzá's sacred well, mecca of countless pilgrimages from Central America and the Mexican plateau, were thrown jade and metal offerings. Humans were also sacrificed. Dredgings of the well in modern times have yielded a valuable collection of artifacts. See Donald Ediger, *The Well of Sacrifice* (1971).

Chicherin, Georgi Vasilyevich (gēôr'gē vəsē'lyəvĭch chēchä'rĭn), 1872–1936, Russian diplomat. Of noble origin, he entered the Russian foreign office but resigned (1904) after joining the Social Democratic party. He was in London during the October Revolution of 1917, was arrested for "enemy associations" after the Russian armistice with Germany, and was finally released by the British authorities. He returned to Russia in Jan., 1918, as Trotsky's aide and soon succeeded him as foreign commissar. An able diplomat, Chicherin successfully ended the diplomatic isolation of the USSR by gaining formal recognition for his country from W European nations. He negotiated the Treaty of Rapallo (see RAPALLO, TREATY OF, and GENOA, CONFERENCE OF) with Germany in 1922. He ceased to conduct foreign affairs in 1928 because of illness and was succeeded by his assistant, Maxim LITVINOV, in 1930.

Chichester (chĭ'chĭstər), municipal borough (1971 pop. 20,547), county town of West Sussex, S England. Chichester is an agricultural and yachting center and has some light industry. The Regnum of the Romans, it was conquered by Ælla and his sons, who landed near Selsey in 477 and later (c.491) founded the kingdom of the South Saxons. In the Middle Ages Chichester was an important port, trading in wheat and wool. A portion of the medieval walls still stands. The 13th-century cathedral stands upon the site of an ancient monastery. Chichester has a teacher training college and a theological college.

Chichi, island, Japan: see BONIN ISLANDS.

Chichibu (chē'chēbo͞o), city (1970 pop. 60,867), Saitama prefecture, central Japan, on the Ara River. It is a center for agricultural products and for the manufacture of silk fabrics. The city's Chichibu (Shinto) Shrine is a major tourist attraction.

Chichicastenango (chē"chēkästänäng'gō), town, SW Guatemala. In the heart of the highlands, Chichicastenango became the spiritual center of the QUICHÉ after their defeat (1524) by Pedro de Alvarado. The town, often called Santo Tomás, is quaint and charming, with a maze of winding streets surrounding the main plaza, the site of one of the most colorful town markets in Central America. In the Dominican monastery (founded 1542) was discovered the famous Popul-Vuh manuscript of Maya-Quiché mythology. There are several excellent collections of Indian relics, especially of carved jade. Chichicastenango is popular with tourists.

Ch'i-ch'i-ha-erh (chē-chē-här) or **Tsitsihar** (tsē'-tsē'här'), city (1970 est. pop. 1,500,000), S central Heilungkiang prov., China, a port on the Nen River near the Great Khingan Mts. It is connected by rail with Harbin, Shen-yang (Mukden), and Ta-lien (Dairen) and is a processing center for soybeans, grain, and sugar beets. Manufactures include locomotives, machine tools, paper products, and cement. The adjacent town of Fu-la-erh-chi (Fularki) has steel works and plants that make heavy machinery. Ch'i-ch'i-ha-erh was founded in 1691 as a Chinese fortress and was formerly the capital of Hokiang and Heilungkiang provs.

Chichimec (chēchēmĕk'), general term for the peoples of the Valley of Mexico between the periods of TOLTEC ascendancy and AZTEC ascendancy. Before the 11th cent. the Chichimec were nomadic peoples on the northern fringes of the valley. Although Aztec tradition has it that they were part of the Chichimec, the Aztecs were actually farmers and military aids to the Toltecs. The Chichimec period (c.950–1300) was one of intertribal warfare and political confusion, but it prepared the way for the tributary empire of the Aztec.

chickadee (chĭk'ədē"), small North American bird of the TITMOUSE family. The black-capped chickadee (*Parus atricapillus*), lively and gregarious, is a permanent resident over most of its range in the East. Both sexes have black caps, gray backs and wings, and fluffy white to buff underparts. They often swing upside down from branch tips, searching for the insects that form more than half their diet. Their call note gives the bird its name. Other species are the Carolina, the boreal, or brown-capped (of the Northeast), and the western chestnut-backed chickadees. Chickadees are classified in the phylum CHORDATA, subphylum Vertebrata, class Aves, order Passeriformes, family Paridae.

Chickahominy (chĭkəhŏm'ĭnē), river, c.90 mi (140 km) long, rising NW of Richmond, Va., and flowing SE to the James River. In the Civil War there was heavy fighting (1862) along its banks.

Chickahominy Indians, North American Indians whose language belongs to the Algonquian branch of the Algonquian-Wakashan linguistic stock (see AMERICAN INDIAN LANGUAGES). They were members of the Powhatan Confederacy. The Chickahominy were among the first Indian peoples with whom the English settlers in Virginia became acquainted.

chickaree: see SQUIRREL.

Chickasaw Indians (chĭk'əsô), North American Indians whose language belongs to the Muskogean branch of the Hokan-Siouan linguistic stock (see AMERICAN INDIAN LANGUAGES). They occupied N Mississippi and were closely related in language and culture to the Choctaw. The Chickasaw warred constantly with the Choctaw, the Creek, the Cherokee, and the Shawnee. The decline of the Chickasaw can be traced to the conflict for control of interior North America between France and Great Britain. Probably because British traders were established in their country before the settlement of Louisiana, the Chickasaw fought on the side of Great Britain, and French attempts to make peace with them were unsuccessful. After 1834 they moved, according to treaty arrangements, to Oklahoma, where they constituted one of the Five Civilized Tribes. See A. M. Gibson, *The Chickasaws* (1971).

Chickasha (chĭk'əshā), city (1970 pop. 14,194), seat of Grady co., S central Okla., on the Washita River; inc. 1898. It lies in an agricultural and oil-producing area. Chickasha has an industrial park; the city's manufactures include mobile homes, transistor and microradio components, lenses, and shock absorbers. The Oklahoma College of Liberal Arts is in Chickasha.

chicken: see POULTRY.

chickenpox or **varicella** (vâr"əsĕl'ə), infectious disease usually occurring in childhood. It is believed to be caused by the same herpes virus that produces shingles. Chickenpox is highly communicable and is characterized by an easily recognizable rash consisting of blisterlike lesions that appear two to three weeks after infection. Usually there are also low fever and headache. When the lesions have crusted over, the disease is believed to be no longer communicable; however most patients simultaneously exhibit lesions at different stages of eruption. Chickenpox is usually a mild disease requiring little treatment other than medication to relieve the troublesome itching, but care must be taken that the rash does not become secondarily infected by bacteria. Pneumonia and encephalitis are rare complications.

chick-pea, annual plant (*Cicer arietinum*) of the family Leguminosae (PULSE family), cultivated since antiquity for the somewhat pealike seeds, which are often used as food and forage, principally in India and the Spanish-speaking countries. The seeds are boiled or roasted and have been substituted for coffee. Other names are *ceci,* garbanzo, and gram pea. Chick-peas are classified in the division MAGNOLIOPHYTA, class Magnoliopsida, order Rosales, family Leguminosae.

chickweed: see PINK.

Chiclayo (chēklä'yō), city (1969 est. pop. 135,000), capital of Lambayeque dept., NW Peru. On the coastal desert between the Andes and the Pacific, Chiclayo may go years at a time with no rainfall. However, by utilizing short Andean streams for irrigation, Chiclayo raises considerable sugarcane and a major part of the country's rice.

chicle (chĭk'əl), name for the gum obtained from the latex of the sapodilla tree (*Achras zapota*), a tropical American evergreen. The sapodilla (known also by many other common names) is widely cultivated in tropical regions, including S Florida, for its fruit, which is plum-sized with translucent yellow-brown flesh. Large-scale cultivation of the tree for latex is impractical because it can be tapped only infrequently and varies widely in yield. Chicle is collected during the rainy season from wild trees in the rain forests. Natives, called *chicleros,* cut zigzag gashes in the tree trunk and collect the sap in bags. The collected material is boiled until it reaches the correct thickness and is then molded into blocks. These are exported, chiefly to the United States, for use in making CHEWING GUM. Unsystematic and excessive tapping of the sapodilla (especially in the Yucatán peninsula, where it was most abundant) is leading to its depletion and has necessitated increasing use of chicle substitutes from other latex-producing plants.

Chico (chē'kō), city (1970 pop. 19,580), Butte co., N Calif., in a region noted for its almond production; inc. 1872. Principal manufactures are processed almonds, matches, and wood products. California State Univ. at Chico and a U.S. botanical experiment station are in the city, and a junior college is in nearby Durham. Lassen Volcanic National Park lies to the northeast.

Chicopee (chĭk'əpē), industrial city (1970 pop. 66,676), Hampden co., SW Mass., at the confluence of the Chicopee and the Connecticut rivers; settled c.1641, set off from Springfield 1848, inc. as a city 1890. It includes the villages of Willimansett, Fairview, Aldenville, Chicopee Center, and Chicopee Falls. Rubber and rubber products, sporting goods, machinery, and firearms are among the city's manufactures. The College of Our Lady of the Elms is there. The author Edward Bellamy was born and lived in Chicopee Falls.

chicory or **succory,** Mediterannean herb (*Cichorium intybus*) of the family Compositae (COMPOSITE family), naturalized in North America, where the tall stalks of usually blue flowers are common along waysides and are known as blue-sailors. It is extensively grown in Europe for its root, which, roasted and powdered, is used as a coffee substitute and adulterant. Chicory is also used as a potherb and salad plant; the common type that is blanched for salads is witloof, or French endive. True endive (*C. endivia*), a salad vegetable since antiquity, is cultivated in several broad-leaved and curly-leaved varieties. It is also called escarole. Chicory is classified in the division MAGNOLIOPHYTA, class Magnoliopsida, order Asterales, family Compositae.

Chicoutimi (shĭko͞o'tĭmē"), city (1971 pop. 33,893), S Que., Canada, at the confluence of the Chicoutimi and Saguenay rivers. The city is the cultural and economic center of the Saguenay area. It has aluminum plants and pulp and paper mills. A Jesuit mission was established there in 1676. In the city is a branch of the Université de Québec.

Chicoutimi, river, c.100 mi (160 km) long, rising in the Laurentian Mts. and flowing N into Lake Kenogami, then E into the Saguenay River at Chicoutimi. A hydroelectric facility on the falls (50 ft/15 m high) just above Chicoutimi supplies power to the region's aluminum and wood-processing industries.

Chidambaram (chĭdŭm'bərəm), town (1971 pop. 48,819), Tamil Nadu state, SE India. It markets rice and produces textiles, cement, and brassware. Its temples are among the oldest examples of Dravidian art. Annamalai Univ., a leading school of S India, is in the town.

Chidley, Cape, headland on the north coast of Labrador, E Canada, at the entrance to Hudson Strait, named by the explorer John Davis in 1587.

Chidon (kī'dŏn): see PEREZ-UZZA.

chief or **chieftain,** political leader of a band, tribe, or confederation of tribes. At the simpler levels of social organization, the band or tribe usually lacks centralized authority and is ruled by the totality of adult males or of family or CLAN heads. Sometimes a temporary headman is chosen for a special occasion such as a hunting or war party. When authority is concentrated in one individual on a more permanent basis, the chief may have limited functions, such as the organization and supervision of work parties, religious ceremonies, or the collection and distribution of goods. A community may possess several chiefs among whom various functions are divided. Chieftainship may be achieved through inherent qualities of leadership, through the display of powers considered supernatural (see SHAMAN), through rank or wealth, or through hereditary succession. The power of chiefs is usually checked by custom and by kinship allegiances. The term *chief-*

dom is sometimes used in political anthropology to designate a particular degree of social organization, intermediate between tribe and state. See L. P. Mair, *Primitive Government* (2d ed. 1964); Morton Fried, *The Evolution of Political Society* (1967); Marshall Sahlins, *Tribesmen* (1968); Elman Service, *Primitive Social Organization* (2d ed. 1971).

Chiemsee (kēm'zā), lake, 31 sq mi (80 sq km), SE West Germany, SE of Munich; the largest lake entirely within West Germany. It is drained by the Alz River. Many resorts are along its shores. On the largest of three islands is a palace built by Louis II of Bavaria in imitation of Versailles.

Ch'ien-fo-tung: see TUN-HUANG, China.

Chiengmai: see CHIANGMAI, Thailand.

Ch'ien Lung (chyĕn lo͞ong), 1711–99, reign title of the fourth emperor (1735–96) of the Ch'ing dynasty, whose given name was Hung-li. Under his vigorous military policy, China attained its maximum territorial expanse; SINKIANG in the west was conquered, and Burma and Annam in the south were forced to recognize Chinese suzerainty. He restricted Western merchants to Canton in 1759, and he rejected British overtures for expanded trade and diplomatic ties in 1793. Ch'ien Lung was a patron of scholarship and the arts; some of China's finest porcelain and cloisonné were produced for his collections, and vast anthologies were edited, partly to censor seditious references to the Manchus. Despite the surface splendor of cultural achievement and imperial expansion, his reign in later years was characterized by growing official corruption, loss of military efficiency, and fiscal imbalance. See S. A. Hedin, *Jehol: City of the Emperors* (1932); L. C. Goodrich, *The Literary Inquisition of Ch'ien Lung* (1935); E. H. Pritchard, *The Crucial Years of Early Anglo-Chinese Relations, 1750–1800* (1936).

Ch'ien-tang (chēēn-täng) or **Tsientang,** river, 285 mi (459 km) long, Chekiang prov., SE China. An important commercial artery, it flows NE to the East China Sea at Hangchow. The tide rushing into the river from the bay causes a bore from 5 to 15 ft (1.5–4.6 m) high, which sweeps past Hangchow and menaces shipping in the harbor.

Chieti (kyĕ'tē), city (1971 pop. 50,976), capital of Chieti prov., Abruzzi region, central Italy, on the Pescara River, near the Adriatic Sea. It is a commercial and industrial center. Manufactures include textiles, iron goods, and construction materials. The city occupies the site of the Roman Teate Marrucinorum, of which ruins remain. Chieti was in the duchy of Benevento (7th cent.), fell to the Normans (1078), and thereafter was in the kingdom of Naples. It has a fine Romanesque cathedral (11th cent.), a 14th-century tower, and a university. The order of the Theatine Brothers (founded 1524) takes its name from the ancient Roman town.

Chifeng: see CH'IH-FENG, China.

chiffon, plain-weave, lightweight, sheer, transparent fabric made of cotton, silk, or man-made fiber; it is made of fine, highly twisted, strong yarn. Chiffon is difficult to handle, but it drapes and wears well and is very durable despite its light weight. It is piece-dyed or piece-printed and may be given a soft or stiff finish. Among its uses are in evening dresses, formal blouses, trimmings, and scarfs.

Chigasaki (chĭgä'sä'kē), city (1970 pop. 129,621), Kanagawa prefecture, central Honshu, Japan, on Sagami Bay. It is a fashionable resort with a large electronics industry.

chigger, minute, six-legged, reddish larva of the harvest MITE, one of various RED BUGS widely distributed throughout the world and common in the S United States. Attaching itself by its mouthparts to the skin of its vertebrate host, the chigger injects saliva that destroys cells and may cause an intense irritation known as red-bug dermatitis. The food of the chigger consists of the cellular contents and tissue fluid of the host. Certain Oriental species carry minute organisms (rickettsias) that cause scrub typhus, a disease of man. The chigger is sometimes confused with the CHIGOE, or jigger, a burrowing flea. Chiggers are classified in the phylum ARTHROPODA, class Arachnida, order Acarina, family Trombidiidae.

Chigirin (chĭgĭrēn'), Ukr. *Chyhyryn*, city, S central European USSR, in the Ukraine, on the Tyasmin River, a tributary of the Dnepr. It has food-processing plants and various light industries. Founded in 1589 as a fortress, Chigirin served as the residence of the hetman of Ukraine from 1649 (when it was so designated by the Treaty of Zborov between Hetman Bohdan CHMIELNICKI and the Polish king) until 1687. It was thus the capital of right-bank UKRAINE. The city passed to Russia in 1795.

Chignecto (shĭgnĕk'tō), isthmus connecting N.S., Canada, with the Canadian mainland, between Chignecto Bay and Northumberland Strait. It is c.17 mi (27 km) across at its narrowest point near Amherst, the chief city of the isthmus.

chigoe (chĭg'ō) or **jigger,** small parasitic FLEA of tropical America and the S United States. Man and his domestic animals are the main hosts. The fertilized female bores into the flesh (usually of the feet or legs) and feeds on the blood causing a painful, pustulous sore. She retains her eggs in her abdomen, which swells to the size of a pea. The eggs are expelled outside the host and hatch in the soil, undergoing complete metamorphosis. The chigoe is sometimes confused with the CHIGGER. The chigoe is classified in the phylum ARTHROPODA, class Insecta, order Siphonaptera.

Chigwell, urban district (1971 pop. 53,620), Essex, SE England. It is a residential suburb of London. Portions of Epping and Hainault forests are in the district. The Chigwell public school was founded in 1629. Part of the urban district was included in Redbridge, a borough of Greater London, in 1965.

Ch'ih-feng or **Chifeng** (both: chûr-fŭng), city, W Liaoning prov., China. It is an agricultural distribution center, trading in wool, furs, hides, and grain. Coal and gold mines are nearby. It was called Ulan Hada by the Mongols, but in about 1778 it was colonized by the Chinese. Before the 1969–70 redistricting it was in the Inner Mongolian Autonomous Region.

Chihli: see HOPEH, China.

Chihli, Gulf of, China: see PO HAI.

Chihuahua (chēwä'wä), state (1970 pop. 1,730,012), 94,831 sq mi (245,612 sq km), N Mexico, on the border of N.Mex. and Texas. The city of Chihuahua is the capital. Largest of the Mexican states, Chihuahua is divided into two regions—the mountains of the Sierra Madre Occidental to the west, and the vast, cactus-and-greasewood desert basins, broken by scattered barren ranges, to the north and east. In extreme E Chihuahua and W Coahuila is a desolate basin, the Bolsón de Mapimí. Chihuahua is a leading national mineral producer; the mines of the Sierra Madre yield silver, gold, copper, lead, and manganese and constitute the state's most valuable industry. Cattle raising on the wide plains, which was practiced from the 16th cent. until it was virtually halted by the depredations of Francisco Villa, has now been revived. Long considered unsuitable for agriculture, the state has seen reclamation of some river valleys, notably that of the Conchos. The newly irrigated areas and upland mountain valleys produce grains, cotton, sugarcane, and tropical fruits. Chihuahua is now one of Mexico's chief agricultural states. Some timber is cut in the mountains. Chihuahua was first known to the Spanish through Cabeza de Vaca, and after the settlement of Durango in 1562 by Francisco de Ibarra, Chihuahua and Durango were called Nueva Vizcaya. Chihuahua became a state after the Mexican revolution against Spain. During the 19th cent. the Apache and Yaqui Indians kept the inhabitants in a recurrent state of terror; today the Tarahumara Indians inhabit some of the remote regions of Chihuahua. Of considerable importance to Chihuahua's economic and political development was the westward expansion of the United States; during the 19th and early 20th cent. foreign investment was considerable, with the border city of JUÁREZ as the commercial link. Chihuahua was occupied by American forces in the Mexican War and played a prominent part in the turbulent years following the revolution in 1910. In 1961, in an attempt to open some of the most valuable timber and mining lands in the nation, Mexico inaugurated the 560-mi (901-km) Chihuahua-Pacific RR, which borders the gigantic Barranca del Cobre (Copper Canyon). At Casas Grandes, in NW Chihuahua, is a vast archaeological site. See study by R. H. Schmidt (1973).

Chihuahua, city (1970 pop. 288,657), capital of Chihuahua state, N Mexico. It lies in a valley almost encircled by hills. Chihuahua is the only large rail and commercial center of a vast northern area. Although agriculture is important, the city's economy depends chiefly on nearby mines; smelting and other mining processes constitute the main industries. Founded in the early 18th cent., Chihuahua prospered despite Indian raids. The revolutionist Hidalgo y Costilla was executed in the city in 1811. Chihuahua was occupied briefly by U.S. forces in 1846 and served as the headquarters of Benito Juárez until French troops took it in 1865; it now has many American residents. There are several good examples of 18th-century colonial architecture, including the aqueduct.

Chihuahua (chəwä'wə), a breed of small TOY DOG probably of oriental origin and introduced into Mexico by Spanish settlers. It stands about 5 in. (12.7 cm) high at the shoulder and weighs from 1 to 6 lb (0.5–2.7 kg). There are two varieties: the smooth, with a short, close-lying, glossy coat, and the long-coated, with soft-textured, flat or slightly wavy hair that forms a fringe of longer hair on the neck, legs, and tail. The coat may be any color but is usually tan. Named after the state of Chihuahua, Mexico, this tiny dog was long believed to have been indigenously Mexican. However, there exist no archaeological remains to support this belief; the animal generally claimed to be the Chihuahua depicted in Toltecan and Aztecan art and described in the writings of early explorers of Mexico is most probably a variety of rodent. It is much more likely that the ancestors of the breed were brought by Spanish merchants by way of their trade route from China, where the practice of dwarfing both plants and animals has had a long history. Today the Chihuahua is widely popular as a house pet. See DOG.

Chikamatsu, Monzaemon (môn'zäĕmōn' chē"-kämä'tso͞o), 1653–1725, the first professional Japanese dramatist. Chikamatsu wrote primarily for the puppet stage in the Tokugawa shogunate. His literary work is divided into historical romances (*jidaimono*) and domestic tragedies of love and duty (*sewamono*). Author of 110 *joruri* [puppet plays] and 30 kabuki plays, he profoundly influenced the development of the modern Japanese theater. Among his best-known works are the *Kokusenya-kassen* [battles of Coxinga], a historical drama concerned with the conquests of a famous Chinese warlord, and the domestic tragedy *Shinju Ten no Amijima* [the love suicides at Amijima]. See *Major Plays of Chikamatsu* (tr. by Donald Keene, 1961); Donald Keene, *Bunraku, The Art of the Japanese Puppet Theatre* (1965).

Child, Francis James, 1825–96, American scholar, b. Boston, grad. Harvard, 1846. At Harvard he was professor of rhetoric (1851–76) and English literature (1876–96). He greatly influenced modern methods of Chaucer study. He is best known, however, for his *English and Scottish Popular Ballads* (5 vol., 1883–98). This is a major source on folklore in which Child defined, with examples, some 305 types of ballads, including complete textual variations.

Child, Sir John, d. 1690, English administrator in India. In 1680 he was appointed the British East India Company's agent at Surat, then the company's main factory (i.e., trading station) in W India. In 1685, Sir John moved the company's seat of government from Surat to Bombay, and in 1686 he was given authority over all the company's possessions in India. His tyrannical methods alienated many; his defeat by the Mogul emperor led to a demand that he be removed from India, but he died before the issue was settled. Sir John's activities were supported in England by **Sir Josiah Child**, 1630–99, who was possibly his brother. A merchant and early mercantilist, he made a fortune supplying the navy and from 1681 to 1690 virtually ruled the East India Company, of which he was deputy governor (1684–86, 1688–90) and governor (1681–83, 1686–88). His *New Discourse of Trade* (final form, 1693) was an early plea for some of the principles of free trade. See study by William Letwin (1959).

Child, Lydia Maria, 1802–80, American author and abolitionist, b. Lydia Maria Francis, Medford, Mass. She edited (1826–34) the *Juvenile Miscellany*, a children's periodical. She and her husband (David Lee Child, whom she married in 1828) were devoted to the antislavery cause; she wrote widely read pamphlets on the subject in addition to editing (1841–49) the *National Anti-Slavery Standard,* a New York City weekly newspaper. Other writings include several historical novels and a book on the history of religions. Her *Frugal Housewife* (1829) went through many editions. See her letters (with introduction by J. G. Whittier, 1883, repr. 1970); biographies by H. G. Baer (1964) and Milton Meltzer (1965).

child abuse, physical maltreatment of children by parents or guardians. Such treatment often results in physical or mental impairment and is sometimes fatal. By the 1970s in the United States there were over 60,000 reported cases per year, a rate that probably represents only a fraction of actual occurrence. Children in child abuse cases are generally less than three years of age. The most common characteristic of child abusers is a history of physical abuse in their own childhood. A number of universities have undertaken child abuse prevention programs. In 1973 the U.S. Congress authorized funds for a program directed at prevention and treatment of child abuse.

child actors. A distinction should be made between child actors who fill the ordinary subsidiary children's roles and those who emerge in periods when performing children become a dominant fad. An example of the latter is the boys' companies of the Elizabethan period. These companies dominated the English stage from c.1576 to c.1610. Many had their origins in grammar and choir schools connected with cathedrals. Particularly well-known were the Children of Paul's and the Children of the Chapel. The companies often performed plays by important authors such as John Lyly and Ben Jonson. In Shakespeare's *Hamlet*, Rosencrantz describes these troupes to Hamlet:

> ". . . but there is, sir, eyrie of children,
> little eyases, that cry out on the top of question
> and are most tyrannically clapped for't. These
> are now the fashion. . . ."

During the first quarter of the 18th cent. children were commonly advertised as novelties on the English stage. The famous French dancer and actress Marie Sallé appeared as a child at the theater in Lincoln's Inn Fields in 1716 and 1717. It became the fashion at that time to present children who had never acted before. In 1804 a great sensation on the London stage was caused by 13-year-old William Henry West Betty, known as "Young Roscius." He played roles such as Richard III and Hamlet and had a multitude of successors (e.g., Infant Hercules, Infant Billington). Many famous adult performers of the late 19th and early 20th cent. had earlier careers as child stars (e.g., Maud Adams, Helen Hayes, and Buster Keaton). However, the American movies of the 1920s and 30s created a craze for exasperatingly cute child actors who often sang and danced; among them were Jackie Cooper, Shirley Temple, Freddie Bartholomew, and Jane Withers. A sinister caricature of the Hollywood moppet is found in Nathanael West's novel *The Day of the Locust* (1939) in the character Adore Loomis, a velvet-suited, sadistic child star who precipitates a riot in which he himself is kicked to death. The careers of many child film actors—Deanna Durbin, Margaret O'Brien, Bobby Driscoll, Claude Jarman, Jr., and Hayley Mills—ended before they reached adulthood. The most noted example of a short-lived career is undoubtedly that of Baby LeRoy, who achieved stardom at eight months and retired when three years old. Other child stars like Jackie Cooper, Judy Garland, Mickey Rooney, Roddy McDowall, and Elizabeth Taylor managed successfully to weather the transition to maturity. A superb performance by a child can be extremely affecting and appealing, e.g., Skip Homeier as a young Nazi in *Tomorrow, the World* (play; film, 1944), Patty Duke as the child Helen Keller in *The Miracle Worker* (play; film, 1962), and Tatum O'Neal as a juvenile con artist in *Paper Moon* (film, 1973). See Marc Best, *Those Endearing Young Charms* (1971).

childbirth: see BIRTH.

Childe, Vere Gordon, 1892–1957, British archaeologist, b. Australia. An Oxford graduate, he taught at the Univ. of Edinburgh (1927–46) and the Univ. of London (1946–56). He gained renown for his monumental synthesis of European prehistory, *The Dawn of European Civilization* (1925, 6th ed. 1957), and *The Prehistory of European Society* (1958). His studies in Asian archaeology led to *New Light on the Most Ancient East* (1929, rev. ed. 1953), and he interpreted human history in two popular works, *Man Makes Himself* (1937, rev. ed. 1951) and *What Happened in History* (1942).

Childebert I (chĭl'dəbərt), d. 558, Frankish king, son of CLOVIS I. On his father's death (511) he and his three brothers shared equally in the Frankish kingdom. His capital was at Paris. When his brother Clodomir died (524), he and another brother CLOTAIRE I murdered Clodomir's sons and seized his lands. With Clotaire he shared in the reconquest and partition of Burgundy and Provence (534) and unsuccessfully campaigned in Spain (542).

Childebert II, 570–95, Frankish king of Austrasia (575–95) and Burgundy (593–95), son of Sigebert I and BRUNHILDA. His mother actually ruled for him. Chaos and warfare marked his reign.

Childeric I (chĭl'dərĭk), c.436–481, Merovingian king of the Salian Franks (c.457–481), a Germanic tribe; son of Meroveus and father of Clovis I. Information on him is mostly legendary. His rule was that of a tribal chieftain. He defeated (463) the Visigoths at Orléans as an ally of the Roman general Aegidius. Subsequently he defeated the Saxons and the Alemanni. His tomb, containing armor and ornaments, was discovered in 1653 at his capital, near Tournai, Belgium.

Childers, Robert Erskine (chĭl'dərz), 1870–1922, Irish politician and author. Born into a Protestant family, he was a clerk in the House of Commons (1895–1910). Gradually becoming convinced of the need for Irish Home Rule, he resigned to work for it, engaging in gun-running for the Irish Volunteers in 1914. After serving in the British forces during World War I, he represented the Irish cause at Versailles and was a member of the Irish delegation that negotiated the treaty with Britain (1921). By this time he was opposed to anything other than republic status for Ireland and urged rejection of the treaty. He fought in the Irish Republican Army in the civil war that followed the creation of the Irish Free State, and was court-martialed and shot as a traitor in 1922. Childers wrote on Irish politics and on military matters, but his best-known work is *Riddle of the Sands* (1903, repr. 1971), a spy novel. His son, **Erskine Hamilton Childers,** 1905–74, became a naturalized Irish citizen and a member of the Dáil in 1938. He held a succession of cabinet posts in the Fianna Fáil governments from 1944 on and in 1973 was elected president of Ireland.

child labor, use of young workers in factories, farms, and mines. Child labor was first recognized as a social problem with the introduction of the factory system in late 18th-century Great Britain. In the Eastern and Midwestern United States, child labor became a recognized problem after the Civil War, and in the South after 1910. Children had formerly been apprenticed or had worked in the family, but in the factory their employment soon constituted virtual slavery, especially among British orphans. This was mitigated by acts of Parliament in 1802 and later. Similar legislation followed on the European Continent as countries became industrialized. Legislation concerning child labor in other than industrial pursuits, e.g., in agriculture, has lagged. Nearly all member nations of the International Labor Organization regulate the employment of children in industry; most also regulate commercial work; some, work in the street trades and a few, agricultural and household work. Despite such regulation attempts, children constitute from 2% to 10% of the labor force in parts of Africa, Asia, Latin America, and the Middle East. Although most European nations had child labor laws by 1940, the material requirements necessary during World War II brought many children back into the labor market. In the United States congressional child labor laws were declared unconstitutional by the Supreme Court in 1918 and 1922. A constitutional amendment was passed in Congress in 1924 but was not approved by enough states. International efforts also failed. The First Labor Standards Act of 1938 set a minimum age limit of 18 for occupations designated hazardous, 16 for employment during school hours for companies engaged in interstate commerce, and 14 for employment outside of school hours in nonmanufacturing companies. See Walter Trattner, *Crusade for the Children* (1970); also annual reports of the National Child Labor Committee.

children, delinquent: see JUVENILE DELINQUENCY.

children, dependent. Until the end of feudalism religious institutions provided the only organized care for children orphaned, deserted, neglected by their parents (see FOUNDLING HOSPITAL), or born into such poverty that their parents could not support them. In England the poor law (1601) recognized the state's obligation to the needy. Under this law overseers of the poor could apprentice older children and provide for younger ones by farming them out, putting them in poorhouses, or giving home relief. Until about the end of the 18th cent. in both Great Britain and the English colonies in North America, the chief methods were still indenture (binding the child out to a master who expected a return in labor for expenses) or placing them in poorhouses. Children were sometimes indentured as infants and were not free until they were 21 years old or more. About 1800 an orphanage was organized in New York City, the first of many in the United States. Although only a small percentage of these institutions have ever been publicly administered, in most areas they later came under city and state regulation. In the 1850s the Children's Aid Society of New York began sending dependent children from Eastern cities to homes in the West. One criticism of this work—that it separated children permanently from their relatives—was met later by the foster home system; in such homes children can be placed whose parents are temporarily unable to care for them, as well as children who are orphaned or deserted. The tendency in orphanages has for some time been away from regimentation and institutionalism. In current ideal circumstances, each child's situation is evaluated individually, and if he cannot remain with his own family he is placed in a foster home or child care institution, depending on which type of care is best suited to his needs and personality. Following the enactment in 1911 of a Missouri law authorizing financial assistance to the needy parents, similar laws were enacted by other states. By the time of the enactment of the Social Security Act in 1935, most states had such legislation. The Social Security Act provided for Federal grants matching those made by states to aid the parents of dependent children under approved statewide plans. These grants are now administered at the national level by the Community Services Administration of the U.S. Dept. of Health, Education, and Welfare. State and local departments of public welfare administer these programs locally. An issue was raised in the 1970s over whether or not so-called illegitimate children were qualified to receive aid. The U.S. Supreme Court ruled in 1973 that these children could not be denied such aid. On an international level the United Nations International Children's Emergency Fund (UNICEF) was established in 1946 to supply aid for the emergency needs of children in devastated countries. To date, it has helped feed children in over 50 nations; besides food aid, UNICEF also staffs projects to prevent the spread of disease among children. See SOCIAL SECURITY and CHILD WELFARE. See Winifred Bell, *Aid to Dependent Children* (1965).

children's book illustration. Among the first picture books intended for children is Comenius' *Orbis Pictus*, a primerlike text written in Latin about 1657 or 1658. Earlier works meant for adults but suitable for children include the Japanese *Scroll of Animals* (12th cent.) with animated sketches by Toba Soja and the first English edition of Aesop's *Fables*, printed by William Caxton in 1484 and illustrated with woodcuts. John Newbery included woodcuts in *The Renowned History of Little Goody Two Shoes* (1765). The earliest illustrators of children's books were usually anonymous, but with the appearance of Thomas BEWICK'S art for *Pretty Book of Pictures for Little Masters and Misses; or, Tommy Trip's History of Beasts and Birds* (1799), well-known artists began to receive credit for their work in this field. William BLAKE printed, engraved, and handcolored his own *Songs of Innocence* (1789). *The Butterfly's Ball* (1807), by William Roscoe, was illustrated by William MULREADY, and illustrations for the first English version of *Grimm's Fairy Tales* (1824) were created by George CRUIKSHANK. John TENNIEL'S remarkable drawings for Lewis Carroll's *Alice's Adventures in Wonderland* (1865) remain unsurpassed. His art creates a visual framework through which the characters of the story come to life. Illustrations for children's books usually enhanced or explained the text, but in the latter quarter of the 19th cent. three artistic giants, Walter CRANE, Kate GREENAWAY, and Randolph CALDECOTT, gave a new dimension to illustration. They produced the picture storybook in which interdependent text and illustration are given equal emphasis. Crane's nursery-song prints in *Baby's Bouquet* (1908) combine soft colors with bold composition. Greenaway's *Under the Window* (1878) is enhanced by delicate garden colors. In the 1870s and 80s Caldecott's nursery books displayed harmonious linear composition and warm color. The exquisite watercolors in Beatrix Potter's *Peter Rabbit* books reveal her careful observation of small wild animals. The grandeur and dignity of Howard PYLE'S portraits intensify the heroic adventures of *Robin Hood* (1883) and *Men of Iron* (1890). Two of Pyle's students were Jessie Wilcox, who illustrated Robert Louis Stevenson's *Child's Garden of Verses* (1905) and N. C. WYETH, whose dramatization of individuals and landscape enriched *Treasure Island* (1917), *Robinson Crusoe* (1920), and many other works. The master illustrator Arthur RACKHAM produced a host of magnificent books beginning in 1900 with *The Fairy Tales of Grimm.* His work is noted for brilliant use of color and dramatic, detailed composition. Ernest Shepard's drawings for A. A. Milne's *Winnie-the-Pooh* (1926) and for an edition of Kenneth Grahame's *Wind in the Willows* (1931) are warm and humorous. After a decline during the early 1920s, the golden age of the picture book began with the publication of Wanda Gág's *Millions of Cats* (1928). In 1938 the American Library Association instituted the Caldecott Medal for the most distinctive American picture book for children. The first recipient was Dorothy Lathrop for *Animals of the Bible* (1937). A number of major illustrators whose works are still popular emerged in the 1930s. Kurt Wiese illustrated Kipling's *Mowgli Stories* (1936). Helen Sewell employed a realistic style for *The First Bible* (1934). Maud and Miska Petersham's *The Christ Child* (1931) and Jean de Brunhoff's broadly drawn, delightful *Story of Babar, the Little Elephant* (1931) were among the outstanding books of the 30s. Robert Lawson's *Ben and Me* (1939) was the first of many witty books that he wrote and illustrated, including *Rabbit Hill* (1944) and *The Fabulous Flight* (1949). Dr. Seuss's popular, cleverly drawn books for young children began with *And to Think that I Saw It on Mulberry Street* (1937). Boris Artzybasheff illustrated *Aesop* and *The Seven Simeons* (both 1937) with bold woodcuts. In the next decade Robert McCloskey produced superb illustrations for *Make Way for Ducklings* (1941). Garth Williams's realistic, expressive drawings brought to life E. B. White's *Stuart Little* (1945) and *Charlotte's Web* (1952). The painter Maxfield PARRISH created a series of glowing and colorful illustrations for a children's version of *The Arabian Nights* (1947). Wesley Dennis created powerful watercolors for many horse books by Marguerite Henry. The first book in the charming *Madeleine* series, written and illustrated in a broad, painterly style by Ludwig Bemelmans, appeared in 1939; his *Parsely* (1953), the story of a moose, incorporates a colorful catalog of wild flowers. Marcia Brown's *Puss in Boots* (1952) is light and whimsical. During the 1960s a number of seldom-used techniques were introduced, and color printing was much improved. Drawing was freed from the constraints of realistic representation, and fantastic imagery flourished. Photography enriched texts, as in Astrid Sucksdorff's *Chendru* (1960). Illustrations combining graphic art and collage graced Ezra Jack Keats's *The Snowy Day* (1962) and Leo Lionni's *Inch by Inch* (1960). Outstanding folk and fairy tales in a picture-book format include Adrienne Adams's *Shoemaker and the Elves* (1960) and Evaline Ness's *Tom Tit Tot* (1965). A landmark in illustrated books of the 1960s is Maurice Sendak's *Where the Wild Things Are* (1963), depicting a surreal and menacing world of make-believe creatures. Sendak's *Higgelty Piggelty Pop; or, There Must Be More to Life* (1967) is a fantasy reminiscent of Tenniel's work. His *In the Night Kitchen* (1970) depicts a dream world in robust detail; it was the first children's book to portray nudity. Sendak's style has had a profound influence on contemporary illustration, as in Harriet Pincus's droll figures for Carl Sandburg's *The Wedding Procession of the Rag Doll and the Broom Handle and Who Was in It* (1967) and Mercer Mayer's comic *A Boy, a Dog, a Frog, and a Friend* (1967). Mayer's book spawned a number of books in which the story is carried entirely by pictures. In the mid-1960s a new kind of picture book emerged in which the illustrations dominate the text. Ben Montresor's illustrations for *Cinderella* (1965) and for Stephen Spender's *The Magic Flute* (1966) are based on his opera stage designs and incorporate the glittering color of that medium. Brian Wildsmith made expressive use of intense, jewellike colors for many works including La Fontaine's *The Lion and the Rat* (1963) and *Little Wood Duck* (1972). Among artists who choose to interpret a single type of book to which their styles are best suited, is Nancy Ekholm Burkert, whose specialty is fantasy and fairy tales; in *Snow-White and the Seven Dwarfs* (1972) her sweeping design and minute detail recall the works of Rackham. Margot and Harve Zemach illustrate and retell folk stories, including the rollicking *Duffy and the Devil* (1973). By the 1970s children's book illustration had developed into an artistic feast of incredible variety and richness, expressive of a particularly imaginative range of individual creativity. See Bettina Hürlimann, *Picture Book World* (1965); R. S. Freeman, *Children's Picture Books* (1967); Brian Doyle, *The Who's Who of Children's Literature* (1968); Miriam Hoffman and Eva Samuels, *Authors and Illustrators of Children's Books* (1972).

Children's Crusade: see CRUSADES.

children's literature. The earliest of what came to be regarded as children's literature was first meant for adults. Among this ancient body of oral literature were myths and legends created to explain the natural phenomena of night and day and the changing seasons. Ballads, sagas, and epic tales were told by the fireside or in courts to an audience of adults and children eager to hear of the adventures of heroes. Many of these tales were later written down and are enjoyed by children today. The first literature deliberately written for children was intended to instruct them. During the Middle Ages the Venerable Bede, Aelfric, St. Aldhelm, and St. Anselm all wrote school texts in Latin, some of which were later used in schools in England and colonial America. More enjoyable and enduring fare came later when William Caxton, England's first printer, published *Aesop's Fables* (1484) and Sir Thomas Malory's *Morte d'Arthur* (1485). The HORNBOOK, invented at the end of the 15th cent., taught children the alphabet, numerals, and the Lord's Prayer. Alphabet books were popular in battledore and in CHAPBOOK form. *The New England Primer* (c.1691) taught the alphabet along with prayers and religious exhortations. The first distinctly juvenile literature in England and the United States consisted of gloomy and pious tales—mostly recounting the deaths of sanctimonious children—written for the edification of Puritan boys and girls. Out of this period came one classic for both children and adults, John Bunyan's *Pilgrim's Progress* (1678). Later works written for adults but adapted for children were Daniel Defoe's *Robinson Crusoe* (1719) and Jonathan Swift's *Gulliver's Travels* (1726). In 1729 the English translation of Charles Perrault's *Tales of Mother Goose* became popular in England. A collection of MOTHER GOOSE rhymes was published in 1765 by John Newbery, an English author and bookseller. Newbery was the first publisher to devote himself seriously to publishing for children. Among his publications were *A Pretty Little Pocket Book* (1744) and *The Renowned History of Little Goody Two Shoes* (1765). Pirated editions of Newbery's works were soon published in the United States by Isaiah Thomas and others. By the end of the 18th cent., juvenile literature, partly under the influence of Locke and Rousseau, had again become didactic. This time the didacticism was of an intellectual and moralistic variety, as evidenced in the sober, uplifting books of such authors as Thomas Day, Mary Sherwood, and Maria Edgeworth in England and in the United States by Samuel Goodrich (pseud. Peter Parley) and Martha Finley (pseud. Martha Farquarson), who wrote the famous *Elsie Dinsmore* series. Contrasting with this movement was 19th-century romanticism, which produced a body of literature that genuinely belonged to children. For the first time children's books contained fantasy and realism, fun and adventure, and many of the books written at that time are still popular today. Folk tales collected in Germany by the brothers Grimm were translated into English in 1823. The fairy stories of Hans Christian Andersen appeared in England in 1846. At the end of the 19th cent. Joseph Jacobs compiled English folk tales. Andrew Lang, a folklorist, began a series of fairy tales. Edward Lear's *Book of Nonsense* (1846) and Robert Louis Stevenson's *Child's Garden of Verses* (1885) set the style for much of the poetry written for children today. Lewis Carroll's twin masterpieces *Alice's Adventures in Wonderland* (1865) and *Through the Looking Glass* (1872) combine lunacy and fantasy with satire and word games. Victorian family life is realistically depicted in Louisa May Alcott's *Little Women* (1868), whereas Mark Twain's *Adventures of Tom Sawyer* (1876) and Robert Louis Stevenson's *Treasure Island* (1880) emphasize adventure; all three books present fully developed characters. At the turn of the century several children's magazines were being published, the most important being the *St. Nicholas Magazine* (1887-1943). Translations widened the world of the English-speaking child from the 19th cent. on; popular translated works include J. D. Wyss's *Swiss Family Robinson* (tr. from the German, 1814); Carlo Collodi's *Pinocchio* (tr. from the Italian, 1892); Felix Salten's *Bambi* (tr. from the German, 1928); Antoine de Saint Exupéry's *Little Prince* (tr. from the French, 1943); Astrid Lindgren's *Pippi Longstocking* (tr. from the Swedish, 1950); and Herta von Gebhardt's *The Girl from Nowhere* (tr. from the German, 1959). The contributions and innovations of the 19th and 20th cent. have achieved a distinct place in literature for children's books and have spawned innumerable genres of children's literature. New collections of tales that reach back to the oral roots of literature have come from Europe, Asia, Africa, and the Caribbean. Fantasy for children includes L. Frank Baum's *Wonderful Wizard of Oz* (1900), A. A. Milne's *Winnie-the-Pooh* (1927), P. L. Travers's *Mary Poppins* (1934), J. R. R. Tolkien's *The Hobbit* (1937), Lloyd Alexander's *Book of Three* (1964), E. B. White's *Charlotte's Web* (1952) and *The Trumpet of the Swan* (1970), and such works of science fiction as Madeleine L'Engle's *A Wrinkle in Time* (1962) and C. S. Lewis's *Narnia* series. Popular collections of humorous verse are Laura Richards's *Tirra Lirra* (1932), Hilaire Belloc's *Cautionary Verses* (1941), John Ciardi's *Reason for the Pelican* (1959), and Arnold Spilka's *Rumbudgin of Nonsense* (1970). Adventure and mystery are found in such works as Armstrong Sperry's *Call It Courage* (1941) and E. L. Konigsburg's *From the Mixed-Up Files of Mrs. Basil E. Frankweiler* (1968). The novel for children now includes many of the literary, psychological, and social elements found in its adult counterpart. Books with sophisticated emphasis on plot, mood, characterization, or setting are Kenneth Grahame's *Wind in the Willows* (1908), Esther Forbes's *Johnny Tremain* (1944), Joseph Krumgold's *And Now Miguel* (1953), and Scott O'Dell's *Island of the Blue Dolphins* (1961). Mature treatment of the emotions of growing up characterizes Irene Hunt's *Up a Road Slowly* (1966), whereas William Armstrong's *Sounder* (1970) realistically portrays the experiences of a black sharecropper and his family. During the 1960s and 70s "socially relevant" children's books appeared, treating subjects like death, drugs, sex, urban crisis, environment, and female liberation. Some critics consider these books as didactic as the children's books of the 17th and early 19th cent. Another trend has been books written by children, especially poetry. Richard Lewis's *Miracles* (1966) is a collection of poems written by children of many countries. Large numbers of nonfiction books are now published, completing the cycle of instruction begun in the Middle Ages. The Newbery Medal, an award for the most distinguished work of literature for children, was established by Frederic Melcher in 1922; in 1938 he established a second award, the Caldecott Medal, for the best picture book of the year. An international children's book award, the Hans Christian Andersen Award, was given in 1970 for the first time to an American, Maurice Sendak, in recognition of his contribution to children's literature. Magazines that review and discuss children's literature are *The Horn Book, The Bulletin of the Center for Children's Books,* and the *School Library Journal* in the United States and *The Junior Bookshelf* in Great Britain. See also CHILDREN'S BOOK ILLUSTRATION. See Anne Carrol Moore, *My Roads to Childhood* (1939); Annis Duff, *Bequest of Wings* (1944); Lillian Smith, *The Unreluctant Years* (1953); Paul Hazard, *Books, Children, and Men* (4th ed. 1960); Bettina Hürlimann, *Three Centuries of Children's Books in Europe* (1967); Shela Egoff, G. T. Stubbs, and L. F. Ashley, *Only Connect* (1969); Cornelia Meigs, *A Critical History of Children's Literature* (rev. ed. 1969); Jean Karl, *From Childhood to Childhood* (1970); May Hill Arbuthnot and Zena Sutherland, *Children and Books* (4th ed. 1972).

child welfare, services provided for the care of disadvantaged children. Foundling institutions for orphans and abandoned children were the earliest attempts at child care, usually under religious auspices. At first the goal was to provide minimum physical subsistence, but services have been expanded to include social and psychological help. In the late 18th cent., a movement developed around the idea that children should not simply be regarded as small adults, and such educators as Rousseau, Pestalozzi, and Froebel were discussing children's special needs at the same time that the Industrial Revolution was exploiting CHILD LABOR. In the 19th cent. many institutions were organized, either under religious auspices or through private charity, to take care of children who were orphaned, destitute (see CHILDREN, DEPENDENT), or handicapped. In child-welfare legislation, the British Children's Charter Act of 1908 and the Ohio Children's Code Commission of 1911 marked a new era. The idea that it was the responsibility of the community to provide children with the advantages that their parents could not supply is a 20th-century development. In this category are free school lunches; medical, dental, and psychiatric services and child guidance clinics in schools; playgrounds; children's courts; special schools for handicapped children; and care in foster families for children of broken homes. Infant and child clinics are often provided by municipalities. Many welfare agencies finance summer camps for both healthy and handicapped children. In the United States child welfare services are administered through the Community Services Administration within the U.S. Dept. of Health, Education, and Welfare. Since 1909 decennial child-welfare conferences have been held at the White House. Under the Social Security Act (1935), the Federal government makes grants to states with approved plans of assistance to dependent children. In addition to those programs, a series of new child-welfare programs were passed by Congress in the 1960s (e.g., the Child Nutrition Act, the Head Start Program, and the Foster Grandparent Program). The International Union for Child Welfare was founded in 1920 with the aim of organizing relief for child victims of major international and national disasters. The United Nations International Children's Emergency Fund (UNICEF) was established in 1946 to alleviate malnutrition and to help reestablish children's services destroyed in the war. See Jean Packman, *Child Care Needs and Numbers* (1968); Dorothy Zietz, *Child Welfare* (2d ed. 1969); Alfred Kadushin, *Child Welfare Services* (1970); Lela Costin, *Child Welfare* (new ed. 1972).

Chile (chĭl'ē, Span. chē'lā), republic (1972 pop. 10,044,940), 292,256 sq mi (756,945 sq km), S South America, west of the continental divide of the Andes mts. SANTIAGO is the capital and the largest city. A long narrow strip of land (no more than c.265 mi/430 km wide) between the Andes and the Pacific Ocean, Chile stretches c.2,880 mi (4,630 km) from near lat. 18°S to Cape Horn (lat. 56°S), including at its southern end the Strait of Magellan and TIERRA DEL FUEGO, an island shared with Argentina. Chile is bordered by Peru on the north, Bolivia on the northeast, and Argentina on the east. In the Pacific Ocean, which forms the nation's western and southern borders, are Chile's several island possessions, including EASTER ISLAND, the JUAN FERNÁNDEZ islands, and the Diego Ramírez islands. Chile also claims a sector of Antarctica. The country is composed of three distinct and parallel natural regions—from east to west, the Andes, the central lowlands, and the Coast Ranges. The Chilean Andes contain many high peaks and volcanoes; Ojos del Salado (22,539 ft/6,870 m high) is the second highest point of South America. Chile is located along an active zone in the earth's crust and experiences numerous earthquakes, some of great magnitude. The climate, which varies from hot desert in the north through Mediterranean-type in the central portion to the cool and humid marine west coast type in the south, is influenced by the cold Peruvian (or Humboldt) Current along the coast of N Chile and by the Andes. Precipitation increases southward; the desert in the north is practically rainless, while S Chile receives abundant precipitation throughout the year. However, along the coast of N Chile high humidity and dense fogs modify the desert climate. The Andes are an orographic barrier, and the western slopes and the peaks receive much precipitation; permanently snow-capped mountains are found along Chile's length. The rivers of Chile are generally short and swift flowing, rising in the well-watered Andean highlands and flowing generally west to the Pacific Ocean; the Loa and Baker rivers are the longest, but those in the central portion of the country are much more important because of their use for irrigation and power production. In N Chile is the southern portion of the extensive desert zone of W South America. It is occupied mainly by the sunbaked Desert of ATACAMA, which, toward the south, gradually becomes a semiarid steppe with limited vegetation. The barren landscape of the north extends from the coast to the Andes, where snow-capped peaks tower above the desert. The Loa River is N Chile's only perennial stream. The region's scanty population is concentrated along the coast and in oases; the ports of IQUIQUE and ANTOFAGASTA (the chief link between Bolivia and the Pacific), the mining towns of ARICA and CHUQUICAMATA, and the industrial town of LA SERENA are the chief population centers. The people of the region are almost totally dependent on supplies from the outside. N Chile, the economic mainstay of the nation, is rich in a variety of minerals, including copper, nitrates, iron, manganese, molybdenum, gold, and silver. Chuquicamata, the world's largest copper-mining center, produces much of Chile's output. The middle portion of the country, roughly between lat. 30°S and 38°S, has a Mediterranean-type climate and fertile soils, and is the nation's most populous and productive region as well as the political and cultural center. It contains Chile's largest cities—Santiago, VALPARAISO, and CONCEPCIÓN. Mineral deposits (in particular copper, coal, and silver) are found in central Chile, and the rivers, especially the Bío-Bío, have been harnessed to generate electricity. The region, the most highly industrialized section of Chile, produces a large variety of manufactured products, especially in and around Santiago, Concepción, and Valparaiso (which is also Chile's chief port). Between the Andes and the Coast Ranges is the Vale of Chile, a long valley divided into basins by Andean spurs. The valley is the heart of the republic, having the highest population density and the highest agricultural and industrial output. The valley's rich alluvial soils account for nearly all of Chile's agricultural production. S Chile, extending from the Bío-Bío River to Cape Horn, is cold and humid, with dense forests, heavy rainfall, snow-covered peaks, glaciers, and islands. Sections of this region, which is in the direct path of moist westerly winds, receive more than 100 in. (254 cm) of precipitation annually. Because of subsidence of the earth's crust, the Coast Ranges and the central lowlands have been partially submerged, forming the extensive archipelago of S Chile, an area of craggy islands (notably CHILOÉ), numerous channels, and deep fjords. The Chilean lake district is a noted resort area. Although all of S Chile is forested, only the drier northern part has exploitable timber resources; PUERTO MONTT and TEMUCO are major timber-handling centers. The rest of the region is a virtually untouched wilderness of mid-latitude rain forest. Because of the climate, agriculture is limited; oats and potatoes are the chief crops. Livestock raising (cattle and pigs) is an important activity. A portion of extreme S Chile lies in the rain shadow of the Andes and is covered by natural grasslands; extensive sheep grazing is carried on, with wool, mutton, and skins the chief products. This area also yields petroleum. More than half of S Chile's small population is found on the island of Chiloé. VALDIVIA, a port on the Pacific Ocean, is the fourth largest industrial center of Chile; PUNTA ARENAS on the Strait of Magellan is the world's southernmost city. The majority of Chile's population is mestizo, a result of frequent intermarriage between early Spanish settlers and native Indians. Many Chileans are also of German, Italian, Irish, British, or Yugoslav ancestry. Three small indigenous groups are still distinguishable—the ARAUCANIAN INDIANS of central Chile (the largest and long the strongest group), the Changos of N Chile, and the Fuegians of Tierra del Fuego. By the 1970s, Chile was predominantly urban; more than a third of the total population was concentrated in and around Santiago and Valparaiso. Chile is overwhelmingly Christian, with more than 85% of the people at least nominally Roman Catholic. Spanish is the country's official language. The country has one of the highest literacy rates (about 85%) of South America, the result of a well-established education system at all levels. The economy is based on the export of minerals, which accounts for more than 85% of the total value of exports. (Chile is the world's second largest producer of copper.) The country has great potential for the development of hydroelectric power, which already accounts for more than half of its electrical output. Although agriculture is the main occupation of about a third of the population, it only accounts for about 10% of the national wealth and produces less than half of the domestic needs; the production of an adequate food supply remains Chile's major economic problem. Wheat, potatoes, corn, sugar beets, and oats are the chief crops; a variety of vegetables, fruits, and grains are grown in the Vale of Chile, the country's primary agricultural area. The vineyards of the valley are the basis of Chile's growing wine industry. Sheep raising is the chief pastoral occupation, providing wool and meat for domestic use and for export. Fishing is an important economic activity; Chile consumes the largest amount of fish of any South American nation. Since World War I, Chile has developed an industrial capacity to process its raw materials and to manufacture various consumer goods. The major industrial products are processed food, fish meal, textiles, iron and steel, paper, lumber, chemicals, and leather goods. Chile's economic growth has long been hindered by high inflation, which has greatly cut down the country's spending power. Chile's main imports are food, machinery, and transportation equipment. The chief trading partners are the United States, West Germany, Great Britain, Japan, and Argentina.

History. Before the arrival of the Spanish in the 16th cent., the Araucanian Indians had long been in control of the land. Diego de ALMAGRO, who was sent by Francisco Pizarro from Peru to explore the southern region, led a party of men through the Andes into the central lowlands of Chile but was unsuccessful (1536) in establishing a foothold there. In 1540, Pedro de VALDIVIA marched into Chile and, despite stout resistance from the Araucanians, founded Santiago (1541) and later established La Serena, Concepción, and Valdivia. In spite of discouragement and incessant warfare with the Indians the Spanish persevered and succeeded. The Indians were pacified, but violent outbreaks occurred; the Araucanians remained hostile until near the end of the 19th cent. Although Chile was unattractive to the Spanish because of its isolation from Peru to the north and its lack of precious metals (copper was discovered much later), the Spanish developed a pastoral society there based on large ranches and haciendas worked by Indians; the yields were shipped to Peru. During the long colonial era, the mestizos became a

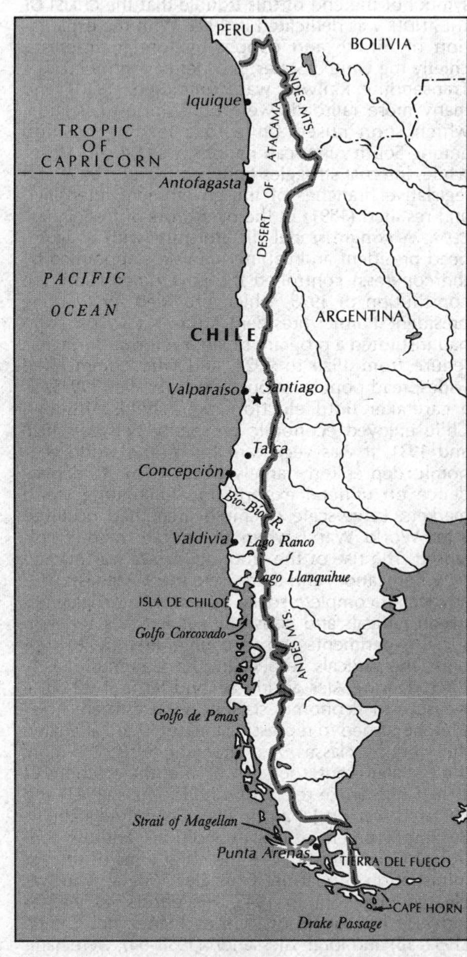

tenant farmer class, called inquilinos; although technically free, most were in practice bound to the soil. During most of the colonial period Chile was a captaincy general dependent upon the viceroyalty of Peru, but in 1778 it became a separate division virtually independent of Peru. Territorial limits were ill-defined and were the cause, after independence, of long-drawn-out boundary disputes with Peru, Bolivia, and Argentina. The movement toward independence began in 1810 under the leadership of Juan MARTÍNEZ DE ROZAS and Bernardo O'HIGGINS. The first phase (1810-14) ended in defeat at RANCAGUA, largely because of the rivalry of O'Higgins with José Miguel CARRERA and his brothers. In 1817, José de SAN MARTÍN, with incredible hardship, brought an army over the Andes from Argentina to Chile. The following year he won the decisive battle of MAIPÚ. O'Higgins, who had been chosen supreme director, formally proclaimed Chile's independence Feb. 12, 1818, at Talca and established a military autocracy that characterized the republic's politics until 1833; O'Higgins ruled Chile from 1818 until 1823, when strong opposition to his policies forced him to resign. During this time the British expatriot Lord Cochrane, commanding the Chilean navy, cleared (1819-20) the coast of Spanish shipping, and in 1826 the remaining royalists were driven from Chiloé island, their last foothold on Chilean soil. The colonial aristocracy and the clergy had been discredited because of royalist leanings. The army, then, plus a few intellectuals, established a government devoid of democratic forms. Yet with the centralistic constitution of 1833, fashioned largely by Diego PORTALES on Chile's particular needs, a foundation was laid for the gradual emergence of parliamentary government and a long period of stability. During the administrations of Manuel BULNES (1841-51) and Manuel MONTT (1851-61) the country experienced governmental reform and material progress. The war of 1866 between Peru and Spain involved Chile and led the republic to fortify its coast and build a navy. Chileans obtained the right to work the nitrate fields in the Atacama, which then belonged to Bolivia. Trouble over the concessions led in 1879 to open war (see PACIFIC, WAR OF THE). Chile was the victor and added valuable territories taken from Bolivia and Peru; a long-standing quarrel also ensued, the

TACNA-ARICA CONTROVERSY, which was finally settled in 1929. Chile also became involved in serious border troubles with Argentina; it was as a sign and symbol of the end of this trouble that the CHRIST OF THE ANDES was dedicated in 1904. With the exploitation of nitrate and copper by foreign interests, chiefly the United States, prosperity continued. The Transandine Railway was completed (1910), and many more railroads were built. Industrialization, which soon raised Chile to a leading position among South American nations, was begun. Meanwhile, internal struggles between the executive and legislative branches of the government intensified and resulted (1891) in the overthrow of José BALMACEDA. A congressional dictatorship (with a figurehead president and cabinet ministers appointed by the congress) controlled the government until the constitution of 1925, which provided for a strong president. Former president Arturo ALESSANDRI (who had instituted a program of labor reforms during his tenure from 1920 to 1924, and who commanded widespread popular support) was recalled (1925) as a caretaker until elections were held. Although Chile enjoyed economic prosperity between 1926 and 1931, it was very hard hit by the world economic depression, largely because of its dependence on mineral exports and fluctuating world markets. Large-scale unemployment had occurred after World War I when the nitrate market collapsed. The rise of the laboring classes was marked by unionization, and there were many Marxists who advocated complete social reform. The struggle between radicals and conservatives led to a series of social experiments and to counterattempts to suppress the radicals (especially the Communists) by force. During Alessandri's second term (1932–38) a measure of economic stability was restored; however, he turned to repressive measures and alienated the working classes. A democratic-leftist coalition, the Popular Front, took power after the elections of 1938. Chile broke relations with the Axis (1943) and declared war on Japan in 1945. Economic stability, the improvement of labor conditions, and the control of Communists were the chief aims of the administration of Gabriel González Videla, who was elected president in 1946. His efforts, as well as those of his successors, Carlos Ibáñez del Campo (1952–58) and Jorge Alessandri (1958–64), were hampered by chronic inflation and repeated labor crises. In the 1964 presidential election (in which Eduardo FREI MONTALVO was elected) and in the 1965 congressional elections, the Christian Democratic party won overwhelming victories over the Socialist-Communist coalition. Frei made advances in land reform, education, housing, and labor. Under his so-called Chileanization program, the government assumed a controlling interest in U.S.-owned copper mines while cooperating with U.S. companies in their management and development. In 1970, Salvador ALLENDE GOSSENS, head of the Popular Unity party, a coalition of leftist political parties, won a plurality of votes in the presidential election and became the first Marxist to be elected president by popular vote in Latin America. Allende, in an attempt to turn Chile into a socialist state, nationalized many private companies, instituted programs of land reform, and, in foreign affairs, sought closer ties with Communist countries. His policies were resisted from the start by many factions within Chilean society. Continuing, widespread domestic problems, including spiraling inflation, lack of food and consumer goods, and stringent government controls, led to a series of violent strikes and demonstrations. As the situation worsened, the traditionally neutral Chilean military began to pressure Allende; he yielded to some of their demands and appointed military men to several high cabinet positions. In Sept., 1973, the armed forces staged a coup that resulted in Allende's death (by suicide, according to the military junta that succeeded him) and in the execution, detention, or expulsion from Chile of thousands of people. Gen. Augusto Pinochet Ugarte took control of the country, promising a more moderate economic policy and the restoration of a pro-Western foreign policy. However, in 1974, the economy continued to deteriorate, even though the government sought to return private enterprise to Chile by denationalizing many industries and by compensating businesses taken over by the Allende government. Work proceeded on the drafting of Chile's third constitution, which was to include articles preventing the election of a minority government. In June, 1974, Pinochet became the undisputed leader of Chile by assuming the position of head of state. In July, Chile's 25 existing provinces were reorganized into 12 regions and the Santiago metropolitan area. See Luis Galdames, *A History of Chile* (tr. 1941, repr. 1964); H. R. Pocock, *The Conquest of Chile* (1967); E. H. Korth, *Spanish Policy in Colonial Chile* (1968); J. F. Petras, *Politics and Social Forces in Chilean Development* (1969); A. U. Hancock, *A History of Chile* (1893, repr. 1971); Salvatore Bizarro, *Historical Dictionary of Chile* (1972); Régis Debray, *The Chilean Revolution: Conversations with Allende* (tr. 1972); R. R. Kaufman, *The Politics of Land Reform in Chile, 1950–1970* (1972); D. J. Morris, *We Must Make Haste Slowly: The Process of Revolution in Chile* (1973); Kenneth Medhurst, ed., *Allende's Chile* (1973).

Chileab (kĭl'ēăb), son of David and Abigail. 2 Sam. 3.3. Daniel: 1 Chron. 3.1.

Chile saltpeter: see SODIUM NITRATE.

chiliasm: see MILLENNIUM.

chili con carne (chĭl'ē kŏn kär'nē) [Span.,=hot peppers with meat], Mexican food popular in the United States and now manufactured and canned commercially. It consists mainly of beef, beans, chilies (see PEPPER), garlic, and spices, although the ingredients may be varied.

Chi-lin (jē-lĭn) or **Kirin** (kē'rĭn'), city (1970 est. pop. 1,200,000), central Kirin prov., China, on the Sungari River. It is a shipping port, a railroad junction, and a commercial and industrial center, with large chemical plants. Oil is refined, and fertilizer, cement, lumber, and sugar are also produced. Chi-lin was the capital of Kirin prov. until 1954. It was formerly called Yung-ki.

Chilion (kĭl'yŏn), Ruth's brother-in-law. Ruth 1.2,5; 4.9.

Chilkoot Pass, alt. c.3,500 ft (1,070 m), in the Coast Mts., on the British Columbia–Alaska line. It was long used by the Chilkoot Indians as a link between the Pacific coast and the Yukon River valley; the first non-Indian traversed the pass in 1878. After the Klondike gold strike (1896), the pass became a much-used route to the interior. See Archie Satterfield, *Chilkoot Pass: Then and Now* (1973).

Chillán (chēyän'), city (1970 pop. 102,361), capital of Ñuble prov., S central Chile. Located in Chile's central valley, the city is a leading agricultural and commercial center. Founded in the 16th cent., it was destroyed by earthquake and flood in 1751 but was rebuilt and played a prominent role in the revolution against Spain. Bernardo O'Higgins, the liberator of Chile, was born in Chillán. One of the world's worst earthquakes leveled Chillán in 1939, claiming 10,000 lives. The city was subsequently rebuilt.

chill hardening: see HARDENING.

Chillicothe (chĭl"ĭkŏth'ē), city (1970 pop. 24,842), seat of Ross co., S central Ohio, on the Scioto River; inc. 1802. It is the trade and distribution center of a farming area that specializes in raising cattle and hogs and growing corn. Long noted for its large paper mills, Chillicothe also manufactures aluminum cooking utensils, shoes, floor tiles, and railroad-car springs. Founded in 1796 by settlers from Virginia, Chillicothe derives its name from the Shawnee Indian word meaning "principal town." In 1800 it became the capital of the NORTHWEST TERRITORY; from 1803 to 1810 and from 1812 to 1816 it was the capital of Ohio. Chillicothe grew in the 19th cent. as an inland port on the Ohio and Erie Canal and a pork packing center. During World War I, Camp Sherman, a large Army training base, was built in Chillicothe; after the war a veterans hospital, still in use, was built on part of the site. Adena State Memorial, the home of Thomas Worthington, Ohio's first U.S. Senator and sixth governor, and Ross County Historical Society Museum, which contains exhibits of pioneer crafts and rifle making, are in Chillicothe. Just outside the city is Mound City Group National Monument, containing prehistoric Indian burial mounds. (See NATIONAL PARKS AND MONUMENTS, table.) Chillicothe also has a state prison and a branch of Ohio Univ.

Chillingworth, William, 1602–44, English theologian. He was converted to Roman Catholicism and in 1630 went to Douai to study. Under the influence of his godfather, William Laud, he abjured that faith in 1634, and took holy orders (1638) in the Church of England. In 1638 he published *The Religion of Protestants a Safe Way to Salvation,* a defense of the Protestant view that the Bible is the sole authority in matters of religion and that the right of interpretation is reserved to the individual. He served as chaplain in the king's army in the civil war, was taken prisoner (1643), and died in detention. See study by R. R. Orr (1967).

Chilliwack (chĭl'ĭwăk), city (1971 pop. 9,135), SW British Columbia, Canada, on the Fraser River. It is an agricultural, dairying, and logging center. The main industry is food processing.

Chilmad (kĭl'măd), city or state that traded with Tyre. Ezek. 27.23.

Chiloé (chēlōā'), island (3,241 sq mi/8,394 sq km), a part of Chiloé prov., off S Chile. It is separated from the mainland by the Corcovado and Ancud gulfs and the Chacao channel. It is the largest of the Chilean islands and the only one that has been successfully settled. A rainy climate favoring the growth of wet and dense evergreen forests makes it one of the world's last virgin frontiers. Nevertheless the settlers have been able to raise wheat and potatoes, and to export timber. The population is concentrated around Ancud, the capital, and Castro; the former was totally destroyed and the latter badly damaged by an earthquake in 1960. Wrested from the Indians by the Spanish in 1567, Chiloé was the last stronghold of Spanish royalists, who were not driven out until 1826.

Chilon (kĭ'lŏn), 6th cent. B.C., one of the SEVEN WISE MEN OF GREECE. He was a Spartan and brought greater strictness to Spartan training. As an ephor (c.556 B.C.) he strengthened the power of that position, and for the first time the ephors directed policy with the king.

Chilpancingo (chēl"pänsēng'gō), city (1970 pop. 56,904), capital of Guerrero state, S Mexico. Nearby aboriginal ruins indicate that the city was once the center of a culture higher than the Aztec. Its full name is Chilpancingo de los Bravos, in honor of its heroes in the war against Spain—three brothers, of whom Nicolás Bravo was most prominent. During the war, the Congress of Chilpancingo, convened in 1813 by Morelos y Pavón, briefly established a constitutional republic based on the reforms of Hidalgo y Costilla.

Chilperic I (chĭl'pərĭk), d. 584, Frankish king of Neustria (561–84), son of Clotaire I. He feuded bitterly with his brother SIGEBERT I, who had inherited the E Frankish kingdom that came to be known as Austrasia. Their struggle became savage after Chilperic and his mistress and future wife, FREDEGUNDE, murdered (567) Chilperic's second wife, Galswintha; she was the sister of Sigebert's wife, BRUNHILDA. In the wars between the two brothers, Sigebert overran Neustria before his death (575). Later, Chilperic was murdered, probably at the instigation of Brunhilda. The feud was inherited by Chilperic's son and successor, CLOTAIRE II.

Chiltern Hills, range of chalk hills, c.45 mi (70 km) long and 15 to 20 mi (24–32 km) wide, S England, NW of London, extending NE from Goring Gap. Its highest elevation is Coombe Hill (852 ft/260 m), SE of Aylesbury. Chiltern timber supports the local furniture industry. Roman works have been found in the hills.

Chiltern Hundreds, the obsolete (since the 19th cent.) administrative districts of Stoke, Burnham, and Desborough in Buckinghamshire, S central England. The stewardship of the Chiltern Hundreds is an obsolete office with only a nominal salary. It is, however, legally an office of profit under the crown and, as such, may not be held by a member of Parliament. Since members of Parliament may not resign, "applying for the Chiltern Hundreds" or for the similarly obsolete stewardship of the Manor of Northstead is the method by which a member gives up his seat.

Chi-lung (jē-lo͝ong), **Kilung,** or **Keelung** (both: kē'-), city (1969 pop. 317,780), N Taiwan, on the East China Sea. Because of its excellent harbor it is the principal port and naval base of Taiwan. Shipbuilding is an important industry. Chemicals, machinery, fertilizers, and marine products are also produced. Coal and gold are mined nearby. The city has extensive rail connections and is a major commercial center. Occupied by the Spanish in 1626, it passed (1641) to the Dutch, who lost it to invading Chinese under KOXINGA in 1662. It passed to the Manchus in 1683. The port was opened to Western trade in 1860. Captured by the Japanese in 1895 and renamed Ki-run, Chi-lung remained under their rule until 1945.

chimaera (kĭmēr'ə), cartilaginous marine fish, related to the sharks. Also called ratfishes, chimaeras are found in temperate oceans throughout the world, mostly in deep water. They have large heads, long, thin, ratlike tails, and large, fanlike pectoral fins. In many species there is a poison spine in front of the first dorsal fin. Their slippery skins are black, gray, or silver, often with stripes or spots. The largest reach a length of about 6½ ft (2 m). Chimaeras resemble sharks in certain fundamental respects: They have cartilage skeletons, males have claspers for internal fertilization of females, and females lay eggs encased in leathery cases. However, they resemble the bony fishes in having the upper jaw fused to the skull, the gill slits opening into a single chamber, a bony covering, or operculum, over the gill slits, and separate anal and urogenital openings. A distinctive feature of chimaeras is the presence of extra claspers in the male, one in front of each pelvic fin and a prominent one on the forehead. The function of these appendages is not known, but they are thought to play a role in courtship. Chimaeras form the subclass Holocephali of the phylum CHORDATA, subphylum Vertebrata, class Chondrichthyes.

Chimay, princesse de: see TALLIEN, THÉRÉSA CABARRUS.

Chimborazo (chēmbōrä'sō), inactive volcano, 20,577 ft (6,272 m) high, central Ecuador; the highest in Ecuador. Its summit is always snow-capped. First explored by Alexander von Humboldt in 1802, it was first scaled in 1880 by Edward Whymper. It is frequently associated with nearby Cotopaxi, although the two volcanoes have different shapes.

chime, in music: see BELL.

Chimera: see BELLEROPHON and TYPHON.

Chimham (kĭm'hăm), Barzillai's son. 2 Sam. 19.37,38,40. The "habitation of Chimham" was a place near Bethlehem. Jer. 41.17.

Chimkent (chĭmkyĕnt'), city (1970 pop. 247,000), capital of Chimkent oblast, Central Asian USSR, in Kazakhstan, on the Turkistan-Siberia RR. It has large zinc and lead smelters and machine, chemical, and textile industries. Founded in the 12th cent., Chimkent was a Kokand fortress before it was taken by Russia in 1864.

Chimmesyan Indians: see TSIMSHIAN INDIANS.

Chimney Rock National Historic Site: see NATIONAL PARKS AND MONUMENTS (table).

chimney swallow: see SWIFT.

chimpanzee, an APE, genus *Pan,* of the equatorial forests of central and W Africa. The common chimpanzee, *Pan troglodytes,* lives N of the Congo River. Full-grown animals of this species are up to 5 ft (1.5 m) tall and weigh about 150 lb (68 kg); they have an arm spread of up to 9 ft (2.7 m) and are much stronger than humans. They are covered with long, black hair over most of the body and have naked faces ranging in color from nearly white to nearly black. The pygmy chimpanzee, *P. paniscus,* lives south of the Congo. It is much smaller and more slenderly built, with a black face. Chimpanzees spend much time on the ground, where they walk on all fours, using the soles of the feet and the knuckles of the hands; they can also stand on two legs and sometimes walk this way for short distances, especially when carrying things. They climb trees in pursuit of food and for nesting and can swing by their hands from one branch to the next. Their diet consists largely of fruit and other plant matter, but they also hunt and eat small animals, including monkeys. They use and even make tools; for example, they collect termites using twigs that they have gathered and stripped of leaves. Chimpanzees move about the forest in bands of varying composition, usually numbering six to ten individuals. There is a social hierarchy among the males of a group, and they engage in dominance contests involving much screaming and stamping. Family groups consist of mothers and children; females mate with many males during their fertile periods. A single infant is born every two or three years; young chimpanzees ride about on their mothers' backs. Under ideal circumstances chimpanzees may live 50 years. Chimpanzees are noisy, excitable animals both in the wild and in captivity. They may develop affection for humans, but are likely to become dangerous after maturing in captivity. They are considered the most intelligent of apes; they have excellent memories and reasoning powers and enjoy performing. Although they are incapable of speech beyond their own simple system of cries, captive chimpanzees have been taught to communicate in a language using visual rather than verbal symbols. Because of their close relationship to humans they are often used for medical and behavioral experimentation. Chimpanzees are classified in the phylum CHORDATA, subphylum Vertebrata, class Mammalia, order Primates, family Pongidae. See G. H. Bourne, *The Chimpanzee* (6 vol., 1973); Jane Van Lawick-Goodall, *In the Shadow of Man* (1971); R. M. Yerkes, *Chimpanzees: A Laboratory Colony* (1943, repr. 1971).

Chimu (chēmōō'), ancient Indian civilization on the desert coast of N Peru. It is believed to have begun c.1200. The MOCHICA, an earlier civilization, was previously known as early Chimu or proto-Chimu. After the decline of the Mochica (c.800), there was a long transition period about which relatively little is known except that it was probably influenced by TIAHUANACO. The Chimu were urban dwellers and apparently had a powerful military and a complex, well-organized social system. They built many well-planned cities; the largest and most impressive was their capital, CHAN CHAN. The Chimu exerted considerable influence on the Cuismancu empire, centered at CHANCAY. The last phases of Chimu civilization were contemporaneous with the rise of the INCA empire, by which it was absorbed c.1460. See V. W. Wolfgang, *The Desert Kingdoms of Peru* (1965); E. P. Lanning, *Peru Before the Incas* (1967).

Ch'in (chĭn), dynasty of China, which ruled from 221 B.C. to 207 B.C. The word *China* is derived from Ch'in, the first dynasty to unify the country. The Ch'in, a vigorous people from the northwest, moved into the rich plain of the Wei River in the 4th cent. B.C. By 221 B.C. the Ch'in army, led by Prince Cheng, had unified China by conquering the warring feudal states of the late CHOU period. The prince took the title Shih Hwang-ti [first emperor] and established his capital near modern Sian, Shensi prov. In all matters of state he was counseled by Li Ssu (d. 208 B.C.), a brilliant Chinese scholar. Until Shih Hwang-ti died in 210 B.C. he was engaged in vast projects. He had built much of the Great Wall (see CHINA, GREAT WALL OF), had extended his empire W to Kweichow, N to Kansu, and S to Tonkin in what is now North Vietnam, and had made his capital the most splendid city of China. He also built a network of roads and canals that converged on the capital. To centralize his administration he abolished feudalism and established the pyramidal governmental system that has been the model for later unifying dynasties. He attempted to unify Chinese culture by standardizing the written language and to combat traces of the feudal past by destroying all philosophical works, especially those of Confucius. Shih Hwang-ti was succeeded by a weakling son, who was quickly overthrown (207 B.C.). Soon after, the HAN dynasty came to power in China. See Derk Bodde, *China's First Unifier* (1938, repr. 1967); Leonard Cottrell, *The Tiger of Ch'in* (1962).

Chin, dynasty of China (265–420): see TSIN.

China, Mandarin *Chung Hua Jen Min Kung Ho Kuo* [central glorious people's united country; i.e., people's republic], country (1974 est. pop. 800,000,000), 3,691,502 sq mi (9,561,000 sq km), E Asia. This article concerns mainland China, now called the People's Republic of China; the Republic of China, or Nationalist China, is on the island of TAIWAN (see separate article). The capital of mainland China is PEKING. The most populous country in the world and the second largest (after the USSR), China has a 4,000-mi (6,400-km) coast that fronts on the Yellow Sea, the East China Sea, and the South China Sea. It is elsewhere bounded on the E by the USSR and North Korea, on the N by the USSR and the Mongolian People's Republic, on the W by the USSR and Afghanistan, and on the S by Pakistan, India, Nepal, Sikkim, Bhutan, Burma, Laos, and North Vietnam. Off the coast is the large island of HAINAN. China comprises 21 provinces (ANHWEI, CHEKIANG, FUKIEN, HONAN, HOPEH, HUNAN, HUPEH, KANSU, KIANGSI, KIANGSU, KWANGTUNG, KWEICHOW, SHANSI, SHANTUNG, SHENSI, SZECHWAN, TSINGHAI, YÜNNAN, and, in MANCHURIA, HEILUNGKIANG, KIRIN, and LIAONING) and five autonomous regions (TIBET, the INNER MONGOLIAN AUTONOMOUS REGION, the NINGSIA HUI AUTONOMOUS REGION, the KWANGSI CHUANG AUTONOMOUS REGION, and the Sinkiang Uigur Autonomous Region [see SINKIANG]). China may be divided into the following geographic regions: the 12,000-ft-high (3,660-m) Tibetan plateau, bounded in the N by the Kunlun mountain system; the Tarim and Dzungarian basins of Sinkiang, separated by the Tien Shan mts.; the vast Inner Mongolian tableland; the eastern highlands and central plain of Manchuria; and what has been traditionally called China proper. This last region, which contains some four-fifths of the country's population, falls into three divisions. North China, which coincides with the Huang Ho (Yellow River) basin and is bounded in the S by the Tsingling mts., includes the loess plateau of the northwest, the N China plain, and the mountains of the Shantung peninsula. Central China, watered by the Yangtze River, includes the basin of Szechwan, the central Yangtze lowlands, and the Yangtze delta. South China includes the plateau of Yünnan and Kweichow and the valleys of the Si and Canton rivers. To the extent that a general statement about the climate of such a large country can be made, China may be described as wet in the summer and dry in the winter. Regional differences are found in the highlands of Tibet, the desert and steppes of Sinkiang and Inner Mongolia, and in China proper. There the Tsingling mts. are the major dividing range not only between semiarid N China and the more humid central and S China but also between the grain-growing economy of the north and the rice economy of the south; overpopulation in the south, due to migrations from the north, has often prompted emigration to SE Asia and elsewhere. Agriculture is by far the leading occupation in China, involving about 80% of the population, although extensive rough, high terrain and large arid areas—especially in the west and north—limit cultivation to only about 11% of the land surface. Except for the oasis farming in Sinkiang and Tsinghai, some irrigated areas in Inner Mongolia and Kansu, and sheltered valleys in Tibet, agricultural production is restricted to the east. China is the world's largest producer of rice, sweet potatoes, kaoliang, millet, barley, peanuts, and tea. Those, together with wheat (in which China ranks third in world production), other grains, corn, soybeans, and potatoes, are the most important crops. Cotton is the most valuable cash crop, followed by oilseeds, silk, tea, tobacco, ramie, jute, hemp, sugarcane, and sugar beets. Livestock raising on a large scale is confined to the border regions and provinces in the north and west; it is mainly of the nomadic pastoral type. China ranks third in world production of sheep and fifth in cattle production. Horses, donkeys, and mules are work animals in the north, while oxen and water buffalo are used for plowing chiefly in the south. Hogs and poultry are widely raised in China proper, furnishing important export staples, such as hog bristles and egg products. Fish supply most of the animal protein in the diet, and both inland and marine fishing are important. China is one of the world's major mineral-producing countries; there has been extensive exploration since 1950 and significant new deposits have been found. Coal is the most abundant mineral (China ranks with the United States and the USSR in production and reserves); high-quality, easily-mined coal is found throughout the country, but especially in the north and northeast. China also has extensive iron-ore deposits; the largest mines are at AN-SHAN and PEN-CH'I, in Liaoning prov. China used to import about 90% of its petroleum, but new fields were discovered in the 1960s, and the country is approaching self-sufficiency in crude oil. Refining operations are being improved. Offshore exploration has become important; massive deposits off the coasts are believed to exceed all the world's known oil reserves. China's leading export minerals are tungsten (China has the world's largest supply), antimony, tin, molybdenum, bismuth, mercury, magnesite, and salt. China is among the world's three top producers of tin, tungsten, antimony, and magnesite, and ranks second (after the United States) in the production of salt, seventh in manganese, and eighth in lead ore. There are large deposits of uranium in the northwest, especially in Sinkiang; new mines have also opened in Kiangsi and Kwangtung provs. Aluminum is found in many parts of the country; the largest reduction plant is at FU-SHUN, in Liaoning prov. China also has deposits of gold, zinc, copper, fluorite, asbestos, phosphate rock, pyrite, and sulfur. Coal is the single most important energy source; coal-fired thermal electric generators provide close to 70% of the country's electric power. China has extensive hydroelectric energy potential, notably in Yünnan, W Szechwan, and E Tibet. Hydroelectric projects are in all the provinces served by major rivers where near-surface coal is not abundant. Perhaps the most spectacular project is the huge dam at the San-men Gorge on the Huang Ho. Important industrial products are manufactures that serve agriculture (farm machinery, fertilizers, etc.), as well as machine tools, iron and steel, textiles, processed foods, and building materials. Before 1945 heavy industry was concentrated in the northeast (Manchuria), but important centers have now been established in other parts of the country, notably in SHANGHAI and WUHAN. Since the 1960s the emphasis has been on regional self-sufficiency, and many factories have sprung up in rural areas. The iron and steel industry is organized around eight major centers (including An-shan, one of the world's largest), but thousands of small iron and steel plants have also been established throughout the country. Brick, tile, cement, and food-processing plants are found in almost every province. Shanghai and CANTON are the traditionally great textile centers, but many new mills have been built, concentrated mostly in the cotton-growing provinces of N China and along the Yangtze River; the largest mill is now in Wu-han.

The domestic handicraft industry produces most of the consumer goods and such export products as porcelain and lacquer articles. Most of China's large cities, e.g. Shanghai, TIENTSIN, and Canton, are also the country's main ports. Other leading ports are rail termini, such as LÜ-TA (a conurbation of LÜ-SHUN, formerly Port Arthur, and TA-LIEN), on the South Manchuria RR, and CH'ING-TAO, on the line from CHI-NAN. In the northeast (Manchuria) are large cities and rail centers, notably SHEN-YANG (Mukden), HARBIN, and CH'ANG-CH'UN. Great inland cities include Peking and the river ports of NANKING, CHUNGKING, and Wu-han. T'AI-YÜAN and HSI-AN are important centers in the less populated interior, and LAN-CHOU is the key communications junction of the vast northwest. Rivers and canals (notably the Grand Canal, which connects the Huang Ho and the Yangtze rivers) remain important transportation arteries. The east and northeast are well served by railroads and highways, and there are now major rail and road links with the interior. There are railroads to North Korea, the USSR, the Mongolian People's Republic, and North Vietnam, and road connections to Pakistan, India, Nepal, and Burma. Although a British crown colony, HONG KONG has long been a major maritime outlet of S China. The Han Chinese (so called for the Han dynasty) make up approximately 94% of the total population. They are linguistically homogeneous in the north, where they speak Mandarin dialects (the basis of the new national language of China), while in the south Cantonese, Wu, and Hakka are only a few of the many dialects spoken (some 108 dialects are spoken in Fukien prov. alone). The written language is universal; Chinese ideographs are common to all the dialects. The non-Chinese groups represent only 6% of the population, but the interior regions in which they live constitute more than half of the total area of the country. Among the main non-Chinese minorities are the Chuang, a Thai-speaking group, found principally in Kwangsi; the Uigurs, who live mainly in Sinkiang; the Hui (Muslims), found chiefly in Ninghsia; the Yi (Lolo), who live on the borders of Szechwan and Yünnan; the Tibetans, concentrated in Tibet and Tsinghai; the Miao, widely distributed throughout the mountainous areas of S China; the Mongols, found chiefly in the Mongolian steppes; and the Koreans, who are concentrated in Manchuria. The Manchus have been sinicized and are now considered as Han. The constitution of the People's Republic of China provides for religious freedom, but religious practice is not encouraged; traditionally, Confucianism, Buddhism, Taoism, and ancestor worship were practiced in an eclectic mixture with varying appeals. Islam, the largest monotheistic sect, is found chiefly in the northwest. Christianity, which had a small number of adherents, has been repressed.

Origins and History. The fossils of *Sinanthropus pekingensis* (see MAN, PREHISTORIC) found in N China are the earliest discovered protohuman remains in NE Asia. About 20,000 years ago, after the last glacial period, modern man appeared in the Ordos desert region. The subsequent culture shows marked similarity to that of the higher civilizations of Mesopotamia, and some scholars argue a Western origin for Chinese civilization. However, since the 2d millennium B.C. a unique and fairly uniform culture has spread over almost all of China. The substantial linguistic and ethnological diversity of the south and the far west result from their having been infrequently under the control of central government. China's history is traditionally viewed as a continuous development with certain repetitive tendencies, as described in the following general pattern. The area under political control tends to expand from the E Huang Ho and Yangtze basins, the heart of Chinese culture, and then, under outside military pressure, to shrink back. Conquering barbarians from the north and the west supplant native dynasties, take over Chinese culture, lose their vigor, and are expelled in a surge of national feeling. Following a disordered and anarchic period a new dynasty may arise. Its predecessor, by engaging in excessive warfare, tolerating corruption, and failing to keep up public works, has forfeited the right to rule—in the traditional view, he has lost "the mandate of Heaven." The administrators change, central authority is reestablished, public works constructed, taxation modified and equalized, and land redistributed. After a prosperous period disintegration reappears, inviting barbarian intervention or native revolt. Although traditionally supposed to have been preceded by the semilegendary HSIA dynasty, the SHANG dynasty (c.1523–1027 B.C.) is the first in documented Chinese history. During the succeeding, often turbulent, CHOU dynasty (c.1027–256 B.C.), CONFUCIUS, LAO-TZE, and MENCIUS lived, and the literature that until recently formed the basis of Chinese education was written. The use of iron was the main material advance. The semibarbarous CH'IN dynasty (221–207 B.C.) first established the centralized imperial system that was to govern China during stable periods. The Great Wall (see CHINA, GREAT WALL OF) was begun in this period. The native HAN dynasty period (202 B.C.–A.D. 220), traditionally deemed China's imperial age, is notable for long peaceable rule, expansionist policies, and great artistic achievement. The THREE KINGDOMS period (A.D. 220–65) opened four centuries of warfare among petty states and of invasions of the north by the barbarian Hsiung-nu (Huns). In this inauspicious time China experienced rapid cultural development. Buddhism, which had earlier entered from India, and Taoism, a native cult, grew and seriously endangered Confucianism. Indian advances in medicine, mathematics, astronomy, and architecture were adopted. Art, particularly figure painting and decoration of Buddhist grottoes, flourished. Feudalism partly revived under the TSIN dynasty (265–420) with the decay of central authority. Under the SUI (581–618) and the T'ANG (618–906) a vast domain, much of which had first been assimilated to Chinese culture in the preceding period, was unified. The civil service examination system based on the Chinese classics and a renaissance of Confucianism were important developments of this brilliant era. Its fresh and vigorous poetry is especially noted. The end of the T'ang was marked by a withdrawal from conquered border regions to the center of Chinese culture. The period of the Five Dynasties and the Ten Independent States (906–60), chaotic and depraved, was followed by the SUNG dynasty (960–1279), a time of scholarly studies and artistic progress, marked by authentication of the Confucian literary canon and the improvement of printing techniques through the invention of movable type. The poetry of the Sung period was derivative, but a new popular literary form, the novel, appeared at that time. Neo-Confucianism developed systematically. Gunpowder was first used for military purposes in this period. While the Sung ruled central China, barbarians—the Khitai, the Jurchen, and the Tangut—created northern empires that were swept away by the MONGOLS under JENGHIZ KHAN. His grandson KUBLAI KHAN, founder of the YÜAN dynasty (1260–1368), retained Chinese institutions. The great realm of Kublai was described in all its richness by one of the most celebrated of all travelers, Marco POLO. Improved roads and canals were the dynasty's main contributions to China. The MING dynasty (1368–1644) set out to restore Chinese culture by a study of Sung life. Its initial territorial expansion was largely lost by the early 15th cent. European trade and European infiltration began with Portuguese settlement of MACAO in 1557 but immediately ran into official Chinese antiforeign policy. Meanwhile the MANCHU peoples advanced steadily south in the 16th and the 17th cent. and ended with complete conquest of China by 1644 and with establishment of the CH'ING (Manchu) dynasty (1644–1912). Under emperors K'ang Hsi (reigned 1662–1722) and CH'IEN LUNG (reigned 1735–96), China was perhaps at its greatest territorial extent.

Foreign Intervention in China. The Ch'ing opposition to foreign trade, at first even more severe than that of the Ming, relaxed ultimately, and in 1834, Canton was opened to limited overseas trade. Great Britain, dissatisfied with trade arrangements, provoked the OPIUM WAR (1839–42), obtained commercial concessions, and established EXTRATERRITORIALITY. Soon France, Germany, and Russia successfully put forward similar demands. The Ch'ing regime, already weakened by internal problems, was further enfeebled by European intervention, the devastating TAI-PING REBELLION (1848–65), and Japan's military success in 1894–95 (see SINO-JAPANESE WAR, FIRST). Great Britain and the United States promoted the Open Door Policy—that all nations enjoy equal access to China's trade; this was generally ignored by the foreign powers, and China was divided into separate zones of influence. Chinese resentment of foreigners grew, and the BOXER UPRISING (1900), encouraged by Empress TZ'U HSI, was a last desperate effort to suppress foreign influence. Belated domestic reforms failed to stem a revolution long-plotted, chiefly by SUN YAT-SEN, and set off in 1911 after the explosion of a bomb at Wu-ch'ang. With relatively few casualties, the Ch'ing dynasty was overthrown and a republic was established. Sun, the first president, resigned early in 1912 in favor of YÜAN SHIH-K'AI, who commanded the military power; Yüan established a repressive rule, which led Sun's followers to revolt sporadically. Early in World War I, Japan seized the German leasehold in Shantung prov. and presented China with TWENTY-ONE DEMANDS, designed to make all of China a virtual Japanese protectorate. China was forced to accept a modified version of the Demands, although the treaties were never ratified by the Chinese legislature. China entered World War I on the Allied side in 1917, but at the Versailles peace conference was unable to prevent Japan from being awarded the Shantung territory. Reaction to this provision in the Versailles treaty led to Nationalist flare-ups and the May Fourth Movement of 1919. At the Washington Conference (1921–22), Japan finally agreed to withdraw its troops from Shantung and restore full sovereignty to China. The Nine-Power Treaty, signed at the Conference, guaranteed China's territorial integrity and the Open Door Policy. Meanwhile, Yüan had died in 1916 and China was disintegrating into rival warlord states. Civil war raged between Sun's new revolutionary party, the KUOMINTANG, which established a government in Canton and received the support of the southern provinces, and the national government in Peking, supported by warlords (semi-independent military commanders) in the north. As cultural ferment seethed throughout China, intellectuals sought inspiration in Western ideals; HU SHIH, prominent in the burgeoning literary renaissance, began a movement to simplify the Chinese written language. Labor agitation, especially against foreign-owned companies, became more common, and resentment against Western religious ideas grew. In 1921, the Chinese Communist party (see COMMUNIST PARTY, in China) was founded. Failing to get assistance from the Western countries, Sun made an alliance with the Communists and sought aid from the USSR. In 1926, CHIANG KAI-SHEK led the army of the Kuomintang northward to victory. Chiang reversed Sun's policy of cooperation with the Communists and executed many of their leaders. Thus began the long civil war between the Kuomintang and the Communists. Chiang established (1928) a government in Nanking and obtained foreign recognition. A Communist government was set up in the early 1930s in Kiangsi, but Chiang's continued military campaigns forced (1934) them on the LONG MARCH to the northwest, where they settled in Shensi. Japan, taking advantage of China's dissension, occupied Manchuria in 1931 and established (1932) the puppet state of MANCHUKUO (see SINO-JAPANESE WAR, SECOND). While Japan moved southward from Manchuria, Chiang chose to campaign against the Communists. In the "Sian Incident" (Dec., 1936), Chiang was kidnapped by Nationalist troops from Manchuria and held until he agreed to accept Communist cooperation in the fight against Japan. In July, 1937, the Japanese attacked and invaded China proper. By 1940, N China, the coastal areas, and the Yangtze valley were all under Japanese occupation, administered by the puppet regime of WANG CHING-WEI. The capital was moved inland to Chungking. After 1938, Chiang resumed his military harrassment of the Communists, who were an effective fighting force against the Japanese. With Japan's attack (1941) on U.S. and British bases and the onset of World War II in Asia, China received U.S. and British aid. The country was much weakened at the war's close. The end of the Japanese threat and the abolition of extraterritoriality did not bring peace to the country. The hostility between the Chinese Nationalists and the Communists flared into full-scale war as both raced to occupy the territories evacuated by the Japanese. The United States, alarmed at the prospect of a Communist success in China, arranged through ambassadors Patrick J. Hurley and George C. Marshall for conferences between Chiang and the Communist leader MAO TSE-TUNG, but these proved unsuccessful. When the Russians withdrew from Manchuria, which they had occupied in accordance with agreements reached at the YALTA CONFERENCE, they turned the Japanese military equipment in that area over to the Chinese Communists, giving them a strong foothold in what was then the industrial core of China. Complete Communist control of Manchuria was realized with the capture of Shen-yang (Mukden) in Nov., 1948. Elsewhere in the country, Chiang's Nationalists, supplied by U.S. arms, were generally successful until 1947, when the Communists gained the upper hand. Sweeping inflation, increased police repression, and continual famine weakened public confidence in the Nationalist government, and much of the population came to at least passively support the Communists. Peking fell to the Communists without a fight in Jan., 1949, followed (April–Nov., 1949) by the major cities of Nanking, Han-k'ou, Shanghai, Canton, and Chungking. In Aug., 1949, when little Nationalist resistance remained, the U.S. Dept. of State announced that no further aid would be given to Chiang's government. The Communists, from their capital at Peking, proclaimed a central people's government on Oct. 1, 1949. The seat of the Nationalist government was moved to Taiwan in Dec., 1949. The new Communist government was immediately recognized by the USSR, and shortly thereafter by Great Britain, India, and other nations. Recognition was, however, refused by the United States, which maintained close ties with Taiwan. By April, 1950, the last pockets of Nationalist resistance were cleaned out, and all of mainland China was secure for the Communists.

Communism in China. The Communists brought the soaring inflation under control and effected a more equitable distribution of food. A land-reform program was launched, and police control was tightened. During the first five-year plan (1953–57), agriculture was collectivized and industry was nationalized. With USSR assistance, construction of many modern large-scale plants was begun, and railroads were built to link the new industrial complexes of the north and northwest. On the international scene, Chinese Communist troops took possession of Tibet in Oct., 1950. That same month Chinese forces intervened in the KOREAN WAR to meet a drive by United Nations forces toward the Manchurian border. Large-scale Chinese participation in the war persisted until the armistice of July, 1953, after which China emerged as a diplomatic power in Asia. CHOU EN-LAI became internationally known through his role at the Geneva Conference of 1954 and at the Bandung Conference of 1955. The Great Leap Forward, an economic program aimed at making China a major industrial power overnight, was underway by 1958. It featured the expansion of cooperatives into communes, which disrupted family life but offered a maximum use of the labor force. The program was not successful. The worst weather conditions in a century brought three successive crop failures (1959–61), with the ensuing food shortages dramatizing the dangers of neglecting agricultural development while emphasizing industrial expansion. The industrialization program, pushed too fast, resulted in the overproduction of inferior goods and the deterioration of the industrial plant. A severe blow was the termination of Soviet aid in 1960 and the withdrawal of Soviet technicians and advisers—events that revealed a growing ideological rift between China and the USSR. The rift, which began with the institution of a destalinization policy by the Soviets in 1956, widened considerably after the USSR adopted a more conciliatory approach toward the West in the COLD WAR. There were massive military buildups along the USSR-Chinese border, and border clashes erupted in Manchuria and Sinkiang. Meanwhile, hostility continued between Communist China and the Nationalist government of Chiang Kai-shek, who pledged himself to the reconquest of the mainland. The Communist government insisted upon its right to Taiwan, but the United States made clear its intention to defend that island against direct attack, having even given (1955) a qualified promise to defend the Nationalist-held offshore islands of Quemoy and Matsu as well. China's relations with other Asian nations, at first cordial, were affected by China's encouragement of Communist activity within their borders, the suppression of a revolt in Tibet (1959–60), and an undeclared border war with India in late 1962 over disputed territory. In the VIETNAM WAR, China provided supplies, armaments, and technical assistance as well as militant verbal support to North Vietnam. In the late 1960s and early 1970s the emphasis of China's foreign policy changed from revolutionary to diplomatic; new contacts were established, and efforts were made to improve relations with many governments. China continued to strengthen its influence with other underdeveloped nations, extending considerable economic aid to countries in South America, Africa, and Asia. Important steps in Chinese progression toward recognition as a world power were the successful explosions of China's first atomic bomb (1964) and of its first hydrogen bomb (1967), and the launching of its first satellite (1970). Internal dissension and power struggles were revealed in such domestic crises as the momentous Cultural Revolution (1966–69); the death (1971) in an airplane crash of defense minister LIN PIAO while he was allegedly fleeing to the Soviet Union after an abortive attempt to assassinate Mao and establish a military dictatorship; and a major propaganda campaign launched in 1973, which mobilized the masses against such widely ranging objects of attack as Lin Piao, the teachings of Confucius, and cultural exchanges with the West. Economically, the emphasis in the 1960s and early 1970s was on agriculture. After the Cultural Revolution, economic programs were initiated featuring the establishment of many small factories in the countryside and stressing local self-sufficiency. Both industrial and agricultural production records were set in 1970, and, despite serious droughts in some areas in 1972, output continued to increase steadily. Long-standing objections to the admission of Communist China to the United Na-

The key to pronunciation appears on page xi.

tions were set aside by the United States in 1971; that October, Communist delegates were seated as the representatives of all China and, despite the opposition of the United States, which favored a "two-China" membership, the Nationalist delegation was expelled. A breakthrough in the hostile relations between the United States and Communist China came with the dramatic visit of President Richard M. Nixon to Peking in Feb., 1972. Although U.S. support of Taiwan remained a sensitive issue, the visit resulted in a joint agreement to work toward peace in Asia and to develop closer economic, cultural, and diplomatic ties. Political power in the People's Republic of China resides in the Chinese Communist party, which operates through the government structure; the party has been dominated since the 1930s by Mao Tse-tung. Although Mao resigned his position as chairman of the People's Republic during the failures of the Great Leap Forward, as chairman of the central committee of the Communist party he remains the most powerful political figure in China. (Liu Shao-ch'i, who succeeded Mao as chairman of the Republic in 1959, was deposed during the Cultural Revolution.) Chou En-lai, premier and chief administrator of the country, is now second only to Mao in the power hierarchy. A new constitution, adopted in Jan., 1975, abolished the position of head of state and enhanced the power of Mao and Chou. For aspects of Chinese culture not treated in this article, see CHINESE ARCHITECTURE; CHINESE ART; CHINESE LITERATURE; CHINESE MUSIC. See Hu Chang-tu et al., *China: Its People, Its Society, Its Culture* (1960); C. K. Yang, *Religion in Chinese Society* (1961); A. D. Barnett, *China on the Eve of the Communist Takeover* (1963) and *Communist China: The Early Years, 1949–1955* (1963); K. S. Latourette, *The Chinese: Their History and Culture* (4th rev. ed. 1964); Henry McAleavy, *The Modern History of China* (1967); F. H. Schurmann and Orville Schell, *The China Reader* (3 vol., 1967); Werner Eichhorn, *Chinese Civilization* (tr. 1968); Jack Gray, *Chinese Communism in Crisis: Maoism and the Cultural Revolution* (1968); E. H. Schafer et al., *Ancient China* (1968); F. H. Schurmann, *Ideology and Organization in Communist China* (2d ed. 1968); L. C. Goodrich, *A Short History of the Chinese People* (4th ed. 1969); Hilda Hookham, *A Short History of China* (1969); Tuan-shêng Ch'ien, *The Government and Politics of China* (1950, repr. 1970); Wolfgang Franke, *China and the West* (tr. 1967), and *A Century of Chinese Revolution, 1851–1949* (tr. 1970); I. C. Y. Hsü, *The Rise of Modern China* (1970); Owen Lattimore et al., *Pivot of Asia: Sinkiang and the Inner Asian Frontiers of China and Russia* (1950, repr. 1970); Joseph Needham, *Science and Civilization in China* (4 vol., 1954–70); T. R. Tregear, *An Economic Geography of China* (1970); Lucien Bianco, *Origins of the Chinese Revolution, 1915–1949* (1971); J. K. Fairbank, *The United States and China* (3d ed. 1971); R. H. Solomon, *Mao's Revolution and Chinese Political Culture* (1971); O. E. Clubb, *Twentieth Century China* (2d ed. 1972); C. P. Fitzgerald, *The Southern Expansion of the Chinese People* (1972); Theodore Shabad, *China's Changing Map* (rev. ed. 1972); Edgar Snow, *Red China Today: The Other Side of the River* (rev. ed. 1971) and *The Long Revolution* (1972); Yuan-li Wu, *China: A Handbook* (1973); Roderick MacFarquhar, *The Origins of the Cultural Revolution* (Vol. I of a projected 3 vol. series, 1974).

China, Great Wall of, fortifications, c.1,500 mi (2,400 km) long, winding across N China from Kansu prov. to Hopeh prov. on the Yellow Sea. The wall, running mostly along the southern edge of the Mongolian plain, was erected to protect China from northern nomads. It is an amalgamation of many walls built in ancient times; the first unified wall was built in the 3d cent. B.C. by the CH'IN dynasty. Laborers were conscripted from all over China to build it, and many of them died during the project. The wall's present form dates substantially from the Ming dynasty (1368–1644). It averages 25 ft (7.6 m) in height and is 15 to 30 ft (4.6–9.1 m) thick at the base, sloping to 12 ft (3.7 m) at the top. Guard stations and watchtowers are placed at regular intervals. The eastern part of the wall is earth and stone faced with brick, but in the west it is merely an earth mound. Successive invasions of China from the north demonstrated that the Great Wall had little military utility. Since 1949 a section N of Peking has been reconstructed and is open to visitors.

china clay, one of the purest of the clays, composed chiefly of the mineral KAOLINITE. Usage of the terms *china clay* and *kaolin* is not well defined; sometimes they are used synonymously for a group of similar clays, and sometimes kaolin refers to those obtained in the United States and china clay to those that are imported. Some authorities term as china clays only the more plastic of the kaolins. China clays are much used in the ceramic industry, especially in fine porcelains, because they can be easily molded, have a fine texture, and are white when fired. These clays are also used as a filler in making paper. In the United States, deposits are found in Georgia, North Carolina, and Pennsylvania and in smaller quantities in some other states; in Europe they are found especially in England (in Cornwall) and in France.

China grass: see NETTLE.

China Incident: see SINO-JAPANESE WAR, SECOND.

china marks, potter's trademark or signature, incised in the plastic clay before firing or printed before glazing on the bottom of the piece to identify it as his product. The practice was adopted by pewterers and silversmiths for establishing the genuineness of their wares. Books on pottery or porcelain usually include a list of the china marks of the important factories.

Chi-nan (jē-nän) or **Tsinan** (tsĭn'än'), city (1970 est. pop. 1,500,000), capital of Shantung prov., E China. It lies 3 mi (4.8 km) S of the Huang Ho (Yellow River) and is a railroad junction on the network linking Shanghai and Nanking with Tientsin; it has connections to Ch'ing-tao and Yen-t'ai. Chi-nan is a light and heavy industrial center with textile mills, food-processing establishments, machine shops, paper mills, and plants making trucks, agricultural machinery, chemicals, and fertilizer. An ancient walled city, Chi-nan was a provincial center as early as the 12th cent. It fell to the Communists in Sept., 1948, with the loss of some 75,000 Nationalist troops. Chi-nan is the seat of Chi-nan Technical Univ., a medical college, and two technical institutes.

chinaware, hard, white, translucent pottery with soft GLAZE, known as PORCELAIN. It originated in China but is now produced in various countries. Its composition is of kaolin and petuntse.

Chincha: see ICA.

chinch bug, small North American BUG, *Blissus leucopterus,* of the seed bug family. It feeds on small grains, corn, and other grasses, sucking the plant juices and doing much damage to crops, particularly in the Midwest. The adults, about 1/8 in. (3.5 mm) long, have black bodies with black and white wings, red legs, and red spots at the bases of the antennae. Both long- and short-winged forms occur. There are two generations a year. The adults overwinter in sheltered places, emerging in spring to feed on early maturing grains, such as wheat and oats. They lay their eggs on the bases of the grasses or in the ground, and the nymphs, or larvae (see INSECT), emerge in about a week. Red when they emerge, the nymphs mature in five stages, turning gray or brown. They feed on the same grasses as their parents. When they reach the adult stage, in about six weeks, they migrate on foot to later-maturing grains, such as corn, which are still tender; there they lay the eggs that give rise to the second generation of the season. The BEDBUG, a member of a different bug family, is sometimes called chinch in the South. Chinch bugs are classified in the phylum ARTHROPODA, class Insecta, order Hemiptera, family Lygaeidae.

chinchilla (chĭnchĭl'ə), small burrowing rodent of South America. It lives in colonies at high altitudes (up to 15,000 ft/4,270 m) in the Andes of Bolivia, Chile, and Peru. One of the costliest of all furs, its soft gray pelt has been valued since the days of the Inca. The wild chinchilla was nearly exterminated before protective laws were passed. At one time over 200,000 pelts were exported from Chile. Wild chinchilla coats have cost as much as $100,000. Chinchillas are now raised on farms in South America and the United States, and this has resulted in lower prices for the skins, which are still considered among the most valuable. Chinchillas are classified in the phylum Chordata, subphylum Vertebrata, class Mammalia, order Rodentia, family Chinchillidae.

Ch'in chiu-shao (chĭn chyo͞o-shou), c.1202–1261, Chinese mathematician. He pioneered in the study of indeterminate analysis in his *Mathematical Treatise in Nine Sections* of 1247. The text existed only in manuscript form for several centuries and still has not been fully translated or investigated. Like many traditional Chinese mathematical works, it reflects a Confucian administrator's concern with calendrical, mensural, and fiscal problems.

Chinchón, Luis Jerónimo Fernández de Cabrera Bobadilla Cerda y Mendoza, conde de (lo͞oēs' hārō'nēmō fārnän'dās dā käbrā'rä bōbä*th*ē'yä sär'dä ē mĕndō'sä kōn'dā dā chĕnchōn'), d. 1647, viceroy of Peru (1629–39). He sent Cristóbal de Acuña on the Teixeira expedition down the Amazon. In 1638, Chinchón's wife, suffering from persistent fever, was treated with a native remedy made from quinaquina bark. As a result, the malaria-curing qualities of quinine became known in Europe. Linnaeus called the genus of quinine-producing trees *Cinchona* in her honor.

chinchona: see CINCHONA.

Chindaswinth (chĭn'dəswĭnth), d. 653, Visigothic king of Spain (642–53). His reign began violently as factions of the nobility sought to dominate royal policy. Chindaswinth prevailed and together with his son RECCESWINTH, whom he admitted to joint rule in 649, inaugurated a program designed to reduce the differences between his Visigothic and Spanish-Roman subjects. He is therefore sometimes designated by historians as a "Romanist" as opposed to a "Gothic nationalist." Unification of the diverse population was furthered by legislation. Chindaswinth seems to have been responsible for revoking the BREVIARY OF ALARIC, the compilation of Roman law principles for only Roman subjects, promulgated by Alaric II in 506. Instead he began the compilation of a code fusing Roman and Germanic law and binding upon all subjects. Eventually promulgated by Recceswinth c.654, it was known as the *Liber iudiciorum* (later as the *Liber* or *Forum iudicum*).

Chinde (chĭn'də), city (1960 pop. 25,617), E central Mozambique, on the Zambezi River delta. Founded c.1890, it served as the chief port for Malawi and Zambia when they were British colonies. It is now an export center for sugarcane.

Chindwin (chĭn'dwĭn), river, c.550 mi (890 km) long, rising in the hills of N Burma and flowing generally S into the Irrawaddy (of which it is the chief tributary) at Myingyan. It is an important commercial waterway.

Chinese, subfamily of the Sino-Tibetan family of languages (see SINO-TIBETAN LANGUAGES), which is also sometimes grouped with the Tai, or Thai, languages in a Sinitic subfamily of the Sino-Tibetan language stock. Chinese comprises a number of variants; those that are mutually unintelligible are considered separate languages by some linguists but are classed among the many dialects of Chinese by others. The most widespread form of Chinese is Mandarin, which may be regarded as modern standard Chinese. It has several dialects and is spoken by about 655 million people in central and N China, claiming more native speakers than any other language (English is second, with 265 million speakers). Almost one person in six speaks Mandarin Chinese as his mother tongue. Originally the language of the court at Peking during the imperial period, Mandarin was then called *kuan hua* [official speech]. After the Nationalists seized control in 1911, the name was changed to *kuo yü* [national tongue]. The Communists have renamed the language *p'u t'ung hua* [generally understood speech]. It is thought that at least 70% of the people of mainland China now speak *p'u t'ung hua.* Mandarin is the official language of both Communist China and Nationalist China. It is also employed as an official language, along with four others, by the United Nations. Other leading forms of Chinese include Wu, the tongue of more than 55 million people in Kiangsu and Chekiang provs.; Fukienese, with some 50 million speakers distributed in Fukien prov., Taiwan, and SE Asia; Cantonese, spoken by 55 million persons residing in Kwangsi and Kwangtung provs., Hong Kong, SE Asia, and the United States; Hakka, the language of 20 million in Kwangtung and Kiangsi provs.; and Amoy-Swatow, the mother tongue of 15 million in Fukien and Kwangtung provs., Taiwan, and the South Pacific. The various forms of Chinese differ least in grammar, more in vocabulary, and most in pronunciation. Like the other Sino-Tibetan languages, Chinese is tonal; i.e., different tones distinguish words otherwise pronounced alike. The number of tones varies in different forms of Chinese, but Mandarin has four tones: a high tone, a rising tone, a tone that combines a falling and a rising inflection, and a falling tone. When Chinese is transcribed into the Roman alphabet, a superscript number is often attached to each word to designate its tone. For example, *ta* pronounced with the first, or high, tone (written as *ta*^{1}) means "assist" or "raise"; *ta* with the second, or rising, tone (*ta*^{2}) means "answer"; *ta* with the third, or falling and rising, tone (*ta*^{3}) signifies "strike" or "do"; and *ta* with the fourth, or falling, tone (*ta*^{4}) means "great." Again like the other Sino-Tibetan languages, Chinese is strongly monosyllabic. Chinese often uses combinations of monosyllables that result in polysyllabic compounds having different meanings from their individual elements. For example, the word for "explanation," *shue[1] ming[2]*, combines *shue[1]* ("speak") with *ming[2]* ("bright"). These compounds can embrace three and even four monosyllables: *shuo[1] ch'u[1] lai[2]*, the word for "describe," is made up of *shuo[1]* ("speak"), *ch'u[1]* ("out"), and *lai[2]* ("come"). This practice has greatly increased the Chinese vocabulary and also makes it much easier to grasp the meaning of spoken Chinese words. Grammatically, Chinese lacks inflection to indicate person, number, gender, case, tense, voice, and so forth. Suffixes are commonly used to denote some of these features. For example, the suffix *-le* is a sign of the perfect tense of the verb. Subordination and possession can be marked by the suffix *-te*. The position and use of a word in a sentence may determine its part of speech and its meaning. The Chinese writing system developed more than 4,000 years ago; the oldest extant examples of written Chinese are from the 14th or 15th cent. B.C., when the Shang dynasty flourished. Chinese writing consists of an individual character or ideogram for every syllable, each character representing a word or idea rather than a sound; thus, problems caused by homonyms in spoken Chinese are not a difficulty in written Chinese. The written language is a unifying factor culturally, for although the spoken languages and dialects may not be mutually comprehensible in many instances, the written form is universal. The characters are written in columns that are read vertically and from right to left, although the Communists on the mainland permit horizontal lines that read from left to right. This difficult system of writing has proved to be an obstacle to mass literacy, for one needs to know at least several thousand characters to read a newspaper and even more to read literary works. In an attempt to deal with this problem, Communist China in 1956 introduced a plan to simplify a large number of commonly used characters. This was intended as a transitional phase until a workable alphabet could be devised and adopted. Also in 1956 an alphabet based on Roman letters was developed in mainland China. However, its purpose was the phonetic transcription of Chinese characters rather than the replacement of them. Since alphabetic writing requires a standardized spoken language, the local differences in the pronunciation of Chinese present a serious obstacle to the development of a satisfactory alphabet. The People's Republic of China is making a great effort to standardize the pronunciation of Mandarin, which is essentially a spoken language, and to have it adopted throughout China. The Peking dialect of Mandarin was chosen because it is already the most widely used. The literary language of Chinese differs greatly from the spoken form. Known as *wenyen*, the literary language is the same for all variants of Chinese as far as vocabulary, grammar, and the system of writing are concerned, but pronunciation differs locally according to the dialect. Under Nationalist leadership a movement began in 1917 to employ the popular, everyday speech (called *paihua*) in literature instead of *wenyen*. Since 1949, under the Communists, *paihua* has been used for all writing, including governmental, commercial, and journalistic texts as well as literary works. See Bernhard Karlgren, *The Chinese Language* (tr. 1949); J. F. De Francis, *Beginning Chinese* (rev. ed. 1963) and *Advanced Chinese* (1966); Iakov Brandt, *Introduction to Literary Chinese* (1964); F. X. Keelan, *Chinese Characters Explained* (1967); H. C. Fenn et al., *Speak Mandarin* (3 vol., 1967); Paul Kratochvil, *The Chinese Language Today* (1968); C. F. Hockett and Chaoying Fang, *Spoken Chinese* (new ed. 1973).

Chinese architecture. As a result of wars and invasions, there are few existing buildings in China predating the Ming dynasty (1368–1644). Insubstantial construction, largely of wood and rice-paper screens, also accounts for the tremendous loss. One early structure that remains is the Great Wall (see CHINA, GREAT WALL OF). The background of Chinese architecture has been clarified to some extent as a result of the increase of archaeological activity since the Communists came to power in 1949. Discoveries in 1952 near Hsi-an have brought to light a complete Neolithic village near Pan-p'o. Two kinds of mud-walled dwellings were found—of round and rectangular shapes. As in later construction, buildings were usually oriented to the south, probably as a protection against the north wind. As early as the neolithic period, a basic principle of Chinese architecture was already established, wherein columns spaced at intervals, rather than walls, provided the support for the roof. Walls came to serve merely as enclosing screens. Although the typical Chinese roof was probably developed in the Shang (c.1523–1027 B.C.) or the Chou (1027–c.256 B.C.) period, its features are unknown to us until the Han dynasty (202 B.C.–A.D. 220). Then it appeared in the form that we recognize today as a hallmark of Chinese architecture—a graceful, overhanging roof, sometimes in several tiers, with upturned eaves. The roof rests on a series of four-part brackets, which in turn are supported by other clusters of brackets set on columns. Decorative possibilities were soon realized in the colorful glazed tiling of roofs and the carving and painting of brackets, which became more and more elaborate. During the Han dynasty the characteristic ground plan was developed; it remained relatively constant through the centuries, applied to palaces and temple buildings in both China and Japan. Surrounded by an exterior wall, the building complex was arranged along a central axis and was approached by an entrance gate and then a spirit gate. Behind them in sequence came a public hall and finally the private quarters. Each residential unit was built around a central court with a garden. Based on imperial zoos and parks, the private residential garden soon became a distinctive feature of the walled complex and an art form in itself. The garden was laid out in a definite scheme, with a rest area and pavilions, ponds, and semi-planned vegetation. Evidence of early architectural development is provided by representations in Han bronze vessels, tomb models, carvings, and tiles. In the first centuries after Christ, the coming of Buddhism did not strongly affect the Chinese architectural style. Although there was considerable building activity, temples continued to be constructed in the native tradition. The only distinctly Buddhist type of building is the PAGODA, which derived from the Indian STUPA. Several masonry pagodas are extant that date from the 6th cent. In the T'ang period (618–906), pagodas were usually simple, square structures; they later became more elaborate in shape and adornment. In the 11th cent. a distinctive type of pagoda was created in the Liao territory. Built in three different stages, with a base, a shaft, and a crown, the structure was surmounted by a spire. Its plan was often octagonal, possibly as a result of the influence of Tantric Buddhism in which the cosmological scheme was arranged into eight compass points rather than four. One of the finest Liao structures is the White Pagoda at Ch'eng-te. Through the T'ang and Sung dynasties, Chinese architecture retained the basic characteristics already developed in the Han, although there was a greater technical mastery and a tendency toward rich adornment and complexity of the system of bracketing. Though little survives of the wooden structures, our knowledge of their appearance comes from detailed representations in painted scrolls, especially by the Li school of artists in the T'ang period and their followers (see CHINESE ART). Extant monuments in Japan, profoundly influenced by Chinese architecture, also reflect the progress of Chinese building techniques. Examples are the 7th-century monastery of Horyu-ji and the 8th-century monastery of Toshodai-ji. In the Ming period the complex of courtyards, parks, and palaces became labyrinthian in scope. Little remains of the imperial palaces at Nanking, the capital of the Ming dynasty until 1421. Peking then became the capital, and its group of imperial buildings, known as the Forbidden City, remains a remarkable achievement. Around its main courtyard and many smaller courts are grouped splendid halls, galleries, terraces, and gateways. White marble, wall facings of glazed terra-cotta, roofs of glazed and colored tiles, and woodwork finished with paint, lacquer, and gilding unite to create an effect of exceptional richness. Notable among these buildings is the group constituting the Temple of Heaven, including the Hall of the Annual Prayers (added in the late 19th cent.), a circular structure on a triple platform surmounted by a roof in three tiers covered with tiles of an intense blue glaze. Since the late 19th cent. the Chinese have adopted European architectural styles. Under Communist rule they have tended to imitate modern Soviet buildings. The trend is toward the impressively massive and the clearly functional in public buildings (e.g., the Great Hall of the People, 1959; Peking). In such buildings only in the detailing around window frames and doorways can traditional features still be seen. See Johannes Prip-Moller, *Chinese Buddhist Monasteries* (1937); D. G. Mirams, *A Brief History of Chinese Architecture* (1940); A. C. H. Boyd, *Chinese Architecture and Town Planning* (1962); N. I. Wu, *Chinese and Indian Architecture* (1963); Laurence Sickman and Alexander Soper, *The Art and Architecture of China* (3d ed. 1968); Michèle Pirazzoli-t'Serstevens, *Living Architecture: Chinese* (1971).

Chinese art, the oldest in the world, has its origins in remote antiquity. (For the history of Chinese civilization, see CHINA.) Excavations in Kansu and Honan have revealed a Neolithic culture with painted pottery that exhibits dynamic swirling or lozenge-shaped patterns. Our knowledge of ancient Chinese art is largely limited to works in pottery, bronze, bone, and jade. Excavations in the city of AN-YANG have yielded numerous ritual bronze vessels that indicate a highly advanced culture in the SHANG dynasty in the 2d millennium. The art of bronze casting of this period is of such high quality that it suggests a long period of prior experimentation. It constitutes the clearest extant record of stylistic development in the Shang, CHOU, and Early HAN dynasties. The adornment of the bronzes varies from the most meager incision to the most ornate plastic embellishment and from the most severely abstract to some naturalistic representations. The Later Han dynasty marks the end of the development of this art, although highly decorated bronze continued to be produced, often with masterly treatment of metal and stone inlays. The advent of Buddhism (1st cent. A.D.) brought a need for art of a different character. Works of sculpture, painting, and architecture of a more distinctly religious nature were created. The human figure, which had appeared rarely in ancient Chinese art, now became most important. Sculpture as an isolated art prior to Buddhism survives chiefly in tomb carvings and monumental tomb guardians in stone. With Buddhism, the representation of the Buddha and of the bodhisattvas became the great theme of sculpture. The forms of these figures came to China from India by way of central Asia, but in the 6th cent. A.D. the Chinese artists succeeded in developing a national style in sculpture. This style reached its greatest distinction early in the T'ANG dynasty. Figures, beautiful in proportion and graceful in gesture, show great precision and clarity in the rendering of form, with a predominance of linear rhythms. Gradually the restraint of the 7th cent. gave way to more dramatic work. For about 600 years Buddhist sculpture continued to flourish; then in the MING dynasty sculpture ceased to develop in style. After this time miniature sculpture in jade, ivory, and glass, of exquisite craftsmanship, but lacking vitality of inspiration, was produced in China, as in Japan. The origins of Chinese painting are lost. Although the arts thrived during the Han dynasty, little painting remains except for tomb decorations in Manchuria and N Korea, some skillfully painted LACQUER ware, and tiles. It is only from the 5th cent. A.D. that we can trace a clear historical development. Near TUN-HUANG, more than a hundred caves (called the Caves of a Thousand Buddhas) contain Buddhist frescoes and scrolls dating mainly from the late 5th to the 8th cent. They show, first, simple hieratic forms of Buddha and of the bodhisattvas and, later, crowded scenes of paradise. The elegant decorative motifs and certain figural elements reveal a Western influence. While Chinese painting never consistently followed the rigid laws of Western PERSPECTIVE, a highly organized system of representing objects in space was evolved. Rendering of natural effects of light and shade is almost wholly absent in this art, which relies rather on its incomparable mastery of line and silhouette. One of the earliest artists about whom anything is known is the 4th-century master KU K'AI-CHIH, who is said to have excelled in portraiture. The art of figure painting reached a peak of excellence in the T'ang dynasty (618–906). Historical subjects and scenes of courtly life were popular, and the human figure was portrayed with a robustness and monumentality unequalled in Chinese painting. Animal subjects were also frequently represented. The 8th-century artist Han Kan is famous for his painting of horses. The T'ang dynasty also saw the rise of the great art of Chinese landscape painting. Lofty and craggy peaks were depicted, with streams, rocks, and trees carefully detailed in brilliant greens and blues. These paintings were usually executed as brush drawing and color washes. Little if anything remains of the work of such famous masters as YEN LI-PEN, Tung Yuan, Wu Tao-tzu, and Wang Wei. In the SUNG dynasty (960–1279), landscape painting reached its greatest expression. A vast yet orderly scheme of nature was conceived, reflecting contemporary Taoist and Confucian views. Sharply diminished in scale, the human figure did not intrude upon the magnitude of nature. The technique of ink monochrome was developed with great skill; with the utmost economy of pictorial means, suggestion of mood, misty atmosphere, depth, and distance were created. During the Sung dynasty the monumental detail began to emerge. A single bamboo shoot, flower, or bird provided the subject for a painting. Among those who excelled in flower painting was the Emperor Hui-tsung, who founded the imperial academy. Hundreds of painters contributed to its glory, including LI T'ANG, HSIA KUEI, and MA YÜAN. Members of the Ch'an (Zen) sect of Buddhism executed paintings often sparked by an intuitive vision. With rapid brushstrokes and ink splashes, they created works of vigor and spontaneity. With the ascendance of the YÜAN dynasty (1260–1368), painting reached a new level of achievement, and under Mongol rule many aspects cultivated in Sung art were brought to culmination. The human figure assumed greater importance, and landscape painting acquired a new vitality. Still-life compositions came into greater prominence, especially bamboo painting. During this time, much painting was produced by the literati, gentlemen scholars who painted for their own enjoyment. Under some of the emperors of the MING dynasty (1368–1644), a revival of learning and of older artistic traditions was encouraged and connoisseurship was developed. We are indebted to the Ming art collectors for the preservation of many paintings that have survived into our times. Bird and flower pictures exhibited the superb decorative qualities so familiar to the West. TUN CH'I-CH'ANG, SHEN CHOU, and Tai Chin are but a few of the many great masters of this period. Under the CH'ING dynasty (1644–1912) a high level of technical competence was maintained, particularly in the applied arts, until the 19th cent., when the output became much more limited. The famous four Wangs imitated the great Yüan masters. Among painters of small-scale landscapes, CHU TA was outstanding as an artist of remarkable personal vision. However, there was little innovation in painting. Throughout the history of Chinese painting one characteristic has prevailed—the consummate handling of the brushstroke. Paintings were executed in a dry or wet-brush technique, with an incredible versatility, ranging from swirling patterns to staccato dots. The mastery of brushwork was directly related to calligraphy, traditionally regarded by the Chinese as an art form. Reliance on calligraphic techniques, however, produced a sterile art of overworked formulas in painting of the 19th cent. Elegant inscriptions and poems were often included within the painting, which took the form of a hand scroll, hanging scroll, or an album leaf, made of silk or paper. The fine art of Chinese pottery making followed to some degree the development of painting, reaching its highest perfection in the Sung dynasty and its extreme technical elaboration and decorative style in the Ming. In ENAMEL ware, lacquer ware, JADE, IVORY, textiles, and many other of the so-called minor arts, the world owes an incalculable debt to China. The influence of Chinese art upon other cultures has been profound; it has extended to the Muslim countries and, since the 14th cent., to Western Europe. Western influence on Chinese art has been evident since the late 17th cent., but not of major significance until comparatively recent times. The 19th cent. produced no major Chinese masters but many competent traditionalists. Early 20th-century artists copied Western styles without real comprehension, and attempts to combine them with Chinese subject matter were largely unsuccessful. After the Communists came to power in 1949, the graphic arts useful to political propaganda were encouraged, and Western influence in the arts was strictly discouraged. Within the limits of government restrictions two painters, Li K'o-jan and Ch'eng Shih-fa, have produced works of considerable individuality. Chinese artists working outside China, including Tseng Yu-ho in Hawaii and Chao Wu-chi in France, have produced abstract works based on calligraphy that reveal some Western influence. See articles on individual artists, e.g., MA YÜAN. See Laurence Sickman and Alexander Soper, *The Art and Architecture of China* (1956); Osvald Sirén, *Chinese Painting* (7 vol., 1956–58); P. C. Swann, *Chinese Monumental Art* (tr. 1963); William Willett, *Foundations of Chinese Art* (1965); Michael Sullivan, *The Arts of China* (rev. ed. 1973).

Chinese Communist party: see COMMUNIST PARTY, in China.

Chinese examination system, civil service recruitment method and educational system employed from the Han dynasty (206 B.C.–A.D. 220) until it was abolished by the Ch'ing dowager empress Tz'u Hsi in 1905 under pressure from leading Chinese intellectuals. The concept of a state ruled by men of ability and virtue was an outgrowth of Confucian philosophy. The examination system was an attempt to recruit men on the basis of merit rather than on the basis of family or political connection. Because success in the examination system was the basis of social status and because education was the key to success in the system, education was highly regarded in traditional China. If a person passed the provincial examination, his entire family was raised in status to that of scholar gentry, thereby receiving prestige and privilege. The texts studied for the examination were the Confucian classics. In the T'ang dynasty (618–906) the examination system was reorganized and more efficiently administered. Because some scholars criticized the emphasis on memorization without practical application and the narrow scope of the examinations, the system underwent further change in the Sung dynasty (960–1279). WANG AN-SHIH reformed the examination, stressing the understanding of underlying ideas and the ability to apply classical insights to contemporary problems. In the Ming dynasty (1368–1644) the commentaries of the Sung Neo-Confucian philosopher CHU HSI were adopted as the orthodox interpretation of the classics. Although only a small percentage of students could achieve office, students spent 20 to 30 years memorizing the orthodox commentaries in preparation for a series of up to eight examinations for the highest degree. By the 19th cent. the examination system was regarded as outdated and inadequate training for officials who faced the task of modernizing China. After it was abolished, mass education along with a Western type curriculum was promoted. See W. T. DeBary, ed., *Sources of Chinese Tradition* (1960); Wolfgang Franke, *The Reform and Abolition of the Traditional Chinese Examination System* (1960); J. M. S. Meskill, *The Chinese Civil Service* (1963); E. A. Kracke, Jr., *Civil Service in Early Sung China, 960–1067* (1968); I. C. Y. Hsu, *The Rise of Modern China* (1970).

Chinese exclusion, policy of prohibiting immigration of Chinese laborers to the United States; initiated in 1882. From the time of the U.S. acquisition of California (1848) there had been a large influx of Chinese laborers to the Pacific coast. They were encouraged to emigrate because of the need for cheap labor, and were employed largely in the building of transcontinental railroads. By 1867 there were some 50,000 Chinese in California, most of them manual laborers. Their numbers continued to increase after the conclusion in 1868 of the Burlingame Treaty with China, which guaranteed the right of Chinese immigration; it did not, however, grant the right of naturalization. In the following decades a great deal of anti-Chinese sentiment arose in California, partly because the growing American labor force had to compete with cheap Chinese labor and partly because many Americans were opposed to further immigration by what they considered to be an inferior people. In 1877 anti-Chinese riots occurred in San Francisco. Efforts were made to ban Chinese immigration, and in 1879 Congress passed a bill to that effect. It was vetoed, however, by President Hayes on the grounds that it violated the Burlingame Treaty. In 1880 a new treaty with China was concluded; it allowed the United States to regulate, limit, or suspend the entry of Chinese labor, but not to prohibit it. In 1882, however, the Chinese Exclusion Act banned immigration of Chinese laborers for 10 years. Some of the later acts (1888 and 1892) were flat violations of the 1880 treaty. A new treaty was signed in 1894 by which China agreed to exclusion of Chinese laborers for 10 years. When that period expired, Congress continued the exclusion unilaterally until the immigration law of 1924 excluded, in effect, all Asians. In 1943 the acts were repealed when a law was signed setting an annual immigration quota of 105 and extending citizenship privileges to Chinese. See R. D. McKenzie, *Oriental Exclusion* (1928); S. C. Miller, *The Unwelcome Immigrant* (1969); B. L. Sung, *The Story of the Chinese in America* (1971).

Chinese literature. It is not known when the current system of writing Chinese first developed. The oldest written records date from about 1400 B.C. in the period of the SHANG dynasty, but the elaborate system of notation used even then argues in favor of an earlier origin. From short inscriptions on bone and tortoiseshell (used for divination), characters standing for individual words have been deciphered and are traceable through many notations to modern forms. Most of the oldest surviving works of literature were not written until the later centuries of the CHOU dynasty (c.1027–256 B.C.). At this time was written most of what scholars of the Han dynasty (202 B.C.–A.D. 220) made into the canonical literature of CONFUCIANISM (which also included their own commentaries), although the current versions of these works, traditionally classified as the *Wu Ching* [five classics], contain later interpolations. The *Wu Ching*, traditionally attributed to CONFUCIUS either as author or compiler, consist of diverse books. The *Ch'un Ch'iu* [spring and autumn annals] is an unadorned chronology of Lu, Confucius's native state. The I CHING [classic of changes] explains, often in a mystifying way, a system of divination, based upon the study of 64 hexagrams of whole and broken lines. The *Li Chi* [book of rites] describes ceremonials and an ideal Confucian state. The *Shu Ching* [classic of documents or book of history] contains historical records, many of them known to be later forgeries. While some of these works contain verse, the main collection of poety in the *Wu Ching* is the *Shih Ching* [classic of songs or book of odes], made up of 305 poems. Written in simple rhyming stanzas, they tell of the peasant's life, of love, and of the wars of the feudal states. During the SUNG dynasty (960–1279), selections from the *Li Chi* and two other works were formed into the *Shih Shu* [four books]; they were thought to embody the quintessence of Confucian teachings. They are the *Ta Hsüeh* [great learning] and the *Chung Yung* [doctrine of the mean] from the *Li Chi*, the *Lun Yü* [analects of Confucius], and the *Book of Mencius* (see MENCIUS). Other important early books include the *Tao Te Ching* [classic of the way and its power], traditionally ascribed to LAO-TZE and the work of CHUANG-TZE. These two books, which form the chief literature of TAOISM, probably circulated in their present form from the 2d cent. B.C. The early Chinese books originally appeared in the cumbersome form of strips of bamboo. Silk was substituted as a writing material in the 2d cent. B.C.; and the invention of paper in the 2d cent. A.D. was responsible for a great increase in books. The method of printing whole pages from wooden blocks was discovered under the T'ang dynasty (618–906) and was perfected and in widespread use by the 10th cent.; it permitted an enormous increase in the number of copies available of any book. In time the literary and vernacular languages diverged sharply. Literary style was exceedingly concise and unmatched for its vigor, richness, and symmetry. Historical and literary allusions abounded, and finally special dictionaries were required for their elucidation. In poetry the freedom of the Chou period was followed by minutely prescribed forms. The lines, which rhymed, had to be matched syllable by syllable in both part of speech and intonation. By the T'ang period the prosodic rules no longer suited the spoken structure of the everyday language; they continued to be observed in spite of changes in pronunciation. It is generally agreed that China's greatest poetry was written in the T'ang dynasty. WANG WEI, LI PO, TU FU, PO CHÜ-I are masters of this period. In the succeeding Sung dynasty SU TUNG-P'O was perhaps the foremost poet. Translations of T'ang and Sung poetry strongly influenced the modern imagist school in English (see IMAGISTS). Chinese lyrics are generally very short, unemphatic and quiet in manner, and limited to suggesting a mood or a scene by a few touches rather than painting a detailed picture. Intellectual themes and narratives are comparatively rare. Many varieties of learned prose have also been written in China. Notable for accuracy and objectivity are the series of dynastic histories produced since Han times; the famous *Shih Chi* [records of the historian] (c.100 B.C.) by SSU-MA CH'IEN, served as their model. Chinese lexicography developed in response to the multiplication of characters. The last of a great series of dictionaries (still in standard use) was produced in the reign of K'ang Hsi (1662–1722). So-called encyclopedias, actually extracts from existing works, have been occasionally compiled; one such work of the MING dynasty (1368–1644) ran to over 11,000 short volumes and appeared in three manuscript copies. While the literati were cultivating polite literature during the T'ang and Sung periods, prose and verse of a popular nature began to appear. It was written in the spoken vernacular rather than in the classical literary language, and scholars regarded it with scorn. Springing from story cycles made familiar by professional storytellers, this vernacular literature first emerged as a full-fledged art in the drama of the Yüan dynasty (1260–1368) (see ORIENTAL DRAMA). It later developed into the great novels of the Ming period that followed. Both the drama and the novel proved immensely popular. Thus the 13th cent. witnessed the emergence of the resources of the living language of the people. The vernacular novels, although they had their roots in the Yüan epoch, took shape gradually during the Ming era until they were finally given their finished form, perhaps anonymously by some talented traditional scholar. An early and outstanding example of the novel is the *San Kuo Chih Yen I* (tr. *San Kuo, or*

Romance of the Three Kingdoms, 1925) set in the THREE KINGDOMS period (220–265), which recounts heroic deeds and chivalrous exploits. Another historical romance is the *Shui Hu Chuan* (tr. *All Men Are Brothers,* 1937), a picaresque tale of men forced by the venality of officials to become bandits. The *Hsi Yu Chi* (tr. *Monkey,* 1943) is an allegorical tale, full of the supernatural, concerning the adventures of a Buddhist pilgrim on a journey to India. The *Chin P'ing Mei* (tr. *The Golden Lotus,* 1939) by contrast portrays domestic life and amorous intrigue, and is marked by realistic incident and the interplay of human relationships. The greatest Chinese novel is, however, considered to be *Hung Lou Meng* (tr. *Dream of the Red Chamber,* 1958), an 18th-century work chiefly by the hand of TS'AO MSÜEH-CH'IN. With an unrivaled gift for subtle characterization and plot construction, the author recounts the declining fortunes of an aristocratic family. After the republican revolution authors turned away from the classical modes of composition, and many writers (notably HU SHIH and LUSIN) advocated writing in the paihua vernacular. The change in Chinese education from preoccupation with the classic literature to scientific and technological subjects reduced mastery of the traditional literary skills as did the abolition of the civil service examinations for official posts, which had been based on a knowledge of the Four Books of the Confucian canon. The use of characters instead of an alphabet persisted, however; this made older writings accessible and permitted the Chinese, who speak widely different dialects, amounting to different languages, to communicate with one another. The use of paihua has proved especially effective in prose. Translations of Western books frequently appeared in China, and the novelists of the republican period were greatly influenced by European writers. Among the most distinguished writers of modern China are Lusin (1881–1936), Kuo Mo-jo, Mao Tun, Lao She (1899–1966), Shen Ts'ung-wen, and Pa Chin. Under the Communist government, Chinese literature has suffered from the government-sponsored concept of SOCIALIST REALISM. A pioneering translator of the classic Confucian and Taoist texts is James Legge, whose works, still standard, appear in many volumes. More recent translations of individual classics include Arthur Waley, tr., *The Book of Songs* (1937); and *The Analects of Confucius* (1938); Richard Wilhelm and C. F. Baynes, tr., *The I Ching or Book of Changes* (1950); Bernhard Karlgren, tr., *The Book of Odes* (1950); W. I. Ch'an, tr., *The Way of Lao Tzu* (1963); W. A. C. H. Dobson, tr., *Mencius* (1963); and Burton Watson, tr., *The Complete Works of Chuang Tzu* (1968). General anthologies of Chinese literature in translation include Lin Yutang, ed., *The Wisdom of China and India* (1942) and Cyril Birch, ed., *Anthology of Chinese Literature* (2 vol., 1961–72). Collections of short stories, new and old, include Edgar Snow, ed., *Living China: Modern Chinese Stories* (1936), and Christopher Levenson, Wolfgang Bauer, and Herbert Franks, tr., *The Golden Casket: Chinese Novellas of Two Millennia* (1964). Anthologies of Chinese poetry include Witter Bynner and K. H. Kiang, tr., *The Jade Mountain: A Chinese Anthology, Being Three Hundred Poems of the T'ang Dynasty* (1929); David Hawkes, tr., *Ch'u Tz'u: The Songs of the South, an Ancient Chinese Anthology* (1959); A. R. Davis, ed., *The Penguin Book of Chinese Verse* (1962); S. S. Liu, tr., *One Hundred and One Chinese Poems* (1967) and Burton Watson, ed., *Chinese Rhyme-Prose* (1971). Bibliographical guides to translations and criticisms of modern Chinese literature include Martha Davidson, comp., *A List of Published Translations from Chinese into English, French, and German* (2 vol., 1952–57); and T. L. Yuan, comp., *China in Western Literature: A Continuation of Cordier's Bibliotheca Sinica* (1958). See also J. R. Hightower, *Topics in Chinese Literature: Outlines and Bibliographies* (1950); Burton Watson, *Early Chinese Literature* (1962); Lai Ming, *A History of Chinese Literature* (1964); W. C. Liu, *An Introduction to Chinese Literature* (1966); C. T. Hsia, *A History of Modern Chinese Fiction* (1961) and *The Classic Chinese Novel* (1968); and H. L. Boorman, ed., *Biographical Dictionary of Republican China* (4 vol., 1967–71).

Chinese music can be traced back as far as the third millennium B.C. Manuscripts and instruments from the early periods of its history are not extant, however, because in 212 B.C., Shih Hwang-ti of the Ch'in dynasty caused all the books and instruments to be destroyed and the practice of music to be stopped. Certain outlines of ancient Chinese music have nevertheless been ascertained. Of primary significance is the fact that the music and philosophy of China have always been inseparably bound; musical theory and form have been invariably symbolic in nature and remarkably stable through the ages. The single tone is of greater significance than melody; the tone is an important attribute of the substance that produces it. Hence musical instruments are separated into eight classes according to the materials from which they are made—gourd (sheng); bamboo (panpipes); wood (*chu,* a trough-shaped percussion instrument); silk (various types of zither, with silk strings); clay (globular flute); metal (bell); stone (sonorous stone); and skin (drum). Music was believed to have cosmological and ethical connotations comparable to those of Greek music. The failure of a dynasty was ascribed to its inability to find the proper *huang chung,* or tone of absolute pitch. The *huang chung* was produced by a bamboo pipe that roughly approximated the normal pitch of a man's voice. Other pipes were cut, their length bearing a definite mathematical ratio to it. Their tones were divided into two groups—six male tones and six female. These were the *lüs,* and their relationship approximated the Pythagorean cycle of fifths. Legend ascribes their origin to birdsong, six from that of the male bird and six from that of the female, and the tones of the two sets were always kept separate. The *lüs* did not constitute a scale, however. The scale of Chinese music is pentatonic, roughly represented by the black keys on a piano. From it, by starting on different notes, several modes may be derived. The melody of vocal music is limited by the fact that melodic inflection influences the meaning of a word. Likewise, quanititative rhythms are not easily adaptable to the Chinese language. Several types of notation were used. Singers used the syllabic symbols for the five notes of the pentatonic scale, as did players of pipes. Players of the stone and bell chimes, which were tuned to the *lüs,* used symbols that represented the pitch names of the *lüs.* Players of flutes and zithers used a kind of tablature. None of this notation indicated rhythm. The ancient Chinese hymns were slow and solemn and were accompanied by very large orchestras. Chamber music was also highly developed. Chinese opera originated in the 14th cent. as a serious and refined art. Throughout the political and social turmoil following World War I, Western (classical and popular) and Japanese sources dominated Chinese music. At present, Western concepts of harmony are in active use but are generally applied to vocal genres, such as cantatas and music dramas, which have educational as well as musical value. The Peking Opera has produced numerous new works since 1949, most of them concerning political topics. It is one of the few forums of traditional performance style, although there is an ongoing effort directed by the Peking Institute of National Music to preserve the few remainders of ancient musical practice. See Curt Sachs, *The Rise of Music in the Ancient World* (1943); J. H. Levis, *Foundations of Chinese Musical Art* (2d ed. 1964); Elizabeth Halson, *Peking Opera* (1966); bibliography by Fredric Lieberman (1970).

Chinese Nationalist party: see KUOMINTANG.

Chinese Turkistan: see SINKIANG.

Chinese white: see ZINC OXIDE.

Ch'ing (chĭng) or **Manchu** (măn″cho͞o', măn'cho͞o″), dynasty of China that ruled from 1644 to 1912. It was established by the MANCHU, a people of Manchuria, who invaded China and captured Peking in 1644. All China was occupied and the remnants of the Ming dynasty destroyed by 1659, but disorders in S China and Taiwan were not finally suppressed until 1683. The Manchu introduced few important changes in China. One notable political innovation, however, was the system of administration involving joint Manchu-Chinese control of military and civil affairs. Emperor K'ang Hsi (reigned 1661–1722) consolidated the Manchu regime by suppressing (1673–81) rebellions and defeating the Mongols and Tibetans. When Jesuit missionaries appeared he issued (1692) an edict of toleration. Under Emperor CH'IEN LUNG (reigned 1735–96), China attained its maximum territorial expansion. China's wealth and luxury goods, notably porcelain and silk, attracted the attention of European maritime powers, but the dynasty was at first opposed to trade. In 1759 an imperial edict allowed maritime trade only at the port of Canton. By the 19th cent. Great Britain had established profitable trade relations with China, but its repeated attempts (1793, 1816, 1834) to obtain a liberal trade policy were unsuccessful. British dissatisfaction over trade restrictions, as well as the insularity of the Manchu officials, precipitated the OPIUM WAR (1839–42). China's defeat in the war resulted in the cession of Hong Kong to Great Britain and the establishment of EXTRATERRITORIALITY for other Western nations. The Manchu regime, already weakened by Western encroachments, was further enfeebled by internal rebellions. The Taiping Rebellion (1850–65) nearly brought the dynasty to an end. However, the Manchu regime suppressed the major rebellions and embarked on a policy of diplomatic, technological, and military modernization led by Tseng Kuo-fan (1811–72) and Li Hung-chang (1823–1901). These statesmen played important roles in the T'ung Chih restoration (1862–74), during which the dynasty tried to restore the traditional order by reasserting Confucian social values. China yielded to Western demands for permanent diplomatic representation in Peking (1860) and continued to suffer territorial encroachments. Russia occupied Ili, Japan incorporated the Ryukyu islands, France made Annam a protectorate, and Great Britain completed its annexation of Burma. The First Sino-Japanese War (1894–95) deprived China of its control over Korea, and the war was followed by the partition of mainland China into foreign spheres of influence. The general agreement was that Great Britain should predominate in the Yangtze valley, France in the extreme south, and Russia in Manchuria. After the Russo-Japanese War (1904–5), Japan took over Russia's sphere. Efforts to strengthen the dynasty against foreign imperialism were undertaken by K'ang Yu-wei (1858–1927) with the support of the emperor KUANG HSU. These efforts, however, were frustrated by the dowager empress TZ'U HSI, who aborted the reform movement in a coup d'état (1898). She supported the BOXER UPRISING, however, in a vain attempt to dislodge the foreign powers (1898–1900). Following foreign suppression of the Boxers, Tz'u Hsi changed course and allowed some moderate educational and administrative reforms. However, the dynasty acted slowly upon the demand of intellectuals, social leaders, and progressive provincial governors for a national assembly and a change to constitutional monarchy. From abroad Sun Yat-sen led a movement for revolutionary overthrow of the Manchus and establishment of a republic. His coalition, which included moderate leaders in S China, revolutionary students who had returned from the West, and military officers finally overthrew the dynasty in the Revolution of 1911. With the collapse of the Ch'ing, China abandoned its 2,000-year tradition of monarchic rule in favor of a republican form of government. See S. Y. Teng and J. K. Fairbank, *China's Response to the West* (1954); Franz Michael, *The Origin of Manchu Rule in China* (1965); Albert Feuerwerker, *Approaches to Modern Chinese History* (1967); Henry McAleary, *The Modern History of China* (1968); I. C. Y. Hsü, *The Rise of Modern China* (1970).

Chingford: see WALTHAM FOREST.

Chinghai: see TSINGHAI, China.

Ch'ing Hai, lake, China: see KOKO NOR.

Chingola (chĭng-gō'lä), city (1972 est. pop., with suburbs, 130,000), N central Zambia. It is a copper-mining center, located on the COPPERBELT.

Ch'ing-tao (chĭng-dou) or **Tsingtao** (tsĭng'tou', chĭng'dou'), city (1970 est. pop. 1,900,000), SE Shantung prov., E China, on the Yellow Sea. With an excellent ice-free harbor, it is a major port of China, connected by rail with Yen-t'ai and Chi-nan. The leading industrial city of Shantung, it has textile mills, food-processing and tobacco-processing establishments, machine shops, paper mills, and plants making diesel locomotives and railroad cars, tires, fertilizers, rubber products, chemicals, and metal items. Leased to Germany in 1898 as part of the Kiaochow territory, Ch'ing-tao became the administrative center of the leasehold and developed into a modern city. The Japanese held it from 1914 to 1922. Ch'ing-tao was a marine and naval base for the United States from 1945 to 1949, when it was abandoned and fell to the Communists. In the city are an astronomical observatory, two marine museums, Shantung Univ., Ch'ing-tao Technical Univ., a medical college, and several technical institutes.

Ching-te-chen (jĭng-dŭ-jŭn) or **Fowliang** (fo͞o'lēäng'), city (1970 est. pop. 300,000), NE Kiangsi prov., China, on the Chang River. It is world famous for its fine porcelain, made since the Han dynasty (202 B.C.–A.D. 220) from the white clay, kaolin, found near P'o-yang lake to the west. Coal is mined in the region. The city reached its greatest fame under the Northern Sung dynasty (c.1000), when it supplied porcelain to the royal household. It declined after heavy damage in the Taiping Rebellion.

Chinhae (chēn'hă'), city (1970 est. pop. 92,000), SE South Korea, on the Korea Strait. It is an important fishing port and naval base.

Chin Hills, mountain range, W Burma, along the boundary between Burma and Assam, India. It rises to 10,018 ft (3,053 m) in Mt. Victoria. The range is covered with pine and teak forests. The Chin Hills Special Division (c.14,000 sq mi/36,260 sq km; 1969 est. pop. 354,000), a mountainous region dotted with small villages, is inhabited by Chin tribes, a Tibeto-Burman people. Falam is the capital. This district is a special division of Burma and has become largely autonomous, with representatives in the Burmese cabinet.

Chin-hua (jĭn-hwä) or **Kinhwa,** town, central Chekiang prov., SE China. A transportation hub on the Chekiang-Kiangsi RR, Chin-hua has been famous for two centuries for its hams. Other products are fertilizer, machine tools, and textiles.

Ch'in-huang-tao or **Chinwangtao** (both: chĭn-wäng-dou), city, NE Hopeh prov., China, on the Po Hai, an arm of the Yellow Sea. It is an ice-free port in an important coal area.

Chi-ning (jē-nĭng) or **Tsining,** city, Inner Mongolian Autonomous Region, China. It is an important railroad center at the junction of the system connecting Peking and Lan-chou, with the line traversing the Mongolian People's Republic to the USSR. Industries include meat-packing, tanning, and the production of textiles.

Chinju (chĕn'jōō'), city (1970 pop. 121,622), capital of South Kyongsang prov., S South Korea. It is a transportation and agricultural center, with industries producing food products and textiles.

Chinkiang: see CHEN-CHIANG.

Ch'in Ling, mountain range, China: see TSINLING.

Chinmoy: see GHOSE, CHINMOY.

Chinnampo: see NAMPO, North Korea.

Chinnereth (kĭn'ərĕth) or **Chinneroth** (-rōth). **1** See GALILEE, SEA OF. **2** Town, near the Sea of Galilee. Deut. 3.17; Joshua 11.2; 19.35. Cinneroth: 1 Kings 15.20.

Chino (chē'nō), city (1970 pop. 20,411), San Bernardino co., S Calif.; founded 1887, inc. 1910. It is the business and processing center of a diversified farming (notably dairying) area. Mobile homes, plumbing hardware, machine products, and wool items are manufactured. A state prison is located in Chino; nearby is a state game-bird farm.

chinoiserie (shēnwäzrē'), decorative work produced under the influence of Chinese art, applied particularly to the more fanciful and extravagant manifestations. Intimations of Eastern art reached Europe in the Middle Ages in the porcelains brought by returning travelers. Eastern trade was maintained during the intervening centuries, and the East India trading companies of the 17th and 18th cent. imported Chinese lacquers and porcelains. Dutch ceramics quickly showed the influence of Chinese blue-and-white porcelains. In the middle of the 18th cent. the enthusiasm for Chinese objects affected practically every decorative art applied to interiors, furniture, tapestries, and *bibelots* and supplied craftsmen with fanciful motifs of scenery, human figures, pagodas, intricate lattices, and exotic birds and flowers. In France the Louis XV style gave especial opportunities to chinoiserie, as it blended well with the established ROCOCO. Whole rooms, such as those at Chantilly, were painted with compositions in chinoiserie, and Watteau and other artists brought consummate craftsmanship to the style. Thomas Chippendale, the chief exponent in England, produced a unique and decorative type of furniture. The craze early reached the American colonies. Chinese objects, particularly fine wallpapers, played an important role in the adornment of rooms, and especially in Philadelphia the style had a pronounced effect upon design. See study by Hugh Honour (1961).

Chinon (shēnôN'), town (1968 pop. 5,435), Indre-et-Loire dept., W central France, in Touraine, on the Vienne River. Chinon was an important medieval town and many buildings (notably three churches) from that period are preserved. Its castle, overlooking the river, consists of three distinct fortresses built from the 11th to the 15th cent.—the Château Saint-Georges, the Château du Milieu, and the Château du Coudray. The builders of the castle included Philip II of France, Richard I of England (the Lion-hearted), and Henry II of France (who died there in 1559). In the Château du Milieu in 1429 Joan of Arc presented herself to Charles VII of France and correctly identified him although he was disguised. In La Devinière, a nearby hamlet, stands the house where the poet Rabelais was born (c.1490).

chinook (shĭnōōk', chĭ-), warm, dry air mass that descends the eastern slopes of the U.S. and Canadian Rocky Mts. after having lost moisture by condensation over the western slopes. Chinooks occur mainly in winter. They sometimes replace the cold continental air mass over the western plains, causing rapid melting of snow and temperature increases as great as 40°F (4°C) within a few hours. Similar winds occurring in the Alps and elsewhere are known as foehn winds. The term *chinook* was originally applied by Oregon settlers to a moist Pacific wind blowing from the direction of a Chinook Indian camp.

Chinook Indians, North American Indian tribe of the Penutian linguistic stock. Altogether twelve main tribes spoke Chinook languages; all were in the Columbia River valley. The Chinook themselves were on the lower extremity of the river and, with the Clatsop Indians, constituted the now extinct Lower Chinook branch of the linguistic stock (see AMERICAN INDIAN LANGUAGES). The village was their main social unit, and a wealthy chief might control several. The Chinook practiced head flattening, and slavery was common. Their food consisted mostly of fish, roots, and berries. They were skilled with canoes, were noted traders, and practiced the custom of POTLATCH. They lacked the totemic art and the secret societies of their neighbors. They were well known to the traders on the Pacific coast in the late 18th cent. and a corrupted form of their language known as Chinook jargon served as a trade language from the Columbia River to Alaska.

Chinook jargon, LINGUA FRANCA of early traders on the Northwest Coast of the United States and Canada. It included Chinook, Nootka, English, and French words, with various borrowings.

chinquapin (chĭng'kəpĭn) [Algonquian], name for certain American species of the CHESTNUT genus of the family Fagaceae (BEECH family) and for a related species, the golden chinquapin (*Castanopsis chrysophylla*), an evergreen of the Pacific states. The common chinquapin is *Castanea pumila,* native to the E United States. Its wood and fruit are used like those of the chestnut. The bush chinquapin (*C. alnifolia*) has a more southern range. Chinquapin is classified in the division MAGNOLIOPHYTA, class Magnoliopsida, order Fagales, family Fagaceae.

chintz (chĭnts) [probably Hindustani,=variegated], originally a painted or stained calico from India. Esteemed for its bright colors and designs, it was used in Europe for bedcovers and draperies. Reproductions of Indian designs and also original patterns were soon produced. Especially noted was toile de Jouy, manufactured from 1700 to 1843 at Jouy, near Paris. Both flower motifs and characteristic pictorial scenes are prized by collectors and imitated in modern prints. Modern chintz is usually made up of bright prints on a light background.

Chinwangtao: see CH'IN-HUANG-TAO, China.

Chioggia (kyôd'jä), city (1971 pop. 49,288), Venetia, NE Italy, on a small island at the southern end of the Lagoon of Venice (an arm of the Gulf of Venice), connected to the mainland by a bridge. It is an important fishing port and has a steel industry. In 1379-80 several naval battles were fought off Chioggia in the war between Venice and Genoa. The liberation of the town from the Genoese turned the war in favor of Venice. Old houses and churches, canals, and sailboats help make Chioggia a picturesque tourist spot.

Chios, Greece: see KHÍOS.

Chipewyan Indians, North American Indians of the ATHABASCAN branch of the Nadene linguistic stock (see also AMERICAN INDIAN LANGUAGES). Scattered Chipewyan groups ranged W Canada between Great Slave Lake and the Churchill River. They were nomadic hunters in rivalry with the Woodland Cree. They are not to be confused with the Chippewa or Ojibwa Indians.

chipmunk, rodent of the family Sciuridae (SQUIRREL family). The chipmunk of the E United States and SE Canada is of the genus *Tamias.* The body of the common Eastern chipmunk, *Tamias striatus,* is about 5 to 6 in. (13-15 cm) long; the upper parts are reddish brown or grayish brown with a median black stripe and two black stripes separated by a whitish band along each side. The tail, 4 to 5 in. (10-13 cm) long, is hairy and flattened. Food is transported in the expansible cheek pouches. Chipmunks make underground burrows, often with concealed entrances beneath stone walls or trees. Although chipmunks are usually found near the ground, they are excellent climbers. In its northern range the chipmunk goes underground about the end of October, but sleeps deeply only during the coldest period. Food for the winter is stored in the burrow. Chipmunks eat nuts, seeds, berries, and insects. Although they are numerous, these animals are not serious threats to crops. The typical life span is 5 years. The chipmunks of W North America belong, like those of E Asia, to the genus *Eutamias.* Chipmunks are classified in the phylum CHORDATA, subphylum Vertebrata, class Mammalia, order Rodentia, family Sciuridae.

Chippawa (chĭp'əwô), village (1966 pop. 3,877), S Ont., Canada, just above Niagara Falls. It was first settled in 1794 and was the scene of an American victory (1814) in the War of 1812.

Chippendale, Thomas, 1718-79, celebrated English cabinetmaker. His designs were so widely followed that a whole general category of 18th-century English furniture is commonly grouped under his name. Chippendale's *Gentleman and Cabinet-Maker's Director,* an illustrated trade catalog first published in 1754, was widely influential in England and America. Among the numerous pieces stamped with his style, it is possible to assign unquestionably to his own workshop only those for which the original bills still remain, as in the case of Harewood House and Nostell Priory, whose furnishings were created by him. While he based his work upon the general Queen Anne and Georgian characteristics of sober design and thoroughly fine construction, retaining many of the early 18th-century details, Chippendale's distinction was to introduce many other forms. For these he used three outside inspirations—Chinese, Gothic, and contemporaneous French ROCOCO. The first two resulted naturally from the general mid-18th-century enthusiasms for CHINOISERIE decoration and pseudo-Gothic architecture. Chippendale's name is emphatically identified with the extensive variety of chair types that he developed—from geometrical to Chinese, lattice, or sumptuously carved and interlaced forms. Chippendale's varied output also included desks; mirror frames; hanging bookshelves; settees, with which he was especially successful; china cabinets and bookcases, frequently with fretted cornices and latticework glazed doors; and tables with delicately fretted galleries and distinctive cluster-column legs of Gothic inspiration. The last phase of his career shows the influence of the designs of Robert Adam. Chippendale's style, quickly imported to America, was imitated by a number of expert cabinetmakers. See studies by Oliver Brackett (1924) and Anthony Coleridge (1968).

Chippewa (chĭp'əwə), river, c.200 mi (320 km) long, rising in several forks in the lake region of N Wis., and flowing SW to the Mississippi, which it enters at the foot of Lake Pepin. Eau Claire and Chippewa Falls are on its banks. The river was once important in the lumbering industry.

Chippewa Falls, city (1970 pop. 12,351), seat of Chippewa co., W central Wis., on the Chippewa River; settled 1837, inc. as a city 1869. Originally a lumbering town, Chippewa Falls once had the world's largest sawmill. Today it is a trade and transportation center in a region of beef- and dairy-cattle farms. Its industries include meat packing and the manufacture of shoes, plastics, tools, and dies. Wissota State Park, which includes Lake Wissota, Wisconsin's largest artificial lake, is nearby.

Chippewa Indians: see OJIBWA INDIANS.

Chirchik (chĭrchĕk'), city (1970 pop. 107,000), Central Asian USSR, in Uzbekistan. It is an industrial center with large chemical plants and machinery factories. There is a chain of hydroelectric stations on the Chirchik River. The city was founded in 1932 on the site of the village of Kirgiz-Kulak.

Chiricahua Indians: see APACHE INDIANS.

Chiricahua National Monument: see NATIONAL PARKS AND MONUMENTS (table).

Chirico, Giorgio de (jōr'jō dā kē'rēkō), 1888-, Italian painter, b. Vólos, Greece. Chirico developed his enigmatic vision in Munich and Italy and from 1911 to 1915 he worked and exhibited in Paris. His powerful, disturbing paintings employ steep perspective, mannequin figures, empty space, and forms used out of context to create an atmosphere of mystery and loneliness. His work exercised a considerable influence on early surrealist painters but was never successfully imitated. In Ferrara, Chirico developed what he termed metaphysical painting, in which he consciously exploited the symbolism of his art. Chirico is represented in leading galleries throughout the world. See his memoirs (tr. 1972); studies by J. T. Soby (1955, repr. 1967) and Isabella Far (tr. 1971).

Chiron (kī'rŏn), in Greek mythology, centaur, son of Cronus. He was a renowned sage, physician, and prophet. Among his pupils were Hercules, Achilles, Jason, and Asclepius. When Hercules accidentally wounded Chiron, the pain was so great that Chiron surrendered his immortality to Prometheus and died. Zeus then set him among the stars as the constellation Sagittarius.

chiropody: see PODIATRY.

chiropractic (kīrəprăk'tĭk) [Gr.,=doing by hand], medical practice based on the theory that all disease results from a disruption of the functions of the nerves. The principal source of interference is thought to be displacement (or subluxation) of vertebrae of the spine, although other areas such as joints and muscle tissue may also be the sites of nerve interference. The method of treatment is by adjustment of displaced vertebrae. The chiropractor seeks to relieve the pressure on the nerves and thereby remove the cause of some specific ailment. Massage and manipulation by hand, exercise, and the application of heat, cold, and light are some of the healing techniques used. The early chiropractors believed that psychic energy, a force beyond human understanding, flowed from the brain, through the nerves, to all parts of the body and that it was interference with this force that caused disease. In 1953 the theory was revised to state that the health of body tissues is controlled by nerve impulses, and that interference in the nerve impulses causes disease. Chiropractic was introduced in the United States by D. D. Palmer in 1895 and carried on by his son, Bartlett Joshua Palmer. There are institutions for training students in the profession of chiropractic, which has legal recognition in the United States and in many other parts of the world. See B. J. Palmer, *Text Book on the Palmer Technique of Chiropractic* (1920); A. E. Homewood, *The Chiropractor and the Law* (1965); H. S. Schwartz, ed., *Mental Health and Chiropractic* (1971).

chiru: see ANTELOPE.

Chiryu (chēryo͞o'), city (1970 pop. 41,896), Aichi prefecture, S central Honshu, Japan. The city was formed in 1970 by the merger of a number of smaller towns.

Chishima: see KURIL ISLANDS.

Chisholm, Shirley Anita St. Hill (chĭz'əm), 1924–, U.S. Congresswoman (1969–), b. Brooklyn, N. Y. An expert on early childhood education, she worked (1959–64) as a consultant to the New York City bureau of child welfare before serving (1964–68) in the state assembly. Elected (1968) to the U.S. House of Representatives as a Democrat, Chisholm became the first black woman to serve in that body. She quickly gained national attention as a vocal critic of the war in Vietnam and the House seniority system and as an outspoken advocate of the interests of the urban poor. An active member of the black Congressional caucus, Chisholm made an unsuccessful bid for the 1972 Democratic presidential nomination. She is the author of *Unbought and Unbossed* (1970) and *The Good Fight* (1973).

Chisholm Trail, route over which vast herds of cattle were driven from Texas to the railheads in Kansas after the Civil War. It took its name from Jesse Chisholm, a part-Cherokee Indian trader who, in the spring of 1866, drove his wagon, heavily loaded with buffalo hides, through the Indian territory that is now Oklahoma to his trading post near Wichita, Kansas, the wheels cutting deep ruts in the prairie. These marked a route followed for almost two decades by traders and by drovers bringing cattle to shipping points and markets in Kansas. Hundreds of thousands of Texas longhorns were driven over the trail annually, and it became celebrated in frontier lore and cowboy ballads. With the development of railroads and the introduction of wire fencing, the trail fell into disuse, although traces of it can still be seen. See studies by Wayne Gard (1954) and B. J. Fletcher (1968).

Chishti, Muin ad-Din Hasan (mo͞oēn' äd-dĭn häsän' chĭsh'tē), 1142–1236, Indian Muslim saint, b. Seistan, Iran. He founded a Sufi mystic order in India. After traveling extensively in the Middle East and Central Asia he went to Lahore, then later settled in Ajmer. His splendid mausoleum there is an important center of pilgrimage.

Chisinau: see KISHINEV, USSR.

Chislon (kĭs'lŏn), Benjamite. Num. 34.21.

Chisloth-tabor (kĭs'lŏth-tā'bər), town, N Palestine, plausibly identified with Iksal, W of Mt. Tabor, Israel. Joshua 19.12. See also CHESULLOTH.

chi-square test: see STATISTICS.

Chistopol (chēstô'pəl), city (1970 pop. 60,000), Tatar Autonomous SSR, E European USSR, on the Kama River. It is a grain-trading center and has machinery plants. Chistopol was chartered in 1781.

Chisum, John Simpson (chĭz'əm), 1824–84, American cattleman, b. Tennessee. In 1837 he moved with his family to Texas. He had no formal education but worked as a builder and contractor, building the first courthouse in Paris, Texas. In 1854 he entered the cattle business; beginning in 1866, in partnership with Charles Goodnight, he drove herds into New Mexico, Colorado, and Wyoming, selling them to government food contractors for Indian reservations. When, in 1883, he established his ranch near Roswell, N.Mex., he became one of the first cattlemen in that region, and his became one of the largest herds. He was a prominent figure in the Lincoln co. cattle war, and at one time Billy the Kid was employed by him; however, Chisum cooperated with the authorities to end lawlessness in the cattle business.

Chiswick Press: see WHITTINGHAM, CHARLES.

Chita (chētä'), city (1970 pop. 241,000), capital of Chita oblast, SE Siberian USSR, at the confluence of the Chita and Ingoda rivers and on the Trans-Siberian RR. Machines and food-processing equipment are manufactured. Founded in 1653, Chita was a place of exile of the 19th-century Decembrist rebels.

Ch'i-t'ai (chē-tī) or **Kitai** (kē'tī'), town and oasis, N Sinkiang Uigur Autonomous Region, China, in the Dzungarian basin. It is a road hub and a trading center (furs, skins, raisins, and tea). Gold mines are nearby.

chitin (kī'tən), main constituent of the shells of arthropods. Chitin, a POLYSACCHARIDE analogous in chemical structure to CELLULOSE, consists of units of a glucose derivative (*N*-acetyl-D-glucosamine) joined to form a long, unbranched chain. Like cellulose, chitin contributes strength and protection to the organism. In arthropods the chitinous shell, or exoskeleton, covers the surface of the body, does not grow, and is periodically cast off (molted). After the old shell is shed, a new, larger shell is secreted by the epidermis, providing room for future growth. The chitin is rigid except between some body segments and joints where it is thin and allows movement of adjacent parts. Chitin is also found in the cell walls of some fungi.

chiton (kī'tən), common name for rock-clinging marine mollusks of the class Amphineura. Chitons are abundant on rocky coasts throughout most of the world, from the intertidal zone to a depth of about 1,200 ft (400 m). They range in length from ½ in. to

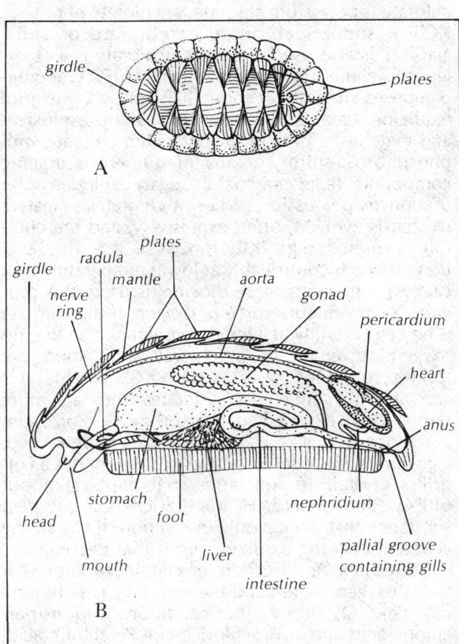

A. *Dorsal view of a chiton, representative mollusk of the class Amphineura*

B. *Internal anatomy of a chiton*

12 in. (1.2–30 cm), according to the species, but most are 1 to 3 in. (2.5–7.5 cm) long. The body of a chiton is low and oval; it is covered dorsally by a slightly convex shell consisting of eight linearly arranged overlapping plates. The shell may be dull or brightly colored. Most of the lower surface consists of a broad, flat foot with which the chiton clings to hard surfaces, often so tightly that a sharp instrument is needed to pry it loose. When dislodged, a chiton rolls into a ball. Beneath the shell is the characteristic molluscan mantle, a fleshy outfolding of the body wall. The lower edge of the mantle, called the girdle, extends below the edge of the shell and aids the foot in gripping. The girdle may be very wide and extend upward over the shell; in some species it is smooth or covered with scales, hairs, or spines that give the animal a shaggy appearance. The many gills are arranged in two rows within the mantle, one on either side of the body. The mouth, located on the ventral surface in front of the foot, contains a toothed, tonguelike scraping organ, the radula. Chitons crawl slowly by means of muscular undulations in the foot. Most are herbivorous, feeding on algae scraped from rocks and shells with the radula; some are carnivorous or omnivorous. Most feed at night and shelter under rock ledges by day. Chitons are classified in the phylum MOLLUSCA, class Amphineura, order Polyplacophora.

Chitose (chētō'sä), city (1970 pop. 56,118), Hokkaido prefecture, central Hokkaido, Japan, on the Chitose River. It is a communications center with a major airport.

Chitré (chētrā'), city (1970 pop. 12,379), S Panama, near the Gulf of Panama. It is a district capital on the Pan-American Highway and is the commercial and processing center for an agricultural area.

Chittagong (chĭt'əgŏng), city (1969 est. pop. 437,200), capital of Chittagong division, SE Bangladesh, on the Karnafuli River near the Bay of Bengal. An important rail terminus and administrative center, it is the chief port of Bangladesh, with modern facilities for oceangoing vessels. Jute, tea, and skins and hides are the major exports; imports include cotton and other piece goods, machinery, and construction materials. Offshore oil installations were set up during the 1960s. Besides an oil refinery and oil-blending plants, the city has large cotton- and jute-processing mills, tea and match factories, chemical and engineering works, an iron and steel mill, and fruit-canning, leather-processing, and shipbuilding industries. Power for Chittagong's industry is supplied by the Karnafuli hydroelectric project. The port was known to the civilized world by the early centuries A.D. and was used by Arakan, Arab, Persian, Portuguese (who called it Pôrto Grande), and Mogul sailors. Originally part of an ancient Hindu kingdom, Chittagong was conquered (9th cent.) by a Buddhist king of Arakan. It passed (13th cent.) to the Mogul empire, was retaken (16th cent.) by the Arakans, and again became part of the Mogul empire in the 17th cent. British control began in 1760. In the city are notable Hindu temples, Buddhist ruins, several fine examples of Mogul art, a university (founded 1966), and many arts and professional colleges. The **Chittagong Hill Tracts District** occupies a narrow coastal strip of parallel ranges along the Bay of Bengal and the Indian and Burmese frontiers. Valuable timber, bamboo, and cane forests, which cover the upper reaches of the hills, support a paper industry. Cotton, rice, tea, and oilseeds are raised in the valleys between the hills, and natural gas deposits lie along the shore. The cottage industries of the hill people produce woven cotton goods and bamboo nets and baskets.

Chittenden, Thomas, 1730–97, governor of Vermont, b. East Guilford, Conn. After moving to Vermont in 1774, he was active in the Windsor Convention, which declared (1777) Vermont independent. He and Ira Allen drew up the constitution, and Chittenden was elected (1778) first governor. He remained one of the Allen party, and he held office (except 1789–90) through Vermont's period of independence and early statehood until a few weeks before his death.

Chittim (kĭt'ĭm), variant of KITTIM.

Chittoor (chĭto͞or'), city (1971 pop. 63,041), Andhra Pradesh state, SE India, in the Poini River valley. Chittoor is on the Bangalore-Madras highway. It is a market for grain, sugarcane, and peanuts. The city is surrounded by mango and tamarind groves, and cattle are bred in the area. Chittoor, a district administrative center, was a British military post until 1884.

Chiu-chiang (jēō-jēäng) or **Kiukiang,** city (1970 est. pop. 120,000), N Kiangsi prov., China, on the Yangtze River, near P'o-yang lake. A major river port, it is connected by rail with Nan-ch'ang. In a major tea-growing area, it is a large processing, marketing, and shipping point. Other exports include rice, tobacco, cotton, ramie cloth, and tungsten ore. Machine tools are manufactured. The city was held by the Taipings from 1850 to 1854. It became a treaty port with a British concession in 1861. Chiu-chiang has notable botanical gardens and an arboretum. Just south is the wooded mountain of Lü Shan, the location of the resort of Ku-ling and of the White

Deer Cave, in which Chu Hsi (Chu Hi), the 13th-century Confucian philosopher, lived and taught.

Chiun (kī'ən), idol worshiped by the Hebrews in the wilderness. Amos 5.26. Remphan: Acts 7.43.

Ch'iung-shan (chēōōng-shän) or **Kiungshan** (kyōōng'shän',jeōōng-), city, on Hainan island, S Kwangtung prov., China. It was the chief town of the island until absorbed by Hai-k'ou (which is now the largest town). Formerly a treaty port, Ch'iung-shan became part of the People's Republic of China in 1950.

Chiusi (kyōō'sē), Lat. *Clusium*, Etruscan *Chamars*, town (1971 pop. 8,756), in Tuscany, central Italy, in the Apennines. Chiusi was one of the 12 sovereign towns of ancient Etruria; its semilegendary king LARS PORSENA is said to have marched from there against Rome (c.500 B.C.). The town was taken by Rome (c.225 B.C.). Many Etruscan ruins have been found, including tombs dating from the 5th cent. B.C., and there is an excellent Etruscan museum. There are also Christian catacombs.

chivalry (shĭv'əlrē), system of ethical ideals that arose from FEUDALISM and had its highest development in the 12th and 13th cent. Chivalric ethics originated chiefly in France and Spain and spread rapidly to the rest of the Continent and to England. They represented a fusion of Christian and military concepts of morality and still form the basis of gentlemanly conduct. Noble youths became pages in the castles of other nobles at the age of 7; at 14 they trained as squires in the service of knights, learning horsemanship and military techniques, and were themselves knighted usually at 21. The chief chivalric virtues were piety, honor, valor, courtesy, chastity, and loyalty. The knight's loyalty was due to the spiritual master, God; to the temporal master, the suzerain; and to the mistress of the heart, his sworn love. Love, in the chivalrous sense, was largely platonic; as a rule, only a virgin or another man's wife could be the chosen object of chivalrous love. With the cult of the Virgin Mary, the relegation of noblewomen to a pedestal reached its highest expression. The ideal of militant knighthood was greatly enhanced by the Crusades. The monastic orders of knighthood, the KNIGHTS TEMPLARS and the KNIGHTS HOSPITALERS, produced soldiers sworn to uphold the Christian ideal. Besides the battlefield, the TOURNAMENT was the chief arena in which the virtues of chivalry could be proved. The code of chivalrous conduct was worked out with great subtlety in the courts of love that flourished in France and in Flanders. There the most arduous questions of love and honor were argued before the noble ladies who presided (see COURTLY LOVE). The French military hero BAYARD was said to be the last embodiment of the ideals of chivalry. In practice, chivalric conduct was never free from corruption, increasingly evident in the later Middle Ages. Courtly love often deteriorated into promiscuity and adultery, pious militance into barbarous warfare. Moreover, the chivalric duties were not owed to those outside the bounds of feudal obligation. The outward trappings of chivalry and knighthood declined in the 15th cent., by which time wars were fought for victory and individual valor was irrelevant. Artificial orders of chivalry, such as the Order of the Golden Fleece (1423), were created by rulers to promote loyalty; tournaments became ritualized, costly, and comparatively bloodless; and the traditions of knighthood became obsolete. Medieval secular literature was primarily concerned with knighthood and chivalry. Two masterpieces of this literature are the *Chanson de Roland* (c.1098; see ROLAND) and *Sir Gawain and the Green Knight* (see PEARL, THE). ARTHURIAN LEGEND and the CHANSONS DE GESTE furnished bases for many later romances and epics. The work of CHRÉTIEN DE TROYES and the ROMAN DE LA ROSE also had tremendous influence on European literature. The endless chivalrous and pastoral romances, still widely read in the 16th cent., were satirized by Cervantes in *Don Quixote*. In the 19th cent., however, the romantic movement brought about a revival of chivalrous ideals and literature. For the lyric poetry of the age of chivalry, see TROUBADOURS; TROUVÈRES; MINNESINGER. See also ORDERS OF KNIGHTHOOD. See Sidney Painter, *French Chivalry* (1940); Léon Gautier, *Chivalry* (tr. 1965); R. W. Barber, *The Knight and Chivalry* (1970); C. T. Wood, *The Age of Chivalry* (1970).

chive: see ONION.

Chkalov: see ORENBURG, USSR.

Chladni, Ernst Florens Friedrich (ĕrnst flō'rĕns frē'drĭkh kläd'nē), 1756–1827, German physicist. An authority on acoustics, he made studies of the transmission of sound in various gases and of vibrating plates of glass and metal covered with sand, on which were formed the so-called Chladni figures, or acoustic figures. He invented a musical instrument that he called the euphonium. Chladni also studied meteorites and proposed that they are of extraterrestrial origin.

Chloe (klō'ē), Corinthian woman in whose house there were Christians. 1 Cor. 1.11.

chloral hydrate (klōr'əl hī'drāt), central nervous system DEPRESSANT that is widely used as a hypnotic, or sleep-inducing drug. Chloral hydrate is the common ingredient, along with alcohol, in what are popularly known as knockout drops or Mickey Finns; the combination can induce acute intoxication and coma.

chloramine: see HYDRAZINE.

chloramphenicol (klōr"ămfĕn'əkōl"), ANTIBIOTIC effective against a wide range of gram-negative and gram-positive bacteria (see GRAM'S STAIN). It was originally isolated from a species of *Streptomyces* bacteria. Chloramphenicol's antibiotic activity results from its interference with protein synthesis in invading microbes. However, it is a very toxic substance, its most serious and potentially lethal effect being depression of red blood cell production in bone MARROW; cases of leukemia were also attributed to early use of chloramphenicol. Because of its toxicity, chloramphenicol is rarely prescribed for infections that can be treated by other antibiotics. It is used to treat typhoid fever, some forms of meningitis, cholera, rickettsial infections such as Rocky Mountain spotted fever and typhus, and diseases caused by the psittacosis group of bacteria. Chloramphenicol is commonly used in biological research to study protein synthesis. Chloromycetin is a trade name for chloramphenicol.

chlorate and **perchlorate,** SALTS of chloric acid, $HClO_3$, and perchloric acid, $HClO_4$, respectively. A chlorate may be formed (together with the corresponding chloride) by heating the hypochlorite; e.g., $3Ca(ClO)_2 \rightarrow Ca(ClO_3)_2 + 2CaCl_2$. This reaction takes place when chlorine gas is passed into a hot aqueous solution of a metal hydroxide; the hypochlorite is formed and decomposes almost immediately. Commercially, a chlorate is derived when a hot aqueous metal chloride solution is decomposed by electrolysis, forming chlorine gas at the anode and metal hydroxide at the cathode (with evolution of hydrogen); the chlorine reacts with the hydroxide to form the hypochlorite, which decomposes to form the chlorate. The most industrially important chlorate is potassium chlorate, or chlorate of potash, $KClO_3$; sodium chlorate, or chlorate of soda, $NaClO_3$, is also used. Potassium chlorate is a colorless crystalline substance that melts at 356°C and decomposes violently at about 400°C. It is a powerful oxidizing agent and is used in making explosives and matches; a mixture of potassium chlorate with phosphorus, sulfur, or any of numerous organic compounds (e.g., charcoal or sugar) explodes upon friction or percussion. When a chlorate is heated, oxygen is evolved, often explosively, and the chloride is formed; e.g., $2KClO_3 \rightarrow 2KCl + 3O_2$. The reaction proceeds controllably at lower temperatures if a catalyst, e.g., manganese dioxide, is used; this provides a convenient source of oxygen. If the chlorate is heated carefully at a lower temperature so that no oxygen is given off, the perchlorate and chloride are formed; e.g., $4KClO_3 \rightarrow 3KClO_4 + KCl$. Perchlorates are safer to handle than chlorates; they are more stable when exposed to heat or shock. Potassium perchlorate, $KClO_4$, is perhaps most widely used, e.g., in matches, fireworks, and explosives. It is a colorless crystalline substance that melts at about 610°C. Chloric acid, $HClO_3 \cdot 7H_2O$, is a colorless substance that occurs only in solution. It is a strong acid and a strong oxidizing agent that decomposes if heated above 40°C. Under certain conditions it forms oxygen, water, and the explosive gas chlorine dioxide, ClO_2; under other conditions it forms perchloric acid and hydrochloric acid. Perchloric acid, $HClO_4$, is a volatile, unstable, colorless liquid that is a strong, corrosive acid and a powerful oxidizing agent, especially when hot. It explodes if heated to about 90°C or on contact with combustible materials. The monohydrate, $HClO_4 \cdot H_2O$, is fairly stable and forms needlelike crystals that melt at 50°C. It explodes if heated to 110°C. The dihydrate, $HClO_4 \cdot 2H_2O$, is a stable liquid that boils at 200°C. Perchloric anhydride, or chlorine heptoxide, Cl_2O_7, is a colorless, oily liquid that boils at 82°C without exploding but that may be detonated by shock; it can be prepared by adding phosphorus pentoxide to cold perchloric acid. The perchlorate free radical (chlorine tetroxide, ClO_4) can be prepared by adding bromine to silver perchlorate; it is extremely reactive and unstable.

chlordane (klōr'dān): see INSECTICIDE.

chloric acid: see CHLORATE.

chloride, chemical compound containing chlorine. Most chlorides are salts that are formed either by direct union of chlorine with a metal or by reaction of hydrochloric acid (a water solution of HYDROGEN CHLORIDE) with a metal, a metal oxide, or an inorganic base. Chloride salts include SODIUM CHLORIDE (common salt), POTASSIUM CHLORIDE, CALCIUM CHLORIDE, and AMMONIUM CHLORIDE. Most chloride salts are readily soluble in water, but MERCUROUS CHLORIDE (calomel) and SILVER CHLORIDE are insoluble, and lead chloride is only slightly soluble. Some chlorides, e.g., antimony chloride and bismuth chloride, decompose in water, forming oxychlorides. Many metal chlorides can be melted without decomposition; two exceptions are the chlorides of gold and platinum. Most metal chlorides conduct electricity when fused or dissolved in water and can be decomposed by ELECTROLYSIS to chlorine gas and the metal. Chlorine forms compounds with the other halogens and with oxygen; when chlorine is the more electronegative element in the compound, the compound is called a chloride. Thus, compounds with bromine and iodine are bromine chloride, BrCl, and iodine chloride, ICl, but compounds with oxygen or fluorine (which are more electronegative than chlorine) are oxides (e.g., chlorine dioxide, ClO_2) or fluorides (e.g., chlorine fluoride, ClF) respectively. Many organic compounds contain chlorine, as is indicated by common names such as carbon tetrachloride, methylene chloride, and methyl chloride. However, in the nomenclature system for organic chemistry adopted by the International Union of Pure and Applied Chemistry (IUPAC), the presence in a compound of chlorine bonded to a carbon atom is indicated by the prefix or infix *chloro;* thus, carbon tetrachloride is tetrachloromethane, methylene chloride is dichloromethane, and methyl chloride is chloromethane.

chloride of lime: see BLEACHING POWDER.

chlorinated hydrocarbon insecticide: see INSECTICIDE.

chlorine (klōr'ēn, klôr'-) [Gr.,=green], gaseous chemical element; symbol Cl; at. no. 17; at. wt. 35.453; m.p. −100.98°C; b.p. −34.6°C; density 3.2 grams per liter at STP; valence −1, +1, +3, +5, +7. Chlorine is a greenish-yellow poisonous gas with a disagreeable, suffocating odor; it is about two and one-half times as dense as air. Only fluorine among the nonmetals is more chemically active. Chlorine belongs to the HALOGEN family of elements, found in group VIIa of the PERIODIC TABLE. The gas is composed of diatomic molecules (Cl_2) with molecular weight 70.906. Chlorine is soluble in water; its aqueous solution, called chlorine water, consists of a mixture of chlorine, hydrochloric acid, and hypochlorous acid; only a part of the chlorine introduced actually goes into solution, the major part reacting chemically with the water. Chlorine water has strong oxidizing properties resulting from the oxygen set free when the unstable hypochlorous acid decomposes. Chlorine reacts readily with hydrogen to form hydrogen chloride; it burns if ignited in a hydrogen atmosphere and, if unignited, can form explosive mixtures with hydrogen; it also unites with the hydrogen in compounds such as turpentine, a hydrocarbon. In the presence of moisture it combines directly with certain metals, such as copper and iron, to form CHLORIDES. Iron ignites when heated in a chlorine atmosphere. With metals and oxygen, chlorine forms several CHLORATES; it also combines with many nonmetals and certain radicals. Because of its activity chlorine does not occur uncombined in nature, but its compounds are numerous and abundant. Sodium chloride (common salt) is present in seawater, salt wells, and large salt deposits, often in association with other chlorides. Chlorine is produced commercially chiefly by the electrolysis of sodium chloride, either molten or in solution. Other chlorides are sometimes employed. Chlorine can also be prepared from hydrochloric acid by oxidation of the hydrogen chloride (Deacon's process) and from bleaching powder. Chlorine is used in water purification; as a DISINFECTANT and as an antiseptic (mercuric chloride); and in the manufacture of bleaching powder (chloride of lime), dyes, and explosives. Chlorinated hydrocarbons have been used extensively as pesticides; some examples are DDT (see separate article), dieldrin, aldrin, endrin, lindane, chlordane, and heptachlor. These compounds resist degradation and have become very troublesome environmental pollutants. Carbon tetrachloride and trichloroethylene are used as solvents. The Freon refrigerants are hydrocarbons that have been reacted with chlorine and fluorine. Chlorine is an important constituent of many poison gases. It is used in such compounds as calomel, CHLOROFORM, and CHLORAL HYDRATE, which are used in medicine. It is also employed in the extraction of bromine from seawater. It is used in preparing some synthetic rubbers, in petroleum refining, and to prepare pure hydrochloric acid (see HYDROGEN CHLORIDE). Chlorine was discovered in 1774 by K. W. SCHEELE, who thought it was a compound of oxygen; it was named and identified as an element by Sir Humphry DAVY in 1810.

chloroform (klôr'əfôrm) or **trichloromethane** (trī''klōrōmĕth'ān), $CHCl_3$, volatile, colorless, nonflammable liquid that has a sweetish taste and a somewhat pungent odor; it boils at 61.2°C. It dissolves freely in ethanol and ether but does not mix with water. Chloroform is produced by reaction of chlorine with ethanol and by the reduction of carbon tetrachloride with moist iron. It was once used as a general anesthetic in surgery but has been replaced by less toxic, safer anesthetics, such as ether. Chemically, it is employed as a solvent for fats, alkaloids, iodine, and other substances. When exposed to sunlight and air it reacts to form phosgene, a poisonous gas.

Chloromycetin (klōr''ōmīsēt'ən), trade name for CHLORAMPHENICOL.

chlorophyll (klôr'əfĭl''), green pigment that gives most plants their color and enables them to carry on the process of PHOTOSYNTHESIS. Chemically, chlorophyll consists of two compounds, chlorophyll *a* and chlorophyll *b;* both contain carbon, hydrogen, oxygen, nitrogen, and magnesium, but in slightly differing proportions. The molecular structure of the chlorophylls is similar to that of the heme portion of hemoglobin, except that the latter contains iron in place of magnesium. Within the photosynthetic cells of plants the chlorophyll is in the chloroplasts—small, roundish, dense protoplasmic bodies that contain the grana, or disks, where the chlorophyll molecules are located. Chloroplasts have been likened to electric batteries, in which the flat chlorophyll molecules are the plates and the grana are the cells. Associated with the chlorophyll in the chloroplasts are two yellow pigments, carotene and xanthophyll. Chlorophyll is the only substance in nature that can trap and store the energy of sunlight. The light used is mainly the red and blue-violet portions of the visible spectrum; the green portion is not absorbed and, reflected, gives chlorophyll its characteristic color. Although all the details of this energy-trapping process are not yet known, it has been shown that when light (in packets called photons, or quanta) is absorbed by the complex chlorophyll molecules, certain electrons are excited, i.e., raised to a higher energy level than normal. The excited electrons are led away by so-called electron-carrier molecules (one of which has been found to contain vitamins B and K), go through a series of reactions in which energy is given up bit by bit, and finally return to the chlorophyll molecule. The energy thus made available is used to "recharge" molecules of ADENOSINE TRIPHOSPHATE, the storehouse of chemical energy used in photosynthesis. The chloroplasts also form another energy-rich phosphorus compound, called $TPNH_2$, using hydrogen from naturally dissociated water. The evolutionary advantage to plants of being independent of special sources of hydrogen is enormous, and this independence can be considered responsible not only for the spread of plants to all parts of the earth but of animals as well, since they depend on plants for food and oxygen. Recently it was discovered that the chloroplasts contain DNA (see NUCLEIC ACID), the genetic code-bearing chemical found in genes.

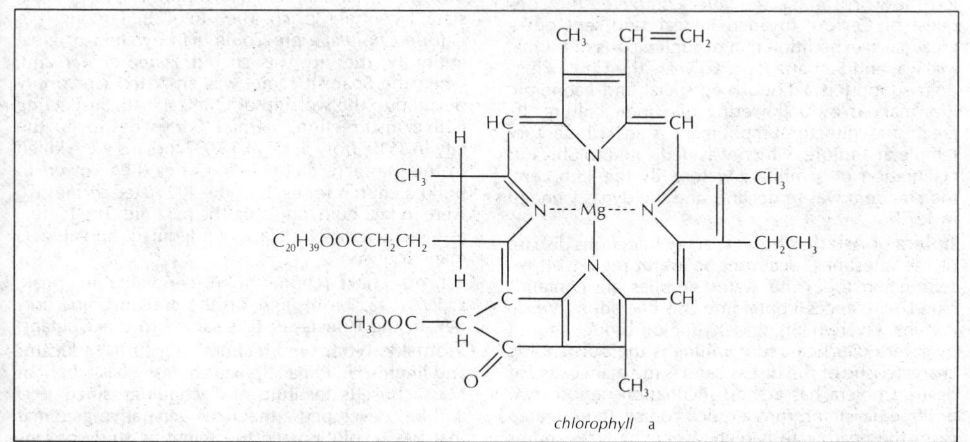

chlorophyll a

Chlorophyta (klōrŏf'ətə), division of the plant kingdom consisting of the photosynthetic organisms commonly known as green ALGAE and the stoneworts. The organisms are largely aquatic or marine plants consisting of one to several cells; a few types are terrestrial, occurring on moist soil, on the trunks of trees, on moist rocks, and even in snowbanks. Various species are highly specialized, some living exclusively on turtles, sloths, or within the gill mantles of marine mollusks. Cells of the Chlorophyta contain organelles called CHLOROPLASTS, in which photosynthesis occurs; the photosynthetic pigments chlorophyll *a* and chlorophyll *b,* and carotenoids, are the same as those found in higher plants and are found in similar proportions. There is no differentiation into specialized tissues among members of the division, even though the plant body, or thallus, may consist of several different kinds of cells. In some groups the reproductive cells, or gametes, are found in the two forms, eggs and sperm; in others all gametes are identical in appearance (isogametes). The zygote resulting from fertilization is neither attached to the parent plant nor dependent upon it; it develops directly into a new plant.

Class Chlorophyceae (green algae). This group contains the largest number of species of the division; it is the most diversified, ranging from common pond scums to the bright green seaweeds. The green algae vary from single cells to long strings and filaments, flat plates (the common sea lettuce), and even hollow tubes. In their diversity of structure and methods of reproduction, the green algae seem to represent many different evolutionary lines, which are brought together into one class largely for reasons of convenience. The cell wall of the green algae usually consists of CELLULOSE, which forms a compact inner layer, often in combination with other carbohydrate components. There is also usually a gelatinous or slimy outer layer secreted by the cell. The nucleus is well-organized and resembles that of higher plants. The chloroplasts, which show a wide variety of shapes and structure, generally possess a body called a pyrenoid, in which starch is stored. Some groups of green algae produce oil as well as starch. The vegetative cells of many of the unicellular green algae, as well as many isogametes, sperms, and forms known as zoospores, have flagella and are motile. The flagella are whiplike structures attached to a special organ in the cytoplasm. Green algae reproduce by both asexual and sexual methods. In asexual reproduction, a normal vegetative cell becomes modified to produce up to 64 flagellated, asexual zoospores. The zoospores are released through a pore in the sporangium wall, and, after swimming around for some time, they lose their flagella and become normal vegetative cells. Similar asexual spores, but without flagella, called aplanospores, are produced in many species. Sexual reproduction in green algae is extremely varied. In its simplest form, two unicellular vegetative cells fuse to form a zygote, which, after MEIOSIS, produces four spores, each of which develops directly into a new vegetative cell. In another reproductive process, one vegetative cell, or gametangium, gives rise to from 4 to 16 smaller cells, which function as gametes. Both isogamy (production of similar cells that function as gametes) and heterogamy (production of distinct eggs and sperms) are common in the group. Both types of reproduction and almost all imaginable intergradations occur in green algae species. The zygote produced by fertilization may either germinate at once to produce new vegetative plants, or develop a thick and resistant wall, and become a zygospore capable of resisting unfavorable environmental conditions. There are about 7,000 species of green algae.

Class Charophyceae (stoneworts). The stoneworts are an isolated, highly modified group of Chlorophyta, of great fossil age, dating as far back as the Devonian period. They are included within the Chlorophyta largely because their physiology and pigmentation is similar to that of the green algae. The plants consist of a complex, branched thallus with an erect stemlike structure and many whorls of short branches. They occur in shallow, fresh or brackish water, and especially in water rich in calcium, where they become stiff and lime-encrusted. Sexual reproduction in stoneworts is by fusion of unlike gametes, i.e., egg and sperm. The only two genera, *Chara* and *Nitella*, have relatively few species, which are not particularly varied, a fact that may reflect their great geological age. See G. M. Smith, *Freshwater Algae of the United States* (2d ed. 1950).

chloropicrin (klōr''əpĭk'rĭn), colorless oily liquid used as a POISON GAS. It is a powerful irritant, causing lachrymation, vomiting, bronchitis, and pulmonary edema; lung injury from chloropicrin may result in death. Trace amounts in the air cause a burning sensation in the eyes, which serves as a warning of exposure. Chloropicrin is more toxic than chlorine but less toxic than PHOSGENE. It is relatively inert and does not react with the chemicals commonly used in gas masks. It has been extensively used as a vomiting gas by the military. It is also used industrially in small amounts as a warning agent in commercial fumigants and as an insecticide and disinfectant for grain. Chloropicrin has the formula CCl_3NO_2. It boils at 112°C with partial decomposition to phosgene and nitrosyl chloride.

chloroplast, a complex, discrete green structure, or organelle, contained in the CYTOPLASM of plant cells. Chloroplasts are reponsible for the green color of almost all plants and are lacking only in plants that do not make their own food, such as fungi and nongreen parasitic or saprophytic higher plants. The chloroplast is generally flattened and lens-shaped and consists of a body, or stroma, in which are embedded from a few to as many as 50 submicroscopic bodies—the grana—made up of stacked, disklike plates. The chloroplast contains chlorophyll pigments, as well as yellow and orange carotenoid pigments. Chloroplasts are thus the central site of the photosynthetic process in plants. The chloroplasts of algae are simpler than those of higher plants, and may contain special, often conspicuous, starch-accumulating structures called pyrenoids.

chloroprene (klōr'əprēn'') or **2-chloro-1,3-butadiene,** colorless liquid organic compound used in the synthesis of neoprene and certain other RUBBERS. The structure of the chloroprene molecule is very similar to that of isoprene; the molecule contains two double bonds and is readily polymerized.

chlorpromazine (klōrpräm'əzēn''), one of a group of tranquilizing drugs called PHENOTHIAZINES that are useful in halting psychotic episodes. Chlorpromazine, sold under the trade name Thorazine, is often used to reduce the severe ANXIETY and agitation and the overactivity of some forms of SCHIZOPHRENIA.

Chmielnicki or **Khmelnitsky, Bohdan** (both: bəkhdän' khmĕlnēt'skē), c.1595–1657, hetman (leader) of Ukraine. An educated member of the Ukrainian gentry, he early joined the Ukrainian Cossacks. Elected (1648) hetman of the ZAPOROZYE Cossacks, he led their rebellion against oppressive Polish rule. At first successful, the revolt grew into a national revolution of the Ukrainian people. Two treaties (1649, 1651) with Poland—the second less satisfactory than the first—were broken by the Poles, and the war dragged on. As compromise with Poland proved to be impossible, Chmielnicki's objective came to be an independent Ukrainian state; for aid he turned to Czar Alexis of Russia. In 1654 at Pereyaslavl (renamed Pereyaslav-Khmelnitski in 1944), Ukraine was proclaimed a protectorate of Moscow and recognized as autonomous. The alliance ultimately led to the destruction of Ukrainian autonomy; its immediate result was resumption of the war, ending only in 1667 with the Treaty of Andrusov, which partitioned Ukraine between Poland and Russia. See George Vernadsky, *Bohdan, Hetman of Ukraine* (1941).

Choate, Joseph Hodges, 1832–1917, American lawyer and diplomat, b. Salem, Mass.; nephew of Rufus Choate. After being admitted (1855) to the bar, he moved to New York City. His legal career lasted over

50 years and included many famous cases; his brilliant presentation of cases won him an unrivaled reputation. Choate twice helped to arouse New York City to defeat Tammany Hall—in 1871, when the Tweed Ring was exposed, and again in 1894. He was president (1894) of the New York state constitutional convention and helped win public approval of the new constitution. In 1899 President William McKinley appointed him ambassador to Great Britain, and he served for six years with distinction, helping to promote Anglo-American friendship. In 1907 he headed the American delegation to the Second Hague Conference. See his autobiography, *Boyhood and Youth* (1917); biographies by T. G. Strong (1917) and E. S. Martin (2 vol., 1920).

Choate, Rufus, 1799–1859, American lawyer and Congressman, b. Essex co., Mass.; uncle of Joseph Hodges Choate. Admitted to the bar in 1823, Rufus Choate gained national reputation as a lawyer and as an orator. He served (1830–34) in the U.S. House of Representatives and sat (1841–45) in the U.S. Senate, completing the unexpired term of his friend Daniel Webster. See biography by C. M. Fuess (1928, repr. 1970).

Chocano, José Santos (hōsā' sän'tōs chōkä'nō), 1875–1934, Peruvian poet and revolutionary, one of the leaders of MODERNISMO. He gave an *indianista* (pro-Indian) slant to modernism, as in the poem "¿Quién sabe?" (1913). His most popular volume, *Alma América* [the soul of America] (1906) led Rubén Darío, the greatest of the *modernistas,* to develop native themes. Chocano was a notorious rake and a strident nationalist. Vigorous, eloquent, at times bombastic, Chocano did not restrict himself to *modernista* forms. Well-known collections of his poetry are *Fiat Lux* (1908) and *Primicias de oro de Indias* [first fruits of gold from the Indies] (1934). Having killed a political enemy, Chocano moved to Chile where he was himself murdered.

chocolate, general term for the products of the seeds of the CACAO or chocolate tree, used for making beverages or confectionery. The flavor of chocolate depends not only on the quality of the cocoa nibs (the remainder after the seeds are fermented, dried, and roasted) and the flavorings but also on a complex process of grinding, heating, and blending. The chocolate liquid formed in an intermediate stage is used in the confectionery trade as a covering for fruits, candies, or cookies, or the process may be continued and the resulting smooth mass of chocolate molded, cooled, and packaged as candy. It should be hard enough to snap when broken, have a mellow flow when melting, be free of gritty particles, and have a rich, dark color and an aromatic smell and flavor. The making of chocolate confectionery is in itself a well-developed industry of considerable commercial importance, employing highly specialized processes and machinery. A chocolate beverage was known to the Aztecs and through Spanish explorers found (c.1500) its way into Europe. In 1657 a shop was opened in London where chocolate was sold at luxury prices, sometimes as high as 15*s.* a pound. It became a fashionable drink; many shops sprang up to become centers of political discussion and grow into famous clubs, such as the Cocoa Tree. Chocolate was first manufactured in the United States at Milton Lower Mills, near Dorchester, Mass., in 1765. About 1876, M. D. Peter of Vevey, Switzerland, perfected a process of making milk chocolate by combining the cocoa nib, sugar, fat, and condensed milk. It is a popular ingredient in custards, puddings, pastry, cakes, mousses, ice creams, and sauces as well as in confectionery. The United States has the world's largest chocolate-manufacturing industry. See P. P. Gott, *All About Candy and Chocolate* (1958); B. W. Minifie, *Chocolate, Cocoa and Confectionery* (1970).

Choctaw Indians (chŏk'tô), North American Indians whose language belongs to the Muskogean branch of the Hokan-Siouan linguistic stock (see AMERICAN INDIAN LANGUAGES). They formerly occupied central and S Mississippi with some outlying groups in Alabama, Georgia, and Louisiana. Choctaw culture was similar to that of the Creek and Chickasaw Indians, who were their enemies in repeated wars. The Choctaw economy, unlike that of the Chickasaw, was based on agriculture, and the Choctaw were perhaps the most competent farmers in the Southeast. Friendly toward the French colonists, the Choctaw were their allies in wars against other tribes. After being forced to cede their lands in Alabama and Mississippi, they moved (1832) to the Indian Territory in Oklahoma, where they became one of the Five Civilized Tribes. See Angie Debo, *The Rise and Fall of the Choctaw Republic* (3d ed. 1967); A. H. DeRosier, *The Removal of the Choctaw Indians* (1971); W. D. Baird, *Peter Pitchlynn: Chief of the Choctaws* (1972).

Choderlos de Laclos: see LACLOS, PIERRE AMBROISE FRANÇOIS CHODERLOS DE.

Chodowiecki, Daniel Nikolaus (dä'nēēl nē'kōlous khôdôvyĕts'kē), 1726–1801, German painter and engraver, b. Danzig. He was the most popular illustrator of his day in Prussia. *The Departure of Jean Calas* (1767) is his most famous painting. It is as an engraver, however, that Chodowiecki is best known. His book illustrations include designs for Schiller's *Räuber,* Cervantes's *Don Quixote,* Goldsmith's *Vicar of Wakefield,* and Shakespeare's works.

Chofu (chō'fo͞o), city (1970 pop. 157,488), Tokyo Metropolis, E central Honshu, Japan, on the Tuma River. It is a residential suburb of Tokyo.

choir [O.Fr.] **1** A group of singers; traditionally the chorus organized to sing in a church. Usually, Roman Catholic, Anglican, and Lutheran choirs are composed of men and boys, but occasionally in these churches and customarily in other Protestant churches men and women form the choir. **2** That division of an organ usually used to accompany the singers, played from the lowest manual on the console. **3** A section of a chorus or orchestra, as the contrasted choirs of polychoral music, or brass choir, woodwind choir. **4** That part of a church reserved for the singers and the officiating clergy in a cathedral or abbey; the same area in a parish church is the chancel: see STALL.

choir stall: see STALL.

Choiseul, César, comte Du Plessis-Praslin, duc de (säzär' kôNt dü plĕsē-prälăN' dük də shwäzöl'), 1598–1675, marshal of France, diplomat, and soldier. He served as ambassador to Turin and commanded the army in Lombardy during the Thirty Years War. In the FRONDE he sided with Cardinal Mazarin and defeated the vicomte de TURENNE at Rethel (1650). Choiseul negotiated the Anglo-French alliance of 1670.

Choiseul, Étienne François, duc de (ātyĕn' fräNswä'), 1719–85, French statesman. After successful service in the army he entered the diplomatic service and gained support from Mme de POMPADOUR. As ambassador to Vienna (1757) he strengthened the Austrian alliance by conducting first negotiations toward the marriage of Marie Antoinette with the future Louis XVI. Later, in his capacity as minister of foreign affairs (1758–70), Choiseul negotiated the FAMILY COMPACT and the Treaty of Paris at the end of the Seven Years War, and he annexed Lorraine (1766) and Corsica (1768). As minister of war (1761–70) and of the navy (1761–66) he reorganized the fighting forces and introduced reforms. He supported the publication of the *Encyclopédie* and aided suppression of the Jesuits, which weakened his position at court. A clique surrounding King Louis XV's mistress, Mme Du Barry, caused his exile from court (1770). See his memoirs (1790); biography by R. H. Soltau (1909).

chokecherry: see CHERRY.

chokedamp: see DAMP.

Chola (chō'lə), S Indian dynasty, whose kingdom was mainly on the Coromandel Coast. Its chief capitals were at Kanchi (Kanchipuram) and TANJORE. The Chola kingdom was one of the three of ancient Tamil tradition, but the dynasty had been virtually submerged for centuries when at the end of the 9th cent. A.D. it rose again. Under the famous rulers Rajaraja I (reigned 985–1014) and Rajendra I (reigned 1014–42) Chola power reached its zenith. The former conquered Kerala and occupied N Ceylon (now Sri Lanka); the latter completed the conquest of Ceylon, invaded Bengal, and sent out a great naval expedition that occupied parts of Burma, Malaya, and Sumatra. For 300 years the Chola kingdom supported a flourishing social and economic life, marked by a flowering of Hindu culture. Its greatest architectural monument is an 11th-century temple at Tanjore, which was dedicated to Shiva in celebration of a military victory. By the 13th cent. the kingdom was in decline, and the dynasty ended in 1279.

cholera or **Asiatic cholera,** acute infectious disease of the intestines, occurring in warm regions. It results when food and water supplies are contaminated with feces containing the bacterium *Vibrio comma.* Overwhelming dehydration brought about by severe diarrhea and vomiting is the outstanding characteristic of the disease and is the main cause of death. Cholera has a short incubation period (two or three days) and runs a quick course. In untreated cases the death rate is high, averaging 50%, and as high as 90% in epidemics, but with effective treatment the death rate is less than 3%. The intravenous replacement of body fluids and essential electrolytes and the restoration of kidney function are more important in therapy than the administration of antibacterial drugs. In regions of Asia where public sanitation is poor the disease is still endemic or epidemic.

cholesterol (kəlĕs'tərōl''), fatty substance found in the body tissues of vertebrates; it is only sparingly soluble in water, but much more soluble in some organic solvents. A STEROID, large concentrations of cholesterol are found in the brain, spinal cord, and liver. The liver is the most important site of cholesterol biosynthesis, although other sites include the adrenal glands and reproductive organs. By means of several enzymatic reactions, cholesterol is synthesized from ACETIC ACID; it then serves as the major

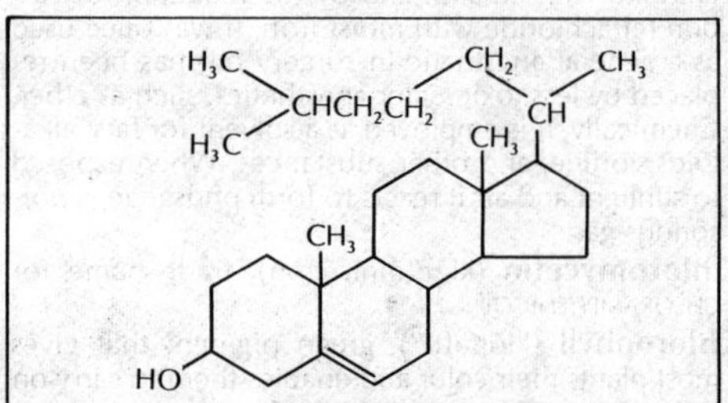

H_3C CH_2 CH_3 $CHCH_2CH_2$ CH H_3C CH_3 CH_3 HO

cholesterol

precursor for the synthesis of vitamin D at the surface of the skin, of the various steroid HORMONES, including CORTISOL, CORTISONE, and ALDOSTERONE in the ADRENAL GLANDS, and of the sex hormones progesterone, estrogen, and testosterone. Cholesterol is secreted in the liver secretion BILE; it sometimes crystallizes in the GALL BLADDER to form gallstones. The insolubility of cholesterol in water is also a factor in the development of atherosclerosis, the pathological deposition of plaques of cholesterol and other LIPIDS on the inside of major blood vessels that is associated with heart disease (see CORONARY HEART DISEASE). Unfortunately, the relationship between cholesterol and heart disease is not completely understood; although it has been shown that decreasing the amount of saturated, or animal, fats in the diet will cause a decrease in serum lipid and cholesterol levels, it has not yet been experimentally established that a reduction of serum lipids will actually delay atherosclerosis or coronary artery disease.

Cholet (shôlā'), city (1968 pop. 41,766), Maine-et-Loire dept., W France, in Poitou, on the Maine River. Cholet, a livestock market, has textile, metallurgical, and other industries. It was totally destroyed during the VENDÉE wars.

choline: see VITAMIN.

Cholon (chōlôn', Fr. shôlôN'), city, since 1932 part of SAIGON, South Vietnam, on the right bank of the Saigon River, a tributary of the Dong Nai. Adjacent to Saigon, with which it is connected by rail, road, and canal waterways, Cholon is an industrial center with many rice mills and factories. Founded c.1780 by Chinese immigrants seeking to escape the civil disorders of Annam, it became a busy trading port long before Saigon was developed by the French. It is still largely a Chinese city, containing around two thirds of South Vietnam's entire Chinese population. Heavy fighting there during the 1968 Tet offensive in the VIETNAM WAR severely damaged the city.

Cholula (chōlo͞o'lä), city (1970 pop. 20,913), Puebla state, E central Mexico. The site of the famous *Teocali de Cholula,* a pre-Columbian pyramid of great antiquity, the city was an old Toltec center and, when the Spanish came, was an Aztec sacred city devoted to the worship of Quetzalcoatl. Suspecting native insurrection, Hernán Cortés destroyed the city in 1519; from 5,000 to 10,000 Indians were killed in the massacre of Cholula. Cortés then vowed to build a church for each of the 400 Aztec shrines; 70 were in fact built, one atop the pyramid. The picturesque city remains a place of pilgrimage and attracts many tourists.

Chomo Lhari (chŏmōlhŭ'rē, chōməlhä'rē), peak, 23,997 ft (7,314 m) high, on the Bhutan-China border, in the Himalayas. It is sacred to the Tibetans.

Chomsky, Noam (nōm chŏm'skē), 1928–, educator and linguist, b. Philadelphia. Chomsky has taught at Massachusetts Institute of Technology since 1955 and has developed a theory of generative grammar that has revolutionized the scientific study of language. Instead of starting with minimal sounds, as the structural linguists had, Chomsky began his abstract analysis of language, set out in his doctoral dissertation *Syntactic Structures* (1957), with the rudimentary or primitive sentence. This formed his basis for deriving innumerable syntactic combinations by means of a complex series of transformational rules. His other principal linguistic works include *Current Issues in Linguistic Theory* (1964), *Aspects of a Theory of Syntax* (1965), *Cartesian Linguistics* (1966), *The Sound Pattern of English* (with Morris Halle, 1968), *Language and Mind* (1972), and *Studies on Semantics in Generative Grammar* (1972). Among his political writings are *American Power and the New Mandarins* (1969), *At War with Asia* (1970), and *Peace in the Middle East?* (1974).

Chomutov (khô'mo͞otôf), Ger. *Komotau,* city (1970 pop. 40,561), NW Czechoslovakia, near the East German border. Chomutov is an industrial center in a lignite-mining region and has steelworks and industries manufacturing machine tools, chemicals, paper, and glass. Chartered in 1396, it was disputed by Roman Catholics and Protestants in the 16th cent. In the city are the 13th-century Church of St. Catherine and a 16th-century town hall with a museum.

Chonan (chŭn'än'), city (1970 est. pop. 78,000), W South Korea. It is a railroad hub and a mining and agricultural center.

chondrite: see METEORITE.

Chone (chō'nä), town (1962 est. pop. 12,800), W Ecuador. Cacao, ivory nuts, and panama hats are shipped through Chone.

Chongjin or **Chungjin** (both: chŭng'jĕn'), Jap. *Seishin,* city, NE North Korea, an ice-free port on the Sea of Japan. It was developed in the 1930s by the Japanese as an iron and steel center. The city has metallurgical plants, chemical factories, sawmills, and fish canneries.

Chongju (chŭng'jo͞o'), city (1970 pop. 143,944), capital of North Chungchong prov., W central South Korea. It is a transportation hub and a marketing and processing center for the surrounding agricultural region. Rice milling, the production of fertilizers and textiles, and the brewing of sake (rice wine) are the city's major industries.

Choniates, Michael: see ACOMINATUS, MICHAEL.

Choniates, Nicetas: see ACOMINATUS, NICETAS.

Chonju (chŭn'jo͞o'), city (1970 est. pop. 263,000), capital of North Cholla prov., SW South Korea. It is a transportation and agricultural center in the heart of the country's most densely populated and richest rice-growing area. Food processing and textile manufacturing are the chief industries. The city was the capital of the Hu Paekju dynasty (892–936). The founder of the Yi dynasty, Korea's last imperial line, is buried in Chonju.

Chopin, Frédéric François (frādārēk' fräNswä' shôpăN'), 1810–49, composer for the piano, b. near Warsaw, of French and Polish parentage. With his lyrical, often melancholy, compositions, he brought romantic piano music to unprecedented heights of expressiveness. A prodigy as a pianist and a composer, he began performing at aristocratic salons in Warsaw, and in 1826 he began fulltime studies at the Warsaw Conservatory. After concert appearances in Vienna and Munich, he settled in Paris, where he gave his first concert in 1831. Although he remained always devoted to Polish culture and artists, he never returned to his homeland. In Paris he became closely associated with the principal composers, artists, and literary figures of his time. He was a virtuoso interpreter of his own works, but his dislike of playing in public made him prefer teaching and composing to the concert stage. In 1836, Liszt introduced him to Mme Dudevant, better known by her pen name GEORGE SAND, with whom he spent the winter of 1838–39 in Majorca; there, despite worsening pulmonary illness, he wrote his 24 preludes, which are counted among his finest compositions. The stormy affair with the novelist lasted until 1847, by which time Chopin's illness had developed into tuberculosis. He made a last concert tour through Great Britain in 1848. Chopin established the piano as a solo instrument free from choral or orchestral influence. Even in the piano concertos in E Minor (1833) and in F Minor (1836), the orchestra is completely dominated by the piano. Other major works include the sonatas in B Flat Minor (1840) and B Minor (1845), and two sets of études (1833, 1837). Because of their highly romantic quality, some of his works have become known by descriptive titles that he did not give them; they were published simply as nocturnes, scherzos, ballades, waltzes, impromptus, fantasies, and the like. Polish nationalism is evident in his many polonaises and mazurkas. His last concert was a benefit performance for Polish refugees, and at his funeral in Paris, Polish soil was strewn on his grave. See his selected correspondence ed. by B. E. Sydow (1962); biographies by F. Niecks (2 vol., 1888, repr. 1973), H. Weinstock (1949), and A. Walker, ed. (1966); studies by G. Abraham (1939), André Gide (1949), and D. Branson (1972).

Chopin, Kate O'Flaherty (shō''păn'), 1851–1904, American author, b. St. Louis. Of Creole-Irish descent, she married (1870) a Louisiana businessman and lived with him in Natchitoches parish and New Orleans. In these places she acquired an intimate knowledge of Creole and Cajun life, upon which she was to draw in many of her stories. After her husband's death in 1883, she returned with their six children to St. Louis and there began to write. Two collections of tales, *Bayou Folk* (1894) and *A Night in Acadie* (1897) earned her a reputation as a local colorist, but her novel *The Awakening* (1899) caused a storm of criticism because of its treatment of feminine sexuality. In depicting objectively a woman's confused groping toward self-understanding and self-acceptance, Chopin seemed to threaten the mores of her time although she did not explicitly attack them. Largely ignored for the next 60 years, her work is now praised for its literary merit as well as for its remarkable independence of mind and feeling. See her complete works, edited by Per Seyersted (2 vol., 1969) and the biography by Per Seyersted (1969).

choragic monuments (kərăj'ĭk, -rāj'-, kō-) [Gr.,= of the choragus, the chorus leader], small decorative structures erected in ancient Greece to commemorate the victory of the leader of a chorus in the competitive choral dances. The prize for the competition, a tripod, was placed on the monument, and the date and the name of the performer were usually inscribed. The best known is that of Lysicrates (c.335 B.C.), still standing in Athens, a graceful circular structure showing one of the early uses of Corinthian columns.

chorale (kōräl'), any of the traditional hymns of the German Protestant Church. The form was developed after the Reformation to replace the PLAINSONG of the earlier service and as a means of congregational participation in the liturgy. Early chorales were mainly translations of Latin hymns set to folksong melodies. The chorale is strophic, written in simple language, and has a simple melody, but its phrasing and metrical structure are less regular than those of the English hymn. J. S. Bach reworked nearly 400 existing chorales and composed 30 new ones. The major development of the form was thereby concluded although there were some 19th-century additions to the repertory.

Chor-ashan (kôr-ā'shăn), one of the places to whose inhabitants David sent spoils of war. 1 Sam. 30.30. See ASHAN.

Chorazin (kōrā'zĭn), city NW of the Sea of Galilee, denounced by Jesus. Mat. 11.21; Luke 10.13.

chord, in geometry, straight line segment both end points of which lie on the circumference of a circle or other curve; it is a segment of a SECANT. A chord passing through the center of a circle is a diameter. In the same circle or in equal circles, equal chords subtend equal arcs and equal central angles.

chord, in music, two or more simultaneously sounding pitches. In tonal music the fundamental chord is called the triad. It consists of three pitches, two at the interval of seven semitones and a third either three or four semitones from the lower, forming respectively the major or minor triad.

Chordata (kôrdā'tə,-dä'-), phylum of animals having a notochord, or dorsal stiffening rod, as the chief internal skeletal support at some stage of their development. Most chordates are vertebrates (animals with backbones), but the phylum also includes some small marine invertebrate animals. The three features unique to chordates and found in all of them at least during early development are: the notochord, composed of gelatinous tissue and bound by a tough membrane; a tubular nerve cord (or spinal cord), located above the notochord; and gill slits leading into the pharynx, or anterior part of the digestive tract (the throat, in higher vertebrates). In addition, all have blood contained in vessels, and the tunicates and vertebrates have a ventrally located heart. All have a postanal tail, that is, an extension beyond the anus of the notochord or backbone and of the body-wall musculature, containing no internal organs. In vertebrates—animals of the subphylum Vertebrata—a backbone of bone or cartilage segments called vertebrae develops around the notochord; its upward projections partially surround the nerve cord. In many fishes and in early fossil amphibians and reptiles the notochord persists in the adult and is enclosed by the vertebrae; in higher vertebrates, however, it disappears during embryonic development. There are two invertebrate subphyla: the Urochordata, or TUNICATES, and the Cephalochordata, or lancelets. A third invertebrate group, comprising the acorn worms and their relatives, shows affinities with chordates and has sometimes been considered a chordate subphylum, but is now often classified in a phylum of its own, the HEMICHORDATA.

Subphylum Urochordata. The tunicates are marine, filter-feeding animals. The most prominent tunicates are the sea squirts (class Ascidiacea), which show affinities to other chordates only in the juvenile stage. Adult sea squirts are sessile (attached), globular or tubular animals, often with prominent incurrent and excurrent siphons; many kinds grow in colonies. Most of the body of the adult is occupied by a very large pharynx with numerous gill slits that act as a sieve for food. Water taken into the incurrent siphon enters the pharynx and passes out through the gill slits, leaving food particles trapped in the pharynx. A groove in the pharynx called the endostyle secretes mucus that traps the particles and conveys them into the digestive tract; the movement of the mucus is caused by the action of cilia. Water leaves the atrium, a sac surrounding the pharynx, by way of the excurrent siphon. Thus the gill slits in tunicates serve a feeding function, not a respiratory function. The sea squirt larva is a free-swimming animal resembling a tadpole. The head, which will become the entire body of the adult, contains a rudimentary brain and sense organs, a small pharynx and digestive tract, and a ventral heart. Incurrent and excurrent openings are located at the top of the head. The tail is a muscular appendage that functions as a swimming organ. It contains a hollow nerve tube (connected to the brain), and a notochord that extends into the head and keeps the animal from telescoping when its muscles contract. When the larva is ready to undergo metamorphosis it attaches to an object head downward. The tail, notochord, and nerve cord degenerate, the pharynx enlarges, and the other organs shift in position; the incurrent and excurrent openings develop siphons. There are two other classes of tunicates, both consisting of small planktonic animals. The salps (Thaliacea) metamorphose into barrel-shaped adults that swim by muscular contractions. The larvaceans (Larvacea) are neotenous, that is, they achieve sexual maturity and reproduce without losing the larval form. Many zoologists believe that tunicates of the sea squirt type were the first chordates and that the larval tail, with its notochord and nerve chord, was evolved as a means of dispersing their larvae. According to this theory, the later chordates, including the vertebrates, are descended from neotenous tunicates that, like the larvaceans, failed to assume the adult form.

Subphylum Cephalochordata. This class includes the several species of lancelets, or amphioxi, small, fish-like, filter-feeding animals found in shallow water. A lancelet has a long body, pointed at both ends, with a large notochord that extends almost from tip to tip and is present throughout life. At one end is a mouth surrounded by prominent bristles and leading into a pharynx. The pharynx has gill slits, an endostyle similar to that of a sea squirt, and an atrium surrounding the pharynx. Water enters the mouth and leaves through the gill slits, and food is trapped in the pharynx. The dorsal, tubular nerve cord is slightly enlarged in the anterior region, forming a rudimentary brain. Nerves extend from the nerve chord to other parts of the body. The muscles, as in fishes, are a series of cone-shaped blocks that fit into each other like stacked paper cups. This is the most primitive occurrence of the segmental body wall structure characteristic of lower vertebrates. The colorless blood moves forward through a ventral vessel and back through a dorsal vessel, in the typical chordate pattern. There is no major heart, although many small enlargements of the vessel serve the function of hearts. There are no blood cells and no respiratory pigments. The excretory system, like that of many invertebrates, consists of segmentally arranged nephridia; there is no kidney. The gonads, unlike those of any other chordate, are numerous and segmentally arranged.

Subphylum Vertebrata. Vertebrates constitute the vast majority of living chordates, and they have evolved an enormous variety of forms. The backbone of vertebrates protects the nerve cord and serves as the axis of the internal skeleton. The skeleton provides strength and rigidity to the body and is an attachment site for muscles. The vertebrae in the middle region of the trunk give rise to pairs of ribs, which surround and protect the internal organs. A cartilaginous or bony case encloses the brain. Bone is a substance unique to vertebrates. It was formerly thought that vertebrates with cartilage skeletons (cyclostomes and sharklike fishes) were descended from early vertebrates that had not yet developed bone. However, very primitive fishes with bone skeletons are known from the fossil record, so lack of bone is now believed to be a degenerate rather than a primitive feature. All but the most primitive vertebrates, known as jawless fishes, have jaws and paired appendages. The fishes and, to a lesser extent, the amphibians and reptiles, show a segmental arrangement of the muscles of the body wall and of the nerves leading to them. There are eight vertebrate classes. Four are aquatic, and may be grouped together as the superclass Pisces, or FISH; four are terrestrial or (in the case of amphibians) semiterrestrial, and may be grouped as the superclass Tetrapoda, or four-footed animals. Fishes breathe water by means of gills located in internal passages, although they may also have lungs as supplementary air-breathing organs. Most move through the water by weaving movements of the trunk and tail. All have fins, and most have two sets of paired fins (pelvic and pectoral). Tetrapods breath air, usually by means of lungs, and never have gills as adults, although the amphibians go through a gilled, water-breathing stage. Except where the appendages have been lost, as in snakes, all have two pairs of limbs, generally used for locomotion; these are homologous to the pelvic and pectoral fins of fish.

Class Agnatha. The Agnatha, or jawless fishes, are the oldest known vertebrates. The only surviving members of this class are the HAGFISH and LAMPREYS, known as cyclostomes. Cyclostomes have long, slender bodies with dorsal, ventral, and caudal (tail) fins, all in the median plane. Although in their lack of jaws or paired lateral appendages they represent a very primitive stage of vertebrate development, the modern cyclostomes are highly adapted for their particular ways of life. The hagfish is a specialized scavenger, and the lamprey is a parasite on other fishes. The lamprey has a round mouth without skeletal supports, a rasping tongue, and a single, dorsally located nostril. The gill passages are enlarged to form pouches and are lined with gill filaments that serve as a surface for the exchange of respiratory gases; in vertebrates the gill passages have acquired a respiratory function. In cyclostomes, as in all fishes, water is taken in through the mouth and expelled through the gill passages; as water passes over the thin-walled gill filaments, dissolved oxygen diffuses into the blood, and carbon dioxide diffuses out. The lamprey has a notochord extending from the head to near the tip of the tail. A few cartilaginous blocks around the notochord constitute the bare rudiments of a backbone; a cartilage framework supports the gill region, and there is a rudimentary cartilage braincase. The meagerness of the skeleton is considered a degenerate, not a primitive condition. The larva of the marine lamprey is a small animal, resembling a lancelet, that uses the pharynx and gill passages for filter-feeding. It metamorphoses into the adult form before migrating to the sea. The extinct relatives of the cyclostomes, called ostracoderms, were jawless fishes with bony armor and in some cases a well-developed bony skeleton.

Class Placodermi. The placoderms, an entirely extinct group of armored fishes, were the first jawed vertebrates. Jaws enabled vertebrates to become predators, an important factor in the later development of active, complex forms. The placoderms were also the first vertebrates to have the two pairs of lateral appendages (supported by pelvic and pectoral girdles) that characterized all later vertebrate groups. These primitive paired fins gave rise to the pelvic and pectoral fins of modern fishes and to the limbs of four-footed animals. The ostracoderms are thought to have given rise to both the sharklike and the bony fishes.

Class Chondrichthyes. The almost exclusively marine SHARKS, RAYS, and CHIMAERAS of the class Chondrichthyes have skeletons made of cartilage. The mouth, equipped in most sharks with numerous sharp teeth, is located on the underside of the head. Passages called gill arches lead from the pharynx to the exterior and are lined with gill filaments. The gill arches are supported by gill bars. Except in chimaeras, the external gill slits are not covered and are conspicuous on the surface of the body. The jaw consists of two distinct pieces; the upper part is not fused to the braincase as in higher vertebrates. The tail is asymmetrical, curving upward in a shape found in early fossil fishes and thought to be primitive. There is no lung or swim bladder. The skin is studded with toothlike structures called denticles. Sharks have typical vertebrate kidneys that excrete a very dilute urine consisting mostly of water; presumably the earliest vertebrates (ancestral to sharks) evolved in fresh water, where this function is necessary to maintain the correct concentration of the physiologically important salts in the tissues against the tendency for them to be diluted by the inward diffusion of water. In marine species, on the other hand, it is necessary to prevent the concentration of those salts from increasing. Although the kidneys of sharks pump out water, their body fluids contain ammonia in concentrations high enough to make the osmotic pressure equal to that of sea water; this prevents the inward diffusion of salts. Sharks have internal fertilization and lay large eggs, well supplied with yolk and protected by leathery shells. In a few species the eggs are hatched within the body.

Class Osteichthyes. The bony fish of the class Osteichthyes are the predominant class of living fishes. In this group the bony skeleton has been retained and lungs and swim bladders have evolved. Early bony fishes evolved in fresh water under conditions of periodic drought and stagnation and developed an internal, moisture-retaining organ, the lung, for gas exchange. Those fishes gave rise to two lines of descendants. Members of one line, the fleshy-finned fish, had thick fins with supporting bones, used for crawling. The only survivors of that group are the coelacanth, or LOBEFIN, which has a vestigial lung and crawls on the sea floor, and the freshwater LUNGFISHES of drought-ridden areas, which can crawl over land in search of water and even live out of water for several years. Early fleshy-finned fish gave rise to the first land vertebrates, the amphibians. The second line, the ray-finned fish, constitutes the predominant modern group. Ray-finned fish are highly specialized for aquatic life; they have developed thin, lightweight fins supported by slender rays, and used only for balance and steering. The lung, a ventral outpocketing of the pharynx, was no longer necessary as these fish invaded fresh waters and oceans throughout the world; it shifted to a dorsal position and evolved into a hydrostatic organ called the swim bladder, or air float. The swim bladder, along with the strong, lightweight skeletal construction, makes ray-finned fishes much lighter-bodied than sharks. The gill passages of ray-finned fishes resemble those of sharks, but have a bony covering, called the operculum, over the external gill slits. Ray-fins have a typical vertebrate kidney which, in freshwater forms, maintains the proper salt concentration in the tissues by excreting excess water. In the marine forms the activity of the kidney is offset by the activity of salt-secreting glands; in addition, the kidney may be modified so as to produce a more concentrated urine. The heart, like that of sharks, has two chambers, and there is no separation of oxygenated and deoxygenated blood in the circulatory system. A few primitive ray-fins (the sturgeon, the paddle fish, and the bowfin) have asymmetrical tails and thick scales regarded as primitive in construction. The higher ray-fins, or teleosts, have more or less symmetrical tail fins extending above and below the vertebral column, and typical fish scales made of very thin layers of bone. Most marine teleosts produce enormous numbers of small eggs that are externally fertilized and float in plankton; only a few of these survive. In many species there is a larval stage that is quite dissimilar to the adult. Teleosts have evolved a tremendous variety of forms and occupy very diverse ecological niches, both freshwater and marine.

Class Amphibia. The AMPHIBIANS, the first vertebrates to have limbs, evolved during the Devonian period. They are only partially terrestrial: Their externally fertilized eggs are laid in fresh water, and they go through a gilled, aquatic larval stage (the tadpole stage) before metamorphosing into land-living adults. The skin of the adult is water-permeable, and the animal must live in a moist environment to prevent desiccation. The adult usually breathes by means of lungs, although some breathe directly through the skin. The heart is a three-chambered structure that creates a partial separation between oxygenated blood, destined for the body tissues, and depleted blood, destined for the lungs; this provides better oxygenation than a system in which the two kinds of blood mix. There are only three groups of amphibians living today. The SALAMANDERS are closest to the basic amphibian stock in form and in method of locomotion. Although supported by limbs, they move with a wriggling motion similar to that of a fish. The FROGS and TOADS are specialized for jumping, with long, muscular hind legs, while the tropical CAECILIANS are burrowing forms that have lost all but vestigial traces of their limbs.

Class Reptilia. The REPTILES, which evolved from amphibians during the Carboniferous period, were the first vertebrate group to become entirely independent of water. This was made possible by the development of a scaly, water-resistant skin and of the terrestrial, or amniote, type of egg found in all higher land vertebrates. The amniote egg has an elaborate series of internal membranes (one of which is called the amnion) surrounding a pool of liquid in which the embryo develops; the membranes prevent desiccation and allow inward diffusion of oxygen. Reptilian eggs have porous shells and large amounts of yolk. Fertilization is internal. In most cases the eggs are laid unhatched; in a few species they are retained and hatched in the body. Reptiles, including such forms as turtles and sea snakes that have returned to an aquatic life, are air-breathing at all stages, and nearly all lay their eggs on land. Gill passages appear, as in birds and mammals, only in the embryo. During the Mesozoic era, reptiles were exceedingly diverse and numerous. The reptilian DINOSAURS included the largest terrestrial animals that have ever lived, as well as many smaller forms. There were also flying and aquatic

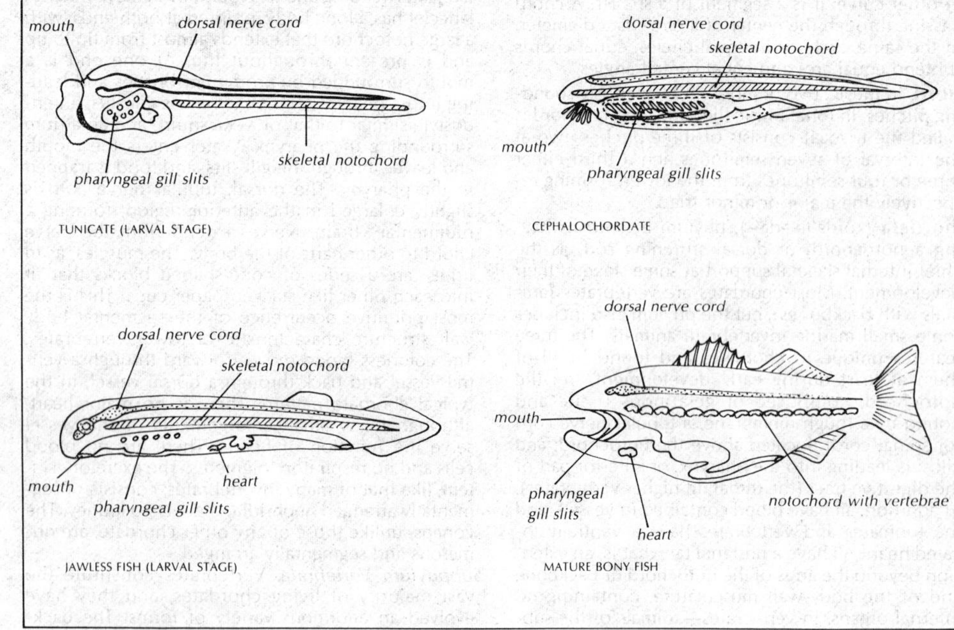

Common features in representative groups of the phylum Chordata

reptiles. With the rise of the early mammals the decline of the reptiles began. The only large and successful modern group of reptiles is the order of LIZARDS and SNAKES. Snakes are descended from lizards, but have lost their limbs. Reptiles, like fish and amphibians, are cold-blooded, that is, they have little ability to regulate their body temperature, which approaches that of the environment. The reptiles gave rise to the two warm-blooded vertebrate groups, the birds and the mammals.

Class Aves. The BIRDS evolved from reptiles in the Jurassic period. Their front limbs are modified into wings, and the breastbone is greatly enlarged to support flight muscles. They have an insulating covering of feathers, which has been an important factor in their ability to regulate body temperature. The other advance that enabled birds to become warm-blooded was the evolution of a four-chambered heart, making the circulatory system a complete double circuit: oxygenated blood is pumped from the lungs to the tissues, and deoxygenated blood is pumped from the tissues to the lungs. The only major group besides insects to invade the air, birds are much less restricted by external temperature requirements than cold-blooded animals, and they have spread throughout every part of the world. They live in many kinds of habitat and have evolved a diversity of forms. Some have become flightless terrestrial animals, while others are aquatic, using their wings for swimming instead of or in addition to flying. Fertilization is internal. The eggs of birds are similar to those of reptiles, but parental care of the eggs and young is highly developed.

Class Mammalia. The MAMMALS also arose from reptiles in the Jurassic period and are now the dominant form of terrestrial vertebrate life. Like the birds, they have a four-chambered heart and a double-circuit circulatory system, and are able to regulate body temperature. In the case of mammals the insulating covering is provided by hair, a feature unique to the class, although in a few forms (particularly in marine species) nearly all the hair is lost, and insulation is provided by fat. A second distinguishing characteristic of mammals is the production of milk by the females for the nourishment of the young. All mammals have internal fertilization, and all but the most primitive (the egg-laying MONOTREMES of Australia) bear live young. The mammalian egg contains little yolk. In the MARSUPIALS the young are born at an extremely undeveloped stage and continue to develop in a milk-supplied pouch. In the vastly more numerous placental mammals nourishment is passed from the circulatory system of the mother to that of the embryo by means of a placenta, and the young are born well-developed. Most mammals have highly evolved sense organs and larger brains than other vertebrates. As a group they display great adaptability to a variety of conditions and have spread to all regions of the world. The earliest placental mammals were small animals of the INSECTIVORE type, but adaptive radiation has resulted in great diversity of forms and ways of life. Some mammals are predators; others are herbivores with specialized digestive systems. Some have taken up an aquatic existence and a few marine forms (whales and sirenians) even give birth at sea. Members of one group, the bats, have developed membranous wings supported by elongated fingers and lead an aerial existence. The PRIMATES, the group that includes man, are fairly close to the original mammalian type in general structure (for example, they have five fingers and toes and walk flat on the sole of the foot), but they have undergone great evolutionary advances in the development of the brain, vision, and manual dexterity. See M. T. Jollie, *Chordate Morphology* (1962); C. K. Weichert, *Anatomy of the Chordates* (4th ed. 1970).

chorea (kərē'ə, kō-) or **St. Vitus' dance,** acute disturbance of the central nervous system characterized by involuntary muscular movements of the face and extremities. The disease, known also as Sydenham's chorea (not to be confused with Huntington's chorea, a hereditary disease of adults), is usually, but not always, a complication of RHEUMATIC FEVER. Sydenham's chorea, a disease of children, especially females, usually appears between the ages of 7 and 14. Facial grimacing and jerking movements persist for 6 to 10 weeks and sometimes recur after months, or even years. Eventually the symptoms disappear. Although there is no specific treatment, sedatives and tranquilizers are helpful in suppressing the involuntary movements.

choriocarcinoma: see NEOPLASM.

Chorley, municipal borough (1971 pop. 31,609), Lancashire, NW England. Manufactures include cotton goods and cotton mill machinery, rayon goods, rubber products, and footwear. Nearby is Leyland, one of England's chief automotive centers.

Chorotega (chōrōtä'gä), aboriginal Indians and language group of Honduras, Nicaragua, and Costa Rica. Little is known of the Chorotega, primarily because of the absence of extensive ruins. Contemporaneous with the Maya to the northwest, they inhabited principally the ULÚA River valley and the MOSQUITO COAST. With other tribes to the south and the CHIBCHA of Colombia, they formed a cultural link between the peoples of the Andean area and those of Mexico. The Chorotega were probably democratic, with a chief chosen by elected council. Chorotega culture became extinct in the Spanish colonial period.

chorus, in the drama of ancient Greece. Originally the chorus seems to have arisen from the singing of the DITHYRAMB, and the dithyrambic chorus allegedly became a true dramatic chorus when THESPIS in the 6th cent. B.C. introduced the actor. First the chorus as a participating actor tied the histrionic interludes together; later, as a narrator, it commented on the action and divided it, creating acts. And as tragedy developed the chorus shrank in size and actors increased in number. Aeschylus began with a chorus of 50, but the number was soon decreased to 12. Sophocles used a chorus of 15. In the 3d cent. B.C. the comic chorus contained only seven persons and in the 2d cent. B.C. only four, the tragic chorus having disappeared altogether. The chorus had ceased to play a vital part in the drama; Euripides assigned to it lyrics not necessarily integrated with the action. Ultimately it was dispensed with in comedy as well.

chorus, in music, large group of singers performing in concert; a group singing religious music is a CHOIR. The term *chorus* may also be used for a group singing or dancing together in a musical or in ballet. By extension it is also used to mean the refrain of a song. Choral music has stemmed from religious and folk music, both usually having interspersed solo and group singing. The chorus as a musical form is integral to opera, and since the 19th cent. it has also been integrated into compositions such as the symphony. Some modern choral groups, such as the Welsh singers, groups presenting spirituals, and the Don Cossack singers, continue the folk-chorus tradition. Others are intentionally formed to present all sorts of group vocal works. Choral societies grew numerous in the 19th cent., especially in Great Britain, the United States, and Germany. Some are created for special purposes, such as festival choruses, many oratorio societies, social and school groups (including GLEE clubs), and the Bach Choir of Bethlehem, Pa. In the United States, two men who did much to promote choral singing in the 19th cent. were William BILLINGS and Theodore Thomas. After 1940 there was a marked increase in the popularity of choral groups, usually organized for stage performance; some of these have specialized in concert versions of opera.

chorus frog: see TREE FROG.

Chorzów (hô'zhōōf), city (1970 pop. 151,338), S Poland. A rail junction and a center of the Katowice mining and industrial region, it has iron, steel, and nitrogen plants, zinc foundries, and factories producing heavy machinery. Formerly known as Krolewska Huta (Ger. *Königshütte*), it passed from Germany to Poland in 1921. The city has a huge sports stadium.

Chosen: see KOREA.

Choshi (chō'shē), city (1970 pop. 90,415), Chiba prefecture, central Honshu, Japan, on the Kashimada Sea at the mouth of the Tone River. It is a fishing center and the major port of Chiba prefecture. Great quantities of soy are produced in Choshi.

Chosroes: see KHOSRU.

Chotts, Plateau of the (shŏts) [Arab.,=salt lake], plateau region of the Atlas Mts., alt. c.3,500 ft (1,070 m), N Algeria, N Africa. The plateau is c.125 mi (200 km) wide in the west, narrowing in the east to become a series of valleys. Enclosed by the Tell Atlas in the north and the Saharan Atlas in the south, the region has interior drainage, a semiarid climate, and is dotted with salt lakes and salt flats. Its grasslands support nomadic herding. The name is also spelled Shotts.

Chou (jō), dynasty of China, which ruled, according to traditional dates, from 1122 B.C. to 256 B.C. or, according to some modern scholars, from c.1027 B.C. to 256 B.C. The pastoral Chou people migrated from the Wei valley NW of the Yellow River c.1027 B.C. and overthrew the SHANG dynasty. From their capital near modern Sian they dominated the N China plain between Manchuria and the Yangtze valley. By 800 B.C., however, the local lords had become strong enough to form separate states, especially in the north and at the mouth of the Yangtze. In later times the state of Ch'u controlled the middle Yangtze valley, and the border state of Ch'in grew in the northwest. In the 6th cent. B.C. the states of Wu and Yüeh became major powers. An anarchic period (403 B.C.–221 B.C.) of warring states followed, during which the Chou gave up their power to the emerging CH'IN dynasty. Despite political disorder, the Chou era was the classical age of China: CONFUCIUS, Mo-ti, LAO-TZE, MENCIUS, and Chuang-tze lived then. Contemporary writings, notably the *Five Classics* (see CHINESE LITERATURE) and archaeological evidence picture the Chou civilization. Iron implements were introduced from W and central Asia and the ox-drawn plow was first used. Chou society was sharply divided between the aristocratic warrior class and the peasant masses and domestic slaves. Writers of the anarchic period that followed it pictured the early Chou as an age of well-ordered beneficent feudalism, but this may merely reflect their own desire for political unity. See Arthur Waley, *Three Ways of Thought in Ancient China* (1939); H. G. Creel, *The Birth of China* (1954) and *Confucius and the Chinese Way* (1960).

Chouans (shōō'ənz, Fr. shwäN) [from Norman French,=owls], peasants of W France who rose against the French Revolutionary government in 1793. One of their first leaders was Jean Cottereau, traditionally nicknamed Jean Chouan, marquis de La Rouerie [John the Owl, marquess of Mischief], and the Chouans supposedly used the hoot of an owl as a signal. The movement eventually merged with the contemporary rising in the VENDÉE. The name Chouannerie continued to be used in reference to the fierce guerrilla warfare that lasted until put down by Napoleon. The so-called Petite Chouannerie persisted until 1815, when Napoleon was forced to divert troops from Waterloo to quell it. Honoré de Balzac's novel *Les Chouans* pictures these people vividly.

Chou En-lai (jō ĕn-lī), 1898–, Chinese Communist leader. A member of a noted Mandarin family, he was educated in China at the American-supported Nankai Middle School, and later attended (1917–19) a university in Japan. His youthful participation in radical movements brought him several months' imprisonment in Tientsin. After his release he studied (1920–22) in France. A founder of the Chinese Communist party, he established (1922) the Paris-based Chinese Communist Youth Group, an organization for expatriate Chinese students. He lived for a few months in England and then studied in Germany. Chou returned (1924) to China and joined Sun Yat-sen, who was then cooperating with the Communists. He served (1924–26) as deputy director of the political department at the Whampoa Military Academy, of which CHIANG KAI-SHEK was commandant. After the NORTHERN EXPEDITION began, he worked as a labor organizer. In 1927 he directed a general strike in Shanghai that laid the city open to Chiang's Nationalist forces. Soon after, Chiang broke with the Communists, executing many of his former allies, and Chou became a fugitive from the Kuomintang. Chou held prominent military and political posts in the Chinese Communist party, and he participated in the LONG MARCH (1934–35) of the Communist army to NW China. During the partial Communist-Kuomintang rapprochement (1936–46) he was the chief Communist liaison officer. In 1949, with the establishment of the People's Republic of China at Peking, Chou became premier and foreign minister. He headed the Chinese Communist delegation to the Geneva Conference of 1954 and to the Bandung Conference (1955). In 1958 he relinquished the foreign ministry but retained the premiership. A practical-minded administrator, Chou has maintained his position through all of Communist China's ideological upheavals, including the Great Leap Forward (1958) and the Cultural Revolution (1966–70). He is believed to be largely responsible for China's reestablishment of contacts with the West in the early 1970s.

Chou-k'ou-tien: see PEKING.

Chou-shan Archipelago (jō-shän), NE Chekiang prov., China, in the East China Sea, at the entrance to Hangchow Bay. It includes the main island of Chou-shan and about 100 lesser islands; Ting-hai on Chou-shan is the major population center. The archipelago forms the richest fishing grounds off the China coast. The island of Puto (P'u-t'o) was a sacred center of Buddhism, with many ancient temples and monasteries.

Chouteau (shōōtō'), family of American fur traders. **René Auguste Chouteau,** 1749–1829, b. New Orleans, accompanied (1763) his stepfather, Pierre LACLEDE, on a trading expedition to the Illinois country and established (1764) the post that became St. Louis. He continued as chief assistant to Laclede until the latter's death in 1778, when he took over the management of Laclede's trading interests. Friendly relations with the Osage Indians enabled him to extend the business considerably; from 1794 to 1802 he held a monopoly on the Osage trade. When the United States acquired Louisiana, Chouteau became a territorial judge and later served as Federal commissioner in negotiating treaties with various Indian tribes. His half-brother, **Jean Pierre Chouteau,** 1758–1849, b. New Orleans, also devoted himself to the fur trade. He worked for René Auguste for many years and extended the trade into present-day Oklahoma, where he established (1796) the first permanent white settlement at Salina. After becoming (1804) U.S. agent for the Osage, he struck out on his own and with others founded (1809) the St. Louis Missouri Fur Company. One of the wealthiest men in St. Louis, he spent the last years of his life on a large plantation outside the city. Two of his sons, Auguste Pierre and Pierre, continued in the fur trade. **Auguste Pierre Chouteau,** 1786–1838, b. St. Louis, who graduated from West Point in 1806, resigned (1807) from the army and became (1809) a member of the St. Louis Missouri Fur Company, taking part in several expeditions. He served as a captain of the territorial militia in the War of 1812. While on a trading expedition to the upper Arkansas River in 1817, he was captured by the Spanish and imprisoned at Santa Fe for several months. After his release he continued to trade with the Osage and made his home at Salina, Okla. In 1832 he led a party including Washington Irving from St. Louis to his post; the journey is described by Irving in *Tour of the Prairies* (1835). **Pierre Chouteau,** 1789–1865, b. St. Louis, early entered his father's business and accompanied him on several expeditions until 1813, when he and a partner formed their own merchandising and Indian trading firm. In 1831 he became a member of Bernard Pratte and Company, which was the Western agent of the AMERICAN FUR COMPANY. With the withdrawal of John Jacob Astor from the American Fur Company in 1834, Pratte, Chouteau and Company bought all the Missouri River interests of the old company. Reorganized (1838) as Pierre Chouteau, Jr., and Company, its business extended from the Mississippi to the Rockies and from Texas to Minnesota until its dissolution in 1864. One of the most powerful men in the West, Chouteau also invested heavily in railroads, rolling mills, and mining. He became one of the leading financiers of his time and lived his later years in New York City.

chow chow, breed of powerful NONSPORTING DOG whose origins are obscure but whose development was accomplished many centuries ago in China. It stands from 18 to 20 in. (45.7–50.8 cm) high at the shoulder and weighs from 50 to 60 lb (22.7–27.2 kg). Its abundant double coat consists of a soft, woolly underlayer and a dense, straight topcoat that stands out from the body. It may be any solid color. The ancestors of the chow chow are believed by some to have been the mastiff of Tibet and the Samoyed. However, because it is the only breed possessing a black tongue, other authorities contend that it is a basic breed and the progenitor of the Samoyed, the Keeshond, the Norwegian elkhound, and the Pomeranian. Whatever the truth of its origins, it was used as an all-purpose hunting dog in China 2,000 years ago. Its name derives from the pidgin-English term for miscellaneous cargo, of which the dog formed a part, brought from China to England in the late 18th cent. It is raised as a companion and house pet. See DOG.

chowder, stew of fish or shellfish with potatoes, onions, and pork (usually salt pork), thickened with crumbled hard bread. It has probably been known in some form to most fishing communities. The name *chowder* seems to have originated from the French word *chaudière* (a large heavy pot used by fishermen to cook soups and stews). The name probably was carried to the French Canadian coasts and traveled from there to New England (noted for its clam chowder) and then south. Each locality on the eastern coast of the United States has its favorite recipe, based on the kinds of fish and vegetables available. The name is extended to include a mixture of vegetables only.

Chozeba (kōzē'bə): see ACHZIB **2.**

Chrétien de Troyes or **Chrestien de Troyes** (both: krātyăN' də trwä), fl. 1170, French poet, author of the first great literary treatments of the ARTHURIAN LEGEND. His narrative romances, composed c.1170–c.1185 in octosyllabic rhymed couplets, include *Érec et Énide; Cligès; Lancelot, le chevalier de la charette; Yvain, le chevalier au lion;* and *Perceval, le conte del Graal,* unfinished (see PARSIFAL). Chrétien drew on popular legend and history, and imbued his romances with the ideals of chivalry current at the 12th-century court of Marie de Champagne, to which he was attached. His other surviving works include imitations of Ovid and *Guillaume d'Angleterre,* a non-Arthurian narrative. Translations of the Arthurian romances are included in W. W. Comfort's edition (1913) and in R. S. and L. H. Loomis, *Medieval Romances* (1957). See R. S. Loomis, *Arthurian Tradition & Chrétien de Troyes* (1949); P. Haidu, *Aesthetic Distance in Chrétien de Troyes* (1968); U. T. Holmes, *Chrétien de Troyes* (1970).

Christ: see JESUS.

Christadelphians (krĭs"tədĕl'fēənz) [Gr.,=brothers of Christ], small religious denomination founded in the United States in 1848 by John Thomas. Its members live by the Scriptures and await the second coming of Christ on earth, who, they believe, will establish a theocracy with its center in Jerusalem. There is no ordained ministry. Christadelphians do not believe in the Trinity or the existence of hell. They do not vote, hold public office, or participate in war. There are c.16,000 members in the United States and c.20,000 members in Canada.

Christchurch, municipal borough (1971 pop. 31,373), Hampshire, S central England, on Christchurch Bay at the confluence of the Avon and Stour rivers. Its industries include aircraft manufacturing and salmon fishing. Christchurch is also a resort. The town's history dates back to Anglo-Saxon times. Its name derives from the church that was part of the Augustinian priory founded there before the Norman conquest of England. In 1974, Christchurch became part of the new nonmetropolitan county of Dorset.

Christchurch, city (1971 pop. 165,637; urban agglomeration 257,505), E South Island, New Zealand, at the base of Banks Peninsula. It is the second largest city in New Zealand. Industries include tanning, meat-packing, and woolens manufacturing. Lyttleton, nearby, is the port for Christchurch. The Univ. of Canterbury was founded in the city in 1873. There are Roman Catholic and Anglican cathedrals. Hagley Park contains botanical gardens and museums.

christening: see BAPTISM.

Christian I, 1426–81, king of Denmark (1448–81), Norway (1450–81), and Sweden (1457–64), count of Oldenburg, and founder of the Oldenburg dynasty of Danish kings. In 1460 he also succeeded to SCHLESWIG AND HOLSTEIN; the terms of the settlement have been cited to justify both Danish and German claims to SCHLESWIG-HOLSTEIN. A weak monarch despite the vastness of his lands, he made large concessions to the nobles, particularly in his German dominions, and barely controlled Sweden (see KALMAR UNION). His attempts to assert his authority in Sweden ended in 1471 with his defeat at Brunkeberg, near Stockholm, by Sten STURE (the elder). He was succeeded by his son John.

Christian II, 1481–1559, king of Denmark and Norway (1513–23) and Sweden (1520–23), son and successor of King John. After several unsuccessful attempts, he asserted claim to Sweden by force. However, his wholesale massacre of Swedish nobles at Stockholm (1520) alienated the Swedes, who raised Gustavus Vasa to the throne as GUSTAVUS I, thus ending the KALMAR UNION. In Denmark, Christian earned the hatred of the nobles and high clergy by thorough reforms in favor of the lower and middle classes, by inviting Lutheran preachers to Copenhagen, and by placing Sigbrit, mother of his Dutch mistress, in charge of the finances of the realm. In 1523 the nobles rebelled (particularly in Jutland), deposed Christian, and chose his uncle, Frederick I, as king. Christian fled, but in 1532 he was captured while attempting to recover the throne. He was imprisoned until his death. A gifted and educated ruler despite his despotic methods, Christian II did much to advance learning in Denmark.

Christian III, 1503–59, king of Denmark and Norway (1534–59). At the death of his father, Frederick I, his election was delayed because he was a Lutheran. The German city of LÜBECK invaded Denmark to reinstate the deposed CHRISTIAN II, and the minor nobility then forced the election of Christian III in 1534 to preserve Danish autonomy. Christian III allied with GUSTAVUS I of Sweden to defeat Lübeck in 1536. That victory broke the power of the Hanseatic League and made the Danish fleet supreme in northern waters. Christian established (1536) Lutheranism in Denmark and imposed it on Norway. Never elected king by the Norwegians, he declared Norway a dependency of Denmark. His son Frederick II succeeded him.

Christian IV, 1577–1648, king of Denmark and Norway (1588–1648), son and successor of Frederick II. After assuming (1596) personal rule from a regency, he concentrated on building the navy, industry, and commerce. He rebuilt OSLO and renamed it Christiania. Aroused when CHARLES IX of Sweden asserted authority over Lapland, he made war on Sweden (the so-called Kalmar War, 1611–13) and largely dictated the peace. In the THIRTY YEARS WAR, urged on by England, France, and the Netherlands, he invaded (1625) Germany to defend Protestantism. Defeated (1626) by TILLY at Lutter, he was driven back in 1627. Schleswig, Holstein, and Jutland were overrun and plundered; Stralsund was besieged by the imperial troops under WALLENSTEIN. Christian, with the help of Gustavus II of Sweden, raised the siege of Stralsund, but in 1629 he signed with Holy Roman Emperor Ferdinand II a separate peace that was lenient to Denmark. His anti-Swedish policy brought on a war with Sweden (1643–45) in which Christian lost the Norwegian provinces of Jamtland and Harjedalen. His son Frederick III succeeded him.

Christian V, 1646–99, king of Denmark and Norway (1670–99), son and successor of Frederick III. His minister, GRIFFENFELD, who until his fall in 1676 dominated Christian's reign, made the monarchy absolute. Christian fought (1675–79) an unsuccessful war with CHARLES XI of Sweden. He was succeeded by his son Frederick IV.

Christian VII, 1749–1808, king of Denmark and Norway (1766–1808), son and successor of Frederick V. Shortly after his accession his mental illness made him dependent on his physician, STRUENSEE, who in 1770 caused the dismissal of Johann Hartwig Ernst BERNSTORFF and in 1771 became an all-powerful minister. After Struensee's downfall (1772), Christian's marriage with Caroline Matilda, sister of George III of England, was annulled. Andreas Peter BERNSTORFF became chief minister in 1773, and after 1784 Christian's son and successor, Frederick VI, acted as regent. Widespread liberal reforms were enacted under the direction of Bernstorff and Prince Frederick, notably the abolition of serfdom.

Christian VIII, 1786–1848, king of Denmark (1839–48), nephew of Christian VII; successor of Frederick VI. As governor and king (May–Oct., 1814) of Norway he accepted a liberal Norwegian constitution that is still in use with some modifications. His reign brought prosperity to Denmark. The nature of Danish rule in the duchies of SCHLESWIG-HOLSTEIN became a prominent issue in 1846. His son Frederick VII succeeded him.

Christian IX, 1818–1906, king of Denmark (1863–1906). A member of the cadet line of Sonderburg-Glücksburg, he succeeded Frederick VII, last of the direct line of Oldenburg. The London Conference of 1852 had settled on him the contested succession to the duchies of SCHLESWIG-HOLSTEIN, but in 1863 Christian accepted parliament's annexation of Schleswig to the Danish crown. This precipitated war (1864) with Prussia and Austria, in which Christian lost Schleswig, Holstein, and Lauenburg. In 1866 the Danish constitution was revised, granting the upper chamber more power than the lower. During Christian's reign there was continual liberal agitation for a more democratic constitution. He was succeeded by his son Frederick VIII. A younger son became king of Greece as George I.

Christian X, 1870–1947, king of Denmark (1912–47) and Iceland (1912–44), son and successor of Frederick VIII and brother of King Haakon VII of Norway. He granted (1915) a new constitution that included the enfranchisement of women. During the German occupation (1940–45) of Denmark, the king defied German authority and was placed (1943) under house arrest. He became a symbol of national resistance. In 1944, Iceland severed all ties with the Danish crown. Christian's son Frederick IX succeeded him.

Christian Brothers: see JOHN BAPTIST DE LA SALLE, ST.

Christian Catholic Church, religious denomination founded (1896) in Chicago by John Alexander DOWIE. Its members are sometimes known as Zionites. The church has its center in ZION, Ill., which Dowie founded (1901) as a religious community. In addition to religious and educational activities in

Zion, the founder started various industries on a co-operative basis, an undertaking that was built up by Wilber Glenn Voliva, who became general overseer upon the deposition of Dowie in 1905. Zion is no longer exclusively a religious community. The church extensively supports foreign missions. See Rolvix Harlan, *John Alexander Dowie and the Christian Catholic Apostolic Church in Zion* (1906).

Christian Churches: see CONGREGATIONALISM; DISCIPLES OF CHRIST.

Christian Endeavor, association in evangelical Protestant Churches for strengthening spiritual life and promoting Christian activities among its members. The first Young People's Society of Christian Endeavor was started in 1881 by Dr. Francis E. CLARK in Portland, Maine. Within a few years the organization had become not only interdenominational but international, and a world union was formed in 1895, with Clark as president. Started primarily as a youth movement, the association now includes all age groups and numbers in the millions. Many denominations are represented in the association's membership.

Christiania: see OSLO, Norway.

Christian iconography: see under ICONOGRAPHY.

Christianity, religion founded in Palestine by the followers of JESUS Christ. One of the world's major religions, it predominates in Europe and the Americas, where it has been a powerful historical force and cultural influence, but it also claims adherents in virtually every country of the world. The central teachings of traditional Christianity are that Jesus is the Son of God, the second person of the TRINITY of God the Father, the Son, and the HOLY GHOST; that his life on earth, his crucifixion, RESURRECTION, and ascension into heaven are proof of God's love for man and his forgiveness of man's sins; and that by faith in Christ man may attain salvation and eternal life (see CREED). This teaching is embodied in the BIBLE, specifically in the New Testament, but Christians accept also the Old Testament as sacred and authoritative Scripture. Christian ethics derive to a large extent from the Jewish tradition as presented in the Old Testament, particularly the TEN COMMANDMENTS, but with some difference of interpretation based on the practice and teachings of Jesus. Christianity may be further generally defined in terms of its practice of corporate worship and rites that usually include the use of SACRAMENTS and that are usually conducted by a trained clergyman within an organized church. There are, however, many different forms of worship, many interpretations of the role of the organized clergy, and many variations in polity and church organization within Christianity. In the two millennia of its history Christianity has been plagued by schism, based on doctrinal and organizational differences. Today there are three broad divisions, Roman Catholic, Orthodox Eastern, and Protestant; but within the category of Protestantism, there is a particularly large number of divergent denominations. Because of the complexity of these differences this article will describe the history of Christianity only to 1054, when the schism between Eastern and Western churches became final. Separate articles detail the history and doctrines of the ROMAN CATHOLIC CHURCH and ORTHODOX EASTERN CHURCH and of the other churches of ancient origin, the ARMENIAN CHURCH, the Coptic Church (see COPT), the JACOBITE CHURCH, and the NESTORIAN CHURCH. In the 16th cent. another major schism took place in the Western Church with the Protestant REFORMATION. For the Protestant churches, see PROTESTANTISM and articles on the separate churches. For the 20th-century movement that seeks to end the divisiveness in Christianity and achieve reunion, see ECUMENICAL MOVEMENT.

Early Christianity. Christianity is in a direct sense an offshoot of JUDAISM, because Jesus and his immediate followers were Jews living in Palestine and Jesus was believed by his followers to have fulfilled the Old Testament prophecies of the MESSIAH. Following a trend of proselytization in the Judaism of that period Christianity was from its beginnings expansionist. Its early missionaries (the most notable of whom was St. PAUL, who was also responsible for the formulation of much Christian doctrine) spread its teachings through Asia Minor to Alexandria and to Greece and Rome. MISSIONS have remained a major element in Christianity to the present day. For the first three centuries of Christianity, history is dependent on apologetic and religious writings; there are no chronicles (see PATRISTIC LITERATURE). Historians differ greatly on how far back the 4th-century picture of the church (which is quite clear) can be projected, especially respecting organization by bishops (each bishop a monarch in the church of his city), celebration of a LITURGY entailing a sacrament and a sacrifice, and claims by the bishop of Rome to be head of all the churches (see PAPACY). There is evidence for these features in the 2d cent. A first problem for Christians was how to resist attempts to interpret the new beliefs in old pagan terms (e.g., Gnosticism) or to incorporate them in some inclusive system (e.g., Manichaeism). The earliest sectarian deviations were those of Marcion and of Montanism (2d cent.). They were handled resolutely by the church; the teachers of novelty were expelled (excommunicated). For 250 years it was a martyrs' church; the persecutions were official, legally motivated by refusal of Christians to worship the state and the Roman emperor. The chief persecutions were under Nero, Domitian, Trajan and the other Antonines, Maximin, Decius, Valerian, and Diocletian and Galerius. In 313, Constantine I and Licinius announced toleration of Christianity in the Edict of Milan. In the East the church passed from persecution directly to imperial control (caesaropapism), inaugurated by Constantine, enshrined later in Justinian's laws, and always a problem for the Orthodox churches. In the West the church remained independent because of the weakness of the emperor and the well-established authority of the bishop of Rome. For 300 years after A.D. 275 the church in the East was occupied with doctrinal controversies—Arianism, Nestorianism, Monophysitism, and Monotheletism. These arguments concerned the relationship of Jesus Christ to God and to man. Decisions were made at a series of general councils of bishops (see COUNCIL, ECUMENICAL); at them was composed the Nicene Creed, the official orthodox summary. These centuries saw a series of Christian writers of unequaled influence (the Fathers of the Church): Origen, St. Athanasius, St. Basil the Great, St. Gregory of Nyssa, St. Gregory Nazianzen, St. John Chrysostom, and Theodoret writing in Greek; St. Ambrose, St. Jerome, and St. Augustine writing in Latin. Origen and St. Jerome had a special role in the church's work of determining and preserving the text of the Bible. From the 3d cent. an element was MONASTICISM, first well organized by St. Basil. In the West it was a central feature in the missionary work of St. Martin (Gaul, 4th cent.) and St. Patrick (Ireland, 5th cent.), and it received definitive shape from St. Benedict and St. Gregory the Great, who thereby generated an activity of continuing vitality in the Roman Catholic Church. German invasions slowed the conversion of Western Europe (e.g., that of England was recommenced in the 6th cent.). All the first invaders were Arian, but the Franks (with Clovis) adopted orthodox Christianity, a fact that probably helped to consolidate their rule. Out of this kingdom came Pepin and Charlemagne, who, by alliance with the papacy and proclamation of an empire (800), charted an ideal of the Middle Ages. In the 7th and 8th cent. the Eastern Church lost to Islam all Asia except Asia Minor. Alienation from the West was exacerbated by the bitter struggle over ICONOCLASM; ecclesiastical animosity between Rome and Constantinople came to a head in the schism of the 9th cent. and attained a sort of legal permanence in 1054 (see LEO IX, SAINT). Eastern and Western Christendom were already in the 9th cent. two different cultures; their one common tie was the Christian doctrine—even worship and practices were very different. From this time it is customary to distinguish Christian history in its Eastern and Western streams as that of the Orthodox Eastern and the Roman Catholic churches. See Philip Hughes, *History of the Church* (3 vol., rev. ed. 1949); K. S. Latourette, *History of the Expansion of Christianity* (7 vol., 1937–45; repr. 1970), *History of Christianity* (1953, repr. 1962), and *Christianity through the Ages* (1965); Jules Lebreton and Jacque Zeiller, *A History of the Early Church* (4 vol., 1944–46; repr. 1962); Hans Lietzmann, *The History of the Early Church* (4 vol., tr. 1961; repr. 1967); Asher Finkel, *The Pharisees and the Teacher of Nazareth* (1964); J. G. Davies, *The Early Christian Church* (1965); R. M. Grant, *Augustus to Constantine* (1970).

Christian of Anhalt, 1568–1630, prince of ANHALT (1603–30). He was a firm Calvinist and a skilled diplomat. As adviser to Frederick IV, elector palatine, he sought to build a strong Protestant alliance against the Catholic states and achieved limited success with the formation (1608) of the PROTESTANT UNION. Christian guided Frederick's son and successor, Frederick V (FREDERICK THE WINTER KING) and arranged his election (1619) to the Bohemian throne in place of the Roman Catholic king, FERDINAND II, also Holy Roman emperor. Supported by the Catholic League under Elector MAXIMILIAN I of Bavaria, Ferdinand sent an army to subdue the Bohemian rebels. When military aid that Christian counted on was not forthcoming, Christian was utterly defeated at the battle of the White Mountain. He was put under the imperial ban, but was pardoned in 1624.

Christian of Brunswick or **Christian of Halberstadt,** 1599–1626, Protestant military leader in the THIRTY YEARS WAR, titular bishop of Halberstadt (1616–23). One of the first allies of Frederick the Winter King, elector palatine of the Rhine, he took up arms in defense of the Palatinate in 1621. Defeated (1622) by the imperial commander TILLY, he went to the Netherlands. Christian then advanced into Germany but had to retreat, and Tilly turned the retreat into a rout at Stadtlohn (1623). While serving with CHRISTIAN IV of Denmark, he was defeated a third time (1626).

Christian Reformed Church, denomination formed after the secession of a group from the REFORMED CHURCH IN AMERICA in 1857. Colonists from Holland who began settling in Michigan in 1846 generally became members of the Reformed (Dutch) church there. A number of these immigrants, dissatisfied with the doctrinal laxity and practices of that church, separated from it in 1857 and united in a new congregation at Holland, Mich. Later other congregations of this "True Holland Reformed Church" were formed in neighboring states. Missionary work in Holland led many Dutch immigrants to join this church upon their arrival in the United States. In 1882, after a new secession movement in the Reformed Church in America, caused by the General Synod's refusal to condemn Freemasonry, a considerable addition to the church was made. In 1890 it adopted the name Christian Reformed Church; in that year it was joined by the True Reformed Dutch Church (1822) of New York and New Jersey. Its constitution is an adaptation of that approved by the Synod of Dort (1619). Its doctrines are drawn mainly from those of the Reformed Church in Holland. The church is very active in mission work both in the United States and abroad. See the centennial publication *One Hundred Years in the New World* (1957); study by Henry Beets (1946).

Christians, name taken by the followers of several evangelical preachers on the American frontier, notably James O'Kelley, Abner Jones, and Barton W. STONE, all of whom were antisectarian. Some congregations joined the DISCIPLES OF CHRIST, a body with similar emphasis founded by Thomas and Alexander CAMPBELL, and the name Christians continued to be applied often to members of the Disciples' church. Other congregations of Christians united as a separate body that ultimately took the name of the Christian Church; this was merged in 1931 with the Congregational churches and the merged group became known as the Congregational Christian churches (see CONGREGATIONALISM). See also CHRISTIANITY.

Christian Science, religion founded upon principles of divine healing and laws expressed in the acts and sayings of Jesus Christ, as discovered and formulated by Mary Baker EDDY and practiced by the Church of Christ, Scientist. Christian Scientists deny the reality of the material world, a denial that guides not only their ultimate concerns, but also their everyday life. They argue that illness and sin are illusions, to be overcome by the mind; thus, they refuse medical help in fighting sickness. The occasion of Mary Baker Eddy's discovery of divine healing was her immediate recovery of life and health when in 1866 she read an account of healing by Jesus in the New Testament. In 1875 her *Science and Health* (later published as *Science and Health, with Key to the Scriptures*), the only authorized textbook of Christian Science, was published. In 1879 she established the Church of Christ, Scientist. In Boston in 1892 was organized the First Church of Christ, Scientist—the Mother Church, of which Christian Science churches throughout the world are branches. Each individual church is self-governing and self-supporting, but all accept the tenets framed by the founder and incorporated in the *Church Manual.* Upon her death in 1910, the administrative power was assumed, as laid down in the *Manual,* by the Christian Science Board of Directors. An extremely strong organization, the board enabled Christian Science to grow steadily in numbers and scope of activity during the first third of the 20th cent. Of the numerous publications issued, the most important include the *Christian Science Monitor,* a daily newspaper; the *Christian Science Quarterly;* the *Christian Science Sentinel;* and the *Christian Science Journal.* These are published by the Christian Science Publishing Society. Other activities are conducted by a board of education and a board of lectureship. The churches have no individual pastors. Services are conducted by two readers, one reading from the Scriptures, the other from *Science and Health.* All churches use the same lessons at the same time. The teachings are drawn from the life and words of Jesus Christ. Although most Christian Scientists are in the United States, the religion is found in most countries with large Protestant populations. A great percentage of its adherents are women. No membership figures have been published since 1936, when there were over 250,000 members in the United States. Declining membership is indicated by the decreasing number of churches and societies listed since about 1950. See Robert Peel, *Christian Science: Its Encounter with American Culture* (1958); C. S. Braden, *Christian Science Today* (1959, repr. 1969); Stephen Gottschalk, *The Emergence of Christian Science in American Religious Life* (1974).

Christianshåb (krĭs'tyäns-hôp), town (1969 pop. 1,588) in Christianshåb dist. (1969 pop. 1,841), W Greenland, on Disko Bay. The town was founded in 1734. It has a shrimp-canning factory.

Christian socialism, term used in Great Britain and the United States for a kind of socialism growing out of the clash between Christian ideals and the effects of competitive business. In Europe, it usually refers to a party or trade union directed by religious leaders in contrast to socialist unions and parties. The movement was begun in England in 1848, after the failure of CHARTISM. Influenced by Carlyle, Southey, Coleridge, and the Fourierists, rather than by Marx, such men as John Ludlow, Frederick Denison MAURICE, and Charles KINGSLEY sought to encourage the laboring masses and the church to cooperate against capitalism. They published periodicals and tracts, promoted workingmen's associations, founded (1854) a workingmen's college, and helped achieve some general reforms. Though their experiments in producers' cooperation failed, their traditions were carried on by the Fabian Society, by adherents of guild socialism, and by several Roman Catholic groups. The movement in the United States was organized with the formation (1889) of the Society of Christian Socialists, although there had been earlier activity by Washington GLADDEN, Richard Theodore ELY, and others. Other church groups joined or aided the socialist movement, but within the churches the movement was concerned more with the application of social gospel to immediate industrial and social problems than with political socialism. See C. E. Raven, *Christian Socialism, 1848–1854* (1920, repr. 1968); James Dombrowski, *The Early Days of Christian Socialism in America* (1936, repr. 1965).

Christians of Saint John: see MANDAEANS.

Christiansted (krĭs'chənstĕd"), town (1970 pop. 2,966), chief city of St. Croix, one of the U.S. Virgin Islands. It is a shipping port for sugar and rum; tourism is the leading industry. Founded in 1733, Christiansted served briefly as capital of the Danish West Indies.

Christie, Dame Agatha, 1891–, English detective story writer. In 1932 she married the archaeologist Sir Max MALLOWAN and accompanied him on several excavations in the Middle East. Christie is the author of over 80 books, most of them featuring either of her two famous detectives—Hercule Poirot, the egotistical Belgian, and Jane Marple, the elderly spinster. Her works, noted for their skillful plots, include the novels *The Mysterious Affair at Styles* (1920), *The Murder of Roger Ackroyd* (1926), *Death on the Nile* (1937), *And Then There Were None* (1940), *Death Comes as the End* (1945), *Funerals Are Fatal* (1953), *The Pale Horse* (1962), *Passenger to Frankfurt* (1970), and *Elephants Can Remember* (1973); and the plays *The Mouse Trap* (1952), one of the longest running plays in theatrical history, and *Witness for the Prosecution* (1954). Christie has also published novels under the pseudonym Mary Westmacott. She was named Dame Commander, Order of the British Empire, in 1971.

Christie's, English firm of art auctioneers and appraisers, one of the largest clearinghouses in the world for art objects of all kinds. Since its founding in 1766 by James Christie, its name has been a symbol of luxury in the English-speaking world. See M. C. Marillier, *Christie's, 1766–1925* (1926); Denys Sutton, *Christie's since the War, 1945–1958* (1959).

Christina, 1626–89, queen of Sweden (1632–54), daughter and successor of Gustavus II. From her father's death (1632) until 1644 she was under a regency headed by Chancellor Axel OXENSTIERNA. Her early devotion to state affairs soon gave place to other interests, especially a zeal for learning. She attracted many foreign artists and scholars—including Descartes—to her court. Music and literature, especially the poetry of Jorge Stiernhielm (1598–1672), were encouraged. On her favorites she lavished titles, lands, and money, and by the end of her reign half of the crown lands had been given away. Her distaste for marriage caused her to designate her cousin Charles (later Charles X) as her successor. Weary of her duties and the growing antagonism of the nobles, and attracted to Catholicism, Christina abdicated in 1654. She left Sweden attired as a man, was received into the Catholic Church at Innsbruck in 1655, and settled at Rome. Her eccentricity and financial incompetence kept her affairs in continual disorder. On the death (1660) of Charles X, Christina returned to Sweden; she hoped to regain her throne but failed. She again went to Sweden in 1667 but was refused entrance into Stockholm because of her religion. She died in Rome and was buried at St. Peter's. See biographies by M. L. Goldsmith (1933), Alfred Neumann (tr. 1935), Sven Stolpc (1960, tr. 1966), C. H. J. Weibull (1960, tr. 1966), and Georgina Masson (1968).

Christine de Pisan: see PISAN, CHRISTINE DE.

Christmas [Christ's Mass], in the Christian calendar, feast of the nativity of Jesus Christ (Dec. 25). In liturgical importance it ranks after Easter, Pentecost, and EPIPHANY (Jan. 6). The observance probably does not date earlier than A.D. 200 and did not become widespread until the 4th cent. The date was undoubtedly chosen for its nearness to Epiphany, which, in the East, originally included a commemoration of the nativity. The date of Christmas coincides closely with the winter solstice, a time of rejoicing among many ancient cultures. Christmas, as the great popular festival of Western Europe, dates from the Middle Ages. In England after the Reformation the observance became a crux between Anglicans and other Protestants, and the celebration of Christmas was suppressed in Scotland and in much of New England until the 19th cent. The Yule Log [*Yule*, from O.E., = Christmas], the boar's head, the goose (in America the turkey), decoration with holly, hawthorn, wreaths, mistletoe, and the singing of carols (especially by waits) are all typically English (see CAROL). Gifts at Christmas are also English; elsewhere they are given at other times, as at Epiphany in Spain. Christmas cards first appeared c.1846. The current concept of a jolly Santa Claus was first made popular in New York in the 19th cent. (see NICHOLAS, SAINT). The Christmas tree was a tradition from the Middle Ages in Germany. The crib (*crèche*) with the scene at Bethlehem was popularized by the Franciscans. A familiar religious observance is the midnight service in Roman Catholic and some Protestant churches. See ADVENT and TWELFTH NIGHT. For an account of medieval and modern Yuletide customs, see Miles Hadfield and John Hadfield, *The Twelve Days of Christmas* (1961).

Christmasberry or **toyon** (tō'yən), evergreen tree or shrub (*Photinia arbutifolia*) of the family Rosaceae (ROSE family), found on the Pacific coast of North America. Its white flowers are followed by bright red berries; with its handsome leaves, it is used on the Pacific coast as a Christmas green. It is also called California holly. Most other species of *Photinia*, sometimes cultivated, are native to the Far East. Christmasberry is classified in the division MAGNOLIOPHYTA, class Magnoliopsida, order Rosales, family Rosaceae.

Christmas fern: see FERN.

Christmas Island (1969 pop. 3,500), 60 sq mi (155 sq km), in the Indian Ocean, c.200 mi (320 km) S of Java. The majority of the inhabitants are Chinese and Malays who work the extensive deposits of phosphate of lime. The island was annexed by Great Britain in 1888 and became part of the former STRAITS SETTLEMENTS in 1889. In 1958 it passed under Australian administration.

Christmas Island, largest atoll in the Pacific (1968 pop. 367), 222 sq mi (575 sq km), in the LINE ISLANDS, a part of the British colony of the GILBERT AND ELLICE ISLANDS. The island is worked as a copra plantation by the British government, and most of the inhabitants work in the industry. The atoll was discovered by Capt. James COOK in 1777, annexed by Great Britain in 1888, and included in the Gilbert and Ellice Islands colony in 1919. British nuclear tests were conducted on the atoll in 1957 and 1958 and U.S. tests in 1962. The United States claims sovereignty over Christmas Island.

Christmas rose: see HELLEBORE.

Christ of the Andes, statue of Christ commemorating a series of peace and boundary treaties between Argentina and Chile. Dedicated March 13, 1904, it stands in USPALLATA PASS, high in the Andes, on the Argentine-Chilean boundary. A tablet (added in 1937) bears in Spanish the inscription: "Sooner shall these mountains crumble into dust than Argentines and Chileans break the peace sworn at the feet of Christ the Redeemer."

Christophe, Henri (äNrē' krĕstôf'), 1767–1820, Haitian revolutionary leader. A freed Negro slave, he aided TOUSSAINT L'OUVERTURE in the liberation of Haiti and was army chief under DESSALINES. When the latter declared himself emperor, Christophe took part (1806) in a successful plot against his life and was elected president of the republic. Christophe, a pure-blooded Negro, then waged a savage and inconclusive struggle with Alexandre PÉTION, the champion of mulatto supremacy, who retained control of S Haiti. In 1811, entrenching himself in N Haiti, Christophe declared himself king as Henri I and entered upon an energetic but tyrannical reign. He created an autocracy patterned after the absolute monarchies of Europe. Compulsory labor enriched his fiefdom. Christophe surrounded himself with lavish, and sometimes ludicrous, magnificence; the pomp and splendor of his reign are still shown by the ruins of the citadel of La Ferrière, a formidable fortress on top of a mountain, surrounded by precipitous cliffs, and of the fabulous palace of Sans Souci, at Cap Haïtien, his capital. In 1820, when he was suffering from partial paralysis, revolts broke out. In despair, Christophe committed suicide. See his correspondence with Thomas Clarkson, ed. by E. L. Griggs and C. H. Prator (1952, repr. 1968); biography by Hubert Cole (1967); J. W. Vandercock, *Black Majesty* (1928); Charles Moran, *Black Triumvirate: A Study of L'Ouverture, Dessalines, Christophe* (1957).

Christopher, Saint [Gr., = Christ bearer), 3d cent.?, martyr of Asia Minor. His characteristic legend is that one day when he was carrying a little child over a river, he felt the child's weight almost too great to bear. The child was Jesus, carrying the world in his hands. Hence St. Christopher is usually represented as a giant, with the Holy Child on his shoulder; he leans on a staff. He is the patron of travelers, hence the practice of wearing his medal on journeys. His name was dropped from the liturgical calendar in 1969. Feast: July 25.

Christ's-thorn, name for several Old World plants popularly said to have composed the crown of thorns. It is applied most often to two members of the family Rhamnaceae (BUCKTHORN family): (1) the Jerusalem thorn (*Paliurus spina-christi*), which is a spiny shrub or small tree with curious fruit resembling a miniature head under a wide-brimmed hat; and (2) a variety of jujube. Christ's-thorn is classified in the division MAGNOLIOPHYTA, class Magnoliopsida, order Rhamnales, family Rhamnaceae.

Christus or **Cristus, Petrus** (both: pē'trəs krĭs'təs), fl. 1444–c.1473, Flemish painter; a follower and probably a pupil of the Van Eycks. In 1444 he became a free citizen of Bruges, where he remained until his death. Christus was successful in the rendering of geometric perspective and became noted for his fine, introspective treatment of figures, particularly in portraiture. Many of his works show a simplification of the compositions of Jan van Eyck, and there are traces of the influence of Roger van der Weyden. Among the paintings ascribed to Christus are the portraits of Edward Grymestone (Earl of Verulam Coll., England); *Lamentation* and a portrait of an unknown Carthusian monk (both: Metropolitan Mus.); *Lamentation* (Brussels); and *Nativity* (National Gall. of Art, Washington, D.C.).

Christy, Edwin P., 1815–62, American showman, b. Philadelphia. He established c.1846 in Buffalo, N.Y., a company of minstrels that came to be known as Christy's Minstrels. The company, although not the first of its kind, crystallized the pattern of the MINSTREL SHOW—the interlocutor, the semicircular arrangement of white performers in blackface, the end man, and the variety act. For over 10 years Christy had great success all over the United States and in England. He retired in 1854, and the group continued under the direction of George N. Harrington, who assumed the name Christy. Some of the songs of Stephen FOSTER were published bearing Christy's name as author and composer.

chromatic aberration: see ABERRATION, in optics.

chromatic scale, in music: see SCALE.

chromatid (krō'mətəd): see CHROMOSOME; CROSSING OVER.

chromatin: see CHROMOSOME.

chromatography (krō"mətŏg'rəfē), resolution of a chemical mixture into its component compounds by passing it through a system that retards each compound to a varying degree; a system capable of accomplishing this is called a chromatograph. The retarding system can be a surface adsorbant, such as silica, alumina, cellulose, or charcoal, capable of reversibly adsorbing the compounds (see ADSORPTION). In column chromatography the adsorbant is packed into a column and a solution of the mixture is added at the top. An appropriate solvent is passed through the column, washing, or eluting, the compounds down the column. A polar substance that is adsorbed very tightly to the surface will be efficiently retarded by the column, while a nonpolar substance will elute very rapidly. By varying the nature of the solid adsorbant and the eluting solvent, a wide variety of resolutions, even of very similar substances, can be carried out. The earliest compounds separated by column chromatography were highly colored, hence the name *chromatography* [Gr.,= color recording]. For analytical purposes a layer of the adsorbant can be spread on a glass plate. The plate is spotted with a solution of the mixture by means of a thin capillary tube, and the solvent is allowed to evaporate. An eluting solvent is then allowed to move up the plate by capillary action, drawing the components of the mixture along by varying degrees. The plate is developed by spraying it with an oxidizing agent, so that each component becomes charred and appears as a dark spot on the plate. The location and size of the spots serve to identify and measure the relative quantities of the components. As in column chromatography, polar substances will not elute as well and will remain nearer the bottom of the plate, while nonpolar substances will elute to the top. This process is called thin-layer chromatography (TLC). In paper chromatography a procedure similar to TLC is used except that the cellulose in the paper acts as the adsorbant. The gas chromatograph (GC) is a system consisting of a liquid with a high boiling point impregnated on an inert solid support as the stationary phase and helium gas as the mobile phase. The stationary phase is packed into a thin metal column and helium gas is allowed to flow through it. The column is attached to an injection port, and the entire system is heated in an oven. A solution of the mixture is injected into the column through the injection port by means of a syringe and is immediately volatilized. The helium gas then sweeps the components out of the column and past a detector. The polarity of the compounds and their volatility determines how long they are retained by the column. When each component passes the detector, a peak is registered on a recorder. From the relative areas under the peaks, the relative quantities of the components can be obtained. By varying the polarity of the column and its temperature, many different resolutions can be carried out. Since the capacity of GC columns is very low, the gas chromatograph is used chiefly as an analytical tool, although it can be used for preparative purposes as well. For compounds that cannot be volatilized readily, the liquid chromatograph (LC) can be used instead of the GC. The stationary phase consists of a finely powdered solid adsorbant packed into a thin metal column and the mobile phase consists of an eluting solvent forced through the column by a high-pressure pump. The mixture to be analyzed is injected into the column and monitored by a detector. Many different LC packings and eluting solvents are available to achieve the desired resolution. In gel-permeation chromatography, compounds are separated on the basis of their molecular size. Porous beads of the gel are packed into a column and the mixture is added at the top in an appropriate solvent. Large molecules move straight down the column, while small molecules stick in the pores and are retarded. For compounds that can exist as IONS, ion-exchange chromatography can be used to separate them from neutral or oppositely charged compounds. The mixture is added to a column packed with a porous, insoluble resin which has a negatively charged (anionic) group attached to it and an unattached, positively charged (cationic) counterion. A cation from the mixture will exchange with the positive counterion of the resin and will be retarded while neutral and anionic substances are not affected. Ion-exchange resins with exchangeable anions work in a similar manner. Electrophoresis can also be used as an effective tool for analyzing mixtures of ions. A strip of paper or a column of polymeric gel, saturated with an electrolyte, is set up so that it spans two solutions containing electrodes. The mixture to be analyzed is spotted onto the paper or gel and the two electrodes are connected to a high-energy power source (about 5,000 volts). Positive ions will migrate in one direction and negative ions in the other. The greater the charge on the ion, the farther it will migrate. This method is especially useful for the resolution of mixtures of proteins.

chromite (krō'mīt), dark brown to black mineral. It is an iron-chromium oxide, $FeCr_2O_4$, with traces of magnesium and aluminum. It crystallizes in the isometric system, but crystals are rare, and it usually occurs as irregular masses and small grains. The only commercial source of chromium and its compounds, chromite is also used in the manufacture of refractories. The principal countries producing chromite are the USSR, South Africa, Rhodesia, the Philippines, and Turkey.

chromium (krō'mēəm) [Gr.,=color], metallic chemical element; symbol Cr; at. no. 24; at. wt. 51.996; m.p. about 1890°C; b.p. 2482°C; sp. gr. about 7.2 at 20°C; valence +2, +3, +6. Chromium is a silver-gray, lustrous, brittle, hard metal that can be highly polished. It is found in group VIb of the PERIODIC TABLE. It does not tarnish in air, but burns when heated, forming the green chromic oxide. When combined with oxygen, besides yielding chromic oxide, which is used as a pigment, it forms chromic anhydride (the red trioxide and anhydride of chromic acid). With other metallic elements, e.g., lead and potassium, together with oxygen, it forms the chromates and dichromates. These compounds are salts of chromic acid and are used as pigments in paints, in dyeing, and in the tanning of leather. Chrome yellow, a pigment, consists largely of lead chromate. Other chrome colors are black, red, orange, and green. In the chrome process for tanning leather, a dichromate is used, and chromium hydroxide, a basic compound of chromium, hydrogen, and oxygen, is precipitated and held in the leather. The hydroxide is used also as a MORDANT in dyeing cloth. A mixture of potassium dichromate and sulfuric acid is used as a powerful agent for cleaning laboratory glassware. Chromium is a comparatively rare element, never occurring by itself in nature but always in compounds. Its chief source is the mineral chromite, which is composed of iron, chromium, and oxygen and is found principally in the USSR, South Africa, Rhodesia, Turkey, and the Philippines. The element, in the form of chromic oxide, gives the greenish tint to the emerald and the aquamarine. Metallic chromium is prepared by reduction of the oxide by aluminum or by carbon. It is used in PLATING other metals because of its hardness and nontarnishing properties. In alloys with other metals it contributes hardness, strength, and heat resistance. Its most important use is in the steel industry, where it is a constituent of several alloy steels, e.g., chromium steel or chrome steel. Stainless steel contains from 11% to 18% chromium. An alloy of nickel and chromium, often called Nichrome, is widely used as a heating element in electric toasters, coffeepots, and other appliances. Stellite is an extremely hard alloy of cobalt, chromium, and tungsten, with small amounts of iron, silicon, and carbon; it is used in metal cutting tools and for wear-resistant surfaces. A similar alloy, with molybdenum instead of tungsten, is used in surgical tools since it does not react with body fluids. Chromium was discovered in 1797 by L. N. Vauquelin.

chromoprotein: see PROTEIN.

chromosome (krō'məsōm''), structural carrier of hereditary characteristics, found in the nucleus of every cell and so named for its readiness to absorb dyes. The term *chromosome* is usually reserved for the structure when it is condensed and readily visible during cell division (see MITOSIS). At other times the chromosome appears as a fibrous structure, called the chromonema, consisting of accumulations (called chromomeres) of chromatin, the dye-absorbing material. During nuclear division, when each chromosome splits, each of the duplicate chromosomes is called a chromatid. A certain number of chromosomes is characteristic of each species of plant and animal; e.g., the human has 46 chromosomes, the potato has 48, and the fruit fly *Drosophila* has 8. Each of these chromosome numbers is the so-called diploid number, i.e., the number found in the somatic (body) cells and in the germ cells that give rise to the gametes, or reproductive cells. When the germ cells divide in the two-step process of MEIOSIS, the chromosomes are separated in such a way that each daughter cell receives a haploid (half the diploid) number of chromosomes. Fusion of the male and female gametes in fertilization restores the diploid number in the fertilized egg, or zygote, which thus contains two sets of homologous chromosomes, one from each parent. The principal constituents of the chromosomes are nucleoproteins containing deoxyribonucleic acid, or DNA (see NUCLEIC ACID). Chromosomes appear microscopically as a linear arrangement of genes, the factors that determine the inherited characteristics of all living organisms. The very large chromosomes in the salivary gland cells of *Drosophila* and other insects have furnished valuable material for the study of GENETICS.

chromosphere (krō'məsfēr'') [Gr.,=color sphere], layer of rarefied gases in the solar atmosphere; it measures 6,000 mi (9,700 km) in thickness and lies between the photosphere (the sun's visible surface) and the corona (its outer atmosphere). The flash spectrum has been a valuable tool in the study of the chromosphere. This SPECTRUM is obtained just before a solar eclipse reaches totality and is formed from the thin arc of the sun disappearing behind the moon's disk. An analysis of the emission lines gives information about the height of the chromosphere and the heights at which various elements exist in it. Using the flash spectrum, scientists find that the chromosphere is composed primarily of hydrogen, causing its visible reddish tint, and of helium, oxygen, calcium, iron, and titanium in lesser amounts. In itself, it consists of three distinct layers which decrease in density and increase abruptly in temperature. The lower chromosphere is about 10,800°F (6,000°C), the middle rises to 90,000°F (50,000°C), and the upper part, merging into the lower corona, reaches 1,800,000°F (1,000,000°C). At 600 mi (1,000 km) above the photosphere, the chromosphere separates into cool, high-density columns, called spicules, and hot, low-density material. The spicules, each about 500 mi (800 km) in diameter, shoot out at 20 mi per sec (32 km per sec) and rise as high as 10,000 mi (16,000 km) before falling back. Any point on the sun will erupt a spicule at the rate of about once every 24 hr. Other types of solar activity are found to occur in the chromosphere. The elements of each layer are sometimes distributed in bright, cloudlike patches called plages, or flocculi, and in general are located along the same zones as sunspots and fluctuate with the same 11-yr cycle; the relationship between the two is not yet understood. Most spectacular of the solar features are the streams of hot gas, called prominences, which shoot out thousands or even hundreds of thousands of miles from the sun's surface at velocities as great as 250 mi per sec (400 km per sec). Two major classifications are the quiescent and the eruptive prominences. Quiescent prominences bulge out from the surface about 20,000 mi (32,000 km) and can last days or weeks. Eruptive prominences are thin flames of gas often reaching heights of 250,000 mi (400,000 km); they occur most frequently in the zones containing sunspots. Dark strandlike objects called filaments were discovered on the disk and were originally thought to be a special kind of feature. These are now known to be prominences seen against the bright background of the photosphere. Until the middle of the 19th cent. prominences could be viewed extending from the edge of the sun's disk only during a solar eclipse. However, in 1868 a method of observing them with a SPECTROSCOPE at any clear time of day was developed, and in 1930 the invention of the CORONAGRAPH allowed them to be continuously photographed. Another phenomenon occurring in the chromosphere is the solar flare, a sudden and intense brightening of a plage which lasts an average of 15 minutes. This feature is also associated with sunspots, although its nature is not well understood. Flares are found to disrupt magnetic compasses and radio signals on the earth.

chronicle, official record of events, set down in order of occurrence, important to the people of a nation, state, or city. Almanacs, *The Congressional Record* in the United States, and the *Annual Register* in England are chronicles. From ancient times rulers have made certain that written records of their achievements proclaimed their glory to posterity. King Alfred of England was perhaps the first to encourage objectivity. The ANGLO-SAXON CHRONICLE, in lively English prose, notes the inauspicious beginnings of the British navy in A.D. 897: while pursuing the Danes, Alfred's long boats ran aground at low tide. Other chronicles of literary as well as historical interest are Tacitus' *Annals* (1st cent. A.D.); Bede's *Historia Ecclesiastica Gentis Anglorum* (7th cent.), Geoffrey of Monmouth's *Historia Regum Britanniae* (c.1135), and Holinshed's *Chronicles of England, Scotland, and Ireland* (1577). Modern developments of the form include the daily metropolitan NEWSPAPER, which provides exhaustive coverage of a panorama of events, from space exploration to kitchen range experimentation; and such codifications of journalistic sources as *The New York Times Index* and the *New York Times Idea Bank*—the latter a computerized *Index*, which makes any name or fact instantly available.

chronicle plays, dramas based upon 16th-century chronicles of English, particularly those of Edward HALL and Raphael HOLINSHED. These plays became very popular late in the reign of Elizabeth I, when, in a burst of patriotism, the public became interested in the history of their country. Starting as loosely structured depictions of events featuring large casts, battle scenes, and much pageantry, the chronicles evolved into narratives of the events of the reign of a single king. Christopher Marlowe depicted the reign of Edward II whereas Shakespeare treated the histories of kings from Richard II to Henry VIII. His *Henry IV,* Parts I and II, and *Henry V* are marked by complex characterizations and comic subplots.

Chronicles or **Paralipomenon** (pâr″əlĭpŏm′ĭnŏn) [Gr.,=things left out], two books of the Old Testament, originally a single work in the Hebrew canon, called First and Second Chronicles in the Authorized Version, where they occupy the 13th and 14th places, and called First and Second Paralipomenon in Greek versions and in the Roman Catholic Bible. The books are a history of the Jewish kingdom under David (1 Chron. 10–29) and Solomon (2 Chron. 1–9) and, after the division of the kingdom, of the southern kingdom of Judah, including the Babylonian captivity (2 Chron. 10–36). The work commences with a collection of genealogies from Adam until the time of Saul (1 Chron. 1–9) and ends with the decree (538 B.C.) of the Persian king Cyrus restoring the Jews (2 Chron. 36.22–23). Thus the historical material parallels (and supplements) part of the narrative of First and Second Samuel and First and Second Kings, but from the point of view of one who adheres strictly to the house of David and to the worship in the Temple. Like Kings, these books quote their sources constantly. Originally Chronicles formed one book with Ezra and Nehemiah. For views of the higher criticism, see OLD TESTAMENT. See J. C. Whitcomb, *Solomon to the Exile: Studies in Kings and Chronicles* (1971).

chronometer, instrument for keeping highly accurate time, used especially in navigation. Before the advent of radio time signals it was the only device that provided the time accurately enough for a ship at sea to determine its longitude. A mechanical chronometer is a spring-driven escapement timekeeper, like a watch, but its parts are more massively built. Changes in the tension of the spring caused by variations in temperature are compensated for by devices included in it. Some modern chronometers are electronic, using the vibrations of a quartz crystal to regulate the rate at which a time-indicating display moves.

chrysalis (krĭs′əlĭs): see PUPA.

chrysanthemum (krĭsăn′thəməm), name for a large number of annual or perennial herbs of the genus *Chrysanthemum* of the family Compositae (COMPOSITE family), some cultivated in the Orient for at least 2,000 years. A chrysanthemum is the floral emblem of the imperial family of Japan, and, sharing the honor with the cherry blossom, it is the national flower; the highest officials are honored by orders of the chrysanthemum. The flower heads are mostly late blooming and of various shades of red, yellow, and white; they range from single daisylike to large rounded or shaggy heads. Chrysanthemums were introduced to England in the late 18th cent., and today innumerable named horticultural types exist. Most are varieties of *C. morifolium*, a species of indeterminate origin and no longer known in the wild form. Chrysanthemums rank with roses in commercial importance as cut flowers and pot and garden plants. The pyrethrum, feverfew, marguerite, and daisy belong to the same genus. Chrysanthemum is classified in the division MAGNOLIOPHYTA, class Magnoliopsida, order Asterales, family Compositae.

Chryseis (krīsē′ĭs), in the *Iliad,* girl captured by Agamemnon. When ransom efforts failed, her father, the priest Chryses, appealed to Apollo, who promptly sent a plague to terrorize the Greek army; it continued until Chryseis was given up. Agamemnon took Briseis from Achilles to replace Chryseis.

chryselephantine (krĭs″ĕləfăn′tĭn, -tīn), Greek sculptural technique developed in the 6th cent. B.C. Sculptures, especially temple colossi, were made with an inner core of wood overlaid with ivory, to simulate flesh, and gold, to represent drapery. The great Parthenon Athena, now lost, was chryselephantine.

Chrysippus (krĭs′ĭpəs), c.280–c.207 B.C., Greek Stoic philosopher, b. Soli, Cilicia. He was a disciple of Cleanthes and succeeded him as head of the Academy in Athens. After Zeno, the founder of STOICISM, Chrysippus is considered the most eminent of the school. He systematized Stoicism and reconciled the factions that threatened to split the school. Chrysippus wrote with exquisite logic but also gave great weight to prophecy and the irrational. Only fragments of his work survive. See J. B. Gould, *The Philosophy of Chrysippus* (1970).

Chrysler, Walter Percy, 1875–1940, American industrialist, founder of the Chrysler Corp., b. Wamego, Kansas. He began as a machinist's apprentice and rose within the industry to become vice president in charge of operations of the General Motors Corp. in 1919. In 1920 he undertook the reorganization of the Willys Overland and Maxwell companies and in 1924 brought out the first Chrysler car. Within a short time he had made his company one of the largest of the automobile industry.

chrysoberyl (krĭs′əbĕr″ĭl) [Gr.,=golden beryl], a beryllium aluminate used as a gem. It has a vitreous luster and is transparent to translucent. The more valuable CAT'S-EYE is a variety of chrysoberyl. Another variety, alexandrite, was first discovered in the Ural Mts. of Russia, on the birthday of Czar Alexander II, for whom it was named. It is remarkable in that it is green by daylight and raspberry red under artificial light. It was popular in imperial Russia, both because of its association with the czar and because red and green were the colors of the empire. It is now found chiefly in Sri Lanka (formerly Ceylon) and Brazil.

chrysolite: see OLIVINE.

Chrysoloras, Manuel (krĭsəlôr′əs), c.1355–1415, Greek teacher and writer, b. Constantinople. Traveling to Italy on a diplomatic mission, he became celebrated for his teaching and introduced Greek literature into Florence and other Italian cities. Among his works were a Greek grammar and translations of Plato and Homer. His pupils included a number of the finest early Renaissance scholars. Through Chrysoloras's teaching, the culture of classical Greece became the foundation of humanist studies in the West.

Chrysophyta (krəsŏf′ətə), division of the plant kingdom consisting of four rather diverse classes of algae, of which the class containing the DIATOMS is the largest and best known. All four classes are placed together in this division because of their similar physiological behavior and structural composition. In the Chrysophyta, the cell walls, in the form of two overlapping shells, are rarely composed of cellulose, but instead usually contain large quantities of silica. The two flagella, when they occur, are usually dissimilar. The plants, which are photosynthetic, are yellowish green to golden brown because of the presence of large amounts of carotenoid pigments (xanthophylls) relative to the amount of chlorophyll. The chlorophyll pigment differs in type and amount from that of the green algae (division CHLOROPHYTA). The photosynthetic pigments are found in cell structures known as CHLOROPLASTS. The food storage products of chrysophytes consist of oils and complex polysaccharides; such products are unique to this group and are most closely related to those of the brown algae (division Phaeophyta). With the exception of diatoms, the four classes of chrysophytes are of little value in the plant-to-fish food chain. Class Chloromonadophyceae (chloromonads), class Xanthophyceae (yellow-green algae), and class Chrysophyceae (golden algae) comprise relatively small groups of marine and freshwater algae, largely single-celled plankton but occasionally colonial or filamentous. Class Bacillariophyceae contains the diatoms, single-celled or occasionally colonial, golden brown algae found commonly and abundantly in both fresh and salt water. Asexual reproduction of diatoms occurs by mitotic cell division, after which each daughter cell keeps one of the two overlapping shells, producing a new shell to fit within the old one (see MITOSIS). The manner of sexual reproduction varies according to the group of diatoms. With over 10,000 known species, the diatoms form the largest single and natural group of algae; they constitute most of the marine plankton that occurs in the colder seas and are thereby the prime food source for marine animals higher on the food chain. Moreover, since the silicon shells of diatoms are totally nonbiodegradable, they accumulate indefinitely in bottom deposits; through the geological ages they have formed layers of diatomaceous earth several hundreds of feet thick that are of considerable importance for many industrial purposes.

chrysoprase (krĭs′əprāz) [Gr.,=golden leek], apple-green variety of CHALCEDONY, used as a gem. The color is caused by the presence of nickel compounds. Silesia was long the chief source of chrysoprase. More recently it has been obtained in California and Oregon and in Australia.

Chrysorrhoas: see JOHN OF DAMASCUS, SAINT.

Chrysostom: see JOHN CHRYSOSTOM, SAINT.

chrysotile: see SERPENTINE.

Ch'üan-chou (chüän-jō) or **Tsinkiang,** town (1970 est. pop. 130,000), SE Fukien prov., China, on an inlet of Formosa Strait. Local handicrafts, machine tools, and fertilizer are produced. Ch'üan-chou has been identified with Zaiton (Zaitun or Zayton), which was the departure point for Marco Polo's return journey. The Overseas Chinese Univ. is in the town.

Chuang-tze or **Chuang-tzu** (jwäng-dzŭ, -dzōō), (c.369–c.286 B.C.) Chinese Taoist writer. Little is known about his life. He was a native of the state of Meng, on the border of presentday Shantung and Honan provinces, and is said to have lived as a hermit. The collection of essays attributed to him, called the *Chuang-tze*, is distinguished by its brilliant and original style, with abundant use of satire, paradox, and seemingly nonsensical stories. Chuang-tze emphasizes the relativity of all ideas and conventions that are the basis of judgments and distinctions; he puts forward as the solution to the problems of the human condition, freedom in identification with the universal Tao, or principle of Nature. He is less political in his orientation than the earlier Taoist LAO-TZE. He is also called Chuang Chou. See his complete works, tr. by Burton Watson (1968).

Chub (kŭb), an African people. Ezek. 30.5. This may be a textual error for Lub (i.e., LUBIM).

chub: see MINNOW.

Chubut (chōōbōōt′), river, c.500 mi (805 km) long, rising in the Andes of SW Argentina and flowing E across Chubut prov. to the Atlantic Ocean at Rawson. The Chico River is its chief tributary. Sheep raising and fruit growing are important along the river's lower course.

Chu-chiang: see CANTON, river.

Chu-chou or **Chuchow** (both: jōō-jō), town (1970 est. pop. 350,000), E central Hunan prov., China, on the Hsiang River. It is a railroad center for lines running north-south and east-west, with large railway building and repair shops. Trucks and fertilizers are also manufactured, uranium is processed, and lead and zinc are mined nearby.

chuckwalla: see IGUANA.

chuck-will's-widow: see GOATSUCKER.

Chudskoye, Lake (chōōtskŭ′yə), or **Lake Peipus** (pī′pəs), Estonian *Peipsi Järv*, c.1,390 sq mi (3,600 sq km), dividing the Estonian Republic from W Pskov oblast, NW European USSR. Its southern section is known as Lake Pskov. Lake Chudskoye, which is navigable, empties through the Narva River into the Gulf of Finland. The Russian coastal population engages in fishing. On the frozen strait between Lake Chudskoye and Lake Pskov, Alexander Nevsky defeated the Livonian Knights in 1242.

Chufut-Kale (chōōfōōt′-kəlyĕ′) [Turk.,=Jews' city], ruined fortress and town, S European USSR, in the Ukraine, in the Crimea. While under Turkish rule (1475–1783), it was the center of the Jewish sect of Karaites. Jewish inscriptions date back to 1203, and the region was probably the last refuge of the Crimean Khazars.

Chugach Mountains (chōō′găch), one of the Pacific coastal ranges, S Alaska, extending from the St. Elias Mts., on the Alaska-Yukon border, NW to the Manuska River. Mt. Marcus Baker, 13,176 ft (4,016 m), is the highest peak. Rugged, with forested lower slopes (the southern slope is a national forest) and glacier-covered summits, the Chugach are a barrier for movement inland from the coast. The Richardson Highway, a north-south road running from the coast to Fairbanks, Alaska, and the Copper River are the only corridors through the range.

Chuguchak: see T'A-CH'ENG, China.

Chu Hsi (jōō shē), 1130–1200, Chinese philosopher of Neo-Confucianism. While borrowing heavily from Buddhism, his new metaphysics reinvigorated Confucianism. According to Chu Hsi, the normative principle of human nature is pure and good. Expressed in concrete form human nature is less than perfect, but it can be refined through self-cultivation based on study of the classics. His thought was orthodox during the Yüan, Ming, and Ch'ing dynasties. For 600 years students memorized his classical commentaries until the CHINESE EXAMINATION SYSTEM was abolished in 1905. See J. P. Bruce, *Chu Hsi and His Masters* (1923).

Chukchi Peninsula (cho͝ok'chē), northeastern extremity of Asia, terminating in Cape Dezhnev, Far Eastern USSR. Washed by the E Siberian and Chukchi seas in the northeast, the peninsula is the eastern extension of the Anadyr mountain range. It is also known as Chukotsk. It is included in the **Chukchi National Okrug** (1970 pop. 101,000). The capital is the village of Anadyr. A large portion of the inhabitants are Chukchi; the rest are Yakut, Eveny, Koryak, Eskimo, and Russians. The Chukchi language is of the Hyperborean family. The people are of two groups, seminomadic hunters and coast-dwelling fishermen. The okrug's coastline lies along the North Sea shipping route. There is mining (tin, lead, zinc, gold, and coal), hunting and trapping, reindeer raising, and fishing. Formed in 1930, the okrug is now part of the Magadan oblast.

Chukotsk: see CHUKCHI PENINSULA, USSR.

Chulalongkorn (cho͞o'lälông'kôrn) or **Rama V** (rä'mä), 1853–1910, king of Siam (1868–1910). Educated in part by a British governess, Anna Leonowens, and an English tutor, he greatly advanced the Westernization of Siam (present-day Thailand) begun by his father, King Mongkut. He departed from tradition by traveling abroad—to Singapore, Java, and India in 1871 and to Europe in 1897. He abolished slavery, simplified court etiquette, initiated the practice of sending young Siamese abroad for training, set up schools, reorganized the administration of justice, laid the foundations of a sound financial policy, and built public works. He also was responsible for the centralization of Siamese administration that checked the independence of the hereditary provincial chieftains (1892). The total effect of Chulalongkorn's reforms and of the foreign policy he directed was to preserve Siam as an independent state at a time when the rest of SE Asia was falling subject to France and Great Britain.

Chula Vista (cho͞o'lə), city (1970 pop. 67,901), San Diego co., S Calif., on San Diego Bay; inc. 1911. Citrus fruits and vegetables are grown in the area, and aircraft engines and men's slacks are manufactured in the city. A junior college is there.

Chulym (cho͞olĭm'), river, c.1,075 mi (1,730 km) long, Krasnoyarsk Kray, S central Siberian USSR. It rises in the eastern slopes of the Kuznetsk Ala-Tau and flows N and W through Krasnoyarsk Kray and Tomsk oblast into the Ob. Its lower course is navigable. Another Chulym River, 140 mi (225 km) long, in SW Siberia, feeds Lake Chany.

Chumashan Indians (cho͞o'măshən), North American Indian group, formerly on the Pacific coast in the vicinity of Santa Barbara, Calif., and on three islands of the Santa Barbara archipelago. Their canoes were quite large, and their culture was more maritime than other California Indians. Spanish missions were established among them in the late 18th cent. Their practice of abortion, in addition to their being forced out by Spanish settlers, led to their extinction. They were sometimes called the Santa Barbara Indians.

Chun (kŭn), in the Bible: see BEROTHAI.

Chunchon (cho͞on'chŭn'), city (1970 pop. 122,672), capital of Kangwon prov., N South Korea. It is an important market town and rice-processing center. Textiles, silk yarn, and raw silk are also produced. Tungsten, mica, and fluorspar are mined nearby. Chunchon was the capital of the kingdom of Maek (250 B.C.–A.D. 660) and was later absorbed by Silla (see KOREA).

Ch'ung-ch'ing: see CHUNGKING, China.

Chungjin: see CHONGJIN, North Korea.

Chungju (cho͝ong'jo͞o'), city (1970 pop. 87,227), central South Korea. Chungju is an important agricultural center.

Chungking (cho͝ong'kĭng') or **Ch'ung-ch'ing** (cho͝ong-chĭng), city (1970 est. pop. 3,500,000), SE Szechwan prov., China, at the junction of the Yangtze and Chia-ling rivers. The commercial center of W China, it commands a large river trade. Surrounded on three sides by water, it is situated on a rock promontory; all supplies from the river front must be carried by stairway or inclined railway. A flourishing industrial city, it has railroad shops, shipyards, a large-scale integrated steel complex, cotton and silk mills, chemical and cement plants, food-processing establishments, machine shops, paper mills, and a developing motor vehicle industry. Large coal and iron mines are nearby. Chungking was opened as a treaty port in 1891. In Nov., 1937, just before the Japanese capture of Nanking in the Second Sino-Japanese War, the capital of China was transferred to Chungking, where it remained until the end of hostilities. During that time administrative agencies, educational institutions, and industrial plants from all over the country were relocated in Chungking, and the population more than tripled. The city was taken by the Communists on Nov. 30, 1949. Its many institutions of higher learning include Chungking Univ., Chungking Technical Univ., and a medical college.

Chung-shan (jo͝ong-shän) or **Shekki** (shĕ'kē'), town, S Kwangtung prov., SE China, near Macao. It is situated on Chung-shan island (sometimes called Macao island), and has sugar refineries. Sun Yat-sen was born there.

Chuquet, Nicolas (nēkôlä' shükā'), c.1450–1500, French mathematician, probably b. Paris. Little is known of Chuquet's life. At Lyons in 1484 he composed a manuscript on the science of numbers, which was finally published in two parts in 1880 and 1881. The first part, called the "Triparty," was a treatise on algebra and contained the first use of the RADICAL sign with an index (as in $\sqrt[3]{\ }$); the second part contained the statement of, and the replies to, a set of 156 mathematical problems.

Chuquicamata (cho͞o"kēkämä'tä), town, N Chile, on the western slopes of the Andes. At an elevation of 10,435 ft (3,181 m), Chuquicamata has one of the world's largest copper mines. The extensive open-pit mining of the region dates to 1915.

Chur (ko͞or), Fr. *Coire*, Romansh *Cuera*, city (1971 pop. 31,193), capital of Grisons canton, E Switzerland, on the Plessur River. Chur is an important transportation junction. Manufactures include foodstuffs (especially chocolate), textiles, and metal products. Chur was capital of the Roman province of Rhaetia. In the 5th cent. it became an episcopal see; the bishops were later made princes of the Holy Roman Empire. The temporal power of the prince-bishops was limited (c.1465) by the townspeople and later, when the Reformation was accepted (1524–26), ended altogether. Outstanding buildings are a restored 8th-century church, the Renaissance episcopal palace, the cathedral (begun 12th cent.), and the Rhaetian Museum (of folklore). Most of the inhabitants speak Romansh. The Swiss painter Angelica Kauffmann was born in Chur.

Church, Benjamin, 1639–1718, New England colonial soldier in KING PHILIP'S WAR, b. Plymouth, Mass. He took a leading part in the Great Swamp Fight (Dec., 1675), W of Kingston, R.I., and finally hunted down and killed Philip in Aug., 1676.

Church, Frederick Edwin, 1826–1900, American landscape painter of the HUDSON RIVER SCHOOL, b. Hartford, Conn., studied with Thomas Cole at Catskill, N.Y. He traveled and painted in North and South America and in Europe and excelled in panoramic scenes. He preferred to paint exotic and foreign landscapes instead of the native scenery favored by other members of the school. His large canvases are noted for the accuracy and clarity of the scenery portrayed, and for a crystalline rendering of light. Church is represented in the Metropolitan Museum; the New York Public Library; the National Academy of Design, New York City; and the Corcoran Gallery.

Church, Sir Richard, 1784–1873, British army officer. After varied service, he organized a Greek regiment to defend (1812–15) the Ionian Islands, and in 1827 he was made generalissimo of the Greek insurgents in the Greek War of Independence. Residing in Greece, he subsequently engaged in politics there and was made (1854) a general in the Greek army.

Church, Richard William, 1815–90, English Anglican clergyman. He was educated at Oxford, where he became a follower of John Henry Newman. As dean of St. Paul's (1871–90) he did much to disseminate High Church doctrine. His book *The Oxford Movement* (1891) was long the authoritative work on the subject. In 1846 he helped found the *Guardian*, an Anglican newspaper. See his life and letters (ed. by his daughter, 1894).

church [probably Gr.,=divine], aggregation of Christian believers. The traditional belief has the church the community of believers, living and dead, headed by Jesus Christ, who founded it in the apostles. This is the doctrine of the mystical body of Christ (Eph. 1.22–23). Some divisions speak of the church militant (the living), the church suffering (the dead in purgatory), and the church triumphant (the saints of heaven). The church is said to be recognizable by four marks (as in the Nicene Creed): it is one (united), holy (producing holy lives), catholic (universal, supranational), and apostolic (having continuity with the apostles). In the Orthodox Eastern Church, the Roman Catholic Church, and the Church of England, crucial importance is attached to the unbroken tradition, as handed down through the Holy Ghost (see APOSTOLIC SUCCESSION); with this doctrine goes the apostolic power to administer grace through the SACRAMENTS. Certain men of the Reformation rejected the doctrine of apostolic succession and substituted for the authority of the church the authority of Scripture alone. Protestants generally interpret the oneness of the church in a mystical sense; the true church is held to be invisibly present in all Christian denominations. The ecumenical movement in recent years has stimulated fresh study on the doctrine of the church.

church [Gr. *kuraikon*=belonging to the Lord], in architecture, a building for Christian worship. The earliest churches date from the late 3d cent.; before then Christians, because of persecutions, worshiped secretly, especially in private houses. In Rome and some other cities Christians worshiped at the martyrs' tombs in the underground cemeteries, or CATACOMBS. The catacomb chapel influenced the furnishing of churches, particularly the CRYPT. The BASILICA form came to be standard in Western Europe, while in the East the norm became the square church of BYZANTINE ARCHITECTURE, derived from the shape of the Greek cross. The interior of the Eastern church is characterized by an image screen (iconostasis) rendering the sanctuary invisible to the lay worshipers, except that the ALTAR may be seen through the doors of the screen. In the West, modifications of the basilica were developed in ROMANESQUE ARCHITECTURE and in GOTHIC ARCHITECTURE. BAROQUE architecture produced innovations in ecclesiastical design in the 17th cent. Western churches in general have an east-west ORIENTATION with the altar at the eastern end. In America, Colonial architects developed an austerely beautiful type of spired church, patterned after the works of Christopher WREN and James Gibbs. Churches differ in importance according to their constitution and the position in the hierarchy of their clergy, the CATHEDRAL being the bishop's church. See CHAPEL; ABBEY; HAGIA SOPHIA; SAINT PETER'S CHURCH; articles on other important churches.

church and state. There have been several phases in the relationship between the Christian church and the state. The uncompromising refusal of the early Christians to accord divine honors to the Roman emperor was the chief cause of the imperial persecutions of the church. After CONSTANTINE I gave it official status, the church at first remained fairly autonomous, but during the 4th cent. the emperor began to figure increasingly in religious affairs. In the East in the 6th cent., Justinian was ruler of church and state equally, and thereafter the ORTHODOX EASTERN CHURCH in the Byzantine Empire was in confirmed subservience to the state. This domination of state over church is called Erastianism, after the theologian ERASTUS. When the empire began to disintegrate, the power of the state over the church declined; and under the Ottoman sultans the situation was reversed to the extent that the patriarchs of Constantinople were given political power over the laymen of their churches. In Russia the Orthodox Church was quite dominated by the state. In the West different factors were in play. After 400 there was no central power in the West, but there was a central ecclesiastical power, the see of Rome, which had claimed primacy from the earliest times. The barbarian invasions and the ensuing anarchy resulted in a tremendous growth in the power of the PAPACY. With the appearance of strong political powers in Europe, particularly the HOLY ROMAN EMPIRE and the kingdom of France, a struggle began between the papacy and the temporal rulers. The principal contention was over INVESTITURE, but underlying it was violent disagreement as to the proper distribution of power; theories ranged from the belief that emperor or king, as ruler by divine right, should control church as well as state (a theory known also as caesaropapism) to the belief that the pope, as vicar of God on earth, should have the right of supervision over the state. The centuries-long struggle was highlighted by such bitter clashes as those between Pope Gregory VII and Holy Roman Emperor Henry IV, between Pope Innocent III and Emperor Frederick II and King Philip II of France, and between Pope Boniface VIII and King Philip IV of France. The conflict of GUELPHS AND GHIBELLINES began as part of the imperial-papal struggle. The nearest the papacy ever came to Erastianism was in the period during which the popes resided at Avignon, where they were virtually at the beck and call of the French kings. After the return of the papacy to Rome the popes generally maintained independence of temporal powers but on occasion were either influenced or coerced by king or emperor. The contest in England was perhaps no less bitter than on the Continent, but it was more sporadic. LANFRANC and ANSELM contended against King WILLIAM II, St. THOMAS À BECKET against Henry II. The REFORMATION introduced a great number of complicated factors into the relations of church and state. Different solutions have been found, ranging from the establishment of one particular church (as in England and the Scandinavian countries) to the total separation of church and state (as in the United States). The patterns of relation between church and state remain a living issue in today's society. See B. D. Hill, ed., *Church and State in the Middle Ages* (1970); Walter Ullmann, *The Growth of Papal Government in the Middle Ages* (3d. ed. 1970).

In the British Isles. The most extreme form of Erastianism is seen in the Church of England (see ENGLAND, CHURCH OF), of which the monarch is supreme head. This situation derives from the strongly political character of the Protestant Reformation in England. It is notable that in the early history of religious dissent, the Puritans (see PURITANISM) did not wish to end the Established Church; their aim was rather to capture and control it. The church was not disestablished after the ENGLISH CIVIL WAR; Anglicanism, or Episcopalianism, was merely replaced by a Presbyterian establishment (although the latter was a dead letter from the beginning). After the Restoration (1660) of the monarchy, measures were taken against the Puritans that for the first time actually excluded them from the Church of England as NONCONFORMISTS. They and the Roman Catholics were the victims of religious and civil disabilities (gradually reduced) into the 19th cent. Although the state has taken less and less interest in supervising the Church of England, the connection is still very real; e.g., revisions of the BOOK OF COMMON PRAYER must be approved by Parliament, and appointments to all bishoprics are made by the monarch, acting on the advice of the prime minister. John CALVIN tended to a view directly opposed to that of the reforming English monarchs; in Geneva he set up a virtual theocracy with the state subordinate to the church. The Presbyterian churches have, therefore, maintained a stand for freedom of the church, and the Church of Scotland (see SCOTLAND, CHURCH OF) is much less under state control than is the Church of England. See T. G. Sanders, *Protestant Concepts of Church and State* (1964).

In the United States. The Presbyterians in the British North American colonies helped in the struggle against the institution of an established church, particularly in Virginia. More important, however, was the broad principle of religious toleration forwarded by Roger WILLIAMS and others. This principle, befitting the heterogeneity of the colonies, ultimately triumphed against both the virtual theocracy of the New England Puritans and the conservative Established Church of the Southern colonists. The American idea of separation of church and state—complete noninterference on both sides—emerged. In the United States today there is a minimum of friction between church and state. The practical line of demarcation, however, continues to create problems, and any seeming transgression by either institution causes a tremendous outcry. Education has been a fertile field of controversy; debates have arisen over such questions as religious education in tax-supported schools and public aid to parochial schools. See study by A. P. Stokes and Leo Pfeffer (3 vol., 1950; rev. ed., 1 vol., 1964); J. F. Wilson, ed., *Church and State in American History* (1965); Leo Pfeffer, *Church, State, and Freedom* (rev. ed. 1967).

On the Continent. In Europe, as in Latin America, the concept of separation of church and state is different from that in the United States, particularly in predominantly Roman Catholic countries. The wars of the Reformation produced, in the Peace of Augsburg (1555), a formula of *cuius regio, eius religio* [whose the region, his the religion], by which the ruling prince determined the religion of his territory. The compromise, curiously contrary to the idea of a universal Christian church, even more curiously corresponded to the principle practiced in Asia (e.g., the Buddhism of Asoka). It more or less prevailed in Europe after the Thirty Years War and the Peace of Westphalia (1648). Religion thus in a certain sense became a national affair, particularly in Protestant countries. The internationalism of the Roman Catholic Church, however, prevented nationalization in Catholic countries, despite such movements as GALLICANISM in France. The church, when recognized as the state church, exercised considerable influence on the government of the state. More important, perhaps, was the fact that the church and its religious orders owned much property and exerted considerable economic influence. The CONCORDAT was used as a means of regulating the relation of church and state and delimiting the spheres of respective influence. Of the modern concordats perhaps the most famous was Napoleon I's Concordat of 1801. The opponents of clerical influence in the state, the anticlericals, in the 19th cent. agitated for the removal of clerical influence. To them the separation of church and state meant the ending of the establishment of the church and complete noninterference of the church in affairs of state but not noninterference of the state in such matters as church property and religious education. The clerical parties, on the other hand, fought to maintain establishment and property and (to some extent) the enforcement of ecclesiastical law by the civil arm. One of the most bitter of these contests took place in France, where ultimately the anticlericals triumphed, notably in the *Lois des associations* (1905), which in effect placed the church under subjection to the state. The contests were also bitter in Latin America, particularly in Mexico, where the church wielded an enormous influence. This struggle led under Plutarco E. Calles to the practical abolition of the church in Mexico and the harrying of priests in the 1920s; adjustments since that time have tended to an approximation of the complete noninterference rule prevalent in the United States. In Germany the relations of church and state reached a crucial point in the KULTURKAMPF of Otto von BISMARCK. Adolf Hitler, although he signed a concordat, undertook to reduce both Roman Catholic and Protestant churches to instruments of the National Socialist government. In Italy, the LATERAN TREATY, agreed to by Pius XI in 1929, ended the so-called Roman Question and secured recognition of the pope as a sovereign apart from the Italian government. In the Soviet Union, especially in its early period, the Communist party fostered much antireligious propaganda. A large percentage of the churches were closed. The Constitution of 1936, however, guaranteed freedom of religious worship, and the Russian Orthodox Church was subsequently revived. In 1944 two state-controlled councils were established to supervise religion; one regulates the affairs of the Russian Church, the other those of the other Christian denominations and of the Muslim, Jewish, and Buddhist groups. Similar systems of state control exist in many other Communist countries. See A. H. Dalton, *Church and State in France 1300–1907* (1907, repr. 1972); E. C. Helmreich, *A Free Church in a Free State? The Catholic Church: Italy, Germany, France 1864–1914* (1964); J. L. Mecham, *Church and State in Latin America* (rev. ed. 1966); H. H. Stroup, *Church and State in Confrontation* (1967).

Churches of Christ, conservative body of Protestant Christians. Its founders were originally members of the DISCIPLES OF CHRIST who gradually withdrew from that body beginning c.1840. They objected to the use of musical instruments in the church and to the introduction of new titles and more power for the pastors. Each church is entirely self-governing. The Bible, especially the New Testament, is considered its complete and sufficient authority. The Churches of Christ, highly evangelistic, have emerged as one of the largest Christian denominations in the United States, especially strong in the South and the West. They were first listed as a separate group in the U.S. census of religious bodies of 1906. They claim a membership of c.2,400,000.

Churches of God in North America, evangelical and orthodox Christian bodies, Arminian in faith (see ARMINIANISM), with certain Baptist doctrines. Each local church has a council consisting of the pastor and of elders elected by the congregation. Baptism by immersion and the Lord's Supper, with the attendant ceremony of foot washing, are the principal ordinances. The Bible is the sole rule of faith and practice. The movement originated during revivals held by John Winebrenner, of Harrisburg, Pa. Opposition to his evangelistic methods led to his eventual exclusion in 1825 from the German Reformed Church. In 1830 the General Eldership of the Church of God was organized by the independent congregations of Winebrenner's founding. Later this became the General Eldership of the Churches of God in North America. Originally in Maryland and Pennsylvania, the churches are now found elsewhere in the United States.

Churchill, Charles, 1731–64, English poet and satirist. Upon his family's insistence he took religious orders in 1756, but life as a London dandy suited him more, and he resigned his curacy. His first poem and perhaps his best work, *The Rosciad* (1761), a satire on the leading actresses and actors of the day, was an immediate success. His other works include *The Prophecy of Famine* (1763), a highly topical political satire, and *An Epistle to William Hogarth* (1763), attacking Hogarth for his heartless portrait of John Wilkes. See his works (ed. by Douglas Grant, 1956); study by W. C. Brown (1953).

Churchill, John: see MARLBOROUGH, JOHN CHURCHILL, 1ST DUKE OF.

Churchill, Lord Randolph Henry Spencer, 1849–95, English statesman; son of the 7th duke of Marlborough. A sincere Tory and a founder (1883) of the Primrose League, dedicated to upholding national institutions, he was nonetheless opposed to the traditional structure of Conservative rule. On entering (1874) the House of Commons, he began to attack the Conservative ministry with the incisive rhetoric for which he became famous. During William Gladstone's Liberal ministry (1880–85) he allied with other Tory independents to form the so-called "Fourth Party," which advocated a new conservatism, more democratic and more receptive to the need for social and political reforms. Acquainted with some of the problems of Ireland, having accompanied his father, the viceroy, there (1876–80), he was committed to continued union but recognized the extent of maladministration and was opposed to coercive measures. Churchill's appointment (1884) as chairman of the National Union of Conservative Associations and his advocacy of increased popular participation in the party organization, provoked a breach with the aristocratic leadership of Lord Salisbury, but Churchill's popularity necessitated Salisbury's acceptance of him into the new Tory government in 1885. He was secretary of state for India (1885–86) and chancellor of the exchequer and leader of the House of Commons (1886). His first budget implicitly criticized the entire foreign policy by its proposed drastic cuts in funds for the armed services. It was rejected by the cabinet and Churchill resigned. There was no effort at reconciliation and, unexpectedly, no popular outcry. Churchill continued as a member of Parliament but had no further active political role. In his last years he was crippled by illness. His American wife, Jennie Jerome, whom he married in 1874, was a leader in London society. She was the author of *Reminiscences* (1908) and two plays, *Borrowed Plumes* (1909) and *The Bill* (1912). She died in 1921. See biographies of Lord Randolph Churchill by their son, Winston S. Churchill (1906, repr. 1952) and R. R. James (1959); Brian Roberts, *Churchills in Africa* (1970); biographies of Jennie Jerome by Anita Leslie (1969) and R. G. Martin (2 vol., 1969–71).

Churchill, Sarah: see MARLBOROUGH, SARAH CHURCHILL, DUCHESS OF.

Churchill, Winston, 1871–1947, American novelist, b. St. Louis, grad. Annapolis, 1894. He wrote several popular historical novels including *Richard Carvel* (1899), *The Crisis* (1901), and *The Crossing* (1904). His later books, such as *Coniston* (1906), *The Inside of the Cup* (1913), and *The Dwelling-Place of Light* (1917), reflected his interest in social, religious, and political problems.

Churchill, Sir Winston Leonard Spencer, 1874–1965, British statesman, soldier, and author; son of Lord Randolph Churchill. Educated at Harrow and Sandhurst, he became (1894) an officer in the 4th hussars. On leave in 1895 he saw his first military action in Cuba as a reporter for London's *Daily Graphic.* He served in India and in 1898 fought at Omdurman in the Sudan under Kitchener. Having resigned his commission, he was sent (1899) to cover the South African War by the *Morning Post,* and his accounts of his capture and imprisonment by the Boers and his escape raised him to the forefront of English journalists. He was elected to Parliament as a Conservative in 1900, but he subsequently switched to the Liberal party and was appointed undersecretary for the colonies in the cabinet of Sir Henry Campbell-Bannerman. He was (1908–10) president of the Board of Trade, and as home secretary (1910–11) originated important labor exchange and old age pension acts. Becoming first lord of the admiralty (1911), he presided over the naval expansion that preceded World War I. Discredited by the failure of the Dardanelles expedition, which he had championed, Churchill lost (1915) his admiralty post and served for a time on the front lines in France. Returning to office under Lloyd George, he served as minister of munitions (1917), secretary of state for war and for air (1918–21), and colonial secretary

(1921–22). In the last capacity he helped negotiate the treaty that set up the Irish Free State. After two defeats at the polls he returned to the House of Commons, once more as a Conservative, and held office (1924–29) as chancellor of the exchequer. His revaluation of the pound (1925) undoubtedly worsened the economic situation (as John Maynard KEYNES pointed out) and thus was a factor leading to the general strike of 1926. He advocated aggressive action to end the strike and thus earned the lasting distrust of the labor movement. Out of office from 1929 to 1939, Churchill wrote and remained in the public eye with his support for Edward VIII in the abdication crisis of 1936 and with his vehement opposition to the Indian nationalist movement. He also issued unheeded warnings of the threat from Nazi Germany. When World War II broke out (Sept., 1939), Neville Chamberlain appointed him first lord of the admiralty. The following May, when Chamberlain was forced to resign, Churchill became prime minister. His stirring oratory, his energy, and his stubborn refusal to make peace until Adolf Hitler was crushed were crucial in rallying and maintaining British resistance to Germany during the grim years from 1940 to 1942. He met President Franklin Roosevelt at sea (see ATLANTIC CHARTER) before the entry of the United States into the war, twice addressed the U.S. Congress (Dec., 1941; May, 1942), twice went to Moscow (Aug., 1942; May, 1944), visited various battle fronts, and attended a long series of international conferences (see CASABLANCA CONFERENCE; QUEBEC CONFERENCE; CAIRO CONFERENCE; TEHERAN CONFERENCE; YALTA CONFERENCE; POTSDAM CONFERENCE). The British nation supported the vigorous program of his coalition cabinet until after the surrender of Germany. Then in July, 1945, Britain's desire for rapid social reform led to a Labour electoral victory, and Churchill became leader of the opposition. In 1946, on a visit to the United States, he made a controversial speech at Fulton, Mo., in which he warned of the expansive tendencies of the USSR (he had distrusted the Soviet government since its inception, when he was a leading advocate of Western intervention to overthrow it) and coined the expression "Iron Curtain." Churchill returned to power in 1951, and his government ended nationalization of the steel and auto industries but maintained most other socialist measures instituted by the Labour government. In 1953 he was honored with a knighthood and in the same year was awarded the Nobel Prize in Literature, not only for his writing but also for his oratory. After another Conservative electoral victory (1955), the aging prime minister retired from the leadership of his party, although he retained a seat in Parliament until 1964. Churchill was undoubtedly one of the greatest public figures of the 20th cent. Extraordinary vitality, imagination, and boldness characterized his whole career. His weaknesses, such as his opposition (except in the case of Ireland) to the expansion of colonial self-government, and his strengths, evidenced by his brilliant war leadership, sprang from the same source—the will to maintain Britain as a great power and a great democracy. His biographical and autobiographical works include *Lord Randolph Churchill* (1906), *My Early Life: A Roving Commission* (1930), and the study of his ancestor *Marlborough* (4 vol., 1933–38). *Blood, Sweat, and Tears* (1941) is one of a number of volumes of collected speeches. *World Crisis* (4 vol., 1923–29) is his account of World War I. *The Second World War* (6 vol., 1948–53) was followed by *A History of the English-speaking Peoples* (4 vol., 1956–58). See his complete speeches edited by R. R. James (8 vol., 1974); the multivolume study by his son Randolph Churchill and Martin Gilbert (1966–); biographies by Reginald Thompson (1963), Violet Bonham-Carter (1965), and Lord Moran (1966); A. J. P. Taylor and others, *Churchill Revised: A Critical Assessment* (1968); R. R. James, *Churchill: A Study in Failure, 1900–1939* (1970); Henry Pelling, *Churchill* (1974); R. W. Thompson, *Generalissimo Churchill* (1974).

Churchill. 1 River, c.600 mi (970 km) long, issuing as the Ashuanipi River from Ashuanipi Lake, SW Labrador, Canada, and flowing in an arc north, then southeast through a series of lakes to Churchill Falls and McLean Canyon. It then runs NE past Goose Bay and through Melville Lake and Hamilton Inlet to the Atlantic Ocean near Rigolet. The river has the greatest hydroelectric power potential of any river in North America, and Churchill Falls is the site of one of the world's largest hydroelectric power plants. Formerly known as the Hamilton River, it was renamed (1965) in honor of Sir Winston Churchill. **2** River, c.1,000 mi (1,610 km) long, issuing from Methy Lake, NW Sask., Canada, and flowing southeast, east, and northeast across the lowlands of N Saskatchewan and N Manitoba to Hudson Bay at Churchill. It meets the Beaver River, its chief tributary, at Lac Île-à-la-Crosse. Once a famous fur-trade route, it was discovered (1619) by Jens Munck, a Scandinavian sent by Christian IV, king of Denmark and Norway, to search for the Northwest Passage. In 1717 the Hudson's Bay Company established a trading post, later called Fort Prince of Wales, near the mouth of the river. A massive stone fort replaced the post in 1732 and served for many years as the British stronghold in the region. Captured (1782) by the French under Jean La Pérouse, the fort was regained by the British and renamed Fort Churchill; its ruins are preserved in Fort Prince of Wales National Historic Park. Exploration of the upper reaches of the river was carried on by the Frobishers, Peter Pond, and Alexander Henry, all of the North West Company. A hydroelectric power station on the upper river supplies power for mining operations in Manitoba. The modern port of Churchill (1966 pop. 1,878), at the mouth of the river, is the western terminus (est. 1929) of the Hudson Bay Railway. There, in the short summer navigation season, grain from the Prairie Provinces is shipped abroad. See James Knight's journal, *The Founding of Churchill*, ed. by J. F. Kenney (1932); S. F. Olson, *The Lonely Land* (1961).

Churchill Downs, Ky.: see LOUISVILLE.

Churchill Falls, once spectacular waterfalls of the upper Churchill River, 245 ft (75 m) high, SW Labrador, Canada; known as Grand Falls until renamed (1965) in honor of Sir Winston Churchill. The falls were discovered (1839) by John McLean, a trader of the Hudson Bay Company, and were rediscovered in 1891, after having been generally forgotten because of their remote location. Four miles (6.4 km) above the falls, the Churchill River narrows to 200 ft (61 m) and negotiates a series of rapids before dropping into McLean Canyon, from which sheer cliffs rise several hundred feet on either side. The river flows 12 mi (19 km) through the canyon over a series of rapids. The total drop from the rapids above the main falls to the end of McLean Canyon is 1,038 ft (316 m). Because of their isolated location and harsh surroundings, the falls never became a tourist attraction. Churchill Falls is the site of the world's largest underground power plant, which has one of the largest hydroelectricity-generating capacities (5,225,000 kw) in the world. It was put into operation in June, 1972, and most of the power is sent to the Montreal vicinity. The falls are expected to dry up as the power plant approaches full operation, since greater amounts of water will be diverted to drive the nearby underground turbines.

church music. 1 Music intended for performance as part of services of worship. With few exceptions, music is essential to the ritual of every religion; the singing of prayers and portions of Scripture is part of Judaeo-Christian tradition, and a large number of melodies for specific parts of the liturgy were embodied in the medieval collection of church music called Gregorian chant. Additional musical settings of liturgy from later times to the present have added to the liturgical repertory. Such customary interpolations in the service as the motet, chorale, and hymn have achieved an integral place in many church services. This is also true of the Anglican anthem and was at one time true of the Lutheran cantata. See ANTHEM; ANTIPHON; CANTATA; CHANT; CHORALE; HYMN; MASS; MOTET; PLAINSONG. **2** Music intended for performance in a church outside of the regular worship service. This may include works taken from the repertory above as well as music of religious content, e.g., oratorios or sacred cantatas and instrumental music which is not specifically secular in nature. See CANTATA; CAROL; ORATORIO. See Erik Routley, *Twentieth-Century Church Music* (1964); E. H. Fellowes, *English Cathedral Music* (5th ed. 1969); Edward Dickinson, *Music in the History of the Western Church* (1902, repr. 1970).

Church of Christ, Scientist: see CHRISTIAN SCIENCE.

Church of England: see ENGLAND, CHURCH OF.

Church of God: see ADVENTISTS.

Church of the Brethren: see BRETHREN.

Church of the Nazarene, U.S. Protestant denomination established in 1908 through the union of the Church of the Nazarene, based in California, the Association of Pentecostal Churches, a New England group, and the Holiness Church of Christ whose origin was mainly in the Southwest. An evangelical group, the Nazarenes believe in entire sanctification, that is, that God "extirpates man's sinful nature" and removes the ability to sin after conversion. Local churches are autonomous in matters of worship and evangelism, but a representative body maintains Sunday schools, Bible colleges, publishing enterprises, and other activities. See C. T. Corbeth, *Our Pioneer Nazarenes* (1958); and T. C. Smith, *Called unto Holiness* (1962).

Church Slavonic, language belonging to the South Slavic group of the Slavic subfamily of the Indo-European family of languages (see SLAVIC LANGUAGES). Although it is still the liturgical language of most branches of the Orthodox Eastern Church, Church Slavonic is extinct today as a spoken tongue. In its earliest period, from the 9th to 11th cent. A.D., this language is variously termed Old Church Slavonic, Old Church Slavic, or Old Bulgarian. The year 1100 is the conventional dividing line between the ancestor, Old Church Slavonic, and its descendant, the later Church Slavonic, which flourished as the literary language of a number of Slavic peoples before the 18th cent. Old Church Slavonic was created in the 9th cent. by St. Cyril and St. Methodius for their translation of the Gospels and other religous texts. Scholars disagree as to which spoken Slavic dialect was chosen by the two saints as the basis for the language of their translations. In any case, because this dialect was inadequate for their purpose, they had to enrich and transform it, drawing on the vocabulary and syntax of Greek. Old Church Slavonic is the first Slavic language known to have been recorded in writing. Two alphabets were devised for it, the Glagolitic and the Cyrillic. Tradition makes St. Cyril the inventor of both, although this view has been questioned; and both alphabets are said to have been derived in part from the Greek. The earliest suriving documents in Old Church Slavonic date from the 10th and 11th cent. In time, as the South and East Slavic tongues influenced this literary language in their respective regions, three major forms of the later Church Slavonic arose: Bulgarian, Serbian, and Russian. For various historical reasons, Russian Church Slavonic eventually became the dominant form. The Western Slavs were not caught up in this development, since they came under the domination of the Roman Catholic Church after the 11th cent. At first employed for religious writings, Church Slavonic later came to be used in secular compositions as well. Today it is written in the Cyrillic alphabet. See Grigore Nandris, *Handbook of Old Church Slavonic* (1959); H.G. Lunt, *Old Church Slavonic Grammar* (4th ed. 1966).

Churchyard, Thomas, 1520?–1604, English author. In his youth he was page to Henry Howard, earl of Surrey. He spent most of his life as a professional soldier, serving in Scotland, Flanders, and France. His best-known work, the poem *Shore's Wife*, was contributed to the 1563 edition of the *Mirror for Magistrates*. Much of his work reflects his war experiences, most notably the narrative poems, *Wofull Warres in Flaunders* (1578) and *General Rehearsall of Warres* (1579).

churn: see BUTTER.

Churriguera, José Benito (hōsā' bānē'tō chōōr-rēgā'rä), 1665–1725, Spanish architect and sculptor. A native of Madrid, he won fame for his design (1689) of the great catafalque for Queen Maria Luisa and for his ornate retables, characterized by twisted columns and elaborate leafwork. After 1690 he served as architect of the Cathedral of Salamanca, although he returned to Madrid after 1699. There he built a private palace (now the Academia de San Fernando) for the banker Don Juan de Goyeneche and also designed for him the urban complex Nuevo Baztán, including the glassworks, palace, and church. Associated with him were his brothers Joaquin and Alberto. Much of the architectural work of the Churrigueras has been subsequently altered. The term **Churrigueresque** (chûr''ĕgərĕsk') describes the architecture of the late 17th and early 18th cent. in Spain, marked by extravagance of design and capricious use of Renaissance motives; the architects of the period used architectural forms to produce free and theatrical contrasts of line and surface with extreme richness and exuberance. The facade of the cathedral at Murcia illustrates the style's full expression. The Churrigueresque manner was an important influence on the Spanish colonial work in the United States and in Mexico, where the mission buildings are frequently naïve examples of that style, much modified by lack of trained workmen.

Churubusco, battle: see CONTRERAS.

Chusan Archipelago: see CHOU-SHAN ARCHIPELAGO, China.

Chushan-rishathaim (kyōō'shăn-rĭshəthā'ĭm), Mesopotamian king, conqueror and oppressor of Israel. Judges 3.8–10.

Chu Shih-chieh (jo͞o shŭ-jĕ), fl. 1280–1303, Chinese mathematician. He contributed to the study of arithmetic and geometric SERIES and to that of finite differences. His two mathematical works, *Introduction to Mathematical Studies* and *Precious Mirror of the Four Elements*, were lost for a time in China and were recovered only in the 19th cent.

Chusovaya (cho͞osəvī'ə), river, c.460 mi (740 km) long, E European USSR. It rises in the central Urals and flows northwest through a major industrial region to join the Kama River at Perm, site of the Kama hydroelectric station. The Chusovaya is navigable c.250 mi (400 km).

Chu Ta (jo͞o dä), c.1626–c.1705, Chinese painter, also known as Pa-ta Shan-jen. He is said to have been a descendant of the imperial Ming family. Becoming a monk after the fall of the dynasty, he suffered from dumbness for a number of years and was known for his fits of madness and eccentric behavior. Despite his afflictions he became a founder of the school of painting known as Ch'ing. Most of his works are small-scale spontaneous studies of nature. His brush strokes, which seem free and careless at first glance, are filled with vitality and descriptive power. His works may be seen at the British Museum; Freer Gallery, Washington, D.C.; and Museum of Fine Arts, Boston.

Chu Teh (jo͞o dŭ), 1886–, Chinese Communist soldier and leader. He was graduated (1911) from the Yünnan military academy and served in various positions with armies loyal to Sun Yat-sen. Stationed in Szechwan prov., he took up the life of a warlord from 1916 to 1920. In 1922 he went to Europe, where he met Chou En-lai and joined the Chinese Communist party. He studied political science at the Univ. of Göttingen but was expelled (1925) from Germany for radical activities. He returned to China by way of the USSR, and in 1927, when Chiang Kai-shek purged the Communists from the Kuomintang, Chu led an uprising in Nanchang and fled with troops to S Kiangsi prov. He joined forces there with Mao Tse-tung. When the Communist position became untenable, Chu led (1934–35) his section of the Red Army on the LONG MARCH to the northwest. In the Second Sino-Japanese War he was commander in chief of all Communist forces, a position he retained after the establishment (Sept., 1949) of the People's Republic of China in Peking. In 1954, Chu left his military position to serve (1954–59) as deputy chairman of the People's Republic of China. He later (1959–) became chairman of the National People's Congress, Communist China's major legislative body.

Chuvash Autonomous Soviet Socialist Republic (cho͞ovāsh'), autonomous republic (1970 pop. 1,224,000), 7,066 sq mi (18,301 sq km), E central European USSR, in the middle Volga valley. CHEBOKSARY is the capital. The region, consisting largely of the Chuvash plateau, is wooded steppe. There are peat bogs and deposits of limestone, dolomite, clays, sands, and phosphorites. Grain, potatoes, flax, hemp, fruit, and sugar beets are grown, and livestock is raised. With about one third of the area in forests, both lumbering and woodworking are important occupations. Among the republic's other industries are oil and natural gas refining, metalworking, and food and flax processing. Chuvash make up some 70% of the population and Russians (who are mostly urban) around 25%; there are Mordvinian, Tatar, and Ukrainian minorities. The Chuvash, descendants of the medieval Bulgars, represent a mixture of Finnish and Mongolian peoples. They speak a Turkic language and adhere to Orthodox Christianity. Their wood carving is notable. Conquered by the Mongols in the 13th and 14th cent., the Chuvash came under Russian rule in 1552. The Chuvash Autonomous Oblast was established in 1920; it became an autonomous republic in 1925.

Chuza (kyo͞o'zə), steward of Herod Antipas. Luke 8.3.

Chuzenji (cho͞ozān'jē), mountain lake, c.5 sq mi (13 sq km), Tochigi prefecture, central Honshu, Japan, in Nikko National Park. The lake is famed for its beauty. The Kegon waterfall (350 ft/107 m high) spills from the lake's outlet. On the shore stands the ancient Buddhist temple of Chuzenji. The lake is also called Satsu-no-umi [Sea of Happiness].

chyme (kīm), semiliquid substance found in the stomach and resulting from the partial digestion of food by the salivary enzyme amylase, the gastric enzyme pepsin, and hydrochloric acid. Secretion of hydrochloric acid by the stomach makes the chyme strongly acidic. The rhythmic muscular action of the stomach wall (peristalsis) moves the chyme into the duodenum, the first section of the small intestine, where it stimulates the release of secretin, a hormone that increases the flow of pancreatic juice as well as bile and intestinal juices. Chyme also stimulates the release of cholecystokinin, a hormone that primarily increases the flow of bile but also increases the proportion of digestive enzymes in the pancreatic juice.

chymotrypsin (kī"mōtrĭp'sĭn), proteolytic, or protein-digesting, ENZYME active in the mammalian intestinal tract. It catalyzes the HYDROLYSIS of PROTEINS, degrading them into smaller molecules called PEPTIDES. Peptides are further split into free AMINO ACIDS. Chymotrypsin is produced in the pancreas as the inactive, or zymogen, form chymotrypsinogen. Along with other digestive enzymes of the pancreas, chymotrypsinogen is carried in the PANCREATIC JUICE through the pancreatic duct into the duodenum. There chymotrypsinogen is activated by another enzyme, trypsin, and by molecules of active chymotrypsin. Partly because it was one of the first enzymes available commercially in crystalline form, chymotrypsin has been studied extensively.

Cialdini, Enrico (ănrē'kō chäldē'nē), 1811–92, Italian general and diplomat. During the wars leading to Italian unification he fought in Sardinian service in the campaigns of 1848–49 and 1859 against Austria and, invading the Papal States in 1860, won at Castelfidardo. He led the siege of Gaeta and, after the surrender of Francis II of Naples in 1861, was made duke of Gaeta. Cialdini was (1861–62) civil and military commissioner of the former kingdom of Naples and became (1864) a senator. He succeeded (1866) La Marmora as commander in the Austro-Prussian War. He was (1876–81) ambassador to France until his retirement.

C.I.A.M. (Congrès internationaux d'architecture moderne). Founded in 1928 by Hélène de Mandrot, Sigfried GIEDION, and LE CORBUSIER, C.I.A.M. sought to divert architecture from academic preoccupations. The organization was the major instrument for propagating avant-garde ideas in architecture and town planning during the periods from 1930 to 1934 and between 1950 and 1955. The early congresses stressed rigid functional zoning and a single type of urban housing; at subsequent meetings members reacted against inflexible and mechanical concepts of orderly planning. Internal conflict led to the group's eventual collapse after the Dubrovnik congress of 1956.

Ciano, Galeazzo (gälāät'tsō chä'nō), 1903–44, Italian foreign minister and Fascist leader; son of Admiral Costanzo Ciano, conte di Cortellazzo. He entered on a diplomatic career, married (1930) Mussolini's daughter Edda, and became foreign minister in 1936. He helped to create the Rome-Berlin Axis and the military pact with Germany and was in part responsible for the attack on Greece in 1940. In 1943 he was dismissed as foreign minister and made ambassador to the Vatican. At the meeting of the Fascist grand council that preceded Mussolini's dismissal (1943) by the king, Ciano voted against the Duce. He was later arrested by the Germans, transferred to the Fascist authorities in N Italy, and executed for high treason. See his diaries (1946).

Ciardi, John (chēär'dē), 1916–, American poet, b. Boston, grad. Tufts College (B.A., 1938), Univ. of Michigan (M.A., 1939). His poetry, noted for its wit and perception, includes *Homeward to America* (1940), *Live Another Day* (1949), *I Marry You* (1958), *In the Stoneworks* (1961), and *Lives of X* (1971). He has also written *How Does A Poem Mean?* (1960); verse translations of Dante's *Inferno* (1954) and *Purgatorio* (1970); and *Dialogue With an Audience* (1963), reprints of his pieces for *The Saturday Review*, with readers' replies.

Cibber, Colley, 1671–1757, English dramatist and actor-manager. Joining the company at the Theatre Royal in 1690, Cibber became successful as a comedian, playing the fops of Restoration comedy. His first play, *Love's Last Shift* (1696), is a landmark in the history of the theater and is regarded as the first sentimental comedy. Of his 30 dramas, *She Wou'd and She Wou'd Not* (1702), *The Careless Husband* (1704), and *The Nonjuror* (1717) are the most notable. From 1710 to 1740 he was the manager of Drury Lane. He was appointed poet laureate in 1730. An extremely unpopular, social-climbing, and insolent man, he was ridiculed by the critics and bitterly attacked by Pope, who made him the hero of the final version of *The Dunciad*. Cibber's *Apology* (1740) is a mine of information about the theater of this period. See R. H. Barker, *Mr. Cibber of Drury Lane* (1939); Leonard Ashley, *Colley Cibber* (1965). Both his son, **Theophilus Cibber,** 1703–58, and his daughter, Charlotte (Cibber) Clarke, d. 1760?, went on the stage with some success, earning wild and eccentric reputations in the tradition of the family. The wife of Theophilus, **Susannah Maria (Arne) Cibber,** 1714–66, sister of the composer Thomas Augustine Arne, sang in opera and appeared with great success in tragic roles.

Cibber or **Cibert, Caius Gabriel** (both: sĭb'ər), 1630–1700, Danish-English sculptor. Cibber was appointed carver to the king's closet for his services to William III of England. He worked for a time for Sir Christopher Wren. Cibber is best known for his statues *Melancholy* and *Raving Madness*, both in London. He also executed sculptures (destroyed) for the Royal Exchange and other works now at Chatsworth.

Cibola: see MARCOS DE NIZA; CORONADO, FRANCISCO VÁSQUEZ DE.

cicada (sĭkā'də), large, noise-producing INSECT of the order Homoptera, with a stout body, a wide, blunt head, protruding eyes, and two pairs of membranous wings. The front wings, which are longer than the rear pair, extend beyond the insect's abdomen. Male cicadas have platelike membranes on the thorax, which they vibrate like drum heads, producing a loud, shrill sound. Females of most species are mute. Characteristic songs are produced by members of different species; each also produces a noise indicating irritation, and some have special courtship songs. There are about 2,000 cicada species distributed throughout the tropical and temperate regions of the world; they are most numerous in the Orient and the Australian region. There are about 180 species in North America; adults of these species range from approximately 1 to 2 in. (2.5–5 cm) in length. The periodical cicadas (*Megacicada* species), found in the eastern half of the continent, have the longest known life cycles of any insect. Because of their periodic appearance they are often called locusts, although they are not related to true locusts. Their life cycle takes 17 years in northern species (the so-called 17-year locusts) and 13 years in southern species; the two types overlap in parts of the United States. The female deposits her eggs in slits that she cuts in young twigs. In about six weeks the wingless, scaly larvae, or nymphs, drop from the tree and burrow into the ground, where they remain for 13 or 17 years, feeding on juices sucked from roots. The nymphs molt periodically as they grow; finally the full-grown nymphs emerge at night, climb tree trunks and fences, and shed their last larval skin. The winged adults, which generally emerge together in large numbers, live for about one week. Different broods mature at regular intervals, so that at least one colony is conspicuous in some part of the United States each year, and even in a given locality a brood may appear every few years. Other North American cicadas (*Tibicen* species and others) are known as dog-day cicadas, or harvest flies, because the adults appear in late summer. Their life cycle is thought to be similar to that of the periodical cicadas, but in most species it is completed in two years. Cicada larvae do little damage, but when adults appear in large numbers their egg-laying may damage young trees. Cicadas are sometimes kept for their song in the Orient, as they were in ancient Greece. They are classified in the phylum ARTHROPODA, class Insecta, order Homoptera, family Cicadidae.

cicely: see SWEET CICELY.

Cicero (Marcus Tullius Cicero) (sĭs'ərō) or **Tully,** 106 B.C.–43 B.C., greatest Roman orator, famous also as a politician and a philosopher. He studied law and philosophy at Rome, Athens, and Rhodes. His political posts included those of curule aedile (69 B.C.), praetor (66 B.C.), and consul (63 B.C.). He was always a member of the senatorial party, and as party leader he successfully prosecuted CATILINE. Later he was unable to prove that he had legal sanction to execute five members of Catiline's group, and on the charge of illegality he was exiled (58 B.C.) by his personal enemy, CLODIUS. He was recalled by Pompey the following year and was hailed as a hero. Strongly opposed to Julius CAESAR, Cicero was a leader of the party that caused him to convene (56 B.C.) the triumvirate at Lucca. In 51 B.C. he was governor of Cilicia, and on his return he joined Pompey against Caesar. After the civil war Caesar forgave Cicero, and he lived in honor at Rome under the dictatorship. He did not take part in the assassination of Caesar, but he applauded it. He and Marc ANTONY were bitter enemies, and Antony attacked Cicero in the senate. Cicero replied in the *First Philippic* and the *Second Philippic*, in which he sought to defend the republic. When Octavian (later AUGUSTUS) took Rome, he allowed Antony to put Cicero's name among those condemned, and Cicero was put to death on Dec. 7, 43 B.C. To the modern reader probably the most interesting of Cicero's voluminous writings are his letters to Atticus, his best friend; to Quintus, his brother; to Brutus, the conspirator; to Caelius, another close friend; and to miscellaneous persons. They reveal more of Roman life and political manners than does any other source. His philosophical works, which are generally stoical, include *De amicitia* [on friendship]; *De officiis* [on duty]; *De senectute* [on old age] or *Cato Major; De finibus* [on ends], a dialogue on the good; *The Tusculan Disputations*; and *De natura deorum* [on the nature of the gods], an attack on various philosophies, especially Epicureanism. His rhetorical works are of less general interest. *De oratore*, addressed to his brother, is a kind of handbook for the young orator; *Brutus* is an account of Roman oratory; and *Orator* is a discussion of the ideal orator. The most widely read of Cicero's works are his orations, which have become the standard of Latin. The most famous of these are the *Orations against Catiline*, on the occasion of the conspiracy, and the *Philippics* against Antony. Other famous speeches are *Against Verres, On the Manilian Law, On Behalf of Archias, On Behalf of Balbus*, and *On Behalf of Roscius*. Cicero's literary and oratorical style is of the greatest purity, and his reputation as the unsurpassed master of Latin prose has never waned. See Loeb ed. of his works (28 vol., 1912–58); his letters (tr. 1969); studies by T. A. Dorey (1965), David Stockton (1971), and D. R. S. Bailey (1972).

Cicero, Quintus Tullius, c.102 B.C.–43 B.C., Roman general; brother of Cicero the orator. After service in Asia he accompanied Julius Caesar to Britain (55 B.C.); wintered in Gaul (54 B.C.), where he fought off the attacks of Ambiorix; and went to Cilicia (51 B.C.) as legate with his brother. He fought for Pompey in the battle of Pharsala. He was proscribed and killed with his brother.

Cicero, town (1970 pop. 67,058), Cook co., NE Ill., an industrial and residential suburb adjoining Chicago; inc. 1867.

cichlid (sĭk'lĭd), common name for members of the family Cichlidae, several hundred species of spiny-finned freshwater fishes of moderate or small size, native to Africa, S Asia, Mexico, and Central and South America. Cichlids are found in tropical waters, where they occupy the same ecological niche as their colder water relatives, the SUNFISHES. The larger species are food fish of some importance, and small species are popular as aquarium fish. Cichlids are noted for the care they give their young; the eggs are laid in a basin hollowed in the sand and, until they hatch, are stored in the mouth of either the male or the female, depending on the species. Cichlids are classified in the phylum CHORDATA, subphylum Vertebrata, class Osteichthyes, order Perciformes, family Cichlidae.

Cid or **Cid Campeador** (sĭd, Span. thēth kämpäāthōr') [Span.,=lord conqueror], d. 1099, Spanish soldier and national hero, whose real name was Rodrigo (or Ruy) Díaz de Vivar. Under Ferdinand I and Sancho II of Castile he distinguished himself while fighting against the Moors, but Alfonso VI distrusted him and banished (1081) him from Castile. Entering the service of the Moorish ruler of Saragossa (a course not unusual among Castilian nobles of his time, in accord with the rights of a free lord in feudal society), he fought against Moors and Christians alike. In 1094 he conquered the kingdom of Valencia, which he ruled until his death. His widow Jimena surrendered the kingdom to the Almoravids in 1102. The Cid's exploits have been much romanticized. *The Song of the Cid*, an anonymous Old Spanish work of the 12th cent., has served as basis for numerous treatments, notably the plays by Guillén de Castro y Bellvís and Pierre Corneille. See Ramón Menéndez Pidal, *The Cid and His Spain* (2 vol., 1929, tr. 1934, repr. 1971); Stephen Clissold, *In Search of the Cid* (1965).

cider, in Europe, fermented juice of apples; in the United States, unfermented apple juice, unless allowed to ferment, in which case it is known as hard cider. Selected apples are grated in a mill, and the juice is expressed and, for hard cider, fermented and filtered. The commercial product is usually pasteurized or treated with preservatives and is frequently blended to balance the chief constituents, sugar, malic acid, and tannin. In France cider is made principally in Normandy and Brittany. It is at its best after a year or two in cask. English cider from the southern and western counties is noted and rivals beer as a popular alcoholic beverage. Cider is popular also in Germany, Spain, and Switzerland. Perry is a similar beverage made from pears.

Ciego de Ávila (syā'gō dā ä'vēlä), city (1970 pop. 60,910), Camagüey prov., central Cuba. An important processing center in a sugarcane region, it is also Cuba's leading producer of pineapples and oranges. Cattle raising is another major industry. The city has excellent road and rail communications. Ciego de Ávila was founded in the late 16th cent.

Cienfuegos (syānfwā'gōs), city (1970 pop. 85,248), Las Villas prov., central Cuba, a port on the Caribbean Sea. It is the marketing and processing center of a region producing sugarcane, tobacco, coffee, and rice, and it has rum distilleries. Sugar is the chief export. Established in 1819 by French emigrants from Louisiana and named for one of the original founders, Cienfuegos was destroyed by a tropical storm in 1825 and later rebuilt. In 1957 members of its naval academy staged an unsuccessful revolt against Cuban dictator Fulgencio Batista. Reported Soviet efforts to build a submarine base at the Cienfuegos harbor in 1970 ceased after the U.S. government expressed strong opposition.

Cierva, Juan de la (hwän dā lä thyār'vä), 1895–1936, Spanish aeronautical engineer, inventor of a rotary-wing aircraft called an autogiro. He flew his first autogiro in 1923 and crossed the English Channel in an improved model in 1928. See his *Wings of Tomorrow* (1931).

Cieszyn: see TESCHEN.

Cieza de León, Pedro (pā'thrō dā thēā'thä dā lāōn'), 1518?–1560, Spanish soldier and explorer in South America. His *Chronicle of Peru* is one of the most richly detailed accounts of the Spanish conquest. See *El Inca*, abr. Eng. tr. (1959) by Harriet de Onís.

cigar and cigarette, tubular rolls of TOBACCO designed for smoking. Cigars consist of filler leaves held together by binder leaves and covered with a wrapper leaf, which is rolled spirally around the binder. Cigarettes consist of finely shredded tobacco enclosed in a paper wrapper, and they often have a filter tip at the end; they are usually shorter and narrower than cigars. In pre-Columbian times, Indians of the West Indies and in parts of Central and South America smoked tobacco and other plant products in the form of rolls similar to the modern cigar or cigarette. Spanish travelers to the Americas introduced the cigar to Spain by the late 1500s, whence it spread to other European countries. Spanish words such as *claro, colorado, maduro, panetela*, and *perfecto* are used to describe the color, shape, and quality of cigars. Havana cigars made of fine Cuban leaf are highly esteemed. The United States and most European countries have large cigar industries. The stogie, a slender roll usually made without binder, is named for Conestoga, Pa., where a cigar factory was established in the early 1800s. The cheroot, originally made in India and Manila, is of uniform thickness with both ends clipped. Cigars, except for very fine grades, have been made by machine since about 1902; cigarettes, since the last quarter of the 19th cent. The cigarette industry has increased phenomenally in the 20th cent., especially since World War I. The composition of cigarettes in the United States has changed; at first, imported Turkish tobacco was favored, then, the tobacco of Virginia. Since World War I, the most important U.S. commercial blends have consisted of the following types of tobacco: the flue-cured type (the most widely used), grown in Virginia, the Carolinas, Georgia, and Florida; Burley and Maryland, both air-cured types; and Turkish tobacco, added for its desired aroma and low nicotine content. Tobacco smoke contains nicotine, carbon dioxide, carbon monoxide, ammonia, aldehydes, and a number of organic tarry compounds. The use of filter-tipped cigarettes increased in the United States after medical reports in the early 1950s suggested a link between lung cancer and cigarette smoking. In 1964 the U.S. Surgeon General issued a report that condemned cigarettes as causing cancer and several respiratory diseases. Despite this report and other deterrents such as antismoking campaigns, a ban on television advertising, and warning labels on packages, cigarette consumption has continued to increase. By the early 1970s, Americans consumed about 550 billion cigarettes a year. See Zino Davidoff and Gilles Lambert, *The Connoisseur's Book of the Cigar* (tr. 1969); Susan Wagner, *Cigarette Country* (1971).

Cignani, Carlo, Conte (kär'lō kōn'tā chēnyä'nē), 1628–1719, Italian historical painter of the Bolognese school. He was a pupil of Francesco Albani. The influence of Guido Reni, Carracci, and particularly of Correggio is apparent in much of his fresco work. His notable paintings include *The Entry of Paul III into Bologna* (painted for the public palace at Bologna); *Pera and Cimon* (Vienna); *The Power of Love* (ducal palace, Parma); and his masterpiece, the colossal *Assumption of the Virgin*, in the dome of the cathedral at Forlì, on which he worked for 20 years.

Cilicia (sĭlĭsh'ə), ancient region of SE Asia Minor, in present S Turkey, between the Mediterranean and the Taurus range. It included a high and barren plateau, Cilicia Trachia or Cilicia Tracheia, and a fertile plain, Cilicia Pedias. The area was under the domination of the Assyrian Empire before it became part of the Persian Empire. Greeks early settled on the coast, and Cilicia was hellenized to a great extent. In the Hellenistic period the region was disputed by the Seleucid kings of Syria and the Ptolemaic kings of Egypt. Tarsus and Seleucia (not to be confused with the port of Antioch) were the principal cities. They flourished after the region became part of the Roman Empire (a portion in 102 B.C., but most of it only after Pompey's campaign against the pirates there in 67 B.C.). Later Cilicia was included in the Byzantine Empire and in the 8th cent. was invaded by the Arabs. In 1080, Prince Reuben set up an Armenian state there, which became a kingdom in 1098 and is generally called Little Armenia. The Armenians cooperated with the rulers of the neighboring Latin Kingdom of Jerusalem. They maintained their independence against the Turks until 1375, when the Mamelukes conquered them. (For the later history of the region, see ARMENIA.) Cilicia is mentioned in the Bible (Acts 6.9; 21.39; 22.3; Gal. 1.21). See Mary Gough, *Travel into Yesterday* (1954).

Cilician Gates (sĭlĭsh'ən), Turk. *Külek Boğazı*, mountain pass, S Turkey, leading across the Taurus range. Known to the ancients as the Pylae Ciliciae, it follows the gorge of the Gökoluk River. The gates have served for centuries as a natural highway linking Anatolia with the Mediterranean coast.

Cima, Giovanni Battista (jōvän'nē bät-tē'stä chē'mä), c.1459–c.1517, Venetian painter, called Cima da Conegliano. Influenced by Giovanni Bellini and Antonello da Messina, he created many fine altarpieces in the best tradition of Venetian coloring and landscape. Many of his paintings have remained in Venice. There are notable altarpieces of the *Madonna and Saints* in Vicenza and in Conegliano and one of *St. Peter, Martyr* in Milan. In the United States he is represented by numerous works, including a *Madonna and Saints* and *St. Jerome* (National Gall. of Art, Washington, D.C.); two paintings of the *Madonna* (Walters Art Gall., Baltimore); and two Bacchic scenes (Philadelphia Mus.).

Cimabue, Giovanni (jōvän'nē chēmäbōō'ā), d. c.1302, Florentine painter, whose real name was Cenni di Pepo or Peppi. The works with which his name is associated constitute a transition in painting from the strictly formalized Byzantine style, hitherto prevalent in Italy, to the freer expression of the 14th cent. Cimabue retained most of the old conventions but introduced greater naturalism in his treatment of figures. He was master of mosaics at the cathedral in Pisa, where a *St. John* is attributed to him. Other attributions include a fresco, *Madonna with Saints and Angels* (lower church of St. Francis in Assisi); frescoes representing the four evangelists, scenes from the lives of the Virgin and St. Peter, scenes from the Apocalypse, and the Crucifixion (all in the upper church of St. Francis in Assisi); and *Madonna Enthroned* (Uffizi). A major work credited to him, a *Crucifixion* (Santa Croce), was badly damaged in the flood that ravaged Florence in 1966. Cimabue is said to have been the teacher of Giotto. See studies by Eugenio Battisti (1966) and Alfred Nicholson (1932, repr. 1972).

Cimarosa, Domenico (dōmĕ'nēkō chēmärô'zä), 1749–1801, Italian operatic composer. He wrote almost 80 operas, which were successfully produced in Rome, Naples, Vienna, and St. Petersburg. His works, of which *Il matrimonio segreto* (1792) is the best known, are good examples of pure opera buffa. He also wrote serious operas and church and instrumental music notable for its clear and Mozartean effect.

Cimarron, river, 698 mi (1,123 km) long, rising in NE N.Mex., and flowing generally E to the Arkansas River, W of Tulsa, Okla. The river winds through a thinly populated area where cattle and wheat are raised. Sections of its bed are dry during most of the year.

Cimarron, Territory of, now the Panhandle of Okla. It was settled in the early 1800s by cattle ranchers, many of them squatters. To protect their claims they attempted, in 1887, to create a separate territorial government at Beaver, Okla. After subsequent efforts toward this end failed in the U.S. Congress, Cimarron became part of the Oklahoma Territory in 1890.

Cimber (Lucius Tillius Cimber), d. after 44 B.C., one of the assassins of Julius CAESAR. He presented the petition that was used as a pretext to approach Caesar and held his hands or his toga as CASCA stabbed.

Cimbri: see GERMANS.

Cimmerians (sĭmēr'eənz), ancient people of S Russia of whom little is actually known. They are mentioned in Homer, but they emerge into history only in the 8th cent. B.C. when they were driven by the Scythians from their former home in Crimea and came to the region around Lake Van (in present-day E Turkey). Defeated (634 B.C.) by the Scythians, the Cimmerians swept across Asia Minor, plundering Lydia and breaking the power of Phrygia. The biblical GOMER may be the eponym of the Cimmerians, and they are mentioned in the inscriptions of the Assyrians, with whom they warred.

Cimon (sī'mən), d. 449 B.C., Athenian general and statesman; son of Miltiades. He fought at Salamis and shared command (with Aristides) of the fleet sent to rescue the Asiatic Greek cities from Persian domination. From 478 to 477 he helped Aristides form the Delian League. He conquered Skíros, subdued Asia Minor, and in 468 defeated the Persian sea and land forces on the Eurymedon River. On the death of Aristides he led the Athenian aristocratic and pro-Spartan party and was its chief statesman in succession to Themistocles. He was later sent into exile, from which he was recalled in 451 to conclude a peace with Sparta. He died while besieging Citium, in Cyprus.

Cîmpina (kŭm'pēnä), town (1970 est. pop. 25,000), S central Rumania, in Walachia. It is a major petroleum center; chemicals and oil-drilling equipment are also produced. The city is connected by oil pipeline with Ploiesti and with the port of Constanta on the Black Sea.

Cîmpulung (kəmpŏŏlŏŏng'), town (1970 est. pop. 27,000), S central Rumania, in Walachia, on the southern slope of the Transylvanian Alps. A commercial center, it has industries producing textiles and paper. It is also a summer resort. Founded in the 12th cent. by German colonists, Cîmpulung became the capital of Walachia in the 13th cent. The town has a 13th-century monastery with a tower and a 14th-century church (restored 17th-18th cent.).

cinchona (sĭngkō'nə) or **chinchona** (chĭngkō'nə), name for species of the genus *Cinchona,* evergreen trees of the MADDER family native to the Andean highlands from Bolivia to Colombia and also to some mountainous regions of Panama and Costa Rica. The trees are now cultivated elsewhere for the commercially valuable "Peruvian bark," the source of QUININE. Several species yield quinine and several other antimalarial alkaloids. The trees were named in honor of the countess of Chinchón who, legend says, was cured of a fever in 1638 by a preparation of the bark. At her instigation the bark was collected for malaria sufferers and later exported to Spain. Indians, however, had long used it for medicinal purposes. It is sometimes called Jesuits' bark because of the part the Jesuits played in its dispersal. So successful were the Dutch and English in transplanting cinchona to Java and India that until World War II these countries, especially Java, grew practically the entire commercial supply. The bark of the uprooted tree is beaten loose, peeled by hand, and dried quickly to prevent the loss of alkaloids. Final extraction is conducted in factories, chiefly in the United States or Europe. Cinchona is classified in the division PINOPHYTA, class Pinopsida. See M. L. Duran-Reynals, *The Fever Bark Tree* (1946); P. E. Thompson and L. M. Werbel, *Antimalarial Agents* (1972).

Cincinnati (sĭnsənăt'ē, -năt'ə), city (1970 pop. 452,524), seat of Hamilton co., extreme SW Ohio, on the Ohio River opposite Covington, Ky.; inc. as a city 1819. The third largest city in the state, Cincinnati is the industrial, commercial, and cultural center for an extensive area including numerous suburbs in Ohio and Kentucky. It is also a port of entry with a large river front and good transportation facilities. Machine tools, transportation equipment (automobiles and parts, truck bodies, aircraft engines), radar equipment, electrical machinery, metal goods, and cosmetics are the chief manufactures. Cincinnati was founded in 1788 as Losantiville; in 1790 Arthur St. Clair, the first governor of the Northwest Territory, renamed it Cincinnati for the Society of Cincinnati, a group of Revolutionary War officers. It was the first seat of the legislature of the Northwest Territory and a busy transshipping center for early settlers. After the opening of the Ohio and Erie Canal (c.1832), the city developed as a shipping point for farm products and meat. A crime wave, the result of corrupt politics and lax law enforcement, provoked the Cincinnati riot in March, 1884, and G. B. Cox, a political boss, gained firm control of the city. A reform movement culminated in the establishment (1924) of the city-manager type of government (notable managers were Clarence A. Dykstra and Clarence O. Sherrill). The Univ. of Cincinnati, Edgecliff College, Xavier Univ., and several other educational institutions are in the city. William Howard Taft and his son Robert A. Taft were born in Cincinnati, where the Taft family has long been prominent. Cincinnati's landmarks are the Taft Museum; Eden Park, with the Cincinnati Art Museum; a museum of natural history; and zoological gardens. The city also has a symphony orchestra, a music conservatory, an art academy, and a large public library. Cincinnati suffered disastrous floods in 1884 and 1937, but Federal and state flood-control projects have now greatly reduced the danger.

Cincinnati, Society of the [Lat. pl. of CINCINNATUS], organization formed (1783) by officers of the Continental Army just before their disbanding after the American Revolution. The organization, with a constitution drafted by Gen. Henry Knox, was founded for fraternal, patriotic, and allegedly nonpolitical purposes. George Washington was made president of the national society, and auxiliary state societies were organized. Membership was limited to officers of the Continental Army, certain officers of the French army that assisted the Continentals, and the eldest male descendants of both. The society provoked much opposition among the zealous Republicans of the time, who attacked it as the beginning of an aristocratic military nobility. The Tammany societies of New York, Philadelphia, and other cities were founded partly in opposition to it. Beginning in 1893 a successful revival of many of the defunct state organizations was made, and the society is still active as a patriotic service organization. It has about 2,500 members in one French and 13 U.S. branches. See W. S. Thomas, *The Society of the Cincinnati, 1783-1935* (1935); E. E. Hume, ed., *General Washington's Correspondence concerning the Society of the Cincinnati* (1941).

Cincinnati, University of, at Cincinnati; coeducational; founded 1819 as Cincinnati College, incorporated 1870 as a municipal university, opened 1873, affiliated with the state university system 1968. The College-Conservatory of Music merged with the university in 1962 and includes the former College of Music (est. 1878) and Conservatory of Music (est. 1867). The Art Academy of Cincinnati and Hebrew Union College-Jewish Institute of Religion are affiliated schools.

Cincinnati Art Museum, Cincinnati, Ohio. Founded in 1877 by the Women's Art Museum Association, the museum opened in 1886. Its collections contain examples spanning 3,000 years of artistic production. Works from Mesopotamia and medieval Europe are featured. The museum's European paintings include works by El Greco, Murillo, Mantegna, Tiepolo, and Titian. The museum also houses outstanding collections of oriental art and musical instruments.

Cincinnatus (Lucius or Titus Quinctius Cincinnatus) (sĭnsĭnā'təs, -năt'əs), fl. 5th cent. B.C., Roman patriot. He was consul in 460 B.C. and dictator twice (458 and 439). According to tradition, in his first dictatorship he came from his farm to defeat the Aequi and Volscians, who were threatening the city from the east and southeast. He returned from battle, resigned his dictatorship, and went home to his farm. In 439 he came out of retirement to put down the plebeians. The separation of legend from history in Cincinnatus' story is impossible.

Cinderella, heroine of one of the most famous folktales in the world. She is rescued from a life of drudgery by her fairy godmother and eventually marries a handsome prince. The story (dating back to 9th-century China) exists in 500 versions in Europe alone; it was included by both Charles Perrault and the Grimm brothers in their collections of tales.

cinema: see MOTION PICTURES.

cinematography: see MOTION PICTURE PHOTOGRAPHY.

cineraria (sĭn"ərâr'ēə): see GROUNDSEL.

Cinna (Lucius Cornelius Cinna) (sĭn'ə), d. 84 B.C., Roman politician, consul (87 B.C.-84 B.C.), and leader of the popular party. Shortly after Cinna's first election, SULLA left Rome to fight against Mithradates VI of Pontus, having received from Cinna and Cinna's colleague Gnaeus Octavius a promise to maintain Sulla's reforms. When Sulla was safely out of Italy, Cinna revived certain anti-Sullan proposals; the conservatives opposed Cinna and expelled him from the city. Cinna promptly collected Roman soldiers and Italians in S Italy, called MARIUS from Africa, and returned to Rome. Cinna and Marius declared themselves consuls, and a great slaughter of Sulla's followers took place. After Marius' death Cinna remained consul. When Sulla defeated Mithradates and set out for Rome, Cinna and Cneius Papirius CARBO raised an army to oppose him, but before the civil war began, Cinna was murdered in a mutiny at Brundisium. His daughter Cornelia was the first wife of Julius Caesar. See Harold Bennett, *Cinna and His Times* (1923). Cinna's son **Lucius Cornelius Cinna,** fl. 44 B.C., was a praetor who expressed approval of Caesar's assassination.

Cinna (Caius Helvius Cinna), d. 44 B.C., Roman tribune. At the funeral of Julius Caesar the mob mistook him for Lucius Cornelius Cinna and killed him. He was probably the minor poet Cinna, a friend of Catullus and author of the epic *Smyrna* (of which fragments survive).

cinnabar (sĭn'əbär), mineral, the sulfide of mercury, HgS. Deep red in color, it is used as a pigment (see VERMILION), but principally it is a source of the metal mercury. It is mined in Spain, Italy, and in the United States in California. The mercury is obtained from it by roasting, the sulfur combining with oxygen and passing off as sulfur dioxide.

cinnamon, name for trees and shrubs of the genus *Cinnamomum* of the family Lauraceae (LAUREL family). Cinnamon spice comes chiefly from the Ceylon cinnamon (*C. zeylanicum*), now cultivated in several tropical regions. It is obtained by drying the central part of the bark and is marketed as stick cinnamon or in powdered form. The waste and other parts are used for oil of cinnamon, a medicine and flavoring. Cassia, cassia bark, or Chinese cinnamon (*C. cassia*) was used in China long before true cinnamon but is now considered an inferior substitute. Cinnamon and cassia (often confused) have been favorite spices since biblical times, used also as perfume and incense. Cinnamon trade successively passed (with political control of Ceylon, now Sri Lanka) to the Portuguese, Dutch, and British. *C. camphora* is the source of CAMPHOR. Cinnamon is classified in the division MAGNOLIOPHYTA, class Magnoliopsida, order Magnoliales, family Lauraceae.

cinnamon vine: see YAM.

Cinneroth (sĭn'ərŏth): see CHINNERETH **2.**

Cino da Pistoia (chē'nō dä pēstô'yä), 1270-1337?, Italian jurist and poet, whose full name was Guittoncino dei Sinibaldi, or Sighibuldi. A friend of Dante and Petrarch, he wrote treatises on jurisprudence as well as numerous lyrics and sonnets dealing with the psychology of love. His verse, musical and tender, foreshadows the work of Petrarch. For translations, see D. G. Rossetti, *The Early Italian Poets* (1904 ed.).

Cinq Mars, Henri Coëffier Ruzé d'Effiat, marquis de (äNrē' kōĕfyā' rüzā' dĕfyä' märkē' də săN-mär'), 1620-42, French conspirator. Introduced at court by Cardinal Richelieu at an early age, Cinq Mars rapidly rose in King Louis XIII's favor and was made master of the horse. He joined in a conspiracy with Frédéric Maurice de BOUILLON and Gaston d'ORLÉANS against the cardinal. The discovery of a secret treaty they had signed with Spain led to their arrest, and Cinq Mars and his friend, François de Thou, were executed. The conspiracy formed the basis of Alfred de Vigny's novel *Cinq-Mars* and Gounod's opera of the same name. See Philippe Erlanger, *Richelieu and the Affair of Cinq-Mars* (tr. 1971).

cinquefoil (sĭngk'foil) [O.Fr.,=five leaves], name for any plant of the widely distributed genus *Potentilla* of the family Rosaceae (ROSE family), chiefly herbs of north temperate and subarctic regions. Most cinquefoils are perennial; many but not all of them have leaves of five leaflets, for which they are also called five-finger. The flowers are most often yellow. Most North American species are native to cooler regions of the W United States. The shrubby cinquefoil (*P. fruticosa*) and the silverweed (*P. anserina*) are common wildflowers in the West and the Northeast; they are thought to be naturalized from the Old World. These and other species are sometimes cultivated in rock gardens. Silverweed is one of the species reputed to have medicinal powers, hence the Latin name of the genus [*potens*=powerful]. Cinquefoil is classified in the division MAGNOLIOPHYTA, class Magnoliopsida, order Rosales, family Rosaceae.

Cinque Ports (sĭngk) [O. Fr.,=five ports], name applied to an association of maritime towns in Sussex and Kent, SE England. They originally numbered five: Hastings, Romney (now New Romney), Hythe, Dover, and Sandwich. The association was informally organized in the 11th cent., and a formal charter was drawn up in the 13th cent. In the 12th cent., Winchelsea and Rye were added with privileges and duties similar to those of the founding members. Later, neighboring places were added as "limbs" or "members." The Cinque Ports reached the peak of their significance during the Anglo-French struggle in the 14th cent. The main duty of the ports was the provision of ships and men for protection against invasion at a time when England had no permanent navy. (The ports form an arc along the coast most likely to receive an invasion from the European continent.) In return the crown allowed the members various privileges, such as exemption from taxation and from certain laws governing municipalities. The highest officer of the chartered organization was the lord warden of the Cinque Ports, who had extensive civil, military, and naval duties. His official residence was at Walmer Castle, near Deal. After Henry VII (1485–1509) founded the royal navy, the association declined. It contributed only five ships to defeat the Spanish Armada in 1588. Today the Cinque Ports court of admiralty still has some maritime jurisdiction. The office of lord warden still exists but has no real power.

Cinthio: see GIRALDI, GIOVANNI BATTISTA.

Cinto, Monte (môn'tā chĕn'tō), peak, 8,891 ft (2,710 m) high, NW Corsica, France, NW of Corte. It is the highest point on Corsica.

Cintra, Port. *Sintra* (sēn'trə), town (1960 pop. 20,321), Lisboa dist., W Portugal, in Estremadura. The region has orange groves and vineyards as well as marble quarries, but Cintra is known primarily for its beautiful mountain location. The view is superb, and Cintra has been rapturously described not only by Portuguese writers but also by Byron and other foreigners. It flourished as a Moorish city, and there are still ruins of a Moorish castle. With Lisbon it was permanently retaken from the Moors by Alfonso I in 1147 and thereafter was a favorite residence of the Portuguese monarchs. Cintra has a royal palace (15th–16th cent.) and an old convent surrounded by a lovely park. Near the town, in the Peninsular War, the Convention of Cintra was agreed upon (1808) by the French, British, and Portuguese.

Cinzio: see GIRALDI, GIOVANNI BATTISTA.

CIO: see AMERICAN FEDERATION OF LABOR AND CONGRESS OF INDUSTRIAL ORGANIZATIONS.

Cione, Andrea di: see ORCAGNA.

cipher: see CRYPTOGRAPHY.

circadian rhythm: see RHYTHM, BIOLOGICAL.

Circassia (sərkăsh'ēə), historic region, encompassing roughly the area between the Black Sea, the Kuban River, and the Caucasus, now largely the KRASNODAR KRAY of SE European USSR. The Circassians are a Muslim people, whose Russian name is Cherkess and whose native name is Adyge. They are now officially classified as three peoples: the Kabarda, in the Kabardino-Balkar ASSR; the Circassians or Cherkess, in the Karachay-Cherkess Autonomous Oblast; and the Adyge, in the Adyge Autonomous Oblast. The term Circassian has sometimes been incorrectly applied to all the mountain peoples of the N Caucasus. Known in antiquity, they inhabited the western side of the Caucasus and the Crimea and were known to the Greeks as the Zyukhoy. They were Christianized in the 6th cent. A.D. but adopted Islam in the 17th cent. after coming under the rule of the Ottoman Empire. In 1829 the Ottoman Turks were forced to cede Circassia to Russia. At this time the Circassians occupied almost the entire area between the main Caucasian range, the Kuban River, and the Black Sea. In the many Russo-Turkish wars in the first half of the 19th cent., the Circassians bitterly fought the Russians. After the Russian conquest of the area, many Circassians migrated to Turkey (1861–64). The men were warlike, proud, and handsome; the women were famous for their beauty, and many were sold into slavery in Turkey. There are today large Circassian groups in Turkey, Syria, and Jordan.

Circe (sûr'sē), in Greek mythology, enchantress; daughter of Helios. She lived on an island, where she decoyed sailors and treacherously changed them into beasts. According to the *Odyssey*, she changed the companions of Odysseus into swine, but with the aid of Hermes, Odysseus forced her to break the spell. In post-Homeric legend she bore Odysseus a son, Telegonus, who unwillingly killed his father.

circle, closed plane curve consisting of all points at a given distance from some fixed point, called the center. A circle is a CONIC SECTION cut by a plane perpendicular to the axis of the cone. The term *circle* is also used to refer to the region enclosed by the curve, more properly called a circular region. The radius of a circle is any line segment connecting the center and a point on the curve; the term is also used for the length *r* of this segment, i.e., the common distance of all points on the curve from the center. Similarly, the circumference of a circle is either the curve itself or its length of ARC. A line segment whose two ends lie on the circumference is a chord; a chord through the center is the diameter. A secant is a line of indefinite length intersecting the circle at two points, the segment of it within the circle being a chord. A tangent to a circle is a straight line touching the circle at only one point, the point of contact, or tangency, and is always perpendicular to the radius drawn to this point. A circle is inscribed in a polygon if each side of the polygon is tangent to the circle; a circle is circumscribed about a polygon if all the vertices of the polygon lie on the circumference. The length of the circumference C of a circle is equal to π (see PI) times twice the radius distance r, or $C=2\pi r$. The area A bounded by a circle is given by $A=\pi r^2$. Greek geometry left many unsolved problems about circles, including the problem of squaring the circle, i.e., constructing a square with an area equal to that of a given circle, using only a straight edge and compass; it was finally proved impossible in the late 19th cent. (see GEOMETRIC PROBLEMS OF ANTIQUITY). In modern mathematics the circle is the basis for such theories as inversive geometry and certain non-Euclidean geometries. The circle figures significantly in many cultures. In religion and art it frequently symbolizes heaven, eternity, or the universe.

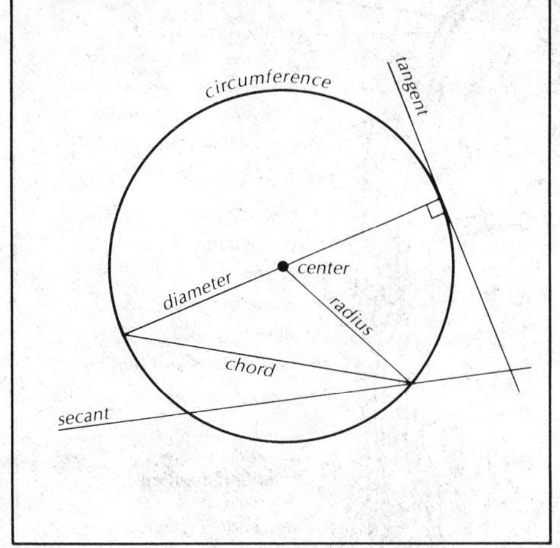

Circle

Circleville, city (1970 pop. 11,687), seat of Pickaway co., S central Ohio, on the Scioto River, in a farm area; inc. 1853. Corn, hogs, and poultry are processed in the city. Circleville was laid out in 1810 within the remains of a circular fort allegedly erected by mound builders. Its growth was spurred by the building of the Ohio and Erie Canal.

circuit, electric: see ELECTRIC CIRCUIT.

circuit breaker, electric device that, like a fuse, interrupts an electric current in a circuit when the current becomes too high. The advantage of a circuit breaker is that it can be reset after it has been tripped; a fuse must be replaced after it has been used once. When a current supplies enough energy to operate a trigger device in a breaker, a pair of contacts conducting the current are separated by preloaded springs or some similar mechanism. Generally, a circuit breaker registers the current either by the current's heating effect or by the magnetism it creates in passing through a small coil. Because it is usual for an electric arc to form between the contacts when a breaker opens, some means must be provided for preventing rapid erosion of the contacts. Normally this is done by opening the contacts fast enough to make the arc of short duration. The U.S. National Electric Code now requires that circuit breakers be used in all new home installations. Breakers for this service are usually of the thermally actuated type.

circuit rider, itinerant preacher of the Methodist denomination who served a "circuit" consisting usually of 20 to 40 "appointments." The circuit system, devised by John Wesley for his English societies in their formative period and developed in America by Francis Asbury, proved especially adapted to the conditions of the American frontier and came into its own in the trans-Allegheny region. Its success was a factor in establishing Methodism in America. The circuit rider, traveling usually on horseback because it was economical and suited to the forest pathways, preached nearly every day and twice on Sundays, thus covering his circuit every four or five weeks. His appointments were usually in pioneer cabins, schoolhouses, or tavern barrooms. The circuit rider often had a limited education, but he was usually an effective preacher and lived a very self-sacrificing life. See E. K. Nottingham, *Methodism and the Frontier* (1941, repr. 1966); W. W. Sweet, *The Methodists, 1783–1840* (1946, repr. 1964).

circulatory system, group of organs that transport blood and the substances it carries to and from all parts of the body. The circulatory system consists of vessels that carry the blood, and a muscular pump, the HEART, that drives the blood. Of the vessels, the ARTERIES carry blood away from the heart; the main arterial vessel, the aorta, branches into smaller arteries, which in turn branch repeatedly into still smaller vessels and reach all parts of the body. Within the body tissues, the vessels are microscopic CAPILLARIES through which gas and nutrient exchange occurs (see RESPIRATION). Blood leaving the tissue capillaries enters converging large vessels, the VEINS, to return to the heart and lungs. The human heart is a four-chambered organ with a dividing wall, or septum, that separates it into a right heart for pumping blood from the returning veins into the lungs, and a left heart for pumping blood from the lungs to the body via the aorta. The circulatory system can be considered as composed of two components, the systemic circulation, which serves the body as a whole except for the lungs, and the pulmonary circulation, which carries the blood to and from the lungs. In the systemic circulation, purified oxygenated blood from the lungs returns to the heart from two pairs of pulmonary veins, a pair from each lung. It enters the left atrium, which contracts when filled, sending blood into the left ventricle. The bicuspid, or mitral, valve controls blood flow into the ventricle. Contraction of the powerful ventricle forces the blood under great pressure into the aortic arch and on into the aorta. The aorta branches into the coronary arteries, which nourish the heart muscle itself, and three major arteries from the aortic arch that supply the head, neck, and arms. The other major arteries branching off from the aorta are the renal arteries, which supply the kidneys; the celiac axis and superior and inferior mesenteric arteries, which supply the intestines, spleen, and liver; and the iliac arteries, which supply the lower trunk and become the femoral and popliteal arteries of the thighs and legs, respectively. The arteries contain fibrous tissue to regulate BLOOD PRESSURE and flow. Blood pressure, the lateral pressure on the walls of the arteries, is controlled by several factors including force of contraction of the heart, elasticity of the arterial walls, blood volume and thickness, and the resistance of the arterioles and capillaries. Within the tissues the small arterioles shade into capillaries, vessels about the diameter of a red blood cell, which form a network facilitating exchange of gases and nutrients. In addition, a system of shunts allows blood to bypass the capillary beds and helps to regulate body temperature. At the far end of the network, the capillaries converge to form venules, which in turn form veins. The inferior vena cava returns blood to the heart from the legs and trunk; it is supplied by the iliac veins from the legs, the hepatic veins from the liver, and the renal veins from the kidneys. The subclavian veins, draining the arms, and the jugular veins, draining the head and neck, join to form the superior vena cava. The two vena cavae, together with the coronary veins, return blood low in oxygen and high in carbon dioxide to the right atrium of the heart. Veins lack muscle tissue but many, especially in the limbs, contain one-way valves that prevent backward flow of blood. In the heart, the blood is pumped from the right atrium into the right ventricle; the tricuspid valve controls flow into the right venticle. The contraction is simultaneous with that of the left atrium. The right ventricle contracts to force blood into the lungs through the pulmonary arteries. In the lungs oxygen is picked up and carbon dioxide eliminated, and the oxygenated blood returns to the heart via the pulmonary veins, thus completing the circuit. In pulmonary circulation the arteries carry oxygen-poor blood and the veins oxygen-rich blood; the

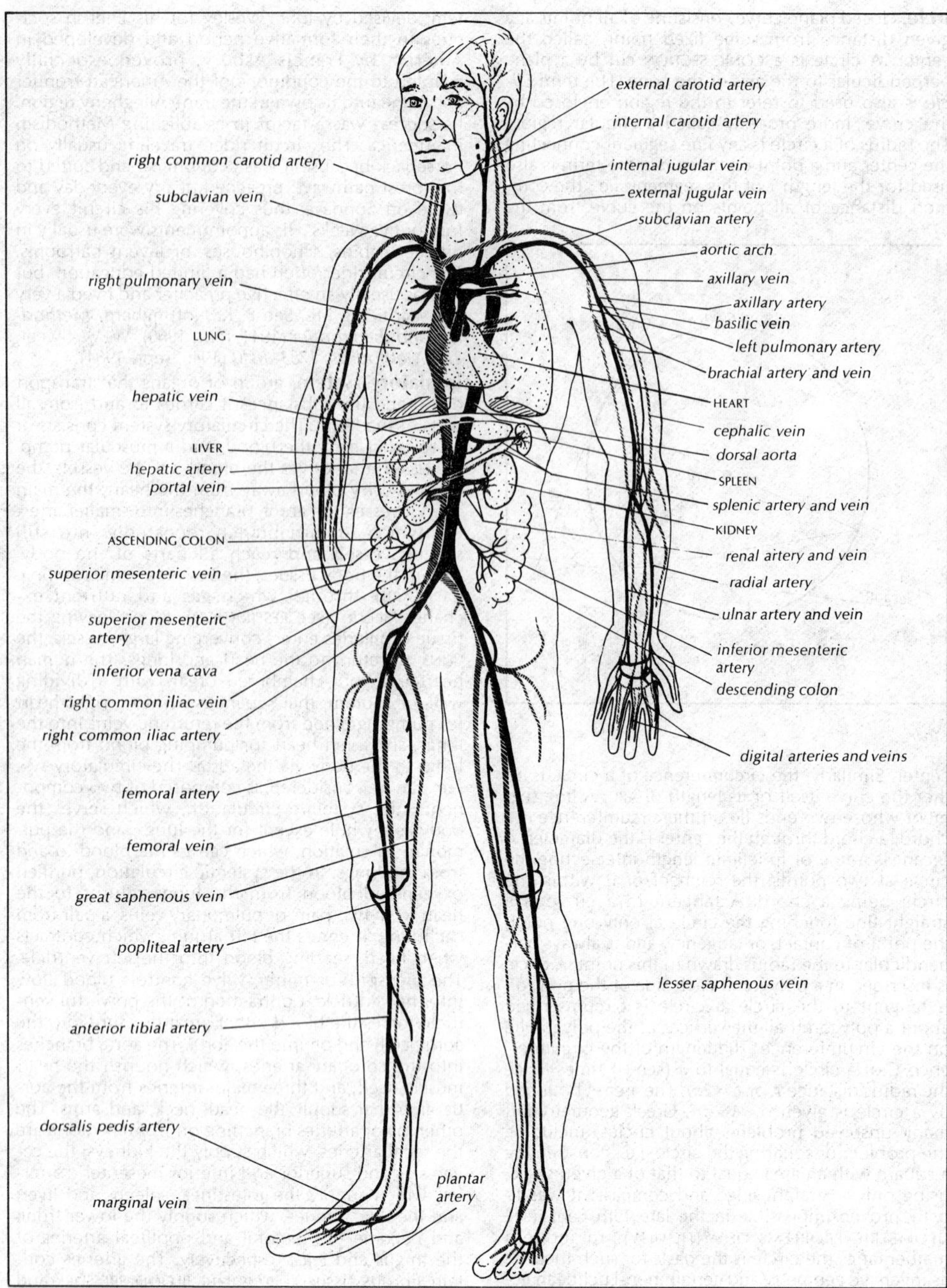

Circulatory system

terms *vein* and *artery* refer to vessels carrying blood to or away from the heart and not to the gas content of the blood carried. The organs most intimately related to the substances carried by the blood are the kidneys, which filter out nitrogenous wastes and regulate concentration of salts; the SPLEEN, which removes worn red blood cells and produces white blood cells, or lymphocytes; and the LIVER, which contributes clotting factors to the blood, helps to control blood sugar levels, also removes old red blood cells and, receiving all the veins from the intestines and stomach, detoxifies the blood before it returns to the vena cava (see URINARY SYSTEM). An auxiliary system, the LYMPHATIC SYSTEM, is composed of vessels that collect lymph from body tissues. Carried to converging vessels of increasing size, the lymph enters the thoracic duct and is emptied into a large vein near the heart. Disorders of the circulatory system result in diminished flow of blood and diminished oxygen exchange to the tissues. Acute impairment of blood flow to the heart muscle itself (heart attack) or to the brain (stroke) are most dangerous. Blood supply is also impeded in such conditions as ARTERIOSCLEROSIS and high blood pressure; low blood pressure resulting from injury (SHOCK) is manifested by inadequate blood flow. Structural defects of the heart affecting blood distribution may be congenital or caused by many diseases; e.g., RHEUMATIC FEVER. See also HEART DISEASE; HYPTERTENSIVE HEART DISEASE.

circumcision (sûr″kəmsĭzh′ən), operation to remove the foreskin covering the glans of the penis. It dates back to prehistoric times and was widespread throughout the Middle East as a religious rite before it was introduced among the Hebrews presumably by Abraham. It is performed by Jews on the eighth day after the birth of the male child, unless postponed for reasons of health. It is also practiced among Muslims and by peoples in many parts of the world. Explanations of the origin of circumcision are entirely conjectural. It is related to rites of initiation. Among Jews it is considered to involve membership in the community and to be a sign of the covenant between God and man. The decision that Christians need not practice circumcision is recorded in Acts 15; there was never, however, a prohibition of circumcision, and it is practiced by Coptic Christians. It is widely practiced in modern times as a sanitary measure. Female circumcision, in the form of excision of the labia minora and clitoris (clitoridectomy), is known in Islam and in certain tribes of Africa, South America, and elsewhere.

circumpolar star, star whose DIURNAL CIRCLE lies completely above or completely below an observer's horizon. A star whose diurnal circle lies above the horizon never sets, even though it cannot be seen during the day. Designation of a star as circumpolar depends on the observer's latitude. At the equator no star is circumpolar. At the North or South Pole all stars are circumpolar, since only one half of the celestial sphere can ever be seen. For an observer at any other latitude a star whose declination is greater than 90° minus the observer's latitude will be circumpolar, appearing to circle the celestial pole and remaining always above the horizon. A constellation made up entirely of circumpolar stars is also called circumpolar. From most of the northern United States (above lat. 40°N) the Big Dipper is circumpolar.

circus [Lat.,=ring, circle], associated historically with the horse and chariot races and athletic contests known in ancient Rome as the Circensian games. The Roman circus was a round or oval structure with tiers of seats for spectators, enclosing a space in which the races, games, and gladiatorial combats took place. Underneath were dressing rooms, dens for wild beasts, and rooms where properties were stored. The Circus Maximus, presumably built in the reign of Tarquin I (c.616–c.578 B.C.), and rebuilt by Julius Caesar, is said to have had a seating capacity of 350,000. Other famous *circi* of Rome were the Circus Flaminius (221 B.C.); the Circus Neronis, of Caligula and Nero, at which many Christians perished; and the Circus Maxentius. The circus of Septimius Severus at Constantinople and many others were often scenes of riot and bloodshed between factions of charioteers. The games, aside from races, were brutal and bloody, and for this reason the Greeks, even under Roman domination, never really accepted the circus. The modern circus, which originated in performances of equestrian feats in a horse ring strewn with sawdust, dates from the closing years of the 18th cent. The circus is a nomadic tent show, with trained animals, acrobats, and clowns. The main tent, known as the big top, is usually surrounded by various concessions and sideshows with freaks and wild animals. Even before 1830, traveling circuses were common in the United States and in England. After 1869 two rings were used in the main tent and the three-ring circus, as we know it today, was initiated by James A. Bailey. The most celebrated circus in America was "The Greatest Show on Earth" of P. T. BARNUM, which, in merging with Bailey's, became Barnum and Bailey's. On Bailey's death in 1907 the circus was purchased by Ringling Brothers, and in 1919 the two circuses were combined. In its heyday from 1880 to 1920, the traveling circus has declined in recent years. See studies by H. R. North and Alden Hatch (1960); E. C. May (1932, repr. 1963); C. P. Fox and Tom Parkinson (1970); Marian Murray (1956, repr. 1973).

cire perdue (sēr pĕrdü′) [Fr.=lost wax], sculptural process of hollow casting in metal. A model is made in plaster or clay, coated with wax in which the finer details are executed, and covered with a mold of perforated plaster or clay. It is then heated until the wax melts and runs out the holes, and molten metal (usually bronze) is poured in the mold at the top until the metal fills the space formerly occupied by the wax. When cool, the mold is broken, the core removed, and the metal is sometimes filed and polished (chased). The chief advantage of this process is that it takes far less metal than the method of solid casting, and the danger of cracking during the cooling process is lessened. The method, probably of Egyptian origin, was introduced into Greece in the 6th cent. B.C. by Rhoecus and Theodorus of Samos and was used extensively from the 5th cent. The *Zeus of Artemisium* (National Mus., Athens) and the *Charioteer of Delphi* (Delphi Mus.), both hollow casts, are the finest of the few Greek bronzes that have survived. In use throughout the world, *cire perdue* was introduced in China c.200 B.C. and was employed later in casting the Benin bronzes of Africa. The great bronze masterpieces of the Renaissance were produced by this process (see the autobiography of Benvenuto Cellini for a detailed account). The method has enjoyed a recent revival, primarily for jewelry making, although it has been supplemented by other processes. See H. Jackson, *Lost Wax Bronze Casting* (1972); G. Pack, *Jewelry Making by the Lost Wax Process* (1968).

cirrhosis (sərō′səs), degeneration of tissue in an organ resulting in fibrosis, with nodule and scar formation. The term is most often used in relation to the liver, since that organ is most often involved in cirrhosis. The most prevalent form of cirrhosis of the liver, portal cirrhosis, appears in middle-aged males with a history of chronic alcoholism and is caused by protein deficiency (specifically choline), a type of malnutrition common in alcoholics. Protein deprivation is also responsible for KWASHIORKOR, a nutritional deficiency with symptoms resembling those of cirrhosis of the liver. Biliary cirrhosis is a type caused by disruption of bile flow and is more common in women. Failure of liver function results in gastrointestinal disturbances, emaciation, enlargement of the liver and spleen, jaundice, accumulation of fluid in the abdomen and other tissues of the body, and obstruction of the venous circulation with distention of the veins. It is not uncommon for greatly distended veins in the esophagus to rupture and cause massive hemorrhage. Treatment is supportive—a diet with adequate protein (except where ammonia poisoning is a factor), vitamin supplements, transfusions to replace any blood loss, and removal of accumulated fluid.

cirrocumulus: see CLOUD.

cirrostratus: see CLOUD.

cirrus: see CLOUD.

Cirta: see CONSTANTINE, Algeria.

Cis (sĭs), same as KISH 1.

Cisalpine Republic (sĭsăl'pīn), Italian state created by Napoleon Bonaparte in 1797 by uniting the Transpadane and Cispadane republics, which he had established (1796) N and S of the Po River. The new republic included the former duchies of Milan, Parma, and Modena, the legations of Bologna and Ferrara, and the Romagna. By the Treaty of Campo Formio (1797), Austria recognized the republic, to which were added the Venetian territories W of the Adige (including Bergamo and Brescia), the duchy of Mantua, and the formerly Swiss Valtellina. The republic was in fact subject to France, and its constitution was based on the French model. In 1799 the Austro-Russian armies occupied it, but Bonaparte recovered it in 1800. By the Treaty of Lunéville (1801) its nominal autonomy was restored. In 1802 it became the Italian Republic and in 1805, with the addition of Venetia, the Napoleonic kingdom of Italy. It was broken up by the Congress of Vienna (see VIENNA, CONGRESS OF) in 1815.

***cis*-butenedioic acid** (sĭs-byo͞o"tĕndī'ōĭk), IUPAC name for maleic acid; see FUMARIC ACID.

Cisleithania: see AUSTRO-HUNGARIAN MONARCHY.

Cisneros, Francisco Jiménez de: see JIMÉNEZ DE CISNEROS, FRANCISCO.

Cispadane Republic: see CISALPINE REPUBLIC.

Cistercians (sĭstûr'shənz), monks of a Roman Catholic religious order founded (1098) by St. Robert, abbot of Molesme, in Cîteaux [*Cistercium*], Côte-d'Or dept., France. They reacted against the laxity in the Cluniac order. The particular stamp of the Cistercians stems from the abbacy (c.1109–1134) of St. STEPHEN HARDING. The black habit of the Benedictines was changed to an unbleached white, and the Cistercians became known as White Monks. St. BERNARD OF CLAIRVAUX is often regarded as their "second founder." Through a return to strict asceticism and a life of poverty, the Cistercians sought to recover the ideals of the original Benedictines. They expanded greatly, especially during St. Bernard's lifetime, and at the close of the 12th cent. there were 530 Cistercian abbeys. The life and writings of St. Bernard were their guiding influence. They considered farming the chief occupation for monks and led Europe in the development of new agricultural techniques. (In England the Cistercians were important in the growth of English wool culture.) The Cistercians were the first to make large use of lay brothers, conversi, who lived in the abbey under a separate discipline and aided the monks in their farm system. In the 13th cent. relaxation of fervor blunted Cistercian importance, and by 1400 they had ceased to be prominent, their place being taken by the Dominican and Franciscan friars. Of later reform attempts, the most important was the movement begun at La Trappe, France (17th cent.); those accepting the greater austerities were known popularly as TRAPPISTS, officially titled (after 1892) Cistercians of the Stricter Observance [Lat. abbr., *O.C.S.D.*], as distinct from Cistercians of the Common Observance [Lat. abbr., *S.O.* Cist.]. Today the difference is not great. The unit of Cistercian life is the abbey. Its members compose a permanent communal entity, with the abbeys joined in loose federation. Cistercian nuns (founded in the 12th cent.) have rules and customs paralleling those of the monks; they lead contemplative lives in complete seclusion from the world. A 17th-century reform of Cistercian nuns produced the remarkable development of PORT-ROYAL. Famous Cistercian abbeys include Cîteaux, Clairvaux, Fountains, Rievaulx, and Alcobaça. See A. J. Luddy, *The Order of Cîteaux* (1932); Louis Bouyer, *The Cistercian Heritage* (tr. 1958); M. B. Pennington, ed., *The Cistercian Spirit* (1970).

Citadel, The—The Military College of South Carolina, at Charleston; state supported; primarily for men; chartered 1842 as The Citadel, opened 1843. From 1882 to 1910 it was named the South Carolina Military Academy. The cadets are subject to military regulations.

Cîteaux: see CISTERCIANS.

Cithaeron (sĭthē'rən), Gr. *Kithairón*, mountain range, c.10 mi (16 km) long, central Greece, between Boeotia in the north and Attica in the south. It rises to 4,623 ft (1,409 m). The range was the scene of many events in Greek mythology and was especially sacred to Dionysius.

cithara: see KITHARA.

cithern: see CITTERN.

Citium (sĭsh'ēəm), ancient city of Cyprus, on the southeast coast, the modern Larnaca. Of Mycenaean origins, it was a major port with valuable saltworks and was an important center under Phoenician and Assyrian rulers. It is identical with the biblical KITTIM. Zeno was born there. It is also known as Cition.

citizen, member of a state, native or naturalized, who owes ALLEGIANCE to the government of the state and is entitled to certain rights. The citizen may be said to enjoy the most privileged form of NATIONALITY; he is at the furthest extreme from nonnational residents of a state (see ALIEN), but he may also be distinguished from nationals with a subject or servile status (e.g., slaves or serfs). (It should be noted, however, that in Great Britain and some other constitutional monarchies a citizen is called a subject.) The term *citizen* originally designated the inhabitant of a town. In ancient Greece property owners in the CITY-STATES were citizens and, as such, might vote and were subject to taxation and military service. Citizenship in the Roman Empire was at first limited to the residents of the city of Rome and was then extended in A.D. 212 to all free inhabitants of the empire. Under feudalism in Europe the concept of national citizenship disappeared. In time, however, city dwellers purchased the immunity of their cities from feudal dues, thereby achieving a privileged position and a power in local government; these rights were akin to those of citizenship and supplied much of the content of later legislation respecting citizenship. Modern concepts of national citizenship were first developed during the American and French revolutions. Today each country determines what class of persons are its citizens. In some countries citizenship is determined according to the *jus sanguinis* [Lat., = law of blood], whereby a legitimate child takes its citizenship from its father and an illegitimate child from its mother. In some countries the *jus soli* [Lat., = law of the soil] governs, and citizenship is determined by place of birth. These divergent systems may lead to conflicts that often result in dual nationality or loss of citizenship (statelessness). Although the Constitution of the United States, as written in 1787, uses the word *citizen* and empowers Congress to enact uniform NATURALIZATION laws, the term was not defined until the adoption (1868) of the FOURTEENTH AMENDMENT, which gave citizenship to former Negro slaves. As this amendment indicates, the United States generally follows the *jus soli*. However, Congress has also recognized, subject to strict rules, the principle of *jus sanguinis* so that children born of American parents abroad are citizens during their minority and can retain this citizenship at majority if they meet certain conditions. Until the 1940s the United States recognized several classes of nationals who were not citizens, e.g., Filipinos and Puerto Ricans. Today, however, all U.S. nationals are citizens. The United States recognizes the right of voluntary EXTRADITION, and in 1967 the Supreme Court ruled that citizenship can be lost only if freely and expressly renounced; Congress does not have the power to take it away.

citrange (sĭ'trənj): see ORANGE.

citric acid or **2-hydroxy-1,2,3-propanetricarboxylic acid,** $HO_2CCH_2C(OH)(CO_2H)CH_2CO_2H$, an organic carboxylic acid containing three CARBOXYL GROUPS; it is a solid at room temperature, melts at 153°C, and decomposes at higher temperatures. It is responsible for the tart taste of various fruits in which it occurs, e.g., lemons, limes, oranges, pineapples, and gooseberries. It can be extracted from the juice of citrus fruits by adding calcium oxide (lime) to form calcium citrate, an insoluble precipitate that can be collected by filtration; the citric acid can be recovered from its calcium salt by adding sulfuric acid. It is obtained also by fermentation of glucose with the aid of the mold *Aspergillus niger* and can be obtained synthetically from acetone or glycerol. Citric acid is used in soft drinks and in laxatives and cathartics. Its salts, the citrates, have many uses, e.g., ferric ammonium citrate is used in making BLUEPRINT paper. Sour salt, used in cooking, is citric acid.

citric acid cycle, series of chemical reactions carried out in the living cell; in most higher animals, including man, it is essential for the oxidative METABOLISM of GLUCOSE and other simple sugars. The breakdown of glucose to carbon dioxide and water is a complex set of chemical interconversions called carbohydrate CATABOLISM, and the citric acid cycle is the second of three major stages in the process, occuring between GLYCOLYSIS and oxidative PHOSPHORYLATION. This cycle is also known as the Krebs cycle, in recognition of the German chemist Hans Krebs, whose research into the cellular utilization of glucose contributed greatly to the modern understanding of this aspect of metabolism. The common designation for this series of reactions, citric acid cycle, is derived from the first product generated by the sequence of conversions, i.e., CITRIC ACID. The reactions are seen to comprise a cycle inasmuch as citric acid is both the first product and the final reactant, being regenerated at the conclusion of one complete set of chemical rearrangements. Citric acid is a so-called tricarboxylic acid, containing three carboxyl groups (COOH). Hence the citric acid cycle is sometimes referred to as the tricarboxylic acid (TCA) cycle. The citric acid cycle begins with the condensation of one molecule of a compound called oxaloacetic acid and one molecule of acetyl CoA (a derivative of coenzyme A; see COENZYME). The acetyl portion of acetyl CoA is derived from pyruvic acid, which is produced by the degradation of glucose in glycolysis. After condensation, the oxaloacetic acid and acetyl CoA react to produce citric acid, which serves as a substrate for seven distinct enzyme-catalyzed reactions that occur in sequence and proceed with the formation of seven intermediate compounds, including succinic acid, fumaric acid, and malic acid. Malic acid is converted to oxaloacetic acid, which, in turn, reacts with yet another molecule of acetyl CoA, thus producing citric acid, and the cycle begins again. Each turn of the citric acid cycle produces, simultaneously, two molecules of carbon dioxide and eight atoms of hydrogen as by-products. The carbon dioxide generated is an ultimate end product of glucose breakdown and is removed from the cell by the blood. The hydrogen atoms are donated as hydride ions to the system of electron transport molecules, which allow for oxidative phosphorylation. In most higher plants, in certain microorganisms, such as the bacterium *Escherichia coli*, and in the algae, the citric acid cycle is modified to a form called the glyoxylate cycle, so named because of the prominent intermediate, glyoxylic acid.

Citrine, Walter McLennan Citrine, Baron (sĭtrēn'), 1887–, English trade union leader. An electrician, he became district secretary of the electrical trade union in 1914 and rose to be general secretary of the Trades Union Congress in 1926, president of the International Federation of Trades Unions in 1928, and president of the World Trade Union Conference in 1945. A skillful organizer, he led the conservative wing in labor and became powerful in the Labour government of Clement Attlee. He was created baron in 1946 and was chairman of the Central Electricity Authority (1947–57). His writings include *My Finnish Diary* (1940), *In Russia Now* (1942), and *British Trade Unions* (1942). See his autobiography, *Two Careers* (1967).

citron (sĭt'rən), name for a tree (*Citrus medica*) of the family Rutaceae (ORANGE family), and for its fruit, the earliest of the CITRUS FRUITS to be introduced to Europe from the Orient. The small evergreen tree is now cultivated commercially in the Mediterranean region and, to a lesser extent, in the West Indies, Florida, and California. The large fruit has a rough and furrowed surface and a thin outer rind of yellowish-green color. The inner rind is thick, white, and tender, and the pulp is small and acid. The juice is sometimes used as a beverage or syrup. The rind, candied and preserved, is used in confectionery and cookery. The name is also applied to a small variety of watermelon with a thick rind, used to make preserves. Citron is classified in the division MAGNOLIOPHYTA, class Magnoliopsida, order Sapindales, family Rutaceae.

citronella, common name for a grass, *Cymbopogon nardus*, the source of oil of citronella, used in perfumes and soaps and as an insect repellent. The plant, with bluish green, lemon-scented leaves, is cultivated in Java and Sri Lanka. Citronella is classified in the division MAGNOLIOPHYTA, class Liliatae, order Cyperales, family Gramineae.

citrus fruits, widely used edible fruits of plants belonging to *Citrus* and related genera of the family Rutaceae (ORANGE family). Included are the tangerine, citrange, tangelo, orange, pomelo, GRAPEFRUIT, LEMON, LIME, CITRON, and KUMQUAT. Almost all the species bearing edible fruits are small trees native to SE Asia and the East Indies. The citron was introduced to the Mediterranean area from the Orient before Christian times; the others were spread chiefly by the Arabs during the Middle Ages. Introduced throughout Europe during the Crusades, they were brought by Portuguese and Spanish explorers to the West Indies, whence they were introduced into North and South America. Commercially they are now the most important group of tropical and subtropical fruits in the world. The fruits are rich in vitamin C (ascorbic acid), various fruit acids (especially CITRIC ACID), and fruit sugar. The rind, which contains numerous oil glands, and the fragrant blossoms of some species are also a source of essential oils used for perfumes and similar products. See H. J. Webber and L. D. Batchelor, ed., *The Citrus Industry* (2 vol., 1943–48); H. H. Hume, *Citrus Fruits* (rev. ed. 1957); J. T. Hopkins, *Fifty Years of Citrus* (1960).

Città Vecchia (chĕt-tä' vĕk'kyä) [Ital.,=old city], **Città Notabile,** or **Notabile** (nōtä'bēlä), Maltese **Mdina** (əmdē'nä), town, central Malta. It was the capital of Malta until supplanted by VALLETTA (1570). The town has a large 17th-century cathedral, the old palace of the grand masters of the Knights of Malta (Knights Hospitalers), and catacombs, some of which are pre-Christian.

cittern (sĭt'ərn), stringed musical instrument of the guitar family having an oval body, a flat back, and a fretted neck (see FRETTED INSTRUMENT). Its strings, made of wire and varying in number, were plucked.

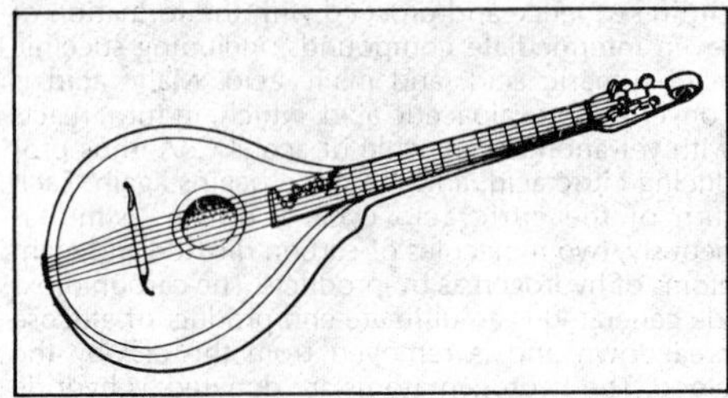

Cittern

It was first made in the Middle Ages and at that time was usually called citole or sitole. The name *cittern* was given it in the 16th cent. in England, where, as in all western Europe, it was very popular until the early part of the 18th cent. It has also been called cister, cistre, cithern, cithren, citharen, cetera, cither, cithara, gittern, and sittron.

city, densely populated urban center, larger than a village or a town, whose inhabitants are engaged primarily in commerce and industry. In the legal sense, in the United States a city is an incorporated municipality. Cities have appeared in diverse cultures, e.g., among the Aztecs, Maya, and Inca, in China and India, and in Mesopotamia and Egypt. In all these civilizations the cities were the centers of internal change and development. The history of ancient Europe is that of the Greek cities and of Rome (see CITY-STATE). From the decline of Rome the cities were in eclipse, and in Western Europe their role as centers of learning and the arts passed to the monasteries. The 11th cent. saw the resurgence of vigorous cities, first in Italy and then in northern Europe, due mainly to a revival of trade; by the 13th cent., with the decline of feudalism, the dynamic life of the Middle Ages was centered in the cities. From that time dates the importance of the great modern cities, e.g., Milan, London, Paris, and the Hanseatic cities. The giant modern city is a product of the Industrial Revolution, which introduced large-scale manufacturing. Sheer size made old problems of urban life acute; some of them, such as sanitation, utilities, and distribution, have been better solved than others, such as HOUSING and transport. As urban life came to furnish more remunerative and varied employment opportunities, rural populations increasingly were attracted, and by the 20th cent. some nations were faced with shortages of agricultural workers. Among movements to reform urban life some aim at abolishing cities as known today; this is the tradition exemplified by William Blake, Henry Thoreau, William Morris, Eric Gill, and Lewis Mumford. There are also less radical designs, like rational city planning and the development of rapid transit to distant suburbs. There have been many reforms aimed at restoring community life for the rootless strangers so frequent in modern cities; such is a common function of settlement houses, community centers, and other philanthropic and cooperative enterprises. Statistical study of cities is difficult, because figures are usually given by political units and rarely is an entire urban area a single, exclusive political unit. Cities are often complex, with subcities within them; e.g., the Newark area falls inside the New York metropolis. The word *megalopolis* is sometimes used to describe the great swath of communities stretching N and S of New York City from Boston to Washington, D.C. In Great Britain the term *conurbation* refers to a cluster of urban areas such as the one centered in London. There are similar complexes of cities in Asia, notably that of WU-HAN in China. See CITY GOVERNMENT; LOCAL GOVERNMENT. See Henry Pirenne, *Medieval Cities* (tr. 1925, repr. 1956); Gustave Glotz, *The Greek City and Its Institutions* (tr. 1929, repr. 1965); Max Weber, *The City* (tr. 1958); Otis Duncan et al., *Metropolis and Region* (1960); Lewis Mumford, *The City in History* (1961); P. M. Hauser, ed., *The Study of Urbanization* (1965); Jane Jacobs, *The Economy of Cities* (1969); Stephan Thernstrom and Richard Sennett, ed., *Nineteenth-Century Cities* (1969); W. A. Robson and D. E. Regan, ed., *Great Cities of the World* (3d ed., 2 vol., 1972); D. R. Gordon, *City Limits* (1973).

City College of the City University of New York; coeducational; est. 1847 as the Free Academy; called the College of the City of New York (CCNY) 1866–1929 (see NEW YORK, CITY UNIVERSITY OF). It includes schools of education, liberal arts, and technology. Its former school of business administration became BARUCH COLLEGE in 1968. Residents of New York City are admitted free to the baccalaureate program.

city government, political administration of urban areas. The English tradition of incorporating urban units (cities, boroughs, villages, towns) and allowing them freedom in most local matters is general in the United States (see CITY; LOCAL GOVERNMENT). The traditional U.S. city government had a mayor and council, whose members (aldermen) represented districts (wards). As the complexity of urban life increased in the 19th cent., the old system became less efficient: problems included overlapping of old offices with new, poor methods of accounting and taxation, and much blatant graft. Hence there arose movements for municipal reform, which have become a recurrent feature of American political life. They have familiarized Americans with a gallery of such political figures as William M. TWEED of New York City, Frank HAGUE of Jersey City, and William Hale THOMPSON of Chicago (see BOSSISM). Although the urban political machine has, in most cities, lost its former power, the traditional type of city government, also known as the independent executive type, remains the most common urban governmental form. It is often subdivided into the strong mayor type (e.g., New York City) and the weak mayor-strong council type (e.g., Los Angeles). Reform efforts, however, have resulted in the development of two fairly widespread alternative governmental types. The commission form has a board, both legislative and administrative, usually elected nonpartisan and at large. First adopted by Galveston, Texas, (1901), this system achieved great popularity in the early 1900s, but many cities (e.g., Buffalo and New Orleans) later abandoned it. The city manager plan gives the administration to one professional nonpolitical director. The system has gained in popularity; notable examples are in Staunton, Va., the first (1908), and Cincinnati, Ohio. A perennial problem of U.S. urban government is the division of urban areas among several independent city governments, survivals of old separate communities. The Eastern metropolises all provide examples, aggravated in some (e.g., New York City and Philadelphia), where state lines run through the heart of the metropolitan area. Attempts at efficiency have produced such organizations as the Port Authority of New York and New Jersey, a corporation set up by joint action of New York state and New Jersey, and assigned specific powers formerly held by local governments. Another problem besetting city government is the migration of middle-class families to the suburban areas, thus shrinking the tax base and financial resources of the cities. In the rest of the English-speaking world and wherever else there is much local self-government, American forms and problems are paralleled. Elsewhere, as typically in France, the local officers, albeit elected mayor and councillors, are largely figureheads, serving mainly to carry out the regulations of the central bureaucracy. See C. M. Kneier, *City Governments in the United States* (3d ed. 1957); L. I. Ruchelman, *Big City Mayors* (1969); C. R. Adrian, *Governing Urban America* (4th ed. 1972). W. A. Robson and D. E. Regan, eds., *Great Cities of the World* (2 vol., 1972).

city manager: see CITY GOVERNMENT.

City of David, epithet of BETHLEHEM, the birthplace of David, and of JERUSALEM, his capital.

city of refuge: see SANCTUARY.

City of Refuge National Historical Park: see NATIONAL PARKS AND MONUMENTS (table).

city planning, process of planning for the improvement of urban centers in order to provide healthy and safe living conditions, efficient transport and communication, adequate public facilities, and aesthetic surroundings. Planning that also includes outlying communities and highways is termed regional planning. Many ancient cities were built from definite plans. The fundamental feature of the plans of Babylon, Nineveh, and the cities of ancient Greece and of China was a geographical pattern of main streets running north and south and east and west, with a public square or forum in the center. This gridiron plan was also followed by the Romans, as in Lincoln and Chester in England; in all their towns the Romans emphasized drainage and water supply and practiced zoning. In medieval cities, built with military security in mind, the only relief from the extremely narrow streets was the space formed by municipal and church squares. The living conditions of the poorer citizens were given little attention. With the Renaissance came the truly monumental views—wide avenues and long approaches creating vistas of handsome buildings. The new aim is seen first in special sections of a city, such as Michelangelo's grouping on the Capitoline at Rome and Bernini's piazza of St. Peter's. In most European cities through the 17th and 18th cent. there was fragmentary replanning of medieval streets. After the fire of 1666 in London, Sir Christopher WREN devised a superb plan for a complete rebuilding of the city, but the plan unfortunately was not carried out. In the 18th cent., Mannheim and Karlsruhe, Germany, were laid out geometrically; Emmanuel Héré planned Nancy, France; John Wood produced grand architectural streets and squares at Bath; and the new part of Edinburgh was laid out. In the early 19th cent. John Nash planned certain sections of London; central Vienna was improved; and Baron HAUSSMAN remodeled Paris to produce the celebrated boulevard system with its spokes-and-hub design. Legislation that enabled cities to make and carry out planning designs was enacted earlier in Europe than in the United States. Such laws were passed in Italy in 1865, in Sweden in 1874, and in Prussia and Great Britain in 1875. Planning in Great Britain was especially concerned with slum elimination; its greatest exponent was Sir Patrick GEDDES. At the turn of the century Sir Ebenezer HOWARD was the founder of the modern garden city movement. The first English GARDEN CITY, Letchworth, was begun in 1903. In the United States, early New England towns, formally disposed along wide elm-lined central roadways or commons, exhibit a conscious planning. Annapolis, Md., Philadelphia, and Paterson, N.J., were built after plans; but the most celebrated example is the city of Washington D.C., laid out according to the plan devised (1971) by Pierre Charles L'ENFANT, under the supervision of George Washington and Thomas Jefferson—a rectangular plan with diagonal main thoroughfares superimposed and the Capital as the central feature. In the 19th cent. Frederick Law OLMSTED was a pioneer in city planning, especially in developing parks. State legislation enabling cities to appoint planning commissions and in some cases giving them authority to carry out the plans began in Pennsylvania in 1891. The work of Daniel Hudson Burnham for the World's Columbian Exposition in Chicago, 1893, was a stimulus to city planning, and Burnham, with Edward Bennett, drew up a plan for Chicago, much of which was put into execution. In 1901 a commission composed of Burnham, Charles Follen McKim, and Frederick Law Olmsted, Jr., devised a scheme for the modern development and beautification of Washington, D.C., adhering to L'Enfant's original plan as a basis for all new operations. A wide influence on planning in U.S. cities was exerted by the ZONING laws adopted in New York City in 1916, which controlled the uses of each district in the city and regulated the areas and heights of buildings in relation to street width. The important Regional Survey of New York and Environs, completed in 1929, took into consideration legal and social factors as well as internal transit problems and various modes of approach to the metropolitan area. Governmental efforts to provide employment during the depression of the 1930s led to the building (under the Federal Resettlement Administration) of three experimental model communities—Greenbelt, Md., Greendale, Wis., and Greenhills, Ohio. Among the many subsequent planned communities, built by private developers are Columbia, Md., and Reston, Va. The increase of traffic and crowding together of tall buildings have crippled the street plans of many cities—especially U.S. cities that have been handicapped by their rectangular or checkerboard layouts. Contemporary examples of planned cities include BRASÍLIA, the federal capital of Brazil; ROTTERDAM, main seaport of the Netherlands, and CHANDIGARH, the joint capital of the Indian states of Hariana and Punjabi Suba. In the larger U.S. cities, physical deterioration, crowding, and complex socioeconomic factors have produced vast slums. Most urban renewal programs of the mid-20th cent. were aimed at clearing these slums through the demolition of decayed buildings and the construction of low-income and middle-income housing projects. It was found, however, that the mere replacement of old buildings with new structures did not eliminate slum conditions. In contrast to traditional planning, which concentrated on improving the physical aspects of buildings and streets, modern city planning is increasingly concerned with the social and economic aspects of city living. The process of city planning is a highly complex, step-by-step procedure, usually involving a series of surveys and studies, development of a land-use plan and transportation plan, preparation of a budget, and approval of a unified master plan by various agencies or legislative bodies. City planners are usually part of an urban planning board or governmental agency that must take into account the characteristics and long-range welfare of the people of a particular urban community—their employment opportunities, income levels, need for transportation, schools, shopping areas, hospitals, parks and recreational facilities. The city planner is faced with the problems of traffic, congestion, and pollution; he must also consider the availability of police, fire, and sanitation services, the limitations posed by zoning and other regulations, and the problems of funding. In recent years, residents of many communities have demanded greater participation in the planning of their own neighborhoods, and some planners have worked closely together with community groups during various stages of the planning process. See Jane Jacobs, *The Death and Life of Great American Cities* (1961, repr. 1969); Lewis Mumford, *The City in History* (1961, repr. 1966); J. W. Reps, *The Making of Urban America* (1965); E. N. Bacon, *Design of Cities* (1966); Frederick Gibberd, *Town Design* (5th ed. 1967); W. H. Whyte, *The Last Landscape* (1968); Françoise Choay, *The Modern City: Planning in the Nineteenth Century* (1969); Hila Colman, *City Planning* (1971).

city-state, in ancient Greece, autonomous political unit consisting of a city and surrounding countryside. The Greek word *polis* meant both city and city-state. From the beginning of Greek history to its climax in the 5th and 4th cent. B.C., the Greeks were organized into city-states, of which there were several hundred. Since the city-state was autonomous, different states—and the same state at different times—had a variety of governments, ranging from absolute monarchy to pure democracy. Only citizens participated in the government, or in the religious, social, and economic life of the city-state, and citizenship was limited to those born of citizen parents. A large proportion of the population of the city-state consisted of slaves. The degree of participation by the citizens in government was often limited by class distinctions. The government usually consisted of an assembly and council; the former predominated in democracies, the latter in oligarchies. Although the various city-states combined into religious or military federations under the hegemony of one city-state, these never endured for long, and Greece was left open to foreign attack by large centralized states to which it eventually became subject. See A. E. Zimmern, *The Greek Commonwealth* (5th rev. ed., 1931, repr. 1973); Gustave Glotz, *The Greek City and Its Institutions* (ed. by N. Mallinson, 1930, repr. 1969); Victor Ehrenberg, *The Greek State* (2d rev. ed., 1969, repr. 1972).

Ciudad [Span., = city]. For cities whose names begin thus but are not so listed, see under the following name; e.g.; for Ciudad Juárez, see JUÁREZ.

Ciudad Bolívar (syōōthäth' bōlē'vär), city (1970 est. pop. 110,000), capital of Bolívar state, E Venezuela, an inland port on the Orinoco River. It is the commercial center of the eastern llanos, the Orinoco basin, and the GUIANA HIGHLANDS. Wood products and leather are produced, and hides, cattle, and gold are exported. The city was founded in 1764 and called Angostura. The congress of Angostura (1819) made Simon BOLÍVAR president of Venezuela and later in the same year decreed the formation of the republic of Greater Colombia, with Bolívar as president. The city's Angostura suspension bridge (2,336 ft/712 m long; completed 1967) is the longest in South America.

Ciudad Guzmán: see GUZMÁN, Mexico.

Ciudad Juárez: see JUÁREZ, Mexico.

Ciudad Porfirio Díaz, Mexico: see PIEDRAS NEGRAS.

Ciudad Real (thyōōthäth' räăl'), city (1970 pop. 41,708), capital of Ciudad Real prov., central Spain, in New Castile, on a fertile plain between the Jabalón and Guadiana rivers. It is an agricultural market place, with farm-related industries. Ciudad Real was founded by Alfonso X of Castile in the 13th cent.; during the Peninsular War, the French defeated (1809) the Spanish in a battle nearby. The city preserves some of its medieval flavor; it has several notable Gothic churches.

Ciudad Rodrigo (rôthrē'gō), town (1970 pop. 13,320), Salamanca prov., central Spain, in León, on the Agueda River near the Portuguese border. It is a trade center for a cattle-raising area. Originally a Roman settlement, the town was abandoned and reestablished in the 12th cent. as a fortress. It has preserved its medieval flavor and has been declared a historic monument.

civet (sĭv'ət) or **civet cat,** any of a large group of mostly nocturnal mammals of the Old World family Viverridae (civet family), which also includes the MONGOOSE. Civets are not true cats, but the civet family is related to the cat family (Felidae). Most civets have catlike bodies, long tails, and weasellike faces. Their fur may be gray or brown, and may be marked in various patterns. All civets have scent-producing glands, located in a double pouch near the genitals. The fatty yellow secretion of these glands has a distinctive musky odor used for territorial marking. Commercially, this substance is known as civet and is used as a perfume fixative. Civet can be removed from captive animals every 14 to 20 days. Some civet species are hunted for their fur. The ground-living, or true, civets form a distinctive group within the family; these animals have a highly carnivorous diet. Most have dark spots and ringed tails. They include several Asian species (genus *Viverra*) and one African species (*Civettictis civetta*). Best known is the Indian civet, *V. zibetha,* of S Asia, from which most of the civet for perfume is derived. It has tawny fur with black spots and black bands on the tail. It is about 30 in. (76 cm) long, excluding the 20-in. (42-cm) tail, and about 15 in. (38 cm) high at the shoulder; it weighs up to 25 lb (11 kg). Its musk glands are greatly enlarged. Some of the ground-living civets are called linsangs and genets. The palm civets form another distinct group within the civet family. These are arboreal, largely fruit-eating animals of Africa and Asia; they are classified in several genera. The North American spotted skunk is sometimes popularly called civet but is not closely related to civets. Civets are classified in the phylum CHORDATA, subphylum Vertebrata, class Mammalia, order Carnivora, family Viverridae.

civics, branch of learning that treats of the relationship between the citizen and his society and state, originally called civil government. In an educational sense it involves passing the tradition of the community to new generations with a view to establishing civic allegiance. With the large immigration into the United States in the latter half of the 19th cent., civics became a subject in the secondary schools and colleges through the influence of the National Education Association and other organizations.

Civil Aeronautics Board (CAB), independent agency of the executive branch of the U.S. Federal government. It was established by Congress in 1938 as the Civil Aeronautics Administration and charged with the encouragement and development of civil aviation and the formulation of economic and safety rules in air traffic. The Federal Aviation Act of 1958 transferred the safety-rulemaking function to the Federal Aviation Administration. The CAB authorizes all carriers and air routes, must approve all rates, and passes on any agreement between airlines. Its five members are appointed by the President with the consent of the Senate.

civil defense, nonmilitary activities designed to protect civilians and their property from enemy actions in time of war. A civil defense program usually includes measures taken during peace (e.g., building home shelters or air raid warning practice), measures to warn civilians of an impending attack, to protect them during attack, and to save their lives and property after attack. Civil defense grew in proportion to the use of aircraft in modern warfare; thus, warning and protection systems were primitive in World War I and greatly improved in World War II, when both sides engaged in the strategic bombing of civilian populations. After World War II the existence of nuclear weapons, the development of long-range bombers and missiles, and the ever-present possibility of war encouraged the establishment of comprehensive civil defense systems. The principal U.S. civil defense agency was established by executive order in 1950, and in 1961 civil defense functions were transferred to the Defense Dept. The civil defense program in the United States has included the formulation of rescue and survival plans, the stockpiling of food and equipment, and the encouragement of home shelter construction. Early warning of attack is provided by chains of radar stations built across Canada. Opinion in the United States has been divided over the value of civil defense programs. Opponents of civil defense have maintained that, given the destructiveness of modern weapons, warning and shelter systems are useless and merely encourage war hysteria. Proponents of civil defense have asserted that, since a major danger from a nuclear attack is radioactive fallout, an adequate shelter program can save the lives of a large portion of the population. With the beginnings of a détente with the Soviet Union and the People's Republic of China in the 1970s, interest in civil defense in the United States, which peaked at the height of the cold war, had begun to decline. However, most industrialized countries still maintain some form of civil defense.

civil engineering: see ENGINEERING.

Civilian Conservation Corps (CCC), established in 1933 by the U.S. Congress as a measure of the New Deal program. The CCC provided work and vocational training for unemployed single young men through conserving and developing the country's natural resources. At its peak in 1935, the organization had more than 500,000 members in over 2,600 camps. These were usually operated by the War Dept., but the men were not subject to military control. In 1939 the CCC was made part of the Federal Security Agency. Beginning in 1940, greater emphasis was placed on projects aiding national defense. Against President Franklin D. Roosevelt's request, Congress abolished the CCC in 1942.

Civilis (Julius Civilis) (sĭvī'lĭs), fl. A.D. 70, Batavian chief who chose the unsettled period at the fall of NERO to raise a revolt in Germany, which quickly spread to Gaul (A.D. 69–A.D. 70). Its chief effect was to remove from VITELLIUS, who was struggling with VESPASIAN, any real support from Gaul. After Vespasian became emperor, he sent the Roman general Cerialis to put down the revolt. The rebels were treated with great consideration, and many entered the Roman service. Civilis' fate, however, is unknown.

civilization, culture with a relatively high degree of elaboration and technical development. The term *civilization* also designates that complex of cultural elements that first appeared in human history between 8,000 and 6,000 years ago. At that time, on the basis of agriculture, stock-raising, and metallurgy, intensive occupational specialization began to appear in the river valleys of SW Asia. Writing appeared, as well as relatively dense urban aggregations that accommodated administrators, traders, and other specialists. The specific characteristics of civilization are: food production (plant and animal domestication), metallurgy, a high degree of occupational specialization, writing, and the growth of cities. Such characteristics have emerged in several parts of the prehistoric world: Mesopotamia, Egypt, China, Greece, Rome, India, Highland Peru and Bolivia, the valley of Mexico, and Guatemala. They were never fully realized in America north of the Rio Grande prior to European colonization.

civil law. As used in this article, the term *civil law* signifies a modern legal system based upon ROMAN LAW, as distinguished from COMMON LAW. In common usage, however, it also means the rules that govern private legal affairs; in this sense civil law contrasts with public law and criminal law. With a few exceptions, the countries on the continent of Europe, the countries that were former colonies of such continental powers (e.g., the Latin American countries), and other countries that have recently adopted Western legal systems (e.g., Japan) follow civil law. It is also the foundation for the law of Quebec prov. and of Louisiana. Modern countries that do not adhere to the civil law (this includes all states of the United States except Louisiana) for the most part were founded by England and apply the system of common law prevailing there. The law that had been in force throughout the Roman Empire when it controlled most of Europe and the Middle East was to some extent supplanted by GERMANIC LAWS when Germanic tribes carried out their great conquests. The principle of personal (as opposed to territorial) law was observed by the invaders, however, and thus the former Roman subjects and their descendants were permitted to follow the Roman law (*leges romanorum*) in their affairs with one another. The great CORPUS JURIS CIVILIS of Justinian, complied in the 6th cent. and in use in the Byzantine Empire, served also to keep the old law alive. The medieval church, too, was an important guardian of Roman law, for much of the law used by the church was based upon Roman principles and concepts. Germanic law, although at first adequate, did not have legal concepts that suited the commercial requirements of the late Middle Ages, and there was then heavy borrowing of Roman ideas. As part of a concurrent revival of interest in classical culture, the late 11th and the 12th cent. saw the resumption of systematic study of Roman law, chiefly in N Italy (notably at Bologna, where IRNERIUS gave the first lectures in Roman law), in S France, and in Spain. Extensive glosses and commentaries on the *Corpus Juris Civilis* and on other classical texts were produced. Through the agency of scholars and of judges trained in Roman law principles, these principles (though stongly modified) came to be observed in national courts in all classes of legal disputes, although for a long time courts of local jurisdiction continued to enforce customary law. Scholars of Roman law enjoyed increasing prestige; by 1500 the *Corpus Juris Civilis* had become the basis of legal science throughout Western Europe. The next step, emulating the systematizing of Justinian, was to state these principles in exact, ordered form, i.e., as a CODE. The CODE NAPOLÉON (1804), the most famous of such works, had many successors. In England there was some interest in Roman law during the Renaissance; there, however, the early centralization of the legal system and the existence of an independent class of lawyers with an interest in the law as administered in the courts ensured the triumph of the common law. Nevertheless, civil law influenced the common law in the fields of admiralty law, testamentary law, and domestic relations, and civil law became the basis for the whole system of EQUITY. The tendency of civil law is to create unified legal systems by working out with maximum precision the conclusions to be drawn from basic principles. The civil law judge is bound by the provisions of the written law, and not by previous judicial interpretations. The traditional civil law decision states the applicable provision from the code or from a relevant STATUTE and the judgment is based upon that provision. See A. T. Von Mehren, *The Civil Law System* (1957); A. N. Yiannopoulos, ed., *Civil Law in the Modern World* (1965).

civil liberty: see LIBERTY.

civil rights, rights that a nation's inhabitants enjoy by law. A distinction is usually recognized between civil liberties and civil rights. The former refers to negative restraints upon government; civil rights pertain to positive acts of government designed to protect persons against arbitrary or discriminatory treatment by government or individuals. The charter of the United Nations states as a central goal the expansion of both civil liberties and civil rights. In the United States civil rights are usually thought of in terms of the specific rights guaranteed in the Constitution: freedom of religion, of speech, and of the press, and the rights to due process of law and to equal protection under the law. Since the Civil War, much of the concern over civil rights in the United States has focused on efforts to extend these rights more fully to blacks. The first legislative attempts to grant blacks a political and legal status equal to that of whites were the Civil Rights Acts of 1866, 1870, 1871, and 1875. Those acts bestowed upon blacks such freedoms as the right to sue and be sued, to give evidence, and to hold real and personal property. The 1866 act was of dubious constitutionality and was reenacted in 1870 only after the passage of the FOURTEENTH AMENDMENT. The third Civil Rights Act (1871) attempted to guarantee to the blacks those social rights that were still withheld. It penalized innkeepers, proprietors of public establishments, and owners of public conveyances for discriminating against blacks in accommodations, but was invalidated by a decision of the Supreme Court in 1883 on the ground that these were not properly civil rights and hence not a field for Federal legislation. After the Civil Rights Act of 1875 there was no more Federal legislation in this field until the Civil Rights Acts of 1957 and 1960, although several states passed their own civil rights laws. The struggle to expand civil rights for blacks has been led by the National Association for the Advancement of Colored People, the Congress of Racial Equality, the Urban League, the Southern Christian Leadership Conference, and others. The civil rights movement, led especially by Martin Luther King, Jr., in the late 1950s and 1960s and the executive leadership provided by President Lyndon Baines Johnson, encouraged the passage of the most comprehensive civil rights legislation to date, the Civil Rights Act of 1964; it prohibited discrimination for reason of color, race, religion, or national origin in places of public accommodation covered by interstate commerce, i.e., restaurants, hotels, motels, and theaters. Besides dealing with the desegregation of public schools, the act, in Title VII, forbade discrimination in employment (Title VII also prohibited discrimination on the basis of sex). In 1965 the Voting Rights Act was passed, which placed Federal observers at polls to ensure equal voting rights, and the Civil Rights Act of 1968 dealt with housing and real estate discrimination. In addition to congressional action on civil rights, there has been action by other branches of the government. The most notable of these were the Supreme Court decisions in 1954 and 1955 declaring racial segregation in public schools unconstitutional, and the court's rulings in 1955 banning segregation in publicly financed parks, playgrounds, and golf courses. In the 1960s women began to organize around the issue of their civil rights. By the early 1970s over 40 states had passed equal pay laws, and in 1972 the Senate adopted an equal rights amendment; if ratified by 38 states it would prohibit all discrimination based on sex. See A. J. M. Milne, *Freedom and Rights* (1968); Chester Antieau, *Federal Civil Rights Acts* (1971); A. L. Del Russo, *International Protection of Human Rights* (1971); H. J. Abraham, *Freedom and the Courts* (1972); T. R. Brooks, *The Walls Come Tumbling Down* (1974).

civil service, entire body of those employed in the civil administration as distinct from the military and excluding elected officials. The term was used in designating the British administration of India, and its first application elsewhere was in 1854 in England. Modern civil service personnel are usually chosen by examination and promoted on the basis of merit ratings. In democratic nations recruitment and advancement procedures are designed to divorce the civil service from political patronage. The use of competitive examinations to select civil officials was begun in China during the Han dynasty (206 B.C.–A.D. 220), and expanded to include all important positions during the Sung dynasty (960–1279; see CHINESE EXAMINATION SYSTEM). In the West, however, selection of civil administrators and staff on the basis of merit examinations is a late development. Despite important contributions to administrative structure and procedure, the Roman Empire seems to have recruited and promoted officials largely on the basis of custom and the judgement of superiors. The establishment of the modern civil service is closely associated with the decline of feudalism and the growth of national autocratic states. In Prussia, as early as the mid-17th cent., Frederick William, elector of Brandenburg, created an efficient civil administration staffed by civil servants chosen on a competitive basis. In France similar reforms preceded the Revolution, and they were the basis for the Napoleonic reforms that transformed the royal service into the civil service. Development of a professional civil service came several decades later in Great Britain and the United States. Owing doubtless in part to the spoils system so strongly established in the Jacksonian era, the United States lagged far behind other nations in standards of civil service competence and probity. Agitation for reform began shortly after the Civil War. In 1871, Congress authorized the President to prescribe regulations for admission to public service and to appoint the Civil Service Commission, which lasted only a few years. The scandals of President Grant's administration lent weight to the arguments of reformers George W. Curtis, Dorman B. EATON, and Carl SCHURZ. President Hayes favored reform and began to use competitive examinations as a basis for appointment to office. The assassination of President Garfield in 1881 by a disappointed office seeker precipitated the passage of the Pendleton Act in 1883, reestablishing the Civil Service Commission after a nine-year lapse. The commission draws up the rules governing examinations for those positions that Congress places in the classified civil service. All Presidents since Cleveland have expanded the classified list, and the great majority of Federal employees during peacetime are now classified. In 1939 the merit system was extended to sections of state administration receiving Federal grants. The Hatch Act of 1940 forbade campaign contributions by officeholders with the intention of divorcing the civil service from politics. Appointive power is shared by the President, who appoints the heads of all government departments and may remove his appointees at will; by Congress, which controls its own employees; and by the Civil Service Commission and departmental appointing officers, in whose charge are vacancies in the classified service. Important changes were made in the structure of the U.S. civil service as a result of the reports issued (1949, 1955) by the two commissions known as the Hoover Commission. The organization of the government bureaucracy was streamlined by the creation of the General Services Administration, combining the operations and activities of some 60 government agencies. Of the world's civil services, the most outstanding on several counts is still the British, extremely powerful because of its permanency, its extensive grants of power from Parliament, and its reputation for absolute honesty, although it is criticized for a lack of flexibility and for class exclusiveness in its upper ranges. A Civil Service Commission and the beginnings of a system of competitive examinations were established in Great Britain in 1855, and the influential Whitley Councils, representing both government employees and administrators in questions dealing with service conditions, were set up after World War II. British civil servants are strictly excluded from politics. In Communist nations, on the other hand, the official party and the civil service tend to interpenetrate. The secretariat of the League of Nations and of the United Nations are possible precursors of an international civil service. See W. A. Robson, *The Civil Service in Britain and France* (1956); Paul Van Riper, *History of the United States Civil Service* (1958); E. A. Kracke, *The Civil Service in Britain and France* (1968); F. C. Mosher, *Democracy and the Public Service* (1968); Alan Gartner et al., ed., *Public Service Employment* (1973).

civil time, local TIME based on Greenwich mean time. Civil time may be formally defined as mean SOLAR TIME plus 12 hr; the civil day begins at midnight, while the mean solar day begins at noon. Civil time is usually not used, since it depends on the observer's longitude; instead, STANDARD TIME, which is the same throughout a given time zone, is generally adopted.

civil war, English: see ENGLISH CIVIL WAR.

civil war, in Roman history: see MARIUS and SULLA; POMPEY and Julius CAESAR.

Civil War, in U.S. history, conflict (1861–65) between the Northern states (the Union) and the Southern states that seceded from the Union and formed the CONFEDERACY. It is generally known in the South as the War between the States and is also called the War of the Rebellion (the official Union designation), the War of Secession, and the War for Southern Independence. The name Civil War, although much criticized as inexact, is most widely accepted. It is, in fact, somewhat misleading, since the war was not a class struggle, but a sectional combat having its roots in such complex political, economic, social, and psychological elements that historians still do not agree on its basic causes. It has been characterized, in the words of William H. Seward, as the "irrepressible conflict." In another judgment the Civil War was viewed as criminally stupid, an unnecessary bloodletting brought on by arrogant extremists and blundering politicians. Both views accept the fact that in 1861 there existed a situation that, rightly or wrongly, had come to be regarded as insoluble by peaceful means. Earlier, in the days of the American Revolution and of the adoption of the Constitution, differences between North and South were dwarfed by their common interest in establishing a new nation. But sectionalism steadily grew stronger. In the 19th cent. the South remained almost completely agricultural, with an economy and a social order largely founded on Negro slavery and the plantation. These mutually dependent institutions produced the staples, especially cotton, from which the South derived its wealth. The North had its own great agricultural resources, was always more advanced commercially, and was also expanding industrially. Hostility between the two sections grew perceptibly after 1820, the year of the MISSOURI COMPROMISE, which was intended as a permanent solution to the issue in which that hostility was most clearly expressed—the question of the extension or prohibition of slavery in the Federal territories of the West. Difficulties over the tariff (which led John C. CALHOUN and South Carolina to NULLIFICATION and to an extreme STATES' RIGHTS stand) and troubles over internal improvements were also involved, but the territorial issue nearly always loomed largest. In the North moral indignation increased with the rise of the ABOLITIONISTS in the 1830s. Since Negro slavery was unadaptable to much of the territorial lands, which eventually would be admitted as free states, the South became more anxious about maintaining its position as an equal in the Union. Southerners thus strongly supported the annexation of Texas (certain to be a slave state) and the Mexican War and even agitated for the annexation of Cuba. The COMPROMISE OF 1850 marked the end of the period that might be called the era of compromise. The deaths in 1852 of Henry CLAY and Daniel WEBSTER left no leader of national stature, but only sectional spokesmen, such as W. H. SEWARD, Charles SUMNER, and Salmon P. CHASE in the North and Jefferson DAVIS and Robert TOOMBS in the South. With the KANSAS-NEBRASKA ACT (1854) and the consequent struggle over "bleeding" Kansas the factions first resorted to shooting. The South was ever alert to protect its "peculiar institution," even though many Southerners recognized slavery as an anachronism in a supposedly enlightened age. Passions aroused by arguments over the FUGITIVE SLAVE LAWS (which culminated in the DRED SCOTT CASE) and over slavery in general were further excited by the activities of the Northern abolitionist John BROWN and by the vigorous proslavery utterances of William L. YANCEY, one of the leading Southern FIRE-EATERS. The "wedges of separation" caused by slavery split large Protestant sects into Northern and Southern branches and dissolved the WHIG PARTY. Most Southern Whigs joined the DEMOCRATIC PARTY, one of the few remaining, if shaky, nationwide institutions. The new REPUBLICAN PARTY, heir to the FREE-SOIL PARTY and to the LIBERTY PARTY, was a strictly Northern phenomenon. The crucial point was reached in the presidential election of 1860, in which the Republican candidate, Abraham LINCOLN, defeated three opponents—Stephen A. DOUGLAS (Northern Democrat), John C. BRECKINRIDGE (Southern Democrat), and John BELL of the CONSTITUTIONAL UNION PARTY. Lincoln's victory was the signal for the SECESSION of South Carolina (Dec. 20, 1860), and that state was followed out of the Union by six other states—Mississippi, Florida, Alabama, Georgia, Louisiana, and Texas. Immediately the question of Federal property in these states became important, especially the forts in the harbor of Charleston, S.C. (see FORT SUMTER). The outgoing President, James BUCHANAN, a Northern Democrat who was either truckling to the Southern, proslavery wing of his party or sincerely attempting to avert war, pursued a vacillating course. At any rate the question of the forts was still unsettled when Lincoln was inaugurated, and meanwhile there had been several futile efforts to reunite the sections, notably the CRITTENDEN COMPROMISE offered by Sen. J. J. Crittenden. Lincoln resolved to hold Sumter. The new Confederate government under President Jefferson Davis and South Carolina were equally determined to oust the Federals.

Sumter to Gettysburg. When, on April 12, 1861, the Confederate commander P. G. T. BEAUREGARD, acting on instructions, ordered the firing on Fort Sumter, hostilities officially began. Lincoln immediately called for troops to be used against the seven seceding states, which were soon joined by Arkansas, North Carolina, Virginia, and Tennessee, completing the 11-state Confederacy. In the first important military campaign of the war untrained Union troops under Irvin MCDOWELL, advancing on Richmond, now the Confederate capital, were routed by equally inexperienced Confederate soldiers led by Beauregard and Joseph E. JOHNSTON in the first battle of BULL RUN (July 21, 1861). This fiasco led Lincoln to bring up George B. MCCLELLAN (1826–85), fresh from his successes in W Virginia (admitted as the new state of WEST VIRGINIA in 1863). After the retirement of Winfield SCOTT in Nov., 1861, McClellan was for a few months the chief Northern commander. The able organizer of the Army of the Potomac, he nevertheless failed in the PENINSULAR CAMPAIGN (April–July, 1862), in which Robert E. LEE succeeded the wounded Johnston as commander of the Confederate Army of Northern Virginia. Lee planned the diversion in the Shenandoah Valley, which, brilliantly executed by Thomas J. (Stonewall) JACKSON, worked perfectly. Next to Lee himself Jackson, with his famous "foot cavalry," was the South's greatest general. Lee then went on to save Richmond in the SEVEN DAYS BATTLES (June 26–July 2) and was victorious in the second battle of Bull Run (Aug. 29–30), thoroughly trouncing John POPE. However, he also failed in his first invasion of enemy territory. In September, McClellan, whom Lincoln had restored to command of the defenses of Washington, checked Lee in Maryland (see ANTIETAM CAMPAIGN). When McClellan failed to attack the Confederates as they retreated, Lincoln removed him again, permanently. Two subsequent Union advances on Richmond, the first led by Ambrose E. BURNSIDE (see FREDERICKSBURG, BATTLE OF) and the second by Joseph HOOKER (see CHANCELLORSVILLE, BATTLE OF), ended in resounding defeats (Dec. 13, 1862, and May 2–4, 1863). Although Lee lost Jackson at Chancellorsville, the victory prompted him to try another invasion of the North. With his lieutenants Richard S. EWELL, James LONGSTREET, Ambrose P. HILL, and J. E. B. (Jeb) STUART, he moved via the Shenandoah Valley into S Pennsylvania. There the Army of the Potomac, under still another new chief, George G. MEADE, rallied to stop him again in the greatest battle (July 1–3, 1863) of the war (see GETTYSBURG CAMPAIGN). In the meantime, with the vastly superior sea power built up by Secretary of the Navy Gideon WELLES, the Union had established a blockade of the Southern coast, which, though by no means completely effective, nevertheless limited the South's foreign trade to the uncertain prospects of blockade-running. In cooperation with the army the Union navy also attacked along the coasts. The forts guarding New Orleans, the largest Confederate port, fell (April 28, 1862) to a fleet under David G. FARRAGUT, and the city was occupied by troops commanded by Benjamin F. BUTLER (1818–93). The introduction of the ironclad warship (see ERICSSON, JOHN; MONITOR AND MERRIMACK) had revolutionized naval warfare, to the ultimate advantage of the industrial North. On the other hand, CONFEDERATE CRUISERS, built or bought in England (see ALABAMA CLAIMS) and captained by men such as Raphael SEMMES, destroyed or chased from the seas much of the U.S. merchant marine. Britain never formally recognized the Confederacy (neither did France) and maintained peaceful relations with the Union despite the provocation late in 1861 of the TRENT AFFAIR, which was adroitly handled by Secretary of State Seward. Charles Francis ADAMS (1807–86) at London and John BIGELOW at Paris were able diplomats, but probably more important in winning popular support for the Union in England and France was the EMANCIPATION PROCLAMATION, which Lincoln issued after Antietam. This act appeased for a time the anti-Lincoln radical Republicans in Congress, among them Benjamin F. WADE, Zachariah CHANDLER, Thaddeus STEVENS, and Henry W. DAVIS, with whom Secretary of the Treasury Salmon P. Chase and Secretary of War Edwin M. STANTON were allied. Not all Unionists were abolitionists, however, and the Emancipation Proclamation was not applied to the border slave states: Delaware, Maryland, Kentucky, and Missouri had all remained loyal. For Lincoln and kindred moderates, such as Postmaster General Montgomery BLAIR, the restoration of the Union, not the abolition of slavery, remained the principal objective of the war. The Union victories at Gettysburg and Vicksburg in July, 1863, marked a definite turning point in the war. Both sides now had seasoned, equally valiant soldiers, and in Lee and Ulysses S. GRANT each had a superior general. But the North, with its larger population and comparatively enormous industry, enjoyed a tremendous material advantage. Both sides also resorted to conscription, even though it met some resistance (see DRAFT RIOTS). Again, under Stanton, successor to Simon CAMERON, the overall administration of the Union army was more efficient. Problems of organization still remained, however, and Henry W. HALLECK continued in the difficult role of military adviser, with the title of general in chief. The Joint Congressional Committee on the Conduct of the War, organized in Dec., 1861, attempted to influence the actions as well as the appointment of Union generals (its efforts were particularly strong on behalf of Hooker). The chairman, Benjamin F. Wade, was frequently at odds with Lincoln, and the committee's investigations and high-handed actions lowered morale among the Union forces.

Grant and Sherman Lead to Victory. That the "war was won in the West" has become axiomatic. There the rivers, conveniently flowing either north (the Cumberland and the Tennessee) or south (the Mississippi), invited Union penetration, as they did not in Virginia. In Feb., 1862, the Union gunboats of Andrew H. FOOTE forced the Confederates to retire from their post FORT HENRY on the Tennessee to their stronghold on the Cumberland, FORT DONELSON. There, on Feb. 16, 1862, Grant, commanding the Army of the Tennessee, won the first great Union victory of the war, and Nashville promptly fell without a struggle. Farther down the Tennessee, Grant was lucky to escape defeat in a bloody contest (April 6–7) with Albert S. JOHNSTON and Beauregard (see SHILOH, BATTLE OF). Minor Union successes at Iuka (Sept. 19) and CORINTH (Oct. 3–4) followed, while the counterinvasion by the Confederate Army of Tennessee under Braxton BRAGG was stopped by Don Carlos BUELL at Perryville, Ky. (Oct. 8, 1862). Willian S. ROSECRANS, Buell's successor, then stalked Bragg through Tennessee, fought him to a standoff at MURFREESBORO (Dec. 21, 1862–Jan. 2, 1863), and finally, by outmaneuvering him, forced the Confederate general to withdraw S of Chattanooga. Union gunboats had cleared the upper Mississippi (see ISLAND NO. 10; FORT PILLOW), leading to the fall of Memphis on June 6, 1862. Grant's VICKSBURG CAMPAIGN, at first stalled by the raids of Confederate cavalrymen Nathan B. FORREST and Earl Van Dorn, was pressed to a victorious end in a brilliant movement in which the navy, represented by David D. PORTER, also had a hand. The Union now controlled the whole Mississippi, and the trans-Mississippi West was severed from the rest of the Confederacy. The fighting in that area (see WILSON'S CREEK; PEA RIDGE; PRAIRIE GROVE; ARKANSAS POST) had held Missouri for the Union and led to the partial conquest of Arkansas, but after the fall of Vicksburg, the war there, with the exception of the unsuccessful Union Red River expedition of Nathaniel P. BANKS and a last desperate Confederate raid into Missouri by Sterling PRICE (both in 1864), was largely confined to guerrilla activity. Back on the Georgia-Tennessee line in Sept., 1863, Bragg, having temporarily halted his retreat, severely jolted the Federals, who were saved from a complete rout by the magnificent stand of George H. THOMAS, the Rock of Chickamauga (see CHATTANOOGA CAMPAIGN). Grant, newly appointed supreme commander in the West, hurried to the scene and, with William T. SHERMAN, Hooker, and Thomas's fearless troops, drove Bragg back to Georgia (Nov. 25). Since Knoxville, occupied in September, withstood Longstreet's siege (Nov.–Dec.), all Tennessee, hotbed of Unionism, was now safely restored to the Union. In March, 1864, Lincoln, for many years an admirer of Grant, made him commander in chief. Leaving the West in Sherman's capable hands, Grant came east, took personal charge of Meade's Army of the Potomac, and engaged Lee in the WILDERNESS CAMPAIGN (May–June, 1864). Outnumbered but still spirited, the Army of Northern Virginia was slowly and painfully forced back toward Richmond, and in July the tenacious Grant began the long siege of PETERSBURG. Although Jubal A. EARLY won at MONOCACY (July 9), threatening the city of Washington, the Confederates were unable to repeat Jackson's successful diversion of 1862, and Philip H. SHERIDAN, victorious in the grand manner at CEDAR CREEK (Oct. 19), virtually ended Early's activities in the Shenandoah Valley. For his part, Sherman, opposed first by the wily Joe Johnston and then by John B. HOOD, won the ATLANTA CAMPAIGN (May–Sept., 1864). On the political front, a movement within the Republican party to shelve Lincoln had collapsed, and, with Andrew JOHNSON, his own choice for Vice President over the incumbent Hannibal HAMLIN, the President was renominated in June, 1864. The Democrats nominated McClellan, who still had a strong popular following, on an ambiguous peace platform (largely dictated by Clement L. VALLANDIGHAM, leader of the COPPERHEADS), which the ex-general repudiated. Even so Lincoln was easily reelected. After the fall of Atlanta, which had contributed to Lincoln's victory, Sherman's troops made their destructive march through Georgia. Hood had failed to draw Sherman back by invading Union-held Tennessee, and after the battle of Franklin (Nov. 30) Hood's army was almost completely annihilated by Thomas at Nashville (Dec. 15–16, 1864). Sherman presented Lincoln with the Christmas gift of Savannah, Ga., and then moved north through the Carolinas. Farragut's victory at Mobile Bay (Aug. 5, 1864) had effectively closed that port, and on Jan. 15, 1865, Wilmington, N.C., was also cut off (see FORT FISHER). After Sheridan's victory at FIVE FORKS (April 1), the Petersburg lines were breached and the Confederates evacuated Richmond (April 3). With his retreat blocked by Sheridan, Lee, wisely giving up the futile contest, surrendered to Grant at APPOMATTOX COURTHOUSE on April 9, 1865. The surviving Confederate armies also yielded when they heard of Lee's capitulation.

The New Nation. The long war was over, but for the victors the peace was marred by the assassination of Abraham Lincoln, the greatest figure of the war. The ex-Confederate states, after enduring the further unpleasantness of RECONSTRUCTION with its corruption and vindictiveness, were readmitted to the Union, which had been saved and in which slavery was now abolished. The Civil War brought death to more Americans than did any other war, including World War II. Photographs by Mathew B. BRADY and others reveal some of the horror behind the statistics. The war cost untold billions and nourished rather than canceled the hatreds and intolerance that persisted for decades. It established many of the patterns, especially a strong central government, which are now taken for granted in our national life. Virtually every battlefield, with its graves, is either a national or a state park. Monuments commemorating Civil War figures and events are conspicuous in almost all sizable Northern towns and are even more numerous in the Upper South. Notable fictional treatments of the war are Stephen Crane's *Red Badge of Courage* (1896) and Margaret Mitchell's *Gone with the Wind* (1936), and there is one outstanding work in verse—Stephen Vincent Benét's *John Brown's Body* (1928). The quantity of historical literature on the Civil War is enormous, and there is no single, adequate bibliographical guide. For bibliographies, see Allan Nevins et al., ed., *Civil War Books: A Critical Bibliography* (2 vol., 1967-69). On the causes of, and events leading up to, the war, see A. C. Cole, *The Irrepressible Conflict, 1850-1865* ("History of American Life" series, Vol. VII, 1934; rev. ed. 1938, repr. 1971); G. F. Milton, *The Eve of Conflict* (1934); A. O. Craven, *The Coming of the Civil War* (1942, new ed. 1957) and *Civil War in the Making* (1959, repr. 1968). Standard, older works on the military phase are C. C. Buel and R. U. Johnson, ed., *Battles and Leaders of the Civil War* (4 vol., 1877; new ed. 1956); J. C. Ropes, *The Story of the Civil War* (2 vol., 1898-99; completed by W. R. Livermore, 1913); Sir Frederick Maurice, *Statesmen and Soldiers of the Civil War* (1926). *R. E. Lee: A Biography* (4 vol., 1934-35) and *Lee's Lieutenants* (3 vol., 1942-44), both by Douglas Southall Freeman, and *Lincoln Finds a General* (5 vol., 1949-59), by K. P. Williams, are definitive in their respective fields. See also T. L. Livermore, *Numbers and Losses in the Civil War in America, 1861-1865* (1901, new ed. 1957, repr. 1969); J. F. Rhodes, *History of the Civil War, 1861-1865* (1917, new ed. 1961); J. B. McMaster, *A History of the People of the United States during Lincoln's Administration* (1927); E. C. Smith, *The Borderland in the Civil War* (1927, repr. 1970); R. S. Henry, *The Story of the Confederacy* (1931, rev. ed. 1957); C. R. Fish, *The American Civil War: An Interpretation* (1937); Margaret Leech, *Reveille in Washington* (1941); Allan Nevins, *Ordeal of the Union* (8 vol., 1947-71); Bruce Catton, *A Stillness at Appomattox* (1953) and other studies; Benjamin Quarles, *The Negro in the Civil War* (1953, repr. 1968); L. M. Starr, *Bohemian Brigade* (1954); J. B. Mitchell, *Decisive Battles of the Civil War* (1955); R. S. West, Jr., *Mr. Lincoln's Navy* (1957); Shelby Foote, *The Civil War* (2 vol., 1958-63); M. M. Boatner, *The Civil War Dictionary* (1959); *American Heritage Picture History of the Civil War* (ed. by R. M. Ketchum et al., 1960); R. F. Nichols, *The Stakes of Power* (1961); Virgil Jones, *The Civil War at Sea* (3 vol., 1960-62); J. M. McPherson, *The Negro's Civil War* (1965); J. G. Randall, *The Civil War and Reconstruction* (2d ed., with David Donald, 1969). See also the bibliographies in separate articles on the major events of the war.

Civitali, Matteo (mät-tē'ō chēvētä'lē), 1436-1501, Italian sculptor and architect, born and worked in Lucca, where his work is best represented. Trained in Florence, he executed elaborate tomb sculptures of biblical figures in the Chapel of San Giovanni Battista in Genoa Cathedral.

Civitavecchia (chē'vētä-věk'kēä), city (1971 pop. 43,434), in Latium, W central Italy, on the Tyrrhenian Sea. The harbor, favored by Trajan (early 2d cent. A.D.), is still the chief port of Rome. It also handles traffic for the Terni industrial area and is the main maritime link with Sardinia. Industries of the city include fishing and petroleum refining. The arsenal in Civitavecchia was built by Bernini, and Michelangelo directed the final stages of the construction of the powerful citadel (begun 1508, nearly destroyed in World War II).

Cl, chemical symbol of the element CHLORINE.

Clackmannanshire (klăkmăn'ənshĭr), county (1971 pop. 45,553), 55 sq mi (142 sq km), central Scotland, at the head of the Firth of Forth. ALLOA is the administrative center. Clackmannanshire is the smallest county in area in Scotland. Part of the Ochil Hills are in the north. The county has an important coal industry, as well as dairy and grain farming and sheep raising. In 1975 Clackmannanshire became part of the Central region.

Clacton, urban district (1971 pop. 37,942), Essex, E central England. It is a seaside resort situated on high cliffs. The Norman Church of St. John was restored there in 1865.

Claflin, Tennessee: see WOODHULL, VICTORIA (CLAFLIN).

Claiborne, William (klā'bərn), c.1587-c.1677, Virginia colonist, b. Westmorland co., England. He emigrated to Virginia in 1621 as official surveyor and then served as secretary of state (1626-37, 1652-60) of that colony. He traded with the Indians, explored near the head of Chesapeake Bay, and established a fort and settlement on Kent Island in the Chesapeake. He opposed the grant of Maryland to Lord Baltimore, and after Baltimore's order (1634) for his arrest, Claiborne undertook armed resistance from his stronghold. Claiborne went (1637) to England to justify his conduct, but the issue was decided in favor of Lord Baltimore. In 1642, Claiborne was made treasurer of Virginia, and several years later, claiming the authority of Parliament, he invaded Maryland and drove out the governor, Leonard Calvert. He controlled Maryland for several years and was a member (1652-57) of its governing commission.

Claiborne, William Charles Coles, 1775-1817, governor of Louisiana, b. Sussex co., Va. He began law practice in Sullivan co., Tenn., and was appointed a judge of the state supreme court in 1796. As a Congressman (1797-1801) he supported Jefferson, and in 1801 the President made him governor of Mississippi Territory. In 1803, Claiborne was one of the commissioners appointed to receive Louisiana from France after the Louisiana Purchase, and he was governor (1804-12) of the newly organized Territory of Orleans. American government was not well received by the Creoles, and Claiborne had many quarrels with legislators and others. He was also criticized for his apparent approval of the questionable activities of Gen. James WILKINSON. However, when the Territory of Orleans was admitted to the Union in 1812 as the state of Louisiana, Claiborne was elected governor and served until 1816. In 1817 he was elected to the U.S. Senate but died before he could take his seat. See Dunbar Rowland, ed., *Official Letterbooks of W. C. C. Claiborne, 1801-1816* (6 vol., 1917).

Clair, René (rənā' klâr), 1898-, French film director, writer, and producer. Clair's films, notable for fantasy and satire, first received international attention in 1930. His *Sous les toits de Paris* (1929), one of the first artistic "talkies," was followed by *Le Million* (1931) and *À Nous la liberté* (1932). *The Ghost Goes West,* made in England in 1936, *Les Belles de Nuit* (1952), and *Les Fêtes Galantes* (1965) are among his notable films. In 1962 he was elected to the French Academy, the first film director to be so honored. See his *Reflections on the Cinema* (tr. 1953) and *Cinema Yesterday and Today,* ed. by R. C. Dale (1972).

Clairaut, Alexis Claude (älěksēs' klōd klěrō'), 1713-65, French mathematician. He assisted P. L. M. de Maupertuis in measuring (1736) a degree of an arc of a meridian in Lapland. He is noted for his work on differential equations and on curves and for formulating Clairaut's theorem dealing with geodesic lines on the surface of an ellipsoid.

Claire, Ina, 1892?-, American actress, b. Washington, D.C., originally named Ina Fagan. Claire began her stage career in 1909, impersonating Sir Harry LAUDER. Noted for her gay and elegant style, she performed in vaudeville and in many successful shows on Broadway and in London, including *The Quaker Girl, Ziegfeld Follies,* and *The Confidential Clerk.* Among her few films were *The Awful Truth* (1929), *Ninotchka* (1939), and *Claudia* (1942).

Clairton, city (1970 pop. 15,051), Allegheny co., SW Pa., an industrial suburb of Pittsburgh, on the Monongahela River; settled 1770, inc. 1903. Its extensive steelworks turn out a great variety of products. Coal mines and oil wells are also found in the area, and coke, coke by-products, and chemicals are important manufactures.

clairvoyance (klâr"voi'əns), power to perceive, as though visually, objects or persons not discernible through the ordinary sense channels. Clairvoyance may occur in a supposedly normal state (second sight) or more generally in a trance induced by various agencies, such as drugs, fasting, illness, or crystal gazing. See SPIRITISM and PARAPSYCHOLOGY.

Clallam Indians (klăl'əm), North American Indians whose language belongs to the Salishan branch of the Algonquian-Wakashan linguistic stock (see AMERICAN INDIAN LANGUAGES). They formerly occupied the south shore of Puget Sound, in the present state of Washington.

clam, common name for certain BIVALVE mollusks, especially for marine species that live buried in mud or sand and have valves (the two pieces of the shell) of equal size. The oval valves, which cover the right and left sides of the animal, are hinged together at the top by an elastic ligament. Clams burrow by means of a muscular foot, located at the front end, which can be extruded between the valves. The head, located within the shell, is rudimentary, without eyes or antennae. Water containing oxygen and food particles enters through an incurrent siphon; waste-containing water is expelled through an excurrent siphon. The two tubes project from the end opposite the foot and may be united in a single structure called the neck. The sexes are usually separate. Eggs and sperm are deposited in the water; the fertilized egg develops into a free-swimming larva without a shell, which may not attain the adult form for several months. Clams are highly valued as food. The soft-shell clam, or steamer (*Mya arenaria*), of both coasts of North America, is one of the most popular eating clams. The hard-shell clam (*Mercenaria mercenaria*), abundant from the Gulf of St. Lawrence to Texas, was called *quahog* by some Indians, who used the violet portion of the shell for wampum. Small hard-shell clams are called littlenecks, or cherrystones. The razor clam (*Ensis*), shaped like an old-fashioned straight razor, burrows rapidly and swims by means of its foot. The Atlantic razor clam, found from Labrador to W Florida and prized for its flavor, may attain lengths of 10 in. (25 cm). The Eastern surf clam (*Spisula solidissima*) frequents sandy bottoms in shallow water from Labrador to North Carolina and is much used for bait. There are also several Pacific surf clams. Other Pacific clams include the succulent Pismo clam (*Tivela stultorum*), found from mid-California southward and protected by law from overdigging, and the GEODUCK of the Pacific Northwest, which may weigh as much as 12 lb (5.4 kg). The valves of many small clams are familiar seashells, such as those of the pea-sized amethyst gem clam. The GIANT CLAM of the S Pacific Ocean may reach a weight of 500 lb (227 kg) and a length of 5 ft (150 cm). There are two families of freshwater bivalves called clams. The small freshwater clams (family Sphaeriidae) are hermaphroditic; they retain the fertilized eggs in a brood pouch and bear young with shells. The large freshwater clams (family Unionidae) are also called freshwater MUSSELS; the nacreous inner layer of their shells is a source of mother-of-pearl. The larvae of these clams are parasitic on the gills of fish. The term *clam* is sometimes used synonymously with *bivalve;* in this sense it includes the OYSTERS, SCALLOPS, and marine mussels. Clams are classified in the phylum MOLLUSCA, class Pelecypoda.

Clamart (klämär'), suburb SW of Paris (1968 pop. 55,299), Hauts-de-Seine dept., N central France. There are pharmaceutical laboratories, a tobacco factory, and nurseries in the town. Fruits and vegetables are grown, and tourism is important. On the outskirts of Clamart are an airplane factory and a military airfield.

clam shrimp: see SHRIMP.

clamworm: see ANNELIDA; WORM.

clan, social group based on actual or alleged unilateral descent from a common ancestor. Such groups have been known in all parts of the world and include some that claim the parentage or special protection of an animal, plant, or other object (see TOTEM). They also include such familiar groups as the Highland clans of Scotland (the English word *clan* comes from Gaelic). Most clans stress mutual obligations and duties. Clan descent is traced in one line only, male or female. The word *clan* has by some been restricted to those descended through the mother (matrilineal) in contrast to the GENS, descended through the father (patrilineal). The word *sib* has been much used to cover both types. A clan includes several family groups. Most clans are exogamous and regard marriages among their members as incest. A clan is distinguished from a lineage in that a clan merely claims common ancestry; a lineage can be traced to a common progenitor. A clan may have several lineages. Several clans may be combined into a larger social group called a phratry. If a tribe includes two clans or phratries, each clan or phratry is called a moiety. See Sir Iain Moncreiffe, *The Highland Clans* (1967).

Clanricarde, Ulick de Burgh, 5th **earl and marquess of** (yōō'lĭk də bûrg, klănrĭk'ərd), 1604-57, Irish Catholic nobleman. He assisted James Butler, 12th earl of ORMONDE, in his attempt, during the English civil war, to unite Catholic and Protestant royalists and hold Ireland loyal to Charles I. When Ormonde left Ireland (1650), he named Clanricarde his deputy. Clanricarde made peace (1652) with Oliver Cromwell at the request of Charles II.

clapboard (klăb'ərd), board used for the exterior finish of a wood-framed building and attached horizontally to the wood studs. The word, in its original and strict use, refers to a product of New England; boards of similar type made elsewhere are termed siding. Clapboards are particularly characteristic of the United States, having been steadily used since the earliest years of the colonial settlements. Each clapboard overlaps the one below it, leaving a few inches exposed to the weather. White pine is considered the best wood for clapboards; cedar, cypress, and spruce are also used.

Clapham, Sir John Harold, 1873-1946, English economic historian. He was lecturer, professor and administrator at Cambridge from 1908 to 1943. Outstanding among his many authoritative, classic works on British economic history are *An Economic History of Modern Britain* (2d ed., 3 vol., 1931-38) and *The Bank of England* (1944). Other books include *The Economic Development of France and Germany, 1815-1914* (4th ed., 1936), a comparative study, and *A Concise Economic History of Britain, from the Earliest Times to 1750* (1949), a useful standard survey.

Clapham Sect, group of English social reformers, active c.1790-1830, so named because their activities centered on the home in Clapham, London, of Henry Thornton and William Wilberforce. Most of the members were evangelical Anglicans and members of Parliament. They included Zachary Macaulay, Thomas Babington, John Venn, James Stephen, and Hannah More. Known as the "Saints," they worked for the abolition of the slave trade and slavery, improvement of prison conditions, and other humane legislation. They published a journal, the *Christian Observer*, and helped to found several missionary and tract societies, including the British and Foreign Bible Society and the Church Missionary Society. See E. M. Howse, *Saints in Politics* (1952, repr. 1971).

Clapp, Verner, 1901-72, American librarian, b. Johannesburg, South Africa. After studying philosophy at Harvard, Clapp worked for the Library of Congress (1922-1956), becoming chief assistant librarian in 1947. He also did much work for the United Nations and served as chairman of the U.S. Library Mission to Japan (1947-48). From 1956 to 1967 he was president of the Council on Library Resources. He has written *The Future of the Research Library* (1963) and *Copyright: A Librarian's View* (1968).

Clapperton, Hugh, 1788-1827, British explorer, b. Annan, Scotland. After serving with the British navy in East India and Canada he made two journeys to W Africa. On the initial journey (1822-25) he was one of the first Europeans to reach Lake Chad (Feb. 4, 1823). He traveled through the Hausa states and collected much information about Kano and Sokoto. Clapperton's second expedition sought to discover the mouth of the Niger River. Before he could accomplish this task he died near Sokoto on April 13, 1827. His servant, R. L. Lander, returned to England with his records, which were published (1829) as the *Journal of a Second Expedition into the Interior of Africa*. See Henry Williams, *Quest beyond the Sahara* (1965).

Clare or **Clara, Saint,** 1193?-1253, Italian nun of Assisi, devoted from her youth to St. FRANCIS, to whom she took a vow of poverty. She led a life of great austerity. She organized her companions into the Franciscan nuns, or Poor Clares, and struggled a long time for the preservation of the primitive poverty of her order. Feast: Aug. 12.

Clare, John, 1793-1864, English nature poet. He is numbered among the romantic poets. His *Poems Descriptive of Rural Life and Scenery* (1820) brought him a brief period of fame. Subsequent volumes included *The Village Minstrel* (1821) and *Rural Muse* (1835). Throughout his life he suffered fits of melancholy, which were intensified by financial difficulties and bad health. In 1837 he was declared insane and committed to an asylum. See biographies by J. W. Tibble and A. Northgrave (2d ed. 1972) and Frederick Martin (1865, repr. 1973); studies by Mark Storey, ed. (1973) and J. M. Todd (1973).

Clare, John Fitzgibbon, 1st **earl of,** 1749-1802, Irish statesman. He was (1783-89) attorney general of Ireland and in 1789 became lord chancellor. A resolute upholder of the Protestant ascendancy in Ireland, he denounced the Catholic Relief Act of 1793 and helped to thwart Lord Fitzwilliam in his move toward Catholic Emancipation. He was instrumental in effecting the Act of Union (1800) between England and Ireland. Clare, who was created earl in 1795, was so unpopular in Ireland that his funeral was broken up by a mob.

Clare, Richard de: see PEMBROKE, RICHARD DE CLARE, 2D EARL OF.

Clare, county (1971 pop. 74,844), 1,231 sq mi (3,188 sq km), W Republic of Ireland, between Galway Bay and the Shannon River. The county town is Ennis. The terrain is broken and hilly, with many bogs and lakes, and the coastline is especially rugged; much of the land is completely barren. Fishing is carried on, and sheep, cattle, pigs, and poultry are raised. Chief crops are oats and potatoes. Woolens are produced, and there are flour mills and slate quarries. The population has declined steadily for more than 100 years. The region came under the control of the Anglo-Norman Clare family in the 13th cent.

Clare Island, c.6 sq mi (15 sq km), Co. Mayo, W Republic of Ireland, at the entrance to Clew Bay. There are ruins of a 13th-century Carmelite abbey and of the 16th-century castle of Grania or Grace O'Malley, queen of the island.

Claremont. 1 City (1970 pop. 23,464), Los Angeles co., S Calif., in a citrus farm area at the foot of the San Gabriel Mts.; inc. 1907. It is mainly residential. The Claremont Colleges, a theological school, and a large botanical garden are there. **2** City (1970 pop. 14,221), Sullivan co., SW N.H., in a farm and dairy area, on the Sugar River near its junction with the Connecticut; inc. 1764. It is a summer resort and has plants manufacturing shoes, textiles, machinery, and paper. The oldest Roman Catholic church in the state (begun 1823) is there, and in nearby West Claremont is Union Church, the state's oldest Episcopal church (begun 1773). A replica of a pre-Revolutionary fort complex is nearby.

Claremont Colleges, at Claremont, Calif.; including five liberal arts and sciences colleges and a graduate school; founded 1925, known until 1961 as the Associated Colleges at Claremont. Their history began with Pomona College (inc. 1887, opened 1888; coeducational), which centers its curriculum in the social sciences and humanities. Scripps College (chartered 1926, opened 1927; for women) has a noted humanities program. Claremont Men's College (chartered and opened 1946) concentrates on preparing students for careers in business and government. Harvey Mudd College (inc. 1955, opened 1957; coeducational) stresses science and engineering. Pitzer College (founded 1963; for women) emphasizes the liberal arts. The Claremont Univ. Center (1925) is the central coordinating institution and the graduate school.

Clarence, George, duke of, 1449-78, son of Richard, duke of York, and brother of EDWARD IV. In defiance of Edward, Clarence married Isabel Neville and joined her father, Richard Neville, earl of WARWICK, in rebellion against the king in 1469-70. He deserted that party in 1471, however, and was reconciled with Edward. In 1478, exasperated by Clarence's continued factiousness, Edward had him attainted for treason by Parliament. He was sent to the Tower of London, where he was secretly executed. It was rumored that he was drowned in a butt of malmsey wine.

Clarence, Lionel, duke of, 1338-68, third son of Edward III of England. His marriage (1352) to Elizabeth de Burgh gained him the title and lands of the earl of Ulster. Governor of Ireland from 1361 to 1367, he presided (1366) at the assembly where the notorious Statute of Kilkenny was adopted, forbidding marriage between the English settlers and the Irish. Clarence died soon after his later marriage to Violante Visconti. His daughter, Philippa, married Edmund Mortimer, 3d earl of March. Their granddaughter, Anne Mortimer, married Richard, earl of Cambridge, and their son, Richard, duke of YORK, derived his claim to the throne through his descent from Lionel.

Clarendon, Edward Hyde, 1st **earl of** (klâr'əndən), 1609-74, English statesman and historian. Elected (1640) to the Short and Long parliaments, he was at first associated with the opposition to CHARLES I and helped prepare the impeachment of the earl of Strafford. The increasing radicalism of the opposition, however, led him to offer his services to the king, whom he aided by drafting a reply to the Grand Remonstrance. After the outbreak of the civil war, Hyde was appointed (1643) chancellor of the exchequer, and he represented (1645) Charles in the unsuccessful Uxbridge negotiations to end the war. Hyde followed Prince Charles (later CHARLES II) into exile in 1646 and became one of his chief advisers. Pursuing Hyde's policy, Charles awaited the appearance of a strong, friendly faction in England and successfully negotiated his own restoration (1660) without foreign aid. After Charles's return to England, Hyde became (1660) lord chancellor and was created earl of Clarendon (1661). Clarendon hoped to achieve a lenient religious settlement that would conciliate the Puritans, but his wishes were overborne by the militantly Anglican Cavalier Parliament, which passed the ironically named CLARENDON CODE. He was unjustly blamed by the public for the sale (1662) of Dunkirk to the French and for the second DUTCH WAR (which he opposed), and he was unpopular with the licentious Restoration court. In 1667, Charles dismissed him from office, using him as a scapegoat for military failures and financial breakdown in the Dutch War. Impeachment proceedings were begun, and Clarendon fled England to live the remainder of his life in exile. As a statesman he was consistent and moderate, never wavering from his early views on constitutional monarchy but blind to new political forces created by the English civil war. Through the marriage (1660) of his daughter Anne to the duke of York (later James II), Clarendon was the grandfather of two queens, Mary II and Anne. His renowned *History of the Rebellion* (standard ed., 6 vol., 1888), written partly from memory and partly from documents, is an indispensable account of the civil war. See his autobiography (1857); study by B. H. G. Wormald (1951, repr. 1964).

Clarendon, George William Frederick Villiers, 4th **earl of,** 1800-1870, British statesman. He was ambassador (1833-39) to Spain during the difficult period of the Carlist war and then lord privy seal (1839-41). As lord lieutenant of Ireland (1847-52), he made efforts to ease disorder and distress during the famine. He was foreign secretary (1853-58) during the Crimean War, held together the French alliance with England, and was one of the negotiators of the Peace of Paris (1856). He was twice again foreign secretary (1865-66, 1868-70), and during the latter period he laid the foundation for the settlement of the ALABAMA CLAIMS of the United States. See biography by H. E. Maxwell (1913); George Villiers, *Vanished Victorian* (1938).

Clarendon, Constitutions of, 1164, articles issued by King HENRY II of England at the Council of Clarendon defining the customs governing relations between church and state. In the anarchic conditions of the previous reign, the church had extended its jurisdiction in various ways, and it was the king's object to curb the growth of ecclesiastical power by securing the assent of the English prelates to this codification, which he claimed represented the practices followed during the reign of his grandfather, Henry I. The majority of the 16 articles dealt with church authority and the competence of ecclesiastical courts, while others defined the extent of papal authority in England; and they were in fact a fair statement of earlier customs. However, several articles were contrary to canon law, and controversy centered on two clauses in particular: that which provided for the secular punishment of clerics convicted of crime in the ecclesiastical courts (already a major point at issue between the king and the archbishop of Canterbury, THOMAS À BECKET) and that which forbade appeals to Rome without royal consent. After much debate, the English prelates assented to the Constitutions at Clarendon, but after the pope had condemned the codification, Becket repudiated his agreement. When the bitter quarrel between the king and his archbishop ended (1170) in Becket's murder, Henry felt compelled to amend the Constitutions, explicitly revoking the two controversial clauses. However, for the most part the Constitutions of Clarendon remained in effect as part of the law of the land. See A. L. Poole, *From Domesday Book to Magna Carta, 1087-1216* (2d ed. 1955).

Clarendon Code, 1661-65, group of English statutes passed after the Restoration of Charles II to strengthen the position of the Church of England. The Corporation Act (1661) required all officers of incorporated municipalities to take communion according to the rites of the Church of England and to abjure the Presbyterian covenant. The Act of Uniformity (1662) required all ministers in England and Wales to use and subscribe to the Book of Common Prayer; nearly 2,000 ministers resigned rather than submit to this act. The Conventicle Act (1664) forbade the assembling of five or more persons for religious worship other than Anglican. The Five-Mile Act (1665) forbade any nonconforming preacher or teacher to come within 5 mi (8.1 km) of a city or corporate town where he had served as minister. These laws, named after Edward Hyde, earl of CLARENDON, chief minister of Charles II at the time of their passage, decreased the following of numerous dissenting sects, especially the Presbyterians. Clarendon himself opposed their enactment, but after their passage he worked for their enforcement. Charles II, to court popularity with dissenters and to ease the position of Roman Catholics (with whom he was in sympathy), attempted to interfere with the operation of these laws by his unsuccessful declarations of indulgence in 1662 and 1672. As a political device to weaken the Whigs, the Clarendon Code was largely superseded by the TEST ACT of 1673, although some of the statutes, in modified form, remained in force for some time.

Clarens (kläräN'), village, Vaud canton, W Switzerland, on the Lake of Geneva. A resort near Montreux, Clarens was once the residence of Lord Byron. The Clarens region is immortalized in Rousseau's *Nouvelle Héloïse.*

claret: see WINE.

Clarín: see ALAS, LEOPOLDO.

clarinet, musical wind instrument of cylindrical bore employing a single reed. The clarinet family comprises all single-reed instruments, including the saxophone. The predecessor of the modern clarinet was the simpler chalumeau, which J. C. Denner of Nuremberg improved (c.1700) into the clarinet. It was accepted into the orchestra during the 18th

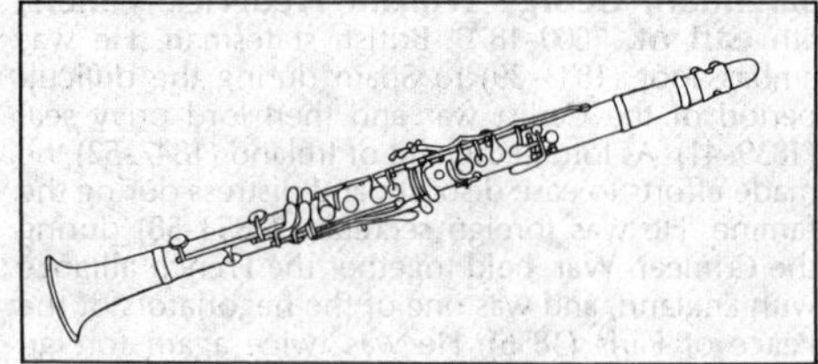

Clarinet

cent., and Mozart used it extensively. Major improvements of the key system during the 19th cent. employed the principles of Theobald Boehm. The clarinets in B flat and A are the standard orchestral instruments. The higher, shriller E flat clarinet is also a band instrument and is used occasionally in the orchestra. Of the larger clarinets, the B flat bass clarinet is the most important. The E flat alto and the E flat contrabass clarinets are mainly band instruments. Clarinets were once made in other keys, but all of these instruments are now obsolete. The basset-horn, a type of alto clarinet, was much used by Mozart and was revived by Richard Strauss. The clarinet is a TRANSPOSING INSTRUMENT. See F. G. Rendall, *The Clarinet* (3d rev. ed. 1971).

Clark, Abraham, 1726–94, political leader in the American Revolution, signer of the Declaration of Independence, b. Elizabethtown (now Elizabeth), N.J. After holding several local offices, Clark became, at the beginning of the American Revolution, a member and later secretary of the New Jersey committee of safety. He was a member (1775) of the New Jersey provincial congress, which appointed him (1776) delegate to the Continental Congress. Clark served three terms in Congress (1776–78, 1779–83, 1787–89), and in the interim periods he served in the New Jersey legislature.

Clark, Alvan, 1804–87, American astronomer and maker of astronomical lenses, b. Ashfield, Mass. In 1846 the firm of Alvan Clark & Sons was established at Cambridgeport, Mass.; it became famous as the manufacturer of the largest and finest telescope lenses. The first achromatic lenses made in the United States were produced there. Clark's son, **Alvan Graham Clark,** 1832–97, b. Fall River, Mass., became a partner in the business. Among lenses made under his direction are the 26-in. lens at the U.S. Naval Observatory, Washington, D.C.; the 36-in. lens at Lick Observatory, California; and the 40-in. lens at Yerkes Observatory, Wisconsin, which is the largest refracting telescope in the world. The younger Clark discovered a number of double stars as well as the companion star of Sirius.

Clark, Champ, 1850–1921, American legislator, b. near Lawrenceburg, Ky. His full name was James Beauchamp Clark. After a career as lawyer, newspaper editor, and politician in Missouri, he was (1893–95, 1897–1921) a member of the U.S. House of Representatives, becoming (1907) Democratic leader. He organized (1910) the successful fight against Speaker Joseph Cannon and his arbitrary control of legislative procedure. Clark served as speaker from 1911 to 1919. At the Democratic convention in 1912 he was the leading candidate for the Democratic nomination for President until William Jennings Bryan shifted his support to Woodrow Wilson. See his autobiographical *My Quarter Century of American Politics* (1920, repr. 1969).

Clark, Francis Edward, 1851–1927, American Congregational clergyman, founder of CHRISTIAN ENDEAVOR. He was born of American parents in Aylmer, Que., and was graduated from Dartmouth College in 1873. While serving as pastor of the Williston Congregational Church in Portland, Maine, he organized (1881) the first Young People's Society of Christian Endeavor. He was a lifelong leader in this movement.

Clark, George Rogers, 1752–1818, American Revolutionary general, conqueror of the Old Northwest, b. near Charlottesville, Va.; brother of William Clark. A surveyor, he was interested in Western lands, served (1774) in Lord Dunmore's War, and later went to what is now Kentucky for the OHIO COMPANY. In 1776 he secured the Virginia legislature's assertion of sovereignty over the Kentucky region, thereby obtaining military and financial support. He returned in time to repel British and Indian attacks on Harrodsburg, Ky., and other posts. In 1778 he made plans for aggressive action against the British in the Old Northwest and, going to Virginia, persuaded Gov. Patrick Henry and his council to send an expedition. At its head, he swept into the Illinois country and took the British-held settlements of KASKASKIA, CAHOKIA, and VINCENNES. The British under Gen. Henry Hamilton advanced from Detroit and retook Vincennes after Clark had left. Winter and Ohio floods halted Hamilton there, but Clark and his men, defying cruel conditions of cold and hardship, braved the flooded bottom lands to return to Vincennes. With the heroic aid of Francis Vigo, François Bosseron, and Father Gibault, he struck at the British fort and surprised and captured Hamilton and the garrison in Feb., 1779. After this, the greatest of his exploits, Clark hoped to capture Detroit, but adequate supplies never came from Virginia to the fort he had built (Fort Nelson, where Louisville now stands), and he remained inactive. In 1782 the British and the Indians disastrously defeated the Kentuckians in the battle of Blue Licks. The ensuing unrest led Clark, who had not taken part in the battle, to lead another expedition northward against the Indians and again establish control of the region. His services had been rewarded by the rank of brigadier general in the Virginia militia, and he was made an Indian commissioner. In 1786 he led another expedition against the Indians in Ohio. His own narrative of the capture of Vincennes is in Milo M. Quaife, ed., *The Capture of Old Vincennes* (1927). See biographies by J. A. James (1928, repr. 1970) and John Bakeless (1957); A. W. Derleth, *Vincennes: Portal to the West* (1968).

Clark, John, 1766–1832, governor of Georgia (1819–23), b. Edgecomb co., N.C. As a boy he served with his father, Elijah Clarke, in the American Revolution and afterwards won distinction as an Indian fighter. He became the hero and leader of the democratic frontiersmen of Georgia in their political struggle with the planters of the coast and the wealthy farmers of the uplands. As governor, he proposed (1821) an amendment to the state constitution to provide for the popular election of governors; it was finally adopted in 1824.

Clark, Jonas Gilman, 1815–1900, founder of Clark Univ., b. Hubbardston, Mass. After a long career in business and finance, he became interested in higher education, making extended trips of observation abroad and interviewing American college presidents. In 1887 he founded Clark Univ. at Worcester, Mass., with an endowment of $1 million, to which, by his will, was added his residuary estate for the establishment of Clark College, the undergraduate school.

Clark, Kenneth Bancroft, 1914–, American educator and psychologist, b. Panama Canal Zone, grad. Howard (B.A., 1935) and Columbia (Ph.D., 1940). He taught psychology at Howard (1937–38), Hampton Institute (1940–41), and the City College of New York (since 1942). Clark was the author of a study on racial discrimination that was cited by the U.S. Supreme Court in its 1954 school desegregation ruling. An early leader in the civil rights movement, he founded the Northside Center for Child Development and Harlem Youth Opportunities Unlimited (HARYOU, 1962). His works include *Prejudice and Your Child* (1955) and *Dark Ghetto* (1965).

Clark, Kenneth MacKenzie (Lord Clark of Saltwood), 1903–, English art historian. After working with Bernard Berenson in Florence, Clark was keeper of the department of fine art at the Ashmolean Museum, Oxford (1931–34). From 1934 to 1945 he was the director of the National Gallery, London, and thereafter Slade professor of fine arts at Oxford until 1950 and from 1961 to 1962. He became chairman of the Arts Council of Great Britain from 1955 to 1960. Among Clark's outstanding writings are two studies on Leonardo da Vinci, *The Drawings at Windsor Castle* (1935, with Carlo Pedretti) and *Leonardo da Vinci* (2d ed. 1952); a study of the paintings of Piero della Francesca (2d ed. 1969); *Landscape into Art* (1949); *The Nude* (1955); *Rembrandt and the Italian Renaissance* (1966); and *The Romantic Rebellion* (1974). His cultural survey *Civilisation* (1970) is based on his popular lecture series for television. See his bibliography, ed. by R. M. Slythe (rev. ed. 1971).

Clark, Lewis Gaylord, 1808?–1873, American editor and writer, b. near Syracuse, N.Y. He was the editor (1834–60) of the *Knickerbocker Magazine* and made it a leading literary publication of its day. He wrote *Knickerbocker Sketch-Book* (1845) and *Knick-Knacks from an Editor's Table* (1852). His twin brother, **Willis Gaylord Clark,** 1808?–1841, was co-editor (1834–41) of the *Knickerbocker.* His *Literary Remains* (1844) includes the sketches and verse that he contributed to the magazine. See *The Letters of Willis Gaylord Clark and Lewis Gaylord Clark* (ed. by L. W. Dunlop, 1940).

Clark, Mark Wayne, 1896–, U.S. general, b. Madison Barracks, N.Y. A West Point graduate, he served as a captain in World War I and rose to become (1940) army ground forces chief of staff. During World War II, he commanded (1943–44) the U.S. 5th Army in N Africa and in Italy, became (1944) Allied commander in Italy, and was promoted (1945) to full general. He served (1945) as head of the U.S. occupation forces in Austria. From May, 1952, to Oct., 1953, he was supreme commander of UN forces in Korea and also commander of U.S. forces in the Far East. Retiring from the army, he served (1954–66) as president of The Citadel, at Charleston, S.C. *Calculated Risk* (1950) and *From the Danube to the Yalu* (1954) are his memoirs of World War II and of the postwar period.

Clark, Ramsey, 1927–, Attorney General of the United States (1967–69), b. Dallas, Texas; son of Tom Campbell Clark. Admitted to the bar in 1951, William Ramsey Clark practiced law in Dallas. After serving as Assistant Attorney General in charge of the lands division (1961–65), Deputy Attorney General (1965–66), and acting Attorney General (Oct., 1966–Feb., 1967), he was appointed by Lyndon B. Johnson to succeed Nicholas Katzenbach. As Attorney General, Clark proved to be a vigorous defender of civil liberties and civil rights; he opposed the use of government wiretaps and initiated the first Northern school desegregation case. He later became active in the antiwar movement, and he visited North Vietnam in 1972. In 1974 he was the Democratic candidate for the U.S. Senate from New York but was defeated by Jacob K. Javits. Clark wrote *Crime in America* (1970). For an account of his career as Attorney General, see *Justice* by Richard Harris (1970).

Clark, Tom Campbell, 1899–, U.S. Attorney General (1945–49), Associate Justice of the U.S. Supreme Court (1949–67), b. Dallas, Texas; father of Ramsey Clark. He received his law degree from the Univ. of Texas. A protégé of Tom Connally, a Democratic Senator from Texas, Clark became (1937) special assistant to the Attorney General, coordinated (1942) war relocation of the West Coast Japanese, and headed the antitrust division (1943) and the criminal division (1945) of the Dept. of Justice. As Attorney General, he was noted for suits against trusts and disloyal groups. He was appointed (Aug., 1949) by President Harry S. Truman to the Supreme Court bench as successor to Frank Murphy. His opinions on the court were generally conservative on criminal and civil rights and control of alleged subversives. Clark retired from the court in 1967 after his son, Ramsey, was named U.S. Attorney General.

Clark, Walter, 1846–1924, American jurist, b. Halifax co., N.C., grad. Univ. of North Carolina (A.B., 1864; A.M., 1867). He entered the Confederate army at 15 and was commended for gallantry in action at Antietam and Fredericksburg. Clark was appointed (1885) judge of the superior court and elected (1889) to the supreme court of North Carolina, where he served until his death. He gained a national reputation for his independent decisions and supported many progressive causes in addresses and articles. Clark prepared an *Annotated Code of Civil Procedure,* annotated 164 volumes of *Supreme Court Reports,* edited 16 volumes of the *State Records of North Carolina,* and did other writing and translating. See his *Papers* (ed. by A. L. Brooks and H. T. Lefler, 2 vol., 1948–51); biography by A. L. Brooks (1944).

Clark, William, 1770–1838, American explorer, one of the leaders of the LEWIS AND CLARK EXPEDITION, b. Caroline co., Va.; brother of George Rogers Clark. He was an army officer (1792–96), serving in a number of Indian engagements. In 1803 he was chosen by his friend Meriwether Lewis to accompany the overland expedition to the Pacific. His observations of nature enlarged the findings of the expedition; his journals and maps recorded its history. In 1807, after the expedition had returned, Clark was appointed superintendent of Indian affairs, with headquarters at St. Louis, and from 1813 to 1821 he was governor of Missouri Territory. During the War of 1812, he led (1814) an expedition against the British and Indians in the upper Mississippi valley; upon reaching Prairie du Chien, Wis., he built Fort Shelby. Later, with Auguste Chouteau, he negotiated a number of important treaties with the Indians and aided in suppressing the Winnebago and Black Hawk uprisings. He was again superintendent of Indian affairs from 1821 until his death. See bibliography under LEWIS AND CLARK EXPEDITION.

Clark, William Andrews, 1839–1925, U.S. Senator and copper magnate, b. Fayette co., Pa. He moved to Montana, where he amassed a large fortune from the development of copper mines. He wielded immense power and had a long feud with Marcus DALY for control of the copper deposits and of political forces—virtually for control of Montana. Clark had political ambitions and was president of the Montana constitutional conventions of 1884 and 1889 but was defeated in the 1888 campaign to be territorial delegate to Congress. Daly blocked Clark's moves skillfully; and, although Clark claimed election as one of Montana's first Senators, the Senate instead seated his Republican opponent. In 1893 the state legislature was deadlocked, and Montana was left with only one Senator. After another deadlock in 1899, Clark was declared elected only to resign when confronted by a Senate investigation and a pending resolution to void his election. In 1901 he was duly elected and this time served his term and retired. He tied the exploitation of copper to Eastern capital, winning over such brilliant rivals as F. Augustus Heinze, and was powerful in copper development in Arizona as well as in Montana. See W. D. Mangam, *Clarks: An American Phenomenon* (1941).

Clark, William Smith, 1826–86, American educator, b. Ashfield, Mass., grad. Amherst, 1848, and studied chemistry and botany at Göttingen (Ph.D., 1852). He taught at Amherst until the Civil War, fought in many battles, and emerged from the struggle a brigadier general. He was elected to the Massachusetts General Court in 1864, 1865, and 1867 and while there secured the location at Amherst of the Massachusetts Agricultural College (the present-day Univ. of Massachusetts). He was president of this institution from 1867 to 1879, helped organize its work, and taught botany and horticulture. He went to Japan (1876–77) to establish the Imperial College of Agriculture at Sapporo.

Clark, Willis Gaylord: see CLARK, LEWIS GAYLORD.

Clark College: see ATLANTA UNIV. CENTER.

Clarke, Charles Cowden, 1787–1877, English lecturer and author. He was a close friend of Keats, who was a pupil of Clarke's father. Clarke's lectures on Shakespeare were published as *Shakespeare Characters* (1863). He and his wife, **Mary Victoria (Novello) Cowden Clarke,** 1809–98, wrote *Recollections of Writers* (1878), and she compiled *The Complete Concordance to Shakespeare* (1844–45). See study by R. D. Altick (1948, repr. 1973).

Clarke, James Freeman, 1810–88, American Unitarian clergyman and author, b. Hanover, N.H. While in charge of the Unitarian church in Louisville, Ky. (1833–40), he was for three years editor of the *Western Messenger.* He helped found the Church of the Disciples in Boston in 1841 and was its pastor until 1888, except in the years from 1850 to 1854. He was (1867–71) a nonresident professor in the Harvard Divinity School. The Transcendental Club, with such members as Bronson Alcott and Emerson, included Clarke, and he was active in the anti-slavery, woman-suffrage, and other reform movements. Among his books, influential in their day, were *Ten Great Religions* (2 vol., 1871–83), *Orthodoxy: Its Truths and Errors* (1866), and *Essentials and Non-Essentials in Religion* (1878). See biography by E. E. Hale (1891, repr. 1968), which includes a fragmentary autobiography; study by A. S. Bolster (1954).

Clarke, John, 1609–76, one of the founders of Rhode Island, b. Westhorpe, Suffolk, England. He emigrated to Boston in 1637 and shortly thereafter joined Anne HUTCHINSON (with whom he had sided in the antinomian controversy) and William CODDINGTON in founding (1638) Portsmouth on Aquidneck (Rhode Island). The next year, he and Coddington withdrew to found Newport, where he was both physician and Baptist pastor. Clarke favored the 1647 union of the Aquidneck settlements with Providence and Warwick and in 1651 went with Roger Williams to England to defend the union against Coddington's attacks. They were successful, and Williams soon returned. Clarke remained in England and was influential in securing the liberal charter of 1663. On his return to Rhode Island he served (1664–69) in the general assembly and was thrice elected deputy governor. His *Ill Newes from New England* (1652) was an arraignment of Massachusetts authorities for their hostility to religious liberty.

Clarke, Mary Victoria (Novello) Cowden: see under CLARKE, CHARLES COWDEN.

Clarke, Samuel, 1675–1729, English philosopher and divine. His chief interest was rational theology, and, although a critic of the deists, he was in sympathy with some of their ideas. He supported the theories of Newton and argued with Leibniz in defense of the existence of absolute space. Clarke maintained that ethical law is as constant as mathematical law. His published works include many translations, lectures, sermons, and commentaries. His treatise *The Scripture Doctrine of Unity* appeared in 1712. The Leibniz correspondence was published in 1717.

Clarke, Walter, c.1638–1714, colonial governor of Rhode Island, b. Newport, R.I. He was deputy governor (1679–86, 1700–1714) and was three times governor (1676–77, 1686, 1696–98) of Rhode Island. He is chiefly remembered for his refusal to surrender the Rhode Island charter upon the demand of Sir Edmund ANDROS.

Clarksburg, city (1970 pop. 24,864), seat of Harrison co., N central W.Va., at the confluence of Elk Creek and the West Fork of the Monongahela River; inc. 1795. It is an industrial and shipping center for an area of coal mines, oil and natural gas fields, and grazing lands. Glass and glass products are the chief manufactures. The city was an important Union supply base in the Civil War, and remains of Federal earthworks are preserved in Lowndes Hill park. A two-year branch of Salem College is in Clarksburg. The city is the birthplace of Stonewall Jackson; a plaque designates the site.

Clarksdale, city (1970 pop. 21,673), seat of Coahoma co., NW Miss., on the Sunflower River; inc. 1882. It is a processing and distributing center for a cotton producing area. Its manufactures include paper, conveyor belts, house trailers, locks, and rubber products.

Clarkson, Thomas, 1760–1846, English abolitionist. He devoted most of his life to agitation against slavery, and the voluminous information that he gathered on the slave trade helped to influence Parliament. With William WILBERFORCE he shares the chief credit for the act of 1807 abolishing the British slave trade. His best-known books are a history of Parliament's abolition of the slave trade (1805) and a memoir of William Penn (1813). See his correspondence with Henri Christophe, ed. by E. L. Griggs and C. H. Prator (1952, repr. 1968); biography by E. L. Griggs (1936).

Clarksville. 1 Town (1970 pop. 13,806), Clark co., S central Ind., on the Ohio River, opposite Louisville, Ky.; founded 1784 by George Rogers Clark. Soap is the chief manufacture. **2** City (1970 pop. 31,719), seat of Montgomery co., NW Tenn., on the Cumberland and Red rivers, in a farm, livestock, and tobacco region; platted 1784, inc. as a city 1855. It is an important market and processing center for dark and burley tobacco. Its industries include meat-packing and the manufacture of snuff, footwear, tires, and air-conditioning equipment. Austin Peay State Univ. is in Clarksville. Part of U.S. Fort Campbell is within the city limits.

Clark University, at Worcester, Mass.; coeducational; chartered 1887, opened as a graduate school 1889. It was the second graduate school to be formed in the United States. Its undergraduate college (est. 1902) was integrated with the university in 1920.

clary: see SAGE.

class, in taxonomy: see CLASSIFICATION.

class action, in law, device that permits one or more people to sue or to be sued as the representative of a large group of people interested in the matter. In most types of suits all members of the class are bound by the decision, even if they do not appear. It is permitted in Federal and most U.S. state courts. Certain requirements must be met, e.g., the class must be so large that individual suit would be impractical, and the named parties who bring the suit must adequately represent the class. Class actions have been successfully used in civil rights cases. They are more controversial when a small sum, e.g., $60, is sought by each member and the main financial benefactor will be the lawyer.

classicism, term that, when applied generally, means clearness, elegance, symmetry, and repose produced by attention to traditional forms. It is sometimes synonymous with excellence or artistic quality of high distinction. More precisely, the term refers to the admiration and imitation of Greek and Roman art, architecture, and literature; the stylistic features and aims most particularly admired include restraint, simplicity, balance, unity of design, and a strong sense of form. Conversely, the term implies the absence of subjectivity, emotionalism, and excessive enthusiasm. Because the principles of classicism were derived from the rules and practices of the ancients, the term came to mean the adherence to specific academic canons. The first major revival of classicism, designated neoclassicism, occurred during the Renaissance. As a result of the intensified interest in Greek and Roman culture, especially the works of Plato and Cicero, classical standards were reinstated as the ideal norm. In Florence, Cosimo de' Medici gathered a circle of humanists (see HUMANISM) who collected, studied, expounded, and imitated the classics. A group of Latin literary stylists called the "Ciceronians" would not use any word not found in Cicero's writings. Other writers espoused simpler styles described by Dionysus of Halicarnassus and by Quintilian. Among these were Francis Bacon, who not only reintroduced the empirical method to scientific investigation, but did much to establish plain classical style in the writing of English prose. In applying the same theories to poetry, Ben Jonson did much to correct the artificiality of Petrarchan convention. Also important were the epigrams and *carpe diem* lyrics inspired by the GREEK ANTHOLOGY and other classical writings. Renaissance painters whose works reflect the classical influence include Mantegna, Raphael, and Michelangelo. It is generally thought that neoclassicism found its highest English expression in the Augustan period (during the reign of Queen Anne), particularly in the writings of Dryden and Pope. In France, the Pléiade (see under PLEIAD) had so set the tone for French letters by the end of the 16th cent. that it was natural for the playwrights Corneille and Racine to be ruled by the *Poetics* of Aristotle. In Germany, the classical stream was deflected in the last quarter of the 18th cent. by the period of STURM UND DRANG, but it was revived later in the century when Goethe and Schiller wrote classical drama and Haydn, Mozart, and Beethoven utilized the principles of classical form in their music. The Napoleonic revival of the idea of the Roman Empire brought with it a new international burst of imitation in architecture (see CLASSIC REVIVAL) and painting (whose foremost exponents were David and Ingres). In 20th-century Europe and America there has been a renewed interest in Greek literature, and classical models have been somewhat revived, as in the work of Ezra Pound and T. S. Eliot. These men, as well as many of the proponents of new criticism (see CRITICISM), have, in their rejection of impressionism and ROMANTICISM, stressed neoclassical restraint in their writings. In art, classical elements can be found in the paintings of Cézanne and the cubists and in the architectural designs of such men as Miës van der Rohe. Spearheading the 20th-century neoclassical revival in music, a reaction to romanticism, were Prokofiev, Stravinsky, and Bartók. See T. S. Eliot, *What Is a Classic?* (1946); Gilbert Highet, *The Classical Tradition* (1949, repr. 1957); P. O. Kristeller. *Renaissance Thought* (1961); W. J. Bate, *From Classic to Romantic* (1961); Gilbert Murray, *The Classical Tradition in Poetry* (1927, repr. 1968); Charles Rosen, *The Classical Style: Haydn, Mozart, Beethoven* (1971); R. R. Bolgar, ed., *Classical Influences on European Culture* (1971).

classic revival, widely diffused phase of taste (known as neoclassic) which influenced architecture and the arts in Europe and the United States during the last years of the 18th and the first half of the 19th cent. The era was characterized by enthusiasm for classical antiquity and for archaeological knowledge, stimulated by the excavations of Roman remains at Pompeii and Herculaneum and by the commencement of archaeological investigation in

Greece by James Stuart and Nicholas Revett in 1751. The results were embodied in their joint work, *Antiquities of Athens,* of which the first volume (1762) is considered to have been responsible for a changed direction in taste. Stuart's garden temple in Greek Doric style (1758) at Hagley, England, was the first example of Greek revival design in Western Europe; but the utilization of Greek material was generally delayed until the latter part of the revival, while the earlier phase confined itself to Roman models. In France the imitation of ancient Rome predominated in the crystallizing of the Empire style sponsored by Napoleon. In the United States, after the Revolution, this same spirit served in the formation of a style for public buildings. Thomas Jefferson's design for the Virginia state capitol (1785) at Richmond marks the return to the monumental Roman temple for inspiration. In America the Greek phase, known as neo-Grec or Greek revival, achieved its first expression, and an exceedingly influential one, in the Bank of Pennsylvania, Philadelphia (1799); it was designed by Benjamin H. Latrobe to imitate a Greek Ionic temple. The Roman and the Greek aspects of the classic revival eventually allied themselves in a Greco-Roman form. The influence of the revival was felt everywhere in Europe and particularly in Great Britain. But in no country did it dominate as in the United States, where classic colonnades were appended to state capitols and to modest farm houses throughout the land. After the Civil War its severe later phase was extinguished by the romantic styles of the Victorian period. Among the important buildings of the American classic revival are the Washington monument, Baltimore (1815), by Robert Mills; Bank of the United States, Philadelphia (1819–24), by William Strickland; campus buildings, Univ. of Virginia (1817–26), by Thomas Jefferson; Merchants' Exchange, Philadelphia (1832–34), by William Strickland; main building, Girard College, Philadelphia (1833–47), by T. U. Walter; and dome and wings of the Capitol at Washington (1851–65), by T. U. Walter. See Talbot Hamlin, *Greek Revival Architecture in America* (1944); D. Wiebenson, *Sources of Greek Revival Architecture* (1969).

classification, in biology, the systematic categorization of organisms into a coherent scheme. The original purpose of biological classification, or systematics, was to organize the vast number of known plants and animals into categories that could be named, remembered, and discussed. Modern classification has the additional purpose of attempting to show the evolutionary relationships among organisms. A system based on categories that show such relationships is called a natural system of classification; one based on categories assigned for convenience, without regard to significant relationships, is called artificial. (For example, a classification of flowers by color is an artificial system.) Modern classification is part of the broader science of taxonomy, the study of the relationships of organisms, which includes collection, preservation, and study of specimens, and analysis of data provided by various areas of biological research. Nomenclature is the assigning of names to organisms and to the categories in which they are classified. The broadest division of organisms is into kingdoms. Traditionally there have been two kingdoms, Animalia and Plantae, but many unicellular and simple multicellular organisms are not easily classified as either plants or animals. In 1866 the zoologist Ernst Heinrich HAECKEL proposed a third kingdom, the Protista, to include all protozoans, algae, fungi, and bacteria. His proposal found fairly wide acceptance in the 20th cent.; however, as the protists include fundamentally dissimilar organisms, a fourth kingdom, the Monera, has been proposed for the bacteria and blue-green algae, which differ from all other organisms in that they lack well-defined cell nuclei. Five- and six-kingdom systems have also been proposed. Kingdoms are divided into a hierarchical system of categories called taxa (sing. taxon). The taxa are, from most to least inclusive: phylum (usually called *division* in botany), class, order, family, genus, and species. Where these divisions are not adequate for making necessary distinctions, intermediate divisions are added, such as suborder and superfamily. The species, the fundamental unit of classification, consists of populations of genetically similar, interbreeding or potentially interbreeding individuals. If two populations of a species are completely isolated geographically and therefore evolve separately, they will be considered two species once they are no longer capable of mixing genetically if brought together. In a few cases interbreeding is possible between members of closely related but clearly distinct species—for example, horses, asses, and zebras can all interbreed. However, the offspring of such crosses are usually sterile, so that the two groups are nonetheless kept separate by their genetic incompatibility. Populations within a species that show recognizable, inherited differences from one another but are capable of interbreeding freely are called subspecies, races, or varieties. The genus (pl. genera) is a grouping of similar, closely related species. For example, the domestic cat and the bobcat are species of the genus *Felis;* dogs, wolves, and jackals belong to the genus *Canis.* Often the genus is an easily recognized grouping with a popular name; for example, the various oak species, such as black oak and live oak, form the oak genus (*Quercus*). Similarly, genera are grouped into families, families into orders, orders into classes, and classes into phyla or divisions. The lower a taxon is in the hierarchy, the more closely related are its members. The earliest known system of classification is that of Aristotle, who attempted in the 4th cent. B.C. to group animals according to such criteria as mode of reproduction and possession or lack of red blood. Aristotle's pupil Theophrastus classified plants according to their uses and their methods of cultivation. Little interest was shown in classification until science became a focal area of activity in the 17th and 18th cent., when botanists and zoologists began to devise the modern scheme of categories. The designation of groups was based almost entirely on superficial anatomical resemblances. Before the idea of EVOLUTION there was no impetus to show more meaningful relationships among species; the species was thought to be uniquely created and fixed in character, the only real, or natural, taxon, while the higher taxa were regarded as artificial means of organizing information. However, since anatomical resemblance is an important indication of relationship, such early classification efforts resulted in a system that in many areas approximated a natural one and (with much modification) is still used. The most extensive work was done in the mid-18th cent. by Carolus LINNAEUS, who devised the presently used system of nomenclature. As biologists came to accept the work of Charles DARWIN in the second half of the 19th cent., they began to stress the significance of evolutionary relationships for classification. Although comparative anatomy remained of foremost importance, other evidence of relationship was sought as well. Paleontology provided fossil evidence of the common ancestry of various groups; embryology provided comparisons of early development in different species, an important clue to their relationships. In the 20th cent., evidence provided by genetics and physiology became increasingly important. Recently there has been much emphasis on the use of biochemistry in taxonomy, as in the comparison of the serum proteins of different animal species. Computers are increasingly used to analyze data relevant to taxonomy. A modern branch of discipline, called numerical taxonomy, uses computers to compare very large numbers of traits without weighting any type of trait—in contrast to the traditional view of certain characteristics as more significant than others in showing relationships. For example, the structure of flower parts is considered more significant than the shape of the leaves in flowering plants because leaf shape appears to evolve much more quickly, with very dissimilar forms sometimes occurring in species with a recent common ancestor. Much of the science of taxonomy has been concerned with judging which traits are most significant. If new evidence reveals a better basis for subdividing a taxon than that previously used, the classification of the group in question may be revised, although there is often disagreement among taxonomists about such revisions. The present system of binomial nomenclature identifies each species by a scientific name of two words, Latin in form and usually derived from Greek or Latin roots. The first name (capitalized) is the genus of the organism, the second (not capitalized) is its species. The scientific name of the white oak is *Quercus alba,* while red oak is *Quercus rubra.* The first name applies to all species of the genus—*Quercus* is the name of all oaks—but the entire binomial applies only to a single species. Many scientific names describe some characteristic of the organism (*alba*= white; *rubra*=red); many are derived from the name of the discoverer or the geographic location of the organism. Genus and species names are always italicized when printed; the names of other taxa (families, etc.) are not. When a species (or several species of the same genus) is mentioned repeatedly, the genus may be abbreviated after its first mention, as in *Q. alba.* Subspecies are indicated by a trinomial; for example, the southern bald eagle is *Haliaeetus leucocephalus leucocephalus,* as distinguished from the northern bald eagle, *H. leucocephalus washingtoniensis.* The advantages of scientific over common names are that they are accepted by speakers of all languages, that each name applies only to one species, and that each species has only one name. This avoids the confusion that often arises

EXAMPLES OF SYSTEMATIC CLASSIFICATION

<table>
<tr><th>COMMON NAME</th><th>SPECIES NAME</th><th>GENUS</th><th>FAMILY</th><th>ORDER</th><th>CLASS</th><th>PHYLUM (DIVISION)</th><th>KINGDOM</th></tr>
<tr><td>Man</td><td>Homo sapiens</td><td>Homo</td><td>Hominidae</td><td rowspan="2">Primates</td><td rowspan="2">Mammalia</td><td rowspan="4">Chordata</td><td rowspan="6">Animalia</td></tr>
<tr><td>Rhesus monkey</td><td>Macaca mulatta</td><td>Macaca</td><td>Cercopithecidae</td></tr>
<tr><td>Leopard frog</td><td>Rana pipiens</td><td rowspan="2">Rana</td><td rowspan="2">Ranidae</td><td rowspan="2">Anura</td><td rowspan="2">Amphibia</td></tr>
<tr><td>Wood frog</td><td>Rana sylvatica</td></tr>
<tr><td>Long-winged grasshopper</td><td>Dissosteira longipennis</td><td>Dissosteira</td><td>Acrididae</td><td>Orthoptera</td><td>Insecta</td><td rowspan="2">Arthropoda</td></tr>
<tr><td>Black widow spider</td><td>Latrodectus mactans</td><td>Latrodectus</td><td>Theridiidae</td><td>Araneae</td><td>Arachnida</td></tr>
<tr><td>White clover</td><td>Trifolium repens</td><td>Trifolium</td><td>Leguminosae</td><td rowspan="2">Rosales</td><td rowspan="2">Magnoliopsida</td><td rowspan="3">Magnoliophyta</td><td rowspan="6">Plantae</td></tr>
<tr><td>Black cherry</td><td>Prunus serotina</td><td>Prunus</td><td>Rosaceae</td></tr>
<tr><td>Wood lily</td><td>Lilium philadelphicum</td><td>Lilium</td><td>Liliaceae</td><td>Liliales</td><td>Liliatae</td></tr>
<tr><td>Ponderosa pine</td><td>Pinus ponderosa</td><td>Pinus</td><td>Pinaceae</td><td>Coniferales</td><td>Pinopsida</td><td rowspan="2">Pinophyta</td></tr>
<tr><td>Ginkgo tree</td><td>Ginkgo biloba</td><td>Ginkgo</td><td>Ginkgoaceae</td><td>Ginkgoales</td><td>Ginkgoopsida</td></tr>
<tr><td>Haircap moss</td><td>Polytrichum juniperum</td><td>Polytrichum</td><td>Polytrichaceae</td><td>Polytrichales</td><td>Musci</td><td>Bryophyta</td></tr>
</table>

from the use of a common name to designate different things in different places (for example, see ELK), or from the existence of several common names for a single species. There are two international organizations for the determination of the rules of nomenclature and the recording of specific names, one for zoology and one for botany. According to the rules they have established, the first name to be published (from the work of Linnaeus on) is the correct name of any organism, unless it is reclassified in such a way as to affect that name (for example, if it is moved from one genus to another). In such a case definite rules of priority also apply. See G. G. Simpson, *Principles of Animal Taxonomy* (1961); Arthur Cronquist, *Evolution and Classification of Flowering Plants* (1968); Ernst Mayr, *Principles of Systematic Zoology* (1969); O. T. Solbrig, *Principles and Methods of Plant Biosystematics* (1970); A. J. Cain, *Animal Species and Their Evolution* (3d ed. 1971); Nicholas Jardine and Robin Sibson, *Mathematical Taxonomy* (1971); Theodore Savory, *Animal Taxonomy* (1972); D. W. Shimwell, *The Description and Classification of Vegetation* (1972); D. H. Valentine, ed., *Taxonomy, Phytogeography, and Evolution* (1972).

Clatsop Indians, North American Indians of the Penutian linguistic stock (see AMERICAN INDIAN LANGUAGES). They lived on the Northwest coast S of the Columbia River.

Clauda, Greece: see GÁVDHOS.

Claude, Jean (zhäN klōd), 1619–87, French Protestant theologian. As Protestant pastor at Paris, Claude received considerable attention for his disagreements with the Roman Catholic apologist Jacques Bossuet, Pierre Nicole, and the Jansenist Antoine Arnauld. He was expelled from France after the revocation of the Edict of Nantes.

Claudel, Paul (pōl klōdĕl'), 1868–1955, French dramatist, poet, and diplomat. He was ambassador to Tokyo (1921–27), Washington, D.C. (1927–33), and Brussels (1933–35). Claudel's writings deal largely with man's inner spirit, and reveal the influence of his profound and mystical Catholicism. His early plays were inspired by the French symbolists, notably by Rimbaud. Perhaps his finest play is *L'Annonce faite a Marie* (1912, tr. *Tidings Brought to Mary,* 1916). Among his other dramas is the lengthy *Le Soulier de satin* (1929, tr. *The Satin Slipper,* 1931). In his theatrical works Claudel combined extensive use of symbols—primarily religious—and exotic backgrounds with the techniques of pantomime, ballet, music, and the cinema. The rich lyric verse of *Cinq Grandes Odes* (1910) marks his highest poetic achievement. His prose works include *Art poétique* (1906) and writings on the Bible. See study by R. Burchan (1966).

Claude Lorrain (klōd lôrăN'), whose original name was **Claude Gelée** or **Gellée** (zhəlā'), 1600–1682, French painter, b. Lorraine. Claude was the foremost landscape painter of his time. In Rome at about 12 years of age he was employed as a pastry cook for the landscape painter Augustino Tassi, whose apprentice he soon became. He traveled in Italy and France, and returned to settle permanently in Rome by 1627. Under the patronage of Pope Urban VIII he rapidly rose to fame. His poetic treatment of landscape raised this subject matter to eminence alongside the more esteemed religious and historical genres. Claude's paintings became so popular and widely imitated that in order to avoid forgeries, he began to record his compositions in a notebook of drawings (Duke of Devonshire Coll., Chatsworth). Engravings of them were later made and published as the *Liber veritatis* (1777). His early works reflect the late mannerist style of Tassi and that of the northerners Brill and Elsheimer. Although he began by using the traditional device of compartmentalized stages—foreground, middleground, and background—in his later landscapes he opened up unlimited vistas, introducing lyrical variations of light and atmosphere. In *The Expulsion of Hagar* (1668; Munich) he defied conventional composition for strong effect. In his later works light was the primary subject. It dissolved forms, drawing the eye into vast panoramas of land and sea. Claude's harbor scenes and views of the Roman countryside exercised a lasting influence on the art of landscape painting. Poussin was indebted to him, as was Richard Wilson, and he was consciously emulated two centuries later by J. M. W. TURNER. Claude's work is best represented in England. It can be seen in the National Gallery, London; the Doria Palace, Rome; the Louvre; the Prado; and in many American collections, including the museums of New York City, Boston, Kansas City, St. Louis, and San Francisco. See study by Marcel Röthlisberger (1961).

Claude Michel: see CLODION.

Claudia (klôd'ēə), Christian who sent greetings to Timothy. 2 Tim. 4.21.

Claudian (Claudius Claudianus) (klôd'ēən), d. 404?, last notable Latin classic poet. Probably born in Alexandria, he flourished at court under Arcadius and Honorius. Besides panegyrics, idyls, epigrams, and occasional poems, he wrote several epics, the most ambitious of which is the *Rape of Proserpine,* perhaps inferior to his epic attack *Against Rufinus.* He has been highly regarded as a vigorous, skillful, and imaginative writer. See T. Hodgkin, *Claudian, the Last of the Roman Poets* (1875); study by Alan Cameron (1970).

Claudius I (Tiberius Claudius Drusus Nero Germanicus) (klôd'ēəs), 10 B.C.–A.D. 54, Roman emperor (A.D. 41–A.D. 54), son of Nero Claudius Drusus Germanicus and thus nephew of TIBERIUS. When CALIGULA was murdered (A.D. 41), the soldiers found Claudius, who had been of little importance, hiding in abject terror behind a curtain in the palace. They hauled him forth, and the Praetorians proclaimed him emperor. This act offended the senators, who never forgave Claudius. It also made him favor the army. He annexed Mauretania and landed in A.D. 43 in Britain, which he made a province. Agrippa's kingdom of Judaea and the kingdom of Thrace were reabsorbed into the empire, and the authority of the provincial procurators was extended. He caused MESSALINA, his third wife, to be executed and was in turn supposedly poisoned by her successor, AGRIPPINA II, after she had persuaded him to pass over his son BRITANNICUS as heir in favor of NERO, her son by a former husband. Claudius was much reviled by his enemies and historians have accused him of being only a tool in the hands of his freedmen-secretaries and his wives; there are indications, however, that he had considerable administrative ability. Claudius' literary works are lost. He is the chief figure in two novels by Robert Graves, *I, Claudius* (1934) and *Claudius the God* (1935). See studies by Arnaldo Momigliano (tr. 1962) and V. M. Scramuzza (1940).

Claudius II (Marcus Aurelius Claudius), d. 270, Roman emperor (268–70), called Gothicus. A successful general under Valerian, Claudius put down the revolt in which GALLIENUS was killed. He succeeded Gallienus and went to the East to resist the Goths who were overrunning the empire. In 269, Claudius overwhelmed the Goths at Naissus (now Nis, Yugoslavia). He died of the plague the following year and was succeeded by AURELIAN.

Claudius, ancient Roman gens. **Appius Claudius Sabinus Inregillensis** or **Regillensis** was a Sabine; he came (c.504 B.C.) with his tribe to Rome. While consul (495), he caused the withdrawal of the plebeians to the sacred mount because of his severe interpretation of the laws of debt. His Sabine name was Attius Clausus. **Appius Claudius Crassus** was decemvir (451–449 B.C.). He seems to have sought to placate the plebeians and was known as a lawgiver, but his career ended in failure. Legend says that his attempt to rape VIRGINIA caused a revolt in which he was killed and which led to the fall of the decemvirs. **Appius Claudius Caecus,** while censor (312–308 B.C.), increased the role taken by the lower classes in public affairs. He was consul (307 and 296) and later persuaded the senate to reject the peace proposals of PYRRHUS. He constructed the first Roman aqueduct and began construction of the Appian Way. **Publius Claudius Pulcher,** while consul (249 B.C.), attacked the Carthaginian fleet at Drepanum and was defeated. It was believed that he was defeated because he threw the sacred chickens into the sea. **Appius Claudius Pulcher,** d. c.48 B.C., campaigned in Asia (72 B.C.). He became praetor (57 B.C.), propraetor in Sardinia (56 B.C.), consul (54 B.C.), and proconsul of Cilicia (53 B.C.). He sought through Pompey the assistance of his rival Cicero to secure his acquittal from impeachment for bribery. He joined Pompey in the civil war and died in Euboea before the battle at Pharsala. For Publius Claudius Pulcher, see CLODIUS.

Claudius Lysias (lĭs'ēəs), official at Jerusalem who saved Paul from the mob. Acts 23,24.

Clausel or **Clauzel, Bertrand** (bĕrträN' klōzĕl'), 1772–1842, marshal of France. Having served in the French Revolutionary Wars and in the Napoleonic campaigns, particularly in the Peninsular War, he was created count (1813). He joined Napoleon in the Hundred Days (1815) and after the Restoration spent some time in exile in the United States, returning (1820) to France to become a deputy of the opposition. After the July Revolution he was sent to Algeria as commander in chief (1830) and was made marshal (1831). Again commander in chief and governor general in Algeria (1835–37), he was blamed for French reverses there.

Clausewitz, Karl von (kärl fən klou'zəvĭts), 1780–1831, Prussian general and writer on military strategy. He served in the Rhine campaigns (1793–94), won the regard of Gerhard von Scharnhorst at the Berlin Military Academy, and served in the wars against Napoleon Bonaparte. In the service of Russia from 1812 until 1814, he helped negotiate the convention of Tauroggen (1812), which prepared the way for the alliance of Prussia, Russia, and Great Britain against Napoleon. Later he reentered the Prussian army, fought at Waterloo, and was appointed (1818) director of the Prussian war college. His masterpiece, *On War,* was unfinished and was published after his death. The doctrines expounded in it, including that of total war (that all citizens, territory, and property of the enemy nation should be attacked in every way possible) and that of war itself as a political act (a continuation of diplomacy by other means, in which political leaders of the state must determine the war's scope and objectives and exercise control of its direction) had an enormous effect on military strategy and tactics.

Clausius, Rudolf Julius Emanuel (rōō'dôlf yōō'lyōōs āmä'nōōĕl klou'zēōōs), 1822–88, German mathematical physicist. A pioneer in the science of thermodynamics, he introduced the concept of entropy and restated the second law of thermodynamics: heat cannot of itself pass from a colder to a hotter body. He applied his researches on heat, electricity, and molecular physics to the development of the kinetic theory of gases and in formulating a theory of electrolysis wherein he states that electric forces are merely directing agents in the interchange of ions. A professor at the Polytechnic Institute, Zurich (1855–67), and at the universities of Würzburg (1867–69) and Bonn (from 1869), he wrote *Die Potentialfunktion und das Potential* (1859) and *Die mechanische Wärmetheorie* (1865–67; tr. *The Mechanical Theory of Heat,* 1879).

Clausthal-Zellerfeld (klous'täl-tsĕl'ərfĕlt), town (1970 pop. 14,821), Lower Saxony, E West Germany, a resort in the Harz mts. Its manufactures include textiles and wood products. The town was once a center for the mining of copper, zinc, and lead ores.

Clauzel, Bertrand: see CLAUSEL, BERTRAND.

Claverhouse, John Graham of: see DUNDEE, JOHN GRAHAM OF CLAVERHOUSE, 1ST VISCOUNT.

clavichord (klăv'ĭkôrd), keyboard musical instrument invented in the Middle Ages. It consists of a small rectangular wooden box, placed upon a table or upon legs, containing a sounding board and a set

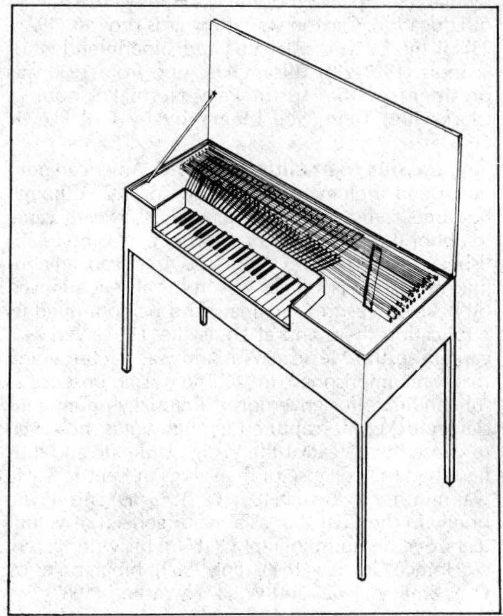

Clavichord

of strings. Keys caused the strings to be struck with small wedges of metal called tangents, which not only set the string into vibration but determined its vibrating length by means of a sort of fretting (see FRETTED INSTRUMENT). Thus one string sufficed for about four keys. Early in the 18th cent., clavichords were built with a string for each key; such instruments were more expensive and harder to tune, but gradually supplanted the older ones. The clavichord became musically important in the 16th cent. and remained popular until the end of the 18th cent.

when it was displaced by the pianoforte. It is a drawing room instrument with a delicate, expressive tone. See Philip James, *Early Keyboard Instruments* (1930); Denis Matthews, ed., *Keyboard Music* (1972).

Clavière, Étienne (ātyĕn′ klävyĕr′), 1735–93, French financier. A merchant and banker of Geneva, he participated (1782) in the popular revolution at Geneva and was forced to leave when the aristocrats returned to power in the same year. He settled in Paris. During the French Revolution Clavière was an adviser to the comte de Mirabeau on financial policy and had a part in the issuing of ASSIGNATS. He was finance minister in the king's Girondist cabinet of March–June, 1792. Clavière fell with the GIRONDISTS and committed suicide rather than face the Revolutionary Tribunal.

Clavijero, Francisco Javier (fränsēs′kō hävyĕr′ klävĕhā′rō), 1731–87, Mexican scholar and historian. A Jesuit, he taught in Mexico until the expulsion of the order (1767). From his refuge in Italy he wrote several works, the most important being *The History of Mexico* (tr. 1787), which shows an immense knowledge of Indian languages, customs, and history.

Clavius, Cristoph (krĭs′tôf klä′vēəs), 1537–1612, German astronomer and mathematician. He entered the Jesuit order in 1555 and studied at Coimbra and Rome. He taught mathematics at the Collegio Romano from 1565. In a commentary on Euclid (1574) and other works, Clavius collected mathematical knowledge, adding some proofs and methods of his own; he helped spread elements of modern algebraic notation such as the plus sign and parentheses. His *Commentary on the Sphere of Sacrobosco* (1581), which had many editions, was the standard astronomical text of his time. In 1582 his proposed reform of the calendar was adopted by Pope Gregory XIII. In the last years of his life he confirmed Galileo's telescopic observations, although he did not accept them as proof of the Copernican theory.

Clawson, city (1970 pop. 17,617), Oakland co., SE Mich., a residential suburb between Pontiac and Detroit; settled c.1833, inc. 1920.

Claxton, Philander Priestly, 1862–1957, American educator, b. Bedford co., Tenn., grad. Univ. of Tennessee (B.A., 1882; M.A., 1887) and studied at Johns Hopkins Univ. and in Germany. After several years' experience as a superintendent of schools in North Carolina, he taught at the North Carolina State Normal and Industrial College (1893–1902) and later was professor of education at the Univ. of Tennessee (1902–11). He served (1911–21) as U.S. commissioner of education, his administration being distinguished by marked expansion of the activities of the Bureau of Education. Claxton was afterwards provost (1921–23) of the Univ. of Alabama and superintendent of schools (1923–29), Tulsa, Okla., and from 1930 was president of the Austin Peay Normal School in Clarksville, Tenn. See biography by C. L. Lewis (1948).

Clay, Cassius Marcellus, 1810–1903, American politician and diplomat, b. Madison co., Ky. Although he came from a slaveholding family, Clay early came to abhor the institution of slavery. In 1845 he established at Lexington, Ky., the *True American,* an abolitionist paper. His press was in his absence moved by his enemies to Cincinnati, and he continued its publication there and at Louisville. He served as a captain in the Mexican War and was captured and for a time imprisoned. In 1851 he was an unsuccessful candidate for governor of Kentucky on an antislavery ticket; he captured enough votes, however, to cause the defeat of the Whig candidate and thus hastened the collapse of the Whigs in Kentucky. He was minister to Russia (1861–62, 1863–69) and served briefly in the Civil War as a major general of volunteers. See his autobiography (1866); his writings, ed. by Horace Greeley (1848, repr. 1969); biographies by D. L. Smiley (1962) and W. H. Townsend (1967).

Clay, Cassius Marcellus, Jr.: see ALI, MUHAMMAD.

Clay, Clement Claiborne, 1816–82, U.S. Senator (1853–61), b. Huntsville, Ala. A legislator and then a judge in his native state, he was twice elected to the U.S. Senate and became an ardent defender of the states' rights doctrine. He left the Senate upon Alabama's secession and entered the Confederate senate, refusing the appointment as Secretary of War in the Confederacy. In 1864 he was sent by Jefferson Davis with two others on a diplomatic mission to Canada, which was intended to open peace negotiations with the Federal government. Lincoln finally decided not to see him, and after a year in Canada, Clay returned to the South. After the assassination of Lincoln, he was accused of having taken part in a plot in Canada against Lincoln's life and also of having planned raids across the border, and a reward was offered for him. He gave himself up, was held at Fortress Monroe for almost a year without trial, and then was freed. His wife, Virginia Clay-Clopton, wrote *A Belle of the Fifties* (1904), a description of their Washington, D.C., home when it was a gathering place of capital society.

Clay, Henry, 1777–1852, American statesman, b. Hanover co., Va. His father died when Henry was four years old, and Clay's formal schooling was limited to three years. His stepfather secured (1792) for him a clerk's position in the Virginia high court of chancery. There he gained the regard of George WYTHE, who directed his reading. Clay also read law under Robert Brooke, attorney general of Virginia, and in 1797 he was licensed to practice. Moving in the same year to Lexington, Ky., he quickly gained wide reputation as a lawyer and orator. He served (1803–6) in the Kentucky legislature and was (1805–7) professor of law at Transylvania Univ. Having spent the short session of 1806–7 in the U.S. Senate, he returned (1807) to the state legislature, became (1808) speaker, and remained there until he was chosen to fill an unexpired term (1810–11) in the U.S. Senate. In 1810 he was elected to the U.S. House of Representatives and served (1811–14) as speaker. As spokesman of Western expansionist interests and leader of the "war hawks," Clay stirred up enthusiasm for war with Great Britain and helped bring on the War of 1812. He resigned (1814) from Congress to aid in the peace negotiations leading to the Treaty of Ghent. He again served (1815–21) in the House, again was speaker (1815–20), and began to formulate his "American system," a national program that ultimately included Federal aid for internal improvements and tariff protection of American industries. In 1821, Clay, to pacify sectional interests, pushed the MISSOURI COMPROMISE through the House. In the House for the last time (1823–25), he once more became (1823) speaker, and he did much to augment the powers of that office. In this session he secured the western extension of the NATIONAL ROAD and, against much opposition, eloquently carried through the Tariff of 1824. As a candidate for the presidency in 1824, Clay had the fourth largest number of electoral votes, and, with no candidate having a majority, the election went to the House, where the three highest were to be voted upon. It became Clay's duty to vote for one of his rivals. Despite the Western interests of Andrew JACKSON and despite the instructions of Kentucky to vote for him, Clay's dislike for the military hero was so intense that he voted for John Quincy ADAMS. When President Adams appointed Clay Secretary of State, Jackson's friends cried "corrupt bargain" and charged Clay with political collusion. Evidence has not been found to prove this, but the accusation impeded Clay's future political fortunes. As Secretary of State (1825–29), he secured congressional approval—which came too late for the American delegates to attend—of U.S. participation in the Pan American Congress of 1826. In 1828, Clay again supported Adams for President, and Jackson's success bitterly disappointed him. Although he intended to retire from politics, Clay was elected (1831) to the U.S. Senate and now led the National Republicans, who were beginning to call themselves Whigs (because they opposed Jackson's "tyranny"). Hoping to embarrass Jackson, Clay led the opposition in the Senate to the President's policies, but when the election came Jackson was overwhelmingly reelected. Clay's chagrin was buried in the crisis developing over the tariff. South Carolina's NULLIFICATION of the tariffs of 1828 and 1832 as well as Jackson's threats of armed invasion of that state allowed Clay to gain politically—working, even at the cost of his own protectionist views, toward a compromise with the John C. CALHOUN faction, he helped to promote the Compromise Tariff of 1833. Clay opposed the Jackson regime at every turn, particularly on the bank issue. When Jackson had the deposits removed (1833) from the BANK OF THE UNITED STATES to his "pet banks," Clay secured in the Senate passage of a resolution—later expunged (Jan., 1837) from the record—censuring the President for his act. Refusing to run for President in 1836, Clay continued his opposition tactics against Van Buren's administration and fought the SUBTREASURY system in vain. In 1840, Clay lost the Whig nomination to William H. Harrison, mainly because of Thurlow Weed's adroit politics. Clay supported Harrison and, when Harrison was elected, was offered the post of Secretary of State, but he chose to stay in the Senate. He now planned to reestablish the Bank of the United States, but the unexpected accession of John TYLER to the presidency and his vetoes of Clay's bills caused Clay to resign his Senate seat. In 1844 he ran against James K. POLK, an avowed expansionist. Earlier Clay had publicly opposed the annexation of Texas, and he restated his position in the "Alabama letters," agreeing to annexation if it could be accomplished with the common consent of the Union and without war. This maneuver probably lost him New York state, with which he could have won the election. His failure was crushing for him and for the Whig party. In 1848 his party refused him its nomination, feeling that he had no chance, so that his presidential aspirations were never fulfilled. He reentered (1849) the Senate when the country faced the slavery question in the territory newly acquired by the Mexican War. Clay denounced the extremists in both North and South, asserted the superior claims of the Union, and was chiefly instrumental in shaping the COMPROMISE OF 1850. It was the third time that he saved the Union in a crisis, and thus he has been called the Great Pacificator and the Great Compromiser. Publication of his papers (ed. by James Hopkins) was begun in 1959. See also his works (7 vol., 1896); biographies by Carl Schurz (1887, repr. 1968), Glyndon Van Deusen (1937), and Bernard Mayo (1937, repr. 1966).

Clay, Lucius DuBignon, 1897–, American general, b. Marietta, Ga. A graduate of West Point and an engineering officer, he held many army administrative posts and became (1944) deputy director of the office of War Mobilization and Reconversion. Clay was (1945–47) deputy chief of the U.S. military government in Germany before he directed operations in the Berlin blockade as U.S. military governor (1947–49). Clay retired from the army as a full general in May, 1949, to enter private business. After the closing of the borders between East and West Berlin by the Communists, he served (Sept., 1961–May, 1962) as President Kennedy's personal representative in Berlin with the rank of ambassador. He wrote *Decision in Germany* (1950).

clay, common name for a number of fine-grained, earthy materials that become plastic when wet. The individual clay particles are always smaller than 0.004 mm. Clays often form colloidal suspensions when immersed in water, but the clay particles flocculate (clump) and settle quickly in saline water. Clays are easily molded into a form that they retain when dry, and they become hard and lose their plasticity when subjected to heat. Chemically, clays are hydrous aluminum silicates, ordinarily containing impurities, e.g., potassium, sodium, calcium, magnesium, or iron, in small amounts. Clay consists of a sheet of interconnected silicates combined with a second sheetlike grouping of metallic atoms, oxygen, and hydroxyl, forming a two-layer mineral such as KAOLINITE. Sometimes the latter sheetlike structure is found sandwiched between two silica sheets, forming a three-layer mineral such as vermiculite. Clays are divided into two classes: residual clay, found in the place of origin, and transported clay, also known as sedimentary clay, removed from the place of origin by an agent of erosion and deposited in a new and possibly distant position. Residual clays are most commonly formed by surface weathering, which gives rise to clay in three ways—by the chemical decomposition of rocks, such as granite, containing silica and alumina; by the solution of rocks, such as limestone, containing clayey impurities, which, being insoluble, are deposited as clay; and by the disintegration and solution of shale. One of the commonest processes of clay formation is the chemical decomposition of FELDSPAR. In the lithification process, compacted clay layers can be transformed into shale. Under the intense heat and pressure that may develop in the layers, the shale can be metamorphosed into slate. From prehistoric times, clay has been indispensable in architecture, in industry, and in agriculture. As a building material, it is used in the form of BRICK, either sun-dried (adobe) or fired. Clays are also of great industrial importance, e.g., in the manufacture of TILE for wall and floor coverings, of porcelain, china, and earthenware, and of pipe for drainage and sewage. Properties of the clays used in such products that must be taken into consideration include plasticity, shrinkage under firing and under air drying, fineness of grain, color after firing, hardness, cohesion, and capacity of the surface to take decoration. On the basis of such qualities clays are variously divided into classes or groups; products are generally made from mixtures of clays and other substances. The purest clays are the CHINA CLAYS and kaolins. "Ball clay" is a name for a group of plastic, refractory clays used with other clays to improve their plasticity and to increase their strength. Bentonites are clays composed of very fine particles derived usually from volcanic ash. They are composed chiefly of the hydrous magnesium-calcium-aluminum silicate called montmorillonite. Highly absorbent, bentonite is much used in foundry work for facing the molds and preparing the molding sands for casting metals. The less absorbent bentonites are used chiefly in the oil industry, e.g., as filtering and deodorizing agents in the refining of petroleum and, mixed with other materials, as drilling muds to protect the cutting bit while drilling. Other uses are in the making of fillers, sizings, and dressings in construction, in clarifying water and wine, in purifying sewage, and in the paper, ceramics, plastics, and rubber industries. Clay is one of the three principal types of soil, the other two being sand and loam. A certain amount of clay is a desirable constituent of soil, since it binds other kinds of particles together and makes the whole retentive of water. Excessively clayey soils, however, are exceedingly difficult to cultivate. Their stiffness presents resistance to implements, impedes the growth of the plants, and prevents free circulation of air around the roots. They are cold and sticky in wet weather, while in dry weather they bake hard and crack. Clods form very often in clayey soils. Clays can be improved by the addition of lime, chalk, or organic matter; sodium nitrate, however, intensifies the injurious effects. In spite of their disadvantages, the richness of clay soils makes them favorable to the growth of crops that have been started in other soil. See also FULLER'S EARTH. See R. E. Grim, *Clay Mineralogy* (2d ed. 1968); R. W. Grimshaw, *The Chemistry and Physics of Clays and Allied Ceramic Materials* (4th ed. 1971).

clay pan: see HARDPAN.

Clayton, Henry De Lamar, 1857–1929, U.S. Congressman, b. Barbour co., Ala. A Democrat, he was a member of the House of Representatives from 1897 to 1915 and later a Federal district judge. He is chiefly remembered as the author of the CLAYTON ANTITRUST ACT.

Clayton, John Middleton, 1796–1856, American statesman, b. Sussex co., Del. Admitted (1819) to the bar, he practiced at Dover, Del., held many state offices, and was twice (1828, 1845) elected to the U.S. Senate. In the presidential election of 1848 he gave his support to Zachary Taylor and was rewarded with the position of Secretary of State, an office he held until Taylor's death in 1850. As Secretary of State he negotiated the CLAYTON-BULWER TREATY, which checked British expansion in Central America and temporarily settled a rivalry that had brought England and the United States into conflict. He reentered the Senate in 1852.

Clayton, city (1970 pop. 16,222), seat of St. Louis co., E central Mo., a suburb of St. Louis; inc. 1919.

Clayton Antitrust Act, 1914, passed by the U.S. Congress as an amendment to clarify and supplement the SHERMAN ANTITRUST ACT of 1890. It was drafted by Henry De Lamar Clayton. The act prohibited exclusive sales contracts, local price cutting to freeze out competitors, rebates, interlocking directorates in corporations capitalized at $1 million or more in the same field of business, and intercorporate stock holdings. Labor unions and agricultural cooperatives were excluded from the forbidden combinations in the restraint of trade. The act restricted the use of the INJUNCTION against labor, and it legalized peaceful strikes, picketing, and boycotts. It declared that "the labor of a human being is not a commodity or article of commerce." Organized labor was as heartened by the act as it had been dejected by the doctrine of the DANBURY HATTERS' CASE, but judicial construction soon made the labor provisions of the act meaningless. The Clayton Antitrust Act was the basis for a great many important and much-publicized suits against large corporations. Later amendments to the act strengthened its provisions against unfair price cutting (1936) and intercorporate stock holdings (1950).

Clayton-Bulwer Treaty, concluded (April 19, 1850) at Washington, D.C., between the United States, represented by Secretary of State John M. Clayton, and Great Britain, represented by the British plenipotentiary Sir Henry Bulwer. American and British rivalries in Central America, particularly over a proposed isthmian canal, led to the treaty. Its most important article provided "that neither . . . will ever obtain or maintain for itself any exclusive control over the said ship canal . . . that neither will ever erect or maintain any fortifications commanding the same . . . or occupy, or fortify, or colonize or assume, or exercise any dominion over Nicaragua, Costa Rica, the Mosquito coast [in present-day Honduras and Nicaragua], or any part of Central America." Although the treaty was soon ratified by the Senate, it was one of the most unpopular in U.S. history, viewed by some as a betrayal of the Monroe Doctrine. Successive Secretaries of State tried in vain to secure modifications that would enable the United States to build its own canal and exercise, under restrictions, political control over it, but it was not until 1901, with the HAY-PAUNCEFOTE TREATIES, that this end was finally achieved. See M. W. Williams, *Anglo-American Isthmian Diplomacy, 1815–1915* (1916, repr. 1965).

Clazomenae (kləzŏm'ĭnē), ancient city of W Asia Minor, 20 mi (32 km) W of present-day İzmir, Turkey. It was one of the 12 Ionian cities of Asia Minor. The city was founded on the mainland but was later moved to a small island, and Alexander the Great built a causeway to it. The town continued to flourish through the Hellenistic and Roman periods. It was the birthplace of the philosopher Anaxagoras and was famous for its black-figure pottery and its terra-cotta sarcophagi.

Cleanthes (klēăn'thēz), 3d cent. B.C., Greek philosopher, head of the Stoic school following Zeno.

Clearchus (klēär'kəs), d. 401 B.C., Spartan officer, celebrated as the leader of the Ten Thousand (see ANABASIS). Sent in 410 to govern Byzantium, he made himself unpopular by his harsh discipline, and Alcibiades took the city in 408 B.C. Clearchus later returned and made himself virtual ruler, thereby incurring the anger of the Spartans, who forced him to leave (403). He sought refuge with Cyrus the Younger of Persia, who used him to recruit and later command the Greek mercenary force in support of Cyrus' claim to the throne. At CUNAXA, Clearchus fought boldly, but Cyrus' forces were defeated. After the battle he led the Greek force (the Ten Thousand) in retreat, but was lured into a conference by TISSAPHERNES and treacherously murdered. The story of the retreat was made famous by Zenophon.

clearcutting: see FORESTRY.

Clearfield, city (1970 pop. 13,316), Davis co., N Utah; inc. 1922. Hill Air Force Base and a naval supply depot are the major employers.

clearing, in banking, the periodic settling of bankers' claims against each other. For that purpose local banks form clearinghouse associations. Clearinghouses are said to have existed in Florence by A.D. 800. They were certainly perfected in Lyons by 1463, and their use was widespread in 18th-century Europe. The first modern clearinghouse was either at Edinburgh (1760) or at London (1773); clearinghouses were then established in Dublin (1846), New York (1853), Paris (1872), and Berlin (1883). Before the introduction of clearinghouses each bank periodically sent runners to other banks to adjust claims bilaterally. The clearinghouse instead holds meetings of representatives of all banks in a given area to adjust claims and is thus a major labor-saving device. The New York Clearing House, for example, clears checks, stock certificates, and coupons several times daily. Each bank sends a delivery clerk and a settling clerk to the house; they bring with them bundles of checks and other obligations due their banks from other banks, each bank being represented by a separate package. Lists of such obligations are handed to an inspector before clearing begins; the total of the lists is the total amount to be settled that day. When clearing begins, each delivery clerk passes from one desk to another, depositing on each his bank's claims upon the bank represented at that desk. When a settling clerk at any one desk has received all his packages, he draws up a statement of the demands made upon his bank, as shown by the totals of the packages. He sends the statement to the manager of the clearinghouse, along with the total that his bank is owed. When all settling clerks have finished, the accounts are examined and proved, and the manager certifies the amounts that each bank owes to and is entitled to receive from the other banks. The balance (debit or credit) for each bank is forwarded to the Federal Reserve bank, which adjusts the accounts of each bank. All packages of claims are accepted at the clearinghouse desks without examination; they are later carried back to the banks receiving them and are there examined. If any claims are found invalid, the banks concerned rectify the error without using the clearinghouse. Dues, usually in proportion to the number of transactions presented by each bank per year, support the clearinghouse. With the consent of the clearing association, nonmembers may be permitted to clear through members. Intercity balances in the United States are settled on the books of the Federal Reserve banks daily by telegraphic transfers. Clearing is practiced also by stock and commodity exchanges. International claims are settled by clearing unions, groups of central banks and other major financial institutions. The most famous such group is the European Payments Union (created 1950). See F. P. Thomson, *Money in the Computer Age* (1968).

Clear Lake, 65 sq mi (168 sq km), W Calif., in wooded hills NW of San Francisco. It is the largest freshwater lake entirely within California and is a fishing resort. Mt. Konochti rises nearly 3,000 ft (910 m) on the west shore.

clearstory: see CLERESTORY.

Clearwater, residential and resort city (1970 pop. 52,074), seat of Pinellas co., W Fla., on the Pinellas peninsula, on Clearwater Bay and the Gulf of Mexico; inc. 1891. Its thriving tourist industry dates from 1896. A landscaped causeway connects the city proper with a 4-mi (6.4-km) long island of white sand beaches fronting on the Gulf. Several national corporate headquarters are in the city. Clearwater was settled after the establishment there of Fort Harrison in 1841. It is linked with Tampa by a causeway across Old Tampa Bay to the east. It is the seat of Clearwater Christian College and a junior college, and has an art center, a theater, and many recreational facilities.

Clearwater, river, c.190 mi (305 km) long, rising in several branches in the Bitterroot Range, N Idaho, and flowing west to join the Snake River at Lewiston, Idaho. The gold-mining era in Idaho began in 1860, when gold was discovered and mining camps were set up on the river's southern fork.

cleavage, tendency of many minerals to split along definite smooth planar surfaces determined by their crystal structure. The directions of these surfaces are related to weaknesses in the atomic structure of the mineral and are always parallel to a possible crystal face. The property of cleavage is useful in identifying a mineral species. The tendency for certain varieties of metamorphic and sedimentary rock to split along more or less smooth surfaces is sometimes referred to as rock cleavage. Flagstone, slate, and schist are noted for this property, which arises from the parallel alignment of fine, platy mineral grains themselves displaying cleavage.

Cleaveland, Moses, 1754–1806, American pioneer, b. Canterbury, Conn. After serving (1777–81) in the American Revolution, he practiced law in his native town and entered (1787) the state legislature. When the Connecticut Land Company purchased (1795) land in the WESTERN RESERVE region of Ohio, Cleaveland was chosen as one of the directors and surveyors of the company. In 1796 he led a party of men to the mouth of the Cuyahoga River, where he determined to develop the main settlement. The surveyors named the site Cleaveland, which name it bore until c.1830, when it became Cleveland.

Cleburne, Patrick Ronayne (klē'bərn), 1828–64, Confederate general, b. Co. Cork, Ireland. He emigrated to America in 1849 and was practicing law in Helena, Ark., when the Civil War broke out. Cleburne, who had served in the British army, was made a brigadier general in March, 1862. He commanded a brigade at Shiloh (April), and a division at Richmond (Aug.) and Perryville, Ky. (Oct.). Promoted to major general (Dec.), he distinguished himself further at Murfreesboro and in the campaigns around Chattanooga and Atlanta. Cleburne was one of the most persistent of the group of Southern generals who advocated that slaves be freed and used as soldiers. His last service was in the Tennessee campaign of 1864; he was killed at the battle of Franklin (Nov.). See biography by Howell and Elizabeth Purdue; Ella Lonn, *Foreigners in the Confederacy* (1940, repr. 1965).

Cleburne, city (1970 pop. 16,015), seat of Johnson co., N Texas; inc. 1907. It is a rail, processing, and medical center in a farming area. The city has huge railroad shops, cotton mills, limestone-processing plants, and factories producing a variety of products. Two rodeos are held there annually. A state park is nearby.

Cleef or **Cleve, Joos van** (yōs vän klāf, klā'və), c.1485–1540, early Flemish portrait painter. Much of his life was spent in Antwerp. He is often identified with the Master of the Death of the Virgin from altarpieces in Munich and Cologne. Portraits of Henry VIII (Hampton Court) and Francis I (Johnson Coll., Philadelphia) are attributed to him. A sentimental *Holy Family* by Joos is in the National Gallery, London.

Cleethorpes (klē'thôrps), municipal borough (1971 pop. 35,785), in the Parts of Lindsey, Lincolnshire, E central England, on the Humber River estuary. It is a popular resort, with many recreational facilities. The nearby Church of Old Clee was dedicated in 1192 by the bishop of Lincoln. In 1974, Cleethorpes became part of the new nonmetropolitan county of Humberside.

clef, in music: see MUSICAL NOTATION.

cleft palate, incomplete fusion of bones of the palate, resulting in a lack of separation between the oral and nasal cavities. The cleft may be confined to the soft palate at the back of the mouth; it may include the hard palate, or roof of the mouth; or it may extend through the gum and lip, producing a gap in the teeth and a HARELIP. The condition appears to be hereditary but not under the control of a single pair of genes. An infant cannot develop proper suction for drinking, and there is the danger of milk entering the nasal cavity and being aspirated into the lungs. Formula must be carefully placed at the back of the tongue for normal swallowing to take place. Ear infection may result from food or fluid passing from the nasal cavity to the middle ear by way of the Eustachian tubes. Proper speech articulation is difficult unless the cleft is surgically closed. The proper time for such an operation is in dispute; some authorities prefer early closure, before the cleft interferes with development of normal speech habits, while others prefer to wait for several years until facial growth has been completed.

Cleisthenes, fl. 510 B.C., Athenian statesman. He was the head of his family, the ALCMAEONIDAE, after the exile of Hippias, and with Spartan help had made himself undisputed ruler of Athens by 506 B.C. He established a more democractic constitution by weakening the clan system and the local parties and by organizing the districts into political rather than social divisions. The Alcmaeonidae thus became leaders of a democratic party, a reorientation making them anti-Spartan instead of pro-Spartan as earlier. An attempt of his rival, Isagoras, to overturn the reforms of Cleisthenes after Cleisthenes had been sent into exile failed, and Cleisthenes was recalled. Sparta aided Isagoras, and Spartan hatred of the Alcmaeonidae began with Cleisthenes. The name also appears as Clisthenes.

Cleiveland, John: see CLEVELAND, JOHN.

clematis (klĕm'ətĭs), any plant of the large genus *Clematis* (sometimes subdivided into three or four genera), widely distributed herbs or vines of the family Ranunculaceae (BUTTERCUP family), many of them native. The vines are the more popular and are usually profuse bloomers; some have an irritating juice, leafstalks serving as tendrils, and small dry fruits with a feathery taillike appendage. The flowers are varied in shape and color. Most popular in North America are the Jackman clematis (*C. jackmanii*), a large purple hybrid, and the Japanese clematis (*C. paniculata*) with small white flowers. Some clematises are called virgin's-bower, traveler's-joy, leatherflower, and old-man's-beard. Clematis is classified in the division MAGNOLIOPHYTA, class Magnoliopsida, order Ranunculales, family Ranunculaceae.

Clemenceau, Georges (zhôrzh klāmäNsō'), 1841–1929, French political figure, twice premier (1906–9, 1917–20), called "the Tiger." He was trained as a doctor, but his republicanism brought him into conflict with the government of Napoleon III, and he went (1865) to the United States, where he spent several years as a journalist and a teacher. Returning to France in 1869, he was mayor of Montmartre in Paris after the overthrow (1870) of Napoleon III. His political career, beginning in revolution, continued to be a stormy one punctuated by verbal and physical duels. As a Socialist, he opposed the moderate Léon GAMBETTA; drove Jules FERRY from power; and first supported but then bitterly opposed General BOULANGER. A member of the chamber of deputies from 1876, he failed to win reelection in 1893 after being implicated in the Panama Canal scandal, and then unjustly accused of being in the pay of the British. During the next nine years he devoted himself to journalism, writing a daily article in *La Justice*, and founding (1900) *Le Bloc.* He was a passionate defender of Alfred Dreyfus in the DREYFUS AFFAIR. In 1902, Clemenceau was elected senator, and in 1906 he became minister of the interior and then premier. During his tenure the first crisis over MOROCCO was settled and the alliance with Great Britain strengthened. Clemenceau's harsh measures against strikers caused his final breach with the Socialists. In 1909 his cabinet fell and Aristide BRIAND became premier. In the next years Clemenceau vigorously attacked Germany and pressed for military preparedness. His newspaper, *L'Homme libre* (after its suppression in 1914, *L'Homme enchaîné*) attacked the government for defeatism even after the outbreak of World War I. Succeeding Paul PAINLEVÉ as premier in Nov., 1917, Clemenceau formed a coalition cabinet in which he was also minister of war. He renewed the dispirited morale of France and pushed the war vigorously until the final victory. Leading the French delegation at the Paris Peace Conference, Clemenceau was the main antagonist of Woodrow WILSON; he regarded the Versailles Treaty as inadequate in guaranteeing the security of France. Ironically, he was defeated in the presidential election of 1920 because of what was regarded as his leniency toward Germany. Alexandre Millerand succeeded him as premier. Clemenceau retired to his native Vendée, where he wrote *In the Evening of My Thought* (tr. 1929) and other works. See biographies by Geoffrey Bruun (1943, repr. 1962) and J. H. Jackson (1946, repr. 1962); Wythe Williams, *The Tiger of France* (1949).

Clemens, Samuel Langhorne: see TWAIN, MARK.

Clement I, Saint, or **Clement of Rome,** d. A. D. 97?, pope (A.D. 88?–A.D. 97?), martyr; successor of St. Cletus. He may have known the apostles Peter and Paul, and after them he was the most esteemed figure in the church. His letter to the church at Corinth was considered canonical by some until the 4th cent. It is notable for the authority Clement assumes in resolving the factionalism that was afflicting the Corinthians and in enjoining the need for order in the church. St. Clement was the first Christian writer to use the myth of the phoenix as an allegory of the Resurrection. Many writings have been wrongly attributed to him, particularly the so-called Second Epistle of St. Clement to the Corinthians. He is represented in frescoes in the Church of San Clemente, Rome. He was succeeded by St. Evaristus. Feast: Nov. 23. See J. A. Kleist, tr., *The Epistles of St. Clement of Rome and St. Ignatius of Antioch* (1946).

Clement III, antipope: see GUIBERT OF RAVENNA.

Clement IV, d. 1268, pope (1265–68), a Frenchman named Guy le gros Foulques; successor of Urban IV. He was a lay adviser of King Louis IX of France, but after his wife's death he entered the church. As pope he continued the struggle against the HOHENSTAUFEN by confirming the agreement with CHARLES I (Charles of Anjou) that gave Charles the crown of Naples, by raising an army for him, and by investing him with the kingdom. When CONRADIN attacked Charles, Clement had a crusade preached against him. He was a strong opponent of nepotism, and he was the patron of Roger BACON. He was succeeded by Gregory X.

Clement V, 1264–1314, pope (1305–14), a Frenchman named Bertrand de Got; successor of Benedict XI. He was made archbishop of Bordeaux by BONIFACE VIII, who trusted him; surprisingly, he was also in some favor at the court of PHILIP IV, even though Philip and the pope were archenemies. He was crowned pope at Lyons in Philip's presence and lived the rest of his life in France. In 1309 he settled at Avignon, beginning the long, controversial residency of the PAPACY there. The pontificate of Clement is one long chronicle of dictation by the French king. Although Clement effectively squelched Philip's effort to have Boniface posthumously condemned as a heretic—an act that would have been disastrous to the papacy—he supported Philip in the infamous suppression of the KNIGHTS TEMPLARS. He called the Council of Vienne (1311; see VIENNE, COUNCIL OF) to settle the issue and to deal with questions of heresy and church reform. He opposed Philip by supporting the election and coronation (1312) of Henry VII as Holy Roman emperor, but later renounced Henry for his policies in Italy. The *Constitutiones Clementinae,* issued by the pope in 1313, are important in canon law. He was succeeded by John XXII.

Clement VI, 1291–1352, pope (1342–52), a Frenchman named Pierre Roger; successor of Benedict XII. His court was at Avignon. He had been archbishop of Sens, archbishop of Rouen, and cardinal (1338). The principal event of his pontificate was the PLAGUE known as the Black Death (1348–50); Clement did what he could for sufferers. He tried to stem the wave of anti-Semitism brought on by the plague, and he did much to protect the Jews. In Roman affairs Clement at first favored Cola di RIENZI, then helped to defeat him. He had a quarrel with Holy Roman Emperor LOUIS IV over the annulment of Margaret Maultasch's marriage; the struggle was aggravated by enmity between the pope and the German archbishops, caused by the elevation of Prague into an archbishopric, detaching it from Mainz. The years before the Black Death were the heyday of papal AVIGNON, which Clement purchased (1348) from JOANNA I. Clement spent extravagantly, had an elegant court, patronized the arts, and vastly favored his relatives. He was completely pro-French. He was succeeded by Innocent VI.

Clement VII, antipope (1378–94): see ROBERT OF GENEVA.

Clement VII, c. 1475–1534, pope (1523–34), a Florentine named Giulio de' Medici; successor of Adrian VI. He was the son of Giuliano de' Medici, who was the younger brother of Lorenzo de' Medici; Clement was therefore first cousin of Pope Leo X. In 1513 he became a cardinal and as archbishop of Florence, was noted as a reformer. He was a chief supporter and adviser of Adrian in his attempts to reform the church. As pope, however, he proved to be unaware of the menace of Lutheranism to the church and certainly not the man for the opening battles of the Reformation. His relations with Holy Roman Emperor CHARLES V were never very cordial, since Clement allied himself with FRANCIS I of France in the League of Cognac (1526). As a result of his hostility to the emperor, the imperial troops under Charles de Bourbon attacked Rome in 1527, sacked the city, and held the pope for some months. Eventually (1529) peace was achieved between Clement and Charles V, and he crowned Charles emperor. About 1527 the first stage of the struggle of HENRY VIII of England against the church began. Clement's behavior in the matter of the divorce and the dispensations for a new marriage has been called vacillating, but when the situation became critical, he put the irreproachable Cardinal CAMPEGGIO in charge of the case with Cardinal Wolsey. Later canon lawyers have steadily maintained that, whether he was influenced by Charles V or not, Clement followed the only course possible on legal grounds. He was a patron of Raphael, Michelangelo, and Benvenuto Cellini. He was succeeded by Paul III.

Clement VIII, 1536–1605, pope (1592–1605), a Florentine named Ippolito Aldobrandini; successor of Innocent IX. He reversed the policy of his predecessors by allying the Holy See with France rather than with Spain, which had assumed a dictatorial attitude over the papacy. Clement absolved HENRY IV of France after his abjuration of Protestantism, and the two rulers were thereafter on most friendly terms. Clement was distinguished for his piety, and he labored for the improvement of the clergy and of the charitable institutions of Rome. His confessors were St. PHILIP NERI and BARONIUS, whom he created cardinal. He was succeeded by Leo XI.

Clement XI, 1649–1721, pope (1700–1721), an Italian (b. Urbino) named Giovanni Francesco Albani; successor of Innocent XII. He was known in his youth for his prodigious learning and brilliance. He became cardinal in 1690. As pope he was involved in the struggle between France and Austria over the throne of Spain; he recognized PHILIP V but later was forced into recognizing Charles of Hapsburg, the other claimant. The chief spiritual concern of his pontificate was that of Jansenism (see under JANSEN, CORNELIS). The brief *Vineam Domini* (1705) condemned the Jansenist ideas on papal infallibility, and in 1713 he issued the bull *Unigenitus,* which condemned certain other Jansenist propositions. He was succeeded by Innocent XIII.

Clement XIV, 1705–74, pope (1769–74), an Italian (b. near Rimini) named Lorenzo Ganganelli; successor of Clement XIII. He was prominent for many years in pontifical affairs at Rome, and he was created cardinal in 1759. He was a Conventual Franciscan. He inherited from his predecessor the hostility of every state of Catholic Europe. Clement XIV's part in the suppression of the Jesuits (see JESUS, SOCIETY OF) has been greatly discussed; he was probably pressured into it. The suppression removed the pope's only independent support and put the church wholly into the hands of the secular princes. He was succeeded by Pius VI.

Clement, one of Paul's co-workers. Philip. 4.3. He is traditionally identified with St. Clement.

Clément, Jacques (zhäk klāmäN'), 1567–89, French Dominican monk, assassin of HENRY III of France. An adherent of the LEAGUE, he thought Henry a danger to the Church because of his recognition of a Protestant successor. Clément was killed by the king's attendants immediately after the stabbing.

Clemente, Roberto Walker, 1934–72, Puerto Rican baseball player, b. Carolina, Puerto Rico. He played his entire major league career with the Pittsburgh Pirates (1955–72) and was the mainspring of their successes for 18 years. He was one of 11 players to reach the 3,000-hit plateau. A right fielder, Clemente was capable of throwing out a runner from his knees. He had a lifetime batting average of .317 and hit 240 home runs. He died in an airplane crash while attempting to take food and medicine to earthquake victims in Nicaragua in Dec., 1972. He is a national hero in Puerto Rico.

Clementi, Muzio (mōō'tsēō klāmĕn'tē), 1752–1832, Italian composer, pianist, and conductor. He wrote more than 100 piano sonatas, which set the definitive form, and he had an enormous influence on almost everything concerning the piano. Educated in Italy, he went (1766) to England to live and study. In 1773 he caused a sensation in London as a pianist, and he conducted the Italian Opera there from 1777 to 1780. In 1781 he went on a concert tour of Europe, which climaxed in a piano contest with Mozart, who disparaged his talents. He returned to London in 1782 and, except for tours on the Continent, spent the rest of his life there. Clementi amassed a fortune as performer, conductor, and proprietor of a piano factory and publishing house. Teacher of many musicians, including the pianists J. B. Cramer and John Field and the composer Meyerbeer, he is especially remembered for his series of études, *Gradus ad Parnassum* (1817); he also wrote several symphonies. See catalog by A. Tyson (1967).

Clement of Alexandria (Titus Flavius Clemens), d. c.215, Greek theologian. Born in Athens, he traveled widely and was converted to Christianity. He studied and taught at the catechetical school in Alexandria until the persecution of 202. ORIGEN was his pupil there. He probably died in Caesarea, Cappadocia. Clement was one of the first to attempt a synthesis of Platonic and Christian thought; in this his successors in the Alexandrian school were more successful. Only a few works survive. The *Address to the Greeks* (*Protrepticus*) sets forth the inferiority of Greek thought to Christianity. Appended to the *Tutor (Pedagogus)* are two hymns, among the earliest Christian poems. His homily, *Who Is the Rich Man? Who Is Saved?* is a well-written fragment. The *Miscellanies* (*Stromateis*) is a collection of notes on Gnosticism. He attacked Gnosticism, but he himself has been called a Christian Gnostic. Although Clement remained entirely orthodox, in his writing he strove to state the faith in terms of contemporary thought. He was long venerated as a saint, but PHOTIUS, in the 9th cent., regarded Clement as a heretic. Because of Photius's contentions the name of Clement was removed from the Roman martyrology. See studies by E. F. Osborn (1957), W. E. G. Floyd (1971), S. R. Lilla (1971), and Morton Smith (1973).

Clement of Rome: see CLEMENT I, SAINT.

Clements, Frederic Edward, 1874–1945, American plant ecologist and pioneer in the study of succession (see ECOLOGY), b. Lincoln, Nebr., grad. Univ. of Nebraska, 1894. From 1917 to 1941 he was in charge of ecological research at Carnegie Institution, Washington. Among his works are *Research Methods in Ecology* (1905), *Plant Succession and Indicators* (1928, repr. 1973), *Flower Families and Ancestors* (1928, with Edith Clements), *Plant Ecology* (1929, with J. E. Weaver), and *The Genera of Fungi* (1931, repr. 1965, with C. L. Shear).

Clemson University, mainly at Clemson, S.C.; coeducational; land-grant; state supported; opened in 1893 as a college, gained university status in 1964. There are branches at Greenville and Sumter. The university includes programs in textile and computer research and maintains an institute in forestry, wildlife science, and marine biology.

Cleobis: see BITON.

Cleobulus (klēəbyōō'ləs), fl. 6th cent.? B.C., one of the SEVEN WISE MEN OF GREECE, tyrant of Lindus on Rhodes, and a writer of verse. He was said to have first put riddles in literary form.

Cleomedes (klē"ōmē'dēz, klē"ə-), fl. 2d cent., Greek astronomer. In a treatise on the circular theory of heavenly bodies, he recorded several hypotheses, e.g., the earth's spherical form and the moon's revolutions, which were established by later scientists.

Cleomenes I (klēŏm'ĭnēz), d. c.489 B.C., king of Sparta after 518 B.C. In accordance with Sparta's policy of helping oligarchies in other states at the expense of the tyrants or the people, Cleomenes joined the Athenians in ousting the tyrant Hippias, but to Cleomenes' dismay CLEISTHENES, the principal Athenian aristocrat, sided with the people and took the power (510 B.C.). Twice Cleomenes attacked democratic Athens. The first time he expelled Cleisthenes, who, however, quickly returned to power, thus halting Spartan influence. The second time Corinth checkmated Sparta by refusing to help in an attack that would have disturbed the balance of power. Cleomenes' reputation for ruthlessness is due chiefly to his attack (c.494 B.C.) on Argos, in which he slaughtered 6,000 Argives—an exploit that gave Sparta hegemony in S Greece for many years.

Cleomenes III, c.260–219 B.C., king of Sparta (235–221 B.C.). He was probably the most energetic king Sparta ever had, a conscious imitator of AGIS III. In his determined effort to restore the prestige of the city, he began (227 B.C.) a war against the ACHAEAN LEAGUE and was successful in many battles. At home his reforms were revolutionary: the kingship was made the supreme power, the ephorate was abolished, and the citizenship was widely extended, apparently to decrease the danger of discontent and to ally the people with the king. Cleomenes came to his downfall suddenly in 222 B.C. (or possibly 221 B.C.) when the Achaean League, allied with ANTIGONUS III of Macedon, routed the Spartan army. Cleomenes fled to Egypt to the protection of his patron, Ptolemy III. Imprisoned by Ptolemy's successor, he escaped, but, failing in an attempt to stir up a revolt in Alexandria, he committed suicide.

Cleon (klē'ən), d. 422 B.C., Athenian political leader. The son of a tanner, he had little education; nevertheless, he was a gifted speaker. He began his political career with a series of relentless attacks on PERICLES. He was antagonistic to Sparta and successfully opposed (425 B.C.) Sparta's peace proposals. In the same year he was given command of the Athenian force blockading Sphacteria (an island at the mouth of the Bay of Pylos) and was brilliantly successful against the Spartans. Three years later he was given another command against the Spartans at Amphipolis, but he failed and was killed in action. His reputation as a vulgar and unprincipled demagogue is chiefly due to accounts by his enemies Thucydides and Aristophanes.

Cleopas (klē'ōpəs), one of the two who met the risen Jesus on the way to Emmaus. Luke 24.18. Perhaps the same as CLEOPHAS.

Cleopatra (klēəpă'trə, -pä'-,-pā'-), 69 B.C.–30 B.C., queen of Egypt, one of the great romantic heroines of all time. Her name was widely used in the Ptolemaic family; there were many earlier Cleopatras. The daughter of Ptolemy XI, she was married at the age of 17 (as was the family custom) to her younger brother PTOLEMY XII. The force and character of the royal pair was, however, concentrated in the alluring (though apparently not beautiful) and ambitious queen. She led a revolt against her brother, and, obtaining the aid of Julius Caesar, she won the kingdom, although it remained a vassal of Rome. Her young brother-husband was accidentally drowned in the Nile. She then married her still younger brother PTOLEMY XIII, but she was the mistress of Caesar and followed him to Rome; there she bore a son, Caesarion (later PTOLEMY XIV), who was said to be his. Returning to Egypt after the murder of Caesar and the battle of PHILIPPI, she was visited (42 B.C.) by Marc ANTONY, who had come to demand an account of her actions. He fell hopelessly in love with her, and Cleopatra, conscious of her royalty and even her claims to divinity as the pharaoh's daughter, seems to have hoped to use Antony to reestablish the real power of the Egyptian throne. They were married in 36 B.C. Most of the Romans feared and hated Cleopatra, and Octavian (later AUGUSTUS) undertook to destroy the two lovers. Antony and Cleopatra were defeated off Actium in 31 B.C., and, returning to Alexandria, they undertook to defend themselves in Egypt. When they failed, Antony committed suicide by falling on his sword. Cleopatra, faced by the cold and unmoved Octavian, also killed herself. Her schemes failed, but her ambition, capability, and remarkable charm have left a great impression on history. Shakespeare's *Antony and Cleopatra,* based on Plutarch, describes the tragic end of the queen's career, and Dryden's *All for Love: or, The World Well Lost* is a reworking of Shakespeare. *Caesar and Cleopatra,* the comedy by G. B. Shaw, deals with the early years of her story. See biographies by Jack Lindsay (1971) and Michael Grant (1973); study by H. Volkmann (tr. 1958).

Cleopatra's Needles, name in popular use for two obelisks of red granite from Egypt. Originally erected at Heliopolis (c.1475 B.C.) by Thutmose III, they were transported to Alexandria (c.14 B.C.) under Augustus and in the 19th cent. were sent separately as gifts of Ismail Pasha to England (1878) and the United States (1880). The British OBELISK, 68.5 ft (20.9 m) high, stands on the Thames embankment in London. The American one, 69.5 ft (21.2 m) high, is in Central Park in New York City. The hieroglyphic inscriptions of Thutmose III and Ramses II covering its sides have suffered more from erosion, because of air pollution, in the few years ... came to the Western world than in the ... ries before it left Egypt.

Cleophas (klē'ōfəs), husband of one of the ... who stood at the foot of the Cross. John 19.25. ... is apparently Mary the mother of St. James the Le... Mat. 27.56; Mark 15.40. But the father of James the Less is Alphaeus. Mat. 10.3; Mark 3.18; Luke 6.15. An explanation is that Cleophas is the Aramaic form and Alphaeus the Greek form of the same name. Some identify CLEOPAS with Cleophas.

clepsydra (klĕp'sĭdrə) or **water clock,** ancient device for measuring time by means of the flow of water from a container. A simple form of clepsydra was an earthenware vessel with a small opening through which the water dripped; as the water level dropped, it exposed marks on the walls of the vessel that indicated the time that had elapsed since the vessel was full. More elaborate clepsydras were later developed. Some were double vessels, the larger one below containing a float that rose with the water and marked the hours on a scale. A form more closely foreshadowing the clock had a cord fastened to the float so that it turned a wheel, whose movement indicated the time. A further step was the use of gear wheels and a turning pointer. It is believed that clepsydras were used in Egypt c.2000 B.C.; from Egypt they were introduced into Greece and later from there into Rome.

clerestory or **clearstory** (both: klĕr'stōr"ē), a part of a building whose walls rise higher than the roofs of adjoining parts of the structure. Pierced by windows, it is chiefly a device for obtaining extra light.

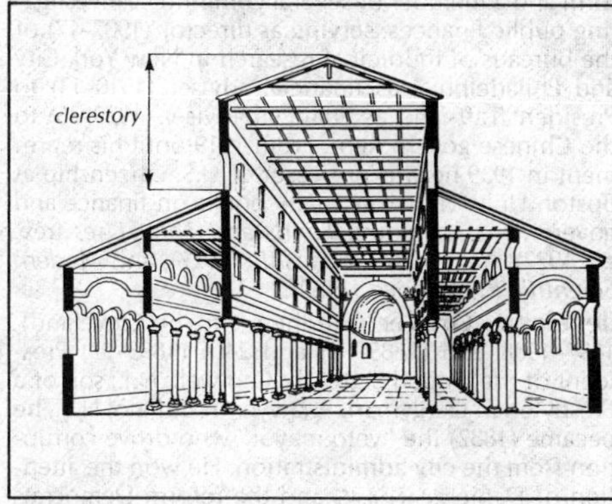

Clerestory

It had an early use in certain Egyptian temples, as at Karnak, and was used later in the great halls of Roman basilicas. It became a characteristic element of medieval churches, receiving its fullest development in churches of the Gothic period.

clergy: see MINISTRY; MONASTICISM; ORDERS, HOLY.

clergy, benefit of: see BENEFIT OF CLERGY.

Clergy Reserves, those lands set apart in Upper and Lower Canada under the British Constitutional Act of 1791 "for the support and maintenance of a Protestant clergy." "Protestant clergy" was interpreted to mean the clergy of the Church of England. This interpretation was fiercely upheld by John Strachan and others but dissatisfied other Protestant denominations and became an issue in the Rebellion of 1837. The method of allotting reserves kept discontinuous plots out of cultivation and prevented settlement and the expansion of roads. An act of 1840 by the assembly of Upper Canada provided for the sale and distribution of the reserves, but this was disallowed by the British government. In 1854 the government finally passed a law secularizing the reserves, but the Anglican and Presbyterian churches retained the endowments that had been granted them.

Clericus, Johannes: see LE CLERC, JEAN.

Clerk-Maxwell, James: see MAXWELL, JAMES CLERK.

Clermont-Ferrand (klĕrmôN'-fĕräN'), city (1968 pop. 148,896), capital of Puy-de-Dôme dept., central France, in Auvergne, ... industrial center, hon... tire factories, and of i... The capital of the for... was formed in 1731 b... Montferrand. Clermo... near the site of Gergo... against Julius Caesar i... destroyed. An episco... was the site of several... of 1095, where Pope... Crusade (see CRUSAD...

situated near the Puy de Dôme peak. It is built largely of the dark volcanic rock of the region. The Gothic Cathedral of Notre-Dame (13th-14th cent.) and the Romanesque Church of Notre-Dame du Port (12th cent.) are among the notable buildings. Blaise Pascal was born in Clermont-Ferrand. There is a university (founded 1854) in the city.

Cletus (klē'təs) or **Anacletus, Saint** (ănəklē'təs), d. A.D. 88?, pope (A.D. 76?-A.D. 88?), martyr, a Roman; successor of St. Linus and predecessor of St. Clement I. He is mentioned in the Canon of the Mass. Feast: April 26.

Cleve, Joos van: see CLEEF, JOOS VAN.

Cleveland, Barbara Villiers, duchess of (vĭl'ərz, vĭl'yərz), 1641-1709, mistress of King Charles II of England. She became Charles's mistress at Breda in 1660 and returned with him to England at the Restoration. The king made her husband, Roger Palmer, earl of Castlemaine. Lady Castlemaine was the arch-enemy of the earl of Clarendon, the lord chancellor, and her glee at his downfall (1667) is recorded in Pepys' diary. She was made duchess in 1670, but by 1671 had been supplanted in Charles's affections by Louise de Kérouaille (the future duchess of Portsmouth). She had borne the king several children. See biographies by Margaret Gilmour (1941) and Allen Andrews (1970).

Cleveland, Frederick Albert, 1865-1946, American economist, b. Sterling, Ill., studied at DePauw Univ. and at the Univ. of Chicago, Ph.D. Univ. of Pennsylvania, 1900. He taught at the Univ. of Pennsylvania (1900-1903) and was professor of finance at New York Univ. (1903-5). He was a leader in budget reform and a member of several committees investigating public finances, serving as director (1907-17) of the bureaus of municipal research in New York City and Philadelphia, as financial adviser (1910-13) to President Taft, and as financial adviser (1929-35) to the Chinese government. From 1919 until his retirement in 1939 he was professor of U.S. citizenship at Boston Univ. He wrote many books on finance and government, including *Funds and Their Uses* (rev. ed. 1922), *American Citizenship* (1927), and *Modern Scientific Knowledge* (1929).

Cleveland, Grover (Stephen Grover Cleveland), 1837-1908, 22d (1885-89) and 24th (1893-97) President of the United States, b. Caldwell, N.J.; son of a Presbyterian clergyman. A lawyer in Buffalo, N.Y., he became (1882) the "veto mayor" who drove corruption from the city administration. He won the attention of Daniel MANNING and the reform Democrats and was elected governor of New York. Cleveland further built his reputation as an enemy of machine politics by breaking violently with the Tammany leader, John KELLY, and supporting the bills prepared by Theodore Roosevelt to improve the government of New York City. By 1884 he was a national figure, and he was nominated as Democratic "clean-government" candidate for President to oppose James G. BLAINE. Cleveland, hated by Tammany and favored by political reformers, got the votes of many reform Republicans—the "mugwumps," who voted against their party. The campaign was notably bitter and was marked by the "Rum, Romanism, and Rebellion" speech of a Blaine supporter, which deeply offended Roman Catholics and may have swung the vote to Cleveland in the key state of New York. Cleveland as President continued his independent, conscientious, but conservative course. He did not go far enough in civil service reform to satisfy the zealots, but at the same time by keeping Republican government employees who were not "offensive partisans" he offended the Democratic spoilsmen. Cleveland was continually at odds with the Republican-controlled Senate. The surplus revenue accumulating in the treasury largely because high Civil War tariffs were still in force fostered much "pork barrel" legislation. Cleveland vetoed such laws and argued for a lower tariff, devoting the whole of his annual message to Congress in 1887 to the question. The tariff was a major issue in the 1888 election. Cleveland received a popular majority but lost the electoral majority to his Republican opponent, Benjamin HARRISON. A romantic note in his first administration was his marriage (1886) in the White House to his former ward, Frances Folsom. In 1889 he retired to private life as a New York City lawyer, but opposition to measures of the Republican administration, notably the McKinley Tariff Act of 1890, [illegible]ought him a new following. In 1892 he was again [illegible]ed President. The Panic of 1893 struck a hard [illegible] his administration. Though the more radical [illegible]s saw salvation in free coinage of silver, [illegible]dent President sought to improve the [illegible]ation by securing repeal of the SHERMAN SILVER PURCHASE ACT with the help of conservative Republicans. Cleveland still urged lower tariffs, although the best opportunity had passed, since the treasury now had a deficit rather than a surplus. The Wilson Bill, embodying Cleveland's tariff ideas, passed the House of Representatives but was so altered by Senator A. P. GORMAN and other protectionist Democrats that Cleveland, in disgust, refused to sign it. The rift between the President and the radical Democrats widened, especially over the gold standard, which Cleveland upheld. In the Pullman strike in 1894, Cleveland, on the grounds that the movement of U.S. mail was being halted by the strikers under Eugene V. DEBS, sent troops into the area over the protest of Gov. J. P. ALTGELD of Illinois. The strike was broken by the use of Federal injunctions and the arrest of the strike leaders. In foreign affairs both of Cleveland's administrations were marked by a strong stand on the VENEZUELA BOUNDARY DISPUTE, which called forth a statement greatly enlarging the scope of the Monroe Doctrine. He refused to recognize the government set up in Hawaii by a revolution that was engineered by Americans who expected speedy annexation to the United States (although he recognized the republic in 1894), and he tried to discourage support of the revolutionists in Cuba. The more radical wing of the Democrats—the silver Democrats—got control of the party in 1896 and nominated William Jennings Bryan, repudiating Cleveland. His strong second term had put him at odds with many (he was nicknamed the Great Obstructionist), and his *Presidential Problems* (1904) was mainly a defense of his own attitude on some of the major issues. Cleveland's independence and conscientiousness in office marked him as a man of courage and personal integrity. See biographies by Robert McElroy (1923), Allan Nevins (1932), H. S. Merrill (1957), and R. G. Tugwell (1968).

Cleveland or **Cleiveland, John,** 1613-58, English poet and political satirist. He served the royalist cause both as soldier and poet. His best-known work was *The Rebel Scot* (1644). Though his contemporary fame was great, and his works originally went through 20 editions, he is known today chiefly for the lyrics "Fuscara" and "Mark Antony." See editions of his poems by J. M. Berdan (1911) and by Brian Morris and Eleanor Withington (1967).

Cleveland, nonmetropolitan county (1972 est. pop. 567,000), NE England, created under the Local Government Act of 1972 (effective 1974). It is composed of the county boroughs of Harlepool and Teesside and parts of the former counties of Durham and Yorkshire (North Riding).

Cleveland. 1 City (1970 pop. 13,327), seat of Bolivar co., NW Miss., in the rich delta cotton country; inc. 1886. It is a farm market center (rice and soybeans are also grown in the area), and its manufactures include pharmaceuticals, aluminum doors, tiles, and pens and pencils. The city is the seat of Delta State College and has a coliseum. **2** City (1970 pop. 750,879), seat of Cuyahoga co., NE Ohio, a port of entry on Lake Erie at the mouth of the Cuyahoga River; laid out (1796) by Moses Cleaveland, chartered as a city 1836. Ohio's largest city and the tenth largest in the United States (1970), it is a great ore port, a large Great Lakes shipping point, and one of the nation's leading iron and steel centers. In addition to many metallurgical manufactures, it has chemical, oil-refining, electrical, automobile, garment, and food-processing industries. There are also numerous research firms; the National Aeronautics and Space Administration has a large research center there, and the research laboratory headquarters of the General Electric Company are in nearby Nela Park. Cleveland grew rapidly after the opening of the first section of the Ohio and Erie Canal in 1827 and the arrival of the railroad in 1851. Its central location midway between the coal and oil fields of Pennsylvania and (via the Great Lakes) the Minnesota iron mines spurred its industrialization; it was there that John D. Rockefeller began his oil dynasty. Cleveland is the seat of Case Western Reserve Univ., Cleveland State Univ., John Carroll Univ., Notre Dame College, St. John College of Cleveland, Ursuline College, Ohio College of Podiatric Medicine, St. Mary Seminary, the Cleveland Institute of Art, the Cleveland Institute of Music, and a large community college. The many points of interest include the Mall (civic center); the Terminal Tower; the Western Reserve Historical Society Museum; the museum of natural history, with a planetarium; Wade Park, with the Cleveland Museum of Art and the Fine Arts Garden; Rockefeller Park, enclosing the Shakespeare and Cultural Gardens; Severance Hall, where concerts of the Cleveland Symphony Orchestra are performed; Gordon Park, with an aquarium; a museum of historical medicine; and Cleveland zoo. The city also has a fine public library. The Cleveland *Plain Dealer* is a nationally known newspaper. In Lake View Cemetery are the graves of James A. Garfield, Mark Hanna (who made his fortune in Cleveland), John Hay, and John D. Rockefeller. Although the city has been a leader in urban renewal and slum clearance projects, it was plagued during the 1960s by racial disorders, especially in the Hough and Glenville sections; riots in the summer of 1968 resulted in 11 deaths and much property damage. See W. H. Alburn and M. R. Alburn, *This Cleveland of Ours* (4 vol., 1933); E. J. Benton, *Cultural Story of an American City: Cleveland* (3 vol., 1943-46); E. H. Chapman, *Cleveland: Village to Metropolis* (1964). **3** City (1970 pop. 20,561), seat of Bradley co., SE Tenn., in a farm and timber area; inc. 1838. Lee College and two junior colleges are there. Cleveland is headquarters of Cherokee National Forest.

Cleveland Heights, city (1970 pop. 60,767), Cuyahoga co., NE Ohio, a residential suburb of Cleveland; inc. 1903. It is known for its beautiful homes. Forest Hills Park, once part of an estate owned by John D. Rockefeller, offers recreational facilities.

Cleveland Orchestra, one of the foremost orchestras in the United States. It gave its first performance in 1918 under the direction of Nikolai Sokoloff, who was conductor until 1933. In its early years the orchestra played in the Cleveland Masonic Temple, but in 1931 it moved into Severance Hall, the gift of John L. Severance. Sokoloff was succeeded as conductor by Artur Rodzinski (1933-43) and Erich Leinsdorf (1943-44), but the orchestra's peak of fame was achieved under the direction of George SZELL (1946-71). Szell, a perfectionist and disciplinarian, brought the orchestra to international attention, leading it on several European tours. He was succeeded by Lorin Maazel.

Cleveland State University, at Cleveland, Ohio; coeducational; founded 1964, incorporating Fenn College (est. 1923). The university consists of six colleges, including graduate studies and law. Among its research facilities are an Institute of Urban Studies and a Computer Center.

Cleves (klēvz), Ger. *Kleve* or *Cleve,* city (1970 pop. 43,447), North Rhine-Westphalia, W West Germany, near the Dutch border. Its manufactures include shoes and food and tobacco products. It is a rail junction and popular resort. Among its noteworthy buildings are the collegiate church (14th-15th cent.), which contains the tombs of the dukes of Cleves, and the 11th-century Schwanenburg [Ger.,= swans' castle], which is associated with the legend of Lohengrin.

Cleves, duchy of, former state, W West Germany, on both sides of the lower Rhine, bordering on the Netherlands. Cleves was the capital. A county from late Carolingian times, it acquired (late 14th cent.) the county of Mark, in Westphalia, and in 1417 was made a duchy. In 1521, Duke John III of Cleves inherited through marriage the duchies of Jülich and Berg and the county of Ravensberg. His daughter, Anne of Cleves, was married in 1540 to Henry VIII of England. In 1609 the male line became extinct, and a complicated dynastic quarrel for the succession followed. Brandenburg acquired (1614) Cleves, Mark, and Ravensberg; the Palatinate-Neuburg line of the Bavarian house of Wittelsbach took Jülich and Berg. The succession was not finally settled until 1666, when the Treaty of Cleves confirmed the division. Cleves was held by France during the French Revolutionary Wars and in 1815 was returned to Prussia.

Clew Bay, inlet of the Atlantic Ocean, c.15 mi (25 km) long and 10 mi (16.1 km) wide, Co. Mayo, W Republic of Ireland. There are about 300 islands in the eastern part of the bay, some of which are cultivated. Clare Island is at the entrance.

Clews, Henry, c.1836-1923, American financier, b. England. He emigrated to the United States c.1850 and joined an import business as a junior clerk. In 1859 he cofounded the banking firm that later became Livermore, Clews, and Company, the second largest marketer of Federal bonds during the Civil War. His own firm, Clews and Company, was formed in 1877. Refusing public office, he nevertheless organized the "Committee of 70," which deposed the Tweed Ring in New York City. He served as President Grant's economic consultant in Japan and wrote and lectured widely on diverse social, political, and economic issues. He wrote *Fifty Years in Wall Street* (1908).

Cliburn, Van (Harvey Lavan Cliburn) (klī'bərn), 1934-, American pianist, b. Shreveport, La. Until

1951, Cliburn studied with his mother, a concert pianist. He later became a pupil of Rosina Lhévinne at the Juilliard School of Music. Cliburn was catapulted to fame as winner of the 1958 International Tchaikovsky Piano Competition in Moscow. His superb technique and romantic interpretations are especially well-suited to Romantic music.

Clichy (klēshē'), suburb N of Paris (1968 pop. 52,704), Hauts-de-Seine dept., N central France. It is a modern industrial city with iron works; automobile parts, metal products, machinery, and plastics are also manufactured. Clichy was once a residence of Merovingian kings and was called Clippiacum in Latin. Dagobert I, king of the Franks, also resided there (7th cent.). The Church of St. Vincent de Paul, named for the saint who was parish priest to Clichy, is a major landmark.

click beetle, common name for members of the widespread BEETLE family Elateridae. Also called elater beetle, the click beetle has a hinge across the front of the body that allows it to flex, and a spine-and-groove arrangement on the underside of the body that provides a snapping mechanism. When a click beetle is turned on its back it cannot right itself by rolling onto its short legs. It arches its body upward so that only the ends touch the ground, then straightens suddenly, causing the spine to slide into the groove. This sends the beetle spinning through the air and produces a loud click. If the beetle lands on its back again it repeats the performance. A click beetle also snaps its body when it is picked up, which may cause the predator to drop it. Click beetles have long, flat bodies, generally rectangular, but curved at the ends. They range in length from 1/4 in. to 4 in. (6.4–102 mm); most are black or brown. Most adults are nocturnal leaf-eaters. The larvae, called WIREWORMS, are destructive to a large variety of plants. Some tropical click beetles are brilliantly luminescent. Click beetles are classified in the phylum ARTHROPODA, class Insecta, order Coleoptera, family Elateridae.

cliff dwellers, American Indians of the Anasazi culture who were builders of the ancient cliff dwellings found in the canyons and on the mesas of the U.S. Southwest, principally on the tributaries of the Rio Grande and the Colorado River in New Mexico, Arizona, Utah, and Colorado. It was once thought that these ruins were the work of an extinct aboriginal people, but it has been established that they were built (11th–14th cent.) by the ancestors of the present PUEBLO INDIANS. The dwellings were large communal habitations built on ledges in the canyon walls and on the flat tops of the mesas. Access to the cliffs was very difficult and thus highly defensible against nomadic predatory tribes such as the Navaho. The cliff dwellers were sedentary agriculturists who planted crops in the river valleys below their high-perched houses. They were experts at irrigating the fields. Their lives were organized on a communal pattern, and the many kivas (see KIVA) show that their religious ceremonies were like those of the Pueblo Indians today. Many of the dwellings are now in national parks. Some of the better-known ones are those of the Mesa Verde National Park, in Colorado, where there are more than 300 dwellings; Yucca House National Monument, also in Colorado; Hovenweep National Monument, in Utah; and Casa Grande, Montezuma Castle, and Wupatki national monuments, in Arizona. See William Current, *Pueblo Architecture of the Southwest* (1971).

Clifford, Clark McAdams, 1906–, U.S. government official, b. Fort Scott, Kansas. Admitted to the bar in 1928, he engaged in private practice before serving (1944–46) in the U.S. navy during World War II. As special adviser (1946–50) to President Harry S. Truman, Clifford was influential in foreign policy and defense matters, helping to formulate the Truman Doctrine (1947) and the legislation that created (1949) the Department of Defense. He also planned Truman's successful campaign strategy in 1948. After a period of private law practice, Clifford served (1961–63) as a foreign policy adviser to President John F. Kennedy and then became (1963) chairman of the Foreign Intelligence Advisory Board. In this capacity he supervised all U.S. espionage operations and played a crucial role in determining U.S. military policy in Vietnam. Clifford also served (1968–69) as Secretary of Defense in Lyndon B. Johnson's cabinet.

Clifford of Chudleigh, Thomas Clifford, 1st Baron (chŭd'lē), 1630–73, English statesman. Member (1667–73) of the CABAL at Charles II's court, he held a number of offices, rising to be acting secretary of state and lord treasurer (1672). He was created Baron Clifford in 1672. Henry Bennet, earl of Arlington, and Clifford, both alleged Roman Catholics, knew of the secret clauses of the Treaty of Dover (1670), which provided for the reestablishment of Roman Catholicism in England. He was forced to resign by passage of the Test Act (1673), which excluded Roman Catholics from office. He died soon afterward, possibly by suicide.

Cliffside Park, borough (1970 pop. 14,387), Bergen co., NE N.J., on the palisades above the Hudson River, opposite New York City; inc. 1895. A residential suburb, it has some light industry.

Clifton, industrial city (1970 pop. 82,437), Passaic co., NE N.J., on the Passaic River; settled 1685, set off from Passaic and inc. 1917. It has steel, textile, chemical, and electronic industries.

climacteric: see MENOPAUSE.

climate, average weather condition over a long period of time, taking into account temperature, precipitation (see RAIN), HUMIDITY, WIND, barometric pressure, and other phenomena. The major influence governing the climate of a region is its latitude, and this is modified by one or more secondary influences including position relative to land and water masses, altitude, TOPOGRAPHY, prevailing winds, OCEAN currents, and prevalence of cyclonic storms. A broad latitudinal division of the earth's surface into climatic zones includes the equatorial zone, or DOLDRUMS, characterized by high temperatures with small seasonal and diurnal change and heavy rainfall; the subtropical, including the trade-wind belts and the HORSE LATITUDES, a dry region with uniformly mild temperatures and little wind; the intermediate, the region of the prevailing westerlies that, because of several secondary influences, displays wide temperature ranges and marked changeability of weather; and the polar, a region of short summers and long winters, where the ground is generally perpetually frozen (see PERMAFROST). The transitional climate between those of the subtropical and intermediate zones, known as the Mediterranean type, is found in areas bordering the Mediterranean Sea and on the west coasts of continents. It is characterized by mild temperatures with moderate winter rainfall under the influence of the moisture-laden prevailing westerlies and dry summers under the influence of the horse latitudes or the trade winds. Climatic types combining the basic factor of latitude with one or more secondary influences include the continental and the marine. Except in the equatorial region, the continental type is marked by dry, sunny weather with low humidity and seasonal extremes in temperature; noteworthy are the Sahara (with the highest temperature on record, 136°F, or 58°C, at Tripoli) and Siberia (with the lowest recorded surface temperature, −93.6°F, or −70°C, at Verkhoyansk). The marine is characterized by small annual and diurnal temperature variation and by copious rainfall on the windward side of coastal highlands and mountainous islands; notable is the mean annual precipitation of 451 in. at Mt. Waialeale, Hawaii. The coastal, or littoral, climate is one in which the direction of the prevailing winds plays a dominant role—the east coasts having generally the heavier rainfall in the trade-wind belts, the west coasts in westerly belts. Both coasts have a climate resembling the continental during the season when the wind is blowing from the interior of the continent. An instance of the coastal type, in which the precipitation is accentuated by the nearness of a mountain barrier, is the west coast of North America from Alaska to Oregon, where the mean annual precipitation averages 80 to 100 in., almost all of it falling during the winter months. Also included are the mountain and plateau climates, where elevation is the dominant factor (the temperature decreasing about 3°F per 1,000 ft., or 5.5°C per 1000 m, of ascent and rainfall increasing with altitude up to about 6000 ft/1800 m, then decreasing with further elevation). Climatology, the science of climate and its relation to plant and animal life, is important in many fields, including agriculture, aviation, medicine, botany, zoology, geology, and geography. The effect of climate on man is sometimes thought to explain the relatively greater development of lands having a variable climate, usually in middle latitudes, where the annual temperature range is conducive to both mental and physical activity. Changes in climate affect the plant and animal life of a given area. Fossils of animals discovered in North America, Greenland, and Siberia and the presence of coal beds in North America and Europe, on one hand, and evidence of glaciation in these same areas, on the other, indicate that they must have experienced alternately warmer and colder climates than they now possess. Despite yearly fluctuations of climatic elements, there has been, apparently, little overall change during recorded history. Climatic cycles (... weather elements that recur with conside... larity) have been claimed to exist; the 35-ye... postulated by Eduard Brückner, German geogra... and meteorologist, was well investigated in Europ... and an 11-year sunspot cycle has been advanced. There is currently much concern that human activities are changing the earth's climate in harmful ways. For example, some scientists believe that the release of large quantities of gases and particulates into the atmosphere from the burning of fuel and from industrial processes is at least partly responsible for a slight lowering of mean temperatures throughout the world. If the trend continues, another ice age may be triggered. See Robert Silverberg, *The Challenge of Climate* (1969); H. H. Lamb, *Climate: Present, Past and Future* (Vol. I, 1972).

Climax, Saint John: see JOHN CLIMAX, SAINT.

climax community: see ECOLOGY.

climbing perch or **walking fish,** member of the labyrinth fish family, adapted to living in oxygen-depleted water or on dry land. It is not related to the true perch. Labyrinth fishes are spiny-finned fishes of Africa and SE Asia, which have a labyrinthine chamber over the gills that enables them to absorb and retain atmospheric oxygen. Members of some species can remain out of water for several days and will even suffocate (drown) if held under water. The climbing perch, *Anabas testudineus,* of SE Asia, is brown and reaches a length of 10 in. (25 cm). Climbing perches travel in search of water when their ponds dry up; they walk with jerky movements, supported by the spiny edges of the gill plates and propelled by the fins and tail. They are said to climb low trees. The family also includes the PARADISE FISHES, the BETTA, and the GOURAMI; all are popular aquarium fishes. The land-walking MUDSKIPPER is of a different family. Climbing perches are classified in the phylum CHORDATA, subphylum Vertebrata, class Osteichthyes, order Perciformes, family Anabantidae.

climbing plant, any plant that in growing to its full height requires some support. Climbing plants may clamber over a support (climbing rose), twine up a slender support (hop, honeysuckle), or grasp the support by special processes such as adventitious aerial roots (English ivy, poison ivy, trumpet creeper), tendrils (see TENDRIL), or hook-tipped leaves (gloriosa lily, rattan). Some climbing plants when not supported become trailing plants (English ivy). Climbing types are to be found in nearly every group of plant, e.g., the ferns (climbing fern), palms (rattan), grasses (some bamboos), lilies (gloriosa lily), and cacti (night-blooming cereus). Tropical kinds—usually called lianas—are particularly abundant. A sturdy vine may strangle a supporting tree, and then, as the strangler fig, become a tree itself.

Clinch, river, c.300 mi (480 km) long, formed by the junction of two forks in SW Va., and flowing generally SW across E Tenn. to the Tennessee River at Kingston. Its waters and those of its tributary, the Powell, are used to make a reservoir at Norris Dam; at its mouth the Clinch forms Watts Bar Reservoir. The river is thus an important part of the system of the Tennessee Valley Authority. In late colonial days the Clinch was one of the routes for settlers going to Tennessee.

cline, in biology, any gradual change in a particular characteristic of a population of organisms from one end of the geographical range of the population to the other. Gradients of characteristics usually accompany, and are responses to, environmental gradients; for example, a mountain range features gradients from top to bottom such as a temperature gradient (colder to warmer) and a humidity gradient (wetter to drier). In species of birds and mammals, there is usually a cline in body size, with smaller individuals in warm climates and larger individuals tending to be found in colder climates.

Clingmans Dome, mountain, Tenn.: see GREAT SMOKY MOUNTAINS.

clinic, name for an institution providing medical diagnosis and treatment for ambulatory patients. The forerunner of the modern clinic was the dispensary, which dispensed free drugs and served only those who could not afford to pay a fee. Dispensaries began to appear in London toward the end of the 17th cent. In the United States the first dispensary was founded in Philadelphia in 1786 through the efforts of Benjamin Rush. Another was established in New York City in 1791, and one in Boston in 1796. Home care was often provided by the early clinics, but later they evolved as places for treatment of those who could visit them. As the clinic movement grew and concern for public health increased, facilities for providing diagnosis and treatment improved. Present-day clinics are maintained by private and city hospitals, by city health departments, by industrial and labor organizations, and by groups of private physicians. Some clinics specialize in vaccination and other measures to prevent infectious disease. Some are established to promote the health of babies and mothers. Others exist to facilitate the diagnosis of tuberculosis or cancer so that these diseases may be treated as early as possible. There are also clinics concerned with mental health. Clinics designated as health centers offer all the health services that are considered essential. They provide free, comprehensive service for people who cannot afford private care. In some areas mobile units travel from place to place providing various kinds of medical and dental care. Clinics maintained by industrial and labor organizations are often free for members, but others charge a nominal fee; in hospital clinics the fee is usually based on the individual's ability to pay.

Clink, district in Southwark, a Greater London borough, England. The Clink prison was used from the 13th cent. as a detention place for heretics. Its name is now a slang term for a prison or jail.

Clinton, De Witt, 1769-1828, American statesman, b. New Windsor, N.Y.; son of James CLINTON. He was admitted (1790) to the New York state bar but soon became secretary to his uncle, George CLINTON, first governor of the state, and in that position (1790-95) he gained considerable political experience and influence at an early age. In 1797 he entered the state legislature. As a U.S. Senator (1802-3), Clinton introduced the Twelfth Amendment to the Constitution and opposed sentiment for hostilities against Spain. In 1803 he became mayor of New York City, and in 10 annual terms (between 1803 and 1815) he promoted public education, city planning, city fortifications, public sanitation, and relief for the poor. While mayor he was successful in dictating the nomination of two governors. Clinton also held office as state senator (1806-11) and lieutenant governor (1811-13). He advocated removal of the political disabilities of Roman Catholics, abolition of slavery, and amelioration of severe punishment for debt and misdemeanors. He ran unsuccessfully for President against James Madison in 1812, with support from both Federalists and Republicans. As canal commissioner after 1810, Clinton sponsored the ERIE CANAL and the Champlain-Hudson Canal. From 1817 to 1823 he was governor. Clinton continued to give constant support to the canal projects, but in 1824, after suffering temporary political reverses and through the opposition of the ALBANY REGENCY and TAMMANY, he was deprived of his post as canal commissioner. Again governor from 1825 until his death, Clinton celebrated the completion of the canals and promoted public and normal schools, manufacturing, and legal reform. See biography by Dorothie Bobbé (1933, rev. ed. 1962); H. L. McBain, *De Witt Clinton and the Origin of the Spoils System* (1907, repr. 1967); Dixon Ryan Fox, *Decline of Aristocracy in the Politics of New York* (1919, repr. 1965).

Clinton, George, c. 1686-1761, colonial governor of New York (1743-53), b. England; father of Sir Henry Clinton. He entered (1708) the British navy and rose to the rank of admiral in 1747. Through family connections, Clinton was appointed (1741) governor of New York and arrived in the colony in 1743. Under the influence of James DeLancey he tried to conciliate the assembly and acquiesced on the issue of increased legislative control over revenues. Clinton later quarreled with DeLancey; his attempts to regain his lost powers failed; and his administration resulted in a permanent weakening of royal government in New York. Clinton was recalled (1753) to England and later served (1754-60) in Parliament.

Clinton, George, 1739-1812, American statesman, Vice President of the United States (1805-1812), b. Little Britain, N.Y. Before he was 20 he served on a privateer and, in the French and Indian War, accompanied the regiment of his father, Charles Clinton, in the expedition against Fort Frontenac led by John Bradstreet. After studying law in New York City he began practice in Ulster co. and was elected (1768) to the provincial assembly, where he became a leader of the anti-British faction. In 1775, Clinton was elected one of the state's delegates to the Second Continental Congress. Military duties as a brigadier general in the Continental Army prevented his signing the Declaration of Independence. Clinton's defense of the Hudson, although courageous, resulted in the capture of Fort Clinton and Fort Montgomery by the British general, Sir Henry CLINTON. Under the new state constitution, which George Clinton helped to frame, he was elected (June, 1777) the first governor of New York state. His energy and leadership as governor for six successive terms (1777-95) led to his being called the father of New York state. He managed trade and public welfare problems ably, and he successfully settled the Indian troubles in W New York. He advanced New York's claims to the NEW HAMPSHIRE GRANTS (now Vermont), initiated action on building canals (later realized by his nephew, De Witt CLINTON), and unsuccessfully fought the transfer from New York to the United States of the right to collect duties at the port of New York. An advocate of state sovereignty, Clinton was one of the chief opponents of the Federal Constitution, writing seven letters against ratification, signed Cato, in the New York *Journal.* These were answered by Alexander HAMILTON in his letters, signed Caesar, in the *Daily Advertiser.* Clinton's views on the Constitution were opposed by a rapidly growing party, the Federalists, under the leadership of John JAY. Jay, running against Clinton for governor, lost the election of 1792 only by a questionable manipulation of returns on the part of the Clintonians, and in 1795 Jay won with ease, Clinton having declined to become a candidate. As a result of his alliance with the Livingstons and Aaron Burr, Clinton became governor for a seventh term in the Republican triumph of 1800. In 1804 he was elected Vice President for President Jefferson's second term. He sought the presidency in 1808, having won support for that office in previous elections, but again he received only the vice presidency, this time under James Madison. See his *Public Papers* (ed. by Hugh Hastings and J. A. Holden, 10 vol., 1899-1914); E. W. Spaulding, *His Excellency George Clinton* (1938, repr. 1964) and *New York in the Critical Period, 1783-1789* (1932, repr. 1960).

Clinton, Sir Henry, 1738?-1795, British general in the American Revolution, b. Newfoundland; son of George Clinton (1686?-1761). He was an officer in the New York militia and then in the Coldstream Guards. He had distinguished himself in America by service in the French and Indian Wars long before he arrived in Boston in 1775 with the reinforcements for Gov. Thomas Gage. He took part in the battle of Bunker Hill (1775), commanded (1776) an unsuccessful expedition against Charleston, S.C., and served under Sir William HOWE in the battle of Long Island, in the occupation of New York, and at White Plains. In 1777 he headed the British occupation of Rhode Island. When Howe moved on Philadelphia, Clinton assumed the command of New York. He did not fulfill the part expected of the New York command in the British strategy that resulted in defeat with the SARATOGA CAMPAIGN; he advanced up the Hudson valley, capturing the patriot strongholds of Fort Clinton (strongly defended by James Clinton) and Fort Montgomery, but after burning Kingston he turned back. Sir Henry (knighted 1777) succeeded Howe in the supreme command in America in 1778. Acting on orders from London, he evacuated Philadelphia and, after Washington's attempt to halt him failed (see MONMOUTH, BATTLE OF), he reached New York. He complained that Lord George Germain did not answer his requests for supplies and twice tried to resign. In Dec., 1779, he left Baron KNYPHAUSEN in command in New York and redeemed his failure of 1776 by capturing Charleston (1780). After placing Cornwallis in command in the Carolinas, he returned to New York. In 1781, expecting Washington to attack, he remained in New York too long and failed to aid Cornwallis in the YORKTOWN CAMPAIGN. He resigned and was succeeded by Sir Guy CARLETON. He was later (1794-95) governor of Gibraltar. He recorded his campaigns from 1775 to 1782 (published in 1954 as *The American Rebellion,* ed. by W. B. Willcox). Cornwallis criticized his account, and the controversy between the two continued until Clinton's death. See W. B. Willcox, *Portrait of a General* (1964).

Clinton, James, 1733-1812, American Revolutionary general, b. Orange co., N.Y.; brother of George Clinton and father of De Witt Clinton. He served in the French and Indian Wars and early in the Revolution took part in the disastrous Quebec campaign. His most noted exploit was his heroic but futile defense of Fort Clinton (near Kingston, N.Y.) against the British drive up the Hudson valley under Sir Henry CLINTON in 1777. James Clinton later fought (1779) with Gen. John Sullivan against the Indians and served at Yorktown (1781).

Clinton. 1 Resort town (1970 pop. 10,267), Middlesex co., S Conn., on Long Island Sound; settled 1663, set off from Killingworth and inc. 1838. A monument commemorates the early years of the school that later became Yale Univ. **2** City (1970 pop. 34,719), seat of Clinton co., E central Iowa, on the Mississippi, in a rich corn and livestock area; inc. 1859. An industrial and rail center, it has food-processing (especially corn) and diverse manufacturing industries. Clinton grew as a lumbering town and in the 1880s was the greatest sawmill center in the Midwest. Two junior colleges are there. **3** Industrial town (1970 pop. 13,383), Worcester co., E central Mass., on the Nashua River, near Wachusett Reservoir, in a farm and wooded area; settled c.1654, set off from Lancaster and inc. 1850. Once an important textile center, it now has chemical and metallurgical industries.

Clio: see MUSES.

clipper, type of sailing ship, designed for speed. Long and narrow, the clipper had the greatest beam aft of the center; the bow cleaved the waves; and the ship carried, besides topgallant and royal sails, skysails and moonrakers—a veritable cloud of sails. The type originated in the United States. Baltimore clippers and Atlantic packet ships were the forerunners of the true Yankee clipper, which may be said to have emerged with the *Ann McKim,* completed in Baltimore in 1833. The Yankee clipper was brought to perfection by Donald McKay of Boston, who built such vessels as the *Flying Cloud,* the *Glory of the Seas,* and the *Lightning.* U.S. and British clippers came to be known as China clippers because they utilized their speed to carry on a flourishing China trade in tea and opium. Clippers sailed from the U.S. Atlantic coast around Cape Horn to California in the days of the gold rush. They steadily reduced the time for their long voyages and held famous races. The clipper came into being only after its finally successful rival, the steamship, was engaging in transoceanic voyages. In the early days the clipper easily outran the plodding steam vessel, but, ironically, the improved steamship began to forge ahead even as some of the fastest and most beautiful clippers were being built. When the *Cutty Sark,* one of the swiftest and most celebrated British clippers, was completed at Dunbarton, Scotland, in 1869, the era of the commercial sailing ship had nearly come to an end. See Howard I. Chapelle, *The History of American Sailing Ships* (1935).

Clipperton Island, uninhabited atoll, c.2 sq mi (5.2 sq km), in the Pacific Ocean, c.800 mi (1,290 km) SW of Mexico. It was used as a base by John Clipperton, an English pirate. The French claimed it in 1858, the Americans held it for a time in the Spanish-American War, and Mexican troops occupied it in 1897. The conflict between France and Mexico was referred to the king of Italy for arbitration in 1908. The award was made (1931) in favor of France, and Mexico surrendered the island in 1932.

Clisson, Olivier de (ōlēvyā' də klēsôN'), 1336-1407, French soldier, b. Brittany. He fought on the English side in the War of the BRETON SUCCESSION but entered the French service as companion in arms to Bertrand Du Guesclin. In 1380 he became constable of France. He defeated (1382) the insurgents of Ghent under Philip van ARTEVELDE at Roosebeke. One of the MARMOUSETS, he made use of his position to satisfy his boundless avidity; he became one of the richest men of his time. After King Charles VI became (1392) insane, Clisson retired to Brittany, where he served as guardian of the duchy after the death (1399) of Duke John de Montfort.

Clisthenes: see CLEISTHENES.

Clive, Kitty (Catherine Raftor), 1711-85, English singer and actress. She made her debut (c.1728) at Drury Lane under the management of Colley Cibber and worked for many years with David Garrick, with whom she never got along. Her charm, wit, and vivacity, linked with a fine singing voice, brought her great success in light comedy and farce. She was a friend of Samuel Johnson; of Fielding, in whose plays and adaptations she appeared; and of Horace Walpole, who gave her a cottage, Clive's-Den, upon her retirement. There she held an informal salon and wrote several farces. She was painted by Hogarth.

Clive, Robert, Baron Clive of Plassey (plăs'ē), 1725-74, British soldier and statesman. He went to India in 1743 as a clerk for the British East India Company and entered the military service of the company in 1744; he soon distinguished himself in the fighting against the French. Clive's brilliant capture of Arcot (1751) and the relief of the siege of Trichinopoly (1752) thwarted DUPLEIX, who had been on the verge of achieving French hegemony in S India. In 1757, Clive, then governor of Fort St. David near Madras, recovered Calcutta from the nawab of Bengal, Siraj-ud-daula. Then, after defeating the nawab at Plassey, he replaced him with the more compliant Mir Jafar. Bengal thus passed under effective British control, and Clive became the first governor. His victories over the Dutch at Biderra (1759) consolidated the British position as the dominant European power in India. Returning (1760) to England, he was given an Irish peerage as Baron Clive of Plassey. As governor of Bengal again from 1765 to 1767, Clive greatly reduced corruption and inefficiency in a formerly disordered administration and reached a settlement with the states of Bihar and Orissa. But his assumption of the right to collect the revenues of those states involved the company in the complexities of wide territorial administration, which it was ill equipped to handle. This was one of the factors that eventually led the British government to assume responsibility for British rule in India. After his return to England, Clive was bitterly attacked by politicians and others and was accused by Parliament of peculation. He was acquitted (1773) after a long investigation, but, broken in health, he committed suicide. See the famous *Essay on Clive* by T. B. Macaulay; biography by A. M. Davies (1939); H. H. Dodwell, *Dupleix and Clive* (1920, repr. 1967); R. J. Minney, *Clive of India* (rev. ed. 1957); G. B. Malleson, *Lord Clive and the Establishment of the English in India* (1962); Michael Edwardes, *Plassey: The Founding of an Empire* (1970).

cloaca (klōā'kə), in biology, enlarged posterior end of the digestive tract of some animals. The cloaca, from the Latin word for *sewer,* is a single chamber into which passes solid and liquid waste materials as well as the products of the reproductive organs, the gametes. Cloacas are found in amphibians, reptiles, birds, and lower mammals; higher mammals have a separate rectal outlet, the anus. The term *cloaca* is also used for analogous chambers in many invertebrates, such as animals of the phylum Aschelminthes.

clock, instrument for measuring and indicating time. Predecessors of the clock were the SUNDIAL, the HOURGLASS, and the CLEPSYDRA. The operation of a clock depends on a stable mechanical oscillator, such as a swinging pendulum or a mass connected to a spring, by means of which the energy stored in a raised weight or coiled spring advances a pointer or other indicating device at a controlled rate. It is not definitely known when the first mechanical clocks were invented. Some authorities attribute the first weight-driven clock to Pacificus, archdeacon of Verona in the 9th cent. Gerbert, a learned monk who became Pope Sylvester II, is often credited with the invention of a mechanical clock, c.996. Mechanical figures that struck a bell on the hour were installed in St. Paul's Cathedral, London, in 1286; a dial was added to the clock in the 14th cent. Clocks were placed in a clock tower at Westminster Hall, London, in 1288 and in the cathedral at Canterbury in 1292. In France, Rouen was especially noted for the skill of its clockmakers and watchmakers. One of the most famous clocks is in the cathedral of Strasbourg; the clock was first placed in the cathedral in 1352, and in the 16th cent. it was reconstructed. In the 19th cent. a new astronomical clock similar to the first two clocks was constructed. Its elaborate mechanical devices include the Twelve Apostles, a crowing cock, a revolving celestial globe, and an automatic calendar dial. Probably the early clock closest to the modern ones was that constructed in the 14th cent. for the tower of the palace (later the Palais de Justice) of Charles V of France by the clockmaker Henry de Vick (Vic, Wieck, Wyck) of Württemburg. Until the 17th cent. few mechanical clocks were found outside of cathedral towers, monasteries, abbeys, and public squares. The early clocks driven by hanging weights were bulky and heavy. When the coiled spring came into use (c.1500), it made possible the construction of the smaller and lighter-weight types. By applying Galileo's law of the pendulum, the Dutch scientist Christiaan Huygens invented (1656 or 1657) a pendulum clock, probably the first. Early clocks used in dwellings in the 17th cent. were variously known as lantern clocks, birdcage clocks, and sheep's-head clocks; they were of brass, sometimes ornate, with a gong bell at the top supported by a frame. Before the pendulum was introduced, they were spring-driven or weight-driven; those driven by weights had to be placed on a wall bracket to allow space for the falling weights. These clocks, probably obtained chiefly from England and Holland, were used in the Virginia and New England colonies. Clocks with long cases to conceal the long pendulums and

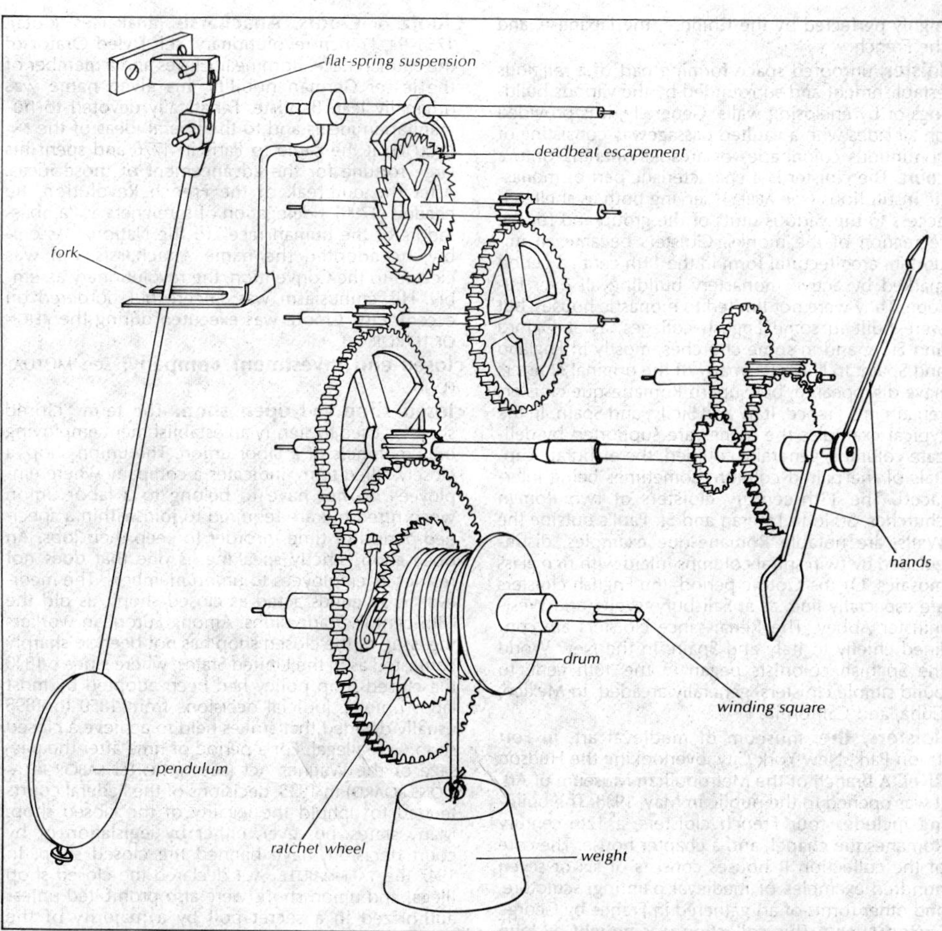

A pendulum clock: Weight-driven clock mechanism

weights came into use after the mid-17th cent.; these were the forerunners of the grandfather clocks. With the development of the craft of cabinetmaking, more attention was concentrated on the clock case. In France the tall cabinet clocks, or grandfather clocks, were often of oak elaborately ornamented with brass and gilt. Those made in England were at first of oak and later of walnut and mahogany; simpler in style, their chief decoration was inlay work. Among the well-known clocks of the world are the clock known as Big Ben in the tower next to Westminster Bridge in the British Houses of Parliament and the tower clock in the Metropolitan Life Insurance Company building, New York City. Electric clocks were made in the second half of the 19th cent. but were not used extensively in homes until after c.1930. The hands of an electric clock are driven by a synchronous electric motor supplied with alternating current of a stable frequency. The quartz clock, invented c.1929, uses the vibrations of a quartz crystal to drive a synchronous motor at a very precise rate. Some quartz clocks have an error of less than one thousandth of a second per day. The ATOMIC CLOCK is even more precise. See WATCH. See C. W. Drepperd, *American Clocks & Clockmakers* (2d ed. 1958); H. A. Lloyd, *The Complete Book of Old Clocks* (1965); Brooks Palmer, *A Treasury of American Clocks* (1967); Eric Bruton, *Clocks and Watches, 1400–1900* (1967); F. J. Britten, *Old Clocks and Watches and Their Makers* (8th ed. 1973); Kenneth Welch, *The History of Clocks and Watches* (1972).

Clodia (klō'dēə), fl. 1st cent. B.C., Roman matron, famous among the ancient Romans for her beauty; sister of Publius CLODIUS. She was suspected of murdering her husband, Quintus Caecilius Metellus Celer (see METELLUS, family), and she accused her lover, Marcus Caelius Rufus, of trying to murder her. According to tradition one of her many lovers was the poet CATULLUS; if this is true then it was she whom he immortalized as Lesbia.

Clodion (klōdēôN') or **Claude Michel** (klōd mēshĕl'), 1738–1814, French rococo sculptor. He executed several important commissions under Louis XVI but is best remembered for his bas-reliefs and small figure groups in bronze and terra-cotta representing fauns, nymphs, and children. He is represented in the Louvre and in the Metropolitan Museum.

Clodius (Publius Clodius Pulcher) (klō'dēəs), d. 52 B.C., Roman politician. He belonged to the Claudian gens (see CLAUDIUS), and his name is also written as Publius Claudius Pulcher. He was brother to Appius Claudius Pulcher and to the notorious Clodia. In 62 B.C. he created a tremendous scandal when, disguised as a woman, he entered the house of Julius Caesar at the time of the women's mysteries of Bona Dea. CICERO prosecuted him for sacrilege, but Clodius, probably by heavy bribery, won an acquittal. The results were that Caesar divorced his wife POMPEIA, and Cicero earned Clodius' unswerving hatred. In 58 B.C., Clodius was tribune of the people, put into office by the First Triumvirate (Caesar, Crassus, and Pompey) probably under the mistaken impression that he would be a tool. Instead, he proved himself a demagogue, seeking popularity in every way. He exiled Cicero on specious charges arising from the conspiracy of Catiline, and he sent Cato the Younger to Cyprus. Clodius spent much of his money in organizing gangs of bullies to intimidate the city. The tribune MILO (initially supported by Pompey) organized a conservative gang, and Rome was plagued with bloody rioting until Clodius was killed by Milo's gang. His irresponsible actions had prepared the way for the civil war of Caesar and Pompey.

Clogher (klŏkh'ər), rural district (1971 pop. 9,554), Co. Tyrone, central Northern Ireland, on the Blackwater River. A religious center since St. Patrick's time, Clogher is the seat of a Protestant bishop; its cathedral was rebuilt in the 18th cent. and restored in 1956. The cathedral of the Roman Catholic bishop of Clogher is at Monaghan, Republic of Ireland.

cloisonné (kloizənā', -sənā'), method of enamel decoration of metal surfaces, such as vases and jewel boxes. Metal filaments (which form the *cloisons* or separating elements) are attached at right angles to the surface outlining the design to be used. These miniature compartments are filled with colored enamel in paste form, and the object is then heated in order to fuse the enamel to the surface and develop its transparency and permanent colors. When finished, the enamel and *cloisons* are closely joined in a smooth, even surface showing the pattern in various colors defined by the metal partitions which prevented their fusing with one another. Probably invented in the Middle East, cloisonné has been highly perfected by the Chinese, the Japanese, and the French.

cloister, unroofed space forming part of a religious establishment and surrounded by the various buildings or by enclosing walls. Generally, it is provided on all sides with a vaulted passageway consisting of continuous colonnades or arcades opening onto a court. The cloister is a characteristic part of monastic institutions (see ABBEY), serving both as sheltered access to the various units of the group and for the recreation of the monks. Cloisters became an important architectural form in the 11th cent., a period marked by active monastery building all over Europe. They were not limited to monastic houses, but were built in some English colleges, as at Oxford and Eton, and in some churches, mostly in England and Spain. In N France many of the original cloisters have disappeared, but superb Romanesque cloisters remain in S France, Italy and Sicily, and Spain. In the typical examples the arches are supported by delicate columns, generally coupled, the elaborate capitals of the paired columns sometimes being interlaced. The 13th-century cloisters of two Roman churches, St. John Lateran and St. Paul's outside the Walls, are notable Romanesque examples, distinguished by twin spiral columns inlaid with rich glass mosaics. Of the Gothic period, the English cloisters are especially fine, as at Salisbury, Wells, and Westminster Abbey. The Renaissance cloisters are confined chiefly to Italy and Spain. In the New World the Spanish colonists began in the 16th cent. to build simple cloisters, generally arcaded, in Mexico, Cuba, and California.

Cloisters, the, museum of medieval art, in Fort Tryon Park, New York City, overlooking the Hudson River. A branch of the Metropolitan Museum of Art, it was opened to the public in May, 1938. The building includes four French cloisters, a 12th-century Romanesque chapel, and a chapter house. The core of the collection it houses consists of six or seven hundred examples of medieval painting, sculpture, and other forms of art gathered in France by George Grey BARNARD. This collection was bought by John D. Rockefeller, Jr., in 1925, and presented to the Metropolitan Museum. Later additions to it include a series of 15th-century tapestries, *Hunt of the Unicorn;* a tapestry series of the 14th cent., *The Nine Heroes;* the famous *Mérode Altarpiece* by Robert Campin; and the Bury St. Edmunds ivory crucifix. See J. J. Rorimer, *The Cloisters* (3d ed. 1963) and *Medieval Monuments at the Cloisters* (rev. ed. 1972).

Clomid (klō'mĭd): see FERTILITY DRUG.

clone, group of organisms, all of which are descended from a single individual through asexual reproduction, as in a pure cell culture of bacteria. Except for changes in the hereditary material that come about by MUTATION, all members of a clone are genetically identical. Laboratory experiments in cloning have resulted in the development of a frog from a cell of an existing animal, and the laboratory fertilization and early development of human eggs; such experiments have raised questions about the eventual possibility of cloning of identical humans from cells of a preexisting individual.

Clonmacnoise (klŏnmăknoiz'), village, Co. Offaly, central Republic of Ireland, on the Shannon River. The monastery founded (548) on the site by St. Kieran became the most famous in Ireland. It survived 1,000 years of raids and invasions, until it was destroyed by the English in 1552. Today there are ruins of a cathedral (first built 904), several churches, two round towers, three sculptured crosses, over 200 inscribed stones, and a castle (built 1214). The ruins comprise a national monument. The annual feast of St. Kieran is held at Clonmacnoise.

Clonmel (klŏnmĕl'), municipal borough (1971 pop. 11,630), administrative center of South Riding, Co. Tipperary, S Republic of Ireland, on the Suir River. Footwear, cider, enamelware, tubular steel furniture, perambulators, and canned meat are produced there. It is also a tourist center with good hunting and salmon fishing. Clonmel was once a stronghold of the powerful Anglo-Norman Butler family. Oliver Cromwell captured it in 1650. There are a number of restored ecclesiastical sites. Laurence Sterne was born in Clonmel.

Clontarf (klŏntärf'), suburb of Dublin, Co. Dublin, E Republic of Ireland. It was the scene of a decisive defeat (1014) of the Danes by the Irish under Brian Boru, who himself was killed in the fighting. Clontarf Castle was built in 1835 on the site of an ancient castle that belonged successively to the Knights Templars and the Knights Hospitalers.

Clootz or **Cloots, Anacharsis** (änäkärsēs' klōts), 1755–94, French revolutionary, self-styled Orator of the Human Race. Born near Cleves and a member of the lesser German nobility, his given name was originally Jean Baptiste. Fanatically devoted to humanitarian ideals and to the liberal ideas of the ENCYCLOPÉDIE, he came to Paris in 1776 and spent his large fortune for the advancement of those ideas. After the outbreak of the French Revolution, he headed (1790) a delegation of foreigners as "ambassadors of the human race" to the National Assembly; he adopted the name Anacharsis and was elected to the Convention, the revolutionary assembly. His enthusiasm was sincere but bordered on eccentricity. Clootz was executed during the REIGN OF TERROR.

closed-end investment company: see MUTUAL FUND.

closed shop and **open shop.** The term "closed shop" is used to signify an establishment employing only members of a labor union. The union shop, a closely allied term, indicates a company where employees do not have to belong to a labor union when hired but are required to join within a specified period of time in order to keep their jobs. An open shop, strictly speaking, is one that does not restrict its employees to union members. The medieval trade guilds acted as closed shops, as did the 18th-century trade clubs. Among European workers the issue of the closed shop has not been so sharply contested as in the United States, where since c.1840 the closed-shop policy had been adopted by most labor unions. Judicial decisions from 1850 to 1898 usually decided that strikes held to achieve a closed shop were illegal. For a period of time after the passage of the Wagner Act (see NATIONAL LABOR RELATIONS BOARD) in 1935, decisions of the Federal courts tended to uphold the legality of the closed shop. Many states, however, either by legislation or by court decision, have banned the closed shop. In 1947 the TAFT-HARTLEY ACT declared the closed shop illegal and union shops were also prohibited unless authorized in a secret poll by a majority of the workers; it was amended (1951) to allow union shops without a vote of the majority of the workers. Thereafter, a campaign was begun by business leaders in certain industries to have so-called right-to-work laws enacted at the state level. More than one third of the states passed such laws, the effect being to declare the union shop illegal. It is argued in favor of the closed shop that unions can win a fair return for their labor only through solidarity, since there is always—except in wartime—an oversupply of labor; and that, since all employees of a plant share in the advantages won through collective bargaining, all workers should contribute to union funds. Arguments in favor of the open shop are that forcing unwilling workers to pay union dues is an infringement of their rights; that union membership is sometimes closed to certain workers or the initiation fee so high as to be an effective bar to membership; and that employers are deprived of the privilege of hiring competent workers or firing incompetent ones. See J. E. Johnsen, comp., *The Closed Shop* (1942), a summary of the arguments on both sides; J. R. Dempsey, *The Operation of the Right to Work Laws* (1958, repr. 1961); W. E. J. McCarthy, *The Closed Shop in Britain* (1964).

closet drama, a play that is meant to be read rather than performed. Precursors of the form existed in classical times. Plato's *Apology* is often regarded as tragic drama rather than philosophic dialogue. The dialogues of Cicero, Strabo, and Seneca were probably declaimed rather than acted, since only the comic theater survived transplantation from Greece to Rome. Closet dramas were particularly popular in the early 19th cent. when melodrama and burlesque dominated the theater, and poets attempted to raise dramatic standards by reviving past traditions. Byron's *Manfred* (1817) and Shelley's *The Cenci* (1819) imitate Shakespeare, and Goethe's *Faust* (Part I, 1808; Part II, 1832) draws in part on the Elizabethan tradition. Milton's *Samson Agonistes* (1671) and Shelley's *Prometheus Unbound* (1819) are based on Greek tragedies. Notable among other closet dramas are Robert Browning's *Strafford* (1837) and *Pippa Passes* (1841).

Clotaire I (klōtâr'), d. 561, Frankish king, son of CLOVIS I. On his father's death (511) he and his brothers received equal shares of the Frankish kingdom. His capital was at Soissons. In 524 he and his brother CHILDEBERT I divided the kingdom of their deceased brother Clodomir, whose children they murdered. With his brother Theodoric he conquered Thuringia. In 534 Clotaire and Childebert seized and divided the First Kingdom of Burgundy, and in 542 they attacked the Visigoths of Spain but were repulsed before Saragossa. The deaths of Theodebald, Theodoric's grandson (555), and of Childebert (558) made Clotaire sole king of the Franks. His sons Chilperic I and Sigebert I inherited Neustria and Austrasia respectively; his sons Charibert and GUNTRAM divided the remainder of the kingdom.

Clotaire II, d. 629, Frankish king, son of CHILPERIC I and FREDEGUNDE. He succeeded (584) his father as king of Neustria, but his mother ruled for him until her death (597). In 613, after the death of his cousin Theodoric II, king of AUSTRASIA, he was called in by Austrasian nobles to assume rule. He thus became king of all the Franks. He put BRUNHILDA to death, restored peace with the help of the nobility, and was compelled to grant (614) a charter giving far-reaching privileges to nobles and clergy. He was also forced to agree that each of the component parts of the Frankish lands, Austrasia, Neustria, and Burgundy, was to have its own mayor of the palace; the mayors of the palace were the chief royal administrators. In 623 he sent his son DAGOBERT I to be king of Austrasia. Dagobert later succeeded to all the Frankish lands.

clotbur: see COCKLEBUR.

clothes moth, name for several species of moths of the family Tineidae, whose larvae feed on wool, furs, feathers, upholstery, and a variety of animal products. Clothes moths are of Old World origin. Those commonest in North America are the case-bearing clothes moth, *Tinea pellionella,* and the webbing clothes moth, *Tineola bisselliella.* The adults are yellowish or buff moths, often called millers, with a wingspread of about ½ in. (1.2 cm). They lay 100 to 150 eggs on the material which is to provide food for the larvae; they do not feed on fabrics themselves. The larva of the case-bearing clothes moth makes an open-ended case out of food fibers and its own silk; it feeds and pupates (see INSECT) within the case. The webbing clothes moth larva makes no case, but when it pupates it builds a cocoon of silk and fibers. The life cycle is completed most rapidly at average room temperature and about 75% humidity. The tapestry, or carpet, moth, *Trichophaga tapetzella,* attacks upholstery. Fumigation, sunning, cleaning, brushing, and cold storage help to prevent damage. Clothes moths are classified in the phylum ARTHROPODA, class Insecta, order Lepidoptera, family Tineidae.

clothing: see COSTUME.

Clotho: see FATES.

cloth of gold, fabric woven wholly or partly of gold threads. From remote times gold has been used as material for weaving either alone or with other fibers. In India tapestries were made from gold threads as fine as silk. Cloth of gold was woven on Byzantine looms from the 7th to the 9th cent. and on those of Sicily, Cyprus, Lucca, and Venice in the 10th cent. Some narrow webs were woven in England, as well as palls of gold and silver cloth. Cloths of estate were magnificent gold tissues used to canopy or cover thrones. Baldachin, or fine cloth with gold warp and silk weft, was used ceremonially and also for rich clothing. The use of gold textiles and embroideries in the Middle Ages is illustrated by the pageantry at the meeting of the FIELD OF THE CLOTH OF GOLD (1520). Gold thread for weaving and embroidery is still made in India, Delhi alone producing many miles per annum, working in the ancient manner. Gold or silver gilt wire is drawn through holes, successively smaller, in a specially devised metal plate, and is used either round or flattened. Modern metallic cloth, known as lamé, is commonly made of a core yarn wound with a thin metal thread, or lamé. Various artificial metallic cloths are also produced.

Clotilda, Saint, d. 545, Frankish queen. She converted her husband, CLOVIS I, to Christianity and built with him in Paris the Church of the Apostles Peter and Paul, later renamed (10th cent.) Sainte-Geneviève. After her husband's death she spent her life caring for the poor. Feast: June 3.

cloud, aggregation of minute particles of water or ice suspended in the air. Clouds are formed when air containing water vapor is cooled below a critical temperature called the DEW point and the resulting moisture condenses into droplets on microscopic dust particles (condensation nuclei) in the atmosphere. The air is normally cooled by expansion during its upward movement. Clouds are occasionally produced by a reduction of pressure aloft or by the mixing of warmer and cooler air currents. Upward flow of air in the atmosphere may be caused by convection resulting from intense solar heating of

Approximate heights of some types of clouds

the ground; by a cold wedge of air (cold front) near the ground causing a mass of warm air to be forced aloft; or by a mountain range at an angle to the wind. A classification of cloud forms was first made (1801) by French naturalist Jean Lamarck. In 1803, Luke Howard, an English scientist, devised a classification that was adopted by the International Meteorological Commission (1929). His designations for three primary cloud types, cirrus, cumulus, and stratus, and their compound forms, are still widely used in modified form. The classification used today comprises four main divisions: high clouds, 20,000 to 40,000 ft (6,100–12,200 m); intermediate clouds, 6,500 to 20,000 ft (1,980–6,100 m); low clouds, near ground level to 6,500 ft (1,980 m); and clouds with vertical development, 1,600 ft to over 20,000 ft (490–6,100 m). High cloud forms include *cirrus*, detached clouds of delicate and fibrous appearance, without shading, generally white in color, often resembling tufts or featherlike plumes, and composed entirely of ice crystals; *cirrocumulus* (mackerel sky), composed of small white flakes or very small globular masses, arranged in groups, lines, or ripples; and *cirrostratus*, a thin whitish veil, sometimes giving the entire sky a milky appearance, which does not blur the outline of the sun or moon but frequently produces a halo. Intermediate clouds include *altocumulus*, a layer or patches composed of flattened globular masses arranged in groups, lines, or waves, with individual clouds sometimes so close together that their edges join; and *altostratus*, resembling thick cirrostratus without halo phenomena, like a gray veil, through which the sun or the moon shows vaguely or is sometimes completely hidden. Low clouds include *stratocumulus*, a cloud layer or patches composed of fairly large globular masses or flakes, soft and gray with darker parts, arranged in groups, lines, or rolls, often with the rolls so close together that their edges join; *stratus*, a uniform layer resembling fog but not resting on the ground; and *nimbostratus*, a nearly uniform, dark grey layer, amorphous in character and usually producing continuous rain or snow. Clouds having vertical development include *cumulus*, a thick, detached cloud, generally associated with fair weather, usually with a horizontal base and a dome-shaped upper surface that frequently resembles a head of cauliflower and shows strong contrasts of light and shadow when the sun illuminates it from the side, and *cumulonimbus*, the thunderstorm cloud, heavy masses of great vertical development whose summits rise in the form of mountains or towers, the upper parts having a fibrous texture, often spreading out in the shape of an anvil, and sometimes reaching the STRATOSPHERE. Cumulonimbus generally produces showers of rain, snow, hailstorms, or thunderstorms. Cloudiness (or proportion of the sky covered by any form of cloud), measured in tenths, is one of the elements of climate. WEATHER is called clear when the sky is less than 3/10 clouded, partly cloudy when it is 3/10 to 7/10 clouded, and cloudy when it is more than 7/10 clouded; the extremes are cloudless and overcast. The cloudiness of the United States averages somewhat less than 50% (i.e., the country receives somewhat more than 50% of the possible sunshine); the Great Lakes region and the coast of Washington and Oregon have the greatest cloudiness (60–70%), and the SW United States—Arizona and adjacent areas—are the least cloudy (10–30%). In aviation, the base of any cloud layer that, when considered in combination with clouds below, results in a cover of more than 6/10 of the celestial dome, is termed the *ceiling*. See A. H. Gordon, *Elements of Dynamic Meteorology* (1962); R. S. Scorer, *Clouds of the World* (1972).

cloud chamber, device used to detect ELEMENTARY PARTICLES and other ionizing radiation. A cloud chamber consists essentially of a closed container filled with a supersaturated vapor, e.g., water in air. When ionizing radiation passes through the vapor, it leaves a trail of charged particles (ions) that serve as condensation centers for the vapor, which condenses around them. The path of the radiation is thus indicated by tracks of tiny liquid droplets in the supersaturated vapor. The cloud chamber was invented c.1900 by C. T. R. Wilson. In the type devised by him, which is often called the Wilson cloud chamber, air or another gas is saturated with water

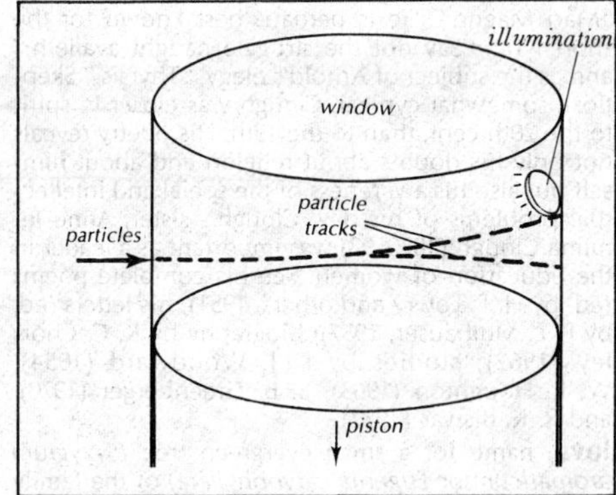

Simplified cloud chamber: A supersaturated vapor is created by withdrawing the piston. Particles enter the chamber and leave visible tracks by ionizing air molecules, which serve as condensation nuclei to form cloud droplets.

vapor and enclosed in a cylinder fitted with a transparent window at the top and a piston or other pressure-regulating device at the bottom. When the pressure in the chamber is suddenly reduced, e.g., by lowering the piston, the gas-vapor mixture is cooled, producing supersaturation. Cloud chambers of this design are sometimes called the pulsed type, since they do not maintain a continuous state of supersaturation of the vapor. A more recent design is the diffusion cloud chamber. In this device a large temperature difference is maintained between the top and bottom of the chamber, usually by cooling the bottom of the chamber with dry ice. The gas in the chamber, usually air, is saturated with a vapor, usually alcohol; the air-vapor mixture cools as it diffuses toward the cool bottom, becoming supersaturated. If the gas is kept saturated with a fresh supply of vapor, e.g., by an alcohol-soaked pad inside the top of the chamber, the operation of the chamber can be essentially continuous. One disadvantage of the cloud chamber is the relatively low density of the gas, which limits the number of interactions between ionizing radiation and molecules of the gas. For this reason physicists have developed other particle detectors, notably the BUBBLE CHAMBER and the SPARK CHAMBER.

Clouet, Jean (zhäN klo͞oā'), called **Janet** or **Jehannet,** c.1485–1540, portrait and miniature painter. He was court painter and valet de chambre to the French king Francis I. He is thought to have been Flemish and may have been related to Jehan Cloët, painter to the duke of Burgundy in the late 15th cent. None of the work attributed to Jean Clouet can be proved to have been his. It includes portraits of Francis I (Louvre), the dauphin Francis (Antwerp), and Charles de Cossé (Metropolitan Mus.); seven miniature portraits (Bibliothèque nationale); and a large number of portrait drawings, all of the highest quality. The drawings are characterized by a geometric simplicity of form and softness of modeling. His son, **François Clouet,** c.1510–c.1572, also called Janet or Jehannet, inherited his father's talent and position, serving as court painter successively under Francis I, Henry II, Francis II, and Charles IX. His work is unsurpassed in clarity and precision of draughtsmanship. He enjoyed a high reputation and was patronized by all the notables of the court. Attributed to him are two portraits of Francis (Uffizi; Louvre); portraits of Catherine de' Medici (Versailles), Elizabeth of Austria (Louvre), and Charles IX (Vienna); and one thought to be of Diane de Poitiers (called *Lady in Her Bath,* National Gall., Washington, D.C.). There are also a large number of portrait drawings preserved in Chantilly and in the Bibliothèque nationale and the Cabinet des Estampes, Paris. See his complete drawings, miniatures, and paintings, ed. by Peter Mellen (1971).

Clough, Arthur Hugh (klŭf), 1819–61, English poet. He was educated at Rugby and Balliol College, Oxford, where he became friends with Matthew Arnold. After graduation (1941) he was fellow and tutor of Oriel College until 1848 when he resigned. During the next few years he traveled on the Continent. In 1852, inspired by his friendship with Emerson, he went to Harvard and lectured. He pursued a civil service career until his health failed in 1860. His first published work, *The Bothie of Toper-na-Vuolich,* a narrative in hexameters, appeared in 1848, followed by *Ambarvalia,* a collection of lyrics, in 1849. His posthumous poems include "Amours de Voyage," the dialogues "Dypsichus," and the tales "Mari Magno." He is perhaps best known for the short lyric, "Say not the struggle naught availeth," and as the subject of Arnold's elegy, "Thyrsis." Skeptical, somewhat cynical, Clough was closer in spirit to the 20th cent. than to the 19th. His poetry reveals not only his doubts about religion and about himself but also his awareness of the social and intellectual problems of his day. Clough's sister, Anne Jemima Clough (1820–92) was important as a leader in the education of women. See his complete poems (ed. by H. F. Lowry and others, 1951); his letters (ed. by F. L. Mulhauser, 1957); biography by K. C. Chorley (1962); studies by F. J. Woodward (1954), W. E. Houghton (1963), E. B. Greenberger (1970), and R. K. Biswas (1972).

clove, name for a small evergreen tree *(Syzygium aromaticum* or *Eugenia caryophyllata)* of the family Myrtaceae (MYRTLE family) and for its unopened flower bud, an important spice. The buds, whose folded petals are enclosed in four toothlike lobes of the calyx, are gathered by hand, dried, and marketed either whole or ground for culinary purposes. Clove oil, obtained by distillation, is widely used in synthetic vanilla and other flavorings as well as in perfumes; it is often considered medicinal and antiseptic. The spicy fragrance of cloves was used by the Chinese (c.3d cent. B.C.) and by the Romans, but the first instance of finding the tree growing wild was recorded by the Portuguese when they discovered the Spice Islands. The Portuguese and then the Dutch held the clove trade in monopoly, eliminating the tree from all but a single island, until the late 18th cent. Today cloves are products also of other tropical areas, e.g., the West Indies and islands off E Africa such as Madagascar and Zanzibar. Clove is classified in the division MAGNOLIOPHYTA, class Magnoliopsida, order Myrtales, family Myrtaceae.

clover, any plant of the genus *Trifolium,* leguminous hay and forage plants of the family Leguminosae (PULSE family). Most of the species are native to north temperate or subtropical regions, and all the American cultivated forms have been introduced from Europe. Red clover *(T. pratense),* the state flower of Vermont, was the leading leguminous hay crop of the northeastern regions until it was surpassed by alfalfa. It is frequently seeded with timothy. Swedish, or alsike, clover *(T. hybridum)* is similarly used in the same area. The common white, or Dutch, clover *(T. repens)* is also cultivated at times but is considered a weed in fields and pastures, where it spreads rapidly. Its dried flower and seed heads have been used for making bread during famines in Ireland and the leaves are eaten as salad in some parts of the United States. The clovers are excellent honey plants. Other plants are sometimes called clover, e.g., the related melilot, or SWEET CLOVER. Clover was used by the Greeks in garlands and other decorations. The druids held it sacred. It is said to have been the early emblem of Ireland from which the shamrock is derived, and it is an emblem of the Trinity. English and American poets have celebrated it. A four-leaved clover is thought to bring good luck. See also LESPEDEZA; TREFOIL. Clover is classified in the division MAGNOLIOPHYTA, class Magnoliopsida, order Rosales, family Leguminosae. See bulletins of the U.S. Dept. of Agriculture.

Clovio, Giorgio Giulio (jôr'jō jo͞o'lyō klō'vyō), 1498–1578, Italian illuminator, miniaturist, and painter, also called Macedo or Il Macedone because of his Macedonian origin. He studied at Rome with Giulio Romano and at Verona under Girolamo de' Libri, from whom he learned illuminating. Clovio was employed by Louis II of Hungary, Cardinal Farnese at Rome, and other princely patrons. Among the best known of the many works ascribed to him are the illuminations for the *Book of the Hours of the Blessed Virgin,* his masterpiece; the manuscript biography of Frederick, duke of Urbino (Vatican Library); Cardinal Grimani's *Commentary on the Epistle to the Romans* (Soane Mus., London); *The Victories of Emperor Charles V* (British Mus.); and the Farnese *Breviary* (Pierpont Morgan Library, New York).

Clovis I (klō'vĭs), c.466–511, Frankish king (481–511), son of Childeric I and founder of the Merovingian monarchy. Originally little more than a tribal chieftain, he became sole leader of the Salian FRANKS by force of perseverance and by murdering a number of relatives. In 486 he defeated the Roman legions under Syagrius at Soissons, virtually ending Roman domination over Gaul. He then subdued the Thuringians. After his marriage (493) to the Burgundian princess CLOTILDA, he had his children baptized but was not immediately converted himself. In 496, while locked in battle with the Alemanni, he vowed to become a Christian if he gained the victory. Clovis defeated the Alemanni and was baptized, reputedly with 3,000 of his followers, by St. Remi, bishop of Rheims. Thereafter Clovis was the champion of orthodox Christianity against the Arian heretics, the Burgundians, and the Visigoths. He attacked the Burgundians (500) at Dijon and the Visigoths (507) under ALARIC II at Vouillé. When he died, he was master of most of Gaul—except Burgundy, Gascony, Provence, and Septimania—and of SW Germany. Shortly before his death he probably had the Salian Law revised and put into writing. Clovis united all Franks under his rule, gained the support of the Gallic clergy, made Paris his base of operations, and extended his conquests into Germany. He thus laid the foundation, which even 400 years of chaos and misrule could not destroy, of the French monarchy and foreshadowed the conquests of Charlemagne. He was succeeded by his four sons, THEODORIC I, Clodomir, CHILDEBERT I, and CLOTAIRE I. See the history of GREGORY OF TOURS; Ferdinand Lot, *The End of the Ancient World and the Beginnings of the Middle Ages* (1927; tr. 1953, repr. 1961).

Clovis. 1 City (1970 pop. 13,856), Fresno co., S central Calif., near the foothills of the Sierra Nevada range; inc. 1912. It is a trade center in a farm and vineyard area. **2** City (1970 pop. 28,495), seat of Curry co., E N.Mex., near the Texas line; inc. 1909. It is a railroad division point, the trade center of a cattle and irrigated farm area (with large stockyards), and the home of Cannon Air Force Base, a tactical air command facility. A junior college is in Clovis, and a state park is nearby. A huge county fair and a rodeo are annual events there.

clown, a jester or buffoon, in a circus or a pantomime: see FOOL.

clubfoot or **talipes** (tăl'əpēz''), deformity in which the foot is twisted out of position. Maldevelopment is usually congenital, although it can result from injury or disease (e.g., poliomyelitis) after birth. It can affect one or both feet. Often the foot is twisted downward, with the heel and toe turning inward, causing only part of the foot—the heel, the toes, or the outer margin—to touch the ground; walking is difficult or impossible. Correction can be made in infancy by manipulation, braces, and casts; in severe cases only surgery can correct the condition.

club moss, name generally used for the living species of the class Lycopodiopsida, a primitive subdivision of vascular plants. The Lycopodiopsida reached their zenith in the Carboniferous period, when they reached the size of trees, and contributed to the coal deposits then being formed. They are now close to extinction. Although they resemble the mosses, they are considered to be evolutionarily more advanced because they are vascular. Club mosses are usually creeping or epiphytic and often inhabit moist places, especially in tropical and subtropical forests. They reproduce by means of spores, either clustered into small cones or borne in the axils of the small scalelike leaves. The principal genera are *Lycopodium* and *Selaginella.* Some species of *Lycopodium* are called ground pine or creeping cedar, especially those that resemble miniature hemlocks with flattened fan-shaped branches, and are often used for Christmas decorations. The spores of *L. clavatum* are gathered and sold as lycopodium powder, or vegetable sulfur, a highly inflammable yellow powder sometimes used for pharmaceutical purposes (e.g., as an absorptive powder) and in fireworks. *Selaginella* species, often incorrectly called *Lycopodium,* are frequently grown as ornamentals. One of the best known is a RESURRECTION PLANT. Club mosses constitute the division LYCOPODIOPHYTA, class Lycopodiopsida.

clubroot, disease of cabbages, turnips, radishes, and other plants belonging to the family Cruciferae (MUSTARD family). It is induced by a slime mold that attacks the roots, causing, in the cabbage, undeveloped heads or a failure to head at all. Clubroot can be partially or in some cases completely controlled by the application of lime (if the soil is very acid), by rotation of crops, and by soil sterilization. The disease is also called finger-and-toe from the swollen shape it gives to roots. Slime molds (class Myxomycetes) are classified in the division FUNGI.

club rush: see CATTAIL; SEDGE.

Cluj (klo͞ozh), Hung. *Kolozsvár,* Ger. *Klausenburg,* city (1970 est. pop. 203,000), W central Rumania, in Transylvania, on the Someşul River. The largest city in Transylvania and the second largest in Rumania, it is the administrative center of an agricultural and mineral-rich area. Its diverse manufactures include machinery, metal products, electrical equipment, chemicals, textiles, and footwear. The city is also a noted educational center with two universities, a branch of the Rumanian Academy of Sciences, a fine arts institute, a polytechnic institute, and several scientific research centers. Cluj was founded by German colonists in the 12th cent. and became a thriving commercial and cultural center in the Middle Ages. It was made a free city in 1405 by the king of Hungary. Stephen Bathory founded (1581) a Jesuit academy there, and the city became (16th cent.) the chief cultural and religious center of Transylvania. It was incorporated into Austria-Hungary in 1867 and was transferred to Rumania in 1920. Hungarian forces occupied the city during World War II. Landmarks include the 14th-century Gothic Church of St. Michael, the house where King Matthias I of Hungary was born (1440), and the ruins of an 11th-century church. Cluj is also noted for its botanical gardens. About half the population is Hungarian.

clumber spaniel, breed of medium-sized SPORTING DOG developed in France and perfected at Clumber Park, an English estate. It stands about 17 in. (43.2 cm) high at the shoulder and weighs between 50 and 60 lb (22.7–27.2 kg). Its dense coat of straight, silky hair is lemon and white or orange and white and forms long, luxuriant fringes, or feathers, on the chest and legs. The heavy-boned, low, short body of the clumber resembles no other spaniel and suggests early crossbreeding with the basset hound. The tail is docked. Although a slow worker, the clumber makes an excellent hunter and retriever when trained. See DOG.

Cluniac order, medieval organization of BENEDICTINES centered at the abbey of CLUNY, France. Founded in 910 by the monk Berno, the abbey's unique constitution provided it freedom from lay supervision and (after 1016) from jurisdiction of the local bishop. With its independence thus guaranteed, Cluny became the fountainhead of the most far-reaching religious reform movement in the Middle Ages. During its height (c.950–c.1130) it was second only to the papacy as the chief religious force in Europe. Hundreds of priories were opened, and many Benedictine abbeys were reformed, some joining the strict Cluniac obedience. In all, nearly 1,000 houses located in many countries were under obedience to the abbot of Cluny. Many Cluniac monks became bishops and through provincial synods were thus able to spread reform in church life throughout Europe. Churches were built, the liturgy was beautified, and schools were opened. Cluny stoutly supported the popes (and was itself under papal protection) and served vitally in the great reform program of Pope St. Gregory VII, particularly in the matter of church independence from lay control. Cluniac zeal diminished in the 12th cent., and the order fell into a state of wealthy decline as the reforming initiative was taken up by the Cistercians. The French Revolution suppressed the remnants of the order and destroyed the abbey at Cluny. The highly centralized organization of the Cluniacs had a permanent effect on Western monasticism.

Cluny (klo͞o'nē, Fr. klünē'), former abbey, E France, in the present Saône-et-Loire dept., founded (910) by St. Berno, a Burgundian monk. He and his successors, all vigorous reformers, made their abbey the center of the CLUNIAC ORDER. Cluny became one of the chief religious and cultural centers of Europe. The abbey remains presently house a national school of arts and trades. The abbey church (10th cent. in part), once the largest church in the world, and the churches of Notre Dame (13th cent.) and of St. Marcellus (12th cent.) are there.

Cluny Museum, 14th- and 15th-century Gothic and Renaissance structure in Paris, built by Pierre de Chaslus, abbot of Cluny, and rebuilt by Jacques d'Ambroise. The site is that of the ancient Roman baths of Emperor Julian. Acquired by the nation after the Revolution, it was subsequently purchased by the antiquarian Du Sommerard, who installed his collection of art objects of the Middle Ages and the Renaissance. The city of Paris purchased the entire property at Du Sommerard's death (1842) and presented it to the state. The museum's 24 galleries display a variety of medieval works, with emphasis on carved wood, metalwork, textiles, and stained glass. A number of superb tapestries of the 15th and 16th cent., produced in Flanders and the Loire valley, are among the museum's greatest treasures.

Clurman, Harold, 1901–, American director, manager, critic, and author, b. New York City. In his early years he acted in minor roles, becoming associated with New York's Group Theatre as founder and managing director in 1931. After his debut as a director with *Awake and Sing,* he became known for his direction of works by Tennessee Williams, Arthur Miller, Eugene O'Neill, and William Inge, among many others. Clurman has written much theater criticism and several books, including *The Fervent Years* (1945), a history of the Group Theatre. See his *On Directing* (1972) and *All People are Famous* (1974).

Clusium: see CHIUSI, Italy.

cluster, in astronomy: see STAR CLUSTER; GALAXY.

clutch, in automobiles: see TRANSMISSION.

Clwyd (klo͞o'ĭd), nonmetropolitan county (1972 est. pop. 354,000), N Wales, created under the Local Government Act of 1972 (effective 1974). It comprises the former county of FLINTSHIRE and portions of the former counties of Denbigh and Merioneth.

Clwyd, river, c.30 mi (50 km) long, rising in Clwyd (Denbighshire), N Wales. It flows N through the Vale of Clwyd to the Irish Sea at Rhyl. The vale is notable for its excellent pastureland.

Clyde, Colin Campbell, Baron: see CAMPBELL, COLIN, BARON CLYDE.

Clyde, principal river of SW Scotland, 106 mi (171 km) long, rising in the Southern Uplands and flowing generally NW through Glasgow to the Firth of Clyde. It drains c.1,480 sq mi (3,830 sq km). The lower Clyde, traversing the heart of Clydeside (Scotland's great population, industrial, and shipbuilding region), is the main route of commercial water traffic in Scotland. The river has been deepened and widened and is navigable for oceangoing vessels to Glasgow. It is connected with the Firth of Forth by the Forth and Clyde Canal. Clydeport, which includes the docks at Glasgow, Clydebank, and Greenock, is an important general cargo, ore, oil, and container port. Erskine Bridge (1,000 ft/305 m long; opened 1970), between Clydebank and Renfrew, is one of the world's longest cable-stayed bridges. A 10-lane bridge (opened 1970) crosses the Clyde at Glasgow. The middle course of the river flows through Clydesdale, a noted farming and orchard region. Bonnington (9,840-kw capacity) and Stonebyres (5,680-kw capacity) are hydroelectric power stations at the Falls of the Clyde near Lanark. The **Firth of Clyde,** c.50 mi (80 km) wide and 2 to 25 mi (3.2–40 km) wide, an arm of the North Channel, extends SW from Dunoon to Ailsa Craig. It is rimmed by yacht basins, summer resorts, and small ports. Bute, Arran, and the Cumbraes are the chief islands.

Clydebank, burgh (1971 pop. 48,296), Dumbartonshire, W central Scotland, on the north bank of the Clyde River. The chief industry is shipbuilding. The ocean liners *Queen Mary* and *Queen Elizabeth* were built there. In 1975, Clydebank became part of the Strathclyde region.

Clydesdale horse, breed of DRAFT HORSE developed in Scotland. It closely resembles the SHIRE HORSE, although it is not as heavy. The Clydesdale is characterized by its graceful, springy step. Initially imported by the United States from Canada, the breed became widely popular owing to its good disposition. It was particularly favored by merchants, who used it to spectacular advantage in the transportation of commercial goods. It is still retained today by horse buffs and private patrons. It averages about 16 hands (64 in./160 cm) high, weighs around 1,800 lb (800 kg), and is characteristically colored rich brown or bay. It has white markings on the face and on the legs, which have luxurious feathering around the fetlocks.

Clymene (klĭm'ənē), in Greek mythology. **1** Daughter of the Titan Oceanus. The wife of Iapetus, she bore him Atlas, Prometheus, Epimetheus, and Menoetius. **2** Nymph, wife of Helios and mother of Phaëthon.

Clymer, George (klī' mər), 1739–1813, American political leader, signer of the Declaration of Independence, b. Philadelphia. A prosperous merchant, he ardently supported the colonial cause before the American Revolution and served (1775–76) as one of the Continental treasurers. In 1776 he served as delegate to the Continental Congress, where he signed the Declaration of Independence. He was again (1780–83) a delegate to the Continental Congress. Clymer was the first president of the Bank of Philadelphia, and he helped to organize the Bank of North America. While in the Pennsylvania legislature (1785–88), he wrote a report leading to penal code reforms. Clymer, a delegate to the Federal Convention, was a member (1789–91) of the first U.S. Congress.

Clytemnestra (klī''təmnĕs'trə), in Greek mythology, the daughter of Leda and Tyndareus. Homer described her as the noble-minded wife of Agamemnon, persuaded to infidelity by the tyrant Aegisthus. However, the Greek tragedians, most specifically Aeschylus, depicted her as remorseless and vengeful. She was the mother by Agamemnon of Orestes, Electra, and Iphigenia. She conspired with Aegisthus to murder Agamemnon on his return from the Trojan War, giving various justifications, most notably the sacrifice of Iphigenia by Agamemnon at the onset of the war. Orestes, who had been living in exile, returned and revenged the death of his father by killing his mother and Aegisthus.

Cm, chemical symbol of the element CURIUM.

CMP (cytidine monophosphate): see CYTOSINE.

CN, ordinary TEAR GAS. The chemical name for CN is chloroacetophenone.

Cnidaria (nīdâr'ēə) or **Coelenterata** (səlĕntərä'tə), phylum of invertebrate animals comprising the SEA ANEMONES, CORALS, JELLYFISH, and hydroids. Cnidarians are radially symmetrical (see SYMMETRY, BIOLOGICAL). The mouth, located at the center of one end of the body, opens into a gastrovascular cavity, which is used for digestion and distribution of food; an anus is lacking. Cnidarians are further characterized by having a body wall composed of three layers: an outer epidermis, an inner gastrodermis, and a middle mesogloea. Tentacles encircle the mouth and are used in part for food capture. Specialized stinging structures, called nematocysts, are a characteristic of the phylum and are borne in the tentacles and often in other body parts. These contain a coiled fiber that can be extruded suddenly. Some nematocysts contain toxic substances and are defense mechanisms, while others are adhesive, helping to anchor the animal or to entangle prey. Two body forms and two life styles are characteristic of the Cnidaria (see POLYP AND MEDUSA). The sessile hydroid, or polyp, form is more or less cylindrical, attached to its substratum at its aboral (opposite the mouth) end, with the mouth and surrounding tentacles at the upper, oral, free end. Colonies of hydroids comprise several different types of individuals: some function in feeding; some in defense; and some in reproduction. The motile jellyfish, or medusoid form, is flattened, with the tentacles usually located at the body margin. The medusoid's convex aboral surface is oriented upward, and the concave oral surface is oriented downward. With few exceptions, the cnidarians are marine. There are over 9,000 known living species; fossil records of cnidarians date back to the Ordovician era. Cnidarians are carnivorous, the major part of their diet consisting of crustaceans. Animals in this phylum have no specialized excretory or respiratory organs and posess a primitive nervous system. Both sexual and asexual reproduction occur. There are three classes of cnidarians.

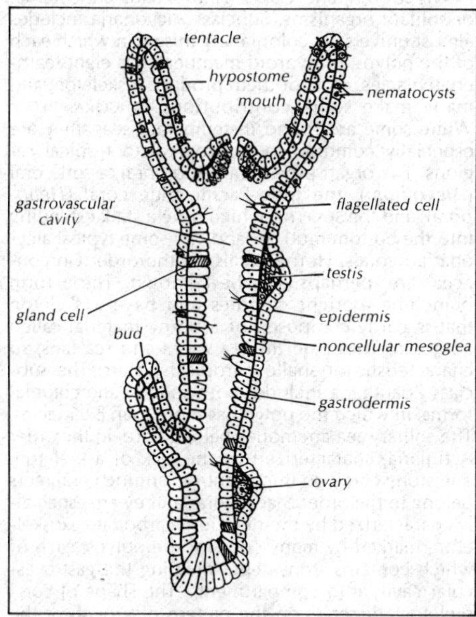

Internal anatomy of Hydra, *representative of the phylum Cnidaria*

Class Hydrozoa. The Hydrozoa include solitary or colonial cnidarians, which have a noncellular mesoglea, lack tentacles within the gastrovascular cavity, and have no gullet. As a rule, the hydroid stage predominates in the life cycle, although in some the jellyfish stage is larger. The order Hydroida includes the many small, colonial hydroids so often seen clinging to wharfs and submerged objects along the sea coasts everywhere, economically important because they foul surfaces. The order also includes solitary hydroids, some reaching several inches in height. One, in the genus *Branchiocerianthus,* is said to reach 8 or 9 ft (244–274.5 cm) in length. The common fresh-water genus *Hydra* also belongs to this order, as does the fresh-water jellyfish, genus *Craspedacusta,* and the commonly studied hydroid jellyfish, genus *Gonionemus.* There are also pelagic hydroid colonies, unusual in having one very large hydroid member, which lives with its mouth downward and its aboral surface upward, like a jellyfish. The aboral end is equipped with a projecting sail. *Velella,* the purple sailor, is an example. The order Milleporina includes colonial organisms that form a massive, porous exoskeleton, somewhat resembling corals. They are sometimes abundant in tropical seas and may contribute to coral reef formation. The order Siphonophora includes often large, floating colonies made up of members of varying form and function. Typical is *Physalia,* the Portuguese man-of-war. Its colorful float is a gas-filled member of the colony and attains lengths up to 1 ft (30 cm). Other members of the colony hang downward from the lower surface of the float; some of these have very powerful nematocysts able to cause severe physiological reaction in swimmers coming in contact with them. These organisms are able to kill sizable fish with their tentacles.

Class Scyphozoa. Cnidarians of class Scyphozoa have a predominant jellyfish stage. They are characterized by a cellular mesoglea and tentacles in their gastrovascular cavity. All of the largest jellyfish belong to this class. The common *Aurelia aurita* is seen in bays and harbors, sometimes in large numbers. It is pallid, unlike some of the more colorful species in the genus *Cyanea.* Stalked jellyfish, the Stauromedusae, are unusual members of the Scyphozoa; they are found attached to seaweed, especially in cooler marine habitats. The order Rhizostomea includes jellyfish in which the original mouth has closed, and which have many subsidiary mouths found in frilled oral arms. *Cassiopaeia* is a well-known example, living in warmer, shallow waters, where it is often found lying on the bottom upside down, exposing its green algal symbionts to the sun.

Class Anthozoa. Class Anthozoa includes Cnidaria that have no jellyfish stage. This is the largest class of cnidarians, containing over 6,000 species. A gullet extends for a short distance into the gastrovascular cavity, and septa are present, which increase the surface for digestion and absorption. Anthozoa are flower animals, including a great many beautiful and colorful organisms, e.g., the SEA ANEMONE, SEA PANSY, SEA FAN, and CORAL. Anthozoans are colonial or solitary organisms. Subclass Alcyonaria includes almost universally colonial organisms in which each of the polyps, or hydroid members, has eight feathery tentacles. Most of them produce a skeleton, and many make some contributions to CORAL REEFS. While some are found in temperate seas, they are especially common in subtropical to tropical regions. The organ pipe coral (*Tubipora*), a soft coral (*Alcyonium*), the Indo-Pacific blue coral (*Heliopora*), and the SEA PENS, which have a stalk extending into the bottom mud or sand, are some typical alcyonarian corals. Horny corals, of the order Gorgonacea, are, perhaps, the best known. These form branching, upright colonies and have a skeleton that is partly composed of a horny material called gorgonin. These are the SEA WHIPS and sea fans, so characteristic of shallow tropical waters. The subclass Zoantharia includes both solitary and colonial forms, in which the polyp has more than 8 tentacles. The solitary sea anemones belong here, in the order Actiniaria, characterized by the lack of a skeleton. The stony corals so important in forming coral reefs belong to the order Madreporaria; they are especially characterized by their calcium carbonate exoskeleton, marked by many cups for the polyps, each of which contains stony septa dividing the gastrovascular cavity into compartments. The shape of coral skeletons depends on the pattern of growth of the colony. For example, in brain corals the polyps are arranged linearly; in the eyed coral (*Oculina*) the polyps are separated from each other by spaces, giving the skeleton a pitted appearance. The burrowing anemone, *Cerianthus*, lives in burrows in the sand and has a greatly elongated body. It is characteristic of the order Ceriantharia. See W. J. Rees, ed., *The Cnidaria and Their Evolution* (1966).

Cnidus or **Cnidos** (both: nī'dəs), ancient Greek city of Caria, SW Asia Minor, on Cape Krio, in present SW Asiatic Turkey. It was partly on the peninsula and partly on an island that had been created by cutting through the peninsula. One of the cities of the Dorian Hexapolis, it sought to maintain its independence but fell (540 B.C.) under Persian rule. It had a large trade, particularly in wine, and was also noted for its medical school and other institutions of learning. One of the most famous statues of the ancient world, Aphrodite by Praxiteles, was there. In the waters off Cnidus the Athenians under Conon defeated the Spartans under Pisander in 394 B.C. Cnidus retained its importance in Roman times and is mentioned in the Bible (Acts 27.7; 1 Mac. 15.23).

Cnossus or **Knossos** (both: nŏs'əs), ancient city of Crete, on the north coast, near modern Iráklion. The site was occupied long before 3000 B.C., and it was the center of an important Bronze Age culture. It is from a study of the great palace, as well as other sites in Crete, that knowledge of the MINOAN CIVILIZATION has been drawn. The city was destroyed before 1500 B.C. (possibly by earthquake) and was splendidly rebuilt only to be destroyed again c.1400 B.C., probably at the hands of invaders from the Greek mainland. This marked the end of Minoan culture. Cnossus later became an ordinary but flourishing Greek city, and it continued to exist through the Roman period until the 4th cent. A.D. In Greek legend it was the capital of King Minos and the site of the labyrinth. The name also appears as Cnosus and Knossus. See Sir A. J. Evans, *Palace of Minos* (4 vol., 1921–35); Leonard Cottrell, *Bull of Minos* (1953); E. L. Bennett, *The Knossos Tablets* (1956); L. R. Palmer, *A New Guide to the Palace of Knossos* (1969).

Co, chemical symbol of the element COBALT.

coach dog: see DALMATIAN.

Coachella Valley (kō″əchĕl'ə), arid region, SE Calif., N of the Salton Sea. Water is brought into the region by artesian wells and by the Coachella Canal (123 mi/198 km long), a branch of the All-American Canal built between 1938 and 1948; more than 100,000 acres (40,500 hectares) have been irrigated. Truck crops, dates (90% of U.S. production), citrus fruits, and alfalfa are grown in the region.

coachwhip snake: see RACER.

coagulation (kōăg″yo͝olā'shən), the collecting into a mass of minute particles of a solid dispersed throughout a liquid (a sol), usually followed by the precipitation or separation of the solid mass from the liquid. The casein in milk is coagulated (curdled) by the addition of acetic acid or citric acid. The albumin in egg white is coagulated by heating. The clotting of blood is another example of coagulation. Coagulation usually involves a chemical reaction. Lyophobic particles (see COLLOID) lose their electric charge by reacting with oppositely charged particles. Lyophilic particles undergo a reaction that causes them to lose their solubility. In either case coagulation occurs. The formation of a gel by evaporation or cooling of a sol is usually called gelation rather than coagulation.

Coahuila (kōäwē'lä), state (1970 pop. 1,140,959), 58,067 sq mi (150,394 sq km), N Mexico, on the northward bulge of the Rio Grande, S of Texas. SALTILLO is the capital. In the eastern part of the state, where peaks of the Sierra Madre Oriental rise, are quantities of silver, copper, lead, iron, and zinc. Coahuila is Mexico's chief coal-producing state and a leading national producer of iron and steel. Lumbering is important, and northeast of the mountains, in the drainage area of the Rio Grande, there is considerable cattle raising. Across W Coahuila and E Chihuahua lie vast and arid plains (some of them recently irrigated), which are broken by barren mountains; most notable of these plains is the Bolsón de Mapimí, extending into Chihuahua. South of the Bolsón is a fertile lake region, center of a vast inland basin, which absorbs rivers with no outlet to the sea. A considerable portion of the LAGUNA DISTRICT lies in this area. TORREÓN is the chief metropolis. Coahuila produces cotton, corn, grapes, and most temperate grains and tropical fruits. Exploration of the territory began in the 16th cent. but was hampered by Indian hostility. After playing some part in the war against Spain, Coahuila was combined (1830) with Texas, a proceeding that caused dissatisfaction among the American minority and contributed to the Texas Revolution (1835–36). During the Mexican War, Saltillo was of strategic importance, and the battle of Buena Vista was fought nearby. Joined with Nuevo León by the constitution of 1857, Coahuila regained its separate status in 1868. The revolutionary leaders Francisco I. Madero and Venustiano Carranza were born in the state.

coal, fuel substance of plant origin, largely or almost entirely composed of carbon with varying amounts of mineral matter. There is a complete series of carbonaceous fuels, which differ from each other in the relative amounts of moisture, volatile matter, and fixed carbon they contain. Of the carbonaceous fuels, those containing the largest amounts of fixed carbon and the smallest amounts of moisture and volatile matter are the most useful to man. The lowest in carbon content, *peat,* is followed in ascending order by LIGNITE and the various forms of coal—subbituminous coal or black lignite (a slightly higher grade than lignite), bituminous coal, semibituminous (a high-grade bituminous coal), semianthracite (a low-grade anthracite), and anthracite. Lignite and subbituminous coal, because of the high percentage of moisture they contain, tend to crumble on exposure to the air. Bituminous coal, being more consolidated, does not crumble easily; it is a deep black in color, burns readily, and is used extensively as fuel in industries and on railroads and in making COKE. Anthracite, which is nearly pure carbon, is very hard, black, and lustrous, and is extensively used as a domestic fuel. Cannel coal, a dull, homogeneous variety of bituminous coal, is composed of pollen grains, spores, and other particles of plant origin. It ignites and burns easily, with a candlelike flame, but its fuel value is low. Coal is found in beds or seams interstratified with shales, clays, sandstones, or (rarely) limestones. It is usually underlaid by an underclay (a layer of clay containing roots of plants). The vegetable origin of coal is supported by the presence in coal of carbonized fibers, stems, leaves, and seeds of plants, which can be detected with the naked eye in the softer varieties and with the microscope in harder coal. Sometimes carbonized tree stumps have been found standing in layers of coal. The general interpretation of these facts is that coal originated in swamps similar to present-day peat bogs and in lagoons, probably partly from plants growing in the area and partly from plant material carried in by water and wind. From the thickness of coal seams, it is assumed that the coal swamps were located near sea level and were subject to repeated submergence, so that a great quantity of vegetable matter accumulated over a long period of time. The initial processes of disintegration and decomposition of the organic matter were brought about by the action of bacteria and other microorganisms. Peat, the first product formed, is altered to form lignite and coal through metamorphism. The pressure of the accumulated layers of overlying sediments and rock upon the submerged plant matter forced out much of the water and caused some of the volatile substances to escape and the nonvolatile carbon material to form a more compact mass. The greater the stress exerted in the process of metamorphism, the higher was the grade of coal produced. Cannel coal was probably formed in ponds, rather than in lagoons or swamps, as it occurs in lenticular masses and is frequently found to contain fossil fish. Coal was formed chiefly in the CARBONIFEROUS PERIOD of geologic time, but valuable deposits date also from the Permian, Triassic, Jurassic, Cretaceous, and Tertiary periods. The chief coal fields of the United States are the Appalachian (from N Pennsylvania into Alabama), the Eastern Interior (Illinois, Kentucky, and Indiana), the Northern Interior (Michigan), the Western Interior (Iowa, Kansas, Missouri, Oklahoma, and Arkansas), the Rocky Mountain (Colorado, Wyoming, Utah, New Mexico, Montana, and North Dakota), the Pacific (Washington), and the Gulf Coast (Texas, Arkansas, and Louisiana). In Europe the chief coal-producing countries are Germany, Great Britain, Russia, Poland, France, and Belgium. There are valuable coal fields in China, India, South Africa, and Australia, but few in South America. See Wilfrid Francis, *Coal* (1954); D. W. van Krevelen, *Coal* (2d ed. 1962); I. A. Williamson, *Coal Mining Geology* (1967).

coalfish: see COD.

coal gas, gas obtained in the destructive distillation of soft coal, as a by-product in the preparation of COKE. Its composition varies, but in general it is made up largely of hydrogen and methane with small amounts of other hydrocarbons, carbon monoxide (a poisonous gas), carbon dioxide, and nitrogen. It is used as a fuel and illuminant.

coal mining, physical extraction of coal resources to yield coal; also, the business of exploring for, developing, mining, and transporting coal in any form. Strip mining is the process in which the overburden (earth and rock material overlying the coal) is removed to expose a coal seam or coal bed. Excavators either dispose of the overburden or store the waste material for replacement after the coal has been extracted. Once exposed, the coal is usually removed in a separate operation. Surface soil is often stripped separately and spread back onto the reclaimed surface. The environment can also be protected by seeding or planting grass or trees on the fertilized restored surface of a strip mine. The term *strip mining* is most often used in reference to coal mining, although the process may also be used to extract certain metallic ores as well. Sometimes the terms *open-pit, open-cast,* or *surface mining* are used in the same sense, although they usually refer to metalliferous mining or the mining of other minerals. Underground coal mining is the extraction of coal from below the surface of the earth. The coal is worked through tunnels, passages, and openings that are connected to the surface for the purpose of the removal of the coal. Mechanical equipment breaks the coal to a size suitable for haulage. Alternatively, the coal is drilled, and the resultant holes are loaded with explosives and blasted in order to break the coal to the desired size. In order to protect the miners and equipment in an underground coal mine, much attention is paid to maintaining and supporting a safe roof or overhead ceiling for the extraction openings. Long-wall mining is a method of underground mining believed to have been developed in Shropshire, England, near the end of the 17th cent. A long face, or working section, of coal, some 600 ft (180 m) in length, is operated at one time. The miners and machinery at the working face are usually protected by hydraulic jacks or mechanical props which are advanced as the coal is extracted. The excavated, or gob, area is either allowed to cave in, or is filled in by waste material called stowing. The Anderton shearer is a widely used coal cutter and loader for long-wall mining. It shears coal from the face as it moves in one direction and loads coal onto an armored conveyor as it travels back in the opposite direction. It is ordinarily used for coal seams greater than 3.5 ft (9.1 cm) in thickness.

Coalsack: see MILKY WAY.

coal tar, product of the destructive distillation of bituminous coal. Coal tar can be distilled into many fractions to yield a number of useful organic products, including benzene, toluene, xylene, naphthalene, anthracene, and phenanthrene. These substances, called the coal-tar crudes, form the starting point for the synthesis of numerous products—notably dyes, drugs, explosives, flavorings, perfumes, preservatives, synthetic resins, and paints and stains. The residual pitch left from the fractional distillation is used for paving, roofing, waterproofing, and insulation.

Coalville, urban district (1971 pop. 28,334), Leicestershire, central England. Coalville is a modern town in the center of the Leicestershire coal field. Besides coal mining, there are hosiery, footwear, and plastics industries.

Coamo (kwä'mō), town (1970 pop. 12,077), S central Puerto Rico, on the Coamo River. It is the trade center of a sugar and tobacco region and has garment factories. The town was founded in the 16th cent.

coast, land bordering an ocean or other large body of water. The line of contact between the land and water surfaces is called the shoreline. It fluctuates with the waves and tides. Sometimes the terms *coast* and *shore* are used synonymously, but often *shore* is interpreted to mean only the zone between the shorelines at high tide and low tide, and *coast* indicates a strip of land of indefinite width landward of the shore. Classically, coasts have been designated as submergent if they resulted from a rise in the relative sea level and emergent if they resulted from a decline. Young submergent coasts usually are irregular and have deep water offshore and many good harbors, either bays or estuaries. Much of the coast of New England and most of the Atlantic coast of Europe are young submergent coasts according to this classification scheme. Gradually the submergent coast, subjected to erosive attacks of the ocean and other agents, becomes mature. Headlands are worn back to form cliffs, at the base of which deposits of eroded material accumulate as fringing beaches; spits and bars also grow up from material that is carried by currents and deposited in deeper water. The shoreline is called mature when it is smooth, the headlands having been cut away and the bays either filled up or closed off by spits. Emergent shorelines usually have shallow water for some distance offshore. Such shorelines are found along the Atlantic coast of the SE United States and along part of the coast of Argentina, near the Río de la Plata. This classification system does not adequately describe many coasts, partly because many of them exhibit features of both submergence and emergence. Because of these and other problems a classification system that is based on the most recent and predominant geologic agent forming the coast has become popular. Under this scheme, there are essentially two major types of coasts. Primary coasts are youthful coasts formed where the sea rests against a land mass whose topography was formed by terrestrial agents. These coasts include land erosion coasts (Maine), volcanic coasts (Hawaii), deposition coasts (Nile Delta coast), and fault coasts (Red Sea). Secondary coasts are formed chiefly and most recently by marine agents, and may even be primary coasts that have been severely modified by wave action. These coasts include wave erosion coasts, marine deposition coasts, and coasts built by organisms (reefs and mangrove coasts). The nature of the coastline of a country or a state is an important factor in its economic development because it relates to defense, fishing, recreation, and overseas commerce. See C. A. M. King, *Beaches and Coasts* (2d ed. 1972).

coast guard, special naval force assigned to seaboard duties. Its primary responsibilities usually consist in suppressing contraband trade and aiding vessels in distress. The British coast guard was established just after the Napoleonic Wars for the purpose of preventing smuggling. When the Coast Guard Act of 1856 put this task under the direction of the admiralty, the British coast guard was reorganized to perform coast-watching and lifesaving duties. In the United States a coast guard was formed in 1915 when an act of Congress combined the Revenue Cutter Service with the Life Saving Service. The cutter service had been established by Congress in 1790, at the suggestion of Alexander Hamilton, to prevent smuggling; until the creation of the navy it was the only U.S. armed service afloat. The Life Saving Service developed some years later (see LIFESAVING). The U.S. coast guard subsequently absorbed the Lighthouse Service (1939) and the Bureau of Marine Inspection and Navigation (1942). In peacetime the coast guard is under the jurisdiction of the Dept. of Transportation; in wartime, and for such other periods as the President may direct, it is under the control of the navy. In addition to its rescue and antismuggling activities, the service enforces navigation rules and maintains jurisdiction over the regulations concerning the construction and equipment of merchant ships and over the licensing of merchant marine officers and seamen. It also operates and maintains weather ships, an ice patrol in the N Atlantic, and various navigational aids, including lighthouses, lightships, buoys, and loran stations. The Coast Guard Academy, for the training of officers, is located in New London, Conn. See studies by M. F. Willoughby (1957), H. R. Kaplan (1972), and Gene Gurney (1973).

Coast Mountains, range, W British Columbia and SE Alaska, extending c.1,000 mi (1,610 km) parallel to the Pacific coast, from the mountains of Alaska near the Yukon border to the Cascade Range near the Fraser River. Mt. Waddington (13,260 ft/4,042 m) is the highest peak. The geologically complex range, composed mainly of metamorphic rocks, slopes steeply to the Pacific Ocean, where the shoreline is deeply indented by fjords. The Coast Mts. have been heavily eroded by mountain glaciers; numerous rivers, including the Fraser, the Skeena, and the Stikine, have cut deep gorges across the range. The average annual precipitation of c.90 in. (230 cm) makes the region one of the wettest parts of Canada. Its slopes are heavily forested, and lumbering is important. In the Coast Mts. is Kemano, one of Canada's largest hydroelectric plants. The Coast Mts. are sometimes confused with the geologically distinct COAST RANGES.

coast protection, methods used to protect coastal lands from erosion. Beaches can exist only where a delicate dynamic equilibrium exists between the amount of sand supplied to the beach and the inevitable losses caused by wave erosion. Various activities of man have upset this equilibrium, decidedly increasing the rate of erosion of the shorelines. For example, the plethora of dams constructed across major drainage systems has served to entrap sediment that would normally reach the coastal zone, imperiling the existence of beaches by cutting off their natural sand supply. Mining of beach sand has removed millions of tons of sand from coasts and drastically upset the balance between natural supply and losses. Historically, man has considered coast protection a local problem, and has attacked the problem by building structures to inhibit the transportation of sand from his local area. However, it has been learned that building structures to solve a local erosion problem may extend and intensify the erosion problem along nearby beaches, requiring the construction of structures along an entire coast. For example, many structures block littoral drift, which is a movement of sand parallel to the coast, both on the beach and offshore, caused by waves. The blockage results in a depletion of sand downcurrent from the structure. Several different kinds of structures are built. Sea walls are constructed at the edge of the shore facing the ocean waves. Designed to protect only the beach areas behind them, they cause an increased loss of sediment in front of and beneath them. BREAKWATERS are long piers built offshore parallel to the shoreline; they are designed to provide calm anchorages in an area behind them called a wave shadow. At the breakwater off Santa Monica, Calif., the wave shadow impeded the littoral drift, producing a deposition of sand behind the breakwater and extensive erosion of the beach downcurrent. Groins are lines of rock or pilings constructed perpendicular to the shoreline. They act as a partial barrier to littoral drift, trapping sand on the updrift side and causing erosion on the downdrift side. Jetties are often built at river mouths and harbor entrances, projecting out into the ocean to direct and confine littoral currents and to prevent silting of the harbor entrance. Jetties cause the same problems of downdrift erosion as groins. In some instances it has been necessary to pump the sand trapped by the structure to adjacent beaches downdrift. Efforts have also been made to prevent erosion using the natural materials at hand. Artificial dunes have been built by bulldozing sand back from the beach or by placing snow fences to trap windblown sand. Since beaches themselves are effective in dissipating wave energy, one remedy to the lack of a sand supply is to pump sand directly onto the beach from interior or offshore zones. Unlike other manmade structures, artificial beaches do not harm the shore downdrift.

Coast Ranges, series of mountain ranges along the Pacific coast of North America, extending from SE Alaska to Baja California; from 2,000 to 20,000 ft (610-6,100 m) high. The ranges include the St. Elias Mts. in SE Alaska and SW Yukon, which have the highest elevations; a partially submerged portion that forms the islands off the coast of SE Alaska and British Columbia; the Olympic Mts. in Washington; the Coast Ranges in Oregon; the Klamath Mts., Coast Ranges, and Los Angeles Ranges in California; and the Peninsular Range in Baja California. The Coast Ranges are rugged, geologically young mountains, formed by faulting and folding and are composed mainly of granitic rock; the northern third is glaciated. N of San Francisco the ranges are humid and thickly forested; the southern parts are dry and covered with brush and grass. Lumbering, mining, and tourism are important.

Coatbridge, burgh (1971 pop. 52,131), Lanarkshire, S central Scotland. In Coatbridge a variety of iron and steel products are manufactured. In 1975, Coatbridge became part of the Strathclyde region.

Coates, Albert, 1882-1953, Russian-English conductor and composer, b. St. Petersburg, studied at the Leipzig Conservatory under Nikisch. After conducting in Germany (1906-10), he returned to Russia and conducted at St. Petersburg until 1917. In 1919 he settled in England where, except for brief teaching assignments in the United States, he remained until 1946, when he moved to the Union of South Africa. Although he was a prolific composer, his works have seldom been performed. Among them are the operas *Samuel Pepys* (1929), *Pickwick* (1936), and *Van Hunks and the Devil* (1952).

Coatesville, city (1970 pop. 12,331), Chester co., SE Pa., on Brandywine Creek, in a farm area; settled c.1717, inc. as a city 1916. It is a steel center. Joseph Hergesheimer wrote about this region in *The Three Black Pennys.* A U.S. veterans hospital is there. The Revolutionary battle of BRANDYWINE (Sept. 11, 1777) was fought to the south of the city; the area is now a state park.

coatimundi (kōä'tēmŭn"dē) or **coati,** omnivore of North and South America related to the RACCOON. The coatimundi has a long snout, an elongated body, and a long bushy tail banded with dark rings. The coat color varies from yellowish brown or reddish brown to black. The males are significantly larger than the females and may be more than 50 in. (127 cm) long and may weigh up to 25 lb (11 kg). Active both day and night, the coatimundi is a forest dweller and an agile tree climber. It eats lizards, birds, and fruit and uses its long mobile snout to grub for insects and roots. On the ground, its short forelegs give it a bearlike gait as it lumbers along with its tail erect. Females and their young travel in bands, but males are solitary and join the band only in the mating season. The young, typically four to six in number, are born following a gestation period of about seventy-seven days. The species *Nasua nanica* is native to SW United States. *N. rufa,* the ringtailed coatimundi, is a related species that ranges from Mexico to Peru. Coatimundis are often raised as pets in Mexico. They are classified in the phylum CHORDATA, subphylum Vertebrata, class Mammalia, order Carnivora, family Procyonidae.

coat of arms: see BLAZONRY and HERALDRY.

Coatzacoalcos (kwätsäkwäl'kōs), city (1970 pop. 73,563), Veracruz state, E central Mexico, at the mouth of the Coatzacoalcos River. It is a port on the Gulf of Campeche, as well as the northern terminus of rail traffic across the Isthmus of Tehuantepec. Highway communications are also good. The city is an important commercial center. Oil, sulfur, and timber are exported, and the port facilities have been enlarged to enable Coatzacoalcos to handle foreign trade.

coaxial cable: see CABLE.

cobalamin: see COENZYME; VITAMIN.

Cobalt (kō'bôlt), town (1971 pop. 2,197), E Ont., Canada, NE of Sudbury, near Lake Timiskaming. Cobalt deposits were discovered in 1903. The town is also the center of one of the world's richest silver districts. The town has a mining museum.

cobalt, metallic chemical element; symbol Co; at. no. 27; at. wt. 58.9332; m.p. 1495°C; b.p. about 2870°C; sp. gr. 8.9 at 20°C; valence +2 or +3. Cobalt is a silver-white, lustrous, hard, brittle metal. It is a member of group VIII of the PERIODIC TABLE. Like iron, it can be magnetized. It is similar to iron and nickel in its physical properties. The element is active chemically, forming many compounds, e.g., the series of cobaltous and cobaltic salts and the complex cobalt ammines derived from cobaltic salts and ammonia. Cobalt yellow, green, and blue are pigments of high quality that contain cobalt; another blue pigment, smalt, is made by powdering a fused mixture of cobalt oxide, potassium carbonate, and sand; these pigments are often used for coloring glass and ceramics. Cobalt chloride, used as an invisible ink, is almost colorless in dilute solution when applied to paper. Upon heating it undergoes dehydration and turns blue, becoming colorless again when the heat is removed and water is taken up. The element rarely occurs uncombined in nature but is often found in meteoric metal. It is a constituent of the minerals COBALTITE and SMALTITE and of other ores, usually in association with other metals. Pure cobalt metal is prepared by reduction of its compounds by aluminum (the Goldschmidt process), by carbon, or by hydrogen. It is a component of several alloys, including the high-speed steels carboloy and stellite, from which very hard cutting tools are made. It is a component of some stainless steels, and of high-temperature alloys for use in jet engines. Alnico, an alloy of cobalt, aluminum, nickel, and other metals, is used to make high-strength permanent magnets. As an element in the diet of sheep, cobalt prevents a disease called sway-back and improves the quality of the wool. A radioactive isotope, cobalt-60 (with gamma ray emission 25 times that of radium), is prepared by neutron bombardment. It is used for cancer therapy and in industry for detecting flaws in metal parts. See HYDROGEN BOMB. Cobolt was discovered in 1735 by Georg Brandt, a Swedish chemist.

cobalt bomb: see HYDROGEN BOMB.

cobaltite (kōˈbôltīt, kōbôlˈtīt), opaque, silver-white, sometimes reddish or grayish mineral of the pyrite group, a compound of cobalt, arsenic, and sulfur, CoAsS. It occurs in crystals of the cubic system, also in compact to granular masses. It is an important ore of cobalt, found chiefly in Sweden, Norway, Zaïre, and Ontario (Canada).

Cobb, Howell, 1815-68, American politican, b. Jefferson co., Ga. In 1837 he became solicitor general of the western judicial circuit of Georgia, a district populated largely by small farmers of Unionist sentiments. He championed their cause and from 1843 to 1851 represented them in the House of Representatives. He was elected floor leader of the Democrats in 1848 and speaker in 1849. Cobb united with the Whigs in Georgia to win approval of the Compromise of 1850. His followers and the Whigs formed the short-lived Constitutional Union party, which elected him to the governorship (1851-53). Cobb was returned to Congress in 1855, and in 1857 President Buchanan appointed him Secretary of the Treasury. After Lincoln's election he resigned, advocated secession, and was chairman of the convention in Montgomery, Ala., that organized the Confederacy. In the Civil War he rose to the rank of major general (1863) but saw little active fighting. See Horace Montgomery, *Howell Cobb's Confederate Career* (1959).

Cobb, Irvin Shrewsbury, 1876-1944, American author, b. Paducah, Ky. He was a noted New York humorist and columnist. Although he wrote over 60 books, Cobb is best known for his humorous stories of Kentucky local color, first collected in *Old Judge Priest* (1915). Among his other books of humor are *Speaking of Operations* (1916) and *Red Likker* (1929). See his autobiography, *Exit Laughing* (1942); study by F. G. Neuman (1934, repr. 1974).

Cobb, Lee J., 1911-, American actor, b. New York City. He first performed with the Pasadena (Calif.) Playhouse in 1929 and made his Broadway debut in *Crime and Punishment* (1935). Cobb created the role of Willy Loman in Arthur Miller's *Death of a Salesman* (1948-49; repeated for television in 1965). He performed Shakespeare in New York, including *The Merchant of Venice* and *King Lear.* His films include *On the Waterfront* (1954), *Twelve Angry Men* (1957), and *The Brothers Karamazov* (1958).

Cobb, Thomas Reade Rootes, 1823-62, American lawyer, b. Jefferson co., Ga.; brother of Howell Cobb. Admitted to the bar in 1842, he edited 20 volumes of the Georgia supreme court reports (1849-57), prepared *A Digest of the Statute Laws of the State of Georgia* (1851), and compiled (1858-61) a new state criminal code. Cobb was a militant secessionist. In the Georgia secession convention he was chairman of the committee that wrote a new state constitution (1861) and helped write the Confederate Constitution. In the Civil War he organized and led Cobb's Legion. Promoted to brigadier general in Nov., 1862, he was killed at Fredericksburg the following month.

Cobb, Ty (Tyrus Raymond Cobb), 1886-1961, American baseball player, b. Narrows, Ga. In 1905 he joined the Detroit Tigers as center fielder and in his 24 years in the American League was one of the most spectacular and brilliant players of the game. Cobb, called the "Georgia Peach" by his admirers, had a .367 lifetime batting average, made 4,191 major-league hits, stole 892 bases, and won 12 batting championships. He was (1921-26) manager of the Detroit team played (1927-28) with the Philadelphia Athletics, and then retired from baseball. He was the first elected (1936) member of the National Baseball Hall of Fame. See his autobiography (1961).

Cobbett, William (kŏbˈĭt), 1763?-1835, British journalist and reformer. The son of a farm laborer, he ran away from home at 14 and later joined the British army. He resigned in order to expose abuses in the military forces, but, unable to prove his accusations, he fled to France to escape suit and thence went to the United States. In America, in his *Observations on Priestley's Emigration* (1794), *Porcupine's Gazette* (1797-99), and other pamphlets and periodicals, Cobbett defended the British monarchy and praised aristocratic government in preference to democracy. His outspoken and skillful disparagement of French Jacobinism and of the pro-French party in the United States made him a major target of the Jeffersonian Republicans. Dr. Benjamin RUSH secured a $5,000 verdict against him for libel in 1799, and shortly afterward Cobbett returned to England. As the threat of French Jacobinism dwindled, Cobbett's Tory patriotism gave way to a deep concern for the condition of the working classes, especially rural workers, in the rapidly industrializing English society, and by 1807 he had become a Radical. His *Political Register,* begun in 1802 and published intermittently throughout the remainder of his life, was one of the greatest reform journals of the period and achieved an unparalleled influence among the working classes. For his attacks on the use of flogging as military punishment he was fined and imprisoned (1810-12). Severe financial difficulties forced him to sell his *Parliamentary Debates* to Hansard's printing firm, (see HANSARD). After the passage (1817) of the Gagging Acts to suppress radicalism and to hinder the circulation of reform literature, Cobbett fled once again to the United States. He settled on a farm on Long Island and wrote his famous *Grammar of the English Language* (1818). Returning to England in 1819, he became a central figure in the agitation for parliamentary reform, but he also found time to write many books, the most important of which, *Rural Rides* (1830), comprises a classic portrayal of the situation of the rural worker. After the Reform Bill was passed in 1832, Cobbett was elected to Parliament, where he became a member of the Radical minority. See biographies by G. D. H. Cole (3d. ed. 1947, repr. 1971), G. K. Chesterton (1926), J. W. Osborne (1966), and James Sambrook (1973).

Cobden, Richard (kŏbˈdən), 1804-65, British politician, a leading spokesman for the MANCHESTER SCHOOL. He made a fortune as a calico printer in Manchester. A firm believer in free trade, after 1838 he devoted himself to the formation and work of the ANTI-CORN-LAW LEAGUE. Campaigning both inside and outside Parliament (to which he was elected in 1841), he finally won over Sir Robert PEEL, and the corn laws were repealed in 1846. After 1849, Cobden concerned himself chiefly with foreign policy, advocating nonintervention in Europe and an end to imperial expansion. He became unpopular for his opposition to the Crimean War (1854-56) and lost his parliamentary seat in 1857. Reelected in 1859, he negotiated (1859-60) the "Cobden Treaty" for reciprocal tariffs with France. Like his close associate John BRIGHT, he favored the North in the Civil War in the United States (which he had twice visited). His many speeches, letters, and pamphlets have been published. See biographies by John Morley (1882) and J. A. Hobson (1919, new ed. 1968); study by D. Read (1967).

Cóbh (kōv) [Irish,=cove], urban district (1971 pop. 6,049), Co. Cork, S Republic of Ireland, on the south shore of Great Island in Cork Harbour. Originally called Cove of Cork, the town was renamed Queenstown upon being visited by Queen Victoria in 1849. The name Cóbh was resumed in 1922. There are large docks and stations of naval stores. Situated on slopes above the harbor and having a fine climate, Cóbh has become a seaside resort. It is the headquarters of the Royal Cork Yacht Club, the oldest yacht club in the world (founded in the early 18th cent.), and there is an annual regatta. Steel is manufactured nearby at Haubowline Island.

Cobham, John Oldcastle, Lord: see OLDCASTLE, SIR JOHN.

Coblentz, William Weber (kōˈblĕnts), 1873-1962, American physicist, b. North Lima, Ohio, grad. Case School of Applied Science (B.S., 1900) and Cornell (Ph.D., 1903). From 1905 to 1945 he was physicist with the National Bureau of Standards. He was the first to verify Planck's law, and he conducted valuable researches on infrared and ultraviolet radiation, the measurement of stellar radiation and planetary temperatures, and the optical properties of iodine.

Coblenz, West Germany: see KOBLENZ.

COBOL [from COmmon Business-Oriented Language], symbolic language used for programming a COMPUTER for business applications.

Cobourg Peninsula, c.50 mi (80 km) long and 25 mi (40 km) wide, N Northern Territory, Australia, E of Melville Island. It is a reserve for native flora and fauna.

cobra, name for African and Asian snakes of the family Elapidae that are equipped with inflatable neck hoods. The family also includes the African MAMBAS, the Asian kraits, the New World CORAL SNAKES and a large number of Australian snakes. All members of the family are poisonous and have short, rigid fangs attached at the front of the mouth. Cobras are found in most of Africa and in S Asia. They are nocturnal hunters, and most feed on small mammals, birds, and frogs. Females of all but one species lay eggs. The hood, which serves as a warning device, consists of loose skin around the neck; when the snake is excited it spreads the hood by extending the underlying long, movable ribs, and inflating it with air from the lungs. The king cobra (*Ophiophagus hannah*), or hamadryad, largest of all venomous snakes, is found in S Asia; it may reach a length of 18 ft (5.5 m) and feeds chiefly on other snakes. The Indian cobra (*Naja naja*), a common snake of the same region, is usually 4 to 5 ft (1.2-1.6 m) long; its large hood is marked on the back by a pattern of figures resembling eyes. It preys on rats and is therefore often found in houses. The Indian cobra and the Egyptian cobra (*Naja haja*) are often displayed by snake charmers. The cobras appear to respond to the music played by the charmer, but, like all snakes, they are deaf, and only follow the movements of the charmer. As cobras do not strike accurately during the day, charmers are seldom bitten. Most cases of snakebite from cobras occur when humans walking barefoot at night disturb the animal. Cobra venom is not as toxic as that of some other members of the family; the fatality rate among human victims is thought to be about 10%. Some African cobras can eject a spray of venom through the openings of the fangs, aiming accurately to a distance of at least 6 ft (1.8 m). Among these is the ringhals (*Hemachatus hemachatus*) of S Africa, which aims the spray at the eyes of the victim, causing great pain and sometimes blindness. The ringhals is the only cobra that bears live young. Cobras are classified in the phylum CHORDATA, subphylum Vertebrata, class Reptilia, order Squamata, family Elapidae.

Cobre, El (ĕl kōˈbrā), town (1970 pop. 3,952), SE Cuba, in a high valley of the Sierra Maestra. Once famous for rich copper mines (hence the name El Cobre), it is now chiefly noted for a shrine to Our Lady of Charity (La Virgen de la Caridad del Cobre), Cuba's patron saint. Guerrilla warfare raged in the neighboring mountains during Fidel Castro's revolution.

Coburg (kōˈbŏŏrk), city (1970 pop. 42,619), Bavaria, E central West Germany, on the Itz River. It has metal, glass, and ceramics industries and is known for its toys and Christmas ornaments. Mentioned in the 11th cent., Coburg in 1353 passed to the house of WETTIN. It was the alternate capital (with Gotha) of Saxe-Coburg-Gotha from 1826 to 1918 and joined Bavaria in 1920. The large ducal castle (16th cent.) was the residence of Martin Luther in 1530. The city has a modern convention hall (1962).

Coburg Peninsula, Australia: see COBOURG PENINSULA.

Coburn, Alvin Langdon, 1882-, American photographer, b. Boston. Coburn began making photographs at eight and by 1905 had become renowned for his thoughtful, perceptive portraits of European literary and artistic celebrities. Living and working in England most of his life, he produced superb photogravures of urban and marine scenes and landscapes that were widely published and exhibited. See his autobiography (1966).

coca (kōˈkə), common name for shrubs of the genus *Erythroxylon*, particularly *E. coca*, of the family Erythroxylaceae, and found abundantly in upland regions and on mountain slopes of South America, as well as in Australia, India, and Africa. Certain South American Indians chew the leaves mixed with an alkali, lime, which acts with saliva to release the drug COCAINE from the leaves. In the low doses used by the Indians, the drug acts as a STIMULANT and an appetite depressant with physiological effects similar to those of TOBACCO. Until the time of the Spanish conquest, only the Inca aristocracy was privileged to chew the coca leaves, but afterwards, the Spanish encouraged the enslaved Indians all to use coca in order to get them to endure long periods of heavy labor and physical hardships. A cocaine-free extract of coca leaves is used in some soft drinks. Coca, a different plant than the cocoa plant CACAO, is grown commercially in Sri Lanka (Ceylon), Java, and Taiwan. Coca is classified in the division MAGNOLIOPHYTA, class Magnoliopsida, order Linales, family Erythroxylaceae.

cocaine (kōkān′, kō′kān), alkaloid drug derived from the leaves of the COCA shrub. Cocaine acts as an anesthetic, depressing nerve endings and nerve trunks; however, it also stimulates the central NERVOUS SYSTEM, producing, in humans, euphoric effects, hallucinatory experiences, and temporary increases in physical energy. The drug's stimulatory effects make it psychologically habit-forming, but the body does not develop tolerance to the drug, i.e., does not need increasing doses to achieve the original effect. Withdrawal from habitual use of cocaine is characterized by severe depression, which acts to encourage return to use of the drug. Long-term use can result in digestive disorders, weight loss, general physical deterioration, and marked deterioration of the nervous system. Cocaine has been found to induce nervous system aberrations, including a PSYCHOSIS that is characterized by the common delusion that ants or other insects are crawling along or under the skin. Habitual injection of cocaine frequently results in skin abscesses. A combination of cocaine and MORPHINE or HEROIN, known as a speedball, is used by some drug addicts (see DRUG ADDICTION AND DRUG ABUSE).

Cocceius, Johannes (kŏksē′əs), 1603–69, German theologian, whose surname was originally Koch or Koken. Born in Bremen, he went to Holland, where he was professor at Francken and Leiden. He produced many learned writings, among them his great dictionary of the Hebrew language (1669), often reprinted. Cocceius held a theory of life based upon the Bible. He made the biblical COVENANT between God and man the central idea of his theology. In his examination of the Old Testament he found Jesus Christ prefigured throughout. His followers, Cocceians, perpetuated and emphasized his teachings.

coccidioidomycosis (kŏksĭd″ēoi″dōmīkō′sĭs), systemic fungal disease (see FUNGUS INFECTION) endemic to arid regions of the Americas. Its original site is in the respiratory tract, from which it can spread to the skin, bones, and central nervous system. Manifestions of the disease range from complete absence of symptoms to systemic infection and death. Coccidioidomycosis is contracted by inhaling dust infected with the fungal spores. The soil that supports *Coccidioides* spores is indigenous to dry, hot geographical areas; SW United States, Argentina, and Paraguay are areas of high incidence of infection. In 60% of the cases no clinical evidence of the disease is present and the only recognizable sign is a positive skin test; in 15% symptoms resembling those of influenza occur; and in 25% more serious signs such as swelling of the knees, weakness, pleural pain, and prostration occur. Diagnosis is made upon positive cultural identification of the virus. Although an antifungal drug is effective in some cases, there is no specific treatment except for bed rest.

coccyx (kŏk′sĭks): see SPINAL COLUMN.

Cochabamba (kōchäbäm′bä), city (1971 est. pop. 180,000), alt. c.8,400 ft (2,560 m), capital of Cochabamba dept., W central Bolivia, the second largest city in Bolivia. It is a commercial center in an agricultural region that ships grains, fruits, and cattle. Industries produce goods mainly for local consumption. Founded in 1574, the city was called Villa de Oropeza and was renamed in 1786. Cochabamba has many historical buildings, including a convent, with five paintings by the Spanish artist GOYA, and a monument to the women of the city who fought and died in the Bolivian war of independence (1815). Cochabamba also has a university.

Cochin, Charles Nicolas (shärl nēkôlä′ kôshăN′), 1715–90, French engraver, designer, writer on art, and painter to the French court. His works, more than 1,500 in number, include historical subjects, such as the *Marriage of the Dauphin*, vignettes and frontispieces, book illustrations, and pencil and crayon portraits.

Cochin (kō″chĭn′), former princely state, 1,493 sq mi (3,867 sq km), SW India, on the Arabian Sea. Now part of Kerala state, the region of Cochin has one of the highest population densities in India. Agriculture is the chief economic activity; rice, coconuts, tapioca, pepper, and vegetable oils are produced. Ernakulam was the former capital and **Cochin** (1971 pop. 438,420) the chief port. The finest port S of Bombay, Cochin has a naval base and shipbuilding industry. Tires, paper, chemicals, and tiles are manufactured. After Vasco da Gama visited Cochin (1502), the Portuguese established a settlement there. The Dutch captured it in 1663 and the British in 1795. In adjoining Mattancheri there is a community of descendants of Jews expelled from Portugal in the 16th cent.

Cochin China (kō′chĭn, kŏ′-), Fr. *Cochinchine*, historic region (c.26,500 sq mi/68,600 sq km) of South Vietnam, SE Asia. The capital and chief city was SAIGON. Cochin China was bounded by Cambodia on the northwest and north, by the historic region of ANNAM on the northeast, by the South China Sea on the east and south, and by the Gulf of Siam on the west. It included the rich MEKONG delta, one of the world's great rice-growing regions, and, in the northeast, the southern spurs of the Annamese Cordillera, where rubber, coffee, tea, oil palm, and sugarcane plantations were established. Only the Plaine des Joncs [reed plain] and the mangrove-covered Ca Mau peninsula were not cultivated. Cochin China was originally part of the KHMER EMPIRE. In the 17th cent. the Annamese (later called Vietnamese) gradually infiltrated through the mouths of the Mekong, increasing their commercial influence until in the middle of the 18th cent. they became masters of the region. After the French occupied Saigon (1859), Annam ceded to France both E Cochin China (1862) and W Cochin China (1867). Unlike the other sections of Indochina, which were French protectorates under native rulers, Cochin China was administered by the French as a colony; thus, French influence was strongest there. After World War II the status of Cochin China became a major issue in the relations between France and Vietnam. Constituted (1946) as an independent republic within the Federation of Indochina, Cochin China was later (1949) permitted by the French to join with Annam and Tonkin in Vietnam. After 1954, when Vietnam was partitioned, Cochin China became the heartland of South Vietnam; it was later divided into several provinces.

cochineal (kŏchĭnēl′, kŏch′ĭnēl), natural dye obtained from an extract of the bodies of the females of a scale insect (*Coccus cacti*) found on certain species of cactus, especially *Nopalea coccinellifera*, native to Mexico and Central America. The insects' bodies contain the pigment called carminic acid, which is obtained by subjecting a mass of the crushed insects to steam or dry heat; such large numbers of the insects are needed to produce a small amount of dye that the cost is high. Once commonly used as a scarlet-red mordant dye for wool and as a food color, cochineal has been largely replaced by synthetic products. It is used chiefly now as a biological stain.

Cochise (kōchēs′, kōchē′sā), c.1815–1874, chief of the Chiricahua group of APACHE INDIANS in Arizona. He was friendly with the whites until 1861, when some of his relatives were hanged by U.S. soldiers for a crime they did not commit. Afterward he waged relentless war against the U.S. army and became noted for his courage, integrity, and military skill. His friendship with Thomas JEFFORDS became the key to peace. In 1872, Gen. Oliver Otis HOWARD, the Indian commissioner, requested Jeffords to accompany him to Cochise's mountain stronghold. As a result of the peace talks, Cochise agreed to live on the reservation that Howard promised would be created from the chief's native territory. After the death of Cochise, however, his people were removed to another reservation. The southeastern-most county of Arizona is named for him.

cochlea (kŏk′lēə): see EAR.

Cochrane, Thomas: see DUNDONALD, THOMAS COCHRANE, 10TH EARL OF.

Cock or **Kock, Hieronymus** (both: hē″ərō′nĭməs kôk), 1510–70, Flemish painter and engraver. In Antwerp he was the first great publisher of prints and made numerous plates after Bruegel, Bosch, and Floris.

Cockaigne or **Cockayne, Land of** (both: kŏkān′), legendary country described in medieval tales, where delicacies of food and drink were to be had for the taking. *The Land of Cockaygne* is a 13th-century English poem satirizing monastic life.

cockatoo: see PARROT.

Cockburn, Sir Alexander James Edmund, 1802–80, British jurist. He was called to the bar in 1829, and a volume of reports on election cases (1832) brought him into national prominence as a trial lawyer. He was made recorder for Southampton (1841) and was elected to Parliament from there (1847). He was noted particularly for his defense advocacy, one of his most famous successes being the acquittal (1843) of Daniel McNaghten, who had killed Sir Robert Peel's secretary, on grounds of insanity; the "McNaghten rules" became the basic definition of criminal responsibility in most English-speaking jurisdictions. In Parliament, Cockburn successfully defended Lord Palmerston's handling of the "Don Pacifico" dispute (1850). He served as attorney general (1851–56) and was chief justice of common pleas (1856–59) and lord chief justice (1859–80), presiding over the famous TICHBORNE CASE.

Cockburn, Sir George, 1772–1853, British admiral. He served in the Mediterranean, and in the War of 1812 he participated in the Chesapeake Bay expeditions and in the burning of Washington. He conveyed Napoleon I in the *Northumberland* to St. Helena, remaining there as governor (1815–16).

Cockburn Island: see MANITOULIN ISLANDS.

cockchafer: see JUNE BEETLE.

Cockcroft, Sir John Douglas, 1897–1967, English physicist, educated at the Univ. of Manchester and at St. John's College, Cambridge. He was a fellow of St. John's College (1928–46) and professor of natural philosophy at Cambridge (1939–46). After serving (1941–44) as chief superintendent of the Air Defence Research and Development Establishment, he directed (1944–46) the atomic energy division of the National Research Council of Canada and became (1946) the director of the British Atomic Energy Research Establishment. The 1951 Nobel Prize in Physics was awarded jointly to Cockcroft and E. T. S. Walton for their pioneer work in transmuting atomic nuclei by bombarding elements with artificially accelerated atomic particles. He was knighted in 1948.

Cockerell, Charles Robert (kŏk′ərəl), 1788–1863, English architect, archaeologist, and writer. While excavating at Bassae, Aegina, and other sites in Italy, Greece, and Asia Minor, he studied the remains of ancient architecture and designed restorations for the temple of Zeus at Agrigento, Sicily. In 1819 he was appointed surveyor of St. Paul's Cathedral, London, and in 1833 he became chief architect of the Bank of England, designing the buildings at Bristol, Liverpool, and Manchester and making alterations in the London branch. From 1840 to 1857 he served as professor of architecture in the Royal Academy and during 1860–61 was president of the Royal Institute of British Architects. His works include the Taylor buildings, Oxford; Hanover Chapel, London; and the National Monument, Edinburgh. He completed the interior of St. George's Hall, Liverpool. Most of Cockerell's works bear the stamp of the CLASSIC REVIVAL, of which he was a notable exponent.

cocker spaniel, breed of small SPORTING DOG developed from English cocker spaniels brought to the United States in the 1880s. It stands from 14 to 15 in. (35.6–38.1 cm) high at the shoulder and weighs about 25 lb (11.3 kg). Its silky, flat, or wavy coat is moderately long and forms fringes, or feathers, on the underside of the body and on the legs, chest, and ears. The coat may be of any solid color or a combination of two or more colors (parti-colored), such as white with red or tan markings or black and tan. The tail is docked. The smallest of the sporting-dog breeds, cockers can be trained to flush game and retrieve. According to some authorities their name derives from their proficiency at hunting woodcocks. They have also been exceptionally popular as house pets. See DOG.

cockfighting, sport of pitting gamecocks against each other. Popular in Asia, in Latin America, and in some areas of the United States, it is an ancient form of amusement, having been practiced in Persia, Greece, and Rome. It has long been opposed by the clergy and by humane groups. Massachusetts passed (1836) the first law in the United States forbidding cockfighting; most other states have since taken similar action. Great Britain prohibited cockfighting by law in 1849. There are several forms of cockfighting, including the single battle and the round-robin tournament. The jousts are usually held in a small circular pit into which the gamecocks—specially bred and trained for fighting—are placed beak to beak by their handlers and then released. Local rules prevail, and a combatant is defeated when he refuses to fight, is unable to fight, or is killed. Metal spurs sometimes are attached to the fowl's natural spurs to make action deadlier.

cockle, common name applied to the heart-shaped, jumping or leaping marine BIVALVE mollusks, belonging to the order Eulamellibranchia. The brittle shells are of uniform size, are obliquely spherical, and possess distinct radiating ridges, or ribs, which aid the animal in gripping the sand. The mantle has three distinct apertures (inhalant, exhalant, and pedal) through which the inhalant and exhalant siphons and the foot protrude. The cockle lives in sand and mud in shallow water, often in brackish inlets. It burrows until only the siphons project, pulling in water from which the animal strains the minute planktonic organisms on which it feeds. All cockles are hermaphroditic. In order to accomplish the characteristic jumping form of forward locomotion, the large, powerful, muscular foot is bent backward beneath the shell and then straightened. In most adults, the foot is about as long as the greatest length of the shell. Several species of cockles are considered by man to be good, edible clams. In the British Isles, great numbers of cockles are taken annually for food from densely populated beds. These beds have been known to migrate in units, probably in response to changes in currents. *Protothaca staminea,* the rock cockle, is among the best known and most widely used for food. It usually does not exceed 3 in. (7.5 cm) in length. Rock cockles are poor diggers and inhabit packed mud, or gravel mixed with sand, usually 8 in. (20 cm) below the surface. They are found on the Pacific Coast near the rocky shores of bays and estuaries. Those inhabiting the open coast during the summer months should not be eaten because they may be infected with toxin-producing organisms. *P. semidecussata,* the Japanese littleneck clam, is smaller but considered to be better-flavored than the rock cockle. The shell is more elongated, with a brownish to bluish banding on one end. It inhabits an environment similar to that of *P. staminea* and is widespread in Puget Sound, Wash.; British Columbia; and San Francisco and Tomales Bay, Calif. Unlike the genus *Protothaca,* the basket cockles (*Clinocardium nuttalli,* or *Cardium corbis*) are good diggers and have a large foot. Lacking siphon tubes, basket cockles burrow only slightly beneath the surface and inhabit sand flats, particularly along the Pacific Coast. They are considered good eating clams but are too few in number to be widely marketed. They are most abundant in British Columbia and in Puget Sound, Wash., with fewer found south as far as Baja California and north as far as the Bering Sea. The hard shell cockles, genus *Chione,* are found from San Pedro, Calif., S into Mexico. The giant Atlantic cockle, *Dinocardium robustum* (*Cardium magnum*), reaches 5 in. (12.5 cm) in diameter and is found along the Atlantic Coast from Virginia to Brazil. It has shells with toothed margins, strikingly colored in yellowish brown with spots and transverse stripes of chestnut or purple. Cockles are classified in the phylum MOLLUSCA, class Pelecypoda, order Eulamellibranchia.

cocklebur or **clotbur,** any species of the genus *Xanthium,* widely distributed coarse annual plants of the family Compositae (COMPOSITE family). They are often persistent weeds; the two-seeded oval burrs are particularly troublesome to sheep growers and the very young plants are poisonous to livestock. Cockleburs are often confused with burdock. Cockleburs are classified in the division MAGNOLIOPHYTA, class Magnoliopsida, order Asterales, family Compositae.

cock of the plains: see GROUSE.

cock-of-the-rock: see COTINGA.

Cockpit Country, hilly region on the plateau of Jamaica, c.200 sq mi (520 sq km), W central Jamaica. Composed of limestone rock, the region has many sink holes, caverns, and subterranean streams.

Cockran, William Bourke, 1854–1923, American political leader, b. Co. Sligo, Ireland. He emigrated to New York City at the age of 17 and in 1876 was admitted to the bar. At first opposed to Tammany Hall, W. Bourke Cockran later joined (1883) the organization, although he subsequently remained independent in action. He supported the gold standard and William McKinley in 1896, anti-imperialism and William Jennings Bryan in 1900, and Theodore Roosevelt's Bull Moose ticket in 1912. As a member (1887–89, 1891–95, 1904–9, and 1921–23) of the U.S. House of Representatives, Cockran was a supporter of organized labor and an opponent of restrictions on immigration. He defended Thomas J. Mooney in 1918. See biography by James McGurrin (1948, repr. 1972).

Cockrell, Francis Marion, 1834–1915, Confederate general and U.S. Senator, b. Johnson co., Mo. Enlisting as a private with Confederate forces in the Civil War, he became a brigadier general in 1863. Cockrell's Brigade was a famous unit in the Western fighting. After the war Cockrell entered Democratic politics, and in 1874, Missouri elected him to the U.S. Senate, where he served until 1905. See biography by Francis Marion Cockrell II (1962).

cockroach or **roach,** name applied to approximately 3,500 species of flat-bodied, oval INSECTS forming the suborder Blattaria of the order Orthoptera. Cockroaches have long antennae, long legs adapted to running, and a flat extension of the upper body wall that conceals the head. They range from 1/4 in. to 3 in. (.6–7.6 cm) in length. Some cockroaches have two pairs of well-developed wings, the front pair covering the hind pair when at rest; others have reduced wings or none at all. In some species only the wings of the female are reduced or absent. Many species are able to fly well, although the familiar household species do not fly. Most cockroaches are shiny brown or black, but bright yellows, reds, and greens occur in some tropical species. Cockroaches are night-active insects and most live in damp places; most are omnivorous scavengers. They are worldwide in distribution but are most numerous in the tropics. Most species live in the wild in their native regions, e.g., the wood cockroaches, species of the genus *Parcoblatta,* found under forest litter in the NE United States. A few tropical and subtropical species that have been introduced into the temperate zone have become residents in human homes, where they multiply rapidly and are serious pests. They invade food supplies and emit foul-smelling glandular secretions. Their shape enables them to use tiny cracks as hiding places. They are popularly believed to be carriers of human diseases, although this has not been proved. The large, dark Oriental cockroach, *Blatta orientalis,* is a cosmopolitan household species. The smaller German cockroach, or Croton bug, *Blattella germanica,* native to Europe, is the common urban cockroach of the NE United States. The American cockroach, *Periplanata americana,* is a large light-reddish species that invades houses in the S United States. Cockroaches reproduce sexually. Their eggs are encased in capsules called oothecae, which in some species remain attached to the abdomen of the female until the eggs hatch. In a few species the ootheca is retained within the body of the female and the young are born live. Young resemble the adults except in size. The group as a whole is extremely old; fossil evidence indicates its extreme abundance during the Carboniferous period, about 350 million years ago. These ancient cockroaches were able to fly and were probably the first flying animals. Cockroaches are classified in five families of the phylum ARTHROPODA, class Insecta, order Orthoptera, suborder Blattaria.

cockscomb: see AMARANTH.

cocksfoot: see ORCHARD GRASS.

cocktail, short mixed drink originating in the United States and served as an appetizer. It generally has a basis of gin, whisky, rum, or brandy combined with vermouth or fruit juices and often flavored with bitters or grenadine. It is blended by stirring or shaking in a vessel containing cracked ice. The term is also applied to nonalcoholic beverages served as appetizers, e.g., tomato juice cocktail, and also to mixed, cut-up fruits and to shellfish and oysters served with a sharp sauce.

Cocoa, city (1970 pop. 16,110), Brevard co., E Fla., on the Indian River (a lagoon), a segment of the Intracoastal Waterway; inc. 1895. It is a tourist center in a region where citrus fruits are grown. An 8-mi (12.9 km) causeway leads from the city over Indian River to Merritt Island, Cocoa Beach, and Cape Canaveral. Brevard Community College is in Cocoa. Patrick Air Force Base is nearby.

cocoa: see CACAO.

coconut, fruit of the coco PALM (*Cocos nucifera*), a tree widely distributed through tropical regions. The seed is peculiarly adapted to dispersal by water since the large pod holding the nut is buoyant and impervious to moisture. The trees therefore establish themselves naturally on small islands and low shores bordering the tropic seas. The tree grows to a height of from 60 to 100 ft (18–30 m), with a smooth cylindrical stem marked by the ringlike scars of former leaves. It bears at the top a crown of frondlike leaves and yellow or white blossoms. The number of nuts varies; a well-cared-for tree may yield 75 to 200 or more annually. The mature fruit as it comes from the tree is encased in a thick, brown fibrous husk. The nut itself has a hard woody shell, with three round scars at one end; the embryo lies against the largest scar and emerges through it as a developing plant. Through this easily punctured spot the milk of the young coconut may be drained. Its constantly growing commercial value has led to extensive cultivation of the coconut, especially in the Malay Archipelago, Sri Lanka, and India. A few are found in the southern extremity of Florida. The coco palm is one of the most useful trees in existence, every part of it having some value. The fruit, either ripe or unripe, raw or cooked, is a staple food in the tropics; the terminal bud, called palm cabbage, is considered a delicacy, and the inner part of young stems is also eaten. The milk of the young nut is a nutritious drink. A sweet liquid obtained from the flower buds ferments readily and is used as a beverage, both when fresh and when distilled to make arrack; it may be boiled down to make various palm sugars, e.g., jaggery. The leaves are used for making fans, baskets, and thatch. The coir (coarse fibers obtained from the husk) is made into cordage, mats, and stuffing; it becomes more buoyant and elastic than hemp in salt water. The hard shell and the husk are used for fuel. The fibrous center of the old trunk is also used for ropes, and the timber, known as porcupine wood, is hard and fine-grained and takes a high polish. From the nutshells are made containers of various kinds—cups, ladles, and bowls—often highly polished and ornamentally carved. The root is chewed as a narcotic. Commercially the greatest value of the coconut lies in the oil, which is extracted from the dried kernels of the fruit. The nuts when ripe are apt to spoil or become rancid. Therefore when they are gathered they are broken open and the flesh is dried and exported under the name of copra. The oil content of copra ranges from 50% to 70% depending upon the method of drying. The coconut and the olive are the earliest recorded sources of vegetable oil. Coconut oil, the major type of palm oil, has been extracted by mortar and pestle in the Orient since antiquity. Primitive methods of drying and expressing the copra are giving way to modern machinery, such as rotary driers and hydraulic presses. The residue, known as coco cake, makes excellent cattle food, as it usually contains a remnant of from 6% to 10% of oil. Large quantities of shredded or desiccated coconut made from copra and many whole coconuts are exported for use chiefly in the making of cakes, desserts, and confectionery. Coconuts are classified in the division MAGNOLIOPHYTA, class Liliatae, order Arecales, family Palmaceae.

cocoon: see PUPA.

Cocopa Indians (kōkō'pə), North American Indians whose language belongs to the Yuman branch of the Hokan-Siouan linguistic stock (see AMERICAN INDIAN LANGUAGES). They formerly lived near the mouth of the Colorado River and in the mountains of S California. Since there was little wild game in the area, the Cocopa cultivated corn, melons, pumpkins, and beans. Some were moved to a reservation in California, and some to Mexico, where they are known as the Cucupá.

Cocos Islands (kō'kōs) or **Keeling Islands,** two separate atolls comprising 27 coral islets (1970 pop. 611), 5.5 sq mi (14.2 sq km), in the Indian Ocean, c.1,400 mi (2,250 km) SE of Sri Lanka. They are under Australian administration. Discovered in 1609 by Capt. William Keeling of the East India Company, the Cocos were settled in 1826 by Alexander Hare, an Englishman. A second settlement was founded in 1827 by John Clunies-Ross, a Scottish seaman, who landed with a boatload of Malay sailors. In 1857 the islands were annexed to the British crown. Queen Victoria granted the lands to the Clunies-Ross family in 1886 in return for the right to use any land on the island for public purposes. In 1903 the islands were included in the STRAITS SETTLEMENTS, and in 1955 they were placed under Australian administration. Only three of the islands are inhabited: West Island, which has an airport and the largest community of Europeans; Home Island, headquarters of the Clunies-Ross Estate; and Direction Island, which has an aviation-marine base. The economy is based on the production of copra and on aviation and government facilities maintained by the Australian government.

Cocteau, Jean (zhäN kôktō'), 1889–1963, French writer, visual artist, and filmmaker. Cocteau's versatility in the arts is unrivaled in the 20th cent. He experimented audaciously in almost every artistic medium, becoming a leader of the French avant-garde in the 1920s. His first great success was the novel *Les Enfants Terribles* (1929), which he made into a film in 1950. Surrealistic fantasy suffuses his films and many of his novels and plays. Among his best dramatic works are *Orphée* (1926) and *La Machine infernale* (1934, tr. 1936), in which the Orpheus and Oedipus myths are surrealistically adapted to modern circumstances. His films include *The Blood of a Poet* (1933), *Beauty and the Beast* (1946), and *Orphée* (1949). Among other works are ballets, sketches, monologues, whimsical drawings, and the text (written with Stravinsky) for the opera-oratorio *Oedipus Rex* (1927). See his autobiography; comp. from his writings by Robert Phelps (tr. 1970); biographies by Frederick Brown (1968), Elizabeth Sprigge and Jean-Jacques Kihm (1968), and Francis Steegmuller (1970); Margaret Crosland, ed., *Cocteau's World* (tr. 1972).

Cocx, Gonzales: see COQUES, GONZALES.

Cocytus (kōsī'təs): see HADES.

cod, member of the large family Gadidae, comprising extremely important and abundant food fishes. The cods include the hake and the haddock, all found in the N Atlantic and Pacific. The cod was extremely important to the economic and social growth of New England; it has been used as a Massachusetts state emblem. All cods are bottom-feeders with soft fins; the large ventral fins are located under or in front of the pectorals rather than behind them as in other fishes. The Atlantic cod varies in color but has two distinct phases, gray-green and reddish brown. Its average weight is 10 to 25 lb (4.5–11.3 kg), but specimens weighing up to 200 lb (90 kg) have been recorded. About 30,000 tons of cod are caught annually. Cods feed on mollusks, crabs, starfish, worms, squid, and small fish. Some migrate south in winter to spawn. A large female lays up to five million eggs in mid-ocean, a very small number of which survive. The Pacific cod is found N of Oregon. Small cod prepared in strips for cooking is called scrod. The tomcod resembles a young Atlantic cod with long, tapering ventral fins. It rarely exceeds 15 in. (37.5 cm) in length and lives close to shore. There is also a Pacific tomcod. The pollack, also called coalfish or green cod, is a plump olive-green cod found in cool waters on both sides of the Atlantic. Pollacks have forked tails and pale lateral lines and grow to 3 ft (90 cm) and 30 lb (13.6 kg); 10,000 tons are taken yearly. The haddock is the most important food fish of Atlantic waters, the annual catch amounting to 50,000 tons, most of which is marketed frozen. It is also found in colder European waters. Haddocks are also bottom-feeders but are found in deeper water (up to 100 fathoms). They are smaller than cods, reaching a top weight of 30 lb (13.6 kg) and length of 3 ft (90 cm) and have black lateral lines and dark side patches. Finnan haddie is lightly smoked haddock. The burbot is the only freshwater cod, found deep in northern streams and lakes. It has a single barbel on its chin. A similar burbot is found in Europe and Asia. Lings and hakes, closely related to the cod, are fishes of commercial importance found in warmer waters. They are slenderer than the cod and have weak tails but are strong swimmers, preying on crustaceans and small fish. Cods are classified in the phylum CHORDATA, subphylum Vertebrata, class Osteichthyes, order Gadiformes, family Gadidae. See A. C. Jensen, *The Cod* (1972).

Coddington, William, 1601–78, one of the founders of Rhode Island, probably b. Boston, England. He came to America in 1630 as an officer of the Massachusetts Bay Company and was its treasurer from 1634 to 1636. He supported Anne HUTCHINSON in the antinomian controversy. With her, John CLARKE, and other Puritan exiles, he purchased the island of Aquidneck (Rhode Island) from the Narragansett Indians and founded Portsmouth (1638). Deposed (1639) as leader of the settlement by Hutchinson and Samuel GORTON, Coddington withdrew with Clarke and founded NEWPORT. The two towns were joined under Coddington's governorship in 1640. He opposed, however, the union with the mainland settlements of Providence and Warwick, which took place in 1647 under a patent received in 1644 by Roger WILLIAMS. The commission Coddington received in 1651 to govern for life Aquidneck and neighboring Conanicut Island was denounced by the island people, and Williams and Clarke succeeded in having it revoked in 1652. Coddington remained influential in Newport affairs and was governor of the united colony of Rhode Island and Providence Plantations in 1674, 1675, and 1678.

code, in communications, set of symbols and rules for their manipulation by which the symbols can be made to carry information. By this extended definition all written and spoken languages are codes. While these are sufficient and actually quite efficient in transmission of information, they are at times ambiguous and are highly inefficient for telecommunications. For example, a circuit capable of carrying a voice message, e.g., a telephone circuit, could carry several times as much information if that information were represented as telegraphic code. Special codes are also used for representing data inside a computer. Generally speaking, INFORMATION THEORY shows that for any particular application there is an optimum code; it does not, unfortunately, tell how to devise the code. For use in a COMPUTER, information is encoded as strings of binary digits; for telegraphic work, codes such as the MORSE CODE, consisting of a series of dots and dashes or marks and spaces, are used. Certain arbitrary codes are used to ensure secrecy of communication; although the eavesdropper may have access to the message, he does not know the rules by which the symbols are associated and cannot convert the message into a form he can understand. See CRYPTOGRAPHY; SIGNALING.

code, in law, in its widest sense any body of legal rules expressed in fixed and authoritative written form. A STATUTE thus may be termed a code. Codes contrast with customary law (including COMMON LAW), which is susceptible of various nonbinding formulations, as in the legal opinions of judges. The earliest codes (e.g., the Roman TWELVE TABLES) met the popular demand that oral regulations be written down so that legal chicanery might be prevented. In later Roman law, however, the term *code* acquired its modern meaning of a precisely formulated statement of the principles underlying some branch of law (e.g., contracts) or an entire legal system. One of the greatest codes was the Roman CORPUS JURIS CIVILIS. In Europe, in the late 18th cent., after the general adoption of CIVIL LAW by the continental countries, jurists asserted that similar codes were needed, and the parent modern European codification, the CODE NAPOLÉON, appeared (1804) and was followed by many others. The civil law code is an attempt to determine in advance what legal exigencies will arise and to furnish the means for meeting them. Basic legal principles (e.g., that contracts express the will of the parties) are worked out in systematic detail and great attention is given to consistency. The movement for codification, however, has been largely unsuccessful in countries where common law prevails, such as the United States, despite the argument that the principles of common law are sometimes uncertain and often contradict one another. Advocates of the common law assert that civil law makes possibly futile attempts to predict and control the course of developments. In the United States the term code is sometimes also applied to the statutes of a state or of the Federal government edited so as to eliminate duplication and inconsistencies and arranged under appropriate headings.

Code Civil: see CODE NAPOLÉON.

codeine (kō'dēn), alkaloid found in OPIUM. It is a NARCOTIC whose effects, though less potent, resemble those of MORPHINE. An effective cough suppressant, it is mainly used in cough medicines. Like other narcotics, codeine is addictive. See DRUG ADDICTION AND DRUG ABUSE.

Code Napoléon (kôd näpôlāôN') or **Code Civil** (sēvēl'), first modern CODE of France, promulgated by Napoléon I in 1804. The work of J. J. Cambacérès and a commission of four appointed by Napoleon I in 1800 was important in making the final draft. The Code Napoléon embodied the private law of France (i.e., law regulating relations between individuals) and, as modified by amendments, it is still in force in that country. It is a revised form of the ROMAN LAW, i.e., the CIVIL LAW, which prevailed generally on the Continent. It shows, of course, many specific French modifications, some based on the GERMANIC LAW that had been in effect in N France. The code follows the Institutes of the Roman CORPUS JURIS CIVILIS in dividing civil law into personal status (e.g., marriage), property (e.g., easements), and the acquisition of property (e.g., wills), and it may be regarded as the first modern analogue to the Roman work. Not only was it applied by Napoleon to the territories under his control—N Italy, the Low Countries, and some of the German states—but it exerted a strong influence on Spain (and ultimately on the Latin American countries) and on all European countries except England. It was the forerunner, in France and elsewhere, of codifications of the other branches of law, including civil procedure, commercial law, and criminal law. Quebec prov. and the state of Louisiana owe much of their law to the Code Napoléon. In addition to the Code Civil, Napoleon was responsible for four other codes: the Code of Civil Procedure (1807), Commercial Code (1808), Code of Criminal Procedure (1811), and the Penal Code (1811).

codling moth (kŏd'lĭng), small moth, *Carpocapsa pomonella,* whose larva is the destructive apple worm. Of European origin, it is now found wherever apples are grown. The adult moth is gray with brown markings and has a wingspan of about ¾ in. (1.8 cm). The ¾-in. larva is pinkish, with a brown head. There are several generations a year; the early eggs are deposited on leaves and the later ones directly on the developing fruit. The larvae feed inside the fruit and pupate (see INSECT) on the bark of the tree. Apple worms also attack pears, quinces, and English walnuts. The codling moth is classified in the phylum ARTHROPODA, class Insecta, order Lepidoptera, family Olethreutidae.

cod-liver oil, yellowish oil obtained from the liver of the codfish. The oil is rich in vitamin A and vitamin D (calciferol). It was long used as a preventive and cure for RICKETS in Baltic and Scandinavian countries, where fish is a dietary staple. However, it was not until the 1920s that doctors in the U.S. finally recognized its therapeutic usefulness. More palatable synthetic vitamins have largely replaced cod-liver oil as dietary supplements, and almost all the milk sold in the United States and Europe now contains added vitamins A and D. See VITAMIN.

codon: see NUCLEIC ACID.

Codreanu, Corneliu Zelea (kôrnĕ'lyŏŏ zĕl'yä kôdrĕä'nŏŏ), 1899–1938, Rumanian political leader and anti-Semitic terrorist. Active in the Rumanian student movement against leftists and liberals, he founded (1927) and led the militant, fascist IRON GUARD until his conviction for treason in 1938. He shot and killed the prefect of Iaşi in 1924 and instigated the murder of Premier Ion Duca in 1933. Both times he was acquitted. Shortly after his imprisonment in 1938, he and 13 of his followers were killed, allegedly while trying to escape.

Codrington, Sir Edward (kŏd'rĭngtən), 1770–1851, British admiral. He held various commands in the French Revolutionary and Napoleonic wars, taking part in the battle of Trafalgar (1805) and serving (1810–13) in the Mediterranean. He commanded the combined British, French, and Russian fleet that in 1827 destroyed the Turkish and Egyptian fleets in the battle of NAVARINO.

Cody, William Frederick: see BUFFALO BILL.

Cody (kō'dē), city (1970 pop. 5,161), seat of Park co., NW Wyo., on the Shoshone River in a sheep, cattle, and irrigated farm area; founded and inc. 1901 by William F. Cody (Buffalo Bill). It is a tourist resort at the eastern entrance to Yellowstone National Park, with dude ranches and a colorful old frontier town flavor. Oil from the Big Horn Basin is refined there. Cody is headquarters for the Shoshone National Forest. Of interest are the Buffalo Bill Historical Center, containing Cody memorabilia; the Whitney Gallery of Western Art, housing a notable collection of art of the Old West; and an annual rodeo. Shoshone Canyon and the Shoshone project are nearby.

Coe College, at Cedar Rapids, Iowa; United Presbyterian; coeducational; founded 1851 as Cedar Rapids Collegiate Institute, chartered 1881 under its present name.

coeducation, instruction of both sexes in the same institution. The economic benefits gained from joint classes and the increasing participation of women in industrial, professional, and political activities have influenced the spread of coeducation. There were scattered examples of coeducation in the late 17th cent. in Scotland and in the American Colonies, but there was no general trend until the great expansion of public education between 1830 and 1845 in the developing W United States. The distance between schools in that region and the small number of pupils caused elementary schools to admit girls. The movement spread naturally to the secondary schools during the reorganization of public education after the Civil War. Oberlin College gave degrees to both men and women as early as 1837, but it was the development of state universities during the post-Civil War era that standardized collegiate coeducation. During the late 1960s a number of formerly all-male and all-female colleges, including in 1969 Yale, Princeton, and Vassar, became coeducational. See Thomas Woody, *A History of Women's Education in the United States* (4th ed. 1929, repr. 1966).

Coehoorn, Menno van (mĕ'nō vän kōō'hôrn), 1641–1704, Dutch military engineer and nobleman. He invented a portable bronze siege mortar called the coehorn. He was considered in his day a rival of Vauban in the construction of fortresses. He served (1702–3) in the army of the duke of Marlborough in the War of the Spanish Succession. The name also appears as Coehorn or Cohorn.

coelacanth: see LOBEFIN; FISH.

Coelenterata (sĭlĕn"tərā'tə), another name for the phylum CNIDARIA.

Coele-Syria: see BIQA, AL.

Coello, Claudio (klou'dyō kōä'lyō), c.1642–1693, Spanish baroque painter. As court painter to Charles II he decorated many churches and public buildings of Madrid. His most famous work is the monumental altarpiece for the sacristy of the Escorial, filled with portraits and allegorical figures.

coelom (sē'ləm), fluid-filled body cavity, found in animals, which is lined by cells derived from MESODERM tissue in the EMBRYO, and which provides for free, lubricated motion of the viscera. In animals of the phyla ANNELIDA, MOLLUSCA, and ARTHROPODA, the mesoderm forms as a mass of tissue from special embryonic cells between an outer layer, the ECTODERM, and an inner layer, the ENDODERM. The coelom then forms as a result of the splitting and hollowing out of the mesodermal mass. In animals of the phyla ECHINODERMATA and CHORDATA, the mesoderm arises as the lining of folds developing from the endoderm, and the spaces within these folds form the coelom. The structure of the embryonic coelom is relatively simple; in an adult other organs push into the coelomic cavity, and it is also subdivided into compartments, e.g., the pericardial cavity, in which the heart develops.

coendou (kōĕn'do͞o): see PORCUPINE.

coenzyme, any one of a group of relatively small organic molecules required for the catalytic function of certain ENZYMES. A coenzyme may either be attached by covalent bonds to a particular enzyme, or exist freely in solution, but in either case it participates intimately in the chemical reactions catalyzed by the enzyme. Often a coenzyme is structurally altered in the course of these reactions, but it is always restored to its original form in subsequent reactions catalyzed by other enzyme systems. ADENOSINE TRIPHOSPHATE (ATP) is a coenzyme of vast importance in the transfer of chemical energy derived from biochemical oxidations. Other NUCLEOTIDES (formed from URACIL, CYTOSINE, GUANINE, and inosine) have also been found to act as coenzymes. For example, uridine triphosphate—a derivative of uracil—has been demonstrated to be of great importance in the metabolism of carbohydrates, as in the biosynthesis of glycogen and sucrose. Those coenzymes that have been found to be necessary in the diet are vitamins. One such compound, biotin, is a member of the B complex; it was first isolated in 1935 from dried egg yolk, and its structure was established in 1942. Biotin is usually found attached to a lysine residue in certain enzymes, where it participates in reactions involving the transfer of carboxyl (−COOH) groups; one such reaction is essential for the synthesis of fatty acids. Another group of coenzymes is the cobalamin family; one member, cyanocobalamin (vitamin B_{12}) is known to be essential in the diet, although its role in metabolism remains obscure. Closely related cobalamins seem to be involved in the biosynthesis of methionine and methane. The complicated cyanocobalamin molecule was reported in 1973 to have been synthesized; it was first isolated from liver some 25 years prior to that date. Coenzyme A has been shown to participate in a variety of biochemical reactions, all involving acyl groups such as the acetyl unit; it is, for instance, associated with the pivotal first step of the Krebs cycle (see CITRIC ACID CYCLE) in which an acetyl unit (the breakdown product of carbohydrates) is introduced into the cycle to be converted eventually into carbon dioxide, water, and chemical energy. Coenzyme A is derived from adenine, ribose, and pantothenic acid (a vitamin of the B complex). The two flavin coenzymes, riboflavin mononucleotide (FMN) and flavin adenine dinucleotide (FAD), occur universally in living organisms and play important roles in biochemical oxidations and reductions. They are usually found tightly bound to certain enzymes (flavoproteins) and are derived from riboflavin (vitamin B_2). Glutathione, a tripeptide consisting of residues of glutamic acid, cysteine, and glycine, is known to act as a coenzyme in a few enzymatic reactions, but its importance may lie in its role as a nonspecific reducing agent within the cell. It is hypothesized that glutathione serves to maintain the biological activity of certain proteins by keeping selected cysteine sidechains in the reduced thiol form, thereby not allowing these residues to oxidize and cross-link with one another to form cystine residues (unnecessary cross-links often result in distortions of protein structure). Heme, a complicated molecule containing iron in the ferrous state, serves as a coenzyme in a variety of biochemical processes. It forms an essential part of the structure of HEMOGLOBIN and participates intimately in the uptake and release of oxygen by this protein. (In this case the use of the word "coenzyme" may be inappropriate in that often hemoglobin is not considered to be an enzyme, since it does not catalyze a chemical reaction.) Heme is an important part of the CYTOCHROMES, enzymes that catalyze the biochemical oxidations and reductions involved in the production of chemical energy in the form of ATP, and heme is also associated with the various enzymes that catalyze the cleavage of peroxides. Lipoic acid seems to be involved in the removal of carboxyl groups from α-keto acids and in the transfer of the remaining acyl groups to various acceptors. Lipoic acid in fact transfers the acetyl group of pyruvic acid to coenzyme A. Like biotin, lipoic acid is commonly found attached to lysine residues within certain enzymes. It was first reported to have been purified and isolated in crystalline form in 1953. The nicotinamide nucleotides were the first coenzymes to be detected (1904) in extracts of a living organism. Nicotinamide adenine dinucleotide (NAD) and nicotinamide adenine dinucleotide phosphate (NADP) are derived from adenine, ribose, and nicotinic acid, or niacin (a vitamin of the B complex) and are important intermediates in the biochemical oxidations and reductions that provide chemical energy within the cell. Both NAD and NADP can be reduced by accepting a hydride ion (H^-, a proton with two electrons) from an appropriate donor; the resulting NADH and NADPH can then be oxidized back to their original states by transferring their hydride ions to various acceptors. In this fashion electron pairs (and protons) are shuttled about in the cell from high energy donors to lower energy acceptors. As a general rule, NADPH donates its hydride ions to biosynthetic processes, such as the fixing of carbon dioxide to make carbohydrates during the dark reaction of photosynthesis. NADH, on the other hand, donates its hydride ions to systems such as the cytochromes, which eventually donate them to oxygen to make (with the addition of a proton) water, producing chemical energy in the form of ATP as a by-product; the process is not yet completely understood. Pyridoxal phosphate is a coenzyme that is essential for many enzymatic reactions, almost all of which are associated with amino acid metabolism; it is, for example, involved in the synthesis of tryptophan, a derivative of pyridoxine (another vitamin of the B complex). The coenzyme tetrahydrofolic acid is derived in humans from the B-complex vitamin folic acid. This coenzyme and its close relatives participate in the transfer of various carbon fragments from one molecule to another; they are, for instance, involved in the synthesis of methionine and thymine. Thiamine pyrophosphate is derived from another B-complex vitamin, thiamine. This coenzyme often plays a role in the removal of carboxyl (−COOH) groups from organic acids, releasing the carbon and oxygen atoms as carbon dioxide (CO_2). This coenzyme, for example, helps to remove a carboxyl group from pyruvic acid, leaving behind an acetyl group, which it donates to lipoic acid; the lipoic acid then transfers the acetyl group to coenzyme A, which finally inserts it into the beginning of the Krebs cycle. This important three-step enzymatic process requires the participation of three coenzymes; hundreds of other biochemical reactions require coenzymes as well, and this serves to explain the great significance of those molecules in the functioning of living organisms. In the case of human beings, it also serves to explain the importance of proper dietary intake of vitamins, which provide the only source of certain "building blocks" for several of these coenzymes. See VITAMIN.

coercion, in law, the unlawful act of compelling a person to do, or to abstain from doing, something by depriving him of the exercise of his free will, particularly by use or threat of physical or moral force. In many states of the United States, statutes declare a person guilty of a misdemeanor if he, by violence or injury to another's person, family, or property, or by depriving him of his clothing or any tool or implement, or by intimidating him with THREAT of force, compels that other to perform some act that the other is not legally bound to perform. Coercion may involve other crimes, such as ASSAULT. In the law of contracts, the use of unfair persuasion to procure an agreement is known as DURESS; such a contract is void unless later ratified. At common law, one who commits a crime under coercion may be excused if he can show that the danger of death or great bodily harm was present and imminent. However, coercion is not a defense for the murder or attempted murder of an innocent third party.

Cœur, Jacques (zhäk kör), c.1395–1456, French merchant prince and adviser of King Charles VII, who made him chief of finances and sent him on important diplomatic missions. His reforms restored order to the confused financial situation brought about by the Hundred Years War. Cœur established French trade in the Levant, employed agents throughout the Orient, owned factories and mines in France and abroad, and rivaled the great Italian merchant republics. Through his monopolies he amassed a fabulous fortune, but he spent a large part of it to finance the campaigns that ultimately drove the English from France. In 1451 he was arrested on the charge, concocted by his debtors and enemies, of having poisoned Agnès SOREL. He was sentenced (1453), after an unfair trial, to imprisonment and a fine of several million francs. In 1454–55 he escaped to Rome. He died in Chios while leading a papal fleet against the Turks. His house in Bourges, which still stands, is one of the finest examples of secular medieval architecture. See A. B. Kerr, *Jacques Cœur* (1927).

Coeur d'Alene (kûrdəlān'), city (1970 pop. 16,228), seat of Kootenai co., N Idaho, near the Wash. line; inc. 1907. It is a tourist and lumbering center situated on Coeur d'Alene Lake W of the Coeur d'Alene Mts.—the gateway to a beautiful summer and winter resort area. The city has numerous lumber mills, grass seed farms, and plants making electronic items and prefabricated homes. Fort Coeur d'Alene (later Fort Sherman) was established there in 1876. The city (named after a tribe of Indians that inhabited the area) grew around the fort after the discovery (1883) of the fabulously rich silver, lead, and zinc lodes and after the mining boom of 1884. For the tumultuous early history of the city, see WESTERN FEDERATION OF MINERS. The city is the headquarters of Coeur d'Alene National Forest and the seat of a junior college.

Coeur d'Alene Indians, North American Indians whose language belongs to the Salishan branch of the Algonquian-Wakashan linguistic stock (see AMERICAN INDIAN LANGUAGES). They occupied N Idaho and were also called the Skitswish. Long known as a peaceful group, the Coeur d'Alene were placed on reservations after an encounter with U.S. forces in 1858; they now number some 500 on a reservation in Idaho.

Cœur de Lion: see RICHARD I, king of England.

coffee, a tree, its seeds, and the beverage made from them. The Arabian coffee tree (*Coffea arabica*) is an evergreen shrub or small tree of the family Rubiaceae (MADDER family). It is believed to be native to Ethiopia but was introduced into Arabia, probably during the 15th cent. Borne in the axils of the smooth, ovate leaves are clusters of fragrant white flowers that mature into deep red fruits about ½ in. (1.27 cm) long. The fruit, sometimes called a cherry, is a drupe, and usually contains two seeds, the coffee beans. Sometimes only one seed develops; the fruit is then called a peaberry. Varieties of Arabian coffee have long provided the bulk of the world's supply. Coffee requires a hot, moist climate with a rainfall of at least 50 in. (127 cm) and a rich soil; it thrives on well-drained slopes, particularly where the soil is of volcanic origin. It can be grown from sea level to c.6,000 ft (1,830 m). The better grades are generally produced above 1,500 ft (460 m). Frost is injurious. The plants are propagated from seed. Other taller vegetation is usually planted to control the amount of sunlight reaching the coffee trees and to protect them from the elements. A coffee tree produces its maximum yield sometime between the 5th and the 10th year and continues to bear for about the next 30 years. Other species of some commercial importance are Liberian coffee (*C. liberica*) and Congo coffee (*C. robusta*). Wide variations in production and demand have caused frequent surpluses disastrous to planters, laborers, and the national economy of producing countries. Experiments designed to employ the surplus for industrial purposes have shown the possibility of making such coffee derivatives as cattle fodder, alcohol, fusel oil, caffeine, and glycerin. A coffee quota agreement (1940), administered by the Inter-American Coffee Board (1941), attempts to stabilize the market by allocating the U.S. importation of coffee from Latin America. A considerable quantity of coffee is exported as parchment coffee (seeds within the husk-like covering, from which the outer pulp has been removed) to be finally cleaned and roasted at points of distribution. Heat acts upon the essential oils, developing the aroma and flavor. Roasts range from light brown to the very dark, almost charred, Italian roast. A wide variety of machines and theories for making coffee all aim to preserve the aroma. Whatever the method used, the prime requirements are properly roasted, freshly ground coffee, freshly boiling water, and absolute cleanliness of utensils, as coffee is easily contaminated by foreign odors. "Turkish" coffee, finely powdered and heavily sweetened, is drunk unfiltered by most Eastern peoples. Westerners favor clear coffee. The French use for breakfast café au lait, coffee combined with scalded milk. The unique mocha from the Yemen region of Arabia and some Sumatra, Java, and Colombian coffees are prized by connoisseurs. Various adulterants, including CHICORY, carrots, parsnips, iris root, beans, rice, and cereals, roasted and ground, may usually be detected by soaking in cold water, which is not discolored by genuine coffee beans. Opinion has differed as to the value of coffee. It has become a popular beverage because of its aroma and the exhilarating and fatigue-allaying properties of its CAFFEINE constituent, to which is attributed a medicinal value in cases of shock, pneumonia, and poisoning. Taken in excess it may cause irritability, depression, and indigestion. The early history of coffee is shrouded in legend. Known in Ethiopia before A.D. 1000, it is believed to have been used first as a food; a ball of the crushed fruit molded with fat was a day's ration for certain African nomads. Later, wine was made from the fermented husks and pulps. Coffee made from the ground and roasted beans was used in Arabia by the 15th cent. and spread to Egypt and Turkey. Despite early suppression on religious and political grounds, it rapidly became a universal beverage of Arabs. At first opposed by Italian churchmen as an infidel drink, it was Christianized by Pope Clement VIII and by the mid-17th cent. it had reached most of Europe. Although introduced in North America c.1668, coffee took first place as the staple American beverage only after tea had met with popular disapproval following the Boston Tea Party. The production of instant coffee, experimented with as early as 1838, was started (1867) by Gail Borden in Illinois. It became increasingly popular after World War II. Coffee is classified in the division MAGNOLIOPHYTA, class Magnoliopsida, order Rubiales, family Rubiaceae. See W. H. Ukers, *All about Coffee* (2d ed. 1938). **Coffeehouses** dispensed coffee before it was made in the home in Arab countries and in Europe and America and were known as centers for gossip, gambling, and literary and political discussions. Periodically government restrictions were imposed in the belief that coffeehouses were meeting places of political malcontents. Will's Coffee House in London was famous as a resort of wits and poets. Johnson, Addison, Steele, Sheridan, Dryden, Swift, Goldsmith, Hogarth, and other notables were the centers of coteries in the houses they frequented. In France also the spread of the coffeehouse was rapid and influenced the development of literature and of the stage.

coffee tree, Kentucky, common name for the plant species *Gymnocladus dioica,* a tree of the family Leguminosae (PULSE family). The seeds of the woody pods have been used as a substitute for coffee.

cofferdam, temporary barrier for excluding water from an area that is normally submerged. Made commonly of wood, steel, or concrete sheet piling (see PILE), cofferdams are used in constructing the foundations of dams, bridges, and similar subaqueous structures and for temporary drydocks. If double sheeting is utilized, the space between the sheets is usually filled with clay and gravel. When great strain or pressure is likely to be encountered, as in deep water, the pneumatic CAISSON is preferred to the cofferdam. See Lazarus White and E. A. Prentis, *Cofferdams* (2d ed. 1956).

Coffeyville, city (1970 pop. 15,116), Montgomery co., SE Kansas, on the Verdigris River near the Okla. line, in a farm and oil area; inc. 1872. It is a trading and distributing center, with oil refineries and plants producing foundry and machine-shop products, inorganic chemicals, power transmission equipment, and milk and dairy items. With the coming of the railroad (1870), Coffeyville grew as a cattle-shipping point. Oil and natural gas were discovered in the area in 1902. The city was the scene (1892) of a famous shoot-out with the notorious Dalton gang during an attempted bank robbery. Of interest are the Dalton graves and the Dalton Museum. A junior college is there.

Coffin, Henry Sloane, 1877–1954, American Presbyterian clergyman, b. New York City. He was pastor of the Madison Ave. Presbyterian Church in New York City (1905–26), lecturer (1904–9), associate professor of pastoral theology (1909–26), and president (1926–45) of Union Theological Seminary. He was moderator (1943–44) of the General Assembly of the Presbyterian Church in the U.S.A. His works include *The Meaning of the Cross* (1931), *God's Turn* (1934), *Religion Yesterday and Today* (1940), *God Confronts Man in History* (1947), and *Communion through Preaching* (1952). See biography by M. P. Noyes (1964).

Coffin, Levi, 1798–1877, American abolitionist, b. North Carolina. In 1826 he moved to the Quaker settlement of Newport (now Fountain City), Ind., where he kept a store until 1847. His home became a leading station of the UNDERGROUND RAILROAD, of which he was styled "president." See his *Reminiscences* (3d ed. 1898, repr. 1968).

coffin, closed receptacle for a corpse. Its purpose is usually to protect and to aid preservation of the body, although in the past some have believed that it may confine the spirit of the deceased. Bark, skins, and mats were commonly used in primitive societies to wrap the body prior to burial. Peoples living near rivers or oceans often buried their dead in canoes, and hollowed oak coffins have been found in the Bronze Age BARROW. The Chaldaeans and the early Greeks enclosed a corpse in clay, sealing the coffin by firing it. The largest known stone coffins (see SARCOPHAGUS) are Egyptian. Wood and papier-mâché were also used in Egypt for mummy chests. Coffins lined with metal, usually lead, came into use in the Middle Ages. Most coffins used in the Western world today are made of elm or oak and are lined with bronze, copper, lead, or zinc.

Coggan, Donald (Frederick Donald Coggan), 1909–, English Protestant clergyman. Educated at Cambridge and ordained in 1934, Coggan began his ministerial career as curate of a London working-class church. He held academic posts in Toronto and London before becoming bishop of Bradford (1956) and archbishop of York (1961). A critic of apartheid and advocate of greater official tolerance for homosexuals, Coggan was appointed in 1974 to succeed Michael Ramsey as archbishop of Canterbury.

Cognac (kônyäk'), city (1968 pop. 22,062), Charente dept., W France, in Angoumois, on the Charente River. The French brandy to which Cognac gives its name has been manufactured and exported from the city since the 18th cent. The city was the birthplace of Francis I and was a Huguenot stronghold in the 16th cent.

Cogswell, Joseph Green, 1786–1871, American librarian and bibliographer, b. Ipswich, Mass. After studying abroad, Cogswell taught mineralogy and geology at Harvard and became librarian in 1821. In 1823 he helped to found the Round Hill School at Northampton, Mass. He superintended the Astor Library in New York City (now part of the New York Public Library) and was librarian from 1848 to 1861 and trustee to 1864. He prepared an alphabetical and analytic catalog for the library, which was printed at his own expense and was the basis for the later card catalog.

Cohan, George Michael (kōhăn', kō'hăn, kō'ən), 1878–1942, American showman, b. Providence, R.I. As a child he appeared in vaudeville as one of "The Four Cohans" with his father, mother, and sister, Josephine. He eventually wrote the act and was the business manager. *The Governor's Son* (1901) was his first attempt at Broadway; *Little Johnny Jones* (1904) was his first success. Cohan wrote the book, music, and lyrics for 20 musicals; he was the producer, director, and most often the star. His inimitable style set the pattern of fast-moving, flippant and gay musicals; his characters were often modeled after real persons. Such shows as *Forty-five Minutes from Broadway* (1906), *Broadway Jones* (1912), *Hello, Broadway* (1914), and *The Song and Dance Man* (1923), and such songs as "The Yankee Doodle Boy," "Give My Regards to Broadway," and "You're a Grand Old Flag" show his preoccupation with flag-waving patriotism. Through his long career he had only one partner, Sam H. HARRIS. In 1913, Cohan revolutionized the mystery farce with his dramatization of Earl Derr Bigger's novel *Seven Keys to Baldpate.* He was an excellent adapter and play doctor; he described his adaptations as "Cohanized." His song "Over There," written during World War I, is now a classic. As an actor he was noted for his debonair characterizations; his performances in O'Neill's *Ah, Wilderness!* (1934) and as the President in *I'd Rather Be Right* (1937) were particularly notable. He made his last public appearance in his own play *Return of the Vagabond* (1940). See his *Twenty Years on Broadway* (1925, repr. 1971); biography by Ward Morehouse (1943).

Cohen, Hermann, 1842–1918, German philosopher. He was a founder of the Neo-Kantian Marburg school and was known for his commentaries on Kant. His own works include *Logik der reinen Erkenntnis* (1902), *Ethik des reinen Willens* (1904), and *Aesthethik des Gefühls* (1912). See *Reason and Hope: Selections from the Jewish Writings of Hermann Cohen* (tr. Eva Jospe, 1971).

Cohen, Morris Raphael, 1880–1947, American philosopher, b. Minsk, Russia, grad. College of the City of New York, 1900, Ph.D. Harvard, 1906. He emigrated to the United States in 1892. At first an instructor in mathematics at the College of the City of New York, Cohen transferred to the department of philosophy, where he taught from 1912 until 1938, becoming famous for his use of Socratic irony. He then taught at the Univ. of Chicago until 1942. His influence, through his students and his books, has been far-reaching, and he is considered one of the most important American philosophers since William James. Cohen's most important books are *Reason and Nature* (1931, rev. ed. 1953) and *Law and the Social Order* (1933). Other works include *A Preface to Logic* (1944), *The Faith of a Liberal* (1945), and *American Thought: A Critical Sketch* (1954). See his autobiography, *A Dreamer's Journey* (1949); biography by L. C. Rosenfield (1962); study by C. F. Delaney (1969).

cohesion: see ADHESION AND COHESION.

Cohn, Ferdinand (fĕr'dĕnänt kōn), 1828–98, German botanist. He is considered a founder of the science of bacteriology. From his early studies of microscopic life he developed theories of the bacterial causes of infectious disease and recognized bacteria as plants. He aided Robert Koch in preparing Koch's famous work on anthrax. Cohn's writings cover such diverse subjects as fungi, algae, insect epidemics, and plant diseases.

Cohnheim, Julius (yo͞o'lyo͝os kōn'hīm), 1839–1884, German experimental histologist and pathologist. In a relatively brief life Cohnheim made a series of remarkable contributions to the rapidly developing science of pathology. In 1863 he completed important studies on the sugar-forming ferments of the salivary glands and pancreas. Subsequently, he joined Rudolf Virchow at the Pathological Institute in Berlin. Perhaps his most impressive study resulted in the final clarification of the mechanisms of inflammation and suppuration; he demonstrated the migration of leukocytes through blood-vessel walls, thus destroying Virchow's contention that no such passage, or diapedesis, takes place. He also studied venous thrombosis, the embryonic-rest theory of neoplasm formation, atypical leukemias, and experimental tuberculosis.

Cohoes (kəhōz'), city (1970 pop. 18,613), Albany co., E N.Y., near Albany, at the confluence of the Mohawk and Hudson rivers; settled by the Dutch 1665, inc. 1869. Its manufactures include textiles (made there since 1840), knitted goods, paper products, boats, and electrical appliances. The world's first power-operated knitting mill was opened there in 1832. The Van Schaick Mansion (1735), built by the son of Cohoes's first settler, was used as headquarters by Gen. Horatio Gates during the Revolutionary War.

cohosh (kōhŏsh'), name for several plants, among them BANEBERRY and a species of BUGBANE, both of the family Ranunculaceae (BUTTERCUP family), and blue cohosh, a member of the family Berberidaceae (BARBERRY family). Both families are classified in the division MAGNOLIOPHYTA, class Magnoliopsida, order Ranunculales.

coiffure: see HAIRDRESSING.

coil: see INDUCTOR; SOLENOID.

Coimbatore (kwĭmbətôr'), town (1971 pop. 353,469), Tamil Nadu state, SE India. Commanding the approach to the Palghat Gap, the major pass through the Western Ghats, it was important in the wars of HAIDAR ALI and Tippoo Sahib. The British obtained undisputed possession of Coimbatore in 1799. The town is now a district administrative center and a junction of rail lines linking the east and west coasts of India. Glassware, fertilizer, electrical goods, cement, and synthetic gems are produced. Coimbatore is also a market for tea, cotton, cardamom, cinchona, and teak.

Coimbra (kōēm'brə), city (1970 municipal pop. 108,046), capital of Coimbra dist., W central Portugal, on the Mondego River, in Beira Litoral. The old capital of Beira, it is a market center with small industries but is known chiefly for its history and for the famous university, which was founded (1292) by King Diniz in Lisbon but was moved temporarily to Coimbra in 1308 and permanently in 1540. Coimbra, then known as Conimbriga, was an important town in Roman days. It continued to flourish down through Moorish times and after its Christian recovery (1047) by Ferdinand I of León. It became the capital of Alfonso I, first king of Portugal, and continued as an important royal residence after the capital was transferred to Lisbon in the 13th cent. There is a fine 12th-century cathedral. Inés de Castro was murdered there (1355).

coin, piece of metal, usually a disk of gold, silver, nickel, bronze, copper, or a combination of such metals, stamped by authority of a government as a guarantee of its value and used as MONEY. Coinage was probably invented independently in Lydia or in the Aegean Islands and in China before 700 B.C. and in India in the 4th cent. B.C. The earliest known example is an electrum coin (c.700 B.C.) of Lydia. Roman coinage dates from about the 4th cent. B.C. The first coins struck in the American colonies were issued by the Massachusetts Bay colony. The first U.S. MINT was established in 1792. Mottoes used on many U.S. coins are "E Pluribus Unum" (1795) and "In God We Trust" (1864). Early coins were die-struck by hand and showed many individual variations. Standardized coins date from the use (in the 17th cent.) of a mill and screw machine (invented c.1561). Coins are usually stamped from rolled metal blanks, are milled, and have a design impressed upon them between the upper and lower dies of a coining press. Milled or lettered edges have been used since the 17th cent. to discourage the removal of slivers of metal, especially from gold or silver coins. No American gold coins have circulated since 1934, when the United States abandoned the domestic gold standard. Starting in 1965, the U.S. Treasury ceased to put silver in all newly minted dimes and quarters. Previously, both coins had contained large amounts of silver. At the same time, the silver content of the half-dollar was reduced from 90% to 40%. See also NUMISMATICS.

Cointreau: see CURAÇAO, liqueur.

Cojutepeque (kōhōōtāpā'kā), city (1968 est. pop. 13,000), central El Salvador. It is north of a volcano of the same name and is on the Inter-American Highway. The city is a commercial and processing center for agricultural produce.

Coke, Sir Edward (ko͝ok), 1552–1634, English jurist, one of the most eminent in the history of English law. He entered Parliament in 1589 and rose rapidly, becoming solicitor general and speaker of the House of Commons. In 1593 he was made attorney general. His rival for that office was Sir Francis Bacon, thereafter one of Coke's bitterest enemies. He earned a reputation as a severe prosecutor, notably at the trial of Sir Walter Raleigh, and held a favorable position at the court of King James I. In 1606 he became chief justice of the common pleas. In this position (after 1613), and as chief justice of the king's bench, Coke became the champion of common law against the encroachments of the royal prerogative and declared null and void royal proclamations that were contrary to law. Although his historical arguments were frequently based on false interpretations of early documents, as in the case of the Magna Carta, his reasoning was brilliant and his conclusions impressive. His constant collisions with the king and the numerous enmities he developed—especially that with Thomas Egerton, Baron ELLESMERE, the chancellor—brought about his fall. Bacon was one of the foremost figures in engineering his dismissal in 1616. By personal and political influence, Coke got himself back on the privy council and was elected (1620) to Parliament, where he became a leader of the popular faction in opposition to James I and Charles I. He was prominent in the drafting of the Petition of Right (1628). His most important writings are the *Reports*, a series of detailed commentaries on cases in common law, and the *Institutes*, which includes his commentary on Littleton's *Tenures*. See W. H. Lyon and Herman Block, *Edward Coke* (1929); C. D. Bowen, *The Lion and the Throne* (1957).

Coke, Thomas (ko͝ok, kōk), 1747–1814, English clergyman and early bishop of the Methodist Episcopal Church in America. After taking orders (1777) in the Church of England, he openly allied himself with the Methodists. He was president of the Irish conference in 1782 and two years later was ordained as superintendent for America by John WESLEY. When Coke was styled bishop shortly after the American conference of 1784, the change was not approved by Wesley. Coke visited America nine times, the last time in 1803. Always deeply interested in Methodist missionary work, he sought (1813) an appointment by the government as bishop of India, agreeing to return to the Established Church. As the request was not granted, he himself secured funds for a Methodist mission, but died on the way to Ceylon. See biographies by W. A. Candler (1923) and J. A. Vickers (1969).

Coke, Thomas William (ko͝ok), 1754–1842, English agricultural reformer, known as Coke of Holkham. He improved breeds of cattle, sheep, and hogs on his country estate and greatly promoted improved methods of breeding and husbandry. He was a member of Parliament for more than 50 years and in 1837 was made earl of Leicester.

coke, hard, gray, massive, porous fuel prepared by the destructive DISTILLATION of bituminous COAL, much used when a porous fuel with few impurities and high carbon content is desired, as in the BLAST FURNACE. Coke bears the same relation to coal as does charcoal to wood. The preparation of coke in beehive ovens results in the loss of volatile by-products. Only a small amount is still made by this method. For industrial purposes, coke is prepared in retorts or furnaces of silica brick, and the by-products (chiefly ammonia, coal tar, and gaseous compounds) are saved. Petroleum coke is the solid residue left by the cracking process of oil refining. Natural coke, or carbonite, is formed by METAMORPHISM from bituminous coal when intrusive igneous rock cuts across a vein of coal.

cola or **kola,** tropical tree (genus *Cola*) of the family Sterculiaceae (STERCULIA family), native to Africa but now grown in other tropical regions. The fruit is a pod containing seeds from which is obtained CAFFEINE, an essential oil. Cola nuts are chewed as a stimulant by the native population and are exported for commercial use in soft drinks and medicines. Colas are classified in the division MAGNOLIOPHYTA, class Magnoliopsida, family Sterculiaceae.

Colatina (ko͞olətē'nä), city (1970 pop. 105,157), Espiritu Santo state, E central Brazil, on the Doce River. The state's chief agricultural center, Colatina is one of the leading coffee producers of Brazil.

Colbert, Charles: see CROISSY, CHARLES COLBERT, MARQUIS DE.

Colbert, Claudette (klōdĕt' kôlbĕr'), 1905–, American movie actress, b. Paris, France; her original name was Claudette Chauchoin. Distinguished by her rosy cheeks, hearty laugh, and curly bangs, Colbert is particularly adept at sophisticated comedy. Her films include *It Happened One Night* (1934), *Private Worlds* (1935), *Since You Went Away* (1944), and *Parrish* (1961). She has often appeared on the stage.

Colbert, Jean Baptiste (zhäN bätēst'), 1619–83, French statesman. The son of a draper, he was trained in business and was hired by Cardinal MAZARIN to look after his financial affairs. On his deathbed, Mazarin recommended Colbert to King Louis XIV, who made him comptroller general of finances (1665). Colbert helped to procure the downfall of the superintendent of finances, Nicolas FOUQUET, for mismanagement. As Louis XIV's minister, Colbert scaled down the public debt by repudiating some obligations and reducing the value of others and set up a system of accounts in order to keep the government within its income. His efforts to make taxes more equal had little success in the face of localism and tradition. Colbert's aim was to make France economically self-sufficient. One of the most successful practitioners of MERCANTILISM, he encouraged the growth of industry through subsidies and tariff protection, rigidly regulated the qualities and prices of manufactured and agricultural products, tried to break down trade barriers within France, initiated a vigorous road-building program, and restricted the use of natural resources. In 1669 he was made secretary of state for naval affairs. He constructed shipyards, arsenals, and harbors, among them Brest and Rochefort, and began the construction of a large navy as a first step in the development of commerce and colonization. Colbert contributed significantly to the splendor of Louis XIV's reign by patronizing the arts and sciences. He founded the Academy of Sciences and the Paris Observatory and promoted the French Academy. His efforts at economy were soon menaced by the extravagance of the king, and the opening of Louis XIV's wars began the decline of Colbert's power and the ascendancy of the marquis de LOUVOIS. It was Colbert's commercial policy, however, that, by challenging Dutch commercial strength, contributed to the DUTCH WAR of 1672–78. To meet military expenses, Colbert was obliged to resort to increased taxation, the sale of offices, borrowing, and the anticipation of future revenues. His new taxes caused serious disturbances. Despite his unpopularity at the time of his death, Colbert was later ranked among the greatest of French statesmen. See E. C. Lodge, *Sully, Colbert and Turgot* (1931, repr. 1970); C. W. Cole, *Colbert and a Century of French Mercantilism* (1939).

Colborne, John: see SEATON, JOHN COLBORNE, 1ST BARON.

Colby, Bainbridge, 1869–1950, U.S. lawyer and public official, b. St. Louis. Upon graduation (1891) from Columbia law school, he began law practice in New York City and became active in Republican politics. He left the party with Theodore Roosevelt (1912) to found the National Progressive party. During World War I he served on the U.S. Shipping Board and he became (March, 1920) Secretary of State in President Wilson's cabinet. He became a close confidant of Wilson, with whom he practiced law (1921–22) after Wilson's term of office ended. See his *Close of the Wilson Administration and the Final Years* (1930).

Colby College, at Waterville, Maine; coeducational; est. 1813, opened 1818. The school, principally a liberal arts college, adopted its present name in 1899. Its library includes the papers of Edwin Arlington Robinson.

Colchester (kōl'chĭstər, –chĕs"tər), municipal borough (1971 pop. 76,145), Essex, SE England, on the Colne River. It is a grain and cattle market. The oyster fisheries of the Colne are important; an annual event is the October oyster feast. Other industries are flour milling, malting, and the making of boilers, gas engines, shoes, and farm machinery. Colchester was one of the great cities of pre-Roman Britain, the capital of the ruler Cunobelin (Shakespeare's Cymbeline). It became an important Roman colony and was the particular object of attack (A.D. 61) by Boadicea. To the Anglo-Saxons the place was known as Colneceaster. The WITENAGEMOT met there in 931. During the ENGLISH CIVIL WAR the town was taken (1648) after a long siege by parliamentarians under Baron Fairfax of Cameron. Of interest are the Roman walls (more completely preserved than elsewhere in England) and the massive Norman castle, part of which houses a museum of Roman antiquities. Colchester has a military base.

colchicine (kŏl'chəsēn"), alkaloid extracted from plants of the genus *Colchicum* and especially from the corms of the autumn crocus, *Colchicum autumnale* (see MEADOW SAFFRON). The metabolic effect of colchicine is not known, but it is thought that it may decrease production of lactic acid and prevent accumulation of uric acid crystals in the body, making it useful in the treatment of gout. Colchicine and derivatives such as demecolcine inhibit MITOSIS, or cell division. As a mitotic poison, it inhibits rapidly proliferating cells and has been used in cancer therapy and as an IMMUNOSUPPRESSIVE DRUG. Colchicine has also been used to visualize chromosomes photomicrographically and to induce mutations experimentally.

Colchis (kŏl'kĭs), ancient country on the eastern shore of the Black Sea and in the Caucasus region. Centered about the fertile valley of the Phasis River (the modern Rion), Colchis corresponds to the present-day region of Mingrelia in the Georgian SSR. In Greek legend it was the home of Aeëtes and Medea, the land where the Golden Fleece was sought by JASON and the Argonauts. Greek trading posts were established in Colchis, but the land remained independent until conquered (c.100 B.C.) and held briefly by Mithradates VI of Pontus. After the time of Trajan to the end of the Roman Empire, Rome exerted considerable influence on the region.

cold, common, catarrhal infection of the upper respiratory tract sometimes confined to the mucous membrane of the nose, at other times involving that of the throat and larynx as well. The cold is the most common human ailment; most Americans suffer from one to three colds per year, children from the ages of one to five being the most susceptible group. Although the incidence of colds is higher in winter, exposure to chilling or dampness is considered to be of little significance. Colds are frequently accompanied by fever and usually general discomfort. The causative agent may be one of 50 to 60 viruses, called rhinoviruses, to which, it seems, almost no one is immune. The congested and discharging mucous membrane may become a fertile ground for a secondary bacterial invasion that may spread to the bronchi and lungs or to the ears, sinuses, or mastoid processes. There is as yet no known cure or preventive for the common cold, although some are of the opinion that large doses of VITAMINS, especially vitamin C, may be helpful preventives. Treatment involves adequate intake of fluids to prevent dehydration and aspirin to relieve pain and fever. When necessary, nasal sprays are used to shrink swollen membranes and syrups to treat severe coughs. Antibiotics are used only in treatment and prevention of secondary bacterial infection. Uncomplicated infections usually last from three to ten days.

Colden, Cadwallader (kōl'dən), 1688–1776, colonial scholar and political leader of New York, b. Ireland, of Scottish parents. After studying medicine in London, Colden arrived (1710) in Philadelphia to practice. He moved (1718) to New York, where he was appointed (1720) surveyor general. He was named (1721) to the governor's council and became increasingly influential during the administration of George Clinton (1686–1761), the colonial governor, whose official papers and addresses Colden in large part prepared. After 1761 he was lieutenant governor of New York, and he became more and more unpopular among the radicals opposed to the British measures. In his 55 years of active public life, Colden was able to make himself one of the most learned men in the colonies. He studied Newton's principles and wrote his own critique, *The Principles of Action in Matter* (1751). He became a botanist of the new Linnaean system of classifying flora (as did his daughter, Jane Colden) and made significant contributions to the medical literature of the colonies. He also published his *History of the Five Indian Nations* (1727), a valuable source on the Iroquois tribes. His letter books (1877–78) and letters and papers (7 vol., 1918–23) were published by the New-York Historical Society. See biography by A. M. Keys (1906, repr. 1971).

cold frame, in horticulture, sun-heated board frame covered with a removable top of glass or other transparent material and sunk into the ground. The top may be solid or slatted or screened for shade. The cold frame is used to start seedlings in early spring (four to six weeks before the average frost-free date), to harden seedlings or plants removed from greenhouses or hotbeds, and to protect plants during the winter. A HOTBED is an artificially or naturally heated cold frame.

cold sore: see HERPES SIMPLEX.

cold storage: see REFRIGERATION.

Coldstream, burgh (1971 pop. 1,270), Berwickshire, SE Scotland, on the English border. General Monck raised troops there in 1660 for his march into England that resulted in the restoration of Charles II to the throne. The regiment became known as the Coldstream Guards, one of the regiments of guards of the royal household. Coldstream, like Gretna Green, was a marriage resort from 1754 to 1856. In 1975, Coldstream became part of the Borders region.

cold type, any method of preparing matter for PRINTING that employs a typewriter, a special keyboard machine, or photocomposition rather than the metal (hot type) used in letterpress composition. Reproduction is usually by a photographic process.

cold war, term used to describe the shifting struggle for power and prestige between the Western powers and the Communist bloc from the end of World War II until the early 1960s. Of worldwide proportions, the conflict was tacit in the ideological differences between COMMUNISM and capitalist DEMOCRACY. Mutual suspicion had long existed between the West and the USSR, and friction was sometimes manifest in the Grand Alliance during World War II. After the war the West felt threatened by the continued expansionist policy of the Soviet Union, and the traditional Russian fear of incursion from the West continued. Communists seized power in Eastern Europe with the support of the Red Army, the Russian occupation zones in Germany and Austria were sealed off by army patrols, and threats were directed against Turkey and Greece. Conflict sometimes grew intense in the UNITED NATIONS, which was at times incapacitated by the ramifications of the cold war, at others effective in dealing with immediate issues. In a famous speech (1946) at Fulton, Mo., Sir Winston Churchill warned of an implacable threat that lay behind a Communist "iron curtain." The United States, taking the lead against the expansion of Soviet influence, rallied the West with the Truman Doctrine, under which immediate aid was given to Turkey and Greece. Also fearing the rise of Communism in war-torn Western Europe, the United States inaugurated the European Recovery Program, known as the MARSHALL PLAN, which helped to restore prosperity and influenced the subsequent growth of the European Community. During the cold war the general policy of the West toward the Communist states was to contain them (i.e., keep them within their current borders) with the hope that internal division, failure, or evolution might end their threat. In 1948 the Soviet Union directly challenged the West by instituting a blockade of the western sectors of Berlin, but the United States airlifted supplies into the city until the blockade was withdrawn (see BERLIN AIRLIFT). The challenges in Europe influenced the United States to reverse its traditional policy of avoiding permanent alliances; in 1949 the United States and 11 other nations signed the North Atlantic Treaty (NATO; see NORTH ATLANTIC TREATY ORGANIZATION). The Communist bloc subsequently formed (1955) the WARSAW TREATY ORGANIZATION as a counterbalance to NATO. Meanwhile, in Asia, the Communist cause gained great impetus when the Communists under MAO TSE-TUNG gained control of mainland China in 1949. The United States continued to support Nationalist China, with its headquarters on Taiwan. President Truman, fearing the appeal of Communism to the peoples of Asia, Africa, and Latin America, created the Point Four program, which was intended to help underdeveloped areas. Strife continued, however, and in 1950 Communist forces from North Korea attacked South Korea, precipitating the KOREAN WAR. Chinese Communist troops entered the conflict in large numbers, but were checked by UN forces, especially those of the United States. The focus of the cold war in Asia soon shifted to the southeast. China supported insurgent guerrillas in Vietnam, Laos, and Cambodia; the United States, on the other side, played a leading role in the formation of the SOUTHEAST ASIA TREATY ORGANIZATION and provided large-scale military aid, but guerrilla warfare continued. The newly emerging nations of Asia and Africa (see AFRO-ASIAN BLOC) soon became the scene of cold-war skirmishes, and the United States and the Soviet Union (and later China) competed for their allegiance, often through economic aid; however, many of these nations succeeded in remaining neutral. Hopes for rapprochement between the Soviet Union and the West had been raised by a relaxation in Soviet policy after the death (1953) of Joseph STALIN. Conferences held in that period seemed more amiable, and hopes were high for a permanent ban on nuclear weapons. However, the success of the Soviet artificial satellite Sputnik in 1957, attesting to Soviet technological know-how, introduced new international competition in space exploration and missile capability. Moreover, both Soviet Premier Nikita KHRUSHCHEV and U.S. Secretary of State John Foster Dulles grimly threatened "massive retaliation" for any aggression, and the Soviet Union's resumption (1961) of nuclear tests temporarily dashed disarmament hopes. While Khrushchev spoke of peaceful victory, extremists in both camps agitated for a more warlike course, even at the risk of nuclear catastrophe. China began to accuse the USSR of conciliatory policies toward the West, and by the early 1960s ideological differences between the two countries had become increasingly evident. The cold-war struggle continued in Southeast Asia, in the Middle East (see CENTRAL TREATY ORGANIZATION), in Africa (see ZAÏRE), in Latin America (where the United States supported the ALLIANCE FOR PROGRESS to counter leftist appeal), and in Europe, where the East German government erected the BERLIN WALL in late 1961 to check the embarrassing flow of East Germans to the West. In 1962 a tense confrontation occurred between the United States and the Soviet Union after U.S. intelligence discovered the presence of Soviet missile installations in Cuba. Direct conflict was avoided, however, when Premier Khrushchev ordered ships carrying rockets to Cuba to turn around rather than meet U.S. vessels sent to intercept them (see CUBAN MISSILE CRISIS). It was obvious from this and other confrontations that neither major power would risk nuclear war. Meanwhile, during the late 1950s and early 60s both European alliance systems began to weaken somewhat; in the Western bloc, France began to explore closer relations with Eastern Europe and the possibility of withdrawing its forces from NATO. In the Soviet bloc, Rumania took the lead in departing from Soviet policy. U.S. involvement in the Vietnam War in Southeast Asia led to additional conflict with some of its European allies and diverted its attention from the cold war in Europe. All these factors combined to loosen the rigid pattern of international relationships that was responsible for the cold war, and it appeared to have ended. See D. F. Fleming, *The Cold War and Its Origins, 1917–1960* (1961); J. A. Lukacs, *A New History of the Cold War* (3d ed. 1966); T. W. Wilson, Jr., *Cold War and Common Sense* (1962); Gabriel Kolko, *The Politics of War* (1968); J. L. Gaddis, *The United States and the Origins of the Cold War, 1941–1947* (1972).

Coldwell, Major James William, 1888–1974, Canadian political leader, b. England. He went to Canada in 1910 and became a school administrator in Regina, Sask. He was a leader of the province's Farmer-Labour party (1932–35) and helped to found the Co-operative Commonwealth Federation (CCF; see NEW DEMOCRATIC PARTY), a leftist party. As the CCF candidate, Major (his given name) Coldwell was elected (1935) to the Canadian House of Commons. He was a Canadian delegate to the San Francisco conference in 1945 and to the UN General Assembly in 1946. He became parliamentary leader of his party in 1940 and national president in 1942, holding both posts until 1960. When the New Democratic party was formed in 1961, he became its honorary president. His *Left Turn, Canada* (1945) discusses the CCF's objectives.

Cole, George Douglas Howard, 1889–1959, English economist, labor historian, and socialist. Educated at Oxford, he was long associated with the university and held a professorship from 1944 to 1957. For many years a leading exponent of GUILD SOCIALISM, he later returned to his original Fabianism, acting as chairman of the Fabian Society from 1939 to 1946 and becoming its president in 1952. His many books, mainly on labor and socialism, range from popular works to scholarly studies. Among his original works of enduring value are *A Short History of the British Working Class Movement* (3 vol., 1927; rev. ed. 1948), *The British Common People* (with Raymond W. Postgate, 1939; rev. ed. *The British People,* 1947), and *A History of Socialist Thought* (5 vol. in 7, 1953–60). See biography by L. P. Carpenter (1973). With his wife, **Margaret Isabel (Postgate) Cole,** 1893–, he wrote over 30 detective stories as well as works on economics and politics. Her works include *Beatrice Webb* (1945), *The Story of Fabian Socialism* (1961), and a biography of her husband (1971). She edited Beatrice Webb's important diaries.

Cole, Margaret Isabel (Postgate): see COLE, GEORGE DOUGLAS HOWARD.

Cole, Thomas, 1801–48, American landscape painter, b. England. He arrived in the United States in 1818 and moved to Ohio, where he was impressed by the beauty of the countryside. In 1825 he went to New York, where his landscape paintings began to be appreciated. Largely self-taught, he depicted the scenery of the Hudson River valley and the Catskills, which he discovered on long walking trips, becoming a leader of the HUDSON RIVER SCHOOL. In 1829 he went to Europe, where he spent some time sketching in England and Italy. In Paris he greatly admired the landscapes of Claude Lorrain. After he returned to New York, he was commissioned (1832) to paint his five famous allegorical scenes, farfetched and neoclassical in style, known as the *Course of Empire* (N.-Y. Historical Soc., New York City). This series and the *Expulsion from the Garden of Eden* (Mus. of Fine Arts, Boston) reflect his strong moralizing tendencies, combined with elements of fantasy; they are far less successful than his landscapes. Other works, such as *Oxbow* (Metropolitan Mus.) and *Catskill Mountains* (Mus. of Art, Cleveland), reveal his joy in the grandeur of nature. See biography by L. L. Noble (1964).

Cole, Timothy, 1852–1931, American wood engraver, b. London. He came to the United States as a child. Cole learned his trade in Chicago and later moved to New York, where in 1873 he began his 40-year association with the *Century Magazine* (then *Scribner's*). He was a pioneer and consummate craftsman in the white line technique of wood engraving, which allowed a more faithful reproduction of the works of European masters and popular contemporary painters. *Dutch and Flemish Masters* (1901) is one of the books that he engraved.

Coleraine (kōlrān'), municipal borough (1971 pop. 14,871), Co. Londonderry, N Northern Ireland, near the mouth of the Bann River. Coleraine is a port. Its industries include distilling, linen milling, the curing of ham and bacon, bog iron mining, and salmon fishing. There is also a large chemical fiber plant. In 1613, James I gave the site of the town to the corporations of the City of London for development.

Coleridge, Hartley (kōl'rĭj), 1796–1849, English author; eldest son of Samuel Taylor Coleridge. Reared in the household of the poet Southey after the estrangement of his parents, Hartley Coleridge went to Oxford and gained a fellowship at Oriel. His shy and melancholy nature, however, curtailed a very promising university career. He was dismissed from Oriel for intemperance and went to London. There he wrote and tutored private pupils. His *Biographia Borealis,* a series of very sound critical biographies, appeared in 1833. The same year he published a small volume of poems, including some beautiful sonnets, which established his literary reputation. Shortly thereafter, he retired to the Lake District, where he remained until his death. In 1840 he edited the dramatic works of Massinger and Ford. His brother Derwent published the remainder of his literary works in 1851. See his letters (ed. by E. L. Griggs and G. E. Griggs, 1936); biography by Lawrence Hanson (1939, repr. 1962).

Coleridge, Samuel Taylor, 1772-1834, English poet and man of letters, b. Ottery St. Mary, Devonshire; one of the most brilliant, versatile, and influential figures in the English romantic movement. Son of a clergyman, he was a precocious, dreamy child. He attended Christ's Hospital school in London and was already formidably erudite upon entering Cambridge in 1791. His erratic university career was interrupted by his impulsive enlistment in the dragoons, from which his brothers managed to extricate him. In 1794 he met the poet Robert SOUTHEY, who shared his political and social idealism, and together they planned to establish a small utopian community, which they called a pantisocracy, on the banks of the Susquehanna River in the United States. The plan failed to materialize for practical reasons. In 1795, Coleridge married Sarah Fricker, the sister of Southey's fiancée, with whom he was never happy. They settled in Nether Stowey in 1797, and shortly thereafter William WORDSWORTH and his sister Dorothy moved into a house nearby. Although Coleridge had been busy and productive, publishing both poetry and much topical prose, it was not until his friendship with Wordsworth that he wrote his best poems. In 1798, Coleridge and Wordsworth jointly published the volume *Lyrical Ballads*, whose poems and preface made it a seminal work and manifesto of the romantic movement in English literature. Coleridge's main contribution to the volume was the haunting, dreamlike ballad "The Rime of the Ancient Mariner." This long poem, as well as "Kubla Khan" and "Christabel," written during the same period, are Coleridge's best-known works. All three poems make use of exotic images and supernatural themes. "Dejection: An Ode," published in 1802, was the last of Coleridge's great poems. It shows the influence of (or affinity to) some poetic ideas of Wordsworth, notably the meditation upon self and nature and upon the relationships among emotion, sense experience, and understanding. While an undergraduate Coleridge had begun to take laudanum (an opium derivative then legal and widely used) for his ailments, and he was addicted by about 1800. That year, after having traveled with Wordsworth in Germany, Coleridge moved with his family to Keswick in the Lake District. He continued his studies and writings on philosophy, religion, contemporary affairs, and literature. In 1808 he separated from his wife permanently, and from 1816 until his death he lived in London at the home of Dr. James Gilman, who brought his opium habit under control. Coleridge worked for many years on his *Biographia Literaria* (1817), containing accounts of his literary life and critical essays on philosophical and literary subjects. It presents Coleridge's theories of the creative imagination, but its debt to other writers, notably the German idealist philosophers, is often so heavy that the line between legitimate borrowing and plagiarism becomes blurred. This borrowing tendency, evident also in some of his poetry, together with Coleridge's notorious inability to finish projects—and his proposal of impractical ones—made him a problematic figure. His lifelong friend Charles Lamb called him a "damaged archangel." Indeed, 20th-century editorial scholarship has unearthed additional evidence of plagiarism; thus, Coleridge is still a controversial figure. However, the originality and beauty of his best poetry and his enormous influence on the intellectual and aesthetic life of his time is unquestioned. He was reputedly a brilliant conversationalist, and his lectures on Shakespeare remain among the most important statements in literary criticism. His *Confessions of an Enquiring Spirit* (ed. by his nephew H. N. Coleridge) was published posthumously in 1840. See his collected letters, ed. by E. L. Griggs (6 vol., 1956-71); *Notebooks: 1794-1808*, ed. by Kathleen Coburn (4 vol., 1957-61); collected works, ed. by Kathleen Coburn (5 vol., 1969-72); biographies by E. K. Chambers (1938), Lawrence Hanson (1938, repr. 1962), and W. J. Bate (1968); studies by J. D. Campbell (1894), Carl Woodring (1961), Marshall Suther (1965), and Norman Fruman (1972); J. L. Lowes, *The Road to Xanadu* (rev. ed. 1964); R. L. Brett, ed., *Coleridge* (1973). His daughter, **Sara Coleridge,** 1802-52, has literary standing in her own right. Her translation of *An Account of the Abipones* (1822) shows a great facility in both Latin and English. Her best work is *Phantasmion* (1837), a fairy tale. See her *Memoir and Letters* (1873, repr. 1974); biography by E. L. Griggs (1941, repr. 1973).

Coleridge-Taylor, Samuel, 1875-1912, English composer; son of a Negro physician of Sierra Leone and an Englishwoman. He studied violin and composition at the Royal College of Music in London. He wrote many songs, orchestral works, piano pieces, and some chamber music but is best known for his cantatas, particularly the *Hiawatha* trilogy (1898-1900) and *A Tale of Old Japan* (1911). See J. F. Coleridge-Taylor, *Genius and Musician* (1943).

Colet, John (kŏ'lĭt), 1467?-1519, English humanist and theologian. While studying on the Continent (1493-96), Colet became interested in classical scholarship and in theories of education. After his residency at Oxford as a lecturer, in 1505 he became dean of St. Paul's Cathedral, London. He planned the new St. Paul's School (1509) and endowed it from his private fortune. With William Lily, the school's first headmaster, and Erasmus, he collaborated on a Latin grammar that was later called the Eton grammar and used by generations of schoolboys. Colet did not, himself, break with the Roman Church, but his ideas on church reform were influential later. Most of his writings were unpublished until the late 19th cent. See biography by J. H. Lupton (2d ed. 1961); Frederic Seebohm, *The Oxford Reformers* (1913, repr. 1971).

Colette (Sidonie Gabrielle Colette) (sēdōnē' gäbrēĕl' kōlĕt'), 1873-1954, French novelist. Colette gained wide fame with her numerous novels, characterized by their sensitive observations—particularly of women—and their intimate, semiautobiographical style. Her early series of novels, published in collaboration with her first husband, Willy (pseud. of Henry Gauthier-Villars), include *Claudine at School* (1900, tr. 1930) and *The Innocent Wife* (1903, tr. 1934). Among many later novels written on her own are *The Vagrant* (1910, tr. 1912), *Chéri* (1920, tr. 1929), *The Cat* (1933, tr. 1936), and *Gigi* (1945). After being divorced in 1906, Colette worked on the music-hall stage until 1914. Her marriage to Henri de Jouvenel also ended in divorce, but her last years were enriched by the companionship of her third husband, Maurice Goudeket. Colette was the first woman to be president of the Goncourt Academy and the second to be made a grand officer of the French Legion of Honor. See *Earthly Paradise*, a collection of her autobiographical writings, ed. by Robert Phelps (1966); biographies by Maria le Hardouin (tr. 1958), Margaret Davies (1961), and Margaret Crosland (1973); studies by Elaine Marks (1960) and R. D. Cottrell (1974).

coleus, common name for a genus of plants with large colorful leaves native to tropical Asia and Africa. Several species are grown as houseplants. Plants of the genus *Coleus* are in the family Labiatae (MINT family).

Colfax, Schuyler (skī'lər kōl'făks), 1823-85, Vice President of the United States (1869-73), b. New York City. He moved in boyhood to Indiana. First a Whig editor, he later helped to organize the Republican party in Indiana. He served in the U.S. House of Representatives (1855-69), being speaker from 1863 to 1869. In 1868 he was elected Vice President under Ulysses S. Grant. Colfax was involved in the CRÉDIT MOBILIER OF AMERICA scandal, which ended his political career. See biography by W. H. Smith (1952).

Colgate, William (kōl'gāt), 1783-1857, American manufacturer and philanthropist, b. England. Arriving as a youth in the United States in 1795, Colgate learned candlemaking in Baltimore and New York. In 1806 he set up a tallow factory in New York and later engaged in soapmaking. In 1847 he moved his factory to Jersey City and by 1850 began producing fancy soaps and toilet preparations. He helped organize several Bible societies, including the American Bible Society (1816), and contributed amply to the institution later called Colgate Univ.

Colgate University, at Hamilton, N.Y.; primarily for men; chartered 1819, opened 1820 as Hamilton Literary and Theological Institution, a Baptist seminary; renamed Madison Univ. 1846, assumed present name 1890. Colgate is principally a liberal arts college.

Col-hozeh (kŏl-hō'zĕ), Judahite of Nehemiah's time. Neh. 3.15; 11.5.

colic, intense pain caused by spasmodic contractions of one of the hollow organs, e.g., the stomach, intestine, gall bladder, ureter, or oviduct. The cause of colic is irritation, and the irritant may be a stone (as in the gall bladder or ureter), an irritant food or gas (in the stomach and intestines), appendicitis, or implantation of an embryo in an oviduct. Intestinal colic in infancy is sometimes attributed to gas formed by excessive swallowing of air or inadequate digestion of milk. Treatment of colic is relative to the cause.

Coligny, Gaspard de Châtillon, comte de (gäspär' də shätēyôN' kôNt də kōlēnyē'), 1519-72, French Protestant leader. A nephew of Anne, duc de MONTMORENCY, he came to the French court at an early age. He distinguished himself at Ceresole (1544) in the Italian Wars, was promoted colonel general of infantry, and in 1552 became admiral of France. He organized two unsuccessful colonies (1555, 1562) in the New World (see RIO DE JANEIRO; RIBAUT, JEAN). In 1557 he defended Saint-Quentin against the Spaniards, but he was taken prisoner and was not released until 1559. In the same year he made public profession of his conversion to Protestantism. He argued for the Protestant cause with CATHERINE DE' MEDICI at the time of the conspiracy of Amboise (1560; see AMBOISE, CONSPIRACY OF). With Louis I de CONDÉ he commanded the Huguenots (French Protestants) after the murder of Protestants at Vassy (1562) and also in the second of the Wars of Religion (1567-68). An unsuccessful attempt to capture Coligny and Condé at Noyers (1568) brought on the third war, in which Coligny became sole leader, nominally as adviser to the young Henry of Navarre (later King HENRY IV of France). Defeated at Moncontour, he was victor at Arnay-le-Duc (1570) and negotiated the Treaty of Saint-Germain (1570). Reconciled with Catherine and King CHARLES IX (1571), he became the king's favorite adviser. To weaken Catholic Spain he proposed that France aid the Low Countries, which were in rebellion against Spanish rule. Catherine, alarmed at the possibility of war with Spain, also feared that Coligny's increasing influence would weaken her own hold on the king. On Aug. 22, 1572, Coligny escaped the assassination ordered by Catherine and by Henri de GUISE; two days later, however, he was murdered in the massacre of Huguenots instigated by Catherine (see SAINT BARTHOLOMEW'S DAY, MASSACRE OF). See Sir Walter Besant, *Gaspard de Coligny* (1879); Eugène Bersier, *Coligny: The Earlier Life of the Great Huguenot* (1884).

Colima (kōlē'mä), state (1970 pop. 240,235), 2,010 sq mi (5,206 sq km), SW Mexico, on the Pacific Ocean. The capital is COLIMA; the port is MANZANILLO. The smallest in population and one of the smallest in area of the Mexican states, Colima is wedged between Jalisco, which nearly surrounds it, and Michoacán. It includes the islands of Revilla Gigedo off the coast. Most of the state lies within the cool highlands of the Sierra Madre Occidental. The smoking volcano, Colima (12,631 ft/3,850 m high), and the neighboring peak, Nevado de Colima (14,235 ft/4,339 m high), are just across the border in Jalisco. Cotton, sugarcane, and rice grow on tropical plains along Colima's coast, and some of Mexico's finest coffee is cultivated on the mountain slopes. Livestock raising is an important occupation. Iron, copper, and some gold are mined in Colima. The state's economic development has been hindered by inadequate communications. Once part of the ancient Aztec kingdom of Colima, the region was conquered by the Spanish in the 16th cent. Wars between conservative and liberal forces during the 19th cent. brought much fighting to the state.

Colima, city (1970 pop. 64,851), capital of Colima state, SW Mexico. It is a marketing and processing center for the surrounding agricultural region. The city was founded in 1523 by the Spanish explorer Gonzalo de Sandoval.

Colin, Alexander: see COLINS, ALEXANDER.

Colines, Simon de (sēmôN' də kôlēn'), d. 1546, Parisian printer. He was associated with the elder Henri ESTIENNE and continued his work. Colines used elegant roman and italic types and a Greek type, with accents, that was superior to its predecessors. He is believed to have designed some of his types; some were designed by Geofroy TORY. His books, often small in format, are superbly crafted.

Colins, Colin, or **Colyn, Alexander** (älĕksäN'drə kôlăN'), c.1527-1612, Flemish sculptor. He brought European court mannerism to Germany, where he directed the sculpture on the Ottheinrichsbau (1562) in Heidelberg. He designed the sculpture for the tomb of Ferdinand II and executed most of the reliefs in marble on the tomb of Maximilian I, both at Innsbruck.

Coliseum: see COLOSSEUM.

collage (kəläzh', kō-) [Fr.,=pasting], technique in art consisting of cutting and pasting natural or manufactured materials to a painted or unpainted surface—hence, a work of art in this medium. The art of collage was initiated in 1912 when Picasso pasted a section of commercially printed oilcloth to his cubist painting, *Still Life with Chair Caning* (Mus. of Modern Art, New York City). Collage elements appear in works by Gris, Braque, Malevich, Dove, and the futurist artists. A basic means of Dada and surrealist art, it was used by Arp, Schwitters, and Ernst. Collage is related to the newer art of assemblage, in which the traditional painted canvas has been abandoned in favor of the assembling of bits of material, which are sometimes additionally painted or carved. See studies by Harriet Janis and Rudi Blesh (rev. ed. 1967), Herta Wescher (1968, tr. 1971), and Norman Laliberté (1972).

collagen (kŏl'əjən), any of a group of proteins found in skin, ligaments, tendons, bone and cartilage, and other CONNECTIVE TISSUE. Collagen is composed of groups of white inelastic fibers with great tensile strength. These fibers are made up of fine fibrils, which are in turn composed of even finer filaments, visible through the electron microscope. Collagen protein contains an unusually high percentage of the amino acids PROLINE and hydroxyproline. X-ray diffraction studies provide evidence that the protein is a coiled chain with periodic, i.e., repeating, arrangement of its amino acids. Cartilage is composed of fibrous collagen in an amorphous gel. The organic (nonmineral) content of bone is made up largely of collagen fibers with calcium salt crystals lying adjacent to each segment of the fiber; the fibers and salt crystals combined form a structure with compressional and tensile strength comparable to that of reinforced concrete. A group of diseases, often termed collagen, or connective tissue, diseases, involve a variety of alterations in the connective tissue fibers; rheumatoid arthritis, rheumatic fever, lupus, and scleroderma are included in this group. Some of these diseases may involve an autoimmune response, in which the immune mechanism injures or destroys the individual's own tissues (see IMMUNITY). Collagen dissolved in boiling water becomes denatured to form GELATIN.

collagen disease: see AUTOIMMUNE DISEASE; COLLAGEN.

collar, decorative strip on the neckline of a garment; modified necklace. Metal circlets, usually twisted, known as torques date from the Bronze Age and are worn by many primitive peoples. The Egyptians fashioned beaded yokes to wear as collars. In the 14th cent. neck chains called livery collars were worn as badges of alliance or fealty; neck chains were also worn as insignia of European orders of knighthood. The medieval gorget, or chin band, circled the neck and enveloped the throat; the habit of conservative orders of nuns retains this feature. Small ruffles began to appear at the neck and wrists c.1530. The ruff, a circular fluted collar of starched linen, made its first appearance in Spain c.1540. It later became a heart- or fan-shaped winglike extension that covered the back and shoulders and rose above the coiffure; it was made of fine linen or lace with matching cuffs and was often embroidered. The standing ruff gave way (c.1635) to broad, falling collars of lace and later of linen. In the late 17th cent. neckcloths and cravats led the way to the stiff wing collar of the 1890s, to the clerical collar, and to the present-day fashion in ascots and neckties for men. Women's collars have varied widely from softly draped fichus and wide berthas to the high, tight collars of the 1890s. Modern collars are generally formed as inseparable parts of dresses and shirts.

collards: see KALE.

collateral, something of value given or pledged as security for payment of a loan. Collateral consists usually of financial instruments, such as stocks, bonds, and negotiable paper, rather than physical goods, although the latter may also be accepted as such. In case of default, the creditor may sell the collateral and apply the money thus acquired to payment of the debt, charging the debtor with any deficiency or crediting him with any surplus. The borrower may usually substitute other collateral for that held by the lender if it is acceptable to the latter. Such a privilege is particularly useful to borrowers who buy and sell securities. Merchandise collateral—such as negotiable warehouse receipts, bills of lading, and trust receipts—is also used, as is personal collateral, including deeds, mortgages, leases, and other rights in real estate. Other collateral may include bills of sale of movable goods, such as crops, machinery, furniture, and livestock, and savings-bank passbooks.

collect (kŏl'ĕkt) [Late Lat.,=meeting], in Western liturgies, short prayer proper to an occasion, often asking a particular favor. In the Roman Catholic Church the collect is said, typically, at Mass just before the epistle and at vespers. It occurs correspondingly in the Anglican and Lutheran liturgies. Many collects are very ancient, especially those of the Sundays and major feasts. Their language is terse.

collective bargaining, in labor relations, procedure whereby an employer or employers agree to discuss the conditions of work by bargaining with representatives of the employees, usually a labor union. Its purpose may be either a discussion of the terms and conditions of employment (wages, work hours, job safety, or job security) or a consideration of the collective relations between both sides (the right to organize workers, recognition of a union, or a guarantee of no reprisals against the workers if a strike has occurred). The merits of collective bargaining have been argued by both opponents and proponents of the process; the former maintain that it deprives the worker of his individual liberty to dispose of his service, while the latter point out that without the union's protection the worker is subject to the dictation of the employer. As an essential process in labor relations, collective bargaining was first developed in Great Britain in the 19th cent. It has since become an accepted practice in most Western countries with a high level of industrialization. See Guy Farmer, *Collective Bargaining in Transition* (2 vol., 1967); M. S. Rukeyser, *Collective Bargaining* (1968); Russell A. Smith, *Collective Bargaining and Labor Arbitration* (1970); W. H. Hutt, *The Strike-Threat System* (1973).

collective farm, an agricultural producer's cooperative. No one definition fits all collective farms. They vary from nation to nation and also within nations. In the Soviet Union, Stalin in 1929 initiated widespread forced collectivization of agriculture. During that year agricultural land was ruthlessly confiscated, and small landowners were forced on pain of death or deportation to go into a kolkhoz [Rus.,= collective farm]. By Feb., 1930, one half of the peasant farms had been collectivized. Widespread resentment of collectivization brought about some modification of the system under the Collective Farm Charter (1935). A mixed system of private and socialized enterprise was put into effect, and members of the collectives were permitted some individual property, including a plot of land and a few farm animals. By 1938 collectivization in the Soviet Union was almost complete; there were 240,000 kolkhozy holding 99.3% of formerly private land under cultivation. Prices paid for the agricultural products of the kolkhozy were set by the state, which also decreed what was to be grown. Collectivization had been instituted by Stalin to modernize agriculture, to secure a reliable food supply, to free capital for industrial production, and to release labor for heavy industry. The program was partly successful, although agricultural production is a continuing problem in the Soviet Union. In 1950, to tighten control over the collectives, a program of amalgamating them into larger units was begun. By 1972 the number of kolkhozy had been reduced from 254,000 to 32,300. The size of collective farms roughly tripled, and in 1972 the average collective had approximately 7,500 acres (3,000 hectares) under cultivation. In 1958 new agricultural measures, designed to woo the farmer-worker, abolished the system of requisition and substituted direct state purchases at higher prices. In 1969 the Collective Farmers' Congress met for the first time in 34 years. It approved new collective farm measures including the increase of the size of private plots, guaranteed income and a unified system of social insurance. In the '70s collective farmers were insured profits on various agricultural commodities as incentive for increased farm production. In the early 1970s, about half of the cultivated land in the U.S.S.R was in collective farms; most of the rest was held by state farms. The commune of Communist China is similar to the collective farm in the Soviet Union. It is more strictly organized, embracing a wider range of activities, putting greater emphasis on collective living, and including nonagricultural workers. Collectivization of agriculture in Communist China began in 1955 and met little resistance. By 1956, 96% of all the households engaged in agriculture had been included in cooperatives. The system of cooperatives failed to free the labor and capital needed for industrial expansion, and in 1958 the commune system was established. Twenty to thirty cooperatives comprising over 20,000 members and 40 to 100 villages were merged into each commune. The land and equipment of the former cooperatives and any property and cash that the peasants had been permitted to withhold from the 1955 collectivization became the property of the commune. An independent economic and administrative unit controlled the labor force and all means of production within each commune and provided central management of industry, commerce, education, agriculture, and military affairs. The workers performed both industrial and agricultural tasks and supported a complete military unit. They lived in communal buildings and took their meals as a community. They used communal nurseries, bathing facilities, barbershops, and similar service facilities. Wages and perquisites were controlled by the state, and all products were marketed through state agencies. By Jan. 1, 1959, 99% of all Chinese farm workers were members of a commune. The larger collective units, however, turned out to be less efficient in terms of management. This inefficiency, coupled with natural disasters and the effects of statistical misstatements made by the government, led in the early '60s to deemphasis in China on collective farming. Communes were decentralized, and in some instances land was broken up into private farms placing an emphasis on private incentive. The collective farms in Israel are of three kinds: the moshav ovdim, a worker's settlement; the kibbutz, a commune; the moshav shitufi, a modified collective. In all, the land, held in the name of the Jewish people by the Jewish National Fund, is rented on long-term lease at nominal fees. In the moshav ovdim each family works its own plot and retains any income from it. To hire labor is forbidden. Produce is marketed collectively, and consumer goods are bought collectively. In the kibbutz, best known of the collectives and most important economically, all property except specified personal possessions is collectively owned, planning and work are collective, and collective living is the rule. Work crews are headed by elected foremen. Work is exacted on the basis of ability, and goods distributed according to need. A biweekly town meeting is the final authority of the kibbutz. Elected officials implement the policy of the kibbutz and administer economic and social affairs. The 300-odd kibbutzim of Israel have combined in a number of federations expressive especially of ideological belief. Although only about 5% of Israel's population hold membership in the kibbutzim, they wield considerable political influence. The moshav shitufi, a late development in collectives in Israel, holds property communally, and its members work collectively. Community living is not required of members. Communal farming efforts have not proved markedly popular in North America, although numerous attempts have been and continue to be undertaken (see COMMUNE; COMMUNISTIC SETTLEMENTS). A noted exception is the agricultural-based colonies of HUTTERITES, who, as a result of persecution in central Europe, emigrated to South Dakota in 1874. They have increased in population and economic prominence to include some 20,000 members, living in over 200 separate colonies in the Dakotas, Montana, Minnesota, Washington, and the Canadian provinces of Alberta, Manitoba, and Saskatchewan. See Geoffrey Hudson et al., *The Chinese Commune* (1960); Eilyahu Kanovsky, *The Economy of the Israeli Kibbutz* (1966); R. C. Stuart, *The Collective Farm in Soviet Agriculture* (1972).

Collège de France (kôlĕzh' də fräNs), institution of higher learning founded in Paris, France, in 1529 by FRANCIS I at the instigation of Guillaume BUDÉ. It was founded to encourage humanistic studies and has always been independent of any university and free from supervision. Its lectures are open to the public without matriculation or fee. It gives no examinations and grants no certificates or degrees. Now its range of studies encompasses numerous humanistic and scientific fields. Its faculty includes many distinguished scholars.

College of Arms: see HERALD'S COLLEGE.

College of Physicians and Surgeons: see COLUMBIA UNIV.

College of the City of New York: see CITY COLLEGE; NEW YORK, CITY UNIV. OF.

College Park. 1 City (1970 pop. 18,203), Clayton and Fulton counties, NW Ga., a residential suburb of Atlanta; inc. 1891. Georgia Military Academy (1900) is there. **2** City (1970 pop. 26,156), Prince Georges co., W central Md., a residential suburb of Washington, D.C.; settled 1745, inc. 1945. It is the seat of the Univ. of Maryland, and its economy is centered on the university, research institutions, and electronics plants.

colleges and universities, institutions of higher education. Universities differ from colleges in that they are larger, have wider curricula, are involved in research activities, and grant graduate and professional as well as undergraduate degrees. Universities generally consist of groups of schools, faculties, or colleges. They arose in the 12th and 13th cent. as a means of providing further training in the professions of law, theology, and medicine, and as centers of study for the rediscovered works of Aristotle and the Arab scholars. Of the earliest universities, Salerno (9th cent.) and Montpellier (13th cent.) specialized in medicine; Bologna (1088) in law; and Paris (12th cent.) in theology. Students and faculty were originally organized in guildlike groups. The student groups, known as "nations" and comprising students from particular localities, gradually diminished in power, however, as the faculty, by virture of its control over teaching and graduation, became more powerful. In the Middle Ages, universities usually originated through royal or ecclesiastical initiative or through migrations of students from other universities. The migrations were sometimes influenced by political events. Oxford Univ., for example, was founded (12th cent.) by English students from the Univ. of Paris who were forced to leave that institution as a result of conflicts between England and France; similarly, the university at Leipzig was founded (15th cent.) by German scholars who were driven out of Prague by John Huss's Czech national movement. The medieval universities often had many thousands of students and played an important role in public affairs. Among the famous institutions founded were Salamanca (c.1230), Prague (1348), Vienna (1365), Uppsala (1477), Leiden (1575), and Moscow (1755). The oldest universities in the New World, both founded in 1551, are Mexico Univ. and San Marcos of Lima. In the 19th cent. many governments reorganized and nationalized universities, as in Italy after unification (1870), in Spain (1876), and in France, where 17 autonomous regional universities were established after 1876. By 1900 many universities were secularized in administration and curriculum, and religious tests had been largely eliminated (in England by act of Parliament in 1871). Women have generally been admitted to universities since about 1870 (see COEDUCATION). In the United States, modern universities developed during the late 19th cent. from the expansion of private colleges and the establishment of state tax-supported universities, largely as a result of the Morrill Act (1862), by which public lands were granted to the states for the formation and support of state agricultural and mechanical schools (see LAND-GRANT COLLEGES AND UNIVERSITIES). Another important influence at that time was the founding of institutions (e.g., JOHNS HOPKINS UNIV.) devoted to graduate study and research. They were modeled on the German universities, with their separate graduate and professional schools each devoted to a particular area of study. In the 20th cent. universities have played an increasingly important role in scientific and technical research, largely as a result of social and governmental demands for these services. The nationalization and bureaucratization of research functions has been especially marked in the United States, where various government agencies dispense large amounts of money to both public and private universities for research purposes. The Federal government also provides direct aid to various categories of students, especially veterans. Since World War II there has been worldwide proliferation of new universities, expansion of old ones, and merging of small institutions into larger university systems. Educational reforms in Japan, for example, have decreed that there be at least one national university in each of 46 sections of the country, so that there are now more than 70 such institutions. The 1960s saw the establishment of seven new universities in Great Britain, while the period from 1948 to 1970 saw the State Univ. of New York grow from a small group of teacher training colleges into a multicampus system with more than 135,000 students.

Colleges. Like universities, colleges first appeared in the Middle Ages; the earliest were founded in 12th-century Paris. Originally the college served as an endowed residence hall for university scholars, but later it absorbed much of the university's activity. It was in England, at Oxford and Cambridge, that the college became the principal center of learning, with the university serving mainly to examine candidates and confer degrees. The Industrial Revolution brought a demand for scientific and technical education, and separate technical colleges (e.g., Yorkshire Science College in Leeds) were founded. Moreover, extension lectures, sponsored by the universities, created a demand for educational centers in remote areas. Degrees, however, continued to be conferred by the universities with which the colleges were affiliated. It was in America that the liberal arts college first appeared extensively as a separate institution. In the 17th and early 18th cent., numerous colleges were established in the colonies, primarily to train young men for the ministry. Notable were Harvard (1636; Puritan), William and Mary (1693; Anglican), Yale (1701; Congregationalist), Princeton (1746; New Lights Presbyterian), Columbia (1754; Anglican), Brown (1765; Baptist), and Rutgers (1766; Dutch Reformed). By 1810 many small colleges had been established in the United States. Later in the same century a number of women's colleges were founded. Notable early women's colleges were Mt. Holyoke (1837), Elmira (1853), Vassar (1861), Wellesley (1871), Smith (1871), and Bryn Mawr (1881). Another development of the 19th cent. was the growth of normal schools, which later became teachers colleges (see TEACHER TRAINING). Though the curricula and ideals of American colleges continued to be influenced by English schools, the American colleges, stimulated by the German university system and by the increasing demand for technical instruction, began to expand their facilities to include graduate and professional schools. By the 20th cent. many American colleges had become universities, and by the middle of the century universities were giving out twice as many bachelor's degrees as were the traditional liberal arts colleges. In an attempt to reassert the importance of the colleges, many of them have been empowered to grant graduate degrees, especially the master's degree. The COMMUNITY COLLEGE movement has been important in expanding opportunities for higher education. OPEN ENROLLMENT has made college training available to a larger segment of high-school graduates. Still another innovation has been the establishment of cluster colleges, a number of specialized institutions clustered on one campus in order to provide the personalized education that is characteristic of the small college without sacrificing the quality and diversity of the university. The University of California at Santa Cruz (est. 1965) has such a cluster-college system.

Bibliography. See Abraham Flexner, *Universities: American, English, and German* (1923, repr. 1968); Donald G. Tewksbury, *The Founding of American Colleges and Universities before the Civil War* (1932, repr. 1969); Hastings Rashdall, *Universities of Europe in the Middle Ages* (3 vol., 1936, repr. 1958); Edward Bradby, *The University Outside Europe* (1939, repr. 1970); Lynn Thorndike, *University Records and Life in the Middle Ages* (1944, repr. 1971); Mark Van Doren, *Liberal Education* (1959); Frederick Rudolph, *The American College and University* (1962); Nevitt Sanford, *The American College: A Psychological and Social Interpretation of Higher Education* (1962); Sidney S. Letter, ed., *New Prospects for the Small Liberal Arts College* (1968); Michael Beloff, *The Plateglass Universities* (1970); World Year Book of Education series, *Higher Education in a Changing World* (ed. by Brian Holmes and David G. Scanlon, 1971); Russel I. Thackrey, *The Future of the State University* (1971).

Colleges of the Seneca, The: see HOBART COLLEGE.

College Station, city (1970 pop. 17,676), Brazos co., E central Texas, in a livestock and cotton region; inc. 1938. Texas Agricultural and Mechanical Univ. is there.

Colleoni, Bartolomeo (bärtōlōmĕ'ō kōl-lāō'nē), 1400–1475, Italian soldier of fortune. A CONDOTTIERE, Colleoni fought in the wars between Venice and Milan, often changing sides and distrusted by both. In 1454 he deserted Milan for the last time and became generalissimo of Venice, a post he held until his death. The beautiful Colleoni Chapel is in his native city, Bergamo, and the celebrated equestrian statue of him by VERROCCHIO is in Venice.

Collett, Camilla (Wergeland) (kämē'lä vĕr'gəlän kôl'ĕt), 1813–95, Norwegian novelist; sister of Henrik Wergeland. Her feminist novels include *The Governor's Daughters* (1854–55), the first Norwegian psychological novel, and the charming *In the Long Nights* (1862). She devoted her life and work to the emotional and social emancipation of women.

collie, breed of large, agile WORKING DOG developed in Scotland during the 17th and 18th cent. It stands from 22 to 26 in. (55.9–66 cm) high at the shoulder and weighs from 50 to 75 lb (22.7–34 kg). There are two varieties of collie; it is thought that originally the rough-coated or long-haired type herded sheep in the torturous climate of the northern Scottish hills while the less weatherproof smooth-coated collie drove cattle to market. Both varieties may be sable and white, blue merle, tricolored (black, tan, and white), or white. Although no thoroughly documented explanation of the origin of the collie's name is ever likely to be set forth, the following is probably the most reasonable. A type of sheep once found in the Scottish Highlands had black markings, either on the face or legs, and was called the "Colley" sheep. The dog that was bred and trained to herd these sheep was known as the "Colley dog," and, later, as the "collie." Today it is one of the most popular farm dogs and pets in the United States. See DOG.

Collier, Jeremy, 1650–1726, English clergyman. Collier was imprisoned as one of the NONJURORS, who refused to pledge allegiance to William III and Mary II. He later was outlawed (1696) for absolving on the scaffold two of those involved in the assassination plot against William. Collier's principal fame comes from his *Short View of the Immorality and Profaneness of the English Stage* (1698) and *Ecclesiastical History of Great Britain* (1708, 1714). In 1713 he was ordained a nonjuring bishop. See Anthony Rose, *The Jeremy Collier Stage Controversy* (1966).

Collier, John, 1884–1968, American social worker, anthropologist, and author, educated at Columbia and the Collège de France. After holding several positions in community organization and social work training, he became active in American Indian affairs in 1922. Collier was editor of the magazine *American Indian Life* from 1926 until 1933, when he was appointed commissioner of Indian Affairs, a position he held for 12 years. In addition to works in verse, he wrote *Indians of the Americas* (1947) and *On the Gleaming Way* (1962, orig. pub. 1949 as *Patterns and Ceremonials of the Indians of the Southwest).*

Collier, John Payne, 1789–1883, English critic, editor, and forger. The marginal notes and signatures supposedly discovered by him on original documents, especially those concerned with Shakespeare, were later exposed as having been forged by him while in the service of the duke of Devonshire. His authentic work included *A Bibliographical and Critical Account of the Rarest Books in the English Language* (1865) and the reprinting of early English tracts.

colligative properties, properties of a SOLUTION that depend on the number of solute particles present but not on the chemical properties of the solute. Colligative properties of a solution include freezing point (see FREEZING), BOILING POINT, osmotic pressure (see OSMOSIS), and solvent VAPOR PRESSURE. By measuring these properties and comparing them with the corresponding properties of the pure solvent, it is possible to determine the number of particles of solute present in the solution. If the mass of solute present is also known, the number-average MOLECULAR WEIGHT can be calculated by dividing the mass of solute by the number of particles present to obtain the average mass per particle.

Collingdale, borough (1970 pop. 10,605), Delaware co., SE Pa., a suburb of Philadelphia; inc. 1891.

Collingswood, borough (1970 pop. 17,422), Camden co., SW N.J.; settled 1682 by Quakers, inc. 1888. It has some light industry.

Collingwood, Cuthbert Collingwood, Baron: see TRAFALGAR, BATTLE OF.

Collingwood, Robin George, 1889–1943, English philosopher and historian. From 1908 he was associated with Oxford as student, fellow, lecturer in history, and professor of philosophy. Collingwood believed that philosophy should be rooted in history rather than in formal science, and he attempted to correlate creative endeavor with historical experience rather than to sensation. He was also significant as a historian. In *Roman Britain* (1936) and in some 150 monographs he brilliantly reconstructed that ancient era from his study of coins and inscriptions. For his philosophical thought, see *Speculum Mentis* (1924), *An Essay on Philosophic Method* (1933), *Principles of Art* (1938), and *The Idea of History* (1946). See Alan Donagan, *The Later Philosophy of R. G. Collingwood* (1962); Lionel Rubinoff, *Collingwood and the Reform of Metaphysics* (1970).

Collingwood, city (1971 pop. 20,906), Victoria, SE Australia, a suburb of Melbourne. It has woolen and hosiery mills and footwear industries.

Collingwood, town (1971 pop. 9,775), S Ont., Canada at the south end of Georgian Bay, an arm of Lake Huron. Collingwood has one of the largest shipbuilding plants and one of the largest dry docks on the Great Lakes.

Collins, Anthony, 1676–1729, English theologian; a friend of John Locke. He set forth the position of the deists and defended the cause of rational theology. His *Discourse of Free Thinking* (1713) was answered by many clergymen and was satirized by Jonathan Swift. His *Philosophical Inquiry Concerning Human Liberty* (1715) is an excellent presentation of the determinist position, the theory that all events are determined by prior causes. See study by James O'Higgins (1970).

Collins, Edward Trowbridge, 1887-1951, American baseball player, b. Millerton, N.Y., grad. Columbia, 1907. One of the game's great second basemen, he was active in the American League for 25 years, playing with the Philadelphia Athletics (1906-14, 1927-30) and the Chicago White Sox (1915-26). During his major league career he stole 743 bases and made 3,313 base hits for a lifetime batting average of .333. Collins was elected to the National Baseball Hall of Fame in 1939.

Collins, Michael, 1890-1922, Irish revolutionary leader. He spent the years from 1907 to 1916 in England, during which period he joined the Fenian movement. He took part in the Easter Rebellion in Dublin in 1916 and was imprisoned for the rest of the year. One of the SINN FEIN members who set up the DÁIL EIREANN in 1919, he led the Irish Republican Army in the guerrilla campaign against British rule that eventually forced the British government to sue for a truce. Although a convinced republican, Collins, with Arthur GRIFFITH, negotiated and signed the treaty (1921) that set up the Irish Free State (see IRELAND) because he felt it the best settlement with England possible at that time. He was finance minister in Griffith's government for a brief time before being assassinated by extremist republicans. See biographies by Frank O'Connor (1937), Rex Taylor (1958), Eoin Neeson (1968), Michael O'Donovan (rev. ed. 1969), and Margery Forester (1971).

Collins, Wilkie (William Wilkie Collins), 1824-89, English novelist. Although trained as a lawyer, he spent most of his life writing, producing some 30 novels. He is best known for two mystery stories, *The Woman in White* (1860) and *The Moonstone* (1868), which are considered the first full-length detective novels in English and among the best of their genre. He was a friend of Dickens, in whose periodical *Household Words* many of Collins's novels first appeared. See biographies by M. P. Davis (1956) and W. H. Marshall (1970).

Collins, William, 1721-59, English poet. He was one of the great lyricists of the 18th cent. While he was still at Oxford he published *Persian Ecologues* (1742), which was written when he was 17. Unstable and weak-willed, he never chose a profession and was constantly in debt until he inherited money from an uncle. He won no popularity during his lifetime, and his career was curtailed by insanity. A precursor of the 19th-century romantics, Collins wrote exquisite verse that emphasized mood and imagination. Among his best odes are "To Evening," "To Simplicity," and the one beginning "How sleep the brave." See biographies by P. L. Carver (1967) and H. W. Garrod (1928, repr. 1973); study by O. Doughty (1964).

Collinsville, city (1970 pop. 17,773), Madison co., SW Ill.; settled 1817, inc. 1872. It is a former coal-mining center where food products and women's garments are now manufactured. Nearby are the Cahokia Mounds State Park, with its Indian earthworks, and a campus of Southern Illinois Univ.

Collodi, Carlo (kär'lō kōl-lô'dē), pseud. of **Carlo Lorenzini** (lōräntsē'nē), 1826-90, Italian author. A prolific journalist, he also wrote didactic tales for children, the most famous of which is *Pinocchio: the Story of a Puppet.* First written (1880) for the *Giornale dei bambini*, the story appeared in book form in 1883 and soon became one of the most widely read juvenile classics. Collodi, however, received little for it. The first English translation (1892) was followed by others in innumerable editions; perhaps the best is that by M. M. Sweet (1927). An animated film version (1940) of *Pinocchio* was made by Walt Disney.

collodion (kəlō'dēən), solution of PYROXYLIN in a mixture of alcohol and ether. Upon exposure to air, the solvents evaporate, leaving a thin, colorless, elastic film on any surface upon which the collodion has been spread. Collodion is the forerunner of the lacquer paints that are now widely used in the automobile industry.

colloid (kŏl'oid) [Gr.,=gluelike], a mixture in which one substance is divided into minute particles (called colloidal particles) and dispersed throughout a second substance. The mixture is also called a colloidal system, colloidal solution, or colloidal dispersion. Familiar colloids include fog, smoke, homogenized milk, and ruby-colored glass. Colloidal particles are larger than molecules but too small to be observed directly with a microscope; however, their shape and size can be determined by electron microscopy. In a true solution the particles of dissolved substance are of molecular size and are thus smaller than colloidal particles; in a coarse mixture (e.g., a suspension) the particles are much larger than colloidal particles. Although there are no precise boundaries of size between the particles in mixtures, colloids, or solutions, colloidal particles are usually on the order of 10^{-7} to 10^{-5} cm in size. The presence of colloidal particles has little effect on the COLLIGATIVE PROPERTIES of a solution. One way of classifying colloids is to group them according to the phase (solid, liquid, or gas) of the dispersed substance and of the medium of dispersion. A gas may be dispersed in a liquid to form a foam (e.g., shaving lather or beaten egg white) or in a solid to form a solid foam (e.g., styrofoam or marshmallow). A liquid may be dispersed in a gas to form an aerosol (e.g., fog or aerosol spray), in another liquid to form an emulsion (e.g., homogenized milk or mayonnaise), or in a solid to form a gel (e.g., jellies or cheese). A solid may be dispersed in a gas to form a solid aerosol (e.g., dust or smoke in air), in a liquid to form a sol (e.g., ink or muddy water), or in a solid to form a solid sol (e.g., certain alloys). A further distinction is often made in the case of a dispersed solid. In some cases (e.g., a dispersion of sulfur in water) the colloidal particles have the same internal structure as a bulk of the solid. In other cases (e.g., a dispersion of soap in water) the particles are an aggregate of small molecules and do not correspond to any particular solid structure. In still other cases (e.g., a dispersion of a protein in water) the particles are actually very large single molecules. A different distinction, usually made when the dispersing medium is a liquid, is between lyophilic and lyophobic systems. The particles in a lyophilic system have a great affinity for the solvent, and are readily solvated (combined, chemically or physically, with the solvent) and dispersed, even at high concentrations. In a lyophobic system the particles resist solvation and dispersion in the solvent, and the concentration of particles is usually relatively low. The Scottish chemist Thomas Graham discovered (1860) that certain substances (e.g., glue, gelatin, or starch) could be separated from certain other substances (e.g., sugar or salt) by DIALYSIS. He gave the name *colloid* to substances that do not diffuse through a semipermeable membrane (e.g., parchment or cellophane) and the name *crystalloid* to those which do diffuse and which are therefore in true solution. Another property of colloid systems that distinguishes them from true solutions is that colloidal particles scatter light. If a beam of light, such as that from a flashlight, passes through a colloid, the light is reflected (scattered) by the colloidal particles and the path of the light can therefore be observed. When a beam of light passes through a true solution (e.g., salt in water) there is so little scattering of the light that the path of the light cannot be seen and the small amount of scattered light cannot be detected except by very sensitive instruments. The scattering of light by colloids, known as the Tyndall effect, was first explained by the British physicist John Tyndall. When an ultramicroscope (see MICROSCOPE) is used to examine a colloid, the colloidal particles appear as tiny points of light in constant motion; this motion, called BROWNIAN MOVEMENT, helps keep the particles in suspension. ABSORPTION is another characteristic of colloids, since the finely divided colloidal particles have a large surface area exposed. The particles of a colloid selectively absorb ions and acquire an electric charge. All of the particles of a given colloid take on the same charge (either positive or negative) and thus are repelled by one another. If an electric potential is applied to a colloid, the charged colloidal particles move toward the oppositely charged electrode; this migration is called electrophoresis. If the charge on the particles is neutralized, they may precipitate out of the suspension. A colloid may be precipitated by adding another colloid with oppositely charged particles; the particles are attracted to one another, coagulate, and precipitate out. Addition of soluble ions may precipitate a colloid; the ions in sea water precipitate the colloidal silt dispersed in river water, forming a delta. A method developed by F. G. Cottrell reduces air pollution by removing colloidal particles (e.g., smoke, dust, and fly ash) from exhaust gases with electric precipitators. Particles in a lyophobic system are readily coagulated and precipitated, and the system cannot easily be restored to its colloidal state. A lyophilic colloid does not readily precipitate and can usually be restored by the addition of solvent. Thixotropy is a property exhibited by certain gels. A thixotropic gel appears to be solid and maintains a shape of its own until it is subjected to a shearing (lateral) force or some other disturbance. It then acts as a sol and flows freely. Common thixotropic gels include oil well drilling mud, certain paints and printing inks, and certain clays. Quick clay, which is thixotropic, has caused landslides in parts of Scandinavia and Canada. There are two basic methods of forming a colloid: reduction of larger particles to colloidal size, and condensation of smaller particles (e.g., molecules) into colloidal particles. Some substances (e.g., gelatin or glue) are easily dispersed (in the proper solvent) to form a colloid; this spontaneous dispersion is called peptization. A metal can be dispersed by evaporating it in an electric arc; if the electrodes are immersed in water, colloidal particles of the metal form as the metal vapor cools. A solid (e.g., paint pigment) can be reduced to colloidal particles in a colloid mill, a mechanical device that uses a shearing force to break apart the larger particles. An emulsion is often prepared by homogenization, usually with the addition of an emulsifying agent. The above methods involve breaking down a larger substance into colloidal particles. Condensation of smaller particles to form a colloid usually involves chemical reactions—typically displacement, hydrolysis, or oxidation and reduction.

Collot d'Herbois, Jean Marie (zhäN märē' kōlō' dĕrbwä'), 1750-96, French revolutionary, originally an actor and playwright. At first he favored a constitutional monarchy; his *Almanach du Père Gérard* (1791) was criticized for its royalist tinge, although its patriotism won a competition sponsored by the Jacobins. He then grew more radical; elected to the Convention, he supported Robespierre, persecuted the Girondists, and suppressed the counterrevolutionary attempts at Lyons in a blood bath. Although he turned against Robespierre on 9 Thermidor (July 27, 1794), he fell in the Thermidorian reaction and was deported to French Guiana.

collotype (kŏl'ətīp"): see PRINTING.

collusion, conspiracy to defraud a person of his legal rights or to obtain some illegal objective by misusing the forms of law. In suits for divorce, collusion is a conspiracy between the husband and the wife, or one or both of these and a third party, to obtain a DIVORCE on manufactured testimony, usually on pretense of adultery. Such a conspiracy is a bar to divorce.

Collyer, Robert, 1823-1912, American Unitarian clergyman, b. England. By trade a blacksmith, Collyer became a Methodist preacher in 1849. He emigrated to the United States in 1850 and settled near Philadelphia, where for a time he combined his labors as a blacksmith with preaching. In 1859, Collyer became a Unitarian and founded the Unity Church in Chicago, where he served as pastor (1860-79). In 1879 he became minister of the Church of the Messiah, New York City. He was widely known as a lecturer. *Clear Grit* (1913) contains some of his lectures, addresses, and poems. Among his many other works are *The Life That Now Is* (1871) and *Father Taylor* (1906). See biography by J. H. Holmes (1917).

Colman, Norman Jay, 1827-1911, American agriculturist and lawyer, b. near Richfield Springs, N.Y., grad. Univ. of Louisville law school, 1851. He promoted the passage of the Hatch Act (1887), which authorized the creation of agricultural experiment stations. As commissioner of agriculture (1885-89) he was influential in causing the Dept. of Agriculture to be made an executive department (1889) represented in the cabinet; he was the first Secretary of Agriculture.

Colman, Ronald, 1891-1958, British stage and film actor. Dignified in demeanor and voice, Colman created an image of kindness, humor, erudition, and romantic appeal. His films include the silent *Stella Dallas* (1927), and the sound films *Raffles* (1931), *Arrowsmith* (1932), *A Tale of Two Cities* (1936), *Lost Horizon* (1937), *The Prisoner of Zenda* (1937), *Random Harvest* (1943), and *Champagne for Caesar* (1949). Colman and his wife, Benita Hume, starred in the television series of the 1950s, *The Halls of Ivy.*

Colmar or **Kolmar** (both: kôlmär'), city (1968 pop. 59,550), capital of Haut-Rhin dept., E France, in Alsace, on the Lauch River and the Logelbach Canal. Colmar has textile and other industries. It became a free city of the Holy Roman Empire in 1226, and Louis XIV made it the capital of Alsace in 1673. The old section of Colmar retains its medieval architecture. St. Martin's Church (13th and 15th cent.) contains the *Madonna of the Rose Arbor* by Martin Schongauer, who lived in Colmar all his life. The Unterlinden Museum, in a convent dating from the

13th-14th cent., is outstanding; it contains the Isenheim altarpiece by Mathias Grünewald and numerous masterpieces of the Rhenish school of the 15th cent.

Cologne (kəlōn'), Ger. *Köln,* city (1970 pop. 848,352), North Rhine-Westphalia, W West Germany, on the Rhine River. It is a commercial and industrial center, a rail and road junction, and a river port. Its manufactures include iron, steel, heavy machinery, chemicals, textiles, printed materials, and eau de cologne. A Roman garrison in the 1st cent. B.C., Cologne was made a Roman colony in A.D. 50 by Emperor Claudius, who named it *Colonia Claudia Ara Agrippinensis* for his wife, Agrippina. The city passed under Frankish control in the 5th cent. The episcopal see, established there in the 4th cent., was made an archdiocese under Charlemagne. Its archbishops, who later ruled a strip of land on the west bank of the Rhine as princes of the Holy Roman Empire, acquired great power and ranked third among the ELECTORS. The archbishops' constant feuds with the lay citizenry resulted in the transfer (mid-13th cent.) of their residence to nearby Brühl, then to Bonn. Cologne was self-governing after 1288, became a free imperial city in 1475, and, as a member of the Hanseatic League, flourished as a commercial center until the 16th cent. Its decline was hastened by the expulsion of the Jews (15th cent.) and the restrictions imposed on Protestants (16th cent.). Cologne was seized by the French in 1794, and the archbishopric was officially secularized in 1801. The city passed to Prussia in 1815, and in 1821 the archdiocese was reorganized. In the 19th cent. Cologne prospered again as an industrial center and as the main transit port and depot of NW Germany. The industrial town of Deutz (noted for the manufacture of motors), on the east bank of the Rhine, was united with Old Cologne, on the west bank. Old Cologne, with its numerous historic buildings, was severely damaged by aerial bombardment in World War II. The famous Gothic cathedral, the largest in northern Europe, was closed from the end of the war until 1956. It contains the relics of the WISE MEN OF THE EAST and the paintings of Stephen Lochner. The cathedral was begun in 1248 on the site of an older church, but the nave and the two spires (each spire 515 ft/157 m high) were built according to the original plans between 1842 and 1880. Other historic buildings in the city include the Romanesque churches of St. Maria im Kapitol, of St. Gereon, of the Holy Apostles, and of St. Andreas (where Albertus Magnus, the 13th-century scholastic, is buried); the Gothic and Renaissance city hall; and the *Gürzenich* (1441–44), formerly a meeting place of the city's merchants and now a concert hall. Impressive modern structures include the opera house and the radio and television broadcasting stations. As the center of West German Catholicism, Cologne has long been famous for its impressive religious processions and for its exuberant Mardi Gras celebrations. The city figures prominently in German romantic literature. Cologne is the seat of a university (founded 1388; discontinued 1798; reestablished 1919) and numerous museums, including those of painting, ethnology, and municipal history.

Colomb or **Colombe, Michel** (both: mĕshĕl' kôlôN'), c.1430–1512, French sculptor, one of the masters of the French Renaissance. Few of his works survive. His name is associated with the execution of the tomb of Francis II, duke of Brittany (completed 1507; Nantes). A relief by Colomb, *St. George and the Dragon* (Louvre), shows a high degree of imagination and skill.

Colomb-Béchar: see BÉCHAR, Algeria.

Colombes (kôlôNb'), city (1968 pop. 80,616), Hauts-de-Seine dept., N central France, on the Seine River. An industrial suburb of Paris, Colombes has fuel refineries, foundries, and publishing houses. A 16th-century church and a sports arena are in the city.

Colombey-les-deux-Églises (kôlôNbā'-lā-döz-āglēz'), town (pop. 391), Haute-Marne dept., NE France. The home and grave site of Charles de Gaulle are there.

Colombia (kəlŭm'bēə, Span. kōlōm'byä), republic (1973 est. pop. 22,750,000), 439,735 sq mi (1,138,914 sq km), NW South America. The capital is BOGOTÁ. The only South American country with both a Caribbean and a Pacific coastline, Colombia is bounded on the NW by Panama, on the NE by Venezuela, on the S by Ecuador and Peru, and on the SE by Brazil. Colombia has both torrid jungles and majestic, snow-capped mountains. By far the most prominent physical features are the three great Andean chains that fan north from Ecuador. The Andean interior is the heart of the country, where in pre-Columbian days the highly advanced CHIBCHA lived. It has the largest concentration of population

and is the area of large-scale cultivation of coffee, Colombia's major crop. Of the three principal Andean ranges, the Western Cordillera is of the least economic importance. One of Colombia's major cities, CALI, lies just east of the range, in the upper Cauca valley. The Central Cordillera has a towering chain of volcanoes (e.g., Tolima) and is the divide between the valleys of the Magdalena and the Cauca rivers. It was until the 19th cent. a backward region, but with improved transportation, the introduction of coffee culture, the exploitation of high-grade coal reserves, and an enormous increase of the white population, its cities of MEDELLÍN and MANIZALES have become the economic and industrial core of the republic. A third major city in the Central Cordillera is ARMENIA. The Eastern Cordillera is the longest chain. Its western slopes yield coffee, and in its intermontane basins grains and cattle are raised. The area is rich in iron, coal, and emeralds. Among the leading cities of the highland basins are TUNJA, BUCARAMANGA, and CÚCUTA, in addition to Bogotá. To the E of the Andes lies more than half of Colombia's territory, a vast undeveloped lowland. The plains are crossed by navigable rivers, tributaries of the Orinoco and Amazon systems. The northern section consists of savannas (the LLANOS), which are devoted to a large extent to cattle and sheep grazing. VILLAVICENCIO, at the region's western end, is its major urban center. The dense jungles of the extreme southeast are of negligible economic importance. LETICIA is the country's southernmost town, and its only port on the Amazon River. A fourth mountain chain, the Cordillera del Chocó, runs parallel to the Pacific N of BUENAVENTURA. The range's slopes yield dyewoods and hardwoods, rubber, tagua nuts (vegetable ivory) and other forest products, and gold and platinum. On the Pacific are the ports of Buenaventura and TUMACO, terminus of a pipeline from the oil-rich area of Putumayo across the mountains. Colombia's chief ocean ports, however, lie on the Caribbean coast to the north: SANTA MARTA, CARTAGENA, and BARRANQUILLA. At Mamonal, adjacent to Cartagena, is the terminus of the pipeline from the Barrancabermeja oil fields. In the north, separating the La Guajira peninsula from the rest of the country, is the magnificent Sierra Nevada de Santa Marta, which contains Colombia's highest peak, Pico Cristóbal (18,947 ft/5,775 m). The difficult terrain in Colombia limits the availability of road and rail transportation and makes air and water travel especially important. Agriculture is the chief source of income in Colombia. An extremely wide variety of crops is grown, depending on altitude, but coffee is by far the major crop and its price on the world market has affected Colombia's economic health. Among the commercial crops, coffee is grown between elevations of 3,000 and 6,000 ft (914 and 1,829 m); bananas, cotton, sugarcane, oil palm, and tobacco are grown at lower elevations. Between 6,000 and 10,000 ft (1,829 and 3,048 m) potatoes, beans, grains, and temperate zone fruit and vegetables are grown. Colombia is rich in minerals, including petroleum, iron, coal, gold, silver, platinum, and emeralds. The saltworks at Zipaquira, near Bogotá, are world famous. The manufacturing sector of the economy has expanded greatly in recent decades, although it is heavily dependent on imported materials. Beverages and processed foods, textiles, metal products, and chemicals are the chief manufactures. Coffee is the main export; others include petroleum and related products, cotton, bananas, and sugar. Various manufactured goods lead the imports. The United States and West Germany are the chief trade partners. In 1969, Colombia joined the Andean Group, an economic organization of South American nations. About two thirds of Colombia's population are mestizos; less than one fifth are of pure European descent. Indians live in the major cities and the remote areas. The small Negro population is concentrated along the coasts and in the Magdalena and Cauca valleys. Spanish is the official language. The population is overwhelmingly Roman Catholic. There are universities in all the major cities. Colombia is governed under an 1886 constitution. The president serves a four-year term. The legislature, subservient to the president, consists of a senate and chamber of deputies. The members are apportioned among the departments (states) and popularly elected for four-year terms. The supreme court is chosen by the president and the legislature. The Conservative and Liberal parties, formed in the 1800s, dominate political life. To insure stability, the two formed the National Front Coalition in 1957 and agreed to divide the major offices between them and alternate in the presidency. The coalition, which ended in late 1973, was challenged in the 1960s by the Popular National Alliance, formed by the former dictator Rojas Pinilla. After the Spanish conquest the area of present-day Colombia formed the nucleus of New Granada (for colonial history, see NEW GRANADA). The struggle for independence was, as in all Spanish-American possessions, precipitated by the Napoleonic invasion of Spain. The revolution was, however, foreshadowed by the rising of the COMUNEROS. Prominent among the first revolutionary leaders was Antonio NARIÑO, who took part in the uprising at Bogotá on July 20, 1810. The revolution was to last nine years before the victory of Simón BOLÍVAR at BOYACÁ (1819) secured the independence of Greater Colombia (Span., *Gran Colombia*). The new state Bolívar created included what is now Venezuela, Panama, and (after 1822) Ecuador, as well as Colombia. Cúcuta was chosen as capital. While Bolívar, who had been named president, headed campaigns in Ecuador and Peru, the vice president, Francisco de Paula SANTANDER, administered the new nation. Political factions soon crystallized. Santander advocated a union of federal sovereign states, while Bolívar championed a centralized republic. Although Bolívar's authority prevailed by and large in the constitutional assembly (1828), Greater Colombia soon fell apart. In 1830, Venezuela and Ecuador became separate nations. The remaining territory emerged as the republic of New Granada. Through the 19th cent. and into the 20th cent. political unrest and civil strife reappeared constantly. Strong parties developed along conservative and liberal lines; the conservatives favored centralism and participation by the church in government and education, and the liberals supported federalism, anti-clericalism, and some measure of social legislation and fiscal reforms. Civil war frequently erupted between the factions. During the 19th and early 20th cent. three statesmen stand out—Tomás Cipriano de MOSQUERA, Rafael NÚÑEZ, and Rafael REYES. While Mosquera was president, a treaty was concluded (1846) granting the United States transit rights across the Isthmus of Panama. A new constitution in 1858 created a confederation of nine states called Granadina. Three years later (1861) under Mosquera, the country's name was changed to the United States of New Granada and in 1863 to the United States of Colombia. The antifederalist revolution of 1885 led one year later, during the presidency of Núñez, to the formation of the republic of Colombia and enactment of a conservative constitution. In 1899, five years after Núñez's death, civil war of unprecedented violence broke out and raged for three years. As many as 100,000 people were killed before the Conservatives emerged victorious. Another humiliation occurred when, after the United States had acquired the right to complete the Panama Canal (although the agreement was later rejected by the Colombian congress), the republic of Panama declared and, aided by the United

States, achieved its independence from Colombia (1903). During the semidictatorial administration (1904–9) of Reyes, internal order was restored and the country's trade and productivity were vigorously expanded. Reyes, nevertheless, had to resign because of discontent over his handling of the Panama issue. Soon afterward Colombia recognized (1914) Panama's independence in exchange for rights in the Canal Zone and the payment of an indemnity from the United States. For the next four decades political life remained fairly peaceful, although there was economic and social unrest in the 1920s and 1930s. Colombia settled (1917) its boundary disputes with Ecuador, and in 1934 a border clash with Peru over the town of Leticia was settled by the League of Nations in Colombia's favor. Under the leadership of the liberals Olaya Herrera (1930–34), Alfonso López (1934–38), and Eduardo Santos (1938–42), wide-ranging reforms were enacted. Colombia participated in World War II on the Allied side. During the war years, internal divisions worsened. The Liberals split and in the 1946 elections presented two candidates, enabling the Conservatives to win. In 1948, while an Inter-American Conference was being held in Bogotá, the leftist Liberal leader Jorge Eliécer Gaitán, under whom the party had reunited, was assassinated, precipitating violent riots and acts of vandalism. The death of Gaitán exacerbated the enmity between social groups and plunged the country into a decade of civil strife, martial law, and violent rule that cost hundreds of thousands of lives. Political violence turned into sheer criminality (*la violencia*), particularly in rural areas. An archconservative dictator, Laureano Gómez, took power in 1950, when the Liberals put forward no candidate. In 1953, Gómez was ousted by a coup led by Gustavo ROJAS PINILLA, the head of the armed forces. Repressive measures continued, fiscal reforms failed, the country was plunged into debt, and Rojas Pinilla became implicated in scandalously corrupt schemes. A military junta, backed by liberals and conservatives alike, ousted Rojas Pinilla in 1957. The following year Alberto LLERAS CAMARGO became president, elected under the National Front coalition agreement. The National Front presidential candidate of 1970, Misael PASTRANA BORRERO, won very narrowly over Rojas Pinilla, who returned to politics as the champion of the underprivileged. Colombia's economy began to recover from the setbacks of the early 1970s as economic diversification and incentives to lure foreign capital into the country were initiated. However, a high inflation rate continued to impede economic growth. In 1974 the Liberal party candidate Alfonso López Michelsen won the first presidential election following the end of the National Front. See Gerardo Reichel-Dolmatoff, *Colombia* (1965); J. L. Payne, *Patterns of Conflict in Colombia* (1968); Orlando Fals-Borda, *Subversion and Social Change in Colombia* (rev. ed., tr. 1969); A. E. Havens and W. L. Flinn, *Internal Colonialism and Structural Change in Colombia* (1970); T. E. Weil and others, *Area Handbook for Colombia* (1970); W. P. McGreevey, *An Economic History of Colombia, 1845–1930* (1971); J. M. Henao and Gerardo Arruba, *History of Colombia* (tr. 2 vol., 1938; repr. 1972).

Colombo, Emilio (āmē'lyō kōlôm'bō), 1920–, Italian political leader. He was elected a member of the constituent assembly in 1946 and a parliamentary deputy for the Christian Democratic party in 1948. During a lengthy tenure in associate cabinet posts, he helped initiate some of Italy's basic postwar reforms, including land redistribution, nationalization of electrical utilities, and a program of government aid for the development of the impoverished south. He is credited with having written much of the Treaty of Rome, which established the European Economic Community (Common Market) in 1958. After serving as minister of the treasury from 1963 to 1970, he became premier in Aug., 1970. His coalition government fell in Jan., 1972, but he continued to hold successive cabinet posts.

Colombo (kəlŭm'bō), largest city (1971 pop. 562,442) and capital of Sri Lanka (Ceylon), a port on the Indian Ocean near the mouth of the Kelani River. The original Sinhalese name, *Kalantotta* ("Kelani ferry"), was corrupted to *Kolambu* by Arab traders and was changed to *Colombo* by the Portuguese. The city's major sections are the old area of narrow streets and colorful market stalls; the modern commercial, business, and government area around the 16th-century Portuguese fort; and Cinnamon Gardens, a wealthy residential and recreational area. Colombo has one of the world's largest man-made harbors and is a popular port of call for passenger ships. Most of Sri Lanka's foreign trade passes through the port. There are also modern facilities for containerized cargo. Gem cutting and ivory carving are among Colombo's specialties; other industries include food and tobacco processing, metal fabrication, engineering, and the manufacture of chemicals, textiles, glass, cement, leather goods, clothing, furniture, and jewelry. An oil refinery is on the city's outskirts. Colombo was probably known to Greco-Roman, Arab, and Chinese traders more than 2,000 years ago as an open anchorage for oceangoing ships. Muslims settled there in the 8th cent. A.D. The Portuguese arrived in the 16th cent. and built a fort to protect their spice trade. The Dutch, also coveting this trade, gained control in the 17th cent. In 1796, Colombo passed to the British, who made it the capital of their crown colony of Ceylon in 1802. In the 1880s, Colombo replaced GALLE as Ceylon's chief port and became a major refueling and supply center for merchant ships on the Europe–Far East route. Colombo served as an Allied naval base in World War II and was made the capital of independent Ceylon in 1948. The Colombo Plan, an international program to aid the economic development of Asian nations, was launched at a conference there in 1950. Two faculties of the Univ. of Sri Lanka, several colleges and research institutes, an observatory, a national museum, Independence Hall (1948), and numerous churches, mosques, and Buddhist and Hindu temples are in Colombo; on the outskirts are two Buddhist universities. About half the city's population is Sinhalese; there are also Tamils, Moors, and small European and Indian communities.

Colombo Plan: see INTERNATIONAL GOVERNMENTAL ORGANIZATIONS.

Colón (kōlōn'), city (1970 pop. 25,986), Matanzas prov., W central Cuba. It is a rail hub and commercial center for the surrounding agricultural region. Colón's sugar industry reached its heyday in the middle 19th cent. and has since declined. The city was founded in 1818.

Colón, city (1970 pop. 67,695), Panama, at the Caribbean end of the Panama Canal. Colón, the second largest city in Panama, is surrounded by, but not part of, the Canal Zone. Cristóbal, within the zone, is a suburb. Colón is an important port and commercial center. It was made a free trade zone in 1953. The city was founded in 1850 by Americans working on the trans-Panama railroad and was named Aspinwall until 1890. The city was often scourged by yellow fever until the sanitary work associated with the construction of the canal was completed under W. C. Gorgas.

colon, in anatomy: see INTESTINE.

colon, in writing: see PUNCTUATION.

Colonia (kōlō'nyä), city (1963 pop. 12,839), capital of Colonia dept., S Uruguay, on the Río de la Plata. It is a resort city, a port, and the trade center for a rich agricultural region. The city, founded by the Portuguese in 1680, was bitterly contested before being ultimately secured by the Spanish. Colonia has many fine examples of colonial architecture.

Colonial architecture: see AMERICAN ARCHITECTURE.

Colonial Conference, British: see IMPERIAL CONFERENCE.

Colonial Heights, city (1970 pop. 15,097), in, but not part of, Chesterfield co., SE Va.; inc. as a city 1948. Metal awnings and paint are manufactured, tires are retreaded, and whiskey is bottled in the city. Of particular interest is the Violet Bank Library and Museum and the giant cucumber tree in front of it. In 1864, during the Civil War, Gen. Robert E. Lee made his headquarters under the tree while directing the defense of besieged Petersburg (across the Appomattox River from Colonial Heights).

Colonial National Historical Park, 9,430 acres (3,816 hectares), SE Va., mainly on the peninsula between the York and James rivers; created 1930 as Colonial National Monument, renamed 1936. The park embraces a historic region that includes YORKTOWN, JAMESTOWN, WILLIAMSBURG, and Cape Henry (added 1939; see HENRY, CAPE); the Colonial Parkway, part of the park, links the three old towns. Archaeological and historical studies as well as reconstruction of old places of interest have been carried on.

colonial preference: see TARIFF.

colonization, extension of political and economic control over an area by a state whose nationals have occupied the area and usually possess organizational or technological superiority over the native population. It may consist simply in a migration of nationals to the territory, or it may be the formal assumption of control over the territory by military or civil representatives of the dominant power (see COLONY). Overpopulation, economic distress, social unrest, and religious persecution in the home country may be factors that cause colonization, but IMPERIALISM, more or less aggressive humanitarianism, and a desire for adventure or individual improvement are also causes. Colonization may be state policy, or it may be a private project sponsored by chartered corporations or by associations and individuals. Before colonization can be effected, the indigenous population must be subdued and assimilated or converted to the culture of the colonists; otherwise, a modus vivendi must be established by the imposition of a treaty or an alliance. As early as the 10th cent. B.C., the Phoenicians founded trading posts throughout the Mediterranean area and later exercised political dominion over these commercial colonies. The Greeks, from a desire for wealth or as a result of the expulsion of a political faction or the defeated inhabitants of a city, established colonies in Asia Minor and Italy, spreading Hellenic culture and stimulating trade. Greek colonies were patterned after the parent state and were at first subject to its jurisdiction. Colonization was an integral part of Roman policy, providing land for the poor, supporting Roman garrisons, and again spreading Roman culture. In their colonization the Romans sought to assimilate the native culture into their own, and in some cases they bestowed Roman citizenship upon natives of the colony. Medieval colonization began with the Crusades and was mainly Italian. The Venetians and Genoese established commercial colonies along trade routes and exercised strict supervision over them. The Portuguese and Spanish became great colonizing nations at the end of the Middle Ages. Portuguese colonization, which received impetus from the development of greatly improved methods of navigation, began with the establishment of trading ports in Africa and the East, while the Spanish concentrated most of their efforts in the Americas. Both the Spanish and the Portuguese exercised strict governmental control over their colonies and used them primarily as a basis for rich commerce with the parent government. They discouraged them from becoming economically self-sufficient. In the late 16th and early 17th cent., the English, Dutch, and French began to undertake colonization through the agency of CHARTERED COMPANIES. The greatest of these private trading companies was the British EAST INDIA COMPANY, which played a vital role in the history of the BRITISH EMPIRE. The French generally adhered to mercantilist theory in establishing their colonies, using them mainly for the economic advantage of France. The English colonists in North America, however, were, in many respects, virtually independent of the parent country, the most serious restriction being the establishment of a trade monopoly by the home government through the NAVIGATION ACTS. Because their territory was suitable for settlement, rather than exploitation, the residence of the British colonists in America tended to be permanent. The increase in overseas trade and colonial consumption helped to stimulate the INDUSTRIAL REVOLUTION, which in turn, because of the increased technological superiority afforded Europe, especially Great Britain, and because of the greater desire for markets and raw materials, gave added impetus to colonization and made it easier to accomplish. Although Great Britain lost most of its North American colonies as a result of the American Revolution, other acquisitions (most notably in India) soon made it the greatest colonial power in the world. The French, stripped of one colonial empire in the colonial wars of the 18th cent., established another in the 19th cent. Germany emerged as an industrial empire in the late 19th cent., but found the colonies of other powers closed to German products and, therefore, embarked upon its own colonial adventures. Japan, also recently industrialized, followed the same path. These ambitions helped to bring on World Wars I and II. Germany was stripped of its colonies after the first conflict; Japan lost its colonies after the second. Modern colonization, frequently preceded by an era in which missionaries and traders were active, has been largely exploitative. Moreover, it has not in the long run proved directly lucrative to the colonial power, because it has involved a heavy drain on the treasury of the home government. Colonization in its classical form is rarely practiced today and is widely considered to be immoral. Most former colonies, especially those in Africa and Asia, have achieved independence from the imperial powers. See MANDATES; TRUSTEESHIP, TERRITORIAL. See D. K. Fieldhouse, *The Colonial*

Empire (1965); C. Verlinden, *The Beginnings of Modern Colonization* (1970); J. H. Parry, *Trade and Dominion* (1971).

Colonna (kōlôn'nä), noble Roman family that played a leading part in the history of Rome from the 12th to the 16th cent. They were hereditary enemies of the ORSINI family and generally sided with the Ghibellines, or antipapal faction, against the popes. **Sciarra Colonna,** d. 1329, a bitter enemy of Pope BONIFACE VIII, was excommunicated, fled to the court of King Philip IV of France, and led, with Chancellor Nogaret, the French expedition that captured (1303) Boniface. As senator of Rome, Sciarra supported Holy Roman Emperor LOUIS IV during his Italian expedition and bestowed the imperial crown on him in 1328, but he was forced into exile when Louis departed shortly afterwards. Despite its antipapal attitude, the family produced in Pope MARTIN V (Oddone Colonna) one of the most successful advocates of papal authority. **Fabrizio Colonna,** d. 1520, was a general of the HOLY LEAGUE against King Louis XII of France. His daughter was Vittoria Colonna (see separate article). **Prospero Colonna,** 1452–1523, Fabrizio's cousin, also fought the French in the Italian Wars and defeated them (1522) at La Bicocca. **Marcantonio Colonna,** 1535–84, duke of Paliano, commanded the papal forces in the battle of Lepanto (1571) against the Turks. Many other members of the family distinguished themselves in the service of the Holy See and of Spain. Three lines of the family, all of princely rank, are still in existence. The Colonna Palace in Rome was begun by Martin V.

Colonna, Vittoria, marchesa di Pescara (vētô'rēä kōlôn'nä märkā'zä dē pāskä'rä), 1492–1547, Italian poet; daughter of Fabrizio Colonna. Her love for her husband, Ferrante d'Avalos, is the subject of part of her lamenting verse. After his death (1525) she lived in convents, devoting herself to religious reform. The larger part of her work treats religious themes. In her later years she was a close friend of Michelangelo. For a translation of her verse, see Lorna de' Lucchi, *An Anthology of Italian Poems* (1922).

colonnade (kŏlənād'), a row of columns usually supporting a roof. There are generally two rows of columns or one row and a wall. Colonnades were

Colonnade

popular with the Greeks and Romans, who employed them in the STOA and the PORTICO; they have continued to be used throughout the Middle Ages, the Renaissance, and modern times. See COLUMN.

Colonne, Édouard (ādo͞oär' kōlôn'), 1838–1910, French conductor and violinist. He appeared as a conductor in Europe and England and was for several years first violinist of the Paris Opéra. In 1873 he founded in Paris the Concert national, which later became known as the Colonne Concerts.

Colonsay (kŏl'ənzā), island, 17 sq mi (44 sq km), Argyll, NW Scotland, one of the Inner Hebrides. Crofting and cheese making are the main occupations. Colonsay is separated from Oronsay by a narrow sound.

colony, any nonself-governing territory subject to the jurisdiction of a usually distant country. The term is also applied to a group of nationals who settle in a foreign country or territory but retain political or cultural connections with their parent state. Colonies in the first sense are traditionally classified as either colonies of settlement or colonies of exploitation. A colony of settlement is usually founded in an uninhabited or sparsely inhabited region and one that is climatically congenial to the settlers. There the colonists often recreate the features of the home government, modifying them to suit new conditions. Colonies of exploitation are established for the purpose of exploiting a region rich in resources or with commercial possibilities. Such colonies often have dense native populations. Colonists in a colony of exploitation will consist chiefly of military and administrative officers and commercial and financial representatives. The use of slaves and forced labor has often been a feature of such colonies. In a colony of exploitation, the government tends to be highly centralized and is frequently upheld by the presence of a strong police force or army; in a colony of settlement, there is generally rapid evolution from a purely military or autocratic government to autonomy or incorporation within the parent state. Since the 18th cent., colonial problems and their settlement have played a central role in European diplomacy and international relations. Strategic considerations, diplomatic rivalries, and the search for markets all led to a dramatic growth in European colonial holdings in the 19th cent. (See COLONIZATION and IMPERIALISM.) In the late 19th cent., Great Britain began granting autonomy to some of its colonies, ultimately resulting in the transformation of the BRITISH EMPIRE into the COMMONWEALTH OF NATIONS. In the 20th cent., many colonial areas came under international supervision through the MANDATES system, or its successor, the trusteeship system (see TRUSTEESHIP, TERRITORIAL). The nature of the French empire was changed profoundly with the creation (1946) of the FRENCH UNION and its reorganization (1958) as the FRENCH COMMUNITY. By the early 1970s most of the former colonies of the Western European powers had become independent nations. Of those that had not, most were autonomous in internal affairs and many remained colonies by choice. The most notable exceptions were the Portuguese colonies, which, despite nationalist uprisings, remained under direct Portuguese rule. However, in 1974, following the overthrow of the Caetano regime, Portugal began to divest itself of its colonies. For bibliography, see under COLONIZATION and IMPERIALISM.

colophon (kŏl'əfŏn") [Gr.,=finishing stroke]. Before the use of printing in Western Europe a manuscript often ended with a statement about the author, the scribe, or the illuminator. The first printed book to have a comparable concluding statement was the Mainz Psalter, crediting the printer and giving the date printed (1457) in its last paragraph. After this, a printed book commonly ended with a statement of the kind, now called a colophon. The information came to be given on the title page after c.1520. The name colophon is applied also to a printer's mark or a publisher's device on a title page or elsewhere.

color, effect produced on the eye and its associated nerves by light waves of different wavelength or frequency. Light transmitted from an object to the eye stimulates the different color cones of the retina, thus making possible perception of various colors in the object. When white light passes through a glass PRISM, it is separated into a band of colors called a SPECTRUM. Since the colors that compose sunlight or white light have different wavelengths, the speed at which they travel through the glass differs. The colors of the visible spectrum, called the elementary colors, are red, orange, yellow, green, blue, indigo, and violet; red light, having the longest wavelength, travels more rapidly through the glass than blue light, which has a shorter wavelength. Color is therefore a property of light that depends on wavelength. When light falls on an object, some of it is absorbed and some is reflected. The apparent color of an object depends on the wavelength of the light that it reflects; e.g., a red object observed in daylight appears red because it reflects only the waves producing red light. The color of a transparent object is determined by the wavelength of the light transmitted by it. An opaque object that reflects all wavelengths appears white; one that absorbs all wavelengths appears black. Black and white are not generally considered true colors; black is said to result from the absence of color, and white from the presence of all colors mixed together. Colors whose beams of light in various combinations can produce any of the color sensations are called primary, or spectral, colors. The process of combining these colors is said to be "additive"; i.e., the sensations produced by different wavelengths of light are added together. The additive primaries are red, green, and blue-violet. White can be produced by combining all three primary colors. Any two colors whose light together produces white are called complementary colors, e.g., yellow and blue-violet, or red and blue-green. When pigments are mixed, however, the resulting sensations differ from those of the transmitted primary colors, the process in this case being a "subtractive" one, since the pigments subtract or absorb some of the wavelengths of light. Magenta (red-violet), yellow, and cyan (blue-green) are called subtractive primaries, or primary pigments. A mixture of blue and yellow pigments yields green, the only color not absorbed by one pigment or the other. A mixture of the three primary pigments produces black. The scientific description of color, or colorimetry, involves the specification of all relevant properties of a color either subjectively or objectively. The subjective description gives the hue, saturation, and lightness or brightness of a color. Hue refers to what is commonly called color, i.e., red, green, blue-green, orange, etc. Saturation refers to the richness of a hue as compared to a gray of the same brightness; in some color notation systems, saturation is also known as chroma. The brightness of a light source or the lightness of an opaque object is measured on a scale ranging from dim to bright for a source or from black to white for an opaque object (or from black to colorless for a transparent object). In some systems, brightness is called value. A subjective color notation system provides comparison samples of colors rated according to these three properties. In an objective system for color description, the corresponding properties are dominant wavelength, purity, and luminance. Much of the research in objective color description has been carried out in cooperation with the Commission Internationale de l'Eclairage (CIE), which has set standards for such measurements. In addition to the description of color according to these physical and psychological standards, a number of color-related physiological and psychological phenomena have been studied. These include color constancy under varying viewing conditions, color contrast, afterimages, and advancing and retreating colors. Color has long been used to represent affiliations and loyalties and as a symbol of various moods and qualities. A well-known use of the symbolism of color is in the liturgical colors of the Western Church, according to which the color of the vestments varies through the ecclesiastical calendar; e.g., purple (i.e., violet) is the color of Advent and Lent; white, of Easter; and red, of the feasts of the martyrs. See also LIGHT; PAINTING; PROTECTIVE COLORATION; VISION. See R. M. Evans, *An Introduction to Color* (1948); Faber Birren, *Creative Color* (1961); Günter Wyszecki and W. S. Stiles, *Color Science* (1967).

Colorado (kŏlərăd'ə, -răd'ō, -rä'dō), state (1970 pop. 2,207,259) 104,247 sq mi (270,000 sq km), W central United States, one of the Rocky Mt. states, admitted as the 38th state of the Union in 1876 (and therefore known as the "Centennial State"). DENVER is the capital, by far the largest city, and the center of state activity. Other major cities are COLORADO SPRINGS, PUEBLO, LAKEWOOD, AURORA, and BOULDER. Colorado is bounded on the N by Wyoming and Nebraska, on the E by Nebraska and Kansas, on the S by Oklahoma and New Mexico, and on the W by Utah. The plains of Colorado's eastern section are part of the High Plains section of the Great Plains. On their western edge the plains give way to the foothills of the Rocky Mts., which run north-south through central Colorado. The mountains are divided into several ranges that make up two generally parallel belts, with the Front Range and a portion of the Sangre de Cristo Mts. on the east and the Park Range, Sawatch Mts., and San Juan Mts. on the west. Mt. Elbert (14,433 ft/4,399 m) is the highest peak in the U.S. Rocky Mts. The mountain ranges are separated by high valleys and basins called parks. These include North Park, Middle Park, South Park, and San Luis Park. The Continental Divide runs north-south along the Rocky Mts. in Colorado. One of the most scenic states in the country, Colorado's parks include Rocky Mountain National Park, Black Canyon of the Gunnison National Monument with its narrow gorge cut by the Gunnison River, Dinosaur National Monument in NW Colorado, and Great Sand Dunes National Monument in S central Colorado. Mesa Verde National Park, once the home of Indian CLIFF DWELLERS, is located in the southwestern corner of the state, a beautiful but formidable area of mesas and canyons. Most of W Colorado is occupied by the Colorado Plateau, where many canyons have been formed by the action of the Colorado, Gunnison, and other rivers. Colorado has a mean elevation of c.6,800 ft (2,070 m) and has 51 of the 80 peaks in North America over 14,000 ft (4,267 m) high, thus laying claim to the name "top of the world." Melting snows from the mountains form important river systems that nourish the water-hungry lands of the Southwest. A broad timber belt, largely coniferous and mostly protected as national forest reserves, acts as a huge reservoir. The mighty Colorado River originates in Rocky Mountain National Park, and the headwaters of the North Platte, South Platte, Arkansas, and Rio Grande also gather in Colorado's mountains. The average annual rainfall in Colorado is only 16.6 in. (42.2 cm), but by means of irrigation the state has been able to develop otherwise unusable land and ranks high among the states in irrigated acres. The COLORADO-BIG THOMPSON PROJECT and the Fryingpan-Arkansas project are two major water-diversion systems that carry water by tunnel across the Continental Divide to farms on the plains of E Colorado. Agriculture, especially the raising of cattle and sheep, is economically important in the state. Crops, which include wheat, hay, corn, and sugar beets, accounted for less than a quarter of all farm income in 1970. In the 1950s manufacturing displaced agriculture as the major source of income in the state. Food processing is the main industry. Other important industries include the manufacture of nonelectrical equipment, transportation equipment, and electrical equipment; printing and publishing; and the production of stone, clay, and glass products, fabricated metals, chemicals, and lumber. Tourism also plays a vital role in the economy. Colorado's climate, colorful scenery, and extensive recreational facilities attract millions of visitors to the state annually. Besides fine hunting and fishing and skiing there are many special events held in the state, including rodeos and fairs. Gold, the lure to exploration and settlement of Colorado, was the first of many useful minerals to be discovered there. In 1970 molybdenum was the most valuable mineral produced in the state; Colorado has the world's largest known deposit of that mineral. Other leading minerals are petroleum, coal, sand and gravel, and uranium. Gold is no longer mined extensively. Large coal and oil deposits provide considerable resources for the generation of electricity. Hydroelectric power is also used, although on a smaller scale. Colorado's earliest inhabitants were the BASKET MAKERS, Indians who settled in the mesa country before the beginning of the Christian era. Later Indians known as cliff dwellers inhabited the area, building their pueblos in canyon walls. The first white man to enter the region was probably the Spanish conquistador Francisco Vásquez de Coronado in the 16th cent. Spain subsequently claimed (1706) the territory, although no Spanish settlements were established there. The search for gold lured Juan María Rivera into the San Juan valley in 1765, and in 1776 the Franciscan friars Silvestre Vélez de Escalante and Francisco Atanasio Domínguez journeyed through part of what is now Colorado. Part of the area was also claimed for France as part of the Louisiana Territory. At the end of the French and Indian Wars (1763), France secretly ceded the Louisiana Territory, including much of Colorado, to Spain. The French regained the whole area in 1800 by the secret Treaty of San Ildefonso concluded with Spain (see SAN ILDEFONSO, TREATY OF). There were still few white men when the United States bought the area N of the Arkansas River and E of the Rocky Mts. in the Louisiana Purchase of 1803. The Federal government sent expeditions to Colorado under Zebulon M. Pike (1806), Stephen H. Long (1819–20), and John C. Frémont (1842–43 and 1845). These expeditions generated some public interest in the new territory, and they explored routes opened earlier by the famous MOUNTAIN MEN, trappers, and fur traders who included William H. Ashley, James Bridger, Jedediah S. Smith, Kit Carson, and the Bent brothers. Bent's Fort, in Colorado, was one of the best-known Western trading posts. Settlement in the area did not begin, however, until the United States acquired the remainder of present-day Colorado from Mexico by the Treaty of Guadalupe Hidalgo in 1848. In the early 1800s a small farming settlement had been established in the San Luis valley, but most settlers pushing westward across the Great Plains continued on to the more fertile lands of Oregon, Washington, and California. It was the discovery of gold that first brought large numbers of white men to Colorado. Prospectors led by Green Russell discovered gold in 1858 at Cherry Creek, where the city of Denver now stands. The next year John Gregory made a great strike on the site of present-day Central City, and the lusty, lawless days of the mining boom began. At the time of the gold rush the area in which the gold fields were located was part of the U.S. Kansas Territory. A group of miners organized the gold fields as Arapahoe co. of Kansas Territory. The region was divided into districts, and miners' and people's courts were set up to provide quick justice. The miners sought separate territorial status in 1859 and formed the illegal Territory of Jefferson, which operated until the bill for territorial status was passed by Congress in 1861. William Gilpin, the first territorial governor, chose the name Colorado [Span.,=red or colored]. Measures proposing statehood for Colorado were introduced in the U.S. Congress in 1864, and again in 1866 and 1867 when they were vetoed by Andrew Johnson. A bill granting Colorado's statehood was finally passed by Congress in 1876. It was also in the 1860s and 1870s that Colorado's settlers achieved peace with the Indians of the area. When the first white settlers came to Colorado, Ute Indians lived in the mountain areas, while Comanche, Cheyenne, Arapaho, and Kiowa Indians roamed the Great Plains. Intertribal warfare between plains and mountain Indians was continuous. The tribes of the plains combined their forces in 1840 to halt the invasion of their homelands and hunting grounds by white settlers, and Indian massacres and lootings were accompanied by the subsequent reprisals carried out by white men. The Federal government tried and failed to achieve peace with the Indians. The warfare finally culminated in the defeat of the Indians after the Indian Wars (1861–69) and the Buffalo War (1873–74). The Ute Indians of the mountains also raided white settlements until a Ute chief, Ouray, brought peace to the tribe in 1873 (there was a brief outbreak of hostilities in 1879) through the cession of Ute territory to the United States. Today, Colorado's Indians live mainly on the Southern Ute reservation and in the Denver area. While Colorado was seeking to establish a government and to deal with the Indian problem, the state's mining boom was in sharp decline. The surface gold had been extracted in the middle 1860s, and mining areas became, and in many cases remain, studded with ghost towns—the machinery abandoned and shacks deserted. Other towns, such as Central City with its famous opera house dating from the city's days of opulence, managed to stay alive. The completion (1870) of a railroad link from Denver to the Union Pacific in Cheyenne, Wyo., and later railroad construction helped to stimulate the extension of farming and the growth of huge cattle ranches as well as to encourage an influx of settlers. In 1870, Nathan C. Meeker, former agricultural editor for the New York *Tribune*, established an agricultural community, Union Colony, at Greeley (named for Horace Greeley). The community constructed Colorado's first large irrigation canal. Between 1870 and 1880 population increased almost five-fold. Denver briefly became the largest receiving market for sheep, and a smelting industry was established. In the 1870s the discovery of silver-bearing lead carbonite ore at Leadville started a new mining boom. Prosperity was short-lived, however, for in the 1890s, despite a rich silver strike at Creede and the discovery of the state's richest gold field at Cripple Creek, Colorado suffered a depression. In 1893 the U.S. government stopped buying silver in order to restore confidence in the nation's currency, which had been placed on the gold standard in 1873. The silver market subsequently collapsed, dealing a severe blow to Colorado's economy. Labor conflicts, disputes over railway franchises, and warfare between sheep and cattle interests also plagued the state at the turn of the century. Many of labor's battles in this period were fought in the mines of Colorado, and the lawlessness and ruthlessness that prevailed among both employers and miners were reminiscent of the early days of the mining camps. When the silver market broke, Colorado turned politically to fusion Populist-Democratic leaders advocating a return to bimetallism. The free-silver movement, however, was unsuccessful, and by 1910, with the improvement of national economic conditions, Colorado settled down to a predominantly agricultural economy. The establishment of large national parks in the early 1900s provided an additional source of revenue in tourism. During World War I the price of silver soared again and the economy prospered. The stock-market crash of 1929 and the droughts of 1935 and 1937 brought hardship to many. The economy recovered again during World War II, when the state produced food and valuable minerals and metal products for the war effort. Since the mid-1960s Colorado has experienced a large influx of new residents and rapid urban growth and development, especially along a strip (c.150 mi/240 km long) centered on Denver and stretching from Fort Collins and Greeley in the north to Pueblo in the south. Colorado's state government is based on the constitution drawn up in 1876 and since amended. The governor of the state is popularly elected and serves for a term of four years. The legislature is made up of a senate with 35 members elected for four-year terms and a house of representatives with 65 members elected for two-year terms. Colorado is represented in the U.S. Congress by two Senators and five Representatives and has seven votes in the electoral college. Since the decline of populism in the state in the early part of the 20th cent., neither the Republican nor Democratic party has consistently dominated Colorado state politics. In 1974, Richard D. Lamm, a Democrat, was elected governor. Among Colorado's institutions of higher learning are the Univ. of Colorado, at Boulder; the Univ. of Denver, at Denver; Colorado State Univ., at Fort Collins; and the United States Air Force Academy, at Colorado Springs. See Robert Emmitt, *The Last War Trail* (1954); Perry Eberhart, *Guide to the Colorado Ghost Towns and Mining Camps* (1959); Caroline Bancroft, *Colorful Colorado: Its Dramatic History* (1959); Federal Writers' Project, *Colorado: A Guide to the Highest State* (1941, repr. 1970); P. F. Dorset, *The New Eldorado: The Story of Colorado's Gold and Silver Rushes* (1970); Le Roy R. Hafen, *Colorado: The Story of a Western Commonwealth* (1970); C. W. Casewit, *Colorado* (1973).

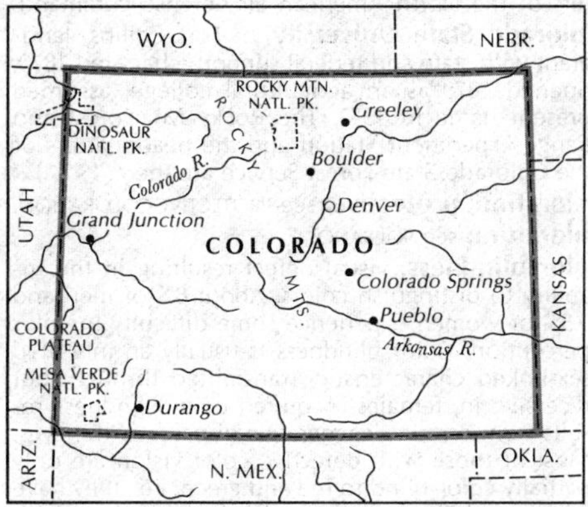

Colorado (kōlōrä'thō), river, c.550 mi (885 km) long, rising from tributaries in the Andes and flowing SE across S central Argentina to the Atlantic Ocean. It marks the northern limit of Patagonia. It is also a rough boundary between the commercial agriculture to the north and ranching to the south. The Colorado is unnavigable and frequently overflows its banks in the spring.

Colorado (1 kŏlərăd'ə, -răd'ō, -rä'dō 2 kŏlərä'də, -rä'də). 1 Great river of SW United States, 1,450 mi (2,334 km) long, rising in the Rocky Mts. of N Colo., and flowing generally SW through Colo., Utah, Ariz., between Nev. and Ariz., and Ariz. and Calif., and then into Mexico, emptying into the Gulf of California; drains c.244,000 sq mi (631,960 sq km). The Gunnison, Green, San Juan, and Little Colorado are the main tributaries of the upper basin of the Colorado; the Gila is the chief tributary of the lower basin. Silt deposited by the Colorado has formed a great delta across the northern part of the Gulf of California, cutting off the head of the gulf; Salton Sea is a remnant of the severed part. The mouth of the river was seen by Francisco de Ulloa in 1539; the lower part was explored by Hernando de Alarcón in 1540. The river flows through c.1,000 mi (1,610 km) of canyons, of which the most spectacular is the Grand Canyon. Many national parks, monuments, and recreational areas are located along the river banks. The Colorado's waters are used for power and irrigation, especially by means of the Colorado River storage project, the Colorado-Big Thompson project, Hoover Dam, Davis Dam, Imperial Dam, the All-American Canal, Parker Dam, and Glen Canyon Dam. Controversies over water rights on the Colorado have long raged between the United States and Mexico and among the bordering states; treaties and compacts now regulate the river's use. 2 River, 894 mi (1,439 km) long, rising in the Llano Estacado, NW Texas, and flowing SE to Matagorda Bay, an inlet of the Gulf of Mexico; drains c.41,500 sq mi (107,485 sq km). Destructive floods, which prevented private development of the river for power, led the Texas legislature to set up the Lower, Central, and Upper Colorado River authorities to undertake projects for flood control, power plants, and irrigation. The Lower Colorado River Authority, with Federal assistance, has been especially active, building five major dams (Buchanan, Roy Inks, Alvin J. Wirtz, Marble Falls, and Mansfield). These projects have benefited a large part of Texas, including the city of Austin. The scenic section of the river above Austin, which includes the lakes formed by the dams, is called Highland Lakes Country. The Central Colorado River Authority has constructed many small irrigation dams and also has jurisdiction over several city reservoirs. The Upper Colorado River Authority regulates the upper Colorado and the several branches of the Concho, a principal tributary.

Colorado, University of, mainly at Boulder; state supported; coeducational; chartered 1861, opened 1877. It has a branch at Colorado Springs and a large general and psychopathic medical center in Denver; it also operates the High Altitude Observatory at Climax. The university museum has a noted collection of materials and specimens relating to the natural history of the Southwest and the Rocky Mountain regions.

Colorado-Big Thompson project, constructed by the U.S. Bureau of Reclamation to divert water from the headstreams of the Colorado River to irrigate c.720,000 acres (291,400 hectares) of land in NE Colorado and to supply power; built 1938–56. Water is diverted by several dams, notably Granby Dam on the Colorado and Green Mt. Dam on the Blue River. Water is stored in Granby Reservoir, Shadow Mt. Lake, and Grand Lake before it is pumped through the Alva B. Adams Tunnel (13 mi/21 km long), to fall down the eastern slope of the Continental Divide into the Big Thompson River, a tributary of the South Platte. Dams near Fort Collins and Estes Park divert the water for use. Flatiron (71,500-kw capacity), Estes (45,000 kw), Pole Hill (33,250 kw), and Green Mt. (21,600 kw) dams generate power.

Colorado College, at Colorado Springs, Colo.; coeducational; chartered and opened 1874.

Colorado National Monument: see NATIONAL PARKS AND MONUMENTS (table).

Colorado Plateau, physiographic region of North America, c.150,000 sq mi (388,500 sq km), SW United States, in Arizona, Utah, Colorado, and New Mexico. It is characterized by broad plateaus, ancient volcanic mountains at altitudes of c.5,000 to 13,000 ft (1,520–3,960 m), and deeply dissected great canyons carved into nearly horizontal and often brightly colored sedimentary and volcanic rocks; the GRAND CANYON of the Colorado River is part of the region. Indian reservations occupy about one third of the mostly semiarid and sparsely vegetated area; about one half of the public land is used for grazing. Ancient cliff dwellings at Mesa Verde and Canyon de Chelly are of archaeological interest. The region has a number of U.S. national parks and monuments.

Colorado potato beetle: see POTATO BEETLE.

Colorado River storage project, a multipurpose plan, undertaken by the U.S. Bureau of Reclamation in 1956, to control the flow of the upper Colorado and its tributaries and to aid in the development of the rugged, remote upper Colorado River basin; includes parts of Wyo., Utah, Colo., Ariz., and N.Mex. The Colorado River Compact of 1922 established the division between the upper and lower basins and stipulated that the upper basin's water consumption be contingent on the delivery of a set amount of water to the lower basin. Since the flow of the Colorado is erratic, a storage project was needed to maintain an even flow of water to the lower basin in dry years. A series of dams regulates stream flow, provides storage reservoirs, creates hydroelectric power, and irrigates both new and previously developed acreage. The four major units of the project are GLEN CANYON DAM, on the Colorado River in Arizona; FLAMING GORGE DAM, on the Green River in Utah; NAVAJO DAM, on the San Juan River in New Mexico; and the Curecanti dams on the Gunnison River in Colorado. The three reservoirs of the Curecanti unit are included in the Curecanti National Recreation Area (see NATIONAL PARKS AND MONUMENTS, table). There are 11 authorized participating projects, including the CENTRAL UTAH PROJECT.

Colorado School of Mines, at Golden; state supported, coeducational; chartered 1874. It was one of the first mineral engineering schools in the United States. It owns extensive experimental and research facilities, field laboratories, and an experimental mine at Idaho Springs. See J. R. Morgan, *A World School: The Colorado School of Mines* (1955).

Colorado Springs, city (1970 pop. 135,060), seat of El Paso co., central Colo., on Monument and Fountain creeks, at the foot of Pikes Peak; inc. 1886. It is a beautiful residential and year-round vacation and health resort city, with thriving industries producing a wide variety of products. The town of El Dorado (later Colorado City) was founded on Fountain Creek by gold miners in 1859. In 1871, Gen. William Palmer and the Denver and Rio Grande RR established the modern city of Fountain Colony nearby; the name was changed to Colorado Springs because of the many mineral springs in the area. The city grew as a summer and health resort, absorbing the earlier community of Colorado City in 1917. Today it is the seat of Colorado College and the headquarters of Pike National Forest. The United States Air Force Academy is nearby, and to the south are U.S. Fort Carson (est. 1942) and Ent Air Force Base, headquarters of the North American air defense command.

Colorado State University, at Fort Collins; land-grant with state and federal support; chartered 1870, opened 1879 as an agricultural college, assumed present name in 1957. The Rocky Mt. Forest and Range Experiment Station and the headquarters of the Colorado State Forest Service are there.

coloration, protective: see PROTECTIVE COLORATION.

coloratura: see SOPRANO.

color blindness, visual defect resulting in the inability to distinguish colors. About 8% of men and 0.5% of women experience some difficulty in color perception. Color blindness is usually an inherited sex-linked characteristic, transmitted through, but recessive in, females. Acquired color blindness results from certain degenerative diseases of the eyes. Most of those with defective color vision are only partially color-blind to red and green, i.e., they have a limited ability to distinguish reddish and greenish shades. Those who are completely color-blind to red and green see both colors as a shade of yellow. Completely color-blind individuals can recognize only black, white, and shades of gray. Color blindness is usually not related to visual acuity; it is significant, therefore, only when persons who suffer from it seek employment in occupations where color recognition is important, such as airline pilots, railroad engineers, and others who must recognize red and green traffic signals. Tests for color blindness include identifying partially concealed figures or patterns from a mass of colored dots and matching skeins of wool or enameled chips of various colors.

color field painting: see POST-PAINTERLY ABSTRACTION.

color index, in astronomy, difference between a star's apparent photographic MAGNITUDE (B) and apparent visual magnitude (V), as measured with standardized photographic plates. Color index is defined as zero for a white star (SPECTRAL CLASS A0). The color index is positive for stars redder than a white star and negative for stars bluer than a white star. In effect, measuring the color index is equivalent to measuring the difference between the amount of blue light and red light that the star radiates.

Colossae (kəlŏs'ē), ancient city of SW Phrygia, Asia Minor, S of the Maeander (modern Menderes) River, in W Turkey, 4 mi (6.4 km) E of Denizli. It flourished as a trading town until eclipsed by neighboring Laodicea. The area around Colossae was famous for fantastic theological theories in early Christian times. Although Paul himself never went there, he addressed his epistle to the COLOSSIANS through his fellow worker, Epaphras, who lived at Colossae.

Colosseum or **Coliseum** (both: kŏləsē'əm), Ital. *Colosseo,* common name of the Flavian Amphitheater in Rome, near the southeast end of the Forum, between the Palatine and Esquiline hills. Begun by Vespasian, A.D. c.75, and completed by his son Titus in A.D. 80, it is the most imposing of Roman antiquities. The vast four-storied oval is 617 ft (188 m) by 512 ft (156 m), much of which is still standing; it had tier on tier of marble seats accommodating c.45,000 spectators. It encloses an arena measuring 250 ft (76 m) by 151 ft (46 m) where gladiatorial combats were held (see GLADIATORS) until 404. According to tradition, persecuted Christians were thrown there to beasts. The Colosseum has been damaged several times by earthquakes. See John Pearson, *Arena: The Story of the Colosseum* (1974).

Colossians (kəlŏsh'ənz), epistle of the New Testament, the 12th book in the usual order. It was written to the Christians of Colossae and Laodicea (1.2; 4.16) by St. PAUL when he was a prisoner, probably in Rome (A.D. c.60). The writing was provoked, apparently, by the appearance in the churches addressed of some sort of gnostic doctrine involving angels (2.18). Colossians is like EPHESIANS in tone, especially in the emphasis on the doctrine of the mystical body of Christ (1.15–20; 1.24–25; 2.9–10). This book contains several well-known passages, on the apostleship of St. Paul (1.24–29), on baptism (2.12–15), and on death and resurrection "with Christ" (2.20–3.4).

colossus (kəlŏs'əs), name given, in antiquity, to a statue of very great size. In Egypt were many colossuses, 50 to 60 ft (15.2 to 18.3 m) high. The Athena Parthenos on the Acropolis at Athens and the Zeus in the temple at Olympia in Greece were other examples. The **Colossus of Rhodes,** one of the seven wonders of the ancient world, was a large bronze statue, destroyed in antiquity, of the sun god, Helios, in the harbor of Rhodes. It was built at least in part by Chares of Lindus (Rhodes) between 292 and 280 B.C. Its height probably was something over 100 ft (30.5 m). The bronze had been taken from the machines and tools left behind by DEMETRIUS I after his unsuccessful siege of Rhodes. According to popular but erroneous legend it stood astride the harbor with the ships passing between its legs. Its actual location was on a promontory overlooking the harbor, and the representational type is well known from images on coins of the same period. Among colossuses of later times the Great Buddha at Kamakura, Japan, and the Bartholdi Statue of Liberty in New York harbor are notable. Of two colossal figures of Christ in South America, one is at Rio de Janeiro, and the other, the CHRIST OF THE ANDES, on the boundary between Argentina and Chile.

Colquhoun, Patrick (kōhōōn'), 1745–1820, British economist and statistician, b. Scotland. Active in civic affairs in Glasgow (where he founded the chamber of commerce) and London, he became known for his *Treatise on the Police of the Metropolis* (1795, 7th ed. 1806), written from his experience as a police magistrate. The most noted of his works is the *Treatise on the Population, Wealth, and Resources of the British Empire* (1814), in which he set forth statistical estimates of the distribution of national income. His figures, demonstrating the exploitation of the working classes, long influenced social and economic reformers.

Colt, Samuel, 1814–62, American inventor, b. Hartford, Conn. In 1835–36, he patented a revolving-breech pistol and founded at Paterson, N.J., the Patent Arms Company, which failed in 1842. An order for 1,000 revolvers from the U.S. government in 1847 in the Mexican War made possible the reestablishment of his business. He later built the Colt's Patent Fire-Arms Manufacturing Company factory at Hartford. Colt also invented a submarine battery used in harbor defense and a submarine telegraph cable. His revolving-breech pistol became so popular that today the word Colt is sometimes used as a generic term for the revolver. See biography by W. B. Edwards (1953).

Colter, John (kōl'tər), c.1775–1813, American trapper and guide, b. Virginia. In 1803 he enlisted in the Lewis and Clark expedition and in 1806, on the return trip, was granted a discharge to join a party of trappers. The following year, on his way to St. Louis, he met the expedition of Manuel Lisa and was engaged to guide the party to the mouth of the Big Horn, where a post was built. Lisa sent Colter on a mission to the Crow Indians. His exact route is not certain, but he is believed to have crossed, alone and on foot, the Wind River Mts. and the Teton range, and he may have been the first white man to see the region that he traversed (now included in Yellowstone National Park). He was severely wounded in a battle between the Crow and Blackfoot Indians, but he escaped and made his way back to the post. In 1809 he guided an expedition of the St. Louis Missouri Fur Company to the Three Forks of the Missouri, returning to St. Louis in 1810. He furnished very valuable data to Clark, who was compiling maps for the report of the Lewis and Clark expedition. See biographies by Stallo Vinton (1926) and Burton Harris (1952).

colter: see PLOW.

Colton, Walter (kōl'tən), 1797–1851, American editor, writer, and clergyman, b. Rutland co., Vt. He became a naval chaplain in 1831. His books *Ship and Shore* (1835), *A Visit to Constantinople and Athens* (1836), and *Deck and Port* (1850) are based upon his naval experiences. In 1846 he was appointed chief judge of Monterey, Calif. and founded the *Californian,* California's first newspaper. Colton's book *Three Years in California* (1850) is an excellent historical account of this period.

Colton, city (1970 pop. 19,974), San Bernardino co., S Calif., a suburb of San Bernardino, in a rich citrus and farm area; inc. 1887.

Coltrane, John, 1926–67, American jazz musician, b. Hamlet, N.C. He began playing tenor saxophone as an adolescent. Coltrane worked with numerous big bands before emerging in the mid-1950s as a major stylist while playing with Miles DAVIS. Originally influenced by Lester YOUNG, Coltrane displayed dazzling technical brilliance coupled with ardent emotion in his playing. His style was at once sonorous and spare. From the late 1950s until his death he was considered the outstanding tenor and soprano saxophonist of the jazz avant-garde.

coltsfoot, Eurasian perennial herb (*Tussilago farfara*) of the family Compositae (COMPOSITE family), now a widespread weed in most northern lands. The scaly flower stalk bears a yellow flower head and downy, somewhat dandelionlike fruits. The leaves—appearing after the flowers—are large and vaguely heart shaped. Coltsfoot was long a popular cough remedy. Other plants are sometimes called coltsfoot, e.g., the related winter heliotrope, or sweet coltsfoot (*Petasites fragrans*), an ornamental. Coltsfoot is classified in the division MAGNOLIOPHYTA, class Magnoliopsida, order Asterales, family Compositae.

colugo (kəlo͞o'gō): see FLYING LEMUR.

Colum, Padraic (pă'drĭk kŏl'əm), 1881-1972, Irish-American author, b. Longford, Ireland. He was active in the IRISH LITERARY RENAISSANCE and helped to found the Abbey Theatre. His verse includes *Wild Earth* (1907), *The Story of Lowry Maen* (1937), and *Collected Poems* (1953). He also wrote children's stories based on Irish folklore. His wife was **Mary (Maguire) Colum,** 1880?-1957, Irish-American critic, b. Sligo, Ireland. Her autobiography, *Life and the Dream* (1947), vividly describes various literary circles.

Columba, Saint, or **Saint Columcille** (kŏl'əmkĭl) [Irish,=dove of the church], 521-97, Irish missionary to Scotland, called the Apostle of Caledonia. A prince of the O'Donnells of Donegal, he was educated at Moville and Clonard. In Ireland he founded the monastery schools of Derry (545), Durrow (553), and Kells (c.554). In 563, Columba and several companions sailed to evangelize Scotland. They landed at IONA, where they established their center. Thence they went about the Highlands and the northern Lowlands spreading the gospel. Before Columba's death N Scotland was entirely Christian. St. Columba ranks with St. Patrick and St. Bridget as one of the three patron saints of the Irish; he is supposed to be buried with them at Downpatrick. Feast: June 9. See Hugh De Blacam, *The Saints of Ireland* (1942).

Columban, Saint (kəlŭm'bən), c.540-615, Irish missionary to the continent of Europe, also called Columbanus. He was trained in the abbey at Bangor. He and 12 companions, including St. Gall, sailed to France (c.585), where they set out to eradicate the general impiety that had grown up under the successors of Clovis. He went into seclusion in the Vosges, and c.590 he founded the abbey at LUXEUIL. His Celtic practices and austerities eventually alienated both ecclesiastical and civil powers. Involved in the hostility between Queen Brunhilda and the Frankish bishops, he was generally feared by them all and was exiled. He went (610) to Switzerland and to Bregenz, seeking to reestablish Christianity there. Hostile reaction caused him to go (612) to Milan. At BOBBIO he set up an abbey. There he died and lies buried. St. Columban was a considerable scholar, and all his foundations became known for their learning. He composed a rule for monks, which was later completely replaced by the longer and less austere rule of St. Benedict. Feast: Nov. 21 and, in Ireland, Nov. 23. See the classic work of Montalembert, *The Monks of the West* (1861); Francis MacManus, *Saint Columban* (1962); Brendon Lehane, *The Quest of Three Abbots* (1968).

Columbia. 1 City (1970 pop. 58,804), seat of Boone co., central Mo.; inc. 1826. The trade center of a farm and coal area, it is best known as the seat of the Univ. of Missouri and Stephens College. The Missouri School of Religion and a junior college are also there. The city is a medical center, with the university hospital, a state cancer hospital, and a state regional mental health clinic. There are houses dating from c.1820. **2** Industrial borough (1970 pop. 11,237), Lancaster co., SE Pa., on the Susquehanna River; settled by Quakers c.1730, inc. 1814. The borough was originally called Wright's Ferry; its name was changed in 1789 when it narrowly missed Congressional selection as the permanent U.S. capital. One of the world's largest concrete arch bridges spans the Susquehanna there. **3** City (1970 pop. 113,542), state capital, and seat of Richland co., central S.C., at the head of navigation on the Congaree River; inc. 1805. It is the largest city in the state and an important trade and commercial point in the heart of a rich farm region. Its industries include printing and the manufacture of textiles, clothing, plastics, electronic equipment, office machinery, and glass and stone products. A trading post flourished nearby in the early 18th cent. In 1786 the site was chosen for the new state capital because of its central location; the legislature first met in its new quarters in 1790. During the Civil War, Sherman's army entered Columbia on Feb. 17, 1865. That night most of the city was burned by drunken Union soldiers and was almost totally destroyed. An educational center, Columbia is the seat of the Univ. of South Carolina, Benedict College, Columbia College, a Lutheran theological seminary, and a Bible college. Also in the city are the state penitentiary, a state hospital, and a U.S. veterans hospital. Notable buildings include the statehouse (begun 1855, damaged in 1865, completed 1901), Woodrow Wilson's boyhood home (1870), and several antebellum houses. Also of interest are the South Carolina Archives Building; the Columbia Museum of Art and Science; and the Midlands Exposition Park, with historical exhibits. Adjacent to the city is U.S. Fort Jackson, a major infantry training center. Lake Murray (formed by the dammed Saluda River) is nearby. **4** City (1970 pop. 21,471), seat of Maury co., central Tenn., on the Duck River; inc. 1817. Once a noted mule market and racing horse center, it is now the trade and processing hub of a fertile area producing beef cattle and burley tobacco and a shipping point for the region's limestone and phosphate deposits. Columbia's many fine antebellum homes include the James K. Polk House (1816). A junior college and a state vocational training center are there. A national jubilee for Tennessee walking horses is held in the city every June.

Columbia, river, c.1,210 mi (1,950 km) long, rising in Columbia Lake, SE British Columbia, Canada. It flows first NW in the Rocky Mt. Trench, then hooks sharply about the Selkirk Mts. to flow S through Upper Arrow Lake and Lower Arrow Lake and receive the Kootenai River (spelled Kootenay in Canada) before entering the United States after a course of 465 mi (748 km). It continues S through Washington and just below the mouth of the Spokane River is forced by lava beds to make a great bend westward before veering south again, running the while entrenched in a narrow valley through the Columbia Plateau. Its chief tributary, the Snake River, joins it just before it turns west again. The Columbia then forms part of the Washington-Oregon border before entering the Pacific Ocean through a wide estuary W of Portland, Oregon. The Columbia River has created regal gorges by cutting through the Cascades and the Coast Ranges; it is fed by the Cowlitz and Willamette rivers, which drain the Puget trough between those ranges. Grand Coulee, now a reservoir in the COLUMBIA BASIN PROJECT, was a former stream channel of the Columbia River. It was created during the Ice Age when the Columbia's course was blocked by ice, forcing it to cut a new channel through the Columbia Plateau. When the ice receded the river resumed its former channel. The Columbia River, commanding one of the great drainage basins of North America (c.259,000 sq mi/670,800 sq km), was discovered by Robert Gray, an American explorer, in 1792 and is named for his vessel, the *Columbia.* It was first actually entered by a British naval officer, William R. Broughton, later the same year. Long before this time the Indians were fishing salmon from the river; today fish are still caught there, but heavy settlement along the river and its tributaries, the construction of dams, and human use have reduced the salmon runs. The first whites to arrive overland were the members of the Lewis and Clark expedition and the fur traders (notably David Thompson of the North West Company and the founders of Astoria). The river was the focus of the American settlement that created Oregon, and the river was itself sometimes called the Oregon River or the River of the West. Irrigation was begun early, and some tributaries were used to water cropland and orchards, as in, e.g., the valleys of the Wenatchee and Yakima rivers. After 1932 plans gradually developed to use the Columbia River to its ultimate possibility and the Columbia basin project was established. Its purpose is to establish flood control, which would alleviate the destruction seen in the Columbia's greatest flood, that of 1894, and somewhat lesser but damaging floods, such as that of 1948; to improve navigation; to extend irrigation in order to make optimum use of the water of the Columbia and its tributaries; and to produce hydroelectric power to supply the Pacific Northwest. There are six Federal and five non-Federal dams on the Columbia River. Grand Coulee (the key unit of the Columbia basin project) and Chief Joseph Dam, on the river's upper course, provide power, flood control, and irrigation. Priest Rapids, Wanapum, Rock Island, Rocky Reaches, and Wells dams are on the middle course; all are among the largest non-Federal hydroelectric facilities in the United States. Bonneville, The Dalles, John Day, and McNary dams, on the lower course, were designed as power, flood control, and navigation projects; these dams provide a 328-mi (528-km) slack-water navigation channel up the Columbia River from the Pacific Ocean to the Snake River. With these Federal projects and non-Federal dams on the Columbia, hydroelectric plants on the river have a potential generating capacity of about 21 million kw. The development of hydroelectric power has had a significant effect on the economic pattern of the Pacific Northwest. See U.S. Dept. of the Interior, Bureau of Reclamation, *The Columbia River* (1947); J. V. Krutilla, *The Columbia River Treaty; The Economics of an International River Basin Development* (1967).

Columbia, District of: see WASHINGTON, D.C.

Columbia basin project, central Wash., a multipurpose development of the U.S. Bureau of Reclamation providing irrigation, hydroelectric power, and flood control. Its key unit, the GRAND COULEE DAM, provides the project with power and pumps the waters of the Columbia River into an irrigation system comprising a series of lakes, reservoirs, and numerous canals. Irrigation was begun in 1948 and will eventually cover more than 1,000,000 acres (404,700 hectares) on the Columbia plateau S of Grand Coulee Dam. In 1969 the project had an installed hydroelectric power generation capacity of 2,333,000 kw. O'Sullivan Dam (200 ft/61 m high; 19,000 ft/5,791 m long; completed 1949) on Crab Creek, the project's southernmost dam, is one of the largest earthfill dams in the United States and impounds Potholes Reservoir.

Columbia College: see COLUMBIA UNIV.

Columbia Heights, city (1970 pop. 23,997), Anoka co., SE Minn., a residential suburb adjoining Minneapolis, on the Mississippi River; inc. 1921. It has many varied manufactures.

Columbian Exposition: see WORLD'S COLUMBIAN EXPOSITION.

Columbia Plateau, physiographic region of North America, c.100,000 sq mi (259,000 sq km), NW United States, between the Rocky Mts. and the Cascade Range in Washington, Oregon, and Idaho. Most of the plateau is underlaid by deposits, more than 10,000 ft (3,048 m) thick in places, of lava (mainly basalt) interbedded with sedimentary rock; older rocks outcrop in the Blue and Wallowa mts. Young lavas, scattered cinder cones, volcanic ash, and barren landscapes (including CRATERS OF THE MOON NATIONAL MONUMENT) are features of the Snake River plain in the south. Older, decayed lavas, much modified by accumulations of loess, occur in the north in the Columbia basin section; coulees (dry river canyons) and scablands (extensively eroded basalt surfaces), both carved by glacial meltwaters, are features of the region. The Columbia Plateau is an important agricultural and grazing area and is a major source of hydroelectric power.

Columbia sheep, medium-wool breed developed in the United States using Lincoln and Rambouillet sheep crosses. The breed was developed primarily for the Western ranges but is also used successfully in farm flocks. Columbias are white-faced, hornless, and relatively large in size and are prolific breeders.

Columbia University, mainly in New York City; founded 1754 as King's College by grant of King George II. Its first president was Samuel JOHNSON (1696-1772), a clergyman, who held classes in the schoolhouse of Trinity Church. The administration of his successor, Myles COOPER, was interrupted by the American Revolution; the college was closed but was reopened as Columbia College (1784). Title was first vested in the regents of the Univ. of the State of New York but in 1787 it was transferred to the trustees of the college, who elected William Samuel JOHNSON president. In 1857, under Charles King (1789-1867), the college moved to a site at Madison Ave. and 49th St.; in 1897, under Seth Low, the move was made to Morningside Heights. The gradual addition of professional and graduate schools resulted in the assumption of the name Columbia Univ. in 1896; in 1912 the name became Columbia Univ. in the City of New York. Columbia College remained the undergraduate school. The school of medicine (est. 1767) was absorbed into the independent College of Physicians and Surgeons (chartered 1807), which in turn was absorbed into the university in 1891. Also included in the university are the schools of law (1858), architecture (1896), and engineering (1896), the school of mines (founded 1864; now included in the school of engineering), and the three graduate faculties—political science (1880), philosophy (1890), and pure science (1892). The university system includes Teachers College (founded 1888, chartered 1889), Barnard College for women (est. 1889), the College of Pharmacy (est. 1892), and the Columbia School of Social Work (formerly the New York School of Social Work, est. 1898 as a summer school, affiliated with Columbia in 1940 and included within the university in 1959). The school of journalism was established in 1912 and that of business in 1916. In addition there are schools of public health, library service, international affairs, and the School of General Studies (est. 1947; adult undergraduate college; formerly the university extension, est. 1904). Much of Columbia's work in the fields of political science and international relations is carried on through a large group of research institutes (e.g., the East Asian, the European, and the Russian institutes). At Irvington-on-Hudson, N.Y., are the university's botanical and biological field stations. At Palisades, N.Y., the university operates the Lamont Geological Laboratory, which has extensive facilities for research in geophysics, geochemistry, and oceanography. The university library system, among the nation's largest, has many important manuscripts and rare book collections. Columbia is affiliated with the Marine Biological Laboratory at Woods Hole, Mass. Notable presidents of Columbia include F. A. P. BARNARD, Nicholas Murray BUTLER, and Dwight D. Eisenhower. Grayson Kirk was president from 1953 to 1969 and was succeeded by Andrew Cordier. In 1970, William J. McGill was appointed president. Columbia Univ. Press was founded in 1893. For histories of the various schools, see the volumes published in the Bicentennial series of Columbia Univ. See J. L. Avorn, et al., *Up Against the Ivy Wall* (1969); *University on the Heights*, ed. by Wesley First (1969).

Columbine: see COMMEDIA DELL' ARTE.

columbine (kŏl'əmbīn), any plant of the genus *Aquilegia,* perennials of the family Ranunculaceae (BUTTERCUP family), popular both as wild flowers and as garden flowers. Columbines have delicate and attractive foliage and flower petals with long spurs that secrete nectar. The common Eastern red-and-yellow-flowered wild columbine (*A. canadensis*), frequenting rocky places, is also called rockbell; it is a favorite of hummingbirds, and the Indians made an infusion of the seeds for headache and fever. The blue-and-white-flowered *A. coerulea* of the Rockies is the state flower of Colorado. The common European columbine (*A. vulgaris*), blue, white, or purple flowered and escaped from gardens in the United States, has been the source of many of the garden kinds—some double and of various soft colors. Columbine is classified in the division MAGNOLIOPHYTA, class Magnoliopsida, order Ranunculales, family Ranunculaceae.

columbium, former name of the chemical element NIOBIUM.

Columbus, Christopher, Ital. *Cristoforo Colombo* (krēstô'fōrō kōlôm'bō), Span. *Cristóbal Colón* (krēstō'bäl kōlōn'), 1451–1506, discoverer of America, b. Genoa, Italy. He spent some of his early years at his father's trade of weaving and later became a seaman on the Mediterranean. Shipwrecked near the Portuguese coast in 1476, he made his way to Lisbon, where his younger brother, Bartholomew, an expert chart maker, lived. Columbus, too, became a chart maker for a brief time in that great maritime center during the golden era of Portuguese exploration and discovery. Engaged as a sugar buyer in the Portuguese islands off Africa (the Azores, Cape Verde, and Madeira) by a Genoese mercantile firm, he met pilots and navigators who believed in the existence of islands farther west. It was at this time that he made his last visit to his native city, but he always remained a Genoese, never becoming a naturalized citizen of any other country. Returning to Lisbon, he married (1479?) the wellborn Dona Filipa Perestrello e Moniz. By the time he was 31 or 32, Columbus had become a master mariner in the Portuguese merchant service. It is thought by some that he was greatly influenced by his brother, Bartholomew, who may have accompanied Bartholomew Diaz on his voyage to the Cape of Good Hope, and by Martín Alonso Pinzón, the pilot who commanded the *Pinta* on the first voyage. Columbus was but one among many who believed one could reach land by sailing west. His uniqueness lay rather in the persistence of his dream and his determination to realize this "Enterprise of the Indies," as he called his plan. Seeking support for it, he was repeatedly rebuffed, first at the court of John II of Portugal and then at the court of Ferdinand and Isabella of Spain. Finally, after eight years of supplication by Columbus, the Spanish monarchs, having conquered Granada, decided to risk the enterprise. On Aug. 3, 1492, Columbus sailed from Palos, Spain, with three small ships, the *Santa María,* commanded by Columbus himself, the *Pinta* under Martín Pinzón, and the *Niña* under Vicente Yáñez Pinzón. After halting at the Canary Islands, he sailed due west from Sept. 6 until Oct. 7, when he changed his course to the southwest. On Oct. 10 a small mutiny was quelled, and on Oct. 12 he landed on a small island (Watling Island; see SAN SALVADOR) in the Bahama group. He took possession for Spain and, with impressed natives aboard, discovered other islands in the neighborhood. On Oct. 27 he sighted Cuba and on Dec. 5 reached Hispaniola. On Christmas Eve the *Santa María* was wrecked on the north coast of Hispaniola, and Columbus, leaving men there to found a colony, hurried back to Spain on the *Niña.* His reception was all he could wish; according to his contract with the Spanish sovereigns he was made "admiral of the ocean sea" and governor general of all new lands he had discovered or should discover. Fitted out with a large fleet of 17 ships, with 1,500 colonists aboard, he sailed from Cádiz in Oct., 1493. His landfall this time was made in the Lesser Antilles, and his new discoveries included the Leeward Islands and Puerto Rico. The admiral arrived at Hispaniola to find the first colony destroyed by Indians. He founded a new colony nearby, then sailed off in the summer of 1494 to explore the southern coast of Cuba. After discovering Jamaica he returned to Hispaniola and found the colonists, interested only in finding gold, completely disorderly; his attempts to enforce strict discipline led some to seize vessels and return to Spain to complain of his administration. Leaving his brother Bartholomew in charge at Hispaniola, Columbus also returned to Spain in 1496. On his third expedition, in 1498, he was forced to transport convicts as colonists, because of the bad reports on conditions in Hispaniola and because the novelty of the New World was wearing off. He sailed still farther south and made his landfall on Trinidad. He sailed across the mouth of the Orinoco River (in present Venezuela) and realized that he saw a continent, but without further exploration he hurried back to Hispaniola to administer his colony. In 1500 an independent governor arrived, sent by Isabella and Ferdinand as the result of reports on the wretched conditions in the colony, and he sent Columbus back to Spain in chains. The admiral was immediately released, but his favor was on the wane; other navigators, including Amerigo VESPUCCI, had been in the New World and established much of the coast line of NE South America. It was 1502 before Columbus finally gathered together four ships for a fourth expedition by which he hoped to reestablish his reputation. If he could sail past the islands and far enough west he hoped he might still find lands answering to the description of Asia or Japan. He struck the coast of Honduras in Central America and coasted southward along an inhospitable shore, suffering terrible hardships, until he reached the Gulf of Darien. Attempting to return to Hispaniola, he was marooned on Jamaica. After his rescue, he was forced to abandon his hopes and return to Spain. It is true the Vikings (see LEIF ERICSSON and THORFINN KARLSEFNI) had previously discovered America (c.1000), but their knowledge had been converted into saga, never acted upon by navigators, so that Columbus was no less a discoverer. Although his voyage was of great importance and marked the beginning of American history, Columbus died in neglect, almost forgotten. Historians have disputed for centuries his skill as a navigator, but it has been recently proved that with only dead reckoning Columbus was unsurpassed in charting and finding his way about unknown seas. See J. M. Cohen, comp., *The Four Voyages of Christopher Columbus* (1969); biographies by S. E. Morison (1942), Salvador de Madariaga (1967), and E. D. S. Bradford (1973).

Columbus. 1 City (1970 pop. 155,028), seat of Muscogee co., W Ga., at the head of navigation on the Chattahoochee River; settled and inc. 1828 on the site of a Creek Indian village. The second largest city in the state, Columbus is a port of entry situated at the foot of a series of falls that extend more than 30 mi (48 km) and provide extensive water power. An important industrial and shipping center with many giant textile mills (the first was built in 1838), it also has iron works, food-processing plants, and factories producing lumber, chemicals, crushed granite, furniture, hospital equipment, concrete, wood and rubber products, and beverages. Columbus, carved out of the wilderness, was built according to plan and remained a busy river port until the arrival of the railroads in the 1850s. Its river traffic has been revitalized with the completion of a series of locks and dams providing access to the Gulf of Mexico. During the Civil War, Columbus was an important Confederate industrial center. It was captured by Federal troops one week after Lee's surrender at Appomattox. Its industrial growth received added impetus in the early 20th cent. with the development of hydroelectric power plants. There are many antebellum homes in the city, and its oldest section has been marked for restoration and preservation. Columbus College is there, and just south of the city is Fort Benning. **2** City (1970 pop. 26,457), seat of Bartholomew co., S central Ind., on the East Fork of the White River; inc. 1821. Its many manufactures include automotive parts, diesel engines, castings, metal furniture, electric controls, and plastic components. In the Civil War, Columbus served as a depot for Union armies. Both the railroads and the war brought industries, which remain to this day. The city is known for its outstanding architecture, including buildings designed by world famous architects from the late 1930s onward. **3** City (1970 pop. 25,795), seat of Lowndes co., NE Miss., on the Tombigbee River; inc. 1821. The trade, processing, and shipping center of a large cotton, livestock, dairy, and timber area, it also has marble works and garment factories. Franklin Academy, the first free school in the state, now part of the public school system, was opened in 1821. Mississippi State College for Women and Columbus Air Force Base are there. A pilgrimage for tourists to the city's many beautiful antebellum homes is conducted each year. **4** City (1970 pop. 15,471), seat of Platte co., E central Nebr., in a prairie region, at the confluence of the Loup and Platte rivers; inc. 1857. It is a railroad, manufacturing, and trade center for a livestock, dairy, and grain area and is the headquarters for the Loup River power project. A junior college is there. **5** City (1970 pop. 540,025), state capital and seat of Franklin co., central Ohio, on the Scioto River; inc. as a city 1834. It is a port of entry, a rail, highway, and air focal point, and a major industrial and trade center in a rich farm region. Its many manufactures include household appliances, aircraft and missiles, automatic controls, foundry and machine-shop products, glass items, processing equipment, and coated fabrics. Columbus was laid out as state capital in 1812, but did not take over the government from Chillicothe until 1816. Its growth was stimulated by the development of transportation facilities—a feeder canal to the Ohio and Erie Canal, which was opened in 1831; the National Road, which reached the city in 1833; and the railroad, which arrived in 1850. Today the city is the seat of Ohio State Univ., Capital Univ., Ohio Dominican College, a business university, state schools for the deaf and blind, and Battelle Memorial Institute (for industrial research in metallurgy, the graphic arts, ceramics, and other fields). Landmarks include the state capitol; the state office building, with the state library; the Columbus Gallery of Fine Arts; the library and museum of the state archaeological and historical society; the headquarters of the American Rose Society, with one of the world's largest rose gardens; Camp Chase Confederate cemetery, with the graves of soldiers who died in the Civil War prison camp there; and the vast state fair grounds. Also in the city are U.S. Fort Hayes (est. 1863) and a state penitentiary. Columbus has an international airport. See H. S. Hunker, *Industrial Evolution of Columbus, Ohio* (1958); R. D. McKenzie, *The Neighborhood: A Study of Local Life in the City of Columbus, Ohio* (1923, repr. 1970).

Columbus Day, holiday commemorating Christopher Columbus's discovery of America. It has been traditionally celebrated on Oct. 12 throughout most of the United States, parts of Canada, and in several of the Latin American republics. In the United States, however, since the observation in 1971 of the Uniform Holiday Act, it is celebrated on the Monday nearest to Oct. 12.

Columcille, Saint: see COLUMBA, SAINT.

Columella (Lucius Junius Moderatus Columella), fl. 1st cent. A.D., Latin writer on agriculture, b. Gades (now Cádiz), Spain. Of his work there remains the 12-volume *De re rustica,* treating general husbandry, the care of domestic animals, and farm management. The 10th book, modeled on Vergil, is in hexameters. A short essay on trees also survives. Columella's Latin is facile and elegant, and his information is surprisingly practical and accurate.

column, vertical architectural support, circular or polygonal in plan. A column is generally at least four or five times as high as its diameter or width; stubbier freestanding masses of masonry are usually called piers or pillars. The shape, proportions, and materials of columns vary widely. Columns arranged in a row form a colonnade. Early forms of masonry columns can be seen in the rock-cut tombs at Beni Hassan in Egypt, with their polygonal shafts and block capitals. In fully developed Egyptian architecture the columns were of gigantic size, spaced very closely together, and were reserved for inner courtyards and halls. In the Aegean area, in pre-Hellenic times, the column type known to have been used is one with a cushionlike cap and with its shaft tapering downward. Subsequent types were the archaic forms of Doric, developed by the Dorians after their coming (before 1000 B.C.) into the region. By the 7th cent. B.C. this Greek Doric had been established in its design. The columns of classical architecture represent the attempt to design proportionings and details that would create maximum structural harmony. It is in the Greek temples of the Periclean Age (5th cent. B.C.), notably in the Parthenon, that the ideal was obtained. In Greek, Roman, and Renaissance architecture the various column types, taken together with the entablatures that they support, form the classical ORDERS OF ARCHITECTURE. The classical column has the three fundamental elements of base, shaft, and capital. The shaft has a gradual upward tapering (entasis), and the capital that crowns it provides a decorative and structural transition between the circular column and the rectangular entablature. The Doric, Ionic, and Corinthian column types advanced toward perfect proportions and details and formed the basis for the columnar architecture of the Romans. Although Greek columns always had vertical channels or flutes cut in their shafts, those of the Romans were often without them. In Greek buildings the columns were usually structurally indispensable, but the Romans and later the Renaissance and modern architects used them often also as a decorative feature, mostly following fixed rules of proportions. The columns of Romanesque, Byzantine, and Gothic buildings were usually structural elements and were without canons of proportioning. The capitals of the Romanesque and Gothic were often variously decorated with plant and animal forms. The columns of Chinese and Japanese architecture are circular or polygonal wood posts, with bases but without capitals, having instead an ornamented projecting bracket. In Indian architecture columns exhibit great variety of detail: shafts, bases, and capitals are often intricately ornamented. In modern construction most columns are of either steel or reinforced concrete. See DORIC ORDER; IONIC ORDER; CORINTHIAN ORDER; CAPITAL.

columnist, newspaper, the writer of a department appearing regularly in the press, usually under a constant heading. Although originally humorous, the column in many cases has supplanted the editorial for authoritative opinions on world problems. Usually independent of the policy of his paper, the columnist is allowed to criticize political and social institutions as well as persons. Well-known American columnists include Eugene Field, George Ade, Bert Leston Taylor (B. L. T.), Finley Peter Dunne, Don Marquis, Heywood Broun, Ernie Pyle, F. P. Adams (F. P. A.), Drew Pearson, Dorothy Thompson, Arthur Krock, David Lawrence, Westbrook Pegler, Walter Lippmann, James Reston, Joseph and Stewart Alsop, Russell Baker, Mary McGrory, William F. Buckley, Tom Wicker, and Art Buchwald. Noted columnists in other newspaper departments include the gossip columnists Walter Winchell, Louella Parsons, and Suzy Knickerbocker; advice-to-the-lovelorn columnists Dorothy Dix, Ann Landers, and Abigail van Buren; economic columnists Paul Samuelson and Sylvia Porter; and sports columnists Grantland Rice, Paul Gallico, and Red Smith.

Colville, river, c.375 mi (600 km) long, rising in the De Long Mts. of the Brooks Range, NW Alaska, and flowing across the tundra, east then north, to the Arctic Ocean. All of its major tributaries rise on the north slope of the Brooks Range. The river, frozen for most of the year, floods each spring as ice on its upper course melts. Umiat is the chief village along its banks. Coal, oil, and natural gas are found in the valley.

Colville Indians, North American Indians whose language belongs to the Salishan branch of the Algonquian-Wakashan linguistic stock (see AMERICAN INDIAN LANGUAGES). Reduced to a few hundred by 1872, they were placed on a reservation in NE Washington; since that time their numbers have markedly increased, so that by the 1970s they numbered some 3,000.

Colvin, Sir Sidney (kōl'vĭn), 1845-1927, English man of letters. Slade professor of fine arts at Cambridge and keeper of prints at the British Museum, he was a friend of Robert Louis Stevenson, whose works and letters he edited. Colvin wrote several studies on literature and art, including *Early Engraving and Engravers in England* (with A. M. Hind, 1905) and *John Keats: His Life and Poetry* (1917). See his *Memories and Notes of Persons and Places* (1921); E. V. Lucas, *The Colvins and Their Friends* (1928, repr. 1971).

Colwyn Bay (kŏl'wĭn), municipal borough (1971 pop. 25,535), Denbighshire, N Wales. It is a popular seaside resort. In 1974, it became part of the new nonmetropolitan county of Clwyd.

coly: see MOUSEBIRD.

Colyn, Alexander: see COLINS, ALEXANDER.

coma, deep state of unconsciousness from which a person cannot be aroused even with the most painful stimuli. It may be caused by severe head or brain injury, APOPLEXY, DIABETES, poisoning with morphine or barbiturates, SHOCK, or HEMORRHAGE. It occurs just before death in many diseases. It is dangerous to force food, fluids, or any medication by mouth on a comatose patient. It is important to keep air passages open. Treatment is directed to the cause of the condition.

coma, in astronomy: see ABERRATION OF STARLIGHT; COMET.

Comanche Indians, North American Indians belonging to the Shoshonean group of the Uto-Aztecan branch of the Aztec-Tanoan linguistic stock (see AMERICAN INDIAN LANGUAGES). They originated from a Basin-type culture and eventually adopted a Plains culture. They separated from the Shoshone Indians and migrated southward in the late 1600s, appearing in New Mexico around 1705. In the late 18th cent. and early 19th cent. their range included SE Colorado, SW Kansas, W Oklahoma, and N Texas. The Comanche were excellent horsemen and inveterate raiders, often pushing far S into Mexico. They were extremely warlike and effectively prevented white settlers from passing safely through their territory for more than a century. They are said to have killed more whites in proportion to their own numbers than any other Indian tribe. They were associated with the Kiowa, the Cheyenne, and the Arapaho in a loose confederacy. The Comanche, however, considered themselves superior to their associates, and their language served as the trade language for the area. The sun dance, a common feature among Plains Indians, was not an important part of Comanche culture; they probably introduced the peyote ritual to the Plains tribes. Never a large group despite their wide range, they were greatly reduced by warfare and disease. They now number approximately 3,000 on individually owned land in Oklahoma. See Ernest Wallace and E. A. Hoebel, *Comanches, The Lords of the South Plains* (1952); J. E. Harston, *Comanche Land* (1963); A. C. Greene, *The Last Captive* (1972); T. R. Fehrenbach, *Comanches: the Destruction of a People* (1974).

Comayagua (kōmäyä'wä), town (1961 pop. 8,473), W central Honduras. Founded in 1537, Comayagua was the most important city of colonial Honduras. In the political struggle following independence from Spain (1821), Comayagua, the Conservative stronghold, rivalled TEGUCIGALPA, seat of the Liberal faction. The cities alternated as capital of the republic, but in 1880 Tegucigalpa became the permanent capital. Today Comayagua is the center of an agricultural and mining region. It has a fine colonial cathedral and other colonial landmarks.

comb, toothed implement for arranging, confining, or ornamenting the hair. Specimens made of ebony, boxwood, bone, ivory, or metal have been found among the relics of ancient Egypt, Greece, and Rome. In the Middle Ages combs were not used by the mass of the people. The Renaissance saw the increased popularity of the comb for ornamental as well as for practical use. Still made by hand at that time, combs were delicately carved and jeweled. It was at that time also that tortoise shell was first used. With the coming of the periwig (c.1660), combs became fashionable for men, as did the practice of combing one's hair in public. The first factory in the United States to manufacture combs was established (1759) at Newberry, Mass.; horn was the most popular material used. In modern methods of combmaking, a plate of a size sufficient for two combs is cut (usually with a die) so that the teeth of one comb are formed by the interstices of the other. The name also refers to tools for graining painted work, for pressing home the weft in a primitive loom, and for carding or combing fibers in preparation for spinning.

Combe, William, 1741-1823, English satirist and miscellaneous writer, b. Bristol. His writing was mainly hack work, issued anonymously to avoid seizure of the proceeds by his many creditors. He is chiefly remembered for the "Dr. Syntax" series (3 vol., 1812-21), for which he wrote doggerel verse to accompany the illustrations of Thomas Rowlandson. See biography by H. W. Hamilton (1968).

Combes, Émile (āmēl' kôNb), 1835-1921, French statesman. An able politician of the left democratic group, he was minister of education under Léon Bourgeois (1895-96) and, succeeding René Waldeck-Rousseau, was (1902-5) premier and minister of interior and religion. Anticlericalism, growing out of the DREYFUS AFFAIR, was rampant, and Combes rigorously enforced the law of 1901 requiring religious associations to seek government authorization. He abolished religious education and initiated the separation of church and state in France; abrogation of the CONCORDAT OF 1801 was formalized in 1905 in a law introduced by Aristide BRIAND. Combes was a member of the Briand cabinet in World War I.

Combin, Grand (gräN kôNbăN'), peak, 14,164 ft (4,317 m) high, Valais canton, S Switzerland, in the Pennine Alps, near the Italian border.

combination, in business: see TRUST.

combinations, in mathematics: see PROBABILITY.

combine, harvesting machine that "combines" the operations of harvesting and THRESHING grain. Although its widespread use did not occur until the 1930s, the combine was in existence as early as 1830. The original combines were traction-powered and were drawn by horses, or later, driven by steam and internal-combustion engines. Self-propelled units appeared in the 1940s and are rapidly being adopted worldwide. Modern units feature dust-free, air-conditioned cabs and can handle up to 100 acres (41 hectares) of grain per day. Originally developed for cereal grains, the combine is now used for legumes, forage grasses, sorghum, and corn. The basic operations of a combine include cutting the standing crop, gathering it up, threshing the seed from the stem, separating out the chaff, collecting the seed in a hopper for delivery to a truck, and returning the straw to the ground. The combine has replaced the farm machines known as the REAPER; the binder, which cut and bound a harvested crop into bundles ready for threshing; and the thresher. See O. H. Friesen, *Combines Operation and Adjustment* (1972).

combing, process that follows CARDING in the preparation of fibers for spinning, lays the fibers parallel, and removes noils (short fibers). The modern combing machine is a specialized carding machine. Combing produces a fine sliver suitable for drawing out and spinning into strong, smooth yarn. The process, used for long staple cottons and worsted yarn, is expensive, since up to 25% of the card sliver is eliminated. Hackling is a form of combing, often by hand, used for linen.

combining weight, the proportion (by weight) in which a chemical element combines with other elements to form compounds. The determination of combining weights was a very important part of early chemical endeavor. The atomic theory of John DALTON (see ATOM) was based in part on his determinations of combining weights, which he called atomic weights. Combining weights were usually measured by early chemists on a scale in which hydrogen had a combining weight of 1. See EQUIVALENT WEIGHT.

comb jelly, common name for oval transparent organisms of the phylum CTENOPHORA, especially of the genus *Pleurobrachia*.

combustion, rapid chemical reaction of two or more substances with a characteristic liberation of heat and light; it is commonly called burning. The burning of a fuel (e.g., wood, coal, oil, or natural gas) in air is a familiar example of combustion. Combustion need not involve oxygen; e.g., hydrogen burns in chlorine to form hydrogen chloride with the liberation of heat and light characteristic of combustion. Combustion reactions involve OXIDATION AND REDUCTION. Before a substance will burn, it must be heated to its ignition point, or kindling temperature. Pure substances have characteristic ignition points. Although the ignition point of a substance is essentially constant, the time needed for burning to begin depends on such factors as the form of the substance and the amount of oxygen in the air. A finely divided substance is more readily ignited than a massive one; e.g., sawdust ignites more rapidly than does a log. The vapors of a volatile fuel such as gasoline are more readily ignited than is the fuel itself. The rate of combustion is also affected by these factors, particularly by the amount of oxygen in the air. The nature of combustion was not always clearly understood. The ancient Greeks believed fire to be a basic element of the universe. It was not until 1774 that the French chemist A. L. LAVOISIER performed experiments that led to the modern understanding of the nature of combustion. See SPONTANEOUS COMBUSTION; HEAT OF COMBUSTION. See C. J. Hilado, *Smoke and Products of Combustion* (1973).

Comecon: see COUNCIL FOR MUTUAL ECONOMIC ASSISTANCE.

Comédie Française (kōmādē' fräNsĕz') or **Théâtre Français** (tāä'trə fräNsā'), state theater of France, on the Rue de Richelieu, Paris. It is sometimes known as La Maison de Molière. The Comédie Française was officially established by Louis XIV (1680), his decree merging the two French companies of comedians at Paris, the troupe of the Hôtel Guénégaud (see MOLIÈRE and BÉJART) and the troupe of the HÔTEL DE BOURGOGNE. The following year an annual grant of 12,000 livres was allotted from the royal treasury, and a new theater was built for the company. In the Revolution its actors were scattered and the theater closed. By decree of Napoleon in 1803 the institution was revived, and the company was organized along lines that have been continued into the present. The system has no stars; all the permanent members, called *sociétaires* or associates, enjoy the same status, roles being apportioned by common agreement. The company continues to perform the finest works of French drama in a varied, yet sometimes heavily traditional repertory. In 1900 fire destroyed the historic building, but most of the works of art and all the archives were saved, and the theater was rebuilt.

comedy, literary work that aims primarily at amusement. Unlike TRAGEDY, which seeks to engage profound emotions and sympathies, comedy strives to entertain chiefly through criticism and ridicule of man's customs and institutions. Although usually used in reference to the drama (see DRAMA, WESTERN; ORIENTAL DRAMA), the term is also applied to such non-dramatic works as Dante's religious poem, *The Divine Comedy.* Dramatic comedy grew out of the boisterous choruses and dialogue of the fertility rites of the feasts of the Greek god Dionysus. What became known to theater historians as Old Comedy in ancient Greece was a series of loosely connected scenes (using a chorus and individual characters) in which a particular situation was thoroughly exploited through FARCE, fantasy, satire, parody, and political propaganda, the series ending in a lyrical celebration of unity. Reaching its height in the brilliantly scathing plays of Aristophanes, Old Comedy gradually declined in favor of a less vital and imaginative drama. Middle Comedy, of which no plays are extant, emphasized social themes. In New Comedy, generally considered to have begun in the mid-4th cent. B.C., the plays were more consciously literary, often romantic in tone, and decidedly less satirical and critical. Menander was the most famous writer of New Comedy and was closely imitated by the Latin dramatists Plautus and Terence. During the Middle Ages the Church strove to keep the joyous and critical aspects of the drama to a minimum, but comic drama survived in medieval folk plays and festivals, in the Italian COMMEDIA DELL' ARTE, in mock liturgical dramas, and in the farcical elements of miracle and morality plays. With the advent of the Renaissance, a new and vital drama emerged. In England in the 16th cent. the tradition of the INTERLUDE, developed by John Heywood and others, blended with that of Latin classic comedy, eventually producing the great Elizabethan comedy. Finding its early expression in the work of Nicholas Udall and John Lyly, Elizabethan comedy reached its highest expression in the plays of Shakespeare and Ben Jonson. Shakespeare, whose comedies ranged from the farcical to the tragicomic, was the master of the romantic comedy, while Jonson, whose drama was strongly influenced by the classical tenets, wrote caustic, rich satire. In France, after the Middle Ages, the classical influence was combined with that of the commedia dell' arte in the drama of Molière, one of the greatest comic and satiric writers in the history of the theater. This combination is also present in the plays of the Italian Carlo Goldoni. After a period of suppression during the Puritan Revolution, the English comic drama reemerged with the witty, frequently licentious, consciously artificial comedy of manners of Etherege, Wycherley, Congreve, and others. At the close of the 17th cent., however, such stern reaction had set in against the bawdiness and frivolity of the Restoration stage that English comedy descended into what has become known as sentimental comedy. This drama, which sought more to evoke tears than laughter, had its counterpart in France in the *comédie larmoyante.* In the later 18th cent. a resurgence of the satirical and witty character comedies was found in the plays of Sheridan and Goldsmith. After an almost complete lapse in the 19th cent., good comedy was again brought to the stage in the comedies of manners by Oscar Wilde and in the comedies of ideas by George Bernard Shaw. In the late 1880s the great Russian dramatist Anton Chekhov began writing his subtle and delicate comedies of the dying Russian aristocracy. The 20th cent. has witnessed several distinct trends in comedy: the sophisticated and witty comedy of manners, initiated by Wilde and carried on by Noel Coward, S. N. Behrman, Philip Barry and others; the romantic comic fantasy of such playwrights as James M. Barrie and Jean Giraudoux; the native Irish comedy of J. M. Synge, Lady Gregory, Sean O'Casey, Brendan Behan, and Brian Friel; the musical comedy, descending from 18th-century ballad operas and the comic operas of W. S. Gilbert and A. S. Sullivan (see MUSICALS); the slick, satirical, and professional comedy of George S. Kaufman, Moss Hart, and Neil Simon; the nihilistic, highly unconventional comedy, containing both comic and tragic elements, of dramatists of the theater of the absurd such as Eugene Ionesco and Samuel Beckett; and the so-called "black comedy," often concerning topics like racism, sexual perversion, and murder, of playwrights such as Joe Orton, Bruce Jay Friedman, and Jules Feiffer. For further information see separate entries on the dramatists mentioned in this article. See Elmer Blistein, *Comedy in Action* (1964); B. N. Schilling, *The Comic Spirit* (1965); J. W. Krutch, *Comedy and Conscience after the Restoration* (rev. ed. 1949, repr. 1967); H. T. E. Perry, *Masters of Dramatic Comedy* (1939, repr. 1968); Walter Sorell, *Facets of Comedy* (1972).

Comenius, John Amos (kōmē'nēəs), Czech *Jan Amos Komenský,* 1592–1670, Moravian churchman and educator, last bishop of the Moravian Church. Comenius advocated relating education to everyday life by emphasizing contact with objects in the environment and systematizing all knowledge. He did not regard religion and science as incompatible. Teaching was to be in the vernacular rather than in Latin, and languages were to be learned by the conversational method. He worked for a universal system of education offering equal opportunities to women. His *Didactica magna* (1628–32; tr. by M. W. Keatinge, 1896; 2d ed., Pt. I, 1910, Pt. II, 1923, repr. 1967) contains an exposition of these principles. He also wrote *Janua linguarum reserata* (1631; tr. *The Gate of Tongues Unlocked,* 1659) and *Orbis sensualium pictus* (1658; tr. *The Visible World,* 1659), one of the earliest illustrated books for children. His collected works were first published in 1867. See biography by F. H. Hay (1973); S. S. Laurie, *John Amos Comenius* (1892, repr. 1973); W. S. Monroe, *Comenius and the Beginnings of Educational Reform* (1900, repr. 1971).

comet [Gr.,=long haired], celestial body of small mass consisting mainly of gases and moving under the sun's gravitational influence. Comets visible from the earth can be seen for periods ranging from a few days to several months. They were long regarded with awe and even terror and were often taken as omens of unfavorable events. Although the occurrence of many comets had been recorded, it was not until 1705 that the return of one was predicted. In that year Edmund Halley concluded that the comet observed in 1682 was the same one that had been described in 1531 and 1607, and he predicted that it would return again in late 1758 or early 1759. The comet returned in the spring of 1759 and again in 1835 and 1910 (see HALLEY'S COMET). Ordinarily a comet contains a small, bright nucleus surrounded by a nebulous envelope of luminous gases called the coma; this luminosity is caused by the molecules absorbing the ultra-violet radiation of the sun. According to the ice-conglomerate theory proposed by F. L. Whipple in 1949, the nucleus consists of ice and other frozen gases with particles of heavier substances interspersed throughout, thus being in effect a large, dirty snowball. As the comet approaches the sun, particles and gases from the nucleus and coma are driven off, usually forming a tail which can extend as much as 100 million mi (160 million km) in length. The tail, pushed by the SOLAR WIND, always streams out in the direction opposite the sun; i.e., it follows the head as the comet approaches the sun and precedes it as the comet passes perihelion (its closest point to the sun) and moves away. Near the sun a comet can change drastically in size and shape, with the head contracting as material flows into the tail; it may even split in two, as Biela's comet did in 1846. The average size of the comet head is about 80,000 mi (130,000 km) in diameter, while some as small as 10,000 mi (16,000 km) and as large as 1,400,000 mi (2,250,000 km) in diameter have been observed. Whereas the volume of a comet is enormous, its mass is estimated to be no more than one millionth that of the earth. Most of the mass is contained in the nucleus and coma. The nucleus itself is small, ranging from one mile to a few thousand miles in diameter. The origin of comets is still uncertain. They were once thought to have originated outside the solar system; however, modern theories suggest they were formed with the formation of the solar system and are permanent members of it. According to the storage-cloud hypothesis of J. H. Oort, a shell of more than 100 billion comets surrounds the solar system at a distance of as much as 150,000 times the distance from the earth to the sun. While in this huge storage cloud, the comets move very slowly; a passing star, however, may change their orbits enough to force some of them into the inner part of the solar system. Some comets appear to have parabolic orbits (see PARABOLA); these orbits may send them past the sun once and then back to the storage cloud. Of the 130 comets with known periods of revolution, about 60 revolve in highly elongated orbits with periods ranging from a hundred to thousands of years. The others return at shorter intervals. About 45 comets have periods of less than 10 years and reach aphelion (the orbital point farthest from the sun) near the planet Jupiter; these have been captured into their smaller orbits by Jupiter's gravitational attraction. As comets lose material with successive passages near the sun, they fade in brightness. Some may break up, leaving a stream of meteoroids (see METEOR) scattered over their orbital path; when the earth passes through this path, a meteor shower is observed. See B. M. Middlehurst, ed., *The Moon, Meteorites, and Comets* (1963); R. S. Richardson, *Getting Acquainted with Comets* (1967); Willey Ley, *Visitors from Afar: The Comets* (1969).

comic strip, combination of cartoon with a story line, laid out in a series of pictorial panels across a page and concerning a continuous character or set of characters, whose thoughts and dialogues are indicated by means of "balloons" containing written speech. As a form of communication the comic strip medium goes back to the Middle Ages, with the BAYEUX TAPESTRY retracing the hostilities leading to the Battle of Hastings. In the 18th and early 19th cent., balloons were used regularly in the satirical cartoons of William Hogarth and Thomas ROWLANDSON; continuity was also utilized by Rowlandson in his *Tours of Dr. Syntax* (1812–21). The comic strip form can be employed to convey a variety of messages (e.g., advertisements). However, the term "comic strip" in its strictest sense refers to syndicated newspaper features that appear daily in single rows of three or four panels, printed in black and white, and weekly in two to four consecutive rows of panels, forming a page, and printed in color in the Sunday comic sections. The immediate ancestor of the newspaper comic strip was the CARTOON, popular in the late 19th cent. Although there is evidence of comic strips appearing in newspapers as early as 1892, it is the year 1896 that commonly marks the birth of the genre in the American press, with *The Yellow Kid* as its first true representative. This feature, consisting of the weekly antics of a little boy in a bright yellow nightgown, was created by Richard Felton Outcault for the Sunday supplement of Joseph Pulitzer's New York *World.* The popularity of *The Yellow Kid* resulted in an immediate increase in the *World*'s circulation. William Randolph Hearst soon succeeded in hiring Outcault for his own New York *Journal,* while Pulitzer hired another artist, George LUKS, to continue the feature in the *World.* The resulting rivalry between the two *Yellow Kids* not only produced the phrase "yellow journalism," but also emphasized the powerful influence of the comic strip as a circulation builder for newspapers. Rudolph Dirks, in the *Katzenjammer Kids* (1897), was the first to make consistent use of a sequence of panels to tell his stories. With the creation of such pioneering strips as *Happy Hooligan* (1899), by Frederick Burr OPPER, Charles ("Bunny") Schultze's *Foxy Grandpa* (1900), Outcault's *Buster Brown* (1902), and James Swinnerton's *Little Jimmy* (1905), all the essential components of the comic strip (e.g., regularity of cast, use of sequence of panels and speech-balloons) were refined and securely established. During their early days, comic strips appeared exclusively as weekly features in the Sunday supplement. In 1907, Bud Fisher created the first successful daily strip with his *Mutt and Jeff.* Because syndicates distributed plates of their comic features to many newspapers, the characters acquired national readership. The enormous influence of comic strips on the public was first demonstrated by "Buster Brown" fashions early in the 20th cent., and it is still evidenced today by the proliferation of "Peanuts" products. Until the mid-1920s comic strips were true to their name, since they were all intended to raise a laugh in the reader. In 1924, Roy Crane, with *Wash Tubbs* (later retitled *Captain Easy*), added an important new dimension to the comic strip: adventure and suspense—which had previously existed, but in burlesque form, in Charles W. Kahles's popular strip, *Hairbreadth Harry* (1906). Some of the earliest examples of this new genre—invariably drawn in a more realistic style than the early "funnies"—were *Tim Tyler's Luck* (1928), by Lyman Young, *Tarzan* (1929), first drawn by Harold Foster, and *Buck Rogers* (1929), by Phil Nowlan and Dick Calkins. These led to such enduring classics as Chester Gould's *Dick Tracy* (1931), Milton Caniff's *Terry and the Pirates* (1934), and Alex Raymond's *Flash Gordon* (1934), and culminated in the most consciously artistic strip of all, Harold Foster's *Prince Valiant* (1937). Some comic strips have proved effective vehicles for political messages: *Little Orphan Annie* (1924), by Harold Gray, extolled free enterprise and conservatism, while the satirical *Pogo* (1949), by Walt Kelly, aimed barbs at the enemies of liberalism. Social satire and intellectual humor have made some strips favorites with adults and university students: *Little Nemo in Slumberland* (1906), by Winson McCay and *Krazy Kat* (1911), by George Herriman were forerunners of these, and they led to Al Capp's *Li'l Abner* (1934), *Pogo, Peanuts* (1950), by Charles SCHULZ, Johnny Hart's *B.C.* (1958), Brant Parker's and Johnny Hart's *Wizard of Id* (1964), and Russell Myer's *Broom Hilda* (1970). Experiments with book-length strips led, in the 1930s, to the comic book, a magazine aimed primarily at a juvenile audience—unlike comic strips, which are intended for the entire family—that at first reprinted entire episodes of newspaper strips but eventually evolved its own characters, e.g., *Superman* (1938), by Jerry Siegal and Joe Shuster, *Batman* (1939), by Bob Kane, and *Captain America* (1941), by Joe Simon and Jack Kirby. Adventure, crime, and war comics eventually elicited complaints from parents, teachers, and clergymen about the portrayal of violence and crime in a product intended for children. In 1954 publishers formed a Comics Code Authority to administer self-censorship standards, thus averting government action. One of the most significant developments of the 1960s was the emergence of comic strip clubs and associations, in the United States and in Europe, whose members collect vintage strips, write critical studies about them, and publish the results of their research in specialized journals. They hold conventions where classic comic material is bought, sold, and traded, and where panel discussions, slide shows, and lectures are given on the subject of comic strips. See Coulton Waugh, *The Comics* (1947); S. D. Becker, *Comic Art in America* (1959); George Perry and Alan Aldridge, *The Penguin Book of Comics* (1967); Pierre Couperie and M. C. Horn, *A History of the Comic Strip* (1968); Walter Herdeg and David Pascal, ed., *The Art of the Comic Strip* (1972).

Comilla (kōmĭl'ə), town (1961 est. pop. 54,500), E Bangladesh, on the Gumti River. An administrative center on the main railroad and highway linking Chittagong with Dacca, it is a collection point for hides and skins and has a noted cottage industry in cane and bamboo basketry. Comilla has three colleges affiliated with the Univ. of Dacca.

Comines, Philippe de (fēlēp' də kōmēn'), c.1447–c.1511, French historian, courtier, and diplomat. In 1472 he left the service of Charles the Bold of Burgundy to enter that of Louis XI of France, who rewarded him richly. After Louis's death he plotted against Charles VIII and was banished from court. He later regained favor, accompanied Charles to Italy, and was briefly ambassador to Venice. His *Mémoires sur les règnes de Louis XI et de Charles VIII* (available in many editions and translations) is a historical and literary work of the highest rank. It contains striking portraits of Charles the Bold, Louis XI, and Charles VIII and is penetrating in its analysis of men, motives, and institutions. His name is also spelled Commines and Commynes. See his memoirs, ed. by Samuel Kinser (2 vol., tr. 1968 and 1973).

Cominform (kŏm'ĭnfôrm) [acronym for Communist Information Bureau], information agency organized in 1947 and dissolved in 1956. Its members were the Communist parties of Bulgaria, Czechoslovakia, France, Hungary, Italy, Poland, Rumania, the Soviet Union, and Yugoslavia. The Cominform attempted to reestablish information exchanges among the European Communist parties that had lapsed since the dissolution (1943) of the COMINTERN. Its decisions were not binding, nor was membership obligatory for Communist parties. It was not a reconstitution of the Comintern, only a setting up of information contacts. Its chief function was the publication of materials designed to demonstrate the unity of its members. In 1948 the Cominform expelled the Yugoslav Communist party because of the defiance by Marshal TITO of Soviet supremacy. In 1956, as a gesture of reconciliation with Tito, the Cominform was dissolved.

Comintern (kŏm'ĭntərn) [acronym for Communist International], name given to the Third INTERNATIONAL, founded at Moscow in 1919. Vladimir Ilyich Lenin feared a resurgence of the Second, or Socialist, International under non-Communist leadership. The Comintern was established to claim Communist leadership of the world socialist movement. The delegates to the first congress were mainly Russians, with some members of left-wing socialist splinter groups who happened to be in the Soviet Union and one German (who abstained on the crucial vote of establishing the organization). Gregory ZINOVIEV was the first president of the Comintern. The second congress laid down (1920) the "Twenty-one Conditions" for membership, firmly establishing a differentiation between the socialist parties of the center and the Communist parties of the left. The Comintern gained strength during the 1920s, but its efforts to foment revolution, notably in Germany, were unsuccessful. In 1935 the Comintern abandoned the membership policies established under the "Twenty-one Conditions" and began to form coalitions, or popular fronts, with bourgeois parties. In 1936, Germany and Japan concluded the so-called Anti-Comintern Pact, ostensibly to protect the world from the Third International. The pact was renewed in 1941 with 11 other countries as signatories. In order to allay the misgivings of its allies in World War II, the Soviet Union dissolved the Comintern in 1943. See K. E. McKenzie, *The Comintern and World Revolution, 1928–1943* (1964); M. M. Drachkovitch, ed., *The Comintern* (1966); Branko Lazitch and M. M. Drachkovitch, *Biographical Dictionary of the Comintern* (1973).

comma: see PUNCTUATION.

Commack (kō'măk), uninc. town (1970 pop. 22,507), Suffolk co., SE N.Y., on central Long Island. It is chiefly residential.

Commagene (kŏməjē'nē), ancient district of N Syria, on the Euphrates River and S of the Taurus range, now in SE Asiatic Turkey. Its metropolis, Samosata, was founded by Samos, the king of Commagene, c.150 B.C. The fertile agricultural district was made part of the Assyrian Empire and later of the Persian Empire. In the period after Alexander the Great, it gradually assumed independence under the Seleucid kings of Syria, and its governor, Ptolemy, revolted in 162 B.C., declaring absolute independence. The ruling dynasty of independent Commagene was related to the Seleucids. In 64 B.C., King Antiochus I, a Roman ally, had his territory enlarged with the addition of Commagene by Pompey, but when he aided the Parthians he was deposed in 38 B.C. by Antony. Commagene was annexed by Tiberius (A.D. 17) but a new king, Antiochus IV, was instated by Caligula (A.D. 38), was soon deposed, and then reinstated (A.D. 41) by Claudius. Finally Vespasian permanently annexed Commagene (A.D. 72). The territory was invaded by KHOSRU I of Persia in 542, but he withdrew the same year when his campaign was checked by BELISARIUS.

Commager, Henry Steele (kŏm'ĭjər), 1902–, American historian, b. Pittsburgh, Pa. He received his Ph.D. from the Univ. of Chicago in 1928 and taught history at New York Univ. (1926–38) and Columbia (1938–56), where he was made adjunct professor in 1956; that same year he was appointed professor at Amherst. His writings, often in collaboration with other historians, are extensive. Among them are *The Growth of the American Republic* (with Samuel E. Morison, 1930; 6th ed., rev. and enl., 2 vol. 1969), *Theodore Parker* (1936, 2d ed. 1947, reissue 1960), *Our Nation* (with Eugene C. Barker, 1941), *Majority Rule and Minority Rights* (1943), *The American Mind* (1950), *Freedom, Loyalty, and Dissent* (1954), and *The Era of Reform* (1960). He edited *Documents of American History* (1934, 8th ed. 1968), *The Heritage of America* (with Allan Nevins, 1939; rev. and enl. ed., 1949), *Readings in American History* (with Allan Nevins, 1939), *America in Perspective: The United States through Foreign Eyes* (1947), *The St. Nicholas Anthology* (1948), *The Spirit of 'Seventy-six* (with R. B. Morris, 1958), and *The Atlas of the Civil War* (1950). Commager is also editor of the multivolume "Rise of the American Nation" series. See the biographical essays in *Freedom and Reform*, ed. by H. M. Hyman and L. W. Levy (1967).

Commander Islands: see KOMANDORSKI ISLANDS, USSR.

Commandments, Ten: see TEN COMMANDMENTS.

commando, small military raiding and assault unit, first employed by the Boers in the South African War (1899–1902). However, it was not until 1940, when the British organized a number of such units, that the term came into wide use. Made up of handpicked volunteers, specifically trained for dangerous work, these units were employed in missions throughout World War II. Some of the most celebrated of the commando operations were the raids on Field Marshal Rommel's headquarters (1941) and on St. Nazaire (1942) and the capture (1944) of the Dutch island of Walcheren. The U.S. army's ranger battalions were somewhat similar and were also popularly called commandos. After World War II, the American rangers and the British army's commandos were disbanded, but the British Royal Marine Commandos remained active and were employed in the Korean war and the Suez operation. During the Arab-Israeli conflicts, commando raids were common on both sides. See GUERRILLA WARFARE.

commedia dell' arte (kōm-mā'dēä dĕl-lär'tā), popular form of comedy employing improvised dialogue and masked characters that flourished in Italy from the 16th to the 18th cent. Its influence on European drama is inestimable and can be seen especially in French pantomime and in the English harlequinade. Probable roots are found in the *Fabulae Atellanae* of the Oscans and Romans and in the Byzantine mimes of the Eastern Roman Empire. Little remains to evaluate the original performances, although *scenarii* (synopses of plot), *concetti* (stock rhetorical speeches for every emotion), and *lazzi* (stock comic business that could be employed) are recorded. The ensemble companies generally performed in Italy, although a company called the *comédie-italienne* was established in Paris in 1661. The characters or "masks," in spite of changes over the years, retained much of their original flavor. Often the actor became so associated with his part that he used the name of his character in everyday life. Most important were the *zanni*, or servant types. They were the plot weavers, and their job was to arouse laughter. Arlecchino, or Harlequin, was the most famous of this type. An acrobat and a wit, he was always childlike and amorous. He wore a black, cat-like mask and motley colored clothes, which were later patterned with red, blue, and green diamonds. He carried a bat or wooden sword, the ancestor of the slapstick. His crony, Brighella, was more roguish and sophisticated. A cowardly villain, he would do anything for money. Figaro and Molière's Scapino are descendants of this type. Pedrolino, the martyr type, was a white-faced, moonstruck dreamer. The French PIERROT is his descendant. Pagliaccio, the forerunner of today's clown, was closely akin to Pedrolino. Pulcinella, as seen in the English PUNCH AND JUDY shows, was dwarfish and cruel, a humpback with a crooked nose, the deformed bachelor who chased pretty girls. Pantalone or Pantaloon was a caricature of the Venetian merchant, rich and retired, mean and miserly, with a young wife or an adventurous daughter. Wearing baggy trousers, he had a pointed beard, and his chin was thrust forward. Il Dottore (the doctor), his only friend, was a walking caricature of learning, pompous and fraudulent. He was dressed in black. He survives in the works of Molière. Il Capitano (the captain) was a caricature of the professional soldier, usually of the Spanish type, bold and swaggering, but cowardly. He was replaced by Scarramuccia or Scaramouche, who was much more agile. Dressed in black and carrying a pointed sword, he was the Robin Hood of his day. The Inamorato (the lover) went by many names. The matinee idol of his time, he had to be handsome and eloquent in order to speak the love declamations. He wore no mask. The Inamorata, whether she be prima donna or seconda donna, was his female counterpart. Isabella ANDREINI was the most famous. Her servant, or soubrette, usually called Columbine, was the beloved of Harlequin. Witty, bright, and given to intrigue, she developed, along with Harlequin, into such characters as Harlequine and Pierrette. La Ruffiana was an old woman, either the mother or a village gossip, who thwarted the lovers. Cantarina and Ballerina often took part in the comedy, but for the most part their job was to add variety to the performance by singing, dancing, or playing a musical instrument. None of the women wore masks. The commedia dell' arte survived the early 18th cent. only by means of its vast influence on written dramatic forms. See Allardyce Nicoll, *Masks, Mimes, and Miracles* (1931); K. M. Lea, *The Italian Popular Comedy* (2 vol., 1934, repr. 1962); Winifred Smith, *Commedia Dell' arte* (rev. ed. 1964); P. L. Duchartre, *The Italian Comedy* (tr. 1928, repr. 1965).

commensalism, relationship between members of two different species of organisms in which one individual is usually only slightly benefited, while the other member is not affected at all by the relationship. For example, some flatworms live attached to the gills of the horseshoe crab, obtaining bits of food from the crab's meals; the crab is apparently unaffected. In many cases commensalism cannot be distinguished from parasitism (see PARASITE). See also COMPETITION; SYMBIOSIS.

Commerce, city (1970 pop. 10,536), Los Angeles co., S Calif., a suburb of Los Angeles; inc. 1960. An important transportation hub for S California, Commerce is the home of several large corporations; manufactures range from telephones to chemicals. In 1927, Charles A. Lindbergh landed *The Spirit of St. Louis* at the old Vail Field in Commerce while on a nationwide tour following his transatlantic flight.

commerce, traffic in goods, usually conceived as nondomestic trade. Engaged in by all peoples from the earliest times, it has been carried on in some areas and by some peoples more than others, because of special advantages or aptness. The Egyptians, the Sumerians and later inhabitants of Mesopotamia, the Cretans, the Syrians, the Phoenicians, the Greeks, the Arabs, and the Western Europeans have excelled in commerce, tapping the resources of the East, Oceania, the Americas, and Africa. The center of commerce has shifted from the Mediterranean to the North Sea and the Atlantic. The Crusades did much to widen European trade horizons and prefaced the passing of trade superiority from Constantinople to Venice and other cities of N Italy. In the 15th and 16th cent. with the sudden expansion of Portugal and Spain the so-called commercial revolution reached a climax. In N and central Europe, the earlier supremacy of the Hanseatic League, the Rhenish cities, and the cities of N France and Flanders was eclipsed by the rise of national states. Antwerp began its long career of glory when the Spanish were losing hegemony, and the Dutch briefly triumphed in the race for world commerce in the 17th cent. The Dutch in turn gave way to a British-French rivalry that by 1815 left Great Britain paramount. The Industrial Revolution of the 18th and the 19th cent. further aided the development of commerce. The rise of the CHARTERED COMPANY under the auspices of the national state had much to do with the expansion of trade, as did the modern corporation, which later displaced the chartered company. World commerce was also aided materially by the invention of the astrolabe, the mariner's compass, and the sextant; by the development of iron and steel construction; by the application of steam to both land and water transport; and by the more recent development of communication devices such as the telephone, telegraph, cable, and radio and of inventions such as refrigeration, the gasoline engine, the electric motor, and the airplane. The theory of commerce as imposed by the national state has varied from the MERCANTILISM of the 17th and 18th cent. and the protective tariff of the 19th and 20th cent. to the free trade that Britain long upheld. After World War II recognition of the need for commercial expansion led to the creation of regional systems such as the COMMON MARKET. In general there was a twofold development. On the one hand there was a reduction of regional trade barriers. And on the other there was a tendency for the Communist and capitalist countries to bar trade with each other; by the 1970s, however, commerce between the two blocs had been greatly expanded. See Miriam Beard, *A History of Business* (2 vol., 1938; repr. 1962–63); H. L. Adelson, *Medieval Commerce* (1962); C. S. Belshaw, *Traditional Exchange and Modern Markets* (1965); William Culican, *The First Merchant Venturers* (1967); Jan Pen, *A Primer on International Trade* (1967); R. S. Lopez, *The Commercial Revolution of the Middle Ages* (1971).

Commerce, United States Department of, Federal executive department charged with promoting U.S. economic development and technological advancement. In Feb., 1903, the Congress established a Department of Commerce and Labor empowered to investigate and report upon the operations of corporations engaged in interstate commerce (with the exception of common carriers). The first secretary was G. B. CORTELYOU. In 1913 the Department of Labor was established as a separate executive department, while the functions of the Department of Commerce were expanded; the chief officer of each department, the Secretary, received cabinet rank. Among its tasks are taking of censuses, promotion of American business at home and abroad, establishing standard weights and measures, and issuing patents and registering trademarks. Agencies under control of the Secretary of Commerce include the Economic Development Administration, the Bureau of the Census, the National Oceanic and Atmospheric Administration, the Office of Minority Business Enterprise, the National Bureau of Standards, the Patent Office, the Maritime Administration, and the Bureau of International Commerce.

Commerce City, city (1970 pop. 17,407), Adams co., N central Colo., an industrial suburb of Denver; inc. 1952.

commercial law, the laws that govern business transactions, except those relating to the transportation of goods (see MARITIME LAW). Commercial law developed as a distinct body of jurisprudence with the beginning of large-scale trade. Formal documents and other evidences of regularized trade practices were known in Egypt and Babylonia. In many parts of the ancient world foreign merchants, through treaty arrangements or other agreements, were allowed to regulate their affairs and adjudicate their own disputes without interference from local authorities. They tended to settle in special sections of commercial cities where they might follow their own religions, laws, and customs. ROMAN LAW incorporated features of the already developed commercial law, which, however, was no longer handled separately in special courts but was treated simply as part of the whole legal system. The barbarian invasions of Europe caused such social disruption that it was not until late in the Middle Ages that long-range commerce again became possible in Europe and merchants were once more able to determine the rules and regulations under which they could safely operate. In the cities of N Italy and S France the merchant class frequently dominated the state and could enact the needed rules as legislation. In other parts of Europe associations of merchants bought protection from powerful lords or kings who granted them safe conduct and permitted them to conduct fairs and to establish regulations and methods of enforcement (see HANSEATIC LEAGUE). Both classes of merchants established special courts where summary judgment was granted with little regard for the technicalities of procedure and doctrine in the regular courts and without the use of lawyers. The term "law merchant" was applied to the substantive principles that eventually emerged from this quasi-judicial activity. The law merchant developed later in England than on the Continent, and it was not fully established there until the mid-16th cent., when English trade with the New World began to assume importance. In England the law was administered by special courts having jurisdiction only over those engaged in trade; these were the courts of piepoudre [Fr., *pied poudré*=dusty foot, an allusion to the dusty shoes of merchant judges who perhaps had been trudging the roads]. The royal courts in early days refused to hear merchants' suits, but in the 17th cent. they reversed this position and obtained exclusive jurisdiction. At first, however, the litigants were required to present proof of the law merchant in each case. The uncertainty and delay that resulted from this requirement demanded reform, and in the 18th cent. Lord Chief Justice Mansfield made the law merchant a part of the COMMON LAW and abolished the requirement of special proof. The United States adopted the principles prevailing in England in the late 18th cent. On the continent of Europe commercial law remains a separate subject matter with its special courts. It has been argued that the continental system is superior in that it distinguishes the business affairs of formally established enterprises from those entered into casually by private persons. The Anglo-American system, on the other hand, has been defended as affording no favoritism to any form of business activity. However, in commercial countries of both systems there has been a considerable increase in the extensive use of commercial arbitration that is in many ways comparable to the former private courts of merchants. The American states have adopted almost uniform commercial statutes that considerably facilitate the flow of trade throughout the nation. See F. R. Sanborn, *The Origins of Early English Maritime and Commercial Law* (1930); J. G. Pease, *The Law of Markets and Fairs* (1958); F. A. Whitney, *The Law of Modern Commercial Practices* (1959).

commercial paper, type of short-term negotiable instrument, usually an unsecured promissory note, that calls for the payment of money at a specified date. Because it is not backed by collateral, commercial paper is usually issued by major firms whose credit-rating is so good that their notes are immediately accepted for trading. The notes are sold at a discount and mature in from three to six months. Commercial paper is an important source of cash for the issuing firm; it supplements bank loans and is usually payable at a lower rate of interest than the prime discount rate. Strictly speaking, it includes only those instruments that are used in commerce in place of money, as distinguished from paper used in investment, personal, estate, speculative, and public transactions. In addition to promissory notes, commercial paper may include drafts, bills of exchange and checks, acceptances, bills of lading, warehouse receipts, orders for delivery of goods, and express orders. See. A. O. Greef, *The Commercial Paper House in the United States* (1939); N. D. Baxter, *The Commercial Paper Market* (1969).

commercial revolution, in European history, a fundamental change in the quantity and scope of commerce. In the later Middle Ages steady economic expansion had seen the rise of towns and the advent of private banking, a money economy, and trading organizations such as the HANSEATIC LEAGUE. Under the new national monarchies, most notably those of Portugal, Spain, the Netherlands, and England, markets grew wider and more secure. Commercial expansion was supported by technical improvements in seafaring, and from about 1450 explorations were made, first to Africa, then to the Orient and the New World. By the mid-16th cent. the Oriental carrying trade had been wrested from the Arabs, and Eastern goods poured into Europe. From the New World came gold and silver, which in less than a century more than doubled European prices and greatly stimulated economic activity. The focus of commerce shifted from Mediterranean to Atlantic ports, CHARTERED COMPANIES were organized, and continued improvements in navigation and ship construction speeded long voyages. As a world-wide trade evolved, the principles of MERCANTILISM were adopted, and local trade barriers were abrogated, stimulating internal commerce. Modern credit facilities also appeared; new institutions included the state bank, the bourse, and the futures market, and the promissory note and other new media of exchange were created. Quickened commercial activity brought economic specialization, thus leading to the transformations in production associated with modern capitalism. By 1700 the stage was set for the INDUSTRIAL REVOLUTION. See H. A. Miskimin, *The Economy of Early Renaissance Europe, 1300–1460* (1969); Joseph Gies, *Merchants and Moneymen* (1972); M. M. Postan, *Medieval Trade and Finance* (1973).

Commines, Philippe de: see COMINES, PHILIPPE DE.

commission government: see CITY GOVERNMENT.

committee, one or more persons appointed or elected to consider, report on, or take action on a particular matter. Because of the advantages of a division of labor, legislative committees of various kinds have assumed much of the work of legislatures in many nations. Standing committees are appointed in both houses of the U.S. Congress at the beginning of every session to deal with bills in the different specific classes. Important congressional committees include those on ways and means; appropriations; interstate commerce; and military, naval, and foreign affairs. The number, but not the scope, of the committees was much reduced in 1946. Since then there has been a large increase in the number of subcommittees, which have become steadily more important. Members of committees are in effect elected by caucuses of the two major parties in Congress; the majority party is given the chairmanship and majority on each committee, and chairmanships, as well as membership on important committees, are gained by seniority. The presiding officer of either house may appoint special committees, including those of investigation, which have the power to summon witnesses and compel the submission of evidence. The presiding officers also appoint committees of conference to obtain agreement between the two houses on the content of bills of the same general character. The American legislative committee system conducts most congressional business, through its powers of scrutiny and investigation of government departments. In France the constitution of the Fifth Republic permits each legislative chamber to have no more than six standing committees. Because these committees are large, unofficial committees have formed that do much of the real work of examining bills. As in the U.S. government, these committees are quite powerful because of their ability to delay legislation. In Great Britain devices such as committees of the whole are used in the consideration of money bills and there are large standing committees of the House of Commons; but legislative committees have not traditionally been very important in the system of government. Recently attempts have been made to form specialized committees. See L. A. Froman, *The Congressional Process* (1967); George Goodwin, Jr., *The Little Legislatures* (1970); Barbara Hinckley, *The Seniority System in Congress* (1971).

Committee for Industrial Organization: see AMERICAN FEDERATION OF LABOR AND CONGRESS OF INDUSTRIAL ORGANIZATIONS.

Committee of Public Safety: see REIGN OF TERROR.

Commodity Credit Corporation: see AGRICULTURAL SUBSIDIES.

commodity market, organized traders' exchange in which standardized, graded products are bought and sold. Commodity markets in the United States are open for trading in about 30 commodities, ranging from wheat and cotton to silver and platinum. Most trading is done in futures contracts, i.e., agreements to deliver goods at a set time in the future for a price established at the time of the agreement. Futures trading allows both HEDGING to protect against serious losses in a declining market and speculation for gain in a rising market. For example, a seller may sign a contract agreeing to deliver grain in two months at a set price. If the grain market declines at the end of two months, the seller will still get the higher price quoted in the futures contract. If the market rises, however, speculators buying grain stand to profit by paying the lower contract price for the grain and reselling it at the higher market price. Spot contracts, a less widely used form of trading, call for immediate delivery of a specified commodity and are often used to obtain the goods necessary to fulfill a futures contract.

Commodus (Lucius Aelius Aurelius Commodus) (kŏm'ədəs), 161–192, Roman emperor (180–192), son and successor of MARCUS AURELIUS. In 180, reversing his father's foreign policy, he concluded peace with the German and the Sarmatian tribes and returned to his licentious pleasures in Rome. There he vaunted his strength in gladiatorial combats and decreed that he should be worshiped as Hercules Romanus. He changed his own name to Marcus Commodus Antoninus and wanted to rename the city of Rome after himself. Many plots to assassinate him failed, but eventually, on the order of his advisers, he was strangled by a wrestler. PERTINAX succeeded him.

Common Cause, U.S. organization that seeks a "reordering of national priorities and revitalization of the public process to make our political and governmental institutions more responsive to the needs of the nation and its citizens." It was established in 1970 by John W. Gardner as the successor organization to the Urban Coalition Action Council, which was founded in 1968. Common Cause calls itself the "national citizens lobby." It supports a large number of political reforms, including abolition of the Congressional seniority system, and a limitation on national campaign spending and political contributions. It has sponsored voter registration drives throughout the nation and has worked for a liberalization of registration requirements. Common Cause has been especially effective in employing lawsuits as a weapon of political reform. In the early 1970s its legal actions were an integral part of the mostly successful drive to force disclosure of those individuals and corporations that had anonymously contributed money to the 1972 presidential campaign. Located in Washington, D.C., the group has about 110,000 members.

common-ion effect, decrease in solubility of an ionic SALT, i.e., one that dissociates in solution into its IONS, caused by the presence in SOLUTION of another solute that contains one of the same ions as the salt. The common-ion effect is an example of CHEMICAL EQUILIBRIUM. For example, silver chloride, AgCl, is a slightly soluble salt that in solution dissociates into the ions Ag^+ and Cl^-, the equilibrium state being represented by the equation $AgCl_{solid} \rightleftharpoons Ag^+ + Cl^-$. According to LE CHÂTELIER'S PRINCIPLE, when a stress is placed on a system in equilibrium, the system responds by tending to reduce that stress. In the system taken as an example, if another solute containing one of those ions is added, e.g., sodium chloride, NaCl, which supplies Cl^- ions, the solubility equilibrium of the solution will be shifted to remove more Cl^- from the solution, so that at the new equilibrium point there will be fewer Ag^+ and Cl^- ions in solution and more AgCl precipitated out as a solid.

common law, system of law that prevails in England and in countries colonized by England. The name is derived from the medieval theory that the law administered by the king's courts represented the common custom of the realm, as opposed to the custom of local jurisdiction that was applied in local or manorial courts. In its early development common law was largely a product of three English courts—King's Bench, Exchequer, and the Court of Common Pleas—which competed successfully against other courts for jurisdiction and developed a distinctive body of doctrine. The term "common law" is also used to mean the traditional element in the law of any common-law jurisdiction, as opposed to its statutory law or legislation (see STATUTE), and to signify that part of the legal system that did not develop out of EQUITY, maritime law, or other special branches of practice. The distinctive feature of common law is that it represents the law of the courts as expressed in judicial decisions. The grounds for deciding cases are found in precedents provided by past decisions, as contrasted to the CIVIL LAW system, based on statutes and prescribed texts. Early common law was somewhat inflexible; it would not adjudicate a case that did not fall precisely under the purview of a particular WRIT and had an unwieldy set of procedural rules. Except for a few types of lawsuit in which the object was to recover real or personal property, the only remedy that it provided was money DAMAGES; equity was created partly to overcome these deficiencies. Until comparatively recent times there was a sharp division between common law (or legal jurisprudence) and equity (or equitable jurisprudence). In 1848 the state of New York enacted a code of civil procedure (drafted by David Dudley FIELD) that merged law and equity into one jurisdiction. Thenceforth, actions at law and suits in equity were to be administered in the same courts and under the same procedure. The Field code reforms were adopted by most states of the United States, by the Federal government, and by the United Kingdom (in the Judicature Act of 1873). Besides the system of judicial precedents, other characteristics of common law are trial by JURY and the doctrine of supremacy of the law. Originally, supremacy of the law meant that not even the king was above the law; today it means that acts of governmental agencies are subject to scrutiny in ordinary legal proceedings. Judicial precedents derive their force from the doctrine of *stare decisis* [Lat.,=stand by the decided matter], i.e., that the previous decisions of the highest court in the jurisdiction are binding on all other courts in the jurisdiction. Changing conditions, however, soon make most decisions inapplicable except as a basis for analogy, and a court must therefore often look to the judicial experience of the rest of the English-speaking world. This gives the system flexibility, while general acceptance of certain authoritative materials provides a degree of stability. Nevertheless, in many instances, the courts have failed to keep pace with social developments and it has become necessary to enact statutes to bring about needed changes; indeed, in recent years statutes have superseded much of common law, notably in the fields of commercial, administrative, and criminal law. Typically, however, in statutory interpretation the courts have recourse to the doctrines of common law. Thus increased legislation has limited but has not ended judicial supremacy. All Canada except Quebec and all of the United States except Louisiana, Puerto Rico, and the Virgin Islands follow common law. U.S. statutes usually provide that the common law, equity, and statutes in effect in England in 1603, the first year of the reign of James I, shall be deemed part of the law of the jurisdiction. Later decisions of English courts have only persuasive authority. See O. W. Holmes, *The Common Law* (1881; new ed., ed. by M. DeWolfe Howe, 1963, repr. 1968); T. F. Plucknett, *Concise History of the Common Law* (5th ed. 1956); Harold Potter, *Historical Introduction to English Law and Its Institutions* (4th ed. 1958); A. R. Hogue, *Origins of the Common Law* (1966); R. C. van Caenegem, *The Birth of the English Common Law* (1973).

Common Market, officially the European Economic Community (EEC), established (1957) by a treaty between Belgium, France, Italy, Luxembourg, the Netherlands, and West Germany (Federal Republic of Germany). It is headquartered in Brussels, Belgium. In 1961, Great Britain, the Republic of Ireland, Norway, and Denmark began negotiations for membership, but these were ended in 1963 at the insistence of France. Another attempt failed in 1967. By 1972, however, negotiations were successful and the four applicants were invited to join by signing the Treaty of Accession. Great Britain, the Republic of Ireland, and Denmark formally joined in 1973, but Norway's electorate rejected the bid. Greece and Turkey and a number of African countries are associate members. The most important step in the creation of the EUROPEAN COMMUNITY, the Common Market has as its aim the eventual economic union of its member nations, ultimately leading to political union. Steps in this program include the gradual elimination of all internal tariff barriers and establishment of a common tariff system, the free movement of labor and capital, the abolition of trusts and cartels, and the development of joint and reciprocal policies on labor, social welfare, agriculture, transport, and foreign trade. Steps toward economic union have included the following: the establishment, in 1962, of common price levels for agricultural products; the removal, 1968, of customs duties; and the agreement, in 1969, to move toward monetary union. A first step in the direction of political union was the 1970 agreement to meet twice a year for foreign policy consultations. See F. B. Jensen and Ingo Walter, *The Common Market* (1965); Uwe Kitzinger, *The European Common Market and Community* (1967); A. E. Walsh and John Paxton, *The Structure and Development of the Common Market* (1968); R. C. Mowat, *Creating the European Community* (1973); Charles Ransom, *The European Community and Eastern Europe* (1973).

Commons, John Rogers, 1862–1945, American economist, b. Hollansburg, Ohio, grad. Oberlin, 1888. Influenced by the other social sciences, Commons tried to broaden the scope of economics, especially in his noted *Legal Foundations of Capitalism* (1924) and *Institutional Economics* (1934). He was also interested in immediate social problems, chiefly those dealing with labor, and served on many government commissions. Commons was one of the editors of *A Documentary History of American Industrial Society* (10 vol., 1910–11) and *History of Labor in the United States* (4 vol., 1919–35). See his autobiography, *Myself* (1934); biography by L. G. Harter (1962).

Commons, House of: see PARLIAMENT.

commonwealth, form of administration signifying government by the common consent of the people. To Locke and Hobbes and other 17th-century writers the term meant an organized political community similar to what is meant in the 20th cent. by the word *state.* Certain states of the United States are known as commonwealths (Massachusetts, Pennsylvania, Virginia, and Kentucky), and the federated states of Australia are known collectively as the Commonwealth of Australia. In the same collective sense, the now independent components of the former British Empire and Britain's remaining dependencies are described as the COMMONWEALTH OF NATIONS. The **Commonwealth** in English history was the government set up by the victorious army power following the English civil war and the execution (1649) of King Charles I. The Commonwealth was dominated from the outset by Oliver CROMWELL, who by the Instrument of Government (1653) was made lord protector of the Commonwealth. The subsequent government is usually known as the PROTECTORATE, though the Commonwealth formally continued until Restoration in 1660.

Commonwealth Fund, foundation established (1918) by Mrs. Stephen V. Harkness "for the welfare of mankind." Its headquarters are in New York City. In 1970 its assets were estimated at over $113 million. Contributing in its first 20 years to the early development of child guidance clinics and the strengthening of rural hospitals and health departments, the fund later emphasized the broadening and integration of medical education, experimental health services, and medical research. Fellowships are offered to graduate students and civil servants from the British Commonwealth for study in the United States, and fellowships for advanced training in medicine and allied fields are given to aid teaching and research.

Commonwealth games, series of amateur athletic meets held among citizens of countries in the Commonwealth of Nations. Originated (1930) as the British Empire games, the series is held every four years and is patterned after the Olympic games. The meets have been: 1930, Hamilton, Canada; 1934, London; 1938, Sydney, Australia; (no games in 1942 and 1946 due to World War II); 1950, Auckland, New

Zealand; 1954, Vancouver, Canada; 1958, Cardiff, Wales; 1962, Perth, Australia; 1966, Kingston, Jamaica; 1970, Edinburgh, Scotland; 1974, Christchurch, New Zealand. Competition is in badminton, boxing, cycling, fencing, shooting, swimming, track and field, weight lifting, and wrestling.

Commonwealth of Australia: see AUSTRALIA.

Commonwealth of Nations, voluntary association of Great Britain and its dependencies, certain former British dependencies that are now sovereign states and their dependencies, and the associated states (states with full internal government but whose external relations are governed by Britain). At its foundation under the Statute of Westminster (see WESTMINSTER, STATUTES OF) in 1931, the Commonwealth was composed of Great Britain, the Irish Free State (now the Republic of Ireland), Canada, Newfoundland (since 1949 part of Canada), Australia, New Zealand, and South Africa. As of 1974 the other sovereign members (with date of entry) were: India (1947), Sri Lanka (as Ceylon, 1948), Ghana (1957), Malaysia (as Federation of Malaya, 1957), Nigeria (1960), Cyprus (1961), Sierra Leone (1961), Tanzania (as Tanganyika, 1961), Jamaica (1962), Trinidad and Tobago (1962), Uganda (1962), Kenya (1963), Malawi (1964), Zambia (1964), Malta (1964), The Gambia (1965), Singapore (1965), Guyana (1966), Botswana (1966), Lesotho (1966), Barbados (1966), Mauritius (1968), Swaziland (1968), Western Samoa (1970), Tonga (1970), Fiji (1970), Bangladesh (1972), the Bahamas (1973), and Grenada (1974). Ireland, South Africa, and Pakistan withdrew in 1949, 1961, and 1972, respectively. Nauru became a special member in 1968. The associated states in 1974 were: Antigua (1967); St. Kitts-Nevis (1967); Dominica (1967); St. Lucia (1967); and St. Vincent (1969). Brunei and (nominally) Rhodesia have statutes similar to those of associated states. The purpose of the Commonwealth is consultation and cooperation. The sovereign members retain full authority in all domestic and foreign affairs, although Britain generally enjoys a traditional position of leadership in certain matters of mutual interest. Members (Canada is the sole exception) are part of the sterling monetary exchange area. There are other economic ties in the fields of trade, investment, and development programs for new nations. A set of trade agreements (begun at the Ottawa Conference in 1932) between Britain and the other members gives preferential tariff treatment to many raw materials and manufactured goods that the Commonwealth nations sell in Britain. There is great concern that Britain's entry (1973) into the European COMMON MARKET may disrupt these economic ties and threaten the viability of the Commonwealth. Periodically there are meetings of Commonwealth heads of government, but no collective decision made at these meetings is considered binding. In 1965 a Commonwealth Secretariat was set up, with headquarters in London. See BRITISH EMPIRE. See W. B. Hamilton, ed., *A Decade of the Commonwealth, 1955–1964* (1965); J. D. B. Miller, *The Commonwealth in the World* (3d ed. 1965); Zelman Cowen, *The British Commonwealth of Nations in a Changing World* (1965); *The Commonwealth Office Yearbook* (annual, from 1967); Nicholas Mansergh, *The Commonwealth Experience* (1969).

commune, in agriculture: see COLLECTIVE FARM.

commune (kŏm'yo͞on), in medieval history, collective institution that developed in continental Europe after the fall of the Roman Empire. Because of the importance of the commune in municipal government, the term is also used to denote a town itself to which a charter of liberties was granted by the sovereign or feudal overlord. Although in most cases the development of communes was inextricably connected with that of the cities, there were rural communes, notably in France and England, that were formed to protect the common interests of villagers. To build defenses, regulate and improve trade, raise taxes, and maintain order, organization of an urban area was necessary. The earliest attempts at united action of the burghers involved the forming of associations in which the burghers swore an oath binding themselves together in a personal bond of mutual support and defense. The communes grew in power and, as autonomous corporate entities, became extremely influential in organizing city government. By the late 12th cent., when cities were well established, all who chose to live in them had to take an oath acknowledging the authority of the communes. Because the town was located on land belonging to a king or emperor (see FEUDALISM), the town owed allegiance to its lord and paid him tribute and, in wartime, service or money payment. Suzerains often favored the communes as sources of wealth and confirmed their rights in liberal charters. Disputes, nevertheless, frequently arose between communes and their overlords. In the struggle between kings and nobles, the kings usually strengthened the communes and sought alliances with them. However, in the 16th and 17th cent., when European states (notably France and Spain) became centralized, the privileges of the communes were gradually withdrawn. The extent of their liberties and the details of their organization varied widely. A common feature was the elected council. The magistrates were usually called *consoli, podestàs,* and *capitouls* in Italy and S France, *échevins* and *jurés* in N France and the Low Countries, *Senatoren* and *Ratsherren* in Germany. Corporations and guilds gained a prominent share in the government. Militia insured the defense. The earliest communes arose in N and central Italy. In the struggle between emperors and popes, the communes forming the LOMBARD LEAGUE gained a great deal of independence and became almost synonymous with the cities themselves. In the 14th cent., however, the communes were usurped by local tyrants. The commune of ROME was established by Arnold of Brescia in 1144. In the Low Countries, e.g., in FLANDERS, communes arose very early and enjoyed very wide privileges. In S France, AVIGNON, ARLES, and TOULOUSE were outstanding examples of self-governed communes, as BARCELONA was in Spain. In Germany, cities such as FRANKFURT, COLOGNE, NUREMBERG, AUGSBURG, and LÜBECK became republics immediately subject to the emperor (imperial and free imperial cities). Others, such as MAGDEBURG, held charters that became models for numerous towns in N Germany, Bohemia, and Moravia. See W. F. T. Butler, *The Lombard Communes* (1906, repr. 1969); Henri Pirenne, *Medieval Cities* (tr. 1925, repr. 1969); M. V. Clarke, *The Medieval City State* (1926, repr. 1966); J. H. Mundy and Peter Riesenberg, *The Medieval Town* (1959).

Commune of Paris, insurrectionary governments in Paris formed during (1792) the FRENCH REVOLUTION and at the end (1871) of the FRANCO-PRUSSIAN WAR. In the French Revolution, the commune represented the will of the urban workers and small tradesmen against that of the upper bourgeoisie and the agrarian provinces. The commune virtually engineered the storming of the Tuileries and the arrest of the king on Aug. 10, 1792, thus precipitating the downfall of the French monarchy. For the next two years the commune, led by Pierre CHAUMETTE and Jacques HÉBERT, was, along with the Committee of Public Safety, a major power in the French state. Through the bloc of deputies known as the MOUNTAIN the commune also dominated the National Convention. During the REIGN OF TERROR, however, many leaders of the commune were executed (1794), and when the moderates gained control of the Convention (1794–95), they broke the commune's power. At the end of the Franco-Prussian War, in 1871, the Parisians opposed the national government, headed by Adolphe THIERS and the National Assembly at Versailles, as too conservative and too ready to accept a humiliating peace with Prussia. Thiers, after failing to disarm the Parisian national guard, fled (March, 1871) to Versailles, and the Parisians elected a municipal council, the commune of 1871. Meanwhile, the victorious Prussians affected neutrality. The Versailles troops began a siege of Paris (the second siege of the city in three months). The *communards,* whose aims included economic reforms, represented many shades of political opinion—followers of Louis BLANQUI, of Pierre PROUDHON, and of the Marxist First International as well as radical republicans of the 1793 Jacobin tradition, such as Louis DELESCLUZE. As the long siege drew to an end, the Versailles troops entered the city despite the desperate defense of the *communards,* who threw up barricades, shot hostages (including the archbishop of Paris), and burned the Tuileries palace, the city hall, and the palace of justice. On May 28 the commune was finally defeated. Severe reprisals followed, with more than 17,000 people executed, including women and children. Numerous persons were deported or imprisoned. Communes were also formed and suppressed in other cities in 1871, notably in Saint-Étienne, Le Creusot, Marseilles, and Toulouse. Memories of the bloody Paris repression embittered political relations between liberals and conservatives for many years afterward. See studies by E. S. Mason (1930, repr. 1967), Frank Jellinek (1937, repr. 1965), Alistair Horne (1965 and 1971), and Stewart Edwards (1971).

communicable diseases, illnesses caused by microorganisms and transmitted from an infected person or animal to another person or animal. Some diseases are passed on by direct or indirect contact with infected persons or with their excretions. Most diseases are spread through contact or close proximity because the causative bacteria or viruses are airborne; i.e., they can be expelled from the nose and mouth of the infected person and inhaled by anyone in his vicinity. Such diseases include diphtheria, scarlet fever, measles, mumps, whooping cough, influenza, and smallpox. Some infectious diseases can be spread only indirectly, usually through contaminated food or water, e.g., typhoid, cholera, dysentery. Still other infections are introduced into the body by animal or insect carriers, e.g., rabies, malaria, encephalitis, Rocky Mountain spotted fever. The human disease carrier, i.e., the healthy person who may himself be immune to the organisms he harbors, is also a source of transmission. Some infective organisms require rather special circumstances for their transmission, e.g., sexual contact in syphilis and gonorrhea, injury in the presence of infected soil or dirt in tetanus, infected transfusion blood or instruments in serum hepatitis and sometimes in malaria. A disease such as tuberculosis may be transmitted in several ways—by contact (human or animal), through food or eating utensils, and by the air. Control of communicable disease depends upon recognition of the many ways transmission takes place. It must include isolation or even quarantine of persons with certain diseases. Proper antisepsis (see ANTISEPTIC) should be observed in illness and in health. Immunologic measures (see IMMUNITY) should be utilized fully. Education of the population in rules of public health is of great importance both in the matter of personal responsibility (disposal of secretions, proper handling and preparation of food, personal hygiene) and community responsibility (safe water and food supply, garbage and waste disposal). Animal and insect carriers must be controlled, and the activities of human carriers must be limited.

communication, transfer of information, such as thoughts and messages, as contrasted with transportation, the transfer of goods and persons (see INFORMATION THEORY). The basic forms of communication are by signs (sight) and by sounds (hearing; see LANGUAGE). The reduction of communication to writing was a fundamental step in the evolution of society for, in addition to being useful in situations where speech is not possible, writing permits the preservation of communications, or records, from the past. It marks the beginning of recorded history. Whereas the rise of BOOK PUBLISHING and JOURNALISM (see also NEWSPAPER and PERIODICAL) facilitated the widespread dissemination of information, the invention of the TELEGRAPH, the RADIO, the TELEPHONE, and TELEVISION made possible instantaneous communication over long distances. With the installation of the submarine CABLE and improvements in short-wave radio technology, international communication was greatly improved and expanded. In 1962 several types of communications satellites were launched. Three years later, in 1965, Early Bird, or Intelsat I, the first in a series of advanced communications satellites, was launched (see SATELLITE, ARTIFICIAL). The 20th-cent. development of mass media has played a major role in changing social, economic, political, and educational institutions. In the United States, radio and television communication is controlled by the FEDERAL COMMUNICATIONS COMMISSION. The international phases of transport and communications are under the direction of the Office of Transport and Communications of the Dept. of State. The UN maintains its International Telecommunication Union (ITU), which has three functions—to maintain and extend international cooperation for the improvement and rational use of telecommunication, to promote the development and efficient use of technical facilities, and to harmonize the actions of nations. Telecommunication has been defined by international agreement as any emission, transmission, or reception of signs, signals, sounds, and writing. See BROADCASTING. See Colin Cherry, *On Human Communication* (1962); T. H. Crowley and others, *Modern Communications* (1962); H. M. McLuhan, *The Medium is the Message* (1967); B. H. Bagdikian, *The Information Machines* (1971); Hadley Read, *Communication: Methods for all Media* (1972); John Tebbel, *The Media in America* (1974).

communications satellite, artificial SATELLITE that functions as part of a global radio-communications network. Echo, the first communications satellite, was launched in Aug., 1960. It was an uninstrumented inflatable sphere that passively reflected radio signals back to earth. Later satellites carried with them electronic devices for receiving, amplifying, and rebroadcasting signals to earth. Relay, launched by the National Aeronautics and Space Administration (NASA), was the basis for Telstar, a commercially sponsored experimental satellite. Earth-synchronous orbits were used by NASA's Syncom and its Earlybird, the world's first commercial communications satellite. Such satellites orbit with a period of 24 hr, so that they remain over a single spot on the earth's surface. In 1962, the U.S. Congress passed the Communications Satellite Act, which created the COMMUNICATIONS SATELLITE CORP. (COMSAT). COMSAT participated in an international consortium, which launched four series of Intelsat satellites, beginning with Earlybird in 1965.

Communications Satellite Corporation (COMSAT), organization incorporated (1962) by an act of Congress to establish a commercial system of international communications using artificial satellites. Although government sponsored, it was financed by a public stock issue. The launching in 1965 of its first satellite, Early Bird, inaugurated a trans-Atlantic service; a similar link with Asia was established some 18 months later. Along with representatives of more than 80 other nations, COMSAT is a member of the International Telecommunications Satellite Consortium (INTELSAT). Through member-company satellites and its many earth stations around the world, the consortium provides for international communications via telephone and television. See COMMUNICATIONS SATELLITE.

communion: see EUCHARIST; LORD'S SUPPER.

communism, fundamentally, the system of social organization in which property (especially real property and the means of production) is held in common. Thus, the EJIDO system of the Mexican Indians and the property-and-work system of the INCA were both communist, although the former was a matter of more or less independent communities cultivating their own lands in common and the latter a type of community organization within a highly organized empire. In modern usage, the term *Communism* (written with a capital *C*) is applied to the movement that aims to overthrow the capitalist order by revolutionary means and to establish a classless society in which all goods will be socially owned. The theories of the movement come from Karl MARX, as modified by Vladimir Ilyich LENIN, leader of the successful Communist revolution in Russia. Communism, in this sense, is to be distinguished from socialism, which (as the term is commonly understood) seeks similar ends but by evolution rather than revolution.

Origins of Communism. Communism as a theory of government and social reform may be said, in a limited sense, to have begun with the ancient Greek idea of the Golden Age, a concept of a world of communal bliss and harmony without the institution of private property. Plato, in his *Republic,* outlined a society with communal holding of property; his concept of a hierarchical social system including slavery has by some been called "aristocratic communism." The Neoplatonists revived the idea of common property, which was also strong in some religious groups such as the Jewish ESSENES and certain early Christian communities. These opponents of private property held that property holding was evil and irreligious and that God had created the world for the use of all mankind. The first of these ideas was particularly strong among Manichaean and Gnostic heretics, such as the Cathari, but these concepts were also found in some orthodox Christian groups (e.g., the Franciscans). The MANORIAL SYSTEM of the Middle Ages included common cultivation of the fields and communal use of the village commons, which might be vigorously defended against the lord. It was partly to uphold these common rights, threatened by early agrarian capitalism, that the participants in the Peasants' Revolt (1381) in England and the insurgents of the Peasants' War in 16th-century Germany advocated common ownership of land and of the means of production. In the 16th and 17th cent. such intellectual works as Sir Thomas More's *Utopia* proposed forms of communal property ownership in reaction to what the authors felt was the selfishness and depredation of growing economic individualism. In addition, some religious groups of the early modern period advocated forms of communism, just as had certain of the early Christians. The Anabaptists under Thomas MÜNZER were the real upholders of communism in the Peasants' War, and they were savagely punished for their beliefs. This same mixture of religious enthusiasm and economic reform was shown in 17th-century England by the tiny sect of the DIGGERS, who actually sought to put their theories into practice on common land. Capitalism, reinforced by the INDUSTRIAL REVOLUTION, which began in the 18th cent., brought about the conditions that gave rise to modern communism. Wages, hours, and factory conditions for the new industrial class were appalling, and protest grew. Although the French Revolution ended without satisfying radical demands for economic egalitarianism, the voice of François BABEUF was strongly raised against economic inequality and the power of private property. For his class consciousness and his will to revolution he has been considered the first modern communist. Although he was guillotined, his movement (Babouvism) lived on, and the organization of his secret revolutionary society on the "cell" system was to be developed later as a means of militant revolution. In the early 19th cent. ardent opponents of industrial society created a wide variety of protest theories. Already what is generally known as utopian communism had been well launched by the comte de SAINT-SIMON. In this era a number of advocates gathered followers, founded small cults, and attempted to launch COMMUNISTIC SETTLEMENTS, particularly in the United States. Most notable among such men were Robert OWEN, Étienne CABET, and Charles FOURIER. Pierre Joseph PROUDHON, although he did not adopt the principle of common ownership, exercised great influence by his attacks on the evils of private property. A host of critics and idealistic revolutionists arose in Germany. More important was the survival or revival of Babouvism in secret French and Italian revolutionary societies, intent on overthrowing the established governments and on setting up a new, propertyless society. It was among them that the terms *communism* and *socialism* were first used. They were used vaguely and more or less interchangeably, although there was a tendency to use the term *socialist* to denote those who merely stressed a strong state as the owner of all means of production, and the term *communist* for those who stressed the abolition of all private property (except immediate personal goods). Among the chief leaders of such revolutionary groups were the Frenchmen Louis BLANC and (far more radical) Louis Auguste BLANQUI, both of whom played important roles in the February Revolution of 1848. The year 1848 was also marked by the appearance of *The Communist Manifesto* of Karl Marx and Friedrich ENGELS, the primary exposition of the socioeconomic doctrine that came to be known as MARXISM. It postulated the inevitability of a communist society, which would result when economic forces (the determinants of history) caused the class war; in this struggle the exploited industrial proletariat would overthrow the capitalists and establish the new classless order of social ownership. Marxian theories and programs soon came to dominate left-wing thought. Although the German group (founded in 1847) for which *The Communist Manifesto* was written was called the Communist League, the Marxist movement went forward under the name of SOCIALISM; its 19th-century history is treated in the article under that heading and under SOCIALIST PARTIES, in European history.

The Growth of Modern Communism. The modern form of Communism (written with a capital *C*) began to develop with the split (1903) within the Russian Social Democratic Labor party into factions of BOLSHEVISM AND MENSHEVISM. The more radical wing, the Bolsheviks, were led by Lenin and advocated immediate and violent revolution to bring about the downfall of capitalism and the establishment of an international socialist state. The triumph of the Bolsheviks in the RUSSIAN REVOLUTION of 1917 gave them the leadership in socialist action. They constituted the Communist party in 1918 (see COMMUNIST PARTY, in the USSR). Meanwhile World War I had shaken the socialist movement as a whole by splitting those who cooperated with the governments in waging the war from those who maintained a stand for revolution against all capitalist governments. Chief among the stalwart revolutionists were the Communist party in Russia and the SPARTACUS PARTY (later the Communist party) in Germany. The establishment of a working socialist state in Russia tended to give that country leadership, and Leninism grew stronger. Communist revolts immediately after the war failed in Germany, and the briefly successful Communist state under Béla KUN in Hungary was also repressed with great bloodshed. The revolutionary socialists now broke completely with the moderate majority of the movement. They withdrew from the Second INTERNATIONAL and formed (1919) the Third International, or COMINTERN, in 1919. Henceforth, the term *Communism* was applied to the ideology of the parties founded under the aegis of the Comintern. Their program called for the uniting of all the workers of the world for the coming world revolution, which would be followed by the establishment of a dictatorship of the proletariat and state socialism. Ultimately there would develop a harmonious classless society, and the state would wither away. The Communist parties were organized on a hierarchical basis, with active cells of members as the broad base; they were made up only of the elite—those approved by the higher members of the party as being reliable, active, and subject completely to party rule. Communist parties were formed in countries throughout the world and were particularly active in trying to win control of labor unions and in fomenting labor unrest. Despite the existence of the Comintern, however, the Communist party in the USSR adopted, under Joseph STALIN, the theory of "socialism in one country," which asserted the possibility of building a true Communist system in one country alone. This departure from Marxist internationalism was challenged by Leon TROTSKY, whose theory of "permanent revolution" stressed the necessity of world revolution. After Trotsky was expelled (1929) from the Soviet Union, he founded a Fourth, or Trotskyist, International to rival the Comintern. Stalin's program of building the Soviet Union as the model and base of Communism in the world had the effect of tying Communist and Soviet policy even more closely together, an effect intensified by the "monolithic unity" produced by the party purges of the 1930s. It became clearly evident in that decade that in practice Communism, contrary to the hopes of theorists and intellectuals, had created in the USSR a giant totalitarian state that dominated every aspect of life and denied the ideal of individual liberty. Except for the small Mongolian People's Republic, no other Communist state was created before World War II. The Chinese Communist party was founded in 1921 and began a long struggle for power with the KUOMINTANG. However, it received little aid from the USSR, and it was not to achieve its goal until 1949. In the late 1920s and early 30s the Communist parties followed a policy of total hostility to the socialists, and in Germany this was one factor that facilitated the rise of the Nazis. In 1935, however, the Comintern dictated a change in policy, and the Communists began to work with other leftist and liberal parties for liberal legislation and government, as in the Popular Front government in France. In World War II the USSR became an ally of the Western capitalist nations after Germany attacked it in 1941. As part of its cooperation with the Allies, the USSR brought about (1943) the dissolution of the Comintern. Hopes for continued cooperation, intrinsic in the formation of the United Nations, were dashed, however, by a widening rift between the Soviet bloc and the Western democracies, especially the United States, after the war (see COLD WAR). Communism had been vastly strengthened by the winning of many new nations into the zone of Soviet influence and strength in Eastern Europe. Governments strictly modeled on the Soviet Communist plan were installed in the "satellite" states—Albania, Poland, Czechoslovakia, Hungary, Bulgaria, and East Germany. A Communist government was also created under Marshal TITO in Yugoslavia, but Tito's independent policies led to the expulsion of Yugoslavia from the COMINFORM, which had replaced the Comintern, and Titoism was labeled deviationist. By 1950 the Chinese Communists held all of China except Taiwan, thus controlling the most populous nation in the world. A Communist administration was also installed in North Korea, and fighting between the People's Republic of Korea (Communist) and the southern Republic of Korea exploded in the KOREAN WAR (1950–53), fought between Communist and United Nations troops. Other areas where rising Communist strength provoked dissension and in some cases actual fighting include Malaya, Laos, many nations of the Middle East and Africa, and, especially, Vietnam, where the United States intervened to aid the South Vietnamese regime against Communist guerrillas and North Vietnam (see VIETNAM WAR). In many of these poor countries, Communists attempted, with varying degrees of success, to unite with nationalist and socialist forces against Western imperialism. After the death of Stalin in 1953 some relaxation of Soviet Communist strictures seemed to occur, and at the 20th party congress (1956) Premier Nikita Khruschchev denounced the methods of Stalin and called for a return to the principles of Lenin, thus presaging some change in Communist methods, although none in fundamental ideology. A resurgence of nationalist feeling within the Soviet bloc—vividly demonstrated by the bloodily suppressed Hungarian uprising of 1956—ultimately forced some acknowledgment from the USSR. However, while it began to allow some limited freedom of action to the Eastern European countries, the invasion of Czechoslovakia in 1968 demonstrated its determination to prevent serious challenges to its domination. Communist parties in Western countries, on the other hand, especially in Italy, have felt more free to set their own policy. When in 1961 the USSR attacked Albania for Stalinism, China came strongly to Albania's defense. Ideological differences between China and the USSR became increasingly apparent in the 1960s and 70s, with China portraying itself as a leader of the underdeveloped world against the two superpowers, the United States and the Soviet Union. While both the USSR and China sought better relations with the United States in the 1970s, it appeared that the differences between the two major Communist powers would increase rather than decrease. See N. A. Berdyaev, *The Origin of Russian Communism* (tr. 1937, repr. 1960); Max Beer, *The General History of Socialism and Social Struggles* (2 vol., tr. 1957); Donald Zagoria, *The Sino-Soviet Conflict* (1962, repr. 1964); Z. K. Brzezinski, *Ideology and Power in Soviet Politics* (rev. ed. 1967); F. W. Houn, *A Short History of Chinese Communism* (1967); G. F. Hudson, *Fifty Years of Communism: Theory and Practice, 1917–1967* (1968); Helmut Gruber, *International Communism in the Era of Lenin* (1969); Raya Dunajevskaya, *Marxism and Freedom* (3d ed. 1971); Leonard Schapiro, *The Communist Party of the Soviet Union* (2d ed. 1971); R. C. Goldston, *Communism: A Narrative History* (1972); W. S. Sworakowski, *World Communism: A Handbook* (1973); D. A. Hyde, *Communism Today* (1973).

communistic settlements, communities practicing common ownership of goods. Communistic settlements were known in ancient and medieval times, but the flowering of such groups occurred in the 19th cent. in the United States, where a number of German pietistic sects established such communities as the AMANA CHURCH SOCIETY, Iowa; Harmony, Pa. (see HARMONY SOCIETY); and ZOAR, Ohio. Similar settlements were founded by the Shakers, Mormons, Mennonites, Dukhobors, and Jansenites. Unique religious settlements were the Oneida Community (see under ONEIDA, N.Y.); Hopedale, Mass.; and the Brotherhood of the New Life, N.Y. (see HARRIS, THOMAS LAKE). Another group were non-Christian, often antireligious and utopian. The leading communities within this group were of two types, those founded by the followers of Robert OWEN (including NEW HARMONY, Ind., and NASHOBA, Tenn.) and the numerous ones (notably BROOK FARM, Mass.) formed on the principles of Charles FOURIER. Belonging to neither of these groups were the Icarian settlements, led by Étienne CABET, and the anarchistic villages of Josiah WARREN. The religious groups, unified by strong faith and authority, tended to prosper and outlive the secular groups; the latter, however, often attracting brilliant and original personalities, provided a ferment of new thought. The chief attempts since the 19th cent. at setting up such colonies have been in Israel, where there are a number of successful agricultural collectives (see COLLECTIVE FARM). See A. F. Tyler, *Freedom's Ferment* (1944, repr. 1962); R. M. Kanter, *Commitment and Community* (1972).

Communist party, in China. Founded in 1921 by Chen Tu-hsiu and Li Ta-chao, professors at Peking Univ., the party was under strong COMINTERN influence from its beginnings. The Chinese Communist party became formally allied with the KUOMINTANG in 1923; by 1925 Communists held many top posts in the Kuomintang organization. CHIANG KAI-SHEK forced a reduction in Communist power in March, 1926, but the party maintained the Kuomintang alliance at the insistence of the USSR. In April, 1927, Chiang Kai-shek drove the Communists, led by CHOU EN-LAI, from SHANGHAI and executed many of their leaders; in July the party formally resigned from the Kuomintang government at Wuhan and went underground, and the long conflict between the party and the Kuomintang began. In Aug., 1927, MAO TSE-TUNG led the peasants of Hunan prov. in the Autumn Crop Uprising, a popular rebellion that was bloodily suppressed. One branch of the party secretly maintained itself in the cities; a short-lived Communist commune was established at Canton in Dec., 1927. In the rural hinterland Mao Tse-tung and CHU TEH established (1927) a precarious soviet in Kiangsi prov. Several other rural soviets were set up in Hunan, Anhwei, and Hupei provs. By 1931, Mao was in control of the official soviet government at Juichin; radical land-reform policies were followed to gain the support of the peasants. A Red Army, under the leadership of Mao and Chu Teh, was recruited from the peasantry of Kiangsi. Eventually driven from their southern base by Chiang's military campaigns, many thousands of Communists trekked north on the LONG MARCH and set up headquarters at YEN-AN in Shensi prov. There the party organization was strengthened, factories were built, and the civil war with Chiang's forces continued. In Sept., 1937, after a two-year effort to promote Chinese unity in the face of further Japanese aggression (see SINO-JAPANESE WAR, SECOND), the Communists obtained a limited truce from Chiang Kai-shek and accepted his nominal authority, although they retained actual military and political control over large areas in the northwest. The truce with the Kuomintang broke down in 1939, but Communist guerrillas remained the only really effective force against the Japanese in N China. When World War II ended in 1945, the Communists controlled wide rural areas in N and central China and moved quickly to gain control of Manchuria. From 1945 to 1949 party membership swelled as Communist armies took city after city from the Nationalists. After the People's Republic of China was set up in 1949, the party became the administrative and policymaking center of the government. For the changes wrought by the Communist regime in China, see CHINA. See J. E. Rue, *Mao Tse-tung in Opposition, 1927–1935* (1966); Shanti Swarup, *A Study of the Chinese Communist Movement* (1966); F. W. Houn, *A Short History of Chinese Communism* (1967); K. T. Chang, *The Rise of the Chinese Communist Party, 1921–1927* (1971).

Communist party, in the USSR, officially the Communist party of the Soviet Union. It exercises all effective power within the country, and, as the oldest and for a long time the only ruling Communist party in the world, it wields considerable (and in some cases controlling) influence over the Communist parties of other countries (see COMMUNISM). It presently has about 14,700,000 members (out of a total estimated population of 246,000,000) and more than 375,000 party units throughout the USSR. Marxist socialism (see MARXISM) took root in Russia in the 1880s. Led by Georgi PLEKHANOV, a small group of Marxists formed (1883) the League for the Emancipation of Labor, stressing the revolutionary capabilities of the growing industrial proletariat. Other groups were soon founded, the largest of which was the Jewish *Bund*, and in 1898 they united to form the Russian Social Democratic Labor party. The second party congress (1903) in Brussels and London split into factions of BOLSHEVISM AND MENSHEVISM. The Bolsheviks, led by Vladimir Ilyich LENIN, demanded a highly disciplined, centralized, and dedicated revolutionary elite rather than a mass party. These principles guided the Bolsheviks before the 1917 revolution and remain the basis for the present Russian Communist party. When the RUSSIAN REVOLUTION began in March, 1917, the Bolsheviks were unprepared, and under the provisional government they played a minor role. When Lenin returned from exile in April, he called for seizure of power, despite opposition within the party. The Bolsheviks gained strength in key areas, capitalizing on mass discontent, and in November they were able to seize control. With a total party membership of about 200,000, they faced the problem of governing alone or sharing power. Lenin and Leon TROTSKY demanded party dictatorship and destroyed all opposition from Mensheviks and other socialist groups. During the civil war (1918–20) the Bolshevik party—from 1918 the All-Russian Communist party—was at the height of its revolutionary ardor. Despite seemingly impossible tasks, it strengthened the party apparatus on all levels. After the death of Lenin (1924) dissident elements in the party were silenced as Joseph STALIN emerged as Lenin's successor. In the party congresses of the 1920s debates were stormy and some intraparty democracy was still evident, but the 16th party congress in 1929 demonstrated Stalin's virtual supremacy. The party, called from 1925 the All-Union Communist party (Bolsheviks), still had at this time a strongly urban character. One purpose of the massive agricultural collectivization launched in 1929 was to strengthen the party in rural areas. By 1933 there were more than 3,500,000 party members and candidates, many newly recruited from rural areas. Then there began the series of purges that turned the 1930s into a reign of terror. The former leaders of the party—Trotsky, BUKHARIN, ZINOVIEV, KAMENEV, RYKOV, and others—were accused of treason. A series of spectacular show trials were held; almost all the defendants were executed or exiled. As the purges drew to a close by 1938, party membership had declined to 1,920,000. There was an immediate upturn in membership with the approach of World War II; in the period after the war membership grew more slowly. In the 1960s the tendency was once more to broaden the base of membership. The Stalinist period, from 1930 until 1953, was characterized by a repressive and omnipotent dictatorship over all Soviet citizens, including party members. The party as an organization lost influence, while its leaders gained absolute power. Party congresses were infrequent. In 1952 the party was renamed the Communist party of the Soviet Union. Decisions were made by Stalin alone, and the fortunes of party members depended upon his whims. Unbounded adulation was accorded him. However, at the 20th party congress (1956, three years after Stalin's death) Premier Nikita KHRUSHCHEV testified that the beliefs long held in the West about Stalin's crimes were true. The subsequent campaign of de-Stalinization reached a climax at the 22d party congress in 1961, and Stalin's body was removed from its place of honor in a mausoleum in Red Square. After the death of Stalin, Georgi MALENKOV at first appeared to hold power, but ultimately Khrushchev emerged as the successor, holding by 1958 the highest posts in both party and government—first secretary of the party and chairman of the council of ministers. The purge (1957–58) of the "antiparty group" of Malenkov, Vyacheslav MOLOTOV, Lazar Kaganovich, and Nikolai BULGANIN strengthened his position. Khrushchev, however, was suddenly removed in 1964 because of dissatisfaction with both his foreign and domestic policies. He was replaced by a so-called collective leadership whose leading members were Leonid BREZHNEV and Alexei KOSYGIN. By the 1970s, Brezhnev, general secretary of the party, had clearly emerged as the dominant figure but with less personal power than Khrushchev had held. The Communist party is organized so that its units parallel the territorial hierarchy of state administration as well as all institutions such as the press, education, armed forces, and agriculture. Through these institutions the party can effectively control the making and implementation of policy. A small core of party members is made up of full-time paid professional workers; the rest hold regular jobs in addition to fulfilling their party obligations. Each party committee has a small ruling body called a bureau or presidium, the leading member of which is the first secretary. The smallest party cell may consist of only three members in a factory, school, or office. The highest body, elected by the party congress, is the central committee, of which the ruling body is the presidium (formerly politburo). Membership in the party is determined in a severe selection process, involving recommendations from party members and a period of trial during which a candidate must prove his ability. A major source of new party members is the Young Communist League (Komsomol), an organization of youths from the ages of 14 to 28. It presently has over 30 million members. Komsomol is patterned after the Communist party and is strictly controlled to realize the goals of indoctrinating Soviet youth with the aims of the party, carrying out specific party tasks, and training future party members. See Herbert Marcuse, *Soviet Marxism* (1958, repr. 1968); R. T. Fisher, *Pattern for Soviet Youth: A Study of the Congresses of Komsomol, 1919–1954* (1959); J. S. Reshetar, Jr., *A Concise History of the Communist Party* (rev. ed. 1964); Merle Fainsod, *How Russia is Ruled* (rev. ed. 1965); T. H. Rigby, *Communist Party Membership in the U.S.S.R., 1917–67* (1968); D. J. R. Scott, *Russian Political Institutions* (4th ed. 1969); Leonard Schapiro, *The Communist Party of the Soviet Union* (2d ed. 1971).

Communist party, in the United States, political party that espouses the Marxist-Leninist principles of COMMUNISM. The first Communist parties in the United States were founded in 1919 by dissident factions of the Socialist party. The larger, which called itself the Communist party of America, consisted of many of the former foreign language federations of the Socialist party, in particular the Russian Federation and the former Michigan Socialist party. The other, named the Communist Labor party, was led by Benjamin Gitlow and John REED. The parties immediately became subject to raids by agents of Attorney General A. Mitchell PALMER and local authorities. These raids resulted in a sharp drop in party membership and, in Jan., 1920, forced the Communists to go underground. In May, 1921, under strong pressure from the Third (Communist) International, or Comintern, the Communist groups in the United States were united under the name of the Communist party of America. The Comintern also forced a change in policy from a militant revolutionary one to one stressing the need to work through established labor organizations and to develop a mass following. Accordingly, in Dec., 1921, the Communists organized the Workers party of America, as a legal, acknowledged organization, and by 1923 the underground party had ceased to function. Attempts were made to work through the growing farmer-labor movement of the early 1920s, but they failed in the face of opposition from most farmer-labor leaders and from the Progressive leader, Senator Robert LaFollette. Unsuccessful Communist-led strikes among textile workers in Passaic, N.J. (1926), in New Bedford, Mass. (1928), and among New York City garment workers (1926) also lessened Communist influence in trade unions. During this period two factions developed within the party. One, led by Jay LOVESTONE, was generally socialist in background and concerned with political theory. The other, led by William Z. FOSTER and Earl BROWDER, was more syndicalist in background and interested in union activity. These two groups alternated in party leadership until 1929, when the Comintern ordered that the Foster group be placed in control to carry out the new policy line established at its Sixth World Congress (1928). The party was renamed the Communist party of the United States of America. The new period, called the Third Period, saw the development of the theory of "social fascism," by which labor and socialist leaders were denounced as more dangerous enemies of the workers than the fascists. During this period the American Communists also made a major appeal for Negro support, calling for the creation of a Negro republic in the South, on the grounds that Negroes were a national, not a racial, minority. The adoption of the new party line coincided with the beginning of the depression of 1929, and as the economic crisis grew, Communist membership increased. However, the policies of that time isolated the Communists both in politics and in the unions, so that despite increased membership and some success in organizing the unemployed, the party's influence remained small. In 1935 the Seventh World Congress of the Comintern announced another change of direction. It now stressed the need for a "popular front," a movement to create political coalitions of all antifascist groups. In the United States, the Communists abandoned opposition to the New Deal; they reentered the mainstream of the trade union movement and played an important part in organizing new unions for the Congress of Industrial Organizations (CIO), for the first time gaining important positions of power in the union movement. As antifascist activists they attracted the support of many non-Communists during this period. However, the party's attacks on Nazi Germany ended abruptly with the signing of the Hitler-Stalin nonaggression pact in Aug., 1939, and World War II, which immediately followed, was denounced as an "imperialist" war caused by Great Britain and France. American defense preparations and aid to the Western democracies were vigorously opposed as "war-mongering," and Communist-dominated unions were quick to go out on strike. In June, 1941, when Germany attacked Russia, the character of the war, for the Communists, was changed overnight from "imperialist" to "democratic." The party, under the leadership of Earl Browder, now went all out in its support of the war. Strikes were opposed as a hindrance to the war effort, and in 1944 the U.S. Communist party "disbanded" as a political party to become the Communist Political Association. In 1945, however, Browder's policy was attacked as being one of the "right deviationism," and he was replaced by William Foster. This change in line and the beginning of the COLD WAR brought the party, which had achieved relative respectability during the war, under renewed attack. In 1948 the Communists supported the presidential candidacy of Henry A. Wallace on the PROGRESSIVE PARTY ticket, but he obtained only slightly more than a million votes. Communist influence in labor unions came under increasing attack. The Taft-Hartley Act of 1947 denied the facilities of the National Labor Relations Board to unions that failed to file affidavits avowing that their officers were not Communists, and in 1949-50 the CIO expelled unions that were still Communist-dominated. In March, 1947, President Truman barred Communists or those aiding or sympathetic to Communism from employment in the executive branch of the Federal government. The sensational confessions of former Communists, such as Whittaker CHAMBERS, and increasing evidence of Communist espionage led to highly publicized investigations by Congress (especially by the House Un-American Activities Committee and the Senate Subcommittee on Government Operations), the Federal Bureau of Investigation, and Federal grand juries. In Oct., 1949, 11 top Communist leaders were convicted on charges of conspiring to advocate the overthrow of the U.S. government. In June, 1951, the Supreme Court found the Smith Act of 1940, under which the convictions had been obtained, constitutional, and the government proceeded to bring many lesser Communist officials to trial. In 1950 the McCarran Internal Security Act required that all Communist and Communist-dominated organizations register with the Federal government the names of all members and contributors, and the Communist Control Act of 1954 further strengthened the provisions of the McCarran Act by providing severe penalties for Communists who failed to register, denying collective bargaining power to Communist-dominated unions, and taking away the "rights, privileges and immunities" of the Communist party as a legal organization. At the same time many states passed "little Smith Acts," with such provisions as the requirement of loyalty oaths from state employees and the denial of a place on the ballot to Communist parties. This was also the period of Senator Joseph McCarthy's hysterical search for Communists in all branches of government. In 1956, Nikita Khrushchev's denunciation of Stalin's excesses, along with the Russian suppression of the Hungarian revolt in that same year, created new schisms in the U.S. Communist party, which lost thousands of members. The Supreme Court has upheld many of the provisions of the Smith and McCarran acts as they apply to the leadership of the Communist party, but several decisions of the 1960s substantially voided sanctions against the rank and file except where some active conspiracy against U.S. security is proved. As a result the party resumed open activities in 1966 and ran presidential candidates in the elections of 1968 and 1972. In 1972 it claimed about 17,000 dues-paying members. The material on American Communism is voluminous and is listed in three bibliographies: Fund for the Republic, Inc., *Bibliography on the Communist Problem in the United States* (1955); Robert F. Delaney, *The Literature of Communism in America* (1962); and Joel Seidman, ed., *Communism in the United States* (1969). For two works registering official views of the American Communist party in different periods, see Earl R. Browder, *What is Communism?* (1936) and William Z. Foster, *History of the Communist Party of the United States* (1952; repr. 1968). See James Oneal and G. A. Werner, *American Communism: A Critical Analysis of Its Origins, Development and Programs* (1947, rev. ed. 1972); Irving Howe and Lewis Coser, *The American Communist Party; A Critical History* (1958, repr. 1962); Theodore Draper, *American Communism and Soviet Russia* (1960); Joseph Starobin, *American Communism in Crisis, 1943-1957* (1972).

community chest, cooperative organization of citizens and social welfare agencies in a city. Also known as a united fund, it has two purposes, to raise funds through an annual campaign for its member agencies and to budget the funds raised. The fund is administered by the community chest or united fund itself, or as a joint endeavor with a community welfare council; to represent the idea of administering, as well as collecting, the funds, the national association in 1927 took the name Community Chests and Councils. Today the organization's official name is the United Way of America. The idea of cooperative collecting for charitable purposes originated in Liverpool, England (1873), and, in the United States, in Denver (1887). In 1900 the Cleveland chamber of commerce went a step further and assumed responsibility for endorsing the agencies seeking funds; 13 years later Cleveland brought almost all its welfare organizations together in the Cleveland Welfare Council. The name *community chest* was coined in Rochester, N.Y., in 1913. See J. R. Sealey et al., *Community Chest: A Case Study in Philanthropy* (1957).

community college, public institution of higher education. Community colleges are characterized by a two-year curriculum that leads to either the associate degree or transfer to a four-year college. The transfer program parallels the first two years of a four-year college. The degree program generally prepares students for direct entrance into an occupation. Because of their low tuition, local setting, and relatively easy entrance requirements, community colleges have been a major force in the post-World War II expansion of educational opportunities in the United States. Their privately owned counterparts are known as junior colleges. See Edmund J. Gleazer, Jr., *This is the Community College* (1968); C. R. Monroe, *Profile of the Community College* (1972).

commutation of sentence, in criminal law, reduction of a sentence for a criminal act by action of the executive head of the government. Like PARDON, commutation of sentence is a matter of grace, not of right; it is distinguished from pardon, however, in that the conviction of crime is not nullified. The commutation, hence, may be granted on condition that the criminal observe certain restrictions for the balance of his original sentence. Many states have statutes providing for commutation of sentence as a reward for good conduct during imprisonment. Once earned, the commutation becomes a matter of right and may be enforced by court action.

commutative law, in mathematics, law holding that for a given binary operation (combining two quantities) the order of the quantities is arbitrary; e.g., in addition, the numbers 2 and 5 can be combined as $2+5=7$ or as $5+2=7$. More generally, in addition, for any two numbers a and b the commutative law is expressed as $a+b=b+a$. Multiplication of numbers is also commutative, i.e., $a\times b=b\times a$. In general, any binary operation, symbolized by $\circ$, joining mathematical entities A and B obeys the commutative law if $A\circ B=B\circ A$ for all possible choices of A and B. Not all operations are commutative; e.g., subtraction is not since $2-5\neq 5-2$, and division is not since $2/5\neq 5/2$.

commutator, device used in an electric GENERATOR to convert the alternating current produced in the generator into direct current before the current is sent into an external circuit; it is basically a rotary switching device synchronized with the frequency of the alternating current. Commutators are also used in electric MOTORS to switch currents in order to maintain magnetic polarities necessary to keep the shafts of the motors turning.

Commynes, Philippe de: see COMINES, PHILIPPE DE.

Comnenus (kŏmnē'nəs), family name of several Byzantine emperors—ISAAC I, ALEXIUS I, JOHN II, MANUEL I, ALEXIUS II, and ANDRONICUS I—who reigned in the 11th and 12th cent., and of the historian, Princess ANNA COMNENA. Though unable to turn back the forces that contributed to the eventual downfall of the BYZANTINE EMPIRE, they were generally able rulers. Hellenism was revived during the family's reign, and contact with the West was increased. A branch of the family founded the empire of Trebizond (see TREBIZOND, EMPIRE OF) after the fall of Constantinople in 1204.

Como (kō'mō), city (1971 pop. 97,395), capital of Como prov., Lombardy, N Italy, at the southwest end of Lake Como, near the Swiss border. It is primarily a tourist center. Originally a Roman colony, Como became an independent commune in the 11th cent. and was frequently at war with, and ruled by, Milan. It later came under Spanish and Austrian control and was liberated by Garibaldi in 1859. In the Middle Ages and the Renaissance, craftsmen, architects, and sculptors from Como (the *maestri comacini*) were renowned throughout Italy. The city has a remarkable marble cathedral (14th-18th cent.), a 13th-century city hall, and several Romanesque churches.

Como, Lake (kō'mō), Ital. *Lago di Como* or *Lario*, c.56 sq mi (145 sq km), 30 mi (48 km) long and from ½ to 2½ mi (0.8-4 km) wide, in Lombardy, N Italy. Lake Como is a natural widening of the Adda River, which feeds and drains the lake. Situated in the foothills of the Alps, the lake is one of the most beautiful of Europe. It is a tourist resort, and handsome villas line its shores. Lecco, Como, Varennes, and Bellagio are principal towns.

Comodoro Rivadavia (kōmōthō'rō rēvätha'vyä), town (1970 pop. 78,479), Chubut prov., S Argentina, on the Gulf of San Jorge, an inlet of the Atlantic Ocean. The major center of oil production in Argentina, it is connected by a 1,100-mi (1,770-km) pipeline with Buenos Aires. The town is under military administration, and a government-owned corporation runs the oil wells.

Comonfort, Ignacio (ēgnä'syō kōmōnfôrt'), 1812-63, Mexican general and president (1855-58). He was one of the leaders in the liberal Revolution of AYUTLA, which in 1855 overthrew SANTA ANNA and installed Juan ÁLVAREZ in the presidency. Comonfort became acting president upon the resignation of Álvarez; with his cabinet, particularly Benito JUÁREZ and Miguel LERDO DE TEJADA, he continued the anticlerical liberal program and embodied it in the constitution of 1857. In Dec., 1857, Comonfort, elected under the new constitution, took office as president. The reform program created a furor and awoke rebellion. Comonfort, a half-hearted liberal, attempted to make his position more moderate and was deserted by the liberals. He allowed the conservatives to seize power, then turned against them. Unsupported by either party and opposed by public opinion, he resigned and fled (Jan., 1858) to the United States. He returned to fight against the French invaders and was killed in battle.

Comoro Islands (kŏm'ərō), French overseas territory (1970 est. pop. 267,000), 838 sq mi (2,170 sq km), an archipelago in the Indian Ocean, at the northern end of the Mozambique Channel, between the Malagasy Republic and Mozambique. The capital and largest city is MORONI. The Comoro Islands comprise the four main islands of Grande Comore—on which Moroni is located—Anjouan, Mayotte, and Mohéli, and numerous coral reefs and islets. They are volcanic in origin and have a tropical climate. African peoples are most numerous in the population, although there are many Arabs and Indians in the towns; overpopulation is a problem. Most of the people are Muslim. French is the official language, but Arabic and Swahili are widely spoken. The islands' economy is largely agricultural; the main farming areas are held by foreign companies and feudalistic local landowners. Vanilla, copra, cocoa, sisal, cloves, and essential oils are the major crops and exports. Rice, machinery, and petroleum are the main imports. The islands were populated by successive waves of immigrants from Africa, Indonesia, Madagascar, and Arabia. In 1841 the French persuaded the king of Mayotte to cede Grande Comore. The other islands were ceded between 1866 and 1909. All were occupied by the British during World War II. In 1946 the islands were granted administrative autonomy within the French Union. The territorial assembly voted in Dec., 1958, to remain in the French Republic as an overseas territory. By 1968 internal self-government was achieved. In 1973 negotiations with France led to an agreement for the islands' eventual independence. The territory is represented in the French National Assembly by two deputies and in the Senate by one senator.

Compactata: see HUSSITES.

compactor, device used to compress garbage to a relatively small volume so as to facilitate its handling and disposal. Essentially the device consists of a mechanical press that acts to reduce the size of garbage in its container. Environmentally it is advantageous in that it may be used as a substitute for the incinerator, which often generates air pollution. However, compacting makes it more difficult to separate waste materials for recycling.

companies, chartered: see CHARTERED COMPANIES.

Companys, Luis (lo͞oēs' kōmpä'nēs), 1883–1940, Spanish politician; Catalan nationalist leader. After the Spanish monarchy fell (1931), he proclaimed an autonomous Catalan republic within the Spanish republic and in 1933 was elected president of CATALONIA. Pressed by extremists, in 1934 he declared Catalonia fully independent, but this separatist revolt failed and Companys was jailed. The leftist electoral victory of 1936 brought him back to power, and he headed the Catalan government throughout the civil war. In 1939 he fled to France, but German occupation forces returned him to Spain in 1940, and he was executed.

company union: see UNION, LABOR.

comparative anatomy: see ANATOMY.

compass. 1 In mathematics, an instrument for making circles and measuring distances. Frequently called a pair of compasses, it consists of two metal legs with one end of each attached to a pivot to form a V-shaped device. The free ends are pointed; a pen or pencil may be substituted for one of the points. **2** In navigation, an instrument for determining direction. The mariner's compass consists of a magnetic needle freely suspended so that in the earth's magnetic field it turns to align itself with the magnetic north and south poles. Declination is the angle between the magnetic needle and the geographical meridian. Use of the compass by the early Chinese is probably legendary. The first known reference in European literature dates from the 12th cent. Another more accurate form of navigational compass is the gyrocompass. It consists essentially of a rapidly spinning, electrically driven rotor, suspended in such a way that its axis automatically points along the geographical meridian. The gyrocompass is unaffected by magnetic influences. This compass came into wide use in warships and aircraft during the Second World War. See GYROSCOPE.

compass plant or **rosinweed,** large, coarse North American perennial plant (*Silphium laciniatum*) of the family Compositae (COMPOSITE family), found chiefly in open grasslands. The deeply cut leaves tend to point north and south. It has been used medicinally and is sometimes cultivated. Other plants of similar leaf orientation are sometimes called compass plants. Compass plant is classified in the division MAGNOLIOPHYTA, class Magnoliopsida, order Asterales, family Compositae.

compensation, workmen's: see WORKMEN'S COMPENSATION.

competition, in biology, relationship between members of the same or different species in which individuals are adversely affected by those seeking the same living requirements, such as food or space. Intraspecific competition, i.e., competition between members of the same species, is illustrated by some species of birds and mammals, the males of which set up territories from which all other males of the same species are excluded. In interspecific competition members of different species compete for the same ecologically limiting factors, such as a food source. Not all relationships between organisms are competitive; for example, the commensal relationship between members of different species is noncompetitive (see COMMENSALISM).

competition, in economics, rivalry in supplying or acquiring an economic service or good. Sellers compete with other sellers, and buyers with other buyers. Competition among merchants in foreign trade was common in ancient times, but among local retail dealers and among producers it is largely modern, a characteristic of mercantile and industrial expansion after the Middle Ages. By the 19th cent. classical economic theorists had come to regard competition, at least within the national state, as a natural outgrowth of the operation of SUPPLY AND DEMAND. The price of an item was seen as ultimately fixed by the confluence of the two forces. Early capitalist economists argued that supply and demand pricing worked better without any effort at regulation or control. Their model of perfect competition was marked by absolute freedom of trade, widespread knowledge of market conditions, easy access of buyers to sellers, and the absence of all action restraining trade by agencies of the state. Under such conditions no single buyer or seller could materially affect the market price of an item. After c.1850, practical limitations to perfect competition became evident as industrial and commercial combinations, cooperatives, and trade unions arose to hamper it. Some governments attempted to impose competition by legislation, e.g., the SHERMAN ANTITRUST ACT of 1890, but the litigation involved in enforcing such legislation proved cumbersome and uncertain. A later development was government acceptance of the existence of industrial and commercial combinations, together with an effort to apply regulation, administered either by the state or by the industries themselves. Such a view was inherent in the development of the CARTEL in Germany and in the fact that governments have accepted the existence of practical monopolies in the field of public utilities (see UTILITY, PUBLIC). Copyrights, patents, and FAIR-TRADE LAWS also tend to reduce competition. See A. R. Burns, *Decline of Competition* (1936); John K. Galbraith, *American Capitalism: The Concept of Countervailing Power* (rev. ed. 1956, repr. 1962); M. S. Massel, *Competition and Monopoly* (1962, repr. 1964).

Compiègne (kôNpyĕ'nyə), city (1968 pop. 29,700), Oise dept., N France, in Île-de-France, on the Oise River. It is an industrial center with varied manufactures; a large glassworks is located in the suburbs. As far back as the Merovingian period (7th cent.), Compiègne had been the site of royal gatherings; from the 17th to 19th cent. French monarchs used it as a summer residence. The forest of Compiègne was a royal hunting ground. Joan of Arc was captured (1430) by the Burgundians at Compiègne. In a railroad car in the forest the armistice ending World War I was signed; in 1940, Hitler forced the French to surrender in the same car (which was later taken to Germany and destroyed). The large 15th-century palace, other old structures, and the place's historic connotations attract many tourists.

complement: see IMMUNITY.

complementarity principle, physical principle enunciated by Niels Bohr in 1928 stating that certain physical concepts are complementary. If two concepts are complementary, an experiment that clearly illustrates one concept will obscure the other complementary one. For example, an experiment that illustrates the particle properties of light will not show any of the wave properties of light. This principle also implies that only certain kinds of information can be gained in a particular experiment. Other information that is equally important cannot be measured simultaneously and is lost. In rigorous terms the principle states that it is impossible to give simultaneously a space-time description of atomic entities and also a set of mathematical, causal laws describing such entities. The QUANTUM THEORY shows that these two descriptions are statistically related alternatives, complementary and mutually exclusive. A space-time description is limited by the UNCERTAINTY PRINCIPLE, while a causal description in mathematical form can only be stated in terms of other variables. See Werner Heisenberg, *The Physical Principles of the Quantum Theory* (1930, repr. 1949).

complex, term originated by C. G. Jung to indicate a group of feelings and memories resulting from early highly emotional experiences that occupy a dominant but unconscious position in the mind of an individual. Although repressed from consciousness, a complex nevertheless continues to exert a prevailing influence over mental activity and behavior. To the extent that complexes dominate personality, they indicate a disturbed state of consciousness, or what Jung called splinter psyches. Therapists try to bring the complexes into consciousness and release their energy for productive use. See INFERIORITY COMPLEX; OEDIPUS COMPLEX.

complex ion, charged molecular aggregate (see ION), consisting of a metallic atom or ion to which is attached one or more electron-donating molecules. In some complex ions, such as sulfate, SO_4^{-2}, the atoms are so tightly bound together that they act as a single unit. Many complex ions, however, such as tetrammine zinc (II), $Zn(NH_3)_4^{+2}$, are only loosely aggregated and tend to dissociate in a water solution until an equilibrium is established between the complex ion and its components (see CHEMICAL EQUILIBRIUM). Such complex ions, or coordinated complexes as they are also called, generally consist of a positively charged central metal atom or ion, like the zinc in tetramine zinc, surrounded by electron-donating, or basic, groups called LIGANDS; in the tetrammine zinc complex, the NH_3 groups are the ligands. The number of bonds connecting the ligands to the central atom or ion is its coordination number, or ligancy. Transition metals (see TRANSITION ELEMENTS) are especially suited for forming complex ions because they have filled or partially filled electron orbitals that can participate in bonding the ligands to the metal. The bonding holding the ligands to the central atom or ion is similar to covalent bonding between atoms but is more complex (see CHEMICAL BOND). All the ligands surrounding the central ion need not be the same, and some positions can be occupied by solvent molecules. Because ligands remain in a fixed position around a central atom or ion, in many complexes different ISOMERS, or arrangements, of the ligand groups are possible. When there are four or more ligands around a central atom, different stereoisomers, or spatial configurations, are possible (see STEREOCHEMISTRY). Many complex ions are colored; the specific color of a complex depends on both the central atom or ion and the ligands. For example, when cobaltous chloride is dissolved in water, a pale pink solution, sometimes called invisible ink, results because of the presence of the hydrated cobaltous ion, $Co(H_2O)_6^{+2}$; this solution does not show up well on paper, but if the paper is heated to drive the water off, visibility improves because of the formation of a blue tetrachlorocobalt (II)$^{-2}$ complex. Some of the more important complex ions are vitamin B_{12}, chlorophyll, and the heme component of hemoglobin, in which the central metal ions are cobalt, magnesium, and iron, respectively, and the ligands are complex organic systems. Many enzymes contain a metal ion about which parts of the protein are coordinated.

complex number: see NUMBER.

complex variable analysis, branch of MATHEMATICS that deals with the CALCULUS of functions of a complex variable, i.e., a variable of the form $z=x+iy$, where x and y are real and $i=\sqrt{-1}$ (see NUMBER). A FUNCTION $w=f(z)$ of a complex variable z is separable into two parts, $w = g_1(x,y) + ig_2(x,y)$, where g_1 and g_2 are functions of the real variables x and y. The theory of functions of a complex variable is concerned mainly with functions that have a derivative at every point of a given domain of values for z; such functions are called analytic, regular, or holomorphic. If a function is analytic in a given domain, then it also has continuous derivatives of higher order and can be expanded in an infinite SERIES in terms of these derivatives (i.e., a Taylor's series). The function can also be expressed in the infinite series

$$f(z)=a_0 + a_1(z - z_0) + a_2(z - z_0)^2 + \cdots + a_n(z - z_0)^n + \cdots,$$

where z_0 is a point in the domain. Also of interest in complex variable analysis are the points in a domain, called singular points, where a function fails to have a derivative. The theory of functions of a complex variable was developed during the 19th cent. by A. L. Cauchy, C. F. Gauss, G. F. B. Riemann, K. T. Weierstrass, and others.

composite, common name for the Compositae, by far the largest family of vascular plants, totaling an estimated 950 genera and perhaps 20,000 species. They are distributed over most of the earth and in almost all habitats and climates. North American genera number about 230, of which 20 are believed to be naturalized from Europe. The greatest number of composites are herbaceous, some are shrubs, and a few are small trees or climbing plants, chiefly tropical. In the typical composite flower (e.g., the sunflower), what appears to be a single flower is in reality a head of many small flowers. Petallike flowers of the outer ring are called ray flowers and are often sterile. These constitute the more conspicuous part of the head and are adapted in a variety of ways (e.g., in size and color) to attract insects for pollination and to serve as a landing platform for them. The central portion of the head is composed of disk flowers, minute tubular florets nearly always containing both stamens and pistils. The entire composite head is supported by a series of bracts (modified leaves), which arise from the base of the flower stalk and are collectively termed the involucre. The FRUITS of composites are achenes. Many are remarkably adapted for dispersal by animals—e.g., the many burr plants of the family, such as the burdock and cocklebur—or by wind, e.g., the dandelion and goldenrod. Although numerous individual variations exist among the composites, the general flower plan makes the plants readily identifiable and represents the highest evolutionary specialization of flower structure of all dicotyledonous plants. In effect, the community of flowers in a composite head performs by a division of labor the same functions as a single flower in other plants. As a flower structure it ensures pollination, and the effective dispersal variations have made the family widespread and predominant. Taxonomic distinctions within the family are not always clear; botanists sometimes subdivide the Compositae into several families (e.g., the thistle, chicory, and ragweed families) or, more frequently, into tribes. The composite group includes many common weeds and wild flowers, especially late summer and autumn flowers. The pollen of many species causes hay fever. This large family is of minor economic importance. A few species are used for food, usually as salad plants—e.g., lettuce, endive and chicory, salsify, and dandelion; the artichoke is the only commercial table vegetable. Many composites have been used in medicinal preparations. The family is most valuable for its ornamentals. Among the well-known and numerous cultivated species are the asters, daisies, chrysanthemums, marigolds, and zinnias. The composite family is classified in the division MAGNOLIOPHYTA, class Magnoliopsida.

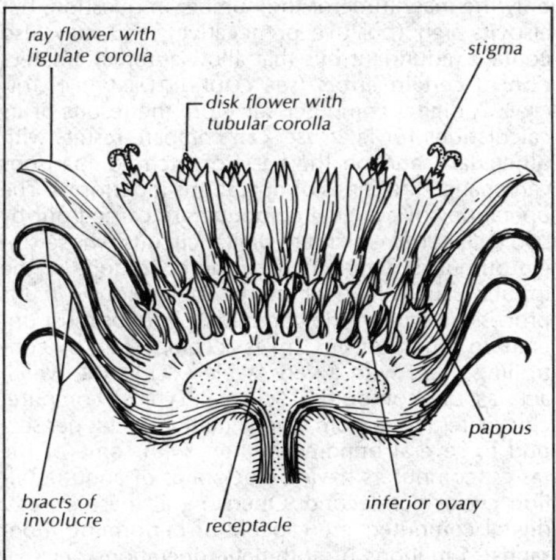

Cross section of a sunflower, a member of the composite family

composite order: see CORINTHIAN ORDER.

composition, in art, the organization of forms and colors within the work of art. In traditional sculpture this means the arrangement of masses and planes. In representational painting it means the grouping of forms on a two-dimensional plane in depth. In abstract painting forms are generally composed on planes parallel to the picture surface. In illusionistic works (see ILLUSIONISM) with advanced PERSPECTIVE, forms are arranged to accord with the laws of depth perception. Triangular groupings were favored in Renaissance art both for reasons of symmetry and for symbolic connotations of the Trinity.

composition, in ancient and medieval law, a sum of money paid by a guilty party as satisfaction to the family of the person he injured or killed. Failure to make the payment might justify retaliation in kind against the offender or his family. In earliest times, the payment was made as a result of a mutual agreement between the parties, but later it was imposed by law. In many societies the amount paid varied according to the rank of the person injured or slain. Composition reflected a transition from a system of feuds or blood revenge (see VENDETTA) to one where socially dangerous acts are primarily a concern of the state rather than of private persons and their families alone. The exaction of the payment recognized the outrage to the person and the family as the prime offense, but it tended to discourage disorder by providing a substitute for retributive killing or other violence. When, in addition to composition, a fine had to be paid to the state, the dangerous act approached the modern conception of a crime (see CRIMINAL LAW). This institution was known in all Germanic cultures, including Anglo-Saxon England, and was widespread in many parts of the world. It is still practiced in certain Middle Eastern countries. An example of composition is wergild [Old Eng., = man's price], the payment made by a murderer to the family of a murdered person. Wergild was often paid to the king for loss of a subject and to the lord of the manor for the loss of a vassal as well as to the family of the deceased. The term *composition* is also used to refer to an agreement between an insolvent debtor and his creditor, whereby the creditor for some consideration, such as an immediate payment of a portion of the debt, waives the remainder and considers his claim fully satisfied.

composition board, wood product produced in the form of a board or sheet, formed of cellulose fibers or particles derived from wood or other sources, and used principally as a building material. The oldest type of composition board is a relatively dense material known as hardboard, discovered accidentally in 1924 by the American scientist William Mason. After obtaining wood fibers by using high-pressure steam, Mason attempted to dry a matlike mass of them in a steam press. Because of a faulty valve, the press remained hot longer than had been planned and thus the first piece of hardboard was formed. In other forms of composition board the fibers are not as closely packed, and the density is correspondingly lower. Some of these boards find application as insulating and soundproofing materials. Other similar types are treated with waterproofing material, e.g., asphalt applied under pressure, and are usable as the sheathing of buildings. Such materials typically have a resistance to shearing forces exceeding that of plywood. Particle board, another form of composition board, is made by binding wood particles ranging in size from flakes to sawdust together with a suitable adhesive, such as a plastic resin, and pressing or extruding them to form sheets. Particle board is used as a cheaper substitute for plywood in some applications; but even though it has a higher density, it is less resistant to puncture and the effects of weather. When properly veneered it is suitable for making furniture. In its raw form it makes an excellent subflooring for dry locations.

compost, substance composed mainly of partly decayed organic material that is applied to fertilize the soil and to increase its HUMUS content; it is often used in vegetable farming, home gardens, flower beds, lawns, and greenhouses. Compost usually is made from plant materials (e.g., grass clippings, vegetable tops, garden weeds, hay, tree leaves, sawdust, and peat) together with manure and some soil; lime, SUPERPHOSPHATES, and nitrogen fertilizers are often added with manure to reinforce the compost and hasten its decomposition.

Compostela, Santiago de, Spain: see SANTIAGO DE COMPOSTELA.

compound, in chemistry, a substance composed of ATOMS of two or more ELEMENTS in chemical combination, occurring in fixed, definite proportion and arranged in a fixed, definite structure. A compound has unique properties that are distinct from the properties of its elemental constituents and of all other compounds. One familiar chemical compound is water, a liquid that is nonflammable and does not support combustion. It is composed of two elements: hydrogen, an extremely flammable gas; and oxygen, a gas that supports combustion. A compound differs from a mixture in that the components of a mixture retain their own properties and may be present in many different proportions. The components of a mixture are not chemically combined; they can be separated by physical means. A mixture of hydrogen and oxygen gases is still a gas and can be separated by physical methods. If the mixture is ignited, however, the two gases undergo a rapid chemical combination to form water. Although the hydrogen and oxygen can occur in any proportion in a mixture of gases, they are always combined in the exact proportion of two atoms of hydrogen to one atom of oxygen when combined in the compound water. Another familiar compound is sodium chloride (common salt). It is composed of the silvery metal sodium and the greenish poisonous gas chlorine combined in the proportion of one atom of sodium to one atom of chlorine. Water is a molecular compound; it is made up of electrically neutral MOLECULES, each containing a fixed number of atoms. Sodium chloride is an ionic compound; it is made up of electrically charged IONS that are present in fixed proportions and are arranged in a regular, geometric pattern (called crystalline structure) but are not grouped into molecules. The atoms in a compound are held together by chemical bonding (see CHEMICAL BOND). A compound is often represented by its chemical FORMULA. The formula for water is H_2O and for sodium chloride, NaCl. The FORMULA WEIGHT of a compound can be determined from its formula. The MOLECULAR WEIGHT of a molecular compound can be determined from its molecular formula. Two or more distinct compounds that have the same molecular formula but different properties are called ISOMERS. Compounds are formed from simpler substances by CHEMICAL REACTION. Some compounds can be formed directly from their constituent elements, e.g., water from hydrogen and oxygen: $2H_2+O_2 \rightarrow 2H_2O$. Other compounds are formed by reaction of an element with another compound; e.g., sodium hydroxide (NaOH) is formed (and hydrogen gas released) by the reaction of sodium metal with water: $2Na+2H_2O \rightarrow 2NaOH+H_2\uparrow$. Compounds are also made by reaction of other compounds; e.g., sodium hydroxide reacts with hydrogen chloride (HCl) to form sodium chloride and water: $HCl+NaOH \rightarrow NaCl+H_2O$. Complex molecules such as proteins are formed by a series of reactions involving elements and simple compounds. Compounds can be decomposed by chemical means into elements or simpler compounds. Water is broken down into hydrogen and oxygen by electrolysis. Candle wax, a mixture of hydrocarbons, is changed in the candle flame by combustion (with oxygen) to a mixture of the simpler compounds carbon dioxide (CO_2) and water. Life is based on numerous reactions in which energy is stored and released as compounds are produced and decomposed.

compound eye: see EYE.

compressed air, air whose volume has been decreased by the application of pressure. Air is compressed by various devices, including the simple hand pump and the reciprocating, rotary, centrifugal, and axial-flow compressors. Compressed air exerts an expansive force that can be controlled and used in various devices including tires, air brakes, caissons, and diving suits. As a source of power it is used to operate PNEUMATIC TOOLS, e.g., pneumatic hammers and drills and spraying equipment. It is widely employed for cleaning dust and dirt out of mechanical equipment. It is used also in mining, tunneling, and the manufacture of explosives, since it is not a fire hazard. Compressed air is in readily available supply and is easily stored and transported.

compression, external stress applied to an object or substance, tending to cause a decrease in volume (see PRESSURE). Gases can be compressed easily, solids and liquids to a very small degree if at all. Water, for example, is practically incompressible, thus making it especially useful for HYDRAULIC MACHINES. According to the KINETIC-MOLECULAR THEORY OF GASES, when the molecules of a gas are brought close enough together by compression, the gas (under certain conditions of temperature) undergoes LIQUEFACTION. This principle is applied commercially to several gases, including liquid oxygen and the so-called bottled gas (a mixture of hydrocarbons) used as a fuel. Boyle's law deals with the decrease in the volume of a gas in relation to the increase of pressure upon it (see GAS LAWS). The ability or the degree to which an internal-combustion engine reduces the volume of its fuel mixture preparatory to firing is called its compression. Also, a region of high pressure in a fluid is called a compression; thus sound waves are said to propagate at compressions and rarefactions (regions of low pressure) of their medium, such as air.

Compromise of 1850. The annexation of Texas to the United States and the gain of new territory by the Treaty of Guadalupe Hidalgo at the close of the Mexican War (1848) aggravated the hostility between North and South concerning the question of the extension of SLAVERY into the territories. The antislavery forces favored the proposal made in the Wilmot Proviso to exclude slavery from all the lands acquired from Mexico. This, naturally, met with violent Southern opposition. When California sought (1849) admittance to the Union as a free state, a grave crisis threatened. Also causing friction was the conflict over the boundary claims of Texas, which extended far westward into territory claimed by the United States. In addition, the questions of the slave trade and the FUGITIVE SLAVE LAWS had long been vexing. There was some fear that, in the event of strong antislavery legislation, the Southern states might withdraw from the Union altogether. The possibility of the disintegration of the Union was deprecated by many but was alarming to some, among them Henry CLAY, who emerged from retirement to enter the Senate again. President TAYLOR was among those who felt that the Union was not threatened; he favored admission of California as a free state and encouragement of New Mexico to enter as a free state. These sentiments were voiced in Congress by William H. SEWARD. John C. CALHOUN and other Southerners, particularly Jefferson DAVIS, maintained that the South should be given guarantees of equal position in the territories, of the execution of fugitive slave laws, and of protection against the abolitionists. Clay proposed that a series of measures be passed as an omnibus compromise bill. Support for this plan was largely organized by Stephen A. DOUGLAS. The measures were the admission of California as a free state; the organization of New Mexico and Utah territories without mention of slavery, the status of that institution to be determined by the territories themselves when they were ready to be admitted as states (this formula came to be known as POPULAR SOVEREIGNTY); the prohibition of the slave trade in the District of Columbia; a more stringent fugitive slave law; and the settlement of Texas boundary claims by Federal payment of $10 million on the debt contracted by the republic of Texas. These proposals faced great opposition, but Daniel WEBSTER greatly enhanced the chances for their acceptance by his famous speech on March 7, 1850. Taylor's death and the accession of conservative Millard FILLMORE to the presidency made the compromise more feasible. After long debates and failure to pass the omnibus bill, Congress passed the measures as separate bills in Sept., 1850. Many people, North and South, hailed the compromise as a final solution to the question of slavery in the territories. However, the issue reemerged in 1854 with the KANSAS-NEBRASKA ACT, and seven years later the factions were fighting the Civil War. See E. C. Rozwenc, *The Compromise of 1850* (1957); Holman Hamilton, *Prologue to Conflict* (1964).

Compton, Arthur Holly, 1892–1962, American physicist, b. Wooster, Ohio, grad. College of Wooster (B.S., 1913), Ph.D. Princeton, 1916. He was professor and head of the department of physics at Washington Univ., St. Louis (1920–23), and professor of physics at the Univ. of Chicago (1923–45), where he helped to develop the atomic bomb. He returned to Washington Univ. where he was chancellor (1945–53) and professor (from 1953). For his discovery of the COMPTON EFFECT he shared with C. T. R. Wilson the 1927 Nobel Prize in Physics. In addition to his work on X rays he made valuable studies of cosmic rays. His writings include *X Rays and Electrons* (1926; 2d ed., with S. K. Allison, *X-Rays in Theory and Experiment*, 1935), *The Human Meaning of Science* (1940), and *Atomic Quest* (1956). See his *Cosmos of Arthur Holly Compton*, ed. by Marjorie Johnston (1968) and *Scientific Papers*, ed. and with an introd. by R. S. Shankland (1973).

Compton, Karl Taylor, 1887–1954, American physicist, b. Wooster, Ohio, grad. College of Wooster (Ph.B., 1908), Princeton (Ph.D., 1912); brother of A. H. Compton. He taught at Princeton from 1915 to 1930 (as professor from 1919) and was president of the Massachusetts Institute of Technology from 1930 to 1948. From 1948 to 1949 he was chairman of the research and development board of the National Military Establishment. He did notable research on photoelectricity, radar, ionization of gases, ultraviolet spectroscopy, and electric arcs.

Compton, city (1970 pop. 76,611), Los Angeles co., S Calif., a residential and industrial suburb between Los Angeles and Long Beach; inc. 1888. It has aircraft, electronic, oil, chemical, and steel industries. A junior college is there.

Compton-Burnett, Dame Ivy, 1892–1969, English novelist. Educated at the Univ. of London, she lived quietly in London for most of her life. She was named a Dame Commander of the British Empire in 1967. Ivy Compton-Burnett's unconventional novels of the Edwardian gentry reveal beneath their irony, satire, and wit an embittered, frightful world of hypocrisy and cruelty. Her writings are noted for their lack of plot, their absence of description and characterization, and their almost complete reliance on articulate, highly stylized conversations. Among her most notable works are *Brother and Sister* (1929), *A House and Its Head* (1935), *Manservant and Maidservant* (1947), *Mother and Son* (1955), *The Mighty and Their Fall* (1961), and *The Last and the First* (1971). See biography by Elizabeth Sprigge (1973); study by Charles Burkhart (1965).

Compton effect [for A. H. Compton], increase in the wavelengths of X rays and gamma rays when they collide with and are scattered from loosely bound electrons in matter. This effect provides strong verification of the quantum theory since the theoretical explanation of the effect requires that one treat the X rays and gamma rays as particles or photons (quanta of energy) rather than as waves. The classical treatment of these rays as waves would predict no such effect. According to the quantum theory a photon can transfer part of its energy to a loosely bound electron in a collision. Since the energy of a photon is proportional to its frequency, after the collision the photon has a lower frequency and thus a longer wavelength. The increase in the wavelength does not depend upon the wavelength of the incident rays or upon the target material. It depends only upon the angle that is formed between the incident and scattered rays. A larger scattering angle will yield a larger increase in wavelength. The effect was discovered in 1923. It is used in the study of electrons in matter and in the production of variable energy gamma-ray beams.

compurgation (kŏm″pərgā′shən), in medieval law, a complete defense. A defendant could establish his innocence or nonliability by taking an oath and by getting a required number of persons to swear they believed his oath. Compurgation, also called wager of law, was found in early Germanic law and in English ecclesiastical law until the 17th cent. In common law it was substantially abolished as a defense in felonies by the Constitutions of Clarendon (1164). Compurgation was still permitted in civil actions for debt, however, and vestiges of it survived until its final abolition in 1833. It is doubtful whether compurgation ever existed in America.

computer, device capable of performing a series of calculations or logical operations without human intervention. Although such devices as the ABACUS and the desk CALCULATING MACHINE have limited calculating capacities, the computer is characterized by the number and complexity of operations it can perform and by its ability to store, retrieve, and process data. Computers are of two types, analog and digital. An analog computer is designed to process data in which the variable quantities vary continuously (see ANALOG CIRCUIT); it translates the relationships between the variables of a problem into analogous relationships between electrical quantities, such as current and voltage, and solves the original problem by solving the equivalent problem, or analog, that is set up in its electrical circuits. Because of this feature, analog computers are especially useful in the simulation and evaluation of dynamic situations, such as the flight of a space capsule or the changing weather patterns over a certain area. The key component of the analog computer is the OPERATIONAL AMPLIFIER, and the computer's capacity is determined by the number of amplifiers it contains (often over 100). A digital computer is designed to process data in numerical form (see DIGITAL CIRCUIT); its circuits perform directly the mathematical operations of addition, subtraction, multiplication, and division. The numbers operated on by a digital computer are expressed in the BINARY SYSTEM; binary digits, or bits, are 0 and 1, so that 0, 1, 10, 11, 100, 101, etc. correspond to 0, 1, 2, 3, 4, 5, etc. Binary digits are easily expressed in the computer circuitry by the presence (1) or absence (0) of a current or voltage. A string of such bits is sometimes called a digital word; it may specify not only the magnitude of the number in question, but also its sign (positive or negative), and may also contain redundant bits that allow automatic detection of certain errors (see CODE; INFORMATION THEORY). A digital computer can store the results of its calculations for later use, can compare results with other data, and on the basis of such comparisons can change the series of operations it performs. The operations of a digital computer are carried out by LOGIC CIRCUITS, which are digital circuits whose single output is determined by the conditions of the inputs, usually two or more. The various circuits processing data in the computer's interior must operate in synchronism; this is accomplished by controlling them with a very stable OSCILLATOR, which acts as the computer's "clock." Typical computer clock rates range from several million cycles per second to several hundred million, with some of the fastest computers having clock rates of about a billion cycles per second. Operating at these speeds, digital computers are capable of performing thousands to millions of arithmetic operations per second, thus permitting the rapid solution of problems so long that they would be impossible for a human to solve by hand. In addition to the arithmetic or logic circuitry and a small number of registers that hold intermediate results, the heart of the computer also contains the central processor—circuitry that decodes the set of instructions, or program, and causes it to be executed—and the storage unit, or memory, where results or other data are stored for periods of time ranging from a small fraction of a second to many months. Since the central processor can operate no faster than the rate at which data is fed to it, it is important that access to this internal memory be very rapid. The basic elements of such a memory are usually either magnetic cores, which store one bit of information according to the direction in which the cores are magnetized, or electronic circuits, which store one bit by being switched either on or off. Magnetic cores have the advantage of not needing power to maintain stored data, but they operate more slowly than electronic circuits. Both are costly and require means for regenerating stored data that would otherwise be lost at various times. For this reason most computers are also equipped with bulk storage systems using equipment such as magnetic tape, magnetic disks, magnetic drums, punched paper tape, or punched paper cards. In a system using magnetic tape the information is stored by a specially designed TAPE RECORDER somewhat similar to one used for recording sound. In disk and drum systems the principle is the same except that the magnetic medium lies in a closed path, or track, on the surface of a disk or cylinder, with a separate magnetic head serving each track. Of these systems disks are the fastest and most efficient. Drum systems operate about as fast but are wasteful of space; this defect has rendered them virtually obsolete. Paper tapes and cards suffer from the same problem as magnetic tape, namely that a good deal of search time may be needed to find a particular item of data, and they operate even more slowly than tape. Before a computer can be used to solve a given problem, it must first be programmed, that is, prepared for solving the problem by being given a set of instructions, or program. Each instruction in the program is a simple, single step, telling the computer to perform some arithme-

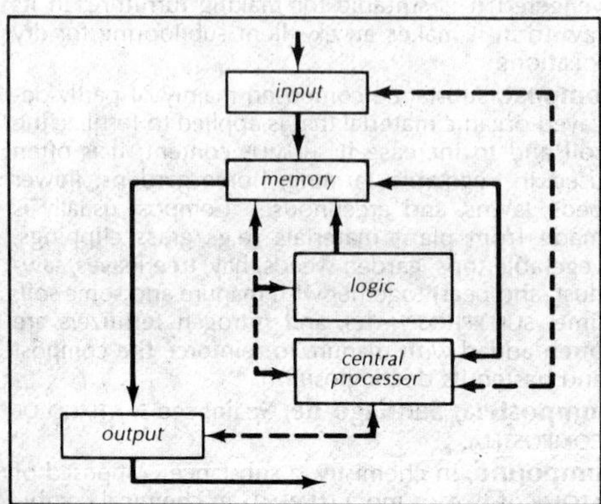

Schematic diagram of a computer system: Data flow is indicated by solid lines; control signals are indicated by dashed lines.

tic operation, read the data from some given location in the memory, compare two numbers, or take some other action. The program is entered into the computer's memory exactly as if it were data, and on activation, the machine is directed to treat this material in the memory as instructions. Other data may then be read in and the computer can carry out the program to solve the particular problem. Since computers are designed to operate with binary numbers, all data and instructions must be represented in this form; the machine language, in which the computer operates internally, consists of the various binary codes that define instructions together with the formats in which the instructions are written. Since it is time-consuming and tedious for a programmer to work in actual machine language, an intermediate programming language, or assembly language, designed for the programmer's convenience, is used for the writing of most programs. The computer is programmed to translate a given assembly language into machine language and then solve the original problem for which the program was written. Assembly languages vary from machine to machine. Certain programming languages are universal, varying little from machine to machine. These are usually designed for particular types of problems. For example, FORTRAN is for scientific and mathematical use, COBOL for business use, PL/1 for general use, and ALGOL for mathematical use. The various programs by which a computer controls aspects of its operations, such as those for translating data from one form to another, are known as software, as contrasted with hardware, which is the physical equipment comprising the installation. Once a program has been prepared, it must be fed into the computer through the machine's input facilities. This is accomplished most often by means of written language, either on paper, in which case it is called hard copy, or on the face of a cathode-ray tube, in which case it is called soft copy. Human beings communicate with the computer by means of teletypewriters, machines that punch paper cards and tapes for presentation to the computer, and special devices such as GRAPHIC TERMINALS. Generally, the slowest operations that a computer must perform are those of transferring data, particularly when the data is received from or delivered to a human being. In large installations, this problem is often alleviated by using small computers to handle data input and output for a larger one. In a fairly recent development known as time-sharing, a single fast computer serves a number of remote data terminals. The computer switches from one terminal to another so quickly that many different users at different terminals can use the computer at the same time without any one of them being aware of the others. Human beings may also communicate with the computer directly through its control panel; however, except for initiating and concluding long periods of operation this is very wasteful, as a vast amount of computing time is lost in the time it takes a human being to respond to an output message. In most moderate to large installations the moment-to-moment control of the machine resides in a special software program called an operating system, or supervisor. Other forms of software include assemblers and compilers for programming languages. Software is of great importance; the usefulness of a highly sophisticated array of hardware can be severely compromised by the lack of adequate software. Advances in the technology of INTEGRATED CIRCUITS has spurred the development of smaller computers, sometimes called minicomputers. These, because of their relatively low cost, are increasingly being used in place of analog computers for single-purpose operation. They are also good for general use in small installations. Except for tasks requiring human creativity, the applications of the digital computer are virtually limitless, such limitations as there are being principally related to difficulty in acquiring adequate data for the computer or in reducing the data to numbers. This is an area of continuing research for new applications and improvements in hardware and software. American scientist Vannevar Bush built a mechanically operated device, called a differential analyzer, in 1930. It was the first general-purpose analog computer. In the 19th cent. British mathematician Charles Babbage designed, but did not build, a mechanical digital device capable of processing information as a modern computer does. The first information-processing digital computer actually built was the Automatic Sequence Controlled Calculator, or Mark I computer. Completed in 1944, this electromechanical device was designed by American engineer Howard Aiken. In 1946 the Electronic Numerical Integrator and Computer, or ENIAC, was put into operation. Using thousands of electron tubes, it was the first electronic digital computer. In the late 1950s transistors replaced electron tubes in computers, allowing a reduction in the size and power consumption of computer components. During this period FORTRAN and ALGOL, and later COBOL, were introduced. In the 1960s hybrid computers were formed by connecting analog computers to digital ones. Later integrated circuits were developed that allowed further reduction in component size and increase in reliability. See John Pfeiffer, *The Thinking Machine* (1962); Jeremy Bernstein, *The Analytic Engine: Computers—Past, Present and Future* (1963); D. G. Fink, *Computers and the Human Mind* (1966); R. R. Fenichel and J. Weizenbaum, ed., *Computers and Computation: Readings from Scientific American* (1971); Irving Adler, *Thinking Machines* (rev. ed. 1973); Craig Fields, *About Computers* (1973); J. M. Adams, *Computers* (1973); R. C. Dorf, *Computers and Man* (1974).

computer music, music composed or performed with the aid of a computer. For composition, the computer is programmed to select or reject elements from a pre-established, digitally represented sound domain. The result is either transcribed into conventional musical notation or electrically synthesized. Sound production consists of a digital program effecting filters and/or oscillators to generate electrical signals whose parameters—amplitude, frequency—can be heard as sound events when they are transcribed onto magnetic tape, amplified, and played through loudspeakers. The Columbia-Princeton Electronic Music Studio is a major center for the production of computer music.

Comstock, Anthony, 1844–1915, American morals crusader, b. New Canaan, Conn. He served with the Union army in the Civil War and was later active in advocating the suppression of obscene literature. He was the author of the comprehensive New York state statute (1868) forbidding immoral works, and in 1873 he secured stricter Federal postal legislation against obscene matter. That same year he organized the New York Society for the Suppression of Vice. As secretary of the society until his death, Comstock was responsible for the destruction of 160 tons of literature and pictures. For his liberal enemies he became the symbol of licensed bigotry and for his supporters the symbol of stalwart defense of conventional morals. Comstock also inspired the Watch and Ward Society of Boston. See biographies by Heywood Broun and Margaret Leech (1927) and De Robinge Bennett (repr. 1971).

Comstock, Henry Tompkins Paige: see COMSTOCK LODE.

Comstock Lode, richest known U.S. silver deposit, W Nevada, on Mt. Davidson in the Virginia Range. It is said to have been discovered in 1857 by Ethan Allen Grosh and Hosea Ballou Grosh, sons of a Pennsylvania minister and veterans of the California gold fields who died under tragic circumstances before their claims were recorded. Henry T. P. Comstock, known as Old Pancake, was a sheepherder and prospector who took possession of the brothers' cabin and tried to find their old sites. He and others searching for gold laid claim to sections of the Comstock (1859) but soon sold them for insignificant sums. The lode did not become really profitable until its bluish sand was assayed as silver. News of the discovery then spread rapidly, attracting promoters and traders as well as miners, and the lode was the scene of feverish activity. Among early arrivals was William Morris Stewart, who later became one of Nevada's first senators. Camps and trading posts in the area became important supply centers, and Virginia City, a mining camp on the mountain, was for several decades the "capital" of the lode and a center of fabulous luxury. Great fortunes were made by the "silver kings," John W. Mackay, James Graham Fair, James C. Flood, and William S. O'Brien, and by Adolph Sutro, George Hearst, and Eilley Orrum Bowers. Silver determined the economy and development of Nevada until exhaustion of the mines by wasteful methods of mining and the demonetization of silver started a decline in the 1870s. By 1898 the Comstock was virtually abandoned. See Grant Smith, *History of the Comstock Lode* (1943); George Lyman, *The Saga of the Comstock Lode* (1934, repr. 1971); Lucius Beebe and Charles Clegg, *Legends of the Comstock Lode* (4th ed. 1956).

Comtat Venaissin (kəNtä' vənäNsăN') or **Comtat,** region of SE France, Vaucluse dept., comprising the territory around AVIGNON. Well-irrigated, it is a truck-farming and fruit-growing area. Comtat Venaissin was given by King Philip III to Pope Gregory X in 1274. Succeeding French kings sought to regain the region, but it remained in papal hands until 1791, when a plebiscite was held and the inhabitants voted to reunite with France. The region's historic capital was CARPENTRAS.

Comte, Auguste (ōgüst' kôNt), 1798–1857, French philosopher, founder of the school of philosophy known as POSITIVISM, educated in Paris. From 1818 to 1824 he contributed to the publications of Saint-Simon, and the direction of much of Comte's future work may be attributed to this association. Comte was primarily a social reformer. His goal was a society in which individuals and nations could live in harmony and comfort. His system for achieving such a society is presented in his *Cours de philosophie positive* (1830–42; tr. *The Course of Positive Philosophy,* 1896 ed.). In this work Comte analyzes the relation of social evolution and the stages of science. He sees the intellectual development of man covered by what is called the Law of the Three Stages—theological, in which events were largely attributed to supernatural forces; metaphysical, in which natural phenomena are thought to result from fundamental energies or ideas; positive, in which phenomena are explained by observation, hypotheses, and experimentation. The sciences themselves are classified on the basis of increasing complexity and decreasing generality of application in the ascending order: mathematics, astronomy, physics, chemistry, biology, and sociology. Each science depends at least in part on the science preceding it; hence all contribute to sociology (a term that Comte himself originated). A sociology developed by the methods of positivism could achieve the ends of harmony and well-being which Comte desired. Another work, *Le Système de politique positive* (1851–54; tr. *System of Positive Polity,* 1875–77), placed religion above sociology as the highest science; it was, however, a religion shorn of metaphysical implications, with humanity as the object of worship. For a modern edition of part of this work see *A General View of Positivism* (1957). Important among his other writings are *Catechisme positiviste* (1852, tr. 1858) and *Synthèse subjective* (1856). Published posthumously were his *Testament* (1884) and his letters (1902–05). See R. L. Hawkins, *Auguste Comte and the United States, 1816–1853* (1936) and *Positivism in the United States, 1853–1861* (1938); F. S. Marvin, *Comte, the Founder of Sociology* (1937, repr. 1965).

comuneros (kōmōōnä'rōs), in Spain and Spanish America, citizens of a city or cities when organized to defend their rights against arbitrary encroachment of government. The first great revolt of *comuneros* in Spain was the uprising (1520–21) of the *comunidades* (autonomous cities) of Castile against the measures of Emperor CHARLES V. In Spanish America, the revolt of the *comuneros* of Paraguay, led by ANTEQUERA Y CASTRO against Gov. Diego de los Reyes Balmaseda and continuing against viceregal and Jesuit opposition from 1723 to 1735, was one of the first considerable democratic uprisings of Latin America. In the *comunero* insurrection of New Granada (1780–81), 60 cabildos rejected new taxes and sought reforms.

Comus (kō'məs), in late Roman legend, god of mirth and revelry. A follower of Dionysus, he was represented as a drunken youth bearing a torch. In Milton's poetic masque, *Comus,* he is the mischievous son of Bacchus and Circe.

Comyn, John (kŭm'ĭn), d. c.1300, Scottish nobleman, known as the Black Comyn. In 1286 he became one of the six regents for MARGARET MAID OF NORWAY and, as such, agreed to the treaty of 1290, by which Margaret was to marry the eldest son of Edward I of England. After her death, he was at first a claimant for the vacant throne but then supported the claim of his brother-in-law, John de BALIOL, who was awarded the crown by Edward I of England in 1292. Comyn joined Baliol in his revolt against Edward but submitted to the English king in 1296. The name also appears as Cumming.

Comyn, John, d. 1306, Scottish nobleman. He was called the Red Comyn, to distinguish him from his father, the Black Comyn. Aiding his uncle, John de BALIOL, in the struggle against Edward I, he was for a time held hostage by the English. After the rout of the Scottish troops at Falkirk (1298), he was appointed one of the guardians of the realm. He renewed the struggle with Edward, but surrendered in 1304 on condition that he could retain his lands. He was murdered at Dumfries by Robert the Bruce (later ROBERT I), probably because Robert feared him as a rival claimant to the throne. The name also appears as Cumming.

Conakry (kŏn'əkrē), city (1972 pop. est., with suburbs, 290,000), capital of Guinea and its Conakry region, SW Guinea, a port on the Atlantic Ocean. Located on Tombo island and connected with the mainland by a causeway, Conakry is Guinea's largest city and its administrative, communications, and economic center. Its economy revolves largely around the port, which has modern facilities for handling and storing cargo, and from which Guinea's chief exports, alumina and bananas, are shipped. A railroad connects Conakry with Kankan, E Guinea, and roads run to the Ivory Coast, Senegal, and Mali. The few local manufactures include food products and beverages; iron ore and bauxite were mined nearby until the late 1960s. In 1887, Conakry was occupied by French forces. Its main growth dates from World War II, and today it is a modern city with wide boulevards and fine botanical gardens. The Polytechnical Institute of Conakry (1963) and a school of administration are located there.

Conaniah (kŏn''ənī'ə), Levite of Josiah's time. 2 Chron. 35.9.

Conant, James Bryant (kō'nənt), 1893–, American educator, b. Dorchester, Mass., grad. Harvard (B.A., 1913; Ph.D., 1916). Except for a brief period in the army (1917–19), Conant taught chemistry at Harvard from 1916 until 1933, serving as chairman of the department during the last three years. He was president of Harvard from 1933 until his resignation in 1953. Conant was chairman (1941–46) of the National Defense Research Committee; in 1953 he was appointed U.S. High Commissioner for Germany and later served as ambassador to West Germany (1955–57). He directed a number of extensive investigations of American education and has published widely in the field. Conant's writings include *Education in a Divided World* (1948), *Modern Science and Modern Man* (1952), *Education and Liberty* (1953), *Slums and Suburbs* (1961), *The Comprehensive High School* (1967), *Scientific Principles and Moral Conduct* (1967), and his autobiography, *My Several Lives* (1970).

Conant, Roger, 1592–1679, one of the founders of Massachusetts, b. East Budleigh, Devonshire, England. He was a salter in London before he went to Plymouth in 1623. Conant lived at Nantasket from 1624 to 1625, when he was appointed to manage the Dorchester Company's settlement on Cape Ann. In 1626, with about 20 settlers, he founded Salem (Naumkeag) and later was the leading citizen of Beverly, which was incorporated (1668) largely because of his efforts. See biography by C. K. Shipton (1944).

Conant, Thomas Jefferson, 1802–91, American biblical scholar and editor of many translations of books of the Bible. He aided in the revision of the English Bible completed in 1881.

conceit, in literature, fanciful or unusual image in which apparently dissimilar things are shown to have a relationship. The Elizabethan poets were fond of Petrarchan conceits, which were conventional comparisons, imitated from the love songs of Petrarch, in which the beloved was compared to a flower, a garden, or the like. The device was also used by the METAPHYSICAL POETS, who fashioned conceits that were witty, complex, intellectual, and often startling, e.g., John Donne's comparison of two souls with two bullets in "The Dissolution." Samuel Johnson disapproved of such strained metaphors, declaring that in the conceit "the most heterogeneous ideas are yoked by violence together." Such modern poets as Emily Dickinson and T. S. Eliot have used conceits.

concentration, in chemistry, measure of the relative proportions of two or more quantities in a MIXTURE. Concentration may be expressed in a number of ways. The simplest statement of the concentrations of the components of a mixture is in terms of their percentages by weight or volume. Mixtures of solids or liquids are frequently specified by weight percentage concentrations, such as alloys of metals or mixtures used in cooking, whereas mixtures of gases are usually specified by volume percentages. Very low concentrations may be expressed in parts per million (ppm), as in specifying the relative presence of various substances in the atmosphere. In addition to these means of expressing concentration, several others are defined especially for describing SOLUTIONS: molarity, molality, mole fraction, formality, and normality. Some of these define the concentration of the solute in reference to the amount of solvent, others in reference to the total amount of solution. The molarity of a solution is the number of MOLES of solute per liter of solution; e.g., a solution of glucose in water containing 180.16 grams (1 gram-molecular weight, or mole) of glucose per liter of solution is referred to as one molar (1 *M*). The molality of a solution is the number of moles of solute per 1,000 grams of solvent; a solution prepared by dissolving 180.16 grams of glucose in 1,000 grams of water is one molal (1 *m*). The mole fraction of a solution is the ratio of moles of solute to the total number of moles in the solution. Since ionic compounds, such as sodium chloride, NaCl, do not occur as molecules, their concentrations cannot be expressed in terms of molarity, molality, or mole fraction. Instead, the concentration of an ionic compound in solution may be given by its formality, the number of gram-formula weights of the compound per liter of solution; e.g., a solution containing 58.44 grams (one gram-formula weight) of NaCl per liter of solution is one formal (1 *F*). In considering the reactions of certain solutions in combination, for example the NEUTRALIZATION of acids and bases, a useful expression of the concentration is the normality of each solution, the number of gram-equivalent weights of solute per liter of solution (see EQUIVALENT WEIGHT); e.g., a solution containing 49.04 grams (one gram-equivalent weight) of sulfuric acid, H_2SO_4, per liter of solution is one normal (1 *N*). Concentrations of solutions may also frequently be given in terms of the weight of solute in a given volume of solvent or solution. The concentration of a solute is very important in studying chemical reactions because it determines how often molecules collide in solution and thus indirectly determines the rates of reactions and the conditions at equilibrium (see CHEMICAL EQUILIBRIUM).

concentration camp, prison created outside the normal prison system for particular categories of people, usually for political reasons. After Adolf Hitler's rise to power in 1933, concentration camps were set up throughout Germany for detaining persons, especially Jews and Communists, considered undesirable by the Nazis (see NATIONAL SOCIALISM). No legal procedure was required for commitment. Inmates performed hard labor under the supervision of SS guards notorious for their brutality. During World War II concentration camps mushroomed throughout German-occupied Europe. Of the millions of people of many nationalities detained in them, a large proportion died of mistreatment, malnutrition, and disease. Several camps were extermination camps. In the best known of these—Majdanek, Treblinka, and Oswiecim (Auschwitz), in Poland—more than 6 million men, women, and children (mostly Jews and Poles) were killed in gas chambers. Documented proof of these horrors, used in later war-crimes trials, includes unmentionable details of sadism, sometimes perpetrated under the guise of medical experiments. Among the most notorious camps liberated by U.S. and British troops in 1945 were Buchenwald, Dachau, and Belsen. The term *concentration camp* has also been used to include forced-labor camps in which political prisoners are confined and any camps used to confine minority groups.

Concepción (kōnsĕpsēōn'), city (1970 pop. 189,929), capital of Concepción prov., S central Chile, near the mouth of the Bío-Bío River. It is an industrial and commercial center and one of Chile's major cities. Its port, Talcahuano, just north of the city, ships the products of the surrounding rich agricultural region. Concepción's industries produce glass, textiles, sugar, hides, and steel. Founded in 1550 by Pedro de Valdivia, the Spanish conqueror of Chile, the city was besieged and destroyed by the Araucanian chief Lautaro in 1554–55. It was completely destroyed by earthquakes in 1570, 1730, 1751, 1835, and 1939, and was severely damaged in 1960. Its numerous rebuildings have given Concepción a modern appearance. Points of interest include the Plaza Independencia and a university.

Concepción del Uruguay (dĕl o͞oro͞ogwī'), city (1970 pop. 73,720), Entre Ríos prov., NE Argentina, a port on the Uruguay River. It ships the grain and beef of the surrounding region. The city was founded in 1778 and was twice the capital of Argentina in the 19th cent. It was the scene of a revolt (1870) that culminated in the assassination of ex-president Justo José de Urquiza.

conceptualism, in philosophy, position taken on the problem of UNIVERSALS, initially by Peter ABELARD in the 12th cent. Like nominalism it denied that universals exist independently of the mind, but it held that universals have an existence in the mind as concept. These concepts are not arbitrary inventions but are reflections of similarities among particular things themselves, e.g., the concept male reflects a similarity between Paul and John. This similarity shows that universals are also patterns in God's mind according to which he creates particular things. Slightly modified, this view becomes the position of moderate REALISM, the classical medieval solution to the controversy. For a modern statement of conceptualism, see C. I. Lewis, *Analysis of Knowledge and Valuation* (1946, repr. 1962).

concert, in music, public performance of a group of musical compositions. Originally the word referred simply to a group of musicians playing together; concerts by a solo performer are properly called recitals. The earliest recorded public concerts were organized by a London violinist, John Banister, in 1672. Many orchestral concerts were given in the 18th cent., and early in the 19th cent., which saw great development of concert life, public concerts of chamber music were given. In the American colonies, the first concert on record took place in Boston in 1731.

concertina (kŏnsûrtē'nə), musical instrument whose tone is produced by free reeds. It was invented by Sir Charles Wheatstone in 1829. It is a

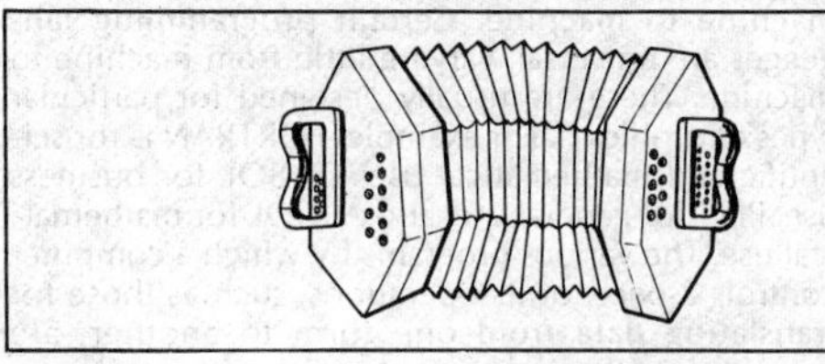

Concertina

chromatic instrument similar to the ACCORDION, but its bellows are attached to hexagonal blocks having handles and buttons (finger pistons), and it is smaller. It is mainly associated with popular music.

concerto (kənchâr'tō), musical composition usually for an orchestra and a soloist or a group of soloists. In the 16th cent. the term was applied to music for an ensemble, either vocal or instrumental. At the end of the century it referred to music in which two ensembles contested with each other. By 1750 it meant music contrasting a full ensemble with soloists in alternation. The form known as *concerto grosso* is characterized by a small group of solo players contrasted with the full orchestra. Giuseppe Torelli (1658–1709) and VIVALDI established the *concerto grosso* in three movements, while CORELLI used four or more. These three composers were active in the development of all forms of the concerto in the baroque period. J. S. Bach's six Brandenburg concertos and the concertos of Handel represent the fullest development of the baroque type. Toward the end of the 18th cent. the solo concerto displaced the *concerto grosso*. Mozart established the classical concerto in three movements, the first of which is a sonata as in a symphony, for solo instrument and orchestra. Beethoven expanded the dimensions of this form, giving greater importance to the orchestra. In the 19th cent. Liszt unified the concerto by using the same themes in all movements. He was one of numerous composers to use the concerto form as a showcase for virtuoso display in the solo. The concerto repertory is strongest in works for piano and violin as the solo instrument. In the 20th cent. renewed interest in the *concerto grosso* has been manifested by such composers as Hindemith, Bartók, and Bloch. See A. J. B. Hutchings, *The Baroque Concerto* (1961); Abraham Veinus, *The Concerto* (rev. ed. 1964); D. F. Tovey, *Essays in Musical Analysis: Concertos* (1936, repr. 1972).

Concert of Europe, term used in the 19th cent. to designate a loose agreement by the major European powers to act together on European questions of common interest. The concert emerged after the Congress of Vienna (1814–15) and included the QUADRUPLE ALLIANCE powers of Great Britain, Austria, Prussia, and Russia, and, as of 1818, France as well. It aimed to preserve peace by concerted diplomatic action reinforced by periodic conferences dealing with problems of mutual concern.

concerto grosso: see CONCERTO.

conch, common name for certain marine GASTROPOD mollusks having a heavy, spiral shell, the whorls of which overlap each other. In conchs the characteristic gastropod foot is reduced in size and the operculum, a horny plate located on the foot and used to seal the shell opening in many gastropods, has the appearance and function of a claw. During locomotion, the operculum secures a foothold in the sand, and the conch jumps forward by means of the quick contraction of a retractor muscle called the columella muscle. Thus the conch lacks the creeping motion of most gastropods. The king conch, *Strombus gigas*, found in the warmer waters of the Atlantic, Caribbean, and Gulf of Mexico, has a shell 10 to 12 in. (25–30 cm) long and may weigh up to 5 lb (2.3 kg). Similar in size and distribution is the queen conch, *Cassis cameo*. Its shell has been used in Europe to carve cameos. Conch shells range in color from white to red; they have been used by man to fashion a number of items, such as buttons, ornaments, or the crude trumpets made from the shell of the trumpet conch, *Charonia tritonis*. This conch is similar in shape to the king and queen conchs but is much more slender and reaches a length of 20 in. (50 cm). *C. tritonis* is found in the Gulf of Mexico and the Indian Ocean. The largest conch and also one of the largest univalves in the world is the horse conch, *Pleuroploca gigantea*, having a shell length of 24 in. (60 cm). It is found along the Atlantic Coast from North Carolina to Brazil. The body can retreat entirely into the shell and remain there for months if unfavorable conditions prevail. An unusual conch shell is that of the spider conch, *Lambis lambis*, which has leglike projections. Spider conchs are voracious carnivores, common on coral reefs. They also feed on algae, as do the king conchs. Most conchs are carnivorous, feeding on bivalve mollusks; some are scavengers as well. They inhabit tropical waters and have been used as a food source for man. The conch is classified in the phylum MOLLUSCA, class Gastropoda, order Mesogastropoda.

Conchos (kōn'chōs), river, c.350 mi (560 km) long, rising in S Chihuahua state, N Mexico, and flowing N and NE to the Rio Grande. Dams along its middle course provide water for extensive cotton oases just south of the city of Chihuahua.

conciliation: see MEDIATION.

Concini, Concino (kōnchē'nō kōnchē'nē), d. 1617, Florentine adventurer, favorite of MARIE DE' MEDICI, queen of France, who made him marshal of France (1613). In 1610 he was made marquis d'Ancre. He exerted great influence after the death of Marie's husband, Henry IV, and succeeded the duke of Sully as minister. His greed and his spy system won him the hatred of all classes. His efforts to weaken the nobility provoked an unsuccessful revolt (1615) led by Henri II de CONDÉ. In 1617, Louis XIII had Concini assassinated. His wife, Leonora Galigaï (1571?–1617), lady in waiting and favorite of the queen, was beheaded and burned for sorcery.

Concord (**1**, **2**, **3**, kŏng'kərd, **4** kŏn'kôrd"). **1** Residential city (1970 pop. 85,164), Contra Costa co., W central Calif., in an oil and farm region; settled c.1852, inc. 1905. Electronic equipment is made. The city is the eastern terminus for rapid transit to the San Francisco Bay area. A junior college is there, and a U.S. naval ammunition depot is nearby. **2** Town (1970 pop. 16,148), Middlesex co., E Mass., on the Concord River; inc. 1635. Electronic and wood products are made. The site of the Revolutionary battle of Concord on April 19, 1775 (see LEXINGTON AND CONCORD, BATTLES OF), is marked by Daniel Chester French's bronze *Minuteman*. Concord has many fine old houses, some opened as memorials to noted occupants—Emerson, the Alcotts, Hawthorne, and Thoreau. An antiquarian museum and the Old Manse, built in 1769 by Emerson's grandfather and made famous by Thoreau, and the place where Ephraim Bull developed the Concord grape are there. **3** City (1970 pop. 30,022), state capital and seat of Merrimack co., S central N.H., on the Merrimack River; settled 1725–27, inc. as Rumford, Mass., in 1733 (Count RUMFORD later took his title from this name) and as Concord, N.H., in 1765. Famous for its granite, the city also has a printing industry and plants making leather goods, electrical equipment, furniture, stone and clay products, textiles and apparel, metalware, and food. It became the state capital in 1808, and its growth was further aided by the building of the Middlesex Canal in 1815. St. Paul's school (preparatory) and the house of Franklin Pierce (now a museum) are in Concord. Mary Baker Eddy was born a few miles away, at Bow. **4** City (1970 pop. 18,464), seat of Cabarrus co., central N.C., near the edge of the Piedmont; settled 1796, inc. 1837. Located in a livestock and grain area, it is also a thriving cotton textile center. In addition to a great variety of cotton goods, its manufactures include foods and metal products. Gold discovered nearby in 1799 started the North Carolina gold rush. Concord is the seat of Barber-Scotia College.

Concord, river, c.15 mi (24 km) long, NE Mass., a short tributary of the Merrimack, which it joins at Lowell. On April 19, 1775, colonial militia fired some of the first shots of the American Revolution at the British over a bridge across the river at Concord, Mass. Henry David THOREAU's first book, *A Week on the Concord and Merrimack Rivers* (1849), records a boat trip with his brother.

concordat (kŏnkôr'dăt), formal agreement, specifically between the pope, in his spiritual capacity, and the temporal authority of a state. Its juridical status is now generally accepted as being a contract between CHURCH AND STATE and as such it is a treaty governed by international laws. The term *concordat* has also been applied to other agreements; thus, in the Swiss Confederation before 1848 federal decisions were called concordats. The fundamental antithesis between church and state found particularly violent expression in the quarrels over INVESTITURE during the Middle Ages and gave rise to the practice of concluding concordats. The earliest agreement to be called a concordat (see WORMS, CONCORDAT OF, 1122) was a dual proclamation rather than a bilateral act. The Concordat of 1516 between Pope Leo X and King Francis I of France, which abolished the Pragmatic Sanction of Bourges (see PRAGMATIC SANCTION), gave the king the right to nominate bishops, abbots, and priors but reserved to the pope the right of confirmation and special rights of appointment. That right was revoked at the States-General of Orléans in 1561, and the struggle between GALLICANISM and ULTRAMONTANISM was resumed, to last until the French Revolution. The CONCORDAT OF 1801, most famous of all concordats, regulated the status of the church in France for a century. In the 19th and 20th cent. numerous concordats were concluded. The appointment of bishops still remained an important issue, but the advance of secularism gave increasing importance to the status of religious education, monastic orders, and church property and to the seemingly conflicting loyalties of Roman Catholics to the state and to the church. In the Catholic countries of Latin America the conflicts and adjustments between church and state gave rise to a number of concordats. The concordat of 1855 with Austria gave vast rights to the church, but it was abrogated by Austria upon the proclamation of papal infallibility. The KULTURKAMPF between Otto von Bismarck and the papacy ended (1887) with a modus vivendi, which was a tentative agreement and not called a concordat. The status of the papacy in Italy was regulated in 1929 by the LATERAN TREATY. The threat of National Socialism (Nazism) to the Roman Catholic Church prompted the concordat of 1933 with Adolf Hitler, who violated it from the start. In Spain, where Francisco Franco had abrogated the concordat of 1931, a provisional agreement with the Vatican over the appointment of bishops was reached in 1941. After World War II a number of concordats (notably that with Poland) were abrogated by Communist regimes. A new concordat with Spain was signed in 1953.

Concordat of 1801, agreement between Napoleon Bonaparte and Pope Pius VII that reestablished the Roman Catholic Church in France. Napoleon, wishing to consolidate his position and to end the confusion in church affairs created by the French Revolution, took the initiative in negotiating the agreement. By its terms Roman Catholicism was recognized as the religion of most French citizens. Archbishops and bishops were to be nominated by the government, but the pope was to confer the office. Parish priests were to be appointed by the bishops, subject to government approval. Confiscated church property, most of which had been sold to private persons, was not to be restored, but the government was to provide adequate support for the clergy. To implement the concordat Napoleon issued (1802) the so-called Organic Articles; these restated the traditional liberties of the Gallican church (see GALLICANISM) while increasing Napoleon's control of church activities. The Organic Articles were not agreed to by the pope, and he did not consider them binding. A century later, anticlericalism, intensified by the Dreyfus Affair, led to the imposition of severe restrictions on the church by the government of Émile COMBES. Anticlericalism culminated in 1905 in the formal repudiation of the concordat, thereby separating CHURCH AND STATE. In Alsace and Lorraine, however, the Concordat of 1801 remained in force even after their recovery (1918) from Germany by France.

Concorde, Place de la (pläs də lä kôNkôrd'), large square, Paris, France. It is bounded by the Tuilleries gardens; the Champs Élysées; the Seine River; and a facade of buildings divided by a vista of the Madeleine Church. The Pont de la Concorde, a monumental bridge, leads from the Place to the other side of the Seine. The square was designed by Jacques Gabriel and built between 1755 and 1792. It was originally planned as a monument to the then ruling Louis XV, whose statue stood in the center, and was called "Place Louis XV." In 1792 the statue was torn down, the square renamed "Place de la Révolution," and a guillotine set up, transforming the area into a site of mass executions. Under the Directory the name "Concorde" was adopted (although during the Bourbon restoration of 1815–30 "Place Louis XV" was revived). The central obelisk, a gift of the Egyptian viceroy, was erected in 1836. The fountains were constructed between 1836 and 1846.

Concordia (kōng-kôr'thyä), city (1970 pop. 110,401), Entre Ríos prov., NE Argentina, a port on the Uruguay River. One of the chief towns in the Argentine Mesopotamia, it exports preserved meat, mate, quebracho, and grain and is the distributing center of a farm and stock-raising district. Concordia was founded in 1832.

concrete, structural masonry material made by mixing broken stone or gravel with sand, cement (see CEMENT, HYDRAULIC), and water and allowing the mixture to harden into a solid mass. The cement is the chemically active element, or matrix; the sand and stone are the inert elements, or aggregate. The use of artificial masonry similar to modern concrete dates from a remote period but did not become a standard technique of construction until the Romans adopted it (after the 2d cent. B.C.) for roads, immense buildings, and engineering works. The concrete of the Romans, formed by combining pozzuolana (a volcanic earth) with lime, broken stones, bricks, and tuff, was easily available and had great durability (the Pantheon of Rome and the Baths of Caracalla were built with it). It proved suitable for temples, basilicas, the forum, and baths; enormous spaces could be roofed without lateral thrusts by vaults cast in the rigid homogeneous material. Concrete was unknown for centuries after the fall of Rome. Scientifically proportioned concrete formed with cement is an invention of modern times, the name not being used until c.1830. Modern portland cement has revolutionized the production and potentialities of concrete and has superseded the natural cements, to which it is vastly superior. Concrete used without strengthening is termed mass, or plain, concrete and has the structural properties of stone—great strength under compressive forces and almost none under tensile ones. F. Joseph Monier, a French inventor, found that tensile weakness could be overcome if steel rods were embedded in a concrete member. The new composite material was called reinforced concrete, or ferroconcrete. It was patented in 1857, and a private house in Port Chester, N.Y., first demonstrated (1857) its use in the United States. By the mid-20th cent. it had become a widely used structural material, rivaled only by steel. Reinforced concrete was improved by the development of prestressed concrete—concrete containing cables that are placed under tension before or after the concrete hardens. Another improvement, thin-shell construction, takes advantage of the inherent structural strength of certain geometric shapes, such as hemispherical and elliptical domes; in thin-shell construction great distances are spanned with very little material. The component materials of concrete are mixed in varying proportions, according to the strength required and the function to be fulfilled. The ideal mixture is that which solidifies with the minimum of voids, the mortar and small particles of aggregate filling all interstices. A typical proportioning is 1:2:5, i.e., one part of cement, two parts of sand, and five parts of broken stone or gravel, with the proper amount of water for a pouring consistency. For hardening into the required shape, the mixture is poured into wood or steel molds, called forms. Among the advantages of concrete as a building material are its adaptability to widely varied structural needs, its practically universal availability, its fire resistance, and the ease with which it can be used. The perfecting of reinforced concrete has profoundly influenced structural techniques and architectural forms throughout the world. See E. S. de Mare, ed., *New Ways of Building* (3d ed. 1958); A. A. Raafat, *Reinforced Concrete in Architecture* (1958); Peter Collins, *Concrete: The Vision of a New Architecture* (1959); A. M. Neville, *The Properties of Concrete* (1963); J. J. Waddell, *Concrete Construction Handbook* (1968).

concrete music: see ELECTRONIC MUSIC.

concretion, mass or nodule of mineral matter, usually oval or nearly spherical in shape, and occurring in sedimentary rock. It is formed by the accumulation of mineral matter in the pore spaces of the sediment, usually around a fossil or fossil fragment acting as a nucleus. Most concretions are very dense and compact, and are usually composed of calcite, silica, or iron oxide. The material making up the concretion is believed to come from the surrounding rock, being redeposited around the nucleus. Concretions range in diameter from a fraction of an inch to many feet, although most are but a few inches in diameter. Perhaps the best known are the flint nodules found in chalk deposits such as those at Dover, England. Concretions having radiating cracks filled with mineral matter are called turtle stones, or septaria.

Condamine, La: see MONACO.

Condé (kôNdā'), family name of a cadet branch of the French royal house of BOURBON. The name was first borne by **Louis I de Bourbon, prince de Condé,** 1530–69, Protestant leader and general. He fought the Spanish at Metz (1552) and Saint-Quentin (1557) but won little favor at court. After his conversion to Protestantism he became involved in the Conspiracy of Amboise (1560; see AMBOISE, CONSPIRACY OF) and escaped execution only through King Francis II's premature death. He was restored to favor by the regent, Catherine de' Medici, but took command of the Huguenots in the Wars of Religion (see RELIGION, WARS OF) and was captured at Dreux (1562). Released in 1563, he once more took up arms in 1567 and was killed at the battle of Jarnac. His son, **Henri I de Bourbon, prince de Condé,** 1552–88, was also a Huguenot general. **Henri II de Bourbon, prince de Condé,** 1588–1646, French political leader, son of Henri I, was forced to leave France (1609) because of the attentions paid his wife by King Henry IV. He returned in 1610 and in 1615 formed a conspiracy against Concino Concini, who dominated the government of the regent, MARIE DE' MEDICI, but he was bought off and later imprisoned (1616–19). Afterward he made his peace with the government, fought against the Protestants in the religious wars, and in 1643 became a member of the council of regency for King Louis XIV. His elder son, Louis II (see CONDÉ, LOUIS II DE BOURBON, PRINCE DE) was known as the Great Condé. Another son, Armand, founded the cadet branch of CONTI. Both sons and a daughter, Mme de LONGUEVILLE, were leaders in the FRONDE. Louis II's great-grandson, **Louis Joseph de Bourbon, prince de Condé,** 1736–1818, fought with distinction in the Seven Years War. At the beginning of the French Revolution he emigrated and fomented counterrevolutionary action. He formed a corps known as the army of Condé, which he allied with the Austrians. In 1797 he offered his services to Russia; in 1800 he entered English pay, but he was obliged to dissolve his army in 1801. He returned to France at the Restoration. His son, **Louis Henri Joseph de Bourbon, prince de Condé,** 1756–1830, followed his father into exile, fought in his army, and headed an unsuccessful revolt in the Vendée during the Hundred Days. He died, probably by suicide. His son was the ill-fated Louis Antoine Henri de Bourbon-Condé, duc d'ENGHIEN. See H. E. P. L. d'Aumale, *History of the Princes de Condé in the XVIth and XVIIth Centuries* (1863–64, tr. 1872).

Condé, Louis II de Bourbon, prince de, 1621–86, French general, called the Great Condé; son of Henri II de Condé. Among his early victories in the Thirty Years War were those of Rocroi (1643), Freiburg (1644), Nördlingen (1645), and Lens (1648). In the series of outbreaks known as the FRONDE he was at first loyal to the court, but his later intrigues and ambitions caused his arrest in 1650. This precipitated the Fronde of the Princes against Cardinal MAZARIN, chief councillor of state during the regency of ANNE OF AUSTRIA. The nobles forced Mazarin to release Condé (1651), who became leader of the rebellious army of the princes and allied himself with Spain against France. After the disintegration of the Fronde and the return to power of Mazarin, Condé was (1653–58) commander of Spanish forces against France. In the final stage of the war he was defeated (1658) in the Battle of the Dunes (see DUNES, BATTLE OF THE). After the Peace of the Pyrenees (1659) between France and Spain, he was pardoned and returned to court. He fought in the Dutch War for King Louis XIV, defeating William of Orange at Seneff (1674) and forcing Raimondo Montecucculi to retreat from the Rhine (1675). His last years were spent in retirement at Chantilly. See Walter FitzPatrick, *The Great Condé* (1873).

condensation, in physics, change of a substance from the gaseous (vapor) to the liquid state (see STATES OF MATTER). Condensation is the reverse of VAPORIZATION, or change from liquid to gas. It can be brought about by cooling, as in DISTILLATION, or by an increase in pressure due to a decrease in volume. Certain natural phenomena, such as dew, fog, mist, and clouds, are the result of the condensation of water vapor in the atmosphere; the formation of DEW illustrates well the fundamental principles involved in such phenomena. The explanation of condensation can be found in the KINETIC-MOLECULAR THEORY OF GASES. As heat is removed from a gas, the molecules of the gas move more slowly, and as a result, the INTERMOLECULAR FORCES are strong enough to pull the molecules together to form droplets of liquid. Similarly, reducing the volume of the gas reduces the average distance between molecules and thus favors the intermolecular forces tending to pull them together.

condensed milk: see MILK.

condenser, in electricity, obsolete term for CAPACITOR. The part of a DISTILLATION apparatus or other apparatus that causes the CONDENSATION of a gas is also called a condenser.

Condillac, Étienne Bonnot de (ātyĕn' bônō' də kôNdēyăk'), 1715–80, French philosopher who developed the theory of sensationalism (i.e., that all knowledge comes from the senses and that there are no innate ideas). He took holy orders, and in 1768 he became a member of the French Academy of Sciences. His major works were *Essai sur l'origine des connaissances humaines* (1746) and *Traité des sensations* (1754). In these he tried to simplify Locke's theory of knowledge by arguing that all conscious experience is simply the result of passive sensations. In spite of this reduction of consciousness to the passive reception of sensation he nevertheless retained the Cartesian dualism of soul and body. He thus attempted to harmonize his deterministic psychology with his religious profession. See Z. Q. Schaupp, *The Naturalism of Condillac* (1926); I. F. Knight, *The Geometric Spirit* (1968).

conditioning: see LEARNING.

condor, common name for certain American vultures, found in the high peaks of the Andes of South America and the Coast Range of S California. Condors are the largest of the living birds, nearly 50 in. (125 cm) long with a wingspread of from 9 to 10 ft (274–300 cm). Voracious eaters, they prefer carrion but will attack living animals as large as deer. Two eggs are laid in a sketchy cliff nest of twigs; the young are unable to fly until they are about a year old. The Andean condor, *Vultur gryphus,* has black plumage with white wing patches and a white neck ruff. The lead-colored head and neck are bare; the male has a comb and wattles. The rare California condor, or California vulture, *Gymnogyps californianus,* is all black with white wing bands. Condors, particularly the California species, are extremely rare and on the verge of extinction. The California condor only lays one egg and does not breed until at least six years old. Condors are classified in the phylum CHORDATA, subphylum Vertebrata, class Aves, order Falconiformes, family Cathartidae.

Condorcet, Marie Jean Antoine Nicolas Caritat, marquis de (mărē' zhäN äNtwän' nēkôlä' kärētä' märkē' də kôNdôrsā'), 1743–94, French mathematician, philosopher, and political leader, educated at Rheims and Paris. He became a member of the Academy of Sciences in 1769 and of the French Academy in 1782. His work on the theory of probability (1785) was a valuable contribution to mathematics. Condorcet took part in the Revolution, but, opposing the extremes of the Jacobins, he was condemned and died in prison. His best-known work is *Esquisse d'un tableau historique des progrès de l'esprit humain* (1795; tr. *Sketch for a Historical Picture of the Progress of the Human Mind,* 1955). In that work Condorcet traced human development through nine epochs to the French Revolution and predicted in the 10th epoch the ultimate perfection of man. See studies by A. E. Burlingame (1930) and J. S. Schapiro (1934, repr. 1963).

condottiere (kōndōt-tyā'rā) [Ital.,=leader], leader of mercenary soldiers in Italy in the 14th and 15th cent., when wars were almost incessant there. The condottieri hired and paid the bands who fought under them. They dealt directly with the cities or states that requested their services and were responsible solely to them. They fought for the highest bidder, passing easily from one lord to another; this game proved dangerous and even fatal to more than one. Some condottieri had small states of their own, either inherited or acquired. The most famous were the Attendolos (founders of the SFORZA family), COLLEONI, CARMAGNOLA, and Sir John de HAWKWOOD. See studies by J. J. Deiss (1966) and Geoffrey Trease (1971).

conducting, in music, the art of unifying the efforts of a number of musicians simultaneously engaged in musical performance. In the Middle Ages and Renaissance the conductor was primarily a time beater, maintaining the measure or *tactus* of polyphonic music with his hand or a roll of music paper. During the baroque era the harpsichordist, playing the *basso continuo,* was the conductor. When the *continuo* disappeared, the first violinist, even today called concertmaster, became the leader or shared the function with a keyboard player. A few 18th-century conductors, such as Johann STAMITZ (1717–57) of the Mannheim orchestra, achieved a high standard of performance. The custom of beating time with a stick (baton) on a music stand or table originated in France. This noisy practice was irritating to the listener. It actually caused the death of the composer LULLY who struck his own foot with his baton, resulting in an abscess that killed him. The beating technique was altered and a more subtle manner was used by Beethoven, Mendelssohn, and Spohr. In his classic treatise *Über das Dirigieren* [concerning directing], Wagner laid down the principles of modern conducting, and under his influence Hans von BÜLOW became the first of the virtuoso conductors. A generally conventional set of gestures is used for beating time, a downstroke marking the beginning of a measure. The baton remains popular although a few conductors, notably STOKOWSKI, prefer not to use it. Modern conducting is highly individual and requires great musical understanding, a thorough knowledge of instruments and of the concert repertory, a clear mastery of the baton and hand gestures, and a human sympathy for the performers. See Hermann Scherchen, *Handbook of Conducting* (tr. 1933); A. C. Boult, *A Handbook on the Technique of Conducting* (7th ed. 1951); Carl Bamberger, *The Conductor's Art* (1965); H. C. Schonberg, *The Great Conductors* (1967).

conduction, transfer of HEAT or ELECTRICITY through a substance, resulting from a difference in TEMPERATURE between different parts of the substance, in the case of heat, or from a difference in electric POTENTIAL, in the case of electricity. Since heat is ENERGY associated with the motions of the particles making up the substance, it is transferred by such motions, shifting from regions of higher temperature, where the particles are more energetic, to regions of lower temperature. The rate of heat flow between two regions is proportional to the temperature difference between them and the heat conductivity of the substance. In solids, the molecules themselves are bound and contribute to conduction of heat mainly by vibrating against neighboring molecules; a more important mechanism, however, is the migration of energetic free electrons through the solid. Metals, which have a high free-electron density, are good conductors of heat, while nonmetals, such as wood or glass, have few free electrons and do not conduct as well. Especially poor conductors, such as asbestos, are used as insulators to impede heat flow (see INSULATION). Liquids and gases have their molecules farther apart and are generally poor conductors of heat. Conduction of electricity consists of the flow of CHARGES as a result of an electromotive force, or potential difference. The rate of flow, i.e., the electric current, is proportional to the potential difference and to the electrical conductivity of the substance, which in turn depends on the nature of the substance, its cross-sectional area, and its temperature. In solids, electric current consists of a flow of electrons; as in the case of heat conduction, metals are better conductors of electricity because of their greater free-electron density, while nonmetals, such as rubber, are poor conductors and may be used as electrical insulators, or DIELECTRICS. Increasing the cross-sectional area of a given conductor will increase the current because more electrons will be available for conduction. Increasing the temperature will inhibit conduction in a metal because the increased thermal motions of the electrons will tend to interfere with their regular flow in an electric current; in a nonmetal, however, an increase in temperature improves conduction because it frees more electrons. In liquids and gases, current consists not only in the flow of electrons but also in that of ions. A highly ionized liquid solution, e.g., salt water, is a good conductor. Gases at high temperatures tend to become ionized and thus become good conductors (see PLASMA), although at ordinary temperatures they tend to be poor conductors. See ELECTROCHEMISTRY; ELECTROLYSIS; SUPERCONDUCTIVITY.

conductus: see MOTET.

cone or **strobilus** (strŏb'ələs), in botany, reproductive organ of the gymnosperms (the conifers, cycads, and ginkgos). Like the flower in the angiosperms (flowering plants), the cone is actually a highly modified branch; unlike the flower, it does not have sepals or petals. Usually separate male (staminate, or pollen) cones and female (ovulate, or seed) cones are borne on the same plant. Each of the numerous scales, or sporophylls, of the staminate cone bears POLLEN-producing anthers and each female-cone scale bears ovules in which egg cells are produced. In the pine, a typical conifer, the staminate cones are small and short-lived; they are borne in clusters at the top of the tree. At the time of pollination, enormous numbers of pollen grains are released; those that land accidentally on female-cone scales extend pollen tubes part way into the ovule during one growing season but usually do not reach the stage of actual fertilization until the next year. The cones that are commonly observed are the seed cones, which are normally hard and woody although in a few the scales are fleshy at maturity. The terms *strobili* and *cones* are also applied to the comparable structures of the horsetails and club mosses.

cone or **conical surface,** in mathematics, surface generated by a moving line (the generator) that passes through a given fixed point (the vertex) and continually intersects a given fixed curve (the directrix). The generator creates two conical surfaces—one above and one below the vertex—called nappes. If the directing curve is a CONIC SECTION (e.g., a circle or ellipse) the cone is called a quadric

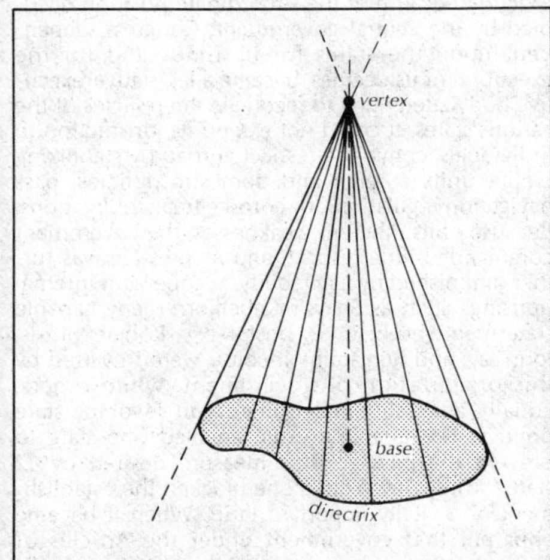

Cone

cone. The commonest type of cone is the right circular cone, a quadric cone in which the directrix is a circle and the line drawn from the vertex to the center of the circle is perpendicular to the circle. The generator of a cone in any of its positions is called an element. The solid bounded by a conical surface and a plane (the base) whose intersection with the conical surface is a closed curve is also called a cone. The altitude of a cone is the perpendicular distance from its vertex to its base. The lateral area is the area of its conical surface. The volume is equal to one third the product of the altitude and the area of the base. The frustum of a cone is the portion of the cone between the base and a plane parallel to the base of the cone cutting the cone in two parts.

coneflower, name for several American wild flowers of the family Compositae (COMPOSITE family). The purple coneflowers (genus *Echinacea*) are found E of the Rockies. They are sometimes grown as garden plants, as are the similar yellow coneflowers, or rudbeckias (see BLACK-EYED SUSAN). Coneflowers are classified in the division MAGNOLIOPHYTA, class Magnoliopsida, order Asterales, family Compositae.

Conegliano, Cima da: see CIMA, GIOVANNI BATTISTA.

Conemaugh (kŏn'əmô"), river c.70 mi (110 km) long, rising in the Allegheny Mts. and flowing NW to the Allegheny River, SW Pa. Federal flood-control works on the river and its tributaries include Conemaugh River Dam (160 ft/49 m high; 1,265 ft/386 m long; completed 1952).

Conestoga Indians (kŏnəstō'gə), North American Indians of the Iroquoian branch of the Hokan-Siouan linguistic stock (see AMERICAN INDIAN LANGUAGES). In the 17th cent. they lived on the lower reaches of the Susquehanna River and about the head of Chesapeake Bay, and they were sometimes called Susquehannocks. From this area they were driven southward and westward by attacks from the Iroquois Confederacy. The few survivors of this warfare were massacred by whites inflamed by accounts of the Indian War then raging (1763) along the Pennsylvania frontier.

Conestoga wagon, heavy freight-carrying vehicle of distinctive type that originated in the Conestoga region of Pennsylvania c.1725. It was used by the farmers to carry heavy loads long distances before there were railroads to convey produce to markets. Later it was used to carry manufactured goods across the Alleghenies to frontier stores and settlements and to bring back the frontier produce. This means of transporting goods by WAGON TRAIN developed into a major business employing thousands of wagons before the railroads crossed the mountains c.1850. The larger Conestoga wagons, usually drawn by six horses, carried loads up to eight tons. The bottom of the wagon box was curved, rising at both ends, so that in going up and down hills the goods would shift less easily and the tailgate would be subjected to less strain. The same curve was carried out in the white hood, at first made of hempen homespun and later of canvas, which rose up and out at each end, covering the front and rear openings with a poke bonnet effect to keep out sun, rain, and dust. The wagons were striking and graceful vehicles as they moved over the hills and were often called "ships of inland commerce." An arch of bells was fastened to the hames of each horse. The drivers usually rode the left wheel horse and are credited with originating the American custom of turning out to the right. The PRAIRIE SCHOONER was a modification of the Conestoga wagon. See study by G. Shumway and H. C. Frey (3d ed. 1968).

coney or **cony** (both: kō'nē), name used for the RABBIT (*Oryctolagus*) and for its fur; more often, for the PIKA, a small rodent found at high altitudes in both hemispheres; and for the HYRAX, a small herbivorous, hoofed animal of Africa and SW Asia. The last is probably the coney referred to in the Bible (Ps. 104.18; Prov. 30.26).

Coney Island (kō'nē), beach resort and amusement center of S Brooklyn borough of New York City, SE N.Y., on the Atlantic Ocean. The tidal creek that once separated the island from the mainland has been filled in, making the area a peninsula. More than a million persons throng to Coney Island on hot weekends and holidays, attracted by the beach, the 2-mi (3.2-km) boardwalk, the New York Aquarium, and the many other entertainment devices, eating places, and souvenir stands. High-rise apartments have replaced much of the amusement area since the 1950s.

confectionery, delicacies or sweetmeats that have sugar as a principal ingredient, combined with coloring matter and flavoring and often with fruit or nuts. In the United States it is usually called candy, in Great Britain, sweets or boiled sweets. Sweetmeats, long known in the Orient and to the Egyptians, were at first preserved or candied fruits, probably made with honey. One of the earliest functions of candy was to disguise unpleasant medicine, and prior to the 14th cent. confections were sold chiefly by physicians. Medieval physicians often used for this purpose sugarplate, a sweetmeat made of gum dragon, white sugar, and rosewater, beaten into a paste. One of the earliest confections still surviving is marzipan, known throughout Europe; it is made of almonds or other nuts, pounded to a paste and blended with sugar and white of egg. In the Middle Ages it was sometimes molded into fancy shapes and stamped with epigrams. Sugarplums, made of boiled sugar, were known in England in the 17th cent., but it was not until the 19th cent. that candy-making became extensive. The display of British boiled sweets at the national exhibition of 1851 stimulated manufacture in other countries, especially in France. In the United States in the middle of the 19th cent. about 380 small factories were making lozenges, jujube paste, and stick candy, but most fine candy was imported. With the development of modern machinery and the increasing abundance of sugar, confectionery making became an important industry. In the early 1970s annual candy sales in the United States had reached around $2 billion. Candy is roughly divided into two classes, hard and soft; the distinction is based on the fact that sugar when boiled passes through definite stages during the process of crystallization. Fondant, or sugar cooked to the soft stage, is the basis of most fancy candies, such as chocolate creams. See P. P. Gott, *All about Candy and Chocolate* (1958); B. W. Minifie, *Chocolate, Cocoa and Confectionery* (1970).

Confederacy, name commonly given to the **Confederate States of America** (1861–65), the government established by the Southern states of the United States after their SECESSION from the Union. (For the events leading up to secession and for the military operations of the Confederacy in the conflict between North and South which followed, see CIVIL WAR.) South Carolina, the first Southern state to secede (Dec. 20, 1860) after the election of the Republican President Abraham Lincoln, was soon followed out of the Union by six more states—Mississippi, Florida, Alabama, Georgia, Louisiana, and Texas. On Feb. 4, 1861, delegates from these states (except the Texans, who were delayed) met at Montgomery, Ala., and organized a provisional government. The Convention passed over the radical secessionists, R. B. Rhett and W. L. Yancey, and elected (Feb. 9) Jefferson DAVIS of Mississippi and Alexander H. STEPHENS of Georgia president and vice president respectively. The Convention also drafted a constitution (adopted on March 11) and functioned as a provisional legislature pending regular elections. The constitution closely resembled the Constitution of the United States, even repeating much of its language, but naturally had STATES' RIGHTS provisions. Slavery was "recognized and protected," but the importation of slaves "from any foreign country other than the slave-holding States or Territories of the United States of America" was prohibited. The general welfare clause of the old Constitution was omitted, protective tariffs were forbidden, and for most appropriations a two-thirds vote of congress was required. There were other, less important, departures from the U.S. Constitution, e.g., the president and vice president were to be elected for six years, but the president was not "reeligible"; members of the president's cabinet might not be granted seats in either house of the Confederate congress to discuss legislation affecting their departments; and amendment to the constitution (by two thirds of the states, with congress having no voice) was made easier. The new government seized or pressed its claims for U.S. property within its domain, especially forts and arsenals, and, when the Union declined to surrender Fort Sumter, ordered the firing (April 12–13) that formally began the hostilities. Lincoln's immediate call for troops brought four more Southern states—Arkansas, North Carolina, Virginia, and Tennessee—into the Confederacy, which now comprised 11 states. The border slave states of Maryland, Kentucky, and Missouri remained in the Union although they contained many Southern sympathizers; Confederate state governments were established at Neosho, Mo., and Russellville, Ky., in opposition to the official governments. In May it was decided to transfer the capital from Montgomery to Richmond, Va., because of Virginia's prestige; that move, considering Richmond's proximity to the North, has generally been regarded as a serious mistake. The new constitution was ratified (the approval of only five states was needed), general elections for congress and for presidential electors (as under the Federal Constitution) were held in Nov., 1861, and on Washington's birthday in 1862, the "permanent" government was inaugurated at Richmond. Davis and Stephens had been chosen without opposition to head it. Judah P. BENJAMIN, successively attorney general, secretary of war, and secretary of state, was the most important figure in Davis's cabinet. Only two other men remained in the cabinet for its entire brief existence—Stephen R. MALLORY, secretary of the navy, and John H. REAGAN, postmaster general. The story of the Confederacy is essentially the story of the loss of the Civil War. Even with its early military triumphs, the Confederacy experienced trying days. It never won recognition as an independent government, although Southerners had been confident that "king cotton" would bring this about. In 1861 they instituted an embargo on the export of cotton and voluntarily limited cultivation of the staple on the theory that these self-imposed and unofficial restrictions would make a cotton-hungry England eager to acknowledge the new nation that could supply in abundance the most important raw material in Britain's industrial system. The British, however, were well provided with cotton from previous boom years, and when their stocks finally were depleted, other sources of supply became available. Furthermore, Lincoln's EMANCIPATION PROCLAMATION enhanced the Union cause in the eyes of the average Briton, and the British government, no matter how pro-Confederate some of its individual members were, was not disposed to fly in the face of popular opinion. The CONFEDERATE CRUISERS built or bought in England were a scourge to the U.S. merchant marine, and later at the settlement of the ALABAMA CLAIMS, Great Britain was adjudged partly responsible for their depredations; but beyond this the Confederate missions of James M. MASON, John SLIDELL, William L. YANCEY, and others in Europe achieved little. Napoleon III would probably have followed Britain in recognizing the Confederacy, but not even the Confederate offer to recognize the French-dominated government of Maximilian in Mexico could induce the emperor to go off on this diplomatic venture alone. On the other hand, both the British and French recognized the blockade of the South, which the Union had proclaimed at the beginning of the war. This was particularly galling to Southerners because at first the blockade was not very effective; it is estimated that not more than a tenth of the ships running the blockade in 1861 were captured. But as the war progressed the blockade became more effective, and by 1865 one of every two blockade runners was being taken. When, in Oct., 1863, Davis expelled the British consuls who had remained in the South, the Confederacy had resigned itself to European nonrecognition, which was mostly influenced by the rising tide of Union successes in the war. The Confederate army early found that volunteers alone were insufficient, and the first conscription law was passed in April, 1862. By a later act (Feb., 1864), white men within the ages of 17 and 50 were drafted into military service. Provisions permitting the hiring of substitutes and exempting one owner or overseer for each 20 Negroes were highly unpopular among the yeomanry, who grumbled about "a rich man's war and a poor man's fight." Joseph E. BROWN and Zebulon B. VANCE, the governors of Georgia and North Carolina, led the denunciation of conscription and further berated Davis for the assumption of state troops into the Confederate army, the suspension of the writ of habeas corpus, and the Confederate tax program. Their extreme states' rights views represented a logical development of the theory that had led the Southern states to secede, but their insistence on maintaining these views at a time when unity was imperative was an added factor in the Confederate defeat. The fact that Brown, Vance, and others like them were able men and no less set on victory than was Davis only emphasizes this glaring deficiency in the nature of the Confederacy. Moreover, from the very beginning, the Confederacy was in bad financial condition, lacking in both specie and banks. It had difficulty in negotiating loans and was forced to finance its operations through issues of paper money, which by 1864 reached $1 billion in face value, more than twice that of the greenbacks issued by the Union. The gold value of these notes declined dangerously. Christopher G. MEMMINGER, secretary of the treasury, was forced to resign in 1864, but the situation was beyond the abilities of any man. With the men at war, the women of the Confederacy carried on at home. They did not face wholesale death as did the soldiers in the field, yet they knew war; it was brought to them in the mighty Union invasion of 1864–65. Feeling the pinch of the Union blockade and already lacking the bare necessities of life—shoes, iron goods, paper, clothing—because the South was nonindustrial (the armies were kept supplied with ammunition, but beyond that industry was negligible), they now saw their country devastated by Union forces such as those led by Sherman and Sheridan. Many, both men and women, cried for peace, but the Union price was too great (see HAMPTON ROADS PEACE CONFERENCE) and most Southerners hung on grimly. Benjamin's proposal that Negroes who willingly enlisted in the fight be freed indicates how desperate affairs became before the Confederacy collapsed. That the Confederacy was able to continue the war as long as it did is a tribute to its stout soldiers and a few brilliant commanders, notably Robert E. Lee. For the South, less populous than the North and largely made up of scattered agricultural communities, defeat was inevitable. The heroic aspect of the South's struggle was tarnished by its retention and defense of the institution of slavery, yet it long revered the "lost cause" of the Confederacy as its greatest tradition. See Jefferson Davis, *The Rise and Fall of the Confederate Government* (1881, abr. ed. 1961); F. L. Owsley, *King Cotton Diplomacy* (1931, new ed. 1959); R. S. Henry, *The Story of the Confederacy* (1931, rev. ed. 1957); C. H. Wesley, *The Collapse of the Confederacy* (1937, repr. 1968); J. G. Randall, *The Civil War and Reconstruction* (1937; rev. ed. by David Donald, 1961); E. M. Coulter, *The Confederate States of America, 1861–1865* ("A History of the South" series, Vol. VII, 1950); Clement Eaton, *A History of the Southern Confederacy* (1954); M. W. Wellman, *They Took Their Stand: the Founders of the Confederacy* (1959); W. B. Yearns, *The Confederate Congress* (1960); C. P. Roland, *The Confederacy* (1960); H. S. Commager, *The Defeat of the Confederacy* (1964); E. M. Thomas, *The Confederacy as a Revolutionary Experience* (1971).

Confederate cruisers, in U.S. history, warships constituting the South's seagoing navy. At the outbreak of the Civil War the United States ranked next to Great Britain in merchant marine. Since almost all of the tonnage belonged to the North, the Confederacy set out to destroy it. Privateering flourished only briefly because the increased effectiveness of the Union blockade forestalled attempts to bring prizes into Southern ports for adjudication. But in the course of the war some 18 cruisers, known as Confederate cruisers, were engaged in this activity. Only eight achieved results of any consequences. Of these, the *Florida*, the *Alabama*, and the *Shenandoah* were outstanding. The *Florida*, built in Liverpool in 1861–62, began her active career in Jan., 1863. Commanded by John N. Maffitt and later by Charles M. Morris, the *Florida*, along with several of her captures that were in turn commissioned Confederate cruisers, took about 60 prizes. She was captured by the U.S.S. *Wachusett* in the harbor of Bahia, Brazil in Oct., 1864. The most famous of the cruisers was the *Alabama*, also built at Liverpool in 1861–62. Under the command of Raphael Semmes she took almost 70 prizes. Her damage to U.S. shipping was valued at more than $6 million in the settlement of the ALABAMA CLAIMS. In a famous naval action off Cherbourg, France, on June 19, 1864, the *Alabama* was sunk by the U.S.S. *Kearsarge*. The *Shenandoah*, bought at London in 1864, was commanded by James I. Waddell. Many of her 38 prizes, principally Pacific whalers, were taken after the fall of the Confederacy, of which Waddell was not apprised until Aug., 1865. On returning to England the *Shenandoah* reverted to the United States. The indirect damage inflicted on the U.S. carrying trade by the cruisers had far more effect than the direct losses they caused. Insurance rates rose, and hundreds of ships transferred to foreign flags, especially to Great Britain's. The raiders were in good part responsible for the decline of the nation's merchant marine. See G. W. Dalzell, *The Flight from the Flag* (1940); Murray Morgan, *Dixie Raider* (1948); Edward Boykin, *Ghost Ship of the Confederacy* (1957); W. N. Still, Jr., *Iron Afloat* (1971).

Confederate States of America: see CONFEDERACY.

Confederation, Articles of, in U.S. history, ratified in 1781 and superseded by the Constitution of the United States in 1789. The imperative need for unity among the new states created by the American Revolution and the necessity of defining the relative powers of the CONTINENTAL CONGRESS and the individual states led Congress to entrust the drafting of a Federal constitution to a committee headed by John Dickinson. In the Articles of Confederation submitted by the committee to the Second Continental Congress, on July 12, 1776, three points provoked much argument—the apportionment of taxes according to population, the granting of one vote to each state, and the right of the Federal government to dispose of public lands in the West. After several revisions were made, however, this constitution, with a preamble and 13 articles, was adopted by Congress on Nov. 15, 1777. In their final form, the Articles retained the vote by states, but based the apportionment of taxes on the value of buildings and land, and specified that no state should be deprived of territory for the benefit of the United States. The preamble and Article 1 established a perpetual union of the Thirteen Colonies under the style of the United States of America. Article 2 asserted that each state retained its sovereignty and every right not expressly delegated to the central government, while Article 3 characterized the confederation as a "league of friendship," for common defense. In Article 4, the free inhabitants of each state were granted the privileges of free citizens in all the states, extradition was provided for, and it was stipulated that full faith and credit be given the records, acts, and judicial proceedings of the courts of one state in the courts of every other state. Article 5 provided that each state send annually not less than two nor more than seven delegates to Congress, though each state was to have only one vote. Article 6 left the conduct of war to Congress, and Article 7 empowered the state legislatures to appoint military officers up to and including the rank of colonel. Article 8 provided that the charges of war and other expenses incurred for the common defense should be defrayed out of a common treasury. Besides placing the conduct of foreign affairs in the hands of Congress, Article 9 authorized a system of settling disputes between states, granted Congress partial control over the currency, sanctioned the establishment of post offices by Congress, and established the Committee of the States, with one delegate from each state, to sit in recess of Congress. The authority of the central government was drastically restricted by this article, which forbade Congress to engage in war, negotiate treaties or alliances, coin money, emit bills of credit, or borrow and appropriate money without obtaining the consent of a majority of the states. Provisions for the functioning of the Committee of the States and for the possible admission of Canada were made in Articles 10 and 11. Article 12 stated that pecuniary obligations of Congress were to be deemed a charge against the United States. Article 13 stipulated that the Articles of Confederation were to be unanimously ratified by the states before going into effect and that no alteration could be made unless agreed to both by Congress and by the legislature of every state. By 1779 all the states had ratified the Articles except Maryland, which refused its assent until states claiming territory NW of the Ohio River relinquished their claims, thus guaranteeing the equitable right of all states to the Western lands. When New York, followed by Virginia and Connecticut, offered to cede to Congress its claims to Western territory, Maryland ratified (March 1, 1781) the articles. While this constitution was a contribution to the techniques of government and a step toward national unity, most American historians hold that the Articles of Confederation proved wholly unsatisfactory because of the subordinate position occupied by the central government. Congress, dependent upon the states for its funds and for the execution of its decrees, became a legislative-executive body attempting to reconcile the policies of the various states. It could not extend its jurisdiction to individuals, command respect abroad by stabilizing credit, unify foreign and domestic policies, pass navigation regulations, or enforce treaty obligations. Because of its inherent weaknesses, the government commanded little respect, and its prestige was further diminished by its inability to cope with internal uprisings such as Shays's Rebellion. Many capable statesmen who held key posts—e.g., Robert Morris, John Jay, and Benjamin Lincoln—were thwarted by this organization of government, while others, equally able, shunned Congress in favor of state politics. The unanimity rule enabled one state to prevent the passage of a measure desired by 12 states. Thus, New York alone blocked the establishment of a vitally important tariff. When it became apparent that government under the Articles of Confederation was, in the words of George Washington, "little more than the shadow without the substance," agitation for a stronger Federal government began. This agitation resulted in the Annapolis Convention of 1786 and the FEDERAL CONSTITUTIONAL CONVENTION of 1787, which drafted the Constitution of the United States. Perhaps the most significant event of the Confederation period was the adoption of the Ordinance of 1787 concerning the Northwest Territory. See Allan Nevins, *The American States during and after the Revolution, 1775–1789* (1924, repr. 1971). A more favorable view of the Articles of Confederation is given in the scholarly studies of Merrill Jensen, *The Articles of Confederation* (1940, repr. 1963) and *The New Nation* (1950, repr. 1962). See also study by S. A. Pleasants III (1968).

Confederation of the Rhine, league of German states formed by Emperor Napoleon I in 1806 after his defeat of the Austrians at AUSTERLITZ. Among its members were the newly created kingdoms of Bavaria and Württenberg (see PRESSBURG, TREATY OF), the grand duchies of Baden, Hesse-Darmstadt, and Berg, and a number of other principalities. Eventually nearly all the German states except Austria and Prussia joined the confederation. The members disavowed their allegiance to the Holy Roman Empire, and Francis II, already styled emperor of Austria, relinquished the title Holy Roman emperor in 1806. Napoleon attempted to influence the internal as well as the foreign affairs of the confederation, but recurring international crises diverted his efforts. After Napoleon's retreat from Russia (1812–13), its members, by changing sides in the war, caused the collapse of the confederation.

Confessing Church, Ger. *Bekennende Kirche*, German Protestant movement. It was founded in 1933 by Martin NIEMOELLER as the Pastors' Emergency League and was systematically opposed to the Nazi-sponsored German Christian Church. The immediate occasion for the opposition was the attempt by the Nazis soon after their rise to power to purge the German Evangelical Church of converted Jews and to make the church subservient to the state. At the Synod of Barmen (May, 1934) the Confessing Church set up an administration and proclaimed itself the true Protestant Church in Germany. After the arrest of many of its ministers the church was forced underground. Eventually the more moderate Lutheran Council replaced it as the most effective opponent to the Nazi regime. After the war Niemoeller and his followers continued as a separate group within the German Evangelical Church. The group is governed by representatives from each territorial church (the Council of Brethren) and its doctrines are based on the Barmen declaration and the Reformation creeds. See A. C. Cochrane, *The Church's Confession under Hitler* (1962).

confession, in law, formal admission of criminal guilt. It is usually obtained in the course of examination by the police or prosecutor or at the trial. For a confession to be admissible against an accused it must have been procured voluntarily after the person was told of his rights (see MIRANDA VS. ARIZONA). If a confession is obtained by torture or by a false promise of immunity from prosecution made by a responsible party, it is inadmissible. A signed confession is prima facie voluntary, and the accused must introduce proof that it was extorted if he wishes to prevent its introduction at the trial. Usually a person who does not plead guilty may not be convicted solely on the basis of his confession.

confessional literature derives from a central ritual of the Christian faith, confession of one's sins. The *Confessions* of St. Augustine, an autobiographical account of Augustine's struggle against the pagan world view of his times (4th–5th cent. A.D.), and his ultimate conversion to Christianity, is the first important example of confessional literature—"I sinned when as a boy I preferred those empty to those more profitable studies. 'One and one, two; two and two, four;' this was to me a hateful singsong: 'the wooden horse lined with armed men' and 'the burning of Troy' . . . were the choice spectacle of my vanity." Probably the best modern example of religious confessions is Thomas Merton's *The Seven Story Mountain* (1948). Not all confessional literature is religious. Jean-Jacques Rosseau's *Confessions* (1781) reveal the author as he is, not as he ought to be: "Two almost incompatible things are united in me, how I don't know; a very ardent temperament . . . and ideas slow to burn . . . It might be said that my heart and my mind do not belong to the same individual." Thomas De Quincey's *Confessions of an English Opium Eater* (1822) and F. Scott Fitzgerald's *The Crack-Up* (1936) follow this tradition. The intimate, autobiographical poetry of poets like Robert Lowell, Sylvia Plath, and Anne Sexton has been termed "confessional poetry." Confessional literature is not always autobiographical. Such novels as Chateaubriand's *Memoirs d'outre-tombe* (1849), Dostoyevsky's *Notes From The Underground* (1864), André Gide's *L'immoraliste* (1930), Saul Bellow's *Herzog* (1964), and Philip Roth's *Portnoy's Complaint* (1969) are the confessions of fictional narrators whose sins may or may not resemble those of their creators.

Confession of Augsburg: see CREED **4.**

confessions of faith, Protestant: see CREED **4, 5, 6.**

confirmation, Christian rite in which the initiation into the church that takes place by BAPTISM is confirmed. In the Roman Catholic and Orthodox Eastern churches, it is a SACRAMENT by which a Christian is strengthened in his faith. In the Lutheran and Anglican churches it is universally used, but it is not a sacrament (except among High Anglicans). In the East it is conferred by the priest on the newly baptized person of whatever age. In the West it is ordinarily an episcopal function, and the recipient has reached a canonical age of discretion. Confirmation consists of the laying on of hands and anointing with chrism, a mixture of oil and balm; Anglicans and Lutherans have abandoned the anointing. Some other Protestant churches use the term *confirmation* for the ceremony of admitting baptized persons into full church membership. Scriptural passages cited as authority for confirmation include Acts 8.14–17; 19.

conflict of laws, that part of the law in each state, country, or other jurisdiction that determines whether, in dealing with a particular legal situation, the law of some other jurisdiction will be recognized or given effect. An alternative term, widely used in Europe, is "private international law." An example of a situation that might involve the different laws of two places is that of a contract signed in one state and mailed to another. Complications may arise if one of the states provides that a contract so delivered is effective once mailed, while the other state provides that it is not effective until received. The rules of conflicts of law that a court applies in these disputed situations are commonly designed to decide the case by the law of the territory having the closest connection with the transaction. An often expressed ideal is that of making the decision the same regardless of where the case is decided. In the United States the existence of many states with legal rules often at variance makes the subject of conflict of laws especially urgent. The Supreme Court ruled in 1938 that each Federal court must apply the conflict of laws rules of the state in which it sits. Certain provisions of the U.S. Constitution deprive the states of complete freedom to determine how they will decide cases in this field. Most important is Article 4, Section 1, which provides, in part, "Full Faith and Credit shall be given in each State to the Public Acts, Records, and judicial Proceedings of every other State." The U.S. Supreme Court has interpreted this provision as requiring each state to treat as valid any judgment rendered by another state that had jurisdiction and to lend its powers of enforcement to the judgment; the sole exception is that the courts of one state do not enforce claims arising under the penal law of another (see EXTRADITION). Jurisdiction in this context is defined as the capacity of the state to interpose its authority in a transaction because of intimate connection with it. There are especially difficult jurisdictional problems in the field of divorce. The chief problem occurs when only one of the parties appears and the other is merely notified of the action. In such cases the Supreme Court has ruled that the state had jurisdiction to divorce if the party appearing was domiciled there. The court has defined DOMICILE as the place where a person is living with the ultimate intention of making it his home. A person who obtains a divorce under these circumstances may claim alimony in any state and is immune from the charge of bigamy if there is a remarriage. The most important attempt in antiquity to deal with the problem of conflict of laws was the *jus gentium* [law of nations] of the Romans: a system of laws applied to all free foreigners. The founder of the modern study of conflict of laws was the medieval jurist, Bartolus of Sassoferrato (1314–57). See W. W. Cook, *The Logical and Legal Basis of the Conflict of Laws* (1942); P. C. Jessup, *Transnational Law* (1956); S. A. Bayitch, *Conflict of Laws* (1968).

Confraternity of Christian Doctrine: see BIBLE.

Confucianism (kənfyo͞o'shənĭzəm), moral and religious system of China. Its origins go back to the *Analects* (see CHINESE LITERATURE), the sayings attributed to CONFUCIUS, and to ancient commentaries, including that of MENCIUS. In its early form (before the 3d cent. B.C.) Confucianism was entirely a system of ethical precepts for the proper management of society. It envisaged man as essentially a social creature who is bound to his fellows by *jen*, a term often rendered as "sympathy," or "human-heartedness." *Jen* is expressed through the five relations—sovereign and subject, parent and child, elder and younger brother, husband and wife, and friend and friend. Of these, the filial relation is usually stressed. The relations are made to function smoothly by an exact adherence to *li*, a term denoting a combination of etiquette and ritual. In at least some of these relations a person may be superior to some and inferior to others. If in his subordinate status he wishes to be properly treated he must—applying a principle similar to the Golden Rule—treat his own inferiors with propriety. Correct conduct, however, proceeds not through compulsion, but through a sense of virtue inculcated by observing suitable models of deportment. The ruler, as the moral exemplar of the whole state, must be irreproachable, but a strong obligation to be virtuous rests upon all men. It was recognized by the early philosophers that the millennial "great commonwealth," the union of mankind under ethical rule, would take a long time to achieve. It might be constantly advanced, however, by practicing the "rectification of names." This is a critical examination of the degree to which the behavior of a functionary or an institution corresponds to its name; thus, the title of king should not be applied to one who exacts excessive taxes, and the criticism of the undeserving claimant should force him to reform. In the 1st cent. A.D. began the practice of offering sacrifices and other veneration to Confucius in special shrines; it continued into the 20th cent. Confucianism had often to contend with supernatural religious systems, notably TAOISM and BUDDHISM, and at times, especially from the 3d to the 7th cent., it suffered a virtual eclipse. Under the T'ang dynasty (618–906) it enjoyed a renascence and was the state religion. In the Sung dynasty (960–1279) occurred the development of neo-Confucianism. Neo-Confucian thinkers formulated a system of metaphysics (which was not a part of older Confucianism), drawing on Taoist and Buddhist ideas; they were particularly influenced by ZEN BUDDHISM. Nevertheless they did not accept the Taoist search for immortality or the otherworldly ideals of Buddhism, remaining faithful to the practical and socially concerned Confucian spirit. The neo-Confucian eclecticism was unified and established as an orthodoxy by Chu Hsi (1130–1200), and his system dominated subsequent Chinese intellectual life. His metaphysics is based on the concepts of *li*, or principle of form in manifold things, and the totality of these, called the "supreme ultimate" (*t'ai chi*). During the Ming dynasty, the idealist school of Wang Yang-ming (1472–1529) put a stress on meditation and intuitive knowledge. The overthrow (1911–12) of the monarchy, with which Confucianism had been closely identified, led to the disintegration of Confucian institutions and a decline in Confucian traditions, a process accelerated after the Communist revolution (1949). See Richard Wilhelm, *Confucius and Confucianism* (tr. 1931, repr. 1970); J. C. Shryock, *The Origin and Development of the State Cult of Confucius* (1932, repr. 1966); Lin Yutang, *The Wisdom of Confucius* (1943); H. G. Creel, *Confucius: The Man and the Myth* (1949, repr. 1972); Liu Wu-chi, *Confucius: His Life and Time* (1955, repr. 1972); Shigeki Kaizuka, *Confucius* (tr. 1956); F. C. Hsu, *Confucianism* (1966); D. H. Smith, *Confucius* (1973).

Confucius (kənfyo͞o'shəs), Chinese *K'ung Fu-tse*, c.551–479? B.C., Chinese sage. Positive evidence concerning the life of Confucius is scanty. Modern scholars base their accounts largely on the *Analects*, a collection of sayings and short dialogues apparently collected by Confucius's disciples, and discard most of the later legends. Confucius was born in the feudal state of Lu, in modern Shantung prov. Distressed by the constant warfare between the Chinese states and by the venality and tyranny of the rulers, he urged a system of morality and statecraft that would preserve peace and afford the people the stable, just government they required. He gathered about him a number of disciples, some of whom occupied high positions, although Confucius himself, possibly because of his extremely outspoken manner toward his superiors, was at most granted an insignificant sinecure. From about his 55th to his 65th year he toured several neighboring states, but he was still unable to induce any ruler to grant him high office so that he might introduce his reforms. Later tradition depicts Confucius as a man who, seeking to restore an older social order, made special study of ancient books. It was said that he was a minister of state and the author (or at least the editor) of the *Wu Ching* [five classics] (see CHINESE LITERATURE). His supposed doctrines are embodied in Confucianism. For bibliography, see CONFUCIANISM.

congenital heart disease, any defect in the HEART present at birth. There is evidence that some congenital heart defects are inherited. However, most commonly, the defect is caused by environmental conditions in the uterus like the presence of certain drugs or viruses that reach the fetus via the maternal circulation, e.g., infection of the mother with rubella (German measles) virus during the first trimester of pregnancy causes a high rate of congenital heart lesions and other malformations. Among the most common congenital heart disorders are malformations in the valves and the persistence of structures that are normally closed off at birth, i.e., the ductus arteriosis (fetal blood vessel that shunts blood from the pulmonary vein to the aorta, bypassing the heart) and the foramen ovale (opening between the left and right atria of the fetal heart). If the malformation is severe, it will produce various symptoms of insufficient heart function, such as cyanosis (bluish tinge to the skin), dyspnea (difficulty in breathing), fatigue, and abnormal heartbeat; valvular deformities predispose the patient to bacterial infection of the endocardium (see ENDOCARDITIS). Less severe malformations may not produce noticeable symptoms until later in life, and some may not require any medical attention. Many congenital heart defects that are debilitating can now be corrected surgically. Other congenital anomalies, such as mongolism, are present in about 20% of cases of congenital heart disease.

congestive heart failure, inability of the heart to expel sufficient blood to keep pace with the metabolic demands of the body. In the healthy individual the heart can tolerate large increases of workload for a considerable length of time. Cardiac failure results from conditions, e.g., coronary, hypertensive, and rheumatic heart disease, that interfere with the nutrition and oxygenation of the heart muscle itself. Congestive heart failure develops in 50% to 60% of patients with such disorders, and it can be either acute or chronic. If the heart has time to compensate the heart muscle may become hypertrophic (enlarged). Eventually the great demand for oxygen by the heart muscle cells cannot be met, and cell death results. Either the left or right ventricle alone may fail first, although combined failure is most common and almost always eventually occurs. Left ventricular failure is marked by shortness of breath (dyspnea), often accompanied by cough; pulmonary congestion and edema are evident. Failure of the right ventricle produces systemic edema, reflecting hepatic and visceral engorgement. Treatment of cardiac failure usually includes long-term restrictions on diet and activity. Digitalis is often prescribed to increase the speed and force of cardiac contractions. Diuretics are used to remove excess sodium and water from the body.

conglomerate, corporation whose asset growth, often very rapid, comes largely through the acquisition of, or merger with, other firms whose products are largely unrelated to each other or to that of the parent company. Merger to gain monopoly ("horizontal integration") was notable at the turn of the century; somewhat later, acquisition of suppliers or buyers ("vertical integration") became fairly common. Conglomerates did not emerge until the 1960s, when they quickly became popular among investors. Their stock prices often rose spectacularly; sometimes, however, they fell just as spectacularly. Economic advantages attributed to the conglomerate include protection against overspecialization, availability of management expertise, and reduced cost due to greater productive capacity.

conglomerate, in geology, sedimentary ROCK composed largely of pebbles or other rounded particles whose diameter is larger than 2 mm (.08 in.). Essentially a cemented gravel, conglomerates are formed along beaches, as glacial drift, and in river deposits. Conglomerates formed of angular shaped pebbles are called breccias.

Congo (kŏng'gō) or **Zaïre** (zäēr'), great river of equatorial Africa, c.2,720 mi (4,380 km) long, formed by the waters of the Lualaba River and its tributary, the Luvua River, and flowing generally N and W through Zaïre to the Atlantic Ocean. The second longest river of Africa and one of the longest in the world, the Congo River drains c.1,425,000 sq mi (3,690,750 sq km) including all of Zaïre and parts of the Congo Republic, Cameroon, Central African Republic, Burundi, Tanzania, Zambia, and Angola. The Lualaba River, considered to be the upper Congo River, rises in SE Zaïre, flows north over rapids and falls to Bukama, and thence across a vast plain and through a series of marshy lakes (Kabwe, Kabele, Upemba) to receive the Luvua River at Ankoro. The Luvua River has its most remote source in the Chambeshi River, which rises in N Zambia and flows southwest into swamps around Lake Bangweulu; it emerges from the swamps as the Luapula River, continues N along the Zaïre-Zambia border into Lake Mweru, exits from there as the Luvua River, and continues NW to the Lualaba River. A third major headstream is the Lukuga River, which drains from Lake Tanganyika and joins the Lualaba River near Kabalo. From Kabalo, the Lualaba River flows N to Kisangani in a varied course marked by a deep and narrow gorge (the Gates of Hell) below Kongolo, a navigable stretch from Kasongo to Kibombo, a section of rapids and falls from Kibombo to Kindu, a shallow but navigable section from Kindu to Ubundu, and a section of seven cataracts—known as Stanley Falls—between Ubundu and Kisangani that marks the end of the Lualaba and the beginning of the Congo River proper. Below Kisangani, the Congo flows west and southwest, in a great curve unbroken by falls or rapids for about 1,090 mi (1,750 km) to Kinshasa. For most of its middle section the Congo is from 4 to 10 mi (6.4–16.1 km) wide, with many islands and sandbars. Because its many large tributaries (including the Lomami, Kasai, Lulonga, Ubangi, Aruwimi, Itimbiri and Mongala rivers) drain areas with alternating rainy seasons on either side of the equator, the Congo has a fairly constant flow throughout the year. Between Bolobo and Kwamouth the Congo narrows in width to between 1 mi and 1½ mi (1.6–2.4 km) but, c.350 mi (560 km) from its mouth, widens to form lakelike Stanley Pool (Malebo Pool), on which Kinshasa and Brazzaville are located. From the western end of Stanley Pool, the Congo descends 876 ft (267 m) in a series of 32 rapids, known as Livingstone Falls, to the port of Matadi. Below Matadi (83 mi/134 km inland) the Congo is navigable by ocean-going vessels and, despite such hazards as the whirlpools of the Devil's Cauldron, shifting sandbars, and sharp bends in the river, forms one of the largest natural harbors in Africa. The river is tidal to Boma, c.60 mi (100 km) upstream. The Congo River enters the Atlantic Ocean between Banana Point, Zaïre, and Sharks Point, Angola, and dredging is required to keep a navigable channel open. The river is continued offshore by a c.500 mi (800 km) long submarine canyon that is c.4,000 ft (1,220 m) deep. With railroads to bypass major falls (Matadi-Kinshasa; Kisangani-Ubundu; Kindu-Kongolo), the Congo River and its tributaries form a system of navigable waterways c.9,000 mi (14,480 km) long, along which move much of central Africa's copper, palm oil kernels, cotton, sugar, and coffee. The chief ocean port is Matadi, with its associated oil port, Ango Ango; the chief river ports are Kinshasa and Kisangani. River steamers operate throughout the year between Kinshasa and Kisangani. The Congo River is Africa's largest potential source of hydroelectric power; the most valuable site is along Livingstone Falls, where the first phase of the Inga Power Project was begun in 1972. The mouth of the Congo River was visited (1482) by Diogo Cão, the Portuguese navigator. It became known as the Zaïre River (a corruption of the local name Mzadi meaning "great water") and was later referred to as the Congo River (for the Kongo kingdom located near its mouth); it was renamed Zaïre River by the government of Zaïre in 1971. The Congo's lower course was traced upstream as far as Isangila by a British force under Capt. J. K. Tuckey in 1816, and its upper headwaters by the missionary David Livingstone, who followed the Lualaba River to Nyangwe in 1871. The journalist Henry Stanley traveled from Nyangwe to Isangila and on to Boma during his great transcontinental journey (1874–77), thus proving the headwaters to be tributaries of the Congo River and not sources of the Nile as hypothesized by Livingstone. See W. H. Bentley, *Pioneering on the Congo* (2 vol. 1900, repr. 1970), Sir Harry Hamilton Johnston, *The River Congo, From its Mouth to Bólóbó* (3d ed. 1884, repr. 1970).

Congo, Belgian: see ZAÏRE.

Congo, kingdom of the: see KONGO, KINGDOM OF THE.

Congo, People's Republic of the, republic (1973 est. pop. 1,130,000), 132,046 sq mi (342,000 sq km), W central Africa. BRAZZAVILLE is the capital. The Congo is bordered on the W by Gabon; on the N by Cameroon and the Central African Republic; on the E and SE by Zaïre; and on the SW by Cabinda, a Portuguese exclave, and by the Atlantic Ocean. The

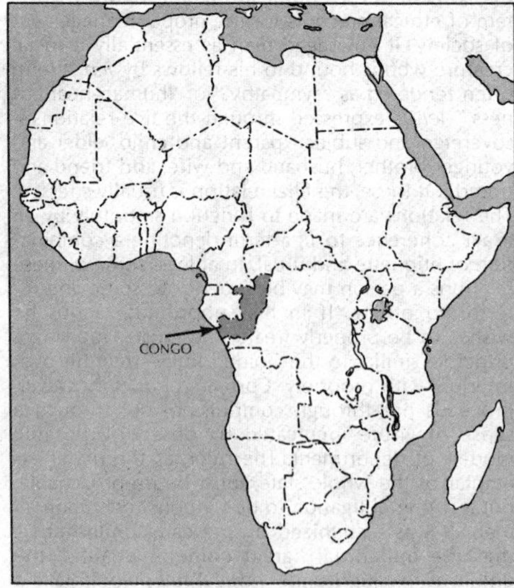

terrain is covered mainly by dense tropical rain forest, with stretches of wooded savanna. Tributaries of the Congo and Ubangi rivers, which separate the Congo from Zaïre, flow through the country. The climate is hot and rainfall is heavy. The Congo serves as the transport and commercial hub of central Africa, with economically important road, river, and rail systems connecting inland areas with the Atlantic. The country's internal road network is inadequate, however, and has hampered economic development. Agriculture and forestry are the chief economic activities in the Congo. The major subsistence crops are cassava and yams. Sugarcane and tobacco, raised primarily on plantations, are the leading export crops, followed by coffee, cocoa, palm products, and groundnuts. Timber is also a major export. Diseases restrict cattle raising, and fishing is not well developed. Industry is limited mainly to the processing of agricultural and forest products, and is concentrated in Brazzaville and Pointe-Noire (both port cities) and in the Niari valley. Mining is increasingly important, with potash and oil the principal exports; petroleum resources are being rapidly depleted, however. The Bakongo, the major ethnic group in the Congo, are mostly farmers or traders; they are Bantu-speaking, as are the other principal tribes, the Bateke, the Mbochi, and the Sanga. Pygmies live in the north, and Vili people dwell along the coast. A majority of the Congolese people practice traditional animist religions; the rest are primarily Christian. French is the country's official language. Pygmies, migrating from the Zaïre region, were probably the first inhabitants of what is now the Congo. They were followed by the Bakongo, the Bateke, and the Sanga, who arrived in the 15th cent. After the coastal areas were explored by the Portuguese navigator Diego Cão in 1482, commerce developed between the Europeans and the coastal African states, which raided the interior for slaves to trade. Portuguese traders predominated throughout the 17th cent., although French trade centers were established (mainly at Loanga), and English and Dutch merchants sought commercial opportunities. Europeans penetrated inland in the late 19th cent., with Pierre Savorgnan de Brazza leading major expeditions in 1875 and 1883. In 1880 he negotiated an agreement with the Bateke to establish a French protectorate over the north bank of the Congo River. Between 1889 and 1910, the Congo (called the French Congo and later the Middle Congo) was administered primarily by French companies that held concessions to exploit the area's rubber and ivory resources. Scandals over the decimation of the African population through forced labor and porterage broke out in 1905 and 1906. France restricted the role of the concessionaires in 1907, and in 1910 the Congo became a colony in French Equatorial Africa. Renewed forced labor and other abuses sparked an African revolt in 1928. The Free French forces made the Congo a bastion of their struggle against the Germans and the Vichy regime during World War II. In 1946, the region was granted a territorial assembly and representation in the French parliament. In the French constitutional referendum of 1958, the Congo opted for autonomy within the French Community. Full independence was achieved on Aug. 15, 1960, with Fulbert Youlou as the first president. Forced to resign after a revolt in 1963, he was succeeded by Alphonse Massamba-Débat. In 1964 the new president founded a Marxist-Leninist party and proclaimed a noncapitalist path of economic development. A Five-Year Plan was initiated, and the state sector of the economy in agriculture and industry was expanded. Tensions between the government and the army grew, and in 1968, Marien Ngouabi, an army commander, seized power. He followed his predecessor's socialist policies, but created his own Marxist-Leninist type of party, the Congolese Workers party. An attempted coup in Feb., 1972, provided Ngouabi with a reason to purge opponents. In June, 1973, a new constitution was approved by referendum; it provided for popularly elected national, regional, and local assemblies. Despite radical rhetoric and close links with Communist countries, the Congo has retained close ties with France; it remains in the French franc zone and is an associate member of the European Common Market. The Congo is a member of a customs union with Gabon, the Central African Republic, Chad, and Cameroon, all of which share a central bank and a common currency. See André Gide, *Travels in the Congo* (tr. 1927); Samir Amin and Catherine Coquery-Vidrovitch, *Histoire économique du Congo, 1880–1968* (1969); G. C. McDonald, *Area Handbook for People's Republic of the Congo* (1971).

Congo, Republic of the: see ZAÏRE.

Congo eel: see SALAMANDER.

Congo Republic: see CONGO, PEOPLE'S REPUBLIC OF THE.

Congregationalism, type of Protestant church organization in which each congregation, or local church, has free control of its own affairs. The underlying principle is that each local congregation has as its head Jesus Christ alone and that the relations of the various congregations are those of fellow members in one common family of God. Congregationalism eliminated bishops and presbyteries. The movement to which the name came to be applied began in the 16th and 17th cent. in England, in a revolt against the formalized worship, unregenerate membership, and state control of the Established Church. Those holding such views found themselves unable to remain within the Church of England. Robert BROWNE published in 1582 the first theoretical exposition of Congregational principles and expressed the position of some of those SEPARATISTS. Churches established on such lines were started very early in the 17th cent. in Gainsborough and Scrooby, but government opposition drove them into exile in Holland. Not until the Protectorate did the Congregationalists make much progress. About that time the name INDEPENDENTS was first introduced, a term long common in Great Britain (it is still used in Wales) but seldom used in America. In 1658, when the Savoy Synod met in London, over 100 churches were represented. With the Restoration came repression for the Independents, partly relieved by the Toleration Act of 1689. A marked tendency among English Congregationalists in the 19th cent. was toward combination in larger fellowship. Churches of this denomination formed a union in Scotland in 1812, in Ireland in 1829; in 1831 the Congregational Union of England and Wales was established. The Congregational Union and the Evangelical Union were united in 1896. Membership in Congregational churches in Great Britain has declined in the 20th cent. They have been active in ecumenical activities, and in 1972 most British Congregationalists and Presbyterians merged to form the United Reform Church. Congregationalism was carried to America in 1620 by the Pilgrims, who were members of John Robinson's congregation in Holland, originally of Scrooby, England. In America, Congregationalism reached its greatest public influence and largest membership. In New England numerous communities were established based on Congregational-type religious principles. In 1648 in the CAMBRIDGE PLATFORM a summary of principles of church government and discipline was drawn up. Congregationalists took a leading part in the GREAT AWAKENING that, in New England, was started in 1734 by the preaching of Jonathan EDWARDS. As the country expanded, Congregational churches were established in the newly opened frontier regions. In 1810 the American Board of Commissioners for Foreign Missions began its work; in 1826 the American Home Missionary Society was formed. These were followed, in 1846, by the American Missionary Association, primarily devoted to missionary work among blacks and Indians. The early part of the 19th cent. brought the Unitarian secession, when over 100 churches left the main Congregational body. Congregational churches began to meet in local and then in statewide conferences, out of which developed (1871) the National Council of the Congregational Churches of the United States. But each local church remained free to make its own declaration of faith and free to decide its own form of worship; in the conduct of the local church each member was granted an equal voice. The principal assistants of the pastor are the deacons. In education Congregationalists were always prominent, but the institutions of their founding—Harvard (1636), Yale (1701), Williams, Amherst, Oberlin, and many others—have been free from sectarianism. The trend toward broader fellowship and larger cooperation was notably indicated in the merging in 1931 of the National Council of the Congregational Churches of the United States and the General Convention of the Christian Church (see DISCIPLES OF CHRIST) to form the General Council of the Congregational and Christian Churches of the United States. The National Association of Congregational Christian Churches was formed in 1955 and had about 85,000 members in the early 1970s. A move to unite the Congregational Christian Churches with the Evangelical and Reformed Church was approved by the councils of the two denominations in 1957, forming the UNITED CHURCH OF CHRIST. See Williston Walker, *The Creeds and Platforms of Congregationalism* (1907, repr. 1960); G. G. Atkins and F. L. Fagley, *History of American Congregationalism* (1942); D. T. Jenkins, *Congregationalism* (1954); A. A. Rouner, Jr., *The Congregational Way of Life* (1960); Horton Davies, *The English Free Churches* (2d ed. 1963); M. L. Starkey, *The Congregational Way* (1966).

Congress, Library of: see LIBRARY OF CONGRESS.

Congress of Industrial Organizations: see AMERICAN FEDERATION OF LABOR AND CONGRESS OF INDUSTRIAL ORGANIZATIONS.

Congress of Racial Equality (CORE), civil rights organization founded (1942) in Chicago by James Farmer. Dedicated to the use of nonviolent direct action, CORE seeks to promote better race relations and to end all discriminatory policies in the United States. Its earliest activities were directed toward the desegregation of restaurants and other public accommodations in Chicago. It later expanded its program of nonviolent sit-ins to public accommodations in the South. CORE first gained national recognition through its sponsorship (1961) of the Freedom Rides, a series of confrontatory bus rides throughout the South by interracial groups of CORE members and supporters. The program, ultimately successful, was designed to end segregation on interstate bus routes. CORE was one of the sponsors of the massive 1963 civil rights march on Washington. In 1966, James Farmer resigned as national director of CORE and the organization's program became somewhat more separatist, concentrating on black voter registration in the South and on community problems, including slum housing and police mistreatment, in the North. See study by August Meier and Elliot Rudwick (1973).

Congress of the United States, the legislative branch of the Federal government, instituted (1789) by Article 1 of the CONSTITUTION OF THE UNITED STATES, which prescribes its membership and defines its powers. Congress is composed of two houses—the Senate and the House of Representatives.

The Senate. The Senators, two from each state, have six-year terms and were chosen by the state legislatures until 1913, when the Seventeenth Amendment, providing for their direct popular election, went into effect. Actually, many states, especially in the West, had already in effect adopted this reform through the use of the direct PRIMARY. The terms of one third of the Senators expire every two years. A Senator must be at least 30 years old, a U.S. citizen of not less than nine years standing, and a resident of the state in which he is elected. The Senate is presided over by the Vice President of the United States, who has no part in its deliberations and may vote only in case of a tie; in his absence his duties are assumed by a president pro tempore, elected by the Senate.

The House of Representatives. Members of the House of Representatives are apportioned among the states according to their populations in the Federal census. Every state is entitled to at least one Representative. States that are entitled only to one (Alaska, Delaware, Nevada, North Dakota, Vermont, and Wyoming, by the 1970 census) have a Representative at large, i.e., one elected by the whole state. The legislatures of those states entitled to more than one Representative have been required since 1842 to divide their states into congressional districts. When a reapportionment is made and until a new districting is carried out, a state whose quota is changed may also elect Representatives at large. Representatives are chosen for two-year terms, and the entire body comes up for reelection every two years. A Representative must be 25 or older, a U.S. citizen of at least seven years standing, and a resident of the state in which he is elected. Although without a vote, one resident commissioner from Puerto Rico and one delegate from the District of Columbia sit in the House. The presiding officer of the House, the speaker, is elected by the members of the House and may designate any member of the House to act in his absence. In 1910 a revolt against the powerful speaker, Joseph Gurney CANNON, resulted in the transfer of much of the power and influence of that office to the House committees.

Joint Activities. In both houses the work of preparing and considering legislation is done by standing committees, and in addition there are special committees in each house as well as joint committees with bicameral membership. The two houses have an equal voice in legislation, but revenue bills must originate in the House of Representatives. Bills, after having been passed by each house separately, must be signed by the President within 10 days of their submission, or they become law automatically, unless Congress is not in session. If vetoed by the President, a bill may become law only by its repassage by a two-thirds majority in each house. The Constitution requires a regular annual meeting of Congress, which, since the passage of the Twentieth Amendment in 1933, begins on Jan. 3 each year. The President may call an extra session of Congress or of either house. Only the House of Representatives may impeach the President or other Federal officers and the Senate alone has the authority to try impeachments, but each house is the judge of the qualifications of its own members. The Senate must ratify all treaties by a two-thirds vote and confirm important presidential appointments to office, including cabinet members, judges of Federal courts, and high-ranking officers of the armed forces. Because of this and because it is the smaller body and its members enjoy longer terms of office and virtually unlimited debate, the Senate is regarded as the more powerful of the two houses. Congress, as a whole, reached the zenith of its power during RECONSTRUCTION. The proceedings of each house are recorded in the *Congressional Record.* Throughout its history many critics have charged that Congress operates under antiquated machinery and processes that are inadequate. Procedural reforms proposed include the adoption of a rule of relevancy in Senate debate, electric voting in the House, joint hearings on similar bills, liberalizing the methods by which a bill may be discharged from committee for consideration, and abolishing seniority as the basis for committee chairmanships. See E. S. Griffith, *Congress: Its Contemporary Role* (4th ed. 1967); S. C. Patterson, comp., *American Legislative Behavior* (1968); Roger Davidson, *The Role of the Congressman* (1969); N. W. Polsby, *Congress and the Presidency* (2d ed. 1971); Louis Fisher, *President and Congress* (1972); Aage Clausen, *How Congressmen Decide* (1973); John Kingdon, *Congressmen's Voting Decisions* (1973).

Congreve, William, 1670–1729, English dramatist, b. near Leeds, educated at Trinity College, Dublin, and studied law in the Middle Temple. After publishing a novel of intrigue, *Incognita* (1692), and translations of Juvenal and Persius (1693), he turned to writing for the stage. His first comedy, *The Old Bachelor* (1693), produced when he was only 23, was extremely successful and was followed by *The Double Dealer* (1693) and *Love for Love* (1695). In 1697 his only tragedy, *The Mourning Bride*, was produced. About this time Congreve replied to the attack on his plays made by Jeremy COLLIER, who in a famous essay attacked the English stage for its immorality and profaneness. Congreve reached his peak with his last play, *The Way of the World* (1700), which has come to be regarded as one of the great comedies in the English language. The leading female roles in Congreve's plays were written for Anne BRACEGIRDLE, who was probably his mistress. He never married. After 1700, Congreve did little literary work, perhaps because of the cool reception accorded his last play or because of his failing health—he suffered from gout. He subsequently held various minor political positions and enjoyed the friendships of Swift, Steele, Pope, Voltaire, and Sarah, duchess of Marlborough. The plays of Congreve are considered the greatest achievement of Restoration comedy. They are comedies of manners, depicting an artificial and narrow world peopled by characters of nobility and fashion, to whom manners, especially gallantry, are more important than morals. Congreve's view of mankind is amused and cynical. His characters are constantly engaged in complicated intrigues, usually centering around money, which involve mistaken identities, the signing or not signing of legal documents, weddings in masquerade, etc. His plays are particularly famous for their brilliance of language; for verbal mastery and wit they have perhaps been equalled only by the comedies of Oscar Wilde. See his works (ed. by F. W. Bateson, 1930); biographies by D. C. Taylor (1931), J. C. Hodges (1941), M. E. Novak (1971), and E. W. Fosse (1888, repr. 1973); David Mann, ed., *A Concordance to the Plays of William Congreve* (1973).

Coniah (kōnī'ə): see JEHOIACHIN.

conical surface: see CONE.

conic section or **conic** (kŏn'ĭk), curve formed by the intersection of a plane and a right circular CONE (conical surface). The ordinary conic sections are the CIRCLE, the ELLIPSE, the PARABOLA, and the HYPER-

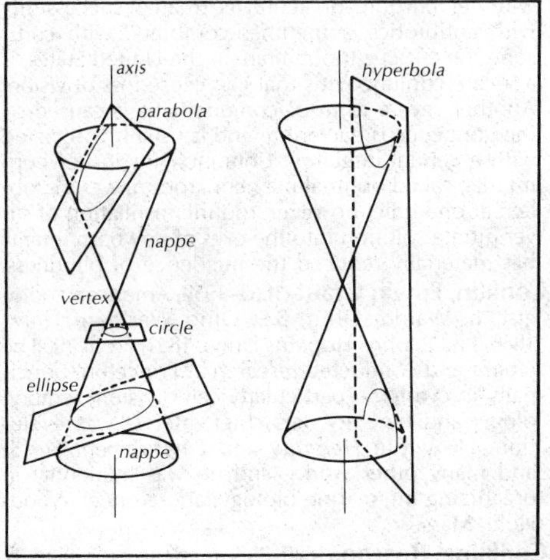

Conic sections

BOLA. When the plane passes through the vertex of the cone, the result is a point, a straight line, or a pair of intersecting straight lines; these are called degenerate conic sections. There are many examples of the conic sections, both in nature and in technology. The orbits of planets and satellites are elliptical, and parallel reflectors (e.g., in telescopes) are parabolic in shape.

conifer (kŏn'ĭfûr) [Lat.,=cone-bearing], tree or shrub of the order Coniferales, e.g., the PINE, MONKEY-PUZZLE TREE, CYPRESS, and SEQUOIA. Most conifers bear cones and most are evergreens, though a few, such as the LARCH, are deciduous. Some have globular fruits, e.g., the YEW. Conifers are widely distributed over the world but are mostly found in the highlands of temperate regions. The conifers, the gingkos, and the cycads comprise the three most important classes of gymnosperms, i.e., plants without true flowers. Conifers are classified in the division PINOPHYTA, class Pinopsida.

Coningh, Philips de: see KONINCK, PHILIPS DE.

Coningham, Sir Arthur (kŭn'ĭng-əm), 1895-1948, British air marshal, b. Australia. During World War I, he served first in the New Zealand army and then joined (1916) the Royal Flying Corps, a forerunner of the Royal Air Force. He remained in the air force and became air vice marshal after the outbreak of World War II. He commanded the tactical air support forces in North Africa (1941-43), during the invasion of Sicily and S Italy (1943-44), and during the Normandy landings (1944-45). He became air marshal in 1946 and retired in 1947.

Coninxloo or **Koninksloo, Gillis van** (both: gĭl'ĭs văn kō'nĭngkslō), 1544-1607, Flemish landscape painter. His *Judgment of Midas* (Dresden), *Latona* (Hermitage, Leningrad), and above all the *Landscape with Figures* (Liechtenstein Gall., Vienna) are fine examples of his art. Coninxloo's paintings, characterized by fantasy, warm tones, and refined realism, were important for the transmission of a Venetian type of landscape to the North.

coniometer: see KONIMETER.

Conjeeveram, India: see KANCHIPURAM.

conjugation: see INFLECTION.

conjugation, in genetics: see RECOMBINATION.

conjunction, in astronomy, alignment of two celestial bodies as seen from the earth. Conjunction of the moon and the planets is often determined by reference to the sun. When a body is in conjunction with the sun, it rises with the sun, and thus cannot be seen; its ELONGATION is 0°. The moon is in conjunction with the sun when it is new; if the conjunction is perfect, an ECLIPSE of the sun will occur. Mercury and Venus, the two inferior planets, have two positions of conjunction. When either lies directly between the earth and the sun, it is in inferior conjunction; when either lies on the far side of the sun from the earth, it is in superior conjunction.

conjunction, in English, PART OF SPEECH serving to connect words or constructions, e.g., *and, but,* and *or.* Most languages have connective particles similar to English conjunctions.

conjunctivitis (kənjəngtəvī'təs), catarrhal inflammation of the membrane that covers the eyeball and lines the eyelid, usually acute, caused by a bacillus or virus. Commonly called pinkeye, mild conjunctivitis usually causes redness, discharge, and itching of the membrane. If left untreated it usually clears up in 8 to 10 days. Conjunctivitis may also be associated with upper respiratory infection or with childhood diseases such as measles. The disorder, whether chronic or acute, is treated successfully with antibiotics, sometimes combined with cortisone. TRACHOMA, though rare in the United States, is a severe conjunctivitis that can cause loss of vision. Another severe form of conjunctivitis is caused by the gonococcus bacterium and is usually associated with a genital infection. Conjunctivitis in newborn infants, called ophthalmia neonatorum, was a problem at one time; however, routine instillation of silver nitrate solution into the eyes of newborn infants has materially reduced the incidence of blindness.

Conklin, Edwin Grant, 1863-1952, American zoologist, b. Waldo, Ohio, B.S. Ohio Wesleyan Univ., 1886, Ph.D. Johns Hopkins Univ., 1891. From 1908 he taught and conducted research at Princeton, principally in cytology (particularly cell division), embryology, and heredity. His chief interest was evolution. He wrote *Heredity and Environment* (1915) and many other works, and he was influential in organizing the marine biology laboratory at Woods Hole, Mass.

Conkling, Roscoe, 1829-88, American politician, b. Albany, N.Y. On his admission to the bar in 1850, he was immediately appointed district attorney of Albany. The son of Alfred Conkling, Congressman and Federal judge, he became a U.S. Representative (1859-63, 1865-67) and Senator (1867-81) and undisputed leader of the Republican party in New York. Conkling's machine was built upon Federal patronage, which was entirely his during the Grant administrations. But in 1878, President Hayes, an advocate of civil service reform, removed two Conkling lieutenants, Chester A. ARTHUR and Alonzo B. CORNELL, from the management of the New York customhouse in defiance of Conkling, who claimed that a Senator had the right to control Federal patronage in his state. Conkling was reelected, and another lieutenant, Thomas C. PLATT, became his colleague in the Senate, while Cornell won the governorship. Conkling headed the third-term movement for Grant in 1880 and placed him in nomination at the Republican national convention. Although his Old Guard or "Stalwart" faction was unsuccessful, he prevented the nomination of James G. BLAINE, his bitter personal enemy. The deadlocked convention chose James A. GARFIELD as a compromise candidate, and Chester A. Arthur was named for Vice President as a sop to the "Stalwarts." Conkling gave Garfield only lukewarm support but claimed afterwards that the President-elect had promised him the patronage in return. Garfield denied this and further antagonized Conkling by making Blaine Secretary of State. When an anti-Conkling man was appointed collector of the port of New York, Conkling resigned from the Senate in protest. Platt soon followed his leader, earning for himself the nickname "Me Too." The two expected vindication through reelection by the state legislature, but both were defeated. Conkling then retired to the private practice of law, in which he was highly successful. See biography by his nephew, A. R. Conkling (1889); study by David M. Jordan (1971).

Connacht: see CONNAUGHT, Ireland.

Connally, John Bowden (kŏn'əlē), 1917-, U.S. public official, b. Floresville, Texas. A lawyer, he became associated with Lyndon B. Johnson, managed the latter's successful senatorial campaign in 1948, and later served as Johnson's administrative assistant. He was named Secretary of the Navy in 1961, but he resigned (1962) to campaign for the governorship of Texas and was elected. When President John F. Kennedy was assassinated in Dallas, Connally was accompanying him and was wounded. He was twice reelected governor, serving until 1968. A conservative Democrat, he was chosen (1971) by President Richard M. Nixon as Secretary of the Treasury and was instrumental in bringing about the institution of a 90-day wage-price freeze in Aug., 1971. In May, 1972, Connally resigned from the cabinet to aid the President's reelection. The following year Connally joined the Republican party and served as a special adviser to the President after the resignation of key aides as a result of the WATERGATE AFFAIR. He left the White House shortly after that, however, and in July, 1974, was himself indicted for accepting a bribe from milk producers before the 1972 election. See studies by Charles Ashman (1974) and A. F. Crawford and Jack Keever (1974).

Connaught, Arthur William Patrick Albert, duke of (kŏn'ôt), 1850-1942, English prince; son of Queen Victoria and Prince Albert, brother of Edward VII. Trained for a military career, he served in Egypt (1882) and India (1886-90) and as commander in chief in the Mediterranean (1907-9). He was (1911-16) governor general of Canada. His son, **Prince Arthur of Connaught,** 1883-1938, was (1920-23) governor general of South Africa.

Connaught or **Connacht** (both: kŏn'ôt, kŏn'əkht), province (1971 pop. 389,763), 6,611 sq mi (17,122 km), W Republic of Ireland, comprising the counties of MAYO, SLIGO, LEITRIM, ROSCOMMON, and GALWAY. It was one of the ancient kingdoms of Ireland, whose rulers, the O'Connors, were supplanted by the Anglo-Norman De Burghs in the 13th cent.

Conneaut (kŏn'ēŏt''), city (1970 pop. 14,552), Ashtabula co., extreme NE Ohio, on Lake Erie, near the Pa. line; settled 1799, inc. 1834. It is a port of entry—an important ore-receiving port and a limestone and coal loading center—and a vacation resort. Conneaut has a railroad museum, with antiques of the steam era.

Connecticut (kənĕt'ĭkət), state (1970 pop. 3,031,709) 5,009 sq mi (12,973 sq km), NE United States, southernmost of the New England states, one of the Thirteen Colonies. HARTFORD is the capital and the largest city, with BRIDGEPORT and NEW HAVEN next in size. Rectangular in outline, the state extends c.90 mi (145 km) from east to west and c.55 mi (90 km) from north to south; it is bounded on the N by Massachusetts, on the E by Rhode Island, on the S by Long Island Sound, and on the W by New York. Connecticut is divided into two roughly equal sections, usually called the eastern highland and the western highland. These sections are separated by the Connecticut valley lowland. The Connecticut River, which flows through only the northern half of the valley, veers off to the southeast at Middletown in central Connecticut. Along the Long Island Sound there is a low, rolling coastal plain. The western highland, with the Taconic Mts. and the Litchfield Hills, is more rugged than the eastern highland. A few isolated peaks in the west are more than 2,000 ft (610 m) high. The Thames and the rivers emptying into it drain the eastern highland, and the Housatonic, with its chief tributary, the Naugatuck, drains the western highland. Though famed for its rural loveliness, Connecticut is heavily industrialized and derives most of its economic wealth from its industries. Textiles, typewriters, silverware, sewing machines, clocks, and watches are among Connecticut's many industrial products. The state's principal industries produce transportation equipment, nonelectrical and electrical machinery, fabricated metals, primary metals, and chemicals. Firearms and ammunition, first produced in Connecticut at the time of the American Revolution, are still manufactured in the state. Groton is an important center for submarine building. Agriculture accounts for only a small share of income in the state; dairy products, eggs, and tobacco are the leading farm items. High-grade broadleaf tobacco, used in making cigar wrappers, has been a speciality of Connecticut agriculture since the 1830s. Largely shade-grown in the fertile Connecticut valley, it remains a valuable crop although production has been adversely affected by new methods of cigar production. Many varieties of fish, as well as oysters, lobsters, and other shellfish, are caught in Long Island Sound, but the fishing industry is small. Few minerals are produced; stone, sand, and gravel account for most income derived from mining. Insurance is an important industry in Connecticut, and Hartford is one of the world's largest insurance centers, with the home offices of many insurance companies located in the city. In 1614, Adriaen Block, a Dutchman, sailed through Long Island Sound and discovered the Connecticut River. The Dutch built a small fort in 1633 on the site of present-day Hartford, but they abandoned it in 1654 as English settlers moved into the area in increasing numbers. Edward Winslow of Plymouth Colony was apparently the first Englishman to visit (1632) Connecticut, and in 1633 members of the Plymouth Colony established a trading post on the site of WINDSOR. This small Pilgrim enterprise was soon absorbed by Puritan settlers from the Massachusetts Bay Company. These settlers had been attracted to the area by the excellent reports brought back by one of their members, John Oldham, in 1633. Oldham returned to the Connecticut area in 1634 and established still another trading post, which became WETHERSFIELD. The following year Puritans flocked in great numbers to the Connecticut valley. In 1636, Thomas Hooker and his congregation left Newtown (present-day Cambridge, Mass.) and settled near the Dutch trading post that had been established on the site of present-day Hartford. Although some of the migrants, like Hooker, had chafed under the restrictive laws of the Massachusetts Bay colony, it was the desire for more and better land rather than religious differences that prompted the Puritan migration. Their departure was without bitterness, and the Connecticut venture had the official blessing of the Massachusetts Bay colony. Land was purchased

from the natives, who were on the whole friendly. The PEQUOT INDIANS resisted white settlement, but they were defeated by the English under John Mason (c.1600-1672) and John Underhill (c.1597-1672) in the short Pequot War of 1637. Not until King Philip's War in 1675-76 was there further serious trouble with the Indians. In 1638-39 representatives of the three Connecticut River towns—Hartford, Windsor, and Wethersfield—met at Hartford and formed the colony of Connecticut. They also adopted the FUNDAMENTAL ORDERS, which established a government for the colony. Under these statutes any householder who had taken a Trinitarian oath of fidelity to the commonwealth was admitted to the town meeting, which acted on local affairs and voted for deputies to the colony's General Court. However, "admitted inhabitants" could not themselves be deputies unless the General Court or a magistrate considered them worthy to be "freemen," and probably less than a third achieved that distinction. Those freemen elected to the General Court, which met at Hartford, chose the magistrates, one of whom was selected to be governor (John Haynes was the first). The governor had to be a member of some approved congregation, and his authority was dwarfed by the great power of the General Court, which exercised both legislative and judicial functions. A second colony, Saybrook, had been established at the mouth of the Connecticut River in 1835 by a group of Englishmen. The colony's founders (who included Viscount Saye and Sile and Baron Brooke, for whom the colony was named) subsequently became embroiled in politics at home during the ENGLISH CIVIL WAR (1642-52) and sold the Saybrook settlement to Connecticut colony in 1644. Connecticut's population expanded gradually, and by 1662 the colony included over a dozen towns, including Saybrook, NEW LONDON, FAIRFIELD, and NORWALK as well as East Hampton and Southampton on Long Island. Another Puritan settlement, New Haven, was established in 1638. It was not connected with Connecticut colony. Theophilus Eaton and John Davenport, a pastor, were the leaders of the settlement, which was initially founded as a trade center. New Haven was an extreme Puritan theocracy. Its freemen, unlike those of Connecticut colony, had to be church members, and a select group among them formed the General Court, which drew up the settlement's laws. New Haven was unique among the Puritan colonies in denying its people trial by jury. The towns of Milford, Guilford, Stamford, Southold (on Long Island), and Branford were dominated by New Haven and in 1643 formed with the mother town a loose confederation called New Haven colony. In 1643, New Haven and Connecticut colonies joined with Massachusetts Bay colony and Plymouth colony to form the NEW ENGLAND CONFEDERATION, a loose union for mutual defense against attack by Indians or by the Dutch who at that time still maintained a fort in the Hartford area. In 1660 the restoration of Charles II to the English throne caused alarm in the New Haven and Connecticut settlements because neither colony had obtained a charter for its establishment and thus had no legal standing in England as colonies. Connecticut sent its governor, John Winthrop (1606-76), to London to secure a royal charter for the colony. In 1662, Winthrop obtained the charter, by which Connecticut not only won its legal right to exist as a corporate colony but also acquired New Haven. Most of the towns within the New Haven colony quickly affirmed the union, but New Haven itself bitterly resisted absorption until, faced with the even more unpleasant prospect of becoming part of the proprietary grant to the west given (1664) to the duke of York, it formally submitted on Jan. 5, 1665. The duke of York surrendered his claim to New Haven in return for the Long Island towns formerly incorporated into the New Haven colony. Connecticut's size varied little after that time, though there were boundary squabbles with Massachusetts, Rhode Island, and New York for many years thereafter. Connecticut's new charter confirmed the Fundamental Orders and subsequent laws so that government went on much as before, except for a brief interruption from 1687 to 1689 when the English tried to assert control over the colony and dispatched an administrator, Sir Edmund Andros, to Connecticut. Andros sought to recover the charter from the colonists, who hid it in an oak tree that came to be known as the Charter Oak. In 1708, Congregationalism was established as the official religion of the colony by the Saybrook Platform, and a modified Presbyterian type of church government was adopted. In 1708 the General Court also passed a limited toleration act, and later the Anglicans (1727), the Baptists, and the Quakers (1729) were exempted from contributing to the support of the Established Church. However, other dissenting groups that lacked the political influence in England possessed by the Anglican, Baptist, and Quaker sects were treated harshly. Connecticut thus occupied a position midway between the more autocratic ecclesiastical system of Massachusetts and the liberal one of Rhode Island. Nevertheless religious harmony generally prevailed until the 1730s, when the GREAT AWAKENING split the Congregational Church into radical and conservative factions. Connecticut's agrarian economy was gradually being transformed, as a small but vigorous merchant class arose. Most of Connecticut's trade, which was based on the exportation of agricultural products and the importation of manufactured goods, was controlled by New York and Boston merchants. Connecticut's ports on Long Island Sound, however, maintained commercial relations with the West Indies, and the colony came to resent England's increasingly burdensome commercial and colonial policy. The years from 1750 to 1776 saw much bitter disagreement between radicals and conservatives in the colony, and in 1766 the radicals managed to oust the governor, Thomas Fitch, and four of his assistants. The conservatives never recovered their power in colonial days. Most of the conservative Congregationalists ultimately supported the patriot cause, but the Anglicans made up the bulk of the state's die-hard Tories. In 1776, the patriot governor, Jonathan Trumbull, was reelected almost unanimously (Connecticut and Rhode Island were the only colonies privileged to elect their chief executives), and he was the only governor of any colony to be retained in office after the outbreak of the American Revolution. There was little fighting in Connecticut during the Revolution—skirmishes at Stonington (1775), Danbury (1777), New Haven (1779), and New London (1781)—but the state was the principal supply area for the Continental Army. After the war the state relinquished (1786) to the United States its claims to western land, except the WESTERN RESERVE, an area in present-day Ohio. The claim was retained until part of the land was given to Connecticut citizens in 1792 and the remainder sold in 1795. In 1799, Connecticut's long dispute with Pennsylvania over the WYOMING VALLEY was finally settled. Connecticut was one of the first states to approve the Federal Constitution (see FEDERAL CONSTITUTIONAL CONVENTION). The Embargo Act of 1807, passed during the administration of Thomas Jefferson, was vehemently denounced throughout New England; the ports on Long Island Sound and on the Connecticut River had developed a lively carrying trade with which the embargo interfered. The War of 1812 was also so unpopular that New England Federalists, meeting at the HARTFORD CONVENTION in late 1814, considered secession. Soon thereafter, in early 1815, the war was ended and the Federalist party subsequently declined as a result of its participation in the Hartford Convention, which some considered to have been a treasonable meeting. In 1818 the Jeffersonians came into power in the state, and a new constitution, replacing the old charter of 1662, was adopted. It disestablished the Congregational Church and greatly extended the franchise, although universal manhood suffrage was not proclaimed until 1845. Meanwhile, after Connecticut's shipping industry had been ruined by the embargo and the war, the state turned to manufacturing. Artisans and craftsmen had become increasingly numerous in late colonial days, and from native iron ore Connecticut forges had produced guns for the patriot soldiers. Modern mass production had its beginning in the state when Eli Whitney, probably the best known of Connecticut's inventors, established (1798) at New Haven a firearms factory that began making guns with standardized, interchangeable parts. Earlier, in 1793, he had invented and manufactured the cotton gin at New Haven. The manufacture of notions (buttons, pins, needles, metal goods, and clocks) gave rise to the enterprising "Yankee peddler," who, with horse and team, covered the nation hawking his wares. Connecticut's insurance industry also developed during this period, and in 1810 the Hartford Fire Insurance Company was established. Connecticut, which had placed limitations on slavery in 1784 and abolished it in 1848, supported the Union during the Civil War with nearly 60,000 troops and an able Secretary of the Navy, Gideon Welles. During and after the war, industry expanded greatly. Immigration provided a cheap labor supply as English, Scottish, and many Irish immigrants, who had arrived in large numbers even before the war, were followed by French Canadians and, in the late 19th and early 20th cent., by Italians, Poles, and others. During World Wars I and II Connecticut prospered, providing munitions and other supplies for the war effort. However, between the two wars the Great Depression left many unemployed in the state. Connecticut's industries have continued to grow and develop since the end of World War II, and in 1954 the world's first nuclear-powered submarine was launched at Groton. Prior to 1965, Connecticut's constitution provided for a bicameral legislature with a house of representatives elected on the basis of geographical distribution. No town or city had less than one or more than two representatives, thus the larger cities were underrepresented. The 1965 constitution remedied this situation by providing for the election of both houses of the general assembly, as the legislature is called, on the basis of election districts apportioned according to population. Connecticut's state senate has 36 members and its house of representatives has 177; members of both houses are elected for two-year terms. The state executive branch is headed by a governor elected for a term of four years; Ella T. GRASSO, a Democrat, was elected governor in 1974. Connecticut is represented in the U.S. Congress by six Representatives and two Senators and has eight electoral votes. In recent decades political power in the state has generally shifted back and forth between Democrats and Republicans. The Connecticut shore is a popular summer resort area, and the protected waters of Long Island Sound lure boating enthusiasts to the state. Another prominent summer attraction is the Stratford Shakespeare Festival, which has been operating since 1965. Institutions of higher learning in Connecticut include Yale Univ., at New Haven; Trinity College, at Hartford; Wesleyan Univ., at Middletown; the Univ. of Connecticut, at Storrs; and the UNITED STATES COAST GUARD ACADEMY and Connecticut College, at New London. See Federal Writers' Project, *Connecticut: A Guide to Its Roads, Lore, and People* (1938); Stewart H. Holbrook, *The Yankee Exodus* (1950); Albert E. Van Dusen, *Connecticut* (1961); R. J. Purcell, *Connecticut in Transition: 1775-1818* (1963); J. Niven, *Connecticut for the Union* (1965); R. L. Bushman, *From Puritan to Yankee* (1967); William Bixby, *The Connecticut Guide* (1974).

Connecticut, river, longest river in New England, 407 mi (655 km) long, rising in Connecticut Lakes, N N.H., and flowing S along the Vt.-N.H. line, then across Mass. and Conn. to enter Long Island Sound at Old Saybrook, Conn.; drains c.11,000 sq mi (28,500 sq km). There are many rapids and falls on the river; Holyoke Falls, the highest, drops 57 ft (17 m). The river is navigable to Hartford, Conn. The Connecticut Valley is one of the best agricultural regions in New England. World-famous cigar binder and wrapper tobacco are grown in the lower part of the valley; truck farming and dairying are also important. Waterpower resources led to the rise of industrial cities in the 1800s, and the valley became a major manufacturing region; large centers include Holyoke and Springfield, Mass., and Windsor, Conn. There are several hydroelectric facilities on the river. Floods and hurricanes caused great damage in the valley in 1938 and 1953; in the latter year, the Connecticut River Flood Control Compact was established and has since sponsored the building of flood-control devices on the river.

Connecticut, University of, mainly at Storrs; coeducational; land grant and state supported; chartered and opened 1881 as Storrs Agricultural School. It became a college in 1893 and a university in 1939. The schools of medicine, law, insurance, and social work are in Hartford. There are two-year branch campuses at Hartford, Waterbury, Stamford, Groton, and Torrington. The Storrs Agricultural Experiment Station is noteworthy.

Connecticut College, at New London; coeducational; chartered 1911 (as Thames College, name changed the same year to Connecticut College for Women), opened 1915. In 1959 men were admitted for graduate work and the school became known by its present name. In 1969 the undergraduate college became coeducational. A 313-acre (127-hectare) arboretum and a plant hormone laboratory are noteworthy.

Connecticut Reserve: see WESTERN RESERVE.

Connecticut Wits or **Hartford Wits,** an informal association of Yale students and rectors formed in the late 18th cent. At first they were devoted to the modernization of the Yale curriculum and declaring the independence of American letters. In their political views they were conservative Federalists, and they attacked their more liberal opponents in jointly written satirical verses—*The Anarchiad* (in the New Haven *Gazette,* 1786–87), *The Political Greenhouse* (in the *Connecticut Courant,* 1799), and *The Echo* (in the *American Mercury,* 1791–1805). Members of the group at various times were Joel Barlow, Timothy Dwight, David Humphreys, John Trumbull, Lemuel Hopkins, Richard Alsop, and Theodore Dwight. See studies by V. L. Parrington (1926, repr. 1969) and Leon Howard (1943).

connective tissue, supportive tissue widely distributed in the body, characterized by large amounts of intercellular substance and relatively few cells. The intercellular material, or matrix, is produced by the cells and gives the tissue its particular character. Connective tissue is diversified in function and may be divided into four categories according to the type of matrix. In connective tissue proper (which forms the framework for most organs) the matrix is soft. In CARTILAGE it is firm but flexible. The intercellular substance of BONE, which is high in mineral salts, is rigid. BLOOD and lymph have a fluid matrix. Three kinds of fibers generally form the supportive material in connective tissue proper. White, or collagenous, fibers vary in size and are composed of fine, parallel fibrils; reticular fibers are small, branching fibers that take on a meshlike pattern; yellow, or elastic, fibers are highly flexible and are capable of branching and anastomosing (or opening) directly into one another. Loose, or areolar, connective tissue is composed of all three of the above fibers; it supports most of the organs in the body and is widely distributed under the skin. The type of connective tissue that forms TENDONS, LIGAMENTS, and FASCIA is composed mainly of collagenous fibers. It is known as compact tissue. Reticular connective tissue forms the bone marrow and the framework for lymphoid tissue. Adipose, or fat, tissue serves as a cushion for various organs and as a fat reservoir. The colored area of the eye, or iris, is composed of pigmented connective tissue.

Connellsville, city (1970 pop. 11,643), Fayette co., SW Pa., on the Youghiogheny River in the Allegheny Mts.; settled c.1770, inc. as a borough 1806, as a city 1911. A major producer of coal and coke, the city also has railroad shops; its manufactures include glass, iron, and steel products. The attack upon Henry C. Frick by the anarchist Alexander Berkman occurred (1892) in Connellsville during the HOMESTEAD STRIKE. A branch of Pennsylvania State Univ. is just south of the city.

Connelly, Marc (Marcus Cook Connelly), 1890–, American dramatist, b. McKeesport, Pa. He is best known for his folk play *The Green Pastures* (1930), a fantasy of Biblical history presented in terms of the life of the Southern Negro; it was based on Roark Bradford's book *Ol' Man Adam an' His Chillun* (1928). Connelly also collaborated with George S. Kaufman on the plays *Dulcy* (1921), *To the Ladies* (1922), *Merton of the Movies* (1922), and *Beggar on Horseback* (1924). At the age of 74 Connelly published his first novel, *A Souvenir from Quam* (1965), which satirizes spy stories. See his memoirs (1968).

Connemara (kŏnəmär′ə), wild, mountainous region, Co. Galway, W Republic of Ireland, lying between the Atlantic Ocean and Loughs Corrib and Mask. There are many mountains, lakes, streams, and glens. It is a well-known vacation area. Most of the villages are found along the coast; Clifden is the chief town. The peat bogs of S Connemara are major fuel sources. Particularly famous is the hardy breed of ponies peculiar to the region.

Connersville, city (1970 pop. 17,604), seat of Fayette co., E central Ind., on the Whitewater River, in a farm area; founded 1813 by John Connor (who had been kidnapped from his white parents and raised by Indians), inc. as a city 1870. Nearby are a bird sanctuary of the state Audubon Society, a state park, and several historic covered bridges.

Connolly, Cyril, 1903–74, English critic and editor. He began his career as a journalist. With Stephen SPENDER he founded *Horizon* (1940–49), a small literary magazine that reflected Connolly's own iconoclastic and mordant attitudes toward contemporary society. Among his works are *Rock Pool* (1935), a satirical novel that ranks with the best of Huxley and Waugh; *Enemies of Promise* (1938), an autobiography of ideas; *The Unquiet Grave* (1944), a potpourri of critical commentaries and aphorisms; *The Condemned Playground* (1945) and *Previous Convictions* (1964), both collections of literary essays; and *The Modern Movement: 100 Key Books From England, France, and America, 1880–1950* (1965).

Connolly, James, 1870–1916, Irish nationalist and socialist. An advocate of revolutionary SYNDICALISM, he went (1903) to the United States, where he helped to organize the Industrial Workers of the World (IWW). Returning to Ireland, he became an organizer of the Belfast dock workers. He helped James LARKIN to organize the Irish Transport and General Workers Union and, during the great lockout of the Dublin transport workers in 1913, organized a citizen army. Convinced that the triumph of Irish nationalism was a prerequisite for the success of Irish socialism, he joined the Easter Rebellion of 1916. He was wounded, court-martialed, and executed. See two selections from his writings: *Socialism and Anatomy* (with intro. and notes by Desmond Ryan, 1948) and *The Workers' Republic* (ed. by Desmond Ryan, 1951); biography by C. D. Greaves (1972).

Connolly, Maureen, 1934–1969, American tennis player, b. San Diego, Calif. She became, at 16, the youngest player to win the U.S. national singles. She successfully defended the U.S. title (1952, 1953), won the Wimbledon championship (1952, 1953, 1954), and completed a grand slam of the world's four major titles in 1953 with the French and Australian championships. Little Mo, as she was known, was one of America's greatest woman tennis players. She broke her leg in a horseback accident and was forced to retire (1955).

Connor, Ralph: see GORDON, CHARLES WILLIAM.

Conon, 3d cent. B.C., Greek astronomer and mathematician of Samos. He traveled in the western part of the Greek world making astronomical observations, then settled at Alexandria. He was a student of solar eclipses and discovered the constellation Coma Berenices. His mathematical studies included an investigation of conic intersections.

Cononiah (kŏn″ōnī′ə), Levite of Hezekiah's reign. 2 Chron. 31.12,13.

Conowingo Dam (kŏn″əwĭng′gō), 4,648 ft (1,417 m) long, 102 ft (31 m) high, on the Susquehanna River, NE Md.; completed 1928. It is one of the largest nonfederal hydroelectric power plants in the United States, with a 474,480-kw capacity. Conowingo Lake, formed by the dam, extends 14 mi (23 km) upstream.

conquistador (kŏnkwĭs′tədôr, Span. kōng-kē″-stäthôr′), military leader in the Spanish conquest of the New World in the 16th cent. Francisco PIZARRO, the conqueror of Peru, and Hernán CORTÉS, the conqueror of Mexico, were the greatest of the conquistadors. The name is frequently used to mean any daring, ruthless adventurer. See Paul Horgan, *Conquistadors in North American History* (1963); F. A. Kirkpatrick, *The Spanish Conquistadores* (2d ed. 1967).

Conrad I, d. 918, German king (911–18). As duke of Franconia he distinguished himself by military exploits and in 911 was elected successor to LOUIS THE CHILD by the Franconian, Saxon, Bavarian, and Swabian lords. Although supported by the bishops, he was unable to maintain strong central government. His reign was plagued by feuds and rebellions by the great feudal lords. Lorraine broke away and acknowledged CHARLES III of France; the Swabians continued warfare till Conrad's death; the duke of Bavaria, expelled, returned successfully. Conrad's most able foe was Henry the Fowler, duke of Saxony. Despite the enmity, Conrad's own deathbed advice was that Henry succeed him. Henry was elected (919) as HENRY I. Conrad's failure to avert the continued Hungarian invasions and his alienation of the nobility increased provincial autonomy and almost dissolved the kingdom.

Conrad II, c.990–1039, Holy Roman emperor (1027–39) and German king (1024–39), first of the Salian dynasty of the Holy Roman Empire. With the end of the Saxon line on the death of HENRY II, the succession passed to the matrilineal descendants of OTTO I, and Conrad, a Franconian noble, was elected (1024) as German king. Although the hereditary principle in Germany was strong enough to secure his election, it did not ensure Conrad support throughout the empire. His accession was contested by his stepson, Ernest of Swabia, and by the Lotharingians (see LOTHARINGIA) and the Italians. After the collapse of the revolts of Ernest and the Lotharingians, Conrad brought N Italy into submission (1026–27) and was crowned emperor at Rome. He suppressed two more revolts (1027, 1030) by Ernest and won (1031) Lusatia from Poland. In 1034 he annexed the kingdom of Burgundy (see ARLES, KINGDOM OF) under the terms of a treaty (1006) between Rudolf III, last independent king of Arles, and Holy Roman Emperor Henry II. In 1036, Conrad returned to Italy, where war was raging between the greater and the lesser nobles. He deposed Archbishop Aribert of Milan, a powerful ally of the great nobles, and made the fiefs of the lesser nobles hereditary by issuing (1037) the Constitution of Pavia. In Germany also Conrad favored the small nobility, thus reversing the policy of Otto I and Henry II, who had depended for support on the Church. He promoted the servile classes to administrative office, thus building a new hereditary class of *ministeriales* to replace the ecclesiastics in the civil service. Conrad's administration was economical, and he encouraged commerce by granting market and mint privileges. At his death, his son HENRY III ascended the throne at the height of its wealth and power.

Conrad III, c.1093–1152, German king (1138–52), son of Frederick, duke of Swabia, and Agnes, daughter of Holy Roman Emperor Henry IV; first of the HOHENSTAUFEN dynasty. He joined his brother Frederick, who had been defeated in the imperial election of 1125 by Lothair of Saxony (Holy Roman Emperor LOTHAIR II), in rebelling against Lothair. Set up as antiking to Lothair in 1127, he went to Italy (1128) and, despite excommunication by Pope Honorius II, was crowned king at Milan. He subsequently failed to make any progress as king and submitted to Lothair in 1135. After Lothair's death he was elected king by the nobles and ecclesiastics who were afraid to increase the power of Lothair's son-in-law, HENRY THE PROUD of Bavaria. Conrad deprived Henry of his duchies, giving Saxony to ALBERT THE BEAR and Bavaria to Leopold of Austria. A civil war broke out and was continued after Henry's death by his brother Guelph (or Welf) and the Saxons, who supported Henry's young son HENRY THE LION. From this strife emerged the opposing parties of the Guelphs and the Ghibellines, representing the Hohenstaufen. A short-lived truce was made in 1142. At Christmas, 1146, Conrad was induced by St. Bernard of Clairvaux to join in the Second Crusade (see CRUSADES) with Louis VII of France. He left in 1147, took part in the unsuccessful siege of Damascus, and returned in 1149. Conrad was never crowned by the pope, and therefore was not confirmed as Holy Roman emperor. His ambitions for the imperial crown and against Roger II of Sicily were thwarted by Guelph, who was subsidized by Roger, and by Henry the Lion, who claimed the duchy of Bavaria. Conrad was succeeded by his nephew, Holy Roman Emperor Frederick I.

Conrad IV, 1228–54, German king (1237–54), king of Sicily and of Jerusalem (1250–54), son of Holy Roman Emperor FREDERICK II. He was elected (1237) king of the Romans at his father's instigation after Frederick had deposed Conrad's older brother Henry in Germany. Archbishop Siegfried II of Mainz was regent for Conrad until 1241, when he was replaced by Henry Raspe, count of Thuringia. The struggle for supremacy between Frederick and Pope INNOCENT IV resulted in the election (1246) of Raspe as antiking at the behest of the pope. Germany was plunged into disorder; after Raspe's death (1247) WILLIAM, COUNT OF HOLLAND became antiking. When Frederick II died (1250) Conrad carried on the struggle with the pope, who was determined to bring about the downfall of the house of HOHENSTAUFEN and to rule in Italy. In 1251, Conrad went to Italy in order to subdue the pope's supporters. He had some successes, but Innocent IV refused to give up his scheme for papal control in Italy. He offered the crown of Sicily to RICHARD, EARL OF CORNWALL, and to Charles of Anjou (later CHARLES I, king of Naples and Sicily), who both refused, and to King Henry III of England for his second son, Edmund. He accepted. In 1254 Conrad was excommunicated. Just as war was about to erupt he died of fever. It was left for his son, CONRADIN, to witness the final downfall of the house of Hohenstaufen.

Conrad, d. 1192, Latin king of Jerusalem (1192), marquis of Montferrat, a leading figure in the Third Crusade (see CRUSADES). He saved Tyre from the Saracens and became (1187) its lord. In 1189 he joined GUY OF LUSIGNAN at the siege of AKKO, but a year later he sought to displace Guy as king of Jerusalem. To establish a claim to the crown he married Isabella, daughter of Amalric I. A compromise (1191) between the two men was short lived. In 1192, Conrad was acknowledged as king, but a few days later he was assassinated, probably by Muslim fanatics. The royal title passed to the two later husbands of his widow—Henry, count of Champagne (1192–97), and AMALRIC II.

Conrad, Joseph, 1857–1924, English novelist, b. Poland, originally named Jósef Teodor Konrad Walecz Korzeniowski. He is considered one of the greatest novelists and prose stylists in English literature. In 1874, Conrad went to sea and later joined (1878) an

English merchant ship, becoming (1884) a master mariner as well as a British citizen. Retiring from the merchant fleet in 1894, he began his career as a novelist, and all of his novels are written in English, an acquired language. His notable early works include *The Nigger of the Narcissus* (1897), *Lord Jim* (1900), and the novellas *Youth* (1902), *Heart of Darkness* (1902), and *Typhoon* (1903). The novels *Nostromo* (1904), *The Secret Agent* (1907), *Under Western Eyes* (1911), and *Chance* (1913) are regarded by many as Conrad's greatest works. Of his later works, *Victory* (1915) is the best known. He also collaborated on two novels with Ford Madox FORD, *The Inheritors* (1901) and *Romance* (1903). Marked by a distinctive, opulent prose style, Conrad's novels combine realism and romanticism. Their backgrounds shift from the sea to politics to society. Conrad was a genius in the creation of atmosphere and character; the impact of various situations was augmented by his expert use of symbolism. He portrayed acutely the conflict between primitive cultures and modern civilization and was particularly adept at delineating people suffering from isolation, loneliness, and moral deterioration. See his complete works (26 vol., 1924-26); biographies by Jocelyn Baines (1960) and Ford Madox Ford (1965); studies by Richard Curle (1968), J. A. Palmer (1968), and Bruce Johnson (1971); bibliography by T. G. Ehrsam (1969).

Conrad, Michael Georg (mĭkh'äĕl gä'ôrk kôn'rät), 1846-1927, German critic and novelist. With Karl Bleibtreu, he founded (1885) the journal *Gesellschaft* as a rallying point for German writers of the naturalistic school. Conrad espoused the cause of Zola with great enthusiasm. His works include a volume of criticism, *Madame Lutetia* (1883), and a naturalistic novel of Munich life, *Was die Isar rauscht* [What the Isar murmurs] (1887).

Conradin (kŏn'rədĭn), 1252-68, duke of Swabia, titular king of Jerusalem and Sicily, the last legitimate HOHENSTAUFEN, son of Holy Roman Emperor CONRAD IV. While Conradin was still a child in Germany, his uncle MANFRED made himself (1258) king of Sicily. When Manfred died the kingdom was seized (1266) by CHARLES I (Charles of Anjou). Young Conradin went to Italy in an attempt to recover his kingdom. Several cities rallied to his support, but he was defeated (1268) by Charles at Tagliacozzo. He was captured and executed at Naples.

Conrad of Marburg, d. 1233, German churchman. He was confessor (1225-31) of St. ELIZABETH of Hungary and administrator of her husband's benefices in his absence. His zeal against heresy earned him appointment (1231) as first papal inquisitor in Germany. His harshness made him much disliked, and he was murdered.

Conrad the Red, d. 955, duke of Lotharingia (Lorraine) (944-53). A Franconian adherent of the German king Otto I (later Holy Roman emperor), he was made duke of Lotharingia and married Otto's daughter Liutgard. He accompanied (951) his father-in-law to Italy against BERENGAR II. Remaining in Italy as Otto's representative, he concluded a peace treaty with the defeated Berengar. Otto, however, considered the treaty too lenient and drastically revised it. The discontented Conrad then led a revolt against Otto with Otto's son, Ludolf, and Frederick, archbishop of Mainz. Expelled (953) from his duchy, Conrad allied (954) with the Hungarians, who were invading the empire. When the invasion united the people behind Otto, Conrad submitted. He fought with valor under Otto at the Lechfeld but was killed in the battle.

Conrad von Hötzendorf, Franz, Graf (fränts gräf kôn'rät fən hö'tsəndôrf), 1852-1925, Austro-Hungarian field marshal. He served (1906-11, 1912-17) as chief of staff and led the Austro-Hungarian armies in World War I. After his dismissal in 1917 because of his opposition to the peace plans of Emperor Charles I, he held (1917-18) an Austro-Hungarian command on the Italian front. See his memoirs (5 vol., 1921-25).

Conroe (kŏn'rō), city (1970 pop. 11,969), seat of Montgomery co., SE Texas; inc. 1885. Long a pine-lumbering town, it prospered after oil was discovered there in 1932. The Conroe oil field is now one of the major producing fields in the state. Other natural resources in the area are timber, clays, and gas. Farm products include beef and dairy cattle and feed for livestock and poultry.

Consalvi, Ercole (ārkô'lā kōnsäl'vē), 1757-1824, Italian cardinal and papal diplomat. In his first term (1800-1806) as secretary of state for Pope Pius VII he negotiated the CONCORDAT OF 1801 with Napoleon Bonaparte (later Emperor Napoleon I). Despite Consalvi's astute diplomacy, Napoleon annexed the papal states in 1809. Consalvi was compelled to go to Paris, where his refusal to attend Napoleon's second marriage (1809) resulted in exile at Reims. Reinstated as secretary of state after Napoleon's second abdication (1814), Consalvi vainly struggled against reactionary elements to reform the administration of the Papal States.

consanguinity (kŏn"săng-gwĭn'ĭtē), state of being related by blood or descended from a common ancestor. This article focuses on legal usage of the term as it relates to the laws of marriage, descent, and inheritance; for its broader anthropological implications, see INCEST. Consanguinity is to be distinguished from affinity, which is the relation of a person, through marriage, to the consanguineous relatives of his spouse. Marriage between persons in lineal consanguinity (persons in the direct line of descent, such as father and daughter) and between brothers and sisters is void under common law, church law, and under statute. Whether or not marriages between persons of collateral consanguinity (those having a common ancestor but not related in direct line of descent) are prohibited as incestuous depends on statutory provision and judicial interpretation. In more than half the states of the United States, marriage between first cousins is prohibited by law, and the Roman Catholic Church and the Orthodox Eastern Church have strict rules on consanguinity as an impediment to marriage. Statutes in the United States discard affinal relationship as an impediment to marriage. Whether incestuous marriages are void or voidable in the United States depends on local statutes and their interpretation. In the law of descent and inheritance, the concept of consanguinity is most important in the area of intestate succession. Most states award the wife of a man who dies intestate a certain share of the estate, even though there exists neither lineal nor collateral consanguinity between the spouses. See G. B. L. Arner, *Consanguineous Marriages in the American Population* (1908, repr. 1969); B. D. Inglis, *Family Law* (2d ed., 2 vol., 1968-70).

Conscience, Hendrik (hĕn'drĭk kôNsēäNs'), 1812-83, Flemish novelist, a founder of modern Flemish literature. His many historical novels were romantic but powerful, in the tradition of Scott; outstanding is *De Leuw van Vlaenderen* (1831, tr. *The Lion of Flanders,* 1885). In later years Conscience devoted his talents to moralistic social novels and idealized stories of Flemish village life. Among these are *The Poor Nobleman* (1851, tr. 1856) and *Ricke ticke tack* (1851, tr. 1856). His work enjoyed a great vogue in the United States in the late 1800s.

conscience, sense of moral awareness or of right and wrong. The concept has been variously explained by moralists and philosophers. In the history of ETHICS, the conscience has been looked upon as the will of a divine power expressing itself in man's judgments, an innate sense of right and wrong resulting from man's unity with the universe, an inherited intuitive sense evolved in the long history of the human race, and a set of values derived from the experience of the individual. Psychologists also differ in their analyses of the nature of conscience. It is variously believed to be an expression of values differing from other expressions of value only in the subject matter involved, a feeling of guilt for known or unknown actions done or not done, the manifestation of a special set of values introjected from the example and instruction of parents and teachers, and the value structure that essentially defines the personality of the individual. As a practical matter, the consciences of different people within a society or from different societies may vary widely.

conscientious objector, person who, on the grounds of conscience, resists the authority of the state to compel military service. Such resistance, emerging in time of war, may be based on membership in a pacifistic religious sect, such as the Society of Friends (Quakers), the Dukhobors, or Jehovah's Witnesses, or on personal religious or humanitarian convictions. Political opposition to the particular aim of conscription, such as that maintained by the Copperheads during the Civil War, by radical groups during World War I and, to a more limited extent, during World War II, and by large numbers during the Vietnam War, is usually considered in a separate category. The problem of conscientious objectors, although present in different forms since the beginning of the Christian era, became acute in World Wars I and II because of the urgent demands for manpower of the warring governments. The United States and Great Britain allowed members of recognized pacifistic religious groups to substitute for combat service: (1) noncombatant military service, (2) nonmilitary activity related to the war effort, or (3) activity considered socially valuable. Pacifists without recognized claim to exemption were liable to harsher treatment, and about 5,000 conscientious objectors were imprisoned in the United States between 1940 and 1945. The postwar Selective Service Act, passed in 1948 and amended in 1951, required that conscientious objection be based on religious belief and training that included belief in a Supreme Being. In 1970 the Supreme Court removed the religious requirement and allowed objection based on a deeply held and coherent ethical system with no reference to a Supreme Being. In 1971 the Supreme Court refused to allow objection to a particular war, a decision affecting thousands of objectors to the Vietnam War. Some 50,000-100,000 men are estimated to have left the United States to avoid being drafted to serve in that war. See G. C. Field, *Pacifism and Conscientious Objection* (1945); M. Q. Sibley and P. E. Jacob, *Conscription of Conscience* (1952, repr. 1965); Lillian Schlissel, ed., *Conscience in America* (1968); G. C. Zahn, *War, Conscience, and Dissent* (1967); Michael Ferber and Staughton Lynd, *The Resistance* (1971).

consciousness, in psychology, a term commonly used to indicate a state of being aware of the environment. In Freudian psychology, conscious behavior largely includes cognitive processes of the ego, such as thinking, perception, and planning, as well as some aspects of the superego, such as conscience. Other activities, such as those stemming from primitive and instinctive needs, are under UNCONSCIOUS control. In this view, all behavior has an unconscious aspect. Some psychologists deny the distinction between conscious and unconscious behavior; others use the term consciousness to indicate all the activities of an individual that constitute the personality. See also DEFENSE MECHANISM; PSYCHOANALYSIS.

conscription, compulsory enrollment of personnel for service in the armed forces. Although obligatory service in the armed forces existed in ancient Greece and Rome and during the Middle Ages in Europe, conscription in the modern sense of the term dates from the French Revolution, when the idea was introduced that every able-bodied man in a nation was a potential soldier and that he could by means of conscription be made to serve in the armed forces; the militia of Greece and Rome, though compulsory, were organized at local levels for brief periods of time. Conscription enabled Napoleon to mold his tremendous fighting forces, and compulsory peacetime recruitment was introduced (1811-12) by Prussia. Mass armies, raised at little cost by conscription, led to the mass warfare of the Napoleonic Wars. The institution of conscription, which was increasingly justified by statesmen on grounds of national defense and economic stimulation, spread to other European nations in the 19th cent. In England compulsory military service was employed in the Anglo-Saxon fyrd as early as the 9th cent.; this arrangement, however, was always at a local level and when the British Empire began expanding after the 16th cent., professional soldiers were relied upon. At the outbreak of World War I, Great Britain adopted conscription and used it again in World War II; it was abolished in 1962. Though little used in the United States prior to the Civil War, conscription was used by both sides in that war. Conscription, or the draft, was not used again until World War I (see SELECTIVE SERVICE). Peacetime conscription was introduced in 1940, and draftees fought in World War II, the Korean War, and the Vietnam War. During the Vietnam War conscription became a highly controversial issue; it was abolished by Congress in 1973. All major military powers of the 20th cent. have used conscription as a means of raising their armed forces. Conscription differs from IMPRESSMENT, which is the forcible mustering of recruits. Largely strongarm in technique, impressment preceded conscription historically and though for a time it was a means of enforcing conscription it has generally passed from use.

consecration: see ORDERS, HOLY.

consent, in law, active acquiescence or silent compliance by a person legally capable of consenting (see AGE OF CONSENT). It may be evidenced by words or acts or by silence when silence implies concurrence. Actual or implied consent is necessarily an element in every CONTRACT and every agreement. In criminal charges, the consent of the party injured (if not obtained by FRAUD or DURESS) is a defense for the accused, unless a third party or the state is injured.

conservation, in art: see ART CONSERVATION AND RESTORATION.

conservation laws, in physics, basic laws that together determine which processes can or cannot occur in nature; each law maintains that the total value of the quantity governed by that law, e.g., mass or energy, remains unchanged during physical processes. Conservation laws have the broadest possible application of all laws in physics and are thus considered by many scientists to be the most fundamental laws in nature. Most conservation laws are exact, or absolute, i.e., they apply to all possible processes; a few conservation laws are only partial, holding for some types of processes but not for others. By the beginning of the 20th cent. physics had established conservation laws governing the following quantities: energy, mass (or matter), linear MOMENTUM, angular momentum, and electric charge. When the theory of RELATIVITY showed (1905) that mass was a form of energy, the two laws governing these quantities were combined into a single law conserving the total of mass and energy. With the rapid development of the physics of ELEMENTARY PARTICLES during the 1950s, new conservation laws were discovered that have meaning only on this subatomic level. There are three absolute laws relating to the creation or annihilation of particles belonging to three different groups: the BARYON class of particles and the electron and muon families of particles in the LEPTON class. According to these conservation laws, particles of a given group cannot be created or destroyed except in pairs, where one of the pair is an ordinary particle and the other is an ANTIPARTICLE belonging to the same group. Two partial conservation laws that have been discovered for particles, governing the quantities known as strangeness and isotopic spin. Strangeness is conserved during the so-called strong interactions and the electromagnetic interactions, but not during the weak interactions associated with particle decay; isotopic spin is conserved only during the strong interactions. One very important discovery has been the link between conservation laws and basic symmetries in nature. For example, empty space possesses the symmetries that it is the same at every location (homogeneity) and in every direction (isotropy); these symmetries in turn lead to the invariance principles that the laws of physics should be the same regardless of changes of position or of orientation in space. The first invariance principle implies the law of conservation of linear momentum, while the second implies conservation of angular momentum. The symmetry known as the homogeneity of time leads to the invariance principle that the laws of physics remain the same at all times, which in turn implies the law of conservation of energy. The symmetries and invariance principles underlying the other conservation laws are more complex, and some are not yet understood. Three special conservation laws have been defined with respect to symmetries and invariance principles associated with inversion or reversal of space, time, and charge. Space inversion yields a mirror-image world where the "handedness" of particles and processes is reversed; the conserved quantity corresponding to this symmetry is called space parity, or simply PARITY, *P*. Similarly, the symmetries leading to invariance with respect to time reversal and charge conjugation (changing particles into their antiparticles) result in conservation of time parity, *T*, and charge parity, *C*. Although these three conservation laws do not hold individually for all possible processes, the combination of all three is thought to be an absolute conservation law, known as the *CPT* theorem, according to which if a given process occurs, then a corresponding process must also be possible in which particles are replaced by their antiparticles, the handedness of each particle is reversed, and the process proceeds in the opposite direction in time. It is expected that further research will discover more conservation laws and reveal their basis in fundamental symmetries of the physical world. Thus, conservation laws provide one of the keys to our understanding of the universe and its material basis. See K. W. Ford, *The World of Elementary Particles* (1963); J. J. Sakurai, *Invariance Principles and Elementary Particles* (1964); R. P. Feynman, *The Character of Physical Law* (1967); Martin Gardner, *The Ambidextrous Universe: Left, Right, and the Fall of Parity* (rev. ed. 1969); W. L. Scott, *History of Science Library: Conflict Between Atomism and Conservation Theory 1644–1860* (1970).

conservation of natural resources, the wise use of the earth's resources by man. The term *conservation* came into use in the late 19th cent. and referred to the management, mainly for economic reasons, of such valuable natural resources as timber, fish, game, topsoil, pastureland, and minerals, and also to the preservation of forests (see FORESTRY), wildlife (see WILDLIFE REFUGE), parkland, WILDERNESS, and WATERSHED areas. In recent years the science of ECOLOGY has clarified the workings of the BIOSPHERE; i.e., the complex interrelationships among man, other animals, plants, and the physical environment. At the same time burgeoning population and industry and the ensuing POLLUTION have demonstrated how delicately balanced ecological relationships are and how easily they can be disrupted (see AIR POLLUTION; WATER POLLUTION; SOLID WASTE). Today, conservation of natural resources is embraced in the much broader conception of conserving the earth itself by protecting its capacity for self-renewal. Particularly complex are the problems of nonrenewable resources such as oil and coal (see ENERGY, SOURCES OF) and other minerals in great demand. Conservation practice was first included in U.S. government policy with the creation in 1871 of a U.S. commissioner of fish and FISHERIES. The Forestry Bureau of the Dept. of Agriculture created the first national forest reserve in 1891. The Irrigation Division in the U.S. Geological Survey developed into the Bureau of Reclamation. The Geological Survey has cataloged and classified the resources of the public domain. In 1906 an act protected the Alaskan fisheries. Conservation as part of a total approach to the use of natural resources was first introduced by President Theodore Roosevelt and his chief forester, Gifford Pinchot. They popularized the philosophy of conservation, inspired a widespread movement, and gave impetus to much legislation. In 1907, President Roosevelt appointed the Inland Waterways Commission, which emphasized the connection between forests, water supply, and stream flow. In 1909 he appointed the National Conservation Commission, which published the first inventory of the country's natural resources. Roosevelt in 1907 also began to withdraw large areas of Western public land from sale and settlement, so that their resources might be investigated, and he also set apart forest reserves, following the example of President Cleveland. Approximately one fifth of all standing timber is held by the government. Reclamation of eroded lands, begun in 1880, was aided by the Newlands Act of 1902, withdrawing areas of water supply from future settlement. In 1920 the development of water power on navigable streams was placed under the control of the Federal Power Commission. The National Park Service was created in 1916. In the 1930s the erosion of much arable land in the Midwest revealed the need for land reclamation and for conservation in general. The National Industrial Recovery Act of 1933 contained provisions for conservation. The Civilian Conservation Corps, founded in 1933 to relieve unemployment, furnished the personnel for many conservation projects. The Tennessee Valley Authority, set up in 1933, was an outstanding attempt to apply principles of conservation, soil reclamation, and electrification to an entire area. The New Deal era as a whole was outstanding for legislation on conservation. By 1960 the Soil Conservation Service, established in 1935, covered 95% of all farms and ranches in the United States. By the same year, under the Conservation Reserve Program, some 28 million acres of cropland had been returned to grass and forest cover. Throughout the 1950s attention was focused on the problem of conservation of water resources, particularly in the Southwest. In the 1960s pollution problems came to the fore in all industrialized countries. In the United States numerous laws were passed to protect the environment and its resources (see ENVIRONMENTALISM). In 1972 the United Nations held a conference on the human environment in Stockholm that drew up conservation principles for all nations. The UN Conference on the Law of the Sea, begun in 1974, will attempt to establish guidelines for conserving the food and mineral resources of the earth's oceans and the seabed. See Frank Graham, Jr., *Man's Dominion: The Story of Conservation in America* (1971); David W. Ehrenfeld, *Conserving Life on Earth* (1972).

conservation of wildlife: see WILDLIFE REFUGE; ENDANGERED SPECIES; CONSERVATION OF NATURAL RESOURCES.

conservatism, in politics, the desire to maintain, or conserve, the existing order. Conservatives value highly the wisdom of the past and are generally opposed to widespread reform. Modern political conservatism emerged in the 19th cent. in reaction to the overwhelming political and social changes associated with the eras of the French Revolution and the Industrial Revolution. By 1850 the term *conservatism*, probably first used by Chateaubriand, was generally used to define the politics of the RIGHT. The original tenets of European conservatism had already been formulated by Edmund BURKE, Joseph de MAISTRE, and others. They emphasized preserving the power of king and aristocracy, maintaining the influence of landholders against the rising industrial bourgeoisie, limiting suffrage, and continuing ties between CHURCH AND STATE. From the conservative view that social welfare was the responsibility of the privileged stemmed the passage of much humanitarian legislation, in which English conservatives usually led the way. In the late 19th cent. great conservative statesmen, notably Benjamin DISRAELI, exemplified the conservative tendency to resort to moderate reform in order to preserve the foundations of the established order. By the 20th cent. conservatism was being redirected by erstwhile liberal manufacturing and professional groups who had achieved many of their political aims and had become more concerned with preserving them from attack by groups not so favored by the political and social system. The new conservatism lost its predominantly agrarian and semifeudal bias, and accepted democratic suffrage, advocated economic LAISSEZ FAIRE, and opposed extension of the welfare state. This form of conservatism is best seen in highly industrialized nations, where it has been flexible and receptive to moderate change. Conservatism should therefore be distinguished both from a reactionary desire for a past age and the radical right-wing ideology of FASCISM and National Socialism. See Peter Viereck, *Conservatism: From John Adams to Churchill* (1956); Russell Kirk, *The Conservative Mind* (rev. ed. 1960); C. L. Rossiter, *Conservatism in America* (2d ed. 1962).

Conservative party, British political party. The Conservatives are a continuation of the historic TORY party. The name was used by George Canning as early as 1824 and was first popularized by John Wilson Croker in the *Quarterly Review* in 1830. The REFORM BILL of 1832, which created some 500,000 new middle-class voters, marked the advent of the new party. The 19th-century Conservatives, like their Tory predecessors, were defenders of the established Church of England. They supported aristocratic government and a narrow franchise. They attempted, by passing factory acts and moderating the poor law of 1834, to ease hardships stemming from the Industrial Revolution, but they had no comprehensive plan to cope with its widespread dislocations. They were stronger in rural than in urban areas and were defenders of agricultural interests. Sir Robert PEEL, in his Tamworth Manifesto (1834) and after, attempted to make the party attractive to the new business classes. But his repeal (1846) of the CORN LAWS brought about an angry reaction from protectionist agricultural interests, led by Lord George Bentinck and Benjamin DISRAELI, and resulted in a party split. The "Peelites" eventually merged with the LIBERAL PARTY, and the Conservatives were hampered by the loss to the Liberals of able young leaders like William Gladstone. In the heyday (1846–73) of free trade and anti-imperial sentiment, the Conservatives were out of office, except for three brief ministries, until the Disraeli government of 1874–80. Disraeli's strong imperialism and his wooing of a broadened electorate with plans for reform, a program known as "Tory democracy," was attractive in a period of depression and increasing imperial competition. After the Reform Bill of 1884 campaign organizations like the Primrose League and the development of the caucus gave the Conservatives greater solidarity and cohesion. They gained additional strength as a result of the secession (1886) from the Liberal party of the Liberal Unionists, who, like the Conservatives, opposed HOME RULE for Ireland. (In 1912 the Liberal Unionists formally merged with the Conservative party.) The party was in office under the 3d marquess of SALISBURY (1886–92; 1895–1902) and Arthur BALFOUR (1902–5). Efforts by Lord Randolph CHURCHILL to implement further domestic reforms in the tradition of Tory democracy were unsuccessful under Salisbury's leadership, but the popular imperialistic emphasis remained. In this period the party was gradually drawing closer to middle-class business interests, but the insistence of Joseph CHAMBERLAIN on a program of tariff reform, including imperial preference, split the party and resulted (1906) in failure at the polls. Conservatives were next in office as part of the coalition government during World War I.

The Modern Conservative Party. In 1922 the Conservatives refused to continue the coalition, and under

Andrew Bonar LAW they emerged victorious at the polls. With the Liberals in decline and the LABOUR PARTY still developing, the Conservatives entered a period of almost continuous hegemony. They held office from 1922 to 1929, interrupted only by a brief Labour ministry in 1924. They were the dominant power in the National governments of Ramsay MACDONALD (1931-35), Stanley BALDWIN (1935-37), and Neville CHAMBERLAIN (1937-40). Under the long leadership of Baldwin (1922-37), the party spoke for the interests of business, the aristocracy, the professional and white-collar classes, and farmers. They lost prestige by the failure of the appeasement policy of Chamberlain toward Nazi Germany, but the country rallied to his successor, Sir Winston CHURCHILL. Triumph in war preceded electoral defeat (1945), owing to popular demand for urgently needed social reform, which the Conservatives would not carry through. Returning to office (1951) under Churchill, the Conservatives displayed a sense of pragmatic modernity in accepting many of the social reforms instituted by the Labour government. The party's majority in the House of Commons was increased in 1955, and Sir Anthony EDEN became (1955) prime minister upon Churchill's retirement. Popularity diminished temporarily during the SUEZ CANAL crisis, but favorable economic conditions and the political skill of Harold MACMILLAN, who headed the government after Eden's retirement (1957), resulted in a solid electoral victory in 1959. Under the leadership of Sir Alec DOUGLAS-HOME, who succeeded Macmillan (1963), the party lost narrowly to the Labour party in 1964, and then, with Edward HEATH as leader, it lost again in 1966. Returning to power in 1970, Heath and the Conservatives faced the problems of a stagnant economy and a declining international political position. The party, in response, moved to curb the power of trade unions and encouraged more economic self-reliance. In foreign affairs, it continued the policy of restricting Great Britain's Commonwealth and international roles while expanding ties with Western Europe, as demonstrated by Britain's entry (1973) into the European Common Market. In Feb., 1974, in the middle of a severe economic crisis and a confrontation with striking coal miners, whose wage demands the government considered inflationary, Heath called a general election, in which the Conservatives lost their majority in the House of Commons. Since Labour did not win a majority either (although it secured more seats), Heath at first sought to remain in office by forming a coalition government with the Liberals. The Liberals, however, refused to participate in such a government, thus forcing Heath's resignation. The Conservatives lost again in the election of Oct., 1974. See studies by Arthur Bryant (1929) and R. B. McDowell (1959); R. T. McKenzie, *British Political Parties* (2d ed. 1963); J. D. Hoffman, *The Conservative Party in Opposition, 1945-51* (1964); E. J. Feuchtwanger, *Disraeli, Democracy and the Tory Party* (1968); Robert Blake, *The Conservative Party from Peel to Churchill* (1970).

Consett, urban district (1971 pop. 35,391), Durham, NE England. There are coal mines, iron and steel plants, and nurseries in Consett. The district has associations with the Roman, Saxon, and Norman conquests. A German colony of swordmakers settled in Consett in the 17th cent.

Conshohocken (kŏn″shəhŏk′ən), industrial borough (1970 pop. 10,195), Montgomery co., SE Pa., on the Schuylkill River, in a fertile farm area that also has clay pits; inc. 1850.

Considérant, Victor Prosper (vĕktôr′ prōspâr′ kôNsēdärăN′), 1808-93, French socialist; follower of Charles FOURIER. In 1837, at the death of Fourier, he became the acknowledged leader of Fourierism. He edited Fourierist newspapers, including the *Philanstère* and the *Phalange,* and published works on the subject, notably a digest of Fourier's writings, *Destinée sociale* (2d ed. 1847-49). As a member of the national assembly, he took part in the JUNE DAYS insurrection (1848) and was forced to leave Paris and live in Belgium. At the request of Albert Brisbane, Considérant tried unsuccessfully to establish (1855-57) a Fourierist colony in Texas. His several books include *Principes du socialisme* (1847), an argument favoring Fourierism over other kinds of socialism. See biography by Maurice Dommanget (1929).

consideration, in law: see CONTRACT.

consols, contraction of *consol*idated annuities, a bond issue designed to consolidate two or more outstanding issues, used in reference to British government stock. Public borrowing began in England with the establishment of the Bank of England and the national debt (1693-94), and the growth of the debt produced a confusing variety of stocks. Prime minister Henry Pelham began to consolidate existing stocks in 1751. The consolidated stocks had a fixed rate of interest, or annuity, payable by the Bank of England, with premiums to be paid if the market conditions justified such payments. Consols bore no maturity date and were redeemable on call by the government. During the late 19th and early 20th cent., consols constituted the major part of the national debt and were thus a reliable index to the state of national credit.

conspiracy, in law, agreement of two or more persons to commit a criminal or otherwise unlawful act. At COMMON LAW, the crime of conspiracy was committed with the making of the agreement, but present-day statutes require an overt step by a conspirator to further the conspiracy. It is not necessary for guilt that the act be fully consummated. Many acts that would not be criminal if accomplished by an individual alone may nevertheless be the object of a conspiracy. With the rise of the labor movement in the 19th cent., British and American courts used this against unions; courts held that while an individual employee might lawfully abstain from work, the concerted stoppage of a group of employees, as in a strike, might be criminal. In 1875, Britain passed a law exempting unions from prosecution for conspiracy, and in 1932 the U.S. Congress passed a law that limited the power of Federal courts to restrain union activity. Other controversial aspects of conspiracy laws include the modification of the rules of EVIDENCE and the potential for a dragnet. A statement of a conspirator in furtherance of the conspiracy is admissible against all conspirators, even if the statement includes damaging references to another conspirator, and often even if it violates the rules against hearsay evidence. The conspiracy can be proved by circumstantial evidence. Any conspirator is guilty of any substantive crime committed by any other conspirator in furtherance of the enterprise. It is a Federal crime to conspire to commit any activity prohibited by Federal statute, whether or not Congress imposed criminal sanctions on the activity itself. An individual injured by a conspiracy may sue the conspirators to recover damages. See P. W. Winfield, *The History of Conspiracy and Abuse of Legal Procedure* (1921); Milton Handler, *Contract, Combination or Conspiracy* (1953).

Constable, Henry, 1562-1613, English poet. After graduating from Cambridge in 1580 he went to Paris, where the atmosphere was more congenial for one of Roman Catholic faith. There he wrote *Diana* (1592), a volume of sonnets. In addition he was the author of four pastorals that appeared in *England's Helicon* (1600) and *Spiritual Sonnets* (1815). Constable's work is considered to have had an important influence on the development of the sonnet.

Constable, John, 1776-1837, English painter, b. Suffolk. Constable and Turner were the leading figures in English landscape painting of the 19th cent. Constable became famous for his landscapes of Suffolk, Hampstead, Salisbury, and Brighton. The son of a prosperous miller, he showed artistic talent while very young but did not devote himself to art until he was 23, when he went to London to study at the Royal Academy. Influenced by the 17th-century landscape painters Ruisdael and Claude Lorrain, his poetic approach to nature paralleled in spirit that of his contemporary, the poet Wordsworth. Constable's direct observations of nature and his free use of broken color were extraordinary in his day. He received but modest recognition in England, being tardily admitted to the Royal Academy in 1829. His work was more popular in France. In 1824, his *View on the Stour* (1819) and *The Hay Wain* (1821; National Gall., London) were exhibited at the Salon in Paris, winning gold medals. His work made a profound impression on the French romantics including the young Delacroix and Bonington. Later his painting affected the Barbizon school and, more indirectly, the general course of French 19th-century landscape art. Today he is especially admired for the spontaneous, vigorous, and very complete sketches made as preparatory exercises for large paintings (e.g., *Weymouth Bay;* National Gall., London). In the United States he is represented in the Metropolitan Museum and the Frick Collection, New York City, and in the galleries of Philadelphia, Toledo, and Chicago. Splendid examples of his work are contained in the National Gallery, London and the Victoria and Albert Museum. See catalogue of the latter collection by Graham Reynolds (1960); C. R. Leslie, *Memoirs of the Life of John Constable* (enl. ed. 1937); collections of his letters by P. Holmes (1931) and R. B. Beckett (1962); biography by Basil Taylor (1973); studies by Sir C. J. Holmes (1902) and Carlos Peacock (rev. ed. 1972).

Constance, 1154-98, Holy Roman empress, wife of Holy Roman Emperor HENRY VI; daughter of King Roger II of Sicily. She was named heiress of Sicily by her nephew King William II. On his death, however (1189), the Sicilian nobles, wishing to prevent German rule in Sicily, chose Constance's nephew TANCRED of Lecce as William's successor. Henry VI conducted an unsuccessful campaign (1191) against Tancred during which Constance was captured but soon released. After Tancred's death (1194) Henry was crowned king of Sicily. When he died (1197) all of Italy revolted against German rule. In order to save the throne of Sicily for her infant son Frederick (later Holy Roman emperor as FREDERICK II), Constance renounced the German kingship for Frederick and had him crowned (1198) king of Sicily. She was regent for her son; before her death she named Pope Innocent III his guardian.

Constance, Ger. *Konstanz,* city (1970 pop. 61,160), Baden-Württemberg, S West Germany, on the Rhine River at the western end of the Lake of Constance (Bodensee), and near the Swiss border. Its manufactures include textiles, chemicals, and electrical equipment. The city is also a tourist center. Constance was founded as a Roman fort in the 4th cent. A.D. and became an episcopal see at the end of the 6th cent. The bishops became powerful and held large territories, including much of Baden-Württemberg and Switzerland, as princes of the Holy Roman Empire. In Constance in 1183, Emperor Frederick I recognized the LOMBARD LEAGUE. Located on a trade route between Germany and Italy, Constance became a free imperial city in 1192. During the Council of Constance (1414-18), John Huss was burned at the stake. In 1531 the city, which had accepted the Reformation, joined the Schmalkaldic League. Emperor Charles V, after defeating the League, deprived Constance of its free imperial status and gave it to his brother, later Emperor Ferdinand I. Constance was in Austrian hands from 1548 until it was ceded (1805) to Baden. The bishopric was suppressed in 1821, and the diocese was abolished in 1827. Among the numerous historic buildings in Constance are the cathedral (11th cent.; additions 15th and 17th cent.); the Council building (1388); and a former Dominican convent (now a hotel), the birthplace (1838) of Graf von Zeppelin, the soldier and aviator. Constance is the seat of a university.

Constance, Council of, 1414-18, council of the Roman Catholic Church, some of its sessions being reckoned as the 16th ecumenical council. It was summoned to end the Great Schism (see SCHISM, GREAT) in which three men were claiming to be pope—GREGORY XII (since recognized as canonical pope), John XXIII (see COSSA, BALDASSARRE), and Benedict XIII (see LUNA, PEDRO DE). Reform of Christian life and extirpation of heresy were also aims of the convocation, which was called by John at the insistence of Holy Roman Emperor SIGISMUND. Sigismund chose Constance, an imperial city, as the meeting place. During the council enormous crowds visited the city; there was much pageantry. The first session was in Nov., 1414, the 45th and last was on April 22, 1418. The council was dominated by theologians, especially French, who held the conciliar theory (i.e., that councils held supreme power in the church and that even the pope was subject to their edicts) that had appeared at the Council of Pisa (see PISA, COUNCIL OF). Instead of the traditional assembly of bishops, the council was organized as a convention of nations (German, Italian, French, and English; the Spanish entered later), each nation having one vote. The decisions were made in caucuses of the nations between sessions. The convention declared in the Articles of Constance (April 6, 1415) that it was an ecumenical council and supreme in the church. Next it declared John deposed (May 29, 1415). Gregory XII, meanwhile, sent legates with a formal decree to convene a council; this was accepted by the convention, which then ceremonially declared the council convened; at the same time Gregory resigned the papacy (July 4, 1415). Benedict provided a hard problem; he would abdicate only if allowed to name his successor. At last, after a trial held in his absence, he was deposed (July 26, 1417). This ended the schism. An elaborate method of electing the new pope was adopted, and the conclave soon agreed on MARTIN V (Nov. 11, 1417). The council, however, had already provided a plan to perpetuate its rule over the church by calling for frequent councils; furthermore, the modest reforms enacted by the council seemed designed to limit the pope's power of taxation and to protect the interests of the national clergy. Martin agreed to all enactments of the council—except, Catholic theologians argue, the council's extreme claim to supremacy—and signed concordats embodying these reforms with Germany, England, and the Latin countries. John Huss and Jerome of Prague were tried and burned at the stake for heresy. St. Bridget of Sweden was canonized. The conciliarists John Gerson and Pierre d'Ailly were among the figures prominent at the council. Church theologians tend to regard as ecumenical in character only those sessions of the council meeting after the convocation by Gregory XII, or the sessions following the election of Martin V. See E. F. Jacob, *Essays in the Conciliar Epoch* (rev. ed. 1963); Brian Tierney, *Foundations of Conciliar Theory* (1955); L. R. Loomis, *The Council of Constance* (1961).

Constance, Lake of, Ger. *Bodensee*, lake, 208 sq mi (539 sq km), bordering on Switzerland, West Germany, and Austria. It is 42 mi (68 km) long and has a maximum depth of 827 ft (252 m). The lake is fed and drained by the Rhine River and divides near the city of Constance into two arms, Untersee and Überlinger See. The main body of the lake is called the Obersee. Fruit is grown on the lake's fertile shores, and wine making and fishing are major industries. The chief towns and cities of the lake are Constance, Friedrichshafen, and Lindau, all in West Germany; Bregenz in Austria; and Rorschach in Switzerland. Remains of lake dwellings have been found.

Constans I (kŏn'stănz), b. 320 or 323, d. 350, Roman emperor, youngest son of Constantine I. At his father's death in 337 he received Italy and Africa as well as Pannonia and Dacia, while his brothers, CONSTANTINE II and Constantius II, received other portions of the empire. Trouble arose among them, and in 340 Constantine invaded Italy to win some of Constans' territory. Constantine was, however, killed in an ambush, and Constans was left to rule until his extortions and infamous conduct led to his assassination 10 years later.

Constans II (Constans Pogonatus), 630–68, Byzantine emperor (641–68), son and successor of Constantine III and grandson of Heraclius I. Early in his reign Armenia and Asia Minor were invaded by the Muslims, who challenged Byzantine supremacy at sea, took Cyprus, and threatened Sicily and Constantinople. An able and vigorous ruler, he sought to end the religious controversy centering about MONOTHELETISM by issuing a decree (648) forbidding its discussion. This involved him in conflict with Pope MARTIN I, whom he finally had arrested and banished. Constans campaigned (658) in the Balkans against the Slavs, and in 662 he moved to Italy, with the purpose of establishing his capital at Rome, but fought with little result against the Lombards and finally settled (663) at Syracuse. From there he directed a successful resistance to the Muslims. Constans extended the administrative reorganization of the empire begun by HERACLIUS. Assassinated, he was succeeded by his son, Constantine IV.

Constant, Benjamin (Henri Benjamin Constant de Rebecque) (äNrē' bäNzhămăN' kôNstäN' də rəbĕk'), 1767–1830, French-Swiss political writer and novelist, b. Lausanne. His affair (1794–1811) with Germaine de STÄEL turned him to political interests. He accompanied her to Paris in 1795 and served (1799–1801) as a tribune under the first consul, Napoleon. When Mme de Stäel was expelled (1802), however, he went into exile with her, spending the following 12 years in Switzerland and Germany. In 1813 he published a pamphlet attacking Napoleon and urging constitutional government and civil liberties. On Napoleon's return from Elba, however, Constant accepted office under him. After Napoleon's final defeat at Waterloo and the restoration of the Bourbons, Constant continued his political pamphleteering, calling for a constitutional monarchy. He served (1819–22, 1824–30) in the chamber of deputies. Constant gained a great reputation as a liberal publicist, and his funeral (shortly after the July Revolution, 1830, which he had supported) was the occasion for great demonstrations. His most important work, the introspective and semi-autobiographical novel, *Adolphe* (1816, tr. 1959), is highly regarded for its style. Parts of his correspondence and journals have been published, the latter as *Le Journal intime* (1887–89) and *Le Cahier rouge* [the red notebook] (1907). The discovery of an unfinished novel, *Cécile* (1951; tr. 1953), has contributed to a new appreciation of Constant's literary merit. See studies by E. W. Schermerhorn (1924, repr. 1970), Harold Nicolson (1949), and W. W. Holdheim (1961).

Constant, Paul Henri Benjamin, baron d'Estournelles de: see ESTOURNELLES DE CONSTANT.

Constanța (kônstän'tsä), city (1970 est. pop. 172,000), SE Rumania, on the Black Sea. It is the administrative center of DOBRUJA and a major railroad junction and industrial city, but its chief importance derives from its role as Rumania's main seaport. Petroleum (brought by pipeline from the Ploieşti oil fields), grain, and lumber are the leading exports. Besides handling general overseas trade, Constanța is important in the transit traffic with Hungary and Czechoslovakia. It also serves as Rumania's major naval and air base and as a seaside resort. The city was founded in the 7th cent. B.C. as the Greek colony of Tomi and came under Roman rule in 72 B.C. Ovid lived in exile there. Constantine I (4th cent. A.D.) named the city Constantiniana and made it an episcopal see. It was captured by the Turks in 1413. Rumania acquired it in 1878. There are several synagogues and mosques, an Orthodox cathedral, and a statue of Ovid, as well as many Roman and Byzantine remains. The regional archaeological museum and the marine biology station are also of interest.

Constant de Rebecque, Henri Benjamin: see CONSTANT, BENJAMIN.

Constantine I or **Constantine the Great** (kŏn'stəntēn, -tīn), 288?–337, Roman emperor, b. Naissus (present-day Nis, Yugoslavia). He was the son of CONSTANTIUS I and St. HELENA and was named in full Flavius Valerius Constantinus. When his father was made caesar (subemperor), Constantine was left at the court of the emperor DIOCLETIAN, where he was under the watchful eye of GALERIUS, who was caesar with Constantius. When Diocletian and MAXIMIAN resigned in 305, Constantius and Galerius became emperors. Constantius requested that Constantine be sent to him in Britain, and Galerius reluctantly complied. Constantius died at York the next year. There, his soldiers proclaimed Constantine emperor, but much rivalry for the vacated office ensued. In Italy, MAXENTIUS, supported by the Romans and by his father Maximian, vied with SEVERUS and Galerius. Constantine, accepting the lesser title of caesar from Galerius, remained aloof while Maxentius and Maximian defeated Severus and Galerius. Constantine made an alliance with Maximian, marrying Maximian's daughter Fausta and recognizing Maxentius after a fashion. When Maximian, in dispute with his son, fled to Constantine, Constantine received and sheltered him until Maximian, in an attempt to regain the throne, undertook (310) a revolt against Constantine's rule in Gaul. Unsuccessful against Constantine, Maximian was forced to commit suicide. Constantine, having already declared against Maxentius and ignoring the fact that Galerius had recognized LICINIUS in the East, now considered himself emperor. When Galerius died in 310, still another claimant to the imperial throne appeared in MAXIMIN (d. 313), who allied himself with Maxentius against the alliance of Licinius and Constantine. While Licinius attacked Maximin, Constantine moved into Italy against Maxentius. The rivals for Italy met (312) at the Milvian or Mulvian Bridge over the Tiber near Rome. Before the battle Constantine, who was already sympathetic toward Christianity, is said by Eusebius of Caesarea to have seen in the sky a flaming cross inscribed with the words, "In this sign thou shalt conquer." He adopted the cross and was victorious. Maxentius was routed and killed. The battle is regarded as a turning point for Christianity. In 313 Constantine and his fellow emperor, Licinius, met at Milan and there issued the so-called Edict of Milan, confirming Galerius' edict of 309, which stated that Christianity would be tolerated throughout the empire. The edict in effect made Christianity a lawful religion, although it did not, as is sometimes believed, make Christianity the official state religion. No longer having Maximin to contend with, Licinius challenged Constantine, and a brief struggle followed. Constantine, victorious, took (315) control over Greece and the Balkans, and the uneasy peace that followed lasted until 324, when Licinius again vied with Constantine. This time Licinius lost his throne and ultimately his life. Constantine was now sole ruler of the empire, and in a reign of peace he set about rebuilding the strength of old Rome. Constantine continued to tolerate paganism and even to encourage the imperial cult. At the same time, however, he endeavored to unify and strengthen Christianity. In 314 he convened a synod at Arles to regulate the Church in the West, and in 325 he convened and presided over a council at Nicaea to deal with the troubles over Arianism (see NICAEA, FIRST COUNCIL OF). Thus Constantine evolved the idea of the ecumenical COUNCIL. In 330 he moved the capital to Byzantium, which was rebuilt as CONSTANTINOPLE, a city predominantly Christian and dedicated to the Virgin. He seems to have favored compromise with Arianism, and in 335, in defiance of the Council of Tyre, he exiled St. ATHANASIUS. As the founder of the Christian empire, Constantine began a new era. He was an absolute ruler, and his reign saw the culmination of the tendency toward despotic rule, centralized bureaucracy, and separation of military and civil powers evolved by Diocletian. Constantine's legal reforms were marked by great humanity, perhaps a result of Christian influence. Though he had done much to unify the empire, at his death Constantine divided it again, providing for his three surviving sons and also to some extent for the sons of his half brother. These nephews were soon killed (though others, notably Julian the Apostate, survived), but complex contests ensued between Constans I, Constantine II, and Constantius II. Historians differ greatly in their assessments of Constantine's motives and the depth of his Christian conviction. Early Christian writers portray him as a devout convert, although they have difficulty explaining his execution in 320 (on adultery charges) of Crispus, his son by his first wife, and FAUSTA, his wife. Some later historians see him as a political genius, expediently using Christianity to unify his empire. An intermediate interpretation pictures him as a pagan gradually converted to Christianity (he was baptized on his deathbed), using his new belief for personal ends much as earlier emperors had used the imperial cult. The chief contemporary historians of Constantine's reign are Lactantius and Eusebius. See biographies by Norman H. Baynes (1931, repr. 1972), L. B. Holsapple (1942), A. H. M. Jones (rev. ed. 1962), John Holland Smith (1971), and F. G. Slaughter (1972); C. B. Coleman, *Constantine the Great and Christianity* (1914); G. P. Baker, *Constantine the Great and the Christian Revolution* (1930, repr. 1967).

Constantine II, 316–40, Roman emperor, son of Constantine I. When the empire was divided at the death (337) of Constantine I, among the brothers Constantius II, Constans I, and Constantine II, Constantine II received Britain, Gaul, and Spain. Maintaining that he had been cheated, he demanded some of the territory given CONSTANS I. In an invasion of Italy intended to win some of that territory, he was killed in an ambush.

Constantine IV, c.652–685, Byzantine emperor (668–85), son and successor of Constans II. He defended Constantinople against the annual naval attacks of the Muslims, who finally withdrew in 678; GREEK FIRE was a conspicuous weapon in the defense. Severely defeated (679) by the Bulgars, Constantine ceded them territory S of the Danube, where they founded a kingdom. In 680 he summoned the Third Council of Constantinople, which briefly reestablished peace between the Eastern and Western churches by condemning MONOTHELETISM. Constantine was succeeded by his son, Justinian II.

Constantine V (Constantine Copronymus), 718–75, Byzantine emperor (741–75), son and successor of LEO III. An able general and administrator, he fought successfully against the Arabs, Slavs, and Bulgars, improved the water supply of Constantinople, forcibly resettled the city after a great plague, and continued his father's financial and religious policies. In 754 he summoned a synod at Constantinople, which sustained ICONOCLASM. He rigidly enforced a decree forbidding the use of images in worship, and he opposed monasticism. A serious result of this policy was the loss of Rome and, ultimately, of Italy to the Byzantines. Pope Zacharias broke with Constantine, and Pope Stephen II placed Rome under the protection of PEPIN THE SHORT. Constantine was succeeded by his son Leo IV.

Constantine VI, b. c.770, Byzantine emperor (780–97), son and successor of Leo IV. His mother, IRENE, was regent until 790, when she was deposed by a military revolt. Constantine recalled her in 792 and made her joint ruler. His subsequent acts of cruelty and his divorce and immediate remarriage (795) alienated his supporters. In 797, Irene deposed her son, had him blinded, and assumed the imperial title. Constantine died in obscurity during the reign (820–29) of Michael II. In his minority the Second Council of Nicaea, which restored icon veneration, took place (787). Constantine fought indecisively against the Bulgarians and the Arabs.

Constantine VII (Constantine Porphyrogenitus), 905–59, Byzantine emperor (913–59). He acceded after the brief reign of his uncle Alexander, who succeeded Constantine's father, Leo VI. A regency (913–20) was followed by the rule (920–44) of the usurper ROMANUS I. In 945, Constantine expelled the sons of Romanus and began his personal rule. His main interests lay in legal reforms, in the fair redistribution of land among the peasants, and in the encouragement of art and learning. He was succeeded by his son, Romanus II. See study by Arnold Toynbee (1973).

Constantine XI (Constantine Palaeologus), d. 1453, last Byzantine emperor (1449–53), brother and successor of John VIII. To secure Western aid against the Turkish assault on what remained of the empire, he proclaimed (1452) the union of the Western and Eastern Churches. No help came, however, and in 1453 Constantine, with some 8,000 Greeks, Venetians, and Genoese, faced 150,000 Turkish besiegers under Sultan Muhammad II. After almost two months of heroic defense, directed by the emperor, the city and the empire fell. Constantine died fighting with the last of his men.

Constantine I, 1868–1923, king of the Hellenes, eldest son of George I, whom he succeeded in 1913. Married to Sophia, sister of the German emperor William II, he opposed the pro-Allied policy of the Greek premier, Eleutherios VENIZELOS, and was forced to abdicate in 1917 under Allied military pressure. His second son, ALEXANDER, succeeded to the throne. Recalled (1920) on Alexander's death, he continued the war against Turkey, although the Allies withdrew their support from Greece. The Turkish victory at İzmir caused a military rebellion, and Constantine in 1922 was again deposed and exiled. His eldest son, George II, succeeded. Constantine is also known as Constantine XII.

Constantine II, 1940–, king of the Hellenes; also known as Constantine XIII. He was appointed regent in 1964 and succeeded to the throne the same year on the death of his father, King Paul I. In 1967, after a military junta had seized political power in Greece, Constantine made an abortive attempt to overthrow the generals. When the coup failed, he and his family fled into exile. The junta declared him formally deposed in June, 1973, and established a republic. In Dec., 1974, after the overthrow of the junta, the Greek voters chose not to restore the monarchy.

Constantine (Konstantin Pavlovich) (kənstəntyēn' päv'ləvĭch), 1779–1831, Russian grand duke, second son of Czar Paul I and brother of Alexander I and Nicholas I. On the death of Alexander I (1825), Constantine was next in line for succession to the throne. However, in 1822 he had secretly renounced his claim in favor of Nicholas in return for Alexander's permission to divorce his first wife and marry a Polish countess. The arrangement was not made public and some confusion resulted concerning the succession. A group known as the DECEMBRISTS took advantage of the situation and attempted to seize power under the slogan "Constantine and Constitution." Nicholas quelled the uprising. During the entire episode Constantine remained in Poland, where he had been commander in chief and virtual governor since 1815. The severity of his administration there led to the Polish uprising of 1830. Constantine died before the rebellion was suppressed.

Constantine, d. 411, Roman general. He was proclaimed emperor by the Roman troops in Britain in 407 and led a revolt in Gaul and Spain against the Western emperor Honorius. He conquered part of Gaul and, through his son Constans, took Spain. Constantine forced recognition from Honorius as joint emperor, but his triumph was short. The counterrevolt of GERONTIUS halted him, and he was defeated by Honorius' general Constantius (later Emperor CONSTANTIUS III). Constantine was beheaded. His withdrawal of Roman troops from Britain had greatly weakened the Roman hold on that island.

Constantine, Learie (kŏn'stăntīn''), 1902–71, West Indian cricket player and the first black man to sit in the British House of Lords; b. Trinidad. The son of a sugar plantation foreman, he became world famous as a cricket player in the 1920s and 30s. He settled in England (1929), and after World War II studied law and was called to the bar. Returning to Trinidad, he began a career in public service, first as minister of works and transport and then as Trinidad's high commissioner in London (1962–64). He was knighted in 1962 and raised to the peerage in 1969.

Constantine (kŏn'stəntēn), ancient *Cirta,* city (1966 pop. 253,649), capital of Constantine dept., NE Algeria, on the gorge of the Rhumel River. A major inland city, it is the railhead of a prosperous and diverse agricultural area. Constantine is also a center of the grain trade and has flour mills, a tractor factory, and industries producing textiles and leather goods. Products made by local artisans are economically important. Founded by Carthaginians (who called it Sarim Batim), Constantine became the capital and commercial center of Numidia and was named Cirta [the city]. Under Roman rule it was a major grain-shipping point and one of the wealthiest cities of Africa. Destroyed (A.D. 311) during the war preceding the accession of Constantine I, it was rebuilt by Constantine himself and renamed in his honor. The city was pillaged by the Vandals in the 5th cent. and later became an object of contention among various Muslim dynasties. The Turks captured it in the 16th cent. and made it a provincial capital. By the time of the French conquest in 1837 the district governor of Constantine had become virtually independent of the Ottoman Empire. Modern Constantine is the seat of a Roman Catholic bishop, a university, and a Muslim school of higher education.

Constantine, Donation of, Lat. *Donatio Constantini,* also called the *Constitutum Constantini,* forged document, probably drafted in the 8th cent. It purported to be a grant by Roman Emperor Constantine I of great temporal power in Italy and the West to the PAPACY. Its purpose was apparently to enhance papal territorial claims in Italy by giving them greater antiquity. The document also recognized the spiritual authority of the popes, but this statement had no weight, since at no time was it argued in the Roman Catholic Church that spiritual authority could emanate from the emperor. It was not, as a matter of fact, ever of great practical value, nor was it, as is sometimes asserted, universally accepted in the Middle Ages. It owes its great fame to the fact that the scholar Lorenzo VALLA demonstrated the falsity of the document by critical methods that became the model for later textual criticism and are said by some to be the beginning of modern textual criticism. See Lorenzo Valla, *Treatise on the Donation of Constantine* (tr. by C. B. Coleman, 1922; repr. 1971).

Constantine Nikolayevich (nēkôläyä'vĭch), 1827–92, grand duke of Russia; brother of Czar Alexander II. Constantine supported all the reforms instituted by his brother, who gave him command of the fleet and made him governor general of Poland in 1862. There his conciliatory policy could not prevent the insurrection of 1863 against Russian rule. He resigned and in 1865 was appointed president of the state council. He retired from state service in 1881.

Constantine the Great: see CONSTANTINE I, Roman emperor.

Constantinople, former capital of the BYZANTINE EMPIRE and of the OTTOMAN EMPIRE, since 1930 officially called İstanbul (for location and description, see ISTANBUL). It was founded (A.D. 330) at ancient BYZANTIUM as the new capital of the Roman Empire by Constantine I, after whom it was named. The largest and most splendid European city of the Middle Ages, Constantinople shared the glories and vicissitudes of the Byzantine Empire, which in the end was reduced to the city and its environs. Although besieged innumerable times by various peoples, it was taken only three times—in 1204 by the army of the Fourth Crusade (see CRUSADES), in 1261 by Michael VIII, and in 1453 by the Ottoman Sultan Muhammad II. Defended by GREEK FIRE, it was also well fortified. An early inner wall was erected by Constantine I, and the enlarged Constantinople was surrounded by a triple wall of fortifications, begun (5th cent.) by Theodosius II. Built on seven hills, the city on the Bosporus presented the appearance of an impregnable fortress enclosing a sea of magnificent palaces and gilded domes and towers. In the 10th cent., it had a cosmopolitan population of about 1 million. The Church of HAGIA SOPHIA, the sacred palace of the emperors (a city in itself); the huge hippodrome, center of the popular life; and the Golden Gate, the chief entrance into the city; were among the largest of the scores of churches, public edifices, and monuments that lined the broad arcaded avenues and squares. Constantinople had a great wealth of artistic and literary treasures before it was sacked in 1204 and 1453. Virtually depopulated when it fell to the Ottoman Turks, the city recovered rapidly. The Ottoman sultans, whose court was called the Sublime Porte, embellished Constantinople with many beautiful mosques, palaces, monuments, fountains, baths, aqueducts, and other public buildings. After World War I the city was occupied (1918–23) by the Allies. In 1922 the last Ottoman sultan was deposed and Ankara became (1923) the new capital of Turkey.

Constantinople, First Council of, 381, second ecumenical council. It was convened by Theodosius I, then emperor of the East and a recent convert, to confirm the victory over Arianism. The council drew up a dogmatic statement on the Trinity and defined Holy Spirit as having the same divinity expressed for the Son by the Council of Nicaea 56 years earlier. That statement has been lost, but the work of the council established the orthodox teaching of the Trinity as it is held today. The traditional belief ascribing the present form of the Nicene Creed (see CREED) to this council has been questioned by modern scholars. The council condemned all varieties of Arianism along with the new heresy, Apollinarianism. The sessions, which were attended only by bishops of the East, lasted two months. Gregory Nazianzen was reinstated as bishop of Constantinople and then made president of the council when its first president, Meletius of Antioch, died. Gregory resigned when the council disregarded his wishes and elected Flavian of Antioch as Meletius' successor at Antioch. One canon of the council, making the bishop of Constantinople second only to the pope in precedence, was not admitted in the West until the Fourth Lateran Council (1215).

Constantinople, Second Council of, 553, regarded generally as the fifth ecumenical council. It was convened by Byzantine Emperor Justinian I to settle the dispute known as the Three Chapters. In an attempt to reconcile moderate Monophysite parties to orthodoxy, Justinian had issued (544) a declaration of faith. The last three chapters anathematized the writings of THEODORE OF MOPSUESTIA, THEODORET of Cyrus, and Ibas for NESTORIANISM. While the charge was true of their writings to a certain extent, the Council of Chalcedon had cleared those men of any personal heresy. Justinian's edict had the effect of slighting the council and encouraging MONOPHYSITISM; it was deeply resented in the West. Pope VIGILIUS, resisting at first, was constrained to support the edict. Under pressure from the Western bishops he then reversed himself. In retaliation, Justinian called a council at Constantinople; it was attended by only six Western bishops, boycotted by Vigilius, and dominated by Justinian and the Eastern bishops. The council approved the imperial edict and seems to have censured Vigilius. The pope was forced to ratify the council's work the following year. The West, in general, was slow in recognizing it as an ecumenical council, though ultimately it was accepted, chiefly because of the orthodoxy of its pronouncements.

Constantinople, Third Council of, 680, regarded by Roman Catholic and Orthodox Eastern churches as the sixth ecumenical council. It was convoked by Byzantine Emperor Constantine IV to deal with MONOTHELETISM. The council was attended by more than 150 bishops from all over the world, and it was presided over by the papal legates. It condemned Monotheletism very clearly by defining the orthodox faith as the acceptance of a separate will and operation in each of the natures of Christ. It also condemned several churchmen as Monothelites, among them an earlier pope, HONORIUS I. The condemnation of Honorius is a much-discussed point in church history. The Orthodox Church accepts as an ecumenical part of the Third Council of Constantinople the Oriental Council of 692, summoned by Justinian II, son and successor of Constantine. It is called in the West the Trullan Synod because it met in the Trullo, i.e., in the dome of the palace, or the Quinisext Synod [Lat.,=fifth-sixth] because it is considered in the East to supplement the fifth and sixth ecumenical councils. The Trullan Synod was entirely legislative, and its principal work was the pronouncement of the obligation to observe the canons of the Apostolic CONSTITUTIONS. There was apparently in the legislation an anti-Western tone, and certain practices of the West were condemned.

Constantinople, Fourth Council of, 869–70, regarded as the eighth ecumenical council by the modern Roman Catholic Church. It has never been accepted by the Orthodox Church, which instead recognizes the council of 880 that supported PHOTIUS. The council of 869 was convoked at the suggestion of Basil I, the new Byzantine emperor, to confirm the restoration of St. IGNATIUS OF CONSTANTINOPLE to the see that Photius had resigned. Only 12 bishops attended at first, and attendance never exceeded 103. The legates of Pope Adrian II presided. Photius had already been condemned, without a hearing, at a Roman synod. At Constantinople his defense was cut short, and when he refused to sign his own condemnation, he was excommunicated. The result of these councils was to intensify the bitterness between East and West.

Constantinople, Latin Empire of, 1204–61, feudal empire established in the S Balkan Peninsula and the Greek archipelago by the leaders of the Fourth Crusade (see CRUSADES) after they had sacked (1204)

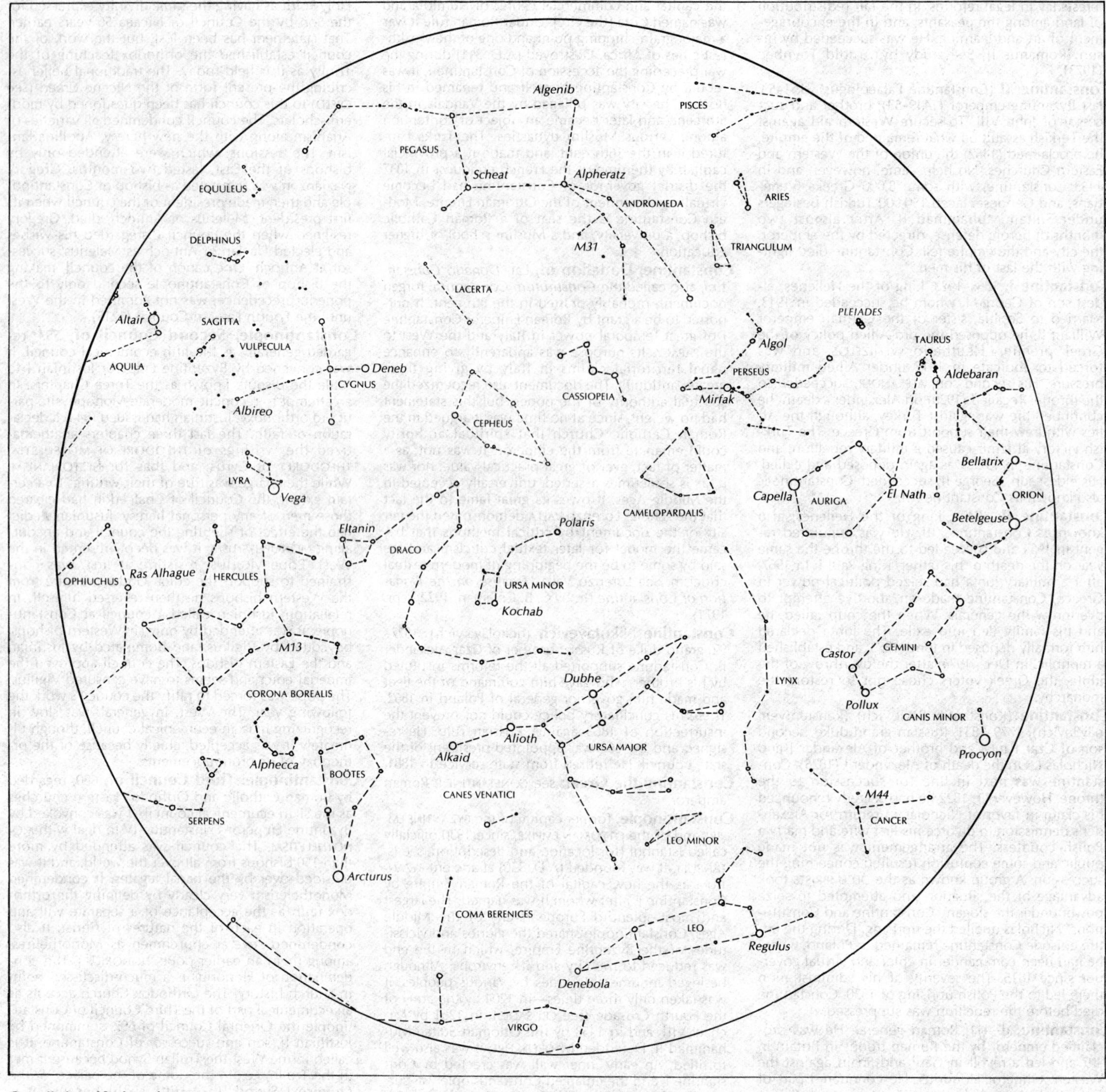

Constellations: Northern sky

Constantinople; also known as the empire of *Romania* (not to be confused with the modern nation Rumania). Its secular and ecclesiastic governments were carefully divided among the Crusaders and their Venetian creditors. It was on both sides of the Dardanelles; its rulers were also suzerains of the kingdom of Thessalonica, the principality of Achaia, and other fiefs. BALDWIN I, HENRY OF FLANDERS, Peter of Courtenay and his wife, Yolande, ROBERT OF COURTENAY, JOHN OF BRIENNE, and BALDWIN II were rulers. The empire declined immediately after its creation, being beset by the Greek emperors of Nicaea (see NICAEA, EMPIRE OF) and despots of Epirus (see EPIRUS, DESPOTATE OF), by the Bulgars under IVAN II (Ivan Asen), by the Turks, by discord among the Westerners, and by Greek resistance. In 1222, Thessalonica fell to the despot of Epirus. By 1224 the Nicaean Emperor JOHN III had recovered Asia Minor. Constantinople, nearly captured by Ivan Asen in 1234, fell to Emperor MICHAEL VIII in 1261. Venice, however, retained possession of most of the Greek isles, the duchy of Athens passed under Catalan rule, and Achaia stayed in the hands of the VILLEHARDOUIN family until 1278. See William Miller, *The Latins in the Levant* (1908, repr. 1964); D. E. Queller, ed., *The Latin Conquest of Constantinople* (1971).

Constantinus Africanus (kŏn″stəntī′nəs ăfrĭkā′nəs), c.1010–1087, medical translator and Benedictine monk. The life of Constantinus before his arrival at Salerno c.1070 is obscure. According to the monk who wrote his biography, Constantinus was born in Carthage, traveled extensively in North Africa and various parts of Asia for four decades, and accumulated everywhere manuscripts on medicine and other sciences. Ejected from Carthage as a magician, he fled to Salerno, where he remained for several years before retiring in 1076 to Monte Cassino. There he spent his remaining years in great activity; among the 30-odd works attributed to him are translations of HIPPOCRATES, GALEN, Isaac Judaeus, and Haly Abbas.

Constantius I (Constantius Chlorus) (kənstăn′shəs), c.250–306, Roman emperor (305–6). A career general, he gave up St. HELENA to marry Theodora, the daughter of MAXIMIAN. He was made caesar (subemperor) under Maximian in 293 and gained prestige when his forces defeated the rebel CARAUSIUS. He went to Britain in 296, where he put down a rebellion of Carausius' successor, Allectus. Returning to Gaul, he defeated the Alemanni in 298. His vigor and his moderation made him popular with the people of the colonies as well as with his soldiers. The two emperors, Diocletian and Maximian, abdicated in 305, and Constantius and Galerius became emperors. The next year, however, Constantius died at York. On his death the imperial throne was claimed by his son Constantine (CONSTANTINE I), but the office was long contested.

Constantius II, 317–61, Roman emperor, son of Constantine I. When the empire was divided (337) at the death of Constantine, Constantius II was given rule over Asia Minor, Syria, and Egypt, while his brothers, Constans I and Constantine II, received other portions. He gained prestige by fighting successfully against the Persians. When in 350 the murder of Constans I threw the West into disorder, Constantius II defeated the usurping Magnentius, a German who had been a commander under Constans I, and became sole emperor. He delegated much power to his cousin Julian (JULIAN THE APOSTATE) in Gaul. When a new dispute erupted with the Persians, Constantius ordered Julian to the East, but Julian's men revolted and proclaimed (360) Julian emperor in the West. Constantius died in the Persian campaign in Cilicia, naming Julian as his successor. A confirmed Arian, Constantius vigorously repressed paganism and was involved in a struggle with St. Athanasius.

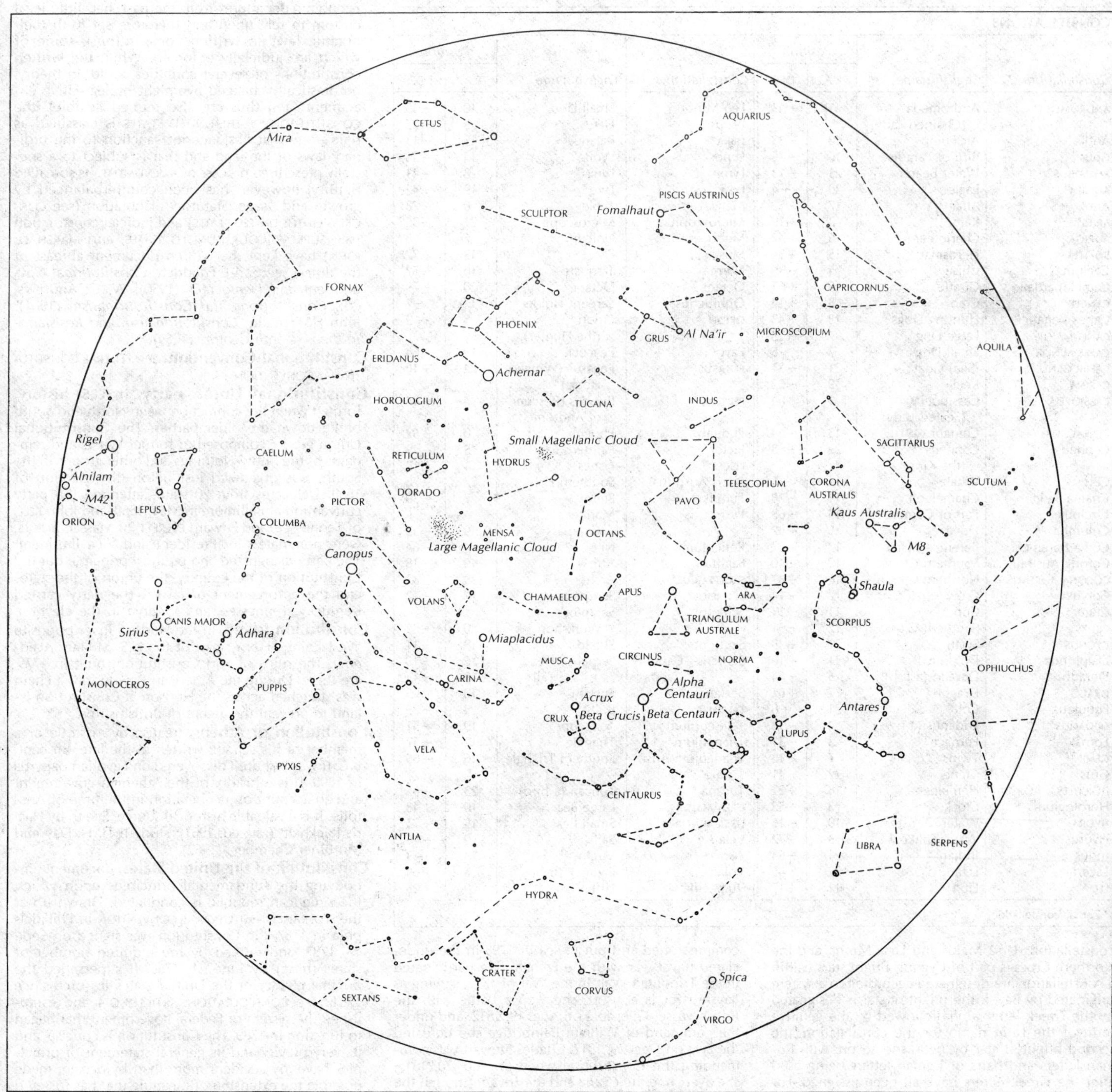

Constellations: Southern sky

Constantius III, d. 421, Roman emperor of the West (421). In 411, as general of HONORIUS, he defeated Gerontius and Constantine; thereafter he was the virtual ruler of the West. Aspiring to the hand of Honorius' sister GALLA PLACIDIA, he vied with his rival, ATAULF, the Visigothic king, and drove him from Gaul into Spain shortly after Ataulf's marriage (414) to Galla Placidia. In 416, after Ataulf was assassinated, he made peace with the new Visigothic king, Wallia, and in 417 he married Galla Placidia. He was the prime mover in granting (418) local government to Gaul and in settling (419) the Visigoths in Aquitaine. In 421 Galla Placidia persuaded Honorius to make Constantius coemperor, but Constantius died a few months after his accession. He was the father of Valentinian III.

Constellation, U.S. frigate, launched in 1797. She was named by President Washington for the constellation of 15 stars in the U.S. flag of that time. The frigate was built to serve against the pirates of the Barbary States, but after the outbreak (1798) of hostilities between the United States and France, she was stationed in Caribbean waters. After the *Constellation,* commanded by Thomas Truxtun, encountered and captured (Feb., 1799) the vessel *Insurgente,* she won (Feb., 1800) a hard-fought victory over another French frigate, the *Vengeance.* The *Constellation* was blockaded at Norfolk, Va., during the War of 1812, but further victories followed in the Mediterranean in 1815. Rebuilt in 1853–55, the *Constellation* was used against Confederate commerce cruisers in the Civil War and later served (1873–93) as a training ship at Annapolis, Norfolk, and Philadelphia. She became the ship with the longest period of service in the navy when she saw duty as flagship of the U.S. Atlantic fleet during World War II. She is preserved at Baltimore. See study by H. I. Chapelle and L. D. Polland (1970).

constellation (kŏnstĭlā'shən), in common usage, group of stars that are imagined to form a configuration in the sky; properly speaking, a constellation is a definite region of the sky in which the configuration of stars is contained. Identifiable groupings of bright stars have been recognized and named since ancient times, the names corresponding to mythological figures (e.g., Perseus, Andromeda, Hercules, Orion), animals (e.g., Leo the Lion, Cygnus the Swan, Draco the Dragon), or objects (e.g., Libra the Balance, Corona the Crown). Ptolemy listed 48 constellations in his *Almagest* (2d cent. A.D.). As systematic observations were extended to the entire southern sky from the 17th cent. on, more constellations were added to the list by J. Bayer, N. L. de Lacaille, and others. For example, Ptolemy's 48th constellation, Argo Navis, representing a ship, was divided into four smaller constellations corresponding to different parts of the ship. The final list consists of 88 constellations, each associated with a definite region of the sky. Thus, the entire CELESTIAL SPHERE is divided, with the boundaries fixed by international agreement, along lines of right ascension (R.A.) and declination (Dec.). See EQUATORIAL COORDINATE SYSTEM. The 12 constellations located along or near the ECLIPTIC, the apparent path of the sun through the heavens, are known as the constellations of the ZODIAC; the remaining constellations are officially classified as northern (28 constellations) or southern (48 constellations). The accompanying table lists the constellations according to their official Latin names, with the English equivalents and the approximate positions given. In some cases the English name is not an exact translation of the Latin; e.g., the English name for the constellation Pictor reflects the fact that the figure in the constellation is not the painter himself but his easel. Certain familiar star groups are not listed as constellations because they form only part of a larger constellation; the Big Dipper and Little Dipper are parts of the

CONSTELLATIONS

Constellation	English name	Position R.A.	Position DEC.	Constellation	English name	Position R.A.	Position DEC.
ANDROMEDA	Andromeda (Chained Lady)	1^h	+43°	Leo Minor	Small Lion	10	+35
Antlia	Air Pump	10	−33	Lepus	Hare	5	−23
Apus	Bird of Paradise	16	−75	LIBRA*	Balance	15	−13
AQUARIUS*	Water Bearer	23	−13	Lupus	Wolf	15	−36
AQUILA	Eagle	20	+4	Lynx	Lynx	8	+41
Ara	Altar	17	−52	LYRA	Lyre	19	+42
ARIES*	Ram	2	+19	Mensa	Table	6	−78
AURIGA	Charioteer	6	+42	Microscopium	Microscope	21	−36
BOÖTES	Herdsman	15	+34	Monoceros	Unicorn	7	−8
Caelum	Chisel	5	−39	Musca	Fly	13	−72
Camelopardalis	Giraffe	5	+67	Norma	T-square	16	−52
CANCER*	Crab	8	+14	Octans	Octant	20	−79
Canes Venatici	Hunting Dogs	13	+43	Ophiuchus	Serpent Holder	17	−7
CANIS MAJOR	Large Dog	7	−23	ORION	Orion (the Hunter)	5	+2
CANIS MINOR	Small Dog	7	+5	Pavo	Peacock	19	−64
CAPRICORNUS*	(Sea) Goat	21	−21	PEGASUS	Pegasus (Winged Horse)	22	+18
CARINA	Keel	9	−62	PERSEUS	Perseus (Rescuer of Andromeda)	4	+44
CASSIOPEIA	Cassiopeia (Seated Lady)	1	+64	Phoenix	Phoenix	0	−52
CENTAURUS	Centaur	13	−44	Pictor	Painter's Easel	5	−49
Cepheus	Cepheus (the King)	22	+68	PISCES*	Fishes	1	+12
Cetus	Whale	1	−6	Piscis Austinus	Southern Fish	22	−28
Chamaeleon	Chameleon	11	−78	Puppis	Stern	7	−39
Circinus	Pair of Compasses	15	−65	Pyxis	Mariner's Compass	9	−32
Columba	Dove	5	−32	Reticulum	Net	4	−64
Coma Berenices	Berenice's Hair	13	+22	Sagitta	Arrow	19	+18
Corona Australis	Southern Crown	19	−40	SAGITTARIUS*	Archer	19	−32
CORONA BOREALIS	Northern Crown	16	+31	SCORPIUS*	Scorpion	17	−32
Corvus	Crow	12	−14	Sculptor	Sculptor's Workshop	0	−32
Crater	Cup	11	−13	Scutum	Shield	19	−11
CRUX	Southern Cross	12	−61	Serpens—Caput	Serpent—Head	16	+10
CYGNUS	Swan	21	+48	Cauda	Tail	18	−13
Delphinus	Dolphin	21	+18	Sextans	Sextant	10	−5
Dorado	Dorado (a fish)	5	−64	TAURUS*	Bull	4	+25
DRACO	Dragon	17	+61	Telescopium	Telescope	19	−51
Equuleus	Colt	21	+8	Triangulum	Triangle	2	+32
ERIDANUS	Eridanus (a river)	4	−18	Triangulum Australe	Southern Triangle	16	−65
Fornax	Furnace	3	−31	Tucana	Toucan (a bird)	23	−63
GEMINI*	Twins	7	+18	URSA MAJOR	Large Bear	10	+48
Grus	Crane	22	−41	URSA MINOR	Small Bear	15	+73
HERCULES	Hercules	18	+22	Vela	Sails	9	−46
Horologium	Clock	3	−53	VIRGO*	Virgin	13	−3
HYDRA	Water Monster	10	−16	Volans	Flying Fish	8	−69
Hydrus	Water Snake	3	−72	Vulpecula	Little Fox	20	+25
Indus	Indian	21	−54				
Lacerta	Lizard	22	+45				
LEO*	Lion	11	+17				

* Zodiac constellation.

constellations Ursa Major and Ursa Minor, and the Northern Cross is part of Cygnus. Bright stars within a constellation are designated according to a system originated by Bayer: the brightest star is designated by the Greek letter *alpha* followed by the genitive form of the Latin name for the constellation, the second brightest star by *beta*, and so on, with Roman letters and pairs of Roman letters being used after the Greek letters have all been assigned. For example, the brightest star in Taurus, Aldebaran, is designated Alpha Tauri, the second brightest, Elnath, is designated Beta Tauri, and so on. Some stars have changed in brightness since Bayer's time, so that the alphabetical order does not necessarily indicate their present relative brightness. In a few cases, e.g., Ursa Major, the assignment of a Bayer name is according to position rather than brightness.

constipation, infrequent or difficult passage of feces. Constipation may be caused by the lack of adequate roughage or fluid in the diet, prolonged physical inactivity, certain drugs, or emotional disturbance. Sudden unexplained changes in bowel habits can be a symptom of a serious disorder (such as lower intestinal obstruction by a growth) and should receive medical attention. Most cases of constipation can be relieved by following a diet that includes adequate roughage and fluid and by establishing regular habits of evacuation. The continued use of laxatives is inadvisable. Daily bowel movements are not essential; many persons suffer from the harm caused by constant use of laxatives and enemas in an effort to establish the desired regularity.

Constitution, U.S. 44-gun frigate, nicknamed *Old Ironsides.* She was perhaps the most famous vessel in the history of the U.S. navy. Authorized by Congress in 1794, she was launched in 1797 and was commissioned and put to sea in 1798 in the undeclared naval war with the French. She participated in the Tripolitan War. In the War of 1812, serving as flagship for Isaac HULL, she won a battle with the British vessel *Guerrière* on Aug. 19, 1812, and under the command of William Bainbridge she defeated the *Java* on Dec. 29, 1812. Charles Stewart was commanding the *Constitution* when on Feb. 20, 1815, she overcame the *Cyane* and the *Levant* (though the *Levant* was later recaptured by the British). The *Constitution* was condemned (1830) as unseaworthy, but public sentiment, aroused by Oliver Wendell Holmes's poem "Old Ironsides," saved the ship from dismantling, and she was rebuilt in 1833. She was laid up at the Portsmouth navy yard in 1855 and was there used as a training ship. In 1877 she was rebuilt, and the next year she crossed the Atlantic. In 1897 she was stored at the Boston navy yard, and in 1925, under authorization of Congress, she was rebuilt by public subscription. She is now maintained at the Boston navy yard. See James Barnes, *Naval Actions of the War of 1812* (1896); Ira N. Hollis, *The Frigate Constitution* (1901); Elliot Snow, *On the Deck of "Old Ironsides"* (1932); T. P. Horgan, *Old Ironsides* (1963); J. E. Jennings, *Tattered Ensign* (1966).

constitution, fundamental principles of government in a nation, either implied in its laws, institutions, and customs or embodied in one document or in several. In the first category—customary and unwritten constitutions—is the British constitution, which is contained implicitly in the whole body of common and statutory law of the realm and in the practices and traditions of the workings of the government. Because it can be modified by an ordinary act of PARLIAMENT, the British constitution is often termed flexible. In the 18th, 19th, and 20th cent. many countries, having made sharp political and economic departures from the past, had little legal custom to rely upon and therefore set forth their organic laws in written constitutions—some of which are judicially enforced. While the written constitutions of several countries could, in theory, be drastically changed overnight by legislative enactment (and thus are also termed flexible), the CONSTITUTION OF THE UNITED STATES is classified as rigid—one that has superior sanction to the ordinary laws of the land and that is subject to a specially prescribed process of AMENDMENT. Its so-called rigidity, however, has been counterbalanced by growth and usage. Statutory elaboration (see CONGRESS OF THE UNITED STATES) and judicial construction (see SUPREME COURT, UNITED STATES, and MARSHALL, JOHN) have kept the written document abreast of the times. See Carl J. Friedrich, *Constitutional Government and Democracy* (1950); W. G. Andrews, ed., *Constitutions and Constitutionalism* (1961); John H. Franklin, *Constitutionalism and Resistance in the Sixteenth Century* (1969).

Constitutional Convention: see FEDERAL CONSTITUTIONAL CONVENTION.

Constitutional Union party, in U.S. history, formed when the conflict between North and South broke down the older parties. The Constitutional Union group, composed of former Whigs and remnants of the Know-Nothings and other groups in the South, was organized just before the election of 1860. Delegates from 20 states attended the party convention at Baltimore in May, 1860, and John BELL, of Tennessee, and Edward EVERETT, of Massachusetts, were nominated for President and Vice President. The party recognized "no political principle but the Constitution of the country, the union of the states and the enforcement of laws." The party carried Kentucky, Tennessee, and Virginia in the election.

Constitution Island, in the Hudson River opposite West Point, SE N.Y.; part of the U.S. Military Academy. The ruins of Fort Constitution, built in 1775, are there. During the American Revolution, a chain was stretched across the Hudson at Constitution Island to prevent the ascent of British ships.

Constitution of Athens, treatise by Aristotle or a member of his school, written in the late 4th cent. B.C. It was lost until discovered on Egyptian papyrus in 1890. It is a history of the Athenian government and an account of its operation in the time of Aristotle. It is a valuable historical source. See tr. by Harris Rackham (rev. ed. 1961); study by J. H. Day and Mortimer Chambers (1962).

Constitution of the United States, document embodying the fundamental principles upon which the American republic is conducted. Drawn up at the FEDERAL CONSTITUTIONAL CONVENTION in Philadelphia in 1787, the Constitution was signed on Sept. 17, 1787, and ratified by the required number of states (nine) by June 21, 1788. It superseded the original charter of the United States in force since 1781 (see CONFEDERATION, ARTICLES OF) and established the system of Federal government that began to function in 1789. The Constitution is concise, and its very brevity and its general statement of principles have, by accident more than by design, made possible the extension of meaning that has fostered growth. There are seven articles and a Preamble; 26 amendments have been adopted. The Preamble does not confer power, but its first words, "We the People of the United States," describe the source of the powers conferred by the rest of the Constitution and have been used by the advocates of a strong union arguing against the proponents of STATES' RIGHTS. The Preamble also states the purpose of the document. One of the statements of purpose, "to . . . promote the general welfare," has been of great importance in the 20th cent. in upholding social legislation, for which no warrant could be found in the enumerated powers of Congress. The first three articles set up the three-fold separation of powers, said to have been modeled on Montesquieu's study of the British government. In actuality this separation has been weakened by the granting of greater powers to the President and his administrative agencies, which now have legislative and judicial as well as executive functions. Article 1 provides for the establishment of the bicameral Congress composed of the Senate and the House of Representatives. The various powers of the Congress and the respective houses, together with their methods of election, are enumerated in the article. The Seventeenth Amendment, passed in 1916, instituted the direct popular election of Senators and removed the power of their election from the state legislatures as had originally been provided in Article 1. Section 4 of Article 1

TEXT* OF THE

CONSTITUTION OF THE UNITED STATES

PREAMBLE

We, the people of the United States, in order to form a more perfect union, establish justice, insure domestic tranquillity, provide for the common defense, promote the general welfare, and secure the blessings of liberty to ourselves and our posterity, do ordain and establish this Constitution for the United States of America.

ARTICLE I

SECTION I

All legislative powers herein granted shall be vested in a Congress of the United States, which shall consist of a Senate and House of Representatives.

SECTION II

[1] The House of Representatives shall be composed of members chosen every second year by the people of the several States, and the electors in each State shall have the qualifications requisite for electors of the most numerous branch of the State legislature.

[2] No person shall be a Representative who shall not have attained to the age of twenty-five years, and been seven years a citizen of the United States, and who shall not, when elected, be an inhabitant of that State in which he shall be chosen.

[3] Representatives and direct taxes shall be apportioned among the several States which may be included within this Union, according to their respective numbers, which shall be determined by adding to the whole number of free persons, including those bound to service for a term of years, and excluding Indians not taxed, three-fifths of all other persons. The actual enumeration shall be made within three years after the first meeting of the Congress of the United States, and within every subsequent term of ten years, in such manner as they shall by law direct. The number of Representatives shall not exceed one for every thirty thousand, but each State shall have at least one Representative; and until such enumeration shall be made, the State of New Hampshire shall be entitled to choose three; Massachusetts, eight; Rhode Island and Providence Plantations, one; Connecticut, five; New York, six; New Jersey, four; Pennsylvania, eight; Delaware, one; Maryland, six; Virginia, ten; North Carolina, five; South Carolina, five; and Georgia, three.

[4] When vacancies happen in the representation from any State, the executive authority thereof shall issue writs of election to fill such vacancies.

[5] The House of Representatives shall choose their Speaker and other officers, and shall have the sole power of impeachment.

SECTION III

[1] The Senate of the United States shall be composed of two Senators from each State, chosen by the legislature thereof for six years; and each Senator shall have one vote.

[2] Immediately after they shall be assembled in consequence of the first election, they shall be divided as equally as may be into three classes. The seats of the Senators of the first class shall be vacated at the expiration of the second year, of the second class at the expiration of the fourth year, and of the third class at the expiration of the sixth year, so that one-third may be chosen every second year; and if vacancies happen by resignation or otherwise during the recess of the legislature of any State, the executive thereof may make temporary appointments until the next meeting of the legislature, which shall then fill such vacancies.

[3] No person shall be a Senator who shall not have attained to the age of thirty years, and been nine years a citizen of the United States, and who shall not, when elected, be an inhabitant of that State for which he shall be chosen.

[4] The Vice-President of the United States shall be President of the Senate, but shall have no vote, unless they be equally divided.

[5] The Senate shall choose their other officers and also a President pro tempore in the absence of the Vice-President, or when he shall exercise the office of President of the United States.

[6] The Senate shall have the sole power to try all impeachments. When sitting for that purpose, they shall be on oath or affirmation. When the President of the United States is tried, the Chief Justice shall preside; and no person shall be convicted without the concurrence of two-thirds of the members present.

[7] Judgment in cases of impeachment shall not extend further than to removal from office, and disqualification to hold and enjoy any office of honor, trust, or profit under the United States; but the party convicted shall, nevertheless, be liable and subject to indictment, trial, judgment, and punishment, according to law.

SECTION IV

[1] The times, places, and manner of holding elections for Senators and Representatives shall be prescribed in each State by the legislature thereof; but the Congress may at any time by law make or alter such regulations, except as to the places of choosing Senators.

[2] The Congress shall assemble at least once in every year, and such meeting shall be on the first Monday in December, unless they shall by law appoint a different day.

SECTION V

[1] Each House shall be the judge of the elections, returns, and qualifications of its own members, and a majority of each shall constitute a quorum to do business; but a smaller number may adjourn from day to day, and may be authorized to compel the attendance of absent members, in such manner, and under such penalties, as each House may provide.

[2] Each House may determine the rules of its proceedings, punish its members for disorderly behavior, and with the concurrence of two-thirds, expel a member.

[3] Each House shall keep a journal of its proceedings, and from time to time publish the same, excepting such parts as may in their judgment require secrecy, and the yeas and nays of the members of either House on any question shall, at the desire of one-fifth of those present, be entered on the journal.

[4] Neither House, during the session of Congress, shall, without the consent of the other adjourn for more than three days, nor to any other place than that in which the two Houses shall be sitting.

SECTION VI

[1] The Senators and Representatives shall receive a compensation for their services, to be ascertained by law and paid out of the Treasury of the United States. They shall, in all cases except treason, felony, and breach of the peace, be privileged from arrest during their attendance at the session of their respective Houses, and in going to and returning from the same; and for any speech or debate in either House they shall not be questioned in any other place.

[2] No Senator or Representative shall, during the time for which he was elected, be appointed to any civil office under the authority of the United States, which shall have been created, or the emoluments whereof shall have been increased during such time; and no person holding any office under the United States shall be a member of either House during his continuance in office.

SECTION VII

[1] All bills for raising revenue shall originate in the House of Representatives; but the Senate may propose or concur with amendments as on other bills.

[2] Every bill which shall have passed the House of Representatives and the Senate shall, before it become a law, be presented to the President of the United States; if he approve he shall sign it, but if not he shall return it, with his objections, to that House in which it shall have originated, who shall enter the objections at large on their journal and proceed to reconsider it. If after such reconsideration two-thirds of that House shall agree to pass the bill, it shall be sent, together with the objections, to the other House, by which it shall likewise be reconsidered, and if approved by two-thirds of that House it shall become a law. But in all such cases the vote of both Houses shall be determined by yeas and nays, and the names of the persons voting for and against the bill shall be entered on the journal of each House respectively. If any bill shall not be returned by the President within ten days (Sundays excepted) after it shall have been presented to him, the same shall be a law, in like manner as if he had signed it, unless the Congress by their adjournment prevent its return, in which case it shall not be a law.

[3] Every order, resolution or vote to which the concurrence of the Senate and House of Representatives may be necessary (except on a question of adjournment) shall be presented to the President of the United States; and before the same shall take effect shall be approved by him, or being disapproved by him, shall be repassed by two-thirds of the Senate and House of Representatives, according to the rules and limitations prescribed in the case of a bill.

SECTION VIII

[1] The Congress shall have power to lay and collect taxes, duties, imposts and excises, to pay the debts and provide for the common defense and general welfare of the United States; but all duties, imposts and excises shall be uniform throughout the United States;

[2] To borrow money on the credit of the United States;

[3] To regulate commerce with foreign nations, and among the several States, and with the Indian tribes;

[4] To establish an uniform rule of naturalization, and uniform laws on the subject of bankruptcies throughout the United States;

[5] To coin money, regulate the value thereof, and of foreign coin, and fix the standard of weights and measures;

* Modern usage in spelling, punctuation, and capitalization has been employed.

[6] To provide for the punishment of counterfeiting the securities and current coin of the United States;

[7] To establish post offices and post roads;

[8] To promote the progress of science and useful arts by securing for limited times to authors and inventors the exclusive right to their respective writings and discoveries;

[9] To constitute tribunals inferior to the Supreme Court;

[10] To define and punish piracies and felonies committed on the high seas and offenses against the law of nations;

[11] To declare war, grant letters of marque and reprisal, and make rules concerning captures on land and water;

[12] To raise and support armies, but no appropriation of money to that use shall be for a longer term than two years;

[13] To provide and maintain a navy;

[14] To make rules for the government and regulation of the land and naval forces;

[15] To provide for calling forth the militia to execute the laws of the Union, suppress insurrections, and repel invasions;

[16] To provide for organizing, arming and disciplining the militia, and for governing such part of them as may be employed in the service of the United States, reserving to the States respectively the appointment of the officers, and the authority of training the militia according to the discipline prescribed by Congress;

[17] To exercise exclusive legislation in all cases whatsoever over such district (not exceeding ten miles square) as may, by cession of particular States and the acceptance of Congress, become the seat of the Government of the United States, and to exercise like authority over all places purchased by the consent of the legislature of the State in which the same shall be, for the erection of forts, magazines, arsenals, dockyards, and other needful buildings;

[18] To make all laws which shall be necessary and proper for carrying into execution the foregoing powers, and all other powers vested by this Constitution in the Government of the United States, or in any department or officer thereof.

SECTION IX

[1] The migration or importation of such persons as any of the States now existing shall think proper to admit shall not be prohibited by the Congress prior to the year one thousand eight hundred and eight, but a tax or duty may be imposed on such importation, not exceeding ten dollars for each person.

[2] The privilege of the writ of habeas corpus shall not be suspended, unless when in cases of rebellion or invasion the public safety may require it.

[3] No bill of attainder or ex post facto law shall be passed.

[4] No capitation or other direct tax shall be laid, unless in proportion to the census or enumeration hereinbefore directed to be taken.

[5] No tax or duty shall be laid on articles exported from any State.

[6] No preference shall be given by any regulation of commerce or revenue to the ports of one State over those of another; nor shall vessels bound to or from one State be obliged to enter, clear or pay duties in another.

[7] No money shall be drawn from the Treasury but in consequence of appropriations made by law; and a regular statement and account of the receipts and expenditures of all public money shall be published from time to time.

[8] No title of nobility shall be granted by the United States; and no person holding any office of profit or trust under them shall, without the consent of the Congress, accept of any present, emolument, office, or title of any kind whatever from any king, prince, or foreign state.

SECTION X

[1] No State shall enter into any treaty, alliance, or confederation; grant letters of marque and reprisal; coin money; emit bills of credit; make anything but gold and silver coin a tender in payment of debts; pass any bill of attainder, ex post facto law or law impairing the obligation of contracts, or grant any title of nobility.

[2] No State shall, without the consent of the Congress, lay any imposts or duties on imports or exports, except what may be absolutely necessary for executing its inspection laws; and the net produce of all duties and imposts, laid by any State on imports or exports, shall be for the use of the Treasury of the United States; and all such laws shall be subject to the revision and control of the Congress.

[3] No State shall, without the consent of Congress, lay any duty of tonnage, keep troops and ships of war in time of peace, enter into any agreement or compact with another State or with a foreign power, or engage in war, unless actually invaded or in such imminent danger as will not admit of delay.

ARTICLE II

SECTION I

[1] The executive power shall be vested in a President of the United States of America. He shall hold his office during the term of four years, and together with the Vice-President, chosen for the same term, be elected as follows:

[2] Each State shall appoint, in such manner as the legislature thereof may direct, a number of Electors, equal to the whole number of Senators and Representatives to which the State may be entitled in the Congress; but no Senator or Representative, or person holding an office of trust or profit under the United States, shall be appointed an Elector.

[3] The Electors shall meet in their respective States and vote by ballot for two persons, of whom one at least shall not be an inhabitant of the same State with themselves. And they shall make a list of all the persons voted for, and of the number of votes for each; which list they shall sign and certify, and transmit sealed to the seat of government of the United States, directed to the President of the Senate. The President of the Senate shall, in the presence of the Senate and House of Representatives, open all the certificates, and the votes shall then be counted. The person having the greatest number of votes shall be the President, if such number be a majority of the whole number of Electors appointed; and if there be more than one who have such majority, and have an equal number of votes, then the House of Representatives shall immediately choose by ballot one of them for President; and if no person have a majority, then from the five highest on the list the said House shall in like manner choose the President. But in choosing the President the votes shall be taken by States, the representation from each State having one vote; a quorum for this purpose shall consist of a member or members from two-thirds of the States, and a majority of all the States shall be necessary to a choice. In every case, after the choice of the President, the person having the greatest number of votes of the Electors shall be the Vice-President. But if there should remain two or more who have equal votes, the Senate shall choose from them by ballot the Vice-President.

[4] The Congress may determine the time of choosing the Electors and the day on which they shall give their votes, which day shall be the same throughout the United States.

[5] No person except a natural-born citizen, or citizen of the United States at the time of the adoption of this Constitution, shall be eligible to the office of President; neither shall any person be eligible to that office who shall not have attained to the age of thirty-five years, and been fourteen years a resident within the United States.

[6] In case of the removal of the President from office, or of his death, resignation, or inability to discharge the powers and duties of the said office, the same shall devolve on the Vice-President, and the Congress may by law provide for the case of removal, death, resignation, or inability, both of the President and Vice-President, declaring what officer shall then act as President, and such officer shall act accordingly until the disability be removed or a President shall be elected.

[7] The President shall, at stated times, receive for his services a compensation, which shall neither be increased nor diminished during the period for which he shall have been elected, and he shall not receive within that period any other emolument from the United States or any of them.

[8] Before he enter on the execution of his office he shall take the following oath or affirmation:

"I do solemnly swear (or affirm) that I will faithfully execute the office of President of the United States, and will to the best of my ability preserve, protect, and defend the Constitution of the United States."

SECTION II

[1] The President shall be Commander-in-Chief of the Army and Navy of the United States, and of the militia of the several States when called into the actual service of the United States; he may require the opinion, in writing, of the principal officer in each of the executive departments, upon any subject relating to the duties of their respective offices, and he shall have power to grant reprieves and pardons for offenses against the United States, except in cases of impeachment.

[2] He shall have power, by and with the advice and consent of the Senate, to make treaties, provided two-thirds of the Senators present concur; and he shall nominate, and, by and with the advice and consent of the Senate, shall appoint ambassadors, other public ministers and consuls, judges of the Supreme Court, and all other officers of the United States whose appointments are not herein otherwise provided for, and which shall be established by law; but the Congress may by law vest the appointment of such inferior officers, as they think proper, in the President alone, in the courts of law, or in the heads of departments.

[3] The President shall have power to fill up all vacancies that may happen during the recess of the Senate, by granting commissions which shall expire at the end of their next session.

SECTION III

He shall from time to time give to the Congress information of the state of the Union, and recommend to their consideration such measures as he shall judge necessary and expedient; he may, on extraordinary occasions, convene both Houses, or either of them, and in case of disagreement between them with respect to the time of adjournment, he may adjourn them to such time as he shall think proper; he shall receive ambassadors and other public ministers; he shall take care that the laws be faithfully executed, and shall commission all the officers of the United States.

SECTION IV

The President, Vice-President and all civil officers of the United States shall be removed from office on impeachment for and conviction of treason, bribery, or other high crimes and misdemeanors.

ARTICLE III

SECTION I

The judicial power of the United States shall be vested in one Supreme Court, and in such inferior courts as the Congress may from time to time ordain and establish. The judges, both of the Supreme and inferior courts, shall hold their offices during good behavior, and shall, at stated times, receive for their services a compensation which shall not be diminished during their continuance in office.

SECTION II

[1] The judicial power shall extend to all cases, in law and equity, arising under this Constitution, the laws of the United States, and treaties made, or which shall be made, under their authority; to all cases affecting ambassadors, other public ministers, and consuls; to all cases of admiralty and maritime jurisdiction; to controversies to which the United States shall be a party; to controversies between two or more States; between a State and citizens of another State; between citizens of different States; between citizens of the same State claiming lands under grants of different States, and between a State, or the citizens thereof, and foreign states, citizens, or subjects.

[2] In all cases affecting ambassadors, other public ministers and consuls, and those in which a State shall be party, the Supreme Court shall have original jurisdiction. In all the other cases before mentioned the Supreme Court shall have

appellate jurisdiction, both as to law and fact, with such exceptions and under such regulations as the Congress shall make.

[3] The trial of all crimes, except in cases of impeachment, shall be by jury; and such trial shall be held in the State where the said crimes shall have been committed; but when not committed within any State, the trial shall be at such place or places as the Congress may by law have directed.

SECTION III

[1] Treason against the United States shall consist only in levying war against them, or in adhering to their enemies, giving them aid and comfort. No person shall be convicted of treason unless on the testimony of two witnesses to the same overt act, or on confession in open court.

[2] The Congress shall have power to declare the punishment of treason, but no attainder of treason shall work corruption of blood or forfeiture except during the life of the person attainted.

ARTICLE IV

SECTION I

Full faith and credit shall be given in each State to the public acts, records, and judicial proceedings of every other State. And the Congress may by general laws prescribe the manner in which such acts, records, and proceedings shall be proved, and the effect thereof.

SECTION II

[1] The citizens of each State shall be entitled to all privileges and immunities of citizens in the several States.

[2] A person charged in any State with treason, felony, or other crime, who shall flee from justice, and be found in another State, shall, on demand of the executive authority of the State from which he fled, be delivered up, to be removed to the State having jurisdiction of the crime.

[3] No person held to service or labor in one State, under the laws thereof, escaping into another, shall, in consequence of any law or regulation therein, be discharged from such service or labor, but shall be delivered up on claim to the party to whom such service or labor may be due.

SECTION III

[1] New States may be admitted by the Congress into this Union; but no new State shall be formed or erected within the jurisdiction of any other State; nor any State be formed by the junction of two or more States or parts of States, without the consent of the legislatures of the States concerned as well as of the Congress.

[2] The Congress shall have power to dispose of and make all needful rules and regulations respecting the territory or other property belonging to the United States; and nothing in this Constitution shall be so construed as to prejudice any claims of the United States or of any particular State.

SECTION IV

The United States shall guarantee to every State in this Union a republican form of government, and shall protect each of them against invasion, and on application of the legislature, or of the executive (when the legislature cannot be convened), against domestic violence.

ARTICLE V

The Congress, whenever two-thirds of both Houses shall deem it necessary, shall propose amendments to this Constitution, or, on the application of the legislatures of two-thirds of the several States, shall call a convention for proposing amendments, which in either case shall be valid to all intents and purposes as part of this Constitution, when ratified by the legislatures of three-fourths of the several States, or by conventions in three-fourths thereof, as the one or the other mode of ratification may be proposed by the Congress; provided that no amendment which may be made prior to the year one thousand eight hundred and eight shall in any manner affect the first and fourth clauses in the Ninth Section of the First Article; and that no State, without its consent shall be deprived of its equal suffrage in the Senate.

ARTICLE VI

[1] All debts contracted and engagements entered into, before the adoption of this Constitution, shall be as valid against the United States under this Constitution as under the Confederation.

[2] This Constitution, and the laws of the United States which shall be made in pursuance thereof, and all treaties made, or which shall be made, under the authority of the United States, shall be the supreme law of the land; and the judges in every State shall be bound thereby, anything in the Constitution or laws of any State to the contrary notwithstanding.

[3] The Senators and Representatives before mentioned and the members of the several State legislatures, and all executive and judicial officers both of the United States and of the several States, shall be bound by oath or affirmation to support this Constitution; but no religious test shall ever be required as a qualification to any office or public trust under the United States.

ARTICLE VII

The ratification of the conventions of nine States shall be sufficient for the establishment of this Constitution between the States so ratifying the same.

AMENDMENT I

Congress shall make no law respecting an establishment of religion, or prohibiting the free exercise thereof; or abridging the freedom of speech or of the press; or the right of the people peaceably to assemble, and to petition the government for a redress of grievances.

AMENDMENT II

A well-regulated militia being necessary to the security of a free State, the right of the people to keep and bear arms shall not be infringed.

AMENDMENT III

No soldier shall, in time of peace, be quartered in any house without the consent of the owner, nor in time of war, but in a manner to be prescribed by law.

AMENDMENT IV

The right of the people to be secure in their persons, houses, papers, and effects, against unreasonable searches and seizures, shall not be violated, and no warrants shall issue but upon probable cause, supported by oath or affirmation, and particularly describing the place to be searched, and the persons or things to be seized.

AMENDMENT V

No person shall be held to answer for a capital, or otherwise infamous crime, unless on a presentment or indictment of a grand jury, except in cases arising in the land or naval forces, or in the militia, when in actual service in time of war or public danger; nor shall any person be subject for the same offense to be twice put in jeopardy of life or limb; nor shall be compelled in any criminal case to be a witness against himself, nor be deprived of life, liberty or property, without due process of law; nor shall private property be taken for public use without just compensation.

AMENDMENT VI

In all criminal prosecutions, the accused shall enjoy the right to a speedy and public trial, by an impartial jury of the State and district wherein the crime shall have been committed, which district shall have been previously ascertained by law, and to be informed of the nature and cause of the accusation; to be confronted with the witnesses against him; to have compulsory process for obtaining witnesses in his favor, and to have the assistance of counsel for his defense.

AMENDMENT VII

In suits at common law, where the value in controversy shall exceed twenty dollars, the right of trial by jury shall be preserved, and no fact tried by a jury shall be otherwise re-examined in any court of the United States, than according to the rules of the common law.

AMENDMENT VIII

Excessive bail shall not be required, nor excessive fines imposed, nor cruel and unusual punishments inflicted.

AMENDMENT IX

The enumeration in the Constitution of certain rights shall not be construed to deny or disparage others retained by the people.

AMENDMENT X

The powers not delegated to the United States by the Constitution, nor prohibited by it to the States, are reserved to the States respectively, or to the people.

AMENDMENT XI

The judicial power of the United States shall not be construed to extend to any suit in law or equity, commenced or prosecuted against one of the United States by citizens of another State, or by citizens or subjects of any foreign state.

AMENDMENT XII

[1] The Electors shall meet in their respective States and vote by ballot for President and Vice-President, one of whom, at least, shall not be an inhabitant of the same State with themselves; they shall name in their ballots the person voted for as President, and in distinct ballots the person voted for as Vice-President, and they shall make distinct lists of all persons voted for as President and of all persons voted for as Vice-President, and of the number of votes for each; which lists they shall sign and certify, and transmit sealed to the seat of the government of the United States, directed to the President of the Senate. The President of the Senate shall, in the presence of the Senate and House of Representatives, open all the certificates and the votes shall then be counted. The person having the greatest

number of votes for President shall be the President, if such number be a majority of the whole number of Electors appointed; and if no person have such majority, then from the persons having the highest numbers not exceeding three on the list of those voted for as President, the House of Representatives shall choose immediately, by ballot, the President. But in choosing the President the votes shall be taken by States, the representation from each State having one vote; a quorum for this purpose shall consist of a member or members from two-thirds of the States, and a majority of all the States shall be necessary to a choice. And if the House of Representatives shall not choose a President whenever the right of choice shall devolve upon them, before the fourth day of March next following, then the Vice-President shall act as President, as in the case of the death or other constitutional disability of the President.

[2] The person having the greatest number of votes as Vice-President shall be the Vice-President, if such number be a majority of the whole number of Electors appointed; and if no person have a majority, then from the two highest numbers on the list the Senate shall choose the Vice-President; a quorum for the purpose shall consist of two-thirds of the whole number of Senators, and a majority of the whole number shall be necessary to a choice. But no person constitutionally ineligible to the office of President shall be eligible to that of Vice-President of the United States.

AMENDMENT XIII

SECTION I

Neither slavery nor involuntary servitude, except as a punishment for crime whereof the party shall have been duly convicted, shall exist within the United States, or any place subject to their jurisdiction.

SECTION II

Congress shall have power to enforce this article by appropriate legislation.

AMENDMENT XIV

SECTION I

All persons born or naturalized in the United States, and subject to the jurisdiction thereof, are citizens of the United States and of the State wherein they reside. No State shall make or enforce any law which shall abridge the privileges or immunities of citizens of the United States; nor shall any State deprive any person of life, liberty or property, without due process of law; nor deny to any person within its jurisdiction the equal protection of the laws.

SECTION II

Representatives shall be apportioned among the several States according to their respective numbers, counting the whole number of persons in each State, excluding Indians not taxed. But when the right to vote at any election for the choice of Electors for President and Vice-President of the United States, Representatives in Congress, the executive and judicial officers of a State, or the members of the legislature thereof, is denied to any of the male inhabitants of such State, being twenty-one years of age, and citizens of the United States, or in any way abridged except for participation in rebellion or other crime, the basis of representation therein shall be reduced in the proportion which the number of such male citizens shall bear to the whole number of male citizens twenty-one years of age in such State.

SECTION III

No person shall be a Senator or Representative in Congress, or elector of President and Vice-President, or hold any office, civil or military, under the United States or under any State, who, having previously taken an oath as a member of Congress, or as an officer of the United States, or as a member of any State legislature, or as an executive or judicial officer of any State, to support the Constitution of the United States, shall have engaged in insurrection or rebellion against the same, or given aid or comfort to the enemies thereof. But Congress may, by a vote of two-thirds of each House, remove such disability.

SECTION IV

The validity of the public debt of the United States, authorized by law, including debts incurred for payment of pensions and bounties for services in suppressing insurrection or rebellion, shall not be questioned. But neither the United States nor any State shall assume or pay any debt or obligation incurred in aid of insurrection or rebellion against the United States, or any claim for the loss or emancipation of any slave; but all such debts, obligations, and claims shall be held illegal and void.

SECTION V

The Congress shall have power to enforce, by appropriate legislation, the provisions of this article.

AMENDMENT XV

SECTION I

The right of citizens of the United States to vote shall not be denied or abridged by the United States or by any State on account of race, color, or previous condition of servitude.

SECTION II

The Congress shall have power to enforce this article by appropriate legislation.

AMENDMENT XVI

The Congress shall have power to lay and collect taxes on incomes, from whatever source derived, without apportionment among the several States, and without regard to any census or enumeration.

AMENDMENT XVII

SECTION I

The Senate of the United States shall be composed of two Senators from each State, elected by the people thereof, for six years; and each Senator shall have one vote. The electors in each State shall have the qualifications requisite for electors of the most numerous branch of the State legislatures.

SECTION II

When vacancies happen in the representation of any State in the Senate, the executive authority of such State shall issue writs of election to fill such vacancies: Provided, that the legislature of any State may empower the executive thereof to make temporary appointments until the people fill the vacancies by election as the legislature may direct.

SECTION III

This amendment shall not be so construed as to affect the election or term of any Senator chosen before it becomes valid as part of the Constitution.

AMENDMENT XVIII

SECTION I

After one year from the ratification of this article the manufacture, sale or transportation of intoxicating liquors within, the importation thereof into, or the exportation thereof from the United States and all territory subject to the jurisdiction thereof, for beverage purposes, is hereby prohibited.

SECTION II

The Congress and the several States shall have concurrent power to enforce this article by appropriate legislation.

SECTION III

This article shall be inoperative unless it shall have been ratified as an amendment to the Constitution by the legislatures of the several States, as provided in the Constitution, within seven years from the date of the submission hereof to the States by the Congress.

AMENDMENT XIX

SECTION I

The right of citizens of the United States to vote shall not be denied or abridged by the United States or by any State on account of sex.

SECTION II

Congress shall have power to enforce this article by appropriate legislation.

AMENDMENT XX

SECTION I

The terms of the President and Vice-President shall end at noon on the 20th day of January, and the terms of Senators and Representatives at noon on the 3d day of January, of the years in which such terms would have ended if this article had not been ratified; and the terms of their successors shall then begin.

SECTION II

The Congress shall assemble at least once in every year, and such meeting shall begin at noon on the 3d day of January, unless they shall by law appoint a different day.

SECTION III

If, at the time fixed for the beginning of the term of the President, the President-elect shall have died, the Vice-President-elect shall become President. If a President shall not have been chosen before the time fixed for the beginning of his term or if the President-elect shall have failed to qualify, then the Vice-President-elect shall act as President until a President shall have qualified; and the Congress may by law provide for the case wherein neither a President-elect nor a Vice-President-elect shall have qualified, declaring who shall then act as President, or the manner in which one who is to act shall be selected, and such person shall act accordingly until a President or Vice-President shall have qualified.

SECTION IV

The Congress may by law provide for the case of the death of any of the persons from whom the House of Representatives may choose a President whenever the right of choice shall have devolved upon them, and for the case of death of any of the persons from whom the Senate may choose a Vice-President whenever the right of choice shall have devolved upon them.

SECTION V

Sections I and II shall take effect on the 15th day of October following the ratification of this article.

SECTION VI

This article shall be inoperative unless it shall have been ratified as an amendment to the Constitution by the legislatures of three-fourths of the several States within seven years from the date of its submission.

AMENDMENT XXI

SECTION I

The eighteenth article of amendment to the Constitution of the United States is hereby repealed.

SECTION II

The transportation or importation into any State, territory, or possession of the United States for delivery or use therein of intoxicating liquors, in violation of the laws thereof, is hereby prohibited.

SECTION III

This article shall be inoperative unless it shall have been ratified as an amendment to the Constitution by conventions in the several States, as provided in the Constitution, within seven years from the date of the submission hereof to the States by the Congress.

AMENDMENT XXII

SECTION I

No person shall be elected to the office of President more than twice, and no person who has held the office of President, or acted as President, for more than two years of a term to which some other person was elected President shall be elected to the office of President more than once. But this Article shall not apply to any person holding the office of President when this Article was proposed by the Congress, and shall not prevent any person who may be holding the office of President, or acting as President, during the term within which this Article becomes operative from holding the office of President or acting as President during the remainder of such term.

SECTION II

This article shall be inoperative unless it shall have been ratified as an amendment to the Constitution by the legislatures of three-fourths of the several States within seven years from the date of its submission to the States by the Congress.

AMENDMENT XXIII

SECTION I

The District constituting the seat of Government of the United States shall appoint in such manner as the Congress may direct:

A number of electors of President and Vice-President equal to the whole number of Senators and Representatives in Congress to which the District would be entitled if it were a State, but in no event more than the least populous State; they shall be in addition to those appointed by the States, but they shall be considered, for the purposes of the election of President and Vice-President, to be electors appointed by a State; and they shall meet in the District and perform such duties as provided by the twelfth article of amendment.

SECTION II

The Congress shall have power to enforce this article by appropriate legislation.

AMENDMENT XXIV

SECTION I

The right of citizens of the United States to vote in any primary or other election for President or Vice-President, for electors for President or Vice-President, or for Senator or Representative in Congress, shall not be denied or abridged by the United States or any State by reason of failure to pay any poll tax or other tax.

SECTION II

The Congress shall have power to enforce this article by appropriate legislation.

AMENDMENT XXV

SECTION I

In case of the removal of the President from office or of his death or resignation, the Vice-President shall become President.

SECTION II

Whenever there is a vacancy in the office of the Vice-President, the President shall nominate a Vice-President who shall take office upon confirmation by a majority vote of both Houses of Congress.

SECTION III

Whenever the President transmits to the President pro tempore of the Senate and the Speaker of the House of Representatives his written declaration that he is unable to discharge the powers and duties of his office, and until he transmits to them a written declaration to the contrary, such powers and duties shall be discharged by the Vice-President as Acting President.

SECTION IV

Whenever the Vice-President and a majority of either the principal officers of the executive departments or of such other body as Congress may by law provide, transmit to the President pro tempore of the Senate and the Speaker of the House of Representatives their written declaration that the President is unable to discharge the powers and duties of his office, the Vice-President shall immediately assume the powers and duties of the office as Acting President.

Thereafter, when the President transmits to the President pro tempore of the Senate and the Speaker of the House of Representatives his written declaration that no inability exists, he shall resume the powers and duties of his office unless the Vice-President and a majority of either the principal officers of the executive department or of such other body as Congress may by law provide, transmit within four days to the President pro tempore of the Senate and the Speaker of the House of Representatives their written declaration that the President is unable to discharge the powers and duties of his office. Thereupon Congress shall decide the issue, assembling within forty-eight hours for that purpose if not in session. If the Congress, within twenty-one days after receipt of the latter written declaration, or, if Congress is not in session, within twenty-one days after Congress is required to assemble, determines by two-thirds vote of both Houses that the President is unable to discharge the powers and duties of his office, the Vice-President shall continue to discharge the same as Acting President; otherwise, the President shall resume the powers and duties of his office.

AMENDMENT XXVI

SECTION I

The right of citizens of the United States, who are eighteen years of age or older, to vote shall not be denied or abridged by the United States or by any State on account of age.

SECTION II

The Congress shall have power to enforce this article by appropriate legislation.

---

gives the states power over the conduct of Federal elections but permits the Congress to alter such regulations at any time. In 1842 the Congress imposed the district system on the United States. In 1962 the Supreme Court dealt with proper apportionment of election districts and in its decision in *Baker* vs. *Carr* allowed voters to go into a Federal court to force equitable representation in a state legislature. This decision was, however, based on the equal protection clause of the Fourteenth Amendment. Later, the court ruled (1964) that state legislative apportionment must reflect the one-man one-vote principle. As a legislative body Congress has certain inherent powers. Among these are the power to investigate pursuant to legislative needs. Congressional investigations have led to a great many court decisions concerning the right of a witness before a Congressional committee to refuse to testify even when granted immunity from prosecution. Section 8 of Article 1 lists the enumerated powers of the Congress. The clause of this section, the "commerce clause," which grants the Congress the right to "regulate commerce with foreign nations, and among the several States," has, in the 20th cent., been used as a strong argument for the expansion of government power. Since the historic case of GIBBONS VS. OGDEN, the commerce clause has been the battleground over which much of the struggle for and against increased Federal regulation of private enterprise has been fought. Until the late 1930s Congress exercised its powers under the clause solely with reference to transportation. But after a series of dramatic reversals by the Supreme Court, Congress began to enter areas that had previously been controlled only by the states. The commerce clause is now the source of important peacetime powers of the national government and an important basis for the judicial review of state actions. Besides its enumerated and inherent powers, the Congress has implied powers under Article 1 "to make all laws which shall be necessary and proper for carrying into execution" the enumerated or expressed powers. Sections 9 and 10 of Article 1 contain guarantees of the writ of HABEAS CORPUS, prohibit bills of attainder and ex post facto laws, and also improve certain limitations on state power. Article 2 creates the executive branch of government headed by the President, elected, along with the Vice President, for a term of four years (see PRESIDENT; ELECTORAL COLLEGE). The Twenty-second Amendment (1951) provides that no person may be elected President more than twice. The Twenty-third Amendment (1961) permits District of Columbia residents to vote in presidential elections. Since the adoption of the Constitution there have been two conflicting views of Article 2. The first is that the powers of the President are limited to those enumerated in the article. The opposite view is that the President is given executive power not limited by the provisions of the rest of the article. Every President has had to make the choice of interpretations for himself. Article 3 provides for a judiciary and defines TREASON. Besides its enumerated powers, the judiciary has the inherent authority to interpret laws and the Constitution with an authority that must be deferred to. Article 3 also guarantees trial by jury in criminal cases and lays the basis for Federal jurisdiction. The Eleventh Amendment (1798), which prohibits suits against any state by citizens of another state or foreigners (see SOVEREIGNTY), was passed in reaction to the Supreme Court's accepting jurisdiction of a suit against a state by a citizen of another state. Article 4, dealing with the relations of the states (see CONFLICT OF LAWS), provides that "Full faith and credit shall be given in each State to the public acts, records, and judicial proceedings of every other State." Section 2 prohibits any state from discriminating against citizens of other states in favor of its own and provides for the extradition of criminals. The article guarantees a republican form of government to every state and provides for the admission of new states as well as the government of territories. Article 5 provides for amending the Constitution (see AMENDMENT). Article 6 establishes the supremacy of the Federal Constitution and laws in case of conflict with those of the states. This clause is the heart of the Federal system. Article 6 also provides for an oath of office for members of the three branches of the Federal government and the states and specifically forbids any religious qualification for office. Article 7 declares that the Constitution should go into force when ratified by nine states. The Constitution has undergone gradual alteration with the growth of the country. Some of the 26 amendments were brought on by Supreme Court decisions. The first 9 amendments, which constitute the Bill of Rights, were added, however, within two years of the signing of the Federal Constitution in order to ensure sufficient guarantees of individual liberties. The Bill of Rights applied only to the Federal government. But since the passage of the FOURTEENTH AMENDMENT (1868), many of the guarantees contained in the Bill of Rights have been extended to the states through the "due process" clause of the Fourteenth Amendment. The First Amendment guarantees the freedom of worship, of speech, of the press, of assembly, and of petition to the government for redress of grievances. This amendment has been the center of controversy in recent years in the areas of free speech and religion. The Supreme Court has held that freedom of speech does not include the right to refuse to testify before a Congressional investigating committee and that any organized prayer in the public schools violates the First Amendment. The Second Amendment guarantees the right to bear arms openly—adopted with reference to state militias. Freedom from the quartering of soldiers without the consent of the owner of the house is guaranteed by the Third Amendment. The Fourth Amendment guarantees against unreasonable search and seizure. This safeguard has only recently been extended to the states. The Fifth Amendment provides that no person shall be held for "a capital or otherwise infamous crime" without indictment, be twice put in "jeopardy of life or limb" for the same offense, be compelled to testify against himself, or "be deprived of life, liberty or property, without due process of law." The privilege against self-incrimination has been the center of a great deal of controversy as a result of the growth of Congressional investigations. The phrase "due process of law," which appears in the Fifth Amendment, is also included in the Fourteenth Amendment. As a result there has been much debate as to whether both amendments guarantee the same rights. Those in favor of what is termed fixed due process claim that all the safeguards applied against the Federal government should be also applied against the states through the Fourteenth Amendment. The supporters of the concept of flexible due process are willing only to impose those guarantees on the states that "are implicit in the concept of ordered liberty." The Sixth Amendment guarantees the right of a speedy and public trial by an impartial jury in all criminal proceedings, while the Seventh Amendment guarantees the right of trial by jury in all common-law suits "where the value in controversy shall exceed twenty dollars," and the Eighth Amendment prohibits excessive bail and fines and "cruel and unusual" punishment. The Ninth Amendment states that "The enumeration in the Constitution of certain rights shall not be construed to deny or disparage others retained by the people." By the Tenth Amendment, generally considered with the first nine (they all went into effect in 1791), "The powers not delegated to the United States by the Constitution, nor prohibited by it to the States, are reserved to the States respectively, or to the people." Powers reserved to the states are often termed "residual powers." This amendment, like the commerce clause, has been a battleground in the struggle against states' rights and for Federal supremacy. The Eleventh Amendment has already been discussed under Article 3. The Twelfth (1804) revised the method of electing President and Vice President. The Thirteenth (1865), Fourteenth (1868), and Fifteenth (1870) amendments, arising out of the Civil War and Reconstruction, abolish slavery and guarantee civil rights and the suffrage to U.S. citizens, including former slaves. The Sixteenth Amendment (1913) authorizes the INCOME TAX. The Seventeenth has been described under Article 1. The Eighteenth (1919)—repealed by the Twenty-first (1933)—introduced PROHIBITION. The Nineteenth (1920) grants WOMAN SUFFRAGE. The Twentieth (1933) abolishes the so-called lame-duck Congress and alters the date of the presidential inauguration. The Twenty-second and the Twenty-third amendments have been discussed under Article 2. The Twenty-fourth Amendment (1964) outlaws the poll tax and any other tax as a requirement for voting in primaries and elections for Federal office. The Twenty-fifth (1967) establishes the procedure for filling the office of Vice President between elections and for governing in the event of presidential disability. The Twenty-sixth (1971) lowers the voting age in all elections to 18. In 1972 an amendment prohibiting all legal forms of discrimination based on sex was submitted to the states for ratification. The wording of the Constitution is general, necessitating interpretation, and any short summary is only rough and approximate. From its very beginnings, the Constitution has been subject to violent controversies, not only in interpretation of some of its phrases, but also between the "loose constructionists" and "strict constructionists." The middle of the 19th cent. saw a tremendous struggle concerning the nature of the Union and the extent of states' rights. The Civil War decided the case in favor of the advocates of strong union, and since that time the general tendency has been toward the centralization and strengthening of Federal power. See C. A. Beard, *An Economic Interpretation of the Constitution* (1913, repr. 1965); C. H. McIlwain, *Constitutionalism, Ancient and Modern* (rev. ed. 1947, repr. 1958); Edward Dumbauld, *The Bill of Rights and What It Means Today* (1957) and *The Constitution of the United States* (1964); A. H. Kelly and W. A. Harbison, *The American Constitution* (4th ed. 1970); E. S. Corwin, *The Constitution and What It Means Today* (13th rev. ed. 1973); Rexford Tugwell, *The Emerging Constitution* (1974).

Constitutions, Apostolic, late 4th-century compilation, in eight books, of administrative canons for the clergy and the laity and of guides for worship. They were supposed to be works of the apostles, but actually included the greater part of the *Didascalia Apostolorum,* a lost Greek treatise of 3d-century origin, most of the DIDACHE, and fragments from Hippolytus and Papias. The work concludes with a collection of 85 moral and liturgical canons known as the "Apostolic Canons," a portion of which became part of canon law of the Western Church. The work is thought to be of Syrian origin. The whole is a valuable primary source on early church history and practice.

constructivism, Russian art movement founded c.1913 by Vladimir Tatlin (1885–1956), related to the movement known as SUPREMATISM. After 1916 the brothers Naum (Pevsner) Gabo and Antoine Pevsner gave new impetus to Tatlin's art of purely abstract constructions. Their sculptural works derived from cubism and futurism, but had a more architectonic emphasis, related to the technology of the society in which they were created. The Soviet regime at first encouraged this new style. However, beginning in 1921, constructivism (and all modern art movements) were officially disparaged as unsuitable for mass propaganda purposes. Gabo and Pevsner went into exile, while Tatlin remained in Russia. In theatrical scene design constructivism spread beyond Russia through the efforts of Vsevolod MEYERHOLD. See George Rickey, *Constructivism* (1967).

consubstantiation: see LORD'S SUPPER.

consul, title of the two chief magistrates of ancient Rome. The institution is supposed to have arisen with the expulsion of the kings, traditionally in 510 B.C., and it was well established by the early 4th cent. B.C. The consuls led the troops, controlled the treasury, and were supreme in the government. At first only patricians were eligible, but in 367 B.C. the Licinian law opened the office to plebeians. Before becoming consul a man generally had to have experience as quaestor, aedile, and praetor, and the minimum age for a consul was normally set at 40 or 45. Ex-consuls became provincial governors as proconsuls. The year was identified by the names of the two consuls in office during that time. Under the empire the title of consul was continued, but only as a title of honor, sometimes conferred on infants or small boys.

consular service, organized body of public officers maintained by a government in the important ports and trade centers of foreign countries to protect the persons and interests of its nationals and to aid them in every possible way. Consuls are officially recognized by a foreign state through the issuance of an authorization known as an exequatur, which may be revoked by the admitting state at any time. The many duties of U.S. consuls in foreign states include promoting and protecting American commercial interests; issuing passports and verifying citizenship; certifying the sanitary conditions of the cargo, crew, and passengers of vessels leaving for U.S. ports; and mediating with local officials in cases of legal matters involving American citizens. The consular service was once strictly distinguished from the DIPLOMATIC SERVICE, but because of the interrelated duties of the two branches, the Rogers Act of 1924 consolidated both into the Foreign Service of the Department of State. The Department of Commerce and the Department of the Treasury may place commercial attachés at a consulate office to aid in gathering statistics and promoting trade. The persons of consuls enjoy immunity and EXTRATERRITORIALITY in all matters pertaining to their official functions, and the premises of consulates are likewise privileged. Such privileges are granted either by courtesy or through special consular treaties.

Consulate, 1799–1804, in French history, form of government established after the coup d'etat of 18 Brumaire (Nov. 9–10, 1799), which ended the DIRECTORY. Three consuls were appointed to rule France—Napoleon Bonaparte (see NAPOLEON I), Emmanuel Joseph SIEYÈS, and Roger Ducos. Sieyès and Ducos were soon replaced by Jean Jacques Régis de CAMBACÉRÈS and C. F. LEBRUN, and the Consulate became little more than a scheme for autocratic government by Bonaparte, who was made first consul for life in 1802 and emperor in 1804.

Consumer Affairs, Office of, agency of the U.S. Department of Health, Education, and Welfare; established 1971. The office advises and represents the President on matters of consumer interest and analyzes and coordinates activities of the Federal government in the area of consumer protection. It conducts investigations and surveys on matters of consumer interest, takes action on individual consumer complaints, makes available to the public information the government has acquired in making its own purchases, and presses for legislation to protect the consumer.

Consumers' League, National, organization designed to promote better conditions among workers by encouraging the purchase of articles made and sold under good working conditions. The movement started in England (1890); the U.S. group was founded (1899) by Florence Kelley and her followers. The league undertook to investigate factories and to educate consumers in purchasing habits. For many years the league used a label for goods which had passed inspection, and many consumers learned to purchase only those goods thus labeled. Many of the objectives of the league are now a matter of law, e.g., shorter hours, a minimum wage, payment for overtime, and the abolition in most states of child labor. It has a membership of about 15,000. See Maud Nathan, *Story of an Epoch-making Movement* (1926).

Consumers' Union, product testing and rating organization founded (1936) to provide consumers with information and counsel regarding major retail goods and services. Through its monthly *Consumer Reports* (circulation c.2 million), the union reports on a diverse range of products, from major appliances and automobiles to health-care and family-planning aids. The organization, whose headquarters is in Mount Vernon, N.Y., also represents consumer interests at government hearings.

consumption, in economics, utilization of goods and services. Consumption may be considered either productive or unproductive. Productive consumption involves wealth used in the process of producing other wealth (e.g., the use of materials and capital to produce other goods), and unproductive consumption involves using wealth for the direct satisfaction of human wants. In a second sense, consumption is viewed as a basically subjective phenomenon, with individual utility, or satisfaction, assuming primary importance. The foremost economist associated with the subjective view was Jeremy Bentham (1748–1832), whose English followers long sought to measure quantitatively the utility provided by consumption. The process of consumption is central to any system of economics; Adam Smith made it the sole end of production. Production, the wholesale and retail trades, and consumption are closely linked, and the exchange of goods and services for money along the various stages from the producer to the ultimate consumer is the foundation of modern capitalist economy. Advertising is today the chief means by which manufacturers and retailers seek to increase consumption, leading many to contend that modern consumption is often governed by false needs. Since the introduction of the theories of John Maynard KEYNES, contemporary economics has increasingly concerned itself with studying total consumption, in the hope that a better understanding of its relationship to national income would lead to effective governmental control of the business cycle. Experience has shown that through taxation the modern government is often able to regulate the amount of its citizenry's disposable income, thus ultimately affecting the nation's total consumption. See E. W. Gilboy, *Primer on the Economics of Consumption* (1968); Thomas Mayer, *Permanent Income, Wealth, and Consumption* (1973).

contact lens, thin plastic lens worn between the eye and eyelid that may be used instead of eyeglasses. Actors, models, and others wear them for appearance, and athletes use them for safety and convenience. Contact lenses may also be used to correct certain abnormalities of the eye that cannot be corrected by regular glasses. A. E. Fick, a Swiss physician, made the first contact lens in 1887. The heavy glass lenses exerted an uncomfortable pressure on the eyeball, covered the entire eye surface, and were difficult to fit. In 1938 the first plastic contact lens was made by Theodore E. Obrig from a newly discovered methylmethacrylate plastic, known as Plexiglas or Lucite, that could be molded into shape. He also devised a quick way to fit the lens that did not involve months of trial and error. The major drawback was that a solution placed between the lens and eye had to be changed every few hours because the wearer's tears could not circulate beneath the lens. In 1950 the corneal contact lens was introduced. It covered only the cornea of the eye, floated on the tears of the wearer, and could be worn all day without difficulty. Recent improvements include a flexible lens that shortens the initial period of adjustment for the wearer and a porous lens that does not have to be removed each day.

contact process: see SULFURIC ACID.

contagious diseases: see COMMUNICABLE DISEASES.

Contarini (kōntärē'nē), ancient Venetian family, including eight doges, a cardinal, and several artists. The most celebrated member was **Andrea Contarini,** 1300?–1382. He was doge (1368–82) at the time of the War of CHIOGGIA between Venice and Genoa; he proved his patriotism by melting his gold and silver plate and mortgaging his lands to raise money for the state.

contempt, in law, interference with the functioning of a legislature or court. In its narrow and more usual sense, contempt refers to the despising of the authority, justice, or dignity of a court. A **contempt of court** can be classified as civil or criminal, direct or constructive. Civil and criminal contempts are distinguished by the function of the punishment—if it is to vindicate judicial authority, the contempt is criminal; if it is to enforce the rights and remedies of a party, the contempt is civil. A direct contempt is one committed in the presence of the court while it is in session. A constructive contempt is one that is committed at a distance from the court and that tends to obstruct or defeat the administration of justice. A refusal to answer a question when directed to answer by a judge is a direct criminal contempt. Disobeying an INJUNCTION or a court order that a judgment (e.g., ALIMONY) be satisfied is a civil contempt. A major distinction is whether the court needs to hear evidence to determine if a contempt was committed. Direct criminal contempts may be punished summarily by fine or imprisonment; civil and constructive criminal contempts can also be punished by fine or imprisonment, but the accused must be granted a hearing. A contempt arising over comment on a court case involves an apparent danger to freedom of expression, and some jurisdictions require indictment and trial by jury. In the United States, Congress can punish for **contempt of Congress** behavior that occurred during legislative proceedings and that threatened legislative power. Congress must act before it adjourns, and any imprisonment can last no longer than that session. State legislatures also have limited powers to punish for contempt. See R. L. Goldfarb, *Contempt Power* (1963, repr. 1971).

Conti (kôNtē'), cadet branch of the French royal house of BOURBON. Although the title of prince of Conti was created in the 16th cent., the founder of the continuous line was **Armand de Bourbon, prince de Conti,** 1629–66, son of Henry II de Condé (see under CONDÉ, family) and brother of Louis II de Bourbon, prince de Condé, with whom he was in rivalry. Disappointed in his expectation of a cardinal's hat, Armand led rebel armies during the first FRONDE; his brother supported the government. Later they joined together in the second Fronde. Armand was reconciled (1653) with the court and married (1654) a niece of Cardinal Mazarin. He was given command of the army in the Italian and Spanish campaigns (1654–57). Toward the end of his life he turned to religious mysticism and retired (1657) to his estates, where he wrote several theological and moral treatises. He was a friend and protector of Molière. His eldest son, Louis Armand I de Bourbon, died while young, and his next son, **François Louis de Bourbon, prince de Conti,** 1664–1709, succeeded. His debauchery and his mockery of Louis XIV caused him to be banished (1683) to Chantilly. He then joined the Hungarian campaign of Charles V of Lorraine. Later he returned to Louis XIV's service and fought in the Dutch War. In 1697 he competed unsuccessfully with Augustus II (Frederick Augustus I, elector of Saxony) for the Polish throne. **Louis François de Bourbon, prince de Conti,** 1717–76, French general, grandson of François, served in the War of the Austrian Succession under General Belle-Isle in Bavaria, and in 1744 he received command of the army in Piedmont. He also distinguished himself in the campaigns in Germany (1745) and Flanders (1746). He resigned his commission in 1747 and for a while was a candidate for the Polish throne. Disliked by Mme de POMPADOUR, however, he lost favor at court. In opposition to the king, he supported the PARLEMENT against René Nicolas de MAUPEOU; later he opposed the reforms of A. R. J. Turgot. He was a writer and a friend of Jean Jacques Rousseau. His son, the last of the line, **Louis François Joseph, prince de Conti,** 1734–1814, fought in the Seven Years War, notably at the battles of Hastenbeck (1757) and Krenfeld (1758). He was the only prince of the blood to favor the edicts of Maupeou (1771). He signed the protests of the princes in 1789 and left France, but he returned in 1790. He was arrested in 1793 and detained at Marseilles. In 1795 he was exiled to Spain.

continent, largest unit of land on the EARTH. The continents include Eurasia (conventionally regarded as two continents, EUROPE and ASIA), AFRICA, NORTH AMERICA, SOUTH AMERICA, AUSTRALIA, and ANTARCTICA. The continents are not distributed regularly over the earth's surface. More than two thirds of the continental regions are in the Northern Hemisphere, rimming the Arctic Ocean. South America and Africa project into the Southern Hemisphere as southward-pointing triangles, forming extensive peninsular regions separating the Atlantic, Pacific, and Indian oceans. In addition, the continents are antipodal to the OCEAN basins, i.e., ocean basins are found on the opposite parts of the earth from continental masses. There is an antipodal relationship between the continental Antarctic region and the Arctic Ocean; and the Pacific Ocean comprises virtually an entire hemisphere of ocean water, while a hemisphere dominated by land is centered in NW Europe. The continental areas bounded by the sea level contour comprise about 29% of the earth's surface. However, from a geological point of view, the submerged continental shelves are also parts of the continents. Inclusion of the shelf area increases the extent of the continents to 34% of the globe. Geologically and topographically the continents are exceedingly complex and variable in detail, yet certain large-scale structural and topographic features appear to be common to all. Generally, the continents contain vast interior plains or plateaus, underlain by a basement complex of igneous and metamorphic rocks of PRECAMBRIAN age. In some places, the basement complex is exposed at the surface, where it is often called the shield, or craton. The Canadian Shield area of E Canada is the exposed basement complex of North America. Portions of shield areas are covered with veneers of flat-lying sedimentary rocks of younger age. The interior plains are frequently surrounded on one or more sides by ranges of mountains. These mountains are largely composed of younger sedimentary rocks that have been intricately folded and faulted and are approximately aligned parallel to the coasts. They also display abundant evidence of volcanic activity and large-scale igneous intrusions. In the United States the folded Appalachian Mts. lie to the east of the interior plains and the Rocky Mts. to the west. The Rockies are huge granitic masses that pushed upward through overlying sedimentary rocks which were then eroded away. How the continents originated has been a continuous major problem of geology. The oldest continental rocks dated by radioactivity are 3.98 billion years old, which suggests that the continents and oceans are probably permanent features of the earth's surface. Although the continental regions have been periodically covered by shallow seas, they appear never to have been the sites of ocean depths. Radioactive dating has also revealed that the rocks of the continental shields occur in large belts, with structures similar to those found in more recent mountain ranges. The oldest rocks are found in the interior, central portion of a shield. These discoveries suggest that the central shield areas of continents originally formed close to the time that the earth's crust first solidified and that the process of continental formation, or accretion, is continuing today. Accretion occurs on the edge of a continent where huge plates of the earth's crust are converging. The rocks in the area of convergence are crushed by the plates and thrown up against the continents in the form of mountains (see PLATE TECTONICS). The continents are composed mainly of granitic rocks, called sial (from a contraction of the names of the two chief constituent elements, silicone and aluminum). Underlying the ocean floor and the sial layer of the continents are denser basaltic rocks called sima (a contraction of silicon and magnesium). The sial and sima form the crust of the earth. Below the crust lies a region of the earth called the mantle. Although the crust is entirely solid, evidence indicates that part of the mantle consists of semimolten rocks on which the continents and ocean basins, in effect, are floating. A condition of gravitational balance, called isostasy, exists between different parts of the earth's crust. The theory of isostasy claims that the continental crust floats higher than the oceanic crust because the former is composed of a thick layer of lower density rocks while the latter is composed of a thin layer of higher density rocks. It is believed that isostatic adjustments for changes in mass distribution on the earth's surface occur through a flow of semimolten materials deep in the earth. These materials cause a compensatory uplift of mountains and plateau areas as erosion wears them down. The mass of eroded material is added to and thus depresses the continental shelves and the ocean floor. Adjustments to maintain equilibrium also accompany such mass changes as the growth and melting of ice sheets on continents. The average land elevation is c.2,700 ft (820 m) above sea level, the highest point on any continent being the summit of Mt. Everest at 29,028 ft (8,848 m), and the lowest point being the surface of the Dead Sea at 1,292 ft (394 m) below sea level. See CONTINENTAL DRIFT.

Continental Congress, 1774–89, Federal legislature of the Thirteen Colonies and later of the United States in the AMERICAN REVOLUTION and under the Articles of Confederation (see CONFEDERATION, ARTICLES OF). Indignation against England's colonial policy reached fever pitch in the colonies after the passage (1774) of the INTOLERABLE ACTS, and the Sons of Liberty and the committees of correspondence promoted the idea of an intercolonial assembly similar to the one held (1765) in 1765 at the time of the STAMP ACT. The **First Continental Congress** (Sept. 5–Oct. 26, 1774) was made up of delegates from all the colonies except Georgia. It met in Carpenter's Hall, Philadelphia, and Peyton Randolph was chosen to preside. The meeting's general purpose was to express colonial grievances against British policy, and only a few radical members considered the possibility of breaking with England. The plan of Joseph GALLOWAY for reconciling Great Britain and the colonies under a new imperial scheme was introduced but rejected. The session's most important act was the creation of the Continental Association, which forbade importation and use of British goods and proposed prohibition of colonial exports. Several petitions of grievances, written principally by John DICKINSON, were sent to the king, and the meeting was adjourned until May 10, 1775. Smoke from the battles of Lexington and Concord (April 19, 1775) had scarcely cleared when the **Second Continental Congress** met on the appointed day in Philadelphia. Armed conflict strengthened the radical element, but only gradually did the delegates swing toward independence. A Continental army was created to oppose the British and, through the agency of John ADAMS, George Washington was appointed (June 15, 1775) commander in chief. The reconciliation plan offered (1775) by Lord North's government was tabled. A diplomatic representative, Silas DEANE, was sent (March, 1776) to France. American ports were opened in defiance of the Navigation Acts. Finally, the momentous step was taken: Congress on July 4, 1776, adopted the DECLARATION OF INDEPENDENCE. The Congress, a young and unsteady organization, had little money and poor means of obtaining more. Nevertheless, it struggled to press the conduct of the war while moving, under force of military circumstances, from place to place; it met at Philadelphia (1775-76), Baltimore (1776-77), Philadelphia again (1777), Lancaster, Pa. (1777), York, Pa. (1777-78), and Philadelphia once more (after 1778). There was friction between Congress and the military leaders, and the soldiers, contemptuous (sometimes justly) of the politicians, constantly agitated for their pay and their rights. The Congress, jealous of its powers, frequently hindered Washington in his strategy. After the war ended and the Articles of Confederation took force, the quality of Congressional membership declined, since state offices were more desirable; and the Congress itself eventually dissolved. The Congress of the postwar period has, however, been underrated by many. Though shackled by the weaknesses of the Federal structure, which sharply curtailed its power and particularly its ability to raise funds, the Congress can be credited with some accomplishments—notably the Ordinance of 1787, which set up the Northwest Territory; decision of the WYOMING VALLEY territorial dispute; and adoption of the decimal system of currency. See *Journals of the Continental Congress* (34 vol., 1904-37); *Letters of Members of the Continental Congress* (ed. by E. C. Burnett, 6 vol., 1921-33; repr. 1963); E. C. Burnett, *The Continental Congress* (1941, repr. 1964); Lynn Montross, *The Reluctant Rebels: the Story of the Continental Congress, 1774-1789* (1950, repr. 1970).

Continental Divide, the "backbone" of a continent. In North America, from N Alaska to New Mexico, it is the great ridge of the Rocky Mts., which separates westward-flowing streams from eastward-flowing waters. In SW New Mexico the divide crosses an area of low relief; it becomes more distinct in N Mexico, where it follows the Sierra Madre Occidental. In the United States it has sometimes been called the Great Divide, a name also occasionally used to designate the whole Rocky Mt. system, especially the southern section where the high, rugged ranges presented an almost impenetrable barrier to westbound explorers and settlers. Glacier, Yellowstone, and Rocky Mt. national parks lie on the Continental Divide.

continental drift, geological theory that the positions of the continents on the earth's surface have changed considerably through geologic time. The first comprehensive and modern theory of continental drift was put forth by the German meteorologist Alfred Wegener in 1912. He cited as evidence the jigsaw fit of the opposing Atlantic coasts, particularly in the region of the coast of Brazil and the Gulf of Guinea of Africa. Wegener was particularly exacting and detailed in correlating geological and paleontological similarities on the two sides of the Atlantic to strengthen his argument. On the basis of the correlations he believed that late in the Paleozoic era, which ended 225 million years ago, all the continents were united into a vast supercontinent, which he called Pangaea. Later, Pangaea broke into two supercontinental masses—Laurasia to the north, and Gondwanaland to the south. The present continents began to split apart early in the next era, the Mesozoic, drifting to their present positions. As additional evidence he cited the unusual presence of coal deposits in South Polar regions and of glacial features in present-day equatorial regions. He also pointed out that a plastic layer in the interior of the earth must exist to accommodate vertical adjustments caused by the creation of new mountains and by the wearing down of old mountains by erosion (see CONTINENT). He postulated that the earth's rotation caused horizontal adjustment of rock in this plastic layer, exerting forces against the roots of the continents. These forces send the continents drifting on the "sea" of the basaltic ocean floor on which they rest. The mystery of mountain building was thus explained by Wegener as resulting from frictional drag along the leading edges of the drifting continents. Wegener's theory stirred considerable controversy throughout the 1920s, but was not generally accepted, particularly by American geologists, and later became the butt of ridicule. In 1954 the theory of continental drift was revived when a group of British geophysicists reported on magnetic studies of rocks from many places and from each major division of geologic time. They found that for each continent, the magnetic pole had apparently changed position through geologic time, forming a smooth curve (or pole path); they called this phenomenon polar wandering. Surprisingly, they found that each continent had its own pole path, and that the pole paths for Europe and North America could be made to coincide by closing the Atlantic Ocean, thus bringing the continents together. They could explain these findings only by assuming continental movements. See PLATE TECTONICS. See Hitoshi Takeuchi et al., *Debate About the Earth* (1967); D. H. Tarling, *Continental Drift* (1971); J. T. Wilson, ed., *Continents Adrift: Readings From Scientific American* (1972).

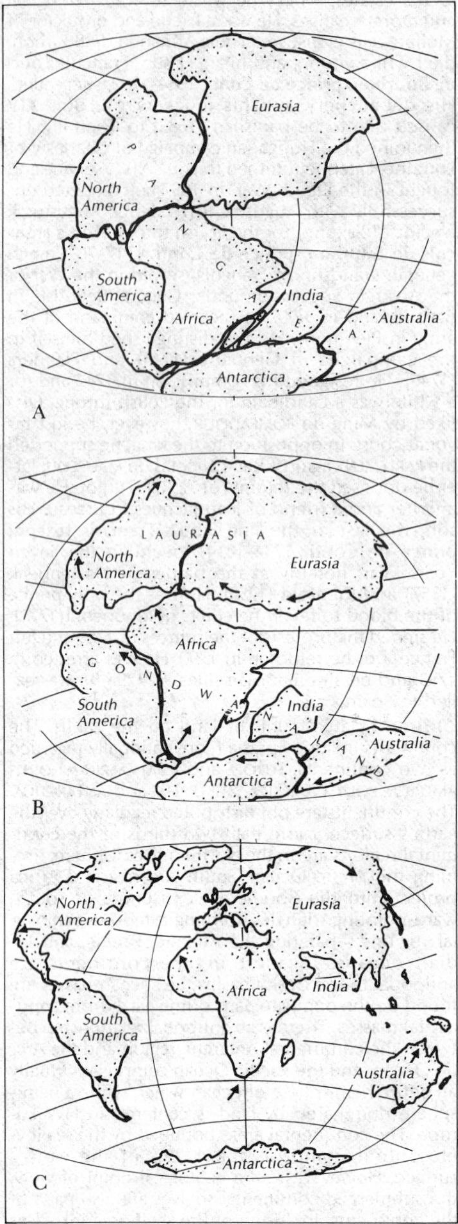

Continental drift (arrows indicate the direction of motion of the landmasses)

A. *Proposed reconstruction of the original, single supercontinent, Pangaea, indicating the major present landmasses*

B. *Proposed reconstruction of the supercontinents, Laurasia and Gondwanaland*

C. *The landmasses in their present positions*

continental shelf: see OCEAN.

Continental System, scheme of action adopted by NAPOLEON I in his economic warfare with England from 1806 to 1812. Economic warfare had been carried on before 1806, but the system itself was initiated by the BERLIN DECREE and extended by the Warsaw Decree (1807), the MILAN DECREE (1807), and the Fontainebleau Decree (1810), which forbade trade with Great Britain on the part of France, her allies, and neutrals. Napoleon expected that the unfavorable trade balance and loss of precious metals would destroy England's credit, break the Bank of England, and ruin English industry. Great Britain retaliated by the ORDERS IN COUNCIL, which forbade nearly all trade between England and any nation obeying the Berlin Decree. One of the most dramatic results of the commercial warfare was the English bombardment of neutral COPENHAGEN (1807) and the seizure of the Danish fleet. England had control of the sea, and large-scale smuggling thrived all along the European coast (with U.S. privateers taking a large part in the illegal trade). Napoleon himself issued special licenses for trade bringing in colonial goods on the payment of duties. Napoleon's Russian campaign of 1812 was brought on by Russia's refusal to conform to the decrees, and the war between England and the United States, known as the WAR OF 1812, was to some extent a result of the economic warfare. But so difficult was the enforcement of the system that in his effort to impose it on Russia, Napoleon had to violate it in France. Napoleon's failure, although it delayed the introduction of the Industrial Revolution in France, resulted in the creation of several new industries on the Continent, notably the manufacture of beet sugar. See F. E. Melvin, *Napoleon's Navigation System* (1919); E. F. Heckscher, *The Continental System* (1922).

continuation school: see VOCATIONAL EDUCATION.

contour or **contour line,** line on a map connecting points of equal elevation above or below mean sea level. It is thus a kind of isopleth, or line of equal quantity. Contour lines are drawn on maps with a uniform interval of vertical distance separating them (usually 10, 20, 50, or 100 ft on American maps) and thus outline the landform configuration, or relief. They may be visualized as representing shorelines if sea level were raised in small increments. Thus the tops of hills, which would appear as separate islands, are shown as a series of closed circular contours; valleys, which would appear as elongate bays, are shown as contour lines converging toward a point at the head of the valley. Since on steep slopes there is little horizontal distance between points greatly different in height, contour lines indicating such terrain are close together; contour lines of gentle slopes are more widely separated. Maps employing contour lines are called contour, or relief, maps although they are popularly called topographic maps (see TOPOGRAPHY) in the United States. Certain conventions are employed on these maps to assist the user. Contours indicating land elevations are printed in brown with every fifth contour drawn thicker and labeled with its elevation; those indicating depths of bodies of water are printed in blue. Hachure lines, pointing downslope, are attached to contour lines in order to emphasize a depression with a steep gradient. In the past, contour maps were made from ground surveys, but today they are constructed from stereographic aerial photographs after ground parties have established the precise location and elevation of selected reference points.

contraband, in international law, goods necessary or useful in the prosecution of war that a belligerent may lawfully seize from a neutral who is attempting to deliver them to the enemy. The term is sometimes also applied to the goods carried into a country by SMUGGLING. The penalty for carrying contraband goods is the confiscation of the goods and often also of the vessel (see PRIZE). Neutral ships guilty of direct assistance to the enemy may be treated as enemy ships. International law has not precisely defined all classes of goods that are contraband of war per se. Munitions are certainly absolute contraband, but the status of food and other conditional contraband at least indirectly needed for war is often in doubt. At the second (1907) of the HAGUE CONFERENCES a vain attempt to define the classes of contraband was made. In World War I many powers at first agreed to abide by the terms of the Declaration of London (see LONDON, DECLARATION OF) respecting contraband, but in time unconditional BLOCKADE of all goods was adopted. At the beginning of World War II the belligerents drew up lists of absolute and conditional contraband, but the total absorption of the economy in warfare led to the prohibition, so far as possible, of all shipping to the enemy. See P. C. Jessup, *The Early Development of the Law of Contraband of War* (1933).

contrabassoon, large, deep-toned instrument of the oboe family, also called double bassoon. Its tube, over 16 ft (5 m) long, is doubled upon itself four times. It was first made by Hans Schreiber of Berlin in 1620. Handel, Haydn, and Beethoven used it for special effects, but it was characterized by faulty intonation until a German, Wilhelm Heckel, in the late 19th cent. made the type generally used today.

contraception: see BIRTH CONTROL.

contract, in law, a promise, enforceable at law, to perform or to refrain from some specified act. In a general sense, all civil obligations fall under TORT or contract law. Torts are usually characterized as violations of duties that have been entirely established by law. In contracts, on the other hand, the parties determine, at least in part, what their obligations to one another will be. This article considers contracts in general; special types are given separate articles, e.g., NEGOTIABLE INSTRUMENT, INSURANCE, and DEED. For a contract to be valid both parties must indicate that they agree to its terms. This is accomplished when one party submits an offer that the other accepts within a reasonable time or a stipulated period. If the terms of the acceptance vary from the offer, that acceptance legally constitutes a counteroffer; the original offering party may then accept it or reject it. At any time prior to acceptance, the offer may be rescinded on notice unless the offering party is bound by a separate option contract not to withdraw. If the parties conduct their negotiations by mail or telegraph, the contract is ordinarily concluded on the day the acceptance is dispatched; in some jurisdictions, however, the offering party may revoke any time prior to receipt of the acceptance at his usual place of business. Only those terms expressed in the contract can be enforced; secret intentions are not recognized. For a contract to be binding it must not have an immoral or a criminal purpose or be against PUBLIC POLICY. Other criteria for the enforcement of contracts have varied. In the earliest type of enforceable promises it was the form of the contract (e.g., a sealed instrument) or the ceremony accompanying its execution that marked the essence of the transaction; contracts not sealed or not dignified by ceremonies held a lesser status and were therefore not always enforceable. The importance of promises in commercial and industrial society produced a new criterion, and generally a promise is now enforceable only if it is made for some consideration, i.e., in exchange for some action or for another promise. In some jurisdictions statutes have made certain promises enforceable without consideration, e.g., promises to pay debts barred by the statute of limitations. To be enforceable, applicable contracts must also comply with the Statute of Frauds (see FRAUDS, STATUTE OF) , a law that exists in some form in every jurisdiction. Since a contract is an agreement, it may be made only by parties with the capacity to reach an understanding. Therefore, the insane and the feeble-minded are unable to make binding contracts. Until the late 19th cent. married women were also without contractual capacity, because at common law they were considered the creatures of their husbands and without wills of their own (see HUSBAND AND WIFE); this disability has been removed by statute all but universally. Minors are not bound by their contracts, but they are responsible for the value of goods received in contracts made for necessities of life. Otherwise, a minor may denounce his contracts at any time and on attaining majority may elect whether to affirm or repudiate them (see AGE OF CONSENT). A contract must also be the uncoerced agreement of the parties; thus, if it is procured by DURESS or FRAUD it is void. While a contract is still wholly or partly unperformed it is termed executory; contracts may terminate, however, in ways other than by being fully executed. If the object of the contract becomes impossible or unlawful, if the parties make a novation (a new superseding agreement), or if the death of one party prevents him from rendering personal services he had agreed to perform, the contract is terminated. The injured party may also treat the contract as a nullity if the other party refuses to perform. The law provides several remedies for breach of contract. The most usual is money DAMAGES for the loss incurred. In cases where some action other than the payment of money was contracted for, a court may grant the plaintiff an INJUNCTION ordering specific performance. If one party may be unjustly enriched by a contract that he then repudiates, restitution may be required. A typical example of this is ordering a minor who revokes a contract to restore the things of value that he obtained. In some jurisdictions a contract made for the benefit of a third party may be enforced by the beneficiary against the defaulting party. See A. L. Corbin, *Contracts* (1952); studies by G. C. Cheshire (7th ed. 1969) and F. Kessler (2d ed. 1970).

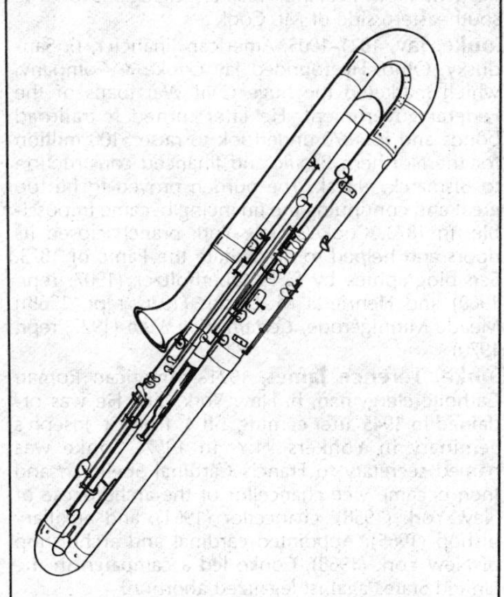
Contrabassoon

contract bridge: see BRIDGE.

contraction, in physics: see EXPANSION.

contraction, in writing: see ABBREVIATION.

contralto (kəntrăl'tō), female voice of lowest pitch. Originally, the term denoted a second voice set against (*contra*) a high voice (*alto*); thus, a second high voice. Since most second parts were for a high male voice or a low woman's voice, the term came to mean a low woman's voice. See also ALTO; COUNTERTENOR; VOICE.

Contreras (kōntrā'räs), village, central Mexico, near Mexico City, site of an important battle (Aug. 19–20, 1847) of the Mexican War. Gen. Winfield Scott, continuing his advance after the battle of Cerro Gordo, approached Mexico City. The Mexicans under General Santa Anna were drawn up for defense. Scott sent out a reconnaissance party under Gideon Pillow, who mistakenly ordered an attack that ended by isolating some of his advance troops. The situation seemed desperate, but brilliant night tactics, supported by reestablishment of communications by Robert E. Lee, prepared the way for a daybreak attack. Santa Anna was forced to retire to Chapultepec. Fierce fighting took place later on that same day at Churubusco, closer to Mexico City, where Mexican troops temporarily stemmed the U.S. advance.

controlled atmosphere storage, practice of storing articles in enclosures in which the atmospheric conditions such as temperature, pressure, humidity, and atmospheric composition, are optimized to prevent undesired changes in or deterioration of the stored articles. Refrigeration is a simple example of controlled atmosphere storage. Machine parts are often stored in air that is as dry as possible to protect them from rust. Substances that react readily with oxygen are often stored in atmospheres of nitrogen, carbon dioxide, or other relatively inert gases. Various fruits such as bananas and oranges are shipped and stored in an atmosphere of ethylene dioxide to retard their ripening.

control surface: see AIRFOIL.

control systems, combinations of components (electrical, mechanical, thermal, or hydraulic) that act together to maintain actual system performance close to a desired set of performance specifications. Open-loop control systems (e.g., automatic toasters and alarm clocks) are those in which the output has no effect on the input. Closed-loop control systems (e.g., thermostats, engine governors, and aircraft and spacecraft automatic control systems) are those in which the output has an effect on the input in such a way as to maintain the desired output value. See FEEDBACK.

Contucci, Andrea: see SANSOVINO, ANDREA.

convection, mode of heat transfer in fluids (liquids and gases). Convection depends on the fact that, in general, fluids expand when heated and thus undergo a decrease in DENSITY (since a given volume of the fluid contains less matter at a higher temperature than at the original, lower temperature). As a result, the warmer, less dense portion of the fluid will tend to rise through the surrounding cooler fluid, in accordance with ARCHIMEDES' PRINCIPLE. If heat continues to be supplied, the cooler fluid that flows in to replace the rising warmer fluid will also become heated and also rise. Thus, a current, called a convection current, becomes established in the fluid, with warmer, less dense fluid continually rising from the point of application of heat and cooler, denser portions of the fluid flowing outward and downward to replace the warmer fluid. In this manner, heat eventually may be transferred to the entire fluid. Convection currents are widely observed in both liquids and gases. Many aspects of weather are connected with convection currents. For example, when a portion of the atmosphere becomes heated by contact with a warm area of land, it rises into the cooler, higher altitudes, with the result that some of the moisture carried with it may be condensed to form clouds and precipitation. Man has used convection currents for heating and ventilation since ancient times. Both hot-air and hot-water heating systems use convection to transfer heat through the entire structure being heated. Convection currents also assist in the ventilation of mines.

convector: see HEATING.

convent: see MONASTICISM.

convention, in U.S. politics, a gathering of delegates to nominate candidates for elective office and to formulate party policy. They are held at the national, state, and local levels. Conventions for nominating candidates for state offices were first held in the early 19th cent. The first national convention was held by the Anti-Masonic party in Baltimore in 1831. Formerly the candidates for President and Vice President were always selected by a caucus, i.e., a meeting of influential members of Congress from each party intended to promote the candidate favored in Congress. The Democrats soon followed the lead of the Anti-Masonic party, and in 1832 Andrew Jackson became the first successful candidate to be nominated at a national convention. The Republican party held its first national convention in 1856, when John Frémont was chosen as the presidential candidate. In the past, candidates were often selected only after many ballots had been taken. This was especially true of the Democratic party, which, until 1936, had required successful nominees to win two thirds of the delegates' votes. Thus, Stephen Douglas was nominated on the 59th ballot in 1860, Woodrow Wilson on the 46th ballot in 1912, and John W. Davis on the 103d ballot in 1924. The difficulty of gaining agreement on a candidate at conventions led to a unique feature of the American political scene: the DARK HORSE—a candidate with little or no formal support before the opening of the convention, who succeeded in gaining the nomination. Since 1960, however, national conventions have tended to ratify front-runner candidates rather than select from among evenly matched rivals. Although today the acceptance speech of the nominee is the recognized climax of the convention, it was not until Franklin Delano Roosevelt flew to Chicago to accept the Democratic nomination in 1932 that a nominee accepted the nomination in person. The organization of a national convention is the responsibility of the party's national committee, which begins making arrangements for the accommodation of hundreds of delegates and the administration of the convention at least a year in advance. Balloting at both the Republican and Democratic conventions is by states, and only one person at any time has the right to cast the votes for his state. Delegates are chosen by a variety of methods, including primary elections, state and local conventions, or state and local committee meetings. Although the two parties follow the same basic pattern of basing representation on the population of the state and the party's strength within the state, the Democratic party introduced a series of reforms after the 1968 convention that modified its traditional delegate selection system. A quota system, assuring proportional representation for women, youths, and blacks was used for the 1972 convention but subsequently discarded in favor of a general commitment to minority representation. A more lasting change was the abolition of the unit rule, which had been in effect since 1832 and which had required state delegations to cast their votes as a bloc for a single candidate. National political conventions have been criticized by members of both parties, especially those committed to some type of national presidential primary election. See P. T. David et. al., *The Politics of National Party Conventions* (rev. ed. 1964); N. W. Polsby and A. B. Wildavsky, *Presidential Elections* (3d ed. 1971).

conversation piece: see PORTRAITURE.

Converse, Frederick Shepherd, 1871–1940, American composer, b. Newton, Mass., studied with J. K. Paine and G. W. Chadwick and in Germany with Rheinberger. His *Pipe of Desire* (Boston, 1906) was performed at the Metropolitan Opera House, New York City, in 1910; it was the first American opera performed there. His orchestral works include *Flivver Ten Million* (1927) and *American Sketches* (1929). He was dean of the faculty (1930–38) of the New England Conservatory of Music.

conversion, in psychology: see DEFENSE MECHANISM; HYSTERIA.

convertiplane: see VERTICAL TAKEOFF AND LANDING AIRCRAFT.

convict labor, work of prison inmates. Until the 19th cent., labor was introduced in prisons chiefly as an added punishment and was often unproductive. Such work is now considered a necessary part of the rehabilitation of the criminal; it is also useful in keeping discipline and reducing the costs of prison maintenance. The main types of work in prison communities are maintenance activities, outdoor public works (farming, road building, reforestation), and industrial labor. Considered a source of cheap labor, convicts were formerly put to work on contract, lease, or piecework bases for private industries. In recent decades these methods have been condemned, and prison industries are devoted chiefly to the production of goods to be used in state institutions. Because of competition with nonprison labor, interstate commerce in the products of convict labor has also been restricted in the United States since 1934. Wages are paid in many state and Federal prisons in the United States and in many European countries. The notorious chain gangs of some Southern states, in which convicts were chained and forced to do heavy labor, have declined but have not disappeared. Work release programs have been introduced with some success in France, Norway, Sweden, and the United States, whereby convicts are allowed to work outside prisons in private industry during the latter part of their prison terms; for this work the convict receives the same wages as nonprison workers.

convolvulus (kənvŏl'vyələs): see MORNING GLORY.

convulsion, sudden violent involuntary contraction of the muscles of the body, often accompanied by loss of consciousness. It is not known what causes the abnormal impulses from the brain that result in convulsive seizures, since the disturbance may arise in normal brain tissue as well as in diseased or injured tissue. Convulsions may occur in such conditions as epilepsy, poisoning, high fever (especially in young children), disturbances of calcium or phosphorus metabolism, alkalosis, diabetes, oxygen insufficiency, and a low blood-sugar content, as well as in local irritation or injury of the brain. Persons undergoing convulsions should be guarded against self-injury (see EPILEPSY). Otherwise, treatment must be directed to the underlying cause.

Conway, Henry Seymour, 1721-95, English soldier and politician; nephew of Robert Walpole. Early in his life he entered upon concurrent and distinguished military and parliamentary careers. He fell into disfavor with George III for defending John WILKES and was dismissed (1764) from his commands. He served (1765-68) as a secretary of state and voiced his dislike of the STAMP ACT. In 1782 he helped bring about Lord North's resignation for his handling of the struggle with the North American colonies.

Conway, Sir Martin: see CONWAY OF ALLINGTON, WILLIAM MARTIN CONWAY, 1ST BARON.

Conway, Moncure Daniel, 1832-1907, American author and preacher, b. Stafford co., Va. An ardent abolitionist, Conway lectured in England during the Civil War in the interests of the North. Brought up as a Methodist, he became a Unitarian minister and later a preacher of free thought. Besides editing and contributing essays to periodicals, he was the author of over 70 books, including a biography of Thomas Paine (1892), whose works he also edited (4 vol., 1894-96). See his autobiography (1904); biography by M. E. Burtis (1952); L. D. Easton, *Hegel's First American Followers* (1966).

Conway, Thomas, 1735-1800?, general in the Continental army in the American Revolution, b. Ireland. Educated in France, he was an officer in the French army before coming (1777) to America. He fought valiantly as a leader of colonial forces at Germantown, but George Washington attempted to block his promotion from brigadier to major general as unfair to officers with longer service. Congress nevertheless appointed him major general (Dec., 1777) and made him inspector general of the army. His part in the intrigue known as the CONWAY CABAL was small, but he lost his command, resigned (1778), and returned to France.

Conway, city (1970 pop. 15,510), seat of Faulkner co., central Ark., in a farm and cotton area; inc. 1873. It is a trade and industrial center. Conway was settled (c.1865) near the site of a French trading post (c.1770). It is the seat of Hendrix College and the State College of Arkansas. A lock and dam on the nearby Arkansas River are tourist attractions. Conway Lake offers excellent hunting and fishing.

Conway, municipal borough (1971 pop. 12,158), Caernarvonshire, N Wales, at the mouth of the Conway River. Conway is a picturesque town with several notable old structures. A high wall (13th cent.) encloses the old town, and there is a 13th-century church and a 13th-century castle. The Royal Cambrian Academy of Art occupies the Elizabethan mansion Plas Mawr. In 1974, Conway became part of the new nonmetropolitan county of Gwynedd.

Conway Cabal, 1777, intrigue in the American Revolution to remove George Washington as commander in chief of the Continental Army. Washington had been defeated at Brandywine and Germantown, and Horatio GATES was flushed with success by his victory in the Saratoga campaign. Some Congressmen and army officers favored Gates as commander in chief. Gen. Thomas CONWAY, personally irritated with Washington, wrote a letter to Gates severely criticizing Washington. James WILKINSON of Gates's staff quoted to William ALEXANDER (Lord Stirling) a phrase purportedly from this letter, and Alexander repeated it to Washington, who sent the quotation to Gates without comment. Gates wrote an elaborate defensive reply and sent it to Washington through Congress. Public opinion supported Washington, and the plot—if such it was—came to nothing. As it turned out, the much-quoted phrase was not in Conway's letter at all, and his name has been unfairly used to designate the cloudy scheme.

Conway of Allington, William Martin Conway, 1st Baron, 1856-1937, English explorer, art historian, and writer. Conway filled several university positions and in 1918-31 represented the combined English universities as Conservative member in the House of Commons. He began mountain climbing at 16 and conducted expeditions of exploration in Spitsbergen (1896-97) and the Bolivian Andes (1898). His numerous books on art and exploration include *Mountain Memories* (1920), *Art Treasures of Soviet Russia* (1925), and *Giorgione as a Landscape Painter* (1929).

Conwell, Russell Herman, 1843-1925, American Baptist minister and lecturer, b. Worthington, Mass. After practicing law, he was ordained (1879) and went to Philadelphia as a minister. He was founder and first president of Temple Univ., a college for working people that opened in 1884. For over 60 years Conwell was active as a lecturer. See biography by A. R. Burr (1917).

cony: see CONEY.

Cooch Behar (ko͞och bĭhär'), former princely state, now part of West Bengal state, E India. It lies in a low, poorly drained plain. Rice, tobacco, and jute are grown. Big-game hunting is practiced. The chief town, **Cooch Behar** (1971 pop. 53,734), is a district administrative center and market town.

Cook, David J., 1840-1907, American law enforcement officer, b. near La Porte, Ind. He moved (1855) with his family to Kansas, went (1859) to the Colorado gold fields, and returned to enlist (1861) in the Union army in the Civil War. Army service as a sort of military policeman led him to found the volunteer Rocky Mountain Detective Association to suppress outlawry in Colorado, and he had a long career as marshal, sheriff, and police chief, mostly around Denver. He brought many train, bank, and express-company robbers to justice, helped to quell the Ute Indian revolt of 1878, and was arbitrator in the mine strike at Leadville in 1880. See his reminiscences (new ed. 1958); biography by W. R. Collier and E. V. Westrate (1936).

Cook, Ebenezer, fl. 1708, American author. Virtually nothing is known about his life. He is the author of *The Sot-Weed Factor* (1708), a satirical poem concerning an Englishman's visit to Maryland. *Sotweed Redivivus* (1730), a treatise on tobacco production, is also attributed to him. Cook is the central character in *The Sot-Weed Factor* (1960), a novel by John BARTH.

Cook, Frederick Albert, 1865-1940, American explorer and physician, b. Sullivan co., N.Y. Cook early became interested in the arctic and accompanied the expedition of Robert E. PEARY in 1891-92 as surgeon. Later he accompanied the Belgian expedition (1897-99) to Antarctica and made other polar voyages. In 1906, after unsuccessful attempts to reach the summit of Mt. McKinley, Cook remained behind when most of the party returned. He later announced that he and a companion had successfully scaled the peak; this assertion was afterward proved to be fraudulent. In 1907 he set out with an expedition for the arctic, and on Sept. 1, 1909, he emerged into civilization again, claiming that he had reached the North Pole in April, 1908. A few days later Peary announced that he had reached the pole in April, 1909, and accused Cook of fraud. The argument was sensational. Cook was deprived of some of the honors that had been accorded him and disappeared from the public eye for a time. Later he was involved in an oil-field promotion scheme in Texas and served five years (1925-30) of a 14-year sentence for having used the mails to defraud. To the end of his life, however, and in the face of a generally hostile public, Cook fought for vindication of his polar and Mt. McKinley claims and even filed several libel suits. He was supported by some well-known explorers as well as some ardent admirers. Cook defended his claims in *My Attainment of the Pole* (1911) and *Return from the Pole* (ed. by F. J. Pohl, 1951). See Theon Wright, *The Big Nail* (1970); Hugh Eames, *Winner Lose All* (1973).

Cook, George Cram: see GLASPELL, SUSAN.

Cook, James, 1728-79, English explorer and navigator. After an apprenticeship to a firm of shipowners at Whitby, he joined (1755) the royal navy. He surveyed the St. Lawrence Channel (1760) and the coasts of Newfoundland and Labrador (1763-67). Cook was commissioned a lieutenant in command of the *Endeavour* and sailed (1768) on an expedition to chart the transit of Venus; he returned to England in 1771, having also circumnavigated the globe and explored the coast of New Zealand, which he accurately charted for the first time, and the coast of E Australia. He commanded (1772-75) an expedition to the South Pacific of two ships, the *Resolution* and the *Adventure*. On this expedition he disproved the rumor of a great southern continent, explored the Antarctic Ocean and the New Hebrides, discovered New Caledonia, and by the observance of strict dietary and hygienic rules prevented scurvy, heretofore the scourge of long voyages. Capt. Cook sailed again in 1776 and, after a year in the South Pacific, rediscovered the Sandwich Islands and unsuccessfully searched the northwest coast of North America for a passage to the Atlantic. On the return voyage he was killed by natives on the Hawaiian Islands. See definitive edition of his journals, ed. by J. C. Beaglehole (Vol. I-III, 1955-67; Vol. IV in prep.); selections from journals, ed. by A. G. Price (1958, repr. 1969); biographies by Christopher Lloyd (1952, repr. 1957), Alan Villiers (1967), and J. C. Beaglehole (1974); Alan Moorehead, *The Fatal Impact* (1966); bibliography by Maurice Holmes (1968).

Cook, Sir Joseph, 1860-1947, Australian statesman, b. England. A leader of the Free Trade party, he served as prime minister (1913-14) and later as minister of the navy (1917-21) and high commissioner to London (1921-27). He was Australian representative at the Paris Peace Conference and a delegate (1922-26) to the League of Nations.

Cook, Thomas, 1808-92, English travel agent. In Leicester in 1841 he founded the travel agency that bears his name. The idea of the guided tour met with quick success, and by 1852 Cook had moved his office to London. Shortly thereafter he set up (1856) his Circular Tour of Europe, and 10 years later he was arranging tours of the United States. His most spectacular achievement was the transportation of an entire expeditionary force (18,000 men) up the Nile for the attempted relief of Gen. Charles George GORDON in 1884.

Cook, Mount, 12,349 ft (3,764 m) high, on South Island, New Zealand, in the Southern Alps; highest peak of New Zealand. Tasman Glacier is on the southeastern side of Mt. Cook.

Cooke, Jay, 1821-1905, American financier, b. Sandusky, Ohio. He founded Jay Cooke & Company, which marketed the huge Civil War loans of the Federal government. He later turned to railroad bonds and in 1870 undertook to raise $100 million for the Northern Pacific and financed construction to Bismarck, N.Dak. The burden proved to be too great and continuing the financing became impossible. In 1873, Cooke's New York branch closed its doors and helped to precipitate the Panic of 1873. See biographies by E. P. Oberholtzer (1907, repr. 1968) and Henrietta M. Larson (1936, repr. 1968); Meade Minnigerode, *Certain Rich Men* (1927, repr. 1970).

Cooke, Terence James, 1921-, American Roman Catholic clergyman, b. New York City. He was ordained in 1945 after earning a B.A. from St. Joseph's Seminary in Yonkers, N.Y. In 1957, Cooke was named secretary to Francis Cardinal Spellman and then became vice chancellor of the archdiocese of New York (1958), chancellor (1961), and auxiliary bishop (1965). Appointed cardinal and archbishop of New York (1968), Cooke led a campaign in the United States against legalized abortion.

Cookeville, city (1970 pop. 14,270), seat of Putnam co., N central Tenn.; inc. 1854. It is a farm trade center with plants making filters, automobile accessories, brushes, clothing, and heating elements. Tennessee Technological Univ. is there.

Cook Islands, group (1970 est. pop. 22,000), 90 sq mi (234 sq km), South Pacific, SE of Samoa. It comprises two main groups, the Lower Cook islands (RAROTONGA, Mangaia, Atiu, Aitutaki, Mauke, Mitiaro, and Manuae and Te-Au-o-tu) and the Northern Cook islands (Nassau, Palmerston, Penrhyn, MANIHIKI, Rakahanga, Pukapuka, and Suwarrow). Avarua on Rarotonga is the administrative center of the group. Fruit juices, citrus fruits, clothing, copra, tomatoes, pearl shell, handicrafts, and jewelry are the principal exports. Most imports come from New Zealand. The Cook islanders are Maoris, a branch of the Polynesian race; they generally work their own land. The southern islands were probably occupied by the Polynesians c.1,500 years ago. Spaniards visited the islands in the late 16th and early 17th cent. Capt. James COOK sighted some of the islands in 1773; others were not discovered until the 1920s. The London Missionary Society was a powerful influence in the southern islands during the 19th cent. The group was proclaimed a British protectorate in 1888 and was annexed by New Zealand in 1901. Although under New Zealand sovereignty, the Cook Islands achieved internal self-government in 1965. The government consists of a prime minister, a cabinet, a 22-member elected legislature, and a 15-member House of Arikis (hereditary chiefs). The latter is a purely consultative body whose members are appointed by the New Zealand High Commissioner for one-year terms. New Zealand remains responsible for foreign affairs and defense, and the Cook islanders are citizens of New Zealand. The islands were formerly called the Hervey Islands.

Cook Strait, channel, c.15 mi (24 km) wide, between North Island and South Island, New Zealand. It was discovered in 1770 by Capt. James Cook.

Cooley, Charles Horton, 1864–1929, American sociologist, b. Ann Arbor, Mich., grad. Univ. of Michigan (B.A., 1887; Ph.D., 1894); son of Thomas M. Cooley. He taught in the sociology department at the Univ. of Michigan after 1892, although his degree was in economics. Cooley's major contribution to the field of sociology was his conceptualization of the "looking-glass self" (a concept that emphasizes the social determination of the self) and primary groups—e.g., the family, the play group, or the neighborhood. He wrote *Human Nature and the Social Order* (1902, rev. ed. 1922), *Social Organization* (1909), *Social Process* (1918), and *Sociological Theory and Social Research* (1930).

Cooley, Thomas McIntyre, 1824–98, American jurist, b. near Attica, N.Y. He was a judge (1864–85) of the supreme court of Michigan and was the first chairman (1887–91) of the Interstate Commerce Commission. His best-known work is *A Treatise on the Constitutional Limitations Which Rest upon the Legislative Power of the States* (1868, 8th ed. 1927). Cooley argued that the U.S. Constitution contained not only direct limitations on the power of the states (e.g., the prohibition in Article I, Section 10, against a state's impairing the obligations of contract) but also implied limitations that could be deduced from the political theory underlying the Constitution. For example, from the division of American governments into executive, legislative, and judicial branches he inferred the freedom of the judiciary from legislative interference. Cooley's study was highly influential in the early interpretation of the due process clause of the FOURTEENTH AMENDMENT to the Constitution. He also wrote extensively on the law of torts and taxation. See C. E. Jacobs, *Law Writers and the Courts* (1954, repr. 1973)

Coolgardie, Australia: see EAST COOLGARDIE GOLDFIELD; KALGOORLIE.

Coolidge, Calvin, 1872–1933, 30th President of the United States (1923–1929), b. Plymouth, Vt. John Calvin Coolidge was a graduate of Amherst College and was admitted to the bar in 1897. He practiced (1897–1919) law in Northampton, Mass., entered state politics as a Republican, and rose steadily in the party. He served (1910–11) as mayor of Northampton, was a member of the Massachusetts state senate from 1912 to 1915 (its president after 1914), and was (1916–19) lieutenant governor before serving (1919–21) as governor. Coolidge rose to national prominence when he used the militia to end the Boston police strike in 1919. In 1920 he was nominated as Republican candidate for the vice presidency and was elected with Warren G. Harding. After Harding died, Coolidge took (Aug. 3, 1923) the oath of office as President. Untouched by the scandals of the Harding administration, he was easily elected to a full term in 1924. His personal honesty and New England simplicity appealed to the American people, and his unquestioning faith in the conservative business values of laissez faire reflected the national mood. Coolidge's policies were aggressively pro-business. Through his appointees he transformed the Federal Trade Commission from an agency intended to regulate corporations into one dominated by big business. He twice vetoed (1927, 1928) the McNary-Haugen bill to aid agriculture and pocket-vetoed (1928) a bill for government operation of the Muscle Shoals hydroelectric plant. The presence in his cabinet of Herbert C. Hoover and Andrew W. Mellon added to the business tone of his administration, and Coolidge supported Mellon's program of tax cuts and economy in government. Through his public statements he encouraged the reckless stock market speculation of the late 1920s and left the nation unprepared for the economic collapse that followed. Coolidge chose not to seek renomination in 1928. After leaving office he retired to Northampton to write newspaper and magazine articles and his autobiography (1929). As first lady, his wife, Grace A. Goodhue Coolidge, was much admired for her poise and charm. A selection of his press conferences was edited by H. H. Quint and R. H. Ferrell (1964). See biographies by C. M. Fuess (1940), D. R. McCoy (1967), Jules Abels (1969), and W. A. White (1938, repr. 1973).

Coolidge, William Augustus Brevoort, 1850–1926, American mountaineer and historian of the Alps, b. New York City. A graduate of Exeter College, Oxford, and life fellow and later modern history tutor at Magdalen College, he ascended nearly all the highest Alpine peaks. He spent most of his life in England and Switzerland. His books include *The Alps in Nature and History* (1908).

Coolidge, William David, 1873–1975, American physical chemist, b. Hudson, Mass., grad. Massachusetts Institute of Technology, 1896. He joined the General Electric Company in 1905 and served as director of its research laboratory (1932–40) and as vice president and director of research (1940–44). He made special studies of X rays, invented an X-ray tube, and invented and developed ductile tungsten.

Coolidge Dam, 249 ft (76 m) high, 920 ft (280 m) long, on the Gila River, SE Ariz.; built 1927–28. It irrigates c.100,000 acres (40,470 hectares), half of which are Indian lands in San Carlos Reservation. San Carlos Reservoir, formed behind the dam, lies above old Indian burial grounds and the former camp of Geronimo.

coolie labor, term applied to unskilled laborers from Asia, especially from India and China. With the discontinuance of slavery, the use of Chinese and Indian contract labor in British and French colonies increased. Indenture of Indian coolies was usually for a term of five years, in return for wages, certain benefits, and the cost of passage; the terms were enforceable by penal sanctions. At the expiration of their terms, the laborers were free to reindenture or to seek other employment. They frequently became peasant proprietors, although they were entitled to return passage to India. The practice was discontinued by the British Indian government, which in 1922 prohibited assisting the emigration of unskilled laborers, except to a few countries. Emigration of Chinese coolies began c.1845, although it was nominally prohibited before 1859. Between these dates the conditions were notoriously bad; the victims were shipped mainly to Cuba and Peru, where they died by the thousands. In 1859, Britain arranged with Canton for legal emigration to the British West Indies and elsewhere on five-year contracts. In 1860 an Anglo-Chinese convention sanctioned such emigration to British territory, and the regulations were agreed to by the other powers in similar conventions. The British Chinese Passenger Act of 1885 regulated British ships in the trade and resulted in the traffic's falling mainly into the hands of the Portuguese, under whom it resembled the African slave trade. In 1904, Great Britain arranged with China the hiring of 50,000 Chinese laborers to work the Transvaal gold mines. In the 19th cent. large numbers of Chinese laborers went to California and Australia. Opposition in Australia to this influx of cheap labor resulted in the passage of the Emigration Restriction Act for the gradual elimination of Asians from Australia, by providing that no one should be permitted to enter the country who failed to write 50 words in any prescribed language. Coolie labor was important in building the first U.S. transcontinental railroad, but this type of immigration into the United States was practically ended by the Chinese Exclusion Act of 1888 and by stringent Federal laws against contract laborers. In 1904, Canada began to exclude coolie labor by charging a head tax of $500. See P. C. Campbell, *Chinese Coolie Emigration to Countries within the British Empire* (1923, repr. 1971).

cooling system, type of heat exchanger commonly incorporated in engines to reduce the heat generated by friction and by combustion of the fuel. Engines of the internal-combustion type generate heat in the cylinders to such an extent that, if they are not cooled, the lubricating oil will be burned and serious damage will be done to the various parts through unevenness of expansion. Most internal-combustion engines are either water- or air-cooled. Around each cylinder and cylinder head of a water-cooled engine is a hollow jacket through which water is circulated to draw heat from the engine. The heated water is passed into a radiator connected to the jackets. The radiator transfers heat to the atmosphere from its large surface area, over which air is drawn by a fan and also, in a motor vehicle, by the vehicle's motion. The cooled water then returns to the jackets around the engine. In order to speed the initial warmup of the engine, thermostatic valves prevent water from entering the radiator until the engine reaches its correct operating temperature. In very cold weather the water may freeze, cracking the radiator. To prevent this, the water is mixed with certain chemicals (see ANTIFREEZE). In air-cooled engines a large cooling surface is provided by means of a number of fins which, as part of the cylinders and the cylinder heads, help to dissipate the heat. Air is caused to flow over the fins by the motion of the engine, if on a motor vehicle, or by a fan, or by both. Sometimes the heated water from the jackets of internal combustion engines or from other sources is cooled in a cooling tower. The water is sprayed into the tower where it mixes with air, heat being dissipated when some of the water evaporates. The rest of the water is recirculated. Large sources of waste heat such as power plants use cooling towers to avoid thermally polluting lakes and rivers by sending hot water into them. Rapidly moving machinery is frequently kept cool, as well as being lubricated, by running it in an oil bath. In a rocket engine the exit nozzle is sometimes cooled by the fuel passing through coils around it to the combustion chamber. Cooling systems in buildings are so devised as to purify the air and regulate its water content as well as to cool it (see AIR CONDITIONING). See also VENTILATION.

Coomaraswamy, Ananda Kentish (ä"nəndä' kĕn'tĭsh ko͞omä"rəswä'mē), 1877–1947, art historian, b. Ceylon (now Sri Lanka). Coomaraswamy was active in educational movements in India. After 1917 he became keeper of Indian and Islamic arts in the Museum of Fine Arts, Boston. He is credited with having built up the museum's great Far Eastern collection. He was critical of Western institutions and sought, as in his *Am I My Brother's Keeper?* (1947), to apply to them standards derived from Oriental philosophy and history. Among his other books are *Dance of Siva* (1918), *History of Indian and Indonesian Art* (1927), *Elements of Buddhist Iconography* (1935), and *The Transformation of Nature in Art* (3d ed. 1956). See the bibliography of his writings in I. K. Bharatha, ed., *Art and Thought* (1947); study by R. F. Livingston (1962).

Coon, Carleton Stevens, 1904–, American anthropologist, archaeologist, and educator, b. Wakefield, Mass., grad. Harvard 1925, Ph.D. 1928. From 1925 to 1939 he was engaged in fieldwork and anthropological research in Arabia, the Balkans, and N Africa, where he discovered (1939) the remains of a Neanderthal man. He taught (1934–48) at Harvard and in 1948 became professor of anthropology at the Univ. of Pennsylvania and curator of ethnology at the University Museum there. Coon became a controversial figure with the publication of *The Origin of Races* (1962), in which he argued that certain races had reached the *Homo sapiens* stage of evolution before others; he said this would explain why different races achieved different levels of civilization. His other writings include *The Seven Caves* (1957), *The Story of Man* (2d ed. 1962), *The Living Races of Man* (1965), and *The Hunting Peoples* (1971).

coon: see RACCOON.

coon cat, name for a breed of large domestic CATS (also called Maine cats), for the COATIMUNDI, and for the CACOMISTLE.

coonhound, black-and-tan, breed of large HOUND developed in the United States. It stands from 23 to 27 in. (58–69 cm) high at the shoulder and weighs from 70 to 85 lb (32–38 kg). The dense, short coat is coal black with tan markings above the eyes and on the muzzle, chest, and legs. The black-and-tan is descended from the old Virginia (American) foxhound and is bred especially for proficiency in hunting raccoons and opossums. It is a slow but methodical trailer, scenting with its nose to the ground much like a bloodhound. Once it has treed its quarry it gives voice until the hunter arrives. There are other varieties of coonhound closely related to the black-and-tan and also originally descended from the foxhound, e.g., the Walker, Trigg, redbone, bluetick, and Plott, but only the black-and-tan is recognized as a separate breed by the American Kennel Club. See DOG.

Coon Rapids, city (1970 pop. 30,505), Anoka co., SE Minn., on the Mississippi River; inc. 1952. It is a suburb of Minneapolis-St. Paul. It has an aerospace research facility and plastic and metallurgical industries. A junior college is there.

Cooper, Alexander: see under COOPER, SAMUEL.

Cooper, Alfred Duff, 1st **Viscount Norwich of Aldwick,** 1890-1954, British statesman and diplomat. Elected to Parliament as a Conservative (Unionist) in 1924, he served as secretary of state for war (1935-37) in the coalition cabinet and was first lord of the admiralty in 1938 when he resigned in protest against the Munich Pact. He returned to the cabinet as minister of information (1940-41) under Winston Churchill. Appointed resident minister of Far Eastern affairs in Singapore in Dec., 1941, he was recalled the following month, shortly before Singapore fell to the Japanese. From 1944 to 1947 he served as ambassador to France. He was raised to the peerage in 1952. Among his writings is an autobiography, *Old Men Forget* (1953).

Cooper, Anthony Ashley: see SHAFTESBURY, ANTHONY ASHLEY COOPER, 1ST EARL OF.

Cooper, Gary (Frank James Cooper), 1901-61, American film actor, b. Helena, Mont. His first important starring role in *A Farewell to Arms* (1933) was followed by such films as *Mr. Deeds Goes to Town* (1936), *Pride of the Yankees* (1942), *For Whom the Bell Tolls* (1943), and *Saratoga Trunk* (1944). Best known to his public as the shy, lanky man of the West, he won Academy Awards for his performances in *Sergeant York* (1941) and *High Noon* (1952). His later films include *Vera Cruz* (1954), *Friendly Persuasion* (1956), and *They Came to Cordura* (1959).

Cooper, James Fenimore, 1789-1851, American novelist, b. Burlington, N.J. He was the first important American writer to draw on the subjects and landscape of his native land in order to create a vivid myth of frontier life. In 1790 Cooper's family moved to Cooperstown, N.Y., a frontier settlement founded by his father near Otsego Lake. Sent to Yale at 13, Cooper was dismissed for a disciplinary reason in his third year. Soon after he went to sea; commissioned as a U.S. midshipman, he served until 1811, at which time he married and settled as a gentleman farmer. Cooper's literary career, which covers a period of 30 years and includes more than 50 publications, began in 1820 with the appearance of *Precaution.* Imitative of the English novel of manners, this book failed to gain an audience; but his next work, *The Spy* (1821), a patriotic story of the American Revolution, was an immediate success. With *The Pioneers* (1823), the first of the famous *Leatherstocking Tales,* and *The Pilot* (1823), an adventure of the high seas, Cooper's reputation as the first major American novelist was established. In 1826 he went to France, nominally as American consul at Lyons. He spent several years abroad, publishing such novels as *The Red Rover* (1827), *The Wept of Wish-ton-Wish* (1829), and *The Water-Witch* (1830), romances of American life on land and sea. In *Notions of the Americans* (1828) he defended his country to European critics; but upon his return home, repelled by what he saw as the abuses of American democracy, Cooper became the staunch social critic of American society. Such works as *The American Democrat* (1838) and the fictional *Homeward Bound* and its sequel, *Home as Found* (both 1838), express the conservative, aristocratic social views that made him quite unpopular; his later life was filled with many quarrels and lawsuits over his works. In his most important novels, the group comprising the *Leatherstocking Tales*—which in order of the narrative are *The Deerslayer* (1841), *The Last of the Mohicans* (1826), *The Pathfinder* (1840), *The Pioneers* (1823), and *The Prairie* (1827)—Cooper skillfully dramatized the clash between the frontier wilderness and the encroaching civilization. Named for their chief character, the forthright frontiersman Natty Bumppo, nicknamed Leatherstocking, the *Leatherstocking Tales* are notable for their descriptive power, their mastery of native background, and their romanticized portrayal of the American Indian. His later works include the novels *Afloat and Ashore* and its sequel, *Miles Wallingford* (both 1844), and the Littlepage trilogy—*Satanstoe* (1845), *The Chainbearer* (1845), and *The Redskins* (1846)—a study of the conflict between the landholding and the propertyless classes in New York state, in which Cooper shows himself a traditional defender of the rights of property. Although Cooper has been criticized for his extravagant plots, his conventional characters, and his stilted dialogue, he nevertheless remains the first great American novelist, a vital and original writer of romances of the wilderness and of the sea and an astute critic of the growing and stumbling American democracy. See his correspondence (ed. by his grandson, J. F. Cooper, 2 vol., 1922, repr. 1971); biographical and critical studies by James Grossman (1949), R. E. Spiller (1931, repr. 1963), George Dekker (1967), T. R. Lounsbury (1882, repr. 1968), and J. P. McWilliams, Jr. (1972); bibliography by R. E. Spiller and P. C. Blackburn (1934, repr. 1969).

Cooper, Myles, 1737?-1785, 2d president of King's College (now Columbia Univ.), b. England, educated at Oxford. He was ordained a priest in 1761 and went to King's College (1762) as professor of moral philosophy and assistant to the president. In 1763 he was made president, succeeding Samuel Johnson. Although his early administration was marked by the founding of a grammar school, a medical school, and a hospital, with changes in the curriculum and great increase in prestige, the college experienced hardships during the American Revolution. Cooper was an active and vocal Loyalist, and in 1775 he was forced to flee before the patriots' hatred to a British warship in New York harbor. He returned to Oxford and lived out his life in England.

Cooper, Peter, 1791-1883, American inventor, industrialist, and philanthropist, b. New York City. After achieving success in the glue business, Cooper, with two partners, erected (1829) the Canton Iron Works in Baltimore. There he constructed the *Tom Thumb,* one of the earliest locomotives built in the United States. His success in trials on the Baltimore & Ohio RR probably saved that pioneer line from bankruptcy. During the next 20 years, Cooper expanded his holdings, becoming a leader in the American iron industry, and in 1870 he was awarded the Bessemer gold medal for rolling the first iron for fireproof buildings. Cooper invented and patented other practical devices and processes. His faith in the success of the Atlantic cable led him to invest heavily in the New York, Newfoundland, and London Telegraph Company after banks refused to finance the operation. He was president of this company for 20 years while he headed the North American Telegraph Company, which controlled more than half of the telegraph lines in the country. An outstanding leader in the civic affairs of New York City, Cooper led the successful fight to secure a public school system and did much to improve several of the municipal departments. His lasting monument is COOPER UNION in New York City, built after his own plans to provide for education for the working classes. He supported the GREENBACK PARTY in national politics, and in 1876 he was the party's presidential candidate, polling over 80,000 votes. Many of his addresses were collected in *Ideas for a Science of Good Government* (1883, repr. 1971). Abram S. HEWITT was his son-in-law, Peter Cooper Hewitt his grandson. See biographies by R. W. Raymond (1901), Allan Nevins (1935, repr. 1967), and E. C. Mack (1949).

Cooper, Samuel, 1609-72, one of the greatest English miniaturists. A student of Hoskins, he worked in London from c.1642. He painted portraits of numerous celebrated Englishmen. His draftsmanship and unusual use of lighting made his vellum-on-card head-and-shoulder paintings remarkable. Specimens of his work are to be found at Windsor Castle; in the collections of the duke of Buccleuch and the duke of Devonshire (the latter containing the famous portrait of Cromwell familiar through engravings); in the Victoria and Albert Museum, London; in the Rijks Museum; and in the Metropolitan Museum of Art. His brother, **Alexander Cooper,** d. 1660, was for many years miniature painter at the court of Queen Christina of Sweden.

Cooper, Thomas, 1759-1839, American scientist, educator, and political philosopher, b. London, educated at Oxford. His important works include *Political Essays* (1799); the appendixes to the *Memoirs of Dr. Joseph Priestley* (2 vol., 1806), in which he reviews Priestley's life and works at length; *Lectures on the Elements of Political Economy* (1826); *Treatise on the Law of Libel* (1830); and (as editor) *The Statutes at Large of South Carolina* (5 vol., 1836-39). Cooper emigrated to the United States in 1794 and, settling near his friend Joseph Priestley in Northumberland, Pa., was his partner in scientific research. As a supporter of the Jeffersonian opposition to the Federalists, he wrote many political pamphlets, especially against the Alien and Sedition Acts of 1798. Convicted under the acts, he was imprisoned and fined $400; after his death this fine was repaid to his heirs. He taught at Dickinson College and the Univ. of Pennsylvania and was president (1820-33) of South Carolina College (now the Univ. of South Carolina). See Dumas Malone, *The Public Life of Thomas Cooper* (1926); J. N. Ireland, *A Memoir of the Professional Life of Thomas Abthorpe Cooper* (1888, repr. 1970).

Co-operative Commonwealth Federation: see NEW DEMOCRATIC PARTY.

Cooperative Extension Service, in the United States, publicly supported, informal adult education and development organization. Established in 1914, it consists of three levels of organization—Federal, state, and county. Its overall objective is to plan, execute, and evaluate learning experiences that will help people acquire the understanding, the abilities and capabilities, attitudes, and skills essential for solving farm, home, and community problems. This objective is met through educational programs that make use of research findings emanating primarily from the U.S. Dept. of Agriculture and the state land-grant colleges and universities.

cooperative movement, series of organized activities that began in the 19th cent. in Great Britain and later spread to most countries of the world, whereby people organize themselves around a common goal, usually economic. The term usually refers more specifically to the formation of nonprofit economic enterprises for the benefit of those using their services. An old and widespread form is the consumers' cooperative, in which people organize for wholesale or retail distribution, usually of agricultural or other staple products. Traditionally, membership is open, and anyone may buy stock. Goods are sold to the public as well as to members, usually at prevailing market prices, and any surplus above expenses is turned back to the members. Money is saved through direct channeling of goods from producer to consumer. Producers' cooperatives are manufacturing and distributive organizations, commonly owned and managed by the workers. Another development in such cooperatives has been the acquisition of failing manufacturing plants by labor unions, who run them on a cooperative basis. Agricultural cooperatives usually involve cooperation in the processing and marketing of produce and in the purchase of equipment and supplies. Actual ownership of land is usually not affected, and in this way the agricultural cooperative differs from the COLLECTIVE FARM. Agricultural cooperatives are often linked with cooperative banks and CREDIT UNIONS, which constitute another important type of cooperative. There is also cooperative activity in insurance, medical services, housing, and other fields. The origin of cooperative philosophy is found in the writings and activities of Robert OWEN, Louis Blanc, Charles FOURIER, and others. Its early character was revolutionary, but under the impact of such movements as Christian Socialism this aspect diminished. After some early 19th cent. experiments, consumers' cooperation took permanent form with the establishment (1844) of the ROCHDALE SOCIETY OF EQUITABLE PIONEERS in England. The cooperative movement has since had considerable growth throughout Great Britain and the Commonwealth, where local cooperatives have been federated into national wholesale and retail distributive enterprises and where a large proportion of the population has membership. Foods are the chief products handled, with insurance and banking activities next in importance. Outstanding examples of cooperative organization are found in the Scandinavian countries, Israel, the People's Republic of China, the Soviet Union, and France. In 1918, the Scandinavian Cooperative Wholesale Society was founded to allow these countries the opportunity to buy food products from other countries jointly. Throughout rural and urban Scandinavia, marketing and consumer cooperatives are common. In Israel, more than 50% of the rural population is organized into agricultural cooperatives. After the successful Communist revolution in China in 1949, large-scale efforts toward cooperative organization were begun; by the mid-1950s more than 90% of all craftsmen were in cooperatives, and by 1958 all agriculture was cooperatively organized. The Soviet Union, which organized its economy along cooperative lines earlier than China, did not achieve the rapid success of the Chinese. France, with a long history of cooperative attempts for both consumers and producers, has gained the most success with agricultural cooperatives (e.g., over 80% of all French grain is sold through cooperatives). The cooperative movement began in the United States in the 19th cent., first among workers and then among farmers. The National Grange, a farmers cooperative was founded in 1867 and later exercised considerable political influence (see GRANGER MOVEMENT). Today the major types of cooperatives include those of farmers, wholesalers, and consumers, as well as insurance, banking and credit, and rural electrification cooperatives (the growth of the latter two facilitated by loans from the Federal government). Although cooperatives are more prevalent in the rural areas of the United States, by the early 1970s a large increase in cooperative apartment buildings and supermarkets in urban areas was evident. An international alliance for the dissemination of cooperative information was founded in 1895. Since then there has been increasing international collaboration among the various kinds of cooperatives and a growing trend toward the establishment of international cooperative distribution. See Laszlo Valko, *International Handbook of Cooperative Legislation* (1954); International Labor Organization, *Cooperative Management and Administration* (1960); H. J. Voorhis, *American Cooperatives* (1961); F. C. Helm, *The Economics of Co-operative Enterprise* (1968); E. P. Roy, *Cooperatives; Today and Tomorrow* (1969).

Cooperstown, residential village (1970 pop. 2,403), seat of Otsego co., E central N.Y., on the Susquehanna River and Otsego Lake; inc. 1807. It was founded by William Cooper, who brought his family there in 1787. His son, James Fenimore Cooper, made his home in Cooperstown after his return from abroad in 1833, and the region is described in his *Leatherstocking Tales.* Fenimore House is the headquarters of the New York State Historical Association. Other museums include Cooperstown Indian Museum; Farmers' Museum; and the National Baseball Hall of Fame and Museum, commemorating the founding (1839) of baseball there by Abner Doubleday. Glimmerglass State Park is nearby.

Cooper Union, accredited institution of higher education; in New York City; coeducational; chartered and opened in 1859. Founded by Peter Cooper, it pioneered in evening engineering and art schools; day schools were added in 1900. Today it includes the School of Engineering and Science, the School of Art and Architecture, and the Division of Adult Education. There are no tuition, application, matriculation, or graduation fees for U.S. residents. The Cooper-Hewitt Museum of decorative art and design was founded in 1897 as part of Cooper Union by Sarah, Eleanor, and Amy Hewitt, granddaughters of Peter Cooper. In 1967 the museum, still located in New York City, became an independent division of the Smithsonian Institution.

Coorg (ko͝org), former state, 1,593 sq mi (4,126 sq km), Karnataka state, SW India. Macara was the capital. Situated mainly in the hilly Western Ghats, the Coorg region produces coffee and timber; rice is the principal lowland crop. An independent Hindu dynasty ruled Coorg from the late 16th cent. until it was annexed by the British in 1834. It was administered by a British chief commissioner until India became independent in 1947.

Coornhert, Dirck Volckertszoon (dûrk vôl'kərtzōn kôrn'hârt), 1522–90, Dutch humanist. His translation (1561) of the first 12 books of the *Odyssey* is considered the first major poetic work of the Dutch Renaissance. Coornhert also translated Cicero, Boccaccio, Seneca, and Boethius. His comedies, morality plays, and a philosophical treatise (1586) express his stoic and humanistic ideas. Coornhert, who had witnessed the methods of the Inquisition, was an active supporter of religious tolerance; his pamphlet (1585) on this subject led to his imprisonment and exile. He eventually returned to Holland and died at Gonda.

Coos (kō'ŏs), island in the Aegean Sea, the present-day KOS. Acts 21.1.

Coosa (ko͞o'sə), river, 286 mi (460 km) long, rising in NW Ga. and flowing SW through E Ala., joining the Tallapoosa near Montgomery, Ala., to form the Alabama River. Locks and dams make the river navigable for barges to Rome, Ga. Jordan, Lay, and Mitchell dams on the river generate electricity.

Coos Bay (ko͞os), city (1970 pop. 13,466), Coos co., SW Oregon, a port of entry on Coos Bay; founded 1854 as Marshfield, inc. 1874, renamed 1944. Lumbering, shipping, tourism, fishing, and canning are important industries. Coos Bay is one of the world's largest lumber-shipping ports. A junior college is in the city.

coot, common name for a marsh bird related to the rail and the gallinule and found in North America and Europe. The American coot *(Fulica americana),* or mud hen, is sooty gray with a white bill, black head and neck, and white wing edgings and tail patch. It has lobed toes and is a skillful swimmer and diver but takes flight awkwardly, pattering the water to gain impetus. It eats aquatic plants. Some scoter ducks are called coots. The European species inhabits the northern regions; there are seven species in South America alone. The horned coot is found high in the Andes. Coots are classified in the phylum CHORDATA, subphylum Vertebrata, class Aves, order Gruiformes, family Rallidae.

copaiba (kōpā'bə, -pī'-), oleoresin (see RESIN) obtained from several species of tropical South American trees of the genus *Copaifera.* The thick, transparent exudate varies in color from light gold to dark brown, depending on the ratio of resin to essential oil. Copaiba is used in making varnishes and lacquers.

copal (kō'pəl), RESIN produced by certain trees of tropical and subtropical regions. It is procured chiefly in fossil and semifossil form, but some is also obtained from living trees. Most copals come from leguminous trees of the PULSE family, e.g., the Congo copal and other African types (mostly of the *Copaifera* species) and the South American copals (chiefly *Hymenaea courbaril*). East Indian or Manila copal is extracted from a pine *(Agathis alba).* A source of hard-surfaced lacquers and varnishes, copals are no longer widely used commercially.

Copán (kōpän'), ruined city of the MAYA, W Honduras, near the village of Copán. Noted for fine sculptured stelae and in particular for the Hieroglyphic Stairway (containing nearly 2,000 glyphs), Copán was, perhaps, the center of knowledge where Mayan astronomical learning, as applied to chronology, achieved its most accurate expression.

Cope, Edward Drinker, 1840–97, American paleontologist and comparative anatomist, b. Philadelphia, studied at the Academy of Natural Sciences, Philadelphia, and at the Smithsonian Institution. His large collection of fossil mammals is now at the American Museum of Natural History. His many published works include *The Vertebrata of the Tertiary Formations of the West* (1883), a report on the F. V. Hayden survey in which he served as geologist and paleontologist. Cope believed that evolution arose from an organism's inner urge to attain a higher state of being. See biography by H. F. Osborn and H. A. Warren (1931).

Copeau, Jacques (zhäk kôpō'), 1879–1949, French theatrical producer and critic. A founder (1909) and editor (1912–14) of the *Nouvelle Revue française,* he established the experimental Théâtre du Vieux Colombier in Paris (1913–24) in order to produce poetic drama of artistic worth. Copeau, an influential figure in the modern theater, encouraged many young dramatists and actors and also introduced the use of symbolic scene design. See Wallace Fowlie, *Dionysus in Paris* (1960).

Copenhagen (kō'pənhā"gən), Dan. *København,* city (1971 pop. 625,678), capital of Denmark and of Copenhagen co., E Denmark, on E Sjaelland and N Amager islands and on the Øresund. It is a major commercial, fishing, and naval port and is Denmark's chief commercial, industrial, and cultural center. It is also a rail hub. Manufactures include pharmaceuticals, processed food, beer, textiles, plastics, marine engines, furniture, and the celebrated COPENHAGEN WARE. There are also iron foundries and large shipyards. Copenhagen was a trading and fishing center by the early 11th cent. It was fortified (1167) by Archbishop Absalon and was chartered (1254) by the bishop of Roskilde. The city was twice destroyed by the Hanseatic League but successfully resisted (1428) a third attack. Copenhagen replaced Roskilde as the Danish capital in 1443. The city exacted tolls from all ships passing through the Øresund until 1857. Having resisted (1658–59) a Swedish siege, Copenhagen was relieved by the Dutch. In 1660 peace between Denmark and Sweden was negotiated there. The city had expanded considerably in the 16th and 17th cent. as its trade grew, and it continued to develop in the 18th cent. as industries such as textile making and tobacco processing brought added prosperity. Copenhagen became involved in the war between Napoleonic France and England in the early 19th cent. The news that Denmark, by a secret convention, was about to join Napoleon's CONTINENTAL SYSTEM and to join in the war on England led the British government to decide to send an expeditionary force to seize the Danish fleet, which already had been mauled (1801) in the battle of Copenhagen. When the Danes refused to surrender, the British landed troops in 1807 and severely damaged Copenhagen by bombarding it. However, the city recovered quickly after the Napoleonic Wars, and its industrial base grew rapidly in the 19th cent. In World War II, Copenhagen was occupied (1940–45) by the Germans, and its shipyards were bombed by the Allies. The city itself was only slightly damaged, and it retained the charm and design that had resulted in its being called "the Paris of the North." The inner harbor of Copenhagen is the channel that divides Sjaelland and Amager islands. From the harbor extends a narrow arm, the Nyhavn [new harbor], lined with picturesque old houses and closed off by Kongens Nytorv, an irregular square from which the main arteries of the city radiate. The Charlottenborg Palace (17th cent.) and the royal theater (opened 1874) are on Kongens Nytorv. Other famous landmarks of the city include Amalienborg Square, enclosed by four 18th-century palaces, one of which has been the royal residence since 1794; the citadel (c.1662); the city hall (1894–1905); the famous round tower, which the astronomer Tycho Brahe (1546–1601) used as an observatory; and the Cathedral of Our Lady (c.1209; rebuilt in the early 19th cent.), with sculptures by Albert B. Thorvaldsen (1768–1844). The island of Slotsholmen, surrounded by a moat on three sides and by the harbor on the fourth, supports an impressive complex of buildings, notably Christiansborg Palace (18th cent.; restored 1916), erected on the site of Archbishop Absalon's original castle and now housing the Danish parliament, supreme court, and foreign office; the Thorvaldsen Museum (opened 1848); and the stock exchange (17th cent.). Favorite spots in the city include the Tivoli amusement park (opened 1843) and the waterfront Langelinie Promenade, near which is the famous statue of Hans Christian Andersen's *Little Mermaid.* Copenhagen is the seat of a university (founded 1479), a technical university (1829), an engineering college, and a college of veterinary science and agriculture. Frederiksberg and Gentofte are Copenhagen's largest suburbs and, although independent municipalities, are intimately tied to the life of the city. Frederiksberg is the seat of the Royal Copenhagen Porcelain factory (established 1651).

Copenhagen, battle of, 1801, an important incident of the FRENCH REVOLUTIONARY WARS. In Dec., 1800, Denmark joined Russia, Sweden, and Prussia in declaring the armed neutrality of the northern powers in the French Revolutionary Wars and in announcing that they would not comply with the British rules on neutral navigation. England considered this a threat and, without declaring war, sent a fleet under admirals Sir Hyde PARKER and Horatio NELSON into the Baltic. On April 2, 1801, Nelson attacked the Danish fleet at the roadsteads of Copenhagen. During the battle he deliberately fixed the telescope to his blind eye, thus ignoring Parker's signal to discontinue action, and destroyed the Danish fleet after a hard battle.

Copenhagen ware, several types of pottery, both underglaze and overglaze, produced in Copenhagen since c.1760. At that time a Frenchman, Louis Fournier, made soft-paste chinaware in the French style. Hard porcelain was introduced in 1775, when pieces with classical figures were in high favor. The Royal Copenhagen Porcelain factory and other factories have produced especially fine tableware and fluted porcelain of the blue Danish pattern. The modern white underglaze porcelain was first made by Arnold Krog in the late 19th cent. and was found to be well adapted to animal and figure sculptures.

copepod: see CRUSTACEAN.

Copernican system, first modern European theory of planetary motion that was heliocentric, i.e., that placed the sun motionless at the center of the solar system with all the planets, including the earth, revolving around it. Copernicus developed his theory in the early 16th cent. from a study of ancient astronomical records. He retained the ancient belief that the planets move in perfect circles and therefore, like Ptolemy, he was forced to utilize epicycles to explain deviations from uniform motion (see PTOLEMAIC SYSTEM). Thus, the Copernican system was technically only a slight improvement over the Ptolemaic system. However, making the solar system heliocentric removed the largest epicycle and explained retrograde motion in a natural way. By liberating astronomy from a geocentric viewpoint, Copernicus paved the way for KEPLER'S LAWS of planetary motion and Newton's embracing theory of universal GRAVITATION, which describes the force that holds the planets in their orbits.

Copernicus, Nicholas (kōpûr'nĭkəs), Pol. *Mikołaj Kopérnik*, 1473–1543, Polish astronomer. After studying astronomy at the Univ. of Kraków, he spent a number of years in Italy studying various subjects, including medicine and canon law. He lectured c.1500 in Rome on mathematics and astronomy; in 1512 he settled in Frauenburg, East Prussia, where he had been nominated canon of the cathedral. There he performed his canonical duties and also practiced medicine. But the work that immortalized him is *De revolutionibus orbium coelestium*, in which he set forth his beliefs concerning the universe, known as the COPERNICAN SYSTEM. That treatise, which was dedicated to Pope Paul III, was probably completed by 1530 but was not published until 1543, when Copernicus was on his deathbed. Modern astronomy was built upon the foundation of the Copernican system. See his complete works, ed. by Edward Rosen (Vol. I, 1973); *Three Copernican Treatises*, ed. by Edward Rosen (3d ed. 1971); studies by S. P. Mizwa (1943, repr. 1969), Angus Armitage (1938, repr. 1971), and Fred Hoyle (1973); Barbara Bienkowska, ed., *The Scientific World of Copernicus* (1973).

Copi, Irving Marmer (kŏp'ē), 1917–, American philosopher, b. Duluth, Minn., grad. Univ. of Mich., 1938, Ph.D. 1948. He was a philosophy professor at the Univ. of Illinois (1947–48) and the Univ. of Michigan (1948–69) before going to the Univ. of Hawaii (1969). Primarily interested in logic, he is the author of *The Theory of Logical Types* (1971), *Introduction to Logic* (4th ed. 1972), and *Symbolic Logic* (4th ed. 1973).

Copiague (kō"pāg'), uninc. residential town (1970 pop. 19,578), Suffolk co., SE N.Y., on the south shore of Long Island.

Copiapó (kōpyäpō'), city (1970 pop. 51,809), capital of Atacama prov., N central Chile, on the Copiapó River. An industrial city at the southern edge of the Desert of Atacama, Copiapó has industries that ship and process the copper, gold, and silver of the surrounding region. The city was founded in 1540 by Pedro de VALDIVIA, the Spanish conqueror of Chile.

Copland, Aaron (kōp'lənd), 1900–, American composer, b. Brooklyn, N.Y. Copland was a pupil of Rubin Goldmark and of Nadia Boulanger, who introduced his work to the United States when she played his Symphony for Organ and Orchestra in 1925. Although his earliest works show European influences, the American character of the greater part of his compositions is evident in his use of jazz and of American folk tunes, as in the short piece for chamber orchestra, *John Henry* (1940). Copland's many ballets include *Billy the Kid* (1938), *Rodeo* (1942), and *Appalachian Spring* (1944). He composed music for the films *Of Mice and Men* (1939), *Our Town* (1940), *The Red Pony* (1948), and *The Heiress* (1949). His major orchestral works are *El Salon Mexico* (1936) and the Third Symphony (1946). Copland wrote a song cycle, *12 Poems of Emily Dickinson*, and a quartet for piano and strings (both 1950), *Canticle of Freedom* for chorus and orchestra (1955), and a tone poem *Inscape* (1967). With Roger Sessions he founded the Copland-Sessions Concerts (1928–31) and in 1932 organized the American Festivals of Contemporary Music at Yaddo, Saratoga Springs, N.Y. He has lectured extensively and received many awards. His writings include *What to Listen for in Music* (1939, rev. ed. 1957), *Copland on Music* (1960), and *The New Music: 1900–1960* (rev. ed. 1968). See biographies by Arthur Berger (1953) and Arnold Dobrin (1967); study by J. F. Smith (1955).

Copley, John Singleton (kŏp'lē), 1738–1815, American portrait painter, b. Boston. Copley is considered the greatest of the American old masters. He studied with his stepfather, Peter Pelham, and undoubtedly frequented the studios of Smibert and Feke. At 20 he was already a successful portrait painter with a mature style remarkable for its brilliance, clarity, and forthright characterization. In 1766 his *Boy with the Squirrel* was exhibited in London and won the admiration of Benjamin West, who urged him to come to England. However, he remained for eight years longer in America and worked in New York City and Philadelphia as well as in Boston. In 1774 he visited Italy and then settled in London, where he spent the remainder of his life, enjoying many honors and the patronage of a distinguished clientele. In England his style gained in subtlety and polish but lost most of the vigor and individuality of his early work. He continued to paint portraits but enlarged his repertoire to include the enormous historical paintings which constituted the chief basis of his fame abroad. His large historical painting *The Death of Lord Chatham* (Tate Gall., London) gained him admittance to the Royal Academy. His rendering of a contemporary disaster, *Brook Watson and the Shark* (Mus. of Fine Arts, Boston), stands as a unique forerunner of romantic horror painting. However, his reputation today rests largely upon his early American portraits which are treasured not only for their splendid pictorial qualities but also as the most powerful graphic record of their time and place. Portraits such as those of Nicholas Boylston and Mrs. Thomas Boylston (Harvard Univ.), Daniel Hubbard (Art Inst., Chicago), Governor Mifflin and Mrs. Mifflin (Historical Society of Pennsylvania, Philadelphia), and Paul Revere (Mus. of Fine Arts, Boston) are priceless documents in which the life of a whole society seems mirrored. Among his finest later portraits are the curiously distorted image of Samuel Adams (Mus. of Fine Arts, Boston) and the group portrait of the Copley family (privately owned). The Museum of Fine Arts, Boston, has an excellent collection of his works. Copley's son became Baron Lyndhurst in 1827. See catalog with biography by J. D. Prown (1966); biographies by J. T. Flexner (rev. ed., 1948) and A. V. Frankenstein (1970).

Copley, John Singleton (1772–1863): see LYNDHURST, JOHN SINGLETON COPLEY, BARON.

copolymer: see POLYMER.

Coppard, Alfred Edgar, 1878–1957, English author. Almost entirely self-educated, he worked at several clerical positions. His tales, written in a poetic and fanciful vein, include *Adam and Eve and Pinch Me* (1921), *Nixey's Harlequin* (1931), and *Dark-eyed Lady* (1947). He also wrote lyric verse that includes *Hips and Haws* (1922), *Pelagea* (1926), and *Cherry Ripe* (1935). See his collected tales (1948).

Coppée, François (fräNswä' kôpā'), 1842–1908, French poet and dramatist. He won fame with the one-act comedy *Le Passant* (1869, tr. 1881), in which Sarah Bernhardt made her first successful appearance. His early verse, as in *Le Reliquaire* (1866), linked him with the PARNASSIANS; his later work, as in *Les Humbles* (1872), is sentimental and tells of the sorrows of the poor. *La Bonne Souffrance* (1898), a religious novel, was written after his return to Catholicism.

Copper, river, c.300 mi (480 km) long, rising in the Wrangell Mts., SE Alaska, and flowing S through the Chugach Mts. to the Gulf of Alaska. The Indians obtained copper from the deposits near the upper river; these deposits attracted the attention of the Russians and later the Americans, but exploration was difficult because of the river's currents and the glaciers near its mouth. The great Kennecott mine (discovered 1898) was finally developed and was reached by the building (1908–11) of the Copper River and Northwestern RR from Cordova, following the river along part of its lower valley. The mine was abandoned in 1938.

copper, metallic chemical element; symbol Cu [Lat. *cuprum*=copper]; at. no. 29; at. wt. 63.54; m.p. 1083°C; b.p. 2595°C; sp. gr. 8.96 at 20°C; valence +1 or +2. Copper is a reddish metal with a face-centered cubic crystalline structure. It is malleable, ductile, and an extremely good conductor of both heat and electricity. It is softer than iron but harder than zinc and can be polished to a bright finish. It is found in group Ib of the PERIODIC TABLE, together with silver and gold. Copper has low chemical reactivity. In moist air it slowly forms a greenish surface film (usually a mixture of carbonate, sulfate, hydroxide, and oxide) called PATINA; this coating protects the metal from further attack. Copper dissolves in hot concentrated hydrochloric or sulfuric acid but is little affected by cold solutions of these acids; it also dissolves in nitric acid. Salt water corrodes copper, forming a chloride. The chief commercial use of copper is based on its electrical conductivity (second only to that of silver); about half the total annual output of copper is employed in the manufacture of electrical apparatus and wire. Copper is also used extensively as roofing, in making copper utensils, and for coins and metalwork. Copper tubing is used in plumbing, and, because of its high heat conductivity, in heat-exchanging devices such as refrigerator and air-conditioner coils. Powdered copper is sometimes used as a pigment in paints. An important use of copper is in alloys such as BRASS, BRONZE, GUN METAL, MONEL METAL, and GERMAN SILVER. The most important chemical compound of copper is COPPER SULFATE pentahydrate, also called bluestone or blue vitriol. Other compounds include PARIS GREEN, BORDEAUX MIXTURE, a cyanide, a chloride, oxides, and a basic carbonate. Verdigris is basic copper acetate. Compounds of copper are widely used as insecticides and fungicides; as pigments in paints; as mordants in dyeing; and in electroplating. Small amounts of copper are found uncombined, particularly near Lake Superior in Michigan. Copper ores are found in various parts of the world. In the United States (the chief producer of copper) ores are mined in Arizona, Utah, Montana, New Mexico, Nevada, and Michigan. Copper ores are also found in Canada, South America (in Chile and Peru), S central Africa, the Soviet Union (in the Ural Mts.), and to a limited extent in Europe and the British Isles. The principal ore of copper is CHALCOPYRITE, a sulfide of copper and iron, also called copper pyrite. Other important ores are chalcocite, or copper glance, a shiny lead-gray copper sulfide; bornite, a lustrous reddish-brown sulfide of copper and iron; cuprite, a red cuprous oxide ore; and MALACHITE, a bright green carbonate ore. AZURITE is a blue crystalline basic carbonate of copper found with other copper ores. Chrysocolla is a bluish-green copper silicate ore. Copper metal is prepared commercially in various ways. Copper sulfide ores, usually containing only 1% to 2% copper, are concentrated to 20% to 40% copper by the FLOTATION PROCESS. They are then usually roasted to remove some of the sulfur and other impurities, and then smelted with iron oxide in either a blast furnace or a reverberatory furnace to produce copper matte, a molten solution of copper sulfide mixed with small amounts of iron sulfide. The matte is transferred to a converter, where it is treated by blowing air through it to remove the sulfur (as sulfur dioxide, a gas) and the iron (as a slag of ferrous oxide). The resulting copper is 98% to 99% pure; it is called blister copper because its surface is blistered by escaping gases when it solidifies during casting. Most copper is further purified by ELECTROLYSIS. The blister copper is refined in a furnace and cast into anodes. Thin sheets of pure copper are used as cathodes. A solution of copper sulfate and sulfuric acid is used as the electrolyte. When the anode and cathode are immersed in the electrolyte and an electric current is passed, the anode is dissolved in the electrolyte and pure copper metal is deposited on the cathode. Soluble impurities, usually nickel and arsenic, remain dissolved in the electrolyte. Insoluble impurities, often including silver, gold, and other valuable metals, settle out of the electrolyte; they may be collected and purified. Copper oxide ores are usually treated by a different process, called leaching, in which the copper in the ore is dissolved in a leaching solution (usually dilute sulfuric acid); pure copper is recovered by electrolysis. Alternatively, the solution is treated with iron to precipitate the so-called cement copper, which is impure. Another important source of copper is secondary (scrap) copper, which is produced from discarded copper and copper alloys. Copper is present in minute amounts in the animal body and is essential to normal metabolism. It is a component of hemocyanin, the blue, oxygen-carrying blood pigment of lobsters and other large crustaceans. It is needed in the synthesis of hemoglobin, the red, oxygen-carrying pigment found in the blood of humans, although it is not a component of hemoglobin. Copper and some of its alloys have been known to man since the BRONZE AGE. One of the first metals known to man, free copper was probably mined in the Tigris-Euphrates valley as long ago as the 5th cent. B.C. Cyprus, from which the metal's name ultimately comes, was the primary source of copper in the ancient world.

Copper Age: see BRONZE AGE.

copperas: the heptahydrate of FERROUS SULFATE.

Copperas Cove (kŏp'ərəs), town (1970 pop. 10,818), Coryell co., central Texas. A farm and ranch center, it grew with the establishment of nearby U.S. Fort Hood.

Copperbelt, mining region, N central Zambia, central Africa. A natural extension of the mineral-rich region of SHABA, the Copperbelt is one of the richest sources of copper in the world. Cobalt, selenium, silver, and gold are also produced.

copperhead, poisonous snake, *Ancistrodon contortrix*, of the E United States. Like its close relative, the water moccasin, the copperhead is a member of the PIT VIPER family, and detects its warm-blooded prey by means of a heat-sensitive organ behind the nostril. The body, which may reach a length of 4 ft

(120 cm), is hazel brown with chestnut-colored crossbands above and pinkish white with dark spots below. The head is a pale copper color. Copperheads inhabit rocky areas with thick underbrush, even in heavily populated regions. They feed chiefly on small mammals, but will also capture large insects, frogs, and other snakes. They are most active in late afternoon and early evening. The young are born alive. Copperheads are not aggressive and usually attempt escape when threatened, but they strike swiftly if startled or attacked. The bite causes severe pain and illness in humans but is seldom fatal. Copperheads are classified in the phylum CHORDATA, subphylum Vertebrata, class Reptilia, order Squamata, family Crotalidae.

Copperheads, in the American Civil War, a reproachful term for those Northerners sympathetic to the South, mostly Democrats outspoken in their opposition to the Lincoln administration. They were especially strong in Illinois, Indiana, and Ohio, where Clement L. VALLANDIGHAM was their leader. The KNIGHTS OF THE GOLDEN CIRCLE was a Copperhead secret society. The term was often applied indiscriminately to all Democrats who opposed the administration. It afforded an opportunity for impugning the loyalty of those who opposed Lincoln's policies, either military or civil (e.g., the suspension of habeas corpus), and it was not until years after the Civil War that the Democratic party succeeded in living down the association. See Wood Gray, *The Hidden Civil War* (1942); F. L. Klement, *The Copperheads in the Middle West* (1960).

Coppermine, river, 525 mi (845 km) long, rising in Lac de Gras, central Mackenzie dist., Northwest Territories, Canada, and winding northwest to enter the Arctic Ocean at Coronation Gulf. Its many falls gives it great hydroelectric power potential. Coppermine, a trading post, is at its mouth.

copper pyrites: see CHALCOPYRITE.

copper sulfate, common name for the blue crystalline heptahydrate of CUPRIC SULFATE, in which copper has valence +2. It may also refer to cuprous sulfate (Cu_2SO_4), in which copper has valence +1.

Coppet (kôpā'), village, Vaud canton, SW Switzerland, on the Lake of Geneva. It is noted for its château, once the residence of Jacques Necker and his daughter, Mme de Staël.

copra: see COCONUT.

Copt (kŏpt), member of the native Christian minority (5%–10%) of Egypt. Copts are not ethnically distinct; they are a cultural remnant, i.e., the Christians who have not been converted to Islam in the 14 centuries since the Muslim invasion. The **Coptic language,** now extinct, was the form of the ancient Egyptian language spoken in early Christian times; by the 12th cent. it was superseded by Arabic. Most Copts belong to the **Coptic Church,** an autonomous Christian sect that officially adheres to MONOPHYSITISM, which was declared (451) a heresy by the Council of Chalcedon. The church is in communion with the Jacobite Church (also Monophysite), but a traditionally close relationship to the Church of Ethiopia was dissolved in 1961 when it declared itself independent of the Coptic patriarch. In rites and customs the Coptic Church resembles other Oriental churches; however, Copts circumcise their infants before baptism and observe certain Mosaic dietary laws. Coptic, Greek, and Arabic languages are all used ceremonially. The chief bishop, the patriarch of Alexandria, is in direct succession to the 5th-century patriarchs who embraced Monophysitism. Among the Copts a small minority are in communion with the pope; these "Catholic Copts" have their own organization and churches but share the rites and practices of the Coptic Church. This community began to develop in the 18th cent. Protestant missions have had some success among the Copts. Besides Copts there are Orthodox communities in Egypt, mainly Greek and Syrian; the Orthodox patriarch of Alexandria traces his succession to the Catholic patriarchs of the 5th cent. There are also many Catholic Syrians, mainly Melchites and Maronites. See Donald Attwater, *The Christian Churches of the East* (2 vol., 1947–48); Edward Wakin, *A Lonely Minority: The Story of Egypt's Copts* (1963); Murād Kāmil, *Coptic Egypt* (1968); O. F. A. Meindarus, *Christian Egypt, Faith and Life* (1970).

Coptic art, Christian art in the upper Nile valley of Egypt. Reaching its mature phase in the late 5th and 6th cent., the development of Coptic art was interrupted by the Arab conquest of Egypt between 640 and 642. Its subsequent course was marked by the influence of Islamic art and a repetition of earlier forms. In contrast with the aristocratic taste prevailing in cosmopolitan Alexandria, which was in close touch with the leading artistic centers of the Roman Empire, older and deeply ingrained traditions remained in force in the upper Nile valley, where an intensely religious culture drew its following chiefly from the lower classes. Coptic art is characterized by a high degree of stylization verging on abstraction. Forms are flattened out, and individual motifs acquire bold simplicity and decorative character. Subject matter represents both Christian and Roman sources. Remains of wall paintings reveal scenes from the Old and New Testaments and images of the Mother and Child. Some of the archaeological sites are El-Bagawat, Oxyrhynchus, Sakkara, Bawit, and Antinoë. Representative examples of Coptic art are in sculpture, textiles, ivory, and illumination. Coptic architecture, as shown in the 5th-century White and Red monasteries near Sohag, showed traces of local Egyptian traditions. See K. Wessel, *Coptic Art: The Early Christian Art of Egypt* (1965).

Coptos (kŏp'təs, -tŏs) or **Coptus** (kŏp'təs), ancient city of Egypt, on the right bank of the Nile, c.27 mi (43 km) N of modern Luxor. Remains of the Temple of Min, patron god of Coptos, have been found there as well as relics from the time of Ramses II and Thutmose III. The town was of importance in Hellenistic times, when it was the terminus of a caravan route to Berenice on the Red Sea. It was built up by Augustus, fell to the Blemmyes in the 3d cent. A.D., and was almost destroyed by Diocletian in A.D. 292. The present-day village of Qift is on the site.

copying processes: see PRINTING; PHOTOCOPYING.

copyright, right granted by statute to the author or originator of certain literary, artistic, and musical productions whereby for a limited period of time he controls the use of the product. He may reproduce the work himself or license another to do so. He receives royalties (payments) on each performance of his work or each copy that is sold. Except for limited measures taken in Roman times, protection of rights in literary property did not appear necessary in Europe before the invention of printing from movable type in the 15th cent. The sovereign asserted his control over printing by issuing patents or privileges to individuals or by organizing publishers' guilds with monopoly rights. Through such devices the state was able to censor heresy and sedition, while at the same time fostering literature. The guilds kept order among their members and were supposed to prevent pirating. In England this function was assigned to the Stationers' Company (chartered 1556), comprising a hundred or so printers and booksellers. The only protection that the common law extended to the author was against publication of his work without his permission; once he allowed publication, the work passed completely out of his control. The first English copyright act (1710), while not abolishing the common-law right, allowed the author to copyright his work for 14 years (with a like period of renewal) and required deposition of copies and a notice that the work was copyrighted. That law was the model for the earliest American copyright statute, passed in 1790 pursuant to Article 1, Section 8 of the U.S. Constitution. The American statute in force today was passed in 1909. It provides for a term of 28 years and a single renewal of the term. Material for copyright must be deposited with the Library of Congress. Literary matter, periodicals, maps, photographs, works of art, textile and other designs, sound recordings, musical compositions, and photoplays may be copyrighted. In the United States prior to 1891, when a special foreign copyright law was passed, it was almost impossible for books by foreign authors to be copyrighted. The most popular British books were published in cheap unauthorized editions, and the writers often received no royalties. After 1891 material in foreign languages was easily copyrighted in the United States; material in English, however, could not be copyrighted if it was imported, unless, in addition, type was set and material printed and bound in the United States. Most of the major countries of the world, with the exception of the United States, however, adhered to the Bern Convention, effective in 1887 and since modified. It provides that literary material copyrighted in any signatory country automatically enjoys copyright in all the signatory countries. The Universal Copyright Convention (UCC), which had as one main purpose bringing the United States into a general system of international copyright, was signed at Geneva on Sept. 6, 1952. It was accepted by the United States in 1954 and came into effect Sept. 16, 1955. The U.S. copyright law was modified to conform to the convention, notably by elimination of procedural steps for the establishment of U.S. copyright in works published in other signatory countries and of the requirement that works in the English language by foreign authors must be manufactured in the United States to obtain U.S. copyright protection. Other countries accept the U.S. principle of formal notice of copyright. The United Nations Educational, Scientific, and Cultural Organization played a leading part in the negotiations for the UCC. Most of the Western nations and many of the Asian nations subscribe to it. The Soviet Union signed in 1973. See Margaret Nicholson, *A Manual of Copyright Practice for Writers, Publishers, and Agents* (2d ed. 1956, repr. 1970); Richard Wincor, *How to Secure Copyright* (rev. ed. 1957); A. J. Clark, *The Movement for International Copyright in 19th Century America* (1960); L. R. Patterson, *Copyright in Historical Perspective* (1968); H. F. Pilpel and M. D. Goldberg, *Copyright Guide* (4th ed. 1969).

Coquelin, Benoît Constant (bənwä' kôNstäN' kôklăN'), 1841–1909, French actor, known as Coquelin aîné [the elder]. He made his debut at the Comédie française in 1860 and achieved fame in classic comic roles, such as the valets in Molière's plays and Beaumarchais's *Figaro*. He made an extensive tour of Europe and America in 1886. In 1897 he created his greatest characterization, the title role in Rostand's *Cyrano de Bergerac*, at the Théâtre de la Porte-Saint-Martin, which he also managed. In 1900 he toured the United States with Sarah Bernhardt and returned to Paris to play opposite her in Rostand's *L'Aiglon*. Highly critical and analytical toward his art, and believing in simulated rather than real emotions, he wrote *L'Art et le comédien* (1880) and *Les Comédiens, par un comédien* (1882); his approach led to an interesting debate with Sir Henry IRVING on techniques of acting. His brother, **Ernest Alexandre Honoré Coquelin,** 1848–1909, known as Coquelin cadet [the younger], acted at the Comédie française after 1868. At his best in secondary comic roles, he was also popular for his monologues and several amusing books written under the pseudonym Pirouette.

Coquerel, Athanase Laurent Charles (ätänäz' lōrăN' shärl kôkrĕl'), 1795–1868, French Protestant clergyman, noted for his eloquence as a preacher. From 1832 he was pastor of the Reformed Church in Paris. He founded and edited liberal periodicals. Among his publications are *Biographie sacrée* (1825–26), *L'Orthodoxie moderne* (1842), and *Christologie* (1858). His son **Athanase Josué Coquerel,** 1820–75, was also a well-known Protestant minister in Paris. From 1849 to 1870 he edited the *Lien*. In 1852 he helped to found the *Nouvelle Revue de théologie*. Among his works are *Jean Calas et sa famille* (1857) and *Histoire de l'Église réformée de Paris* (1860).

Coques or **Cocx, Gonzales** (gōnzä'lĕs kōks), 1614–84, Flemish portrait painter, active in Antwerp and England. He excelled in painting diminutive portraits and family groups of the aristocracy with meticulously executed backgrounds. The elegance of his paintings won him the title "the little Van Dyck." Coques is represented in the galleries of Berlin, Dresden, Paris, London, Vienna, and Philadelphia.

Coquilhatville, Zaïre: see MBANDAKA.

coquilla nut (kōkē'yə, kōkēl'yə), [Span.,=little coconut], fruit of a Brazilian PALM (*Attalea funifera*), closely related to the coconut palm. Its fruit, 3 to 4 in. (7.6–10.2 cm) long, is very hard, of a richly streaked brown, and capable of taking a fine polish; it is used in cabinetwork and for such turned articles as bellpulls, umbrella handles, and walking-stick knobs. A stiff, wiry, bright chocolate-colored leaf fiber, called piassava or piassaba, obtained from this and similar palms, is exported. It is used in making brooms and rope. The nut is also a source of palm oil. Coquilla nuts are classified in the division MAGNOLIOPHYTA, class Liliatae, order Arecales, family Palmae.

Coquimbo (kōkēm'bō), city (1970 pop. 55,360), N central Chile. On a beautiful sheltered bay of the Pacific, it is the port for LA SERENA. Exports are chiefly agricultural produce and minerals. In 1922, Coquimbo was severely damaged by a tidal wave following an earthquake.

coral, small, sedentary, marine animal, related to the sea anemone, but characterized by a skeleton of horny or calcareous material. The skeleton itself is also called coral. Although most corals form colonies by budding, there are some solitary corals; in both types the individual animals, called polyps, resemble the sea anemone in form. In the large group known as stony corals, or true corals (Madreporaria), each polyp secretes a cup-shaped skeleton, the theca, around itself. Some solitary corals of that group may reach a diameter of 10 in. (25 cm); in the colonial forms the individual polyps are usually under 1/8 in. (3 mm) long, but the colonies may be enormous. The body of each polyp is saclike, consisting of a wall of jellylike material surrounding a digestive cavity, with a single opening, the mouth, at the unattached end. The mouth is surrounded by tentacles used to capture small prey, and is invaginated to form a pharynx leading into the body cavity. Thin sheets of tissue (mesentaries) extend radially from the wall to the pharynx, dividing the cavity. A second set of radial divisions is created by folds (septa) of the outer skeleton and body wall, which extend upward from the floor of the body cavity. Reproduction occurs both sexually and by budding. Sexual reproduction is by means of eggs and sperm that are produced in the mesentaries and shed into the water. Fertilization results in a free-swimming larva, which attaches to a surface and secretes a skeleton, becoming (in colonial forms) the parent of a new colony. As new polyps are produced by budding they remain attached to each other by thin sheets of living tissue as well as by newly secreted skeletal material. The great variety in the form of various colonial corals, which may be treelike and branching, or rounded and compact, depends chiefly on the method of budding of the particular species. In the brain corals, for example, each theca merges with the one next to it on either side, forming long rows of polyps separated by deep channels. In some of the branching corals the polyps occupy small, discrete pits on the surface of the skeleton. As a colonial coral produces more polyps the lower members die, and new layers are built up on the old skeleton, forming a large mass. In tropical and subtropical regions, these massive corals, along with other plants and animals, may form a CORAL REEF. Most of the reef-forming corals belong to the stony coral group. The soft corals (Alcyonaria) are a group of soft, often feathery forms, with skeletons composed of calcareous or horny particles imbedded in the body wall. Each polyp of a soft coral has eight tentacles. Among the well-known soft corals are the SEA PEN, SEA PANSY, whip coral, and organpipe coral. The precious red coral (*Corallium*) of the Mediterranean Sea, used for jewelry, also belongs to that group. The spicules of its skeleton are fused together. Although corals grow in both warm and temperate climates, they are most abundant in warm, shallow water; over 200 coral species are found in the Great Barrier Reef of Australia. In many shallow-water species the polyps contain unicellular plants, which may provide the high oxygen concentration required by such corals. Stony and soft corals are classified in the phylum CNIDARIA, class Anthozoa.

coral bells: see SAXIFRAGE.

Coral Gables, city (1970 pop. 42,494), Dade co., SE Fla., on Biscayne Bay; inc. 1925. Founded at the height of the Florida land boom, Coral Gables is mainly residential and is a splendid example of a planned city. Electronic equipment, processed meat, and furniture are among its products. Coral Gables is the headquarters for various Inter-American business organizations. The Univ. of Miami is in the city.

coralline algae: see RHODOPHYTA.

coral reefs, limestone formations produced by living organisms, found in shallow, tropical marine waters. In most reefs, the predominant organisms are stony CORALS, colonial cnidarians that secrete an exoskeleton of calcium carbonate (limestone). The accumulation of skeletal material, broken and piled up by wave action, produces a massive calcareous formation that supports the living corals and a great variety of other animal and plant life. Although corals are found both in temperate and tropical waters, reefs are formed only in a zone extending at most from 30°N to 30°S of the equator; the reef-forming corals do not grow at depths of over 100 ft (30 m) or where the water temperature falls below 72°F (22°C). Corals are not the only, and in some cases not even the major, reef-forming organisms. Calcium carbonate is also deposited by coralline algae, the protozoan FORAMINIFERANS, some mollusks, echinoderms, and tube-building annelid worms. However, any reef formed by a biological community is usually called a coral reef. Geologically, coral reefs are classified into three main types. Fringing reefs are coral platforms that are more or less continuous with the shore and exposed at low tide. Barrier reefs are separated from the shore by a wide, deep lagoon or surround a lagoon that has a central island. An atoll is a reef surrounding a lagoon that has no central island, with passages through the reef to the sea. It is generally believed that fringing reefs formed as a result of upward and outward growth of corals that became established on rocks near shore; there is disagreement about the nature of barrier reef and atoll formation. Charles Darwin postulated a progression from fringing reef to barrier reef to atoll, as a result of a slow, steady sinking of the sea floor that creates a lagoon and a simultaneous upward and outward growth of coral. Where entire volcanic islands sink, only the reef remains above water, forming an atoll. Not all scientists accept Darwin's proposal, but most current theories involve subsidence of the sea floor. Changes of the ocean level may also be involved. Sediments accumulate on the lagoon side of atolls and support vegetation; in time the entire lagoon may fill, creating an island. Many such atolls and islands, common in the Pacific and Indian oceans, are inhabited. The Great Barrier Reef of NE Australia is the largest known complex of coral reefs. It is 10 to 90 mi (16–145 km) wide and about 1250 mi (2010 km) long, and is separated from the shore by a lagoon 10 to 150 mi (16–240 km) wide. See Robert Silverberg, *The World of Coral* (1965).

coral-root: see ORCHID.

Coral Sea, southwest arm of the Pacific Ocean, between Australia, New Guinea, and the New Hebrides. The Great Barrier Reef lies along its western edge. During World War II it was the scene of a major U.S. victory against the Japanese in 1942; the battle, fought by aircraft near the Louisiade Archipelago, checked the southward expansion of the Japanese.

coral snake, name for poisonous New World snakes of the same family as the Old World COBRAS. About 30 species inhabit Mexico, Central America, and N South America; two are found in the United States. The Eastern coral snake (*Micrurus fulvius*), or harlequin snake, is found in the SE United States and N Mexico. It is a burrowing snake with a small, blunt head and a cylindrical body, averaging 2½ ft (75 cm) in length. The body is ringed with bands of black, red, and yellow; the tail has yellow and black rings only. The Sonoran, or Western, coral snake (*Micruroides euryxanthus*) is a rather rare species found in the SW United States and NW Mexico. It is about 18 in. (45 cm) long and has much broader bands of yellow than those of the Eastern species. Coral snakes can be distinguished from a number of similarly colored harmless snakes by the fact that they are the only ones with red bands touching yellow ones. The venom of coral snakes, like that of cobras, acts on the nervous system and causes paralysis; the mortality rate among humans who are bitten is high. However, coral snakes are infrequently encountered because of their burrowing habits, and they seldom bite unless handled. They feed on other snakes and on lizards. Coral snakes are classified in the phylum CHORDATA, subphylum Vertebrata, class Reptilia, order Squamata, family Elapidae.

Coram, Thomas (kôr'əm), 1668?–1751, English philanthropist and colonizer. He lived for some years in Massachusetts, working as a shipbuilder. On his return to England he became (1732) a trustee of James Oglethorpe's Georgia colony and sponsored (1735) a colony in Nova Scotia for unemployed artisans. He established the London Foundling Hospital (1739), a pioneer institution of its kind. See biography by Herbert Compston (1918).

Corbett, James John, 1866–1933, American boxer, b. San Francisco. "Gentleman Jim" Corbett won (1892) the heavyweight boxing championship from John L. SULLIVAN at New Orleans and lost (1897) the title to Robert L. FITZSIMMONS at Carson City, Nev. He failed (1900, 1903) to regain the title in fights with James J. Jeffries. Corbett also appeared on the stage and in films and wrote *The Roar of the Crowd* (1925).

Corbière, Tristan (trĕstäN' kôrbyĕr'), 1845–75, French poet, born Édouard Joachim Corbière. He spent most of his life on the coast of Brittany, living a Bohemian existence and suffering chronic illness. His passion for the sea is expressed in his early poems *Gens de mer* [men of the sea], which were collected in *Les Amours jaunes* (1873, tr. 1954). Corbière's style combines vernacular elements with complex, intimate emotion and constantly reflects his internal pain. Verlaine brought his work to the attention of the literary world, and, in the 20th cent., the surrealist writers claimed him as an ancestor.

Corbin, Margaret, 1751–1800, American Revolutionary heroine, b. Franklin co., Pa. Upon the death of her husband in the attack on Fort Washington (Nov. 16, 1776), she commanded his cannon until she was seriously wounded. She was the first woman to be pensioned (1779) by the government. In 1916 her remains were moved from Highland Falls, N.Y., to West Point, where a monument was erected in her honor.

corbina (kôrbē'nə): see CROAKER.

Corby, urban district (1971 pop. 47,716), Northamptonshire, central England. Situated over one of the world's largest ironstone fields, Corby has grown rapidly since the 1930s, when new techniques of steel production were developed. The manufacture of steel tubing is the chief industry.

Corcoran, William Wilson (kôr'kərən), 1798–1888, American financier, philanthropist, and art collector, b. Georgetown, D.C. After becoming a successful banker, he retired in 1854 and devoted himself to his philanthropic activities, which included gifts to many educational and religious institutions, as well as the founding of the Louise Home for Women in Washington. His chief gift was the **Corcoran Gallery of Art,** in Washington, which had as its nucleus Corcoran's art collection. The present marble building, designed by Ernest Flagg, was opened in 1897. The gallery has collections of paintings, sculpture, and ceramics, as well as an art school.

Corcoran Gallery of Art: see under CORCORAN, WILLIAM WILSON.

Corcyra: see KÉRKIRA, Greece.

cordage, collective name for rope and other flexible lines. It is used for such purposes as wrapping, hauling, lifting, and power transmission. Early man used strips of hide, animal hair, and plant materials. Hemp and flax were formerly standard in Europe and America but were largely replaced in the 19th cent. by hard fibers, especially Manila hemp and sisal. In the 20th cent. the natural fibers have been replaced in many applications by synthetic fibers such as nylon and polyester. The fibers are straightened, usually by combing, then spun into yarn. Twine, which is sometimes called cord, is formed by wrapping two or more yarns together. By twisting together a number of yarns, a strand is formed. By twisting together three or more strands, a rope is produced. A cable-laid rope is formed from three or more ropes. In general a synthetic fiber rope lasts much longer and is much stronger than a natural fiber rope. Steel wire, often with a fiber core, is also used for rope.

Corday, Charlotte (Marie Anne Charlotte Corday d'Armont) (kōrdā', mărē' än shärlôt', därmôN'), 1768–93, assassin of Jean Paul MARAT. Although of aristocratic background, she sympathized with the GIRONDISTS in the French Revolution and felt that Marat, in his persecution of the Girondists, was acting as the evil genius of France. She resolved to emulate the action of Brutus and destroy the "tyrant." Leaving her native Normandy for Paris, she gained an audience with Marat by promising to betray the Girondists of Caen and stabbed him (July 13, 1793) in his bath. She was guillotined. See Austin Dobson, *Four Frenchwomen* (1923); Joseph Shearing (pseud. of G. M. V. C. Long), *The Angel of the Assassination* (1935).

Cordele (kôrdēl'), city (1970 pop. 10,733), seat of Crisp co., S central Ga., on a branch of the Flint River; founded and inc. 1888. It is a shipping, commercial, and processing center located in a timber and farm area. Watermelons, cotton, peanuts, corn, and cantaloupes are grown there.

Cordeliers (kôrdəlyā'), political club of the French Revolution. Founded (1790) as the Society of the Friends of the Rights of Man and of the Citizen, it was called after its original meeting place, the suppressed monastery of the Cordeliers (Franciscan Recollects). In 1792–93 the club was instrumental in the destruction of the GIRONDISTS, or moderates. Its early leaders, such as Georges DANTON, having withdrawn, the club drifted to the extreme left under the influence of Jean Paul MARAT and Jacques René HÉBERT. Controlling the Paris commune, the extremists, or Hébertists, were a threat to the power of Maximilien ROBESPIERRE, who had them executed during the REIGN OF TERROR. The club dissolved after Hébert was executed (March, 1794).

cordial: see LIQUEUR.

Cordier, Andrew Wellington, 1901–, American educator and public official, b. Canton, Ohio. He studied at Manchester College in Indiana, where he later taught (1923–44). He also studied at the Univ. of Chicago and at the Graduate Institute of International Studies in Geneva. After working briefly for the U.S. Dept. of State (1944–46) he began a long association with the United Nations, where he was until 1962 executive assistant to the UN secretaries general. He was a chief negotiator for the United Nations in the Congo in 1960. In 1962 he became dean of the School of International Affairs (SIA) at Columbia. When Grayson Kirk resigned, he served as acting president (1968–69) and then as president (1969–70) of Columbia, subsequently returning to his post at SIA until 1972.

Cordilleras (kôrdĭl'ərəz, Span. kōrdēyä'räs) [Span., originally=little string], general name for the entire chain of mountain systems of W North America, extending from N Alaska to Nicaragua. The Cordilleras include the Rocky Mts., the ranges of the Great Basin, the Sierra Nevada, the Coast Ranges, and the Sierra Madre. The name Cordilleras was first applied to the similar systems of W South America, where the mountains stretching from Panama to Cape Horn are known locally as the Cordillera de los Andes (Andes Mts.). Some geographers use the term *cordillera* for any extensive group of mountain systems.

cordite: see POWDER.

Córdoba, Francisco Fernández de: see FERNÁNDEZ DE CÓRDOBA, FRANCISCO.

Córdoba, Gonzalo Fernández de: see FERNÁNDEZ DE CÓRDOBA, GONZALO.

Córdoba (kôr'dōvä), city (1970 pop. 798,663), capital of Córdoba prov., central Argentina, on the Río Primero. It is the third largest city of Argentina and a cultural and commercial center. Near the city on the Primero is one of the most important dams in South America. Irrigation has transformed the surrounding countryside, formerly devoted to cattle ranches, into orchards, grain fields, and vineyards. Córdoba exports wheat, cattle, lumber, and minerals, and there are some small industries. The city is also a popular tourist and health resort. Córdoba was founded in 1573 and prospered during colonial times as a link on the commercial route between Buenos Aires and Chile. The advent of the railroad in the 19th cent. increased prosperity. Many buildings in the city date from colonial times. Most notable are the cathedral and the former city hall (now a police headquarters). The university (founded 1613) made Córdoba an early intellectual center of South America. The city also has an observatory and several museums.

Córdoba, city (1970 pop. 60,944), Veracruz state, E central Mexico. It is the commercial and processing center of a fertile coffee, sugarcane, and tropical fruit region. Sugar milling is the chief industry. The city is also a popular tourist spot. Córdoba was founded in 1617. The Spanish viceroy O'Donojú and the Mexican revolutionary Agustín de ITURBIDE signed a treaty there in 1821 that established Mexico's independence.

Córdoba or **Cordova,** city (1970 pop. 235,632), capital of Córdoba prov., S Spain, in Andalusia, on the Guadalquivir River. Modern industries in the city include brewing, distilling, textile manufacturing, and metallurgy. Of Iberian origin, Córdoba flourished under the Romans, then passed to the Visigoths (572) and the Moors (711). Under the Umayyad dynasty it became the seat (756–1031) of an independent emirate, later called caliphate, which included most of Muslim Spain. The city was then one of the greatest and wealthiest in Europe, renowned as a center of Muslim and Jewish culture and admired for its architectural glories—notably, the great mosque, begun in the 8th cent., which is one of the finest of all Muslim monuments, and for its gold, silver, silk, and leather work. The city reached its zenith under Abd ar-Rahman III but declined after the fall of the Umayyads and became subject to Seville in 1078. Ferdinand III of Castile conquered it in 1236; in 1238 the great mosque became a cathedral. Córdoba never recovered its former splendor, but remained famous for its work in gold, silver, and leather. It was sacked by the French in 1808 and sided with Franco early (1936) in the civil war. The Senecas, Lucan, Averroës, and Maimonides were born in Córdoba. There is a university in the city.

Cordova, Spain: see CÓRDOBA.

corduroy, a cut filling-pile fabric with lengthwise ridges, or wales, that may vary from fine (pinwale) to wide. Extra filling yarns float over a number of warp yarns that form either a plain-weave or twill-weave ground. After the fabric is woven the floating yarns are cut, and the pile is brushed and singed to produce a clear cord effect. Originally a cotton fabric, it may also be made of man-made fibers such as rayon, polyester, or acrylic. Among its uses are in the manufacture of trousers, coats, and slip covers.

Core (kō'rē), variant of KORAH.

Corelli, Arcangelo (ärkän'jālō kōrĕl'lē), 1653–1713, Italian composer and violinist. Famed for his virtuosity and his elegant style of composition, he spent most of his life in Rome, where he was court violinist to Cardinal Ottoboni. His violin technique was perpetuated by his many students and in his sonatas for violin with harpsichord, among which is the well-known set of variations on the air *La Follia.* He also helped to establish the typical form of the concerto grosso (see CONCERTO). See Marc Pincherle, *Corelli: His Life, His Work* (tr., 1956).

Corelli, Franco (fräng'kō), 1923?–, Italian tenor. He made his debut at Spoleto in 1952 as Don José in Bizet's *Carmen.* In 1961 he made his debut with the Metropolitan Opera, singing Manrico in Verdi's *Il Trovatore.* Since then he has been a leading tenor with the Metropolitan, extraordinarily popular, and famed for the great volume of his voice. He is particularly noted for his performances as Calaf in Puccini's *Turandot* and as Cavaradossi in *Tosca.*

Corelli, Marie (kərĕl'ē), pseud. of **Mary Mackay,** 1855–1924, English novelist. Her popular, highly moralistic books, written in flamboyant, pretentious prose, include *A Romance of Two Worlds* (1886), *Thelma* (1887), *Barabbas* (1893), and *The Sorrows of Satan* (1895). She was Queen Victoria's favorite novelist. See biographies by Eileen Bigland (1953) and W. S. Scott (1955).

coreopsis (kōrēŏp'sĭs), or **tickseed,** names for species of *Coreopsis,* a chiefly North American genus of the family Compositae (COMPOSITE family). They are easily cultivated annuals or perennials with daisylike heads of flowers in various colors—commonly yellow or variegated. Garden kinds are sometimes called calliopsis. Coreopsis is classified in the division MAGNOLIOPHYTA, class Magnoliopsida, order Asterales, family Compositae.

Corfu, Greece: see KÉRKIRA.

corgi: see CARDIGAN WELSH CORGI; PEMBROKE WELSH CORGI.

Cori, Carl Ferdinand (kôr'ē), 1896–, and his first wife, **Gerty Theresa (Radnitz) Cori,** 1896–1957, American biochemists. They were both born in Czechoslovakia and received M.D. degrees (1920) from German Univ. of Prague. In 1920 they were married, and in 1922 they came to the United States, where they later (1928) were naturalized. Carl Cori was professor of pharmacology and biochemistry (1931–66) at the school of medicine at Washington Univ., St. Louis, and Gerty Cori was professor of biological chemistry at the same institution (from 1947), with which she also had been associated from 1931. For their contributions to biochemistry, especially their research on carbohydrate metabolism and enzymes, the Coris shared with B. A. Houssay the 1947 Nobel Prize in Physiology and Medicine. Since 1966, Carl Cori has served as visiting lecturer at Massachusetts General Hospital, Boston.

coriander (kōr"ēăn'dər), strong-smelling Old World annual herb *(Coriandrum sativum)* of the family Umbelliferae (CARROT family), cultivated for its fruits. Dried coriander seed contains an aromatic oil used as a flavoring, as a medicine, and in liqueurs. The seed itself is used as a spice similarly to that of the related caraway and cumin. Coriander is classified in the division MAGNOLIOPHYTA, class Magnoliopsida, order Umbellales, family Umbelliferae.

Corinna (kərĭn'ə), fl. c.500? B.C., Greek poet of Tanagra. The 4th-century spelling of her text has caused some scholars to identify her as Hellenistic. Her verse, fragments of which remain, dealt with mythological themes and was written in Boeotian dialect.

Corinth, Lovis (lō'vēs kô'rĭnt), 1858–1925, German painter and graphic artist. He studied in Paris and Munich, joined the Berlin secession group, and later succeeded Max Liebermann as president. His early work was naturalistic in approach. Corinth was antagonistic toward the expressionist movement, although after a stroke in 1911 his style loosened and took on many expressionistic qualities. His colors became more vibrant, and he created portraits and landscapes of extraordinary vitality and power. A self-portrait is in the Museum of Modern Art, New York City. See catalog by the New York Gallery of Modern Art (1964).

Corinth (kŏr'ĭnth) or **Kórinthos** (kô'rĭnthôs), city (1971 pop. 20,733), capital of Corinth prefecture, S Greece, in the NE Peloponnesus, on the Gulf of Corinth. It is a port and major transportation center trading in olives, tobacco, raisins, and wine. Founded in 1858 after the destruction of Old Corinth by an earthquake, it was rebuilt after another earthquake in 1928. It formerly was known as New Corinth. Old Corinth, just southwest of modern Corinth, is now a village. Strategically situated on the Isthmus of Corinth and protected by the fortifications on the ACROCORINTHUS, Corinth was one of the largest, wealthiest, most powerful, and oldest cities of ancient Greece. Dating from Homeric times, it was conquered by the Dorians. In the 7th and 6th cent. B.C., under the tyrants Cypselus, his son Periander, and their successors, it became a flourishing maritime power. Syracuse, Kérkira, Potidaea, and Apollonia were among its colonies. The natural rival of Athens, Corinth was traditionally allied with Sparta. Athenian assistance to the rebellious Corinthian colonies was a direct cause of the PELOPONNESIAN WAR (431–404 B.C.). During the Corinthian War (395–387 B.C.), however, Corinth joined with Athens against the tyrannical rule of Sparta. After the battle of Chaeronea (338 B.C.) Corinth was garrisoned by Macedonian troops. It became (224 B.C.) a leading member of the ACHAEAN LEAGUE and in 146 B.C. was destroyed by the victorious Romans. Julius Caesar restored it (46 B.C.) and also reestablished the ISTHMIAN GAMES. Corinth was again laid waste by the invading Goths (A.D. 395) and by an earthquake in 521. Early in the 13th cent., Corinth was conquered by Geoffroi I de Villehardouin as a sequel to the Fourth Crusade. It was taken by the Ottoman Turks in 1458, and in 1687 was seized by Venice, which lost it to the Turks in 1715. In 1822 it was captured by Greek insurgents. Ancient ruins at Old Corinth include the market place, fountains, the temple of Apollo, and a Roman amphitheater. Paul preached here, and wrote two epistles to the infant Corinthian church.

Corinth, city (1970 pop. 11,581), seat of Alcorn co., extreme NE Miss., near the Tenn. line, in a livestock and farm area; founded c.1855. Manufactures include telephone equipment, textiles, clothing, and dairy products. During the Civil War, Corinth was a strategic railroad center, abandoned to Gen. H. W. Halleck's Union army in May, 1862, after the battle of Shiloh. General Rosecrans repulsed the Confederates under generals Earl Van Doren and Sterling Price in heavy fighting there, Oct. 3–4, 1862. Corinth National Cemetery (est. 1866) has 6,000 graves.

Corinth, Gulf of, inlet of the Ionian Sea, c.80 mi (130 km) long and from 3 to 20 mi (4.8–32 km) wide, indenting central Greece and separating the Peloponnesus from the Greek mainland. It is connected with the Saronic Gulf by the 4-mi (6.4-km) Corinth Canal (which cuts across the Isthmus of Corinth at sea level), and with the Gulf of Pátrai by the Ríon Strait. The city of Corinth lies on the gulf's southeastern shore.

Corinth, Isthmus of, c.20 mi (32 km) long and 4–8 mi (6.4–12.9 km) wide, connecting central Greece (Attica and Boeotia) with the Peloponnesus, between the Gulf of Corinth and the Saronic Gulf. It is crossed by the Corinth Canal, built between 1881 and 1893, which connects the Aegean and the Adriatic seas. Parallel to the canal are ruins of the ancient Isthmian Wall, which was restored (3rd–6th cent. A.D.) by Byzantine emperors to defend the Peloponnesus. Near the eastern end of the wall are ruins of the sanctuary of Poseidon where the ISTHMIAN GAMES were played.

Corinthian order, most ornate of the classic orders of architecture. It was also the latest, not arriving at full development until the middle of the 4th cent. B.C. The oldest known example, however, is found in the temple of Apollo at Bassae (c.420 B.C.). The Greeks made little use of the order; the chief example is the circular structure at Athens known as the CHORAGIC MONUMENT of Lysicrates (335 B.C.). The temple of Zeus at Athens (started in the 2d cent. B.C. and completed by Emperor Hadrian in the 2d cent. A.D.) was perhaps the most notable of the Corinthian temples. The Greek Corinthian, aside from its distinctive capital, is similar to the Ionic but the column is somewhat more slender. The capital, which may have been especially devised for circular structures, is of uncertain origin. Callimachus is the legendary originator of the design. The delicate foliated details make plausible an original in metalwork. The Romans used the Corinthian order in numerous monumental works of imperial architecture. They gave it a special base, made carved additions to the cornice, and created numerous capital variations, utilizing florid leafage and sometimes human and animal figures. The prevailing form of Roman Corinthian is seen in the Pantheon and the Maison Carrée, and it was embodied in the order as later systematized by the Italian writers of the Renaissance (e.g., Vignola). The capital joined acanthus leaves and volutes, scroll-shaped forms, in an intricate combination and Renaissance sculptors and metalworkers, especially in Italy, France, and Spain, found in its complexity a medium for their full virtuosity. The volutes either became mere light scrolls or were replaced by birds, rams' heads, or grotesque figures. The composite order, so named by the 16th-century codifiers, is actually only a variation of the Corinthian, devised by the Romans as early as the 1st cent. A.D. by forming a capital in which were combined both Corinthian foliage and the volutes and echinus, or rounded molding, of the four-cornered type of Ionic. For the other Greek orders see DORIC ORDER and IONIC ORDER.

Corinthians (kərĭn'thēənz), two epistles of the New Testament, the seventh and eighth books in the usual order. They were written to the church at Corinth by St. PAUL. First Corinthians, written probably at Ephesus early in A.D. 55, is one of the longest and most important epistles. The first main part (1.10–4.21) attacks factionalism at Corinth, giving as its remedy the mystery of the Cross (1.18–3.4) and showing the true nature of Christian ministry (3.5–4.5). St. Paul then condemns several practices—incest (5), litigation among Christians (6.1–11), and fornication (6.12–20). He answers questions on marriage and celibacy (7), on the scandal involved in eating meat previously offered in pagan sacrifices (8; 10), and on the veiling of women in church (11.3–16). The rest of the epistle contains five famous passages—the institution of the Eucharist (11.20–34); the doctrine of the mystical body of Christ, i.e., Christian believers conceived as a unity (12); an eloquent panegyric on Christian love (13); the functions of prophecy among Christians (14); and a splendid chapter on Christ's resurrection (15). The epistle closes with a discussion of practical plans (16). Second Corinthians is shorter; it was written perhaps within a year of the other, probably from Macedonia. Its burden is Paul's apostleship, his authority, and his motives. After particulars of his relations with the Corinthians (1.15–2.17), there follow statements about the Christian ministry (3–4.6) and about Paul's motives rooted in personal union with Jesus (4.7–6.10); these lead to an exhortation (6.11–7.16). A digression (8–9) follows about collection of alms for poor Christians of Jerusalem. The last portion of the epistle contains a magnificent defense of the apostle's mission, citing his authority (10) and recounting his behavior (11–12.13). The announcement of an impending visit of the apostle to Corinth ends the book. Many critics consider the epistle (on internal evidence) to represent the accidental combination of two letters, the last four chapters being then separate from the rest. See Walter Schmithals, *Gnosticism in Corinth* (tr. 1971); John Reuf, *Paul's First Letter to Corinth* (1972).

Corinthian War (395 B.C.–86 B.C.), armed conflict between Corinth, Argos, Thebes, and Athens on one side and Sparta on the other. Angered by Sparta's tyrannical overlordship in Greece after the Peloponnesian War, several Greek states took advantage of Sparta's involvement in war with Persia to challenge Spartan supremacy. With Persian aid, Athens was able to build a fleet, refortify its port, and eventually recover the islands of Lemnos (now Límnos), Scyros (now Skíros), and Imbros (now İmroz). Unable to fight a war on two fronts, Sparta withdrew its forces from Asia Minor. Meanwhile, Antalcidas, the Spartan agent in Persia, attempted to bring about peace with Persia and halt Persian support to the rebellious Greek states. He persuaded Artaxerxes II to agree to the so-called King's Peace, or Peace of Antalcidas, but the terms were those of the Persian king. Cyprus and the Greek city-states in Asia Minor were returned to Persia; the Athenians were forced to give up their conquests except Lemnos, Imbros, and Scyros; and the Greek city-states (except those in Asia Minor) were to be independent, thus eliminating combinations such as the Theban-dominated Boeotian League, which had fought against Sparta. Sparta interpreted the terms of peace to justify interference in the Greek states, which eventually revolted against its domination, thus bringing about the Spartan defeat by Thebes at LEUCTRA in 371 B.C.

Corinto (kōrēn'tō), town (1970 est. pop. 12,985), NW Nicaragua, on the Pacific Ocean. It is a railroad terminus and Nicaragua's leading port. Coffee, sugar, hides, and woods are exported. U.S. marines landed in Corinto in 1912, and it has a U.S. naval base.

Coriolanus (Gnaeus Marcius Coriolanus) (kôr"ēəlā'nəs), Roman patrician. He is said to have derived his name from the capture of the Volscian city Corioli. According to legend he was expelled from Rome because he demanded the abolition of the people's tribunate in return for distributing state grain to the starving plebeians. He joined the Volscians and led (491? B.C.) them in an attack on Rome. Only the tears of his wife and his mother caused him to spare the city. The angry and frustrated Volscians put him to death. Plutarch tells the story, and Shakespeare's *Coriolanus* is based on Plutarch.

coriolis effect [for G. G. Coriolis], tendency for any moving body on or above the earth's surface, e.g., an ocean current or an artillery round, to drift sideways from its course because of the earth's rotation. In the Northern Hemisphere the deflection is to the right of the motion; in the Southern Hemisphere it is to the left. The coriolis deflection of a body moving toward the north or south results from the fact that the earth's surface is rotating eastward at greater speed near the equator than near the poles, since a point on the equator traces out a larger circle per day than a point on another latitude nearer either pole. A body traveling toward the equator with the slower rotational speed of higher latitudes tends to fall behind or veer to the west relative to the more rapidly rotating earth below it at lower latitudes. Similarly, a body traveling toward either pole veers eastward because it retains the greater eastward rotational speed of the lower latitudes as it passes over the more slowly rotating earth closer to the pole. The coriolis effect on a body traveling east or west results from the fact that centrifugal force due to rotation acts directly outward at right angles to the axis of rotation and thus has a horizontal component relative to the earth's surface at all points other than those on the equator. A body traveling eastward relative to the earth's surface has an eastward rotational speed equal to the sum of the earth's speed and its own speed; it therefore experiences a greater centrifugal force, whose horizontal component deflects it toward the south. A body traveling westward relative to the earth's surface has an eastward rotational speed equal to the difference of the earth's speed and its own speed; it experiences a smaller centrifugal force than the earth below it and thus tends to fall inward toward the axis of rotation. The horizontal component of this deflection is toward the north. In most man-operated vehicles continuous course adjustments mask the coriolis effect so that it is generally ignored in these cases. It is, however, extremely important to account for the coriolis effect when considering projectile trajectories, terrestrial wind systems, and ocean currents.

Cork, Richard Boyle, 1st earl of: see BOYLE, RICHARD, 1ST EARL OF CORK.

Cork, county (1971 pop. 351,735), 2,881 sq mi (7,462 sq km), SW Republic of Ireland. CORK is the county town. Largest of the Irish counties, it has a rocky and much-indented coast line (Bantry, Dunmanus, Roaringwater, Courtmarsherry, Clonakilty, and Youghal bays, and Kinsale and Cork harbors). The interior has wild rugged mountains rising as high as 2,239 ft (682 m) and fertile valleys (notably of the Bride, the Blackwater, the Lee, and the Bandon). The main occupations are farming (dairying, raising livestock, and growing grains and sugarbeets) and fishing. Manufacturing is centered around the city of Cork. CÓBH is an important transatlantic harbor. There are prehistoric remains (dolmens and stone circles) and ruins of medieval abbeys and churches.

Cork, county borough (1971 pop. 128,235), county town of Co. Cork, S Republic of Ireland, on the Lee River near its mouth on Cork Harbour. The oldest part of the town is on an island between the north and south branches of the Lee, now crossed by numerous bridges. Exports are largely farm produce (dairy products, grain, livestock), cloth, and fish. Imports include coal, raw materials, fertilizers, grain, machinery, and automobile parts. Automobiles, rubber, leather, cotton, and woolen goods, paint, processed foods, flour, and whiskey are manufactured. St. Finbarr is supposed to have founded an abbey on the site early in the 7th cent. In the 9th cent. the Danes occupied Cork and walled it. Dermot MacCarthy ousted the Danes and in 1172 swore allegiance to Henry II of England. Oliver Cromwell occupied Cork in 1649, and the duke of Marlborough in 1690. Many public buildings were destroyed in the nationalist disturbances of 1920, and the SINN FEIN lord mayor was murdered by the constabulary. Terence MacSwiney succeeded him and died in jail in London after a hunger strike. Educational institutions include University College (constituent college of the National Univ. of Ireland) and a school of art. The Protestant St. Finbarr's Cathedral (designed by William Burges), the Roman Catholic cathedral, the Church of St. Ann, and the Carnegie library are noteworthy.

cork, protective, waterproof outer covering of the stems and roots of woody plants. Cork is a specialized secondary tissue produced by the cork cambium of the plant (see MERISTEM). The regularly arranged walls of cork cells are impregnated with a waxy material, called suberin, that is almost impermeable to water or gases. Cork is buoyant in water because of the presence of trapped air in the cavities of the waterproof dead cells. It is also resilient, light, chemically inert, and, because of the suction cup action of the cut cells, adhesive. These qualities make cork valuable for bottle stoppers, insulating materials, linoleum, and many household and industrial items. See CORK OAK.

cork oak, name for an evergreen species of the oak genus *(Quercus)* of the family Fagaceae (BEECH family). The cork oak *(Q. suber)* is native to the Mediterranean region, where most of the world's commercial supply of CORK is obtained. It is cultivated elsewhere as an ornamental and has been introduced into warmer regions of the United States because of its economic value. The bark of the tree is stripped off (about every 10 years) and then processed for shipment as commercial cork. There is a cork layer in all trees but it is not as extensive or valuable as in the cork oak. Cork oak is classified in the division MAGNOLIOPHYTA, class Magnoliopsida, order Fagales, family Fagaceae.

corkwood: see BOMBAX.

corm, short, thickened underground stem, usually covered with papery leaves. A corm grows vertically, producing buds at the upper nodes and roots from the lower surface. Corms serve as organs of food storage and in some plants (e.g., crocus and gladiolus) of asexual reproduction; they are often mistakenly called bulbs.

Cormenin, Louis Marie de La Haye, vicomte de (lwē mārē' də lā ā vēkôNt' də kôrmənăN'), 1788–1868, French politician, jurist, and pamphleteer. He held minor offices under Napoleon, and after 1828 he sat almost continuously in the chamber of deputies. Under the pseudonym Timon he wrote numerous pamphlets against the government of Louis Philippe and in favor of liberal reforms. After the 1848 Revolution, Cormenin was influential in drawing up the new republican constitution. His works include the legal compilation *Questions de droit administratif* (1822), *Le Livre des orateurs* (1836), and *Entretiens de village* (1846).

cormorant (kôr'mərənt), common name for large aquatic birds, related to the gannet and the pelican, and found chiefly in temperate and tropical regions, usually on the sea but also on inland waters. Cormorants are 2 to 3 ft (61–92 cm) long, with thick, generally dark plumage and green eyes. The feet are webbed, and the bill is long with the upper mandible terminally hooked. Expert swimmers, cormorants pursue fish under water. In the Orient they are used by fishermen who collar the leashed birds to prevent them from swallowing the catch. The double-crested cormorant of the Atlantic coast, Brandt's cormorant of the Pacific coast, and the red-faced cormorant, *Phalacrocorax urile,* are common forms. The glossy black European cormorant is widely distributed in the Northern Hemisphere. A South American cormorant is a source of guano. The great cormorant nests high in trees or, as in other species, on steep, rocky sea cliffs. Two to six eggs per clutch are laid by the female. The young are born blind, and the parents feed the nestlings with half-digested food which is dropped into the nests. Later, the young birds poke their heads into the gullet of the adults to feed. Cormorants are long-lived; a banded one was observed after 18 years. Cormorants are classified in the phylum CHORDATA, subphylum Vertebrata, class Aves, order Pelecaniformes, family Phalacrocoracidae.

corn, in botany. The name *corn* is given to the leading cereal crop of any major region. In England, corn means wheat; in Scotland and Ireland, oats. The grain called corn in America is Indian corn or maize (*Zea mays*). The plant is a GRASS that was domesticated and cultivated in America long before Europeans reached the New World. It is so changed from the ancestral wild grass that this has not been identified with certainty, and it has been so adapted to cultivation that it never reverts to a wild state; it requires the care of man. It is probably a complex hybrid of several related New World grasses, e.g., teosinte (*Euchlaena mexicana*), a tropical American fodder plant in which the seeds are not united in a cob. The Indians had many varieties of corn, e.g., sweet corn, popcorn, and corn for corn meal. White, yellow, red, and blue corn were grown as distinct strains. The easily produced and readily identifiable strains of corn have made it a favorite subject for experimental genetics. The development of hybrid corn seed, now the basis of an independent, large-scale business, was an early (beginning of the 20th cent.) and revolutionary introduction of the principles of theoretical science into practical agriculture. At first ridiculed, the scientifically developed hybrids now represent almost all commercially grown corn types. They have resulted in higher yields, increased sugar and lowered starch content, and uniform plants bred to specification for mechanical harvesting. As human food, corn is eaten fresh or ground for meal. It is the basic starch plant of Central and Andean South America, where it is still hand ground on metates to be made into tamales, tortillas, and other staple dishes. In the S United States it is familiar as hominy, mush, and grits. Starch, sugar, and oil are also extracted for many products, but corn's chief use is as animal fodder. It is the primary feed grain of the United States (the world's largest producer), where more than half the annual crop is so used. In Europe this is almost the only use of corn. Corn was introduced by 17th-century explorers to all parts of the Old World, where it is now an important agricultural item. The part of the United States where most of the corn is grown, including Ohio, Illinois, Indiana, Missouri, Kansas, Iowa, and Nebraska, is known as the Corn Belt. The corn plant has a pithy noded stalk supported by prop roots. The staminate (male) flowers form the tassel at the top of the plant. The pistillate (female) flowers are the kernels on the cob, which is enclosed by a leafy husk beyond which extend threadlike styles and stigmas (the silk), which catch the pollen. The corn plant with its ornamental tassel and ears has been a motif of American art since prehistoric times. See H. A. Wallace and W. L. Brown, *Corn and Its Early Fathers* (1956); H. T. Walden, *Native Inheritance: The Story of Corn in America* (1966); G. E. Inglett, *Corn* (1970).

Cornaro, Caterina (kätärē'nä kōrnä'rō), 1454–1510, queen of Cyprus. A celebrated Venetian beauty, she was married in 1472 to James II of Cyprus, who was eager to secure Venetian support. Venice was in turn interested in intervening in the affairs of the island. James II died in 1473, and his infant son, James III, in 1474. Caterina reigned amidst diplomatic intrigue and hostilities of native anti-Venetian factions until Venice forced her to abdicate (1489) and took Cyprus. Caterina returned to Venice and retired to Asolo. There she held a small but brilliant court, depicted by Pietro Bembo in his Platonic dialogue, *Gli Asolani*. A famous portrait of her by Titian is in the Uffizi.

Corn Belt, major agricultural region of the U.S. Midwest where corn acreage exceeds that of any other crop. Located in the north central plains, it is centered in Iowa and Illinois and extends into S Minnesota, SE South Dakota, E Nebraska, NE Kansas, N Missouri, Indiana, and W Ohio. Large-scale commercial and mechanized farming prevails in this region of deep, fertile, well-drained soils and long, hot, humid summers. The belt produces more than half of the U.S. corn crop. Corn is raised mainly as feed for livestock, especially hogs, which are the main source of cash income. Winter wheat, soybeans, and alfalfa are also important crops in the area.

corn borer or **European corn borer,** common name for the larva of a moth of the family Pyralidae, introduced from S Europe into the Boston area in 1917. The corn borer, *Ostrinia nubilalis,* has steadily spread southward into the Gulf States and northward and westward across the continent to the Rocky Mts. It also still occurs in most of Europe and parts of Asia. The full-grown larva is about 1 in. (2.5 cm) long, with a dark brown head and pinkish body. It is a major pest of all types of corn, its host preference, but also attacks many other cultivated crops, (e.g., sorghum, soybeans, and potatoes) and flower plants (e.g., dahlias, asters, and gladioli). The newly hatched yellowish larvae cause damage by feeding on the leaves of the host plant; older larvae bore into the stalk thereby severely weakening the plant and causing ear damage, which results in a loss in yield and reduction of quality. The full-grown larvae overwinter in cornstalks, corncobs, and debris on the ground. Adults emerge in the spring and are brownish with zigzag streaks across the tips of the forewings. There are sometimes more than one generation per year depending on an increased length of the host's growing season. Control of these pests is complicated by the fact that the larvae also infest common weeds and wild grasses growing near the cornfields. For insecticidal control, see bulletins of the U.S. Dept. of Agriculture. Corn borers are classified in the phylum ARTHROPODA, class Insecta, order Lepidoptera, family Pyralidae.

Cornbury, Edward Hyde, Viscount, 1661–1723, colonial governor of New York and New Jersey (1702–8). He deserted the army of James II and ingratiated himself with William of Orange (William III). Appointed governor by William, he became extremely unpopular, and his administration was a period of turmoil in both provinces. After his removal, he was imprisoned for debt in New York, but upon becoming 3d earl of Clarendon in 1709 he was able to free himself and return to England. See Herbert L. Osgood, *The American Colonies in the Eighteenth Century,* Vol. II (1924).

cornea: see EYE.

corn earworm or **cotton bollworm,** destructive larva of a moth, *Heliothis zea.* Also known as tomato fruitworm, the larva attacks a variety of crops, boring into and feeding on the developing fruits—tomatoes, corn kernels, or cotton bolls. The adult moth is pale yellow. It is classified in the phylum ARTHROPODA, class Insecta, order Lepidoptera, family Noctuidae.

Corneille (Cornelis van Beverloo) (kôrnā'yə), 1922–, Belgian painter. Corneille was a member of CoBrA, the European group allied with ABSTRACT EXPRESSIONISM. His work is characterized by linear, weblike configurations that often form broken representational elements.

Corneille, Pierre (pyĕr kôrnā'yə), 1606–84, French dramatist, ranking with Racine as a master of French classical tragedy. Educated by Jesuits, he practiced law briefly in his native Rouen and moved to Paris after the favorable reception of his first play, *Mélite* (1629), a comedy. His first trágedy, *Médée* (1635), was followed by *Le Cid* (1637). This masterpiece, based on a Spanish play about the CID, took Paris by storm; "beautiful as the *Cid*" became a French proverb. However, Jean Chapelain composed a paper for the newly founded French Academy that attacked the play as plagiaristic and faulty in construction, and thereafter Corneille adhered to classical rules. Among the finest of his score of tragedies that followed are *Horace* (1640), *Cinna* (1640), and *Polyeucte* (1643). The comedy *Le Menteur* (1643) had great success. Corneille's tragedies exalt the will at the expense of the emotions; his tragic heroes and heroines display almost superhuman strength in subordinating passion to duty. At his best, Corneille was a master of the grand style, powerful and majestic. His last plays are marred by monotonous declamation. Corneille's old age was embittered by the rise of Racine, who replaced him in popular favor. See study by D. A. Collins (1966).

cornel: see DOGWOOD.

Cornelia, fl. 2d cent. B.C., Roman matron, daughter of Scipio Africanus Major. She was the wife of Tiberius Sempronius Gracchus and mother of the GRACCHI. She refused to remarry after her husband's death, devoting herself to her children, whom she educated well and inspired with a sense of civic duty and a desire for glory. When a wealthy patrician woman spoke of her jewels, Cornelia pointed to her two sons, saying, "These are my jewels!" Whether she supported the revolutionary tendencies of her sons or tempered them is debated by historians.

cornelian: see CARNELIAN.

cornelian cherry: see DOGWOOD.

Cornelius, Saint, d. 253, pope (251–253); successor of St. Fabian. His rule was marked by the support of St. Cyprian and the opposition of the antipope NOVATIAN, and by the problem of readmitting to the church Christians who apostasized during persecution. Cornelius was martyred under Gallus. He was succeeded by St. Lucius I. He is mentioned in the Canon of the Mass. Feast: Sept. 16.

Cornelius, centurion of an Italian cohort stationed at Caesarea, one of the first Gentile converts and traditionally first bishop of Caesarea. Acts 10.

Cornelius, Peter (pā'tər kôrnā'lēŏŏs), 1824–74, German composer and poet; follower of Liszt and Wagner. He wrote music criticism, songs, and poetry but is best known for his operas *Der Barbier von Bagdad* (1858) and *Der Cid* (1865).

Cornelius, Peter von, 1783–1867, German painter. He studied at Düsseldorf and in Rome, where he joined the German NAZARENE group and collaborated with other members in the decoration of the Casa Bartoldy. In 1820 he was commissioned by Louis I of Bavaria to paint the fresco decorations in the Glyptothek, Munich. *The Last Judgment* was one of his fresco decorations for the Ludwigskirche, Munich. Cornelius believed that art should express noble ideals, and he disdained to work from nature. His favorite themes were religious or philosophical. In addition to his painting, Cornelius produced illustrations for *Faust* and the *Nibelungenlied* and designs for the decoration of the royal mausoleum, done for Frederick William II of Prussia.

Cornelius Nepos: see NEPOS, CORNELIUS.

Cornell, Alonzo B. (kôrnĕl'), 1832–1904, American businessman and politician, b. Ithaca, N.Y. Cornell was a director (1868–99) and vice president (1870–76) of the Western Union Telegraph Company, founded by his father, Ezra Cornell. A supporter of Senator Roscoe CONKLING, he was surveyor of customs (1869–73) at the port of New York, chairman (1870–78) of the Republican state central committee, and speaker (1873) of the New York assembly. President Grant, just before leaving office, appointed him naval officer in the New York customhouse. President Hayes, in an attempt to wrest control of the port of New York customhouse from the Conkling machine, brought pressure upon him to resign because of his official party connection. Cornell refused, and though strongly supported by Conkling, he and Chester A. Arthur, the collector of the port of New York, were removed in 1878. Cornell was promptly chosen governor of New York for the term 1880–83. He modernized the state finances, made good appointments, and vetoed much extravagant legislation. By not taking sides in the patronage fight between President Garfield and Conkling in 1881, he contributed to Conkling's defeat in the legislature and was himself defeated for renomination as governor. He wrote a biography of his father (1884). See his public papers (3 vol., 1880–82).

Cornell, Ezra, 1807–74, American financier and founder of CORNELL UNIVERSITY, b. Westchester Landing, N.Y. Cornell, who began life as a laborer, was of an ingenious mechanical bent and had a shrewd business mind. He aided in constructing (1844) the telegraph line between Baltimore and Washington, D.C., over which Samuel F. B. Morse sent the first test message. Having devised the method of stringing wires on poles, he entered into line construction in the East and the Midwest. He was founder, director, and for a time the largest stockholder of the Western Union Telegraph Company, which was formed in 1855 to end cutthroat competition in the field. His interest in agricultural education led to his association in the New York senate with Andrew Dickson WHITE, and together they mapped and secured legislation for founding (1865) Cornell Univ., with a charter embracing many of Cornell's ideas. He made many gifts to the university, including an initial $500,000, and was responsible for the successful financial returns on the university's Federal land grant. See biographies by his son, Alonzo Cornell (1884), and Philip Dorf (1952, abr. ed. 1965).

Cornell, Joseph, American artist, 1903–73, b. Nyack, N.Y. Cornell is best known for his surrealist-influenced shadow boxes. These are small constructions, within glass-fronted, shallow boxes or frames, made of found objects, maps, photographs, and engravings. Their selection and arrangement are nostalgic and personally symbolic. Cornell's *Hôtel du Nord* (c.1953; Whitney Mus., New York City) is a representative work.

Cornell, Katharine, 1898–1974, American actress, b. Berlin. Cornell made her debut in 1916 with the Washington Square Players. In 1921 she married Guthrie McClintic, a producer-director. From their first production together, *The Green Hat* in 1925, they proved to be a successful team, with such productions as *The Barretts of Wimpole Street* (1931, repeated on television, 1956), *Saint Joan* (1936), *Candida* (1937), *The Doctor's Dilemma* (1941), and *The Three Sisters* (1942). She was among the first major American performers to form a repertory company; she took several entire New York casts and productions on the road. Cornell played Mrs. Patrick Campbell in *Dear Liar* on Broadway in 1960. After McClintic's death in 1961, Cornell retired from the theater. See her autobiography (1939); Guthrie McClintic, *Me and Kit* (1955).

Cornell University, mainly at Ithaca, N.Y.; with land-grant, state, and private support; coeducational; chartered 1865, opened 1868. It was named for Ezra CORNELL, who donated $500,000 and a tract of land. With the help of state senator Andrew D. WHITE, who became Cornell's first president, it was made the state land-grant institution. Cornell University Medical College, affiliated with New York Hospital, Bellevue Hospital, and the Memorial Center for Cancer and Allied Diseases, is in New York City. The university operates an aeronautical laboratory at Buffalo, the New York Agricultural Experiment Station (Geneva), and the Cornell Agricultural Experiment Station (Ithaca), and is affiliated with the Brookhaven National Laboratories (Long Island). Of note on Cornell's campus are the U.S. plant, soil, and nutrition laboratory, the Savage school of nutrition, and the laboratory of nuclear physics, which includes a reactor and a synchotron. In Puerto Rico the university operates a large radar station for investigations of the upper atmosphere and outer space. The colleges of agriculture, home economics, veterinary medicine, and the school of industrial and labor relations are divisions of the State University of New York. See M. G. Bishop, *A History of Cornell* (1962); K. C. Parsons, *The Cornell Campus* (1968); R. F. Howes, *A Cornell Notebook* (1971).

corner, securing of all or nearly all the supply of any commodity or stock so that its buyers are forced to pay exorbitant prices. Corners may be planned deliberately or may be brought about unintentionally, as through a fight for controlling interest in a corporation's stock. In the first type the operator acquires control of the particular commodity or shares and then induces other operators to promise to sell the commodity or stock by raising the market price to an unusually high level. The cornerer purchases such promises to sell. When the cornerer thinks he can make the biggest profit, he withdraws all his shares from the market, and those who have promised to sell find themselves "cornered"; that is, they have to buy stock from the cornerer at his own price to fulfill their contracts. The cornerer sets the price just low enough to keep the dealers from repudiating their contracts. To be successful, cornerers must have enough money to buy the necessary amount of shares or commodity. The Bible describes Joseph's corner of the grain in Egypt. A famous deliberate corner was Jim Fisk's and Jay Gould's corner of the U.S. gold supply in 1869; the move was frustrated when the Federal government placed its own gold supply on sale. A notable illustration of the unintentional corner was that on the stock of the NORTHERN PACIFIC RAILWAY in 1901. Deliberate corners and other forms of price manipulation on the various stock and commodity exchanges are now illegal in the United States. The Securities and Exchange Commission, the New York Stock Exchange, and the Dept. of Agriculture seek to prevent corners.

Corner Brook, city (1971 pop. 26,309), W central N.F., Canada, on the Humber River. It is Newfoundland's second largest city and has a large pulp and paper mill. Nearby is Gros Morne National Park.

cornet, brass wind musical instrument, created in France about 1830 by adding valves to the post horn. It is usually in B flat and is the same size as the B flat trumpet, but has a more conical bore. The cornet, a TRANSPOSING INSTRUMENT, has a less brilliant tone but greater agility than the trumpet. It has long been a

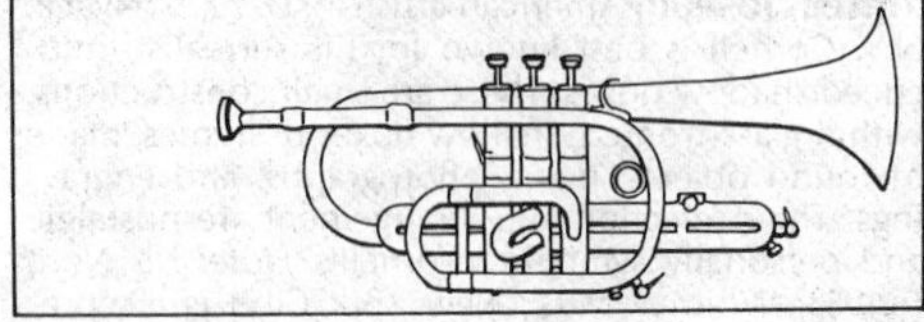

Cornet

standard instrument in bands. In the orchestra, especially in France, the cornet is used with the trumpet. It should not be confused with the cornett, an instrument of the Middle Ages and Renaissance, which used a cup mouthpiece on a wooden or ivory body supplied with fingerholes similar to those on woodwinds. A bass cornett, the serpent, so called because of its twisted shape, was used until the early 19th cent.

cornflower, common herb (*Centaurea cyanus*) of the family Compositae (COMPOSITE family). It is a garden flower in the United States but a weed in the grainfields of Europe. It is called bluebottle or bluet in England and bluebonnet in Scotland; in North America the cornflower shares with other plants the names ragged robin, bachelor's-button, or ragged sailor. The long-stemmed blue heads of the flowers, having radiating bottle- or vase-shaped florets, yield a juice which, mixed with alum, has been used as a dye. Cornflowers are classified in the division MAGNOLIOPHYTA, class Magnoliopsida, order Asterales, family Compositae.

cornice (kôr'nis), molded or decorated projection that forms the crowning feature at the top of a building wall or other architectural element; specifically, the uppermost of the three principal members of the classic ENTABLATURE, hence by extension any similar crowning and projecting element in the decorative arts. The term is also employed for any projection on a wall that is provided to throw rainwater off the face of the building. The cornice undoubtedly had its origin in the primitive eave projection: the Greek Doric and Ionic cornices recall early wooden roof forms, and the Egyptian cavetto-and-fillet cornice is a derivation of the overhanging papyrus stalks that formed the eaves of primitive shelters. The cornice early lost its structural significance and became a stylized decorative element; in the Greek and Roman eras it assumed firmly standardized forms in the classical orders that were retained, with variations, through the Renaissance and later periods. As an element in the classical entablature the cornice is composed of the cymatium, or crown molding, above the corona, the projecting flat member, which casts the principal shadow; in this shadow, and supporting the corona, are a group of moldings called the bed molds, which may be elaborated with dentils. The Corinthian and Composite cornices are further embellished with modillions, or brackets, under the corona; the soffit of the Doric corona is decorated with square, flat projections called mutules, having guttae, or small knobs, hanging from their lower surfaces.

Corning, city (1970 pop. 15,792), Steuben co., S N.Y., on the Chemung River, in a dairy and vineyard region; settled 1788, inc. as a city 1890. The glass industry, for which the city is famous, began there in 1868, and the Corning glass museum is a major tourist attraction today. A junior college and a museum of western art are located in the city, and a number of state parks are in the area. In 1972, in the wake of Hurricane Agnes, the city was heavily damaged by floodwaters from the Chemung River.

Cornish, dead language belonging to the Brythonic group of the Celtic subfamily of the Indo-European family of languages. See CELTIC LANGUAGES.

Cornish hen or **Cornish chicken,** breed of POULTRY that originated in Cornwall, England, but gained prominence only after it was established in the United States. Its body shape is quite different from that of other chickens. Both males and females have short legs and broad muscular breasts. Although relatively slow-growing, the Cornish hen has excellent meat qualities and is used extensively in breeding programs today. Its cross with the fast-growing PLYMOUTH ROCK CHICKEN is responsible for most of the broiler and frier types currently on the market. An increasingly popular form of Cornish poultry, marketed for its delicious meat, is the Rock Cornish game hen. This is actually a standard meat-type chicken packaged at a smaller size.

Cornish literature. The literature of the Celtic language of Cornwall, which disappeared before 1800, consists largely of a few MIRACLE PLAYS, mostly of the 15th cent. With the exception of the *Life of St. Meriasek,* they are usually on biblical subjects. The plays closely resemble Breton drama. Also surviving is the Middle Cornish narrative poem *The Passion of Our Lord.* See R. M. Longsworth, *The Cornish Ordinalia* (1967); Edwin Norris, ed., *Ancient Cornish Drama* (2 vol., 1859; repr. 1968).

corn laws, regulations restricting the export and import of grain, particularly in England. As early as 1361 export was forbidden in order to keep English grain cheap. Subsequent laws, numerous and complex, forbade export unless the domestic price was low and forbade import unless it was high. The purpose of the laws was to assure a stable and sufficient supply of grain from domestic sources, eliminating undue dependence on foreign supplies, yet allowing for imports in time of scarcity. The corn law of 1815 was designed to maintain high prices and prevent an agricultural depression after the Napoleonic Wars. Consumers and laborers objected, but it was the criticism of manufacturers that the laws hampered industrialization by subsidizing agriculture that proved most effective. Following a campaign by the ANTI-CORN-LAW LEAGUE, the corn laws were repealed by the Conservative government of Sir Robert Peel in 1846, despite the opposition of many of his own party, led by Lord George Bentinck and Benjamin Disraeli. With the revival of protectionism in the 20th cent., new grain restriction laws have been passed, but they have not been as extensive as those of earlier times. See D. G. Barnes, *A History of English Corn Laws from 1660 to 1846* (1930, repr. 1965).

Corno, Monte (mōn'tā kōr'nō), highest peak of the Apennines, c.9,560 ft (2,910 m) high, in the Gran Sasso d'Italia range, Abruzzi, central Italy. It is snow-capped for most of the year.

Cornouaille (kôrnwī'), district of Brittany, NW France, comprising parts of Finistère, Côtes-du-Nord, and Morbihan depts. The name was probably brought by Britons who fled Cornwall at the time of the Anglo-Saxon invasions (c.500).

Cornplanter, c.1740-1836, chief of the Seneca Indians. The son of an Indian woman and a white father, he acquired great influence among the Seneca Indians and in the American Revolution led war parties for the British against the colonial forces, particularly against Gen. John Sullivan in New York. He later favored friendship with the whites and signed the Treaty of Fort Stanwix (1784). He was given a grant of land on the Allegheny River, where he lived to a very old age. His views were opposed by the energetic RED JACKET but supported by HANDSOME LAKE (Cornplanter's half brother).

corns and calluses, thickenings of the outer layer of SKIN where there is irritation or constant pressure. Corns are cone-shaped with their points protruding into the dermis, or inner layer of skin. They usually have hard, shiny surfaces surrounded by red, painful areas. Soft-surfaced corns sometimes develop between overlapping toes where there is an accumulation of moisture. Treatment of corns is directed at the relief of irritation or pressure, e.g., wearing properly fitted shoes; they can also be softened by pastes and ointments or removed by a physician. Calluses typically involve only the outermost layers of skin and are not usually painful; they tend to disappear once the source of irritation has been removed. See BUNION.

cornstarch, material made by pulverizing the ground, dried residue of corn grains after preparatory soaking and the removal of the embryo and the outer covering. It is used as laundry starch, in sizing paper, in making adhesives, and in cooking. DEXTRIN, corn syrup, and corn sugar are produced by the hydrolysis of cornstarch. See STARCH.

Cornu, Marie Alfred (märē' älfrĕd' kôrnü'), 1841–1902, French physicist. From 1867 he was professor at the École polytechnique, Paris. He measured the velocity of light and made important contributions to spectrum analysis, astronomy, and optics. Cornu's spiral, a curve for calculating light intensities in Fresnel diffraction, is named for him.

cornucopia (kôr"nyōōkō'pēə), in Greek mythology, magnificent horn that filled itself with whatever meat or drink its owner requested. Some legends designate it as a horn of the river god Achelous, others as a horn of the goat Amalthaea. It is often represented as filled with fruits and flowers and has become the symbol of plenty.

Cornwall, Barry, pseud. of **Bryan Waller Procter,** 1787–1874, English author. His sentimental songs were much in vogue during his lifetime. Included among Cornwall's longer works are *Dramatic Scenes* (1819) and *Mirandola* (1821), a tragedy. He enjoyed the friendship of many of the notable men of his time, including Charles Lamb, of whom he wrote a biography which appeared in 1866. He was the father of the poet Adelaide Procter. See his *Literary Recollections* (ed. by R. W. Armour, 1936); biography by R. W. Armour (1935).

Cornwall, county (1971 pop. 379,892), SW England. The county town is BODMIN. Cornwall is a peninsula bounded seaward by the English Channel and the Atlantic Ocean and landward by Devonshire. It terminates in the west with the rugged promontory of Lands End. The region is a low-lying plateau, rising to its greatest height at Brown Willy (1,375 ft/419 m) in Bodmin Moor. The principal rivers are the Tamar, which forms most of the border with Devonshire, the Fowey, the Fal, and the Camel. In the beautiful river valleys are productive vegetable and dairy farms. The uplands are used for sheep and cattle pasturage. The climate is mild and moist, with subtropical vegetation along the southern coast. Cornwall is an important source of china clay. Various types of fish are caught, including pilchard, which are not plentiful elsewhere in Britain. Cornwall has produced many of Britain's finest sailors. Engineering, ship repairing, and rock quarrying are the only industries. Cornish tin and copper mines were known to ancient Greek traders, and during World War II the old mines were reworked. Cornwall's climate, the picturesque coastal towns (Penzance, Falmouth, and St. Ives), and the romance of its past, interwoven with Arthurian legend and tales of piracy, have made the region popular with tourists. Cornwall's history has been somewhat distinct from that of the rest of England. The Cornish language, related to the Welsh and Breton tongues, did not die out until the 18th cent. The county long resisted Saxon penetration. It was organized in the 14th cent. as a duchy. (The monarch's eldest son is the Duke of Cornwall.) Cornwall was slow to accept the Reformation. In 1549 thousands of Cornishmen marched to defend the Roman Catholic Church service. In the 18th cent. the Wesleyan movement took a firm hold in Cornwall, which has remained predominantly Methodist until the present day. In 1974, Cornwall was reorganized as a nonmetropolitan county.

Cornwall, manufacturing city (1971 pop. 47,116), SE Ont., Canada, on the St. Lawrence River. Its principal manufactures are cotton and rayon textiles, paper, chemicals, and electronic equipment. The headquarters of the Canadian St. Lawrence Seaway Authority are in Cornwall. The historical Indian village of St. Regis is across the river on the Quebec-New York boundary.

Cornwallis, Charles Cornwallis, 1st Marquess, 1738–1805, English general and statesman. He was commissioned an ensign in the British army in 1756 and saw service in Europe in the Seven Years War. As a member of Parliament (which he entered in 1760), he opposed the tax measures that helped bring on the AMERICAN REVOLUTION. When the war came, however, he placed himself at the king's service and was sent (1776) to America. He served under Gen. William Howe at the battle of Long Island, in the New Jersey campaigns, and at the battle of Brandywine, acquitting himself with credit in all the engagements. In 1778, Cornwallis became second in command to Sir Henry CLINTON, British commander in America. Two years later Cornwallis began the fateful CAROLINA CAMPAIGN, which led directly to the YORKTOWN CAMPAIGN and the major British defeat that in 1781 ended the fighting. Cornwallis was not held responsible for the disaster and in 1786 became governor general of India. There he reformed the civil service and the judiciary and distinguished himself in the campaigns against TIPPOO SAHIB of Mysore. He was created a marquess in 1792 and returned to England in 1794. In 1798, Cornwallis was sent to Ireland as viceroy and commander in chief, and he was stern in repressing the rebellion there in the same year. He worked to achieve the Act of Union (1800), which initiated the unhappy experiment of uniting the Irish and British parliaments, but he resigned (1801) with William Pitt when George III refused to accept CATHOLIC EMANCIPATION. Cornwallis was then commissioned British minister plenipotentiary and helped to draw up the Treaty of Amiens (1802), which temporarily halted the war with Napoleonic France. In 1805 he was again appointed governor general of India, but he died two months after his arrival there. See his correspondence (ed. by Charles Ross, 3 vol., 1859); Arthur Aspinall, *Cornwallis in Bengal* (1931); Frank and Mary Wickwire, *Cornwallis: the American Adventure* (1970).

Coro (kō'rō), city (1970 est. pop. 56,000), capital of Falcón state, NW Venezuela, 7 mi (11.3 km) from the Caribbean Sea, and at the base of the Paraguaná peninsula. The development of the oil industry on the peninsula stimulated rapid expansion of the city. Coffee, hardwoods, hides, and tobacco are exported through its port of La Vela. Founded in 1527, Coro became the base for Spanish explorations into the interior. From 1528 to 1546 it was mortgaged by the Spanish to a German banking house, and during this time German adventurers explored the region.

corolla: see PETAL.

corollary: see THEOREM.

Coromandel Coast (kŏrōmăn'dəl), east coast of Tamil Nadu and Andhra Pradesh states, SE India, stretching more than 400 mi (644 km) from Point Calimere, opposite the northern tip of Sri Lanka to the delta of the Krishna River. Its major cities, Nagapattinam, Pondicherry, and Madras, are ports. The inland coastal plain is bounded by the Eastern Ghats and includes the valleys of the Krishna, Penner, and Cauvery rivers. The name probably stems from Cholomandalam, i.e., land of the Cholas, an empire that ruled the region from the 9th to the 12th cent.

Corona (kərō'nə), city (1970 pop. 27,519), Riverside co., S Calif.; inc. 1896. Citrus fruits are processed and castings, plywood paneling, fiberglass insulation, pipes, valves, and mobile homes are manufactured in the city. Cleveland National Forest is on Corona's western boundary.

corona, luminous envelope surrounding the SUN, outside the chromosphere. The corona is visible only at the time of totality during a total eclipse of the sun. It then appears as a halo of light with an irregular outer edge, radiating from the sun's surface and contrasting with the dark lunar disk that it borders. It is divided into the inner corona, a ring of pale-yellow light against which crimson prominences are outlined, and the outer corona, a pearly white halo that extends far out into space. Scientists are nearly in accord in believing that it consists of extremely fine particles of matter and that its luminosity results partly from sunlight reflected by the particles and partly from its own light. By means of the CORONAGRAPH, the corona can be studied and photographed in full daylight. At its base, the corona has a temperature of 1,000,000°C and is completely ionized. Studies have shown that the corona extends throughout the solar system. Just above the chromosphere, the corona is almost static, rising very slowly. Its velocity increases with increasing distance from the sun; near the earth it is moving with supersonic speed and is known as the SOLAR WIND.

Corona Borealis (bôrēăl'əs) [Lat., = the northern crown], northern CONSTELLATION lying between Hercules and Boötes. Its name derives from the crown Bacchus gave Ariadne when she was deserted by Theseus. The constellation is a small arc of bright stars, of which the brightest is Alphecca (Alpha Coronae Borealis). Corona Borealis reaches its highest point in the evening sky in early July.

Coronado, Francisco Vásquez de (frănthēs'kō väs'kāth dā kōrōnä'thō), c.1510–1554, Spanish explorer in the Southwest. He went to Mexico with Viceroy Antonio de Mendoza and in 1538 was made governor of Nueva Galicia. The viceroy, dazzled by the report of Fray MARCOS DE NIZA of the great wealth of the Seven Cities of Cibola to the north, organized an elaborate expedition to explore by sea (see ALARCÓN, HERNANDO DE) and by land. Coronado, made captain general, set out in 1540 from Compostela, crossed modern Sonora and SE Arizona, and reached Cibola itself—the Zuñi country of New Mexico. He found neither splendor nor wealth in the Indian pueblos. Nevertheless he sent out his lieutenants: Pedro de Tovar visited the Hopi villages in N Arizona, García López de Cárdenas discovered the Grand Canyon, and Hernando de Alvarado struck out eastward and visited Acoma and the pueblos of the Rio Grande and the Pecos. Alvarado came upon a Plains Indian nicknamed the Turk, who told fanciful tales of the wealthy kingdom of QUIVIRA to the east. Coronado, still hopeful, spent a winter on the Rio Grande not far from the modern Santa Fe, waged needless warfare with the Indians, then set out in 1541 to find the promised land of Quivira under the lying guidance of the Turk. Just where the party went is not absolutely certain, but it is generally thought they journeyed in the Texas Panhandle, reached Palo Duro Canyon (near Canyon, Texas), then turned N through Oklahoma and into Kansas. They reached Quivira, which turned out to be no more than Indian villages (probably of the Wichita), innocently empty of gold, silver, and jewels. The Spanish turned back in disillusion and spent the winter of 1541–42 on the Rio Grande, then in 1542 left the northern country to go ingloriously back to Nueva Galicia and into the terrors of the MIXTÓN WAR. In 1544, Coronado was dismissed from his governorship and lived the rest of his life in peaceful obscurity in Mexico City. He had found no cities of gold, no El Dorado; yet his expedition had acquainted the Spanish with the PUEBLO INDIANS and had opened the Southwest. Subsidiary expeditions from Nueva Galicia to S Arizona and Lower California make the scope of Coronado's achievement even more astonishing. See F. W. Hodge and T. Hays Lewis, ed., *Spanish Explorers in the Southern United States,* Vol. II (1907); G. P. Hammond and Agapito Rey, ed., *Narratives of the Coronado Expedition* (1940); A. Grove Day, *Coronado's Quest* (1940, repr. 1964); Herbert E. Bolton, *Coronado on the Turquoise Trail* (1949).

Coronado (kŏr"ənä'dō), city (1970 pop. 20,910), San Diego co., S Calif., on a peninsula on the west side of San Diego Bay; inc. 1890. It is a well-known beach resort. Adjacent to the city are a large U.S. naval air station and a naval amphibious base. Points of interest include the Hotel del Coronado, a state historical monument.

Coronado National Memorial: see NATIONAL PARKS AND MONUMENTS (table).

coronagraph (kərō'nəgrăf), device invented by the French astronomer B. Lyot (1931) for the purpose of observing the CORONA of the sun and solar prominences occurring in the CHROMOSPHERE. Because of the intense light of the sun, the PHOTOSPHERE, corona, and chromosphere can ordinarily be seen only during a total ECLIPSE. The coronagraph consists of two refracting telescopes in tandem. A solid disk placed in front of the prime focus of the first telescope plays the part of the moon and eclipses the sun's image in the telescope so that only the outer layers of the sun's atmosphere are focused by the second telescope onto photographic film. A monochromatic filter is also used to improve optical clarity and remove chromatic aberration.

coronary artery disease, condition that results when the coronary arteries are narrowed or occluded, most commonly by atherosclerotic deposits of fibrous and fatty tissue. A coronary thrombosis (heart attack) is precipitated when the lumen of an artery, usually already narrowed by atherosclerosis, is completely blocked by a thrombus (blood clot). Coronary artery disease is the commonest underlying cause of cardiovascular disability and death. Men are affected about four times as frequently as women; before the age of 40 the ratio is eight to one. Other predisposing factors are hypertension, diabetes, high cholesterol levels, and heavy cigarette smoking. The primary symptom of the condition is ANGINA PECTORIS, a pain that radiates in the upper left quadrant of the body.

coronary heart disease: see CORONARY ARTERY DISEASE.

coronation, ceremony of crowning and anointing a sovereign on his or her accession to the throne. Although a public ceremony inaugurating a new king or chief had long existed, a new religious service was added when Europe became Christianized. The service, derived from Old Testament accounts of the anointing of Saul and David by Samuel, helped to alter the concept of kingship, because anointment was thought to endow a prince with divine blessing and some degree of priestly (possibly even divine) character. In England, from the coronation (973) of Edgar, the ceremony included a coronation oath, anointment, investiture, enthronement, and homage. The pageantry of the English coronation, which since 1066 has taken place in Westminster Abbey, is still that of medieval times. In France, Pepin the Short, first king of the Carolingian line, was twice anointed by popes, partly to legitimize his supersession of the Merovingian dynasty. Later the French coronation came to resemble the English form, which was probably introduced into France in the 10th cent. The custom whereby the Holy Roman emperor was crowned by the pope dates from the coronation of Charlemagne on Christmas Day, 800. The anointing of the emperor by the pope was instituted by Louis I in 816. In 1804, Napoleon I brought Pope Pius VII to Paris to crown him in Notre Dame cathedral; but, in a famous episode, he seized the crown from the pope's hands and crowned himself.

Coronel (kōrōnĕl'), city (1970 pop. 73,568), S central Chile, a port on the Pacific Ocean. It is a major coaling station and a shipping point for the coal from nearby mines. In a naval engagement off Coronel on Nov. 1, 1914, during World War I, German Admiral Graf von Spee defeated a British squadron under Sir Christopher Cradock, a triumph offset later by the battle of the Falklands.

coroner, judicial officer responsible for investigating deaths occurring through violence or under suspicious circumstances. The office has been traced to the late 12th cent. Originally the coroner's duties were primarily to maintain records of criminal justice and to take custody of all royal property. In England this second function persists in his jurisdiction over TREASURE-TROVE. In his present-day work of determining cause of death, the coroner proceeds by means of the INQUEST whenever there is doubt. In several of the United States the coroner has been replaced by the medical examiner, who can only conduct POST-MORTEM EXAMINATIONS, and who works in cooperation with the public prosecutor.

coronet (kŏr'ənĕt, kŏrənĕt'), head attire of a noble of high rank, worn on state occasions. It is inferior to the crown. British peers wear their coronets at the coronation of their sovereign. Although dukes wore coronets to mark their rank by the 14th cent., it was in the reign of Elizabeth I that individual patterns were adopted for other peers, and barons received distinguishing insignia in 1661. The coronet of a duke is bordered by 8 strawberry leaves; that of a marquess, by 4 strawberry leaves alternating with 4 silver balls (sometimes called pearls) on low points; that of an earl, by 8 strawberry leaves alternating with 8 silver balls on high points; that of a viscount, by 16 silver balls on the rim; that of a baron, by 6 silver balls on the gold rim.

Corot, Jean-Baptiste Camille (zhäN-bätēst' kämē'yə kōrō'), 1796–1875, French landscape painter, b. Paris. Corot was one of the most influential of 19th-century painters. The son of shopkeepers, he worked in textile shops until 1822, when he began to study painting. The classical landscape painters Michallon and Bertin were his teachers. In 1825 he made his first trip to Italy, during which he painted calm, solid, and exquisitely composed groups of Roman buildings (e.g., *View of the Farnese Gardens,* 1826; Phillips Coll., Washington, D.C.). Upon his return to France he lived mostly in the Ville d'Avray, which formed the subject of many of his celebrated paintings, including two in the Metropolitan Museum. He worked in Italy again in 1834 and 1843, and traveled in Switzerland, Holland, and England. Corot exhibited regularly at the Salon from 1827. His work lay outside the contemporary controversy concerning classicism and romanticism and, indeed, outside the theories of the Barbizon school, with which his name is often linked. Corot's landscapes celebrate the countryside without idealizing the peasant or romanticizing farm labor. He used sketches made directly from nature to aid his studio compositions, sometimes painting entire landscapes outdoors. In Rome he created works notable for their simplicity of form and clarity of lighting, such as the *Colisseum* and the *Forum* (both: Louvre). His later landscapes, more lyrical in tone and painted primarily in shades of gray and green, were more popular. His delicate handling of light is especially evident in *Femme à la Perle* (Louvre) and *Interrupted Reading* (Art Inst., Chicago). Today Corot's work is highly valued, his figure studies and portraits being particularly sought after. His work is represented in most of the prominent galleries of England, France, and the United States. See studies by Jean Leymarie (tr. 1966) and Yvon Taillandier (tr. 1967).

corporal punishment, physical chastisement of an offender. It may include the death penalty (see CAPITAL PUNISHMENT), but the term usually refers to such practices as flogging, mutilation, branding, and confinement in the pillory or stocks. Until c.1800 most crimes were punished thus (rather than by imprisonment) in many parts of the world. Flogging was especially prevalent, being used also to keep order among the institutionalized insane and in the schools as well as in armed forces. A movement against the use of corporal punishment was led in the late 17th cent. by American Quakers who achieved local reforms in Pennsylvania and New Jersey. The 18th cent. saw a reaction against the whole concept of violent punishment and the substitution of what were considered more humane methods. The effectiveness of corporal punishment has been questioned by modern criminologists and educators. Flogging, however, is still used in some countries, including the Republic of South Africa, and is used, often unofficially, to maintain discipline within some British and American prisons. Corporal punishment, usually caning or spanking, is also common in the schools of many areas of the United States and Great Britain, although the practice appears to be declining.

corporation, in law, organization enjoying legal personality for the purpose of carrying on certain activities. Most corporations are businesses for profit; they are usually organized by three or more subscribers who raise capital for the corporate activities by selling shares of STOCK, which represent ownership and are transferable. Besides business corporations, there are also charitable, cooperative, municipal, and religious corporations, all with distinctive features. In the United States all governmental units smaller than a state (e.g., counties, cities) are municipal corporations. Certain religious functionaries (e.g., Roman Catholic archbishops) legally are corporations sole. The legal personality of a corporation is symbolized by its seal and its distinctive name. As a legal person, the corporation continues in existence when the organizers lose their connection with it. In most cases its liability is limited to the assets it possesses and creditors may not seize property of persons associated with the corporation as stockholders or otherwise. Legal personality gives the corporation many of the capacities of a natural person; e.g., it can hold property and can even commit crimes (for which it may be fined and its directors imprisoned). The corporate form was known in Rome, although the notion of its personality was not fully developed. In Norman England and on the Continent in medieval times, municipal and ecclesiastical corporations were common. In the overseas trade expansion of the 16th and 17th cent., associates bought shares in a ship, or its cargo, and divided the profits while spreading the risk. The Muscovy Company (chartered 1555) and the Dutch East India Company (chartered 1602) were perhaps the earliest trading companies with what came later to be called permanent capital. The initial British colonization of America and the appropriation of India were basically achieved through the use of government-chartered trading corporations. The failure of the MISSISSIPPI SCHEME and the SOUTH SEA BUBBLE, both in 1720, led to reforms and stricter fiscal regulation of corporations. New corporations were created in the Industrial Revolution to finance larger economic units, such as railways and steam-driven machinery in factories. Until 1844 incorporation in England continued to be a matter of special grant by the king or Parliament. In general, the history of corporations in America has been marked by the abdication of state control over corporations. The modern concept of corporate power is that the rights of the participants as well as the conduct of the enterprise must be the subject of managerial discretion. The salient characteristic of the modern corporation is the separation of management from ownership. In the United States the state legislatures became the chief authorities to grant charters to corporations, although the Federal government incorporates in a limited field. Federal charters were granted to both of the Banks of the United States, to certain railroads after the Civil War, and to the Communications Satellite Corporation (Comsat). Corporations owned by the Federal government and financed by government appropriations include the Federal Deposit Insurance Corporation, the Community Credit Corporation, and various corporations established to meet emergencies and later liquidated. At first states passed a special act for each incorporation, but in 1811, New York state enacted a general incorporation law enabling the secretary of state to give charters. Since the DARTMOUTH COLLEGE CASE of 1819, when a charter was held to be a binding contract between a state and a corporation, unalterable and unamendable by the state without the corporation's consent, fewer perpetual charters have been granted, the right of the legislature to alter or annul being specifically reserved in the charter. Variability in state incorporation laws and the ability of corporations incorporated in one state to do business in all other states have allowed corporations to incorporate in the state or states having the most lenient incorporation laws—formerly New Jersey but, since 1913, Delaware, Maryland, and Maine. A more recent type of corporation is the holding company, organized to buy a controlling interest in other corporations. The amount of cash needed to control a concern is lessened by pyramiding holding companies. This is done by creating a company to hold a voting control of one or more operating companies. A third company is created to hold a controlling interest in the second, and so on. The control of the last holding company is sufficient to control all; and such control, because of the scattering of stock among many small holders, may need the ownership of only 10% or 20% of the stock available. The large business corporation has strongly influenced the control of property in the modern world. Approximately 100 corporations are thought to own half of the total corporate wealth of the United States; they are typically controlled by a small minority of the stockholders. There are several methods employed by small groups of stockholders to gain control of large corporations. These include pooling of the majority of stock in the hands of trustees having the power to vote it and the use of proxies (agents for the actual stockholders pledged to vote for particular candidates for managerial positions). Proxies are generally successfully used because stockholders rarely attend meetings or name proxies other than those suggested to them by management. See also TRUST. See A. A. Berle and G. C. Means, *The Modern Corporation and Private Property* (1932, rev. ed. 1968); E. S. Mason, ed., *The Corporation in Modern Society* (1960, repr. 1966); W. L. Warner, *The Corporation in the Emergent American Society* (1962); P. F. Drucker, *The Concept of the Corporation* (rev. ed. 1972); Herman Kahn, ed., *The Future of the Corporation* (1974).

corporation tax, imposts levied by federal, state, or local governments against corporations, their income, or their peculiar attributes, such as charters, capitalization, dividends, and franchises. In the United States such taxes were brought about by the difficulty of taxing corporate bonds and stocks and by the growth of corporations beyond state bounds, with consequent difficulty of assessment and taxation. Such special state corporation taxes now include fees and licenses for incorporation or for an increase in capitalization or for filing the corporation's charter in another state; taxes on gross earnings; taxes on tonnage and financial instruments or transactions; franchise taxes; capital stock taxes; and net income taxes. In 1909 the Federal government imposed an excise tax on net incomes of U.S. corporations. That tax was superseded by a corporation INCOME TAX after the Sixteenth Amendment (1913). In Great Britain in 1920 a tax was levied on corporations, including foreign companies of limited liability doing business in the United Kingdom, but exempting the profits of corporations receiving income from other corporations already taxed. In both the United States and Great Britain, EXCESS PROFITS TAX has generally been imposed only during wartime. See Séan Réamonn, *The Philosophy of the Corporate Tax* (1970); B. I. Bittker, *Federal Income Taxation of Corporations and Shareholders* (3d ed. 1971); Hugo Nurnburg, *Cash Movements Analysis of the Accounting for Corporate Income Taxes* (1971).

corporative state, economic system inaugurated by the Fascist regime of Benito Mussolini in Italy. It was adapted in modified form under other European dictatorships, among them Adolf Hitler's National Socialist regime in Germany and the Spanish regime of Francisco Franco. Although the Italian system was based upon unlimited government control of economic life, it still preserved the framework of capitalism. Legislation of 1926 and later years set up 22 guilds, or associations, of employees and employers to administer various sectors of the national economy. These were represented in the national council of corporations. The corporations were generally weighted by the state in favor of the wealthy classes, and they served to combat socialism and syndicalism by absorbing the trade union movement. The Italian corporative state aimed in general at reduced consumption in the interest of militarization. See Roland Sarti, *Fascism and the Industrial Leadership in Italy, 1919–1940* (1971).

corposant: see SAINT ELMO'S FIRE.

corpus callosum: see BRAIN.

Corpus Christi (kôr'pəs krĭs'tē), city (1970 pop. 204,525), seat of Nueces co., S Texas; inc. 1852. It is a busy port of entry on Corpus Christi Bay at the entrance to Nueces Bay (an inlet at the mouth of the Nueces River); the main cargoes handled are cotton, oil, grain, and chemicals. The city is a petroleum and natural gas center, with much heavy industry. It has oil refineries, smelting plants, chemical works, and food-processing establishments, as well as a large shrimp fleet and an important fishing industry. Excellent sports-fishing facilities, beaches, and a mild climate make Corpus Christi a well-known tourist center. It is the gateway to Padre Island National Seashore. Tradition holds that the bay was named by the Spanish explorer Alonzo Alvarez de Pineda who discovered it on Corpus Christi Day in 1519, but there is evidence that it was named instead by the first settlers, who arrived from the lower Rio Grande valley in the 1760s. In 1839, Col. H. L. Kinney founded a trading post there, and traders, adventurers, and ne'er-do-wells collected in a raffish colony on land claimed by both Texas and Mexico. The small port and terminus for overland wagon-train traffic boomed during the Mexican War. It was briefly captured by the U.S. navy in the Civil War and later served as a supply and shipping point for sheep and cattle. It developed industrially after the discovery of oil in the area and the completion (1926) of a deepwater channel past Mustang Island. Its remarkable growth is evidenced by a spectacular bridge (235 ft/72 m high; completed 1959) over the harbor entrance and by a large dam on the Nueces River that has increased the city's water supply. The city has many historical points of interest and is the seat of a junior college and of the Univ. of Corpus Christi. A huge naval air-training station, also containing a major U.S. army helicopter maintenance facility, is on the southern shore of the bay. The city has suffered from occasional hurricanes; it is now partially protected from flooding by a sea wall 12,300 ft (3,749 m) long, built between 1939 and 1941 to a height 14 ft (4 m) beyond the high-water mark of a devastating 1919 hurricane.

Corpus Christi [Latin,=body of Christ], feast of the Western Church, observed on the Thursday after Trinity Sunday (or on the following Sunday). It commemorates the founding of the sacrament of the Eucharist, supplementing the anniversary on MAUNDY THURSDAY. The feast was established generally in 1264, with an office by St. Thomas Aquinas, which includes the splendid hymn PANGE LINGUA. In medieval times it was celebrated with pageants and the performance of MIRACLE PLAYS.

Corpus Juris Civilis (kôr'pəs jŏŏ'rĭs sĭvĭ'lĭs), most comprehensive code of ROMAN LAW and the basic document of all modern CIVIL LAW. Compiled by order of Byzantine Emperor Justinian I, the first three parts appeared between 529 and 535 and were the work of a commission of 17 jurists presided over by the eminent jurist Tribonian. The Corpus Juris was an attempt to systematize Roman law, to reduce it to order after over 1,000 years of development. The resulting work was more comprehensive, systematic, and thorough than any previous work of that nature, including the THEODOSIAN CODE. The four parts of the Corpus Juris are the Institutes, a general introduction to the work and a general survey of the whole field of Roman law; the Digest or Pandects, by far the most important part, intended for practitioners and judges and containing the law in concrete form plus selections from 39 noted classical jurists such as Gaius, Paulus, Ulpian, Modestinus, and Papinian; the Codex or Code, a collection of imperial legislation since the time of Hadrian; and the Novels or Novellae, compilations of later imperial legislation issued between 535 and 565 but never officially collected. Because it was published in numerous editions, copies of this written body of Roman law survived the collapse of the Roman empire and avoided the fate of earlier legal texts—notably those of the great Roman jurist Gaius. With the revival of interest in Roman law (especially at Bologna) in the 11th cent., the Corpus Juris was studied and commented on exhaustively by such scholars as IRNERIUS. Jurists and scholars trained in this Roman law played a leading role in the creation of national legal systems throughout Europe, and the Corpus Juris Civilis thus became the ultimate model and inspiration for the legal system of virtually every continental European nation. The name Corpus Juris Civilis was first applied to the collection by the 16th-century jurist Denys Godefroi. See H. F. Jolowicz, *Historical Introduction to the Study of Roman Law* (2d ed. 1952) and *Roman Foundations of Modern Law* (1957); A. T. Von Mehren, *The Civil Law System* (1957).

Correggio (kərĕj'ō), c.1494–1534, Italian painter, whose real name was Antonio Allegri, called Correggio for his birthplace. He learned the rudiments of art from his uncle Lorenzo Allegri. His early works were greatly influenced by the divergent styles of Mantegna and Leonardo da Vinci, as evidenced in the *Marriage of St. Catherine* (National Gall. of Art, Washington, D.C.) and *Madonna of St. Francis* (Dresden). Correggio's first important commission (1518) was the decoration of the convent of San Paolo at Parma. He handled the erudite allegorical program with exuberance. Depicting an impressive array of gods in the lunettes, he added a group of capricious *putti* (male infants) to the dome. Correggio painted many other mythological scenes including the sensual *Io* (Vienna); *Danae* (Borghese Gall., Rome); and *Antiope* (Louvre). In 1520 he began to fresco the dome of St. John the Evangelist, Parma, with the *Ascension of Christ*. A few years later he was working on his most famous project, *Assumption of the Virgin*, in the dome of the cathedral in Parma. The Virgin is encircled by an elaborate network of apostles, patriarchs, and saints, all emerging from the clouds. Correggio used daring foreshortening in his execution of the figures. His illusionistic ceiling decorations were widely imitated in the 17th cent. Pervaded by a sense of grace and tenderness, his paintings are characterized by their soft play of light and color. Other famous works are *Madonna of St. Jerome* (Parma), *Adoration of the Child* (Uffizi), and *Madonna and Saints* (Philadelphia Mus.). See his frescoes, ed. by A. Q. Ghidiglia (1964); biography by C. Ricci (1930); studies by A. E. Popham (1957) and E. Panofsky (1961).

Correggio (kōr-rĕd'jō), town (1971 pop. 20,301), in Emilia-Romagna, N central Italy. It is an agricultural market and a cheese-manufacturing center. It was the seat of a small principality of the Da Correggio family (12th–17th cent.), whose palace is a good example of 16th-century architecture. The painter Antonio Allegri was born there (1494) and was called Correggio after the town.

Corregidor (kərĕ'gĭdôr"), historic fortified island (c.2 sq mi/5 sq km), at the entrance to Manila Bay, just off Bataan peninsula of Luzon island, the Philippines. From the days of the Spanish, Corregidor and its tiny neighboring islets—El Fraile, Caballo, and Carabao—guarded the entrance to Manila Bay, serving as an outpost for the defense of Manila. The Spanish also maintained a penal colony on Corregidor. When the Americans acquired the Philippine Islands after the Spanish-American War (1898), they elaborately strengthened those defenses. Corregidor was honeycombed with tunnels to serve as ammunition depots, and Fort Mills and Kindley Field were established. Fort Drum was built on El Fraile, Fort Hughes on Caballo, and Fort Frank on Carabao. The new fortifications were deemed so formidable that Corregidor became known as the Gibraltar of the East, or "the Rock." In the early phase of World War II, Corregidor's batteries guarded the entrance to Manila Bay—denying that splendid harbor to the Japanese for five months—and protected the flank of the large U.S.-Filipino army concentrated on Bataan peninsula. During those months Corregidor was subjected to one of the most intense continuous bombardments of the entire war. Its surface was churned to rubble, and the garrison was forced into the caves and tunnels. After the fall of Bataan, about 10,000 U.S. and Filipino troops under Lt. Gen. Jonathan M. Wainwright fought gallantly on for a month. They were hopelessly cut off from all supplies and aid. Corregidor was finally invaded early in May, 1942, and the garrison was forced to surrender. The island was recaptured in March, 1945, by U.S. paratroopers and shore landing parties. It is now a national shrine. See James and William Belote, *Corregidor: The Saga of a Fortress* (1967).

correspondence principle, physical principle, enunciated by Niels Bohr in 1923, according to which the predictions of the QUANTUM THEORY must correspond to the predictions of the classical theories of physics when the quantum theory is used to describe the behavior of systems that can be successfully described by classical theories. Technically this principle means that the results of a quantum theory analysis of a problem that involves the use of very large quantum numbers must agree with the results of a classical physics analysis. Such correspondence is known as the classical limit of the quantum theory. Ordinarily the quantum theory is used to describe the behavior of bodies that are so small that they cannot be seen under an optical microscope, while the theories of classical physics are used to analyze the behavior of large-scale bodies. The correspondence principle provided an important theoretical basis for the development of a detailed correlation between the newer quantum theory and the classical physics that preceded it.

Corrèze (kôrĕz'), department (1968 pop. 237,858), S central France, in LIMOUSIN. TULLE is the capital.

Corrib, Lough (lŏkh kŏr'ĭb), lake, 68 sq mi (176 sq km), Counties Galway and Mayo, W Republic of Ireland. The irregularly shaped lake, which is 27 mi (43 km) long, drains into Galway Bay through the Corrib River. It is connected by a partly subterranean channel with Lough Mask to the north. Lough Corrib is an important transportation route; it is also a major brown-trout fishery.

Corrientes, city (1970 pop. 137,823), capital of Corrientes prov., NE Argentina, a port on the Paraná River. It is the commercial center of a rich pastoral and agricultural region. The city exports the cattle, timber, and agricultural products of the province. An important cultural center, it has several institutions of higher education, museums, and historical monuments. Corrientes was founded in 1588 and survived fierce Indian attacks during the late 16th and early 17th cent. In 1762 an uprising of the *comuneros* [townspeople] against the colonial governor foreshadowed the wars of independence from Spain. The city and province were among the first to rebel (1844) against Juan Manuel de Rosas.

Corrievrekin or **Corryvreckan** (both: kŏr'ēvrĕkən), whirlpool in Corrievrekin passage N of Jura island, Argyllshire, W Scotland.

corrosion, atmospheric oxidation of metals (see OXIDATION AND REDUCTION). By far the most important form of corrosion is the rusting of IRON. Rusting is essentially a process of oxidation in which iron combines with water and oxygen to form rust, the reddish-brown crust that forms on the surface of the iron. Rust, a chemical compound, is a hydrated ferric oxide $Fe_2O_3 \cdot nH_2O$, where n is usually $1\frac{1}{2}$. The chemical mechanism of rusting is not fully known, but is thought to involve oxidation of metallic iron to ferrous ion (Fe^{++}) and reaction of the ferrous ion with oxygen and water to form rust. The reaction is catalyzed by water, acids, and metals (e.g., copper and tin) below iron in the ELECTROMOTIVE SERIES. Because iron is so widely used, e.g., in building construction and in tools, its protection against rusting is important. Although metals (e.g., aluminum, chromium, and zinc) above iron in the electromotive series corrode more readily than iron, their oxides form a tenuous coating that protects the metal from further attack. Rust is brittle and flakes off the surface of the iron, continually exposing a fresh surface. Rusting can be prevented by excluding air and water from the iron surface, e.g., by painting, oiling, or greasing, or by plating the iron with a protective coating of another metal. Metals used for plating include chromium, nickel, tin, and zinc. Zinc plating is called galvanizing. Many alloys of iron are resistant to corrosion. Stainless steels are alloys of iron with such metals as chromium and nickel; they do not corrode because the added metals help form a hard, adherent oxide coating that resists further attack. The iron hulls of ships can be protected against rusting by attaching magnesium strips to the underside of the vessel. An electric current is generated, with the magnesium and iron acting as electrodes and seawater acting as the electrolyte. Because magnesium is above iron in the electromotive series, it serves as a "sacrificial anode" and is oxidized in preference to the iron. This is called cathodic protection, since the iron serves as the cathode and thus escapes oxidation. This method is also used to protect the pipes of electric generating plants where salt water is used as a coolant.

corrosive sublimate: see MERCURIC CHLORIDE.

corrupt practices, in politics, fraud connected with elections. The term also refers to various offenses by public officials, including bribery, the sale of offices, granting of public contracts to favored firms or individuals, and granting of land or franchises in return for monetary rewards. Election fraud may consist of efforts to influence or intimidate the voter or to tamper with the official BALLOT or election count. To eliminate these practices nearly all democratic nations have passed laws that attempt to safeguard the honesty of political campaigns and elections. In Great Britain the Acts of 1883 and 1918, frequently amended, define election abuses and limit political spending by or on behalf of candidates for Parliament. In the United States individual states have their own election laws, and they preceded Congress in enacting corrupt practices acts. In large cities of the United States election fraud has historically been associated with political machines (see BOSSISM), while in the S United States it was historically used to deprive the Negro of political power. On the Federal level, the Corrupt Practices Act of 1925, the Hatch Act of 1940, parts of the Taft-Hartley Act of 1947, and the campaign financing legislation of 1974 have all tried to regulate campaign finances by limiting amounts spent and the size and source of campaign gifts, by requiring disclosure of expenditure, and by public financing of presidential elections. In 1968, in the wake of several scandals, both the Senate and the House established ethics committees and adopted codes of conduct that required members to file reports on their income and campaign contributions. In 1972, Congress passed legislation limiting the amount of money presidential and congressional candidates could spend in their campaigns; the law also required that all contributions and expenditures exceeding $100 be publicly reported. Revelations of political sabotage and espionage financed through secret campaign funds during the 1972 presidential election (see WATERGATE AFFAIR) led to renewed efforts on the state and Federal levels to regulate campaign finances. The most immediate result was the 1974 law limiting the amount that can be spent in campaigns and providing for a measure of public financing of national elections. The term has also been applied to businesses and labor unions, in the former case for price fixing, and in the latter for misappropriation of funds or the rigging of union elections. See Alexander Heard, *The Cost of Democracy* (1960, repr. 1967); H. E. Alexander, *Regulation of Political Finance* (1966) and *Money in Politics* (1972); E. M. Epstein, *Corporations, Contributions, and Political Campaigns* (1968); George Thayer, *Who Shakes the Money Tree? American Campaign Financing Practices from 1789 to the Present* (1973).

Corryvreckan, whirlpool: see CORRIEVREKIN, Scotland.

corsair: see PIRACY.

corset, article of dress designed to support or modify the figure. Greek and Roman women sometimes wrapped broad bands about the body. In the Middle Ages a short, close-fitting, laced outer bodice or waist was worn. By the 16th cent. it had become a tight inner bodice, sometimes of leather, stiffened with whalebone, wooden splints, or steel; fashion demanded the slenderest possible waist in contrast with the enormous farthingales and stuffed breeches that were worn. Stays and tight lacing were made for both men and women from the 17th through the 19th cent., except for a brief period following the French Revolution. By 1900 the corset had become primarily a female garment, and it was gradually modified to conform to the natural lines of the body. Today the garment that most closely resembles the corset is termed a girdle.

Corsica (kôr'sĭkə), Fr. *Corse,* island (1968 pop. 269,831), 3,367 sq mi (8,721 sq km), a department of metropolitan France, SE of France and N of Sardinia, in the Mediterranean Sea. AJACCIO, the capital, and BASTIA are the chief towns and ports. The island is largely mountainous, culminating in Monte Cinto (8,891 ft/2,710 m). Principal rivers are the Golo, Tavignano, Liamone, Gravone, Tarova, and Profiano. Olive oil, wine, and timber are the main exports. Much wheat and cheese are produced, and sheep are raised. Communications are poor. Much of the island is wild, covered by undergrowth, or maquis; the flowers of the maquis produce a fragrance that carries far out to sea and has earned for Corsica the name "the scented isle." The maquis long provided ideal hideouts for bandits, and banditry was not fully suppressed until the 1930s. Blood feuds between clans also persisted into modern times. Most Corsicans speak a dialect akin to Italian. After having belonged to the Romans (3d cent. B.C.–5th cent. A.D.), the Vandals, the Byzantines, and the Lombards, the island was granted (late 8th cent.) by the Franks to the papacy. It was threatened by the Arabs from c.800 to 1100. In 1077, Pope Gregory VII ceded Corsica to Pisa. Pisa and Genoa and later Genoa and Aragón battled for Corsica. In the mid-15th cent. the actual administration of the island was taken up by the Bank of San Giorgio in Genoa; Genoese rule was harsh and unpopular. Later unrest was typified by the episode of "King" Theodore I (see NEUHOF, THEODOR, BARON VON). In 1755, Pasquale PAOLI headed a rebellion against Genoa, but its success resulted only in the cession (1768) of Corsica to France. One consequence of the transfer was the French citizenship of Napoleon I, who was born in 1769 at Ajaccio. With British support Paoli expelled the French in 1793, and in 1794 Corsica voted its union with the British crown. The French (under Napoleon) recovered it, however, in 1796, and French possession was guaranteed at the Congress of Vienna (1815). French rule brought education and relative order, but economic life remained agrarian and primitive. In World War II, Corsica was occupied by Italian and German troops. Late in 1943 the population revolted, and, with the assistance of a Free French task force, the Axis forces were driven out. A postwar exodus of population caused the French government to announce a program of economic development in the 1950s. The island has developed a tourist industry. In 1958 a right-wing coup similar to that in Algiers contributed to the return to power of Charles de Gaulle in France.

Corsicana (kôrsĭkăn′ə), city (1970 pop. 19,972), seat of Navarro co., E central Texas; inc. 1848. It is an oil center with wells and refineries and additional industries that depend on the cotton, small grains, and Hereford cattle produced in the surrounding blackland farm area. The discovery of oil when a city water well was being dug (1894) caused dismay at first but led to the drilling (1895) of the first commercial oil well W of the Mississippi and the building (1898) of the first refinery in Texas. In Corsicana are a junior college and Pioneer Village, a complex of restored log structures.

Cort, Henry, 1740–1800, English inventor. He revolutionized the British iron industry with his use of grooved rollers to finish iron, replacing the process of hammering, and through his invention of the puddling process. This process involved stirring the molten pig iron in a reverbatory furnace until the decarburizing action of the air produced a loop of pure metal.

Cortázar, Julio (ho͝o′lyō kōrtä′zär), 1914–, Argentine novelist, poet, essayist, and short-story writer, b. Brussels. A student of SURREALISM, he creates a cruel and despairing world full of fantasy and satire. Life is often depicted as a maze or game from which man must extricate himself. His works include *Final del juego* (1956; tr. *End of the Game,* 1967), *Historias de cronopios y de famas* (1962; tr. *Cronopios and Famas,* 1969), *Rayuela* (1963; tr. *Hopscotch,* 1966), *Sixty-two: A Model Kit* (1972; tr. 1972), and *All Fires the Fire and Other Stories* (tr. 1973).

Cortelyou, George Bruce (kôr′təlyo͞o), 1862–1940, American public official and business executive, b. New York City. He taught school, and after learning stenography, he became secretary to several New York City and Federal officials. Appointed (1895) stenographer to President Cleveland, Cortelyou became secretary to Presidents McKinley (1900) and Theodore Roosevelt (1901). He also served under Roosevelt as Secretary of Commerce and Labor (1903–4), Postmaster General (1905–7), and Secretary of the Treasury (1907–9). He then left government service and became prominent as an executive of public-utility companies.

Corte Real or **Corte-Real, Gaspar** (gəshpär′ kôr′tə rĕäl′), c.1450–1501?, Portuguese explorer. Sent by King Manuel I to search for the Northwest Passage, he is said to have discovered Greenland in 1500 and may have touched on the North American coast. He made a second voyage with his brother Miguel in 1501. He then sent Miguel home and continued his exploration, sailing southwest along the present U.S. coast. Gaspar Corte Real was lost. In 1502 Miguel Corte Real went in search of him but was also lost. The brothers certainly reached Newfoundland and made sweeping discoveries, but the results were inconclusive. See H. P. Biggar, *Voyages of the Cabots and the Corte-Reals* (1903).

Cortés, Hernán, or **Hernando Cortez** (kôrtĕz′, Span. ārnän′, ārnän′dō kōrtās′), 1485–1547, Spanish CONQUISTADOR, conqueror of Mexico. He went to Hispaniola (1504) and later (1511) accompanied Diego de VELÁZQUEZ to Cuba. In 1518 he was chosen to lead an expedition to Mexico. Although Velázquez later sought to recall his commission, Cortés sailed in Feb., 1519. In Yucatán he rescued a Spaniard who had learned the Mayan language; after a victory over Indians in Tabasco, Cortés acquired the services of a female slave Malinche—baptized Marina—who knew both Maya and Aztec. Having proceeded up the coast, Cortés founded Villa Rica de la Vera Cruz and was chosen captain general by the cabildo; thus he discarded Velázquez's authority and became responsible only to Charles V. Cortés, learning that the Aztec empire of MONTEZUMA was honeycombed with dissension, assumed the role of deliverer and rallied the coastal Totonacs to his standard; he also began negotiations with Montezuma. Scuttling his ships to prevent the return of any Velázquez sympathizers to Cuba, he began his famous march to Tenochtitlán (modern Mexico city), capital of the Aztec empire. He defeated the Tlaxcalan warriors, then formed an alliance with the so-called republic of Tlaxcala; practically destroyed CHOLULA; and arrived at Tenochtitlán in Nov., 1519. There the superstitious Montezuma received the Spanish as descendants of the god Quetzalcoatl. Cortés seized his opportunity, took Montezuma as a hostage, and attempted to govern through him. In the spring of 1520, Cortés went to the coast, where he defeated a force under Pánfilo de NARVÁEZ. Pedro de ALVARADO, left in command, impetuously massacred many Aztecs, and soon after Cortés's return the Aztecs besieged the Spanish. In the ensuing battle, Montezuma was killed. The Spanish, seeking safety in flight, fought their way out of the city with heavy loss on the *noche triste* [sad night] (June 30, 1520). Still in retreat, they defeated an Aztec army at Otumba and retired to Tlaxcala. The next year Cortés attacked the capital, and after a three-month siege Tenochtitlán fell (Aug. 13, 1521). With it fell the Aztec empire. As captain general, Cortés extended the conquest by sending expeditions over most of Mexico and into N Central America. In 1524–26, Cortés himself went to Honduras, killing CUAUHTÉMOC, the Aztec emperor, on the expedition. In Cortés's absence his enemies gradually triumphed, and after his return his power was made more fictitious than real by the audiencia. Although on his visit to Spain (1528–30) Cortés was made marqués del Valle de Oaxaca, Charles V refused to name him governor. Returning to Mexico, he vainly sent out maritime expeditions, frustrated more than once by Nuño de GUZMÁN. Subsequently he quarreled with the viceroy, Antonio de MENDOZA, and in 1540 he again sought justice in Spain. There, neglected by the court, he died. The best-known contemporary account of the conquest is that of Bernal Díaz del Castillo. See the letters of Cortés (Eng. ed. by F. A. MacNutt, 1908); W. H. Prescott, *Conquest of Mexico* (1937); studies by Salvador de Madariaga (1942, repr. 1969) and H. R. Wagner (1944, repr. 1969).

Cortes (kôr′tĕz, Span. kōr′tās), representative assembly in Spain. The institution originated (12th–13th cent.) in various Spanish regions with the Christian reconquest; until the 19th cent. the local cortes of Leon, Castile, Aragón, Catalonia, Navarre, Valencia, and other states met separately. The three estates—clergy, nobility, and burghers—voted the taxes, recognized the kings upon their accession, and indirectly exercised some legislative influence. The cortes of Aragón and Catalonia were particularly powerful. After the consolidation of the royal power (15th cent.) and the unification of Spain, the cortes were seldom convoked except to pay homage, and their powers were curtailed. The first national Cortes of Spain met at Cádiz in 1810 in the Peninsular War, the Spanish war of liberation from Napoleonic rule. They voted (1812) a liberal constitution, later (1814) revoked by Ferdinand VII. Thereafter the status of the Cortes frequently changed in its struggle for power with the king. At the fall of the monarchy in 1931, a constituent Cortes promulgated a republican constitution, and the Cortes was the parliament of Spain until 1939. Under Francisco Franco's dictatorship a Cortes was preserved but stripped of effective legislative power. Under the Portuguese monarchy various legislative bodies were known as cortes.

cortex, in botany, term generally applied to the soft tissues of the leaves, stems, and roots of plants. Cortical cells of the leaves and outer layers of the stems of nonwoody plants contain chloroplasts, and are modified for food storage (usually in the form of starch) in roots and the inner layers of stems and seeds. Because of the combination of its soft texture (especially after cooking) and its role as a food storage tissue, the cortex is the predominant plant tissue eaten by man and other animals.

Cortez, Hernando: see CORTÉS, HERNÁN.

corticosteroid drug (kôr″təkōstâr′oid), any one of several synthetic or naturally occurring substances with the general chemical structure of STEROIDS. They are used therapeutically to mimic or augment the effects of the naturally occurring corticosteroids, which are produced in the cortex of the ADRENAL GLAND. Corticosteroids are very powerful drugs affecting the entire system; even corticosteroids used on large areas of skin for long periods are absorbed in sufficient quantity to cause systemic effects. Corticosteroids, as well as ADRENOCORTICOTROPIC HORMONE (ACTH), the pituitary gland substance that stimulates the adrenal cortex, have modifying effects on many diseases. Some corticosteroid derivatives mimic the action of the naturally occurring steroid hormone ALDOSTERONE, causing increased sodium retention and potassium excretion. Others have the same effects as the naturally occurring steroids CORTISONE and CORTISOL, which are classed as glucocorticoids; these affect carbohydrate and fat metabolism, reduce tissue inflammation, and suppress the body's immune defense mechanisms. Cortisone and hydrocortisone are used to treat ADDISON'S DISEASE, a disorder caused by underproduction of the adrenal cortex hormones. These and synthetic steroids are extensively used to treat arthritis and other rheumatoid diseases including rheumatic heart disease. They are also used in some cases of autoimmune diseases such as systemic lupus erythematosus, in severe allergic conditions such as asthma, in allergic and inflammatory eye disorders, in some respiratory diseases, and in some leukemias and cancers. The anti-inflammatory, itch-suppressing, and vasoconstrictive properties of steroids make them useful when applied to the skin to relieve diseases such as eczema, psoriasis, and insect bites. Because corticosteroids lower the resistance to infection, patients on steroid therapy cannot be vaccinated for smallpox or immunized. The administration of corticosteroids also causes underproduction of the natural hormones by the adrenal cortex, and so ACTH or corticosteroid therapy must always be withdrawn gradually. In addition, when used in large doses for long periods of time, the drugs can cause atrophy of the adrenal cortex. Side effects of steroid therapy include glaucoma, excess hair growth, and imbalance of many substances, including calcium, nitrogen, potassium, and sodium. Many of the synthetic corticosteroids, such as prednisone, prednisolone, triamcinolone, and betamethasone, are more potent than the naturally occurring compounds.

corticosterone (kôr″təkōstĕr′ōn), steroid HORMONE secreted by the outer layer, or cortex, of the ADRENAL GLAND. Classed as a glucocorticoid, corticosterone helps regulate the conversion of amino acids into carbohydrates and glycogen by the liver, and helps stimulate glycogen formation in the tissues. Corticosterone is similar in structure, although somewhat less potent, than the other glucocorticoids CORTISOL and CORTISONE. It is produced in response to stimulation by the pituitary substance ADRENOCORTICOTROPIC HORMONE (ACTH). In some species, but not in humans, corticosterone is the predominant glucocorticoid secreted by the adrenal. It is a precursor in the synthesis of ALDOSTERONE, another adrenal cortical steroid.

corticotropin (kôr″təkōtrŏp′ən): see ADRENOCORTICOTROPIC HORMONE.

Cortina d'Ampezzo (kōrtē′nä dämpĕd′zō), town (1971 pop. 8,574), in Venetia, NE Italy, in the heart of the DOLOMITES. It is an international winter sports center. The 1956 winter Olympic games were held there.

cortisol (kôr′tĭsôl″), or hydrocortisone, steroid HORMONE that in humans is the major circulating hormone of the cortex, or outer layer, of the ADRENAL GLAND. Like CORTISONE, cortisol is classed as a glucocorticoid; it stimulates liver glycogen formation while it decreases the rate of glucose utilization in body cells. A main effect of cortisol is to reduce the reserves of protein in all body cells except cells of the liver and gastrointestinal tract. It also makes fatty acids available for metabolic use. Cortisol is synthesized and secreted by the adrenal cortex in response to the stimulating substance ADRENOCORTICOTROPIC HORMONE (ACTH). In turn, cortisol is the major regulator of ACTH production in the pituitary gland; it acts by negative feedback inhibition, i.e., a rise in the level of cortisol in the blood inhibits ACTH secretion by the pituitary. Cortisol is more potent than cortisone with respect to metabolic and anti-inflammatory effects.

cortisone (kôr'tĭsōn"), steroid HORMONE whose main physiological effect is on carbohydrate metabolism. It is synthesized from CHOLESTEROL in the outer layer, or cortex, of the ADRENAL GLAND under the stimulation of ADRENOCORTICOTROPIC HORMONE (ACTH). Cortisone is classed as a glucocorticoid with CORTISOL and CORTICOSTERONE; its effects include increased glucose release from the liver, increased liver glycogen synthesis, and decreased utilization of glucose by the tissues. These actions tend to counter the effects of INSULIN and may aggravate or mimic diabetes in sufficiently high doses. Cortisone also exerts an effect on salt retention in the kidneys similar to that of ALDOSTERONE, although it is not as potent. The hormone causes increased breakdown of proteins and decreased protein synthesis, and large doses given over a long period of time may result in inhibited growth in children or weakening of bones and wasting of muscles in adults. The principal medical use of cortisone comes from its anti-inflammatory and anti-allergic effects; it is extremely useful in the treatment of innumerable diseases including asthma and other allergic reactions, arthritis, and various skin diseases. Cortisone is necessary to maintain life and enable the organism to respond to stress; failure of the adrenal glands to synthesize cortisone (Addison's disease) or surgical removal of the adrenals is fatal unless cortisone is given as replacement therapy. Although less cortisone is manufactured in the body than either cortisol or corticosterone and although cortisone is less potent than cortisol, the term cortisone is often used collectively to include the other glucocorticoids, both the naturally occurring and the synthetic compounds such as prednisone. Small quantities of cortisone were first isolated from animal adrenals in 1935-36. A method of manufacture, involving laboratory synthesis from an acid of BILE, was developed, and in 1949 cortisone was first offered commercially. The specific mechanisms by which cortisone and similar compounds act are still poorly understood.

Cortissoz, Royal (kôrtē'sōz), 1869-1948, American critic and lecturer on art. He was the New York *Herald Tribune* art critic from 1891 and was noted for his lectures at the Metropolitan Museum and at other museums throughout the United States. He wrote biographies of Augustus Saint-Gaudens (1907), John La Farge (1911), and Whitelaw Reid (1921), as well as *Art and Common Sense* (1913), *American Artists* (1923), *Personalities in Art* (1925), and *The Painter's Craft* (1930).

Cortland, city (1970 pop. 19,621), seat of Cortland co., central N.Y., in a fertile farm area; settled 1791, inc. as a city 1900. Fish line, metal products, and automotive and aircraft parts are among the manufactures. The State Univ. College at Cortland is a major employer, and a junior college is in nearby Groton.

Cortona, Pietro Berrettini da (pyā'trō bār-rĕt-tē'nē dä kōrtō'nä), 1596-1669, Italian baroque painter and architect, b. Cortona. The Barberini family commissioned him to paint frescoes for the vast ceiling of their palace in Rome, which resulted in the exuberant *Allegory of Divine Providence and Barberini Power* (1633-39). The work, filled with swirling clouds and figures, was one of the most influential of baroque decorative schemes. It is a paramount example of baroque ILLUSIONISM. In Florence he executed frescoes of the *Four Ages* and the rich ceiling decoration in the Pitti Palace, the *Allegories of the Virtues and Planets.* In these seven rooms the ceilings are unified with the structure of the rooms by stucco ornamentation. Pietro's pupil Ciro Ferri (1634-89) completed the work in the Pitti Palace. Almost equally ornate were Pietro's early architectural designs, such as that for the church of SS. Martina e Luca (1635-50) in Rome, which Pietro finished at his own expense. Later he turned to a greater simplification and massiveness in the facades of Santa Maria della Pace (1656-57) and Santa Maria in Via Lata (1658-62). His architectural works are among the most significant of the baroque period.

Cortona (kōrtō'nä), town (1971 pop. 22,377), Tuscany, central Italy. It is an agricultural and tourist center. One of the 12 important Etruscan cities, Cortona later (310 B.C.) united with Rome. The town passed to Florence in the early 15th cent. Landmarks include the Romanesque cathedral (remodeled during the Renaissance), the Palazzo Pretorio (13th cent.), and the Church of San Francesco (begun 1245). The Diocesan Museum contains paintings by Luca SIGNORELLI (who was born in Cortona), Fra ANGELICO, and others.

Cortot, Alfred Denis (älfrĕd' dənē' kôrtō'), 1877-1962, French pianist and conductor. Among his appearances as a conductor were those at Bayreuth from 1898 to 1901. He joined the faculty of the Paris Conservatory in 1907 and in 1919 founded the École normale de Musique, Paris. For many years he played trios with Jacques Thibaud and Pablo Casals.

Çorum (chôro͝om'), city (1970 pop. 55,890), capital of Çorum prov., N central Turkey. It is the trade center for a farm region where grains, fruits, sheep, and goats are raised. The city's manufactures include copper and leather goods. Important Hittite remains have been found there.

Corumbá (ko͝oro͞omba'), city (1970 pop. 81,838), Mato Grosso state, SW Brazil, on the Paraguay River. A river port and a junction point on the railroad to Bolivia, it is a trade center for a large pastoral region. Corumbá exports leather and meat products and has varied light industries. Founded as a military outpost and colony in 1778, it became strategically important with the opening of the Paraguay River to international trade after the Paraguayan War (1865-70). Nearby are the buttes of Morro do Urucum, which contain vast iron and manganese deposits.

Coruña, La (lä kōro͞o'nyä), city (1970 pop. 189,654), capital of La Coruña prov., NW Spain, in Galicia. It is a busy Atlantic port, a distribution center for the surrounding farm area, and a summer resort spot. It has shipyards, metalworks, and an important fishing industry. La Coruña reached its height as a port and a textile center in the late Middle Ages. The Armada sailed from its harbor in 1588. The city was sacked by Sir Francis Drake in 1598. In the Peninsular War it was the scene of the battle (1809) in which Sir John Moore was killed. The city was a focus of antimonarchist sentiment during the 19th cent. Chief landmarks are a 13th-century church and the Roman Torre de Hércules, now a lighthouse. Glazed window balconies, or *miradores,* are characteristic of La Coruña.

corundum (kərŭn'dəm), mineral, aluminum oxide, Al_2O_3. The clear varieties are used as gems and the opaque as ABRASIVE materials. Corundum occurs in crystals of the hexagonal system and in masses. It is transparent to opaque and has a vitreous to adamantine luster. The transparent gem varieties are colorless, pink, red, blue, green, yellow, and violet; the common varieties are blue-gray to brown. Emery is a common corundum, used as an abrasive and distinguished by its impurities of magnetite and hematite. The chief corundum gems are the RUBY (red) and the SAPPHIRE (blue). Yellow, pink, green, and white stones are also called yellow, pink, green, and white sapphires. Corundum gems are also made synthetically. The chief sources of natural corundum are Burma, Sri Lanka (formerly Ceylon), India, Thailand, Republic of South Africa, Tanzania, and the United States (North Carolina, Georgia, and Montana). Most of the emery is mined in Naxos and the other Cyclades and in Asia Minor.

Corvallis (kôrvăl'ĭs), city (1970 pop. 35,153), seat of Benton co., NW Oregon, on the Willamette River; inc. 1857. It is a food-processing hub in the heart of the fertile Willamette valley. It is also a research center, especially in forestry. Corvallis is the seat of Oregon State Univ. and the headquarters for Siuslaw National Forest. Nearby are a junior college, a state game farm, and a national wildlife refuge.

corvée (kôrvā'), under the feudal system, compulsory, unpaid labor demanded by a lord or king and the system of such labor in general. There were national and local variations, but in broad terms the corvée proper included work on the lord's portion of the manorial property and many attendant duties. Military service also came under the general terms of the corvée. The corvée included both regular and exceptional demands. "Real" corvée referred to the duties attached to the ownership or tillage of certain lands; "personal" corvée referred to the duties of specific individuals. Highly developed during the feudalization of the late Roman Empire, the corvée system was an integral part of the nonmoneyed social and economic system of the Middle Ages, but towns and all individuals who were able liberated themselves when possible by money payment instead of services. In France the royal corvée, compulsory work on public roads, was introduced in the 18th cent. Both the royal and the seignorial corvée bore heavily and almost exclusively upon the peasants and helped cause the French Revolution. Austria abolished the last European corvée system in 1848.

corvette, small warship, classed between a frigate and a sloop-of-war. Corvettes usually were flush-decked and carried fewer than 28 guns. They were widely employed in escorting convoys and attacking merchant ships during the great naval wars of the late 18th and early 19th cent., but corvettes passed from use with the transition from sail to steam. At the beginning of World War II the term was reintroduced to designate a small vessel of about 1,000 tons displacement, armed with depth charges and a single 4-in. (10.2-cm) gun. In the early years of the war, large numbers of these vessels were employed by the British and Canadian navies as convoy escorts in the North Atlantic; later they were supplanted by the larger, faster, and better-armed frigates.

Corvinus, Matthias: see MATTHIAS CORVINUS.

Corvo, Baron: see ROLFE, FREDERICK WILLIAM.

Corwin, Thomas, 1794-1865, American politician, b. Bourbon co., Ky. A lawyer, he was an Ohio legislator in the 1820s, a U.S. Representative (1831-40), and governor of Ohio (1840-42). In the U.S. Senate (1845-50) Corwin, a Whig, violently opposed the Mexican War. He was Secretary of the Treasury (1850-53) under President Fillmore, and although not entirely approving of the Republican position on slavery, he reentered the House (1859-61) as a member of that party. He was minister to Mexico from 1861 to 1864. See biography by Josiah Morrow (1896).

Cory, William Johnson, 1823-92, English poet and classicist. He was assistant master at Eton from 1845 to 1872. His verse, of which *Ionica* (1858) is the best known, consists primarily of imitations and translations of the Greek and Latin poets. See his *Letters and Journals* (ed. by F. W. Cornish, 1897).

Coryate, Thomas (kŏr'ēāt), 1577?-1617, English traveler. Grotesque in appearance, he became part of the household of Henry, the oldest son of James I, where he was a sort of unofficial court jester. In 1608 he went on a journey that covered much of Europe and resulted in the publication of his *Crudities* (1611), a strange mixture of travel observations and poetry. In 1612 he set out again, voyaged in Asia Minor and Egypt, then back to Palestine and E to Persia and India, where he died in 1617. His letters from India were published in 1616 and 1618; some are reprinted in *Early Travels in India* (ed. by Sir William Foster, 1921). See biography by Michael Strachan (1962).

Cos, Greece: see KŌS.

Cosa, Juan de la (hwän dā lä kō'sä), c.1460-1510, Spanish navigator. He sailed with Columbus in 1492 (as pilot of the flagship *Santa María*) and again in 1498. After accompanying Alonso de Ojeda in 1499, he drew (1500) a world map (a manuscript copy exists in Madrid) that seems to be the first to question the identification with Asia of the new lands and to furnish evidence that the Cabots coasted farther S along the Atlantic shore than other documents reveal. In 1501 he was with BASTIDAS, and later (1504) he again explored the northern coast of South America. Securing for Ojeda a commission to colonize and explore that coast, Cosa accompanied him (1509) to the site of Cartagena and was there killed by the Indians.

Cosam (kō'săm), ancestor of St. Joseph, in Luke's genealogy. Luke 3.28.

Cosenza (kōzān'tsä), city (1971 pop. 101,908), capital of Cosenza prov., Calabria, S Italy, at the confluence of the Busento and Crati rivers. It is an agricultural and industrial center. Manufactures include textiles, furniture, and lumber. The chief city of the ancient Brutii, it was taken by the Romans in 204 B.C. According to tradition, Alaric I (c.370-410 A.D.), the Visigothic king, was buried in the bed of the Busento at Cosenza. The city has suffered from numerous earthquakes. A castle built by Emperor Frederick II dominates the old part of the city.

Cosgrave, William Thomas (kŏs'grāv), 1880-1965, Irish statesman. A member of SINN FEIN, he fought in the Easter Rebellion of 1916 and was sentenced to life imprisonment. Freed a year later, he was elected to the British Parliament and joined in setting up the DÁIL EIREANN in 1919. He became minister of local government in the revolutionary cabinet. Cosgrave supported the treaty (1921) that set up the Irish Free State (see IRELAND) and, after the deaths of Arthur Griffith and Michael Collins, he was elected president. In 1932, when the republicans won the election, Cosgrave became opposition leader. In 1944 he resigned the leadership of his Fine Gael, or United

Ireland, party. His son, **Liam Cosgrave,** 1920–, entered the Dáil as a Fine Gael member in 1943 and served as minister of commerce and industry (1948–54) and of external affairs (1954–57). He became leader of the party in 1965, and in March, 1973, following the general election, he was made prime minister. In the face of continuing deterioration of the political situation in Northern Ireland, Cosgrave supported the British government in its establishment of a coalition executive there and its plans for a Council of Ireland to link the governments of the republic and the North.

Coshocton (kəshŏk'tən), city (1970 pop. 13,747), seat of Coshocton co., central Ohio, where the Tuscarawas and Walhonding rivers meet to form the Muskingum; inc. 1833. A warlike tribe of Delawares had a village there of the same name; in 1764 the expedition of Col. Henry Bouquet freed a number of white prisoners and established a peace treaty. Of interest is the Roscoe Village, a restored canal town on the Ohio-Erie Canal.

Cosimo de' Medici: see MEDICI, COSIMO DE'.

cosine, in trigonometry, relation defined in a right triangle for one of the acute angles (A) as the ratio of the length of the side adjacent to that angle (b) to the length of the hypotenuse (c), or $\cos A = b/c$. The concept may be extended to any plane triangle, in which case the Law of Cosines is found to hold: $a^2 = b^2 + c^2 - 2bc \cos A$, where a, b, and c are the lengths of the sides and A is the angle opposite side a; analogous relationships hold for angles B and C opposite sides b and c respectively. In general, the cosine function $\cos x$ may be expressed as an infinite SERIES, $\cos x = 1 - x^2/2! + x^4/4! - x^6/6! + \cdots$, where $n! = 1 \cdot 2 \cdot 3 \cdots n$. See TRIGONOMETRY.

Cosmati work: see MOSAIC.

cosmetics, preparations externally applied to change or enhance the beauty of skin, hair, nails, lips, and eyes. The use of body paint for ornamental and religious purposes has been common among primitive peoples from prehistoric times (see BODY-MARKING). Ointments, balms, powders, and hair dyes have also been used from ancient times. Many cosmetics originated in the Orient, but their ingredients and use are first recorded in Egypt; ancient tombs have yielded cosmetic jars (called kohl pots) and applicators (called cosmetic spoons). The Egyptians used kohl to darken their eyes; a crude paint was used on the face, and fingers were often dyed with henna. Greek women used charcoal pencils and rouge sticks of alkanet and coated their faces with powder, which often contained dangerous lead compounds. Beauty aids reached a peak in imperial Rome—especially chalk for the face and a rouge called fucus—and ladies required the services of slaves adept in their use. Many cosmetics survived the Middle Ages, and Crusaders brought back rare Eastern oils and perfumes. In the Renaissance, cosmetics, usually white-lead powder and vermilion, were used extravagantly. From the 17th cent. recipes and books on the toilette abounded. Professional cosmetologists began to appear, and luxurious prescriptions often included a bath in wine or milk. At its height by 1760, the use of cosmetics virtually disappeared with the advent of the French Revolution. The year 1900 saw a revival of their use, accompanied by the manufacture of beauty aids on a scientific basis in France. Since then the industry has grown to tremendous proportions with products manufactured for every conceivable use. In the United States, cosmetics intended for interstate commerce are controlled under the Federal Food, Drug, and Cosmetic Act of 1938.

cosmic rays, radiation of very high energy reaching the earth from outer space. Primary cosmic rays consist mostly of protons (nuclei of hydrogen atoms), some alpha particles (helium nuclei), and lesser amounts of nuclei of carbon, nitrogen, oxygen, and heavier atoms. These nuclei collide with nuclei in the upper atmosphere, producing secondary cosmic rays of protons, neutrons, mesons, electrons, and gamma rays of high energy, which in turn hit nuclei lower in the atmosphere to produce more particles (see ELEMENTARY PARTICLES). These cascade processes continue until all the energy of the primary particle is dissipated. The secondary particles shower down through the atmosphere in diminishing intensity to the earth's surface and even penetrate beneath it. The size of the shower indicates the energy of the primary ray, which may be as high as 10^{11} billion electron volts (Bev) or more, almost a billion times higher than the highest energy yet produced in a man-made particle accelerator; however, cosmic rays of lower energy predominate. Cosmic rays have long been used as a source of high-energy particles in the study of nuclear reactions. The positron, the MUON, the PION (or pi MESON), and some of the so-called strange particles were initially discovered in studies of this radiation. Cosmic rays were first found to be of extraterrestrial origin by V. F. Hess c.1911; they were so named in 1925 by R. A. Millikan, who did extensive research on them. Since then much more pertinent information has been collected, but the origin of cosmic rays remains unknown. It is believed that some cosmic rays are produced in solar flares; however, the majority seem to come from interstellar space, probably from within our GALAXY, the MILKY WAY system. The nature of the acceleration processes by which the primary particles achieve great velocities (very nearly the speed of light) is still highly speculative but may be uncovered in the future from information gathered from spacecraft. See J. E. Hooper and Morton Scharff, *Cosmic Radiation* (1958); B. B. Rossi, *Cosmic Rays* (1964).

cosmology, area of science that aims at a comprehensive theory of the creation, evolution, and present structure of the entire physical UNIVERSE. The earliest theories (see PTOLEMAIC SYSTEM) assumed that the earth was the center of the universe. With the acceptance of the heliocentric, or sun-centered, theory (see COPERNICAN SYSTEM), the nature and extent of the solar system began to be realized. In the 18th cent. William Herschel and other astronomers showed that the bright, nebulous band of light called the MILKY WAY is composed of a vast collection of STARS separated by enormous distances. This system of stars came to be called a galaxy and was thought to constitute the entire universe with the sun at or near its center. By studying the distribution of globular STAR CLUSTERS the American astronomer Harlow Shapley was able to give the first reliable indication of the size of the galaxy and the position of the sun within it. Modern estimates show it to have a diameter of about 100,000 LIGHT-YEARS with the sun at the edge of the disk, about 30,000 light-years from the center. During the first two decades of the 20th cent. astronomers came to realize that some of the faint hazy patches in the sky, called NEBULAS, are not within our own galaxy, but are separate galaxies at great distances from the Milky Way. After studying the red shifts (see DOPPLER EFFECT) in the spectral lines of the distant galaxies, the American astronomers Edwin Hubble and M. L. Humason concluded that the universe is expanding with the galaxies flying away from each other at great speeds. According to HUBBLE'S LAW, the expansion of the universe is approximately uniform. The greater the distance between any two galaxies, the greater their relative speed of separation. Today the most widely accepted picture of the universe is a system of billions of galaxies, most of them clustered in groups of hundreds or thousands, spread over a volume with a diameter of at least 10 billion light-years, and all receding from each other with the speeds of the most widely separated galaxies approaching the speed of light. On a more detailed level there is great diversity of opinion, and cosmology remains a highly speculative and controversial science. Present models of the universe hold two fundamental premises: the cosmological principle and the dominant role of GRAVITATION. The cosmological principle states that if a large enough sample of galaxies is considered, the universe looks the same from all positions and in all directions in space. The second point of agreement is that gravitation is the most important force in shaping the universe. However, on the vast scale of the entire universe, Newton's law of universal gravitation, which served science for nearly 300 years, has proved inadequate. According to Einstein's general theory of RELATIVITY, which is a geometric interpretation of gravitation, matter produces gravitational effects by actually distorting the space about it; the curvature of space is described by a form of NON-EUCLIDEAN GEOMETRY. A number of cosmological theories satisfy both the cosmological principle and general relativity. The two general types of theories are the big-bang hypothesis and the steady-state hypothesis, with many variations on each basic approach. According to big-bang theories, at the beginning of time all of the matter and energy in the universe was concentrated in a very small volume that exploded, and the resultant expansion continues today. This explosion is dated between 8 and 13 billion years ago. The original temperature of the universe was as high as 10 billion degrees, and the original composition was pure hydrogen. In the primeval fireball (the violent initial stages of expansion lasting only a few hours), some of the hydrogen was converted into helium by fusion; the relative abundance of hydrogen and helium in the oldest stars is being used as a test of the theory. After many millions of years the expanding universe, at first a very hot gas, thinned and cooled enough to condense into individual galaxies and then stars. In one widely held version of the big-bang theory, the universe is oscillating. The pull of gravitation tends to slow its expansion, eventually halting and then reversing it; this leads to a collapse back to the initial, ultrahigh-density conditions followed by another explosion. According to the steady-state theories, the universe expands, but new matter is continuously created at all points in space left by the receding galaxies. The theories imply that the universe has always expanded, with no beginning or end, at a uniform rate and that it always will expand and maintain a constant density. The continuous creation of matter violates one of the central and best-established laws of physics, the conservation of energy (see CONSERVATION LAWS, in physics). For meeting this objection to the steady-state theory, proponents suggest that the laws of physics, which were discovered by experiments in terrestrial laboratories, may not hold true for the universe at large. They also claim that the constants of physics are not really fixed but change slowly over very long periods of time as the universe evolves. Several spectacular discoveries since 1950, owing largely to the development of RADIO ASTRONOMY, have shed new light on the problem. This branch of astronomy studies the radio waves emitted by stars and galaxies rather than their visible light. Optical and radio astronomy complemented each other in the discovery of the quasars and the radio galaxies. Quasars are starlike objects and radio galaxies are star systems, both of which radiate prodigious amounts of energy as radio waves and hence are detectable at very great distances. It is believed that the energy reaching us now from some of these objects was emitted as long as 8 billion years ago, not long after the creation of the universe, if the big-bang theory is correct. Evidence that the radio galaxies and quasars were more numerous and more intense in the remote past supports the big-bang hypothesis and makes the steady-state theory untenable in its original form. Further evidence for the big-bang theory was the discovery in the 1960s that feeble radio noise is received from every part of the sky. This background radiation has the same intensity and distribution of frequencies in all directions and thus is not associated with any individual celestial object. Rather, all space is believed to be uniformly filled with the background radiation in much the same way as an oven is filled with thermal energy (heat). The radiation filling space has a BLACK BODY temperature of three degrees above absolute zero and is interpreted as the electromagnetic remnants of the primordial fireball, stretched to long wavelengths by the expansion of the universe. However, some recent evidence may support a modified version of the steady-state cosmology. The centers of certain galaxies eject huge amounts of matter and infrared radiation in sudden bursts; this process may require new energy sources. This intense activity suggests the continuous occurrence of "little big bangs" at certain points in space, creating new galaxies that could maintain a steady-state universe. See George Gamow, *Matter, Earth and Sky* (2d. ed. 1965); J. E. Charon, *Cosmology* (tr. 1970); D. W. Sciana, *Modern Cosmology* (1971).

cosmonaut: see ASTRONAUT.

cosmos (kŏz'məs), any plant of the tropical American genus *Cosmos* of the family Compositae (COMPOSITE family). *C. bipinnatus*, of Mexico, and others are cultivated in many varieties for their showy flowers in shades of red, yellow, and white. Cosmos is classified in the division MAGNOLIOPHYTA, class Magnoliopsida, order Asterales, family Compositae.

cosmotron: see PARTICLE ACCELERATOR.

Cossa, Baldassarre (bäldäs-sär'rā kôs'sä), c.1370–1419, Neapolitan churchman, antipope (1410–15; see SCHISM, GREAT) with the name John XXIII. He had a military career before entering the service of the church. He was made a cardinal by Boniface IX (1402) and proved himself able, especially in financial matters. In 1408 he deserted Gregory XII and helped to bring about the Council of Pisa (see PISA, COUNCIL OF) to end the schism between the Roman and the Avignon popes. The council, declaring both Gregory XII and Benedict XIII deposed, set up a third claimant, Alexander V. On Alexander's death a year later, Cardinal Cossa was elected. Of the three rival "popes," John had by far the greatest following. He immediately sought the aid of SIGISMUND and helped elect Sigismund Holy Roman emperor. John allied himself with LOUIS II of Anjou (later king of Naples) to make war on LANCELOT of Naples and his ally Gregory XII. An ineffective council at Rome (1412–13) was followed by the Council of Constance (see CONSTANCE, COUNCIL OF), which John convened under pressure from Sigismund. At the opening of the council he reluctantly promised (1415) to abdicate if his rivals would do so. Then, surreptitiously, he fled to the lands of his ally Frederick of Hapsburg. He was forced to return. The council formally deposed him, and he submitted. He was held prisoner in Germany until released by Martin V in 1418; he returned to Italy. He died cardinal bishop of Tusculum. In his lifetime he had a reputation for unscrupulousness and self-aggrandizement.

Cossa, Francesco, or **Francesco del Cossa** (fränchĕs'kō dĕl kôs'sä), c.1435–1477?, Italian painter. He was a leading representative of the Ferrarese school and was regarded, with Ercole de'Roberti, as the founder of the Bolognese school. His principal works include *The Glorification of March, April, and May,* frescoes in the Schifanoia Palace, Ferrara; some admirable portraits of the artist's contemporaries; *Madonna Enthroned* (Bologna); *Madonna and Child with Angels, St. Liberal,* and *St. Lucy* (National Gall. of Art, Washington, D.C.); and an altarpiece representing scenes from the life of St. Vincent Ferrer (National Gall., London, and the Vatican). See Benedict Nicolson, *The Painters of Ferrara* (1950).

Cossacks (kŏs'ăks, -əks), Rus. *Kazaki,* Ukr. *Kozaky,* peasant-soldiers in the Ukraine and in several regions of the former Russian Empire who, until 1918, held certain privileges in return for rendering military service. The first Cossack companies were formed in the 15th cent., when the Ukraine, then part of the unified Polish-Lithuanian state, took independent measures to defend itself against the devastating Tatar raids. The Ukrainian Cossacks, of heterogeneous background, were chiefly Russians and Poles and included many runaway serfs. By the 16th cent. they had settled along the lower and middle Dnepr River (for their history to 1775, see ZAPOROZHYE). Similar communities grew up on the Don (see DON COSSACKS) and its tributaries. They were all organized on principles of political and social equality, and originally were virtually autonomous. Each community elected an ataman as its head, while an assembly of all the Cossacks chose the hetman. The Cossacks gave shelter to refugees from Poland and Russia and took part in peasant revolts in the Ukraine and Russia in the 17th and 18th cent. Open struggle ensued between the Cossacks and the Polish and Russian governments. By the late 18th cent. the Cossacks had lost most of their political autonomy and had been made the privileged military class, integrated with the Russian military forces. Under the last czars they were often used to quell strikes and other disturbances. The primary unit of Cossack organization, the village, was largely self-governed until 1918. Land was held in common by the village. But an 1869 law, which allowed officers and civil servants to own land as personal property, contributed to the breakup of the traditional cohesiveness of Cossack village life. In the 19th cent. the Russian government began to organize new Cossack units so that by the early 20th cent. there were 11 Cossack communities, each named for its location—Don, Kuban, Terek, Astrakhan, Ural, Orenburg, Siberia, Semirechensk, Transbaikalia, Amur, and Ussuri. Following the Bolshevik Revolution (1917), the majority of the Cossacks fought against the Soviet armies in the civil war of 1918–20. In 1920 the Soviet government abolished all their privileges and between 1928 and 1933 the Cossack communities were forcibly collectivized. In 1936, however, the Cossack party regained status, being allowed to form several cavalry divisions in the Russian army. Although the Cossack communities were incorporated into the Soviet administrative system, their traditions and customs continue to survive, notably on the Don and Kuban rivers. See studies by P. J. Huxley-Blythe (1964), Philip Longworth (1969), and V. G. Glazkov (1972).

Cossimbazar (kəsĭm'bəzär''), town (1971 pop. 6,306), West Bengal state, E central India. It was one of the chief overseas ports of Bengal from the 16th to the 18th cent., when Calcutta surpassed it.

Costa, Isaäc da (ē'sä-äk dä kô'stä), 1798–1860, Dutch poet and historian, b. Amsterdam, of an aristocratic Sephardic Jewish family. Deeply influenced by Bilderdijk, he entered (1822) the Reformed Church, and much of his poetry is fervently Christian. Da Costa's period of poetic maturity is placed between the publication of his political poem *Vijf-en-twintig Jaren* [twenty-five years] in 1849, which revealed unusual social consciousness, and the appearance of the narrative poem *De Slag bij Nieuwpoort* [the battle of Nieuport] in 1859. He was a distinguished scholar in Protestant biblical theology and the classics. His work on Jewish history was translated into English as *Israel and the Gentiles* (1855).

Costa, Lorenzo (lōrĕn'tsō kō'stä), 1460–1535, Italian painter of the Ferrarese and Bolognese schools. Trained in the manner of such painters as Tura and Cossa, he modified the strident Ferrarese style when he became a partner of Francia. His art became softer and more symmetrical. Among his paintings are the *Madonna and Child with the Bentivoglio Family* and the *Triumphs of Petrarch* in San Giacomo Maggiore, the *Madonna with Saints* in San Petronio, and the *Madonna* in San Giovanni in Monte, all in Bologna. His *Three Saints* is in the Metropolitan Museum.

Costa, Lúcio (lo͞o'syo͞o kô'stə), 1902–, Brazilian architect. As the principal designer of the city of Brasília (1957), Costa is known for his use of reinforced concrete in designs that combine traditional and modern forms. In Rio de Janeiro, the block of apartments in Guinle Park (1948–54) typifies his streamlined work. The Ministry of Education and Health (1937–42) exhibits his understanding of the effect of climatic considerations on architectural design.

Costa Brava (kō'stä brä'vä), a strip of coast, Gerona prov., NE Spain, in Catalonia, near the French border on the Mediterranean. The area has enjoyed a booming tourist industry since the end of World War II.

cost accounting: see ACCOUNTING.

Costa e Silva, Artur da (ərto͞or' dä ko͞osh'tə ē sēl'və), 1902–69, president of Brazil (1967–69). An army general, he participated in the coup that deposed (1964) President Goulart. He served as war minister (1964–66) under President Castelo Branco and succeeded him in office. He attempted to introduce social and economic reforms, but political criticism of his military regime mounted. In Dec., 1968, he dismissed congress, imposed news censorship, and proceeded to rule by decree. He was incapacitated by a cerebral hemorrhage in Aug., 1969, at which time a military triumvirate took over the government. He died in December of that year.

Costa i Llobera, Miguel (mēgĕl' kō'stä ē lyōbä'rä), 1854–1922, Catalonian poet and orator. In 1888 he was ordained a priest in Rome, where he developed a love of Latin literature. Costa i Llobera's works are serious and contemplative, and they exerted a strong influence on Catalonian literature in general. His masterpiece is *Horacianes* [poems in the manner of Horace] (1906). Among his other works are *De l'agre de la terra* [from the bitterness of the earth] (1897) and *Tradiciones i fantasies* [traditions and fantasies] (1903).

Costa Mesa (kŏs'tə mā'sə), city (1970 pop. 72,660), Orange co., S Calif.; inc. 1953. Boatbuilding and the manufacture of electronic equipment and tools are the major industries; there are also research laboratories. Orange Coast College and Southern California College are in the city, and the Univ. of California at Irvine is adjacent.

Costa Rica (kŏs'tə rē'kə), republic (1970 pop. 1,710,083), 19,575 sq mi (50,700 sq km), Central America. The capital is SAN JOSÉ; other important cities are ALAJUELA, HEREDIA, PUNTARENAS (the Pacific port), and CARTAGO. Costa Rica is bounded on the N by Nicaragua, on the E by the Caribbean Sea, on the SE by Panama, and on the S and W by the Pacific Ocean. One of the most stable countries in Latin America, Costa Rica has a long democratic tradition, a literacy rate of over 90%, and no army. The coastal plains are low, hot, and heavily forested. Bananas, cocoa, and sugarcane are cultivated there. In the northwest is the Nicoya peninsula, a semiarid plain where cattle and grain are raised. A massive cordillera, with peaks over 12,000 ft (3,658 m) high, cuts the country from northwest to southeast. Within it, under the shadow of volcanoes such as Irazú, lies the central plateau (*meseta central*), with a perennially spring-like climate. This plateau is the heart of the country, where coffee is cultivated and most of the population and market facilities are located. Costa Rica is an agricultural country. Coffee, bananas, cocoa, and sugar are exported, and machinery, chemicals, foodstuffs, and fuels are imported. The population is largely of Spanish descent. The country is governed under the 1949 constitution. The president, a strong executive, serves a four-year term and may not be immediately reelected. The unicameral legislature is also elected for four years. There is universal adult suffrage, and voting is compulsory.

History. Although Columbus skirted the Costa Rican coast in 1502, the Spanish conquest did not begin until 1563, when Cartago was founded. The region

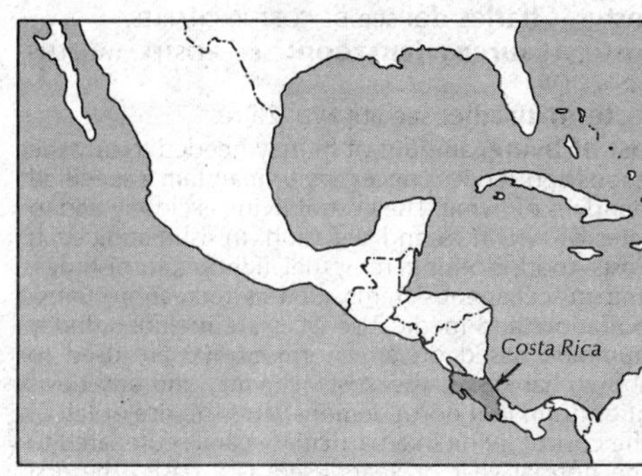

was administered as part of the captaincy general of Guatemala. Few of the native Indians survived, and the colonists, unable to establish a hacienda system based on Indian labor, generally became small landowners. From Cartago, westward expansion into the plateau began in the 18th cent. Costa Rica became independent from Spain in 1821. From 1822 to 1823 it was part of the Mexican Empire of Augustín de Iturbide. It then became part of the CENTRAL AMERICAN FEDERATION until 1838, when the sovereign republic of Costa Rica was proclaimed. In 1857, Costa Rica participated in the defeat of the filibuster William WALKER, who had taken over Nicaragua. The cultivation of coffee, introduced in the 19th cent., led to the creation of a landed oligarchy that dominated the country until the administration of Tomás GUARDIA (1870–82). In 1874, Minor Cooper KEITH founded LIMÓN and introduced banana cultivation. Keith also started the United Fruit Company. Later many tracts had to be abandoned because of leaf blight, and, after World War II, United Fruit started new plantations on the Pacific coast; these have been worked by Negroes from Jamaica. Costa Rica's history of orderly, democratic government began in the late 19th cent. The pattern was broken in 1917, when Federico Tinoco overthrew the elected president, Alfredo González. The United States opposed Tinoco, and he was deposed in 1919. Costa Rica cooperated with the United States during World War II and after the war joined the United Nations and other international organizations. In 1948 there was a second breakdown of the political system. In a close presidential election Otilio Ulate appeared to have defeated the former president, Dr. Rafael Calderón. But the incumbent, Teodoro Picado, accused Ulate's supporters of fraud and obtained a congressional invalidation of the election. A six-week civil war ensued, at the conclusion of which a junta led by José Figueres Ferrer, a backer of Ulate, assumed power. Picado was exiled. Forces from Nicaragua backed Picado, and the Organization of American States (OAS) was called upon to mediate between the two countries. In 1949 a new constitution was adopted, and the junta transferred power to Ulate as the elected president. Figueres was elected his successor in 1953. In UN-supervised elections in 1958, Mario Enchadi Jiménez defeated Figueres's candidate. Politics remained stable in the 1960s. In 1963, Costa Rica joined the Central American Common Market. Figueres was again elected president in 1970. The Irazú volcano erupted in 1963–64 and caused serious damage to agriculture. Another volcano, Arenal, erupted in 1968 for the first time in hundreds of years, killing many. In 1973 a serious drought led to a state of emergency. Daniel Oduber Quiros was elected president in 1974, but the ruling National Liberation Party lost its majority in the legislature for the first time in 25 years. See Ricardo Fernández Guardia, *History of the Discovery and Conquest of Costa Rica* (1913); C. L. Jones, *Costa Rica and Civilization in the Caribbean* (1935, repr. 1967); D. G. Munro, *The Five Republics of Central America* (1918, rep.1967); H. I. Blutstein et al., *Area Handbook for Costa Rica* (1970); J. P. Bell, *Crisis in Costa Rica: The 1948 Revolution* (1971); C. F. Denton, *Patterns of Costa Rican Politics* (1971); B. H. English, *Liberación Nacional in Costa Rica* (1971).

Costa y Martínez, Joaquín (hwäkēn' kōs'tä ē märtē'nāth), 1846–1911, Spanish jurist, economist, and sociologist. He wrote works on Spanish law and economics and was the founder of modern Spanish sociology. Among the first to accurately criticize Spain's agrarian economy, he founded the Liga Nacional to promote agricultural reform. After the disaster of the Spanish-American War (1898), he entered politics and later joined the republicans. He refused to sit in the Cortes when elected in 1904, declaring that Spain could recover prestige and prosperity only through a national revolution.

Coster, Charles de: see DE COSTER, CHARLES.

Coster, Laurens Janszoon: see KOSTER, LAURENS JANSZOON.

Costermansville: see BUKAVU, Zaïre.

cost of living, amount of money needed to buy the goods and services necessary to maintain a specified standard of living. The cost of living is closely tied to rates of INFLATION and deflation. In estimating such costs, food, clothing, rent, fuel, lighting, furnishings, and miscellaneous items such as recreation, transportation, and medical services are included. Index numbers based on any norm of 100 are used to show changes in the cost of living, and any deviation from that norm demonstrates the rise or fall of the cost of living in a particular year as compared to the normal year or years used as a basis. The first attempt to gather data on the cost of living in the United States was made by the U.S. Bureau of Labor Statistics in 1890. During World War II and immediately following it, many employers established systems of wage changes based on changes in the cost of living, but such attempts were denounced by labor spokesmen as establishing a "fixed" standard of living. However, an agreement using the cost of living index as a basis for the determination of wage rates was signed in May, 1948, between General Motors and the United Automobile Workers of America. Since then many other unions, recognizing the security provided by a cost of living adjustment during times of rising prices, have also had such clauses included in their contracts. People living on social security and pension benefits are among those most affected by changes in the cost of living; their incomes are generally fixed and thus unable to adjust to changing prices. Since World War II the cost of living in most countries of the world has, except for minor interruptions, steadily increased. See bibliography under STANDARD OF LIVING.

costs, legal: see DAMAGES.

costume, distinctive forms of clothing including official or ceremonial attire such as ecclesiastical VESTMENTS, coronation robes, academic gowns, ARMOR, and theatrical dress. The use of ornament preceded the use of protective garments; its purpose was to emphasize social position by a great display of trophies, charms, and other valuables and to enhance attractiveness. Superstition, caste distinction, and climatic necessity all have been influential in the evolution of dress. The ancient Egyptian costume for men was first a wrapped loincloth and later a kilt or skirt of pleated and starched white linen. Egyptian women first wore the *kalasiris,* a one-piece, narrow sheath of transparent linen, which was later adopted by men as the tunic. The Egyptian costume evolved into a highly decorative mode of dress characterized by the use of fluted linen, of jewelry (especially the beaded yoke COLLAR), and of COSMETICS and PERFUME; the WIG was also worn. The basic Greek garment, noted for its simplicity and graceful draping, consisted of the chiton and girdle. Roman dress, influenced by that of the Greeks, was simple and dignified; the toga, which was worn over the tunic, was the distinctive garment of the Roman citizen. The change from ancient to medieval costume began (c.400) with the disintegration of the Roman Empire. Roman dress, which had previously assimilated the elaborate features of Byzantine dress, was gradually affected by the austere costume of the barbaric invader. Both men and women wore a double tunic; the under tunic, or chemise, had long tight sleeves (a feature that remained until the 17th cent.) and a high neck; the girded wool overtunic, or robe, often had loose sleeves. A mantle, or indoor cloak, was also worn. After 1200 a great variety of fine fabrics from the East were available as a result of the Crusades, and the elegant dress of feudal Europe was evolved. With the introduction of various ways of cutting the basic garment, FASHION, or style, began. A long, girded tunic, then called the cote or cotte, continued to be worn over the chemise by both men and women; a surcote (sleeveless and with wide armholes) was often worn over it. At this time family crests, or coats of arms (see BLAZONRY; HERALDRY; CREST), became popular, and parti-colored garments came into vogue. Proper fit was increasingly emphasized, and by 1300 tailoring had become important and BUTTONS had become useful as well as ornamental. The belted cote-hardie, with a close-fitting body and short skirt, was worn over a tighter, long-sleeved doublet and a chemise. And, as men's legs were now exposed, HOSE were emphasized. The introduction (c.1350) of the houppelande, or overcoat, marked the first real appearance of the collar. Over a chemise and corset women wore a gown with a V neck and a long, flowing train; the front of the skirt was often tucked into the high-waisted belt. In its extreme, the style of the period was typified by profuse dagging (scalloped edges), exaggerated, hanging sleeves, pointed slippers, and fantastic headdresses (see HEADDRESS and VEIL). After 1450 there was a reversal in fashion from the pointed Gothic look to the square look of the Renaissance. The style in its exaggerated form is best represented in Holbein's paintings of the English court of Henry VIII. Men's costume had wide, square shoulders with puffed sleeves, padded doublets, bombasted upperstocks, or trunk hose, short gowns (cloaks), and square-toed shoes. The doublet, now sleeveless, was worn over the shirt (formerly the chemise) and under the jerkin. Women wore a square-necked gown with the bodice laced up the front and attached to the gathered skirt at the hips; the front of the skirt was often open, to reveal decorative petticoats. These, together with a preference for rich, heavy materials, especially velvet, and a fad for profuse slashing and puffing of the under material seen through the slash, created a massive and bulky appearance. In Elizabethan England (c.1550) the costume was stiffened, and the appearance was less bulky. Both men and women wore the characteristic "shoulder wings," pointed stomacher, and starched ruff and cuffs made of LACE. Materials were heavy and lustrous and considerable ornamentation was used. Men wore a short cape, and their trunk hose were unpadded, longer, and generally made in sections, or paned. Women wore exaggerated farthingales, or hoops. The early 17th-century English costume was less formal, with a softer line created by satin and silk materials. The period of the Cavalier and Puritan is captured in the court paintings of Van Dyck and in the early work of Rembrandt. Men characteristically wore pantaloon breeches (full trunk hose), high boots, a broad, falling lace or linen collar and cuffs, and a full cloak. In women's costume, the arms began to be displayed and necklines were lower. The bodice was finished with a wide, round collar, or bertha, at the neck, and a flared, pleated, or ruffled skirtlike section, or peplum, was added at the waist. The apron was often a permanent part of the skirt. In England after 1660, the dress of the Restoration period became extravagantly decorative, using ribbons, flounces, and feathers. The dandies of the period wore petticoat breeches, full-sleeved cambric shirts, and bolerolike doublets. Sir Peter Lely's court paintings show excellent examples of such costume. In the 18th cent., France, under the rule of Louis XIV, became the costume center of the world, with Mme Pompadour, Mme du Barry, and Marie Antoinette successively dictating the fashions of the day; it was the age of the wig, of rococo settings, of delicate pastels and flower-patterned silks, and of EMBROIDERY. Early in the century, Rousseau's ideas affected style of dress. Women's costume became graceful and pastoral; the pointed bodice, tightly laced, was finished with a triangular scarf, or fichu, at the neck, and sleeves were ruffled at the elbow. The bell-shaped hoop appeared c.1710, and c.1735 side hoops, or panniers, were popular. Women's costume, which at this period became extremely formal, was gradually softened into a romantic look (as in portraits by Gainsborough) that anticipated the EMPIRE STYLE. The 18th-century man first wore a knee-length cassock that buttoned all the way down over an equally long waistcoat, and buckled knee breeches. As the century progressed, the waistcoat became shorter, the skirt of the coat began to form tails, the collar became higher, and the sleeves and breeches became tighter. The Empire style, associated in early 19th-century France with Josephine, was an attempt to recapture classic simplicity. Women wore a thin muslin dress with a high waist, a low round neck, and puffed short sleeves. Men wore a short-waisted cutaway coat with tails, a high collar, and large lapels and military boots; plain-colored wools became predominant. The whole male appearance was strikingly military. After 1815 women, emphasizing their fragility, achieved the hourglass shape with an extremely tight corset. Their dresses had wide collars, sloping shoulders, leg-of-mutton sleeves, and full skirts. Men wore the frock coat, which was fitted and had a skirt that reached the knees, and trousers were introduced and generally adopted. After 1840, Victorian women wore layers of decorative crinoline and, after 1855, the hoop; sleeves were bell-shaped, and waist and necklines were pointed. Though men still wore the tailcoat and frock coat, the sack coat, sometimes worn without the vest, was becoming popular for everyday wear. In general, men's clothes were becoming looser and more tubular and were predominantly of somber broadcloth. After 1865 the bustle became fashionable for women; at this time, too, women first wore a tailored jacket with collar and lapels—the forerunner of the suit. The growing emphasis on sports, especially tennis and golf, was beginning to affect costume. Knee breeches, called knickerbockers or knickers, came into fashion for men, and sweaters became popular. After 1890 women most often wore the suit or the shirtwaist with balloon sleeves and wasp waist: the dress of the Gibson girl. Men's suits had square shoulders and straight waists and were usually of serge or tweed; the tuxedo was used for formal wear. After 1910, as women's feet and legs began to be exposed, shoes were colored to match the outfit. The nightgown, for women, gave way for a time to pajamas. The popularity of sportswear for men increased; the open-necked shirt was worn and trousers were cuffed and creased. Women's dress after 1914 was characterized by straight lines, e.g., the floor-length hobble skirt and the flapper's boyish, short-skirted costume and matching accessories were popular in the 1920s. The following decades produced radical changes in women's wear, from the flowing skirts of the 30s and the box-jacketed suits of the 40s to the sack dress of the early 60s. Since then the fluctuating hemline has been the predominant concern of fashion. The abbreviated miniskirt has vied for popularity with the full-length maxi and the calf-length midi in coats, skirts, and dresses. Women's clothing has become less restrictive and more casual than in previous eras. The pants suit currently leads in popularity for comfort and elegance. During the 1960s men's clothing underwent revolutionary changes in color and fabric, becoming flamboyant for the first time in the 20th cent. The flaring of trouser cuffs in the 1970s was a major modification in shape. Traditional national dress in Western European countries has generally given way to standardized modes, although traditional costume is still associated with national celebrations and pageantry. The typical costume—a gathered peasant skirt, a full blouse with puffed sleeves, and a laced bodice—is colorful and picturesque, often elaborately fashioned and embroidered, and augmented by kerchief, headdress, and apron. Costume in the Orient had until recently remained unchanged for centuries. In the Arab countries both men and women have for centuries wrapped themselves in voluminous flowing robes that indicate the tribe and status of the wearer by means of style, color, and richness. The people of Malaysia wrap themselves in a loose skirt, or sarong. Chinese dress has been distinguished by the use of magnificent textiles and embroidery and of pearls and jade—all symbolic of rank and wealth. Men and women of the Peoples' Republic of China wear dark-colored trouser suits, whereas in Nationalist China a sheath dress with mandarin collar and side slits in the skirt has become characteristic of women's clothing. Japanese men and women have widely adopted Western modes of dress but many women retain the characteristic kimono and *tabi* (socks) or geta (wooden clogs). India, too, has traditional costumes dictated by religion or caste. Women in general wear the long draped fabric, or sari, sandals, and profuse jewelry. Exquisite muslins and "painted" cottons have from antiquity been notable features of Indian garments. The term *costume* also includes accessories, such as the SHOE, HAT, GLOVE, PURSE, CORSET, HANDKERCHIEF, FAN, UMBRELLA, CANE, and JEWELRY; styles of wearing the hair (see HAIRDRESSING) and BEARD; and primitive methods of BODY-MARKING and attaching ornaments to the body. See table of fashion designers under FASHION. See Millia Davenport, *The Book of Costume* (2 vol. in 1, 1962); Blanche Payne, *History of Costume* (1965); James Laver, *The Concise History of Costume and Fashion* (1969); Geoffrey Squire, *Dress and Society* (1974).

Cosway, Richard (kŏz'wā), 1740?-1821, English miniaturist. His work was elegant and modish and became highly popular in his day. There is a collection of his works in Windsor Castle. Perhaps best known is the portrait of Mme du Barry. A self-portrait is in the National Portrait Gallery, London. Cosway was married to the miniaturist Maria Hadfield. See biography by G. C. Williamson (1897).

Cotabato (kōtäbä'tō), city (1970 est. pop. 51,900), Cotabato prov., W Mindanao, the Philippines, near the mouth of the Mindanao River on Moro Gulf. It has long been a Muslim center. Its port serves a vast, fertile farm area which, as the object of a government colonization program, has had a great population increase since World War II. Cotabato prov. is a focus of coffee cultivation and has important pineapple and peanut crops. Rubber is also produced, and lumbering is a major industry. The provincial capital is Pagalungan.

Côte-d'Or (kōt-dôr), department (1968 pop. 421,192), E France, largely in Burgundy, partly in Champagne. DIJON is the capital.

Cotentin (kôtäNtăN'), region of N France, in Normandy, roughly coinciding with the peninsula formed by Manche dept. and extending into the English Channel. CHERBOURG is the chief port, and there are numerous fishing ports. The lambs of the Cotentin breed of sheep are highly esteemed for their meat. Cattle are also raised in the region. Much of the land is divided by hedgerows into small fields and apple orchards. An old Norman county, Cotentin takes its name from its historic capital, Coutances.

Côtes-du-Nord (kōt-dü-nôr), department (1968 pop. 506,102), NW France, in Brittany, on the English Channel. Saint-Brieuc is the capital.

cotinga (kōtĭng'gə), any of the New World tropical birds of the family Cotingidae. Cotingas range from N Argentina to the southern border of the United States; most are forest species and inhabit the highest treetops. Although there is great variation in appearance among these birds, all have broad bills with slightly hooked tips, rounded wings, and strong short legs. Some species are dull-colored, with little difference between males and females; in many species, however, the males are brightly colored and have curiously modified wing and head feathers. The umbrella birds (genus *Cephalopterus*), found from Central America to Argentina, have a black, umbrellalike crest, which is raised and expanded during courtship displays, and feathered throat wattles nearly as long as the bird itself. The bellbirds (genus *Procnias*), found from Central America to Argentina, have a distinctive bell-like call; they are marked by feather-studded, fleshy protuberances drooping over their bills. Both the male and the female cock-of-the-rock (genus *Rupicola*) are marked by a fan-shaped crest of feathers, which extends from bill tip to the top of the head. There are two cock-of-the-rock species; in *R. rupicola*, of the Guianas, the male is golden-orange with black wings and tail, while in *R. peruviana*, of the Andes, the male is bright red with similar markings. In both species the female is olive brown. The cock-of-the-rock, a terrestrial bird, performs a communal mating ritual in which males go through stylized stances and acrobatics. There are about 90 species of cotingas classified in 33 genera of the phylum CHORDATA, subphylum Vertebrata, class Aves, order Passeriformes, family Cotingidae.

Cotman, John Sell, 1782–1842, English landscape painter and etcher. He was a leading representative of the Norwich school. Cotman studied in London and in 1806 settled in Norwich where he opened an art school. He suffered periods of melancholia throughout his life. He took up etching c.1810 and produced several series of etchings of English, and later French, antiquities. His *Liber Studiorum* (1838) is an outstanding work in this medium. For the last nine years of his life he was a drawing master at King's College, London. Although Cotman's work was but little appreciated in his day, it is now highly prized for its fine color, decorative and structural qualities, and sustained poetic mood. He is best known for his watercolors and drawings, of which the British Museum possesses many, including the famous *Greta Bridge*. Cotman's oil paintings are in many British galleries. See catalog by V. G. R. Rienaecker (1953); biography by S. D. Kitson (1937).

Cotonou (kōtōno͞o'), city (1970 est. pop. 111,000), capital of Atlantique dept., S Dahomey, on the Gulf of Guinea. It is Dahomey's chief seaport and commercial center. Cotonou's airport and road and rail connections also make it the transportation and communications hub of Dahomey. The city has small-scale industries; manufactures include palm oil and cake, peanut oil, textiles, cement and other construction materials, aluminum sheet, beverages, and processed seafood. Motor vehicles and bicycles are assembled, and there are sawmills in the city. Cotonou is a distribution center for petroleum products. Drilling for offshore oil is carried on nearby. Cotonou was originally a small state that was dominated by the kingdom of DAHOMEY from the 18th cent. In 1851 the French made a treaty with the Dahomean king Gezo that allowed them to establish a trading post at Cotonou. In 1883 the French navy forcibly occupied the city to forestall British ambitions in the area. Britain confirmed France's right to Cotonou in 1885. The port was enlarged and modernized in the 1960s. Cotonou has research institutes concerned with textiles, tropical agriculture, and geology.

Cotopaxi (kōtōpăk'sē), active volcano, 19,347 ft (5,897 m) high, N central Ecuador. A symmetrical snowcapped cone, it is one of the most beautiful peaks of the Andes and one of the highest volcanoes in the world. It is continuously active, and frequent eruptions have caused severe damage. Cotopaxi was first scaled by Wilhelm Reid in 1872.

Cotrone: see CROTONA.

Cotswold Hills, range, mainly in Gloucestershire, W England, extending c.50 mi (80 km) NE from Bath; Cleeve Cloud (c.1,080 ft/330 m) is the highest point. Its crest line forms the Thames-Severn watershed. The region is famous for Cotswold sheep and for its picturesque stone houses. Noteworthy are the many megalithic monuments and long barrows. Among the ruins is Hailes Abbey, founded in 1246. The Cotswold Games were held there from the 17th to the 19th cent.

Cotswold sheep, large, white-faced, hornless breed with a broad, flat back, moderately deep body, heavy fleece, and long, coarse wool hanging in ringlets. It was originated in the Cotswold Hills in England. The Cotswold is often crossed with the Merino and Rambouillet breeds. In the United States it is found mostly in the Northwest.

cottage cheese, unripened soft cheese, also known as pot cheese, baker's cheese, Dutch cheese, or smearcase. It is produced chiefly in the United States. Cottage cheese is made of pasteurized skim milk, which is set with a starter of lactic acid bacteria. The curd and whey are separated by low heat. The curd is stirred and seasoned with salt, cream, and, in some localities, molasses or sugar. The use of skim milk yields a cheese low in fat and vitamin A. When sold commercially, it is sometimes mixed with bits of fruits or raw vegetables.

Cottage Grove, village (1970 pop. 13,419), Washington co., SE Minn., near the St. Croix River; inc. 1965. Machined-metal products are among the manufactures.

cottage industry: see SWEATING SYSTEM.

Cottbus or **Kottbus** (both: kôt'bo͝os), city (1970 pop. 82,897), capital of Cottbus district, E East Germany, on the Spree River. It is an industrial center and rail junction. Manufactures include textiles, metal products, and processed food. Cottbus developed as a market center in the late 12th cent. and passed to Brandenburg in the mid-15th cent. It was annexed, with the rest of LUSATIA, by Saxony in 1635 and was taken by Prussia in 1815.

Cottereau, Jean: see CHOUANS.

Cotton, Charles, 1630–87, English author. He is chiefly remembered for his contribution to his friend Izaak Walton's *Compleat Angler* (5th ed. 1676). His pleasant, unaffected verse includes "An Ode to Winter" and "The Retirement." He also wrote burlesques of Vergil (1664) and Lucian (1665) and a translation of Montaigne's *Essays* (1685–86).

Cotton, George Edward Lynch, 1813–66, English clergyman and educator, grad. Trinity College, Cambridge, 1836. From 1837 until 1852 he was an assistant master at Rugby and is the "young master" in Thomas Hughes's *Tom Brown's School Days*. He later became (1852) headmaster of Marlborough College and after 1858 served as bishop of Calcutta, where he did extensive missionary work and established numerous schools for Eurasian children. See memoir by his wife (1871).

Cotton, John, 1584–1652, Puritan clergyman in England and Massachusetts, b. Derbyshire, educated at Cambridge. Imbued with Puritan doctrines, he won many followers during his 20 years as vicar of the rich and influential parish of St. Botolph's Church, Boston, Lincolnshire. He was summoned to appear before the High Court of Commission (1632), but instead of appearing he resigned and fled. Some of his followers sailed (1633) with him to Massachusetts Bay, where the young city of Boston was so named primarily to honor him. He and John Winthrop were the leading figures of the colony, and Cotton was chiefly responsible for the exile of Anne HUTCHINSON, because of her antinomian doctrines, and for the expulsion of Roger WILLIAMS. He was one of the molders of the Congregational Church, and his arguments in such treatises as *The Keys of the Kingdom of Heaven* (1644), *The Way of the Churches of Christ in New England* (1645), and *The Way of the Congregational Churches Cleared* (1648) were influential in his day. He was a firm believer in the right of the Congregational minister to dictate to the faithful, and thus he has been viewed as a strong upholder of theocracy. His *Milk for Babes* (1646) was a well-known catechism for children. His daughter was the wife of Increase MATHER and the mother of Cotton MATHER. See biographies by Larzer Ziff (1962) and Everett Emerson (1965).

Cotton, Sir Robert Bruce, 1571–1631, English antiquarian. The Cottonian collection of books, manuscripts, coins, and antiquities became a part of the British Museum when it was founded in 1753. Cotton collected especially Hebrew and Greek manuscripts and Anglo-Saxon charters. An unprinted classified catalog of the collection is in the Harleian MSS of the British Museum. Cotton was an antiroyalist parliamentarian whose opinions brought him two terms in prison. His magnificent library was sealed in 1630 and remained so until after his death.

Cotton, Thomas Henry (Henry Cotton), 1907–, British golfer, b. Cheshire, England. Although a professional at 17, Cotton did not achieve international recognition until he won the British Open in 1934. He again won this title in 1937 and in 1948, in addition to three British Professional Golf Association crowns and many European championships. Cotton played on three British Ryder Cup teams and twice was captain. He wrote *The Game of Golf* (1949).

cotton, most important of the vegetable fibers. Cotton has been spun, woven, and dyed since prehistoric times. It formed the staple clothing of India, Egypt, and China. Hundreds of years before the Christian era cotton textiles were woven in India with matchless skill, and their use spread to the Mediterranean countries. In the 1st cent. Arab traders brought fine MUSLIN and CALICO to Italy and Spain. The Moors introduced the cultivation of cotton into Spain in the 9th cent. Fustians and dimities were woven there and in the 14th cent. in Venice and Milan, at first with a linen warp. Little cotton cloth was imported to England before the 15th cent., although small amounts were obtained chiefly for candlewicks. By the 17th cent. the East India Company was bringing rare fabrics from India. Before the arrival of the white man in the New World, cotton was skillfully spun and woven into fine garments and dyed tapestries. Cotton fabrics found in Peruvian tombs are said to belong to a pre-Inca culture. In colors and texture, the ancient Peruvian and Mexican textiles resemble those found in Egyptian tombs. Cotton cultivation began in America in the Jamestown colony (1607). Since the early days of the republic, the United States has been the world's leading producer of cotton. The invention (1793) of the cotton gin, a machine for separating seeds from fiber, and the mechanization of textile production marked the Industrial Revolution and suddenly brought cotton into world prominence to supersede flax and wool textiles. The manufacture of cotton goods is a great industry, second only to that of Great Britain (where it centers about Lancashire). For some years American manufacture was chiefly in New England; today an increasing number of mills are located in the Southern cotton-producing states, the so-called Cotton Belt. Cotton has played a significant historical role in world industry. The reliance of British mills on imported cotton fiber influenced that country's accession to the Monroe Doctrine, and its need for the large African and Indian markets for cotton goods dictated much of its sea-domination policy as an imperial nation. In the United States, cotton brought about the one-crop economy of the Deep South and was a principal economic cause of the Civil War. The passing of slavery, always an adjunct of the cotton plantations, and the exhaustion of the soil pushed the Cotton Belt to the West. Large cotton-producing countries such as Brazil, Egypt, and India (the second largest world producer) have used cotton exports to offset an unfavorable balance of trade. China and the USSR rank after the United States and India in total annual production. All cotton-producing nations have depended on an abundance of cheap labor; although mechanical cultivating and picking devices have long been known, they have been perfected for widespread use (especially in the United States) only since World War II. The cotton plant belongs to the genus *Gossypium* of the family Malvaceae (MALLOW family). It is generally a shrubby plant having broad three-lobed leaves and seeds in capsules, or bolls; each seed is surrounded with downy fiber, white or creamy in color and easily spun. The fibers flatten and twist naturally as they dry. Cotton is of tropical origin but is most successfully cultivated in temperate climates with well-distributed rainfall. In the United States nearly all the commercial cotton crop comes from varieties of upland cotton (*G. hirsutum*), but small quantities are obtained from sea-island and American-Egyptian cotton (both belonging to the species *G. barbadense*). *G. arboreum* and *G. herbaceum* are the chief cultivated species in Asia. Cotton is planted annually by seed in furrows; the plants are thinned and weeded during the spring growing season. Diseases and insect pests are numerous; of these the most destructive is the BOLL WEEVIL, which causes enormous losses. Sea-island cotton, valued for its silky fibers, was the leading type before the advent of this insect, to which it is particularly susceptible. When mechanical pickers are employed, a chemical defoliant is used to make the leaves drop so that only the cotton bolls are left on the plant for stripping. In the ginhouse the cotton is separated from the seeds by a COTTON GIN and then baled. The usual plantation bale, weighing 500 lb (227 kg), is covered with jute and bound with iron hoops. The U.S. Dept of Agriculture has established official standards for grades of cotton. The manufacture of cotton into cloth involves many processes—CARDING, COMBING, and SPINNING, which bring the raw fiber to a yarn or thread strong enough for weaving. Innumerable commodities are made from cotton. From the lint (the fiber separated from the seed) come the major products, chiefly TEXTILE and YARN goods, cordage, automobile-tire cord, and plastic reinforcing. The linters (short cut ends left on the seed after ginning and later removed by specialized processing) are a valuable source of CELLULOSE products. Cotton hulls are used for fertilizer, fuel, and packing; fiber from the stalk is used for pressed paper and cardboard. Production of the chief by-product, cottonseed oil, has assumed the importance of a separate industry since its establishment in the late 19th cent. The oil content of cotton seeds is about 20%. After being freed from the linters, the seeds are shelled and then crushed and pressed or treated with solvents to obtain the crude oil. In its highly refined state, cottonseed oil is employed as salad and cooking oil, for cosmetics, and especially in the manufacture of margarine and shortenings. Paint makers use it to some extent as a semidrying oil. Less refined grades are used in the manufacture of soap, candles, detergents, artificial leather, oilcloth, and many other commodities. The cottonseed oil industry is becoming increasingly important to cotton growers as cotton fiber finds greater competition in the cheaper and stronger synthetic fibers. Cotton is classified in the division MAGNOLIOPHYTA, class Magnoliopsida, order Malvales, family Malvaceae. See D. S. Hamby, ed., *The American Cotton Handbook* (2 vol., 3d ed. 1965–66); W. H. Fortenberry, *The Story of Cotton* (1967); Clifford Shaw and Frank Eckersley, *Cotton* (1967); J. L. Sinclair, *The Production, Marketing, and Consumption of Cotton* (1968).

Cotton Belt, major agricultural region of the SE United States where cotton is the main cash crop. Located on the Atlantic and Gulf coastal plains and on the Piedmont upland, it extends through North Carolina, South Carolina, Georgia, Alabama, Mississippi, W Tennessee, E Arkansas, Louisiana, E Texas, and S Oklahoma, and also into small areas of SE Missouri, SW Kentucky, N Florida, and SE Virginia. The belt has the climatic conditions necessary for cotton to thrive—high temperatures, from 30 to 55 in. (76.2–139.7 cm) annual rainfall, and a 200-day growing season. A modified plantation system exists there. The Cotton Belt, no longer continuous, is made up of many separate intensive production areas; corn, wheat, soybeans, peanuts, beans, and livestock are important in the intervening areas. Until the invention of the cotton gin in 1793, the Cotton Belt was confined to the coastal areas of South Carolina and Georgia; by the mid-1800s, it extended from S Virginia to E Texas. Post-Civil War reforms, soil depletion, and the boll weevil combined to push cotton west. Increasing amounts of irrigated cotton are grown in W Texas, S New Mexico, S Arizona, and S California, where aridity makes it easier to control insect pests. Texas, Mississippi, and Arkansas are the leading producers of cotton in the belt; California ranks after Texas nationally. See BLACK BELT; IMPERIAL VALLEY.

cotton gin, machine for separating cotton fibers from the seeds. The charkha, used in India from antiquity, consists of two revolving wooden rollers through which the fibers are drawn, leaving the seeds. A similar gin was early used in the S United States for long-staple cotton. In the modern roller gin, rollers covered with rough leather draw out the fibers, which are cut off by a fixed knife pressed against the rollers. This type of gin cleans only about two bales per day, but it does not snarl or break the fibers. The saw gin, invented by the American inventor Eli Whitney in 1793 and patented in 1794, consisted of a toothed cylinder revolving against a grate that enclosed the seed cotton. The teeth caught the fibers, pulling them from the seeds; the fibers were then removed from the cylinder by a revolving brush. This device, especially suited to short- and medium-staple cotton, has been mechanized and is used in commercial plants that are also called gins, where the fiber is conveyed from farm wagon to baler by air suction. Such plants have one or more gin stands, each with a series of from 70 to 80 circular saws set on a shaft. The fibers, freed from dirt and hulls, are pulled through a grid by the saw teeth to remove the seeds. The fibers are removed from the saw teeth by a revolving brush or by a blast of air (in more modern plants) and are then carried by air blast or suction to a condenser and finally to the baling apparatus.

cotton grass, common name for SEDGES of the genus *Eriophorum*.

cottonmouth: see WATER MOCCASIN.

cottonseed oil: see COTTON.

cottontail rabbit, animal of the order Lagomorpha, which includes the hares and rabbits, except for the domestic, or European, RABBIT, which is in a separate species. Members of the genus *Sylvilagus,* cottontails have large ears and short legs and move with a scurrying or scampering gait. Unlike the European rabbit, they do not dig their own burrows but make a nest in a depression in the ground. Unlike hares, they seek protection in hiding rather than in swift flight. The cottontail ranges from the southern border of Canada to N Argentina. There are six races. Cottontails are a common source of TULAREMIA, or rabbit fever. They are classified in the phylum CHORDATA, subphylum Vertebrata, class Mammalia, order Lagomorpha, family Leporidae.

cottonwood: see WILLOW.

Cottrell, Leonard, 1913–, British author and archaeologist, grad. King Edward's Grammar School, Birmingham. He was a commentator, writer, and producer for the British Broadcasting Corporation until 1960, when he resigned to devote himself to writing. During World War II he was stationed in the Mediterranean with the Royal Air Force as a war correspondent. Among his many books are *The Bull of Minos* (1958), *The Great Invasion* (1958), *Realms of Gold* (1963), *Egypt* (1965), and *Lost Civilizations* (1974). He was the editor of the *Concise Encyclopaedia of Archaeology* (1965).

Coty, René (rənā' kōtē'), 1882–1962, French president (1954–59). From 1923 to 1940 he served in the legislature, first as a deputy and then as a senator. In 1940, when France fell to the Germans, he voted to hand all power to Marshal Pétain. After a wartime spent in retirement, Coty returned to the legislature and in Dec., 1953, was elected president as a compromise candidate. In the crisis of May, 1958, he threatened resignation if Charles De Gaulle were not made premier; he left office with the creation (1959) of the Fifth Republic.

cotyledon (kŏt"əlēd'ən), in botany, a leaf of the embryo of a SEED. The embryos of flowering plants, or ANGIOSPERMS, usually have either one cotyledon (the monocots) or two (the dicots). Seeds of gymnosperms, such as pines, may have numerous cotyledons. In some seeds the cotyledons are flat and leaflike; in others, such as the bean, the cotyledons store the seed's food reserve for germination and are fleshy. In most plants the cotyledons emerge above the soil with the seedling as it grows.

couch grass, name for several grasses, among them QUACK GRASS.

Coucy, Robert de (rōbĕr' də ko͞osē'), d.1311, French architect, celebrated for his part in the building of Rheims Cathedral, which he carried on as master of the works after the death of Hugues Libergier in 1263. Probably the Robert de Coucy traditionally known as the original architect of Rheims Cathedral, after the fire of 1211, was his father; their separate works on the cathedral have been confused.

Coudé focus: see TELESCOPE.

Coudert, Frederic René (ko͞odâr'), 1832–1903, American lawyer and public official, b. New York City. He practiced law in New York City and for many years was counsel in the United States for the French, Italian, and Spanish governments. He was (1880) a member of the international conference at Bern for the codification of the law of nations, served (1893–95) as counsel for the United States in the Bering Sea fur-seal arbitration at Paris, and was (1896–98) a member of the Venezuela Boundary Commission. He was active in political reform movements in New York City and was a trustee of many educational institutions.

Coué, Émile (āmēl' kwā), 1857–1926, French psychotherapist. He is remembered for his formula for curing by optimistic autosuggestion, "Day by day, in every way, I am getting better and better." His teaching achieved a vogue in England and the United States in the 1920s.

Coues, Elliott (kouz), 1842–99, American ornithologist, b. Portsmouth, N.H., grad. Columbian College, later Columbian Univ. and now George Washington Univ. (B.A., 1861; M.D., 1863; Ph.D., 1869). He served as an army surgeon in the Civil War and as naturalist on government surveys and taught (1877–87) at Columbian Univ. He was a founder of the American Society for Psychical Research and a leader in the theosophist movement. He wrote *Key to North American Birds* (1872), *Birds of the Northwest* (1847), *Fur-bearing Animals* (1877), and *Birds of the Colorado Valley* (1878); he edited the journals of Lewis and Clark (1893), Zebulon M. Pike (1895), and Alexander Henry and David Thompson (1897).

cougar: see PUMA.

cough, sudden forceful expiration of air from the lungs caused by an involuntary contraction of the muscles controlling the process of breathing. The cough is a response to some irritating condition such as inflammation or the presence of mucus (sputum) in the respiratory tract, as in infectious disease, or to heavy dust or industrial or tobacco smoke. Coughing may also be a reflex action to factors outside the respiratory tract; diseases that are not respiratory in nature (e.g., congestive heart failure or mitral valve disease) often bring on coughing. If there is mucus or a foreign substance in the respiratory tract, the cough should not be hindered since by this action the offending matter is expelled from the body. If, however, the cough becomes exhausting, sedation is indicated.

Coughlin, Charles Edward (kŏg'lĭn), 1891–, Roman Catholic priest in the United States, b. Ontario, Canada, grad. Univ. of Toronto, 1916. After study at St. Michael's College, Toronto, he was ordained (1916) and became (1926) pastor of the Shrine of the Little Flower at Royal Oak, Mich. In the 1930s he made radio addresses in which he criticized such diverse groups as U.S. bankers, trade unionists, and Communists. In 1934 he organized the National Union for Social Justice, which denounced President Franklin Delano Roosevelt's New Deal policies and advocated such measures as silver inflation as well as the nationalizing of banks, utilities, and natural resources. Coughlin also published a magazine, *Social Justice,* in which he expressed pro-Nazi opinions and made increasingly anti-Semitic remarks directed especially at Jewish members of Wall Street. The magazine was barred from the mails by the U.S. government for violation of the Espionage Act and ceased publication in 1942. Father Coughlin was meanwhile silenced by his superiors but continued his parish duties.

Coulanges, Numa Denis Fustel de: see FUSTEL DE COULANGES, NUMA DENIS.

Coulee Dam National Recreation Area: see NATIONAL PARKS AND MONUMENTS (table).

Coulomb, Charles Augustin de (ko͞o'lŏm, ko͞olŏm', Fr. shärl ōgüstăN' də ko͞olôN'), 1736–1806, French physicist. In 1789 he retired from his posts as military engineer and as superintendent of waters and fountains and devoted himself to continuing his scientific research. He was known for his work on electricity, magnetism, and friction, and he invented a magnetoscope, a magnetometer, and a torsion balance that he employed in determining torsional elasticity and in establishing COULOMB'S LAW. The unit of quantity of electric charge, the coulomb, is named in his honor. See study by C. S. Gilmor (1971).

coulomb (ko͞o'lŏm), abbr. coul or C, unit of electric CHARGE. The absolute coulomb, the current U. S. legal standard, is the amount of charge transferred in 1 second by a current of 1 AMPERE; i.e., it is 1 ampere-second. The international coulomb, which was the legal standard before 1950 and upon which the definition of the ampere was formerly based, is defined as the amount of charge that, when passed through a water solution of silver nitrate under certain standard conditions, will cause the deposit of a certain mass (approximately 1.1 mg) of metallic silver; 1 international coul equals 0.999835 absolute coul.

Coulomb's law (ko͞o'lŏmz), in physics, law stating that the electrostatic force between two charged bodies is proportional to the product of the amounts of charge on the bodies divided by the square of the distance between them. If the bodies are oppositely charged, one positive and one negative, they are attracted toward one another; if the bodies are similarly charged, both positive or both negative, the force between them is repulsive (see CHARGE, ELECTRIC). Coulomb's law applies exactly only when the charged bodies are much smaller than the distance separating them and therefore can be treated approximately as point charges. When combined with principles of quantum physics, Coulomb's law helps describe the forces that bind electrons to an atomic nucleus, that bind atoms together into molecules, and that hold together solids and liquids. The law was deduced in 1785 by C. A. de Coulomb from experimental measures of the forces between charged bodies; the experiments were made using his torsion balance.

council, ecumenical (ĕk″yo͞omĕn'ĭkəl) [Gr.,=universal], in Christendom, council of church authorities accepted by the church as the official voice, also called general council. The utterances of such a council are called canons, the first being usually a detailed statement of the common faith. The acceptance of the canons is unequal; thus, Roman Catholics regard them as binding (canonical) only when a pope has subsequently ratified them, and many canons of several councils have never been accepted. The following is the list of the general councils recognized by Roman Catholics (the numbering is the customary one, and the opening year is given): (1) 1 Nicaea, 325; (2) 1 Constantinople, 381; (3) Ephesus, 431; (4) Chalcedon, 451; (5) 2 Constantinople, 553; (6) 3 Constantinople, 680; (7) 2 Nicaea, 787; (8) 4 Constantinople, 869; (9) 1 Lateran, 1123; (10) 2 Lateran, 1139; (11) 3 Lateran, 1179; (12) 4 Lateran, 1215; (13) 1 Lyons, 1245; (14) 2 Lyons, 1274; (15) Vienne, 1311; (16) Constance, 1414; (17) Basel and Ferrara-Florence, 1431, 1438; (18) 5 Lateran, 1512; (19) Trent, 1545; (20) 1 Vatican, 1869; (21) 2 Vatican, 1962. (See separate article on each council; e.g., NICAEA, FIRST COUNCIL OF.) The Orthodox Eastern Church recognizes the first seven and counts the Trullan Synod of 692 as an ecumenical extension of the Third Council of Constantinople. The first council was the model for the rest. The common purpose of the first eight councils was to determine whether specific theological novelties were orthodox or heretical (not orthodox). The rest of the councils, all held in Western Europe, have dealt chiefly with church discipline and morals. Two of them, the Second Council of Lyons and the Council of Ferrara-Florence, were occupied with abortive attempts at reconciliation between East and West. In the Great Schism arose the conciliar theory, which held that an ecumenical council is superior to the pope; that theory was in its heyday at the Council of Constance (see SCHISM, GREAT). The Council of Trent, convened to deal with the Protestant Reformation, was probably the most far-reaching in its effects. The traditional opinion is that when the bishops of the world unite to define belief in the light of what they have received from their predecessors, God will protect them from error. This is a manifestation of the infallibility of the teaching church, and papal infallibility is compared to it in the definition published by the First Vatican Council (see INFALLIBILITY). Two famous councils that claimed in vain to be ecumenical are the Robber Council of Ephesus (see EUTYCHES) and the Council of Pisa in the Great Schism. Pope John XXIII established as one of the principal themes of the Second Vatican Council the reunion of all Christians with the Church of Rome. Protestants, rejecting the teaching authority of the church, do not regard ecumenical councils and their canons as binding on the conscience. Protestant observers, however, have officially attended the last two councils. The ECUMENICAL MOVEMENT among Protestants is not to be confused with an ecumenical council, although they share a similar aim. See studies by Lorenz Jaeger (tr. 1961), Philip Hughes (1961), Francis Dvornik (1961), and E. F. Jacobs (rev. ed. 1963).

Council Bluffs, city (1970 pop. 60,348), seat of Pottawattamie co., SW Iowa, on and below bluffs overlooking the Missouri River, opposite Omaha, Nebr.; inc. 1853. It was the site of an Indian trading post and of a Pottawattamie Indian mission before 1846, when it was settled by Mormons and named Kanesville. When the Mormons departed in 1852, the settlement was renamed Council Bluffs. An important supply point during the gold rush (1849-50), Council Bluffs was made the eastern terminus of the Union Pacific RR in 1863. The city is now an important trade and industrial center for a large agricultural area. It has grain elevators, and its manufactures include processed foods, cast-iron pipes, farm equipment, electronic equipment, and fabricated metals. Among the points of interest in the city are Dodge House, a national historic landmark and the former home of Gen. G. M. Dodge, founder of the Union Pacific RR; the Lewis and Clark monument, which commemorates the meeting held near there in 1804 between U. S. explorers Lewis and Clark and the Indians; and the Lincoln monument, built in honor of Abraham Lincoln's visit to Council Bluffs in 1859. Iowa Western Community College is there, and Lake Manawa State Park lies entirely within the city limits. An extensive levee system along the Missouri River protects the part of the city below the bluffs.

Council for Mutual Economic Assistance (COMECON or CMEA), international governmental organization for the coordination of economic policy among certain Communist nations. Its members include Albania (which has not participated since 1961), Bulgaria, Cuba, Czechoslovakia, East Germany, Hungary, Mongolia, Poland, Rumania, and the Soviet Union. Yugoslavia participates in matters of mutual interest but is not a member. First formed in 1949, the council was relatively dormant until 1954. In 1956 its activities were greatly expanded, and in 1959 a formal charter was ratified giving COMECON the same international status as the European Free Trade Association and the Common Market. To meet the challenge of these Western associations, COMECON undertook large-scale measures for organization of industrial production and coordination of economic development by conducting a series of five-year plans (1956-60, 1961-65, 1966-70, and 1971-75). During the first 15 years of its existence, trade among COMECON countries and foreign trade increased by over 400%. However, growth of both types of trade declined after that period.

Council of Europe: see INTERNATIONAL GOVERNMENTAL ORGANIZATIONS.

Council of Foreign Ministers, Council of Ten, etc.: see FOREIGN MINISTERS, COUNCIL OF; TEN, COUNCIL OF; etc.

counselor at law: see ATTORNEY.

counterfeiting, manufacturing spurious coins, paper money, or evidences of governmental obligation (e.g., bonds) in the semblance of the true. There must be sufficient resemblance to the genuine article to deceive a person using ordinary caution. The offense may be regarded as a special variety of FORGERY. The crime affects property but was historically considered to be an interference with the administration of government. Hence, under an early English statute (1350), counterfeiting the king's seal or his gold and silver coinage was a grave crime against the state amounting to high TREASON and was punishable by death. The statute left unchanged the common-law misdemeanors of counterfeiting copper coinage and passing counterfeit foreign currency. Other early statutes were directed against debasing the coinage by clipping or filing off the edges to sell the metal. By the 19th cent. counterfeiting was considered a felony rather than a form of treason. Article 1, Section 8, of the U.S. Constitution authorizes Congress to "provide for the punishment of counterfeiting the Securities and current Coin of the United States." Under that power, statutes have been enacted making criminal the counterfeiting of the currency and bonds of the United States, of the evidences of indebtedness (e.g., checks) of the Federal Reserve System, of postage stamps, and of foreign money used for exchange. Under its powers to define and punish offenses of international law and its powers to control interstate and foreign commerce, Congress has passed legislation against the counterfeiting of foreign money and securities within the United States. Nearly every state now has statutes against counterfeiting. Since its establishment in 1865 the U.S. Secret Service has been the primary agency in the combating of counterfeiters in the United States. To commit the crime of counterfeiting one does not necessarily have to make a whole coin or bill. It may be accomplished by plating coins, by raising the amount of a bill, or by any other alteration calculated to deceive the recipients. To retain counterfeit money or government obligations knowingly is also a criminal offense, regardless of how possession was acquired. The knowing utterance (passing) of counterfeit currency or securities is also criminal. For the further protection of the currency and of postage stamps, statutes forbid making certain types of photographs (e.g., in color) where there would be danger of deception. See Lynn Glaser, *Counterfeiting in America* (1968).

counterglow: see GEGENSCHEIN.

counterpoint, in music, the art of combining melodies each of which is independent though forming part of a homogeneous texture. The term derives from the Latin for "point against point," meaning note against note in referring to the notation of PLAINSONG. The academic study of counterpoint was long based on *Gradus ad Parnassum* (1725, tr. 1943) by Johann Joseph Fux (1660-1741), an Austrian theorist and composer. This work formulates the study of counterpoint into five species—note against note, two notes against one, four notes against one, syncopation, and florid counterpoint, which combines the other species. Countless textbooks have followed this method, but since the early 20th cent. several theorists have based their courses in counterpoint on a direct study of 16th-century contrapuntal practice. The early master composers of contrapuntal music include PALESTRINA, LASSO, and BYRD. Polyphonic forms were later given a most brilliant and sophisticated expression during the BAROQUE era in the works of J. S. BACH. See also POLYPHONY; IMITATION. See Walter Piston, *Counterpoint* (1947); Humphrey Searle, *Twentieth Century Counterpoint* (1954); Kent Kennan, *Counterpoint* (2d ed. 1972).

Counter Reformation: see REFORMATION, CATHOLIC.

countertenor, a male singing voice in the ALTO range. Singing in this range requires a special vocal technique called falsetto. Countertenor singers were required during the Renaissance and Baroque periods because social and religious conventions restricted women from public singing. See also CASTRATO.

country and western music, American popular music form originating in the Southeast (country music) and the Southwest and West (western music). The two regional styles coalesced in the 1920s when recorded material became available in rural areas, and they were further consolidated after musicians from various sections met and mixed during service in World War II. The primary difference between the two styles is that country music is simpler and uses fewer instruments, relying on guitar, fiddle, banjo, and harmonica, whereas the music of the Southwest tends toward steel guitars and big bands whose style verges on swing (e.g., The Light Crust Doughboys). Country and western music is directly descended from the folk songs, ballads, and popular songs of the English, Scottish, and Irish settlers of the southeastern seaboard of the United States. Its modern lyrics depict the emotion and experience of rural and (currently) urban poor whites; they often tell frankly of illicit love, crime, and prison life. Over the last 50 years country and western music has gained a nationwide audience. Since 1924 the "Grand Ole Opry," a Saturday night performance featuring country and western singers, has broadcast weekly from Nashville, Tenn. Many of the musicians have been influenced by black blues and GOSPEL MUSIC, but the performers and audience are almost all white. Leading performers include Hank Williams, Jimmy Rogers, Johnny Cash, Tex Ritter, June Carter, the Carter family, Merle Haggard, Loretta Lynn, Jim Reeves, Tammy Wynette, Eddie Arnold, Charlie Pride (a black man), and Charlie Rich. See Bill C. Malone, *Country Music USA* (1968); Paul Hemphill, *The Nashville Sound* (1971).

Counts, George Sylvester, 1889-1974, American educator, b. near Baldwin City, Kansas, grad. Baker Univ., 1911, Ph.D. Univ. of Chicago, 1916. He taught in the educational departments of several universities before joining the faculty of Teachers College, Columbia Univ., in 1927. A strong advocate of teachers' unions, he ran for public office on the American Labor party ticket and was president (1939-42) of the AMERICAN FEDERATION OF TEACHERS. His works include *The American Road to Culture* (1930), *The Prospects of American Democracy* (1938), *The Challenge of Soviet Education* (1957), and *Education and the Foundations of Human Freedom* (1962). See study by G. L. Gutek (1971).

county [from Fr. *comté*,=domain of a count], division of LOCAL GOVERNMENT in the United States, Great Britain, and many Commonwealth countries. The county developed in England from the shire, a unit of local government that originated in the Saxon settlements of the 5th cent. By the 11th cent. the shire system was fully established throughout most of England, with each shire being ruled by a shire-reeve, or sheriff, appointed by the crown. By the 14th cent. the office of justice of the peace had developed; in each county a court of three or four justices, also appointed by the king, assisted the sheriff in the administration of local affairs. With the passage of the Local Government Act of 1888, power passed from the king's appointed officials to the newly created county councils, elected by local residents. The county system of government was adopted in most of the nations settled by the British. Throughout the English-speaking world, for example, most courts are still organized by counties. In the United States there are approximately 3,000 counties, most of which are either rural or suburban. Louisiana, influenced by the French, has parishes, which are essentially similar to counties. The major functions of county government in the United States include law enforcement, the recording of deeds and other documents, and the provision and maintenance of public works such as roads and parks. See H. S. Duncombe, *County Government in America* (1966); J. C. Bollens, *American County Government* (1969).

coup (ko͞o) [Fr.,=blow], among North American Indians of the Plains culture, a war honor, awarded for striking an enemy in such a way that it was considered an extreme act of bravery. Coups were awarded according to the degree of recklessness involved; the most reckless, such as striking an armed enemy with the bare hand, counted highest. Killing an enemy, wounding him, scalping him, or stealing his horse or gun—all these were coups of value. Recital of the deeds was an important social function, and a warrior with many coups held a high status and was honored at feasts, ceremonials, and in the tribe. After warfare had ceased, coups became transferable property, passing from the old men to the younger, who needed coups to acquire warrior status in the tribe.

Couper, James Hamilton (ko͞o'pər), 1794–1866, American planter of Georgia, grad. Yale, 1814. Influential in promoting agricultural research and experimentation, he was a pioneer in the cultivation of rice, long-staple cotton, and sugarcane and introduced new plants, including Bermuda grass.

Couperin, François (fräNswä' ko͞opərăN'), 1668–1733, French harpsichordist and composer, called "le Grand" to distinguish him from the other musicians in his family. His harpsichord music, in its charm, delicacy, and graceful ornamentation, represents the culmination of French rococo. He published four books of harpsichord suites (1713–30), which generally consisted of short, highly ornamental pieces, with descriptive titles such as *Les Abeilles, Les Papillons, La Voluptueuse,* and *Le Rossignol en amour.* His style of harpsichord playing, formulated in *L'Art de toucher de clavecin* (1716), influenced the keyboard technique of Bach. Couperin also composed much religious and chamber music and works for the organ. He was organist (1685–1733) at St. Gervais, Paris, a position held by members of the Couperin family from c.1650 until 1826. In 1693, Couperin was chosen by Louis XIV as one of the organists of the royal chapel, and later he was made music master of the royal family and harpsichordist at the royal court. The Couperin line of musicians had begun with three brothers—Louis (c.1626–1661), an organist, violinist, and composer of harpsichord suites, which are characterized by a vigorous, frequently dissonant style; François (c.1631–c.1701), a harpsichordist and violinist; and Charles (1638–79), an organist, the father of Couperin le Grand. The line extended to the great-grandsons of François, the second brother—Pierre Louis (1755–89) and François Gervais (1759–1826), who were organists at St. Gervais. See biography by P. Brunold (1949).

Couperus, Louis Marie Anne (lwē märē' än ko͞opā'-ro͞os), 1863–1923, Dutch novelist. In his early works he emphasized with graceful irony the determining forces of man's past and environment; this fatalism characterizes all his novels. Couperus is best known for the realistic family saga *De Boeken der kleine Zielen* (4 vol., 1901–3; tr. *The Book of the Small Souls,* 4 vol., 1914–18). Other works include symbolic fairy tales and verse.

Courbet, Gustave (güstäv' ko͞orbā'), 1819–77, French painter, b. Ornans. He studied in Paris, learning chiefly by copying masterpieces in the Louvre. An avowed realist, Courbet was always at odds with vested authority, aesthetic or political. In 1847 his *Wounded Man* (Louvre) was rejected by the Salon, although two of his earlier pictures had been accepted. He first won wide attention with his *After Dinner at Ornans* (Lille) in 1849. The next year he exhibited his famous *Funeral at Ornans* and *Stonebreakers* (both: Louvre). For his choice of subjects from ordinary life, and more especially for his obstinacy and audacity, his work was reviled as offensive to prevailing politics and aesthetic taste. Enjoying the drama, Courbet rose to defend his work as the expression of his newfound political radicalism. His statements did nothing to recommend the work to his enemies. In 1855, Courbet exhibited the mammoth, self-congratulatory *Painter's Studio* (Louvre). Attacked by academic painters of every persuasion, he set up his own pavilion where he exhibited 40 of his paintings and issued a manifesto on realism. Within the next decade he triumphed as the leader of the realist school. His influence became enormous, reaching its height with his rejection of the cross of the Legion of Honor offered him by Napoleon III in 1872. Under the Commune, Courbet was elected to the chamber and in consequence was later held responsible, fined, and imprisoned for the destruction of the Vendôme column. In 1873 he fled to Switzerland, where he spent his few remaining years in poverty. Although his aesthetic theories were not destined to prevail, his painting is greatly admired for its frankness, vigor, and solid construction. Courbet is represented in galleries throughout France and the United States. The Metropolitan Museum has more than 20 of his works. See biography by Jack Lindsay (1974); study by T. J. Clark (1973).

Courbevoie (ko͞orbvwä'), city (1968 pop. 58,283), Hauts-de-Seine dept., N central France, on the Seine River. An industrial suburb of Paris, Courbevoie manufactures automobiles, bicycles, perfumes, and pharmaceuticals. There are also electrical industries, foundries, and copper works. The Avenue du Général de Gaulle, which runs through Courbevoie, is a continuation of the CHAMPS ÉLYSÉES of Paris.

Courcelle, Daniel Rémy, sieur de (dänyĕl' rāmē' syör' də ko͞orsĕl'), d.1698, governor of New France (1665–72). He arrived with the intendant Jean Talon, and together they inaugurated a period of peace and prosperity. Courcelle led (1666) an unsuccessful winter raid on the Mohawk Indians, but a campaign in Sept., 1666, under the marquis de Tracy and Courcelle induced the Iroquois to conclude a peace that was kept for a number of years. In 1671 he led to Lake Ontario an expedition that chose the site for a fort later established as Fort Frontenac. While governor, Courcelle instituted militia service for all males and supported the expeditions of Robert de La Salle and Louis Jolliet. Ill health led him to request his recall to France in 1672, and the comte de Frontenac took his place as governor. Courcelle was later appointed governor of Toulon, where he died.

coureurs de bois (ko͞orör' də bwä) [Fr.,=woods runners], unlicensed traders during the French regime in Canada. Traders were required to be licensed, but to only a favored few were licenses granted. The *coureurs de bois* defied regulations and ventured into the Canadian wilderness. Although they stimulated the growth of the fur trade and the exploration of Canada, their defiance caused problems for the government of New France and contributed to poor relations with the Indians, to whom they sold liquor. Toward the end of the 17th cent. it was estimated that one third of the able-bodied men of the colony were *coureurs de bois,* although this may be an exaggeration.

Courier, Paul Louis (Paul Louis Courier de Méré) (pōl lwē ko͞oryā' də mārā'), 1772–1825, French political writer and classical scholar. His translation (1810) of the Greek text of *Daphnis and Chloë* is considered excellent. After the Bourbon restoration, which he opposed, he devoted himself to writing trenchant political pamphlets, the best known of which are *Simple Discours* (1821), for which he was jailed, and *Le Pamphlet des pamphlets* (1824), remarkable for its stylistic brilliance. His memoirs and letters (1828) have the same original charm that makes his literary works memorable. He was murdered, presumably by one of his servants.

courlan (ko͞or'lən): see LIMPKIN.

Courland or **Kurland** (both: kûr'lănd, Ger. ko͞or'länt), Lettish *Kurzeme,* historic region and former duchy, W European USSR, in Latvia, between the Baltic Sea and the Western Dvina River. It is an agricultural and wooded lowland. Yelgava (Ger. *Mitau*), the historic capital, and Liepaya (Ger. *Libau*) and Ventspils (Ger. *Windau*), the Baltic seaports, are the chief cities. The early Baltic tribes—Letts and Kurs—who inhabited the region were subjected in the 13th cent. by the LIVONIAN BROTHERS OF THE SWORD. In 1561 the order disbanded and its grand master became the first duke of Courland, under Polish suzerainty. In the Northern War (1700–21), it was taken (1701) by Charles XII of Sweden. Empress Anna, who was, by marriage, duchess of Courland before her accession in Russia, forced (1737), the nobles of Courland to elect her favorite, Ernst Johann von Biron, their duke. Russian influence became paramount, and with the third partition of Poland (1795) the duchy passed to Russia. In 1918, Courland was incorporated into Latvia, except for a strip of the southern coast that went to Lithuania. In independent LATVIA (1918–40), Courland was divided into two provinces, Kurzeme and Zemgale.

Courland Lagoon: see KURSKY ZALIV, USSR.

Cournand, André Frederic (ko͞or'nănd), 1895–, American physician and physiologist, b. France, B.A. Sorbonne, 1913, M.D. Univ. of Paris, 1930. He emigrated to the United States in 1930 and was naturalized in 1941. He was associated with the College of Physicians and Surgeons, Columbia, after 1935 and became a full professor in 1951. He shared with Werner Forssmann and Dickinson W. Richards the 1956 Nobel Prize in Physiology and Medicine for work in developing cardiac catheterization. This technique, whereby a catheter is inserted through a vein into the heart, facilitates study of both the diseased and healthy heart and, in many cases, aids in determining the advisability of heart surgery.

Cournot, Antoine Augustin (äNtwän' ōgüstăN' ko͞ornō'), 1801–77, French mathematician and economist. He developed mathematical theories of chance and probability and was one of the first to attempt the application of mathematics to economic problems. His writings include *Researches into the Mathematical Principles of the Theory of Wealth* (1838, tr. 1897).

Courrèges, André: see under FASHION.

Court, Antoine (äNtwän' ko͞or), 1696–1760, French Protestant preacher, called the Restorer of Protestantism in France. He was successful in reorganizing the remnants of the persecuted Calvinists in France. With a price on his head, he escaped to Lausanne in 1730, where he spent the remainder of his life directing the theological seminary that he founded.

Court, Margaret, 1942–, Australian tennis player. Playing tennis from age eight, she rose to prominence in the game in the early 1960s under her original name, Margaret Smith. Ranked first in world standings six times since 1962, she retired in 1966, but returned to the game after marriage in 1968, and in 1970 became the second woman (Maureen Connolly was the first) to win the grand slam. In 1973 she was defeated by Bobby RIGGS in a nationally televised match but went on to win her fifth U.S. Open championship later that year. See *The Margaret Smith Story* written with Don Lawrence (1965).

court, in law, official body charged with administering justice. The term is also applied to the judge or judges who fill the office and to the courtroom. Distinct courts originate when legal relations are no longer entirely a private matter. Thus, courts do not exist in a society governed by VENDETTA, and they are of little consequence in one where COMPOSITION for wrongs is the rule. The most ancient courts known, e.g., those of Egypt and Babylonia, were semiecclesiastical institutions that used religious rituals in deciding issues. In Greece the functions of a court were chiefly undertaken by assemblies of the people that heard the arguments of orators. In Rome there was a clear evolution of the court system from priestly beginnings to a wholly secular, hierarchal organization staffed by professional jurists (see ROMAN LAW). Western Europe (after the collapse of Rome) and Anglo-Saxon England had mainly feudal courts of limited territorial authority, administering customary law, which differed in each locale. In England, after the Norman Conquest (1066), royal authority was gradually extended over the feudal lords, and by the early 13th cent., although purely local courts had not been abolished, there was established the supremacy of the central courts that had evolved from the Curia Regis [Lat.,=king's court], namely, the Court of EXCHEQUER, the Court of Common Pleas, and King's Bench. The Court of Common Pleas heard cases between ordinary subjects of the king, while King's Bench acted as a court of appeals and heard cases involving persons of high rank. Soon itinerant royal courts were established to spare civil litigants the labor and expense of going to the capital at Westminster and to afford hearings to persons held on criminal charges in county jails. By the 14th cent. the principal function of the central courts was to hear appeals from the circuit courts. Unity was at least temporarily disrupted by the emergence (16th cent.) of EQUITY as a distinctive body of law administered by the chancery. The conflict of jurisdiction continued to some extent until 1875, when the Judicature Act of 1873 went into effect. It provided for a supreme court of judicature, comprising the high court of justice and the court of appeal. The high court of justice (with jurisdiction over England, Wales, and Northern Ireland) is divided, purely for administrative purposes, into three divisions: chancery; probate, divorce, and admiralty; and King's (or Queen's) Bench. Appeals may in some instances be taken from the court of appeals to the House of Lords. The judicial committee of the privy council hears appeals from overseas territories still under British domain and from Commonwealth countries. In the United States there are two distinct systems of courts, Federal and state. Each is supreme in its own sphere, but if a matter simultaneously affects the states and the Federal government, the Federal courts have the decisive power. The district court is the lowest Federal court. Each state constitutes at least one district, and some of the more populous states contain as many as four districts. There are 10 circuit courts of appeals (each with jurisdiction over a definite territory) and a court of appeals for the District of Columbia; these hear appeals from the district courts. There are, in addition, various specialized Federal courts, including the Court of Tax Appeals and the Court of Claims. Heading the Federal court system is the U.S. SUPREME COURT. The court systems of the states vary to some degree. At the bottom of a typical structure are local courts that only have authority in specific jurisdiction (e.g., court of the justice of the peace, POLICE COURT, and court of PROBATE). County courts, or the equivalent, exercising general criminal and civil jurisdiction, are on the next level. All states have a highest court of appeals, and some also have intermediate appellate courts. In a few states separate courts of equity persist. In addition to law courts there are ecclesiastical courts, arbitral tribunals (e.g., for labor cases), administrative tribunals (e.g., of the Interstate Commerce Commission), and courts-martial (see MILITARY LAW). See CONFLICT OF LAWS. See Harold Potter, *Historical Introduction to English Law and Its Institutions* (4th ed. 1958, repr. 1969); Lewis Mayers, *The American Legal System* (rev. ed. 1964); R. M. Jackson, *The Machinery of Justice in England* (5th ed. 1967); H. J. Abraham, *The Judicial Process* (2d ed. 1968); Herbert Jacob, *Justice in America* (2d ed. 1972).

Courteline, Georges (zhôrzh ko͞or″təlĕn′), 1858–1929, French writer. His prolific humorous and satiric works include sketches, plays, tales, and novels. Bourgeois attitudes are ridiculed in his comedy *Boubouroche* (1892, tr. 1961); official red tape is satirized in his sketches *Messieurs les ronds-de-cuir* (1893, tr. *The Bureaucrats,* 1928); and the pitfalls of justice in the courts are hilariously exposed in *Hortense, couche-toi* (1897, tr. *Hold on, Hortense,* 1961) and *L'Article 330* (1900, tr. 1961).

Courtenay, William (kôrt′nē), c.1342–1396, English prelate, archbishop of Canterbury (1381–96). He was important for his condemnation of the doctrines of Wyclif and for suppressing the Lollards.

courtly love, philosophy of love and code of lovemaking that flourished in France and England during the Middle Ages. Although its origins are obscure, it probably derived from the works of Ovid, various Oriental ideas popular at the time, and the songs of the troubadours. According to the code, a man falls passionately in love with a married woman of equal or higher rank. Before his love can be declared, he must suffer long months of silence; before it can be consummated, he must prove his devotion by noble service and daring exploits. The lovers eventually pledge themselves to secrecy and to remain faithful despite all obstacles. In reality, courtly love was little more than a set of rules for committing adultery. It was more important as a literary invention, expressed in such works as Chrétien de Troyes's *Lancelot* (12th cent.), Guillaume de Lorris's *Roman de la Rose* (13th cent.), and Chaucer's *Troilus and Criseyde* (14th cent.). In these works it was the subjective presentation of the lovers' passion for each other and their consideration for other people that transformed the code of courtly love into one of the most important literary influences in Western culture. See CHIVALRY. See Denis de Rougemont, *Love in the Western World* (tr. 1956); C. S. Lewis, *The Allegory of Love* (1936, repr. 1958).

court-martial: see MILITARY LAW.

Court of Justice: see EUROPEAN COMMUNITY.

Courtrai: see KORTRIJK, Belgium.

courts of love: see CHIVALRY and COURTLY LOVE.

court system in the United States, judicial branches of the Federal and state governments charged with the application and interpretation of the law. The U.S. court system is unique in that it is divided into two administratively separate systems, the Federal and the state, each of which is independent of the executive and legislative branches of government. Such a dual court system is a heritage of the colonial period. By the time the U.S. Constitution had first mandated (1789) the establishment of a Federal judiciary, each of the original Thirteen Colonies already had its own comprehensive court system based on the English model. Thus, the two systems grew side by side and came to exercise exclusive jurisdiction in some areas and overlapping, or concurrent, jurisdiction in others. Of the two systems, the Federal is by far the less complicated. According to Article III of the Constitution, "The judicial Power of the United States, shall be vested in one supreme Court, and in such inferior Courts as the Congress may from time to time ordain and establish." In accordance with this directive, the Federal judiciary is divided into three main levels. At the bottom are the Federal district courts, which have original jurisdiction in most cases of Federal law. Made up of 91 districts, the Federal district court system has at least one bench in each of the 50 states, as well as one each in the District of Columbia and Puerto Rico. There are from 1 to 24 judges in each district, and, as with most Federal jurists, district court judges are appointed by the President and serve for life. Cases handled by the Federal district courts include those relating to alleged violations of the Constitution or other Federal laws, maritime disputes, cases directly involving a state or the Federal government, and cases in which foreign governments, citizens of foreign countries, or citizens of two or more different states are involved. Directly above the district courts are the United States courts of appeals, each made up of one or more district courts. Established by Congress in 1891, the court of appeals system is composed of 10 judicial circuits throughout the 50 states plus one in the District of Columbia. There are from three to nine judges in each circuit. In addition to hearing appeals from their respective district courts, the courts of appeals have original jurisdiction in cases involving a challenge to an order of a Federal regulatory agency, such as the Securities and Exchange Commission. The highest level court in the Federal system is the Supreme Court of the United States, the only Federal court explicitly mandated by the Constitution. Since 1869 it has been composed of one Chief Justice and eight Associate Justices. The Supreme Court sits in Washington, D.C., and has final jurisdiction on all cases that it hears. The high court may review decisions made by the U.S. courts of appeals, and it may also choose to hear appeals from state appellate courts if a Constitutional or other Federal issue is involved. The Supreme Court has original jurisdiction in a limited number of cases, including those that involve high-ranking diplomats of other nations. In addition the Federal judiciary maintains a group of courts that handle certain limited types of disputes. Included among such special Federal courts are the U.S. court of claims, which adjudicates claims against the U.S. government, and the U.S. customs court, which passes upon customs disputes. Special court judges, unlike those in the three main levels of the Federal judiciary, do not serve for life. The U.S. armed forces have courts-martial for cases involving military personnel (see MILITARY LAW). The system of state courts is quite diverse; virtually no two states have identical judiciaries. In general, however, the states, like the Federal government, have a hierarchically organized system of general courts along with a group of special courts. The lowest level of state courts, often known generically as the inferior courts, may include any of the following: magistrate court, municipal court, justice of the peace court, police court, traffic court, and county court. Such tribunals, often quite informal, handle only minor civil and criminal cases. More serious offenses are heard in superior court, also known as state district court, circuit court, and by a variety of other names. The superior courts, usually organized by counties, hear appeals from the inferior courts and have original jurisdiction over major civil suits and serious crimes such as grand larceny. It is here that most of the nation's jury trials occur. The highest state court, usually called either appellate court, state court of appeals, or state supreme court, generally hears appeals from the state superior courts and, in some instances, has original jurisdiction over particularly important cases. A number of the larger states, such as New York, also have appellate courts that are intermediate between the superior courts and the state's highest court. Additionally, a state may have any of a wide variety of special tribunals, usually on the inferior court level, including juvenile court, divorce court, probate court, family court, and small claims court. In all, there are more than 1,000 state courts of all different types, and their judges, who may be either appointed or elected, handle the overwhelming majority of trials held in the United States each year.

court tennis, indoor racket and net game of ancient origin. It is believed to have originated (about the 14th cent.) in medieval France and is the forerunner of most modern racket games. In its early days the sport was known as royal tennis because of the interest it held for French and English royalty. Enjoying varying degrees of popularity over the years, the sport was first played in the United States in 1876. Court tennis is played on an indoor, cement court 110 ft by 38 ft (33.53 m by 11.58 m), which is surrounded by four walls 30 ft (9.14 m) high. A player hits the ball—made of tightly wound cloth—with a 16-oz (.45-kg), 27-in. (68.5-cm) racket over the center net and plays the surface of the floor, the walls, and the ceiling to put the ball out of reach of the opponent. The scoring is intricate, and hitting the ball into wall openings also wins points. See Allison Danzig, *The Racquet Game* (1930).

Coushatta Indians: see ALABAMA INDIANS.

Cousin, Jean (zhäN ko͞ozăN′), c.1490–c.1560, celebrated French painter, designer, and sculptor. To him have been attributed the designs for the windows of various churches of Sens and Paris and a painting, *Eva Prima Pandora* (Louvre). He also designed tapestries for the Cathedral of Langres. Much of his work has been confused with that of his son **Jean Cousin,** c.1522–c.1594, who also designed stained glass. He illustrated the *Livre de fortune* (1568), and engravings of Ovid's *Metamorphoses* (1570) have been attributed to him. The influence of mannerism is apparent in his principal surviving painting, *The Last Judgment* (Louvre).

Cousin, Victor (vēktôr′), 1792–1867, French educational leader and philosopher, founder of the eclectic school. He lectured at the Sorbonne from 1814 until 1821, when political reaction forced him to leave. Recalled to teaching in 1828, Cousin was named in 1830 to the council of public instruction and was made councillor of state. In 1832 he became a peer of France, and in 1840 he accepted the position of minister of public instruction. He became virtually the national arbiter of educational and philosophical matters. His chief works in education were the complete reorganization and centralization of the primary system and the establishment of a policy of philosophical freedom in the universities. As an eclectic, Cousin sought to develop a system that combined the psychological insights of Maine de Biran, the common sense of the Scottish school, and the idealism of Hegel and Schelling. He argued that each of these philosophies contains an element of truth that can be grasped by intuition. Cousin's approach to philosophy was historical, and he introduced the study of the history of philosophy into the French academic course. His works include *Fragments philosophiques* (1826), *Du vrai, du beau et du bien* (1836; tr. *Lectures on the True, the Beautiful, and the Good,* 1854), *Cours de l'histoire de la philosophie* (8 vol., 1815–29), various studies of educational systems, and a brilliant translation of Plato. See George Boas, *French Philosophies of the Romantic Period* (1925); W. V. Brewer, *Victor Cousin as a Comparative Educator* (1971).

Cousin-Montauban, Charles Guillaume Marie: see PALIKAO, CHARLES GUILLAUME.

Cousins, Samuel, 1801–87, English mezzotint engraver. He is famous for his interpretations in mezzotint of the work of Sir Thomas Lawrence, but his plates, over 200 in number, also include reproductions of the work of Thomas Gainsborough, Sir Joshua Reynolds, Sir John Millais, and Sir Edwin Landseer. See biography by Alfred Whitman (1904).

Cousteau, Jacques Yves (zhäk ēv ko͞ostō′), 1910–, French naval officer. In 1943, with Émil Gagnan, he invented the self-contained underwater breathing apparatus (scuba), or aqualung. He founded (1945) the French navy's undersea research group and in 1957 was made director of the oceanographic museum of Monaco. He also helped develop the bathyscaphe. Since 1951 he has gone on annual oceanographic expeditions and has written numerous books and made several documentary films recording his trips. His publications include *The Silent World* (with Frédéric Dumas, 1953), *The Living Sea* (with James Dugan, 1963), *World Without Sun* (ed. by James Dugan, 1965), *The Shark* (with Philippe Cousteau, 1970), *Life and Death in a Coral Sea* (with Philippe Diolé, 1971), and *The Whale* (with Philippe Diolé, 1972). Among his films are *World Without Sun* (1964), *Desert Whales* (1970), and *Tragedy of Red Salmon* (1970).

Coustou (ko͞ostoo′), family of French sculptors. **Nicolas Coustou,** 1658–1733, studied with his uncle, Antoine Coysevox, with whom he later collaborated on the decorations at Marly and at Versailles. He became rector and chancellor of the Académie royale. Among his best-known works are *La Seine et la Marne* (Tuileries Gardens) and the bas-relief, *Passage du Rhin* (Louvre). His brother, **Guillaume Coustou,** 1677–1746, also studied with Coysevox and in Rome. Returning to Paris, he worked at Versailles and at Marly. He is famous for his colossal group, *The Ocean and the Mediterranean,* at Marly, and above all for his exuberant *Horses of Marly* at the entrance of the Champs Élysées, Paris. His son **Guillaume Coustou,** the younger, 1716–77, was also a noted sculptor.

Cousy, Robert Joseph (ko͞o'zē), 1928–, American basketball player, b. New York City. He compiled an outstanding record with the Boston Celtics in the National Basketball Association (NBA). He was the league's finest backcourt player, a brilliant playmaker, and a leading scorer. He was chosen for the NBA all-star squad for 10 straight years and played in 12 all-star games. After his retirement in 1963 he was basketball coach at Boston College (1963–69) and then coach of the NBA's Cincinnati Royals (later the Kansas City–Omaha Kings; 1969–73).

Coutchiching (ko͞o"chĭchĭng'): see PRECAMBRIAN ERA.

Couthon, Georges (zhōrzh ko͞otôN'), 1755?–1794, French revolutionary. An able lawyer, he was elected to the Legislative Assembly (1791) and to the Convention (1792). He became (1793) an important member of the Committee of Public Safety, the dictatorial body that ruled France in 1793 and 1794 under Maximilien ROBESPIERRE. He generally supported Robespierre in the REIGN OF TERROR. Although partially paralyzed, he led the army that took (1793) Lyons from the counterrevolutionists. As commissioner there he proved most humane, in contrast with his successor Jean Marie Collot d'Herbois. Couthon fell with Robespierre in the coup d'etat of 9 THERMIDOR (July 27, 1794) and was guillotined.

Couture, Thomas (tômä' ko͞otür'), 1815–1879, French academic painter. He was a pupil of Gros and Delaroche. He achieved fame with his vast orgy painting, *Romans in the Decadence of the Empire* (1847; Louvre). Acquiring a great reputation as a teacher, he wrote two treatises on painting. Puvis de Chavannes, Manet, and Fantin-Latour worked in his studio at various times.

couvade (ko͞oväd'), imitation by the father of many of the concomitants of childbirth, at the time of his wife's parturition. The father may go to bed, retire into seclusion, and observe taboos and restrictions. Among the theories that have been advanced to account for the couvade is that during this period, the father has to be cautious to avoid an injury that could be transmitted to the baby by sympathetic magic. Another is that the father asserts his paternity by appearing to take part in the delivery. A third explanation is that the father simulates the wife's activities in order to get evil spirits to focus on him rather than her. In extreme form, men may mimic the pain and process of childbirth. The practice of couvade has been noted since antiquity into modern times and in such widely dispersed places as Africa, China, Japan, India, and among the Indians of both North and South America.

Couve de Murville, Maurice (mōrēs' ko͞ov də mürvēl'), 1907–, French politician and diplomat. An expert in public finance, he entered the diplomatic service after World War II, serving as ambassador to Egypt, the United States, and West Germany. As minister of foreign affairs in Charles de Gaulle's administration (1958–68), he pursued the Gaullist policy of keeping France out of NATO military operations and preventing Great Britain from becoming a member of the Common Market. He served briefly as finance minister (May–July, 1968) and then as premier until June, 1969.

Couzens, James (kŭz'ənz), 1872–1936, U.S. Senator, industrialist, and philanthropist, b. Ontario, Canada. He moved (1887) to Detroit, and after he entered (1903) into partnership with Henry Ford, he became vice president and general manager of the Ford Motor Company. In 1919 he sold his interests to the Fords for $35 million. As mayor (1919–22) of Detroit, Couzens installed municipal street railways. Serving (1922–36) in the U.S. Senate, he acted with the Progressive Republicans, advocating such measures as high, graduated income taxes and public ownership of utilities. He established the Children's Fund of Michigan with $10 million, gave $1 million for relief in Detroit, and began a loan fund for the physically handicapped. His support of the New Deal cost him (1936) the senatorial renomination. See biography by Harry Barnard (1958).

Covadonga (kōvä*th*ōn'gä), village, Oviedo prov., N Spain, in Asturias. A battle fought nearby sometime between 718 and 725 was the first victory of the Christians over the Moors; it had great symbolic significance in the Christian reconquest of Spain. The village attracts many tourists. Legend says that a cave near Covadonga was the refuge of King PELAYO. The cave's chapel dates from the 8th cent.

covalent bond (kō"vā'lənt): see CHEMICAL BOND.

Covarrubias, Miguel (mēgāl' kōvär-ro͞o'bēäs), 1902–1957, American artist and writer, b. Mexico City. Largely self-taught, he went to New York City in 1923 and won prompt recognition as a brilliant illustrator, stage designer, and caricaturist. His drawings and caricatures for *Vanity Fair* and the *New Yorker* are superb examples of his early work. He also was a noted muralist and lithographer. In the late 1920s he became interested in ethnology. His first major book, *The Island of Bali,* appeared in 1937. He later wrote three excellent studies of the life and art of the American Indians, *Mexico South* (1946), *The Eagle, the Jaguar, and the Serpent* (1954), and *Indian Art of Mexico and Central America* (1957).

covenant (kŭv'ənənt), agreement entered into voluntarily by two or more parties to do or refrain from doing certain acts. In the Bible and in theology the covenant is the agreement or engagement of God with man as revealed in the Scriptures. In law a covenant is a contract under seal or an agreement by deed. In Scottish history the various pacts among the religious opponents of episcopacy were called covenants; those who agreed to the pacts were the COVENANTERS. The idea of the covenant between God of Israel and His people is fundamental to the religion of the Old Testament. God promised man specific good if man gave God the obedience and love due Him. In the covenant of God and Noah, He agreed never again to destroy man by a flood and set the rainbow in the sky as the sign of the covenant. Gen. 9. The covenants with Abraham, Isaac, and Jacob established Israel as God's chosen people and promised Canaan to them. Gen. 17; 26.1–5; 28.10–15; 32.24–32. The culmination of God's covenants with Israel comes in His promises and delivery of the Law of Moses. This provides the theme of Exodus, Leviticus, Numbers, and Deuteronomy. The great covenant with Israel is called in Christian theology the Old Covenant, because Jesus is believed to have come to fulfill it and set up a new and better covenant. Mat. 5.17, 18; Gal. 4; Heb. 8–10. This theology is behind the conventional names of the two parts of the Bible; for *testament* in the expressions "Old Testament" and "New Testament" is derived from a Latin mistranslation of a Greek word used in the Septuagint for *covenant.* In Protestant theology the covenant is especially prominent in the teaching of Johannes COCCEIUS. In English common law, covenants are agreements entered into by deed. One of the parties promises to perform or not to perform certain acts, or states that something has or will be done, or has not or will not be done. Covenants are bound by the same rules as other contracts and are variously classified. There are affirmative, alternative, auxiliary, collateral, concurrent, declarative, dependent, executory, express, and independent covenants, and covenants in law are covenants for title, covenants of seizin, covenants of warranty, and others. The express promise contained in a covenant is its most characteristic feature and distinguishes it from a bond, which is a simple record of indebtedness. The sealing and delivery of a covenant is an essential element of its validity. The covenantor is the party bound to perform the stipulation of a covenant; the covenantee is the party in whose favor the covenant is made.

Covenanters (kəvənăn'tərz), in Scottish history, groups of Presbyterians bound by oath to sustain each other in the defense of their religion. The first formal Covenant was signed in 1557, signaling the beginning of the Protestant effort to seize power in Scotland. It was renewed thereafter at times of crisis, most notably in the 17th cent. The National Covenant of 1638 aimed to unite the Scots in opposition to the episcopal innovations of King Charles I and William LAUD, especially the use of the English Book of Common Prayer. The Covenanters successfully resisted the king's armies in the BISHOPS' WARS (1639–40). In the ENGLISH CIVIL WAR they supported the parliamentary party only after the English Parliament had accepted (1643) the Solemn League and Covenant, which provided for the establishment of a Presbyterian state church in England and Ireland as well as in Scotland. After the first civil war, however, the Independents in the English army secured control of affairs and prevented implementation of the Covenant. The Scots, therefore, concluded the agreement known as the "Engagement" with Charles I, by which the king agreed to establish Presbyterianism in England if restored to the throne. As a result, the Covenanters fought for Charles I in the second civil war and, after his execution (1649), they fought for Charles II, who also subscribed (1650) to the Solemn League and Covenant. They were subdued, however, by Oliver Cromwell's conquest of Scotland (1650–51). After the Restoration (1660), Charles II resumed his father's effort to impose episcopacy in Scotland. The Covenanters were subjected to alternate attempts to conciliate them and to hunt them down. The result was a series of new compacts of resistance among them and new attempts to suppress them. A rebellion in 1679, which culminated in a rout at Bothwell Bridge, was met with harsh repression, as was the resistance of Richard CAMERON and his followers, who issued the Sanquhar Declaration in 1680. The troubles ended with the Glorious Revolution of 1688, which restored the Presbyterian Church in Scotland. See studies by J. K. Hewison (1908) and J. D. Douglas (1964).

Covent Garden (kŭv'ənt), area in London containing the city's principal fruit and garden market and the Royal Opera. The market was established in 1671 by Charles II on the site of the abbot of Westminster's convent garden, from which the present area's name is derived. In 1974 the entire market was removed to a new site at Nine Elms on the South Bank of the Thames near Vauxhall. The Royal Opera was erected on the site of the Theatre Royal built in 1732 by John RICH and later managed by the KEMBLE family. After being repaired and enlarged in 1787, the theater burned down in 1808 and was replaced, only to burn down again in 1856. It was rebuilt in 1858 to house opera and ballet. The Royal Ballet began performing at the Royal Opera in the spring of 1946. See studies by E. B. Chancellor (1930), Harold Rosenthal (1958), and Clemence Dane (1964).

Coventry (kŏv'əntrē), county borough (1971 pop. 334,839), Warwickshire, central England. It is an industrial center noted for automobile production; tractors, airplanes, machine tools, synthetic textiles, electrical equipment, and engineering products are also made. Lady GODIVA and her husband founded a Benedictine abbey in the town in 1043. By the 14th cent. Coventry, a flourishing market and textile-weaving town, was one of the five largest towns in England. The entire central portion of Coventry, including the 14th-century Cathedral of St. Michael, was destroyed in an 11-hour air raid in Nov., 1940. A new cathedral, alongside the ruins of the old one, was completed in 1962. Of interest are a statue of Lady Godiva; St. Mary's Hall (1340–42, with 15th-century additions); Holy Trinity Church (13th cent.), with a spire 237 ft (72 m) high; the spire (230 ft/70 m high) of Christ Church; and Ford's Hospital, a restored Tudor almshouse. Coventry's educational institutions include the Univ. of Warwick, Lancaster College of Technology, Coventry College—a teacher training school, and two old public schools. In 1974, Coventry became part of the new metropolitan county of West Midlands.

Coventry, town (1970 pop. 22,947), Kent co., W R.I.; settled 1643, set off from Warwick and inc. 1741. Formerly a noted lace center, it still has textile industries, but today glass, chemicals, and pharmaceuticals are also important. Coventry's many historic structures include the Payne house (1668) and Nathanael Greene's homestead (1770).

Coventry Plays: see MIRACLE PLAY.

cover crop, green temporary crop grown to prevent or reduce erosion and to improve the soil by building up its organic content. Green-manure crops are usually classed as cover crops. In orchards a cover crop is sometimes used to check the growth of some fruits when they reach maturity by supplying a plant that will compete with the tree for the nutriment in the soil. Cover crops are often the first means used to rehabilitate land that has become run down as the result of poor farming practices and neglect. Leguminous plants (e.g., clovers, vetches, and soybeans) and nonleguminous (e.g., rye, barley, wheat, and turnips) are used. See CATCH CROP.

Coverdale, Miles, 1488–1569, English translator of the BIBLE, educated at Cambridge. Coverdale was ordained (1514) and entered the house of Augustinian friars at Cambridge. He became an advocate of ecclesiastical reform, and his preaching against confession and images forced him to reside abroad. In 1535, Coverdale published an English translation of the entire Bible, probably largely with the aid of German versions, Tyndale's Pentateuch and New

Testament, and the Vulgate. He was a principal collaborator in the Great Bible (1539) and edited that of 1540, known as Cranmer's Bible. On the fall (1540) of Thomas Cromwell, Coverdale again went to the Continent, but he returned (1548) and enjoyed high favor under Edward VI, serving as bishop of Exeter from 1551 to 1553. On Mary's accession he lost his bishopric and again left England. After Elizabeth's succession, he resumed his life in England, where he was widely known for his eloquent sermons and addresses. Coverdale was rector of St. Magnus, London Bridge, from 1563 to 1566. See his writings and letters (ed. by George Pearson, 2 vol., 1844–46); Henry Guppy, *Miles Coverdale and the English Bible* (1935).

covered wagon: see CONESTOGA WAGON; PRAIRIE SCHOONER.

Covilhã (ko͞ovēlyəN'), town (1970 municipal pop. 60,768), E central Portugal, in Beira Baixa. It had a famous fair in medieval times and is still a trade center as well as a textile milling town.

Covina (kōvē'nə), city (1970 pop. 30,380), Los Angeles co., S Calif.; inc. 1901. Citrus fruits are processed, and medical supplies and fabricated-metal products are made. The area was settled in 1842, citrus crops were introduced in 1886, and the citrus industry reached its peak in the 1930s when Covina was one of the world's largest producers.

Covington. **1** City (1970 pop. 10,267), seat of Newton co., N central Ga.; inc. 1854. It is a processing and market center in a cotton area. Natural and synthetic textiles are manufactured in the city. Points of interest include antebellum homes spared by Sherman in his march (1864) to the sea. **2** City (1970 pop. 52,535), seat of Kenton co., N central Ky., at the confluence of the Ohio and Licking rivers; inc. 1815. It is an industrial center, connected by bridges with Cincinnati across the Ohio and Newton across the Licking. There are tobacco and meat-packing establishments and plants making a great variety of products, including paper, sheet metal, metal fabricators, machine tools, and electrical equipment. A ferry and a tavern were established there c.1801, and the city was first settled in 1812. Among its points of interest are the suspension bridge to Cincinnati (designed by J. A. Roebling); Devou Park, with a museum of natural history; Cathedral Basilica of the Assumption; the tiny Monte Casino chapel; the Garden of Hope; and the Carneal House (1815). Frank Duveneck was born in Covington, and the city has a museum devoted to his paintings. The artist and naturalist Daniel Carter Beard was also born in Covington and lived there. Thomas More College (formerly Villa Madonna College) is in nearby Fort Mitchell. The greater Cincinnati airport is also in the area. **3** City (1970 pop. 10,060), seat of Alleghany co. but politically independent, W central Va., near the W. Va. line, on the Jackson River in a valley surrounded by mountains; laid out 1819, inc. as a city 1952. Paper, furniture, chemical fibers, and film are manufactured in Covington. Nearby Humpback Bridge (built 1835, used until 1929) is the only covered bridge of its construction left in the United States. There is excellent hunting and fishing in the area, and a state park is nearby.

cow: see CATTLE; DAIRYING.

Cowansville, town (1971 pop. 11,920), S Que., Canada, on the Yamaska River, SE of Montreal. It is a manufacturing town producing textiles, furniture, electronic equipment, and chemicals.

Coward, Sir Noel, 1899–1973, English playwright, actor, composer, and director, b. Teddington. Onstage from the age of 12, Coward gained prominence in 1924 acting in his *Vortex.* His name soon became synonymous with urbanity, sophistication, incomparable wit, and a certain sentimentality. The characters in his 27 plays are usually rich, vain, spoiled, and snobbish couples, who express themselves with a brittle badinage that covers the suffering they undergo together or apart. Coward's success was such that five of his plays were hits in London in 1925. The best-known of his theater works include *Fallen Angels* (1925), *Hay Fever* (1925), *Easy Virtue* (1925), *Private Lives* (1930), *Cavalcade* (1931), *Design for Living* (1932), *Conversation Piece* (1934), and *Blithe Spirit* (1941). He also wrote revues, sketches, musical comedies, operettas, and 281 songs. His major films include the romantic masterpiece *Brief Encounter* (1946) and the patriotic film *In Which We Serve* (1942), for which he was director, actor, and producer. Coward wrote short stories and a novel, *Pomp and Circumstance* (1960), performed in cabaret, made recordings, and wrote three autobiographical works, *Present Indicative* (1937), *Middle East Diary* (1945), and *Future Indefinite* (1954). His *Song at Twilight* (1966) is an autobiographical drama about the agony of an aging homosexual writer who has had to write dishonestly about himself. The play initiated a tremendous revival of interest in Coward's works. See biographies by Robert Greacen (1954), Sheridan Morley (1969), and Charles Castle (1973).

cowbird, New World bird of the blackbird and oriole (hangnest) family. The male eastern, or common, cowbird is glossy black, about 8 in. (20 cm) long, with a brown head and breast; the female is gray. Most cowbirds lay their eggs in the nests of smaller bird species, victimizing especially vireos, sparrows, and flycatchers. Sometimes the alien egg is ejected or buried under a new nest floor or the nest is abandoned, but usually the host bird incubates the egg and feeds the voracious intruder while its smaller offspring are starved or crowded out. Cowbirds eat seeds but feed chiefly on insects, following behind grazing cattle in order to capture the insects stirred up in this way—hence the name *cowbird* and the earlier name *buffalo bird.* Related birds are the bronzed, the California, the dwarf, the Nevada, and the red-eyed cowbirds. Cowbirds are classified in the phylum CHORDATA, subphylum Vertebrata, class Aves, order Passeriformes, family Icteridae.

cowboys, in American history. **1** Tory marauders, adherents to the British cause in the American Revolution, who fought in the contested area of Westchester co., N.Y. Their opposite numbers, who favored the Revolutionary cause and who operated in the same territory at the same period, were called skinners. **2** Mounted men employed as herders on cattle ranches of the American West. They were more important and picturesque in the days before the vast ranches were fenced, when their duties consisted of driving cattle to pasture and water, branding them at the roundup, protecting them from wild animals and thieves, and driving them to the shipping point. See RODEO. See Emerson Hough, *The Story of the Cowboy* (1897, repr. 1970); J. B. Frantz and J. E. Choate, Jr., *The American Cowboy, the Myth and the Reality* (1955, repr. 1968); John A. Lomax and Alan Lomax, *Cowboy Songs and Other Frontier Ballads* (rev. ed. 1966).

Cowell, Henry Dixon, 1897–1965, American composer and pianist, b. Menlo Park, Calif., largely self-educated, studied musicology in Berlin (1931–32). He experimented with new musical resources; in his piano compositions he introduced the tone cluster, played with the arm or the fist, and wrote compositions to be played directly on the strings of the piano. Cowell founded (1927) *New Music,* a quarterly for the publication of music by contemporary American and European composers. In 1932, with the help of Leon Theremin, he invented the rhythmicon, a device that produces various rhythms and cross-rhythms mechanically, for which he wrote a concerto (1932). An interest in counterpoint produced the five *Hymns and Fuguing Tunes* (1941–45). He also wrote symphonies, piano pieces, band music, and vocal and chamber music, and edited *American Composers on American Music* (1933). See his *New Musical Resources* (1930, repr. 1969).

Cowes (kouz), urban district (1971 pop. 18,895), Isle of Wight, S England. A resort town with lovely promenades, it is also the main port of the island and the center for yachting in the British Isles. Cowes became the headquarters of the Royal Yacht Club in 1838, and fashionable regattas are held annually. Industries include shipbuilding and aircraft works. Queen Victoria died in Osborne House in East Cowes. In 1974, Cowes became part of the new nonmetropolitan county of Isle of Wight.

cowfish: see TRUNKFISH.

Cowl, Jane, 1890–1950, American actress, playwright, and producer, b. Boston, Mass. Cowl's stage career began in 1903 with *Sweet Kitty Bellairs.* Between 1917 and 1935 she was a leading lady nearly every season, appearing in *The Road to Rome, Romeo and Juliet, Lilac Time,* and *Smilin' Through,* among others. Cowl coauthored six successful plays and performed on radio, in films (e.g., *The Garden of Lies,* 1915, and *Payment on Demand,* 1950), and on television.

Cowley, Abraham (ko͞o'lē, kou'-), 1618–67, one of the English METAPHYSICAL POETS. He published his first volume of verse, *Poetical Blossoms* (1633), when he was 15. While a student at Cambridge, Cowley wrote three plays and began the scriptural epic *Davideis* (1656), in which he developed the use of the couplet as a vehicle for narrative verse. As a result of the Puritan uprising he left Cambridge and in 1656 went to France, where he served as secretary and royalist agent for Queen Henrietta Maria. Cowley's principal works include *The Mistress* (1647), a love cycle written in the manner of John Donne; *Poems* (1656), including the Pindaric odes and the elegies on Richard Crashaw and William Hervey; and *Verses on Several Occasions* (1663), including "To the Royal Society," an ode recalling his earlier prose tract *Proposition for the Advancement of Experimental Philosophy* (1661). See Samuel Johnson's essay in *Lives of the English Poets* (1778); biographies by A. H. Nethercot (1931, repr. 1967) and J. G. Taaffe (1972); study by R. B. Hinman (1960).

Cowley, Hannah, 1743–1809, English poet and dramatist. One of the DELLA-CRUSCANS, she contributed under the name Alma Matilda sentimental verse to the *World.* Her most successful comedy was *The Belle's Stratagem* (produced in 1780).

Cowley, Malcolm (kou'lē), 1898–, American critic and poet, b. Belsano, Pa., grad. Harvard, 1920. He lived abroad in the 1920s and knew many writers of the "lost generation," about whom he wrote in *Exile's Return* (1934) and *Second Flowering* (1973). For many years he wrote a book-review column for the *New Republic.* His works include *The Blue Juniata* (1927) and *A Dry Season* (1942), poems; *The Literary Situation* (1954), a critical analysis; and *Many Windowed Houses: Collected Essays on Writers and Writing* (1970).

cow lily: see WATER LILY.

Cowloon: see HONG KONG.

cowpea, black-eyed pea, or **black-eyed bean,** annual leguminous plant (*Vigna sinensis*) of the family Leguminosae (PULSE family). Native to the Old World, it was introduced in the early 18th cent. to the S United States, where it is now much used in Southern cooking and, especially, as a CATCH CROP and a major forage plant. The cowpea is also grown commercially in India and China and is sometimes called China bean. Cowpeas are classified in the division MAGNOLIOPHYTA, class Magnoliopsida, order Rosales, family Leguminosae.

Cowpens National Battlefield: see NATIONAL PARKS AND MONUMENTS (table).

Cowper, William (ko͞o'pər, kou'-), 1731–1800, English poet. Physically and emotionally unfit for the professional life, he was admitted to the bar but never practiced. After a battle with insanity, Cowper retired to the country, taking refuge with the family of Mrs. Mary Unwin, whose life-long devotion to him he celebrates in "To Mary." Most of his country life was spent at Olney, where he met John Newton, the ardent evangelical preacher. He contributed to Newton's *Olney Hymns* (1779) several poems, including the two commencing "Oh for a closer walk with God" and "God moves in a mysterious way." His hymns, while expressing the hope of the new humanitarian religious revival, often gave way to religious despair and self-distrust. After Newton left Olney, Cowper, having recovered from another period of insanity, turned to writing about simple homely subjects, producing his famous long poem, *The Task* (1785). Its descriptions of the sights and sounds of country life foreshadowed 19th-century romanticism. Cowper's sweet-tempered, playful moods found a way into many of his poems, the most notable being "The Diverting History of John Gilpin." He also made a relatively unsuccessful translation of Homer (1791). After the death of Mrs. Unwin in 1796, his old malady returned, and he wrote little except the anguished poem, "The Castaway." His letters are considered among the most brilliant in English literature. See his verse and letters selected by B. Spiller (1968); biography by D. Cecil (1947); study by J. A. Roy (1914, repr. 1972).

Cowper, William Cowper, 1st Earl (ko͞o'pər), 1664?–1723, English jurist. He became lord keeper of the great seal in 1705 and in 1706 took a leading part in negotiating the union of England with Scotland. He was the first lord chancellor of Great Britain (1707–10), and presided at the trial of Henry SACHEVERELL, though he disapproved the action. He was forced out of office with the Whigs in 1710. Cowper wrote (1714) a tract on political parties to convince George I that the Whigs alone were loyal to the Glorious Revolution and the Act of Settlement. He was lord chancellor again (1714–18) and contributed much to the modern system of equity.

Cowper's gland: see REPRODUCTIVE SYSTEM.

cowpox, infectious disease of cows caused by a virus related to the virus of smallpox. Also called variola, it is characterized by pustular lesions on the teats and udder. Cowpox is transmitted by contact, inducing a mild infection of the hands in persons who milk infected cows. The fact that such persons had immunity to smallpox led Edward JENNER to attempt VACCINATION with this virus, instead of using the dangerous method of vaccinating with material from the sores of smallpox. Jenner's method was successful and is the basis of the modern vaccination against smallpox. Horses and sheep may contract a similar disease.

cowrie or **cowry** (both: kou'rē), common name applied to marine gastropods belonging to the family Cypraeidae, a well-developed family of marine snails found in the tropics. Cowries are abundant in the Indian Ocean, particularly in the East Indies and the Maldive Islands. Species of cowries inhabit the waters around S California and the warm waters southward from the SE United States. They characteristically have massive, smooth, shiny shells with striking patterns and colors. The upper surface is round and the lower flat. When alive, the cowrie's shell is usually concealed by its large mantle; as the cowrie creeps along the ocean bottom, the mantle envelops the shell. As the body grows, the inner whorls of the shell are dissolved, and the dissolved lime is then used to enlarge the outer whorl of the shell. Some shells have been used for money, e.g., those of the money cowrie, *Cypraea moneta.* The shells of various species are used also for personal adornment and in some primitive cultures indicate the rank of the wearer. The smooth brown cowrie, *Cypraea spadicea,* inhabits the protected outer coast and mud flats in S California, often as far north as Newport, Calif. The most prized cowrie for a shell collector is the tiger cowrie, *Cypraea tigris,* which grows to 4 in. (10 cm) in length and whose shell is considered by some to be the most lustrous shell of the South Pacific. Having the appearance of a tiger skin, it is white with many brown spots. Cowries are classified in the phylum MOLLUSCA, class Gastropoda, order Mesogastropoda, family Cypraeidae.

cowslip, name for plants of the BORAGE, MARSH MARIGOLD, and PRIMROSE families.

Cox, David, 1783–1859, English landscape painter, a follower of John Constable. He is best known for his watercolors of Welsh scenery, of which he produced a great number. Cox is well represented in the British and the Victoria and Albert museums and in the Birmingham Art Gallery. See biographies by N. N. Solly (1875) and William Hall (1881); study by F. G. Roe (1946).

Cox, Jacob Dolson, 1828–1900, Union general in the Civil War and American statesman, b. Montreal, of a New York City family. Admitted to the Ohio bar in 1853, he was active in organizing the new Republican party there and served (1859–61) in the state senate. Cox, made a brigadier general of volunteers early in the Civil War, served ably in the Kanawha valley and Antietam campaigns and commanded in West Virginia (1862–63) and Ohio (April–Dec., 1863). He later led a corps in the Atlanta campaign (1864), fought at Nashville (Dec., 1864), and finished his service with Sherman in North Carolina. He had risen to be a major general of volunteers and, returning home a hero, was elected governor of Ohio for the term 1866–68. Because he supported President Andrew Johnson on Reconstruction against the radical Republicans, he was not renominated. Nevertheless U. S. Grant, on assuming the presidency, made Cox his Secretary of the Interior. This was one of Grant's few good appointments. Cox, however, advocated and practiced civil service reform and opposed the President on other points, notably the move to annex Santo Domingo. The Republican spoilsmen had long been hostile to him, and in Oct., 1870, Cox resigned from the cabinet and became identified with the Liberal Republicans. He later served one term in Congress (1877–79), was dean of the Cincinnati Law School for 16 years beginning in 1881, and also served as president of the Univ. of Cincinnati from 1885 to 1889. He wrote ably on military affairs. His books include *Atlanta* (1882), *The Battle of Franklin* (1897), *The March to the Sea* (1898), and *Military Reminiscences of the Civil War* (1900). Kenyon Cox was his son.

Cox, James Middleton, 1870–1957, American political leader and journalist, b. Butler co., Ohio. After serving on the editorial staff of the Cincinnati *Enquirer,* he bought the Dayton (Ohio) *Daily News* (1898) and subsequently acquired several other papers in different states. He served in the U.S. House of Representatives (1909–13). As governor of Ohio (1913–15, 1917–21) he became prominent as a supporter of President Wilson. Nominated in 1920 as presidential candidate by the Democratic party with Franklin Delano Roosevelt as his running mate, Cox, a staunch supporter of the League of Nations, was soundly defeated by Warren G. Harding. See his autobiography, *Journey through My Years* (1946).

Cox, Kenyon, 1856–1919, American painter, draftsman, and art critic, b. Warren, Ohio. He studied in Cincinnati, at the Pennsylvania Academy of the Fine Arts, and with Carolus-Duran and Gérôme in Paris. He worked in New York City, where he became an influential teacher at the Art Students League and the National Academy of Design. His portraits, figure pieces, and murals are academic in style. He painted murals for the Library of Congress, the state capitols of Iowa and Minnesota, and the public library of Winona, Minn. His portrait of Saint-Gaudens is in the Metropolitan Museum. Cox's writings on art include *Old Masters and New* (1905), *The Classic Point of View* (1911), and *Concerning Painting* (1917).

Cox, Samuel Sullivan, 1824–89, American statesman and legislator, b. Zanesville, Ohio. He traveled widely, practiced law, and was a newspaper editor before serving (1857–65) as a Congressman from Ohio. He moved (1865) to New York City and served again (1869–85) in the U.S. Congress. Cox argued for reforms in the civil service, worked to extend the scope of the census, and championed legislation for the development of the West. After serving (1885–86) as minister to Turkey, he again entered (1886) Congress. Among his books are *A Buckeye Abroad* (1852), *Puritanism in Politics* (1863), and *Three Decades of Federal Legislation* (1885). See biography by David Lindsey (1959).

Coxe, Tench, 1755–1824, American political economist, b. Philadelphia. He entered his father's mercantile business in 1776, but after 1790, when he became assistant to Alexander Hamilton, the Secretary of the Treasury, he remained in public office, although he never attained an important office. A firm believer in a balanced national economy, he supported Hamilton in his efforts to put the finances of the country on a sound basis. Politically, however, he was Anti-Federalist. He assisted Jefferson on two reports to Congress—one on fisheries, the other on foreign commerce. In Coxe's *Enquiry into the Principles on Which a Commercial System for the United States of America Should Be Founded* (1787), he first urged the necessity of an economy balanced between agriculture and manufacturing. He advocated especially the culture and manufacture of cotton. Many of his essays are collected in his *Views of the United States* (1794). His *Statement of the Arts and Manufactures of the United States of America . . . 1810* is an official digest of the census data collected in that year. See study by Harold Hutcheson (1938).

Coxetter, Louis Mitchell (kŏk'sətər), 1818–73, Confederate privateersman and blockade-runner, b. Nova Scotia. He settled in Charleston, S.C., and in the Civil War he captained the ship *Jefferson Davis,* which captured 10 prizes in 1861. When, because of the increasing effectiveness of the Union blockade, profiteering declined, Coxetter turned to blockade-running, at which he was equally successful.

Coxey, Jacob Sechler (kŏk'sē), 1854–1951, American social reformer, b. Selinsgrove, Pa. He began his career as a stationary engineer, later turning to the scrap-iron business and then to sandstone quarrying in Massillon, Ohio. Interested in the problem of the unemployed, he advocated public works, financed by fiat money, as a remedy. He was Republican mayor (1931–33) of Massillon but was an unsuccessful candidate for many major public offices, including the presidency in 1932 and 1936. He was most famous, however, as the leader of **Coxey's Army,** a band of jobless men who marched to Washington, D.C., following the Panic of 1893, to petition Congress for measures that they hoped would relieve unemployment and distress. Coxey was aided by Carl Browne, a skilled agitator with curious religious notions. By wide advertising Coxey gathered more than 100 men and left Massillon with them on Easter Sunday, 1894, intending to reach Washington for a May Day demonstration. The "army," named the Commonweal of Christ by Browne, was met by crowds in every city through which it passed. It had an anticlimactic and ineffectual ending when, reaching Washington with c.500 men instead of the proclaimed 100,000, its leaders were arrested for walking on the Capitol lawn. Coxey's was only one of several industrial "armies" that in those months started from different sections of the country for the capital. See D. L. McMurry, *Coxey's Army* (1929, repr. 1970).

Coyoacán: see MEXICO, city.

coyote (kī'ōt, kīō'tē) or **prairie wolf,** small, swift WOLF, *Canis latrans,* native to W North America. It is found in deserts, prairies, open woodlands, and brush country; it is also called brush wolf. The coyote resembles a medium-sized dog, with a narrow, pointed face, long, thick, tawny fur and a black-tipped bushy tail. Adult males have a head and body length of about 35 in. (89 cm), with a 14-in. (36-cm) tail; they stand 21 in. (53 cm) at the shoulder and usually weigh about 30 lb (14 kg). The cry of the coyote, heard in the early evening, is a series of high-pitched yelps. Coyotes live in pairs, and both parents care for the young; they make their dens in roots of trees, rock crevices, or in ground burrows made by other animals. They are largely nocturnal, but are also seen in the day. They hunt alone, in pairs, or in small groups. Omnivorous feeders, they prey on a variety of small animals, sometimes cooperating to attack larger mammals; they also eat plant matter, carrion, and garbage. They can maintain a speed of 35 mi (56 km) per hour while chasing prey. Coyotes are responsible for destroying some domestic livestock, but they are valuable scavengers and destroyers of rodents. There has almost always been a bounty on coyotes somewhere in the United States, and many thousands are killed each year. Despite this, coyotes have not been reduced in number, and their range has actually increased in the past century. Common in the central and W United States, they range N to Alaska, S to Central America, and E to the Great Lakes; they are occasionally seen even in New England. They are classified in the phylum CHORDATA, subphylum Vertebrata, class Mammalia, order Carnivora, family Canidae.

Coypel (kwäpĕl'), family of French painters. **Noël Coypel,** 1628–1707, director of the Académie de France à Rome and later of the Académie royale de péinture et de sculpture in Paris, was employed on the decorations of the palaces of the Louvre, Tuileries, Fontainebleau, and Versailles. One of his best-known paintings is the *Martyrdom of St. James* (Notre-Dame de Paris). He was succeeded as director of the Académie royale by his son, **Antoine Coypel,** 1661–1722, who was made court painter in 1716. His Aeneid series, painted for the Palais-Royal, are among the foremost expressions of high baroque decoration in France. His work combined the pedantry of classical taste with the melodrama of baroque trompe-l'œil (illusionistic) effects. He was also an accomplished etcher.

coypu: see NUTRIA.

Coysevox, Antoine (äNtwän' kwäzvō'), 1640–1720, French sculptor. He enjoyed the patronage of Louis XIV and produced a great part of the sculpture at Versailles. His *Winged Horses,* at the entrance to the Tuileries gardens, and his portrait and memorial sculptures show free, vigorous, and original treatment. The bust of Condé (Le Havre), that of Colbert (Versailles), and the tomb of Mazarin (Louvre) are notable works.

Coz (kŏz), Judahite. 1 Chron. 4.8.

Cozbi (kŏz'bī), Midianite woman whom Phinehas killed. Num. 25. 6–18.

Cozens, Alexander (kŭz'ənz), c.1717–1786, English draftsman and writer, b. Russia. Cozens is thought to have been the first principal English master to work entirely with landscape subjects. He invented a system of "blot" drawings using accidental blots on drawing paper to aid his imagination by suggesting a landscape that could be further developed. In the 1950s his work was exhibited as that of a precursor of the ABSTRACT EXPRESSIONISTS. He expounded his blot system in his treatise, *A New Method of Assisting the Invention in Drawing Original Compositions of Landscape* (c.1785). His son, **John Robert Cozens,** 1752–97, English watercolor landscape artist, is best known for his poetic paintings of the Alps and Italy. His work had an influence on both Turner and Girtin. Examples of his watercolors are in the Victoria and Albert Museum, the Tate Gallery, and the British Museum (all: London). See A. P. Oppé, *Alexander and John Robert Cozens* (1953).

Cozzens, James Gould, 1903–, American novelist, b. Chicago. His novels usually concern upper-middle-class professional men who are faced with moral dilemmas that require partial compromise with their ideals. All Cozzens's works are characterized by meticulous craftsmanship and an objective, almost clinical style. Among his important novels are *The Last Adam* (1933), *The Just and the Unjust* (1942), *Guard of Honor* (1948; Pulitzer Prize), *By Love Possessed* (1957), and *Morning, Noon, and Night* (1968).

Cr, chemical symbol of the element CHROMIUM.

crab, CRUSTACEAN with an enlarged cephalothorax covered by a broad, flat shell called the carapace. Extending from the cephalothorax are the various appendages: five pairs of legs, the first pair bearing claws (or pincers), are attached at the sides; two eyes on short, movable stalks, two short antennules, two longer antennae, and numerous mouthparts are attached at the front; at the rear the tiny abdomen is bent under the cephalothorax. Crabs are chiefly marine, but some are terrestrial for long periods. They are omnivorous; some are scavengers and others predators. The abdomen of the female, wider and flatter than that of the male, forms an apronlike structure that continuously circulates water over the eggs that are carried on her underside. The free-swimming larva, which hatches in about two weeks, is easily recognized by the large spine that projects from its carapace. After several molts, the young crab settles to the bottom and begins to take on adult features. Crabs tend to move sideways, although they are capable of locomotion in all directions. Swimming crabs have the last pair of legs flattened to form paddles; of these the BLUE CRAB of the Atlantic coast of the United States is much used for food. It is marketed as a soft-shelled crab after it has molted and before the new shell has hardened. Females of the oyster and mussel crabs live inside the shells of bivalve mollusks. Often seen scurrying about near their burrows in muddy banks are the FIDDLER CRABS, the males of which have one much enlarged claw used in defense and in courtship rituals. The sand, or ghost, crabs build burrows high up on the sand into which they seem to vanish. The sluggish, long-legged spider crabs are often disguised by the algae, barnacles, and sea anemones that attach themselves to the carapace. The giant spider crab of Japan, the largest living arthropod, has legs about 4 ft (22 cm) long and a carapace over 1 ft (30 cm) wide. The closely related kelp crabs are found in kelp beds in the Pacific. The name king crab is applied to the largest (up to 15 lb/6.8 kg) of the edible crabs, found in the N Pacific and marketed canned or frozen, and also to the HORSESHOE CRAB, which is not a crustacean. True crabs are classified in the phylum ARTHROPODA, class Crustacea, order Decapoda. See also HERMIT CRAB.

Crab, The, English name for CANCER, a CONSTELLATION.

crabapple: see APPLE.

Crabb, George, 1778–1851, English writer and philologist. He is known for his *Dictionary of English Synonyms* (1816) and his *History of English Law* (1829).

Crabbe, George, 1754–1832, English poet, b. Aldeburgh, Suffolk. After practicing medicine for a short time, he went to London in 1780, hoping to earn money by his writing. He was befriended by Edmund Burke, whose generous assistance aided in the publication of *The Library* (1781). He took orders in 1781 and held various livings, becoming rector at Trowbridge in 1814. *The Village* (1783), his most famous work, is a grim picture of rustic life, written partly in reply to Goldsmith's nostalgic *Deserted Village.* His bleak, realistic descriptions of life led Byron to call him "nature's sternest painter, yet the best." His other works include *The Parish Register* (1807), *The Borough* (1810), *Tales* (1812), and *Tales of the Hall* (1819). See biographies by his son (ed. by E. M. Forster, 1932; repr. 1949) and R. L. Chamberlain (1965); study by Arthur Pollard (1972).

crabgrass, name for any of several GRASS species of the genus *Digitaria*, and especially the species *D. sanguinalis.* Crabgrass is a common lawn weed, especially in the S and E United States. The grass has branching stems that may reach a length of 3 ft (91 cm) and flowers borne on purple spikes. It is sometimes cut for hay.

Crab Nebula, diffuse gaseous NEBULA in the constellation Taurus; cataloged as M1 or NGC 1952. It is the remnant of a SUPERNOVA observed in 1054 by the Chinese and Japanese. The nebula is a strong emitter of radio waves and X rays. At its center is an optical PULSAR.

Crabtree, Lotta, 1847–1924, American actress, b. New York City. A protégée of Lola MONTEZ, she became, while still a child, a favorite in California mining camps with her sprightly singing, dancing, and reciting. In 1867 she scored her first success in New York City in a dramatization of Dickens's *Old Curiosity Shop,* and thereafter she performed in burlesque and comic pieces, captivating large audiences. She retired in 1891. See biography by David Dempsey (1968).

cracking of petroleum: see PETROLEUM.

Craddock, Charles Egbert, pseud. of **Mary Noailles Murfree,** 1850–1922, American novelist, b. near Murfreesboro, Tenn. She wrote her best works about the mountain people of Tennessee, most notably *The Prophet of the Great Smoky Mountains* (1885). Her novels combined romantic descriptions of landscape with realistic rendering of local dialect. She also wrote a series of Southern historical novels, including *Where the Battle Was Fought* (1884). See biography by E. W. Parks (1941); study by Richard Cary (1971).

Cradock, town (1970 pop. 22,329), Cape Province, SE South Africa, on the Great Fish River; founded as a frontier outpost in 1811. It is a trade and distribution center. Cradock's Dutch Reformed church was built (1868) as a replica of St. Martin's-in-the-Fields in London. Olive Schreiner, the South African author and feminist, lived in Cradock and is buried outside the town.

crafts: see ARTS AND CRAFTS.

Craig, Edward Gordon, 1872–1966, English scene designer, producer, and actor. The son of Ellen TERRY, Gordon Craig began acting with Henry Irving's Lyceum company (1885–97). Feeling that the realism in vogue was too limiting, he turned to scene design and developed new theories. He strove for the poetic and suggestive in his designs in order to capture the essential spirit of the play. His ideas gave new freedom to scene design, although many were impractical in execution. Among his notable productions were *The Vikings* and *Much Ado about Nothing* (both in 1903 for Ellen Terry) and *Hamlet* (with the Moscow Art Theatre in 1912). At Florence, Italy, he founded (1913) the Gordon Craig School for the Art of the Theatre; he also edited a magazine, *The Mask* (1908–29). He wrote *On the Art of the Theatre* (1911, rev. ed. 1957), *The Theatre Advancing* (1921), *Scene* (1923), and biographies of Henry Irving (1930) and Ellen Terry (1931). See his memoirs (1957); biographies by his son Edward Craig (1968) and by Denis Bablet (1966).

Craig, James: see CRAIGAVON, JAMES CRAIG, 1ST VISCOUNT.

Craig, Sir James Henry, 1748–1812, British soldier, governor of Canada (1807–11), b. Gibraltar. He served in the British army from 1763, fighting in the American Revolution and later holding posts in Africa and India. In 1807 he was appointed governor of Canada and lieutenant governor of Lower Canada (Quebec). His lack of sympathy with representative government and with the French Canadians found expression in his dissolution (1809) of the assembly of Lower Canada and in the imprisonment of the sponsors of the newly established journal *Le Canadien.* His arbitrary methods served only to consolidate the position of the French Canadians. Craig was replaced for reasons of health by Sir George Prevost.

Craig, John, 1512?–1600, Scottish minister of the Reformation. He joined the Dominican order, but through reading the *Institutes* of Calvin, he adopted Protestantism. Imprisoned at Rome for heresy, he escaped (1559) and went to Vienna, where he preached before Archduke Maximilian. Returning to Scotland in 1560, he shortly became the colleague of John Knox in Edinburgh. Chaplain to James VI after 1579, he was the author of the *King's Confession* (1581), upon which was based the National Covenant of 1638. See Craig's *Short Summe of the Whole Catechisme* (1581, ed. by T. G. Law, 1883).

Craigavon, James Craig, 1st **Viscount** (krāgăv'ən), 1871–1940, Irish statesman. He worked with Edward CARSON in rousing the Protestants of Ulster against HOME RULE in the crisis preceding World War I. He organized the Ulster Volunteers to resist any attempt to enforce Home Rule. In 1921 he became prime minister of the newly established government of Northern Ireland, a position he held until his death. He was created a viscount in 1927. See biography by St. John Ervine (1949).

Craigavon, urban district (1971 pop. 12,594), Co. Armagh, S central Northern Ireland. Craigavon was designated one of the NEW TOWNS in 1962, primarily to stimulate economic growth. Rubber products are made there.

Craigie, Sir William A., 1867–1957, British lexicographer, b. Dundee, Scotland. Educated at the Univ. of St. Andrews, Craigie studied Scandinavian languages at Copenhagen before beginning in 1893 his career as lecturer at St. Andrews and as lecturer and professor at Oxford. Generally considered the foremost lexicographer of his time, he was engaged on the *New English Dictionary* (commonly called the *Oxford Dictionary*) after 1897 and was joint editor from 1901 to 1933. Craigie was persuaded to come to the United States and was the chief editor of *A Dictionary of American English on Historical Principles* (issued in parts after 1936; published as 4 vol., 1938–43). He also edited other dictionaries, made critical editions of texts, and wrote monographs and textbooks on the English language.

Craik, Dinah Maria Mulock (krāk), 1826–87, English author. She is best known for the moralistic novel *John Halifax, Gentleman* (1856) and for the children's classics *The Adventures of a Brownie* (1872) and *The Little Lame Prince* (1875).

Craiova (kräyŏ'vä), city (1970 est. pop. 175,000), SW Rumania, in Walachia, on the Jiu River, a tributary of the Danube. It is the administrative and industrial center of the agricultural and mineral-rich Oltenia region and is an important market for grain. Machine building, food processing, and the manufacture of electrical equipment are the chief industries. Built on the site of a Roman settlement, Craiova became the capital of Oltenia in 1492. It was destroyed by an earthquake in 1790 and burnt by the Turks in 1802. An agreement signed in the city in 1940 returned S Dobruja to Bulgaria. Craiova has a university (est. 1966) and other institutions of higher learning, a state philharmonic orchestra, and several museums containing prehistoric and Roman relics. The 17th-century St. Demetrius church (restored 18th cent.) and the 19th-century palace are also of interest.

crake: see RAIL.

Cram, Ralph Adams, 1863–1942, American architect, b. Hampton Falls, N.H. An ardent exponent of Gothic architecture, Cram produced many collegiate and ecclesiastical works in a neo-Gothic style. Among these are part of the reconstruction of the Cathedral of St. John the Divine in New York City; the graduate school and chapel at Princeton; and buildings at Williams, Phillips Exeter Academy, Rice Univ., and the U.S. Military Academy at West Point. After the withdrawal of B. G. GOODHUE in 1914, the architectural firm with which he was associated was known as Cram and Ferguson.

Cramer, Johann Baptist (yōhän' bäptĭst' kräm'ər), 1771–1858, German pianist and piano teacher. He studied (1779–81) with Clementi in London. From 1788 he toured as a pianist, achieving international distinction. After teaching (1832–45) in Munich and Paris, he returned to London. He wrote many sonatas and several piano concertos, but he is remembered for 84 technical studies (1804).

cramp, painful uncontrollable contraction of a muscle or group of muscles. The type that results from cold, strain, or disturbance of circulation (as experienced by swimmers) is eased by massage and the application of heat. Cramp in the abdominal or skeletal muscles brought on by hard physical exertion in extremely high temperatures (e.g., in miners, stokers, or firemen) because of loss of salt from the body during profuse perspiration can last for hours or days if untreated. Such cramps are considered to be a type of HEAT EXHAUSTION. A cool atmosphere and the replacement of salt and water orally or intravenously is required, and application of heat is not recommended. Heat cramps in persons who do heavy labor can be prevented by the addition of salt to drinking water or by taking salt tablets. Contraction of muscles in a hollow organ is known as COLIC. A stitch in the side is due to a cramp in the muscles between the ribs.

Cranach or **Kranach, Lucas** (both: lo͞o'käs krä'näkh), the Elder, 1472–1553, German painter and engraver. He settled in Wittenberg c.1504 and was court painter successively under three electors of Saxony. There he maintained a flourishing workshop and was twice burgomaster. Cranach was a friend of Luther, whose doctrine he upheld in numerous paintings and woodcuts, and he has been called the painter of the Reformation. He was a rapid and prolific painter, and the work turned out by his studio is uneven in excellence. Naïve and fanciful, often awkward in draftsmanship, it has, nonetheless, freshness and originality and a warm, rich color. His portraits are particularly successful. Among his best-known works are *Repose in Egypt* (Gemäldgalerie, Staatliche Mus., Berlin-Dahlem); *Judgment of Paris* (Staatliche Kunsthalle, Karlsruhe); *Adam and Eve* (Courtauld Inst., London); and *Crucifixion* (Weimar). This last contains figures of Luther and Cranach. His many famous protraits include those of Elector John Frederick and *Self-Portrait* (Uffizi). Cranach was also an accomplished miniaturist. He produced a few copperplates and designs for woodcuts. See study ed. by E. Ruhmer (1963). His son and pupil **Lucas Cranach,** the Younger, 1515–86, continued the tradition of his father whose workshop, signature, and popularity he inherited. Their work is often indistinguishable.

cranberry, name for low creeping evergreen BOG plants of the genus *Oxycoccus* of the family Ericaceae (HEATH family). Cranberries are considered by some botanists to be species of the blueberry genus

Vaccinium. The tart red berries are used for sauces, jellies, pies, and beverages. The European or small cranberry is found in North America, but the cranberry of commercial cultivation is the native American or large cranberry (*O.* or *V. macrocarpus*). This cranberry has been in cultivation since c.1840, chiefly in New Jersey, Massachusetts, and Wisconsin bogs that are especially prepared for annual flooding. The cranberry is prevalent on Cape Cod and is the chief export crop of Massachusetts. The serving of cranberry sauce with the Thanksgiving turkey is traditional in the United States. Other species of the genus are also called cranberry, but are of less importance. The unrelated high-bush cranberry or cranberry tree belongs to the family Caprifoliaceae (HONEYSUCKLE family). Cranberries of the heath family are classified in the division MAGNOLIOPHYTA, class Magnoliopsida, order Ericales, family Ericaceae. The family Caprifoliaceae is in the order Dipsacales.

Cranbrook, city (1971 pop. 12,000), SE British Columbia, Canada. It is a lumbering center.

Cranbrook Foundation, at Bloomfield Hills, Mich.; est. and endowed by George G. and Ellen Booth in 1927. It includes a noted academy of art, an institute of science, Christ Church (Episcopal), Brookside School (elementary; coeducational), Cranbrook School (preparatory; for boys; 1927), Kingswood School (preparatory; for girls; 1931). Most of the buildings were designed by Eliel Saarinen; many statues by Carl Milles are also there.

Crandell, Prudence, 1803–89, American educator and abolitionist, b. Hopkinton, R.I. In 1831 she opened a school for girls in Canterbury, Conn. Her decision to admit a Negro was protested, and in 1833 she decided to devote the school entirely to the education of Negro girls. She was arrested and tried, the judgment against her being reversed on appeal in 1834. In that year she gave up her work, married the Rev. Calvin Philleo, and moved to the Middle West.

Crane, Hart (Harold Hart Crane), 1899–1932, American poet, b. Garrettsville, Ohio. He published only two volumes of poetry during his lifetime, but those works established Crane as one of the most original and vital American poets of the 20th cent. His extraordinarily complex poetry, with its rich imagery, verbal ingenuity, and meticulous craftsmanship, curiously combines ecstatic optimism with a sense of haunted alienation. *White Buildings* (1926), his first collection of poems, was inspired by his experience of New York City. His most ambitious work is *The Bridge* (1930), a series of closely related long poems on the United States in which the Brooklyn Bridge serves as a mystical unifying symbol of civilization's evolution. Crane's personal life was anguished and turbulent. After an unhappy childhood during which he was torn between estranged parents, he held a variety of uninteresting jobs, always, however, returning to New York City and his writing. An alcoholic and a homosexual, he was constantly plagued by money problems and was often a severe trial to friends who tried to help him. In 1931 he won a Guggenheim Fellowship and went to Mexico to work on a long poem about Latin America; a year later, returning to the U.S., the poem not even started, he jumped overboard from his ship and was drowned. His collected poems were published in 1933. See his letters ed. by T. S. W. Lewis (1974); biographies by Philip Horton (new ed. 1957) and John Unterecker (1969); studies by H. A. Leibowitz (1968) and M. D. Uroff (1974).

Crane, Stephen, 1871–1900, American novelist, poet, and short-story writer, b. Newark, N.J. Often designated the first modern American writer, Crane is ranked among the authors who introduced realism into American literature. The 14th child of a Methodist minister, he grew up in Port Jervis, N.Y., and briefly attended Lafayette College and Syracuse Univ. He moved to New York City in 1890 and for five years lived in poverty as a free-lance writer. His first novel, *Maggie: A Girl of the Streets* (1893), a grimly realistic story of slum life, was unpopular but gained the young writer the friendship of Hamlin Garland and William Dean Howells. Crane's next novel, *The Red Badge of Courage* (1895), brought him wide and deserved fame. Set during the Civil War, the novel traces the development of a young recruit, Henry Fleming, through fear, illusion, panic, and cowardice, to a quiet, humble heroism. This remarkable account of the emotions of a soldier under fire is all the more amazing since Crane had never been in battle. On the strength of the novel he served as a foreign correspondent in Cuba and in Greece. Around 1897 he married Cora Taylor, who ran a brothel in Florida; this marriage, coupled with Crane's unorthodox personality, aroused scandalous rumors including those that he was a drug addict and a satanist. Because of this unfair slander Crane spent his last years abroad; he died of tuberculosis in Germany at the age of 28. Crane was a superb literary stylist who emphasized irony and paradox and made innovative use of imagery and symbolism. Thus, although realistic, his works are highly individual. In addition to his novels he wrote superb short stories and poems. The title stories of *The Open Boat and Other Tales* (1898) and *The Monster and Other Stories* (1899) are considered among the finest stories in English. His two books of epigrammatic free verse, *The Black Rider* (1895) and *War Is Kind* (1899), anticipated several strains of 20th-century poetry. Crane's collected works were published in 12 volumes (1925–26). See his letters, ed. by R. W. Stallman and Lillian Gilkes (1960); biographies by John Berryman (1950) and R. W. Stallman (1968); studies by D. G. Hoffman (1957), Eric Solomon (1966), Milne Holton (1972), and R. M. Weatherford, ed. (1973); bibliography by R. W. Stallman (1972).

Crane, Walter, 1845–1915, English designer, illustrator, and painter. As a painter he is grouped with the later Pre-Raphaelites, but he is better known for his illustrations of the works of Spenser and of Hawthorne's *Wonder Book* and Grimm's *Fairy Tales.* Seeking with William MORRIS to ally art with everyday life, he designed textiles, glass windows, tapestries, and house decorations. Crane's interest in socialism is expressed in his cartoons for *Commonweal* and *Justice.* In 1888 he founded the Arts and Crafts Exhibition Society of London. See his memoirs, *An Artist's Reminiscences* (1907); study by P. G. Konody (1902).

crane, large wading bird found in marshes in the Northern Hemisphere and in Africa. Although sometimes confused with herons, cranes are more closely related to rails and limpkins. Cranes are known for their loud trumpeting call that can be heard for miles and for the rhythmic dances they perform during mating season, when both males and females can be seen jumping high into the air. They eat small animals, grain, and other vegetable matter. The North American whooping crane, a white bird almost 5 ft (152 cm) tall, is nearly extinct, partly because the population increases slowly, even in protected environments; the female crane lays only two eggs per year. The sandhill crane, about 4 ft (122 cm) tall with gray plumage, is becoming rare; it winters W of the Mississippi River. The little brown crane breeds mainly in N and W North America. The Florida crane is brownish gray with a reddish, warty head. Cranes are classified in the phylum CHORDATA, subphylum Vertebrata, class Aves, order Gruiformes, family Gruidae.

crane, hoisting machine for lifting heavy loads and transferring them from one place to another, ordinarily over distances of not more than 200 ft (60 m). For longer distances a truck or trailer is apt to prove more economical; the chief advantages of a crane are its long reach and the great heights to which it can lift loads. Cranes actuated by either manual or animal power have been in use from early times. Modern cranes are of varied types and sizes; they may be actuated by steam, electricity, diesel, or hydraulic power as well as by manual power, and they are indispensable in industries where heavy materials are handled constantly. The overhead traveling crane, a type of bridge crane, is used inside buildings or in outdoor storage yards. Two or more parallel girders span its working area. Another girder, called the bridge, stretches between them and rolls along them on wheels; this girder, in turn, supports a carriage from which a lifting attachment is lowered by pulleys. On a stacking crane the pulleys are replaced by a stiff, rotating column on which a pair of forks ride up and down. The gantry crane, another type of bridge crane, has a bridge supported by vertical structures that move along tracks. Gantries are used on piers or in shipyards. The jib crane has a horizontal load-supporting boom fastened to a rotating vertical column, either attached to a wall or extending from floor to ceiling; when the column is held only at the bottom it is called a pillar crane. The derrick is a crane equipped either with a vertical mast held by struts, as on barges, or with guy wires, as in building construction. The boom is attached to the bottom of the mast by a pivot and is raised and lowered by a cable reaching from the top of the mast to the end of the boom. A crawler crane is a self-propelled crane that moves on caterpillar treads.

crane fly, true FLY resembling a mosquito, often called daddy longlegs because of its six long, delicate legs. (The HARVESTMAN, also called daddy longlegs, belongs to an unrelated order.) Most species of crane flies have a single pair of wings and slender bodies. They feed upon plant substances and frequent damp places in pastures and meadows. Crane flies belong to the phylum ARTHROPODA, class Insecta, order Diptera, family Tipulidae.

crane's-bill: see GERANIUM.

cranial index: see CEPHALIC INDEX.

cranium: see SKULL.

crank, mechanical linkage consisting of a bar attached to a pivot at one of its ends in such a way that it is capable of rotating through a complete circle about the pivot. One of the principal uses of a crank is to turn reciprocating, or back and forth, motion into rotary motion or vice versa. A bell crank is one designed to change the direction of a linear motion.

Cranmer, Thomas (krăn'mər), 1489–1556, English churchman under HENRY VIII; archbishop of Canterbury. A lecturer in divinity at Jesus College, Cambridge, he is said to have come to the attention of the king in 1529 by suggesting that Henry might further his efforts to achieve a divorce from KATHARINE OF ARAGÓN by collecting opinions in his favor from the universities. Cranmer went (1530) to Rome to argue the king's case and was (1532) an ambassador to Holy Roman Emperor Charles V. In 1533, Henry named him archbishop of Canterbury, and as soon as the appointment was confirmed by the pope, Cranmer proclaimed that Henry's marriage to Katharine was invalid. A few days later he crowned Anne BOLEYN as Henry's queen. Completely subservient to the king's will, Cranmer declared Anne's marriage invalid in 1536. He promoted Henry's marriage (1540) to Anne of Cleves and the divorce from her, and was later (1542) one of the accusers of Catherine Howard. Cranmer was strongly influenced by the German Reformation. With his friend Thomas CROMWELL, he endorsed the translation of the Bible into English and was influential in procuring a royal proclamation (1538) providing for a copy in every parish church. However, as long as Henry VIII lived, the archbishop could promote no significant doctrinal changes. The situation changed with the accession (1547) of the young EDWARD VI, and Cranmer shaped the doctrinal and liturgical transformation of the Church of England during Edward's reign. He was responsible for much of the first BOOK OF COMMON PRAYER (1549) and compiled the revised prayer book of 1552, which contains the most famous examples of Cranmer's sonorous prose, with the aid of prominent reformers from the Continent. His Forty-two Articles (1553), though never formally adopted, formed the basis of the Thirty-nine Articles (see CREED 5). Cranmer supported the claims of Lady Jane GREY after Edward's death. Upon the accession (1553) of the Roman Catholic Queen Mary I, he was tried for treason, then convicted of heresy, stripped of his preferments, and condemned. A few days before his death he recanted, but when asked to repeat the recantation in public at the stake, he refused and thrust the hand that had written it into the fire. See biographies and studies by F. C. Hutchinson (1951, repr. 1966), Theodore Maynard (1956), and J. G. Ridley (1962, repr. 1966).

crannog: see LAKE DWELLING.

Crannon, Greece: see LAMÍA.

Cranston, industrial city (1970 pop. 73,037), Providence co., central R.I., a residential suburb of Providence; inc. as a town 1754, as a city 1910. Its manufactures include machinery, chemicals, textiles, and beer. The city was named for Samuel Cranston, a colonial governor of Rhode Island. In the 19th cent. Cranston was an important textile center. The Friends Meeting House (1729) and several pre-Revolutionary buildings remain standing.

crape: see CREPE.

crape myrtle: see LOOSESTRIFE.

crappie: see SUNFISH.

craps: see DICE.

Crapsey, Adelaide (krăp'sē), 1878–1914, American poet, b. Brooklyn, N.Y., grad. Vassar, 1901; daughter of Algernon Sidney Crapsey. After teaching in girls' schools she became an instructor at Smith College. A slender volume, *Verse,* which won high praise from critics, appeared a year after her early death from tuberculosis; a new edition with 20 additional poems was issued in 1934. Her special contribution to verse form is the cinquain—a compressed five-line verse resembling the Japanese haiku in its fragile precision and expressive delicacy. See biography by M. E. Osborn (1933).

Crapsey, Algernon Sidney, 1847–1927, American Episcopal clergyman, b. Fairmont, Ohio. In 1879 he became rector of St. Andrew's Church, Rochester, N.Y., which under his administration was known for its social work. In 1906 he was expelled from the ministry for heresy because of beliefs concerning the physical being and life of Christ. His books include *Religion and Politics* (1905), *The Rise of the Working Class* (1914), *The Ways of the Gods* (1920), and the autobiographical *Last of the Heretics* (1924).

craquelure (krăklo͝or'), hairline surface cracking of paintings into characteristic patterns determined by age, climatic conditions, and the materials used in the work. Cracking was so common in works by 18th-century English painters that it became known as *craquelure anglaise.* Forgers and restorers often imitate craquelure to enhance the look of authenticity in their works.

Crashaw, Richard (krăsh'ô), 1612?–1649, one of the English METAPHYSICAL POETS. He was graduated from Cambridge in 1634 and remained there as a fellow at Peterhouse until the Puritan uprising, when he fled to the Continent (1643). Though he was the son of an ardent Puritan clergyman, by 1646 he had converted to Roman Catholicism. He served for several years as an attendant to Cardinal Palotto, who finally procured him a minor post at the shrine of Loreto, Italy, in April, 1649. Four months later Crashaw died of a fever. Although he wrote secular poetry in Latin and Greek as well as English, his fame rests on his intense religious poetry. His strange mixture of sensuality and mysticism is unusual in English literature and has been compared to the baroque art of Italy and Spain. The principal volume of his work is *Steps to the Temple* (1646), enlarged to include *Delights of the Muses* (1648). See his complete poems ed. by G. W. Williams (1972); studies by Austin Warren (1957), G. W. Williams (1963), and M. F. Bertonasco (1971).

Crassus (krăs'əs), ancient Roman family, of the plebeian Licinian gens. It produced men who achieved great note in the 2d cent. and 1st cent. B.C. One of the well-known members was **Lucius Licinius Crassus,** d. 91 B.C., a noted orator and lawyer (much admired by Cicero). He was a strict follower of constitutional forms, and he and Scaevola as consuls in 95 B.C. proposed a law—called the Licinian Law, the Lex Licinia, or the Lex Licinia Mucia—to banish from Rome Latins who had gained Roman citizenship by illegal means (or what the law set as illegal means). This greatly aggravated anti-Roman sentiment among the allies and helped bring on the Social War. **Publius Licinius Crassus,** d. 87 B.C., was consul in 97. He was the financial backer of the Roman colony of Narbo (modern Narbonne) in Gaul and achieved fame by his victories in Spain after his consulship. He was a partisan of SULLA and, after being proscribed by the followers of Marius, committed suicide. His son, **Marcus Licinius Crassus,** d. 53 B.C., was the best-known member of the family. He was a man of considerable charm and almost unbounded avarice and ambition. He was a partisan of Sulla and commanded some of Sulla's forces. He was also a highly successful dealer in real estate, and bought property that was confiscated or deserted in the period of the bloody Sullan proscriptions. He became the principal landowner in Rome by organizing his private fire brigade, buying burning houses cheap, and then putting out the fire. He gained immense prestige—along with POMPEY—for suppressing the uprising of SPARTACUS. They were both consuls together in 70 B.C., and Crassus' rivalry and jealousy of Pompey grew. He was involved in plotting against Catiline, apparently secretly encouraging the conspiracy but not directly participating in it. He and Julius CAESAR drew closer together, Crassus hoping to use Caesar's ability, Caesar (deep in debt) hoping to use Crassus' money. Caesar, seeing that he needed stronger support than Crassus, created (60 B.C.) the First Triumvirate—Crassus, Pompey, and Caesar. With Crassus' envy of Pompey and Pompey's scorn of Crassus, the arrangement worked only because of Caesar's consummate ability in handling men. Crassus seems to have backed the political maneuvers of the notorious Clodius, and trouble was stirred up between Crassus and Pompey. Caesar called both of them to Lucca, where in 56 B.C. a conference reaffirmed the alliance. Crassus and Pompey were again consuls together in 55. Crassus managed to get Syria assigned for his proconsular service in 54. Avid for military glory, he left even before his term as consul was up to undertake a campaign against the Parthians. His ambition outran his ability. After early successes, his army was completely routed at Carrhae (modern Haran) by Parthian archers in 53 B.C. Crassus in this disgrace was treacherously murdered, and Caius Cassius Longinus had difficulty in saving even the remnants of the army.

crater, circular, bowl-shaped depression on the earth's surface. (For a discussion of lunar craters, see MOON.) Many of the largest craters are formed by the impact of meteorites. Impacting at speeds in excess of 10 mi/sec (16 km/sec), a meteorite creates pressures on the order of millions of atmospheres, creating shock waves that blast out a circular hole and often destroy the meteorite. Berringer Crater, Arizona, c.¾ mi (1⅕ km) in diameter and 600 ft (180 m) deep, is probably the best-known crater of this type. Others include Chubb Crater, Quebec, Lake Bosumtwi, Ghana, and Brent Crater, Ontario. Two major impact events have occurred in the 20th cent., both in Siberia. In 1908 near Lake Baykal one occurred that caused vast destruction of timber from its blast, and the other in 1947 at Sikhote-Alin also caused great damage. Craters are also commonly formed at the surface opening, or vent, of erupting volcanoes, particularly of the type called cinder cones, where the lava is extruded rather explosively. Virtually all volcanoes display a crater, called a sink, around the vent that is believed to be a collapse feature caused by molten lava subsiding as an eruption phase diminishes. Volcanic craters formed in these ways are relatively small, usually less than 1 mi (1.6 km) in diameter, and represent only a small fraction of the cone's diameter at the base. A caldera is a much larger crater, ranging from 3 to 18 mi (5–30 km) in diameter, and represents a considerable fraction of the volcano's basal diameter. Most calderas are formed by the collapse of the central part of a cone during great eruptions. A few small calderas have been formed by explosive eruptions in which the top of a volcano was blown out. Some volcanic craters are created by a combination of these events. Formed thousands of years ago, the caldera that contains Crater Lake, Oregon, is 6 mi (9.7 km) in diameter. In recent times, caldera-producing eruptions occurred at Krakatoa, Indonesia, in 1883 and Katmai, Alaska, in 1912. See ASTROBLEME; TEKTITE; VOLCANO.

Crater Lake National Park, 160,290 acres (64,869 hectares), SW Oregon, in the Cascade Range; est. 1902. Crater Lake, 20 sq mi (52 sq km), lies in a huge pit that was created when the top of a prehistoric volcano was blown off by a violent eruption. The second-deepest lake (1,932 ft/589 m) in North America, Crater Lake is 6 mi (9.6 km) wide, lies 6,164 ft (1,879 m) above sea level, and is surrounded by cliffs that are from 500 to 2,000 ft (152–610 m) high. Having no inlet or outlet, the lake was formed by rain and snowfall, and its waters are maintained by precipitation. The lake was discovered in 1853 by prospectors, who called it Deep Blue Lake because of the intense blue of the water; it was renamed Crater Lake in 1869. A scenic highway follows the rim of the crater. Wizard Island, a cinder cone 776 ft (237 m) high, near the lake's western shore, was also formed by volcanic activity.

Craters of the Moon National Monument, 53,545 acres (21,665 hectares), S central Idaho; est. 1924. This region, composed of several closely grouped volcanoes, is suggestive of a telescopic view of the moon. Volcanic activity dating back c.20,000 years has left behind cinder cones, tree molds, craters, and other interesting formations. At one time Indians used the lava caves.

Crates (krā'tēz), fl. 449 B.C., Athenian comic poet. He is said to have introduced into comedy themes other than those of personal satire, and he was one of the first to show the comic possibilities of the drunkard. Fragments of his plays survive.

Cratinus (krətī'nəs), d. c.419 B.C., Athenian comic poet. He won the prize at the Athenian drama contest when Aristophanes competed with *The Clouds* and was regarded with Aristophanes and Eupolis as one of the greatest comic poets. He attacked Pericles violently in his plays. Fragments of his plays survive.

craton (krā'tŏn): see CONTINENT.

Craven, Avery Odelle, 1886–, American historian, b. Randolph co., N.C. He received his Ph.D. at the Univ. of Chicago in 1923 and taught at several colleges in the Midwest before he returned in 1928 to Chicago, becoming professor of American history in 1929. Craven is a leader of that school of American historians that holds that the Civil War could have been avoided. His chief works are *Soil Exhaustion as a Factor in the Agricultural History of Virginia and Maryland, 1606–1860* (1926); *Edmund Ruffin, Southerner: a Study in Secession* (1932); *The Repressible Conflict, 1830–1861* (1939); *The Coming of the Civil War* (1942, 2d ed. 1957); *The Rise of Southern Nationalism* (1953); *The Civil War in the Making 1815–1860* (1959); and *An Historian and the Civil War* (1964).

crawfish: see CRAYFISH.

Crawford, Francis Marion, 1854–1909, American novelist, b. Bagni di Lucca, Italy; son of Thomas Crawford. He was educated in the United States and Europe and lived most of his adult life in Italy. The best of his romantic novels of Italy and other countries abroad include *Saracinesca* (1887), *Sant' Ilario* (1889), and *Don Orsino* (1892). He also wrote romances set in the United States.

Crawford, Isabella Valancy, 1850–87, Canadian poet, b. Dublin, Ireland. The remote woodland region of her childhood in Upper Canada is depicted in her long, sentimental poem, "Malcolm's Katie." She died in poverty at age 37, and 20 years after her death her *Collected Poems* (1905) brought recognition of her talent.

Crawford, Joan, 1908–, American movie star, b. San Antonio, Texas, as Lucille le Sueur. Crawford began her career as a Broadway chorus dancer, and in 1926 she began making films. In 1945 she won an Academy Award for her performance in *Mildred Pierce.* Crawford was a top box office attraction for many years. Her best-known films include *Grand Hotel* (1932), *The Women* (1939), and *Humoresque* (1954). Her later films, mostly in the horror genre, include *Berserk* (1967). See her autobiographies (1962 and 1972); study by L. J. Quirk (1970).

Crawford, Ralston, 1906–, American painter, b. St. Catherine's, Ont. Crawford's paintings are marked by precise detail, flat color, and the simplification of form. His works portray the American city and industrial machinery. *Steel Foundry* (1936) and *Grain Elevators from the Bridge* (1942) are in the Whitney Museum, New York City.

Crawford, Ruth, 1901–53, American composer, b. East Liverpool, Ohio. Crawford attended music schools in Jacksonville, Fla., and Chicago. Her most frequently performed composition is a string quartet (1931). She also collected and published American folk music with her husband, the musicologist and composer Charles Seeger, father of the folk singer Pete Seeger.

Crawford, Thomas, 1813–57, American sculptor, b. New York City. He was apprenticed to a wood carver and later worked for a firm of tombstone cutters. He achieved his first success with decorations for the Capitol at Washington, which include the figure above the dome entitled *Armed Freedom,* and the bronze doors and pediment statues for the Senate wing. He designed the Washington monument, Richmond, Va., for which he executed the equestrian figure and the figures of Patrick Henry and Jefferson. A pupil of Thorvaldsen, Crawford was a leading exponent of the Greek Revival movement. He lived and worked in Rome most of his life. He married Louise Cutter Ward, sister of Julia Ward Howe. The novelist Francis Marion Crawford was their youngest son.

Crawford, William Harris, 1772–1834, American statesman, b. Amherst co., Va. (his birthplace is now in Nelson co.). He moved with his parents to South Carolina and later to Georgia. After studying law he practiced at Lexington, Va., and served (1803–7) in the state legislature. In the stormy state political battles of the time, he was the leader of the upcountry forces and allied with the followers of James Jackson and later George M. Troup, leaders of the tidewater region. In a duel Crawford killed a partisan of John Clark, head of the opposite faction, and in another duel was wounded by Clark. In the U.S. Senate (1807–13), Crawford staunchly advocated rechartering the Bank of the United States. From 1813 to 1815 he was minister to France. He was then appointed Secretary of War by President Madison, but in 1816 he was made Secretary of the Treasury, a post he held through both of Monroe's administrations. He had strong support for the presidency in 1816 but disavowed his candidacy. In the presidential election of 1824, Crawford, a leading candidate, finished third in the voting. Since no candidate received a majority of the electoral votes, the election went to the House of Representatives, and John Quincy Adams was finally chosen. Crawford later served as a judge in Georgia. See biographies by P. J. Green (1965) and C. C. Mooney (1974).

Crawford Notch, water gap in the White Mts., N central N.H., through which the Saco River flows. It is named for Abel Crawford, an early settler. The area is a state park (est. 1911).

Crawfordsville, city (1970 pop. 13,842), seat of Montgomery co., W central Ind.; inc. 1866. It is the trading center of an agricultural and dairy region. Major industries include printing and binding and the manufacture of nails and wire, plastic, and metal products. Wabash College and the Lew Wallace Study are in Crawfordsville.

Crawley, new town and urban district (1971 pop. 67,240), Sussex, SE England. Crawley was designated one of the NEW TOWNS in 1946 to alleviate overpopulation in London. There are many industries, including precision engineering. It is a regional retail shopping center. Crawley College of Further Education is there. In 1974, Crawley became part of the new nonmetropolitan county of West Sussex.

Crayer, Gaspar de (gäs'pär də krī'ər), c.1584–1669, Flemish religious and portrait painter. He was greatly influenced by Rubens. While lacking the genius of Rubens, Crayer almost rivaled him in productivity and maintained a high standard of work. His paintings are to be seen in countless Flemish provincial churches and in the museums and churches of Brussels and Ghent.

crayfish or **crawfish,** freshwater CRUSTACEAN smaller than but structurally very similar to its marine relative the LOBSTER, and found in ponds and streams in most parts of the world except Africa. Crayfish grow some 3 to 4 in. (7.6–10.2 cm) in length and are usually brownish green; some cave-dwelling forms are colorless and eyeless. They are scavengers, feeding on decayed organic matter and also on small fish. The swamp crayfish digs a burrow up to 3 ft (91 cm) deep with a water-filled cavity at the bottom in case of drought. The eggs develop while attached to the swimming legs of the female and look like miniature adults when hatched. Although crayfish are not eaten in most parts of the United States, they are consumed in areas in the Mississippi River basin and are used in the Louisiana area in a thick soup called crayfish bisque. They are agricultural pests in the Mississippi Delta area, where they feed on sprouting wheat and corn. A red-clawed species is considered a delicacy in Europe. Crayfish are classified in the phylum ARTHROPODA, class Crustacea, order Decapoda.

crayon, any drawing material available in stick form. The term includes charcoal, conte crayon, chalk, pastel, grease crayon, litho crayon, and children's wax colors. The pigment is often bound with gum tragacanth or wax, and the sticks are wrapped in paper or embedded in wood.

Crazy Horse, d. 1877, Indian chief of the Oglala SIOUX INDIANS. He was a prominent leader in the Sioux resistance to the encroachment of whites in the mineral-rich Black Hills. When Crazy Horse and his people refused to go on a reservation, troops attacked (March 17, 1876) their camp on Powder River. The great war chief was victorious in that battle as well as in his encounter with Gen. George CROOK on the Rosebud River (June 17). Crazy Horse joined SITTING BULL and GALL in defeating George Armstrong CUSTER at the battle of the Little Bighorn (June 25). In Jan., 1877, Gen. Nelson Appleton MILES attacked his camp, and Crazy Horse and his followers spent the remainder of the winter in a state of near starvation. The group, numbering about 1,000, finally surrendered at the Red Cloud agency in May. Imprisoned because of a rumor that he was planning a revolt, Crazy Horse was stabbed to death with a bayonet when attempting to escape. His bravery and skill were generally acknowledged, and he is revered by the Sioux as their greatest leader. See biographies by Mari Sandoz (1942, repr. 1955) and E. A. Brininstool (1949).

crazyweed: see LOCOWEED.

cream cup: see POPPY.

creamery: see DAIRYING.

cream of tartar, white crystalline powder. Chemically it is potassium hydrogen tartrate, $KC_4H_5O_6$, the acidic potassium salt of TARTARIC ACID. It is used as the leavening agent in baking powders. An impure form, called tartar or argol, forms naturally during the fermentation of grape juice into wine and crystallizes in the wine casks.

Crébillon, Prosper Jolyot de (prôspĕr' zhôlyō' də krābēyôN'), 1674–1762, French dramatist. His tragic melodramas, marked by violent plots, include *Idoménée* (1705), *Électre* (1708), and *Rhadamiste et Zénobie* (1711), which is considered his best. After a long retirement he was persuaded by Mme de Pompadour, who was seeking a rival to Voltaire, to write *Catilina* (1748), which was performed with great success. His son **Claude Prosper Jolyot de Crébillon,** 1707–77, wrote witty, ribald tales, notably *Les Égarements du cœur et de l'esprit* (1736) and *Le Sopha* (1742).

crèche (krĕsh, krāsh), representation of the Infant Jesus in the manger, usually surrounded by figures of Mary, Joseph, shepherds, animals, and the Wise Men; also called Christmas Crib. The crèche has been displayed in churches during the period from Christmas Eve to Jan. 6 since the Middle Ages, especially after St. Francis of Assisi instituted the custom in 1223 at Gréccio, Italy. It is a Christmas tradition in many homes. The term *crèche* is also applied to a DAY NURSERY.

Crécy (krāsē'), officially **Crécy-en-Ponthieu** (-äN-pôNtyö'), village, Somme dept., N France. A nearby forest is popular for camping. At Crécy, on Aug. 26, 1346, Edward III of England defeated Philip VI of France in the HUNDRED YEARS WAR. The French forces were armed with crossbows and, although outnumbering the English troops, were overwhelmed by the English longbows. The victory enabled the English to reach Calais. Among the combatants were Edward the Black Prince of England and the blind John of Luxembourg, king of Bohemia, who, fighting for the French, died in the battle. Crécy is also known in English as Cressy.

Credi, Lorenzo di: see LORENZO DI CREDI.

credit, granting of goods, services, or money in return for a promise of future payment. Most credit is accompanied by an INTEREST charge, which usually makes the future payment greater than an immediate payment would have been. The credit system is founded upon the lender's confidence in the borrower or in his COLLATERAL and general possessions. Credit may be classified according to the industry using it, its quality or liquidity, or the length of time for which it is extended. Basically there are two kinds, business and consumer. The chief function of business credit is the transference of capital from those who own it to those who can use it, in the expectation that the profit from its use will exceed the interest payable on the loan. Thus business credit increases the productive power of capital. Consumer credit permits the purchase of retail commodities without the use of cash or with the use of relatively little cash. It is estimated that some 90% of all wholesalers' and manufacturers' sales, and more than 30% of all retail sales are made on a credit basis. In the larger banks, credit-analysis departments determine the amount of credit that may safely be given to loan applicants. Data as to credit risk are supplied by agencies organized for that purpose. The chief agency in the United States is Dun and Bradstreet, formed by a merger (1933) of R. G. Dun & Company (1841) and the Bradstreet Company (1849). If more credit is granted than the community can liquidate, there is inflation; if too little is granted, there is deflation. A lack of business confidence may cause credit to dissolve, thereby contributing to economic crises, panics, and depressions. In BOOKKEEPING, the credit side is the side of the account on which payments are entered; hence, the term *credit* is sometimes applied to the payments themselves. See CREDIT CARD; DEBT; DEBT, PUBLIC; INSTALLMENT BUYING AND SELLING. See F. T. Juster, *Household Capital Formation and Financing, 1897–1962* (1966); W. E. Dunkman, *Money, Credit, and Banking* (1970).

credit, letter of, commercial instrument through which a bank or other financial institution instructs a correspondent institution to advance a specified sum of money to the bearer. The document is called a circular letter of credit when it is not addressed to any particular correspondent. In effect, a letter of credit is a DRAFT, save that the amount is merely stated as a maximum not to be exceeded. Letters of credit, mainly used by travelers, greatly simplify nonlocal business transactions. Those who issue such letters are usually so well known that any bank will honor the letter upon proper identification. Travelers' checks are a modified form of a letter of credit. They are issued in coupons, upon whose face a value is usually expressed in terms of the currency of a particular country. In the United States they are issued by express companies and banks. Circular letters of credit require that each payment, as it is made, be endorsed by the firm making payment so that other banks may know how much of the total credit has been used.

credit card, device used to obtain consumer credit at the time of purchasing an article or service. Credit cards may be issued by a local retailer, such as a department store, or a national retailer, such as one of the major oil companies. They may also be issued by third parties, such as a bank or group of banks, or an express or so-called travel and entertainment company. First popular in California, credit cards spread throughout the United States and much of Western Europe during the late 1960s; between 1965 and 1970 the number of such cards grew from less than 5 million to more than 50 million. Through the revolving charge plan, card holders are able to postpone payment on their purchases by accepting a monthly interest charge. Consumers may also use the major bank cards to obtain short-term personal loans. Credit card issuers get revenue from fees paid by stores that accept their cards and from interest charged on unpaid credit balances. Concern has been voiced over widespread, sometimes unsolicited, distribution of bank credit cards, costly losses and theft of cards, and possible excessive encouragement of consumer debt at high interest rates.

Crédit Mobilier of America (krĕ'dĭt mōbĭlyā', krādē'), ephemeral construction company, connected with the building of the Union Pacific RR and involved in one of the major financial scandals in American history. Oakes AMES, Thomas C. DURANT, and a few other influential stockholders of the Union Pacific organized the Crédit Mobilier under an existing Pennsylvania charter, which they took over. Acting for both the Union Pacific and for their newly created construction company, they made contracts with themselves. Oakes Ames, as head of the Crédit Mobilier, in 1867 assigned contracts to seven trustees to build the remaining 667 mi (1,074 km) of road for a total sum that brought profits variously estimated at from $7 million to $23 million. This process depleted generous congressional grants to the Union Pacific and left it under a heavy debt by the time of its completion in 1869. The scandal became political when Ames (a U.S. Representative), to forestall investigation or interference by Congress, sold or assigned shares of the Crédit Mobilier stock to members of Congress at par, although the shares were worth twice as much at the time. He wrote to Henry S. McComb, an associate, that he had placed the stock "where it will produce the most good to us" and subsequently forwarded a list of Congressmen who had received or were to receive shares. Later friction between Ames and McComb facilitated the publication of these letters in Charles A. Dana's New York *Sun* in the midst of the presidential election campaign of 1872. A subsequent investigation by Congress badly smirched the political reputations of Vice President Schuyler Colfax, Senator James W. Patterson of New Hampshire, Representative James Brooks of New York, and others—most of all, of course, Ames himself. Ames and Brooks were censured by Congress, but there were no prosecutions. See study by J. B. Crawford (1880, repr. 1969).

credit union, cooperative financial institution that makes low-interest personal loans to its members. It is usually composed of persons from the same occupational group or the same local community. Funds for lending come from the sale of shares to members and from the members' savings deposits. Cooperative banking originated in Germany in the middle of the 19th cent.; it was developed by Hermann Schulze-Delitzsch and later was particularly adapted to rural communities by F. W. Raiffeisen. In the United States, the Credit Union National Association (founded 1934) has been instrumental in organizing credit unions. Credit unions are important because they provide loans to blue-collar workers and small farmers, who would otherwise have difficulty securing credit at reasonable interest rates. Under provisions of the Credit Union Act of 1934, U.S. credit unions are chartered by their respective states or by the Federal government. See R. F. Bergengren, *Credit Union, North America* (1940); Jack Dublin, *Credit Unions: Theory and Practice* (2d ed. 1971); J. C. Moody and G. C. Fite, *The Credit Union Movement* (1971).

creed [Lat. *credo*=I believe], summary of basic doctrines of faith. The following are historically important Christian creeds. **1** The Nicene Creed, beginning, "I believe in one God the Father Almighty, maker of heaven and earth, and of all things visible and invisible, and in one Lord Jesus Christ . . . ." It is usually described as a revision by the First Council of Constantinople (381) of the creed adopted at Nicaea in 325, although there are good grounds for the belief that it represents substantially a creed written or used by Eusebius of Caesarea. In the Western Church since the 9th cent. it has differed from the original by the addition of the *Filioque* clause: "And in the Holy Ghost . . . Who proceedeth from the Father *and the Son* . . . ." ("qui ex Patre *Filioque* procedit . . . ."). Over this addition there has been a long controversy between the Orthodox Eastern and Roman Catholic churches. The Nicene Creed is an official creed of Orthodox Eastern, Roman Catholic, and some Protestant churches. **2** The ATHANASIAN

CREED, which is a partial statement of doctrine dealing especially with the Trinity and the Incarnation. **3** The Apostles' Creed, beginning, "I believe in God the Father Almighty, Creator of heaven and earth. And in Jesus Christ . . . ." It does not appear in its present form before 650, but its predecessors probably arose in Rome in the 2d or 3d cent. It has two material differences from the Nicene Creed: the phrase, "He descended into hell," is omitted in the Nicene, and the words "resurrection of the body" are changed to "resurrection of the dead" in the Nicene. It is used by Roman Catholics at various daily services and at baptism; it is also much used by Protestants. **4** The Augsburg Confession (1530), the official statement of the Lutheran churches. It was mainly the work of Philip Melanchthon and was endorsed by Martin Luther for the Diet of Augsburg. **5** The Thirty-nine Articles, which are official in the Church of England. They date in their present form from Elizabeth I's reign, when they were written by a group of bishops. They are Calvinistic in theological emphasis and enounce clearly the royal supremacy in the Church of England. They are included, with occasional modifications, in the prayer books of other churches of the Anglican Communion, including that of the Protestant Episcopal Church of the United States. **6** The Westminster Confession (1645-47), the most celebrated pronouncement of English-speaking Calvinism. It is official in the Church of Scotland, with occasional changes in most of its daughter churches (usually Presbyterian), and among Congregationalists. See P. T. Fuhrmann, *Introduction to the Great Creeds of the Church* (1960); J. H. Leith, *Creeds of the Churches* (1963, repr. 1973).

Cree Indians, North American Indians whose language belongs to the Algonquian branch of the Algonquian-Wakashan linguistic stock (see AMERICAN INDIAN LANGUAGES). They formerly inhabited Manitoba S of the Churchill River. Members of one branch of the Cree, allying themselves with the Siouan Assiniboin Indians, moved southwestward into buffalo territory and became the Plains Cree. It is probable that they introduced the method of hunting buffalo by driving them into enclosures, since the Woodland Cree used this method in hunting deer. The culture and language of the Woodland Cree greatly resembles that of the Ojibwa Indians. A warlike tribe, the Cree were nevertheless friendly toward French and English fur traders, and their history is closely connected with the activities of the Hudson's Bay and the North West companies. They were powerful in the late 18th cent. until smallpox drastically reduced their population. See Leonard Mason, *The Swampy Cree* (1967).

Creek Indians, North American Indian confederacy. The peoples forming it were mostly of the Muskogean branch of the Hokan-Siouan linguistic stock (see AMERICAN INDIAN LANGUAGES). The Creek received their name from early white traders because so many of their villages were located at rivers and creeks. They lived primarily in Alabama and Georgia and were settled, agricultural people. There were more than 50 towns, generally called tribes, in the confederacy, which was formed chiefly for protection against the tribes to the north. Certain villages were set aside for war ceremonies, others for peace celebrations. Each had its annual green corn dance. This festival was a time for renewing social ties and was a period of amnesty for criminals, except murderers. The Creek Confederacy was not ruled by a permanent central government. The structure was a combination of democratic and communistic principles. Decisions by the national council were not binding on towns or individuals who wished to dissent. Nevertheless, civil strife was almost unknown among them. Under this system there was no private ownership of land, although crops were privately owned to a degree. Each owner was required to contribute a certain portion for public use. The Creek impressed the early white men (Hernando De Soto saw them in 1540) by their height, their proud bearing, and their love of ornament. They were hostile to the Spanish and therefore friendly to the British in colonial days, but, frightened by white encroachment and fired by the teachings of the Shawnee chief TECUMSEH, they rebelled in the Creek War of 1813-14. They massacred a large number of whites and blacks at Fort Mims, and Andrew Jackson won part of his reputation by defeating them at the battle of Horseshoe Bend. By a treaty signed in 1814 the Creek ceded approximately two thirds of their land to the United States, and subsequent cessions further reduced their holdings. Eventually they were moved to the Indian Territory, where they became one of the Five Civilized Tribes. A treaty signed by the confederacy in 1889 permitted white settlement of their lands, and there was great bitterness among the Creek. By the early 1970s there were some 17,000 Creek, most of them living in Oklahoma. See J. R. Swanton, *The Early History of the Creek Indians* (1922) and *Social Origins and Social Usages of the Indians of the Creek Confederacy* (1928, repr. 1970); Grant Foreman, *The Five Civilized Tribes* (new ed. 1953, repr. 1966); D. H. Corkran, *The Creek Frontier, 1540-1783* (1967).

Creeley, Robert, 1926-, American poet, b. Arlington, Mass. He has lived and worked in Europe and Latin America and taught English at various universities in the United States. For a time he was editor of the *Black Mountain Review*. Creeley's poems have an effect of purity and elegance, with their intentional reticence, brevity of development, and spare lyricism. His works include *The Island* (1963), a novel; *Poems: 1950-1965* (1965); *Selected Writings* (1966); and *Pieces* (1969).

creeper, common name for members of a family of small, inconspicuous birds related to wrens and nuthatches. They are found in wooded regions of the temperate Northern Hemisphere. A creeper spirals up a tree trunk using its long, stiff tail as a prop and searches out minute insects with its long, downward-curved beak; it then swoops to the base of another tree to begin again. The most widely distributed member of the family is the brown creeper, *Certhia familiaris,* found in North America and Eurasia. It is 5 in. (13 cm) long, brown above and white below. Other North American creepers are the Rocky Mt., Sierra, and California creepers. Some WARBLERS are also called creepers, e.g., the honey creeper. Creepers are classified in the phylum CHORDATA, subphylum Vertebrata, class Aves, order Passeriformes, family Certhiidae.

Creevey, Thomas (krē'vē), 1768-1838, English diarist. His journals and letters record, from the viewpoint of a Whig member of Parliament and minor officeholder, the history and manners of the late Georgian period. See the edition by John Gore (1948).

Creighton, Mandell (măn'dəl krī'tən), 1843-1901, British historian and churchman. He was professor of ecclesiastical history at Cambridge from 1884 until his appointment (1891) as bishop of Peterborough. In 1896 he was made bishop of London. He was a founder of the *English Historical Review* and wrote biographies of Cardinal Wolsey, Queen Elizabeth I, and Simon de Montfort. His masterwork was his *History of the Papacy during the Period of the Reformation* (5 vol., 1882-94; new ed., with title *History of the Papacy from the Great Schism to the Sack of Rome,* 6 vol., 1897; repr. 1968). See biographies by his wife, Louise Creighton (2 vol., 1904), and W. G. Fallows (1964).

cremation, disposal of a corpse by fire. It is an ancient and widespread practice, second only to BURIAL. Although cremation was not practiced in ancient China or Egypt because of religious beliefs, it was noted in Greece as early as 1000 B.C. and was the predominant mode of disposition by the time of Homer. Until the advent of Christianity as the dominant religion in the latter part of the Roman civilization, cremation was widely accepted. Its use is often related to a belief in the properties of fire as a purifying agent. Its object may also be to light the way of the deceased to another world, or to prevent the return of the dead. More practical considerations include the fear of depredation by enemies and, in the modern world, the shortage of land in urban areas. The earliest known method of cremation is the log pyre. In more elaborate practices, pitch and gums are added to the wood. In modern crematories the corpse is exposed not to flames but to intense heat that reduces the body to ashes. Disposal of the ashes varies in different parts of the world. Hindus, for whom cremation is the typical form of disposal, place them in urns or put them in a river, preferably the sacred Ganges. Other methods include burial or scattering. In the Western world the practice of cremation gained new favor with the rise of large cities and of the health hazard associated with crowded cemeteries. In the late 19th cent. the practice was legalized in several European countries and the first crematory in the United States was built. Cremation is expressly forbidden by the Roman Catholic Church. See SUTTEE. For bibliography see FUNERAL CUSTOMS.

Crémazie, (Joseph) Octave (zhôzĕf' ôktäv' krāmäzē'), 1822-79, French Canadian poet, b. Quebec, considered the father of French Canadian poetry. With his brothers he was proprietor of a Quebec bookshop, the gathering place for a literary group that included such figures as F. X. GARNEAU and H. R. CASGRAIN. He and his friends founded a monthly magazine, *Les Soirées canadiennes,* devoted to the perpetuation of French Canadian folklore. In 1855 his poem "Le Vieux Soldat canadien" appeared, bringing Crémazie instant fame. His subsequent poems, which show the influence of French romanticism, are filled with patriotic feeling. In 1862 the poet suffered business difficulties and fled to France, where he lived in poverty under an assumed name. He wrote a journal of the siege of Paris (1870) and died at Le Havre. See his *Œuvres complètes* (1883).

crème de menthe (krĕm də mĭnt, Fr. krĕm də mäNt), a mint-flavored LIQUEUR, either green or white, and often served with finely crushed ice.

Cremer, Sir William Randal (krē'mər), 1828-1908, English pacifist. At first active in trade unionism, he gradually expanded his work and interests, becoming one of the most active advocates of international arbitration. In 1871 he became secretary of the Workmen's Peace Association, a position he held until his death. For his efforts in the cause of international arbitration Cremer was awarded the 1903 Nobel Peace Prize. He gave most of the stipend in trust to the International Arbitration League. He was knighted in 1907. See biography by Howard Evans (1909, repr. 1973).

Crémieux, (Isaac) Adolphe (ēsäk' ädôlf' krāmyö'), 1796-1880, Jewish-French statesman and political writer. A lawyer, he served briefly as minister of justice in the provisional government of 1848 after the overthrow of King Louis Philippe. He supported Louis Napoleon (later Napoleon III) for president, but opposed his coup d'etat (Dec., 1851) and as a result was imprisoned temporarily in 1851. In 1870, after Napoleon III's fall, he became minister of justice in the government of national defense. In this position he eliminated the death penalty for political offenders, abolished slavery in the colonies, and extended full French citizenship rights to the Jews of Algeria. He was president (1876) of the Alliance Israélite Universelle, through which he advocated international Jewish emancipation and founded Jewish schools in Cairo and Alexandria.

Cremin, Lawrence Arthur, 1925-, American educator and historian, b. New York City. He received his Ph.D. from Columbia in 1949 and began teaching at Teachers College, Columbia. He became a member of the history department at Columbia in 1961. In that year Cremin also became Frederick A. P. Barnard professor of education at Teachers College, and in 1974 he was named president of the college. An expert in the field of American educational history, he was commissioned by the U.S. Office of Education to write a comprehensive history of education in the United States. The first volume, *American Education: The Colonial Experience,* appeared in 1970. His other works include *Transformation of the School* (1961) and *The Genius of American Education* (1965).

Cremona (krĭmō'nə, Ital. krāmô'nä), city (1971 pop. 81,983), capital of Cremona prov., Lombardy, N Italy, on the Po River. It is an agricultural market and an industrial center. Originally (3d cent. B.C.) a Roman colony, Cremona was in the Middle Ages an independent commune frequently at war with Milan until its surrender to that city in 1344. It was known in the Middle Ages as a center of learning, in the late Renaissance for a school of painting founded (16th cent.) by Giulio CAMPI, and later (17th-18th cent.) for the violins made by the AMATI, the GUARNERI, the STRADIVARI, and their successors. The cathedral (12th-16th cent.), the tall campanile, the baptistery, the city hall (13th cent.), and the Soldiers' Loggia (13th cent.) adorn Cremona's impressive main square.

creole (crē'ōl), Span. *criollo* (crēōl'yō) [probably from *crío*=child], term originally applied in West Indies to the native-born descendants of the Spanish conquerors. The term has since been applied to certain descendants in the West Indies and the American continents of French, Portuguese, and Spanish settlers. The creoles were distinguished from the natives, the Negroes, and from people born in Europe. A sharp distinction of interest always lay between the creoles, whose chief devotion was to the colony, and the foreign-born officials, whose devotion was to the mother country. Never precise, the term acquired various meanings in different countries. It has biological and cultural connotations. The term was early adopted in the United States in Louisiana, where it is still used to distinguish the descendants of the original French settlers from the Cajuns, who are at least partially descended from the Acadian exiles. The word is also commonly applied to things native to the New

World, such as creole cuisine and creole horses. The term is also used in places distant from the Americas, such as the island of Mauritius, but there it has lost much of its original meaning. The picturesque life of the Louisiana creoles has been ably depicted in the works of Lafcadio Hearn, George Washington Cable, and Grace King. See F. J. Woods, *Marginality and Identity* (1972).

creole language (krēōl'), any language that began as a PIDGIN but was later adopted as the mother tongue by a people in place of the original mother tongue or tongues. Examples are the GULLAH of South Carolina and Georgia (based on English), the creole of Haiti (based on French), and the Papiamento of Curaçao (developed from pidgin Spanish and Portuguese).

Creon (krē'ŏn), a name given to several minor legendary Greek kings. In the legend of Oedipus, Creon is the brother of Jocasta and after the death of Oedipus' sons becomes king of Thebes. In Euripides' *Medea*, Creon is the king of Corinth and is murdered by the vengeful Medea. Apollodorus portrays him as an early king of Thebes who purifies Amphitryon after the murder of his uncle.

creosote (krē'əsōt), volatile, heavy, oily liquid obtained by the distillation of coal tar or wood tar. Creosote derived from beechwood tar has been used medicinally as an antiseptic and in the treatment of chronic bronchitis. Creosote obtained from coal tar is poisonous. It is used chiefly as a preservative for wood, e.g., in fence posts, railroad ties, and telephone poles; it provides protection against fungi, shipworms, and termites. Although wood may be treated by dipping it in hot creosote, greater protection is obtained if the creosote is forced into the wood under pressure.

crepe, thin fabric of crinkled texture, woven originally in silk but now available in all major fibers. There are two kinds of crepe. The hard-finished, typically dyed black and used for mourning (which tends to retain the old spelling *crape*), is made of hand-twisted silk yarn and finished by a rather complex trade process after weaving; the soft crepes include the Canton, or Oriental, weaves (crepes de Chine) in plain or damask weaves. Their crisped or wavy appearance results from the peculiar arrangement of the weft, which is formed of yarn from two different bobbins twisted together in opposite directions or uses alternately a right-twisted and a left-twisted thread.

crepe myrtle: see LOOSESTRIFE.

Crépy, Treaty of (krāpē'), 1544, concluded by Holy Roman Emperor Charles V and King FRANCIS I of France at Crépy-en-Laonnois (formerly spelled Crespy), Aisne dept., N France. The emperor renounced his claim to the duchy of Burgundy and the king renounced his pretensions to Naples, Flanders, and Artois. In a secret treaty signed at the same time, Francis agreed to help the emperor suppress the German Protestants and to restore Geneva, where Calvin had established his state, to the duke of Savoy. He also agreed to support Charles against King Henry VIII.

Créquy or **Créqui, François, chevalier de** (fräNswä' shəvälyā' də krākē'), c.1629–87, marshal of France. Having fought in the Thirty Years War and on the government side in the Fronde, he conducted brilliant campaigns in the War of Devolution (1667–68) and conquered Lorraine in 1670. He refused (1672) to serve under Marshal Turenne in the third Dutch War (1672–78) and was exiled but soon submitted. In 1675, he was captured after his defeat at Konzer Brücke near Trier. Released shortly after, he achieved military renown in Alsace. In 1684, Créquy occupied Luxembourg.

Crerar, Henry Duncan Graham (krēr'är), 1888–1965, Canadian general in World War II. He fought in World War I and later headed the Royal Military College. In 1940 he was made chief of the Canadian general staff. In 1941 he was given command of the Canadian 2d Division Overseas; in 1944 he became commander of the 1st Canadian Corps and was made a full general, serving with distinction during the campaigns in Europe. He retired in 1946.

Crerar, John (krē'rər), 1827–89, American capitalist and philanthropist, b. New York City. Crerar was a manufacturer in Chicago, and gave liberally to many causes. He is remembered chiefly for the **John Crerar Library,** a scientific and technical reference library in Chicago, for which he provided in his will. The library has special collections on medicine, Chinese literature, Dutch history, floriculture, the history of the women's movement, trade unions, and social science in general. It is noted for its fine bibliographical work.

Crerar, Thomas Alexander, 1876–, Canadian political leader. Under his able direction the United Grain Growers, Ltd., of which he was president (1907–29), became one of the most successful farmers' cooperative movements in W Canada. A Liberal, Crerar served (1917–19) as minister of agriculture in Sir Robert Borden's coalition cabinet; he resigned in protest against the government's high tariff policy. He was leader (1920–21) of the new National Progressive party and of the Progressives in the House of Commons, retiring in 1922 to private life. He reentered the political scene as minister of railways and canals (1929–30) in Mackenzie King's Liberal government and later served (1935–45) as minister of mines and resources in King's cabinet. In 1945, Crerar was appointed to the Canadian Senate, serving until 1966.

Cres (tsərĕs'), Ital. *Cherso,* island (1961 pop. 4,113), 158 sq mi (409 sq km), in the Adriatic Sea, off Croatia, NW Yugoslavia. Formerly in Austria-Hungary, it passed to Italy in 1918 and to Yugoslavia in 1947. Fruit growing, fishing, and sheep raising are the chief occupations.

Cresap, Michael (krē'săp), 1742–75, American frontiersman and soldier, b. Allegany co., Md. An Indian fighter, he was accused by Thomas Jefferson and others of massacring the family of the friendly Indian chief Logan and thus starting (1774) Lord Dunmore's War. But this is denied by most modern historians who accept a letter from George Rogers Clark stating that Cresap was with him at the time of the massacre. Cresap fought in the war, and after the American Revolution began he became (1775) captain of a company of riflemen. Cresap drove his men at such a hard pace to support the patriots at Boston—traveling 550 mi (885 km) in 22 days—that he died of exhaustion as a result. See biography by J. J. Jacob (1826, repr. 1971).

Crescens (krĕs'ənz), companion of Paul, a missionary in Galatia. 2 Tim. 4.10.

crescent, emblematic representation of the quarter moon. The crescent and star, ancient Byzantine symbols that became the emblems of Constantinople, were assumed as the standard of the Ottoman Turks after their capture of that city. The crescent surmounted by a cross indicates the origin of the Eastern Orthodox Church. The crescent appears on the flags of various present-day Muslim nations. The emblem is also used in blazonry.

Cresilas or **Kresilas** (both: krĕs'ĭləs), fl. c.450 B.C., Greek sculptor, b. Crete. He worked at Athens. His statue of Pericles is the earliest Greek portrait statue that has been identified.

cresol (krē'sōl), $CH_3C_6H_4OH$, any one of three aromatic alcohols present in coal tar. The three compounds are structural ISOMERS; they may be thought of as hydroxy derivatives of TOLUENE or as methyl derivatives of PHENOL. The names of the three compounds indicate which of the hydrogens on the benzene ring portion of the molecule have been replaced. Two adjacent hydrogens are replaced, one with a methyl group and one with a hydroxyl group, to form *ortho*-cresol, also called 2-hydroxytoluene, or 2-methylphenol. When a single unreplaced hydrogen lies between the two that are replaced, the compound formed is *meta*-cresol, 3-hydroxytoluene, or 3-methylphenol. When the replaced hydrogens lie opposite one another on the ring, the compound formed is *para*-cresol, 4-hydroxytoluene, or 4-methylphenol. Because the boiling points of these three compounds are nearly the same, a separation of a mixture of the three into its pure components is impractical. The mixture of cresols obtained from coal tar is called cresylic acid. The cresols are used in the manufacture of disinfectants and synthetic resins.

Crespi, Giovanni Battista (jōvän'nē bät-tēs'tä krās'pē), c.1575–1632, Italian painter, sculptor, and architect of the Milanese school. He was also called Il Cerano. His paintings are imbued with a highly dramatic religious fervor, described by broad areas of light and shadow and a warm palette. Much of his work is in the Cathedral of Milan, for which he executed paintings of the life of St. Charles Borromeo, and where he became head of the statuary works in 1629.

Crespi, Giuseppe Maria (jōōzĕp'pä märē'ä), 1665–1747, Italian painter of the Bolognese school, called Lo Spagnuolo. He is well represented in and around Bologna. His best-known works are the imposing paintings of the *Seven Sacraments* (1712; Dresden), but he is also noted for his spontaneous rendering of genre scenes. The National Gallery of Art, Washington, D.C., has his *Cupids with Sleeping Nymphs* and other paintings.

Crespi, Juan (hwän), 1721–82, Spanish explorer in the Southwest, a Franciscan. He came to America in 1749, and in 1767 he went to the peninsula of California in charge of Mission Purísima Concepción. In 1769 he joined the expedition of Gaspar de Portolá to occupy San Diego and Monterey and continued up the coast with Portolá. The following year he founded the Mission San Carlos Borromeo, in the present-day Carmel-by-the-Sea, which became his headquarters. He was chaplain of the expedition to the N Pacific conducted by Juan Pérez in 1774. His diaries, published in H. E. Bolton's *Fray Juan Crespi* (1927, repr. 1971), provided valuable records of these expeditions.

Crespin, Régine (rāzhēn' krĕspăN'), 1927–, French soprano. She made her debut at the Paris Opéra in 1951 as Elsa in Wagner's *Lohengrin.* The range, flexibility, and richness of her voice were critically acclaimed after her performance as Kundry in Wagner's *Parsifal* at Bayreuth in 1958. In 1962 she made her American debut at the Metropolitan Opera, singing the Marschallin in Richard Strauss's *Der Rosenkavalier.* She is also noted for her performances in such roles as Charlotte in Massenet's *Werther* and Dido in Berlioz's *The Trojans.*

Crespo, Joaquín (hwäkēn' krās'pō), 1841?–1898, president of Venezuela (1884–86, 1894–98). He served his first term under the dominance of Antonio GUZMÁN BLANCO. In 1892 he led a revolt and established a military dictatorship. His second term was noted for the bitter feelings between the United States and England brought about by the Venezuela Boundary Dispute. When he chose his successor, revolts occurred, and Crespo was killed in the fighting. The next year Cipriano Castro came into power.

Crespy: see CRÉPY, TREATY OF.

cress, name for several plants often used for salads, e.g., the WATERCRESS, garden cress or PEPPERGRASS, and Indian cress or NASTURTIUM.

Cressent, Charles (shärl krĕsăN'), 1685–1768, French cabinetmaker, one of the chief creators of the RÉGENCE STYLE. Although at first a sculptor and bronze craftsman, he studied under the furniture designer Boulle and became official cabinetmaker to the regent Philippe II, duc d'Orléans. Examples of his furniture display a strong and majestic beauty, with subtly curving supports and swelling surfaces. Against their veneers of mahogany and ebony stand lavish relief adornments in superbly modeled gilt bronze—the scrolls, shells, female busts, and dragons typical of régence decoration. Pieces by Cressent are in the Louvre and in the Wallace Collection, London.

Cressida: see TROILUS AND CRESSIDA.

Cressy, Hugh Paulinus (krĕ'sē), 1605–74, English Benedictine monk. He was educated at Oxford and converted to Roman Catholicism in Rome in 1646. His *Exomologesis* (1647) is an apologia for his conversion. His most ambitious work, however, is his *Church History of Brittany, or England* (1668), one of the first attempts at objective church history. He edited the work of several Catholic mystics—Walter Hilton's *Scale of Perfection,* Friar Augustin Baker's *Sancta Sophia,* and the *Revelations of Divine Love* by Juliana of Norwich. Cressy served as chaplain to Catherine of Braganza, wife of Charles II.

crest, in feudal livery, an ornament of the headpiece that afforded protection against a blow. The term is incorrectly used to mean family coat of arms. Crests were widely used in the 13th cent. by feudal chiefs, as they had been by ancient Greek warriors and the Roman centurions. The earlier forms were usually of stuffed leather, gilded, silvered, or painted; later they were of wood or metal. The crest came to be used in HERALDRY, first only by persons of high rank, then by all those entitled to a coat of arms. It surmounts the escutcheon; its colors are those of the coat of arms. The dragon, wivern, and plume of feathers are common crests. The lion, used by Edward III of England, remains the crest of the English sovereigns. See also BLAZONRY.

crested swift: see SWIFT.

Creston, Paul, 1906–, American composer, b. New York City as Joseph Guttoveggio. Creston was largely self-taught in composition. His music is generally tonal and conservative. Among Creston's many works are five symphonies (1941–56), *Two Choric Dances* (1938) for orchestra, two violin concertos (1956, 1970), a concerto for marimba (1940), and a concerto for alto saxophone (1944). Creston is the author of *Principles of Rhythm* (1964).

Crestwood, city (1970 pop. 15,398), St. Louis co., E central Mo., a suburb of St. Louis; inc. as a city 1949. Located in a truck-farming area, it is mostly residential with some light industry. The Thomas Sappington House (1808; restored 1965) is a good example of Federal architecture.

Creswell, John Angel James, 1828-91, U.S. Postmaster General (1869-74), b. Port Deposit, Md. He was a lawyer, U.S. Representative (1863-65), and U.S. Senator (1865-67), but his important work was done later as Postmaster General. He reorganized the Post Office Dept. to meet the expanding needs of the United States. One-cent post cards were introduced, postal treaties were revised, postal laws were recodified, money-order business was facilitated, free delivery was extended, methods of contracting with railways were improved, and the franking privilege was limited. Some reforms that Creswell advocated, such as a postal savings bank and postal telegraph, were adopted later.

Cretaceous period (krĭtā'shəs), third and last period of the MESOZOIC ERA of geologic time (see GEOLOGIC ERA, table). The Cretaceous was marked, both in North America and in Europe, by extensive submergences of the continents. Changes both in the earth's surface and in its flora and fauna brought the Mesozoic to a close. At the beginning of the Lower Cretaceous in North America, the Mexican sea of the late JURASSIC PERIOD spread over Texas, depositing the Trinity sandstone and limestone. Retreating at the end of Trinity time, it returned in Fredericksburg time and inundated Texas, Oklahoma, New Mexico, and parts of Arizona, Kansas, and Colorado. It reached its maximum late in Fredericksburg or early in Washita time, and was drained by a general emergence of land, which brought the Lower Cretaceous to a close. Fredericksburg and Washita deposits were chiefly limestone, but some continental sediments (i.e., sandstone, shale, and conglomerate) mark the late Washita emergence. The Comanchean series of rocks (Trinity, Fredericksburg, and Washita) reaches a thickness of some 1,500 ft (460 m) in central Texas, and is several times as thick in Mexico. The Comanchean seas were probably separated by a land barrier from contemporaneous seas in the California area, where 26,000 ft (7,925 m) of Shastan shales, with sandstone and thin limestone, were laid down. The sediments were derived by rapid erosion from the recently elevated Sierra Nevada and Klamath mts. In Montana, Alberta, and British Columbia the Kootenai deposits of sandstone and sandy shale, which contain workable deposits of good coal, were formed; along the Atlantic coast the unconsolidated sandy clay, gravel, and sand of the Potomac series were deposited. The Upper Cretaceous opened in W North America with the deposition of continental sands (now the Dakota sandstone) over the surface exposed by the Washita retreat. Some of these sands were redistributed by the Colorado sea, which, advancing from Mexico, finally extended to the Arctic. The eastern border of this, the greatest of North American Mesozoic seas, passed through Texas, Kansas, NW Missouri, Iowa, Minnesota, SW Ontario, Manitoba, Saskatchewan, and Mackenzie, while the western border crossed Arizona, Utah, E Idaho, W Montana, British Columbia, Yukon, and NE Alaska. Branches extended eastward into the Gulf and Atlantic coast regions and southward over Mexico and Yucatán. The Colorado deposits are composed chiefly of shales and limestone, but there is chalk in Kansas and South Dakota. Slight shifting of the sea was followed by the deposition of the Montana shale and sandstone and then by withdrawal of the sea. In Laramide time conditions in the West were similar to those of the CARBONIFEROUS PERIOD in other regions: swamps and bogs were formed which later became valuable deposits of COAL. In the Gulf region the Upper Cretaceous progression of rocks is from nonmarine sand and clay, with lignite, to marine sands, chalk or soft limestone, and continental sand, with clay. On the Atlantic coast the late Upper Cretaceous is represented by continental sands, gravel, and clay, with lignite, followed by clays and sands with glauconitic greensands. The Pacific Coast Upper Cretaceous is marine sandstone and shale, with local conglomerate and coal. At the close of the Cretaceous occurred the Laramide revolution—at least two different epochs of mountain building and one of relative quiet. In this disturbance the Rockies and the E Andes were first elevated, and there were extensive flows of lava. The Appalachians, which had been reduced almost to base level by erosion, were rejuvenated, and the seas retreated from all parts of the continent. The intermittent character of the Laramide disturbance makes difficult the demarcation of the Mesozoic and the succeeding CENOZOIC ERA. The Lower Cretaceous opened in NW Europe with the deposition of a continental and freshwater formation, the Wealden sand and clay, best displayed in England. The sea, meanwhile, expanded from the Mediterranean, finally overlaying successive Wealden strata with limestone. There was at the same time an extensive sea in N Europe. At the close of the Lower Cretaceous, there was probably some recession of the seas. In the Upper Cretaceous, a great transgression of seas submerged lands which had been emergent since the Paleozoic. The striking feature of the European Upper Cretaceous is a great chalk deposit, now exposed in the cliffs of the English Channel. In India, the late Upper Cretaceous was marked by an overflow of lava in the Deccan plateau. The area covered by igneous rocks dating from this period now comprises over 200,000 sq mi (518,000 sq km) and was formerly much larger, having been reduced by erosion. Near Bombay the formation is 10,000 ft (3,000 m) thick. The Lower Cretaceous is characterized by a revolution in the plant life with the sudden appearance of flowering plants (angiosperms), such as the beech, fig, magnolia, and sassafras. By the end of the Cretaceous such plants were dominant, the willow, elm, grape, laurel, birch, oak, and maple having made their appearance, besides grass and the sequoias of California. This prepared the way for the dominance of mammals in Cenozoic animal life. The marine invertebrates of the Cretaceous included nautiluses, barnacles, lobsters, and crabs; sea urchins and foraminifers were common; ammonites, though plentiful, were increasingly degenerate. Reptiles reached their climax. New kinds of dinosaurs were Triceratops, Tyrannosaurus, Stegosaurus, Brontosaurus, and Iguanodon. Flying reptiles were highly developed, while in the sea there were ichthyosaurs, plesiosaurs, and mosasaurs. However, by the end of the Cretaceous the dinosaurs became extinct. The rather abrupt disappearance of dinosaurs and other forms of Cretaceous life remains a mystery. The decline in dinosaurs was accompanied by a rise in the mammals, but since the mammals were initially small, it does not appear likely that they were superior predators. Changes in vegetation suggest that the ecological food chain for the large reptiles was disrupted, although this hypothesis is difficult to reconcile with the simultaneous disappearance of huge sea-dwelling reptiles. A worldwide atmospheric change in the oxygen-carbon dioxide ratio may have occurred, caused by the rapid rise of modern plants and other life forms and resulting in climatic changes with which the large dinosaurs could not cope. Of other reptiles there were crocodiles and turtles, while snakes and lizards made their first appearance. The climate of the Cretaceous was apparently fairly mild and uniform, but it is possible that toward the end of the period some variant zones of climate had appeared. By the end of the Cretaceous period, South America and Africa had separated, with the consequent widening of the S Atlantic. The N Atlantic continued to widen, although it appears that Europe, Greenland, and North America were still connected. Madagascar had separated from Africa, while India was still drifting northward toward Asia. Antarctica and Australia had yet to separate.

Cretan bull, in Greek mythology, giant bull that Hercules captured as his seventh labor. Some versions of the legend state that this bull was the same one that carried Europa to Crete; others claim that it was the beautiful white bull loved by Pasiphaë.

Crete (krēt), Gr. *Kriti,* island (1971 pop. 456,642), c.3,235 sq mi (8,380 sq km), SE Greece, in the E Mediterranean Sea, c.60 mi (100 km) from the Greek mainland. The largest of the Greek islands, it extends c.160 mi (260 km) from east to west and marks the southern limit of the Aegean Sea, the southern part of which is also called the Sea of Crete. IRÁKLION is the capital of the Crete governorate and is the island's largest city; KHANIÁ is the only other large city. The rocky northern coast of Crete is deeply indented, and the interior is largely mountainous, culminating in Mt. Ida (8,058 ft/2,456 m). Crete has many small farms, whose chief crops are grains, olives, and oranges, and food processing is its main industry. Sheep, goats, and dairy cattle are also raised. The island has few mineral deposits. Transportation facilities are very limited. Crete had one of the world's earliest civilizations, the MINOAN CIVILIZATION, named after King Minos, the legendary author of Cretan institutions; in the ruined palace at CNOSSUS invaluable finds have been made. The Cretan kingdom reached its greatest power, prosperity, and civilization c.1600 B.C. Later, for reasons still obscure, its power suddenly collapsed; but Crete flourished again after the Dorian Greeks settled on the island in large numbers and established city-states. Among the most powerful of the cities (110 in number, according to Homer) were Cnossus and Cydonia (modern Khaniá). Although important as a trade center, Crete played no significant part in the political history of ancient Greece. It became a pirate haven in the 3d cent. B.C. but was conquered (68 B.C.-67 B.C.) by the Romans under Quintus Metellus. It passed (A.D. 395) to the Byzantines, fell (824) to the Arabs, but was reconquered by Nicephorus Phocas (later Nicephorus II) in 961. As a result of the Fourth Crusade, the island passed to Venice in 1204; and in 1212, after expelling rival Genoese colonists, the Venetians set up a new administration, headed by a duke. Under Venetian rule Crete was generally known as Candia (Iráklion) for the duke's residence. Insurrections against the arbitrary Venetians were frequent, and the Cretans were not displeased at changing masters when the Ottoman Turks conquered (1669) virtually the whole island after a 24-year war. Two offshore island fortresses remained in Venetian hands until 1715. A series of revolts against the Turks in the 19th cent. reached a climax in the insurrection of 1896-97 that led to war (1897) between Greece and Turkey. The European powers intervened in the war, forcing Turkey to evacuate (1898) Crete. An autonomous Cretan state was formed under nominal Turkish rule, but it was governed by a high commission of the occupying powers (England, France, Russia, and Italy). The Cretan national assembly, led by Eleutherios VENIZELOS, declared in favor of union with Greece, but the powers rejected its demand. The Young Turk revolution of 1908, however, enabled the Cretans to proclaim their union with Greece, and in 1909 foreign occupation troops were withdrawn. Cretan representatives were admitted to the Greek parliament in 1912, and in 1913, as a result of the Balkan Wars, Crete was officially incorporated into Greece. The followers of Venizelos controlled Crete during their uprising (1935) against the imminent restoration of the monarchy but were defeated by Gen. George Kondylis. A new revolt (1938) against the dictatorship of John Metaxas was also suppressed. In World War II, Crete was used as a British military and naval base late in 1940. The British and Greek forces on the Greek mainland evacuated to Crete in 1941, but they were quickly overwhelmed by the Germans in a large-scale airborne invasion, the first of its kind. Late in 1944, British ships isolated the German occupation troops, who eventually surrendered. In the postwar period there was some Communist guerrilla activity on the island. See R. F. Willetts, *Ancient Crete* (1965); J. S. Bowman, *Crete* (1969); K. Bramgan, *The Foundations of Palatial Crete* (1970). See also bibliographies under AEGEAN CIVILIZATION and MINOAN CIVILIZATION.

Créteil (krātā'), city (1968 pop. 49,233), capital of Val-de-Marne dept., N central France, on the Marne River. Gold and silver items, pencils, and varnish are produced. A church built in the 12th and 13th cent. is in Créteil.

cretinism, condition produced in infants and children due to lack of thyroid hormone. It usually results from a congenital defect (e.g., absence of the thyroid, presence of only a rudimentary gland, inability of the gland to produce thyroxine). However, it can develop later if there is a lack of iodine in the diet, or if the thyroid is diseased or surgically removed. Cretinism causes very serious retardation of physical and mental development; if the condition is left untreated, growth is stunted and the physical stature attained is that of a dwarf. In addition, the skin is thick, flabby, and waxy in color, the nose is flattened, the abdomen protrudes, and there is a general slowness of movement and speech. If discovered early enough and treated with thyroid extract and sufficient iodine intake throughout life, growth may become normal and mental facility greatly improved. If the condition commences after adulthood it is called MYXEDEMA.

Creusa (krēō͞o'sə), in Greek mythology. **1** Daughter of Erechtheus and wife of Xuthus. Her sons, Achaeus by Xuthus, and Ion by Xuthus or Apollo, are the ancestors of the Achaeans and the Ionians. **2** Princess of Corinth: see JASON and MEDEA. **3** Daughter of Priam and wife of Aeneas. She died fleeing from Troy.

Creuse (krœz), department (1968 pop. 156,876), central France, in the MASSIF CENTRAL. GUÉRET (the capital) and AUBUSSON are the chief towns.

Creusot, Le (lə krœzō'), city (1968 pop. 34,102), Saône-et-Loire dept., E central France, in Burgundy. Situated in a coal-mining region, it is the site of the large Schneider iron and steel mills and munitions factories (founded 1837).

crevasse (krəvăs'), large crack in the upper surface of a GLACIER, formed by tension acting upon the brittle ice. Transverse crevasses occur where the grade of the glacier bed becomes suddenly steeper; longitudinal crevasses, where the glacier spreads over a wider valley or plain. Marginal crevasses are due to the strain built up when the central part moves faster than the sides.

Crèvecoeur, J. Hector St. John (krĕvkör'), 1735–1813, American author and agriculturist, b. France as Michel Guillaume Jean de Crèvecoeur. It is believed that he served under Montcalm in Canada. After traveling in the Great Lakes region and in the Ohio valley and working as a surveyor in Pennsylvania, he settled (c.1769) on a farm in Orange co., N.Y., where he wrote *Letters from an American Farmer* (1782). Other letters, found in 1922, were published as *Sketches of Eighteenth Century America* (1925). The two books give outstanding descriptions of American rural life of the period. He wrote, over the signature Agricola, agricultural articles for American newspapers. He introduced the culture of European crops, notably alfalfa, into America and of the American potato into Normandy. As French consul in New York City (from 1783) he sought to improve commercial relations between France and the United States. He lived in France from 1790. See biography by T. L. Philbrick (1970).

Crewe, Robert Offley Ashburton Crewe-Milnes, 1st **marquess of** (kro͞o"mĭlz'), 1858–1945, British statesman. He succeeded (1885) his father as Baron Houghton and was created earl (1895) and later marquess (1911) of Crewe. A Liberal, he held a succession of high offices, including those of lord lieutenant of Ireland (1892–95), colonial secretary (1908–10), and secretary for India (1910–15). As Liberal leader in the House of Lords from 1908 he played an important role in securing passage of the Parliament Act of 1911, which deprived the Lords of its veto. He was later ambassador to France (1922–28). See biography by James Pope-Hennessy (1955).

Crewe (kro͞o), municipal borough (1971 pop. 51,302), Cheshire, W central England. It is an important railroad junction with large locomotive and car works.

cribbage (krĭb'ĭj), card game played by two persons with a deck of 52 cards and a scoring (pegging) device known as a cribbage board. The board contains four rows of 30 holes each (two rows for each player), plus additional holes, called game holes. Each player gets two pegs to keep the score. The English poet Sir John Suckling (1609–42) is credited with inventing and naming the game. Each king (high card), queen, jack, and ten represents a count of 10 points; each ace, a count of 1; each other card, its index value. Each player receives six cards and lays away two face down to form the crib. The stock is cut by the dealer to produce the starter. Cards are placed face up alternately, nondealer first, in front of the player, who announces the total count. The object of each series is to carry the total of the cards to 31 or as close as possible without exceeding it. A player pegs 1 for laying down the last card in a series before reaching 31, or he pegs 2 for adding a card that makes exactly 31. Points also are scored for making the count 15 and for playing cards in sequence or in pairs. When all the cards have been played, each player pegs additional points for the pairs, sequences, and counts of 15 that can be arranged from the cards in his hand and the starter; the dealer also pegs the score in the crib. Several hands are played until the game is reached when one player pegs 61 points (once around the board) or 121 points (twice around). See Douglas Anderson, *All about Cribbage* (1971).

Crichton, James (krī'tən), 1560?–1583?, Scottish adventurer and scholar, called the Admirable Crichton. A graduate of the Univ. of St. Andrews, he spent some time in France, possibly in military service. By 1579 he was in Italy, where he attracted attention by his scholarly accomplishments and personal charm. Reputedly he spoke 12 languages and displayed amazing erudition and powers of memory in public disputations. He entered the service of a Mantuan nobleman as tutor to his son and was slain by his charge in a street brawl. His fame is due to the extravagant praise given him by Aldus Manutius (grandson of the famous printer of the same name) and by his 17th-century biographer, Sir Thomas Urquhart.

Crick, Francis Harry Compton, 1916–, English scientist, grad. University College, London, and Caius College, Cambridge. From 1940 to 1947 he served as a scientist in the admiralty. He was a visiting lecturer at several institutions in the United States including Brooklyn Polytechnic (1953–54), Harvard (1959), Univ. of Rochester (1959), and Johns Hopkins school of medicine (1960). He shared the 1962 Nobel Prize in Medicine and Physiology with Maurice Wilkins and James Watson for their work in establishing the structure and function of deoxyribonucleic acid (DNA), the key substance in the transmission of hereditary characteristics from generation to generation. See his *Of Molecules and Men* (1967) and J. D. Watson, *The Double Helix* (1968).

cricket, common name of the slender, chirping, hopping INSECTS forming the family Gryllidae in the order Orthoptera. Most crickets have long antennae, muscular hind legs for jumping, and two pairs of fully developed wings. In some subfamilies the wings are reduced or absent. In most subfamilies the males have song-producing, or stridulatory, organs on the front wings. Both sexes possess auditory organs on the forelegs. The stridulatory apparatus is most highly developed in the field crickets and the tree crickets. Members of these subfamilies have a ridged region, which acts as a file, and a hardened region, which acts as a scraper, on each front wing; sound is produced by rubbing the wings together. Crickets occur mostly in the temperate climates. The common field crickets of the United States are species of the genus *Gryllus;* all are brown to black, about 1 in. (2.5 cm) long, and are found in fields and meadows and often in houses. The tree crickets are slender, pale green or whitish insects of trees and shrubs; most U.S. species belong to the genus *Oecanthus.* The rate of chirping of tree crickets increases with increasing temperature. In the snowy tree cricket, *Oecanthus fultoni,* this variation is so regular that if the number 40 is added to the number of chirps per 15-sec interval, the sum is a fair approximation of the temperature in degrees Fahrenheit. Ant-loving crickets are tiny wingless forms 1/8 in. to 1/5 in. (3–5 mm) long that occur in ant nests, where they feed on an oily secretion produced by the ants. Unusual crickets are the mole crickets of the genus *Gryllotalpa.* These nocturnal insects have strong front legs adapted for digging and burrowing rather than strong hind legs for jumping. They live in moist soil. Crickets reproduce sexually, producing from one to three generations per year. The females usually lay eggs in the ground or in soft-stemmed plants during the late summer or fall. The eggs hatch in the spring and the emerging young are similar to the adults except for their smaller size and lack of wings. In addition to the true crickets of the family Gryllidae, some insects of the long-horned GRASSHOPPER family (Tettigoniidae) are also called crickets. These are the cave, or camel, crickets, found throughout the world in dark, moist places, and the stone, sand, or Jerusalem crickets of W North America, found under stones in sandy soil. True crickets belong to the phylum ARTHROPODA, class Insecta, order Orthoptera, suborder Ensifera, family Gryllidae.

cricket, summertime ball and bat game played chiefly in Great Britain and the Commonwealth countries. It is played by two opposing teams of 11 men each on a level, closely cut, green turf preferably measuring about 525 ft (160 m) by about 550 ft (170 m). Two wickets are placed 66 ft (20.12 m) apart near the middle of the field. A wicket consists of two small wooden crosspieces known as bails resting on three wooden stumps 28 in. (71.1 cm) high. At each wicket stands a batsman. If the bowler of the opposing team knocks down the bails of the wicket opposite him, the batsman defending that wicket is retired. In bowling the hard, leather-covered ball, the bowler may not bend his arm, and the ball usually approaches the batsman on one bounce. When the bowler has bowled the ball six times (eight in Australia and South Africa) to the batsman at one wicket, an umpire (there is one at each wicket) calls "over," and another bowler begins bowling to the batsman's partner at the other wicket. The players in the field shift their positions according to which batsman is batting. For his part, the batsman tries to hit the ball with his paddle-shaped bat far enough so that he and his partner may run to exchange places, thereby scoring a run. When the ball is hit for a long distance (in any direction, since there are no foul lines in cricket), several exchanges or runs may be made. (If the ball reaches the boundary of the field on the ground, four runs are scored without the batsmen having to run; similarly, if the ball clears the boundary in the air, six runs are added to the score.) However, if the opposing team recovers the ball in time to knock down the bails of a wicket before the batsman reaches it, he is out. A batsman is also retired if the ball he hits is caught on the fly (as in baseball), and he may be retired for several other more technical reasons. An outstanding batsman may score more than 100 runs, a "century," before being retired, and totals in the 400s have been posted. A game consists of two innings; in one inning all the men of each team bat once in a fixed order (unless a team chooses to retire without completing its batting order); it may take several days to complete one game. The team scoring the most runs wins. Except in case of serious injury, no substitutions are allowed. The origin of cricket is obscure. Some contend that it was invented in France as a derivative of croquet. Most evidence, however, suggests that cricket was developed in medieval England (c.12th–13th cent.). In 1744 the London Cricket Club drew up the first authoritative set of rules. The Marylebone Cricket Club (founded 1787) is one of the world's oldest cricket organizations and is still the international governing body of the game. In Great Britain the principal cricket matches are those between the universities (especially Oxford and Cambridge) and between the largely professional teams representing the English counties. International, or test, matches are played annually, the most famous contest being that between Australia and Britain for the "Ashes." After Australia's surprising victory in the 1882 competition, London's *Sporting Times* displayed an obituary for British cricket whose final lines read: "The body will be cremated, and the ashes taken to Australia." The following year the British vowed to retrieve "the ashes;" thus was born the unusual name of this famous sporting event. In the United States the game was supplanted in popular favor by baseball, a sport derived in part from cricket. See *Wisden Cricketers' Almanack* (1864–); Rowland Bowen, *Cricket: A History* (1970); John Ford, *Cricket: A Social History, 1700–1835* (1972); Gordon Ross, *The History of Cricket* (1972); Peter Smith, *The Observer's Book of Cricket* (1973).

Crile, George Washington (krīl), 1864–1943, American surgeon, b. Coshocton co., Ohio, M.D. Univ. of Wooster medical school (later merged with Western Reserve Univ.), 1887. He taught at the Univ. of Wooster (1889–1900) and at Western Reserve Univ. (1900–1924) and was a founder and director (from 1921) of the Cleveland Clinic Foundation. He worked on hemorrhage and transfusion, surgery of the thyroid, and shock, developing the technique of anociassociation to prevent surgical shock. His works include *Diseases Peculiar to Civilized Man* (1934), *Phenomena of Life* (1936), and *Intelligence, Power, and Personality* (1941).

Crillon, Louis des Balbes de Berton de (lwē dā bälb də bĕrtôN' də krēyôN'), c.1541–1615, French soldier. He fought under François de Guise in the retaking (1558) of Calais; served in the first wars against the Huguenots (1562–70); and fought under John of Austria in his Turkish campaign. Crillon distinguished himself at Lepanto (1571). He sided with King Henry III against the Catholic LEAGUE and was one of the best captains of King Henry IV, under whom he took part in the battle of Ivry and the siege of Paris.

crime: see CRIMINAL LAW; CRIMINOLOGY; GANG; JUVENILE DELINQUENCY; ORGANIZED CRIME.

Crimea (krīmē'ə), Rus. and Ukr. *Krym,* peninsula (1970 pop. 1,814,000), c.10,000 sq mi (25,900 sq km), extreme S European USSR, linked with the mainland by the Perekop Isthmus. The peninsula, administratively part of the Ukraine, is coterminous with the Crimea oblast, of which SIMFEROPOL is the capital. Other major cities include SEVASTOPOL, KERCH, FEODOSIYA, YALTA, and YEVPATORIYA. The peninsula is bounded on the S and W by the Black Sea. The eastern tip of the Crimea is the Kerch peninsula, separated from the Taman peninsula (a projection of the mainland) by the Kerch Strait, which connects the Black Sea with the Sea of Azov. Along the Crimea's northeast shore are a series of shallow, stagnant, but mineral-rich lagoons, known collectively as the Sivash or Putrid Sea, which are linked to the Sea of Azov by the Arabatskaya Strelka. The northern part of the Crimea is a semiarid steppe, drained by a few streams; this region supports fine wheat, corn, and cotton crops. In the south rises the Crimean or Yaila Range (Yaltinskaya Yaila), with its extensive meadows and forests. The tallest peak rises to c.5,000 ft (1,520 m). Protected by steep mountain slopes, the Black Sea littoral, called the "Soviet Riviera," has a subtropical climate and numerous resorts, notably at Yalta and Sochi. In this region are vineyards and fruit orchards; fishing, mining, and the production of essential oils are also important. Heavy industry in the Crimea includes ironworks and plants producing machinery, chemicals, and building materials. In the Crimean Range is one of the USSR's chief astronomical observatories. Known in ancient times as Tauris, the peninsula was the home of the Cimmerian people, called the Tauri. Expelled from the steppe by the Scythians in the 7th cent. B.C., they founded (5th cent. B.C.) the kingdom of Cimmerian Bosporus, which later came under Greek influence. Ionian and Dorian Greeks began to colonize the coast in the 6th cent., and the peninsula became the major source of wheat for ancient Greece. In the 1st cent. B.C., the kingdom of Pontus began to rule the Greek part of the peninsula, which became a Roman protectorate in the 1st cent. A.D. Its Greek name was then Latinized into Chersonesus Taurica. During the next millennium the area was overrun by Ostrogoths, Huns, Khazars, Cumans, and in 1239, by the Mongols of the Golden Horde. Meanwhile, the southern shore was mostly under Byzantine control from the 6th to the 12th cent. Trade relations were established (11th–13th cent.) with Kievan Russia. In the 13th cent. Genoa founded prosperous coastal commercial settlements. After Tamerlane's destruction of the Golden Horde, the Tatars established (1475) an independent khanate in N and central Crimea. In the late 15th cent. both the khanate and the southern coastal towns were conquered by the Ottoman Empire; the Turks called the peninsula Crimea. Although they became Turkish vassals, the Crimean Tatars were powerful rulers who became the scourge of the Ukraine and Poland, exacted tribute from the Russian czars, and raided Moscow as late as 1572. Russian armies first invaded the Crimea in 1736. Empress Catherine II forced Turkey to recognize the khanate's independence in 1774, and in 1783 she annexed it outright; the annexation was confirmed by the Treaty of Jassy (1792). Many Tatars, with their Muslim religion and Turkish language, emigrated to Turkey, while Russians, Ukrainians, Bulgarians, Germans, Armenians, and Greeks settled in the Crimea. During the CRIMEAN WAR (1853–56), parts of the remaining Tatar population were resettled in the interior of Russia. After the Bolshevik Revolution (1917) an independent Crimean republic was proclaimed; but the region was soon occupied by German forces and then became a refuge for the White Army. In 1921 a Tatar Autonomous Soviet Socialist Republic was created (Tatars then constituted about 25% of the population). During World War II, German invaders took the Crimea after an eight-month siege. Accused by the Soviet government of collaborating with the Germans, the Crimean Tatars were forcibly removed from their homeland after the war and resettled in distant parts of the Asian USSR. The republic itself was dissolved (1945) and made into an oblast of the Russian Soviet Federated Socialist Republic; in 1954 it was transferred to the Ukraine. Russians and Ukrainians now constitute most of the Crimea's population.

Crimean War (krīmē'ən), 1853–56, war between Russia on the one hand and Turkey, England, France, and Sardinia on the other. The causes of the conflict were inherent in the unsolved EASTERN QUESTION. The more immediate occasion was a dispute between Russia and France over the Palestinian holy places. Challenging the claim of Russia to guardianship of the holy places, France in 1852 secured from Sultan ABD AL-MAJID certain privileges for the Latin churches. Russian counterdemands were turned down (1853) by the Turkish government. In July, 1853, Russia retorted by occupying the Turkish vassal states of Moldavia and Walachia, and in October, after futile negotiations, Turkey declared war. In March, 1854, England and France, having already dispatched fleets to the Black Sea, declared war on Russia; Sardinia followed suit in Jan., 1855. Austria remained neutral, but by threatening to enter the war on the Turkish side forced Russia to evacuate Moldavia and Walachia, which were occupied (Aug., 1854) by Austrian troops. In Sept., 1854, allied troops landed in the Crimea, with the object of capturing SEVASTOPOL. The Russian fortress, defended by TOTLEBEN, resisted heroically until Sept., 1855. Allied commanders were Lord RAGLAN for the British and Marshal Saint-Arnaud, succeeded later by Marshal Canrobert, for the French. Military operations, which were marked on both sides by great stubbornness, gallantry, and disregard for casualties, remained localized. Famous episodes were the battles of BALAKLAVA and INKERMAN (1854) and the allied capture (1855) of MALAKHOV and Redan, which preceded the fall of Sevastopol. On the Asiatic front the Russians gained advantages and occupied Kars. The accession (1855) of Czar Alexander II and the capture of Sevastopol led to peace negotiations that resulted (Feb., 1856) in the Treaty of Paris (see PARIS, CONGRESS OF). The Crimean War ended the dominant role of Russia in SE Europe; the cooling of Austro-Russian relations was an important factor in subsequent European history. The scandalous treatment of the troops, particularly the wounded, depicted by war correspondents, prompted the work of Florence NIGHTINGALE, which was perhaps the most positive result of the war. See Peter Gibbs, *Crimean Blunder* (1960); W. B. Pemberton, *Battles of the Crimean War* (1962); J. Langdon-Davies, *Crimean War* (1964); A. J. Barker, *The War Against Russia 1854-6* (1970).

criminal law, the branch of law that defines crimes, treats of their nature, and provides for their punishment. A TORT is a wrong committed against an individual; a crime, on the other hand, is regarded as an offense committed against the public, even though only one individual may have been wronged. The real distinction lies in the way a remedy for the wrong is pursued. A tort is a wrong for which the remedy is pursued by, and at the discretion of, the injured individual or his representative, while a crime is a wrong for which the wrongdoer is prosecuted by the state for the purpose of punishment. However, the fact that a particular act has been or may be prosecuted as a crime does not necessarily preclude an injured party from seeking recovery from the offender in a civil action. Crimes are usually classified as TREASON, FELONY, and MISDEMEANOR. The fundamental distinction between felonies and misdemeanors rests with the penalty and the power of imprisonment. In general, a misdemeanor is an offense for which a punishment other than death or imprisonment in the state prison is prescribed by law. The term "degree of crime" refers to distinctions in the culpability of an offense because of the circumstances surrounding its commission. Crimes are sometimes divided according to their nature into crimes mala in se and crimes mala prohibita; the former class comprises those acts that are thought to be immoral or wrong in themselves, or naturally evil, such as murder, rape, arson, burglary, larceny, and the like; the latter class embraces those acts that are not naturally evil but are prohibited by statute because they infringe on the rights of others (e.g., acts in restraint of trade that have been made criminal under antitrust legislation). In the United States, the power to define crimes and set punishment for them rests with the legislatures of the United States, the several states, and the territories, the principal authority being that of the individual states. This power in the states is restricted by the Federal constitution, e.g., in the Fourteenth Amendment and in prohibitions against acts of attainder (an act of attainder is a legislative declaration that a particular individual is guilty of a crime) and against ex post facto laws (laws declaring certain actions to be criminal with retroactive effect). State constitutions may also limit state legislative action. The courts cannot look further into the propriety of a penal statute than to ascertain whether the legislature has the power to enact it. Administrative rules may have the force of law, and violations of such rules are punishable as public offenses, provided that the legislature has made such violations misdemeanors. A common law crime is one punishable under common law, as distinguished from crimes specified by statute. In many U.S. jurisdictions, including some in which comprehensive criminal statutes have been enacted, the common law in relation to crimes and criminal procedure has been recognized by the courts as in force, except insofar as it has been abrogated or repealed, expressly or impliedly, by statute. Thus the state may prosecute crimes that were indictable at common law even though they may not be denominated as such or be provided for by statute. In many other jurisdictions the courts have held the common law as to crimes as being abolished, and no act is punishable as a crime unless it is made so by statute, or unless the act is made punishable as a crime by the constitution; criminal procedure is entirely regulated by statute. There are no common law offenses against the United States, and one may be subject to punishment for crime in a Federal court only for the commission or omission of an act defined by statute or regulation having legislative authority, and then only if punishment is authorized by Congress. In general, crimes must be defined in a penal statute with appropriate certainty and definiteness; the constitutional requirement of due process of law is violated by a criminal statute that fails to give a person of ordinary intelligence fair notice that his contemplated conduct is forbidden by the statute. Except as otherwise provided by statute, to constitute a crime an overt act (actus reus) must be accompanied by a criminal intent (mens rea) or by such negligence as is regarded by law as equivalent to a criminal intent. Motive, or that which leads or tempts the mind to indulge in a criminal act, as distinguished from intent, is neither a crime nor an essential element of a crime. The motive with which an offense was committed is immaterial. Proof of motive may be material in proving that the defendant committed a particular crime, but it is not essential to a conviction. Every accused has the right to avail himself of any and all defenses the law recognizes and permits—e.g., insanity, mistake of fact, or self-defense. An accused having the right to resort to several defenses may make an election as to the one on which he will rely. The fact that one undertakes a crime on the advice, or as the agent, of another is not a defense; on the other hand, except in the case of HOMICIDE, an act that would otherwise constitute a crime may be excused when committed under duress or compulsion that is present, imminent, and impending, and that produces a well-grounded apprehension of death or serious bodily harm if the act is not done (see COERCION). Religious belief is not ordinarily a justification or excuse for the commission of a crime (see BIGAMY). The procedure in criminal cases is substantially the same throughout the United States. The person suspected of crime is taken into custody by a police officer, usually by service of a WARRANT of arrest. The case is first presented to a grand jury, which draws up an INDICTMENT if there is sufficient evidence to justify trial; otherwise it discharges the accused. While action is pending, the party charged may be released on BAIL. Trial is by jury or before a judge alone. The government presents its case (i.e., attempts to prove the allegations of the indictment), through the public prosecutor, usually called the district attorney, while the accused is represented by counsel chosen by himself or appointed by the court. The legal presumption of innocence puts the burden of proving guilt beyond a reasonable doubt on the prosecution, unless, of course, the defendant pleads guilty to the charge. Special rules restricting the introduction of EVIDENCE in criminal trials further protect the defendant. If the accused is adjudged innocent, he is discharged; if he is found guilty, the judge pronounces sentence upon him. (For types of criminal penalties, see CAPITAL PUNISHMENT; CORPORAL PUNISHMENT; PRISON.) If the defendant is convicted, he may file for an APPEAL; if he is acquitted, however, the prosecution cannot appeal the verdict. Generally speaking, this procedure is confined to felonies; misdemeanors, being relatively less serious offenses, are handled in a more summary fashion. It is generally accepted that no court will enforce the criminal law of another jurisdiction, but by means of EXTRADITION a fugitive from justice may be delivered to the competent authorities. For an account of criminal law in ancient and medieval times, see COMPOSITION; VENDETTA. See also MILITARY LAW; MARTIAL LAW; INTERNATIONAL LAW; PIRACY; WAR CRIMES. See Glanville Williams, *Criminal Law* (2d ed., 1961); W. J. Chambliss, ed., *Crime and the Legal Process* (1969); S. H. Kadish, *Criminal Law and Its Processes* (1969).

criminology, the study of crime, its causes, its correction, and its prevention. Although it is generally considered a subdivision of SOCIOLOGY, it also draws on the findings of psychology, economics, and other disciplines that investigate humans and their environment. Most criminologists regard crime as a violation of social rules that have been codified into laws (see CRIMINAL LAW). Since cultures vary in organization and values, what is considered criminal may also vary, although most societies, preliterate or otherwise, have restrictive laws or customs. Crimes against property, long a major concern of Western criminology, acquired new definitions in Communist countries, where private property is limited to consumer goods. In examining the evolution and definition of crime, criminology aims to remove from this category acts that no longer conflict with society's norms and acts that violate the norms without imperiling society. Criminology as a study also embraces environmental, hereditary, or psychological causes, modes of investigation and conviction, and the efficacy of punishment (see PRISON). Determination of the prevalence of crime is difficult because of varying definitions and the fact that much crime is unreported. In the last few decades recorded crime in Western countries has risen. Offenses against property (burglary and theft) have risen in the United States and in other urbanized countries, as have crimes of violence (murder, rape, aggravated assault). Crime rates tend to fluctuate with social trends, rising in times of depression, after wars, and in other periods of disorganization. In the United States ORGANIZED CRIME first became significant during prohibition. Within cities, poverty areas have the highest rates of reported crime, especially among young people (see JUVENILE DELINQUENCY). The high incidence of recidivism (repeated criminality) has led criminologists to suggest the need for more effective penal systems and better analyses of causation. The causes of crime are complex. The idea that criminals can be detected by their physical structure (shape of head, ear lobes, and the like) has been largely discredited. Hereditary physical and psychological traits are generally ruled out as independent causes of crime, but psychological states are believed to determine an individual's reaction to potent environmental influences. Some criminologists assert that certain offenders are born into environments (such as extreme poverty or minority groups in areas where they are discriminated against) that tend to generate criminal behavior. Others argue that since only some persons succumb to these influences, there are additional stimuli. Perhaps the most widely accepted theory in criminology is Edwin Sutherland's theory of differential association, which argues that criminal behavior is learned in small groups. Psychiatry generally considers crime to result from emotional disorders, usually stemming from maladjustment in childhood. The criminal symbolically enacts a repressed wish, or desire, and such crimes as pyromania or kleptomania are specific expressions of personality disorders. Therefore, psychiatrists hold, crime prevention and the cure of offenders are matters of treatment rather than coercion. Criminologists are nearly unanimous in advocating that acts involving narcotics, alcohol, and sexual preferences (known among criminologists as crimes without victims) be removed from the category of crime. In dealing with crime in general the emphasis has gradually shifted from punishment to rehabilitation. Criminologists have worked to increase the use of probation and parole, psychiatric treatment, education in prison, and betterment of living conditions. One major area of crime that was relatively ignored until recent decades is that of white-collar crime, i.e., crimes committed by people of relatively high social status in the regular course of their professional or business careers. The President's Commission on Law Enforcement and Administration of Justice in 1967 concluded that about three times as much property is stolen by white-collar criminals as by other criminals outside of organized crime. See Sheldon Glueck and Eleanor Glueck, *Criminal Careers in Retrospect* (1943, repr. 1966); Hermann Mannheim, ed., *Pioneers in Criminology* (2d ed. 1960, repr. 1972) and *Comparative Criminology* (2 vol., 1965); Don Gibbons, *Society, Crime, and Criminal Careers* (1968); Jürgen Thorwald, *Crime and Science* (1968); Roger Hood, *Key Issues in Criminology* (1970); Edwin Sutherland and Donald Cressey, *Criminology* (8th ed. 1970); Richard Quinney, *The Social Reality of Crime* (1971); Stephen Schafer and William Knudten, *Reader in Criminology* (1973).

Crinoidea: see ECHINODERMATA; SEA LILY.

Cripple Creek, city (1970 pop. 425), alt. 9,375 ft (2,858 m), seat of Teller co., central Colo.; inc. 1892. Now a summer resort, it was once a great gold-mining town. The discovery of gold (1891) on a cattle ranch created one of the richest camps of a major gold-producing area, with a rough and exciting town life. In 1901 the district had an estimated population of 50,000. Although gold production declined after that year, the opening of a drainage tunnel in 1941 reactivated formerly flooded mines and led to the discovery of new veins. Violence marked miners' strikes there in 1893 and 1904. Today the old mines are tourist attractions.

Cripps, Sir Stafford, 1889–1952, British statesman. A brilliant and successful patent and corporation lawyer, he joined the Labour party in 1929 and became solicitor general in 1930, being knighted the same year. He resigned on the formation (1931) of the National government but won a seat in Parliament. He became a leading spokesman of the left wing of the Labour party and in 1939 was expelled from the party for urging a united front with the Communists. Sir Winston Churchill appointed (1940) him ambassador to the Soviet Union and on Cripps's return to England in 1942 made him lord privy seal and leader of the House of Commons. In the same year Cripps was sent to India with a self-government plan (which was rejected by India). Shortly thereafter he became minister of aircraft production. In 1945, Cripps was readmitted to the Labour party and appointed president of the Board of Trade in the new Labour government. He returned to India to negotiate independence in 1946, and the failure of his mission (because of the antagonism between Hindus and Muslims) is often seen as the point at which the partition of India became inevitable. In 1947, Cripps was appointed to the newly created office of minister of economic affairs and within the same year became, in addition, chancellor of the exchequer. Great Britain was in the throes of a severe economic crisis, which Cripps sought to counter with his policy of austerity. By continuing rationing and imposing strict economic controls, he was able to slow inflation while maintaining full employment and without cutting back the government's welfare programs. Despite a vigorous export drive, however, Britain's balance of payments situation remained serious, and in 1949, Cripps most reluctantly devalued the pound by 30%. He retired in 1950. See biography by Colin Cooke (1957).

Cris: see KÖRÖS, river, Rumania.

Crişana-Maramureş (krĭshä'nä-märämōō'rĭsh), historic province, NW Rumania, between Transylvania and Hungary. It covers approximately the present-day regions of Crişana (4,725 sq mi/12,238 sq km) and of Maramureş (4,053 sq mi/10,497 sq km). ARAD, ORADEA, and SATU-MARE are the chief cities. The region occupies the easternmost part of the Hungarian plain and the western foothills of the Transylvanian Alps. It is largely agricultural. Crişana-Maramureş was part of Hungary until 1919 and retains a sizable Hungarian minority.

crisis, economic: see DEPRESSION.

Crispi, Francesco (fränchās'kō krēs'pē), 1819–1901, Italian premier (1887–91, 1893–96), b. Sicily. After participation in the Sicilian revolt of 1848 against the repressive rule of Ferdinand II of Sicily, he went into exile to Piedmont, then to Malta and England, where he met Mazzini, and to France. He returned to Italy and joined GARIBALDI in his expedition to Sicily, which resulted in the proclamation of the kingdom of Italy (1861). A deputy to the Italian parliament from 1861, he was at first a republican, but later became an outspoken monarchist. He was minister of the interior (1877–78) and later premier. Through his personal relations with Bismarck, friendship with Germany was furthered, while Italian relations with France deteriorated. He was much interested in colonial policies; Eritrea in NE Africa was organized under him. Crispi was again premier, when the victory of the Ethiopians over the Italians at Aduwa forced him from office.

Crispus, prominent Corinthian Jew converted by St. Paul. Acts 18.8; 1 Cor. 1.14.

Cristóbal (krēstō'bäl), town (1970 pop. 388), Panama Canal Zone, near the Caribbean end of the canal. Cristóbal is the American residential suburb of Colón.

Cristus, Petrus: see CHRISTUS, PETRUS.

Critias (krĭsh'ēəs, krĭ'tēəs), c.460–403 B.C., Athenian political leader and writer. A relative of Plato, he was an aristocrat and had early training in philosophy with Socrates and wrote poems and tragedies. He is best remembered, however, as one of the Thirty Tyrants imposed on Athens by the Spartans. He was soon at odds with Theramenes, who was put to death. Critias earned a name for rapacity and bloodthirstiness, although Plato seems to have admired him, using him as a speaker in the dialogues *Protagoras, Timaeus,* and *Critias.* When THRASYBULUS led his forces against the Thirty, Critias was killed in battle.

critical angle: see REFRACTION.

critical mass: see CHAIN REACTION.

criticism, the interpretation and evaluation of literature and the arts. It exists in a variety of literary forms: dialogues (Plato, John Dryden), verse (Horace, Alexander Pope), letters (John Keats), essays (Matthew Arnold, W. H. Auden), and treatises (Philip Sydney, Percy Bysshe Shelley). There are several categories of criticism: theoretical, practical, textual, judicial, biographical, and impressionistic. One of the most laborious and exacting kinds is textual criticism, which is the comparison of different texts and versions of particular works with the aim of arriving at an incorrupt "master version." This has been perhaps most familiar over the centuries in biblical criticism. Textual critics of note include St. Augustine and St. Jerome (the Bible), Samuel Johnson and H. H. Furness (Shakespeare), and F. J. Furnival (early English texts). From its beginning criticism has concerned philosophers. Plato raised the question of the authenticity of poetic knowledge in the *Ion,* in which both poet and performer are forced to admit ignorance about the source of their inspiration or the function of their craft. In his *Poetics,* Aristotle focused on tragic drama to discover its effect—the purgation of the audience's emotions (see TRAGEDY). Roman civilization produced two critics who were poets rather than philosophers. Horace declared in the *Ars Poetica* (c.13 B.C.) that poetry must be "dulce et utile"—"sweet and useful." In his *On the Sublime* (1st cent. A.D.) the Greek Longinus presented the view that poetry must be the divinely inspired utterance of the poet's impassioned soul. Interestingly, each of these pronouncements was an accurate description of the author's own work rather than a set of rules for all poetry. Thus, the ancients can be credited with delineating the two major types of criticism: theoretical, which attempts to state general principles about the value of art (Plato, Aristotle), and practical, which examines the particular works, genres, or writers in light of theoretical criteria (Horace, Longinus). Renaissance critics ignored their recent heritage—the medieval attitude toward art as a form of prayer—and looked to the classics, Aristotle's works in particular, for usable models. Philip Sydney maintained in his *Defense of Poetry* (1595) that poetry must engage and uplift the emotions of its audience with "heart ravishing knowledge." In his *Poetics* (1561) the Italian critic Julius Caesar Scaliger transformed Aristotle's description of the dramatic unities of time, setting, and plot into exigencies, strictly adhered to by the neoclassical dramatists of 17th-century France and England. John Dryden, the master critic of Restoration England, upheld neoclassical standards, adding his own emphases. In his *Essay of Dramatic Poesy* (1668) he justified the use of rhyme in tragedy by arguing that drama was the work of a poet, not a transcription of random conversation. In his *Essay on Criticism* (1711) Alexander Pope added an important section on the criticism of critics: those who do their job best always "survey the Whole, not seek slight faults to find." Because the general tone of criticism of this period was prescriptive, it is called judicial criticism. Samuel Johnson's *Lives of the Poets* (1779–81) was the first thorough-going exercise in biographical criticism, the attempt to relate a writer's background and life to his works. The revolution from neoclassicism to romanticism was first outlined by William Wordsworth and Samuel Taylor Coleridge, who emphasized the importance of emotion and imagination in literature. In his Preface to the Second Edition of the *Lyrical Ballads* (1800), Wordsworth described the lyric as "emotion recollected in tranquility," whereas Coleridge, in his *Biographia Literaria* (1817) defined imagination as "the repetition in the finite mind of the eternal act of creation," rather than as a mere mechanical flight of fancy. The radical shift in emphasis was further delineated by John Keats in his letters and by Percy Bysshe Shelley in his *Defense of Poetry* (1821)—"poets are the unacknowledged legislators of the world." Diverse trends marked the criticism of the mid-19th century. The didacticism of Matthew Arnold, who held that the aims of literature should be "high seriousness" and a "criticism of life," was countered by Edgar Allan Poe in *The Poetic Principle* (1850), by Walter Pater in *Studies in the History of the Renaissance* (1873), and by Arthur Symons in *The Symbolist Movement in Literature* (1899). These critics celebrated art for art's sake, with no moral strings attached. Henry James, an important novelist and critic of the novel, stressed the possibilities of point of view for further developing the narrative form in his essay "The Art of Fiction" (1893). The emphasis in criticism of this period on the reaction of the critic to the work under scrutiny led to the use of the term impressionistic criticism. However, as the American critic M. H. Abrams has pointed out in *The Mirror and the Lamp* (1953), all criticism, no matter what its form, type, or provenance, emphasizes one of four relationships: the mimetic, the work's connection to reality; the pragmatic, its effect on the audience; the expressive, its connection to the author; and the objective, the work as an independent, self-sufficient creation. The 20th cent. has been called the Age of Criticism. Such major disciplines as psychology and anthropology, and such ideologies as Christian theology and Marxist dialectic, were found to have valid application to works of literature. Freudian analysis became a tool for literary biographers. Carl Jung's theory of the collective unconscious also became a tool, along with anthropological methodology, for critics like T. S. Eliot (in *The Sacred Wood,* 1920) and Northrop Frye (in *Anatomy of Criticism,* 1957), who sought to trace similarities of pattern in literatures of disparate cultures and ages. I. A. Richards used techniques of psychological measurement to examine reader response with new precision, notably in *Practical Criticism* (1929). By means of the so-called New Criticism—the technique of close reading—such critics as Cleanth Brooks, Allen Tate, Lionel Trilling, John Crowe Ransom, and Robert Penn Warren revived the notion of a poem as an autonomous art object. Notable among academic and journalistic critics who used a combination of critical approaches to enlighten their readers are Edmund Wilson (in such works as *The Triple Thinkers,* 1938), W. H. Auden (in *The Dyer's Hand,* 1962), and George Steiner (in *Language and Silence,* 1970). There have been a variety of critical trends in music and art criticism also. The approach has ranged from practical to theoretical, from G. B. Shaw's music reviews in the London press of the 1880s to treatises like Alfred Einstein's *Mozart* (1945) and Charles Rosen's *Classical Style* (1971). And the spectrum of art criticism includes such works as Robin George Collingwood's *Principles of Art* (1938), André Malraux's *Voices of Silence* (1952), and John Canaday's weekly reviews of museum and gallery exhibits. With the decline of representational art and the rise of cubism, abstract expressionism, and minimal art, art critics seem to have proliferated, with critics like Clement Greenberg, Barbara Rose, and Hilton Kramer among the most influential. Newer areas for critical scrutiny include film, architecture, and urban planning. Notable film critics include James Agee, Andre Bazin, and Pauline Kael. Ada Louise Huxtable's architecture criticism and Louis Mumford's studies of the city have broken new ground for critical scrutiny. See George Saintsbury, *A History of Criticism* (3 vol., 1961); F. C. Crews, *The Pooh Perplex* (1963); René Wellek, *A History of Modern Criticism* (4 vol., 1955–65); W. C. Greene, *The Choices of Criticism* (1965).

Critius (krĭsh'əs), or **Kritios** (krĭt'ēōs), and **Nesiotes** (nēshēō'tēz), fl. 5th cent. B.C., Greek sculptors, in the time of the Persian Wars. They made statues of the Tyrannicides, Harmodius and Aristogiton, who slew the tyrant Hipparchus. The works replaced a group by Antenor taken from Athens by Xerxes and later returned. The originals have disappeared, but a number of Roman reproductions survive. The most complete marble copies are those in the national museum at Naples. Critius, probably a pupil of Antenor, established a school of sculpture at Athens.

Crittenden, George Bibb, 1812–80, Confederate general, b. Russellville, Ky.; son of John J. Crittenden and brother of Thomas L. Crittenden. Upon the outbreak of the Civil War, he left the U.S. army to become a Confederate brigadier general. At MILL SPRINGS (Jan., 1862) he was badly defeated and resigned, but he reenlisted and served without rank for the rest of the war.

Crittenden, John Jordan, 1787–1863, U.S. public official, b. Woodford co., Ky. A Kentucky legislator (1811–17), Crittenden entered the U.S. Senate (1817–19) but resigned to resume state offices. He served as Attorney General under Presidents William H. Harrison and John Tyler (March to Sept., 1841) and Millard Fillmore (1850–53). He replaced Henry Clay when Clay resigned from his Senate seat (1842) and was reelected the next year. During his last term in the Senate (1855–61), Crittenden was foremost in attempting to conciliate North and South (see CRITTENDEN COMPROMISE) and was chairman of the Border States Convention (May, 1868). See study by A. D. Kirwan (1962).

Crittenden, Thomas Leonidas, 1819–93, Union general in the Civil War, b. Russellville, Ky.; son of John J. Crittenden and brother of George B. Crittenden. He served in the Mexican War and was (1849–53) U.S. consul at Liverpool. A major general in the Kentucky militia when the Civil War began, Crittenden became a Union brigadier general (Sept., 1861) and was promoted to major general (July, 1862) for his service at Shiloh. He commanded under Rosecrans at Murfreesboro and in the Chattanooga campaign. After being exonerated for the rout of his corps at Chickamauga, he served for a time in the Army of the Potomac. Crittenden resigned his commission in Dec., 1864, but reentered the army in 1867 and served until 1881.

Crittenden, Thomas Theodore, 1832–1909, governor of Missouri (1881–85), b. Shelby co., Ky.; nephew of John J. Crittenden. In the Civil War he served (1862–65) as lieutenant colonel of a Missouri cavalry regiment in the fighting in Missouri and Arkansas. He was state attorney general in Missouri for a brief period after the war and served in the U.S. House of Representatives (1873–75, 1877–79). As governor, Crittenden brought an end to outlaw activity in the state, especially by breaking up the Jesse JAMES gang. In President Cleveland's second term (1893–97) he was consul general in Mexico City. See *The Crittenden Memoirs* (comp. by H. H. Crittenden, 1936).

Crittenden Compromise, in U.S. history, unsuccessful last-minute effort to avert the Civil War. It was proposed in Congress as a constitutional amendment in Dec., 1860, by Sen. John J. Crittenden of Kentucky with support from the National Union party. Basically, it accepted the boundary between free and slave states that had been set by the MISSOURI COMPROMISE (1820–21), extended the line to California, and assured the continuation of slavery where it already existed. In addition, it advocated slavery in the District of Columbia, upheld the FUGITIVE SLAVE LAW (1850) with minor modifications, and called for vigorous suppression of the African slave trade. At a peace conference called by the Virginia legislature in 1861, the compromise gained support from four border state delegations. Nevertheless, it failed in the House of Representatives in Jan., 1861, by a vote of 113 to 80 and in the Senate in March by a vote of 20 to 19. Its defeat made clear the inevitability of the Civil War. See A. D. Kirwan, *John J. Crittenden: The National Union Party Struggle for the Union* (1962).

Crivelli, Carlo (krēvĕl'lē), b. c.1430, d. after 1493, Venetian painter, who worked chiefly in the Marches. His paintings, notable for their rather harsh conception, include the *Virgin and Child* in the Ascoli Cathedral; a large altarpiece (National Gall., London); and *Coronation of the Virgin* (Brera, Milan). His work reveals a crystalline, linear technique and a fondness for elegant decorative motifs. Works in the United States include three entitled *Pietà* (Mus. of Fine Arts, Boston; Fogg Mus., Cambridge; Detroit Inst. of Arts); several of the *Madonna* (Walters Art Gall., Baltimore; National Gall. of Art, Washington, D.C.; Metropolitan Mus.); and *St. George on Horseback* (Gardner Mus., Boston).

Crna Gora: see MONTENEGRO, Yugoslavia.

Croaghpatrick (krō'äpăt'rĭk, krō'äkh-), mountain, 2,510 ft (765 m) high, Co. Mayo, W Republic of Ireland, near Clew Bay. Legend connects it with St. Patrick, and its summit has long been a place of pilgrimage.

croaker, member of the abundant and varied family Sciaenidae, carnivorous, spiny-finned fishes including the weakfishes, the drums, and the whitings. The croaker has a compressed, elongated body similar to that of the bass. The name describes the croaking or grunting sounds produced by members of most species, chiefly during the breeding season. Croakers are found in sandy shallows of all temperate and warm seas. They range in weight from the 1-lb (0.5-kg) Atlantic croaker to the 150-lb (68-kg) common drum. The Atlantic croaker, common from Cape Cod to Texas, is an important food fish. The spot-fin croaker is found in the Pacific. The drums, the largest and noisiest croakers, include the red drum, or channel bass, of which over 2 million lb (900,000 kg) are taken per year off Florida; the common, or black, drum, found from New England to the Rio Grande; and the freshwater drum, found in central North America. The whitings, or kingfishes, include the Northern, or king, whiting, or sea mink; the Southern kingfish, or king whiting; and the surf whiting and its Pacific counterpart, the corbina. All average 3 lb (1.4 kg) in weight and 2 ft (60 cm) in length. Croakers are bottom feeders; those mentioned above have sensitive chin barbels to aid in locating their prey. The weakfishes, named for their easily torn flesh, lack barbels; they are also called sea trout. The common weakfish, or squeteague, abundant along the Atlantic coast, grows to 12 lb (5.5 kg) in weight and 3 ft (90 cm) in length. The more southerly spotted weakfish is similar. The white sea bass, weighing up to 60 lb (27 kg), is a Pacific croaker found as far north as Puget Sound. The spot, a small croaker, is commercially important in Virginia and the Carolinas, where the annual catch is estimated at 10 million lb (4.5 million kg) or more. Croakers are classified in the phylum CHORDATA, subphylum Vertebrata, class Osteichthyes, order Perciformes, family Sciaenidae.

Croatia (krōā'shə), Croatian *Hrvatska* (hərvät'skä), constituent republic of Yugoslavia (1971 pop. 4,422,564), 21,824 sq mi (56,524 sq km), NW Yugoslavia. ZAGREB is the capital. The second largest Yugoslav republic, it includes Croatia proper, SLAVONIA, DALMATIA, and most of ISTRIA. There are important seaports at RIJEKA (Fiume), OSIJEK, SPLIT, PULA, ZADAR, ŠIBENIK, and DUBROVNIK. Western Croatia lies in the Dinaric Alps; the eastern part, drained by the Sava and Drava rivers, is mostly low lying and agricultural. The Pannonian plain is the chief farming region. More than one third of Croatia is forested, and lumber is a major export. The region is the leading coal producer of Yugoslavia, and also has deposits of bauxite, copper, petroleum, and iron ore. The republic is the most industrialized and prosperous area of Yugoslavia. Tourism, especially along the Adriatic coast, is important to the economy. The Croats are Roman Catholic and use the Latin alphabet; there are also Serbs, Slovenes, and other minorities in Croatia. A part of the Roman province of Pannonia, Croatia was settled in the 7th cent. by Croats, who accepted Christianity in the 9th cent. A kingdom from the 10th cent., Croatia conquered surrounding districts, including Dalmatia, which was chronically contested with Venice. Croatia's power reached its peak in the 11th cent., but internecine strife facilitated its conquest in 1091 by King LADISLAUS I of Hungary. In 1102 a pact between his successor and the Croatian tribal chiefs established a personal union of Croatia and Hungary under the Hungarian monarch. Although Croatia remained linked with Hungary for eight centuries, the Croats were sometimes able to choose their rulers independently of Budapest. In personal union with Hungary, Croatia retained its own diet and was governed by a ban, or viceroy. After the battle of MOHÁCS in 1526 most of Croatia came under Turkish rule. In 1527 the Croatian feudal lords agreed to accept the Hapsburgs as their kings in return for common defense and retention of their privileges. During the following century Croatia served as a Hapsburg outpost in the defense of central Europe from a Turkish onslaught. The centralizing and Germanizing tendencies of the Hapsburgs, however, severely weakened the power of the Croatian nobility and awakened a national consciousness. During the 19th cent. Hungary imposed Magyarization on Croatia and promulgated (1848) laws that seriously jeopardized Croatian autonomy within the Hapsburg empire. Joseph JELLACHICH, ban of Croatia, had the diet pass its own revolutionary laws, including the abolition of serfdom. Jellachich's forces also marched against the Hungarian revolutionaries in the 1848–49 uprisings in the Hapsburg empire. When the dual Austro-Hungarian monarchy was established in 1867, Croatia proper and Slavonia were included in the kingdom of Hungary, and Dalmatia and Istria in the Austrian empire. The following year Croatia, united with Slavonia, became an autonomous Hungarian crownland governed by a ban responsible to the Croatian diet. Despite the achievement of autonomy in local affairs, Croatia remained restless because of continuing Magyarization. Cultural and political Croat and South Slav organizations arose, notably the Croatian Peasant party, founded in the early 20th cent. With the collapse of Austria-Hungary (1918), the kingdom of Serbs, Croats, and Slovenes (see YUGOSLAVIA) was formed. Serbs dominated the new state, however, and promoted centralization, ignoring Croat desires for a federal structure. Agitation resulted in the assassination (1928) of Stefan RADIČ, head of the Croatian Peasant party. After Radič's successor, Vladimir MAČEK, connived with fascist Italy to form a separate Croatian state, Yugoslavia allowed the formation (1939) of an autonomous *banovina* comprising Croatia, Dalmatia, and parts of Bosnia and Hercegovina. Nevertheless, many Croats, especially members of the Ustachi fascist terrorist organization, insisted on complete independence. When the Germans invaded Yugoslavia in 1941, the Ustachi seized power and declared Croatian independence under Ante Pavelič. Croatia was placed under Italian and later German military control, while the Ustachi dictatorship perpetuated brutal excesses, including the massacre of thousands of Serbs. A large part of the population joined the anti-fascist Yugoslav partisan forces under TITO, himself a native of Croatia. Pavelič fled in the wake of Germany's defeat in 1945, and Croatia became one of the six republics of reconstituted Yugoslavia. Croatian nationalism persisted in Communist Yugoslavia, however. The Ustachi and other émigré nationalist groups remained active abroad; in 1972 a small band of invaders waged a gun battle with Yugoslav border security forces. Meanwhile, the Yugoslav government hoped that a major decentralization reform that took effect in the early 1970s would satisfy Croat demands for increased republican autonomy and thus dampen secessionist sentiment. See Stephen Gazi, *A History of Croatia* (1973).

Croatoan, unexplained letters found (1590) carved on a tree on ROANOKE ISLAND off North Carolina by Governor John White when he returned to the colony from England and discovered the colonists gone. White took the letters to mean that the settlers had moved to Croatoan Island some 50 mi (80 km) away, but no trace of them was ever found. The name, in the form Croatan, is popular in the region and is perhaps best known in the name of Croatan Sound, which connects Pamlico Sound with Albemarle Sound.

Croce, Benedetto (bānādĕt'tō krô'chā), 1866–1952, Italian philosopher, historian, and critic. He lived mostly in Naples, devoting himself to studying and writing. He founded and edited (1903–44) *Critica,* a review of literature, history, and philosophy, which in 1944 became *Quaderni della critica.* Croce was made a senator in 1910 and was minister of education (1920–21). A staunch opposer of Fascism, he lived in retirement until 1943, when he became a leader of the Liberal party. Croce's system of philosophy is related to the idealistic school in that spirit, monistic in manifestation, constitutes the only reality. The general title of the work presenting his system is *Philosophy of the Spirit* (1902–17; tr. 1909–21), which is divided into four parts, *Aesthetic as Science of Expression and General Linguistic, Logic as the Science of Pure Concept, Philosophy of the Practical,* and *History: Its Theory and Practice.* Among his other works are *A History of Italy, 1871–1915* (1927; tr. 1929) and *History as the Story of Liberty* (1938; tr. 1941). See his essays, *My Philosophy* (tr. 1949); studies by A. A. De Gennaro (1961), G. N. G. Orsini (1961), and Bernard Bosanquet (1972).

crochet work (krōshā'), form of knitting done with a hook, by means of which loops of thread or yarn are drawn through other, preceding loops. Crochet stitches are all based on the chain or single crochet, i.e., a single loop. In double crochet the thread is thrown once about the hook before the loop is drawn. All other stitches and patterns are merely varying combinations of the single or double loop. The art finds its highest expression in Irish crochet, done with the finest thread and hooks in intricate patterns, usually displaying a motif of leaves or flowers set in an open weblike ground. Whole garments, as well as trimmings, hats, and bags are made by the skillful Irish needlewomen.

Crocker, Charles, 1822–88, American railroad builder, b. Troy, N.Y. In 1836 he moved with his family to Marshall co., Ind., where he later set up a small foundry. He joined a party to seek gold in California in 1849. He and a brother opened (1852) a store to sell supplies to miners, and as it prospered they started others, later consolidating them in Sacramento. There Crocker met Mark HOPKINS, Hopkins's partner, Collis P. HUNTINGTON, and Leland STANFORD, and with them he organized (1861) the Central Pacific Railroad Company of California. Crocker undertook responsibility for actual construction, completing it in 1869. His difficulty in maintaining an adequate labor force for the arduous work led to his employment of Chinese laborers, who were kept in a state of virtual slavery. In 1871, Crocker sold out his interest to his partners, but in the Panic of 1873 he returned as director and vice president. See Oscar Lewis, *The Big Four* (1938).

Crockett, Davy (David Crockett), 1786–1836, American frontiersman, b. Limestone, near Greeneville, Tenn. After serving (1813–14) under Andrew Jackson against the Creek Indians in the War of 1812, he settled in Giles co., Tenn., and in 1821 was elected to the state legislature. In 1823, Crockett, having moved to the extreme western part of the state, was reelected from his new constituency. When it was jokingly suggested that he should run for Congress, he took the proposal seriously and served three terms in the House (1827–31, 1833–35). His dress, language, racy backwoods humor, and naive yet shrewd comments on city life and national affairs made him a popular figure in Washington. Crockett became a political opponent of Jackson, and the Whigs took him up so assiduously that he became the showpiece of conservatism. Resenting his defeat for reelection in 1835, Crockett left Tennessee for Texas, where he heroically lost his life in the defense of the ALAMO. *A Narrative of the Life of David Crockett* (1834), *An Account of Col. Crockett's Tour to the North and down East* (1834), and *Col. Crockett's Exploits and Adventures in Texas* (posthumous, 1836) were supposedly written by Crockett himself in his own inimitable idiom, but they do not match, either in content or style, those letters which are definitely known to be his. See his *Narrative,* facsimile edition edited by J. A. Shackford and S. J. Folmsbee (1973); study by J. A. Shackford (1956).

crocodile, large, carnivorous REPTILE of the order Crocodilia, found in tropical and subtropical regions. Crocodiles live in swamps or on river banks and catch their prey in the water. They have flattened bodies and tails, short legs, and powerful jaws. The eyes, ears, and nostrils are located near the top of the head and are exposed when the crocodile floats on the surface of the water. The ears and nostrils have valves that close when the animal is submerged. Most crocodiles are more aggressive than the related ALLIGATORS. The two forms are distinguished by the long lower fourth tooth: in crocodiles, but not in alligators, this tooth protrudes on the side of the head when the mouth is closed. The snouts of most crocodiles are narrower than those of alligators. Small crocodiles feed on fish and small aquatic animals; larger ones also catch land mammals and birds that approach the water. Members of some large species sometimes attack and eat humans. The female crocodile deposits her eggs, usually about 20 in number, in a nest of rotting vegetation or in a shallow pit on the river bank, and digs them up when she hears them hatching. In most species the average adult length is between 6 and 10 ft (1.8–3 m). The largest crocodile (the saltwater crocodile) is often 14 ft (4.3 m) long and may exceed 20 ft (6 m) in length. The Nile, American, and Orinoco crocodiles are commonly 12 ft (3.7 m) long, and specimens up to 23 ft (7 m) long have been reported for the last two species. The smallest crocodile (the Congo dwarf crocodile) averages 3½ ft (105 cm) long. With the exception of the two African dwarf crocodiles (*Osteolaemus*) and the so-called false gavial (*Tomistoma*) of Asia, crocodiles are classified in the genus *Crocodylus,* with about a dozen species. The Nile crocodile (*Crocodylus niloticus*) is found in fresh and salt water throughout S and central Africa. In early historic times it ranged N to the Nile delta and the Mediterranean coast. It sometimes attacks humans, as does the saltwater crocodile (*C. porosus*), found on islands and in straits from SE Asia to Australia and Melanesia. The marsh crocodile, or mugger (*C. palustris*), is a freshwater species of India and Ceylon, regarded as sacred in some regions. The American crocodile (*C. acutus*) is found in fresh and salt water in S Florida, the West Indies, Central America, and NW South America. It does not attack humans without provocation. The Orinoco crocodile (*C. intermedius*) is a freshwater species of the Orinoco basin of Colombia and Venezuela. Two smaller species are found in limited areas of Central America and Cuba. Crocodiles are classified in the phylum CHORDATA, subphylum Vertebrata, class Reptilia, order Crocodilia, family Crocodilidae. See also GAVIAL.

crocus: see IRIS.

Croesus (krē'səs), d. c.547 B.C., king of Lydia (560–c.546 B.C.), noted for his great wealth. He was the son of Alyattes. He continued his father's policy of conquering the Ionian cities of Asia Minor, but on the whole he was friendly to the Greeks, and he is supposed to have given refuge to the Athenian statesman Solon. Threatened by CYRUS THE GREAT of Persia, Croesus allied himself with Amasis II of Egypt and Nabonidus of Babylonia against the Persian might, but the alliance was of no avail. Cyrus defeated and captured Croesus, and, according to Herodotus, Croesus cast himself upon a funeral pyre.

crofting: see BLEACHING.

Croghan, George (krō'gən), d. 1782, American Indian agent, b. Ireland. He migrated to North America in 1741 and became (1756) deputy superintendent of Indian affairs under Sir William JOHNSON. Croghan was to a large extent responsible for Johnson's success and reputation among the Indians. In the French and Indian War he caused many tribes to desert the French cause. See biographies by A. T. Volwiler (1926, repr. 1971) and N. B. Wainwright (1959).

Croghan, George, 1791–1849, American military officer, b. near Louisville, Ky.; nephew of George Rogers Clark and William Clark. He won public acclaim and a congressional award for his defense of Fort Stephenson against almost overwhelming enemy forces in the War of 1812. Croghan later served under Zachary Taylor in the Mexican War. See *Army Life on the Western Frontier,* selections from Croghan's official reports ed. by F. P. Prucha (1958).

Croissy, Charles Colbert, marquis de (shärl kôlbĕr' märkē də krwäsē'), c.1625–96, French diplomat, brother of Jean Baptiste Colbert. He entered the service of Cardinal Mazarin and filled many diplomatic posts in Europe in the 1650s and 60s. In 1668 he signed the peace treaty of Aix-la-Chapelle, which ended the War of Devolution. As ambassador to England (1668–74) he negotiated the first treaty of Dover with King Charles II (1670). In 1678 he became president for life of the Parlement of Paris. Becoming minister of state for foreign affairs in 1680, he worked to develop an alliance system for France and was probably instrumental in developing the "chambers of reunion" to aid Louis XIV's expansionist ambitions.

Croix, Carlos Francisco de Croix, marqués de (kär'lōs frănthēs'kō dā krəwä' märkās' dā krəwä'), 1699–1786, Spanish colonial administrator, b. Lille, France. As viceroy of New Spain (1766–71), he was a genial, honest, and industrious official, but the real ruler was José de GÁLVEZ, the Visitor-General. Many reforms were instituted; the Jesuits were expelled (1767); and the natives of NW Mexico were subdued in order to open the California frontier. His nephew, **Teodoro de Croix,** 1730–91, was military commander and provincial governor in Mexico before becoming viceroy of Peru (1784–90). He put into operation the reforms in Indian administration that resulted indirectly from the revolt of Tupac Amaru.

Croker, John Wilson (krō'kər), 1780–1857, British Tory politician and author, b. Ireland. He was a member of Parliament from 1807 to 1832 and secretary of the admiralty from 1810 to 1830. The most famous of his regular contributions as a critic to the *Quarterly Review* was his virulent attack (1818) on Keats's *Endymion.* Croker's best work was his careful edition (1831) of Boswell's *Life of Johnson.* See *Croker Papers* (ed. by L. J. Jennings, 3 vol., 1884; repr. 1972).

Croker, Richard, 1841–1922, American politician, head of TAMMANY Hall from 1886 to 1902, b. Co. Cork, Ireland. He became prominent as Democratic leader of New York City's East Side and as an aide of John KELLY. He was elected (1868) alderman and held minor appointive offices, which increased in importance after Kelly succeeded (1871) William M. Tweed as boss. Croker became Kelly's chief lieutenant, and after Kelly's death (1886) Croker was the acknowledged Tammany boss. Croker was (1889–90) city chamberlain and brought about the elections of Hugh Grant (1888), Thomas F. Gilroy (1892), and Robert Van Wyck (1897) as mayors. The election (1901) of Seth Low as mayor of New York caused Croker's abdication as Tammany leader, and he was succeeded by Charles F. MURPHY. Croker spent the remainder of his life in leisure in England and Ireland. See T. L. Stoddard, *Master of Manhattan* (1931).

Croker, Thomas Crofton, 1798–1854, Irish antiquary, b. Cork. One of the first to collect Irish folklore, he compiled *Fairy Legends and Traditions of the South of Ireland* (1825–28), *Legends of the Lakes* (1829), and *Popular Songs of Ireland* (1837).

Croly, Jane Cunningham, pseud. **Jennie June,** 1829–1901, American journalist and feminist, b. England. She came to the United States at the age of 12 and in 1857 married author and editor David Goodman Croly. She was one of the earliest American newspaperwomen, writing for various New York newspapers under the pseudonym Jennie June. From 1860 to 1887 she edited *Demorest's Quarterly Mirror of Fashion* (later *Demorest's Illustrated Monthly*) and later was part owner of *Godey's Lady's Book.* She specialized in women's features and was among the first journalists who syndicated their articles. In 1856 she called the first women's congress. Twelve years later, in 1868, she founded Sorosis, the only women's club of importance at that time, and in 1889, the New York Women's Press Club. She wrote *The History of the Woman's Club Movement in America* (1898).

Cro-Magnon man (krō"-măg'nŏn), human being that lived about 35,000 years ago. Skeletal remains, associated with artifacts of the Aurignacian culture, were first found (1868) in the rock shelter of Cro-Magnon in Les Eyzies, Dordogne, France. Later finds, differing slightly from each other in skeletal characteristics, were made in a number of caverns in the Dordogne valley, Solutré, and in Spain, Germany, Czechoslovakia, and Poland. Cro-Magnon man is of the same species as modern man (*Homo sapiens*). Unlike NEANDERTHAL MAN, whom he superseded, Cro-Magnon stood straight and was 6 ft (180 cm) or more tall. The head was balanced as in modern man; the forehead was high, the brain large, and the chin well developed. Skillfully made flint and bone tools, shell and ivory jewelry, and polychrome paintings found on the walls of some caves in S France and N Spain indicate an advanced culture. See MAN, PREHISTORIC.

Cromarty, county, Scotland: see ROSS AND CROMARTY.

Cromarty Firth, deep narrow inlet of Moray Firth, c.15 mi (25 km) long, in Ross and Cromarty co., N Scotland. It provides excellent anchorage, its narrow entrance being protected by the headlands of the Sutor rocks, more than 400 ft (122 m) high.

Cromberger, Juan: see PABLOS, JUAN.

Crome, John, 1768–1821, English landscape painter, b. Norwich. Crome was the principal painter of the Norwich school. He is often called Old Crome to distinguish him from his son who painted in the same manner but with less mastery. He was born into poverty but rose to the position of a provincial landscape painter, earning his living by giving drawing lessons and selling an occasional picture. Crome's work was influenced by Gainsborough and by the Dutch masters. His landscapes are notable for simplicity and serenity. Beautiful examples are to be seen in many British galleries and private collections. *Mousehold Heath* and *Poringland Oak* are in the National Gallery, London. The Metropolitan Museum has *The Old Oak* and *Hautbois Common.* Crome's etchings were published after his death under the title *Norfolk Picturesque.* See studies by R. H. Mottram (1931) and D. and T. Clifford (1968).

Cromer, Evelyn Baring, 1st earl of (ĕv'lĭn bâr'ĭng krō'mər), 1841–1917, British administrator in Egypt. Appointed (1877) first British commissioner of the Egyptian public debt office, he directed investigations by France and England into the bankrupt administration of ISMAIL PASHA. After the deposition of Ismail and accession of TEWFIK PASHA, Baring became (1879) British controller general in Egypt. He was (1880–83) finance minister in India and returned to Egypt after Arabi Pasha's nationalist revolt to become British agent and consul general in 1883. Until his resignation in 1907, Baring (created Baron Cromer in 1892 and earl in 1901) was the virtual ruler of Egypt. Faced with the Mahdist rebellion in Sudan, he recommended Egyptian withdrawal and only reluctantly agreed to the appointment of Charles George GORDON to arrange the evacuation. He reformed Egyptian finances, administration, and education; improved the railroads; and developed methods of agriculture and irrigation. After the reconquest (1896–98) of the Sudan, he devised the Anglo-Egyptian system of government. Cromer was a Greek scholar and wrote books on imperial and Egyptian affairs. See biography by L. J. L. Zetland (1932); study by John Marlowe (1970).

cromlech (krŏm'lĕk) [Welsh or Breton,=crooked stone], term that has changed in meaning from its original equivalent to DOLMEN. It later came to be used for a single standing stone and now usually refers to a circle of such stones, as at STONEHENGE.

Crommelynck, Fernand (fĕrnäN' krômələ̆Nk'), 1888?–, Belgian dramatist, b. Brussels. Crommelynck earned his living as an actor before the great success of his tragic farce about jealousy *Le Cocu magnifique* (1921, tr. 1966). Other plays that reveal his expert craftsmanship and strong lyric power include *Le Sculpteur de masques* (1908), *Le Marchand de regrets* (1913), and *Carine* (1930). See the translation of two plays by Marnit Gijsen (1966).

Crompton, Samuel, 1753–1827, English inventor of the mule spinner, or muslin wheel, an important step in the development of fine cotton spinning. Working as a young man in a spinning mill, he knew the defects of the Hargreaves jenny and determined to produce something better. After five years of secret work, he perfected (1779) a machine that combined the features of the jenny and Arkwright's frame and that, in one operation, by drawing, twisting, and winding the cotton, produced a very fine yarn. Crompton, however, was too poor to obtain a patent for his invention and sold his rights for £60. Later Parliament granted him £5,000.

Cromwell, Oliver, 1599–1658, lord protector of England. The son of a gentry family, he entered Cambridge in 1616 but probably left the next year. Cromwell entered Parliament in 1628, standing firmly with the opposition to CHARLES I, and was active in the Short and Long Parliaments (1640), although not a conspicuous leader. During the first civil war (see ENGLISH CIVIL WAR) he rose rapidly to leadership because of his military ability and his genius for organizing and inspiring the parliamentary armies. His own regiment, the Ironsides, distinguished itself at Marston Moor (1644) and in numerous minor engagements. In 1644 he pressed for a thorough reorganization of the parliamentary forces and was appointed (1645) second in command to Sir Thomas Fairfax (later Baron FAIRFAX OF CAMERON) in the resulting New Model Army, which defeated the king at Naseby in 1645. In the quarrel between the army and Parliament following the first civil war, Cromwell, himself an Independent, supported the sectarians in the army and approved the seizure (1647) of Charles from Parliament. However, he favored a moderate settlement with the king (as opposed to the radical proposals of the LEVELERS) until Charles's flight to Carisbrooke (1647) and secret dealings with the Scots caused him to lose all hope of further negotiations with the king. In the second civil war he repelled the Scottish royalist invasion at Preston (1648). His political power was enhanced by the removal of Presbyterian leaders from Parliament in Pride's Purge (see under PRIDE, THOMAS), and at the king's trial (1649) his was the leading voice demanding execution. In 1649, after the proclamation of the republican Commonwealth, Cromwell led a punitive expedition into Ireland, remembered primarily for the massacre of the royalist garrison at Drogheda. He then initiated a policy of systematic dispossession of the Irish, transferring their lands to English landlords. In 1650 he invaded Scotland and routed the Scottish royalists at Dunbar; later he defeated the Scots and Charles II himself at Worcester (1651) and left the rest of the conquest of Scotland to Gen. George Monck. Cromwell, now virtual dictator of the Commonwealth, dissolved the Rump Parliament in 1653 after it had failed to effect reforms demanded by the army and had sought to perpetuate its power. His attempt to replace it by the Nominated (Barebone's) Parliament (see BAREBONE, PRAISE-GOD), appointed by himself from nominations of the Independent congregations, resulted in a reckless, hopelessly divided body that was finally forced to dissolve itself. A group of army officers then drew up the constitutional document known as the Instrument of Government (1653), by which Cromwell became lord protector (see PROTECTORATE). The Parliament of 1654, which was elected under the terms of the same document, wanted to prepare a new constitution and was soon dissolved. After that Cromwell resorted to open military government, dividing England into 11 districts, each administered by a major-general. Another, more amenable Parliament was summoned in 1656, and in 1657 it presented to Cromwell a new constitution known as the Humble Petition and Advice and offered him the crown. He declined the crown but accepted (with some modifications) the Humble Petition, which further increased his power and set up a second legislative chamber. The second session of this same Parliament, however, challenged the new constitution, and Cromwell dissolved it (1658) seven months before his death. Cromwell's foreign policy was governed by the need to expand English trade and prevent the restoration of the Stuarts, and by the desire to build up a Protestant league and enhance the prestige of the English republic. He approved the Navigation Act of 1651, which led to the first (1652–54) of the DUTCH WARS, and he pressed the war against Spain (1655–58) as a means of encroaching on Spanish rights of colonization in America. The Dutch war resulted in several important naval victories for the English under Admiral Robert BLAKE, but the Spanish war, apart from the sinking of a Spanish fleet (also by Blake), brought only Jamaica and imposed a great strain on English finances. Although Cromwell professed love for both toleration and constitutional government, only Jews and non-Anglican Protestants (excepting Quakers) were tolerated during his rule, and he found it impossible to cooperate with Parliament in governing. Opinions of Cromwell have always varied widely. His military skill and force of character are universally recognized. He met the task of holding together the gains of the civil wars and the disharmonious groups in the Puritan party in what seemed the only practical way. This involved cruelty, force, and intolerance, which were evidently alien to him personally. His government, dependent on his own strong character, costly in its foreign policy, and representing a break in English institutions and a minority religious viewpoint, could not survive him long. He was succeeded as protector by his son Richard. See the writings and speeches of Oliver Cromwell (ed. by W. C. Abbott and others, 4 vol., 1937–47); biographies by M. P. Ashley (1969), J. E. C. Hill (1970), C. V. Wedgwood (rev. ed. 1973), and Antonia Fraser (1973); M. P. Ashley, *The Greatness of Oliver Cromwell* (1957, repr. 1966); writings on the period by Samuel Rawson GARDINER and Sir Charles FIRTH.

Cromwell, Richard, 1626–1712, lord protector of England; third son of Oliver Cromwell. He was the eldest surviving son at the death of his father (Sept. 3, 1658), who had nominated him as his successor. Although he had served in Parliament and on the council of state, Richard lacked the energy and experience to manage complicated affairs of state. Army and Parliament struggled for power, and the army forced Richard to dismiss Parliament on April 22, 1659. His Protectorate had actually collapsed, but it continued in name until May 25, when the Rump Parliament, which had reassembled itself, reestablished the Commonwealth. He lived abroad (1660–80) and later in England under an assumed name. A man of integrity and dignity, he was unfortunate in being forced into a situation too difficult for his talents. See biography by R. W. Ramsay (1935); study by E. M. Hause (1972).

Cromwell, Thomas, earl of Essex, 1485?–1540, English statesman. While a young man he lived abroad as a soldier, accountant, and merchant, and on his return (c.1512) to England he engaged in the wool trade and eventually became a lawyer. He entered Parliament in 1523 and soon became legal secretary to Cardinal WOLSEY, for whom he managed the suppression of minor monasteries. He avoided being disgraced with Wolsey in 1529, and by 1531 was serving HENRY VIII as a member of the privy council. By 1532 he had become the king's chief minister and was responsible for drafting most of the acts of Parliament by which the Reformation was effected. He probably originated the idea of making the king supreme head of the Church in England. As Henry's vicar-general after 1535, he supervised (1536–9) the visitation and suppression of monasteries and the confiscation of monastic lands and wealth. Much of Cromwell's unpopularity with the people, demonstrated by the PILGRIMAGE OF GRACE, derived from the ruthlessness of his agents in carrying out that project. He issued injunctions to the clergy, regulating their conduct and duties, assailed the worship of images and relics, and initiated a much-needed system of parish registers. He was made a baron and lord privy seal in 1536, lord great chamberlain in 1539, and earl of Essex in 1540. He negotiated the king's marriage to ANNE OF CLEVES as a means of securing the North German princes as allies against the Catholic Holy Roman emperor Charles V. When Anne proved unattractive and the alliance failed, Henry allowed charges of treason and heresy to be brought against Cromwell by his bitter enemy the duke of Norfolk. Cromwell was condemned by act of attainder and beheaded. See biographies by R. B. Merriman (1902), Theodore Maynard (1950), and A. G. Dickens (1959); G. R. Elton, *The Tudor Revolution in Government* (1953) and *Reform and Renewal* (1973).

Cronaca, Il: see POLLAIUOLO.

Cronin, A. J. (Archibald Joseph Cronin), 1896–, Scottish novelist. He gave up his prosperous London medical practice to devote himself to writing after the success of his first novel, *Hatter's Castle* (1931). His novels, written in a direct simple style, reflect both his religious beliefs as a Roman Catholic and his medical training. He is best known for *The Citadel* (1937), *The Keys of the Kingdom* (1941), *The Green Years* (1944), *Shannon's Way* (1948), and *Pocketful of Rye* (1969).

Cronje, Piet Arnoldus (pēt ärnôld'əs krŏn'yā), 1835?–1911, South African military commander. A Boer, he commanded the Transvaal forces that frustrated the raid against the Transvaal led by Sir Leander Starr Jameson. In the South African War (1899–1902), Cronje conducted the unsuccessful siege of Kimberley. Retreating west before the advance of Lord Roberts, he was surrounded (1900) at Paardeberg and forced to surrender.

Cronkite, Walter, 1916–, American radio and television newsman, b. St. Joseph, Mo. He left the Univ. of Texas to write for the Houston *Press* and later for other Scripps-Howard newspapers. In 1939 he became a wire-service reporter with United Press, serving as a war correspondent (1942–45) and as a reporter at the Nuremberg trials. He joined the Columbia Broadcasting System in 1950 and in 1962 became managing editor and anchorman of "The CBS Evening News with Walter Cronkite." In 1973 a national poll indicated that he was the most trusted newsman in the United States. His books include *Challenges of Change* (1971).

Cronstadt: see KRONSHTADT, USSR.

Cronstedt, Axel Fredrik, Baron (äk'səl frā'drĭk, kro͞on'stĕt), 1722–65, Swedish mineralogist and chemist. In 1751 he discovered in niccolite an impure form of nickel, reported it as a newly discovered element, and proposed the name nickel for it. He was one of the first to recognize the importance of the chemical constituents of minerals and rocks and to use the blowpipe in the study of minerals. He wrote *An Essay towards a System of Mineralogy* (1758; tr., 2d ed., 1788).

Cronus (krō'nəs), in Greek legend, the youngest Titan, son of Uranus and Gaea. With the help of his mother, he led the Titans in the revolt against Uranus and ruled the world. He married his sister Rhea and fathered the great gods—Zeus, Poseidon, Demeter, Hera, Hades, and Hestia. Because he was fated to be overthrown by one of his children, he swallowed them all as infants until Rhea hid Zeus and presented Cronus with a stone wrapped in a blanket, which he ate. Later Zeus tricked him into disgorging his children. Zeus then led the Olympian gods in overthrowing Cronus in the battle called the Titanomachy, described by Hesiod. Cronus and all the defeated Titans, except Atlas, were exiled. Cronus is equated with the Roman Saturn and was probably a god of a pre-Hellenic people.

Crook, George, 1828–90, U.S. general, b. near Dayton, Ohio, grad. West Point, 1852. During the Civil War, Crook commanded a regiment of Ohio volunteers as colonel. After the war he operated so successfully against the Paiute and Snake Indians in Idaho and the Apache in Arizona that he was promoted (1873) to brigadier general in the regular army. Made commander of the Dept. of the Platte in 1875, he was engaged in the hard-fought Sioux War of 1876. In Arizona in 1883, Crook led an expedition into the mountains against a Chiricahua band of the Apache and finally succeeded in persuading GERONIMO to return to the reservation (1884). Later, Geronimo broke his pact and escaped, which led to censure of Crook's policies and his voluntary resignation. From 1888 until his death Crook was major general and commander of the Division of the Missouri. Although his fame rested upon his Indian campaigns, Crook also had a reputation for enlightened patience and integrity in dealing with Indian affairs, preferring negotiation to warfare. See his autobiography (ed. by M. F. Schmitt, 2d ed. 1960) and contemporary accounts by J. F. Finerty (1961) and Charles King (rev. ed. 1964).

Crooked Island: see BAHAMA ISLANDS.

Crookes, Sir William, 1832–1919, English chemist and physicist. After serving at the Radcliffe Observatory, Oxford, and teaching chemistry at Chester Training College, he retired to work in his own laboratory in London. He discovered the element thallium and made special studies of radioactive substances in the course of which he invented the spinthariscope, used to make visible the flashes produced by bombarding a screen with the alpha rays of a particle of radium, and he devised the radiometer, which measures the intensity of radiant energy. He also intensively studied the rare earths and diamonds. Crookes devised spectacles to protect the eyes of glassworkers from damaging rays. One of his chief inventions is the Crookes tube, with which J. J. Thomson, W. C. Roentgen, R. A. Millikan, and others conducted important research. He founded the *Chemical News* in 1859 and was the author of numerous scientific papers and of *Select Methods in Chemical Analysis* (1871). Crookes was also interested in psychical research.

Crookes tube, device invented by Sir William Crookes (c.1875) consisting essentially of a sealed glass tube from which nearly all the air has been removed and through the walls of which are passed two electrodes. When a high voltage is applied between the two electrodes, electrons are emitted from the CATHODE and are accelerated toward the anode. Many of these electrons, or cathode rays (as they are usually called), miss the anode and strike instead the glass wall of the tube, causing it to exhibit fluorescence. The behavior of the rays indicates that they travel in straight lines and exert a pressure on any object placed in their path. The Crookes tube was used by Crookes in a number of experiments and was later used in experiments leading to the discovery of X rays by W. C. Roentgen (1895) and of the electron by J. J. Thomson (1897).

Cropsey, Jasper Francis, 1823–1900, American artist, b. Staten Island, N.Y. Trained as an architect, Cropsey designed two churches in Staten Island and several stations on the Sixth Ave. elevated railway in Manhattan. He was a founder of the American Water Color Society and is noted for his landscapes and Civil War scenes.

croquet (krōkā'), lawn game in which the players hit wooden balls with wooden mallets through a series of 9 or 10 wire arches, or wickets. The first player to hit the posts placed at each end of the field wins. The game developed in France in the 17th cent. and has been popular also, with varying rules, in Great Britain and the United States. Roque (minus the first and last letters of *croquet*) is an American variant devised in 1899. See Paul Brown, *Croquet* (1957); A. G. F. Ross, *Croquet Handbook* (1959); J. W. Solomon, *Croquet* (1966).

Crosby, Bing, 1904–, American singer and film actor, b. Tacoma, Wash., as Harry Lillis Crosby. He sang with dance bands from 1925 to 1930; in 1931 he began work in radio and films and gained enormous popularity for his "crooning" style. In 1944 he won an Academy Award for his performance in *Going My Way*. Crosby's other notable films include *The Country Girl* (1955) and *Stagecoach* (1966). See his autobiography, *Call Me Lucky* (1953); Kathryn Crosby, *Bing and Other Things* (1967).

Crosby, municipal borough (1971 pop. 57,405), Lancashire, NW England, on Liverpool Bay. Formed in 1937 from the urban districts of Great Crosby and Waterloo-with-Seaforth, Crosby is primarily residential. The local history of Crosby dates back more than 1,000 years. The Merchant Taylor's School for boys was founded in 1620. In 1974, Crosby became part of the new metropolitan county of Merseyside.

Cross, Wilbur Lucius, 1862–1948, American educator and public official, b. Mansfield, Conn., grad. Yale (B.A., 1885; Ph.D., 1889). He was instructor (1894–97), assistant professor (1897–1902), and professor (1902–30) of English at Yale, where he also was dean (1916–30) of the graduate school. Cross became well known as a literary critic, edited the *Yale Review* for almost 30 years, and was the author of *The Life and Times of Laurence Sterne* (1909), *The History of Henry Fielding* (1918), and books on the English novel. After he retired (1930) from Yale he turned to politics. As Democratic governor of Connecticut (1931–39), he brought about much reform legislation—abolition of child labor, governmental reorganization, and improved factory laws. See his autobiography, *Connecticut Yankee* (1943).

cross, widely used symbol. In various forms, it can be found in such diverse cultures as those of ancient India, Egypt, and the American Indians. It is found in the megalithic monuments of Western Europe. The most important use is among Christians, to whom it recalls the crucifixion of Jesus and man's redemption thereby. The Christian form of blessing by tracing a cross over oneself or another person or thing originated before A.D. 200. The oldest Christian remains contain drawings of crosses and cruciform artifacts, and the fact that the cross was the Christian emblem before the toleration of Christianity is shown by the vision of CONSTANTINE I. His mother, St. HELENA, is supposed to have found the True Cross at Calvary in 327, and the event is commemorated on May 3 as the Finding of the Cross. Splinters of the relic are widely distributed and honored by Roman Catholics and Orthodox Eastern. In 614, to the scandal of Christendom, Khosru II of Persia took the largest piece of the relic from Jerusalem. It was restored by Heraclius I in 627; the anniversary of this event is Sept. 14, the Exaltation of the Cross. The relic was lost in the Muslim occupation of Jerusalem. Use of the cross was one of the popular practices attacked by Byzantine iconoclasm and vindicated (787) by the Second Council of Nicaea. The crucifix—the cross with the figure of Jesus upon it—had already been established in use; at first, the figure was painted or in bas-relief, a style surviving in the Christian East. Older Western crucifixes often presented the Savior reigning, in robe and crown; the realistic dying figure, dating from the Renaissance, is now universal in Roman Catholicism. Devotion to the cross as a symbol of the Passion is an outstanding development (from the 11th cent.) in the history of Christian thought; it has ever since been an essential part of the public and private religious life of Roman Catholics. Protestants have been generally sparing in using the cross, even in blessings, and have abandoned the crucifix, but the symbolism has been retained in their literature (e.g., in the hymn, *When I Survey the Wondrous Cross*). The cross was the badge of the Crusades and was adopted as the emblem of the Templars, of the Knights Hospitalers (Knights of Malta), and of the Teutonic Knights. It became important in HERALDRY, FLAG designs, and DECORATIONS. There are many shapes of crosses. The Latin cross, the commonest, has upright longer than transom. With two transoms it is called an archiepiscopal or patriarchal cross; with three it is a papal cross. A cross widely used by Slavs and by others of Eastern rites has two transoms and a slanting crosspiece below. The Greek cross has equal arms. St. Andrew's cross is like an X, and the tau cross is like a T. The Celtic, or Iona, cross bears a circle, the center of which is the crossing. The Maltese cross and the swastika (an ancient and widely diffused symbol) are still more elaborate. Examples of artistic effort spent on crosses are seen in the monumental crosses of market, town, and wayside in Europe (e.g., at Cheddar, Malmesbury, and Winchester, England) and in the wayside calvaries of Austria and Brittany. Some of the finest art products of the Celts were stone crosses. (For the later Eleanor Crosses, see ELEANOR OF CASTILE). Processional crosses (on poles) lend themselves to elaboration. Crosses are also worn for personal adornment. Pectoral crosses and necklace crosses have given scope for fine enameling.

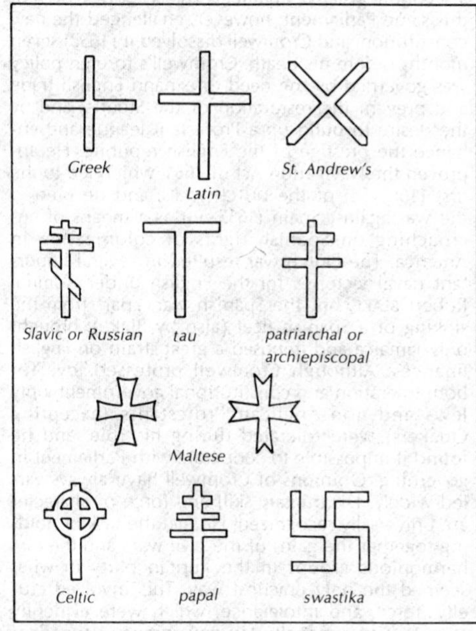

Types of crosses

crossbill, bird of the genus *Loxia*, in the FINCH family. Its bill, crossed at the tips, is specialized for pulling apart pine cones and picking out the seeds. Crossbills are found in the evergreen forests of the Northern Hemisphere, as far south as NW Africa and Guatemala. Two species occur in the United States. The red crossbill (*L. curvirostra*) is found in Europe and in N and central Asia as well as in North America. Males have orange to dull red plumage, with black wings. The white-winged crossbill (*L. leucoptera*) occurs in northern Russia and in North America; the male of this species is rosy red and both sexes are marked with white wing bars. Females of both species are olive-gray and yellow; they lay three to four pale green, brown-spotted eggs, in well-formed nests built in trees. Crossbills are not considered migratory, but they shift their breeding grounds erratically, probably in response to the availability of pine cones. Sometimes they suddenly appear in large numbers in areas where they are rarely seen. They are classified in the phylum CHORDATA, subphylum Vertebrata, class Aves, order Passeriformes, family Fringillidae.

crossbow: see BOW AND ARROW.

cross-examination: see EVIDENCE.

cross-eye: see STRABISMUS.

cross-fertilization: see FERTILIZATION.

Cross-Florida Waterway: see OKEECHOBEE WATERWAY.

crossing over, process in genetics by which the two CHROMOSOMES of a homologous pair exchange equal segments with each other. Crossing over occurs in the first division of MEIOSIS. At that stage each chromosome has replicated into two strands called sister chromatids. The two homologous chromosomes of a pair synapse, or come together. While the chromosomes are synapsed, breaks occur at corresponding points in two of the non-sister chromatids, i.e., in one chromatid of each chromosome. Since the chromosomes are homologous, breaks at corresponding points mean that the segments that are broken off contain corresponding GENES, i.e., alleles. The broken sections are then exchanged between the chromosomes to form complete new units, and each new recombined chromosome of the pair can go to a different daughter sex cell. Crossing over results in RECOMBINATION of genes found on the same chromosome, called linked genes, that would otherwise always be transmitted together. Because the frequency of crossing over between any two linked genes is proportional to the chromosomal distance between them, crossing over frequencies are used to construct genetic, or linkage, maps of genes on chromosomes. MUTATIONS, temperature changes, and radiation all affect crossing over frequency. Under the microscope, a crossover has the appearance of an *X* and is called a chiasma.

crossword puzzle, word game played on a rectangle marked with white and black squares that may or may not form a design; crossword puzzles typically appear in newspapers. Two lists of numbered definitions are given, one for horizontal words, the other for vertical words. The puzzle is solved when all the words are correctly supplied. In the diagramless puzzle, there is no key to the length of the words used. A crossword puzzle inscription has been found on an ancient tomb in Egypt; the puzzle first appeared in the modern world in Great Britain in the 19th cent. as a children's game, and after 1920 it became popular with adults there and in the United States. See ACROSTIC; ANAGRAM.

Croswell case, U.S. court case involving freedom of the press. In 1803, Harry Croswell, the editor of the *Wasp* of Hudson, N.Y., was convicted of libeling President Thomas Jefferson in his newspaper. In his appeal of the conviction to the New York supreme court, Croswell was defended by Alexander Hamilton. In a famous brief, Hamilton argued that freedom of the press consisted in the right to print the truth, if with good motives and for justifiable ends, even if this truth reflected on "the government, magistracy or individuals." Although the court sustained the conviction, the legislature of New York incorporated Hamilton's position into law in 1805. It was the law of libel until 1964, when *New York Times Company* vs. *Sullivan* expanded the protection of the press.

Crothers, Rachel (krŭth′ərz), 1878–1958, American playwright and director, b. Bloomington, Ill., grad. Illinois State Normal Univ., 1892. Her plays, many of which were social comedies treating the ethical problems of women, were notable for their craftsmanship. Among her major successes were *The Three of Us* (1906), *A Man's World* (1909), *He and She* (1911), *Old Lady 31* (1916), *Let Us Be Gay* (1929), and *Susan and God* (1937).

Croton, Italy: see CROTONA.

Crotona (krōtō′nə) or **Croton** (krō′tən), ancient city, S Italy, on the east coast of Bruttium (now Calabria), a colony of MAGNA GRAECIA founded c.708 B.C. There Pythagoras established his school, which exerted a notable political and moral influence. The nearby temple of Hera Lacinia was the religious shrine of Magna Graecia. Crotona's athletes won fame at the Olympic games. The height of the city's prosperity was reached after the army, led by the athlete Milo, destroyed the rival town of Sybaris (510 B.C.). Crotona then became involved in wars and soon declined. It was captured by the Romans in 277 B.C.; until modern times it was never more than a provincial town. It was called Cotrone from the Middle Ages until 1928, when its name was changed to Crotone.

Croton Aqueduct (krō′tən), 38 mi (61 km) long, SE N.Y., carrying water from the Croton River basin to New York City; built 1837–42. It was one of the earliest modern aqueducts in the United States. Water impounded by New Croton Dam (completed 1905) is channeled S to the Bronx, for most of its length in a covered trench along the surface. Water is carried over the Harlem River into Manhattan by Highbridge, a Roman-type aqueduct bridge. New Croton Aqueduct (built 1885–91), 30.5 mi (49 km) long, supplements the flow of Croton Aqueduct. Deep underground tunnels, including one under the Harlem River, channel water from this aqueduct to New York City.

Croton bug: see COCKROACH.

Crotone: see CROTONA.

croup (kro͞op), acute obstructive laryngitis in young children, usually between the ages of three and six. The manifestations are a high-pitched cough and difficulty in breathing, owing to a spasm or swelling of the larynx. The cause can be an acute infection (especially by the influenza virus or diphtheria bacterium), an allergy, a tumor of the larynx, or obstruction by a swallowed object. Treatment depends on the cause; e.g., antibiotics are used in the case of bacterial infections, epinephrine and similar drugs in the case of allergy. The inhalation of steam from a vaporizer or hot-water faucet relieves breathing difficulties in most cases. In severe cases oxygen may be administered, or it may be necessary to cut an opening in the trachea to prevent suffocation.

crow, partially migratory black bird of the same family as the raven, the magpie, the jay, and the rook and the jackdaw of Europe. The American, or common, crow, about 19 in. (49 cm) long, has a wingspread of over 3 ft (92 cm). Crows eat some eggs and nestlings and grain, but destroy many harmful insects and rodents. In winter they gather at night by thousands in communal roosts. Crows, along with the other members of the family Corvidae, are considered to be the most intelligent of all birds. They are easily tamed and can learn to mimic some human sounds. Their throaty "caw" is familiar, although they can also produce a musical warble. The fish crow of the Atlantic and Gulf coasts is smaller than the common crow. The carrion crow of Great Britain is a flesh-eating bird 18 to 20 in. (46–51 cm) long. Crows are classified in the phylum CHORDATA, subphylum Vertebrata, class Aves, order Passeriformes, family Corvidae.

crowberry, evergreen alpine and arctic shrub of the genus *Empetrum* (or, sometimes, other related species), bearing black, red, or purple berrylike fruits. Some are cultivated in rock gardens. Crowberry is classified in the division MAGNOLIOPHYTA, class Magnoliopsida, family Empetiaceae.

crowfoot, name for plants with the leaf or some other part resembling the foot of a crow, particularly the BUTTERCUP.

Crow Indians, North American Indians whose language belongs to the Siouan branch of the Hokan-Siouan linguistic stock (see AMERICAN INDIAN LANGUAGES) and who call themselves the Absaroka, or bird people. They ranged chiefly in the area of the Yellowstone River and its tributaries and were a hunting tribe typical of the Plains cultural area. Their only crop was tobacco, which they used for pleasure and religious purposes. Until the 18th cent. the Crow lived with the HIDATSA INDIANS on the upper Missouri River; after a dispute they migrated westward until they reached the Rocky Mts. The Crow developed a highly complex social system that included, among other things, great care and attention for children. They were enemies of the Sioux and helped the white men in the Sioux wars. See R. H. Lowie, *The Crow Indians* (1935, repr. 1956); Peter Nabokov, *Two Leggings: The Making of a Crow Warrior* (1967).

Crowley, city (1970 pop. 16,104), seat of Acadia parish, SW La.; inc. 1888. It is a shipping, milling, and storing center for one of the nation's largest rice-growing areas and has a rice experiment station. Oil and natural gas wells are located nearby.

crown, circular head ornament, symbolizing sovereign dignity. (For crowns worn by nobles, see CORONET.) The use of the crown as a symbol of royal rank is of ancient tradition in Egypt and the Orient. In ancient Greece and Rome, however, crowns—sometimes made of leaves—were merely wreaths, awarded to victors in athletic or poetic contests or bestowed on citizens in recognition of an act of public service. The crown as used in medieval and modern times is an elaboration of the DIADEM and is generally made of metal, often gold inlaid with precious gems. The crown became thoroughly identified with the functions of monarchy, and the term *crown* is often used in a purely institutional sense, as in crown lands, crown colonies, and crown debt. Among famous crowns of historic interest are the Lombard iron crown, kept at Monza, Italy; the crown of Charlemagne, at Vienna, Austria; and the sacred crown of St. Stephen of Hungary. These are exceptional in that they were used repeatedly over centuries for coronation ceremonies. Most crowns are of recent origin, although the jewels they contain are often taken from older crowns. The ancient crowns of England were destroyed under Oliver Cromwell. There are two crowns used by the British sovereigns: the crown of Edward the Confessor (a much-altered replica of the original crown) is used for the coronation ceremony in Westminster Abbey, and the imperial state crown is worn on state occasions. Crowns are also worn by the consorts and families of sovereigns. The triple crown of the popes, known as a tiara, dates from the 14th cent. Regardless of their actual shape, crowns are usually represented in heraldry as closed at the top by four arched bars called diadems and surmounted by a globe and a cross. In religion and art, a crown symbolizes sovereignty (Rev. 19.12) and also honor, especially the reward of martyrdom (Heb. 2.9).

Crowne, John, c.1640–c.1703, English playwright. The favorite playwright of Charles II, he is remembered for several rather mediocre comedies. Crowne was influenced by the French tradition, particularly by Molière, and the mental states of his characters are more important than plot. Among his plays are *Pandion and Amphigenia* (1665), *Sir Courtly Nice* (1685), and *The Married Beau* (1694).

crown gall: see GALL.

Crown Point. 1 City (1970 pop. 10,931), seat of Lake co., NW Ind.; inc. 1868. Film is processed, and truck conveyors, golf balls, feed grinders, and cabinets are made. **2** Town (1970 pop. 1,857), Essex co., NE N.Y., on Lake Champlain. Crown Point is a summer resort on a historic site. The French realized the strategic importance of this point on the route from New York to Canada and in 1731 began building Fort St. Frederic. In the French and Indian Wars the fort successfully resisted (1755–56) early English attacks but was demolished (1759) before the advance of Jeffrey Amherst. The British began to build Fort Amherst (renamed Fort Crown Point) in 1759. Early in the American Revolution, Crown Point was captured (May 12, 1775) by Seth Warner and a detachment of Green Mountain Boys. After twice changing hands, it was finally abandoned (June 22, 1777) to Gen. John Burgoyne in the Saratoga campaign. Crown Point Reservation, with bathing and fishing facilities, a museum, and ruins of colonial forts, is nearby.

Croydon, borough (1971 pop. 331,851) of Greater London, SE England. The borough was created in 1965 by the merger of the county borough of Croydon with the urban district of Coulsdon and Purley. It has the largest population of the London boroughs. Scientific instruments, internal-combustion engines, and electronic equipment are manufactured, but Croydon is largely residential. Several office buildings have been constructed in the borough, which also has a technical college and a college of art.

crucible, vessel in which a substance is heated to a high temperature, as for fusing or calcining. The necessary properties of a crucible are that it maintain its mechanical strength and rigidity at high temperatures and that it not react in an undesirable way with its contents. PORCELAIN and GRAPHITE are two refractory materials widely used for crucibles, but FIREBRICK can be used as well, especially when vessels of large capacity are needed. The chamber at the bottom of a metal-refining furnace, in which the molten metal collects to be drawn off, is also known as a crucible.

crucifix: see CROSS.

crucifixion, hanging on a CROSS, in ancient times a method of CAPITAL PUNISHMENT. It was practiced widely in the Near East but not by the Greeks. The Romans, who may have borrowed it from Carthage, reserved it for slaves and despised malefactors. They used it frequently, as in the civil wars and in putting down the Jewish opposition. Crucifixion was probably at first a modification of hanging on a tree or impaling on a pole, and from such a connection come the synonyms *tree* and *rood* (i.e., rod or pole) for Jesus' cross. The Romans used mostly the T cross, the Latin cross, or St. Andrew's cross. Most ancient sources describe the cross Jesus died on as a Latin cross, the type most common in the liturgy of the West. It was common practice among the Romans to scourge the prisoner and to require him to carry his cross to the place of crucifixion. The prisoner was either nailed or tied to the cross, and, to induce more rapid death, his legs were often broken. See Mat. 27.24–61; Mark 15.15–47; Luke 23.13–56; John 19.13–42. Crucifixion was abolished when the empire became Christian. See also CALVARY and GOOD THIEF.

Cruden, Alexander, 1701–70, author of a famous biblical concordance, b. Aberdeen, Scotland. He spent most of his life near London. In 1737 he published his *Complete Concordance to the Holy Scriptures,* which went through several editions and is the basis of later biblical concordances.

crude oil: see PETROLEUM.

cruelty, prevention of. In the 19th cent. many laws were passed in Great Britain and the United States to protect the helpless, especially children, lunatics, and domestic animals, from willful and malicious acts of cruelty. At first, cruelty to animals was deemed criminal only when severe enough to constitute a public nuisance. But in 1822 the British Parliament passed the Martin Act for animal protection, and two years later Richard Martin formed the Society for the Prevention of Cruelty to Animals. The Cruelty to Animals Acts of 1849 and 1854 firmly established protection for animals. Not until 1884 was the first British law passed to protect children from cruelty. This movement to protect the helpless soon spread throughout Europe and to the United States, where the American Society for the Prevention of Cruelty to Animals was formed (1866) by Henry Bergh in New York City. The American Humane Association, for the protection of animals and children, was organized in 1877. In the United States, as in Great Britain, protection of children came after that of animals, the first Society for the Prevention of Cruelty to Children having been formed in New York City in 1875. In all states, parents guilty of bodily cruelty to, or moral corruption of, their children may now be lawfully punished, and the children may be taken from them to become wards of the state (see CHILD ABUSE). Societies of both types—for the protection of children and of animals—promote better legislation and enforcement, investigate and report alleged cruelties, establish shelters and sometimes (animal) hospitals, and carry on education against cruelty. While most of these societies are private, philanthropic organizations, some receive public funds. See R. C. McCrea, *The Humane Movement* (1910, repr. 1969); L. G. Housden, *The Prevention of Cruelty to Children* (1955); P. P. Hallie, *The Paradox of Cruelty* (1969); David Bakan, *Slaughter of the Innocents* (1971).

Cruikshank, George (kro͝ok'shăngk), 1792–1878, English caricaturist, illustrator, and etcher; younger son of Isaac Cruikshank (1756–1810), caricaturist. Self-taught, George early gained a reputation for his humorous drawings and political and social satires. He succeeded James Gillray as the most popular caricaturist of his day. Cruikshank illustrated more than 850 books and contributed to such publications as the *Meteor*, the *Scourge*, and the *Satirist*. Among the best of his many illustrations are the famous *Life in London* (in collaboration with his brother); his masterly etchings for Grimm's *German Popular Stories*; and the 12 etchings in Richard Bentley's miscellany, which include the notable illustrations of *Oliver Twist*. In his later years Cruikshank made many drawings depicting the evils of intemperance, such as *The Drunkard's Children, The Bottle*, and *The Gin Trap*. Collections of his works are in the British and the Victoria and Albert museums. See biographies by Blanchard Jerrold (1882) and William Bates (2d. ed. 1972); catalogues by A. M. Cohn (1924) and M. D. George (1949); study, ed. by R. L. Patten (1973).

cruiser, large, fast, moderately armed warship, intermediate in type between the aircraft carrier and the destroyer. During World War II, battle cruisers operated as small battleships, combining in one vessel maximum qualities of gun caliber, armor protection, and speed. Upon the retirement of the BATTLESHIP from the major navies of the world, the cruiser became the largest of the conventionally armed warships in commission. The cruiser's primary mission in modern warfare is to provide antiaircraft defense and gunfire support for aircraft carriers. Light cruisers, lightly armed and very fast, are often employed in scouting, police duties, and other jobs where speed rather than defensive strength is important. The advent of guided missiles as the primary offensive weapon of modern warfare has led to the conversion of many cruisers into guided-missile cruisers. The guided-missile cruiser *Long Beach* (completed 1961) was the first ship since World War II to be constructed for the U.S. navy from keel up as a cruiser; it was also the first nuclear-powered surface fighting ship in the world. See *Jane's Fighting Ships* (pub. annually since 1897); study by S. L. Poole (1970).

crullers: see DOUGHNUTS.

crumhorn, J-shaped, double-reed musical instrument used throughout Europe from the 15th cent. through the 17th cent. It possesses a soft, reedy tone. The reed is enclosed by a wooden cap with a

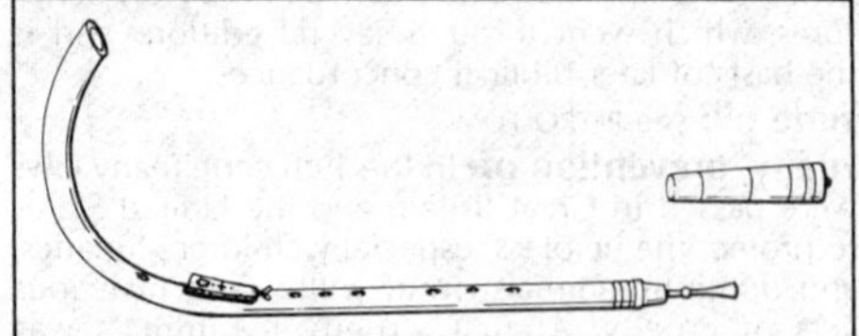

Tenor crumhorn

hole at the top through which the player blows. The cap serves as a wind chamber, which causes the reed to vibrate. The crumhorn is one of the ancestors of the OBOE.

Crump, Edward Hull, 1876–1954, American politician, Democratic boss of Tennessee, b. near Holly Springs, Miss. At first (1905–9) a municipal administrator in Memphis, Tenn., he was later mayor (1909–16, 1939–41) and Congressman (1931–35) from Tennessee. Meanwhile, he built an efficient political machine that dominated the state elections. Crump's boss rule was upset in the 1948 Tennessee Democratic primaries, when his favored candidates for Senator and governor were beaten. See biography by W. D. Miller (1964).

Crusades, series of wars undertaken by European Christians between the 11th and 14th cent. to recover the Holy Land from the Muslims. In the 7th cent., Jerusalem was taken by the caliph UMAR. Pilgrimages (see PILGRIM) were not cut off at first, but early in the 11th cent. the FATIMID caliph Hakim began to persecute the Christians and despoiled the Holy Sepulcher. Persecution abated after his death (1021), but relations remained strained and became more so when Jerusalem passed (1071) from the comparatively tolerant Egyptians to the Seljuk TURKS, who in the same year defeated the Byzantine emperor Romanus IV at Manzikert. Late in the 11th cent., Byzantine Emperor ALEXIUS I, threatened by the Seljuk Turks, appealed to the West for aid. This was not the first appeal of the kind; while it may have helped to determine the time and the route of the **First Crusade,** 1095–99, its precise import is difficult to estimate. Direct impetus was given the crusade by the great speech of Pope URBAN II at the Council

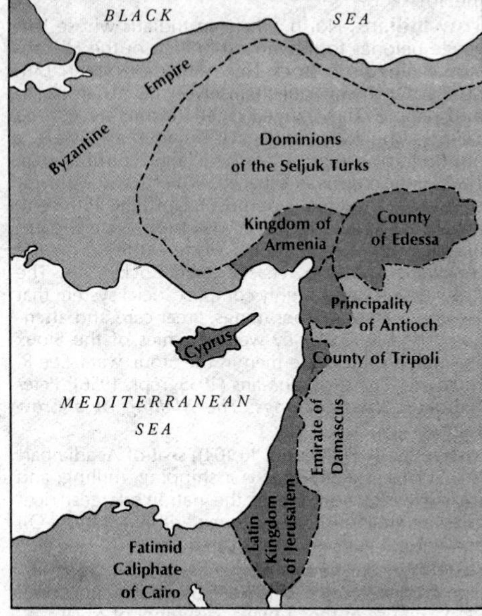

Crusader States (c.1140)

of Clermont (now Clermont-Ferrand), in 1095. Urban exhorted Christendom to go to war for the Sepulcher, promising that the journey would count as full penance and that the homes of the absent ones would be protected by a truce. The battle cry of the Christians, he urged, should be *Deus volt* [God wills it]. From the crosses that were distributed at this meeting the Crusaders took their name. Bishop ADEMAR was designated as papal legate for the crusade, and Count RAYMOND IV of Toulouse was the first of the leaders of the expedition to take the cross. Preached by many wandering preachers, notably PETER THE HERMIT, the movement spread through Europe and even reached Scandinavia. The chief factors that contributed to this enthusiastic response were the increase in the population and prosperity of Western Europe; the high point that religious devotion had reached; the prospect of territorial expansion and riches for the nobles, and of more freedom for the lower classes; the colonial projects of the Normans (directed against the Byzantine Empire as much as against the Muslim world); the desire, particularly of the Italian cities, to expand trade with the East; and a general awakening to the lure of travel and adventure. The conflict between spiritual and material aims, apparent from the first, became increasingly serious. The organized host of the crusade was preceded in the spring of 1096 by several undisciplined hordes of French and German peasants. WALTER THE PENNILESS led a French group, which passed peacefully through Germany and Hungary but sacked the district of Belgrade. The Bulgarians retaliated, but Walter reached Constantinople by midsummer. He was joined there by the followers of Peter the Hermit, whose progress had been similar. A German group started off by robbing and massacring the Jews in the Rhenish cities and later so provoked the king of Hungary that he attacked and dispersed them. The bands that had reached Constantinople were speedily transported by Alexius I to Asia Minor, where they were defeated by the Turks. The survivors either joined later bands or returned to Europe. Alexius began to take fright at the proportions the movement was assuming. When, late in 1096, the first of the princes, Hugh of Vermandois, a brother of Philip I of France, reached Constantinople, the emperor persuaded him to take an oath of fealty. GODFREY OF BOUILLON and his brothers Eustace and Baldwin (later BALDWIN I of Jerusalem), Raymond IV of Toulouse, BOHEMOND I, TANCRED, Robert of Normandy, and Robert II of Flanders arrived early in 1097. At Antioch all except Tancred and Raymond (who promised only to refrain from hostilities against the Byzantines) took the oath to Alexius, which bound them to accept Alexius as overlord of their conquests. Bohemond's subsequent breach of the oath was to cause endless wrangling. The armies crossed to Asia Minor, took Nicaea (1097), defeated the Turks at Dorylaeum, and took Antioch (1098). Their campaign was completed in July, 1099, by the taking of Jerusalem, where they massacred the Muslims and Jews. The election of Godfrey of Bouillon as defender of the Holy Sepulcher marked the beginning of the Latin Kingdom of Jerusalem (see JERUSALEM, LATIN KINGDOM OF). A Latin patriarch was elected. Other fiefs, theoretically dependent on Jerusalem, were created as the crusade's leaders moved to expand their domains. These were the counties of Edessa (Baldwin) and Tripoli (Raymond) and the principality of Antioch (Bohemond). The First Crusade, which thus ended in victory, was the only crusade that achieved more than ephemeral results. Until the ultimate fall (1291) of the Latin Kingdom the brunt of the fighting in the Holy Land fell on the Latin princes and their followers and on the great military orders, the KNIGHTS HOSPITALERS and the KNIGHTS TEMPLARS, that arose out of the Crusades. The later Crusades were for the most part only expeditions to assist those who already were in the Holy Land; they are a single current, and dates are given them only for convenience. The **Second Crusade,** 1147–49, was preached by St. BERNARD OF CLAIRVAUX after the fall (1144) of Edessa to the Turks. It was led by Holy Roman Emperor CONRAD III, whose army set out first, and by King LOUIS VII of France. Both armies passed through the Balkans and pillaged the territory of the Byzantine emperor, MANUEL I, who provided them with transportation to Asia Minor in order to be rid of them. The German contingent, already decimated by the Turks, merged (1148) with the French, who had fared only slightly better, at Acre (Akko). A joint attack on Damascus failed because of jealousy and, possibly, treachery among the Latin princes of the Holy Land. Conrad returned home in 1148 and was followed (1149) by Louis. The Second Crusade thus ended in dismal failure. The **Third Crusade,** 1189–92, followed on the capture (1187) of Jerusalem by SALADIN and the defeat of GUY OF LUSIGNAN, REGINALD OF CHÂTILLON, and RAYMOND of Tripoli at Hattin. The crusade was preached by Pope Gregory VIII but was directed by its leaders—RICHARD I of England, PHILIP II of France, and Holy Roman Emperor FREDERICK I. Frederick set out first, but was hindered by the Byzantine emperor, ISAAC II, who had formed an alliance with Saladin. Frederick forced his way to the Bosporus, sacked Adrianople (Edirne), and compelled the Greeks to furnish transportation to Asia Minor. However, he died (1190) in Cilicia, and only part of his forces went on to the Holy Land. Richard and Philip, uneasy allies, arrived at Acre in 1191. The city had been besieged since 1189, but the siege had been prolonged by dissensions between the two chief Christian leaders, Guy of Lusignan and CONRAD, marquis of Montferrat, both of whom claimed the kingship of Jerusalem. The city was nevertheless starved out by July, 1191; shortly afterward Philip went home. Richard removed his base to Jaffa, which he fortified, and rebuilt Ascalon (Ashqelon), which the Muslims had burned down. In 1192 he made a three-year truce with Saladin; the Christians retained Jaffa with a narrow strip of coast (all that remained of the Latin Kingdom of Jerusalem) and the right of free access to the Holy Sepulcher. Antioch and Tripoli were still in Christian hands; Cyprus, which Richard I had wrested (1191) from the Byzantines while on his way to the Holy Land, was given to Guy of Lusignan. In Oct., 1192, Richard left the Holy Land, thus ending the crusade. Pope INNOCENT III launched the **Fourth Crusade,** 1202–4, which was totally diverted from its original course. The Crusaders, led mostly by French and Flemish nobles and spurred on by FULK OF NEUILLY, assembled (1202) near Venice. To pay some of their passage to Palestine they aided Doge Enrico Dandolo (see under DANDOLO, family) and his Venetian forces in recovering Zara (Zadar) on the Dalmatian coast from the Hungarians. The sack of Zara (1202), violently denounced by the pope, prefaced more serious political schemes. Alexius (later ALEXIUS IV), son of the deposed Byzantine emperor Isaac II and brother-in-law of PHILIP OF SWABIA, a sponsor of the crusade, joined the army at Zara and persuaded the leaders to help him depose his uncle, ALEXIUS III. In exchange, he promised large sums of money, aid to the Crusaders in conquering Egypt, and the union of the Roman and the Eastern churches. The actual decision to turn on Constantinople was largely brought about by Venetian pressure. The fleet arrived at the Bosporus in 1203; Alexius III fled, and Isaac II and Alexius IV were installed as joint emperors while the fleet remained outside the harbor. In 1204, ALEXIUS V overthrew the emperors. As a result the Crusaders stormed the city, sacked it, divided the rich spoils with the Venetians according to a prearranged plan, and set up the Latin Empire of Constantinople (see CONSTANTINOPLE, LATIN EMPIRE OF). There followed the pathetic interlude of the **Children's Crusade,** 1212. Led by a visionary French peasant boy, Stephen of Cloyes, children embarked at Marseilles, hoping that they would succeed in the cause that their elders had betrayed. According to later sources, they were sold into slavery by unscrupulous skippers. Another group, made up of German children, went to Italy; most of them perished of hunger and disease. Soon afterward Innocent III and his successor, Honorius III, began to preach the **Fifth Crusade,** 1217–21. King Andrew II of Hungary, Duke Leopold VI of Austria, JOHN OF BRIENNE, and the papal legate Pelasius were among the leaders of the expedition, which was aimed at Egypt, the center of Muslim strength. Damietta (Dumyat) was taken in 1219 but had to be evacuated again after the defeat (1221) of an expedition against Cairo. The **Sixth Crusade,** 1228–29, undertaken by Holy Roman Emperor FREDERICK II, was simply a peaceful visit, in the course of which the emperor made a truce with the Muslims, securing the partial surrender of Jerusalem and other holy places. Frederick crowned himself king of Jerusalem, but, occupied with Western affairs, he did nothing when the Muslims later reoccupied the city. THIBAUT IV of Navarre and Champagne, however, reopened (1239) the wars, which were continued by Richard, earl of Cornwall. They were unable to compose the quarrels between the Knights Hospitalers and Knights Templars. In 1244 the Templars, who advocated an alliance with the sultan of Damascus rather than with Egypt, prevailed. A treaty (1244) with Damascus restored Palestine to the Christians, but in the same year the Egyptian Muslims and their Turkish allies took Jerusalem and utterly routed the Christians at Gaza. This event led to the **Seventh Crusade,** 1248–54, due solely to the idealistic enterprise of LOUIS IX of France. Egypt again was the object of attack. Damietta fell again (1249); and an expedition to Cairo miscarried (1250), Louis himself being captured. After his release from captivity, he spent four years improving the fortifications left to the Christians in the Holy Land. The fall (1268) of Jaffa and Antioch to the Muslims caused Louis IX to undertake the **Eighth Crusade,** 1270, which was cut short by his death in Tunisia. The **Ninth Crusade,** 1271–72, was led by Prince Edward (later EDWARD I of England). He landed at Acre but retired after concluding a truce. In 1289 Tripoli fell to the Muslims, and in 1291 Acre, the last Christian stronghold, followed.

Heritage of the Crusades. After the fall of Acre no further Crusades were undertaken in the Holy Land, although several were preached. Already, however, the term *crusade* was also being used for other expeditions, sanctioned by the pope, against heathens and heretics. ALBERT THE BEAR and HENRY THE LION led (1147) a crusade against the WENDS in NE Germany; Hermann von SALZA in 1226 received crusading privileges for the Teutonic Knights against the Prussians; the pope proclaimed (1228) a crusade against Emperor Frederick II; and several crusades were fought against the ALBIGENSES and the Hussites (see HUSSITE WARS). War against the Turks remained the chief problem of Eastern Europe for centuries after 1291. Campaigns akin to crusades were those of John HUNYADI, JOHN OF AUSTRIA (d. 1578), and JOHN III of Poland. In their consequences, the crusades in Europe were as important as those in the Holy Land. However, although the Crusades in the Holy Land failed in their chief purpose, they exercised an incalculable influence on Western civilization by bringing the West into closer contact with new modes of living and thinking, by stimulating commerce, by giving fresh impetus to literature and invention, and by increasing geographical knowledge. The crusading period advanced the development of national monarchies in Europe, because secular leaders deprived the pope of the power of decision in what was to have been the highest Christian enterprise. In the Levant the Crusades left a lasting imprint, not least on the Byzantine Empire, which was disastrously weakened. Physical reminders of the Crusades remain in the monumental castles built by the Crusaders, such as that of AL KARAK. The chief material beneficiaries of the Crusades were Venice and the other great Mediterranean ports. The ideal of chivalry was also developed by the Crusades. The chief collection of sources is *Recueil des historiens des croisades* (ed. by the Académie des Inscriptions et Belle-Lettres, 16 vol., 1841–1906); several chronicles are translated in the "Records of Civilization" series. Outstanding among eyewitness acounts are those of WILLIAM OF TYRE, RICHARD OF DEVIZES, Geoffroi de VILLEHARDOUIN, Jean de JOINVILLE, ANNA COMNENA, and Nicetas Acominatus. Treatments in English include Ernest Barker, *The Crusades* (1923, repr. 1971); A. S. Atiya, *The Crusade in the Later Middle Ages* (1938, repr. 1970); Steven Runciman, *A History of the Crusades* (3 vol., 1951–54, repr. 1962–66); K. M. Setton, ed., *A History of the Crusades* (2 vol., 1955–62, repr. 1969).

Crusca, Accademia della: see ACCADEMIA DELLA CRUSCA.

crusher, machine used to reduce materials such as ore, coal, stone, and slag to particle sizes that are convenient for their intended uses. Crushers operate by slowly applying a large force to the material to be reduced. Generally this is accomplished by catching it between jaws or rollers that move or turn together with great force. Reduction in size is generally accomplished in several stages, as there are practical limitations on the ratio of size reduction through a single stage.

Crusius, Christian August (krĭs'tēän ou'go͝ost kro͞o'zēo͞os), 1715–75, German philosopher and theologian. He was educated at the Univ. of Leipzig, where he became professor of philosophy (1744) and theology (1750). He opposed the philosophies of G. W. Leibniz and Christian Wolff and strongly influenced the early writings of Immanuel KANT. None of his many works has been translated into English.

crustacean (krŭs"tā'shən), primarily aquatic arthropod of the class Crustacea. Most of the 26,000 crustacean species are marine, but there are many freshwater forms. The few groups that inhabit terrestrial areas have not been particularly successful in an evolutionary sense; most require very humid environments in order to survive. Crustaceans can be divided according to size into two main groups. The larger group includes the familiar SHRIMP, CRAYFISH, LOBSTERS, and CRABS, all belonging to the order Decapoda, as well as the BARNACLES that constitute the subclass Cirripėdia. The smaller group includes species that are either microscopic or range up to a few inches (about 5 cm) in size. Most of the smaller marine forms can be found in plankton (see MARINE BIOLOGY) and thereby occupy an important position in the marine food chain; for example, the very large crustacean order Copepoda supplies the food of a still larger crustacean order the Euphausids, which in turn constitutes krill, the principal food of baleen whales. Other copepods supply food for small fish, and still others exist as parasites on the skin and gills of fish. Best known of the smaller freshwater crustaceans are members of the genus *Daphnia* (water fleas), the fairy shrimp (a phyllopod that swims inverted), and *Cyclops* (a copepod). The order Isopoda includes the only large group of truly terrestrial crustaceans. Known as wood lice, sow bugs, or pillbugs, these small animals can be found under the bark of trees, beneath stones and rocks, and in other damp places. When disturbed they curl up armadillolike, withdrawing into the exoskeleton. All crustaceans have bilaterally symmetrical bodies covered with a chitinous exoskeleton, which may be thick and calcareous (as in the crayfish) or delicate and transparent (as in water fleas). Since it does not grow, the exoskeleton must be periodically molted when the animal undergoes metamorphosis (typically from free-swimming larva to adult) or simply outgrows its shell. The free-swimming larva characteristic of crustaceans, called a nauplius larva, has an unsegmented body, a median eye, and three pairs of appendages. Like other arthropods, adult crustaceans have segmented bodies and jointed legs; the segments are usually grouped into a recognizable head, thorax, and abdomen. In the majority of larger crustaceans the head and thorax are fused into a cephalothorax, which is protected by a large shield-like area of the exoskeleton called the carapace. The head bears two pairs of antennae, usually one median eye and two lateral eyes, and three pairs of biting mouthparts—the mandibles and the two pairs of maxillae. Crustacean appendages have undergone extensive adaptation for various tasks such as swimming, sensory reception, and walking. Many species have the first pair of thoracic appendages modified into claws and pincers. The gills are generally attached at the bases of the thoracic appendages, and the beating of the appendages creates a flow of water over the gills that facilitates respiration. Reproduction is sexual, and in most forms the sexes are separate. In many species the eggs are brooded beneath the abdominal segments of the female. Crustaceans constitute the class Crustacea of the phylum ARTHROPODA.

Cruveilhier, Jean (zhäN krüvĕyā'), 1791–1874, French physician. The first professor of pathology at the Univ. of Paris (from 1836), he introduced the descriptive method into the study of that field. He was the first to describe multiple sclerosis adequately. His works include *The Anatomy of the Human Body* (2 vol., 1829–42; tr. 1844).

Crux (kro͞oks) [Lat., = cross], small but brilliant southern CONSTELLATION whose four most prominent members form a Latin cross, the famous Southern Cross. The long arm of the cross, terminating in the brightest member, ACRUX (Alpha Crucis), points almost directly at the south celestial pole. Two other stars, MIMOSA (Beta Crucis) and Gacrux (Gamma Crucis) are also among the brightest in the sky. Also

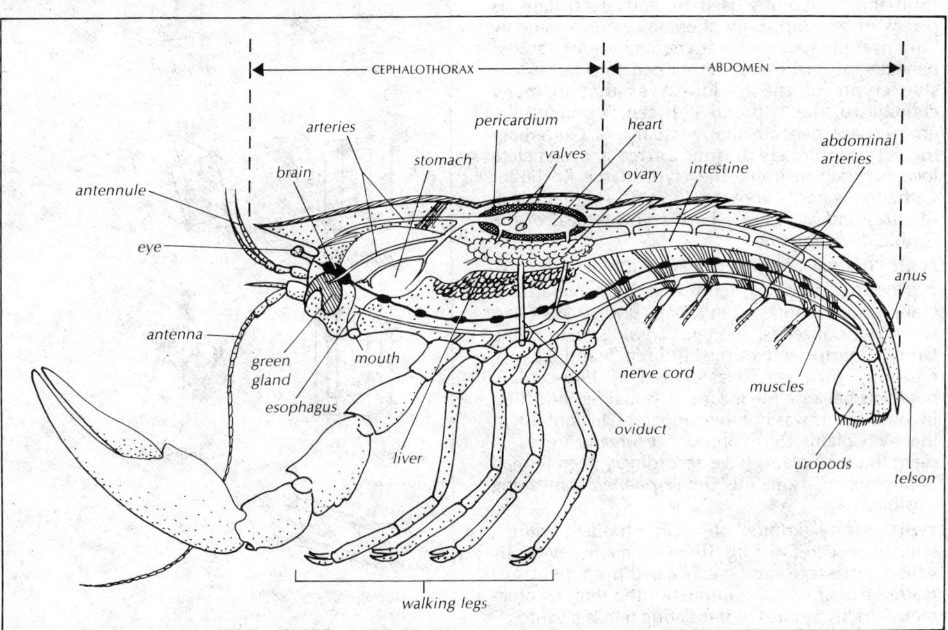

Internal anatomy of a female crayfish, representative of the class Crustacea

in Crux is the Coalsack, a famous dark nebula. Crux reaches its highest point in the evening sky in May; its location in the far southern sky makes it visible most of the year to southern observers but not at all to observers north of about 25°N lat.

Cruz, Juana Inés de la: see JUANA INÉS DE LA CRUZ.

Cruz, Juan de la: see JOHN OF THE CROSS, SAINT.

Cruz, Ramón de la (rämōn' dä lä kro͞oth), 1731–94, Spanish dramatist. He wrote tragedies and adapted French and Italian plays, but he owes his fame to his *sainetes*, some 450 masterly one-act comedies that depict the life of the middle and lower classes. His work freed the awakening Spanish drama from foreign influence.

cryogenics: see LOW-TEMPERATURE PHYSICS.

cryolite or **kryolite** (both: krī'əlīt) [Gr.,=frost stone], mineral usually pure white or colorless but sometimes tinted in shades of pink, brown, or even black and having a luster like that of wax. Chemically, it is a double fluoride of sodium and aluminum, Na_3AlF_6. Its principal use is as a flux in the smelting of aluminum. It is used also as a source of soda, aluminum salts, fluorides, and hydrofluoric acid (by the action of sulfuric acid). It was discovered in Greenland in 1794 and occurs almost nowhere else. Cryolite has been produced synthetically.

cryosurgery (krī'ōsûr"jərē), bloodless surgical technique using a supercooled probe to destroy diseased tissue. Liquid nitrogen circulating through the instrument cools it to temperatures as low as −196°C. Tissue destroyed on contact with the probe is removed by natural body processes. The method has proved successful in removal of tonsils, tumors, hemorrhoids, and cataracts, and in treating various brain disorders. Surgeons have been successful in treating PARKINSONISM with the cryogenic probe; the small areas of the brain that are believed responsible for the symptoms can be frozen temporarily at 0°C and thawed if the symptoms do not disappear. When the correct location is found, the tissue can be quickly supercooled and destroyed.

cryotron (krī'ōträn"), magnetically controlled electronic switching device that operates at extremely low temperatures; it is designed to supplant, in part, the transistor in special electronic equipment (e.g., the computer). One type of cryotron consists of a straight wire (the gate) around which a wire coil (the control coil) is wound. Kept at temperatures near absolute zero, both wires become superconductors (see LOW-TEMPERATURE PHYSICS; SUPERCONDUCTIVITY), but when current is passed through the coil, a magnetic field is induced that causes the gate to lose its superconductivity, thus switching off the current through it. Another type of cryotron uses conducting films in place of the wires to increase the switching speed. The cryotron is so minute that many of these devices can be packed into a very small area, thereby greatly increasing the degree of control.

crypt (krĭpt) [Gr.,=hidden], vault or chamber beneath the main level of a church, used as a meeting place or burial place. It undoubtedly developed from the catacombs used by early Christians as places of worship. Early churches were commonly built over the tombs of martyrs. Such vaults, located beneath the main altar, developed into the extensive crypts of the Middle Ages that in many churches of the 11th and 12th cent. occupied the entire space beneath the sanctuary. At Canterbury the 12th-century crypt forms a large and complete lower church in itself. The crypt of the Rochester Cathedral is partly above ground. The cathedrals at Chartres and at Bourges have crypts typical of the Gothic development.

cryptococcosis: see FUNGUS INFECTION.

cryptogam, in botany, term used to denote a plant that produces spores, as in ALGAE, FUNGI, MOSSES, and FERNS, but not seeds. The term *cryptogam,* from the Greek *kryptos,* meaning "hidden," and *gamos,* meaning "marriage," was coined by 19th-century botanists because the means of sexual reproduction in these plants was not then apparent. In contrast, in the seed plants the reproductive organs are easily seen; the seed plants have accordingly been termed *phanerogams,* from the Greek *phaneros,* meaning "visible."

cryptography (krĭptŏg'rəfē) [Gr.,=hidden writing], science of secret writing. There are many devices by which a message can be concealed from the casual reader, e.g., invisible writing, but the term cryptography strictly applies to translating messages into cipher or code. The science of breaking codes and ciphers without the key is called cryptanalysis. Cryptology is the science that embraces both cryptography and cryptanalysis. In enciphering, each letter of the message is replaced by another letter or figure; in encoding, syllables, words, or whole sentences are treated. The code is the agreed upon set of rules whereby messages are converted from one form to another. The beginnings of cryptography can be traced to the hieroglyphs of early Egyptian civilization (c.1900 B.C.). Ciphering has always been considered vital for diplomatic and military secrecy; the Bible is replete with examples of ciphering, and many figures throughout history have written in ciphers, including Julius Caesar, Charlemagne, Alfred the Great, Mary Queen of Scots, and Louis XIV. Francis Bacon's celebrated biliteral cipher (1605) was an arrangement of the letters *a* and *b* in five-letter combinations, each representing a letter of the alphabet. This code illustrates the important principle that a code employing only two different signs can be used to transmit information. In the 20th cent. mathematical theory and computer science have both been applied to cryptanalysis. As the science of cryptology becomes increasingly sophisticated, most nations have found it necessary to develop special governmental bureaus to handle diplomatic and military security, e.g., the National Security Agency in the United States. See Helen Gaines, *Cryptanalysis* (1956); David Kahn, *The Codebreakers* (1967); J. R. Wolfe, *Secret Writing: The Craft of the Cryptographer* (1970).

Cryptophyta, small division of the plant kingdom, consisting of only one class and one order of photosynthetic, unicellular, flagellate ALGAE of both fresh water and marine habitats. There are only a few genera and fewer than 90 species, most of them rare. The cells are somewhat flattened and often asymmetric in shape. The cell wall, when present, may be of cellulose, and is often in the form of a sheath called a lorica. The cell chloroplasts contain CAROTENES, the photosynthetic pigments chlorophyll *a* and chlorophyll *c,* and pigments unique to this division, the brown or yellow xanthophylls, which give the cells a brownish color.

crypts of Lieberkühn: see DIGESTIVE SYSTEM.

Crystal, city (1970 pop. 30,925), Hennepin co., SE Minn., a suburb of Minneapolis.

crystal, a solid body bounded by natural plane faces that are the external expression of a regular internal arrangement of constituent atoms, molecules, or ions. The particles in a crystal occupy positions with definite geometrical relationships to each other. The positions form a kind of scaffolding, called a crystalline lattice; the atomic occupancies of lattice positions are determined by the chemical composition of the substance. The formation of a crystal by a substance passing from a gas or liquid to a solid state, or by going out of solution (by precipitation or evaporation), is called crystallization. A crystalline substance is uniquely defined by the combination of its chemistry and the structural arrangement of its atoms. In all crystals of any specific substance the angles between corresponding faces are constant (Steno's Law, or the First Law of Crystallography). Crystalline substances are grouped, according to the type of symmetry they display, into 32 classes. These in turn are grouped into seven systems on the basis of the relationships of their axes, i.e., imaginary straight lines passing through the ideal centers of the crystals. Crystals may be symmetrical with relation to planes, axes, and centers of symmetry. Planes of symmetry divide crystals into equal parts (mirror images) that correspond point for point, angle for angle, and face for face. Axes of symmetry are imaginary lines about which the crystal may be considered to rotate, assuming, after passing through a rotation of 60°, 90°, 120°, or 180°, the identical position in space that it originally had. Centers of symmetry are points from which imaginary straight lines may be drawn to intersect identical points equidistant from the center on opposite sides. The crystalline systems are cubic, or isometric (three equal axes, intersecting at right angles); hexagonal (three equal axes, intersecting at 60° angles in a horizontal plane, and a fourth, longer or shorter, axis, perpendicular to the plane of the other three); tetragonal (two equal, horizontal axes at right angles and one axis longer or shorter than the other two and perpendicular to their plane); orthorhombic (three unequal axes intersecting at right angles); monoclinic (three unequal axes, two intersecting at right angles and the third at an oblique angle to the plane of the other two); trigonal, or rhombohedral (three equal axes intersecting at oblique angles); and triclinic (three unequal axes intersecting at oblique angles). In all systems in which the axes are unequal there is a definite axial ratio for each crystal substance. Crystals differ in physical properties, i.e., in hardness, cleavage, optical properties, heat conductivity, and electrical conductivity. These properties are important since they sometimes determine the use to which the crystals are put in industry. For example, crystalline substances that have special electrical properties are much used in communications equipment. These include quartz and Rochelle salt, which supply voltage upon the application of mechanical force (see PIEZOELECTRIC EFFECT), and germanium, silicon, galena, and silicon carbide, which carry current unequally in different crystallographic directions (semiconductor rectifier). See SOLID; SOLID STATE PHYSICS. See F. C. Phillips, *An Introduction to Crystallography* (1970); J. D. Dana, *Manual of Mineralogy* (18th ed., rev. by C. S. Hurlbut, Jr., 1971).

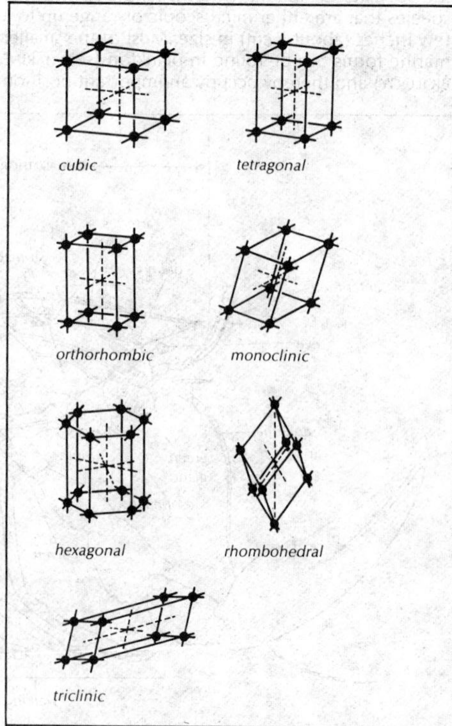

Types of crystal

crystal gazing, form of DIVINATION in which a medium achieves CLAIRVOYANCE by staring steadily into a clear surface, such as a crystal ball, a pool, a mirror, or other bright object. It is in such a state that the crystal gazer is supposedly able to perceive persons or events that are distant in time or space. This ancient and widespread practice has its origin in the belief that certain objects have supernatural powers. In recent times the crystal ball has been used by some spiritualists as a vehicle through which contact is made with the dead. Colloquially, the term is often used to describe any irresponsible or unfounded prediction about the future. See SPIRITISM.

Crystal Lake, city (1970 pop. 14,541), McHenry co., NE Ill., in a dairy farm and lake resort area; inc. 1874. Electrical components, drills, and tools are manufactured. A junior college is there.

Crystal Palace, building designed by Sir Joseph PAXTON and erected in Hyde Park, London, for the Great Exhibition in 1851. In 1854 it was removed to Sydenham, where, until its damage by fire in 1936, it housed a museum of sculpture, pictures, and architecture and was used for concerts. In 1941 its demolition was completed because it served as a guide to enemy bombing planes. The building was constructed of iron, glass, and laminated wood. One of the most significant examples of 19th-century, proto-modern architecture, it was widely imitated in Europe and America.

Cs, chemical symbol of the element CESIUM.

CS, chemical compound (orthochlorobenzalmalonitrile) used in riot control and, by the military, as a harassing agent. The compound is dispersed as an aerosol or as a finely divided powder. Exposure to CS causes intense pain in the eyes and upper respiratory tract; the pain spreads to the lungs and gives the sensation of suffocation. In humid weather CS may cause severe blistering of the skin. Heavy exposure to the compound may cause serious lung damage, resulting in death. Nonetheless, CS is less toxic than many other TEAR GASES. CS was first synthesized in the 1920s by Ben Carson and Roger Staughton; the compound's name is derived from their initials.

Csaba: see BÉKÉSCSABA, Hungary.

Csepel (chĕ'pĕl), island, c.100 sq mi (260 sq km), 30 mi (48 km) long, in the Danube, N central Hungary, just S of Budapest. In the northern section are the city and harbor of the same name, and there is an international free port. An industrial suburb of Budapest, the city of Csepel has ironworks and steelworks, an oil refinery, munitions factories, and motorcycle works. The rest of the island is agricultural.

Ctenophora (tĭnŏf'ərə), a small phylum of exclusively marine, solitary invertebrate animals, commonly known as sea walnuts or comb jellies. Ctenophores are characterized by eight unique rows (combs) consisting of ciliated plates called ctenes, which are radially arranged on the spherical body surface. The animals swim weakly, powered by those structures. The two hemispheres of the ctenophore body are marked by a mouth, or oral pole, on the underside, and an opposite aboral pole, on which is located the statocyst, a unique sense organ controlling equilibrium. Most ctenophores resemble biradially symmetrical (see SYMMETRY, BIOLOGICAL) jellyfish (phylum CNIDARIA) but lack the cnidarian whorl of tentacles around the mouth, and all but one species (*Euchlora rubra*) lack nematocysts, specialized stinging cells. Ctenophores, which are all carnivorous, have specialized adhesive cells called

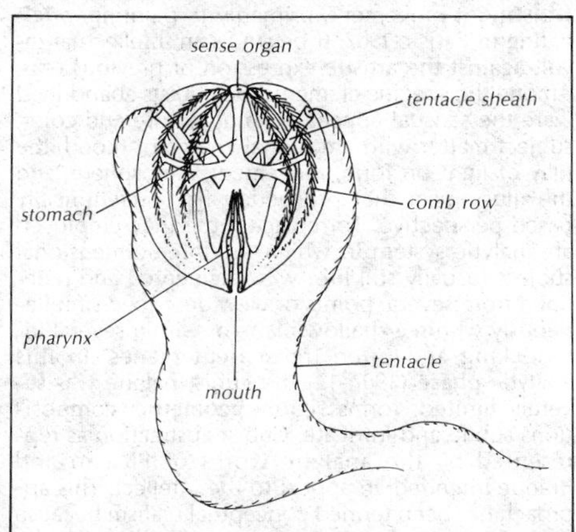

Pleurobrachia, *representative of the phylum Ctenophora*

colloblasts, used to capture planktonic animals on which the ctenophores feed. Less than one hundred species are known, but many become locally abundant and are ecologically significant. They vary from less than ¼ in. (0.6 cm) to over 1 ft (30.5 cm) long. Most are transparent, but pale pinks, reds, violets, and oranges are also known in some species. All ctenophores are bioluminescent, the production of light originating in the walls of the eight canals. The phylum is also characterized by hermaphroditism. There are two classes, Tentaculata and Nuda.

Class Tentaculata. Members of this class are characterized by having tentacles, typically two feathery ones that can be retracted into specialized sheaths. In some, there are smaller, secondary tentacles, and the primary tentacles are reduced. This class includes the small, oval sea gooseberries (genus *Pleurobrachia*), common on both Atlantic and Pacific coasts. The more flattened species of the genus *Mnemiopsis*, about 4 in. long (10 cm), is common on the upper Atlantic coast; it has a large mouth and feeds mainly on larval mollusks and copepods. This species is especially brilliantly luminescent. The similar, but larger, genus *Leucothea* is abundant on the Pacific coast. Venus's girdle (genus *Cestum*) is a flattened, ribbonlike form reaching over 1 yd (91 cm) in length, and found in tropical waters.

Class Nuda. This class includes species that have no tentacles. Typical is the large-mouthed genus *Beroe*, which feeds on jellyfish and other ctenophores. See P. A. Maglitsch, *Invertebrate Zoology* (1967); M. S. Gardiner, *The Biology of Invertebrates* (1972).

Ctesias (tē'shēəs, tē'sēəs), fl. 400 B.C., Greek historian and physician of Cnidus. He lived many years in the Persian court. He tended Artaxerxes II when he was wounded in the battle of Cunaxa (401 B.C.). In 398 he was sent by the Persians as envoy to Evagoras and Conon. Of Ctesias' histories only Photius' abridgments of *Persica* and *Indica* remain; in them Ctesias hoped to show Herodotus' unreliability.

Ctesibius (tĭsĭb'ēəs), fl. 2d cent. B.C., Alexandrian Greek inventor. He reputedly was the first to discover and apply the expansive power of air as a motive force. Among the inventions ascribed to him are a water clock (clepsydra), a hydraulic organ, and a force pump.

Ctesiphon, ruined ancient city, 20 mi (32 km) SE of Baghdad, Iraq, on the left bank of the Tigris opposite Seleucia and at the mouth of the Diyala River. After 129 B.C. it was the winter residence of the Parthian kings. Ctesiphon grew rapidly and was of renowned splendor. The Romans captured it in warring against Parthia. It became the capital of the Sassanids in c.224 and a center of Nestorian Christianity. In 637 it was taken and plundered by the Arabs who renamed it, along with Seleucia, Al Madain; it was abandoned by them when Baghdad became the capital of the Abbasids. Its site marks the farthest advance of Great Britain against the Ottoman Empire (Turkey) in World War I. It is now noted for its impressive ruins.

CTP (cytidine triphosphate): see CYTOSINE.

Cu, chemical symbol of the element COPPER.

Cuala Press (ko͞o'lä), private printing press founded in Dundrum, Ireland, in 1902 by Elizabeth and Lily Yeats, the sisters of William Butler Yeats. Called the Dun Emer Press until 1908, it began as part of a larger company whose purpose was to provide employment for Irish women. Until it ceased operation in the late 1940s, the press followed a program of publishing works by contemporary Irish writers and new editions and translations of Irish classics. Its publications emphasized literary merit rather than fine printing. Among the authors whose works were published by the Cuala Press are Yeats, Lionel Johnson, Lady Gregory, John Millington Synge, John Masefield, and Louis MacNeice.

Cuanza or **Kwanza** (both: kwän'zä), river, 600 mi (966 km) long, rising in central Angola and flowing NW and W to the Atlantic. Its lower course, which is navigable for c.160 mi (260 km), was the original route of Portuguese penetration into N Angola. The large Cambambe project, on the lower Cuanza, produces hydroelectric power and supplies water for irrigation. Sugarcane is grown in the lower Cuanza valley.

Cuauhtémoc (ko͞o-outā'môk), d. 1525, Aztec emperor. Succeeding the brother of MONTEZUMA II in 1520, Cuauhtémoc failed to unite the Indian city-states of the Valley of Mexico against the Spanish after the expulsion of Hernán CORTÉS from TENOCHTITLÁN. He courageously defended his capital, but was taken prisoner when it fell (1521) after a three-month siege. Tortured to reveal his treasure, Cuauhtémoc replied that it lay at the bottom of the lake—where the Spaniards had perished with it in their flight from Tenochtitlán on the *noche triste* [sad night]. Cortés took Cuauhtémoc with him on his march to Honduras and, accusing the Aztec of treason, had him hanged. The name occurs also as Cuauhtemoctzín, Guatémoc, Guatemozín, and Quauhtémoc.

Cuautla (kwou'tlä), city (1970 pop. 67,869), Morelos state, S Mexico, in the Cuautla River valley. It is a highway junction and the heart of a sugarcane and rice district. Cuautla's hot springs and lovely scenery make it a popular resort and tourist attraction. Historically, Cuautla is famous for the heroic defense made there in 1812 by patriot forces under José María Morelos y Pavón, who cut through Spanish besieging forces. The city is sometimes called Ciudad Morelos.

Cuba (kyo͞o'bə, Span. ko͞o'bä), republic (1970 pop. 8,553,395, including the Isle of Pines), 44,218 sq mi (114,524 sq km), consisting of the island of Cuba and numerous adjacent islands. HAVANA is the capital. Cuba is the largest and westernmost of the West Indies and lies strategically at the entrance of the Gulf of Mexico, with the western section only 90 mi (145 km) S of Key West, Fla. The south coast is washed by the Caribbean Sea, the north coast by the Atlantic Ocean, and in the east the Windward Channel separates Cuba from Haiti. The shores are often marshy and are fringed by coral reefs and cays. There are many fine seaports—Havana (the chief import point), MATANZAS, CÁRDENAS, NUEVITAS (the chief export point), SANTIAGO DE CUBA, CIENFUEGOS, and GUANTÁNAMO (a U.S. naval base since 1903). Of the many rivers, only the Cauto is important. Cuba has three mountain regions: the wild and rugged Sierra Maestra in the east, rising to 6,560 ft (2,000 m) in the Pico Turquino; a lower range, the scenic Sierra de los Órganos, in the west; and the Sierra de Trinidad, a picturesque mass of hills amid the plains and rolling country of central Cuba, a region of vast sugar plantations. The rest of the island is level or rolling. The topography, the semitropical

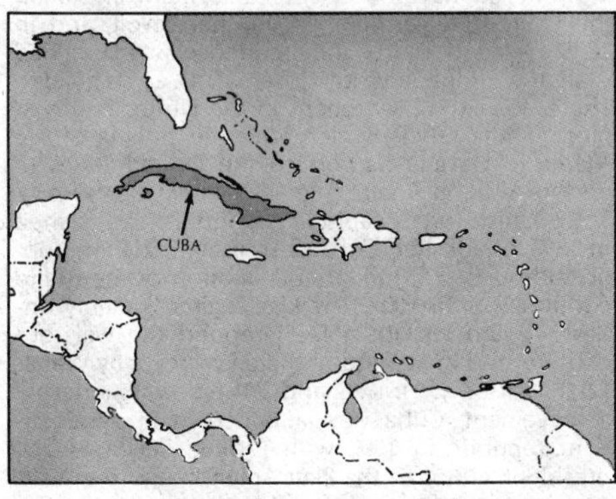

and generally uniform climate, and the soil are suitable for various crops, but sugarcane has been dominant since the late 18th cent.; it is grown on about two thirds of all crop land. Attempts at diversification have been only partially successful; the program of agrarian reform established by the revolutionary government of Fidel Castro failed to solve the problems arising from a one-crop economy, and sugar and its derivatives still account for about 85% of the value of all exports. Cattle raising is second in production value. An excellent tobacco is grown, especially in the VUELTA ABAJO region of Pinar del Río, and coffee, rice, corn, citrus fruits, and sweet potatoes are important. However, the emphasis on export crops (sugar and to a lesser degree tobacco) necessitates the importation of much food. Large-scale fishing operations have been encouraged under the Castro regime, and that industry is now one of the largest in Latin America; Cuban fishing fleets operate from Greenland to Argentina. Manufacturing is centered chiefly in the processing of agricultural products; sugar-milling has long been the largest industry, and Cuba is also known for its tobacco products. Some consumer goods (textiles, fertilizer, cement, etc.) are also manufactured. Mining has never been of major importance, although Cuba's nickel deposits are among the largest in the world. Extraction is difficult because of the presence of other metals in the nickel ore, but production has nevertheless increased considerably and nickel is now the country's second most valuable export item (after sugar). Large amounts of copper, chromite, and manganese are also mined, as well as lesser quantities of salt, lead, zinc, gold, silver, and oil. Limestone, clay, gypsum, and sulfur production easily meet the country's needs. There are immense iron reserves, but problems of extraction and purification are even greater than with nickel, and iron production is still almost negligible. The island was discovered in 1492 by Christopher Columbus. The Spanish conquest began in 1511 under the leadership of Diego de VELÁZQUEZ, who founded BARACOA and other major settlements. Cuba served as the staging area for Spanish explorations of the Americas. As an assembly point for treasure fleets, it offered a target for French and British buccaneers, who attacked the island's cities incessantly. The native ARAWAK Indians soon died off and were replaced as laborers by Negro slaves, who contributed much to the cultural evolution of the island. The white element was continuously replenished by immigration, chiefly from Spain but also from other Latin American countries. Despite pirate attacks and the trade restrictions of Spanish mercantilist policies, Cuba, the Pearl of the Antilles, prospered. In the imperial wars of the 18th cent. other nations coveted the Spanish possession, and in 1762 a British force under George Pocock and the earl of Albemarle captured and briefly held Havana. Cuba was returned to Spain by the Treaty of Paris in 1763 and remained Spanish even as most of Spain's possessions became (early 19th cent.) independent republics. The slave trade expanded rapidly, reaching its peak in 1817. Sporadic slave revolts were brutally suppressed by the Spaniards. Desires for Cuban independence increased when representation at the Spanish Cortes, granted in 1810, was withdrawn, yet neither internal discontent nor filibustering expeditions (1848–51) led by Narciso LÓPEZ, achieved results. The desire of U.S. Southerners to acquire the island as a slave state also failed (see OSTEND MANIFESTO). Cuban discontent grew and finally erupted (1868) in the TEN YEARS WAR, a long revolt that ended

(1878) in a truce, with Spain promising reforms and greater autonomy. Spain failed to carry out most of the reforms, although slavery was abolished (1886) as promised. Revolutionary leaders, many in exile in the United States, planned another revolt, and in 1895 a second war of independence was launched with the brilliant writer José MARTÍ as its leader. There was strong sentiment in the United States in favor of the rebels, which after the sinking of the *Maine* in Havana harbor led the United States to declare war on Spain (see SPANISH-AMERICAN WAR). The Spanish forces capitulated, and a treaty, signed in 1898, established Cuba as an independent republic, although U.S. military occupation of the island continued until 1902. The U.S. regime, notably under Leonard WOOD, helped rebuild the war-torn country, and the conquest of yellow fever by Walter REED, Carlos J. FINLAY, and others was a heroic achievement. Cuba was launched as an independent republic in 1902 with Estrada Palma as first president, although the Platt Amendment (see PLATT, ORVILLE HITCHCOCK), reluctantly accepted by the Cubans, kept the island under U.S. protection and gave the United States the right to intervene in Cuban affairs. U.S. investment in Cuban enterprises increased, and plantations, refineries, railroads, and factories passed to American (and thus absentee) ownership. This economic dependence led to charges of "Yankee imperialism," strengthened when a revolt headed by José Miguel GÓMEZ led to a new U.S. military occupation (1906-9). William Howard TAFT and Charles MAGOON acted as provisional governors. After supervising the elections, the U.S. forces withdrew, only to return to guarantee order in the Negro insurrection of 1912. Sugar production increased, and in World War I the near-destruction of Europe's beet-sugar industry raised sugar prices to the point where Cuba enjoyed its "dance of the millions." The boom was followed by collapse, however, and wild fluctuations in prices brought repeated hardship. Politically, the country suffered fraudulent elections and increasingly corrupt administrations. Gerardo MACHADO as president (1925-33) instituted vigorous measures, forwarding mining, agriculture, and public works, then abandoned his great projects in favor of suppressing opponents. Machado was overthrown in 1933, and from then until 1959 Fulgencio BATISTA Y ZALDÍVAR, a former army sergeant, dominated the political scene, either directly as president or indirectly as army chief of staff. With Franklin Delano Roosevelt's administration a new era in U.S. relations with Cuba began: Sumner WELLES was sent as ambassador, the Platt Amendment was abandoned in 1934, the sugar quota was revised, and tariff rulings were changed to favor Cuba. However, economic problems continued, complicated by the difficulties of U.S. ownership of many of the sugar mills and the continuing need for diversification. In March, 1952, shortly before scheduled presidential elections, Batista seized power through a military coup. Cuban liberals soon reacted, but a revolt in 1953 by Fidel CASTRO was abortive. In 1956, however, Castro landed in Oriente prov. and took to the Sierra Maestra, where, aided by Ernesto "Che" GUEVARA, he reformed his ranks and waged a much publicized guerrilla war. The United States withdrew military aid to Batista in 1958; with Cuba a tinder box and his army demoralized, Batista finally fled on Jan. 1, 1959. Castro, supported by young professionals, students, urban workers, and some farmers, was soon in control of the nation. Castro's social revolution began in a burst of popular enthusiasm, but many groups were soon disillusioned. Massive executions, often summary, of so-called war criminals were followed by dismissal, resignation, and frequent incarceration of prominent revolutionists such as Hubert Matos, who disagreed with Communist tendencies in the regime. Private press, radio, and television were first muzzled and then completely suppressed. Land reform was pushed energetically, but little land was apportioned to individual farmers; by 1970 the state owned almost 70% of the farmland. Industrial reform meant essentially confiscation. The expropriation of U.S. landholdings, banks, and industrial concerns, and an intensive program of vilification against the United States, led to the breaking (Jan., 1961) of diplomatic relations by the U.S. government. That same year Castro openly proclaimed his allegiance with the Communist camp. The Soviet Union replaced the United States as major trading partner, and since 1961 massive Soviet aid has maintained Cuba's economic and military security. Meanwhile Cuban exiles were pouring into the United States by the thousands; one result of their activities was the preparation of an invasion force (trained mostly in Florida and Guatemala under the supervision of the U.S. Central Intelligence Agency) which landed on Girón Beach in the Bay of Pigs, Cuba, in April, 1961. It was quickly crushed—a debacle especially humiliating to the United States because of its involvement. Cuba's significance as a pawn in the COLD WAR was further dramatized the following year when the USSR began to buttress Cuba's military power and to build missile bases on the islands. In a dramatic confrontation President John F. Kennedy demanded (Oct., 1962) the dismantling of the missiles and ordered naval vessels to blockade the island, preventing further importation of offensive weapons. After a period of great world tension, during which several Soviet vessels turned away from Cuba, Soviet Premier Khrushchev (despite fiery denunciations by Castro and by Chinese Communists) agreed to withdraw the missiles. Shortly before Christmas, 1962, Castro released over 1,000 prisoners captured during the Bay of Pigs invasion in exchange for considerable quantities of food and medicine. His relations with other Latin American countries were harmed by his openly announced intention of spreading his revolution to those countries by guerrilla warfare. In Feb., 1962, the ORGANIZATION OF AMERICAN STATES (see also PAN-AMERICANISM and PUNTA DEL ESTE) formally excluded Cuba from its council, and by Sept., 1964, all Latin American nations except Mexico had broken diplomatic and economic ties with Cuba. After the death (1967) of Guevara while engaged in guerrilla activity in Bolivia, Cuban attempts to encourage revolution in other countries abated, and by the early 1970s the Castro government exhibited an interest in regaining the friendship of the Latin American nations and resumed diplomatic relations with several of them. In Cuba, Castro has remained in firm control; most of the thousands who had opposed him have fled the island (between Dec., 1965, and April, 1973, a Cuban government-controlled airlift carried more than 250,000 people between Havana and Miami, Fla.), and, despite economic disappointments, he is tremendously popular with the poorer people, who make up the bulk of the population. Perhaps his greatest success has been in increasing educational opportunities and dramatically reducing illiteracy. The principal institutions of higher learning are the Univ. of Havana (founded 1728, reorganized 1943 and 1960), in Havana; Universidad de Oriente, in Santiago de Cuba; and Central Universidad de las Villas, in Santa Clara. See W. F. Johnson, *The History of Cuba* (4 vol., 1920); Elie Abel, *The Missile Crisis* (1966); C. A. Chapman, *A History of the Cuban Republic* (1927, repr. 1969); R. R. Fagen, *The Transformation of Political Culture in Cuba* (1969); R. E. Ruíz, *Cuba, the Making of a Revolution* (1970); H. I. Blutstein et al., *Area Handbook for Cuba* (1971); K. S. Karol, *Guerrillas in Power* (tr. 1971); Carmelo Mesa-Lago, ed., *Revolutionary Change in Cuba* (1971); Andrew Salkey, *Havana Journal* (1971); Bertram Silverman, comp., *Man and Socialism in Cuba* (1971); Hugh Thomas, *Cuba, the Pursuit of Freedom* (1971); L. E. Aguilar, *Cuba 1933* (1972); R. E. Bonachea and N. P. Valdés, ed., *Cuba in Revolution* (1972); P. S. Foner, *The Spanish-Cuban American War and the Birth of American Imperialism, 1895-1902* (2 vol., 1972); Lowry Nelson, *Cuba* (1972).

Cubango, river, Angola: see OKAVANGO, river.

Cuban missile crisis, 1962, major cold war confrontation between the United States and the Soviet Union. After the BAY OF PIGS INVASION, the USSR increased its support of Fidel Castro's Cuban regime, and in the summer of 1962, Nikita Khrushchev secretly decided to install ballistic missiles in Cuba. When U.S. reconnaissance flights revealed the clandestine construction of missile launching sites, President Kennedy publicly denounced (Oct. 22, 1962) the Soviet actions. He imposed a naval blockade on Cuba and declared that any missile launched from Cuba would warrant a full-scale retaliatory attack by the United States against the Soviet Union. On Oct. 24, Russian ships carrying missiles to Cuba turned back, and when Khrushchev agreed (Oct. 28) to withdraw the missiles and dismantle the missile sites, the crisis ended as suddenly as it had begun. The United States ended its blockade on Nov. 20, and by the end of the year the missiles and bombers were removed from Cuba. See D. L. Larson, ed., *The Cuban Crisis of 1962* (1963); Elie Abel, *The Missile Crisis* (1966, repr. 1968); Robert F. Kennedy, *Thirteen Days* (1969, repr. 1971); G. T. Allison, *Essence of Decision* (1971); Abram Chayes, *The Cuban Missile Crisis* (1974).

Cubberley, Ellwood Patterson, 1868-1941, American educator, b. Andrews, Ind., grad. Univ. of Indiana, 1891, Ph.D. Columbia, 1905. He was a pioneer writer in the history of American education and served as president (1891-96) of Vincennes Univ. and as superintendent of schools (1896-98) in San Diego, Calif. In 1898 he joined the faculty of Stanford, becoming professor of education in 1906 and in 1917 dean of the school of education, which he administered until his retirement in 1933. His works include *Changing Conceptions in Education* (1909), *The History of Education* (1920), *Public School Administration* (1929), and *Public Education in the United States* (rev. and enl. ed. 1947). See J. B. Sears and A. D. Henderson, *Cubberley of Stanford* (1957); study by L. A. Cremin (1965).

cube, in geometry, regular solid bounded by six equal squares. All adjacent faces of a cube are perpendicular to each other; any one face of a cube may be its base. The dimensions of a cube are the lengths of the three edges which meet at any vertex. The volume of a cube is equal to the product of its dimensions, and since its dimensions are equal, the volume is equal to the third power, or cube, of any one of its dimensions. Hence, in arithmetic and algebra, the cube of a number or letter is that number or letter raised to the third power. For example, the cube of 4 is $4^3=4\times4\times4=64$. The problem to construct a cube with a volume equal to twice that of a given cube using only a compass and a straightedge is known as the problem of the duplication of the cube and is one of the famous GEOMETRIC PROBLEMS OF ANTIQUITY. The cube, or hexahedron, is one of only five regular polyhedra (see POLYHEDRON).

cubeb: see PEPPER.

cubism, art movement, primarily in painting, originating in Paris c.1907. It began as an intellectual revolt against the artistic expression of previous eras. Among the specific elements the cubists abandoned were the sensual appeal of paint texture and color, subject matter with emotional charge or mood, the play of light on form, movement, atmosphere, and the illusionism that proceeded from scientifically based perspective. To replace these they employed an analytic system in which the three-dimensional subject (usually still life) was fragmented and redefined from several points of view described simultaneously within a shallow plane or within several interlocking and often transparent planes. In this analytic phase (1907-12) the cubist palette was severely limited, forms rigidly geometric, compositions subtle and intricate. Cubist abstraction as represented by the analytic works of Picasso and Braque intended an appeal to the intellect. This approach has been termed conceptual realism because the cubists sought to show everyday objects as the mind, not the eye, perceives them—from all sides at once. During the later, synthetic phase of cubism (1913 through the 1920s), paintings were composed of fewer and simpler forms based to a lesser extent on natural objects. Brighter colors were employed, and many artists introduced the *trompe l'oeil* element of COLLAGE. The works of Juan Gris are most representative of this phase. The major exponents of cubism included Picasso, Braque, Jean Metzinger, Gris, Duchamp, and Léger. Although few painters remained faithful to its tenets, many profited from its discipline. The several sources of cubist inspiration included the later work of Cézanne; the geometric forms and compressed picture space in his paintings appealed especially to Braque, who developed them in his own works. African sculpture, particularly mask carvings, had enormous influence in the early years of the movement. Picasso's *Demoiselles d'Avignon* (1907; Mus. of Modern Art, New York City) is one of the most significant examples of this influence. Within this revolutionary composition lay much of the basic material of cubism. The cubist break with the tradition of imitation of nature was completed in the works of Picasso, Braque, and their many groups of followers. The major segments of the cubist movement included the Montmartre-based Bâteau-Lavoir group of artists and poets (Max Jacob, Guillaume Apollinaire, Gertrude and Leo Stein, Modigliani, Picabia, Delaunay, Archipenko, and others); the Puteaux group of the *Section d'Or* salon (J. Villon, Léger, Picabia, Kupka, Marcoussis, Gleizes, Apollinaire, and others); the Orphists (Delaunay, Duchamp, Picabia, and Villon); and the experimenters in collage who influenced cubist sculpture (Laurens and Lipchitz). Although the cubist groups were largely dispersed after World War I, their collective break from visual realism had an enriching and decisive influence on the development of 20th-century art. It provided a new stylistic vocabulary and a technical idiom that remain forceful today. See also ORPHISM and articles on individual artists, e.g., GRIS. See Guillaume Apollinaire, *The Cubist Painters* (1913, tr. 1949); D. H. Kahnweiler,

The Rise of Cubism (1915, tr. 1949); A. H. Barr, Jr., *Cubism and Abstract Art* (1936, repr. 1966); Robert Rosenblum, *Cubism and Twentieth-Century Art* (rev. ed. 1967); Douglas Cooper, *The Cubist Epoch* (1971).

Cuchulain (ko͞o'ho͝olĭn), Irish legendary hero of Ulster, of prodigious strength and remarkable beauty. He is the central figure of the Ulster legends, the greatest work of which is the *Táin Bó Cúalnge* [the cattle raid of Cooley]. The great feature of this is Cuchulain's stand at a ford on the boundary of Ulster, where he defended single-handedly his province against the armies of the rest of Ireland.

cuckoo, common name for members of the extensive avian family Cuculidae, including the ani and the roadrunner (*Geococcyx californianus*), widely distributed in temperate and tropical regions. Cuckoos are slender-bodied, long-tailed birds with medium to stout down-curved bills, pointed wings, short legs (except in the terrestrial species), and dull (usually grayish brown or rufous) plumage. They are generally insectivorous and arboreal. Of the parasitic Old World cuckoos, the common European cuckoo, *Cuculus canorus,* is typical. The female visits the nests of smaller birds, selecting those whose eggs match hers in color, and replaces an egg of the host with one of her own; she usually lays four or five eggs, each at 48-hr intervals and each in a different nest. The young cuckoo, being larger than its nest mates, displaces them from the nest and becomes the sole recipient of its foster parents' care. Each species of Old World cuckoo has its own unique pattern of parasitism, and different species choose different host species for their eggs. The cuckoo is referred to in the Bible, by Aristotle and Pliny, in mythology, and in English poetry. Its nesting habits have given us the word *cuckold,* and its simple but musical song, which gives it its name, was used by Beethoven in his Pastoral Symphony and is also imitated in the cuckoo clock. The American cuckoos look like attenuated pigeons; they are not parasitic and build flimsy nests of twigs. Typical are the black-billed and yellow-billed (*Coccyzus americanus*) cuckoos, known for their low, chuckling call notes. They frequent and breed at the edges of deciduous woodlands, either species tending the young of the other. These birds are valued as destroyers of harmful insects—particularly the tent caterpillar, which few other birds will eat. There are also western and southern species. Most gregarious of the cuckoos are the anis of the American tropics. The groove-billed ani, from 12 to 14 in. (30–35 cm) long, has black plumage with a faint purple gloss. Anis nest colonially, several females together laying as many as 25 eggs in the same nest, and they may breed at any time of the year. Of the ground cuckoos, the roadrunner, or chaparral cock, of the southwest deserts is best known. It feeds mostly on small snakes and lizards, which it pounds to death with its heavy bill and swallows headfirst. The roadrunner speeds over the ground at up to 15 mi (40.3 km) per hr with its long tail extended horizontally, its head down, and its ragged crest erect. Roadrunners are weak fliers and nonmigratory. They build coarse nests in thorny bushes; because they lay at intervals, both eggs and young may appear together in the nest. Also included in the cuckoo family are the coucals, medium to large in size, slow-flying, mostly terrestrial birds of the tropics from Africa to Australia, e.g., the black concal, *Centropus grilli.* Cuckoos are classified in the phylum CHORDATA, subphylum Vertebrata, class Aves, order Cuculiformes, family Cuculidae.

cucumber, fruit of *Cucumis sativus,* a species of GOURD whose many varieties are descended from a plant native to Asia and Africa. Cucumber is classified in the division MAGNOLIOPHYTA, class Magnoliopsida, order Violales, family Curcurbitaceae.

cucumber tree: see MAGNOLIA.

Cucupá Indians: see COCOPA INDIANS.

Cúcuta (ko͞o'ko͞otä), city (1968 est. pop. 167,400), capital of Norte de Santander dept., NE Colombia, near the Venezuelan border, on the eastern cordillera of the Colombian Andes. An industrial city, Cúcuta is the center of a rich coffee, oil, and mineral region. The city was founded in 1733. Simón BOLÍVAR captured Cúcuta in 1813 and set out from there on his march to CARACAS. At Cúcuta the constituent congress of 1821 met to draft the constitution of Greater Colombia (present-day Venezuela, Ecuador, and Colombia). The city was rebuilt after an earthquake in 1875.

Cudahy, Michael (kŭd'əhē), 1841–1910, American meat packer, b. Co. Kilkenny, Ireland. He went (1849) to Milwaukee and after 1856 worked for meat-packing firms. In the 1870s he introduced refrigeration into the meat-packing industry. He became a partner of Philip D. Armour and later, with his brother John, established a packing company in Omaha, Nebr.

Cudahy, city (1970 pop. 22,078), Milwaukee co., SE Wis., an industrial suburb of Milwaukee, on Lake Michigan; inc. 1906. It was founded in 1892 by John and Patrick Cudahy as a site for their meat-packing enterprise, which remains a major industry. The city also produces pipe fittings, valves, drop forgings, packaging and bottling machinery, cranes, and truck seats.

Cuddalore or **Kudalur** (both: kŭdəlôr'), town (1971 pop. 101,345), Tamil Nadu state, SE India. It is a port on the Bay of Bengal and a district administrative center. Peanut products, cashew nuts, and sugar are the chief exports. Fort St. David, a stronghold of Tippoo Sahib, is a notable architectural monument in Cuddalore.

Cuddapah (kŭd'əpä), city (1971 pop. 66,238), Andhra Pradesh state, S central India. It is a district administrative center and a market for peanuts, cotton, tumeric, and onions. Paint and varnish are manufactured, and asbestos and barite are processed. Melons from the district are famous. The city was part of the Chola empire (11th–15th cent.). Muslims conquered it in 1565, and the British took control in 1800.

Cudworth, Ralph, 1617–88, English theologian and philosopher. He was a noted representative of the CAMBRIDGE PLATONISTS. Cudworth's most ambitious work, *The True Intellectual System of the Universe,* was never completed. The first part, a critique of atheistic materialism, appeared in 1678, and two parts were published posthumously as *A Treatise concerning Eternal and Immutable Morality* (1731) and *A Treatise on Freewill* (1838). In his works Cudworth attacked the materialistic philosophy of Hobbes and maintained the belief that moral ideas are innate in man. See study by J. A. Passmore (1951).

Cuenca (kwĕng'kä), city (1970 est. pop. 77,300), alt. c.8,000 ft (2,440 m), S central Ecuador. Founded in 1557, Cuenca is in one of the richest agricultural basins of the Ecuadorian Andes and is the commercial center of S Ecuador. The chief industry is weaving of Panama hats. Cuenca is known as the "marble city" because of its many fine buildings, including the cathedral, government palace, and university.

Cuenca, city (1970 pop. 34,485), capital of Cuenca prov., E central Spain, in New Castile, at the confluence of the Huecar and Júcar rivers, c.3,000 ft (910 m) above sea level. This historic town retains its medieval character in the narrow streets, clustered houses, and bridges; the modern, industrial section (timber trade, furniture, pottery, paper, leather) called Curretaria, extends onto the Huecar plain. The city was taken (1177) from the Moors by Alfonso VIII of Castile. Cuenca was badly damaged in the Peninsular War and the Second Carlist War. It has a notable Gothic cathedral (begun 13th cent.). Nearby is the Ciudad Encantada [enchanted city], a fantastic labyrinth of eroded rocks.

Cuénod, Hugues (üg kwänō'), 1902–, Swiss tenor. Cuénod was educated in Lausanne, Basel, and Vienna. Noted for his interpretation of works ranging from Monteverdi to Stravinsky, he was still performing in his 70s.

Cuernavaca (kwārnävä'kä), city (1970 pop. 159,909), capital of Morelos state, S Mexico, in the Cuernavaca Valley. The city has flour mills and beverage, textile, and cement industries. Cuernavaca is also a popular tourist and health resort. In the city are beautiful churches, monasteries, a 16th-century Franciscan convent, a palace built by Hernán Cortés and now decorated with murals by Diego Rivera, and a formal garden that was frequented by Emperor Maximilian and Empress Carlotta. Nearby is the Toltec ruin, Xochicalco, built over limestone caves.

cuesta (kwĕs'tə), asymmetric ridge characterized by a short, steep escarpment on one side, and a long, gentle slope on the other. The steep side exposes the edge of erosion-resistant rock layers that form the cuestas. They are usually formed by erosion in plains areas underlain by gently dipping sedimentary rock layers. Cuestas have a more gentle dip than similar structures called HOGBACKS. Along the U.S. Atlantic and Gulf coastal plains are found a series of low subdued cuestas composed of seaward-dipping and poorly cemented Cretaceous and Tertiary sandstones, while the intervening lowlands are underlain by impermeable clays. These conditions produce ideal structures for artesian water supply systems, which have been extensively tapped by coastal cities. A well-known example of a cuesta is the Niagara cuesta that runs westward across W New York State and Ontario, then swings northward, forming the peninsula between Lake Huron and Georgian Bay, and finally curves southward, forming the Door Peninsula between Green Bay and Lake Michigan. Following withdrawal of the last Pleistocene ice sheet about 10,000 years ago, Niagara Falls first formed where the Niagara River crosses the Niagara cuesta at Lewiston, N.Y., and Queenston, Ont. Since then, the falls have migrated nearly 7 mi (11 km) southward as a result of undercutting and rockfall, leaving the steep-walled Niagara Gorge to mark its path.

Cueva, Beatriz de la (bäätrēs' dā lä kwā'vä), d. 1541, governor of Guatemala. After the death of her husband, Pedro de ALVARADO, she maneuvered her own election and became the only woman to govern a major American political division in Spanish times. A young, beautiful, and ambitious woman who styled herself the Hapless One (*La Sin Ventura*), she was drowned a few weeks after assuming office in the destruction of Ciudad Vieja by a mysterious flood from the volcano AGUA.

Cueva, Juan de la (hwän), 1550?–1610?, Spanish dramatist, one of the precursors of Lope de Vega. He spent the years from 1574 to 1577 in Mexico. Of his 14 plays, the most famous is the comedy *El infamador* [the scoundrel] (1581). Cueva rejected traditional dramatic unities and introduced national themes to the stage, laying the foundation for the national drama of Spain's Golden Age. His innovations included employing a variety of meters and reducing the comedy to four acts. See study by R. F. Glenn (1973).

Cui, César Antonovich (tsāzär' äntô'nôvĭch küē'), 1835–1918, Russian composer and critic, a military engineer by profession. As a music critic in St. Petersburg and Paris, he championed the group of nationalist Russian composers known as The FIVE, consisting of Rimsky-Korsakov, Balakirev, Mussorgsky, Borodin, and himself. Of these, he was the least distinctive composer. He was largely self-taught, and his best works are songs and short salon pieces, which avoid the technical deficiencies of his operas and orchestral music. See V. I. Seroff, *The Mighty Five* (1948); M. O. Zetlin, *The Five* (tr. 1959).

Cuiabá (ko͞oyəbä'), city (1970 pop. 100,865), capital of Mato Grosso state, W Brazil, at the head of navigation on the Cuiabá River. Founded in the gold rush of the early 18th cent., it has been the state capital since 1818. The city is a trading center for an extensive cattle-raising and agricultural area. Economic development has been hampered by Cuiabá's isolation and by the shortage of labor. The chief means of communication is still the riverboat.

Cuismancu: see CHANCAY.

Cujas or **Cujacius, Jacques** (zhäk küzhäs', kyo͞ojā'shəs), 1522–90, French jurist and scholar of Roman law. He taught at Toulouse, Bourges, and elsewhere. Unlike previous scholars, he was relatively unconcerned with the practical applications of Roman law and wished primarily to study the ancient texts in their relation to history and literature. He is often considered the founder of the historical school of jurisprudence. Much of his critical effort was directed toward reconstructing in the original form the excerpts from eminent Roman jurists quoted in the Corpus Juris Civilis. Cujas prepared critical editions of works of Ulpian and Paulus.

Culbertson, Ely (ē'lē kŭl'bərtsən), 1891–1955, American authority on contract bridge, b. Rumania. His father was an American engineer then living in Rumania, and his mother was of Russian parentage. Culbertson introduced the first successful system of bidding in contract bridge, wrote numerous books on the game, edited *Bridge World* magazine, wrote a widely read newspaper column on bridge, and won many bridge tournaments. After World War II he wrote and lectured on world peace, setting forth his plans in the book *Must We Fight Russia?* (1946). See his autobiography, *The Strange Lives of One Man* (1940), and his *Contract Bridge for Everyone,* ed. by Victor Mollo (rev. ed. 1969).

Culdees (kəldēz') [Irish,=servants of God], ancient monks of Ireland and Scotland, appearing after the 8th cent. Little is known of their origin, and their relationship to the monks of the Celtic Church, e.g., at Iona, is unclear. They were originally anchorites, but by the time of the reforms of St. Malachy (12th cent.) they had become secular canons living in community. They gained a reputation for extreme laxness. The last Culdee community, at Armagh, was disbanded in 1541.

Culebra Cut: see PANAMA CANAL.

Culiacán (ko͞olēäkän'), city (1970 pop. 358,812), capital of Sinaloa state, W Mexico, on the Culiacán River. It is situated on a hot coastal plain that produces tropical fruits, sugarcane, cotton, beans, and maize; cattle-raising is also important. Fine oysters come from the city's Pacific port, Altata. Culiacán, founded in 1531, figured prominently in the early Spanish colonial period as a point of departure for northern expeditions, notably that of Francisco Coronado in 1540. Within the city are numerous plazas, an impressive cathedral, and luxuriant tropical gardens.

Cullen, Countee (koun'tē'), 1903–46, American poet, b. New York City, grad. New York Univ. 1925, M.A. Harvard, 1926. A major writer of the Harlem Renaissance—a flowering of Negro artistic and literary talent in the 1920s—Cullen wrote poetry inspired by American Negro life. His technique was conventional, modeled on that of John Keats, and his mood passed from racial pride and optimism in the 1920s to sadness and disappointment in the 1930s. Among his volumes of verse are *Color* (1925), *Copper Sun* (1927), *The Ballad of the Brown Girl* (1927), and *On These I Stand* (1947). See bibliography by Margaret Penny (1971).

Cullman, city (1970 pop. 12,601), seat of Cullman co., N Ala.; inc. 1875. It is a shipping and trade center for a cotton, timber, and dairy region. Cullman College is there, and St. Bernard College is nearby. Cullman was settled in 1873 by immigrants from Germany.

Culloden Moor (kəlŏd'ən, -lō'dən), moorland in Inverness-shire, NE Scotland, in the Highland region. There, on April 16, 1746, English forces under the duke of Cumberland defeated the Highlanders under Prince Charles Edward Stuart, thus ending the Jacobite uprising of 1745.

Cullum, George Washington (kŭl'əm), 1809–92, American army officer, b. New York City, grad. West Point, 1833. In the Civil War, Cullum was made a brigadier general of volunteers (Nov., 1861) and served as chief of staff to General Halleck (1861–64) and as superintendent of West Point (1864–66). He is chiefly known for his excellent *Biographical Register of the Officers and Graduates of the U.S. Military Academy* (1850; 3d ed., 3 vol., 1891), which furnishes sketches of the graduates of West Point.

culminate, in astronomy, the maximum height in the sky reached by a celestial body on a given day. At the culminate the body is crossing the observer's CELESTIAL MERIDIAN and is said to be in upper TRANSIT.

Culpeper, Thomas Culpeper, 2d Baron, 1635–89, English colonial governor of Virginia. In 1673, with the earl of Arlington, he was granted all lands in Virginia not previously patented. In addition, Culpeper was granted (1675) the right of succession to the governorship of Virginia and soon replaced Sir William Berkeley. He remained in England and ruled through deputies until 1680, when Charles II required him to go in person to Virginia. His general pardon of all those who had participated in Bacon's Rebellion made him popular for a brief time, but after about four months he returned to England. When disturbances arising out of the low price of tobacco broke out in the colony, he was threatened with removal unless he remained in Virginia. During his second stay (1682–83) Culpeper hanged some of the planters who had destroyed tobacco plants and quarreled violently with the burgesses. Upon leaving the colony again in 1683 he was deprived of the governorship. However, in 1688 he procured from James II a renewal in perpetuity of his vast Northern Neck proprietary (see FAIRFAX OF CAMERON, THOMAS FAIRFAX, 6TH BARON).

cult, ritual observances involved in worship of, or communication with, the supernatural or its symbolic representations. A cult includes the totality of ideas, activities, and practices associated with a given divinity or social group. It includes not only ritual activities but also the beliefs and myths centering on the rites. The objects of the cult are often things associated with the daily life of the celebrants. The English scholar Jane Harrison pointed out the importance of the cult in the development of religion. Sacred persons may have their own cults. The cult may be associated with a single person, place, or object or may have much broader associations. There may be officials entrusted with the rites, or anyone who belongs may be allowed to take part in them.

cultivation, tilling or manipulation of the soil, done primarily to eliminate weeds that compete with crops for water and nutrients. Cultivation may be used in crusted soils to increase soil aeration and infiltration of water; it may also be used to move soil to or away from plants as desired. Cultivation among crop plants is best kept at a minimum; excessive cultivation can be harmful as it may cause root pruning and loss of soil water due to increased evaporation.

cultivator, agricultural implement for stirring and pulverizing the soil, either before planting or to remove weeds and to aerate and loosen the soil after the crop has begun to grow. The cultivator usually stirs the soil to a greater depth than does the HARROW. See CULTIVATION.

culture, in anthropology, the way of life of a society. The scientific use of the term was established by Sir Edward Burnett Tylor in the late 19th cent. The concept of culture has proved so useful that it has spread to the other social sciences, to the humanities, and to the biological sciences. The concept of culture is used to distinguish human societies from animal groups. The customs, ideas, and attitudes shared by a group, which make up its culture, are transmitted from generation to generation by learning processes rather than biological inheritance. Adherence to these customs and attitudes is regulated by systems of rewards and punishments peculiar to each culture. Language and other symbolic media are the chief agents of culture transmission, but many behavior patterns are acquired through experience alone. A pattern of cultural universals is found in all societies. It includes such human institutions as social organization, religion, structure, economic organization, and material culture (tools, weapons, clothing). Societies are differentiated according to the degree of complexity of cultural organization. Basically, each human group has its own distinctive culture, but a complex society may contain subcultures determined by national origin, religion, or social status. Conversely, a common culture may be adopted by several different societies through peaceful or enforced culture contact. This involves acculturation, the process whereby the members of one group adopt the customs of another. The spread of culture traits through direct or indirect contact among groups is called diffusion. A culture area is the territory within which a certain configuration of culture traits is to be found. The two theories of culture that have dominated anthropological thought in the 20th cent. are the structural-functional theory derived from Bronislaw Malinowski and the pattern-process theory derived from Franz Boas. Structural-functional theory focuses on social structure, while pattern-process theory emphasizes cultural patterns. Each theory attempts to explain all aspects of culture, and each is applied to all cultures. All anthropologists, however, recognize certain broad evolutionary sequences in the cultural history of mankind, particularly in the technological and economic spheres. These stages of development have not occurred everywhere at the same time, nor have all cultures passed through all of them. One or more stages may be skipped through culture contact or acculturation. The first stage is that of the food collectors—fishers, hunters, and vegetation gatherers who live in small migratory groups, following the food supply and camping in caves or temporary shelters, as in the Paleolithic and Mesolithic periods. The next stage is that of the food producers, who have learned to domesticate plants and animals and who live in settled villages; an example is the culture of the Neolithic period. This stage leads to the rise of urban centers, as in the great historic civilizations of the world. In classifying a contemporary culture according to its stage of development, its technological level should not be considered alone. The food collectors of the 20th cent., such as the Australian aborigines, cannot be equated with the Paleolithic hunters of 25,000 years ago, for the Paleolithic systems of kinship and religion, for example, were quite different. See Ruth Benedict, *Patterns of Culture* (1934); A. L. Kroeber and Clyde Kluckhohn, *Culture: A Critical Review of Concepts and Definitions* (1952); Margaret Mead, ed., *Cultural Patterns and Technical Change* (1953); Ralph Linton, *The Tree of Culture* (1955); Jack Lindsay, *A Short History of Culture* (1962); Ashley Montagu, ed., *Culture* (1968); P. L. Wagner, *Environments and Peoples* (1972).

Culver City, city (1970 pop. 31,035), Los Angeles co., S Calif., a residential suburb of Los Angeles; inc. 1917. It is a center of the U.S. motion-picture industry, which began in the city c.1915. The city's chief industrial products are electronic and aerospace equipment. West Los Angeles Univ. College of Law, a private law school, and a junior college are in Culver City. Directly south of the city is Los Angeles International Airport.

Culver's root: see FIGWORT.

Cumae (kyo͞o'mē), ancient city of Campania, Italy, near Naples. According to Strabo, it was the earliest Greek colony in Italy or Sicily, and it seems to have been founded c.750 B.C. by Chalcis. The area has yielded earlier non-Greek archaeological finds. Cumae founded a number of colonies and grew to be a great power. It repulsed Etruscan and Umbrian attacks, but fell in the late 5th cent. B.C. to the Samnites. Cumae supported Rome in the 2d cent. B.C. and adopted Roman culture; ultimately its inhabitants became Roman citizens. As neighboring cities rose to power, Cumae declined, although it did not disappear until the 13th cent. A.D. There are extensive Greek and Roman ruins, and the cavern where the famed Cumaean Sibyl (the priestess of Apollo mentioned by Vergil) uttered her prophecies may still be seen.

Cumaná (ko͞omänä'), city (1970 est. pop. 100,000), capital of Sucre state, NE Venezuela, on the Manzanares River near its mouth on the Gulf of Cariaco, an inlet on the Caribbean Sea. Coffee, tobacco, cacao, and sugar are exported. Founded in 1521 to exploit the pearl fisheries near Margarita island, Cumaná was often raided by the Dutch and British in the 16th and 17th cent. Frequently a victim of earthquakes, the city was severely damaged in 1929.

Cumans or **Kumans** (both: ko͞o'mänz), nomadic East Turkic people, identified with the Kipchaks (or the western branch of the Kipchaks) and known in Russian as Polovtsi. Coming from NW Asiatic Russia, they conquered S Russia and Walachia in the 11th cent., and for almost two centuries warred intermittently with the Byzantine Empire, Hungary, and Kiev. They founded a nomadic state in the steppes along the Black Sea, and were active in commerce with the Orient and Venice. In the early 12th cent. the main Cuman forces were defeated by the Eastern Slavs. The Mongols decisively defeated the Cumans c.1245. Some were sold as slaves, and many took refuge in Bulgaria and also in Hungary, where they were gradually assimilated into the Hungarian culture. Others joined the khanate of the Golden Horde (also called the Western Kipchaks), which was organized on the former Cuman territory in Russia.

Cumberland, Richard, 1631–1718, English philosopher. He was bishop of Peterborough from 1691. In his *De legibus naturae* [on natural laws] (1672) he first propounded the doctrine of utilitarianism and opposed the egoistic ethics of Thomas Hobbes.

Cumberland, Richard, 1732–1811, English dramatist; great-grandson of the 17th-century philosopher Richard Cumberland. His family connections earned him a clerical position with the British board of trade. The author of over 40 plays, he was most successful with his sentimental comedies, the best of which are *The Brothers* (1769) and *The West Indian* (1771). He also wrote two seldom read novels, *Arundel* (1789) and *Henry* (1795), and an autobiography (1806–7).

Cumberland, William Augustus, duke of, 1721–65, British general; third son of George II. Entering the army shortly before the outbreak (1740) of the War of the Austrian Succession, he was defeated by the French at Fontenoy (1745). Returning to England to put down the 1745 rising of the JACOBITES, he defeated Prince Charles Edward Stuart at Culloden Moor (1746) and earned the nickname "the Butcher" by his ruthless punishment of the rebels. Once more on the Continent, he averted the fall of Maastricht but was again defeated by the French in 1747. In the Seven Years War he signed (1757) a capitulation to the French (the Convention of KLOSTERZEVEN) for which he was dismissed. See two biographical studies by Evan Charteris (1913, 1925).

Cumberland, county (1971 pop. 71,497), 1,520 sq mi (3,937 sq km), N England, bordering on the Irish Sea to the west, Solway Firth to the north and west, and Scotland to the north. The county town is CARLISLE. The region, with adjacent Westmorland and N Lancashire, includes the area known as the LAKE DISTRICT. Cumberland is largely mountainous in the south and central area and low in the west, east, and north. Scafell Pike (3,210 ft/978 m) is the highest point in England. The chief streams are the Derwent, the Eden, and the Esk. Cumberland is a pastoral region (sheep and cattle grazing) with some crop farming. Coal and iron mining are important along the west coast. Other industries are quarrying (granite, limestone, and slate), chemical and textile manufacturing, and smelting. Tourism is important in the Lake District. There are nuclear-power plants at Windscale and Calder Hall. In 1974, Cumberland became part of the new nonmetropolitan county of Cumbria. The district has remains of the great walls built during the Roman occupation. Cumberland was the scene of many centuries of border strife between England and Scotland.

Cumberland. **1** City (1970 pop. 29,724), seat of Allegany co., NW Md., on the North Branch of the Potomac; settled 1750, inc. 1815. It is an important railroad and shipping center for a coal-mining area. Its manufactures include textiles, synthetic fibers, tires, glass, metal products, petrochemicals, propellants, and plastics. Cumberland grew around the site of a trading post established (1750) by the Ohio Company at a natural gateway through the Appalachians to the Ohio valley. Fort Cumberland (built 1754) was the base of operations for the ill-fated Braddock expedition (1755) against the French and Indians and the site of Washington's first military headquarters (1757). The city became the eastern terminus of the Cumberland Road, or NATIONAL ROAD; a division point for the Baltimore & Ohio RR; and the western terminus of the Chesapeake and Ohio Canal (completed 1850), which now runs through Green Ridge State Forest. Other local attractions include the old toll gate house (1833) and the Narrows, a magnificent gorge through the Appalachians to the Ohio valley. A junior college is in the city and Frostburg State College is to the west. **2** Town (1970 pop. 26,605), Providence co., NE R.I., on the Blackstone River and the Mass. line; included in Massachusetts until 1746, inc. as a R.I. town 1747. Its manufactures include textiles and metal and fiber-glass products. The Ballou Meetinghouse dates from c.1740.

Cumberland, river, 687 mi (1,106 km) long, rising in E Ky., and winding generally SW through Ky. and Tenn., then NW to the Ohio River near Paducah, Ky.; drains c.18,500 sq mi (47,910 sq km). Locks and canals make the river navigable for small craft for much of its length. The river's upper course flows through the rugged, forested coal-mining region of SE Kentucky, where its valley is a main transportation route. The central section of the river passes through the Nashville Basin, an agricultural region and the site of Nashville, Tenn. The Tennessee Valley Authority markets hydroelectric power produced by dams on the Cumberland and its tributaries, including Wolf Creek Dam, Ky. (270,000-kw capacity), which impounds Lake Cumberland; Dale Hollow Dam (54,000 kw); Center Hill Dam (135,000 kw); and Barkley Dam (130,000 kw). The Cumberland valley was the scene of several important Civil War battles (see FORT DONELSON).

Cumberland Gap, natural passage through Cumberland Mt., near the point where Virginia, Kentucky, and Tennessee meet. The gap was formed by the erosive action of a stream that once flowed there. It was discovered and named in 1750 by Dr. Thomas Walker, leader of a land company exploration party. Daniel Boone's WILDERNESS ROAD ran through the gap. A strategic point in the Civil War, the gap was held alternately by Confederate and Union forces. Cumberland Gap National Historic Park was established there in 1955 (see NATIONAL PARKS AND MONUMENTS, table).

Cumberland Island National Seashore, Ga.: see NATIONAL PARKS AND MONUMENTS, table.

Cumberland Plateau or **Cumberland Mountains,** southwestern division of the Appalachian Mt. system, extending northeast to southwest through parts of West Virginia, Virginia, Kentucky, and Tennessee into N Alabama; Black Mt., Ky., is the highest point (4,145 ft/1,263 m). On the east the plateau rises sharply from the Great Valley of E Tennessee; on the west the slope is rough and broken. The plateau is the source of the Cumberland River and several tributaries of the Tennessee. The surrounding region, which is sparsely populated, yields various minerals, especially coal. The coal is strip-mined; the removal of surface material and the building of unsightly spoil dumps have killed vegetation and interfered with stream flow by causing accelerated erosion and flooding. Cumberland Gap provides a natural passage through Cumberland Mt., a ridge of the plateau.

Cumberland Presbyterian Church, branch of the Presbyterian Church in the United States founded in 1810. In 1906 many of its congregations were united with the main body of the church. It began as a revival movement in the "Cumberland country," a newly settled region of Kentucky and Tennessee. The Negro members organized separate churches, and in 1869 they were legally set apart as the Colored Cumberland Presbyterian Church. The church has a combined membership of c.90,000.

Cumberland Road: see NATIONAL ROAD.

Cumberland Valley, 75 mi (121 km) long and from 15 to 20 mi (24–32 km) wide, part of the great Appalachian valley, between the Potomac and Susquehanna rivers, W Md. and S Pa. It is a fertile farming area that is now becoming urbanized; Chambersburg and Carlisle, Pa., and Hagerstown, Md., are in the valley.

Cumbernauld, new town and burgh (1971 pop. 31,784), in the detached, eastern portion of Dunbartonshire, Glasgow. Cumbernauld, the 15th of Britain's NEW TOWNS, was designated in 1955 to alleviate Glasgow's growth problems. Its population target was set at 70,000, anticipating that 80% of the immigrants would come from Glasgow. Cumbernauld's industries include food processing and the manufacture of adding machines and adhesive products. It was the first new town in which automobile traffic was adequately anticipated and provided for. Wherever possible, vehicular roads were completely separated from pedestrian ways. Under the local government act of 1973, Cumbernauld was included in the new region of Strathclyde.

Cumbria, nonmetropolitan county (1972 est. pop. 476,000), extreme NW England, created under the Local Government Act of 1972 (effective 1974). It is composed of the county boroughs of Barrow-in-Furness and Carlisle; the former counties of Cumberland and Westmorland; and parts of the former counties of Lancaster and Yorkshire (West Riding).

Cumbrian Mountains, mountains of the Lake District, NW England; Scafell Pike (3,210 ft/978 m) is the highest point. Studded with lakes and narrow valleys, the range extends through Cumberland, Westmorland, and N Lancashire.

cumin or **cummin** (both: kŭm'ĭn), low annual herb (*Cuminum cyminum*) of the family Umbelliferae (CARROT family), long cultivated in the Old World for the aromatic seedlike fruits. The fruits resemble the related caraway and are similarly used in cooking. Cumin is an ingredient of curry powder; the oil is used for liqueurs and in veterinary practice and was formerly used in medicine. Cumin is mentioned in the Bible. For black cumin, see LOVE-IN-A-MIST. Cumin is classified in the division MAGNOLIOPHYTA, class Magnoliopsida, order Umbellales, family Umbelliferae.

Cumming, John: see COMYN, JOHN.

cummings, e e (Edward Estlin Cummings), 1894–1962, American poet, b. Cambridge, Mass., grad. Harvard, 1915. His poetry, noted for its eccentricities of typography, language, and punctuation, usually seeks to convey a joyful, living awareness of sex and love. Among his 15 volumes of poetry are *Tulips and Chimneys* (1923), *Is 5* (1926), and *95 Poems* (1958). A prose account of his war internment in France, *The Enormous Room* (1922), is considered one of the finest books ever written about World War I. Cummings was also an accomplished artist whose paintings and drawings were exhibited in several one-man shows. See his *Complete Poems, 1913–1962* (2 vol., 1972); studies by B. A. Marks (1964) and Norman Friedman, comp. (1972).

Cummings, Homer Stillé, 1870–1956, American lawyer, U.S. Attorney General, b. Chicago. He practiced law in Stamford, Conn., where he was mayor three times. He rose to prominence in the state Democratic organization, served as a state representative on the Democratic National Committee, (1900–1925), and was chairman of the National Committee (1919–20). When Thomas J. Walsh, whom President Franklin Delano Roosevelt had named Attorney General, died just before the inauguration in 1933, Cummings was given a temporary appointment to fill the position. The appointment was made permanent in April, 1933, and he served until 1939.

cummingtonite (kŭm'ĭngtənīt): see AMPHIBOLE.

Cummins, Albert Baird, 1850–1926, U.S. Senator from Iowa (1909–26), b. Green co., Pa. He studied law in Chicago and in 1878 joined his brother in practice in Des Moines. As governor of Iowa (1901–8), Cummins worked to break up railroad domination in politics and to inaugurate progressive policies in the state. He was elected (1908) to the U.S. Senate and was co-author there of the Esch-Cummins Transportation Act of 1920.

cumulonimbus: see CLOUD.

cumulus: see CLOUD.

Cunard, Sir Samuel (kyōōnärd'), 1787–1865, Canadian pioneer of regular transatlantic steam navigation, b. Halifax, N.S. The son of a United Empire Loyalist, he became a leading businessman of Nova Scotia and engaged in banking, lumbering, shipping, and shipbuilding enterprises. His fleet at one time numbered some 40 vessels. He was interested in the development of steam navigation and owned shares in the *Royal William*, the first Canadian steamer to cross the Atlantic (1833) from Canada to England. When the British government invited bids (1838) for carrying mail to and from Liverpool, Halifax, and Boston, Cunard went (1839) to England and presented to the admiralty such carefully considered plans for a line of steamships that he received the contract. In association with others, he formed the British and North American Royal Mail Steam Packet Company, which in 1840 placed four ships in operation, establishing the first regular steamship service between the continents. This was the beginning of the noted Cunard Line. See F. E. Dodman, *Ships of the Cunard Line* (1955).

Cunaxa (kyōōnăk'sə), ancient town of Babylonia, near the Euphrates River, NE of Ctesiphon. It was the scene of a battle (401 B.C.) between CYRUS THE YOUNGER and ARTAXERXES II, described by XENOPHON in the *Anabasis*. CLEARCHUS, Spartan mercenary leader under Cyrus, chose to attack the Persian left wing (under Tissaphernes), which he completely routed and pursued. When he and his Ten Thousand returned, they found that Cyrus had fought hard in the center, had broken Artaxerxes' bodyguard, but in the moment of victory had been killed. Cyrus' army, demoralized, had broken up, and the Persians had taken the field. The retreat of the Ten Thousand northward is the most famous feature of the campaign.

cuneiform (kyōōnē'ĭfôrm) [Lat.,=wedge-shaped], system of WRITING developed before the last centuries of the 4th millennium B.C. in the lower Tigris and Euphrates valley, probably by the Sumerians. The characters consist of arrangements of wedgelike strokes generally impressed with a stylus on wet clay tablets, which were then dried or baked. The history of the script is strikingly parallel to that of the Egyptian HIEROGLYPHIC (see also ALPHABET and INSCRIPTION). The normal Babylonian and Assyrian writing used a large number (300–600) of arbitrary cuneiform symbols for words and syllables; some

pictograph original	pictograph as positioned in later cuneiform	early Babylonian cuneiform	Assyrian	meaning
				heaven god
				earth
				woman
				to drink
				fish
				sun day
				donkey
				orchard
				to plow to till

Examples of the development of cuneiform

had been originally pictographic. There was an alphabetic system, too, making it possible to spell a word out, but because of the adaptation from Sumerian, a different language, there were many ambiguities. A single symbol could be used to represent a concept, an object, a simple sound or syllable, or to indicate the category of words requiring additional definition. Cuneiform writing was used outside Mesopotamia also, notably in ELAM and by the Hittites (see ANATOLIAN LANGUAGES). There are many undeciphered cuneiform inscriptions, apparently representing several different languages. Cuneiform writing declined in use after the Persian conquest of Babylonia (539 B.C.), and after a brief renaissance (3d–1st cent. B.C.) ceased to be used in Mesopotamia. A very late use of cuneiform writing was that of the Persians, who established a syllabary for Old Persian. This is the writing of the Achaemenids (mid-6th cent. B.C.–4th cent. B.C.), whose greatest monument is that of Darius I at Behistun. Key discoveries of cuneiform inscriptions have been made at Nineveh, Lagash, Erech, Tel el Amarna, Susa, and Boğazköy. Two great names in the interpretation of cuneiforms are those of Sir Henry C. RAWLINSON and G. F. GROTEFEND. See Edward Chiera, *They Wrote on*

Clay (1956); S. A. B. Mercer, ed., *A Sumero-Babylonian Sign List* (with Assyrian; 1918, repr. 1966); J. D. Prince, *Assyrian Primer* (1909, repr. 1966).

Cunene or **Kunene** (both: ko͞onä'nə), river, rising in W central Angola and flowing c.750 mi (1,200 km) S and W to the Atlantic Ocean. Its lower course forms part of Angola's border with South West Africa.

Cuneo (ko͞o'nāō), city (1971 pop. 54,505), capital of Cuneo prov., Piedmont, NW Italy, on the Stura River, near the Maritime Alps. It is an agricultural and industrial center and a transportation junction. Manufactures include textiles, beer, and chemical fertilizers. Silkworms are raised. A possession of the house of Savoy after 1382, Cuneo endured numerous sieges (especially in 1799, when it fell to Austrian and Russian forces).

Cunha, Euclides da (ā"o͞oklē'dĭsh dä ko͞o'nyə), 1866–1909, Brazilian writer. After his military service, Cunha became a civil engineer and a journalist. He wrote several historical works but is remembered for only one book, *Os sertões* (1902, tr. *Rebellion in the Backlands*, 1944), an account of a rebellion against the Brazilian government led by a religious fanatic, Antônio Conselheiro, in 1896–97. The book is a pessimistic narrative, embellished with lengthy descriptions of the Brazilian landscape and living conditions; it is primarily concerned with the state of mankind in Brazil. Its power and sincerity counterbalance its complexity of style and racist doctrine.

Cunha, Tristão da (trēshtouN'), c.1460–1514?, Portuguese navigator. His most important voyage was undertaken in 1506, when he set out with 15 ships for India. He discovered three volcanic islands in the S Atlantic, one of which is named for him. After taking Socotra off Arabia, in the hope of establishing control over the Red Sea, he went on to India, while Afonso de ALBUQUERQUE, under secret royal orders, detached part of the fleet. On his return to Portugal, Tristão da Cunha carried out a diplomatic mission at the papal court. A son, **Nuno da Cunha** (1487–1539), was governor of India and captured Basra in 1529.

Cunningham, Sir Alexander, 1814–93, English archaeologist and army engineer; son of Allan Cunningham. He retired (1861) as a major general after 30 years of service with the Bengal engineers and then was head (1861–65, 1870–85) of the archaeological survey of India. In 1867 he was knighted. Among his books are *Bhilsa Topes* (1854), a history of Buddhism based on architectural remains; *The Ancient Geography of India* (1871, 2d ed. 1924), of which only one volume was written; *The Book of Indian Eras* (1883); and *Coins of Ancient India* (1891). His collection of rare coins is in the British Museum. See study by Abu Imam (1966).

Cunningham, Allan, 1784–1842, Scottish author. His collection of *The Songs of Scotland, Ancient and Modern* (4 vol., 1825) included his own "A Wet Sheet and a Flowing Sea," one of the best-known sea ballads. His six-volume *Lives of the Most Eminent British Painters, Sculptors, and Architects* appeared from 1829 to 1833.

Cunningham, Andrew Browne, 1st **Viscount Cunningham of Hyndhope** (hīnd'hōp), 1883–1963, British admiral. A long-seasoned naval officer—he fought in the South African War and World War I—Cunningham was (1939–42) commander in the Mediterranean, which he kept open to the British. He was later naval commander in the expedition against N Africa (1942–43), commander in chief of the Allied naval forces in the Mediterranean (1943), and first sea lord and chief of the naval staff (1943–46). He retired and was created viscount in 1946. See his memoirs, *A Sailor's Odyssey* (1951); biography by Oliver Warner (1967).

Cunningham, Imogen, 1883–, American photographer, b. Portland, Oregon. Cunningham began taking pictures in 1901. After study abroad she opened a studio in Seattle in 1910 and for six decades has produced strong, exquisite portraits. Cunningham was a member of the Group *f/64* (see PHOTOGRAPHY, STILL). In the late 1920s she began her celebrated series of plant photographs. These exhibit an unsurpassed pristine sensuality. See *Imogen Cunningham: Photographs* (Univ. of Washington, 1970).

Cunningham, Merce, 1922?–, American dancer and choreographer, b. Centralia, Wash. Cunningham studied with Martha GRAHAM and was a soloist in her company from 1940 to 1955. He formed his own company in 1950 and began to create dances to the music of avant-garde composers, including John Cage. His best-known works include *Suite by Chance* and *Symphonie pour un homme seul* (both, 1952), which reveal his spare, expressive style. Cunningham is particularly noted for his solo dances.

Cunninghame Graham, Robert Bontine (kŭn'ĭngəm), 1852–1936, British politician and author. He lived as a cattle rancher in Argentina and traveled widely in Latin America, Morocco, and Spain. He served (1886–90) as a Liberal member of Parliament from Scotland, took part in early labor politics, and, with James Keir Hardie, founded (1888) the Scottish Labour party. Later he was first president (1928) of the Scottish Nationalist party. His writings include collections of sketches and tales, such as *The Ipané* (1899) and *Rodeo* (1936), and historical studies of Spanish conquistadors. See biography by Hugh MacDiarmid (1952).

Cuno, Wilhelm (vĭl'hĕlm ko͞o'nō), 1876–1933, German chancellor (Nov., 1922–Aug., 1923). A businessman, he headed a nonpartisan conservative ministry. His attempt to establish a moratorium on German reparations payments and his program of passive resistance to French occupation of the Ruhr both failed. During his term of office inflation reached huge proportions.

Cunobelinus: see CYMBELINE.

Cuoco, Vincenzo (vēnchän'tsō ko͞o-ô'kō), 1770–1823, Italian political philosopher. A lawyer, he was exiled (1799) from Naples for his part in establishing the PARTHENOPEAN REPUBLIC. In the Napoleonic era he was counselor to Joseph Bonaparte and minister of finance under Joachim Murat. His *Historical Essay on the Neapolitan Revolution of 1799* (1801) predicted Italy's gradual reunification; the views presented became central to the philosophy of the Risorgimento. He also wrote a study on the Italian Renaissance and one on ancient Greek settlements in Italy.

Cupar (ko͞o'pər), burgh (1971 pop. 5,604), county town of Fife, E Scotland. There are printing and engineering works and beet sugar refineries. Linen and flax textiles are made. In 1975, Cupar became part of the Fife region.

Cupid: see EROS.

cupric (kyo͞o'prĭk), COPPER in the +2 VALENCE state.

cupric sulfate or **copper (II) sulfate,** chemical compound, $CuSO_4$, taking the form of white rhombohedral crystals or amorphous powder. It decomposes at 650°C to cupric oxide (CuO). It is fairly soluble in water and when dissolved forms the pentahydrate, $CuSO_4 \cdot 5H_2O$, the form that is most familiar. The pentahydrate can be collected as blue triclinic crystals; it is also known as blue vitriol. It loses part of its water of crystallization when heated to 110°C and fully dehydrates at 150°C. Cupric sulfate is used in copperplating, in dyeing (as a mordant), in wet-cell batteries, in pigments, and in insecticides, fungicides, and algicides. It is insoluble in alkali solutions, a property used in the preparation of Bordeaux mixture; lime (calcium hydroxide) is added to moist cupric sulfate, forming a basic cupric sulfate precipitate (a mixture of cupric sulfate and cupric hydroxide). The anhydrous sulfate is used to detect the presence of water in certain organic liquids; it turns into the blue pentahydrate, e.g., when added to alcohol that contains water. Cupric sulfate is prepared by the action of warm dilute SULFURIC ACID (oil of vitriol) on COPPER metal or cupric oxide; it is also a by-product of copper sulfide ore refining. It occurs naturally in the minerals chalcanthite (the pentahydrate), hydrocyanite (the anhydrous sulfate), and brochantite (a basic sulfate, $CuSO_4 \cdot 3Cu(OH)_2$).

cuprous (kyo͞o'prəs), COPPER in the +1 VALENCE state.

Curaçao (kyo͞o'rəsō, ko͞oräsou'), island (1969 est. pop. 143,800), 178 sq mi (461 sq km), largest of the Netherlands Antilles, in the Dutch West Indies. Willemstad is the capital of the Netherlands Antilles, which also includes the islands of Bonaire, Aruba, Saba, St. Eustatius, and the southern half of St. Martin. Curaçao is semiarid; most of the plant life is of desert character. Oil refining is the principal industry, and the island has some of the world's largest refineries, receiving oil from the enormous reserves at nearby Lake Maracaibo, Venezuela. Other island industries include tourism (Curaçao is a free port), shipbuilding, and the manufacture of cement, paint, and tiles. Discovered by Alonso de Ojeda and Amerigo Vespucci in 1499, Curaçao was not settled by the Spanish until 1527. The Dutch captured it in 1634 and remained in possession except for a brief period of British rule during the Napoleonic Wars. As native Arawak Indians died out, many African slaves were imported. The present population is about 85% mestizo, with Negro, Indian, Spanish, and Dutch elements. In the 18th cent. Curaçao was a base for a flourishing Dutch entrepôt trade. Prosperity declined after the abolition of slavery in 1863 but revived with the introduction of the petroleum industry in the early 20th cent. Curaçao was the scene of severe racial strife and rioting in 1969.

curaçao (kyo͞orəsō'), a LIQUEUR, sweet or dry, distilled from dried orange peel and spirits and flavored with rum. Originally made by the Dutch on the island of Curaçao off the coast of Venezuela from an orange native to the island, it is now produced principally in the Netherlands. Grand Marnier and Cointreau are varieties of curaçao made with cognac.

curare (kyo͞orär'ē), any of a variety of substances originally used as arrow poisons by South American Indians in hunting and in warfare. The main active substance of curare, tubocurarine, is an alkaloid extracted from *Chondodendron tomentosum, Strychnos toxifera*, and other plant species. The poison produces muscle paralysis by interfering with the transmission of nerve impulses at the receptor sites of all skeletal muscle. Muscles with many nerves, such as eye muscles, are affected first. In recent years curare has been put to medical use. When given in small quantities with general ANESTHESIA, especially in abdominal surgery, curare insures the desired relaxation of muscle tissue with a minimal concentration of the anesthetic, lessening the possibilities of anesthesia-induced complications. Curare is also used to relieve spastic paralysis, to treat some mental disorders, and to induce muscle relaxation for the setting of fractures.

curassow (kyûr'əsō"), common name for the largest members of an order of game birds called pigeon-toed fowls, which includes the white-crested guan and the rufous-bellied chachalaca, *Ortalis wagleri*. These gregarious roosting birds, found from Texas to Argentina, vary from 20 to 40 in. (50–100 cm) in length and are brownish to olive-green in color. They feed on fruit, vegetation, and insects. Curassows are larger than other members of the family and have an erect crest and bright orange or yellow bills. The great curassow, *Crax rubra*, is found from Mexico to Ecuador. The meat of these birds is a delicacy. Although none are found in the Dutch West Indies, their name is taken from the island of Curaçao. They are easily tamed. Curassows are classified in the phylum CHORDATA, subphylum Vertebrata, class Aves, order Galliformes, family Cracidae.

curculio (kərkyo͞o'lēō), name applied to various WEEVILS (members of the snout beetle family, or Curculionidae), especially those that attack fruit. The term is sometimes limited to the acorn and nut weevils of the genus *Curculio*, characterized by extremely long beaks adapted for boring. There are 44 *Curculio* species in North America, including pests of hickory, pecan, and hazelnut. The females, whose beaks may be twice as long as their bodies, lay their eggs in holes bored in the nuts. The larvae feed on the nuts, later pupating (see INSECT) in the soil. The plum curculio, *Conotrachelus nenuphar*, is a serious pest of peach, plum, cherry, and apple, causing deformed and prematurely falling fruit. In spring the adults leave their winter shelter in piles of rubbish and fly to blossoming or early fruiting trees, where they feed for a week or more before mating. Eggs are laid in the fruit in slits made by the female, and the larvae feed for two to three weeks before pupating in the ground. Curculios are classified in the phylum ARTHROPODA, class Insecta, order Coleoptera, family Curculionidae.

Curecanti National Recreation Area: see NATIONAL PARKS AND MONUMENTS (table).

curfew [O.Fr.,=cover fire], originally a signal, such as the ringing of a bell, to damp the fire, extinguish all lights in the dwelling, and retire for the night. The custom originated as a precaution against fires and was common throughout Europe in the Middle Ages. The curfew has most recently been used in times of turbulence, such as revolution or civil disorders. It is a restrictive measure forcing all persons into their homes to reduce activity against the government or the occupying force. In some communities it has been applied to curb juvenile delinquency.

Curia Regis: see PARLIAMENT.

Curia Romana: see CARDINAL.

Curiatii: see HORATII.

Curicó (ko͞orēkō'), city (1970 pop. 59,621), capital of Curicó prov., central Chile, near the Mataquito River. Founded in 1743, Curicó is the metropolis of a flourishing agricultural region noted for livestock raising. The town was rebuilt after an earthquake destroyed it in 1928.

Curie (kürē'), family of French scientists. **Pierre Curie,** 1859–1906, scientist, and his wife, **Marie Sklo-**

dowska Curie, 1867–1934, chemist and physicist, b. Warsaw, are known for their work on radioactivity and on radium. Pierre Curie's early work dealt with crystallography and with the effects of temperature on magnetism; he discovered (1883) and, with his brother Jacques Curie, investigated piezoelectricity (a form of electric polarity) in crystals. Marie Sklodowska's interest in science was stimulated by her father, a professor of physics in Warsaw. In 1891 she went to Paris to continue her studies at the Sorbonne. In 1895 she married Pierre Curie and engaged in independent research in his laboratory at the municipal school of physics and chemistry where Pierre was director of laboratories (from 1882) and professor (from 1895). Following A. H. Becquerel's discovery of radioactivity, Mme Curie began to investigate uranium, a radioactive element found in pitchblende. In 1898 she reported a probable new element in pitchblende, and Pierre Curie joined in her research. They discovered (1898) both polonium and radium, laboriously isolated one gram of radium salts from about eight tons of pitchblende, and determined the atomic weights and properties of radium and polonium. The Curies refused to patent their processes or otherwise to profit from the commercial exploitation of radium. For their work on radioactivity they shared with Becquerel the 1903 Nobel Prize in Physics. The Sorbonne created (1904) a special chair of physics for Pierre Curie; Marie Curie was appointed his successor after his death in a street accident. She also retained her professorship (assumed in 1900) at the normal school at Sèvres and continued her research. In 1910 she isolated (with André Debierne) metallic radium. As the recipient of the 1911 Nobel Prize in Chemistry she was the first to be awarded a second Nobel Prize. She was made director of the laboratory of radioactivity at the Curie Institute of Radium, established jointly by the Univ. of Paris and the Pasteur Institute, for research on radioactivity and for radium therapy. During World War I she devoted her energies to providing radiological services for hospitals. In 1921 a gram of radium, a gift from American women, was presented to her by President Harding; this she accepted in behalf of the Curie Institute. A second gram, presented in 1929, was given by Mme Curie to the newly founded Curie Institute in Warsaw. Among the numerous and valuable writings of the Curies are Marie Curie's doctoral dissertation, *Radioactive Substances* (1902, 2 vol., tr. 1961); *Traité de radioactivité* (1910); *Radioactivité* (1935); and her biography of Pierre Curie (1923, tr. 1923). Pierre Curie's collected works appeared in 1908. A biography of Marie Curie was written by a daughter, Ève Curie (tr. 1937). The Curies' other daughter, Irène (see under JOLIOT-CURIE, family), was also a scientist. See biography by Robert W. Reid (1974).

curing: see FISH CURING.

Curitiba (kōōrētē'bä), city (1970 pop. 608,417), capital of Paraná state, SE Brazil. It was founded in 1654 but was of little significance until the late 19th and early 20th cent., when immigrants (chiefly Germans, Italians, and Slavs) began to develop the Paraná hinterland. A commercial and processing center for an expanding agricultural and ranch area, Curitiba exports coffee, maté, lumber, and livestock products through the Atlantic port of Paranaguá, c.70 mi (110 km) away. The city grew rapidly after 1950; modern buildings house the state university, the state public library, and the governor's offices.

curium (kyōōr'ēəm), radioactive chemical element; symbol Cm; at. no. 96; mass no. of most stable isotope 247; m.p. about 1340°C; b.p. unknown; sp. gr. 13.5 (calculated); valence +3 or +4. Curium is a silvery metal. It is chemically reactive and resembles gadolinium in its chemical properties, although it has a more complex crystalline structure. It is a member of the ACTINIDE SERIES in group IIIb of the PERIODIC TABLE. Thirteen isotopes of curium are known. Curium-242, prepared by neutron bombardment of americium-241, has a half-life of 163 days; curium-247, the most stable isotope, has a half-life of about 16 million years. Some curium isotopes are available in multigram quantities. Oxides, fluorides, a chloride, a bromide, and an iodide of curium have been prepared. Curium is intensely radioactive; it is about 3,000 times as radioactive as radium. It is also very toxic when absorbed in the body because it accumulates in the bones and disrupts the formation of red blood cells. Curium was first produced by the bombardment of plutonium-239 with alpha particles in a cyclotron at the Univ. of California at Berkeley. Identified in 1944 by G. T. SEABORG, R. A. James, and A. Ghiorso, it was named for Pierre and Marie Curie, the noted pioneers in the study of radioactivity. The metal was first isolated as the hydroxide by L. B. Werner and I. Perlman in 1947.

curlew (kûr'lōō), common name for large shore birds of both hemispheres, generally brown and buff in color and with decurved bills. There are eight species, belonging to the genus *Numenius.* The long-billed curlew, *N. americanus,* its bill almost one third the body length (about 2 ft/61 cm), is now rare in the E United States; it frequents salt marshes, prairies, and tidal creeks in the West. In summer it eats locusts and other injurious insects. The Hudsonian and the nearly extinct Eskimo curlews migrate from arctic breeding grounds to South America. The bristle-thighed curlew summers and nests in Alaska and winters on South Pacific islands, where it feeds on the eggs of other birds. The curlew makes a nonstop flight between breeding grounds. Some of the godwits and ibises are called curlews. Curlews are classified in the phylum CHORDATA, subphylum Vertebrata, class Aves, order Charadriiformes, family Scolopacidae.

Curley, James Michael, 1874–1958, American political leader, b. Boston. He held many municipal offices, served (1902–3) in the Massachusetts legislature, and became a power in the Democratic party of Boston before he served (1911–14) in the U.S. House of Representatives. Curley—whose colorful personality and shrewd political manipulations steadily increased his popularity—served three terms as mayor of Boston (1914–18, 1922–26, 1930–34) before he was governor of Massachusetts (1935–37) and again U.S. Congressman (1943–46). After Curley was once more elected (1945) mayor of Boston, he was convicted (1946–47) of mail fraud. He served (1947) five months in prison before his sentence was commuted by President Truman. After he fulfilled his duties as mayor (1947–50) and was defeated (1949) for reelection to that post, Curley was given (1950) a full pardon by Truman. See his autobiography (1957).

curling, winter sport, similar in principle to bowls and quoits, played on an ice court by teams of four. Each player hurls a squat, circular stone—weighing 38 lb (17.2 kg), dished on bottom and top and having a top handle for the player's grip—at the tees, or fixed goals, which are placed 38 yd (35 m) apart. Around each tee a circle is drawn with a radius of 6 ft (1.8 m). Each player is provided with a crampit, or spiked metal plate, to get a foothold on the ice, and a broom to sweep the ice in front of the swerving stone—one of the eye-catching features of the game. The players on both teams alternately send the stones toward one tee; the stones lying nearest the tee at the end of play count toward the score. The play is then made toward the opposite tee. Curling is a major winter sport of Scotland, where it was played perhaps as early as the 16th cent. The Royal Caledonia Curling Club, founded in 1838, is the governing body of the sport. Curling is also popular in Canada and is played to some extent in the United States and other countries.

curly-coated retriever, breed of large SPORTING DOG conjectured to be descended from the water spaniel and the retrieving setter. It stands about 23 in. (58 cm) high at the shoulder and weighs about 65 lb (30 kg). Its dense coat is tightly curled all over and may be black or liver in color. Easily trained as an efficient and hardy retriever on land and water, the curly-coated retriever is uncommon in the United States. See DOG.

Curragh, the (kûr'əkh), undulating plain or common, 4,885 acres (1,977 hectares), Co. Kildare, E Republic of Ireland. It has been a military camp since 1646. The Curragh racecourse is Ireland's most famous horse-racing center. The region gave its name to the Curragh Incident or "Mutiny," in which many British army officers resigned (March, 1914) in an attempt to avoid possible operations in Ulster to enforce HOME RULE.

Curran, John Philpot (kŭr'ən), 1750–1817, Irish statesman and orator. He became the best-known trial lawyer in Dublin when he was still very young and entered the Irish Parliament in 1783. He fought for CATHOLIC EMANCIPATION and vigorously opposed the repressive policy of the British government in Ireland. He was defense lawyer for the leaders of the UNITED IRISHMAN after the 1798 rebellion. He opposed the parliamentary union (1800) of Ireland with England, but refused to support acts of open rebellion. Subsequently he sat in the privy council of the United Kingdom. His daughter, Sarah, was in love with Robert EMMET, who was captured and hanged when he came to Dublin to visit her. Their tragic love affair inspired Thomas Moore's verses beginning, "She is far from the land where her young hero sleeps" and "Oh! breathe not his name."

currant, northern shrub of the family Saxifragaceae (SAXIFRAGE family), of the same genus (*Ribes*) as the gooseberry bush. The tart berries of the currant may be black, white, or red; the white gooseberry becomes purple when mature. Both, especially the larger European species, are eaten fresh and also used in preserves, sauces, and pies. Because the plants act as a host to blister RUST, their cultivation in America is discouraged, and in regions of infection the wild species are eradicated. American Indians used dried currants in making PEMMICAN, but the "dried currant" of commerce is a raisin. Indian currant is a name for a West Coast species and for the coralberry of the honeysuckle family. Native species of gooseberry are sometimes cultivated in gardens. Currant is classified in the division MAGNOLIOPHYTA, class Magnoliopsida, order Rosales, family Saxifragaceae.

currency: see MONEY.

current, electric, net movement or flow of electric charge from one point to another or across some boundary. See ALTERNATING CURRENT; DIRECT CURRENT; ELECTRICITY.

Currie, Sir Arthur William, 1875–1933, Canadian commander in World War I. He made a distinguished record for himself in World War I as a brigade and division commander, particularly at Ypres (1915) and Vimy Ridge (1917), where he was knighted on the battlefield. Promoted to lieutenant general, he commanded the Canadian Corps, which played key roles in the assaults on the Amiens salient and the Hindenburg Line, from June 1917 until the end of the war. In 1919 he became Canada's first full general. From 1920 until his death he was principal and vice chancellor of McGill Univ.

Currier & Ives, American lithographers and print publishers, who produced highly popular hand-colored prints of contemporary scenes and events in American life. **Nathaniel Currier,** 1813–88, b. Roxbury, Mass., founded the business in New York City in 1835, and in 1857 formed a partnership with the able artist and businessman **James Merritt Ives,** 1824–95, b. New York City. The prints, in which were depicted horses, yachts, trains, newsworthy events, and scenes of nature and outdoor recreation, have become prized collectors' items. Both Currier's and Ives's sons followed their fathers in the business, which was eventually liquidated in 1907. See H. T. Peters, *Currier & Ives, Printmakers to the American People* (1929, special ed. 1942); John L. Pratt, ed., *Currier & Ives Chronicles of America* (1968).

Curry, Jabez Lamar Monroe, 1825–1903, American educator, b. Lincoln co., Ga., grad. Univ. of Georgia, 1843. He studied law at Harvard and later became a member of the Alabama legislature, then of Congress (1857–61) and of the Confederate Congress (1861–64). After the Civil War, Curry served as president of Howard College (1865–68), as professor of English and public law at Richmond College (1868–81), and as U.S. minister to Spain (1885–88). After 1881, as administrative agent of the Peabody Fund for Southern Education, Curry established state normal schools and fostered better rural schools throughout the South, further extending his work after 1890 as agent of the Slater fund for Negro schools. He became (1901) supervising director of the Southern Education Board. See biography by E. A. Alderman and A. C. Gordon (1911); study by J. P. Rice (1949).

Curry, John Steuart, 1897–1946, American painter, b. Dunavant, Jefferson co., Kansas. He spent his youth on his father's farm. In 1916 he entered the Kansas City Art Institute and later studied in Chicago and New York and in Paris. His early paintings of Kansas life, such as *Baptism in Kansas,* aroused interest by their simple and authentic character. He often chose typically American subject matter, from rural life to circus scenes, which he depicted with a dramatic flair. In addition to his oil paintings he is well known for his murals, such as those in the Dept. of Justice Building in Washington, D.C., and the statehouse in Topeka, Kansas. See L. E. Schmeckebier, *John Steuart Curry's Pageant of America* (1943).

curry [Malayalam], condiment much used in India and elsewhere in the Orient, in combination with rice, meat, and a variety of other dishes. It is compounded of such spices as turmeric, fenugreek, cloves, cumin, ginger, black and cayenne pepper, coriander, and caraway. When the pungent leaf of an East Indian tree of the rue family is included, the curry powder is used not only as a stimulating flavor, but also for medicinal purposes. Curry paste is made from the slightly acid, jellylike pulp of the tamarind pod, combined with a variety of spices. The Western commercial curry powder is a spice compound.

Cursor Mundi (kûr'sôr mŭn'dī), a long religious epic in Middle English relating the history of the world as recorded in the Old and New Testaments. This anonymous poem (written c.1300) is a useful record of the northern English dialect of the period. See edition by the Early English Text Society (7 pts., 1874-93; Pt. 3 repr. 1966).

Curtea-de-Arges (ko͝or'tää-dä-är'zhĕsh), town (1966 pop. 16,424), S central Rumania, in Walachia, on the southern slope of the Transylvanian Alps. A district administrative and trade center, it has industries producing tiles and textiles. Curtea-de-Arges served (1330-1430) as the seat of the dukes of Walachia and became (18th cent.) an Orthodox bishopric. Its 16th-century Byzantine cathedral (rebuilt 19th cent.) became the burial place of the kings of Rumania.

Curtin, John, 1885-1945, Australian political leader. A labor union secretary, he edited (1917-28) a labor weekly and was later a member of the lower house—from 1928 to 1941, except for three years. He became Labour party leader. As wartime prime minister (1941-45), he vigorously organized the defense of Australia in World War II, working closely with the United States; he also helped plan closer cooperation within the British Commonwealth of Nations. He died in office.

Curtis, Benjamin Robbins, 1809-74, American jurist, Associate Justice of the U.S. Supreme Court (1851-57), b. Watertown, Mass. After studying law at Harvard, he practiced at Northfield, Mass., and served in the state legislature. Appointed to the Supreme Court by President Fillmore, he wrote one of the two dissenting opinions in the DRED SCOTT CASE and resigned from the court because of the bitter feelings engendered by the case. One of the nation's leading lawyers, he was chief counsel to Andrew Johnson at the President's impeachment trial. See biography by his son B. R. Curtis (1879, repr. 1970), which includes a memoir by G. T. Curtis.

Curtis, Charles, 1860-1936, Vice President of the United States (1929-33), b. near North Topeka, Kansas. Of part Indian background, Curtis lived for three years on a Kaw reservation. After studying law with a Topeka attorney, he was admitted to the bar (1881) and entered Republican politics in Kansas. He served in the U.S. Congress (1892-1906), where he championed Indian rights to self-government by sponsoring the Curtis Act (1898). He served in the U.S. Senate from 1907 to 1913 and from 1915 to 1929. He was a fiscal conservative and generally supported farm and veterans' benefits. After an unsuccessful bid for the Republican presidential nomination, he became Herbert Hoover's running mate in 1928. Once elected, he played little part in the administration, but in 1932 he again ran with Hoover in his unsuccessful try for a second term. See biography by Marvin Ewy (1961).

Curtis, Cyrus Hermann Kotzschmar, 1850-1933, American publisher and philanthropist, b. Portland, Maine. He started his first periodical, *The People's Ledger*, in Boston in 1872. Later, in Philadelphia he started a periodical called the *Tribune and Farmer*. The women's column of this paper was so successful that in 1883 it became *The Ladies' Home Journal*; under the editorship of Curtis's son-in-law, Edward W. BOK, it soon became the most important magazine of its kind. Curtis founded (1890) the Curtis Publishing Company and in 1897 purchased the *Saturday Evening Post*, which, with his editor George Horace LORIMER, he built up to a position of eminence. *Country Gentleman* was bought in 1911. In 1913 he purchased the Philadelphia *Public Ledger*. This was the first of his newspaper ventures. Among others purchased were the Philadelphia *Press* (1920), the New York *Evening Post* (1924), and the Philadelphia *Inquirer* (1930). His newspapers were never as successful as his magazines, and he eventually had to sell three of them at a loss. Throughout his life, Curtis donated money to hospitals, museums, and schools. See E. W. Bok, *A Man from Maine* (1923).

Curtis, George Ticknor, 1812-94, American lawyer and writer, b. Watertown, Mass. A highly successful patent attorney, Curtis served in the Massachusetts legislature (1840-43) and as U.S. commissioner at Boston under the Fugitive Slave Act of 1850. He was one of the defense counsel in the Dred Scott Case. Closely associated with Daniel Webster, he was one of the "Cotton Whigs" who became Democrats. He wrote biographies of Daniel Webster (1870) and James Buchanan (1883), and many legal treatises. His *Constitutional History of the United States . . . to the Close of the Civil War* (Vol. I, 1889; Vol. II, ed. by J. C. Clayton, 1896), his most notable work, is the classic Federalist interpretation of the Constitution.

Curtis, Samuel Ryan, 1805-66, Union general in the Civil War, b. Clinton co., N.Y., grad. West Point, 1831. Curtis won a decisive victory at Pea Ridge (1862) and was therefore promoted to major general. He commanded the Dept. of Missouri (1862-63), the Dept. of Kansas (1864-65), and the Dept. of the Northwest (1865). His last services (1865-66) were in negotiating treaties with the Indians and in reporting on the construction of the new Union Pacific RR.

Curtis Institute of Music, in Philadelphia; coeducational; founded 1924 by Mary Louise Curtis Bok (later Mrs. Efrem Zimbalist) and named for her father, Cyrus Curtis. The institute operates entirely on a scholarship basis, with a faculty made up principally of concert artists. The library includes the Burrell collection of Wagnerian materials.

Curtiss, Glenn Hammond, 1878-1930, American inventor and aviation pioneer, b. Hammondsport, N.Y. He was a member of Alexander Graham Bell's Aerial Experiment Association (1907-9). In 1908 he made the first public flights in the United States, and in 1909 he established the first flying school there. His greatest triumph was his then daring and spectacular flight from Albany to New York City in 1910. In 1911, Curtiss invented ailerons, which he attached to his newly developed seaplane. He organized (1916) the Curtiss Aeroplane and Motor Corp., which built many planes for the Allied nations during World War I. After the war Curtiss continued to contribute radical improvements in the design of both planes and motors. See biographies by C. C. Roseberry (1972) and Clara Studer (1937, repr. 1972).

curve, in mathematics, a line no part of which is straight; more generally, it is considered to be any one-dimensional collection of points, thus including the straight line as a special kind of curve. In analytic geometry a plane curve is usually considered as the graph of an equation or function, and the properties of curves are seen to depend largely on the degree of the equation in the case of algebraic curves (i.e., curves with algebraic equations) or on the particular function in the case of transcendental curves (i.e., curves whose equations are not algebraic). For examples of plane curves, see CIRCLE; ELLIPSE; HYPERBOLA; PARABOLA. A twisted or skew curve is one that does not lie all in one plane, e.g., the helix, a curve having the shape of a wire spring. A thorough treatment of space curves requires the techniques of DIFFERENTIAL GEOMETRY.

Curzon of Kedleston, George Nathaniel Curzon, 1st Marquess (kûr'zən), 1859-1925, British statesman. Entering Parliament as a conservative in 1886, he showed early brilliance in politics and was undersecretary of state for India (1891-92) and undersecretary for foreign affairs (1895-98). Travels in Asia resulted in several books—*Russia in Central Asia* (1889), *Persia and the Persian Question* (1892), and *Problems of the Far East* (1894). As viceroy (1898-1905) of India he achieved important reforms in administration, education, and currency and set up (1901) the North-West Frontier Province. He also partitioned (1905) Bengal, an action that angered the Hindus. He resigned after a quarrel with Lord Kitchener, commander of the army in India, who was supported by the home government. After his return to England, he became (1907) chancellor of Oxford Univ. and was created (1911) an earl (raised to marquess in 1921). During World War I he served in the coalition cabinets of Asquith and Lloyd George. As foreign secretary (1919-24), he presided over the Conference of Lausanne (see under LAUSANNE, TREATY OF), disapproved of the French occupation of the Ruhr, and paved the way for the Dawes plan for settling German war reparations. He expected to succeed Andrew Bonar Law as prime minister in 1923 and was bitterly disappointed at being passed over. See biographies by Lord Ronaldshay (1928) and Kenneth Rose (1969); David Dilks, *Curzon in India* (2 vol., 1969).

Cusa, Nicholas of: see NICHOLAS OF CUSA.

Cusco, Peru: see CUZCO.

cuscus: see PHALANGER.

Cush (kŭsh). **1** Asiatic nation, perhaps the same as one of similar name in E Mesopotamia. Gen. 10.8; 1 Chron. 1.10. **2** Benjamite opposed to David. Ps. 7, title. **3** Ancient kingdom of NUBIA, in the present Sudan, which flourished from the 11th cent. B.C. to the 4th cent. A.D. The rulers of Cush overran Upper Egypt (mid-8th cent. B.C.) as far as Thebes. PIANKHI conquered the rest of Egypt (Lower Egypt) from Tefnakhte. TIRHARKA was defeated in the Delta by the Assyrians, and the Cushites lost control of Egypt. The Cushite capital was transferred from NAPATA to MEROË; Meroë was a prosperous state until the 4th cent. A.D., when it fell to the Ethiopians and was abandoned. There is a theory that the people of Meroë moved westward and introduced ironcasting techniques to the Lake Chad area. See A. J. Arkell, *A History of the Sudan to A.D. 1821* (1955).

Cushan (kyo͞o'shăn), obscure name in Hab. 3.7. Some identify it with the Asiatic or the African Cush.

Cushi (kyo͞o'shī). **1** Messenger of Joab. 2 Sam. 18.19-33. **2** Ancestor of one of Jehoiakim's courtiers. Jer. 36.14. **3** Zephaniah's father. Zeph. 1.1.

Cushing, Caleb, 1800-1879, American statesman, b. Salisbury, Mass. After practicing law he served in the Massachusetts state legislature and later in Congress (1835-43). A loyal Whig, he chose to stand by John Tyler, after the death of President William H. Harrison, rather than follow Henry Clay in his opposition program. As the first American commissioner to China, Cushing negotiated (1844) the opening of the ports of China to U.S. trade. He remained prominent in politics, engineered (1852) the nomination of Franklin Pierce at the Democratic convention of 1852, and served efficiently as Pierce s Attorney General (1853-57). Secession convinced him that conciliation was impossible, and he supported Lincoln. He later acted (1871-72) as counsel for the United States at the arbitration of the Alabama claims and was (1874-77) minister to Spain. See biography by C. M. Fuess (1923, repr. 1965).

Cushing, Harvey Williams, 1869-1939, American neurosurgeon, b. Cleveland, B.A. Yale, 1891, M.D. Harvard, 1895. Associated with Johns Hopkins (1896-1912), Harvard (1912-32), and Yale (1933-37), he was noted for his great contributions to brain surgery and also as a teacher and an author. For his life of Sir William Osler he won the 1925 Pulitzer Prize in biography. Among his other works are a famous treatise on the pituitary body, as well as *Tumors of the Nervus Acusticus* (1917), *Intracranial Tumours* (1932), and the autobiographical *From a Surgeon's Journal, 1915-1918* (1936). See biographies by J. F. Fulton (1946) and E. H. Thomson (1950). **Cushing's disease** was first described by him. It is a disorder attributed to hyperactivity of the cortex of the adrenal glands and affects women more than men. The symptoms include obesity (moonface, an accumulation of fat at the back of the neck called buffalo hump, and abdominal protrusion), hypertension, hirsutism, and easy bruisability. Treatment is by removal of one or both adrenal glands or, if the pituitary body is involved, by X-ray therapy or by surgery.

Cushing, Luther Stearns, 1803-56, American lawyer, b. Lunenburg, Mass., grad. Harvard law school, 1826. His best-known work is his short *Manual of Parliamentary Practice* (1844; many later editions), usually known as *Cushing's Manual*. It is still used in the United States in conducting meetings and legislative activities. Cushing's fuller treatment of the subject is *Elements of the Law and Practice of Legislative Assemblies* (1856).

Cushing, William Barker, 1842-74, Union naval hero in the Civil War, b. Delafield, Wis., educated at Annapolis. Cushing became noted for a series of daredevil exploits, particularly for his sinking of the Confederate warship *Albemarle* at Plymouth, N.C., in Oct., 1864. In Jan., 1865, he took part in the seizure of Fort Fisher. See biography by R. J. Roske and Charles Van Doren (1957, repr. 1973).

Cushing's disease: see CUSHING, HARVEY WILLIAMS.

Cushitic (kəshĭt'ĭk), group of languages belonging to the Hamitic subfamily of the Hamito-Semitic family of languages. See HAMITO-SEMITIC LANGUAGES.

Cushman, Charlotte Saunders (ko͝osh'mən), 1816-76, one of the first outstanding American actresses, b. Boston. Cushman turned from opera to drama and in 1835 first played Lady Macbeth, the role in which she was said to be unequaled. Her portrayals of Romeo and Hamlet won her popular favor, but her most celebrated role was Meg Merrilies in Scott's *Guy Mannering*. An actress of dramatic power and regal bearing, she was the first of her profession to be elected to the Hall of Fame (1915). See biography by Joseph Leach (1970).

Cushman, Pauline, 1835-93, Union spy in the Civil War, b. New Orleans. She became an actress at 18 in New York City. In 1863 she was banished to Confederate lines as a supposed Southern sympathizer, when in reality she had already performed valuable services for Union intelligence in Louisville and

Nashville. Captured with compromising papers upon her, she was taken to Gen. Braxton Bragg, court-martialed, and sentenced to be hanged. However, in the hasty departure (June, 1863) of the Confederates from Shelbyville, Tenn., she was left behind and was thus able, for the last time, to help the Union cause with information about Confederate strength and plans. Dressed in a Federal uniform, she lectured afterwards about her experiences. Her later life was unhappy, and she committed suicide in San Francisco.

custard-apple, common name for members of the Annonaceae, a family of shrubs, woody vines, and small trees of the tropics. The custard-apples (*Annona squamosa* and *A. reticulata*) and other members of the family bear a soft, sweet fruit much eaten in the tropics and have been transplanted from the Americas to the Old World. The pawpaw, or papaw (*Asimina triloba*), one of the few temperate species remaining from the more extensive range of the family in the past, is a shrub or small tree of E North America which also bears a sweet edible fruit. The name pawpaw is sometimes applied to the PAPAYA, an unrelated plant. The custard-apple family is classified in the division MAGNOLIOPHYTA, class Magnoliopsida, order Ranales.

Custer, George Armstrong, 1839–76, American army officer, b. New Rumley, Ohio, grad. West Point, 1861. He fought in the Civil War at the first battle of Bull Run, distinguished himself as a member of General McClellan's staff in the Peninsular campaign, and was made a brigadier general of volunteers in June, 1863. The youngest general in the Union army, Custer ably led a cavalry brigade in the Gettysburg campaign. He fought in Virginia in the great cavalry battle at Yellow Tavern and in General Sheridan's Shenandoah Valley campaign. Made a divisional commander in Oct., 1864, he defeated (Oct. 9) Gen. Thomas L. Rosser at Woodstock. After dispersing the remnants of Gen. Jubal A. Early's command at Waynesboro on March 2, 1865, he was in the advance in pursuit of Lee's army beyond Richmond. Custer received the Confederate flag of truce, was present at the surrender at Appomattox Courthouse, and was promoted major general of volunteers. His record (he had also been brevetted a major general in the regular army), considering his youth, was one of the most spectacular of the war. In the reorganization of the U.S. army after the war Custer was assigned to the 7th Cavalry with the rank of lieutenant colonel, and he remained the acting commander of this regiment until his death. In 1867 he was court-martialed and removed from command for leaving his command at Fort Wallace, Kansas, without permission, but in Sept., 1868, he was reinstated, mostly through the efforts of Sheridan, with whom he had always been a favorite. In massacring the Cheyenne and their allies at the battle of the Washita (Nov., 1868), he was accused of abandoning a small detachment of his men, who were annihilated by the Indians. He served (1873) in Dakota Territory and in 1874 commanded the expedition into the Black Hills that led to renewed hostilities with the Sioux. In the comprehensive campaign against the Sioux planned in 1876, Custer's regiment was detailed to the column under the commanding general, Alfred H. Terry, that marched from Bismarck to the Yellowstone River. At the mouth of the Rosebud, Terry sent Custer forward to locate the enemy while he marched on to join the column under Gen. John Gibbon. Custer came upon the Indian encampment on the Little Bighorn on June 25 and decided to attack at once. Not realizing the overwhelming numerical superiority of the Indians, most of whom lay concealed in ravines, he divided his regiment into three parts, sending two of them, under Major Marcus A. Reno and Capt. Frederick W. Benteen, to attack farther upstream, while he himself led the third (over 200 men) in a direct charge. The Indians killed every one of them. Reno and Benteen were themselves kept on the defensive, and not until Terry's arrival was the extent of the tragedy known. The men (except Custer, whose remains were reinterred at West Point) were buried on the battlefield, now a national monument in Montana. Custer's spectacular death made him a popular but controversial hero, still the subject of much dispute as to his actions and character. Custer wrote *My Life on the Plains* (1874), and his wife, **Elizabeth Bacon Custer,** 1842–1933, who devoted much of her life to upholding his memory, wrote *Boots and Saddles* (1885), *Tenting on the Plains* (1887), and *Following the Guidon* (1890). See biographies by Frazier Hunt (1928) and Jay Monaghan (1959, repr. 1971); Charles A. Windolph, *I Fought with Custer* (as told to Frazier and Robert Hunt, 1947); W. A. Graham, *The Story of the Little Big Horn: Custer's Last Fight* (1959); E. I. Stewart, *Custer's Luck* (1955, repr. 1971).

Custer Battlefield National Monument: see LITTLE BIGHORN, river; NATIONAL PARKS AND MONUMENTS (table).

Custine, Adam Philippe, comte de (ädäN′ fēlēp′ kôNt də küstēn′), 1740–93, French general. He served in the Seven Years War and in the American Revolution. Elected to the States-General (1789), he served in the French Revolutionary Wars and in 1792 took Frankfurt and Mainz. His failure in the campaign of 1793 led to accusations of treason, and he was guillotined.

Custis, George Washington Parke, 1781–1857, American dramatist, b. Mt. Airy, Md., educated at the College of New Jersey (now Princeton). The grandson of Martha Washington, he grew up at Mt. Vernon and became heir to part of the Washington estate. He wrote several plays, including *The Indian Prophecy* (1827), *Pocahontas* (1830), and *The Railroad* (1830). Custis also wrote *Recollections and Private Memoirs of Washington* (1860).

Custis-Lee Mansion, Va.: see ARLINGTON HOUSE NATIONAL MEMORIAL.

custom, habitual group pattern of behavior that is transmitted from one generation to another and is not biologically determined. Since societies are perpetually changing, no matter how slowly, all customs are basically impermanent. If short-lived, they are more properly called fashions. Customs form the core of human CULTURE and are stronger and more persistent in preindustrial societies than in industrial ones, in rural than in urban areas. When formalized in the social or religious sphere it leads to ETHICS, and when enforced in the sphere of rights and duties, custom leads to LAW. See FOLKWAYS; MORES.

customs duty: see TARIFF.

Custoza (ko͞ostô′tsä) or **Custozza** (-tôt′tsä), village, Venetia, N Italy, near Verona. It was the scene of an Austrian victory over Sardinia in 1848 (see RISORGIMENTO) and of an Austrian victory over Italy in 1866 (see AUSTRO-PRUSSIAN WAR).

Cutch: see KUTCH.

cutch: see CATECHU.

Cuth (kŭth) or **Cuthah** (kyo͞o′thə), ancient city of Mesopotamia, near Babylon. The inhabitants, when settled in Samaria, introduced the worship of NERGAL. In later times the Jews called the Samarians Cuthites (2 Kings 17.24, 30).

Cuthbert, Saint, c.635–687, Celtic monk, bishop at Lindisfarne (685–86). He spent some time in the monastery at Ripon. When St. WILFRID introduced the Roman computation of Easter there, he left, but later he accepted the change. Cuthbert preached for some years in his native Scotland, especially to the Picts of Galloway. He became prior at Lindisfarne (see HOLY ISLAND) but after some years resigned (676) to live in solitary retreat on Farne Island. With great reluctance, he accepted (685) the bishopric of Bernicia at Lindisfarne, retiring to Farne for his last weeks. His relics were taken to Durham later. Feast: March 20. See Bertram Colgrave, *Two Lives of Saint Cuthbert* (1940, repr. 1969).

cutlass fish: see MACKEREL.

Cutler, Manasseh (mənăs′ə), 1742–1823, American clergyman, scientist, and one of the organizers of the OHIO COMPANY OF ASSOCIATES, b. Killingly, Conn. A student of both law and theology, he was admitted to the bar in 1767 and was ordained (1771) pastor of the Congregational Church at Hamilton, Mass. He also studied medicine and became a practicing physician. In science Cutler used both the telescope and microscope and contributed his observations to the *Proceedings* of the American Academy of Arts and Sciences, of which he was a member. His botanical papers, taken together, form the first systematic description and classification of New England flora. He aided (1786) in forming the Ohio Company and in 1787 was sent as agent to the Continental Congress to secure a grant of land on the Ohio River for settlement. By skillful lobbying he succeeded in negotiating the land purchase. He also promoted the ORDINANCE OF 1787, which provided for the establishment of territorial government in the area. He was (1801–5) a member of the U.S. House of Representatives. Cutler wrote, in addition to his scientific papers, *Description of Ohio* (1787, repr. 1896). See W. P. Cutler and J. P. Cutler, *Life, Journals, and Correspondence of Rev. Manasseh Cutler* (1888).

Cutler Ridge, uninc. town (1970 pop. 17,441), Dade co., SE Fla., a residential suburb of Miami.

cutlery, various types of implements for cutting, preparing, and eating food. In addition to different kinds of knives and the steels to sharpen them, the term usually encompasses forks and spoons. The history of cutlery probably begins with the shell and the sharp flint used for cutting. The primitive craft of chipping flint began by improving naturally sharp edges, e.g., the chipped flint knives of the Neolithic period. Knives were made of copper and bronze when those metals came into use. Finally steel and alloys of steel have displaced other materials for the blades of instruments for cutting. The early generalized cutting instrument has been differentiated into specialized instruments of wide variety, e.g., the sword, the razor, and shears. Table knives were introduced c.1600; until then, individuals brought to the table their own knives, which served also as daggers. The penknife was originally a knife for pointing quill pens. The pocket knife, with the blade folding into the handle, was invented c.1600. The cutler's craft or industry was long marked by the successful resistance of the handicraftsman to mass production. Small shops, with from one workman to a half dozen, were characteristic. Certain localities have become known for the excellence of their cutlery. In Spain, the Toledo blade was famous when the sword was an important weapon. Solingen, in Germany, and Sheffield, in England, have been noted for their cutlery since the Middle Ages. The best knives are forged from high-carbon steel. Cheaper grades are beveled from steel bars thick in the center and tapering toward the edges or are stamped from sheets of metal. In hollow-ground blades, the sides are concave. For stainless blades, the steel is usually partly replaced by, or coated with, chromium. Scissors blades commonly are either cast in molds or stamped. Most razor blades are die-stamped. See G. I. Lloyd, *The Cutlery Trades* (1913, repr. 1968); J. B. Himsworth, *Story of Cutlery, from Flint to Stainless Steel* (1954).

Cuttack (kətăk′), city (1971 pop. 194,036), Orissa state, E central India. Founded in the 10th cent., it was long famous for gold and silver filigree work. Cuttack is now an important trade center for rice and jute.

Cutter, Charles Ammi, 1837–1903, American librarian, b. Boston. Cutter cataloged the library of the Harvard Divinity School and in 1860 was appointed as the assistant to the librarian of Harvard. As librarian of the Boston Athenaeum (1868–93) he was a pioneer in subject cataloging. The Athenaeum catalog (5 vol., 1874–82) served as a model for later dictionary catalogs. His *Rules for a Dictionary Catalog* (1875) was the first work of its kind. Cutter's system of classification, *Expansive Classification* (1891–93), used the alphabet instead of numbers; it was the basis of the Library of Congress classification. From 1893 until his death Cutter was librarian of the Forbes Library, Northampton, Mass.

cutter, small, one-masted sailing vessel, with a rig similar to that of a SLOOP except that it usually has a sliding bowsprit and a topmast. From 1800 to 1830 cutters were in service between England and France. They were also employed to pursue smugglers, their speed and easy handling fitting them admirably for the task. These revenue cutters were so well known that the name was applied to the revenue vessel even after steam had replaced sails, and vessels of the coast guard are still called cutters. The name is also used for a heavy rowboat carried on large ships.

cutting, in horticulture, part of a plant stem, leaf, or root cut off and used for producing a new plant. It is a convenient and inexpensive method of propagation, not possible for all plants but used generally for grapes; chrysanthemums; verbenas (stem cuttings); blackberries (root cuttings); African violets (leaf cuttings); and for many other plants. Cuttings, as soon as they are made, are usually placed in moist sand, frequently heated from below; if taken in the fall, as hardwood cuttings of trees or shrubs, they are kept in unheated sand over the winter and planted in the spring. The word *cutting* alone usually means stem cutting; *slip* is a common synonym. The general availability today of rooting hormones and misting devices has made possible the propagation by cuttings of many kinds of plants that had not previously responded favorably. See G. W. Adriance and F. R. Brison, *Propagation of Horticultural Plants* (2d ed. 1955).

cuttlefish, common name applied to cephalopod mollusks that have 10 tentacles, or arms, 8 of which have muscular suction cups on their inner surface and 2 that are longer and can shoot out for grasping prey, and a reduced internal shell enbedded in the enveloping mantle. The body is short, broad, and flattened. Cuttlefish are carnivorous and excellent at capturing prey with their arms. Although good swimmers, they are not as fast as the related SQUIDS, but like the squids cuttlefish have lateral fins used as stabilizers and for steering and propulsion. They swim by jet propulsion, forcibly expelling water through a siphon. During the day they lie buried in the bottom of the ocean; at night they swim and hunt for food. Except for the squid genus *Loligo*, cuttlefish have the best cephalopod eyes, which are highly complex. When disturbed, cuttlefish eject a cloud of dark brown ink from an ink sac for protection. The ink gland and ink sac are specializations of the rectal gland. The ink is composed mostly of melanin and has been used as the artist's pigment, sepia. All cuttlefish are dioecious, i.e., the sexes are separate. The common, worldwide, deep-water cuttlefish, genus *Spirula*, is considered a "living fossil" because it possesses a remnant of the external shell of the ancient cephalopods. These cuttlefish have a small, coiled internal shell containing a bubble of gas (nitrogen), which serves as a float in the ocean. The European cuttlefish, *Sepia officinalis*, possesses a degenerate internal shell composed of lime, which is popularly called cuttlebone. Within the narrow spaces between the thin septa of the shell are fluid and gas (mostly nitrogen), which give the organism buoyancy. These cuttlefish are found in the Mediterranean and E Atlantic. The cuttlebone is used for pet birds as a source of lime salts. *Sepia* are able to undergo a complex of color changes ranging from pink to brown with varying stripes and spots, usually displayed when they are disturbed. The eggs, deposited singly and attached by a stalk to objects on the ocean bottom, are extremely large, up to .6 in. (15 mm) in diameter. The smallest cuttlefish, *Idiosepius*, inhabits tide pools and attains a length of .6 in. (15 mm). Cuttlefish are classified in the phylum MOLLUSCA, class Cephalopoda, order Sepioidea.

cutwork: see LACE.

cutworm, name for the larvae of many moths of the family Noctuidae (owlet moths). These larvae, or caterpillars, feed at night on the stems and roots of young plants, often cutting them off near the surface of the ground. They hide in soil by day. They attack a wide variety of field crops in low-lying areas; an average cutworm feeding on corn consumes 65 sq in. (410 sq cm) of foliage during its development. Most species pupate (see INSECT) underground. Many species overwinter in the pupal stage, the adults emerging in the spring and laying eggs from which the larvae hatch in summer. The number of generations occurring during the summer varies with the species and the climate. Cutworms are classified in the phylum ARTHROPODA, class Insecta, order Lepidoptera, family Noctuidae.

Cuvier, Georges Léopold Chrétien Frédéric Dagobert, Baron (zhôrzh lāôpôld' krātyăN' frādārēk' dägōbĕr' bärôN' küvyā'), 1769–1832, French naturalist, b. Montbéliard, studied at the academy of Stuttgart. From 1795 he taught in the Jardin des Plantes. He became permanent secretary (1803) of the Academy of Sciences and later was made chancellor of the Univ. of Paris. A pioneer in the science of comparative anatomy, he originated a system of zoological classification that comprised four phyla based on differences in structure of the skeleton and organs. His reconstruction of the soft parts of fossils deduced from their skeletal remains greatly advanced the science of paleontology. The flying reptile pterodactyl was identified and named by Cuvier. He rejected the theory of evolution in favor of CATASTROPHISM. Cuvier held various high posts in the government and did much to develop higher education in France. Among his more important works are *Tableau élémentaire de l'histoire naturelle des animaux* (1798); *Mémoires sur les espèces d'éléphants vivants et fossiles* (1800); with A. M. C. Dumeril and G. L. Duvernoy, *Leçons d'anatomie comparée* (5 vol., 1801–5); *Recherches sur les ossements fossiles des quadrupèdes* (1812); and *Le Règne animal destribué d'après son organisation* (1817). See study by William Coleman (1964).

Cuvilliès, François de (fräNswä' də küvēyĕs'), 1695–1768, French architect, decorator, and engraver. He introduced into Germany the ROCOCO style of decoration then popular in France. He became architect to Charles Albert, elector of Bavaria, and, when the latter became Emperor Charles VII (1742), was appointed architect to the imperial court. His two foremost works, both at Munich, were the Residenz-Theater (1751–53) and the pavilion called the Amalienburg, in the park of Nymphenburg. The brilliant interiors of the pavilion represent the highest achievements of German rococo decoration.

Cuxhaven (ko͝oks'häfən), city (1970 pop. 44,564), Lower Saxony, N West Germany, at the mouth of the Elbe River. A North Sea fishing and passenger port, it is also a summer resort. Its manufactures include machinery and textiles. From 1394 to 1937, Cuxhaven was held by Hamburg; in the 20th cent. it became a docking place for oceangoing vessels.

Cuyahoga (kī"əhō'gə), river, c.80 mi (130 km) long, flowing SW through Cuyahoga Falls, then N to Lake Erie, NE Ohio, forming part of Cleveland harbor. By the late 1960s, the Cuyahoga was one of the most polluted rivers in the United States and was a major cause of Lake Erie's deterioration.

Cuyahoga Falls, city (1970 pop. 49,678), Summit co., NE Ohio, on the Cuyahoga River; inc. 1836. On its course through the city the river drops 220 ft (67 m) through a series of falls and rapids. A suburb of Akron, Cuyahoga Falls is both residential and industrial, with a milk plant and factories that make metal products, rubber goods, and machinery.

Cuyp or **Kuyp** (both: koip), family of Dutch painters of Dordrecht. **Jacob Gerritszoon Cuyp,** 1594–c.1651, pupil of Abraham Bloemaert, was a portrait and landscape painter. His stepbrother and pupil, **Benjamin Cuyp,** 1616–52, painted figure compositions and peasant scenes in the style of Rembrandt. **Aelbert Cuyp,** 1620–91, son and pupil of Jacob, was one of the foremost Dutch landscapists. He first painted still lifes, interiors with figures, and animals but later specialized in the pastoral landscapes for which he is famous. They are characterized by breadth and simplicity of treatment and richness of color and light. Many of his best works are in England. Representative are his *Piper with Cows* and *Promenade* (Louvre) and *Horseman and Cows in a Meadow* (National Gall., London). The Metropolitan Museum contains six landscapes.

Cuyuna, iron range in Minnesota: see MESABI.

Cuza, Alexander John (ko͞o'zä), or **Alexander John I,** 1820–73, first prince of Rumania (1859–66), b. Moldavia. An officer who participated in the 1848 revolution and in the political struggle for the union of the principalities, he was elected prince of both Moldavia and Walachia in 1859, and in 1862 he was recognized by Turkey as sovereign of the united principalities, thenceforth known as Rumania. In 1864 he emancipated the serfs and allowed peasants to acquire land, thereby alienating the powerful landlords. His educational and legal reforms included the founding of the universities of Bucharest and of Iaşi and the promulgation of penal and civil codes. In 1866, conspirators, taking advantage of the country's financial difficulties, discontent over the agrarian policy, and Cuza's scandalous personal life, forced him to abdicate. He went into exile, first to Paris, later to Vienna, Florence, and Heidelberg.

Cuzco or **Cusco** (both: ko͞o'skō), city (1969 est. pop. 105,000), alt. 11,207 ft (3,416 m), capital of Cuzco dept., S Peru, at the confluence of the Huatanay and Tullamayo rivers. Predominantly Indian in population, it is a trading center for agricultural produce and for woolen textiles produced in the Cuzco mills. Cuzco was founded, according to legend, by MANCO CAPAC, first of the Inca rulers. The city had massive palaces and temples (most notably the Temple of the Sun, now the site of a Dominican convent), which were lavishly decorated with gold medallions and ornaments. When Francisco PIZARRO entered the city in 1533, it was plundered; and on its ruins the conquerors and their descendants built the colonial city, using the ancient walls (many of which are still visible) as foundations for new buildings. The cathedral and church of La Merced is the most notable of Cuzco's many churches. A severe earthquake in 1950 destroyed much of the city, but most of the historic buildings have been restored. The National University of Cuzco is in the city; nearby are the ruins of the Inca fortress SACSAHUAMÁN.

Cwmbran (ko͝ombrän'), urban district (1971 pop. 31,614), Monmouthshire, SE Wales. Cwmbran was created under the New Town Act of 1946 to house employees of the nearby steelworks. In 1974, Cwmbran became part of the new nonmetropolitan county of Gwent.

cyanamide process: see AMMONIA.

cyanide, chemical compound containing the CYANO GROUP, —CN. Cyanides are salts or esters of HYDROGEN CYANIDE (hydrocyanic acid, HCN) formed by replacing the hydrogen with a metal (e.g., sodium or potassium) or a radical (e.g., ammonium or ethyl). The most common and widely used cyanides are those of sodium and potassium; they are often referred to simply as "cyanide." Both are white, crystalline, chemically active compounds. They are used as insecticides, in making pigments, in metallurgy (e.g., electroplating and case hardening), and in refining gold and silver by the CYANIDE PROCESS. Organic cyanides are called nitriles. The ethyl ester of hydrogen cyanide (CH_3CH_2CN) is called variously ethyl cyanide, propionitrile, propane nitrile, nitrilopropane, and cyanoethane; propane nitrile is the approved name in the nomenclature system for organic chemistry adopted by the International Union of Pure and Applied Chemistry (IUPAC). Most cyanides are deadly poisons that cause respiratory failure. Symptoms of cyanide poisoning include an odor of bitter almond on the breath, dizziness, convulsions, collapse, and, often, froth on the mouth. In case of cyanide poisoning a doctor should be summoned immediately. If the poison was swallowed, vomiting should be induced. Artificial respiration should be used if needed.

cyanide process or **cyanidation,** method for extracting GOLD from its ore. The ore is first finely ground and may be concentrated by flotation; if it contains certain impurities, it may be roasted. It is then mixed with a dilute solution of sodium cyanide (or potassium or calcium cyanide) while air is bubbled through it. The gold is oxidized and forms the soluble aurocyanide complex ion, $Au(CN)_2^{-1}$. (Silver, usually present as an impurity, forms a similar soluble ion.) The solution is separated from the ore by methods such as filtration, and the gold is precipitated by adding powdered zinc. The precipitate usually contains silver, which is also precipitated, and unreacted zinc. The precipitate is further refined, e.g., by smelting to remove the zinc and by treating with nitric acid to dissolve the silver. The cyanide process was developed (1887) by J. S. MacArthur and others in Glasgow, Scotland. It is now the most important and widely used process for extracting gold from ores.

cyanocobalamin: see COENZYME; VITAMIN.

cyanogen (sīăn'əjən), NCCN, colorless, flammable, extremely poisonous gas with a characteristic odor somewhat like that of hydrogen cyanide. It melts at −35°C, boils at −21°C, and is soluble in water, ethanol, or ether. It is chemically very active.

cyano group (sī'ənō), in chemistry, FUNCTIONAL GROUP that consists of a carbon atom joined to a nitrogen atom by a triple bond; it can be joined to an atom or another group by a single bond to the carbon atom. When a cyano group is joined to hydrogen, it forms HYDROGEN CYANIDE. When it is joined to a metal, it forms a metal CYANIDE. When it is joined to an ALKYL GROUP or ARYL GROUP, it forms a nitrile. When two cyano groups are joined directly to one another, they form the CYANOGEN molecule, NCCN. Both the cyano group and hydrogen cyanide have been found in interstellar space.

cyanosis (sī"ənō'sĭs), bluish coloration of the skin, mucous membranes, and nailbeds, resulting from a lack of oxygenated hemoglobin in the blood. It is the symptom of many disorders, including various pulmonary and heart diseases and many congenital heart defects (see BLUE BABY). Cyanosis that is caused by slowed circulation through peripheral blood vessels results in a bluish tinge only on the cool portions of the body (fingertips, nose, ears). In such cases the capillary blood gives up more than normal amounts of oxygen. Although this type of cyanosis can be caused by reduced cardiac output (e.g., in congestive heart failure), the most common causes are nervous tension and exposure to cold. Another type of cyanosis results from poisoning, either by nitrates in contaminated food or water or by certain chemicals and drugs.

cyanotype: see BLUEPRINT.

Cyaxares (sīăk'sərēz), d. 585 B.C., king of Media (c.625–585 B.C.). His name also appears as Umakishtar and Huyakhshtara. In the course of his reign he raised the kingdom of the Medes to a major power in the Middle East. Cyaxares reorganized Median military forces, developing the cavalry especially, and renewed war with Assyria. He captured and leveled (614) Ashur and after joining forces with Nabopolassar of Babylonia as well as with the Scythians, who were former enemies, besieged Nineveh, occupying and pillaging the city in 612. Fighting continued (612–605) in N Mesopotamia and ended in the defeat of the Assyrians, with Cyaxares claiming Assyria proper as Media's share of the spoils. Hostilities later erupted between Media and the neighboring kingdom of Lydia in the northwest; they lasted from 590 to 585, ending in a stalemate. Cyaxares was succeeded by his son ASTYAGES.

Cybele (sĭb'əlē), in ancient Asiatic religion, GREAT MOTHER OF THE GODS. The chief centers of her early worship were Phrygia and Lydia. In the 5th cent. B.C. her cult was introduced into Greece, where she was associated with Demeter and Rhea. The spread of her cult to Rome late in the 3d cent. B.C. was marked chiefly by her Palatine temple. Cybele was primarily a nature goddess, responsible for maintaining and reproducing the wild things of the earth. As guardian of cities and nations, however, she was also entrusted with the general welfare of the people. She was attended by the Corybantes and Dactyls, who honored her with wild music and dancing. At her annual spring festival, the death and resurrection of her beloved ATTIS were celebrated. She frequented mountains and woodland areas and was usually represented either riding a chariot drawn by lions or seated on a throne flanked by two lions. Cybele is frequently identified with various other mother goddesses, notably Agdistis.

cybernetics, term coined by American mathematician Norbert Wiener to refer to the general analysis of CONTROL SYSTEMS and COMMUNICATION systems in living organisms and machines. In cybernetics, analogies are drawn between the functioning of the brain and nervous system and the COMPUTER and other electronic systems. The science overlaps the fields of neurophysiology, INFORMATION THEORY, computing machinery, and AUTOMATION. See SERVOMECHANISM. See Norbert Wiener, *Cybernetics* (1961) and *The Human Use of Human Beings* (1967); F. H. Fuchs, *The Brain as a Computer* (1973).

cycad (sī'kăd), any plant of the order Cycadales, tropical and subtropical palmlike evergreens. The cycads, ginkgos, and conifers comprise the three major orders of gymnosperms, or cone-bearing plants (see CONE and PLANT). The cycads first appeared in the Permian period. They are the most primitive of the living seed-bearing plants and in many ways resemble the ferns. Some have tuberous underground stems, with the crown of leathery, glossy, fernlike leaves springing from ground level; others have a columnar stem, usually 6 to 10 ft (1.8–3.1 m) high (though the corcho of Cuba reaches 30 ft/9.1 m), and are often mistaken for palms. There are nine genera composed of less than 100 species, some found in very restricted areas. Many cycads (e.g., the fern palm of the Old World tropics and the nut palm of Australia) bear edible nutlike fruits. The pith of the coontie (*Zamia floridana*) yields a starch called Florida ARROWROOT or SAGO; the coontie is often called sago palm. Cycads are grown as ornamentals in warm regions and in greenhouses. The cycads are classified in the division PINOPHYTA, class Cycadopsida.

Cyclades (sĭ'klədēz) Gr. *Kikládhes* [Gr.,=circular], island group (1971 pop. 86,337), c.1,000 sq mi (2,590 sq km), SE Greece, a part of the Greek archipelago, in the Aegean Sea stretching SE from Attica. The name was originally used to indicate those islands forming a rough circle around DELOS. The Cyclades include about 220 islands of which TÍNOS, ÁNDROS, MÍLOS, NÁXOS, KÉA, PÁROS, Serifos, Ios, Kithnos, and Thira are the most important. HERMOUPOLIS, on Síros, is the chief town and administrative center of the group. Largely mountainous, with a dry and mild climate, the islands produce wine, fruit, wheat, olive oil, and tobacco, and attract many tourists. Iron, manganese, and sulfur are mined, and marble is quarried. In 1829 the Cyclades passed from the Ottoman Empire to Greece.

Cycladic art (sĭklăd'ĭk), Bronze Age art of the central Aegean Cycladic islands. Early tomb remains include several types of jugs, pots, and bowls decorated in geometric designs, as well as figural sculptures made of marble. The latter are predominantly female fertility figures of many sizes, restrained in expression and refined in execution. They are frontal and geometric in style. Figures of musicians have also been discovered. In pottery of the 17th cent. B.C., found at Phylakopi in Melos, considerable Minoan influence is discernible. Cycladic art was absorbed by the Mycenaens c.1400 B.C. See Pierre Demargne, *Aegean Art* (tr. 1964); Colin Renfrew, *The Emergence of Civilization* (1972).

cyclamate, any member of a group of salts of cyclamic acid (cyclohexanesulfamic acid). The sodium and calcium salts were commonly used as artificial sweeteners until 1969, when their use was banned by the U.S. Food and Drug Administration after reports that ingestion of large quantities of cyclamates appeared to cause cancer in some animals. There is no evidence that cyclamates are associated with cancer in humans.

cyclamen: see PRIMROSE.

cycle, in astronomy, period of time required for the recurrence of some celestial event. The length of a cycle may be measured relative to the sun or to the fixed stars (see SIDEREAL TIME). A frequently observed cycle is the DAY, during which the sun seems to circle around the earth due to the earth's rotation on its axis; although the length of the day varies, the average day is defined as exactly 24 hr of MEAN SOLAR TIME. Another important cycle is the YEAR, during which the earth completes an orbit of the sun. The solar year is measured from one vernal EQUINOX to the next and is equal to 365 days, 5 hr, 48 min, 46 sec of mean solar time (see CALENDAR). The sidereal year, measured relative to the stars, differs in length from the solar year due to the PRECESSION OF THE EQUINOXES. The moon goes through a cycle of phases as it orbits the earth, completing a cycle from one full moon to the next in about 29½ days, or one lunar month (see SYNODIC PERIOD). The moon completes an orbit of the earth relative to the stars in one sidereal month, which is about 2 days shorter than the lunar month. Every 18 years, 11⅓ days the earth, moon, and sun are in very nearly the same relative positions; for this reason, solar and lunar ECLIPSES recur in a cycle with this period. This cycle was known to the Chaldeans (fl. 1000–540 B.C.) and was called the saros by them. HALLEY'S COMET reappears in a cycle whose period is about 75 years. Astronomers also make use of various other cycles, e.g., those of sunspots and variable stars.

cyclic AMP: see ADENOSINE MONOPHOSPHATE.

cyclic compound, any one of a class of compounds whose molecules contain a number of atoms bonded together to form a closed chain or ring. If all of the atoms that form the ring are the same, the compound is said to be homocyclic; if not, the compound is called heterocyclic. Cyclohexane and benzene are homocyclic hydrocarbons; furfural is heterocyclic, as is pyridine. A cyclic compound that behaves chemically like the open-chain aliphatic compounds is said to be alicyclic; cyclohexane is such a compound. Many cyclic compounds exhibit the special properties characteristic of the aromatic compounds.

cyclohexane (sī"kləhĕk'sān), C_6H_{12}, colorless liquid hydrocarbon. It is a cyclic alkane that melts at 6°C and boils at 81°C. It is nearly insoluble in water. Cyclohexane is found naturally to some extent in petroleum but is prepared commercially by catalytic hydrogenation of benzene. It is widely used as a solvent and in making certain compounds used in the preparation of nylon.

cyclone, atmospheric pressure distribution in which there is a low central pressure relative to the surrounding pressure. The resulting pressure gradient, combined with the CORIOLIS EFFECT, causes air to circulate about the core of lowest pressure in a counterclockwise direction in the Northern Hemisphere and in a clockwise direction in the Southern Hemisphere. Near the surface of the earth, the frictional drag on the air moving over land or water causes it to spiral gradually inward toward lower pressures, still in the same rotational sense. This inward movement of air is compensated for by rising currents near the center, which are cooled by expansion when they reach the lower pressures of higher altitudes. The cooling, in turn, greatly increases the relative humidity of the air, so that a general characteristic of "lows" is cloudiness and high humidity; they are thus often referred to simply as storms. According to the theory first proposed by the Norwegian physicist Vilhelm Bjerknes, the extratropical, or middle-latitude, cyclone originates as a wave, or perturbation, in the POLAR FRONT separating the cold polar easterly winds from the warmer prevailing winds farther toward the equator. This wave, once induced by the opposing air currents, is accentuated by the rotational sense of the circulation, which pumps warm, moist air toward the pole around the eastern side of the cyclone center and cold, dry air toward the equator to the west of the center. Such wave cyclones often intensify, expanding the radius of the affected area to 500 mi (805 km) or more, while reducing atmospheric pressure, especially toward the center. Tropical cyclones, formed over warm tropical oceans, are not associated with FRONTS, as are the middle-latitude wave cyclones, nor are they as large as the latter. A tropical cyclone that has matured to a severe intensity is called a HURRICANE when it occurs in the Atlantic Ocean or adjacent seas, a typhoon when it occurs in the Pacific Ocean or adjacent seas, or simply a cyclone or tropical cyclone when it occurs in the Indian Ocean region. Cyclones in middle latitudes move generally from west to east along with the prevailing winds and cover 500 to 1,000 mi (800–1,610 km) each day; tropical cyclones usually move toward the west with the flow of the trade winds during their formative stages, then curve toward the poles around the subtropical ANTICYCLONES.

Cyclopean (sīkləpē'ən), name often applied to a primitive method of masonry construction of prehistoric times, found chiefly in Greece, Italy, and the Near East. The term is derived from Cyclopes, the mythological beings who were supposed to have built walls in this manner. The massive Cyclopean walls were usually made of huge, rough boulders, laid upon one another; the interstices were filled with stones, and the walls were bound with a clay mortar. These walls were characteristic of MYCENAEAN CIVILIZATION. Remaining examples are found at Cnossus, Mycenae, Tiryns, and Athens. There are many Cyclopean remains from Etruscan architecture. Similar examples are seen in China, Japan, and Peru.

cyclopropane, C_3H_6, a gaseous hydrocarbon. It is a cyclic alkane, its three carbon atoms being joined together in a ring. The angle between successive carbon-carbon bonds in the ring is only 60°, much less than that between successive carbon-carbon bonds in a normal open-chain alkane; the cyclopropane molecule is thus said to be "strained." Many reactions of cyclopropane involve breaking one of the carbon-carbon bonds in the ring, which opens the ring and relieves the strain. Cyclopropane is prepared commercially by the reaction of 1,3-dichloropropane with zinc. It is a potent, widely used inhalation anesthetic. Cyclopropane allows the transport of more oxygen to the tissues than do other common anesthetics and also produces greater skeletal muscle relaxation. It is not irritating to the respiratory tract. Because of the low solubility of cyclopropane in the blood, postoperative recovery is usually rapid but nausea and vomiting are common. See ANESTHESIA.

Cyclops (sī'klŏps), plural **Cyclopes** (sīklō'pēz), in Greek mythology, immense one-eyed beings. They appear in at least two distinct traditions. According to Hesiod the Cyclopes were smiths, the sons of Uranus and Gaea. They were imprisoned in Tartarus by their father and again by their brother Cronus. In return for their freedom they gave Zeus the thunderbolt that aided him in overthrowing Cronus. In Homer the Cyclopes are a lawless, barbarous people, one of whom (POLYPHEMUS) Odysseus encounters in his wanderings.

cyclosis (sīklō'sĭs), streaming of cytoplasm within a living cell without deformation of the external cell membrane. In some plant cells there is a rapid rotatory cytoplasmic movement, which is limited to the peripheral parts of the cell next to the cell wall; chloroplasts and granules move in this stream. This movement may be increased by light, and is dependent on temperature and *p*H. Auxins, or growth hormones, may also increase the rate of movement. Specialized cell components, microtubules, may direct the flow or may serve as a framework upon which the streaming occurs. Examples of cells in which cyclosis can be seen are the leaf cells of small aquatic plants, such as *Elodea*, and root hair cells of many plants. In some of the Protozoa, e.g., the ciliates, slower cyclotic movements function in moving digestive vacuoles through the cell body.

cyclostome (sī'kləstōm"), jawless fish, member of the Cyclostomata, the only living order of the vertebrate class Agnatha (see CHORDATA). This group includes the HAGFISH and the lamprey. The name also applies to members of the order Cyclostomata of the invertebrate phylum ECTOPROCTA, class Gymnolaemata.

cyclotron: see PARTICLE ACCELERATOR.

Cydonia, Crete: see KHANIÁ.

Cygnus (sĭg'nəs) [Lat.,=the swan], northern CONSTELLATION located SE of Draco and NW of Pegasus. It was depicted as a bird by most ancient cultures. It is sometimes called the Northern Cross because five of its brightest stars form a huge Latin cross. Its most famous star is DENEB, at the head of the cross, forming a large triangle with Vega in Lyra and Altair in Aquila. Cygnus reaches its highest point in the evening sky in September.

cylinder, in mathematics, surface generated by a line moving parallel to a given fixed line and continually intersecting a given fixed curve called the directrix; each line of the family of lines forming the cylinder is called a ruling, or generator. If the directrix is a CONIC SECTION (e.g., a circle or a parabola), the cylinder is called a quadric cylinder. The commonest type of cylinder is the right circular cylinder, in which the directrix is a circle and the lines forming the cylinder are all perpendicular to the plane of

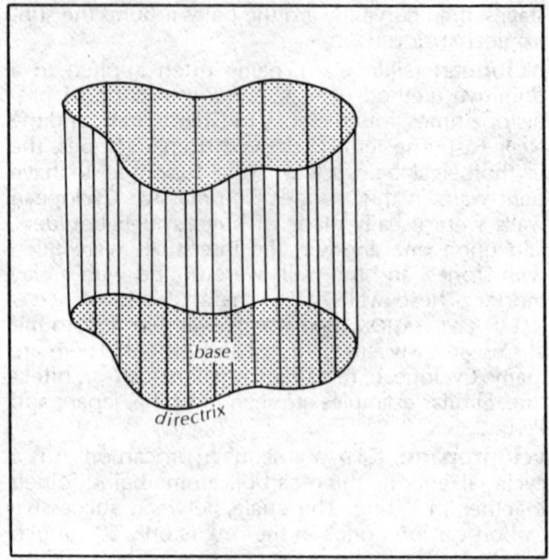

Cylinder

the circle. The solid bounded by a cylindrical surface and two parallel planes intersecting the surface in closed curves is also called a cylinder. The perpendicular distance between the planes is the altitude of the cylinder. The volume of the cylinder is equal to the product of the altitude and the area of the base (the area enclosed by either closed curve).

cymbals (sĭm'bəlz), percussion instruments of ancient Oriental origin. They consist of a pair of slightly concave metal plates which produce a vibrant sound of indeterminate pitch. Known in Europe since the Middle Ages, they were introduced

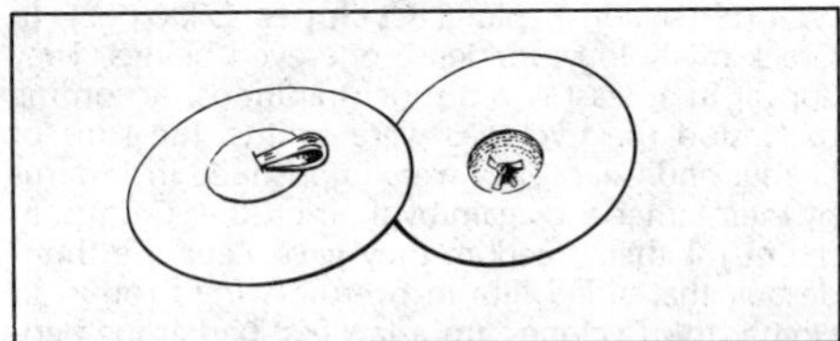

Cymbals

into the European orchestra by Nikolaus Adam Strungk in 1680, but were generally used for exotic effects until the 19th cent. In the orchestra, cymbals have leather handles and are clashed by sweeping them past each other sideways or played by means of a foot pedal. A single cymbal may be struck by wooden or felt drumsticks. Jazz drummers use cymbals of several sizes with a wide variety of playing techniques.

Cymbeline (sĭm'bəlēn) or **Cunobelinus** (kyo͞o″-nōbĭlī'nəs), d. A.D. c.40, British king. His conquest of the Trinovantes (of Essex) made him the wealthiest and most powerful ruler in SE England. After his death his kingdom was divided between his sons Togodumnus and CARACTACUS. Cymbeline gives his name, but little else, to Shakespeare's *Cymbeline.*

Cyme (sī'mē), ancient Greek city of W Asia Minor, on the Ionian Sea and N of the present Smyrna in W Asiatic Turkey. It was the largest and most important of the 12 cities of Aeolis. In the late 5th cent. B.C., Cyme struggled to be free of Persian domination but was only intermittently successful. Later it was a city of the Seleucids and ultimately of Rome.

Cymru and **Cymry:** see WALES.

Cynewulf (kĭn'əwo͝olf), fl. early 9th cent.?, Old English religious poet of Northumbria or Mercia. Four poems have been ascribed to him on the evidence of his signatures in runes in the text of each of these poems. The poems, all more explicitly didactic than any earlier works, are: *Juliana, The Ascension, Elene,* and *The Fates of the Apostles.* Other poems, formerly thought his, are now attributed to poets of the "Cynewulf school." See *The Poems of Cynewulf* (tr. by C. W. Kennedy, 1949).

Cynics (sĭn'ĭks) [Gr.,=doglike, probably from their manners and their meeting place, the Cynosarges, an academy for Athenian youths], ancient school of philosophy founded c.440 B.C. by ANTISTHENES, a disciple of Socrates. The Cynics considered virtue to be the only good, not just the highest good as Socrates had asserted. To them, virtue meant a life of self-sufficiency, of suppression of desires and restriction of wants. The Cynics paraded their poverty, their antagonism to pleasure, and their indifference to others, thereby gaining a reputation for fanatical unconventionality. After Antisthenes the principal Cynics were DIOGENES of Sinope and Crates, his pupil. The Cynics, who survived until the 6th cent. A.D., influenced the Stoics, with whom they shared some philosophical objectives (see STOICISM).

Cynthus: see GIRALDI, GIOVANNI BATTISTA.

Cypress, city (1970 pop. 31,026), Orange co., S Calif.; inc. 1956. Forest Lawn-Cypress, a branch of the famous cemetery in Glendale, Calif., is a major employer. A junior college is there, and the Los Alamitos Naval Air Station is just outside the city limits.

cypress, common name for members of the Cupressaceae, a widely distributed family of coniferous shrubs and trees, several yielding valuable timber. The major genera are *Juniperus* (JUNIPER), *Thuja* (ARBORVITAE), and *Cupressus* (the true cypresses). Species of the latter, found in S Europe, the Far East, and W North America, are resinous evergreens with a fragrant, durable wood and scalelike leaves. The Monterey cypress (*C. macrocarpa*) is native to a limited region around the Bay of Monterey, Calif., but is cultivated in many parts of the world. It is sometimes planted as a hedge. The cypress of classical literature is the European *C. sempervirens* or Italian cypress. It has since early times been symbolic of mourning and, more recently, of immortality. The gates of St. Peter's at Rome, which stood for 1,100 years, were made of its wood. The funereal, or mourning, cypress (*C. funebris*) of China, with "weeping" branches, is a popular ornamental elsewhere. American trees of the genus *Chamaecyparis* of the same family are also called cypresses. Important as timber trees are the Lawson cypress, or Port Orford cedar (*C. lawsoniana*), and the Nootka, Sitka, or Alaska yellow cypress (*C. nootkatensis*), both of NW North America. *C. thyoides,* called white cedar in E North America, is a smaller tree also used for lumber. The lumber called cypress in the S United States is chiefly from trees of the family Taxodiaceae (BALD CYPRESS family). The true cypress family is classified in the division PINOPHYTA, class Pinopsida, order Coniferales.

Cyprian, Saint (sĭp'rēən), 200?–258, Father of the Church, bishop of Carthage (c.248). A disciple of Tertullian, he was far less a purist than his master. Converted in his middle age, he rose quickly to become the most powerful bishop in Africa. His vigorous championing of Pope St. Cornelius against the attacks of NOVATIAN averted a dangerous schism. Many Christians had apostasized under the persecution of the Roman emperor Decius. Novatian and his sect maintained these could not be received back into the church. Cyprian concurred with Pope Cornelius (and Calixtus I before him), calling for strictness but ultimate forgiveness for the truly contrite. The schism occasioned his important treatise, *De unitate ecclesiae,* in which he argues for the authority of the bishop as ground for the church's unity. He recognized the preeminence of the Church of Rome, but fell into sharp dispute with Pope Stephen I on the validity of baptism conferred by heretics or schismatics; Cyprian believed persons so baptized had to be rebaptized upon entering the church. The question was settled in favor of the Roman teaching, after Cyprian's martyrdom in the persecution of Valerian. He is mentioned in the canon of the Mass. Feast: Sept. 16. See G. S. Walker, *The Churchmanship of Saint Cyprian* (1969).

Cyprus (sī'prəs), Gr. *Kypros,* republic (1971 est. pop. 634,000), 3,578 sq mi (9,267 sq km), an island in the E Mediterranean Sea, c.40 mi (60 km) S of Turkey and c.60 mi (100 km) W of Syria. The capital is NICOSIA. Other important cities are FAMAGUSTA, LARNACA, and LIMASSOL. Two mountain ranges traverse the island from east to west; the highest point is Mt. Olympus (6,406 ft/1,953 m), in the southwest. Between the ranges lies a wide plain, the chief agricultural region. Crops include grapes (used for wine making), cereals, olives, tobacco, citrus fruits, and cotton. Sheep and goats are raised, and silkworms are cultivated. Fishing is an important livelihood. Among the mineral resources are pyrites, ocher, chrome, asbestos, gypsum, umber, and copper. Nearly 80% of the population are Greek Cypriots and about 18% are Turkish Cypriots. The constitution, in effect since 1960, provides for a president and vice president, elected by the Greek and Turkish communities, respectively. There is a bicameral legislature, and the Greek and Turkish communities also have their respective communal chambers, which exercise authority over religious, educational, and cultural affairs. Excavations have proved the existence of a Neolithic culture on Cyprus in the period from 4000 B.C. to 3000 B.C. Contact with the Middle East and, after 1500 B.C., with Greece greatly influenced Cyp-

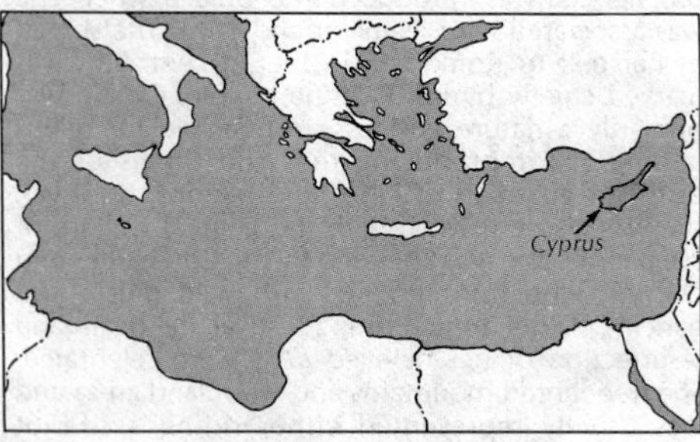

riot civilization. Phoenicians settled on the island c.800 B.C. Cyprus subsequently fell under Assyrian, Egyptian, and Persian rule. Alexander the Great conquered it in 333 B.C., after which the island again became an Egyptian dependency until its annexation by Rome in 58 B.C. Ancient Cyprus was a center of the cult of Aphrodite. After A.D. 395 Cyprus was ruled by the Byzantines until 1191, when Richard I of England conquered it. In 1192, Richard bestowed the island on GUY OF LUSIGNAN. In 1489, Cyprus was annexed by Venice. The Turks conquered it in 1571. At the Congress of Berlin (1878) the Ottoman Empire placed Cyprus under British administration, and in 1914 Britain annexed it outright. Under British rule the movement among the Greek Cypriot population for union (*enosis*) with Greece was a constant source of tension. Agitation flared into violence in 1954, and in 1955 a Greek Cypriot organization (EOKA), led by Col. George Grivas, launched a campaign of widespread terrorism. Tension and terror mounted, especially after British authorities deported (1956) MAKARIOS III, spokesman for the Greek Cypriot nationalists. The conflict, tantamount to civil war, was aggravated by Turkish support of Turkish Cypriot demands for partition of the island. Negotiations (1955) among Britain, Greece, and Turkey on the status of Cyprus broke down completely. Finally in 1959, a settlement was reached. It provided for Cypriot independence in 1960 and for the terms of the constitution. Treaties precluded both *enosis* and partition. Elections (1959) made Makarios president (he was reelected in 1968 and 1973) and Fazil Kutchuk vice president. In 1961, Cyprus joined the Commonwealth of Nations and the United Nations. But trouble continued. Large-scale fighting between Greek and Turkish Cypriots erupted several times in the 1960s and a Greco-Turkish war was narrowly averted. A UN peacekeeping force was sent in 1965. In March, 1970, there was an attempt on Makarios's life by radical Greek Cypriots. The government was also fearful of a possible coup led by Grivas, who favored *enosis.* Turkish Cypriots demanded official recognition of their organization (which exercised de facto political control in the 30 Turkish enclaves) and the stationing of Turkish troops on the island to offset the influence of the Cypriot national guard, which was dominated by officers from Greece. Greek Cypriots interpreted the proposal as amounting to partition. Grivas returned to Cyprus in 1971 to rekindle the EOKA movement. Acts of violence against the government increased and were met in 1973 by an effort to suppress the guerrillas by the national police force (which had been created by Makarios to counter the national guard). Grivas died in Jan., 1974, and although the movement was split between hardliners and moderates, it continued to be dominated by Greek officers. In July, 1974, following a large-scale national police assault on the EOKA, the Makarios government was overthrown (July 15) by the national guard. Nikos Sampson, a Greek Cypriot newspaper publisher, acceded to the presidency. Although first reported to have been killed, Makarios escaped abroad by way of the British military base at Akrotiri. Both Greece and Turkey mobilized their armed forces. Citing its obligation to protect the Turkish Cypriot community, Turkey invaded (July 20) N Cyprus. The invasion precipitated the fall of the military regime in Athens and also resulted in the resignation of Sampson. He was replaced by Glafkos Clerides, the Greek Cypriot president of the house of representatives. A UN-sponsored ceasefire was arranged on July 22, and Turkey was permitted to retain military forces in the areas it had captured. Negotiations between Turkey, Greece, and Cyprus were begun in Geneva in an attempt to arrange a settlement. Despite the ceasefire, Turkish forces continued to advance on the island. With the breakdown of the negotiations, Turkey renewed (Aug. 14) full-scale attacks against Greek Cypriot positions. In response to the Turkish presence in the northern third of Cyprus, the Cyprus Liberation Army was formed by members of the EOKA and the national guard. After five months in exile, Makarios returned (Dec., 1974) to Cyprus and promised to work for peace between Greek and Turkish Cypriots. See G. F. Hill, *History of Cyprus* (4 vol., 1940–52); Gordon Home, *Cyprus, Then and Now* (1960); Stanley Kyriakides, *Cyprus: Constitutionalism and Crisis Government* (1968); Hugh Dominic Purcell, *Cyprus* (1969); E. K. Keefe et al., *Area Handbook for Cyprus* (1971).

Cyrankiewicz, Józef (yo͞o'zĕf sĭrănkyă'vĭch), 1911–, Polish political leader. Active in the Polish resistance after the German invasion in 1939, he was arrested in 1941 and spent the remainder of the war in concentration camps. He was a member of the Polish Socialist party from 1932 and became secretary general of its central executive committee in 1946. In 1947 he became premier. Upon the formal merger of the Socialists and Communists in 1948, Cyrankiewicz was named secretary of the central committee of the new United Polish Workers' party. Vice premier (1952–54), he held the premiership again from 1954 to 1970, proving himself flexible under both Stalinist and anti-Stalinist regimes. He was instrumental in quelling the 1956 Poznań uprising but remained in power even during the more tolerant regime of Władysław Gomułka. In 1970, however, he resigned in the wake of serious riots over inflation. Cyrankiewicz was made titular head of state, and in 1972 he was removed from all important political positions.

Cyrano de Bergerac, Savinien (sävēnyăN' sĕrānō' də bĕrzhəräk'), 1619–55, French novelist. Satirizing the customs and beliefs of his time, he wrote two fantastic romances about visits to the moon and sun—*L'Autre Monde; ou, Les Estats et empires de la lune* (1657) and *Les Estats et empires du soleil* (1662); these usually appear together, as in the translation by Richard Aldington, *Voyages to the Moon and the Sun* (new ed. 1962). Cyrano's swaggering personality, evinced by the many duels he fought over insults to his unusually large nose, was romanticized by Edmond Rostand in the verse drama *Cyrano de Bergerac* (1897). See study by E. Harth (1970).

Cyrenaica (sĭrənā'ĭkə, sīrə-), historic region, E Libya, bordering on the Mediterranean Sea. BENGASI, Al Marj, DARNAH, and TOBRUK are the chief cities. The Greeks colonized N Cyrenaica in the 7th cent. B.C., founding numerous settlements. In the mid-1st cent. B.C., Cyrenaica became a Roman province. In A.D. 115–16 there was a large-scale but unsuccessful revolt of Jewish settlers. When Rome was divided (4th cent.) into the Eastern and Western empires, Cyrenaica came under the Byzantines, who, however, exercised little control over the region. In 642 the Arabs conquered Cyrenaica and many of them settled in the region from the 9th to 11th cent. The Ottoman Turks captured the area in the mid-16th cent. The SANUSI Muslim brotherhood was founded (1843) in Cyrenaica and gained many adherents there. For the history of Cyrenaica after the Ottoman conquest, see LIBYA.

Cyrenaics (sĭrĭnā'ĭks, sī-), one of the minor schools of Greek philosophy, flourishing in the late 4th and early 3d cent. B.C. Cyrenaic philosophy taught that present individual pleasure is the highest good. It is thus an early version of HEDONISM, but its importance in philosophy declined in favor of the later version of EPICURUS. It drew upon certain of Socrates' ethical views and also upon aspects of the view of knowledge held by the Sophists. ARISTIPPUS of Cyrene, its founder, held that since each person can know only his own sensations, there can be no universal standard of what is pleasurable—hence, all pleasures are equally valuable. His followers modified this doctrine by distinguishing between greater and lesser pleasures. Theodorus held man's happiness to be a state of cheerfulness, while Anniceris stressed the pleasures of friendship, society, and patriotism. Hegesias (called the Death-Persuader) taught that a happy life is pure illusion and that the complete suppression of pain, i.e., death, is the only end worth pursuing.

Cyrene (sīrē'nē), ancient city near the northern coast of Africa, in Cyrenaica (now E Libya). It was a Greek colony founded (c.630 B.C.) by Aristoteles of Thera, who became king of Cyrene as Battus. For eight generations the monarchs were alternately named Battus and Arcesilas. Having important commerce with Greece, the little city-state flourished. Other cities were founded in Cyrenaica, notably Barca, but Cyrene retained power. In the late 6th cent. Cyrene submitted to the Persians under CAMBYSES II, but later (after 480 B.C.) became independent again. Although the city became subject to Alexander the Great in 331 and was later practically annexed by the Ptolemies of Egypt, it seems to have had nominal independence until the marriage of Berenice (d. 221?), daughter of Cyrene's king, to PTOLEMY III. Cyrene remained part of the Ptolemaic kingdom until 96 B.C. It was later the center of a Roman province. Under the Roman emperor Trajan there were Jewish uprisings, which were severely punished, and Cyrene declined. At its prime Cyrene was a large and beautiful city and an intellectual center noted for its schools of medicine and philosophy. Aristippus, Callimachus, Eratosthenes, and Synesius were born here. Extensive ruins include the temple of Apollo (dating from the 7th cent. B.C.), the agora, the capitol, the acropolis, and the theater.

Cyril, Saint (Saint Cyril of Alexandria), d. 444, patriarch of Alexandria (412–44), Doctor of the Church, known for his animosity toward heretics and heathens. He drove the Jews from Alexandria, and under his rule HYPATIA was killed. The great episode in his career was his struggle against NESTORIANISM, which culminated in the Council of Ephesus in 431 (see EPHESUS, COUNCIL OF). There Cyril presided and had the full support of Pope CELESTINE I. He returned triumphant, but he continued to be opposed by the Antiochene bishops, who tended toward Nestorianism; consequently, they stayed out of communion with Alexandria, and so with the church, for two years. In 433, Cyril consented to a compromise with Antioch by declaring that Christ had two natures, human and divine, and that in speaking of one nature he meant one Person. St. Cyril wrote much on theology, particularly on the problem of the Trinity. His doctrines, though deemed orthodox in his time, were in a sense a preface to those of EUTYCHES and of MONOPHYSITISM. Feast: Feb. 9.

Cyril and Methodius, Saints, d. 869 and 884, respectively, Greek missionaries, brothers, called Apostles to the Slavs and fathers of Slavonic literature. Their history and influence are obscured by conflicting legends. After working among the KHAZARS, they were sent (863) from Constantinople by Patriarch Photius to MORAVIA. This was at the invitation of Prince Rostislav, who sought missionaries able to preach in the Slavonic vernacular and thereby check German influence in Moravia. Their immediate success aroused the hostility of the German rulers and ecclesiastics. Candidates from among their converts were refused ordination, and their use of the vernacular in the liturgy was severely criticized. According to one source, when Photius was excommunicated by Rome the brothers were called there. Their orthodoxy was established, and the use of Slavonic in the liturgy was approved. Cyril died while in Rome, but Methodius, consecrated by the pope, returned to Moravia and was made archbishop of Sirmium. Despite the papal sanction the Germans contrived to have him imprisoned, and, though released two years later, his effectiveness appears to have been blocked. His last years were spent translating the Bible and ecclesiastical books into Slavonic. His influence in Moravia was wiped out after his death but was carried to Bulgaria, Serbia, and Russia, where the southern Slavonic of Cyril and Methodius is still the liturgical language of both Roman Catholic and Orthodox churches. The **Cyrillic alphabet** used in those countries today, traditionally ascribed to St. Cyril, was probably the work of his followers. It was based probably by Cyril himself upon the glagolithic alphabet, which is still used by certain Yugoslav Catholics. Feast: July 7. See R. L. Wilken, *Judaism and the Early Christian Mind* (1971).

Cyril Lucar: see LUCARIS, CYRIL.

Cyrus the Great (sī'rəs), d. 529 B.C., king of Persia, founder of the greatness of the ACHAEMENIDS and of the Persian Empire. According to Herodotus, he was the son of an Iranian noble, the elder Cambyses, and a Median princess, daughter of Astyages. Many historians, following other ancient writers (such as Ctesias), deny this genealogy, and the whole of Cyrus' life is encrusted with legend. Cyrus overthrew Astyages, king of the Medes, sometime between 559 B.C. and 549 B.C. He entered Ecbatana and, taking over the Median kingdom, began to build a great empire after the Assyrian model. Cyrus' objectives were to gain power over the Mediterranean coast, secure Asia Minor, and civilize the east. Croesus of Lydia, Nabonidus of Babylonia, and Amasis II of Egypt tried to build a strong alliance against him, but to no avail. He defeated and captured CROESUS (546 B.C.), and Lydia became a satrapy under the Persian government. The Chaldaean empire of Babylonia fell to Cyrus in 538 B.C. He did not conquer Egypt, but he prepared the way for later Persian victories there. Cyrus demanded the surrender of the Greek cities that had been under Lydia, and they also became satrapies of Persia. Cyrus was much admired by the Jews, whom he favored, placing them in power in Palestine. His motive was probably to create a buffer state between Persia and Egypt, but the result was a rehabilitation of Israel. He figures prominently in the Bible (e.g., 2 Chron. and Ezra), is viewed as God's appointed agent (Isa. 40–48), and is approved by Daniel (Dan. 6.28). Cyrus was admired as a liberator rather than a conqueror, because he respected the customs and religions of each part of his vast empire. The exact limits of Cyrus' eastern conquests are not known, but it is possible that they reached as far as the Peshawar region. He used Susa, Ecbatana, and Babylon as his capitals but was buried at Pasargadae, where he had built a splendid palace. At his death his son Cambyses succeeded him, despite the ambitions of another son, Smerdis.

Cyrus the Younger, d. 401 B.C., Persian prince, younger son of Darius II and Parysatis. He was his mother's favorite, and she managed to get several satrapies in Asia Minor for him when he was very young. His friendship toward LYSANDER helped Sparta achieve victory in the Peloponnesian War. Cyrus was at court when Darius died (404 B.C.) and was accused (probably justly) by TISSAPHERNES of a plot to murder his elder brother and the legitimate heir, ARTAXERXES II. Cyrus was saved only by the pleas of his mother and was restored to his satrapies. He began careful plans for a rebellion. He collected an army and through CLEARCHUS hired a large troop of Greek mercenaries (the Ten Thousand) for the campaign. On the pretext of setting out to put down brigands in Pisidia, the army was marched E from Sardis to Tarsus and then into Syria. Tissaphernes rushed to court with the news, and Artaxerxes set out to meet the rebels. Many of Cyrus' men threatened mutiny when they learned of his true intent, but they were won over by his charm and bravery and proceeded to fight. Cyrus was killed in the battle of CUNAXA. The loss was followed by the heroic retreat of the Ten Thousand. The revolt of Cyrus and the battle of Cunaxa were the basis for Xenophon's celebrated prose history, *Anabasis*.

cyst, abnormal sac in the body, filled with a fluid or semisolid and enclosed in a membrane. Cysts can be congenital but are usually acquired, the most common locations being the skin and the ovaries. Sebaceous cysts of the skin, known as blackheads or whiteheads, occur when dirt or other material blocks the oil glands of the skin, preventing secretions from escaping. Retention cysts develop in glandular organs when ducts are blocked, commonly in kidney tubules, mammary glands, and sweat glands. Most cysts cannot be cured except by surgical removal.

cysteine (sĭs'tēn), organic compound, one of the 22 α-AMINO ACIDS commonly found in animal PROTEINS. Only the L-stereoisomer participates in the biosynthesis of mammalian protein. It is particularly abundant in the proteins of hair, hooves, and the KERATIN of the skin. Cysteine is an extremely important constituent of proteins because of the reactive thiol group (containing hydrogen and sulfur) on its side chain. This group is said to participate in the catalytic reactions of certain enzymes, such as that of papain, the enzyme from papaya latex used to make commercial meat tenderizers. The thiol group of one cysteine residue is capable of combining with the thiol group of another to form a disulfide bridge, either linking two peptide chains together, as in the case of INSULIN, or causing a single peptide chain to fold back on itself, making a loop. This latter effect on the secondary structure of proteins is evidently of great importance in maintaining the

H
H—C—SH
H_2N—C—C(=O)OH
H

cysteine

proper configuration of both structural proteins and enzymes. It is often said that a permanent, the process used to change one's hairstyle, evidently acts by breaking, rearranging, and re-forming disulfide bridges in the proteins making up hair. Two cysteine

cystine

molecules linked together by a disulfide linkage make up the amino acid cystine, often occurring as a separate entry in lists of common amino acids. A major complication of cystinuria, an inherited metabolic disease, one of whose symptoms is a twentyfold to thirtyfold increase in urinary excretion of cystine, is the precipitation of this relatively insoluble amino acid in the kidney, impairing its function. A similar sort of renal failure often accompanies cystinosis, another inherited disease. Cystine was isolated from a urinary calculus in 1810 and from horn tissue in 1899. The reduction of cystine to cysteine was reported in 1884 and the structures of the two amino acids were proved by chemical synthesis in 1903–4. Neither cysteine nor cystine is essential to the diet of man; cystine and cysteine are interconvertible, and cysteine is made in the body from SERINE and METHIONINE.

cystic fibrosis (sĭs'tĭk fībrō'sĭs), inherited disorder of the exocrine glands (see GLAND), affecting mainly infants and children. The disorder causes the ducts of these glands to become blocked by thick mucus and excessive fiber formation. The glands behind the blocked ducts continue to secrete substances, which cause them to become swollen, forming cysts. The abnormally sticky secretions chiefly obstruct the pancreas, lungs, and liver. The disease also causes the sweat glands to secrete excessive salt, causing heat prostration in hot weather. Symptoms, which vary according to the severity of the condition and the glands involved, include a distended abdomen, diarrhea, bulky, foul-smelling stools, and malnutrition. Milder cases generally exhibit repeated incidence of respiratory infections. Treatment consists of dietary adjustment (low fat) and the administration of vitamins, pancreatin, and antibiotics to ward off secondary infections. Special measures are necessary to decrease the viscosity of pulmonary secretions. Severe cases are usually fatal.

cystine: see CYSTEINE.

cystitis (sĭstī'tĭs), acute or chronic inflammation of the urinary BLADDER. In young people the disease occurs more often in females and frequently results from bacterial invasion from the adjacent rectum and genital organs. Among older persons males are more often affected because of a higher frequency of urinary tract obstruction. Other predisposing factors are pregnancy, diabetes, and various systemic disorders. Usual symptoms are frequent urination with burning pain; the appearance of blood in the urine; pain in the pubic area; and sometimes chills and fever. Treatment is with antibiotics.

Cythera, Greece: see KÍTHIRA.

cytochrome (sī'təkrōm"), protein containing heme (see COENZYME) that participates in the phase of biochemical respiration called oxidative PHOSPHORYLATION. Cytochromes act as carriers of hydride ions (sometimes considered to be the equivalent of electron pairs) in the series of complex enzymes known as the electron transport chain. As the hydride ions or their equivalent travel along the electron transport chain, each cytochrome is in turn reduced (accepts a hydride ion or pair of electrons) and then oxidized (donates the hydride ion or pair of electrons to the next acceptor in the chain); in the process the iron atom in the cytochrome heme shuttles between the ferrous and ferric states. The cytochromes were discovered in 1886.

cytokinesis: see MITOSIS.

cytology (sītŏl'əjē), in biology, the study of the structure of all normal and abnormal components of cells and the changes, movements, and transformations of such components. The discipline includes cytogenics, cytochemistry, and microscopic anatomy, investigated with the use of various microscopes such as light, phase, interference, and electron microscopes. Cells are studied directly in the living state (phase microscopy) or are killed (fixed) and prepared for viewing (embedded, sectioned, and stained) on light or electron microscopes.

cytoplasm: see PROTOPLASM.

cytosine (sī'tōsēn"), organic base of the PYRIMIDINE family. It was isolated from the NUCLEIC ACID of calf thymus tissue in 1894. A suggested structure for cytosine, published in 1903, was confirmed in the same year when that base was synthesized in the laboratory. Combined with the sugar ribose in glycosidic linkage, cytosine forms a derivative called cytidine (a nucleoside), which in turn can be phosphorylated with from one to three phosphoric acid groups, yielding the three NUCLEOTIDES CMP (cytidine monophosphate), CDP (cytidine diphosphate), and CTP (cytidine triphosphate). Analogous nucleosides and nucleotides are formed from cytosine and deoxyribose. The nucleoside derivatives of cytosine perform important functions in cellular metabolism. CTP acts as a COENZYME in both carbohydrate and lipid metabolism; it can readily donate one of its phosphate groups to adenosine diphosphate (ADP) to form ADENOSINE TRIPHOSPHATE (ATP), an extremely important intermediate in the transfer of chemical energy in living systems. CTP is the source of the cytidine found in ribonucleic acid (RNA) and deoxycytidine triphosphate (dCTP) is the source of the deoxycytidine in deoxyribonucleic acid (DNA). Thus cytosine is intimately involved in the preservation and transfer of genetic information.

Cytoxan (sītŏk'sĭn), trade name for the drug cyclophosphamide, used to inhibit growth of tumors and rapidly proliferating cells. It is used in the treatment of leukemia, Hodgkin's disease, and lymphosarcoma and other solid tumors. A drug of great specificity, Cytoxan is activated in the body by the enzymes in certain types of tumors. Because it is also activated in such tissues as blood plasma and liver, it is a highly toxic substance. Nevertheless, it is a potent and useful chemotherapeutic agent.

Cyzicus (sĭz'ĭkəs), ancient city, NW Turkey, at the neck of the Cyzicus Peninsula. Strategically located, it rivaled Byzantium in commercial importance. Founded (756 B.C.) by Greek colonists from Miletus, it was a member of the Delian League. In 410 B.C., Alcibiades defeated a Spartan fleet off Cyzicus, and in 74 B.C. the city withstood a siege by Mithridates VI of Pontus. As a reward for its loyalty, it became a free city under Roman rule. In A.D. 675 the town was pillaged by the Arabs and then used as a base for a siege of Constantinople. There are ruins of a large temple built by Roman Emperor Hadrian and of other public buildings.

Czartoryski (chärtôrĭs'kē), Polish princely family. Although of ancient lineage, it rose to prominence only in the 17th cent., and in the 18th cent. during the reign of the Saxon kings of Poland it virtually ruled the country. **Prince Michael Czartoryski,** 1697–1773, was grand chancellor of Lithuania. His brother, **Prince Augustus Czartoryski,** d. 1782, was palatine of Polish Russia. Failing in their efforts to reform the Polish constitution, the brothers fell out with King Augustus III and, securing the support of Catherine II of Russia, succeeded in elevating their nephew, Stanislaus Poniatowski, to the Polish throne as STANISLAUS II after Augustus's death. **Prince Adam Jerzy Czartoryski,** 1770–1861, grandson of Michael, was a hostage at the Russian court after the failure of the Polish insurrection in 1794. There he befriended the future czar, Alexander I, who after his accession appointed Czartoryski (1803) foreign minister. He resigned in 1806 but remained a close adviser of Alexander, whom he accompanied to the Congress of Vienna and from whom he obtained the Polish constitution of 1815 after Alexander was recognized as king of Poland by the congress. Opposing the later Polish policy of Alexander and Nicholas I, Czartoryski took part in the insurrection of 1830 and headed (1830–31) the provisional government. When it fell, he emigrated to Paris, where until his death he was the leader of the Polish aristocratic party. He was (1803–23) curator of the university at Vilna and greatly improved the Polish school system. He left memoirs (tr. 1888). See Marian Kukiel, *Czartoryski and European Unity* (1955).

Czech language (chĕk), in the past sometimes also called Bohemian, member of the West Slavic group of the Slavic subfamily of the Indo-European family of languages (see SLAVIC LANGUAGES). One of the official languages of Czechoslovakia, it is spoken by about 10 million people, of whom nine million reside in Czechoslovakia and one million in the United States. Grammatically, Czech has seven cases (nominative, genitive, dative, accusative, locative, instrumental, and vocative) for nouns, pronouns, and adjectives. It is not necessary to use personal pronouns with verbs since person and number are clearly shown by the verb endings; however, personal pronouns may be used for emphasis. In the pronunciation of Czech the stress always falls on the first syllable of a word, but this accentuation is not shown by any diacritical marks. A sharp distinction is made between long and short vowels, an acute accent (´) being used to indicate a long vowel. A hook or inverted circumflex (ˇ) over a consonant is the sign that the consonant is palatalized, that is, pronounced softly. The earliest surviving record of Czech is in the form of glosses in a Latin manuscript of the 11th cent. A.D. The period of Old Czech, the oldest stage of the language, is usually placed in the 11th to 14th cent. At that time there were many dialects. A Czech literature began to take shape in the 13th cent. Standardization of the spelling and pronunciation of the language occurred during the Middle Czech period of the 15th and 16th cents., largely as a result of the work of John HUSS, the celebrated Czech religious reformer, who made the Prague dialect the basis of his far-reaching linguistic reforms. The modern period of Czech began in the 17th cent. The domination of the Czechs by the Hapsburg rulers of Austria from 1620 to 1918 seriously hampered the development of the Czech language and literature, although a national literary revival began in the 18th cent. However, after independence was regained in 1918, the language and literature of Czechoslovakia again began to flourish. A modified version of the Roman alphabet is used for writing Czech. See William E. Harkins, *A Modern Czech Grammar* (1953); Reginald G. A. de Bray, *Guide to the Slavonic Languages* (rev. ed. 1969).

Czech Legion, military force of about 40,000 to 50,000 men, composed mostly of Czech and Slovak Russian prisoners of war and deserters from the Austro-Hungarian army who enrolled in the Russian army during World War I. Constituted with the consent of the Russian revolutionary government set up in 1917, the legion took a minor part in fighting the Germans and Austrians. After Russia left the war as a result of the peace of Brest-Litovsk in 1918, an agreement between the legion and the Bolshevik regime in Russia allowed for the evacuation of the legion via the Trans-Siberian RR and its eventual transfer to the Franco-German front. During its evacuation, the legion reluctantly became involved in the Russian civil war, fighting mostly on the anti-Bolshevik side, and controlled in mid-1918 much of the vital railroad line. However, plans (favored by some Allied officials) to use the legion for intervention against the Soviet regime never materialized.

Czech literature dates from the 10th cent. The legends of St. Wenceslaus (10th cent.) were written in OLD CHURCH SLAVONIC. Until c.1400, Czech literature consisted mainly of Latin chronicles (Cosmas of Prague, 1125) and of Czech hymns, tales of chivalry, and romances in verse. The 15th cent. witnessed a poetic flowering that paralleled increasing national consciousness. In 1394, Smil Flaska of Pardubice initiated modern realistic Czech literature with an allegorical admonition in verse, *New Council.* In a similar vein were the sermons of Tomáš Štítný (c.1331–c.1401) and the works of the peasant mystic Petr Chelčický (*The Net of the True Faith,* 1440–43). The language reforms of John Huss helped to make Czech an effective literary language for the writers of the Renaissance, as in the works of the humanists, in the religious and secular writings of the Moravian bishop Jan Blahoslav (1503–71), and in the histories of Veleslavin (1545–99). The crowning glory of the age was the Kralice Bible, translated by the Czech Brethren and published from 1579 to 1593. The Thirty Years War (1618–48) brought wholesale destruction of Czech literary works followed by repression of national life. In the 17th cent. the great educator COMENIUS (Jan Amos Komenský), like many other Czechs, worked in exile, and the language was gradually reduced to little more than a peasant dialect. In the 18th cent. men like the philologists Josef DOBROVSKÝ and Josef Jungmann helped to rehabilitate writing in Czech. Jan KOLLÁR led the Pan-Slavic revival in the early 19th cent., while Karel Hynek MÁCHA, considered the foremost Czech poet, expressed a Byronic romanticism developed further by the novelist Božena Němcova and the poet Karel J. Erben. Pan-Slavism and romanticism dominated Czech literature in the first half of the 19th cent. František PALACKÝ highlighted Slavic scholarship. The 13th-century Slavic texts produced by Václav Hanka (1791–1861) were proved spurious;

they became, however, part of the Czech literary tradition and remained influential. In the later 19th cent., when the poetry of Svatopluk ČECH, Jan NERUDA, and Joseph V. SLÁDEK and the novels of Alois Jirásek achieved fame, literature was oriented toward the intellectual and the bourgeois. After 1890 realism gained force with the writings of the influential critic Thomas Masaryk. Proletarian and rural themes were developed, and writers such as Jaroslav VRCHLICKÝ, J. S. MACHAR, Petr BEZRUČ, and Otokar BŘEZINA won fame at home, while Karel ČAPEK brought Czech literature into the mainstream of world letters. In the period from 1918 to 1938 Czech literature was the most cosmopolitan of the Slavonic literatures; at the same time native themes were cultivated. A dominant trend was the movement away from the intellectual and the individual toward the abstract and the hedonistic. Jaroslav HAŠEK produced his classic war satire, *The Good Soldier Schweik* (4 vol., 1920–23), and Franz Kafka dominated the literary circles of Prague. The German occupation saw the destruction of Czech literary art and the death of many outstanding figures. After World War II a reorientation of Czech writing toward Russia ensued, and SOCIALIST REALISM became dominant in Czech literature. Postwar novelists of note include Egon Hostovský and Jan Drda. Some relaxation of the strictures of socialist realism was evident in the 1950s and 60s. See František Chudoba, *A Short Survey of Czech Literature* (1924); W. E. Harkins, ed., *Anthology of Czech Literature* (1953); Milada Součková, *A Literature in Crisis* (1954) and *The Czech Romantics* (1958); Paul Selver, ed., *An Anthology of Czechoslovak Literature* (1929, repr. 1969).

Czechoslovakia (chĕk″ōslōväk′ēə), Czech *Československo* (chĕs′kōslōvĕn″skō), federal republic (1973 est. pop. 14,500,000), 49,370 sq mi (127,869 sq km), central Europe. It is bounded by East Germany and Poland on the north, West Germany on the west, Austria and Hungary on the south, and the USSR on the east. Natural boundaries are formed by the Carpathian and Sudetes mts. in the north, the Erzgebirge range (Krušne Hory) in the northwest, the Bohemian Forest in the west, and the Danube River in the south. Since the country is landlocked, the chief rivers—the Danube, the Elbe, the Vltava (Moldau), and the Oder—are of great economic importance. There are three main geographic regions: the Bohemian plateau, the Moravian lowland, and mountainous Slovakia. The country has a continental climate. The republic, founded in 1918 as the AUSTRO-HUNGARIAN MONARCHY fell apart, comprises Slovakia and the traditional Czech lands of Bohemia, Moravia, and Czech Silesia. PRAGUE is the federal capital. Other important cities are BRNO, BRATISLAVA, OSTRAVA, PLZEŇ, KOŠICE, and OLOMOUC. The population is largely Slavic, consisting chiefly of Czechs (about two thirds of the total) and Slovaks (a little less than one third). There are small minorities of Hungarians (565,000 in 1969), Germans (110,000), Poles (72,000), and Ukrainians (59,000). Czech and Slovak are the official languages. Catholicism is the majority religion, but there are large Protestant (notably Hussite) groups in Bohemia and Moravia, and Orthodox Eastern and Uniate churches in Slovakia. The churches have been persecuted by Communist authorities. Czechoslovakia is highly industrialized, although historically Slovakia has been less advanced economically than Bohemia, and much recent effort has been directed toward reducing the disparity. More than one third of the total labor force is in industry. The major manufactured goods include machinery, transportation equipment, and other metal goods; iron and steel; chemicals; food products; and textiles and footwear. The country has large reserves of bituminous coal and lignite and some iron ore and other minerals, but iron must be imported to meet industrial needs. Agriculture accounts for only a small part of Czechoslovakia's national income and employs well under one fifth of the labor force, but it is highly developed and efficient. Ninety percent of the farmland is collectivized, and half of it is devoted to grains. Major crops are sugar beets, potatoes, fodder, wheat, barley, and oats. Additional grain must be imported. Czechoslovakia has extensive forests, particularly in Slovakia. Most of the country's trade is with the USSR and Eastern Europe. The main imports are fuel, raw materials, and foodstuffs. The main exports are manufactured goods such as machinery, transportation equipment, and textiles. (For history prior to 1918 as well as more detailed geographic and economic information, see BOHEMIA; MORAVIA; SLOVAKIA.) The creation of Czechoslovakia was the culmination of the long struggle of the Czechs against their Austrian rulers. It was largely accomplished by the nation's first and second presidents, T. G. MASARYK and

Eduard BENEŠ. The union of the Czech lands and Slovakia was officially proclaimed in Prague on Nov. 14, 1918; the Treaty of St. Germain (Sept., 1919) formally recognized the new republic. Ruthenia was added by the Treaty of Trianon (June, 1920). Because Czechoslovakia inherited the greater part of the industries of the Austro-Hungarian Monarchy, it was economically the most favored of the Hapsburg successor states. Benefiting from a liberal, democratic constitution (1920) and led by able statesmen, the new republic appeared to have a bright future. Redistribution of some of the estates of the former nobility and the church generally improved the living conditions of the peasantry. In foreign policy Czechoslovakia relied on its friendship with France and on its LITTLE ENTENTE with Yugoslavia and Rumania. Yet the new state was far from being a stable unit. With its antagonistic and nationalistic ethnic elements, it reflected the inherent weakness of the Hapsburg empire. The Czechs and Slovaks had separate histories and greatly differing religious, cultural, and social traditions. The constitution of 1920, which set up a highly centralized unitary state, failed to take into account the important problem of national minorities. The Germans and Magyars of Czechoslovakia openly agitated against the territorial settlements. Although the constitution provided for autonomy for Ruthenia, in practice autonomy was constantly postponed. The Slovak People's party accused the Czech government of having denied Slovakia promised autonomous rights. Hitler's rise in Germany, the German annexation of Austria, the resulting revival of revisionism in Hungary and of agitation for autonomy in Slovakia, and the appeasement policy of the Western powers left Czechoslovakia without allies, exposed to hostile Germany and Hungary on three sides and to unsympathetic Poland on the fourth. The nationality problem led to a European crisis when the German nationalist minority, led by Konrad Henlein and vehemently backed by Hitler, demanded the union of the predominantly German districts with Germany. Threatening war, Hitler extorted through the MUNICH PACT (Sept., 1938) the cession of the Bohemian borderlands (Sudetenland). Poland and Hungary obtained territorial cessions shortly thereafter. Beneš resigned the presidency in October and was succeeded by Emil Hacha. In Nov., 1938, the truncated state, renamed Czecho-Slovakia, was reconstituted in three autonomous units—Bohemia and Moravia, Slovakia, and Ruthenia. In March, 1939, Hitler forced Hacha to surrender Czecho-Slovakia to German control and made Bohemia and Moravia into a German "protectorate." Slovakia gained nominal independence as a satellite state. Ruthenia was awarded to Hungary. After the outbreak of World War II, Beneš set up a provisional government in London, and Czech units fought with the Allied forces. Except for the brutalities of the German occupation, Czechoslovakia suffered relatively little from the war. In April, 1944, Soviet forces, accompanied by a Czech coalition government headed by Beneš, and American troops entered Czechoslovakia; the fall (May 12, 1945) of Prague marked the end of military operations in Europe. Soviet and American troops were withdrawn later in the year. At the Potsdam Conference of 1945 the expulsion of about 3,000,000 Germans from Czechoslovakia and an exchange of minorities between Czechoslovakia and Hungary were approved. The country's pre-1938 territory was restored, except for Ruthenia, which was ceded to the USSR. In the elections of 1946 the Communists emerged as the strongest party (obtaining one third of the votes) and became the dominant party in the coalition headed by the Communist Klement Gottwald. Beneš was elected president. Soviet pressure prevented Czechoslovakia from accepting Marshall Plan aid (June, 1947). During the summer of 1947, the Communists began a campaign of political agitation and intrigue that gave them complete control of the government in Feb., 1948. In March, Jan MASARYK, the non-Communist foreign minister, died in mysterious circumstances. After the adoption of a new constitution (Beneš resigned rather than sign it), a new legislature was elected and enacted a program for nationalizing the economy. Czechoslovakia became a Soviet-style state. Political and cultural liberty was curtailed, and purge trials were conducted from 1950 to 1952. Riots occurred in 1953, reflecting economic discontent. A very modest liberalization trend was begun in response but was reversed in Nov., 1957, when Antonin Novotný became president. In 1960 a new constitution was enacted. Another cautious movement toward liberalization was initiated in 1963. Restrictions on the press, education, and cultural activities were eased, and local authorities received increased economic autonomy. Profit considerations were introduced into the economy. Czechoslovakia became celebrated internationally for its experimental theater work and its many fine films. But political power remained the exclusive possession of a small circle in the Communist party. That factor, the sluggishness of the economy (despite the reforms), and Slovak resentment over Novotný's Czech-dominated administration, produced the startling developments of 1968. Alexander Dubček, a Slovak, replaced Novotný as party leader in January; Ludvik Svoboda became president in March. Under Dubček democratization went further than in any other Communist state. Press censorship was reduced, and the restoration of a genuinely democratic political life seemed possible. Slovakia was granted political autonomy. Seriously alarmed at what it construed to be a threat to Soviet security and to the supremacy within the USSR of the Soviet Communist party, the USSR with its Warsaw Pact allies invaded Czechoslovakia in Aug., 1968. Dubček and other leaders were taken to Moscow. Despite opposition by the populace, the USSR forced the repeal of most of the reforms. A revised constitution was promulgated. (Slovakian autonomy was retained.) In April, 1969, Dubček was replaced as party leader, and in June, 1970, he was expelled from the party. In the early 1970s there were many efforts to stamp out dissent, including mass arrests, union purges, and religious persecution. Under the 1968 constitution, Czechoslovakia is a federal republic. The two component parts are the Czech Socialist Republic, with its capital in Prague, and the Slovak Socialist Republic, with its capital at Bratislava. There is a bicameral federal legislature elected every five years. The federal president, who is elected by the legislature, appoints the premier and ministers. Each republic has a council and assembly. The federal government deals with defense, foreign affairs, and certain economic matters. The Communist party, which is the actual source of power in the country, heads the National Front, which also includes figurehead political groups, trade unions, and youth organizations. See historical studies by R. J. Kerner (1940) and S. H. Thomson (2d ed. 1953, repr. 1965); Vratislav Bušek and Nicolas Spulber, ed., *Czechoslovakia* (1957); Miloslav Rechcigl, Jr., ed., *Czechoslovak Contribution to World Culture* (1964) and *Czechoslovakia Past and Present* (2 vol., 1968); Z. A. B. Zeman, *Prague Spring* (1969); William Shawcross, *Dubcek* (1970); G. Golan, *The Czechoslovak Reform Movement* (1971) and *Reform Rule in Czechoslovakia* (1972); Vojtech Mastny, *The Czechs under Nazi Rule* (1971); Ivan Sviták, *The Czechoslovak Experiment, 1968–1969* (1971); Vera Olivova, *The Doomed Democracy* (tr. 1972).

Czernin, Ottokar, Graf (ô′tōkär gräf chĕr′nĭn), 1872–1932, Austro-Hungarian foreign minister. He was an adviser to Archduke Francis Ferdinand. As foreign minister (1916–18) he sought a negotiated peace, but was unwilling to abandon Austrian war aims in Italy and the Balkans. He was one of the negotiators of the Treaty of BREST-LITOVSK. Czernin was dismissed after the private peace-making attempts of Emperor CHARLES I, extended through Prince SIXTUS OF BOURBON-PARMA, were dramatically disclosed by the French premier, Clemenceau.

Czernowitz: see CHERNOVTSY, USSR.

Czerny, Karl (chĕr′nē), 1791–1857, Austrian pianist; pupil of Beethoven and teacher of Liszt. He is known for his technical studies for the piano; his numerous other works are seldom performed.

Częstochowa (chĕN″stəkô′və), city (1970 pop. 187,613), S Poland, on the Warta River. It is an important railway and industrial center, known especially for its iron and steel plant and iron-smelting works. Other industries include sawmilling, papermaking, and the manufacture of metals, chemicals, and textiles. Iron ore is mined in the vicinity. Częstochowa is a celebrated religious center, and a world-famous place of pilgrimage. Its monastery stands on the Jasna Gora [mountain of light] and contains an image of Our Lady, supposedly painted by St. Luke and brought to Częstochowa in the 14th cent. In 1655, when Charles X of Sweden overran Poland, the prior and a handful of soldiers defended the monastery and its relic for 40 days until the Swedes abandoned the siege. Fired by what they thought to be a miracle, the Polish people rose to successful resistance. The event figures prominently in Henryk Sienkiewicz's novel *The Deluge.* The monastery was again defended against the Swedes in 1702. Venerated as the "Queen of Poland," the image became the national symbol of Poland.

Czolgosz, Leon F. (chŏl′gŏsh), c. 1873–1901, American anarchist, b. Detroit, Mich. He shot and killed William McKinley in Buffalo on Sept. 6, 1901, saying that the President was "an enemy of good working people." Czolgosz was later adjudged sane and was executed.

Czuczor, Gergely (gĕr′gĕlĭ tso͞o′tsôr), 1800–1866, Hungarian philologist and poet, a Benedictine monk. With John Fogarasi he compiled a Hungarian dictionary (completed 1861). He also wrote folk poetry and popular epics. Czuczor was imprisoned (1849–51) for his poem *The Alarm* (1848), which called Hungary to violent revolt against Austrian rule.

D

D, fourth letter of the ALPHABET. It corresponds to the Greek delta. It is a usual symbol for a voiced dental or, as in English, alveolar stop. The capital represents in MUSICAL NOTATION a note in the scale and in Roman numerals the number 500.

Dabareh (dăb'ərĕ), same as DABERATH.

Dabbasheth (dăb'əshĕth), border city of Zebulun. Joshua 19.11.

dabchick: see GREBE.

Daberath (dăb'ērăth), town, N Palestine, probably the present-day Dabburiya (Israel), on the slope of Tabor E of Nazareth. Joshua 19.12; 1 Chron. 6.72. Dabareh: Joshua 21.28.

Dablon, Claude (klōd däblôN'), 1619?–1697, French Jesuit missionary in North America. He went from France to Canada in 1655 and worked first among the Onondaga Indians in New York, then (1661) among the Cree Indians in the Hudson Bay region. In 1669 he went to take charge of the Western missions, with headquarters at Sault Ste Marie. He accompanied Father ALLOUEZ on one exploring journey in the Green Bay-Fox River country. Made superior of the Jesuits in Canada, he served from 1670 to 1680 and from 1686 to 1693 and was director of the great expansion of missionary and exploring work done by the Jesuits.

Dabo, Leon (dä'bō), 1868–1960, American painter, b. Detroit. He worked with John La Farge, studied in Paris under Puvis de Chavannes, and was influenced by Whistler and by Japanese landscape painting. Dabo's own landscapes of Hudson River scenes often employ mists and silvery half-lights. He painted numerous pictures of the sea, and his murals (1902) in the Church of St. John the Baptist, Brooklyn, N.Y., are well known. He also designed stained-glass windows. Dabo was one of the organizers of the Armory Show in 1913.

Dąbrowa Górnicza (dôNbrô'vä gôrnē'chä), Ger. *Dombrowa,* city (1970 pop. 61,660), SE Poland, on the Czarna Przemsza River, a tributary of the Vistula. It is a railway junction and a center of the Katowice mining and industrial region. Coal mining in the area dates from 1796. Metals, machine tools, glass, and electric motors are manufactured in the city. Dąbrowa Górnicza passed to Prussia in 1795 and to Russia in 1815. During the 19th cent. it was an important center for research in mining and metallurgy. The city reverted to Poland in 1919.

Dąbrowska, Marja (mär'yä dôNbrôf'skä), 1892–1965, Polish sociologist and novelist. Dąbrowska worked as a militant publicist to further social and economic reform. Her works of fiction, including the epic novel *Nights and Days* (1932–34) and *The Crossroads* (1937), treat the problems of social change. Her short stories (1955) criticize the Communist regime. See study by Zbigniew Folejewski (1967).

Dąbrowski, Jan Henryk (yän hĕn'rĭk dôNbrôf'skē), 1755–1818, Polish general. He distinguished himself in the insurrection led by Kosciusko in 1794. After its failure he went to France and organized (1797) a Polish legion, which he commanded in Napoleon's Italian campaign. In 1806, Napoleon had him recruit an army in Poland, and he subsequently distinguished himself in Napoleon's campaigns against Prussia, Austria, and Russia. Returning to Poland in 1813, Dąbrowski entered the service of Czar Alexander I and began to organize the new Polish army. He retired in 1816. His name is sometimes spelled Dombrowski.

Dacca (dăk'ə), city (1972 est. pop. 1,500,000), capital of Bangladesh, on a channel of the Dhaleswari River, in the heart of the world's largest jute-growing region. It is the industrial, commercial, and administrative center of Bangladesh, with an active trade in jute, rice, oilseeds, sugar, and tea. The city comprises three distinct sections: an old area of narrow streets and crowded bazaars; a modern part, called Ramna, with government and diplomatic establishments, hotels, and educational and cultural facilities; and a residential and industrial community N and W of Ramna. Between Dacca and its nearby river port of Narayanganj lies Bangladesh's greatest industrial concentration. Manufactures include textiles, cotton saris, jute products, paper, chemicals, hosiery, shoes, matches, soap, and glass. There are also printing and engineering plants. Dacca is famous for its cottage industries (especially confectioneries) and handicrafts (particularly gold and silver filigree work, embroidery, and shell carving). In the late 19th cent., competition from British cloth virtually put an end to the manufacture of Dacca's world-renowned muslins. Dacca's history dates back to A.D. c.1,000, but the city achieved its glory as the 17th-century Mogul capital of Bengal. English, French, and Dutch industrialists set up factories there in the 17th and 18th cent., and Dacca passed under British rule in 1765. It became the capital of East Pakistan in 1947. The city was surrendered by the Pakistani army to Indian troops in Dec., 1971, and a few days later became capital of the provisional government of Bangladesh. Landmarks include the Dakeshwari ["hidden goddess"] temple, from which the city's name probably derives; the Bara Katra palace (1644); the Lal Bagh fort (1678); and several beautiful mosques. The Univ. of Dacca (founded 1921) and other higher educational facilities and agriculture research institutes are also in the city. The surrounding district is a very densely populated and fertile agricultural region that is subject to heavy monsoon floods.

dace: see MINNOW.

Dachau (dä'khou), city (1970 pop. 32,349), Bavaria, S West Germany, on the Amper River; chartered in 1391. It is a rail junction and has industries that manufacture machinery, electrical equipment, and textiles. There is a 16th-century castle. Nearby was (1933–45) an infamous Nazi CONCENTRATION CAMP, which today has a number of memorials and a museum.

dachshund (däks'ho͝ond, -ənd, dăsh'-), breed of small, short-legged HOUND developed in Germany over hundreds of years. It stands from 5 to 9 in. (13–23 cm) high at the shoulder and weighs from 5 to 20 lb (2–9 kg). There are six varieties of dachshund: the smooth haired, with a short, glossy coat; the long-haired, with a soft and silky coat; the wirehaired, with a short, harsh coat; and miniatures of each of these types. The color may be black or chocolate marked with tan, or various shades of solid red. Originally bred to hunt badgers, the dachshund was later used on a wide variety of small ground game. The 12-lb (5-kg) miniature variety was perfected to hunt hares. Today the dachshund is raised primarily as a house pet. See DOG.

Dachstein, peak, Austria: see SALZKAMMERGUT.

Dacia (dā'shə), ancient name of the European region corresponding roughly to modern Rumania (including Transylvania). It was inhabited before the Christian era by a people who were called Getae by the Greeks and were called Daci by the Romans. They were a people of advanced material culture, with a tribal organization. Augustus claimed them as tributary allies but the Daci paid little heed, and Domitian, after inconclusive campaigns against them, was forced (A.D. 90) to pay them tribute to keep them quiet. TRAJAN invaded Dacia in A.D. 102 and again in 105. He established a large number of colonies, and Dacia became a Roman province. The Goths invaded (250–70) the region, and Aurelian was obliged to concede Dacia. It was the Roman colonists in Dacia who formed the Latin-speaking nucleus that established the Romance tongue Rumanian, which is still spoken in that region.

Dacko, David (däk'ō), 1932–, president of the Central African Republic (1960–66). He succeeded his cousin, Barthélémy BOGANDA, as head of government in 1959 and worked for a federation of the territories of French Equatorial Africa. When this project collapsed, he led the country to full independence and was elected president (1960). His inability to solve the republic's economic problems and the government's corruption led to his removal in a 1966 coup.

Da Costa, Isaäc: see COSTA, ISAÄC DA.

Da Costa, Uriel: see ACOSTA, URIEL.

Dacron, trademark for a polyester fiber. Dacron is a condensation polymer obtained from ethylene glycol and terephthalic acid. Its properties include high tensile strength, high resistance to stretching, both wet and dry, and good resistance to degradation by chemical bleaches and to abrasion. The continuous filament yarn is used in curtains, dress fabrics, high-pressure fire hoses, men's shirts, and thread. The staple fiber is ideal for mixing with wool in men's and women's suits, as well as in dress fabrics, knitted wear, and washable woven sportswear.

Dada (dä'dä) or **Dadaism** (dä'däĭzəm), international nihilistic movement among European artists and writers that lasted from 1916 to 1922. Born of the widespread disillusionment engendered by World War I, it originated in Zürich with the poetry of the Rumanian Tristan Tzara. Dada attacked conventional standards of aesthetics and behavior and stressed absurdity and the role of the unpredictable in artistic creation. In Berlin, Dada had political overtones, exemplified by the caricatures of George Grosz. The French movement was more literary in emphasis; it centered around Tristan Tzara, André Breton, Louis Aragon, Jean Arp, Marcel Duchamp, Francis Picabia, and Man Ray. The latter three artists carried the spirit of Dada to New York City. Typical were the elegant collages devised by Arp, Kurt Schwitters, and Max Ernst from refuse and scraps of paper, and Duchamp's celebrated *Mona Lisa* adorned with a mustache and a goatee. Dada principles were eventually modified to become the basis of SURREALISM in 1924. The literary manifestations of Dada were mostly nonsense poems—meaningless random combinations of words—which were read in public. See Hans Richter, *Dada: Art and Anti-Art* (1965); Robert Motherwell, ed., *The Dada Painters and Poets* (1951, repr. 1967); A. H. Barr, ed., *Fantastic Art, Dada, Surrealism* (1947, repr. 1968); W. S. Rubin, *Dada, Surrealism, and Their Heritage* (1968).

Daddah, Moktar Ould (mo͝okh'tär o͞old däd'dä), 1924–, president of Mauritania (1961–). A lawyer, he held a number of government posts before becoming (1958) premier when Mauritania joined the French Community. After Mauritania gained its independence, he became president.

Daddi, Bernardo (bārnär'dō däd'dē), fl. 1312–48, Italian painter of the Florentine school. First influenced by his contemporary Giotto, he soon adopted the delicate line and lyrical expression of the Sienese painters, especially the Lorenzetti. Among his dated works are a triptych (1328) in the Uffizi and an altarpiece (1333) in the Ospedale Bigallo, Florence. In the United States there are numerous paintings attributed to Daddi. These include panels of the *Madonna and Child* in the National Gallery of Art, Washington, D.C.; the Walters Art Gallery, Baltimore; and the Gardner Museum, Boston. See Richard Offner, *A Corpus of Florentine Painting* (Sec. III: Vol. III, 1930; Vol. VIII, 1958).

daddy longlegs, name applied to the HARVESTMAN, an arachnid, and to the CRANE FLY, an insect.

Dadra and Nagar-Haveli (dä'drä, nä'gär-hävä'lē), union territory (1971 pop. 74,165), 188 sq mi (487 sq km), E central India, on the Arabian Sea. Portugal colonized these two enclaves in the mid-16th cent. India occupied them in 1954. Despite a ruling by the International Court of Justice at The Hague that upheld Portugal's claim to the areas, they were incorporated into India as a single union territory in 1961.

Daedalus (dĕd'ələs), in Greek mythology, craftsman and inventor. After killing his apprentice Talos in envy, he fled from Greece to Crete. There, at the order of King Minos, he built the Minotaur's labyrinth. When Minos refused to let him leave Crete, Daedalus built wings of wax and feathers for himself and his son Icarus. Together they flew away, but Icarus flew too close to the sun and fell to his death when the wax melted. Daedalus escaped to Sicily.

daffodil: see AMARYLLIS.

Dagenham: see BARKING; REDBRIDGE.

Dagestan Autonomous Soviet Socialist Republic (dăgəstăn'), autonomous region (1970 pop. 1,429,000), c.19,400 sq mi (50,250 sq km), SE European USSR, bounded on the E by the Caspian Sea. MAKHACHKALA (the capital) and DERBENT are the chief cities. Dagestan in the south consists mainly of parts of the Caucasus mts. Except for the Caspian plain and the Nogai steppe and the irrigated lowlands in the north, the terrain is one of steep mountains divided by valleys. Difficulty of access has left most of Dagestan's mineral resources untapped; however, important quantities of oil and natural gas have been extracted along the coast. The irrigated lowlands support winter wheat, corn, sunflowers, fruits, and wine grapes. The republic's major industries produce canned fruit, wine, oil, machines, chemicals, textiles, and wood products. The Samur, Sulak, and other rivers provide hydroelectric power. Dagestan's terrain has encouraged the development of a multiplicity of ethnic groups, most of whom are Muslim. About half the population consists of indigenous Caucasian mountain peoples (Avars, Lezghians, Darghins, Lakhs); the rest is made up of Turkic (notably Kumyks) and Iranian groups (especially Tats), and, in the cities, Russians and Ukrainians. An ancient area of human settlement, Dagestan belonged to Caucasian Albania in the 1st millennium B.C. It was later invaded by Huns, Persian Sassanids, and, in the 7th cent. A.D., by Arabs, who introduced Islam. Taken by the Turks in the 11th cent. and the Mongols in the 13th cent., the region became the center of a struggle between Turkey and Persia in the 15th cent. It was a Persian province when Russia annexed it by the Treaty of Gulistan in 1813. Muslim mountaineers resisted Russian domination until 1859, and a new revolt erupted in 1877, during the Russo-Turkish war of that year. Dagestan came under Soviet rule in 1920 and in 1921 was made an autonomous republic.

Dagobert I (dăg'ōbûrt), c.612–c.639, Frankish king, son and successor of King Clotaire II. His father was forced to appoint Dagobert king of the East Frankish kingdom of Austrasia at the request of PEPIN OF LANDEN, mayor of the palace, and Arnulf, Bishop of Metz, who effectively ruled in Austrasia. After Clotaire's death (629) Dagobert reunited Aquitaine with Austrasia and Neustria and became king of all the Franks. He was, however, forced by popular demand to give (634) Austrasia its own king in the person of his son, Sigebert III. The last of the MEROVINGIANS to exercise personal rule, he made himself independent of the great nobles, especially of Pepin of Landen. Dagobert maintained a brilliant court and extended his suzerainty over the Basques and the Bretons.

Dagon (dā'gŏn), god of fertility, widely worshiped in the Near East, particularly in Canaan. In the Old Testament he is mentioned as one of the chief deities of the Philistines. Judges 16.23–30; 1 Sam. 5.1–5; 1 Chron. 10.8–10; 1 Mac. 10.83,84; 11.4.

Daguerre, Louis Jacques Mandé (lwē zhäk mäNdā' dägâr'), 1789–1851, French scene painter and physicist, inventor of the daguerreotype, a photograph produced on a silver-coated copper plate treated with iodine vapor. Known first for his illusionistic painted stage sets, Daguerre attracted further attention as the inventor and exhibitor, with C. M. Bouton, of the diorama (pictorial views seen with changing lighting), shown at the Diorama in Paris. In 1829 his experiments with the daguerreotype were joined with those of J. Nicéphore NIÉPCE, who had been doing related work since 1814. Until Niépce's death in 1833 they worked together on the photographic process. Daguerre completed the invention of the daguerreotype alone, and in 1839 it was made public and ceded to the Academy of Sciences, only a few weeks before the rival invention of the calotype was announced by William Henry Fox TALBOT. The daguerreotype was introduced into the United States by J. W. DRAPER and S. F. B. MORSE. See study by Helmut and Alison Gernsheim (rev. ed. 1968).

Daguesseau, Henri Françis: see AGUESSEAU, HENRI FRANÇOIS D'.

Dahl, Michael (däl), 1656–1743, Swedish portrait painter. In 1688, after traveling on the Continent, he settled in England. After the death of KNELLER in 1723, Dahl enjoyed an enormous popularity, painting Queen Anne and members of the aristocracy. Beyond a surface artificiality, Dahl's work reflects a considerable humanity. His paintings are to be seen in the National Portrait Gallery, London (e.g., *Self-Portrait*, 1691), and in Windsor Castle.

Dahlak Archipelago (däläk' ärkĭpĕl'əgō), island group, Ethiopia, in the Red Sea off Messewa. There are 2 large and 124 small islands. The pearl fisheries there were known to the Romans and still produce a few pearls. In the 7th cent. the group formed an independent Muslim state, but it was subsequently conquered by Yemen and, later, by the Ottoman Turks.

Dahlberg, Edward (däl'bərg), 1900–, American novelist, critic, and essayist, b. Boston, grad. Columbia, 1925. The illegitimate son of an itinerant hairdresser, he spent much of his childhood in Kansas City where his mother ran the Star Ladies' Barbershop. His childhood experiences were recreated in his first novel, *Bottom Dogs* (1930). Dahlberg has lived mostly in Europe. His works include the novel *Those Who Perish* (1934); volumes of mystical literary criticism such as *Do These Bones Live?* (1941); and studies of ancient societies such as *The Carnal Myth* (1968). See his autobiographical *Because I Was Flesh* (1964) and *The Confessions of Edward Dahlberg* (1971).

Dahlberg, Erik Jönsson, Count (ā'rēk yön'sən däl'-bĕrg), 1625–1703, Swedish military engineer, field marshal, and architect. In 1658 he conveyed the army of CHARLES X of Sweden across the frozen Little and Great Belt straits in a daring march on Copenhagen. As governor of Livonia, he held Riga through two sieges. His volume of architectural engravings is a valuable record of Sweden's monuments.

Dahlgren, John Adolphus Bernard (dăl'grən), 1809–70, American naval officer, b. Philadelphia. Appointed a midshipman in 1826, he had a long and honorable naval career. In charge of ordnance at the Washington navy yard after 1847, he expanded the ordnance facilities and designed the 9-in. (22.9-cm) and 11-in. (27.9-cm) guns that came to be called Dahlgrens. In the Civil War, Dahlgren received command of the Washington navy yard and soon became also chief of the Bureau of Ordnance. Promoted to rear admiral in 1863, he served as commander of the South Atlantic Blockading Squadron, cooperated (1863) with Gen. Q. A. Gillmore in the unsuccessful attempt to take Charleston, helped to place troops in Florida in 1864, cooperated with Sherman in taking Savannah, and in Feb., 1865, helped to occupy Charleston. He later held high posts and wrote widely on naval ordnance. See biography by his wife, Madeleine V. Dahlgren (1882).

dahlia (dăl'yə, dăl'-), [for Anders Dahl, 1751–89, Swedish botanist and pupil of Linnaeus], any plant of the genus *Dahlia* of the family Compositae (COMPOSITE family), tuberous-rooted perennials native to Mexico and Guatemala and widely cultivated in gardens. Most of the several thousand horticultural varieties have been developed from the single species (*D. pinnata*) of garden dahlia introduced into cultivation in England c.1800, but other species and hybrids, e.g., the cactus dahlia (*D. juarezii*) are also grown. Dahlias are stout and rather woody plants, some species reaching the stature of small trees, with late-blooming flowers in a wide range of colors and sizes. The tubers of the garden dahlia are one source of fructose, used by diabetics. Dahlias are classified in the division MAGNOLIOPHYTA, class Magnoliopsida, order Asterales, family Compositae.

Dahlmann, Friedrich Christoph (frē'drĭkh krĭs'tôf däl'män), 1785–1860, German historian. He was dismissed from his professorship at Göttingen for protesting (1837) the abrogation of the constitution by King Ernest Augustus of Hanover. He later taught at Bonn, and he was prominent in the Frankfurt Parliament (1848–49). His *Quellenkunde der deutschen Geschichte* [sources of German history] (1830), enlarged in many subsequent editions, is an indispensable aid to the study of German history.

Dahna: see RUB AL KHALI.

Dahomey (dəhō'mē, Fr. däōmā'), republic (1973 est. pop. 2,870,000), 43,483 sq mi (112,622 sq km), W Africa, bordering on Togo in the west, on Upper Volta and Niger in the north, on Nigeria in the east, and on the Bight of Benin (an arm of the Gulf of Guinea) in the south. PORTO-NOVO is the capital and COTONOU the largest city and chief port; other towns include ABOMEY, OUIDAH, and PARAKOU. Dahomey falls into four main geographic regions: in the south is a narrow coastal zone (1–3 mi/1.6–4.8 km wide) fringed on the north by a series of interconnected lagoons and lakes with only two outlets to the sea (at Grand-Popo and Cotonou). Behind the coastal region is a generally flat area of fertile clay soils; this is crossed by the wide Lama marsh, through which flows the Ouémé River. In NW Dahomey is a region of forested mountains (the Atacora; highest point c.2,150 ft/655 m), from which the Mekrou and Alibori rivers flow NE to the Niger River (which forms part of the country's northern border). In the northeast is a highland region covered mostly with savanna and containing little fertile soil. Dahomey's population is made up of black Africans, who are divided into four main linguistic groups—the Ewe, the Yoruba, the Voltaic, and the Fulani. The Ewe-speakers, who live in the south, in-

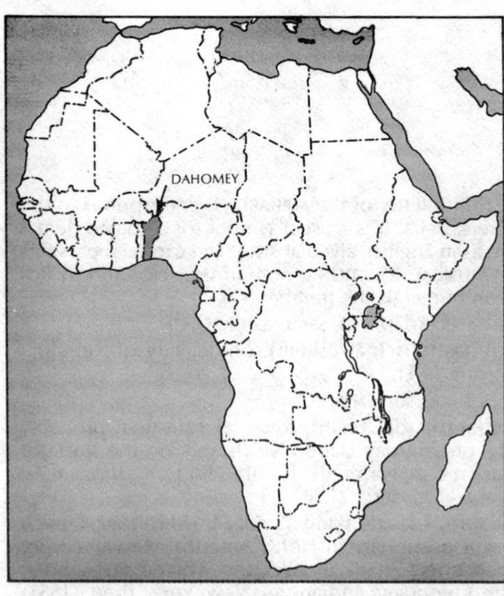

clude the Fon, or Dahomey (Dahomey's largest single ethnic group), Aja, Peda, and Chabe subgroups. The Yoruba live in the southeast near Nigeria, the group's main homeland. The Voltaic-speakers live in central and N Dahomey and include the Bariba and Somba subgroups. The Fulani live in the north. French is the country's official language. Most of the inhabitants follow traditional religious beliefs: 15% are Christian (largely Roman Catholic) and 13% (living mostly in the north) are Muslim. The economy of Dahomey is overwhelmingly agricultural, with the majority of workers engaged in subsistence farming. The chief crops are manioc, maize, cassava, millet, sorghum, groundnuts, pulses, cacao, cotton, and palm nuts and kernels. Large numbers of goats, sheep, and pigs are raised. There is a sizable freshwater fishing industry, and some sea fish are also caught. Most of Dahomey's few manufactures are either processed agricultural goods or basic consumer items; the main products include palm oil, palm-kernel oil, palmetto, soap, textiles, footwear, jute sacks, cement, and ginned cotton. The country's mineral resources, which include petroleum (discovered offshore in 1968), chromite, low-quality iron ore, ilmenite, and titanium, have not as yet been exploited on a large scale. Dahomey has limited rail and road systems, and they are almost exclusively in the southern and central parts of the country. Rail lines run along the coast and from the coast to Parakou and to Pobé; a line from Parakou to Niger is planned for the late 1970s. The chief imports are textiles, clothing, machinery, electrical equipment, foodstuffs, motor vehicles, tobacco, and metals; the principal exports are palm products, cotton, groundnuts, and cacao. The annual cost of imports usually far exceeds earnings from exports. The leading trade partners are France, the Netherlands, Nigeria, and the United States. Dahomey is an associate member of the European Common Market.

History. Little is known about the history of N Dahomey. In the south, according to oral tradition, a group of Aja migrated (12th or 13th cent.) eastward from Tado on the Mono River and founded the village of Allada. Later, Allada became the capital of Great Ardra, a state whose kings ruled with the consent of the elders of the people. Great Ardra reached the peak of its power in the 16th and early 17th cent. A dispute (c.1625) among three brothers over who should be king resulted in one brother, Kokpon, retaining Great Ardra. Another brother, Do-Aklin, founded the town of Abomey, and the third, Te-Agdanlin, founded the town of Ajatche or Little Ardra (called Porto-Novo by the Portuguese merchants who traded there). The Aja living at Abomey organized into a strongly centralized kingdom with a standing army and gradually mixed with the local people, thus forming the Fon, or Dahomey, ethnic group. By the late 17th cent. the Dahomey were raiding their neighbors for slaves, who were then sold (through coastal middlemen) to European traders. By 1700, about 20,000 slaves were being exported annually, especially from Great Ardra and Ouidah, located on what was called the SLAVE COAST. In order to establish direct contact with the European traders, King Agaja of Dahomey (reigned 1708–32), who began the practice of using women as soldiers, conquered most of the south (except Porto-

Novo). This expansion brought Dahomey into conflict with the powerful Yoruba kingdom of OYO, which captured Abomey in 1738 and forced Dahomey to pay an annual tribute until 1818. However, until well into the 19th cent. Dahomey continued to expand northward and to sell slaves. Dahomey's involvement in the slave trade had declined temporarily in the late 18th cent., severely dislocating the kingdom's economy. The economy revived under King Gezo (reigned 1818–58), who built up the army and raided Oyo, which had been weakened by civil wars, for slaves. He also began to trade palm products to French merchants established on the coast. In 1850, Great Britain sent a mission under Consul Beecroft to Gezo in an unsuccessful attempt to have the king cease trading slaves. In 1851, Gezo signed a commercial treaty with France. His successor, King Gelele (reigned 1858–89), pursued an aggressive policy toward his neighbors and vigorously engaged in the slave trade, thus in part causing Britain to annex Lagos in 1861. In 1862, Richard Burton, the British explorer, visited Gelele. In 1863, Porto-Novo accepted a French protectorate, hoping thereby to offset Dahomey's power. During the 1880s, as the scramble for Africa among the European powers accelerated, France tried to secure its hold on the Dahomey coast in order to keep it out of German or British hands. King Behanzin (reigned 1889–93) attempted to resist the French advance, but in 1892–93 France defeated Dahomey, established a protectorate over it, and exiled Behanzin to Martinique. During the period 1895–1898 the French added the northern part of present-day Dahomey, and in 1899 the whole colony was made part of FRENCH WEST AFRICA. Under the French a port was constructed at Cotonou, railroads were built, and the output of palm products increased. In addition, elementary school facilities were expanded, largely under the auspices of Roman Catholic missions. In 1946, Dahomey became an overseas territory with its own parliament (whose authority was limited to relatively unimportant local matters) and representation in the French national assembly. In 1958, Dahomey became an autonomous state within the FRENCH COMMUNITY, and on Aug. 1, 1960, it became fully independent. The country's first president was Hubert Maga, whose main support came from Parakou and the north and who was allied with Sourou Migan Apithy, a politician of Porto-Novo. Independent Dahomey has been plagued by governmental instability, caused by economic (especially fiscal) troubles, ethnic rivalries (especially between inhabitants of the north and south), and social unrest. In 1963, following demonstrations by workers and students, the armed forces staged a successful coup d'etat, putting Justin Ahomadegbé into power (in alliance with Apithy). In 1965 the military replaced this government with one headed by Col. Christophe Soglo. Soglo was ousted in late 1967, and a younger army officer, Lt. Col. Alphonse Alley, came to power with the goal of reestablishing civilian rule. Elections in May, 1968, were held under a cloud of suspicion (important politicians were not allowed to take part), and the results were subsequently disallowed. Later in 1968, Dr. Émile Zinsou was made president, and he gave way in 1969 to Lt. Col. Paul-Émile de Souza. Dahomey tried to hold elections in 1970, but severe disagreement between northern and southern politicians led to their cancellation. Instead, a three-man presidential council (consisting of Maga, Ahomadegbé, and Apithy) was formed; each member was to lead the country for two years. The first leader was Maga, who in May, 1972, was replaced without incident by Ahomadegbé. However, in Oct., 1972, the military again intervened, toppling Ahomadegbé and installing an 11-man government headed by Maj. Mathieu Kerekou. This was Dahomey's 11th change of government since 1960. See M. J. Herskovits, *Dahomey: An Ancient West African Kingdom* (2 vol., repr. 1967); Karl Polanyi and Abraham Rotstein, *Dahomey and the Slave Trade: An Analysis of an Archaic Economy* (1966); W. J. Argyle, *The Fon of Dahomey* (1966); I. A. Akinjogbin, *Dahomey and Its Neighbours, 1708–1818* (1967); Robert Cornevin, *Histoire du Dahomey* (1962) and *Le Dahomey* (2d ed. 1970).

daibutsu (dī'bo͝otso͞o) [Jap.,=great Buddha], Japanese name applied to colossal statues of Buddha, usually over 16 ft (5 m) in height. The most notable are those at Nara, Kamakura, and Kyoto. The bronze daibutsu at Nara, which has been restored many times, is 53 ft (16 m) high and dates from the 8th cent. The famous bronze Buddha of Kamakura of 1252 is 37 ft (11 m) high. The Buddha of Kyoto, originally made in 1586, has been destroyed and reconstructed many times; the present wooden statue is an unfinished replica from the 19th cent.

Daiches, David (dā'chēz), 1912–, English critic, b. Sunderland, grad. Edinburgh Univ. (M.A., 1934); Oxford (M.A., 1935; D. Phil., 1938). While teaching at various English universities he has written many valuable works of criticism. They include *The Novel and the Modern World* (1939), *A Study of Literature* (1948), *A Critical Approach to Literature* (1956), *A Critical History of English Literature* (1960), and *More Literary Essays* (1968). He has also written studies of Burns, Milton, Scott, Lawrence, and Virginia Woolf, and a biography of Charles Edward Stuart, *The Last Stuart: The Life and Times of Bonnie Prince Charlie* (1973).

Dáil Éireann (dôl ā'rôn, dīl âr'ən) [Irish,=diet of Ireland], the popular representative body of the Oireachtas, or National Parliament, of the Republic of Ireland. The second chamber, the Saenad Éireann, or Senate, has very limited powers, and the executive, as represented by the prime minister, is responsible to the Dáil, whose members are elected by universal adult suffrage. The members of the first Dáil were elected in Dec., 1918, ostensibly to the British Parliament, but they established themselves as a separate revolutionary body. It first convened at Mansion House, Dublin, in Jan., 1919, and proclaimed the Irish republic. The Dáil existed precariously until the creation of the Irish Free State in 1921, and established itself firmly in the period of civil war that followed. See also IRELAND; SINN FEIN. See study by J. L. McCracken (1958); Basil Chubb, *The Government and Politics of Ireland* (1970).

Daimiel (dīmyĕl'), town (1970 pop. 17,710), Ciudad Real prov., central Spain, in New Castile. It is an important farm center, with industries producing metal and alcoholic beverages. The town's Gothic church once belonged to the Knights Templars.

Daimler, Gottlieb (dām'lər, Ger. gôt'lēp dīm'lər), 1834–1900, German engineer, inventor, and pioneer automobile manufacturer. His improvements in the internal-combustion engine, made in the 1880s, contributed largely to the development of the automobile industry. In 1890 he founded the Daimler Motor Company at Cannstatt, Germany.

daimyo (dī'myô) [Jap.,=great name], the great feudal landholders of Japan, the territorial barons as distinguished from the kuge, or court nobles. Great tax-free estates were built up from the 8th cent. onward by the alienation of lands to members of the imperial family who could not be supported at court. These estates were administered by territorial barons, or the daimyo. By the 12th cent. certain daimyo had become more powerful than the emperor himself. One, YORITOMO, became the first SHOGUN and forcefully revised this situation by setting up a centralized feudal system. The power of the shogun disintegrated during the fierce civil wars of the 14th, 15th, and 16th cent., but in the early 17th cent. IEYASU completed the reunification of Japan. The daimyo who supported Ieyasu before the decisive battle of Sekigahara (1600) became the fudai, or hereditary vassals, and his opponents were known as tozama, or outside lords. The tozama, who controlled the rich western fiefs, were generally viewed with suspicion by the shogun and were excluded from office in the central government. Ieyasu's descendants, the TOKUGAWA shoguns, deployed the daimyo and shifted their fiefs to retain power in the central government. In the 18th and early 19th cent. the daimyo, with their tastes for luxury and need for show in long stays at the court, were hard pressed by the limits of their incomes (in general, tax revenue from peasants and merchants in their fief). They tended to sink deeper and deeper in debt, especially to the merchants of Tokyo and Osaka, while their social and economic usefulness approached the vanishing point. The daimyo were advised by a council of elders consisting of their highest-ranking vassals. The civil and military administration of the daimyo domains were staffed by the samurai. Pressured by their advisers, who argued that the Tokugawa regime was too weak to counter the Western threat, tozama barons of W Japan (notably Satsuma, Chosho, Tosa, and Hizen) joined the imperial court to overthrow the shogun in the MEIJI RESTORATION (1868). Convinced of the need to establish a centralized administration, these daimyo returned their fiefs to the emperor (1869). By 1871 all daimyo had lost their feudal privileges.

Dairen: see TA-LIEN, China.

dairying, industry concerned with producing, processing, and distributing milk and milk products. Ninety percent of the world's milk is obtained from cows; the remainder comes from goats, buffaloes, sheep, reindeer, yaks, and other ruminants. In the United States, 20% of the gross national income from agriculture is derived from dairying; Wisconsin, Minnesota, and New York are the most important dairy states. About one third of the milk produced is used for BUTTER, almost as much for market MILK, and the remainder is devoted to farm uses and the making of CHEESE, concentrated milks, ice cream, and by-products such as dried milk solids (e.g., LACTOSE and CASEIN). Commercial dairy products are processed or manufactured and then marketed by creameries, some of which, especially in Denmark, are farmers' cooperatives. Modern dairying dates from 1850, its development paralleling the growth of urban populations. Large-scale dairying was stimulated by the invention of specialized machines, notably the cream separator (see SEPARATOR, CREAM); by research in chemistry, physics, and bacteriology; by the discovery of PASTEURIZATION; by the introduction of the test devised by American agricultural chemist S. M. Babcock for determining the fat content of milk; by improved refrigeration and transportation; by the increase in output resulting from the scientific study of the breeding and feeding of CATTLE; by the greater consumption of dairy products resulting from increased knowledge of their nutritional value; and by the discovery of new uses for the by-products of factory operation. See J. G. Davis, *A Dictionary of Dairying* (2d ed. 1955, suppl. 1965); J. T. Schlebecker, *A History of American Dairying* (1967); K. N. Russell, *The Principles of Dairy Farming* (6th ed. 1972).

Daisetsu-zan (dīsā'tso͞o-zäN), group of volcanic peaks, central Hokkaido, Japan, rising to 7,513 ft (2,290 m) at Asahi-dake. They are part of Daisetsuzan National Park (895 sq mi/2,318 sq km; est. 1934), the largest national park in Japan.

daisy [O.E.,=day's eye], name for several common wild flowers of the family Compositae (COMPOSITE family). The daisy of literature, the true daisy, is *Bellis perennis,* called in the United States English daisy. This is a low European plant, cultivated in the United States mostly in the double form, with heads of white, pink, or red flowers. The English daisy, which closes at night, has long been considered the flower of children and of innocence. A purple species native to the lower Mississippi basin is called Western daisy (*Astranthum* or *Bellis integrifolium*). The common, often weedy, daisy of the United States (*Chrysanthemum leucanthemum*), called also white, or oxeye, daisy, is native to Europe but naturalized in America. The white daisy is one of the plants named marguerite, but the usual marguerite in cultivation is *C. frutescens,* a bushy perennial with white or lemon-yellow flowers, native to the Canary Islands and called also Paris daisy. Among other plants called daisy, yellow daisy is a synonym for the BLACK-EYED SUSAN; Michaelmas daisy, for an ASTER. The seaside daisy and daisy fleabane are species of the FLEABANE genus. Daisies are classified in the division MAGNOLIOPHYTA, class Magnoliopsida, order Asterales, family Compositae.

Daito (dī'tō), city (1970 pop. 93,136), Osaka prefecture, SW Honshu, Japan. It is a residential suburb of Osaka.

Dakar (dəkär', dä-), city (1973 est. pop. 585,000), capital of Senegal, W Senegal, on Cape Verde Peninsula, a port on the Atlantic Ocean. Situated in a market-gardening region, Dakar is Senegal's largest city and its administrative, communications, and economic center. Manufactures include refined sugar, peanut oil, fertilizers, cement, and textiles. Artisans make garments, furniture, and jewelry. The city is the busiest port in W Africa, serving Mali and Mauritania as well as Senegal, and has modern facilities for handling and storing goods. Dakar grew up around a French fort built in 1857 to protect the merchants and residents of nearby Gorée Island (now a Dakar suburb). The first major pier was completed in 1866. Dakar's importance increased significantly after 1855, when a railroad linked it with the Senegal River. In 1887 it was made a commune, along with Gorée, Rufisque, and St. Louis; the communes together elected a deputy to the French National Assembly. Dakar replaced St. Louis as the capital of French West Africa in 1902. In 1923 a new railroad linked Dakar with interior peanut-growing areas and the Niger River. In 1940, Free French forces under Gen. Charles DeGaulle fought unsuccessfully to free Dakar from Vichy control, but in late 1942 U.S. forces occupied the city and stayed to the end of World War II. Dakar was the capital of the short-lived (1959–60) Mali Federation. Today it is a modern city with a European appearance. Nearby are sandy beaches and a zoological and forest park. Dakar's Roman Catholic cathedral (inaugurated

1929) is the seat of an archbishop. The Univ. of Dakar (1949), the National School of Administration, a school for librarians, and a UN-administered institute of economic development and planning are in the city. It is also the site of the famous Institut fondamental d'Afrique noire, which promotes scholarly research in many fields. The city hosts many international conferences on artistic and scholarly topics. Dakar's Yoff international airport is the main stopping point for flights from Europe to South America.

Dakota Indians: see SIOUX INDIANS.

Daladier, Édouard (ädo͞oär' dälädyā'), 1884–1970, French politician, a Radical Socialist. After World War I he was a member of successive French cabinets. He was premier from Jan. to Oct., 1933, and again from Jan. to Feb., 1934, when the STAVISKY AFFAIR, which did not implicate him personally, caused serious riots in Paris and forced his resignation. In April, 1938, Daladier obtained the premiership and was also minister of national defense. He did his best to nullify the social and economic legislation enacted by the four previous cabinets and signed (Sept., 1938) the MUNICH PACT. From 1939 he was also minister of war and foreign affairs. He resigned as premier in March, 1940, because his failure to aid Finland's defense against Russia was unpopular, but he remained in the cabinet until the French collapse (June) in World War II. Arrested by the Vichy government in 1940, he was a defendant at the war-guilt trial at RIOM (1942), was interned by the Germans, and was liberated in 1945. Daladier was elected to the national assembly in 1946. He sat in the assembly until 1958.

Dalaiah (dăl″āī'ə), descendant of David. 1 Chron. 3.24.

Dalai Lama: see TIBETAN BUDDHISM.

Dalälven (däl'ĕl″vən), river, c.325 mi (520 km) long, Kopparberg co., W central Sweden, in the mountains along the Norwegian border. It flows SE to Avesta, then NE into the Gulf of Bothnia at Skutskar. The Västerdalälven is its chief tributary. The river passes through the Siljan agricultural region and the Bergslagen and Domnarvet iron-mining districts. Numerous cascades furnish power for industries.

Da Lat (dä lät), city (1968 est. pop. 84,000), South Vietnam, in the central highlands, alt. c.5,000 ft (1,520 m). Developed by the French as a health resort and hunting center, it is a modern city surrounded by mountains that rise to 7,380 ft (2,249 m). Coffee, tea, tobacco, and temperate-zone vegetables are commercially grown. The plateaus north of the city are considered one of the world's great hunting grounds; the big game includes elephants, bears, tigers, and leopards. Da Lat is linked by highway with Saigon and is on a branch rail line from the coastal city of Phan Rang. It has an airport. In the city are the Univ. of Da Lat and a noted military academy.

Dalberg, Emmerich Joseph (Emeric Joseph, duc de Dalberg) (ĕmərĕk' zhōzĕf' dälbârk'), 1773–1833, French diplomat of German origin; nephew of Karl Theodor von Dalberg. The foreign minister of Baden, he entered (1810) the service of French Emperor Napoleon I, who made him a duke and a councillor of state. A follower of Charles Maurice de TALLEYRAND, he served (1814) in the provisional government formed after the fall of Paris and supported the recall of the BOURBONS. In recompense he was made French plenipotentiary at the Congress of Vienna.

Dalberg, Karl Theodor, Freiherr von, 1744–1817, German statesman, of an ancient noble family prominent in imperial service. He was archbishop-elector of Mainz (1802–3) and, as such, archchancellor of the Holy Roman Empire. In 1803 the seat of the archbishopric was moved to Regensburg. A faithful collaborator of Napoleon I, Dalberg became (1806–13) prince-primate of the CONFEDERATION OF THE RHINE and grand duke of Frankfurt (1810–13). Dalberg was known for his humane and enlightened outlook.

Dalcroze, Émile Jaques: see JAQUES-DALCROZE.

Dale, David, 1739–1806, Scottish cotton manufacturer and philanthropist. In 1785 he built New Lanark, a cotton mill and model community that provided his employees with good housing and schools. He was succeeded at New Lanark by his son-in-law, Robert OWEN, who later made the community world famous. Dale withdrew in 1770 from the Church of Scotland, founding the Old Independents, or Dalites, whom he served as minister.

Dale, Sir Henry Hallett, 1875–1968, English scientist. For his study of acetylcholine as agent in the chemical transmission of nerve impulses he shared with Otto Loewi the 1936 Nobel Prize in Physiology and Medicine. He also investigated the pharmacology of ergot and histamine shock. He was director of the National Institute for Medical Research (1928–42), professor of chemistry and director of the Davy-Faraday Laboratory at the Royal Institution (1942–46), and president of the Royal Society (1940–45) and of the British Association for the Advancement of Science (1947). In 1932 he was knighted. His writings include *Adventures in Physiology* (1953) and *Autumn Gleanings* (1954).

Dale, Sir Thomas, d.1619, acting governor (May–Aug., 1611, 1614–16) of the Virginia colony. Sent by the London Company to restore order, he arrived (1611) in Virginia with three ships of settlers and governed until another fleet under Sir Thomas Gates arrived four months later. When Governor Gates departed (1614) Dale again ruled. Although Dale's administration was severe, famines, epidemics, insubordination, and Indian attacks were overcome; private holdings were instituted; cultivation of tobacco was begun; and the colony was settled in a more favorable location at Henrico. Upon his return to England, Dale received command of a fleet bound for India, fought the Dutch en route, and died soon after arrival.

D'Alembert, Jean le Rond: see ALEMBERT.

D'Alembert's principle (dăl'əmbâr″), in mechanics, principle permitting the reduction of a problem in dynamics to one in statics. This is accomplished by introducing a fictitious force equal in magnitude to the product of the mass of the body and its acceleration, and directed opposite to the acceleration. The result is a condition of kinetic equilibrium. Jean le Rond d'Alembert, a French mathematician, introduced the principle in 1742 and established it the next year in his *Traité de dynamique.* The principle shows that Newton's third law of motion applies to bodies free to move as well as to stationary bodies.

Daley, Richard Joseph, 1902–, U.S. political leader, b. Chicago. Admitted to the bar in 1933, he entered politics and served as a Democrat in the state assembly (1936–38) and the state senate (1939–46) and as director of revenues for Illinois (1949–50) before being elected (1955) mayor of Chicago. His long tenure both as mayor and as chairman (from 1953) of the Cook County Democratic party enabled him to build an extremely powerful political machine. Although often accused of unscrupulous political practices, Daley proved to be an efficient administrator. He achieved national notoriety in 1968 when Chicago police used brutal tactics to subdue demonstrators during the Democratic National Convention. See biographies by W. F. Gleason (1970) and Mike Royko (1971).

Dalhousie, James Andrew Broun Ramsay, 1st **marquess of** (dălho͞o'zē, -hou'-), 1812–60, British statesman. After serving as president of the Board of Trade (1845–47) he was governor general of India (1847–56). He annexed the Punjab (1849) after the British victory in the second Sikh War and lower Burma (1852) after the second Burma war. He also expanded British control by peaceful methods, annexing seven princely states on the basis of lapse (i.e., when the Indian rulers left no direct male heirs) and one state, Oudh, on the grounds of misgovernment. At the same time Dalhousie developed public works; planned the railway system, with which began heavy British investment in Indian economic development; encouraged western education; and instituted reforms in Hindu social practices, including authorizing the remarriage of widows. Dalhousie's policy of annexation was a factor in the outbreak of the INDIAN MUTINY, but he must be accounted one of the ablest and most effective governors general of India. He was created marquess in 1849. See his letters (1910, repr. 1973); biography by W. W. Hunter (1890, repr. 1961); study by M. A. Rahim (1963).

Dalhousie University (dălhou'zē), at Halifax, N.S., Canada; nonsectarian; coeducational; founded 1818 by the 9th earl of Dalhousie. Except for a few years between 1838 and 1845, Dalhousie did not function as a university until 1863. It has faculties of arts and science, graduate studies, dentistry, law, medicine, and health professions, as well as schools of nursing, physiotherapy, physical education, dental hygiene, and pharmacy. It has research institutes in public affairs, medicine, mental retardation, pharmacy, pathology, and oceanography. The Univ. of King's College (founded 1789) is associated with it.

Dali, Salvador (sälväthōr' dä'lē), 1904–, Spanish surrealist painter. At first influenced by FUTURISM, Dali began in 1924 to imitate the Italian CHIRICO. By 1929 he had become a leader of SURREALISM. His precise style enhanced the nightmare effect of his paintings. Among his best-known works is *Persistence of Memory* (1931; Mus. of Modern Art, New York City). In 1940 Dali emigrated to the United States. He wrote *The Secret Life of Salvador Dali* (1942). Dali has also made surrealist ventures in films, advertising, and the ballet. See his diary, ed. by Michel Déon (tr. 1965); studies by J. T. Soby (1946, repr. 1970) and Carlton Lake (1969).

Dalin, Olof von (o͝o'lôv fən dälēn'), 1708–63, Swedish historian, poet, and journalist, the foremost figure of the Swedish Enlightenment. In his successful career in the civil service, Dalin served as royal librarian (1737–39), tutor to the future Gustavus III (1750–56), royal historiographer (1755–56), and king's councillor (1763). His periodical, the *Swedish Argus* (1733–34), helped to introduce the Enlightenment in Sweden and won for Dalin the title "the Voltaire of the North." Dalin's prose masterpiece, the allegorical *Tale of the Horse* (1740), uses folk material to satirize the relations between the Swedish people (the horse) and the monarchy (the master). Most of his writings were more notable as skillful imitations than as creative efforts. They include essays, plays, lyric poetry, and humorous prose, all highly regarded in his time. His *History of the Swedish Kingdom* (4 vol., 1746–62) ridiculed confused theories of Sweden's Gothic origins.

Dallapiccola, Luigi (lo͞oē'jē däl″läpēk'kōlä), 1904–, Italian composer, b. Pisino, Istria (then Austria, now Yugoslavia). Dallapiccola was in an Austrian detention camp during World War I, and, because his wife is Jewish, he suffered persecution under Mussolini. He was the first Italian composer of atonal music. His strong interest in vocal music is revealed in his operas *The Prisoner* (1944–48) and *Odysseus* (1968); the oratorio *Job* (1950); and the Christmas Concerto (1956) for soprano and orchestra. He has also written instrumental concertos, ballets, and orchestral works.

Dallas, Alexander James, 1759–1817, U.S. Secretary of the Treasury (1814–16), b. Jamaica, West Indies. He went (1783) to Philadelphia, practiced law, and was secretary of state (1791–1801) and U.S. district attorney (1801–14) in Pennsylvania. Appointed Secretary of the Treasury by President Madison, Dallas succeeded to the office near the close of the War of 1812, when treasury affairs were in an extremely critical conditon. He pushed Congress to levy taxes heavier than any previously borne in the United States and asked for the reestablishment of the BANK OF THE UNITED STATES. Under Dallas's administration confidence in U.S. currency was restored. After securing Madison's veto on the first bank bill, which did not suit him, Dallas largely dictated the second bill, which John C. Calhoun forced through Congress; it became law in 1816. See biographies by his son George Mifflin Dallas (1871) and Raymond Walters, Jr. (1943, repr. 1969).

Dallas, George Mifflin, 1792–1864, American statesman, Vice President of the United States (1845–49), b. Philadelphia; son of Alexander James Dallas. He read law, was admitted (1813) to the bar, and was secretary to Albert Gallatin. After serving as solicitor (1815–17) of the Bank of the United States, Dallas was city attorney (1817–19) and mayor (1819) of Philadelphia. An active Democrat, he was appointed (1829) U.S. district attorney for E Pennsylvania, then served as a U.S. Senator (1831–33), as attorney general of Pennsylvania (1833–35), and as minister to Russia (1837–39). He returned to his law practice, and a sharp political rivalry developed between him and James Buchanan in Pennsylvania. In 1844, Dallas was elected Vice President on the Democratic ticket along with James K. Polk. Dallas was later appointed (1856) minister to Great Britain and was succeeded (1861) in that post by Charles Francis Adams. Dallas conducted the negotiations leading to the Dallas-Clarendon Convention, signed in 1856, which set a basis for the settlement of difficulties in Central America. He also secured from Great Britain a disavowal of the right of search, a historic matter of dispute. He wrote a biography (1871) of his father. See his letters from London (1869) and his diaries (1892) while a minister to Great Britain and Russia.

Dallas, city (1970 pop. 844,401), seat of Dallas co., N Texas, on the Trinity River near the junction of its three forks; inc. 1871. Its manufactures include cotton-processing machinery, textiles, leather goods, and aircraft and electronic equipment. Oil is refined, and there are meat-packing plants. Founded c.1841, Dallas was early populated by French artisans and gentlemen who abandoned the nearby Fourierist community, La Réunion. Dallas developed as a cotton market in the 1870s. Later it became the financial (particularly insurance) and commercial center of the Southwest. In 1970 the metropolitan area (including such places as Grand Prairie and Garland), included over 1.5 million people. A branch of the Univ. of Texas, a theological seminary, and the schools of dentistry and nursing of Baylor Univ. are in Dallas. A noted fashion center, the city is also known for its museums, its musical activities, and its interest in literature and the drama (the Dallas Theatre Center boasts the only public theater ever designed by Frank Lloyd Wright). The city is served by an expanding reservoir system utilizing the waters of the Trinity River. The annual Texas State Fair is held in Dallas. President John F. Kennedy was assassinated in Dallas on Nov. 22, 1963. The Dallas–Fort Worth Regional Airport, the largest commercial airport in the world, was opened in 1974.

Dalles, The, Oregon: see THE DALLES.

Dalling and Bulwer, Baron: see BULWER, WILLIAM HENRY LYTTON EARLE, BARON DALLING AND BULWER.

Dalmanutha (dălmənyōō'thə), a place, probably on the W shore of the Sea of GALILEE, where Jesus came apparently to be tempted by the PHARISEES. Mark 8.11. In a parallel passage it is mentioned as Magadan. Mat. 15.39. The place is unidentified, and Dalmanutha may have resulted from the misreading of Magadan or MAGDALA.

Dalmatia (dălmā'shə), Serbo-Croatian *Dalmacija,* historic region of Yugoslavia and province of Croatia, extending along the Adriatic Sea, approximately from Rijeka (Fiume) to the Gulf of Kotor. SPLIT is the provincial capital; other cities include ZADAR (the historic capital), ŠIBENIK, and DUBROVNIK. Except for a coastal lowland, Dalmatia is generally mountainous, rising to the Dinaric Alps. The coast, which is famed for its scenic beauty and its resorts, has many bays and excellent harbors protected by a chain of islands. Although Dalmatian rivers are mostly unnavigable, they supply a substantial portion of Yugoslavia's hydroelectricty. Agriculture, fishing, and tourism are the principal economic activities. There is also industry and mining in the region. The bulk of the population consists of Roman Catholic Croats; there are also Eastern Orthodox Serbs and some Italians (mainly at Zadar and nearby cities). Long in conflict with Rome, Dalmatia was definitively subdued by Augustus (35 B.C.–33 B.C.) and was incorporated with part of Illyria as a Roman province. It was overrun by the Ostrogoths (5th cent. A.D.), reconquered by the Byzantine Empire (6th cent.), and settled, except in the coastal cities, by the Slavs in the 7th cent. By the 10th cent. it was divided between the kingdoms of Croatia (north) and Serbia (south), while Venice held several ports and islands. After several centuries of struggle, chiefly between Venice and the crowns of Hungary and Croatia, the coastal islands and most of Dalmatia, except Dubrovnik, were under Venetian control by 1420. Hungary retained the Croatian part, which in 1526 passed to the Turks but was recovered by the Treaty of Karlowitz (1699). The Treaty of Campo Formio (1797) gave Venetian Dalmatia to Austria, and the Treaty of Pressburg (1805) gave it to France. It was first attached to Napoleon's Italian kingdom but in 1809 was incorporated into the Illyrian provs. (see ILLYRIA). The Congress of Vienna restored (1815) it to Austria, where it was made (1861) a crown land, with its capital at Zara. By the secret Treaty of London (1915) the Allies promised Dalmatia to Italy in return for Italian support in World War I. In Dec., 1918, it became part of the newly established kingdom of Serbs, Croats, and Slovenes (after 1929 Yugoslavia), but Italy continued to claim Dalmatia. The Treaty of Rapallo (1920) gave Dalmatia to Yugoslavia, except for Zara and several islands, which subsequently passed to Italy. During World War II, Italy held most of Dalmatia, and after the war it was returned to Yugoslavia. The Italian peace treaty of 1947 gave Yugoslavia the islands that had been ceded to Italy after World War I.

Dalmatian (dălmā'shən), breed of hardy, strong-bodied NONSPORTING DOG probably developed in the Austrian province of Dalmatia (now Yugoslavia) several hundred years ago. It stands from 19 to 23 in. (48.3–58.4 cm) high at the shoulder and weighs from 35 to 50 lb (15.9–22.7 kg). Its short, dense, hard coat is glossy white with black or dark-brown spots. Long associated with horses and valued for its speed, endurance, and dependable nature, the Dalmatian has also been called the coach dog and the firehouse dog. In addition to its historical service as protector and companion to carriages, it has also successfully assumed many other roles, e.g., sentinel, draft animal, shepherd, sporting dog, and circus performer. Today it is largely raised as a companion and pet. See DOG.

Dalmáu, Luis (lōōēs' dälmou'), fl. 1428–60, Spanish primitive painter, court painter to Alfonso of Aragon. His only undisputed work, *Virgin with Councilors* (Barcelona), shows the influence of Jan van Eyck, which indicates that he may have visited Flanders.

Dalny: see TA-LIEN, China.

Daloa (dä'lwä), town (1967 est. pop. 42,150), W central Ivory Coast. It is the market center for a fertile region producing coffee, kola nuts, cacao, rice, cassava, cotton, and timber. The French established a post in Daloa in 1904.

Dalou, Aimé-Jules (ĕmā'-zhül dälōō'), 1838–1902, French sculptor. He was popular under the Third Republic. Dalou studied with Carpeaux and was later exiled (1871–79) to England for his revolutionary sentiments. He taught in London. His best-known works are his *Triumph of the Republic* (Place de la Nation, Paris), his reliefs for the chamber of deputies, and his *Silenus* and monument to Delacroix (both: Luxembourg Gardens). His work was baroque in its sources although his style is often considered naturalistic. Dalou was particularly skilled in portraiture.

Dalphon (dăl'fən), one of Haman's sons. Esther 9.7.

Dalrymple, James: see STAIR, JAMES DALRYMPLE, 1ST VISCOUNT.

Dalrymple, John: see STAIR, JOHN DALRYMPLE, 1ST EARL OF, and STAIR, JOHN DALRYMPLE, 2D EARL OF.

Dalton, Hugh (Edward Hugh John Neale Dalton) (dôl'tən), 1887–1962, British politician and economist. He was educated at Cambridge and at the London School of Economics, where he became a lecturer. He was elected a Labour member of Parliament in 1924. As undersecretary of state for foreign affairs he represented (1929) Britain at the League of Nations and negotiated the evacuation of British and French troops from the Rhineland. On losing his seat in Parliament (1931) he continued to teach at the Univ. of London, wrote widely, and worked against the Labour party's policy of opposition to rearmament. He served in the coalition war cabinet as minister of economic warfare (1940–42) and president of the Board of Trade (1942–45) and in the postwar Labour government as chancellor of the exchequer (1945–47). He resigned when his budget proposals were leaked. He remained in the Labour government, however, and was active in politics until 1957. He was created a baron (a life peerage) in 1960. See his memoirs (3 vol., 1953–62).

Dalton, John, 1766–1844, English scientist. He revived the ATOMIC THEORY, which he formulated in the first volume of his *New System of Chemical Philosophy* (2 vol., 1808–27). He had already applied the concept to a table of atomic weights (1803), in a paper (1805) on the absorption of gases, and in developing his famous law of partial pressures, known also as DALTON'S LAW. His interest in weather conditions led him to keep daily records from 1787 and to write *Meteorological Observations and Essays* (1793). Dalton, himself afflicted with color blindness, investigated (c.1794) the condition, known also as Daltonism. From 1793 he taught mathematics and physical sciences at New College, Manchester. He was a member of the Royal Society (from 1822) and in 1825 received its medal for his work on the atomic theory. See study by Arnold Thackray (1972).

Dalton, city (1970 pop. 18,872), seat of Whitfield co., extreme NW Ga., in the Appalachian valley; inc. 1847. It is a highly industrialized city in a farm area; its large tufted-textile industry was begun in the late 1800s. In the Civil War, Dalton (Confederate headquarters after the Chattanooga campaign) fell to Sherman in the Atlanta campaign (1864). A junior college is there. The Chickamauga and Chattanooga National Military Park is nearby.

Dalton plan: see PROGRESSIVE EDUCATION.

Dalton's law [for John Dalton], physical law that states that the total pressure exerted by a homogeneous mixture of gases is equal to the sum of the partial pressures of the individual gases. The partial pressure of a gas is the pressure it would exert if all the other gases in the mixture were absent.

Daly, Arnold, 1875–1927, American actor, b. Brooklyn, N.Y. He first appeared on the stage in 1892. Inspired by Richard Mansfield's production of *The Devil's Disciple* (1897–98), Daly determined to present Shaw on the American stage, and in 1903 he came into prominence when he played successfully in *Candida.* His production of *Mrs. Warren's Profession* (1905) caused an uproar and the arrest of the principal actors, but they were immediately acquitted. The following year Daly toured with *Arms and the Man* and *The Man of Destiny.* See biography by B. H. Goldsmith (1927).

Daly, Augustin, 1838–99, American theatrical manager and dramatist, b. Plymouth, N.C. After 1859 he was drama critic for several New York City newspapers and adapted many plays from French and German. In 1867 he made his debut as manager with his melodrama *Under the Gaslight,* and in 1869 he opened his first theater, the Fifth Avenue. A few years later he established the famous Daly's Theatre on Broadway, with a company headed by John Drew and Ada Rehan. Here he presented, along with his own adaptations, magnificent productions of Shakespearean comedies. In 1893 he established a London theater, known later as Daly's, where he took his company annually. His meticulous concern with details earned him both devotion for his inspired direction and hatred for his paternalistic handling of his company. See biography by J. F. Daly (1917); Marvin Felheim, *The Theatre of Augustin Daly* (1956).

Daly, Marcus, 1841–1900, American copper magnate, b. Ireland. He went to New York City at 15 and later moved to California, where he worked as a miner. He was employed by the "silver kings," J. G. Fair and J. W. Mackay, at the Comstock Lode. In 1876 he was sent by a large company to investigate the silver mines at Butte, Mont. Discovering that there was rich copper beneath the silver, he purchased the Anaconda silver mine and tested the copper. Then, with the backing of George Hearst and others, he quietly bought up neighboring mines and formed a mining company. He built a smelter at Anaconda and connected it by rail with Butte. He was so successful that Anaconda became almost a household word in the United States. Daly purchased coal mines to fuel his furnaces, bought forests to supply his timber, and built power plants to supply the mines. He also established a number of banks. His great rival was William A. CLARK, and their bitter struggle for control kept the copper industry in turmoil; the contest for power included other men, notably F. Augustus HEINZE. Though Daly himself did not seek public office, his effective political machine thwarted Clark's ambitions for many years. The feud dominated Montana politics and economy. Daly also established a newspaper, the influential Anaconda *Standard.* See C. G. Glasscock, *The War of the Copper Kings* (1935, repr. 1971).

Daly City, city (1970 pop. 66,922), San Mateo co., W Calif., a suburb of San Francisco; inc. 1911. Settled in 1906 by refugees from the San Francisco earthquake, Daly City is still primarily residential. The "Cow Palace," scene of the 1964 Republican national convention, is there. Daly City is the southern terminus of the Bay Area Rapid Transit System.

Dalyell or **Dalzell, Thomas** (both: dăl'yəl, dēēl'), 1599?–1685, Scottish soldier; also called Dalziel of Binns. He fought for Charles II at the battle of Worcester (1651), was captured, escaped, and took service in Russia. Returning to Scotland after the Restoration (1660), he became commander of the forces charged with suppressing the COVENANTERS.

Dam, Henrik (hăn'rēk däm), 1895–, Danish biochemist. He identified vitamin K in 1934 and later investigated the role of vitamin E in nutrition. The 1943 Nobel Prize in Physiology and Medicine was awarded jointly to Dam and to E. A. Doisy for their work on vitamin K. In 1946, Dam became professor of biochemistry at the Polytechnic Institute, Copenhagen, and in 1956 he became head of the biology division of the Danish Fat Research Institute.

dam, barrier, commonly across a watercourse, to hold back water, often forming a reservoir or lake. Dams are made of timber, rock, earth, masonry, or concrete or of combinations of these materials. Timber is seldom used in dams because timbers are impermanent and their height is limited. Rock-fill dams consist of an embankment of loose rock with either a core impervious to water (e.g., clay) or a watertight face on the upstream side. Earth dams may be either simple embankments of earth or embankments reinforced with a core of cement or with an upstream surface made watertight. Masonry and concrete dams are either gravity dams or arch dams (either single-arch or multiple-arch). Gravity dams are dependent upon their own weight for resistance to the pressure of the water. Single-arch dams are curved upstream and are usually constructed in narrow canyons or gorges where the rocky side walls are strong enough to withstand the tremendous thrust of the dam that is caused by the pressure of the water. Dams of the multiple-arch type consist of a number of single arches supported by buttresses. Dams have been constructed from early times to provide a ready supply of water for irrigation and other purposes. One of the earliest large dams for this purpose was a marble structure built c.1660 in Rajputana (Rajasthan), India. Many modern dams are constructed for multiple purposes, e.g., to provide for irrigation, to aid flood control, and to furnish power for hydroelectric plants. Some dams are built to improve the navigability of waterways. In the 20th cent. many dams have been constructed in the United States (see CENTRAL VALLEY PROJECT; MISSOURI RIVER BASIN PROJECT; TENNESSEE VALLEY AUTHORITY). The tallest dam in the United States is the OROVILLE DAM. Located in California, it is 770 ft (235 m) high. The largest dam in total volume in the United States is the FORT PECK DAM, which is located in Montana. A large dam in the Panama Canal Zone forms GATÚN LAKE. Notable dams are found in Egypt across the Nile (see ASWAN) and along many other important rivers, e.g., the Dnepr, Tigris, Euphrates, Indus, Ganges, Huang Ho, and Zambezi (see KARIBA DAM). A dam used only to impound water is often called a barrage. See A. H. Cullen, *Rivers in Harness: The Story of Dams* (1962); Norman Smith, *A History of Dams* (1970).

damages, money award that the judgment of a court requires the defendant in a suit to pay to the plaintiff as compensation for the loss or injury inflicted. Damages are the form of legal redress most commonly sought. With a few exceptions, English courts of law traditionally afforded only this remedy, while the grant of damages in courts of EQUITY was solely incidental to other relief, such as INJUNCTION. The purpose of damages is to compensate the injured party for the loss that he has suffered and will probably suffer from the defendant's illegal conduct. Thus, in a suit for physical injuries the plaintiff may seek recovery for the pain he endured and his accrued medical expenses and for probable loss of earnings due to disability during the period of his incapacity. In suing for breach of contract the plaintiff need not prove the extent of his loss if the contract specified the "liquidated" damages, i.e., the probable loss from breach. Where there is a question as to the amount of damages, the jury usually makes the assessment. While the ordinary object of damages is simply to compensate the injured party to the extent of the injury, where there was fraud or deliberate wrongdoing, exemplary or punitive damages may be allowed. Many statutes thus provide for double or treble damages. In some instances where the extent of the loss cannot be determined or the injury is slight, nominal damages (e.g., a penny) may be granted. Usually the losing party is required to reimburse the winning party for having put him to legal expense. In England reasonable counsel fees are recoverable, while in the United States only those expenses fixed by statute are recoverable. In some states of the United States, however, even the winning party may be required to pay compensation if by delay or other improper conduct he added to his opponent's legal costs. When damages and legal costs are awarded they become a LIEN on the debtor's property, which the creditor may seize and sell if the debtor does not meet his obligation. In some states, if the debtor attempts to put his property out of reach, an injunction ordering him to pay may be issued.

damalisk, name for African antelopes of the genus *Damaliscus,* closely related to the hartebeest. Damalisks are slenderly built and rather horselike in form; they are common grazing animals of the African grasslands. They vary in color from deep reddish brown to tan; many have black markings on the face and body. The horns sweep back, up, and inward, in the form of a lyre. Different common names are applied to the different species and races. The sassaby, *Damaliscus lunatus,* is a large damalisk, standing nearly 4 ft (120 cm) at the shoulder; it is found in N South Africa. Blesbok and bontebok are names for the two races of the small S African damalisk, *D. dorcas;* both stand under 3½ ft (105 cm) tall and are deep red with white patches on the face and rump. Both the blesbok and the bontebok are extinct in the wild but are preserved on farms and in parks. The three races of *D. korrigum,* found in E, central, and W Africa, are known respectively as the tiang, topi, and korrigum. A rare damalisk species, *D. hunteri,* is known as Hunter's hartebeest; its long, narrow face resembles that of the true hartebeests. It is now restricted to a small area of Kenya and Somalia. Damalisks are classified in the phylum CHORDATA, subphylum Vertebrata, class Mammalia, order Artiodactyla, family Bovidae.

Daman, India: see GOA, DAMAN, AND DIU.

Damanhur (dämänho͝or'), city (1970 est. pop. 161,400), capital of Buhayrah governorate, N Egypt, in the Nile River delta. It is a communications center and a market for cotton and rice. In Roman times it was called Hermopolis Parva.

Damar: see DHAMAR, Yemen.

Damaris (dăm'ərĭs), woman converted at Athens. Acts 17.34.

Damas, Léon (lāôN' dämä'), (Léon-Gentran Damas), 1912–, French poet, b. French Guiana. With Léopold SENGHOR and Aimé CÉSAIRE he was one of the first supporters of negritude, a black consciousness movement. His poetry mirrors his intense personality; it is agitated and syncopated in both syntax and graphic representation on the page. Anthologies of his verse include *Black-Label* (1956) and *Pigments* (1962). His *African Songs of Love, War, Grief, and Abuse* (1961) contains brief verses sympathetically portraying village life in Guiana. He has also published an autobiographical work, *Return to Guiana* (1938).

Damascene, John: see JOHN OF DAMASCUS, SAINT.

damascening (dăməsēn'ĭng) or **damaskeening** (-skēn'ĭng), the art of decorating iron, steel, or bronze with inlaid threads of gold or silver, or producing a watered effect in forging, as in sword blades, gun barrels, and various metal objects. The method, long practiced in the Middle East as well as in China and Japan, was highly developed in Italy. The inlay forms a delicate and intricate pattern upon the contrasting background. The whole fabric is penetrated by the ornamental treatment, so that grinding does not remove it.

Damascus (dəmăs'kəs), Arabic *Dimashq* or *ash-Sham,* city (1970 est. pop. 835,000), capital of Syria and of its Damascus governorate, SW Syria, on the eastern edge of the Anti-Lebanon mts. It is Syria's largest city and its administrative, financial, and communications center. Damascus stands in the oasis of Ghouta on the margins of the Syrian Desert, and is bisected by the Barada River. Manufactures include textiles, metalware, refined sugar, glass, furniture, cement, leather goods, preserves, confections, and matches. The city is served by a railroad, highways, and an international airport. Located in a strategic spot commanding the Barada River and transdesert routes, Damascus has been inhabited since prehistoric times and is reputedly the oldest continuously occupied city in the world. There was a city on its site even before the time (c.2000 B.C.) of ABRAHAM (Gen. 14.14; 15.2). Damascus was probably held by the Egyptians before the Hittite period (2d millennium B.C.) and was later ruled by the Israelites and ARAM. TIGLATHPILESER III made it (732 B.C.) a part of the Assyrian Empire. From the 6th to the 4th cent. B.C. it was a provincial capital of the Persian Empire until it passed (332 B.C.) without a struggle to the armies of Alexander the Great. After Alexander's death the Seleucids (see SELEUCIA) gained control of the city, although the Ptolemaic dynasty of Egypt tried to wrest it from them. When Seleucid power waned, TIGRANES of Armenia took Damascus; but after his surrender to the Romans, Damascus passed (64 B.C.) into the Roman Empire under Pompey. One of the cities of the DECAPOLIS confederacy, it was generally under Roman influence until the breakup of the empire. Damascus became a thriving commercial city, noted for its woolen cloth and grain, and was early converted to Christianity. It was on the road to Damascus that PAUL (d. 67) experienced his dramatic conversion, and it was from Damascus that he escaped persecution by being lowered down the wall in a basket (Acts 9; 2 Cor. 11.32). The Roman emperor THEODOSIUS I had a Christian church built there (A.D. 379) on the foundations of the Roman temple of Zeus (1st cent. A.D.). After the permanent split (395) of the Roman Empire, Damascus became a provincial capital of the Byzantine Empire. However, the Arabs, who had attacked and sporadically held the city since before the time of Paul, occupied it permanently in 635. The city was then gradually converted to Islam, and the Christian church built by Theodosius was rebuilt (705) as the Great Mosque. Damascus was the seat of the caliphate under the Umayyads from 661 until 750, when the Abbasids made Baghdad the center of the Muslim world. Damascus thereafter fell prey to new conquerors—the Egyptians, the Karmathians, and the Seljuk Turks (1076). Although the Christian Crusaders failed in several attempts to annex the city, they ravaged the rich alluvial plain several times while the Saracen rulers, notably NUR AD-DIN (1118–74) and SALADIN (1137?–1193), were absent on campaigns. Damascus continued to prosper under the Saracens; its bazaars sold brocades (damask), wool, furniture inlaid with mother of pearl, and the famous swords and other ware of the Damascene metalsmiths. In 1260 the city fell to the Mongols under HULAGU KHAN, and it was sacked c.1400 by TAMERLANE, who took away the swordmakers and armorers. In 1516, Damascus passed to the Ottoman Turks, and for 400 years it remained in the Ottoman Empire. There was a massacre of Christians by Muslims in 1860, and in 1893 a disastrous fire damaged the Great Mosque. In World War I, Col. T. E. LAWRENCE helped to prepare the British capture of Damascus; it was entered (1918) by British Field Marshal ALLENBY and Emir Faisal (later King FAISAL I of Iraq). After the war the city became the capital of one of the French Levant States mandated under the League of Nations. In 1925–26, Damascus joined with the DRUSES in revolt against the French, who shelled and badly damaged the city. During World War II, Free French and British forces entered Damascus, which became capital of independent Syria in 1941. When Syria and Egypt joined to form the UNITED ARAB REPUBLIC in 1958, Cairo was made the capital, with Damascus the capital of the Syrian region. Syria withdrew from the United Arab Republic in 1961. Damascus Univ. (1923), Damascus Oriental Institute of Music (1950), a technological institute (1963), an industrial school (1964), and the national museum (1919) are in Damascus. The old city lies south of the Barada, and the new town (greatly extended since 1926) lies north of the river. Points of interest include the Great Mosque (one of the largest and most famous mosques in the Muslim world), the quadrangular citadel (originally Roman; rebuilt 1219), a 16th-century Muslim monastery, and Azm palace (1749; now a museum and center for the study of Islamic art and architecture). The biblical "street which is called Straight" (Acts 9.11) still runs in the old city from the east to the west gate, flanked by bazaars. See Colin Thubron, *Mirror to Damascus* (1967).

Damascus ware, early siliceous-glazed semiporcelain produced in Damascus. The most common decoration is in blue and black. However, purple, sage green, and, rarely, a red can be found. Made mainly in the 14th cent., it arrived in Europe via Venice as the container of exotic foods. After the contents were eaten, the bowls were kept as treasured possessions.

damask (dăm'əsk) [from Damascus], fabric of silk, wool, linen, cotton, or man-made fibers, with a pattern formed by the weaving; e.g., the ground may be in twill weave, and the contrasting design in satin. True damasks are flat and reversible, thus differing from brocades. Splendid patterns, silks, and dyes were used by the Damascus weavers, sometimes with the addition of gold or silver thread. Fine linen table damask is one of the most beautiful examples of the modern weavers' art, in both pattern and texture. Double damask has more picks, or threads, to the inch than single; compound damask has one or two warps and two fillings.

Damasus I, Saint (dăm'əsəs), c.305–384, pope (366–84), a Spaniard; successor of Liberius. His election was opposed by the Arian Ursinus (antipope 366–67). The Roman emperor Valentinian I had Ursinus exiled and decreed that all religious cases must come before the pope. Damasus ruled with vigor, addressing the entire church with authority. He encouraged the papal secretary St. Jerome in his work on the Vulgate, and undertook to memorialize the early martyrs by placing inscriptions on their tombs. He was succeeded by St. Siricius. Feast: Dec. 11.

Damavand or **Demavend** (both: dĕm'əvĕnd), volcanic cone, 18,934 ft (5,771 m) high, in the Elburz range, N Iran; highest peak in Iran. A permanently snow-covered volcano of recent geologic origin, it emits gases and small quantities of sulfurous materials; lava flows have impounded local streams, creating many small lakes. There are mineral springs and fruit orchards on Damavand's slopes. The mountain is the traditional scene of the feats performed by such legendary heroes of ancient Persia as Rustam and Faridun; it was immortalized in the great epic poem, the *Shahnameh.*

d'Amboise, Jacques: see AMBOISE, JACQUES D'.

Dambul (dämbo͞ol') or **Dambulla** (dämbo͞ol'ə), village, central Sri Lanka (Ceylon). It has notable cave temples of the 1st cent. B.C. and is a place of Buddhist pilgrimage. There is a recumbent Buddha figure 47 ft (14 m) long.

Damiani, Pietro: see PETER DAMIAN, SAINT.

Damien, Father (dā'mēən, dämyăN'), (Damien de Veuster), 1840–89, Belgian missionary priest, originally named Joseph de Veuster. He went to Hawaii (1864) as a Picpus Father (Father of the Sacred Heart of Jesus and Mary). He was ordained (1864) in Honolulu and worked among the islanders for several years. In 1873, at his request, he was sent to the lepers' colony on Molokai island, where he labored until his death from leprosy. Attention was called to Father Damien by a tract in his defense by R. L. Stevenson, *An Open Letter to the Reverend Dr. Hyde,* addressed to a minister who had made some slanderous insinuations against Father Damien shortly after his death. In 1936 his body was removed in great state from Molokai to Antwerp. See biography by Gavan Daws (1973).

Damietta: see DUMYAT, Egypt.

Damocles (dăm'əklēz), in classical mythology, courtier at the court of Dionysius I. He so persistently praised the power and happiness of Dionysius that the tyrant, in order to show the precariousness of rank and power, gave a banquet and had a sword suspended above the head of Damocles by a single hair. Hence the expression "the sword of Damocles" to mean an ever-present peril.

Damodar (dä'mōdär), river, 370 mi (595 km) long, rising in Bihar state, E India, and flowing SE through West Bengal state to join the Hooghly River below Calcutta. Its dams supply electricity to Calcutta and the Hooghlyside industrial district.

Damoh (dəmō'), town (1971 pop. 59,993), Madhya Pradesh state, central India. It is a district administrative center and a market for metal products, handwoven cloth, soap, cattle, and oilseed.

Damon and Pythias (dā'mən, pĭth'ēəs), two youths whose loyalty to each other symbolizes true friendship. Pythias, condemned to death for plotting against Dionysius I of Syracuse, was given leave to arrange his affairs after Damon pledged to give his own life if his friend did not return. When Pythias returned just in time to take his own place for execution, Dionysius was so impressed by their loyal friendship that he released them both.

Damophon (dăm'əfŏn), fl. 2d cent. B.C., Greek sculptor of Messene. He is remembered for colossal heads of Demeter and Artemis, found in Arcadia. He was a skilled worker in ivory and gold.

damp, in mining, any mixture of gases in an underground mine, especially oxygen-deficient or noxious gases. The term *damp* probably is derived from the German *dampf,* meaning fog or vapor. Several distinct types of damp are recognized. Firedamp is METHANE and other flammable gases, often mixed with air; it results from the decomposition of coal or other carbonaceous materials. Explosive mixtures of firedamp with air usually contain from 1% to 14% methane. The mixture of gases that remains after a firedamp explosion is called afterdamp; it consists chiefly of carbon dioxide and nitrogen. Chokedamp is any mixture of oxygen-deficient mine gases that causes suffocation. (In England, carbon dioxide is called chokedamp.) Several methods are used for detection of damps. The Davy SAFETY LAMP is one of the earliest detection devices. The color and height of the lamp flame indicate the amount of firedamp present; if the flame is extinguished, chokedamp is present. Canaries were formerly kept in mines; the birds are overcome by relatively small quantities of noxious gases, and their death warned the miners of the presence of damps. Special colorimetric detectors are now used. The methanometer is a special portable instrument used to detect firedamp.

Dampier, William (dăm'pēr), 1651?–1715, English explorer and buccaneer. He fought (1673) in the Dutch War, managed a plantation in Jamaica, then worked with logwood cutters in Honduras (1675–78). After taking part in a buccaneering expedition against Spanish America (1679–81), he sailed from Virginia in 1683 on a piratical voyage along the coast of Africa, across the Atlantic, and around Cape Horn to prey on Spanish cities on the west coast of South America. The party split up, and Dampier joined a group that crossed to the Philippines. Dampier was marooned (probably voluntarily) on the Nicobar Islands. After many hardships, he returned to England in 1691. He published an account of his experiences in *A New Voyage round the World* (1697), supplemented by *Voyages and Descriptions* (1699), which included *Discourse of Trade-Winds,* a masterly treatise on hydrography. Dampier was made a naval officer and commanded an expedition (1699–1701) to Australia, New Guinea, and New Britain (which he discovered to be an island and named). Other discoveries included Dampier Archipelago and Dampier Strait. His vessel, the *Roebuck,* finally foundered off Ascension island. Dampier commanded an unsuccessful privateering expedition (1703–7) in the course of which Alexander SELKIRK was voluntarily marooned. Dampier's account was published in his *Voyage to New Holland* (Part I, 1703; Part II, 1709). Though an excellent hydrographer and navigator, he proved an incompetent commander, guilty of drunkenness and overbearing conduct. He was pilot to Woodes Rogers on a voyage around the world (1708–11). See editions of Dampier's writings by John Masefield (1906) and Sir Albert Gray (1927, repr. 1968); biographies by Joseph Shipman (1962) and Christopher Lloyd (1966).

Damrosch, Frank Heino (hī'nō dăm'rŏsh), 1859–1937, German-American conductor and educator, attended the College of the City of New York; son of Leopold Damrosch. In 1885, after a few years in Denver, he became chorus master and assistant conductor of the Metropolitan Opera, New York City, remaining in that position until 1891. He organized the Musical Art Society, an a cappella chorus, in 1893. He supervised (1897–1905) the music of the public schools of New York and conducted (1898–1912) the Oratorio Society and the Symphony Concerts for Young People. His most important work was the founding in 1905, with James Loeb, of the Institute of Musical Art (later a unit of the Juilliard School), which he directed until 1933. See biography by L. P. Stebbins and R. P. Stebbins (1945).

Damrosch, Leopold, 1832–85, German conductor. After taking a degree in medicine, he became (1857) first violinist in the ducal orchestra at Weimar, where he was a friend of Liszt and Wagner. In 1871 he came to New York City, where he founded the Oratorio Society in 1873 and the New York Symphony Society in 1878, conducting both until his death. He introduced (1884) German opera at the Metropolitan, New York City, and led American premières of works by Brahms and Wagner.

Damrosch, Walter Johannes, 1862–1950, German-American conductor and composer; son of Leopold Damrosch. At his father's death in 1885, he finished the season as conductor of the Metropolitan Opera, New York City, and conducted there with Anton Seidl until 1891. In 1894 he organized the Damrosch Opera Company, which introduced opera in many American cities. In 1900 he returned to the Metropolitan for two seasons. After a season with the New York Philharmonic, he conducted the New York Symphony. When the two orchestras merged, he stayed on as the director, leaving in 1927 to devote his time to radio broadcasting. His outstanding contribution in that field was his series of children's concerts during school hours. He also composed music for the theater and several operas, notably *Cyrano de Bergerac* (1913) and *The Man Without a County* (1937).

damselfish, common name for members of the large family Pomacentridae, marine fishes of tropical waters. Common in the West Indies and along the Florida coasts are the sergeant-major, named for its vertical stripes, and the reef fish, found among coral reefs. The clownfish and blue devil are popular aquarium species. Males of this family guard the eggs zealously. Damselfishes rarely grow to more than 6 in. (15 cm) in length. Certain damselfishes are found associated with sea anemones, which are injurious to the fishes' predators, and which afford protection to the damselfish. Damselfish are classified in the phylum CHORDATA, subphylum Vertebrata, class Osteichthyes, order Perciformes, family Pomacentridae.

damselfly: see DRAGONFLY.

Damville, Henri, comte de: see MONTMORENCY, HENRI, DUC DE, the elder.

Dan. **1** Son of Jacob and Bilhah and founder of one of the 12 tribes of Israel. Their allotment in SW Palestine was the smallest, and its occupants, the Amorites, were most hostile. This hostility caused the larger part of the tribe to march north where they established themselves. They shared the lot of the northern Hebrews. Gen. 30.6; 46.23; 49.16,17; Ex. 31.6; Num. 1.38,39; 2.25,31; 10.25; 26.42; Deut. 27.13; 33.22; Judges 1.34; 5.17,18; Joshua 19.40–48; 1 Chron. 12.35; 27.22; 2 Chron. 2.14. **2** City, northernmost landmark of Palestine, hence the expression "from Dan to BEERSHEBA." Its original name was Laish or Leshem; it was renamed by the conquering Danites. Gen. 14.14; Deut. 34.1; Joshua 19.47; Judges 18.29; 1 Sam. 3.20; 1 Kings 15.20; 2 Chron. 16.4; 30.5. See DANJAAN. **3** Communal settlement in Israel, near the source of the Dan River.

Dana, Charles Anderson (dā'nə), 1819–97, American newspaper editor, b. Hinsdale, N.H. He was a member of the BROOK FARM community for five years. In 1847 he began 15 years on the New York *Tribune,* most of that time as managing editor. When Dana's views on the conduct of the Civil War became too militant for the editor, Horace Greeley, Dana resigned. His reports as a special investigator in the West for the War Dept. helped to build up official confidence in General Grant. In 1864, Dana became Assistant Secretary of War. His *Recollections of the Civil War* (1898) are valuable. He is best remembered for his great career as editor of "the newspaperman's newspaper," which began in 1868 when Dana became editor and part owner of the New York *Sun.* Though his editorials were erratic—he denounced the corruption in Grant's administration and refused to support labor unions and civil service reform—and often cynical, as a news editor he established high standards of readability and maintained a famous staff of writers. He also wrote *The Art of Newspaper Making* (1895) and *Eastern Journeys* (1898). See biography by C. J. Rosebault (1931); study by Candace Stone (1938, repr. 1969).

Dana, Francis, 1743–1811, American diplomat, b. Charlestown, Mass. Son of a prominent lawyer, he was himself a lawyer. He went as a colonial agent to England, then served as a delegate to the Massachusetts provincial council (1776–80) and the Continental Congress (1776–78), before accompanying (1779) John Adams on his mission to Paris. In 1780, Dana was sent to Russia. Although he stayed at St. Petersburg for two years (1781–83), he was never recognized or accredited. He later was a justice of the Massachusetts supreme court (1785–1806), becoming chief justice in 1791. Richard Henry Dana (1787–1879) was his son. See biography by W. P. Cresson (1930).

Dana, James Dwight, 1813–95, American geologist, b. Utica, N.Y., grad. Yale, 1833. He was the geologist and mineralogist on the U.S. expedition to the antarctic regions and the South Seas commanded by Charles Wilkes (1838–42). Dana's reports, published in large folio volumes with elaborate plates and an atlas, included *Zoophytes* (1846), *Geology* (1849), and *Crustacea* (1852–55). He became editor with Benjamin Silliman of the *American Journal of Science* and in 1846 succeeded Silliman at Yale as professor of natural history and geology. Revisions of his *System of Mineralogy* (1837) and *Manual of Geology* (1862) long remained standard works, and his *Corals and Coral Islands* (1872) and *Characteristics of Volcanoes* (1890) were authoritative. See biography by D. C. Gilman (1899, repr. 1973).

Dana, John Cotton, 1856–1929, American librarian and museum director, b. Woodstock, Vt. He was a lawyer and a civil engineer before joining the staff of the Denver (Colo.) Public Library in 1889, where he instituted the first branch for children. In 1902 Dana became head of the Newark (N.J.) Public Library, which under his direction offered new services to the public including a branch for businessmen. In 1909 the Newark Museum was founded, with Dana as its director until 1929. Dana was a pioneer in library advertising and in library printing and was one of the founders of the Special Libraries Association and its first president. He was president (1895–96) of the American Library Association. Among his many publications are *A Library Primer* (1899) and *The New Museum* (1917).

Dana, Richard Henry, 1787–1879, American poet and essayist, b. Cambridge, Mass.; son of Francis Dana. After studying law, he was admitted to the bar in 1811. Critic and poet, Dana was a founder and editor of the *North American Review* and also contributed to other periodicals. His best-known poem, *The Buccaneer,* appeared in 1827. See his collected *Poems and Prose Writings* (1850). His son, **Richard Henry Dana,** 1815–82, b. Cambridge, Mass., was also a writer and a lawyer. After spending two years (1831–33) at Harvard, he shipped as a common sailor around Cape Horn to California. The narrative of this voyage, published as *Two Years before the Mast* (1840), was written to secure justice for the sailor and has become an American classic of the days of sailing ships. Returning to Harvard, Dana graduated in 1837 and entered law practice. He handled many maritime cases and published *The Seaman's Friend* (1841), a standard manual of the law of the sea. Active in politics, he helped found the Free-Soil party. See his journal, ed. by R. F. Lucid (3 vol., 1968); biography by C. F. Adams (1890).

Danaë (dăn'āē), in Greek legend, daughter of Acrisius. When it was prophesied that Danaë's son would kill Acrisius, her father imprisoned her in a brass tower. However, Zeus came to her in the form of a shower of gold, and she bore him a son, PERSEUS. Acrisius put Danaë and Perseus into a chest and threw them into the sea, but they floated safely to land and the prophecy was eventually fulfilled.

Da Nang (dənăng', dän äng), formerly **Tourane** (tŏŏrän', -rän'), city (1968 est. pop. 334,000), NE South Vietnam, a port on the South China Sea. The second largest city in South Vietnam, it has an excellent deepwater harbor (dredged and improved by the United States) and is a busy commercial port on the railroad from Saigon to the demarcation line in the north. Its commercial airport, also modernized by the United States, is one of the largest in the area. A cotton mill is in the city. Da Nang Bay was the scene (1535) of the first landing of Europeans in Vietnam. The city was originally ceded to France by ANNAM in 1787 and became (after 1858) a French concession. It was the site of a huge U.S. military base during the Vietnam War. A copper seam is at Duc Bo, just south of the city, and coal and gold have been mined c.30 mi (50 km) to the southwest.

Danann: see TUATHA DE DANANN.

Danaüs (dăn'āəs), in Greek mythology, son of Belus and Anchinoe and twin of Aegyptus. Danaüs, who had 50 daughters, the Danaïds, and Aegyptus, who had 50 sons, ruled Libya and Arabia. When Belus died the brothers quarreled, and Danaüs fled with his daughters to Argos in Greece. There he became so powerful a ruler that the Greeks called themselves the Danai after him. Nevertheless, Aegyptus' sons pursued them and besieged Argos, demanding the Danaïds in marriage. Danaüs, forced to consent, instructed his daughters to kill their husbands on the wedding night. All obeyed but one; Hypermnestra spared Lynceus, who in some versions of the legend killed Danaüs and became king himself. For their crime the other Danaïds were condemned in Hades to the eternal task of filling a sieve with water. The *Suppliants* of Aeschylus is the first and only extant play of a trilogy dealing with the daughters of Danaüs.

Danbury, city (1970 pop. 50,781), Fairfield co., SW Conn., in a farm area; settled 1685, inc. as a city 1889. Its hat industry dates from 1780. Other manufactures include electronic equipment, plastics, machinery, and furniture. An early military depot, Danbury was the object of Gen. William Tryon's 1777 raid, which, although repulsed, resulted in the destruction of much of the village and the death of David Wooster; Wooster is buried in Wooster Cemetery. The famous Danbury Hatters' Case (1902) resulted in a U.S. Supreme Court ruling (1908) prohibiting boycotts by labor unions. In the city are Western Connecticut State College and a Federal prison. Among the old homes the David Taylor House (1750) and the Dodd House (1770)—both included in the Scott-Fanton Museum—are noteworthy. Danbury was the subject of lectures and writings by James Montgomery Bailey. It is also known for its state fairs, held annually since the early 1800s.

Danbury Hatters' Case, decided in 1908 by the U.S. Supreme Court. In 1902 the hatters' union instituted a nationwide boycott of the products of a nonunion hat manufacturer in Danbury, Conn., and the manufacturer brought suit against the union for unlawfully combining to restrain trade in violation of the Sherman Antitrust Act. The Supreme Court held that the union was subject to an INJUNCTION and liable for the payment of treble damages. This precedent for Federal court interference with labor activities was later modified by statutes.

Danby, Francis, 1793–1861, British historical and landscape painter. He painted many romantic and imaginary scenes and excelled in depicting sunrise and sunset. A good example of his work is *Conway Castle* (British Mus.). See study by Eric Adams (1973).

Danby, Thomas Osborne, earl of, 1631–1712, English statesman. Under the patronage of the 2d duke of Buckingham, he was appointed treasurer of the navy (1668), a privy councilor (1672), and lord treasurer (1673–78). A staunch royalist, he was also a fervent Anglican and thus opposed to alliance with France. He ended (1674) England's participation in the third Dutch War and arranged (1677) the marriage of Princess Mary to the Dutch William of Orange. However, while telling Parliament that he was raising money for war with France, he was at the same time negotiating reluctantly at Charles II's behest for a French alliance (1677). Impeached for treasonable communications with the French (1678), he was imprisoned (1679–84). Danby's firm Protestantism led him to support the opposition to James II, and he was a signatory of the request (1688) to William and Mary to become sovereigns. Despite his suspected Jacobite sympathies, he continued to be influential under the new monarchs; in 1690 he was made president of the council. Impeached again (1695), in connection with a bribe from the East India Company, he resigned. Although exonerated and restored to royal favor, he did not return to office. He was created marquis of Carmarthen in 1689 and duke of Leeds in 1694. See biography by Andrew Browning (3 vol., 1944–51).

Dance, George, the elder, 1700?–1768, English architect. Among his public buildings in London, the most important is the Mansion House (1739–52), now regarded as a debased example of the neo-Palladian style. He built the churches of St. Botolph, Aldgate, and St. Leonard, Shoreditch. His son, **George Dance,** the younger, 1741–1825, also an architect, studied in Italy. In 1768 he became one of the four original members of the Royal Academy. He was a powerful and inventive designer, as evidenced in his renowned Newgate Prison (1770–78). Among his many other London works were designs for Finsbury Square and for Alfred Place and Crescent. Sir John SOANE was his pupil. See study by Dorothy Stroud (1972).

dance [Old High Ger. *danson*=to drag, stretch], the art of precise, expressive, and graceful human movement, usually performed in accord with musical accompaniment. Dancing developed as a natural expression of united feeling and action. Many primitive dances have survived in the FOLK DANCE of modern times. American Indian dances illustrate most of the purposes of primitive dancing and are usually of a ritualistic and ceremonial nature: the war dance, expressing prayer for success and thanksgiving for victory; the dance of exorcism, performed by medicine men to drive out evil spirits; the dance of invocation, calling on the gods for help in farming, hunting, the fertility of men and animals, and other tribal concerns; initiation dances for secret societies; mimetic dances, illustrating events in tribal history, legend, or mythology; dances representing cosmic processes; and, more rarely, the dance of courtship, an invocation for success in love. The dance of religious ecstasy, in which hypnotic or trancelike states are induced (a characteristic phenomenon of the Orient and of Africa), was represented in America by the remarkable GHOST DANCE. American Indian dancing is always performed on the feet, but in many islands of the Pacific and in the Orient some of the dances are performed in a sitting posture, only the hands, arms, and upper parts of the body being used. Ancient Egyptian dances, often of a religious character, were derived from primitive African forms. In Greece the choral dance in honor of Dionysus played a part in the development of the drama. In India dance and drama have usually been related, both generally having religious significance. An elaborate code of movements of the arms and hands (mudras), expressive use of the face and especially of the eyes, and a sinuous posturing of the body are important features of Indian classical dancing, among the best-known examples being Kathakali and the Bharata Natyam, both of S India. The early dances of Japan, probably influenced by ancient Chinese forms, became institutionalized with the establishment of a national school of dancing in the 14th cent. Soon the dance became associated with the famous no drama (see ORIENTAL DRAMA). Secular dances are performed by the GEISHA. In medieval Europe the repeated outbreaks of dance mania, a form of mass hysteria sometimes caused by religious frenzy and usually associated with epidemics of bubonic plague, are reflected in the allegory of the dance of death (see DEATH, DANCE OF). Dancing as a social activity and a form of entertainment is of relatively recent origin. During the Middle Ages, especially in France, dancing was a feature of the more enlightened and convivial courts. Some medieval dances, such as the *volta*, precursor of the waltz, became the sources of modern dance steps. In the 16th cent. two types of dance were popular, the solemn and stately dances performed at the court of Charles IX and the lively peasant dances. The BALLET first appeared in Italian courts in the 16th cent., and it became popular in France, especially during the reign of Louis XIV. Among the formal dances of the 17th cent. were the courante, SARABAND, pavan, MINUET, GAVOTTE, quadrille (or contredanse), and cotillion. Music, which had developed to accompany dancing, had, by this time, evolved many forms and rhythms no longer associated with the dance. French dances made their way to England in the 17th cent. where variations of the MORRIS DANCE were frequently performed in villages and small towns. Popular national dances include the MAZURKA and POLONAISE from Poland; the czardas from Hungary; the FANDANGO, BOLERO, *seguidilla, and* FLAMENCO from Spain; the TARANTELLA and saltarello from Italy; the WALTZ and galop from Germany; the polka and schottische from Bohemia; the strathspey and HIGHLAND FLING from Scotland; the HORNPIPE from England; and the JIG from Ireland. The United States initiated the barn dance, Virginia reel, clog dance, cakewalk, and Paul Jones in the 19th cent., the two-step c.1890, the turkey trot (one-step) c.1900, and the fox-trot c.1912. The popularity of JAZZ in the early 1920s produced a number of new social dances, of which the most popular was the CHARLESTON. From South America came the Argentine tango and the Brazilian maxixe and samba; from Cuba, the rumba, conga, and mambo. Since the 1920s America has seen a wave of dance crazes, among them the Lindy Hop of the 1930s, the boogie woogie and jitterbug of the 1940s, the cha cha and rock and roll of the 1950s, and the twist, frug, and various frenzied discothèque and go-go dances of the 1960s. Tap dancing and ballroom and adagio dancing have won wide popularity as entertainment and have been featured frequently in musical stage shows and movies. See MODERN DANCE. See Lincoln Kirstein, *Book of the Dance* (rev. ed. 1942); Curt Sachs, *World History of the Dance* (tr. 1937, repr. 1963); Walter Sorell, *The Dance through the Ages* (1967); Anatole Chujoy and P. W. Manchester, ed., *The Dance Encyclopedia* (rev. ed. 1967); Walter Terry, *The Dance in America* (rev. ed. 1971); Gaston Vuillier, *A History of Dancing from the Earliest Ages to Our Own Time* (1898, repr. 1973).

dance of death: see DEATH, DANCE OF.

Dance Theatre of Harlem, the first black classical ballet company. The group was founded in Harlem, New York City, by Arthur MITCHELL of the New York City Ballet, the first black premier danseur in history. The company began as a school for 30 students in the summer of 1968. Classes were conducted with the doors open so that passersby could watch the students at the barre; at the end of that summer the school had 400 students. To encourage them to become professional performers as soon as possible, Mitchell began taking his students on lecture-demonstration tours in 1969, and by 1970 had a professional company of 20 ready for their debut at the 1971 festival at Spoleto, Italy. After two European tours and three national tours, the company had its successful first full season in New York City in 1974. It is noted for graceful and vigorous performances of works by George Balanchine, Jerome Robbins, Antony Tudor, and Mitchell. The school was given a permanent home by Alva Gimbel in 1971 and offers extensive courses in ballet and related arts to all who are interested, regardless of age.

Dandarah (dän'dərä) or **Dendera** (dĕn'-), town, N Egypt, on the Nile River. Nearby is the site of the ancient Greek city of Tentyra. There is a large, well-preserved temple of Hathor (1st cent. B.C.), which contained a zodiacal table now in the Louvre museum in Paris, and a temple of Isis, which contains cultist inscriptions.

dandelion [Eng. form of Fr.,=lion's tooth], any plant of the genus *Taraxacum* of the family Compositae (COMPOSITE family), perennial herbs of wide distribution in temperate regions. The dandelion has a rosette of deep-toothed leaves (the name is usually attributed to this) and a bright yellow flower followed in fruit by a round head of white down, an adaptation for wind distribution of the seedlike fruits. The common dandelion (*T. officinale*) is native to Europe but widely naturalized. Although it is considered in the N United States chiefly as a lawn pest because of the easily dispersed seeds and the deep root, it is also cultivated both for medicine and for food. The young leaves resemble chicory and are used for salad greens and as a potherb, especially in Europe. The roots may be roasted and used as a coffee substitute. The flower heads are utilized for dandelion wine and are good forage for bees. In medicine the roots are dried and used chiefly as a bitter tonic and laxative. The Russian dandelion (*T. kok-saghyz*) has been cultivated for the milky juice typical of the genus, as a potential source of rubber. Dandelions are classified in the division MAGNOLIOPHYTA, class Magnoliopsida, order Asterales, family Compositae.

Dandie Dinmont terrier (dăn'dē dĭn'mŏnt), breed of hardy, long-bodied TERRIER developed in England and Scotland and first recorded as a distinct type in the very early 18th cent. It stands from 8 to 11 in. (20.3–27.9 cm) high at the shoulder and weighs from 18 to 24 lb (8.1–10.9 kg). The double coat consists of a mixture of soft and harsh hair about 2 in. (5.1 cm) long that gives it a crisp but not wiry texture and appearance. Its color may be pepper or mustard. Like most of the other terriers from England's northern Border districts, the Dandie Dinmont was bred to go to ground (i.e., go into an animal's den or underground shelter) in the hunting of such game as otters, badgers, and foxes. Today it is raised principally as a pet. See DOG.

Dandolo (dän'dōlō), ancient Venetian family that produced four doges, many admirals, and other prominent citizens. **Enrico Dandolo,** c.1108-1205, became doge in 1192. He is considered the founder of the Venetian colonial empire. In the Fourth Crusade (see CRUSADES) he acted to divert the Crusaders in 1202 to Zara (see ZADAR) and in 1203 to Constantinople. Though aged and blind, he commanded the fleet in the capture (1204) of Constantinople and secured for Venice the most valuable share of the spoils and of the conquered Greek territories. In 1205 he and Emperor BALDWIN I of Constantinople were defeated near Adrianople by the Bulgars. Baldwin having been captured, Dandolo led the remnants of the Latin forces back to Constantinople, where he soon died. **Andrea Dandolo,** c.1307-1354, doge of Venice (1343-54), was professor of jurisprudence at Padua before his election. He subdued rebellious Zara, fought successfully against Genoa, and reorganized the laws of Venice. He wrote a chronicle of Venetian history and was a friend of Petrarch.

dandruff, excessive flaking of skin from the scalp. In some cases the excess of scales may be due to dryness; usually, however, it is the sign of a skin disease, such as SEBORRHEA or a fungus infection, and should, if persistent and serious, be treated by a dermatologist.

Dandy, Walter Edward, 1886-1946, American neurosurgeon. Having studied with Harvey Cushing at Johns Hopkins Univ., Dandy soon made himself a notable figure in the developing specialty of neurosurgery. His introduction of ventriculography in 1918 and, later, of encephalography was of the utmost importance in making possible more accurate diagnosis and localization of tumors of the brain and intracranial tissues. Dandy also devised new instruments and operative procedures for the treatment of hydrocephalus, neuralgias, and other disturbances of the cranial nerves.

Dane, Clemence, pseud. of **Winifred Ashton,** 1888-1965, English novelist and playwright. She was an artist, teacher, and actress before she turned to writing. Her first novel, *A Regiment of Women* (1917), is a compelling study of the hothouse emotional life in a girls' school. *Legend* (1919), concerns a young girl who devotes her life to her deranged father; Dane made it into a play called *Bill of Divorcement* (1921), which starred Katherine Cornell. Dane wrote many other novels and plays.

Danegeld (dăn'gĕld"), medieval land tax originally raised to buy off raiding Danes and later used for military expenditures. In England the tribute was first levied in 868, then in 871 by ALFRED, and occasionally thereafter. Under ÆTHELRED (978-1016) it became a regular tax, and was collected by later rulers until the 12th cent., when it was converted into TALLAGE.

Danelaw (dăn'lô"), originally the body of law that prevailed in the part of England occupied by the Danes after the treaty of King ALFRED with Guthrum in 886. It soon came to mean also the area in which Danish law obtained; according to the treaty the boundary between England and Danelaw ran "up the Thames, and then up the Lea . . . to its source, then straight to Bedford and then up the Ouse to Watling Street." The Danelaw comprised four main regions: Northumbria; the areas around and including the boroughs of Lincoln, Nottingham, Derby, Leicester, and Stamford; East Anglia; and the SE Midlands. Though the English kings soon brought the Danelaw back under their rule, they did not attempt to interfere with the laws and customs of the area, many of which survived until after the Norman Conquest. See Dorothy Whitelock, *The Norman Conquest: its Setting and Impact* (1968); F. M. Stenton, *The Free Peasantry of the Northern Danelaw* (1969) and *Anglo-Saxon England* (3d ed. 1971).

Danforth, Thomas, 1703-86, American pewterer, founder of a family of celebrated pewterers, b. Taunton, Mass. In 1733 he opened a pewter shop in Norwich, Conn., where he made a wide variety of pewter tableware of excellent form, quality, and workmanship, using marks in the English mode. His descendants carried on the Danforth tradition for more than a century.

Dangerfield, Thomas, 1650?-1685, English conspirator. Several times imprisoned for criminal activities, he was employed (1679) by Roman Catholics to aid the victims of the Popish Plot (see OATES, TITUS) by conjuring up a Protestant plot against Charles II. He turned on his employers, however, and incriminated them in the so-called Mealtub Plot (1679), another nonexistent conspiracy against the king. Though his victims were acquitted, he continued his libels against Catholics. He was murdered when returning from the pillory following his conviction for perjury.

Dangerous Archipelago: see TUAMOTU ISLANDS.

Daniel. 1 Prophet, central figure of the book of DANIEL. **2** See CHILEAB. **3** Sealer of the covenant. Ezra 8.2; Neh. 10.6.

Daniel, Antoine (Saint Antony Daniel) (äNtwän' dänyĕl'), 1600-1648, French missionary in the New World, a Jesuit priest. He came in 1632 to Canada and in 1634 went with Father Jean BRÉBEUF as missionary to the Huron Indians. He was killed by the Iroquois. One of the Jesuit martyrs of North America, he was beatified in 1925 and canonized in 1930. Feast: March 16 (among the Jesuits) and Sept. 26.

Daniel, Samuel, 1562?-1619, English poet and historian. He was tutor to William Herbert, 3d earl of Pembroke, and later to Lady Anne Clifford. Eventually he found favor with James I, and in 1603 he was appointed inspector of the Children of the Queen's Revels (a company of boy actors), a position he held for the rest of his life. Daniel is known chiefly for *Delia* (1592), a collection of sonnets. His other poetry includes a narrative, *The Complaint of Rosamund* (1592), and a defense of learning, *Musophilus* (1599). Besides being the author of numerous court masques, he wrote two Senecan tragedies, *Cleopatra* (1594) and *Philotas* (1605). His ardent patriotism and his belief in a strong and absolute monarchy inspired his epic, *The Civil Wars between the Two Houses of Lancaster and York* (1595, enl. ed. 1609). *Defence of Rhyme* (1603?) and a *History of England* (1631) are his major prose works. He was much admired by the 19th-century English romantics for his purity of diction. See study by C. Seronsy (1967).

Daniel, book of the Old Testament, 27th in the order of the Authorized Version (AV), 4th of the books of the Major Prophets. It relates a series of events and visions from the life of Daniel, a Jew of the 6th cent. B.C., who spent his career at the court of Babylon, where he was called Belteshazzar. Some parts of the work occur not in Hebrew but in Western Aramaic, and others are found originally in Greek versions only; the passages peculiar to Greek originals are treated as apocryphal in AV but as canonical in the Greek and the Western canon. The book divides as follows: Daniel and his friends are taken to the Babylonian court, where they remain faithful to the Law (1); a dream of King Nebuchadnezzar is interpreted by Daniel (2); Nebuchadnezzar, demanding divine honors, tries to punish three recalcitrant Jews by burning them in a furnace (3; this chapter includes in the Greek Version the famous Song of the THREE HOLY CHILDREN); a second dream of Nebuchadnezzar is interpreted by Daniel to foretell the king's madness (4); Daniel interprets the handwriting on the wall at Belshazzar's feast (5); he escapes alive from the lions' den (6); Daniel has four apocalyptic visions (7; 8; 9; 10-12). The Greek version of the book has two more chapters (see SUSANNA; BEL AND THE DRAGON). The difference between Greek and Hebrew-Aramaic texts in chapter 3 causes a different numbering; thus, AV 3.24-30, 4.1-3, and 4.4-37 correspond to Douay 3.91-97, 3.98-100, and 4.1-34, respectively. Other biblical allusions to Daniel include Ezek. 14.14-20; 28.3; Mat. 24.15. The book presents many critical problems, not least being the date: most scholars set it in the mid-2d cent. B.C. and believe the stories to be legendary. Several fragments of the book of Daniel were found at Qumran (see DEAD SEA SCROLLS). They show that in the 1st cent. B.C. the book was not yet in the Hebrew canon. See studies by W. A. Criswell (4 vol., 1968-72) and L. J. Wood (1973); see also bibliography under OLD TESTAMENT.

Daniels, Jonathan Worth, 1902-, American newspaper editor and author, b. Raleigh, N.C. In 1925 he joined the staff of the Raleigh (N.C.) *News and Observer,* which was edited by his father, Josephus Daniels. He edited the paper from 1933 to 1942 while his father was ambassador to Mexico, and succeeded to the editorship after Josephus Daniels' death in 1948. The paper ably reflects his views, those of a Southern liberal. Daniels held various official posts, including administrative assistant to President F. D. Roosevelt (1943-45) and U.S. member (1947-53) of the United Nations subcommittee on prevention of discrimination and protection of minorities. He contributed widely to periodicals and wrote a novel, *Clash of Angels* (1930); reportorial books, *A Southerner Discovers the South* (1938) and *Frontier on the Potomac* (1946); a biography of Truman, *The Man of Independence* (1950); and several histories, including *The Time Between the Wars: Armistice to Pearl Harbor* (1966).

Daniels, Josephus, 1862-1948, American statesman, newspaper editor, and author, b. Washington, N.C. He became editor of the Raleigh *State Chronicle* in 1885 (he was admitted to the bar the same year) and in 1894 consolidated three newspapers into the Raleigh *News and Observer.* He was in charge of the Democratic publicity bureau in the presidential campaigns of 1908 and 1912. Throughout both of Wilson's administrations, including the period of World War I, he was Secretary of the Navy. He was much criticized for pacifistic tendencies and administrative inefficiency before the U.S. entry into the war, but his record in 1917-18 quieted these charges. After leaving office, he continued to be a force in both state and national politics. When he was ambassador to Mexico (1933-41), Daniels was influential in improving U.S. relations with Mexico. His books include *Life of Woodrow Wilson* (1924, repr. 1971), and *The Wilson Era* (2 vol., 1944-46). *Tar Heel Editor* (1939), *Editor in Politics* (1941), and *Shirt Sleeve Diplomat* (1947) are autobiographical. See *Roosevelt and Daniels* (ed. by Carroll Kilpatrick, 1952); biography by J. L. Morrison (1966).

Danilo I (Danilo Petrović-Njegoš) (dänē'lo), 1670?-1735, last elected prince-bishop (*vladika*) of MONTENEGRO (1696-1735) and founder of the Petrović-Njegoš dynasty. After coordinating defense operations and settling, at least partially, tribal (family) disputes among his people, Danilo launched a struggle against the Turks in 1711. During his rule political ties between Russia and Montenegro were first established. In 1715, Danilo visited Czar Peter I at St. Petersburg and secured his alliance against the Turks—a journey that became traditional among his successors. He subsequently recovered Zeta from the Turks and restored the monastery at Cetinje. Empowered to choose his successor, Danilo designated his nephew. This became the usual order of succession, the prince-bishops being bound to celibacy.

Danilo II (Danilo Petrović-Njegoš), 1826-60, prince of MONTENEGRO (1851-60). He secularized (1852) his principality (chiefly in order to be able to marry) and transferred his ecclesiastic functions to an archbishop. Danilo and his brother Mirko defeated the Turks at Ostrong (1853) and at Grahovo (1858). Assassinated by a Montenegrin exile, Danilo was succeeded by his nephew, Nicholas I.

Danilova, Alexandra (dänē'lōvä), 1906?-, Russian-American ballerina. In 1923 she entered the Imperial Ballet School, St. Petersburg, and from 1924 to 1929 was a member of Diaghilev's Ballet Russe. From 1938 to 1958, Danilova was prima ballerina of the Ballet Russe de Monte Carlo. She toured with her own company and, after retiring, lectured, choreographed, and taught dance.

Danish language, member of the North Germanic, or Scandinavian, group of the Germanic subfamily of the Indo-European family of languages. The official language of Denmark, it is spoken by about 5 million people, most of whom live in Denmark; however, there are some Danish speakers in Greenland, the Faeroe Islands, Iceland, the Virgin Islands, and the United States. Like the other Scandinavian languages, Danish is derived from Old Norse, and by the first half of the 12th cent. it could be distinguished from the parent tongue (see GERMANIC LANGUAGES; NORSE). Between 1100 and 1800 a number of phonological changes took place in Danish, and the grammar became increasingly simple. The spelling and pronunciation of the language began to be standardized c.1700, and a modern standard Danish can be said to have existed since about 1800, although there are still a number of dialects. Danish grammar is comparatively simple. The noun is inflected only to show the possessive and plural forms and has but two genders, neuter and nonneuter (or common). The meaning of nouns that are otherwise the same can depend on gender. For example, nonneuter *øre* means "coin," whereas neuter *øre* means "ear." Homonyms may also be differentiated in Danish by the use of a *stød,* or glottal stop, which is a sound that results from the closing and opening of the glottis to expel air. Verbs have no personal inflection. Although the vocabulary of Danish is substantially native, many words have been borrowed from other languages, notably from Low German in the 14th to 16th cent.; from High German, Latin, and French in the 16th to 19th cent.; and from English since the late 19th cent. Because of the large number of similar and identical words in Danish, Norwegian, and Swedish, a knowledge of any one of these languages makes it possible to understand the spoken and written forms of the other two. Since c.1100, Danish has used the Roman alphabet, to which three symbols, å (written as *aa* before 1948), æ, and ø, have been added. On the whole, the spelling of Danish is a better guide to pronunciation than is the spelling of English. See L. F. A. Wimmer, *A Short History of the Danish Language* (1897); Danish grammars by Elias Bredsdorff (1959) and Erling Norlev and H. A. Koefoed (3d ed. 1968).

Danish literature. The earliest literature of Denmark is preserved in the runic carvings on nearly 275 stone monuments erected to the Vikings c.850–1050. A number of these are written in alliterative verse. The Danish legends of the heroic period were preserved in the work of SAXO GRAMMATICUS (fl. 12th cent.). With Christianity came the epic poetry of the scholastics, the legends of saints, and theological works written in Latin. The Danish folk song appeared in the 12th cent., stimulated by customs of knighthood and chivalry. Danish literature of the later Middle Ages, primarily in Latin, was formal and ecclesiastical; it included annals, chronicles, legends, and a few poems. The Reformation stimulated religious polemic and satire as well as the literary use of the Danish language. The Danish translation of the New Testament, completed in 1531 by the humanist Christian Pedersen (d. 1554), who also published an edition of Saxo (1514), greatly influenced Danish literature. In 1535, Hans Tausen (1494–1561) translated the Old Testament. From the Reformation also dates modern Danish drama, which was long a medium for religious moralizing. Fine poetry in the Renaissance manner was created in the early 17th cent. by Anders ARREBO, and baroque verse reached its zenith as rendered by the clergyman Thomas Kingo (1634–1703). Ludvig HOLBERG introduced the ideas of the Enlightenment in the 18th cent., and neoclassical poetry, the drama, and the essay flourished, following French and English models. German influence is seen in the verse of the leading poets of the late 18th cent., Johannes EWALD and Jens Baggesen. It was maintained by the romantic school, fathered by Adam OEHLENSCHLÄGER. A transcendent figure in Danish literary culture was N. F. S. GRUNDTVIG; both he and Oehlenschläger influenced the poet and novelist Bernhard INGEMANN. A more aesthetic ideal was promulgated by the dramatist and essayist J. L. HEIBERG; two of his protégés were the philosopher Søren KIERKEGAARD and Hans Christian ANDERSEN, renowned for his fairy tales. Although S. S. Blicher may have been the first Danish realist, the actual breakthrough to realism was inspired by the internationally influential critic Georg BRANDES and was reflected in the novels of J. P. JACOBSEN, H. J. Bang, Karl GJELLERUP, and Hendrik PONTOPPIDAN and in the early verse of H. H. DRACHMANN. By 1900 a lyrical reaction was being led by the poet J. J. JORGENSEN; impressionistic themes became important, but were never the sole fruit of Danish literary endeavor. Both before and after World War I, Martin ANDERSEN NEXØ wrote in a context of proletarian realism, and J. V. JENSEN employed elements of realism and fantasy alike. Fantasy was dominant in the tales of Isak DINESEN, while the theater was enlivened by the dramas of Kaj MUNK and the brilliant stage technique of Kjeld ABELL. The period following World War II saw the passing of a number of great figures and the emergence of Martin Hansen, Aage Dons, Hans Christian Branner, Frank Jager, and Knut Sønderby as outstanding Danish writers. See P. M. Mitchell, *A History of Danish Literature* (2d ed. 1971); F. J. B. Jansen and P. M. Mitchell, ed., *Anthology of Danish Literature* (1972; bilingual).

Danish West Indies: see VIRGIN ISLANDS of the United States.

Danites: see MORMONS.

Dan-jaan (dăn-jā'ən), unidentified city, perhaps the same as DAN **2.** 2 Sam. 24.6.

Dannah (dăn'ə), unidentified town, S Palestine. Joshua 15.49.

Dannecker, Johann Heinrich von (yō'hän hīn'rĭkh fən dän'ĕkər), 1758–1841, German sculptor. He studied with Pajou in Paris and with Canova in Rome. His art shows a revival of classical influence, as well as moderate naturalism. Among his statues are *Sappho, Psyche,* and *Ariadne on a Panther.* He made busts of many noted contemporaries, including Metternich and Schiller.

D'Annunzio, Gabriele (gäbrēĕ'lā dän-nōōn'tsyō) 1863–1938, Italian poet, novelist, dramatist and soldier, b. Pescara. He went to Rome in 1881 and there began his literary career. The richly sensuous imagery of even his early poetry—*Le primavere della mala pianta* [the springtimes of the evil plant] (1880) and *Canto nuovo* [new song] (1882)—displayed his unrivaled literary craftsmanship. His novels—*Il piacere* (1889, tr. *The Child of Pleasure,* 1898), *L'innocente* (1892, tr. *The Intruder,* 1898, and *The Victim,* 1914), *Giovanni Episcopo* (1892, tr. *Episcopo & Company,* 1896), and *Il trionfo della morte* (1894, tr. *The Triumph of Death,* 1896)—show the same creative handling of the Italian language, but the works are shallow and theatrical. The outbreak of World War I found him in France, where he had lived since 1910. He returned to Italy, where his oratory had much to do with persuading Italy to join the Allies, and fought with spectacular daring in the air force. In Sept., 1919, he led an expedition (known as the march on Ronchi) against Fiume, where he established a rule opposed by both the Italian government and the rest of Europe, which lasted until Jan., 1921. His troops in the Fiume raid introduced the black shirt that was to be the uniform of the fascists. D'Annunzio, one of the few writers to be courted by Mussolini, was an early exponent of Fascism. His book *Notturno* (1921) is a moving analysis of sensations and memories during weeks of blindness from which he partially recovered. He added little in later life to the long list of his works. His plays include *Il sogno d'un mattino di primavera* (1897, tr. *The Dream of a Spring Morning,* 1902), *Il sogno d'un tramonto d'autunno* (1898, tr. *The Dream of an Autumn Sunset,* 1904), *La città morta* (1898, tr. *The Dead City,* 1902), and *Francesca* (1902, tr. *Francesca da Rimini,* 1902). Most of these were written during the time of his love affair with Eleonora Duse, which he described with cruel candor in the novel *Il fuoco* (1900; tr. *The Flame of Life,* 1900). Mussolini appointed him (1937) president of the Royal Italian Academy, but he died before taking office. See biography by G. Griffin (1935, repr. 1970); studies by Anthony Rhodes (1960), Giovanni Gullace (1966), and Robert Forcella (4 vol., 1926–37, repr. 1973).

danse macabre: see DEATH, DANCE OF.

Dante Alighieri (dăn'tē, Ital. dän'tā älēgyĕ'rē), 1265–1321, Italian poet, b. Florence. Dante was the author of the *Divine Comedy,* one of the greatest of literary classics. Born into a Guelph family of decayed nobility, Dante moved in patrician society. He was a member of the Florentine cavalry that routed the Ghibellines at Campaldino in 1289. The next year, after the death (1290) of his exalted Beatrice he plunged into intent study of classical philosophy and Provençal poetry. This woman, thought to have been BEATRICE PORTINARI, was Dante's acknowledged source of spiritual inspiration. He married Gemma Donati, had several children, and was active (1295–1300) as councilman, elector, and prior of Florence. In the complex politics of Florence, he found himself increasingly opposed to the temporal power of Pope Boniface VIII, and he eventually allied himself with the White Guelphs. After the victory of the Black Guelphs, he was dispossessed and banished (1302). Exile made Dante a citizen of all Italy; he served various princes, but supported Holy Roman Emperor Henry VII as the potential savior of a united Italy. He died at the court of Guido da Polenta in Ravenna, where he is buried. Dante's reputation as the outstanding figure of Italian letters rests mainly on the *Divine Comedy,* a long vernacular poem in 100 cantos (more than 14,000 lines), composed during his exile. Dante entitled it *Commedia*; the adjective *Divina* was added in the 16th cent. It recounts the tale of the poet's journey through Hell, Purgatory, and Heaven, and is divided accordingly into three parts. In Hell and Purgatory Dante is guided by Vergil, through Heaven, by Beatrice, for whom the poem is a memorial. The work is written in *terza rima,* a complex verse form in pentameter, with interlocking triads rhyming *aba, bcb, cdc,* etc. A magnificent synthesis of the medieval outlook, it pictures a changeless universe ordered by God; its allegorical theme is the gradual revelation of God to the pilgrim. It is also a religious dialogue on the gradations of earthly sin and piety as well as on such topics as predestination and classical philosophy. The symbolism is complex yet highly rational; the verse is musical; and the entire work is one of great imagination. Through his masterpiece Dante established Tuscan as the literary language of Italy, surpassed all previous Italian writers, and gave rise to a vast literature. His works also include *La vita nuova* [the new life] (written c. 1292), a collection of prose and lyrics celebrating Beatrice and illustrating his idealistic concept of love; the *Convivio* (c.1304), an encyclopedic allegory praising both love and science; *De monarchia,* a treatise on the need for kingly dominance in secular affairs; *De vulgare eloquentia,* on rules for the Italian vernacular; and lyrics, eclogues, and epistles. There are numerous translations of the *Divine Comedy,* including those by M. B. Anderson (1921), J. D. Sinclair (3 vol., 1948), and Dorothy Sayers (3 vol., 1963). See biographies by Michele Barbi (tr. 1954) and P. J. Toynbee (ed. by C. S. Singleton, 1965); studies by C. S. Singleton (2 vol., 1954, 1958), Erich Auerbach (tr. 1961), T. G. Bergin (1967 and 1969), J. A. Symonds (1899, repr. 1973), and Benedetto Croce (1922, repr. 1973).

Danton, Georges Jacques (zhōrzh zhäk däNtôN'), 1759–94, French statesman, one of the leading figures of the FRENCH REVOLUTION. A Parisian lawyer, he became a leader of the CORDELIERS early in the Revolution and gained popular favor through his powerful oratory. He held a position under the COMMUNE OF PARIS and was a member of the Legislative Assembly (1791–92), where he championed national defense. Danton took part in the movement that led in Aug., 1792, to the storming of the Tuileries and the overthrow of the monarchy. His leadership of the event is debated. In the new republic he was minister of justice and virtual head of the Provisional Executive Council. Danton sought foreign war in order to spread French institutions to all Europe. A member of the Convention, the national assembly, he dominated the first Committee of Public Safety (April–July, 1793), created by the Convention as the chief governing body of France on the eve of the FRENCH REVOLUTIONARY WARS. When France suffered military reverses, Danton began to advocate a conciliatory foreign policy. He was not included (July, 1793) in the new Committee of Public Safety, and he retired from the capital. He returned in November when financial scandals involving his friends were revealed. Perhaps to help them, he advocated relaxation of emergency measures, particularly the REIGN OF TERROR, and attacked the dictatorship of the committee. Soon after the committee had eliminated the extremists under Jacques René HÉBERT, it turned upon Danton and the "Indulgents" or moderates. On March 30, 1794, Danton and his followers were charged with a conspiracy to overthrow the government. The trial was a mockery, and Danton was guillotined. There has been much controversy as to his character among historians, particularly between Alphonse AULARD, who defended him as a great patriot and statesman, and Albert MATHIEZ, who viewed him as a demagogue and an unscrupulous politician. Actually, Danton revealed all these qualities at various times. See his *Speeches* (tr. 1928); biographies by Louis Madelin (1914, in French), Hermann Wendel (tr. 1935), and Robert Christophe (tr. 1967).

Danube (dăn'yōōb), Czech *Dunaj,* Ger. *Donau,* Hung. *Duna,* Rumanian *Dunarea,* Rus. *Dunai,* Serbo-Croatian and Bulg. *Dunav,* great river of central and SE Europe, c.1,770 mi (2,850 km) long, with a drainage basin of c.320,000 sq mi (828,800 sq km); it is second in length only to the Volga among European rivers. The Danube rises in two sources (the Brege and Brigach rivers) in the Black Forest, SW West Germany, and flows NE across S West Germany past Ulm and Regensburg, where it turns SE to enter Austria at Passau. It continues its southeastern course through Upper and Lower Austria, past Linz and Vienna; this section is particularly famous for its scenery. It then forms the border between Czechoslovakia and Hungary from Bratislava to Szob, where it turns south and flows across the Great Alföld (plain) of central Hungary past Budapest. After entering Yugoslavia above Belgrade, it turns southeast, then east and flows through narrow gorges, forming part of the Yugoslavia-Rumania border. Iron Gate gorge, site of a hydroelectric power dam, is there; the Sip Canal bypasses the rapids in the gorge. After passing the Iron Gate, the Danube broadens again and forms most of the Rumania-Bulgaria border. Near Silistra it leaves the Bulgarian border and turns north, passing through E Rumania to Galaţi, a port city, where the Danube divides into a delta before entering the Black Sea. The delta (c.1,000 sq mi/2,590 sq km) has many lakes and swamps. The northernmost branch of the delta forms the frontier between Rumania and the USSR. The central branch is canalized and is the main shipping route upstream. The Danube receives more than 300 tributaries, notably the Inn, Drava, Tisza, Sava, and Prut. Navigable by barges from Ulm (larger craft from Regensburg), the Danube is a vital traffic artery; in volume, however, Danubian commerce is far below that of the Rhine River. The Danube is linked to the Main and Rhine rivers by the Rhine-Main-Danube Canal; other canals link it with the Oder and Tisza rivers. River navigation is impeded by ice in winter and by varying seasonal water levels. Under the Roman Empire (when it was known as Danubius and, in its lower course, as Ister), the Danube was the northern border against the barbarian world. As Rome declined, the Danubian plains for centuries attracted invading hordes—Goths, Huns, Avars,

Magyars, Pechenegs, Cumans, Mongols, and others. The Danube increased in commercial importance in the era of the Crusades, but commerce suffered (15th-16th cent.) after the Turks gained control of its course from the Hungarian plain to the Black Sea. In the 19th cent. the Danube's economic importance as an international waterway increased. At the end of the Crimean War the Congress of Paris appointed (1856) a Danube navigation commission to clear the delta (below Brăila) of obstructions. By the Treaty of Versailles (1919) the Danube was internationalized and an international commission was set up with jurisdiction over the course from Ulm to Brăila. Germany repudiated the internationalization in 1936 and forced both the navigation (1939) and international (1940) commissions to dissolve. After World War II, delegates from Czechoslovakia, Hungary, Yugoslavia, Rumania, Bulgaria, the USSR, the United States, Great Britain, and France met (1948) at Belgrade to determine the international status of the Danube. When, instead of a general international commission, a body composed of only the seven riparian nations was set up, the three Western nations refused to sign the convention. Subsequently, the seven riparian nations signed a separate agreement establishing a new Danube commission. Austria joined it in 1959 and West Germany followed in 1963. Its seat is now at Budapest.

Danubian Principalities: see MOLDAVIA; WALACHIA.

Danvers, town (1970 pop. 26,151), Essex co., NE Mass.; settled in the 1630s, set off from Salem 1752, inc. as a town 1757. Electrical equipment and shoes are the chief products. The Salem witchcraft incidents began there in 1692; more than half of the victims were from Danvers. Danvers was a center of colonial revolutionary activity. John Greenleaf Whittier spent his later years there, and Israel Putnam was born in Danvers. Numerous buildings of historical and architectural interest are preserved, several dating from the 1600s. There is a state mental hospital in the town.

Danville. 1 City (1970 pop. 42,570), seat of Vermilion co., E Ill., on the Vermilion River at the Ind. line; inc. 1839. It is a commercial and industrial center in a dairy, farm, and coal area. Coal is extensively mined, and the city has railroad shops, meat-packing establishments, lumber and flour mills. Abraham Lincoln maintained a law office in Danville for five years. The city is the seat of a junior college and a U.S. veterans' hospital. Nearby is Kickapoo State Park, with a number of lakes. **2** City (1970 pop. 11,542), seat of Boyle co., central Ky.; settled 1775, inc. 1836. It is a manufacturing center in an agricultural region. One of the oldest settlements in Kentucky, Danville was a seat of government (1784-92) by act of the Virginia legislature. The Kentucky constitutional conventions were held there. Points of interest include Weisiger Memorial State Shrine (the old courthouse square) and the Dr. Ephraim McDowell State Shrine, scene (1809) of the first ovariotomy. Centre College of Kentucky and the first state-supported school for the deaf (opened 1823) are in Danville. **3** City (1970 pop. 46,391), S central Va., on the Dan River; politically independent of, but surrounded by, Pittsylvania co.; founded 1793, inc. 1870. It is a market and processing point for bright leaf tobacco. The city is also known for its huge Dan River textile mill that produces cotton and double-knit goods. During the Civil War, Danville maintained a Confederate quartermaster depot, a hospital, and a prison camp. In April, 1865, Jefferson Davis and his cabinet fled to Danville from Richmond. The Sutherlin Mansion, the "Last Capitol of the Confederacy," is maintained as a historical landmark. Other points of interest include the home of Lady Nancy Witcher (Langhorne) Astor, who was born in Danville; Stratford College; Averett College; and a junior college.

Danzig: see GDANSK, Poland.

Daphnae: see TAHPANHES.

Daphne (dăf'nē), in Greek mythology, a nymph. She was loved by Apollo and by Leucippus, a mortal who disguised himself as a nymph to be near her. When Leucippus betrayed his sex while bathing, the nymphs tore him to pieces. Apollo then pursued Daphne, who prayed to Gaea for aid and was changed into a laurel tree.

daphne, common name for, and genus name of, certain low deciduous or evergreen shrubs native to Eurasia. In the United States several naturalized species are cultivated for their handsome foliage and fragrant flowers, e.g., *D. mezereum* and *D. laureola,* commonly called spurge-laurel and olive-spurge respectively but unrelated to the true spurge or laurel. The dried bark of *D. mezereum* is used medicinally, but the plant itself is poisonous. Daphnes are classified in the division MAGNOLIOPHYTA, class Magnoliopsida, order Myrtales, family Thymelaeaceae.

Daphnis (dăf'nĭs), in Greek mythology, shepherd, the son of Hermes and a nymph. After swearing fidelity to the nymph Nomeia, he was made drunk and seduced by the nymph Chimaera. Nomeia then blinded him. He tried to comfort himself by playing melancholy songs upon the shepherd's pipes, and his friends lamented for him in song. Daphnis was revered as the inventor of pastoral music.

Daphnis and Chloë: see LONGUS.

Da Ponte, Lorenzo (lōrĕnt'sō dä pôn'tā), 1749-1838, Italian poet, librettist, and pioneer in spreading Italian culture in the United States. Forced to leave Venice in 1782 because of scandal, Da Ponte went to Vienna, where he became poet to the Italian theater for nine years. There he wrote the librettos of three of Mozart's operas—*The Marriage of Figaro* (1786), *Don Giovanni* (1787), and *Così fan tutte* (1790)—and many other works. Banished again because of scandal, he wandered through Europe, made an unhappy marriage, and settled in 1791 in London. There he worked as a tutor of Italian, a bookseller, and a librettist to the Drury Lane Theatre, until he went bankrupt in 1804. He set out for America in 1805, but he failed as a grocer in New Jersey. The rest of his life he spent as a celebrated teacher of Italian language and culture (except for an unsuccessful period spent in Pennsylvania selling medicines). He taught nearly 2,000 private pupils and was appointed professor of Italian language and literature at Columbia in 1830. His library, bought by the university when the chair was established in 1825, was the nucleus of its collection of Italian poetry and miscellaneous literature. In 1833 he helped establish the Italian Opera House in New York City, where 28 performances of Italian opera were given before the theater was transferred to other management. The venture represented the first attempt to establish Italian opera permanently in the United States. Da Ponte's last years were marred by poverty and the failure of his Italian opera. He wrote a remarkable collection of memoirs (ed. by Arthur Livingston, tr. 1929) detailing his extraordinary life. See biographies by April Fitzlyon (1955) and J. L. Russo (1922, repr. 1966).

Dara (dā'rə), in the Bible: see DARDA.

Darbhanga (dərbŭng'gə), city (1971 pop. 132,129), Bihar state, NE India, on the Baghmati River. It is a district administrative center in a sugarcane- and tobacco-growing area. Once part of the ancient and medieval Brahman kingdom of Mithila, Darbhanga passed to the Mogul empire in the 14th cent. The British assumed control in 1765. Darbhanga has a mixed Hindu-Muslim population.

D'Arblay, Madame: see BURNEY, FANNY.

Darboux, Jean Gaston (zhäN gästôN' därbo͞o'), 1842-1917, French mathematician. He is known for his work on orthogonal surfaces and for his application of infinitesimal calculus to geometry. From 1880 until his death he held the chair of higher geometry at the Sorbonne and from 1900 was perpetual secretary of the Academy of Sciences.

Darboy, Georges (zhôrzh därbwä'), 1813-71, French churchman, bishop of Nancy (1859-63) and archbishop of Paris (1863-71). In the Franco-Prussian War he behaved heroically, notably in the siege of Paris when he remained in the city to aid the wounded. When the Commune of Paris was set up, he was imprisoned as a hostage and subsequently shot.

Darby, John Nelson, 1800-1882, one of the founders of the PLYMOUTH BRETHREN, b. England. In 1827 he left a curate's post in Wicklow, Ireland, and joined with others in Dublin to found the Brethren. Later he formed congregations on the Continent, in Switzerland, France, and Germany. Between 1859 and 1874, Darby paid a number of visits to the United States and Canada. His followers, especially those on the Continent, came to be called Darbyites or Exclusive Brethren.

Darby, borough (1970 pop. 13,729), Delaware co., SE Pa., a suburb adjacent to Philadelphia; settled by Quakers 1682, inc. 1853. Although residential, it has some manufactures. One of the oldest settlements in the state, it has many colonial landmarks. The Darby Library Company was founded in 1743 by Quakers.

Darcy, Thomas Darcy, Baron, 1467-1537, English nobleman. He served in a number of military expeditions for Henry VII and for the young Henry VIII. He disapproved of Henry VIII's divorce from Katharine of Aragón, and he became involved in intrigues with the agents of Holy Roman Emperor Charles V against Henry. After the outbreak of the rebellion in the N of England known as the PILGRIMAGE OF GRACE (1536), Darcy yielded Pontefract Castle to the rebels and became one of their leaders. He was pardoned at first, but later convicted of treason and beheaded.

Darda (där'də), wise man. 1 Kings 4.31. Apparently the same man as Dara. 1 Chron. 2.6.

Dardanelles (därdənĕlz') or **Çanakkale Boğazı** (chänäk'kälĕ bōäzŭ'), strait, c.40 mi (60 km) long and from 1 to 4 mi (1.6 to 6.4 km) wide, connecting the Aegean Sea with the Sea of Marmara and separating the Gallipoli peninsula of European Turkey from Asian Turkey. It was called the Hellespont in ancient times and was the scene of the legend of HERO and Leander. Its modern name is derived from Dardanus, an ancient Greek city on its Asian shore. Controlling navigation between the Black Sea and the Mediterranean, the Dardanelles and BOSPORUS straits have long been of immense strategic and commercial importance. Ancient Troy prospered at the western entrance to the Hellespont. Xerxes I crossed (c.481 B.C.) the strait over a bridge of boats, as did Alexander the Great in 334 B.C. Throughout the existence of the Byzantine and Ottoman empires the Straits were essential to the defense of Constantinople (İstanbul). By 1402 the Dardanelles were under the control of Ottoman Sultan Beyazid I. Muhammad II began (15th cent.) to fortify the passage, which, with brief interruptions, has remained in Turkish hands until the present. Russian expansion along the Black Sea (from the 18th cent.) and the resulting weakening of the Ottoman Empire became of great concern to the Western powers (see EASTERN QUESTION), notably England and France, which from 1841 joined forces to prevent Russia from gaining control over, or special rights in, the Straits. In 1841, England, France, Russia, Austria, and Prussia agreed to close the Straits to all but Turkish warships in peacetime. This convention was formally reaffirmed by the Congress of Paris (1856) at the end of the Crimean War and, theoretically at least, remained in force until World War I. Early in 1915 an Anglo-French fleet, commanded first by Admiral Carden and later by Admiral Sir John de Robeck, sought unsuccessfully to force the Dardanelles and take Constantinople. A second attempt, known as the GALLIPOLI CAMPAIGN, was also unsuccessful, but after the final Turkish collapse an Allied fleet passed (Nov., 1918) the Straits and occupied Constantinople. The Treaty of Sèvres (1920) with Turkey internationalized and demilitarized the Straits zone, but it was superseded by the Treaty of Lausanne (1923). The zone was restored to Turkey, but was to remain demilitarized; the Straits were to be open to all ships in peacetime and in time of war if Turkey remained neutral; if Turkey was at war, it could not exclude neutral ships. Secretly, however, Turkey soon began to refortify the zone, and in 1936, by the MONTREUX CONVENTION, it was formally permitted to remilitarize it. The Montreux Convention was essentially enforced by Turkey through World War II until Jan., 1945, when it was modified by the opening of unrestricted passage for Allied supplies to the Soviet Union. After the war the Soviet Union sought without success to have the Montreux Convention revised in its favor.

Dardanus (där'dənəs), in Greek mythology, founder of Troy; son of Zeus and the Pleiad Electra. His descendants, the Trojans, were sometimes called the Dardani.

Dardic languages (där'dĭk), group of languages belonging to the Indo-Iranian subfamily of the Indo-European family of languages. See INDO-IRANIAN LANGUAGES.

Dare, Virginia, b. 1587, first white child of English parents to be born in America. She was the daughter of Ananias and Elenor Dare, members of Sir Walter Raleigh's ill-fated colony that settled ROANOKE ISLAND on the North Carolina coast. Since no trace remained of the colony when the relief expedition reached Roanoke in 1591, the child's fate is not known.

Dares Phrygius (dâr'ēz frĭj'ēəs), supposed author of a history of the Trojan War. Dares of Phrygia is mentioned by Homer in the *Iliad* as a priest of Troy. During the Middle Ages he was widely regarded as the author of *De excidio Troiae historia* [history of the destruction of Troy], which reputedly had been translated into Latin in the 5th cent. A.D. This work and the supposed diary of Dictys Cretensis became, through Benoît de Sainte-More's *Roman de Troie,* the most popular sources for medieval stories of the Trojan War.

Dar-es-Salaam (där'-ĕs-sälăm') [Arabic,=haven of peace], city (1967 pop. 272,515), capital of Tanzania, on an arm of the Indian Ocean. It is the country's largest city and its administrative, communications, and economic center. The major industries produce foods and beverages, oil, textiles, clothing, shoes, cement, aluminum products, and pharmaceuticals. Although situated on a lagoon with only limited access to the sea, Dar-es-Salaam is Tanzania's main port; exports include cotton, sisal, coffee, diamonds, and skins and hides. The port can handle oceangoing vessels, but dhows still carry some goods bound for coastal African and SW Asian ports. A railroad runs from Dar-es-Salaam to Kigoma, on Lake Tanganyika, and the Great Uhuru (Tan-Zam) Railway is scheduled to link Dar-es-Salaam with the Zambian Copperbelt by 1975. Dar-es-Salaam has an international airport. Founded in 1866 by the sultan of Zanzibar, who built his summer palace there, Dar-es-Salaam was a small town when German forces occupied it in 1887. In 1891 it became the capital of GERMAN EAST AFRICA, but its main growth began during World War II. Today it is a modern city, with wide, shaded streets. It is the site of the Univ. of Dar-es-Salaam (1961), Kivukoni College (1961), a technical college, a teachers college, a college of business education, a botanical garden, and the National Museum of Tanzania. Several organizations concerned with ending white minority rule in S Africa have headquarters in the city.

Darfur (där'fo͝or), province and former sultanate, W Sudan. The region is mountainous, dominated by the central massif of Jebel Marra, which rises to 10,130 ft (3,088 m). Much of the terrain is dry plateau, and there are sand dunes in the extreme north. The Fur (for whom the area is named) and the Baggara are the major ethnic groups. Darfur's economy is based on subsistence agriculture. Cattle, sheep, and goats are raised in the north. Prehistoric Darfur was inhabited by peoples related to the pre-dynastic Egyptians. The royal family of Cush, which fell c.350 A.D., may have established a dynasty in Darfur. Christian kingdoms emerged in the period between 900 and 1200, but they were destroyed by Muslim incursions from Kanem in the middle 13th cent. Fur, a major black African kingdom probably founded in the 15th cent., pushed aside the Kanem-Bornu rulers in the 17th cent. Fur was conquered by the Egyptians in 1874 and by the Mahdists of Sudan in 1883. With the fall of the Mahdist state in 1898, Darfur became a semiautonomous sultanate under Anglo-Egyptian suzerainty. The sultan attempted to expel the foreign influence during World War I, but his forces were defeated by the British in 1916, and Darfur was incorporated into Sudan as a province.

Dargomijsky, Aleksandr Sergeyevich (əlyĭksän'dər syĭrgä'əvĭch därgōmē'skĭ), 1813–69, Russian composer. He and Glinka brought nationalism to Russian music, strongly influencing the next generation of composers. Among his works are three operas: *Esmeralda,* (1847); *Russalka* (1856); and *The Stone Guest* (1872). See M. D. Calvocoressi and Gerald Abraham, *Masters of Russian Music* (1936).

Dariel, pass, USSR: see DARYAL.

Darien (dâr"ēĕn'), Span. *Darién* (däryān'), eastern part of Panama between the Gulf of Darien on the east and the Gulf of San Miguel on the west. Darien province, heavily forested and sparsely populated, is in the western part of the region. Formerly the name was frequently used to mean the entire isthmus of Panama. In 1513, Vasco Núñez de Balboa led an expedition across Darien and became the first European to view the Pacific Ocean from the New World. Keats referred to this exploit in his poem, "On First Looking Into Chapman's Homer," but confused Balboa with Hernán Cortés.

Darien (dâr'ēĕn"), residential town (1970 pop. 20,411), Fairfield co., SW Conn., on Long Island Sound; settled c.1641, inc. 1820. Many 18th-century houses remain.

Darien Scheme, Scottish project to establish a colony on the Isthmus of Darien. In 1695 the Scottish Parliament passed an act that chartered a company for trading with Africa and the Indies. William PATERSON directed the first efforts of the company to found a colony on the Isthmus of Panama to compete with the Dutch and Spanish for trade. Stock was subscribed in England and Scotland, but opposition by the English government and by the East India Company caused English investors to withdraw. The company's two expeditions (1698, 1699) failed because of poor leadership and equipment, disease, and the hostility of the Spanish; many lives were lost. The failure, with its immense losses to Scottish investors, vividly demonstrated Scotland's commercial disadvantage outside the British realm. By the terms of the Act of Union with England (1707), Scotland secured equality in trade. Investors in the Darien venture were partially indemnified for their losses.

Darío, Rubén (ro͞obĕn' därē'ō), 1867–1916, Spanish American poet, originally named Félix Rubén García Sarmiento, b. Nicaragua. A child prodigy, through reading he acquired a thorough knowledge of Spanish and French cultures, widened during his many years abroad in both South America and Europe as diplomatic representative of various Spanish American countries. He was particularly influenced by the writings of the French Parnassians. Darío was the leader and founder of MODERNISMO, emphasizing perfection of form, musical expression, and an ineffable sadness related to that of symbolist poetry. His influence on contemporary Spanish and Spanish American writers was enormous. *Azul* [blue], written in 1888 when he was 21, revolutionized the whole of Spanish syntax and metrics; it was followed by *Prosas profanas* (1896), a departure from pure form and content to grace, beauty, and exoticism. *Cantos de vida y esperanza* [songs of life and hope] (1905) is concerned with the future of Spanish America. *El canto errante* [the wandering song] (1907) shows Darío's elegance strengthened by considerable power and technical mastery. His profound work "Poema del otoño" [autumn's poem] (1910) is often considered his masterpiece. See his *Selected Poems* (tr. 1965); biography by C. D. Watland (1965); studies by D. A. Fiore (1963) and by Miguel González-Gerth and G. D. Schade, ed. (1970).

Darius I (Darius the Great) (dərī'əs), d. 486 B.C., king of ancient Persia (521–486 B.C.), called also Dariavaush and Darius Hystaspis (after his father, Hystaspes or Vishtaspa). A distant cousin of CAMBYSES II, he succeeded to the throne after the fall of the impostor claiming to be SMERDIS. The first years of his reign were spent in putting down revolts in Persia, Media, Babylonia, and the East. He then proved himself the true successor of CYRUS THE GREAT and one of the most able of the ACHAEMENIDS by revising and increasing Cyrus' use of the satrapies. These provinces were ruled by satraps, who functioned as viceroys and were responsible only to the Great King; the satraps were, however, checked by generals, ministers of home affairs, and secret police, all of whom were responsible to Darius alone. This system proved so efficient that it was later adopted by Alexander the Great and, still later, by the Parthians. Darius also undertook lengthy campaigns; an incursion against the Scythians began in 512 B.C., and it involved taking Thrace and Macedonia and building a bridge across the Danube. He was involved in a dispute with the Greeks after giving refuge to the tyrant HIPPIAS, but more serious quarrels began with the revolt (c.500 B.C.) of the Ionian cities against Persian rule. Having put down the rebels, Darius set out to punish the Greek city-states that had aided in the insurrection (see PERSIAN WARS). His first expedition was turned back by storms; his second met defeat in the memorable battle of Marathon (490 B.C.). Darius consolidated Persian power in the East, including NW India. He continued Cyrus' policy of restoring the Jewish state, and under his auspices the rebuilding of the temple in Jerusalem was completed in 515 B.C. For this reason he is mentioned warmly in Ezra, Haggai, and Zechariah. He left the BEHISTUN INSCRIPTION. Written in old Persian, Babylonian, and Elamite, it provided the key for deciphering Babylonian cuneiform. Upon his death he was succeeded by his son XERXES I.

Darius II, d. 404 B.C., king of ancient Persia (423?–404 B.C.); son of Artaxerxes I and a concubine, hence sometimes called Darius Nothus [Darius the bastard]. His rule was not popular or successful, and he spent most of his reign in quelling revolts in Syria, Lydia (413), and Media (410). He lost Egypt (410), but through the diplomacy of PHARNABAZUS, TISSAPHERNES, and CYRUS THE YOUNGER he secured much influence in Greece in the Peloponnesian War. ARTAXERXES II succeeded Darius, but the succession was challenged by Cyrus the Younger.

Darius III (Darius Codomannus) (kŏdəmăn'əs), d. 330 B.C., king of ancient Persia (336–330 B.C.). A cousin of Artaxerxes III, he was raised to the throne by the eunuch Bagoas, who had murdered both Artaxerxes and his son, Arses; Darius in turn murdered Bagoas. His rule was not stable, however. When ALEXANDER THE GREAT invaded Persia, Darius was defeated in the battle of Issus (333 B.C.) and again in the battle of Gaugamela near Arbela (331 B.C.). For the first time Persia was confronted by a united Greece, and Darius' greatest error was in underestimating Alexander's strength. Darius used the wrong tactics in battle and was forced to flee to Ecbatana and then eastward to Bactria. It was there that the satrap of Bactria, Bessus, had Darius murdered on Alexander's approach and took command himself in the unsuccessful opposition to the Macedonian conqueror. These events brought the Persian Empire to an end and marked the beginning of the Hellenistic period in the E Mediterranean. Darius III is probably the Darius the Persian mentioned in the Bible (Neh. 12.22).

Darius the Mede, in the Bible, king of the Chaldeans after the defeat of Belshazzar; he is called the son of Ahasuerus. He is not easily identified with any known monarch. Dan. 5.31; 9.1; 11.1.

Darjeeling (därjēl'ĭng), town (1971 pop. 42,662), West Bengal state, NE India, near the Sikkim border. Its most famous product is tea. The town is a district administrative center and a market for grains, fruit, and vegetables. Situated at an altitude of c.7,000 ft (2,130 m), Darjeeling is also a Himalayan resort commanding majestic views of Mt. Everest and Kanchenjunga. Many Tibetan refugees who fled from the Chinese army in 1959 live in the vicinity.

Dark Ages: see MIDDLE AGES.

dark horse, in U.S. politics, a person unexpectedly chosen by a major party as a candidate for public office, especially for the presidency. A presidential dark horse is usually chosen at a party national convention and often has acquired only a local or limited reputation at the time of his nomination. He is invariably the offspring of compromise after rival factions have deadlocked the convention. Probably the best-known example of a dark horse is James K. Polk, who was selected at the Democratic convention of 1844 on the ninth ballot, although he had not been nominated until the eighth ballot.

dark-line spectrum: see SPECTRUM.

Darkon (där'kŏn), ancestor of a family who returned with Zerubbabel. Ezra 2.56; Neh. 7.58.

Darlan, Jean François (zhäN fräNswä' därläN'), 1881–1942, French admiral. A career naval officer, he became commander of the French navy in 1939 and joined the VICHY GOVERNMENT in 1940 as minister of the navy. After the fall of Pierre LAVAL, Darlan was made (Feb., 1941) vice premier, foreign minister, and successor-designate to Marshal Pétain; he was the actual head of government. Laval returned to power in April, 1942; Darlan lost his cabinet posts but was given command of the French armed forces. In Algiers during the Allied landing (Nov. 7, 1942) in North Africa, Darlan ordered the cessation of French resistance to the Allies. Although publicly repudiated by Pétain, he assumed control over French N and W Africa in the marshal's name and brought them to the side of the Allies. He was assassinated in December. He was succeeded as high commissioner by Gen. H. H. GIRAUD.

Darley, Felix Octavius Carr, 1822–88, American illustrator, lithographer, and painter, b. Philadelphia. He is best known for his pen-and-ink drawings, which, for their inventiveness, versatility, vigorous style, and technical facility, placed him in the front rank of American illustrators. He illustrated the works of Cooper, Hawthorne, Irving, Longfellow, and others.

Darley, George, 1795–1846, English author and mathematician, b. Ireland. Included among his works are the pastoral drama *Sylvia* (1827), the poem *Nepenthe* (1835), a precursor of 20th-century symbolist poetry; and several books on mathematics. See his letters (ed. with a memoir by C. C. Abbott, 1928).

Darling, Grace Horsley, 1815–42, British heroine. The daughter of a lighthouse keeper on the Farne Islands, she aided her father in rescuing five persons from the wrecked *Forfarshire* in 1838.

Darling, Jay Norwood, 1876–1962, American cartoonist, known as "Ding," b. near Charlevoix, Mich. He worked for the Sioux City, Iowa, *Journal,* for the Des Moines *Register,* and from 1917 to 1949 for the New York *Tribune* (later the *Herald Tribune*). His forceful and witty work won him the Pulitzer Prize for cartoons in 1923 and 1943. Actively interested in the preservation of wildlife, he served as chief (1934–35) of the U.S. Bureau of Biological Survey. He wrote *Ding Goes to Russia* (1931) and *The Cruise of the Bouncing Betsy* (1937). See J. M. Henry, ed., *Ding's Half Century* (1962).

Darling, river, 1,702 mi (2,739 km) long, rising in the Eastern Highlands, NE New South Wales and SE Queensland, Australia, and flowing SW across New South Wales into the Murray River at Wentworth. It is the longest river in Australia. Although it receives numerous tributaries in its upper course, the Darling has dried up on several occasions. The river is used extensively for irrigation. It was discovered in 1828 by Charles Sturt, an English explorer.

Darling Downs, tableland, 27,610 sq mi (71,510 sq km), SE Queensland, Australia, W of the Great Dividing Range. Settled in 1840 by sheep grazers, this grassland region has become an important farming and dairying area; it is in Australia's wheat belt.

Darling Range, Western Australia state, Australia, at the edge of the Western Plateau, extending 200 mi (322 km) parallel with the southwest coast and rising to 1,910 ft (582 m) in Mt. Cooke. Gold and tin are mined there. The suburbs of Perth are on its slopes.

Darlington, county borough (1971 pop. 85,899), Durham, NE England, on the Skerne River near its junction with the Tees River. It is a railroad center, with extensive locomotive works, iron foundries, steel plants, and worsted factories. The locomotive that drew the first passenger train (1825), on the Stockton and Darlington Railway, is preserved in Bank Top Station. St. Cuthbert's Collegiate Church (12th cent.) is noteworthy. Queen Elizabeth College, the College of Technology, and the School of Art are in the borough. In 1974, Darlington became part of the new nonmetropolitan county of Durham.

Darmstadt (därm'shtät), city (1970 pop. 141,224), Hesse, central West Germany. It is a commercial, industrial, and transportation center; its manufactures include chemicals, steel, machinery, and printed materials. Darmstadt was mentioned in the 11th cent. and was chartered in 1330. It passed to the landgraves of HESSE in 1479. The city was severely damaged during World War II. It is the site of a technical university.

Darnah (där'nä) or **Derna** (dĕr'-), city (1970 est. pop. 26,000), NE Libya, a port and former caravan center on the Mediterranean Sea. Farm products and wool are its chief exports. During the Tripolitan War, William Eaton commanded a U.S. force, made up of marines and hired Arab soldiers, that in April, 1805, captured Darnah, then a stronghold of the Barbary pirates.

Darnley, Henry Stuart or **Stewart, Lord,** 1545-67, second husband of MARY QUEEN OF SCOTS and father of James I of England (James VI of Scotland). His mother was Margaret Douglas, the daughter of Archibald Douglas, earl of Angus, and Margaret Tudor, daughter of Henry VII of England; this made Darnley a candidate for succession to the English throne after Elizabeth I. His father was Matthew Stuart, 4th earl of LENNOX. Darnley was born and brought up in England, where his father was in exile. In 1565, at the age of 19, he was allowed by Queen Elizabeth to follow his father to Scotland, and within a short time he married Queen Mary. The motives of the Scottish queen were predominantly political; Darnley was a Catholic and his right of succession to the English throne reinforced Mary's own. However, his handsome appearance and courtly manners must also have impressed Mary because at first she was apparently infatuated with him. The Protestant lords, dismayed at what appeared a Catholic triumph, revolted, but Mary defeated them easily. Within a short time Darnley had shown himself to be a vicious and dissipated man, and Mary denied him the crown matrimonial (which would have given him power equal to Mary's). Wounded in pride and suspicious of Mary's relationship with David RIZZIO, Darnley joined a conspiracy against Rizzio. On March 9, 1566, Darnley and a group of nobles seized Rizzio in the queen's presence and stabbed him to death. They may have hoped simultaneously to shock the pregnant queen into fatal illness, but she defeated the coup by winning over Darnley and escaping from her captors to the help of loyal nobles. Darnley soon found himself without a friend in either camp. Although Mary made efforts toward reconciliation after the birth of their son, Darnley remained intractable, and the council demanded that the queen rid herself of him. Possibly with Mary's knowledge, there was then formed a plot, one of whose leaders was the earl of BOTHWELL. The earl of Morton was later executed for his part in it, and others may have had a hand. Recovering from an illness, Darnley arrived in Edinburgh early in 1567 and lodged in Kirk o' Field, a house just outside the city. On the night of Feb. 9, after a visit from Mary, the house was blown up by gunpowder. In the morning the bodies of Darnley and a page were found strangled in an adjoining garden. Details of the murder remain a historical mystery. Mary's subsequent failure to punish Bothwell and her hasty marriage to him led to the revolt that soon dethroned her.

Darrow, Clarence Seward, 1857-1938, American lawyer, b. Kinsman, Ohio. He first practiced law in Ashtabula, Ohio. In 1888 he moved to Chicago, where he was corporation counsel for several years and conducted the cases that the city brought to reduce transit rates. Later, as general counsel for the Chicago and Northwestern RR, he resigned (1894) to defend Eugene V. DEBS and others in connection with the Pullman strike. The defense was unsuccessful. Darrow soon renounced his lucrative practice to defend the "underdog." A staunch opponent of capital punishment, he exerted his tremendous courtroom skill in behalf of over 100 persons charged with murder; none of his clients was ever sentenced to death. Darrow procured, in 1906, the acquittal of William D. HAYWOOD and his associates on the charge of murdering former Governor Steunenberg of Idaho. He offended many socialists (with whom he had been popularly identified) by introducing a plea of guilty in his defense of the McNamara brothers in the Los Angeles *Times* dynamiting case (1911). Darrow was himself tried for allegedly bribing a juror in the trial, but he was acquitted. In the Chicago "thrill" murder trial (1924) of Nathan Leopold and Richard Loeb he saved the defendants from execution by a plea of temporary insanity. Long an agnostic, Darrow fought fundamentalist religious tenets in the Scopes evolution case (1925; see SCOPES TRIAL). Pitted against William Jennings BRYAN, he defended without success a schoolteacher charged with violating a Tennessee statute prohibiting teaching that man descended from other forms of life. Many felt, nevertheless, that Darrow's examination of Bryan on the witness stand did much to discredit fundamentalist interpretation of the Bible. Among Darrow's books are a novel, *Farmington* (1904); *Crime: Its Cause and Treatment* (1922); and *Attorney for the Damned,* a collection of his defense summations, ed. by Arthur Weinberg (1957). See his autobiography (1932); biographies by Irving Stone (1941, repr. 1971) and Miriam Gurko (1965).

D'Artagnan, Charles de Batz-Castelmore: see ARTAGNAN, CHARLES DE BATZ-CASTELMORE D'.

darter or **anhinga** (ănhĭng'gə), common name for a very slender, black water bird very closely related to the cormorant. It frequents the wooded borders of freshwater lakes, rivers, and swamps in tropical and warm temperate regions—in America, from the SE United States to Cuba and Argentina; in Africa, S of the Sahara desert; in Asia, in the southern regions; and also in Australia and New Guinea. Darters (*Anhinga anhinga*) eat fish, crustaceans, reptiles, and insects, attacking their prey with rapierlike thrusts of their sharp beaks, whence the name darter. Another common name, snake-bird, describes the darter's habit of swimming with its body submerged and only the snakelike head and long, curved neck exposed. In the S United States darters are called water turkeys, for no apparent reason. They nest in small colonies with ibises and herons, building bulky nests lined with leaves. The helpless young are fed by regurgitation. Darters are strong fliers and migrate annually. They are classified in the phylum CHORDATA, subphylum Vertebrata, class Aves, order Pelecaniformes, family Anhingidae.

Dartford, municipal borough (1971 pop. 45,670), Kent, SE England, near London. Its industries include flour milling and the manufacture of paper, drugs, chemicals, and cement. In 1355, Edward III founded an Augustinian convent in Dartford. The rebellion led by Wat TYLER started there in 1381.

Dartmoor Prison, English prison, at Princetown, Devonshire, built (1806-9) to house French captives during the Napoleonic Wars. During the War of 1812 many American prisoners were confined there, and their brutal mistreatment was investigated after the war by an Anglo-American commission that awarded compensation to the families of those who had died there. Between 1812 and 1816 about 1,500 American and French prisoners died in the prison and were buried in a field beyond the prison walls. Unoccupied for over 30 years, Dartmoor was reopened in 1850 as a civilian prison for convicts sentenced to long terms of imprisonment or to hard labor. See A. J. Rhodes, ed., *Dartmoor Prison; A Record of 126 Years of Prisoner of War and Convict Life, 1806-1932* (1933); Tom Tullett, *Inside Dartmoor* (1966).

Dartmouth, city (1971 pop. 64,770), S N.S., Canada, on Halifax harbor, an inlet of the Atlantic Ocean. The city has large sugar and oil refineries, an automobile assembly plant, and a naval research establishment. Dartmouth has expanded greatly in recent decades.

Dartmouth, municipal borough (1971 pop. 5,696), Devonshire, SW England, on the Dart estuary. The principal feature of the town today is the Royal Naval College. The borough has boat-building facilities and is a yachting center. Dartmouth was an important port for the wine trade (12th-15th cent.) with Bordeaux and supplied Edward III with 31 ships for the siege of Calais in the Hundred Years War.

Dartmouth, residential and resort town (1970 pop. 18,800), Bristol co., SE Mass., on Buzzards Bay, in a dairy region; settled c.1650, inc. 1664. Farming, fishing, and summer tourism are its economic mainstays. The town was practically annihilated in King Philip's War but was rebuilt and later became a shipbuilding center.

Dartmouth College, at Hanover, N.H.; mainly for men; chartered 1769, opened 1770, the ninth colonial college (see WHEELOCK, ELEAZAR). Stressing liberal arts, Dartmouth also has schools of business administration and civil engineering. There is also a medical school with a hospital. The college outing club sponsors a famous winter sports carnival. See studies by R. F. Leavens and A. H. Lord (1965) and F. N. Stites (1972).

Dartmouth College Case, decided by the U.S. Supreme Court in 1819. The legislature of New Hampshire, in 1816, without the consent of the college trustees, amended the charter of 1769 to make Dartmouth College public. The trustees brought suit. Daniel Webster argued successfully that the amendment violated the Constitution because the state had impaired "the obligation of a contract." The opinion of the court, delivered by Chief Justice John Marshall, was that a charter was in effect inviolable. The decision made the contract clause of the Constitution a powerful instrument for the judicial protection of property rights against state abridgment. In 1837, Chief Justice TANEY, while not challenging the basic principle, ruled in the CHARLES RIVER BRIDGE CASE that a legislative charter must be construed narrowly and a corporation could claim no implied rights beyond the specific terms of a grant.

Daru, Pierre Antoine, Comte (pyĕr äNtwän' kôNt därü'), 1767-1829, French soldier, administrator, statesman, and writer. He served in the French Revolutionary Wars, was imprisoned during the Reign of Terror, and became chief of the army commissary under Napoleon I, who created him count. His exemplary administration vastly contributed to Napoleon's victories. Daru also filled various cabinet posts under Napoleon and was made a peer after the restoration of the Bourbons. His writings include histories of Venice and Brittany and translations of Horace.

Darusmont, Frances Wright: see WRIGHT, FRANCES.

Darvon: see ANALGESIC.

Darwen (dăr'wĭn, dăr'ĕn), municipal borough (1971 pop. 28,880), Lancashire, NW England. Engineering and the manufacture of wallpaper, paint, and plastics are the major industries. The importance of textiles has declined.

Darwin, Charles Galton, 1887-1962, English physicist and administrator. Educated at Cambridge, he worked under Ernest Rutherford at Manchester, where he collaborated with H. G. J. Moseley in fundamental work on X-ray diffraction by crystals. Following World War I he became a fellow and lecturer at Christ's College, Cambridge, where he and R. H. Fowler developed new methods of statistical mechanics that later served as a foundation for quantum statistics. Professor at Edinburgh from 1924 to 1936 and master of Christ's College from 1936, he directed the National Physical Laboratory during World War II, leaving the post in 1949. The last 15 years of his life were devoted to the study of the sociological implications of the population explosion, as reflected in his book *The Next Million Years* (1953).

Darwin, Charles Robert, 1809-82, English naturalist, b. Shrewsbury; grandson of Erasmus Darwin. He firmly established the theory of organic evolution known as DARWINISM. He studied medicine at Edinburgh and for the ministry at Cambridge but lost interest in both professions during the training. His interest in natural history led to his friendship with the botanist J. S. Henslow; through him came the opportunity to make a five-year cruise (1831-36) as official naturalist aboard the *Beagle.* This started Darwin on a career of accumulating and assimilating data that resulted in the formulation of his concept of evolution. He spent the remainder of his life carefully and methodically working over the information from his copious notes and from every other available source. Independently, A. R. WALLACE had worked out a theory similar to Darwin's. Both men were exceptionally modest; they first published summaries of their ideas simultaneously in 1858. In 1859, Darwin set forth the structure of his theory and massive support for it in the superbly organized *Origin of Species,* supplemented and elaborated in his many later books, notably *The Descent of Man* (1871). Darwin also formulated a theory of the origin of CORAL reefs. See his autobiography (ed. by Nora Barlow, 1958) and *Life and Letters* (ed. by Francis Darwin, 1887; repr., with intro. by G. G. Simpson, 1962); letters of Darwin and Henslow, ed. by Nora Barlow (1967); P. B. Sears, *Charles Darwin: The Naturalist as a Cultural Force* (1950); Jacques Barzun, *Darwin, Marx, Wagner* (rev. ed. 1958); Gerhard Wichler, *Charles Darwin: The Founder of the Theory of Evolution and Natural Selection* (tr. 1961); Alan Moorehead, *Darwin and the Beagle* (1969); Philip Appleman, ed., *Darwin* (1970); D. L Hull, *Darwin and his Critics* (1973).

Darwin, Erasmus, 1731–1802, English physician and poet. During most of his life he practiced medicine in Lichfield and cultivated a botanical garden. He was a prominent member of the Lichfield literary group, which included Anna Seward and Thomas Day. In a long poem, *The Botanic Garden* (1789–91), Darwin expounded the botanical system of Linnaeus. His *Zoonomia* (1794–96), explaining organic life according to evolutionary principles, anticipates later theories. He was the grandfather of Charles Darwin and of Francis Galton. See biography by Desmond King-Hele (1964).

Darwin, Sir Francis, 1848–1925, English botanist, assistant to his father, Charles Robert Darwin. He lectured in botany at Cambridge and was foreign secretary of the Royal Society and president of the British Association. He edited the *Life and Letters of Charles Darwin* (1887) and was knighted in 1913.

Darwin, Sir George Howard, 1845–1912, English astronomer and mathematician; 2d son of Charles Darwin. He was Plumian professor (from 1883) of astronomy and experimental philosophy at Cambridge, and a recognized authority on cosmogony. He wrote *The Tides* (1898) and *Scientific Papers* (5 vol., 1907–16).

Darwin, city (1971 pop. 31,687), capital of the Northern Territory, N Australia, on Port Darwin, an inlet of the Timor Sea. Remotely situated on the sparsely settled north coast, Darwin has no rail connection with any of the major Australian cities. It is important largely because of its convenient position as an air stop on the Singapore-Sydney route. Australian military personnel and their dependents make up a large part of the population. There is a large Chinese quarter dating from the 1870s, when Chinese laborers worked on the cable link to Adelaide. In World War II the city was heavily bombed by the Japanese; later a military airdrome, fuel-oil installations, and a wharf were built, and Darwin became a key Allied base. Originally called Palmerston, the town was renamed (1911) for Charles Darwin because its site had been discovered (1839) during a voyage of Darwin's ship, the *Beagle.* The city was almost completely destroyed by a hurricane in Dec., 1974.

Darwinism, concept of EVOLUTION developed in the mid-19th cent. by Charles Robert DARWIN. Darwin's meticulously documented observations led him to question the then current belief in special creation of each species. After years of studying and correlating the voluminous notes he had made as naturalist on H.M.S. *Beagle,* he was prompted by the submission (1858) of an almost identical theory by A. R. WALLACE to present his evidence for the descent of all life from a common ancestral origin; his monumental *Origin of Species* was published in 1859. Darwin observed (as had Malthus) that although all organisms tend to reproduce in a geometrically increasing ratio, the numbers of a given species remain more or less constant. From this he deduced that there is a continuing struggle for existence, for survival. He pointed out the existence of variations—differences among members of the same species—and suggested that the variations that prove helpful to a plant or an animal in its struggle for existence better enable it to survive and reproduce. These favorable variations are thus transmitted to the offspring of the survivors and spread to the entire species over successive generations. This process he called the principle of natural SELECTION (the expression "survival of the fittest" was later coined by Herbert Spencer). In the same way, sexual selection (factors influencing the choice of mates among animals) also plays a part. In developing his theory that the origin and diversification of species results from gradual accumulation of individual modifications, Darwin was greatly influenced by Sir Charles Lyell's treatment of the doctrine of UNIFORMITARIANISM. Darwin's evidence for evolution rested on the data of comparative anatomy, especially the study of homologous structures in different species and of rudimentary (vestigial) organs; of the recapitulation of past racial history in individual embryonic development; of geographical distribution, extensively documented by Wallace; of the immense variety in forms of plants and animals (to the degree that often one species is not distinct from another); and, to a lesser degree, of paleontology. As originally formulated, Darwinism did not distinguish between acquired characteristics, which are not transmissible by heredity, and genetic variations, which are inheritable. Modern knowledge of heredity—especially the concept of mutation, which provides an explanation of how variations may arise—has supplemented and modified the theory, but in its basic outline Darwinism is now universally accepted by scientists.

Darwin's finches or **Galapagos finches** (gəlä'pəgōs"), species of small finches, constituting the subfamily Geospizinae of the finch family. This group is confined to the Galapagos Islands, with a single species found on Cocos Island, about 600 mi (960 km) to the northeast. The specialization of these finches was one of the important pieces of evidence considered by Charles DARWIN in formulating the theory of EVOLUTION, and is one of the most striking examples of ADAPTIVE RADIATION. Geographically isolated from other finches, and without competition from similar species, these birds have developed highly distinctive anatomical and behavioral characteristics, with each species adapted to a particular ecological niche. The most conspicuous variation is in the size and shape of the bill, which is adapted in the different species for different purposes, such as crushing seeds, pecking wood, and probing flowers for nectar. *Camarhynchus pallidus,* an insect-eating finch, is especially interesting in that it uses twigs and cactus spines, held in its beak, to probe for insects. Darwin proposed that the Galapagos finches evolved on the islands from a single species of finch. Darwin's finches are classified in three genera of the phylum CHORDATA, subphylum Vertebrata, class Aves, order Passeriformes, family Fringillidae, subfamily Geospizinae.

Daryal (däryăl', Rus. dəryäl') or **Dariel** (dărēĕl'), pass, c.3,950 ft (1,204 m) high, SE European USSR, in Georgia, in the central Greater Caucasus mts. below Mt. Kazbek. Situated above the Terek River, it is noted for its wild grandeur. The GEORGIAN MILITARY ROAD crosses the pass, which has long been significant as an invasion route. In ancient times Daryal was called the Gates of Alan or the Caucasian or Iberian Gates. The gorge appears in Lermontov's poem *The Demon.*

Das, Chitta Ranjan (chĭt'tə rŭn'jən däs), 1870–1925, Indian political leader. A lawyer who firmly opposed British rule and defended many Indian nationalists, he idealized traditional Indian life. He supported Mohandas Gandhi's noncooperation movement and was imprisoned in 1921. In 1922 he partially broke with Gandhi and founded the Swaraj [self-rule] party, urging Indians to run for political office so that the British administration might be disrupted from within; Gandhi's influence remained paramount, however. Das was elected mayor of Calcutta in 1924 and appeared to be leaning toward cooperation with the British before his death.

Dase, Ethiopia: see DESSYE.

dash: see PUNCTUATION.

Dashava (dəshä'və), major natural gas producing region of W USSR, mainly in Lvov oblast, W Ukrainian SSR, in the Carpathian foothills. It is linked by pipeline to many centers of W USSR, including Lvov, Kiev, Minsk, and Moscow.

dasheen: see ARUM.

Dasht-e Kavir (dăsht-ēkävēr'), great salt desert, c.500 mi (800 km) long and c.200 mi (320 km) wide, SE of the Elburz mts., N central Iran. It is a huge basin of interior drainage named after the kavirs (salt marshes) located there. The Kavir Buzurg (Great Kavir), c.200 mi (320 km) long and c.100 mi (160 km) wide, lies in the heart of the region; low sandy hills separate it from smaller kavirs. An almost rainless climate with strong surface evaporation has created a crust of salt over the marsh and mud lands. Chemical salts balance the evaporation by drawing moisture from the substrata and the atmosphere. Because its kavirs have properties similar to quicksand, travel in the Dasht-e Kavir is extremely dangerous. It is almost uninhabited and only partly explored; settlement is restricted to the hills and surrounding mountains. Extending S from the Dasht-e Kavir is the **Dasht-e Lut,** a sand and stone desert, c.300 mi (480 km) long and c.200 mi (320 km) wide; it consists of dried-out kavirs and contains a large salt marsh. The two deserts occupy most of the central Iranian plateau.

Dasht-e Lut, Iran: see DASHT-E KAVIR.

dassie: see HYRAX.

dasyure (dăs'ēyŏŏr"), name for several small, predatory MARSUPIALS, or pouched mammals, of the family Dasyuridea, found in Australia, Tasmania, and New Guinea. Typical dasyures, known in Australia as native cats, are furry animals with large eyes, pointed snouts, and long tails. The largest are the size of house cats; most are somewhat smaller. They are variously colored, and most species are spotted. Dasyures hunt by night and are able to climb trees. Once found all over Australia, they are now extinct in many regions. They are not related to true cats. The fierce TASMANIAN DEVIL is a large, atypical dasyure. Dasyures are classified in several genera of the phylum CHORDATA, subphylum Vertebrata, class Mammalia, order Marsupialia, family Dasyuridae.

data communications, application of telecommunications technology to the problem of transmitting data, especially to, from, or between COMPUTERS. In popular usage, it is said that data communications make it possible for one computer to "talk" with another. Telephone circuits are often used, although their relatively limited frequency range makes them rather slow paths for data. This limitation is offset somewhat by their ready availability and relatively low cost. Generally, however, fairly elaborate equipment, such as modems (*mo*dulator-*dem*odulators), is required to coordinate the computer and the telephone circuit. Where cost can be justified, high speed data links are constructed; these are often coaxial cables designed for wide frequency range, or microwave, radio systems.

date, name for a PALM (*Phoenix dactylifera*) and for its edible fruit. Probably native to Arabia and North Africa, it has from earliest times been a principal food in many desert and tropical regions. For some 4,000 years it has been grown near the Tigris and Euphrates rivers. It is cultivated in many other warm regions, including parts of the SW United States and Mexico. The trees sometimes reach a height of 100 ft (30.5 m) and yield fruit for generations. Staminate (male) and pistillate (female) flowers are borne on separate trees, and pollination of those grown commercially is usually done by hand. Seedless dates may be produced without pollination but they are inferior. Heavy, pendant clusters of the sweet, nutritious fruits are produced; the yield after maturity (10 to 15 years) is usually from 100 to 200 lb (45–90 kg) or more per tree annually. Each fruit is 1 to 3 in. (2.54–7.6 cm) long, reddish brown or yellowish brown, and somewhat cylindrical or oblong. When ripe, the bunches of fruit are cut intact from the palm and matured in a warm place. In the Old World a sugar and a fermented drink are made from the sap of the date palm and other species of *Phoenix,* and the seeds are sometimes roasted and used as a coffee substitute or pressed for oil, leaving a residue useful for stock feed. The wood of the trunk is often used in construction and the leaves are used for weaving mats and baskets. Dates are classified in the division MAGNOLIOPHYTA, class Liliatae, order Arecales, family Palmae.

date line, international: see INTERNATIONAL DATE LINE.

Dathan (dā'thən), Levite who, with his brother Abiram and with KORAH, was consumed by fire from heaven. Num. 16.1–35; 26.9,10; Deut. 11.6.

Datia (dŭ'tēä), town (1971 pop. 37,437), Madhya Pradesh state, N central India. It is a district administrative center and a market for food grains and oilseed. Handloom weaving is an important industry. Datia's large square palace (17th cent.) is one of the finest examples of Hindu architecture in N India.

dating, in geology, archaeology, paleontology, and physics, the determination of the actual or relative age of an object, of a natural phenomenon, or of a series of events. Geologic dating is classified commonly as absolute (establishment of the actual age of the earth and its rocks), or relative (determination of the sequence of geologic events). The chief methods for absolute dating include those based on the salinity of oceans, on the rate of erosion of land surfaces, on the thickness of sedimentary rocks, on varved clay, and on radioactivity. The salinity method is based on the assumption that the oceans originally held fresh water and that the rivers carried dissolved salt from weathered rocks to the sea, increasing the salinity of the oceans at a constant rate.

On this basis the age of the earth was estimated to be about 100 million years. Computations for the erosion method of dating are founded on the assumption that it would take 9 million years to produce a major unconformity (erosional surface). In age determinations based on the thickness of sedimentary strata, a rate of deposition of the sediments is postulated and divided into their estimated total thickness. The preceding three methods have been discounted as highly unreliable. The varved-clay method is applied, with fair accuracy, to recent deposits. Streams flowing into still bodies commonly deposit layers (varves) of clay and other fine sediments throughout the year. Those laid down during the fall and winter have a dark color because of the presence of dead vegetation; those deposited during the rest of the year have a light color. By counting each pair of varves the age of the deposit can be determined. The dating method most widely used and accepted is based on the natural RADIOACTIVITY of certain minerals found in rocks. Since the rate of radioactive decay of any particular ISOTOPE is known, the age of a specimen can be computed from the relative proportions of the remaining radioactive material and its decay products. By this method the age of the earth is estimated to be over 3.5 billion years. Some of the radioactive elements used in dating and their decay products are the decay series from uranium-238 to lead-206, uranium-235 to lead-207, thorium-232 to lead-208, rubidium-87 to strontium-87, and potassium-40 to argon-40 and calcium-40. Each radioactive member of these series has a known, constant decay rate, measured by its HALF-LIFE, that is unaffected by any physical or chemical changes. Relative dating is accomplished by marking out the succession in which rocks were deposited, using various surface criteria including raindrops, ripple marks, and mud cracks. Igneous masses are dated according to whether they caused metamorphism in the surrounding rock (proof of emplacement in preexisting rock) or whether sediments were deposited on them after they were formed. Fossils are used in dating, since certain assemblages of species are characteristic of specific periods of geologic time. Pollen analysis, or palynology, incorporates the microscopic examination of fossil pollen grains in peats and lake deposits. From this can be established the succession of the deposits as well as the climate prevalent at the time of deposition. In archaeology and recent geology radioactive carbon-14, which decomposes to nitrogen-14, has been used successfully. Carbon dating is especially useful because all organic matter contains carbon, and thus contains a certain proportion of carbon-14. The fluorine content of fossil bones is an indication of their age because it accumulates from water in the ground at a predictable rate. The discovery of some remains of the Piltdown Man was proved to be a hoax when it was shown that the jaw and skull had different fluorine contents and were therefore of different ages. In dendrochronology the age of a tree can be determined by counting the number of annual rings in its cross section (see CAMBIUM). This method is applied to dating archaeological sites, especially in the SW United States and other dry regions. A special auger is used to secure a core from the trunk of a tree, and the ring pattern is matched with those of trees of known age. The pattern is affected by climatic factors and is distinctive for a particular period. By the use of overlapping patterns, dating by this method has been carried back as far as 3,000 years. See P. M. Hurley, *How Old is the Earth?* (1959); W. L. Stokes, *Essentials of Earth History* (2nd ed. 1965); E. F. Zeuner, *Dating the Past* (4th ed. 1970).

dative (dā'tĭv) [Lat.,=giving], in Latin grammar, the CASE typically used to refer to a secondary recipient of an action. For example, *him* in *I gave him a book* is translated in Latin by a dative case. The Latin dative also has other uses; and the cases called dative in other languages correspond in their grammatical function only in part to that of the Latin.

Daubenton, Louis Jean Marie (lwē zhäN märē' dōbäNtôN'), 1716–1800, French naturalist. He was a professor at the Collège de France from 1778; his work touched on many fields—comparative anatomy, plant physiology, mineralogy, and experimental agriculture. He is known especially for his work on the anatomy of mammals in Buffon's *Histoire naturelle* and is credited with introducing the Merino sheep into France.

D'Aubigné, Jean Henri Merle: see MERLE D'AUBIGNÉ, JEAN HENRI.

Daubigny, Charles-François (shärl-fräNswä' dōbēnyē'), 1817–78, French landscape painter. He went to Italy early in life and later studied in Paris with Paul Delaroche. Although usually classed with the Barbizon school, he never lived in Barbizon. His last 30 years were spent largely in his houseboat on the Seine and the Oise, and he is best known for his pictures of the banks of those rivers. He was particularly successful in his atmospheric depiction of dawn, twilight, and moonlight. His later pictures are handled with great breadth. Monet and Boudin were especially attentive to his work. Daubigny is well represented in the Louvre, the Mesdag Museum (The Hague), the National Gallery (London), and the Metropolitan Museum. Characteristic are his *Return of the Flock—Moonlight, Banks of the Oise,* and *Moonlight.* His son **Karl Pierre Daubigny,** 1846–86, painted in his father's manner.

Daudet, Alphonse (älfôNs' dōdā'), 1840–97, French writer, b. Nîmes (Provence). Daudet made his mark with gently naturalistic stories and novels portraying French life both in the provinces and in Paris. At the age of 16, after his father had suffered financial loss, he was obliged to serve as study master (*maître d'études*) in a school at Cévennes. With the help and encouragement of his older brother, he went to Paris, where he began his literary career with the publication of a small volume of poetry, *Les Amoureuses* (1857). His career was assured with the success of *Lettres de mon moulin* (1869, tr. *Letters from My Mill,* 1900), a group of delightful, Provence-inspired short stories. *Le Petit Chose* (1868) is a semiautobiographical novel touchingly descriptive of his life at boarding school and sometimes compared to Dickens's *David Copperfield.* It was followed in rapid succession by *Aventures prodigieuses de Tartarin de Tarascon* (1872), *Contes du lundi* (1873), *Fromont jeune et Risler aîné* (1874), *Jack* (1876), *Le Nabab* (1877), *Les Rois en exil* (1879), *Numa Roumestan* (1881), *L'Évangeliste* (1883), *Sapho* (1884), *La Belle Nivernaise* (1886), and *L'Immortel* (1888). He was at once objective and personal, and his works, permeated by an engaging sense of humor and a subtle irony, are drawn largely from his own experience. Two volumes of reminiscences, *Souvenirs d'un homme de lettres* and *Trente ans de Paris,* appeared in 1888. See study by M. Sachs (1965). His brother, Louis Marie Ernst Daudet (1837–1921) was a historian. His son was **Léon Daudet,** 1867–1942, author, editor for the Roman Catholic paper *Action française,* and a member of the Goncourt Academy. He was a bitter opponent of the Third Republic and of democracy in general, serving as deputy from 1919 to 1924, but failing to be elected senator in 1927. He wrote a biography of his father, but his most valuable work is probably *Souvenirs des milieux littéraires, politiques, artistiques et médicaux* (6 vol., 1914–21; tr. of selections, *Memoirs of Léon Daudet,* 1925).

Daugava: see DVINA (Western Dvina), river, USSR.

Daugavpils (dou'gäfpēls), Ger. *Dünaburg,* city (1970 pop. 101,000), W European USSR, in Latvia, on the Western Dvina River. It is a rail junction and commercial center. The city's industries produce lumber, food products, iron, and textiles. It was founded (1278) by the Livonian Knights and became a strategic fortress. Passing (1561) to the combined kingdom of Lithuania and Poland, it was ceded to Russia in the first partition of Poland (1772). Daugavpils was a flourishing trade center until World War I. In independent Latvia (1918–40) it was the capital of Latgale prov. Its former (1893–1920) Russian name was Dvinsk.

Daugherty, Harry Micajah (dô'ərtē), 1860–1941, American politician, b. Fayette co., Ohio. He became a successful corporation lawyer in Columbus, Ohio, and served (1890–94) in the state legislature. A leader of the Republican party in his state, he directed Warren G. Harding's successful campaign for the presidential nomination in 1920. Daugherty, rewarded (1921) by Harding with the office of U.S. Attorney General, became the President's confidant and influenced his appointments. He was charged with being implicated in the Teapot Dome affair, and other scandals of the Harding administration. After President Calvin Coolidge forced (1924) his resignation, Daugherty was prosecuted (1927) for alleged conspiracy to defraud the U.S. government, but the case was dismissed after two juries failed to agree. He wrote, with Thomas Dixon, *The Inside Story of the Harding Tragedy* (1932).

Daughters of the American Revolution (DAR), a Colonial patriotic society in the United States, open to women having one or more ancestors who aided the cause in the Revolution. The society was organized (1890) at Washington, D.C., and has its national headquarters at Memorial Continental Hall there. With a membership of about 190,000, the society has done much for the preservation and marking of historic places. In politics, the DAR has been criticized for its conservative policies. There is a similar but unrelated organization known as the Daughters of the Revolution. See studies by Martha Strayer (1958, repr. 1973) and Peggy Anderson (1974).

Daulatabad (doulətəbäd'), village, Andhra Pradesh state, SE India. Its 13th-century fortress is built atop a conical rock c.500 ft (150 m) high. The Chand Minar (1294), a minaret of Turkish style, is one of the outstanding examples of Islamic art in S India. In ancient times the village was called Deogir.

Daumat, Jean: see DOMAT, JEAN.

Daumier, Honoré (ônôrā' dōmyā'), 1808–79, French caricaturist, painter, and sculptor. Daumier was the greatest social satirist of his day. Son of a Marseilles glazier, he accompanied his family to Paris in 1816. There he studied under Lenoir and learned lithography. He soon began to contribute cartoons to the weekly *Caricature.* In 1832 his representation of Louis Philippe as Gargantua caused him six months' imprisonment. Two outstanding lithographs of 1834, *Rue Transnonain* and *Le Ventre législatif* [the legislative paunch] testify to his early direct and bitterly ironic approach. After the suppression of *Caricature* his work appeared in *Charivari,* where he mercilessly ridiculed the bourgeois society of his day in a highly realistic graphic style. Relished as cartoons in his time, Daumier's lithographs, of which he produced almost 4,000, are now considered masterpieces. He also painted about 200 small canvases of power and dramatic intensity that were stylistically similar to his lithographs. Among these are *Christ and His Disciples* (Rijks Mus.); *Republic* (Louvre); *Three Lawyers* (Phillips Gall., Washington, D.C.); the romantic *Don Quixote* and *The Third-Class Carriage* (both: Metropolitan Mus.). Daumier's sculpture includes over 30 small, painted busts. An example of his work in this medium is a statuette in the Walters Art Gallery, Baltimore. In his last years he suffered from increasing blindness. His financial condition was perilous. Corot put at his disposal a cottage in Valmondois, and it was there that Daumier died. See his *Teachers and Students* (tr. 1970); catalog raisonné ed. by K. E. Maison (2 vol., 1968); studies by J. Adhémar (1954), K. E. Maison (1960), O. Larkin (1966), H. P. Vincent (1968), and J. L. Wasserman (1969).

Daun, Leopold Joseph Maria, Graf von (lā'ōpôlt yō'zĕf märē'ä gräf fən doun), 1705–66, Austrian field marshal. He gained distinction in the War of the Austrian Succession. Daun later reorganized the Austrian army and gave the officers corps a new sense of professionalism. In the Seven Years War he defeated the Prussian forces at Kolin (1757) and Hochkirch (1758) but was defeated at Torgau (1760) after being severely wounded. Daun was a leading exponent of the classic war of maneuver.

Dauphin (dô'fĭn), town (1971 pop. 8,891), SW Man., Canada, on the Vermilion River. It is the retail and distribution center for an agricultural, lumbering, and fishing area.

dauphin (dô'fĭn, Fr. dōfăN') [Fr.,=dolphin], French title, borne first by the counts of Vienne (also called Viennois) and later by the eldest son of the king of France, or, if the dauphin came to die before the king, by the dauphin's eldest son. The origin of the title is rather obscure; it probably was the family name of the counts of Vienne, who adopted the dolphin as their heraldic device (12th cent.). Their territory came to be called the dauphiné, or dauphinate, of Vienne, or simply the DAUPHINÉ. Another dauphinate, that of Auvergne, ruled by a branch of the house of Vienne, came into existence when Auvergne broke up in the 12th cent. The title dauphin passed, with the Dauphiné, to the direct heirs of the French kings when (1349) Dauphin Humbert II of Vienne sold the region to King Philip VI of France. When Philip died (1350) his grandson, later King Charles V, became the first heir to the throne to bear the title. After Louis XI the title was merely honorific. Louis Antoine, duc d'Angoulême (1775–1844), son of King Charles X, was the last dauphin. Louis, eldest son of Louis XIV, was known as the Great Dauphin; he was a competent military leader. LOUIS XVII is known as the Lost Dauphin.

Dauphiné (dōfēnā'), region and former province, SE France, bordering on Italy. It is now divided into three departments, Hautes-Alpes, Isère, and Drôme. In the east the Alps culminate in the Barre des Écrins; their magnificent scenery attracts many tourists. The lower districts are fertile and warm, with vineyards and mulberry shrubs (for silk worms). Some iron is mined, and water power is harnessed for industry. Grenoble (the historic capital), Vienne, and Valence are the chief towns. In the kingdom of Provence (879) and after 933 in that of Arles, Dauphiné was nominally part of the Holy Roman Empire. The rulers assumed the title DAUPHIN. In 1349 the area was sold to France by Dauphin Humbert II, who was childless, and for the next century it was governed as a separate province by the eldest son of the king of France. In 1457 it was annexed by the crown.

Daurat or **Dorat, Jean** (both: zhäN dōrä'), 1508?-1588, French classical scholar. He taught (1546-56) at the Collège de Coqueret at Paris. Among his pupils were the poets Ronsard, Du Bellay, Baïf, and Belleau, who included him in the PLÉIADE.

Davanagere (dä'vəng-gĕrĕ), town (1971 pop. 121,018), Karnataka state, SW India. It is on the Bangalore-Poona railroad. Davanagere is a market for blankets, textiles, vegetable oil, and cotton. There is a machine-tool factory in the suburbs. In the late 18th cent., Haidar Ali, ruler of Karnataka (Mysore), gave Davanagere to the Mahratta leader Apoji Ram, who encouraged merchants to settle there.

Davao (dävou'), city (1970 pop. 392,473), Davao del Sur prov., SE Mindanao, the Philippines, at the mouth of the Davao River on Davao Gulf. The chief commercial center and major port of Mindanao, Davao experienced much industrial growth in the 1960s and its population almost tripled. The city serves a prosperous region that produces hemp, coffee, cacao, and timber, and it has an important wood products industry. Before World War II, Davao was noted for its very large Japanese population. The city and port were seized by Japanese landing parties on Dec. 20, 1941, and used as a base for operations in the Dutch East Indies (now Indonesia). In 1945, after most of the Philippines had been liberated, Japanese forces clung stubbornly to the city and its recovery involved heavy fighting. Davao has a land area of 748 sq mi (1,937 sq km), making it one of the largest cities in the world. The volcanic Mt. Apo, highest (9,690 ft/2,954 m) peak in the islands, is within its boundaries. Davao is the seat of the Univ. of Mindanao. Three provinces that horseshoe around Davao Gulf also carry the name Davao: Davao del Sur, Davao del Norte, and Davao Oriental (noted for its iron deposits); their provincial capitals are Digos, Tagum, and Mati, respectively.

D'Avenant or **Davenant, Sir William** (dăv'ənənt), 1606-68, English poet, playwright, and theatrical producer. His life and work bridge the gap between the Elizabethan and Restoration ages. His best plays appeared between 1634 and 1639. They include *The Wits,* a realistic comedy; *The Platonic Lovers,* a romantic comedy of manners; and *Love and Honour,* a tragicomedy, anticipating the Restoration heroic drama. In 1638 he succeeded Ben Jonson as poet laureate. For his services in the royalist cause he was knighted by Charles I in 1643. *Gondibert,* an unfinished epic poem, and seemingly his most ambitious work, was published in 1651. During the Puritan regime Cromwell permitted him to produce a series of plays that are considered to be the first English operas, the best known being *The Siege of Rhodes* (1656; part 2, 1659). After the Restoration he and Thomas Killigrew were given exclusive patents to produce plays. In these few years D'Avenant divided his energy between managing the Duke of York's players and adapting old plays, most notably those of Shakespeare. His historical significance is greater than the intrinsic value of his work. See biographies by Alfred Harbage (1935, repr. 1971) and A. H. Nethercot (1938, repr. 1967).

Davenport, Charles Benedict, 1866-1944, American zoologist, b. Stamford, Conn., Ph.D. Harvard, 1892. As director (1904-34) of the experimental station of Carnegie Institution at Cold Spring Harbor, N.Y., he conducted research in eugenics and heredity. He is especially noted for his work on the genetic factors in human skin pigmentation. He also made anthropometric studies of American troops during World War I.

Davenport, Herbert Joseph, 1861-1931, American economist, b. Wilmington, Vt., Ph.D. Univ. of Chicago, 1898. He taught at the Univ. of Missouri and at Cornell. In *Value and Distribution* (1908) and *The Economics of Enterprise* (1913) he followed the principles of classical economics, attempting to purify them of nonscientific elements. He made contributions to the theories of cost, interest, and taxation.

Davenport, John, 1597-1670, Puritan clergyman, one of the founders of New Haven, Conn., b. Coventry, England, educated at Merton and Magdalen colleges, Oxford. Starting as a Church of England cleric, Davenport turned more and more to nonconformity. As pastor of an influential London parish he fostered the Puritan cause and in 1633 had to flee to Holland. There he also got into theological troubles, and, after returning to England, he and Theophilus EATON headed a party of Puritan colonists who sailed (1637) to New England. In 1638, Davenport led the colonists to a spot chosen by Eaton, and New Haven colony was founded. Davenport was minister in New Haven and a powerful figure in the colony until he lost (1665) the bitter fight to prevent the union of New Haven colony and Connecticut. In 1667 he accepted the call to the First Church in Boston, where new theological disputes caused many of his congregation to secede and form the Third or Old South Church.

Davenport, city (1970 pop. 98,469), seat of Scott co., E central Iowa, on the Mississippi River; inc. 1836. Bridges connect it with the Illinois cities of Rock Island, Moline, and East Moline, and the four communities are known as the Quad Cities. Davenport is an important rail, commercial, and industrial center. Heavy industrial and agricultural equipment are among the city's manufactures. An early trading post was on the site, and the treaty ending the Black Hawk War was signed there in 1832. Davenport prospered with the arrival (1856) of the first railroad to bridge the Mississippi and had a heavy river traffic in the late 19th cent. Today it is the seat of St. Ambrose College, Marycrest College, a junior college, and the Palmer School of Chiropractic (developed by the son of D. D. Palmer). Also in the city are a municipal art gallery; a public museum; a zoo; and several parks, including Credit Island, site of a battle (1814) in the War of 1812. A large roller-gate dam and several locks, built there by the Federal government, raise the water level of the river.

David, Saint, d.588?, patron saint of Wales, first abbot of Menevia (present-day SAINT DAVID'S). He apparently established a strict rule and was a zealous missionary, founding 12 monasteries. His cult, which was popular in Wales from very early days, made the pilgrimage to his shrine important in the Middle Ages. On his feast, March 1, the national Welsh festival is still celebrated. The ancient Welsh form of his name is Dewi.

David, d. c.972 B.C., king of the ancient Hebrews (c.1012-c.972 B.C.), successor of SAUL. His story appears in several narratives in the Old Testament, with repetition and, according to critics, interpolations of later date. Many of the most interesting and beautiful narratives in the Bible deal with the story of David, such as the fight of David and Goliath, the friendship of David and Jonathan, and the revolt of Absalom. To him were ascribed many of the PSALMS. David's reign seems to mark the change of the Jews from a somewhat rude confederation of tribes to a settled national state. Indicative of this is the rise of Jerusalem, to which David moved his capital from Hebron. David is one of the greatest of Hebrew national heroes. His descendants, the House of David, retained the kingdom of Jerusalem until 586 B.C. When the Messianic hope appeared in Israel, it centered in this house, and according to the Gospels, Jesus was of this royal seed. 1 Sam. 16-30; 2 Sam.; Kings 1,2; 1 Chron. 11-29.

David I, 1084-1153, king of Scotland (1124-53), youngest son of Malcolm III and St. Margaret of Scotland. During the reign of his brother Alexander I, whom he succeeded, David was earl of Cumbria, ruling S of the Clyde and Forth rivers. By his marriage to the heiress of the earl of Northumbria he also became earl of Huntingdon and acquired a claim to Northumbria. In the long struggle for the English crown between MATILDA (his niece) and STEPHEN, David fought for Matilda, but his main object was to secure Northumbria for himself. Although he was defeated by Stephen in the Battle of the Standard (1138), Stephen conceded him the earldom. David's internal rule was wise and momentous for Scotland. He made land grants to many Anglo-Norman families, thus providing the kingdom with a new feudal aristocracy. He also encouraged the commercial development of the Scottish burghs and strengthened the church by new foundations and endowments. He was succeeded by his grandson, Malcolm IV. See study by A. M. Mackenzie (1954).

David II (David Bruce), 1324-71, king of Scotland (1329-71), son and successor of Robert I. David's guardians were not strong enough to prevent the invasion (1332) of Scotland by Edward de BALIOL, who, with the support of Edward III of England, was victorious at Halidon Hill (1333). The young king was sent to France, where he was maintained in the Château Gaillard by Philip VI. David returned to rule Scotland in 1341. In 1346 he invaded England to aid the French king and was captured and held prisoner until, in 1357, he was ransomed for the promise of 100,000 marks. Finding the money to pay the ransom (never paid in full) occupied him for most of the rest of his inglorious reign. His nephew Robert II succeeded him.

David, Félicien César (fālēsyăN' săzär' dävēd'), 1810-76, French composer. His tone poem *Le Desert* (1844) and his opera *Lalla-Roukh* (1862) contain Oriental elements, presaging the exoticism of late 19th-century French romantic music.

David or **Davit, Gerard** (both: gā'rärt dä'vĕt), c.1460-1523, Flemish painter, b. Oudewater, Holland. By 1484 he had established himself in Bruges, where he remained until his death. Dependent on the art of earlier Flemish painters, such as Jan van Eyck and the Master of Flémalle, his work displays a uniform tenderness and grace. Among his notable paintings are the *Madonna Enthroned* (Louvre); the *Virgin among the Virgins* (1509, Rouen); the *Mystic Marriage of St. Catherine* (National Gall., London); the *Annunciation* (Metropolitan Mus.); and the *Deposition* (Frick Coll., New York City). See Erwin Panofsky, *Early Netherlandish Painting* (1953).

David, Jacques-Louis (zhäk-lwē' dävēd'), 1748-1825, French painter. David was the virtual art dictator of France for a generation. Extending beyond painting, his influence determined the course of fashion, furniture design, and interior decoration and was reflected in the development of moral philosophy. His art was a sudden and decisive break with tradition, and from this break "modern art" is dated. David studied with Vien, and after winning the Prix de Rome (which had been refused him four times, causing him to attempt suicide by starvation) he accompanied Vien to Italy in 1775. His pursuit of the antique, nurtured by his time in Rome, directed the classical revival in French art. He borrowed classical forms and motifs, predominantly from sculpture, to illustrate a sense of virtue he mistakenly attributed to the ancient Romans. David was consumed by a desire for perfection and by a passion for the political ideas of the French Revolution. He therefore imposed a fierce discipline upon the expression of sentiment in his work. This inhibition resulted in a distinct coldness and rationalism of approach. His reputation was made by the Salon of 1784. In that year he produced his first masterwork, *The Oath of the Horatii* (Louvre), a strong and dramatic statement of the Corneillian concept of moral duty ascendant over personal feeling. This work and his celebrated *Death of Socrates* (1787; Metropolitan Mus.) and *Lictors Bringing to Brutus the Bodies of His Sons* (1789; Louvre) were themes appropriate to the political climate of the time. They secured for David vast popularity and success. Having been admitted to the Académie royale in 1780 and working as court painter to the king, the powerful republican David, upon being elected to the revolutionary Convention, voted for the king's death and for the dissolution of the Académie royale both in France and in Rome. These schools were soon resurrected and generally dominated by David's own theories. In his paintings of the Revolution's martyrs, especially in his *Marat* (1793; Brussels), his iron control is softened and the tragic portraits are moving and dignified. Imprisoned for a time at the end of the Reign of Terror, David emerged to become First Painter to the emperor and foremost recorder of Napoleonic events (e.g., *Napoleon Crossing the Saint Bernard Pass,* 1800; *Coronation of Napoleon and Josephine,* 1805-07; and *The Distribution of the Eagles,* 1810) and a sensitive portraitist (*Mme Récamier,* 1800; Louvre). In this period David reached the height of his influence, but his painting, more than ever the embodiment of neoclassical theory, was again static and deadened in feeling. *The Battle of the Romans and Sabines* (1799; Louvre) was a grandiose exercise in frozen motion. During the Restoration David spent his last years in Brussels. As a portraitist he was at his most distinguished, although he belittled this painting genre. Using living, rather than sculptured, models, he allowed his spontaneous sentiment to be revealed. In these last years his portraits, such as *Antoine Mongez and His Wife Angelica* (1812; Lille) and *Bernard* (1820; Louvre) are enormously vital and in them the seeds of the new romanticism are clearly discernable. See D. L. Dowd, *Pageant-Master of the Republic* (1948); J. Lindsay, *Death of the Hero* (1960); study by H. Rosenau (1948).

David, John Baptist Mary, 1761-1841, French missionary in the United States, b. Brittany. He was educated at Nantes, joined the Sulpicians, and because of the French Revolution emigrated to the United

States. At Bardstown, Ky., he founded a seminary (St. Thomas) and schools for boys and girls. He also established a community of Sisters of Charity at Nazareth, Ky. From 1819 he was bishop coadjutor of Bardstown. Bishop David's devotional works were popular for a generation.

David, Pierre-Jean: see DAVID D'ANGERS.

David (dävēd'), city (1970 pop. 35,680), SW Panama. It is a communications and marketing center. Cattle raising is the principal occupation in the region, but coffee, cacao, and sugar are also produced. David is surrounded by the picturesque highlands of Chiriquí.

David d'Angers or **Pierre-Jean David** (dävēd' däNzhā'; pyĕr-zhäN), 1788–1856, French sculptor. His works are numerous and present national figures, often nude, in statues, busts, reliefs, and medallions. The pediment of the Panthéon in Paris shows a group of distinguished Frenchmen receiving wreaths from the hand of France. Although he was considered a romantic in his day, his style reflects a strong academic training. The Musée David at Angers, his birthplace, has a fine collection of his sculptures.

Davidson, George, 1825–1911, American geographer and astronomer, b. England. From 1845 to 1895 he was on the staff of the U.S. Coast and Geodetic Survey. He was in charge of the charting (1850–60) of the U.S. Pacific coast for navigation purposes, the results of which were recorded in the *Pacific Coast Pilot.* From 1860 to 1866, Davidson surveyed the Delaware River and mapped the district around Philadelphia for fortifications. His survey (1867) of the Alaskan coast resulted in the government publication *Coast Pilot of Alaska* (1869 and later editions). From 1867 to 1887 he had charge of the Survey's work along the coast of W United States; he measured the great base lines known as the Davidson quadrilaterals, upon which the primary triangulation of the Pacific coast states is based. In 1879 he built in San Francisco the first observatory on the Pacific coast. He headed several U.S. expeditions to observe total solar eclipses and the transits of Venus and Mercury. His writings include *The Discovery of San Francisco Bay* (1907), *Francis Drake on the Northwest Coast* (1908), and *The Tracks and Landfalls of Bering and Chirikof* (1901).

Davidson, Jo, 1883–1952, American sculptor, b. New York City. He studied at the Art Students League and the École des Beaux-Arts, Paris. He is known especially for his portrait busts, which display vigorous modeling and psychological insight. Davidson made likenesses of some of the leading figures of the 20th cent., including Woodrow Wilson, Franklin Delano Roosevelt, Mahatma Gandhi, and Albert Einstein. His autobiography, *Between Sittings,* was published in 1951.

Davidson, John, 1857–1909, Scottish poet. After teaching in Scotland he went to London. There, struggling with poverty and illness, he wrote *Fleet Street Eclogues* (1893; Ser. 2, 1896), *Ballads and Songs* (1894), *New Ballads* (1897), literary dramas, and novels. He established a small reputation as a lyric poet, but he earned little money. Despairing, he drowned himself in the ocean near Penzance in 1909. See study by C. V. Peterson (1972).

Davidson, Thomas, 1840–1900, American scholar and philosopher, b. Scotland, grad. Univ. of Aberdeen, 1860. In 1866 he emigrated to Canada and then to the United States. On a visit to London in 1883 he founded the Fellowship of the New Life, out of which the Fabian Society developed. He later established a summer school at his home in the Adirondacks as well as lecture classes for workers in New York City. Davidson acted as tutor, traveled extensively in Europe, and wrote several books on philosophy and education, including *Aristotle and Ancient Educational Ideals* (1892), and *History of Education* (1900). See *The Education of the Wage Earners* (edited by C. M. Bakewell, 1904, repr. 1971); *Memorials of Thomas Davidson* (ed. by W. A. Knight, 1907); William James, *Memories and Studies* (1911).

Davie, Alan, 1920–, Scottish painter, goldsmith, and jazz musician. Davie uses brilliant color dripped and smeared onto the canvas. His powerful imagery is mythological and often brutally violent. His symbolic forms are related to the SURREALISM of Ernst and Miró, but they seem less fantastic than tortured.

Davie, William Richardson, 1756–1820, American Revolutionary soldier and statesman, b. Egremont, Cumberland, England. During the American Revolution he served under Casimir Pulaski and later took part in the Carolina campaign, becoming Gen. Nathanael Greene's commissary general. After the war he practiced law in Halifax, N.C., served (1786–98) in the state legislature, and drew up (1789) the act for establishment of the Univ. of North Carolina. Davie was governor of North Carolina (1798–99) and one of the peace commissioners John Adams sent (1799) to France after the XYZ Affair. See biography by Blackwell Robinson (1957).

Davies, Arthur Bowen, 1862–1928, American painter and lithographer, b. Utica, N.Y., studied at the Art Institute of Chicago and the Art Students League, New York City. In 1893 he traveled in Europe and exhibited successfully on his return. A president of the Society of Independent Artists, he was largely responsible for the famous Armory Show of 1913. He was also a member of the EIGHT. A romantic artist, he favored symbolic pictures of the female nude in idyllic landscapes. Characteristic are his *Maya, Mirror of Illusions* (Art Inst., Chicago) and *The Dawning* (Brooklyn Mus., N.Y.). Less known are his lithographs and watercolors.

Davies, Emily (Sarah Emily Davies) (dā'vĭs), 1830–1921, British feminist, co-founder of Girton College, Cambridge. Educated at home, she became (1862) secretary of a committee to obtain the admission of women to university examinations. Out of this undertaking grew another committee, of which she was also secretary, to form a college for women. The college was organized at Hitchin, Hertfordshire, in 1869 and in 1873 transferred to Cambridge as Girton College. Davies was mistress of the college (1873–75) and its honorary secretary until 1904. From 1866 she was closely associated with the English woman-suffrage movement and was active in organizing the first woman-suffrage petition presented to Parliament by John Stuart Mill in 1866. She wrote *Higher Education of Women* (1866) and *Thoughts on Some Questions Relating to Women* (1910). See Barbara Stephens, *Emily Davies and Girton College* (1927).

Davies, Henry Walford: see DAVIES, SIR WALFORD.

Davies, John: see DAVIES OF HEREFORD, JOHN.

Davies, Sir John (dā'vĭs), 1569–1626, English poet. A successful lawyer, he served as solicitor general and attorney general in Ireland from 1603 to 1619. His works include *Nosce Teipsum* (1599), a long poem on the immortality of the soul; *Orchestra; or, A Poem of Dancing* (1596), an explication of the order of the universe; *Hymns of Astraea* (1599), acrostics on the name Elizabeth Regina; epigrams; sonnets; and tracts on the state of Ireland.

Davies, Joseph Edward (dā'vēz), 1876–1958, American diplomat, b. Watertown, Wis. Admitted to the bar in 1901, he was commissioner of corporations (1913–15) and chairman (1915–16) of the Federal Trade Commission, before serving (1919) as President Wilson's economic adviser at the Paris Peace Conference. He later served as ambassador to the USSR (1937–38), ambassador to Belgium (1938–40), and special assistant (1940) to Secretary of State Cordell Hull. During World War II, Davies was (1942–46) chairman of the President's War Relief Control Board. In 1945 he attended the Potsdam Conference. His book, *Mission to Moscow* (1941), gives a favorable picture of the USSR.

Davies, Sir Louis Henry (dā'vĭs), 1845–1924, Canadian jurist, b. Charlottetown, P.E.I. While a member of the provincial legislature (1872–79), he also served (1876–79) as prime minister of Prince Edward Island. From 1882 to 1901 he sat as a Liberal in the Canadian House of Commons and held a cabinet post from 1896 to 1901. Appointed a judge of the Supreme Court of Canada in 1901, he became chief justice in 1918. He was knighted in 1897.

Davies, Samuel (dā'vēz), 1723–61, American Presbyterian clergyman, b. New Castle co., Del. Ordained as an evangelist, he went in 1747 to Hanover co., Va., where he was soon the center of a revival that became part of the movement known as the GREAT AWAKENING. He went with Gilbert TENNENT to England and Scotland in 1753 to raise funds for the support of the College of New Jersey (now Princeton Univ.) and was its president from 1759 to 1761.

Davies, William Henry, 1871–1940, English poet, b. Wales. Leaving school at a young age, Davies lived for a number of years as a peddler and a beggar in the United States and England. His first attempt at poetry, *The Soul's Destroyer* (1905), printed at his own expense, won the favorable attention of G. B. Shaw. Thereafter Davies's success was assured. *The Autobiography of a Super-Tramp* (1908) describes his vagabond life. Davies was a prolific poet; his favorite themes were nature and the hardships of the poor. See his poems (ed. by Osbert Sitwell, 1942).

Davies of Hereford, John (dā'vĭs), 1565?–1618, English poet. He settled in London about 1600 after spending several years as a writing master at Oxford. His main efforts were religious and philosophical treatises written in verse, the best of which were *Mirum in Modum* (1602) and *Micro-cosmos* (1603). He also wrote *The Scourge of Folly* (1610?), a book of complimentary epigrams on contemporary poets.

Dávila, Pedrarias: see ARIAS DE ÁVILA, PEDRO.

Da Vinci, Leonardo: see LEONARDO DA VINCI.

Davis, Alexander Jackson, 1803–92, American architect, b. New York City. He was the partner of Ithiel Town of New Haven, with whom he designed many important buildings, including the New York Customs House (1832), now the Subtreasury; the Patent Office at Washington, D.C. (1832); and the state capitols of Indiana (1832–35), North Carolina (1831, in association with David Paton), Illinois (1837), and Ohio (1839). The most prolific practitioner of his time, Davis was notably successful in his Greek revival style; he also anticipated, in a New York shop front designed in 1835, the architectural use of iron. He was a founder (1837) of the American Institute of Architects. See R. H. Newton, *Town and Davis, Architects* (1942).

Davis, Benjamin Oliver, 1877–1970, American general, b. Washington, D.C. After study (1897–98) at Howard Univ., Davis served as a lieutenant in the Spanish-American War and in 1899 enlisted in the regular army as a private. He subsequently rose through years of service to become (1940) the first Negro general in the U.S. army. He retired briefly from the army in 1941 but returned to duty as inspector general, retiring finally in 1948.

Davis, Benjamin Oliver, Jr., 1912–, American air force general, b. Washington, D.C.; son of Benjamin Oliver Davis. After study at Western Reserve and Chicago universities, he attended West Point, where he became (1936) the first Negro graduate. He served as an infantry officer, entered the U.S. air force, and completed his flight training in 1942. During World War II he distinguished himself as a combat pilot. In 1954, Davis became the first Negro general in the U.S. air force. He served (1961–65) as director of air power and organization for the air force.

Davis, Bette, 1908–, American film actress, b. Lowell, Mass., as Ruth Elizabeth Davis. A tough, intelligent, compelling actress, and one of the foremost Hollywood stars from 1936 into the late 1940s, Davis began her film career in 1931. She won Academy Awards for *Dangerous* (1935) and *Jezebel* (1938). Her outstanding films include *Of Human Bondage* (1934), *Dark Victory* (1939), *The Old Maid* (1939), *The Man Who Came to Dinner* (1941), *The Corn Is Green* (1945), and *All About Eve* (1950). See her autobiography (1962); biography by Jerry Vermilye (1972).

Davis, Charles Henry, 1807–77, American naval officer and scientist, b. Boston. Appointed a midshipman in 1823, Davis directed operations of the Coast Survey for a time along the New England coast. He established the *American Ephemeris and Nautical Almanac* in 1849 and published several hydrographic studies. In the Civil War he was fleet captain and chief of staff to S. F. Du Pont in the successful expedition (Nov., 1861) against Port Royal, S.C. On May 9, 1862, he replaced A. H. Foote in command of the Upper Mississippi flotilla of gunboats. The next day he repulsed the attack of a Confederate fleet near Fort Pillow, and on June 6 he annihilated the Confederate fleet before Memphis, taking the city the same day. He then joined Farragut in an unsuccessful attempt to take Vicksburg. Davis was chief (1862–65) of the Bureau of Navigation and superintendent (1865–67, 1874–77) of the Naval Observatory. For his victories at Fort Pillow and Memphis he was promoted to rear admiral in Feb., 1863. See biography by his son Charles H. Davis (1899).

Davis, Colin, 1927–, English conductor. Davis began his musical career as a clarinetist; he is a self-taught conductor. After holding various posts in Great Britain, Davis gained wide recognition when he substituted for Otto Klemperer at a performance of Mozart's *Don Giovanni* in 1959. After serving with the Sadler's Wells Opera, he became conductor of the British Broadcasting Corporation Symphony (1967–71) and of the Royal Opera, Covent Garden (1971–). He made his American debut in 1961 with the Minneapolis Symphony. Davis is renowned as a conductor of Mozart and Berlioz.

Davis, David, 1815–86, American jurist, Associate Justice of the U.S. Supreme Court (1862–77), b. Cecil co., Md., grad. Kenyon College, 1832; cousin of Henry Winter Davis. In 1836 he settled as a lawyer in Bloomington, Ill., his home thereafter. From 1848 to 1862 Davis presided over the eighth judicial circuit in Illinois, famous because Abraham Lincoln practiced in its courts. An intimate of Lincoln (the tall, spare Lincoln and the corpulent Davis often bunked together in traveling the circuit), he successfully managed his friend's campaign to secure the Republican nomination for the presidency at Chicago in 1860. Davis and Leonard Swett, another lawyer from the eighth circuit active in Lincoln's cause, gave several political assurances without Lincoln's knowledge (notably one to Simon Cameron of Pennsylvania), which Lincoln reluctantly honored. Lincoln appointed (1862) Davis to the U.S. Supreme Court. Not especially learned in the law, he nevertheless wrote one of the most important opinions in the history of the court in *Ex parte Milligan* (1866). The decision, denouncing arbitrary military power, became famous as one of the bulwarks of civil liberty in the United States. Davis, who did not allow his judicial position to interfere with his political ambitions, was nominated for President by the Labor Reform Convention at Columbus, Ohio, in 1872, but withdrew when he failed to win the nomination of the LIBERAL REPUBLICAN PARTY as well. In 1877 he resigned from the court to serve (1877–83) as U.S. Senator from Illinois. See biography by W. L. King (1960).

Davis, Dwight Filley, 1879–1945, American tennis player and public official, b. St. Louis, grad. Harvard, 1900, and Washington Univ. law school. An outstanding tennis player, Davis donated in 1900 a cup as an international tennis trophy; this donation brought about the annual Davis Cup matches. He held several public offices in St. Louis, and after service in World War I he was Secretary of War (1925–29). He succeeded Henry L. Stimson as governor general (1929–32) of the Philippines. In World War II, Davis served in the army as a major general.

Davis, Elmer, 1890–1958, American newspaperman, radio commentator, and author, b. Aurora, Ind. Davis was a Rhodes scholar (1910–13) at Oxford. For 10 years (1914–24) he was on the staff of the New York *Times.* In 1939 he became radio news analyst for the Columbia Broadcasting System. He soon became noted for his incisiveness, objectivity, and dry humor. During World War II Davis was (1942–45) director of the Office of War Information. From 1945–53 he was radio news analyst with the American Broadcasting Company. His works include *History of the New York Times* (1921), several novels, short stories, and two volumes of essays—*Show Window* (1927) and *Not to Mention the War* (1940). His later writings include *But We Were Born Free* (1954) and *Two Minutes till Midnight* (1955). See Roger Burlingame, *Don't Let Them Scare You* (1961, repr. 1974).

Davis, George Breckenridge, 1847–1914, American army officer and jurist, b. Ware, Mass., grad. West Point, 1871. His early military service was divided between duty on the Western frontier and teaching at West Point. Davis joined the judge advocate general's department in 1888 and was graduated in 1891 from the Columbian Univ. (now George Washington Univ.) law school. He became judge advocate general in 1901. He edited *The War of the Rebellion: Official Records of the Union and Confederate Armies* (4 series, 70 vol. in 128 vol., 1880–1901). In 1896 he returned to West Point and taught law and history until 1901. Davis was an American delegate (1907) to the Second Hague Conference. His other writings include *The Elements of Law* (1897) and *A Treatise on the Military Law of the United States* (1898). He retired as major general in 1911.

Davis, Henry Winter, 1817–65, American political leader, b. Annapolis, Md. He was elected (1854) to the House of Representatives on the Know-Nothing ticket and was twice reelected (1856, 1858) with the aid of the Republican party. He tried to remain neutral on the slavery issue, but in 1860 cast the deciding vote for a Republican as speaker, which enabled the Republicans to organize the House. His action was censured by the Maryland legislature, and he was not reelected. Davis became the leader of the Unionist forces in Maryland in opposition to Governor Hicks, whose sympathies were Southern. Again (1863–65) in Congress, he bitterly attacked Lincoln's gradual assumption of extraconstitutional powers and opposed his Reconstruction program. Davis and Benjamin F. WADE substituted for Lincoln's measures a much more thorough and radical plan of their own and succeeded in forcing it through both House and Senate, only to see it killed by Lincoln's pocket veto (1864). They replied with the Wade-Davis Manifesto, an angry attack on the President's plan and actions. When Davis was defeated, Thaddeus STEVENS took up the fight on the Reconstruction issue. Davis was a magnetic speaker, and at his death was, as a private citizen, virtually dictating the actions of the radical Republicans in Congress. See study by G. S. Henig (1973).

Davis, James John, 1873–1947, American public official, b. Wales. After emigrating (1881) to the United States, he worked as a puddler in ironworks in Pennsylvania and, moving to Elwood, Ind., became active in local politics and labor activities. After 1907 he became well known as director general of the Loyal Order of Moose. He was appointed (1921) Secretary of Labor by President Warren G. Harding, remained at that post until 1930, and served (1930–45) in the U.S. Senate. See his autobiography, *The Iron Puddler* (1922).

Davis, Jefferson, 1808–89, American statesman, President of the Southern Confederacy, b. Fairview, near Elkton, Ky. His birthday was June 3. His parents moved to Mississippi when he was a boy. He was given a classical education at Transylvania Univ. and was appointed to West Point, where he was graduated in 1828. He spent the next seven years in various army posts in the Old Northwest and took part (1832) in the Black Hawk War. In 1835 he married the daughter of Zachary Taylor, but she died three months later. Davis spent the next 10 years in the comparative quiet of a Mississippi planter's life. In 1845 he married Varina Howell. Elected (1845) to the House of Representatives, he resigned in June, 1846, to command a Mississippi regiment in the Mexican War. Under Zachary Taylor he distinguished himself both at the siege of Monterrey and at Buena Vista. Davis was appointed (1847) U.S. Senator from Mississippi to fill an unexpired term but resigned in 1851 to run for governor of Mississippi against his senatorial colleague, Henry S. FOOTE, who was a Union Whig. Davis was a strong champion of Southern rights and argued for the expansion of slave territory and economic development of the South to counterbalance the power of the North. He lost the election by less than 1,000 votes and retired to his plantation until appointed (1853) Secretary of War by Franklin PIERCE. Throughout the administration he used his power to oppose the views of his Northern Democratic colleague, Secretary of State William L. Marcy. Davis favored the acquisition of Cuba and opposed concessions to Spain in the *Black Warrior* and Ostend Manifesto difficulties, and he also promoted a southern route for a transcontinental railroad, therefore favoring the Gadsden Purchase. Reentering the Senate in 1857, he became the leader of the Southern bloc. He took little part in the secession movement until Mississippi seceded (Jan., 1861), whereupon he withdrew from the Senate. He was immediately appointed major general of the Mississippi militia, and shortly afterward he was chosen president of the Confederate provisional government established by the convention at Montgomery, Ala., and inaugurated in Feb., 1861. Elected regular President of the Confederate States (see CONFEDERACY), he was inaugurated at Richmond, Va., in Feb., 1862. Davis realized that the Confederate war effort needed a strong centralized rule. This conflicted with the states' rights policy for which the Southern states had seceded, and, as he assumed more and more power, many of the Southern leaders combined into a anti-Davis party. Originally hopeful of a military rather than a civil command in the Confederacy, he closely managed the army and was involved in many disagreements with the Confederate generals; arguments over his policies raged long after the Confederacy was dead. Lee surrendered without Davis's approval. After the last Confederate cabinet meeting was held (April, 1865) at Charlotte, N.C., Davis was captured at Irwinville, Ga. He was confined in Fortress Monroe for two years and was released (May, 1867) on bail. The Federal government proceeded no further in its prosecution of Davis. After his release he wrote an apologia, *The Rise and Fall of the Confederate Government* (1881). He was buried at New Orleans, but his body was moved (1893) to Richmond, Va. See his papers, ed. by H. M. Monroe, Jr. (Vol. I, 1972); biographies by W. E. Dodd (1907, repr. 1966) and Hudson Strode (4 vol., 1955–66); Varina H. Davis, *Jefferson Davis: A Memoir* (1890); B. J. Hendrick, *Statesmen of the Lost Cause* (1939); R. W. Patrick, *Jefferson Davis and His Cabinet* (1944).

Davis or **Davys, John,** 1550?–1605, English navigator. He made his first voyage in search of the NORTHWEST PASSAGE in 1585, continuing the work of Martin FROBISHER. On this voyage he discovered Cumberland Sound of Baffin Island and made explorations that prepared the way for his later voyages in 1586 and 1587. On the third exploration he sailed through Davis Strait into Baffin Bay and coasted down Baffin Island and across the east end of Hudson Strait. He clarified much of the confusion over the geography of that region. In 1591, Davis sailed S for the Straits of Magellan, and in 1592 he sighted the Falkland Islands. He later made voyages to the East Indies and was killed in a fight with Japanese pirates. A type of quadrant he invented was used for more than a century, and he wrote a manual, *The Seaman's Secrets* (1594). See *The Voyages and Works of John Davis,* ed. by A. H. Markham (1880, repr. 1970); biography by Sir Clements Markham (1889, repr. 1970).

Davis, John William, 1873–1955, American lawyer and public official, b. Clarksburg, W.Va. Admitted (1895) to the bar, he taught (1896–97) at Washington and Lee Univ. and later practiced (1897–1913) in Clarksburg. He served as Congressman (1911–13), U.S. Solicitor General (1913–18), and ambassador to Great Britain (1918–21). After 1921 he practiced law in New York City. He was nominated for President in 1924 on the 103d ballot, when, after a two-week deadlock at the Democratic convention, the forces of Alfred E. Smith and William Gibbs McAdoo agreed to compromise on a third candidate. Hampered by his legal affiliation with large corporations, Davis, even though he carried the South, won only 136 electoral votes and 8,386,500 popular votes. His speeches are collected in *Treaty-making Power in the United States* (1920) and *Party Government in the United States* (1929). See biography by W. H. Harbaugh (1973).

Davis, Miles, 1926–, American jazz musician, b. Alton, Ill. Rising to prominence with the birth of modern jazz in the mid-1940s, Davis became a dominant force in jazz trumpet. He was influential in the development of "cool" jazz in 1949–50, led numerous outstanding small groups through the 1950s and 60s, and produced a successful blend of jazz and ROCK MUSIC in the 1970s. Davis's trumpet and fleugelhorn styles are warmly lyrical and are marked by his brilliant use of mutes.

Davis, Paulina Wright, 1813–76, American lecturer and suffragist, b. Bloomfield, N.Y. Born Paulina Kellogg, she was married in 1833 to a merchant, Francis Wright, who died two years later. In 1849 she was married again, this time to Thomas Davis, who later became a congressman from Rhode Island. She was active in the early antislavery and women's-rights movements. In 1844 she began to lecture women on anatomy and physiology and was instrumental in opening the medical profession to women. In 1853 she founded the first women's-rights paper in the United States, *Una,* and in 1871 she published *A History of the National Women's Rights Movement.*

Davis, Rebecca Harding, 1831–1910, American novelist, b. Washington, Pa. Her early stories, published in the *Atlantic Monthly,* and *Margaret Howth* (1862), the first of her novels dealing with the effects of social problems on individuals, foreshadowed the naturalistic techniques of later 19th-century writers. See her autobiographical *Bits of Gossip* (1904); biography by Gerald Langford (1961).

Davis, Richard Harding, 1864–1916, American author and journalist, b. Philadelphia; son of Rebecca Harding Davis. After attending Lehigh and Johns Hopkins universities, he became a reporter in Philadelphia and later was on the New York *Evening Sun.* His stories and articles were soon attracting attention, and with the publication of *Gallegher and Other Stories* (1891), a collection of tales about a newsboy-detective, his reputation as a fiction writer was established. In 1890 he became managing editor of *Harper's Weekly* and began making trips in its behalf to various parts of the world. As a foreign correspondent he covered all the wars of his day and published several books recording his experiences; his war dispatches were colorful and dramatic, emphasizing heroic acts. Besides collections of short stories, his other writings include the novels *Soldiers of Fortune* (1897) and *The Bar Sinister* (1903) and the plays *The Dictator* (1904) and *Miss Civilization* (1906). See his *Adventures and Letters* (ed. by his brother, C. B. Davis, 1917).

Davis, Stuart, 1894–1964, American painter, b. Philadelphia, studied with Robert Henri in New York City. At the age of 19 he did drawings and covers for *The Masses* and exhibited in the Armory Show. One of the early jazz enthusiasts, Davis is often said to have incorporated its exciting tempos into the vibrant patterns of his paintings. In the 1920s the influence of cubism became apparent in his work. He painted the famous *Eggbeater* series in an attempt to avoid the depiction of natural objects and instead to create an art of abstract forms and planes. During the 1930s he was active in the Artists' Congress, editing *Art Front.* Davis was an articulate spokesman for abstract art. Among his canvases in numerous museums are *Visa* (Mus. of Modern Art, New York City); *Colonial Cubism* (Walker Art Center, Minneapolis); and *Midi* (Wadsworth Atheneum, Hartford, Conn.). See biography by E. C. Goosen (1959); study ed. by D. Kelder (1971).

Davis, William Morris, 1850-1934, American geographer, geologist, and teacher, b. Philadelphia; B.S. Harvard, 1869. He founded (1904) the Association of American Geographers and served three terms as its president. He was on the Harvard faculty from 1879 to 1912 and was visiting professor at the Univ. of Berlin (1908-9) and at the Sorbonne (1911-12). In 1912 he led a transcontinental excursion across the United States sponsored by the American Geographical Society. After 1925 he spent most of his time in the W United States, where he lectured at universities. Davis is responsible for enlarging the scope and systematizing the study of geography; his methods of description and analysis and his use of maps and block diagrams revolutionized the teaching of geography. His major works include *The Coral Reef Problem (1928),* and *Geographical Essays* (1909, repr. 1954). See study by R. J. Chorley, A. J. Dunn, and R. P. Beckinsale, vol. II in *The History of the Study of Landforms* (1973).

Davis, city (1970 pop. 23,488), Yolo co., central Calif.; settled in the 1850s, inc. 1917. Canned foods and steel products are manufactured; the Univ. of California at Davis is there.

Davis, Mount, peak, 3,213 ft (979 m) high, SW Pa., in the Alleghenies; highest point in Pennsylvania.

Davis Cup: see TENNIS.

Davis Mountains, W Tex., SE of El Paso. Old Baldy, 8,382 ft (2,555 m), is the highest peak. Forested slopes, great springs, and deep canyons attract tourists; Davis Mountains State Park is there. On the summit of Mt. Locke, 6,791 ft (2,070 m) high, is the Univ. of Texas McDonald Observatory, with the world's third-largest (107 in./272 cm) reflector telescope. **Fort Davis,** est. 1854 as a border outpost, is now a national historic site (see NATIONAL PARKS AND MONUMENTS, table).

Davisson, Clinton Joseph, 1881-1958, American physicist, b. Bloomington, Ill. He joined the engineering department of the Bell Telephone Laboratories in 1917. Davisson worked on thermionics, magnetism, and electron diffraction. His demonstrations with L. H. Germer in 1927 confirmed Louis de Broglie's theory of the wave nature of moving electrons by means of diffraction by crystals. For this he shared with G. P. Thomson the 1937 Nobel Prize in Physics.

Davis Strait, c.400 mi (640 km) long and c.180 mi (290 km) wide at the narrowest point, between Greenland and Baffin Island, NE Canada, connecting the Atlantic Ocean and Baffin Bay. Large amounts of ice and icebergs move south through the strait. The British explorer John Davis sailed through it in 1587.

Davit, Gerard: see DAVID, GERARD.

Davitt, Michael (dăv'ĭt), 1846-1906, Irish revolutionary and land reformer. He joined the FENIAN MOVEMENT in 1865 and was imprisoned three times by the English for his revolutionary activities. Davitt and Charles Stewart Parnell were the leading figures in the organization of the National Land League in 1879 (see IRISH LAND QUESTION). Influenced by the theories of Henry GEORGE, Davitt broke with Parnell over the question of land nationalization. But he remained an important Irish leader and was instrumental in bringing the Parnell and anti-Parnell factions together in the United Irish League (1898). See his *The Fall of Feudalism in Ireland* (1904); also M. M. O'Hara, *Chief and Tribune* (1919).

Davos (dävôs'), town (1970 pop. 10,238), Grisons canton, E Switzerland, on the Landwasser River. It is a famous winter sports center and a health resort for the tubercular.

Davout, Louis Nicolas (lwē nēkôlä' dävo͞o'), 1770-1823, marshal of France. One of Napoleon's ablest generals, Davout defeated a Prussian army at Auerstedt (1806) and played a brilliant part in the victory at Wagram (1809). He also fought (1812) in the Russian campaign. Napoleon made him duke of Auerstedt, prince of Eckmühl, and gave him political posts including control of N Germany and Poland (1807-9). During the HUNDRED DAYS, Davout was minister of war, and after the final defeat of Napoleon (1815) and the restoration of King Louis XVIII he was for several years deprived of his rank and titles.

Davy, Sir Humphry, 1778-1829, English chemist and physicist. The son of a woodcarver, he received his early education at Truro and was apprenticed (1795) to a surgeon-apothecary at Penzance. While director (1798-1801) of the laboratory of the Pneumatic Institution, Clifton, he investigated the properties of nitrous oxide (laughing gas). He was lecturer (1801) and professor (1802-13) at the Royal Institution, London. His researches in electrochemistry led to his isolation of potassium and sodium in 1807 and of calcium, barium, boron, magnesium, and strontium in 1808. He established the elementary nature of chlorine, advanced the theory that hydrogen is characteristically present in acids, and classed chemical affinity as an electric phenomenon. He was also noted for the invention of a safety lamp for miners and for his lectures on agricultural chemistry (pub. 1813). Knighted (1812) and made a baronet (1818), he was elected (1820) president of the Royal Society. His collected works (9 vol., 1839-40; repr. 1972) include a biographical memoir by his brother, John Davy. See biography by Anne Treneer (1963).

Davy Jones, personification or spirit of the sea. The name is best known in the expression "Davy Jones's locker," meaning the bottom of the sea, to which drowned sailors go.

Davys, John: see DAVIS, JOHN.

Dawes, Charles Gates (dôz), 1865-1951, American statesman and banker, b. Marietta, Ohio. Admitted (1886) to the bar, Dawes practiced law in Lincoln, Nebr., until 1894 and became interested in various gas and electric companies. He was a member of the Republican executive committee in William McKinley's presidential campaign (1896) and served (1897-1901) as comptroller of the Treasury. He organized the Central Trust Company of Illinois in 1902 and became a prominent figure in banking. After the United States entered World War I he was general purchasing agent of the American Expeditionary Force. In 1921 he was appointed director (the first) of the U.S. Bureau of the Budget; in 1923-24 he was head of the reparations committee that advanced the DAWES PLAN as a means of stabilizing postwar German finances. His work was recognized by the award (shared with Sir Austen Chamberlain) of the Nobel Peace Prize in 1925. Dawes served (1925-29) as Vice President under Calvin Coolidge. Herbert Hoover appointed him ambassador to London in 1929, and in 1932 he was made president of the Reconstruction Finance Corporation. His many books include *Notes as Vice President* (1935), *A Journal of Reparations* (1939), and *Journal as Ambassador to Great Britain* (1939). See biography by B. N. Timmons (1953).

Dawes, Henry Laurens, 1816-1903, U.S. Senator (1875-93), b. Cummington, Mass. He was U.S. district attorney for W Massachusetts (1853-57) and a Republican member of the House of Representatives (1857-75). He performed his most important service as chairman of the Senate Committee on Indian Affairs and gave his name to the DAWES ACT and the DAWES COMMISSION.

Dawes, William, 1745-99, figure in the American Revolution, b. Boston, Mass. On the night of April 18, 1775, Dawes rode from Boston, via Brighton Bridge, to Lexington, warning the countryside of the British advance. At Lexington, he was joined by Paul REVERE and Samuel PRESCOTT. On the way to Concord, a British patrol surprised them. Revere was captured; Dawes eluded the English but had to turn back; Prescott reached Concord with the news.

Dawes Act, 1887, passed by the U.S. Congress to provide for the granting of individual landholdings to Indians who would renounce their tribal holdings. Sponsored by H. L. Dawes while he was chairman of the Committee on Indian Affairs, the act sought to absorb the Indians into the body politic of the nation.

Dawes Commission, commission to the Five Civilized Tribes, created by the U.S. Congress in 1893 under the Dawes Act with H. L. Dawes as chairman. Its aim was the reorganization of the INDIAN TERRITORY by securing the assent of the chiefs to the extinguishing of tribal land titles and by allotting lands to individuals.

Dawes Plan, presented in 1924 by the committee headed (1923-24) by Charles G. DAWES to the Reparations Commission of the Allied nations. It was accepted the same year by Germany and the Allies. The Dawes committee consisted of ten representatives, two each from Belgium, France, Great Britain, Italy, and the United States; it was entrusted with finding a solution for the collection of the German REPARATIONS debt, set at almost 20 billion marks. Germany had been lagging in payment of this obligation, and the Dawes Plan provided that the Ruhr area be evacuated by Allied occupation troops, that reparation payment should begin at 1 billion marks for the first year and should rise over a period of four years to 2.5 billion marks per year, that the German Reichsbank be reorganized under Allied supervision, and that the sources for the reparation money should include transportation, excise, and custom taxes. The plan went into effect in Sept., 1924. Although German business picked up and reparations payments were made promptly, it became obvious that Germany could not long continue those huge annual payments. As a result, the YOUNG PLAN was substituted in 1929.

Dawkins, Sir William Boyd, 1837-1929, English geologist and archaeologist. He was a member (1861-69) of the Geological Survey of Great Britain, curator (1870-90) of the Manchester Museum, and professor of geology (from 1872) at Owens College (now Victoria Univ.), Manchester. Noted for his research on fossil mammals and on the antiquity of man, he wrote *Cave Hunting* (1874) and *Early Man in Britain* (1880) and was co-author of *The British Pleistocene Mammalia* (6 vol., 1866-1912). In 1919 he was knighted.

dawn redwood: see SEQUOIA.

Dawson, Sir John William, 1820-99, Canadian geologist and educator, b. Pictou, N.S., studied at the Univ. of Edinburgh. After serving (1850-55) as superintendent of education in Nova Scotia, he was from 1855 to 1893 principal of, and professor of geology at, McGill Univ., where he helped found and develop its Redpath museum of botany and geology. He was knighted in 1884. Dawson was a pioneer in paleobotany. His numerous papers and books, many of them classics in geology, include *Acadian Geology* (1855, 4th ed. 1891), *Air Breathers of the Coal Period* (1863), *Fossil Men* (1880, 3d ed. 1888), and an autobiography, *Fifty Years of Work in Canada* (1901). See biography by C. F. O'Brien (1971). His son, **George Mercer Dawson,** 1849-1901, was a geologist (1873-75) for the North American Boundary Commission. On the staff of the Canadian Geological Survey from 1875, he served as its director from 1895. He did pioneer geological work in the Northwest Territories and in British Columbia and explored the Yukon valley. Dawson, former capital of W Yukon, Canada, was named for him. See biography by L. S. Winslow-Spragge (1962).

Dawson or **Dawson City,** city (1971 pop. 762), W Yukon Territory, Canada, at the confluence of the Yukon and Klondike rivers. It is the trade center of the Klondike mining region and a tourist center. During the gold rush of 1898 Dawson was a boom town, reported to have a population of about 20,000. It was named for George M. Dawson, the Canadian geologist. The territorial capital was moved from Dawson to Whitehorse in 1952.

Dawson Creek, city (1971 pop. 11,885), E British Columbia, Canada, near the Alta. border, on Dawson Creek and NE of Prince George. It is the southern terminus of the Alaska Highway.

Dax (däks), town (1968 pop. 19,348), Landes dept., SW France, in Gascony, on the Adour River. It has long been famous for its hot mineral springs. An aviation school is in the town.

Day, Benjamin, 1838-1916, American printer; son of Benjamin Henry Day. While working in New York City, Day invented a process, utilizing celluloid sheets, for shading plates in the color printing of maps and illustrations. It is known as the Ben Day, or Benday, process. The term "Ben Day" is used as a noun, verb, and adjective.

Day, Benjamin Henry, 1810-89, American journalist. He learned the printer's trade in the office of the Springfield (Mass.) *Republican* and opened a printing office in New York City. Lack of work during a financial depression led him to begin publishing (1833) the New York *Sun.* The first edition consisted of four small pages; he wrote the paper and set the type without assistance. The price of the paper was 1¢; the price of other New York dailies at the time was 6¢. The *Sun* was the first paper in the city to employ newsboys. By 1835, Day claimed a circulation of 19,360, the largest in the world, and in 1838 sold the *Sun* to his brother-in-law, Moses Yale BEACH, for $40,000. In 1842, Day founded the monthly *Brother Jonathan,* which later became the first illustrated weekly in the United States.

Day, Clarence Shepard, 1874-1935, American essayist, b. New York City, grad. Yale, 1896. His biographical sketches of his parents, *God and My Father* (1932), *Life with Father* (1935), and *Life with Mother* (1937), won him popular recognition; incidents from these three books were used by Howard Lindsay and Russel Crouse for the play *Life with Father* (1939), which was one of the longest-running plays in Broadway history. Day's other works include essays, *This Simian World* (1920), and a collection of light verse and drawings, *Scenes from the Mesozoic* (1935).

Day, James Edward, 1914–, U.S. Postmaster General (1961–63), b. Jacksonville, Ill. He practiced law in Chicago, and later became a legal assistant to Gov. Adlai E. Stevenson. He was (1950–53) insurance commissioner of Illinois and in 1953 became an insurance executive. He later moved to Los Angeles, where he was active in California Democratic politics. His appointment as Postmaster General (a deviation from the practice of naming a professional politician) was made by President John F. Kennedy in the belief that Day's business experience had equipped him to handle the mounting deficits of the U.S. postal service. In an attempt to diminish the annual deficit, Day advocated higher rates and introduced new methods. He resigned in 1963 and returned to private law practice. See his *My Appointed Round: 929 Days As Postmaster General* (1965).

Day, John, 1522–84, English printer. At his London shop Day designed and made type for himself, but not for sale. His types included musical notes and the first Anglo-Saxon type. He printed the first English book of church music (1560) and the first English edition of John Foxe's *Book of Martyrs* (1563), though not under that title (see FOXE, JOHN). His edition of Euclid was the first English translation of that work. Day's printer's mark was a rising sun, a sleeper awakening, and the motto, "Arise, for it is Day."

Day, John, 1574?–1640?, English dramatist. Educated at Cambridge, he was one of Philip Henslowe's group of playwrights, collaborating with Thomas Dekker, Henry Chettle, and others. The allegorical masque *The Parliament of Bees,* which was written c.1607 (pub. 1641) is his only important work. His other plays include *The Isle of Gulls* (1606) and *The Travels of Three English Brothers* (1607).

Day, Thomas, 1748–89, English social reformer and author. He supported the American Revolution and the abolition of slavery and was interested in improving the lot of the small farmer. His moralistic *History of Sandford and Merton* (3 vol., 1783–89) contrasts the "natural" education of the virtuous Sandford with the conventional one of the objectionable Merton. In Lichfield he was a member of the literary group centering about Anna SEWARD. See biographies by James Keir (1791, repr. 1970) and S. H. Scott (1935).

Day, William Rufus, 1849–1923, American statesman and Associate Justice of the U.S. Supreme Court (1903–22), b. Ravenna, Ohio. Admitted (1872) to the bar, Day practiced law in Ohio and served (1886–90) as judge of the court of common pleas. He became (1897) assistant to the Secretary of State and then (April, 1898) Secretary of State in the month when war was declared against Spain. He was successful in converting France and Germany from an attitude of seeming hostility to definite neutrality. Made chairman (Sept., 1898) of the U.S. commission to arrange peace after the Spanish-American War, he insisted upon purchase of the Philippines rather than claiming these islands by right of conquest. The treaty therefore provided for the payment of $20 million. Day became (1899) a judge of the U.S. Circuit Court of Appeals, and in 1903 President Theodore Roosevelt appointed him to the Supreme Court. See biography by J. E. McLean (1946).

day, period of TIME for the earth to rotate once on its axis. The ordinary day, or solar day, is measured relative to the sun, being the time between successive passages of the sun over a stationary observer's CELESTIAL MERIDIAN. The length of a solar day varies during the course of a year, so for purposes of time measurement an average, or mean, solar day is used (see MEAN SOLAR TIME), equal to exactly 24 hr. The sidereal day, used by astronomers, is measured relative to the fixed stars rather than the sun (see SIDEREAL TIME); it is about 4 min shorter than the mean solar day. The term *day* is also used to refer to that part of each 24-hr period during which the sun's direct rays are not blocked by the earth, this period of daylight hours extending from sunrise to sunset; the remaining portion of the 24 hr is called *night.* If the plane of the earth's orbit about the sun coincided with the plane of the equator, day and night would each be 12 hr long everywhere on the earth all year long. However, because of the obliquity of the ECLIPTIC, the times of sunrise and sunset vary from day to day, with the result that in the Northern Hemisphere there are long days and short nights in the summer and short days and long nights in the winter. See EQUINOX; SOLSTICE.

Dayak: see DYAK.

Dayan, Moshe (mō'shə dīăn', däyän'), 1915–, Israeli military leader, b. Palestine. After attending Senior Agricultural School in Nahalal, Dayan fought with the Haganah (Jewish militia) throughout the 1930s and with the British Army during World War II. He lost an eye in battle in 1941, necessitating the eye patch that has become his trademark. As Israel's chief of staff (1953–58), he established a reputation as a military strategist by directing the 1956 Sinai campaign. Dayan became minister of agriculture in 1959 and assumed the post of minister of defense in 1964. His reputation was enhanced by Israel's military success in the Six-Day War (1967), but he was blamed for Israel's unpreparedness in the 1973 October War and resigned (May, 1974) with Golda Meir. See biography by Shabtai Teveth (tr. 1973).

day-care center: see DAY NURSERY.

Daye, Matthew (dā), c.1620–1649, British printer in Massachusetts Bay colony; son of Stephen Daye. His name first appears on the almanac for 1647, but it would seem probable that he was employed at the Cambridge Press from its beginning and that the early works produced there under the supervision of Stephen Daye were actually printed by Matthew Daye. See also GLOVER, JOSE.

Daye, Stephen, c.1594–1668, British settler in North America, considered by many to be the first printer in the English American colonies. He came to Massachusetts Bay with his family in 1638 under contract to the Rev. Jose GLOVER, who brought along a printing press. Glover died on the voyage and his widow helped the Dayes set up his press. Daye apparently supervised its establishment and it became the Cambridge Press, the first printing plant in the colonies. From it was issued *The Freeman's Oath,* a broadside published in 1639. It was followed by an almanac and by the Bay Psalm Book (1640), the first book printed in the colonies. Stephen Daye was not a printer, but a locksmith, whereas his son, Matthew Daye, was a trained printer. Matthew may have done the actual printing for the company.

dayflower: see SPIDERWORT.

Day Lewis, Cecil, 1904–72, English author, b. Ireland. While he was still at Oxford, he became associated with a group of leftist poets led by W. H. Auden. After graduation he taught at various schools until 1935 and then decided to devote himself to writing. He was professor of poetry at Oxford from 1951 to 1956. Included among his volumes of poetry are *Collected Poems 1929–1933* (1935), *Overtures to Death* (1938), *Short Is the Time* (1945), *Collected Poems* (1954), *Pegasus and Other Poems* (1957), and *The Whispering Roots and Other Poems* (1970). Lewis was a member of the Communist party from 1935 to 1938, and his early poetry is marked by didacticism and a preoccupation with social themes. His later work, however, is more personal and metaphysical. Besides poetry, C. Day Lewis is noted for the collection of essays *A Hope for Poetry* (1934); for a verse translation of Vergil's *Aeneid* (1952); and for detective stories written under the pseudonym Nicholas Blake. From 1967 to 1972 he was poet laureate of Great Britain. See his autobiography, *The Buried Day* (1960); biography by J. N. Riddel (1971).

daylight saving time. The amount of daylight on a given DAY of the year at a given latitude is fixed. However, the hours of sunrise and sunset vary from day to day. During the summer months, the sun rises earlier and sets later and there are more hours of daylight. Clocks and other mechanical timepieces keep CIVIL TIME, so that if clocks are set ahead in the spring by some amount (usually one hour), the sun will rise and set later in the day as measured by civil time. This provides more usable hours of daylight for activities that are scheduled by civil time and occur in the afternoon and evening, such as outdoor recreation. Daylight saving time can also be a means of conserving lighting power. In the fall, as the period of daylight grows shorter, clocks are set back to correspond to standard time. Benjamin Franklin, when serving as U.S. minister to France, wrote an article recommending earlier opening and closing of shops to save the cost of lighting. In England, William Willett in 1907 began to urge the adoption of daylight saving time. During World War I the plan was adopted in England, Germany, France, and many other countries. In the United States, Robert Garland of Pittsburgh was a leading influence in securing the introduction and passage of a law (signed by President Wilson on March 31, 1918) establishing daylight saving time in the United States. After World War I the law was repealed (1919). In World War II, however, national daylight saving time was reestablished by law on a year-round basis. National year-long daylight saving time was adopted as a fuel-saving measure during the energy crisis of the winter of 1973–74. In late 1974, standard time was reinstituted for the four-month winter period with the fewest daylight hours.

day lily: see LILY.

day nursery or **crèche** (krĕsh), institution for the care of children of working mothers, also known as a day-care center. Originating in Europe in the late 18th and early 19th cent., day nurseries were established in the United States by private charities in the 1850s, the first being the New York Day Nursery (1854). Early day nurseries cared for children of all ages, but problems arising from inadequately trained and motivated staff caused most states to limit day nurseries to serving only children from two to five years old. The women's liberation movement, as well as other social developments of the mid-20th cent., spurred the growth of day nurseries and led to efforts designed to lower the age at which children may be cared for. The federally funded Head Start program (est. 1965) was designed to provide a combination of educational and day-care services to children from poor families. The day nursery should not be confused with the NURSERY SCHOOL, an educational institution with different objectives. See E. S. Beer, *Working Mothers and the Day Nursery* (1947, repr. 1970); E. B. Evans and G. E. Saia, *Day Care for Infants* (1972); Margaret Steinfels, *Who's Minding the Children?* (1974).

Dayr az Zawr (dĕr ăz zôr) or **Deir ez Zor** (-ĕz-), town (1960 pop. 42,036), capital of Dayr az Zawr governorate, E Syria, on the Euphrates River. It is a prosperous farming town, with a cattle-breeding center and an agricultural school. It is also a hub for transdesert travel and has an airport. Salt rock mines are nearby. The modern town was built by the Ottoman Empire in 1867 to curb Arab tribes of the Euphrates region. France occupied Dayr az Zawr in 1921 and made it the seat of a large garrison. It was taken by Britain in 1941, and in 1946 it became part of independent Syria. Another spelling of the town's name is Dayr al-Zur.

Dayton, Robert, 1939–, American artist, b. Pasadena, Calif. Blinded in an accident in 1968, Dayton has experimented since then with odor-emitting gases that resemble pungent body odors. His work, called Aroma-Art, is presented in a sealed chamber where an audience inhales scented air.

Dayton, city (1970 pop. 243,601), seat of Montgomery co., SW Ohio, on the Great Miami River where it is joined by the Stillwater River; inc. 1805. It is a port of entry; the industrial, trade, and distributing point for a fertile farm area; and an aviation center. Its chief products are cash registers, air conditioners, home appliances, and automobile parts and accessories. Dayton grew with the extension of canals (1830s and 40s) and railroads (1850s), and with the industrial demands of the Civil War. It was the first large city to adopt (1913) the city-manager form of government. It was the home of the Wright brothers, who, after their flight near Kitty Hawk, N.C., set up a research aircraft plant in Dayton. The city's educational institutions include Wright State Univ., the Univ. of Dayton, a theological seminary, and a junior college. Among the points of interest are the birthplace of Paul Laurence Dunbar, and Carillon Park, which contains a restored Wright brothers' airplane and a fine carillon tower, with 32 bells. A veterans hospital and home are in Dayton, and Wright-Patterson Air Force Base is nearby. Following a severe flood in 1913, a flood-control system of the Miami valley was established.

Daytona Beach (dātō'nə), city (1970 pop. 45,327), Volusia co., NE Fla., on the Atlantic coast and Halifax River (a lagoon); inc. 1876. The center of a major urban area comprising eight cities, Daytona Beach is a popular year-round resort. Its economy, which was long oriented to tourism, has become more diversified with the growth of space-related industries. The city was founded in 1870 in an area first settled by Spanish Franciscans in the late l6th and 17th cent. Noted for its hard, white beach, Daytona Beach has been the scene of automobile racing since 1902. It is the seat of several institutions of higher education.

Daza, Hilarión (ēläryōn' dä'sä), 1840–94, president of Bolivia (1876–79). Entering the army, Daza rose rapidly in rank, chiefly through the favor of the notorious Mariano Melgarejo (1818–1871). In 1870, Daza turned against his erstwhile protector, helped oust him from office, and then in 1876, Daza seized control. Heading an administration famed for corruption and bacchanalian orgies, he involved Bolivia in the War of the Pacific (see PACIFIC, WAR OF THE) and, after failure as a general in the field, he was deposed and exiled. When he returned from exile in 1894, he was assassinated.

Dazai, Osamu (ōsä'mōō dä'zī), pseudonym of **Tsushima Shuji** (tsōō'shĭmä shōō'jē), 1909–48, Japanese novelist. Considered one of the foremost fiction writers of 20th-century Japan, Dazai was noted for his ironic and gloomy wit, his obsession with suicide, and his brilliant fantasy. In the 1930s and 40s he wrote a number of subtle novels and short stories that are frequently autobiographical in nature. His first novel, *Gyofukuki* (1933), is a grim fantasy involving suicide. His stories, published as *Bannen* [declining years] (1936) describe his sense of personal isolation and his debauchery. In *Otogi Zoshi* (1945) he retold a number of old Japanese fairy tales with vividness and a trenchant wit. The decline of the Japanese nobility after World War II was his theme in *The Setting Sun* (1947, tr. 1956). He depicted a dissolute life in postwar Tokyo in *Bion no Tsuma* (1947). His *No Longer Human* (1948, tr. 1958) was a rephrasing of much autobiographical matter. Dazai committed suicide while working on a novel entitled *Good-bye*.

DC: see DIRECT CURRENT.

D-Day: see NORMANDY CAMPAIGN.

DDT, or 2,2-bis(*p*-chlorophenyl)-1,1,1,-trichloroethane, chlorinated hydrocarbon compound used as an INSECTICIDE. First introduced during the 1940s, it has been used to kill insects that feed on crops and spread disease, e.g., the anopheles mosquito, which carries malaria. Swiss scientist Paul Müller was awarded the 1948 Nobel Prize in Physiology and Medicine for discovering the insecticidal properties of DDT in 1939. However, it is toxic to many animals, including man, and is not easily degraded into nonpoisonous substances. Because of the deleterious effects caused by the accumulation of DDT in the environment, some countries have banned its use.

deacon: see ORDERS, HOLY.

Dead, Book of the: see BOOK OF THE DEAD.

deadly nightshade: see BELLADONNA; NIGHTSHADE.

dead reckoning: see NAVIGATION.

Dead River, 45 mi (72 km) long, rising on the Canadian border, NW Maine, and flowing northeast through a hunting and fishing region to the Kennebec River. Long Falls Dam, on the Dead River, generates hydroelectricity. In 1775, the American general Benedict Arnold followed the course of the river on his march to Quebec.

Dead Sea, salt lake, c.390 sq mi (1,010 sq km), extending c.45 mi (70 km) in the Jordan trough of the Great Rift Valley between the Ghor on the north and Wadi Arabah on the south, on the Israel-Jordan border. The surface of the Dead Sea, 1,292 ft (394 m) below sea level, is the lowest point on earth. Situated between steep, rocky cliffs, 2,500 to 4,000 ft (762–1,219 m) high, the sea is divided by the Al Lisan peninsula into two basins—a larger northern basin c.1,300 ft (400 m) deep, and a smaller southern basin, c.35 ft (11 m) deep. The lake is fed by the Jordan River and a number of small streams; it has no outlet. The inflow has been greatly reduced by the increased use of the waters of the Jordan for irrigation. Since it is located in a very hot and dry region, the Dead Sea loses much water through evaporation; its level fluctuates during the year. One of the saltiest water bodies in the world, the sea supports no life. It yields large amounts of mineral salts; potash and bromine are commercially extracted. The ancient cities of Sodom and Gomorrah were on the southwestern shore; present-day Sodom is the site of mineral-salt extraction works. Biblical names for the Dead Sea include Salt Sea, East Sea, and Sea of the Plain.

Dead Sea Scrolls, documents discovered in 1947, and later, in caves above the waters of the NW Dead Sea. Thus far most scholarly and popular attention has been centered on the scrolls discovered in the first Qumran cave, said to have been found by shepherds. Later finds in neighboring caves have supplied thousands of scroll fragments containing parts of every book of the Hebrew Bible (or Old Testament) except Esther, as well as texts of the Qumran sect and part of apocryphal and pseudepigraphical works. Archaeologists in the vicinity have unearthed a cemetery and a complex of buildings on the site of the Qumran community, and they have demonstrated that the scrolls stored in jars in the first Qumran cave were written or copied between the 1st cent. B.C. and the first half of the 1st cent. A.D. Chief among the scrolls are the two copies of the Book of Isaiah (one complete, the other incomplete; they are almost 1,000 years older than any biblical manuscript known before); a commentary (*midrash*) on the Book of Habakkuk; a copy of the Apocalypse of Lamech (unlike the other scrolls, it is written in Aramaic and not in Hebrew and was at first thought to be the Book of Lamech but is actually a variant form of Genesis, including details and names not in the traditional version); and works written especially by and for the ascetic community of Qumran (a book of the community rules, called frequently *The Manual of Discipline;* an allegorical account of the community, *The War of the Sons of Light with the Sons of Darkness;* and a group of devotional poems, *The Thanksgiving Psalms*). The Qumran community resembled the Essenes and has been identified with them by some scholars. However, the discovery (1964) of a similar scroll at Masada gave rise to the speculation that the Qumran scrolls might be the work of the ZEALOTS, a later revolutionary Jewish sect that led the revolt against Rome in A.D. 66. Startling parallels in expression and thought between the Qumran materials and the New Testament have led to speculation as to the Essene influence on Christianity. A possible textual similarity between a minute scrap of the scrolls and the Gospel of St. Mark could establish the first tie between the Essenes and early Christians. The recent deciphering of the so-called "Temple Scroll" revealed a list of rules of conduct resembling standard Christian ethics. Some have suggested that Jesus or John the Baptist belonged to the community; this has been hotly debated. Other texts, not related to the Qumran scrolls, have been found in the area around the Dead Sea. In the caves at Wadi Murabbaat, c.11 mi (18 km) S of Qumran, were found many documents concerning Bar Kokba's army as well as more biblical manuscripts. At Khirbet Mird, N of the Kidron Valley, manuscripts have been found probably dating from even more ancient times. Israel's 1967 occupation of East Jerusalem caused an ownership dispute—as yet unresolved—and a publication halt that ended in 1973 when the Palestine Archaeological Museum resumed translation of the scrolls. Five volumes of translation, *Discoveries in the Judean Desert* (1957–67) have been published. See Millar Burrows, *The Dead Sea Scrolls* (1955, repr. 1965) and *More Light on the Dead Sea Scrolls* (1958); Lucetta Mowry, *The Dead Sea Scrolls and the Early Church* (1962, repr. 1966); G. R. Driver, *The Judaean Scrolls* (1966); M. A. Larson, *The Essene Heritage* (1967); Edmund Wilson, *The Dead Sea Scrolls, 1947–1969* (1969).

Deadwood, city (1970 pop. 2,409), seat of Lawrence co., W S.Dak., in the Black Hills; settled 1876 after discovery of gold there. It is a tourist center for the Black Hills and a trading hub for a lumbering, stock-raising, and mining region, with ore smelting and refining operations. Built in a narrow canyon, with houses climbing up the steep sides, the city of Deadwood Gulch (so called because the trees had been killed by fire) boomed and waned with the alternate discovery and abandonment of nearby gold and silver mines. Its colorful early history is commemorated in the Adams Memorial Museum, several monuments, and an annual "Days of '76" celebration in August. The graves of such famous Deadwood citizens as Wild Bill Hickok (who was shot in the back in a saloon there during a card game) and Calamity Jane are in Deadwood; the cabin and grave of Deadwood Dick are nearby.

deafness, partial or total lack of hearing. It may be present at birth (congenital) or may be acquired at any age thereafter. Most older persons suffer some degree of hearing loss. A person who cannot detect sound at an amplitude of 20 decibels in a frequency range of from 800 to 1,800 vibrations per sec is said to be hard of hearing. The ear normally perceives sounds in the range of 20 to 20,000 vibrations per sec. There are two principal kinds of deafness. Conductive deafness results from a disturbance in the transmission of sound through the outer and middle ear to the nerve receptors of the inner ear. Perceptive, or nerve, deafness results from damage to the neural receptors of the inner ear, the nerve pathways to the brain (notably the auditory nerve), or the area of the brain that receives sound information. In some cases of deafness both the conductive and the nerve mechanisms are disturbed. Disturbances of the conductive mechanism are often temporary or curable. Many such cases are caused by infection of the ear itself or of the upper respiratory tract—conditions that respond to antibiotic therapy. Foreign bodies or impacted wax can cause hearing loss and must be removed by a physician. In children, a common cause of conductive deafness is excessive lymphoid tissue (adenoids) about the eustachian tube, which interferes with proper ventilation of the middle ear. Removal of such tissue results in a return of normal hearing. In older persons the predominant cause of deafness is otosclerosis, a chronic condition in which spongy bone formation results in fixation of the stapes, the bone that connects the middle ear to the inner ear, and restricts its vibration. Important advances in surgical techniques have led to successful treatment of otosclerosis by replacing the stapes with a combination of grafted tissue, plastic, and wire appliances. Deafness can also be caused by perforation or rupture of the eardrum by a sudden loud noise, by physical puncture, or as a result of an infectious disease. In some such cases the eardrum can be repaired by grafting. Today there are many advanced medical techniques for treating chronic infections of the middle ear, infection of the mastoid, and congenital malformations of the outer and middle ear that, if neglected, might result in deafness. Deafness of the perceptive type is usually permanent. It can be brought about by such diseases as meningitis, syphilis, typhoid, mumps, and measles. Tumors and injury of the brain, the effects of toxic substances, senility, and excessive noise are additional factors that lead to nerve deafness. Continued exposure to loud noise, as in certain industries, can result in damage to the cochlea, or inner ear, causing perceptive deafness. The hearing of patients with perceptive deafness can sometimes be improved if the patient avoids exposure to loud noise, e.g., by wearing protective ear plugs. Most instances of congenital deafness are of the neural, or perceptive, type, including those resulting from rubella or other infections contracted by the mother during the first three months of pregnancy, from erythroblastosis (Rh incompatibility), or from anoxia (lack of oxygen during delivery). Persons whose deafness cannot be relieved by medical or surgical means may be greatly helped by various types of electronic HEARING AIDS. Those with hearing loss that cannot be relieved even by mechanical devices (i.e., those with nerve deafness) can have special training in lip reading. When deafness is present at birth or develops before a child has learned to speak, it is necessary also to provide specialized speech training and perhaps education in "manual speech," in which fingers and hands are the instruments of expression and communication. Schools and trained teachers for the aurally handicapped are now found in every large city in the world. Except for sporadic attempts by clerics in the past centuries, there was no well-organized effort to help the aurally handicapped until the Abbé Charles Michel de l'Epée founded a school for the deaf in Paris in 1755. Samuel Heinicke established another one in Germany in 1778. The first public school for the deaf in the United States was founded (1817) in Hartford, Conn., by Thomas Hopkins Gallaudet; it is now called the American School for the Deaf. Alexander Graham Bell and his father, Alexander Melville Bell, did much to establish the study of speech on a scientific basis and to improve the methods of teaching the aurally handicapped. See Louis DiCarlo, *The Deaf* (1964); J. C. Ballantyne, *Deafness* (2d ed. 1970); E. D. Mindel and Vernon McCay, *They Grow in Silence* (1971).

Deak, Francis, Hung. *Deák Ferenc* (dĕ'äk fĕ'rĕnts), 1803–76, Hungarian politician. A landed proprietor and lawyer, he entered the Hungarian diet in 1833 and became minister of justice after the revolution of March, 1848. He vainly opposed Louis KOSSUTH, trying to prevent an open break with Austria, and upon his failure he withdrew from public affairs. After the defeat (1849) of the Hungarian revolutionists, Deak became the recognized leader of his nation. Though always advocating the continued union of Austria and Hungary, he insisted on the restoration of the Hungarian constitution of 1848, Hungarian territorial integrity, and the recognition of Hungary as a separate kingdom. The government of Emperor Francis Joseph having begun, in 1860, to seek reconciliation with Hungarian national sentiment, Deak in the diet of 1866 cooperated with Julius ANDRÁSSY in drawing up a report on a new constitution. This report was the basis of the negotiations (1867) between Deak and the Austrian chancellor, F. F. Beust, which resulted in the *Ausgleich* [compromise] establishing the AUSTRO-HUNGARIAN MONARCHY. Deak continued to act as a moderating force.

Deakin, Alfred (dē'kĭn), 1856–1919, Australian political leader. He held office in various ministries and aided in the fight for federation of the Australian states. He accomplished a great deal in social legislation, irrigation, defense, and preferential tariffs. At first attorney general of Australia (1901), he later was prime minister in three different fusion governments (1903-4, 1905-8, 1909-10). He wrote authoritative books on irrigation.

Deal, municipal borough (1971 pop. 25,415), Kent, SE England, on the Downs, an important passage for Channel shipping. It is a popular holiday resort. There is some boat building; other industries are brush making, the production of plastics, and precision engineering. Deal was the reputed landing place of Julius Caesar in 55 B.C. and a later member of the CINQUE PORTS. Henry VIII built three castles in the area: Deal Castle, Walmer Castle (seat of the lord warden of the Cinque Ports), and Sandown Castle (now washed away). From the 17th to the early 19th cent., Deal was an important supply and service center for ships anchored at the Downs.

Deal Island, small island, off the western shore of Delmarva peninsula, in Tangier Sound, SE Md. It is an important oyster, clam, and crab shipping and processing center.

Dean, Bashford, 1867-1928, American zoologist and armor expert, b. New York City, grad. College of the City of New York, 1886, Ph.D. Columbia, 1890. He taught zoology at Columbia (1891-1927), served with the U.S. Fish Commission (1889-92, 1900-1901), and was curator of herpetology and ichthyology at the American Museum of Natural History (1903-26). His important works on ichthyology include *Bibliography of Fishes* (1916-23). As an authority on medieval arms and armor he became curator (1903) of the collection at the Metropolitan Museum of Art and made it one of the greatest collections of its kind in the world.

Dean, James, 1931-55, American film actor, b. Fairmount, Ind. After a few stage and television roles, Dean was chosen to play the moody, rebellious son in the film *East of Eden* (1953). He was further identified with restless, inarticulate youth in his second film *Rebel Without a Cause* (1954). Dean was killed when his racing car crashed the day after he finished work on *Giant* (1955). His death set off a worldwide wave of cultist mourning unequalled since the death of Rudolph Valentino. See biographies by David Dalton (1973) and Venable Herndon (1974).

Dean, Jerome Herman (Dizzy Dean), 1911-74, American baseball player, b. Lucas, Ark. His name was originally Jay Hanna Dean. A colorful right-handed pitcher, Dean performed brilliantly (1930-37) for the St. Louis Cardinals of the National League. After his pitching arm was injured he was traded (1938) to the Chicago Cubs but retired three years later. Dean became (1941) a sportscaster on radio and television and was noted for his picturesque descriptions of baseball games. He was elected to the Baseball Hall of Fame in 1953.

Dean, Forest of, ancient royal forest (c.30,000 acres/12,140 hectares), Gloucestershire, W England, between the Severn and the gorges of the Wye River. It was the first (1938) of the National Forest Parks of Great Britain. In the forest are ruins of Roman roads and mines. Today the forest's economic value lies in its collieries, stone quarries, and timber.

Deane, Silas, 1737-89, political leader and diplomat in the American Revolution, b. Groton, Conn. A lawyer and merchant at Wethersfield, Conn., he was elected (1772) to the state assembly and became a leader in the revolutionary cause. He was (1774-76) a delegate to the Continental Congress, which sent (1776) him as diplomatic agent to France. There Deane worked with Pierre de BEAUMARCHAIS in securing commercial and military aid for the colonies, obtaining supplies that were of material help in the Saratoga campaign (1777). He recruited a number of foreign officers, such as the marquis de Lafayette, Casimir Pulaski, Baron von Steuben, and Johann De Kalb. Late in 1776, Congress sent Benjamin Franklin and Arthur Lee to join Deane. Together they arranged (1778) a commercial and military alliance with France. Deane, however, was soon recalled by Congress and was faced with accusations of profiteering made against him by Lee. Embittered, unable to clear himself, and accused as a traitor after publication of some pessimistic private letters, Deane lived the rest of his life in exile. In 1842 Congress voted $37,000 to his heirs as restitution and characterized Lee's audit of Deane's accounts "a gross injustice." See Charles Isham, ed., *The Deane Papers, 1774-1790* (5 vol., 1887-91); biography by G. L. Clark (1913).

Dearborn, Henry, 1751-1829, American general and cabinet member, b. Hampton, N.H. He was a physician and became a captain of militia. When the American Revolution broke out, he led his company in the battle of Bunker Hill. Later he saw distinguished service, accompanying Benedict Arnold in the march against Quebec (where he was captured, but later exchanged), serving in the Saratoga campaign in 1777, wintering at Valley Forge, and fighting in the battle of Monmouth. He led (1779) a regiment in John Sullivan's campaign against Loyalists and Indians in New York and was on General Washington's staff at Yorktown. After the war he settled in Maine, and represented (1793-97) the District of Maine in Congress. As Secretary of War (1801-9) under President Thomas Jefferson he helped form the plan for Indian removal beyond the Mississippi River. At the outbreak of the War of 1812, he became major general in command of the northern frontier from Niagara to the Atlantic coast. His inaction contributed to the British capture of Detroit. Several plans to invade Canada were not even attempted, and although, in 1813, Dearborn took York (now Toronto) and Fort George on the Niagara River, he lost many men and exposed Sackett's Harbor to an almost successful British attack. He was relieved of command in 1813. From 1822 to 1824 he served as minister to Portugal. Fort Dearborn (around which grew the city of Chicago) was named for him.

Dearborn, city (1970 pop. 104,199), Wayne co., SE Mich., on the Rouge River, adjoining Detroit; settled 1795, inc. as a city 1929. The home of the Ford Motor Company, Dearborn is also a major warehousing and distribution center. In addition to automobiles, bricks, steel, tools and dies, and metal products are manufactured there. Largely residential despite its industry, Dearborn is famous for the Edison Institute of Technology, which includes Greenfield Village, birthplace of Henry Ford. Ford's large estate, Fair Lane, designated as a national historic landmark, is now part of the Univ. of Michigan's Dearborn campus. Ford Motor Company is currently developing a "new town" on 2,300 acres (930 hectares) in the center of the city. A veterans hospital and a junior college are in Dearborn.

Dearborn, Fort: see FORT DEARBORN.

Dease, Peter Warren (dēs), 1788-1863, Canadian explorer. He was in the North West Company before its merger with the Hudson's Bay Company and later was a Hudson's Bay Company trader. He was a member of the party of Sir John Franklin's second arctic expedition. Later he and Thomas SIMPSON explored (1836-39) the coast of the Arctic Ocean in Canada and Alaska from the mouth of the Mackenzie River to Point Barrow. They also mapped the southern shores of Victoria and King William islands.

death, cessation of all life (metabolic) processes. Death may involve the organism as a whole (somatic death) or may be confined to cells and tissues within the organism. The physiological death of cells that are normally replaced throughout life is called necrobiosis; the death of cells caused by external changes, such as an abnormal lack of blood supply, is called necrosis. Somatic death is characterized by the discontinuance of cardiac activity and respiration, and eventually leads to the death of all body cells from lack of oxygen, although for approximately six minutes after somatic death—a period referred to as clinical death—a person whose vital organs have not been damaged may be revived. However, achievements of modern biomedical technology have enabled the physician to artificially maintain critical functions for indefinite periods. Especially with recent refinements in organ transplantation technique, the need has arisen to more precisely define medical death, since the death of a donor must be established before transfer of an organ, which often has limited viability after death, can be undertaken. The criterion more and more frequently used to establish somatic death has become the complete cessation of all levels of nervous system activity. Somatic death is followed by a number of irreversible changes that are of legal importance, especially in estimating the time of death. These include RIGOR MORTIS, livor mortis (discoloration of the body due to settling of blood), algor mortis (cooling of the body), autolysis (breakdown of tissue by enzymes liberated by that tissue after death), and putrefaction (invasion of the body by organisms from the gastrointestinal tract). Causes of death in human beings include injury, acute or chronic disease, and neoplasia (cancer). See EUTHANASIA; FUNERAL CUSTOMS; VITAL STATISTICS.

death, dance of, or **danse macabre** (däns məkä'brə, -bər, däns), originally a 14th-century morality poem. The poem was a dialogue between death and representatives of all classes from the pope down. By the 15th cent., pictorial representation with verses illustrating the pictures became common. The dance, in which death as a skeleton or a corpse led his victims, was painted on walls of churchyards and cemeteries. The earliest known fully articulated example of the dance of death was a series of mural paintings (1424-25) in the cloisters of the Church of the Holy Innocents, Paris. The paintings were destroyed in 1669. In 1485, Guyot Marchand published a set of 17 woodcuts, with verses appended, based on the Paris murals; the set went through many editions and established its own genre. The best-known representations of the dance of death are the drawings of Holbein, the younger. Goethe wrote a ballad on the theme, *Der Todtentanz*, and in music Saint-Saëns used it in *Danse macabre*. See facsimile of Guyot Marchand's dance of death (1945); Hans Holbein, *Dance of Death* (1538, new ed. 1972); study by L. P. Kurtz (1934).

death angel: see MUSHROOM.

death rate: see VITAL STATISTICS.

Death Valley National Monument, 1,907,760 acres (772,070 hectares), SE Calif. and SW Nev.; est. 1933. Death Valley, 140 mi (225 km) long, is a deep, arid basin, bordered on the W by the Panamint Range and on the E by the Amargosa Range. In summer the valley has some of the highest air temperatures (134°F/57°C) and ground temperatures (165°F/74°C) in the world. Less than 2 in. (5 cm) of rain falls annually; the small Amargosa River and Furnace Creek disappear into the sands. Salt and alkali flats, unique rock formations, and briny pools are found there. Badwater, in the south central part of Death Valley, is 282 ft (86 m) below sea level, the lowest point in North America; Telescope Peak, in the Panamint Range, is 11,049 ft (3,368 m) high. Death Valley was named by gold seekers who mistakenly undertook to cross this desolate region in 1849 on their way to the California gold fields. The valley itself yielded gold and silver in the 1850s, and in the 1880s borax was discovered and taken out by mule-drawn wagons. In spite of the harsh environment, many small animals and peculiar desert plants are found in Death Valley; they have attracted much scientific attention. The Panamint Indians, an offshoot of the Shoshone, are the only group ever to be self-subsisting in the region. The valley was much publicized by the American adventurer Walter Scott ("Death Valley Scotty"), whose ostentatious home, Scotty's Castle, is a showplace there.

Deauville (dōvēl'), town (1968 pop. 5,232), Calvados dept., N France, on the English Channel. A fashionable resort, it has a famous racecourse and a gambling casino.

De Bakey, Michael Ellis, 1908–, American surgeon. While still at Tulane medical school (M.D., 1932), De Bakey developed an interest in problems relating to heart-lung machines, and he later made refinements in the technique of blood transfusions. In 1948 he became head of surgery at Baylor College of Medicine in Houston and five years later made medical history by performing the first successful carotid endarterectomy. A pioneer in dacron-tube replacements for blood vessels, De Bakey revolutionized the surgery of aneurysms. In 1966 he implanted the first completely artificial heart in man.

De Bary, Heinrich Anton (hīn'rĭkh än'tōn də bärē'), 1831-88, German botanist. He was professor at the universities of Freiburg in Breisgau (1855-66) and Halle (1867-72) and first rector of the Univ. of Strasbourg (from 1872). An authority on the life history of fungi and bacteria, he wrote several standard works in these fields and discovered sexual reproduction in fungi and the alternation of generations in rust fungi. His research established mycology as a science. In 1879, De Bary coined the word *symbiosis*.

debenture (dəbĕn'chər), document acknowledging indebtedness. In Great Britain a debenture is practically the same as a BOND, and debenture stock is similar to preferred stock. In the United States the term is usually employed for a corporation certificate without special security, such as a mortgage, to back it up. Debentures are generally issued by service corporations that have few mortgageable assets, or by blue-chip companies that are stable enough to invite unsecured loans. In a typical debenture, the corporation promises to repay the principal either periodically or on a specified date, and with regular interest. The term is also used for a document by which a government is bound to pay a creditor money due after some condition has been fulfilled.

Debir (dē'bər). **1** King of Eglon. Joshua 10. **2** City, Palestine, WSW of Hebron, on the main caravan route to Egypt. Joshua 10.38; 11.21; 12.13; 21.15; 1 Chron. 6.58. Kirjath-sannah: Joshua 15.49. Kirjath-sepher: Joshua 15.15,16; Judges 1.11,12. **3** Unidentified location, S Palestine, SW of Jericho. Joshua 15.7. **4** Unidentified city, Palestine, E of the River Jordan. Joshua 13.26.

Dęblin (dĕN'blĕn), city (1966 pop. 11,700), E Poland, on the Vistula River. It is a railway junction and one of the main crossings of the Vistula. Founded as a fortress by Czar Nicholas I in 1837, it was captured by the Germans in 1915 but was returned to Poland after World War I.

Deborah (dĕb'ōrə). **1** Judge of Israel, the only woman to hold that office. Under her guidance Barak conquered Sisera and delivered Israel from the tyranny of King Jabin. The triumphant "Song of Deborah" is one of the most brilliant poems in the Bible. Judges 4; 5. **2** Nurse of Rebecca. Gen. 35.8.

De Bow, James Dunwoody Brownson (də bō'), 1820–67, American editor and statistician, b. Charleston, S.C. He became (1844) editor of the *Southern Quarterly Review.* His long article, "The Oregon Question," attracted attention in England and France as well as in America. In 1846 he went to New Orleans, where he began publishing the monthly *De Bow's Review.* He was an ardent secessionist, and his magazine helped shape Southern opinion. Advocating a chair of political economy at the new Univ. of Louisiana, he was appointed to fill it. He was superintendent of the U.S. census of 1850, and his *Statistical View of the United States* (1854) was an abstract and interpretation of the census reports. He also wrote *Encyclopaedia of Trade and Commerce of the United States* (1853), *Industrial Resources and Statistics of the Southwest* (1853), *The Southern States* (1856), and many articles for the eighth edition of *The Encyclopaedia Britannica.* During the Civil War he was chief agent of the Confederate government in the purchase of cotton. See biography by O. C. Skipper (1958).

Debray, Jules Régis (zhül rāzhĕs' dəbrā'), 1940–, French journalist. He went to Cuba, taught philosophy at the Univ. of Havana, and, after lengthy conversations with Fidel Castro, wrote *Revolution in the Revolution?* (1967), a handbook on guerrilla warfare that offered a philosophical justification for the use of violence. In April, 1967, Debray was captured by government troops in Bolivia while accompanying a guerrilla force under Ernesto "Che" Guevara. Tried by a military tribunal, he first insisted that he had accompanied the guerrillas only as a journalist, but then abandoned his defense after learning of the capture and death of Guevara. He was sentenced (1967) to 30 years in prison. Such notables as Charles De Gaulle, Pope Paul VI, André Malraux, and Jean-Paul Sartre petitioned for his release, and he was pardoned in Dec., 1970. He sought refuge in Chile, where he wrote *The Chilean Revolution* (1972) after interviews with Salvador Allende.

Debrecen (dĕ'brĕtsĕn), city (1970 pop. 155,122), E Hungary, the nation's third largest city and the economic and cultural center of the Great Plain (Alföld) region E of the Tisza River. It is also a county administrative center, a road and rail hub, and an industrial city that produces railway cars, agricultural machinery, medical instruments, pharmaceuticals, furniture, and processed foods. Debrecen was traditionally famous for its fairs and livestock markets. Known in the 13th cent., the city grew as a market for cattle and grain. It became the stronghold of Hungarian Protestantism in the 16th cent., and its Calvinist college later formed the nucleus of a university. Under the Turkish occupation of Hungary (16th–17th cent.), Debrecen enjoyed semiautonomous status and often served as a refuge for peasants fleeing the Turks. It was also an important trade center, but the wars in the late 17th cent. between Christian Europe and the Turks ruined the city's economy. Debrecen became the center of Hungarian resistance against Austrian rule in the 19th cent.; and on April 14, 1849, Louis Kossuth proclaimed Hungary's independence in the great church in the heart of Debrecen. Russian troops, who had helped the Hapsburgs crush the Hungarian uprising, occupied the city briefly. Economic revival began in the early 20th cent. In 1944–45, during World War II, Debrecen served as provisional capital of Hungary.

Debre Zeyt (dĕb'rə zāt), town (1970 est. pop. 28,000), Shoa prov., central Ethiopia. It is the headquarters of the Ethiopian air force and is the site of an air force academy. It is also a weekend resort for persons from nearby Addis Ababa.

de Broglie: see BROGLIE.

De Bruyn, Cornelis: see BRUYN, CORNELIS DE.

Debs, Eugene Victor, 1855–1926, American Socialist leader, b. Terre Haute, Ind. Leaving high school to work in the railroad shops in Terre Haute, he became a railroad fireman (1871) and organized (1875) a local of the Brotherhood of Locomotive Firemen. In 1880 he became national secretary and treasurer of the brotherhood, and in 1884 he was elected to the Indiana legislature. He resigned (1892) from the brotherhood and launched (1893), instead of a trade union, an industrial union to include all railroad workers, the American Railway Union, of which he became president. After a successful strike against the Great Northern RR, the American Railway Union participated (1894) in the PULLMAN STRIKE by refusing to service Pullman cars. An injunction, however, was served against the strikers and Federal troops, sent to Illinois by President CLEVELAND over the protest of Illinois governor John P. ALTGELD, broke the strike. Debs and others were convicted of violating the injunction and sentenced to a six-month jail term. While in prison, Debs read widely, including socialist works, and later became a Socialist. In 1898, he helped form the Social Democratic party (renamed the Socialist party in 1901; again renamed Social Democratic in 1972) and was (1900) its presidential candidate, polling 96,000 votes. As candidate (1904) of the Socialist party, he received 402,000 votes. He became editor of the Socialist weekly *Appeal to Reason* and lectured widely. After 1900, he grew more bitter in his attacks on trade unionism and more vehement in advocating the organization of labor by industries. He helped to found (1905) the INDUSTRIAL WORKERS OF THE WORLD, but soon withdrew from the movement. Debs was again the Socialist candidate for President in 1908 and 1912. During World War I, the Socialist party refused to take part in the government war effort and in 1918 Debs, a leading pacifist, was sentenced to a 10-year prison term for publicly denouncing the government's prosecution of persons charged with sedition under the Espionage Act of 1917. Although still in a Federal penitentiary, he was Socialist candidate for President in 1920 and gathered nearly 920,000 votes. He was released (1921) by order of President Harding. But his health was broken, and he accomplished little in his last years, although he was widely revered as a martyr for his principles. See Ray Ginger, *The Bending Cross* (1949, repr. 1969); H. W. Morgan, *Eugene V. Debs: Socialist for President* (1962, repr. 1973); Iris Noble, *Labor's Advocate: Eugene V. Debs* (1966).

debt, obligation in services, money, or goods owed by one party, the debtor, to another, the creditor. When contested, debts are collected by a civil suit upon which the judge renders a judgment, and an execution is levied on the debtor's property. In ancient nations debt was associated with slavery because the insolvent debtor and his household were in many cases turned over to the creditor to perform compulsory services. In early Rome the insolvent was given into custody of the creditor for 60 days prior to his sale as a slave, subject to such treatment as pleased the creditor. That arrangement was mitigated in 494 B.C. by the first of the uprisings of the Roman people; turbulence in Rome afterward was to a large extent occasioned by the desire to restrain creditors. In Greece the reforms of Solon had a similar origin. In Palestine, every 50th year—the year of jubilee—Jewish debtors were freed and their obligations were canceled. Imprisonment for debt, which once crowded prisons, was ended in theory in England and the United States by laws enacted in the 19th cent. However, imprisonment on other charges, such as concealment of assets, in some instances continues the substance of imprisonment for debt. The laws of BANKRUPTCY are designed to apply the resources of debtors to their debts and thereafter to remove such legal obligations.

debt, public, indebtedness of a government expressed in money terms. The indebtedness of a central government is often called the national debt. The debt is differently computed by nearly every nation. Some authorities exclude all government obligations other than those incurred by public borrowing from individuals. About 1800 the idea of a public debt became distinct from the concept of the debts of the sovereign himself. Governments may incur debts for several reasons. They may borrow to meet temporary needs, as when estimated revenue falls below estimated expenditures. Short-term treasury notes, payable by increased taxes or by greater economy, may be issued, but such a debt should not become permanent. Public works, especially when widespread unemployment exists, are another source of public debt and are justified in part by their permanent social utility. The largest public debts are incurred to meet emergencies; such are war debts, arising from the impossibility of financing the extended activities of government by new taxes or from the need to borrow abroad to finance the war effort. Public debts are advantageous in securing part of the national funds at an interest rate lower than that provided by private industry and in founding the financial operations of government on a permanent basis. They also have an expansionary effect on employment and production. The disadvantages are that unjustifiable projects may be undertaken because the full burden of payment is not immediately due; that the government's demands may become so large that the interest rate on government bonds will rise to the point where money is diverted from private enterprise; and that too great a debt may induce governments to depreciate currency or default on obligations. Public loans, the characteristic form of government debts in modern times, may be in the form of short-term instruments, e.g., tax warrants, treasury certificates, treasury notes, and other notes such as those of the FEDERAL RESERVE SYSTEM; long-term government bonds; and various notes that promise yearly payment of interest but without date for payment of principal. The number of those holding government obligations has increased in recent history; but governments in times of stress have often converted bonds to issues carrying lower interest rates, have depreciated the value of currency, or have defaulted entirely on their obligations, with disastrous results for the bondholders. Default on obligations held by foreigners has been a reason offered for past intervention by major powers in Latin America, Africa, and elsewhere. The payment of the public debt improves the national credit. Public debts may be paid by a SINKING FUND or by annuities, but both have the disadvantage of committing the government to fixed annual payments, whether convenient or not. Another method is to use only surplus revenue, setting a permanent appropriation to be paid against principal over and above annual interest rates; thus amortization of the public debt halts when the government has a deficit. The ultimate security of the public debt lies in the willingness of the people to pay and the ability of the government to collect the taxes. The U.S. national debt originated with the Revolution and as of 1975 amounted to more than $400 billion. See E. R. A. Seligman, *Currency Inflation and Public Debts* (1921); William Withers, *The Retirement of National Debts* (1932, repr. 1969); C. C. Abbott, *Management of the Federal Debt* (1946); J. M. Buchanan, *Public Principles of Public Debt* (1958) and *Public Debt in a Democratic Society* (1967).

Deburau or **Debureau, Jean Gaspard** (both: zhäN gäspär' dəbürō'), 1796–1846, French pantomime performer, whose original name was Jan Kaspar Dvorjak, b. Bohemia. He became famous for his introduction of the pantomime character PIERROT at the Théâtre des Funambules. With delicate charm and pathos, he captured the essence of the ever hopeful but always disappointed lover. He is the subject of a play by Sacha Guitry and of Marcel Carné's film, *Children of Paradise* (1944). See biography by Francis Kozik (tr. 1940).

Debussy, Claude Achille (klôd äshēl' dəbüsē'), 1862–1918, French composer, exponent of musical IMPRESSIONISM. He studied for 11 years at the Paris Conservatory, receiving its Grand Prix de Rome in 1884 for his cantata *L'Enfant Prodigue.* After traveling in Europe and Russia, Debussy settled down in Paris in 1887 and devoted himself to composing for the rest of his life. In his music he developed a new fluidity of form and explored unusual harmonic relationships and dissonances. By making use of the whole-tone scale, instead of the traditional scale of Western music, he achieved new nuances of mood and expression, as in his famous tone poem *Prélude à l'après-midi d'un faune* (*Prelude to the Afternoon of a Faun,* 1894). Inspired by a pastoral poem of Mallarmé, it is one of Debussy's most sensuous and evocative orchestral works, lending itself perfectly to ballet. Other outstanding orchestral pieces are his *Nocturnes* (1899) and *La Mer* (*The Sea,* 1905). His piano works exploit to the utmost the subtle coloristic possibilities of the instrument. Among them are *Suite bergamasque* (pub. 1905), containing the popular *Clair de lune; Estampes* (1903); *The Children's Corner* (1908); 24 preludes, including *La Cathédrale engloutie* (1910); and 12 études. He also wrote many exquisite songs and an opera, *Pelléas et Mélisande* (1892–1902), based on the drama by Maeterlinck. See reminiscences of Marguerite Long (tr. 1972); biographies by V. I. Seroff (1956), Edward Lockspeiser (2 vol., 1962–65), and Oscar Thompson (rev. ed. 1965).

Debye, Peter Joseph Wilhelm (dĕbī'), 1884–1966, American physicist, b. the Netherlands. He was professor at the universities of Zürich, Utrecht, Göttingen, Leipzig, and Berlin. In 1940 he came to the United States and served as professor of chemistry at Cornell Univ. (1940–52). For his work on the structure of molecules he received the 1936 Nobel Prize in Chemistry. He is known also for his studies in the conductivity of electricity by salt solutions and in the heat capacity of solids.

decadents, in literature, name loosely applied to those 19th-century, fin-de-siècle European authors who sought inspiration, both in their lives and in their writings, in aestheticism and in all the more or less morbid and macabre expressions of human emotion. In reaction to the naturalism of the European realists, the decadents espoused that art should exist for its own sake, independent of moral and social concerns. The epithet was first applied in the 1880s to a group of self-conscious and flamboyant French poets, who in 1886 published the journal *Le Décadent.* The decadents venerated Baudelaire and the French SYMBOLISTS, the group with whom they are often mistakenly identified. In England the decadent movement was represented in the 1890s by Oscar Wilde, Walter Pater, Ernest Dowson, and Aubrey Beardsley and the writers of the *Yellow Book.* J. K. Huysmans's *À rebours* (1884) and Wilde's *Picture of Dorian Gray* (1891) present vivid fictionalized portraits of the 19th-century decadent—his restlessness, his spiritual confusion, and his moral inversion. See Mario Praz, *Romantic Agony* (tr. 1933); A. E. Carter, *The Idea of Decadence in French Literature* (1958); Maurice Rheims, *The Flowering of Art Nouveau* (1966); Yvor Winters, *Primitivism and Decadence* (1937, repr. 1969).

Decalogue: see TEN COMMANDMENTS.

Decameron: see BOCCACCIO, GIOVANNI.

Decamps, Alexandre Gabriel (älĕksäN'drə găbrēĕl' dəkäN'), 1803–60, French genre and historical painter, engraver, and lithographer. First known for his caricatures and illustrations, he turned to painting in thick impasto and strong color. One of his richest sources was the Orient, which he depicted in vivid detail. His *Good Samaritan* and *Night Patrol at Smyrna* are in the Metropolitan Museum.

decapod (Gr.,=10 feet), name for invertebrate animals of the CRUSTACEAN order Decapoda (phylum ARTHROPODA) including the crabs, the lobsters and crayfish, and the true shrimps, all having five pairs of legs. The name Decapoda was also formerly applied to a very different group of animals, a CEPHALOPOD order including the cuttlefish and squids, characterized by two long and eight short tentacles. The cuttlefish are now classified in the order Sepioidea and the squids in the order Teuthoidea of the class Cephalopoda in the phylum MOLLUSCA.

Decapolis (dĕkăp'əlĭs) [Gr.,=ten cities], confederacy of 10 ancient cities, all E of the Jordan, except Scythopolis. The others were (according to Pliny) Dion, Pella, Gadara, Hippos, Gerasa, Philadelphia, Damascus, Raphana, and Kanatha. The league was constituted after Pompey's campaign (65 B.C.–62 B.C.) as a protection against the Jews and the Arabian tribes and as a customs union. The Roman governor of Syria exercised general supervision of its affairs, and the cities belonging to the league were liable to Roman military service and taxation. The name was used for the general locality, as in the Bible (Mat. 4.25; Mark 5.20; 7.31).

decathlon (dĭkăth'lŏn), in modern OLYMPIC GAMES, a contest composed of 10 track-and-field events. It consists of the broad jump; the high jump; discus throwing; shot putting; javelin throwing; the 100-meter, 400-meter, and 1,500-meter races; the 110-meter hurdle race; and pole vaulting. The decathlon became an Olympic event in 1912 and was generally won by American athletes until 1960. The PENTATHLON is a five-event contest.

Decatur, Stephen (dĕkā'tər), 1779–1820, American naval officer, b. Sinepuxent, near Berlin, Md.; son of a naval officer, Stephen Decatur. After joining the U.S. navy in 1798, he rose to fame in the TRIPOLITAN WAR. In 1804 he and his men stole into Tripoli harbor and destroyed the captured U.S. frigate *Philadelphia.* This daring exploit won Decatur promotion to captain. He helped in the bombardment of Tripoli and, after peace was concluded (1805), negotiated successfully with the bey of Tunis. In 1808 he was one of the judges at the court-martial of James BARRON; thereafter the two men were enemies. In the War of 1812 Decatur commanded three vessels, with the *United States* as his flagship. On Oct. 25, 1812, the *United States* met and captured the British frigate *Macedonian.* Afterward the British blockade held him powerless until Jan., 1815. Then (unaware that the war had ended) he put to sea in the *President,* outran three enemy ships and defeated the fourth, the *Endymion,* but the battle delayed him and he was forced to surrender to the other pursuers. In the so-called ALGERINE WAR in 1815 he used his squadron with vigor to force the dey of Algiers to sign the treaty that ended American tribute to Algeria. As one of the three navy commissioners (1815–20), he was powerful in naval affairs. His opposition to reinstating the unfortunate and disgraced James Barron led to bitter words. Barron challenged him, and in the ensuing duel Decatur was mortally wounded at Bladensburg, Md., on March 22, 1820. Known for his reckless bravery and stubborn patriotism, he is also remembered for the toast, "Our country! In her intercourse with foreign nations may she always be in the right; but our country, right or wrong!" See biographies by C. T. Brady (1900), C. L. Lewis (1937, repr. 1971) and Helen Nicolay (1942).

Decatur. 1 Industrial city (1970 pop. 38,044), seat of Morgan co., N Ala., on the Tennessee River; inc. 1826. It is a commercial and manufacturing center, with shipyards and industries thriving on power supplied by the Tennessee Valley Authority (TVA). Textiles, plastics, chemicals, bricks, tires, and trailers are among the city's manufactures. A settlement known as Rhodes Ferry was there when President James Monroe directed (1820) that a site be selected near a great river to honor Stephen Decatur, who had been killed in a duel; thus Rhodes Ferry became Decatur. The city grew as a cotton center. During the Civil War it was continually raided by Federal forces; only two houses and the imposing state bank (1832) survived. The TVA's largest nuclear power plant is located nearby. The present city was formed (1927) by the union of Decatur and Albany (formerly New Decatur). **2** City (1970 pop. 21,943), seat of De Kalb co., NW Ga., a residential suburb of Atlanta; inc. 1823. Agnes Scott College, Columbia Theological Seminary, and a hospital for crippled children are in the city. On nearby Stone Mountain is a spectacular Confederate memorial featuring carved figures of Gen. Robert E. Lee, Gen. Stonewall Jackson, and Confederate President Jefferson Davis. **3** City (1970 pop. 90,397), seat of Macon co., central Ill., on the Sangamon River (dammed there to form Lake Decatur); inc. 1839. A railroad and industrial center in a rich farm and livestock area, Decatur has railroad repair shops and huge plants for processing corn and soybeans. In addition to food products, the city's manufactures include tires, tractors, machinery, and automobile equipment. Coal deposits underlie the area. Points of interest include the Lincoln Log Cabin Courthouse, where Abraham Lincoln practiced law; Lincoln Square, where he received his first endorsement for the presidential nomination; and the city library, which has a Lincoln collection. The site of Lincoln's first home in Illinois is nearby. The Grand Army of the Republic was organized in Decatur in April, 1866. Millikin Univ. is in the city.

decay of organic matter or **putrefaction,** process whereby heterotrophic organisms, including some bacteria, fungi, saprophytic plants, and lower animals, utilize the remains of once-living tissue as a source of nutrition. The polysaccharides, lipids, nucleic acids, and proteins of dead tissue are broken down into smaller organic molecules, often by enzymes that are secreted into the external environment by the bacteria and fungi that are involved; the breakdown products are then readily absorbed by the heterotrophs and are used both as a source of building blocks for the synthesis of their own polysaccharides, lipids, nucleic acids, and proteins, and as a source of chemical energy, obtained either by FERMENTATION (in an anaerobic environment) or RESPIRATION (in the presence of oxygen). Often during the process of putrefaction, trace elements and nitrogen are released into the environment in forms suitable for uptake by higher plants; this is the basis for the use of decayed organic matter as fertilizer. The disagreeable odor produced as putrefaction takes place is caused by the formation of certain gases, including ammonia and hydrogen sulfide, and certain volatile amines, including putrescine and cadaverine, two products of the breakdown of protein by microorganisms.

Decazes, Élie (ālē' dəkäz'), 1780–1860, French statesman, a favorite of King Louis XVIII, who made him a duke in 1820. A lawyer and judge, Decazes was made minister of police in 1815 and was influential in the French government even before he became (1819) premier. His government maintained a precarious balance between the ultraroyalists and the radicals. His downfall, marking the failure of the moderates, came when the ultraroyalists accused him of complicity in the assassination (1820) of the duc de BERRY. He resigned, but Louis XVIII sent him as ambassador to England (1820–21). Decazes continued to figure in politics until the February Revolution of 1848.

Deccan (dĕ'kăn"), region of India. Sometimes defined as all India S of the Narbada River, it is in a more limited sense the plateau of central peninsular India, including approximately all Karnataka and S Andhra Pradesh, SE Maharashtra, and NW Tamil Nadu. The rich volcanic soil is used for growing cotton. The last of the great Mogul emperors, Aurangzeb, exhausted the power of his empire in a futile attempt (1683–1707) to absorb the region. It was in the Deccan that the Hindus began to regain (early 18th cent.) political and military power in India under Sivaji, leader of the Mahrattas. There in the late 18th cent. the British decisively defeated the French in their struggle for India.

December: see MONTH.

Decembrists, in Russian history, members of secret revolutionary societies whose activities led to the uprising of Dec., 1825, against Czar NICHOLAS I. Formed after the Napoleonic Wars, the groups comprised officers who had served in Europe and had been influenced by Western liberal ideals. They advocated the establishment of representative democracy but disagreed on the form it should take; some favored a constitutional monarchy, while others supported a democratic republic. Their poorly organized rebellion was precipitated by the confusion surrounding the succession to the throne on the death of ALEXANDER I. The more moderate members persuaded several regiments in St. Petersburg to refuse their oath of allegiance to the unpopular Nicholas and to demand that his elder brother, Constantine, who had secretly renounced the throne in 1822, be made czar and grant a constitution. The rebels marched to Senate Square and were crushed by artillery fire. Five of their leaders were later executed. The Decembrists' insurrection made a profound impression on Russia. It led both to the increasing police terrorism of the czarist government and to the spread of revolutionary activity among the educated classes. See M. O. Zetlin, *The Decembrists* (tr. 1958).

decemvirs (dēsĕm'vərz) [Lat.,=ten men], in ancient Rome, group of 10 men appointed to a special judicial or executive capacity. The most famous were those who developed in the 5th cent. B.C. the Laws of the Twelve Tables, the primary Roman code. There was a permanent decemvirate of priests that guarded the Sibylline Books (see SIBYL).

De Chirico, Giorgio: see CHIRICO, GIORGIO DE.

decibel, abbr. dB, unit used to measure the loudness of SOUND. It is one tenth of a bel (named for A. G. Bell), but the larger unit is rarely used. The decibel is a measure of sound intensity as a function of power ratio, with the difference in decibels between two sounds being given by $dB=10\log_{10}(P_1/P_2)$, where P_1 and P_2 are the power levels of the two sounds. The faintest audible sound, corresponding to a sound pressure of about 0.0002 dyne per sq cm, is arbitrarily assigned a value of 0 dB. The loudest sounds that can be tolerated by the human ear are about 120 dB. The level of normal conversation is about 50 to 60 dB. The decibel is also used to measure certain other quantities, such as power loss in telephone lines.

deciduous plant: see TREE.

decimal system [Lat.,=of tenths], numeration system based on powers of 10. A number is written as a row of digits, with each position in the row corresponding to a certain power of 10. A decimal point in the row divides it into those powers of 10 equal to or greater than 0 and those less than 0, i.e., negative powers of 10. Positions farther to the left of the decimal point correspond to increasing positive powers of 10 and those farther to the right to increasing negative powers, i.e., to division by higher positive powers of 10. For example, $4,309=(4\times10^3)+(3\times10^2)+(0\times10^1)+(9\times10^0)=4,000+300+0+9$, and $4.309=(4\times10^0)+(3\times10^{-1})+(0\times10^{-2})+(9\times10^{-3})=4+3/10+0/100+9/1000$. It is believed that the decimal system is based on 10 because humans have 10 fingers and so became used to counting by 10s early in the course of civilization. The decimal system was introduced into Europe c.1300. It greatly simplified arithmetic and was a much-needed improvement over the Roman numerals, which did not use a positional system. A number written in the decimal system is called a decimal, although sometimes this term is used to refer only to a proper FRACTION written in this system and not to a mixed number. Decimals are added and subtracted in the same way as are integers (whole numbers) except that when these operations are written in columnar form the decimal points in the column entries and in the answer must all be placed one under another. In multiplying two decimals the operation is the same as for integers except that the number of decimal places in the product, i.e., digits to the right of the decimal point, is equal to the sum of the decimal places in the factors; e.g., the factor 7.24 to two decimal places and the factor 6.3 to one decimal place have the product 45.612 to three decimal places. In division, e.g., 4.32 |12.8, where there is a decimal point in the divisor (4.32), the point is shifted to the extreme right (i.e., to 432.) and the decimal point in the dividend (12.8) is shifted the same number of places to the right (to 1280), with one or more zeros added before the decimal to make this possible. The decimal point in the quotient is then placed above that in the dividend, i.e., 432.|1280.0; zeros are added to the right of the decimal point in the dividend as needed, and the division proceeds the same as for integers. The decimal system is widely used in various systems employing numbers. The metric system of weights and measures, used in most of the world, is based on the decimal system, as are most systems of national currency.

Děčín (dyĕ'chēn), Ger. *Tetschen,* city (1970 pop. 45,589), Czechoslovakia, in Bohemia, on the Elbe. It includes (since 1950) the city of Podmokly (Ger. *Bodenbach*), which is on the left bank of the Elbe. A center of a coal-mining region, it is also a river port and an industrial center. Founded in 1128, it was incorporated into Czechoslovakia in 1918. The city has a 17th-century castle with a fine library.

Decius (Caius Messius Quintus Decius) (dē'shəs), 201–51, Roman emperor (249–51), b. Pannonia. He was sent by PHILIP (Philip the Arabian) to quell a mutiny, but when the soldiers hailed him as emperor, he marched at their head, defeated and killed Philip near Verona, and accepted the title of emperor, adding Trajan (Traianus) to his name. He undertook to rebuild the state, and in an effort to revive the state religion he persecuted the Christians vigorously. He was killed in the attempt to repel an invasion of the Goths into Moesia and was succeeded by GALLUS.

Decius Mus, Publius (mŭs), name of three Romans, father, son, and grandson, who, according to legend, sacrificed themselves for their country. As a tribune, the father fought (343 B.C.) in the war against the Samnites and, as consul with Manlius Torquatus, commanded in the war with the Latins. Near Mt. Vesuvius he "devoted" himself to the gods and then deliberately exposed himself to death (340 B.C.) in the belief that the enemy would thereby be destroyed by the gods. His son, when consul for the fourth time (295 B.C.), similarly sought death in the battle at Sentinum against the Gauls, Samnites, and Etruscans. His grandson, in the war with Pyrrhus, followed their example at Asculum (279 B.C.), according to Cicero's *Tusculan Disputations.*

Declaration of Independence, full and formal declaration adopted July 4, 1776, by representatives of the Thirteen Colonies in North America announcing the separation of those colonies from Great Britain and making them into the United States. Official acts that colonists considered infringements upon their rights had previously led to the Stamp Act Congress (1765) and to the First Continental Congress (1774), but these were predominantly conservative assemblies that sought redress from the crown and reconciliation, not independence. The overtures of the First Continental Congress in 1774 came to nothing, discontent grew, and as the armed skirmishes at Lexington and Concord (April 19, 1775) developed into the American Revolution, many members of the Second CONTINENTAL CONGRESS of Philadelphia followed the leadership of John Hancock, John Adams, and Samuel Adams in demanding independence. The delegates from Virginia and North Carolina were in fact specifically instructed on independence and on June 7, 1776, Richard Henry Lee called for a resolution of independence. On June 11, John Adams, Benjamin Franklin, Thomas Jefferson, Robert R. Livingston, and Roger Sherman were instructed to draft such a declaration; the actual writing was entrusted to Jefferson. The first draft was revised by Franklin, Adams, and Jefferson before it was sent to Congress, where it was again changed. That final draft was adopted July 4, 1776, and Independence Day has been the chief American patriotic holiday ever since. It is interesting to note, however, that the July 4 document is merely a fuller statement justifying the resolution of independence adopted by Congress July 2, 1776. The Declaration of Independence is the most important of all American historical documents. It is essentially a partisan document, a justification of the American Revolution presented to the world; but its unique combination of general principles and an abstract theory of government with a detailed enumeration of specific grievances and injustices has given it enduring power as one of the great political documents of the West. After stating its purpose, the opening paragraphs (given here in the form used in the engrossed copy) assert the fundamental American ideal of government, based on the theory of NATURAL RIGHTS, which had been held by, among others, John Locke, Emerich de Vattel, and Jean Jacques Rousseau. "We hold these truths to be self-evident, that all men are created equal, that they are endowed by their Creator with certain unalienable Rights, that among these are Life, Liberty and the pursuit of Happiness.—That to secure these rights, Governments are instituted among Men, deriving their just powers from the consent of the governed,—That whenever any Form of Government becomes destructive of these ends, it is the Right of the People to alter or to abolish it, and to institute new Government, laying its foundation on such principles and organizing its powers in such form, as to them shall seem most likely to effect their Safety and Happiness. Prudence, indeed, will dictate that Governments long established should not be changed for light and transient causes; and accordingly all experience hath shewn, that mankind are more disposed to suffer, while evils are sufferable, than to right themselves by abolishing the forms to which they are accustomed. But when a long train of abuses and usurpations, pursuing invariably the same Object evinces a design to reduce them under absolute Despotism, it is their right, it is their duty, to throw off such Government, and to provide new Guards for their future security." Then follows an indictment of George III for willfully infringing those rights in order to establish an "absolute Tyranny" over the colonies. The document states that colonial patience had achieved nothing and therefore the colonists found themselves forced to declare their independence. The stirring closing paragraph is the formal pronouncement of independence and is borrowed from the resolution of July 2. "We, therefore, the Representatives of the united States of America, in General Congress, Assembled, appealing to the Supreme Judge of the world for the rectitude of our intentions, do, in the Name, and by Authority of the good People of these Colonies, solemnly publish and declare, That these United Colonies are, and of Right ought to be Free and Independent States; that they are Absolved from all Allegiance to the British Crown, and that all political connection between them and the state of Great Britain, is and ought to be totally dissolved; and that as Free and Independent States, they have full Power to levy War, conclude Peace, contract Alliances, establish Commerce, and to do all other Acts and Things which Independent States may of right do.—And for the support of this Declaration, with a firm reliance on the protection of divine Providence, we mutually pledge to each other our Lives, our fortunes and our sacred Honor." Not all the men who helped draw up or voted for the Declaration signed it (Robert R. Livingston, for example, did not) nor were all the signers present at its adoption. All the signatures except six (Wythe, R. H. Lee, Wolcott, Gerry, McKean, and Thornton) were affixed on Aug. 2, 1776. The first is that of John Hancock, president of the Continental Congress. The remaining 55 (see individual articles on each) are those of Josiah Bartlett, William Whipple, Matthew Thornton, Samuel Adams, John Adams, Robert Treat Paine, Elbridge Gerry, Stephen Hopkins, William Ellery, Roger Sherman, Samuel Huntington, William Williams, Oliver Wolcott, William Floyd, Philip Livingston, Francis Lewis, Lewis Morris, Richard Stockton, John Witherspoon, Francis Hopkinson, John Hart, Abraham Clark, Robert Morris, Benjamin Rush, Benjamin Franklin, John Morton, George Clymer, James Smith, George Taylor, James Wilson, George Ross, Caesar Rodney, George Read, Thomas McKean, Samuel Chase, William Paca, Thomas Stone, Charles Carroll of Carrollton, George Wythe, Richard Henry Lee, Thomas Jefferson, Benjamin Harrison, Thomas Nelson, Jr., Francis Lightfoot Lee, Carter Braxton, William Hooper, Joseph Hewes, John Penn, Edward Rutledge, Thomas Heyward, Jr., Thomas Lynch, Jr., Arthur Middleton, Button Gwinnett, Lyman Hall, and George Walton. See studies by J. H. Hazelton (1906, repr. 1970), C. L. Becker (1922, repr. 1962), and F. R. Donovan (1968); Dumas Malone, *The Story of the Declaration of Independence* (1954); David Hawke, *A Transaction of Free Men* (1964); Robert Ginsberg, ed., *A Casebook on the Declaration of Independence* (1967).

Declaration of Rights, in British history: see BILL OF RIGHTS.

Declaration of the Rights of Man and Citizen, a fundamental document of French constitutional history, drafted by Emmanuel SIEYÈS, adopted by the Constituent Assembly on Aug. 26, 1789, and embodied in the French constitution of 1791 as a preamble. Its framers were much influenced by the American Declaration of Independence and by the *philosophes* (see ENLIGHTENMENT). The French declaration listed the "inalienable rights" of the individual (a list of duties was, after some debate, omitted by its framers). The rights to "liberty, property, security, and resistance to oppression" and the rights to freedom of speech and of the press were guaranteed. The document asserted the equality of men and the sovereignty of the people, on whom the law should rest, to whom officials should be responsible, and by whom finances should be controlled. Many of its provisions were aimed at specific abuses of the ancien régime. The declaration had immense effect on liberal thought in the 19th cent.

declension: see INFLECTION.

declination, in astronomy, one of the coordinates in the EQUATORIAL COORDINATE SYSTEM. The declination of a celestial body is its angular distance north or south of the celestial equator measured along its HOUR CIRCLE.

decompression chamber, device for adjusting the body from high external pressure to lower, or atmospheric, pressure. Normally, most of the nitrogen inhaled by a person is exhaled without being absorbed. However, as external pressure is increased, e.g., in deep-sea diving, nitrogen is absorbed and carried to the body tissues. As a person returns to normal pressure the nitrogen comes out of solution in the body fluids. If the transition is too rapid, bubbles of nitrogen collect in tissues and joints, where they cause pain and sometimes paralysis (see DECOMPRESSION SICKNESS). The decompression chamber allows for a controlled reduction of pressure so that the nitrogen is expired through the lungs. A typical chamber is a steel cylinder capable of withstanding high internal gas pressures and able to accommodate one or more persons. Two types of devices in current use are the surface and the submersible chambers. The surface decompression chamber is entered by the diver when he emerges from the water. The pressure in the chamber is quickly increased to approximate the pressure experienced by the diver underwater. A gradual decompression is then undertaken. The diver enters the underwater chamber while still submerged, seals the hatch, and is then decompressed slowly as the chamber is hauled to the surface.

decompression sickness, physiological disorder caused by a rapid decrease in atmospheric pressure, resulting in the release of nitrogen bubbles into the body tissues. It is also known as caisson disease, altitude sickness, and the bends. It is an occupational hazard of persons who work under greatly increased atmospheric pressure below the surface of the earth (e.g., divers and laborers who work under compressed air) when their return to normal atmospheric pressure is made too quickly. When the body is subjected to high atmospheric pressure the respiratory gases are compressed and larger amounts are dissolved in the body tissues. During ascent from depths greater than 30 ft (9.1 m), these gases escape as the external pressure decreases. Airplane pilots who go rapidly from normal atmospheric pressure to high altitudes (low atmospheric pressure) in unpressurized aircraft or in aircraft with faulty pressurizing apparatus also encounter the disorder. The decrease in air pressure releases body nitrogen in the form of gas bubbles that block the small veins and arteries and collect in the tissues, cutting off the oxygen supply and causing nausea, vomiting, dizziness, pain in the joints and abdomen, paralysis, and other neurological symptoms. In severe cases there may be shock, total collapse, and, if treatment is not prompt, death. Persons who work under increased atmospheric pressure must make the ascent to normal atmospheric pressure gradually, often through pressurized chambers, a procedure that allows the nitrogen to be released slowly from the blood and expired from the lungs. Inhalation of pure oxygen aids in clearing nitrogen from the body. Those who suffer symptoms of decompression sickness at high altitudes (commonly called aeroembolism) experience relief on returning to an atmospheric pressure normal to them; this and oxygen inhalation will usually effect recovery.

De Coningh, Philips: see KONINCK, PHILIPS DE.

Decorated style, type of construction favored in the second period of English Gothic architecture in the 14th cent. The basic elements of Gothic architecture as developed in the Early English style (late 12th and 13th cent.) were retained; but bar tracery, ornamented molding, and other decorations developed from straight geometric designs into more opulent and curvilinear patterns based on shapes in nature. As the builders' skill advanced, the stone construction became lighter and more spacious, and vaulting attained extraordinary degrees of complication. The style is exemplified in Bristol Cathedral.

Decoration Day: see MEMORIAL DAY.

decorations, civil and military. The practice of bestowing decorations to reward civil and military achievements, particularly those implying valor, dates back at least to the laurel wreaths of the ancient Greeks and Romans and gained prevalence with the medieval custom of conferring knighthood (see KNIGHT). At present, orders of knighthood in the feudal sense, such as the Order of the Bath and the Order of the Garter, still exist in Great Britain. British orders created in modern times—e.g., the Distinguished Service Order (1886), the Royal Victoria Order (1896), the Order of Merit (1902), and the Order of the British Empire (1917)—are decorations for civil and military service rather than true feudal orders. In the rest of Europe the old orders of knighthood, where they still exist, have also tended to lose their feudal connotations. Among the best known orders of chivalry are the Order of the Golden Fleece, created (1429 or 1430) by Philip the Good of Burgundy and conferred by Austria and by Spain; the Danish orders of the Dannebrog (1219) and Elephant (1462); the Italian orders of Annunziata (1362) and of Saints Maurice and Lazarus (1434); the papal order of the Golden Spur (1559); the Prussian orders of the Black Eagle (1701) and Red Eagle (1734); the Swedish Order of the Seraphim (1748); and the Polish orders of the White Eagle and of Polonia Restituta (1919). The French Legion of Honor, created by Napoleon Bonaparte in 1802, is composed of an unlimited number of knights and headed by a grand master (the president of France). In the late 19th cent. countries in many parts of the world followed the lead of the European nations and instituted elaborate systems of honors; in recent decades new African nations have also done so. Most European orders are graded in several classes, and the stars, crosses, ribbons, and other insignia corresponding to different classes vary greatly in aspect and value. Major military decorations include the *Medaille militaire* (France, 1852); the Croix de Guerre (Belgium and France, 1915); the Iron Cross (Germany, 1813; revived in 1939); and the Victoria Cross (Great Britain, 1856). The highest decoration for exceptional heroism in the United States is the Congressional Medal of Honor, instituted in 1861 for the navy and 1862 for the army. Among other decorations awarded by the Congress are the Distinguished Service Cross and Distinguished Service Medal (1917) and the Distinguished Flying Cross (1942). The Purple Heart (created by George Washington, 1782; revived 1932) is awarded for wounds received in action; the silver star and bronze star are awarded, respectively, for heroism and for outstanding service. Oak-leaf clusters (in the navy, gold or silver stars) are marks of repeated awards of the same decoration. In the United States and Great Britain a ribbon, indicating by its colors the corresponding medal, rather than the medal itself, is worn over the left breast pocket of the uniform. In some other countries, e.g., the Soviet Union, the medals themselves are worn suspended on ribbons. Several countries award decorations to entire units; an example is the Presidential Unit Citation in the United States. Campaign ribbons and battle stars are decorations awarded automatically for presence in certain battles or theaters of operations.

decorative arts, term embracing all the fine and applied visual arts. It refers to embellishment, enrichment, or ornamentation in architecture of walls (see ORNAMENT), public buildings and private houses (see INTERIOR DECORATION), metalwork, and woodwork. It is also applied to textiles, pottery, books, and numerous household objects that have surfaces suitable for ornamental DESIGN; to ecclesiastical vestments and appurtenances; and to personal apparel and belongings, including costumes, jewelry, goldwork and silverware, arms and armor, tools, saddles, and automobiles. See articles on individual subjects (e.g., VESTMENTS).

De Coster, Charles Théodore Henri (də kŏs'tər, Fr. shärl tāōdôr' äNrē' də kôstĕr'), 1827–79, Belgian author, b. Munich. His collected legends from Flemish folklore (1857), written in old French style, gained him note as a medievalist. His *Contes brabançons* (1861) was followed by his widely known *La Légende d' Ulenspiegel* (1868, tr. 1918, 1922). This remarkable tale, written in archaic style and recounting the fabulous exploits of Till EULENSPIEGEL, has been compared with the *Gargantua* of Rabelais. However, the book derives more directly from the medieval satiric allegory on Reynard the Fox, apparently originally fashioned in Flanders.

découpage (dā"ko͞opäzh'), any process of decorating surfaces in which paper cutouts made of new materials completely cover the surface. These cutouts are attached to the work by pasting or gluing. The simple techniques involved in this form of COLLAGE make it an easily accessible art form.

De Crayer, Gaspar: see CRAYER, GASPAR DE.

decree, in law, decision of a suit in a court of EQUITY. It is the counterpart in equity of the JUDGMENT in a court of law, although in those jurisdictions where law and equity have merged, judgment is sometimes used to include both. The difference between the two, however, is fundamental. A judgment must be unconditionally for one party or another, but a decree is adaptable to the peculiar necessities of each case and may include rights and duties of both parties. A decree may impose conditions on its enforcement upon either party. The decree may act against the person of the defendant; it is not restricted to the award of money damages. It may contain an INJUNCTION against the performance of certain acts. One of the most familiar of the decrees given by courts of equity is the decree of DIVORCE, adjudicating the dissolution of a MARRIAGE and awarding ALIMONY. Decrees are enforced by proceedings for CONTEMPT of court.

decretals: see CANON LAW.

Dedan (dē'dən), eponym of a people apparently occupying Arabia S of Palestine. The people are called Dedanim or Dedanites. Gen. 10.7; 25.3; Isa. 21.13; Ezek. 27.20. See DODANIM.

Dedekind, Julius Wilhelm Richard (yo͞ol'yo͞os vĭl'hĕlm rĭkh'ärt dā'dəkĭnt), 1831–1916, German mathematician. Dedekind studied at Göttingen under the German mathematician Carl Gauss and in 1852 received his doctorate there for a thesis on Eulerian integrals. In 1858 he went to Zürich as a professor; in 1862 he returned to his home town Brunswick to become a professor there. Dedekind led the effort to formulate rigorous definitions of basic mathematical concepts. Perhaps his best-known contribution is the "Dedekind cut," whereby real numbers can be defined in terms of rational numbers.

Dedham (dĕd'əm), town (1970 pop. 26,938), seat of Norfolk co., E Mass., on the Charles River, a suburb of Boston; inc. 1636. America's oldest frame house, the Fairbanks house (1636), is there, and Dedham is said to have had the first public school in America (1649). The county courthouse was the scene of the Sacco-Vanzetti trial (1921). Horace Mann practiced law in Dedham, and Fisher Ames was born there. See history of Dedham by Frank Smith (1936).

deduction, in LOGIC, form of inference in which particular conclusions are reached by reasoning from certain general principles assumed to be true. For example, if we know that all men have two legs and that John is a man, it is then logical to deduce that John has two legs. This type of reasoning received its classical formulation in the Aristotelian SYLLOGISM and was greatly extended by the development of SYMBOLIC LOGIC. Deduction is the process opposite to INDUCTION. See Hugues LeBlanc and William Wisdom, *Deductive Logic* (1971); R. J. Ackermann, *Modern Deductive Logic* (1971).

Dee, John, 1527–1608, English mathematician and occultist. He was educated at Cambridge. Accused of practicing sorcery against Queen Mary I, he was acquitted and later was a favorite of Queen Elizabeth I, for whom he drew up valuable hydrographical and geographical materials on newly discovered lands. He also made calculations in preparation for adoption of the Gregorian calendar in England, which he vainly sought. He is better remembered, however, for the more sensational side of his career. His interest in crystal gazing, divination, and the occult led to his association with Edward Kelly, who claimed to have dicovered the alchemical secret of transmuting base metal to gold. Dee and Kelly spent several years abroad, patronized by various nobles and monarchs. When Dee finally broke with Kelly and returned to England, he found himself generally shunned and much of his property destroyed. Although he maintained the favor of Elizabeth and was warden of Manchester College (1595–1604), he later retired to seclusion, and died in poverty. Dee wrote extensively, not only concerning his occult experiments but also on mathematics, natural sciences, and astrology. His diary was edited in 1842 by J. O. Halliwell-Phillips. See biographies by Richard Deacon (1968) and Peter J. French (1972).

Dee. 1 River, c.90 mi (140 km) long, rising in the Cairngorms, SW Aberdeenshire, E Scotland, and flowing E past Ballater to the North Sea through an artificial channel at Aberdeen. The channel was constructed (1872) to improve Aberdeen's harbor. Celebrated for its beauty, the Dee also has notable salmon fisheries. **2** River, c.50 mi (80 km) long, rising in N Kirkcudbrightshire, SW Scotland, and flowing generally S to the Irish Sea. There are five power stations in the Dee basin.

Dee, river, c.70 mi (110 km) long, rising in the Cambrian mts., Merionethshire, NW Wales, and flowing NE through Bala Lake, then meandering through a picturesque course NE, N, and NW past Chester to the Irish Sea. At low tide the long, broad, shallow estuary is an expanse of sand, across which the narrow stream flows. Thomas Telford's aqueduct crosses the Dee near Trevor. Sluices at the outlet of Bala Lake control the river's flow.

deed, in law, written document that is signed and delivered by which one person conveys land or other realty (see PROPERTY) to another. A deed may assure the extent of the conveying party's ownership or, if the party is uncertain of the precise extent, he issues a quitclaim (i.e., a sale), without description, of whatever he may own. The formalities with which a deed is invested are designed to make the instrument conclusive evidence of the transaction described and to eliminate the need for further proof. In all states of the United States deeds must be formally delivered and their receipt formally attested. It is possible to deposit a deed with a third party or a court for delivery to the purchaser; this is termed a delivery in escrow. Most states also require that deeds be acknowledged by a duly authorized commissioner and that a copy be deposited with the clerk of the county where the realty is situated. If the formalities are not observed, a deed (or the contract purporting to convey realty) is some, but not conclusive, evidence of the conveyance.

Deep Sea Drilling Project, U.S. program designed to investigate the evolution of ocean basins by core drilling of ocean sediments and underlying oceanic crust. Funded by the National Science Foundation, the project is directed by a consortium of the leading oceanographic institutions in the United States called Joint Oceanographic Institutions for Deep Earth Sampling (JOIDES). Begun in 1964, a test drilling program was completed successfully in 1965. On the strength of this success, plans were developed to construct a seagoing vessel capable of extensive voyages and able to drill through great water depths. In 1968, the *Glomar Challenger,* displacing 10,500 tons and capable of drilling 2,500 ft (760 m) of sediment in 20,000 ft (6,100 m) of water, was leased to JOIDES. Similar in appearance to a freighter, but with a tall well-drilling derrick amidships, the *Glomar Challenger* is equipped with a highly accurate satellite-controlled navigation system and elaborate equipment to position and steady the ship while on station. The scientific operations carried out on board consist of continuous seismic and magnetic surveys while underway, in-hole measurements, and laboratory analysis of the cores recovered. The project has verified that the present ocean basins are relatively young features, the oldest sediments being of Jurassic age. It has confirmed that the sea floor spreads from midocean ridges and is consumed in ocean trenches and other regions. The project has also shown that Europe, North America, Africa, and South America were joined until the Atlantic Ocean opened from the north 200 million years ago; it has determined the extent of deposition of continental sediments by turbid flows of sediment-laden water far out in the Atlantic; and it has discovered that the Mediterranean Sea has periodically dried up in the past. In its first few years, the Deep Sea Drilling Project has made as many fascinating and significant discoveries about the ocean floors and the earth itself as the first telescope did about the heavens.

deep-sea exploration: see OCEANOGRAPHY.

deer, ruminant mammal of the family Cervidae, found in most parts of the world except Australia. The only deer in Africa are small numbers of red deer found in the north in a forested area. Antlers, solid bony outgrowths of the skull, develop in the males of most species and are shed and renewed annually. They are at first covered by the "velvet," a soft, hairy skin permeated by blood vessels; this skin dries and is rubbed off as the antlers mature. The stem of the antler is called the beam, and the branches are the tines. Antlers are used as weapons during breeding-season combats between bucks. In the deer that lack antlers (the MUSK DEER and Chinese river deer) the upper canines are long and serve as weapons. Deer are polygamous. They eat a variety of herbaceous plants, lichens, mosses, and tree leaves and bark. The white-tailed deer that lives in woodlands throughout the United States and in Central America and N South America was a source of food, buckskin, and other necessities for American Indians and white settlers. Deer flesh, called venison, is still considered a delicacy. Slaughter through the years nearly exterminated the whitetail, but it is now restored in large numbers in the E United States and to a lesser extent in the West. In summer its upper parts are reddish brown, in winter grayish. The mule deer exists in reduced numbers from the plains region westward, and the closely related black-tailed deer is a Pacific coast form. Old World deer include the red deer, closely related to the North American WAPITI, the fallow deer, and the axis deer. The barking deer, or muntjac, is a small deer of S Asia. The misleadingly named mouse deer, or CHEVROTAIN, is not a deer, but belongs to a related family. Deer are classified in the phylum CHORDATA, subphylum Vertebrata, class Mammalia, order Artiodactyla, family Cervidae. See also CARIBOU; ELK; MOOSE; PÈRE DAVID'S DEER; REINDEER.

Deere, John, 1804–86, American industrialist, manufacturer of agricultural implements, b. Rutland, Vt. He was one of the pioneers of the steel PLOW industry. A blacksmith by trade, he established (1837) a shop at Grand Detour, Ill. There he was associated with Leonard Andrus in making (1837) the first Grand Detour steel plow. In 1843, Deere and Andrus formed a partnership for the manufacture of plows. The partnership was terminated in 1847, when Deere moved to Moline, Ill. There he established a factory that in time made other farm implements as well as plows and became known throughout the world. The firm was incorporated in 1868 as Deere and Company.

Deerfield. 1 Village (1970 pop. 18,949), Cook and Lake counties, NE Ill., a residential suburb of Chicago; inc. 1903. The huge Sara Lee Bakery is its major industry. Communications and construction equipment are also made. **2** Town (1970 pop. 3,850), NW Mass., on the Deerfield River; inc. 1677. In the Indian massacre of 1704 nearly 50 inhabitants were killed, and most of the survivors were taken to Canada; many were killed on the way. Old Deerfield St. is lined with 18th-century houses. Deerfield Academy, one of the country's foremost private secondary schools, is in the town.

Deerfield, river, 70 mi (113 km) long, rising in S Vt. and flowing S into NW Mass., then SE to the Connecticut River at Greenfield, Mass. The river has extensive hydroelectric facilities.

Deerfield Beach, town (1970 pop. 17,130), Broward co., SE Fla., on the Atlantic coast; inc. 1925.

deerfly: see HORSEFLY.

deerhound: see SCOTTISH DEERHOUND.

Deer Park. 1 Uninc. town (1970 pop. 31,120), Suffolk co., SE N.Y., on Long Island. Primarily residential, it has an aircraft instruments laboratory. **2** City (1970 pop. 12,773), Harris co., S Texas, an industrial suburb of Houston.

Defense, United States Department of, executive department of the Federal government charged with coordinating and supervising all departments, agencies, and functions of the government relating to national security. It is by far the largest of the Federal departments, and each of its three departments—army, navy and air force—is bigger than any other Federal agency. Ever since the department was established, the major portion of the Federal budget has been allocated to the Defense Dept. It was created in 1947 as the National Military Establishment and reorganized as the Dept. of Defense in 1949. The Secretary of Defense—appointed from civilian life by the President with the consent of the U.S. Senate—was empowered to execute the general policies and programs for the National Military Establishment, to assist the President in all national security matters, and to help eliminate unnecessary duplication and overlapping in the fields of military supply, transport, storage, health, and research. The establishment—under civilian control—was made up of a number of subsidiary agencies including the NATIONAL SECURITY COUNCIL (to help integrate domestic, foreign, and military policies), the CENTRAL INTELLIGENCE AGENCY (to coordinate intelligence activities of Federal agencies concerned with national security), and the JOINT CHIEFS OF STAFF. In the face of much controversy and heavy criticism, James V. FORRESTAL pioneered in the organization of the establishment. Under the National Security Act of 1949, the National Military Establishment was redesignated the Dept. of Defense, nine military boards were abolished, and the new offices of Deputy Secretary of Defense and three Assistant Secretaries of Defense were created. The Secretary of the Army, the Secretary of the Navy, and the Secretary of the Air Force—empowered by the act of 1947 to aid in the organization of the establishment—were subordinated (1949) to give the Secretary of Defense full cabinet authority over his department. The effectiveness of the new defense establishment received its first test in the Korean War. It was generally agreed that the department revealed a capability to react quickly to crisis, but there was criticism that too much reliance had been placed on strategic air power and nuclear weapons to the neglect of conventional military forces. During the Eisenhower administration the emphasis on the ability of the defense structure to respond to a nuclear attack with a massive retaliation was continued, despite numerous critics who argued that the United States was being hampered in its ability to fight a limited war against aggression. Under Secretary of Defense Robert S. MCNAMARA (1961–68), the department aimed for a more balanced military program designed to give the defense establishment the flexibility needed to cope with any crisis from brush war to nuclear attack. From its inception, the Dept. of Defense has worked toward the goal of service unification. Although progress in this area was often frustratingly slow and achieved only over considerable opposition, the trend toward centralization has been unmistakable. See C. W. Borklund, *Men of the Pentagon: From Forrestal to McNamara* (1966) and *The Department of Defense* (1968); Adam Yarmolinsky, *The Military Establishment* (1971).

defense mechanism, in psychoanalysis, any of a variety of unconscious personality reactions. By means of such reactions an individual attempts to satisfy his emotional needs: e.g., to establish harmony among conflicting strivings; to reduce feelings of anxiety or guilt arising from wishes, thoughts, and emotions that are not acceptable; or to modify reality to make it more tolerable and acceptable. Defense mechanisms include rationalization—protection of the ego against awareness of antisocial motives by substituting socially acceptable reasons for behavior; repression—preventing unacceptable ideas or impulses from entering the conscious mind; regression—return to infantile behavior and gratification; reaction-formation—denial of unacceptable feelings and simulation of their opposite; projection—the assignment to others of urges and wishes one's own ego repudiates; displacement—release of dangerous impulses in a substitute situation or disguised activity; identification—reacting to another's desires or tendencies as if they were one's own; sublimation (considered a constructive mechanism)—redirection of the libido toward socially valuable ends; and conversion—transformation of a psychological conflict into a physical symptom. See D. R. Miller and G. E. Swanson, *Inner Conflict and Defense* (1966); Anna Freud, *The Ego and the Mechanisms of Defense* (rev. ed. of her writings, Vol. II, 1967).

Deffand, marquise du: see DU DEFFAND.

Defiance, city (1970 pop. 16,281), seat of Defiance co., NW Ohio, at the confluence of the Auglaize and Maumee rivers, in a farm area; settled 1790, inc. 1836. Its manufactures include machinery, food products, and fabricated metal items. Anthony Wayne built Fort Defiance there in 1794. Defiance College is in the city. A Johnny Appleseed festival is held annually.

De Filippo, Eduardo (ādwär'dō dā fēlĭp'pō), 1900–, Neapolitan playwright and actor. De Filippo has often worked with his brother Peppino and sister Titina, also playwrights and actors. In his scores of plays he combines pathos and farce. *Napoli milionaria* (1946) depicts postwar Naples, riddled with ruins and black-market corruption; *Filumena Marturano* (1946) concerns a loving prostitute who coaxes her lover into marriage by refusing to tell him which one of her three children is his. Both plays were made into successful motion pictures, the latter entitled *Matrimonio all'italiana* (*Marriage Italian-Style*, 1964). Among De Filippo's other well-known plays is *Il figlio di Pulcinella* (1957). Most of his plays are collected in *Cantata dei giorni pari* and *Cantata dei giorni dispari* (4 vol., 1951–59). See R. W. Corrigan, *Masterpieces of the Modern Italian Theater* (1967).

deflation: see INFLATION.

Defoe or **De Foe, Daniel** (dĭfō'), 1660?–1731, English writer b. London. The son of a London butcher, and educated at a Dissenters' academy, he was typical of the new kind of man reaching prominence in England in the 18th cent.—self-reliant, industrious, possessing a strong notion of personal and moral responsibility. Although intended for the Presbyterian ministry, he had, by 1683, set himself up as a merchant dealing in many different commodities. In spite of his own considerable savings and his wife's dowry, Defoe went bankrupt in 1692. Although he paid his creditors, he was never entirely free from debt again. His first important publication was *An Essay upon Projects* (1698), but it was not until the poem *The True-born Englishman* (1701), a defense of William III from his attackers, that he received any real fame. An ill-timed satire early in Queen Anne's reign, *The Shortest Way with Dissenters* (1702), an ironic defense of High Church animosity against nonconformists, resulted in Defoe's being imprisoned. He was rescued by Robert Harley and subsequently served the statesman as a political agent. Defoe has been called the father of modern journalism; during his lifetime he was associated with 26 periodicals. From 1704 to 1713 he published and wrote a *Review,* a miscellaneous journal concerned with the affairs of Europe; this was an incredibly ambitious undertaking for one man. He was nearly sixty when he turned to writing novels. In 1719 he published his famous *Life and Strange Surprising Adventures of Robinson Crusoe,* followed by two less engrossing sequels. Based in part on the experiences of Alexander SELKIRK, *Robinson Crusoe* describes the daily life of a man marooned on a desert island. Although there are exciting episodes in the novel—Crusoe rescuing his man Friday from cannibals—its main interest derives from the way in which Crusoe overcomes the extraordinary difficulties of life on the island while preserving his human integrity. *Robinson Crusoe* is considered by some critics to be the first true novel in English. Defoe's great novels were not published under his name but as authentic memoirs, with the intention of gulling his readers into thinking his fictions true. Two excellent examples of his semihistorical recreations are the picaresque adventure *Moll Flanders* (1722), the story of a London prostitute and thief, and an account of the 1665 great plague in London entitled *A Journal of the Plague Year* (1722). His writing is always straightforward and vivid, with an astonishing concern for circumstantial detail. Defoe's other major works include *Captain Singleton* (1720), *Colonel Jack* (1722), *Roxana* (1724), and *A Tour through the Whole Island of Great Britain* (1724–27). In 1724, *A General History of the Pyrates* by a Captain Charles Johnson was published; it was not until 200 years later that Defoe was discovered to be the true author of the work (see edition by Manuel Schonhorn, 1972). See also Defoe's letters, ed. by G. H. Healey (1955); biographies by J. R. Sutherland (2d ed. 1950) and J. R. Moore (1958); studies by G. H. Starr (1965 and 1971), J. R. Sutherland (1971), and Pat Rogers, ed. (1972).

defoliant, any one of several chemical compounds that, when applied to plants, can alter their metabolism, causing the leaves to drop off. In agriculture defoliants are used to eliminate the leaves of a crop plant so they will not interfere with the harvesting machinery. In recent years defoliants have been employed in jungle warfare, notably in Southeast Asia. Their main military objective is to deprive the enemy of cover. In addition they have been used on food crops that have been considered potential sustenance for the enemy. Unfortunately, defoliants are not discriminating chemical weapons. Normally applied from the air, they are difficult to confine to a desired area and may thus contaminate watercourses, with disastrous effects on fish and other aquatic life. Human beings are also known to suffer toxic effects from them. Further, indigenous populations have suffered severe malnutrition when their food crops have been defoliated to prevent their use by the enemy. Possibly the severest and most long-lasting side effect of military defoliation is the disruption of the fragile jungle ecosystem. Contrary to appearances, the soils that underlie rain forests are not abundant in plant nutrients. Therefore, the ecosystem generally functions to conserve and recycle the nutrients that do exist. Any massive disruption, such as killing or interfering with the metabolism of large numbers of plants, inevitably causes large amounts of nutrients to be washed away by rainfall. Also, when sunlight, which would normally be blocked by the leaves, falls on the claylike soil of the jungle, the soil bakes and becomes very hard. These conditions operate against reestablishment of normal vegetation.

De Forest, John William, 1826–1906, American author, b. Seymour, Conn. He served in the Civil War, chiefly as a captain. His vivid accounts of battle scenes in Louisiana and Sheridan's Shenandoah valley campaign, published in *Harper's Monthly,* were among the finest contemporaneous war records. Best known as a novelist, he was the author of *Miss Ravenel's Conversion from Secession to Loyalty* (1867), the first realistic novel of the Civil War, and *Kate Beaumont* (1872), a study of South Carolina culture. See *A Volunteer's Adventures* (ed. by J. H. Croushore, 1946); biography by Frank Bergmann (1971); study by J. F. Light (1965).

De Forest, Lee, 1873–1961, American inventor, b. Council Bluffs, Iowa, grad. Yale, 1896. He was a pioneer in the development of wireless telegraphy, sound pictures, and television. His triode (1906) made practicable transcontinental telephony, both wire and wireless, and led to the foundation of the radio industry. He is frequently called "the father of radio." The first high-powered naval radio stations were designed and installed by him. See his autobiography (1950); biography by I. E. Levine (1964).

Defregger, Franz von (fränts fən dā'frĕgər), 1835–1921, Austrian genre and historical painter. He studied in Munich with Piloty. He is known for his popular pictures of Tyrolean life, which depend largely for their interest on their fine characterization and humor. Good examples are *The Last Summons* and *Zither Player* (both: Vienna).

Degas, Edgar (Hilaire Germain Edgar Degas) (ēlĕr' zhĕrmăN' ĕdgär' dəgä'), 1834–1917, French painter and sculptor, b. Paris; son of a banker. Although prepared for the law, he abandoned it for painting, studying at the École des Beaux-Arts with L. Lamothe, a student of Ingres, and in Italy, copying 15th- and 16th-century masters. He was precociously gifted as a draftsman and a brilliantly subtle and penetrating portraitist (e.g., *Bellelli Family,* 1859; Louvre). He exhibited for six years in the Salon (1865–70), but later ceased showing there and exhibited with the impressionists, whose works he admired although his approach often differed from theirs. An unflagging perfectionist, Degas strove to unite the discipline of classical art with the immediacy of impressionism. Trained in the linear tradition of Ingres, Degas shared with the impressionists their directness of expression and the interest in and portrayal of contemporary life. His favorite subjects were ballet dancers, women at their toilette, café life, and race-track scenes. He made notes and sketches from living models in motion to preserve informality of action and position. From these he organized his finished work in the studio, not directly from nature as his contemporaries did. Moreover, he created many daring compositional innovations. Influenced by Japanese prints and especially by photography, Degas diverged from the traditional ideas of balanced arrangements. He introduced what appeared to be accidental cutoff views, off-center subjects, and unusual angles, all quite carefully planned. Sometimes he effected a remarkable balance by giving special weight to the focus of interest, as in *Woman with Chrysanthemums* (1865; Metropolitan Mus.) and *Foyer of the Dance* (1872; Louvre). Gradually, Degas turned away from the medium of oil painting, perhaps because of his failing eyesight. He produced more freely executed, glowing pastels and charcoal drawings. His works in sculpture include many notable studies of dancers and horses. A number of his paintings and sculptures may be seen in the Metropolitan Museum. Many of his most celebrated works, including *Absinthe, The Rehearsal,* and *Two Laundresses* (1882) are in the Louvre. Ranked among the greatest of French artists, Degas profoundly influenced such later artists as Toulouse-Lautrec and Picasso. See his letters ed. by M. Guérin (tr. 1947); catalogs of his works by J. Rewald (sculpture, 1944), L. Browse (dancers, 1949), D. Cooper (pastels, 1954), J. S. Boggs (portraits, 1962, and drawings, 1966), and E. P. Janis (monotypes, 1968); studies by A. Vollard (tr. 1927), D. C. Rich (1951), and D. Halévy (tr. 1964, repr. 1971).

De Gasperi, Alcide (älchē'dā dā gä'spārē), 1881–1954, Italian premier and a founder of the Christian Democratic party. Born in the Trentino—then under Austria—he represented Italian irredentists in the Austrian parliament and after the transfer of the Trentino to Italy at the end of World War I served (1921–24) as a Catholic deputy in the Italian parliament. After 16 months of imprisonment as an anti-Fascist, De Gasperi received (1931) a position at the Vatican Library; there he organized during World War II the center-right Christian Democratic party. A successor in part to Luigi Sturzo's Popular party, the moderately conservative group condemned the anticlerical tendencies manifest in Italian politics since the Risorgimento. It derived its program from the social teachings of the Roman Catholic Church. After the Italian surrender in 1943 he held several cabinet posts. From 1945 to 1953 he was premier of eight successive coalition cabinets dominated by the Christian Democrats. In 1947, De Gasperi excluded the Communists and left-wing Socialists from the government, and in 1948 his party won a major electoral victory. De Gasperi championed close cooperation with the United States and led Italy into the European Recovery Program and the North Atlantic Treaty Organization.

De Gaulle, Charles (shärl də gōl), 1890–1970, French general and statesman, first president (1959–69) of the Fifth Republic. During World War I he served with distinction until his capture in 1916. In *The Army of the Future* (1934, tr. 1941) he foresaw and futilely advocated for France the mechanized warfare by which Germany was to conquer France in 1940. In World War II he was promoted to brigadier general (1940) and became undersecretary of war in the cabinet of Premier Paul Reynaud. He opposed the Franco-German armistice and fled (June, 1940) to London, where he organized the Free French forces and rallied several French colonies to his movement. He was sentenced to death in absentia by a French military court. The Free French forces were successful in Syria, Madagascar, and N Africa. In June, 1943, De Gaulle became copresident, with Gen. Henri Honoré GIRAUD, of the newly formed French Committee of National Liberation at Algiers. He succeeded in forcing Giraud out of the committee, and in June, 1944, it was proclaimed the provisional government of France. His government returned to Paris on Aug. 26 and was recognized by the principal Allies. He was unanimously elected provisional president of France in Nov., 1945, but he resigned in Jan., 1946, when it became obvious that his views favoring a strong executive would not be incorporated into the new constitution. Many of the rightist elements had gathered under the Gaullist banner, and he became (1947) head of a new party—Rassemblement du Peuple Français [Rally of the French People]—which claimed to speak for all Frenchmen and to be above factional strife but which, nevertheless, took part in subsequent elections. The party had some temporary electoral success, but in 1953 De Gaulle dissolved it and went into retirement. In 1958, after the military and civilian revolt in ALGERIA had created a political crisis in France, he was considered the only leader of sufficient strength and stature to deal with the situation. He became premier with power to rule by decree for six months. During this time a new constitution, which strengthened the presidency, was drawn up (1958). The constitution also provided for the FRENCH COMMUNITY, the first step towards resolving imperial problems. De Gaulle was inaugurated as president of the new Fifth Republic in Jan., 1959. He decided to allow Algeria self-determination. This decision led to several revolts in Algeria by French colonists who opposed independence. Finally, in 1962, an agreement was reached that provided for Algerian independence. In domestic affairs, De Gaulle attempted to restore French national finances by devaluing the franc and creating a new franc worth 100 old francs. Much of De Gaulle's program consisted of an attempt to raise France to its former world stature. He argued for French parity with the United States in NATO decisions and promoted French development of atomic weapons. In 1966, he withdrew French troops from NATO and ordered the withdrawal of NATO military installations from France by April, 1967. He was reelected to a second seven-year term in 1965. Although he rejected limitations on French sovereignty, he supported participation in the Common Market but strongly opposed British membership in it. He fostered ties with West Germany and established diplomatic relations with the People's Republic of China. In May, 1968, student demonstrations protesting French political and educational systems were followed by huge workers' strikes that nearly toppled the Gaullist government. Nevertheless, in elections held in June, the Gaullists were returned to power. In 1969, after being defeated in a referendum on constitutional reform, De Gaulle resigned as president. See his *War Memoirs* (tr., 3 vol., 1955–60) and *Memoirs of Hope* (tr. 1972); biographies by Aidan Crawley (1969), Philippe Masson (1971), and Brian Crozier (1973); P. M. Williams and Martin Harrison, *De Gaulle's Republic* (1960); Alexander Werth, *The De Gaulle Revolution* (1960); Robert Aron, *An Explanation of De Gaulle* (1965); John Hess, *The Case for De Gaulle* (1968); John Newhouse, *De Gaulle and the Anglo-Saxons* (1969); Anthony Hartley, *Gaullism: The Rise and Fall of a Political Movement* (1971); Philippe Alexandre, *The Duel: De Gaulle and Pompidou* (1972).

De Grasse, François Joseph Paul, comte de: see GRASSE, FRANÇOIS JOSEPH PAUL, COMTE DE.

degree, academic, title bestowed upon a student on the fulfillment of certain requirements or given as an honor to an eminent person. The practice of awarding degrees originated in the universities of medieval Europe. The first known degree, granted to doctoral candidates in civil law, was awarded in Italy at the Univ. of Bologna during the 12th cent. From Italy the practice spread throughout Europe, and in the 13th cent. the first bachelor's degree was awarded at the Univ. of Paris. By the time the first colleges were opened in the American colonies, the process of granting degrees was firmly established. Originally there were only a few types of degrees offered by American schools. Today, however, approximately 1,500 types of degrees are granted by academic institutions in the United States. The degrees usually conferred in American universities are Bachelor of Arts (B.A.) or of Science (B.S.), at the end of an undergraduate liberal arts or science course; Master of Arts (M.A.) or of Science (M.S.), at the end of a prescribed postgraduate course in liberal arts or in science. The highest degree conferred by a university is the doctorate: Doctor of Philosophy (Ph.D.), of Medicine (M.D.), of Divinity (D.D.), of Laws (LL.D.). There are numerous other degrees given less frequently, including purely honorary awards such as Doctor of Literature (Litt.D.). Occasionally, traditional degrees are replaced by newer ones. During the 1960s, for example, most American law schools replaced the Bachelor of Laws (LL.B.) with the Juris Doctor (J.D.), even though the actual requirements for the law degree remained substantially the same. The requirements for degrees differ in different institutions. The gowns and insignia worn at academic convocations indicate the degree attained by the wearer or the degree for which he is a candidate; they also indicate the institution awarding the degree.

De Haven, Edwin Jesse (də hā'vən), 1816–65, American arctic explorer. He accompanied Charles Wilkes on the naval exploring expedition that reached Antarctica. In 1850 he was chosen to head an expedition into the arctic regions financed by Henry Grinnell to search for the lost party of Sir John Franklin. Only the graves of three of the lost men were found before dangerous ice forced the expedition to return, but not before De Haven had discovered Grinnell Land on Ellesmere Island.

De Heem, Jan Davidszoon: see HEEM, JAN DAVIDSZOON DE.

Dehmel, Richard (rĭkh'ärt dā'məl), 1863–1920, German poet. An ardent mountain climber and soldier, he expressed his restless temperament in passionate and impressionistic poetry. His verse, often dealing with social problems, represents a revolt against extreme naturalism. Among his works are the poetic collection *Erlösungen* [redemptions] (1891) and the verse novel *Zwei Menschen* [two human beings] (1903).

Dehn, Adolf Arthur (dān), 1895–1968, American painter and illustrator, b. Waterville, Minn. During the 1920s, Dehn became known as a forceful satiric illustrator. Later he concentrated primarily on painting, especially watercolor. Among his major works are *Jimmy Savo and Rope* (Whitney Mus., New York City) and *Butte, Utah* (Mus. of Modern Art, New York City). Dehn is the author of *Water Color Painting* (1945) and *Water Color, Gouache, and Casein Painting* (1955).

De Hooch or **De Hoogh, Pieter:** see HOOCH, PIETER DE.

Dehra Dun (dâr'ə dōōn), city (1971 pop. 170,187), Uttar Pradesh state, N central India. It is a district administrative headquarters and a trade center for surrounding hill areas. In Dehra Dun is the Indian military academy and an institute for research in forestry, with an associated museum and botanical garden. The temple (1699) of Ram Rai, founder of the Hindu Udasi sect of ascetics, is the city's most notable historical building.

dehydrated food: see FOOD PRESERVATION.

Deianira (dēyənī'rə): see HERCULES.

Deidamia (dēĭdā'mēə): see ACHILLES.

Deimos (dī'mŏs), in astronomy, one of the two moons, or natural satellites, of MARS.

Deinotherium: see DINOTHERIUM.

Deira (dē'īrə), old English kingdom between the Humber and the Tyne rivers. In the late 6th cent. it was united with Bernicia, to the north, to form NORTHUMBRIA.

Deirdre (dâr'drə, dēr'-), beautiful heroine of Irish legend. A druid prophesied at her birth that she would bring great misfortunes. Deirdre, chosen to be the wife of Conchobar, king of Ulster, fell in love with Naoise, the son of Usnach, and fled with him and his two brothers to Scotland. After a long idyllic stay there, they were enticed into returning to Ireland by Conchobar, who then treacherously killed the sons of Usnach. Deirdre, her heart broken, died on her lover's grave. This legend was very popular with the writers of the Irish literary renaissance, notably Yeats, Synge, and James Stephens.

Deir ez Zor, Syria: see DAYR AZ ZAWR.

deists (dē'ĭsts), term commonly applied to those thinkers in the 17th and 18th cent. who held that the course of nature sufficiently demonstrates the existence of God. For them formal religion was superfluous, and they scorned as spurious claims of supernatural revelation. Their tenets stemmed from the rationalism of the period, and though the term is not now generally used, the tenor of their belief persists. The term *freethinkers* is almost synonymous. Voltaire and J. J. Rousseau were deists, as were Benjamin Franklin, Thomas Jefferson, and George Washington. See E. R. Pike, *Slayers of Superstition* (1931, repr. 1970); G. A. Koch, *Religion of the American Enlightenment* (1933, repr. 1968).

De-jima, island, Japan: see DE-SHIMA.

De Jong, Petrus Josef Sietse (pā'trüs yō'zəf sēēt'sə də yông), 1915-, Dutch naval officer and politician. Having entered the royal navy in 1931, he served as a submarine commander in World War II and rose in the navy after the war. He was state secretary for defense (1959-63) and then headed the ministry of defense (1963-67). A member of the Catholic party, he served (1967-71) as prime minister and minister of general affairs, ruling a coalition of Christian and conservative parties. He resigned when his coalition lost its ruling majority in general elections. Shortly afterward he was appointed a senator of the upper chamber of parliament.

De Kalb, Johann: see KALB, JOHANN.

De Kalb (dē kălb), city (1970 pop. 32,949), De Kalb co., N Ill., in a farm area; inc. 1861. Vegetables and fruit are canned, and motors, musical instruments, wire screening, electrical equipment, and plastics are manufactured. The growth of the city was stimulated in the 1870s by the development and manufacture of workable barbed wire by a resident, Joseph F. Glidden. De Kalb is the seat of Northern Illinois Univ.

Dekar (dē'kär), father of an officer of Solomon. 1 Kings 4.9.

De Kempener, Pieter: see KEMPENER, PIETER DE.

Deken, Agatha: see WOLFF, ELISABETH.

De Keyser, Thomas: see KEYSER, THOMAS DE.

Dekker, Eduard Douwes (ā'düärt dou'əs dĕ'kər), pseud. **Multatuli** (məltätü'lē), 1820-87, Dutch novelist. His experiences in the Javanese colonial service (1838-57) made him an ardent advocate of reform in colonial administration and were the inspiration of *Max Havelaar* (1860, tr. 1868, 1927), which satirized the grasping spirit, the religion, morals, and government of the Dutch bourgeoisie. His unsparing criticism had tremendous effect in a Holland that had grown intellectually lethargic. See D. H. Lawrence's introduction to Siebenhaar's translation of *Max Havelaar* (1927).

Dekker, Thomas, 1572?-1632?, English dramatist and pamphleteer. Little is known of his life except that he frequently suffered from poverty and served several prison terms for debt. He began his literary career c.1598 working for Philip HENSLOWE. During this period he wrote his most famous play, *The Shoemaker's Holiday* (1600), a delightful domestic comedy concerning the success of Simon Eyre, a master shoemaker who becomes the lord mayor of London. The play is notable for its realistic depiction of everyday life in 17th-century London. After collaborating with John Webster on several plays and with Thomas Middleton on the first part of *The Honest Whore* (1604; Part II, 1630), Dekker turned to writing pamphlets, the most notable being *The Seven Deadly Sins of London* (1606) and *The Gull's Handbook* (1609), a satiric account of the fops and gallants of his day. In 1610 he returned to playwriting, writing separately and in collaboration with Middleton (*The Roaring Girl,* 1611), Philip Massinger (*The Virgin Martyr,* 1622), John Ford, and others. Many of his works, however, have been lost. He was known to have at least partially written over 40 plays, of which about 15 are extant. See edition of his plays by Fredson Bowers (4 vol., 1953-61); study by G. R. Price (1969).

De Koninck, Philips: see KONINCK, PHILIPS DE.

de Kooning, Willem (də kōōn'ĭng), 1904-, American painter, b. Netherlands. De Kooning emigrated to the United States in 1926 and settled in New York City, working on the Federal Arts Project until 1935. He began experiments with abstraction as early as 1928, but continued to produce realistic paintings throughout the 1930s. Influenced by Arshile GORKY, de Kooning forged a powerful abstract style and in the 1940s became a leader of ABSTRACT EXPRESSIONISM. In his monumental series of the early 1950s entitled *Woman,* he reintroduced a representational element. *Woman I* (Mus. of Modern Art, New York City), with its startling ferocity, brought him considerable notoriety. He later reverted chiefly to nonfigurative work but produced more paintings of women during the 1960s. His huge canvases are impulsively executed and charged with great energy. He is married to the painter Elaine Fried de Kooning. See studies by T. B. Hess (1959 and 1967) and Harriet Janis (1960).

de Kruif, Paul (də krīf), 1890-1971, American author, b. Zeeland, Mich., grad. Univ. of Michigan (B.S., 1912). He was bacteriologist at the university from 1912 to 1917. Among his books are *Microbe Hunters* (1926), *The Fight for Life* (1938), and *Hunger Fighters* (1939).

De la Beche, Sir Henry Thomas (də lä bāsh, dĕləbĕsh'), 1796-1855, English geologist. As a result of his private undertaking to prepare a geological map of England, the British government became aware of the need for such mapping. In 1832 his work was subsidized, and in 1835 the Geological Survey was formed with De la Beche as its first director. He wrote several standard works on geology, including *A Geological Manual* (1831, 3d ed. 1833) and *How to Observe Geology* (1835), which he enlarged under the title *The Geological Observer* (1851, 2d ed. 1853). He was knighted in 1842.

Delacroix, Eugène (Ferdinand-Victor-Eugène Delacroix) (fĕrdēnäN'-vēktôr'-özhĕn' dəläkrwä'), 1798-1863, French painter. Delacroix is considered the foremost painter of the romantic movement in France; his influence as a colorist is inestimably great. There is considerable responsible speculation that he was the illegitimate son of Talleyrand. He studied in Guérin's studio with Géricault, who became a major influence on his work. Delacroix enriched his neoclassical training with acute attention to the works of Rubens, Michelangelo, Veronese, and the Venetian school, and later Constable, Bonington, and the English watercolorists. When his first major work, *The Bark of Dante* (Louvre), had been exhibited in the Salon in 1822 and purchased by the government, he was, to his own surprise, recognized as the leader of the opposition to the neoclassical school of David. In temperament and choice of subjects he was a romantic, as revealed by his dramatic interpretation of scenes from mythology, literature, and political, religious, and literary history. But his art was as exuberant and lavish as the baroque, and as unified in composition and grand in conception as the finest neoclassical works. In 1824, much affected by Constable's treatment of light in *The Hay Wain,* Delacroix repainted much of his *Massacre at Chios* (Louvre). The violence of the subject matter and ravishing color of this work and of *The Death of Sardanapalus* (1826; Louvre) were damned by the critics. In England in 1825 he spent several months absorbing English painting and making numerous studies of horses. As a tribute to Byron and the Greek War of Independence he painted *Greece Expiring on the Ruins of Missolonghi* (1827; Bordeaux). Nothing Delacroix perceived was ever wasted. The four months he spent in Morocco in 1832 provided him with visual material that he drew upon for the rest of his life. There he filled seven fat notebooks with brilliant watercolor sketches and notes. His continuing fascination with the exotic was revealed by *Women of Algiers* (1834; Louvre) and *The Jewish Wedding* (1839; Louvre). Delacroix's other major sources were the works and lives of major literary figures. In 1820 he made 17 bizarre and exciting lithographs for Goethe's *Faust.* He used Shakespeare often in several media (e.g., *Hamlet and Horatio in the Graveyard,* 1839; Louvre). Emphasizing the melancholy, he depicted Tasso in the madhouse and the blind Milton. He was inspired by turbulent scenes both from the plays and poems of Byron (e.g., *Combat of the Giaour and the Pasha,* 1827; Art Inst. of Chicago) and from the novels of Scott. Not a religious man himself, Delacroix nevertheless created many strong works on religious themes. A frequenter of the intellectual salons of the day, he portrayed many notable contemporaries, including Paganini (1832; Phillips Coll., Washington, D.C.) and, in 1838, his close friends Chopin (Louvre) and George Sand (Copenhagen). His powerful *Entrance of the Crusaders into Constantinople* (1841; Louvre) is a compelling, epic work of history painting. Of his animals in motion, the watercolor *Tiger Attacking a Horse* (1825-28; Louvre) and *The Lion Hunt* (1861; Art Inst. of Chicago) are characteristic. Delacroix's *Self-Portrait* (1835-37; Louvre) reveals a thin, dynamic, yet reserved countenance. A man of delicate constitution, he possessed indomitable energy and sexual and artistic passion. In draftsmanship, composition, and especially in color his works are consistently exciting. During the last three decades of his life he secured numerous public commissions. His decorations in the Palais Bourbon (1833-47; Paris), the Palais de Luxembourg (1841-46), and the Church of Saint-Sulpice (1853-61) are examples of his genius as a muralist. His work is best represented in the Louvre. Delacroix's enormous involvement in contemporary artistic and intellectual life is recorded in his journal, kept from 1823 to 1854 (tr. by Walter Pach, 1937, repr. 1972). See his selected letters, 1813-63, ed. by J. Stewart (1971); J. Lindsay, *Death of the Hero* (1960); studies by L. F. Johnson (1963) and G. P. Mras (1966).

Delagoa Bay (dĕl"əgō'ə), inlet of the Indian Ocean, c.55 mi (90 km) long and 20 mi (30 km) wide, S Mozambique, SE Africa; Lourenço Marques, the capital and chief port of Mozambique, is on the bay. Delagoa Bay is a large deepwater harbor, with numerous quays to handle oceangoing vessels; railroads lead into the interior. The bay was discovered (1502) by António do Campo, one of Vasco da Gama's captains; the area was first explored (1544) by Lourenço Marques, the Portuguese trader. In the 1700s, Dutch and Austrian trading companies tried to establish posts on the bay; both were driven out by malaria and the Portuguese. In 1787, Portugal built a fort there, around which the town of Lourenço Marques grew. In the mid-1800s, Portugal's claim to the area was challenged by Great Britain and by the Transvaal when it was realized that the bay provided a major access route to the Kimberley diamond mines. The Transvaal recognized Portugal's sovereignty in 1869, and in 1875 France, acting as arbiter, awarded the area to Portugal.

Delaherche, Félix Auguste (fālĕks' ōgüst' dəläärsh'), 1857-1940, French potter. He is considered the greatest ceramist since Bernard Palissy. Working alone in the village of La Chapelle-aux-Pots, he made no duplicates, fired his kiln but once a year, and destroyed every piece with which he was dissatisfied. His works were of dark red stoneware with stylized ornamentation, roughened surface, and sparkling polychrome glazes.

Delaiah (dĕlăī'ə). **1** Chief priest. 1 Chron. 24.18. **2** Ancestor of a family who returned with Zerubbabel. Ezra 2.60; Neh. 7.62. **3** Father of SHEMAIAH **3.** **4** Prince of Jehoiakim. Jer. 36.12,25.

De Lairesse, Gerard: see LAIRESSE, GERARD DE.

de la Mare, Walter (də lə mâr), 1873-1956, English poet and novelist. For many years he worked in the accounting department of the Anglo-American Oil Company. Much of his verse and prose shows delight in imaginative excursions into the shadowed world between the real and the unreal. Included among his books of poetry are *Songs of Childhood* (1902), *The Listeners* (1912), *Peacock Pie* (1913), *Poems for Children* (1930), and *The Fleeting and Other Poems* (1933). His fiction includes *Henry Brocken* (1904), *The Return* (1910), *Memoirs of a Midget* (1921), and *On the Edge* (1930), a collection of somewhat macabre short stories. See studies by H. C. Duffin (1949, repr. 1969) and Forrest Reid (1929, repr. 1970).

Delambre, Jean Baptiste Joseph (zhäN bätēst' zhôzĕf' dəläN'brə), 1749-1822, French astronomer and mathematician. He was a member of the bureau of longitudes from 1795 and professor at the Collège de France from 1807. With P. F. A. Méchain he measured (1791-99) for the French government an arc of the meridian between Barcelona and Dunkirk. He is noted also for astronomical computations, especially a table of the motions of Uranus, and for discovering four formulas in spherical trigonometry (Delambre's analogies). Delambre is known for his historical works, including the six-volume *Histoire de l'astronomie* (1817–27).

De Lancey (də lăn'sē), family of political leaders, soldiers, and merchants prominent in colonial New York. **Étienne De Lancey** or **Stephen De Lancey,** 1663–1741, b. Caen, France, was among the more famous of the Huguenots exiled by the revocation (1685) of the Edict of Nantes. He became one of the wealthiest men in New York City through his activities as a merchant. He married into the Van Cortlandt family and was for 24 years a member of the colonial assembly. His town house, built in 1719, was later sold to Samuel FRAUNCES, who made it a notable tavern in the Revolutionary period. It still stands, probably the most famous of the old buildings on Manhattan island. His son, **James De Lancey,** 1703–60, b. New York City, educated in England, was a noted jurist and one of the most important figures in colonial New York politics. He was a justice (1731–33) and chief justice (1733–60) of the provincial supreme court and served (1753–55, 1757–60) as lieutenant governor. His political dexterity enabled him to control both the council and assembly, and after the suicide of the governor, Sir Danvers Osborne, he assumed control of that office also. He led the De Lancey faction against Gov. George Clinton in politics and against the Livingston faction when that family expressed its Presbyterian opposition to the chartering of King's College (now Columbia Univ.) as an Anglican institution. He was presiding judge at the trial of John Peter Zenger and was president of the Albany Congress (1754). His son, **James De Lancey,** 1732–1800, b. New York City, inherited the leadership of the De Lancey faction and, although he had opposed British colonial policies, was an important Loyalist officer in the American Revolution. He later received $160,000 for his estates, which were confiscated by the patriots. His cousin, **James De Lancey,** 1746–1804, b. New York City, was also a Loyalist during the Revolution. He commanded a cavalry troop in raids outside New York City before fleeing (1782) to Nova Scotia. **Oliver De Lancey,** 1718–85, son of Étienne, b. New York City, was a British officer who served in the last of the French and Indian Wars and in the American Revolution. His son, **Oliver De Lancey,** 1749–1822, b. New York City, was also a British officer in the Revolution, succeeding John André as adjutant general of the British forces in America.

De Land, resort city (1970 pop. 11,641), seat of Volusia co., NE Fla.; inc. 1882. It has dairies, citrus packing plants, and lumber mills. Other products are electrical and electronic parts, wearing apparel, and medical supplies. De Land is the seat of Stetson Univ. Nearby are Indian burial grounds and Ponce de Leon Springs.

Delaney, Shelagh (shē'lə), 1939–, English playwright, b. Salford, Lancashire. Working as an usherette, she found so much fault with the plays of the 1950s that she decided to write a play herself. The result was *A Taste of Honey* (1958), about a young working-class Lancashire girl who refuses to conform to her dreary surroundings. Her other works include *Sweetly Sings the Donkey* (1963), a collection of short stories.

De Langlade, Charles Michel: see LANGLADE.

Delano, Amasa (ăm'əsə dĕl'ənō), 1763–1823, American sea captain, b. Duxbury, Mass. He served in the American Revolution as a soldier at 15 and later as a privateersman. His experiences on the sea in the days of New England's supremacy are recorded in his *Narrative of Voyages and Travels in the Northern and Southern Hemispheres, Comprising Three Voyages Round the World* (1817). See J. B. Connolly, *Master Mariner* (1943).

Delano, city (1970 pop. 14,559), Kern co., S central Calif., in the fertile San Joaquin valley; inc. 1915. The city's economy is based on agriculture and related enterprises, especially vineyards and wineries.

Delany, Martin Robinson (dəlā'nē), 1812–85, American Negro leader, b. Charles Town, Va., (now in West Virginia). The son of free Negroes, he attended a Negro school in Pittsburgh and studied medicine at Harvard. He emphasized the practical aspects of Negro problems. Taking up the cause of emigration (the return of American Negroes to Africa), he was largely responsible for the first National Emigration Convention in 1854 and headed an expedition to the Niger valley. In the Civil War he was an army physician. Later he was in the Freedmen's Bureau, served as a trial judge in Charleston, S.C., and lost (1874) the election for lieutenant governor of South Carolina; he was a stern enemy of corruption. His ideas of race appeared in *Principles of Ethnology* (1879). See biographies by F. A. Rollin (1868, repr. 1969), Dorothy Sterling (1971), and Victor Ullman (1971).

De la Ramée, Louise: see OUIDA.

Delarey or **De la Rey, Jacobus Hercules** (yäkō'bəs hĕr'külĕs dəlärī'), 1847?–1914, Boer general in the South African War. He scored several victories in the early phase of the war and in later guerrilla fighting successfully eluded British traps. Delarey appeared reconciled to the Boer defeat and sat (1907) in the first parliament Great Britain permitted in the Transvaal. At the outbreak of World War I, however, Delarey opposed the government's attack on the German colony of South West Africa. He was killed by a patrol that was rounding up dissidents.

Delaroche, Hippolyte (ēpôlēt' dəlärôsh'), 1797–1856, French historical and portrait painter, known as Paul Delaroche. He studied with Gros. The exhibition of his large *Joas Saved by Josabeth* in 1822 brought him a popularity that continued throughout his life. He devoted himself chiefly to the painting of large historical canvases. *Death of the Duke of Guise* (Chantilly) is a notable example. Romantic in subject and in sentiment, the painting of Delaroche is studied and academic in handling. He was also a popular portraitist.

de la Roche, Mazo (mä'zō də lä rôsh), 1885–1961, Canadian novelist, b. Toronto. Her popular novel, *Jalna* (1927), was followed by a series depicting the history, through 150 years, of the vigorous Whiteoak family who lived at "Jalna." The series includes 16 novels; among them are *Whiteoaks* (1929), *Finch's Fortune* (1931), *Young Renny* (1935), *Whiteoak Harvest* (1936), *Growth of a Man* (1938), *The Building of Jalna* (1944), and *Mary Wakefield* (1949). Her dramatization of *Whiteoaks* was staged in London and New York. De la Roche also wrote plays, children's books, a history of Quebec, and an autobiography, *Ringing the Changes* (1957).

De la Rue, Warren (dĕl'ərōō, dĕlərōō'), 1815–89, British scientist and inventor. Especially noted as an astronomer, he was a pioneer in celestial photography. He adapted the wet-plate process to lunar photography and invented (1858) for Kew Observatory a photoheliograph, the first device to give good solar pictures. His photographs of a solar eclipse in 1860 demonstrated that prominences observed at the sun's edge are of solar origin. De la Rue is known also for his research in chemistry, solar physics, and electrical discharge through gases. His inventions include an envelope-folding machine (1851).

Delaunay, Robert (rōbĕr' dəlōnā'), 1885–1941, French painter. By 1909, Delaunay had progressed from a neo-impressionist phase to cubism, applying cubist principles to the exploration of color. He immediately enlarged cubist themes to include the architecture of cities (e.g., *La Ville de Paris,* 1912; Musée d'Art moderne, Paris). He became a major figure in the movement Apollinaire termed ORPHISM. This amalgam of fauve color, futurist dynamism, and analytical cubism sought to emulate the rhythms but not the appearance of nature. Delaunay is most famous for his series of paintings of the Eiffel Tower; one of them is in the Solomon R. Guggenheim Museum, New York City.

Delavigne, Casimir (käzēmēr' dəlävē'nyə), 1793–1843, French dramatist, poet, and satirist. His first publication, a verse diatribe against the Restoration, *Les Messéniennes* (1818), brought him recognition. His successful plays included comedies, such as *L'Ecole des vieillards* (1823), and tragedies, such as *Les Vêpres siciliennes* (1819), *Le Paria* (1821), *Louis XI* (1832), and *Les Enfants d'Édouard* (1833). After his death, interest in his works declined rapidly.

Delaware (dĕl'əwâr, -wər), state (1970 pop. 548,104), 2,057 sq mi (5,328 sq km), E United States, one of the Middle Atlantic states and one of the Thirteen Colonies. The capital is DOVER, and the only large city is WILMINGTON. Together with Maryland and Virginia, the state occupies the peninsula between Chesapeake Bay and Delaware Bay. Delaware is situated on the northeast portion of the peninsula, facing the Delaware River, which broadens into Delaware Bay; the bay in turn joins the Atlantic Ocean at Cape Henlopen. New Jersey lies across the river and bay from Delaware, which has water along its entire eastern edge; elsewhere Delaware is bounded by Pennsylvania on the north and by Maryland on the west and the south. The second smallest of all U.S. states (only Rhode Island is smaller), Delaware is sometimes called the Diamond State, in reference to its size and the fertility of its soil (which, however, suffered from overuse in the 19th cent. and had to be restored to vigor by scientific farming). No place in the narrow state is very far from water. Many small rivers flow across the state, some flowing E to the Delaware, others W across Maryland to the Chesapeake. In the north the Christina and Brandywine rivers flow into the Delaware; in the south the

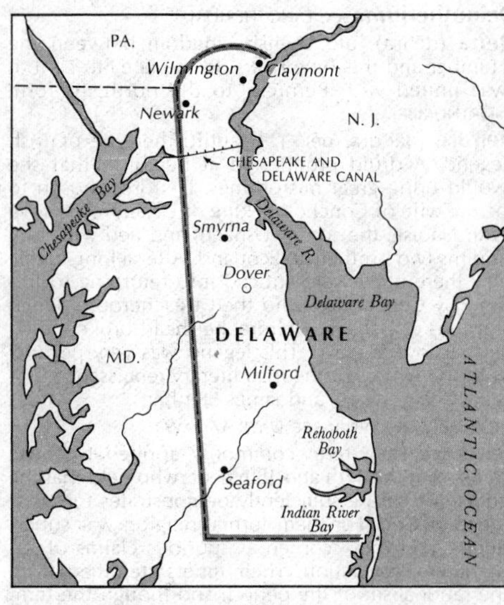

Nanticoke River flows SW to Chesapeake Bay. The climate is equable, and all the land is low-lying, from the sand dunes in the south to the pleasant little hills on the border of Pennsylvania in the north; the average altitude is c.60 ft (18 m), and the highest point, at Centerville (NW of Wilmington and almost on the Pennsylvania border) is only 440 ft (134 m). Delaware is chiefly an industrial state, although agriculture is still important. Industry is heavily concentrated in the north, while farming is carried on throughout the state. Delaware's chief agricultural products are broilers, corn, soybeans, and dairy products. Potatoes and hay are also grown. Much of the state's wealth comes from industries around Wilmington, especially the chemicals industry that was founded by the DU PONT family in the 19th cent. and that has become one of the largest chemical companies in the world. In addition to chemicals and chemical products, industries in Delaware manufacture food products, rubber and plastic products, and primary and fabricated metals. Because of Delaware's lenient laws governing business taxation, some of the nation's largest corporations have their home offices in Wilmington. Delaware has a small fishing industry and the principal species caught are clams, menhaden, oysters, and scup. Long before white men explored the Delaware area, it was inhabited by the DELAWARE INDIANS—notably the Nanticoke in the south and the Minqua in the north. In 1609, Henry Hudson, in the service of the Dutch East India Company, sailed into Delaware Bay. A year later the British captain Sir Samuel Argall, bound for the colony of Virginia, also sailed into the bay. Argall named one of the capes Cape La Warre after the governor of Virginia, Thomas West, Baron De la Warr. From the time of its discovery, the region was contested by the Dutch and English. The first settlement was established by Dutch patroons, or proprietors, in partnership with the Dutch navigator David Pietersen de Vries; it was called Swanendael and was established (1631) on the site of the present-day town of Lewes. However, within a year it was attacked and utterly destroyed by the Indians. This attack notwithstanding, the Indians were generally friendly and willing to trade with the newcomers. The Dutch West India Company, organized in 1623, was more interested in trade on the South River, as the Delaware was called at that time, than in settlement (the North River was the Hudson, in the Dutch colony of New Netherland). Several Dutchmen, interested in settling the area, put their services at the disposal of Sweden and colonized the area for that country. The best known of these was Peter Minuit, who had been governor of New Amsterdam. In 1637–38 Minuit directed the colonizing expedition for the Swedes that organized NEW SWEDEN. Fort Christina was founded in 1638 on the site of present-day Wilmington and was named in honor of the queen of Sweden. The colony grew with the arrival of Swedish, Finnish, and Dutch settlers. English colonists from Connecticut tried to establish trading posts in the Delaware River region and failed, but Dutch interests in the area were not disposed of as easily. Peter Stuyvesant, governor of New Netherland, sailed to the Delaware region in 1651 and established Fort Casimir on the Delaware shore at the site of present-day New Castle. The

Swedes captured the fort by surprise in 1654, but their triumph was brief; Stuyvesant returned with an expedition in 1655 and conquered all New Sweden. The Dutch West India Company sold part of New Sweden to the Dutch city of Amsterdam in 1656 and the rest in 1663. In 1664 the English seized the Dutch holdings on the Delaware. The Dutch recaptured the colony in 1673 and although they held Delaware only briefly, they set up three district courts that marked the beginning of Delaware's division into three counties. The colony was returned to the English in 1674 and remained in their hands until the American Revolution. The English duke of York (later James II) annexed the region to New York, land granted him earlier by Charles II. In 1682 the duke transferred the claim to William Penn, who wanted to secure a navigable water route from his new colony of Pennsylvania to the ocean. The three counties of Delaware thus became the Three Lower Counties (or Territories, as Penn called them) of Pennsylvania. The individual counties were called New Castle, Kent (formerly St. Jones), and Sussex (formerly Hoornkill, also known as Whorekill, and Deale). The English proprietors of Maryland contested Penn's claim to Delaware, and the boundary dispute was not fully settled until 1750. The inhabitants of the Delaware counties were at first unwilling to be joined to the "radical" Quaker colony of Pennsylvania or to have their affairs settled in Philadelphia. They finally accepted the Penn charter of 1701 after provisions were added giving the Three Lower Counties the right to a separate assembly, which first met in 1704. Delaware maintained quasi-autonomy until the American Revolution. The two colonies maintained strong ties, however, and two of Delaware's leading statesmen during the Revolution—Thomas McKean and John Dickinson—were also prominent in Pennsylvania affairs. Although there were many Loyalists in Delaware just prior to the American Revolution, Delaware supported independence, with two of its three delegates to the Continental Congress—Caesar Rodney and Thomas McKean—voting for independence. George Read, the third Delaware delegate, voted against independence, fearing that Loyalist sentiment was too strong in the colonies. However, Read subsequently signed the Declaration of Independence. In 1776 the colony of Delaware became a state, with a president as its chief executive. Regiments from the state rendered valiant service to the patriot cause, especially the Delaware 1st Regiment, which was nicknamed the Blue Hen's Chickens—originally because they carried with them gamecocks bred by a famous hen of Kent and later because they themselves showed the fighting quality of gamecocks. Delaware was a leader in the movement for revision of the form of government under the Articles of Confederation and in 1787 became the first state to ratify the new Constitution of the United States. The late 18th cent. also marked the beginning of industry in Delaware with the establishment of gristmills on the Brandywine and Christina rivers. Wilmington became a center for the manufacture of cloth, paper, and flour—products that helped to build the industrial economy of N Delaware that flourished in the 19th cent. Shortly thereafter, in 1802, Eleuthère Irénée Du Pont established a gun powder mill on the Brandywine River. The state constitution of 1776 was superseded by a new constitution in 1792, which provided that the chief executive be a governor rather than a president. Prior to the Civil War, Delaware was a slave state, but in the early 19th cent. the number of slaves in the state declined, while the number of free Negroes increased. Many citizens of Delaware favored manumission of slaves and belonged to the American Colonization Society, but there were few who sympathized with the growing abolitionist movement and there was strong sentiment for separation of whites and blacks. In the Civil War, Delaware remained loyal to the Union, but pro-Southern feeling increased rather than diminished during the course of the war. Delaware refused to accept an emancipation proposal made by Lincoln in 1861 and did not ratify the Thirteenth, Fourteenth, and Fifteenth amendments to the U.S. Constitution until 1901. Delaware Democrats subsequently became divided, and the Republican Party emerged in 1905 to assume a leading political role for some years. A new state constitution in 1897 reflected the political strength as well as conservatism of Delaware's farmers through provisions that kept the political strength of Wilmington at a minimum and that of rural areas at a maximum. Many European immigrants came to the state in the late 19th and early 20th cent., settling in the Wilmington area. Southern Delaware's population continued to be made up largely of blacks and persons of English origin. Delaware's industries flourished during the 19th cent. as transportation facilities improved. Industry continued to expand in the 20th cent., especially during World Wars I and II. The chemical industry built up by the Du Pont family was broken up by a Federal antitrust suit in 1912. Racial tensions appeared in the state in the 1950s and 60s as Delaware's schools became racially integrated, and after the assassination of Martin Luther King in 1968, rioting erupted in Wilmington. Under the provisions of the 1897 constitution, the governor is elected to a four-year term. The state legislature, called the general assembly, is made up of a senate of 21 members elected to serve for four years and a house of representatives with 41 members elected for two years. In the 1960s the general assembly was reapportioned on the basis of population, thus giving a greater influence to urban areas and reducing the rural influence. Delaware is represented in the U.S. Congress by two Senators and one Representative and has three electoral votes. Neither Democrats nor Republicans have dominated Delaware politics in recent years. Sherman W. Tribbet, a Democrat, was elected governor in 1972. The leading institution of higher education is the Univ. of Delaware, at Newark. The standard history of the early period is Benjamin Ferris, *A History of the Original Settlements on the Delaware* (1846). See J. A. Munroe, *Federalist Delaware, 1775–1815* (1954), and *Delaware: A Student's Guide* (1965); Federal Writers' Project, *Delaware: A Guide to the First State* (1938, rev. ed. 1955, repr. 1973).

Delaware, city (1970 pop. 15,008), seat of Delaware co., central Ohio, on the Olentangy River; inc. as a city 1903. A trade center in a rich farm area, it has some manufacturing. Ohio Wesleyan Univ. is in the city, which is also the birthplace of Rutherford B. Hayes. During the War of 1812, Delaware served as Gen. William Henry Harrison's headquarters.

Delaware, river, c.280 mi (450 km) long, rising in the Catskill Mts., SE N.Y., in east and west branches, which meet at Hancock. It flows SE along the New York–Pennsylvania border to Port Jervis, then between Pennsylvania and New Jersey generally S to Delaware Bay, an estuary (52 mi/84 km long) between New Jersey and Delaware. Reservoirs and dams on its headstreams provide flood control and water supply; part of New York City's water supply comes from the Delaware. The diversion of great amounts of water from the upper Delaware has increased the salinity of Delaware Bay. The Delaware River Basin Compact was formed (1961) to regulate the use of water in the entire river basin. The Delaware River cuts through Kittatinny Mt. near Stroudsburg, Pa., forming the Delaware Water Gap, a scenic resort and recreation area. The lower Delaware River, from Trenton, N.J. (the head of navigation), past Philadelphia, Pa. (an ocean port), to Wilmington, Del., flows through a highly industrialized area; water pollution is a problem there. The Delaware River has long been significant in commerce and now carries a great amount of tonnage. The Chesapeake and Delaware Canal links it with Chesapeake Bay.

Delaware, University of, at Newark, Del.; land-grant and state supported; coeducational; founded 1743 as a Presbyterian school, moved to Newark 1765, and chartered as Newark Academy by the Penns in 1769. It became Newark College in 1833 and was designated a land-grant college in 1870. It was called Delaware College (for men) from 1843 to 1921. In 1921 Delaware College and the affiliated women's college (founded 1913) were merged to form the present institution.

Delaware and Hudson Canal, former waterway, 107 mi (172 km) long, between Honesdale, Pa., and Kingston, N.Y., linking the Delaware and Hudson rivers; built 1825–29 to move coal from the Pennsylvania fields to New York markets. It operated profitably until the 1860s; increasing railroad competition caused its abandonment in 1899. The first locomotive in the United States ran in 1829 on a rail line built to serve the canal.

Delaware and Raritan Canal, abandoned canal, 45 mi (72 km) long, between Bordentown and New Brunswick, N.J., connecting the Delaware and the Raritan rivers; opened in 1834. Once an important inland waterway, it was superseded by the railroads in the latter half of the 19th cent.

Delaware Aqueduct, SE N.Y., 85 mi (137 km) long, carrying water from the Rondout Reservoir, Sullivan co., SE into the New York City water system at the Hillview Reservoir, Westchester co.; built 1937–62. The tunnel taps the Delaware River basin and supplies about 60% of New York City's water. The aqueduct's deep, gravity-flow construction requires little maintenance. The Rondout Reservoir receives water from other Delaware basin reservoirs through a tunnel system.

Delaware Bay: see DELAWARE, river.

Delaware Indians, English name given several closely related North American Indian tribes of the Algonquian branch of the Algonquian-Wakashan linguistic stock (see AMERICAN INDIAN LANGUAGES). In the 17th cent., they lived in what is now New Jersey, Delaware, E Pennsylvania, and SE New York. They called themselves the Lenni-Lenape or the Lenape and were given the name Delaware by the settlers because they lived in the vicinity of the Delaware River. The Delaware evolved into a loose confederacy of three major divisions: the Munsee (wolf), the Unalachtigo (turkey), and the Unami (turtle). They occupied the territory from which most of the Algonquian tribes had originated and were accorded the respectful title of grandfather by these tribes. They traded with the Dutch early in the 17th cent., sold much of their land, and began moving inland to the Susquehanna valley. In 1682 they made a treaty of friendship with William Penn, which he did his best to honor. In 1720 the Delaware fell victim to Iroquois attack and were forced to move into what is now Ohio. The western Delaware sided with the French in the last of the French and Indian Wars, took part in Pontiac's Rebellion, and sided with the British in the American Revolution. Some of the Delaware in Pennsylvania had been converted to Christianity by the Moravians. In 1782 a settlement of these peaceful Christian Indians at Gnadenhutten were massacred by a force of white men. Anthony Wayne defeated and subdued the Delaware in 1794, and by the Treaty of Greenville (1795) they and their allies ceded their lands in Pennsylvania and Ohio to the white men. They crossed the Mississippi River and migrated to Kansas and then to Texas. They were later moved to Indian Territory and settled with the Cherokee. A remarkable history of the Delaware, in the form of pictographs, was located by the French scholar Constantine Samuel Rafinesque in 1836. Known as the *Walum Olum,* it depicted Delaware migrations and changes; its claim to antiquity, however, is somewhat doubtful. See D. G. Brinton, *The Lenâpé and Their Legends* (1884, repr. 1969); M. R. Harrington, *Religion and Ceremonies of the Lenape* (1921); F. G. Speck, *A Study of the Delaware Indian Big House Ceremony* (1931) and *Oklahoma Delaware Ceremonies, Feasts, and Dances* (1937), C. A. Weslager, *The Delaware Indians* (1972).

Delaware Prophet, fl. 18th cent., North American Indian leader. His real name is not known. He began preaching (c.1762) among the Delaware Indians of the Muskingum valley in Ohio. He spoke against intertribal war, drunkenness, polygamy, and the use of magic, and he promised his hearers that if they would but heed his words the Indians would be strong again and able to resist the whites. He prepared symbolic charts of his message on deerskin and left them in various villages to help his converts teach others. The religious fervor spread rapidly and is said to have been an inspiration to Pontiac. After the collapse of Pontiac's Rebellion (1763–66) the cult of the Delaware Prophet waned and was largely superseded by that of the Munsee Prophet, who was in turn succeeded by the Shawnee Prophet.

Delaware River Basin Compact, providing for the utilization and development of the water resources of the Delaware River basin. In 1961 the Federal government and the states of Delaware, Pennsylvania, New Jersey, and New York agreed to form a partnership in a 50-year building program under the supervision of the Delaware River Basin Commission. Dams and reservoirs furnishing hydroelectricity, flood control, recreation, and wildlife refuge are planned. A minimum flow rate was established to prevent saltwater intrusion in the lower river.

Delaware Water Gap, scenic gorge, 2 mi (3.2 km) long, cut by the Delaware River through Kittatinny Mt., on the N.J.-Pa. line; located in a resort area. The gap, parts of the wooded Kittatinny Mt., several islands, and c.40 mi (64 km) of river bank are included in Delaware Water Gap National Recreation Area (see NATIONAL PARKS AND MONUMENTS, table).

De la Warr, Thomas West, 12th Baron (dĕl'əwər), 1577–1618, English colonial governor of Virginia. He saw fighting in the Netherlands and was knighted when serving in Ireland. He succeeded to the peerage in 1602. In 1609 he was appointed first governor of Virginia (Sir Thomas GATES governed as deputy until De la Warr arrived). He sailed in April,

1610, with an expedition including Sir Samuel ARGALL. On his arrival at Jamestown he found the settlers in such dire need that they were ready to return to England. He encouraged them to remain, sent Argall for supplies, and had forts built. Argall, on his voyage, sailed into the bay later called (after the governor) Delaware Bay. Lord De la Warr returned to England, and the colony was governed by Sir Thomas Gates and Sir Thomas Dale. De la Warr in his *Relation . . . of the Colonies Planted in Virginia* (1611) pleaded for the colony. He died during his second voyage to Virginia.

Delbrück, Hans (häns dĕl'brük), 1848–1929, German historian, professor at the Univ. of Berlin. His *Geschichte der Kriegskunst* [history of the art of warfare] (4 vol., 1900–1927) is notable for going beyond technical problems and linking warfare to politics and economics.

Delbrück, Rudolf von (ro͞o'dôlf fən), 1817–1903, German statesman. He served (1857–76) under BISMARCK as president of the chancellery of the North German Confederation (1866–71) and, after 1871, of the German Empire. A protagonist of free trade and liberal economics, he opposed Bismarck's adoption of a protectionist policy in the 1870s and resigned in 1876.

Delcassé, Théophile (tāôfēl' dĕlkäsā'), 1852–1923, French foreign minister. He began his career as a political journalist and then turned to politics. First undersecretary and then minister for the colonies (1893–95), he became foreign minister in 1898 and remained in office until 1905. Commencing with the FASHODA INCIDENT, in which his conciliatory attitude marked the start of a Franco-British *rapprochement*, he greatly influenced the alignment of European powers prior to World War I. The Entente Cordiale with Great Britain (1904), for which he was largely responsible, settled colonial differences between the two nations, particularly in Morocco and Egypt; France agreed to recognize the British occupation of Egypt in return for British acknowledgment of French interests in MOROCCO. This convention opened the way for the Triple Entente (1907) between Great Britain, France, and Russia (see TRIPLE ALLIANCE AND TRIPLE ENTENTE). During Delcassé's tenure as foreign minister, Franco-Russian relations were cemented (1899) by the extension of the Franco-Russian alliance of 1894, and a secret nonaggression treaty was signed (1902) between France and Italy that neutralized Italian membership in the Triple Alliance with Germany and Austria-Hungary. In 1905, Delcassé proposed the establishment of a French protectorate over Morocco. Emperor William II of Germany visited Tangier and proclaimed his country's support of Moroccan independence. Delcassé urged his government to stand firm, but the fear of war with Germany caused the French to oppose Delcassé, and he resigned. Delcassé was later naval minister (1911–13) and foreign minister (1914–15). See biography by C. W. Porter (1936); Christopher Andrew, *Théophile Delcassé and the Making of the Entente Cordiale* (1968).

Del City, city (1970 pop. 27,133), Oklahoma co., central Okla., a residential suburb of Oklahoma City; inc. 1948.

Delderfield, R. F. (Ronald Frederick Delderfield), 1912–73, English writer, b. London. He did not start writing novels until he was 44, after having been a successful playwright and newspaperman. His "old-fashioned" novels are long, panoramic, socio-historical studies of life in the English west country. They include *God Is an Englishman* (1970), *Theirs Was the Kingdom* (1971), and *Give Us This Day* (1973), a trilogy. See his autobiographical *For My Own Amusement* (1972).

Deledda, Grazia (grä'tsēä dälĕd'dä), 1875–1936, Italian novelist, b. Sardinia. Her first work, a collection of short stories, was published when she was 19. She was awarded the Nobel Prize in 1926. Deledda's work is lyric and in part naturalistic, and combines sympathy and humor with occasional touches of violence. Her novels include *Dopo il divorzio* (1902, tr. *After the Divorce,* 1905), *Elias Portolú* (1903), *Cenere* (1904, tr. *Ashes,* 1908), *Canne al vento* [reeds in the wind] (1913), *La Madre* (1920, tr. *The Mother,* 1922), and *La Fuga in Egitto* [flight into Egypt] (1925).

Delémont (dəlāmôN'), Ger. *Delsberg,* town (1970 pop. 11,797), Bern canton, NW Switzerland. A watchmaking center of the Bernese Jura, it was once the residence (1528–1792) of the prince-bishops of Basel. The 18th-century episcopal palace still stands.

De Leon, Daniel (dē lē'ŏn), 1852–1914, American socialist leader. Born on the island of Curaçao of Spanish-American parents, he was educated in Germany and the Netherlands before going (1872) to New York City. There he edited a Spanish newspaper, studied law at Columbia (LL.B., 1876), practiced law for a few years, and then returned to Columbia to lecture (1883–89) on Latin American diplomacy. His interest in labor reform grew, and he joined successively the Knights of Labor (1888), Edward Bellamy's "Nationalist" movement (1889), and the Socialist Labor party (1890). He was Socialist Labor candidate for governor of New York in 1891, and for years he edited the Socialist Labor weekly, *The People.* He was an inflexible and doctrinaire Marxian revolutionist and consequently fell out with most other liberal leaders. He opposed unionization of labor according to trades and led the group that formed the Socialist Trade and Labor Alliance, but his leadership was too radical for some of the members (prominent among them Morris HILLQUIT), who withdrew in 1899 and ultimately formed the Socialist party. De Leon's prestige lessened. He helped to found the INDUSTRIAL WORKERS OF THE WORLD in 1905, but in the quarrel over political action he and his followers were expelled. The rival Workers' International Industrial Union, which he then organized, did not flourish. He wrote a great deal of Socialist polemical literature and translated a work of Karl Marx. See Arnold Peterson, *Daniel De Leon, Social Architect* (2 vol., 1941–53); study by L. G. Raĭskiĭ (1959); Carl Reeve, *The Life and Times of Daniel De Leon* (1972); bibliography by O. C. Johnson (1966).

Delescluze, Louis Charles (lwē shärl dəläklüz'), 1809–71, French journalist and radical republican. In his active career he was often in prison or in exile. He supported the July Revolution of 1830 but came to oppose the regime of King Louis Philippe and took part in the February Revolution of 1848. The conservatism of the new leaders and the bloody suppression of the JUNE DAYS brought him further political disenchantment. A bitter opponent of the Second Empire of NAPOLEON III, he engaged in increasingly radical journalistic attacks on the emperor. After the fall of the empire, Delescluze was elected (1871) to the national assembly, but he resigned to serve in the COMMUNE OF PARIS. He was perhaps the ablest leader in the commune, but he could not save it. When defeat by the government troops became inevitable, Delescluze deliberately placed himself in the line of fire and was killed.

Delft (dĕlft), city (1971 pop. 86,189), South Holland prov., W Netherlands. It has varied industries and is noted for its ceramics (china, tiles, and pottery) known as delftware. Founded in the 11th cent. and chartered in 1246, Delft was an important commercial center until superseded (17th cent.) by Rotterdam. The aspect of old Delft has changed little since Jan Vermeer, who was born and lived there (17th cent.), painted his famous *View of Delft.* The city's notable buildings include a 13th-century Gothic church (Oude Kerk); the Gothic Nieuwe Kerk (15th cent.), with the tombs of William the Silent, who was assassinated in Delft, and Hugo Grotius, who was born there; and the 17th-century town hall. The city has a technical university.

delftware. The earliest delftware was a faïence, a heavy, brown earthenware with opaque white glaze and polychrome decoration, made in the late 16th cent. Some of the earliest imitations of Chinese and Japanese porcelain were made at Delft in the 17th cent. Delft was important as a pottery center from the mid-17th cent. to the end of the 18th cent. By 1850 little of the industry survived. The name *delft* is also often applied to the wares of similar nature made in 17th-century London, Bristol, and Liverpool.

Delhi (dĕl'ē), union territory and city, N central India. The union territory (1971 pop. 4,044,338), 573 sq mi (1,484 sq km), is on the Delhi plain, which is crossed by the Jumna River and stretches between the Indus valley and the alluvial plain of the Ganges. A hot and arid region, with temperatures rising above 110°F (43°C) in the summer, it has extensive irrigation works to support agriculture, the chief occupation. Hindi and Urdu are spoken by more than 90% of the population. NEW DELHI, the capital of India, and Old Delhi are the chief urban centers. The union territory is administered by the minister for home affairs in the central Indian government with the aid of an advisory council composed of the Delhi members of Parliament and others. Throughout India's history the region of Delhi, commanding roads in all directions, was the key to empire. From the earliest times many cities rose and fell there, and within 50 sq mi (130 sq km) S of New Delhi are more important dynastic remains than exist in any other area of the country. The earliest city on the Delhi plain was the semilegendary Indraprastha, mentioned in the Hindu epic MAHABHARATA. Another historic site is the Rajput citadel and town containing the Lal Kot [red fort], erected in 1052; it is sometimes confused with Shah Jahan's Red Fort in Old Delhi. In 1192 the legions of the Afghan warrior Muhammad of Ghor captured the Rajput town, and the DELHI SULTANATE was established (1206). The invasion of Delhi by Tamerlane in 1398 put an end to the sultanate; the Lodis, last of the Delhi sultans, gave way to BABUR, who, after the battle of Panipat in 1526, founded the Mogul empire. The early Mogul emperors favored Agra as their capital, and Delhi became their permanent seat only after Shah Jahan built (1638) the walls of Old Delhi. Among the most famous monuments on the Delhi plain are the 12th-century Kutb Minar and the tomb of Humayan (built 1565–69; it is the architectural prototype of the Taj Mahal at Agra). The city of **Delhi,** or Old Delhi (1971 metropolitan area pop. 3,629,842), on the Jumna River, adjoins New Delhi in the east central part of the territory and is enclosed by high stone walls erected in 1638 by Shah Jahan. Within the walls he built the famous Red Fort—so called for its walls and gateways of red sandstone—that contained the imperial Mogul palace. In the palace is a public audience hall (Diwan-i-Am), where the splendid Peacock Throne stood, and a private audience hall (Diwan-i-Khas), built entirely of white marble and bearing the apt inscription "If there is a heaven on earth, it is this!" Shah Jahan also built the Jama Masjid [great mosque], one of the finest in Islam. Just south of the fort, on the Jumna's bank, is Rajghat, where Gandhi's body was cremated; it is now one of the most revered shrines in India. In the northwest, beyond the old walls, there are residences, hotels and clubs, the Univ. of Delhi, and an amphitheater (built 1911) that marks the site of the ceremony in 1877 in which Queen Victoria was proclaimed empress of India. The present city of Old Delhi did not become important until Shah Jahan (for whom it was sometimes called Shahjahanabad) made it the capital of the Mogul empire in 1638. It was sacked (1739) by the Persian Nadir Shah, who carried off the Peacock Throne. The city was held by the MAHRATTAS from 1771 until 1803, when the British took it. During the INDIAN MUTINY of 1857 it was held for five months by the rebels. It was (1912–31) interim capital of India until New Delhi was officially inaugurated and is today a commercial center.

Delhi Sultanate, first Muslim empire (1192–1398) of India, which at its height (c.1315) encompassed almost the entire subcontinent. It was founded after the Afghan ruler MUHAMMAD OF GHOR defeated PRITHVI RAJ and captured Delhi in 1192. Muhammad dispatched his most capable general, Qutb ud-Din on a tour of conquest in N India. In 1206, Qutb ud-Din proclaimed himself sultan of Delhi and founded a line of rulers called the Slave dynasty, because he and several of the sultans who claimed succession from him were originally military slaves. Iltutmish (1210–35), who erected the QUTB MINAR, and Balban (1266–87) were among the dynasty's most illustrious rulers; they firmly established the empire and repulsed the Mongols on the northwest frontier. Continually faced with revolts, both of conquered territories and of rival families, the Slave dynasty came to an end in 1290. Under the Khalji dynasty (1290–1320), the conquests of Sultan Ala ud-Din Muhammad Khalji brought Muslim dominion in India to the greatest extent it was to reach until the advent of the Mogul empire. Early in the reign of Muhammad Tughluq, founder of the Tughluq dynasty (1325–98), the power of Delhi was acknowledged even in the extreme S of India. His eccentric rule and ferocious temperament provoked a series of revolts, notably that of the Hindu Vijayanagar kingdom in the south, and a steady loss of territory; by his death (1351) the Hindu south had recovered its independence and the Deccan had become a separate Muslim state, the Bahmani kingdom. Under Tughluq's successors the sultanate of Delhi began to disintegrate into several small states. With the sack of Delhi by Tamerlane in 1398, the once great sultanate fell, although local rulers lingered on at Delhi until the invasion of Babur and the MOGUL conquest. See V. D. Mahajan, *The Sultanate of Delhi* (2d ed. 1963).

Delian League, confederation of Greek states under the leadership of Athens. The name is used to designate two distinct periods of alliance, the first 478–404 B.C., the second 378–338 B.C. The first alliance was made between Athens and a number of Ionian states (chiefly maritime) for the purpose of opposing Persia. All the members were given equal vote in a council established in the temple of Apollo at Delos, where the league's treasury was kept. The assessments to be levied on the members were originally fixed by Athens, and the fairness with which these were apportioned contributed much toward maintaining enthusiasm at the start. States willingly contributed funds, troops, and ships to defeat Persia. That object was accomplished, and with the death (465 B.C.) of Xerxes I all immediate danger from the East was over. But at this time an event took place that served to commit the league to a new policy. Naxos attempted to secede, and Athens, taking the leadership from the assembly, forced (c.470 B.C.) Naxos to retain allegiance. Soon Thasos attempted the same maneuver and was likewise subdued (463 B.C.) by the Athenian general Cimon. The Athenians were so successful in their aims, using both force and persuasion, that by 454 B.C. the league had grown to c.140 members. A Spartan invasion was averted in 457 B.C., and Thebes, the traditional enemy of Athens, was subjected (456 B.C.). In 454 B.C., because of the real or pretended danger of Persian attack, the treasury was transported from Delos to the Athenian Acropolis. The league had in effect become an Athenian empire. However, its unity was not very stable, and in 446 B.C. Athens lost Boeotia. Gradually Athens lost its prestige as well as many of its alliances, and, with the Peloponnesian War (404 B.C.), the league came to an end. In 394 B.C., Conon reestablished the Athenian mastery of the sea at Cnidus. Proffers of alliance reached Athens, and in 378 B.C. the second Athenian confederacy was formed. Two years later Athens won a naval victory over Sparta near Naxos; the Athenians and Spartans compromised with a treaty that left Athens supreme on the sea and Sparta supreme on the mainland of Greece. In 371 B.C., Thebes withdrew from the alliance and gained predominance over Boeotian land that had been occupied (387 B.C.) by Sparta. A treaty was made between Athens and Sparta. By 351 B.C., however, the status of the league had been seriously weakened in the north and in the east, and in 338 B.C. the league was utterly destroyed by the victory of Philip II of Macedon in the battle of CHAERONEA.

Delian problem: see GEOMETRIC PROBLEMS OF ANTIQUITY.

Delibes, Léo (lāō' dəlĕb'), 1836–91, French composer. After studying at the Conservatory in Paris, he became an accompanist at the Théâtre-Lyrique in 1853, and, ten years later, at the Paris Opéra. He achieved great success with his ballets, especially *Coppélia* (1870) and *Sylvia* (1876). Delibes also wrote many operettas and several operas, of which *Lakmé* (1883) is the most famous. His music, profusely melodic and vividly orchestrated, is admirably suited for stage performance. He was also an organist and composed religious music.

Delibes, Miguel (mēgĕl' dālē'bās), 1920–, Spanish novelist, short-story writer, and journalist, b. Valladolid. He is a master of description—mainly of provincial and rural atmospheres—and of psychological analysis of characters, drawn from the middle and lower classes. Among his works are *La sombra del ciprés es alargada* [the shadow of the cypress is extended] (1947), *Aún es de día* [it is still day] (1949), *El camino* [the road] (1950), *Diario de un cazador* [diary of a hunter] (1955), *Mi idolatrado hijo Sisí* [my adored son Sisí] (1953), and *El libro de caza menor* [the book of small game] (1964), and *Smoke on the Ground* (tr. 1972). See study by J. W. Diaz (1971).

Delilah (dĭlī'lə), courtesan in the pay of the Philistines who was loved by SAMSON. She learned that his strength lay in his long hair and betrayed him to his enemies by cutting it off. Judges 16.4–20.

delinquency, juvenile: see JUVENILE DELINQUENCY.

deliquescence (dĕl"əkwĕs'əns), conversion of a solid substance into a liquid as a result of absorption of water vapor from the air. Since impurities in a solid lower its melting point, the absorbed water causes a decrease in the normal melting point of the solid. If enough water is absorbed to lower the melting point below room temperature, the solid will deliquesce, or turn to liquid. Lithium sulfide and magnesium iodide are examples of deliquescent salts.

delirium (dĭlĕr'ēəm), temporary state of mental confusion characterized by active, uncontrolled imagination and faulty judgment. It ranges from mere flightiness to a maniacal state and is a symptom in many disorders. Among the causes are intoxication (see DELIRIUM TREMENS), infectious diseases, diseases of the brain itself, exhaustion, drugs, high fever, malnutrition, and metabolic disorders. There is not necessarily any apparent change in the brain structure, although the condition is thought to result from a chemical imbalance in the brain. The underlying cause must be treated, and in the meantime the patient must be protected from injury and quieted if necessary by suitable drugs.

delirium tremens, acute psychosis that may occur after several years of chronic alcoholism. An episode of delirium tremens is usually preceded by disturbed sleep and irritability. The patient becomes confused and delirious, experiences violent trembling and epileptoid seizures, and exhibits maniacal, destructive behavior. The patient also has vivid hallucinations, in which he usually visualizes various forms of animal life or feels them upon his skin. Delirium tremens can be treated and even prevented by the injection of fairly large doses of dextrose, thiamine (vitamin B_1), and insulin and the continued administration of fluids (sodium chloride and sodium lactate) and the B vitamins. The condition is related to the abrupt drop in blood alcohol level after drinking ceases. Tranquilizers, sedatives, and anticonvulsants are also used in treatment.

Delisle, Guillaume (gēyōm' dəlēl'), 1675–1726, French geographer and cartographer. His most important work is a world map (1700), as accurate as the data available at that time permitted and the first map on which the errors of Ptolemy were wholly absent. Delisle is called the founder of modern cartography. He was geographer to Louis XV.

Delitzsch, Franz (fränts dä'lĭch), 1813–90, German Lutheran theologian and Hebraist. He was professor of theology at Rostock from 1846 to 1850, at Erlangen until 1867, and later at Leipzig. He was the author of many commentaries on books of the Old Testament. His son, **Friedrich Delitzsch,** 1850–1922, was an Assyrian scholar and author of works on Assyrian language, literature, and history.

Delium (dē'lēəm), town of ancient Greece, a port in E Boeotia, named for its temple of Apollo similar to the one at Delos. In the Peloponnesian War the Athenians were defeated (424 B.C.) by the Boeotians there; Socrates fought in the battle.

Delius, Frederick (dē'lyəs), 1862–1934, English composer, of German parentage. Influenced by Grieg, Delius combined romanticism and impressionism in his music, which is characterized by rather free structure and rich chromatic harmony. From 1886 to 1888 he studied in Leipzig, where his suite *Florida* (1886) was first performed. His works were appreciated earlier in Germany than in his native land, but recognition in England did come in his later years. Among his finest works are the orchestral pieces *Brigg Fair* (1907), *On Hearing the First Cuckoo in Spring* (1912), and *North Country Sketches* (1914). The best of his six operas is *A Village Romeo and Juliet* (1907). Outstanding also are his choral works *Sea Drift* (1903); *A Mass of Life* (1904–5), with text from Nietzsche's *Thus Spake Zarathustra;* and *Song of the High Hills* (1912). He also composed chamber music, concertos, and songs. In the 1920s Delius became blind and paralyzed but continued to compose and revise with the assistance of an amanuensis, Eric Fenby. His last public appearance was in London in 1929 at a six-day festival of his works organized by Sir Thomas Beecham. See biographies by Claire Delius (1935), Arthur Hutchings (1948), Sir Thomas Beecham (1959), G. Jahoda (1969), and A. Jefferson (1972).

Della Bella, Stefano: see BELLA.

Della Casa, Giovanni: see CASA.

Della-Cruscans (dĕl'ə-krŭs'kənz) [from the Accademia della Crusca, founded for linguistic purity, Florence, 16th cent.], a group of English poets living in Italy at the end of the 18th cent. who published pretentious, sentimental verse in *The Arno* (1784) and *The Florence Miscellany* (1785). Robert Merry, writing as "Della Crusca," Bertie Greatheed, William Parsons, and Mrs. Piozzi, under other names, were the contributors. In England their poetry and that of their followers, including Hannah Cowley, was published in the *World* and collected in the *British Album* (1789–91). Their verses were ridiculed by William Gifford.

Della Porta: see PORTA.

Della Quercia, Jacopo: see QUERCIA.

Della Robbia (dĕl"ə rŏb'ēə, Ital. dĕl'lä rôb'byä), Florentine family of sculptors and ceramists famous for their enameled terra-cotta or faïence. Many of the Della Robbia pieces are still in their original settings in Florence, Siena, and other Italian cities, but the finest collections are in Florence in the cathedral, the Bargello, and the Italian Academy and in London in the Victoria and Albert Museum. **Luca della Robbia,** 1400?–1482, founder of the atelier, was known first as a sculptor in bronze and marble. He was commissioned (1421) to design the choir gallery of the cathedral at Florence. Later he perfected a process for making clay reliefs and figures permanent by coating them with a glaze compounded of tin, antimony, and other substances. A pure religious feeling is expressed in his panels and medallions, where the Madonna and saints and angels appear usually in white on a blue background, sometimes with touches of gold and color in the decorative setting. A *Madonna and Child* is in the Metropolitan Museum. **Andrea della Robbia,** 1435–1525?, nephew and chief pupil of Luca, made a marble altar for a church near Arezzo and extended the use of clay to whole altarpieces (one is in the Church of Santa Croce, Florence), friezes, and fountains. His medallions on the Foundling Hospital, Florence, show simple baby forms (*bambini*) on blue ground, but in many of his medallions the central figures are framed in garlands of richly colored fruits and flowers. *The Virgin in Adoration*, an unglazed terra-cotta relief, is in the National Gallery of Art, Washington, D.C. Andrea della Robbia's sons, **Luca II,** c.1480–1550, **Giovanni,** c.1469–c.1529, and **Girolamo,** c.1488–1566, carried on the family tradition into the 16th cent. See studies by Allan Marquand on the Della Robbias (4 vol., 1973).

Deller, Alfred, 1912–, English COUNTERTENOR. He began his career as a chorister in his parish church. From 1940–47 he was a lay clerk at Canterbury Cathedral, and in 1947 he was appointed to the choir of St. Paul's Cathedral in London. Deller's unusual voice is particularly suited to Renaissance music and to the music of Handel and Purcell. In 1948 he formed the Deller Consort, which presents authentic performances of medieval, Renaissance, and baroque music; the consort has made numerous recordings and performed all over the world. Deller's son, Mark Deller, is also a countertenor, and the two have often performed together.

Dells of the Wisconsin or **The Dells,** scenic part of the Wisconsin River, central Wis., NW of Portage. The river has cut a deep gorge through 8 mi (12.9 km) of sandstone, which is carved into caves, pinnacles, and other curious shapes, often beautifully colored. A state park, The Dells is a major recreation area of the Midwest.

Delmarva, peninsula, c.180 mi (290 km) long, separating Chesapeake Bay on the west from Delaware Bay and the Atlantic Ocean on the east; named for the three states (Delaware, E Maryland, and E Virginia) that occupy it. The western coast of the peninsula is irregular and marshy; the eastern shore is straight with sandy beaches and offshore bars. The Chesapeake and Delaware Canal cuts across Delmarva's narrow neck. The Chesapeake Bay Bridge-Tunnel links Cape Charles, Va., the southern tip of the peninsula, with Norfolk, Va. Poultry raising (Delmarva is the largest producer of broilers in the United States), truck farming, fishing, and tourism are major industries. Dover, Del., and Salisbury, Md., are the main cities of the peninsula.

Delmedigo, Elijah ben Moses Abba (dälmĕ'dĕgō), c.1460–1497, Jewish philosopher and Talmudist, b. Crete, known also as Elijah Cretensis. He emigrated to Italy as a young man. He studied the Jewish, Islamic, Greek, and Latin classics, composing numerous translations and lecturing on philosophy in Padua, where he was the head of the yeshivah. Giovanni Pico della Mirandola was among his Christian pupils, protecting him from his Christian enemies. After Pico's death (1494) he was forced to return to Crete, where he remained until his own death. In the controversy surrounding the question of religion versus philosophy, Delmedigo held that the two were not incompatible, and that any conflict should be resolved in favor of a philosophic interpretation of the religious text. His chief importance in the history of philosophy derives from his making the works of Averroës available in Latin to the Italian philosophers of the Renaissance.

Delmenhorst (dĕl'mənhôrst), city (1970 pop. 63,266), Lower Saxony, N West Germany, near Bremen. Manufactures of this industrial city include textiles, linoleum, processed food, and machinery.

Deloney, Thomas c.1543–c.1600, English ballad writer, fiction writer, and pamphleteer. He was a silk weaver. Deloney's chief works are three prose narratives—*Jack of Newbury, Thomas of Reading,* and *The Gentle Craft* (all c.1597)—relating to the clothier's, weaver's, and shoemaker's crafts respectively. Vivid and humorous, they reproduce bourgeois scenes of contemporary London. Their popularity indicates a certain fatigue with the elaborate prose of authors like John LYLY.

De Long, George Washington, 1844–81, American arctic explorer, b. New York City, grad. Annapolis,

1865. In 1873 he was assigned to the *Juniata,* which was sent to the arctic to search for C. F. Hall's expedition on the *Polaris.* In 1879, backed by the younger James Gordon BENNETT and under the auspices of the U.S. navy, he sailed from San Francisco on the *Jeannette* with a plan to penetrate Bering Strait and attempt a dash to the North Pole. There was then a theory that a current from Japan would speed them north. Instead, the vessel was caught in the ice pack and drifted nearly two years until it was crushed and sank. The men had abandoned ship with provisions, sledges, and boats and now set out southward for Siberia. After reaching open water and embarking in the boats, they were separated. One boat was lost. A second, with De Long in command landed, but only two men sent ahead for aid survived. The third boat, commanded by George W. MELVILLE, reached the Lena delta and was rescued. The next year Melville returned and found the bodies of De Long and his companions, who had perished from cold and hunger. The expedition had proved definitely that Wrangel Island was not the southern tip of a northern continent and had proved essential facts about the polar drift. In traversing nearly 50,000 sq mi (129,500 sq km) of Arctic Ocean territory, De Long had proved that the continental shelf of northern Siberia extends far northward and is dotted by numerous small islands. The expedition was also a demonstration of heroism. De Long's diary was edited by his widow as *The Voyage of the Jeannette* (1884). Melville's account was published as *In the Lena Delta* (1885). See Edward Ellsberg, *Hell on Ice* (1938), a fictionalized account; Emma De Long, *Explorer's Wife* (1938); Adolf Hoehling, *The Jeannette Expedition* (1967, repr. 1969).

Delorme, Marion (märyôN' dəlôrm'), 1613?–1650, French courtesan. Her house was a meeting place for Mazarin's enemies during the FRONDE. Alleged to have married CINQ MARS in secret, she is the chief figure in Victor Hugo's play *Marion Delorme* and a character in Vigny's novel *Cinq-Mars.*

Delorme or **de l'Orme, Philibert** (fēlĕbĕr'), c.1510–1570, French architect. Delorme was one of the greatest architects of the Renaissance, but unfortunately most of his work has been destroyed. Having traveled in Italy from 1533 to 1536, he introduced into France a form of classicism that endured until the mid-18th cent. As court architect to Francis I and Henry II, he designed the tomb of Francis I at Saint-Denis, a chapel at Villers-Cotterets, Château Neuf at Saint-Germain-en-Laye, and part of the palace of Fontainebleau. For Diane de Poitiers, mistress of Henry II, he planned (c.1550) the superb château at Anet. Upon the death of Henry II, Delorme fell into disgrace. During this time he wrote a treatise on architecture, *Nouvelles Inventions pour bien bastir et à petits frais* (1561), in which he proposed that a modern French order be invented that would suit local building conditions. In 1563 he was restored to favor by Catherine de' Medici, who commissioned him to design the Tuileries and the great gallery at Chenonceaux. See study by Anthony Blunt (1958).

Delos (dē'lŏs), island, c.1 sq mi (2.6 sq km), SE Greece, in the Aegean Sea, smallest of the CYCLADES. In Greek mythology, Leto gave birth to Apollo and Artemis on Delos; and the island was particularly sacred to Apollo. Delos was of great commercial and political importance in antiquity. The temple of Apollo there was the seat of the treasury of the DELIAN LEAGUE until it was removed (454 B.C.) to Athens. In the 2d cent. B.C. Delos had a flourishing slave market which continued to thrive even after a slave rebellion c.130 B.C. In 88 B.C. the island was sacked by Mithridates VI of Pontus; it never recovered and Delos was abandoned toward the end of the 1st cent. B.C. It is virtually uninhabited today. Excavations conducted since the 1870s by the French School (Athens) have revealed remains of temples, commercial buildings, theaters, private houses, and numerous inscriptions.

de los Angeles, Victoria (dā lōs än'hālās), 1923–, Spanish soprano, b. Barcelona. After a concert debut in Madrid in 1944, de los Angeles toured Scandinavia, France, England, and South America. Her debut in the United States was made at Carnegie Hall in 1950, and she joined the Metropolitan Opera Company the same year, performing there until 1961. Since then she has toured extensively. Her performances of Catalan folk-song are especially notable.

Delphi (dĕl'fī), locality in Phocis, Greece, near the foot of the south slope of Mt. Parnassus, c.6 mi (10 km) northeast of the port of Cirrha. It was the seat of the Delphic ORACLE, the most famous and most powerful of ancient Greece. The oracle originated in the worship of an earth-goddess, and later legend ascribed it to GAEA. It passed to APOLLO; some stories say he won it by killing the Python, others that it descended to him peacefully through Themis and Phoebe. The Delphic oracle was the preeminent shrine of Apollo, but in winter, when Apollo was absent among the Hyperboreans, it was sacred to Dionysus, who was said to be buried there. The oracle was housed in the great temple to Apollo, first built in the 6th cent. B.C. (it was destroyed and rebuilt at least twice). The oracular messages were spoken by a priestess seated on a golden tripod, who uttered sounds in a frenzied trance; they were interpreted to the questioner by a priest, who usually spoke in verse. Delphi was unique in its universal position in the otherwise fragmented political and social life of Greece. It was the meeting place of the Amphictyonic League, the most important league of Greek city-states, and also the site of the PYTHIAN GAMES. Persons seeking the help of the oracle brought rich gifts, and the shrine grew very wealthy. The prestige and influence of the Delphic oracle prevailed for centuries through all of Greece. During Hellenistic times, however, the importance of the oracle declined. Delphi was frequently pillaged from early Roman times, and the sanctuary fell into decay. One of the art works excavated there is the beautiful 5th-century bronze statue called the Delphic Charioteer (now at the Archaeological Mus., Delphi, Greece).

Delphic oracle: see DELPHI, Greece.

delphinium: see LARKSPUR.

Delray Beach, resort city (1970 pop. 19,366), Palm Beach co., SE Fla., on the Atlantic coast; settled 1895, inc. 1911. Mostly residential, Delray Beach is also the trade center for a citrus-fruit and vegetable-growing region. The city's vast flower farms are noted especially for chrysanthemums and gladiolas. Florida Atlantic Univ. is just S of Delray Beach.

Del Rio (rē'ō), city (1970 pop. 21,330), seat of Val Verde co., W Texas, a port of entry on the Rio Grande opposite Ciudad Acuña, Mexico; founded 1868, inc. 1911. It is the marketing and distributing center for a region known for its sheep, lambs, wool, and mohair. Farms irrigated from the nearby San Felipe Springs also yield alfalfa, truck crops, fruits, and especially grapes. The international bridge to Mexico has made Del Rio important in tourist traffic. Laughlin Air Force Base, a jet training command, is to the east. The spectacular S-shaped international Amistad (Friendship) Dam (dedicated 1969) and its lake on the Rio Grande are 12 mi (19 km) northeast.

Delsarte, François (fräNswä' dĕlsärt'), 1811–71, French teacher of acting and singing. He studied singing (1825–29) at the Paris Conservatoire and appeared as a tenor at the Opéra-Comique, but faulty training had damaged his voice. Delsarte formulated certain principles of aesthetics that he applied to the teaching of dramatic expression. He set up rules coordinating the voice with the gestures of all parts of the body. In 1839 he opened his first *cours d'esthétique appliqué,* and his advice was sought by many famous artists, e.g., Rachel, Henriette Sontag, and W. C. Macready. Steele MACKAYE studied with him in Delsarte's last years and brought to the United States the Delsarte system, to which he had added many of his own ideas, including elements of gymnastics. Some of Delsarte's writings are included in the compilation *Delsarte System of Oratory* (1893). See Percy MacKaye, *Epoch: The Life of Steele MacKaye* (1927).

delta [from triangular shape of the Nile delta, like the Greek letter *delta*], the alluvial plain formed at the mouth of a river where the stream loses velocity and drops part of its load of sediment. No delta is formed if the coast is sinking or if there is an ocean or tidal current strong enough to prevent deposition of sediment. A deltaic plain is usually very fertile but subject to floods. The three main varieties of deltas are the arcuate delta (as that of the Nile), the bird's-foot delta (as that of the Mississippi), and the cuspate delta (as that of the Tiber). The Nile, Mississippi, Orinoco, Niger, Rhine, Rhône, Danube, Kuban, Volga, Ural, Amu Darya, Lena, Indus, Ganges and Brahmaputra, Irrawaddy, Tigris and Euphrates, and Huang Ho (Yellow) rivers are among those that have formed large deltas.

Deluc, Jean André (zhäN äNdrā' dəlük'), 1727–1817, Swiss geologist. During the first half of his life he was engaged mainly in business in Switzerland. He also made scientific excursions in the Alps on whose natural history he was an authority. When his commercial affairs failed in 1773, he emigrated to England where he became reader to Queen Charlotte. He held the doctrine of CATASTROPHISM to explain present geological formations, opposing the view that present processes have acted continuously during past ages. He also made contributions in the field of meteorology.

Deluge (dĕl'yo͞oj), in the Bible, the overwhelming flood that covered the earth and destroyed every living thing except the family of NOAH and the creatures in his ARK. Gen. 6–8; Isa. 54.9; Mat. 24.38; Luke 17.27; Heb. 11.7; 1 Peter 3.20; 2 Peter 2.5. Archaeology has yielded little trace of the biblical flood. Flood stories resembling the biblical story are found in the folklore of many races—American Indians, Fiji Islanders, and Australian aborigines. The earliest known of these stories is Sumerian, one form being found in the record of Berossus (3d cent. B.C.), another on a tablet of the Gilgamesh epic of at least 2000 B.C. See DEUCALION and UR.

delusion, false belief based upon a misinterpretation of reality. It is not, as in a hallucination, a belief or perception with no basis in reality. Delusions vary in intensity, and occasional delusions are not uncommon in normal people. Fixed delusions, however, are characteristic of paranoid reactions and some types of SCHIZOPHRENIA; PARANOIA is characterized by a systematized and elaborate delusional system. The common psychotic delusions include persecution delusions, in which the individual falsely believes himself to be the target of another person's hostility; influence delusions, in which the individual feels he is being interfered with, or controlled by, some remote force, such as cosmic rays or electricity; and delusions of grandeur, in which the individual imagines himself an unappreciated person of great importance. Delusions play an important role in the development of mass hysteria and are of importance to the social psychologist.

Delvaux, Laurent (lōräN' dĕlvō'), 1695–1778, Flemish sculptor. After studying in Rome, Delvaux developed a style that combined French neoclassic and Italian baroque elements. Ornate in the extreme, his works express a marked coldness. Delvaux's *Hercules* is in the Royal Museum of Fine Arts, Brussels.

Delvaux, Paul, 1897–, Belgian painter. Delvaux, influenced by Magritte and Chirico, creates meticulous surreal compositions based on Renaissance ideas of perspective and peopled with self-absorbed somnambulists. Often containing an ironic eroticism, Delvaux's visionary paintings allude to the double standards of Victorian sexual morality. His *Venus Asleep* (1944) is in the Tate Gallery, London.

De Mabuse, Jan: see MABUSE, JAN DE.

demand and supply: see SUPPLY AND DEMAND.

Demas (dē'măs), companion who forsook Paul. Col. 4.14; 2 Tim. 4.10.

Demavend, peak, Iran: see DAMAVAND.

dementia (dĭmĕn'shə) [Lat.,=being out of the mind], reduction of intellectual faculties, however caused, resulting in apathy, confusion, and stupor. In the 17th cent. the term was synonymous with INSANITY; more recently, the term *dementia praecox* has been used as a synonym for SCHIZOPHRENIA. *Dementia* stresses the irreversibility of the intellectual defect and is not generally applied to states of intellectual deterioration that are dynamically determined and may be overcome. Dementia is also distinct from the limited degree of intelligence of the feeble-minded, imbeciles, and idiots in that it entails the deterioration of a previously intact intelligence.

Demerara (dĕmərâr'ə), river, c.200 mi (320 km) long, rising in the Guiana Highlands, E Guyana, and flowing N to the Atlantic Ocean. Georgetown, Guyana's chief port, is at the river's mouth. The Demerara is navigable for oceangoing vessels to Mackenzie, an important exporting center for bauxite and kaolin.

Demerol: see MEPERIDINE; ANALGESIC.

demesne (dĭmān'), land under FEUDALISM kept by the lord for his own use and occupation as distinguished from that granted to tenants. Initially the demesne lands were worked by the serfs in payment of the feudal debt. As the serfs' labor service came to be commuted to money payments, the demesne lands were often cultivated by paid laborers. Eventually many of the demesne lands were leased out either on a perpetual, and therefore hereditary, or a temporary, and therefore renewable, basis so that many peasants functioned virtually as free proprietors after having paid their fixed rents. In England the term *ancient demesne,* sometimes shortened to *demesne,* referred to those lands that were held by the crown at the time (1066) of William the Conqueror and were recorded in the Domesday Book.

The term *demesne* also referred to the demesne of the crown, or royal demesne, which consisted of those lands reserved for the crown at the time of the original distribution of landed property. The royal demesne could be increased, for example, as a result of forfeiture. The lands were managed by stewards of the crown and were not given out in fief.

Demeter (dĭmē'tər), in Greek religion, goddess of harvest and fertility; daughter of Cronus and Rhea. She was the mother of Persephone by Zeus. When Pluto abducted Persephone, Demeter grieved so inconsolably that the earth became barren through her neglect. Searching for her daughter, she wandered to Eleusis, where the ELEUSINIAN MYSTERIES were inaugurated in her honor. She revealed to Triptolemus, an Eleusinian, the art of growing and using corn. The Thesmophoria, a fertility festival held in her honor at Athens, was attended only by women. The Romans identified her with Ceres.

Demetrius I (Demetrius Poliorcetes) (dĭmē'trēəs pŏl"ēôrsē'tēz), c.337–283 B.C., king of Macedon. The son of ANTIGONUS I, he proved himself a very able commander in his father's wars, particularly against Ptolemy I. Though Ptolemy defeated him at Gaza in 312 B.C., Demetrius was able to expel Cassander from Athens; he then defeated Ptolemy off Salamis and took Cyprus. Although he had huge armaments, including new weapons of assault, he failed (305 B.C.) to take Rhodes by sea. When Cassander, Seleucus I, and Lysimachus, fearing the power of Antigonus, allied themselves against him, Antigonus and Demetrius were badly defeated in the battle of Ipsus in 301 B.C., and Antigonus was killed. Demetrius later became reconciled with Seleucus I and regained Athens for himself in 295 B.C. In order to obtain the throne of Macedon he murdered his competitors, including the sons of Cassander, and succeeded (294 B.C.) to the throne. He had his father's ambition to conquer all Asia, but his enemies united against him, and when Lysimachus and Pyrrhus invaded Macedonia he was forced (285 B.C.) to take refuge with Seleucus, who held him until he died. His son, Antigonus II, made good his claim to the throne of Macedon.

Demetrius II, d. 229 B.C., king of Macedon (239–229 B.C.), son of Antigonus II. His reign was a confusion of wars and invasions, mostly concerned with possession of Epirus. The Aetolian League and the Achaean League united against him and defeated him. His heir was his son Philip V.

Demetrius I (Demetrius Soter) (sō'tər), c.187–150 B.C., king of ancient Syria (162–150 B.C.), son of Seleucus IV. He was sent as a hostage to Rome, where he remained during the reigns of his father and his uncle Antiochus IV. After Antiochus died, he was succeeded by his son Antiochus V, but Demetrius escaped (162 B.C.), killed his cousin, and took the throne. He put down the revolt of the general Timarchus in Babylon and set out to crush the Maccabees. The usurper Alexander Balas rose against Demetrius and was supported by the Maccabean party as well as by Egypt and Pergamum. Demetrius was defeated in battle.

Demetrius II (Demetrius Nicator) (nīkā'tər), d. c.125 B.C., king of ancient Syria, son of Demetrius I. He was aided against the usurper, Alexander Balas, by Ptolemy VI (Ptolemy Philometer). He married Ptolemy's daughter, Cleopatra Thea, even though she was already married to Alexander Balas. Demetrius ascended the throne in 146 B.C., but in fighting against the Parthians in 141 he was captured. Before his capture Demetrius reaffirmed Judaean independence, freeing the Jews from Syrian taxation. Tryphon, who served under Alexander Balas as governor of Antioch, had revolted and had put Alexander Balas' infant son, Antiochus Dionysius, on the throne. Two years later Tryphon murdered the boy and took the throne himself. Demetrius, coming back from prison, regained the throne in 128 B.C. He soon lost it again and died in battle at Tyre, fighting a war with Egypt.

Demetrius. **1** Silversmith of Ephesus who stirred up a riot against Paul. Acts 19.23–41. **2** Disciple commended in 3 John 12.

Demetrius, in Russian history: see DMITRI.

Demetrius Phalereus (fəlĕr'o͞os, fəlĕr'ēəs) [Lat.,= of Phalerum], d. c.280 B.C., Athenian orator. He was one of the first Peripatetics and also wrote extensively in history, rhetoric, and literary criticism. He was governor of Athens (317–307 B.C.) under CASSANDER. In 307 B.C., when Demetrius I took Athens, Demetrius Phalereus was overthrown. He escaped to Egypt, where he rose in the favor of Ptolemy I, to whom he is said to have suggested a library. On the accession of Ptolemy Philadelphus, Demetrius again went into exile. He died soon afterward.

De Mézières y Clugny, Athanase (ätänäz' də māzyĕr' ē klünē'), c.1715–1779, explorer and Indian agent in Spanish Louisiana, b. Paris. He went to Louisiana c.1733. When France ceded the territory to Spain he stayed on in the Spanish service. Made lieutenant governor of the Natchitoches dist. (1769), De Mézières, by judicious use of his control of the Indian trade and by tact, kindness, and patience, won the friendship of the previously hostile tribes of the Red River valley and neighboring regions and concluded treaties with them. His valuable reports and diaries are translated in H. E. Bolton's *Athanase de Mézières* (1914).

De Mille, Agnes (də mĭl), 1908?–, American choreographer and dancer, b. New York City; daughter of film director W. C. De Mille and niece of Cecil B. De Mille. After her concert debut in 1928, she went to London and worked with Antony Tudor. There she created the first important American ballet, *Rodeo* (1942). Influenced by the work of Martha Graham and also by the techniques of film-making, she brought ballet form to musical comedy in *Oklahoma!* (1943), and thereafter in such musicals as *Bloomer Girl* (1944), *Carousel* (1945), *Brigadoon* (1947), and *Paint Your Wagon* (1951). She has created dances for the American Ballet Theatre, notably *Fall River Legend* (1948), and for films. De Mille wrote *To a Young Dancer* (1962) and *The Book of the Dance* (1963). See her autobiographies, *Dance to the Piper* (1952), *And Promenade Home* (1958), and *Speak to Me, Dance with Me* (1973).

De Mille, Cecil B., 1881–1959, American movie director and producer, b. Ashfield, Mass. In 1913, together with Samuel Goldwyn, he made the first feature-length film in Hollywood, *The Squaw Man.* In 1915 he came into prominence with his first "spectacle" film, *Carmen.* His films were marked by their epic style and their theatricality, by their mass crowd scenes, and often by their biblical themes. In 1953 he won an Academy Award for *The Greatest Show on Earth.* His biggest and most popular production, *The Ten Commandments* (1956), was a remake of his 1923 film. See his autobiography, ed. by Donald Hayne (1959); biography by Gabe Essoe and Raymond Lee (1970); study by Gene Ringgold and DeWitt Bodeen (1969).

Demirel, Süleyman (sülämän' dĕmĭrĕl'), 1924–, Turkish political leader. A successful engineer, he became leader of the Justice party in 1964, deputy prime minister in Feb., 1965, and prime minister in Oct., 1965. His failure to halt civil anarchy in the form of student riots, leftist agitation, and political terrorism forced the resignation of his centrist government in 1971.

demiurge (dĕm'ēûrj") [Gr.=workman, craftsman], name given by Plato in a half-mythological passage in the *Timaeus* to God the Creator. In GNOSTICISM the Demiurge, creator of the material world, was not God but the Archon, or chief of the lowest order of spirits or aeons. According to the Gnostics, the Demiurge was able to endow man only with psyche (sensuous soul), the pneuma (rational soul) having been added by God. The Gnostics identified the Demiurge with the Jehovah of the Hebrews. In philosophy the term is used to denote a divinity who is the builder of the universe rather than its creator.

democracy [Gr.,=rule of the people], term originating in ancient Greece to designate a government where the people share in directing the activities of the state, as distinct from governments controlled by a single class, select group, or autocrat. The definition of democracy has been expanded, however, to describe a philosophy that insists on the right and the capacity of a people, acting either directly or through representatives, to control their institutions for their own purposes. Such a philosophy places a high value on the equality of individuals and would free people as far as possible from restraints not self-imposed. It insists that necessary restraints be imposed only by the consent of the majority and that they conform to the principle of equality. Democracy first flourished in the Greek CITY-STATE, reaching its fullest expression in ancient ATHENS. There the citizens, as members of the assembly, participated directly in the making of their laws. A system of rotation in executive office existed that gave all citizens their turn. Jurors, who acted in the capacity of both judges and jurors, were chosen by lot. A democracy of this sort was possible only in a small state where the people were politically educated. In addition, it was a limited democracy, since the majority of people in Athens were slaves or noncitizens. Athenian democracy fell before the imperial idea, as did other ancient manifestations of democracy in the early Italian cities and in the early church. In this period and in the Middle Ages, certain concepts crucial to modern Western democracy were developed. One idea was REPRESENTATION. Doctrines of natural law developed into the idea of natural rights, i.e., that all people have certain rights, such as self-preservation, that cannot be taken from them. The idea became allied with that of contract. According to this view, rulers and people were bound to each other by a contract involving reciprocal obligations. If the sovereign failed in his duties or transgressed on natural rights, the people could take back the sovereignty with which they had invested him. This idea, as postulated by John LOCKE, strongly influenced the development of British parliamentary democracy and, as defined in the SOCIAL CONTRACT theory of Jean Jacques ROUSSEAU, helped form the philosophical justification for the American Revolution and the French Revolution. English settlers in America faced frontier conditions that emphasized the importance of the individual and helped somewhat in breaking down class distinctions and prejudices. These and other factors led to a democratic political structure marked by a high degree of individualism and civil liberty. The 19th cent. may be characterized generally as a period when, the philosophy of democracy having triumphed in many Western countries, emphasis was placed on broadening the franchise and improving the machinery for enabling the will of the people to be more fully and directly expressed. The idea that equality of opportunity can be maintained through political democracy alone has long been challenged by socialists and others, who insist that economic democracy through economic equality and public ownership of the major means of production is the only foundation upon which a true political democracy can be erected. In the 20th cent., almost all governments have labeled themselves democracies. However, the classic form of Western democracy, featuring competing political parties and stressing individual rights, has not developed in many areas of the world outside of North America and Western Europe, except for India and Japan. See Harold Laski, *Democracy in Crisis* (1933, repr. 1969); Ernest Barker, *Reflections on Government* (1942, repr. 1967); Walter Lippman, *Essays in the Public Philosophy* (1955); R. A. Dahl, *A Preface to Democratic Theory* (1956, repr. 1963); Sidney Hook, *The Paradoxes of Freedom* (1962); Leslie Lipson, *The Democratic Civilization* (1964, repr. 1969); Herbert Agar, *The Perils of Democracy* (1965); Richard Ketchum, *What Is Democracy?* (1968); Carole Pateman, *Participation and Democratic Theory* (1970); Carl Cohen, *Democracy* (1971); Dorothy Pickles, *Democracy* (1971); Marvin Zimmerman, *Contemporary Problems of Democracy* (1972); M. I. Finley, *Democracy Ancient and Modern* (1973); C. B. MacPherson, *Democratic Theory* (1973).

Democratic party, American political party. When political alignments first emerged in George Washington's administration, opposing factions were led by Alexander HAMILTON and Thomas JEFFERSON. In the basic disagreement over the nature and functions of government and of society, the Jeffersonians advocated a society based on the small farmer; they opposed strong centralized government and were suspicious of urban commercial interests. Their ideals—opposed to those of the FEDERALIST PARTY—came to be known as Jeffersonian democracy, based in large part on faith in the virtue and ability of the common man and the limitation of the powers of the Federal government. This group of anti-Federalists, who called themselves Republicans or Democratic Republicans (the name was not fixed as Democratic until 1828), supported many of the ideals of the French Revolution and opposed close relations with Great Britain. Led by Jefferson and his ally James MADISON, the group had become a nationwide party by 1800, winning the support of Aaron BURR and George CLINTON in New York, of Benjamin RUSH and Albert GALLATIN in Pennsylvania, and of most influential politicians in the South. Jefferson became President in 1800 in an election that has often been called a turning point in American history. With this election emerged an alliance between Southern agrarians and Northern city dwellers, an alliance that grew to be the dominating coalition of the party. With Madison and James MONROE succeeding Jefferson, the party's "Virginia dynasty" held the presidency until 1824. As the Federalist party waned, politics came to consist mainly of feuds within the Democratic Republican organization, such as the opposition of the QUIDS to Madison's election (1808) and the peace ticket led by De

Witt CLINTON (1812). By 1820 the party dominated the nation so completely that Monroe was reelected without opposition. But the foundations for political regrouping were being laid. In 1824 the electoral vote was split between Andrew JACKSON, Henry CLAY, and John Quincy ADAMS; when the election went into the House of Representatives, Clay threw his support to Adams, who won. Jackson was elected in 1828 and in 1832 (when his followers held the first national convention of the Democratic party), but in the great political debates of his administrations, most notably over his dissolution of the Bank of the United States and the NULLIFICATION controversy, opposition to him ultimately coalesced in the WHIG PARTY. Until 1860 the Democrats won all the presidential elections except those of 1840 and 1848, electing Martin VAN BUREN, James K. POLK, Franklin PIERCE, and James BUCHANAN. During this period political debate centered more and more on the bitter question of slavery that was dividing the North and South. With the demise of the Whig party in the election of 1852 and the emergence of the sectional, antislavery REPUBLICAN PARTY in 1854 (succeeding the FREE-SOIL PARTY), the Democrats remained the sole national party. The vital question of the decade between 1850 and 1860 concerned slavery in the territories, and on this issue the Democratic party divided sharply. One group, mainly Northern, led by Stephen A. DOUGLAS, championed the doctrine of POPULAR SOVEREIGNTY, which held that the inhabitants of the territory should decide whether it would be slave or free. Other Northern Democrats (mostly the old BARNBURNERS) swung over to the new antislavery parties. Southern Democrats, led by Robert TOOMBS and Jefferson DAVIS among others, and buttressed by the Supreme Court's decision in the DRED SCOTT CASE, held that slavery must be protected in the territories. At the Democratic Convention of 1860, held in Charleston in April, the party split. The Northern Democrats nominated Douglas, and the Southern Democrats chose John C. BRECKINRIDGE, thus facilitating the victory of Abraham Lincoln. During the Civil War some members of the party were openly sympathetic toward the South (see COPPERHEADS), and the Republicans in postwar years attempted with some success to depict the Democrats as the party of rebellion. Southern leaders associated the defeat of the South and RECONSTRUCTION with the Republican party, and the eleven states of the old Confederacy, with few exceptions, voted Democratic thereafter, giving rise to the "solid South." The years from 1860 to 1912 were lean ones for the party on the national level. In 1876 the Democratic candidate, Samuel J. TILDEN, won a plurality of the popular vote, but the disputed electoral votes of Florida, South Carolina, and Louisiana (states still under Republican control) were awarded to the Republican Rutherford B. HAYES, who became President. Thus only the victories of Grover CLEVELAND (1884 and 1892) broke the Republican control of the presidency during this period. Yet the Democrats often controlled one or both of the houses of Congress in this era and had wide success in the states. In general policy the two parties had much the same complexion from the end of Reconstruction in 1877 until 1896. Traditionally the Democrats were more the party of agrarianism and cheap money and the opponents of protective tariffs, and even the most conservative Democrats were opposed to the control of industry and trade by the trusts and big business. However, radical economic and agrarian schemes were as distasteful to many Democrats as they were to the Republicans. The problem of how to deal with the agrarian appeal of the POPULIST PARTY and with the question of FREE SILVER split the Democrats in Cleveland's second administration. In the convention of 1896 a radical group succeeded in nominating William Jennings BRYAN for President on a platform calling for free silver and supporting other Populist demands. In the election the party suffered its worst popular defeat since 1872, and it appeared doomed by the impossibility of reconciling its diverse elements—Southern farmers, Western farmers, urban industrial classes, and a wealthy few. The Democrats regained the presidency in 1912 under Woodrow WILSON, but only because the candidacy of Theodore Roosevelt on the PROGRESSIVE PARTY ticket diminished the Republican vote. Under Wilson's progressive policy, known as the New Freedom, some fruitful reform was enacted, but the idealism he had inspired waned after World War I. Democratic presidential candidates were defeated in 1920 and in 1924. In 1928 the urban Democrats secured the presidential nomination of Alfred E. SMITH, a Roman Catholic. The issues of religion and prohibition divided the party, and Smith was easily defeated by Herbert Hoover. Nevertheless, the Democrats made key inroads into important urban voting blocs. The economic depression that began in 1929 helped to sweep the Democrats and Franklin Delano ROOSEVELT into office in 1932, and with his New Deal the Democrats were again identified as the party of reform. Roosevelt was reelected in 1936 with the largest plurality in the nation's history, and in 1940 he became the first U.S. President to be elected to a third term. After leading the country for three years in World War II, he was reelected for a fourth term in 1944. Upon his death (April, 1945) he was succeeded by Harry S. TRUMAN. In 1948, despite the withdrawal from the Democratic convention of many Southern Democrats (whose subsequent nominee was J. Strom THURMOND) and despite the candidacy of Henry A. WALLACE, Truman defeated the Republican candidate, Thomas E. Dewey. The Democratic nominee in 1952, Adlai E. STEVENSON, was defeated by Dwight D. Eisenhower, who again defeated Stevenson in 1956. In 1960, John F. KENNEDY narrowly defeated the Republican candidate, Richard M. Nixon, in the presidential race. Upon Kennedy's assassination (1963), Lyndon B. JOHNSON became president and won a landslide victory in 1964 against the conservative Republican Barry Goldwater. His administration was marked by much social welfare and civil rights legislation but above all by the Vietnam War, which split the party and contributed largely to the defeat of Hubert H. HUMPHREY by Richard Nixon in 1968. Another factor in the defeat of Humphrey was the strong third-party showing of the conservative Southern Democrat George C. WALLACE, who ran on the ticket of the American Independent party. The modern Democratic party represents an uneasy alliance among labor, urban, and ethnic minority groups, intellectuals and middle-class reformers, and the traditional Southern Democrats. Wallace's showing in 1968 and a marked swing in the South toward the Republicans showed the strength of Southern disaffection with the national Democratic policies on civil rights, segregation, and economic issues. In 1972 the balance in the party was further upset with the nomination of George MCGOVERN, whose defense and social welfare views proved unacceptable to many labor unions and other groups, while the South continued to swing its support to national Republican candidates. The result was a landslide victory for President Nixon, although the Democrats retained their solid majorities in Congress. The political scandals that emerged during the second Nixon administration (see WATERGATE AFFAIR) and the serious economic problems of the country were important causes for the Democratic gains in the 1974 election; Democrats increased their majorities in both houses of Congress and at the state and local levels. See Charles A. Beard, *Economic Origins of Jeffersonian Democracy* (1915); Arthur M. Schlesinger, Jr., *The Age of Jackson* (1945); H. J. Clancy, *The Democratic Party* (1962); Wilfred Binkley, *American Political Parties* (4th ed. 1962); Paul Ferguson, *The American Party Drama* (1966).

Democritus (dĭmŏk'rĭtəs), c.460–c.370 B.C., Greek philosopher of Abdera; pupil of Leucippus. His theory of the nature of the physical world was the most radical and scientific attempted up to his time. He avoided the abstractions of his predecessors, Anaxagoras (mind) and Empedocles (harmony and discord), by employing consistent mechanistic postulates that required no supernatural intervention. He held that all things were composed of atoms; these he asserted to be tiny particles, imperceptible to the senses, composed of exactly the same matter but different in size, shape, and weight. They were underived, indivisible, and indestructible. Democritus postulated the constant motion of atoms and, on this basis, explained the creation of worlds. He held that the whirling motion caused by the falling of atoms resulted in aggregations—the heavier atoms forming the earth and the lighter ones the heavenly bodies. He taught that what the senses perceive as quality is merely the result of a specific quantitative distribution of atoms. Sense perception yields only confused knowledge, telling us merely how things affect us; thought alone can apprehend the nature of things. Democritus' ethics were moderately hedonistic, teaching that the true end of life is happiness achieved in inner tranquility. See A. T. Cole, *Democritus and the Sources of Greek Anthropology* (1967).

demodulation: see MODULATION.

demography, science of human POPULATION. Demography represents a fundamental approach to the understanding of human society. Its primary tasks are to ascertain the number of people in a given area, to determine what change that number represents from a previous census, to explain the change, and on that basis to estimate the future trend. The demographer also traces the origins of population changes and studies their impact. Demographers compile and analyze data that are useful for understanding various social systems, for example, the average age at first marriage in a given society, or the level of employment.

De Moivre, Abraham: see MOIVRE, ABRAHAM DE.

demon, supernatural being, generally malevolent in character. In general, the more civilized pagan societies came to consider demons as powerful, supernatural beings who lacked the dignity of gods and who, depending on the circumstance, might be either benevolent or malevolent in their dealings with men. Some demons, like the Greek Pan, were nature spirits; others were guardians of the home or fields or watchers over travelers; still others were spirits of disease and insanity or dream spirits. Some demons were considered to be intermediaries between men and the gods. It was not until the development of late Hebraic and Christian thinking that demons came to represent the unqualified malevolence so common in European demonology of the 16th and 17th cent. This period was a high point in the study of demons, in the speculation on their nature, number, and specific fiendishness. The list compiled in 1589 by a demonologist named Binsfield was considered to be highly authoritative; in it he listed the following major demons and their particular evils: Lucifer (pride), Mammon (avarice), Asmodeus or Ashmodai (lechery), Satan (anger), Beelzebub (gluttony), Leviathan (envy), and Belphegor (sloth). The widespread and ancient belief in demons is still a strong force in many regions of the world today. See SPIRITISM; WITCHCRAFT. See R. H. Robbins, *The Encyclopedia of Witchcraft and Demonology* (1959); H. A. Relly, *The Devil, Demonology, and Witchcraft* (1968).

demonetization, governmental withdrawal of the monetary quality from particular coinage or precious metal. By demonetization former money is no longer legal tender, although in certain cases it may still be used as money of exchange, i.e., the actual metallic value may sometimes be accepted in discharge of indebtedness. However, such was not the case with regard to the demonetization (1933) of U.S. gold. The demonetization law stipulated that gold may not lawfully be used in domestic exchange, although it may be purchased for shipment abroad. Other instances of demonetization were the American conversion (1873) of silver into money of exchange and the similar British conversion (1889) of pre-Victorian gold coins. See MONEY.

De Morgan, Augustus, 1806–71, English mathematician and logician, b. India. A noted teacher, he was professor of mathematics (1828–31, 1836–66) at University College (now part of the Univ. of London) and a founder and first president (1865) of the London Mathematical Society. Known as a reformer of logic, he developed a new logic of relations that he summarized in *Syllabus of a Proposed System of Logic* (1860). His works include *An Essay on Probabilities* (1838), *Formal Logic* (1847), *Trigonometry and Double Algebra* (1849), and *A Budget of Paradoxes* (1872).

De Morgan, William Frend, 1839–1917, English artist and novelist; son of Augustus De Morgan. A famous potter, he designed glass and tiles and rediscovered an old process of making colored lusterware. When he was 66 he retired from business and turned to writing novels, which were quite popular and brought him a large income. They include *Joseph Vance* (1906) and *When Ghost Meets Ghost* (1914).

Demosthenes (dĭmŏs'thənēz), 384?–322 B.C., Greek orator, generally considered the greatest of the Greek orators. He was a pupil of Isaeus, and—although the story of his putting pebbles in his mouth to improve his voice is only a legend—he seems to have been forced to overcome a weak voice and delivery. After years of private practice in law, he became a political orator in 351 B.C. when he delivered the first of three *Philippics*. Philip II of Macedon had been steadily building power, and Demosthenes saw clearly the danger to Greek liberty in the great Macedonian state. The *Philippics* (the second in 344, the third in 341) and the three *Olynthiacs* (349), in which he urged aid for Olynthus against Philip, were all directed toward arousing Greece against the conqueror. The third of the *Philippics* is generally considered the finest of his orations. In *On the Peace* (346) Demosthenes urged an end to the Phocian War. In 343 he accused his rival, Aeschines, of accepting Macedonian bribes in a speech entitled (as was Aeschines' defense) *On the False Legation.* Philip triumphed in the battle of Chaeronea (338), and Demosthenes' cause was lost. Although he had many rivals, he was greatly honored by his admirers, but a proposal by Ctesiphon to give Demosthenes a gold crown caused Aeschines to bring suit. Demosthenes roundly defended his own career and attacked that of Aeschines in *On the Crown* (330). The verdict was in favor of Demosthenes. Later he was involved in a complex and obscure affair involving money taken by one of the lieutenants of Alexander the Great; it ended with Demosthenes in exile. After the death of Alexander he was recalled and attempted to build Greek strength to throw off the yoke of Macedon, but he was unsuccessful and Antipater triumphed. Demosthenes fled and took poison before he could be captured. See A. W. Pickard-Cambridge, *Demosthenes and the Last Days of Greek Freedom* (1914); C. D. Adams, *Demosthenes and His Influence* (1927, repr. 1963); W. W. Jaeger, *Demosthenes: The Origin and Growth of His Policy* (1938, repr. 1963).

demotic: see HIEROGLYPHIC.

Dempsey, William Harrison (Jack Dempsey), 1895–, American boxer, b. Manassa, Colo. Dempsey, called the "Manassa mauler," won (1919) the world's heavyweight boxing championship by knocking out Jess Willard at Toledo, Ohio, and lost (1926) the title to James J. (Gene) Tunney at Philadelphia. Seeking to regain the crown at Chicago in 1927, Dempsey again lost a 10-round decision to Tunney in the fight that involved the controversial "long count" in the seventh round. He retired, but made a brief comeback tour in 1931–32. He later devoted himself to business interests and sports promotion. A popular fighter, Dempsey drew enormous crowds, and he became the greatest earner in boxing history; his second bout with Tunney set a record ($2,658,660) in gate receipts. See his autobiography, *Round by Round* (written in collaboration with M. M. Stearns, 1940).

Demuth, Charles (dā'mo͞oth), 1883–1935, American watercolor painter, b. Lancaster, Pa. At the age of 20 he began his art study under William Chase at the Pennsylvania Academy of the Fine Arts. In 1907 and again in 1912, Demuth visited Europe. On returning to the United States he began a series of line-and-wash illustrations for works of Zola, Poe, and Henry James and made drawings of vaudeville performers. He is perhaps best known for his beautiful translucent flower and fruit studies in watercolor. Demuth was one of the first painters to draw inspiration from the geometric shapes of machines and modern technology. There are several works by him in the Art Institute, Chicago, and many in the Columbus Gallery of Fine Arts, Ohio. See biography by Emily Farnham (1971).

Denain (dənăN'), city (1968 pop. 27,973), Nord dept., N France. It has coal fields, ironworks, and steel mills. At Denain in 1712, during the War of the Spanish Succession, the French under Villars defeated the Austrians under Prince Eugene.

denaturation, term used to describe the loss of the native, higher-order structure of PROTEIN molecules in solution. Most globular proteins exhibit complicated three-dimensional folding described as secondary, tertiary, and quaternary structures. These conformations of the protein molecule are reasonably fragile and any factor that alters the precise geometry is said to cause denaturation. The denatured protein is thought to be unfolded with a geometry that approximates a helix of irregular pitch and diameter. Extensive unfolding sometimes causes precipitation of the protein from solution. It should be stressed that denaturation is defined as a major change from the original native state without alteration of the molecule's AMINO ACID sequence, i.e., without cleavage of any of the primary chemical bonds that link one amino acid to another. Treatment of proteins with strong acids or bases, high concentrations of inorganic salts or organic solvents (e.g., alcohol or chloroform), heat, or irradiation all produce denaturation to a variable degree. Loss of three-dimensional structure usually produces a loss of biological activity. Thus, the denatured ENZYME is often without catalytic function. Renaturation is accomplished with varying success, and occasionally with a return of biological function, by exposing the denatured protein to a solution that approximates normal physiological conditions. Denaturation may be studied in the laboratory in any number of ways that monitor the physical properties of protein. Thus measurements of changing viscosity, density, light-scattering ability, and movement in an electrical field all record slight changes in molecular architecture.

denatured alcohol: see ETHANOL.

Denbighshire (dĕn'bēshĭr) or **Denbigh,** county (1971 pop. 184,824), N Wales, bounded on the N by the Irish Sea and on the W by the River Conway. The county town is Denbigh, but WREXHAM, a coal-mining and manufacturing center, is more important; the area's products include iron, coal, steel, blast-furnace bricks, and tinplate. There are light industries in the seaside towns. Sheep, cattle, pigs, and poultry are raised. Dairy products, oats, wheat, barley, and potatoes come from the valleys of the Conway, Clwyd, and Dee rivers. Forestry and tourism (in the Dee valley and the coastal towns, especially at Colwyn Bay) are also important. In 1974, Denbighshire was divided between the new nonmetropolitan counties of Clwyd and Gwynedd.

Denby, Edwin, 1870–1929, U.S. Secretary of the Navy (1921–24), b. Evansville, Ind. President Harding appointed him to the cabinet. In 1924 he was involved in the scandal about the oil reserves (see TEAPOT DOME). He was charged not with fraud but with neglect of duty, and he eventually resigned.

Dendera: see DANDARAH, Egypt.

Dendermonde (dĕndərmôn'də), Fr. *Termonde,* town (1970 pop. 9,000), East Flanders prov., central Belgium, at the confluence of the Dender and Scheldt rivers. Manufactures include carpets and linen. Dendermonde was involved in the wars of the 17th and 18th cent.; in 1667 it held off the French under Louis XIV by opening dikes and flooding the countryside. Of note is the town hall (14th cent.).

dendrite: see NERVOUS SYSTEM; SYNAPSE.

dendrochronology: see DATING.

Deneb (dĕn'ĕb), brightest star in the constellation CYGNUS; Bayer designation Alpha Cygni; 1970 position R.A. $20^h40.4^m$, Dec. +45°10'. It is a white supergiant of SPECTRAL CLASS A2 Ia; its intrinsic brightness (about 60,000 times as luminous as the sun) is the greatest of all the bright stars. Thus, even though it is also one of the most distant bright stars, being about 1,600 light-years from the earth, it has an apparent MAGNITUDE of 1.25, making it one of the 20 brightest. Its name is from the Arabic meaning "hen's tail," referring to its position in the constellation.

dengue fever (dĕng'gā), acute infectious disease caused by a filterable virus and transmitted by the bite of the *Aedes* mosquito. The disease occurs in both epidemic and sporadic form in warm climates (S United States, South America, the Mediterranean countries, India, the Philippines, and the Indonesian islands). The symptoms of dengue fever, following an incubation period of five to eight days, are fever, chills, severe headache, pain in the joints, sweating, and prostration. The fever and symptoms subside in two to four days, but after a remission lasting from a few hours to two days there is another rise in temperature and a generalized rash appears. Convalescence is sometimes prolonged, with weakness and low blood pressure. There is no specific treatment for dengue fever except good nursing care. The disease can be prevented or controlled by eradicating the mosquitoes and destroying their breeding places. Dengue fever is rarely fatal.

Denham, Sir John, 1615–69, English poet and dramatist. His fame rests largely on two works: *Cooper's Hill* (1642), a topographical poem, combining descriptions of scenery with moral reflections, and *The Sophy,* a historical tragedy of the Turkish court, acted in 1641. He served the royalists during the Puritan revolution and as a result was made surveyor general of the royal works. He was knighted in 1661. See ed. of his works by T. H. Banks, Jr. (1928); biography by Brendan O'Hehir (1968).

Den Helder (dŭn hĕl'dər), city (1971 pop. 61,052), North Holland prov., NW Netherlands, on the North Sea. It is the main base of the Netherlands's navy.

denial, mental defense mechanism that operates unconsciously to resolve emotional conflict and to allay anxiety by disavowing thoughts, feelings, wishes, needs, or external reality factors that are consciously intolerable. Reality is regarded as nonexistent or is transformed so that it is no longer unpleasant or painful. The term *denial* used in a psychiatric sense does not apply to a conscious endeavor to repudiate or disown, as in malingering or lying. Referring to the concept of denial as disavowal, Freud distinguished between repression as a defense against internal demands and disavowal as a defense against the claims of external reality; later he used repression to speak of a defense against an emotion and disavowal to refer to a defense against an idea. His daughter, Anna Freud, also specified an external direction for denial, although psychiatrists generally have not thus restricted the term. She further described the widespread occurrence of denial in the fantasies, words, and acts of small children and explained that the mature ego does not continue to make extensive use of denial because it conflicts with the capacity to recognize and critically test reality. Thus, denial is commonly spoken of as a primitive, narcissistic, or immature form of psychic defense appearing in normal children less than 5 years old and in adult dreams and fantasies, but otherwise characteristic of psychosis if frequently relied upon by adults when they are awake and addressing themselves to external reality. This is not to say that denial occurs only in psychotic adults. Aspects of denial of impending death regularly occur in persons who are terminally ill, and denial of what appears to be a hopeless situation can sometimes lead to persistence, exploration, and survival instead of submission. Indeed, there is some evidence that the capability to deny threats to oneself (or delay one's perception of them) or to readily forget failures and other distressing events may be associated with better overall functioning, when not carried to an extreme, than the opposite trait of sensitization to the unpleasant aspects of reality.

Denikin, Anton Ivanovich (əntôn' ēvä'nəvĭch dyĭnyē'kĭn), 1872–1947, Russian general. The son of a serf, he rose from the ranks. After the Bolshevik Revolution in Nov., 1917 (Oct., 1917, O.S.) he joined General KORNILOV, whom he succeeded (1918) as commander of the anti-Bolshevik forces in the south. He gained control of a large part of S Russia, but failed (1919) to capture Moscow. He was driven back by the Soviet army, and his forces were demoralized. In 1920 he resigned his command to General Piotr Nikolayevich WRANGEL. Denikin lived in France until 1946, when he moved to the United States, where he died. See biography by D. V. Lehovich (1974); study by W. G. Rosenberg (1961).

Denis, Saint (dĕn'ĭs, dənē'), fl. 3d cent.?, patron of France. He is said to have been first bishop of Paris and to have died a martyr on MONTMARTRE. His shrine was SAINT-DENIS. The Latin of the name is Dionysius; he was long identified with DIONYSIUS THE AREOPAGITE. Feast: Oct. 9.

Denis, king of Portugal: see DINIZ.

Denis, Maurice (môrēs' dənē'), 1870–1943, French painter and writer on art. His paintings, usually on religious themes, have not proved so influential as his art theories. As the spokesman for symbolism and for the NABIS, Denis proposed his famous definition of painting: "Remember that a picture, before being a battle horse, a nude, an anecdote or what-not, is essentially a flat surface covered with colors assembled in a certain order." In 1919, Denis attempted to revive the teaching of religious art and cofounded the Studios of Sacred Art. His writings include *Théories* (2 vol.; 1920, 1922) and *Histoire de l'art religieux* (1939).

Denison, city (1970 pop. 24,923), Grayson co., N Texas, near the Red River; inc. 1873. It is a rail center with textile mills, garment factories, and plants that manufacture a great variety of products. The town was founded by the railroad in 1872 on the site of an old stagecoach station. Wealth from industry has preserved the beauty of gracious and well-shaded streets, and local funds have converted (1968) the downtown area into a modern shopping park. Dwight D. Eisenhower was born there, and his birthplace is open to visitors. A junior college is in Denison. Lake Texoma, north of the city, is impounded on the Red River by the huge Denison Dam. A state park is at the lake, and a wildlife refuge is also in the area.

Denison Dam, 17,200 ft (5,243 m) long, on the Red River along the Texas-Okla. border, NW of Denison, Texas. The dam, built by the U.S. Corps of Engineers for flood control and hydroelectric power (175,000-kw capacity), was completed in 1944 and impounds **Lake Texoma** (227 sq mi/588 sq km), one of the largest man-made lakes in the United States. The lake is a major recreation area and has two national wildlife refuges along its shores.

Denison University, at Granville, Ohio; coeducational; American Baptist. The school was founded in 1831 as the Granville Literary and Theological Institution. The name was changed in 1845 to Granville College and in 1856 to its present form.

denitrifying bacteria: see NITROGEN CYCLE.

Denizli (dĕnēzlē'), city (1970 pop. 83,583), capital of Denizli prov., W Turkey. Picturesquely situated, it is an agricultural market center and the gateway for excursions by tourists to the nearby ruins of LAODICEA at Lycum and HIERAPOLIS. The city was captured by the Ottoman Turks in 1389. It was badly damaged by earthquakes in 1710 and 1899.

Denmark, Dan. *Danmark,* kingdom (1971 pop. 4,950,597), 16,629 sq mi (43,069 sq km), N Europe, bordering on West Germany in the south, on the North Sea in the west, on the Skagerrak in the north, and on the Kattegat and the Øresund in the east. The southernmost of the Scandinavian countries, Denmark proper includes most of the JUTLAND peninsula; several major islands, notably SJAELLAND, FYN, LOLLAND, FALSTER, LANGELAND, ALS, MØN, BORNHOLM, and AMAGER; and about 450 other islands. The FAEROE ISLANDS and GREENLAND, semiautonomous parts of the Danish realm, lie to the northwest. COPENHAGEN is Denmark's capital, largest city, and chief industrial center; other important cities include Ålborg, Århus, Esbjerg, Frederiksberg, Gentofte, Lyngby, Odense, and Roskilde. Denmark proper is divided into 14 counties. A part of the European plain, the country is almost entirely low-lying, and more than 70% of its land area is cultivated. The North Atlantic Drift (a warm ocean current) usually ensures a relatively mild climate, but occasionally ice closes the Baltic Sea, thus cutting off warmer waters and making the winter quite severe. Almost all the inhabitants of Denmark speak Danish (there are several dialects), and the great majority belong

to the established Lutheran Church. Traditionally an agricultural country, Denmark after 1945 greatly expanded its industrial base so that by the late 1960s manufacturing contributed about 40% of the gross national product and agriculture less than 10%. The main commodities raised are livestock (cattle, pigs, and poultry), root crops (beets, kohlrabi, and potatoes), and cereals (barley, oats, and wheat). There is a large fishing industry, and Denmark possesses a commercial shipping fleet of considerable size. The leading manufactures include food products (especially meat and dairy goods), beer, metals (made almost entirely from imported raw materials, since Denmark has practically no mineral resources), metal goods, chemicals, electrical and electronic equipment, ships, textiles, and furniture. The country also has a growing tourist industry. Denmark's main exports are machinery, meat, and transportation equipment (especially ships); the chief imports are machinery, metals, fuels, and transportation equipment (especially motor vehicles). The country's leading trade partners in the early 1970s were Sweden, West Germany, and Great Britain. In 1972, Denmark (along with Great Britain and Ireland) accepted membership in the European Economic Community (Common Market). Denmark has an excellent system of public education, developed largely in the 19th cent. There are universities at Århus, Copenhagen, and Odense.

History to 1448. The Danes probably settled Jutland by c.10,000 B.C. and later (2d millennium B.C.) developed a Bronze Age culture there. However, little is known of Danish history before the age of the VIKINGS (9th–11th cent. A.D.), when the Danes had an important role in the Viking (or Norse) raids on Western Europe and were prominent among the invaders of England who were opposed by King Alfred (reigned 871–99) and his successors. St. Ansgar (801–65) helped convert the Danes to Christianity; HAROLD BLUETOOTH (d. c.985) was the first Christian king of Denmark. His son, SWEYN (reigned c.986–1014), conquered England. From 1018 to 1035, Denmark, England, and Norway were united under King CANUTE (Knut). The southern part of Sweden (Skåne, Halland, and Blekinge) was, with brief interruptions, part of Denmark until 1658. After Canute's death, Denmark fell into a period of turmoil and civil war. Later, WALDEMAR I (reigned 1157–82) and WALDEMAR II (reigned 1202–41) were energetic rulers who established Danish hegemony over N Europe. With the end of the Viking raids and with the development of a strong and independent church, the nobles were able to impose their will on the weaker kings. In 1282, Eric V (reigned 1259–86) was forced to submit to the Great Charter, which established annual parliaments and a council of nobles who shared the king's power. This form of government persisted until 1660. WALDEMAR IV (reigned 1340–75) again brought Danish power to a high point, but he was humiliated by the HANSEATIC LEAGUE in the Treaty of Stralsund (1370). Waldemar's daughter, Queen MARGARET, achieved (1397) the union of the Danish, Norwegian, and Swedish crowns in her person (see KALMAR UNION). Sweden soon escaped effective Danish rule, and with the accession (1523) of Gustavus I of Sweden the union was dissolved. However, the union with NORWAY lasted until 1814.

Denmark and Norway. In 1448, CHRISTIAN I became king and established on the Danish throne the house of Oldenburg, from which the present ruling family (Schleswig-Holstein-Sonderburg-Glücksburg) is descended. He also united (1460) SCHLESWIG and HOLSTEIN with the Danish crown. The Reformation (early 16th cent.) gradually gained adherents in Denmark, and during the reign of CHRISTIAN III (1535–59) Lutheranism became the established religion. In the late 16th and early 17th cent., Denmark had a brilliant court, with a brisk intellectual and cultural life; the astronomer Tycho Brahe (1546–1601) was a major figure, and the Danish Renaissance style of architecture (strongly influenced by that of the Low Countries) was developed. The division of power in Denmark between the king and the nobles seriously handicapped the country's attempt to gain supremacy in the Baltic region. Denmark was involved in numerous wars with Sweden and other neighbors; the participation of CHRISTIAN IV (reigned 1588–1648) in the Thirty Years War (1618–48) and the wars of FREDERICK III (reigned 1648–70) with Sweden caused Denmark to lose its hegemony in the north to Sweden. The Danish-Swedish Treaty of Copenhagen (1660) confirmed most of the Danish losses imposed by the Treaty of Roskilde (1658). The wars weakened the nobility by reducing its numbers and strengthened the monarchy by increasing the power and importance of the royal army. Frederick III and CHRISTIAN V (reigned 1670–99), aided by their minister Count GRIFFENFELD, were able to make the kingdom an absolute monarchy with the support of peasants and townspeople. Denmark maintained an imperial status by continuing to rule over Iceland and by establishing (late 17th cent.) the Danish West Indies (see VIRGIN ISLANDS). In the NORTHERN WAR (1720–21) against Charles XII of Sweden, FREDERICK IV (reigned 1699–1730) gained some financial awards and the union of ducal Schleswig with royal Schleswig. The later 18th cent. was marked by important social reforms carried out by the ministers Johann Hartwig Ernst BERNSTORFF, Andreas Peter BERNSTORFF, and Johann Friedrich STRUENSEE. Serfdom was abolished (1788), and peasant proprietorship was encouraged. In the French Revolutionary and Napoleonic Wars, Denmark, having sided with Napoleon I, was twice attacked by England (see COPENHAGEN, BATTLE OF; COPENHAGEN). By the Treaty of Kiel (1814), Denmark lost Norway to Sweden and Helgoland to England.

1814 to the Present. In the early 19th cent., Denmark's modern system of public education was started, and there was a flowering of literature and philosophy (led by Hans Christian Andersen and Søren Kierkegaard). As a result of plans for a liberal, centralized constitution, FREDERICK VII (reigned 1848–63) became involved in a war with Prussia (1848–50) over the status of SCHLESWIG-HOLSTEIN. Denmark was defeated and agreed in the London Protocol of 1852 to preserve a special status for the two duchies. In the meantime, a new constitution was promulgated (1849), ending the absolute monarchy and establishing wide suffrage. The new government attempted (1855) to incorporate Schleswig into the Danish constitutional system, and soon after the accession (1863) of CHRISTIAN IX war broke out again (1864), this time with Prussia and Austria. Denmark was defeated badly and lost Schleswig-Holstein. This loss of about one third of the Danish territory was, however, offset by great economic gains that transformed Denmark, in the second half of the 19th cent., from a land of poor peasants into the nation with the most prosperous small farmers in Europe. This change was achieved largely by persuading the farmers to specialize in dairy and pork products rather than in grain (which was more expensive to produce than the grain imported from the United States). The FOLK HIGH SCHOOLS, originated by N. F. S. GRUNDTVIG (1783–1872), played an important role in reeducating the Danish farmers. At the same time, the cooperative movement flourished in Denmark. Electoral reforms (1914–15) granted suffrage to the lower classes and to women and strengthened the lower chamber of the legislature. Denmark remained neutral in World War I and recovered North Schleswig after a plebiscite in 1920. In the interwar period and after World War II, Denmark adopted much social welfare legislation and a system of progressive taxation. Although the Social Democratic government of Denmark had signed a 10-year nonaggression pact with Germany in 1939, the country was occupied by German forces in April, 1940. CHRISTIAN X (reigned 1912–47) and his government remained, but in Aug., 1943, the Germans established martial law, arrested the government, and placed the king under house arrest. Most of the Jewish population (including refugees from other countries) escaped, with Danish help, to Sweden. The Danish minister in Washington, although disavowed by his government, signed an agreement granting the United States military bases in Greenland. Danish merchant vessels served under the Allies, and a Danish resistance force operated (1945) under the supreme Allied command. Denmark was liberated by British troops in May, 1945. After the war, Denmark recovered quickly, and its economy, especially the manufacturing sector, expanded considerably. Denmark became (1945) a charter member of the United Nations and, breaking a long tradition of neutrality, joined the North Atlantic Treaty Organization in 1949. In 1960, Denmark became part of the European Free Trade Association, which it left in 1972 in order to join the European Economic Community.

Government. Denmark is a constitutional monarchy, governed according to the 1953 constitution. Legislative power is vested in the monarch (who is also head of state) in conjunction with the unicameral Folketing (parliament) of 179 elected members. Executive power is exercised by the monarch through his ministers (led by the prime minister), who are responsible to the Folketing and must have the support of the majority of that body. The reigning monarch is Queen Margaret (Margrethe) II, who succeeded her father, King Frederick IX, upon his death in 1972. In the period following 1945, the Social Democratic party has been the leading political party, although at times it has been forced to form a coalition government or to govern as a minority government. In Dec., 1973, a minority Moderate Liberal party government, with Paul Hartling as prime minister, replaced the Social Democrats in power. See Palle Lauring, *A History of the Kingdom of Denmark* (tr., 3d ed. 1968); K. E. Miller, *Government and Politics in Denmark* (1968); W. G. Jones, *Denmark* (1970); Peter Manniche, *Living Democracy in Denmark* (1952, repr. 1970); P. V. Glob, *Denmark: An Archaeological History* (tr. 1971); Stewart Oakley, *A Short History of Denmark* (1972).

Denmark Strait, passage, c.300 mi (480 km) long and 180 mi (290 km) wide at the narrowest point, between Greenland and Iceland. The cold E Greenland current passes through the strait and carries icebergs S into the N Atlantic Ocean.

Dennett, Tyler (dĕn'ĭt), 1883–1949, American historian and educator, b. Spencer, Wis. Dennett was lecturer in American history at Johns Hopkins Univ. (1923–24) and at Columbia (1927–28), chief of the division of publications (1924–29) and historical adviser (1929–31) in the U.S. Dept. of State, and professor of international relations at Princeton (1931–34). As president of Williams (1934–37) he was a sharp critic of the New Deal, but favored the admission of more high school graduates to the institution, saying that a college should not be an exclusive club for the wealthy and wellborn. Disagreement with the board of trustees led to his resignation, and Dennett thereafter devoted himself to writing. He wrote, in addition to numerous articles in magazines and periodicals, *The Democratic Movement in Asia* (1918); *Americans in Eastern Asia* (1922, repr. 1963); *Roosevelt and the Russo-Japanese War* (1925, repr. 1958), and *John Hay* (1933), which won the 1934 Pulitzer Prize for biography. He also edited *Lincoln and the Civil War in the Diaries and Letters of John Hay* (1939).

Dennie, Joseph, 1768–1812, American Federalist journalist, b. Boston. As editor, he made the *Farmer's Weekly Museum* at Walpole, N.H., an influential paper, particularly because of the "Lay Preacher" essays he wrote and printed in it. In Philadelphia he founded the *Port Folio,* which became a leading literary weekly, and edited it under the pseudonym Oliver Oldschool, Esq., from 1801 to 1812. In the *Port Folio* Dennie attacked Jefferson so violently that he was tried for seditious libel in 1805 but was acquitted. Dennie's "Lay Preacher" essays were published in two collections (1796–1817); both editions were published in one volume by H. M. Ellis in 1943. See his letters (ed. by L. G. Pedder, 1936); study by H. M. Ellis (1915, repr. 1971).

Dennis, James Shepard, 1842–1914, American missionary, b. Newark, N.J. He served (1869–92) in Syria and Lebanon, most of the time at the Presbyterian Theological Seminary at Beirut. His *Christian Missions and Social Progress* (1897–1906) and other writings on the mission field were influential.

Dennis, John, 1657–1734, English critic and playwright. Best known for his critical works, which include *Grounds of Criticism in Poetry* (1704) and *An Essay on the Genius and Writings of Shakespeare* (1712), Dennis was also the author of several unsuccessful tragedies. His *Appius and Virginia* (1709) was satirized as bombastic in Pope's *Essay on Criticism.* This led to a vicious response from Dennis, who described Pope as a "hunch-back'd toad." The bitter quarrel between the two men terminated only with Dennis's death.

Denon, Dominique-Vivant, Baron (dōmēnēk'-vēväN bärôN' dənôN'), 1747–1825, French artist, writer, and archaeologist. He had a brilliant career as artist and diplomat under the ancien régime and followed Napoleon on his campaign in Egypt. In 1804 he became director general of museums and was instrumental in bringing foreign masterpieces into the Louvre as the spoils of conquest. His accounts of his travels and his treatise on ancient monuments contain collections of his engravings of works of art. Denon was partly responsible for the design of the Vendôme Column, a monument to Napoleon.

Denonville, Jacques René de Brisay, marquis de (zhäk rənā' də brēzā' märkē' də dənôNvēl'), d. 1710, governor of New France (1685–89). To subdue the Iroquois Indians he led a force of 3,000 French and Indian enemies of the Iroquois into the Seneca country in W New York in 1687 and destroyed their villages. Subsequently, he invited a number of Iroquois to a peace conference, and, betraying them, shipped them off to France as galley slaves. This act so infuriated the Iroquois that they descended the St. Lawrence River in force, massacred the inhabitants in Lachine in 1689, and terrorized the country. Denonville was recalled to France in 1689 and then served as a royal tutor.

density, ratio of the MASS of a substance to its volume, expressed, for example, in units of grams per cubic centimeter or pounds per cubic foot. The density of a pure substance varies little from sample to sample and is often considered a characteristic property of the substance. Most substances undergo expansion when heated and therefore have lower densities at higher temperatures. Many substances, especially gases, can be compressed into a smaller volume by increasing the pressure acting on them. For these reasons, the temperature and pressure at which the density of a substance is measured are usually specified. The density of a gas is often converted mathematically to what it would be at a standard temperature and pressure (see STP). Water is unusual in that it expands, and thus decreases in density, as it is cooled below 3.98°C (its temperature of maximum density). Density often is taken as an indication of how "heavy" a substance is. Iron is denser than cork, since a given volume of iron is more massive (and weighs more) than the same volume of cork. It is often said that iron is "heavier" than cork, although a large volume of cork obviously can be more massive and thus be heavier (i.e., weigh more) than a small volume of iron. See SPECIFIC GRAVITY.

Dent, Edward Joseph, 1876–1957, English musicologist. He studied and taught at Cambridge. Dent wrote biographies of Alessandro Scarlatti (1905), Busoni (1933), and Handel (1934), and many critical works. In 1922 he founded the International Society for Contemporary Music, of which he was president until 1938.

Dentatus (Manius Curius Dentatus) (dĕntā'təs; mā'nēəs kyŏŏr'ēəs), d. 270 B.C., Roman general. As consul (290) he defeated the Samnites, Sabines, and Lucani; in his third consulship (275) he drove PYRRHUS from Italy. Many stories are told of his simplicity and incorruptible honor. He refused to be bribed by Samnite ambassadors, saying that it was more glorious to conquer owners of gold than to possess it himself. He began (272) Rome's second aqueduct, Anio Vetus.

Dent Blanche (däN bläNsh), peak, 14,318 ft (4,364 m) high, Valais canton, S Switzerland, in the Pennine Alps.

dentistry, treatment and care of the teeth and associated oral structures. Dentistry is mainly concerned with tooth decay, disease of the supporting structures, such as the gums, and faulty positioning of the teeth. Egyptian writings dating back to the 18th cent. B.C. contain prescriptions for the treatment of toothache and swelling of the gums. There have been unearthed crowns and bridges made by the Etruscans in the 7th cent. B.C. that are remarkably good. At about that time extraction of teeth was being performed in Asia Minor as a cure for bodily ills and diseases, in recognition of the fact that dental health and general health were closely related. The early skills achieved by the Etruscans, Phoenicians, Egyptians, Greeks, and Romans were largely lost during the Middle Ages, when barbers and roving bands of charlatans practiced an unskilled form of dentistry at marketplaces and fairs. Apparently during that time only one man, Abulcasis, a Spanish Moor, interested himself in dental surgery, leaving behind instruments and theories that were quite advanced for his era, the 10th cent. A.D. Pierre Fauchard, a Frenchman, is considered the father of modern dentistry; by the end of the 17th cent. he was making fillings of lead, tin, or gold, and devising artificial dentures. By the middle of the 18th cent. Philip Pfaff, a German, was making dentures of plaster of Paris, and shortly thereafter the French discovered how to mold porcelain into dentures. The first American to make use of this process was Charles Willson Peale; it was he who made the now-famous set of false teeth for George Washington. As dentistry progressed, the center of accomplishment shifted from Europe to the United States. The first dental school in the world was established in Baltimore in 1840. The first integration of a dental school with a university occurred at Harvard. The development of local and general anesthesia, the invention of the drilling machine, discovery of better substances for filling the teeth (amalgam and gold), and, most important, the ability to devise replacements that closely approximate natural teeth in function and appearance, constructed from porcelain and plastic, contributed much to the rapid growth of dentistry as a science and an art. New developments in dental care include the sometimes controversial practice of adding fluoride to the local water supply (fluoridation) to make teeth more resistant to cavities; annual applications of a clear liquid plastic to children's teeth to make them more decay resistant, a treatment still in the experimental stage; and the implantation of artificial teeth directly into the gums. Dentistry, like medicine and surgery, is practiced in specialized fields: oral surgery, orthodontics (corrective dentistry), periodontics (diseases of the gums), prosthodontics (partial or total replacement), endodontics (treatment of dental pulp chamber and canals), and pedodontics (dental problems of children).

dentition, kind, number, and arrangement of the TEETH of man and other animals. During the course of evolution, teeth were derived from bony body scales similar to the placoid scales on the skin of modern sharks. Tooth structures such as are found in man are restricted to certain vertebrates, i.e., most fish, mammals, and reptiles, and some amphibians. The teeth of sharks, which are primitive vertebrates, are simple conelike structures, sometimes with serrated edges and sometimes flattened for crushing shelled prey. In many lower vertebrates the individual teeth are replaced throughout the animal's life; old tooth loss and new tooth growth follow wavelike patterns down the length of jaw and affect alternate teeth at any one time, so that half the teeth in a region are always functional. Fish and reptiles that have teeth have homodont dentition; that is, all teeth are identical. The mammals have heterodont dentition, or teeth of different basic types, including incisors for nipping or cutting, canines for piercing, and premolars and molars for shearing and grinding. Carnivorous animals have relatively small incisors, used for grasping rather than for cutting; long and strong canines; and relatively thin, sharp premolars and molars, used for severing muscle and other tissues. Herbivorous animals have well-developed incisors, used to cut grass and other vegetation; canines that are either smaller than those of carnivores or absent altogether; and broad, flat premolars and molars for grinding food. In some herbivores, the upper canines are absent, and vegetation is cut by the combined action of the tongue and lower incisors. Omnivorous animals such as man have less specialized dentition. Only part of the dentition of mammals is usually replaced; however, the incisors of rodents grow out at the base as fast as they are worn down at the tip. Teeth, the hardest structures in the body, have been well preserved as fossils and are important in taxonomic studies.

Denton, city (1970 pop. 39,874), seat of Denton co., N Texas; inc. 1866. It is the seat of North Texas State Univ. and Texas Woman's Univ. It is also the processing, trade, and distribution center of a large agricultural area. It has flour mills, food-processing establishments, and plants making building materials, machine tools, and clothing. Denton is known as a city of roses. The North Texas State Fair is held there annually. Nearby are an agricultural experiment station and man-made Lake Lewisville (formerly Lake Dallas) in the Trinity River system.

D'Entrecasteaux Islands (däNtrəkästō'), volcanic group, SW Pacific, SE of New Guinea, part of Papua New Guinea. Comprising the Fergusson, Goodenough, and Normanby islands, the group, with a total land area of c.1,200 sq mi (3,110 sq km), is mountainous and has several extinct volcanoes, hot springs, and geysers. Coconuts and pearl shells are the chief products. The islands were named for the French navigator J. A. B. d'Entrecasteaux.

Dents du Midi (däN' dü mēdē'), mountain group in the Alps, Vaud canton, SW Switzerland, near the French border. It rises to 10,695 ft (3,260 m) in Dent du Midi (Haute Cime) peak.

denture, artificial replacement for natural teeth and surrounding tissue. Dentures are classified as partial or complete. The former are removable and maintained by clasps, or are fixed bridges with crowns cemented over adjacent teeth or over spikes embedded in the jaw. Complete dentures are replacements for all of the teeth of a jaw and are normally held in place by the suction created by saliva and by the close matching of the denture base to the tissues of the mouth. The first-known mention of dentures is found in the 1728 manuscript of Pierre Fouchard, a French dental surgeon often called the father of modern dentistry. Various substances including wood, ivory, and metal have been used in the construction of dentures, but major advances have resulted from the development of synthetic rubbers and plastics. Today dentures are usually composed of porcelain or acryllic teeth mounted in an acryllic base that is tinted to resemble the gums.

Denver, James William, 1817–92, American territorial governor, army officer, and Congressman, b. Winchester, Va. He commanded a company of Missouri volunteers in the Mexican War, then went (1850) to California, where he was state senator and secretary of state before serving (1855–57) as U.S. Representative. President Buchanan appointed him commissioner of Indian affairs (1857) and territorial governor (1858) of troubled Kansas. As governor, Denver established order in the newly discovered Colorado gold mines and helped bring about the separation of Colorado from Kansas (Denver is named for him). In the Civil War he was a brigadier general of volunteers and later he practiced law in Washington, D.C.

Denver, city (1970 pop. 514,678), alt. 5,280 ft (1,609 m), state capital, coextensive with Denver co., N central Colo., on the South Platte River at the mouth of Cherry Creek; inc. 1861. It is the largest city in the state, a port of entry, and a great processing, shipping, and distributing point for an extensive agricultural area. It is also the financial and administrative center of the Rocky Mt. region, and the location of numerous Federal agencies. Denver has stockyards and meat-packing plants, railroad shops, fruit and vegetable canneries, feed and flour mills, and many electronics plants. Foremost among its manufactures are rubber goods and luggage. Tourism is also important. An excellent transportation system (highway, rail, and air) is afforded the many visitors who are attracted by the healthful climate and the beauty of the city and the surrounding area. The city was made territorial capital in 1867. The rich gold and silver strikes of the late 1870s and the 1880s brought prosperity to the city, and it became the metropolis for bonanza kings such as H. A. W. Tabor, who built the Tabor Grand Opera House. In the late 1890s, Denver's development as an important metropolis began. Among the city's educational institutions are the Univ. of Denver, Loretto Heights College, Regis College, Colorado Women's College, Metropolitan State College, the Univ. of Colorado medical school, and three theological seminaries. Points of interest include a park system with many mountain areas; the Denver Art Museum; the Colorado State Historical Museum; a museum of natural history; the state capitol; and the zoological gardens. A U.S. mint, the

Rocky Mountain Arsenal, and the U.S. Army Fitzsimmons General Hospital are there. Nearby is Lowry Air Force Base. See R. L. Perkin, *The First One Hundred Years: An Informal History of Denver and the "Rocky Mountain News"* (1959); S. W. Zamonski, *Fifty-Niners: A Denver Diary* (1961).

Denver, University of, at Denver; coeducational; United Methodist; chartered 1864 and opened as Colorado Seminary by John Evans and others. In 1880 it was reorganized as the Univ. of Denver. It maintains Chamberlin Observatory and, in cooperation with other institutions, high-altitude laboratories at Echo Lake and at Mt. Evans.

deodar or **deodar cedar:** see CEDAR.

deodorizer or **deodorant,** substance used to absorb or eliminate offensive odors. Disinfectants such as hydrogen peroxide, chlorine, and chlorine compounds eliminate odors caused by microorganisms. Adsorbent deodorizers such as activated charcoal and silica gel remove odorous molecules by attracting them to the adsorbent surface. Some substances, such as chlorophyll, eliminate odors by combining chemically with odorous impurities. Glycols, which are disinfectant as well as deodorizing substances, are sprayed into the air to absorb odors. In some industrial processes, odor-containing air is scrubbed, i.e., bubbled through a liquid that dissolves or emulsifies the odorous molecules. In personal hygiene, deodorants may be applied locally on body surfaces. Because most body odor is caused by the action of bacteria on the skin (perspiration is nearly odorless), many deodorants contain antiseptics that destroy bacteria; the antiseptic hexachlorophene is no longer used in deodorants because it has been shown to cause brain damage. An antiperspirant component of deodorant preparations, usually an aluminum salt, blocks the pores through which perspiration is secreted.

department store: see STORE.

De Patinir, De Patenier, or **De Patiner, Joachim:** see PATINIR, JOACHIM DE.

De Pauw, Washington Charles (dĭpô′), 1822–87, American manufacturer, b. Salem, Ind. At first successful at banking, he later established a plate-glass works at New Albany, Ind., which became one of the largest plants in the country. He donated some $300,000 to Indiana Asbury College, which was renamed (1884) DePauw University.

DePauw University, at Greencastle, Ind.; coeducational; United Methodist; est. 1832, chartered 1837. The school opened in 1838 as Indiana Asbury College, and in 1884 the present name was adopted.

De Pere (dĭ pēr), city (1970 pop. 13,309), Brown co., E central Wis., on the Fox River; inc. 1857; De Pere and West De Pere consolidated 1890. A channel 20 ft (6 m) wide allows port traffic from Green Bay as far as De Pere, the last upstream dock. Wood and paper products, industrial plating, aluminum, and metal parts are among the manufactures. A mission, founded there (1671) by Father Allouez, was burned, rebuilt (1685), and used until 1717. De Pere grew in the 19th cent. as a lumber town, port, and commercial center. St. Norbert College is in West De Pere.

Depew, Chauncey Mitchell (dĭpyo͞o′), 1834–1928, American orator, politician, and railroad president, b. Peekskill, N.Y. Admitted to the bar in 1856, he was a Republican member (1862–63) of the state legislature and then secretary of state of New York (1863–65). In 1866 he refused the ministry to Japan in favor of serving the railroad interests of Commodore Vanderbilt. He served as general counsel (1875–82), vice president (1882–85), president (1885–99), and chairman of the board (1899–1928) of the New York Central lines. Noted as an after-dinner speaker, he used his oratorical abilities to deliver nominating speeches at the Republican conventions of 1888 and 1896. He was elected U.S. Senator (1899–1911) but failed to secure reelection in 1910, partly because an investigation of life insurance companies revealed that he received an annual retainer from the Equitable Life Assurance Company. See his memoirs (1922).

Depew, village (1970 pop. 22,158), Erie co., W central N.Y., a suburb of Buffalo; inc. 1894. Printing is a major industry. Depew's diverse manufactures include transportation equipment, chemicals, steel castings, metal stampings, felt and silk items, and prefabricated concrete. Founded in 1892, the village was named for Chauncey M. Depew, a railroad executive and later a U.S. Senator.

depilatory (dĭpĭl′ətôr″ē), substance used to remove hair. In preparing hides for tanning, lime is the chief depilatory. For the removal of superfluous hair from the human body, metal sulfides are used, e.g., barium sulfide, sodium sulfide, calcium hydrosulfide, and strontium hydrosulfide. The powdered material is usually combined with other substances (lime, sugar, chalk, perfume) and made into a paste which is spread on the skin. The hair is dissolved into a gelatinous mass and is removed along with the paste. However, these reagents do not prevent regrowth of hair and are potentially dangerous. Wax depilatories that harden on the skin and pull up the hair by the roots when peeled off delay but do not prevent regrowth of hair. The only permanent method of removing hair is by cosmetic electrolysis, in which a weak electric current, passing through a needle, destroys the hair follicle.

deportation, expulsion of an alien from a country by an act of the government. The term is not applied ordinarily to sending a national into EXILE or to committing one convicted of crime to an overseas penal colony. In international law the right to return an ALIEN to the country to which he owes allegiance (or to any country that will accept him) derives from a government's sovereign control over its own territory. Deportation in the United States is the responsibility of the Immigration and Naturalization Service of the Dept. of Justice. Except for the ALIEN AND SEDITION ACTS of 1798 there was no American deportation law until the enactment in 1882 of a statute aimed at some of the Chinese who had emigrated to the United States. In 1891 the class of deportable aliens was enlarged, and succeeding statutes increased deportable classes to include persons who before their entry into the United States were insane, feeble-minded, illiterate, or diseased in various ways. Proceedings in such cases formerly had to be brought within a limited period after entry. The Immigration and Nationality Act of 1952, however, removed the statute of limitations on any kind of deportation. The largest group of deported persons are those who have entered the country illegally. A deported alien cannot reenter the United States unless he receives special permission from the Attorney General.

depreciation, in ACCOUNTING, reduction in the value of fixed or capital assets, as by use, damage, weathering, or obsolescence. It can be estimated according to a number of methods. In the straight-line method, depreciation is simply seen as a function of time; the cost of the asset, minus its value as scrap, is divided by an estimate of its life. Other methods distribute depreciation over the life of the asset by gradually increasing, or gradually diminishing, installments. The resale value of a machine generally declines most quickly during its early years; thus its depreciation is measured in decreasing installments. The opposite is true of rights of limited duration, such as copyrights and leaseholds, whose value depreciates most quickly as their date of expiration approaches. The technical name for the depreciation of such nonmaterial rights is amortization. The problem of calculating depreciation has special importance because of the need for accuracy in income tax returns. Failure to make allowance for depreciation results in overestimating income. Depreciation of money is brought about by a decline in the price of a particular currency in terms of other currencies, thereby lowering the foreign exchange value of the first currency. See J. D. Coughlan, *Depreciation* (1969).

De Predis, Ambrogio (ämbrō′jō dä prā′dēs) c.1455–c.1506, Milanese painter. He worked under LEONARDO DA VINCI and copied many of his paintings. He also executed several portraits of the Sforzas (National Gall. of Art, Washington, D.C.; Vienna).

depressant, any one of various substances that diminish functional activity, usually by depressing the NERVOUS SYSTEM. BARBITURATES, SEDATIVES, alcohol, and MEPROBAMATE are all depressants. Depressants have various modes of action and effects. Some are primarily used medically to relieve emotion stress, anxiety, and tension; others induce sleep, and still others are used to relieve pain. Depressants also reduce the rate and force of contraction of the heart and are used in the treatment of some forms of HEART DISEASE. Many depressants can induce psychological dependence and addiction (see DRUG ADDICTION AND DRUG ABUSE). Typically, overdosage results in confusion, coma, and convulsions. In many cases, the effects of one depressant are intensified if another depressant is taken at the same time, e.g., if barbiturates are taken with alcohol. Because of their potential for abuse, there are now strict regulations regarding the dispensing of many depressant drugs.

depression, in economics, period of economic crisis in commerce, finance, and industry, characterized by falling prices, restriction of credit, contraction of production, numerous bankruptcies, and a high level of unemployment. A less severe crisis is usually known as a recession or downturn. A short period in which fear takes hold of the minds of businessmen is more properly called a PANIC and does not necessarily occur in every depression; but lack of business confidence is always present in depressions. Depressions usually mark a downward swing in the curve of the business cycle and are caused by a disequilibrium between the quantity of goods produced and the consumers' ability to buy. Overproduction, decreased demand, or a combination of both factors forces curtailment of production, dismissal of employees, and wage cuts. Unemployment and lowered wages further decrease purchasing power, causing the crisis to spread and become more acute. Recovery is generally slow, the return of business confidence being dependent on the development of new markets, exhaustion of the existing stock of goods, or, as recently, remedial action by governments. Depressions now tend to become worldwide in scope because of the international nature of trade and credit. Insufficient numbers of profitable investment outlets, overexpansion of commerce, industry, or agriculture, a stock-market crash, the failure of a great banking or industrial firm, or war may be among the precipitating factors. In antiquity, and even up to the 18th cent., depressions had chiefly noneconomic causes, such as wars and weather-induced crop failures. From c.1700 to 1825 economic crises were in the main speculative or commercial; since 1825 they have been increasingly industrial. The existence of reserve banks, such as in the Federal Reserve System of the United States, created after the panic of 1907, has ameliorated financial and commercial crises. By regulating the discount rate, such banks can help to control loans and investments and hence can help stabilize economic conditions. No central bank of the Federal Reserve System failed in the depression that began in 1929. The economic crises of the 20th cent. saw the entry of governments into large areas of the economy that had previously been in private hands. Job reeducation programs, government employment of the previously unemployed, and increased public welfare responsibilities are among the programs adopted to alleviate depressions. Moreover, by applying Keynesian economic principles to public policy, governments have sought to affect the business cycle directly and prevent depressions. Large-scale public works expenditure (pump priming), tax cuts, and deficit spending during recession are among the measures that have been taken to reduce the severity of periodic economic downturns. See also GREAT DEPRESSION. See J. M. Clark, *Strategic Factors in Business Cycles* (1934); Edwin Frickey, *Economic Fluctuations in the United States, 1866–1914* (1942, repr. 1967), Dixon Wechter, *The Age of the Great Depression, 1929–1941* (1948); W. C. Mitchell, *What Happens during Business Cycles* (1951); J. A. Estey, *Business Cycles* (3d ed. 1956); C. P. Kindleberger, *The World in Depression, 1929–1939* (1973).

depression, in psychiatry, a painful emotional reaction characterized by intense feelings of loss, sadness, worthlessness, failure, or rejection not warranted by an objective view of events. It is distinguished from grief, which is a realistic response to actual loss or suffering. Depression is often a disproportionately intense reaction to difficult life situations, e.g., retirement, business loss, or physical disability. It may be accompanied by such physiological symptoms as tense posture, persistent frowning, slowing of motor and mental activity, fatigue, lack of appetite, and insomnia. The tendency toward self-recrimination, self-punishment, guilt, remorse, and shame, typical of depressed individuals, suggested to Freud that in depression the self becomes the target for anger that cannot be expressed toward others. Suicide, the terminal response to intense, psychoneurotic depression, is an extreme manifestation of destructive feelings that are turned against oneself. In MANIC DEPRESSIVE PSYCHOSIS, periods of intense excitement alternate with periods of acute depression. There is some evidence connecting depressive states with a deficiency of the neurotransmitter substance norepinephrine in the limbic system of the brain.

Depretis, Agostino (ägōstē′nō däprā′tēs), 1813–87, Italian premier. An early supporter of the revolutionary Giuseppe Mazzini, he entered the Sardinian parliament after 1848 and was a leader of the opposition to Camillo Benso di Cavour. He soon became a supporter of monarchism, however, and held several cabinet posts after the foundation (1861) of the Italian kingdom. As leader of the left in parliament, he was premier three times (1876–78, 1878–79, 1881–87). He maintained himself in power by heading coalitions of the moderate elements, a policy known as *transformismo*. Depretis worked for the Triple Alliance of 1882 (see TRIPLE ALLIANCE AND TRIPLE ENTENTE) and instituted moderate reforms.

De profundis (dā prōfo͞on'dēs) [Lat.,=from the depths], one of the penitential psalms, Ps. 130 (or 129). See PSALMS.

depth charge, explosive device used against submarines and other underwater targets, either rolled into the water from rails on the stern of a ship or propelled from depth charge throwers. The charge is detonated by water pressure at a predetermined depth. It does not have to come into actual contact with the target to destroy it, since the concussion can accomplish this if the charge explodes near enough. First used by the British navy in World War I, it was largely responsible for the defeat of the German U-boat campaign.

De Quincey, Thomas, 1785–1859, English essayist. In 1802 he ran away from school and tramped about the country, eventually settling in London. His family soon found him and entered him (1803) in Worcester College, Oxford, where he developed a deep interest in German literature and philosophy. He left Oxford in 1808 without completing his degree and settled (1809) at Grasmere, where he made the acquaintance of Wordsworth. By 1817 the opium habit, which he had begun while at Oxford, had reached its height. He achieved literary eminence with the publication of his *Confessions of an English Opium-Eater* (1822), which first appeared in the *London Magazine* in 1821. It is an account of the progress of his drug habit, including descriptions of the bizarre and spectacular dreams he had while under the influence of opium. He became a prolific contributor to various journals, especially to *Blackwood's,* Edinburgh, after 1825. Among his best works—all written in a polished, highly imaginative, and discursive prose—are "On Murder Considered as One of the Fine Arts," "Suspiria de Profundis," "On the English Mail-Coach," "On the Knocking at the Gate in Macbeth," and *Autobiographic Sketches* (1853). See his letters (ed. by W. H. Bonner, 1936); his diary for 1803 (ed. by H. A. Eaton, 1927); biographies by Edward Sackville-West (1936) and H. A. Eaton (1936, repr. 1972); studies by S. K. Proctor (1943), J. E. Jordan (1952, repr. 1973), and Albert Goldman (1965).

Dera Ghazi Khan (dā'rə gä'zē khän), town (1961 pop. 47,105), E central Pakistan, on the Indus canal. It is an administrative center in a wheat and millet area. The town was founded in the late 15th cent. A college affiliated with Punjab Univ. is there.

Derain, André (äNdrā' dəräN'), 1880–1954, French painter. He studied for a short time under Carrière. Derain's friendship with Vlaminck and Matisse led to his association c.1905 with the fauves. Forceful in his application of pure, bright patches of color, he was for a while prominent as an exponent of FAUVISM. His portrait of Matisse (1905; Philadelphia Mus. of Art) is a characteristic fauvist composition. Early in his career, however, Derain revealed a tendency toward an architectonic arrangement of forms, and his art gradually assumed a more conservative expression. He was influenced by African art and the work of French and Italian primitives. Derain is well represented in American collections, including the Lyman Allyn Museum, New London, Conn., and the Art Institute, Chicago. See study by Denys Sutton (1959).

Dera Ismail Khan (ĭsmīl' khän), town (1961 pop. 46,140), N central Pakistan, c.1 mi (1.6 km) E of the Indus River. A district administrative center, it is known for its lacquered woodwork, glass and ivory ware, mats, and sarongs. The old town, founded in 1469 by a Baluchi chief and named for one of his sons, was washed away by the Indus River; the new town was laid out by Afghan Durrani chiefs in 1823. Oil has been found in the district.

Deraismes, Maria (märēä' dəräm'), 1828–94, French feminist. She was a founder (1869) of the first French society dedicated to improving conditions and securing greater educational advantages for women. Her complete writings were published in 1895.

Derbe (dûr'bē), ancient town of Lycaonia, Asia Minor. Paul and Barnabas fled there from Iconium. Acts 14.6; 16.1; 20.4.

Derbent (dyĭrbyĕnt'), city (1969 est. pop. 61,000), SE European USSR, in Dagestan, on the Caspian Sea. It stands on a narrow strip of land that forms a natural pass (the Caspian or Iron Gates) between the Caucasian foothills and the sea. Orchards and vineyards are cultivated, and fishing is an important occupation. Industries include food processing and the production of textiles and bricks. There are oil and natural gas deposits in the area. Derbent was founded (5th or 6th cent. A.D.) by the Persians as a strategic fortress at the Iron Gates. There are remains of the Caucasian Wall (also called Alexander's Wall), built by the Persians in the 6th cent. as a bulwark against northern invaders. The Arabs, who took Derbent in 728, made it a commercial and cultural center. Passing (1220) to the Mongols and later recovered by Persia, Derbent was briefly held (1722) by Peter I of Russia and was annexed to Russia in 1806. Ancient caravansaries and baths and a mosque (8th cent.) have been preserved.

Derby, Edward George Geoffrey Smith Stanley, 14th **earl of** (där'bē), 1799–1869, British statesman. Although a Whig, he entered (1827) government as George Canning's undersecretary for the colonies. As chief secretary for Ireland (1830–33) under the 2d Earl Grey, he favored firm measures to deal with Irish unrest, but he also supported Irish educational projects. Given the colonial office in 1833, he secured the abolition of slavery but resigned (1834) in a controversy over the government's Irish policy. Having become a Conservative, he served as Peel's colonial secretary (1841–45). Resigning because he opposed repeal of the corn laws, he became leader (with Lord George Bentinck and Benjamin DISRAELI) of the Tory protectionists and headed two brief ministries (1852, 1858–59). Derby formed another government in 1866 with Disraeli as chancellor of the exchequer and leader in the House of Commons. Through Disraeli's initiative and skill the famous REFORM BILL of 1867 was passed. Derby never quite fulfilled the promise of his early brilliance; it was his lieutenant, Disraeli, who modernized the Conservative party in this era. See studies by W. D. Jones (1956) and Robert Stewart (1971).

Derby, Edward Henry Stanley, 15th **earl of,** 1826–93, British politician, son of the 14th earl. Although his political persuasions were more liberal than those of his father, he served in the latter's administrations as undersecretary of state for foreign affairs (1852), the first secretary of state for India (1858–59), and foreign secretary (1866–68). He was foreign secretary again (1874–78) under Benjamin Disraeli, but resigned in protest against Disraeli's intervention in the Russo-Turkish war (1878). Derby later (1880) formally shifted his allegiance to the Liberal party and was colonial secretary (1882–85) under William Gladstone. He broke with the Gladstonian Liberals over the issue of Home Rule for Ireland and led the Liberal Unionists in the House of Lords until his retirement in 1891.

Derby, Elias Hasket, (dûr'bē), 1739–99, American merchant, b. Salem, Mass. He inherited the considerable wealth and maritime business that his father, Richard Derby (1712–83), also of Salem, had acquired in trade with Spain and the West Indies previous to the American Revolution. In the Revolution, Elias increased his wealth by fitting out a number of successful privateersmen. After the war he was a pioneer in exploring new trade routes, his ships being among the first to carry the Stars and Stripes to the Baltic and the Orient. His most lucrative trade was with the island of Mauritius in the Indian Ocean. The success of his enterprises was partly due to his wise selection of captains and supercargoes. His mansion, built in 1797 by Samuel MCINTIRE, was reputed the finest in Salem in its day. His son, Elias Hasket Derby, Jr. (1766–1826), b. Salem, made several remarkable voyages for his father's firm and took over the business after his father's death.

Derby, James Stanley, 7th **earl of,** 1607–51, English nobleman. He sat in the House of Commons (1625–28), took his seat in the House of Lords as Baron Strange in 1628 (succeeding his father as earl of Derby in 1642), and was made lord lieutenant of Wales. He did not take an active part in the Long Parliament, but once civil war became imminent he moved to secure Lancashire for the royalists. His plan, although sound at the time, was rejected by King Charles I, and later royalist attempts to capture northern towns were largely unsuccessful. He was impeached (1642) for high treason and fled (1643) to the Isle of Man. He joined Prince Rupert in invading Lancashire in 1644, but after the defeat of the royalists at Marston Moor he returned to Man, where he harbored royalist fugitives. After refusing (1649) to come to terms with Parliament, he fought for Charles II in the battle of Worcester, was captured, court-martialed, and executed.

Derby, Thomas Stanley, 1st **earl of,** 1435?–1504, English nobleman. During the Wars of the Roses, Stanley was ostensibly a supporter of the Lancastrian Henry VI, but he had Yorkist sympathies, having married Eleanor, sister of the Yorkist Richard Neville, earl of Warwick. In the battle of Blore Heath (1459), Stanley did not use his troops on the king's behalf; and in 1461, after the Yorkist Edward IV had become king, he was appointed chief justice of Cheshire. He managed to hold office continuously under both Edward IV and Richard III, becoming lord steward, a privy councilor, and constable of England—this despite his support of the brief Lancastrian restoration in 1471 and his marriage (1482) to Margaret Beaufort, the mother of Henry Tudor, the Lancastrian claimant to the throne. In the battle of Bosworth (1485) he took the field nominally in support of Richard III but took no part in the fighting; after the battle he crowned his stepson Henry VII on the battlefield. He was created (1486) earl of Derby and remained powerful at court until his death.

Derby (där'bē, dûr'-), county borough (1971 pop. 219,348), county town of Derbyshire, central England, on the Derwent River. Derby is a rail center with large engineering works and repair shops. Manufactures include Rolls-Royce automobiles and airplane engines, pottery (see DERBY WARE), synthetic textiles, machinery, and chemicals. Derby was a Roman settlement and (in the 9th cent.) one of the Five Boroughs of the Danes. England's first silk mill was built there in 1718. Derby is the birthplace of the philosopher Herbert Spencer. Noteworthy are the Cathedral of All Saints, with its Perpendicular tower (1509–27), the Roman Catholic Church of St. Mary (built by A. W. N. Pugin in 1838), the arboretum, the chapel of St. Mary of the Bridge, and a grammar school founded in 1160. There is a technical college and a teacher-training college. In 1974, Derby became part of the new nonmetropolitan county of Derbyshire.

Derby (dûr'bē). **1** Uninc. town (1970 pop. 10,206), Adams co., N central Colo., a suburb of Denver. **2** City (1970 pop. 12,599), New Haven co., SW Conn., at the confluence of the Naugatuck and Housatonic rivers, opposite Shelton; founded 1642 as a trading post, inc. as a city 1893. Its copper industry and pin manufactures date from the 1830s.

Derby (där'bē), English horse race, instituted (1780) by the 12th earl of Derby and held annually at Epsom Downs, near London. The race is open only to three-year-old colts and fillies that must be entered when yearlings. The original course is still used; it is one yard more than one and one-half miles. Hundreds of thousands of spectators view the race each year. Other well-known races, notably the Kentucky Derby (dûr'bē), held each year since 1875 at Churchill Downs, Louisville, Ky., have been named for the English classic.

Derbyshire or **Derby,** county (1971 pop. 884,339), central England. The county town is DERBY. The terrain of the county is flat in the south, rising in the north to more than 2,000 ft (610 m) in the Peak district. The region is drained by the Trent River, with the Dove, the Derwent, and the Wye flowing into it. Much of the county is used for agriculture. Dairy farming and sheep and cattle raising are important occupations. There is also wheat and oat cultivation, as well as market gardening. In the eastern part of the county there are rich coal deposits. Manufacturing of textiles, steel, porcelain, and paper is carried on at Derby, Chesterfield, Alfreton, Glossop, and Ilkeston. In the Anglo-Saxon period Derbyshire was part of the kingdom of MERCIA. There are pre-Roman, Roman, and Norman remains. The great house of the dukes of Devonshire is at CHATSWORTH. In 1974, Derbyshire was reorganized as a nonmetropolitan county.

Derby ware (där'bē), English china produced at Derby since about 1750, when William Duesbury opened a pottery there. The china was close in style to contemporary CHELSEA WARE and BOW WARE, whose factories Derby absorbed in the 1770s. It became Royal Crown Derby in 1890 by permission of Queen Victoria. It was in this ware that the government authorized reproductions of the Rhodian and Persian porcelains in the Victoria and Albert Museum for exhibiting in the provinces. Japanese Imari porcelain also was successfully reproduced. Derby ware is distinguished by delicacy of body and richness of decoration; ivory china and eggshell porcelain are among the types manufactured. There have been a score or more of Derby marks, most of which show a crown over a D, sometimes with crossed swords and six dots, the whole in blue or red.

derelict (dĕr'əlĭkt"), in law, personal PROPERTY abandoned by the owner. It is necessary that there be both the intention to abandon and an external act manifesting this intention. In maritime law, derelict refers to a deserted or abandoned ship, e.g., a wrecked ship from which the crew has fled. SALVAGE may be claimed by those rescuing such a ship.

Derg, Lough (lŏkh dĕrg), in Ireland. **1** Expansion of the Shannon River, 23 mi (37 km) long and 1 to 5 mi (1.6–8 km) wide, W central Republic of Ireland. On the lake is the republic's first (1927) major hydroelectric power plant, with an 85,000-kw capacity. On Holy Island or Iniscaltra are ruins of churches and a round tower. **2** Lake, c.20 sq mi (50 sq km), Co. Donegal, NW Republic of Ireland. Station Island, traditional scene of SAINT PATRICK'S PURGATORY, is a famous place of pilgrimage. Saints' Island has ruins of a monastery.

derivation, in grammar: see INFLECTION.

derivative: see CALCULUS.

dermatitis (dûr″mətī′tĭs), nonspecific irritation of the skin. The causative agent may be a bacterium, fungus, or parasite; it can also be a foreign substance, known as an allergen. Contact dermatitis is an allergic reaction to a substance that comes in contact with the skin, such as soap. Atopic dermatitis, also known as ECZEMA, is a chronic, itching inflammation that tends to run in families susceptible to asthma and hay fever. Stasis dermatitis, or eczema of the legs, is caused by poor circulation and is found in older persons suffering from vascular disorders. When dermatitis is chronic it tends to cause thickening, pigmentation, and scaling, and when acute, a red, itching area of blisters and oozing.

dermatology (dûrmətŏl′əjē), branch of MEDICINE concerned with diagnosis and treatment of diseases and disorders of the SKIN. Dermatologists also study the structure and function of the skin, and the relationship between skin pathologies and malfunctions of other organs of the body. Dermatology often overlaps the practice of other medical specialties, e.g., neurology and internal medicine.

dermis: see SKIN.

Dermot McMurrough or **Diarmiud mac Murchada** (both: dûr′mət məkmûr′ə), 1110–71, Irish king of Leinster. He became involved in a complicated feud, partly because he abducted a neighbor's wife, and in 1166 was defeated and banished by the High King Rory O'CONNOR. Dermot appealed for help to Henry II of England, who refused him direct support but allowed him to enlist a force led by Richard de Clare, 2d earl of PEMBROKE, and other Norman barons in Wales. After Pembroke had invaded (1170) and won much of E Ireland, including Dublin, he married Dermot's daughter, Eva. Although Dermot is remembered chiefly for his treachery, he was also a patron of the compilation of the valuable Irish manuscript, the Book of Leinster.

Derna: see DARNAH, Libya.

Dernburg, Bernhard (bĕrn′härt dĕrn′bo͝ork), 1865–1937, German financier and public official. As colonial director (1906) and colonial secretary (1907–10), he was responsible for reforms improving the economy, educational system, and administration of the German colonies. His efforts (1914–15) to act as German propagandist in the United States were offset by the sinking of the *Lusitania.* Dernburg was finance minister in the Scheidemann cabinet (1919) but resigned in protest against the Treaty of Versailles. He served (1920–30) in the Reichstag.

derrick: see CRANE.

Derry, Northern Ireland: see LONDONDERRY.

Derry, town (1970 pop. 11,712), Rockingham co., SE N.H.; set off from Londonderry 1827. Shoes and wood products are made. Robert Frost farmed in Derry and taught school there.

dervish (dûr′vĭsh) [Pers.,=beggar], the friar or monk of ISLAM. There are numerous societies of dervishes, many of them quite similar to religious orders in Western Christendom, with the important difference that since dervishes do not bind themselves by final vows and are never cloistered, enclosed orders are really unknown. Various groups are characterized by extreme forms of mystical practices, such as those of the howling dervishes and whirling dervishes. Some form of SUFISM is usually the theological basis of dervish sects. There is a strong antinomianism among the dervishes, who claim special dispensation on account of their superior favor with God. The ALMOHADS and ALMORAVIDS were at first dervish orders. See also FAKIR.

Derwent (dûr′wənt), river, c.60 mi (100 km) long, rising in the Pennines, Derbyshire, central England, and flowing SE past Derby to the River Trent. Reservoirs on its headwaters supply water to the cities of the Midlands.

Derwentwater, lake, 3 mi (4.8 km) long and 1 mi (1.6 km) wide, Cumberland, NW England, formed by a widening of the River Derwent. It is surrounded by wooded hills, with the Lodore (c.90 ft/27 m) and Barrow (c.108 ft/33 m) waterfalls at its upper end. Its islands include Lord's Isle, site of the former mansion of the earls of Derwent; Isle of St. Herbert (a 7th-century hermit); and Floating Island, a mass of vegetation, sometimes inundated. The River Derwent flows NW through the Lake District to Solway Firth.

Derzhavin, Gavril Romanovich (gəvrēl′ rəmä′nəvĭch dyĭrzhä′vĭn), 1743–1816, Russian classical poet. His satirical ode to Catherine II, *Felitsa* (1783), won her favor, and he became poet laureate and later Minister of Justice. The *Ode to God* (1784, tr. in B. G. Guerney, *A Treasury of Russian Literature,* 1943) is the most famous of his many lyrics. His poetry and memoirs present a rich and complex portrait of his time. See biography by J. V. Clardy (1967).

DES: see DIETHYLSTILBESTROL.

Desaguadero (dāsägwä*th*ā′rō), river, c.200 mi (320 km) long, flowing SE from Lake Titicaca to Lake Poopó, W Bolivia. It is used for irrigation in its northern course. Its flow diminishes toward the south and its banks become less densely populated.

Desai, Morarji Ranchhodji (môrär′jē ränchō′jē dēsī′), 1896–, Indian political leader. He entered the civil service in 1919 but resigned in 1930 to devote himself to the independence movement, and he was jailed several times for his nationalist activities. After independence he served as an administrator of Bombay (1947–56) before becoming minister of commerce and industry (1956–58) and then minister of finance (1958–63). He returned to the government in 1967 as deputy prime minister and minister of finance, but in 1969 he was maneuvered from office by Indira Gandhi and subsequently became a leader of the right-wing opposition.

Desaix de Veygoux, Louis Charles Antoine (lwē shärl äNtwän′ dəsā′ də vāgo͞o′), 1768–1800, French general in the FRENCH REVOLUTIONARY WARS. He served under J. B. Jourdan and J. V. Moreau on the Rhine and distinguished himself in Napoleon Bonaparte's Egyptian campaign as a soldier and an administrator. He saved the day for Napoleon at Marengo, but he was killed there.

desalination of water: see WATER, DESALINATION OF.

De Sanctis, Francesco (fränchās′kō dā sängk′tēs), 1817–83, Italian historian and literary critic. He was one of the founders of modern Italian literary criticism. He suffered imprisonment for his political views and was exiled to Malta. He was later professor of comparative literature at Naples (1871–77) and supported Cavour, who appointed him minister of education. Important works are his *Saggi critici* [critical essays] (1866) and his *History of Italian Literature* (1871, tr. 1931), a history of Italian national feeling as traced through literature. He also wrote studies of Petrarch (2d ed. 1883) and Leopardi (1885).

Desargues, Gérard (zhärär′ dəzärg′), 1591–1661, French mathematician and engineer, a founder of modern geometry. He discovered the theorems on involutions and transversals known by his name and worked on conic sections. His writings, lost for a time, were republished in 1864. His purely mathematical texts, in French, ed. by René Taton, were republished in 1951.

Des Barres or **Desbarres, Joseph Frederick Wallet** (däbär′), 1721?–1824, British army officer, surveyor, and artist. He was born of French parents (probably in Switzerland), was educated at Basel and in Great Britain, and became a British citizen. He served with British forces in America in the French and Indian War, rendering valuable service as an engineer in the taking of Quebec. He later spent 10 years surveying the coasts of Nova Scotia and another 10 years in London editing his data, incorporating the surveys of others, and supervising the engraving of the plates; the result was *The Atlantic Neptune,* which appeared in successive issues (1777–81) and was used by British seamen in American waters for three generations. The plates are justly famous for their artistic excellence, and they are collector's items; the largest collection is found in the U.S. Library of Congress. Des Barres was later lieutenant governor of Cape Breton (1784–1805) and then of Prince Edward Island (1805–1813). His name also appears as Joseph Frederick Walsh Des Barres.

Descartes, René (rənā′ däkärt′), Lat. *Renatus Cartesius,* 1596–1650, French philosopher and scientist, b. La Haye. He was educated in the Jesuit College at La Flèche and the Univ. of Poitiers, then entered the army of Prince Maurice of Nassau. In 1628 he retired to Holland, where he spent his time in scientific research and philosophic reflection. In 1649 he was invited by Queen Christina to Sweden, but he was unable to endure the rigors of the northern climate and died not long after arriving in Sweden. Even before going to Holland, Descartes had begun his great work, for the essay on algebra and the *Compendium musicae* probably antedate 1628. But it was with the appearance in 1637 of a group of essays that he first made a name for himself. These writings included the famous *Discourse on Method* and other essays on dioptrics, meteors, and analytical geometry. Mathematics was his greatest interest; building upon the work of others, he originated the CARTESIAN COORDINATES and Cartesian curves; he is often said to be the founder of analytical geometry. To algebra he contributed the treatment of negative roots and the convention of exponent notation. It was with the intention of extending mathematical method to all fields of human knowledge that he developed his methodology, the cardinal aspect of his philosophy. He discards the authoritarian system of the scholastics and begins with universal doubt. But there is one thing that cannot be doubted: doubt itself. This is the kernel expressed in his famous phrase, *Cogito, ergo sum* [I think, therefore I am]. From the certainty of the existence of a thinking being, he passed to the existence of God, for which he offered one proof based on St. Anselm's ontological proof and another based on the first cause that must have produced the idea of God in the thinker. Having thus arrived at the existence of God, he reaches the reality of the physical world through God, who would not deceive the thinking mind by perceptions that are illusions. Therefore, the external world, which we perceive, must exist. He thus falls back on the acceptance of what we perceive clearly and distinctly as being true, and he studies the material world to perceive connections. He views the physical world as mechanistic and entirely divorced from the mind, the only connection between the two being by intervention of God. This is almost complete DUALISM. In science, he discarded tradition and to an extent supported the same method as Francis Bacon, but with emphasis on rationalization and logic rather than upon experiences. In physical theory his doctrines were formulated as a compromise between his devotion to Roman Catholicism and his commitment to the scientific method, which met opposition in the churchmen of the day. He made numerous advances in optics, such as his study of the reflection and refraction of light. He wrote a text on physiology, and he also worked in psychology; he contended that emotion was finally physiological at base and argued that the control of the physical expression of emotion would control the emotions themselves. His chief work on psychology is in his *Traité des passions de l'âme* (1649); the development of his philosophy is in *Meditationes de prima philosophia* (1641); his *Principia philosophiae* (1644) is also very important. His influence on philosophy was immense, and was widely felt in law and theology also. Frequently he has been called the father of modern philosophy, but his importance has been challenged in recent years with the demonstration of his great debt to the scholastics. He influenced the rationalists, and Baruch Spinoza also reflects Descartes's doctrines in some degree. The more direct followers of Descartes, the Cartesian philosophers, devoted themselves chiefly to the problem of the relation of body and soul, of matter and mind. From this came the doctrine of occasionalism, developed by Nicolas Malebranche and Arnold Geulincx. See Jacques Maritain, *The Dream of Descartes* (tr. 1944, repr. 1969); A. G. Balz, *Descartes and the Modern Mind* (1952); J. R. Vrooman, *René Descartes* (1970); Hiram Caton, *The Origin of Subjectivity: An Essay on Descartes* (1973).

descent, in anthropology, method of classifying individuals in terms of their various kinship connections. Matrilineal and patrilineal descent refer to the mother's or father's sib (or other group), respectively. Bilateral descent refers to descent derived from both sibs equally. Descent groups are of basic significance in the social structure of most nonindustrial societies. They constitute a series of social groups that dominate the domestic organization and the process of socialization, the use and transfer of property, the settlement of disputes, religious activities such as ancestor worship, and certain political relationships. Some lineage systems extend to the limits of the society itself. The Tiv of E Nigeria, for example, all consider themselves descendants in the male line of an eponymous ancestor, and the genealogy of this progeny defines the complete outline of descent group structure.

Deschanel, Émile (āmĕl' dāshänĕl'), 1819–1904, French author and politician. Of his numerous works the best known are such critical studies as *Études sur Aristophane* (1867) and *Le Romantisme des classiques* (1882). His *Catholicisme et socialisme* (1850) offended Louis Napoleon (later Napoleon III), and Deschanel spent the years 1851–59 in exile. He was made a professor at the Collège de France and a senator in 1881.

Deschanel, Paul Eugéne Louis (pôl ûzhĕn' lwē), 1855–1922, president of the French republic (1920); son of Émile Deschanel. A member of the chamber of deputies from 1885 and several times its president, he was chosen over Georges Clemenceau to succeed Raymond Poincaré as president of France. Ill health soon forced his resignation, and he was succeeded by Alexandre Millerand. Deschanel wrote many political works, notably *Gambetta* (1920) and *La Question sociale* (1898).

Deschutes (dāshōōts'), river, c.240 mi (390 km) long, rising in several lakes in the Cascade Range, W central Oregon, and flowing NE to the Columbia River. The U.S. Bureau of Reclamation has developed the stream and its main tributary, the Crooked River, for power (1,500-kw capacity) and irrigation (c.100,000 acres/40,470 hectares).

descriptive geometry, branch of GEOMETRY concerned with the two-dimensional representation of three-dimensional objects; it was introduced in 1795 by Gaspard Monge. By means of such representations, geometrical problems in three dimensions may be solved in the plane. (Such problems arise in all branches of engineering.) Modern mechanical drawing and architectural drawing are based on the principles of descriptive geometry.

desegregation: see INTEGRATION.

Deseret: see MORMONS; UTAH.

desert, arid region, usually partly covered by sand, having scanty vegetation or sometimes almost none, and capable of supporting only a limited and specially adapted animal population. The so-called cold deserts, caused by extreme cold and often covered with perpetual snow or ice, are quite distinct from the deserts of warm regions; cold deserts cover about one sixth of the world's surface. It is estimated that warm deserts form about one fifth of the land surface of the world. The largest desert regions of the world lie between 20° and 30° north and south of the equator, either where mountains intercept the paths of the trade winds or where atmospheric high-pressure areas cause descending air currents and lack of precipitation. Other factors contributing to the formation of deserts include the amount of sunshine, rate of evaporation of water, and range of temperature. An area having an annual rainfall of 10 in. (25 cm) or less is considered to be a desert. Some deserts have no rain for intervals of several years. Deserts and semideserts exist in some regions having up to about 20 in. (50 cm) of rainfall where evaporation is very high and loss by runoff is great. Temperature ranges in deserts are often extreme. Europe is the only continent without deserts; there are, however, semiarid portions around the Black and Caspian seas, in parts of the Ukraine and N Caucasus. In Asia a great desert, the GOBI, exists in the middle latitudes chiefly because of its remoteness from water. Also in central Asia are the KARA KUM and Kyzyl-Kum deserts. Farther south there are desert areas in NW India and through S Pakistan, Afghanistan, Iran, Iraq, and Arabia; these are largely the result of their situation in a subtropical high-pressure belt and of the distribution of pressure areas that produce cold, dry winds in winter and hot, dry winds in summer. The SAHARA, the largest desert in the world, is in Africa. Second only to the Sahara in area is the desert region of central and W Australia, lying in a high-pressure belt and in the path of the trade winds (which lose much of their moisture on the windward slopes of the east-coast mountains). South America has deserts on the coast and interior of Chile and E of the Andes in Argentina and Patagonia. In North America, deserts are found from N Mexico northward through parts of the SW and W United States. Extreme desert conditions exist in the MOJAVE DESERT, the IMPERIAL VALLEY, and Death Valley (see DEATH VALLEY NATIONAL MONUMENT). The northern plateau region of Mexico and the adjacent portions of Texas, Arizona, and New Mexico have less extreme desert conditions with a quite abundant growth of mesquite, greasewood, creosote bush, yucca, and various species of CACTUS. Middle-latitude deserts are found in parts of the Great Basin. Plants of the desert have leaves and stems adapted to lessen their loss of water, and individual plants are more widely spaced than those in more humid regions; their roots form a spreading network sometimes penetrating to 50 ft (15 m) underground. Among the animals living in deserts of North America are species of squirrels, mice, bats, foxes, rabbits, and deer; reptiles, e.g., the Arizona coral snake, species of rattlesnakes, the desert tortoise, and the horned toad, gila monster, and many other lizards; a number of birds, e.g., the cactus wren, the road runner, species of owls, sparrows, and hawks; and spiders, scorpions, termites, and beetles. See DUNE; OASIS. See J. W. Krutch, *The Voice of the Desert* (1955); D. F. Costello, *The Desert World* (1972); studies by E. C. Jaeger on desert flora and fauna (1957, 1961, 1965).

desertion, in law, the forsaking of a station involving public or social duties without justification and with the intention of not returning. In military law, it is the abandonment of (or failure to arrive at) a place of duty without leave; in time of war, especially in the face of the enemy, desertion is punishable by death. In maritime law, a seaman who abandons a ship without leave is rendered liable to damages and forfeits the wages he has already earned. In family law, desertion is the willful abandonment of the spouse or the children of a marriage without consent of the other party or parties. The refusal to renew cohabitation without justification is also desertion, although in only a few states of the United States is mere abstinence from sexual intercourse considered such. The refusal by a husband to support his wife has been regarded as desertion if he has the means to support her. The wife who refuses to follow her husband when he changes his DOMICILE in good faith deserts him, since the matrimonial domicile is established by the husband's residence. In most states, desertion continued for a certain period is grounds for DIVORCE.

desert lily, common name for the species *Hesperocallis undulata,* a member of the family Liliaceae (LILY family), found in the SW United States.

desert trumpet: see BUCKWHEAT.

De-shima (dā'-shĭmä) or **De-jima** (dā'-jĭmä), artificial island, c.40 acres (16 hectares), Nagasaki prefecture, W Kyushu, Japan, in Nagasaki harbor. It has many docks and is connected by bridge to the city of Nagasaki. Dutch traders were restricted (1641–1858) to this island after Japan closed (17th cent.) its borders to foreign trade.

Desiderio da Settignano (dāzēdē'rēō dä sĕt''-tēnyä'nō), 1428–64, Florentine sculptor, a follower of Donatello. His marble carving, of exquisite delicacy, is best seen in his church decorations and in his busts of women and children. His *Laughing Child* in Vienna is characteristic of his style and charm. His tomb of Carlo Marsuppini in the Church of Santa Croce, Florence, is one of the most beautiful of early Renaissance monuments. The National Gallery of Art, Washington, D.C., has four examples.

Desiderius (dĕsĭdēr'ēəs), d. after 774, last Lombard king in Italy (756–74). The duke of Tuscany, he was chosen king with the support of the pope and of Pepin the Short, who was king of the Franks and whose son Charles (later Emperor Charlemagne) married Desiderius's daughter. Desiderius's alliance with his son-in-law Duke Tassilo of Bavaria and his subsequent interference in Roman affairs incensed Charlemagne, who repudiated (771) his wife and provoked open conflict. Desiderius responded by supporting the claims of the children of Charlemagne's brother Carloman (d. 771), by attacking Pope ADRIAN I, and by occupying several papal cities. Charlemagne invaded (773) Italy, captured (774) Desiderius at Pavia after a long siege, and proclaimed himself king of the Lombards. Desiderius was forced to retire to a monastery at Liège.

design, plan or arrangement of line, form, mass, color, and space in a pattern. A design may be created to serve a functional purpose as in ARCHITECTURE and in industrial designs or else purely to provide aesthetic pleasure. The design may refer to preparatory stages for a work of art (see DRAWING; CARTOON) or it may be extended to include the compositional elements in a finished work of art.

Désirade: see GUADELOUPE.

De Sitter, Willem: see SITTER, WILLEM DE.

Desmarets, Nicolas (nēkōlä' dāmärā'), 1648–1721, French statesman; the nephew of Jean Baptiste Colbert. He became director of finances in 1703 and succeeded Michel CHAMILLART as controller general of finances in 1708. He tried to meet the huge expenses of the War of the Spanish Succession by issuing paper money and instituting an income tax, the *dixième* [Fr.,=tenth]. Those measures only intensified France's financial crisis, first by encouraging speculation that led to inflation and second by placing the burden of taxation on the poor and the middle class while exempting the privileged aristocracy.

Desmarets de Saint-Sorlin, Jean (zhäN dāmärā' də săN-sôrlăN'), 1595–1676, French poet and dramatist. A protégé of Richelieu, he was a founding member of the French Academy. His comedy *Les Visionnaires* (1637) ridicules the sophisticated society of his day. In 1670 he precipitated a controversy over the literary merits of the ancients that foreshadowed the polemics of PERRAULT and BOILEAU-DESPRÉAUX; Boileau attacked him in *L'Art poétique.*

De Smet, Pierre Jean (dē smĕt), 1801–73, Jesuit missionary in the U.S. Pacific Northwest, b. Belgium. He emigrated to the United States in 1821, served his novitiate in Florissant, Mo., and was ordained in 1827. He began (1838) his long missionary career at a mission on the site of Council Bluffs, Iowa. In 1840 he went to Montana with two Flathead Indians who had come to St. Louis in search of a "black robe" (Jesuit), and he established missions in Montana and Idaho. Traveling widely across the Northwest from 1840 to 1846, he won the friendship of various Indian tribes. Later he acted often as mediator between Indian and white—notably in the council at Fort Laramie in 1851 and in the Yakima War of 1858–59. He is said to have advised Brigham Young as to a place for the Mormons to settle, and he was a pacifier in the UTAH WAR. He undertook several peace missions to the Sioux. His books are excellent source material in Western history—*Letters and Sketches* (1843), *Oregon Missions and Travels* (1847), *Western Missions and Missionaries* (1859), and *New Indian Sketches* (1863). See biography by J. U. Terrell (1964).

desmid: see DIATOM.

Des Moines (də moin), city (1970 pop. 200,587), state capital and seat of Polk co., S central Iowa, at the junction of the Des Moines and the Raccoon rivers; inc. as Fort Des Moines in 1851, chartered as Des Moines in 1857. Iowa's largest city, it is an important industrial and transportation center in the heart of the Corn Belt. Printing and publishing, agricultural processing, and the manufacture of machinery, tires, farm implements, recreational vehicles, metal products, and apparel are among its many industries. The city is also the home office of numerous insurance companies. Settled by homesteaders, Des Moines became the capital of Iowa in 1857. It is the seat of Drake Univ., the College of Osteopathic Medicine and Surgery, Open Bible College, and two junior colleges. Places of interest include the capitol (1871–84); the Des Moines Art Center; the Center of Science and Industry; the State Historical, Memorial, and Art Building; the Equitable Building; the state fairgrounds; and c.1700 acres (690 hectares) of parks. The city suffered a severe flood in 1954; dams and reservoirs on the Des Moines River now provide flood control.

Des Moines, river, 535 mi (861 km) long, rising in SW Minn. and flowing SE across Iowa to the Mississippi River at Keokuk, SE Iowa. Flowing through rich farmland, the river floods in the spring and is nearly dry in late September; dams now regulate its flow. It is the main source of water for Des Moines, Iowa.

Desmond, Gerald Fitzgerald, 15th **earl of,** d. 1583, Irish nobleman. He spent his life fighting Thomas Butler, 10th earl of ORMONDE, who represented English interests. He was twice imprisoned in London, but returned both times to continue his struggle. In 1579 he was proclaimed a traitor, and after four years of rebellion, he was captured and killed.

Desmoulins, Camille (kämē'yə dāmōōlăN'), 1760–94, French revolutionary and journalist. His oratory of July 12, 1789, contributed to the storming of the Bastille two days later. His pamphlets and journals, such as *Révolutions de France et de Brabant* (1789), were received with immense enthusiasm. Elected to the Convention (1792), he attacked the GIRONDISTS in the *Histoire des Brissotins;* but late in 1793, after the execution of Girondist leaders, Desmoulins, along with Georges DANTON, counseled moderation, publishing the journal *Le Vieux Cordelier.* He was arrested with Danton and others and was executed. His beautiful wife, Lucile Duplessis, was guillotined shortly after.

Desna (dyĭsnä'), river, c.740 mi (1,190 km) long, W European USSR, partly in the Ukraine. It is a main tributary of the Dnepr. Rising SE of Smolensk, the Desna flows S and SW past Bryansk and Chernigov, joining the Dnepr above Kiev. It is navigable for c.330 mi (530 km) below Novgorod Seversky, Ukraine.

Desnos, Robert (rôbĕr' dĕsnôs'), 1900–45, French poet. Among the best-known surrealist poets, he was one of the chief proponents of so-called automatic writing. He put himself in a trance before writing many of his works. They include *La Liberté ou l'amour* [liberty or love] (1927), *Corps et Biens* [bodies and blessings] (1930), *État de veille* [wakefulness] (1943), *Contrée* [thwarted] (1944), *Félix Labisse* (1945), and *Choix de poems* [choice of poems] (1945). He also wrote a novel, *Le Vin est tiré* [the wine is killed] (1943), and a surrealistic drama, *La Place de L'étoile* (1945). During World War II, Desnos died as a prisoner in the Theresienstadt concentration camp.

De Soto, Hernando (dĭsō'tō, Span. ĕrnän'dō dā sō'tō), c.1500–1542, Spanish explorer in the present-day United States. After serving under Pedrarias in Central America and under Francisco Pizarro in Peru, the dashing young conquistador was made governor of Cuba by Emperor Charles V, with the right to conquer Florida (meaning the North American mainland). He led an expedition that left Spain in 1538 and landed on the Florida coast, probably near Tampa Bay, in 1539. That was the start of an adventure that took him and his band nearly halfway across the continent in search of gold, silver, and jewels, which they never found. After wintering near Tallahassee they went N through Georgia and the Carolinas into Tennessee, then turned S into Alabama, where De Soto was wounded in a battle with Indians. He was so determined to continue his treasure hunt that he refused to inform his men that Spanish vessels were off the coast. In the spring of 1541 they again set forth and were probably the first white men to see and cross the Mississippi (there is strong argument as to the exact spot). A journey up the Arkansas River and into Oklahoma disclosed no treasures, and, discouraged, they turned back to the banks of the Mississippi. There De Soto died; he was buried in the river, so that the Indians, whom he had intimidated and ill-used, would not learn of his death. His men went west again across the Red River into N Texas, then returned to the Mississippi and followed it to the sea. A remnant of the expedition made its way down the coast to arrive at Veracruz in 1543. The chief chronicle of the expedition is by a Portuguese called the Gentleman of Elvas, See biographies by R. B. Cunninghame Graham (1924), Theodore Maynard (1930, repr. 1969), and Bernard Shipp (1831, repr. 1971); study by R. F. Schell (1966); E. G. Bourne, *Narratives of the Career of Hernando de Soto* (1904).

De Soto National Memorial: see NATIONAL PARKS AND MONUMENTS (table).

Desoxyn (dĕsŏk'sĭn), trade name for the drug methamphetamine hydrochloride. See AMPHETAMINE.

Despenser, Hugh le, d. 1265, chief justiciar of England. He joined the barons in their struggle against Henry III and received various offices, becoming chief justiciar in 1260. He lost this office in 1261 but was restored to it in 1263. He fought in the BARONS' WAR and was killed at Evesham in 1265. His son and grandson **Hugh le Despenser,** the elder, 1262–1326, and **Hugh le Despenser,** the younger, d. 1326, became even more prominent. The elder Despenser took part in Edward I's Scottish campaigns and engaged in negotiations with France. On the accession of EDWARD II, Despenser alienated the baronial party by his support of Piers GAVESTON and, on the latter's death (1312), became the chief adviser to the king. After Edward's defeat by the Scots at Bannockburn in 1314, Hugh withdrew from the court. About 1318 the younger Despenser, who had earlier supported the barons, joined his father and the king, soon gaining more influence with Edward than had the elder Hugh. Both Despensers became involved in a quarrel with the barons, who formed a league against them and brought about their banishment in 1321. In 1322, however, they returned to England, and after the baronial defeat at Boroughbridge they were the real rulers of the kingdom. The elder Despenser was created earl of Winchester in 1322. Their rule was notable for several important administrative reforms and the conclusion of peace with Scotland (1323), but their greed was enormous and they were bitterly hated by the barons. Both Despensers were executed after the invasion of Queen ISABELLA in 1326. See J. C. Davies, *The Baronial Opposition to Edward II* (1918, repr. 1967).

Des Périers, Bonaventure (bōnävăNtür' dā pārēā'), c. 1510–1544, French humanist and poet; protégé of Margaret of Navarre. His chief work, *Cymbalum mundi* (1537), a series of four skeptical prose dialogues in the manner of Lucian, was banned because of its attack on Christianity.

Despiau, Charles (shärl dāpēō'), 1874–1946, French sculptor. He studied at the École des Arts décoratifs and the École des Beaux-Arts, Paris, and worked in Rodin's studio (1907–14). His well-constructed, quiescent forms of young women have often been compared with the works of Maillol. Despiau is known for his sensitive portrait busts; his *Mme Derain* (1922) is at the Phillips Gallery in Washington, D.C.

Des Plaines (dĕs plānz), city (1970 pop. 57,239), Cook co., NE Ill., a suburb of Chicago on the Des Plaines River; inc. 1925. Its manufactures include electrical and electronic equipment, chemicals, cylinders, oil products, and cosmetics. It was founded in the 1830s as the town of Rand; the name was changed in 1869; Riverview was annexed in 1925. De Lourdes College is there, and O'Hare International Airport is to the south.

Des Plaines, river, 110 mi (177 km) long, rising in SE Wis., and flowing S and SW through NE Ill., joining the Kankakee River S of Joliet, Ill., to form the Illinois River. The lower Des Plaines is part of the Illinois Waterway.

Desportes, Alexandre-François (älĕksäN'drə-fräNswä' dāpôrt'), 1661–1743, French painter. He is best known for his hunting scenes and paintings of animals. Desportes, who began as a portrait painter, was among the first to paint landscapes from nature; for that practice he was held to be eccentric. His works are in the tradition of careful realism of Flemish still-life paintings. The Louvre and the Wallace Collection, London, have examples of his work.

despotism, government by an absolute ruler unchecked by effective constitutional limits to his power. In Greek usage, a despot was ruler of a household and master of its slaves. The title was applied to gods and, by derivation, to the quasi-divine rulers of the Near East. In the Byzantine Empire, despot was a title of honor of the emperors and their relatives and of vassal princes of the tributary states and dignitaries of the Eastern Church. The Ottoman Empire perpetuated the term as applied to church officials and territorial princes. The 18th-century doctrine of the Enlightenment influenced such absolutist rulers as Frederick the Great of Prussia, Catherine II of Russia, and Holy Roman Emperor Joseph II toward a rule of beneficent intent known as benevolent despotism. However, despot is now a term of opprobrium.

Des Prés, Josquin: see JOSQUIN DESPREZ.

Dessalines, Jean Jacques (zhäN zhäk dĕsälēn'), c.1758–1806, Negro emperor of Haiti (1804–6), born a slave. A shrewd general, he served under TOUSSAINT L'OUVERTURE in the wars that liberated Haiti. His barbaric cruelty against the mulattoes whom Toussaint was unable to control led to a bitter struggle with the mulatto leaders André RIGAUD and Alexandre PÉTION. Dessalines fought brilliantly against the French under Leclerc in 1802, earning the nickname of the Tiger. After the decimation of the French army by yellow fever and the capture of Toussaint, he revolted and overwhelmed the invaders in 1803. Independence was declared Jan. 1, 1804, at Gonaïves and Dessalines chosen governor for life. Later, attempting to emulate Napoleon, he had himself crowned emperor as Jacques I in an ostentatious ceremony. In attempting to reorganize the nation's shattered economy, the ambitious emperor instituted drastic measures, such as forced labor, and accompanied them with despotic and cruel acts. He was ambushed and killed; Henri CHRISTOPHE succeeded him in power.

Dessau (dĕs'ou), city (1970 pop. 98,261), Halle district, central East Germany, at the confluence of the Elbe and Mulde rivers. It is an industrial city, river port, and rail and road transport center. Manufactures include machinery, chemicals, paper, and processed food. Dessau was first known as a German settlement in 1213. In 1603 it became the residence of the line of ANHALT-Dessau. From 1925 to 1932 it was the seat of the Bauhaus art school, headed by Walter Gropius. The city was severely damaged in World War II. The Marienkirche in Dessau, a 16th-century church, has an altarpiece by Lucas Cranach, the younger. The philosopher Moses Mendelssohn was born (1729) in Dessau.

Dessoir, Max (mäks dĕswär'), 1867–1947, German philosopher. He earned doctorates from the universities of Berlin (philosophy, 1889) and Würtzburg (medicine, 1892). He was a professor at Berlin from 1897 until 1933, when the Nazis forbade him to teach. He worked mainly in the area of aesthetics, trying to foster a general science of art. Dessoir understood an aesthetic object to be one occurring either in nature or in art, the parts of which are related to each other with an intensity beyond that of normal experience. He defined five primary forms of aesthetic experience: beauty, ugliness, comedy, tragedy, and the sublime. He saw the role of art as moral and social and regarded "Art for art's sake" as a futile and fatuous maxim. Dessoir was also interested in parapsychology. Among his few works translated into English are *Outlines of the History of Psychology* (tr. 1912) and *Aesthetics and Theory of Art* (tr. 1970).

Dessye (dĕs'yā), Ital. *Dessie,* town (1968 est. pop. 40,600), capital of Wallo prov., central Ethiopia, in the Great Rift Valley. It is an administrative, military, and commercial center.

Destouches, Philippe Néricault (fēlēp' nārēkō' dātōōsh'), 1680–1754, French dramatist. He was known for his moralistic comedies. *Le Glorieux* (1732, tr. 1791), his masterpiece, treats the conflict between the old nobility and the rising bourgeoisie.

destroyer, class of warship very fast relative to its length, generally equipped with torpedos, antisubmarine equipment, and medium-caliber and antiaircraft guns. The newest destroyers are equipped with guided missiles as their chief offensive weapon. The destroyer, originally called the torpedo-boat destroyer, was introduced in 1892 as an answer to the TORPEDO BOAT, but it rapidly replaced that type by taking over its functions. Later, its role as a torpedo launcher declined, and today destroyers have a mainly defensive role; they are used for convoying merchant ships and as escort vessels in a battle fleet. Destroyers were of great importance in World War II; equipped with new electronic devices, they proved highly effective as antisubmarine weapons and, hence, as escorts for convoys. Specialized types include the radar picket destroyer, designed for detection of enemy aircraft and control of friendly combat air patrol, and the minelaying destroyer. The USS *Truxtun* (launched in 1964) was the first of a class of nuclear-powered destroyer-type ships, officially categorized as frigates. See Ewart Brookes, *Destroyer* (1962); E. J. March, *British Destroyers: A History of Development 1892–1953* (1966); *Jane's Fighting Ships* (pub. annually since 1897).

Destutt de Tracy, Antoine Louis Claude, Comte (äNtwän' lwē klōd kôNt dĕstüt' də träsē'), 1754–1836, French philosopher and psychologist. Although active in the Napoleonic government, he was important for his leadership of the ideologists, disciples of Condillac. This group contributed to such later psychological developments as the James-Lange theory of emotions. Starting from Condillac's reduction of consciousness to the reception and combination of sensations, he developed a philosophy of education for post-Revolutionary France. See his *Élémens d'idéologie* (4 vol., 1800–1815).

detective story, type of popular fiction in which a crime, usually a murder, is solved by a detective through the logical interpretation of evidence. Although some critics trace the origins of the genre to such disparate works as Aesop's fables, Chaucer's *Canterbury Tales,* and the Apocrypha, most agree that the detective story, complete with all its conventions, emerged in 1841 with the publication of Edgar Allan Poe's "The Murders in the Rue Morgue." This and all of Poe's "tales of ratiocination" feature the chevalier C. Auguste Dupin, a brilliant amateur detective, who, by a keen analysis of motives and clues, solves crimes that are baffling to the police. The first full-length detective novel is probably Wilkie Collins's *The Moonstone* (1868), which continued Poe's concept of the brilliant detective—although Collins's rose-growing Sergeant Cuff is a policeman—and added an emphasis on the sleuth's idiosyncracies. Charles Dickens's *The Mystery of Edwin Drood* (1870) is a detective novel both intriguing and frustrating because, since the novel is unfinished, its crime is never solved. In 1887, Arthur Conan Doyle published "A Study in Scarlet," which introduced Sherlock Holmes, destined to become the most famous of all literary detectives. This vain and aloof amateur sleuth, with a fondness for pipes, violins, and drugs, solves crimes through extraordinarily perceptive recognition and interpretation of evidence. Like Conan Doyle, subsequent detective-story writers often featured the same detective in several works. Especially popular are G. K. Chesterton's Father Brown, E. D. Biggers's Charlie Chan, S. S. Van Dine's Philo Vance, Rex Stout's Nero Wolfe, Agatha Christie's Hercule Poirot and Miss Marple, Dorothy Sayers's Lord Peter Wimsey, Leslie Charteris's "The Saint," Robert van Gulick's Magistrate Dee, Harry Kemelman's Rabbi David Small, Emma Lathan's John Putnam Thatcher, and Ellery Queen in the works of Frederic Dannay and M.B. Lee. Authors often incorporate the conventions of the detective story into the novel, producing works that are warm, witty, often erudite, and filled with interesting characters and atmosphere. Such authors include Dorothy Sayers, Michael Innes, Josephine Tey, Nicholas Blake, Edgar Wallace, Ngaio Marsh, Philip McDonald, Anna K. Green, Carolyn Wells, Mary Roberts Rinehart, Elizabeth Daly, and Hilda Lawrence. Some detective novels focus on the actions of the police in solving a crime; notable "police procedure" novelists are Freeman Wills Crofts, George Bagby, Ed McBain, and Maj Sjöwall and Per Wahlöö. Dashiell Hammett initiated the "hard-boiled" dectective genre, featuring tough, brash, yet honorable "private eyes" living on the seedy criminal fringe and involved in violent and incredibly complex crimes; other such writers are Raymond Chandler and Ross Macdonald and, adding lurid sex and brutality, James Hadley Chase and Mickey Spillane. In the early 1960s espionage novels became very popular. Usually convoluted in plot, they emphasize action, sex, innovative cruelty, and the moral ambiguity of the spy's world. Noted authors of espionage novels are Graham Greene, Eric Ambler, Ian Fleming, Len Deighton, and John Le Carré. In the subtle and perceptive works of writers such as Georges Simenon and Nicholas Freeling the psychological reasons behind a crime are often emphasized more than the crime's solution. Other writers, notably Julian Symons, extend this emphasis, maintaining that early mysteries, with their country house settings and aristocratic characters, are snobbish and escapist. Attempting to be contemporary and meaningful, these authors probe the psychological and sociological aspects of a crime, often producing grim and uncomfortable conclusions. Despite its conventions, good writers can make the detective novel their own. For example, Agatha Christie is noted for her clever plots, John Dickson Carr for his ingenious "locked room" mysteries, Dick Francis for his depiction of the horse-racing world, and Ruth Rendell for her novels combining character and atmosphere with absorbing police procedure, perceptive sociological and psychological analysis, and a sense of life's tragedy. See GOTHIC ROMANCE. See the annual collections of the best detective stories, ed. by A. J. Hubin; Howard Haycraft, *Murder for Pleasure* (rev. ed. 1968); Jacques Barzun and W. H. Taylor, *A Catalogue of Crime* (1971).

detector, in physics, device for detecting, measuring, and analyzing particles and other forms of RADIATION entering it. Such devices play an important role not only in basic research, as in the study of ELEMENTARY PARTICLES, but also in numerous applications of physics, from uses of radioactive tracers in medicine and biology to prospecting for natural ores that exhibit RADIOACTIVITY. Almost all instruments used for detecting are based either on the ionization of matter caused by radiation or on the LUMINESCENCE it can cause in certain materials. In devices based on ionization (the separation of neutral atoms or molecules into oppositely charged fragments), various methods may be used to convert the ionization to a useful measure of the radiation. In the IONIZATION CHAMBER and the GEIGER COUNTER, the radiation is measured by changes in an external electrical circuit; these changes are due to a current resulting from the increase of charges. In the BUBBLE CHAMBER, CLOUD CHAMBER, and SPARK CHAMBER, ionization is used to make visible the track of the charged particle causing the ionization. By adding a magnetic field across the path of incoming particles, a great deal can be learned about the nature and properties of the particles detected by the chambers; the presence of uncharged particles can be indicated indirectly as well. Another device used in studies of particles records a visible track made in a photographic emulsion. The most important device based on the luminescent effect of radiation is the SCINTILLATION COUNTER. In addition to these larger instruments, there are also small detectors designed to be worn or carried by persons working near sources of potentially dangerous radiation. These are scaled down and sometimes simplified versions of the devices already described. Typical of these small detectors are pocket-size ionization chambers that resemble fountain pens and film detectors, embedded in badges, that register the amount of radiation by the degree of exposure of the film.

detergent (dētûr'jənt, dĭ–), substance that aids in the removal of dirt. Detergents act mainly on the oily films that trap dirt particles. The detergent molecules have a hydrocarbon portion, soluble in oil, and an ionic portion, soluble in water. The detergent acts as an emulsifier, i.e., by bridging the water and oil phases, it breaks the oil into tiny droplets suspended in water. The disruption of the oil film allows the dirt particles to become wet and float away. Soap, the sodium salt of long-chain fatty acids, is a good detergent although it has some disadvantages, e.g., it forms insoluble compounds with certain salts found in hard water thus diminishing its effectiveness, and in acid solutions, frequently used in industry, it is decomposed (thus precipitating the free fatty acid of the soap). Synthetic detergents were produced experimentally in France before the middle of the 19th cent. and were further developed in Germany during World War I. However, not until the 1930s were chemical processes developed that made production in quantity feasible in any country. Synthetic detergents were first developed for commercial use in the 1950s. Detergents are classified as anionic, or negatively charged, e.g., soaps; cationic, or positively charged, e.g., tetraalkyl ammonium chloride, used as fabric softeners; nonionic, e.g., certain esters made from oil, used as degreasing agents in industry; and zwitterionic, containing both positive and negative ions on the same molecule. Detergents are incorporated in such products as dry-cleaning solutions, toothpastes, antiseptics, and solutions for removing poison sprays from vegetables and fruit. Laundry detergent preparations may contain substances called builders, which enhance cleansing; however, phosphate-containing builders have been found to contribute to EUTROPHICATION of waterways and their use has been curtailed. Detergents that can be decomposed by microorganisms are termed biodegradable.

determinant, square array of numbers or other elements representing a specific combination of these elements as a sum (or difference) of products. The order of a determinant is equal to the number of rows or columns that it has. For example, a fifth-order determinant has five rows and five columns. The general second-order determinant

$$\begin{vmatrix} a_{11} & a_{12} \\ a_{21} & a_{22} \end{vmatrix}$$

has the value $a_{11}a_{22}-a_{12}a_{21}$; in this notation the first subscript indicates the row of the element and the second subscript the column. For example, the second-order determinant

$$\begin{vmatrix} 1 & 2 \\ 3 & 4 \end{vmatrix}$$

has the value $(1\times4)-(2\times3)=4-6=-2$. A determinant of order n is indicated by $|a_{ij}|$, where i and j each take on the values 1,2,3, . . . ,n. The value of an nth-order determinant is the sum of all possible products of elements such that no two elements in a given product are in the same row or column. This value may be found more easily by expanding the determinant by minors. The minor A_{ij} of an element a_{ij} of an nth-order determinant is the determinant of order $(n-1)$ formed by deleting the ith row and the jth column of the original determinant. For example, in the determinant

$$\begin{vmatrix} 4 & 2 & 1 \\ 3 & 1 & 2 \\ 5 & 0 & 3 \end{vmatrix}$$

the element a_{21}, whose value is 3, has the minor

$$\begin{vmatrix} 2 & 1 \\ 0 & 3 \end{vmatrix}$$

In expanding a determinant by minors, first the minor of every element in a particular row or column is formed. Products are derived by multiplying each minor by its corresponding element. A plus sign is placed in front of each product if the sum of the row number and column number of its element is even, and a minus sign if the sum is odd. Finally, the signed products are added algebraically. For example, expanding the above determinant by its second row yields:

$$-3\begin{vmatrix} 2 & 1 \\ 0 & 3 \end{vmatrix}+1\begin{vmatrix} 4 & 1 \\ 5 & 3 \end{vmatrix}-2\begin{vmatrix} 4 & 2 \\ 5 & 0 \end{vmatrix}=$$

$$-3(6)+1(12-5)-2(-10)=+9.$$

Determinants of higher order can be evaluated by successive expansions of this type. By choosing rows of columns containing zeros, some terms can be eliminated. There are various rules for transforming a given determinant, which can be used to obtain a row or column most of whose elements are zeros. Determinants have many applications in mathematics and other fields, e.g., in the solution of simultaneous linear equations. A more general type of array with wider applications is the MATRIX.

determinism, philosophical thesis that conditions control the course of events; a doctrine opposed to libertarianism, or belief in freedom of the will. Modern determinism is based on the type of psychology that sees the individual as controlled entirely by his history. The doctrine is opposed by the principle of emergence, which states that truly novel and unpredictable events may occur out of the composite of forces in a situation.

Detmold (dĕt'mōlt), city (1970 pop. 63,266), North Rhine-Westphalia, N central West Germany. Once the capital of Lippe, it is now a furniture-manufacturing center and summer resort. There is a 16th-century castle (now a museum). Nearby is a large monument, Hermannsdenkmal, commemorating the battle (A.D. 9) of the TEUTOBURG FOREST.

detonator (dĕ'tənā"tər), type of EXPLOSIVE that reacts with great rapidity and is used to set off other, more inert explosives. Fulminate of mercury mixed with potassium chlorate is a commonly used detonator. The word is also applied to equipment which, by flame, spark, percussion, friction, or pressure, is used to set off a chemical detonator.

Detroit (dĭtroit', dē–), city (1970 pop. 1,511,482), seat of Wayne co., SE Mich., on the Detroit River and between lakes St. Clair and Erie; inc. as a city 1815. Michigan's largest city and the fifth largest in the nation, Detroit is a port of entry and a major Great Lakes shipping and rail center. Its early carriage industry helped Henry Ford and others to make Detroit the "automobile capital of the world." In addition to the manufacture of automobiles and automobile parts, Detroit's industries include steel mills, drug manufacturers, and food-processing plants. Detroit leads the nation in the production of gray-iron foundry products, metal stampings, and machine tools. It is high among national producers of tires, paint, wire goods, and industrial inorganic chemicals. Extensive salt mines lie under the southwestern section of the city. A French fort and fur-trading settlement founded there in 1701 by Antoine de la Mothe Cadillac and called *Ville d'etroit* [city of the strait] were captured by the British in 1760. Three years later the British withstood a long siege there in PONTIAC'S REBELLION. American control, resulting from JAY'S TREATY, was established in 1796. Detroit was first the territorial and then the state capital from 1805 to 1847. Fire in 1805 nearly destroyed all of the several hundred buildings in the town, but the settlement was rebuilt from a design by Pierre C. l'Enfant. Detroit was surrendered in 1812 by William Hull to British forces under Isaac Brock, but was recovered by William Henry Harrison in 1813. With the development of land and water transportation, the city grew rapidly during the 1830s. It assumed great importance after the mid-19th cent. as a shipping, shipbuilding, and manufacturing center. Among its notable mayors were James Couzens (1919–22) and Frank Murphy (1930–33). In July, 1967, race riots in Detroit caused property damage estimated at $150 million. Wayne State Univ. and the Univ. of Detroit are located there. Detroit has a symphony orchestra, organized in 1914. Points of interest include the Detroit Institute of Arts; a historical museum; a huge civic center, with Cobo Hall, one of the world's largest exhibition buildings; Fort Wayne (1849); and several parks with recreational facilities. Belle Isle in the Detroit River is a park with flower gardens, a conservatory, a children's zoo, and an aquarium. The Ambassador International Bridge (the world's longest international suspension bridge) and a vehicular tunnel link Detroit with Windsor, Ont. See S. Glazer, *Detroit: A Study in Urban Development* (1965); S. Farmer, *A History of Detroit and Wayne County and Early Michigan* (3d rev. ed. 1969); W. H. Ferry, *The Buildings of Detroit* (1969); and F. B. and A. M. Woodford, *All Our Yesterdays: A History of Detroit* (1969).

Detroit, river, 32 mi (52 km) long, flowing from Lake St. Clair S into Lake Erie between Detroit, Mich., and Windsor, Ont.; it forms part of the U.S.-Canada boundary. About 75% of the tonnage on the Great Lakes moves on the river.

Detroit, University of, at Detroit; coeducational; Jesuit; est. 1877 as a college, inc. 1881, became a university 1911. It is affiliated with St. John's Hospital and Providence Hospital in Detroit.

Detskoye Selo: see PUSHKIN, USSR.

Dett, Robert Nathaniel, 1882–1943, American composer and pianist, b. Drummondsville, Que. After receiving degrees from Oberlin College and the Eastman School of Music, Dett studied in Paris with Nadia Boulanger. He wrote many choral and piano pieces, the latter including *Magnolia Suite* (1911) and *Cinnamon Grove Suite* (1927), some of which draw upon his Negro heritage. Dett also arranged and published a collection of Negro spirituals (4 vol., 1936).

Dettifoss (dĕ'tĭfôs), waterfall, in the Jökulsá á Fjöllum River, NE Iceland. Iceland's most impressive fall, it drops 144 ft (44 m) into a long canyon.

Deucalion (dyo͞okā'lēən), in Greek mythology, son of Prometheus and father of Hellen. When Zeus, angered by man's irreverence, flooded the earth, Deucalion, warned by Prometheus, survived by taking refuge with his wife, Pyrrha, in an ark. Later, an oracle told them to cast behind them the bones of their mother (i.e., the stones of the earth). From these stones sprang men and women who repopulated the world.

Deuel (dyo͞o'əl), father of Eliasaph the Gadite. Num. 1.14; 7.42, 47; 10.20. Reuel: Num. 2.14.

deuterium (do͞otēr'ēəm), isotope of HYDROGEN with mass no. 2. The deuterium nucleus, called a deuteron, contains one proton and one neutron. Deuterium is also called heavy hydrogen, and water in which the hydrogen atoms are deuterium is called heavy water (deuterium oxide, D_2O). Deuterons are sometimes used in particle accelerators, and heavy water is used in "swimming pool" nuclear reactors as a moderator.

deuterocanonical books: see OLD TESTAMENT.

Deuteronomy (do͞otərŏn'əmē), book of the Old Testament, last of the five books of the Law (the Pentateuch or Torah) ascribed by tradition to Moses. According to the text it gives the final words of Moses to his people and may be outlined as follows: first, the introductory discourse reviewing the history of Israel since the exodus from Egypt (1–4); second, an address of Moses to the people (5–30), beginning with general principles of morality (5–11) and then continuing with particulars of legislation, including a repetition of the Ten Commandments (12–26), and a concluding exhortation (27–30); third, a chapter of narrative in which Moses delivers the book of the Law to the Levites (31); fourth, the Song of Moses, a hymn (32); fifth, the blessing of Israel by Moses (33); and sixth, the death of Moses (34). The legislation is pointed toward life in the Promised Land, with the eventual foundation of a single lawful sanctuary. Deuteronomy's main theme is absolute monotheism. For critical views on its composition and bibliography, see OLD TESTAMENT.

Deutsch, Babette (doich), 1895–, American poet, b. New York City. Her poems are noted for their technical virtuosity and wide range of tone and subject matter. Her best-known collections include *Animal, Vegetable, Mineral* (1954), *Coming of Age* (1959), and *Collected Poems* (1963 and 1969). She has also written novels, including *Mask of Silenus* (1933), and numerous critical works, such as *Poetry in Our Time* (1954). She is married to Avrahm Yarmolinsky, the critic and scholar.

Deutsch, Gotthard (gôt'härt), 1859–1921, Austrian Jewish scholar and historian. He studied at the rabbinical seminary at Breslau, Germany, and at the Univ. of Vienna (Ph.D., 1881) after which he taught at Brünn in Moravia. In 1891 he went to the United States to become professor of the history and philosophy of religion at the Hebrew Union College at Cincinnati. His contributions to Jewish newspapers and journals, in addition to his many books, made him an outstanding leader of the Jewish community. He was an editor of the *Jewish Encyclopedia*, contributing many articles. His *Philosophy of Jewish History* (1897) and *History of the Jews* (1921) are well known.

Deutscher, Isaac (doi'chər), 1907–67, English writer, b. Poland. Editor (1926–32) of the Communist press in Poland, he was expelled from the party for his anti-Stalinist views. During World War II he escaped to England in 1939, and he served on the staffs of the *Economist* and the *Observer*. Deutscher made notable use of his literary and political acumen in writing a number of excellent works on Soviet topics. Outstanding are his scholarly biography of Stalin (1949) and his trilogy on Trotsky, *The Prophet Armed* (1954), *The Prophet Unarmed* (1959), and *The Prophet Outcast* (1963).

Deutsches Theater (doi'chə tāā'tər), German private theater organization founded in 1883. It became a leader in naturalistic theater style. Under its first director, Adolph L'Arronge, the Deutsches merged with the Freie Bühne (Otto Brahm, director) and in 1884 built its own house in Berlin. The first major success was Schiller's *Don Carlos*. Plays by Sophocles, Calderón, Molière, Shakespeare, and other classical writers were also mounted. During Brahm's directorship modern works by Ibsen and Hauptmann were produced. Max REINHARDT, who succeeded Brahm, won renown as a theatrical innovator. The theater collapsed but was revived after World War I and survived World War II. See biography of Otto Brahm by Maxim Newmark (1937); O. M. Sayler, ed., *Max Reinhardt and his Theatre* (tr. 1924, repr. 1968).

Deutsch-Wagram: see WAGRAM, Austria.

deutzia: see SAXIFRAGE.

Deux-Sèvres (dö-sĕv'rə), department (1968 pop. 326,462), W France, largely in Poitou. Niort is the capital.

De Valera, Eamon (ā'mən dĕ vəlâr'ə), 1882–, Irish statesman, b. New York City. He was taken as a child to Ireland. As a young man he joined the movement advocating physical force to achieve Irish independence and took part in the Easter Rebellion of 1916. He was sentenced to life imprisonment (escaping execution because he was a U.S. citizen) but was released under a general amnesty in 1917. Elected that same year a member of Parliament and president of SINN FEIN, De Valera was arrested again in May, 1918. However, he escaped from prison (Feb., 1919) and went to the United States, where he raised funds for Irish independence. In the meantime he had been elected president of Ireland by the DÁIL EIREANN, the revolutionary parliament that had declared the country independent. In 1920, when he returned to Ireland, the country was in a state of virtual war against British rule. In 1921 the British government opened the negotiations that led to the establishment of the Irish Free State. De Valera, however, repudiated the final treaty because it excluded Northern Ireland and required Irish officeholders to swear allegiance to the British crown. He resigned from the Dáil in Jan., 1922. Nominal leader of the republican intransigents, De Valera greatly deplored the period of civil war that followed. He maintained his opposition to the government, however, and did not enter the Dáil with his party, FIANNA FÁIL, until 1927. In the general election of 1932 his party gained control of the Dáil, and De Valera became head of the government. He immediately abolished the oath of allegiance and refused to pay land annuities to Britain. A tariff war followed that was not ended until 1938. In 1937, De Valera introduced a new constitution declaring Ireland a fully sovereign state. He kept Ireland neutral throughout World War II, refusing to let the British use southern Irish ports and vigorously protesting Allied military activity in Northern Ireland. Fianna Fáil was defeated in the election of 1948, but De Valera returned as prime minister with independent support (1951–54) and with an absolute party majority (1957–59). Hampered by failing vision, in 1959 he moved to the less demanding office of president of the republic, to which he was reelected in 1966. He retired in 1973. See biographies by M. J. MacManus (1946, repr. 1957) and F. P. Longford and T. P. O'Neill (1971); Calton Younger, *A State of Disunion* (1972).

devaluation, decreasing the value of one nation's currency relative to gold or the currencies of other nations. It is usually undertaken as a means of correcting a deficit in the BALANCE OF PAYMENTS. Although devaluation occurs in terms of all other currencies, it is best illustrated in the case of only one other currency. For example, if the United States is losing money in its trade with France, a decision may be made to devalue the U.S. dollar by 10%. Whereas previously one dollar may have been worth about 5.5 francs, a 10% devaluation causes it to be worth only about 5 francs. Such a move causes French products to become more expensive for Americans and U.S. products to become cheaper for Frenchmen. An ounce of French cologne that previously cost 55 francs in France and 10 dollars in the United States may still sell for 55 francs in France but will now cost 11 dollars in the United States. The net result of such a devaluation is that U.S. exports will increase and imports decrease, thus helping to reverse the balance of payments deficit.

developer: see PHOTOGRAPHIC PROCESSING.

Deventer, Sir Jacob Louis van (yä'kōp lo͞oē' fän dĕf'əntər), 1874?–1922, Boer general. In the South African War he commanded guerrilla forces in the Cape Colony. During World War I he helped suppress a Boer extremist outbreak against the government. Deventer also participated in the campaigns against Germany in South West Africa (1914–15) and in former German East Africa (1917–18).

Deventer, city (1971 pop. 66,318), Overijssel prov., E central Netherlands, on the IJssel River. It is an industrial center with machine shops, foundries, textile plants, and carpet manufactures. A member of the Hanseatic League in the Middle Ages, it was a prosperous commercial city and a center of piety and learning; Thomas à Kempis and Erasmus of Rotterdam studied there. Deventer has retained many medieval and Renaissance structures, including the Groote Kerk (church, built 8th cent., and later rebuilt), the Mariakerk (15th cent.), the weighhouse (16th cent.), and the town hall (17th cent.).

Devereux, Robert: see ESSEX, ROBERT DEVEREUX, 2D EARL OF.

devil: see SATAN; DEMON; EXORCISM.

devilfish, name applied to the manta RAY and to an American species of OCTOPUS.

devil's advocate: see CANONIZATION.

devil's-club or **devil's-walking-stick:** see GINSENG.

devil's coach horse: see MANTID.

devil's darning needle: see DRAGONFLY.

Devils Island, Fr. *Île du Diable,* the smallest and southernmost of the Îles du Salut, in the Caribbean Sea off French Guiana. A penal colony founded in 1852, it was used largely for political prisoners, the most celebrated of whom was Alfred Dreyfus. Although conditions were probably not as sordid as in other prison camps in French Guiana, the island's name became synonymous with the horrors of the system. The penal colonies were phased out between 1938 and 1951.

Devils Lake, 1 mi (1.6 km) long, in Devils Lake State Park, central Wis., NW of Madison. The clear, oval-shaped lake is ringed by bluffs, 400 to 500 ft (122–152 m) high. Indian mounds stand on its shores. The lake is a year-round resort.

devil's-paintbrush: see HAWKWEED.

Devils Postpile National Monument: see NATIONAL PARKS AND MONUMENTS (table).

Devils Tower National Monument, 1,347 acres (545 hectares), overlooking the Belle Fourche River, NE Wyo.; first designated U.S. national monument (est. 1906). Devils Tower, 865 ft (264 m) high and narrowing in width from 1,000 ft (305 m) at its base to 250 ft (76 m) at its summit, is a cluster of rock columns formed by the cooling and crystallization of molten matter. Generally acknowledged by geologists to be a remnant of an ancient lava intrusion in sedimentary strata, the exact form of its origin and its relation to the Black Hills is debated. Through the ages the surrounding sedimentary material has been removed by wind and water action, especially that of the Belle Fourche River, leaving the more resistant igneous-rock tower to dominate the skyline. Devils Tower, called Grizzly Bear Lodge and Bad God's Tower by some of the region's Indian tribes, has played a role in shaping Indian legends and folklore. It has long served as a landmark for travelers and explorers. Prairie dogs and other wildlife are found on the grounds of the monument.

De Vinne, Theodore Low (də vĭn'ē), 1828–1914, American printer, b. Stamford, Conn. He learned his trade in the office of the Newburgh (N.Y.) *Gazette* and in 1848 entered the shop of Francis Hart in New York City. In 1858 he was made a junior partner, and after Hart's death in 1877 De Vinne became owner of the business. It continued as Theo. L. De Vinne & Company until 1908, when it was incorporated as the De Vinne Press. De Vinne became the best-known American printer of his day and did much by his writings and by his example of workmanship to advance the cause of good printing. He printed the *Century Magazine* and the *Century Dictionary,* both of them considered fine specimens of the art in that period. He also printed many of the Grolier Club books. He was a close student of types and did much to make American printers type conscious. De Vinne helped to bring reproduction and illustration processes to new standards of excellence. His numerous books include *The Invention of Printing* (1876), *The Practice of Typography* (4 vol., 1900–1904), and *Notable Printers of Italy during the Fifteenth Century* (1910).

Devolution, War of, 1667–68, undertaken by Louis XIV for the conquest of the Spanish Netherlands. On her marriage to Louis, Marie Thérèse, daughter of Philip IV of Spain, had renounced her rights of inheritance in return for a large dowry. Blaming Spain for having failed to pay the stipulated dowry, Louis declared war and invoked an old law of Brabant providing that property might "devolve" upon the children of a first marriage—in this case upon Marie Thérèse (rather than upon Charles II of Spain). The French easily captured (1667) the Spanish Netherlands. The United Provinces, in alarm, formed the TRIPLE ALLIANCE with England and Sweden (Jan., 1668). The French overran Franche-Comté (Feb., 1668) but came to terms with the Triple Alliance in the Treaty of AIX-LA-CHAPELLE (May, 1668).

Devon, England: see DEVONSHIRE.

Devon cattle (dĕv′ən), breed of cattle originated in England and brought to America by colonists as early as 1623. They range in color from deep red to pale chestnut, the most popular being "ruby red." The breed was used for centuries in England for draft animals. In the United States they were raised extensively as a dual-purpose breed, i.e., for both dairy and beef production, until the early 1950s when the emphasis shifted to use as a beef breed.

Devonian period (dĭvō′nēən), fourth period of the PALEOZOIC ERA of geologic time (see GEOLOGIC ERAS, table). It was named (1838) by the geologists Sir Roderick Impey Murchison and Adam Sedgwick for Devonshire, England, where they first investigated rocks formed during the period. At the beginning of the Devonian, the continents were mostly dry land; later a great flood covered large areas of North America and Europe and smaller parts of Africa, South America, and Australia. In the Lower Devonian only the Appalachian and Acadian areas of North America were submerged; formations include limestone and sandstone. These are typically demonstrated near Cumberland, Md. Toward the beginning of the Middle Devonian the Appalachian basin was elevated and the interior was flooded. The seas at their maximum extension became muddy and deposited shales. During the Upper Devonian the seas withdrew, the eastern coast continued to rise, and the Catskill delta was formed. The Cordilleran area of the Far West submerged, depositing from 4,000 to 6,000 ft (1,200–1,800 m) of limestone and shale in Nevada and 2,400 ft (730 m) of quartzites and limestones in Utah. The Devonian period in Europe was marked by considerable volcanic activity and the deposition of two great rock systems: the marine formation of Devonshire, the Rhine valley, and the USSR; and the OLD RED SANDSTONE. The most notable Devonian animals were the fishes, which appeared in great numbers toward the close of the period. Conspicuous types were sharks, armored fishes, lungfishes, and ganoid fishes. Common invertebrates of the Devonian were corals, crinoids, starfishes, sponges, trilobites, and the forerunners of the ammonites. Of land life the chief vestige is the footprint of a primitive salamanderlike amphibian in the Upper Devonian of Pennsylvania. Trees made their first appearance; the Devonian plants were the earliest to be extensively preserved as fossils, but their high degree of development suggests that more primitive forms existed earlier. They were similar to the plants of the succeeding Carboniferous period.

Devon Island, c.20,900 sq mi (54,100 sq km), E Franklin dist., Northwest Territories, Canada, between Baffin and Ellesmere islands.

Devonport, England: see PLYMOUTH.

Devonshire, Spencer Compton Cavendish, 8th **duke of** (kăv′əndĭsh, dĕv′ənshĭr), 1833–1908, British statesman. He became marquess of Hartington in 1858. He frequently held office in Liberal cabinets and by 1880 was recognized as the leader of the conservative (Whig) faction of the Liberal party with regard to social legislation. He led the Liberal Unionists who broke (1886) with Gladstone over Home Rule for Ireland. Devonshire (he became duke in 1891) later (1904) left the Liberal Unionists because the majority of that group, led by Joseph Chamberlain, had come to favor the abandonment of free trade. See biography by Bernard Holland (1911).

Devonshire or **Devon,** county (1971 pop. 896,245), 2,591 sq mi (6,711 sq km), SW England. The county town is EXETER. Devonshire is bounded on the N by the Bristol Channel, on the S by the English Channel, and on the W by Cornwall. It is a land of rolling hills, dominated by DARTMOOR and EXMOOR, upland areas of forests and rugged stone. The Exe and the Tamar (forming the Cornwall border) are the main rivers. PLYMOUTH is the chief port and industrial center for SW England. Devonshire is a farming and pastoral county (for beef and dairy cattle) with some fishing off the coastal towns. Devonshire "clotted" cream and West Country cider are notable products. A considerable woolen industry and export trade flourished from the 12th to the 18th cent. Today some woolen goods, lace, pottery, and marine fixtures are manufactured, and clay is mined. Quiet and picturesque, Devonshire is a popular tourist and vacation center. The county was occupied in Paleolithic times; numerous habitation sites and ceremonial centers have been excavated (see KENT'S CAVERN). Exeter was the westerly outpost of Roman occupation. Devonshire was incorporated into Wessex early in the 8th cent. by King Ine. In Elizabethan times the county reached its greatest maritime importance, and its name is associated with Walter Raleigh, Francis Drake, John Hawkins, and Richard Grenville. From Plymouth, many colonists sailed for America. In 1974 the county was reorganized as the nonmetropolitan county of Devonshire.

De Vos: see VOS.

De Voto, Bernard Augustine (də vō′tō), 1897–1955, American writer and editor, b. Ogden, Utah, grad. Harvard, 1920. He taught at Northwestern Univ. (1922–27) and then at Harvard (1929–36). After 1935 he conducted "The Easy Chair" in *Harper's Magazine* and from 1936 to 1938 was editor of the *Saturday Review of Literature.* His most important writing was in the field of American history and literature. His trilogy, *The Year of Decision: 1846* (1943), *Across the Wide Missouri* (1947), and *The Course of Empire* (1952), is a scholarly and vigorous study of the American West. He was the official editor of the Mark Twain manuscripts at Harvard and published *Mark Twain's America* (1932), *Mark Twain in Eruption* (1940), and *Mark Twain at Work* (1942). His other works include literary studies, *The Literary Fallacy* (1944) and *The World of Fiction* (1950); *The Journals of Lewis and Clark* (1953), which he edited; and several novels. See biography by Wallace Stegner (1974).

Devoy, John (dĭvoi′), 1842–1928, Irish-American journalist and Irish patriot, b. Ireland. He joined the Irish Republican Brotherhood (see FENIAN MOVEMENT) in 1861. For proselytizing within the British army he was sentenced in 1866 to 15 years in prison. He was released in 1871, however, and went to America. He founded (1881) and edited the *Irish Nation* and became one of the leading Irish propagandists in the United States. He organized the rescue of Irish prisoners in Australia in 1875–76 and secured American financial support for the Land League movement. In 1903 he founded the *Gaelic-American.* During World War I he secured much of the financial backing for the Easter Rebellion of 1916. Afterward he backed the Irish Free State against the republican extremists and helped secure a market for its first bonds. See his *Recollections of an Irish Rebel* (1929); Desmond Ryan, *The Phoenix Flame* (1937).

Devrient, Ludwig (lo͝ot′vĭkh dəvrēäN′), 1784–1832, German actor. He abandoned a commercial career in 1804 to join a traveling theatrical company. In Berlin he was a favorite in comedy and tragedy, especially in the works of Shakespeare and Schiller. His three nephews were actors. **Karl August Devrient,** 1797–1872, was popular in heroic and character roles such as Lear, Shylock, and Faust. Karl's brother, **Philipp Eduard Devrient,** 1801–77, directed the Court Theater, Dresden (1844–46), and the Karlsruhe Theater (1852–70). He wrote several plays and also a history of the German stage (1848–74) in five volumes. With his son, Otto, he published translations of Shakespeare's plays. **Gustave Emil Devrient,** 1803–72, was the youngest and most gifted of the three brothers. He excelled in youthful, heroic parts. When he gave Hamlet in London, his portrayal was said to equal that of Edmund Kean.

De Vries: see also VRIES.

De Vries, Hugo (hü′gō də vrēs), 1848–1935, Dutch botanist. He opened a new approach to the study of evolution by using the experimental method to investigate the processes of evolution. His study of discontinuous variations, especially in the EVENING PRIMROSE, led to his rediscovery (reported in 1900) of Mendel's laws of heredity and to the development of the theory of MUTATION, which he expounded in *The Mutation Theory* (1901–3, tr. 1909–10) and in *Plant-Breeding* (1907). He maintained that mutations—sudden, unpredictable, inheritable changes in an individual organism—are the chief method by which new species develop in the course of evolution and that each quality subject to change is represented by a single physical unit (which he called a pangen). De Vries's work on osmosis is also important; he coined the term *isotonic.* He was professor (1878–1918) at the Univ. of Amsterdam, and he established an experimental garden at Hilversum.

dew, thin film of water that has condensed on the surface of objects near the ground. Dew forms when radiational cooling of these objects during the nighttime hours also cools the shallow layer of overlying air in contact with them, causing the CONDENSATION of some water vapor. This condensation occurs because the capacity of air to hold water vapor decreases as the air is cooled. The temperature at which condensation begins, for a sample of air with a given water vapor content, is termed the dew point. If a dew point temperature below 32°F (0°C) is reached, sublimation occurs, i.e., the water vapor converts directly to FROST. Should the surface temperature drop below 32°F after the dew has already collected, the dew may freeze into so-called white dew. Most authorities account for the supply of water vapor as coming from the atmosphere, though some research suggests that it also diffuses up through the soil and then condenses on the ground surface if conditions are favorable. Dew forms most readily on those surfaces that lose heat through radiation most efficiently but are nevertheless insulated from external heat sources. Dew formation is favored by high humidity in the lowest layers of air, which either supplies the moisture or at least inhibits the evaporation of the dew already deposited. Strong winds inhibit dew formation because they mix a larger layer of air, creating a more homogeneous distribution of heat and water vapor; under such circumstances it is unlikely that a sufficiently cool and damp layer of air can form near the ground.

Dewar, Sir James (dyo͞o′ər), 1842–1923, British chemist and physicist, b. Scotland. He was professor of chemistry (from 1877) at the Royal Institution, London, and later was director of the Davy-Faraday Research Laboratory there. He is best known for his work on the properties of matter at very low temperatures (approaching absolute zero) and the liquefaction of gases, in the course of which he invented the Dewar flask and liquefied (1898) and solidified (1899) hydrogen. With Sir Frederick Abel he invented the smokeless explosive cordite. He was knighted in 1904. See his *Collected Papers* (2 vol., 1927); biography by James Crichton-Browne (1923, repr. 1925).

Dewar flask [for Sir James Dewar], container after which the common thermos bottle is patterned. It consists of two flasks, one placed inside the other, with a vacuum between. The vacuum prevents the passage of heat from one flask to the other. For greater efficiency the flasks are silvered to reflect heat. The substance to be kept hot or cold, e.g., liquid air, is contained in the inner flask. See LOW-TEMPERATURE PHYSICS.

dewberry, name for several species of the genus *Rubus* of the family Rosaceae (ROSE family). Dewberry is classified in the division MAGNOLIOPHYTA, class Magnoliopsida, order Rosales, family Rosaceae. See BRAMBLE.

D'Ewes, Sir Simonds (dyo͞oz), 1602–50, English antiquarian, b. Coxden. He collected many old manuscripts and made transcriptions of others with the intention of writing a history of England; these now form part of the Harleian Collection of the British Museum. His valuable collection of the journals of the Parliaments during the reign of Elizabeth I were published in 1682. D'Ewes was a member of the Long Parliament; he sided against Charles I and then against the army and was expelled from Parliament in Pride's Purge (see under PRIDE, THOMAS). Portions of his diary of the period have been edited by Wallace Notestein (1923) and Willson Coates (1942, repr. 1970).

De Wet, Christian Rudolf (də vĕt), 1854–1922, Boer general and statesman. In the South African War he achieved great success, especially in guerrilla fighting; he described his experiences in *The Three Years' War* (1902). After the war De Wet at first favored amity with the British but later supported a separate Boer state. He opposed the entrance of the Union of South Africa into World War I and led (1914) a rebellion. He was captured and sentenced to six years' imprisonment, but after a short time he was pardoned.

Dewey, George, 1837–1917, American admiral, hero of the battle of Manila, b. Montpelier, Vt., grad. Annapolis, 1858. He saw active duty in the Civil War and rose in the navy in service and rank, becoming chief of the Bureau of Equipment in 1889, president of the Board of Inspection and Survey in 1895, and commodore in 1896. He was unpopular with many high-ranking naval commanders, and it seems to have been through the influence of Assistant Secretary of the Navy Theodore Roosevelt and the direct intervention of President McKinley that Dewey was appointed in 1897 to command the Asiatic squadron. When the SPANISH-AMERICAN WAR broke out, Dewey was ready. He sailed to Manila, entered the harbor after midnight on May 1, 1898, and engaged the Spanish fleet at dawn. By noon he had destroyed eight Spanish ships with only eight Americans wounded. Manila was at his mercy, but he waited for reinforcements; meanwhile he brought Emilio Aguinaldo, the Filipino rebel, back from exile to lead a revolution in the Philippines. In maintaining relations with neutral warships at Manila, Dewey had to exercise firmness with the officers of five German ships who would not accede to his blockade rules. When Gen. Wesley Merritt arrived with army forces, the commanders cooperated in capturing Manila. Promoted to admiral of the navy in 1899, he was feted on his return to the United States with almost hysterical enthusiasm and briefly received wide support as a potential presidential candidate. See his autobiography (1913, repr. 1971); Laurin Hall Healy and Luis Kutner, *The Admiral* (1944); Nathan Sargent, *Admiral Dewey and the Manila Campaign* (1947); R. S. West, *Admirals of American Empire* (1948, repr. 1971).

Dewey, John, 1859–1952, American philosopher and educator, b. Burlington, Vt., grad. Univ. of Vermont, 1879, Ph.D. Johns Hopkins, 1884. He taught at the universities of Minnesota (1888–89), Michigan (1884–88, 1889–94), and Chicago (1894–1904) and at Columbia from 1904 until his retirement in 1930. He lectured at the Univ. of Peking in 1912 and 1931, and in 1924 he prepared a report on the reorganization of the schools of Turkey. Dewey's original philosophy, called instrumentalism, bears a relationship to the utilitarian and pragmatic schools of thought. Instrumentalism holds that the various modes and forms of human activity are instruments developed by man to solve his multiple individual and social problems. Since the problems are constantly changing, the instruments for dealing with them must also change. Truth, evolutionary in nature, partakes of no transcendental or eternal reality and is based on experience that can be tested and shared by all who investigate. Dewey conceived of democracy as a primary ethical value, and he did much to formulate working principles for a democratic and industrial society. In education his influence has been a leading factor in the abandonment of authoritarian methods and in the growing emphasis upon learning through experimentation and practice. In revolt against abstract learning, Dewey considered education as a tool that would enable the citizen to integrate his culture and vocation effectively and usefully. He had a profound impact on the progressive school movement. Dewey actively participated in movements to forward social welfare, protect academic freedom, and effect political reform. Among his writings, which are concerned with almost all philosophical fields except metaphysics, are *Psychology* (1887), *The School and Society* (1899; rev. ed. 1915), *Ethics* (with James H. Tufts, 1908), *Democracy and Education* (1916), *Reconstruction in Philosophy* (1920), *Human Nature and Conduct* (1922), *Experience and Nature* (1925), *The Quest for Certainty* (1929), *Art as Experience* (1934), *Logic: the Theory of Inquiry* (1938), *Freedom and Culture* (1939), and *Problems of Men* (1946). See Sidney Hook, ed., *John Dewey: Philosopher of Science and Freedom* (1950); J. J. McDermott, ed., *Philosophy of John Dewey* (2 vol., 1972); H. S. Thayer, *Meaning and Action* (2d ed., 1972); biography by George Dykhuizen (1973); studies by G. R. Geiger (1958, repr. 1974) and Arthur Wirth (1966).

Dewey, Melvil, 1851–1931, American library pioneer, originator of the Dewey decimal system, b. Adams Center, N.Y., grad. Amherst (B.A., 1874; M.A., 1877). A man of originality and of enormous energy, Dewey played an important role in the early days of library organization in the United States. He became acting librarian of Amherst in 1874, and there he evolved his system of classification, using numbers from 000 to 999 to cover the general fields of knowledge and designating more specific subjects by the use of decimal points. From 1883 to 1889 he was librarian of Columbia College where he established the first library training school. As librarian (1889–1906) at the New York State Library at Albany he founded another important library school. His interests extended from spelling reform to organizing the Lake Placid Club, a resort in the Adirondacks. Dewey is credited with the invention of the vertical office file. He was a founder of the American Library Association, the New York State Library Association, and the *Library Journal.* The 18th edition of his *Dewey Decimal Classification and Relative Index* (1876) was published in 1971. See biography by G. G. Dawe (1933); study by Fremont Rider (1944).

Dewey, Thomas Edmund, 1902–71, American political figure, governor (1943–55) of New York, b. Owosso, Mich. Admitted (1925) to the bar, Dewey practiced law and in 1931 became chief assistant U.S. attorney for the Southern District of New York. After briefly serving (1933) as U.S. attorney, he was appointed (1935) special prosecutor to investigate organized crime and was elected (1937) district attorney of New York county. He won a national reputation for "racket-busting." He was the unsuccessful Republican candidate for governor of New York in 1938, but was elected governor in 1942. In 1944 he won the Republican presidential nomination, but he lost the election to Franklin Delano Roosevelt. Reelected (1946) governor, Dewey again ran for President on the Republican ticket in 1948 and, contrary to general expectation, lost the election to Harry S. Truman by a close margin. He was reelected governor of New York in 1950, and resumed private law practice on completion of his term (1955). He wrote *Journey to the Far Pacific* (1952) after a tour of the Far East, and *Thomas E. Dewey on the Two Party System* (1966).

Dewing, Francis, fl. 1716–22, early American engraver, b. England. He came to Boston in 1716 as an engraver and printer, probably one of the first in America. In 1722 he engraved and printed a large map, *The Town of Boston in New England,* by John Bonner.

Dewing, Thomas Wilmer, 1851–1938, American painter, b. Boston, Mass. Dewing studied in Paris with the academician Jules Lefebvre. Returning to New York City in 1880, he produced hazy, atmospheric, impressionistic compositions. His paintings are moody and introspective, e.g., *The Recitation* (1891; Detroit Inst. of Arts), and express the quietude often found in the works of Whistler.

De Wint, Peter, 1784–1849, English landscape painter. He was a leading watercolorist. Most of De Wint's landscapes are distinctly English in subject and treatment, Lincolnshire scenes being favorites. *A Cornfield* and *Landscape with Water* (Victoria and Albert Mus.) are among his best-known works.

De Witt, Jan, and **Cornelius de Witt:** see WITT, JAN DE; WITT, CORNELIUS DE.

De Witt, uninc. town (1970 pop. 10,032), Onondaga co., central N.Y., a suburb of Syracuse.

dew point: see DEW.

Dewsbury, county borough (1971 pop. 51,310), West Riding of Yorkshire, N central England, on the Calder River. It is a commercial center for heavy woolen textiles and has the largest rag-trading market in the world. There are woolen mills and blanket, carpet, and shoddy factories. Other industries are coal mining, engineering, and the manufacture of chemicals. Dewsbury houses several departments of the Dewsbury and Batley Technical and Art College. In 1974, Dewsbury became part of the new metropolitan county of West Yorkshire.

Dexedrine (dĕk'sĭdrēn), trade name for the drug dextroamphetamine sulfate. See AMPHETAMINE.

Dexippus (Publius Herennius Dexippus) (dĕksĭp'əs), fl. 253–276, Greek historian of the Roman period. He commanded Greek troops in an unsuccessful attempt to halt a Gothic invasion in 262. His works, much admired by Photius, included a universal history, a contemporary account of wars against the Goths (preserved largely by Zosimus), and an account of the Diadochi.

Dexter, Timothy, 1747–1806, American merchant and eccentric, b. Malden, Mass. He gained a fortune from the American Revolution by buying up depreciated continental currency that was afterwards reclaimed at full value. He also gained money by shrewd mercantile transactions. He was styled "Lord Timothy Dexter" by his fellows, and he accepted the title. Dexter wrote *A Pickle for the Knowing Ones* (1802), remarkable for the totally individual spelling and the absence of all punctuation. In the second edition he added a page of "stops" so that readers could "peper and salt it as they please." See biographies by J. P. Marquand (1925 and 1960).

dextrin, any one of a number of CARBOHYDRATES having the same general formula as starch but a smaller and less complex molecule. They are polysaccharides and are produced as intermediate products in the HYDROLYSIS of starch by heat, by acids, and by enzymes. Their nature and their chemical behavior depend to a great extent on the kind of starch from which they are derived. For example, some react with iodine to give a reddish-brown color, others a blue, and still others yield no color at all. For commerical use dextrin is prepared by heating dry starch or starch treated with acids to produce a colorless or yellowish, tasteless, odorless powder which, when mixed with water, forms a strongly adhesive paste. It is used widely in adhesives, e.g., for postage stamps, envelopes, and wallpapers, and for sizing paper and textiles.

dextrose: see GLUCOSE.

Deyssel, Lodewijk van (lō'dəvĭk vän dĕ'səl), pseud. of Karel Joan Lodewijk Alberdingk Thijm, 1864–1952, Dutch novelist, critic, and essayist. He was editor of *De Nieuwe Gids* [the new guide], the monthly organ of the progressive literary movement, the "Eighters." His two novels, *De kleine Republiek* [little republic] (1886) and *Een Liefde* [love story] (1887) shocked Dutch society with their explicit naturalism. Deyssel subsequently shifted to mysticism, documenting his evolution in *Van Zola tot Maeterlinck* [from Zola to Maeterlinck] (1895).

Dezful (dĕzfōōl'), city (1966 pop. 84,499), Khuzestan prov., W Iran, on the Dez River, near the site of ancient SUSA. It is the trade center for an irrigated farm region. Petroleum is produced nearby. The city gets its name, which means "citadel bridge," from a bridge built across the Dez by (according to legend) Shapur II. The city is also known as Dizful and Desful.

Dhamar or **Damar** (both: dămär'), town, S central Yemen, in an oasis in the highlands. Dhamar is known for its thoroughbred horses and its ancient Muslim university.

Dhanbad (dän'bäd), city (1971 metropolitan area pop. 433,085), Bihar state, E central India. A new city, Dhanbad serves as a district administrative center. It is located near the Jharia coalfields and is surrounded by man-made lakes. The Indian School of Mines and Applied Geology is in the city.

Dhar (där), town (1971 pop. 36,164), Madhya Pradesh state, central India. It is a district administrative center and a market for cotton, grains, and oilseed. Dhar was the capital of the kingdom of Malwa and a center of Hindu learning from the 9th to 14th cent. The fort (c.1340) and the Hindola Mahal and Jahaj Mahal are notable landmarks.

dharma (där'mə), in Hinduism, the doctrine of the religious and ethical rights and duties of each individual. It refers generally to duty ordained by religion, but may also mean simply virtue, or right conduct. Sacred law is the codification of dharma, and Hinduism is also called Sanatana Dharma [the eternal dharma]. In Buddhism, dharma has two distinct meanings: It refers to religious truth, namely Buddhist teaching as the highest truth; it is also used to denote a quality, a condition of being, or any existing thing or phenomenon.

Dharwar, India: see HUBLI-DHARWAR.

Dhulia (dōōl'yə), city (1971 pop. 137,089), Maharashtra state, W central India, on the Panjhra River. Dhulia is a district administrative center. Cotton and woolen goods are manufactured from the produce of the district.

diabase: see BASALT.

Diabelli, Antonio (äntô'nyō dēäbĕl'lē), 1781–1858, Austrian music publisher. He published works by Beethoven and Schubert and composed the waltz theme of Beethoven's Diabelli Variations.

diabetes or **diabetes mellitus** (məlī'təs), chronic disorder usually caused by a deficient secretion of INSULIN, a hormonal substance produced by the endocrine glands in the PANCREAS, the islets of Langerhans. The exact cause of pancreatic failure is not yet fully understood, but heredity seems to be a factor, as is obesity. Disorders of endocrine glands other than those in the pancreas—e.g., acromegaly and Cushing's syndrome—can also bring on diabetes. The lack of insulin results in an inability to metabolize glucose. The capacity to store glycogen in the liver and the active transport of glucose across cell membranes are impaired. The symptoms are the appearance of sugar in the urine, an increase of sugar in the blood, the passage of urine in large amounts, thirst, hunger, weakness, weight loss, and itching of the skin. Prolonged hyperglycemia (excess blood glucose) leads to increased protein and fat catabolism, a condition that can cause premature vascular degeneration and atherosclerosis. Uncontrolled diabetes leads to diabetic acidosis, which, if not treated promptly, can result in death. About 4% of women and 2% of men in the United States become diabetic. Although the incidence is less frequent among children and adolescents, the onset of diabetes in young people is usually more abrupt, more severe, and more difficult to control. In cases of severe diabetes the patient must generally inject daily doses of insulin. In some cases insulin therapy is either supplemented or replaced by oral medication, including sulfonylurea drugs (see ORINASE) and PHENFORMIN. A common complication of insulin therapy is insulin shock, a hypoglycemic condition that results from an oversupply of insulin in relation to the glucose level in the blood (see HYPERINSULINISM). The treatment of diabetes was revolutionized when F. G. Banting and C. H. Best isolated the hormone insulin in 1921. Until that time control could be attempted only in the mildest forms of the disease. Since the advent of insulin therapy the lives of diabetics have been greatly prolonged. See Arnold Bloom, *Diabetes Explained* (1973).

diadem, in ancient times, the fillet of silk, wool, or linen tied about the head of a king, queen, or priest as a distinguishing mark. Later, it was a band of gold, which gave rise to the crown. In heraldry, the diadem is one of the arched bars that support the crown.

Diadochi (dīăd'əkī) [Gr.,=successors], the Macedonian generals and administrators who succeeded Alexander the Great. The empire of Alexander, the largest that the world had known to that time, was quickly built. At his death in 323 B.C. it disintegrated even more quickly. Alexander's more important followers sought immediately to increase their personal power in a bloody scramble. These men are known as the Diadochi. Chief among them were Antipater, Perdiccas, Eumenes, Craterus, Antigonus (Antigonus I), Ptolemy (Ptolemy I), Seleucus (Seleucus I), and Lysimachus. The first struggle was over the regency; theoretically Alexander's feebleminded brother, Philip, and also Alexander's posthumous son by Roxana had the real claim to the inheritance. Perdiccas had the regency (323-322), in effect if not in name, to which Antipater also had claim. Eumenes supported Perdiccas, while Antigonus, Ptolemy, and Craterus supported Antipater. In 321 battle was joined, and the allies of Antipater won, although Craterus was killed. On the death of Antipater in 319 the struggle was on again in earnest. There were shifting alliances, but in general the chief figure was Antigonus, who, with the help of his son, Demetrius Poliorcetes (Demetrius I of Macedon), attempted to rebuild the empire of Alexander. He failed. Antigonus and Demetrius were finally defeated in the battle of Ipsus (301 B.C.). Already the Diadochi had been declaring themselves kings, Antigonus first and then the others. The contest was carried on to the next generation, with Demetrius fighting successfully against Cassander, the son of Antipater, and it was pursued even further with the wars between the Seleucidae and the Ptolemies. Commonly, however, the period of the Diadochi is said to end with the victory of Seleucus I over Lysimachus at the battle of Corupedion in 281, fixing the boundaries of the Hellenistic world for the next century. This left the descendants of Ptolemy, Seleucus, and Antigonus as the chief claimants to power in the Hellenistic age, and the empire of Alexander was irrevocably split.

Diaghilev, Sergei Pavlovich (syĭrgā' päv'ləvĭch dyä'gĭlyĭf), 1872-1929, Russian ballet impresario and art critic, grad. St. Petersburg Conservatory of Music, 1892. In 1898 he founded an influential journal, *Mir Iskusstva (The World of Art)*. He took a company of Russian dancers to Paris (1909) and, with the assistance of the painters L. N. Bakst and Aleksandr Benois and the choreographer Michel FOKINE, founded Diaghilev's Ballet Russe, a troupe that was to revolutionize the world of dance. Diaghilev's productions were based on the principles of asymmetry and perpetual motion; both music and scene design became an integral part of the dance. An imposing personality, he was associated with dancers of the first rank, such as Vaslav Nijinsky, Tamara Karsavina, Anna Pavlova, Mikhail Mordkin, Alicia Markova, and Anton Dolin. His choreographers included Léonide Massine, Bronislava Nijinska, George Balanchine, and Serge Lifar; Stravinsky, Debussy, Ravel, Dukas, Falla, Milhaud, and Richard Strauss wrote music that was first performed by his company, and Picasso, Chagall, and Derain often worked with him as scene designers. See biographies by B. Kochno (1970) and J. Percival (1971).

diagnosis, determination of the nature of a disease or ailment. A clinical diagnosis based on the medical history and physical examination of the patient is used whenever laboratory tests for the disease cannot be made. Diagnosis by physical examination includes ascertaining temperature, pulse, and blood pressure and involves the use of palpation, or feeling, to detect enlarged organs and other abnormalities; percussion, or tapping, to delineate some of the internal organs; and auscultation, or listening, to interpret sounds from organs such as the heart and lungs. Instruments that facilitate physical examination include the sphygmomanometer for determining blood pressure; the STETHOSCOPE for listening to the heart and lungs; the otoscope for examination of the ear; the OPHTHALMOSCOPE to disclose the inner eye; the laryngoscope and BRONCHOSCOPE to view the larynx, windpipe, and other air passages; the esophagoscope and the gastroscope for viewing the esophagus and the stomach, and the proctoscope and sigmoidoscope, for inspecting the rectum and part of the large intestine. In diagnostic tests the blood, urine, tissues, and other excretions and secretions of the body are examined grossly and microscopically for evidence of chemical imbalance, cellular change, and the presence of pathogenic organisms. X-rays, electrocardiographs, and electroencephalographs (brain tracings) are other diagnostic aids. Exploratory surgery may be used as a last resort to arrive at a precise diagnosis.

dialect, variety of a LANGUAGE used by a group of speakers within a particular speech community. Every individual speaks a variety of his language, termed an idiolect. Dialects are groups of idiolects with a common core of similarities in pronunciation, grammar, and vocabulary. Dialects exist as a continuum in which adjacent dialects are mutually intelligible, yet with increasing isolation between noncontiguous dialects, differences may accumulate to the point of mutual unintelligibility. For example, in the Dutch-German speech community there is a continuous area of intelligibility from Flanders to Schleswig and to Styria, but with Flemish and Styrian dialects mutually unintelligible. Adjacent dialects usually differ more in pronunciation than in grammar or vocabulary. When a dialect is spoken by a large group of speakers of a language, it often acquires prestige, which leads to the development of a standard language. Some countries have an official standard, such as that promoted by the French Academy. Dialects that have prestige, but are not the standard dialect, are termed nonstandard, whereas substandard dialects, such as the provincial dialects in post-revolutionary France, are held in contempt. The first linguistic dialectology focused on historical dialects, written texts serving as the basis for establishing the dialects of a language through the methods of comparative linguistics (see PHILOLOGY). The methods of modern linguistic geography began in late 19th-century Europe with the use of informants rather than texts, and resulted in the first linguistic atlases of France, by Jules Gilliéron, and of Germany, by Georg Wenker. Those techniques were refined in the United States in the preparation of the *Linguistic Atlas of the United States* (Hans Kurath et al., ed.) and its derivative works. In recent years linguists have become increasingly interested in social dialects, such as the languages of social groups within an urban population and the languages of specific occupations (farmers, dockworkers, coal miners, government workers) or life styles (beatniks, drug users, teenagers, feminists). In the United States much work has been done in the area of black English, the common dialect of many Negroes. See also SLANG. See Harold Orton and Eugen Dieth, ed., *Survey of English Dialects* (1962-70); H. B. Allen and G. N. Underwood, *Readings in American Dialectology* (1971); R. H. Bentley and S. D. Crawford, ed., *Black Language Reader* (1973); Hans Kurath, *Studies in Area Linguistics* (1973).

dialectic (dīəlĕk'tĭk) [Gr.,= art of conversation], in philosophy, term originally applied to the method of philosophizing by means of question and answer employed by certain ancient philosophers, notably Socrates. For Plato the term came to apply more strictly to logical method and meant the reduction of what is multiple in our experience of phenomena to the unity of systematically organized concepts or ideas. Immanuel Kant gave the name "Transcendental Dialectic" (the title of one section of his *Critique of Pure Reason*) to his endeavor to expose the illusion of judgments that attempt to transcend the limits of experience. G. W. F. Hegel applied the term *dialectic* to the logical method of his philosophy, which proceeds from thesis through antithesis to synthesis. Hegel's method was appropriated by Karl Marx and Friedrich Engels in their philosophy of DIALECTICAL MATERIALISM.

dialectical materialism, official philosophy of Communism, based on the writings of Karl MARX and Friedrich ENGELS, as elaborated by G. V. PLEKHANOV, V. I. LENIN, and Joseph STALIN. In theory dialectical materialism is meant to provide both a general world view and a specific method for the investigation of scientific problems. The basic tenets are that everything is material and that change takes place through "the struggle of opposites." Because everything contains different elements that are in opposition, "self-movement" automatically occurs; the conflict of opposing forces leads to growth, change, and development, according to definite laws. Communist scientists are expected to fit their investigations into this pattern, and official approval of scientific theories in the USSR is determined to some extent by their conformity to dialectical materialism (see LYSENKO, TROFIM DENISOVICH). Use of these principles in history and sociology is sometimes called historical materialism. Under these doctrines the social, political, and intellectual life of society reflect only the economic structure, since human beings create the forms of social life solely in response to economic needs. Men are divided into classes by their relations to the means of production—land and capital. The class that controls the means of production inevitably exploits the other classes in society; it is this class struggle that produces the dynamic of history and is the source of progress toward a final uniformity. Historical materialism is deterministic; that is, it prescribes that history inevitably follows certain laws and that individuals have little or no influence on its development. Central to historical materialism is the belief that change takes place through the meeting of two opposing forces (thesis and antithesis); their opposition is resolved by combination produced by a higher force (synthesis). Historical materialism has many advocates outside the Communist world. See Gustav Wetter, *Dialectical Materialism* (1958, repr. 1973); Z. A. Jordan, *The Evolution of Dialectical Materialism* (1967); Roger Garaudy, *Marxism in the Twentieth Century* (1970).

dialysis (dīăl'ĭsĭs), in chemistry, transfer of solute (dissolved solids) across a semipermeable membrane. Strictly speaking, dialysis refers only to the transfer of the solute; transfer of the solvent is called OSMOSIS. Dialysis is frequently used to separate different components of a solution. For example, a solution of starch and sodium chloride in water can be separated by placing the mixture in a vessel on one side of a semipermeable membrane and placing pure water on the other side. The smaller particles of sodium chloride (which dissolve in water to form sodium and chloride ions) will diffuse across the membrane; diffusion of the much larger starch particles (which are not truly in solution but are in colloidal suspension) is hindered and may be completely prevented. By continuously or periodically replacing the solvent with fresh solvent, almost all of the sodium chloride can be removed. The method was originated by Thomas Graham, who termed the substance that remained within the membrane a *colloid* and the substance that diffused a *crystalloid*. An extension of the method makes possible the separation of mixed colloids by the use of a semipermeable membrane (usually synthetic) of known selectivity, i.e., one that will permit the diffusion of one colloid and hinder the diffusion of others. Mixed macromolecules, such as proteins, may be similarly separated. By the use of graded semipermeable membranes chosen to allow successively smaller molecules to pass, mixtures can be separated into components of graded ranges of molecular weight. Artificial kidney machines have been developed that make use of dialysis to purify the blood of persons whose kidneys have ceased to function. Such hemodialysis has saved the lives of many persons suffering from renal failure. In such machines, blood is circulated on one side of a semipermeable membrane (often cellophane) while a special dialysis fluid is circulated on the other side. The dialysis fluid must be a solution that closely matches the chemical composition of the blood. Metabolic waste products such as urea and creatinine diffuse through the membrane into the dialysis fluid and are discarded, while loss by diffusion of substances necessary to the body (such as sodium chloride) is prevented by their presence in the dialysis fluid. See DIFFUSION.

diamagnetism: see MAGNETISM.

Diamond, David, 1915-, American composer, b. Rochester, N.Y. Diamond was trained at the Cleveland Institute of Music and the Eastman School; he also studied with Roger Sessions and Nadia Boulanger. He has composed in a variety of styles, beginning with neoclassical works in the 1930s and developing a romantic phase prior to his use of 12-tone technique in the late 1950s. Diamond has written much chamber and vocal music; nine symphonies; music for Shakespeare's *Romeo and Juliet, The Tempest,* and *Timon of Athens;* and *Rounds* (1944), for strings, his best-known work.

diamond, mineral, one of two crystalline forms of the element carbon (see ALLOTROPY), the hardest natural substance known, used as a gem and in industry. It crystallizes in the isometric system (see CRYSTAL) commonly as transparent to translucent white, colorless, yellow, green, blue, or brown octahedrons (the familiar diamond shapes). In addition to the GEM varieties there are bort, which is poorly crystallized or of inferior color and in fragmentary condition, and carbonado (black diamond), which is gray to black and opaque, with poor cleavage. Bort and carbonado are used as abrasives, in the cutting of diamonds, and for the cutting heads of rock drills. The earliest sources of gem diamonds were India and Borneo, where they were found in river alluvium. All the famous diamonds of antiquity were Indian diamonds. In the early 18th cent. similar deposits were found in Brazil, though they may have been known as early as 1670. Since the mid-19th cent. the Brazilian fields, especially those of Bahia, have been important chiefly for the production of carbonados. In 1867 a stone found in South Africa some time before was recognized as a diamond. Within a few years a wild search for diamonds was being carried on there, both in river diggings and inland. In 1870-71 dry diggings, including most of the celebrated mines, were discovered. These dry diggings are volcanic pipes, filled for most of their length with blue ground or kimberlite, an igneous rock consisting largely of SERPENTINE. At the surface the blue ground is weathered to a clay called yellow ground. The discoveries of 1870-71 led to a rush, in the course of which a great number of prospectors staked out claims, securing the diamonds by open-pit or quarry mining. The damage caused by floods and mudslides, unavoidable when there were so many different claims, was an important factor in the series of amalgamations carried on by Cecil RHODES and Barnett BARNATO. Rhodes brought about the merging of their interests in the De Beers Consolidated Mines, Ltd., which established (1889) an effective monopoly over the diamond industry. Loss of diamonds by theft, costing hundreds of thousands of pounds annually, was reduced through the passage of the so-called I. D. B. (Illicit Diamond Buying) Act, which limited the trade to licensed buyers and imposed severe penalties for the mere possession without a license of uncut stones. Thefts were further curtailed by the institution of compounds in which the natives live while employed by the company and which they leave only after being thoroughly searched. Diamantiferous earth is mined both by the open-pit method and by underground mining. After being removed to the surface, it is crushed and then concentrated. Sorting is done by passing the concentrated material in a stream of water over greased tables. The diamond, being largely water repellent, sticks to the grease, but the other minerals retain a film of water, which prevents them from adhering to the grease. The diamonds are then removed from the grease, cleaned, and graded for sale. Well-known diamond mines in South Africa are the Dutoitspan, Bultfontein, De Beers, Kimberley, Jagersfontein, and Premier. Other important diamond-producing countries include Angola, Sierra Leone, Zaïre, South West Africa, Ghana, Tanzania, Brazil, Venezuela, and the USSR. Among famous Indian diamonds have been the Great Mogul, known only through the description of the French jeweler and traveler Jean B. Tavernier; the Orlov, which was originally given to Catherine II of Russia; Koh-i-noor, now among the English crown jewels; and the Regent or Pitt. From the Cullinan, a South African diamond found and presented in 1907 to King Edward VII, 105 stones were cut; two of them were long the world's largest diamonds. Other notable diamonds are the Hope (blue), Dresden (green), and Tiffany (yellow). Most of the major producers belong to a marketing cartel formed to maintain the price of diamonds at a high level. Synthetic diamonds were successfully produced in 1955; a number of small crystals were manufactured when pure graphite mixed with a catalyst was subjected to pressure of about 1 million lb per sq in. and temperature of the order of 5,000°F (3,000°C). Synthetic diamonds are now extensively used in industry. See Samuel Tolansky, *The History and Use of Diamond* (1962); Eric Bruton, *Diamonds* (1971); Victor Argenzio, *Diamonds Eternal* (1974).

Diamond Head, peak, 761 ft (232 m) high, along the rim of an extinct volcano, SE Oahu island, Hawaii. A prominent point in the Honolulu skyline, Diamond Head was designated a national natural landmark to protect its slopes from the commercial development along world-famous Waikiki Beach. U.S. Fort Ruger is at the northern end of the crater's floor. The crater was the site of an ancient Hawaiian burial ground.

Diamond Mountains: see KUMGANG SAN, North Korea.

Diamond Necklace, Affair of the, scandal that took place at the court of King Louis XVI of France just before the French Revolution. An adventuress who called herself the comtesse de La Motte duped Cardinal de ROHAN, the grand almoner, who was out of favor with Queen MARIE ANTOINETTE, into believing that she could regain the queen's regard for him. Mme de La Motte and her accomplices then engineered a sham correspondence between the cardinal and the queen and even arranged an interview between him and a woman impersonating the queen. In the interview the cardinal was led to believe that the queen wished to acquire a diamond necklace of enormous value and that she had chosen him as her confidential agent. When Rohan obtained the necklace from the jewelers, he turned it over to the comtesse; her husband took it to London, where it was broken up for sale. The affair became public after Rohan failed to meet the payments to the jewelers. The cardinal was arrested and tried by the PARLEMENT; he was acquitted but lost his position in court. Mme de La Motte was punished and imprisoned, but she escaped to London, where she wrote her highly questionable memoirs. Alessandro CAGLIOSTRO, at first suspected of complicity, was acquitted. The queen, noted for her extravagance and frivolity, was unjustly implicated in the affair; her enemies hinted that she had schemed to ruin the cardinal or that she had used her favor to obtain the necklace and then refused to pay. The scandal added greatly to her unpopularity at a critical time. A vast literature has grown around the subject, notably Dumas's romance *The Queen's Necklace* and Carlyle's *Diamond Necklace.* See also J. D. Chamier, *The Dubious Tale of the Diamond Necklace* (1939); Frances Mossiker, *The Queen's Necklace* (1961).

Diana, in Roman religion, goddess of the moon, forests, animals, and women in childbirth. She was probably originally a forest goddess and a special patroness of women. She was identified with the Greek Artemis, and at her temple on the Aventine at Rome she was honored as the virgin goddess. Her most famous cult, however, was at Aricia, near Lake Nemi; there she was worshiped as an earth goddess and was associated with fertility rites and with the GREAT MOTHER OF THE GODS.

Diane de France (dyän də fräNs), 1538-1619, duchess of Angoulême; illegitimate daughter of King Henry II of France. She was legitimized in 1547. She was married to François, eldest son of Constable Anne de Montmorency. She worked for the alliance of King Henry III with Henry of Navarre (King Henry IV) and exerted much influence during the reign of Henry IV.

Diane de Poitiers (pwätyā'), 1499-1566, duchess of Valentinois, mistress of King Henry II of France. Noted for her beauty, Diane, who was much older than Henry, retained her influence over him until his death (1559). She maintained friendly relations with the queen, Catherine de' Medici, while completely eclipsing her. In the rivalry for Henry's favor between Anne, duc de MONTMORENCY, and the GUISE family, she took sides against whichever party was more powerful at the moment. She supported the king's anti-Protestant policy. After Henry's death, she was forced to retire from the court. See H. W. Henderson, *The Enchantress* (1928).

Dianthus: see PINK.

diapensia (dīpĕn'sēə), common name for the Diapensiaceae, a family of low evergreen shrubs native to cool and arctic regions of the Northern Hemisphere. The species that are restricted to the New World are found in the E United States. *Galax* is native to woods from Virginia to Georgia; it has spikes of white blossoms (and is sometimes called wandflower), and its leaves are often used as greens by florists. The pyxie, or flowering moss *(Pyxidanthera barbulata),* is a creeping plant of the pine barrens. The diapensia family is classified in the division MAGNOLIOPHYTA, class Magnoliopsida.

diaphragm, large muscle in man and other mammals that acts as a partition between the cavity of the chest and that of the abdomen. It is the chief muscle used in respiration. During exhalation the diaphragm is relaxed and dome-shaped. During inhalation it contracts, pulling downward, and with the combined contraction of the chest muscles allows the chest cavity to expand. Any interference with its free movement, as in the paralysis of poliomyelitis, seriously impedes the function of the lungs and therefore endangers life. In its downward movement the diaphragm also stimulates the stomach and liver and thus aids in the digestive processes. Spasmodic contraction of the diaphragm results in HICCUPS. The diaphragm is also subject to developmental defects, hernia, injury, displacement, and infection.

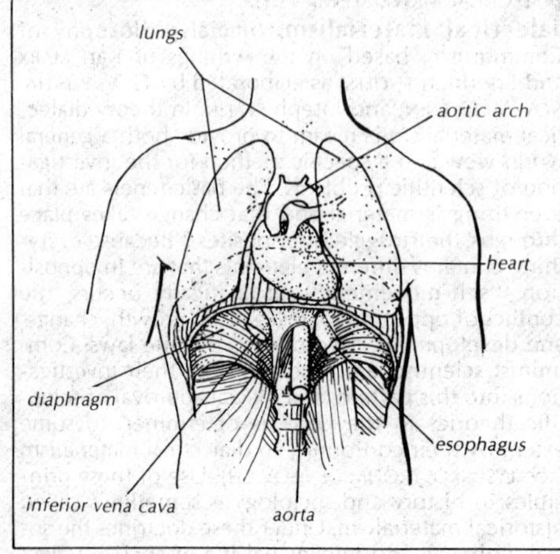

Diaphragm

Diarmuid mac Murchada: see DERMOT MCMURROUGH.

diarrhea (dīərē'ə), frequent discharge of watery feces from the intestines, sometimes containing blood and mucus. It can be caused by excessive indulgence in alcohol or other liquids or foods that prove irritating to the stomach or intestine, by allergy to certain food products, by poisoning with heavy metals, by chemicals such as are found in cathartics, by hyperactivity of the nervous system, and by infection with a virus (intestinal grippe) or with bacteria or their toxins. Diarrhea is a concomitant of many infectious diseases, especially TYPHOID FEVER, bacillary or amebic DYSENTERY, and CHOLERA. Persistent diarrhea may result in severe dehydration and shock. It is therefore necessary to replace the fluid lost by the body. Treatment is with a bland diet and drugs that will decrease the activity of the intestines, as well as with specific measures directed to the underlying cause.

diary [Lat., = day], a daily record of events and observations. As distinguished from memoir (an account of events placed in perspective by the author long after they have occurred), the diary derives its impact from its immediacy, requiring each generation of readers to supply its own perspective. The earliest diaries extant are the Roman *commentarii*—household account books, senators' speech notebooks, Caesar's account of the Gallic Wars. Diaries are of particular interest to historians because they depict everyday life in a particular place and time, often illuminating important historical events. Examples of such diaries are the *Journal d'un bourgeois de Paris,* written by an anonymous French clerk from 1401 to 1431; accounts of daily life in the American colonies by William Bradford, John Winthrop, William Byrd, and Samuel Sewall; Anne Frank's diary (1947, tr. 1953), an account of the early days of World War II by a young German-Jewish girl who died in a concentration camp; and Harold Nicolson's diaries (1964-68), which treat the world situation from 1929 to 1962. A particularly unusual diary is that of the painter Eugène Delacroix (kept from 1822-24, 1847-63), which contains many extraordinary drawings. Among the many diaries of literary and psychological interest the greatest is probably that of Samuel PEPYS. While presenting a detailed portrait of life in 17th-century England, the diary also renders many charming and humorous incidents, the product of Pepys's observant eye and delightful style. It records, for example, the New Year festivities of 1666: "Then to dancing and supper and mighty merry till Mr. Belt came in, whose pain of the tooth-ake made him no company, and spoilt ours." Other important literary diarists are John Evelyn, Jonathan Swift, Dorothy Wordsworth, Jules and Edmund Goncourt, Charles Baudelaire, André Gide, Franz Kafka, Virginia Woolf, and Anaïs Nin, whose 126-volume diary represents her efforts to "unmask the deeper self," so that it might be studied by psychiatrists.

Dias, Antônio Gonçalves: see GONÇALVES DIAS, ANTÔNIO.

Dias, Bartolomeu (bär"to͝olo͝omā'o͞o dē'əsh), d. 1500, Portuguese navigator. He was the first European to round (1488) the Cape of Good Hope, which he called Cabo Tormentoso [cape of storms]. That voyage opened the road to India. Dias accompanied CABRAL on the voyage that resulted in the discovery of Brazil, but he perished in heavy seas off the African coast. He is also called Bartholomew Diaz.

Diaspora (dīăs'pərə) [Gr., = dispersion], term used today to denote the Jewish communities living outside the Holy Land. It was originally used to designate the dispersal of the Jews at the time of the destruction of the Temple (586 B.C.) and the forced exile [Heb., = Galut] to Babylonia (see BABYLONIAN CAPTIVITY). During this period there began to develop certain ideas and institutions that were to form the foundations of Jewish life in exile after the second dispersion (A.D. 135): monotheism, the synagogue, personal accountability for a righteous life, the hope of a return to the Holy Land, and so on. See JEWS; JUDAISM.

diastase (dī'əstās"): see AMYLASE.

diathermy (dī'əthûr"mē), therapeutic measure used in medicine to generate heat in the body tissues. Electrodes and other instruments are used to transmit electric current to surface structures, thereby increasing the local blood circulation and facilitating and accelerating the process of absorption and repair. Diathermy is used for arthritis, bursitis, and other disorders of the tendons and muscles, as well as for certain other conditions requiring tissue repair. Because of the high-frequency current used in shortwave diathermy, care must be taken to avoid burning the patient's skin or injuring the deeper tissues.

diatom (dī'ətŏm", -tōm"), single-celled microscopic form of plant belonging to the group of golden-brown ALGAE. Most diatoms exist singly, although some join to form colonies. They are usually yellowish or brownish, and are found in fresh and salt water, in moist soil, and on the moist surface of other plants. They are most abundant in polar and other cold waters. Some 15,000 species are known. The living matter of each diatom is enclosed in a shell of siliceous material that it secretes. Many of the shells (some are round and some elongated and tapering at both ends) show intricate and beautiful sculpturing. Some diatoms can move over moist surfaces by a streaming of the protoplasm, and some aquatic forms can move about in the water. When the aquatic forms die they drop to the bottom, and the shells, not being subject to decay, collect in the ooze and eventually form the material known as diatomaceous earth (sometimes called kieselguhr). When it occurs in a more compact form as a soft, chalky, light-weight rock, it is called diatomite. Deposits of diatomaceous material, formed under water in past geologic time and now exposed above water, are found in all parts of the world. They are scattered over most of the United States, but productive sources exist chiefly in Oregon, California, Washington, Nevada, Florida, New York, and New Jersey. Diatomite is much used as an insulating material against both heat and sound, in making dynamite and other explosives, and for filters, abrasives, and similar products. Most of the earth's limestone has been deposited by diatoms, and much petroleum is of diatom origin. Diatoms, as the principal constituent of plankton (see MARINE BIOLOGY), are an important food source for fish and other aquatic animals, e.g., the baleen whales. The desmids, a much smaller group of plankton sometimes confused with diatoms, are green algae (division Chlorophyta). They are also usually single cells but are not siliceous and never occur in marine habitats. They are noted for their extraordinary symmetry and geometrical beauty. They are found only in fresh (usually still) water. Diatoms are classified in the division CHRYSOPHYTA, class Bacillariophyceae.

diatomaceous earth: see DIATOM.

Diavolo, Fra: see FRA DIAVOLO.

Diaz, Armando (ärmän'dō dē'äts), 1861–1928, Italian field marshal. In World War I he replaced (1917) CADORNA as chief Italian commander. He defeated (1918) the disintegrating Austro-Hungarian army at Vittorio Veneto and concluded (Nov. 3) the armistice, based on unconditional surrender, with Austria-Hungary. Created duca della Vittoria [duke of victory], he was later minister of war (1922–24).

Diaz, Bartholomew: see DIAS, BARTOLOMEU.

Díaz, Porfirio (pôrfē'ryō dē'äs), 1830–1915, Mexican statesman, a mestizo, christened José de la Cruz Porfirio Díaz. He gained prominence by supporting JUÁREZ and the liberals in the War of the Reform and in the war against the French and Maximilian. Defeated by Juárez in the presidential election of 1871, Díaz charged fraud and led a revolt against the government, which was not completely suppressed until after the inauguration of Sebastián LERDO DE TEJADA. Díaz again lost in the presidential race of 1876. He refused defeat, rose against Lerdo, and gained the presidency. He remained in power until 1911. From 1880 to 1884, Manuel González was president, Díaz having declared for the principle of nonreelection in 1876; later the constitution was altered to permit Díaz's reelection and continuance in office. His rule was ruthless and effective. Incipient revolutions were crushed, and banditry was officially eliminated by incorporating marauders into a state police called the *rurales*. Aspirants for political power were shrewdly matched to leave the president supreme; elections were a mockery. The regime of Díaz saw the growth of material prosperity in Mexico. Foreign capital poured into the country. The natural wealth of Mexico was exploited, principally by foreigners. Roads, railroads, and telegraph lines increased in number. Jose Ives Limantour (1854–1935), the leader of a group, the *Científicos*, who espoused the doctrines of Comte and Spencer, reformed the fiscal system and gave Mexico financial stability. Mexico became a land of peace and prosperity, ruled in the interest of the few. Díaz sold three quarters of the mineral resources of Mexico to foreign interests and apportioned millions of acres among friendly *hacendados*. The peons, far from obtaining social justice, lost more of their communal lands (see EJIDO); half of the entire rural population was bound to debt slavery. Opposition to Díaz grew, and in the last decade of his rule discontent increased rapidly. The announcement in 1909 of his intention to restore democratic rule in Mexico created a sensation, but in 1910, after engineering his reelection as usual, he gave no evidence of carrying out his announced intention. The upshot was a revolution led by Francisco I. MADERO. In 1911, Díaz was forced to flee the country; he died in exile. See biographies by David Hannay (1917, repr. 1970) and Carleton Beals (1932, repr. 1971); J. K. Turner, *Barbarous Mexico* (1969).

Diaz de la Peña, Narciso Virgilio (dyäs də lä pānyä'), 1808–76, French landscape and figure painter of the Barbizon school, b. Bordeaux, of Spanish parents. Mainly self-taught, he was influenced by Delacroix and Théodore Rousseau. He used a heavy, worked-over impasto, and the flickering light of his landscapes influenced Renoir's work. Collections of his paintings are in the Louvre, the Museum of Rheims, and the Metropolitan Museum (which has *A Clearing in the Forest of Fontainebleau*). His *Courtesans* and *Descent of the Bohemians* are at the Museum of Fine Arts, Boston, and his *Valley Marsh* at the Cincinnati Art Museum. See Robert L. Herbert, *Barbizon Revisited* (1962).

Díaz del Castillo, Bernal (bärnäl' dē'äth dĕl kästē'lyō), c.1492–1581, Spanish conquistador and chronicler. He had served in the New World under various commanders—Pedro Arias de Ávila, Diego de Velázquez, Francisco Fernández de Córdoba, and Grijalva—before joining Hernán Cortés in 1519 to serve in the conquest of Mexico. His monumental work, *The True History of the Conquest of New Spain* (1632; tr. by A. P. Maudslay 1928, rev. ed. 1956, and by Albert Idell, 1956; both with variant title), written in his old age in Guatemala, is a fresh, unstudied account of events, scenes, and men he had himself known, with an accent on everyday concerns and on the common soldier. See biographies by R. B. Cunninghame Graham (1915) and Herbert Cerwin (1963).

Díaz Mirón, Salvador (sälvä*th*ōr' dē'äs mērōn'), 1853–1928, Mexican poet. Díaz Mirón's life abounded with revolutionary plots, political quarrels, duels, and vigorous journalistic debates. His early post-romantic poetry was written under the influence of Byron and Victor Hugo, whereas his later verse was exquisitely polished and less emotional in tone. One of his poems, "A Gloria," is thought to have influenced José Santos Chocano and Rubén Darío. His collection *Lascas* [chips from a stone] (1901) marks him as a precursor of MODERNISMO.

Díaz Ordaz, Gustavo (gōōstä'vō dē'äs ōr'däs), 1911–, president of Mexico (1964–70). A lawyer, law professor, and judge, he served in both houses of the federal legislature and was secretary of interior (1958–63). As president, he continued the reform measures begun by his predecessors and furthered close ties with the United States.

Dib, Mohammed (môämĕd' dēb), 1920–, French novelist and poet. In a vigorous, forthright style, he writes about life in his native Algeria. His novel *Dieu en barbarie* [god in barbarity] (1970), takes place immediately after Algeria gained independence from France. Among his other works are two volumes of short stories, *Le Talisman* (1966) and *Au Café*, and two collections of poetry, *Ombre gardienne* [guardian shade] (1961) and *Formulaires* (1970).

dibatag: see ANTELOPE.

Dibdin, Charles, 1745–1814, English song writer and theatrical entrepreneur. His best-known songs are from his ballad operas, such as *The Bells of Aberdovey* from *Liberty Hall* (1785) and *To Bachelors' Hall* and *Tom Bowling* from *The Oddities* (1789).

Diblaim (dĭb'lāĭm, dĭblā'ĭm), father of Hosea's wife, Gomer. Hosea 1.3.

Diblath (dĭb'lăth), variant of RIBLAH **2**.

Dibon (dī'bŏn) or **Dibon-gad,** ancient city, E of the Dead Sea, now a ruin called Dhiban. The MOABITE STONE was found there, and important remains from the Moabite period have been excavated. Num. 21.30; 33.45, 46; Joshua 13.9; Isa. 15.2; Jer. 48.18,22. Dimon: Isa. 15.9. See DIMONA.

Dibri (dĭ'brī), father of SHELOMITH **1.**

Dibrugarh (dĭb'rōōgər), town (1971 pop. 80,344), Assam state, NE India, at the confluence of the Brahmaputra and Bibru rivers. The town is surrounded by hills and is often threatened by monsoon floods. It is a district administrative center and a terminus for rail and river traffic. There are four airfields, which were used by the British against Japanese forces in Burma during World II. Dibrugarh is surrounded by tea plantations and has tea and plywood factories, oilseed mills, and railroad workshops.

Dice: see HORAE.

dice [plural of *die*], small cubes used in games. They are usually made of ivory, bone, wood, plastic, or similar materials. The six sides are numbered by dots from 1 to 6, so placed that the sum of the dots on opposite sides equals 7. Dice much like those used today were found in ancient Egyptian tombs and in the ruins of Babylon. The playing of dice was popular in Greece and even more so in Rome, and dice were used throughout the Middle Ages. In the simplest form of play with dice each player throws, or shoots, for the highest sum. The most popular dice game in the United States is called craps. It is played with two dice; the underlying principle of the game is the fact that the most probable throw is a 7. On the first throw, if a player shoots 7 or 11 (called a natural) he wins and throws again, but if he shoots 2, 3, or 12 (called craps) he loses. If he shoots 4, 5, 6, 8, 9, or 10 that number becomes his point, and he continues to shoot until he makes his point, in which case he wins and retains the dice, or until he shoots a 7, in which case he loses and relinquishes the dice to the next player. Bets may be placed against the thrower or, in side bets, in favor of him. In gambling halls all bets are made with the house either for or against. There are numerous other dice games. See studies by John Scarne and Clayton Rawson (rev. ed., 1962) and H. A. Heritage (1969).

Dickens, Charles, 1812–70, English novelist, b. Portsmouth. The son of a naval clerk, he spent his early childhood in London and in Chatham. When he was 12 his father was imprisoned for debt, and Charles was compelled to work in a blacking warehouse; this double humiliation he never forgot. At 17 he was a court stenographer, and later he was an expert parliamentary reporter for the *Morning Chronicle*. His sketches, mostly of London life (signed Boz), began appearing in periodicals in 1833, and the collection *Sketches by Boz* (1836) was a success. Dickens was then commissioned to write burlesque sporting sketches; the result was *The Posthumous Papers of the Pickwick Club* (1836–37), which promptly made Dickens and his characters, especially Sam Weller and Mr. Pickwick, famous. In 1836 he married Catherine Hogarth, who was to bear him 10 children; the marriage, however, was never happy. Dickens had a tender regard for Catherine's sister Mary Hogarth, who died young, and a lifelong friendship for another sister, Georgina Hogarth. The early-won fame never deserted Dickens. His readers were eager and ever more numerous, and for them Dickens worked, vigorously producing novels, which appeared first in monthly installments and then were made into books. *Oliver Twist* (in book form 1838) was followed by *Nicholas Nickleby* (1839) and by two works originally intended to start a series called *Master Humphrey's Clock: The Old Curiosity Shop* (1841) and *Barnaby Rudge* (1841). He wrote rapidly, sometimes on more than one novel at a time, and usually finished an installment just when it was due. Haste did not prevent his loosely strung and intricately plotted books from being the most popular novels of his day. When he visited America in 1842, he was received with ovations but awakened some displeasure by his remarks on copyright protection and his approval of abolition. He replied with sharp criticism of America in *American Notes* (1842) and the novel *Martin Chuzzlewit* (1843). The first of his Christmas books was the well-loved *A Christmas Carol* (1843); in later years other short novels and stories written for the season followed, notably *The Chimes* and *The Cricket on the Hearth*. Dickens lived in Italy in 1844 and in Switzerland in 1846. *Dombey and Son* (1848) was the first in a string of triumphant novels, including *David Copperfield* (1850), his own favorite novel, which was partly autobiographical; *Bleak House* (1853); *Hard Times*

(1854); *Little Dorrit* (1857); *A Tale of Two Cities* (1859); *Great Expectations* (1861); and *Our Mutual Friend* (1865). In 1856 he bought his long-desired country home at Gadshill. Two years later, because of Dickens's attentions to a young actress, Ellen Ternan, his wife ended their marriage by formal separation. Her sister Georgina remained with Dickens to care for his household and the younger children. Dickens was working furiously, editing and contributing to the magazines *Household Words* (1850-59) and *All the Year Round* (1858-70) and managing amateur theatricals. To these labors he added platform readings from his own works; three tours in the British Isles (1858, 1861-65, 1866-67) were followed by one in America (1867-68). When he undertook another English tour of readings (1869-70), his health broke, and he died soon afterward, leaving his last novel, *The Mystery of Edwin Drood,* unfinished. His grave is in Westminster Abbey. Charles Dickens is one of the giants of English literature. He wrote from his own experience a great deal—the Marshalsea prison dominates *Little Dorrit,* and his father was at least partially the model for Mr. Micawber in *David Copperfield.* Although he was expert at journalistic reporting, he wrote nothing that was not transformed from actuality by his imagination. Sharp depiction of the eccentricities and characteristic traits of people was stretched into caricature, and for generations of readers the names of his characters—Mr. Pickwick, Uriah Heep, Miss Havisham, Ebenezer Scrooge—have been household words. His warmth of feeling sometimes spilled into sentimental pathos, sometimes flowed as pure tragedy. Dickens evoked the sights, sounds, and smells of London, and the customs of his day. He attacked the injustices of the law and social hypocrisy and evils, but after many of the ills he pictured had been cured he gained still more readers. Some critics complain of his disorderliness in structure and of his sentimentality, but none has attempted to deny his genius at revealing the very pulse of life. The old standard biography of Dickens is that by his friend John Forster (3 vol., 1872-74; new ed. 1928, repr. 1966). Full accounts of his life include that by Edgar Johnson (1952, repr. 1965) and a centennial biography by E. W. Tomlin (1970). See his letters ed. by Madeline House and Graham Storey, (3 vol., 1965, 1969, and 1974; 9 more vol. projected); studies by Monroe Engel (1959), A. O. J. Cockshut (1962), George Gissing (1925, repr. 1969), Ivor Brown (1964 and 1970), Steven Marcus (1965), Barbara Hardy (1970), Angus Wilson (1970), A. E. Dyson (1971), and John Carey (1974); Philip Collins, ed., *Dickens: The Critical Heritage* (1971); Philip Hobsbaum, *A Reader's Guide to Charles Dickens* (1973); Michael and Mollie Hardwick, *The Charles Dickens Encyclopedia* (1973).

Dickey, James, 1923-, American poet, b. Atlanta, Ga. After serving in the air force during World War II, he attended Vanderbilt Univ., graduating in 1946. He has been an English teacher and an advertising executive. Dickey's poetry has great energy. He makes use of the ordinary in his verse, joining the natural and mechanical on such topics as war, nature, and machinery. His volumes of poetry include *Into the Stone and Other Poems* (1960), *Buckdancer's Choice* (1965), and *Eye-Beaters, Blood Victory, Madness, Buckhead and Mercy* (1970). He is probably best known for his only novel, *Deliverance* (1969), in which a group of businessmen on a hunting trip are forced to fight for their lives, using only their own physical and mental resources. See his *Self-Interviews* (1970) and *Sorties* (1972).

Dickinson, Edwin, 1891-, American painter, b. Seneca Falls, N.Y. Dickinson's landscape and still-life canvases are romantic works painted in a geometric style with an abundance of realistic detail. *Fossil Hunters* and *Window and Oar* (1955) are in the Whitney Museum in New York City.

Dickinson, Emily, 1830-86, American poet, considered one of the greatest poets in American literature. Her unique, gemlike lyrics are distillations of profound feeling and original intellect, and they stand outside the mainstream of American literary tradition. Dickinson was born in Amherst, Mass., where she spent almost all her life. Her father was a prominent lawyer who was active in civic affairs. His three children (Emily, a son, Austin, and another daughter, Lavinia) thus had opportunities of meeting many distinguished visitors. Emily Dickinson attended Amherst Academy irregularly for six years and Mount Holyoke Seminary for one, and in those years lived a normal life filled with friendships, parties, church, and housekeeping. Before she was 30, however, she began to withdraw from village activities and gradually ceased to leave home at all. While she corresponded with many friends, she eventually stopped seeing them; she often fled from visitors and eventually lived as a virtual recluse in her father's house. Even before her withdrawal she had been writing poetry, and her creative peak seems to have been reached in the period from 1858 to 1862. Although she was encouraged by the critic Thomas Wentworth Higginson, who never comprehended her genius, and Helen Hunt Jackson, who believed she was a great poet, Dickinson published only seven poems during her lifetime. She was an intense, sensitive person who became exhausted by emotional contact with others. Her mode of existence, although circumscribed, was evidently satisfying, even essential, to her. After her death in 1886, Lavinia Dickinson discovered over 1,000 poems in her sister's bureau. For too long Dickinson was treated less as a serious artist than as a romantic figure who had renounced the world after a disappointment in love. This legend, based on conjecture, distortion, and even fabrication, still plagues her biographers. While she wrote love poetry that indicates a strong attachment, it has proved impossible to know the object of it, or even how much of it was fed by her poetic imagination. The chief tension in her work comes from a different source: her inability to accept the orthodox religious faith of her day and her longing for the spiritual comfort of it. Immortality she called "the flood subject," and she alternated confident statements of belief with lyrics of despairing uncertainty that were both reverent and rebellious. Her verse, noted for its aphoristic style, its wit, its delicate metrical variation and irregular rhymes, its directness of statement, and its bold and startling imagery, has had a great influence on 20th-century poetry. Dickinson's posthumous fame began when Mabel L. Todd and Higginson edited and published two volumes of poems (1890, 1891) and some of her correspondence (2 vol., 1894). Other editions of verse followed, many of which were marred by unskillful and unnecessary editing. A definitive edition of her works did not appear until the 1950s, when T. H. Johnson published her poems (3 vol., 1955) and letters (3 vol., 1958); only then was a serious study of her work possible. Valuable biographies of Dickinson include: G. F. Wicher, *This Was a Poet* (1938); Millicent Todd Bingham, *Emily Dickinson: A Revelation* (1954) and *Emily Dickinson's Home* (1955, repr. 1967); Thomas H. Johnson, *Emily Dickinson: An Interpretive Biography* (1955); Jay Leda, *Years and Hours of Emily Dickinson* (2 vol., 1960, repr. 1970); R. B. Sewall, *The Life of Emily Dickinson* (2 vol., 1974). See studies by C. R. Anderson (1960); A. J. Gelpi (1965); D. J. M. Higgins (1967); and W. R. Sherwood (1968).

Dickinson, Goldsworthy Lowes, 1862-1932, English author. He was a pacifist during World War I, and he was later instrumental in the conception of the League of Nations. His political writings include *The International Anarchy, 1904-1914* (1926). He is also known for *The Greek View of Life* (1896), a study of Hellenic society. See his autobiography ed. by Dennis Proctor (1973); biography by E. M. Forster (1934, repr. 1973).

Dickinson, John, 1732-1808, American patriot and statesman, b. Talbot co., Md. After studying law in Philadelphia and in London at the Middle Temple, he developed a highly successful practice in Philadelphia. In 1760 he became speaker of the assembly of the Lower Counties (Delaware), and in 1762 he entered the Pennsylvania legislature. Dickinson led the conservative wing opposing Benjamin Franklin and defending the proprietary system. The Sugar Act and the Stamp Act led him to write a pamphlet (1765) in protest. As a member of the Stamp Act Congress he helped draw up the petitions to the king, but he opposed all violent resistance to the law. The passage of the TOWNSHEND ACTS (1767) led to the colonial nonimportation agreements and the publication of Dickinson's famous *Letters from a Farmer in Pennsylvania,* which appeared in the *Pennsylvania Chronicle* in 1767 and 1768. He pointed out that these laws were inconsistent with established English contitutional principles, but he favored nonimportation agreements and conciliation rather than revolt. Dickinson came to be regarded as the leader of the conservative group, which opposed not only British actions but also the ideas of such radicals as Samuel Adams. He was a delegate to the First Continental Congress and drew up a petition to the king. However, he still hoped for reconciliation even after the opening of hostilities, and he refused to sign the Declaration of Independence. He continued to be the leader of the conservative patriots in Pennsylvania and Delaware and held state posts. His draft formed the basis of the Articles of Confederation (see CONFEDERATION, ARTICLES OF). In 1786 he presided over the Annapolis Convention, and in the subsequent Federal Constitutional Convention, Dickinson was a delegate from Delaware and a leading champion of the rights of the small states. He later wrote vigorously in support of the Constitution. He was one of the founders of Dickinson College. See biographies by C. J. Stillé (1891, repr. 1967) and Edwin Wolf (2d ed. 1967); study by D. L. Jacobson (1965).

Dickinson, Jonathan, 1688-1747, American Presbyterian clergyman, a founder and first president of the College of New Jersey (now PRINCETON UNIVERSITY), b. Hatfield, Mass., grad. Yale, 1706. He was a leading preacher of the Great Awakening in the middle colonies and supported the revivalists or "New Sides" in the ensuing controversy. Convinced of the need of an educational institution to carry forward the ideals of William TENNENT, he obtained a charter (1746) for the College of New Jersey. In 1747 he opened the institution at his house in Elizabethtown (now Elizabeth), N.J.

Dickinson, Preston, 1891-1930, American painter, b. New York City. In New York he studied at the Art Students League. From 1910 to 1915 he traveled in Europe, returning often later in life. His still lifes and landscapes in oil and watercolor are built up of highly colorful planes. He is well represented in museums throughout the United States.

Dickinson. 1 City (1970 pop. 12,405), seat of Stark co., SW N.Dak., on the Heart River; inc. 1919. It is a processing and shipping center for a livestock, dairy, and wheat region. A briquette-producing plant utilizes the area's extensive lignite reserves. Dickinson State College and state experimental livestock and agricultural stations are in the city. 2 Uninc. town (1970 pop. 10,776), Galveston co., S Texas, on a navigable bayou that flows into Galveston Bay. It is a residential community.

Dickinson College, at Carlisle, Pa.; coeducational; Methodist; founded 1773 as The Grammar School, chartered and opened as Dickinson College 1783. It was named for John Dickinson. The Dickinson Law School, an affiliated institution, was established as a department of Dickinson College in 1834 and separately incorporated in 1890.

Dickson, Leonard Eugene, 1874-1954, American mathematician, b. Independence, Iowa, grad. Univ. of Texas, 1893. He studied in Leipzig and Paris and joined the staff of the Univ. of Chicago in 1900. A leading American algebraist, he wrote on invariants and the theory of finite and infinite groups. His chief work is *A History of the Theory of Numbers* (3 vol., 1919-23, repr. 1966).

dictator, originally a Roman magistrate appointed to rule the state in times of emergency; in modern usage, an absolutist or autocratic ruler who assumes extraconstitutional powers. From 501 B.C. until the abolition of the office in 44 B.C., Rome had 88 dictators. They were usually appointed by a consul and were invested with sweeping authority over the citizens, but they were limited to a term of six months and lacked power over the public finances. Dictators were held to strict account for their conduct in office. Lucius Cornelius Sulla and Julius Caesar abolished the limitations to dictatorship and governed unconstitutionally. The Romans abandoned the institution after Caesar's murder. Modern dictators have usually come to power in times of emergency. Frequently they have seized power by coup d'etat, but some, most notably Benito Mussolini in Italy and Adolf Hitler in Germany, achieved office by legal means and once in power overthrew constitutional restraints. In the USSR the "dictatorship of the proletariat" has taken the form of a concentration of power in the hands of the Communist party. Under Joseph Stalin it developed into a personal dictatorship, but after his death there emerged a system of collective leadership. Latin American nations have undergone many dictatorships, usually by military leaders at the head of a junta. See TOTALITARIANISM.

dictionary, published list, in alphabetical order, of the words of a language. In monolingual dictionaries the words are explained and defined in the same language; in bilingual dictionaries they are translated into another language. Modern dictionaries usually also provide phonetic transcriptions, hyphenation, synonyms, derived forms, and etymology. However, a dictionary of a living language can never be complete; old words fall into disuse, new words are constantly created, and those surviving constantly change their meanings. The modern dictionary is often prescriptive rather than descriptive, for it attempts to establish certain forms as preferable. The most remarkable case of this sort is the dictionary of the French Academy, which is widely admired and ignored. The popular American attitude of the 19th cent. toward dictionaries gave them a nearly sacred authority, but in the 20th cent. the dictionary makers themselves began to replace notions of purity (especially based on ETYMOLOGY) by criteria of use, somewhat ahead of analogous developments in GRAMMAR. Because of the unprecedented scientific advances of the 20th cent., scientific terms have come into popular use and consequently have increased the size of general dictionaries. Lexicography is an ancient occupation; dictionaries of many sorts were produced in China, Greece, Islam, and other complex early cultures. The 13th-century *Dictionarius* of John of Garland is the first recorded use of the term to mean word list. Nathan Bailey (d. 1742) was the author of three English dictionaries so much more comprehensive and consistent than any of their predecessors as rightly to be considered the first examples of modern lexicography. His *Universal Etymological English Dictionary* was published in 1721; his larger dictionary, *Dictionarium Britannicum*, was published in 1730. An interleaved copy of this larger work was used by Samuel JOHNSON in preparing *A Dictionary of the English Language*, in two volumes, which appeared in 1755. Johnson's definitions evince his scholarship, humor, judgment, and skill and are basic to later lexicography. William Kenrick, who published a dictionary in 1773, was first to indicate pronunciation with diacritical marks (see ACCENT) and to divide words according to their syllables. The dictionary of Thomas Sheridan (1721-88), an actor, was published in 1780, and the dictionary of John Walker (1732-1807), also an actor, in 1791. In both these dictionaries special care was given to pronunciation, in which for many years Walker's authority received more deference than it merited. The first great lexicographer after Johnson was an American, Noah WEBSTER (1758-1843). The first edition of the book later known as *Webster's Spelling Book* appeared in 1783. For years the annual sales of this book were more than a million copies. To help those who had mastered the *Spelling Book* to continue their education, Webster published his *Compendious Dictionary of the English Language*, in 1806, with concern for "what the English language *is*, and not, how it *might have been made*." His larger dictionary, *An American Dictionary of the English Language*, in two volumes, was published in 1828. Authorized publishers have issued a series of skillful revisions and abridgments that have retained for Webster's dictionaries their popularity. The largest of Webster's dictionaries, called "the Unabridged," appeared as the 5th edition (1846) and included linguistic material that set it apart from previous Webster's dictionaries and made it outstanding. Continually revised, it is currently published in one volume. Another notable one-volume American dictionary was that by Joseph Emerson Worcester (1784-1865), first published in 1830; an edition revised by the author appeared in 1860 and was the first to employ a group of expert consultants, use illustrations, and indicate synonyms in the text. A later one-volume American dictionary was the Funk and Wagnalls *Standard*, completed in 1895. This dictionary listed definitions according to current rather than historical frequency of usage, an innovation that was generally adopted. *The Century Dictionary*, an American dictionary in six volumes, with encyclopedic features, was completed in 1891. Supplementary volumes were *The Century Cyclopedia of Names* (1894) and *The Century Atlas of the World* (1897). In England, progress in lexicography since Walker's time has been notably in the collection and organization of examples of usage. In 1836-37, Charles Richardson (1775-1865) published, in two volumes, a dictionary richer in illustrative examples than any of its predecessors. In 1857 the Philological Society began collecting dated examples of usage. This work of the Philological Society made possible the publication of the dictionary variously known as the *New English Dictionary on Historical Principles*, the *Oxford English Dictionary* (*OED*), and *Murray's Dictionary* (for Sir James A. H. Murray, 1837-1915, one of the editors). Publication of this dictionary began in 1884 and was completed in 1928, 70 years after the collecting of the material began. The 12 volumes and supplement of this monumental and unrivaled lexicon describe the history of some 250,000 English words, incorporating more than 2 million citations of usage in the process of defining a total of nearly 415,000 words. Two major shorter editions are published: *The Concise Oxford Dictionary of Current English* (5th ed. 1964) and the *Shorter Oxford English Dictionary* (3d. ed. 1973). A much less ambitious but notable project is the four-volume *Dictionary of American English on Historical Principles*, edited by Sir William Alexander CRAIGIE at Chicago. It was completed in 1943. Recent advances in lexicography have been made by the frequently revised collegiate or desk dictionary, an up-to-date abridgment of a large, comprehensive work. The *Webster's New Collegiate Dictionary* (8th ed., 1973) is based on *Webster's Third New International Dictionary*, published in 1966. This unabridged version has more than 550,000 entries, probably the largest number ever included in a dictionary of any language. Also notable are several modern American dictionaries of intermediate size, including the *Random House Dictionary* (1966) and the well-illustrated *American Heritage Dictionary* (1969). See R. L. Collison, *Dictionaries of English and Foreign Languages* (2d ed. 1971, a bibliographical guide).

Dicumarol (dīko͞o'mərôl"), trade name for an ANTICOAGULANT used to treat blood clots.

Didache (dĭd'əkē) [Gr.,=teaching], early Christian work written in Greek, called also *The Teaching of the Twelve Apostles*. Dates for its composition suggested by scholars have ranged from A.D. 50 to A.D. 150. Discovered in 1875 by Bryennios, Greek Orthodox metropolitan of Nicomedia, it is an invaluable primary source for the primitive church. The first part is a collection of moral precepts, perhaps based on rabbinical teachings (there are many quotations from the Old Testament); the second portion gives directions for baptism and the Eucharist; the third contains directions for bishops and deacons. The *Didache* may be of composite authorship. A short work, it has been published in English translation in collections of patristic literature.

Diderot, Denis (dənē' dēdərō'), 1713-84, French encyclopedist, philosopher of materialism, and critic of art and literature. He was also a novelist, satirist, and dramatist. Diderot was enormously influential in shaping the rationalistic spirit of the 18th cent. Educated by the Jesuits, he rejected a career in law to pursue his own studies and writing. In 1745 he became editor of the ENCYCLOPÉDIE, enlisting nearly all the important French writers of the ENLIGHTENMENT; they produced the most remarkable compendium up to that time. The best known of his plays is *Le Père de famille* (1758), which became the prototype of the "bourgeois drama." Other highly distinctive works include *La Religieuse* [the nun] (1796), a psychological novel; *Jacques le fataliste* (1796), a rambling novel in the manner of Sterne; and *Le Neveu de Rameau* [Rameau's nephew], a brilliant satire in dialogue. His philosophical writings include his *Pensées philosophiques* (1746) and *Lettre sur les aveugles* [letter on the blind] (1749), which contains the most complete statement of his materialism. Through his *Salons*, articles published in newspapers from 1759, he pioneered in modern art criticism. Diderot's vast correspondence forms a brilliant picture of the period. His later years, until he came to enjoy the patronage of Catherine II of Russia, were filled with financial difficulties. His influence was great, both on his immediate successors, Holbach and Helvétius, and on the writers and thinkers of France, Germany, and England. See his *Selected Writings*, tr. by D. Coltman and ed. by L. G. Crocker (1966); biography by A. M. Wilson (1972); studies by J. M. Morley (1971) and Carol Blum (1974).

Didion, Joan (dĭd'ēŏn), 1934-, American writer, b. Sacramento, Calif., grad. Berkeley, 1956. All her works explore the emptiness and despair of contemporary American life, a condition she views as produced by the disintegration of significant morality and values. Her works include the novels *Run River* (1963) and *Play It As It Lays* (1970) and a collection of magazine pieces, *Slouching Toward Bethlehem* (1968).

Didius Julianus (Marcus Didius Salvius Julianus) (dĭ'dēəs jo͞olēā'nəs), d. 193, Roman emperor (193). He was consul under PERTINAX, on whose death the Praetorian Guard received bids for the position of emperor. Didius bid highest and became emperor. Two months later he was murdered when Septimius SEVERUS, who would not recognize him, bought the support of the Praetorian Guard. Severus succeeded him.

Dido (dī'dō), in Roman mythology, queen of Carthage, who is also called Elissa. She was the daughter of a king of Tyre. After her brother Pygmalion murdered her husband, she fled to Libya, where she founded and ruled Carthage. According to one legend Dido, to escape marriage to the king of Libya, threw herself on a burning pyre. In the *Aeneid*, Vergil tells how she fell in love with Aeneas, who had been shipwrecked at Carthage, and how she destroyed herself on the pyre when, at Jupiter's command, he left to continue his journey to Italy.

Didon, Henri (äNrē' dēdôN'), 1840-1900, French Dominican preacher and writer. He became known as an eloquent preacher, especially for his eulogy on Archbishop DARBOY. He was sent to Corsica by the Dominicans (1880-87) because he was suspected of leaning toward modernistic ideas. His life of Christ, which was widely read, appeared in 1890. His Lent and Advent series of sermons were tremendously popular.

Didot, François (fräNswä' dēdō'), 1689-1757, Parisian printer. The son of a printer, Denis Didot, he was the first of the family to win fame in his craft. His son, **François Ambroise Didot**, 1730-1804, was said by Benjamin Franklin Bache to be the best printer of his time. Bache was apprenticed to Didot by his grandfather, Benjamin Franklin. The scholarly and typographic excellence of Didot's books is unquestioned. Influenced by the work of BASKERVILLE, he designed type in the modern, pseudoclassical style, and his work in turn influenced the work of BODONI. Didot improved the point system of measuring and naming sizes of type, first employed by Pierre Simon Fournier, and secured its general adoption in France. His sons, **Pierre Didot**, 1761-1853, and **Firmin Didot**, 1764-1836, continued the great tradition of the family, producing handsome books, mostly classics, with well-chosen texts that were conscientiously and skillfully edited. The Didot family never overlooked the requirements of students and general readers for good but inexpensive books. Firmin Didot was the first in France to print books from STEREOTYPE plates; the process enabled him to make less expensive books. He improved and named the process. His sons followed him in the family business which is still in operation.

Didrikson, Babe (Mildred Didrikson) (dĭd'rĭksən), 1913-56, American athlete, generally considered the greatest woman athlete of modern times, b. Port Arthur, Texas. At an early age Babe Didrikson excelled in basketball, baseball, and track. In 1932 she won five events, tied for first in another, and finished fourth in still another event in the National AAU track and field championships. Two weeks later she won two events in the Olympic games in Los Angeles with record performances and was disqualified in a third while tied for first. From 1934 on she devoted herself to golf. In 1938 she married George Zaharias, a wrestler. She gained wide notice as Babe Didrikson Zaharias. She won the U.S. Golf Association amateur competition (1946) and 15 tournaments in 1946-47. She was the first American woman to win the British amateur title (1947), and after turning professional in 1947 she won 33 tournaments (including the U.S. Open in 1948, 1950, and 1954) before succumbing to cancer. She wrote *Championship Golf* (1948).

Didymus: see THOMAS, ST.

Didymus Chalcenterus (dĭd'ĭməs kălsĕn'tərəs), fl. 1st cent. B.C., Hellenistic Greek grammarian and expositor. Famous for his prodigious literary output, he supposedly produced over 3,500 works. He collated much of the work of the Alexandrian critics, and though only fragments of his own work are extant, he is probably the source of many surviving classical commentaries.

Didymus of Alexandria, d. c.396, Greek grammarian and theologian, also called Didymus the Blind. His treatise *On the Holy Ghost* was translated by St. Jerome, who studied briefly with him. Although Didymus had been trusted with teaching theology by St. Athanasius, he was condemned for Origenism by the Third Council of Constantinople and the Second Council of Nicaea.

die, any of various devices used for drawing wire, and for blanking, bending, cutting, machine forging, and embossing. Dies used for striking, or stamping, coins and medals are cut in intaglio, one for the front, another for the back, of the coin. Such dies were used as early as c.800 B.C. in Greece. Diemaking, or diesinking, formerly entirely a hand process in which the graver (a cutting tool), riffler (a file), and chisel were employed, has been accelerated in modern times by the use of diemaking machines supplemented by hand finishing. A punch, or male die, is commonly made as the counterpart in relief of the original die, or matrix; both are preserved as models, and duplicates are made from them for working dies. Sheet metal or other material is blanked (cut) out, shaped, or embossed between the dies by power-operated levers or drop hammers, or by DIE-CASTING. The die used for drawing wire or extruding rods is made of hard metal with a hole or a series of progressively smaller holes through which the metal is forced. For making screws or threading pipe a hollow hard metal die with internal threading is used.

die-casting, process by which molten metal is forced by a plunger or compressed air into a metallic die and the pressure maintained until the metal has solidified. Die castings are accurate, are sharply outlined, have a good surface finish, and can be made in complicated designs. Zinc, aluminum, and magnesium alloys are the principal metals used. The high cost of the die usually limits the process to large-scale, high-speed production. Typical products are carburetor bodies and zippers. Type-casting machines are specialized die-casting machines.

Diefenbaker, John George, 1895–, Canadian political leader. Elected to Parliament in 1940, he succeeded George Drew as leader of the Progressive Conservative party in 1956 and in 1957 succeeded the Liberal Louis St. Laurent as prime minister, although his party failed to win a clear-cut majority. In 1958 his party captured more than 75% of the parliamentary seats in the most overwhelming Conservative victory of the century. The Conservatives, however, lost their majority in the 1962 elections, and early in 1963 the Diefenbaker government fell. Diefenbaker was leader of the opposition from 1963 to 1967; he continued to sit in Parliament after he was replaced as leader of the Conservatives.

Diego, Gerardo (hārär'dō dyā'gō), 1896–, Spanish poet, b. Santander. Although he has embraced many new poetic credos, his poetry can be classified into two styles. His traditional poetry of real and sentimental experiences includes *Soria* (1923) and *Versos humanos* [human verses] (1925). A second style, called creationism, produced more dehumanized poetry like *Imagen* [image] (1922) and *Manual de espumas* [manual of foam] (1924). A synthesis of both styles is seen in *Alondra de verdad* [the lark of truth] (1941).

Diégo-Suarez (dyā'gō-swä'rěs) or **Antsirane** (äntsěrä'nā), town (1970 est. pop. 38,600), N Malagasy Republic, at the tip of Madagascar, on Diégo-Suarez Bay. The bay, an arm of the Indian Ocean, is one of the world's finest natural harbors; its location, however, has hindered its development as a major port. Diégo-Suarez is a transshipment point between coastal and ocean vessels, coffee, corn, peanuts, and cattle being the items of export. There are saltworks nearby. The bay was discovered (1543) and named by Diogo Soares, the Portuguese explorer. The area was ceded to France in 1885, at which time the town became the capital of the French colony; France has maintained a naval base there since 1901.

dieldrin: see INSECTICIDE.

dielectric (dī''ĭlěk'trĭk), material that does not conduct electricity readily, i.e., an insulator (see INSULATION). A good dielectric should also have other properties: It must resist breakdown under high voltages; it should not itself draw appreciable power from the circuit; it must have reasonable physical stability; and none of its characteristics should vary much over a fairly wide temperature range. One important application of dielectrics is as the material separating the plates of a CAPACITOR. It has been observed that a capacitor with plates of a given area will vary in its ability to store electric charge depending on the material separating the plates. On the basis of this variation each insulating material can be assigned a dielectric constant. Generally, the dielectric constant of air is defined as 1 and other dielectric constants are determined with reference to it. Other properties of interest in a dielectric are dielectric strength, a measure of the maximum voltage it can sustain without significant conduction, and the degree to which it is free from power losses.

Diem, Ngo Dinh (nō dĭn dyěm), 1901–63, prime minister of South Vietnam (1954–63). A member of an influential Roman Catholic family, he was a civil servant before World War II and was connected with the nationalists during the war. He repeatedly refused high office with the government of BAO DAI until 1954, when he became prime minister. In 1955 he controlled a referendum that abolished the monarchy and emerged as South Vietnam's ruler. With strong backing from the United States, Diem initially made some progress, but his favoritism toward his family and toward Roman Catholics over Buddhists caused substantial criticism by the early 1960s. Opposition grew as Diem's authoritarianism increased and as South Vietnam's position in the VIETNAM WAR deteriorated. With the apparent connivance of the U.S. government, a group of dissident generals staged a coup in 1963, and Diem was murdered during the takeover.

Diemen, Anton van (än'tōn vän dē'mən), 1593–1645, Dutch colonial official. As governor general for the Dutch East India Company in the East Indies after 1636, he captured Ceylon and Malacca from the Portuguese. He sent Abel TASMAN on exploring voyages. Tasman called an island that he found (1642) Van Diemen's Land (now Tasmania).

Dienbienphu (dyěn'byěn'fōō'), former French military base, NW North Vietnam, near the Laos border. It was the scene in 1954 of the last great battle between the French and the Viet Minh forces of HO CHI MINH in Indochina. The French occupied the base by parachute drop in Nov., 1953; this move prevented a Viet Minh thrust into Laos and provided support for indigenous forces opposing the Viet Minh in that area. Although the base could be supplied only by air, the French military felt its position was tenable. Weary of inconclusive guerrilla warfare, they were willing to invite an open Viet Minh attack in an area where their superior weaponry could be used to full advantage. The Viet Minh army, under the command of Gen. Vo Nguyen Giap, chose to engage the French, and by March, 1954, some 49,500 Viet Minh troops had encircled Dienbienphu, where some 13,000 soldiers, under the leadership of Col. (later Gen.) Christian de Castries, were firmly entrenched in strong positions. The first Viet Minh assault came on March 13, and by the end of April, despite massive French air bombardment, the French defense area had been reduced to 2 sq mi (5 sq km). Desperate pleas for U.S. intervention were unsuccessful, and on May 7, after a 56-day siege, the French positions fell. This defeat signaled the end of French power in Indochina. See Vo Nguyen Giap, *People's Army, People's War* (1962); Jules Roy, *The Battle of Dienbienphu* (1963, tr. 1965); Bernard Fall, *Hell in a Very Small Place: The Siege of Dienbienphu* (1966).

diencephalon (dī''ənsěf'əlŏn): see BRAIN.

Diepenbeeck, Abraham van (vän dē'pənbāk''), 1596–1675, Flemish glass painter, book illustrator, and painter. He was active mainly in Antwerp and was strongly influenced by Rubens, who was his teacher.

Dieppe (dēěp'), city (1968 pop. 29,970), Seine-Maritime dept., N France, in Normandy, at the mouth of the Arques River on the English Channel. It is a fishing and commercial port, a manufacturing center, and a beach resort. Channel steamers sail from Dieppe to Newhaven, England. Dieppe was frequently involved in the wars between England and France. In the late 17th cent. it suffered severely from the DRAGONNADES of Louis XIV and an Anglo-Dutch naval bombardment (1694). In World War II, Dieppe was the object of a costly commando attack (Aug. 19, 1942) to test the strength of the German defenses. The Allied forces, mostly Canadians, lost two thirds of their men in casualties. Among the notable buildings of the city are the Church of Saint-Jacques (begun 13th cent.) and a 15th-century château.

diesel engine, type of INTERNAL-COMBUSTION ENGINE invented by the German engineer Rudolf Diesel and patented by him in 1892. Although his engine was designed to use coal dust as fuel, the diesel engine now burns low-cost fuel oil. It does not require a large water supply or a long warming-up period and is highly efficient in converting heat energy into work. Diesels are widely used in both stationary and mobile installations where the power required is between that furnished by the gasoline engine and that of the steam turbine and where the relatively high initial cost can be written off over a long period. For example, diesels having capacities of 100 to 5,000 hp are employed on industrial and municipal electric generators and on continuously operating pumps (e.g., on oil pipelines). Moreover, they occupy relatively little space compared with steam units, since no boiler is needed—a factor of importance aboard ships. The diesel engine differs from the gasoline engine in that the ignition of fuel is caused by compression of air in its cylinders instead of by a spark: the high compression ratio allows the air in the cylinder to become hot enough to ignite the fuel. Because of the high temperatures of operation, a diesel engine must be water-cooled. The construction of the diesel engine is heavier than that of the gasoline engine; there are usually three or more cylinders (supported on a framework and bedplate) and a heavy flywheel. The cylinders are set to work alternately to give a smooth-turning effect, and the flywheel contributes further to smooth action. There are two classes of diesel engines. In the two-stroke, or two-cycle, type there is a complete cycle of operation in every two strokes of a piston. This type of engine requires a supply of compressed air for operating and for starting. In the four-stroke, or four-cycle, type the first downstroke of the piston draws in air, which is compressed on the upstroke to about 500 lb per sq in. (35 kg per sq cm). At the top of the stroke a jet of oil is sprayed in through an injector. The oil is ignited and the rapid expansion of the gas created by the explosion forces the piston down in the working, or firing, stroke. The next upstroke drives the waste gases out through the exhaust valve, and the cycle is complete. The speed and power of the diesel are controlled by varying the amount of fuel injected into the cylinder, not the amount of air admitted as in the gasoline engine. Small and medium-size ships may have several diesels producing as much as 50,000 hp. Heavy-duty land transports such as trains, trucks, buses, and tractors are often diesel-powered. A few automobiles and even some airplanes have had diesel engines. See L. Van H. Armstrong, *The Diesel Engine* (1959); W. R. Nitske and C. M. Wilson, *Rudolf Diesel* (1965); P. O. Black, *Andel's Diesel Engine Manual* (1966); A. W. Judge, *High Speed Diesel Engine* (1967).

Dies irae (dē'äs ē'rā) [Lat.,=day of wrath], hymn of the Roman Catholic Church. A part of the Requiem Mass, it is a powerful description of the Judgment and a prayer to Jesus for mercy. Suggested in part by Zeph. 1.14–16, it was probably written by Thomas of Celano. In 16th-century polyphonic masses it was usually sung to the plain-song melody, but there are a few isolated examples of new music combined with the old melody in masses by minor composers. More recently, it has usually been supplied with new, and frequently intensely dramatic, music, notably by Mozart, Berlioz, and Verdi. It is no longer in general use in Roman Catholic funeral liturgy.

Dieskau, Ludwig August, Baron (lōōt'vĭkh ou'gōōst bärōn' dē'skou), 1701–67, French general in the French and Indian Wars. In 1755 he was sent to take command of French troops in America. He led them and their Indian allies in an attack against British and colonial forces at Lake George and was defeated by the British commander Sir William JOHNSON. Dieskau was captured but was exchanged in 1763.

diet, in German history, an assembly or council. It originated as a meeting of landholders and burghers, convoked by the ruler to discuss the problems of the princely purse. The imperial diet or *Reichstag* of the HOLY ROMAN EMPIRE was a loose assembly of lay and ecclesiastic princes, which met at irregular intervals. The Golden Bull (1356) of Holy Roman Emperor Charles IV solidified its organization into three groups—the ELECTORS, the princes, and the representatives of the imperial cities. With the growth of sovereign states in Germany, the empire came to have less meaning and the diet also declined in importance. The Peace of Westphalia (1648), which ended the Thirty Years' War, confirmed the sovereignty of the individual princes, thus making the diet into a federal body. The diet became a conference of ambassadors rather than a legislature, while the member states (notably Prussia and Austria) grew into strong nations. After 1663 the diet met at Regensburg. Among the most important diets were those of Worms and Cologne (1495, 1512; see MAXIMILIAN I, Holy Roman emperor), and of the REFORMATION—Worms (1521), Speyer (1529), and Augsburg (1530, 1547, 1555). For the federal diet (*Bundesrat*) of 1815–66, which succeeded the imperial diet, see GERMAN CONFEDERATION. For the diet of the German Reich and the German republic, see REICHSTAG. Other parliamentary bodies, including those of Poland, Hungary, Bohemia, the Scandinavian countries, and Japan, have also been called diets.

diet: see NUTRITION.

diethylstilbestrol (dīěth''əlstĭlběs'trōl) or **DES,** nonsteroid female sex HORMONE having the same physiological effects as the steroid hormone ESTROGEN. It is effective when taken orally and is often used medically for estrogen replacement. Diethylstilbestrol is used in the "morning-after" pill, a contraceptive pill which is taken after intercourse. The hormone is implicated in certain types of CANCER; its administration to beef cattle to speed growth is controversial.

Dietikon (dyě'tēkôn), town (1970 pop. 22,705), Zürich canton, N Switzerland, on the Limmat River. It is a suburb of Zürich.

Dietrich, Marlene (mär″lā′nə dē′trĭkh), 1901–, German-American film actress and singer, b. Berlin. Dietrich began her career as a violinist. She then studied drama, appearing on the stage in Vienna and Berlin before her great film success as Lola in *The Blue Angel* (1930). She came to the United States to star in the films of Josef von Sternberg, including *Shanghai Express* (1932) and *Blonde Venus* (1932). Her film image was that of a sultry and ageless femme fatale. During World War II she entertained the U.S. armed forces. After the war she appeared internationally in concerts, in cabarets, and on television.

Dietrich von Bern: see THEODORIC THE GREAT.

Diez, Friedrich Christian (frē′drĭkh krĭs′tyän dēts), 1794–1876, German philologist. A professor at Bonn, Diez is noted as one of the founders of the science of Romanic philology. His great works were a grammar of the Romanic languages (1836; later much enlarged) and a dictionary of the Romanic languages (1853; also much enlarged in later editions).

differential, in the automobile, a set of gears used on the driving (usually rear) axle. The two wheels on the driving axle must be interconnected in order to receive their energy from the same source, the driving shaft; at the same time they must be free to revolve at different speeds when necessary (e.g., when rounding a curve, the outer wheel travels farther and thus must revolve faster than the inner wheel in order to prevent skidding). These two requirements are met by the differential gearing. Furthermore, through it the rotating motion of the driving shaft is transmitted to the axle and the wheels. The axle is in two halves; to each half is attached a wheel at one end and, at the inner end, a gear (see GEAR). The end of the driving shaft is also equipped with a gear. By an ingenious arrangement of these and other gears, together constituting the differential, a difference in speed of the two wheels is compensated for without a loss of tractive force. A disadvantage of the conventional differential is that when one wheel is on a dry and the other on a slippery surface, the differential causes the wheel on the slippery surface to revolve at double speed while the other wheel remains stationary. This hazard can be avoided by use of a limited slip differential, which feeds power to one wheel when the other wheel starts to slip and thus keeps the automobile moving. See R.T. Hinkle, *Kinematics of Machines* (2d ed., 1960).

differential calculus: see CALCULUS.

differential geometry, branch of GEOMETRY in which the concepts of the CALCULUS are applied to curves, surfaces, and other geometric entities. The approach in classical differential geometry involves the use of coordinate geometry (see ANALYTIC GEOMETRY; CARTESIAN COORDINATES), although in the 20th cent. the methods of differential geometry have been applied in other areas of geometry, e.g., in PROJECTIVE GEOMETRY. The properties of a curve in space, **r**, at any point along its length, *s*, may be described in terms of three mutually perpendicular VECTORS of unit length: the tangent vector $\mathbf{t} = d\mathbf{r}/ds$, oriented in the same direction as the curve at the given point and indicating the rate of change of the curve; the normal vector **n**, perpendicular to the curve at the point and indicating the direction of the rate of change of **t**, i.e., the tendency of **r** to bend in the plane containing both **r** and **t**; and the binormal vector **b**, perpendicular to both **t** and **n** and indicating the tendency of the curve to twist out of the plane of **t** and **n**. These three vectors are related by the three formulas of Frenet, which are fundamental to the study of space curves: $d\mathbf{t}/ds = \kappa\mathbf{n}$; $d\mathbf{n}/ds = -\kappa\mathbf{t} + \tau\mathbf{b}$; $d\mathbf{b}/ds = -\tau\mathbf{n}$, where the constants κ and τ are the curvature and the torsion of the curve, respectively. Of special interest are the curves called evolutes and involutes; the evolute of a curve is another curve whose tangents are the normals to the original curve, and an involute of a curve is a curve whose evolute is the given curve. In the analysis of surfaces, points on a surface may be described not only with respect to the three-dimensional coordinates of the space in which the surface is considered but also with respect to an intrinsic coordinate system defined in terms of a system of curves on the surface itself. The curves on the surface that represent the shortest distances between points on the surface are called geodesics; they correspond to straight lines on a plane. Tangent and normal vectors are also defined for a surface, but the relationships between them are more complex than for a space curve (e.g., a surface can have an infinite number of vectors tangent to it at a given point). The results of the theory of surfaces are expressed most easily in the notation of TENSORS. It is found that the total, or Gaussian, curvature of a surface is a bending invariant, i.e., an intrinsic property of the surface itself, independent of the space in which the surface may be considered. Of particular importance are surfaces of constant curvature; planes, cylinders, cones, and other developable surfaces have zero curvature, and the elliptic and hyperbolic planes of NON-EUCLIDEAN GEOMETRY are surfaces of constant positive and negative curvature, respectively. Differential geometry was founded by Gaspard Monge and C. F. Gauss in the beginning of the 19th cent. Important contributions were made by many mathematicians during the 19th cent., including G. F. B. Riemann, E. B. Christoffel, and C. G. Ricci. This work was collected and systematized at the end of the century by J. G. Darboux and Luigi Bianchi. The importance of differential geometry may be seen from the fact that Einstein's general theory of RELATIVITY is formulated entirely in terms of the differential geometry, in tensor notation, of a four-dimensional manifold combining space and time.

differentiation, in biology, series of changes that occur in cells and tissues during development, resulting in their specialization. In plants, unspecialized cells, composing tissue called MERISTEM, differentiate into vascular tissue (xylem and phloem; see WOOD), supportive tissue (sclerenchyma), and storage tissue (parenchyma). In animals, the tissues of the gastrula stage of the EMBRYO, i.e., the ECTODERM, ENDODERM, and MESODERM, differentiate into specialized tissues. See also NOTOCHORD.

diffraction, bending of light around the edge of an obstacle. When light strikes an opaque body, a shadow forms on the side of the body that is shielded from the light source. Ordinarily light travels in straight lines through a uniform, transparent medium, but those light waves that just pass the edges of the opaque body are bent, or deflected. This diffraction results in the INTERFERENCE of the light waves that pass the opaque body, resulting in a fuzzy border region between the shadow area and the lighted area. Upon close examination it can be seen that this border region is actually a series of alternate dark and light lines extending both slightly into the shadow area and slightly into the lighted area. If the observer looks for these patterns, he will find that they are not always sharp. However a sharp pattern can be produced if a single, distant light source, or a point light source, is used to cast a shadow behind an opaque body. Diffraction also occurs and causes interference when light waves interact with a device called a **diffraction grating.** A diffraction grating may be either a transmission grating (a plate pierced with small, parallel, evenly spaced slits through which light passes) or a reflection grating (a plate of metal or glass that reflects light from polished strips between parallel lines ruled on its surface). In the case of a reflection grating, the smooth surfaces between the lines act as narrow slits. The number of these slits or lines is often 12,000 or more to the centimeter (30,000 to the inch). The ruling is generally done with a fine diamond point. Since the light diffracted is also dispersed (see SPECTRUM), these gratings are utilized in diffraction SPECTROSCOPES for producing and analyzing spectra and for measuring directly the wavelengths of lines appearing in certain spectra. The diffraction of X rays by crystals is used to examine the atomic and molecular structure of these crystals. Beams of particles can also exhibit diffraction since, according to the QUANTUM THEORY, a moving particle also has certain wavelike properties. Both electron diffraction and neutron diffraction have been important in modern physics research. Sound waves also undergo diffraction with resulting interference.

diffusion, in chemistry, the spontaneous migration of substances from regions where their concentration is high to regions where their concentration is low. Generally, the greater the difference in concentration, the faster the diffusion. This redistribution of a substance is due to the random motion of the molecules (or atoms or ions) of the substance. Because of the random nature of the motion of molecules, the rate of diffusion of molecules out of any region in a substance is proportional to the concentration of molecules in that region, and the rate of diffusion into the region is proportional to the concentration of molecules in the surrounding regions. Thus, while molecules continuously flow both into and out of all regions, the net flow is from regions of higher concentration to regions of lower concentration. Since an increase in temperature represents an increase in the average molecular speed, diffusion occurs faster at higher temperatures. At any given temperature, small, light molecules (such as H_2, hydrogen gas) diffuse faster than larger, more massive molecules (such as N_2, nitrogen gas) because they are traveling faster, on the average. (See HEAT; KINETIC-MOLECULAR THEORY OF GASES.) According to Graham's law (for Thomas Graham), the rate at which a gas diffuses is inversely proportional to the square root of the density of the gas. Diffusion often masks gravitational effects. For example, if a relatively dense gas (such as CO_2, carbon dioxide) is introduced at the bottom of a vessel containing a less dense gas (such as H_2, hydrogen gas), the dense gas will diffuse upward and the less dense gas will diffuse downward. It is true, however, that at equilibrium the two gases will not be uniformly mixed. There will be some variation in the density and composition of the gas mixture; at the top of the vessel the gas mixture will be slightly less concentrated, and there will be a slight preponderance of molecules of the less dense gas. These differences, which are due to gravity, are almost impossible to measure in the laboratory, although they interact with other factors in determining the distribution of gases in planetary atmosphere. Diffusion is not confined to gases; it can take place with matter in any state. For example, salt diffuses (dissolves) into water; water diffuses (evaporates) into the air. It is even possible for a solid to diffuse into another solid; e.g., gold will diffuse into lead, although at room temperature this diffusion is very slow. Generally, gases diffuse much faster than liquids, and liquids much faster than solids. Diffusion may take place through a semipermeable membrane, which allows some, but not all, substances to pass. In solutions, when the liquid solvent passes through the membrane but the solute (dissolved solid) is retained, the process is called OSMOSIS. Diffusion of a solute across a membrane is called DIALYSIS, especially when some solutes pass and others are retained. Diffusion is important in many life processes. It occurs, for example, across the alveolar membrane of the lung, which separates the carbon-dioxide-rich blood from the oxygen-rich air. Oxygen diffuses across the membrane and becomes dissolved in the blood; carbon dioxide diffuses across the membrane into the air.

diffusion, in optics, the scattering of light when it passes through a colloid, such as fog, or through frosted glass, or when it is reflected from a rough surface.

digallic acid: see GALLIC ACID.

Digby, George: see BRISTOL, GEORGE DIGBY, 2D EARL OF.

Digby, John: see BRISTOL, JOHN DIGBY, 1ST EARL OF.

Digby, Sir Kenelm, 1603–65, English author and man of affairs. He was the son of Sir Everard Digby, a wealthy Roman Catholic, who was hanged for his participation in the Gunpowder Plot. In 1625, Digby secretly married Venetia Stanley, a childhood sweetheart. His *Private Memoirs,* written in 1628 (pub. 1827), is an account of their relationship. The same year he conducted a highly successful privateering raid against a French and Venetian fleet at Scanderoon (now İskenderun, Turkey). A royalist, Digby was imprisoned by Parliament in 1642. On his release he went to France and became chancellor to Queen HENRIETTA MARIA. In 1645 he tried unsuccessfully to gain papal support for Charles I. Allowed to return to England in 1654, he became an agent for Oliver Cromwell for the purpose of securing rights for Catholics. After the Restoration (1660) he remained chancellor to Henrietta Maria but was forbidden at the court. Digby conducted scientific experiments and wrote various scientific, literary, and religious treatises; but he is best known for his publicizing of the "powder of sympathy," which was supposed to heal wounds without direct application. See his memoirs (1968); biographies by J. F. Fulton (1937) and R. T. Petersson (1956).

Digby, Kenelm Henry, 1800–1880, English author, b. Ireland. He converted to Roman Catholicism after his graduation from Cambridge. His principal works are *The Broadstone of Honour* (1822; enl. ed., 4 vol., 1826–27) and *Mores Catholici* (11 vol., 1831–40).

Digest: see CORPUS JURIS CIVILIS.

digestive system, in the animal kingdom, a group of organs functioning in digestion and assimilation of food and elimination of wastes. Virtually all animals have a digestive system. In the vertebrates (phylum CHORDATA, subphylum Vertebrata) the digestive system is very complex. It consists of the gastrointestinal tract (gut), an extensive tube extending from the mouth to the anus, through which the swallowing, digestion, and assimilation of food and the elimination of waste products are accomplished. In the digestive system, ingested food is converted into a form that can be absorbed into the CIRCULATORY SYSTEM for distribution to and utilization by the various tissues of the body. This is accomplished both

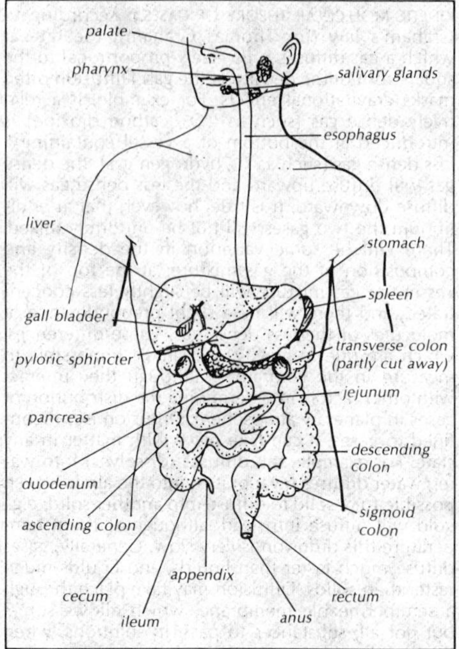

Digestive system

physically, by mastication in the mouth and churning of the stomach, and chemically, by secretions and enzymes of the gastrointestinal tract. Beginning at the MOUTH, all food passes through the alimentary canal (PHARYNX, ESOPHAGUS, STOMACH, and INTESTINES) before it reaches the anus, where undigested matter is eliminated as waste. The outer walls of the digestive tract are composed of layers of muscle and tissue that undergo waves of contraction (peristalsis), thereby pushing the food along its digestive path. The inner lining contains glands that secrete the acids and enzymes necessary to break down food into a form utilizable by the body. Digestion begins in the mouth, where chewing reduces the food to fine texture, and saliva moistens it and begins the conversion of starch into simple sugars by means of an enzyme, salivary AMYLASE. The food is then swallowed, passing through the pharynx and down the muscular esophagus, or gullet, to the expanded muscular pouchlike section of the gastrointestinal tract, the stomach. Specialized cells in the stomach secrete digestive enzymes and GASTRIC JUICES, which act on the partially digested food. The stomach also physically churns and mixes the food. The stomach secretions include the enzyme PEPSIN, which acts on proteins; hydrochloric acid, essential for the action of pepsin; and an enzyme, gastric lipase, which begins the breakdown of fats. The gastric juices of young children contain, in addition to those just mentioned, the enzyme RENNIN, which acts on milk. Some foods, including simple sugars and alcohol, are absorbed directly through the stomach wall and do not remain in the stomach. Most food, however, is not absorbed in the stomach and passes into the duodenum (first section of the small intestine) in the form of a thick liquid called chyme. Digestive enzymes from the PANCREAS and BILE from the LIVER act on the chyme in the duodenum. These enzymes include pancreatic lipase, which breaks down fats into glycerol and fatty acids; pancreatic amylase, which continues the breakdown of starches and most other carbohydrates into disaccharides; and TRYPSIN and erepsin, which break down whole and partially digested proteins (proteoses and peptones) into amino acids, the end products of protein digestion. Bile is essential for emulsifying large fat globules into smaller ones that are more easily digested by pancreatic lipase. In addition, intestinal juices are secreted by small glands in the intestinal wall called the crypts of Lieberkühn. Like the pancreatic juices, intestinal juices contain enzymes that continue the digestion of proteins and fats and also contain three enzymes that break down disaccharides into glucose, galactose, and fructose (simple sugars). The digested food is absorbed into the circulatory and lymphatic systems through small fingerlike projections of the intestinal wall, called villi. Undigested material passes into the large intestine, where most of the water is absorbed and the solid material, or feces, is excreted through the anus. See J. E. Morton, *Guts: The Form and Function of the Digestive System* (1967); H. W. Davenport, *Physiology of the Digestive Tract: An Introductory Text* (3d ed. 1971).

Digger Indians, term indiscriminately applied to many Indians of the central plateau region of W North America, including tribes in Oregon, Idaho, Utah, Arizona, Nevada, and central California. The name is supposedly derived from the fact that they dug roots for food. It has no ethnological significance and was a term of opprobrium.

Diggers, members of a small English religio-economic movement (fl. 1649–50), so called because they attempted to dig (i.e., cultivate) the wastelands. They were an offshoot of the more important group of Puritan extremists known as the LEVELERS. Gerrard Winstanley was the leader of the Diggers and the exponent of their egalitarian and communistic philosophy in his *New Law of Righteousness* (1649). The little band planted the common land at St. George's Hill, Surrey, and at nearby Cobham, but their project was met with suspicion by their neighbors and resistance from the landowners on whose property they encroached. In the spring of 1650 their community was destroyed by mob violence, and the experiment was abandoned. Winstanley's *Law of Freedom* (1652) extended his thesis that English law and institutions should be modified immediately to bring social and economic equality to all men through common ownership of the land. See D. W. Petegorsky, *Left-Wing Democracy in the English Civil War* (1940); G. H. Sabine, ed., *The Works of Gerrard Winstanley* (1941, repr. 1965).

digital circuit, electronic circuit in which the current or voltage, depending on which the devices in the circuit are sensitive to, is kept at one or another of several discrete levels; variation in the range between levels is thus in principle "ignored" by the devices in the circuit. In practical terms, this means that each level is represented by a zone such that any current (or voltage) lying in that zone affects the circuit exactly as if it were at that level. Usually the simplest arrangement is used, in which there are two levels corresponding to "on" and "off"; thus the presence or absence of a pulse of current represents one bit, or binary digit (see INFORMATION THEORY). The data on which a digital circuit operates is expressed as a chain of binary numbers. A digital device, such as a computer, is capable of carrying out arithmetical and logical operations on these numbers. Since most of the physical variables encountered in the real world, e.g., position and temperature, exist in analog form, they are represented electrically by continously varying currents and voltages in ANALOG CIRCUITS. To make digital and analog circuits compatible special convertors are used—either analog-to-digital or digital-to-analog depending on the direction of information flow.

digital computer: see COMPUTER.

digitalis (dĭj"ĭtăl'ĭs), any of several chemically similar drugs used primarily to increase the force and rate of heart contractions, especially in damaged heart muscle. The effects of the drug were known as early as 1500 B.C.; it was later obtained from the foxglove plant, *Digitalis purpurea*, and from fuchsia (see FIGWORT). It was used in the 19th cent. to treat dropsy (EDEMA). Digitalislike substances are found in a wide variety of plants and animals, including the poisons of some toad species. Foxglove remains the main source for the drug used medically today. Chemically, digitalis is composed of a sugar (glycoside), a steroid, and a cyclic ester known as a lactone; the pharmacological activity varies according to differences, occurring naturally or introduced synthetically, in the steroid or sugar portions. Common preparations include digitalis, digitoxin, and digoxin, from foxglove, and ouabain from *Strophanthus gratus*, the ouabaio tree; these vary both in solubility and in rapidity and duration of effect. Digitalis slows the pulse, slows the conduction of nerve impulses in the heart, and increases the amount of blood pumped by the heart. It is used in heart failure and in cardiac arrhythmias. The mechanism by which it acts to enhance heart muscle contraction is not definitely known. Toxic effects include nausea, vomiting, and visual disturbances.

digitoxin: see DIGITALIS.

Digne (dē'nyə), city (1968 pop. 15,778), capital of Alpes-de-Haute, Provence dept., SE France, in Provence. Points of interest include the Notre-Dame-de-Bourg Cathedral (13th–14th cent.) and a museum housing Gallo-Roman artifacts. On the outskirts of the city is a spa with thermal baths.

digoxin: see DIGITALIS.

Dijon (dēzhôN'), city (1968 pop. 145,357), capital of Côte-d'Or dept., E France, the old capital of Burgundy. It is a transportation hub and industrial center with food, metal-products, and electronics industries. Its mustard and cassis (black currant liqueur) are famous. Dijon is also an important shipping point for Burgundy wine. It is at least equally noteworthy for its art treasures. Founded in ancient times, Dijon began to flourish when the rulers of Burgundy made it their residence (11th cent.). Even after Burgundy was reunited with France (late 15th cent.), Dijon remained a thriving cultural center. The orator and writer Bossuet, the composer Rameau, and the dramatist Crebillon were among the notable figures born in the city. Dijon Univ. was founded in 1722. Rousseau's prize-winning entry in an essay contest of the Academy of Dijon in 1749 made him famous. Among the city's valued artworks are the funeral statues of the dukes of Burgundy by Claus Sluter and his disciples, housed in the splendid museum in the town hall that was originally the ducal palace (12th cent.; largely rebuilt 17th–18th cent.). Sluter (d.1406) sculpted the *Well of Moses* at the Chartreuse of Champmol near Dijon; it was largely destroyed in 1793. Other remarkable buildings in Dijon include the Cathedral of St. Bénigne (13th–14th cent.), the Church of Notre Dame (13th cent., in Burgundian Gothic), St. Michael's Church (Renaissance), the Hôtel Aubriot (14th cent.; now containing a museum of Burgundian folklore), and the palace of justice (15th–16th cent.), which once housed the powerful parlement of Burgundy.

dik-dik: see ANTELOPE.

Dike: see HORAE.

dike, in technology: see LEVEE.

Diklah (dĭk'lə), descendant of Noah and son of Joktan. Gen. 10.27; 1 Chron. 1.21.

Dilantin (dĭ'lăntĭn), trade name for diphenylhydantoin, an anticonvulsant drug. The first nonsedative antiepileptic agent, it is still widely used to control the grand mal type of EPILEPSY. It is also useful against types of psychomotor epilepsy, i.e., epilepsy involving bizarre patterns of movement. In some cases Dilantin, in combination with phenobarbital, a BARBITURATE, is more effective than either drug used alone.

Dilean (dĭl'ēən, dĭ'–), unidentified town, SW Palestine. Joshua 15.38.

Dilke, Sir Charles Wentworth (dĭlk), 1843–1911, British statesman. A radical leader in the Liberal party, he helped pass the parliamentary REFORM BILLS of 1884–85 as well as laws giving the municipal franchise to women, legalizing labor unions, and limiting working hours. Dilke's political career was effectively ended in 1885, when he was named as corespondent in a notorious divorce case. See biographies by Stephen Gwynn and G. M. Tuckwell (1917) and Roy Jenkins (rev. ed. 1965).

dill, Old World annual or biennial plant *(Anethum graveolens)* of the family Umbelliferae (CARROT family), of which the pungent, aromatic leaves and seeds are used for pickling and for flavoring sauces, salads, and soups. Dill water (a carminative) and oil of dill are made from the seeds. Dill was formerly used in charms against witchcraft. Dill is classified in the division MAGNOLIOPHYTA, class Magnoliopsida, order Umbellales, family Umbelliferae.

Dillard, James Hardy, 1856–1940, American educator, b. Nansemond co., Va., grad. Washington and Lee Univ., 1876. Professor (1891–1907) of Latin at Tulane, where he was also dean (1904–7) of the academic colleges, Dillard resigned to act as president (1907–31) of the Jeanes Foundation for Negro rural schools. He was director (1910–17) and president (1917–31) of the John F. Slater Fund. He contributed much to the improvement of Negro education and interracial relations. See B. G. Brawley, *Dr. Dillard of the Jeanes Fund* (1930, repr. 1971).

Dillard University, at New Orleans, La.; coeducational; United Church of Christ (Congregationalist) and Methodist; chartered 1930, opened 1935 by combining New Orleans Univ. and Straight College. It was named for James H. Dillard. The Flint-Goodrich Hospital, which offers postgraduate work for doctors, is there.

Dillenius, Johann Jakob (dĭlā'nēəs), 1687–1747, English botanist, of German birth. He published catalogs of the plants of Eltham, Kent, and of Geissen, Germany, and a work on mosses that placed him in the first rank among botanists of his day. A genus of tropical trees, *Dillenia*, was named after him by Linnaeus.

Dillinger, John (dĭl'ĭnjər), 1902-34, American bank robber, probably b. Indianapolis. Paroled after serving a prison term for attempted robbery, Dillinger organized a gang and terrorized the Midwest in 1933. He escaped jail twice, was held responsible for 16 killings, and was declared "public enemy number one" before he was shot (July, 1934) in a Chicago street by FBI agents. See biographies by Robert Cromie and Joseph Pinkston (1962) and by John Toland (1963).

Dillon, Clarence Douglas, 1909–, U.S. Secretary of the Treasury (1961-65), b. Geneva, Switzerland (of American parents). After graduation from Harvard he became a member of the New York Stock Exchange and joined the family investment firm. Dillon became active in Republican politics and in 1953 was appointed ambassador to France. In 1958 he became Under Secretary of State for Economic Affairs and strongly advocated free trade and close cooperation with the Common Market. Despite Dillon's support of the Republican presidential candidate in 1960, President Kennedy chose him as Secretary of the Treasury. Dillon's policies included an overhaul of U.S. foreign trade policy.

Dillon, John, 1851-1927, Irish nationalist. A supporter of Charles Stewart PARNELL, he entered Parliament in 1880 and was arrested several times for his advocacy of boycotting and agrarian agitation. After the Parnell divorce scandal, Dillon led the anti-Parnell faction until the Nationalist party was reunited (1900) under the leadership of John REDMOND. During World War I, Dillon incurred the enmity of Sinn Fein by encouraging military recruiting in Ireland in spite of his opposition to conscription. He succeeded (1918) Redmond in the leadership of the Nationalist party, but his career came to an end after the Sinn Fein victory in the 1918 election.

Dillon, John Forrest, 1831-1914, American jurist, b. Montgomery co., N.Y., M.D. State Univ. of Iowa, 1850. He abandoned medical practice early in his career and was admitted to the Iowa bar in 1852. Dillon was an Iowa state judge (1858-68) and a U.S. circuit judge (1869-79). During his judicial career he wrote *Municipal Corporations* (1872), one of the earliest systematic studies on this subject, and *Removal of Cases from State Courts to Federal Courts* (1876). He was (1879-82) a professor in the Columbia school of law, and president of the American Bar Association from 1891 to 1892.

Dilthey, Wilhelm (vĭl'hĕlm dĭl'tī), 1833-1911, German philosopher. He taught at the universities of Basel, Kiel, Breslau, and Berlin. He was one of the first to claim the independence of the spiritual sciences as distinct from the natural sciences. Dilthey laid down a foundation of descriptive and analytic psychology on which to base a study of philosophy. His principal work is *Einleitung in die Geisteswissenschaften* [introduction to the human studies] (1883). See his monograph, *The Essence of Philosophy* (tr. 1954); studies by H. A. Hodges (1944, repr. 1969), Kurt Müller-Vollmer (1963), and H. N. Tuttle (1969).

DiMaggio, Joseph Paul (dĭmä'jēō), 1914–, American baseball player, b. Martinez, Calif. He joined the New York Yankees of the American League in 1936 and quickly rose to stardom, batting .347 during his second season (1937). He was known for his versatility, fielding talent, and hitting ability. In 1941, "Joltin' Joe," as he was known, established a new record by hitting safely in 56 consecutive games. With the exception of three years (1943-45) in military service, DiMaggio played his entire career with the Yankees; he retired in 1951. He compiled a lifetime average of .325 and hit 361 home runs. He was elected to the Baseball Hall of Fame in 1955. His second wife was Marilyn Monroe. See his autobiography, *Lucky to Be a Yankee* (1946); Al Silverman, *Joe DiMaggio: The Golden Year—1941* (1969).

dime novels, swift-moving, thrilling novels, mainly about the American Revolution, the frontier period, and the Civil War. The books were first sold in 1860 for 10 cents by the firm of Beadle and Adams. The earliest was *Malaeska: The Indian Wife of the White Hunter* (1860), by Anne Stephens, which is said to have sold 300,000 copies in the first year; similar novels sold by the thousands throughout the country and especially in the Civil War camps. Such men as Bruin Adams, Col. Mayne Reid, Col. Prentiss Ingraham, W. F. Cody, and Ned BUNTLINE wrote of their own adventures. Among the most famous series were those about Deadwood Dick, by Edward L. Wheeler, and those about Nick CARTER. After 1880, when imitators entered the field with lurid stories that dealt in blood and thunder, the quality of the dime novel was lowered. Their popularity lasted until the 1890s, when series of stories such as those about the Rover Boys and Frank Merriwell and pulp magazines and the comic strip began to replace them. See Edmund Pearson, *Dime Novels* (1929); Albert Johannsen, *The House of Beadle and Adams and its Dime and Nickel Novels* (3 vol., 1962).

dimension, in mathematics, number of parameters or coordinates required to describe points in a mathematical object (usually geometric in character). For example, the space we inhabit is three-dimensional, a plane or surface is two-dimensional, a line or curve is one-dimensional, and a point is zero-dimensional. By means of a coordinate system one can specify any point with respect to a chosen origin (and coordinate axes through the origin, in the case of two or more dimensions). Thus, a point on a line is specified by a number x giving its distance from the origin, with one direction chosen as positive and the other as negative; a point on a plane is specified by an ordered pair of numbers (x,y) giving its distances from the two coordinate axes; a point in space is specified by an ordered triple of numbers (x,y,z) giving its distances from three coordinate axes. Mathematicians are thus led by analogy to define an ordered set of four, five, or more numbers as representing a point in what they define as a space of four, five, or more dimensions. Although such spaces cannot be visualized, they may nevertheless by physically significant. For example, the quadruple of numbers (x,y,z,t), where t represents time, is sometimes interpreted as a point in four-dimensional space-time (see RELATIVITY). Many features of plane and solid Euclidean geometry have mathematical analogues in higher dimensional spaces.

dimension, in physics, an expression of the character of a derived quantity in relation to fundamental quantities, without regard for its numerical value. In any system of measurement, such as the metric system, certain quantities are considered fundamental, and all others are considered to be derived from them. Systems in which length (L), time (T), and mass (M) are taken as fundamental quantities are called absolute systems. In an absolute system force is a derived quantity whose dimensions are defined by Newton's second law of MOTION as ML/T^2, in terms of the fundamental quantities. Pressure (force per unit area) then has dimensions M/LT^2; work or energy (force times distance) has dimensions ML^2/T^2; and power (energy per unit time) has dimensions ML^2/T^3. In a gravitational system (also called an engineering system), force (F) rather than mass is taken as fundamental, so that the dimensions of derived quantities such as mass, pressure, work, and power are then FT^2/L, F/L^2, FL, and FL/T, respectively. In either type of system, additional fundamental quantities are also defined, such as electric charge and luminous intensity. The expression of any particular quantity in terms of fundamental quantities is known as dimensional analysis and often provides physical insight into the results of a mathematical calculation. Dimensional analysis applies to systems using metric units, English units, or any other system of units. The only important distinction is between absolute and gravitational systems.

dimethylbenzene (dī"mĕthəlbĕn'zēn): see XYLENE.

dimethyl ketone: see ACETONE.

diminishing returns, law of, in economics, law stating that if one factor of production is increased while the others remain constant, the overall returns will relatively decrease after a certain point. Thus, for example, if more and more laborers are added to harvest a wheat field, at some point each additional laborer will add relatively less output than his predecessor did, simply because he has less and less of the fixed amount of land to work with. The principle, first thought to apply only to agriculture, was later accepted as an economic law underlying all productive enterprise. The point at which the law begins to operate is difficult to ascertain, as it varies with improved production technique and other factors. Anticipated by Anne Robert Jacques Turgot and implied by Thomas Malthus in his *Essay on the Principle of Population* (1798), the law first came under examination during the discussions in England on free trade and the corn laws. It is also called the law of decreasing returns and the law of variable proportions. See W. J. Spillman and E. Lang, *The Law of Diminishing Returns* (1924).

Dimitrov, Georgi (gēôr'gē dĭmē'trŏf), 1882-1949, Bulgarian Communist leader. A revolutionary from boyhood, he was a leader in the 1923 Communist uprising against Alexander TSANKOV. When it failed, he fled Bulgaria and continued to work for the Communist cause. In 1933 he was arrested in Berlin for alleged complicity in setting the REICHSTAG on fire. Dimitrov's cool conduct of his defense and the accusations he directed at his prosecutors won him world renown. He was acquitted and went to the USSR, which conferred citizenship upon him. Dimitrov was secretary general of the Comintern from 1934 until its dissolution in 1943. In 1944 he returned to Bulgaria to head the Communist party there, and in 1946 he succeeded Kimon Georgiev as premier. Dimitrov died in Moscow, where he was undergoing medical treatment. See his *The United Front* (1938), *Leipzig 1933* (tr. 1968), and *Selected Works* (3 vol., 1972); biographies by Filip Panaiotov (tr. 1963) and Luka Zulamski (tr. 1968); study by R. J. Pritchard (1972).

Dimitrovgrad (dĭmē'trôvgrät), city (1968 est. pop. 44,000), S Bulgaria, on the Maritsa River. Located on the Sofia-Istanbul RR, the city has one of Bulgaria's largest cement works, as well as several thermoelectric power stations that provide power to coal-mining areas nearby. Several engineering schools are in the city, which is named for Bulgarian Communist leader Georgi Dimitrov.

Dimnah (dĭm'nə), the same as RIMMON **5.**

Dimon (dī'mŏn), the same as DIBON.

Dimona (dĭmō'nə) [Heb.,=wasting], town (1972 pop. 23,700), S Israel, in the Negev Desert. It is the seat of the Negev Nuclear Research Center. Mining and the production of textiles, chemicals, and processed minerals are also important. The town was founded in 1955 and named for ancient Dimonah, which was located nearby (Joshua 15.22). The Dibon of Neh. 11.25 is probably the ancient Dimonah.

Dinah (dī'nə), daughter of Jacob and Leah. Gen. 30.21; 34.1-31.

Dinajpur (dĭnäj'po͝or), town (1961 est. pop. 37,700), N Bangladesh, on the Punarbhaba River. It is an important road junction and the administrative center for a district where rice and sugarcane are grown. A college affiliated with Rajshahi Univ. is in the town. Dinajpur proper, the northeast quarter of the town, where the maharajah of Dinajpur once resided, gave its name to the entire district.

Dinant (dēnäN'), town (1970 pop. 9,747), Namur prov., S Belgium, on the Meuse River. It is a commercial and industrial center, a tourist resort, and the gateway to the nearby limestone Han Grotto. Fortified since Merovingian times, Dinant was noted in the Middle Ages for its metalware. The town belonged to the bishopric of Liège until the French Revolution (1789) and was sacked by Charles the Bold in 1466 in the revolt of Liège. Of note are the Gothic Church of Notre Dame (13th cent.), a citadel (15th cent.; rebuilt in the 19th cent.), and the 17th-century town hall.

Dinard (dēnär'), town (1968 pop. 9,068), Île-et-Vilaine dept., NW France, in Brittany, on an inlet of the English Channel. Formerly a small fishing village, it is now a popular beach resort.

Dinaric Alps (dĭnâr'ĭk), Ital. *Alpi Dinariche,* Serbo-Croatian *Dinara Planina,* mountain system, extending c.400 mi (640 km) along the east coast of the Adriatic Sea from the Isonzo River, NE Italy, through Yugoslavia, to the Drin River, N Albania; it covers one third of Yugoslavia. The highest peak is Jezerce (8,833 ft/2,692 m) in N Albania. The system, linked to the main Alpine group by the Julian Alps, consists of the Dinaric Alps proper, Velebit Mts., Karst plateau, and North Albanian Alps. The partially submerged western part of the system forms the numerous islands and harbors along the Yugoslav coast. The rugged mountains, composed of limestone and dolomite, are a barrier to travel from the coast to the interior; there are no natural passes. Sinkholes and caverns dominate the landscape. The region is sparsely populated and forestry and mining are the chief economic activities.

Dindigul (dĭn'dĭgəl), town (1971 pop. 127,406), Tamil Nadu state, S India. It is a railroad junction and a trade center for hides, food grains, coffee, and spices. Cigars (cheroots) are the principal manufacture.

D'Indy, Vincent (văNsäN' dăNdē'), 1851-1931, French composer. D'Indy was a pupil of César Franck, whom he succeeded as president of the Société nationale de Musique. In 1894, Charles Bordes, Guilmant, and d'Indy founded the Schola Cantorum, Paris, of which d'Indy was composition teacher and, from 1911 until his death, director. His methods of teaching are largely embodied in *Cours de composition musicale* (3 vol., 1903; rev. ed. 1950), of which he was joint author. He also wrote biographies of Franck (1906), Beethoven (1911), and Wagner (1930). D'Indy's compositions include a dramatic legend, *Le Chant de la cloche* (1879–83); several music dramas; *Symphony on a French Mountain Air* for piano and orchestra (1886); the symphonic variations *Istar* (1896); songs; chamber music; piano works; and three additional symphonies.

Dinesen, Isak (ē'säk dē'nəsən), pseud. of **Baroness Karen Blixen,** 1885–1962, Danish author, who wrote primarily in English. In 1914 she married Baron Blixen and went to live in British East Africa, on a coffee plantation. She was divorced in 1921 and took over the management of the plantation where she lived until 1931, when falling coffee prices forced her to return to Denmark. From her experiences she wrote her autobiographical *Out of Africa* (1937). Dinesen is best known for her tales, many of which have eerie, supernatural elements. Her works include *Seven Gothic Tales* (1934), *Winter's Tales* (1943), *Last Tales* (1957), and *Anecdotes of Destiny* (1958). *The Angelic Avengers* (1947), first published in German-occupied Denmark, was a political allegory written under the pseudonym Pierre Andrézel. Writing despite severe illness, Dinesen finished the African sketches *Shadows on the Grass* in 1961. See biography by Parmenia Migel (1967) and studies by E. O. Johannesson (1961), R. W. Langbaum (1964), Frans Lasson and Clara Svendson (1970), and Donald Hannah (1972).

Dingley, Nelson, 1832–99, U.S. Congressman (1881–99), b. Durham, Maine. For many years the editor of the Lewiston (Maine) *Journal,* he was also a state official, serving as governor of Maine (1874–75). His service in the House of Representatives was marked chiefly by his preparation of the highly protective tariff measure called the Dingley Act, which replaced (1897) the Wilson-Gorman Act and remained in force until 1909.

dingo (dĭng'gō), wild dog of Australia, believed to have been introduced thousands of years ago by the aboriginal settlers of that continent. The only large carnivorous mammal found in Australia by the first European colonists, it stands about 24 in. (61 cm) high at the shoulder and has large, erect ears, a wolflike head, and rather long legs. It is usually yellowish red in color, with white markings on the underside, feet, and tip of tail. The dingo mates once a year and has a litter of up to eight pups. In the wild state it howls rather than barks, is nocturnal in its hunting habits, and usually travels in small groups. Although most often its quarry is small animals, the dingo's predation on livestock has caused serious economic loss in some areas of the continent. It has often been kept as a pet by the natives and used by them in hunting. The dingo is classified in the phylum CHORDATA, subphylum Vertebrata, class Mammalia, order Carnivora, family Canidae, genus *Canis,* species *dingo.*

Dingwall, burgh (1971 pop. 4,233), county town of Ross and Cromarty, N Scotland, at the head of Cromarty Firth. It is the market town for eastern Ross and the Black Isle district. In 1975, Dingwall became part of the new Highland region.

Dinhabah (dĭn'əbə), unidentified city of Edom. Gen. 36.32; 1 Chron. 1.43.

Diniz, Port. *Dinis* (dēnēsh'), 1261–1325, king of Portugal (1279–1325), son and successor of Alfonso III. Like his grandfather, Alfonso X of Castile, whose legal works he had translated into Portuguese, Diniz was a poet and a patron of literature. He founded (1290) at Lisbon the university that was later moved to COIMBRA. He also stimulated commerce and industry and encouraged agriculture, giving special favors to nobles who would pursue farming. He is therefore sometimes called *o Lavrador* [the farmer]. Diniz laid down laws to restrict further acquisitions of land by the church, confiscated the lands of the Templars, and generally worked to increase the royal holdings. The reign was relatively peaceful, though at its beginning the king's brother led several unsuccessful revolts, which involved Diniz in a desultory war with Castile. The last years of his reign were darkened by revolts of his son, the later Alfonso IV. All these conflicts were settled by the intervention of Diniz's wife Isabella, better known as St. Elizabeth of Portugal. Diniz is also known in English as Denis or Dionysius.

dinosaur (dī'nəsôr) [Gr.,=terrible lizard], extinct land reptile of the MESOZOIC ERA. The dinosaurs, which were egg-laying animals, ranged in length from 2½ ft (91 cm) to about 90 ft (27 m). Although all dinosaurs were originally classified in a single order, it was later discovered that the group contained two distinct types that could easily be distinguished by certain structural differences. The pelvis in the saurischians (or lizard-hipped) dinosaurs resembled that of the reptiles of today. In the ornithischians (or bird-hipped) dinosaurs the pubic bone of the pelvis had forward and backward extensions and so superficially resembled that of a bird. The jaws and teeth of the two groups also differed. Members of the saurischian order, which included both herbivores and carnivores, had teeth around the entire jaw or confined to the front of the mouth. Ornithischians had teeth along the sides of the jaw, but never in the front; the bones at the front of the mouth sometimes developed into the horny beaks typical of the so-called duck-billed dinosaurs. All ornithischians were herbivores. Fossil remains of dinosaurs have been found in rock strata of every continent, indicating that they differed widely in structure, habitat, and diet. Their intelligence, judged by the size of their brain cavities, was uniformly low. The belief that additional intelligence centers were located in the pelvic or shoulder region (as suggested by enlargements of the spinal cord in these areas) was later proved erroneous. A combination of factors, among which geographic and climatic changes were especially important, probably accounts for their extinction. During the Upper Cretaceous, crustal disturbances resulted in the draining of swamps, destroying the natural habitat of many dinosaurs. Elsewhere the formation of mountains caused colder climates in which reptiles cannot thrive. Some forms in North America had been wiped out by flooding in earlier Cretaceous times. Destruction of herbivorous forms by carnivorous types and the inability of the large, clumsy dinosaurs to compete with the small, fleet mammals, which were gradually becoming more numerous at the time, also contributed to the dinosaurs' extinction. Of the saurischian dinosaurs, some were carnivorous bipeds, such as TYRANNOSAURUS; some, herbivorous quadrupeds, such as BRONTOSAURUS and DIPLODOCUS. Among the ornithischians, IGUANODON was duck-billed, STEGOSAURUS was armored, and TRICERATOPS was horned. See E. H. Colbert, *Dinosaurs* (1961) and *Men and Dinosaurs* (1968); D. F. Glut, *The Dinosaur Dictionary* (1972).

Dinosaur National Monument: see NATIONAL PARKS AND MONUMENTS (table).

Dinotherium (dīnəthēr'ēəm) [Gr.,=terrible beast], extinct mammal related to the elephant, fossil remains of which have been found in Miocene and Pliocene formations of Africa, Europe, and India. It had a short proboscis and a pair of tusks which extended downward, curving backward, from the lower jaw. The name is also spelled Deinotherium. It is classified in the phylum CHORDATA, subphylum Vertebrata, class Mammalia.

Dinwiddie, Robert, 1693–1770, colonial governor of Virginia (1751–58), b. near Glasgow, Scotland. He was collector of customs (1727–38) for Bermuda and surveyor general (1738–51) for the Bahamas, Jamaica, Pennsylvania, Maryland, Virginia, and the Carolinas. Appointed lieutenant governor of Virginia in 1751, he was really the chief executive of the colony, always known as governor, since the two men who held the titular office during his term never came to Virginia. Dinwiddie favored an aggressive policy to forestall the French in the Ohio valley, and late in 1753 he sent George Washington on a mission to Fort Le Boeuf, c.12 mi (19 km) south of the site of Erie, Pa., to warn the French to withdraw from the territory claimed by the British. The French declined to heed Washington's demand, and early in 1754 Dinwiddie dispatched a force of workmen to build a fort at the junction of the Monongahela and Allegheny rivers, generally called the forks of the Ohio. Washington, made a lieutenant colonel of the colonial militia, soon followed with a detachment to protect them. The French drove the workmen away before Washington arrived and then defeated him on July 3, 1754, at FORT NECESSITY. Hostilities in the last of the French and Indian Wars had begun. Dinwiddie worked energetically preparing for Gen. Edward Braddock's campaign and the others that followed, but failed to win the full cooperation of other colonies that he constantly sought. His exertions finally ruined his health, and he left Virginia in 1758. See biography by L. K. Koontz (1970).

Diocletian (Caius Aurelius Valerius Diocletianus) (dī'əklē'shən), 245–313, Roman emperor (284–305), b. Salona, Dalmatia (the modern Split, Yugoslavia). Of humble birth, he obtained high military command under Probus and Aurelian and fought under Carus in Persia. The army proclaimed him emperor after the death of Numerian, and he became sole ruler when CARINUS, joint emperor with Numerian, was murdered by his own officers. In order to repel the Germans he appointed MAXIMIAN augustus (286) and CONSTANTIUS I and GALERIUS caesars (293). The four rulers had their respective capitals at Nicomedia, Mediolanum (modern Milan), Treveri (modern Trier), and Sirmnium. In Diocletian's reign Britain was restored (296) to the empire, the Persians were subjugated (298), and the Marcomanni were expelled from the empire. The persecution of the Christians in the latter part of his reign was a course to which he had been instigated by Galerius. Diocletian abdicated (305), and Maximian resigned at the same time. Diocletian was the first to divide the empire formally and to set up a genuine autocracy with no theoretical checks. The Edict of Diocletian (301) was an economic measure to regulate prices and wages. Its effects, however, were ruinous to agriculture and to the markets. This unsuccessful economic measure and the persecution of the Christians were the only black marks against Diocletian's splendid career, ended by his retirement to his castle at Salona.

Diodati, Giovanni (jōvän'nē dyōdä'tē), 1576–1649, Swiss Calvinist scholar and theologian, of a family of Italian Protestant refugees. He succeeded (1609) Theodore Beza as professor of theology at Geneva. Diodati served (1618) as a deputy to the Synod of Dort, and was chosen to assist in compiling the canons. He is chiefly known for his translation of the Bible into Italian.

diode (dī'ōd), two-terminal electron tube or semiconductor device. A diode has a low resistance to electric current in one direction and a high resistance to it in the reverse direction. This property makes a diode useful as a rectifier, converting alternating current (AC) into direct current (DC). In general, the current flowing through a diode is not proportional to the voltage between its terminals. When the voltage applied in the reverse direction exceeds a certain value, a semiconductor diode "breaks down" and conducts heavily in the direction of normally high resistance. When the reverse voltage at which breakdown occurs remains nearly constant for a wide range of currents, the phenomenon is called avalanching. A diode using this property is called a Zener diode. It can be used to regulate the voltage in a circuit. Semiconductor diodes can be designed to have a variety of characteristics. One such diode, called a varactor, exhibits a capacitance that is proportional to the voltage across it. In another kind, the tunnel diode, the current through the device decreases as the voltage is increased within a certain range; this property, known as negative resistance, makes it useful as an amplifier. A thermistor is a special diode exhibiting a voltage drop that depends on the temperature of the diode. Some diodes are photosensitive; the voltage drop across them depends on the amount of light that strikes them. Another kind, called a light-emitting diode (LED), produces light as current passes through it; some LED's can act as lasers.

Diodorus Siculus (dīədôr'əs sĭk'yōōləs), d. after 21 B.C., Sicilian historian. He wrote, in Greek, a world history in 40 books, ending with Caesar's Gallic Wars. Fully preserved are Books I–V and XI–XX, which cover Egyptian, Mesopotamian, Indian, Scythian, Arabian, and North African history and parts of Greek and Roman history. His compilation is uncritical and unreliable.

dioecious plant (dīē'shəs), plant in which the male and female reproductive structures are found in different individuals, as distinct from a monoecious plant (see HERMAPHRODITE), in which they are found in the same individual.

Diogenes (dīŏj'ənēz), c.412–323 B.C., Greek Cynic philosopher; pupil of Antisthenes. He was born in Sinope and lived in Athens. He taught that the virtuous life is the simple life, and he dramatically discarded conventional comforts, living in a tub. He is said to have thrown away his last utensil, a cup, when he saw a peasant drink from his hands. When Alexander the Great asked what he might do for him, Diogenes said, "Only step out of my sunlight." His daylight quest with a lantern "for an honest man" was probably the most striking expression of his contempt for his generation.

Diogenes Laërtius (lāōr'shēəs), fl. early 3d cent., Greek biographer. Extant is a work in 10 books on the lives and opinions of the philosophers from Thales to Epicurus, with whole books devoted to Plato and Epicurus. His work is an invaluable source of history. See his *Lives of Eminent Philosophers,* tr. by R. D. Hicks (1925, repr. 1966).

Diogenes of Apollonia (ăpəlō'nēə), 5th cent. B.C., Greek philosopher. An eclectic, he reverted to the Milesian tradition of a century earlier in seeking to explain the constitution of all matter in terms of a single basic stuff. He believed, with Anaximenes, that this substance was air and, with Anaxagoras, that a principle of intelligence, or *Nous,* was responsible for governing and diffusing air. Some of Diogenes' extensive work in physiology was preserved by Aristotle.

Diomed (dī'ōmĕd), **Diomede** (-mēd), or **Diomedes** (dī"ōmē'dēz), in Greek legend. **1** Son of Tydeus, he was one of the principal Greek warriors in the Trojan War. Previously he had avenged his father's death in the expedition of the EPIGONI against Thebes. **2** A Thracian king, son of Ares and Cyrene. He was killed during the eighth labor of Hercules while trying to protect his man-eating horses.

Diomede Islands (dī'əmēd), pair of rocky islands in Bering Strait between Alaska and Siberia. The boundary between the United States and the USSR as well as the International Date Line pass between them. They were discovered (1728) by the Danish explorer Vitus Bering on St. Diomede's feast day.

Dion Cassius (Cassius Dio Cocceianus) (dī'ən kăsh'əs), c.155–235?, Roman historian and administrator, b. Nicaea in Bithynia. He was a grandson of Dion Chrysostom. His rise in civil and military office was steady; he became a senator (c.180), praetor (193), consul (220?), proconsul in Africa (224), legate in Dalmatia (226), legate in Pannonia (227), and consul again (229). He was a good commander, but he remained in favor more for his literary works than for his abilities in office. His great work, partially extant, was a history of Rome (written in Greek) from the earliest times until Dion Cassius' own period. Of the original 80 books, 19 survive in full. They are a reputable source for the period of the later republic and the first two centuries A.D. Dion Cassius tried earnestly to study all available sources in the light of a moderate skepticism. He is also called Dio Cassius.

Dion Chrysostom (krĭs'əstəm, krĭsŏs'-), d. after A.D. 112, Greek Sophist and orator [Chrysostom = golden-mouthed], b. Prusa (modern Bursa) in Bithynia. He lived at Rome under Emperor Domitian, who subsequently banished him. He traveled widely, finally returning to Rome in the favor of emperors Nerva and Trajan. He leaned toward the philosophy of the Cynics and Stoics. With Plutarch he shared in the revival of Greek literature in the 1st cent. Extant are 80 orations on literary, political, and philosophical subjects. His name also appears as Dio Cocceianus.

Dione (dīō'nē), in astronomy, one of the 10 known moons, or natural satellites, of SATURN.

Dione, in Greek mythology, earth goddess. In some legends she is the daughter of Oceanus and Tethys; in others she is a Titaness, born to Uranus and Gaea. A goddess also of the oak tree, she was Zeus' first mate and shared with him the oracle at DODONA.

Dionne, Narcisse Eutrope (närsēs' ötrôp' dyôn), 1848–1917, French Canadian historian. He was a prolific writer and produced biographies in French of Samuel de Champlain, Jacques Cartier, Pierre Bédard, and other figures, numerous historical works, and the *Inventaire chronologique,* an invaluable bibliography of books, pamphlets, maps, and periodicals published in or about the province of Quebec (4 vol., 1905–9; supplementary volume, 1912).

Dion of Syracuse (dī'ən), 409?–354? B.C., Sicilian Greek political leader, brother-in-law of Dionysius the Elder, tyrant of Syracuse. He became interested in philosophy through his acquaintance with Plato. Opposed to tyranny, Dion endeavored to set up a moderate system of government with DIONYSIUS THE YOUNGER as the model prince. He thus became unwelcome at court and retired (366 B.C.) to Athens. Learning that Dionysius the Younger had taken measures against him, Dion assembled an armed force and sailed to Sicily. He was well received by the people and in 357 B.C. defeated Dionysius in battle. A rival, Heracleides, procured Dion's exile, but Dion was recalled, and he assumed control. He was murdered by an Athenian, a former companion.

Dionysia: see DIONYSUS.

Dionysius, king of Portugal: see DINIZ.

Dionysius Exiguus (dīənĭsh'ēəs ĕksĭg'yo͞oəs), d. c.545, Roman monk, chronologist, and scholar, a transmitter of Greek thought to the Middle Ages. He made collections of 5th-century papal decrees and the canonical documents of the early church councils. Dionysius, in an attempt to improve the reckoning of the date of Easter, was the first (525) to use our present system of reckoning a date from the time of the birth of Christ (see ERA).

Dionysius of Halicarnassus (hăl"ĭkärnăs'əs), fl. late 1st cent. B.C., Greek rhetorician and historian. He taught at Rome and was one of the most celebrated of ancient critics. Among his extant works are *On the Arrangement of Words, On Imitation, On the Early Orators, On Thucydides,* and *On the Eloquence of Demosthenes. The Art of Rhetoric* attributed to him is probably of later date. Of his longest work, *Antiquities of Rome,* in 20 books, approximately the first half is extant. In it the history of Rome to the 3d cent. B.C. is covered.

Dionysius Periegetes (pĕ"rēəjē'tēz), fl. 300 B.C., Greek poet. He wrote the poem *Description of the Inhabited Earth,* which was popular in antiquity.

Dionysius the Areopagite, Saint (ârēŏp'əjīt), fl. 1st cent. A.D., Athenian Christian, converted by St. Paul. Acts 17.34. Tradition has made him a martyr and the first bishop of Athens. He has been confused with St. DENIS. During the Middle Ages he was revered as the author of certain philosophical writings erroneously attributed to him since the 6th cent. These are ten letters and four treatises (*The Celestial Hierarchy, The Ecclesiastical Hierarchy, The Divine Names, Mystical Theology*) written in Greek, possibly in Palestine, in the late 5th or early 6th cent. It is now customary to refer to their author as Pseudo-Dionysius. Their obscure style was no barrier to their study and repeated translation into Latin, notably by Erigena and Robert Grosseteste. They exerted a lasting influence on the development of SCHOLASTICISM, particularly through St. Thomas Aquinas. The treatises provided a medium for transmission to Western culture of the concepts of Neoplatonism and of the theology of angels. Feast: Oct. 9. See studies by Denys Rutledge (1965) and R. F. Hathaway (1970).

Dionysius the Elder, c.430–367 B.C., tyrant of Syracuse. Of humble origin, he entered politics as a supporter of the poorer classes. Having prompted (400 B.C.) a measure to elect truly democratic generals, he secured for himself one of these generalships. His next move was to arouse distrust of his colleagues, and so well did he succeed that he soon became tyrant. Fundamentally his reign was characterized by a consistent policy of maintaining the obedience of the Syracusans through fear of the constant menace of the Carthaginians, then masters of a large part of Sicily. At the same time he kept alive the enthusiasm of his subjects by expeditions against the cities of the Italian mainland and by his none too successful efforts to repel the Carthaginians. He sided with Sparta against Athenian naval predominance. He wrote tragedies and was patron of the arts.

Dionysius the Younger, fl. 368–344 B.C., tyrant of Syracuse, son of Dionysius the Elder. He ended the war with Carthage and enlisted the support of the professional army. Neither gifted nor trained for administration or warfare, his banishment of DION OF SYRACUSE destroyed his only valid chance of maintaining his influence. In 357 B.C. the Syracusans welcomed Dion, who came to avenge his family for the ill-treatment they had received, and Dionysius fled. The murder of Dion gave Dionysius the opportunity to reestablish himself in his native city, whence he was finally expelled by TIMOLEON in 344 B.C. The remainder of his life was spent chiefly in Corinth, where he is said to have been a teacher of rhetoric. He wrote poetry and philosophy and was a patron of the arts. Dion, with Plato's backing, had attempted to fashion him into the model philosopher king, but failed. Subsequently Dionysius expelled Plato from his court.

Dionysius Thrax [Lat.,=the Thracian], fl. 100 B.C., Greek grammarian of Alexandria. His *Art of Grammar* remained a standard work for centuries and was a model for subsequent grammars.

Dionysus (dīənī'səs), in Greek religion, god of fertility and wine. Legends concerning him are profuse and contradictory. However, he was one of the most important gods of the Greeks and was associated with various religious cults. He was probably in origin a Thracian deity. According to the Orphic legend, he was Dionysus Zagreus, the son of Zeus and Persephone (see ORPHIC MYSTERIES); in other legends he was the son of Zeus and Semele and was reared by the nymphs on Mt. Nysa, where he invented the art of wine making. Having grown to manhood, Dionysus wandered through many lands, teaching men the culture of the vine and the mysteries of his cult. He was followed by an entourage of satyrs, sileni, maenads, and nymphs. There are many stories concerning the denial of his divinity and of the dreadful revenges he took (e.g., ORPHEUS and PENTHEUS). Many festivals were held in honor of Dionysus; most famous were the Lesser or Rural Dionysia (in late December), the Greater or City Dionysia (in late spring), the Anthesteria (in early spring), and the Lenaea (in winter). His characteristic worship was often drunken and orgiastic. Votaries, through music, dancing, and drinking, and through eating flesh and blood of sacrificial animals, attempted to merge their identities with that of the god. Later, however, the worship of Dionysus became more formalized and calm. It was believed that not only could he liberate and inspire man through wine and ecstatic frenzy, but he could endow him directly with divine creativity. Dionysus thus came to be considered a patron of the arts. He was variously represented as a full-grown bearded man, as a beast, and as a delicate, effeminate youth. The Romans identified him with Liber and with Bacchus, who was more properly the god of wine. From the music, singing, and dancing at the festivals of Dionysus developed the DITHYRAMB and ultimately Greek drama.

Diop, Birago (bĕrägō' dyōp), (Birago Ishmael Diop), 1906–, Senegalese author who writes in French. He is best known for his collections of aphoristic stories based on African folk tales, including *Contes d'Amadou Koumba* (1947; tr. *Tales of Amadou Koumba,* 1966). Diop also published a poetry anthology, *Leurres et lueurs* [lures and glimmers] (1960). In addition to writing, he has held several official veterinary posts in Africa and was Senegalese ambassador to Tunisia.

Diophantus (dīəfăn'təs), fl. A.D. 250, Greek algebraist. He pioneered in solving a type of indeterminate algebraic equation; work in this field is known as Diophantine analysis. Only 6 of the 13 books with which he is credited are extant. The standard edition in Greek was edited by Paul Tannery (2 vol., 1893–95). See study and English translation by T. L. Heath (2d ed. 1910, repr. 1964).

Dior, Christian: see under FASHION.

Diori, Hamani (hämän'ē dēôr'ē), 1916–, first president of Niger. He served in the French national assembly (1946–51, 1956–58) and then became Niger's prime minister (1958–60). Leading Niger to complete independence from France in 1960, he assumed the presidency, which he held until 1974 when he was overthrown in a military coup.

Dioscorides, Pedanius (pĭdān'ēəs dīəskôr'ĭdēz), fl. 1st cent. A.D., Greek physician of Anazarbus, Cilicia. While traveling as a surgeon in the Roman army, he collected information on the remedies of the period and wrote a work on materia medica (tr. *The Greek Herbal of Dioscorides,* 1934, repr. 1959) that remained standard for centuries.

Dioscuri: see CASTOR AND POLLUX.

Diotrephes (dīŏt'rĕfēz), ambitious Christian. 3 John 9.

Diourbel (dyo͞orbĕl'), town (1967 est. pop. 36,000), W Senegal, on the railroad from DAKAR to the Niger River in Mali. The market for a peanut-growing region, it produces peanut oil as well as beverages and perfume. Diourbel has a beautiful mosque.

dip, in agriculture, method of treating animals (chiefly livestock) infested with skin parasites such as mites, ticks, and warbles. The animal is dipped into or forced to swim through a tank filled with a solution containing INSECTICIDE. The chemicals used in dips include lindane, rotenone, lime sulphur, and various arsenic compounds. See publications of the U.S. Dept. of Agriculture.

Diphilus (dĭf'ĭləs), fl. 300 B.C., Greek poet of the New Comedy, b. Sinope. His many dramas (perhaps 100) were extensively copied by Plautus and Terence and influenced the entire Roman stage. The fragments of his works that remain reveal his talent for strongly contrasted scenes and brilliant theatrical effects.

diphosgene (dī"fŏz'jēn), colorless liquid developed as a military poison. It boils at 128°C; its vapors have the odor of PHOSGENE. Diphosgene is a lung irritant but is only slightly lachrimatory. Like phosgene, its effects are often delayed. Chemically it is trichloromethylchloroformate, $ClCO_2CCl_3$.

diphtheria (dĭfthēr'ēə), acute contagious disease caused by *Corynebacterium diphtheriae* (Klebs-Loffler bacillus). It begins as a soreness of the throat with fever. The bacteria lodge in the mucous membranes of the throat, producing virulent toxins that destroy the tissue. The resultant formation of a tough gray membrane is one of the most dangerous aspects of diphtheria, since it can spread to the larynx and cause suffocation. The toxins may disseminate to other parts of the body, damaging the tissues of the heart, kidneys, or nerves. Deaths from diphtheria often result from inflammation of the heart. Infection of the nerves can cause inability to swallow and paralysis. Diphtheria usually occurs in children of preschool age. Treatment with antitoxin is begun as early as possible. Penicillin should also be given, particularly to guard against complicating factors such as pneumonia or streptococcal infection. Diphtheria was once a common and dreaded disease with a high mortality rate; it appeared in both epidemic and sporadic form, spreading from the respiratory droplets of infected individuals. To prevent the disease, infants are given a series of three injections of diphtheria toxoid (toxin that has been rendered harmless), often combined with pertussis (whooping cough) and tetanus immunization.

Diplodocus (dĭplŏd'əkəs) [Gr.,=double beam (or rafter)], quadruped vegetarian DINOSAUR found in the Jurassic strata of the United States. It had a small head and a long tail and was probably an amphibious inhabitant of the swamp. Some of these animals reached a length of more than 80 ft (24 m), but were more slender and lighter in weight than the related brontosaur (see BRONTOSAURUS). The Diplodocus is classified in the phylum CHORDATA, subphylum Vertebrata, class Reptilia, order Saurischia.

diploid cell: see MEIOSIS.

diplomatic service, organized body of agents maintained by governments to communicate with one another. Until the 15th cent. any formal communication or negotiation among nations was conducted either by means of ambassadors specially appointed for a particular mission or by direct correspondence among heads of states. This procedure was not always satisfactory, however, and by the mid-16th cent. several countries had established permanent representatives in foreign states. One of the first powers to do this was Venice, which in 1496 appointed two merchants as representatives in London because the journey to England was "very long and very dangerous." Other countries later followed suit, and by the end of the 17th cent. permanent legations had become widespread in Europe. There was no uniformity in titles and status among various ambassadors, however, and agents operating below the ambassadorial level, although influential, were often corrupt. At the Congress of Vienna (1815) this system was corrected, and a classification of diplomatic ranks was adopted. Four grades of diplomatic representatives were recognized: ambassador, papal legate, and papal nuncio; minister plenipotentiary and envoy extraordinary; minister; and chargé d'affaires. This codification went far toward professionalizing the diplomatic service and established it as a branch of the public service in each nation. As the diplomatic service became a regularized institution, its functions began to grow. While the ambassador himself continued to act as a personal representative of his particular head of state, his staff necessarily expanded as various types of attachés were assigned to his embassy. Today secretaries, military, cultural, and commercial attachés, clerical workers, and various experts and advisers are all part of the diplomatic corps. The persons of diplomats enjoy diplomatic immunity, i.e., they are exempt from search, arrest, or prosecution by the government to which they are accredited. This immunity, which derives from the concept of EXTRATERRITORIALITY, is deemed necessary for diplomats to properly carry out their official duties. They are allowed communications and transportation without interference, and their embassy and residence enjoy similar privileges of extraterritoriality. Diplomatic business is generally conducted according to forms long established by custom, including memorandums, informal oral or written notes, or formal notes. Although French was once the universal language of diplomacy, both French and English are used today. The larger countries of the world have permanent diplomatic relations with scores of other nations, whether those nations are considered friendly or unfriendly. If two countries have no diplomatic relations, their interests may be represented by diplomats of other powers, and when two states are at war their interests are usually represented by neutral states. In the event that a nation refuses to admit a diplomat from a foreign nation or demands his recall, the diplomat's government must either comply or break off relations. In the United States, ambassadors are appointed by the President and are subject to the approval of the Senate. Although the CONSULAR SERVICE and the diplomatic service were once separate in the United States, the Rogers Act of 1924 combined the two branches into the Foreign Service. The Foreign Service Act of 1946 reorganized the Foreign Service, raising salary levels and introducing the merit system for promotions to all but appointive positions. Today the Foreign Service is under the control of a Deputy Undersecretary of State, assisted by the Foreign Service Institute. In the 20th cent. there have been numerous meetings of heads of state and foreign ministers and various types of international conferences, all of which have tended to lessen the traditional diplomatic function. Moreover, some claim that modern communications have also changed diplomacy greatly by removing whatever autonomy a diplomat may once have had in making policy decisions. The possibility of immediate telephone or air contact with a superior has allegedly reduced the diplomat to a quasi-messenger. Even if this may appear true, the diplomat continues to serve as an expert adviser, and while not empowered to make final decisions, he greatly influences the decision-making process. See Garrett Mattingly, *Renaissance Diplomacy* (1955); Sir Ernest Satow, *Guide to Diplomatic Practice* (4th ed. 1957); Charles W. Thayer, *Diplomat (1959);* William Barnes, *The Foreign Service of the United States* (1961); Harold Nicolson, *Diplomacy* (3d ed. 1963);F. J. Merli and T. A. Wilson, ed., *Matters of American Diplomacy* (1974).

Dipoenus (dīpē'nəs) and **Scyllis** (sĭl'ĭs), c.580 B.C., Greek sculptors, who worked jointly in ivory, ebony, and probably marble. They are mentioned by Pliny the Elder.

dipole: see POLE, in electricity and magnetism.

dipper, common name for the only aquatic member of the order Perciformes (perching birds) found near cold mountain streams. With their short, stubby wings and tails and their thick brownish plumage, dippers are thought to be closely related to the wrens. There are four species: the brownish gray North American dipper, *Cinclus mexicanus*, called also water ouzel, found from Alaska to Panama; the white-headed dipper of the Andes; the European common dipper, with a white throat and breast, found from Scandinavia to Africa; and the Asian dipper of Siberia and China. Dippers have filmy feathers, large preen glands that provide waterproofing oil, and flaps over the nostrils and a third eyelid to keep out water. They swim well under water, using their wings for propulsion, and eat water insects and larvae, newts, and minnows. Their wrenlike domed nests are built in rock crevices. Dippers are classified in the phylum CHORDATA, subphylum Vertebrata, class Aves, order Perciformes, family Cinclidae.

Dipper, Big, and **Little Dipper:** see URSA MAJOR.

Dirac, Paul Adrien Maurice (dĭrăk'), 1902–, English physicist. He was educated at the Univ. of Bristol and St. John's College, Cambridge, and became professor of mathematics at Cambridge in 1932. In 1928, Dirac published a version of quantum mechanics that took into account the theory of RELATIVITY (see QUANTUM THEORY). One consequence of his theory was the prediction of negative energy states for the electron, implying the existence of an ANTIPARTICLE to the electron; this antiparticle, the positron, was discovered in 1932 by C. D. Anderson. Dirac's equation for the motion of a particle is a relativistic modification of the Schrödinger wave equation, the basic equation of quantum mechanics. For their work Dirac and Erwin Schrödinger shared the 1933 Nobel Prize in Physics. Dirac also received the Copley Medal of the Royal Society in 1952 for this and other contributions to the quantum theory, including his formulation (with Enrico Fermi) of the Fermi-Dirac statistics and his work on the quantum theory of electromagnetic radiation. He wrote *The Principles of Quantum Mechanics* (1930, 4th ed. 1958).

direct action, theory and methods used by certain labor groups to fight employers, capitalist institutions, and the state by direct economic action, without using intermediate organizations. Political measures, such as arbitration, collective bargaining, and trade agreements, are rejected as ineffective. According to the theory, workers, acting as a class, are in a position to exert pressure on capitalist institutions to secure rights. Such measures as the STRIKE, the GENERAL STRIKE, the BOYCOTT, and SABOTAGE—frequently accompanied by physical violence—are the preferred methods for labor disputes; PROPAGANDA and agitation are employed against the government. The specific reforms gained are seen as steps toward the ultimate revolution and toward abolition of capitalism. The theory was developed with the rise of the labor movement in the 19th cent. and was formulated as a definite policy in the early 20th cent. by anti-Marxist radical groups, notably proponents of SYNDICALISM. The method was used in France and spread to other European countries. In the United States the INDUSTRIAL WORKERS OF THE WORLD advocated it. The doctrine was repudiated by the Communists of the Third International, who held to the theory of political action. See William Mellor, *Direct Action* (1920); L. L. Lorwin, *Labor and Internationalism* (1929).

direct current, abbr. DC, a movement of electric charge across an arbitrarily defined surface in one direction only. See ELECTRICITY; GENERATOR.

directing. The modern theatrical director is in complete charge of all the artistic aspects of a dramatic presentation. It is his first task to discover a central mood or idea in the text of the play to be performed that will serve as a unifying determinant for the interpretation of individual scenes and characters. Then he must work out the movement of the actors on stage and the pacing of each line and scene. Finally, he helps plan the lighting, scenery, sound effects, and musical accompaniment for the production. All the director's efforts are aimed at creating a fully unified aesthetic experience. Directing in some form has always existed in the theater. In ancient Greece playwrights trained their chorus and actors, and medieval religious plays had either individual or group directors. During later centuries the stage manager was the forerunner of the director. Prior to the rise of the director in the 19th cent., theatrical productions involved little rehearsing, and the actors simply stood at the front of the stage and declaimed to the audience. In England, Madame VESTRIS and W. C. MACREADY were the first to emphasize the importance of rehearsing, and they also introduced realistic scenery and acting techniques. The 19th-century interest in realism, coupled with far-reaching technical advances, made indispensable the director's function of integrating the various and increasingly complex aspects of play production. The beginning of modern directing is commonly associated with the MEININGEN PLAYERS, a German acting troupe organized in 1874 by George II, duke of Saxe-Meiningen. Under the direction of Ludwig Chronegk, the group worked as a unit, setting an influential example of effective ensemble playing. Leading realistic directors of the late 19th cent. included André ANTOINE in France, Otto BRAHM in Germany, and Constantin STANISLAVSKY in Russia. The most innovative of these was probably Stanislavsky, who stressed ensemble acting and the importance of an actor's absolute identification with his role. Almost as soon as realism gained ascendancy, various antirealistic theatrical movements developed, beginning with Paul Fort's Théâtre d'Art (1890). The theories of Adolphe APPIA in Germany and Edward Gordon CRAIG in England encouraged European directors to experiment with symbolic settings. Even conservative directors such as Harley GRANVILLE-BARKER and Jacques COPEAU soon realized that a realistic setting was not essential to the true rendering of a play's meaning. In addition to producing increased artistic possibilities for directors, the rise of antirealism made the director's practical task of coordinating scene design, lighting, and acting even more essential. A director who experimented successfully with both realism and antirealism was the German Max REINHARDT. Noted for his extravagant productions, he tried to remove the barrier between actors and audience by projecting the stage into the audience and scattering actors among the spectators. During the 1920s there were several important antirealist directors working in Germany and the Soviet Union, notably Vsevolod MEYERHOLD, Alexander Tairov, and Erwin PISCATOR. A disciple of Reinhardt, Piscator worked with the playwright Bertolt BRECHT, whose theories have greatly influenced 20th-century theater. In order to emphasize the social and intellectual content of Brecht's plays, Piscator utilized stylized settings and mechanical devices such as motion pictures. Brecht wished to insure the intellectual receptiveness of his audience by making it continually aware that it was watching a play, not reality. To this end he and Piscator took the opposite of the Stanislavsky technique and schooled their actors to alienate themselves from their roles. During the 19th and early 20th cent., the American theater was dominated by directors specializing in elaborate surface realism, with David BELASCO as their prototype. A break from that tendency was made by the GROUP THEATRE (1931–41), with Cheryl Crawford, Lee Strasberg, and Harold Clurman directing plays of social significance and promulgating Stanislavsky's theories of acting. Strasberg's Actors' Studio produced a generation of theater and film actors devoted to the Stanislavsky technique. During the 1950s and 60s the emergence of the theater of the absurd and the theater of cruelty granted di-

dispensary: see CLINIC.

dispersion, in chemistry, mixture in which fine particles of one substance are scattered throughout another substance. A dispersion is classed as a SUSPENSION, COLLOID, or SOLUTION. Generally, the particles in a solution are of molecular or ionic size; those in a colloid are larger but too small to be observed with an ordinary microscope; those in a suspension can be observed under a microscope or with the naked eye. A coarse mixture (e.g., sand mixed with sugar) is usually not thought of as a dispersion.

dispersion, in physics: see SPECTRUM.

displaced person: see REFUGEE.

displacement, in psychology: see DEFENSE MECHANISM.

Disraeli, Benjamin, 1st earl of Beaconsfield (dĭzrā'lē), 1804–81, British statesman and author. He is regarded as the founder of the modern Conservative party. He was of Jewish ancestry, but his father, the literary critic Isaac D'Israeli, had him baptized (1817) a Christian. In 1826, Disraeli published his first novel, *Vivian Grey*. It was the beginning of a prolific literary career, and his political essays and numerous novels earned him a permanent place in English literature. After a period of foreign travel (1830–31), Disraeli returned to London, where he soon became prominent in society. He attracted attention by his flamboyant dress and affectations. Standing four times for Parliament without success, he was finally elected in 1837 and rapidly developed into an outstanding, realistic, and caustically witty politician. He was a follower of Sir Robert PEEL until 1843, but he then became spokesman for the Young England group of Tories, espousing a sort of romantic and aristocratic Toryism. He emerged as a principal opponent of repealing the corn laws and, after the repeal went through (1846), helped bring down Peel's ministry. At the death of Lord George Bentinck (1848), Disraeli became leader of the Tory protectionists. He now sought to rebuild the party along lines already made clear in his political novels, especially in *Coningsby* (1844) and *Sybil* (1845). Taking a historical view of the constitution, he favored elevation of crown, church, and aristocracy as bulwarks of moderate democracy and social order. In advocating formation of a political partnership with the working classes, Disraeli was attempting to revitalize the old feudal idea of mutual rights and responsibilities of social classes. He was chancellor of the exchequer in the brief governments of the earl of DERBY in 1852 and 1858–59, and after continued opposition during the Liberal governments of Palmerston and Russell, he became chancellor under Derby again in 1866. With consummate political skill Disraeli "educated his party" to pass the fairly radical parliamentary REFORM BILL of 1867, which enfranchised some two million men, largely of the working classes, and greatly benefited his party. Disraeli succeeded Derby as prime minister in 1868 but lost the office to William GLADSTONE in the same year. Disraeli's second ministry (1874–80) enacted many domestic reforms in housing, public health, and factory legislation, but it was more notable for its aggressive foreign policy. The annexation of the Fiji islands (1874) and of the Transvaal (1877), war against the Afghans (1878–79), and the Zulu War of 1879 proclaimed England a world imperial power more clearly than before. So also did Queen Victoria's assumption (1877) of the title of empress of India; Disraeli was a great favorite of the queen's. Disraeli's purchase (1875) of the controlling share of the Suez Canal stock from the bankrupt khedive of Egypt strengthened British Mediterranean interests, which were jealously guarded in the diplomacy during and after the Russo-Turkish War (1877–78). During the war Disraeli supported Turkey diplomatically and by threat of intervention in order to combat Russian influence in the eastern Mediterranean, and he induced Turkey to cede Cyprus to Great Britain. He forced Russia to submit the Treaty of San Stefano to the Congress of Berlin (1878) and there secured treaty revisions that greatly reduced Russian power in the Balkans (see BERLIN, CONGRESS OF). He was created earl of Beaconsfield in 1876. See biographies by W. F. Monypenny and G. E. Buckle (4 vol., rev. ed. 1929; repr. 1968), Cecil Roth (1952), Robert Blake (1966), and R. A. Levine (1968); D. C. Somervell, *Disraeli and Gladstone* (1925); B. R. Jerman, *The Young Disraeli* (1960).

D'Israeli, Isaac, 1766–1848, English critic and historian, b. London; father of Benjamin Disraeli. Born into a wealthy Jewish family, he produced his first poem at the age of 14. His best-known work is *Curiosities of Literature* (6 vol., 1791–1834), a miscellany of literary and historical anecdotes and original material. D'Israeli's five-volume study of Charles I (1828–31) marked a great advance in methods of historical research and earned him the honorary degree of Doctor of Civil Law at Oxford. See study by J. Ogden (1969).

dissenters: see NONCONFORMISTS.

dissociation, in chemistry, separation of a substance into atoms or ions. Thermal dissociation occurs at high temperatures. For example, hydrogen molecules (H_2) dissociate into atoms (H) at very high temperatures; at 5000°K about 95% of the molecules in a sample of hydrogen are dissociated into atoms. Electrolytic dissociation occurs when an ELECTROLYTE is dissolved in a polar SOLVENT. For example, when hydrogen chloride, HCl, is dissolved in water to form hydrochloric acid, most of its molecules dissociate into hydrogen IONS (H^+) and chloride ions (Cl^-). Some pure substances spontaneously dissociate. For example, in pure water some of the molecules dissociate to form hydrogen ions and hydroxyl ions. Dissociation is generally reversible; when the atoms or ions of the dissociated substance are returned to the original conditions, they recombine in the original form of the substance. The dissociation constant is a measure of the extent of dissociation. It is represented by the symbol *K*. In the simplest case, if a substance AB dissociates into two parts A and B and the concentrations of AB, A, and B are represented by [AB], [A], and [B], then $K=[A]\times[B]/[AB]$. The dissociation constant is measured at equilibrium, and its value is usually affected by changes in temperature and concentration.

distaff: see SPINNING.

distemper, in veterinary medicine, highly contagious, catarrhal, often fatal disease of dogs. It also affects wolves, foxes, mink, raccoons, and ferrets. Distemper is caused by a filtrable virus that is airborne; it is also spread by infected utensils, brushes, and clothing. Symptoms are high fever, apathy, and lack of appetite with resulting dehydration and loss of weight. The respiratory and gastrointestinal tracts become involved, and there is vomiting and diarrhea. A dog may recover from the above signs and then develop nervous complications, i.e., convulsions, localized muscular twitches, weakness, and paralysis. Distemper in dogs can be controlled by immunizing each animal as early as possible with a modified live-virus vaccine.

distillation, process used to separate the substances composing a mixture. It involves a change of state, as of liquid to gas, and subsequent CONDENSATION. The process was probably first used in the production of intoxicating beverages. Today, refined methods of distillation are used in many industries, including the alcohol and petroleum industries. A simple distillation apparatus consists essentially of three parts: a flask equipped with a thermometer and with an outlet tube from which the vapor is emitted, a condenser that consists of two tubes of different diameters placed one within the other and so arranged that the smaller (in which the vapor is condensed) is held in a stream of coolant in the larger, and a vessel in which the condensed vapor is collected. The mixture of substances is placed in the flask and heated. Ideally, the substance with the lowest BOILING POINT vaporizes first (see VAPORIZATION), the temperature remaining constant until that substance has completely distilled. The vapor is led into the condenser where, upon being cooled, it reverts to the liquid (condenses) and runs off into a receiving vessel. The product so obtained is known as the distillate. Those substances having a higher boiling point remain in the flask and constitute the residue. Since a perfect separation is never effected, the distillate is often redistilled to increase its purity (hence the expression "double distilled" or "triple distilled"). When the substance with the lowest boiling point has been removed, the temperature can be raised and the process repeated with the substance having the next lowest boiling point. The process of obtaining portions (or fractions) in this way is one type of **fractional distillation.** A more efficient method of fractional distillation involves placing a vertical tube called a fractionating column between the flask and the condenser. The column is filled with many objects on which the vapor can repeatedly condense and reevaporate as it moves toward the top, effectively distilling the vapor many times. The less volatile substances in the vapor tend to run back down the column after they condense, concentrating themselves near the bottom. The more volatile ones tend to reevaporate and keep moving upward, concentrating themselves near the top. Because of this the column can be tapped at various levels to draw off different fractions. Fractional distillation is commonly used in refining petroleum, some of the fractions thus obtained being gasoline, benzine, kerosene, fuel oils, lubricating oils, and paraffin. Another form of distillation involves heating out of free contact with air such substances as wood, coal, and oil shale and collecting separately the portions driven off; this is known as **destructive distillation.** Wood, for example, when treated in this way yields acetic acid, methyl or wood alcohol, charcoal, and a number of hydrocarbons. Coal yields coal gas, coal tar, ammonia, and coke. Ammonia is also obtained by the destructive distillation of oil shale. Many alcoholic beverages are distilled, e.g., brandy, gin, whiskey, and various liqueurs. The apparatus used, called the still, is the same in principle as other distillation apparatus.

Distinguished Service Cross, Distinguished Service Medal, and **Distinguished Service Order:** see DECORATIONS, CIVIL AND MILITARY.

distortion, in electronics, undesired change in an electric signal wave form as it passes from the input to the output of some system or device. In an audio system distortion results in poor reproduction of recorded or transmitted sound. In passing through an electronic device, the amplitude of an input signal may be changed. For example, any voltage that is applied to an amplifier may be increased by a factor of 10. Amplitude distortion occurs when this factor is not the same for all input voltages. Frequency distortion occurs when the amplitudes of the different frequency components of an input signal are changed by a factor that is not the same for all frequencies. Phase distortion occurs when the phase shift that the different frequency components of an input signal undergo is not the same for all frequencies. All three kinds of distortion noticeably lower the quality of television communications, but only the first two are usually noticeable in radio communications.

distribution, in economics, relative amount of goods and services that each worker, employer, or economic group gets from the total produced. Distribution, in that sense, does not refer to the physical MARKETING or circulation of goods, which is part of the process of exchange, but to the relative well-being and economic wealth of persons and groups. By classifying people according to their share of the distribution—usually by means of relative income—a picture of society's stratification system, and thus its structure, may emerge. Inequalities in distribution are also related to inequalities in political power; the economically dominant strata of society tend also to be politically dominant. The DIVISION OF LABOR, which necessitates exchange, causes various problems of distribution. Regions prosper unequally; one industry may get more return from its labor on the common product than another; some workers get more than others. In territorial distribution, inequalities arise from a region's overproduction of the commodity peculiar to it, such as rubber, which cuts the value of that commodity in exchange for others. Underproduction has the reverse effect if it is not due to crop failure, disaster, or other short-term phenomena. Inequalities in distribution among industrial groups making a common product are explained by the relative number employed in each group when compared to the value of what they produce or to the relative amount they get for a specific amount of work. Unequal distribution arises also from inequality in reward to those in the same industrial classification (capitalist, manager, or laborer). The distribution of wealth between the capitalist and manager on the one hand and labor on the other has been the chief source of social strife in the Western world since the French Revolution. Labor unions (see UNION, LABOR), through the use of political and economic pressure, have striven for increased wages at the expense of profits. The distribution of the world's wealth has, since World War II, become a major issue in international politics, especially as those nations that had previously been the undeveloped suppliers of raw materials to the industrialized countries have gained political independence and embarked on development programs. See E. G. Nourse et al., *Distribution of Income in Relation to Economic Progress* (1936); Harold Barger, *Distribution's Place in the American Economy since 1869* (1955).

distributive law. In mathematics, given any two operations, symbolized by * and ∘, the first operation, *, is distributive over the second, ∘, if $a*(b\circ c)=(a*b)\circ(a*c)$ for all possible choices of *a, b,* and *c.* Multiplication, ×, is distributive over addition, +, since for any numbers *a, b,* and *c,* $a\times(b+c)=(a\times b)+(a\times c)$. For example, for the numbers 2, 3, and 4,

$2\times(3+4)=14$ and $(2\times3)+(2\times4)=14$, meaning that $2\times(3+4)=(2\times3)+(2\times4)$. Strictly speaking, this law expresses only left distributivity, i.e., a is distributed from the left side of $(b+c)$; the corresponding definition for right distributivity is $(a+b)\times c=(a\times c)+(b\times c)$.

District of Columbia, Federal district (1970 pop. 756,510), c.70 sq mi (180 sq km), on the east bank of the Potomac River, coextensive with the city of WASHINGTON, D.C. (the capital of the United States). The District was established by congressional acts of 1790 and 1791 and selected by George Washington. It was originally a 10-mi (16.1-km) square (100 sq mi/259 sq km), with Maryland and Virginia granting land on each side of the river, including the town of Georgetown and the county of Alexandria respectively. The "Federal City" was laid out at its center. Alexandria county, at the request of its inhabitants, was returned to Virginia in 1846. The city continued to grow on the east bank of the river and in 1878, when Georgetown became a part of Washington (although it continued to operate as a separate city until 1895), the city of Washington and the District of Columbia became one and the same. Today, although "Washington" is the name known throughout the world, the city is more commonly called "the District" by its own residents.

di Suvero, Mark: see SUVERO, MARK DI.

Dithmarschen (dĭt'märshən), region, SW Schleswig-Holstein, N West Germany, between the Elbe and Eider rivers. It is chiefly an agricultural region, with extensive cattle raising in the west. The eastern portion is a sandy upland. There are oil fields near HEIDE. The region was conquered by Charlemagne, and its population was Christianized. Later in the Middle Ages it became a virtually independent peasant republic. In 1474, Emperor Frederick III incorporated Dithmarschen into Holstein and invested Christian I of Denmark with the fief, but the attempts of the Danish kings and nobles to take possession of the region were repulsed by the peasants until 1559. Dithmarschen passed to Prussia in 1867. The region is also called Ditmarsh.

dithyramb (dĭth'ĭrăm), in ancient Greece, hymn to the god Dionysus, choral lyric with exchanges between the leader and the chorus. It arose, probably, in the extemporaneous songs of the Dionysiac festivals and was developed (according to tradition, by ARION) into the literary form to be found, for example, in the dithyrambs of BACCHYLIDES. In its later development it became freer in its meter and more musical (see the poets PHILOXENUS and TIMOTHEUS). The TRAGEDY seems to have come out of the dithyramb, but the dithyramb was also cultivated after tragedy was invented. See A. W. Pickard-Cambridge, *Dithyramb, Tragedy, and Comedy* (1927, repr. 1962).

Ditmars, Raymond Lee (dĭt'märz), 1876–1942, American naturalist and author, b. Newark, N.J., grad. Barnard Military Academy, 1891. His early skill in preparing insect collections led to his first position in the division of entomology at the American Museum of Natural History; he remained at the museum for about five years and became assistant curator. While serving (1898–99) as a reporter on the New York *Times* he met W. T. Hornaday, who asked him to join the staff of the New York Zoological Park; Ditmars served as curator of reptiles from 1899 and as curator of mammals from 1910. He became a world authority on snakes and through his research, collecting expeditions, and writings contributed greatly to knowledge of reptiles and other animals. His works include *The Reptile Book* (1907), *Reptiles of the World* (1909, rev. ed. 1933), *Snakes of the World* (1931), *Strange Animals I Have Known* (1931), *The Making of a Scientist* (1937), *The Book of Insect Oddities* (1938), and *Field Book of North American Snakes* (1939).

Dittersdorf, Karl Ditters von (dĭt'ərs fən dĭt'ərsdôrf), 1739–99, Austrian composer and violinist. He was a successful opera and symphony composer in Vienna and an important precursor of Mozart in these forms. The comic opera *Doktor und Apotheker* (1786) is his best-remembered work. He also composed numerous symphonies, oratorios, cantatas, violin concertos, and piano works.

Diu, India: see GOA, DAMAN, AND DIU.

diuretic (dī"yərĕt'ĭk), any one of a group of drugs that increase urine formation and rid the body of excess sodium. Diuretics are used to treat diseases in which excess sodium is retained and fluid accumulates, e.g., heart insufficiencies. Some diuretics are used to treat hypertension, or high blood pressure. The two main types of diuretics are mercurial diuretics and thiazides. Carbonic anhydrase inhibitors, which increase excretion of bicarbonate, are also used to increase urine formation. The drug spironolactone acts as a diuretic because it blocks the sodium-retaining effects of the hormone ALDOSTERONE.

diurnal circle, apparent path followed by a star due to the earth's rotation on its axis. The stars appear to move on the CELESTIAL SPHERE in concentric circular paths centered at the celestial poles. Since the earth rotates west to east, the stars appear to move from east to west along their diurnal circles. Stars whose diurnal circles lie completely above the horizon are called CIRCUMPOLAR STARS.

diver, general term used to refer to many diving birds, e.g., the LOON, the GREBE, and some ducks, auks, and penguins.

Dives (dī'vēz) [Lat.,=rich], traditional name of the unnamed rich man of the parable in Luke 16.19–31.

dividend, that part of the net earnings of a corporation that is distributed to its stockholders. Dividend disbursements are based on a percentage of the par value of the stock or are a certain sum per share of no-par-value stock. They become payable only when approved by the board of directors and are usually declared at regular intervals. Obviously, dividends should not be paid unless the company has accumulated a profit or surplus. In the United States, dividends may be paid in property of various kinds, including bonds and stocks of the company or stocks of other companies first acquired for other purposes, in notes, or in cash. Dividends may be paid in stocks when the accumulated profits of a company are to be retained for reinvestment in the business. Dividends in the form of notes, often called scrip dividends, are rare; they are only paid when the company has earnings that it expects to convert into cash before the notes are due. In Great Britain, dividends are payable only in cash. Liquidation dividends are the return of the capital of a business that is being terminated. Enterprises with diminishing assets, such as mines, issue a modified form of liquidation dividend. The dividend from preferred shares of stock is a fixed percentage that must be paid before the remainder of the profit is divided among other shares. If there are not enough profits to pay the whole dividend on preferred stock, future profits may be assigned to pay back those dividends before anything is paid on common stock. Preferred stock is ranked as first and second preferred, according to the priority of its obligations. Preferred dividends differ from interest on bonds in that there is no default if the former are not paid. The term *dividend* is also used to refer to a fractional payment of the amount owed by a bankrupt firm to a creditor.

Dividing Range: see GREAT DIVIDING RANGE.

divination, practice of foreseeing future events or obtaining secret knowledge through communication with divine sources and through omens, oracles, signs, and portents. It is based on the belief in revelations offered to humans by the gods and in extrarational forms of knowledge; it attempts to make known those things that neither reason nor science can discover. Before it spread throughout the Graeco-Roman world, various branches of divination as practiced by the Chaldaeans were considered superior to all the sciences. Among those branches the most significant were the study of the flight of birds, the study of water and water patterns, the study of the entrails of sacrificial animals (haruspication), and the inspection of animals' shoulder blades (scapulimancy). The Greeks placed their greatest trust in the wisdom of the ORACLE. Divination was essential to all the religions of classical antiquity; no state and hardly any individual would have dared undertake a significant action without first consulting the gods. Divination persists to the present day in crystal gazing, palmistry, fortunetelling, and astrology. See W. R. Halliday, *Greek Divination* (1913, repr. 1967); W. B. and L. R. Gibson, *The Complete Illustrated Book of Divination and Prophecy* (1973).

Divine, Father, c.1882–1965, American religious leader, founder of the Peace Mission movement, b. probably near Savannah, Ga., and named George Baker. After preaching in the South, he moved (c.1915) to the North and began styling himself Major M. J. Divine, later Father Divine. Many of his followers believed him to be the personification of God. Although Father Divine was black, his movement, with its missions and its "heavens" for regenerate "angels," was nonsectarian and interracial; it spread beyond New York City, where it had its start in Harlem, to other places in the United States and abroad. After Father Divine's death the movement faltered. See R. A. Parker, *The Incredible Messiah: the Deification of Father Divine* (1937); Sara Harris, *Father Divine* (rev. ed. 1971).

Divine Comedy: see DANTE ALIGHIERI.

Divine Proportion: see GOLDEN SECTION.

divine right, doctrine that sovereigns derive their right to rule by virtue of their birth alone—a right based on the law of God and of nature. Authority is transmitted to a ruler from his ancestors, whom God himself appointed to rule. Because the sovereign was responsible not to the governed, but to God alone, active resistance to a king was a sin ensuring damnation. The doctrine evolved partly in reaction against papal claims to wield authority in the political sphere. In England, King James I and his son Charles I made many claims based on divine right, and a notable exponent of the theory was Sir Robert FILMER. It ceased to be important in England after the Glorious Revolution of 1688. The epitome of the doctrine is found in the rule of Louis XIV of France. See J. N. Figgis, *The Theory of the Divine Right of Kings* (1896, repr. 1965); Fritz Kern, *Kingship and Law in the Middle Ages* (tr. 1939, repr. 1970).

diving, deep-sea, act of descending into deep water, generally with some form of breathing apparatus, and remaining there for an extended period. It is used in fishing for sponges, coral, and pearls; in work on the underwater parts of bridges, docks, and other structures; in examining and repairing the underwater parts of ships; in recovering valuables from sunken ships; in raising sunken ships to the surface; and in certain military operations, including reconnaissance and sabotage. Commercial and military diving, usually with little or no equipment, was known to the early Greeks. In the *Iliad,* Homer describes the use of divers in the Trojan Wars; Greek laws regulating those who dived for sunken treasure are found as early as the 3d cent. B.C. Before the introduction of modern apparatus, diving was done with the aid of a rope and a stone weight; using the rope as a guide for position, the naked diver quickly scooped up whatever commodity was being sought. Some means whereby a diver could stay under water for an extended period early claimed the attention of inventors. Various types of diving dress and underwater armor were devised in the 17th cent., fresh air being supplied by a pipe from the surface, where it was kept above the water by a float. The first practical diving equipment was devised in England by Augustus Siebe early in the 19th cent. His first suit was of the open type, consisting of a helmet attached to a jacket made of waterproof material. Air was pumped to the helmet through a pipe from the surface—air pressure serving to keep the water level below the diver's head and the air finally escaping through open vents at the bottom of the jacket. The diver had to maintain a generally upright position; if he happened to fall there was a great chance of drowning, because the air in the suit was likely to rush out through the vents. To correct this difficulty, Siebe later developed the closed type of diving suit that, with improvements, is still in general use. Instead of the earlier open vents, the closed type of suit had valves that let air out without letting water in, regardless of the diver's position. Modern helmet diving suits usually consist of a waterproof one-piece suit made of canvas and rubber that entirely covers the wearer except for his head and hands. Heavy rubber bands seal the suit at the wrists, leaving the hands free. On his feet the diver wears leaded boots weighing about 40 lb (18 kg), and lead weights are fastened to his chest to maintain equilibrium. Around his waist is a belt for carrying a knife, tools, and other equipment. Covering his head is a metal helmet, which is in two parts, the breastplate and the helmet proper. The breastplate is a metal frame fitting over the shoulders and attached to the suit. The helmet has windows at the sides and front. Air (a mixture of nitrogen and oxygen or of helium and oxygen) is furnished through a flexible and noncollapsible pipe connecting the helmet with the source of air supply. To the diver is attached a lifeline, used for communication and for hauling the diver to the surface. Telephonic communication is also used extensively. Too rapid an ascent from great depths causes the diver to suffer DECOMPRESSION SICKNESS. To prevent this, deep-sea divers either use an all-steel, armored diving suit or breathe a special mixture of nine gases developed by the Swiss mathematician Hannes Keller. While the type of diving described above is widely used, it has the disadvantage of restricting the diver's lateral movement because of his connection to the surface. This fact led to the development of the scuba (acronym for self-contained underwater breathing apparatus). Although there was an early interest in such equipment, the modern scuba was not designed until the first half of the 20th cent. by Jacques Yves COUSTEAU and Emil Gagnan. In 1943 successful tests were made of the new compressed-air breathing apparatus, and it has been widely used since (marketed under the trademark Aqualung). There are three types: open-circuit, closed-circuit, and semiclosed-circuit. In the last two, the air breathed (usually pure oxygen or a combination of oxygen, helium, and nitrogen) is exhaled through a canister containing materials that will remove the exhaled carbon dioxide. The air is then recirculated to the diver for rebreathing. In the open-circuit type the diver exhales the air (usually an oxygen-helium-nitrogen combination, rather than pure oxygen) directly into the water after breathing. Though less efficient than the closed-circuit scuba, the open-circuit type is considered safer and is in wider use. The scuba is designed to deliver air to the diver at the same pressure as that exerted on him by the surrounding water. In this way the diver is able to descend to great depths without feeling the ill effects of high pressure (see SKIN DIVING). A skilled scuba diver with good equipment can descend as deeply as a helmet suit diver. Record-setting dives of over 300 ft (91 m) have been made with scuba gear, although careful scuba divers do not go below about 130 ft (40 m). Beyond this depth a condition known as nitrogen narcosis (popularly called "raptures of the deep") tends to set in. Caused by the narcotic effects of the air's nitrogen at high pressure, the condition is marked by a loss of judgment that often causes the diver to discard parts of his equipment or engage in other dangerously foolish behavior. Nitrogen narcosis also affects helmet suit divers, but not until a depth of about 200 ft (61 m). Several types of large metallic structures have been used as underwater diving vessels since early times. Aristotle, as early as 360 B.C., mentions primitive vessels used by sponge divers. Some were rectangular and others bell-shaped; they were generally open at the bottom, and compressed air was pumped into them to keep out the water, thus enabling men to work within the device. A bathysphere—a hollow, globular steel structure built to withstand tremendous pressure—was designed by Otis Barton and used by him and William BEEBE in undersea exploration in the 1930s. It was followed by Barton's benthoscope. Both vessels, however, were limited by the fact that they had at all times to be attached to a steel cable and winch system. They could go only as far as the longest cable and strongest winch—certainly no more than 10,000 ft (3,048 m). The first free and self-contained diving craft was the bathyscaphe, invented by Auguste PICCARD. His craft, the *Trieste*, descended (1960) to 35,000 ft (10,668 m), the deepest known point in the ocean. See also SUBMARINE. See H. E. Larson, *A History of Self-Contained Diving and Underwater Swimming* (1959); R. F. Marx, *They Dared the Deep* (1967); T. A. Hampton, *The Master Diver and Underwater Sportsman* (1970); Jack Coggins, *Prepare to Dive! The Story of Man Undersea* (1971); J. S. Potter, *The Treasure Diver's Guide* (rev. ed. 1972).

diving, springboard and platform, sport of entering the water from a raised position, often while executing tumbles, twists, and other acrobatic maneuvers. In most dives the upper part of the body enters the water first, and the diver's arms are extended straight out over the head into the water. Body rigidity, vertical entrance into the water, and precise timing are necessary for reasons of safety and form. A poorly executed dive can result in injury ranging from mild skin irritation to bone fracture, depending on the height of the dive. Diving probably originated with the first prehistoric swimmers adventurous enough to take a headfirst plunge into the water. The earliest recorded major diving feat took place in 1871 in England, with competitors diving off London Bridge. Since then competitive diving has become an essential part of most aquatic sports meets. Men's diving became an Olympic event in 1904, and women's diving was added to the program in 1912. As in the related field of SWIMMING, the U.S. diving teams have dominated Olympic competition for many years. Springboard diving takes place on a flexible plank made of wood, aluminum, or steel and measuring 14 to 16 ft (4.3–4.9 m) long by 20 in. (50.8 cm) wide. It extends horizontally over the water at a height of either 1 or 3 m (about 3 ft 3 in. or 9 ft 7 in.). The flexibility of the board allows the diver to jump high into the air and execute a number of acrobatic maneuvers before entering the water. Platform diving (also called high diving) usually occurs on a tower 10 m (32 ft 10 in.) high that is not flexible and does not extend over the water's surface. The height of the tower enables the competitor to perform acrobatics during his descent. It also poses considerable danger to him, because he enters the water at approximately 32 mi (51.5 km) per hr. Both types of diving can be done from a standing or running start, and in competition both are scored on the basis of form, execution, and degree of difficulty of the particular dive. All dives involve one of three basic positions that the diver assumes while executing his twists and somersaults. In the layout, or straight, dive the body is rigidly extended at all times. In the pike, or jackknife, there is bending at the hips but none at the knees. In the tuck position both the knees and hips are bent so that the body assumes a ball shape. In all dives the final entrance position should be rigid and vertical. The racing dive, used for speed in competitive swimming, involves no acrobatics and has a nearly horizontal entrance. See Charles Batterman, *The Techniques of Springboard Diving* (1968); George Eaves, *Diving: The Mechanics of Springboard and Firmboard Techniques* (1969).

diving beetle: see WATER BEETLE.

divining rod or **dowser,** stick used in searching for underground water or minerals. This form of divination is still in common use in many parts of the world. The instrument is typically a forked twig. The operator holds the forked ends of the twig close to his body, with the stem pointing forward. When he walks over a spot under which water or the desired mineral lies, the stem of the divining rod is supposedly pulled down. Impartial research, however, has indicated that successes in this method result mostly from chance and possibly also from a heightened sensitivity to visual cues of which the diviner is unaware.

division, fundamental operation in arithmetic; the inverse of multiplication. Division may be indicated by the symbol $\div$, as in $15 \div 3$, or simply by a fraction, 15/3. The number that is being divided, e.g. 15, is called the dividend and the number dividing into it, e.g. 3, the divisor. The result of division is called the quotient. If the dividend is an exact (integral) multiple of the divisor, then the division will be exact, the quotient being the factor by which the divisor must be multiplied to yield the dividend (in the above example the quotient 5 multiplied by the divisor 3 equals the dividend 15). If the dividend is not an exact multiple of the divisor there will be a remainder expressed as a fraction with the divisor as the denominator; e.g., $\frac{16}{3} = 5\frac{1}{3}$, where $\frac{1}{3}$ is the remainder. A division in which the divisor b is larger than the dividend a is simply indicated by the fraction a/b, with no actual operation being carried out. In terms of multiplication either of the symbols $1/b$ or b^{-1} is called the multiplicative inverse of b with the property that the product of a number and its inverse equals 1, or $b \cdot b^{-1} = 1$. The division of a by b is equivalent to the multiplication of a by the multiplicative inverse of b, i.e., $a \div b = a \cdot (1/b) = a \cdot b^{-1}$; for example, when $a = 25$ and $b = 5$, then $1/b = 1/5$ and $25 \div 5 = 25 \cdot (1/5) = 5$.

division, in taxonomy: see CLASSIFICATION.

divisionism: see POSTIMPRESSIONISM.

division of labor, in economics, the specialization of the functions and roles involved in production. Division of labor is closely tied with the standardization of production, the introduction and perfection of machinery, and the development of large-scale industry. Among the different categories of division of labor are territorial, in which certain geographical regions specialize in producing certain products, exchanging their surplus for goods produced elsewhere; temporal, in which separate processes are performed by different industrial groups in manufacturing one product, as the making of bread by farmers, millers, and bakers; and occupational, in which goods produced in the same industrial group are worked by a number of persons, each applying one or more processes and skills. Modern mass-production techniques are based on the last type. The proficiency attained through experience at one task and the time saved by concentration on one phase of an operation are such that the total production is many times what it would be had each worker made the complete article. The classic example is that given by Adam Smith, advocate of free trade (of which the division of labor is the underlying principle), in which 10 men, each performing one or more of the 18 operations necessary to make a pin, together produce 48,000 pins a day, whereas working separately they could not make 200. Problems created by the division of labor include the monotony of concentration on routine tasks, technological unemployment for people whose skills are not in demand, and eventually chronic unemployment if the economy does not expand quickly enough to reabsorb the displaced labor. Karl Marx, who recognized many of the disadvantages of increased specialization, predicted that those workers displaced by the division of labor would eventually take part in a world-wide proletarian revolution. Each variant of the division of labor has its own peculiar problems of DISTRIBUTION. See Robert A. Brady, *Organization, Automation, and Society* (1961); Émile Durkheim, *The Division of Labor in Society* (tr. 1965); H. R. Bowen and G. L. Mangum, ed., *Automation and Economic Progress* (1967); Tibor Kiss, *International Division of Labour in Open Economies* (1971).

divorce, partial or total dissolution of the MARRIAGE relation by judgment of a court. Partial dissolution is a divorce "from bed and board," a decree of judicial SEPARATION, leaving the parties married while forbidding cohabitation. Total dissolution of the bonds of a valid marriage is what is now usually meant by divorce. It is to be distinguished from a decree of NULLITY OF MARRIAGE, which is a judicial finding that there never was a valid marriage. In England, divorce was originally under the jurisdiction of the ecclesiastical courts. These courts followed the CANON LAW rules. They could grant a divorce from bed and board and could pass on the original validity or nullity of the marriage, but could not grant a total divorce from the marriage bond. This power lay only in Parliament. In 1857, by act of Parliament, judicial courts succeeded to the jurisdiction over nullity and partial dissolution and were given the added power to grant total dissolution of the marriage. In the United States, where ecclesiastical courts were never established, the matrimonial law of England applied by these courts was never received as part of the common law. Consequently, suits for divorce can be brought under authority of statute only. The statutes usually confer on equity courts jurisdiction over divorce. The power to legislate on divorce belongs to the states and not to the Federal government. Although created by a contract between husband and wife, marriage is a legal relation of a particular nature with certain mutual rights and obligations, determined not by agreements but by the general law. In a sense, the state has an interest in every marriage. The parties cannot themselves terminate the relation by a contract of separation. The relation can be dissolved only for what the state deems proper grounds. The public policy of the several states toward divorce is extremely varied. The most common grounds are adultery, DESERTION, and cruelty. Habitual drunkenness, incurable insanity, conviction of a crime, nonsupport, and impotence are some of the less common grounds. Corrupt consent by a party to the conduct of the other party bars a divorce, as does COLLUSION. Forgiveness of the matrimonial offense either express or implied (as by cohabitation) on condition that it not be repeated is a bar to a divorce for that particular offense. The fact that the party seeking the divorce is likewise guilty of the matrimonial offense charged is also a bar. However, since 1970 California has had only two grounds for the dissolution of a marriage—irreconcilable differences and incurable insanity—and no attempt is made to establish which party was at fault. A decree of divorce is valid only if the court rendering the decree has jurisdiction, and jurisdiction is in the main based on the DOMICILE of the parties. Questions as to the validity of a divorce obtained in a foreign country, or in another of the states of the United States are of extreme complexity. An absolute divorce, as contrasted with a decree of nullity, takes effect from the date of the decree. Property rights depending on the marriage, such as DOWER, are cut off if the wife is the guilty party. By the divorce decree the custody of the children is usually given at the discretion of the court to one of the parties, the welfare of the children being the principal consideration. The wife retains the husband's name, although in some states she may choose to resume her maiden name. Both parties are usually at liberty to remarry, although this rule is not invariable, and a time limit within which the parties may not remarry is sometimes imposed. In some jurisdictions, the wife is entitled to ALIMONY at the discretion of the court.

Dix, Dorothea Lynde, 1802–87, American social reformer, pioneer in the movement for specialized treatment of the insane, b. Hampden, Maine. For many years she ran a school in Boston. In 1841 she visited a jail in East Cambridge, Mass., and was shocked at conditions there, especially at the indiscriminate mixing of criminals and the insane. She began inspecting other places in Massachusetts and in 1842 wrote a famous memorial to the state legislature. Her crusades resulted in the founding of state hospitals for the insane in many states, and her influence was felt in Canada and Europe. Dix also did notable work in penology. During the Civil War she was superintendent of women war nurses. See Gladys Brooks, *Three Wise Virgins* (1957); H. E. Marshall, *Dorothea Dix: Forgotten Samaritan* (1937, repr. 1967); S. C. Beach, *Daughters of the Puritans* (1967); Francis Tiffany, *Life of Dorothea Lynde Dix* (repr. 1971).

Dix, John Adams, 1798-1879, American statesman, b. Boscawen, N.H. He served in the War of 1812, was later admitted to the bar, and practiced law in Cooperstown, N.Y. He held high state offices and served (1845-49) as Democratic U.S. Senator from New York. In 1848 he ran on the Free-Soil ticket for governor of New York. President Buchanan appointed him Secretary of the Treasury in 1861, and in his two-month tenure of office, despite secession, he was able to secure loans. He was a major general in the Civil War and later minister to France (1866-69). Dix was prominent in railroad affairs and was made (1863) president of Union Pacific with T. C. Durant as vice president. He was long president of the Erie RR. He served as the Republican governor of New York in 1873 and 1874.

Dix, Morgan, 1827-1908, American Episcopal clergyman, b. New York City; son of John A. Dix. He was rector of Trinity Church in New York City from 1862 to 1908. Among his writings are *Memoirs of John Adams Dix* (1883) and *History of the Parish of Trinity Church in the City of New York* (4 vol., 1898-1906). A fifth part on the rectorship of Dr. Morgan Dix himself was added to the *History* in 1950. See biography by W. A. Swanberg (1968).

Dix, Otto, 1891-1969, German painter and draftsman. Dix fought in World War I and returned to Düsseldorf haunted by the horrors he had witnessed. Associated with the NEW OBJECTIVITY movement in German EXPRESSIONISM, he depicted the sordid world of prostitutes and swindlers with a painful precision and intensity. In 1924 he published *War,* a series of 50 etchings, fantastic visions executed with great clarity. Accused of an attempt on Hitler's life in 1939, he was imprisoned in Dresden and later made prisoner of war by the French. After the war he worked in West Germany.

Dix, Fort: see FORT DIX.

Dixie, Lady Florence Caroline Douglas, 1857-1905, British traveler and writer; daughter of the 7th marquess of Queensberry. She visited Patagonia (1878-79) and wrote *Across Patagonia* (1880), the first of several vivid travel books. She was field correspondent (1879) of the London *Morning Post* in the Zulu War and was instrumental in securing the short-lived restoration (1883) of CETEWAYO, the Zulu king.

Dixon, Thomas, 1864-1946, American novelist, b. Shelby, N.C., grad. Wake Forest College. A militant Southerner, he is best known for his novel *The Clansman* (1905), on which the movie *The Birth of a Nation* (1915) was based.

Dixon, city (1970 pop. 18,147), seat of Lee co., N Ill., on the Rock River; founded 1830, inc. 1857. Electronic equipment, cement, and paper products are manufactured. On the site of the Dixon Blockhouse is a statue of Abraham Lincoln as a youthful captain in the Black Hawk War. Sauk Valley College, a junior college, is in Dixon.

Diyala (dĭyä'lă, -'ə), river, c.275 mi (440 km) long, rising as the Sirvan River in NW Iran and flowing SW through the Zagros mts. into E Iraq, where it enters the Tigris River S of Baghdad. The Diyala is unnavigable, but its valley is an important trade route between Iran and Iraq. A dam on the lower Diyala provides flood control and irrigates the area NE of Baghdad.

Diyarbakır (dēyär"bäkŭr), anc. *Amida,* city (1970 pop. 138,657), capital of Diyarbakır prov., SE Turkey, on the Tigris (Dicle) River. It is the trade center for a region producing grains, melons, cotton, and copper ore. Manufactures of the city include flour, wine, textiles, and machinery. A Roman colony from A. D. 230, the city was taken (mid-4th cent.) by Shapur II of Persia. It was conquered by the Arabs in 638 and later was held by the Seljuk Turks and Persians. The Ottoman Turks captured Diyarbakır in 1515. The city retains the magnificent black basalt fortification walls mainly constructed by Constantine I in the 4th cent.

Dizahab (dĭz'əhăb, dĭ'zə-), unidentified place, on the border of Moab. Deut. 1.1.

Dizful, Iran: see DEZFUL.

dizziness: see VERTIGO.

Djaja Peak (jä'yə), group of peaks in the Sudirman mts., W New Guinea, rising to 16,503 ft (5,031 m), the highest point on New Guinea and in Indonesia. The peaks are snow-covered, but the lower slopes have lush tropical vegetation. It was formerly called Mt. Carstensz and Mt. Sukarno.

Djajapura (jä"yəpŭr'ə), formerly **Sukarnapura** (so͞okär"nəpo͞or'ə), town, capital of Irian Barat (Indonesian New Guinea), Indonesia. A regional trade center and seaport, it is on Humboldt Bay (an inlet of the Pacific) near the border of the Australian territory of New Guinea. Occupied by the Japanese in World War II, it was liberated by U.S. forces in April, 1944, and served as General MacArthur's headquarters. Another former name was Hollandia.

Djakarta or **Jakarta** (both: jəkär'tə, jäkär'tä), formerly **Batavia** (bətā'vēə), city (1971 est. pop. 4,500,-000), capital and largest city of Indonesia, NW Java, at the mouth of the canalized Chiliwong (or Tjiliwung) River, on Djakarta Bay, an inlet of the Java Sea. It is the administrative, commercial, industrial, and transportation center of the country, with food-processing plants, ironworks, automobile-assembly plants, textile mills, chemical factories, tanneries, saw mills, soap factories, and printing establishments. Its port, Tanjungpriok, is the largest in Indonesia, handling most of the country's export-import trade. Exports consist mainly of agricultural, forest, and mining products. The city is divided into two sections—the old town in the north, with Javanese, Chinese, and Arab quarters, and a modern residential garden suburb in the south. With its many canals and drawbridges, Djakarta somewhat resembles a Dutch town. Landmarks include the great architectural monuments built during President Sukarno's long rule—freedom statues, a huge sports complex (financed by the Soviet Union), and the Merdeka Mosque (under construction), which will be the largest Islamic temple in the world. Djakarta is the seat of the Univ. of Indonesia. There are notable museums and several 17th-century houses and churches. The Dutch founded (c.1619) the fort of Batavia near the Javanese settlement of Djakarta, repulsing English and native attempts to oust them. Batavia became the headquarters of the Dutch East India Company and was a major trade center in the 17th cent. It declined in the 18th cent., following rebellions against the Dutch, but prospered again with the introduction of plantation cultivation in the 19th cent. From 1811 to 1814, Djakarta was the center of British rule in Java. Batavia was renamed Djakarta in Dec., 1949, and was proclaimed the capital of newly independent Indonesia. It has an international airport.

Djambi or **Jambi** (both: jäm'bē), city (1961 pop. 113,000), SE Sumatra, capital of Djambi prov., Indonesia, a port at the head of navigation on the Hari River. It is the shipping and commercial center of an area producing oil, rubber, and timber. Djambi State Univ. is there.

Djenné or **Jenné** (both: jĕnā'), town, S central Mali, on the Bani River. It is an agricultural market center. Founded in the 8th cent. by the Songhai, Djenné became in the 13th cent. a great market for gold, slaves, and salt. It rivaled Timbuktu in prosperity and Muslim culture, and many merchants from North Africa were attracted to it. Djenné resisted a series of attacks by the kings of ancient Mali but finally fell c.1473. From the 16th cent. the town declined; it came under French control in the late 19th cent. There are several examples of Moorish architecture, including a fine mosque.

Djerid, Chott (shôt jĕrēd'), salt lake, c.1,900 sq mi (4,920 sq km), W central Tunisia, N Africa. It is now an extensive salt flat with water only in its lower areas.

Djibouti (jēbo͞otē'), town (1970 est. pop. 70,000), capital of the French Territory of the Afars and the Issas, NE Africa, a port on the Gulf of Tadjoura (an inlet of the Gulf of Aden). It is the territory's only sizable town and its administrative center. Its importance results from the large transit trade it enjoys as a terminus of the railroad from Addis Ababa, Ethiopia, to the sea and from its strategic position near the shipping lanes that carry the Suez Canal traffic. Activity at its port declined drastically after the Suez Canal was closed in 1967. The only important industry is the production of salt from the sea. There is a camel market in the town. Djibouti was founded by the French c.1888 and became the capital of French Somaliland in 1892. There was severe rioting in Djibouti in 1967 after the territory voted to retain its ties with France.

Djilas, Milovan (mē'ləvän jē'läs), 1911-, Yugoslav political leader and writer, b. Montenegro. A Communist party member from 1932, he helped Josip Broz Tito organize volunteers to fight in the Spanish civil war. He was active in the Yugoslav resistance in World War II and after the war rose to high posts in party and government. As a top political adviser to Tito and an outspoken critic of Russian attempts to bring Yugoslavia into the Soviet orbit, he was widely regarded as a possible successor to Tito. In 1953 he became a vice president of the federal assembly's executive council. He was about to assume the presidency when, in 1954, he was abruptly dismissed from government service. His support of the Hungarian revolution (1956) brought him a prison term, extended in 1957 upon publication in the West of his influential book criticizing the Communist oligarchy, *The New Class: An Analysis of the Communist System.* Released (1961), he was arrested again in 1962 and finally freed in 1966. He also wrote *Land Without Justice* (1958), *Conversations with Stalin* (tr. 1962), *The Unperfect Society* (tr. 1969), and the novel, *Under the Colors* (tr. 1971). See his *Memoir of a Revolutionary* (tr. 1973).

Djokjakarta: see JOGJAKARTA, Indonesia.

Dmitri (dəmē'trē) or **Demetrius** (dĭmē'trēəs), 1582-91, czarevich, son of Ivan IV (Ivan the Terrible) of Russia. His brother, FEODOR I, succeeded Ivan in 1584, but Boris GODUNOV actually ruled Russia for the period of Feodor's reign (1584-98). Dmitri was killed in 1591, possibly on Boris's orders. Subsequently four pretenders assumed his name. The first, whose origin is unknown, appeared in Poland c.1600; claiming that he was Dmitri, he enlisted the support of Lithuanian and Polish nobles and finally of King Sigismund III of Poland. He invaded Russia in 1604. Boris died suddenly in 1605 and the false Dmitri was crowned as czar. But his favoritism toward Poland and his marriage to Marina Mniszech, a Polish noblewoman, aroused the opposition of the boyars, led by Prince Vasily Shuiski. An insurrection was provoked in Moscow, and Dmitri was killed. Shuiski was made czar as Vasily IV. In 1607 another Dmitri appeared. Aided by the Poles after Marina identified him as her husband, he marched on Moscow and had some success, but in 1610 he was killed. In 1612 a man claiming to be Dmitri's son was put to death by strangling. Another, also claiming to be Dmitri's son, was beheaded in 1613. In that year the chaotic period, known as the Time of Troubles in Russian history, came to an end with the coronation of Michael Romanov, first of the Romanov line, as czar.

Dmitri Donskoi (dəmē'trē dənskoi'), 1350-89, Russian hero, grand duke of Moscow (1359-89). He successfully resisted Lithuanian attempts to invade Moscow, and was the first Russian prince since the Mongol conquest who dared to wage open war on the TATARS. His great victory at KULIKOVO (1380) made him a popular Russian hero, but the Tatars regained their overlordship by their successful surprise attack on Moscow in 1382.

Dmitrov (dəmē'trəf), city (1967 est. pop. 38,000), N central European USSR, on the Moscow Canal. It is a river port and industrial city. Products include machinery, iron, cellulose, reinforced concrete, clothing, and gloves. Dmitrov was founded in 1154. In the 13th cent. it became the capital of an independent duchy that was united with the grand duchy of Moscow in 1472. Landmarks include the 16th-century cathedral of the Borisglebsky Monastery, the 16th-century Uspensky Cathedral, and remains of an old kremlin.

DNA: see NUCLEIC ACID.

Dnepr (dənyĕ'pər) or **Dnieper** (nē'pər), Ukr. *Dnipro,* river, c.1,430 mi (2,300 km) long, W European USSR. One of the longest rivers in Europe and in the USSR, it rises in the Valdai Hills, W of Moscow. It flows generally S past Smolensk, through Belorussia, past Mogilev, then through the Ukraine, past Kiev, Cherkassy, Kremenchug, Dnepropetrovsk, Zaporozhye (site of the DNEPROGES dam), Nikopol, and Kherson into the Black Sea. Between Kremenchug and Nikopol the Dnepr makes a vast bend to the east. It is the main river of the Ukraine. Since the construction (1932) of the Dneproges dam the Dnepr is navigable for virtually its entire course. Its tributaries include the Berezina, the Pripyat, and the Ingulets from the west and the Sozh, the Desna, the Orel, and the Samara from the east. The Dnepr is linked by canal with the Western Bug. Known as Borysthenes to the ancients, the river was (9th-11th cent.) a commercial route for the Slavs and Byzantines.

Dneprodzerzhinsk (dənyĕ″prədzĭrzhĕnsk′), city (1970 pop. 227,000), S European USSR, in the Ukraine, a port on the Dnepr River. It is a major industrial center with iron and steel, machine tool, chemical, and cement plants. Originally called Kamenskoye, it was industrialized in the late 19th cent. and renamed Dneprodzerzhinsk in 1936.

Dneproges (dənyĕprəgĕs′) [Rus. abbr., = Dnepr hydroelectric station], a hydroelectric station, SW European USSR, in the Ukraine, on the Dnepr River near Zaporozhye. It has one of the largest dams and power stations in the USSR. With a capacity of up to 648,000 kw, the hydroelectric station supplies power for the industrial centers of Dnepropetrovsk, Krivoy Rog, and Zaporozhye. More than ½ mi (.8 km) long and 200 ft (61 m) high, the dam raised the level of the Dnepr 123 ft (37 m). Since the completion of the dam and the flooding of the rapids above it, the entire Dnepr has become navigable. The dam was built between 1927 and 1932 and was at first called Dneprostoi. The dam and plant were partially destroyed by retreating Soviet troops during the German invasion of 1941 and then completely destroyed by the Germans as they withdrew in 1943. They were rebuilt between 1944 and 1949.

Dnepropetrovsk (dənyĕ″prəpĕtrôfsk′), city (1970 pop. 863,000), capital of Dnepropetrovsk oblast, S European USSR, in the Ukraine, on the Dnepr River. A hub of rail and water transportation, it is a major industrial center with a huge iron and steel industry based on iron ore from the nearby Krivoy Rog mines and coal from the Donets Basin. The city also has plants producing heavy machinery, chemicals, rolling stock, and food products. Founded in 1787 by Potemkin on the site of a Zaporozhe Cossack village, it was named Ekaterinoslav (Yekaterinoslav) for Catherine II. It was called Novorosiysk from 1791 to 1802 and Katerineslav until 1926, when it was renamed Dnepropetrovsk. The population greatly increased after the completion (1932) of the Dneproges dam and power station. The city was occupied (1941–43) by German forces during World War II. It has art, historical, and zoological museums.

Dneprostroi, hydroelectric station, USSR: see DNEPROGES.

Dnestr (dənyĕ′stər), Ukr. *Dnister,* river, c.850 mi (1,370 km) long, SW European USSR, forming part of the border between the Ukraine and the Moldavian Republic. It rises in the Carpathian Mts., flows generally SE through the SW Ukraine past Galich, Khotin, and Mogilev-Podolski, through the Moldavian Republic past Bendery and Tiraspol, and empties through an estuary into the Black Sea SW of Odessa. It is navigable below Galich; its tributaries include the Sereth and the Stry. The Dnestr formed the Rumanian-Soviet border from 1918 to 1940, when the USSR recovered Bessarabia.

Dnieper: see DNEPR, river, USSR.

Dniester: see DNESTR, river, USSR.

Doab (dō′ăb), term applied in India to a tract of land between two converging rivers. The Doab, unqualified by the names of any rivers, designates the tract in Uttar Pradesh state between the Ganges and Jumna rivers, extending from the Siwalik Hills to the rivers' confluence at Allahabad. This well-irrigated region is the greatest wheat growing area of the state.

Doane, George Washington, 1799–1859, Episcopal bishop of New Jersey (1832–59), b. Trenton, N.J. He acted as rector of St. Mary's Church, Burlington, N.J., and there he established a school for girls, St. Mary's Hall, and Burlington College for boys. A leading high churchman, Bishop Doane was also the author of a number of hymns, including "Softly Now the Light of Day" and "Fling Out the Banner, Let It Float." The *Life and Writings of George Washington Doane* (4 vol., 1860–61) was prepared by his son, **William Croswell Doane,** 1832–1913. He was bishop (1869–1913) of the Episcopal diocese of Albany, and author of the well-known hymn "Ancient of Days."

Dobbs, Arthur, 1689–1765, British colonial governor of North Carolina (1753–65), b. Co. Antrim, Ireland. A member of the Irish House of Commons (1727–30) and surveyor general of Ireland (1730), he wrote *An Essay on the Trade and Improvement of Ireland* (1729), in which he advocated certain land reforms. He also became interested in the search for a Northwest Passage and was largely responsible for the expedition (1741–42) under Christopher Middleton. He was appointed governor of North Carolina in 1753, arriving at the colony a year and a half later. His administration was marked by conflicts with the assembly arising out of his frequent arbitrary assertions of power. A capable administrator, he attempted to serve the interests of both the crown and the colonists and consequently drew the heavy criticism of both. See biography by Desmond Clarke (1958).

Dobbs Ferry, village (1970 pop. 10,353), Westchester co., SE N.Y., on the Hudson River, a suburb of New York City; inc. 1873. It is mostly residential but has a chemical research laboratory. Dobbs Ferry is the site of Livingston Manor, where George Washington and Marshal Rochambeau of France were supposed to have planned the YORKTOWN CAMPAIGN. Mercy College and Miss Masters School for Girls are also there.

Dobell, Sydney Thompson (dōbĕl′), 1824–74, English poet. He is best known for the melodramatic, extravagantly emotional poem *Balder* (1853). In 1855 he published jointly with Alexander Smith (1830–67) some sonnets on the Crimean War.

Döbereiner, Johann Wolfgang (yō′hän vôlf′gäng dö′bərīnər), 1780–1849, German chemist. From 1810 he was professor of the Univ. of Jena. He is known especially for his discovery of similar triads of elements, a step in the development of the PERIODIC LAW. He discovered furfural, worked on the use of platinum as a catalyst, and invented a lighter (known as Döbereiner's lamp) that is ignited by the action of hydrogen on a platinum sponge.

Doberman pinscher (dō′bərmən pĭn′shər), breed of large, compact WORKING DOG originating in Germany c.1890. It stands from 24 to 28 in. (61–71 cm) high at the shoulder and weighs from 60 to 75 lb (27–34 kg). Its short, smooth, close-lying coat may be black, brown, or blue in color with rust red markings above the eyes and on the muzzle, chest, legs, and vent. The Doberman was named for Louis Dobermann of Apolda, Germany, who developed the breed by crossing native German sheepherding-dog stock with the Rottweiler, Manchester terrier, and the old German pinscher. The Doberman was first used as a guard dog and pet. Later, when its great capacity for training was appreciated, it became increasingly popular as a police and war dog. See DOG.

Döblin, Alfred (äl′frĕt döblĭn′), 1878–1957, German novelist and physician. His experiences as a psychiatrist in the workers' district of Berlin served as the basis for his experimental novel *Berlin Alexanderplatz* (1929, tr. 1931), in which he applied the techniques of James Joyce's *Ulysses* to his story of the life of a Berlin worker. Other novels include *Die drei Sprünge des Wang-lun* [the three leaps of Wang-lun] (1915) and *Pardon wird nicht gegeben* (1935, tr. *Men without Mercy,* 1937). Döblin left Germany in 1933, lived in Palestine and the United States, and returned to Germany after World War II.

Dobrée, Bonomy (bŏn′əmē dō′brē), 1891–, English scholar and critic, b. London, grad. Cambridge (B.A., 1921, M.A., 1924). He served with the Royal Artillery in both world wars, attaining the rank of lieutenant-colonel. Dobrée taught at the Univ. of London, Egyptian Univ. in Cairo, and the Univ. of Leeds. Among his numerous works are *Restoration Comedy, 1660–1720* (1924), *Restoration Tragedy, 1660–1720* (1929), *Rudyard Kipling* (1951), *Alexander Pope* (1963), and *From Milton to Ouida* (1970).

Dobrich: see TOLBUKHIN, Bulgaria.

Dobrogea: see DOBRUJA.

Dobromierz, Poland: see HOHENFRIEDEBERG.

Dobrovský, Josef (dô′brôfskē), 1753–1829, Hungarian philologist, of Bohemian parentage. In 1792 the Royal Bohemian Academy of Sciences commissioned Dobrovský to recover Bohemian manuscripts lost in the Thirty Years War. He is the founder of modern Slavonic studies and the father of modern Czech philology and literature. Dobrovský was criticized by scholars when he questioned the authenticity of *The Judgment of Libusha,* the oldest Czech writing, discovered by Hanka in 1817. He wrote much on early Slavic materials.

Dobruja (dō′brŏŏjə, dô′-), Rum. *Dobrogea,* Bulg. *Dobrudza,* historic region, c.9,000 sq mi (23,300 sq km), SE Europe, in SE Rumania and NE Bulgaria, between the lower Danube River and the Black Sea. The chief cities are CONSTANȚA, in Rumania, and TOLBUKHIN and SILISTRA, in Bulgaria. Dobruja comprises a low coastal strip and a hilly and forested inland. Largely agricultural, the region grows cereal crops, has vineyards, and breeds Merino sheep. The largest industrial concentration is in and around Constanța. Tourism is also economically important, particularly in the Rumanian part of Dobruja. The population includes Rumanians, Bulgarians, Turks, and Tatars. Dobruja's original inhabitants were conquered in the 6th cent. B.C. by the Greeks, who founded colonies along the Black Sea coast. The region passed to the Scythians in the 5th cent. B.C. and to the Romans (who made it part of Moesia) in the 1st cent. B.C. As part of the Roman Empire and later of the Byzantine, it suffered frequent invasions from the Goths, Huns, Avars, and other tribes. Part of the first Bulgarian empire (681–1018), it was reconquered by the Byzantines. In 1186 it was included in the second Bulgarian empire. Tatar raids were common in the 13th cent. In the 14th cent. the region became an autonomous state under Walachian prince Dobrotich, from whom the name *Dobruja* derives. Turks conquered the region in 1411, and for the next five centuries it remained a sparsely populated and barely cultivated territory of the Ottoman Empire. In 1878 the Congress of Berlin awarded N Dobruja to Rumania and a strip of land later known as S Dobruja to Bulgaria. As a result of the second Balkan War Bulgaria ceded (1913) S Dobruja to Rumania. The Treaty of Neuilly, signed in 1919 between Bulgaria and the Allies of World War I, gave all of Dobruja to Rumania. In 1940, however, the German-imposed Treaty of Craiova forced Rumania to transfer S Dobruja to Bulgaria.

Dobson, Austin (Henry Austin Dobson), 1840–1921, English poet and essayist. From 1856 to 1901 he was employed in the Board of Trade. His volumes of light verse include *Vignettes in Rhyme* (1873), *Proverbs in Porcelain* (1877), and *At the Sign of the Lyre* (1885). Among his studies of 18th-century England are *Eighteenth Century Vignettes* (3 series, 1892–96) and his biographies of Fielding (1883), Steele (1886), Goldsmith (1888), Richardson (1902), and Fanny Burney (1903). See study by Alban Dobson (1928, repr. 1970).

Dobson, William, 1610–46, English court painter. After the death of Van Dyck, Dobson was made court painter to Charles I and did some interesting court portraits. Some of his works are close to the Venetian High Renaissance style and have allegorical implications. His *Endymion Porter* (National Gall., London) is a strong and characteristic portrait.

dobsonfly, common name for a group of INSECTS of the order Neuroptera, found throughout E North America. The adults may be 5 in. (12.7 cm) long; the male has mandibles half as long as the body. They are soft-bodied insects with a fluttery flight, and are largely nocturnal. Despite their strong jaws, the adults probably do not eat, living only long enough to lay large egg masses near water. The large aquatic larvae, called hellgrammites and much used by fishermen as bait, feed on aquatic insects for three years and then emerge to pupate on land. The closely related alderflies differ from the dobsonflies in their smaller size and diurnal habits. Dobsonflies are classified in the phylum ARTHROPODA, class Insecta, order Neuroptera, family Corydalidae.

Dobzhansky, Theodosius (dôbzhän′skē), 1900–, American geneticist, b. Russia, grad. Univ. of Kiev, 1921. He emigrated to the United States in 1927 and was naturalized in 1937. Dobzhansky taught at the California Institute of Technology (1930–40) and was professor of zoology at Columbia (1940–62), leaving to become associated with the Rockefeller Institute (now Rockefeller Univ.). He conducted much research with *Drosophila* and is known for his basic work in genetics. His writings are of considerable significance and include *Genetics and the Origin of Species* (1937, 3d ed. 1951), a challenging summation of contemporary knowledge of genetics; *Evolution, Genetics, and Man* (1955); and *Mankind Evolving: The Evolution of the Human Species* (1962), which with great wisdom deals with cultural as well as biological evolution. See also *Genetics of the Evolution Process* (1970) and *Genetic Diversity and Human Equality* (1973).

Docetism (dōsĕt′ĭzəm) [Gr., = to appear], early heretical trend in Christian thought. Docetists claimed that Christ was a mere phantasm who only seemed to live and suffer. A similar tendency to deny Jesus' humanity appeared in the teachings of Simon Magus, Marcion, Gnosticism, and certain phases of monarchianism.

dock, in botany: see BUCKWHEAT.

Doctors of the Church: see FATHERS OF THE CHURCH.

documentary: see MOTION PICTURES.

Dodai (dō′dāī, -dī, dŏ′dāī), the same as DODO.

Dodanim (dō′dənĭm, dŏ-) or **Rodanim** (rō′dənĭm, rŏ′-), nation, probably the Rhodians. Gen. 10.4, 1 Chron. 1.7. Dedan in Ezek. 27.15 probably refers to the same.

Dodavah (dŏ′dəvə, dōdā′-), father of ELIEZER **3**.

Dodd, Samuel Calvin Tate, 1836–1907, American lawyer, b. Franklin, Pa. He was admitted to the Pennsylvania bar in 1859. Dodd was employed by the Rockefeller interests and is credited with devising the business TRUST arrangement by which John D. Rockefeller was able to consolidate control of many companies engaged in producing oil. Dodd strongly opposed the Sherman Antitrust Act (1890), and a collection of his addresses, *Trusts* (1900), defends business combinations. He organized (1899) the Standard Oil Company of New Jersey, the result of Rockefeller's consolidations and one of the earliest of the large holding companies. His view that only "unreasonable" combinations in restraint of trade should be illegal was adopted by the Supreme Court in 1911; later revisions of this decision declared certain actions to be unreasonable per se.

Dodd, William, 1729-77, English author. At one time king's chaplain, he ran heavily into debt, forged a bond, and was sentenced to death. Dr. Johnson led a movement to obtain clemency, but Dodd was executed. His best-known work is *The Beauties of Shakespeare* (1752).

Dodd, William Edward, 1869-1940, American historian and diplomat, b. Clayton, N.C. He was professor of history at Randolph-Macon College (1900-1908) and at the Univ. of Chicago (1908-33). From June, 1933, to Dec., 1937, he was ambassador to Germany. Dodd, an admirer of the German culture he knew in his pleasant student days at Leipzig, returned as U.S. envoy with high hopes of improving German-American relations. The Nazis, however, recently come to power, soon alienated him, and he became an outspoken critic of Hitlerism. His historical writings reflect with vigor his passionate devotion to democracy, and he inspired a whole school of historians, who carried on his Jeffersonian and Wilsonian ideals. His works include biographies of Nathaniel Macon (1903, repr. 1970) and Jefferson Davis (1907, repr. 1966), *Statesmen of the Old South* (1911), *Expansion and Conflict* (1915), *The Cotton Kingdom* ("Chronicles of America" series, Vol. XXVII, 1919), *Woodrow Wilson and His Work* (1920, rev. ed. 1932, repr. 1958), *Lincoln or Lee* (1928, repr. 1964), and *The Old South: Struggles for Democracy* (1937). He also edited, with Ray Stannard Baker, *The Public Papers of Woodrow Wilson* (6 vol., 1924-27). See *Ambassador Dodd's Diary, 1933-1938* (ed. by his son, William E. Dodd, Jr., and his daughter, Martha Dodd, 1941). See biography by Robert Dallek (1968).

dodder: see MORNING GLORY.

Doddridge, Philip, 1702-51, English nonconformist minister and noted hymn writer. His *Rise and Progress of Religion in the Soul* (1745) has been much translated. His many hymns include "Awake, My Soul, Stretch Every Nerve" and "O Happy Day, That Fixed My Choice." Doddridge's *Correspondence and Diary* (5 vol., 1829-31) was edited by his great-grandson.

Dodds, Harold Willis, 1889-, American educator, b. Utica, Pa., grad. Grove City College, 1909, M.A. Princeton, 1914, Ph.D. Univ. of Pennsylvania, 1917. He taught economics and political science and became well known as an adviser on electoral procedure to several Latin American governments, particularly Nicaragua (1922-24, 1928) and Cuba (1935). He was adviser (1925-26) to the Commission for the Tacna-Arica Plebiscite and secretary (1920-28) of the National Municipal League. Appointed professor of politics at Princeton in 1927, he was president of that university from 1933 to 1957. His works include *Out of This Nettle, Danger* (1943) and *The Academic President* (1962).

dodecahedron: see POLYHEDRON.

Dodecanese (dōdĕk"ənēs', -nēz, dō"dĕk-), Gr. *Dhodhekánisos,* island group (1971 pop. 121,017), c.1,035 sq mi (2,680 sq km), SE Greece, in the Aegean Sea, between Asia Minor and Crete, comprising the greater part of the group known as the Southern SPORADES. Despite its name ("twelve islands"), it consists of about 20 islands and islets, of which the most important are RHODES, KÓS, KÁRPATHOS, KÁLIMNOS, PÁTMOS, Astipálaia, Kásos, Tilos, Sími, Léros, Nísiros, Khalki, and Kastellórizo. The city of Rhodes, on the largest of the islands, is the administrative seat. Agriculture, livestock raising, fruit growing, and sponge diving are the main occupations. Centers of ancient Greek culture, the Dodecanese were held by the Ottoman Turks from 1522 until 1912, when they were occupied by Italy during the Italo-Turkish War. The islands were captured by the Allies during World War II, and in 1947 they formally passed to Greece.

Dodge, David Low, 1774-1852, American merchant and pacifist, b. Brooklyn, Conn. In 1815 he founded the New York Peace Society, possibly the first such organization to be established. In 1828 other peace societies joined with it to form the American Peace Society; Dodge served as a director and as a member of the executive committee until 1836.

Dodge, Grace Hoadley, 1856-1914, American philanthropist, b. New York City; great-granddaughter of David Low Dodge. She played an important part in the founding of Teachers College of Columbia. She also promoted working girls' clubs and the New York Travelers' Aid Society.

Dodge, Grenville Mellen, 1831-1916, Union general in the Civil War and railroad builder, b. Danvers, Mass. Before the war Dodge, a civil engineer, did railroad work in the West. After he distinguished himself leading a brigade at Pea Ridge (March, 1862), where he was wounded, he was made a brigadier general of volunteers. Dodge's skill in rapidly rebuilding the bridges and railroads destroyed by Confederate forces was of great value to Grant and Sherman in their Western campaigns. Promoted to major general of volunteers (June, 1864), he led a corps in Sherman's Atlanta campaign until he was severely wounded at the siege of Atlanta. After campaigning (1865-66) against the Indians, he left (May, 1866) the army to become chief engineer of the Union Pacific RR. His efficient and rapid construction of that line was his greatest achievement. Dodge was a Republican Congressman from Iowa (1867-69). Throughout his long career he was prominent as a developer of railroads, especially in the Southwest. See biography by S. P. Hirshson (1967).

Dodge, Mary Mapes, 1831-1905, American writer of children's stories, b. New York City. During her lifetime she was the acknowledged leader in the field of juvenile fiction. Her story *Hans Brinker; or, The Silver Skates* (1865) has become a children's classic. From 1873 until her death she edited and contributed to the children's magazine *St. Nicholas;* collections of her work in *St. Nicholas* were published as *Baby Days* (1876) and *Baby World* (1884). Other works include *Irvington Stories* (1864) and *Donald and Dorothy* (1883). See biography by A. B. Howard (1943).

Dodge City, city (1970 pop. 14,127), seat of Ford co., SW Kansas, on the Arkansas River; inc. 1875. The distributing center for a great wheat and livestock area, it also produces agricultural implements and supplies. Laid out in 1872 near Fort Dodge (1864) on the old Santa Fe Trail, it soon flourished as the Santa Fe railhead and became a wild and rowdy cow town; Wyatt Earp and Bat Masterson were among those who helped to curb lawlessness. Fort Dodge is now a soldiers' home. The city hall, formerly located on the site of Boot Hill, an early cowboy burial ground, has been removed to permit enlargement of that tourist attraction. St. Mary of the Plains College and a junior college are in the city. There is an annual rodeo.

Dodgson, Charles Lutwidge: see CARROLL, LEWIS.

Dodo (dō'dō). **1** Father of ELHANAN **1**. **2** Father of the mighty man Eleazar. 2 Sam. 23.9; 1 Chron. 11.12. Dodai: 1 Chron. 27.4. **3** Issacharite. Judges 10.1.

Dodona (dōdō'nə), in Greek religion, the oldest oracle, in inland Epirus, c.50 mi (80 km) E of Corcyra, sacred to Zeus and Dione. It was believed that an old oak tree there became oracular when a black dove, from Egyptian Thebes, settled on it. Priests listened to and interpreted the rustling of the tree's leaves, the cooing of doves, and the clanging of brass vessels that were hung from the tree's branches.

Dodsley, Robert, 1703-64, English publisher and author. He wrote occasional verses, and also several plays, including *The King and the Miller of Mansfield* (1737); a ballad opera,*The Blind Beggar of Bethnal Green* (1741); and the tragedy *Cleone* (1758). He is best known, however, as the publisher of works by Pope, Johnson, Gray, and Goldsmith and as the editor of *A Select Collection of Old Plays* (12 vol., 1744) and *A Collection of Poems by Several Hands* (6 vol., 1748-58). He founded with Burke the *Annual Register* (1758), which still exists.

Doeg (dō'ĕg), agent of Saul in the massacre at Nob. 1 Sam. 21.1-9; 22.6-23; title of Ps. 52.

Doenitz, Karl (dön'ĭts), b. 1891 or 1892, German admiral. He secretly planned a German submarine fleet in the years following the Treaty of Versailles, was given command of submarine operations by Adolf Hitler in 1935, and replaced Admiral Raeder in 1943 as chief naval commander. On the announcement (May 1, 1945) that Hitler was dead and had designated Doenitz his successor, the admiral formed a new cabinet and ordered the unconditional surrender (effective May 7) of Germany to the Allies. His government, at Kiel, was dissolved by the Allies. Doenitz was imprisoned (1946-56) for war crimes. His memoirs appeared in 1958 (tr. 1959).

Doesburg, Theo van (tā'ō văn dōōs'bûrg), 1883-1931, Dutch painter, teacher, and writer. Together with Mondrian he founded the magazine *De Stijl* and successfully proselytized in Europe for the new aesthetic of abstraction, simplicity, clarity, and harmony. He influenced Gropius and taught at the Bauhaus and in Berlin from 1921 to 1923. In 1926 he developed a more dynamic version of *De Stijl* principles, called elementarism. The Museum of Modern Art, New York City, has several of his compositions.

dog, carnivorous, domesticated mammal (*Canis familiaris*) of the family Canidae, to which the wolf, jackal, and fox also belong. The family Canidae is sometimes loosely referred to as the dog family, and its characteristics, e.g., long muzzle, large canine teeth, and long tail, as canine traits. However, the term *dog* usually refers only to the domestic species *Canis familiaris.* Two characteristics distinguish the dog from other canids and, indeed, from all other species of animal life. The first is its worldwide distribution in close association with humans, encompassing both hemispheres from the tropics to the Arctic. The second is the enormous amount of genetic variability found within the species. For example, the Irish wolfhound may stand as high as 39 in. (99.1 cm) at the shoulder, while the Chihuahua's shoulder is usually no more than 6 in. (15.2 cm) from the ground; the silky coat of the Yorkshire terrier may be 2 ft (61 cm) long, while a few breeds of dog (such as the Mexican hairless) are entirely without hair. The evolution of such widely differing breeds has been heavily influenced over the centuries by conscious human selection, in addition to natural evolution. It seems probable that the dog is descended from a wolflike ancestor. True wolves appeared in Europe about one million years ago and in the Americas some 700,000 years later. Dog remains estimated to have been deposited about 10,500 years ago were found in Idaho, and somewhat younger remains (about 9,000 years old) were found at sites in Britain and Turkey. It is probable that the dog was the first animal to be domesticated and that the process occurred independently in a number of different areas of the world, although some sources conclude that the first dogs appeared somewhere in Eurasia. It is thought that the earliest domesticated dogs resembled the present-day dingo, the wild dog of Australia. The dingo is believed to have come to Australia as a domestic dog with the aborigines from Southeast Asia. Although more historical information exists on the forerunners of European dogs (such as the British hounds, terriers, and shepherd dogs) than on those of other areas, there is evidence that dogs have existed in most areas of the world throughout the period of recorded history. One of the oldest known breeds is the basenji, which originated in central Africa and is still used as a hunter by certain tribes in that region. Several distinct breeds were known in ancient Egypt and a mastifflike breed (resembling the Kurdish dog in present-day Iraq) is found in Babylonian illustrations of c.2200 B.C. Dogs have been selectively bred through the centuries for special purposes, notably to pursue and retrieve game, as draft animals, as guides (e.g., for the blind), and as companions. Although dogs possess hearing abilities far superior to man's, their acute sense of smell is probably the sense most utilized. In addition to traditional hunting and tracking, the dog's sense of smell has been put to such diverse uses as the location of exotic foods and the detection of drugs, e.g., in luggage and packages. Attempts to classify dogs probably date from the time of man's discovery that certain canine traits are more desirable than others. The earliest known system of classification, that of the Romans, included categories for house dogs, shepherd dogs, sporting dogs, war dogs, dogs that ran by scent, and dogs that ran by sight. Today there are systems of classification and breeding in most countries of Western Europe and in North America, many using a variation of the standard British system. In the United States, the classification system most frequently encountered is that employed by the American Kennel Club (AKC), which recognizes 116 of the more than 200 known breeds. The breeds are grouped into six classes. In the SPORTING DOG group are pointers, retrievers, setters, and spaniels. These dogs hunt by air scent as opposed to those of the HOUND group, e.g., beagles, foxhounds, and bloodhounds, which track their prey by ground scent. Also classified as hounds are those dogs of the grey-

against the Social Democrats, and in Feb., 1934 he ruthlessly suppressed a Socialist uprising. In April, 1934, Austria became a CORPORATIVE STATE with a one-party, authoritarian system. Dollfuss was assassinated (July 25) by Austrian Nazis, who made an unsuccessful attempt to seize power. See Walter Maass, *Assassination in Vienna* (1972).

Dollier de Casson, François (fräNswä' dôlyā' də käsôN'), 1636–1701, priest and explorer in Canada, b. near Nantes, France. In 1657 he entered the seminary of Saint-Sulpice, Paris, and in 1666 he went as a missionary to Canada. With Father Galinée he set forth (1669) in La Salle's company, bound for the Ohio-Mississippi country, where the two priests planned to carry on missionary activities among the Western Indian tribes. At Lake Ontario they parted from La Salle and went W to Lake Erie; on its north shore they wintered (1669–70), claiming the land in the name of Louis XIV. Prevented by a series of misfortunes from continuing their missionary travels, they decided to go on to Sault Ste Marie and return to Montreal by way of the Ottawa River. In 1671, Dollier de Casson became superior of the seminary at Montreal and later was vicar general of the diocese of Quebec. His history of Montreal from 1640 to 1672 was published in 1868; it was translated into English (1928) by Ralph Flenley, who added a biography.

Döllinger, Johann Joseph Ignaz von (yō'hän yō'-zĕf ĭg'näts fən döl'ĭngər), 1799–1890, German theologian and historian, leader of the OLD CATHOLICS. Ordained in 1822, he was subsequently professor of church history and ecclesiastical law at the Univ. of Munich, chief librarian of the university, and a member of the Academy of Sciences. Between 1845 and 1852 he had considerable influence as representative of the university in the Bavarian chamber and as one of the leading members of the Catholic party in the Frankfurt Parliament. Döllinger devoted his efforts to the cause of a German Catholic Church, independent of the state. Some lectures delivered in Rome (1857) were published in English as *The Church and the Churches; or, The Papacy and the Temporal Power.* This work, subsequently banned, expressed the opinion that the temporal sovereignty was not an essential accompaniment of the papacy. In 1863 followed a work known in English as *Fables Respecting the Popes in the Middle Ages.* When the Vatican Council was in session Döllinger opposed the doctrine of papal infallibility in a series of letters and papers, published under the pseudonym Janus as *The Pope and the Council* (1869). When that doctrine was pronounced a dogma in 1870, he refused to accept it. In 1871 he was defrocked and excommunicated. Although he was in sympathy with the Old Catholics, he never had intended that a separate sect should grow out of the movement, and he never formally became a member of the Old Catholic Church. Despite his excommunication, he continued his academic career; he was made rector of the Univ. of Munich and in 1873 president of the Academy of Sciences. Many of his works were translated into English.

Dollond, John (dŏl'ənd), 1706–61, English optician and inventor. A silk weaver, he taught himself languages, mathematics, and science, becoming a noted scholar as well as a scientist. He invented the achromatic lens, which led to the construction of telescopes free of color fringes, and the heliometer, used in astronomical measurement.

dolmen (dŏl'mĕn, dōl-) [Breton,=stone table], burial chamber consisting of two or more upright stone slabs supporting a capstone or table, typical of the Neolithic period in Europe. See MEGALITHIC MONUMENTS.

Dolomieu, Déodat Guy Silvain Tancrède Gratet de (dāōdä' gē sĕlvăN' täNkrĕd' grätā' də dôlômyö'), 1750–1801, French geologist. He contributed to the study of volcanic geology, especially through examination and comparison of the products of volcanoes. In 1791 he reported on the character of the mineral dolomite, named for him. He wrote several works on his findings during geological journeys, especially in S Europe, and is known for his *Sur la philosophie mineralogique* (1801).

dolomite (dō'ləmīt). **1** Mineral, calcium magnesium carbonate, $CaMg(CO_3)_2$. It is commonly crystalline and is white, gray, brown, or reddish in color with a vitreous-to-pearly luster. The magnesium is sometimes replaced in part by iron or manganese. **2** Carbonate rock composed chiefly of the mineral dolomite, similar to limestone but somewhat harder and heavier. The rock may be metamorphosed into dolomitic marble. Most dolomites probably originated from the partial replacement of the calcium in limestone by magnesium. Its chief uses are as a building stone, for the manufacture of refractory furnace linings, and as basic magnesium carbonate for pipe coverings. Formations of dolomite are very widespread (occurring in Europe, the United States, Africa, Brazil, and Mexico) and notably in the region of the Alps now called the Dolomites, where the rock was first studied by Dolomieu.

Dolomites, or **Dolomite Alps,** Alpine group, N Italy, between the Isarco and Piave rivers, named for the dolomitic limestone of which it is composed. Famous for their strikingly bold outline (a stairstep effect created by erosion of alternate layers of soft and hard rock) and for their vivid colors at sunrise and sunset, the Dolomites are ideal for mountain climbing. Hydroelectricity is produced in the Dolomites. The Marmolada (10,964 ft/3,342 m), the highest peak, has glaciers. Cortina d'Ampezzo and other resorts are among the major tourist centers of Italy.

dolphin, large, swift game fish, *Coryphaena hipparus,* also called dorado. It is of nearly worldwide distribution in warm waters. Its long, slender body is blue, and in the living animal there are luminous shades of gold, green, and purple. The dolphin has a dorsal fin that runs the length of the body and a forked tail. Males, larger than females, may reach a length of nearly 6 ft (1.8 m) and a weight of over 65 lb (30 kg). Dolphins travel alone or in groups, attaining speeds of 35 mi (56 km) per hr. They feed on a variety of fishes, especially flying fish, which they sometimes pursue by leaping out of the water. They are valued as food in Polynesia, where they are known as mahimahi. The term *dolphin* is also applied to a group of aquatic mammals (see DOLPHIN, mammal). The fish known as dolphins are classified in the phylum CHORDATA, subphylum Vertebrata, class Osteichthyes, order Perciformes, family Coryphaenidae.

dolphin, aquatic mammal, any of the small toothed WHALES of the family Delphinidae, numbering more than 50 species. These include the true, or beaked, dolphins, the KILLER WHALE, the pilot whale, and 12 freshwater species found in rivers of South America and S Asia. Most species are highly gregarious. The name *dolphin,* meaning "beaked," is also applied to a species of fish (see DOLPHIN, fish). In the United States dolphins are often mistakenly called porpoises, a name correctly applied to small, blunt-nosed whales of another family. Dolphins breathe air through a single, dorsal blowhole. They are fish-like in form, with streamlined, hairless bodies. Their powerful, horizontal flukes, or tail fins, drive them through or out of the water, while their forefins and dorsal fin are used for steering. Constantly shedding their skins, dolphins accumulate no barnacles or other external parasites. A layer of blubber protects them from cold and seals small wounds. The dolphin's intelligence, playfulness, and friendliness, its built-in smile and merry-looking eyes have been a source of interest and enchantment to human beings from earliest times; it is a common figure in mythology and literature and has been much depicted in art, especially in the posture of its graceful, arched, 30-ft (9-m) leap. Dolphins have long been famous for riding the bows of ships, and it is now known that they also ride the bows of large whales. Today they are valued and exploited as entertainers in more than 40 water shows around the world and have thus become available for extensive study. The best known are the common dolphin (*Delphinus delphis*), of worldwide distribution, and the bottle-nosed dolphin (*Tursiops truncatus*), found in coastal waters of the North Atlantic Ocean and the Mediterranean Sea. The bottlenose has been particularly intensively studied; it is presumed that much of what is known about this species applies to other dolphins and even to the large whales. The common dolphin averages 8 ft (2.4 m) in length and 165 lb (75 kg) in weight. It has a dark blue or black upper body, a white underbody, golden stripes on the sides, and a sickle-shaped dorsal fin. Its pronounced, slim beak, holding 100 teeth, is separated from its snout by a deep groove. A fast swimmer, it travels in large schools in warm waters and is noted for leaping alongside boats for long distances. Its life span is about 50 years. The bottle-nosed dolphin is blue-gray with a dorsal fin and white belly. Its average length is 9 ft (2.7 m) and its average weight 350 lb (160 kg). Its domed forehead, called the melon, contains an oily substance thought to protect the brain case and to act as an acoustic lens. With age the 200 or more teeth of the bottlenose wear down, hence the name *truncatus.* Members of this species live about 25 years. Bottle-nosed dolphins swim in large schools with a social organization and hierarchy, hunting the small fish, crustaceans, squid, and cuttlefish that make up their diet. They have been clocked swimming at 30 mi (48 km) per hour, although 20 to 24 mi (32–39 km) per hour is their usual speed. They can dive 70 ft (20 m) and remain underwater for 15 minutes. They sleep by night, just below the surface of the water, rising for air every three or four minutes. Their aquatic natural enemies are sharks and killer whales; these they attempt to outswim, using complex evasive strategy, or batter to death, acting in a group. If one of their number is injured or sick they make every effort to rescue it, holding it above the water for air. Play behavior is highly developed in the bottlenose from infancy through old age, and in this connection it displays considerable tool-making, tool-using, and manipulative ability; for example, a dolphin has been observed to kill a fish, strip its skeleton, and use the bones, held in the mouth, to pry another fish out of a crevice. Sex play is frequent and is initiated by any individual toward any other, without regard to size, age, sex, relationship, or even species; approaches to human beings and to turtles are common. Courtship and impregnation occur mainly in spring, when males vie for the attention of the females. A single calf, 3½ ft (97 cm) long and weighing 30 lb (14 kg), is born tail first after a gestation of 12 months. The mother or a female assistant bites the umbilical cord in two and pushes the calf to the surface to breathe; it is nursed for one to two years. One female may watch over several calves while the mothers hunt, or during battle. The senses of the bottlenose have been subjected to intensive investigation, as have their intelligence and their remarkable systems of echolocation and communication. In relation to body size, the brain of the adult bottlenose is comparable in size to that of man; it is twice as convoluted and possesses 1½ times as many cells. The bottlenose has partially stereoscopic vision that is keen both in water and in air; when the animal leaps from one medium to the other, its brain corrects for the difference in refractive index. The eye has a glowing layer for night vision and a brownish filter that is lowered over the iris in bright sunlight. The brain has no olfactory lobe and the sense of smell is presumably missing, but the taste buds are well developed and are used to detect underwater chemical traces, as when the dolphin tracks fish. Dolphins produce an enormous variety of sounds, up to frequencies ten times those heard by human beings. The sounds are apparently produced by a complex of anatomical structures including the blowhole with its air sacs and valves. Each dolphin has a signature whistle with which it identifies itself; a calf soon learns to recognize its mother's whistle. Clicking and rapid creaking sounds are the basis of the echolocation mechanism (sonar) with which the dolphin gathers extremely precise information about the size, location, and nature of surrounding objects. Dolphins communicate by means of a demonstrably descriptive language understood by more than one species, using all the sounds in their repertory. They are observed to converse, and it has been repeatedly shown that one animal can convey instructions to another. Computer-aided efforts are being made, so far without success, to learn the dolphin language and to teach dolphins human speech, either in its normal form or translated into whistle combinations. Dolphins are capable of imitation and memorization; they demonstrate foresight, learn from observation, communicate experience, solve complex problems, perform elaborate tasks, and learn multiple procedures simultaneously. Their so-called training is in fact a discipline structured around play, using their natural behavior as the basis for involved maneuvers; they appear to perform primarily for their own enjoyment. In situations of great stress in captivity they have been known to commit suicide by starvation, battering against walls, or drowning. There is no record of a dolphin attacking a person, even while being mistreated, and there are many reports of dolphins rescuing people from drowning. The United States and Soviet navies have spent vast sums to reach a greater understanding of dolphin echolocation, which could have countless military applications. The U.S. navy has trained dolphins to act as messengers to underwater stations, to rescue wounded frogmen and protect them from sharks, and to seek and destroy submarines, using kamikaze methods; this last project has met with considerable public criticism. Until recently dolphins formed the basis of a widespread fishing industry; only the Japanese continue to hunt them for food on a large scale. They are accidentally caught and killed in large numbers in tuna seining operations. Dolphins are classified in the phylum CHORDATA, subphylum Vertebrata, class

Mammalia, order Cetacea, family Delphinidae. See Antony Alpers, *A Book of Dolphins* (1960) and *Dolphins: the Myth and the Mammal* (1961); J. C. Lilly, *Man and Dolphin* (1961) and *The Mind of the Dolphin* (1967); W. N. Kellogg, *Porpoises and Sonar* (1961); K. S. Norris, ed., *Whales, Dolphins and Porpoises* (1966); Eleanore Devine and Martha Clark, *The Dolphin Smile* (1967); Robert Stenuit, *The Dolphin, Cousin to Man* (1968); D. K. and M. C. Caldwell, *The World of the Bottlenosed Dolphin* (1972).

Dolton, village (1970 pop. 25,937), Cook co., NE Ill., on the Calumet River, S of Chicago; settled 1832, inc. 1892. It lies in a truck-farming area. Steel, aluminum products, glass, chemicals, paper bags, and chain belts are manufactured there.

Dom (dōm), peak, 14,942 ft (4,554 m) high, Valais canton, S Switzerland, in the Mischabelhörner group. It is the highest peak entirely in Switzerland.

Domagk, Gerhard (gĕr'härt dō'mäk), 1895-1964, German chemist and pathologist. A teacher successively at the universities of Greifswald and Münster, he became (1927) director of research at the I. G. Farbenindustrie laboratory at Wuppertal. Because of a Nazi decree he was obliged to decline the 1939 Nobel Prize in Physiology and Medicine. In 1947 he received a gold medal in lieu of the prize money. The award was made for his discovery of the efficacy of prontosil, the forerunner of the sulfa drugs, in treating streptococcal infections.

domain, in physics: see MAGNETISM.

Domat, Jean (zhäN dōmä'), 1625-96, French jurist. His *Les Loix civiles dans leur ordre naturel* [civil laws in their natural order] (3 vol., 1689-94) is a restatement of Roman law considered as a system derived from ethical theory and natural theology. It is believed to be the earliest work on the subject to depart from the arrangement of the 6th-century Corpus Juris Civilis. His name is also spelled Daumat. See H. F. Jolowicz, *Roman Foundations of Modern Law* (1957).

Dombrowa: See DĄBROWA GÓRNICZA, Poland.

Dombrowski, Jan Henryk: see DĄBROWSKI.

dome, a roof circular or (rarely) elliptical in plan and usually hemispherical in form, placed over a circular, square, oblong, or polygonal space. Domes have been built with a wide variety of outlines and of various materials. The earliest domes were probably roofed primitive huts and consisted of bent-over branches plastered with mud. Another primitive form, called a beehive dome, is constructed of concentric rings of corbeled stones and has a conical shape. Ancient examples have been found in the tombs of Mycenae and can also still be seen in the folk architecture of Sicily. Although there is evidence of widespread knowledge of the dome, its early use was apparently restricted to small structures built of mud brick. It was the Romans who first fully realized the architectural potentialities of the dome. The Roman development in dome construction culminated in the PANTHEON (2d cent. A.D.). The Romans, however, failed to discover a proper handling of the PENDENTIVE—the device essential to placing a dome over a square compartment—that was finally achieved by the Byzantine builders of HAGIA SOPHIA at Constantinople (A.D. 532-37). The other solution to placing a dome over a square was the SQUINCH, which in the form of stalactites was to receive superb expression in Islamic architecture. Under Byzantine influence the Muslims early adopted the use of the dome, one of their first important monuments being the Dome of the Rock in Jerusalem. They often used the so-called Persian or onion dome. The most celebrated example is the TAJ MAHAL (A.D. 1630) at Agra, India. Both the influence of the Roman Pantheon and of the Byzantine pendentive came to bear on the designers of the Italian Renaissance, and the crossings of many churches of the period were covered by masonry domes on pendentives. Between pendentive and dome a circular drum usually was interposed, serving both to give greater elevation and external importance and as a space for the introduction of windows. By the addition of an outer shell, the exterior came to be independently designed for maximum effectiveness, and the placing of a lantern at the top of this outer shell provided an apex for the entire composition. Celebrated examples are Brunelleschi's octagonal, ribbed dome for the Cathedral of Florence (1420-36); St. Peter's, Rome, designed by Michelangelo, with two masonry shells (completed 1590), internal diameter 137 ft (42 m); the church of the Invalides, Paris, by J. H. Mansart (1706), 90 ft (27 m); St. Paul's Cathedral, London, by Sir Christopher Wren (1675-1710), 112 ft (34 m); and the Panthéon, Paris, by J. G. Soufflot (1775-81), 69 ft (21 m). The last three domes are built with triple shells, the middle shells serving to support the crowning lanterns. In the United States the dome of the Massachusetts state capitol,

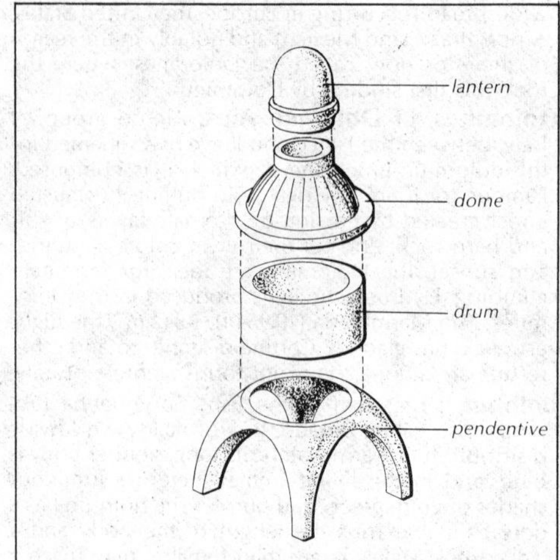

Parts of a dome

designed (1795) by Charles Bulfinch, established the dome as a distinctive feature for numerous later state capitols as well as for the national Capitol at Washington, D. C. The dome of the latter, however, is of cast iron instead of masonry. The design, by T. U. Walter, has an inner diameter of 90 ft (27 m) and possesses great external impressiveness. The dome in modern architecture utilizes such materials of construction as reinforced and thin-shell concrete, glass and steel, plastic, and GEODESIC structures. Important examples have been created by Frank Lloyd WRIGHT, Pier Luigi NERVI, and Buckminster FULLER.

Domenchina, Juan José (hwän hōsā' dōmänchē'nä), 1898-1959, Spanish poet and critic, b. Madrid. He was active in the transition from *modernismo* to the "new poetry." Such early volumes as *Del poema eterno* [from the eternal poem] (1917) and *La corporeidad de lo abstracto* [the substance of the abstract] (1929) are characteristic of his intellectual, abstract, and baroque form of expression. His later poetry *Dédalo* [Daedalus] (1932), *Margen* [the edge] (1933) and *La sombra desterrada* [the exiled shadow] (1949-50) possesses a more human, anguished tone. He died in Mexico, where he had lived in exile since 1939.

Domenichino (dōmānēk'nō) or **Domenico Zampieri** (dōmā'nēkō tsämpyĕ'rē), 1581-1641, Italian painter, b. Bologna. He was one of the principal pupils of the Carracci, beginning as Ludovico Carracci's assistant in Bologna. In 1602 he went to Rome, where he worked with Annibale Carracci in the Farnese Palace. Later he carried out numerous fresco commissions for Roman churches, of which the most important are the *Martyrdom of St. Andrew* in San Gregorio Magno, the *Life of St. Cecilia* in San Luigi de' Francesci (1615-17), and the decoration of Sant' Andrea della Valle (1624-28). The finest easel painting of his early Roman years is the *Last Communion of St. Jerome.* He also worked in Naples, designing frescoes (unfinished) of a more baroque nature for the chapel of San Gennaro in the cathedral. As an adherent of classical doctrine and as an influential landscape painter, Domenichino has a place of considerable importance. See catalog of drawings by J. W. Pope-Hennessy (1948).

Domenico Veneziano (dōmā'nēkō vānätsyä'nō), c.1400-1461, Italian painter. His origin is unknown, although his name suggests that he came from Venice. His art, with rich coloring and detailed landscape settings, has close affinities with northern painting. In Florence he created his most celebrated work, the *St. Lucy Altarpiece* (central panel in the Uffizi). It is one of the first works in which the Madonna and Saints (*Sacra Conversazione*) are brought into the same spatial volume. Domenico reduced the elaborate, formal structure that customarily separated the deity from the saints. Disposing of the Gothic hierarchical order, he introduced the figures in a harmonious group. Other paintings attributed to him are several Madonnas (Settignano; National Gall., London; National Gall. of Art, Washington, D.C.); an exquisite circular painting of the *Adoration of the Magi* (Berlin); and some portraits (National Gall. of Art, Washington, D.C.; Gardner Mus., Boston).

Dome of the Rock: see MOSQUE.

Domesday Book (do͞omz'dā), record of a general census of England made (1085-86) by order of WILLIAM I (William the Conqueror). The survey ascertained the economic resources of most of the country for purposes of more accurate taxation. Royal agents took the evidence of local men in each hundred (county subdivision), the latter acting as inquest jurors. Descriptions of each piece of land, its present and former holders, the holding itself, and the population on it were among the facts recorded. For the thoroughness and speed with which it was taken, the Domesday survey as an administrative measure is unsurpassed in medieval history. Written from the data thus gathered, the Domesday Book is an invaluable historical source. It furnished the material for F. W. Maitland's masterly survey, *Domesday Book and Beyond* (1897), which deals with social and economic conditions in Anglo-Saxon and Conquest times. Many of the Domesday records have been printed by counties in the *Victoria County Histories,* and several portions have been independently published. The name *domesday* is a variant of *doomsday,* meaning day of judgment. See V. H. Galbraith, *The Making of Domesday Book* (1961); R. W. Finn, *The Domesday Inquest and the Making of Domesday Book* (1961) and *Introduction to Domesday Book* (1963).

domestic relations. For psychological and sociological aspects, see MARRIAGE. For legal aspects, see DIVORCE; HUSBAND AND WIFE; PARENT AND CHILD.

domestic science: see HOME ECONOMICS.

domestic service, work performed in a household by someone who is not a member of the family. It was performed by slaves in many early civilizations, e.g., in Greece and Rome. Under the feudal system the work was done by serfs. The guild system required indentured apprentices to perform household duties while learning a trade. With the disappearance of feudalism and guilds, servants were recruited from free wage earners. Domestic service came to be regarded as an unattractive occupation because of the long hours, low wages, poor living conditions, low social status, and dependence on the personal habits of the employer. In the colonies of North America, domestic service was performed by transported convicts, bond servants who sold themselves into service for stated periods to pay their passage, Indians, and black slaves. After the American Revolution indentured servants were largely replaced, except in the South, by free labor. The rapid development of the industrial system in the 19th cent. provided more lucrative employment for native-born labor and coincided with an influx of immigrants, many of whom went into domestic service. The immigration quotas established in 1921 cut down this supply. In the United States domestic servants now participate in social security benefits. In 1950 the old-age insurance system was expanded to include household employees who were regularly employed, and in the social security amendments of 1954 old-age and survivors' insurance were extended to domestic servants regardless of work regularity. Domestic servants, however, remain uncovered by minimum wage legislation. In Great Britain domestic workers are covered by national health and unemployment insurance schemes. The shortage of domestic laborers in most Western countries has been partially offset by the employment of part-time domestics, the use of labor-saving devices, and an increase in the number of restaurants. See George Stigler, *Domestic Servants in the United States, 1900-1940* (1946).

domestic shorthair cat: see CAT.

domicile (dŏm'əsīl"), one's legal residence. This may or may not be the place where one actually resides at any one time. The domicile is the permanent home to which one is presumed to have the intention of returning whenever the purpose for which one is absent has been accomplished. One may simultaneously have a temporary lodging for a short time at one place, a more permanent abode called a residence at another, and a domicile at still another place. Usually the domicile of the husband and father determines that of wife and children. Determining domicile is important in defining the legal status of a person and the nationality of a public corporation (a legal person) under international law.

Dominic, Saint (dŏm'ənĭk), 1170?-1221, Castilian churchman, named Domingo de Gúzmán, founder of the DOMINICANS. He studied at Palencia and became a canon, then prior of canons, of the cathedral of Osma. He and his bishop went (c.1203) to Rome seeking permission to evangelize the Tatars; instead, Pope Innocent III sent them to S France to preach to

Annals of the Four Masters, a history of the world, was compiled between 1632 and 1636.

Donelson, Andrew Jackson (dŏn'əlsən), 1799-1871, American politician, b. Cumberland region of Tennessee. He was brought up at the Hermitage by his uncle, Andrew Jackson. After graduating from West Point he accompanied Jackson as aide-de-camp in the Seminole campaign. He practiced law in Nashville, but again aided Jackson as private secretary in the presidential campaigns of 1824 and 1828. After Jackson's election to the presidency Donelson was his private secretary, and Mrs. Donelson was Jackson's hostess at the White House. Her refusal to accept Mrs. J. H. Eaton (see O'NEILL, MARGARET) socially led to a temporary estrangement between uncle and nephew, but Jackson found himself in need of Donelson's aid and recalled him. In 1844, Donelson was sent as chargé d'affaires to the republic of Texas to conduct negotiations for annexation. After his success in this mission he served (1846-49) as minister to Prussia. In 1856 he ran for Vice President as the Know-Nothing candidate.

Donelson, Fort: see FORT DONELSON.

Donets (dənyĕts'), river, c.650 mi (1,050 km) long, SW European USSR, mainly in the Ukraine. A tributary of the Don, it is also called the North Donets (Rus. *Severny Donets*). It rises NE of Belgorod, which it passes, and flows generally southeast to join the lower Don. Its lower course is navigable.

Donets Basin, abbreviated as **Donbas** or **Donbass** (both: dənbäs'), industrial region (c.10,000 sq mi/ 25,900 sq km), S European USSR, N of the Sea of Azov and W of the Donets River. It is located mainly in Donetsk and Voroshilovgrad oblasts of the Ukraine and extends E into Rostov oblast. The Donets Basin is one of the main coal-producing and steel-manufacturing areas of the USSR and it forms one of the densest industrial concentrations in the world. Based on a rich supply of coal, the Donbas has been extensively developed because of its proximity to markets in European areas of the USSR and to large deposits of ferrous metals in other parts of the E Ukraine (Krivoy Rog, Nikopol). In 1965 the Donbas was the source of more than one half of the coking coal and one third of all the coal produced in the USSR; total coal production in the region that year amounted to 206 million metric tons. Two types of coal predominate in the Donbas: anthracite, in the south and east (used mainly by thermal power stations), and bituminous, in the southwest and north (used mainly for coking). Major coal centers include Shakhty, Shakhertsk, Gorlovka, and Krasnyy Luch. Other minerals besides coal are produced in the region, and there are also heavy-machinery, chemical, and power plants. Major iron- and steel-producing centers are Donetsk, Yenakiyevo, Makeyevka, Kramatorsk, and Kommunarsk. The development of the Donets Basin began c.1870, and by 1913 it was the source of virtually all the coal and more than half of the iron and steel produced in czarist Russia.

Donetsk (dənyĕtsk'), city (1970 pop. 879,000), capital of Donetsk oblast, S European USSR, in Ukraine, on the Kalmius River. The largest industrial center of the DONETS BASIN and one of the largest in the Soviet Union, it has coal mines, iron and steel mills, machinery works, and chemical plants. The city was founded in 1870 as Yuzovka, a metallurgical settlement named after a Scottish industrialist named Hughes. From 1924 to 1961 it was called Stalino.

Dong, Pham Van (făm văn dông), 1906-, prime minister of the Democratic Republic of (North) Vietnam (1954-). He joined the underground Communist movement in the 1920s, was arrested by the French colonial officials, and was released in 1936 after seven years in prison. A close associate of HO CHI MINH, Dong was one of the founders of the Viet Minh, a nationalist organization. After the 1954 agreement with France, which divided Vietnam into North and South, Dong assumed the office of prime minister and also served (1954-61) as minister of foreign affairs. After Ho Chi Minh's death (1969), Dong's position became even more important.

Dongan, Thomas, 1634-1715, colonial governor of New York, b. Co. Kildare, Ireland. He was appointed governor in 1682, and on the instructions of the duke of York (later James II), he called (1683) a legislative assembly; measures, known as the Charter of Liberties and Privileges, were passed granting popular rights and religious toleration. These and subsequent enactments (1684, 1685) were not approved by James II, but were continued by virtue of a permanent charter for New York City secured by Dongan in 1686. He was replaced by Governor Andros in 1688. Dongan became 2d earl of Limerick in 1698. See biography by J. H. Kennedy (1930, repr. 1974).

Dongen, Kees van (kās vän dông'ən), 1877-1968, Dutch painter who worked in Paris. After moving to Paris in 1897, he met Matisse and became an exponent of FAUVISM eight years later. A precocious technician, he produced brilliant figure studies and portraits but soon left the movement to become a fashionable portraitist.

Don Giovanni: see DON JUAN.

Dong Nai or **Donnai** (both: dông'nī'), river, c.300 mi (480 km) long, rising as the Dadung in the mountains of S central South Vietnam. It flows SW past Bien Hoa and joins with the Saigon River below Saigon to form an extensive delta on the South China Sea. There are rapids and waterfalls on its upper reaches.

Dongola (dŏng'gələ), region, part of Northern prov., Sudan. Old Dongola, c.75 mi (120 km) south of the present city of Dongola, was the capital of the Christian kingdom of Makurra or NUBIA, which was first threatened by Muslims from Egypt in 641. It was taken by the Mamelukes in 1275. The first Muslim ruler, a puppet of the Mamelukes, ascended the throne in 1315. His successor gained independence in 1325, but the Muslims reconquered the land in 1366 and the capital was abandoned. Dongola was briefly ruled (1811-20) by Mameluke refugees from Egypt. The Mahdists, in the course of their revolt, held it from 1885 to 1896.

Doniphan, Alexander William (dŏn'ĭfən), 1808-87, American lawyer and soldier, b. Mason co., Ky. He began (1830) to practice law in Lexington, Mo., and served three terms in the state legislature, becoming involved in the Mormon issue. In 1838, Doniphan, as brigadier general of the state militia, was ordered against the Mormons by the governor but flatly refused to carry out orders to execute Joseph Smith and other Mormon leaders. At the opening of the Mexican War he organized a mounted regiment of Missouri volunteers that formed part of Stephen W. Kearny's force in his march on Santa Fe. When Kearny continued to California, Doniphan was left in command in New Mexico, where he subdued and made peace with the Navaho. In Dec., 1846, turning over the command at Santa Fe to Sterling Price, Doniphan, on Kearny's orders, set out with 856 men for Chihuahua to join John Wool's army. Not far along the way his undisciplined but capable fighting outfit routed (Dec. 25) the Mexicans in a farcical engagement at the Brazito River, near El Paso, which was easily occupied. They then pushed on to a point c.15 mi (24 km) N of Chihuahua, where, in the battle of Sacramento (Feb. 28, 1847), they again defeated the Mexicans. Chihuahua was taken the next day. Since Wool was not there as planned, Doniphan began another long march E to Saltillo, which was reached late in May. A few days later Doniphan and his men were commended by Zachary Taylor at Monterrey; then, their terms of enlistment being completed, they went down the Rio Grande, sailed for New Orleans, and returned to Missouri. The entire march, covering some 3,600 mi (5,793 km) and conducted with small loss under adverse circumstances, is one of the famous expeditions in American history. Doniphan, who returned to law practice at Richmond, Mo., opposed secession and favored neutrality for Missouri in 1861. Although offered high command by the Union, he took no active part in the Civil War. See contemporary accounts by Frank S. Edwards (1847, repr. 1966), F. A. Wislizenus (1848, repr. 1969), and Jacob Robinson (1848, repr. 1972); Justin H. Smith, *The War with Mexico* (1919).

Donizetti, Gaetano (gītä'nō dōnēdzĕt'tē), 1797-1848, Italian composer. He studied music in Bergamo and Bologna and achieved success with his first opera, *Enrico di Borgogna* (1818). His early work was influenced by Rossini, but he later developed his own pleasantly melodic, often sentimental, style. Most popular of his more than 60 operas are *Lucrezia Borgia* (1833), *Lucia di Lammermoor* (1835), and *Linda di Chamounix* (1842), all serious operas; *La Fille du régiment* (*The Daughter of the Regiment,* 1840), a French *opéra comique;* and *L'Elisir d'amore* (*The Elixir of Love,* 1832) and *Don Pasquale* (1843), outstanding examples of *opéra buffa.* He also wrote songs, several symphonies, chamber music, oratorios, cantatas, and church music. In 1845 he became paralyzed, and he never composed again.

Don Juan (dŏn wän, jo͞o'ən, Span. dōn hwän), legendary profligate. He has a counterpart in the legends of many peoples, but the Spanish version of the great libertine has become the most universal. At the height of his licentious career, Don Juan seduces the daughter of the commander of Seville and kills her father in a duel. When he later visits a statue of his victim and jeeringly invites it to a feast, the statue comes to life and drags Juan off to hell. The earliest-known dramatization of the story is *El burlador de Sevilla* (1630), attributed to Gabriel Téllez, who wrote under the pseudonym Tirso de Molina. Molière's *Le Festin de Pierre* (1665) and Mozart's opera *Don Giovanni* (1787) are perhaps the most famous treatments of the theme. Among the many other literary works that use the unscrupulous gallant as the hero are Byron's *Don Juan,* Espronceda's *Estudiante de Salamanca,* and Shaw's *Man and Superman.*

donkey: see ASS.

Donnai: see DONG NAI, river, South Vietnam.

Donne, John (dŭn, dŏn), 1572-1631, English poet and divine. He is considered the greatest of the METAPHYSICAL POETS. Reared a Roman Catholic, Donne was educated at Oxford, Cambridge, and Lincoln's Inn. He traveled on the Continent and in 1596-97 accompanied the earl of Essex on his expeditions to Cádiz and the Azores. On his return he became secretary to Sir Thomas Egerton (later Baron Ellesmere), lord keeper of the great seal, and achieved a reputation as a poet and public personage. His writing of this period, including some of his *Songs and Sonnets* (others were written as late as 1617) and *Problems and Paradoxes,* consists of cynical, realistic, often sensual lyrics, essays, and verse satires. Donne's court career was ruined by the discovery of his marriage in 1601 to Anne More, niece to Sir Thomas Egerton's second wife, and he was imprisoned for a short time. After 1601 his poetry became more serious. The two *Anniversaries—An Anatomy of the World* (1611) and *Of the Progress of the Soul* (1612)—reveal that his faith in the medieval order of things had been disrupted by the growing political, scientific, and philosophic doubt of the times. He wrote prose on religious and moral subjects; a polemic against the Jesuits; *Biathanatos* (not published until 1644), a qualified apology for suicide; and the *Pseudo-Martyr* (1610), an argument for Anglicanism. After a long period of financial uncertainty and desperation, during which he was twice a member of Parliament (1601, 1614), Donne yielded to the wishes of King James I and took orders in 1615. Two years later his wife died. The tone of his poetry, especially the *Holy Sonnets,* deepened after her death. After his ordination, Donne wrote more religious works, such as his *Devotions* (1624) and sermons. Several of his sermons were published during his lifetime. Donne was one of the most eloquent preachers of his day. He was made reader in divinity at Lincoln's Inn, a royal chaplain, and in 1621, dean of St. Paul's, a position he held until his death. All of Donne's poetry—his love sonnets and his religious and philosophical poems—is distinguished by a remarkable blend of passion and reason. His love poetry treats the breadth of the experience of loving, emphasizing, in such poems as "The Ecstasie," the root of spiritual love in physical love. The devotional poems and sermons reveal a profound concern with death, decay, damnation, and the possibility of the soul's transcendent union with God. Original, witty, erudite, and often obscure, Donne's style is characterized by a brilliant use of paradox, hyperbole, and imagery. His most famous poems include "A Valediction: Forbidding Mourning," "Go and catch a falling star," "Hymn to God the Father," and the sonnet to death ("Death be not proud"). Neglected for 200 years, Donne was rediscovered by 20th-century critics, and his work has influenced such poets as W. B. Yeats, T. S. Eliot, and W. H. Auden. See biography by R. C. Bald (1970); studies by R. E. Hughes (1968) and R. S. Jackson (1970); centenary volumes edited by P. A. Fiore (1972) and A. J. Smith (1972).

Donnelly, Ignatius, 1831-1901, American author and agrarian reformer, b. Philadelphia. He studied law, was admitted to the bar, and in 1856 moved to Minnesota. There he gained political prominence, was lieutenant governor (1859-63), Congressman (1863-69), and a state legislator. Strongly expounding agrarian reform, he was a founder and leader of the POPULIST PARTY and the author of the ringing preamble to the party platform of 1892. He edited the weekly *Anti-Monopolist* (1874-79) and the Populist *Representative* (1894-1901). His many popular works included *Atlantis: The Antediluvian World* (1882), an erudite but fanciful work on ATLANTIS; *Ragnarok: The Age of Fire and Gravel* (1883); two books arguing that Bacon wrote the Shakespearean plays; and a gloomy Utopian novel, *Caesar's Column* (1891). See biographies by Oscar M. Sullivan (1953) and Martin Ridge (1962).

Donner Party, group of emigrants to California who in the winter of 1846-47 met with one of the most famous tragedies in Western history. The California-bound families were mostly from Illinois and Iowa, and most prominent among them were the two Donner families and the Reed family. In going West they took a little-used route after leaving Fort Bridger and were delayed. They suffered severely in crossing the salt flats W of Great Salt Lake, and dissensions and ill feelings in the party arose when they reached what is today Donner Lake in the Sierra Nevada. They paused (Oct., 1846) to recover their strength, and early snow caught them, falling deep in the passes and trapping them. Their limited food gave out, the cold continued, and the suffering of the group, camped on Alder Creek and Donner Lake, grew intense. A party that attempted to make its way through the snow-choked passes in December suffered horribly. The surviving members of the Donner Party were driven to cannibalism. Finally, expeditions from the Sacramento valley made their way through the snowdrifts to rescue the hunger-maddened migrants. Only about half of the original party of 87 reached California. The survivors later disagreed violently as to the details of (and particularly the blame for) the disaster. See C. F. McGlashan, *History of the Donner Party* (1879, repr. 1966); G. R. Stewart, *Ordeal by Hunger* (1936, new ed. 1960); and an epic poem by George Keithley (1972). **Donner Lake,** named for the party, is today a popular mountain resort near Truckee. There is a monument to the party. Nearby **Donner Pass** has a U.S. weather observatory.

Donnybrook, parish and suburb of Dublin, Co. Dublin, E central Republic of Ireland. It was famous for its annual fair, licensed by King John of England in 1204 and suppressed in 1855 because of its disorderliness. The disorder gave rise to the term "donnybrook," meaning an uproarious brawl.

Donovan, William Joseph (Wild Bill Donovan), 1883–1959, American lawyer, director of the Office of Strategic Services (OSS), b. Buffalo, N.Y. Distinguished service in World War I won him medals and the nickname Wild Bill Donovan. He was prominent in Republican politics and served (1925–29) in the office of the Attorney General. President Franklin Delano Roosevelt sent him on foreign missions, and in 1942 he was made head of the newly created OSS, which he made into a formidable and successful intelligence agency. Donovan, given rank of major general, served until 1945, and later returned to public service as ambassador to Thailand (1953–54). See biography by Carey Ford (1970).

Don Quixote de la Mancha: see CERVANTES SAAVEDRA, MIGUEL DE.

Dooley, Thomas Anthony, 1927–61, American physician and author, b. St. Louis, Mo., grad. Univ. of Notre Dame, M.D. St. Louis Univ., 1953. In 1954, Dooley supervised the care and treatment of thousands of refugees from North Vietnam. He described this experience in *Deliver Us from Evil* (1956). To provide medical care in remote areas he then helped organize the Medical International Corporation (MEDICO), which later became (1962) a service of CARE. His writings include *The Edge of Tomorrow* (1958) and *The Night They Burned the Mountain* (1960).

Doolittle, Hilda, pseud. **H. D.,** 1886–1961, American poet, b. Bethlehem, Pa., educated at Bryn Mawr. After 1911 she lived abroad, marrying Richard ALDINGTON in 1913. In England, under the influence of Ezra Pound, she became associated with the IMAGISTS and developed into one of the most original poets of the group. Volumes of her verse include *Sea Garden* (1916), *Red Shoes for Bronze* (1931), *The Walls Do Not Fall* (1944), and *Bid Me to Live* (1960). See T. B. Swann, *The Classical World of H. D.* (1962).

Doolittle, James Harold, 1896–, American aviator, b. Alameda, Calif. After serving in World War I, he became noted for his speed records and speed tests and then engaged in commercial aviation. In 1940 he was recalled to the army air corps. Doolittle commanded the first bombers that raided (April 18, 1942) Tokyo and other Japanese cities from the aircraft carrier *Hornet.* He later headed the North African Strategic Air Forces and led the 8th Air Force in its massive attacks on Germany. In 1945 he resigned from the army with the rank of lieutenant general to go into business. See biographies by Q. J. Reynolds (1953, repr. 1972) and C. V. Glines (1972).

Doom or **Doomsday:** see JUDGMENT DAY.

Doomsday Book: see DOMESDAY BOOK.

Doon (do͞on), river, c.30 mi (48 km) long, Ayrshire, SW Scotland, flowing NW through Loch Doon (6 mi/9.7 km long) to the Firth of Clyde S of Ayr. Robert Burns celebrated its beauty in his poetry.

Door Peninsula, 80 mi (129 km) long, NE Wis., between Green Bay and Lake Michigan; a canal at Sturgeon Bay bisects the peninsula. Cherry growing and tourism are the chief industries. The peninsula was visited as early as the 17th cent. by French explorers and missionaries.

dopamine (dōp'əmēn), one of the intermediate substances in the biosynthesis of EPINEPHRINE and norepinephrine. See CATECHOLAMINE.

Dophkah (dŏf'kə), desert camp. Num. 33.12.

doping, in electronics: see SEMICONDUCTOR.

Doppler effect, change in the wavelength (or frequency) of energy in the form of waves, e.g., sound or light, as a result of motion of either the source or the receiver of the waves; the effect is named for the Austrian scientist Christian Doppler, who demonstrated the effect for sound. If the source of the waves and the receiver are approaching each other (because of the motion of either or both), the frequency of the waves will increase and the wavelength will be shortened—sounds will become higher pitched and light will appear bluer. If the sender and receiver are moving apart, sounds will become lower pitched and light will appear redder. A common example is the sudden drop in the pitch of a train whistle as the train passes a stationary listener. The Doppler effect is employed in RADAR to sense the velocity of the object under surveillance. In astronomy, the Doppler effect for light is used to measure the velocity and rotation of stars and galaxies along the direction of sight. In the SPECTRUM of nearly every star there are wavelengths, characteristic of atoms, that lie near but not quite coincident to the same wavelengths as measured in the laboratory. The small deviations or shifts are generally due to the relative motion of the celestial object and the earth. Both blue shifts and RED SHIFTS are observed for various objects, indicating relative motion both towards and away from the earth. Such shifts have been used to measure the orbital velocity of the earth, to detect BINARY STARS and VARIABLE STARS, and to detect rotation of other galaxies. The Doppler effect is responsible for the red shifts of distant galaxies, and possibly also of QUASARS, and thus provides the best evidence for the expansion of the universe, as described by HUBBLE'S LAW. In addition to observations of visible light, the Doppler effect for radio waves is utilized by astronomers to determine the velocities of dust clouds in the spiral arms of the Milky Way galaxy. These observations provided the first direct proof that our own galaxy is rotating. The Doppler shift in radar pulses reflected from the surfaces of Venus and Mercury have been analyzed to obtain new values for their periods of rotation about their axes.

Dor or **Dora,** Canaanite seaport, ancient Palestine (modern Israel), N of Caesarea Palestinae. It was never a Jewish city but rather a Phoenician outpost. It was rebuilt by the Romans; still visible are the ruins of a temple and a theater. Later it was fortified by the Crusaders. Joshua 11.2; 12.23; 17.11; Judges 1.27; 1 Kings 4.11; 1 Chron. 7.29; 1 Mac. 15.11,13,25.

dorado: see DOLPHIN (fish).

Dorat, Jean: see DAURAT, JEAN.

Dorati, Antal (äntäl' dōrä'tē), 1906–, Hungarian-American conductor, b. Budapest. Dorati studied with Zoltán Kodály and Béla Bartók. He made his conducting debut at 18 at the Budapest Opera. His first appearance in the United States was with the National Symphony in 1937. Dorati was the conductor of the Dallas (1945–48), Minneapolis (1949–60), and British Broadcasting Corporation (1963–66) symphonies. Since 1966 he has been conductor of the Stockholm Philharmonic. In 1970 he became conductor of the National Symphony in Washington, D.C., as well. Dorati is also a composer but has subordinated composing to conducting. He has made many recordings, and among his major achievements is a complete recording on long-playing records of all of the symphonies of Franz Joseph Haydn.

Dorcas (dôr'kəs) or **Tabitha** (tăb'ĭthə) [Gr. *Dorcas* and Aramaic *Tabitha*=gazelle], Christian woman of Joppa whom St. Peter raised from the dead. She made clothes for the poor. Acts 9.36–43.

Dorchester, Guy Carleton, 1st Baron: see CARLETON, GUY.

Dorchester (dôr'chĭstər), municipal borough (1971 pop. 13,737), county town of Dorset, S central England. Dorchester is a busy agricultural market, especially for sheep and lambs. Printing, leatherworking, brewing, and the manufacture of agricultural machinery are important industries. Nearby is Maiden Castle, a fortification originally built in prehistoric times. In Roman times Dorchester was called Durnovaria; Maumbury Rings was a Roman amphitheater. Baron Jeffreys of Wem held his Bloody Assizes in the town in 1685. It was also the site of the 1834 trial of the "Tolpuddle Martyrs," important in the history of British trade unionism. Thomas Hardy lived in Dorchester, which is the "Casterbridge" of his Wessex novels. In 1974, Dorchester became part of the new nonmetropolitan county of Dorset.

Dorchester, Mass.: see BOSTON.

Dorchester Heights National Historic Site: see NATIONAL PARKS AND MONUMENTS (table).

Dordogne (dôrdô'nyə), department (1968 pop. 374,073), SW France. PÉRIGUEUX is the capital.

Dordogne, river, c.305 mi (490 km) long, rising near the Puy de Sancy in the Auvergne Mts., S central France. It flows southwest to join the Garonne River N of Bordeaux and to form the Gironde. The upper and middle Dordogne valley has become a popular tourist attraction. There are famous vineyards along the river's lower course.

Dordrecht (dôr'drĕkht) or **Dort** (dôrt), city (1971 pop. 100,935), South Holland prov., SW Netherlands, at the point where the Lower Merwede divides to form the Noord and Oude Maas (Old Meuse) rivers. An important rail junction and river port, it has shipyards and manufactures heavy machinery, clothing, and chemicals. Founded in the early 11th cent., Dordrecht was the scene (1572) of the meeting of the Estates of Holland that proclaimed William the Silent stadtholder. The Synod of Dort, held there in 1618–19, condemned the REMONSTRANTS. Dordrecht has a 14th-century Gothic church (Groote Kerk) and an art museum. The statesman Jan de Witt was born there.

Doré, Gustave (güstäv' dôrā'), 1832–83, French illustrator, engraver, painter, and sculptor. He is best known for his highly imaginative and dramatic illustrations. At first he did his own engraving on wood, but as his success grew, his later work was done in collaboration with numerous engravers. His lively illustrations for some 120 books, including *Paradise Lost,* the *Divine Comedy* (1861), *Don Quixote* (1862), the Bible (1866), Balzac's *Droll Tales,* the works of Rabelais, the *Fables* of La Fontaine, and other classics, are still admired. He particularly excelled in weird, fantastic scenes. Less popular today are his works in painting and sculpture. See study by Nigel Gosling (1974).

Doria, Andrea (ändrā'ä dō'rēä), b. 1466 or 1468, d. 1560, Italian admiral and statesman, of an ancient family prominent in the history of Genoa. He started his career as a CONDOTTIERE and in the ITALIAN WARS fought for Francis I of France. In 1528 he fell out with Francis and went over to Charles V, Holy Roman emperor and King of Spain, under the condition that the independence of Genoa be preserved. Doria became (1528) virtual dictator of Genoa, but even under the constitution that he imposed the republican institutions were preserved. He mercilessly suppressed conspiracies against himself (1547, 1548) and ended factional strife. As admiral of the fleet, Doria assisted the Spanish against the Turks and the pirate BARBAROSSA. He helped Charles V in taking Tunis from Barbarossa in 1535 but failed at Algiers in 1541. In 1559 he recovered, with French aid, Corsica for Genoa.

Dorians, people of ancient Greece. Their name was mythologically derived from Dorus, son of HELLEN. Originating in the northwestern mountainous region of Epirus and SW Macedonia, they migrated through central Greece and into the Peloponnesus probably between 1100 and 950 B.C., defeating and displacing the Achaeans. They rapidly extended their influence to Crete and established colonies in Italy, Sicily, and Asia Minor. Sparta and Crete are generally considered as having had the most typical form of Dorian rule—the invaders maintained their separate societies and subjected and enslaved the conquered population. The arrival of the Dorians marked the disruption of the earlier Greek culture and the beginning of a period of decline. Although the cultural level of the Dorians was below that of the Achaeans, the Dorians did contribute to the culture of Greece, e.g., in drama, poetry, sculpture, and especially in the huge stone buildings that marked the beginning of the Doric style of architecture.

Doric order, earliest of the orders of architecture developed by the Greeks and the one that they employed for most buildings. It is generally believed that the column and its capital derive from an earlier architecture in wood. The cornice details, which have a resemblance to carpentry forms, have also led to the theory of its origin in wooden forms. The type had arrived at a definite form in the 7th cent. B.C., but further improvements produced the perfected order of the 5th cent. B.C. as it appeared in the PARTHENON and the PROPYLAEA at Athens. It continued to be used by the Greeks until about the 2d cent. B.C. The Greek Doric column has no base. Its massive shaft, generally treated with 20 flutes, terminates in a simple CAPITAL composed of a group of annulets, a projecting curved molding called the echinus, and a square slab or abacus at the top. The entablature, which is generally about one third the column height, consists of a plain architrave, a frieze ornamented with channeled triglyphs between which are square spaces or metopes sometimes used for sculpture, and a cornice. The cornice has projecting blocks or mutules in its exposed lower surface or soffit, above which is a plain vertical face or corona, finished by a group of crowning moldings. The proportions, heavy in the earliest Doric columns, became more slender in the perfected type, the entasis became less sharp, and the echinus projection was diminished. The Roman Doric, while derived from the Greek, was probably also influenced by a simple and slender column developed by the Etruscans. It was infrequently used, but examples are seen in the Colosseum and the theater of Marcellus. The column differs from the Greek in its addition of a base and in changes in the capital profile. The 16th-century Italians established as a Tuscan order a form of simplified Doric in which the column had a simpler base and was unfluted, while both capital and entablature were without adornments. For the other Greek orders see IONIC ORDER and CORINTHIAN ORDER. See also ORDERS OF ARCHITECTURE.

Dorion, Sir Antoine Aimé (äNtwän' ĕmā' dôryôN'), 1818–91, Canadian politician and jurist, b. Lower Canada (Quebec). In 1854 he was elected to the Canadian Assembly and held several cabinet posts before confederation (1867). Although an opponent of confederation on the grounds that it would imperil French Canadian interests, he accepted it when dominion status had been won. In the Liberal government of Alexander Mackenzie he briefly held (1873) the post of minister of justice, resigning to accept appointment (1874) as chief justice of the court of Queen's Bench, Quebec. Dorion presided over this court until his death.

Doriot, Jacques (zhäk dôryō'), 1888–?, French collaborator during the German occupation of France in World War II. For many years he served as the mayor of Saint-Denis, a Paris suburb. He was also a Communist leader in the chamber of deputies. In 1934 he was expelled from the Communist party for advocating an alliance with other leftist parties. Enormously popular, he was reelected to the chamber of deputies despite his split with the Communists. He soon became a virulent opponent of the Communists and organized (1936) a party on the extreme right, the French Popular party. By that time a strong supporter of Adolf Hitler, Doriot came into his own after the German defeat (1940) of France in World War II. Treated coolly by the Vichy government, but backed by the German occupation authorities, he organized a youth movement, recruited for a French legion to fight Russia, and sought to control the French laborers who had been sent to work in Germany. He fled (1944) to Germany after the overthrow of the Vichy government. Early in 1945 he was reported to have been killed in an air raid.

Doris, small mountainous district, central Greece, inland between the Gulf of Corinth and the Malian Gulf. It was the traditional homeland of the Dorians, who may, in fact, have paused there during their invasion of Greece. Sparta gave Doris military aid during the 5th cent. B.C.

Dorking, urban district (1971 pop. 22,354), Surrey, SE England. It is a market town and residential suburb of London. Leith Hill, the highest point in SE England (965 ft/294 m), is nearby. The composer Ralph Vaughan Williams lived in Dorking and founded the annual Leith Hill music festival.

Dormont, borough (1970 pop. 12,856), Allegheny co., SW Pa., a residential suburb of Pittsburgh; settled c.1790, inc. 1909.

dormouse, name for Old World nocturnal RODENTS of the family Gliridae. There are many dormouse species, classified in several genera. Many resemble small squirrels. Dormice sleep deeply during the day, and European species hibernate for nearly six months of the year; their name is derived from the French *dormir,* "to sleep." Best known is the common dormouse, or hazelmouse, *Muscardinus avellanarius,* of Europe and W Asia, which resembles a mouse with a bushy tail. It is up to 4 in. (10 cm) long excluding the 2-in. (5-cm) tail, with rounded ears, large eyes, and thick, soft, reddish brown fur. Social animals, hazelmice build neighboring nests of leaves and grasses in bushes and thickets. They feed on insects, berries, seeds, and nuts, and are especially partial to hazelnuts. The European, or fat, dormouse, *Glis glis,* is the largest of the family reaching a length of 8 in. (20 cm) excluding the tail; it has a very thick coat of grayish fur and becomes extremely fat in autumn. It is found in forested regions of Europe and W Asia and lives in hollow trees. The ancient Romans raised it in captivity for food. There are many dormouse species in Africa. The spiny dormice of S Asia belong to a different rodent family, the Platacanthomyidae; they have spines mixed with their fur. True dormice are classified in the phylum CHORDATA, subphylum Vertebrata, class Mammalia, order Rodentia, family Gliridae.

Dornoch (dôr'nŏkh, –nŏk), burgh (1971 pop. 838), county town of Sutherlandshire, N Scotland, on Dornoch Firth. It is a summer resort. A former ecclesiastical center, Dornoch has a 13th-century cathedral (rebuilt in the 19th cent.). The last burning for witchcraft in Scotland took place in Dornoch in 1722. In 1975, Dornoch became part of the new Highland region.

Dorpat: see TARTU, USSR.

Dorr, Thomas Wilson, 1805–54, leader of Dorr's Rebellion (1842) in Rhode Island, b. Providence. After studying law under Chancellor Kent in New York he practiced in Providence. Although born of a wealthy Whig family, he became leader of the popular movement for universal manhood suffrage. Rhode Island, still governed under the colonial charter of 1663, restricted the vote to men owning $134 in land. Thus, most of the townspeople, whose numbers had greatly increased with the growth of industry, were disenfranchised. Since the ruling conservatives were deaf to pleas for reform, Dorr's party called a constitutional convention (Oct., 1841). The legislature called a rival convention, which drafted a new constitution, known as the Freemen's Constitution, making some concession to democratic demands. It was defeated in a state referendum by the opposition of the Dorrites. Their own convention drafted the People's Constitution, which was soon overwhelmingly approved in another referendum. Both the conventions and referendums had been extralegal, but the Dorrites claimed that their constitution had been approved in the referendum by a majority of those entitled to vote under the old charter. Early in 1842 both Dorr's followers and the charter government forces elected and organized governments, Dorr heading one and Samuel H. King the other. The Federal government declined to interfere. In May, Dorr resorted to a show of arms. After an abortive assault on the Providence armory, his government collapsed and he fled the state. King declared martial law, many Dorrites were arrested, and the leader himself was indicted for high treason. Minor armed clashes and demonstrations caused much excitement. The conservatives, finally convinced of the strength of Dorr's cause, called yet another convention. A new constitution, greatly liberalizing voting requirements, was accepted by both parties. On its approval by the people in 1843, Dorr returned, was found guilty, and sentenced (1844) to solitary confinement at hard labor for life. The harshness of the sentence was widely condemned, and in 1845 Dorr, broken in health, was released. He was restored to his civil rights in 1851, and in 1854 the court judgment against him was set aside. See Don King, *The Life and Times of Thomas Wilson Dorr* (1859, repr. 1969); A. M. Mowry, *The Dorr War* (1901, repr. 1968); A. M. Schlesinger, Jr., *The Age of Jackson* (1945); M. E. Gettleman, *Dorr Rebellion* (1973).

Dorrego, Manuel (mänwĕl' dôr-rā'gō), 1787–1828, Argentine statesman and soldier, governor of Buenos Aires province (1820, 1827–28). After serving for a time in the War of Independence, he returned (1816) to Buenos Aires and became a journalist. He attacked the government of Juan Martín de Pueyrredón and was banished (1817). Returning to Buenos Aires in 1820, he was provisional governor of the province (July–Sept., 1820). A leading advocate of federalism, he opposed the unitarian administration of Bernardino Rivadavia. After Juan Facundo QUIROGA forced Rivadavia's resignation and the dissolution of the national government, Dorrego became governor of Buenos Aires (Aug., 1827). He accepted (1828) on behalf of the nation the treaty of peace with Brazil. His constitutional government was overthrown (Dec., 1828) by Juan LAVALLE, and Dorrego was summarily executed. This action led to a reprisal by Juan Manuel de ROSAS, who claimed to be Dorrego's avenger.

Dorr's Rebellion: see DORR, THOMAS WILSON.

D'Ors, Eugenio: see ORS, EUGENIO D'.

D'Orsay, Alfred Guillaume Gabriel, count: see ORSAY, ALFRED GUILLAUME GABRIEL, COUNT D'.

Dorset, Charles Sackville, 6th **earl of:** see SACKVILLE, CHARLES.

Dorset, Marion, 1872–1935, American biochemist, b. Columbia, Tenn.; grad. Univ. of Tenn. (B.S., 1893) and Columbian (now George Washington) Univ. (M.D. 1896). He began working as a researcher for the U.S. Dept. of Agriculture in 1894 and became chief of the biochemical division in 1904. He made important discoveries in bacterial toxins, diseases of animals, and disinfectants, and pioneered work in the inspection of meat food products. He was co-discoverer of the virus that causes hog cholera and later developed a serum to prevent it.

Dorset, Thomas Sackville, 1st **earl of:** see SACKVILLE, THOMAS, 1ST EARL OF DORSET.

Dorset sheep, medium-sized breed developed in England; the only major breed in which both rams and ewes are horned. It has been introduced into many areas of the United States, although it has failed to gain widespread popularity there.

Dorsetshire, county (1971 pop. 361,213), SW England, on the English Channel. The county seat is DORCHESTER. The rolling country is crossed by the North Dorset and South Dorset downs, chalk ranges running east and west. The rocky coastline has a fine harbor at POOLE. The fertile valleys (the Vale of Blackmore, the Stour, and the Frome) are devoted to agriculture. Sheep, cattle, pigs, and poultry are raised, and barley, kale, wheat, oats, beans, and peas are grown. There is also dairy farming. Portland and Purebeck marble are quarried in Dorsetshire. The county's pre-Roman antiquities include MAIDEN CASTLE. Dorset was part of the Anglo-Saxon kingdom of WESSEX. Thomas Hardy was born in Dorsetshire and treats the region in some of his novels. In 1974, Dorsetshire was reorganized as a nonmetropolitan county.

Dort, Netherlands: see DORDRECHT.

Dorticós Torrado, Osvaldo (ōsväl'dō dōrtēkōs' tōr-rä'thō), 1919–, president of Cuba (1959–). A prosperous lawyer, he participated in Fidel Castro's revolutionary movement and was imprisoned (1958). He escaped and fled to Mexico, returning to Cuba after Castro's triumph (1959). As minister of laws (1959) in the new government, he played a major role in formulating Cuban policies. He was appointed president the same year. Noted for his intellect and competence, he wielded considerable influence, serving as a member of the secretariat of the central committee of Cuba's Communist party.

Dortmund (dôrt'mŏŏnt), city (1970 pop. 639,634), North Rhine-Westphalia, W West Germany, a port on the Dortmund-Ems Canal. It is an industrial center in the RUHR district. Its manufactures include iron, steel, and beer. Coal is mined nearby. First mentioned c.885, Dortmund flourished from the 13th cent. as a member of the Hanseatic League but later (17th cent.) declined. From the mid-19th cent. the city grew as an industrial center. It was badly damaged during World War II. Outstanding buildings include the Reinold church (begun in the 13th cent.) and a large convention hall (Ger. *Westfalenhalle*), built from 1950 to 1952. The city has a university and a teachers college.

Dortmund-Ems Canal (dôrt'mŏŏnt-ĕms), waterway, 165 mi (266 km) long, NW West Germany, from Dortmund to Emden. Built from 1892 to 1899, it connects the industrial RUHR district with the Ems River and the North Sea. It is connected to the Rhine River by two canals.

Dorus: see HELLEN.

Dorval (dôrväl'), city (1971 pop. 20,469), S Que., Canada, on the south shore of Montreal island and on the St. Lawrence River. It is the site of Montreal international airport.

Dorylaeum (dŏrĭlē'əm), ancient city of N Phrygia, Asia Minor, now in NW Turkey. It was an important trading city of the Romans but later fell to ruins. At this site on July 1, 1097, the Christians of the First Crusade defeated the Seljuk Turks. Many scholars hold that the modern Eskisehir is near the site, but the question has not been settled.

Dos Passos, John Randolph (dəs păs'əs), 1844–1917, American lawyer, b. Philadelphia. He was admitted to the bar in 1865 and moved (1867) to New York City, where he conducted his practice. His *Treatise on the Law of Stockbrokers and Stock Exchanges* (1882) became a standard work. Dos Passos was a pioneer in the organization and development of the modern TRUST company, and in 1891 he helped to organize the American Sugar Refining

Company (the "sugar trust") for H. O. Havemeyer. He opposed the Sherman Anti-Trust Act in *Commercial Trusts* (1901) and vigorously advocated extensive legal reforms in *The American Lawyer* (1907). He was the father of John Roderigo Dos Passos.

Dos Passos, John Roderigo, 1896-1970, American novelist, b. Chicago, grad. Harvard, 1916. His first successful novel, *Three Soldiers* (1921), belonged to the group of socially conscious novels of disillusionment that appeared after World War I. With *Manhattan Transfer* (1925) his major creative period began. Intertwining accounts of a succession of unrelated characters, this novel presents a composite picture of the meaninglessness and decadence of the life of the typical New Yorker of the early 1920s. In his finest achievement, the trilogy *U.S.A.* (1937), composed of *The 42nd Parallel* (1930), *1919* (1932), and *The Big Money* (1936), he developed the kaleidoscopic technique of *Manhattan Transfer*, by skillfully weaving together narration, STREAM OF CONSCIOUSNESS, biographies of representative figures, and quotations from newspapers and magazines, Dos Passos presented the first three decades of the 20th cent. in America. After *U.S.A.* the radical leftwing views that strongly colored his earlier works gave way to a conservative social philosophy. In his second trilogy, *District of Columbia* (1952), which includes *Adventures of a Young Man* (1939), *Number One* (1943), and *The Grand Design* (1949), he defends many of the principles he had previously criticized. In general, his later works lack the power and cohesion of his earlier novels, although *Midcentury* (1961) again skillfully presents the conflicts of contemporary society. His nonfiction works include *Tour of Duty* (1946), *Men Who Made the Nation* (1957), *Mr. Wilson's War* (1963), and *Easter Island: Island of Enigmas* (1971). See his autobiographical *The Best Times* (1967); biographies by J. H. Wrenn (1961) and Melvin Landsberg (1972); study by J. D. Brantley (1968).

Dosso Dossi (dôs'sō dôs'sē), 1479?-1542, Italian painter of the Ferrarese school, whose real name was Giovanni di Niccolò de Luteri. He may have been a pupil of Lorenzo Costa, but was certainly influenced by Giorgione, Titian, and Raphael. He often collaborated with his brother Battista, a landscape painter. Dosso Dossi is first recorded in Mantua, but after 1514 he executed many decorative works for the ducal palace and churches of Ferrara, including frescoes, pictures, and cartoons for tapestries. Both his landscapes and portraits show originality and imagination. He was a friend of Ariosto, who mentions him in *Orlando Furioso*. His works include *Circe in the Woods* (Borghese Villa); *The Three Ages of Man* (Metropolitan Mus.); *The Standard Bearer, Scene from a Legend*, and *Saint Lucretia* (National Gall. of Art, Washington, D.C.). See E. G. Gardner, *The Painters of the School of Ferrara* (1911); Felton Gibbons, *Dosso and Battista Dossi* (1968).

Dost Muhammad (dōst mōōhäm'mäd), 1793-1863, emir of Afghanistan. He and his family struggled to get the emirate for years before he finally succeeded in establishing himself in 1826. He waged continual war with the Sikhs, and trouble with the British, beginning in 1838, led to the first (1839-42) of the Afghan Wars. Defeated, he fled to India, but he later returned, and it was at least with British acquiescence that he regained the throne. Friendly relations were resumed and an agreement was reached in 1855, but Britain firmly refused to support him against the Persians. A strong, capable ruler, he helped to build Afghanistan and sought to play Russian interests against the British.

Dostoyevsky or **Dostoevsky, Feodor Mikhailovich** (fyô'dər mēkhī'ləvĭch dəstəyĕf'skē), 1821-81, Russian novelist, one of the towering figures of world literature. Dostoyevsky was born and raised in Moscow by Russian Orthodox parents. His father, a military surgeon and an alcoholic of harsh, despotic temperament, was brutally slain (1839) by his own serfs. This event haunted Dostoyevsky all his life and perhaps accounts in part for the preoccupation with murder and guilt in his writings. Dostoyevsky attended military engineering school in St. Petersburg and upon graduation entered government service as a draftsman. This career he soon abandoned for writing. His first published work, *Poor Folk* (1846), which brought him immediate critical and public recognition, reveals his characteristic compassion for the downtrodden. His second novel *The Double* (1846), less favorably received, shows the profound insight into human character that dominates his later works. At about this time Dostoyevsky became involved with a group of radical utopians. The discovery of their illegal printing press brought about their arrest and condemnation. The prisoners were reprieved but were forced to take part in a pre-execution ceremony before the reprieve was read to them. Dostoyevsky was sentenced to four years at hard labor in a Siberian penal colony. During this harrowing period he suffered great physical and mental pain, including repeated attacks of epilepsy. The prison experience worked a profound change of heart in him. He abandoned his belief in the liberal, atheistic ideologies of Western Europe and turned wholeheartedly to religion and to the belief that Orthodox Russia was destined to be the spiritual leader of the world. After several years of obligatory military service in Siberia, he was allowed to return to St. Petersburg. With him was the widow he had married in Siberia and her son. Dostoyevsky joined his beloved brother Mikhail in editing the magazine *Time*, which serialized *The Insulted and The Injured* (1861-62) and the record of his experience in the penal colony, *The House of the Dead* (1862). He made several trips to Western Europe. One result was *Winter Notes on Summer Impressions* (1863), reflecting his severely anti-Western attitudes. Financial troubles, combined with a turbulent love affair and a passion for roulette, led to a nightmarish period in Germany, partly described in the short novel *The Gambler* (1866). In 1864 his unhappy marriage ended with the death of his wife. The same year his financial problems increased when his brother died and Dostoyevsky assumed responsibility for the remaining family. In 1867 he married his young secretary, who gave him profound affection and understanding and greatly enriched his later years. *Notes from the Underground* (1864), a detailed study of neurotic suffering, began the greatest period of Dostoyevsky's literary career. *Crime and Punishment*, a brilliant portrait of sin, remorse, and redemption through sacrifice, followed in 1866. His next novel, *The Idiot* (1868), concerns a Christ figure, a meek, human epileptic whose effect on those around him is tragic. *The Possessed* (1871-72) is a violent denunciation of the leftists and revolutionaries that Dostoyevsky had previously admired. In *A Raw Youth* (1875) he described decay within family relationships and the inability of science to deal with the primary need of human beings: a purpose for living beyond the mere struggle for sustenance. Both of these themes are central to the enormously complex plot and character development of his masterpiece, *The Brothers Karamazov* (1879-80), generally thought to be one of the finest novels ever written. A profound psychologist and philosopher, he depicted with remarkable insight the depth and complexity of the human soul. His powerful though generally humorless narrative style, his understanding of the intricacies of character, especially the pathological conscience, and his amplification of sin and redemption made him a giant among novelists and, in the realm of ideas, a precursor of Freudian psychological analysis. Dostoyevsky died of lung hemorrhage complicated by an attack of epilepsy. The translations of his novels by Constance Garnett have long been standard. In recent years new translations have appeared, e.g., those by David Magarshack. See his *Diary of a Writer* (tr. 1949) and diaries and notebooks from 1860 to 1881, ed. by C. R. Proffer (1972); his letters, ed. by E. C. Mayne (1964); the notebooks for his novels, ed. by Edward Wasiolek (5 vol., tr. 1967-71); biographies by E. J. Simmons (1940) and Avrahm Yarmolinsky (1971); studies by Edward Wasiolek (1964), Konstantin Mochulsky (1947, tr. 1967), Vasily Rozanov (1891, tr. 1972), Janko Laurim (1943, repr. 1973), and J. C. Powys (1946, repr. 1973); collection of critical essays, ed. by Rene Wellek (1962).

Dothan (dō'thən), city (1970 pop. 36, 733), seat of Houston co., SE Ala., near the Fla. line, in a timber and peanut-growing area; inc. 1885. It is the industrial and medical center of the region. Manufactures include lumber products, furniture, toys, farming tools, truck and trailer bodies, and textile goods. A nuclear power plant, a state technical junior college, and hot mineral springs are located in Dothan. A national peanut festival is held there every October.

Dothan (dō'thăn) or **Dothaim** (dōthā'ĭm), ancient city, central Palestine, in the uplands NE of Samaria. It was in the vicinity of Dothan that Joseph was sold into slavery and that the Syrians were blinded by Elisha's prayer. The site has been partially excavated. Gen. 37.17; 2 Kings 6.13; Judith 4.6; 7.3,18; 8.3.

Dou, Dow, or **Douw, Gerard** or **Gerrit** (all: gä'rärt, gĕr'ĭt dou), 1613-1675, Dutch genre and portrait painter of Leiden. The son of a glass painter, he was apprenticed to an engraver and worked from 1628 to 1631 in the studio of the young Rembrandt. Although he occasionally borrowed Rembrandt's themes, he was more detailed and meticulous in his execution. His scenes of domestic, middle-class life were tremendously popular and often imitated. Among his most famous works are *Evening Light* (Rijks Mus.), *Young Man* (The Hague), *The Cook* (Louvre), and a self-portrait (Metropolitan Mus.).

Douai (do͞o'ā, do͞oā'), town (1968 pop. 51,567), Nord dept., N France, in French Flanders, on the Scarpe River. It is a major industrial and commercial center of the northern coal region. The chief manufactures are foundry products, wire, boilers, springs, and chemicals. Probably a Roman fortress (*Duacum*) built in the 4th cent., Douai was a possession of the counts of Flanders during the Middle Ages. Because of its prosperity as a center of the cloth trade, the town received a charter (1228) granting some autonomy. With the Hundred Years War (1337-1453) and the resulting curtailment of English wool imports, the town declined and passed in 1384 to the dukes of Burgundy and in 1477 to the Spanish Hapsburgs. Louis XIV seized Douai in 1667, and after the War of the Spanish Succession (1701-14), the town was permanently restored to France by the Peace of Utrecht (1713). Points of interest include the town hall (15th cent.); the belfry (14th cent.); the Palace of Justice (16th and 18th cent.); and St. Peter's Church (16th and 18th cent.). Under the patronage of Philip II of Spain, a Roman Catholic college was established in Douai for English priests. At the college the Old Testament of the Douay Bible was prepared in 1609.

Douaumont (do͞o-ōmôN'), village (1968 pop. 12), Meuse dept., NE France. It was part of the VERDUN battlefield in World War I, and its cemetery, now a national memorial, contains the graves of 300,000 unidentified French soldiers.

double bass, bowed stringed musical instrument, the contrabass of the modern orchestral string section. It originated as a double-bass VIOL, an instrument described as early as 1566. A true double-bass

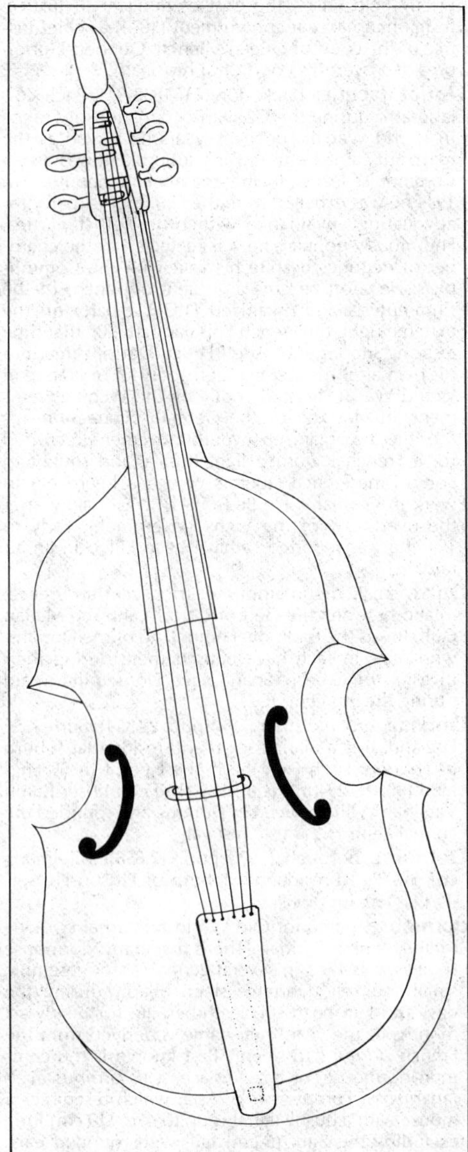

Double bass

VIOLIN appeared during the 18th cent. but was rejected as unwieldy and of poor tonal quality. The present double bass is tuned in fourths and usually has a flat back and sloping shoulders but has never attained a definitive form. The bow, the last to give up its convex shape, was long held palm upward like the viol bow, but the violin style is now customary. The double bass is a TRANSPOSING INSTRUMENT. Indispensable in the orchestra, it also has a place in the dance band. The illustration (opposite page) of the double bass is in proportion to the illustrations accompanying the viol and violin entries.

double bassoon: see CONTRABASSOON.

Doubleday, Abner, 1819-93, alleged originator of BASEBALL and Union general in the American Civil War, b. Saratoga co., N.Y., grad. West Point, 1842. The A. G. Mills commission (1905-8) investigated the origin of baseball and reported that in 1839 Doubleday invented the game at Cooperstown, N.Y.—where the National Baseball Hall of Fame and Museum now stands. The report has been criticized by many, who point out that a children's game similar to baseball had been played long before Doubleday's time. Doubleday served in the Mexican War and in the Civil War. He saw action at Fort Sumter (where he aimed the first shot in defense), Antietam, Fredericksburg, and Gettysburg. He wrote *Reminiscences of Forts Sumter and Moultrie in 1860-61* (1876) and *Chancellorsville and Gettysburg* (1882). See R. S. Holzman, *General "Baseball" Doubleday* (1955).

double solitaire: see SOLITAIRE.

double star: see BINARY STAR.

Double Tenth: see WU-CH'ANG, China.

Doubs (do͞o), department (1968 pop. 426,363), E France, in FRANCHE-COMTÉ, bordering on the Jura mts. and on Switzerland. BESANÇON is the capital.

Doubs, river, c.270 mi (435 km) long, rising in the Jura mts., E France, and flowing northeast, forming part of the French-Swiss border, then looping into W Switzerland before turning back into France where it meanders southwest to empty into the Saône River. Lake of Brenets, a natural widening in the river, is a tourist center; at the northern end of the lake the river drops 88 ft (27 m). The Doubs is heavily canalized and passes through several industrial cities including Montbéliard and Besançon.

Dougga (do͞o'gə), village, Tunisia, SW of Tunis. It is a tourist spot noted for the ruins of the ancient city of Thugga, including a Punic mausoleum (2d cent. B.C.); temples, arches, a theater, a circus, and an aqueduct of Roman times; and a Byzantine fortress.

doughnuts, small sweetened cakes of leavened dough, deep-fried in oil, sometimes called friedcakes or crullers. In some places a distinction is made between a doughnut and a friedcake, the former being made with yeast and the latter with buttermilk and soda or sweet milk and baking powder. The three names are generally used in modern cookbooks without distinction.

Doughty, Sir Arthur George (dou'tē), 1860-1936, Canadian historian and archivist, b. England. As archivist (1904-35) of the dominion, he largely created the archives of the nation. He wrote *The Canadian Archives and Its Activities* (1924). Doughty's historical works include *The Fortress of Quebec* (1904), *The Cradle of New France* (1908), and *The Acadian Exiles* (1915). With Adam Shortt he edited *Documents Relating to the Constitutional History of Canada, 1759-1791* (1907, rev. ed. 1918) and *Canada and Its Provinces* (23 vol., 1913-17).

Doughty, Charles Montagu (dō'tē, dou'tē), 1843-1926, English author and traveler. He is best known for his *Travels in Arabia Deserta* (1888), describing his life among the Bedouins. Now considered a masterpiece of travel literature, the book received little attention until it was reissued in 1921 with an introduction by T. E. LAWRENCE. Doughty's poems include the epic *The Dawn in Britain* (6 vol., 1906). See biography by D. G. Hogarth (1928, repr. 1971).

Doughty, Thomas, 1793-1856, American painter of the HUDSON RIVER SCHOOL, b. Philadelphia. Although self-taught, he was one of the first American landscape painters to win widespread recognition at home and abroad. His paintings, few in number, are mostly of river scenery. Among the best are *On the Hudson* and *A River Glimpse* (Metropolitan Mus.); *A View of the Schuylkill* (Edinburgh Mus.); and others in the Corcoran Gallery, the Brooklyn Museum, and the Pennsylvania Academy of the Fine Arts. See F. A. Sweet, *The Hudson River School* (1945).

Douglas, Archibald, 5th earl of Angus, 1449-1514, Scottish nobleman. He was a member of the faction that allied with Edward IV of England in opposition to the influence of Robert Cochrane, favorite of JAMES III. He won the nickname Bell-the-Cat by personally capturing Cochrane in 1482. He supported Alexander STUART, duke of Albany, in his abortive attempt (1484) to seize the throne, but he retained his position and estates. In 1488 he was a leader in the rebellion that replaced James III with James IV, and he served the latter as lord chancellor from 1493 to 1498. In 1513, Angus is recorded as having advised James of the near certainty of defeat at Flodden Field. His two sons were killed in that battle, and he was succeeded by his grandson.

Douglas, Archibald, 6th earl of Angus, 1489-1557, Scottish nobleman; grandson of Archibald Douglas, 5th earl of Douglas. His marriage (1514) to MARGARET TUDOR alienated the Scottish noblemen and caused Margaret to lose the regency to John STUART, duke of Albany. A struggle for control of the young James V ensued between Angus and Albany, with James's mother, Margaret, favoring first her husband, then Albany. In 1526, Angus seized the young king and held him until James escaped in 1528. Margaret had meanwhile (1527) divorced Angus, and, deprived of his lands because of his alliance with Henry VIII, he left for England. After King James's death in 1542, Angus returned to Scotland, was restored to power, and was soon fighting against England. But he continued to correspond with Henry and to contest the power both of the regent James Hamilton, earl of Arran, and his successor, the dowager queen, Mary of Guise.

Douglas, Archibald, 8th earl of Angus, 1555-88, Scottish nobleman; grandnephew of Archibald Douglas, 6th earl of Angus. During the regency (1572-78) of his uncle, James Douglas, 4th earl of MORTON, he held a number of important positions, but when Morton fell in 1581, Angus was declared guilty of treason and escaped to England. He returned to Scotland (1582) and was reconciled with King James VI. As an ardent Presbyterian, he opposed James STUART, earl of Arran, and in 1584 after an unsuccessful attempt to remove Arran from power, Angus again fled to England. In the next year he took part in another rebellion, which brought about the downfall of Arran.

Douglas, Archibald, 3d earl of Douglas, 1328?-1400?, Scottish nobleman; illegitimate son of Sir James de Douglas, lord of Douglas. In 1361 he became constable of Edinburgh and in 1364 and 1368 he was warden of the Western Marches. He served as ambassador to France in 1369 and 1371. From 1380 until his death he both arranged truces with the English and engaged them in battle. In 1388, at the death of James Douglas, 2d earl of Douglas and Mar, he succeeded to the earldom and the Douglas estates. He had already acquired—by grant, purchase, and inheritance—Galloway and the Bothwell estates. At his death the Douglas family was the most powerful in Scotland.

Douglas, Archibald, 4th earl of Douglas, 1369-1424, Scottish nobleman, called Tyneman [loser]; 2d son of Archibald Douglas, 3d earl of Douglas. In 1390 he married Margaret Stuart, daughter of Robert III. He held Edinburgh against the English when Henry IV invaded in 1400. In 1402 Douglas was tried and acquitted of the murder of David STUART, duke of Rothesay, heir apparent to the throne. Later that year Douglas led a Scottish army against the English and was taken prisoner by Sir Henry PERCY at Homildon Hill. He was then induced to join the Percy conspiracy against Henry IV, but at the battle of Shrewsbury (1403) he was taken prisoner by Henry and held until ransomed in 1408. From 1412 to 1422, Douglas continued his border warfare against England and was a member of several delegations of Scottish nobles who tried, unsuccessfully, to ransom their young king, JAMES I, from the English. In 1423 he and his Scottish contingent joined the French against the English. He was made lieutenant general of the French army and duke of Touraine. In 1424 the allies were defeated at Verneuil, and Douglas was slain.

Douglas, Archibald, 5th earl of Douglas, 1391?-1439, Scottish nobleman; son of Archibald Douglas, 4th earl of Douglas. He fought in France for the French against the English in 1421 and persuaded his father in 1423 to go to France. Although Douglas was one of the Scottish nobles who accompanied JAMES I home when that king returned (1424) from his long English captivity, James so distrusted the Douglas power and loyalty that the earl was twice imprisoned for short times by royal order. After James's death in 1437, Douglas was lieutenant general of the kingdom in the minority of James II and the most powerful man in Scotland.

Douglas, Clifford Hugh, 1879-1952, English engineer and social economist, educated at Cambridge Univ. Author of the economic theory of SOCIAL CREDIT, he became (1935) chief reconstruction adviser to the Social Credit government of Alberta, Canada, but, differing with some of its policies, he shortly resigned. His books include *Economic Democracy* (1920), *Social Credit* (1924), *The Monopoly of Credit* (1931), *The Use of Money* (1935), and *The Alberta Experiment: An Interim Survey* (1937).

Douglas, David, 1798-1834, Scottish botanist. He made several journeys in North America between 1823 and 1834 to study American plants and sent to Scotland more than 200 plants and seeds then unknown in Europe. His journal (1914) is of historical as well as of scientific importance, because he was one of the earliest travelers in the Oregon country and in California. In 1834 he traveled to Puget Sound and the Fraser River and then went to the Hawaiian Islands. The Douglas fir, which he observed c.1825, was named for him. See biography by William Morwood (1973).

Douglas, Gawin (gä'wĭn) or **Gavin** (găv'ĭn), 1474?-1522, Scottish poet and churchman; son of Archibald Douglas, 5th earl of Angus. He is considered one of the great medieval Scottish poets. Douglas was Bishop of Dunkeld. Jealousy held by Scottish nobles toward the Douglas family interrupted his ecclesiastical career, and from 1515 his life was torn by political quarrels. His poetry was largely composed prior to this, in the more peaceful period of his life. *The Palace of Honor* and *King Hart* (i.e., *Heart*; the latter is possibly not his) are allegories of considerable skill, but his best work is his translation of the *Aeneid*. One of the first English translations made directly from the original, Douglas's version is remarkably accurate, and its medieval tone only enhances its charm. The greatest parts of the whole poem, however, are the original prologues to each of the books. Douglas is little read today because the Scottish dialect in which he wrote is extremely difficult to understand. See selections from his work, ed. by D. F. C. Coldwell (1964).

Douglas, George, pseud. of **George Douglas Brown,** 1869-1902, English novelist, b. Scotland. His reputation rests on his single novel, *The House with the Green Shutters* (1901), a somber story of Scottish life. See study by James Veitch (1952).

Douglas, Sir Howard, 1776-1861, British general and colonial administrator. He was a distinguished teacher of military strategy and an important authority on military and naval engineering. After a command in Canada (1795-99), he served intermittently as commandant of the senior department of the Royal Military College and as inspector general of instructions there; in the meantime he participated (1809-12) in the Peninsular War. While governor of New Brunswick (1823-31) he secured a charter for King's College at Fredericton (later the Univ. of New Brunswick) and attempted to settle the Maine boundary dispute with the United States. He was (1835-40) high commissioner of the Ionian Islands, where he introduced a code of laws modeled on a Greek code. He served in Parliament as a Conservative from 1842 to 1847. Douglas's many technical works include treatises on naval gunnery, steam navigation, armor plating, land fortifications, national defense, and naval maneuvers.

Douglas, James, 2d earl of Douglas and Mar, 1358?-1388, Scottish nobleman; son of William Douglas, 1st earl of Douglas and Mar. In 1373 he married Isabel Stuart, daughter of Robert II. With the aid of a French contingent he made raids on the English border in 1385. In the famous battle of OTTERBURN, celebrated in the ballads *Chevy Chase* and the *Battle of Otterburn*, Douglas himself was killed, but his forces were victorious, and his opponent, Sir Henry Percy, was taken captive.

Douglas, James, 9th earl of Douglas, 1426-88, Scottish nobleman, last earl of Douglas. Following the murder of his brother William, the 8th earl, by JAMES II, he led a rebellion against the king in 1452 but was defeated. He soon entered into a conspiracy with the English, and in 1455 he was again defeated by James. Douglas escaped to England, but in 1484 was captured while on a raid on Scotland and was imprisoned the rest of his life. His lands, which had been confiscated, were granted to another branch of the family, headed by the earls of Angus.

Douglas, James (d. 1581): see MORTON, JAMES DOUGLAS, 4TH EARL OF.

Douglas, James (1658-1712): see HAMILTON, JAMES DOUGLAS, 4TH DUKE OF.

Douglas, James (1662-1711): see QUEENSBERRY, JAMES DOUGLAS, 2D DUKE OF.

Douglas, Sir James, 1803-77, Canadian fur trader and colonial governor, b. British Guiana (now Guyana). As a young man, he went to Canada in the service of the North West Company; soon after its merger (1821) with the Hudson's Bay Company, he accompanied the noted John McLoughlin to the Columbia River country. Rising eventually to chief factor, he succeeded (1846) McLoughlin in command of the Hudson's Bay Company territory W of the Rockies. On Vancouver Island, on the site of the present Victoria, he built (1843) Fort Camosun (later Fort Victoria), which became (1849) the western headquarters for the company. In 1851 he was appointed governor of Vancouver Island, and in 1858 he also became governor of the new colony of British Columbia on the mainland. At this time Douglas severed his long association with the Hudson's Bay Company. His governorship, which extended until 1864, was marked by a firm control of the colonies' affairs, made particularly turbulent by the gold rushes to the Fraser River and to the Cariboo region. Shortly before his retirement he was knighted (1863). See biographies by R. H. Coats and R. E. Gosnell (rev. ed. 1926), W. N. Sage (1930), and Derek Pethick (1969).

Douglas, Sir James de, lord of Douglas, 1286?–1330, Scottish nobleman, called the Black Douglas and Douglas the Good; eldest son of William de Douglas, lord of Douglas. In the war of independence against England he joined ROBERT I and made himself the terror of the border, even burning his own castle of Douglas twice to rid it of English garrisons. He led a force at Bannockburn (1314), and was knighted there. In 1327, Douglas almost captured the young Edward III and succeeded in ending the English campaign. After Robert I died, Douglas started with his king's heart in a casket to bury it in Palestine, but he was killed fighting the Moors in Spain. See biography by I. M. Davis (1974).

Douglas, John Sholto: see QUEENSBERRY, JOHN SHOLTO DOUGLAS, 8TH MARQUESS OF.

Douglas, Norman (George Norman Douglas), 1868–1952, British novelist and essayist, b. Scotland. He spent the years from 1894 to 1896 in diplomatic service in Russia but resigned from the foreign service in 1896. His masterpiece, *South Wind* (1917), which is set on Nepenthe, a literary idealization of Capri, satirizes conventional morality. Other works include *Old Calabria* (1915), *In the Beginning* (1927), and *Good-bye to Western Culture* (1930). Written in a witty, conversational style, all Douglas's works reveal his erudition and his genuine appreciation of the Mediterranean area. See biography by Nancy Cunard (1954); studies by R. M. Dawkins (1952) and R. D. Lindeman (1965).

Douglas, Paul Howard, 1892–, U.S. Senator (1949–67), b. Salem, Mass. An economist, he joined the faculty of the Univ. of Chicago in 1920; was active as a government adviser, especially on problems of wages and social security; and served (1939–42) as alderman on the Chicago city council. In 1942 he enlisted in the U.S. marine corps. A Democrat, he was elected to the U.S. Senate in 1948 and reelected in 1954 and 1960. As Senator, he was a leader of liberal Democrats and was prominent in support of labor and social security legislation. He was defeated for reelection in 1966 by Charles Percy, a Republican. His books include *Real Wages in the United States, 1890–1926* (1930), *The Theory of Wages* (1934), *Social Security in the United States* (1936; 2d ed. 1939), and *Ethics in Government* (1952). See his memoirs (1972).

Douglas, Stephen Arnold, 1813–61, American statesman, b. Brandon, Vt. He was admitted to the bar at Jacksonville, Ill., in 1834. After holding various state and local offices he became a U.S. Representative in 1843, and from 1847 until his death was a U.S. Senator. In the Senate, Douglas was made chairman of the Committee on Territories, an all-important post in the next decade because of the growing battle over the issue of slavery in the territories. For the COMPROMISE OF 1850, Douglas drafted the bills instituting territorial government in New Mexico and Utah, whose citizens were left free to act for themselves on all subjects of legislation (including slavery) not inconsistent with the Constitution. This was the essence of Douglas's doctrine of POPULAR SOVEREIGNTY (a phrase he coined later, in 1854), or Squatter Sovereignty, as its opponents contemptuously called it. When, in the early 1850s, expanding settlement and the great desire for a transcontinental railroad to the Pacific focused attention on the Nebraska region, Douglas proposed a bill in which, as in New Mexico and Utah, all questions of slavery were left to the residents of the new territory. A conference of leaders changed the bill to provide for two territories rather than one, and in this form the KANSAS-NEBRASKA ACT became law in 1854. Douglas believed that popular sovereignty would unite the northern and southern wings of the Democratic party and at the same time settle the slavery issue peacefully. But he had not foreseen the bitter contest that would develop between proslavery and Free-State settlers in KANSAS. In his report on the Kansas situation he blamed the organized interference of interests outside the territory for the failure of popular sovereignty. When James Buchanan decided to support the proslavery Lecompton Constitution (see under LECOMPTON), on which only the proslavery forces in Kansas had voted, Douglas rebelled and in one of his major speeches denounced both the Lecompton Constitution and Buchanan, whom he had formerly supported. It was a courageous and spectacular stand, but his enemies held, unfairly, that Douglas was motivated by political expediency, for he was coming up for reelection in 1858. In this Illinois campaign the "Little Giant," as his admirers called him, was pitted against Abraham LINCOLN. The contest was made memorable by the Lincoln-Douglas debates, which first gained Lincoln a national reputation. Of the seven debates, the second, held at Freeport on Aug. 27, 1858, had the most important consequences. There Lincoln shrewdly put to Douglas a question exposing the inconsistency between Douglas's doctrine of popular sovereignty and the U.S. Supreme Court's decision in the Dred Scott Case—"Can the people of a United States Territory, in any lawful way . . . exclude slavery from its limits prior to the formation of a State constitution?" Had Douglas answered No, in line with the Dred Scott decision, he would have offended many of his constituents and doubtless lost his seat in the Senate. As it was, he replied that people of a territory could exclude slavery, since that institution could not exist for a day without local police regulations and these could be legislated only with their approval. The Republicans won a popular majority in the ensuing election, but the Democrats controlled the legislature, and Douglas was returned to the Senate. However, his Freeport doctrine, as his answer to Lincoln's question was styled, had made him anathema to Southern Democrats. Since they controlled the Senate, he was relieved of the chairmanship of the Committee on Territories. The Democratic national convention at Charleston, S.C., in 1860 adopted his recommendations in a platform advocating nonintervention with slavery in the territories; the demands of William L. Yancey that the Federal government protect the institution were thus rejected, and Yancey and other Southern delegates withdrew. Although Douglas led on all 57 ballots taken there for the presidential nomination he was unable to muster the necessary two thirds of the vote, and the convention adjourned. Reconvening at Baltimore, the Democrats finally chose him only after more Southern delegates withdrew to nominate their own candidate, John C. Breckinridge. Douglas won only 12 electoral votes, although he stood second to the victorious Lincoln in the popular count. In the following months Douglas worked hard to effect a compromise between the sections; when that failed and the Civil War broke out, he vigorously supported Lincoln. One of the greatest orators of his day, he made a speaking tour to rally the people of the Northwest in the crisis, but after an eloquent speech at Springfield, he was stricken with typhoid fever and died. Douglas's reputation suffered with the growth of the Lincoln legend. In recent years, however, historians have asserted that he was one of the few men of his era with a truly national vision, and this was both the basis for his honorable attempts to reconcile differences and for his ultimate political failure, because the age was essentially one of bitter sectional controversy. See his letters, ed. by R. W. Johannsen (1961); biographies by Allen Johnson (1908, repr. 1970), G. M. Capers (1959), and R. W. Johannsen (1973); G. F. Milton, *The Eve of Conflict: Stephen A. Douglas and the Civil War* (1934, repr. 1963); Damon Wells, *Stephen Douglas: The Last Years* (1970).

Douglas, William: see LIDDESDALE, WILLIAM DOUGLAS, KNIGHT OF.

Douglas, William, duke of Queensberry: see QUEENSBERRY, WILLIAM DOUGLAS, 4TH DUKE OF.

Douglas, William, 1st earl of Douglas and Mar, 1327?–1384, Scottish nobleman; nephew of Sir James de Douglas, lord of Douglas. About 1348 he returned to Scotland from France and recaptured the Douglas lands from the English. Later he took part in the negotiations for the ransom and release of DAVID II. In 1354 he succeeded to the estates of his father and uncle and to the lands of his kinsman, William Douglas, Knight of LIDDESDALE, whom he had slain. Douglas engaged in French-incited raids on the English border and fought (1356) for the French in the battle of Poitiers. In 1358 he was made earl of Douglas, and after the accession of Robert II he was made justiciar S of the Forth and received the lands of the earl of Fife. At the death of his wife's brother in 1374 he received the lands and title of the earl of Mar. Douglas had an illegitimate son by Margaret Stuart, countess of Angus in her own right. This was George Douglas, who became 1st earl of Angus.

Douglas, William, 6th earl of Douglas, 1423?–1440, Scottish nobleman, eldest son of Archibald Douglas, 5th earl of Douglas. In answer to an invitation from the young James II, who was at that time controlled by Sir William Crichton and Sir Alexander Livingstone, Douglas and his brother visited the royal castle at Edinburgh and were there beheaded. The judicial murder achieved a temporary break in the wealth and power of the Douglas family. William had been 3d duke of Touraine, lord of Galloway and Annandale, and count of Longinville. Now the earldom passed to James Douglas, son of Archibald Douglas, 3d earl of Douglas, and Galloway went to Margaret, sister of the 6th earl, who eventually married William Douglas, 8th earl. The rest of the lands and titles were lost to the family.

Douglas, William, 8th earl of Douglas, 1425?–1452, Scottish nobleman, son of James Douglas, 7th earl of Douglas. By marrying his cousin Margaret Douglas, the Fair Maid of Galloway, he reunited the two chief estates of his family (which had been divided since the execution of the 6th earl). Through the favor of JAMES II he was able to avenge the death of the 6th earl by partially destroying Sir William Crichton and completely ruining Sir Alexander Livingstone. When Douglas defied James, however, the king himself slew him at Stirling Castle. His brother James succeeded to the title.

Douglas, William de, lord of Douglas, d. 1298, Scottish nobleman. His English estates were confiscated (c.1290) by Edward I when he abducted and married a royal ward, Eleanor, widow of William Ferrers. He opposed the candidacy for the Scottish throne of John de BALIOL (1249–1315) because of Baliol's submissive attitude toward Edward, and he was one of the recalcitrant barons who pressed Baliol into revolt. He was captured (1295) when Berwick castle, which he commanded, fell to the English but regained his freedom and his Scottish lands by swearing fealty to Edward. In 1297 he took part in the revolt of Sir William WALLACE and was again captured by the English. He died in the Tower of London. His eldest son was Sir James de Douglas.

Douglas, William Orville, 1898–, American jurist, Associate Justice of the U.S. Supreme Court (1939–), b. Maine, Minn. He received his law degree from Columbia in 1925 and later was professor of law at Yale. A Democrat, Douglas was appointed (1934) to the Securities and Exchange Commission; as chairman (1937–39) he pursued a vigorous policy of reform. He was prominent as a proponent of the New Deal and was appointed to the Supreme Court by President Franklin Delano Roosevelt. He became known on the court for his fervent support of civil rights, conservation, and civil liberties, particularly the First Amendment guarantees of freedom of speech and press. Consistently liberal, in 1953 he granted a stay of execution to Julius and Ethel Rosenberg, who had been convicted of spying for the Soviet Union and were subsequently executed. The House of Representatives made an unsuccessful attempt to impeach Douglas for this act. Among Douglas's books are case books on business law and works on American law and civil rights, including *We The Judges* (1956) and *A Living Bill of Rights* (1961). An advocate of outdoor life and an enthusiastic traveler, Douglas has written many books on these subjects, including *Men and Mountains* (1950), *Russian Journey* (1956), *My Wilderness* (1962), and *The Three Hundred Year War: A Chronicle of Ecological Disaster* (1972). The first volume of his autobiography appeared in 1974. An anthology (1959) of his supreme court opinions was compiled by Vern Countrymen.

Douglas, municipal borough (1970 pop. 20,385), capital of the Isle of Man, Great Britain. It is a popular resort on the Irish Sea, and tourism is the chief industry. There are also light-engineering, knitting, and carpet-weaving factories. The Tower of Refuge, near the harbor entrance, was built in 1832 by William Hillary, founder of the Royal National Lifeboat Institution. The Manx Museum has a collection of the natural history and antiquities of the Isle of Man.

Douglas. 1 City (1970 pop. 12,462), Cochise co., SE Ariz., at the Mexican border; inc. 1905. The mining and smelting of copper have been important since 1900; the city grew around a copper smelter. Douglas is also a ranching center and a border station, with plants that manufacture wearing apparel and electronic parts. Gypsum and tungsten mines and limestone quarries are in the area. The city has a junior college and an international airport. Its sister city is Agua Prieta, Mexico. 2 City (1970 pop. 10,195), seat of Coffee co., S central Ga.; inc. 1895. It is a livestock and tobacco market, with food-processing plants, mobile home manufacturers, and garment factories. A junior college is there.

Douglas and Mar, James Douglas, 2d **earl of:** see DOUGLAS, JAMES, 2D EARL OF DOUGLAS AND MAR.

Douglas and Mar, William Douglas, 1st **earl of:** see DOUGLAS, WILLIAM, 1ST EARL OF DOUGLAS AND MAR.

Douglas fir: see PINE.

Douglas-Home, Sir Alec (dŭg'ləs-hyōōm) (Alexander Frederick), 1903–, British politician. Educated at Eton and Oxford, he was elected to the House of Commons in 1931 as a Conservative. As parliamentary private secretary (1937–39) to Prime Minister Neville Chamberlain, he supported the latter's policy of appeasement toward Nazi Germany. He lost his Commons seat in 1945; reelected in 1950 he resigned (1951) when he succeeded his father's peerage as the 14th earl of Home. He served as minister of state (1951–55), secretary of state for commonwealth relations (1955–60), and leader of the House of Lords (1957–60). As foreign secretary (1960–63), he pursued a policy of détente with the USSR and worked for the establishment of an independent British nuclear deterrent. In Oct., 1963, he became prime minister after Harold Macmillan's resignation, emerging as the controversial compromise choice of a badly divided Conservative party. The first peer to become prime minister since 1902, he renounced his Scottish title for life and took a seat in the Commons. As prime minister, Douglas-Home was handicapped by the divisions within his party. After the Conservative defeat in Oct., 1964, he served as leader of the opposition until July, 1965. He became foreign secretary again when the Conservatives returned to power in June, 1970. He was made a life peer in 1974.

Douglas Point: see KINCARDINE, Ont., Canada.

Douglass, Frederick, c.1817–1895, American abolitionist, b. near Easton, Md. The son of a Negro slave, Harriet Bailey, and an unknown white father, he took the name of Douglass (from Scott's hero in *The Lady of the Lake*) after his second, and successful, attempt to escape from slavery in 1838. At New Bedford, Mass., he found work as a day laborer. An extemporaneous speech before a meeting at Nantucket of the Massachusetts Anti-Slavery Society in 1841 was so effective that he was made one of its agents. Douglass, who had learned to read and write while in the service of a kind mistress in Baltimore, published his *Narrative of the Life of Frederick Douglass* in 1845. Fearing capture as a fugitive slave, he spent several years in England and Ireland and returned in 1847, after English friends had purchased his freedom. At Rochester, N.Y., he established the *North Star* and edited it for 17 years in the abolitionist cause. Unlike Garrison, he favored the use of political methods and thus became a follower of James G. Birney. In the Civil War he helped organize two regiments of Massachusetts Negroes and urged other Negroes to join the Union ranks. During Reconstruction he continued to urge civil rights for Negroes. He was secretary of the Santo Domingo Commission (1871), marshal of the District of Columbia (1877–81), recorder of deeds for the same district (1881–86), and minister to Haiti (1889–91). *Life and Times of Frederick Douglass* (1962) is a revised edition of his autobiography, which has also been published as *My Bondage and My Freedom.* See also biographies by Booker T. Washington (1907), Philip Foner (1964), Benjamin Quarles (1968), and Arna Bontemps (1971); Edmund Fuller, *A Star Pointed North* (1946); P. S. Foner, ed., *Life and Writings of Frederick Douglass* (4 vol., 1950–55).

Douglas spruce: see PINE.

Douhet, Giulio (jōō'lyō dōōā'), 1869–1930, Italian military officer and early advocate of air power. He served in World War I and was court-martialed for criticizing the Italian high command. However, he was later recalled and was promoted (1921) to general. He attracted great attention by maintaining that command of the air could win a war regardless of land or sea power.

Doukhobors: see DUKHOBORS.

Doulton ware (dōl'tən), English pottery produced at Lambeth after 1815, first by John Doulton and his partners, then by his descendants. It won the medal at the Exhibition of 1851 and more than 200 subsequent awards for the perfection of the various products and the beauty of their decoration by skilled artists who signed their work. It includes brown stoneware with graffito or scratched designs; other salt-glaze pieces with black, brown, blue, bronze, green, gray, or white bodies; FAÏENCE; impasto; and Carrara. Sculptured terra-cotta plaques by George Tinworth won additional fame for Doulton ware. Its factories became the Royal Doulton Potteries.

Doumer, Paul (pōl dōōmâr'), 1857–1932, president of the French republic (1931–32). He entered the chamber of deputies in 1888, was governor general of Indochina (1897–1902) and a senator after 1912, and served in several cabinets after World War I. After following Gaston Doumergue as president, he was assassinated by an insane Russian émigré. Albert Lebrun succeeded him.

Doumergue, Gaston (gästôN' dōōmĕrg'), 1863–1937, president of the French republic (1924–31). He entered national politics in 1893 as a Radical Socialist deputy and served in various cabinets before and during World War I. After serving as president he retired, but when the cabinet of Édouard DALADIER fell in Feb., 1934, as a result of the STAVISKY AFFAIR, Doumergue was called on to be the "strong man" of France and to restore order. Premier of a coalition cabinet, he asked for extraordinary powers to meet the financial and political crises. These demands caused the fall of his cabinet, which was succeeded (Nov., 1934) by another under P. E. Flandin.

Dounreay, village, Highland region, N Scotland. A large-scale experimental nuclear breeder reactor is located nearby. A second reactor will be completed in the 1970s.

Doura, ancient city, Syria: see DURA.

Douro (Port. dō'rōō) or **Duero** (Span. dōōā'rō), river, c.475 mi (765 km) long, rising in the Sierra de Urbión, N central Spain. It flows W across N Spain, then southwest to form part of the Spanish-Portuguese border before flowing W across N Portugal to the Atlantic Ocean at Pôrto. One of the longest rivers of the Iberian Peninsula, it drains most of the northern portion of the central plateau; the Tormes, Esla, and Pisuerga rivers are its chief tributaries. Silting, rapids, and deep gorges combine to make the Douro unnavigable. The middle Douro is extensively used for irrigation. Several hydroelectric power plants are along the river. Grapes are the chief crop of the Douro valley, and the Douro estuary is the center of Portuguese wine trade.

douroucouli: see MONKEY.

Douw, Gerard: see DOU.

Dove, Arthur Garfield, 1880–1946, American painter, b. Canandaigua, N.Y. Early in his career he did commercial illustration in New York City. Following a European trip (1907–9), he adopted an abstract style that flowered in the 1930s into fluid, poetic canvases based on forms in nature. Dove has subsequently been recognized as a precursor of the abstract expressionists. Examples of his work are *Rise of the Full Moon* and *Pozzuoli Red* (Phillips Gall., Washington, D.C.).

Dove (dŭv), river, c.40 mi (60 km) long, rising in the Pennines, Derbyshire, central England, and flowing S and SE to the River Trent near Burton upon Trent. It forms much of the Derbyshire-Staffordshire boundary. Its watercourse was a haunt of Izaak Walton and still provides fishing. The rocky and wood-bordered Dovedale, below Hartington, is celebrated by artists and poets.

dove: see PIGEON.

dovekie: see AUK.

Dover, municipal borough (1971 pop. 34,322), Kent, SE England, on the Strait of Dover, beneath chalk cliffs c.375 ft (114 m) high. The small Dour River flows through the town. Dover is a resort and an important port for travel and shipping to the Continent; it was chief among the members of the CINQUE PORTS. The Romans fortified the place and called it Dubris. In Anglo-Saxon times there was also a fort there. In 1216, Dover was defended by Hubert de Burgh against a French attack. In the English civil war it was taken (1642) by the parliamentarians. It was the landing place of Charles II in 1660. Only 21 mi (34 km) from France, Dover was the center of English Channel defense and an important naval base in World War I. For four years in World War II it was a constant target of German long-range guns. In the cliffs a series of subterranean caves and tunnels once used by smugglers were put to use as shelters from 1940 to 1944. Improvement of the extensive harbor took place in the late 19th and early 20th cent. Noteworthy are Shakespeare Cliff (the first coal in Kent was discovered there in 1822); the 13th-century Maison Dieu Hall, hostel of Hubert de Burgh; Dover Castle on the cliffs, of Roman or Saxon origin; the lighthouse in the castle, partly Roman; the Church of St. Mary, also in the castle, of Saxon origin with Roman brick; the barracks; and St. Martin's priory (1332), part of Dover College, a boys' school. In 1974, Dover became part of the new nonmetropolitan county of Kent.

Dover. 1 City (1970 pop. 17,488), state capital, and seat of Kent co., central Del., on the St. Jones River; founded 1683 on orders of William Penn, laid out 1717, inc. as a city 1929. In a rich farming and fruit-growing region, it is a shipping and canning center with varied industries. Dover Air Force Base there, one of the largest air cargo terminals in the world (operated by the Military Air Transport Service), is a major factor in the city's economy. The old statehouse on the green, built in part in 1722 as the county courthouse, has been the capitol since 1777. Numerous historic houses and sites remain. The state museum is in the Old Presbyterian Church (1790). The city is the seat of Delaware State College and two junior colleges. 2 City (1970 pop. 20,850), seat of Strafford co., SE N.H., on the Bellamy, Salmon Falls, and Cocheco rivers near their confluence with the Piscataqua; settled 1623, inc. as a city 1855. The 30-ft (9-m) falls of the Cocheco there have empowered industry since the late 1700s. Among the many manufactures today are shoes, printing presses, office machines, and farm equipment. The first permanent settlement in New Hampshire, Dover was organized in 1633 but grew slowly. Lord SAYE AND SELE and his group had large holdings there from 1633 to 1641. An Indian massacre occurred in 1689. In 1812 the first cotton factory was established and the town thrived as a textile center. Dover's historic attractions include the garrison house (late 1600s); the Hale house (1806), where Lafayette and James Monroe stayed; and a library that was organized in 1792. Jeremy Belknap preached in Dover in the Revolutionary years, and Lincoln made a speech there in 1860. 3 Industrial town (1970 pop. 15,039), Morris co., N central N.J., on the Rockaway River; settled 1722, inc. as a town 1869. In a rich iron ore area, the town grew as an iron-manufacturing center on the old Morris Canal. It still has important iron- and steelworks as well as a great variety of manufactures. The U.S. army Picatinny Arsenal is nearby. A junior college is in the city, and numerous lakes and mountain resorts are in the area. 4 City (1970 pop. 11,516), Tuscarawas co., E Ohio, on the Tuscarawas River, in a farm, coal, and fireclay area; inc. 1867. Electrical equipment, sheet steel, masonite, chemicals, knives, and wire are among its products. Many people of Swiss descent live there, and the annual state Swiss festival is held in Sugarcreek, W of Dover. Nearby Dover and Atwood dams are part of the Muskingum flood control project.

Dover, Strait of, separating Great Britain from France and connecting the English Channel with the North Sea. It is 21 mi (34 km) wide between Dover and Cape Gris-Nez, near Calais, and is called Pas-de-Calais by the French. The Romans called it Fretum Gallicum. The Strait of Dover has been the scene of naval battles: in the 13th cent. Hubert de Burgh defeated the invading French, and in 1588 the Spanish Armada was checked there by the English.

Doves Press (dŭvs), one of the leaders in the revival of the art and craft of making books that occurred in the late 19th and early 20th cent. It was founded at Hammersmith, London, in 1900 by T. J. Cobden-Sanderson and Emery Walker, both of whom had been associated with William Morris in the work of the KELMSCOTT PRESS. The masterpiece of the Doves Press was the Doves Bible (5 vol., 1903). The Doves type, suggested by type used by Nicolas Jenson in the 15th cent., was designed by Emery Walker. The work of the press ended in 1916, when Cobden-Sanderson prevented further use of the type by throwing it into the Thames.

Dovrefjell (dô'vrəfyĕl), mountainous region of S Norway, c.100 mi (160 km) long and 40 mi (60 km) wide, culminating in Snøhetta (7,500 ft/2,286 m high). It is crossed by the Dovre railway and highway and is the source of several important rivers. It is a symbol of steadfastness and independence in Norwegian folklore and literature.

Dovzhenko, Aleksandr (əlyĭksän'dər dōvzhĕn'kō), 1894–1956, Soviet film director, b. Ukraine. He ranks with Eisenstein and Pudovkin as one of the greatest of Soviet filmmakers. *Zvenigord* (1928), *Arsenal*

(1929), and *Earth* (1930), the latter one of the great films of all time, all introduced much film innovation and brought him worldwide fame. *Earth*, however, was denounced by Soviet official critics as "counter revolutionary," and Dovzhenko was forced to reconcile himself to producing films more agreeable to the regime. An early user of MONTAGE, he employed poetic imagery and surrealistic symbols to emphasize human character. Later films include *Life in Blossom* (1947) and *Poem of the Sea* (1956).

Dow, Gerard: see DOU.

Dow, Lorenzo (dou), 1777–1834, American evangelist, b. Coventry, Conn. Although connected at times with the Methodist Church, he was an independent preacher for much of his life, traveling between the North and the South on horseback. By 1830, Dow was nationally known, not only for his eloquence, but for his oddities of manner and dress. He visited Ireland and England, where he introduced camp meetings. See biography by C. C. Sellers (1928).

Dow, Neal, 1804–97, American prohibitionist, b. Portland, Maine. He helped organize the Maine Temperance Union in 1838 and prepared (1851) the famous "Maine Law," which superseded the less rigid prohibition legislation of 1846. As mayor of Portland (1851–59), Dow succeeded with difficulty in making his law operative in that city. He lectured on prohibition throughout the United States, and in 1857 he visited England. He was the Prohibition party's candidate for President in 1880. See his reminiscences (1898) and biography by F. L. Byrne (1961, repr. 1969).

Dowden, Edward (dou'dən), 1843–1913, English critic, b. Ireland. He is best known as a Shakespearean scholar and as a biographer of Shelley (1886). See study by K. R. Ludwigson (1973).

dowel, cylindrical wooden peg used principally to join other pieces of wood by fitting tightly into corresponding holes. Usually the tightness of the fit is improved by the use of glue or some other adhesive. Dowels are often driven into mating holes in masonry or plaster walls to provide an anchor. Occasionally they are also used as pegs on which clothing or other items are hung. The stock from which dowels are cut, cylindrical pieces of wood ranging up to several feet in length, is also called a dowel, or sometimes doweling.

dower, that portion of a deceased husband's real PROPERTY that a widow is legally entitled to use during her lifetime to support herself and their children. A wife may claim the dower if her husband dies without a will or if she dissents from the will. At common law, dower consists of a one-third interest in all the land that the husband owned during the marriage. In many states of the United States dower rights have been abolished and other provisions, especially rights of inheritance, have been made for the widow. Where it still exists, the dower right attaches to the land as soon as it comes into the husband's possession; for that reason it cannot be defeated by a conveyance of the land by the husband in his lifetime unless his wife joins in the deed. If the wife is the guilty party in a divorce or the marriage is annulled, the right of the wife to dower is ended. The husband's lifetime use of his deceased wife's property, a right that is contingent on the birth of lawful issue, is known as curtesy.

Dowie, John Alexander (dou'ē), 1847–1907, founder of the CHRISTIAN CATHOLIC CHURCH, b. Scotland. He emigrated (1860) to Australia, where he was ordained as a Congregational minister. Dowie's teaching included belief in the healing of disease by prayer, and he founded the International Divine Healing Association. Dowie went to the United States in 1888; he founded his church in Chicago in 1896. In 1901, Dowie established Zion, Ill., which was composed of his followers and governed by special regulations laid down by him. Soon his administration was under criticism, and in 1905 he was deposed. See fictionalized biography by Arthur Newcomb (1930).

dowitcher: see SNIPE.

Dowland, John (dou'lănd), 1562–1626, English composer, unsurpassed in his day as a lutanist. His books of *Songs or Ayres* (1597–1603) established him as the foremost song composer of his time. See study by Diana Poulton (1972).

Down, county (1971 pop. 310,617, excluding Belfast, which lies partly within the county), 952 sq mi (2,466 sq km), SE Northern Ireland. The county town is DOWNPATRICK. The shoreline extends along the Irish Sea and is deeply indented by Strangford Lough and Dundrum Bay. The undulating surface rises to the beautiful Mourne Mts. in the south. The chief rivers are the Lagan and the Bann. Agriculture is the most important activity, and the area is extensively cultivated (oats, potatoes, wheat, and flax). There is market gardening in the north. Cattle, sheep, pigs, and poultry are raised. Manufactures include linen, cotton, rayon, clothing, and processed foods. The chief manufacturing towns are Newtownards, NEWRY, Downpatrick, and Banbridge. Fishing is also economically important; herring and whitefish constitute the main catch.

Downers Grove, village (1970 pop. 32,751), Du Page co., NE Ill.; settled 1832, inc. 1873. Its manufactures include baked goods, plastic and metal products, electrical components, and chain belts. The Avery Coonley School, a private, progressive elementary school, and George Williams College, operated by the Y.M.C.A., are there. Argonne National Laboratory is nearby.

Downey, city (1970 pop. 88,445), Los Angeles co., S Calif., a residential and industrial suburb between Los Angeles and Long Beach; inc. 1957. Its many manufactures include metal products, aircraft, missiles, and chemicals.

Downing, Andrew Jackson, 1815–52, American horticulturist, rural architect, and landscape gardener, b. Newburgh, N.Y. With his brother Charles Downing he took over the operation of the nursery that his father had established at Newburgh, and c.1838, Andrew became sole owner. His *Treatise on the Theory and Practice of Landscape Gardening, Adapted to North America* (1841) rapidly became a classic and passed through 10 editions (10th ed., 1921). His *Cottage Residences* (1842) was an attempt to point the way to improvement in the homes of country people. With Charles, Downing published, both in England and the United States, *The Fruits and Fruit Trees of America* (1845), a valuable work that passed through 13 editions in the author's lifetime. From 1846 until his early death he edited the *Horticulturist;* his editorials were in part published as *Rural Essays* (1853). In 1850 he published his *Architecture for Country Houses.* With Calvert VAUX he designed and constructed the homes and gardens of a great number of country estates along the Hudson River. He also planned the grounds for the Capitol, the White House, and the Smithsonian Institution.

Downing, Sir George, 1623–84, English diplomat. A nephew of Gov. John Winthrop of Massachusetts, he was educated at Harvard. He returned (1646) to England, joined the parliamentarians, and was appointed (1649) scoutmaster general (chief of intelligence) of the army in Scotland. In 1657, Oliver Cromwell sent him as ambassador to Holland. He made his peace with Charles II in 1660 and received (1663) a baronetcy after betraying three regicides to the government. He was again ambassador to Holland, where his aggressiveness was a factor in the outbreak (1664) of the second Dutch War. From 1667 to 1671, Downing served as secretary to the treasury commission. As head of the customs commission, he went again to The Hague in 1671 but was expelled in 1672. He amassed enormous wealth and owned Downing St., London, which is named for him. See John Beresford, *The Godfather of Downing Street* (1925).

Downing Street, Westminster, London, England. On the street are the British Foreign Office and, at No. 10, the residence of the first lord of the Treasury, who is usually (although not necessarily) the prime minister of Great Britain. Since nearly all prime ministers from the time of Robert Walpole (18th cent.) have lived at No. 10, it has come to designate the British government.

Downpatrick (doun"păt'rĭk), urban district (1971 pop. 7,403), county town of Co. Down, E Northern Ireland, at the southwest extremity of Strangford Lough. The town has linen mills and is a market for an area where oats and flax are grown and sheep are raised. Hunting is popular in the vicinity. The seat of the diocese of Down, Downpatrick has long been a religious center; St. Patrick is said to have founded a church there c.440. The present cathedral dates from 1790. In the town are remains of Inch Abbey (founded 1180) and of the Monastery of Saul (foundation ascribed to St. Patrick); a large rath and the holy wells of Struell are nearby. Downpatrick has always been a place of pilgrimage, for the collective tomb of Ireland's three great saints—Patrick, Columba, and Bridget of Kildare—has been thought (incorrectly) to be in the town.

Downs, North, and **South Downs,** parallel ranges of chalk hills, SE England. They rise to 965 ft (294 m) at Leith Hill. The North Downs range, extending c.100 mi (160 km) through Surrey and Kent, is cut by the Wey, Mole, Darent, Medway, and Stour rivers. It is separated by The Weald from the South Downs (c.65 mi/100 km long) in Sussex and E Hampshire, which are cut by the Arun, Adur, and Ouse rivers. The Downs provide excellent pasturage for sheep; Southdown sheep are well known.

Downs, The, roadstead, c.8 mi (13 km) long and 6 mi (9.7 km) wide, between North Foreland and South Foreland, off Deal, Kent, SE England, in the English Channel. It is protected, except from strong south winds, by the Goodwin Sands and the coast. Two naval battles were fought nearby—between the Dutch and the Spanish in 1639 and between the British and the French in 1666 (see DUTCH WARS).

Down's syndrome: see MENTAL RETARDATION.

dowry (dou'rē), the property that a woman brings to her husband at the time of the marriage. The dowry apparently originated in the giving of a marriage gift by the family of the bridegroom to the bride and the bestowal of money upon the bride by her parents. It has been a well-established institution among the propertied classes of various lands and times, e.g., in ancient Greece and Rome, India, medieval Europe, and modern continental countries. Generally the husband has been compelled to return the dowry in case of divorce or the death of the wife when still childless. One purpose of the dowry was to provide support for the wife on the husband's death, and thus it was related remotely to the rights of DOWER. In civil-law countries the dowry is an important form of property. In England and the United States (except for Louisiana), the dowry system is not recognized as law.

dowser: see DIVINING ROD.

Dowson, Ernest Christopher, 1867–1900, English poet. He attended Queens College, Oxford, but left in 1888 without taking a degree. Dowson's life was tragic. In 1894 his father died, and his mother committed suicide six months later. Dowson himself was consumptive, alcoholic, and debt-ridden. He died of tuberculosis at the age of 32. One of the fin-de-siècle DECADENTS, Dowson wrote fragile, sensuous poetry voicing regret for the passing of youth and beauty, the denial of love, and the rejection of pleasure. His best-known poem is "Non Sum Qualis Eram Bonae sub Regno Cynarae," with its refrain, "I have been faithful to thee, Cynara! in my fashion." A Roman Catholic, Dowson wrote some very fine religious poetry. He also made some notable translations from the French and wrote a novel and a play. See his works (ed. by Desmond Flower, 1934) and his letters (ed. by Desmond Flower and Henry Maas, 1968); biographies by Thomas B. Swann (1964) and John Mark Longaker (3d ed. 1967).

Doxiades, Constantinos (kônstäntē'nôs dôksyä'thēs), 1913–, Greek urban planner, designer, and consultant on ekistics, the science of human settlements. In Athens, Doxiades has held many official and academic positions in town planning and housing reconstruction. He has lectured extensively in the United States and served as consultant to many organizations and governments. After World War II he created many bold designs for towns and settlements built throughout Greece. His book publications include *Ekistic Analysis* (1946), *March of the People* (1948), and *Between Dystopia and Utopia* (1966).

doxology, sacred statement of praise. In the Psalms the word *hallelujah* is a Hebrew doxology. The best-known doxologies of the Christian church are GLORIA IN EXCELSIS, or the greater doxology; GLORIA PATRI, or the lesser doxology; and the closing stanza of Thomas Ken's morning and evening hymns, beginning, "Praise God from whom all blessings flow," sung to the tune *Old Hundred* from the Genevan Psalter (see HYMN).

Doyle, Sir Arthur Conan, 1859–1930, English author and creator of Sherlock Holmes, b. Edinburgh. Educated at the Royal Infirmary in Edinburgh, he received a medical degree in 1881. In 1887 the first Sherlock Holmes story, *A Study in Scarlet*, appeared in *Beeton's Christmas Annual.* Doyle abandoned his medical practice in 1890 and devoted his time to writing. Other works that involve the sleuthing of the great detective include *The Sign of the Four* (1890), *The Memoirs of Sherlock Holmes* (1894), *The Hound of the Baskervilles* (1902), *The Return of Sherlock Holmes* (1905), *His Last Bow* (1917), and *The Case Book of Sherlock Holmes* (1927). The brilliant and theatrical Holmes solves all his extraordinarily complex cases through ingenious deductive reasoning. His sober, credulous companion, Dr. Watson, narrates all the Sherlock Holmes stories. The Holmes cult has given rise to several notable clubs, of which the Baker Street Irregulars is perhaps the most famous. Doyle also wrote historical romances, including *Micah Clarke* (1889) and *The White Company* (1891). His play *A Story of Waterloo* (1894) was one of Sir Henry Irving's notable successes. Doyle also wrote two political pamphlets justifying England's action in the Boer War. In his later years he became an ardent spiritualist and wrote a *History of Spiritualism* (1926). He was knighted in 1902. See his autobiography (1924); biographies by J. D. Carr (1949, repr. 1973) and Hesketh Pearson (1961); studies by Michael Harrison (1958), J. E. Holroyd (1959), and Vincent Starrett (rev. ed. 1960).

Doyle, Richard, 1824–83, English caricaturist, water colorist, and illustrator. He was the son and pupil of John Doyle, a popular caricaturist. His *Journal* (British Mus.), a book of sketches done at the age 15, shows his extraordinary precocity. He worked on the staff of *Punch* (1843–50), and drew the famous cover design. Doyle illustrated some of Thackeray's works.

D'Oyly Carte, Richard: see CARTE, RICHARD D'OYLY.

DPN, in biochemistry, abbreviation for diphosphopyridine nucleotide, a COENZYME now usually called nicotinamide adenine dinucleotide, or NAD.

Drachenfels (drä'khənfĕls) [Ger.,=dragon's rock], mountain, 1,053 ft (321 m) high, in the SIEBENGEBIRGE, W West Germany, on the Rhine. It is of volcanic origin. In legend, it is the scene of Siegfried's triumph over the dragon. The Drachenburg, a fortress that is now in ruins, was built on the mountain (probably in 1117) by Archbishop Frederick I of Cologne. It was captured by the Swedes (1632) and by the Spaniards (1633) in the Thirty Years War.

Drachmann, Holger Henrik Herholdt (hŏl'gər hănrĕk' hăr'hŏlt drăkh'män), 1846–1908, Danish poet and dramatist. His early work was influenced by the political realism of Georg Brandes; *Poems* (1872) and *Muted Melodies* (1875) are dominated by social consciousness. Drachmann's work was sometimes romantic and lyrical, as in *Vines and Roses* (1879). Besides poetry, he wrote brilliant articles on art and politics, romantic novels, and several popular operettas and plays, including *Once Upon a Time* (1885). Periodic crises in his life altered the nature and direction of his writing many times.

Draco (drā'kō) or **Dracon** (drā'kŏn), fl. 621 B.C., Athenian politician and law codifier. Of his codification of Athenian customary law only the section dealing with involuntary homicide is preserved. From this and from later accounts in the writings of Aristotle and Plutarch it appears that in Athens the penalty of death was prescribed for the most trivial offense. The code adopted the principle that murder must be punished by the state and not by VENDETTA. Though the code was considerably ameliorated by SOLON, its name became a synonym for harsh legislation.

Draco [Lat.,=the dragon], northern CONSTELLATION lying SE of Ursa Minor and N of Lyra and Hercules. It is traditionally depicted as a dragon. Draco contains the bright star Eltanin (Gamma Draconis). Thuban (Alpha Draconis) was the polestar 5,000 years ago, i.e., it was the star nearest the celestial pole, but because of the PRECESSION OF THE EQUINOXES, the polestar is now POLARIS. Draco reaches its highest point in the evening sky in July, and is visible throughout the year for observers north of 40°N lat.

Draconids: see METEOR SHOWER.

Dracula: see STOKER, BRAM.

Dracut (drā'kət), town (1970 pop. 18,214), Middlesex co., NE Mass., near the N.H. line; settled 1664, inc. 1702. The commercial center of a fertile farm region, the town manufactures textiles.

draft, in banking, order by one party to another party to pay a stated sum to the person or firm in whose favor the draft is made. It is similar in form to the ordinary bank CHECK. Often the drawer and the drawee of a draft are the same person. A sight draft is payable immediately on presentation to the drawee; a time draft is payable at a fixed date in the future. A draft is sometimes known as a bill of exchange. It was originally devised to give credit to a customer who intended to pay in the future, but it came to be used to pay foreign debts (see FOREIGN EXCHANGE) because it obviated the bother, expense, and risk of transmitting money. Apparently, drafts were used in early Babylon, Egypt, and Rome, but the earliest clear instance of their use is in Genoa c.1156. Drafts are usually used in commercial transactions in which buyer and seller are distant from each other. The seller draws a draft against the buyer of his goods and sends the draft, together with shipping documents, to his bank. The bank or its agent presents the draft to the buyer for his acceptance of the obligation or for payment. If, in the case of a time draft, the buyer accepts the obligation to pay, he will often put a note to that effect, along with his signature, on the draft. Such an accepted draft is known as a trade acceptance and represents a legal commitment on the part of the buyer to pay the amount stipulated. For military draft, see CONSCRIPTION.

draft horse or **work horse,** any breed of HORSE that is suited to or used for drawing heavy loads. Draft horses originated in central Europe, where their domestication preceded the Roman invasion. Popular breeds include the BELGIAN, CLYDESDALE, PERCHERON, and SHIRE, all of which are extremely large and noted for their strength, endurance, and good disposition.

draft riots, in the American Civil War, mob action to protest unfair Union conscription. The Union Conscription Act of March 3, 1863, provided that all able-bodied males between the ages of 20 and 45 were liable to military service, but a drafted man who furnished an acceptable substitute or paid the government $300 was excused. A defective piece of legislation enforced amid great unpopularity, it provoked nationwide disturbances that were most serious in New York City, where for four days (July 13–16, 1863) there occurred large-scale, bloody riots. Many elements in New York sympathized with the South, and the war had aggravated long-standing economic and social grievances. Aroused by the statements of Gov. Horatio SEYMOUR and other Democratic leaders that the conscription act was unconstitutional, the populace was incited to action. Laborers, mostly Irish-Americans, made up the bulk of a tremendous mob that overpowered the police and militia, attacked and seized the Second Ave. armory containing rifles and guns, and set fire to buildings. Abolitionists and Negroes were especially singled out for attack. Many Negroes were beaten to death, and a Negro orphanage was burned, leaving hundreds of children homeless. Business ceased, and robbing and looting flourished. Since the conscription provision that allowed the rich to buy exemption was especially resented, the Tammany city government voted to pay the necessary $300 for anyone who might be drafted. Meanwhile, New York troops (including the famous 7th Regiment, which had been sent to the front for the Gettysburg campaign) were rushed back, and with the aid of the police, militia, naval forces, and cadets from West Point, they succeeded in restoring order. President Lincoln supported a Democratic-dominated commission that investigated the draft in New York, while Governor Seymour urged both adherence to the conscription act and a court test of its constitutionality (which never came about). In August the draft was peacefully resumed. The privilege of buying one's way out of service was limited (1864) to conscientious objectors. The riots had inflicted property damage of $1.5 million to $2 million, and it has been estimated that total casualties ran as high as 1,000. See B. L. Lee, *Discontent in New York City, 1861–1865* (1943); Irving Werstein, *July, 1863* (1957, repr. 1971); James McCague, *Second Rebellion: The Story of the New York City Draft Riots* (1968); Adrian Cook, *The Armies of the Streets* (1974).

Draga (drä'gä), 1867–1903, queen consort of King ALEXANDER of Serbia. A widow and a lady in waiting to the king's mother, Draga Mašin (Mashin) was accused by general rumor of a shady and promiscuous past. In 1900 the infatuated king shocked his nation by marrying her. Her unpopularity, especially in army circles, was aggravated by the subsequent political measures of the king. In 1903 an army clique, headed by Colonel Alexander Mašin, a brother of the queen's first husband, formed a conspiracy. A regiment occupied the palace, and the king and queen were brutally murdered.

Drago, Luis María (lōōēs' mārē'ä drä'gō), 1859–1921, Argentine statesman, jurist, and writer on international law. As minister of foreign affairs under Julio A. ROCA, he dispatched (Dec. 29, 1902) a note to the Argentine minister at Washington protesting the forcible coercion of Venezuela by Great Britain, Germany, and Italy (see VENEZUELA CLAIMS). This protest set forth the **Drago Doctrine,** intended as a corollary of the Monroe Doctrine. Drago, apparently under the erroneous impression that the European nations were merely attempting to collect unpaid bonds, maintained that no public debt should be collected from a sovereign American state by armed force or through the occupation of American territory by a foreign power. The doctrine was not new in principle, though its concept is narrower than that of the earlier CALVO DOCTRINE, from which it grew. The Drago Doctrine was discussed at the Pan-American Congress of 1906 and was brought before the Hague Conference of 1907, where a modified form offered by Horace PORTER was approved instead.

dragon, mythical beast usually represented as a huge, winged, fire-breathing reptile. For centuries the dragon has been prominent in the folklore of many peoples; thus, its physical characteristics vary greatly and include combinations of numerous animals. The dragon has often been associated with evil. In many legends a dragon had the ability to wreak havoc upon a land and therefore had to be either propitiated by a human sacrifice, or killed; it was also often the guardian of a treasure or a maiden. The highest achievement of a hero in medieval legend was the slaying of a dragon, as in the story of St. George. King Arthur, son of Uther Pendragon (dragon's head), also killed a dragon. The giant red dragon of the Apocalypse (Rev. 12) gave rise to the use of the beast as symbolic of Satan in Christian art and literature. In ancient China the dragon was associated with fertility and prosperity. Many of the beliefs connected with the dragon are echoed in SNAKE WORSHIP.

Dragonetti, Domenico (dōmĕ'nĕkō drăgōnĕt'tē), 1763–1846, Italian double-bass virtuoso. He appeared in opera houses in Europe and after 1794 in concerts in England. He was a friend of Beethoven and Haydn and left to the British Museum a large and valuable collection of manuscripts and old instruments.

dragonfly, any INSECT of the order Odonata, which also includes the damselfly. Members of this order are generally large predatory insects and characteristically have chewing mouthparts and four membranous, net-veined wings; they undergo complete METAMORPHOSIS. Species are found throughout the world except in the polar regions; the greatest variety occurs in the tropics. Dragonflies, which are commonly called horse stingers and devil's darning needles, are strong fliers with elongated bodies; they rest with their wings outstretched. Some are 5 in. (12.7 cm) long. Damselflies are smaller, with slender, often brilliantly colored, bodies and rest with their wings folded back. Both lay eggs on or near water. The nymphs are aquatic and breathe by means of gills located at the end of the abdomen; the gills can also be used for propulsion through the water. The nymphs feed on insect larvae and are an important food for fish and birds. When grown, they crawl up out of the water and molt. Most species produce a single generation each year, with the nymph stage usually overwintering. Both nymphs and adults prey on mosquitoes and other insects and are harmless, indeed beneficial, to humans. Fossil remains of a form from the Permian period, with a wingspread of 2½ ft (76 cm), were found in Kansas. Dragonflies are classified in the phylum ARTHROPODA, class Insecta, order Odonata.

dragonnades or **dragonades** (both: drăgənādz'), name given to a form of persecution of French Protestants, or HUGUENOTS, before and after the revocation (1685) of the Edict of Nantes (see NANTES, EDICT OF) by Louis XIV. It consisted of harassing the Huguenots by billeting soldiers (particularly the rowdy dragoons) in their houses and in disregarding the soldiers' misconduct. The outrages committed against the persons and property of the Huguenots contributed—at least as much as the legal enforcement of the revocation of the edict—to the conversion but also to the mass emigration of Huguenots, so that entire cities and regions were ruined and depopulated.

dragon's blood, name for a red RESIN obtained from a number of different plants. It was held by early Greeks, Romans, and Arabs to have medicinal properties; Dioscorides and other early writers described it. A chief source was *Dracaena cinnabari*, a tree of the lily family. Voyagers to the Canary Islands in the 15th cent. obtained it from another species, *D. draco*. The resin, occurring in beautiful garnet-colored drops when the tree is broken, was well known as the source of varnish for 18th-century Italian violinmakers. Later, dragon's-blood varnishes and medicines were obtained chiefly from the immature fruits of a palm (*Daemonorops draco*) native to Malaya. Although still sometimes used in photoengraving processes, dragon's blood as a coloring material has largely been replaced by synthetics.

Draguignan (drăgēnyäN'), town (1968 pop. 19,465), capital of Var dept., SE France, in Provence. It is a rural town with some medieval remains. The old summer palace of the bishops of Fréjus (18th cent.), now a museum, is there.

drainage, in agricultural practice, the removal of excess water from the soil, either by a system of open ditches, or gravity drains, or by an underground method if the soil texture and the lay of the land demand it. Drainage was practiced in the Nile basin c.400 B.C. and by ancient Roman farmers. Today drains made from cylindrical tiles of clay or concrete, laid several feet underground, are much used in the United States, where an estimated 100 million acres (40.5 million hectares) were drained in 1970. Arterial drainage, using diesel or centrifugal pumps, is employed for large areas. Drainage results in improved soil structure, increased efficiency of phosphorus fertilizer, and reduced loss of nitrogen.

drainage, in mining, removal of water seeping into shafts and other underground mine workings from the surrounding ground. Unless seeping water is removed continually, it may endanger haulage and mining equipment, weaken supporting structures, and, in some instances, flood the mine completely. Water in a mine is drained into sumps, or reservoirs, usually excavated below the lowest working level of the mine, and is then removed by pumps. Methods to minimize seepage include the sealing of visible fissures through which water enters and the injection of concrete into the ground surrounding the shafts.

drainage basin: see CATCHMENT AREA.

Drake, Alfred, 1914–, American singer, actor, and director, b. New York City, originally named Alfred Capurro. Drake first appeared on stage in 1935 in *The Mikado.* The Broadway production of *Oklahoma!* (1943) brought him stardom, followed by leading roles in *Kiss Me Kate* (1948) and *Kismet* (1953). In 1964 he played the king in John Gielgud's production of *Hamlet,* and in 1973 he appeared in the musical *Gigi,* both on Broadway.

Drake, Edwin Laurentine, 1819–80, American oil well driller, b. Greene co., N.Y. In 1858 he was employed to conduct drilling operations and on Aug. 27, 1859, he struck oil near Titusville, Pa., at a depth of 69 ft (21.1 m). Drake's was the first producing oil well in the United States.

Drake, Sir Francis, 1540?–1596, English navigator and admiral, first Englishman to circumnavigate the world (1577–80). He was born in Devonshire, the son of a yeoman, and was at an early age apprenticed to a ship captain. He made voyages to Guinea and the West Indies and in 1567 commanded a ship in a slave-trading expedition of his kinsman, John HAWKINS. On the voyage the Spanish, then in close naval rivalry with the ascendant strength of England, destroyed all but three of the English vessels. In 1572, with two ships and 73 men, Drake set out on the first of his famous marauding expeditions. He took the town of Nombre de Dios on the Isthmus of Panama, captured a ship in the harbor of Cartagena, burned Portobelo, crossed and recrossed the isthmus, and captured three mule trains bearing 30 tons of silver. The voyage brought Drake wealth and fame. For the next few years he commanded the sea forces against rebellious Ireland. In Dec., 1577, he set out with five ships to raid Spanish holdings on the Pacific coast of the New World. He abandoned two ships in the Río de la Plata in South America, and, with the remaining three, navigated the Straits of Magellan, the first Englishman to make the passage. A storm drove them far southward; one ship and its crew were destroyed, and another, separated from Drake's vessel, returned to England. Drake continued alone in the *Golden Hind* up the coast of South America, plundered Valparaiso and smaller settlements, cut loose the shipping at Callao, and captured a rich Spanish treasure ship. Armed now with Spanish charts, he continued north along the coast, looking for a possible passage to the Atlantic, feeling it would be unsafe to retrace his course. Sailing possibly as far north as the present state of Washington with no success, he determined to cross the Pacific. He returned to San Francisco Bay to repair and provision his ship. He named the region New Albion and took possession of it in the name of Queen Elizabeth I. Then crossing the Pacific, he visited the Moluccas, the Celebes, and Java, rounded the Cape of Good Hope, and arrived at Plymouth on Sept. 26, 1580, bearing treasure of extremely high value. Elizabeth endeavored for a time to justify Drake's conduct to Spain, but, failing to satisfy the Spanish, she finally abandoned all pretense and openly recognized Drake's exploits by knighting him aboard the *Golden Hind.* In 1585, Drake commanded a fleet that sacked Vigo in Spain and burned São Tiago in the Cape Verde Islands. Proceeding across the Atlantic, he took Santo Domingo and Cartagena (which were subsequently ransomed), plundered the Florida coast, including the settlement of St. Augustine, and rescued Sir Walter Raleigh's Roanoke colony under Ralph Lane on the Carolina coast. Meanwhile, Spain had begun to prepare for open war. In 1587, Drake entered the harbor of Cádiz with 26 ships and destroyed about 30 of the ships the Spanish were assembling. He had, he said, merely singed the king of Spain's beard and wished to carry out further expeditions against the Spanish ports, but Elizabeth would not sanction his plans. He was a vice admiral in the fleet that defeated the ARMADA in 1588. He was in joint command of an attempted invasion of Portugal in 1589 but failed to take Lisbon. Drake's last expedition, in 1595, undertaken jointly with Hawkins, was directed against the West Indies. This time the Spanish were prepared, and the venture was a complete failure. Hawkins died off Puerto Rico, and Drake shortly afterward, of dysentery, off Portobelo, where he was buried at sea. See biographies by Sir Julien Corbett (1890, repr. 1969) and G. M. Thomson (1972); see also Sir Julien Corbett, *Drake and the Tudor Navy* (2 vol., 1899, repr. 1970); Garrett Mattingly, *The Armada* (1959); K. R. Andrews, *Drake's Voyages* (1967); K. R. Andrews, ed., *The Last Voyage of Drake and Hawkins* (1972).

Drake, Francis Marion, 1830–1903, Union army officer in the Civil War, railroad president, and governor of Iowa (1896–98), b. Rushville, Ill. He helped defend St. Joseph, Mo., against Confederate forces under the command of Gen. Sterling Price. As lieutenant colonel of an Iowa regiment he fought with distinction in the Western campaigns, being brevetted brigadier general of volunteers in Feb., 1865. Admitted to the bar in 1866, Drake was president of the Iowa Southern RR for several years and later headed (1882–98) the Indiana, Illinois & Iowa, which became part of the Chicago & Alton. As governor he called a special session of the general assembly to revise the legal code of Iowa and substantially reformed the state's charitable and penal institutions. Drake Univ. was named for him.

Drake, Joseph Rodman, 1795–1820, American poet and satirist, b. New York City. Under the name "The Croakers," he and his friend Fitz-Greene Halleck wrote a series of light satirical verses for the New York *Evening Post* (1819, first complete ed. 1860). Drake's longest serious poem is "The Culprit Fay" (in *The Culprit Fay and Other Poems,* 1835); his poem "The American Flag" was long a standard patriotic declamation. Halleck's elegy beginning, "Green be the turf above thee," was written upon Drake's death. See F. L. Pleadwell, ed., *The Life and Works of Joseph Rodman Drake* (1935).

Drakensberg Range (drä'kənzbûrg, Afrik. -bĕrkh), South Africa, extending 700 mi (1,127 km) NE-SW in Natal, Lesotho, Orange Free State, and Transvaal. Thabana-Ntlenyana, at 11,425 ft (3,482 m), is the highest point. The mountains are part of the escarpment that forms the southern edge of the central plateau of Africa. Another name for the range is Quathlamba.

Drakes Bay, inlet of the Pacific Ocean, formed by the San Andreas fault, W Calif., NW of San Francisco. Point Reyes forms its outer arm. The bay was visited by Sir Francis Drake in 1579.

Drake University, at Des Moines, Iowa; coeducational; chartered and opened 1881 by the Disciples of Christ; named for Francis M. Drake.

dram: see ENGLISH UNITS OF MEASUREMENT.

Dráma (drä'mä), city (1971 pop. 29,692), capital of Dráma prefecture, NE Greece, in Macedonia. It is the trade center for a tobacco-producing region.

drama, Western. The Western dramatic tradition has its origins in ancient Greece. The precise evolution of its main divisions—TRAGEDY, COMEDY, and SATIRE—is not definitely known. According to Aristotle, Greek drama, or, more explicitly, Greek tragedy, originated in the DITHYRAMB. This was a choral hymn to the god Dionysus and involved exchanges between a lead singer and the chorus. It is thought that the dithyramb was sung at the Dionysia, an annual festival honoring Dionysus. Tradition has it that at the Dionysia of 534 B.C., during the reign of Pisistratus, the lead singer of the dithyramb, a man named Thespis, added to the chorus an actor with whom he carried on a dialogue, thus initiating the possibility of dramatic action. Thespis is credited with the invention of tragedy. Eventually, Aeschylus introduced a second actor to the drama and Sophocles a third, Sophocles' format being continued by Euripides, the last of the great classical Greek dramatists. Generally, the earlier Greek tragedies place more emphasis on the chorus than the later ones. In the majestic plays of Aeschylus, the chorus serves to underscore the personalities and situations of the characters and to provide ethical comment on the action. Much of Aeschylus' most beautiful poetry is contained in the choruses of his plays. The increase in the number of actors resulted in less concern with communal problems and beliefs and more with dramatic conflict between individuals. Accompanying this trend, from the time of Aeschylus to that of Euripides, was a tendency toward realism. The latter playwright's characters are ordinary, not godlike, and the gods themselves are introduced more as devices of plot manipulation (as in the use of the deus ex machina in *Medea,* 431 B.C.) than as strongly felt representations of transcendent power. Utilizing three actors, Sophocles developed dramatic action beyond anything Aeschylus had achieved with only two and also introduced more natural speech. However, he did not lose a sense of the godlike in man and man's affairs, as Euripides often did. Thus, it is Sophocles who best represents the classical balance between the human and divine, the realistic and the symbolic. Greek comedy is divided by scholars into Old Comedy (5th cent. B.C.), Middle Comedy (c.404–c.321 B.C.), and New Comedy (c.320–c.264 B.C.). The sole literary remains of Old Comedy are the plays of Aristophanes, characterized by obscenity, political satire, fantasy, and strong moral overtones. While there are no extant examples of Middle Comedy, it is conjectured that the satire, obscenity, and fantasy of the earlier plays were much mitigated during this transitional period. Most extant examples of New Comedy are from the works of Menander; these comedies are realistic and elegantly written, often revolving around a love-interest. The Roman theater never approached the heights of the Greek, and the Romans themselves had little interest in serious dramatic endeavors, being drawn toward sensationalism and spectacle. The earliest Roman dramatic attempts were simply translations from the Greek. Gnaeus Naevius (c.270–c.199 B.C.) and his successors imitated Greek models in tragedies that never transcended the level of violent melodrama. Even the nine tragedies of the philosopher and statesman Seneca are gloomy and lurid, emphasizing the sensational aspects of Greek myth; they are noted primarily for their inflated rhetoric. Seneca became an important influence on Renaissance tragedy, but it is unlikely that his plays were intended for more than private readings. Although Roman tragedy produced little of worth, a better judgment may be passed on the comedies of Plautus and Terence. Plautus incorporated native Roman elements into the plots and themes of Menander, producing plays characterized by farce, intrigue, romance, and sentiment. Terence was a more polished stylist who wrote for and about the upper classes and dispensed with the element of farce. The Roman preference for spectacle and the Christian suppression of drama led to a virtual cessation of dramatic production during the decline of the Roman Empire. Pantomimes accompanied by a chorus developed out of tragedy, and comic mimes were popular until the 4th cent. A.D. (see PANTOMIME). It is this mime tradition, carried on by traveling performers, that provided the theatrical continuity between the ancient world and the medieval. The Roman mime tradition has been suggested as the origin of the COMMEDIA DELL' ARTE of the Italian Renaissance, but this conjecture has never been proved. While the Christian church did much to suppress the performance of plays, paradoxically it is in the church that medieval drama began. The first record of this beginning is the trope in the Easter service known as the Quem quaeritis. Tropes, originally musical elaborations of the church service, gradually evolved into drama; eventually the Latin lines telling of the Resurrection were spoken, rather than sung, by priests who represented the angels and the two Marys at the tomb of Christ. Thus, simple interpolations developed into grandiose cycles of mystery plays, depicting biblical episodes from the Creation to Judgment Day. The most famous of these plays is the SECOND SHEPHERD'S PLAY. Another important type that developed from church liturgy was the miracle play, based on the lives of saints rather than on scripture. The miracle play reached its peak in France and the mystery play in England. Both types gradually became secularized, passing into the hands of trade guilds or professional actors. The *Second Shepherd's Play,* for all its religious seriousness, is most noteworthy for its elements of realism and farce, while the miracle plays in France often emphasized comedy and adventure (see MIRACLE PLAY). The MORALITY PLAY, a third type of religious drama, appeared early in the 15th cent. Morality plays were religious allegories, the most famous being EVERYMAN. Another type of drama popular in medieval times was the INTERLUDE, which can be generally defined as a dramatic work with characteristics of the morality play that is primarily intended for entertainment. By the advent of the Renaissance in the 15th and 16th cent., most European countries had established native traditions of religious drama and farce that contended with the impact of the newly discovered Greek and Roman plays. Little had been known of classical drama during the Middle Ages, and evidently the only classical imitations during that period were the Christian imitations of Terence by the Saxon nun Hrotswith in the 10th cent. The translation and imitation of the classics occurred first in Italy, with Terence, Plautus, and Seneca as the models. The Italians strictly applied their interpretation of Aristotle's rules for the drama, and this rigidity was primarily responsible for the failure of Italian Renaissance drama. Some liveliness appeared in the comic sphere, particularly in the works of Ariosto and in Machiavelli's satiric masterpiece, *La Mandragola* (1524). The PASTORAL drama—set in the country and depicting the romantic affairs of rustic people, usually shepherds and shepherdesses—was more successful than either comedy or tragedy. Notable Italian practitioners of the genre were Giovanni Battista Guarini (1537–1612) and Torquato Tasso. But the true direction of the Italian stage was toward the spectacular and the musical. A popular Italian Renaissance form was the INTERMEZZO, which presented music and lively entertainment between the acts of classical imitations. The native taste for music and theatricality led to the emergence of the OPERA in the 16th cent. and the triumph of this form on the Italian stage in the 17th cent. Similarly, the commedia dell'arte, emphasizing comedy and improvisation, was more popular than academic imitations of classical comedy. Renaissance drama appeared somewhat later in France than in Italy. Estienne Jodelle's Senecan tragedy *Cleopatre captive* (1553) marks the beginning of classical imitation in France. The French drama initially suffered from the same rigidity as the Italian, basing itself on Roman models and Italian imitations. However, in the late 16th cent. in France there was a romantic reaction to classical dullness, led by Alexandre Hardy, France's first professional playwright. This trend was stopped in the 17th cent. by Cardinal Richelieu, who insisted on a return to classic forms. Richelieu's judgment, however, bore fruit in the triumphs of the French neoclassical tragedies of Jean Racine and the comedies of Molière. The great tragedies of Pierre Corneille, although classical in their grandeur and in their concern with noble characters, are decidedly of the Renaissance in their exaltation of man's ability, by force of will, to transcend adverse circumstances. Renaissance drama in Spain and England was more successful than in France and Italy because the two former nations were able to transform classical models with infusions of native characteristics. In Spain the two leading Renaissance playwrights were Lope de Vega and Pedro Calderón de la Barca. Earlier, Lope de Rueda had set the tone for future Spanish drama with plays that are romantic, lyrical, and generally in the mixed tragicomic form. Lope de Vega wrote an enormous number of plays of many types, emphasizing plot, character, and romantic action. Best known for his *La vida es sueño*, a play that questions the nature of reality, Calderón was a more controlled and philosophical writer than Lope. The English drama of the 16th cent. showed from the beginning that it would not be bound by classical rules. Elements of farce, morality, and a disregard for the unities of time, place, and action inform the early comedies *Gammer Gurton's Needle* and *Ralph Roister Doister* (both c.1553) and the Senecan tragedy *Gorboduc* (1562). William Shakespeare's great work was foreshadowed by early essays in the historical chronicle play, by elements of romance found in the works of John Lyly, by revenge plays such as Thomas Kyd's *Spanish Tragedy* (c.1586)—again inspired by the works of Seneca—and by Christopher Marlowe's development of blank verse and his deepening of the tragic perception. Shakespeare, of course, stands as the supreme dramatist of the Renaissance period, equally adept at writing tragedies, comedies, or chronicle plays. His great achievements include the perfection of a verse form and language that capture the spirit of ordinary speech and yet stand above it to give a special dignity to his characters and situations; an unrivaled subtlety of characterization; and a marvelous ability to unify plot, character, imagery, and verse movement. With the reign of James I the English drama began to decline until the closing of the theaters by the Puritans in 1642. This period is marked by sensationalism and rhetoric in tragedy, as in the works of John Webster and Thomas Middleton, spectacle in the form of the MASQUE, and a gradual turn to polished wit in comedy, begun by Francis Beaumont and John Fletcher and furthered by James Shirley. The best plays of the Jacobean period are the comedies of Ben Jonson, in which he satirized contemporary life by means of his own invention, the comedy of humours. The second half of the 17th cent. was distinguished by the achievements of the French neoclassicists and the Restoration playwrights in England. Jean Racine brought clarity of perception and simplicity of language to his love tragedies, which emphasize women characters and psychological motivation. Molière produced brilliant social comedies that are neoclassical in their ridicule of any sort of excess. In England, Restoration tragedy degenerated into bombastic heroic dramas by such authors as John Dryden and Thomas Otway. Often written in rhymed heroic couplets, these plays are replete with sensational incidents and epic personages. But Restoration comedy, particularly the brilliant comedies of manners by George Etherege and William Congreve, achieved a perfection of style and cynical upper-class wit that is still appreciated. The works of William Wycherley, while similar in type, are more savage and deeply cynical. Later and gentler masters of Restoration comedy were George Farquhar, Oliver Goldsmith, and Richard Brinsley Sheridan. The 18th cent. ushered in the middle-class or domestic drama, which treated the problems of ordinary people. George Lillo's *London Merchant; or, The History of George Barnwell* (1731), is an important example of this type of play because it brought the bourgeois tragic hero to the English stage. Such playwrights as Sir Richard Steele and Colley Cibber in England and Marivaux in France contributed to the development of the genteel, sentimental comedy. While the political satire in the plays of Henry Fielding and in John Gay's *Beggar's Opera* (1728) seemed to offer a more interesting potential than the sentiment of Cibber, this line of development was cut off by the Licensing Act of 1737. The Italian Carlo Goldoni, who wrote realistic comedies with fairly sophisticated characterizations, was also possessed of a tendency toward middle-class moralizing. His contemporary, Count Carlo Gozzi, was more ironic and remained faithful to the spirit of the commedia dell'arte. Prior to the surge of German ROMANTICISM in the late 18th cent., two playwrights stood apart from the trend toward sentimental bourgeois realism. Voltaire tried to revive classical models and introduced exotic Eastern settings, although his tragedies tend to be more philosophical than dramatic. Similarly, the Italian Count Vittorio Alfieri sought to restore the spirit of the ancients to his drama, but the attempt was vitiated by his chauvinism. The STURM UND DRANG in Germany represented a romantic reaction against French neoclassicism and was supported by an upsurge of German interest in Shakespeare, who was viewed at the time as the greatest of the romantics. Gotthold Lessing, Friedrich von Schiller, and Goethe were the principal figures of this movement, but the plays produced by the three are frequently marred by sentimentality and too heavy a burden of philosophical ideas. The romantic movement did not blossom in French drama until the 1820s, and then primarily in the work of Victor Hugo and Alexandre Dumas père, while in England the great Romantic poets did not produce important drama, although both Lord Byron and Percy Bysshe Shelley were practitioners of the CLOSET DRAMA. Burlesque and mediocre MELODRAMA reigned supreme on the English stage. Although melodrama was aimed solely at producing superficial excitement, its development, coupled with the emergence of REALISM in the 19th cent., resulted in more serious drama. Initially, the melodrama dealt in such superficially exciting materials as the gothic castle with its mysterious lord for a villain, but gradually the characters and settings moved closer to the realities of contemporary life. The concern for generating excitement led to a more careful consideration of plot construction, reflected in the smoothly contrived climaxes of the "well-made" plays of Eugène Scribe and Victorien Sardou of France and Arthur Wing Pinero of England. The work of Émile Augier and Alexandre Dumas fils combined the drama of ideas with the "well-made" play. Realism had perhaps its most profound expression in the works of the great 19th-century Russian dramatists: Nikolai Gogol, A. N. Ostrovsky, Ivan Turgenev, Leo Tolstoy, Anton Chekhov, and Maxim Gorky. Many of the Russian dramatists emphasized character and satire rather than plot in their works. Related to realism is NATURALISM, which can be defined as a selective realism emphasizing the more sordid and pessimistic aspects of life. An early forerunner of this style in the drama is Georg Büchner's powerful tragedy *Danton's Death* (1835), and an even earlier suggestion may be seen in the pessimistic romantic tragedies of Heinrich von Kleist. Friedrich Hebbel wrote grimly naturalistic drama in the middle of the 19th cent., but the naturalistic movement is most commonly identified with the "slice-of-life" theory of Émile Zola, which had a profound effect on 20th-century playwrights. Henrik Ibsen of Norway brought to a climax the realistic movement of the 19th cent. and also served as a bridge to 20th-century symbolism. His realistic dramas of ideas surpass other such works because they blend a complex plot, a detailed setting, and middle-class yet extraordinary characters in an organic whole. Ibsen's later plays, such as *The Master Builder* (1892), are symbolic, marking a trend away from realism that was continued by August Strindberg's dream plays, with their emphasis on the spiritual, and by the plays of the Belgian Maurice Maeterlinck, who incorporated into drama the theories of the symbolist poets (see SYMBOLISTS). While these antirealistic developments took place on the Continent, in England Oscar Wilde produced comedies of manners that compare favorably with the works of Congreve, and George Bernard Shaw brought the play of ideas to fruition with penetrating intelligence and singular wit. During the 20th cent., especially after World War I, Western drama became more internationally unified and less the product of separate national literary traditions. Throughout the century realism, naturalism, and symbolism (and various combinations of these) continued to inform important plays. Among the many 20th-century playwrights who have written what can be broadly termed naturalist dramas are Gerhart Hauptmann (German), John Galsworthy (English), John Millington Synge and Sean O'Casey (Irish), and Eugene O'Neill, Clifford Odets, and Lillian Hellman (American). An important movement in early 20th-century drama was EXPRESSIONISM. Expressionist playwrights tried to convey the dehumanizing aspects of 20th-century technological society through such devices as minimal scenery, telegraphic dialogue, talking machines, and characters portrayed as types rather than individuals. Notable playwrights who wrote expressionist dramas include Ernst Toller and Georg Kaiser (German), Karel Čapek (Czech), and Elmer Rice and Eugene O'Neill (American). The 20th cent. also saw the attempted revival of drama in verse, but although such writers as William Butler Yeats, W. H. Auden, T. S. Eliot, and Maxwell Anderson produced effective results, verse drama was no longer an important form in English. In Spanish, however, the poetic dramas of Federico García Lorca are placed among the great works of Spanish literature. Three vital figures of 20th-century drama are the American Eugene O'Neill, the German Bertolt Brecht, and the Italian Luigi Pirandello. O'Neill's body of plays in many forms—naturalistic, expressionist, symbolic, psychological—won him the Nobel Prize in Literature and indicated the coming-of-age of American drama. Brecht wrote dramas of ideas, usually promulgating socialist or Marxist theory. In order to make his audience more intellectually receptive to his theses, he endeavored—by using expressionist techniques—to make them continually aware that they were watching a play, not vicariously experiencing reality. For Pirandello, too, it was paramount to fix an awareness of his plays as theater; indeed, the major philosophical concern of his dramas is the difficulty of differentiating between illusion and reality. World War II and its attendant horrors produced a widespread sense of the utter meaninglessness of human existence. This sense is brilliantly expressed in the body of plays that have come to be known collectively as the theater of the absurd. By abandoning traditional devices of the drama, including logical plot development, meaningful dialogue, and intelligible characters, absurdist playwrights sought to convey modern man's feelings of bewilderment, alienation, and despair—his sense that reality is itself unreal. In their plays man is often portrayed as a dupe, a clown who, although not without dignity, is at the mercy of forces that are inscrutable. Probably the most famous plays of the theater of the absurd are Eugene Ionesco's *Bald Soprano* (1950) and Samuel Beckett's *Waiting for Godot* (1953). The sources of the theater of the absurd are diverse; they can be found in the tenets of SURREALISM, dadaism (see under DADA), and EXISTENTIALISM;

in the traditions of the music hall, VAUDEVILLE, and BURLESQUE; and in the films of Charlie CHAPLIN and Buster KEATON. Playwrights whose works can be roughly classed as belonging to the theater of the absurd are Jean Genet (French), Max Frisch and Friedrich Dürrenmatt (Swiss), Günter Grass (German), Fernando Arrabal (Spanish), and Edward Albee (American). The pessimism and despair of the 20th cent. have also found expression in the existentialist dramas of Jean-Paul Sartre and Albert Camus, in the realistic and symbolic dramas of Arthur Miller, Tennessee Williams, and Jean Anouilh, and in the surrealist plays of Jean Cocteau. Somewhat similar to the theater of the absurd is the so-called "theater of cruelty," derived from the ideas of Antonin Artaud, who, writing in the 1930s, foresaw a drama that would assault its audience with movement and sound, producing a visceral rather than an intellectual reaction. After the violence of World War II and the subsequent threat of the atomic bomb, his approach seemed particularly appropriate to many playwrights. Elements of the theater of cruelty can be found in the brilliantly abusive language of John Osborne's *Look Back in Anger* (1956) and Edward Albee's *Who's Afraid of Virginia Woolf?* (1962), in the ritualistic aspects of some of Genet's plays, in the masked utterances and enigmatic silences of Harold Pinter's "comedies of menace," and in the orgiastic abandon of Julian Beck's *Paradise Now!* (1968); it has, however, probably had its fullest expression in Peter Brooks's production of Peter Weiss's *Persecution and Assassination of Marat as Performed by the Inmates of the Asylum at Charenton under the Direction of the Marquis de Sade* (1964). For further information see national literature articles and articles on individual playwrights, e.g., ALBEE, EDWARD. See Allardyce Nicoll, *World Drama from Aeschylus to Anouilh* (1950); John Gassner, *Masters of the Drama* (3d ed. 1954); Margarette Bieber, *The History of Greek and Roman Theatre* (2d ed. 1961); Barrett Clark, ed., *European Theories of the Drama* (rev. ed. 1965); George Freedley and J. A. Reeves, *A History of the Theatre* (3d ed. 1968); Martin Esslin, *The Theatre of the Absurd* (1961, repr. 1969); John Gassner and Edward Quinn, ed., *The Reader's Encyclopedia of World Drama* (1969); G. E. Wellarth, *The Theatre of Protest and Paradox* (2d ed. 1970); C. J. Stratman, *Bibliography of Medieval Drama* (2d ed. 1972); Sheldon Cheney, *The Theatre* (rev. ed. 1972); Richard Gilman, *The Making of Modern Drama* (1974).

Drammen (drä'mən), city (1970 est. pop. 49,000), capital of Buskerud co., SE Norway, at the head of the Dramsfjord and at the mouth of the Dramselva River. It is a commercial and fishing port and a trade and industrial center. Manufactures include forest products, textiles, and metal goods.

Drancy (dräNsē'), city (1968 pop. 69,528), Seine-Saint Denis dept., N central France. An industrial suburb NE of Paris, Drancy produces automobile brakes, aircraft, and hardware. There are also breweries and printing plants. During World War II, Drancy was the site of a Nazi concentration camp.

Drangiana (drăn''jēā'nə, -ăn'ə), ancient country, part of the Persian Empire, between Aria on the north and Gedrosia on the south. It was conquered (330 B.C.) by Alexander the Great and incorporated into his empire. Drangiana is the modern Seistan region of Afghanistan and E Iran.

Draper, John William, 1811-82, American scientist, philosopher, and historian, b. near Liverpool, England, M.D. Univ. of Pennsylvania, 1836. In 1839 he became professor of chemistry at the Univ. of the City of New York. He helped organize the medical school of the university, became its professor of chemistry and physiology, and in 1850 succeeded as its president. His chief contribution to abstract science was research in radiant energy. His work on the spectra of incandescent substances foreshadowed the development of spectrum analysis, in which his son Henry Draper became a pioneer. Draper's research in the effect of light upon chemicals led him to take up photography. He was said to be the first in New York to use Daguerre's process, announced in 1839, improving it so much that by December of that year he made his first satisfactory photographic portrait. A picture he took (1840) of his sister is the oldest surviving photographic portrait. Draper also made (1839-40) the first photographs of the moon. Most of his papers on radiant energy were republished in his *Scientific Memoirs* (1878). His *Human Physiology* (1856) was the leading textbook of the period in its field, and it contained his own admirable micro-photographs, the first ever published. In 1863 his *History of the Intellectual Development of Europe* was published, and in 1874 his *History of the Conflict between Religion and Science*, a rationalistic classic that aroused great controversy. His other works include *History of the American Civil War* (3 vol., 1867-70) and *Thoughts on the Future Civil Policy of America* (1865). See study by D. H. Fleming (1950, repr. 1972). His son, **Henry Draper,** 1837-82, was a physician by vocation, but he made major contributions in the field of astronomical photography and spectroscopy. He was the first to photograph stellar spectrum lines. See biography by G. F. Barker in National Academy of Sciences, *Biographical Memoirs*, Vol. III (1895).

Draper, Lyman Copeland, 1815-91, American historical collector and librarian, b. Erie co., N.Y. He spent years traveling through an area ranging from New York to Mississippi, gathering the stories of old pioneers and documentary material on frontier history for a projected series of biographies of Western heroes. His extensive collection was deposited with the Wisconsin Historical Society at Madison, of which he was secretary and librarian (1854-86); there he built up one of the notable historical libraries of the country. He founded and edited the first 10 volumes of the society's *Collections* and wrote *King's Mountain and its Heroes* (1881, repr. 1967 and 1971), but never completed the intended biographies. His collection, valuable to many researchers, contains the George Rogers Clark papers and other manuscript sources. See biography by W. B. Hesseltine (1954).

Draper, Ruth, 1884-1956, American monologist, b. New York City. The author of 36 monologues, ranging from farce to tragedy, she played the various characters within each sketch with only a change of costume and props. Her delicate and sophisticated art gained her worldwide acclaim. See study by M. D. Zabel (1960).

Drau: see DRAVA.

draughts: see CHECKERS.

Drava or **Drave** (both: drä'və), Ger. *Drau*, Hung. *Dráva*, river, c.450 mi (720 km) long, rising in the Carnic Alps, N Italy. It flows generally E through S Austria (where it is called the Drau) and enters NW Yugoslavia. It forms part of the Yugoslav-Hungarian border before joining the Danube River E of Osijek. The Mur River is its chief tributary. The lower course of the Drava is navigable.

Dravidian (drəvĭd'ēən), name given to the peoples of S and central India and N Ceylon who speak Dravidian languages. They are so called for purely linguistic reasons; the peoples are of varying racial types. It is thought that Dravidian-speaking peoples may have been spread throughout the Indian subcontinent before the invasions of the ARYANS.

Dravidian languages (drəvĭd'ēən), family of about 20 languages that appears to be unrelated to any other known language family. The Dravidian languages are spoken by approximately 120 million people, living chiefly in S and central India and N Sri Lanka. The four major Dravidian languages are Kanarese (or Canarese), having 18 million speakers; Malayalam, having 15 million speakers; Tamil, with 38 million speakers; and Telugu, with 42 million speakers. Each of these languages has a noteworthy literature of considerable age. Brahui, another of the Dravidian group, has about 200,000 speakers, in Baluchistan. It is thought that the Dravidian tongues are derived from a language spoken in India prior to the invasion of the Aryans c.1500 B.C. Dravidian languages are noted for retroflex and liquid sound types. A distinctive feature is the formation of a comparatively large number of sounds in the front of the mouth. Verbs have a negative as well as an affirmative voice. Gender classification is made on the basis of rank instead of sex, with one class including beings of a higher status and the other beings of an inferior status (to which inanimate objects and sometimes women are assigned). Nouns are declined, showing case and number. In the Dravidian languages great use is made of suffixes (but not of prefixes) with nouns and verbs. There are many words of Indic origin in the Dravidian languages, which in turn have contributed a number of words to the Indic tongues. The Dravidian languages have their own alphabets, which go back to a common source that is related to the Devanagari alphabet used for Sanskrit. Brahui, however, is recorded in the Arabic script. See Thomas Burrow, *A Dravidian Etymological Dictionary* (1961); Kamil Zvelebil, *Comparative Dravidian Phonology* (1970).

drawbridge: see BRIDGE.

drawing, art of the draftsman. In its broadest sense it includes every use of the delineated line and is thus basic to the arts of painting, architecture, sculpture, calligraphy, and geometry. The word *drawing* is commonly used to denote works in pen, pencil, crayon, chalk, charcoal, or similar media in which form rather than color is emphasized. For centuries drawings have been made either as preparatory studies (see CARTOON) or as finished works of art. Preparatory drawings sometimes reveal a vigor and spontaneity lacking in the completed work. Among the many artists acclaimed for their drawings are Leonardo da Vinci, Michelangelo, Dürer, Rubens, Hogarth, Goya, Daumier, Klee, Picasso, and Matisse. Drawings are often used as ILLUSTRATIONS and are reproduced by such processes as ETCHING, ENGRAVING, and LITHOGRAPHY. See Paul Sachs, *Modern Prints and Drawings* (1954); Heribert Hutter, *Drawing: History and Technique* (tr. 1968); K. T. Parker, ed., *Old Master Drawings* (14 vol., 1940, repr. 1970).

drawn work: see LACE.

Drayton, Michael, 1563-1631, English poet. The son of a prosperous tradesman, he received his educational training in the house of Sir Henry Goodere, where he served as page. There he made a lasting friendship with Anne Goodere, the youngest daughter of Sir Henry, who became the "Idea" in his series of sonnets (1593-1619). His work reflects the many poetic fashions of the day. He wrote poems on English history and topography (*England's Heroical Epistles*, 1597-99, and the 15,000-line panoramic *Poly-Olbion*, 1612-22); satires (*The Owl*, 1604, and "The Moon Calf," 1627); a Spenserian, though mock-heroic, fairyland poem (*Nymphidia*, 1627); and the idyllic *Muses' Elysium* (1630). He also wrote scriptural paraphrases, pastorals, popular ballads, myths, and collaborated on plays. See his complete works (ed. by J. W. Hebel et al., 5 vol., 1931-41); studies by B. H. Newdigate (1941) and Oliver Elton (1895, repr. 1974).

dream, mental activity associated with the rapid-eye-movement (REM) period of sleep. It is made up commonly of a number of visual images, i.e., of scenes or thoughts expressed in terms of seeing rather than in those of the other senses or in words. The content of dreams sometimes reflects somatic disturbances, such as toothache and indigestion, or external stimuli, such as the ringing of an alarm clock. Although dreams were once believed to last only a few seconds, it is now believed that they last as long as the dreamer senses that they do; moreover, it has been found that stimuli impulses administered in an REM period are incorporated by the sleeper into a dream sequence. The dream content can often be correlated with body changes during REM sleep, e.g., side-to-side eyeball movement may reflect a dream about watching a passing vehicle. In the newborn, REM sleep accounts for about half the total sleeping time. The proportion gradually decreases with age; electroencephalograph studies, measuring brain electrical activity known to correlate with REM sleep, have shown that the adult dreams for 1½ to 2 hr of every 8-hr period of sleep. Dreaming is necessary to the restorative process of sleep; sleepers deprived of dream-sleep show personality changes, e.g., irritability and loss of coordination. In primitive and ancient cultures dreams played an extensive role, being variously considered as visitations of the gods, prophetic pronouncements, and the meanderings of human souls released by sleep. The dreams of Jacob and Joseph and those of Pharaoh interpreted by Joseph are classic. With the ascendancy of science and rationalism during the 18th and 19th cent. dreams ceased to be considered worthy of speculation. Freud, in his *Interpretation of Dreams* (1900, tr. 1913), was one of the first to reemphasize dreams as keys to the make-up of the individual, worthy of careful and exhaustive scientific study. He distinguished the manifest content of dreams, i.e., the experienced dream image, from the latent content, i.e., the meaning of the dream. The language of dreams is largely visual symbol; some images are of so universal and ancient a nature that the interpretation is standard, and others are significant only through the free ASSOCIATION of the patient in psychoanalysis. Freud believed that the symbolic nature of dreams is a disguise designed to protect the dreamer from recognizing attempts at wish fulfillment, i.e., expression of thoughts and impulses repressed in his conscious life; dreams are believed to protect sleep by draining off the force of emotional disturbances that would otherwise cause a person to awaken. C. G. Jung held that dreams function to reveal the unconscious mind, anticipate future events, and give expression to neglected areas of the dreamer's personality. In Jung's view, dreams are not limited to the infantile wishes of the personal unconscious but may also be shaped by innate mental structures called archetypes that originate in the collective unconscious of the human species. Alfred Adler also emphasized the anticipatory and compensatory function of dreams. See G. S. Hall, *The Meaning of Dreams* (1966); G. E. von Grunebaum and Roger Caillois, ed., *The Dream and Human Societies* (1967); Leopold Caligon and Rollo May, *Dreams and Symbols* (1968).

Drebbel, Cornelis Jacobszoon (kôrnā'lĭs yä'kôpsōn drĕb'əl), 1572–1634, Dutch inventor, physicist, and mechanician. His major inventions were a "perpetual motion" machine and the first navigable SUBMARINE, the air supply of which was renewed by oxygen extracted from saltpeter. His other inventions include thermostats used to make self-regulating ovens, as well as various optical instruments. He also discovered a process for making scarlet dye that was used for many years by the dye industry. See studies by Gerrit Tierie (1932) and L. E. Harris (1961).

dredging, process of excavating materials under water. It is used to deepen waterways, harbors, and docks and for mining alluvial mineral deposits, including tin, gold, and diamonds. The Dutch at an early period cleared their canals of silt with a pole to which was attached a bag held open by a steel ring. The apparatus, operated from the side of a stationary barge, was dragged along the bottom and then emptied into the barge. Modern dredging equipment may be divided into four main classes. The **grab dredge** is used where the amount of excavation is relatively small. It consists of one or more grab buckets, operated by cranes mounted on a vessel or barge or sometimes on the shore. Each bucket has jaws that are hinged together. The bucket is lowered to the bottom with its jaws open and pointing down. When it sinks into the material to be dredged, its jaws close. The material can then be lifted to the surface and discharged into a hopper for removal to a disposal area. The **dipper dredge,** also known as the boom-and-dipper assembly, is similar in appearance to a land power shovel. It is used extensively in canal construction and was employed in the cutting of the Panama Canal. The **ladder-bucket dredge,** a more elaborate type, is generally mounted on a self-propelling vessel built with a longitudinal well in the center, open to the water beneath for a considerable length. Mounted and hinged over the well is a long steel frame, which may be raised or lowered at will; it is equipped with a long string of buckets passing over sprockets at each end. The buckets, operating through the well, scoop up material from the bottom and discharge it into a chute that projects over the vessel's side to a hopper barge moored alongside or into a receiving hopper in the dredge itself. The **suction dredge,** or hydraulic dredge, an entirely different type, is used principally where material such as sand or mud is to be removed. It consists of a flexible pipe connected at one end to a powerful centrifugal pump. At the other, open end there is usually a device designed to break up the material to be dredged. The open end of the pipe is lowered to the bottom, where the material to be dredged is mixed with water, pumped up, and then discharged into hopper barges. There the heavy material settles, and the surplus water is allowed to overflow. Material from these dredges is sometimes pumped through pipes for long distances and used to build up low-lying ground. Hopper barges made to carry away and sink the material brought up by dredges are of a special type. In the space where the material is carried are hinged doors, or flaps, held closed by chains and opening downward. Around the space are watertight compartments to give the barge buoyancy. When the dredge is above the disposal area, the bottom doors are released and the material discharged; the doors are then closed again by winches.

Dred Scott Case, argued before the U.S. Supreme Court in 1856–57. It involved the then bitterly contested issue of the status of slavery in the Federal territories. In 1834, Dred Scott, a Negro slave, personal servant to Dr. John Emerson, a U.S. army surgeon, was taken by his master from Missouri, a slave state, to Illinois, a free state, and thence to Fort Snelling (now in Minnesota) in Wisconsin Territory, where slavery was prohibited by the MISSOURI COMPROMISE. There he married before returning with Dr. Emerson to Missouri in 1838. After Emerson's death, Scott sued (1846) Emerson's widow for freedom for himself and his family (he had two children) on the ground that residence in a free state and then in a free territory had ended his bondage. He won his suit before a lower court in St. Louis, but the Missouri supreme court reversed the decision (thus reversing its own precedents). Scott's lawyers then maneuvered the case into the Federal courts. Since J. F. A. Sanford, Mrs. Emerson's brother, was the legal administrator of her property and a resident of New York, the Federal court accepted jurisdiction for the case on the basis of diversity of state citizenship. After a Federal district court decided against Scott, the case came on appeal to the Supreme Court. In Feb., 1857, the court decided in conference to avoid completely the question of the constitutionality of the Missouri Compromise and to return a verdict against Scott on the ground that under Missouri law as now interpreted by the supreme court of that state he remained a slave despite his previous residence in free territory. However, when it became known that two antislavery justices, John McLean and Benjamin R. Curtis, planned to write dissenting opinions vigorously upholding the constitutionality of the Missouri Compromise (which had, in fact, been voided by the Kansas-Nebraska Act of 1854), the court's Southern members, constituting the majority, decided to consider the whole question of Federal power over slavery in the territories. They decided in the case of *Scott vs. Sandford* (the name was misspelled in the formal reports) that Congress had no power to prohibit slavery in the territories, and Chief Justice Roger B. TANEY delivered the court's opinion that the Missouri Compromise was unconstitutional. Three of the justices also held that a Negro "whose ancestors were . . . sold as slaves" was not entitled to the rights of a Federal citizen and therefore had no standing in court. The court's verdict further inflamed the sectional controversy between North and South and was roundly denounced by the growing antislavery group in the North. See V. C. Hopkins, *Dred Scott's Case* (1951, repr. 1967); S. I. Kutler, ed., *The Dred Scott Decision* (1967); F. B. Latham, *The Dred Scott Decision* (1968).

Dreiser, Theodore (drī'sər), 1871–1945, American novelist, b. Terre Haute, Ind. A pioneer of naturalism in American literature, Dreiser wrote novels reflecting his mechanistic view of life, a concept that held man as the victim of such ungovernable forces as economics, biology, society, and even chance. In his works conventional morality is unimportant, consciously virtuous behavior having little to do with material success and happiness. Dreiser was born into a large, poverty-ridden, and grimly religious family. His education was irregular, but he did manage to spend the year 1889–90 at the Univ. of Indiana. After working as a journalist on several midwestern newspapers, he went in 1894 to New York City, where he was soon writing for and editing magazines. His first novel, *Sister Carrie* (1900), the story of a country girl's rise to material success first as the mistress of a wealthy man and then as an actress, was given limited circulation by its publisher and attacked for its alleged immorality; it was reissued in 1912. *Jennie Gerhardt* (1911), again about a "fallen woman," was also attacked for its lack of morality, but it sold well enough for Dreiser to give up journalism. With these two works, Dreiser started his long battle for the right of the novelist to portray life as he sees it. In *The Financier* (1912), he turned his attention more specifically to American social and economic institutions. This novel, the first of a trilogy that includes *The Titan* (1914) and *The Stoic* (1947), describes the rise to power of a ruthless industrialist. In *The Genius* (1915) and its sequel, *The Bulwark* (1946), Dreiser explores the failings of an American artist. *An American Tragedy* (1925), considered his greatest work, tells of a poor young man's futile effort to achieve social and financial success; the attempt ends in his execution for murder. In his later life Dreiser became interested in socialism, about which he wrote in the nonfictional *Dreiser Looks at Russia* (1928) and *Tragic America* (1931). Among his other works are such collections of short stories as *Free* (1918), *Chains* (1927), and *A Gallery of Women* (1929); and the autobiographies *A Traveler at Forty* (1913), *A Book About Myself* (1922; republished as *Newspaper Days,* 1931), and *Dawn* (1931). See his selected letters (3 vol., 1959); biographies by W. A. Swanberg (1965) and R. H. Elias (rev. ed. 1970); studies by F. O. Matthiessen (1951, repr. 1973), R. D. Lehan (1969, repr. 1974), Ellen Moers (1969), and James Lundquist (1974).

Drenthe (drĕn'tə), province (1971 pop. 372,600), c.1,030 sq mi (2,670 sq km), NE Netherlands, bordering on West Germany in the east. Assen is the capital, and Emmen is the chief industrial center. The province is made up largely of heath country where farming is pursued. Manufactures include food products, textiles, and metal goods. Long subject to the bishops of Utrecht, Drenthe passed (1536) to Emperor Charles V. It was part of the United Provinces of the Netherlands from 1581, but was not entitled to a seat in the States-General until 1796.

Dresden (drĕz'dən), city (1970 pop. 501,508), capital of Dresden district, SE East Germany, on the Elbe River. It is an industrial and cultural center, a rail junction, and a large inland port. Manufactures include precision and optical instruments, chemicals, clothing, processed food, ceramics, and glass. Originally a Slavic settlement called Drezdane, Dresden was settled with Germans by the margrave of Meissen in the 13th cent. From 1485 until 1918 it was the residence of the dukes, then the electors, and later the kings, of Saxony. Prussia occupied Dresden in the Second Silesian War (see AUSTRIAN SUCCESSION, WAR OF THE), but withdrew after the Treaty of Dresden (1745). In the Seven Years War, Dresden was again occupied (1756) by the Prussians. In Aug., 1813, Napoleon I defeated the coalition forces near Dresden in his last great victory before his defeat (Oct., 1813) at Leipzig. In the late 17th and 18th cent., particularly under the electors Frederick Augustus I and Frederick Augustus II (Augustus II and Augustus III as kings of Poland), Dresden became a center of the arts and an outstanding showplace of baroque and rococo architecture. In the late 18th and early 19th cent. it was a leading center of the romantic movement, and in the late 19th and early 20th cent. it was a center of German opera. Ranked as one of the world's most beautiful cities before World War II, Dresden was severely damaged by British and U.S. bombing during the war (Feb., 1945). Among the city's famous landmarks, all damaged in the war, are the city hall, the Zwinger palace and museum, the Hofkirche [court chapel], and the cathedral. Most of the fabulous art collection, acquired by the court in the 18th and 19th cent., was safely kept through the war outside Dresden, but many art objects were afterward moved to the USSR. The city is the seat of a technical university. "Dresden china" was originally made in Dresden, but the factory was moved to MEISSEN in the early 18th cent.

dress: see COSTUME.

Dressler, Marie, 1869–1934, American actress, b. Coburg, Ont., Canada. She appeared on stage and in vaudeville before making her first film, *Tillie's Punctured Romance* (1914). Although she gained fame as a large, good-natured comedienne, she gave a strong performance as a disreputable old alcoholic in *Anna Christie* (1930). Her other films include *Min and Bill* (1931), *Tugboat Annie* (1932), and *Dinner at Eight* (1933).

Dreux (drö), town (1968 pop. 30,815), Eure-et-Loir dept., N central France. It is an industrial center where foundry products, boilers, metal products, radio and television equipment, and automobile paints are manufactured. An old Gallo-Roman city, Dreux belonged to the counts of Vexin and the dukes of Normandy in medieval times. The town changed hands many times before being united with the French crown under Louis XV (18th cent.). Dreux is rich in monuments, among which are St. Peter's Church (13th–17th cent.) and a belfry (16th cent.).

Drew, Daniel, 1797–1879, American railroad speculator, b. Carmel, N.Y. He became a cattle dealer in early life and by 1834 was successful enough to engage in the steamboat business on the Hudson, which he developed rapidly. In 1844, Drew entered Wall St., where he founded the firm of Drew, Robinson & Company. After its dissolution a decade later, he became an independent operator and was bold and scheming in pursuing his goals. In 1857 he forced his way into becoming a director of the ERIE RAILROAD. During the famous "Erie War" (1866–68), Drew manipulated Erie stock so that he and his allies Jay GOULD and James FISK defeated the attempt of Cornelius VANDERBILT to gain control. Sometime later, however, Drew was financially outsmarted by Gould and Fisk. This was the beginning of his downfall, which ultimately led to his complete financial ruin in the Panic of 1873. By 1876 he was bankrupt. In his heyday Drew, a Methodist, contributed to the establishment of several churches, as well as Drew Theological Seminary (now part of Drew Univ.) and Drew Seminary (for girls) at Carmel. See C. F. Adams and Henry Adams, *Chapters of Erie* (1871, repr. 1967); Bouck White, *The Book of Daniel Drew* (1910, repr. 1973).

Drew, George Alexander, 1894–1973, Canadian political leader. A lawyer, he led the Conservative party in Ontario from 1938 and served in the provincial legislature (1939–48) and in the House of Commons (1949–56). From 1943 until he resigned in 1948, Drew was premier of Ontario and minister of education, laying the foundation for extensive educational reforms. From 1948 to 1956 he was national leader of the Progressive Conservative party. He then served (1957-64) as Canadian high commissioner to the United Kingdom.

Drew, John, 1827-62, American actor, b. Dublin. He made his debut in 1846 at the Bowery Theatre, New York, afterward touring various cities and establishing a reputation as an Irish comedian. His career for the rest of his life was bound up in the Arch Street Theatre, Philadelphia, where he maintained a famous stock company, with his wife as co-star. His wife, **Louisa Lane Drew,** 1820-97, b. London, came to the United States as a child and, until her marriage in 1850, acted with such stars as J. B. Booth, Joseph Jefferson, and Edwin Forrest. On her husband's death she assumed management of the Arch Street Theatre until 1892, establishing her reputation as a character actress. She was constantly seen on tour (1880-92) as Mrs. Malaprop in *The Rivals,* which was her best role. A strong-willed woman who spent her entire life on the stage, she ruled her theater and her family with a firm hand. Her three children, John and Sidney Drew and Georgiana Drew (who married Maurice BARRYMORE), had their early training under their mother. See her *Autobiographical Sketch,* with an introduction by John Drew (1899); M. J. Moses, *Famous Actor-Families in America* (1906). Her eldest son, **John Drew,** 1853-1927, b. Philadelphia, began his career in her company. In 1875 he joined the company of Augustin DALY in New York and appeared with Fanny Davenport. Later, with Ada Rehan as co-star, he played with acclaim in Daly's remarkable Shakespearean productions. In 1892 he left Daly, and as one of the first Charles FROHMAN stars, he played in modern comedies with Maude Adams. Distinguished and handsome, he was a romantic actor noted for his versatility in comedy; he was especially praised as Petruchio in *The Taming of the Shrew.* In 1905 he succeeded Joseph Jefferson as president of the Players' Club. He died while on tour in an all-star revival of Pinero's *Trelawney of the Wells.* See his autobiography, *My Years on the Stage* (1922); biographies by E. A. Dithmar (1900) and Peggy Wood (1928).

Drewrys Bluff (dro͝or'ēz), high ground on the southern bank of the James River, E Va., S of Richmond; scene of two engagements in the Civil War. On May 15, 1862, the Confederates, positioned on the bluff, repulsed Union gunboats that were part of Gen. George McClellan's PENINSULAR CAMPAIGN. In May, 1864, Union Gen. Benjamin Butler led the Army of the James up the peninsula against Richmond. Butler was defeated at Drewrys Bluff on May 16, 1864, by a greatly inferior Confederate force under Gen. Pierre Beauregard. Butler's forces then retreated to the village of Bermuda Hundred, where Beauregard bottled them up until Gen. U.S. Grant crossed the James and moved on Petersburg.

Drew University, at Madison N. J.; United Methodist; coeducational; est. and opened 1867, chartered 1867 as Drew Theological Seminary; named for Daniel Drew. With the addition of Brothers College in 1928, it became Drew Univ. It includes a theological school, a graduate school, and a liberal arts college.

Drexel, Anthony Joseph, 1826-93, American banker and philanthropist, b. Philadelphia. He entered (1838) at an early age the well-known banking firm of Drexel and Company, founded by his father, Francis Martin Drexel, an Austrian immigrant. Anthony became a partner, and later under his dominant leadership the firm expanded extensively. Drexel Institute, opened in 1892, was the most important of his many philanthropies.

Drexel Institute of Technology, at Philadelphia, Pa.; coeducational; founded 1891 by Anthony J. Drexel, opened 1892, chartered 1894 as Drexel Institute of Art, Science, and Industry. It was renamed in 1936. Drexel has a work-study program for students in science, engineering, and business administration.

Dreyer, Carl Theodore, 1889-1968, Danish motion picture director. He began making films in Denmark in 1920. Dreyer's *Passion of Joan of Arc* (1928) is widely regarded as one of the classics of the silent screen. It makes extensive use of closeups to suggest the everyday human reality behind historical events. His later works, many of which won international acclaim, include such films as *Vampyr* (1932), *Day of Wrath* (1943), *Ordet* (1955), and *Gertrud* (1964). See studies by Tom Milne (1971) and David Bordwell (1973).

Dreyer, Johan Ludwig Emil (yō'hän lo͝ot'vĭkh ā'-māl drī'ər), 1852-1926, Danish astronomer, b. Copenhagen, who worked in Great Britain. He was assistant astronomer at the earl of Rosse's observatory, Parsonstown (now Birr), Ireland (1874-78), and at the observatory of the Univ. of Dublin (1878-82) and director (1882-1916) of the observatory at Armagh. He compiled the standard *New General Catalogue of Nebulae and Clusters of Stars* (1888; supplements, 1895, 1908), wrote a biography of Tycho Brahe (1890) and *History of the Planetary Systems from Thales to Kepler* (1906), and edited *Second Armagh Catalogue of 3,300 Stars* (1886), the scientific papers of Sir William Herschel (1912), and the first volumes of the collected works of Tycho Brahe (15 vol., 1913-29).

Dreyfus Affair (drā'fəs, drī-). In 1894, Capt. Alfred Dreyfus (1859-1935), a French general staff officer, was convicted of treason *in camera* by a French court-martial and was sentenced to degradation and deportation for life; he was sent to Devils Island for solitary confinement. The case had arisen when a French spy in the German embassy discovered a handwritten *bordereau* [schedule], received by Major Max von Schwartzkoppen, German military attaché in Paris, which listed secret French documents. The army attempted to ferret out the traitor. At this time the French army was the stronghold of monarchists and Catholics and was permeated by anti-Semitism. Suspicion fell on Dreyfus, a wealthy Alsatian Jew, while the press noised accusations of Jewish treason. Dreyfus protested his innocence, but public opinion generally applauded the conviction, and interest in the case lapsed. However, the matter flared up again in 1896 and soon divided Frenchmen into two irreconcilable factions. In 1896, Col. Georges PICQUART, chief of the intelligence section, discovered evidence indicating Major Ferdinand Walsin ESTERHAZY as the real author of the *bordereau.* Picquart was silenced by army authorities, but in 1897 Dreyfus's brother, Mathieu, made the same discovery and increased pressure to reopen the case. Esterhazy was tried (Jan., 1898) by a court-martial and acquitted in a matter of minutes. Émile ZOLA, a leading supporter of Dreyfus, promptly published an open letter to the president of the French republic, Félix Faure, accusing the judges of having obeyed orders from the war office in their acquittal of Esterhazy. Zola was tried for libel and sentenced to jail, but he escaped to England. By this time the case had become a major political issue and was fully exploited by royalist, militarist, and nationalist elements, on the one hand, and by republican, socialist, and anticlerical elements, on the other. The violent partisanship dominated French life for a decade. Among the anti-Dreyfusards were Édouard DRUMONT; Paul Déroulède, who founded a patriotic league; and Maurice BARRÈS. The pro-Dreyfus faction, which steadily gained strength, came to include Georges CLEMENCEAU, in whose paper Zola's letter appeared, Jean JAURÈS, René WALDECK-ROUSSEAU, Anatole FRANCE, Charles PÉGUY, and Joseph REINACH. They were, in part, less concerned with Dreyfus personally, who remained in solitary confinement on Devils Island, than with discrediting the rightist government. Later in 1898 it was discovered that much of the evidence against Dreyfus had been forged by Colonel Henry of army intelligence. Henry committed suicide (Aug., 1898), and Esterhazy fled to England. Revision of Dreyfus's sentence became imperative. The case was referred to an appeals court in September and after Waldeck-Rousseau became premier in 1899, the court of appeals ordered a new court-martial. There was worldwide indignation when the military court, unable to admit error, found Dreyfus guilty with extenuating circumstances and sentenced him to 10 years in prison. However, a pardon was issued by President Émile Loubet, and in 1906 the supreme court of appeals exonerated Dreyfus, who was reinstated as a major and decorated with the Legion of Honor. In 1930 his innocence was reaffirmed by the publication of Schwartzkoppen's papers. The immediate result of the Dreyfus Affair was to unite and bring to power the French political left wing. Widespread antimilitarism and rabid anticlericalism also ensued; army influence declined, and in 1905 Church and state were separated in France. See Joseph Reinach, *Histoire de l'affaire Dreyfus* (7 vol., 1901-11); Alfred Dreyfus and Pierre Dreyfus, *The Dreyfus Case* (tr. 1937); studies by Guy Chapman (1955 and 1972), D. W. Johnson (1966), L. L. Snyder (1972), and D. L. Lewis (1973).

Driesch, Hans Adolf Eduard (häns ä'dôlf ā'do͞oärt drēsh), 1867-1941, German philosopher, b. Bad Kreuznach, grad. (zoology) Univ. of Jena, 1889. His early interest in biology was gradually overshadowed by involvement in philosophy. As an embryologist he had experimented with the eggs of sea urchins and had established that a portion of an early embryo could develop into a complete, though smaller than normal, organism. This contradicted then-current mechanistic theories and led Driesch to develop a theory of vitalism, explaining organic systems in terms of a mysterious self-determining principle rather than in physical or chemical terms. His main work on the subject of vitalism is *The History and Theory of Vitalism* (1905). Driesch joined the Univ. of Heidelberg's philosophy faculty in 1912 and while there wrote *Theory of Order* (1912), *Logic as a Task* (1913), and *Theory of Reality* (1917). He later taught at Cologne and Leipzig but in 1933 was retired by the Nazis.

drift, deposit of mixed clay, gravel, sand, and boulders transported and laid down by glaciers. Stratified, or glaciofluvial, drift is carried by waters flowing from the melting ice of a glacier. The flowing water sorts the particles, generally depositing layers of coarser particles nearer the point of origin. Till, or boulder clay, which makes up the greater part of the drift, is unstratified, consisting of disorganized heaps of rocks that range widely in size. Till is deposited directly by the glacier itself without water transport. The drift may take the form of a DRUMLIN, a KAME, an ESKER, a MORAINE, or an outwash plain; its thickness varies noticeably from place to place and is not dependent upon topographical factors. Presence of drift proved useful in establishing the existence of time periods when large parts of the surface of continents were covered with glaciers (see GLACIAL PERIOD). Large sections of continental Europe and North America are covered by drift.

Driftless Area, c.13,000 sq mi (33,670 sq km), largely in SW Wis. but extending into SE Minn., NE Iowa, and NW Ill. The continental glacier which covered most surrounding regions did not touch this area, which therefore has no glacial drifts. It abounds in caves and sinkholes and has residual, well-drained soil. The Federal government prohibited farming in the Driftless Area until the 1840s because it was an important lead-mining region. In the mid-1800s, the area was settled by European immigrants, who found it similar to their former homelands.

drill, tool used to create a hole, usually in some hard substance, by its rotary or hammering action. Many different tools make up the drill family. The awl is a pointed instrument used for piercing small holes. In its early form it was a thorn or a tool of bone or chipped flint; many prehistoric awls of flint have been found. The gimlet, which consists of a cross handle holding a metal shaft with a screw point, is used for boring small holes. Its principle and that of a similar tool, the auger, were known and used in ancient times, but the tools were much improved in the Middle Ages. The auger has a cross handle containing a shaft that usually ends with a central screw-shaped point; the point acts to pull two knife edges about it into the material to do the actual cutting. Spiral channels extend part way up the shaft to allow chips to be removed from the hole. The term auger is also applied to various augerlike tools. More elaborate types of drills are composed of two main parts: a replaceable device that does the actual cutting, called a bit, and a second device that drives it. Both devices may be referred to as drills. Two common types of rotary bits are the auger and the twist bit. Hand-powered rotary driving devices include the hand drill, which has a crank that transmits turning power to the bit through a gear and pinion, and the bit brace, which is a bow-shaped device that is rotated to turn a bit. Motor-powered rotary driving devices include the drill press and the portable electric drill, both used at home or in industry for cutting holes in such materials as metal, wood, and plastic. The core drill cuts an annular hole through minerals. For a small hole the drill bit contains diamonds, which bore a hole by their abrasive action when they are rotated. A rotary oil well drill uses a bit containing either rolling cutters with hard teeth or a fixed, chisel cutting edge. The percussive types of drill force a bit to move forward by a hammering action that chips away material, instead of cutting or abrading it. For example, an air percussion drill chips through rock with a cross-shaped bit driven by a piston; the similar churn drill is lifted and dropped by cable. One special kind of drill, the fusion drill, creates a hole by melting or flaking minerals with an oxyacetylene torch. An agricultural implement for planting certain seeds or for placing fertilizer in the soil is called a drill. Small drills for gardens are pushed by hand; large drills for field work are drawn by horses or tractors. The agricultural drill is named for its special uses, e.g., the grass drill and the grain drill, or for its construction, as the disk drill and the hoe drill. The fertilizer drill is commonly combined with the seed drill.

drill, monkey: see MANDRILL.

Drin (drēn), river, c.175 mi (280 km) long, formed at Kukës, NE Albania, by the confluence of the White Drin and the Black Drin, which rise in Yugoslavia. It is the largest river of Albania. The Drin flows generally west through deep gorges and then onto the coastal plain before turning south and entering the Adriatic Sea S of Lezhë. North of Lezhë, a distributary (formed 1858–59) diverts some of the flow to the Bojana River. The Drin is not navigable.

Drina (drē'nä), river, c.285 mi (460 km) long, formed by the confluence of the Piva and Tara rivers, S central Yugoslavia. It flows generally N through central Yugoslavia to the Sava River. There are several high dams on the Drina and its headstreams.

Drinkwater, John, 1882–1937, English author. A founder of the Birmingham Repertory Theatre, he was associated with it as actor, director, and general manager for many years. He is best known for his chronicle plays, including *Abraham Lincoln* (1918), *Mary Stuart* (1921), and *Robert E. Lee* (1923). *Bird in Hand,* a highly successful comedy, was produced in 1927. His other works include biographical studies, a novel, and several collections of poems.

dripstone: see STALACTITE AND STALAGMITE.

Driver, Samuel Rolles, 1846–1914, English clergyman and biblical scholar. He was regius professor of Hebrew and canon of Christ Church, Oxford, and from 1876 to 1884 was a member of the Old Testament Revision Committee, set up to work on a revised version of the Bible. His chief work is his *Introduction to the Literature of the Old Testament* (1891). He collaborated with C. A. Briggs and Francis Brown in preparing *A Hebrew and English Lexicon of the Old Testament* (completed 1906).

drives: see LIBIDO.

Drobak (drö'bäk), town, Akershus co., SE Norway, on the Oslofjord. It is a picturesque summer resort and a winter port for Oslo.

Drobisch, Moritz Wilhelm (mō'rĭts vĭl'hĕlm drō'bĭsh), 1802–96, German philosopher and mathematician. He was a teacher at Leipzig and a follower and adherent of Johann Friedrich Herbart. Drobisch's works include *Neue Darstellung der Logik* [new exposition of logic] (1836) and *Empirische Psychologie* (1842).

Drogheda (drô'ədə, droi'də), urban district (1971 pop. 19,744), Co. Louth, E central Republic of Ireland, on the Boyne River. The town is a port that exports agricultural products (especially to Liverpool) and imports coal. There are cement-processing works, breweries, ironworks, and linen, cotton, and lumber mills. Salmon are caught in the Boyne. Drogheda was a Danish stronghold in the 10th cent. In 1394 the Irish princes of Leinster and Ulster submitted there to Richard II. Poynings's Law (see under POYNINGS, SIR EDWARD) was enacted in Drogheda in the 15th cent. Oliver CROMWELL stormed the town in 1649 and massacred the inhabitants. The battle of the BOYNE was fought at Drogheda in 1690. Of the ancient town gates, St. Lawrence's Gate on the east side remains. Magdalen Steeple is all that remains of the Dominican abbey founded in 1224. There are ruins of a priory from the time of Edward I.

Drogobych (drəgô'bĭch), Pol. *Drohobycz,* city (1970 pop. 56,000), Lvov oblast, SW European USSR, in the Ukraine, in the N Carpathian foothills. The major petroleum-refining center of the Borislav oil field, it is linked by an oil pipeline with Borislav and a natural gas pipeline with Dashava. An old Ukrainian settlement, Drogobych belonged to Kievan Russia until the 14th cent., when it passed to Poland. It was taken by Austria in 1772 but reverted to Poland in 1919; in 1939 it was included in the Ukraine.

Drôme (drōm), department (1968 pop. 342,891), SE France. VALENCE is the capital.

dromedary: see CAMEL.

drongo (drŏng'gō), any of the insect-eating Old World birds of the family Dicruridae. Most species have black plumage with an iridescent purple or green shimmer and long, deeply forked tails. They have long pointed wings and stout, hooked bills ornamented with long bristles about the mouth. Most have ornamental crests or head plumes. Drongos range in body length from 7 to 15 in. (18–38 cm); the tail in some species is as long as 28 in. (71 cm). Solitary, arboreal birds of forests, wooded savannas, and fields, drongos are most numerous in S Asia, but also occur in S Africa and NE Australia. Typical of the family is the king crow, *Dicrurus macrocercus,* found from India to Java and Taiwan. Drongos are powerful, aggressive birds and will drive off birds much larger than themselves, incidentally providing protection to more docile species that nest in the same trees. Members of some species follow cattle in order to feed on the associated insects. There are about 20 drongo species, classified in two genera, *Dicrurus* and *Chaetorhynchus,* of the phylum CHORDATA, subphylum Vertebrata, class Aves, order Passeriformes, family Dicruridae.

dropsonde (drŏp'sŏnd''), RADIOSONDE that is dropped by a parachute from a carrier balloon or an aircraft. See WEATHER BALLOON.

dropsy: see EDEMA.

dropwort, name for several herbs, especially a meadowsweet (see SPIRAEA).

Drosophila: see FRUIT FLY.

Droste-Hülshoff, Annette Elisabeth, Freiin von (änĕt'ə ālē'zäbĕt frī'īn fən drôs'tə-hüls'hôf), 1797–1848, German poet. Often called the greatest German woman poet, she has been especially praised for her religious *Das geistliche Jahr* (1850). Also noted are the ballad "Die Schlacht im Loener Bruch" and the fine short novel *Die Judenbuche* (1842, tr. *The Jew's Beech Tree,* in Kuno Francke and W. G. Howard, *The German Classics of the Nineteenth and Twentieth Centuries,* 1913–15). Her masterful verse, romantic in spirit, is free of traditional influence.

Drouais, François-Hubert (fräNswä'-übâr' drōōä'), 1727–75, French painter, a follower of François Boucher, whose style he imitated. Under the patronage of the court he painted portraits of Louis XV, Mme Du Barry, Mme de Pompadour, and many others. He is best known for his portraits of children. His *Count of Artois and His Sister* is in the Louvre.

drought, abnormally long period of insufficient rainfall. Drought cannot be defined in terms of inches of rainfall or number of days without rain, since it is determined by such variable factors as the distribution in time and area of precipitation during and before the dry period. Since ancient times droughts have had far-reaching effects on mankind by causing the failure of crops, natural vegetation, and water supply. Livestock and wildlife, as well as humans, die of thirst and famine; large land areas often suffer damage from dust storms or fire. Drought is thought by some to have caused migrations of early man. In India and China especially drought has periodically brought widespread privation and death. In 1930 lack of rainfall devastated the Great Plains of the United States; the DUST BOWL developed in the 1930s, and its area spread to alarming dimensions (about 50 million acres). During the summer of 1962 much of the eastern part of the country experienced the worst drought in more than 50 years. During the 1970s a severe drought afflicted the countries in the Sahel region in W Africa. Efforts to end a drought include RAINMAKING. See V. P. Subrahmanyam, *Incidence of Continental Drought* (1967); C. S. Russell et al., *Drought and Water Supply* (1970); W. C. Palmer and L. M. Denny, *Drought Bibliography* (1971).

Drouyn de Lhuys, Édouard (ādwär' drōōăN' də lüēs'), 1805–81, French diplomat. He served under the July Monarchy. After the Revolution of 1848, he was president of the committee of foreign affairs, ambassador to London, and three times minister of foreign affairs (1851, 1852–55, 1862–66). He had much to do with the role of Emperor Napoleon III in the Crimean War and the Austro-Prussian War.

Droysen, Johann Gustav (yōhän' gŏŏs'täf droi'zən), 1808–84, German historian. A member of the FRANKFURT PARLIAMENT, he was a leading proponent of German unification under the leadership of his native Prussia. His *Geschichte der preussischen Politik* [political history of Prussia] (14 vol., 1855–86) poses the goal of German unification as the dominant theme of Prussian history. See his *Outlines of the Principles of History* (1858; tr. 1893, repr. 1967).

Drude, Paul Karl Ludwig (poul kärl lōōt'vĭkh drōō'də), 1863–1906, German physicist. Drude first experimented with the physical determinants of optical constants, measuring the optical constants of a variety of substances to an unprecedented degree of accuracy. He worked on the relations among optical constants, electrical constants, and the physical structure of substances, gradually shifting from a mechanical to an electromagnetic viewpoint. From age 26 to his death he edited the journal *Annalen der Physik.*

drug addiction and drug abuse, the chronic or habitual use of any chemical substance to alter states of body or mind for other than medically warranted purposes. Addiction can be specified in purely medical terms, while what constitutes abuse depends on a particular social context. An individual is said to be addicted only if he develops a physical dependence on a given drug; i.e., when the drug dose is decreased or if the drug is discontinued altogether, the addict will experience a withdrawal syndrome, which often includes vomiting, muscle cramps, convulsions, and delirium. With the continued use of an addictive drug, tolerance develops; i.e., constantly increasing amounts of the drug are needed to duplicate the initial effect. If an addict's particular drug is unavailable, withdrawal symptoms can be prevented by using another drug of the same type, a phenomenon known as cross-tolerance. Among the drugs with potential for abuse that affect the nervous system are the NARCOTICS (including OPIUM, its constituent, MORPHINE, and the morphine derivatives HEROIN and METHADONE), the DEPRESSANTS (ALCOHOL, SEDATIVES, and BARBITURATES), the STIMULANTS (COCAINE and AMPHETAMINES), and the PSYCHOTOMIMETIC DRUGS, or hallucinogens (mescaline, psilocybin, and LYSERGIC ACID DIETHYLAMIDE, or LSD). MARIJUANA and HASHISH, once classified as hallucinogens, are now considered to have a different pharmacological effect. True addiction, as opposed to psychological dependence, has been definitely established only for the narcotics and the depressants. It is generally believed that psychotomimetic drugs produce neither physical nor psychological dependence. The absence of addiction does not mean that these drugs are harmless; a traumatic drug experience can produce PARANOIA or trigger other psychotic reactions. Drug use is not always considered drug abuse. For example the stimulant CAFFEINE in coffee and tea is a drug used by millions of people; but because of its relatively mild stimulatory effects and because caffeine does not generally trigger antisocial behavior in users, the drinking of coffee and tea is not generally considered drug abuse. Even narcotics addiction is only seen as drug abuse in certain social contexts. In some undeveloped agrarian countries where the poor use a mild narcotic such as smoked opium, narcotics are not unduly corrosive to social fabric. In contrast, in a technologically advanced nation, with drug laws that make it a criminal offense to obtain and use drugs, a potent narcotic such as heroin is readily abused. The addict obtains his drugs from, and associates with, individuals living in a subculture based on drug use and involving the rituals of obtaining the drug, preparing it, and taking it. There are consequent dangers of HEPATITIS, malnutrition, and contaminated or misrepresented black market drugs. Shoplifting, burglary, prostitution, and other criminal activities are common, since the addict is often unable to find and hold regular employment and must obtain as much as several hundred dollars a day to support his habit. Although narcotics were used as early as 4000 B.C., opium addiction first became a major social problem in the 19th cent. in China. Chinese emigrants to the United States, who were employed to build the transcontinental railroad, brought the opium-smoking habit to the West Coast. During the 19th cent. opium was grown in the United States as well as imported. Along with cocaine, morphine and other opiates were used freely in patent medicines and doctors' prescriptions, and many people became addicted without realizing it. The indiscriminate use of morphine in treating wounded soldiers also produced many addicts. Substitution of morphine addiction for alcohol addiction was considered beneficial by some physicians because alcohol is more destructive to the body and is more likely to trigger antisocial behavior. Today narcotics are the leading cause of death among teenagers in New York City, where half of the nation's more than 300,000 addicts live. Addiction, which began among urban ghetto minorities, spread in the 1960s and 70s to white middle class youth and to American veterans of the Vietnam War. Heroin is the predominant street narcotic. It is a potent morphine derivative that the body converts back into morphine. Heroin was developed as a supposedly nonaddictive alternative to morphine and a cure for addiction. It is sniffed, injected under the skin, or, for maximum effect, injected into a vein (mainlining). The effect sought by the user is euphoria or a lethargic indifference to his personal problems. Some addicts experience a "rush" immediately after heroin injection, a sensation that has been compared to a whole-body orgasm. For the confirmed addict, the principal motive behind each dose is to avoid the agony of withdrawal. Narcotics addicts in otherwise good physical and mental health experience no debilitating physiological effects from their addiction, so long as their drug needs are regularly supplied. The unavailability of legal drug sources causes the addict to turn to the black market, where the prices he pays are as much as fifty times higher than for a pharmaceutical equivalent. The adulterants used to cut, or dilute, black market heroin are often more dangerous than the drug itself; e.g., reported deaths by heroin overdose may actually be caused by the QUININE used to dilute the heroin in a typical street dose. In the United States legal measures against drug abuse were first established in 1875, when opium dens were outlawed in San Francisco. The first national drug law was the Pure Food and Drug Act of 1906, which required accurate labeling of patent medicines containing opium and certain other drugs. In 1914, the Harrison Narcotic Act forbade sale of substantial doses of opiates or cocaine except by licensed doctors and pharmacies. Later, heroin was totally banned. Subsequent Supreme Court decisions made it illegal for doctors to prescribe any narcotic to addicts. By 1970 over 55 Federal drug laws and countless state laws specified a variety of punitive measures, including life imprisonment and even the death penalty. To clarify the situation, the Comprehensive Drug Abuse Prevention and Control Act of 1970 repealed, replaced, or updated all previous Federal laws concerned with narcotics and all other dangerous drugs. While possession was made illegal, the severest penalties were reserved for illicit distribution and manufacture of drugs. The act dealt with prevention and treatment of drug abuse, as well as control of drug traffic. Nevertheless, because obtaining the daily dose is the overriding concern in the addict's existence, laws to regulate or prohibit the use of narcotics have been largely ineffective and counterproductive. The illegality of importation and sale has resulted in an enormously profitable smuggling and black market operation. A kilogram of pure heroin purchased in Europe for $5,000 will be sold on the street for about $1 million, after passing through at least six middlemen. It is now widely believed that attempts to limit drug abuse by police action alone have failed and that success will come only when addiction is treated as a medical problem. The different therapies available for the treatment and rehabilitation of narcotics addicts reflect different theories about the nature of addiction. While the reality of addiction is unquestioned, competent experts disagree on the causes. Psychological theories maintain that there is a distinct addictive personality; sociological theories see the cause in a hopeless and frustrating life situation, as often occurs in the slums; biochemical theories, the most recent attempts at explanation, lay the blame on purely physiological alterations in the brain. The Federal government stresses involuntary incarceration during which detoxification is enforced. Narcotics are withdrawn abruptly ("cold turkey") if dependence and the danger of a severe withdrawal syndrome is still minimal, or by gradually reducing the dose to zero. The first Federal hospital for narcotics addicts was opened in 1935 in Lexington, Kentucky, and tens of thousands of addicts have been treated there. About one third of them were voluntary admissions, and the remainder had been convicted of Federal drug offenses. A voluntary approach is used by therapeutic communities such as Synanon, Daytop, and Phoenix House. Addicts live together under strong social pressure to give up drugs, solve their emotional problems, and become self-reliant. Some therapeutic communities maintain that the addict is never really cured and must remain associated with the community for the rest of his life to prevent relapse and readdiction. Others believe that they can prepare the addict for reentry into normal society. Unfortunately, follow-up statistics show that permanent cures for narcotics addiction are rare. A postwithdrawal syndrome of anxiety, depression, and drug craving is almost universal among former addicts, and most rehabilitated addicts who return to society either become readdicted or become alcoholics. It is fair to say that no cure for narcotics addiction has been found. The alternative to detoxification is a maintenance program in which addicts are regularly supplied with pure, measured doses of a narcotic. No cure is attempted; it is accepted that the addict will always need his narcotic, much as a diabetic will always need his insulin. But with drugs legally supplied free or at nominal cost, the addict need not resort to crime. In Britain, addicts have legally obtained their narcotic of choice by doctor's prescription or at clinics since the 1920s. In the United States, heroin addicts are usually maintained on methadone, a synthetic opiate that itself is addictive. Methadone blocks the effects of heroin; it does not produce as much sedation and euphoria as heroin, so that addicts on methadone can hold jobs and can live reasonably normal lives. Because it is legally available, addicts have no incentive to obtain black market drugs. Of all attempts to treat narcotic addiction, the maintenance programs have had the greatest long-term success. Unfortunately, addicts supplied with drugs may sell them to nonaddicts, thereby spreading the drug habit. In addition, it has been found that deaths from methadone overdose may sometimes exceed deaths from heroin overdose. The most recent developments in treating heroin addiction are the nonaddictive narcotic antagonists such as naloxone and cyclazocine. Like methadone, these drugs block the effects of heroin on the nervous system. Unlike methadone, the antagonists do not reduce the craving for heroin or relieve postwithdrawal anxiety and depression. It is hoped that further research will correct these deficiencies and show the way to a true biochemical cure for addiction that will replace the open-ended maintenance programs. Like narcotics, alcohol is subject to abuse. It is estimated that there are 5.5 million alcoholics among some 80 million social drinkers in the United States (see ALCOHOLISM). Perhaps the most harmful consequences of alcohol abuse for society are the accidents caused by drunken drivers, who are responsible for about half of all highway fatalities. Because alcoholic beverages are legally and plentifully available and because alcohol is a socially acceptable drug, the alcoholic is not forced into black market dealings and criminal activity. Unlike narcotics, alcohol itself is physically harmful to the body, producing brain damage and liver ailments (see CIRRHOSIS). The intoxicating and depressant effects of the barbiturates are almost identical to those of alcohol. A casual barbiturate user can be left with a hangover; an addict can experience convulsions and DELIRIUM TREMENS when the barbiturate is withdrawn. However, since it is easier to swallow a bottle of pills than down a quart of whiskey, the danger of death by overdose is much greater with the barbiturates. Abuse of the barbiturate tranquilizers, which were available without a prescription until the 1940s, began with middle-class adults seeking to relax and allay anxiety. By the 1960s, use of barbiturates as "thrill pills" was common among college-age youth. Despite legal restrictions, production of barbiturates increased 800% between 1942 and 1969; it is estimated that half of these drugs end up in illegal channels. Other frequently abused drugs include central nervous system stimulants, such as cocaine and the amphetamines. In moderate amounts, these stimulants increase stamina, prolong endurance, and improve concentration; they are used by people who need to remain alert over long periods, such as truck drivers and college students. Amphetamines were originally prescribed medically as diet pills, to depress the appetite. Overuse of these stimulants produces extreme agitation, tension, insomnia, hyperactivity, and an illusion of extraordinary efficiency; in addition, the frenetic pace combined with lack of sleep and nourishment is extremely debilitating. Repeated large doses induce a paranoid PSYCHOSIS that sets in during drug use and that is characterized by the sensation that insects are crawling on the skin. There are no physiological withdrawal symptoms associated with the use of stimulant drugs, but the acute depression and fatigue that occur when they are discontinued can create a psychological dependence on them. Taken intravenously, amphetamines are known as speed; the combination of heroin and amphetamines is known as a speedball. Because of a tendency to violent and irrational behavior, amphetamine users are considered the most dangerous segment of the drug subculture by the drug users themselves. There are indications that illicit use of amphetamines is decreasing among young people. The hallucinogens, particularly LSD, have generated the most sensational publicity and misconceptions of all drugs. Much of society's concern with LSD and marijuana is not related to their pharmacological effects, but rather is traceable to these drugs' role as symbols of a deviant youth subculture that is antagonistic to the prevailing ethics of American society. In general, both the dangers and benefits of these drugs have been exaggerated. More than with other drugs, the effects are largely psychological and depend to a large extent on the user's expectation. Disorders in perception and alterations in modes of consciousness are typical reactions. While medical authorities consider LSD-induced states similar to SCHIZOPHRENIA, the drug users themselves consider it the key to a different, if not superior, consciousness. The user of hallucinogens often holds a complex set of mystical beliefs about the drug experience and its role in self-exploration. Long-term use of LSD is rare; on the contrary, use tends to be self-limiting, since the drug's effects become less attractive as they become familiar through repetition. Marijuana and hashish, while often classed with the hallucinogens, do not induce alterations of consciousness except in massive doses. Among a substantial number of people, marijuana is replacing or complementing alcohol as a social amenity. The claim that marijuana leads to use of more potent drugs has never been proved. It seems possible that marijuana may someday join tobacco, coffee, and alcohol as a legal psychoactive substance. See Joel Fort, *The Pleasure Seekers* (1969); Oakley S. Ray, *Drugs, Society, and Human Behavior* (1972); Margaret O. Hyde, ed., *Mind Drugs* (1972); E. M. Brecher and the editors of Consumer Reports, *Licit and Illicit Drugs* (1972); J. M. Singh et al., ed., *Drug Addiction* (2 vol., 1972); N. E. Zinberg and J. A. Robertson, *Drugs and the Public* (1972); Drug Abuse Survey Project, *Dealing With Drug Abuse: A Report to the Ford Foundation* (1972).

drug poisoning, toxic effects caused by an administered drug. Reaction to a drug caused by an allergic sensitivity is not considered drug poisoning. Virtually all drugs, especially in large doses or when taken over long periods of time, can initiate a toxic condition. Certain drugs used in combination, such as alcohol and BARBITURATES, result in an intensified alteration of physiological state that is frequently dangerous. Drugs that affect the nervous system often cause adverse reactions in high concentrations. Alcohol and other nervous system DEPRESSANTS such as barbiturates and NARCOTICS, taken in sufficiently large doses, can result in coma and convulsions. Excessively high doses of stimulants such as AMPHETAMINES result in blurred vision, spasms, heart irregularities, and respiratory failure. In addition, both stimulants and depressants are dangerous because continued use can lead to addiction and tolerance for doses that are high enough to be toxic. Overdosage of an analgesic like ASPIRIN can result in acid-base disturbances, spontaneous bleeding, and convulsions. Virtually all drugs produce some side effects. For example, side reactions with barbiturates may include respiratory depression and skin rashes. Other drugs cause adverse reactions when taken over long periods of time. The antibiotic STREPTOMYCIN taken over long periods can result in deafness, and continued use of aspirin and other SALICYLATES can result in kidney damage and ANEMIA. Some drugs only have toxic effects on sensitive individuals. Psychotomimetic agents such as LYSERGIC ACID DIETHYLAMIDE (LSD) can result in hyperexcitability, coma, and prolonged psychotic states and can cause major personality changes in some users. In susceptible persons even moderate doses of phenothiazine tranquilizers, which are used to calm psychotic patients, can cause such toxic effects as low blood pressure, uncontrollable muscle movements, and various pigmentation and blood cell disorders (see PHENOTHIAZINE).

drug resistance, condition in which infecting BACTERIA are able to resist the destructive effects of drugs such as ANTIBIOTICS and SULFA DRUGS. Drug resistance is a serious public health problem because many disease-causing bacteria are no longer susceptible to previously effective drug therapy. Drug resistance is sometimes established by MUTATION of a GENE, i.e., a mutation may occur in a bacterial cell that alters the cell's sensitivity to a single drug or to chemically similar drugs. Sometimes a bacterium can acquire a drug resistant form of a gene through a mechanism of gene transfer in bacteria called transformation. For example, bacteria sensitive to the antibiotic STREPTOMYCIN become resistant to it when they acquire genetic material that carries the trait for streptomycin resistance. In another type of transferable drug resistance, called infectious drug resistance, a resistance factor, or R factor, is transferred during conjugation, the bacterial mating process. Infectious drug resistance can also be transferred during conjugation between bacterial species. An R factor can carry resistance to several chemically unrelated drugs, and strains of bacteria have acquired simultaneous resistance to such drugs as sulfanilamide, streptomycin, NEOMYCIN, CHLORAMPHENICOL and TETRACYCLINE. Bacteria with various R factors synthesize ENZYMES that inactivate drugs, e.g., many staphylococci are resistant to PENICILLIN because they produce penicillinase, an enzyme that inactivates penicillin. Other R factors may alter the permeability of the bacterial cell membrane, preventing several unrelated drugs from entering the cell. The numbers of R factors are on the increase partly because drug use in humans or animals favors the survival of bacteria that are drug resistant. In species such as *Escherichia coli,* the human intestinal bacterium, and species of *Salmonella,* bacteria containing R factors have increased because drug therapy has become common in humans, and antibiotics are now routinely incorporated into animal feed. These increased numbers of R factors, when transmitted to disease-causing bacteria that subsequently invade the host, can make drug treatment ineffective.

drugs, substances used in medicine either externally or internally for curing, alleviating, or preventing a disease or deficiency. At the turn of the century only a few medically effective substances were widely used scientifically, among them ETHER, MORPHINE, DIGITALIS, diphtheria antitoxin, smallpox vaccine, IRON, QUININE, IODINE, alcohol, and MERCURY. Since then, and particularly since World War II, many important new drugs have been developed, making chemotherapy an important part of medical practice: the ANTIBIOTICS, acting against bacteria and fungi; QUINACRINE and other synthetics acting against malaria and other parasitic infections; cardiovascular drugs, including various digitalislike agents, used in heart disease; DIURETICS, which increase the rate of urine flow; whole blood, plasma, and blood derivatives; ANTICOAGULANTS such as HEPARIN and coumarin (DICUMAROL); various smooth muscle relaxants such as PAPAVERINE, used in heart and vascular diseases; smooth muscle stimulants; immunologic agents, which protect against many diseases and allergenic substances; hormones such as THYROXINE, INSULIN, and ESTROGEN and other sex hormones; CORTISONE and synthetic CORTICOSTEROID DRUGS used in treating inflammatory diseases such as arthritis; vitamins; poison antidotes; and various drugs that act as STIMULANTS or DEPRESSANTS on all or various parts of the nervous system, including ANALGESICS, NARCOTICS, AMPHETAMINES, and BARBITURATES (see ANESTHESIA; PSYCHOPHARMACOLOGY; PSYCHOTOMIMETIC DRUGS). Drugs are obtained from many sources: Many inorganic materials, such as metals, are chemotherapeutic; hormones, alkaloids, vaccines, and antibiotics come from living organisms; and other drugs are synthetic or semisynthetic. Synthetics are often more effective and less toxic than the naturally obtained substances and are easier to prepare in standardized units. There are two marketing classes of drugs: ethical drugs, for which prescriptions are needed, and proprietary drugs, which are sold over the counter without prescription. Many of the latter, such as mouthwashes, gargles, and cold preparations, are only slightly, if at all, effective in curing ailments. Standards for drugs and tests for their identity, quality, and purity are given in the U.S. PHARMACOPOEIA, first published in 1820 and at first revised every 10 years, later every 5 years. The British publish a similar pharmacopoeia. The *National Formulary* published by the American Pharmaçeutical Association gives the composition, description, method of preparation, and dosage for drugs; privately published volumes that give information supplied by drug companies about their drug products are published more frequently. Legislation to safeguard drug purchasers began in the United States with the Pure Food and Drugs Act of 1906; this was superseded by the more inclusive and more stringent Federal Food, Drug, and Cosmetic Act of 1938. Such laws are enforced by the Food and Drug Administration. The 1962 Kefauver-Harris amendments to the Food, Drug, and Cosmetic Act increased the authority of the Food and Drug Administration to regulate testing and marketing of new drugs. The scientific study of drugs, their actions and effects, is PHARMACOLOGY. See Bernard Barber, *Drugs and Society* (1967); P. G. Stecher, ed., *The Merck Index* (8th ed. 1968); H. F. Dowling, *Medicines for Man* (1970); Walter Modell, ed., *Drugs of Choice, 1972-1973* (7th ed. 1972).

druids (drōō'ĭdz), priests of ancient Celtic Britain, Ireland, and Gaul and probably of all ancient Celtic peoples. Information about them is derived almost exclusively from the testimony of Roman authors, notably Julius Caesar, and from Old Irish sagas, supplemented to some extent by archaeological evidence. The druids constituted a priestly upper class in command of a highly ritualistic religion, which apparently centered on the worship of a pantheon of nature deities. Druids were also responsible for the education of the young and generally for the intellectual life of the community; although apparently literate, they taught by oral transmission, and their courses are said to have lasted as long as 20 years. The druids believed in immortality of the soul and, apparently, in its departure at death into another, not earthly, body. Their religious ceremonies seem to have been performed chiefly in tree groves (the oak and the mistletoe that grows on the oak were held sacred) and at river sources and lakes. The druids performed animal, and sometimes human, sacrifices and practiced divination and other forms of magic. Tacitus mentions a Celtic tribe, the Bructeri, that was led by a prophetess, and Irish legend confirms that there were women druids, although their precise role is not known. According to Caesar, the druids in Gaul were organized into a federation or brotherhood that extended across tribal divisions and was headed by an archdruid; they met once a year, probably on the site of Chartres, to arbitrate private and intertribal disputes. They thus wielded great political power and were an important cohesive force among the Celtic tribes. The druids in Gaul were the core of the rebellions against Rome. Their power, although broken by the Romans, finally yielded only to Christianity. In the late 18th and 19th cent. interest in the druids was spurred by archaeological discoveries and by the romantic movement. At first the megalithic monuments of France and Great Britain, notably those at Carnac and Stonehenge, were ascribed to them, but these are now known to predate Celtic culture. See T. R. Kendrick, *The Druids* (2d ed. 1928, repr. 1966); Lewis Spence, *The History and Origins of Druidism* (1949); Nora Chadwick, *The Druids* (1966); Stuart Piggott, *The Druids* (1968).

drum, fish: see CROAKER.

drum, in music, percussion instrument, known in various forms and played throughout the world and throughout known history. Essentially a drum is a frame over which one or more membranes or skins are stretched. The frame is usually cylindrical or conical, but it may have any shape. It acts as a resonator when the membrane is struck by the hand or by an implement, usually a stick or a whisk. The variety of tone and the volume of sound from a drum depend on the area of the membrane that is struck and, more particularly, on the skill of the player. Some of the rhythmic effects of drum playing can be exceedingly complex, especially those of intricate Oriental arrangements. The modern orchestra may have as many as five drums under one player, allowing an impressive range of tones and greater ease of tuning. In Western music the KETTLEDRUM is of special importance. A metal bowl with a membrane stretched over the open side, it is the only drum that can be tuned to a definite pitch. It originated with the Muslims, later being adapted into orchestral music. The kettledrum was formerly tuned by hand screws placed around the edge, but today it is often tuned by a pedal mechanism. The bass drum, especially popular in military bands, is a huge wooden cylinder with a drumhead (membrane) on both ends. The SNARE DRUM (sometimes called the side drum) also has a drumhead at either end; across one end are stretched gut strings wound with wire. These strings rattle when the other end of the drum is beaten. The tenor drum is primarily used in military bands and is normally played with small felt sticks. The tambourine, known from Roman times, is a single-headed small drum, usually with jingles attached to the frame; it is shaken and struck by hand.

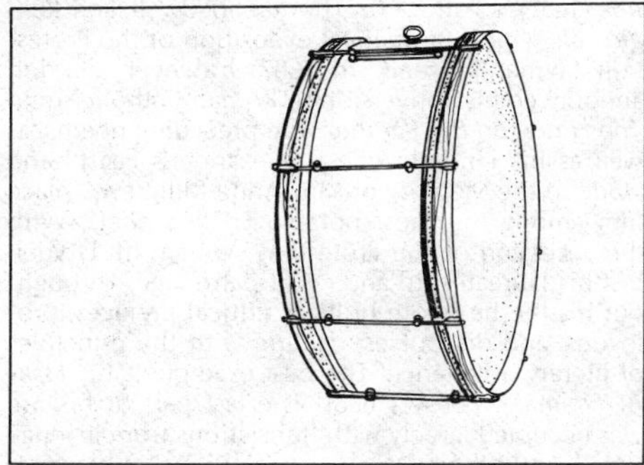

Bass drum

Drumheller, city (1971 pop. 5,446), SE Alta., Canada, on the Red Deer River. It is in an agricultural area with coal mines and oil and gas fields.

drumlin (drŭm'lĭn), smooth oval hill of glacial DRIFT, elongated in the direction of the movement of the ice that deposited it. Drumlins, which may be more than 150 ft (45 m) high and more than ½ mi (.8 km) long, are common in Massachusetts, New York, and Wisconsin.

Drummond, Henry, 1786-1860, English banker, known particularly as one of the founders of the CATHOLIC APOSTOLIC CHURCH. Beginning in 1826, he gathered annually for five years, at his home in Surrey, a group of laymen and clergymen to examine the prophecies in the Scriptures. Out of these meetings grew the organization of the Catholic Apostolic Church under Edward IRVING. Drummond became an apostle of the church in 1832. From 1847 until his death, he was a member of Parliament.

Drummond, Henry, 1851-97, Scottish clergyman and author, educated at the Univ. of Edinburgh. He was a minister of the Free Church and from 1877 a lecturer on science in Free Church College, Glasgow. Deeply interested in the reconciliation of science and religion, he wrote *Natural Law in the Spiritual World* (1883). After travels in Africa he published *Tropical Africa* (1888), and *The Ascent of Man* is a collection of the Lowell Lectures he delivered in Boston in 1893. A sermon, *The Greatest Thing in the World* (1890), has been reprinted many times.

Drummond, James Eric: see PERTH, JAMES ERIC DRUMMOND, 16TH EARL OF.

Drummond, William: see DRUMMOND OF HAWTHORNDEN, WILLIAM.

Drummond, William Henry, 1854-1907, Canadian poet, b. Ireland. For several years he worked and practiced medicine in frontier Canadian communities. There he came to know the French Canadians, whom he celebrated in his best poems, using their own dialect of English. His published volumes include *The Habitant* (1897), *Johnnie Courteau* (1901), *The Voyageur* (1905), and his complete *Poetical Works* (1912).

Drummond light: see CALCIUM OXIDE.

Drummond of Hawthornden, William, 1585-1649, Scottish poet. He was educated at Edinburgh and in France, retiring in 1610 to Hawthornden, where he spent his life as a gentleman of letters. His first volume of verse, *Teares on the Death of Moeliades* (1613), was followed by *Poems* (1616), *Forth Feasting* (1617), and *Flowres of Sion* (1623). The poems in these volumes show a strong Italian, especially Petrarchan, influence. His prose works include *A Cypresse Grove* (1623, an essay on death) and a history of Scotland (1655). The visit of Ben Jonson to Hawthornden (1618-19) resulted in Drummond's notes of Jonson's conversations. See his poetical works ed. by L. E. Kastner (1913, repr. 1969); biography by David Masson (1873, repr. 1969), study by F. R. Fogle (1952).

Drummondville, city (1971 pop. 31,813), S Que., Canada, on the St. Francis River, NE of Montreal. Its manufactures include textiles, paper and wood products, and rubber goods.

Drumont, Edouard (ādwär' drümôN'), 1844-1917, French journalist and anti-Semitic leader. His book, *La France juive* [Jewish France] (1886) and his periodical, *La Libre Parole,* were equally brilliant and virulent. Drumont reached his apex of influence in the DREYFUS AFFAIR.

drupe: see FRUIT.

Drury Lane, street and district of London, at first a place of fine residences, among which was that of the Drury family. It was the site of the original Drury Lane Theatre, which was built by Thomas KILLIGREW in 1663 under a charter from Charles II and called the Theatre Royal. After burning down (1672), the theater was rebuilt (1674) with Christopher Wren as architect. It was again rebuilt (1791-94) and again burned down (1809). The present Drury Lane Theatre was changed according to the design of Benjamin Wyatt in 1812. The oldest English theater still in use, it has at various times housed everything from a circus to opera. See *Reminiscences of Michael Kelly of the King's Theatre and Theatre Royal Drury Lane* (2 vol., 2d ed. 1826, repr. 1968).

Druse, Jebel, Syria: see JABAL AD DURUZ.

Druses (drōō'zĭz), small religious community of hill people in Syria, Lebanon, Israel, and Jordan, numbering about 370,000. They are quite distinct from their neighbors and insist upon the distinction. The Druses, whose religion allows no conversion or intermarriage, have traditionally maintained a cohesiveness among themselves that has only recently been threatened as the younger generation tends to show less interest in the religion. They believe that the sixth Fatimite caliph, Hakim, who in the 11th cent. announced his divinity, is really God and that therefore he is still living but hidden until his time shall come (see FATIMID). Knowledge of the Druse faith is uncertain, since the Druses tend to conceal the tenets of their religion; in fact, most of the Druses themselves have only a superficial knowledge of the religion; the society is divided into the *uqal* [knowers], who make up less than 10% of the population, and the *juhal* [ignorant]. The Druses have their own customs as well as their own beliefs, which vary considerably from both Sunnite and Shiite doctrines of Islam. They were not content with control by the Ottoman sultans, and a long series of wars occurred. The result was that the Turks left them for the most part undisturbed, except for punitive action in retaliation against Druse incursions. Druse opposition to Christians was directed particularly against the MARONITES, and in the 19th cent. the Druses sporadically swept down from their hills to perpetrate bloody massacres of the Christians, notably in the 1860s. These actions helped to prepare the way for French control in Syria and Lebanon—the last thing the Druses desired. After the French mandate was created (1920), they opposed the foreign control and in 1925–27, supported by Syrian nationalists, took Damascus and defied the French until a protracted war had been fought. In World War II, when the British and Free French undertook their campaign against the Vichy government in Syria, the Druses supported them. The independence of Syria was proclaimed in 1941, and in 1944 the Druses of Syria agreed to surrender their autonomous rights in the Jebeal Druz [*jebel*=mountain], as their section of the Hauran is called; thus, theoretically at least, the Syrian Druses became amalgamated with the other Syrians under the country's central government. The Druses, like other groups in the Middle East, have changed in recent times. The powerful feudal families of the past have conceded political power to members of other social classes. In Lebanon, Druses held high political offices in the 1960s and 70s. The Druses in Israel tend to be more assimilated; many have served in the army and are university graduates. See study by P. K. Hitti (1928, repr. 1966).

Drusilla (dro͞osĭl'ə), daughter of Herod Agrippa I, married to Felix the procurator. Acts 24.24.

Drusus (dro͞o'səs), Roman family of the gens Livius. An early distinguished member was **Marcus Livius Drusus,** d. 109? B.C., tribune of the people (122) with Caius Sempronius Gracchus (see under GRACCHI). As a member of the senatorial party he led a successful attack on Gracchus by making more extreme democratic proposals than Gracchus had dared to. By these and other, more unscrupulous tactics, Drusus disgraced Gracchus. In 112, Drusus was made consul by the senatorial party. His son **Marcus Livius Drusus,** d. 91 B.C., was also a leader of the senatorial party. His policy was to win the people and the Italian allies over to the senate, so that the senate might recover from the knights (equites) the control of the courts. By a general increase in the franchise he won the support of the people and of the Italians, but the senate, alarmed over popular unrest, annulled Drusus' laws. The Italians were infuriated, and the SOCIAL WAR between Rome and the Italians broke out. Drusus was assassinated. A member of the family by adoption was LIVIA DRUSILLA, mother of **Nero Claudius Drusus Germanicus,** 38 B.C.–9 B.C., called Drusus Senior; he was the stepson of Augustus. He fought (15 B.C.) against the Rhaetians and gained much credit for his generalship. In 13 B.C.–12 B.C. he was in Gaul pacifying the tribes, and on his return to Rome he was made (11 B.C.) urban praetor. Returning to the provinces, he ravaged Germany E and N of the Rhine. He fortified the Rhine but put the Germans under no permanent subjection. He died in Germany. His brother was the emperor TIBERIUS. He married Antonia Minor, the daughter of Marc Antony, and had three children, GERMANICUS CAESAR, Livilla, and CLAUDIUS I. Tiberius' son, **Drusus Caesar,** d. A.D. 23, called Drusus Junior, served in the provinces—in Pannonia (A.D. 15) and in Illyricum (A.D. 17–A.D. 20). In A.D. 22 he was made tribune. Meanwhile, Sejanus, Tiberius' minister, had become jealous of Drusus' power and tried to turn Tiberius against him. Drusus died the same year, perhaps of poisoning by Sejanus or by his wife under Sejanus' influence.

dryads: see NYMPH.

Dryburgh Abbey (drī'bərə), Premonstratensian abbey, Berwickshire, SE Scotland, on the Tweed below Melrose. Founded in 1150, it was several times destroyed (1322 and 1545) and rebuilt and is now a picturesque ruin, a favorite subject for etching and painting. It belonged at one time to ancestors of Sir Walter Scott and contains his tomb.

dry cell: see CELL, in electricity; BATTERY, ELECTRIC.

dry cleaning, process of cleaning fabrics without water. Special solvents and soaps are used so as not to harm fabrics and dyes that will not withstand the effects of ordinary soap and water. Dry cleaning began in France about the middle of the 19th cent., at first in small plants, where it was done by hand; with the development of specialized machinery it has become an important industry. The danger of fire—at first a constant menace because of the large amounts of flammable materials in use—was largely overcome by concentrating the work in specially designed plants and by the use of a high-boiling petroleum product still commonly used in the United States. Newer chlorinated hydrocarbon synthetic solvents, such as perchlorethylene, are nonflammable but require precautions against their toxic fumes. The process of dry cleaning for ordinary fabrics is to place them in revolving washers where they are washed with the cleansing fluid and a special soap, rinsed with pure cleansing fluid, and then spun to remove most of the fluid. They are then dried with warm air in a tumbler. Delicate fabrics are done by hand. The cleansing fluids are reclaimed and used again. Unusual stains are given an expert test to determine the proper solvent; special stain removers include chloroform, ether, and carbon disulphide.

Dryden, John, 1631–1700, English poet, dramatist, and critic, b. Northamptonshire, grad. Cambridge, 1654. He went to London about 1657 and first came to public notice with his *Heroic Stanzas* (1659), commemorating the death of Oliver Cromwell. The following year, however, he celebrated the restoration of Charles II with *Astraea Redux.* In 1662 he was elected to the Royal Society, and in 1663 he married Lady Elizabeth Howard. His long poem on the Dutch War, *Annus Mirabilis,* appeared in 1667. The following year he became poet laureate. He had a long and varied career as a dramatist. His most notable plays include the heroic dramas, *The Conquest of Granada* (2 parts, 1670–71) and *Aurenz-Zebe* (1675); his blank-verse masterpiece, *All for Love* (1677), a retelling of Shakespeare's *Antony and Cleopatra;* and the comedy *Marriage à la Mode* (1672). His great political satire on Monmouth and Shaftesbury, *Absalom and Achitophel,* appeared in two parts (1681, 1682). It was followed by *MacFlecknoe* (1682), an attack on Thomas Shadwell, and *Religio Laici* (1682), a poetical exposition of the Protestant layman's creed. In 1687, however, Dryden announced his conversion to Roman Catholicism in *The Hind and the Panther.* The preceding poems, as well as his Pindaric odes, "Alexander's Feast" and "Ode to the Memory of Mrs. Anne Killigrew," place him among the most notable English poets. With the accession of the Protestant William III, Dryden lost his laureateship and court patronage. Throughout his life he wrote brilliant critical prefaces, prologues, and discourses, dealing with the principles of literary excellence. The best example is his *Essay of Dramatic Poesy* (1668). The last part of his life was occupied largely with translations from Juvenal, Vergil, and others. A 21-volume edition of his complete works was begun in 1956 under the general editorship of E. N. Hooker and H. T. Swedenberg. See biography by C. E. Ward (1961); studies by L. I. Brevold (1953), Bruce King (1966), Mark Van Doren (1920, repr. 1969), R. D. Hume (1970), James Kinsley and Helen Kinsley, eds., (1971), A. C. Kirsch (1965, repr. 1972), and Earl Miner, ed. (1973).

dry farming, farming system adopted in areas having an annual rainfall of approximately 15 to 20 in. (38.1–50.8 cm)—with much of the rainfall in the spring and early summer—where irrigation is impractical. Seeding rates are used that correspond to the soil water supply; management practices that minimize water loss and soil erosion are also utilized. The land is often summer-fallowed (not used for crops) in alternate years to conserve moisture. Dry-land crops must be either drought-resistant or drought-evasive, i.e., maturing in late spring or fall; special varieties of crops such as wheat, barley, corn, sorghum, and rye are often used.

Drygalski, Erich von (ā'rĭkh fən drĕgäl'skē), 1865–1949, German polar explorer. A professor of geography at the Univ. of Munich, he led an expedition that wintered (1892–93) in W Greenland. From 1901 to 1903 he led the German antarctic expedition in the *Gauss* to explore the unknown area of the Antarctic lying S of the Kerguelen Islands. Despite being trapped by ice for nearly 14 months, Drygalski discovered Kaiser Wilhelm II Land. Subsequently he wrote the narrative of the expedition and edited the voluminous scientific data (18 vol. and 3 atlases, 1905–26).

dry ice: see CARBON DIOXIDE.

drying oil, any of several natural oils which, when exposed to the air, oxidize to form a tough, elastic film. The common drying oils are cottonseed oil (see COTTON), corn oil, soybean oil, TUNG OIL, and LINSEED OIL. Nearly a million pounds of drying oils are used each year in the United States, mainly in paints, varnishes, lacquers, and printer's ink. The first three oils mentioned are more properly called semidrying oils. Linseed oil is the most widely used. Use is recorded as early as A.D. 200 of boiled linseed oil, which dries faster than raw oil. Tung oil is imported from China, and linseed oil mainly from Argentina. Drying oils may also be prepared from various nondrying fish oils (e.g., sardine and herring oils) and from whale oil.

Dryopithecus (drī'ōpəthē'kəs, -pĭth'əkəs), an extinct group of apes. Fossils about 20 million years old have been found in Africa, Asia, and Europe. *Dryopithecus* is generally believed to be ancestral to modern apes and man. PROCONSUL, a group of fossil apes that may have been the ancestor of the chimpanzee, is considered by some authorities to be a subgroup of Dryopithecus.

drypoint, an INTAGLIO printing process in which the lines are scratched directly into a metal plate with a needle; also, the print made from such a plate. Although it is often used in combination with ETCHING, no acid is used for the drypoint. It differs from ENGRAVING in the type of tool employed and the consequent shallowness of the line. In drypoint the burr raised by the needle is usually left on the plate, producing a rich, velvety effect. It is characteristically a sketchy medium suitable for improvisation, but it can also be used to render fine detail. Unless the plate is steel faced, the burr deteriorates rapidly, allowing relatively few good prints to be pulled. Dürer, Rembrandt, Whistler, and Picasso are considered the greatest masters of the technique.

dry rot, fungus disease that attacks both softwood and hardwood timber. Destruction of the cellulose causes discoloration and eventual crumbling of the wood. This frequently results in the collapse of wooden structures such as house flooring, mine shafts, and ship hulls. Because the fungi require moisture for growth, dry rot occurs most often in places where the ventilation is poor or humidity is high or when the wood has been improperly seasoned. In the United States it is most frequently caused by a pore fungus (*Poria incrassata*) and by the dry-rot, or house, fungus (*Merulis lacrymans*). It may be prevented by application of creosote or other preservatives. Dry rot sometimes attacks standing conifers. The name is also used for other fungus diseases that attack the roots or stems of plants (see DISEASES OF PLANTS).

Dry Tortugas (tôrto͞o'gəz), island group, off S Fla., 60 mi (97 km) W of Key West. Named by the Spanish explorer PONCE DE LEÓN in 1513, the islands later became a pirate base. They are famous for their bird and marine life. Loggerhead Key is the largest island. On Garden Key are Fort Jefferson National Monument (see NATIONAL PARKS AND MONUMENTS, table) and a U.S. bird refuge. The island group is also known as Tortugas.

Dual Alliance, 1879–82: see TRIPLE ALLIANCE AND TRIPLE ENTENTE.

dualism, any philosophical system that seeks to explain all phenomena in terms of two distinct and irreducible principles. It is opposed to monism and pluralism. In Plato's philosophy there is an ultimate dualism of being and becoming, of ideas and matter. Aristotle criticized Plato's doctrine of the transcendence of ideas, but he was unable to escape the dualism of form and matter, and in modern metaphysics this dualism has been a persistent concept. In modern philosophy dualism takes many forms. Thus in Immanuel Kant there is an ontological dualism between the phenomenal and noumenal worlds and an epistemological dualism between the passivity of sensation and the spontaneity of the understanding. In psychology occasionalism and interactionism both assumed a dualism of mind and matter. The term also has a theological application, e.g., the Manichaeans explained evil in the world as resulting from an ultimate evil principle, coeternal with good.

Dual Monarchy: see AUSTRO-HUNGARIAN MONARCHY.

Duan, Le: see LE DUAN.

Duane, James (dyo͞oān'), 1733–97, political figure in the American Revolution, b. New York City. Admitted to the bar in 1754, Duane soon gained renown and wealth as a lawyer. Although he took a cautious approach in the prerevolutionary agitation in New York City, his sincere interest in colonial rights won him a seat in the Continental Congress (1774), where he served until 1783. His support of Joseph Galloway's conciliatory plan and his habitual caution in Congress incurred numerous attacks on his patriotism. He served on various Revolutionary committees and helped draft the Articles of Confederation. Toward the close of the war Duane was a member of George Clinton's council and from 1784 to 1789 served as mayor of New York City. He was at the same time state senator and was a member of the convention that ratified the Federal Constitution. From 1789 until his retirement (1794) he was U.S. district judge for New York. Duane, who invested heavily in land in Vermont and W New York, was long an ardent advocate of New York's claims to the New Hampshire Grants. His last years were spent in Duanesburg (in the Mohawk valley), which he was chiefly responsible for establishing in 1765. See biography by E. P. Alexander (1938).

Duane, James Chatham, 1824-97, American army engineer, b. Schenectady, N.Y., grad. Union College, 1844, and West Point, 1848; grandson of James Duane. In the Civil War he organized the engineer equipage of McClellan's army (1861-62) and commanded a battalion of engineers in the Peninsular campaign. Duane was chief engineer of the Army of the Potomac in the Antietam campaign (1862) and from July, 1863, to the end of the war. He was brevetted brigadier general for his service in the siege of Petersburg (1864). After the war he served on numerous engineering commissions and official boards.

Duane, William, 1760-1835, American journalist, b. near Lake Champlain, N.Y., of Irish parentage. He learned the printer's trade in Ireland and in 1787 went to Calcutta, where he edited the *Indian World.* His attacks on the local government there brought about his deportation and the confiscation of his property. Unable to secure redress in England, Duane moved to Philadelphia and joined Benjamin Franklin Bache in editing the *Aurora.* Upon Bache's death (1798), Duane became sole editor. An able and courageous writer, he made the *Aurora* the leading Jeffersonian organ. His acid criticism, however, led to his arrest (1799) under the Alien Act. Acquitted, he was arrested again under the Sedition Act (see ALIEN AND SEDITION ACTS). Charges against him were dismissed when Jefferson came into office. Duane's prosperous journal declined after the removal of the government to Washington, D.C., but it remained influential in local politics. In the War of 1812, Duane served as adjutant general. He retired from the *Aurora* in 1822 and traveled in South America, writing upon his return *A Visit to Colombia in the Years 1822 & 1823* (1826).

Duane, William, 1872-1935, American physicist, b. Philadelphia, grad. Harvard, 1893, Ph.D. Univ. of Berlin, 1897. He taught at the Univ. of Colorado (1898-1907), worked at the Curie radium laboratory in Paris (1907-12), and returned in 1913 to teach at Harvard (as professor of biophysics, 1917-34). He is known for his researches in radioactivity and X rays and their application in radiotherapy.

Duane, William John, 1780-1865, U.S. Secretary of Treasury (June-Sept., 1833), b. Clonmel, Ireland. He emigrated (1796) to Philadelphia with his father, William Duane (1760-1835), and assisted him in publishing the *Aurora* until 1806. An influential lawyer, he served several terms in the Pennsylvania legislature and was powerful in state politics. He was appointed Secretary of Treasury by President Jackson to succeed Louis McLane, who was transferred to the Dept. of State because he refused to remove government deposits from the BANK OF THE UNITED STATES to state banks. When Jackson made this request of Duane, the new Secretary also refused to carry out the transfer and was replaced by Roger B. Taney. Duane defended his own position in his documentary *Narrative and Correspondence concerning the Removal of the Deposites* (1838) and then withdrew from public life.

Duarte (dwär'ta), 1391-1438, king of Portugal (1433-38), eldest of the five sons of John I. He was a "philosopher-king," notable for his legal reforms and as the author of *O leal conselheiro* [the loyal counselor]. Much concerned with exploration, he spurred on his brother Prince HENRY THE NAVIGATOR with encouragement and financial aid. The disastrous defeat (1437) of Henry's expedition against Tangier was the major event of Duarte's reign.

Duarte (dwär'tē), city (1970 pop. 14,981), Los Angeles co., S Calif.; settled c.1841, inc. 1957. It is residential, with light industry and warehousing. The City of Hope National Medical Center is there.

Dubai (do͞obī'), sheikhdom (1968 pop. 59,092), c.1,500 sq mi (3,890 sq km), part of the federation of UNITED ARAB EMIRATES, E Arabia, on the Persian Gulf. Little is known of the early history of Dubai, but it appears to have been a dependency of ABU DHABI until 1833. Along with the other sheikhdoms that now compose the federation, it became a British protectorate in the 19th cent. Dubai became the commercial capital of the sheikhdoms and was an important port of call for British steamers to India. Dubai was at war with Abu Dhabi from 1945 to 1948. Oil was discovered in Dubai in the early 1960s, and production began in 1966. Dubai became part of the United Arab Emirates at its founding in 1971.

Du Barry, Jeanne Bécu, comtesse (zhän bākü' kôNtĕs' dü bärē', do͞obăr'ē), 1743-93, mistress of King Louis XV of France. A courtesan of illegitimate birth, she was the mistress of Jean Du Barry when her beauty attracted (1768) the king's attention. After being nominally married to her lover's brother, Guillaume, comte Du Barry, she was installed at court (1769) and retained her influence until the king's death (1774). Although her position involved her in political intrigues, they were of minor importance. Mme Du Barry was noted for her kindness, and she lacked the ambition of her predecessor, Mme de Pompadour. At the accession of Louis XVI she left the court. She was arrested by the Revolutionary Tribunal on charges of treason (1793) and was guillotined. See biographies by Stanley Loomis (1959), Agnes Stoeckl (1966), and Marion Ward (1968).

Du Bartas, Guillaume de Salluste (gēyōm' də sälüst' dü bärtäs'), 1544-90, French poet. A Huguenot soldier under Henry IV, Du Bartas is known chiefly for his epic poems *La Sepmaine; ou, Creation du monde* (1578) and the unfinished *La Seconde Sepmaine* (1584). In lofty verse they retell the main events of the Bible from a Protestant viewpoint.

Dubawnt (do͞obônt'), river, 580 mi (933 km) long, rising in Wholdaia Lake, SE Mackenzie dist., Northwest Territories, Canada, and flowing NE to Dubawnt Lake (c.1,600 sq mi/4,140 sq km) then E across Keewatin dist. to Baker Lake at the head of Chesterfield Inlet of Hudson Bay.

Dubawnt Lake, one of the largest lakes of Canada, c.1,600 sq mi (4,140 sq km), W Keewatin dist., Northwest Territories. The Dubawnt River flows through it. Located north of the tree line, the lake is icebound most of the summer.

Dubček, Alexander (ä"lĕksän'dĕr do͞ob'chĕk), 1921-, Czechoslovakian political leader. A member of the Slovakian national minority, he was active in the Communist underground in World War II and rose in the party hierarchy after the war, becoming head of the Slovakian Communist party and a member of the presidium of the Communist party's central committee. In 1967 he led the liberal opposition to the party's first secretary, Antonín NOVOTNÝ. In Jan., 1968, Novotný was forced to resign; Dubček succeeded him. In Dubček's brief term in office he relaxed censorship, placed liberal Communists in leading state posts, began to pursue an independent foreign policy, and promised a gradual democratization of Czech political life. The USSR became increasingly alarmed at Dubček's policies, and in Aug., 1968, Soviet and other Warsaw Pact armies invaded Czechoslovakia. Dubček was arrested along with other leaders, taken to Moscow, and forced to consent to the cancellation of key reforms. He retained his post as first secretary, but pro-Soviet elements in the Czech party soon (1969) removed him. After serving briefly as ambassador to Turkey (1969-70), he fell into official disgrace.

Du Bellay, Guillaume (gēyōm' dü bĕlā'), 1491-1543, French diplomat under King Francis I; brother of Jean Du Bellay. He was employed in negotiations regarding the Treaty of Cambrai (1529) between Francis and Holy Roman Emperor Charles V and in negotiations with King Henry VIII of England; he helped Henry secure French support for his divorce from Katharine of Aragón. He was also active in uniting German Protestant princes against Charles V and secured the Treaty of Scheyern (1532) with them. He served as governor of Turin (1537-39) and of the province of Piedmont (1539-42). He left an uncompleted manuscript history of the reign of Francis I.

Du Bellay, Jean (zhäN), 1492-1560, French humanist and diplomat, cardinal of the Roman Catholic Church; brother of Guillaume Du Bellay and patron of his cousin, Joachim Du Bellay. He undertook numerous missions to England, Rome, and Germany for King Francis I. After the accession of Henry II (1547), he lived mostly in Rome. A religious moderate, he was criticized—as was his brother—for being too favorably inclined toward King Henry VIII of England, for whose divorce he secured the support of several French universities.

Du Bellay, Joachim (zhōäshăN'), 1522?-1560, French poet of the Pléiade (see under PLEIAD). He wrote their manifesto, *La Deffence et illustration de la langue francoyse* (1549), which urges the study and emulation of the classics and the use of French as the literary language. His poetic works, broadly imitative of Latin and Italian works, include a collection of sonnets, *L'Olive* (1549); and *Divers jeux rustiques* (1558). He served (1553-57) in Rome as secretary to his cousin, Cardinal Du Bellay; *Les Regrets* (1558) and *Les Antiquités de Rome* (1558) contain some of his finest poems, conveying his impressions of Rome and his nostalgia for his native land. The *Antiquités* were translated by Edmund Spenser. See studies by A. W. Satterthwaite (1960) and L. C. Keating (1971).

Dübendorf (dü'bəndôrf"), town (1970 pop. 19,639), Zürich canton, NE Switzerland. Tobacco products and chemicals are produced in the town.

Dubinsky, David (do͞obĭn'skē), 1892-, American labor leader, president (1932-66) of the INTERNATIONAL LADIES GARMENT WORKERS UNION (ILGWU), b. Brest-Litovsk, Poland. He was a baker in his father's shop in Lodz (then in Russian Poland), and after becoming active in the bakers' union, he was banished (1908) to a Siberian prison. He escaped and reached (1911) the United States, where he became a cloak cutter and joined the ILGWU. He rose rapidly through the ranks of the union and served as president from 1932 until his retirement in 1966. After 1932 he led in the expansion of membership of the ILGWU. Although a vice president of the American Federation of Labor (AFL), he led (1935-36) his union in joining with the Congress of Industrial Organizations (CIO). When the AFL suspended the CIO unions (1936), Dubinsky resigned from the AFL. He opposed, however, the establishment of the CIO on a permanent independent basis, and in 1938 he also broke with it, thus making the ILGWU independent until 1940 when it reaffiliated with the AFL. In 1936 he was one of the founders of the AMERICAN LABOR PARTY in New York State. When it fell under Communist influence, he resigned and helped organize (1944) the LIBERAL PARTY. In 1945 he again became a vice president and member of the executive council of the AFL, retaining the position after it merged with the CIO in 1955. His efforts at ousting corrupt union leaders culminated in the anti-racket codes adopted by the AFL-CIO in 1957. See M. D. Danish, *The World of David Dubinsky* (1957).

Dublin, county (1971 pop. 849,542, including the city of Dublin), 327 sq mi (847 sq km), E central Republic of Ireland, on the Irish Sea. The county is dominated by the great city of Dublin, which is the county seat and capital of the Republic. The area is low-lying in the north and center, rising to the Wicklow Mts. in the south. The chief river is the Liffey, which bisects the city of Dublin and empties into Dublin Bay. There are two islands, Lambay and Ireland's Eye, off the coast. The rural area, upon which the city has increasingly encroached, is devoted to dairy farming and the raising of wheat, barley, and potatoes. Beef cattle are also grazed. Fishing is pursued along the coast. There are several industrial suburban towns; Balbriggan is noted for hosiery manufacture. Organized as a county by King John of England in the early 13th cent., Dublin was the heart of the English PALE and was strongly guarded by castles along its boundaries.

Dublin, Irish *Baile Átha Cliath,* county borough (1971 pop. 566,034), capital of the Republic of Ireland and county town of Co. Dublin, on Dublin Bay at the mouth of the Liffey River. Its harbor, with shipyards, docks, and quays, dates from 1714. Coal from S Wales and England is imported, while agricultural products, whiskey, and stout are the chief exports. The old Royal and Grand canals, connecting Dublin with the interior, have been superseded by railroads for most commercial traffic. Dublin's chief industries are brewing, textile manufacturing (silk making was introduced by Huguenot refugees in the 16th cent.), distilling, shipbuilding, food processing, and the manufacture of foundry products, glass, and cigarettes. Dublin was a Danish town until 1014, when BRIAN BORU defeated the Danes at nearby Clontarf. The Danes established themselves again until Richard Strongbow, 2d earl of PEMBROKE, captured the city for the English in 1170. In 1172, Henry II of England came to Dublin and granted the city to the "men of Bristol"; it became the seat of English government and center of the PALE. In 1209 occurred the Black Monday massacre of English residents. Edward BRUCE unsuccessfully assaulted the town in the early 14th cent. In the ENGLISH CIVIL WAR the city surrendered (1647) to the parliamentarians, and Oliver CROMWELL landed there in 1649. James II held (1689) his last Parliament in Dublin. After winning the battle of the BOYNE, William III entered the city in 1690. From 1782 to 1800, when the Irish Parliament (the so-called Grattan's Parliament) enjoyed temporary independence of England, Dublin experienced a prosperous and stimulating era; many of the city's buildings date from this period. After the Act of Union of 1800, which sent Irish representatives to the British Parliament, many wealthy aristocrats moved from their Dublin mansions to London, and the years of prosperity ended. In the 19th cent. Dublin saw much bloodshed in connection with nationalist efforts to free Ireland from English rule—the insurrection led by Robert EMMET in 1803; the 1867 uprising of the FENIAN MOVEMENT; and the murder (1882) of Lord Frederick Cavendish, chief secretary for Ireland, and his undersecretary in Phoenix Park during terrorist activity and agitation by the Land League. Dublin also became the center of a Gaelic renaissance: the Gaelic League was founded there in 1893, and the ABBEY THEATRE began producing Irish plays. In 1913 the city was paralyzed by strikes, eventually culminating in the Easter Rebellion of 1916. The early troubles of the Irish Free State led to the worst period of bloodshed in Dublin's history (see IRELAND). Today Dublin is the seat of the Irish legislature, the Dáil Éireann, in Leinster House. The Univ. of Dublin or Trinity College (founded 1591) has in its library the famous Book of Kells and a copy of every book published in the British Isles. University College (Roman Catholic) was incorporated in 1909 as part of the National Univ. of Ireland; mastery of the Gaelic language is a requirement for its students. Dublin Castle (c.1220) was the residence of the lords lieutenants of Ireland until 1922 and now houses government offices. The city's earliest church, Christ Church, was founded in 1038; in 1172 Strongbow built a new church (restored 1871-78) on this site, and his tomb is there. St. Patrick's is the national cathedral of the Protestant Church of Ireland; Jonathan SWIFT, buried there, was dean from 1713 to 1745. Kilmainham Hospital, a notable structure that is no longer a hospital, dates from 1679. Dublin has a national museum, noted for its collection of Irish antiquities, and the National Gallery of Art, which has a good collection of old masters.

Dublin. 1 Uninc. town (1970 pop. 13,641), Alameda co., W Calif., a suburb in the San Francisco-Oakland area. Photographic supplies, security equipment, and telephone parts are manufactured, and aircraft research is conducted. 2 City (1970 pop. 15,143), seat of Laurens co., central Ga., on the Oconee River; inc. 1812. It is a commercial and industrial center. Lumbering and the manufacture of wood products are its chief industries.

Dublin, University of, at Dublin, Ireland; founded 1591 by Queen Elizabeth I of England; also called Trinity College, Dublin. It has faculties of arts (humanities); arts (letters); mathematical and engineering sciences; medical, veterinary, and dental sciences; natural sciences; and economic and social studies, as well as schools of business and social studies; dentistry; divinity; education; engineering; law; music; medicine; and veterinary medicine. The university library houses a large collection of ancient and medieval manuscripts, including the Celtic *Book of Kells* (8th cent. A.D.).

Dubna (do͞obnŭ'), town (1970 pop. 44,000), Moscow oblast, central European USSR, near the confluence of the Volga and Dubna rivers. Founded in 1956, it is the seat of the Joint Institute for Nuclear Research. The institute was established at an international conference in Moscow in 1956; its members include most Communist nations.

Dubnow, Simon (do͞ob'nôf), 1860-1941, Jewish historian and ideologist, b. Belorussia. Self-educated, he settled after extensive travels in St. Petersburg, where he taught Jewish history. He was one of the founders and directors of the Jewish Historico-Ethnographical Society there (1909-18) and was asked to prepare several publications by the Bolshevik government, none of which was ever published. In 1922 he moved to Berlin. When Adolf Hitler came to power in 1933, Dubnow went to Riga, Latvia, where he remained at work until killed by the Nazis in Dec., 1941. Among Dubnow's numerous works are *History of the Jews in Russia and Poland* (3 vol., 1916-20) and *History of the Jews* (10 vol., 1925-29; tr. 5 vol., 1967-73), in which he maintained that Jewish survival had resulted from the communal and spiritual independence of Jews in the Diaspora. See biographies by Aaron Steinberg, ed., (1963) and R. M. Seltzer (1970).

Dubois, Guillaume (gēyōm' dübwä'), 1656-1723, French statesman, cardinal of the Roman Catholic Church. A man of humble birth, he was tutor to Philippe II d'ORLÉANS, who, when he became regent, made Dubois councilor of state (1715). In 1718, Dubois became secretary of state for foreign affairs. Reversing the foreign policy of King Louis XIV, he concluded the TRIPLE ALLIANCE of 1717 with England and the Netherlands, and negotiated (1719) marriage contracts between the royal houses of France and Spain. In 1721 he was made a cardinal and in 1722 became chief minister.

du Bois, Guy Pène, 1884-1958, American painter and critic, b. Brooklyn, N.Y.; studied under William Chase and in Paris. In New York City after 1906 he worked as a reporter and art critic for various newspapers and edited *Arts and Decoration.* The wry humor of his early paintings of social manners gives way in later work to more somber presentations of human manners and mores. His paintings include *Morning, Paris Café* (Whitney Mus., New York City) and *Restaurant Number 1* and *Number 2* (Art Inst., Chicago). See his autobiography, *Artists Say the Silliest Things* (1940).

Du Bois, William Edward Burghardt (dəbois'), 1868-1963, American Negro civil rights leader and author, b. Great Barrington, Mass., grad. Harvard (B.A., 1890; M.A., 1891; Ph.D., 1895). Du Bois was an early exponent of full racial equality for Negroes and a cofounder (1909) of the National Negro Committee, which later became the NATIONAL ASSOCIATION FOR THE ADVANCEMENT OF COLORED PEOPLE (NAACP). The formation of the NAACP marked a break between Du Bois, along with other leaders, and Booker T. WASHINGTON, who believed that unskilled Negroes should be educated vocationally in order to achieve economic equality. Du Bois demanded that Negroes should achieve not only economic equality but civil and political equality as well. Although these were quite radical goals at the time, he later (1919) attacked the extremism of Marcus GARVEY, who called for complete black separatism. From 1897 to 1910, Du Bois taught economics and history at Atlanta Univ. In 1910 he became editor of the NAACP magazine, *Crisis,* a position he held until 1932, when he returned to Atlanta Univ. (1932-44). His concern for the liberation of blacks throughout the world led to his active participation in several Pan African Congresses; in 1945, at the Fifth Congress in Manchester, England, he met with the African leaders Kwame Nkrumah and Jomo Kenyatta. In the following years he published several books, and in 1961 he became a member of the Communist party. In the last two years of his life Du Bois lived in Ghana, where he became editor of an *African Encyclopedia for Africans.* His works include *The Souls of Black Folks* (1903), *John Brown* (1909), *Black Reconstruction* (1935), *The World and Africa* (1947), *The Black Flame* (1957-61), and his *Autobiography* (1968). See his correspondence, ed. by Herbert Aptheker (Vol. I, 1973); biographies by F. L. Broderick (1959), Leslie Lacy (1970), and by his wife, Shirley Graham DuBois (1971); studies by E. M. Rudwick (1960, repr. 1968), R. W. Logan (1971), and W. M. Tuttle, ed. (1973).

Du Bois (do͞o'bois, dəbois'), city (1970 pop. 10,112), Clearfield co., W central Pa., in the region of the Allegheny plateau; inc. 1881. The city developed with the advent of extensive lumbering and mining operations and is now the commercial and industrial center of a coal-mining and farming area. Abundant game and fish are found in the vicinity. A junior college is there.

Du Bois-Reymond, Emil (ā'mēl dü bwä-rāmōN'), 1818-96, German physiologist of French descent. A pupil and successor (after 1858) of Johannes Müller at the Univ. of Berlin, he is known especially for his studies of nerve and muscle action, in which he demonstrated that electrical changes accompany muscle action.

Dubos, René Jules (rənā' zhül dübō'), 1901-, American bacteriologist, b. France, Ph.D. Rutgers, 1927. He joined the Rockefeller Institute (now Rockefeller Univ.) in 1927 and became professor there in 1957. From soil bacteria he isolated in crystalline form the agent, one of the ANTIBIOTICS, that destroys the so-called Gram-positive germs and named it gramicidin; this work laid the basis of a new field of chemotherapy. He has written *So Human an Amimal* (1968) and *A God Within* (1972).

Dubrovnik (do͞o'brôvnĭk), Ital. *Ragusa,* city (1971 pop. 58,920), SW Yugoslavia, in Croatia, on a promontory jutting into the Adriatic Sea. It is a seaport and a tourist center. Industries include oil refining, slate mining, and metal working. Dubrovnik was founded in the 7th cent. by Roman refugees fleeing Slav incursions. Later, however, Slavic people settled in the city, which became a link between the Latin and Slavic civilizations. Dubrovnik rose to eminence as a powerful merchant republic. Though it was under the protectorate of the Byzantine Empire until 1205, of Venice until 1358, of Hungary until 1526, and of Turkey until 1806, Dubrovnik remained a virtually independent republic until it was abolished in 1808 by Napoleon I and included in the Illyrian provs. The Congress of Vienna assigned (1815) it to Austria, and in 1918 it was included in Yugoslavia. Medieval Dubrovnik was the center of Serbo-Croatian culture and literature. The city retains much of its medieval architecture, notably the city walls and forts, the customs house, the mint, the 15th-century rector's palace, and the Dominican and Franciscan monasteries, with one of the oldest (founded 1317) pharmacies in Europe.

Dubuffet, Jean (zhäN dübüfā'), 1901-, French painter and sculptor. Dubuffet began his artistic career in 1942. He created primitive, childlike, and humorous effects savagely opposed to established taste. For many works he prepared a thick impasto of materials such as asphalt, pebbles, and glass to enrich the surface texture of his paintings. Among his recent works are numerous large, white, crudely representational sculptures with heavily outlined colored edges and facets. The Museum of Modern Art, New York City, has his *Cow with the Subtile Nose* and *Beard of Uncertain Returns.* See studies by Peter Selz (1962) and Max Loreau (tr. 1973).

Dubuque, Julien (dəbyo͞ok'), 1762-1810, pioneer settler of Iowa, b. Nicolet co., Que. Setting out at a young age for the West, Dubuque reached Prairie du Chien by 1785 and crossed to the Iowa side of the Mississippi, then in Spanish Louisiana. He ingratiated himself with a band of Fox Indians encamped at a site nearby the present-day city of Dubuque, and by a written cession they gave (1788) him sole right to work their lead mines. This right was confirmed, and the first landholdings in Iowa to be given to a private individual were granted to him by Baron Carondelet, governor of Louisiana. For 20 years Dubuque worked the mines and traded in furs, employing Indians and French Canadian settlers. He retained the confidence of the Indians and was buried by them—with the honors of a chief—on a bluff overlooking the city named for him. See biography by Richard Herrman (1922).

Dubuque (dəbyo͞ok'), city (1970 pop. 62,309), seat of Dubuque co., NE Iowa, on the Mississippi River; chartered 1841. It is a trade, industrial, and rail center and a river port for an agricultural and dairy area. It has railroad shops, shipyards, food-processing plants, a brewery, and factories that make cast-iron and sheet-metal products, chemicals, and machinery. One of the oldest cities in the state, it was named for Julien Dubuque, who had settled nearby c.1788. Indian title to the territory ended with the Black Hawk Treaty of 1833, and white settlers began to pour in. Iowa's first newspaper, the Du Buque *Visitor,* was established there in 1836. The town developed first as a mining town, then as a lumbering and milling center. Today it is the seat of the Univ. of Dubuque, Clarke College, and Loras College. Of interest are the library, with a collection of paintings; St. Raphael's Cathedral (1857); the Ham House Museum; and Eagle Point Park. Nearby are Crystal Lake Cave; the U.S. locks and dam on the Mississippi; the grave of Julien Dubuque (with a memorial tower built 1897); and a Trappist monastery, New Melleray Abbey.

Du Cange, Charles du Fresne, sieur (shärl dü frĕn syör dü käNzh), 1610-88, French medieval historian and philologist. He is principally known for his *Glossarium mediae et infimae Latinitatis* [glossary of medieval and late Latin] (1678). It remains the greatest collection ever made of the forms of early medieval Latin and of the oldest Romance languages.

Ducas (dyo͞o'kəs), Greek family and dynasty of Constantinople. Some of its members were Byzantine emperors—Constantine X, Michael VII, ALEXIUS V, and JOHN III.

Ducasse, Isidore (ēzēdôr' dükäs'), 1846-70, French poet who wrote under the name Comte de Lautréamont, or simply Lautréamont. Born in Montevideo, Uruguay, he moved to Paris in 1867, where he lived like a hermit until his death at the age of 24. In 1870 he published a volume of poetry, *Poesies.* He is best known for his only other work, *Les Chants de Maldoror* (1890, tr. 1943), a nightmarish epic poem replete with grotesque, often erotic, imagery. Because of his hallucinatory, nonrepresentational style, Lautréamont was viewed by the surrealists as a progenitor.

Duccio, Agostino di: see AGOSTINO DI DUCCIO.

Duccio di Buoninsegna (do͝ot'chō dē bwōnēnsä'nyä), fl. 1278–1319, early Italian artist, first great painter of Siena. Infusing new life into the stylized Byzantine tradition, he initiated a style intrinsic to the development of the Sienese school—the expressive use of outline. The use of line varied from a vigorous quality in his rendering of narrative scenes to a lyrical and majestic tone in his portrayal of the Madonna and angels. In Siena he is recorded as having decorated some official chests in 1278 and as having painted a book cover in 1285. Also in 1285 he was commissioned to paint a Madonna for Santa Maria Novella, Florence, today identified with the Rucellai Madonna (Uffizi). His most celebrated and only authenticated work is a large altar called the *Maestà* in the Siena cathedral. It was finished in 1311 and was carried to its place by a rejoicing populace. While the main panel of the altar remains in the cathedral, the scattered predelle are now in the galleries of London and Berlin; the Frick Collection, New York City; the National Gallery of Art, Washington, D.C.; and several private collections. Several other works are attributed to Duccio on stylistic grounds, including the design of stained-glass windows in the cathedral at Siena. His influence on Sienese painting is comparable to that of GIOTTO in the development of Florentine art.

Du Cerceau: see ANDROUET DU CERCEAU.

Du Chaillu, Paul Belloni (pōl bĕlōnē' dü shäyü'), c.1831–1903, French-American explorer in Africa. Born probably in Paris, he spent his youth on the west coast of Africa, where his father was a trader in Gabon. There he learned the native languages and became interested in exploring the interior. Arriving in the United States in 1852, he became a citizen and gained the support of the Philadelphia Academy of Natural Sciences for an expedition to explore Gabon. On his explorations (1855–59), he captured many rare birds and animals, some of them previously unknown to science. He brought back the first gorillas to be seen in America. His published account, *Explorations in Equatorial Africa* (1861), upset the previous ideas of the region's geography; Du Chaillu made a second expedition (1863–65) to prove the truth of his account. On this trip he visited many tribes hitherto unknown and verified previous reports of Pygmy people. His book, *A Journey to Ashango-Land* (1867), is an account of this expedition. His subsequent writings include *Stories of the Gorilla Country* (1867), *Wild Life under the Equator* (1868), *My Apingi Kingdom* (1870), and *The Country of the Dwarfs* (1871). He traveled in Scandinavia (1871–78) and published *The Land of the Midnight Sun* (1881) and *The Viking Age* (1889). See biography by Michel Vaucaire (tr. 1930).

Duchamp, Marcel (märsĕl' düshäN'), 1887–1968, French painter, brother of Raymond DUCHAMP-VILLON and half-brother of Jacques VILLON. Duchamp is noted for his cubist-futurist painting *Nude Descending a Staircase,* depicting continuous action with a series of overlapping figures; it was the cause of great controversy when exhibited in 1913 at the New York ARMORY SHOW. Duchamp invented readymades—commonplace objects—e.g., the urinal entitled *Fountain,* which he exhibited as works of art. In 1915 he was a co-founder of a DADA group in New York. After 1920, Duchamp produced a series of elaborate nonfunctional machines. He emigrated to the United States in 1942. Many of his works, including the celebrated symbolic construction *The Bride stripped bare by her Bachelors, even* (1915–23), are at the Philadelphia Mus. of Art. See catalog with study ed. by Anne D'Harnoncourt and Kynaston McShine (1973).

Duchamp-Villon, Raymond (rāmôN' düshäN'-vēyôN'), 1876–1918, French sculptor; brother of the artists Marcel Duchamp and Jacques Villon. From the tradition of Rodin he turned to cubism in 1912. He began to assemble machinelike forms with more than a touch of fantasy. His famous geometrically faceted *Horse* is in the Musée national d'Art moderne, Paris, which contains other of his works. An enlarged cast of the *Horse,* made after the sculptor's death, is in the Museum of Modern Art, New York City.

Duchenne, Guillaume Benjamin Amand (gēyōm' bäNzhämăN' ämäN' düshĕn'), 1806–75, French physician. He is noted for researches on diseases of the muscular and nervous systems and for his pioneer work on the use of electricity in the diagnosis and treatment of disease.

Duchesne, Louis Marie Olivier (lwē märē' ōlēvyā' düshĕn'), 1843–1922, French Roman Catholic ecclesiastic, educator, church historian, and archaeologist. He made a scientific expedition to Mt. Athos, Greece, and to Asia Minor (1874–76). His able thesis, *Étude sur Liber pontificalis,* won (1877) for him the professorship of church history at the Catholic Institute, Paris, which he held for eight years. He founded the *Bulletin critique* (1880) to disseminate his views on theology, history, and philology and edited and published an edition of *Liber pontificalis* (2 vol., 1886–92). Appointed to the directorship of the French school of archaeology at Rome, he there became president of the papal commission to deliberate revising the breviary (1902). Among his works are *Christian Worship: Its Origin and Evolution* (tr. 1903, 5th ed. 1949, repr. 1956), and *Early History of the Christian Church* (3 vol., tr. 1910–24, repr. 1957–60).

Duchesne, Rose Philippine (rōz fēlēpēn'), 1769–1852, French educator in the United States, a Roman Catholic nun, b. Grenoble, France. She entered the order of the Visitation, but was forced (1791) by the antireligious decrees of the French Revolution to leave her convent. In 1804 she joined the Society of the Sacred Heart, which sent her to the United States in 1818. From the convent and school she founded at St. Charles, Mo.—later moved to Florissant, Mo.—she traveled over a wide area, founding schools for girls, doing charitable work, and finally ministering to the Indians. Duchesne was a valiant missionary and a well-known benefactress. She was beatified in 1940. See biography by Louise Callan (1957, abr. ed. 1965).

duck, common name for wild and domestic waterfowl of the family Anatidae, which also includes geese and swans. It is hunted and bred for its meat, eggs, and feathers. Strictly speaking, duck refers to the female and drake to the male. Ducks are usually divided into three groups: the surface-feeding ducks—such as the mallard, wood duck, black duck, and teal—which frequent ponds, marshes, and other quiet waters; the diving ducks—such as the canvasback, scaup, scoter, eider, and redhead—found on bays, rivers, and lakes; and the fish-eating ducks, the mergansers, with slender, serrated bills, which also prefer open water. The surface feeders take wing straight up, while the divers patter along the water's surface in taking off. Ducks make long migratory flights. At the time of the postnuptial molt, the power of flight is temporarily lost, and most of the Northern Hemisphere drakes assume "eclipse" plumage similar to that of the female. The ancestor of all domestic breeds (see POULTRY), except the Muscovy of South American origin, is the mallard, *Anas boscas,* which is found in Europe, Asia, and North America. In the mallard drake a white ring separates the bright-green head and neck from the chestnut breast, the back is grayish brown, the tail white, and the wings have blue patches. The wood duck, *Aix sponsa,* smaller than the mallard, nests in hollow trees; the drake is a varicolored, iridescent ornament to lakes and ponds. The blue-winged, green-winged, and European teals (genus *Querquedula*) are small ducks that fly with great speed. The canvasback, *Fuligula vallisneria,* is hunted widely for its palatable flesh. It has a chestnut head and neck, black bill and chest, and whitish back and underparts. A swift flier, it is also an expert swimmer and diver. It breeds from the Dakotas and Minnesota north and winters on the coastal waters along the entire continent. In northern countries a portion of the down with which the eider ducks line their nests is systematically collected, as are some of the eggs; since the eiders lay throughout the season, these are soon replaced. The mergansers, genus *Mergus,* also called sheldrakes or sawbills, are usually crested. They include the goosander and the smaller red-breasted merganser, both circumpolar in distribution, and the North American hooded merganser, similar to the Old World smew. Because their fish diet gives their flesh a rank taste, they are called by sportsmen "trash ducks." Ducks are classified in the phylum CHORDATA, subphylum Vertebrata, class Aves, order Anseriformes, family Anatidae.

duckbill, fish: see PADDLEFISH.

duckbill, marsupial: see PLATYPUS.

duck hawk: see FALCON.

Duck Lake, small lake, central Sask., Canada, SW of Prince Albert. It was the scene of the first encounter in Riel's Rebellion (see under RIEL, LOUIS) in 1885. A large group of métis (persons of mixed French and Indian descent) under Gabriel Dumont defeated a detachment of Northwest Mounted Police.

duckweed, any plant of the genus *Lemna* and sometimes of related genera. Duckweeds are tiny floating or submerged aquatic plants with reduced roots or none at all. They flower only rarely, and their flowers are small and inconspicuous. Duckweeds grow in freshwater throughout most of the world. They are classified in the division MAGNOLIOPHYTA, class Liliatae, order Arales, family Lemnaceae.

Duclos, Jacques (zhäk düklō'), 1896–, French Communist party leader. Early in his career he joined the French Communist party and in 1931 became party secretary and a member of the political bureau. He served (1926–32, 1936–40) in the chamber of deputies and was (1936–39) its vice president. In World War II he helped organize French resistance during the German occupation and was a principal architect of the Paris uprising of 1944. After the war he served (1945–58) in the national assembly (formerly the chamber of deputies) and was (1946–52) its vice president. Elected senator in 1959, Duclos ran for president in 1969 and won 21% of the vote.

Ducommun, Élie (ālē' dükômöN'), 1833–1906, Swiss journalist and pacifist. He organized (1891) the International Peace Bureau at Bern and shared the 1902 Nobel Peace Prize with C. A. Gobat.

ductility, ability of a metal to be drawn into a fine wire. The cohesion between the molecules of a ductile metal must be sufficient to hold them together as the metal is drawn through a narrow opening in a metal die (see ADHESION AND COHESION). The metal must neither break nor be scraped off during this process. Platinum is a very ductile metal. Steel, copper, and tungsten also have high ductility.

ductless gland: see ENDOCRINE SYSTEM; GLAND.

Du Deffand, Marie de Vichy-Chamrond, marquise (märē' də vēshē'-shäNrôN' märkēz' dü dĕfäN'), 1697–1780, French woman of letters, whose salon was frequented (1753–80) by the leaders of the Enlightenment. Her letters (1766–80) to Horace WALPOLE, whom she loved deeply, are typical of her brilliant, witty correspondence.

Dudevant, Amandine Aurore Lucie Dupin, baronne: see SAND, GEORGE.

Dudinka (do͞odyĕn'kə), city (1970 pop. 20,000), capital of the Taymyr National Okrug, Krasnoyarsk Kray, N Siberian USSR, on the Yenisei River. It is the river port for the Norilsk mining area and is accessible to seagoing ships. It is connected by rail with Norilsk. Founded in 1616 as a winter outpost on the Yenisei, Dudinka became a city in 1951.

Dudley, John: see NORTHUMBERLAND, JOHN DUDLEY, DUKE OF.

Dudley, Joseph, 1647–1720, colonial governor of Massachusetts, b. Roxbury, Mass.; son of Thomas Dudley. In 1682 he was one of the agents sent to England to protest against the threatened loss of the Massachusetts charter. Having found favor in England, Dudley was appointed head of the temporary government in the colony until Sir Edmund Andros arrived (1686) a few months later as governor of all of New England. Under Andros he held several prominent positions, but with Andros's fall (1689) Dudley was sent to England to answer charges brought against him by the colonists. Acquitted of the charges, he was appointed chief of the council of New York (1690–92) and acted as chief justice during the trial of Jacob Leisler. Back in England again, he was elected to Parliament (1701), but soon returned as governor of Massachusetts (1702–15). Dudley raised and directed military expeditions against Canada, but his administration was marked by dissension because of his earlier unpopularity in the colony and his uncompromising attitude. See biography by Everett Kimball (1911). His son, **Paul Dudley,** 1675–1751, b. Roxbury, Mass., rose to considerable prominence as a jurist in spite of his father's unpopularity and the hostility of the Mather faction. He was chief justice of Massachusetts (1745–51) and was well known as a naturalist.

Dudley, Robert: see LEICESTER, ROBERT DUDLEY, EARL OF.

Dudley, Thomas, 1576–1653, colonial governor of Massachusetts, b. England. As a young man he served as a clerk and later as steward to the earl of Lincoln. In 1630 he emigrated to America as deputy governor of the Massachusetts Bay colony and spent the remainder of his life in one public office or another, being elected deputy governor 13 times and serving four terms as governor. He was also a founder and one of the first overseers of Harvard. See biography by Augustine Jones (1899).

Dudley, county borough (1971 pop. 185,535), Worcestershire and Staffordshire, W central England. Dudley's famed iron, coal, and limestone industries have been declining since c.1870. Today industries include engineering works and steelworks, metallurgy, glass cutting, and leatherworking. The town developed around Dudley Castle in the 13th cent. The borough, isolated on an elevated site surrounded by Staffordshire, was greatly enlarged in 1966. The ruins of Dudley Castle are surrounded by a park with a zoo. Dudley has a college of education and a technical college. In 1974, Dudley became part of the new metropolitan county of West Midlands.

Dudok, William (do͞o'dôk), 1884–, Dutch architect. Dudok developed a dignified, widely influential style emphasizing the horizontal and utilizing an asymmetric effect with cubic groupings. As chief architect of the town of Hilversum, he worked almost exclusively in brick. He also designed theaters, stores, and housing projects, including Erasmus House (1937) and the Bijenkorf Store (1929–30) in Rotterdam.

duel, prearranged armed fight with deadly weapons, usually swords or pistols, between two persons concerned with a point of honor. The duel may have originated in the wager of battle, an early mode of trial in which an accused person fought with his accuser under judicial supervision (see ORDEAL). In 887, Pope Stephen VI prohibited the judicial duel and all forms of ordeal. Wager of battle was abolished in France in the mid-16th cent., and the duel in part took its place. The institution later spread to Great Britain and other countries. The duel of honor, which actually evolved in the 16th cent., was very closely linked with the code of chivalry (see KNIGHTHOOD AND CHIVALRY). To initiate a duel the offended party would present a challenge to fight, which had to be accepted or the person challenged would be dishonored. Negotiations were conducted by seconds, who also observed the combat to see that all agreements of the complex ceremony were observed. The object of a duel was not necessarily to kill, and in most cases after the firing of a prescribed number of shots or drawing blood the fight would be stopped. Although dueling was opposed by the churches of various countries, it long persisted among aristocrats, army officers, and others. German students were noted for their duels. Alexander HAMILTON was killed in a duel with Aaron BURR in the United States, and Andrew Jackson took part in several duels. In the United States dueling persisted longest in the Southern states and on the Western frontier. Dueling today has been made illegal by statute in most countries. Killing in the course of a duel is usually considered willful murder, and all persons aiding the principals are guilty with them. See studies by John Atkinson (1964) and Robert Baldrick (1965).

due process of law: see FOURTEENTH AMENDMENT.

Duer, John (dyo͞o'ər), 1782–1858, American jurist, b. Albany, N.Y.; son of William Duer. He studied law in Alexander Hamilton's office and was admitted to the New York bar. In 1821, Duer was a member of the state constitutional convention, and later he served (1825–27) as commissioner to revise the state statutes. Duer became U.S. district attorney for S New York in 1827 but in 1829 resumed his law practice in New York City, becoming an expert on insurance law. He was elected judge of the superior court of New York City in 1849 and chief justice in 1857. Duer's writings, especially his treatise on law and marine insurance (2 vol., 1845–46), gained him a wide reputation.

Duer, William, 1747–99, political leader in the American Revolution and financier, b. Devonshire, England. He served for a time as aide-de-camp to Robert Clive in India, afterward spending some time in the West Indies looking after his father's estates. In 1768 he moved to New York and, having received a contract to supply the royal navy with masts, purchased a tract of timberland above Saratoga on the Hudson. He built a mansion, erected mills, and became a gentleman of influence. Elected (1775) to New York's provincial congress, he served prominently in the state constitutional convention and acted on the Committee of Public Safety. From March, 1777, until Jan., 1779, he was a delegate to the Continental Congress. During the American Revolution he was one of the largest contractors supplying the Continental army. From 1786 to 1789 he was secretary of the Board of the Treasury, and after the Dept. of the Treasury was organized (1789) he became Assistant Secretary under Alexander Hamilton. Duer aided Manasseh Cutler in securing the land grant for the OHIO COMPANY OF ASSOCIATES. A speculator with great holdings, Duer was probably second only to Robert Morris as a financier of the period. His multifold plans did not succeed, however; the government sued him for certain irregularities involved in his work with the Treasury Dept. He was imprisoned for debt, and his ruin is supposed to have helped create the Panic of 1792. Except for a brief period, he spent the rest of his life in prison. See J. S. Davis, *Essays in the Earlier History of American Corporations* (1917, repr. 1965).

Duer, William Alexander, 1780–1858, American jurist and educator, b. Rhinebeck, N.Y.; son of William Duer. He was admitted to the New York bar in 1802 and practiced in New York City and, from 1804 to 1806, in New Orleans. Back in New York, he was a member of the state legislature (1814–20) and a judge of the state supreme court (1822–29). From 1829 to 1842 he was president of Columbia College. There he established scientific courses that did not require the study of Latin, and he increased instruction in modern languages and Hebrew. *A Course of Lectures on the Constitutional Jurisprudence of the United States* (1843, 2d ed. 1856) was based on his course in constitutional law. He also wrote a biography of his grandfather, *Life of William Alexander, Earl of Stirling* (1847). His *Reminiscences of an Old Yorker* was published posthumously in 1867.

Duero, river: see DOURO.

Dufay, Guillaume (gēyōm' düfā'), c.1400–1474, founder and leading composer of the Burgundian school. After his early training in the cathedral choir at Cambrai, he sang in the papal chapel in Rome (1428–33) and later in Florence and Bologna (1435–37). He was in the service of the antipope Felix V for seven years and was a canon of the cathedral of Cambrai, where he lived from 1445 until his death. He traveled a great deal, knew many musical styles, and was highly esteemed by his contemporaries. His music is in the northern French tradition, but contains some Italian and English elements. He composed three-part vocal chansons, masses, songs with instrumental accompaniment, and motets.

Duff, Alexander, 1806–78, Scottish missionary in India. In Calcutta he opened (1830) a mission college which became an important center of education in India; both religious and scientific subjects were taught. Duff was also instrumental in founding the Univ. of Calcutta. In 1844 he helped to launch the Calcutta *Review.*

Duff, Sir Lyman Poore, 1865–1955, Canadian jurist, b. Ontario. A lawyer and judge in British Columbia, he was appointed a judge of the Supreme Court of Canada in 1906, and in 1933 he became chief justice, serving until his retirement in 1944. He was chairman (1931–32) of the Royal Commission on Transportation (popularly called the Duff Commission) appointed to inquire into railroad problems in Canada, and twice (1931, 1943) he was administrator of the government of Canada. He was knighted in 1934.

Duff Cooper, Alfred: see COOPER, ALFRED DUFF.

Dufferin and Ava, Frederick Temple Hamilton-Temple-Blackwood, 1st **marquess of,** 1826–1902, British diplomat. He served on numerous missions abroad, as governor general of Canada (1872–78), ambassador to Russia (1879–81), ambassador to Turkey (1881–82), commissioner to Egypt (1882–83), viceroy of India (1884–88), ambassador to Italy (1888–91), and ambassador to France (1891–96). His administration in India saw the annexation (1886) of Burma and an improvement in relations with the Afghans. See biographies by Alfred Lyall (1905) and Harold Nicolson (1938).

Duffy, Sir Charles Gavan, 1816–1903, Irish-Australian statesman. He founded (1842) the *Nation,* a patriotic Irish literary journal. Duffy agitated for the repeal of the union of Ireland and England, first working with Daniel O'CONNELL and then with the more radical Young Ireland movement. In 1848 he was arrested for advocating rebellion but later was acquitted. Entering Parliament in 1852, he helped to found the Independent Irish party. Disconsolate over the failure of Catholics and Protestants to unite for land reform, he went (1855) to Australia. He entered (1856) the assembly of the Victoria colony, and as minister of land and works (1857–59, 1862–65) he formulated a land act to aid immigrant farmers and check the dominance of squatters. He served (1871–72) as prime minister of Victoria. Duffy was knighted in 1873.

Dufour, Guillaume Henri (gēyōm' äNrē' düfo͞or'), 1787–1875, Swiss general. He served in the French army under Napoleon I, and in 1847 he led the Swiss federal forces to victory against the SONDERBUND. A noted cartographer, he was also the author of several military treatises and histories. Dufour presided over the first Geneva Convention, which established (1864) the International Red Cross.

Dufourspitze, peak: see ROSA, MONTE.

Dufy, Raoul (räo͞ol' düfē'), 1877–1953, French painter, illustrator, and decorator, studied at the École des Beaux-Arts. After meeting Matisse he abandoned his early impressionist style and turned c.1905 to the more spontaneous expression of FAUVISM. For a time he designed fabrics for the dressmaker Paul Poiret and illustrated books, including the writings of Apollinaire, Mallarmé, and Gide. He created his own distinctly urbane mode of painting. Using swift, stenographic brush strokes, he developed a remarkable linear virtuosity and brilliant color. Dufy's glittering landscapes, seascapes, and witty views of society are represented in leading galleries of contemporary art. Typical is his watercolor *The Palm* (Mus. of Modern Art, New York City). See biography by Raymond Cogniat (1962); study by Alfred Werner (1970).

Du Gard, Roger Martin: see MARTIN DU GARD.

Dugdale, Richard Louis (dŭg'dāl), 1841–83, American social investigator, b. Paris. While inspecting (1874) county jails for the New York prison association, he came across the facts that gave him material for his famous study of the Jukes (fictitious name of a real family). The study was published as *The Jukes: A Study in Crime, Pauperism, Disease, and Heredity* (1875). One of the first social investigations of familial feeble-mindedness and criminality, it created a sensation at the time; however, more recent studies have brought Dugdale's assumptions and conclusions about hereditary degeneracy into question. The finding of the manuscript (1911), revealing the actual names of the family, enabled Arthur H. Estabrook to make a comparative study, *The Jukes in 1915.*

Dugdale, Sir William, 1605–86, English antiquarian. His chief works are *Antiquities of Warwickshire* (1656), *The Baronage of England* (1675–76), and the greater part of *Monasticon Anglicanum* (3 vol., 1655–73). The Dugdale Society, founded in 1920, publishes historical manuscripts.

dugong: see SIRENIAN.

Duguay-Trouin, René (rənā' dügā'-tro͞oăN'), 1673–1736, French privateer and naval officer. A member of a Breton family of shipowners, he became (1689) a privateer and was given command of a vessel in 1691. His bravery, the respect he won from his men, and his successes against the English and the Dutch in the wars of King Louis XIV caused him to rise rapidly in command. By 1709 he was reported to have captured 300 merchantmen and 20 warships or privateers. In 1711, in the War of the Spanish Succession, he captured Rio de Janeiro after an 11-day bombardment and forced the city to pay a heavy ransom. As a reward for his services Duguay-Trouin was ennobled by Louis XIV in 1709 and commissioned a lieutenant general in 1728. He left memoirs.

Du Guesclin, Bertrand (bĕrtrăN' dü gĕklăN'), c.1320–80, constable of France (1370–80), greatest French soldier of his time. A Breton, he initially served Charles of Blois in the War of the BRETON SUCCESSION. Charles was supported by the French crown, while his rival was allied with England. In 1356–57, Du Guesclin held Rennes against English attack. Entering the service of King Charles V of France on Charles's accession (1364), he won the brilliant victory of Cocherel over the forces of King CHARLES II of Navarre. The victory forced Charles II into a new peace with the French king. Du Guesclin was captured in the same year at Auray by English forces under Sir John Chandos. Ransomed by Charles V, who placed him at the head of the "free companies," the marauding soldiers who pillaged France after the Treaty of BRÉTIGNY between France and England, De Guesclin was sent to Spain to aid Henry of Trastamara (later HENRY II of Castile) against PETER THE CRUEL. Du Guesclin, though successful in the campaign of 1366, was defeated and captured (1367) by Peter and EDWARD THE BLACK PRINCE at Nájera. In 1369, however, he and Henry won the battle of Montiel, gaining for Henry the throne of Castile. Warfare with England was renewed in 1369, and Du Guesclin reconquered Poitou and Saintonge and pursued (1370–74) the English into Brittany. He disapproved of the confiscation (1378) of Brittany by Charles V, and his campaign to make the duchy submit to the king was halfhearted. An able tactician and a loyal and disciplined warrior, Du Guesclin had reconquered much of France from the English when he died while on a military expedition in Languedoc. See biographies by D. F. Jamison (1864), E. V. Stoddard (1897), and Roger Vercel (tr. 1934).

Duhamel, Georges, (zhôrzh düämĕl'), 1884–1966, French novelist and playwright. From Duhamel's experience as a surgeon during World War I came *Vie des martyrs* (1917, tr. *The New Book of Martyrs,*

1918) and *Civilisation* (1918, tr. 1919). The latter, published under the pseudonym Denis Thévenin, won him the Goncourt Prize. These collections of sketches are noted for their compassionate accounts of human suffering. He was successful as a dramatist; his *Dans l'ombre des statues* was performed in 1912 (tr. *In the Shadow of Statues,* 1914) and *L'oeuvre des athlètes* in 1920. His fiction includes two cycles of novels—*Cycle de Salavin* (1920-32, tr. 1936), about a sensitive eccentric, and *Chronique des Pasquiers* (1933-45, tr. 1937-46), about a bourgeois Parisian family. Essays in *Scènes de la vie future* (1930, tr. *America: the Menace,* 1931), *Querelles de famille* (1931), and *Défense des lettres* (1936, tr. 1939) reflect Duhamel's aversion to the overindustrialization and overmechanization of modern life. He was elected to the French Academy in 1936. See studies by L. C. Keating (1965) and B. L. Knapp (1972).

Duhamel du Monceau, Henri Louis (äNrē' lwē düämĕl' dü môNsō'), 1700-1782, French agriculturist and tree expert. He did experimental work on plant physiology and ecology and wrote *The Elements of Agriculture* (1762, tr. 1764) and other standard works on agriculture and on the distribution and culture of trees and shrubs.

Duhem, Pierre Maurice Marie (pyĕr mōrēs' märē' düĕm'), 1861-1916, French physicist and philosopher and historian of science. After studying at the École Normale Supérieure he taught at Lille (1887-1893), Rennes (1893-1894), and Bordeaux (1894-1916). His extension and application of the thermodynamic potential to topics in chemistry ranks him among the founders of modern physical chemistry. His *Traité d'énergétique générale* (2 vol., 1911) aimed at a generalized, abstract thermodynamics that subsumed classical mechanics. His major philosophical work, *La théorie physique: Son objet, sa structure* (1906; tr. *The Aim and Structure of Physical Theory,* 1954) depreciates pictorial models in favor of an axiomatic approach, according to which a physical theory is not an explanation, but a system of mathematical propositions that represents experimental laws. As a historian Duhem discovered important currents of medieval thought in physics, cosmology, and astronomy, which he saw as precursors of the 17th-century scientific revolution. He set forth this material, hitherto almost unknown, in *Études sur Léonard de Vinci* (3 vol., 1906-1913) and *Le Système du monde* (10 vol., 1913-1959). See study by Armand Lowinger (1941).

Dühring, Eugen Karl (oigān' kärl dü'rĭng), 1833-1921, German philosopher and economist. He practiced law in Berlin until blindness threatened him and then became (1864) docent at the Univ. of Berlin. He was unable to get along with academic authorities, however, and he retired in 1877. A positivist in the manner of Comte and Feuerbach, he looked to the study of man as the basis of his philosophy. His political philosophy rested on the retention of capitalism with the elimination of its abuses through a strong labor movement. He was violently criticized by Engels in *Anti-Dühring* (1877). His works include *Kritische Geschichte der allgemeinen Principien der Mechanik* (1872) and *Cursus der Philosophie* (1875).

duiker (dī'kər, dā'-), name for members of a group of small, light ANTELOPES, found in thick brush and forest over most of Africa. All stand under 25 in. (64 cm) high at the shoulder. They have arched backs, pointed faces, and short, sharp, straight horns; in most species the horns are present in both sexes. Solitary, mostly nocturnal animals, they dive into the brush when threatened; *duiker* means "diver" in Afrikaans. Although primarily browsers, they are less exclusively vegetarian than other antelopes. Their diet includes grasses, leaves, twigs, insects, and snails. The gray, or common, duiker, *Sylvicapra grimmia,* is found from Ethiopia to the Cape of Good Hope and W to Senegal. It stands up to 25 in. and weighs up to 30 lb (14 kg). The local races vary in color from fawn to bluish gray. Females are usually hornless. The many kinds of forest duiker and blue duiker are species of the genus *Cephalophus.* The blue duikers, found in W and central Africa, stand only 14 in. (36 cm) at the shoulder. Duikers are classified in the phylum CHORDATA, subphylum Vertebrata, class Mammalia, order Artiodactyla, family Bovidae.

Duisburg (düs'bo͝ork), city (1970 pop. 454,839), North Rhine-Westphalia, W West Germany, at the confluence of the Rhine and Ruhr rivers. Located in the RUHR district, it is the largest inland port in Europe and a center of West German steel production. Other manufactures include textiles, chemicals, and metal and wood products. Duisburg was a port in Roman times. It passed to the duchy of Cleves in 1290, and in 1614 was acquired, with Cleves, by Brandenburg. Its growth as an industrial center dates from c.1850. As a center of the German armaments industry, the city was heavily bombed during World War II. The Gothic Salvator Church is the burial place of the geographer and cartographer G. Mercator (d. 1594). Wilhelm Lehmbruck, the sculptor, was born in Duisburg, and his works are displayed there in a museum.

Dujardin, Félix (fālĕks' düzhärdăN'), 1801-60, French zoologist. He contributed valuable research on bacteria and on the Infusoria. In 1835 he described protoplasm in unicellular animals, naming it sarcode. He taught at the universities of Toulouse and Rennes.

Dujardin, Karel, 1622-78, Dutch painter and etcher. He studied with Berchem and in Italy. Dujardin was particularly successful in painting landscapes with figures and animals, and he made some 51 fine etchings of similar subjects. His *Charlatans* and *Cavalry* (both: Louvre) are characteristic works.

Dukas, Paul (pōl dükä'), 1865-1935, French composer and critic. He was influenced by both the romanticism of Wagner and the impressionism of Debussy. His compositions are few, the best known being a symphonic poem, *The Sorcerer's Apprentice* (1897), and an opera, *Ariane et Barbe-Bleue* (1907).

Duke, James Buchanan, 1856-1925, American industrialist, processor of tobacco products, b. near Durham, N.C. The Civil War left the Duke family poor, but James and his brother, Benjamin, helped their father in building up a local tobacco-processing business, which soon prospered. Development of cigarette-making machines and extensive advertising gave the Duke company a lead in tobacco manufacturing. Through a long series of mergers with competitors, James Duke organized (1890) and led a trust that, when dissolved by order of the Supreme Court in 1911, controlled 150 factories with a capitalization of $502 million. He left a trust fund to Trinity College that provided for the erection of buildings and facilities; the name of the college was changed to Duke Univ. He also gave large amounts for hospitals, orphanages, and churches. See biographies by J. W. Jenkins (1927, repr. 1971) and J. K. Winkler (1942).

Duke Endowment, institution founded (1924) by industrialist James B. Duke with an endowment of $40 million for philanthropic purposes largely within the states of North Carolina and South Carolina. Beneficiaries are Duke, Furman, and Johnson C. Smith universities, Davidson College, hospitals and orphanages, and rural Methodist churches and ministers in North Carolina. In 1972 its endowment exceeded $430 million.

Duke of York Islands, group of 13 coral islands (1969 est. pop. 5,870), 23 sq mi (60 sq km), SW Pacific, in the BISMARCK ARCHIPELAGO, part of Papua New Guinea. There are several coconut plantations. Duke of York Island is the largest of the group, which was formerly called Neu Lauenburg.

Dukes, Leopold, 1810-91, Hungarian Hebrew scholar. He made a collection of rabbinical proverbs and wrote on the history of Jewish literature, notably of Hebrew poetry in the Middle Ages. He also translated into German Rashi's commentary on the Pentateuch.

Duke University, at Durham, N. C.; coeducational; opened 1838, chartered 1841 as Union Institute in Randolph County. Reorganized 1852 as Normal College, it became (1859) Trinity College (Methodist) and moved to Durham in 1892. It was renamed in 1924 for James B. Duke, who gave it financial assistance. Its research in tobacco culture and medicine is notable.

Dukhobors or **Doukhobors** (both: do͞o'kəbôrz) [Russ.,=spirit wrestlers], religious sect, prominent in Russia from the 18th to the 19th cent. The name was coined by the Orthodox opponents of the Dukhobors, who had originally called themselves Christians of the Universal Brotherhood. They were in doctrine somewhat like the Quakers, rejecting completely priesthood, the sacraments, and the other outward symbols of Christianity. The members came from the lower level of society, primarily farmers; the Dukhobors promoted a communal, absolutely democratic attitude and preached equality. Because they rejected the authority of both state and church, they were persecuted under Catherine II. Alexander I persuaded them to settle near the Sea of Azov. There they built up flourishing agricultural communities. When they did not agree to military conscription, considering it sinful, the government in 1840 forcibly ejected them from their lands and moved them farther east. Again they built thriving communities. In 1887 military conscription was again extended to them and again was resisted. Severe persecution followed and their leader, Peter Veregin, was exiled to Siberia. Leo Tolstoy befriended the Dukhobors and helped enable them to go to Canada. Over 7,000 of them moved (1898-99) to what is now Saskatchewan. Veregin later joined them. Once more their abilities produced flourishing communities, and they spread after 1908 to British Columbia. Frugal, industrious, and abstemious, the Dukhobors built their own roads and their own irrigation projects. Orchards and farms flourished. The sect became a small but important group in the development of W Canada. There were internal divisions, however, primarily over the question of communal ownership of land. The Sons of Freedom stressed ascetic practices, most spectacularly nudism. The Dukhobors in later days had much trouble with the government and with their non-Dukhobor neighbors; this occasionally burst into violence, but was usually expressed in passive resistance. One of the more remarkable forms was the so-called nudist strikes, in which the Dukhobors stripped off their clothing and marched in revolt against governmental decisions. The elder Peter Veregin was killed by a time bomb in 1924, and his son, Peter Veregin, came from Russia to lead the sect. He died in 1939, recommending that the Dukhobors abandon communal life and adjust themselves to Canadian ways. In 1945 the Union of the Dukhobors of Canada was founded, but immediately afterward the Sons of Freedom made themselves a separate organization. See J. F. C. Wright, *Slava Bohu* (1940); H. B. Hawthorn, ed., *Doukhobors of British Columbia* (1955); George Woodcock and Ivan Avakumovic, *The Doukhobors* (1968).

Dulac, Edmund (dyo͞olăk'), 1882-1953, French illustrator of English books. He is known for his imaginative, colorful illustrations of the *Arabian Nights* (1907), Shakespeare's *Tempest* (1908), and *The Rubaiyat* of Omar Khayyam (1909).

Dulany, Daniel (dyo͞olā'nē), 1685-1753, political leader of colonial Maryland, b. Ireland. He emigrated to Maryland c.1703, studied law, and was admitted to the bar. He entered the assembly in 1722 and remained a member for 20 years, becoming a leader of the colonists in opposition to the proprietor. When the proprietor vetoed (1722) a bill passed by the Maryland assembly that would have introduced English statute law into the colony, Dulany denounced his action as a violation of the charter. To win Dulany over, the proprietor appointed him his agent and receiver general in 1733, a judge of admiralty in 1734, and commissary general in 1736. He was also appointed to the council in 1742 and served in that body until his death. His son, **Daniel Dulany,** 1722-97, was educated in England. He gained prominence as a colonial politician in Maryland and was probably the most celebrated lawyer in the American colonies. Dulany opposed the Stamp Act in his *Considerations on the Propriety of Imposing Taxes in the British Colonies.* He lost his popularity, however, when in 1773 he engaged in newspaper controversy with Charles Carroll in defense of the fees exacted by government officials for performing certain services. Dulany was a Loyalist during the Revolution and most of his property was confiscated by the state in 1781. See A. C. Land, *The Dulanys of Maryland* (1955, repr. 1974).

dulcimer (dŭl'sĭmər), stringed musical instrument. It is a wooden box with strings stretched over it that are struck with small mallets. The number of strings may vary. The dulcimer is related to the PSALTERY and to the modern ZITHER. It originated in the Middle

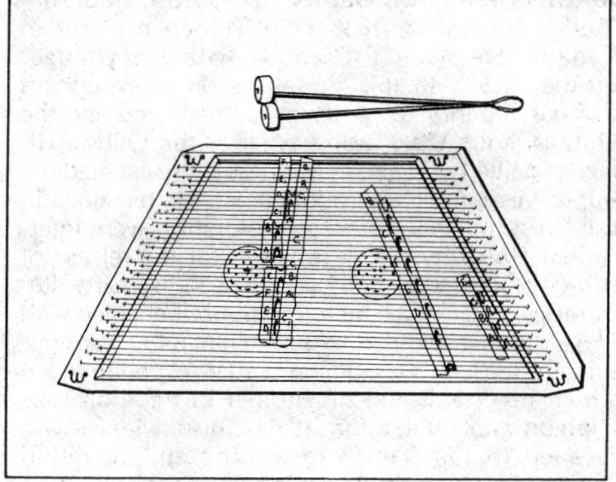

Dulcimer

East and was adopted in Europe in the Middle Ages. The popularity of the dulcimer continued in Western Europe until the 17th cent., when it sharply declined, though a German, Pantaleon Hebenstreit, enlarged it to make an instrument called the pantaleon in the early 18th cent. It is still much used in Eastern Europe in gypsy bands. In Appalachia a plucked dulcimer very similar to the zither is popular. It is comparatively small and is held on the player's lap.

Du Lhut, Daniel Greysolon, sieur: see DULUTH.

Dulles, Allen Welsh (dŭl'əs), 1893–1969, U.S. public official, b. Watertown, N.Y.; brother of John Foster Dulles. He entered (1916) diplomatic service and became (1922) chief of the division of Near Eastern affairs, part of the Dept. of State. In 1926 he resigned to practice law. During World War II he was a prominent member of the Office of Strategic Services. Returning (1951) to government service as deputy director of the CENTRAL INTELLIGENCE AGENCY, Dulles became director in 1953. Under his direction the CIA was strengthened and made a more effective element in the U.S. intelligence system. Dulles resigned in 1961 after a series of events (most notably the Bay of Pigs invasion of Cuba) in which the CIA played a controversial role that aroused much criticism. His works include *Germany's Underground* (1947), *The Craft of Intelligence* (1963), and *Secret Surrender* (1966).

Dulles, John Foster, 1888–1959, U.S. Secretary of State (1953–59), b. Washington, D.C.; grandson of John Watson Foster, Secretary of State under President Benjamin Harrison, and nephew of Robert Lansing, Secretary of State under Woodrow Wilson. A graduate (1908) of Princeton, he was admitted (1911) to the bar and was counsel to the U.S. delegation to the Paris Peace Conference (1919). He soon achieved prominence as an international lawyer and attended various international conferences in the interwar years. He was appointed (1945) adviser to the U.S. delegation at the San Francisco Conference (1945), and served (1945–49) as a U.S. delegate to the United Nations General Assembly. He was appointed (1949) to finish the unexpired term of Senator Robert F. Wagner of New York, but was defeated (1950) in a general election for the seat. In 1951, as ambassador at large, Dulles negotiated the peace treaty with Japan. Appointed (1953) Secretary of State by Dwight D. EISENHOWER, he emphasized the collective security of the United States and its allies and the development of nuclear weapons for "massive retaliation" in case of attack. Regarding Communism as a moral evil to be resisted at any cost, he firmly upheld the Chinese Nationalist defense of islands off the coast of Communist China and initiated the policy of strong U.S. backing for the South Vietnamese regime of Ngo Dinh Diem. Dulles helped develop the Eisenhower doctrine of economic and military aid to maintain the independence of Middle Eastern countries; under its terms U.S. forces were sent to Lebanon in 1958. Dulles resigned from office a month before his death. He wrote *War, Peace, and Change* (1939) and *War or Peace* (1950). See biographies by M. A. Guhin (1972) and Townsend Hoopes (1973); studies by Richard Goold-Adams (1962) and L. L. Gerson (1967); Roscoe Drummond and Gaston Coblentz, *Duel at the Brink* (1960).

Dullin, Charles (shärl dülăN'), 1885–1949, French actor, producer, and director. Dullin was an outstanding member of Copeau's Théâtre du Vieux Colombier. He organized and toured with his own group before opening the Théâtre de l'Atelier in Paris in 1921. There, among other experimental plays, he introduced the work of Pirandello to the French public.

Duluth or **Du Lhut, Daniel Greysolon, sieur** (dəlōōth', Fr. dülüt'), 1636–1710, French explorer in Canada. He went to Canada with his younger brother c.1672. In 1678 he set out on an expedition to Lake Superior to pacify the Indians and end the Ojibwa-Sioux War. Going as far as the Ojibwa village at Mille Lacs Lake in Minnesota, he claimed the upper Mississippi region for France. He remained in the West, but his plans for exploration were interrupted (1680) by the negotiation for the release of HENNEPIN and ACO, members of La Salle's party. Returning to Mackinac, he found himself charged with illegal trading and had to go to France to clear himself. In 1683 he was off on a new expedition, on which he established his brother in trade on Lake Nipigon and built a fort at Kaministikwia. He was recalled to join Perrot in leading an expedition against the Iroquois. Returning to Kaministikwia he prepared to search for the Western Sea, but was again recalled to fight the Iroquois. In 1686 he built Fort St. Joseph on the St. Clair River. He went on his last Lake Superior expedition in 1688. In 1695 he was retired because of lameness. Duluth won the Lake Superior and upper Mississippi region for France; his treatment of the Indians gained their lasting friendship.

Duluth (dəlōōth'), city (1970 pop. 100,578), seat of St. Louis co., NE Minn., at the west end of Lake Superior, at the head of lake navigation and opposite Superior, Wis.; inc. 1870. It is a commercial, industrial, and cultural center of N Minnesota, the second largest port on the Great Lakes, a convention headquarters, and the gateway to a resort region. Huge amounts of grain, iron ore (especially taconite), and bulk cargo are shipped on lake freighters and ocean vessels. Manufactures include steel and cement; metal and wood products; electrical equipment; textiles; and prepared foods. Indian settlements were found there (1670s) by the early explorers and fur traders, including the sieur Duluth (for whom the city was named). Permanent settlement began c.1852. Built largely on rocky bluffs overlooking the lake, the city was at first a trade and shipping center for the timber country. Discovery of iron (1865) in the Mesabi range made it the chief ore-shipping point for the nation's steel mills. With the opening of the St. Lawrence Seaway (1959), it became one of the leading ports on the Great Lakes for the export of grain. It is the seat of the College of St. Scholastica and a branch of the Univ. of Minnesota. It has a civic symphony orchestra. Points of interest include the huge Aerial Lift Bridge, linking the city to 7 mi (11.3 km) of sand beach on Park Point; the Skyline Blvd., winding high above the city for 15 mi (24 km); and Leif Erikson Park, with its replica Viking ship that sailed from Norway in 1922. A U.S. air force base and a U.S. coast guard station are nearby.

duma (dōō'mä), Russian name for a representative body, particularly applied to the Imperial Duma established as a result of the Russian Revolution of 1905. The parliamentary organization of 1906, largely the work of Count WITTE, provided for a state council (an upper house, with some members appointed by the czar and others elected by the nobility, the ZEMSTVOS, the clergy, trade and industry, and the university faculties) and for the Duma (a lower house elected by a system of suffrage that was neither equal nor direct); no law was to be passed without the consent of the Duma. When Czar Nicholas II found that a majority of opposition candidates had been elected in 1906, he dissolved the Duma after 10 weeks. The second Duma (1907), even more hostile to the government, was also dissolved. The third Duma (1907–12) was the product of an electoral change that made it the tool of the government. It did, however, extend the peasants' rights and enact some labor laws. The fourth Duma (1912–17) had a conservative majority; called at rare and brief intervals, it was in constant conflict with the czar. It was dissolved by Nicholas in March, 1917 (Feb., O. S.), but refused to disband. Revolution (see RUSSIAN REVOLUTION) broke out, and the Duma, after electing a provisional committee, disintegrated. The committee and the Petrograd soviet appointed the provisional government. See V. A. Maklakov, *The First State Duma* (tr. 1964); Alfred Levin, *The Second Duma* (2d ed. 1966).

Dumaguete (dōōmägā'tā), city (1970 est. pop. 49,600), capital of Negros Oriental prov., SE Negros, the Philippines. A busy interisland-shipping port at the entrance to Tañon Strait (which separates the islands of Negros and Cebu), it is also a trade and cultural center. Silliman Univ. (founded 1901) and Foundation Univ. are there.

Dumah (dōō'mə). **1** Descendants of Ishmael, an Arabic tribe in the desert of N Arabia. Gen. 25.14; 1 Chron. 1.30. **2** Town, S Palestine. Joshua 15.52. **3** Apparently a symbolic name for Edom. Isa. 21.11.

Dumas, Alexandre (älĕksäN'drə dümä'), known as **Dumas père** (pĕr), 1802–70, French novelist and dramatist. His father (an illegitimate son of the marquis de la Pailleterie and a Negro woman, Louise Cosette Dumas), was a general in the Revolution. Dumas delighted many generations of readers with his highly romantic novels immortalizing the adventures of the Three Musketeers and the Count of Monte Cristo. Largely self-educated, Dumas was a flamboyant youth with a gift for storytelling and a penchant for love affairs. At the age of 20 he obtained a minor post with the duc d'Orléans in Paris, and later he was active in the Revolution of 1830. His first successes were the historical dramas *Henri III et sa cour* (1829), *Christine* (1830), *Antony* (1831), and *La Tour de Nesle* (1832), notable for its evocation of the Middle Ages. After a number of novels, written independently or in collaboration, he produced his great triumphs, *The Three Musketeers* (1844, tr. 1846) and its sequels—*Twenty Years After* (1845, tr. 1846) and *The Vicomte de Bragelonne* (1848–50, tr. 1850?)—and *The Count of Monte Cristo* (1845, tr. 1846), which in its dramatic version was made famous by James O'Neill. Although these historical novels and their successors, written with the aid of numerous collaborators, especially Auguste Maquet, are scorned by critics, who find them lacking in style and characterization, they have had enormous popularity and have been translated into nearly every language. Among his other works are *Queen Margot* (1845, tr. 1845), *The Lady of Monsoreau* (1846, tr. 1847), *The Forty-Five* (1848), *The Black Tulip* (1850), and *The Journal of Madame Giovanni* (tr. 1944). Dumas *père's* incredible output of novels, travel works, memoirs, and historical studies made him wealthy, but he spent more than he earned on a horde of pensioners at his home, "Monte-Cristo," near Saint-Germain. His memoirs (1852–54) end with the year 1832. He was interested in Italian unification, and among his activities was a part in Garibaldi's expedition in 1860. See biography by A. Craig Bell (1950, repr. 1973); A. Maurois, *The Titans* (1957, repr. 1971).

Dumas, Alexandre, known as **Dumas fils** (fēs), 1824–95, French dramatist and novelist, illegitimate son of Dumas Père. He was the chief creator of the 19th-century comedy of manners. His first important play, *La Dame aux camélias* (1852, tr. 1856), known in English as *Camille*, was a sensation. It was based on a partly autobiographical novel of the same title, which he had published in 1848. Portraying a love affair of a courtesan, the play became the vehicle of many famous actresses, and it was the basis of Verdi's opera *La Traviata*. Another successful play, *Le Demi-Monde* (1855, tr. 1858), aroused much discussion because of its portrayal of the disreputable world of French society. In later plays Dumas preached a revolt against romantic morality, the excesses of the wealthy, and bourgeois puritanism and propounded social and psychological questions. His stage works are notable for skillful construction, though the characterizations are somewhat lacking in vitality. His novels include *Tristan le Roux* (1850) and *Diane de Lys* (1853). Among his best plays are also *The Money Question* (1857, tr. 1915), *Le Fils naturel* [the natural son] (1858), *Les Idées de Mme Aubray* (1867), *L'Étrangère* [the strange woman] (1876), and *Denise* (1885). His early essays, *Entr'actes* (1878–79), are mostly on social subjects. In 1874 he was elected to the French Academy. See A. Maurois, *The Titans* (1957, repr. 1971); study by H. Stanley Schwarz (1927, repr. 1971).

Dumas, Jean Baptiste André (zhäN bätēst' äNdrā'), 1800–1884, French organic chemist. He was distinguished for his researches on atomic weights, esters, vapor densities, the oxidation products of alcohols, and the laws of substitution. He taught in several institutions, including the Sorbonne; served as minister of agriculture and commerce, as senator, and as vice president of the High Council of Education; and in 1868 became perpetual secretary of the Academy of Sciences. His works include *Traité de chimie appliquée aux arts* (8 vol., 1828–45).

Dumas fils: see DUMAS, ALEXANDRE (1824–95).

Dumas père: see DUMAS, ALEXANDRE (1802–70).

Du Maurier, George Louis Palmella Busson (dyōō môr'ēā), 1834–96, English artist and novelist, b. Paris of a French father and an English mother. He studied chemistry, but later turned to art for a livelihood. In spite of the loss of one eye when he was a young man, he became a successful illustrator and in 1864 joined the staff of *Punch*. His novels include *Peter Ibbetson* (1892; successfully dramatized in 1915 and later made into an opera by Deems Taylor, which was produced in 1931) and *Trilby* (1894; the story of a young model who, when hypnotized by the musician Svengali, is a great singer). See biography by Leonée Ormond (1969). **Daphne Du Maurier,** 1907–, his granddaughter, is the author of popular novels, including *Jamaica Inn* (1936) and *Rebecca* (1938), and two books on her own family, *Gerald: A Portrait* (1934) and *The Du Mauriers* (1937).

Dumba, Konstantin Theodor (kônstäntēn' tā'ōdôr dōōm'bä), 1856–1947, Austro-Hungarian diplomat. As ambassador (1913–15) to the United States, he was involved with Franz von Papen and Karl Boy-Ed in schemes to sabotage the American munitions industry. Dumba was recalled on President Wilson's request. His memoirs (tr. 1932) present his defense.

Dumbarton (dəmbär'tən), royal burgh (1971 pop. 25,640), county town of Dunbartonshire, W Scotland, at the confluence of the Leven and Clyde rivers. It is a shipbuilding center (the *Cutty Sark* was fitted out there) and has engineering works. Aircraft, bricks, and whiskey are produced. Castles that played an important role in Scottish history were built on Dumbarton Rock, a 250-ft-high (76-m) hill of basalt, from at least the 5th cent., when Dumbarton was the capital of the kingdom of Strathclyde. It became the capital of the earldom of Lennox in the 12th cent. and was granted a royal charter in 1222. Sir John de Monteith, the governor of Dumbarton Castle, betrayed William WALLACE in 1305; Wallace was imprisoned in the castle. In 1975, Dumbarton became part of the new Strathclyde region.

Dumbarton Oaks Conference: see UNITED NATIONS.

Dumbartonshire (dŭm″bar'tənshĭr) or **Dunbartonshire** (dŭn″-), county (1971 pop. 237,518), 241 sq mi (624 sq km), W central Scotland. Dumbarton is the county town. Two burghs, Kirkintilloch and Cumbernauld, are detached from the rest of the county and lie to the east, between Lanarkshire and Stirlingshire. Bearsden and Clydebank are other important burghs. The terrain is mountainous in the northwest with lowland farm belts in the valleys of the Clyde and Leven rivers. Loch Lomond, the largest lake in Great Britain, forms part of the county's eastern border. Oats are the staple crop. There is some dairy farming, and sheep and cattle are raised. The banks of the Leven and the Clyde are industrialized, with shipyards, engineering works, and factories that manufacture office equipment, sewing machines, clothing, alarm clocks, and other products. Balloch, at the southern end of Loch Lomond, has been known since the 18th cent. for its bleaching, dyeing, and calico printing. Bowling is the western terminus of the Forth and Clyde Canal, built in 1790. The first working steamboat, William Symington's *Charlotte Dundas*, was launched there in 1802. Glen Fruin was the site of a clash in 1603 between the MacGregor and Colquhoun clans in which the latter was nearly wiped out. The county has remains of the Wall of ANTONINUS, built A.D. c.140. In the 5th cent. the area was incorporated into the kingdom of Strathclyde, with its center at Dumbarton. Dumbartonshire and parts of Stirlingshire, Renfrewshire, and Perthshire constituted the old Scottish earldom of Lennox that was formed in the 12th cent. In 1975, Dumbartonshire became part of the Strathclyde region.

dumb show, a theatrical pantomime included as part of a drama, especially in Elizabethan works, from the third quarter of the 16th cent. well into the 17th cent. Whether presented as a spectacle, with music, or as a masque with the players as allegorical characters, the dumb show appeared as prologue, between the acts, or during the play itself. It usually either presaged the events of the play or interpreted them as a chorus does.

Dumdum (dŭm'dəm), town (1971 pop. 31,232), West Bengal state, E central India, a suburb of Calcutta. In the 19th cent. its arsenal was the first to manufacture lead-nosed bullets that spread on impact, inflicting a tearing wound. In 1905, Great Britain acceded to the prohibition of dumdum bullets adopted by the first Hague Conference in 1899.

Dumfries (dəmfrēs'), burgh (1971 pop. 29,384), county town of Dumfriesshire, SE Scotland, on the Nith River. The chief manufactures are nitrocellulose, hosiery, knitwear, rubber goods, and canned milk. Dumfries was sacked by the English in 1448, 1536, and 1570. Robert I is said to have killed John COMYN before the altar of Greyfriars Church at Dumfries in 1306. The poet Robert Burns lived in Dumfries (1791-96) and is buried in St. Michael's Church. Craigenputtock, home of the writer Thomas Carlyle, is nearby. In 1975, Dumfries became part of the new Dumfries and Galloway region.

Dumfriesshire (dəmfrēs'shĭr) or **Dumfries,** county (1971 pop. 88,215), 1,074 sq mi (2,782 sq km), SE Scotland. DUMFRIES is the county town. The valleys of the Annan, Nith, and Esk rivers are cultivated (oats, turnips, barley, and potatoes). Cattle, sheep, pigs, and poultry are raised. Limestone and sandstone are quarried near the Solway Firth, and there is salmon fishing. Industries include coal mining, wool spinning, and the manufacture of hosiery, plastics, and rubber goods. Dumfriesshire has a nuclear generating plant. In 1975 Dumfriesshire became part of the new Dumfries and Galloway region.

Dummer, Jeremiah, 1645-1718, early American silversmith and engraver, b. Newbury, Mass. He was apprenticed (1659) to John Hull and set up as a silversmith in Boston c.1666. He held several public offices, was known as a merchant, and engraved plates for currency (in 1710 he printed the first paper money in Connecticut). He may have painted the portraits of himself and his wife and of John Coney, silversmith, and his wife; these bear his inscription. Dummer's silverwork mark is ID enclosed over a fleur-de-lis in a heart or occasionally ID in a rectangle. He is represented in the collections of colonial silver of the Museum of Fine Arts, Boston, and the Metropolitan Museum. See H. F. Clarke and H. W. Foote, *Jeremiah Dummer, Colonial Craftsman and Merchant* (1935).

Dummer, Jeremiah, c.1680-1739, colonial agent for Massachusetts and Connecticut, b. Boston; son of Jeremiah Dummer (1645-1718). He saw little opportunity for business in Boston and settled in England, where he became a prosperous lawyer. He became the agent in England of Massachusetts (1710) and of Connecticut (1712). Dummer helped persuade Elihu Yale, a wealthy English merchant, to donate books and valuable goods to the Collegiate School of Connecticut—which was renamed (1718) Yale College. Dummer himself collected nearly 1,000 books, which were sent to this institution. His most important service for the colonies was his well-reasoned *Defence of the New England Charters* (1721), written to answer the attacks in Parliament. Because Dummer recommended and supported the appointment of the unpopular Samuel Shute as governor of Massachusetts, he was dismissed as colonial agent in 1721 by the Massachusetts General Court and in 1730 by Connecticut.

Dumont, Pierre Étienne Louis (pyĕr ātyĕn' lwē dümôN'), 1759-1829, Swiss jurist and political writer. Dumont knew Mirabeau well and wrote many of his speeches. His *Souvenirs sur Mirabeau* (1832) is a valuable record of the times. An important work of Dumont was his French edition (1802) of Jeremy Bentham's *Introduction to the Principles of Morals and Legislation* (1789).

Dumont (do͞o'mŏnt), borough (1970 pop. 20,155), Bergen co., NE N.J.; settled 1677 by the Dutch, inc. 1894. It is a residential suburb of Hackensack.

Dumont d'Urville, Jules Sébastien César (zhül sābästyăN' säzär' dümôN' dürvēl'), 1790-1842, French navigator. While on duty (1819-20) in the E Mediterranean, he saw and recognized the importance of the newly discovered Venus of Milo and was influential in having the Louvre secure it. In 1822-25, while serving on the *Coqville*, he surveyed the Falklands, New Zealand. In 1826-29 he commanded the *Astrolabe* in a voyage around the world; searching for the ill-fated La Pérouse expedition, he explored the coasts of Australia and many islands of Oceania. With the *Astrolabe* and the *Zelée* he made a second circumnavigation in 1837-40, and in 1840 he penetrated the ice pack S of New Zealand and discovered ADÉLIE COAST in Antarctica.

Dumouriez, Charles François (shärl fräNswä' dümo͞o-rēā'), 1739-1823, French general in the FRENCH REVOLUTIONARY WARS. After fighting in the Seven Years War, he was employed by King Louis XV on several secret missions. His career was fading when the outbreak of the French Revolution opened new prospects for him. Although close to the JACOBINS in 1790, he offered his services to King Louis XVI and became (March, 1792) minister of foreign affairs in a ministry that included several GIRONDISTS and that sought war with Austria. Made minister of war (June, 1792), he resigned to take the marquis de Lafayette's place as an army commander when the latter was charged with treason (Aug., 1792). Dumouriez helped defeat the Prussians at Valmy (Sept., 1792), drove the Austrians from Belgium at Jemappes (Nov., 1792), and invaded the Netherlands (Feb., 1793). Defeated (March) at Neerwinden, he began negotiations with the Austrians, and after turning over to them the commissioners sent from Paris to investigate his defeat he finally (April, 1793) deserted to the Austrian lines. After wandering over Europe, disavowed even by the French royalists, he settled (1800) in England. See his memoirs (both English and French eds., 1794; enlarged French ed., 1823); Arthur Chuquet, *Dumouriez* (1914, in French).

dumping, selling goods at less than the normal price, usually as exports in international trade. It may be done by a producer, a group of producers, or a nation. Intranational dumping, only an occasional practice, is usually done to drive competitors off the market and secure a monopoly, or to hinder foreign competition. In international trade, acute competition from foreign producers often leads to charges of dumping. A policy of dumping depends for its effectiveness on monopolistic influences maintaining a high price in the home market, export bounties, or low import duties in the foreign market. Dumping disturbs those markets that receive dumped goods, and it may drive local producers out of business. Governments may condone, or even sponsor, dumping in other markets for either political reasons or to achieve a more favorable balance of payments. In the late 19th cent., dumping became part of the trade policy of great European cartels, especially German cartels. Britain, France, Japan, and the United States also have practiced dumping. Antidumping legislation was first passed (1904) by Canada. In the United States various tariff acts have been passed to deal with different types of dumping; in particular the 1921 Emergency Tariff Act imposed special duties on goods imported for sale at less than their fair value or cost of production. It was amended by the Customs Simplification Act of 1954. The General Agreement on Tariffs and Trade prohibits dumping and provides for increased import duties to combat the practice. See Contracting Parties to the General Agreement on Tariffs and Trade, *Anti-Dumping and Countervailing Duties* (1958) and *Anti-Dumping Legislation* (1970); study by Jacob Viner (1923, repr. 1966).

Dumyat (do͞omyät') or **Damietta** (dămēĕt'ə), city (1970 est. pop. 98,000), capital of Dumyat governorate, N Egypt, on Lake Manzala near the Mediterranean Sea. It is a manufacturing and trade center. Its products include glassware; cotton, silk, and rayon textiles; and processed rice and fish. Of commercial and strategic importance in the Middle Ages, Dumyat was pillaged by the Byzantines and by the Sicilian NORMANS. It was captured and held by Crusaders from 1219 to 1221 and again (under Louis IX of France) from 1249 to 1250. Dimity, a sheer cotton fabric, was first made there. The city is the seat of Dumyat Institute, a branch of Al Azhar Univ.

Düna: see DVINA (Western Dvina), river, USSR.

Dünaburg: see DAUGAVPILS, USSR.

Dunajec (do͞onä'yĕts), river, 156 mi (250 km) long, rising in the Carpathians, S Poland, and flowing NE past Nowy Sącz into the Vistula River. There are hydroelectric stations at Rożnów (the largest in Poland), Czchów, and Czorsztyn.

Dunant, Jean Henri (zhäN äNrē' dünäN'), 1828-1910, Swiss philanthropist and founder of the International Red Cross, b. Geneva. In 1862 appeared his *Un souvenir de Solférino* (tr. *The Origins of the Red Cross*, 1911), a description of the sufferings of the wounded at the battle of Solferino and a plea for organizations to care for the war wounded. There was an immediate response. Gustave Moynier and the Société genevoise d'Utilité publique took up the cause. An international conference in 1863 led to the conference of 1864 that adopted the Geneva Convention and established the Red Cross. Dunant aided other causes and wrote several books. He shared with Frédéric Passy the first Nobel Peace Prize (1901). See Josephine Rich, *Jean Henri Dunant, Founder of the International Red Cross* (1956); V. K. Libby, *Henry Dunant: Prophet of Peace* (1964); H. N. Pandit, *The Red Cross and Henry Dunant* (1969).

Dunash ben Labrat (do͞o'näsh bĕn lä'brät), 920-90, Hebrew grammarian and poet, b. Fez. He was also called Rabbi Adonim Halevy (ha-Levi). He wrote an exhaustive criticism of Menahem's Hebrew lexicon, adding to and correcting it, and was the first to adapt the Arabic meter to Hebrew poetry.

Dunash ben Tamim (tä'mēm) or **Dunash ibn Tamim,** c.900-c.960, Hebrew scholar, an astronomer and physician of North Africa. A pioneer in the field of scientific comparative philology, he tried to demonstrate that Arabic was merely a corrupt form of the purer Hebrew.

Dunbar, Paul Laurence, 1872-1906, American poet and novelist, b. Dayton, Ohio. The son of former slaves, he won recognition with his *Lyrics of Lowly Life* (1896)—a collection of poems from his *Oak and Ivy* (1893) and *Majors and Minors* (1895). His humorous poems employing Negro folk materials and dialect were especially popular. Other works include the novel *The Sport of the Gods* (1902) and the collection of short stories *Folks from Dixie* (1898), in which he portrayed the lives of Southern Negroes. See his *Complete Poems* (1913); biographies by Benjamin Brawley (1936, repr. 1967) and Addison Gayle (1971); study by Jay Martin, ed. (1974).

Dunbar, William, c.1460-c.1520, Scottish poet. After attending the Univ. of St. Andrews he was attached for some time to the Franciscans, probably as a novice. By 1491 he seems to have been connected with the court of James IV as a poet and minor diplomat. Writing in the traditions of Chaucer and the medieval Scottish poets, Dunbar is notable for the liveliness of his verse, his virtuosity in metrical form, his variety of mood, and his caustic satire. Most of his best poetry seems to have appeared between 1503 and 1508. "The Thistle and the Rose," celebrating the marriage of James IV and Margaret Tudor, and "The Golden Targe" are richly decorative allegories. "The Dance of the Seven Deadly Sins" combines mordant humor and the grotesque. "The Two Married Women and the Widow" is extravagantly ribald, while "The Flyting of Dunbar and Kennedie" shows his gift for satiric invective. Other poems, such as "Of the Nativity of Christ," express genuine religious feeling. One of his best-known poems is the gloomy "Lament for the Makers" with its refrain "Timor mortis conturbat me" [the fear of death throws me into confusion]. See edition of his poems by W. M. Mackenzie (1960); biography by J. W. Baxter (1952); studies by Tom Scott (1966) and Rachel Taylor (1931, repr. 1971).

Dunbar, William, 1749-1810, American scientist in the old Southwest, b. near Elgin, Morayshire, Scotland. He came to America in 1771. Commissioned by President Jefferson to investigate the Ouachita and Red River areas, he wrote the first scientific account of the mineral wells at Hot Springs, Ark. Dunbar set up his own private astronomical observatory with instruments imported from Europe; took the first meteorological observations in the Southwest; studied the rise and fall of the Mississippi and explored its delta; and published his findings on these subjects and on the plants, animals, and Indians of the region in the *Transactions* of the American Philosophical Society.

Dunbar, burgh (1971 pop. 4,586), East Lothian, SE Scotland, on the North Sea. It is a fishing center and seaside resort. Dunbar Castle was held by "Black Agnes," countess of Dunbar, against a six-week siege by the English in 1338. Mary Queen of Scots was abducted to the castle by the earl of Bothwell and stayed there the night before her defeat at Carberry Hill (1567). The 1st earl of Murray razed the castle in 1568. Oliver Cromwell defeated the Scots there in 1650. In 1975, Dunbar became part of the new Lothian region.

Duncan, Isadora, 1878-1927, American dancer, b. San Francisco. She had little success in the United States when she first created dances based on Greek classical art. But in Europe, at Budapest (1903) and at Berlin (1904), and later in London and New York City (1908), she had the triumphs that made her name. An innovator and pioneer in expressionism, she danced barefoot to music that was often not written to be danced. Her costume, an adaptation of the Greek tunic, was complemented by several colored scarves draped from her shoulders. Through her many tours, her schools in Berlin, Paris, Moscow, and London, and her daring and dynamic personality, she had a great influence on modern dance. She was married (1922-23) to the Russian poet Sergei Yesenin. In 1927 she gave her last concert in Paris; she died when her scarf caught in the wheel of her car while she was motoring at Nice. See her autobiography (1927, repr. 1966) and *The Art of The Dance,* ed. by S. Cheney (1928, repr. 1970); biographies by Irma Duncan (1958), W. Terry (1964), and V. Seroff (1971); I. Schneider, *Isadora Duncan: The Russian Years* (tr. 1968).

Duncan, Robert, 1919-, American poet, b. Oakland, Calif. He first attracted notice as a leading poet of the San Francisco renaissance during 1947-49. His lyric style contains private allusions, gaps in syntax, and individualistic spellings. Among his themes are the search for love and the decline of man's faith in the supernatural. His volumes of poetry include *Selected Poems* (1959), *Wine* (1964), *Bending the Bow* (1968), and *Derivations* (1970).

Duncan, Robert Kennedy, 1868-1914, American industrial chemist and educator b. Brantford, Ont., grad. Univ. of Toronto (B.A., 1892). He was professor at the Univ. of Kansas (1906-10) and at the Univ. of Pittsburgh (1910-14). In Kansas he introduced the system of fellowships for research in industrial chemistry that became the basic plan of the Mellon Institute (now part of Carnegie-Mellon Univ.) and greatly furthered the discovery of new products and new processes. He wrote several books for laymen.

Duncan, city (1970 pop. 19,718), seat of Stephens co., SW Okla., in an oil, farm, and cattle area; inc. 1892. Its economy is based chiefly upon the oil industry; there are oil refineries and meat-packing plants in the city. Oil-drilling equipment and clothing are manufactured there. The city is located on the old Chisholm Trail. During the late 19th cent. it was a stopping-off place for cattlemen driving their herds from Texas to the railhead in Abilene, Kansas.

Duncansbay Head or **Duncansby Head,** sandstone cliff, 210 ft (64 m) high, in Caithness, northeastern extremity of the Scottish mainland.

Duncanville, city (1970 pop. 14,105), Dallas co., N Texas, a suburb of Dallas; est. 1882, inc. 1947. It is mostly residential with some light manufacturing.

Dundalk (dəndôk'), urban district (1971 pop. 21,718), county town of Co. Louth, NE Republic of Ireland, near the mouth of the Castletown River at Dundalk Bay. It has a port that exports livestock, barley, and other crops and imports coal. There are tobacco, clothing, and shoe factories, distilleries, breweries, flour mills, linen mills, and fisheries. Dundalk is also a railroad center with facilities for the manufacture and maintenance of railroad equipment. Dundalk has been besieged frequently because of its location at a natural pass into N Ireland.

Dundalk (dŭn'dôlk"), city (1970 pop. 85,377), Baltimore co., NE Md., a suburb of Baltimore, on the Patapsco River; inc. 1946. It has one of the world's largest steel plants and a busy nine-berth marine terminal, operated by the Maryland Port Authority, with direct rail connections. There are also factories making radio and electronic parts, auto bodies, and yachts. The first house built there (1665) was burned by the British after their march on Washington (1814) during the War of 1812. U.S. Fort Holabird is nearby.

Dundas (dŭn'dəs), town (1971 pop. 17,208), S Ont., Canada. It is a suburb of Hamilton and is at the head of the Desjardins Canal, which formerly gave it water connection with Hamilton and other ports. The canal is no longer in use.

Dundee, John Graham of Claverhouse, 1st **Viscount** (klăv'ərəs), 1649?-1689, Scottish soldier, known as Bonnie Dundee. After service abroad under William of Orange (later William III of England), he returned (1678) to Scotland to help in the suppression of the COVENANTERS, a task to which he devoted himself for 10 years. He was second in command of the Scottish force vainly sent to help James II repel William of Orange in 1688, and James made him Viscount Dundee. After James's flight, Dundee raised forces in Scotland to help restore him, but was killed in his hour of victory at KILLIECRANKIE. Loathed by the Covenanters and venerated by the JACOBITES, Dundee has been immortalized in ballads and novels, especially in Sir Walter Scott's song usually called *Bonnie Dundee* and in Scott's *Old Mortality.* See his memorials and letters (ed. by Mark Napier, 1859-62); biographies by C. S. Terry (1905) and A. N. and H. A. N. Taylor (1939).

Dundee, city (1971 pop. 182,084), Angus, E central Scotland, on the Firth of Tay. It is a port and manufacturing city. Jute, cement, sugar, paper, oil, and timber are imported; jute products, linoleum, potatoes, and cattle are exported. Jute processing (using jute imported from Asia) is the largest industry; others include engineering, shipbuilding and repairing, textiles (especially linen), food processing (the marmalade is famous), and the manufacture of brick, plastics, metal products, linoleum, and electrical products. Called the "Scottish Geneva," Dundee was a center of the Reformation and a stronghold of the COVENANTERS in the religious wars. Queen's College, part of the Univ. of St. Andrews, as well as the Tower of St. Mary's Church, a 15th-century steeple, are notable landmarks. There is also a college of art and a technical college. Under the Local Government Act of 1973, Dundee became (1975) part of the Tayside region.

Dundonald, Thomas Cochrane, 10th **earl of,** 1775-1860, British naval commander. He served in the Napoleonic Wars, executing his assignments with a boldness and originality sometimes too radical for the admiralty. Given charge of a British naval force in the Bay of Biscay, he brilliantly succeeded in crippling a French fleet (1809); but he criticized the handling of the fleet by his commander in chief, Lord Gambier, and was discredited when a court-martial acquitted Gambier. In 1814 he was accused, perhaps falsely, of implication in a stock market fraud. Dismissed from the navy, he went to South America, where, as admiral of the Chilean navy, he was prominent in the liberation of Chile and Peru. He aided the newly independent nation of Brazil from 1823 to 1825, and in 1827 he commanded the Greek navy in the war of liberation against Turkey. The next year he returned to England. He received a pardon and was reinstated (1832) in the navy, eventually becoming admiral. See biography by Warren Tute (1965); study by Henry Cecil (1965).

dune, mound or ridge of wind-blown sand formed in arid regions and along coasts. Dunes are common in most of the great deserts of the world. Often a dune begins to form because material is deposited by the wind as it encounters a bush, a rock, or other obstacle to impede its flow. Dunes that are not stabilized by vegetation have a tendency to migrate, driven by the prevailing wind. These free-moving dunes are of two main kinds, transverse and longitudinal, and the characteristic form is maintained in migration. Transverse dunes usually form where wind blows quite constantly from one direction across expanses of loose sand; the windward slope is typically gentle, and the lee side, where the sand blown over the crest seeks its natural angle of repose, is steep. Such dune ridges have a tendency, especially with increasing distance from the source of sand, to break up into individual small hills. One of the commonest forms of these hills is the symmetrical, crescent-shaped, transverse dune called a barkhan; examples can be found at Pismo Beach, Calif., and near Arequipa, Peru. Longitudinal dunes are ridges, with about the same slope on both sides, elongated in the direction of the prevailing wind. They are especially well developed in the African deserts and are also seen in Arizona and in the Imperial Valley, Calif. Coastal blowout dunes, which are approximately U-shaped with their open ends upwind, form along shores where vegetation cover is locally broken. Examples are the dunes along the southern and eastern shores of Lake Michigan. Dunes reaching a height of more than 500 ft (152 m) exist in the Great Sand Dunes National Monument, Colo.; gleaming white dunes of gypsum sand are formed in White Sands National Monument, N.Mex. Sand dunes may cause destruction as they migrate; in France on the coast of the Bay of Biscay they destroyed villages and farmland. In some areas of Europe and the United States this danger has been checked by planting vegetation and by erecting barriers. One value of dunes is their absorption of rain, which helps to raise the level of the water table and thus produces oases in some areas and provides accessible sources of water through rather shallow wells.

Dunedin (dənē'dĭn), city (1971 pop. 82,235), SE South Island, New Zealand, at the head of Otago Harbor. Dunedin is an important port and industrial center. The chief exports are wool, meat, and dairy products. The Univ. of Otago (the first in New Zealand), Knox College, and Anglican and Roman Catholic theological schools and cathedrals are in the city. It was founded in 1848 as a Free Church of Scotland settlement. (*Dunedin* is the Gaelic equivalent of *Edinburgh*).

Dunedin, Scotland: see EDINBURGH.

Dunedin, resort city (1970 pop. 17,639), Pinellas co., W Fla., on the Gulf Coast and St. Joseph Sound (part of the Intracoastal Waterway); founded by Scots in 1870, inc. 1898. It is a processing center for citrus fruit. The city is connected to Dunedin Beach, an island, by a causeway.

Dunes, Battle of the, 1658, decisive engagement fought near Dunkirk in the struggle between France and Spain that had resulted from Spanish intervention in the FRONDE. The Spanish under the command of Don John of Austria and Louis II de Condé lost to the French and their English allies under the command of Turenne.

Dunfermline (dŭnförm'lĭn, dŭm-), burgh (1971 pop. 49,882), Fife, E central Scotland, on the Firth of Forth. It is a center for the manufacture of table linen and terylene, a synthetic fabric, and has silk mills, collieries, and engineering works. The naval base of Rosyth became part of the burgh in 1911. Dunfermline abbey, founded by Malcolm III of Scotland in the 11th cent., holds his remains and those of his wife, St. Margaret, and of Robert I. The palace was a favorite seat of Scottish kings and was the birthplace of Charles I of England. Andrew Carnegie, the industrialist, was born in Dunfermline, which is now the headquarters of the Carnegie Trusts. Carnegie gave the town its library and Pittencrieff Glen, a 60-acre (24-hectare) public park.

dung beetle: see SCARAB BEETLE.

Duniway, Abigail Scott, 1834-1915, American editor and advocate of woman's rights, b. near Groveland, Ill. She went to Oregon with her family in 1852 and the next year married Benjamin Charles Duniway. For many years she edited the *New Northwest* in Portland and through her writings and lectures became recognized as the leader of the woman's movement in the Northwest. For her account of her part in the movement, see *Path Breaking* (1914).

Dunkards: see BRETHREN.

Dunkeld (dŭn″kĕld′), village, Perthshire, central Scotland. It was a center of Celtic Christianity and the seat of the early Scottish kings.

Dunkers: see BRETHREN.

Dunkirk (dŭn′kûrk), Fr. *Dunkerque,* town (1968 pop. 28,082), Nord dept., N France, on the North Sea. It is a leading French port and one of Western Europe's major iron and steel centers. Other important industries are oil production and refining, shipbuilding, food processing, brewing, and the manufacture of textiles and electrical equipment. Among Dunkirk's chief exports are refined petroleum, steel, coal, machinery, cement and other construction materials, and agricultural products. Probably founded c.7th cent. A.D. and often fortified, Dunkirk played a key role in the struggles in Europe that extended over centuries; it was ruled successively by Flanders, Burgundy, Austria, France, Great Britain, and Spain. Ceded briefly in the 1650s to Oliver Cromwell, it was bought back permanently from Charles II by Louis XIV in 1662. The town withstood an Anglo-Dutch bombardment in 1694 and an English siege in 1793. During the 19th cent. improvements were made on the harbor, and Dunkirk grew in commercial importance. During World War II, more than 300,000 Allied troops who were cut off from retreat on land by the German breakthrough to the French Channel ports were evacuated (May 26–June 4, 1940) from Dunkirk. The retreat was carried out by all kinds of available British craft, some manned by civilian volunteers, and was protected by the Royal Air Force. It is considered one of the epic actions of naval history. See Robert Carse, *Dunkirk, 1940: A History* (1970).

Dunkirk, city (1970 pop. 16,855), Chautauqua co., SW N.Y., on Lake Erie; founded c.1800, inc. as a city 1880. It is a port of entry and trades extensively with other Great Lakes ports. Dunkirk, located in the grape belt, produces wines and other grape products. The city also manufactures steel, food products, pet foods, and clothing. In 1946, Dunkirk developed a program to help DUNKIRK, France (for which it was named), recover from World War II. Other U.S. cities later followed Dunkirk's example and established a program, called the One World Plan, to aid war-damaged European cities.

Dún Laoghaire (dōōn lăr′ē, dŭn lâr′ə), borough (1971 pop. 52,990), Co. Dublin, E central Republic of Ireland, on the Irish Sea. It is the main passenger and mail port for Dublin and a seaside resort with yachting and fishing. With the opening of a railroad to Dublin in 1834 and the completion of the port in 1859, Dún Laoghaire grew rapidly. It was known as Kingstown before 1921 and as Dunleary before 1821.

Dunlap, William, 1766–1839, American dramatist and theatrical manager, b. Perth Amboy, N.J. He was first a portrait painter, but inspired by the success of *The Contrast* by Royall Tyler, he began to write plays for the American Company (see HALLAM, LEWIS). His second comedy, *The Father; or, American Shandyism,* produced in 1789, was his first success. *The Fatal Deception; or, The Progress of Guilt* (1794; pub. 1806 as *Leicester*) and *Fontainville Abbey* (1795) are excellent examples of the Gothic romance school. His *André* (1798), a tragedy based on an actual occurrence in the Revolution, was the first native play on American material. He was a partner in the American Company (1796–97) and he later was manager of the Park Theatre, New York City (1798–1805). To meet the demand for new drama, he translated and adapted numerous French and German plays. Dunlap was a founder and secretary of the National Academy of Design. His *History of the American Theatre* (1832) and *History of the Rise and Progress of the Arts of Design in the United States* (1834) are invaluable source books and contain important autobiographical material. Dunlap's diary was edited by D. C. Barck in 1930. See biographies by O. S. Coad (1917, repr. 1962) and R. H. Canary (1970).

Dunleary, Republic of Ireland: see DÚN LAOGHAIRE.

Dunmore, John Murray, 4th **earl of,** 1732–1809, British colonial governor of Virginia, a Scottish peer. Appointed governor of New York in 1770, he remained there for about 11 months before being transferred to Virginia. In 1774 he led the Virginians in an Indian campaign usually known as Lord Dunmore's War. Sending one expedition under Andrew LEWIS west by the Kanawha valley, he personally headed the northern column, which set out from Fort Dunmore at Pittsburgh. Lewis defeated the Indians at Point Pleasant, and Dunmore negotiated a final treaty with them in the Scioto valley. When the news of Lexington and Concord reached Virginia, Dunmore, who twice before had dissolved the house of burgesses for its procolonist stand, removed the colony's gunpowder stores to a man-of-war. The aroused Virginians made him pay for the powder. Threats against his life forced him to take refuge (June, 1775) on shipboard where he declared martial law and sent out loyal troops, who were defeated at Great Bridge on Dec. 9, 1775. In Jan., 1776, he attacked Norfolk from the sea, but in July he was forced to return to England. From 1787 to 1796 he was governor of the Bahamas. See R. G. Thwaites and L. P. Kellogg, ed., *Documentary History of Dunmore's War, 1774* (1905).

Dunmore, borough (1970 pop. 17,300), Lackawanna co., NE Pa., an industrial suburb of Scranton; inc. 1783. It is the center of the anthracite coal-mining region.

Dunmore's War: see DUNMORE, JOHN MURRAY, 4TH EARL OF.

Dunnet Head, sandstone promontory, 341 ft (104 m) high, in Caithness, the northern extremity of the Scottish mainland.

Dunning, John, 1st **Baron Ashburton,** 1731–83, English jurist and politician. He attracted notice in 1762 by his written defense of the British East India Company merchants against their Dutch rivals. He was solicitor general from 1768 to 1770. In Parliament from 1768, he consistently supported the right of free election and petition in the case of John WILKES and in 1780 carried the famous resolution that "the influence of the crown has increased, is increasing, and ought to be diminished." He was created a peer in 1782.

Dunning, William Archibald, 1857–1922, American historian, b. Plainfield, N.J., grad. Columbia (B.A., 1881; Ph. D., 1885). After studying in Berlin, he returned (1886) to spend a lifetime at Columbia, becoming the first Lieber professor of history and political philosophy in 1904. His reputation is twofold: first, his scholarly studies of Reconstruction led the way to a new interpretation of that era in American history; second, his *History of Political Theories* (3 vol., 1902–20) was a brilliant survey of a hitherto unanalyzed field. Dunning not only wrote two superb studies of Reconstruction—*Essays on the Civil War and Reconstruction* (1898, rev. ed. 1904) and *Reconstruction, Political and Economic, 1865–1877* (1907, repr. 1968)—but also inspired and directed the long series of books by his students on Reconstruction in the individual states. He also wrote *The British Empire and the United States* (1914), an excellent survey of Anglo-American relations. One of the founders of the American Historical Association, he was its president in 1913. J. G. de Roulhac Hamilton edited his *Truth in History and Other Essays* (1937).

Dunois, Jean, comte de (zhäN kôNt də dünwä′), c.1403–1468, French general, called the Bastard of Orléans; natural son of Louis, duc d'Orléans. He joined the Armagnacs in the civil war during the reign of King Charles VI and was captured (1418) by the Burgundians (see ARMAGNACS AND BURGUNDIANS). Released in 1420, he entered the service of the dauphin (later King CHARLES VII of France) during the HUNDRED YEARS WAR. Dunois had charge of the defense of Orléans when it was relieved (1429) by Joan of Arc, joined her subsequent campaign, and took part in the coronation of Charles VII. In 1436 he aided in the capture of Paris. He received (1439) the county of Dunois from his half brother Charles, duc d'Orléans. Charles VII later made him count of Longueville. Dunois was prominent in the conquest of Guienne and Normandy in the final years of the Hundred Years War. He participated in the PRAGUERIE against Charles VII and was (1465) a leader of the League of the Public Weal against King LOUIS XI, but each time he regained favor at court.

Dunoyer de Segonzac, André: see SEGONZAC.

Dunsany, Edward John Moreton Drax Plunkett, 18th **Baron** (dənsăn′ē, -sā-), 1878–1957, English author. His life was spent as a soldier and sportsman. Lord Dunsany's plays, often dealing with the fantastic and supernatural, include *The Gods of the Mountain* (1911), *The Golden Doom* (1912), and the one-act play *A Night at an Inn* (1916). His prose works include *A Dreamer's Tales* (1910), *The Book of Wonder* (1912), *My Talks with Dean Spanley* (1936), *The Story of Mona Sheehy* (1937), and *A Glimpse from a Watch Tower* (1946). See biography by Mark Amory (1972).

Dunsinane (dŭn″sĭnān′), westernmost of the Sidlaw Hills, 1,012 ft (308 m) high, Perthshire, central Scotland. On its summit are ruins of a fort, called Macbeth's Castle; it is the traditional scene of Macbeth's final defeat as related by Shakespeare.

Duns Scotus, John (dŭnz skō′təs) [Lat. *Scotus*= Irishman or Scot], c.1266–1308, scholastic philosopher and theologian, called the Subtle Doctor. A native of Scotland, he became a Franciscan and taught at Oxford, Paris, and Cologne. The exact canon of Duns Scotus' work is unknown; the best known of his undoubtedly authentic works are *On the First Principle* and two commentaries on the *Sentences* of Peter Lombard. He put Aristotelian thought to the service of Christian theology and was the founder of a school of SCHOLASTICISM called Scotism, which was often opposed to the Thomism of the followers of St. Thomas Aquinas. In metaphysics, Duns taught the "univocity of being": By this he meant that being must be regarded as the ultimate abstraction that can be applied to everything that exists. He is also known for the use of the "formal distinction," a subtle manner of distinguishing between different aspects of the same thing. The Scotists deny that matter is the principle of individuality and insist that individuation of things is caused by a determination called "haecceitas" or "thisness." According to Scotus, the essence of things as well as their existence depends not on the Divine Intellect but on the Divine Will; his philosophy accordingly is voluntaristic in its entire spirit. It is possible to prove the existence of God, but the ontological proof of St. ANSELM is modified: The idea of God's possible existence involves his necessary existence, but knowledge of that possible existence must be demonstrated from sensible things, i.e., from experience. Scotus taught that the state arose from common consent of the people in a kind of social contract. He also denied that property was ordained by natural law. Scotism has had considerable influence on Roman Catholic thought and has been to some degree sponsored by the Franciscans. See study by C. R. Harris (2 vol., 1959).

Dunstable, John (dŭn′stəbəl), c.1385–1453, English composer. Dunstable is thought to have accompanied his patron, the duke of Bedford, to France. About 60 of his works—nearly all sacred pieces—are extant. He was among the first composers to begin to unify the musical setting of the Mass. Dunstable was the outstanding English composer of his time and influenced composers of the Burgundian school, including Guillaume Dufay and Gilles Binchois. His name is sometimes spelled Dunstaple.

Dunstable (dŭn′stəbəl), municipal borough (1971 pop. 31,790), Bedfordshire, SE England. Located at the meeting point of the ancient Icknield Way and Watling Street, Dunstable is a developing residential and industrial district, with printing plants and extensive automobile works. There are interesting traces of Stone and Bronze Age civilizations, including the Maiden Bower and Five Knolls earthworks; one of the Knolls, excavated in 1926, contained remains and ornaments of a woman of c.2000 B.C. The Priory Church includes part of an Augustinian priory founded with the town in 1131. Whipsnade Zoo is nearby. Dunstable has a College of Further Education.

Dunstan, Saint (dŭns′tən), c.910–88, English monk, archbishop of Canterbury (960–88), b. near Glastonbury. He lived as a monk until called (940) to court by King EDMUND of Wessex. He became (943) abbot of Glastonbury and initiated reforms that proved to be a turning point in English religious life. He was a royal counselor under King EDRED, and the favorable peace with the Danes is credited to him. Unpopular with Edwy, he went to Flanders (956–58), where he witnessed the Benedictine reform then in full sway on the Continent. He was recalled by EDGAR and was appointed bishop of Worcester (958), bishop of London (959), and archbishop of Canterbury. He was not in favor with Æthelred. Dunstan is regarded as one of the greatest Anglo-Saxon saints and has been called one of the makers of England. Feast: May 19. See study by E. S. Duckett (1955).

Dunster, Henry, c.1612–1659, first president of Harvard, b. Lancashire, England, educated at Magdalene College, Cambridge (M.A., 1634). He emigrated to New England in 1640 and was almost at once (Aug. 27, 1640) appointed president of the new college. He formulated its rules and patterned its procedure after the English schools, worked actively for its support, and gave freely of his meager salary for its success. Because of his adoption of Baptist principles he was forced to resign in 1654, and he spent the remainder of his life as a pastor in Scituate, Mass.

duodecimal system: see NUMERATION.

duodenum: see INTESTINE; PANCREAS.

Duong Van Minh: see MINH, DUONG VAN.

Duparc, Henri (äNrē′ düpärk′), 1848–1933, French composer. Duparc studied piano with César Franck and became one of his first composition pupils. A nervous disorder caused him to cease composing in 1885. He spent the rest of his life in Switzerland. Extremely self-critical, Duparc destroyed many of his works, so that only a handful remain. His fame rests entirely on the 14 beautiful songs he wrote between 1868 and 1884. See Sydney Northcote, *The Songs of Henri Duparc* (1949).

Dupleix, Joseph François (zhôzĕf' fräNswä' düplĕks'), 1696–1763, French colonial administrator in India. He went to India in 1721 as an officer of the French East India Company. In 1731 he was appointed governor of Chandernagor, where he made a considerable fortune, and in 1742 he became governor of Pondichéry and was thus the chief official in French India. When the War of the Austrian Succession brought the French and British East India companies into conflict, Dupleix supervised the capture of Madras (1746) and successfully defended Pondichéry, but the Treaty of Aix-la-Chapelle (1748) restored the prewar situation. Dupleix then formed a vast project for establishing French supremacy in India. Intervening in native politics, intrigues, and warfare, he controlled the Carnatic and nearly the entire Deccan by 1751. Soon, however, the British began to regain ground under the leadership of Robert CLIVE, and the French government, anxious to avoid war and uninformed of Dupleix's grandiose schemes, recalled the governor in 1754. With Dupleix, the last hope of a French empire in India vanished. He ended his days in poverty and neglect. See G. B. Malleson, *Dupleix* (1890); Henry Dodwell, *Dupleix and Clive* (1920, repr. 1962); Virginia Thompson, *Dupleix and His Letters* (1933).

Duplessis, Maurice Le Noblet (mōrēs' lə nôblā' düplĕsē'), 1890–1959, Canadian lawyer and political leader. Elected in 1927 to the Quebec legislature, he was leader (1933–35) of the provincial Conservative party. A founder of the Union Nationale, a French Canadian nationalist party, Duplessis became premier and attorney general of the province of Quebec in 1936, when the party was victorious in the elections. He was defeated in 1939 on the issue of Canadian conscription for World War II but was reelected in 1944. He remained in office, as both premier and attorney general of Quebec, until his death.

Du Plessis-Mornay: see MORNAY, PHILIPPE DE.

duplication of the cube: see GEOMETRIC PROBLEMS OF ANTIQUITY.

Du Pont (do͞opŏnt), family notable in U.S. industrial history. The Du Pont family's importance began when Eleuthère Irénée Du Pont (see separate article) established a gunpowder mill on the Brandywine River in Delaware. Development, expansion, and family control of E. I. du Pont de Nemours & Company have been the family's chief concerns, and its prolific members have kept the chemical company well staffed. Outstanding among the Du Ponts was Henry du Pont (1812–89), a West Point graduate and son of the company's founder, who set the basis for the family's cohesiveness; he headed the firm from 1850 to 1889. His son, Lammot I (1831–84), a chemist and inventor, developed a cheap and superior blasting powder and made the Du Pont company a leader in the manufacture of explosives. Later, Pierre Samuel DU PONT (1870–1954) and his cousin Coleman brought about the company's public incorporation, a departure from the long-established family partnership. The Du Ponts have also been active in politics. Coleman increased Delaware's roads, and Pierre contributed heavily to the state's educational system. The Du Pont company today produces synthetic fibers (it pioneered the development of nylon), cellophane, synthetic rubber, chemicals, paint, and other products. One of the largest corporations in the world, it has been the subject of various antitrust investigations; in 1961 the U.S. Supreme Court ordered that the company divest itself of its 23% holding in General Motors. Members of the family continue to hold almost 40% of the stock in the Du Pont company. See W. H. Carr, *The du Ponts of Delaware* (1964).

Du Pont, Eleuthère Irénée (do͞o pŏnt, Fr. älötĕr' ĕrānā' dü pôN), 1772–1834, American gunpowder manufacturer, b. Paris, France; son of Pierre Samuel du Pont de Nemours. At the age of 17, Irénée entered the royal gunpowder works, where Lavoisier taught him the trade. After Lavoisier was forced to leave the plant, Irénée began managing (1791) his father's printing house, where the Du Ponts published counterrevolutionary pamphlets. When the Jacobins suppressed the printing house, Irénée and his family left for the United States to set up a trading and land company. Although he met disillusionment upon reaching (1800) the United States, Irénée soon formulated plans to improve the quality of American gunpowder. In July, 1802, he began constructing his powder works on Brandywine Creek, near Wilmington, Del. Despite lack of capital, Irénée continuously improved his gunpowder and plant and, within a few years, developed an extensive business (now E. I. du Pont de Nemours & Company). His sales were augmented during the War of 1812 and the years following, but his immense debts and family obligations constantly plagued him. He was appointed (1822) a director of the Bank of the United States, and his judgment on developing industries and encouraging agriculture was often sought.

Du Pont, Pierre Samuel, 1870–1954, American industrialist, b. Wilmington, Del., grad. Massachusetts Institute of Technology, 1890. Du Pont worked as a chemist with the family's company, helping to develop smokeless powder. In 1902, Pierre and his two cousins, Alfred and Coleman du Pont, bought E. I. du Pont de Nemours & Company. Pierre became treasurer and later vice president. In 1915, after a group headed by Pierre and including outsiders bought Coleman's stock, Alfred brought suit against Pierre for breach of trust. After four years in court, the case was settled in Pierre's favor, but Alfred and Pierre remained estranged for many years. Under Pierre's presidency (1915–20) the Du Pont company developed scores of chemical manufactures and acquired substantial interests in many other industries, including a large block of General Motors stock. He became president of General Motors in 1920 to protect family interests, but returned to Du Pont as chairman of the board in 1923. He supported Al Smith, and although at first an adherent of Franklin Roosevelt, he later opposed him. See J. K. Winkler, *The Du Pont Dynasty* (1935); Marquis James, *Alfred I. Du Pont, the Family Rebel* (1941); biography by A. D. Chandler and S. Salsbury (1970).

Du Pont, Samuel Francis, 1803–65, American naval officer, b. Bergen Point, N.J.; grandson of Pierre Samuel du Pont de Nemours. Appointed a midshipman in 1815, he saw his first active duty in the Mediterranean (1817) and served in the Mexican War. As commander of the South Atlantic Blockading Squadron in the Civil War, Du Pont directed (Nov., 1861) the successful naval attack against Port Royal, S.C., for which he won a rear admiral's commission. He secured further footholds for the Union on the coasts of South Carolina, Georgia, and Florida. The blockade Du Pont organized was generally successful, except at Charleston. Against Du Pont's advice the Dept. of the Navy ordered him to attack Charleston with ironclad monitors. When the attack failed (April 7, 1863), Secretary of the Navy Gideon Welles blamed Du Pont and, at Du Pont's request, relieved him of his command (July, 1863). A congressional investigation followed, but its findings were inconclusive. See his *Civil War Letters,* ed. by J. D. Hayes (3 vol., 1969); biography by his nephew H. A. du Pont (1926).

Du Pont de Nemours, Pierre Samuel (pyĕr sämüĕl' dü pôN də nəmo͞or'), 1739–1817, French economist, one of the PHYSIOCRATS. Early in his career he attracted the attention of François Quesnay and edited the *Journal de l'agriculture* in 1765–66 and the *Éphémérides du citoyen* from 1768 to 1772. He also edited some of Quesnay's writings under the title *Physiocratie* (1768) and later presented his own views of economy and political philosophy in his *Tableau raisonné des principes de l'économie politique* (1775) and other works. He was also active in practical politics. He became the financial and economic adviser of his friend Anne Robert Jacques Turgot. Under the comte de Vergennes he was one of the diplomats in the long negotiations (1783) after the American Revolution, and he drew up a trade treaty (1786) with Great Britain that expressed his economic principles. In the French Revolution he was an important figure in the Constituent Assembly, especially in financial debates. He opposed the issue of the ASSIGNATS, and as the Revolution moved further to the left he fell under the suspicion of his fellow revolutionists and for a time lived in hiding and issued pamphlets against the "radicals." He emerged into notice in the Directory, but disappointed with the course of events, he immigrated (1799) to the United States, where his son E. I. du Pont set up a powder mill. The elder Du Pont returned to Napoleonic France in 1802, at which time Thomas Jefferson enlisted his aid in negotiations for the Louisiana Purchase. In 1815 he returned to the United States where he died. He corresponded with Jefferson, and his economic theories had some influence on U.S. policy. See biography by Ambrose Sarick (1965).

Düppel: see DYBBØL, Denmark.

Duprat, Antoine (äNtwän' düprä'), 1463–1535, chancellor of France and cardinal. First president of the Paris Parlement (1508), he was a trusted adviser of Louise of Savoy, who appointed him tutor to her son, the future King FRANCIS I. Upon assuming the throne in 1515, Francis I made Duprat chancellor. Duprat negotiated the Concordat with Leo X (1516), which increased the royal authority over the Roman Catholic Church. Using his office to augment the growth of absolute monarchy, he sought to decrease the power of the parlements and reformed the financial system. In 1525 he governed France during the king's brief captivity following the battle of Pavia. His wife having died (1508), Duprat took Holy Orders in 1516 and was made a cardinal in 1527 and papal legate in 1530.

Dupré, Jules (zhül düprā'), 1811?–1889, French landscape painter of the Barbizon school. He excelled in portraying dramatic and tragic aspects of nature. A frequent and honored exhibitor at the Salon, Dupré spent his last years at L'Isle-Adam, where some of his best work was done. His *On the Road* is in the Art Institute of Chicago, and he is represented in many other American galleries.

Dupuytren, Guillaume, Baron (gēyōm' bärôN' düpüētrăN'), 1777–1835, French surgeon. As professor at the Hôtel Dieu, Paris, from 1812, he was noted as diagnostician, lecturer, and surgeon. He wrote on surgery, described a fracture of the fibula and a contraction of the hand that bear his name, and founded the chair of pathological anatomy at the Univ. of Paris. He was made a baron in 1823.

Duque de Caxias (do͞o'kĭ dĭ käsh'yəs), city (1970 pop. 431,345), Rio de Janeiro state, SE Brazil, on Guanabara Bay. It is a commercial and industrial suburb of the city of Rio de Janeiro.

Duquesne, Abraham (äbrä-äm' dükĕn'), 1610–88, French naval officer. In the FRONDE outbreaks, he suppressed a revolt at Bordeaux (1650). As commander of the new French fleet, he distinguished himself in the third of the Dutch Wars, engaging Admiral De Ruyter in the Lipari Islands, and sharing in the victory of Palermo (1676). He fought the Barbary pirates (1681) and bombarded Algiers (1682–83) and Genoa (1684). Although a Protestant, he was created marquis (1681) and was exempted from proscription when the Edict of Nantes was revoked (1685).

Duquesne (dəkān', do͞o-, dyo͞o-), city (1970 pop. 11,410), Allegheny co., SW Pa., on the Monongahela River, opposite McKeesport, in a coal region; settled 1789, laid out 1885 by the Duquesne Steel Company, inc. as a city 1917. Iron and steel are produced in the city.

Duquesne, Fort: see FORT DUQUESNE.

Duquesne University (do͞okān'), at Pittsburgh, Pa; coeducational; Roman Catholic; founded 1878; incorporated 1882 as the Pittsburgh Catholic College of the Holy Ghost. In 1911 the school obtained a university charter and adopted its present name.

Duquesnoy, François (fräNswä' dükĕnwä'), 1594–1643, Flemish sculptor. In 1618 he went to Rome, where he remained most of his life, eventually becoming one of the most sought after sculptors of his day. His small reliefs and statuettes in bronze, ivory, and wax were often inspired by classical art, especially his spirited scenes of children. Among his monumental works are the self-contained figure of *St. Susanna* in Santa Maria di Loreto and the more baroque *St. Andrew* under the dome of St. Peter's.

Dura (do͞or'ə) or **Europus** (yo͞orō'pəs), ancient city of Syria, on the Euphrates River and E of Palmyra, sometimes called Dura-Europus or Dura-Europos. Founded (c.300 B.C.) by a general of Seleucus I, it prospered. In the 2d cent. A.D. the Parthians took Dura, and in A.D. 165 it was taken by Rome and remained a Roman city until it was seized (A.D. c.257) by Shapur I of Persia. Dura was then abandoned to the desert. Modern excavations have yielded rich finds, supplying much information on life, history, and art in Mesopotamia from Hellenistic through Roman times. The name is also spelled Doura. The modern village of Salihiye is on the site. See M. I. Rostovtzeff et al., *Excavations at Dura-Europos* (reports, 1929–59); M. I. Rostovtzeff, *Dura-Europos and Its Art* (1938).

Dura, plain, near Babylon, where Nebuchadnezzar set up a golden image. Dan. 3.1.

duralumin (do͞orăl'yəmĭn, dyo͞o-), alloy of aluminum (over 90%) with copper (about 4%), magnesium (0.5%–1%), and manganese (less than 1%). Before a final heat treatment the alloy is ductile and malleable; after heat treatment a reaction between the aluminum and magnesium produces increased hardness and tensile strength. Because of its lightness and other desirable physical properties, duralumin is widely used in the aircraft industry.

Duran, Carolus: see CAROLUS-DURAN.

Duran, Durand (both: düräN'), or **Durante** (düräNt'), Jewish family of scholars. **Profiat Isaac ben Moshe ha-Levi Duran**, 1350–1414, called Efodi, was born probably in Perpignan, France, but he moved to Catalonia. In 1391, when widespread massacres of Spanish Jews resulted in mass conversions, Duran was one of the many who professed Christianity but in reality remained true to his faith. He ultimately returned openly to Judaism. He wrote a Hebrew grammar and a satiric epistle against Christianity, which was at first accepted by Christian authorities but later burned when its real intent was recognized. **Simon ben Zemah Duran**, 1361–1444, called Rashbatz, was a poet, physician, and Talmudic authority. He fled Spain after the persecutions of 1391 and became rabbi of Algiers. He was the first rabbi to receive a salary. His writings were notably in the field of Hebrew scholastic philosophy.

Durance (düräNs'), river, c.180 mi (290 km) long, rising in SE France at the foot of Montgenèvre Pass on the Italian border and flowing southwest then northwest before entering the Rhône River at Avignon. The upper Durance is used to generate hydroelectricity; the lower river is used for irrigation and for municipal water supply.

Durand, family: see DURAN.

Durand, Asher Brown (dyŏŏrănd'), 1796–1886, American painter and engraver, b. near Newark, N.J. He established a reputation by his engravings of Trumbull's *Signing of the Declaration of Independence,* followed by a series of engraved portraits of eminent contemporaries. After 1835, Durand devoted himself to painting, producing portraits of several of the Presidents. After a year of travel and study in Europe, he turned to landscape painting, becoming a leader of the HUDSON RIVER SCHOOL. At first he was painstaking and meticulous, but later his rendering became more spontaneous. Examples of his work are *In the Woods* and *The Beeches* (Metropolitan Mus.); *Woodland Brook* and *Franconia Notch* (N.Y. Public Library); and *Mountain Forest* (Corcoran Gall.). Durand was a founder of the National Academy of Design, New York City, and its president from 1845 to 1861. Two of his allegorical paintings are there, *Morning of Life* and *Evening of Life.* See biography by his son, John Durand (1894, repr. 1970).

Durand, Charles Auguste Émile: see CAROLUS-DURAN.

Durandus, Gulielmus (gulēēl'məs dyŏŏrăn'dəs), 1237?–1296, French canon jurist. Educated at the Univ. of Bologna, he served several 13th-century popes in various capacities including those of governor of the papal territories of Romagna and the March of Ancona. In 1286 he became Bishop of Mende. Durandus' *Speculum judiciale* [mirror of law] (1271, rev. in 1286 and 1291) is an outline of canon, criminal, and civil law that was long studied. His *Rationale divinorum officiorum* [rationale of the divine office] (c.1286) is an exhaustive treatment, many times reprinted, of the nature and symbolism of the Roman Catholic liturgy. Parts have been translated as *The Symbolism of Churches and Church Ornaments* (1843) and *The Sacred Vestments* (1899). His name appears also as Durand, Durantus, Duranti, and Durantis.

Durango (dŏŏräng'gō), state (1970 pop. 919,381), 47,691 sq mi (123,520 sq km), N central Mexico. The city of DURANGO is the capital. The western half of the state is dominated by the Sierra Madre Occidental. These mountains contain rich silver, gold, lead, mercury, sulfur, iron, and coal mines that extend north into the state of Chihuahua. Durango is a leading national producer of ferrous metals. The semiarid plains of eastern Durango afford good ranching, and livestock raising is a major occupation. Lumbering is also economically important in the state. On the border of Coahuila is the fertile LAGUNA DISTRICT, where vast desert basin lands are irrigated by the Nazas River. Gómez Palacio is the state's chief settlement in this region. Agriculture is important in the Nazas valley; cotton is the chief crop, and wheat, sugarcane, tobacco, corn, and grapes are also grown. Although known early to the Spanish, Durango was not opened up until 1562, when Francisco de Ibarra undertook its exploration and colonization. The early settlers of Durango and Chihuahua (which were then called Nueva Viscaya) suffered frequent Indian attacks, but the mines and grazing lands continued to attract colonists. Durango became a separate state in 1823, shortly after the Mexican revolution against Spain.

Durango, city (1970 pop. 137,000), capital of Durango state, N central Mexico, along the highway linking Mexico City with El Paso, Texas. Minerals are the chief product, but the city is also an agricultural and commercial center. Founded as a mining town in 1563, Durango served as capital of the region of Nueva Viscaya. In the 19th cent. the city suffered frequent scorpion plagues. Durango is the seat of an archbishopric. Nearby is the Cerro del Mercado (640 ft/195 m high), a hill of solid iron ore. Durango's cathedral is a massive example of early 18th-century architecture.

Durango (dŏŏrăng'gō), city (1970 pop. 10,333), seat of La Plata co., SW Colo., on the Animas River; inc. 1881. It is situated in a mountainous region at an altitude of c.6,500 ft (1,980 m). The economy is based on farming, mining, lumbering, and tourism. The mining of carnotite ore for uranium brought about a boom in 1948. Durango is the gateway to Mesa Verde National Park and other recreation areas. Nearby are Aztec ruins. Fort Lewis College is in Durango.

Durant, Henry Fowle (dŏŏrănt', dyŏŏ-), 1822–81, American lawyer and educator, b. Hanover, N.H., grad. Harvard, 1841. Christened Henry Welles Smith, he adopted the name Durant (1851) because he felt there were too many lawyers in Boston named Smith. After the death of his son (1863) he abandoned the law and became an evangelist. In 1870 he obtained a charter for Wellesley College and from that time on devoted himself completely to the college, of which he was officially the treasurer. See biography by Florence Kingsley (1924).

Durant, Thomas Clark, 1820–85, American railroad builder, chief figure in the construction of the Union Pacific RR, b. Lee, Mass. He was successful in building railroads in the Midwest, and, after the Union Pacific was organized (1862) by an act of Congress, John A. DIX was elected president and Durant vice president of the company. The burden of management and money raising was assumed by Durant, and, with much money at his disposal, he helped to secure in 1864 the passage of a bill that increased the land grants and privileges of the railroad. He organized and at first controlled the CRÉDIT MOBILIER OF AMERICA, but later (1867) he lost control of the company to Oakes AMES and his brother. Durant, however, continued on the directorate of the Union Pacific and furiously pushed construction of the railroad until it met the Central Pacific RR on May 10, 1869. The Ames group then procured his discharge. See biography by H. K. Hochschild (1961).

Durant, William James, 1885–, American historian and essayist, b. North Adams, Mass. He received his Ph.D. from Columbia in 1917 and published his doctoral dissertation, *Philosophy and the Social Problem,* in the same year. This was followed by *The Story of Philosophy* (1926), an immediate best seller that opened the way for a school of popularized history. Durant then embarked upon a life-long project, the writing of a comprehensive history of civilization. *The Story of Civilization* (10 vol., 1935–67; vol. 7–10 written with his wife, Ariel Durant) is a monumental work stretching from prehistory to the 18th cent. See also their *The Lessons of History* (1968) and *Interpretations of Life* (1970).

Durant, city (1970 pop. 11,118), seat of Bryan co., S central Okla., in the Red River valley farm area; inc. 1873. It is the commercial and processing center for an agricultural region where peanuts, cotton, wheat, and oil are produced and cattle are raised. Southeastern State College is there, and Lake Texoma and Denison Dam are nearby. The ruins of Fort Washita, on Lake Texoma, include 48 buildings.

Durante, family: see DURAN.

Duras, Marguerite (märgərēt' düräs'), 1914–, French author, b. Saigon, Indochina (now South Vietnam). Often ranked with the exponents of the new novel, or antinovel, Duras has abandoned many of the conventions of the novel form. Her novels often treat existential moments in people's lives. Avoiding the use of descriptive passages, she has her characters reveal themselves through what they say—and do not say. Duras's experience as a film writer and director has influenced her narrative technique. Her novels, many of which have been made into films, include *Un Barrage contre le Pacifique* (1950; tr. *The Sea Wall,* 1952), *Le Marin de Gibraltar* (1952; tr. *The Sailor from Gibraltar,* 1966), *Moderato cantabile* (1958; tr. 1960), *10:30 du soir en été* (1960; tr. *10:30 on a Summer Night,* 1965), and *Détruire, dit-elle* (1969; tr. *Destroy, She Said,* 1970). She wrote the screenplay for Resnais's *Hiroshima Mon Amour* (1959).

Durazzo: see DURRËS, Albania.

Durban (dûr'bən), city (1970 pop. 495,458), Natal prov., E South Africa, on Durban Bay, an arm of the Indian Ocean. Persons of Indian and Pakistani descent make up c.40% of the population. Durban is an industrial center, a major seaport, and a year-round resort. Industries include shipbuilding and ship repairing, petroleum refining, sugar refining, whaling and fishing, automobile assembly, and the manufacture of food products, paint, chemicals, fertilizers, soap, footwear, and textiles. Sugarcane is grown on nearby estates. Durban is the main port for the WITWATERSRAND and is connected by railroad with Johannesburg and other cities on the Rand. Its main exports are manganese and other ores, coal, sugar, and maize. Louis Botha International Airport is nearby. The site of Durban was discovered in 1497 by Vasco da Gama, but was not settled until 1824, when Britons arrived. The city, first called Port Natal, was renamed Durban in 1835 after Sir Benjamin D'Urban, then governor of Cape Colony. In 1842, BOERS besieged British troops in the Old Fort (now a museum) there. Durban became the chief commercial city of Natal after 1887, when the bay was dredged. The city was the site of the national convention (1908–09) that paved the way for the creation in 1910 of the Union of South Africa. Durban is the seat of the Univ. of Natal (1909), the Univ. of Durban (1960; for Asians), Natal College for Advanced Technical Education (1907), and M. L. Sultan College for Advanced Technical Education (1946; for Asians). Also there are Durban Museum and Art Gallery, the Local History Museum, an aquarium, and Greyville Race Course.

Düren (dür'ən), city (1970 pop. 53,620), North Rhine-Westphalia, W West Germany, on the Ruhr River. It is a transportation and industrial center; manufactures include iron, steel, glass, textiles, and chemicals. Düren was a center of Carolingian culture. In 1246 it was given to the count of Jülich by Emperor Frederick II. In 1543 it was captured and burned by the troops of Emperor Charles V. The city was severely damaged during World War II.

Dürer, Albrecht (äl'brĕkht dür'ər), 1471–1528, German painter, engraver, and theoretician, most influential artist of the German school, b. Nuremberg; son of a goldsmith. Dürer was an apprentice, first in his father's workshop and later until 1490 in the studio of the painter Wolgemut. After his bachelor journey, which took him to Colmar, Basel, and Strasbourg, and a trip to Italy in 1494, he established himself permanently in Nuremberg. Through these travels he gained a firsthand acquaintance with the art of Schongauer, the foremost Northern engraver of this time, and while in Italy he was drawn to the art of Mantegna and Bellini. Dürer made a second trip to Italy in 1505, staying in Venice for nearly two years. In 1520 he voyaged to the Netherlands, where he was received as a recognized master—the first German artist to achieve substantial renown beyond the borders of his native country. Dürer's principal accomplishment lay in his resolute acceptance of the discoveries of the Italian Renaissance and in his ability to convert the essence of these discoveries into a form palatable to Northern taste. Whether he was directly acquainted with the art of antiquity, or whether his classical forms derive from Italian intermediaries, is a matter of dispute. Nonetheless, his superbly proportioned figures, particularly in mythological scenes, breathe the spirit of classical antiquity. More gifted as a draftsman than as a painter, he executed a vast number of woodcuts and engravings throughout his career, achieving as a graphic artist an unsurpassed technical mastery and expressive power. Together with an amazingly keen sense of observation for realistic details, Dürer developed a highly rational system of perspective and bodily proportions, but was equally adept at creating visions of terrifying fantasy. A series of large woodcuts of the *Apocalypse* was issued in 1498. Two cycles of the *Passion of Christ* and a *Life of the Virgin* appeared in the first decade of the 16th cent. After 1500, Dürer became more interested in art theory, and his engravings reveal a meticulousness of craftsmanship, with a great richness of detail. In the second decade of the 16th cent. he concentrated more on the translation of lighting and tonal effects into the graphic medium. The artist's investigation of the ideal proportions of the human body culminated in the *Fall of Man* (1514). A friend of some of the leading contemporary humanists, Dürer expressed his humanistic inclinations in such engravings as *Knight, Death, and the Devil* (1513); and *St. Jerome in his Cell,* and *Melencolia I* (both: 1514). Dürer's *Portrait of his Father* (1490) in Florence, and his *Self-Portrait* (1493) in the Louvre are his earliest known paintings. He signed most of his work and made penetrating self-portraits throughout his life, revealing a consciousness of his individuality unusual in German art before his time. Among Dürer's several important altarpieces are the *Paumgärtner Altar* (1502–4) in Munich and the *Feast of the Rose Garlands* (1506) and the *Adoration of the Trinity* (1511) in Vienna. The *Heller Altar,* finished in 1509, was destroyed by fire in the 18th cent. For the Emperor Maximilian I, Dürer was the designer of more decorative projects, including a mammoth woodcut known as the *Triumphal Arch,* a *Triumphal Procession,* and a small prayer book. His sensitive perception of the natural world is shown in a number of drawings and watercolors of plants and animals and in a remarkable series of Alpine landscapes executed in the course of his journey to Italy. As a theoretician, Dürer composed a treatise on human proportions, a work on applied geometry, and a treatise on fortifications. Converted (c.1519) to the cause of Protestantism, he reflected the doctrines of Luther in some of his later works, such as a woodcut of the *Last Supper* (1523) and drawings of saints for an unexecuted altarpiece. Later artists owe much to Dürer—in general, for his power of artistic conception; more specifically, for his iconographical innovations and for his advances in graphic techniques. See catalog of his prints and drawings by the Museum of Fine Arts, Boston (1971); graphics ed. by Charles Talbot (1971); biographies by Erwin Panofsky (4th ed. 1955, repr. 1971) and Marcel Brion (1960); studies by Christopher White (1971), Heinz Lüdecke (1972), and Walter Koschatzy (1974).

duress (dyo͝orĭs´, do͞o´-, do͞orĕs´), in law, actual or threatened violence or imprisonment, by reason of which a person is forced to enter into an agreement or to perform some other act against his will. The constraint or threat of constraint must have been directed toward the person thus compelled or toward the wife, husband, parent, child, or other near relative of the person compelled. Anyone who makes a contract under duress is entitled to void it and be free of its obligations, but in order to release him from the contract duress must be shown to have been such as to overcome his mind and will. However, annoyance and persuasion do not constitute duress. See also COERCION.

D'Urfey, Thomas (dûr´fē), 1653–1723, English song writer and dramatist. His comedies for the stage were forerunners of the ballad opera. In 1719 he published *Wit and Mirth; or, Pills to Purge Melancholy,* which included his own witty, satirical songs and many older tunes adapted to new lyrics. This was a major source for ballad operas, including the tunes of John Gay's *Beggar's Opera.*

Durga: see HINDUISM.

Durgapur (do͝or´gäpo͝or), city (1971 pop. 207,232), West Bengal state, E central India, on the Damodar River. Located in an area of iron and coal mines, the city has an iron and steel plant, completed in 1962 with British aid. Durgapur is a distribution point for hydroelectric power generated by dams on the Damodar.

Durham, John George Lambton, 1st **earl of** (dûr´ əm), 1792–1840, British statesman. A stormy liberal career in Parliament (1813–32), which earned him the nickname Radical Jack, culminated in the important role he played in drafting the Reform Bill of 1832 and forcing it through the House of Lords. After the Canadian rebellion of 1837–38 he was appointed high commissioner and governor general of Canada, with the mission of winning back disaffected Canadian opinion by recommending political reforms. Durham submitted (1839) the *Report on the Affairs of British North America,* which has been called the Magna Carta of the British colonies. Its chief proposal was for the creation of an executive council responsible to the colonial assembly, which would allow Canada self government within the British empire. Other recommendations included reform of the land laws, railroad building to unify the country, and the union of Upper and Lower Canada to improve administration and finance and to extinguish the nationalism of the French Canadians.

Durham, county (1971 pop. 1,408,103), 1,015 sq mi (2,629 sq km), NE England, on the North Sea between the Tees and Tyne rivers. The county seat is Durham, site of one of England's finest Norman cathedrals. The region is low-lying along the coast, rising inland to the Pennines. It is one of the most densely populated counties of England. More than one half of the land area is devoted to agriculture. There is dairy farming, and cattle and sheep are raised. Oats, wheat, barley, potatoes, and turnips are grown. Industry is concentrated along the Tyne and the Tees. Shipbuilding and repairing (also along the Wear River) is very important. Other heavy industries include coal mining (central Durham), engineering, and the production of chemicals, and iron and steel. Electrical goods, clothing, textiles, paint, and plastics are the chief products of Durham's light industry. SUNDERLAND and HARTLEPOOL are important seaports. The area was occupied by the Romans and subsequently became part of the Anglo-Saxon kingdom of NORTHUMBRIA. From pre-Norman times until 1836, the bishops of Durham intermittently exercised palatine powers over the county. The powers were most important during the Middle Ages. In 1974 most of Durham was reorganized as the new nonmetropolitan county of Durham. A small area of NW North Riding of Yorkshire was added to the new county; NE Durham became part of the new metropolitan county of Tyne and Wear, and SE Durham became part of the new nonmetropolitan county of Cleveland.

Durham, municipal borough (1971 pop. 24,744), county town of Durham, NE England, on the sides of a hill nearly encircled by the Wear River. There are small factories producing organs and carpets. Noteworthy is the castle (1072), now occupied by part of the Univ. of Durham (founded 1832). In 995 the relics of St. Cuthbert were brought to Durham (then Dunholme), and a church was built as his shrine. The present cathedral, begun on the same site in 1093, is considered the finest example of Norman architecture in the country. It contains the tomb of the Venerable Bede (d. 735).

Durham (dûr´ăm), city (1970 pop. 95,438), seat of Durham co., N central N.C., in the Piedmont area; inc. 1867. A prominent center for the marketing and processing of tobacco, Durham is a major cigarette manufacturer. It also has textile and hosiery mills and an important insurance industry. The area was settled c.1750. Durham was a hamlet when Gen. Joseph E. Johnston surrendered nearby to Gen. William T. Sherman during the Civil War. After the war the tobacco industry began its great development, with James B. Duke a leading manufacturer. A recent spur to growth has been the establishment (1959) of the 5,000-acre (2,023-hectare) Research Triangle Park, occupying the triangular area between Durham, Chapel Hill, and Raleigh, and utilizing the concentration of university research talent in those three cities. Durham is the seat of Duke Univ. and North Carolina Central Univ. Other points of interest include the Sarah P. Duke Memorial Gardens and the Children's Nature Museum.

Durham, University of, at Durham, England; founded 1832. It has faculties of divinity, arts, social sciences, science, music, education, and law.

Durham cattle: see SHORTHORN CATTLE.

Duris of Samos, fl. 3d cent. B.C., Greek historian. A descendent of ALCIBIADES, Duris was tyrant of Samos for a time. He wrote *Samian Chronicle*—a history of Samos—and a rambling history of Greece and Macedonia covering most of the 4th cent. B.C. and the early years of the 3d cent. B.C. Only fragments of these works survive.

Durkee, John (dûr´kē), 1728–82, American pioneer and Revolutionary officer, b. Windham, Conn. Durkee, a leading member of the Connecticut Sons of Liberty, led the group that forced Jared INGERSOLL to resign at the time of the Stamp Act. Later he led Connecticut settlers into the WYOMING VALLEY, laid out (1769) Wilkes-Barre, and was the leader of the Connecticut faction in the first of the Pennamite Wars. He was captured twice by the Pennsylvanians. In the Revolution he raised a company that fought well at Bunker Hill, and he saw action in other battles, notably Long Island, Trenton, and Monmouth.

Durkheim, Émile (dûrk´hĭm, Fr. āmēl´ dürkĕm´), 1858–1917, French sociologist. His is considered one of the chief founders of modern sociology. Educated in France and Germany, Durkheim taught social science at the Univ. of Bordeaux and later became a professor at the Sorbonne. His view that the methods of natural science can be applied to the study of society was influenced by the positivist philosophy of Auguste COMTE. Durkheim held that the collective mind of society was the source of religion and morality and that the common values developed in society, particularly in primitive societies, are the cohesive bonds of social order. The loss of such values, he felt, leads to social instability and disorientation of the individual, a situation that he believed has contributed to the increase of suicide in modern times. To support his theories he drew extensively on anthropological and statistical materials. His important works include *The Division of Labor in Society* (1893, tr. 1933), *The Rules of Sociological Method* (1895, tr. 1938), *Le Suicide* (1897), and *The Elementary Forms of Religious Life* (1912, tr. 1915). See biography by Steven Lukes (1973); studies by Harry Alpert (1939, repr. 1961), Robert Bierstedt (1966), Dominick La Capra (1972), Steven Lukes (1972), and R. A. Nisbet (1965 and 1974).

Duroc swine (dŭ´rŏk, do͞o´-), breed originating during the 1800s in the NE United States from crosses among a number of red strains existing in that region. One of the most numerous breeds, they are large, rugged, solid-red animals, noted for hardiness and prolificacy.

durra: see SORGHUM.

Durrell, Lawrence, 1912–, British author, b. India, of Irish parents. He has traveled widely, often serving in diplomatic positions, and most of his works are set in exotic locations and convey an extraordinary sense of place. His novel *The Black Book,* which is steeped in an atmosphere of moral decadence, was published in Paris in 1938. Durrell's masterpiece is the tetralogy *The Alexandria Quartet,* consisting of *Justine* (1957), *Balthazar* (1958), *Mountolive* (1958), and *Clea* (1960). Purporting to be a study of the many ramifications of love, the quartet's excellence lies more in its technique—its rich, ornamental language and its evocation of the exotic, frequently bizarre atmosphere of the city of Alexandria, Egypt—than in its analysis of human emotion. Durrell's diplomatic service is reflected in *Bitter Lemons* (1957), *Esprit de Corps* (1958), and *Stiff Upper Lip* (1959), spoofs of diplomatic life, and in *Reflections on a Marine Venus* (1953), *Prospero's Cell* (1960), and *Spirit of Place* (1969), travel books. The novels *Tunc* (1968) and *Numquam* (1970) satirize various kinds of popular fiction. Among Durrell's other works are volumes of poetry including *The Red Limbo Lingo: A Poetry Notebook for 1968–1970* (1971) and *Vega and Other Poems* (1973), and the novel *Monsieur* (1975). See studies by John Unterecker (1965) and G. S. Fraser (1968). Durrell's brother **Gerald Durrell**, 1925–, b. India, is a naturalist, author, conservationist, and zoo director. In 1945, Durrell became a student keeper at the Whipsnade Zoo, London, and two years later he organized and led his first animal-collecting expedition. He has written many witty accounts of his collecting adventures and of the establishment (1958) of the Jersey Wildlife Preservation Trust. The Trust, of which Durrell is founder and director, is a small zoo on the Isle of Jersey dedicated to the preservation of endangered species. His books include *The Overloaded Ark* (1953), *The Bafut Beagles* (1954), *The Drunken Forest* (1956), *My Family and Other Animals* (1957), *A Zoo in My Luggage* (1960), *Catch Me a Colobus* (1972), and *A Bevy of Beasts* (1973).

Dürrenmatt, Friedrich (frē´drĭkh dür´ənmät), 1921–, Swiss playwright and novelist. Dürrenmatt's writings depict a world both comic and grotesque. His plays include the tragic farce *Der Besuch der alten Dame* (1956, tr. *The Visit,* 1958), *Romulus der Grosse* (1949; adapted by Gore Vidal as *Romulus,* 1962), and the comedy *The Physicists* (1962, tr. 1964). His sense of irony is also evident in his novels, which include *The Judge and His Hangman* (1952, tr. 1954), *The Quarry* (1953, tr. 1962), and *The Pledge* (1958, tr. 1959). A volume of his stories, *Der Sturz,* appeared in 1971. See studies by M. B. Peppard (1969) and Armin Arnold (1969, tr. 1972).

Durrës (do͝or´əs), Ital. *Durazzo,* city (1970 pop. 53,000), capital of Durrës prov., W Albania, on the Adriatic Sea. The chief seaport of Albania and the leading commercial and communications center, it has a dockyard, a power plant, and industries that manufacture clothing, foodstuffs, and leather and tobacco products. It is linked by rail with Tiranë and Elbasan. The city exports foodstuffs, chromites, copper ore, petroleum, and bitumen, and imports machinery and industrial goods. Durrës is the seat of a Greek Orthodox metropolitan and, since A.D. 449, of a Roman Catholic archbishopric. Founded (c.625 B.C.) as Epidamnus, a joint colony of Corinth and Corcyra, it became an important trade center. The quarrel between Corinth and Corcyra over Epidamnus helped to precipitate (431 B.C.) the PELOPONNESIAN WAR. Durrës passed to Rome in 229 B.C. and became a military and naval base. Under Roman rule it was known as Dyrrhachium, from which the present name is derived. Pompey made (48 B.C.) a stand there against Caesar. The city passed to the

Byzantine empire in the 8th cent., to the Normans of Sicily in 1185, to Naples in 1272, and to Serbia in 1336. Venice captured it in 1392 and held it until 1501 when it passed to the Turks. Under Turkish rule Durrës declined rapidly and almost disappeared. It was occupied (1912) by the Serbs in the First Balkan War, but was assigned to Albania in 1913. Italy (1915) and Austria (1916-18) also occupied the city. Durrës was the capital of Albania from 1913 to 1920, and revived thereafter as the country's chief seaport. It suffered heavy damage during World War II. The city, with its many mosques, has an Oriental character. Three Byzantine towers and medieval fortifications erected by Venice have survived.

Dur Sharrukin: see KHORSABAD.

durum wheat: see WHEAT.

Duruy, Victor (vĕktôr' dürüē'), 1811-94, French historian. He was a professor at Rheims and Paris, and as minister of public instruction (1863-69) under Napoleon III he encouraged the adoption of the principle of free obligatory elementary education. His best-known work is his *Histoire des Romans* (7 vol., 1870-85; tr., 8 vol., 1883), but he also wrote other popular histories, notably of Greece and France. He was elected to the French Academy in 1884.

Dušan, Stephen: see STEPHEN DUŠAN.

Duse, Eleonora (dōō'zə, Ital. ālāōnô'rä dōō'zā), 1859-1924, Italian actress. Of a theatrical family, she made a successful appearance at 14 as Juliet and in 1878 gained recognition in Augier's *Les Fourchambault.* In 1893, in New York and London, her portrayal of Dumas's *La Dame aux camélias* was considered a rare dramatic event. With her portrayal in 1895, in Paris, of Magda in Hermann Sudermann's *Heimat,* she became the only rival of Bernhardt. For some years a romantic attachment existed between Duse and the Italian poet D'Annunzio, whose plays she was often the first to present and champion. She appeared in the film *Cenere* (1916). A great interpreter of Ibsen, she made her farewell appearance (1923) in his *Lady from the Sea* in New York. Duse's acting was characterized by extreme simplicity and lack of theatrical artifice. She excelled in emotional parts, and her emotional power, however restrained, was tremendous in its effect. A slender woman of melancholy appearance, she was an enigmatic personality who disdained publicity. See biographies by E. A. Rheinhardt (tr. 1930), Frances Winwar (1956), and Jean Stubbs (1971).

Dušek, Jan Ladislav (yän lä'dĕsläf dōō'shĕk), 1760-1812, Czech pianist and composer; pupil of C. P. E. Bach. One of the earliest piano virtuosi, he was famous for his lyrical touch. His piano sonatas foreshadow the works of romantic composers such as Brahms, Schumann, and Chopin.

Dushan, Stephen: see STEPHEN DUŠAN.

Dushanbe (dōōshăn'bə, -shän'-), city (1970 pop. 374,000), capital of the Tadzhik Soviet Socialist Republic, Central Asian USSR. It is a major industrial and cultural center in a rich agricultural area. Coal, lead, and arsenic are mined nearby. A leading cotton textile center, Dushanbe also produces silk, textile machinery, clothing, leather goods, tractor parts, and foodstuffs. The city served as the headquarters for the Emir of Bukhara, a Tadzhik leader who fought the Bolsheviks. It was called Stalinabad from 1929 to 1961. A university and the Tadzhik Academy of Sciences are in the city.

Düsseldorf (düs'əldôrf), city (1970 pop. 663,586), capital of North Rhine-Westphalia, W West Germany, at the confluence of the Rhine and Düssel rivers. It is a major industrial, financial, and commercial center; a busy inland port; and an important rail junction. Its manufactures include iron, steel, machinery, chemicals, textiles, clothing, and paper. Chartered in 1288, Düsseldorf later was (14th-16th cent.) the capital and residence of the dukes of BERG. In 1614 it passed to the Palatinate-Neuburg line of the Bavarian house of Wittelsbach. It was occupied by France in 1795 and in 1815 became part of Prussia. Its industrial growth dates from c.1870. After World War I it was occupied again by France from 1921 to 1925. The city was badly damaged during World War II. Present-day Düsseldorf is an elegant city and a cultural center, with noted theaters and museums and a university. Its famous art academy (founded 1777; reestablished 1819) gave its name in the 19th cent. to the Düsseldorf school, of which Bendemann and Schadow-Godenhaus were representative. Heinrich Heine, the poet, was born (1797) in Düsseldorf.

dust, atmospheric, minute particles slowly settling or suspended by slight currents and existing in varying amounts in all air. There is least dust at high levels over the ocean and most at low levels over cities; dust caused by smoke is a serious urban problem (see AIR POLLUTION). Sources of atmospheric dust are winds blowing over dry earth (plowed fields, deserts, and roads), the various products of combustion, volcanic eruptions, salt spray from the oceans, pollen and other material from plants, and meteoric particles. Dust sometimes settles quickly on surfaces, but vast quantities are carried to the upper layers of the air and suspended there for long periods of time. The effects of a volcanic eruption such as that of Krakatoa in Indonesia have been observed three years after its occurrence. Hygroscopic dust particles (those to which water adheres) are the nuclei of condensation in free air; the nucleus of each droplet in a fog or cloud and of each raindrop and snowflake is one of these invisible particles of inorganic or organic dust. John Aitken, a Scottish physicist who in 1880 invented a device for counting particles in air, first correlated dust particles and condensation. Dust is also chiefly responsible, through its scattering effect upon light (diffusion), for one type of HAZE and for sunrise and sunset colors. The testing of nuclear devices in the atmosphere creates radioactive dust (FALLOUT), a serious hazard to all forms of life.

Dust Bowl, areas of the U.S. prairie states that suffer from dust storms. The storms may smother growing crops, destroy pasturage, and injure health; but their most serious effect is the removal of topsoil. During World War I the high price of wheat and the needs of Allied troops encouraged farmers to grow more wheat by plowing and seeding areas that were formerly used only for grazing. After years of good yields, livestock were returned to graze the area; their hooves pulverized the unprotected soil. In 1934 strong winds blew the soil into huge clouds, and each succeeding year, from December to May, the dust storms have recurred. However, the Dust Bowl, which covered 25,000 sq mi (64,750 sq km) at its greatest extent in the late 1930s, has been shrinking because of increased rainfall, regrassing, and erosion-preventing measures such as contour farming.

dust devil: see WHIRLWIND.

Dustin, Hannah, b. 1657, d. after 1729, New England pioneer. She was captured (1697) in an Indian raid on Haverhill, Mass., and taken up the Merrimack River to a place near modern Concord, N.H. While the Indians were asleep, Hannah and a 10-year-old boy (Samuel Lennardson) killed and scalped 10 of their guards and with another prisoner returned to Haverhill.

Dutch and Flemish literature, written in the standard language of the Low Countries since the Middle Ages. It is conventional to use the term *Dutch* when referring to the language spoken by the people of the modern Netherlands, and *Flemish* when referring to that spoken by the Belgians who use the same language; this is inaccurate in making a distinction that does not truly exist and in attributing to Flanders more than its share. Flourishing from the 12th cent., with French influence stronger than German, Middle Dutch literature shows the same general characteristics as the contemporary vernacular literatures; thus the bourgeois spirit was expressed in the works of Jacob van Maerlant, and in the Dutch versions of *Reynard the Fox;* Hadewijch, John Ruysbroeck, and Gerard Groote spoke the language of MYSTICISM. By the 14th cent., CHIVALRY and SCHOLASTICISM had waned, and by the 15th cent., mysticism was transformed as moral piety. Among the best-known of Dutch medieval dramas are *Mary of Nimmegen* and the morality play *Elckerlijk,* closely related to EVERYMAN. The greatest Dutch figure of the Renaissance, Erasmus, wrote in Latin, but other humanists—Jan van der Noot, Dirck Coornhert, Hendrick Spieghel, and the painter and poet Karel van Mander—used vernacular. Reformation polemics were represented by the Catholic Anna Bijns, and the Protestant Philip van Marnix. With the establishment of the republic and the subsequent commercial prosperity, came the Golden Age of Dutch literature; this is the period of the masters Pieter Hooft and Joost van den Vondel, of the homely verse of Jacob Cats, of the comedies of Gerbrand Bredero, and of the works of Constantijn Huygens. Flemish literature, represented in the 17th cent. by the lyric verse of Justus de Harduyn (1582-1641), the comic drama of Guilliam Ogier (1618-89), and the prose of Adriaen Poirte (1605-74), suffered severe decline in the 18th cent. as French became the more favored language. Dutch literature, too, declined. Pieter Langendijk and Joseph Addison's imitator Justus van Effen, the novelists Elisabeth Wolff and Agatha Deken, were the chief Dutch writers in the 18th cent., in addition to Rhijnvis Feith, the Van Haren brothers, and William Bilderdijk. In the 19th cent., Dutch and Flemish literature expanded on European lines, with the novelists Jacob van Lennep, Anna Bosboom-Toussaint, Eduard Dekker, and the Belgian Hendrik Conscience, and the poets Isâàc Da Costa, Hendrik Tollens, Everhardus Potgieteri, and the Belgians Guido Gezelle, Georges Rodenbach, and Pol de Mont. This was also the period of the sketches of Nicolaas Beets. The 1880s saw a reorientation of Dutch letters under foreign influence, especially under that of French NATURALISM; the parallel Belgian movement began slightly later. By 1900 impressionistic themes were emerging in poetry. Leaders in the new movements were Albert Verwey and Lodewijk van Deyssel in the Netherlands, and August Vermeylen in Belgium. The new forces were seen in the novelists and short-story writers Frederik van Eeden, Louis Couperus, Herman Robbers, Israel Querido, and in the Belgians Stijn Streuvels and Felix Timmermens. Among the better-known poets are Roland Holst, Pieter Boutens, and Herman Gorter in the Netherlands, and Karel van de Woestijne in Belgium. The successful dramatist Herman Heijermans has a special place in 20th-century Dutch literature. After the 1940s, the regional and psychological novel and poetry with a more human content came to typify Flemish literature. A major preoccupation of Dutch authors prior to World War II was the exploration of the subconscious mind. The physician Simon Vestdijk, perhaps the greatest Dutch writer of the 20th cent., wrote psychological novels that revealed the influence of EXISTENTIALISM. His contemporary Gerrit Achterberg explored similar themes of life and death in his powerful poems. The works of postwar Dutch writers, such as Anna Blaman, Alfred Kossman, and Adriaan Van der Veen, reveal the influence of both the Nazi occupation and existentialism. Indeed, the existentialist influence is found even in fictional works of the 1960s in which writers such as Willem F. Hermans, Jan Walkers, and Harry Mullisch express their overpowering sense of absurdity and despair. For further information see separate entries on most of the authors mentioned in this article, e.g. BIJNS, ANNA. See J. A. Russell, *Romance and Realism: Trends in Belgo-Dutch Prose in Literature* (1959); Theodor Weevers, *Poetry of the Netherlands in Its European Context* (1960); R. P. Meijer, *Literature of the Low Countries* (1971).

Dutch art, as a distinct national style, dates from about the turn of the 17th cent., when the country emerged as a political entity and developed a clearly independent culture. During the Middle Ages, Netherlandish art was subject to the leveling influence of the Romanesque and Gothic styles that prevailed throughout Europe. In the 15th and 16th cent. the southern, or Flemish, provinces in general led in quantity and refinement of production and set the artistic pace for the entire region (see FLEMISH ART AND ARCHITECTURE). Consequently, it is difficult to distinguish a development of national traits in the art of the Dutch provinces before the aesthetic florescence of the 17th cent. Moreover, the iconoclasm that attended religious and political upheavals in the mid-16th cent. destroyed much existing work. The earliest known Dutch paintings, by such artists as Geertgen tot Sint Jans and Albert van Ouwater, date from the second half of the 15th cent. and are clearly related to the Flemish tradition of the Van Eycks. In the 16th cent. a profusion of Italian Renaissance motifs appeared especially in decorative sculpture, and centers of sculptural production grew up at Dordrecht, Utrecht, and Breda. In painting, enthusiasm for Italian art, combined with a kind of late revival of Gothicism, resulted in a mixture of mannerist and classicist elements in works by such painters as Cornelis Englebrechtsz (1468-1533), Jacob Corneliszoon van Oostsanen (c.1470-1533), Jan de Mabuse, Jan van Scorel, Maerten van Heemskerck, Hendrik Goltzius, and Cornelis Corneliszoon (1562-1638). At the same time, a continuing native tendency toward sober realism asserted itself in the works of Jan Mostaert, Antonio Moro, and Lucas van Leyden. The current of Italian Renaissance influence persisted well into the 17th cent. and is to be noted especially in the work of the most important sculptor, Hendrik de Keyser, whose style was perpetuated in the work of his sons Willem and Pieter de Keyser. The 12-year truce with Spain (1609-21) introduced a period of unprecedented cultural growth and material prosperity. Calvinist proscription of church art and the absence of extensive state patronage encouraged the development of private easel painting, and a heightened national pride was reflected in the immense popularity of pictures portraying the domestic scene and Dutch burgher activities. With rapid, vigorous brushstrokes Frans Hals captured the expressions of jovial burghers. Many artists devoted themselves primarily to treating special types of material. Among these were Thomas de Keyser and Bartholomeus van der Helst, who were primarily portraitists; their works include many of the large group portraits of officers of corporations and guilds—a type of painting peculiar to Dutch culture. Adriaen van Ostade became well known as a painter of peasant scenes. At Utrecht the 16th-century Italianate tradition persisted in the work of Abraham Bloemaert. The outstanding members of the Utrecht school, notably Gerard van Honthorst, Hendrik Terbrugghen, and Dirck van Baburen, went to Italy and were influenced by Caravaggio in their rendering of large-figured genre groups and isolated half-length figures of musicians and drinkers. With their dramatic rendering of light and shade, these artists, together with the classical and historical painters the Pynas brothers and Pieter Lastman, provided the background for the greatest figure to emerge in the history of Dutch art, Rembrandt van Rijn. His genius was expressed in the whole gamut of subject matter, from portraiture, landscape, and interiors to still life and historical scenes. However, his incredible mastery of all types of painting and the graphic arts was reflected only weakly in the art of his numerous pupils, among whom were Nicholaes Maes, Gerard Dou, and the most talented of his disciples, Carel Fabritius. Toward the middle of the 17th cent. there was increased interest in the rendering of homely domestic scenes and views of urban life, seen in the paintings of Pieter de Hooch, Gabriel Metsu, and Jan Steen. In the 1660s and 70s taste began to favor effects of wealth, elegance, and refinement. A tranquillity of atmosphere pervaded not only works of lesser artists but also the exquisite paintings of Gerard Ter Borch and Jan Vermeer. Landscape became an enormously popular subject, offering full scope to the native tendency toward pictorial realism. The painters depicted their countryside with a sensitivity and unpretentious sincerity that has made the Dutch school of landscape one of the most influential and esteemed of all time. At the beginning of the 17th cent. a mannered, decorative style was carried over from the 16th cent. in the landscapes of Gillis van Coninxloo. A straightforward contemplative realism emerged in work by such artists as Esaias van der Velde and the highly original Hercules Seghers. In the second quarter of the century the landscapes of Jan van Goyen and Salomon van Ruisdael reveal a greater breadth of space and more dynamic composition. The culmination of these tendencies was reached in the art of Jacob van Ruisdael, Aelbert Cuyp, and Meindert Hobbema and in that of the great specialists in marine views, Jan van de Cappelle, Willem van de Velde, and Ludolf Backhuysen. Certain landscapists emphasized animal painting (e.g., Paul Potter) or concentrated on unusual light effects in sunsets and moonlight scenes (e.g., Aert van der Neer). Outstanding painters of still life included Jan Davidszoon de Heem, Willem Claeszoon Heda, and Willem Kalf (1619–93). An outstanding painter of birds and wildlife was Melchior d' Hondecoeter. Also characteristically Dutch as subject matter were architectural interiors. Specialists in this field included Pieter Saenredam and Emanuel de Witte. After the middle of the 17th cent. there was a long period of artistic decline. Even works of the principal artists in the last quarter of the century reveal tendencies toward empty elaboration of effects and pomposity or sentimentality of content. During the 18th cent. a strong wave of French influence encouraged renewed interest in historical and mythological painting and a heavy-handed imitation of rococo elegance. Among the more original 18th-century masters were Jacob de Wit (1695–1754) and Cornelis Troost (1697–1750). Not until the middle of the 19th cent. was there a revival of Dutch artistic culture—marked by the creative production of Jozef Israëls, Anton Mauve, Hendrik Mesdag, Johann Jongkind, and the Maris brothers. The outstanding genius of the second half of the century was Vincent van Gogh, one of the most important figures of the postimpressionist school. During the 20th cent., Dutch painting was strongly influenced by FAUVISM, CUBISM, and EXPRESSIONISM. Piet Mondrian and Theo van Doesburg founded the movement known as de STIJL, which radically altered the development of international design. After World War II, Piet Ouberg (1880–1954) influenced a younger generation of artists with his colorful abstract composition. In 1949 the CoBrA group of avant-garde artists signaled the new tendency toward ABSTRACT EXPRESSIONISM. In the graphic arts an outstanding recent figure is M. C. Escher. In sharp contrast with the vitality of the Dutch school in painting and the graphic arts is its lack of important sculpture. Outstanding among Dutch minor arts is the silverwork and goldwork of the 16th and 17th cent. There was also extensive production and export of ceramic tiles, of which the finest examples date from the late 16th and 17th cent. (See articles on individual artists, e.g., Jacob van RUISDAEL.) On early Netherlandish painting see studies by Erwin Panofsky (2 vol., 1953) and M. J. Friedländer (9 vol. in 10, tr. 1967). See Carel van Mander, *Dutch and Flemish Painters* (tr. 1936); Jakob Rosenberg *et al.*, *Dutch Art and Architecture: 1600 to 1800* (rev. ed. 1972); J. M. Nash, *The Age of Rembrandt and Vermeer* (1972).

Dutch East India Company: see EAST INDIA COMPANY, DUTCH.

Dutch East Indies: see INDONESIA.

Dutch elm disease: see DISEASES OF PLANTS; ELM.

Dutch Guiana: see SURINAM.

Dutch Harbor: see ALEUTIAN ISLANDS.

Dutch language, member of the West Germanic group of the Germanic subfamily of the Indo-European family of languages (see GERMANIC LANGUAGES). Also called Netherlandish, it is spoken by about 12 million inhabitants of the Netherlands, where it is the national language, and by slightly more than 250,000 people in the Western Hemisphere. The written and spoken forms of Dutch differ significantly. For example, written Dutch exhibits far greater formality than spoken Dutch in both grammar and vocabulary. One reason for this divergence is that written Dutch evolved from the Flemish spoken in the culturally advanced Flanders and Brabant of the 15th cent., whereas modern spoken Dutch grew out of the vernacular of the province of Holland, which became dominant after the 16th cent. (see FLEMISH LANGUAGE). Also, written Dutch is relatively uniform, while the spoken language has a number of dialects as well as an official standard form. The Roman alphabet is used for Dutch, and the earliest existing texts in the language go back to the late 12th cent. Among the words with which Dutch has enriched the English vocabulary are: brandy, cole slaw, cookie, cruiser, dock, easel, freight, landscape, spook, stoop, and yacht. Dutch is noteworthy as the language of an outstanding literature, but it also became important as the tongue of an enterprising people, who, though comparatively few in number, made their mark on the world community through trade and empire. See Coenraad Bernardus van Haeringen, *Netherlandic Language Research* (2d ed. 1960); W. Z. Shetter, *An Introduction to Dutch* (3d ed. 1968).

Dutch literature: see DUTCH AND FLEMISH LITERATURE.

Dutchman's-breeches: see FUMITORY.

Dutchman's-pipe: see BIRTHWORT.

Dutch metal: see BRASS.

Dutch New Guinea: see IRIAN BARAT, Indonesia.

Dutch Reformed Church: see REFORMED CHURCH IN AMERICA.

Dutch Wars. 1 1652–54, war between the English and the Dutch. It marked a crisis in the long-standing rivalry between the two nations as leaders in world trade. The crisis was precipitated by English search and seizure of Dutch merchant ships in the course of an unofficial Anglo-Dutch maritime war and, secondarily, by the English Navigation Act of 1651, which was directed against Dutch trade with British possessions. Hostilities were opened (May, 1652) by a sea fight between the British and Dutch admirals, Robert BLAKE and Maarten TROMP. At the beginning of the war Blake broke up the Dutch herring fleet, while George Ayscue successfully waylaid Dutch ships in the English Channel. However, the victory of Tromp over Blake off Dungeness (Nov., 1652) gave the Dutch command of the Channel, and in Jan., 1653, a Dutch treaty with Denmark closed the Baltic to English trade. Meanwhile reforms were introduced into the British navy for greater efficiency, and generals Richard Deane and George Monck were associated with the naval command. Tromp's fleet was forced to retire after an engagement off Portland (Feb., 1653), and the English regained control of the Channel. After Blake's succeeding victory off Gabbard's Shoal (June, 1653) the British were able to blockade the Dutch coast. While Dutch trade was thus effectively cut off, England itself was approaching financial exhaustion. Negotiations were undertaken but failed. On July 31, 1653, Tromp attacked the blockading fleet; he was defeated and killed, but the English ships were forced to return home for refitting. Peace was finally signed in April, 1654. The Dutch agreed to salute the British flag in British seas, to pay compensation for English losses, and to submit territorial claims to arbitration. **2** 1664–67, another war between the English and the Dutch. The first war had humbled, but had not crushed, the Dutch power, which continued to challenge English commercial supremacy, especially in the East Indian trade and in the West African slave trade. In 1664, Robert Holmes raided the Dutch colonies on the coast of Africa, and Richard Nicolls took the Dutch colony of New Netherland (later New York and New Jersey) in North America. War was officially declared by England in March, 1665. The duke of York (later James II) won the battle off Lowestoft (June, 1665), and in September the bishop of Munster, an ally of the English, overran the eastern province of the Netherlands; he was, however, soon expelled. In Jan., 1666, Louis XIV of France declared war on England, yet his interests did not lie on the side of the Dutch, and he took little part in the war. The British fleet under Monck and Prince Rupert was defeated in the Four Days Battle or Battle of the Downs (June 1–4, 1666) by Michiel de Ruyter and Cornelis Tromp, but in August they inflicted a severe defeat on the Dutch and destroyed shipping along the Dutch coast. The plague, the great fire, and disaffection in Scotland made England anxious for peace, and negotiations were undertaken, while Charles II let the fleet fall into a state of unpreparedness that enabled De Ruyter to attack the British ships in the Thames and inflict heavy losses (1667). By the Treaty of Breda (July, 1667) the trade laws were modified in favor of the Dutch, and all conquests of war were retained, with the English receiving New Netherland and Delaware and the Dutch keeping Surinam. At the same time the English and French both gave up their conquered territories. The Treaty of Breda was a blow to English prestige but proved in the long run to English advantage. **3** 1672–78, first of the great wars of Louis XIV of France. It was fought to end Dutch competition with French trade and to extend Louis XIV's empire. Having obtained the support of CHARLES II of England by the secret Treaty of Dover (1670) and allied himself with Sweden (see CHARLES XI) and several German states, Louis overran the southern provinces of the Netherlands (May, 1672). The Dutch stopped his advance on Amsterdam by opening the dikes; about the same time, under the command of De Ruyter, the Dutch defeated the English and French fleets at Southwold Bay. When Dutch peace proposals made at this juncture were spurned by the French, a revolution broke out, and William of Orange (later William III of England) took over Dutch leadership from the ill-fated Jan de WITT (July, 1672). William's attempt to divide the French lines and enter France was countered by the French seizure of Maastricht (1673). By the end of the year the French were forced to retreat, and Spain, the Holy Roman emperor, Brandenburg, Denmark, and other powers entered the war on the side of the Dutch. In 1674, England made peace with the Dutch. Nevertheless, the military situation changed in favor of France. In 1674, Louis II de CONDÉ won the battle of Seneff, while TURENNE was victorious at Sinzheim. The defeats CRÉQUY suffered in 1675 were balanced by the successful naval campaign of Abraham DUQUESNE in 1676, and in 1677 the French defeated William at Cassel and took Freiburg. Peace was negotiated at Nijmegen in 1678. Maastricht was ceded to the Dutch and a trade treaty modified the French restrictive tariffs in favor of the Dutch. By a subsequent treaty with Spain, Louis received Franche-Comté and a chain of border fortresses in return for evacuating the Spanish Netherlands. By a treaty with the Holy Roman emperor (1679), France was confirmed in possession of Freiburg and a part of Lorraine. See C. H. Wilson, *Profit and Power* (1957); Pieter Geyl, *Orange and Stuart, 1641–1672* (1970).

Dutch West India Company, trading and colonizing company, chartered by the States-General of the Dutch republic in 1621 and organized in 1623. Through its agency NEW NETHERLAND was founded. The phenomenal success of the Dutch East India Company was an influential factor in its establishment. The United New Netherland Company, which had been trading around the mouth of the Hudson River for several years, was absorbed into the new company. By the terms of the charter no citizen of the Netherlands could trade with any point on the African coast between the Tropic of Cancer and the Cape of Good Hope or on the American coast between Newfoundland and the Straits of Magellan without the company's permission. The company was responsible to the States-General in larger matters, such as declaring war, but otherwise had almost complete administrative and judicial power in its territory. The company was more interested in conquest than in peaceful trade, and its first concern was to take Brazil from the Portuguese. After 30 years of warfare, however, Brazil was lost. By that time the company had built Fort Orange (1624) on the site of Albany, N.Y., Fort Nassau (1624) on the Delaware River, Fort Good Hope on the site of Hartford on the Connecticut River, and finally Fort Amsterdam (1626), on the southern tip of Manhattan Island, which was the nucleus of the settlement called New Amsterdam, now New York City. England could not then afford to antagonize the Dutch because of wars with France and Spain and so permitted the Dutch settlement to be made on lands that England claimed. New Netherland remained under the control of the company until the English finally conquered it in 1664 (see NEW YORK, state). The company's unsound financial condition led to its reorganization under a new charter in 1674. Thereafter it engaged primarily in the African slave trade, though it still possessed colonies in Guiana. In 1791 its charter expired and was not renewed.

Dutch West Indies: see CURAÇAO.

Dutton, Clarence Edward, 1841-1912, American geologist, b. Wallingford, Conn., grad. Yale, 1860. After service in the army during and after the Civil War, he was a member (1875-91) of the U.S. Geological Survey. Working chiefly in the Rocky Mts. region, he wrote several papers, including geological studies of the high plateaus of Utah (1879-80), the Tertiary history of the Grand Canyon district (1882), and an authoritative report (1890) on the Charleston earthquake of 1886. As head of the division of volcanic geology for the survey, he studied volcanism in Hawaii, California, and Oregon. Dutton was among the earliest advocates of the theory of isostasy (the term was originated by him) stating that the general equilibrium in the crust of the earth is maintained by the flow or yielding of rock beneath it under gravitational stress. His writings include *Earthquakes in the Light of the New Seismology* (1904).

duty, in taxation: see TARIFF; EXCISE TAXES.

Duun, Olav (ō'läv dōōn), 1876-1939, Norwegian novelist. He taught in public schools until 1927. His monumental series of six novels, *The People of Juvik* (1918-23, tr. 1930-35), is a saga of a Norwegian farm family. Later works, including *Floodtide of Fate* (1938, tr. 1960), depict the internal conflict of the individual against a background of impending social catastrophe. Most of his work was written in Landsmaal Norwegian, a rural dialect based on Old Norse.

Duval, Claude (dōōvăl'), 1643-70, English highwayman. Born in Normandy, he went to England at the time of the Restoration (1660) in the train of the duke of Richmond. He led a daring career as a highwayman until he was captured when drunk. He was hanged at Tyburn. Duval was noted for his gallantry to the ladies, and his memorial inscription in the Covent Garden Church begins: "Here lies Du Vall: Reader, if male thou art, Look to thy purse; if female, to thy heart."

Duval, William Pope, 1784-1854, American frontiersman, territorial governor of Florida (1822-34), b. near Richmond, Va. He went to Kentucky as a young man, studied law, and began practicing at Bardstown c.1804. Duval was a U.S. Representative from Kentucky (1813-15) and U.S. judge in East Florida (1821-22). As territorial governor, he accomplished the peaceful removal of the Seminole Indians to the southern district, the compilation and revision of territorial laws, and legislation creating a board of education and improving the schools. He was the original of Washington Irving's "Ralph Ringwood" in *Wolfert's Roost.*

Duvalier, François (fräNswä' düvälyā'), 1907-71, dictator of Haiti (1957-71). A physician, he became director general of the national public health service in 1946 and subsequently served as minister of health and of labor. After opposing Paul Magloire's coup in 1950, he hid in the interior, practicing medicine, until a general political amnesty was granted in 1956. In 1957, with army backing, "Papa Doc," as he was known, was overwhelmingly elected president. Reelected in a sham election in 1961, he declared himself "president for life" in 1964. His regime, the longest in Haiti's history, was a brutal reign of terror; political opponents were summarily executed, and the populace was kept in a state of abject fear by the notorious TONTON MACOUTES. Under Duvalier, the economy of Haiti continued to deteriorate, and the illiteracy rate remained at about 90%. Duvalier nevertheless maintained his hold over Haiti. His practice of voodooism encouraged rumors among the people that he possessed supernatural powers. He died in April, 1971, after arranging for his son, Jean-Claude, to succeed him. See Jean-Pierre Gingras, *Duvalier: Caribbean Cyclone* (1967); Al Burt and Bernard Diederich, *Papa Doc* (1969).

Duvalier, Jean-Claude (zhäN-klōd), 1951–, "president for life" of Haiti (1971–); son of François Duvalier. An undistinguished law student, he was proclaimed president upon the death of his father. Although his inexperience made it seem likely that he would be a mere figurehead for his family and various ambitious ministers, he abruptly dismissed the powerful minister of the interior and of national defense, Luckner Cambronne, in Nov., 1972, and was subsequently firmly in control, although strongly influenced by his mother, Simone Duvalier. Known as "Baby Doc," he brought a more enlightened rule than that of his father, disbanding the dreaded TONTON MACOUTES, increasing political and personal freedoms, and improving the economy by attracting foreign capital, new industries, and restored U.S. aid.

Duveen, Joseph, 1st **Baron Duveen of Millbank,** 1869-1939, English art dealer. Beginning his career in 1886 in his father's firm, Duveen Brothers, he soon expanded the business to mammoth dimensions. He contributed paintings to many museums, notably the National Gallery and the Tate Gallery, both in London. After 1906 he employed Bernard Berenson to authenticate his great acquisitions in Renaissance art. A salesman with an amazing gift of persuasion, Duveen built an empire out of the business of art dealing. He was the most influential agent in the forming of the art collections of Henry Clay Frick, William Randolph Hearst, Henry E. Huntington, Samuel H. Kress, Andrew Mellon, John D. Rockefeller, and Joseph E. Widener. Many of these collections are now in museums. In 1933, Duveen was created baron. See biography by S. N. Behrman (rev. ed. 1972).

Duveneck, Frank (dyōō'vənĕk), 1848-1919, American portrait and genre painter and teacher, b. Covington, Ky., studied in Cincinnati and in Munich. In 1875 he showed a group of his canvases in Boston, where they created a sensation because of their bold brushwork, rich color, and forceful presentation of personality. He taught for many years in Munich and, after 1889, in Cincinnati. His influence on his contemporaries was great, particularly on William Chase and his followers and on the ashcan school. His *Whistling Boy* (Cincinnati Art Mus.) and *Old Woman* (Metropolitan Mus.) are characteristic of his portrait studies.

Duvergier de Hauranne, Jean (zhäN düvĕrzhyā' də ōrän'), 1581-1643, French theologian. He is often called the Abbé de Saint-Cyran from an abbacy he held *in commendam* (i.e., received the revenues from but did not actually administer). A personal friend of Cornelis JANSEN, he collaborated with him and was one of the molders of Jansenism. He was also a close friend of the ARNAULD family, and he was largely responsible for the conversion of PORT-ROYAL into the stronghold of Jansenism. He was the first of the Jansenist controversialists against the Jesuits, and because of his views he antagonized Cardinal Richelieu, who had him imprisoned in 1638. He was released on the cardinal's death in 1642.

du Vigneaud, Vincent (dyōō vēn'yō), 1901–, American biochemist, b. Chicago. He was professor of biochemistry and head of the department at George Washington Univ. school of medicine (1932-38) and at Cornell Univ. medical college (from 1938). His researches involved the chemistry of insulin, protein, and sulphur compounds; and the syntheses of penicillin (1946) and the B-vitamin biotin (1942). He was awarded the 1955 Nobel Prize in Chemistry for his identification and synthesis of two pituitary hormones, oxytocin, used medicinally in obstetrics, and vasopressin, used to treat diabetes.

Duyckinck, Evert Augustus (dī'kĭngk), 1816-78, American editor and biographer, b. New York City, grad. Columbia, 1835. From 1840 to 1842 he edited *Arturus, a Journal of Books and Opinion,* and from 1848 to 1853, with his brother George Long Duyckinck (1823-63), he owned and edited the *Literary World,* the best literary weekly of the period. With his brother he also edited and prepared much of the copy for the *Cyclopedia of American Literature* (2 vol., 1855), which he revised and enlarged in 1866 and which was a standard work in its time.

dvi-manganese: see RHENIUM.

Dvina (dvēnä') or **Northern Dvina,** Rus. *Severnaya Dvina,* river, c.465 mi (750 km) long, N European USSR. It is formed near Veliki Ustyug by the union of the Sukhona and Yug rivers, flows N past Kotlas, then turns northeast, and empties into Dvina Bay, an arm of the White Sea, just below Arkhangelsk. It is connected with the Volga-Baltic Waterway by the Sukhona River and the Northern Dvina Canal.

Dvina or **Western Dvina,** Ger. *Düna,* Lettish *Daugava,* Rus. *Zapadnaya Dvina,* river, c.635 mi (1,020 km) long, NW European USSR. Rising in the Valdai Hills, it flows S and then generally W past Velizh and through Belorussia, past Vitebsk and Polotsk, and through Latvia, past Daugavpils and Riga, into the Gulf of Riga, an arm of the Baltic Sea. It is navigable in its upper course, but, because of rapids, only partly navigable in its lower course. The Dvina's main port is Riga, and the river is connected by canal with the Berezina and the Dnepr rivers.

Dvořák, Antonín (än'tônēn dvôr'zhäk), 1841-1904, Czech composer. He studied at the Organ School, Prague (1857-59) and played viola in the National Theater Orchestra (1861-71) under Smetana. With the performance (1873) of his *Hymnus* he attracted wide attention. In 1884 he went to England to conduct some of his works. While he was director (1892-94) of the National Conservatory, New York, he composed his most famous work, the Symphony in E Minor, Op. 95, *From the New World* (1893). It conveys with great exuberance Dvořák's impressions of American scenes and folk music and at the same time evokes nostalgia for his native land. After his return to Prague he was professor and director of the conservatory there. He drew freely on Czech folk music and materials in his works, which are outstanding for their rhythmic variety, melodic invention, and brilliant instrumentation. They include nine symphonies (two posthumous), as well as symphonic poems, concertos, overtures, string quartets and other chamber music, operas, songs, choral works (mostly religious), and some piano pieces, notable for their freshness of romantic imagination. See biographical studies by Gervase Hughes (1967), John Clapham (1966), and Viktor Fischl, ed. (1943, repr. 1970).

Dvůr Králové nad Labem (dvōōr' krä'lôvā näd lä'bĕm), Ger. *Königinhof,* town (1970 pop. 16,220), NW Czechoslovakia, in Bohemia, on the Labe (Elbe) River. Among its manufactures are cement, cotton and linen textiles, machinery, and beer. Founded in 1139 as a ducal palace, the town was given by King Wenceslaus II of Bohemia to his queen, Elizabeth, in the late 13th cent. In 1817 several manuscripts purported to be early medieval Czech poems were "discovered" at Dvůr Králové nad Labem; one of the scholars who exposed the poems as patriotic forgeries was Thomas G. Masaryk, later the chief founder of independent Czechoslovakia.

dwarf cornel: see DOGWOOD.

dwarf elk: see WAPITI.

dwarfism, condition in which an animal or plant is less than normal in size and lacks the capacity for normal growth. Dwarfism is deliberately produced and perpetuated in certain species (e.g., in breeding miniature dogs and cultivating dwarf plants). Among humans, dwarfism usually results from a combination of genetic factors and endocrine malfunction. It can also be caused, however, by acquired conditions, such as kidney disease. Pituitary dwarfism is caused by an insufficiency of the pituitary growth hormone. Typically, the pituitary dwarf stops growing in early childhood, but retains normal body proportion, mental capacity, and sexual development. This type of dwarf, who is completely normal except for size, is commonly called a midget. CRETINISM is a type of dwarfism accompanied by mental retardation and distortion of the body, resulting from an insufficiency of thyroid hormone. Unlike cretinism and pituitary dwarfism (which are thought to be caused by a combination of heredity and endocrine malfunction), achondroplastic dwarfism is completely hereditary. Typically, the growth of the limbs is stunted, but the trunk is of normal size, and mental capacity is normal. Humans who range in height from 2 to 4 ft (5.08-10.16 cm) are generally classified as dwarfs. However, small size that is an inherited characteristic of race (such as among African Pygmies) is not considered to be dwarfism since the individuals in such groups are physiologically normal. There are many famous dwarfs in legend and in history. They were court favorites from earliest historic times and reached the height of fashion in Europe between the 15th and 17th cent. Although they were considered playthings, they were frequently noted for wit and intrigue. The career of Jeffery Hudson, a dwarf knighted in jest by Charles I, could be matched by that of few adventurers of any period. Most famous in recent times was "General TOM THUMB."

dwarf star: see WHITE DWARF.

dwarf tree, in horticultural practice, a tree artificially kept to a smaller size than is normal for average members of the species. This is usually accomplished either by limiting its root space and food and by careful pruning or by grafting it on the rootstock of a smaller species. Dwarf trees (their culture is an ancient Japanese art called BONSAI) utilize limited space and are grown for ornamental purposes. Dwarf fruit trees are valued for both decoration and fruit production in small gardens. Natural dwarfing occurs among plants growing in areas where only low-growing varieties can survive (see ALPINE PLANTS). See G. E. Severn, *Miniature Trees in the Japanese Style* (1967), Masakuni Kawasumi, *Introductory Bonsai* (1972).

Dwiggins, William Addison, 1880–1956, American type designer, calligrapher, and book designer, b. Martinsville, Ohio. He attained prominence as an illustrator and commercial artist, and he brought to the designing of type and books some of the boldness that he displayed in his advertising work. His typefaces—Electra and Caledonia are most widely used—were specifically designed for linotype composition and have the clean spareness of the motor age. His scathing attack on contemporary book designers in *An Investigation into the Physical Properties of Books* (1919) led to his working with the publisher Alfred A. Knopf. A series of finely conceived and executed trade books followed and did much to increase public interest in book format. Dwiggins was perhaps more responsible than any other designer for the marked improvement in book design in the 1920s and 1930s. He gained recognition as a calligrapher and wrote much on the graphic arts, notably essays collected in *MSS by WAD* (1949), and his *Layout in Advertising* (1928; rev. ed., 1949) remains standard.

Dwight, Harrison Gray Otis, 1803–62, American Congregational missionary to the Armenians, b. Conway, Mass. He served the Armenian population of Constantinople for 30 years. His travels with Eli Smith were recorded in *Researches of Rev. Eli Smith and Rev. H. G. O. Dwight in Armenia* (1833).

Dwight, Henry Otis, 1843–1917, American missionary in Turkey, b. Constantinople, studied at Ohio Wesleyan Univ.; son of Harrison Gray Otis Dwight. In 1867 he returned to Constantinople as secular agent for the American Board of Commissioners for Foreign Missions. From 1872 to 1899 he was editor of the board's Turkish publications. In 1880, Dwight was ordained a Congregational minister. He wrote a number of books and articles on Turkish affairs and edited the *Turkish and English Lexicon* (1890).

Dwight, John, fl. 1671–98, English potter, reputed founder of the Chelsea porcelain factory. The registration in 1671 of his patent for the "Mistery of transparent earthenware . . ." is the first certain recorded event of his life. He is considered to have laid the foundation of the pottery industry in England and to have set a standard not excelled elsewhere. There are examples of his work at the Victoria and Albert Museum and the British Museum.

Dwight, Theodore, 1764–1846, American author, b. Northampton, Mass.; brother of Timothy Dwight and grandson of Jonathan Edwards. A leader of the Federalist party in New England, he became famous for his political pamphlets and articles. As one of the younger CONNECTICUT WITS he proved himself a highly capable satirist. He served in Congress (1806–7), in the Connecticut state council (1809–15), and as secretary of the HARTFORD CONVENTION. He later wrote the journal of the convention (1833).

Dwight, Theodore William, 1822–92, American lawyer, b. Catskill, N.Y., grad. Hamilton College, 1840. He studied at Yale law school and was admitted to the bar in 1845. He was professor of law and later head of the law school at Hamilton. In 1858 he became the sole member of the faculty of the newly established Columbia school of law. Until 1873, when the faculty was enlarged, he taught all private-law subjects and lectured elsewhere extensively. From 1873 until his retirement in 1891 he headed the law faculty. Dwight was particularly interested in prison reform; he collaborated on *A Report on Prisons and Reformatories in the United States and Canada* (1867), served as president of the New York Prison Association, and was (1878) a delegate to the International Prison Congress at Stockholm.

Dwight, Timothy, 1752–1817, American clergyman, author, educator, b. Northampton, Mass., grad. Yale, 1769. He renounced legal for theological studies and after 1783 was pastor for 12 years of a Congregational church at Greenfield Hill, Conn. During his pastorate he became famous throughout New England for his preaching and for the excellent private school he established near his church. One of the leaders of the CONNECTICUT WITS, he tried to modernize the curriculum at Yale. At the death of Ezra Stiles, Dwight was named president of Yale, and from 1795 to 1817 he presided over the college. A great leader and teacher in his day and a strong believer in theocracy and Federalism, he vigorously opposed the rising Republicanism of Connecticut and the nation. His theology owed much to that of his grandfather, Jonathan Edwards. See his *Theology, Explained and Defended* (5 vol., 1818–19) and *Conquest of Canäan* (1788, repr. 1970); biographies by C. E. Cunningham (1942) and Kenneth Silverman (1969).

Dwight, Timothy, 1828–1916, American educator, b. Norwich, Conn., grad. Yale, 1849; grandson of Timothy Dwight (1752–1817). Appointed professor of sacred literature at Yale, he assisted in the reorganization of the divinity school, edited the *New Englander* (1866–74), and served on the American committee on the revision of the Bible (1873–85). In 1886 he succeeded Noah Porter as president of Yale. He expanded the institution, securing the legislative charter that authorized the title *university* instead of *college*, and retired in 1898. He is the author of *Thoughts of and for the Inner Life* (1899) and *Memories of Yale Life and Men* (1903). See Francis Parsons, *Six Men of Yale* (1936, repr. 1971).

Dy, chemical symbol of the element DYSPROSIUM.

Dyak or **Dayak** (both: dī'ăk), name applied to the indigenous peoples of the island of BORNEO, numbering over 1 million. The Dyaks have maintained their customs and mode of life largely uninfluenced by modern civilization. The group is generally divided into the Sea Dyaks, or Iban, who inhabit the coastal areas and rivers; the Land Dyaks of SW Borneo; the Bahau of central and E Borneo; and the Ngadju of S Borneo. In Dyak communities, a few enormous longhouses provide dwelling places for a whole village. Each longhouse has a chief. In clearings made in the jungle, rice, yams, sugarcane, and other crops are grown cooperatively by the people of the entire community. Fishing and hunting (with blowguns and poison darts) supplement the food supply. Dyaks have highly complex animistic and shamanistic religious cults. Intertribal warfare has persisted, with headhunting as an important feature. See Benedict Sandin, *The Sea Dayaks of Borneo before White Rajah Rule* (1968); Derek Freeman, *Report on the Iban* (2d ed. 1970); Robert Pringle, *Rajahs and Rebels* (1970).

Dybbøl (düb'öl), Ger. *Düppel*, village, Sønderjylland co., S Denmark, on the Flensborg Fjord. The Danes were defeated at Dybbøl in 1849 by Saxon and Bavarian troops and in 1864 by the Prussians, who held the village until 1920.

Dyce, Alexander (dīs), 1798–1869, Scottish editor. He is best known for his scholarly editions of the works of Elizabethan and Jacobean dramatists, including those of George Peele, Robert Greene, John Webster, Christopher Marlowe, Beaumont and Fletcher, and a nine-volume edition of Shakespeare (rev. ed. 1864–67).

Dyck, Sir Anthony van: see VAN DYCK, SIR ANTHONY.

Dyck, Christopher van, 1601–c.1672, German designer and maker of printing type, who worked in Amsterdam. Types that he designed were used by the ELZEVIR firm. His roman typeface was of the kind known in England and America as "old style" and on the Continent as "Elzevir." It was sturdy, legible, without much contrast between light and heavy lines, and with inconspicuous serifs. It strongly influenced CASLON and other designers of old-style types.

dye, any substance, natural or synthetic, used to color various materials, especially textiles, leather, and food. Natural dyes are so called because they are obtained from plants (e.g., ALIZARIN, CATECHU, INDIGO, and logwood), from animals (e.g., COCHINEAL, KERMES, and Tyrian purple), and from certain naturally occurring minerals (e.g., OCHER and PRUSSIAN BLUE). They have been almost entirely replaced in modern dyeing by synthetic dyes. Most of these are prepared from coal tar, being formed from an aromatic HYDROCARBON such as benzene, from which indigo is derived (see also ANILINE), or anthracene, which yields alizarin. Although some materials, e.g., silk and wool, can be colored simply by being dipped in the dye (the dyes so used are consequently called direct dyes), others, including cotton, commonly require the use of a MORDANT (see also LAKE). Alizarin is a mordant dye and the color it gives depends upon the mordant used. Dyes are classified also as acidic or basic according to the medium required in the dyeing process. A vat dye, e.g., indigo, is so called from the method of its application; it is first treated chemically so that it becomes soluble and is then used for coloring materials bathed in a vat. When the materials become impregnated with the dye, they are removed and dried in air, the indigo reverting to its original, insoluble form. The process by which a dye becomes "attached" to the material it colors is not definitely known. One theory holds that a chemical reaction takes place between the dye and the treated fiber; another proposes that the dye is absorbed by the fiber. Dyeing is an ancient industry. The Chinese, Persians, and Indians used natural dyes many centuries ago, including indigo, probably the oldest dye in use, and Tyrian purple, derived from a species of snail. The Egyptians prepared some brilliant colors. In the 13th and 14th cent. dyeing assumed importance in Italy; the methods employed were carried to other parts of Europe and, as new dyes became known, the dyeing industry flourished and grew. Cochineal was introduced from Mexico. Finally, in the 19th cent. the work of W. H. Perkin and Adolf von Baeyer produced the first synthetic dyes. See T. S. Gore and others, ed., *Recent Progress in the Chemistry of Natural and Synthetic Colouring Matters* (1962); Stuart Robinson, *The History of Dyed Textiles* (1970).

Dyer, Sir Edward, 1543?–1607, Elizabethan poet. A friend of Sidney and Spenser, he was celebrated in his day as an elegist. His best-known poem is "My Mind to Me a Kingdom Is." See study by R. M. Sargent (1935, repr. 1968).

Dyer, Eliphalet (əlīf'əlĭt"), 1721–1807, American jurist, b. Windham, Conn. After serving in the state legislature for several years, Dyer took part in the French and Indian Wars and later was a member of the governor's council (1762–84) and became (1766) an associate judge of Connecticut's superior court. He was one of the organizers of the SUSQUEHANNA COMPANY and was an active supporter of the company in its attempts to secure confirmation of its lands in the Wyoming Valley. A Connecticut delegate to the Stamp Act Congress (1765), he was later a member (1774–79; 1780–83) of the Continental Congress. Dyer was chief justice of Connecticut from 1789 until 1793.

Dyer, John, 1700?–1758, English nature poet, b. Wales. He is best known for the topographical poem *Grongar Hill* (1726).

Dyer, Mary, d. 1660, Quaker martyr in Massachusetts, b. England. She accompanied (c.1635) her husband to Massachusetts and supported Anne Hutchinson, whom she followed to Rhode Island, where her husband held several public offices. In 1650 she returned to England and there joined the Society of Friends (Quakers). On her return to America (1657) she was arrested in Boston and banished, but twice returned (1659, 1660) to minister to imprisoned Quakers. Twice arrested by Massachusetts authorities and condemned to be hanged both times, she was reprieved in 1659 but was subsequently executed in 1660. See biography by Horatio Rogers (1896).

Dyersburg, city (1970 pop. 14,523), seat of Dyer co., NW Tenn., near the Mississippi River; inc. 1850. It is a processing and industrial center for a rich cotton and farm belt. A junior college is there.

dyer's-weed, name for any of several plants from which dyestuffs are obtained. They include a MIGNONETTE, a BROOM, and species of GOLDENROD.

Dyfed (dĭv'ĕd), nonmetropolitan county (1972 est. pop. 372,000), W Wales, created under the Local Government Act of 1972 (effective 1974). It comprises the former counties of CARDIGANSHIRE, Carmarthenshire, and PEMBROKE.

Dyk, Viktor (vĭk'tôr dĭk), 1877–1931, Czech writer and nationalist. Dyk considered his novels, satires, short stories, plays, and poems as weapons in the struggle to free his country from Austrian rule. A long poem, *The Window* (1920), describes his experiences in an Austrian prison. As a dramatist he is best known for *The Messenger* (1907), which concerns the Czech loss of independence, and for the satirical play, *Andrew and the Dragon* (1920).

Dykh-Tau (dĭkh-tou), peak, c.17,000 ft (5,180 m) high, SE European USSR, in the central Greater Caucasus.

Dykstra, Clarence Addison (dĭk'strə), 1883–1950, American educator and civic administrator, b. Cleveland, grad. Univ. of Iowa, 1903. After graduate work at the Univ. of Chicago, he taught in Pensacola, Fla., was instructor in history and government at Ohio State Univ. (1907–9) and professor of political science at the Univ. of Kansas (1909–18). From 1918 to 1920 he served as executive secretary of the Cleveland Civic League. He later held similar positions in Chicago and Los Angeles. He was also commissioner of water and power in Los Angeles (1923–26) and professor of municipal administration at the Univ. of California at Los Angeles (1923–29). Dykstra was city manager of Cincinnati from 1930 until 1937, when he resigned to become president of the Univ. of Wisconsin. In 1945 he resigned from the Wisconsin presidency to become provost of the Univ. of California at Los Angeles. He served on several government committees.

Dylan, Bob (dĭl'ən), 1941–, American singer and composer, b. Duluth, Minn. as Robert Zimmerman. Dylan learned guitar at the age of 10 and autoharp and harmonica at 15. After a rebellious youth, he moved to New York City in 1960 and was soon recognized as a brilliant artist. Influenced by Huddie LEDBETTER, Bo Diddly, Hank Williams, and Woody GUTHRIE, Dylan had a profound effect on folk and ROCK MUSIC. As a lyricist he captured the cynicism, anger, and alienation of American youth, which reverberated in his harsh vocal delivery and insistent guitar-harmonica accompaniment. Among his many songs of social protest are "Blowin in the Wind" and "The Times They Are A-Changin." Dylan's style has evolved from folk ("Don't Think Twice"), to folk-rock ("Highway 61 Revisited"), to country blues ("Country Pie"). Enigmatic and reclusive, he has become a cult figure who satisfies his followers with an occasional album or, as in 1974, a concert tour. He has published an autobiography, *Bob Dylan, Self-Portrait* (1970), and a novel, *Tarantula* (1971). See biographies by Anthony Scaduto (1972); Craig McGregor, ed., *Bob Dylan: A Retrospective* (1972).

dynamics, branch of MECHANICS that deals with the MOTION of objects; it may be further divided into kinematics, the study of motion without regard to the forces producing it, and kinetics, the study of the forces that produce or change motion. Motion is caused by an unbalanced FORCE acting on a body. Such a force will produce either a change in the body's speed or a change in the direction of its motion (see ACCELERATION). The motion may be either translational (straight-line) or rotational. With the principles of dynamics one can solve problems involving work and energy and explain the pressure and expansion of gases, the motion of planets, and the behavior of flowing liquids and gases. Solids are rigid, having a definite shape, but fluids (liquids and gases) are not, and special branches of dynamics have been developed that treat the particular effects of forces and motions in fluids. These include hydrodynamics, the study of liquids in motion, and aerodynamics, the study of gases in motion. The applications of liquids both at rest and in motion are studied under HYDRAULICS, a branch of engineering closely related to dynamics. The principles of dynamics may also be combined with the study of other phenomena, as in ELECTRODYNAMICS, the study of charges in motion.

dynamite, EXPLOSIVE made from nitroglycerin and an inert, porous filler such as wood pulp, sawdust, kieselguhr, or some other absorbent material. The proportions vary in different kinds of dynamite; often ammonium nitrate or sodium nitrate is added. The mass is usually pressed in cylindrical forms and wrapped in an appropriate material, e.g., paper or plastic. The charge is set off with a DETONATOR. Dynamite was discovered by Alfred B. NOBEL in 1866.

dynamo: see GENERATOR.

dyne (dīn), unit of FORCE in the CGS SYSTEM of units, which is based on the METRIC SYSTEM; an acceleration of 1 centimeter per second per second is produced when a force of 1 dyne is exerted on a mass of 1 gram. In terms of the NEWTON, the force unit in the MKS SYSTEM, 1 dyne equals 0.00001 newtons.

dysentery, inflammation of the intestine characterized by the frequent passage of feces, usually with blood and mucus. The two most common causes of dysentery are infection with a bacillus (see BACTERIA) of the *Shigella* group, and infestation by an AMEBA, *Entamoeba histolytica.* Both bacillary and amebic dysentery are spread by fecal contamination of food and water and are most common where sanitation is poor. They are primarily diseases of the tropics, but may occur in any climate. It is estimated that in some parts of the tropics 80% of the children acquire bacillary dysentery before the age of five; the mortality rate is high among infants and the aged if the infection is not treated, preferably with a broad-spectrum antibiotic. In adults bacillary dysentery usually subsides spontaneously, but treatment is desirable to prevent recurrence. Amebic dysentery is prevalent in regions where human excrement is used as fertilizer; in some such regions over half the population probably harbors the amebic cyst. The cyst is the inactive, resistant stage in which the ameba is transmitted from one host to another; the active form is that which causes damage. Both cysts and active amebas are excreted in the feces of an infected person, but only the cysts are hardy enough to survive outside the body. A person recovering from the infection, or one with an inactive case, passes mostly cysts; such a person is a more likely source of contamination than one with an active case. When cysts are ingested with contaminated food or water they are transformed in the intestine into active amebas. If these remain within the lumen of the intestine they are relatively innocuous, but if they invade the intestinal wall they cause ulceration, dysentery, and usually pain. In severe cases the resulting dehydration may lead to prostration. Amebic dysentery may occur in acute or chronic form. In prolonged infections the amebas may invade the blood vessels of the intestine and be carried to other parts of the body, where they cause amebic abcesses. Abcesses of the liver and brain are especially dangerous; destruction of liver tissue is the most frequent complication of amebic dysentery. Infection by amebas, whether of the intestine alone or of other parts of the body, is called amebiasis. Infections are diagnosed by finding cysts or active amebas in the feces. However, the disease is easily misdiagnosed for several reasons. *Entamoeba histolytica* may be harbored without causing symptoms (although it may be passed on and cause the disease in others); it is easily confused with harmless amebas of the human intestine, especially *Entamoeba coli*; it commonly coexists with bacteria that may in some cases be the cause of the symptoms. A combination of drugs is generally used to treat amebic dysentery: an amebicide to eliminate the organism from the intestinal tract, an antibiotic to eradicate associated bacterial infection, and a drug to combat infection of the liver and other tissues. Preventive measures include the protection of water supplies from contamination and the washing of hands by food handlers.

Dyson, Sir Frank Watson (dī'sən), 1868–1939, English astronomer, b. Ashby-de-la-Zouch, grad. Cambridge. He was astronomer royal of Scotland (1905–10) and of England (from 1910). As director (1910–33) of Greenwich Observatory he greatly expanded its research activities and inaugurated (1928) the wireless transmission of Greenwich time. Noted for his study of solar eclipses, he was an authority on the spectrum of the corona and on the chromosphere; his observations of an eclipse (in Brazil, 1919) confirmed Einstein's theory of the effect of gravity on light. Dyson plotted the motions of many previously uncharted stars. A fellow of the Royal Society from 1901, he was knighted in 1915. His publications include *Astronomy: A Handy Manual* (1910) and *Eclipses of the Sun and Moon* (with Richard Woolley, 1937). See biography by Margaret Wilson (1951).

dyspepsia: see INDIGESTION.

dysplasia: see HIP DYSPLASIA.

dysprosium (dĭsprō'zēəm) [Gr.,=hard to get at], metallic chemical element; symbol Dy; at. no. 66; at. wt. 162.50; m.p. 1409°C; b.p. 2335°C; sp. gr. 8.54 at 25°C; valence+3. Dysprosium is a lustrous silvery metal; it is very soft and can be cut with a knife. It is in group IIIb of the PERIODIC TABLE and is a member of the LANTHANIDE SERIES; all members of this series are RARE-EARTH METALS and resemble one another in their chemical properties. Dysprosium is stable in air at room temperature. It dissolves in both dilute and concentrated mineral acids; forms a white oxide known as dysprosia; and, with other elements, forms several brightly colored salts. It is commonly found with other rare-earth metals in several minerals, including gadolinite and euxenite. Dysprosium and its compounds are among the most highly susceptible to magnetization of all substances and are used in special magnetic alloys. A cermet of dysprosium oxide and nickel is used in nuclear reactor control rods. Dysprosium is used with argon in mercury-vapor lamps to give a higher light output and balance the color spectrum. Although dysprosium was discovered (but not isolated) in 1886 by P. E. Lecoq de Boisbaudran, a French chemist, it did not become available in relatively pure form until the 1950s.

Dzerzhinsk (dzĭrzhĕnsk'), city (1970 pop. 221,000), W European USSR, a port on the Oka River. There are chemical, textile, and cable industries. The city was called Chernorech until about 1919 and Rastyapino until 1929, when it was renamed in honor of Felix Dzerzhinsky, founder of the Soviet secret police.

Dzerzhinsky, Felix Edmundovich (fyĕ'lyĭks ĕdmo͝on'dəvĭch dzĭrzhĕn'skē), 1877–1926, Russian Bolshevik leader, organizer and first chairman (1917–21) of the Cheka (see SECRET POLICE). He was the son of Polish aristocrats. Under his direction, the reign of terror against anti-Bolsheviks reached its height in 1918. Dzerzhinsky also headed the agencies that succeeded the Cheka (the OGPU and the GPU) and held other high posts.

Dzhambul (jəmbo͞ol'), city (1970 pop. 188,000), capital of Dzhambul oblast, Central Asian USSR, on the Talas River and the Turkistan-Siberia RR. Industries include food processing and the manufacture of chemicals, metal products, and leather goods. Founded in the 7th cent., it was called Taraz or Talas. In the 8th and 9th cent. it was ruled by Arabs. From the 10th to the 12th cent. it was the capital of the Karakhan state, and in 1864 it passed to Russia. It was called Aulie-Ata until 1938. Near Dzhambul are two mausoleums (11th and 12th cent).

Dzierżoniów (jēĕrzhô'nyo͞of), Ger. *Reichenbach,* town (1970 pop. 32,900), SW Poland. It is a manufacturing center known for its textiles (especially woolens) and for its machine-building and electrical equipment industries. The town was the site of the signing of two treaties. By the first (1790), Austria promised Prussia to renounce acquisition of Turkish territory. By the second (1813), Austria conditionally consented to join the coalition against Napoleon I.

Dzungaria (zo͝on-gâr'ēə), Mandarin *Chun-ko-erh,* physical region (c.300,000 sq mi/777,000 sq km) of Sinkiang Uigur Autonomous Region, NW China. It is a largely steppe and semidesert basin surrounded by high mountains (the Tien Shan in the south and the Altai in the north). Wheat, barley, oats, and sugar beets are grown, and cattle, sheep, and horses are raised. The fields are irrigated with melted snow from the permanently white-capped mountains. Wu-lu-mu-ch'i (Urumchi) and I-ning (Kuldja) are the main cities; other smaller oasis towns dot the piedmont areas. The population consists of Uigurs, Khazaks, Khirghiz, Mongols, and Chinese; since 1953 there has been a massive influx of Chinese to work on water conservation and industrial projects. The Dzungaria has deposits of coal, iron, and gold, as well as large oil fields. Dzungaria (named for the Dzungar, one of the Mongol tribes) was ruled by a confederation of Western Mongols that established (17th cent.) a large empire in central Asia. The region passed to the Chinese in the mid-18th cent. The Dzungarian Ala-Tau is a mountain chain that lies on the boundary of Sinkiang and Kazakh SSR (see ALA-TAU). At the eastern end of the chain, on the Russian-Chinese border, lies the Dzungarian Gate, which for centuries was used as an invasion route by conquerors from central Asia. The name also appears as Jungaria, Sungaria, or Zungaria.

E

E, fifth letter of the ALPHABET. It is a usual symbol for a mid-front vowel, such as ĕ in the English *step.* A mid-front vowel was represented by Greek epsilon [Gr., = *e* without the aspirate], to which *E* corresponds in form and place (see also H). English ē is pronounced as a diphthong of ĭ and *y*. In MUSICAL NOTATION *E* represents a note in the scale.

e, in mathematics, irrational NUMBER occurring widely in mathematics and science, approximately equal to the value 2.71828; it is the base of natural, or Naperian, LOGARITHMS. The number *e* is defined as the limit of the expression $(1+1/n)^n$ as n becomes infinitely large, or

$$e=\lim_{n\to\infty}(1+1/n)^n.$$

In 1873 the French mathematician C. Hermite proved that *e* was transcendental, i.e., not a ROOT of any algebraic equation; this proof constituted a great contribution to the growth of mathematics. The number *e* is also known as Euler's number, for Leonhard Euler, who discovered the famous formula $e^{i\pi}=-1$, where $i=\sqrt{-1}$, thus expressing the relationship between the numbers *e*, *i*, and π. Many of the expressions of the form e^x, known as the exponential function and often written $\exp(x)$, occur in various applications ranging from statistics to nuclear physics.

Ea (ā'ä) or **Enki** (ĕng'kē), ancient water god of Sumerian origin, worshiped in Babylonian religion. The great benefactor of mankind, Ea was called the lord of wisdom, of magic, and of the arts and sciences. With the sky god Anu and the earth god Enlil, or Bel, he was the third of the great divine triad.

Ead-. For some Anglo-Saxon names beginning thus, see ED-; e.g., for Eadwin, see EDWIN.

Eadmer or **Edmer** (both: ĕd'mər), d. 1124?, English monk and historian. He was in the monastery of Christ Church, Canterbury, when Anselm became archbishop of Canterbury, and his biography of St. Anselm is the basic one. Eadmer's *Historiae novorum* is a history of England from 1066 to 1122 from the ecclesiastical point of view and is excellent of its kind. He was elected archbishop of St. Andrews, but was never consecrated because the Scots refused to accept the spiritual authority of Canterbury. See R. W. Southern, *St. Anselm and His Biographer* (1963).

Eadwig: see EDWY.

Eagels, Jeanne, 1894-1929, American actress, b. Kansas City as Jeanne Aguilar. Eagels first gained fame in 1911 in *Jumping Jupiter.* Noted for her steamy characterizations, she was on stage every season until 1924. Her performance as Sadie Thompson in *Rain* (1922) won her enormous acclaim. Eagels's films include *The Letter* (1929) and *Jealousy* (1929). Her turbulent private life was the subject of a 1957 film.

eagle, common name for large predatory birds of the family Falconidae (HAWK family), found in all parts of the world. Eagles are similar to the buteos, or buzzard hawks, but are larger both in length and in wingspread (up to 7½ ft/228 cm) and have beaks nearly as long as their heads. They are solitary birds, said to mate for life. The nest, or aerie, of twigs and sticks is built at a vantage point high in a tree or on a cliff in a permanent feeding territory and is added to year after year, the refuse of the previous nests decomposing beneath the new additions. The eaglets (usually two) do not develop adult markings until their third year, when they leave parental protection and seek their own mates and territories. The American bald (in the sense of white, as in piebald), or white-headed, eagle (*Haliaetus leucocephalus*) is found in all parts of North America near water and feeds chiefly on dead fish (sometimes robbing the osprey's catch) and rodents. It is dark brown with white head, neck, and tail plumage. The northern species (found chiefly in Canada) is slightly larger than the southern, which ranges throughout the United States. The golden, or mountain, eagle (genus *Aquila*—whence *aquiline,* meaning eaglelike) is widespread in the Northern Hemisphere, in the United States found mostly in the West. In Asia it is trained to hunt small game (see FALCONRY). The adult is sooty brown with tawny head and neck feathers; unlike those of the bald eagle, its legs are feathered to the toes. The gray and Steller's sea eagles (also in the genus *Haliaetus)* are native to colder areas of the Northern Hemisphere; the king or imperial eagle to S Europe and Asia; and the rare monkey-eating eagle to the Philippines. The harpy, or harpy eagle (*Thrasyaetus harpyia*), of Central and South America, the largest (38 in./95 cm long) of the hawks, eats macaws and sloths. It was named for the winged monsters of Greek myth and was called "winged wolf" by the Aztecs. Eagles—impressive both in size and for their fearsome beauty—have been symbols of royal power and have appeared on coins, seals, flags, and standards since ancient times. The eagle was the emblem of one of the Ptolemies of Egypt and was borne on the standards of the Roman armies and of Napoleon's troops. The American bald eagle became the national emblem of the United States by act of Congress in 1782. In folklore the eagle's ability to carry off prey, including children (e.g., the legend of Ganymede), has been exaggerated; even the powerful golden eagle can lift no more than 8 lb (3.6 kg). Eagles are classified in the phylum CHORDATA, subphylum Vertebrata, class Aves, order Falconiformes, family Accipitridae.

Eagle Pass, city (1970 pop. 15,364), seat of Maverick co., W Texas, a port of entry on the Rio Grande opposite Piedras Negras, Mexico; inc. 1918. Linked by highway with Mexico City, it is a tourist resort and a shipping and processing point for vegetables grown in the richly cultivated lowlands along the Rio Grande. The city has also prospered from mineral processing and international trade. The site of a U.S. army camp during the Mexican War, it was on one of the main routes to California during the gold rush. In 1855 trouble with the Mexicans led to the burning of Piedras Negras. Fort Duncan (1849), a base for raids against the Mexicans and the Indians, housed thousands of U.S. troops during the Villa revolution in Mexico just before World War I. Ten buildings from the original fort remain.

Eagleton, Thomas Francis, 1929-, U.S. Senator (1968-), b. St. Louis, Mo. Admitted to the bar in 1953, he entered Democratic politics in Missouri and served as circuit attorney for St. Louis (1957-60), state attorney general (1961-65), and lieutenant governor (1965-68). He was elected to the U.S. Senate in 1967. Eagleton was nominated (July 13, 1972) for the vice presidency on the ticket with Senator George S. McGovern. Shortly thereafter he admitted that he had been three times hospitalized for nervous exhaustion and twice received electric shock therapy. After days of indecision and mounting pressure from the press and party leaders, Eagleton, at first supported by McGovern, withdrew (July 31, 1972) from the ticket at McGovern's request and was replaced by Sargent Shriver. He was reelected to the Senate in 1974.

eaglewood: see ALOES.

Eakins, Thomas (ā'kĭnz), 1844-1916, American painter, photographer, and sculptor, b. Philadelphia, where he worked most of his life. Eakins is considered the foremost American portrait painter and one of the greatest artists of the 19th cent. He studied art at the Pennsylvania Academy of the Fine Arts and anatomy at Jefferson Medical College. In Paris from 1866 until 1870, he studied with Gérôme and Bonnat, and with the sculptor A. A. Dumont. He visited Spain, where he was drawn to the works of Velázquez. From 1870 he taught at the Pennsylvania Academy, where he was harshly criticized for his teaching innovations: he insisted on working from live, nude models, on learning anatomy from dissection, on learning motion by watching athletes perform, and on working in oils. His refusal to abandon the use of nude models forced his resignation in 1886. Eakins sought, above all, to describe honestly the reality of what he saw. He sought to "peer deeper into the heart of American life." He felt that no formula of ideal beauty could compare with what is real, so he refused the temptation to see what, according to fashion, he ought to. His portraits were not flattering; they were penetrating, and they often disappointed his sitters. His painstaking study of anatomy and geometric perspective served his ambition to grasp and define in paint exterior reality, while his remarkable honesty of approach provided him a view of the interior realities of human character. His perception and mode of illumination of the human face are frequently likened to those of Rembrandt. Eakins revived the art of portraiture in the United States and, through his influence as a teacher, founded a native school of American art, visible in the works of his pupils Henri, Sloan, Glackens, and Sterne, and more recently in the work of Andrew Wyeth. Eakins used photography in many ways: as an art in its own right to make powerful studies of family and friends, animals and rural scenes; as an aid to accuracy in painting, either by copying directly or to inspire a related work; and to study motion. He devised for Eadweard MUYBRIDGE a camera which, by means of a revolving disc over the lens, could make several exposures on a single plate, and thereby aid in understanding movement, everyday as well as athletic. Eakins's few works in sculpture include the horses on the Soldiers' and Sailors' Memorial Arch, Brooklyn, N.Y. Only toward the very end of his life was he recognized as a major painter. Among his most notable works are *The Surgical Clinic of Professor Gross* (1875; Jefferson Medical College, Philadelphia), the realism of which caused a scandal when it was finished; *The Clinic of Professor Agnew* (1889; Univ. of Pennsylvania); *The Concert Singer* (1892; Pennsylvania Acad.); *The Chess Players* (1876) and *The Thinker* (1900; both: Metropolitan Mus.); the portraits of Mrs. Frishmuth (1900; Philadelphia Mus.) and Miss Van Buren (1891; Phillips Coll., Washington, D.C.). His pictures of athletes, such as *The Swimming Hole* (1883; Fort Worth Mus., Texas), *Salutat* (1898; Addison Gall., Andover, Mass.), *Max Schmitt in a Single Scull* (1871; Metropolitan Mus.), are especially fine. In a period when many artists were concerned with the exotic or deliberately picturesque, Eakins succeeded in recording the everyday world about him with insight and profound humanity. See illustrated catalogs of his watercolors by D. F. Hoopes (1971) and his photographs by G. Hendricks (1972); studies by Fairfield Porter (1959), S. Schindler (1967), Lloyd Goodrich (1933 and 1970), and Gordon Hendricks (1974).

Ealdhelm, Saint: see ALDHELM, SAINT.

Ealing, borough (1971 pop. 299,450) of Greater London, SE England. The borough was created in 1965 by the merger of the municipal boroughs of Acton, Ealing, and Southall. It is highly industrialized: motor vehicles, scientific instruments, glass, plastics, and engineering products are manufactured. Cardinal Newman went to school in Ealing, and the former French king Louis Philippe taught there. The biologist Thomas Huxley was born in Ealing.

Eames, Wilberforce (ēmz), 1855-1937, American bibliographer, b. Newark, N.J. He joined the staff of the Lenox Library in New York City in 1885 and became its librarian in 1895. After 1911 he was bibliographer of the New York Public Library, of which the Lenox had become a part. Eames was honored for the scholarliness of his work on Americana. See biographies by R. G. Vail (1938) and H. M. Lydenberg (1956).

ear, organ of hearing and equilibrium. The human ear consists of outer, middle, and inner parts. The outer ear is the visible portion; it includes the skin-covered flap of cartilage known as the auricle, or pinna, and the opening (auditory canal) leading to the eardrum (tympanic membrane). The middle ear, separated from the outer ear by the eardrum, contains three small bones, or ossicles, known because of their shapes as the hammer (malleus), anvil (incus), and stirrup (stapes). Air reaches the middle ear through the EUSTACHIAN TUBE, which connects it to the throat. The inner ear, or labyrinth, contains the cochlea, which houses the sound-analyzing cells of the ear, and the vestibule, which houses the organs of equilibrium. The cochlea is a coiled, fluid-filled tube divided into the three canals: the vestibular,

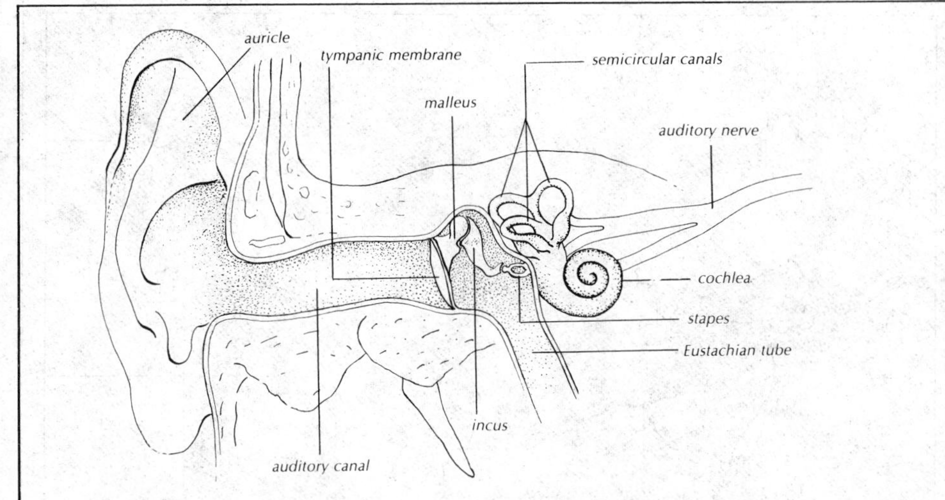

Ear

tympanic, and cochlear canals. The basilar membrane forms a partition between the cochlear canal and the tympanic canal and houses the organ of Corti. Anchored in the Corti structure are some 20,000 hair cells, with filaments varying in length in a manner somewhat analogous to harp strings. These are the sensory hearing cells, connected at their base with the auditory nerve. In the course of hearing, sound waves enter the auditory canal and strike the eardrum, causing it to vibrate. The sound waves are concentrated by passing from a relatively large area (the eardrum) through the ossicles to a relatively small opening leading to the inner ear. Here the stirrup vibrates, setting in motion the fluid of the cochlea. The alternating changes of pressure agitate the basilar membrane on which the organ of Corti rests, moving the hair cells. This movement stimulates the sensory hair cells to send impulses along the auditory nerve to the brain. The exact mechanism by which the movement of the sensory hair cells stimulates nerve impulses is unknown. In addition, it is not known how the brain distinguishes high-pitched sounds from low-pitched sounds. One theory proposes that the sensation of pitch is dependent on which area of the basilar membrane is made to vibrate. How the brain distinguishes between loud and soft sounds is also not understood. Some scientists believe that loudness is determined by the intensity of vibration of the basilar membrane. In a small portion of normal hearing, sound waves are transmitted directly to the inner ear by causing the bones of the skull to vibrate, i.e., the auditory canal and the middle ear are bypassed. This kind of hearing, called bone conduction, is utilized in compensating for certain kinds of deafness (see DEAFNESS; HEARING AID). In addition to the structures used for hearing, the inner ear contains the semicircular canals and the utriculus and sacculus, the chief organs of balance and orientation. There are three fluid-filled semicircular canals: two are in a vertical position and determine vertical body movement such as falling or jumping. The third is in a horizontal position and determines horizontal movements like rotating. Each canal contains an area at its base, called the ampulla, that houses sensory hair cells. The hair cells project into a thick gelatinous mass. When the head is moved, the canals move also, but the thick fluid lags behind, and the hair cells are bent by being driven through the relatively stationary fluid. As in the cochlea, the sensory hair cells stimulate nerve impulses to the brain. The sensory hair cells of the saclike utriculus and sacculus project into a gelatinous material that contains lime crystals. When the head is tilted in various positions, the gelatin and crystals exert varying pressure on the sensory cells, which, in turn, send varying patterns of stimulation to the brain. The utriculus sends indications of the position of the head to the brain and detects stopping and starting. The function of the sacculus is not fully understood.

Earhart, Amelia (âr'härt), 1898–1937, American aviator, b. Atchison, Kansas. She was the first woman to cross the Atlantic by airplane (1928) and the first woman to make a solo flight across the Altantic (1932). She was the first person to fly alone from Honolulu to California (1935). In 1937 she attempted with a copilot, Frederick J. Noonan, to fly around the world, but her plane was lost on the flight between New Guinea and Howland Island; her fate remains a mystery. She was married to G. P. Putnam (1887–1950) in 1931. See biographies by Richard O'Connor (1971) and A. H. Pellegreno (1971).

Earl, Ralph: see EARLE, RALPH.

Earle, John, 1601?–1665, English clergyman and author. The *Microcosmographie* (1628), a collection of witty characterizations, is his most famous work. In 1663 he became bishop of Salisbury.

Earle or **Earl, Ralph,** 1751–1801, American portrait and landscape painter, b. Worcester co., Mass. He is purported to have painted four scenes of the battle of Lexington as an eyewitness, but is best known for his portraits, which may be seen in the museums of Chicago, New York City, Worcester, Mass., and Yale Univ. Earle studied with Benjamin West in London, to the detriment of his previously uncluttered style. His later work shows the influence of Copley. Much of his work is characterized by a monumental gravity and directness, best exemplified by his powerful portrait of Roger Sherman (c.1775; Yale Univ.). The unevenness in his painting is sometimes attributed to his fondness for drink, which finally killed him.

Earlham College, at Richmond, Ind.; Friends; coeducational; founded 1847.

Early, Jubal Anderson, 1816–94, Confederate general, b. Franklin co., Va., grad. West Point, 1837. After fighting against the Seminole in Florida he resigned from the army (1838), studied law, and practiced at Rocky Mount, Va. He fought briefly in the Mexican War. Early voted against secession in the Virginia convention (April, 1861), but when war broke out he became a colonel of Virginia troops. Promoted to brigadier general at the first battle of Bull Run (July, 1861), he fought in all the campaigns (1862–64) of the Army of Northern Virginia. He was prominent at Salem Church (see CHANCELLORSVILLE, BATTLE OF) and in the GETTYSBURG CAMPAIGN (1863). In the WILDERNESS CAMPAIGN (1864) he temporarily commanded A. P. Hill's corps, and when R. S. EWELL was forced to retire, Early assumed command of the 2d Corps. After Cold Harbor, Lee sent Early against Gen. David Hunter, who was threatening Lynchburg. Early drove Hunter westward and then marched down the Shenandoah valley, crossed the Potomac, and moved on Washington. He defeated Lew Wallace in the battle of MONOCACY (July 9, 1864) and was before the capital on July 11. The arrival of troops from Grant's army compelled him to withdraw to Virginia, but later in the month he again crossed the Potomac. His cavalry raided far and wide and burned Chambersburg, Pa., when that town refused to pay a ransom. In Sept., 1864, P. H. SHERIDAN moved against Early and, defeating him at Winchester and Fisher's Hill, drove him up the valley. Early returned and surprised Sheridan's army at Cedar Creek (Oct. 19) but was finally defeated. On March 2, 1865, his small force was overwhelmed by Gen. George Custer, of Sheridan's army, at Waynesboro. Lee, although still confident of Early's ability, was forced by public opinion to remove him. At the end of the war Early fled the country and did not return until 1869. He resumed the practice of law and was associated with Gen. P. G. T. Beauregard in the Louisiana lottery. See his memoirs (1912; new ed. by F. E. Vandiver, 1960); biography by M. K. Bushong (1955); studies by F. E. Vandiver (1960) and E. J. Stackpole (1961).

Early Christian art and architecture. Little is known about Christian art in the first two centuries after the death of Christ. Among the earliest manifestations extant are the early 3d-century paintings on the walls of the catacombs in Rome. Whereas the style resembles that of secular Roman wall painting, the subject matter consists mainly of biblical figures. Jonah, Daniel, and Susanna appear in scenes of miracles through divine intervention. Among the motifs that symbolized the hope of resurrection and immortality are the fish and the peacock. Following the official recognition of Christianity after the Edict of Toleration (313), the scope of Early Christian art was radically enlarged. Elaborate mosaic narrative cycles covered the upper walls, triumphal arch, and apse of basilican churches. Some are preserved in Santa Maria Maggiore and Santa Pudenziana in Rome and Sant'Appollinare Nuovo in Ravenna. The use of gold backgrounds heightens the effect of otherworldliness and transcendence. In contrast to paganism, the Christian faith was bound by the authority of sacred writings, and it placed increasing importance on the production of books and their illumination. Some fragments of the biblical text, written in silver and gold on purple vellum and sumptuously illuminated, are still preserved (see ILLUMINATION). Foremost of these is the Vienna Genesis, a manuscript of the first half of the 6th cent. The sculpture of the stone SARCOPHAGUS was extensively practiced. In some cases subjects similar to those of the catacombs were used; in others, scenes of the life of Christ or more ceremonious compositions were created, showing the enthroned Christ receiving the homage of the apostles. Ivory carvers decorated book covers and reliquary caskets or larger objects, such as the throne of Maximianus in Ravenna, a work of the 6th cent. Before the legal recognition of the new faith in the early 4th cent., Christian places of worship were of necessity inconspicuous and had no fixed architectural form. Afterward, however, imposing cult edifices were erected in many parts of the Roman Empire, especially in its major cities, Rome, Constantinople, Milan, Antioch, and Ravenna. Early Christian builders adapted structures that had long been used in the Hellenistic and Roman worlds. The basilican hall, consisting of a nave flanked by lower aisles and terminated by an apse, was adopted as the standard structure in Christian congregational worship. Sant'Apollinare Nuovo in Ravenna and Santa Sabina in Rome still survive as largely unaltered examples of this type. In Early Christian architecture a distinct emphasis was placed on the centralized plan—of round, polygonal, or cruciform shape. Baptisteries and memorial shrines (martyria) were based on the traditionally centralized Roman funerary monument. Martyria were erected on sites connected with certain events in the life of Christ and other places held to be sanctified by the sacrifice of the martyrs. In such buildings as Saint Peter's in Rome and the Holy Sepulcher in Jerusalem, the martyrium structure and basilica were combined, creating a new formal synthesis of great significance for the religious architecture of the medieval period. A distinct type of Christian art and architecture was evolved in Egypt (see COPTIC ART). In the eastern part of the Roman Empire, the development of the Early Christain tradition was continued under the auspices of the Byzantine emperors (see BYZANTINE ART AND ARCHITECTURE and see Christian iconography under ICONOGRAPHY). See C. R. Morey, *Early Christian Art* (2d ed. 1953); D. T. Rice, *The Beginnings of Christian Art* (1957); Richard Krautheimer, *Early Christian and Byzantine Architecture* (1965); John Beckwith, *Early Christian and Byzantine Art* (1970).

early man: see MAN, PREHISTORIC.

Earn, Loch (lŏkh ûrn), lake, 7 mi (11.2 km) long and 1 mi (1.6 km) wide, Perthshire, central Scotland. Ardvorlich House, on its shore, is the Darlinvarach of Sir Walter Scott's *Legend of Montrose*. Earn River (46 mi/74 km long), the lake's outlet, flows eastward through Strathearn past Comrie, Crieff, and Bridge of Earn into the Firth of Tay.

Earp, Wyatt Berry Stapp, 1848–1929, law officer and gunfighter of the American West, b. Monmouth, Ill. After serving as police officer in Wichita (1874) and Dodge City (1876–77), Kansas, he became an armed guard for Wells, Fargo & Company in Tombstone, Ariz. There, with his brothers Virgil and Morgan and a friend, Doc Holliday, he was involved in the controversial gunfight at the O.K. Corral (Oct. 26, 1881), in which several men were killed. Testimony conflicts as to whether Earp's group had killed a group of criminals or was itself a group of thieves and murderers. Leaving Tombstone in 1882, Earp traveled widely, operating saloons in San Diego, Calif.; Nome, Alaska; and Tonopah, Nev., before settling in

Los Angeles. See biography by Frank Waters (1960); studies by E. E. Ellsworth (1963 and 1964).

earring, a personal adornment, sometimes an amulet, worn attached to the ear lobe. Since prehistoric times the ear has been pierced for the insertion of the earring; certain primitive tribes distort the lobe with plugs several inches in diameter or with heavy stones. Egyptians first wore large gold hoops, which eventually became smaller and supported pendants. In Babylonia and later in Assyria where the earring was worn by men to denote rank, the earring evolved into an exquisite work of the goldsmith's art. In Greece the finely wrought gold earrings often had tinkling pendants. The Romans were first to popularize earrings set with precious stones. Earrings were little used with the headdresses of the Middle Ages, but their use had a vigorous revival during the Renaissance and was also adopted by men; pearls were especially favored. In the 18th cent. the diamond earring became most fashionable; the 19th cent. saw extensive use of the cameo. With the invention (c.1900) of a screw device for attaching the earring, their popularity again increased.

earth, in astronomy and geology, fifth largest planet of the solar system and the only planet definitely known to support life. It is the third in order from the sun, only Mercury and Venus being nearer; the mean distance from the earth to the sun is c.93 million mi (150 million km). The earth rotates from west to east about a line (its axis) that is perpendicular to the plane of the equator and passes through the center of the earth, terminating at the north and south geographical poles. The period of one complete rotation is a day; the rotation of the earth is responsible for the alternate periods of light and darkness (day and night). The earth revolves about the sun once in a period of a little more than 365¼ days (a year). The path of this revolution, the earth's orbit, is an ellipse rather than a circle, and the earth is consequently nearer to the sun in January than it is in July; the difference between its maximum and minimum distances from the sun is c.3 million mi (4.8 million km). This difference is not great enough to affect climate on the earth. The change in seasons is caused by the tilt of the earth's axis to the plane of its orbit, making an angle of c.66.5°. When the northern end of the earth's axis is tilted toward the sun, the most direct rays of sunlight fall in the Northern Hemisphere. This causes its summer season. At the same time the Southern Hemisphere experiences winter since it is then receiving indirect rays. Halfway between, in spring and in autumn, there is a time (see EQUINOX) when all parts of the earth have equal day and night. When the northern end of the earth's axis is tilted away from the sun, the least direct sunlight falls on the Northern Hemisphere. This causes its winter season. The earth is surrounded by an envelope of gases called the atmosphere, of which the greater part is nitrogen and oxygen. Gravitational forces have molded the earth, like all celestial bodies, into a spherical shape. However, the earth is not an exact sphere, being slightly flattened at the poles and bulging at the equator. The equatorial diameter is c.7,926 mi (12,760 km) and the polar diameter 7,900 mi (12,720 km); the circumference at the equator is c.24,830 mi (40,000 km). The surface of the earth is divided into dry land and oceans, the dry land occupying c.57.5 million sq mi (148.9 million sq km), and the oceans c.139.5 million sq mi (361.3 million sq km). Knowledge of the earth's interior has been gathered by three methods: by the analysis of earthquake waves passing through the earth (see SEISMOLOGY), by analogy with the composition of meteorites, and by consideration of the earth's size, shape, and density. Research by these methods indicates that the earth has a zoned interior, consisting of concentric shells differing from one another by size, chemical makeup, and density. The earth is undoubtedly much denser near the center than it is at the surface, because the average density of rocks near the surface is c.2.8, while the average density of the entire earth is c.5.5. The outer shell, or crust, varies from 5 to 25 mi (8 to 40 km) in thickness, and consists of the CONTINENTS and ocean basins at the surface. The continents are composed of rock types collectively called sial, a classification based on their densities and composition. Beneath the ocean basins and the sial of continents lie denser rock types called sima. The sial and sima together form the crust, beneath which lies a shell called the mantle. The boundary between the crust and the mantle is marked by a sharp alteration in the velocity of earthquake waves passing through that region. This boundary layer is called the Mohorovičić discontinuity, or Moho. Extending to a depth of c.1,800 mi (2,900 km), the mantle probably consists of very dense (average c.3.9) rock rich in iron and magnesium minerals. Although temperatures increase with depth, the melting point of the rock is not reached because the melting temperature is raised by the great confining pressure. At depths between c.60 mi and c.125 mi (100 and 200 km) in the mantle, a plastic zone, called the asthenosphere, is found to occur. Presumably the rocks in this region are very close to melting, and the zone represents a fundamental boundary between the moving crustal plates of the earth's surface and the interior regions. The molten magma that intrudes upward into crustal rocks or issues from a volcano in the form of lava may owe its origin to radioactive heating or to the relief of pressure in the lower crust and upper mantle caused by earthquake faulting of the overlying crustal rock. Similarly, it is thought that the heat energy released in the upper part of the mantle has broken the earth's crust into vast plates that slide around on the plastic zone, setting up stresses along the plate margins that result in the formation of

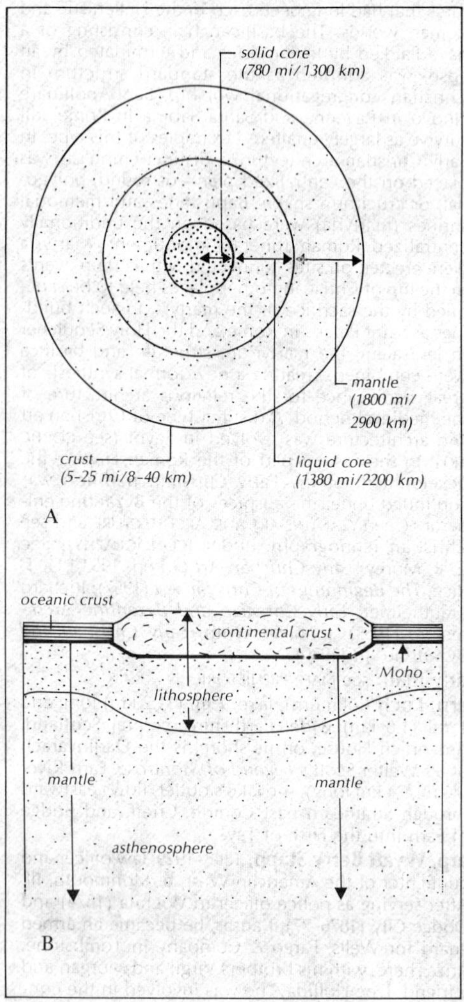

A. *Cross section of the earth, showing its shells*

B. *Detailed cross section of the crust and upper mantle: The lithosphere consists of the hard rock in the crust and upper mantle, lying above the soft rock of the asthenosphere.*

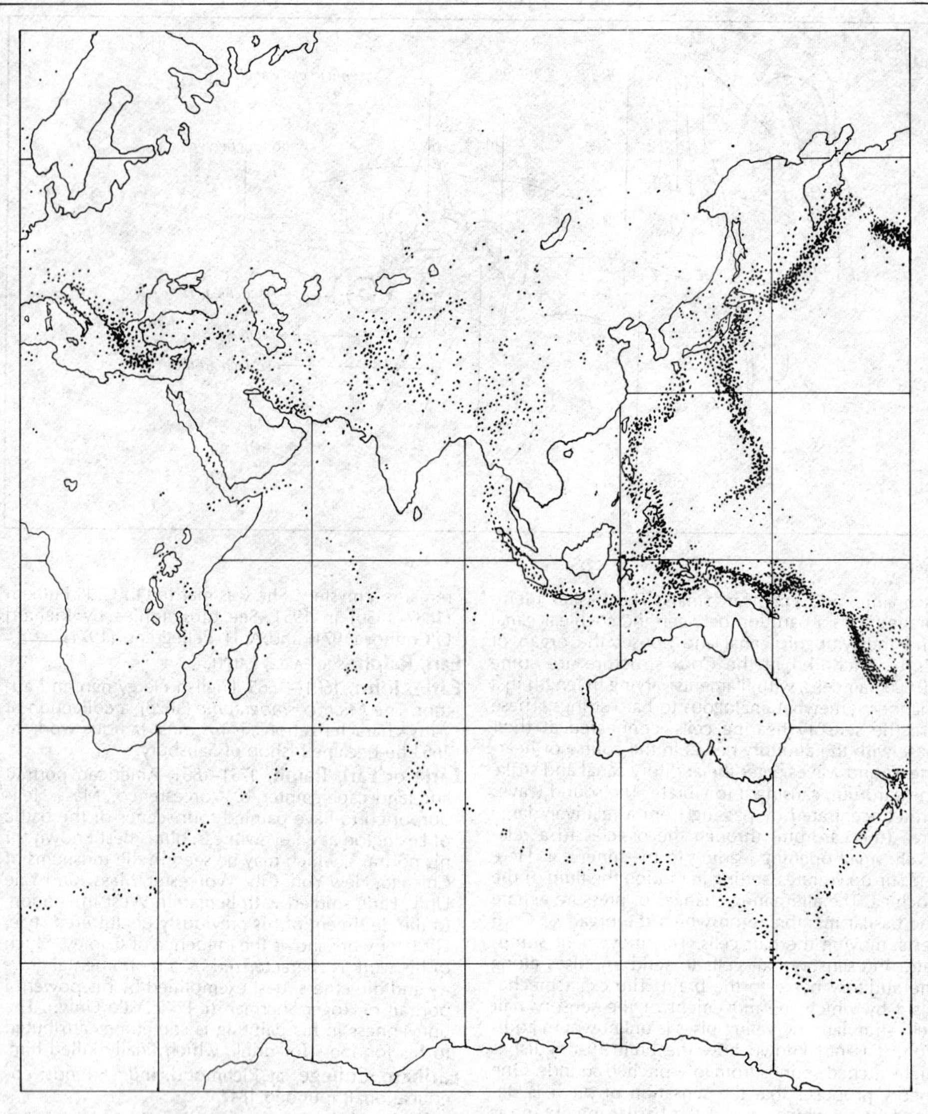

Worldwide pattern of earthquake activity: The dots indicate the epicenters of all earthquakes recorded during a recent 10-year period.

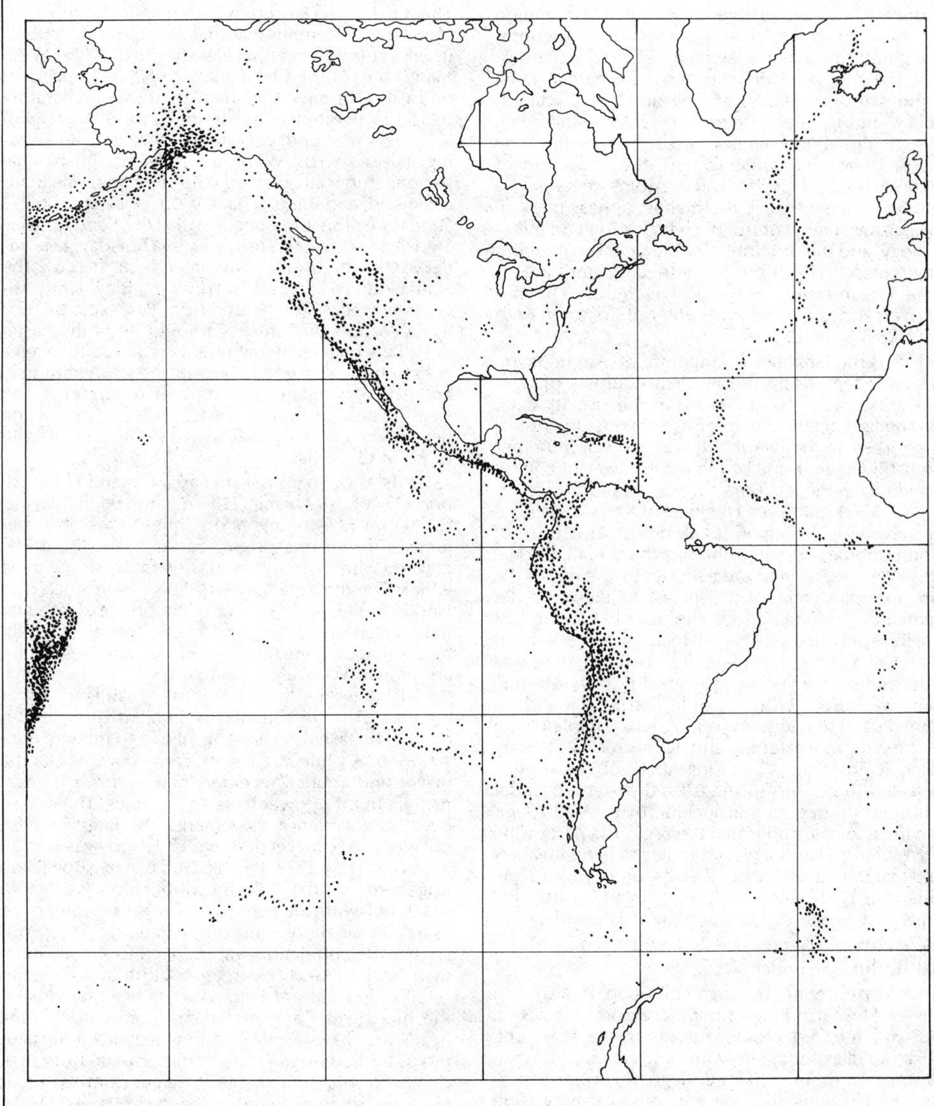

folds and faults (see PLATE TECTONICS). Thought to be composed of iron and nickel, the dense (c.11.0) core of the earth lies below the mantle. The abrupt disappearance of direct compressional earthquake waves, which cannot travel through liquids, at depths below c.1,800 mi (2,900 km) indicates that the outer 1,380 mi (2,200 km) of the core are molten. It is thought, however, that the inner 780 mi (1,260 km) of the core are solid. The earth is estimated to be 4.5 billion to 5 billion years old, based on radioactive dating of lunar rocks and meteorites, which are thought to have formed at the same time. The origin of the earth continues to be controversial. Among the theories as to its origin, the most prominent are gravitational condensation hypotheses, which suggest that the entire solar system was formed at one time in a single series of processes resulting in the accumulation of diffuse interstellar gases and dust into a solar system of discrete bodies. Older and now generally discredited theories invoked extraordinary events, such as the gravitational disruption of a star passing close to the sun or the explosion of a companion star to the sun. See A. W. Poldervaart, *Crust of the Earth* (1955); A. H. Cook and T. F. Gaskell, ed., *The Earth Today* (1961); Harold Jeffreys, *The Earth* (5th ed. 1970); John Guest, *The Earth and Its Satellite* (1971); A. N. Strahler, *The Earth Sciences* (2d ed. 1971); P. J. Wyllie, *The Dynamic Earth* (1971); I. G. Gass et al., ed., *Understanding the Earth* (1972); R. F. Flint, *The Earth and Its History* (1973).

earth, in chemistry, metallic oxide not readily reducible by chemical means, e.g., ALKALINE EARTHS, RARE EARTHS, and ALUMINA . The name is also applied to certain absorbent clays, e.g., FULLER'S EARTH, and to other compounds, e.g., carbonates, silicates, or hydroxides. Many earths were once thought to be ELEMENTS. A. L. Lavoisier was first to suspect that they might be compounds of more basic elements. Earth was one of the four "roots" of the Greek philosopher Empedocles, the other three being air, water, and fire. These substances were first called elements *(stoicheia)* by Plato.

earthenware, form of POTTERY fired at relatively low temperatures, so that the clay does not vitrify (become glassy), as do stoneware and porcelain clays. Occasionally, earthenware is used as a general term for all kinds of pottery.

earthflow: see LANDSLIDE.

earth goddess: see GREAT MOTHER OF THE GODS.

earth pig: see AARDVARK.

earthquake, trembling or shaking movement of the earth's surface. Great earthquakes usually begin with slight tremors, rapidly take the form of one or more violent shocks, and end in vibrations of gradually diminishing force. Most earthquakes are related to compressional or tensional stresses built up at the margins of the huge moving lithospheric plates that make up the earth's surface (see LITHOSPHERE). The immediate cause of most shallow earthquakes is the sudden release of stress along a FAULT, or fracture in the earth's crust, resulting in movement of the opposing blocks of rock past one another. These movements cause vibrations to pass through and around the earth in wave form, just as ripples are generated when a pebble is dropped into water. Volcanic eruptions, rockfalls, landslides, and explosions also result in earthquake vibrations, but most of these are of only local extent. The subterranean point of origin of an earthquake is called its focus; the point on the surface directly above the focus is the epicenter. The effects of the earthquake are strongest in a broad zone surrounding the epicenter; as the ordinary earthquake has several epicenters lying along the plane of the fault, the distribution of these effects shows great irregularity. Seismologists, scientists who deal with the analysis and interpretation of earthquake waves, have deduced the internal structure of the earth from analyses of changes that occur in earthquake waves travelling through the earth's interior (see EARTH). Body waves pass through the earth; they are of two basic types: P, or primary, waves, which are compressional and travel fastest; and S, or secondary, waves, which are transverse, i.e., they cause the earth to vibrate perpendicularly to the direction of their motion. S waves cannot pass through liquids. Waves that pass around the earth on its surface consist of several major types and are called L, or long, waves. They cause destruction near the epicenter because of their churning motion. Since the velocities of the P and S waves are affected by changes in the density and rigidity of the material through which they pass, the boundaries between the regions of the earth known as the crust, mantle, and core have been discerned. The disappearance of S waves below depths of 1,800 mi (2,900 km) indicates that at least the outer part of the earth's core is liquid. Seismographs (see SEISMOLOGY) are used to record P, S, and L waves; the magnitude and intensity of an earthquake is determined by the use of scales, e.g., the RICHTER SCALE and the Mercalli scale. Earthquakes cause uplift or subsidence of a land area and can trigger landslides and TSUNAMIS, all of which may cause loss of life and severe damage to property. The worst damage occurs in urban areas where the L waves can produce destructive vibrations in buildings and break water and gas lines, starting uncontrollable fires. Damage and loss of life results from falling chimneys and parapets and from flying glass. Flexible structures built on bedrock are generally more resistant to earthquake damage than rigid structures built on loose soil. Notable earthquakes have occurred at Lisbon (1755), at Charleston, S.C. (1886), in Assam prov., India (1897 and 1950), in California (1906), at Messina (1908), in Kansu prov., China (1920), in Japan (1923), in Chile (1960), and in Iran (1962). The Lisbon and Chilean earthquakes were accompanied by tsunamis. In 1963, 90% of the city of Skopje, Yugoslavia, was destroyed by a severe earthquake; the damage was so extensive that the government leveled the remaining buildings and began to erect a new city in its place. On Good Friday, 1964, the most severe North American earthquake ever recorded struck Alaska. Besides elevating some 70,000 sq mi (181,300 sq km) of land and devastating several cities, it generated tsunamis that caused damage as far S as California. In 1968 a still more powerful earthquake destroyed 2,000 dwellings in Hokkaido and N Honshu, Japan. In Feb., 1971, movement of the San Fernando fault near Los Angeles rocked the area for 10 sec, thrust parts of mountains 8 ft (2.4 m) upward, killed 64 persons, and caused damage amounting to 500 million dollars. Managua, the capital of Nicaragua, was almost totally destroyed, with great loss of life, by a severe earthquake that struck in Dec., 1972. It is estimated that in the last 4,000 years over 13 million deaths were caused by earthquakes. See PLATE TECTONICS. See D. L. Niddrie, *When the Earth Shook* (1961); W. M. Adams, *Earthquakes* (1964); H. A. Brown *Cataclysms of the Earth* (1967); see also bibliography under SEISMOLOGY.

earthworks, art form developed in the late 1960s and early 70s by Robert SMITHSON, Christo, Robert MORRIS, and others, in which the artist employs the elements of nature in situ. The resulting work, often vast in scale, is subject to all natural changes in temperature, light, wind, etc. Smithson's *Spiral Jetty* (1970), a huge spiral of rock and salt crystal in the middle of the Great Salt Lake, Utah, is a characteristic example of the earthwork form.

earthworm, terrestrial, cylindrical segmented worm of the class Oligochaeta. There are 2,200 earthworm species, found all over the world except in arid and arctic regions and ranging in size from 1 in. (2.5 cm) to the 11-ft (330-cm) giant worms of the tropics. Some earthworms are pallid in color, many are reddish brown to purple, and one Philippine species is bright blue. Earthworms burrow in the ground, swallowing soil from which the organic material is extracted and ground up in the gizzard and depositing the residue as castings outside the burrow. They come to the surface only on cloudy days and at night (hence the name night crawlers) unless they are flooded out by heavy rainfalls. In cold and dry weather they retreat into their burrows and remain dormant. The segments of the earthworm, visible externally as rings, are separated by internal partitions. On each segment are four pairs of bristles, or setae, with which the worm anchors itself to the walls of the burrow, drawing itself forward by rhythmic muscular contractions. There is a nerve cord, with ganglia in each segment and an enlarged cerebral ganglion (a primitive brain) at the anterior end. Although they have no prominent sense organs, earthworms are sensitive to light, touch, vibration, and chemicals. The circulatory system is enclosed in vessels; the blood (which contains hemoglobin) is pumped by muscular contractions of five linearly arranged hearts. Earthworms are hermaphroditic, but they cross-fertilize. Two worms exchange sperm cells during copulation; fertilization occurs after the worm's own eggs and the received sperm are encased in a tough sheath secreted by the clitellum, a conspicuous band of tissue near the anterior end. The sheath slips over the worm's head and is deposited underground, where it serves as a cocoon for the developing young. There is no larval stage; the young hatch as miniature adults. The common American and European earthworm, *Lumbricus terrestris*, up to 10 in. (25 cm) long, with about 150 segments, is used for laboratory dissection and study. Earthworms are also used as live bait and are eaten by some peoples—such as the Maoris, who consider certain species delicacies. The earthworm's greatest service, however, of immense importance to agriculture, is aerating and mixing the soil. Earthworm castings bring to the surface from 7 to 18 tons of soil per acre annually. This invaluable function of the earthworm was first pointed out in a detailed study by Charles Darwin. Earthworms are classified in the phylum ANNELIDA, class Oligochaeta, order Opisthopora.

earwig, common name for any of the smooth, elongated INSECTS of the order Dermaptera. Earwigs are small, with pairs of horny, forcepslike abdominal appendages, larger in the male than in the female, and short, leathery forewings that cover the membranous hindwings when folded. Some of the 900 species lack wings; the winged species rarely fly. Many tropical earwigs are brightly colored and carnivorous, even cannibalistic. The common earwig of temperate climates is native to Europe but has spread widely and seems destined to become cosmopolitan in distribution. Most species feed on plants and some are serious pests; others are predaceous or scavengers. The pincers of the male are used in courtship battles with other males. The female is unusual in that it guards its eggs and tends the young, which molt from 4 to 6 times during METAMORPHOSIS. The superstition that earwigs crawl through the ears and into the brains of sleeping persons probably derives from their nocturnal habits and the tarry or waxy odor of a secretion of their abdominal glands. A fossil earwig links the order to ancient cockroaches. Earwigs are classified in the phylum ARTHROPODA, class Insecta, order Dermaptera.

easement, in law, the right to use the land of another for a specified purpose, as distinguished from the right to possess that land. If the easement benefits the holder personally and is not associated with any land he owns, it is an easement in gross (e.g., a public utility's right to run power lines through another's property). At COMMON LAW an easement in gross could not be transferred, but today it may be transferable. If the easement is held incident to ownership of some land, it is an easement appurtenant (e.g., the right to run a ditch through a neighbor's yard to drain your land). The land subject to the easement appurtenant is the servient estate, the land benefited the dominant estate. If certain conditions are met, the easement passes with the land to the new owner after the sale of either estate. An easement may be created by express agreement of the parties, in which case it must usually be in writing (see FRAUDS, STATUTE OF), or it may be implied by a court from the actions of the parties in certain circumstances.

Easley, city (1970 pop. 11,175), Pickens co., NW S.C., in the foothills of the Blue Ridge Mts.; inc. 1874. Cotton is grown, and clothing, textiles, and textile machinery are manufactured there.

East, Edward Murray, 1879–1938, American biologist, b. Du Quoin, Ill., grad. Univ. of Illinois (B.S., 1900; Ph.D., 1907). He served the agricultural experiment stations at the Univ. of Illinois and in Connecticut, and from 1909 he was professor of experimental plant morphology and of genetics at Harvard. His researches—in part for the Dept. of Agriculture—on the genetics and breeding of corn, tobacco, and potatoes were especially valuable; he was instrumental in revolutionizing American corn growing by applying inbred strain breeding. His works include *Mankind at the Crossroads* (1923) and *Heredity and Human Affairs* (1927); he contributed to and edited *Biology in Human Affairs* (1931).

East African Community, association of Kenya, Tanzania, and Uganda; established 1967; headquarters at Arusha, Tanzania. The purpose of the community is to strengthen and regulate the industrial, commercial, and other relations among these countries and to foster accelerated and balanced development. The East African Common Market forms the main organ of the community. Within it the partner states have pledged to maintain a common customs and excise tariff, abolish trade restrictions, inaugurate a common agricultural policy, harmonize the monetary policies and commercial laws, coordinate economic planning and transportation policy; and to operate common services, including 11 agricultural and medical research institutes, one industrial research organization, the collection of income tax and excise and customs revenues, a court of appeal that is the highest appeal body in the partner states, control of civil aviation and meteorology, and the promotion of literacy. The community replaced (1962) the East African Common Services Organization. See Ingrid Doimi di Delupis, *The East African Community and the Common Market* (1969).

East Anglia (ăng'glēə), kingdom of Anglo-Saxon England, comprising the modern counties of Norfolk and Suffolk. It was settled in the late 5th cent. by Angles. Little is known of its early history, but its large size and the fact that it was protected by fens probably made it one of the most powerful English kingdoms in the late 6th cent. Raedwald of East Anglia (d. 627?) followed Æthelbert of Kent as overlord of S England. He helped EDWIN defeat ÆTHELFRITH of Northumbria and seize the Northumbrian throne. This brief ascendancy was eclipsed by the rise of the kingdom of Mercia, of which East Anglia was a dependency for long periods after 650. In 825 the East Anglians rebelled against Mercia, with the help of EGBERT of Wessex, but thereafter their kingdom was a dependency of Wessex. The great Danish invading army was quartered (865–66) in East Anglia and returned (869) to conquer the kingdom completely, to destroy its monasteries, and to murder its young ruler, St. Edmund. When King Alfred of Wessex first defeated the Danes in the 870s, they retired under Guthrum to an area that included East Anglia, and the treaty of 886 confirmed the region as part of the DANELAW. Its Danes gave aid to later Viking invaders and continued to harass Wessex until Edward the Elder finally defeated their army in 917. After that time, East Anglia was an earldom of England.

East Avon, river: see AVON **2,** river, England.

East Berlin: see under BERLIN.

Eastbourne, county borough (1971 pop. 70,495), East Sussex, SE England. It is a popular resort with a 3-mi (4.8-km) terraced promenade along the sea front. There are glass, soap, brewing, and boatbuilding industries. Eastbourne has a College of Further Education and teacher-training and physical-education colleges for women. Compton Place (1726–27), seat of the Dukes of Devonshire until 1954, is now a school.

East Cape: see CAPE DEZHNEV, USSR.

East Chicago, city (1970 pop. 46,982), Lake co., extreme NW Ind., on Lake Michigan, in the heavily industrialized Calumet region, adjoining Gary, Hammond, and Whiting; inc. 1889. It is the largest port in the state, and its Indiana Harbor on Lake Michigan is connected with the Grand Calumet River by a ship and barge canal. The city has important steelworks. There are also oil refineries, railroad equipment shops, and chemical plants. St. Joseph's College has a campus there.

East China Sea, arm of the Pacific Ocean, c.480,000 sq mi (1,243,200 sq km), bounded on the E by the Kyushu and Ryukyu islands, on the S by Taiwan, and on the W by China. It is connected with the South China Sea by the Formosa Strait and with the Sea of Japan by the Korea Strait; it opens in the N to the Yellow Sea. The Yangtze River empties into the sea, whose main ports are Shanghai, Hangchow, Ningpo, and Fu-chou, China; and Chi-lung, Taiwan.

East Cleveland, city (1970 pop. 39,600), Cuyahoga co., NE Ohio, a suburb of Cleveland; inc. 1911. Mostly residential, it is also the site of a General Electric lamp factory and research laboratory.

East Coolgardie Goldfield (ko͝olgär'dē), Western Australia, SW Australia. It is the richest gold field in Australia. The chief mining center is the town of Kalgoorlie. Coolgardie, of no importance today, was the first gold-rush town in the area. Gold was discovered there in 1892.

East Detroit, city (1970 pop. 45,920), Macomb co., SE Mich., a suburb of Detroit; inc. 1925 as Halfway village, renamed and inc. as a city 1929. It is mostly residential.

Easter [from Old Eng. EASTRE, name of a spring goddess], chief Christian feast, commemorating the resurrection of Jesus Christ after his crucifixion. In the West, Easter is celebrated on the Sunday following the full moon next after the vernal equinox (see CALENDAR); thus, it falls between March 22 and April 25. The Orthodox Eastern Church calculates Easter somewhat differently, so that the Orthodox Easter usually comes several weeks after that of the West. Many dates of the Christian calendar are dependent on Easter. For most Christians there is a preparatory period of penitence, beginning (in the West) with Septuagesima Sunday, 17 days before LENT, and ending in HOLY WEEK. With Easter begins the paschal season, liturgically marked with rejoicing; Alleluia is often said, and the paschal CANDLE is set up. The five Sundays of this time begin with Low Sunday. They are followed by Ascension Day (Thursday; see under ASCENSION) and, 10 days later, by PENTECOST. The Sunday after Pentecost is Trinity Sunday. Until Advent the weeks are counted from Pentecost or Trinity. A feature of Roman Catholic life is the Easter duty, by which every member is required to receive communion sometime between Ash Wednesday and Trinity Sunday. Painting and rolling eggs and wearing new clothes are Easter customs; there is no development of social festivities comparable with those of Christmas.

Easter Island, Span. *Isla de Pascua,* island (1970 est. pop. 1,600), 46 sq mi (119 sq km), South Pacific, c.2,200 mi (3,540 km) W of Chile, to which it belongs. Of volcanic origin, Easter Island is mostly covered with grasslands and is swept by strong trade winds. The inhabitants are of Polynesian stock. The land is fertile, and farming is the principal occupation; sheep are raised, and maize, sweet potatoes, figs, bananas, pineapples, melons, and vegetables are grown. Wool is the only export. Chile regards the island as an integral part of the mainland, not as a colony. The inhabitants are citizens of Chile but do not pay taxes and are not subject to military conscription. A Chilean naval officer is governor, and a mayor and council of elders have a voice in local matters but no power to raise revenues. There have been independence movements, the latest in 1964, but none has succeeded. Easter Island was named on Easter Day, 1722, by the Dutch navigator Jakob Roggeven. At that time the population was about 4,000, but with the spread of European epidemics, especially smallpox, and the marauding of Spanish slavers, the population was reduced to slightly more than 100 by 1887. Chilean annexation in 1888 led to stabilization. Easter Island has long been famous for the hieroglyphs and remarkable monolithic stone heads that have evoked various legends and theories as to their origins. The statues, carved from tufa, a soft volcanic stone, range in height from 10 to 40 ft (3–12 m), some weighing more than 50 tons. Of the various theories explaining the origin and culture of the builders of these monuments, the most recent is that of Thor HEYERDAHL, who holds that fair-skinned invaders from the East carved the monoliths, and that later (c.1680) the present Polynesians conquered the island, unleashing a period of violent strife. An interesting but highly controversial study of the island's riddles from a paleological and psychoanalytic point of view was presented in 1948 by the American psychologist Werner Wolff. A more conservative approach is evident in the excellent studies of the French ethnologist Alfred Métreaux, who maintains that the statues are no more than 500 to 600 years old and that they were built by the Polynesian ancestors of the present inhabitants. Métreaux also disputes several theories linking Easter Island petroglyphs and other inscriptions to Egyptian and ancient Hindu hieroglyphic systems. There is no evidence to support a belief, once widely held, that the island is a remnant of a "lost continent." Chile has declared the entire island a historic monument. See John Dos Passos, *Easter Island* (1971).

Eastern Church: see ORTHODOX EASTERN CHURCH.

Eastern Desert, Egypt: see ARABIAN DESERT.

Eastern Empire: see *Roman Empire* under ROME; BYZANTINE EMPIRE.

Eastern European Mutual Assistance Treaty: see WARSAW TREATY ORGANIZATION.

Eastern Ghats, mts., India: see GHATS.

Eastern Highlands, c.2,400 mi (3,860 km) long, general name for the mountains and plateaus roughly paralleling the east and southeast coasts of Australia (including Tasmania) and forming the Continental Divide (see GREAT DIVIDING RANGE); rises to Mt. Kosciusko (7,316 ft/2,230 m), Australia's highest peak. Rugged, with many gorges and few gaps, the Eastern Highlands long hindered Australia's westward expansion. The slopes are covered with eucalyptus forests. Rich in minerals, the highlands contain most of Australia's coalfields; gold, copper, tin, oil, and natural gas are also extracted. The southern part of the regio is a popular winter resort area. Major segments of the system are the Australian Alps, the New England Range, and the Blue Mts.

Eastern Michigan University, mainly at Ypsilanti, Mich.; coeducational; founded 1849 as a normal school, became Eastern Michigan College in 1956, gained university status in 1959. In 1964 a college of business was added to the three original colleges of arts and sciences, education, and the graduate school. The university maintains various extension centers throughout the state.

Eastern Question, term designating the problem of the fate of European territory controlled by the decaying OTTOMAN EMPIRE (Turkey) in the 18th, 19th, and early 20th cent. The Turkish threat to Europe was checked by the Hapsburgs in the 16th cent., but the Ottoman Turks still controlled the Balkan Peninsula. With the Treaty of Karlowitz (1699), the disintegration of the Ottoman Empire started, and Russia began to push toward the Black Sea. In the 18th cent. France supported the Turks against Russia and Austria. The Eastern Question came into sharp focus during the reign of Czarina CATHERINE II with the first two of the RUSSO-TURKISH WARS (1768-74, 1787-92). At this stage Russia, in alliance with Austria, planned the partition of the Ottoman Empire. Constantinople was the chief prize coveted by Russia, which lacked an adequate warm-water outlet to the sea. These designs aroused alarm in Prussia and, more especially, in Great Britain, which saw its dominance in the Mediterranean threatened by Russian ambitions. (Later it was the strategic importance of the Suez Canal that most concerned Britain.) The formation of a diplomatic alliance by Great Britain, Prussia, and the Netherlands and the Austrian defeats at the hands of the Turks offset Russian successes; yet the first stage of the struggle, terminating with the Treaty of Jassy (1792), left Russia with a foothold on the north shore of the Black Sea. During the Napoleonic era, when attention shifted elsewhere, Russia, after another war with Turkey, again secured favorable terms in the Treaty of Bucharest (1812). Russian conquests against Persia and in the Caucasus were confirmed in the treaties of GULISTAN (1813) and TURKAMANCHAI (1828). These developments and the outbreak of national aspirations among the oppressed peoples of the Balkans again made the Eastern Question a major European problem. The Holy Alliance was committed to defending the territorial integrity of Turkey, but the rival imperialistic interests of the Great Powers, each of which hoped to profit from Ottoman disintegration, soon caused the abandonment of this principle. In the Greek War of Independence (1821-30), both England and Russia assisted the Greek insurgents, each trying to impose its influence on the newly formed state. The Russo-Turkish War of 1828-29, connected with the Greek war, ended successfully for Russia (see ADRIANOPLE, TREATY OF), but the subsequent Russian assistance to Turkey against MUHAMMAD ALI of Egypt, followed by a Russo-Turkish alliance (1833), greatly disquieted Britain and France. Still, the five Great Powers (Britain, France, Russia, Austria, and Prussia) acted in concert in the final settlement of the Egyptian question, and a treaty signed (1840) in London offered international guarantees of the Ottoman Empire's integrity. In 1853, however, rivalry among Britain, France and Russia brought on the CRIMEAN WAR. The treaty that ended it (see PARIS, CONGRESS OF) attempted to deprive Russia of pretexts for intervention, to check Russia's naval power on the Black Sea, and to place the empire under international protection. But Turkey had become the "sick man of Europe," and its disintegration could not be arrested. Events in BOSNIA AND HERCEGOVINA once more led to a Russo-Turkish War (1877-78); the Treaty of SAN STEFANO was so favorable to Russia that Britain went to the verge of war to compel a revision. The congress (see BERLIN, CONGRESS OF) that revised the Treaty of San Stefano marked a setback for Russian influence but created fresh problems. The new Balkan states, dissatisfied with their borders, turned to the individual great powers to back their claims. Austria, allied with Russia in the late 18th cent., had come to fear Russian influence in the Balkans; after its defeat by Prussia in 1866, it had joined in an alliance with Germany (see TRIPLE ALLIANCE AND TRIPLE ENTENTE). Germany, which had assumed the role of "honest broker" at the Congress of Berlin, became increasingly interested in extending its influence over the Ottoman Empire. The German-Austrian *Drang nach Osten* [drive to the East] policy became manifest in the reorganization of the Turkish army by German officers, the construction of BAGHDAD RAILWAY, the crisis over MOROCCO, and the Austrian annexation (1908) of Bosnia and Hercegovina. Russian PAN-SLAVISM in the Balkans and the almost total disappearance of European Turkey in the BALKAN WARS caused Turkey to seek German and Austrian support and to join the Central Powers after the outbreak of World War I. The war destroyed the Ottoman Empire and closed the old Eastern Question, but the problem of maintaining stability in the area once ruled by the empire remained. See Sir J. A. Marriott, *The Eastern Question* (4th rev. ed. 1941, repr. 1956); M. S. Anderson, *The Eastern Question, 1774-1923* (1966) and *The Great Powers and the Near East, 1774-1923* (1970).

Eastern Rumelia: see RUMELIA.

Eastern Turkistan: see SINKIANG.

Easter Rebellion: see IRELAND.

East Flanders, Flemish *Oost-Vlaanderen* (ōst-vlän'dərən), Fr. *Flandre Orientale,* province (1970 pop. 1,310,117), 1,147 sq mi (2,971 sq km), NW Belgium, bordering on the Netherlands in the north. The chief towns are Ghent (the capital), Sint-Niklaas, Aalst, and Oudenaarde. The low-lying province is drained by the Scheldt, Dender, and Leie rivers. It has productive farms and growing industries. Manufactures include textiles and steel. The population is mostly Flemish speaking. For the history of East Flanders, see FLANDERS.

East Friesland (frēz'lənd), Ger. *Ostfriesland,* region and former duchy, c.1,100 sq mi (2,850 sq km), Lower Saxony, NW West Germany, on the North Sea. It includes the East FRISIAN ISLANDS and is separated in the west from the Netherlands by the Dollart, an inlet of the North Sea formed by the Ems estuary. Emden, a port and shipbuilding center, is the region's chief city. The extensive moors and marshlands of East Friesland have been partly reclaimed. Cattle raising, sheep raising, and farming are carried on, and there are fisheries along the coastline. East Friesland became a county of the Holy Roman Empire in 1454, was raised to a duchy in 1654, passed to Prussia in 1744, and—after various transfers during the French Revolutionary Wars—was attached to Hanover in 1815.

East Grand Rapids, city (1970 pop. 12,565), Kent co., SW Mich., a residential suburb of Grand Rapids; inc. 1926.

East Ham: see NEWHAM.

Easthampton, town (1970 pop. 13,012), Hampshire co., W Mass.; inc. 1809. It is primarily a manufacturing town with diversified light industry. Easthampton was settled in 1664. In the 1820s, Samuel Williston founded the town's textile industry. Williston Academy, a boys' preparatory school located in Easthampton, is named for him.

East Hartford, town (1970 pop. 57,583), Hartford co., central Conn., on the Connecticut River opposite Hartford; settled c.1640, inc. 1783. East Hartford is a major trucking and warehousing center. Tobacco is grown and processed and bulk oil is stored and distributed there. Fabricated steel, precision parts, aircraft engines, appliances, brushes, and candy are the chief manufactures.

East Haven, town (1970 pop. 25,120), New Haven co., S Conn., on Long Island Sound, a residential suburb of New Haven, in a farm area; inc. 1785. Points of interest include an early 18th-century stone church and a trolley museum.

East India Company, British, 1600-1874, company chartered by Queen Elizabeth I for trade with Asia. The original object of the group of merchants involved was to break the Dutch monopoly of the spice trade with the East Indies. However, after 1623, when the English traders at Amboina were massacred by the Dutch, the company admitted defeat in that endeavor and concentrated its activities in India. It had established its first factory at Masulipatam in 1611, and it gradually acquired unequaled trade privileges from the Mogul emperors. Although the company was soon reaping large profits from its Indian exports (chiefly textiles), it had to deal with serious difficulties both in England and in India. During the 17th cent. its monopoly of Indian trade was constantly challenged by independent English traders called "interlopers." In 1698 a rival company was actually chartered, but the conflict was resolved by a merger of the two companies in 1708. By that time the company had established in India the three presidencies of Madras, Bombay, and Calcutta. As Mogul power declined, these settlements became subject to increasing harassment by local princes, and the company began to protect itself by intervening more and more in Indian political affairs. It had, moreover, a serious rival in the French East India Company, which under Joseph François DUPLEIX launched an aggressive policy of expansion. The victories (1751-60) of Robert CLIVE over the French made the company dominant in India, and by a treaty of 1765 it assumed control of the administration of Bengal. Revenues from Bengal were used for trade and for personal enrichment. To check the exploitative practices of the company and to gain a share of revenues, the British government intervened and passed the Regulating Act (1773), by which a governor general of Bengal (whose appointment was subject to government approval) was given charge of all the company's possessions in India. Warren HASTINGS, the first governor general, laid the administrative foundations for subsequent British consolidation. By the East India Act of 1784 the government assumed more direct responsibility for British activities in India, setting up a board of control for India. The company continued to control commercial policy and lesser administration, but the British government became increasingly the effective ruler of India. Parliamentary acts of 1813 and 1833 ended the company's trade monopoly. Finally, after the INDIAN MUTINY of 1857-58 the government assumed direct control, and the East India Company was dissolved. See studies by Beckles Willson (1903), Holden Furber (1948, repr. 1970), Lucy Sutherland (1952), and Brian Gardner (1972).

East India Company, Dutch, 1602-1798, chartered by the States-General of the Netherlands to expand trade and assure close relations between the government and its colonial enterprises in Asia. The company was granted a monopoly on Dutch trade E of the Cape of Good Hope and W of the Strait of Magellan. From its headquarters at Batavia (founded 1619) the company subdued local rulers, drove the British and Portuguese from Indonesia, Malaya, and Ceylon, and arrogated to itself the fabulous trade of the Spice Islands. A colony, established (1652) in South Africa at the Cape of Good Hope, remained Dutch until conquered by Great Britain in 1814. The company was dissolved when it became scandalously corrupt and nearly insolvent in the late 18th cent., and its possessions became part of the Dutch colonial empire in the Far East. See Albert Hyma, *The Dutch in the Far East* (1942, repr. 1953); study by Brian Gardner (1972).

East India Company, French, 1664-1769, commercial enterprise planned by Jean Baptiste Colbert and chartered by King Louis XIV for the purpose of trading in the Eastern Hemisphere. It failed to found a colony on Madagascar but established ports on the nearby islands of Bourbon and Île-de-France (now Réunion and Mauritius). By 1719 the company had established itself in India but was near bankruptcy. In that year it was combined under John LAW with other French trading companies to make the Compagnie des Indes (see MISSISSIPPI SCHEME). It resumed independence in 1723. With the decline of the Mogul empire, the French found it necessary to intervene in Indian political affairs to protect their interests. From 1741 the French under Joseph François DUPLEIX pursued an aggressive policy against both the Indians and the English until they ultimately suffered defeat by Robert CLIVE. Despite its apparent success, the French company had never been able to maintain itself financially, and in 1769 it was abolished.

East Indies, name used primarily for Indonesia, but also more widely to include SE Asia. It once referred chiefly to India.

East Kilbride, town (1971 pop. 63,505), Lanarkshire, S central Scotland. Established in 1946 under the New Towns Act to absorb the growing population of GLASGOW, East Kilbride has engineering works and manufactures automobile and aircraft engines, textiles, and electronic equipment. There is a center for engineering research in the town. In 1975, East Kilbride became part of the new Strathclyde region.

Eastlake, city (1970 pop. 19,690), Lake co., NE Ohio, a suburb of Cleveland, on the Chagrin River and Lake Erie; inc. 1949. It has diversified light manufacturing industries.

East Lansing, city (1970 pop. 47,540), Ingham co., S central Mich., a suburb of Lansing, on the Red Cedar River; inc. 1907. It is a residential city and the seat of Michigan State Univ.

Eastleigh, municipal borough (1971 pop. 45,320), Hampshire, S central England; inc. 1936. Its industries include workshops for the British Railways and two large cable factories.

East Liverpool, industrial city (1970 pop. 20,020), Columbiana co., NE Ohio, on the Ohio River near the Pa. and W.Va. borders; settled 1798 as St. Clair, called Fawcett's Town until its incorporation as East Liverpool in 1834. Extensive clay deposits in the area are used in making pottery, brick, and tile. A ceramics center since about 1839, it has a museum housing a historical pottery collection.

East London, city (1970 pop. 118,298), Cape Prov., SE South Africa, on the Indian Ocean. The city grew around a British military post founded in 1847. Its harbor was developed from 1886, and today it is a leading South African port. The main exports are maize, wool, and fruit. East London's manufactures include automobiles, furniture, textiles, clothing, footwear, processed food, and glass. There is a large fishing industry. The city is also a popular seaside resort. East London Museum and a technical college are in the city.

East Longmeadow, town (1970 pop. 13,029), Hampden co., SW Mass., a suburb of Springfield; settled c.1740, set off from Longmeadow and inc. 1894. It is chiefly residential, with some manufacturing industries.

East Lothian (lō'thēən), formerly **Haddingtonshire** or **Haddington,** county (1971 pop. 55,891), 267 sq mi (691 sq km), SE Scotland. The county town is HADDINGTON. In the south are the Lammermuir Hills, which slope gently down to the Firth of Forth on the north. The Tyne is the chief river. The rich lowlands are extensively cultivated (wheat, barley, and potatoes), and the highlands are devoted to sheep grazing. There is fishing, coal mining, and distilling. The county was part of the Anglo-Saxon kingdom of NORTHUMBRIA. It suffered severely in the border warfare (13th-16th cent.) between England and Scotland. Under the Local Government Act of 1973, East Lothian became (1975) part of the Lothian region.

East Lyme (līm), town (1970 pop. 11,399), New London co., SE Conn., on Long Island Sound; settled c.1660, inc. 1839. The town has light diversified industry. Its many colonial houses include the Thomas Lee House (c.1660), which has been restored. A state park is on the Sound.

Eastmain (ēst'mān), river, c.510 mi (820 km) long, rising in the Otish Mts., central Que., Canada, and flowing W into James Bay. Three miles (4.8 km) from its mouth is East Main (founded 1685), one of the oldest Hudson's Bay Company posts.

East Malaysia: see MALAYSIA, FEDERATION OF.

Eastman, George, 1854-1932, American inventor, industrialist, and philanthropist, b. Waterville, N.Y. By mass production of his photographic inventions, Eastman enormously stimulated the development of photography as a popular hobby. He invented a dry-plate process and established (1880) a factory at Rochester, N.Y., for making the plates; he devised a roll film and the Kodak camera (1888) to use it, as well as a process for color photography (1928). The Eastman Kodak Company, founded in 1892, was one of the first firms in America to establish a plant for large-scale production of a standardized product and to maintain a fine chemical laboratory; its progressive welfare program included a profit-sharing plan. Eastman's philanthropies were estimated at over $100 million: the principal recipients were the Univ. of Rochester and the Eastman School of Music, Massachusetts Institute of Technology, Tuskegee and Hampton institutes, Rochester Dental Dispensary, and dental clinics in several European capitals. In 1932 after a long illness Eastman committed suicide. See biography by C. W. Ackerman (1930, repr. 1973).

Eastman, Joseph Bartlett, 1882-1944, U.S. government administrator, b. Katonah, N.Y. President Wilson appointed him in 1919 to the Interstate Commerce Commission. As Federal coordinator of railroads (1933-36), director of the Office of Defense Transportation (1941-44), and a member of the War Production Board, Eastman showed great ability at mobilizing transportation for the good of the nation. At first an advocate of government ownership of railroads, he later modified his views. See his *Selected Papers and Addresses,* ed. by G. L. Wilson (1948); biography by C. M. Fuess (1952); study by Earl Latham (1959).

Eastman, Max, 1883-1969, American author, b. Canandaigua, N.Y., grad. Williams, 1905. For many years a Communist and a leader of American liberal thought, he edited the left-wing periodicals *The Masses* (1913-17) and the *Liberator* (1918-23). His eventual disillusionment with Communism is reflected in such works as *Marxism, Is It Science?* (1940), *Stalin's Russia* (1940), and *Reflections on the Failure of Socialism* (1955). His other works include *Enjoyment of Poetry* (1913), his most popular work; *Enjoyment of Laughter* (1936); and *Poems of Five Decades* (1954). Among his autobiographical works is *Love and Revolution* (1965).

Eastman School of Music: see ROCHESTER, UNIV. OF.

East Massapequa (măsəpēk'wə), uninc. town (1970 pop. 15,926), Nassau co., SE N.Y., on the south shore of Long Island. It is chiefly residential.

East Meadow, uninc. residential city (1970 pop. 46,290), Nassau co., SE N.Y., on W Long Island.

East Moline (mōlēn'), city (1970 pop. 20,832), Rock Island co., NW Ill., an industrial suburb of Moline, on the Mississippi River; inc. 1907. East Moline, Moline, Rock Island, and Davenport, Iowa, are known as the Quad Cities. Farm equipment is made in East Moline. A junior college and a state hospital are in the city.

East Northport, uninc. residential town (1970 pop. 12,392), Suffolk co., SE N.Y., on the north shore of Long Island. A U.S. hospital is there.

Easton. 1 Town (1970 pop. 12,157), Bristol co., E. Mass., in a farm area; settled 1694, inc. 1725. It has a foundry and assorted manufactures. Stonehill College is in suburban North Easton. **2** Industrial city (1970 pop. 30,256), seat of Northampton co., E. Pa., at the junction of the Delaware and Lehigh rivers; founded 1751 by Thomas Penn, inc. as a city 1886. Cement, paper products, electronic equipment, machinery, and steel are among its manufactures. Indian conferences were held there in 1756 and 1761. During canal days Easton was a coal-receiving port in the Pennsylvania Dutch region. Lafayette College, the First United Church of Christ (1776), and the house (1757) of George Taylor, a signer of the Declaration of Independence, are in the city. A park has been constructed along the banks of the old Lehigh Canal. There is a canal museum in the city.

East Orange, city (1970 pop. 75,471), Essex co., NE N.J.; settled 1678, separated from Orange and inc. 1863. A residential city adjacent to Newark, it is the seat of Upsala College.

East Pakistan: see BANGLADESH; PAKISTAN.

East Paterson, borough (1970 pop. 20,511), Bergen co., NE N.J., an industrial suburb of Paterson, on the Passaic River; inc. 1916.

East Peoria, city (1970 pop. 18,455), Tazewell co., N central Ill., on the Illinois River opposite Peoria; inc. 1919. It is a rail and warehousing center for central Illinois. Tractors, earth-moving machinery, and diesel engines are made. A junior college and a U.S. coast guard base are there.

East Point, city (1970 pop. 39,315), Fulton co., NW Ga., an industrial suburb of Atlanta; inc. 1887. Textiles, machinery, fertilizer, chemicals, and paper are among the manufactures. Atlanta Christian College is in East Point.

East Providence, city (1970 pop. 48,151), Providence co., E R.I., on the Providence and Seekonk rivers; inc. as a city 1958. A wholesale and distribution center for petroleum products in the S New England area, East Providence is also the site of factories producing metal goods and machinery. Originally part of Massachusetts, it was organized as a town of Rhode Island in 1862.

East Prussia, Ger. *Ostpreussen,* former province of Prussia, extreme NE Germany. From 1919 to 1939 it was separated from the rest of Germany by the Polish Corridor and the Free City of Danzig (Gdańsk). Königsberg (Kaliningrad) was the capital. East Prussia bordered on Poland and Lithuania in the south and east and stretched to Memel and the Baltic Sea in the north and northeast. In 1945, at the end of World War II, East Prussia was overrun by Soviet troops and about 600,000 of its inhabitants were killed. At the Potsdam Conference (1945), East Prussia was divided by two transfers; the transfers were made permanent by treaties between West Germany and Poland and the USSR that were signed and ratified between 1970 and 1972. The northern part was assigned at Potsdam to the USSR; it includes the cities of Kaliningrad, Sovetsk (Tilsit), Chernyakhovsk (Insterburg), Gusev (Gumbinnen), and Baltiysk (Pilau). The rest was incorporated into Poland as Olsztyn province; this part includes the cities of Olsztyn (Allenstein), Malbork (Marienburg), and Elbląg (Elbing). Most Germans who had not left by the end of the war were expelled by the Polish and Soviet governments shortly after its end. The region of East Prussia has low rolling hills that are heavily wooded, and it is dotted by many lakes (especially in MASURIA). The region is drained by several rivers including the Nemen (Nieman); the Baltic coast is deeply indented by the Vistula Lagoon (Frisches Haff) and by the Gulf of Kursh (Kurisches Haff). In the 13th cent. the TEUTONIC KNIGHTS conquered the region of East Prussia from the Borussi, or Prussians (a people related to the Liths), displaced the original population, and secured the territory as a fief for their order. In 1309, Malbork became the headquarters of the grand master of the Teutonic Knights. In 1466, by the Peace of Torun, the knights ceded Pomerelia (later a part of WEST PRUSSIA) and ERMELAND to Poland and accepted Polish suzereinty over the rest of their domain. In 1525, Grand Master ALBERT OF BRANDENBURG, after secularizing the Teutonic order, took the title "duke of Prussia," remaining under Polish suzerainty. The duchy was inherited (1618) by the elector of Brandenburg. Frederick William, the Great Elector, won full sovereignty over the duchy at the Peace of OLIVA (1660), and in 1701 his son, Frederick III, had himself crowned "king in Prussia" as Frederick I at Königsberg. East Prussia, as the original Prussia came to be called, from 1701 to 1945 shared the history of PRUSSIA. It remained the stronghold of the Prussian landowning and military aristocracy—the Junkers—whose immense estates took up a large part of the province.

East Ridge, town (1970 pop. 21,799), Hamilton co., SE Tenn., a residential suburb of Chattanooga, near the Ga. border; inc. 1921.

East Riding, England: see YORKSHIRE.

East River, tidal strait, 16 mi (26 km) long and 600-4,000 ft (183-1,219 m) wide, connecting Upper New York Bay and Long Island Sound, New York City, and separating the boroughs of Manhattan and the Bronx from Brooklyn and Queens. The East River is linked with the Hudson River at the northern end of Manhattan island by the Harlem River. Roosevelt (formerly Welfare), Wards, Randalls, Rikers, North Brother, and South Brother islands, all located in the East River, have city institutions, parks, and recreation areas. Roosevelt Island was developed as a residential area in the early 1970s. Hell Gate, at the junction of the Harlem and East rivers, was named for its treacherous currents and rocky reefs (now removed). Eight bridges, including the historic Brooklyn Bridge, span the river; subway, railroad, and vehicular tunnels pass beneath it. The New York Naval Shipyard (Brooklyn Navy Yard) was located on the southeastern side of the river from 1801 until 1969, at which time it became a commercial shipyard.

East Rockaway, village (1970 pop. 10,323), Nassau co., SE N.Y., on SW Long Island; settled c.1688, inc. 1900. It is mostly residential with light manufacturing.

East Saint Louis (lo͞o'ĭs), city (1970 pop. 69,996), St. Clair co., SW Ill., on the Mississippi River opposite St. Louis, with which it is connected by five bridges; inc. 1859. It is an important transportation hub, industrial center, and livestock market, with large railroad yards and repair shops, warehouses, and important stockyards (opened 1873). East St. Louis has major chemical and meat-packing industries and factories that produce a great variety of products, chiefly those using the clay, stone, and silica of the area. The first settlement there was in 1765. Cahokia Creek was bridged in 1795, and a ferry across the Mississippi began operation shortly thereafter. The city was plagued by devastating floods until its first dike was completed in 1909. The Old Cathedral (1834) and Old Courthouse (1839) have been preserved. A large state park is adjacent to the city. Just northeast are the CAHOKIA MOUNDS.

East Suffolk, England: see SUFFOLK.

East Sussex, nonmetropolitan county (1972 est. pop. 650,000), extreme SE England, created under the Local Government Act of 1972 (effective 1974). It is composed of the county boroughs of BRIGHTON, EASTBOURNE, and HASTINGS, and parts of the former county of East Sussex.

East Turkistan: see SINKIANG.

Eastview: see VANIER, town, Canada.

Eaton, Amos, 1776-1842, American naturalist, b. Chatham, N.Y., grad. Williams College, 1799. After practicing law for a time, he conducted pioneer geological surveys in Albany and Rensselaer counties, N.Y. (1820-21), and along the Erie Canal (1822-23). His report on the canal was published in 1824. He then became professor at the scientific school opened by Stephen Van Rensselaer (1824) in Troy, N.Y. (now Rensselaer Polytechnic Institute). Besides a number of textbooks, he wrote the *Manual of Botany* (1817; 8th ed., with John Wright, *North American Botany,* 1840) and *An Index to the Geology of the Northern States* (1818). See biography by E. M. McAllister (1941).

Eaton, Dorman Bridgman, 1823-99, American reformer, b. Hardwick, Vt. He was a law partner of William Kent in New York City. His major interests were reform in municipal administration and abolition of the spoils system in national politics. He drafted the Metropolitan Health Law, passed in 1866, which gave New York City its present health department, and drafted bills organizing the New York City fire and dock departments and reorganizing the police department. In 1873 he became chairman of the National Civil Service Commission and with George W. Curtis and Carl Schurz led in gaining support for civil service reform. He drafted the Pendleton Act of 1883, which has remained the basis of the Federal civil service system.

Eaton, John, 1829–1906, American educator, b. Sutton, N.H., grad. Dartmouth, 1854. After serving as a school principal in Cleveland, Ohio, and as superintendent of schools in Toledo, he enrolled at Andover Theological Seminary in 1859. During the Civil War, he served as a chaplain in the Union army and was brevetted brigadier general for his work in caring for the Negroes who entered the Union lines. After the war, as editor of the Memphis *Post* and as Tennessee superintendent of schools (1867–69), he was a strong advocate of free public schools. Appointed (1870) U.S. commissioner of education, he won public and congressional support for the Bureau of Education, which he directed until 1886. Afterward he served (1886–91) as president of Marietta College and in 1899–1900 was in charge of the school system of Puerto Rico.

Eaton, John Henry, 1790–1856, U.S. Senator (1818–29) and Secretary of War (1829–31), b. Halifax co., N.C. After being admitted to the bar, he practiced in Franklin, Tenn., and married Myra Lewis, a ward of Andrew Jackson. Eaton remained close to Jackson and completed (1817) the biography of Jackson begun by John Reid. He was appointed (1818) to the Senate to fill a vacancy and defended Jackson's earlier activities in Florida. Twice elected (1821, 1826) to the Senate, Eaton resigned in 1829 to enter the cabinet. The refusal of Washington society to accept Eaton's second wife (see Margaret O'NEILL) helped to disrupt Jackson's cabinet and led to Eaton's resignation. He was governor (1834–36) of Florida, then was minister (1836–40) to Spain. His refusal to support Van Buren ended his political career.

Eaton, Theophilus, 1590–1658, Puritan leader in Connecticut, one of the founders of New Haven, b. Buckinghamshire, England. A member of the London congregation of John DAVENPORT, he was interested in the Massachusetts Bay Company and other Puritan colonial ventures. In 1637 he went with Davenport and others to Boston, and later that year he led an exploring party that chose the site of a new colony. A small band was left to winter there, and the next spring settlers came, and New Haven was founded. Eaton was the governor and a leading figure of the New Haven colony until his death and was supposedly the chief drafter of the law code of 1656. He was much interested in trade and promoted the unsuccessful attempts of New Haven to found a colony on the Delaware.

Eaton, William, 1764–1811, U.S. army officer, celebrated for his exploit in the Tripolitan War, b. Woodstock, Conn. Captain Eaton was sent to Tunis as consul in 1798 and learned much about the BARBARY STATES. When he returned to the United States in 1804, he had a scheme to win the war against Tripoli by supporting the claimant to the rule of Tripoli, Hamet Karamanli. Somewhat reluctantly, Congress appointed him "navy agent to the Barbary States" and allowed him to try his plan. In Egypt, Eaton persuaded the claimant to undertake the venture and gathered a mixed army of 400 men, including Greeks, Italians, Arabs, and others. With this small band he set off on the long march overland to take Tripoli from the rear, took the seaport of Derna, and might have taken Tripoli if the TRIPOLITAN WAR had not ended with a truce (1805) before he arrived. See biography by F. R. Rodd (1932) and N. B. Gerson (1968); L. B. Wright and J. H. Macleod, *The First Americans in North Africa* (1945, repr. 1969).

Eatontown, borough (1970 pop. 14,619), Monmouth co., E central N.J.; inc. 1926. A residential borough in a truck-farming region, it is named for Thomas Eaton, who built a gristmill there c.1670. The mill's site is now a landmark. Fort Monmouth (est. 1917), a U.S. army base, is in Eatontown.

Eau Claire (ō klâr), city (1970 pop. 44,619), seat of Eau Claire co., W central Wis., on the Chippewa at the mouth of the Eau Claire River, in a hilly lake region; inc. 1872. Manufactures include defense items, kitchen appliances, tires, paper products, and dairy goods. A trading port was there in the late 18th cent. The city grew from several sawmills established on the Eau Claire River in the mid 1800s. It is the seat of the Univ. of Wisconsin at Eau Claire and has a state fish hatchery.

eau de Cologne (ō də kəlōn'), dilute perfume [commonly called cologne in English] introduced c.1709 in Cologne, Germany, by Jean Marie Farina. It was probably a modification of a popular formula made before 1700 by Paul Feminis, an Italian in Cologne, and was based on bergamot and other citrus oils. The water of Cologne was believed to have the power to ward off bubonic plague.

Ebal (ē'bəl). **1** Seirite. Gen. 36.23; 1 Chron. 1.40. **2** The same as OBAL.

Ebal, Mount, Arabic *Jabal Aybal,* 3,084 ft (940 m) high, in the Samarian hills, NW Jordan. On Ebal, according to the Bible, the curses due for the violations of God's commands were delivered. There also, Joshua built the altar and monument inscribed with the Mosaic law. (Deut. 11.29; 27.4, 13; Joshua 8.30–33.)

Eban, Abba (äb'ə ē'bən), 1915–, Israeli statesman, b. Cape Town, South Africa. He was educated at Cambridge Univ., where he became (1938) a lecturer in Oriental literature. During World War II he rose to the rank of major in the British army. In the years preceding Israel's independence, Eban was chief instructor (1944–46) at the Middle Eastern Center for Arab Studies in Jerusalem and worked at the Jewish Agency for Palestine before commencing (1947) his diplomatic career as liaison officer to the UN Special Committee on Palestine. In 1948 he became Israel's charter UN representative and served concurrently as ambassador to the United States from 1950 until his election to the Knesset (Israeli parliament) in 1959. He held various cabinet positions before becoming foreign minister in 1966. In that office he strove for closer ties with the United States and Western Europe. He resigned in 1974 with Golda Meir.

Ebbw Vale (ĕb'o͞o), urban district (1971 pop. 26,049), Monmouthshire, SE Wales. It is an industrial center with steelworks, tin-plate factories, and collieries. Aneurin Bevan, a Labour party leader, was born in Ebbw Vale.

Ebed (ē'bĕd). **1** Father of GAAL. **2** One who returned with Ezra. Ezra 8.6.

Ebed-melech (ēbĕd'-mēlĕk', ē'bĕd-mē'-) [Heb.,= king's slave], King Zedekiah's Ethiopian eunuch through whom Jeremiah was freed from prison. Jer. 38.7–12; 39.17. The name may be a title.

Eben-ezer (ĕb'ən-ē'zər) [Heb.,=stone of help]. **1** Stone set up (near Shen) by Samuel to commemorate the victory over the Philistines. 1 Sam. 7.12. **2** Site of the battle where the Philistines captured the Ark. 1 Sam. 4.1; 5.1.

Eber (ē'bər), variant of HEBER **1.**

Eberhard (ā'bərhärt), d. 939, duke of Franconia; brother of the German king, Conrad I, whom he succeeded as duke. The first to rebel against the centralizing policy of Holy Roman Emperor OTTO I, he was an important member of the successive coalitions against Otto. After Eberhard's death at the battle of Andernach, Otto seized his duchy.

Eberhart, Richard, 1904–, American poet, b. Austin, Minn., grad. Dartmouth (1926) and Cambridge (1929). His poetry, noted for its simplicity and directness, has as a frequent theme the loss of innocence and spontaneity. Among his volumes of poetry are *A Bravery of Earth* (1930), *Burr Oaks* (1947), *Undercliff* (1953), *Collected Poems* (1960), *Selected Poems* (1966), *Shifts of Being* (1968), and *Fields of Grace* (1972). His *Collected Verse Plays* was published in 1962.

Eberle, Abastenia St. Leger (ĕb'ərlē), 1878–1942, American sculptor, b. Webster City, Iowa, studied at the Art Students League, New York City. She produced a number of portrait sculptures and executed several fountains. Much of her work was drawn from her observation of life on the streets of New York. Her *Girl on Roller Skates* is in the Metropolitan Museum.

Ebert, Friedrich (frē'drĭkh ā'bərt), 1871–1925, first president (1919–25) of the German republic. A saddler, he became a trade union leader and a Social Democratic deputy in the Reichstag. In 1913 he became party leader. Ebert supported the war effort during World War I, favored cooperation with MAXIMILIAN, PRINCE OF BADEN, in the critical days of Oct., 1918, and succeeded Maximilian as chancellor when the monarchy collapsed. Ebert would have preferred a parliamentary monarchy to the republic, of which he was elected president in Feb., 1919. As president, he provided strong, nonpartisan leadership. He suppressed the uprising (1919) of the Communist SPARTACUS PARTY and the reactionary putsch (1920) of Wolfgang KAPP. During his presidency Germany accepted the Treaty of Versailles and adopted the Weimar constitution.

Ebetsu (ābā'tso͞o), city (1970 pop. 63,762), Hokkaido prefecture, central Hokkaido, Japan. It is an industrial suburb of Sapporo and the site of a huge electric power company.

Ebiasaph (ēbī'əsăf), variant of ABIASAPH.

Ebionites (ē'bēōnīts) [Aramaic,=poor], Jewish-Christian sect of rural Palestine, of the first centuries after Christ. There were two groups, according to Origen. The Judaic Ebionites held closely to Mosaic law and regarded Jesus as a miracle-working prophet and St. Paul as an apostate. Gnostic Ebionites believed Christ to be a spirit, invisible to men, giving him the title "Prophet of the Truth." See H. J. Schoeps, *Jewish Christianity* (1969).

Ebner-Eschenbach, Marie, Baronin von (märē' bärō'nĭn fən äb'nər-ĕsh'ənbäkh), 1830–1916, Austrian writer. She began writing lyrics and plays with small success, but in middle age achieved fame as a writer of *Novellen.* Her popular works, in the style of "poetic realism," include the novel *Das Gemeindekind* (1887, tr. *The Child of the Parish,* 1893), *Komtesse Muschi* (1885, tr. *The Two Countesses,* 1893), and *Krambambuli* (1894, tr. 1913–15), a dog story.

Éboli, Ana de Mendoza de la Cerda, princesa de (ä'nä t͟hä mändō'thä t͟hä lä thär'dä prēnthā'sä t͟hā ā'bōlē), 1540–92, Spanish noblewoman. After the death (1573) of her husband, Ruy Gómez, principe de Éboli, she is supposed by romantic tradition to have had an affair with Antonio PÉREZ. She was certainly involved in political intrigues with him and shared his disgrace after the murder of Juan de ESCOBEDO. She spent the years after 1579 in prison and enforced retirement. She appears in Schiller's *Don Carlos.*

Éboli (ĕ'bōlē), town (1971 pop. 25,340), in Campania, S Italy. It is an agricultural and industrial center. A medieval castle dominates the town. Nearby are the ruins of Eburum, wnich was colonized by the Greeks, flourished under the Romans, and was destroyed (5th cent. A.D.) by the Visigoths.

ebony, common name for members of the Ebenaceae, a family of trees and shrubs widely distributed in warmer climates and in the tropics. The principal genus, *Diospyros,* includes both ebony and persimmon trees. Ebony wood, valued from ancient times, is hard and dark; it is extensively used for piano keys and in cabinetmaking, especially the black Macassar ebony of India and the East Indies. Several species (notably *D. hirsuta*) that have wood striped with black or with shades of brown are called calamander wood or variegated ebony. Several other unrelated hardwoods are commonly called ebony. Of the many species in the family bearing edible fruit, the best known are the persimmons. *D. virginiana* is native in the United States E of the Mississippi. The Japanese persimmon (*D. kaki*) is cultivated in Japan and China, in the Mediterranean area, and in the warmer regions of the United States. The unripe fruit contains tannic acid, a powerful astringent. Soft and pulpy when ripe, persimmons are difficult to market. Large quantities are eaten on the tree by opossums, whence the name possumwood for the tree. Persimmon wood has a limited use in the manufacture of objects (e.g., golf club heads) requiring hard wood. The ebony family is classified in the division MAGNOLIOPHYTA, order Ebenales, class Magnoliopsida.

Eboracum: see YORK, England.

Eboué, Félix Adolphe (fālĕks' ädôlf' ĕbwā'), 1884–1944, French colonial official. After service in Martinique and in the Sudan, he became France's first black colonial governor. He served as governor of Chad (1938–40), and then as governor general of French Equatorial Africa (1940–44), attempting to develop the economy of the region while retaining a respect for African society and customs.

Ebreo, Leone: see ABRAVANEL, JUDAH.

Ebro (ē'brō, ā'brō), longest river entirely in Spain, c.575 mi (925 km) long, rising in the Cantabrian Mts., N Spain, and flowing southeast between the Pyrenees and the Iberian Mts. past Logroño and Zaragoza. It empties through a wide delta into the Mediterranean below Tortosa. San Carlos de la Rapita, in the delta, is the chief port. The river is of little use for inland navigation because of varying volume. In its middle course the waters are canalized for irrigation. The Jalón, the Gallego, and the Cinca-Segre are the main tributaries. Large hydroelectric power plants in the Ebro system supply c.50% of Spain's hydroelectricity. During the Spanish civil war a great battle, ultimately lost by the Loyalists, was fought along the Ebro (Aug.–Nov., 1938).

Ebronah (ēbrō'nə), wilderness camping place of the Israelites. Num. 33.34,35.

Eça de Queiroz, José Maria (zho͞ozĕ' mərē'ə ā'sə dĭ kārōz'), 1846?–1900, Portuguese novelist. Trained in law and employed in the Foreign Service, he became an ardent admirer of French culture. He brought elements of French naturalism to *O crime do Padre Amare* (1876) and *Os Maias* (1880), ironic portrayals of corruption among the clergy and in high society. Eça de Queiroz rejected the long oratorical sentence traditional in Portuguese prose. His reputation as a major novelist was secured by *A ilustre casa de Ramires* [the illustrious Ramires family] (1900) and *A cidade e as serras* [the city and the mountains] (1901). Sparkling description and profound character analysis are characteristic of his writing. His essays and letters exhibit his urbanity and skeptical humor.

écarté (ā″kärtā'), card game similar to EUCHRE, played by two persons. The pack has 32 cards, seven through ace in each suit; the king is the highest card, and the ace ranks below the jack and above the ten. A trick is won by the higher trump or by the higher card of the suit led. The object of play is primarily to win three tricks.

Ecatepec (ākätāpĕk'), city (1970 pop. 220,918), Mexico state, S central Mexico. It is an industrial center, with ironworks and chemical and paper factories. Ecatepec was the site of an Aztec kingdom established in the 12th cent. The Mexican revolutionary hero Morelos y Pavón was executed by the Spanish at Ecatepec in 1815; a monument to him stands in the city.

Ecbatana (ĕkbăt'ənə, ĕkbətä'nə), capital of ancient MEDIA, later the summer residence of Achaemenid and Parthian kings, beautifully situated at the foot of Mt. Elvend and NE of Behistun. In 549 B.C. it was captured by Cyrus the Great. It possessed a royal treasury and was plundered in turn by Alexander, Seleucus, and Antiochus III. The site has never been thoroughly excavated, since it is covered by the modern city, HAMADAN, Iran, where the traditional tomb of Esther is still honored by the Jewish community. Ecbatana was the Achmetha of Ezra 6.2 and the Apocrypha. It is also called Hangmatana.

eccentric, in mechanics, device for changing rotary to back-and-forth motion. A disk is mounted off center on a shaft. One flat, open, circular end of a rod fits around the edge of the disk; the other end is usually attached to a block that slides in a slot. As the shaft rotates the block slides back and forth, carrying along whatever is attached to it, e.g., a valve. The distance between the center of the shaft and the center of the disk is the eccentricity. The so-called throw may mean either the eccentricity or the distance the block moves, which is twice the eccentricity. Cams and cranks perform the same function as the eccentric, which designers often prefer to the crank for short motions.

eccentricity, in astronomy: see ORBIT.

Eccles, Sir John Carew, 1903–, Australian neurophysiologist. He was educated at the Univ. of Melbourne and at Magdalene College, Oxford. He was director (1937–44) of the Kanematsu Research Institute of Sydney Hospital and taught at the Univ. of Otago in New Zealand and at the Australian National Univ. In 1966 he went to Northwestern Univ. in Evanston, Ill., where he became head of the Institute for Biomedical Research; in 1968 he became head of the research unit of neurobiology at the State Univ. of New York at Buffalo. He shared the 1963 Nobel Prize in Physiology and Medicine with A. L. Hodgkin and A. F. Huxley for work on the transmission of signals from nerve cells.

Eccles, municipal borough (1971 pop. 38,413), Lancashire, NW England, on the Manchester Ship Canal. There are light and heavy engineering, chemical, rubber, plastics, and textile industries. Eccles cakes are famous. The parish church is said to date from 1111, although most of the present building is of the 15th cent. In 1974, Eccles became part of the new metropolitan county of Greater Manchester.

Ecclesiastes (ĕklē″zēăs'tēz), book of the Old Testament, 21st in the order of the Authorized Version. Although traditionally ascribed to Solomon (who is identified as the author in the text), it was clearly written much later; the 3d cent. B.C. is generally accepted, but some scholars set it as late as 160 B.C. It is a philosophical essay, opening with the theme, since "all is vanity," life should be enjoyed (1–7.1). This is followed by passages in praise of wisdom and mercy, with increasing emphasis on the universality of death (7.2–12.7); there is a brief epilogue on the fear of God's judgment (12.8–14). The apparent cynicism is said to have distressed the ancient rabbis; some scholars ascribe to pious correctors a number of the nonpessimistic observations, e.g., 5.1–7. Ecclesiastes is one of the biblical examples of wisdom literature (see WISDOM). For bibliography, see OLD TESTAMENT.

Ecclesiasticus (ĕklē″zēăs'tĭkəs) [Lat. from Gr.,=ecclesiastical], biblical book included in the Old Testament of the Western canon and the Septuagint, but not included in the Hebrew Bible and placed in the Apocrypha in the Authorized Version. It is called also the Wisdom of Jesus the Son of Sirach. A prologue states that the book was composed in Hebrew by one Jesus, son of Sirach, and translated into Greek by his grandson. The date of the translation may be 132–131 B.C. The date of the composition of the original Hebrew text is 200–180 B.C. The excellence of wisdom is the theme of Ecclesiasticus. The bulk of the book is given over to instructive apothegms, but there are eloquent passages. Such are the praise of wisdom beginning at 14.20 and leading into a protest against determinism (15.11–20), the praise of wisdom put in her own mouth (24), and the praise of God for the works of nature (42–43). This leads into the praise of the famous men of Israel (44–50). The book closes (51) with a psalm. Although more than half of the Hebrew version has been recovered, there is much textual variation. The book is a good example of wisdom literature (see WISDOM). For bibliography, see APOCRYPHA.

eccrine gland: see SWEAT.

Ecevit, Bülent (bülĕnt' ĕjĕvĭt'), 1925–, Turkish political leader and journalist. An editor for *Ulus*, the organ of the Republican People's party, he was elected to parliament (1957–60 and again from 1961) and served (1961–65) as minister of labor. He led the left-of-center faction of the Republican People's party and was the party's secretary general from 1966 to 1971. In 1972, Ecevit succeeded İsmet İnönü as party chairman, promising a democratic-socialist program. In Jan., 1974, he became premier of a coalition government. Following the overthrow in July, 1974, of the Cypriot leader Archbishop MAKARIOS by the Greek officers of the Cypriot National Guard, Ecevit mobilized Turkish troops and launched an attack on Cyprus to protect that country's Turkish minority. His action brought about the fall of the Greek Cypriot rebel government, and, indirectly, the fall of the junta in Greece itself. Strains in his coalition caused Ecevit's resignation in Sept., 1974.

Ecgberht: see EGBERT.

Echandi Jiménez, Mario (mär'yō āchän'dē hēmā'nās), 1915–, president of Costa Rica (1958–62). A lawyer, he served as ambassador to the United States (1950–51, 1966–68), as foreign minister (1951–53), and in the national assembly (1953–58). He was a conservative president, introducing a cautious economic program designed to increase productivity and reduce the national debt. He ran again for president in 1970, losing to former President José Figueres Ferrer.

Echegaray, José (hōsā' āchāgärī'), 1832–1916, Spanish dramatist, mathematician, physicist, economist, and politician. He taught science, practiced engineering, and devoted his later life to economics and politics, holding several cabinet posts. From 1874 to 1905, Echegaray wrote 68 plays, becoming the leading Spanish playwright of his day. He shared the 1904 Nobel Prize in Literature with Frédéric Mistral. Among his best-known works are *O locura o santidad* (1876, tr. *Folly or Saintliness*, 1895) and *El gran Galeoto* (1881, tr. *The Great Galeoto*, 1895). Echegaray's early plays were chiefly romantic; as the realistic problem play came into vogue, however, he adapted his work to the prevailing style, and his melodramatic theater became satiric and sensational in tone.

Echeverría, Esteban (āstā'bän ā″chävärē'ä), 1805–51, Argentine romantic poet, prose writer, and revolutionary propagandist. After five years in Europe he introduced romanticism in Argentina in his poem *Elvira* (1832). Although he excelled as a prose writer, it was as a poet that he deeply influenced later writers, particularly through his poetic depiction of the South American landscape. His most successful poem, "La Cautiva," which extols the pampas, appeared in *Rimas* (1837). Echeverría was the leading spirit in the Asociación de Mayo, a secret society founded to combat the dictator Jean Manuel de Rosas. He spent the last years of his life in exile in Montevideo.

Echeverría Álvarez, Luis (lōōēs' āchāvār-rē'ä äl'väräs), 1922–, president of Mexico (1970–). A lawyer, he was formerly a law professor. As a member of the predominant Institutional Revolutionary party, he held numerous party and government posts beginning in the 1940s. As secretary of the interior (1964–69), he gained prominence for his stern handling of student riots during the 1968 Olympic games in Mexico City. Although he faced no strong challenge in the presidential election, he campaigned strenuously, traveling widely and discussing social and economic problems. As president, he launched reforms that aroused considerable conservative opposition. He introduced agricultural technical assistance programs, promoted public works, and furthered Mexican control of industries by placing limits on foreign investment.

Echidna: see TYPHON.

echidna (ĭkĭd'nə) or **spiny anteater,** primitive animal of the order Monotremata, the egg-laying mammals. A short-legged, grayish brown animal, the echidna is covered with sharp quills and can protect itself by rolling into a tight bristly ball. It may reach 18 in. (46 cm) in length. Padded soles and stout claws make it a clumsy walker but a strong and rapid burrower. The echidna has only a rudimentary tail and lacks both external ears and teeth. With its sensitive muzzle and long sticky tongue it probes for ants and termites. It is nocturnal and hibernates in winter. There are two genera and several species of echidna; all are native to the sandy and rocky areas of New Guinea, E Australia, and Tasmania. Females produce one or two eggs, which are deposited in a rudimentary marsupial pouch. The newly hatched young remain in the pouch, feeding on a milky fluid, until their spines begin to grow. Echidnas are not closely related to true anteaters, which are higher mammals. They are classified in the phylum CHORDATA, subphylum Vertebrata, class Mammalia, order Monotremata.

Echinodermata (əkī″nōdûr'mətə) [Gr.,=spiny skin], phylum of exclusively marine bottom-dwelling invertebrates, having external skeletons of calcareous plates just beneath the skin. The plates may be solidly fused together, as in the SEA URCHIN, loosely articulated to facilitate movement, as in the SEA STAR (starfish), or reduced to minute spicules in the skin, as in the SEA CUCUMBER. The skin usually has warty projections or spines, or both. Echinoderms display pentamerous radial symmetry, that is, the body can be divided into five more or less similar portions around a central axis. Unlike other radially symmetrical animals, they develop from a bilaterally symmetrical larva and retain some degree of bilateral symmetry as adults. There is no head; the surface containing the mouth (the underside, in sea stars and most others) is called the oral surface, and the opposite side, which usually bears the anus, the aboral surface. The body cavity contains a system of water-filled canals unique to echinoderms. Called the water-vascular, or ambulacral, system, it connects with the tube feet, or podia, which are extensions of the body wall that protrude through holes in the skeleton. The areas with such holes are called ambulacra. The tube feet usually have suction cups on their tips and are used primarily for locomotion in most echinoderms, but may also function in feeding, respiration, and sensory reception. The water-vascular system consists of a circular passageway, the ring canal, that surrounds the digestive tract and five radial canals that radiate from the ring canal like spokes of a wheel. Each radial canal underlies an ambulacral area. The ring canal is usually connected to a porous plate in the body wall, the madreporite, by a lime-walled tube called the stone canal. The position of the madreporite varies in the different groups. Seawater enters the system through the madreporite. Short lateral canals equipped with valves lead from the radial canals into the tube feet. A muscular, water-filled bulb, the ampulla, is connected to each tube foot. When the valve closes and the ampulla contracts, water is squeezed into the tube foot, causing the foot to extend. The foot is retracted by the contraction of the attached muscles, thereby forcing the water back into the ampulla. Sea stars, sea cucumbers, and sea urchins move by alternately extending and retracting groups of tube feet, gripping with the suction cups and pulling themselves along. Because the tube feet are very thin-walled, their surface is suitable for the diffusion of oxygen into the body cavity and the diffusion outward of carbon dioxide and wastes. The tube feet perform at least part of the respiratory function in most echinoderms; however, many groups have developed auxiliary respiratory structures. Echinoderms have no special excretory organs. Circulation occurs in an open system of channels and sinuses and in the body cavity, which is lined with flagellated cells that create an internal current. The cavity contains large phagocytic cells (amoebocytes) that function in the transport of food and the storage of insoluble wastes. There is a simple nervous system sensitive to temperature, light, and vibrations, with the various body projections serving as sensory receptors. Echinoderms

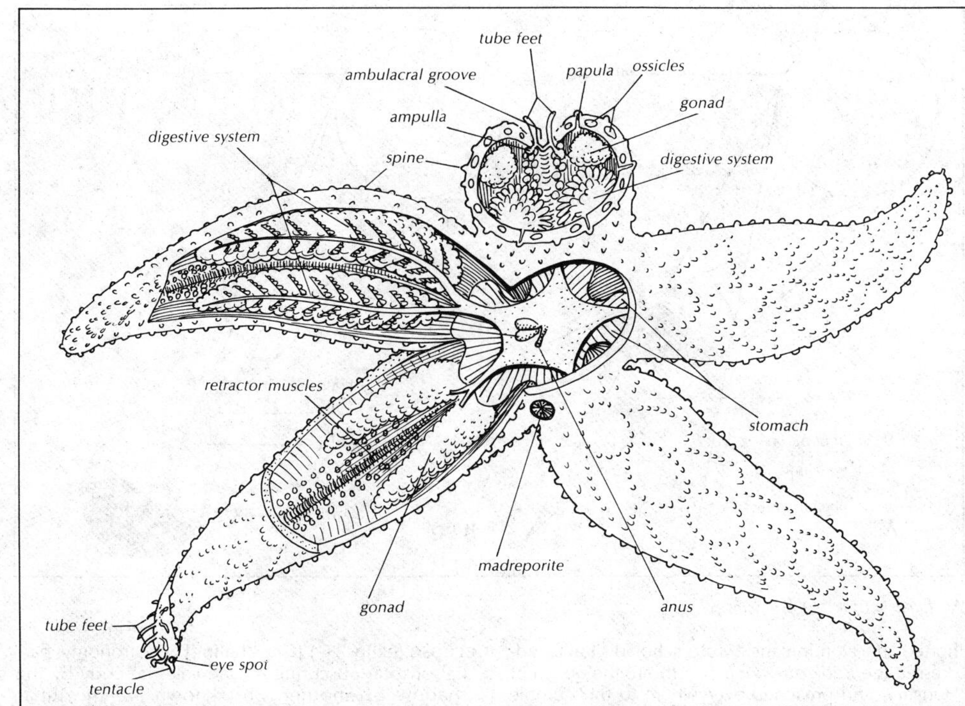

Internal anatomy of a sea star, representative of the phylum Echinodermata

have extensive powers of regeneration of lost or injured parts. They reproduce sexually, and nearly all species have separate sexes. Fertilization is external; the gametes are simply shed into the water at spawning time. The floating embryo develops into a ciliated, free-swimming, bilaterally symmetrical larva, which undergoes metamorphosis into the radially symmetrical adult. There are five living classes of echinoderms.

Class Asteroidea. Sea stars, or starfish, vary in shape from nearly circular, to pentagonal, to the familiar starlike and flowerlike forms with five or more tapering arms. The arms are extensions of the body rather than appendages; each contains an extension of the body cavity, a radial canal, and body organs. Each arm has an ambulacral groove on the undersurface; in the furrow of the groove is the ambulacral area, or ambulacrum, with holes for the tube feet. The margins of the groove have sharp spines that can close over the ambulacrum. The tip of each arm bears a short tentacle that functions as a sensory receptor for chemical and vibratory stimuli, and a red pigment spot that serves as a simple eye. The exoskeleton consists of a latticework of lime ossicles, or plates, between which project thin-walled fingerlike extensions called papulae. The papulae and the tube feet are the principal sites of respiratory exchange. In some groups of sea stars there are also body wall projections called pedicellaria, equipped with tiny pinchers that are operated by muscles and are used to clean the body surface and capture very small prey. Sea stars crawl about on rocks or muddy bottoms, feeding on a variety of living and dead animals. Many feed largely on bivalve mollusks and are notorious as destroyers of commercial oyster beds. In most species there are two gonads in each arm; at spawning time these nearly fill the arms. The swimming larva settles and goes through a sessile (attached) stage while changing to the adult form.

Class Ophiuroidea. The BRITTLE STARS, or serpent stars, are so called for their long, slender, fragile arms, which are set off sharply from the circular, pentagonal, or slightly star-shaped body disk. The arms of brittle stars are flexible and appear jointed because of the conspicuous plates of the exoskeleton. They bear a row of spines along each edge. In one group, the basket stars, they are repeatedly branched, forming a large mass of tentaclelike limbs. Each arm contains a radial canal (or one of its branches), but it does not contain body organs. The small tube feet, which project from the undersides of the arms, function mainly as sensory receptors. Brittle stars feed on detritus and small organisms raked into the mouth with the arms. The mouth leads to a large, saclike stomach that fills most of the body cavity. There is no intestine or anus, and solid waste is extruded through the mouth. The stomach is folded into ten pouches, between which lie ten respiratory sacs that open by slits onto the aboral surface. The cells lining the sacs have flagellae, which create a current of water moving in and out. Respiratory exchange occurs chiefly through the thin lining of the sacs.

Class Echinoidea. Echinoids—SEA URCHINS, heart urchins, and SAND DOLLARS—are echinoderms without arms and with a spiny shell, or test, formed of tightly fused skeletal plates. The sea urchins (regular echinoids) are hemispherical in shape, round on top and flat on the lower surface. They have very long, prominent spines and are often brightly colored. The test of a sea urchin is divided into ten parts from pole to pole, like the sections of an orange. Five of these are ambulacra, with openings for tube feet; these alternate with wider sections, called interambulacra, that lack tube feet. However, spines and pedicellaria are found over the entire surface of the test. Urchins move by pushing against the substratum with the spines and extruding the tube feet in the direction of movement. If turned over they can right themselves by means of the tube feet on the aboral surface. The mouth, located in the center of the undersurface, is surrounded by a thickened region bearing five pairs of short, heavy tube feet and five pairs of bushy gills. Within the mouth is an elaborate five-sided jaw structure called Aristotle's lantern that can be partially extruded from the mouth. It is able to grind up calcareous exoskeletons of plants and animals. The anus is at the center of the aboral surface and is surrounded by a thin-walled area without skeletal plates. Sand dollars and heart urchins (irregular echinoids) have a dense covering of short spines, and locomotion is exclusively by movement of the spines. There are two groups of podia-bearing ambulacra, one arranged in a petallike pattern on the upper surface and the other forming a similar pattern on the lower surface. The upper tube feet function as respiratory organs (there are no gills around the mouth), and the lower ones are specialized for gathering food particles. Sand dollars are extremely flattened and oval in outline; the anus is on the oral surface. Heart urchins are somewhat flattened and are heart-shaped; a deep ambulacral groove running from top to bottom creates a secondary bilateral symmetry. The anus is on the aboral surface, opposite the groove.

Class Holothuroidea. The sea cucumbers are long-bodied echinoderms with the mouth at or near one end and the anus at or near the other. Because of their elongation along the oral-aboral plane, they lie on their sides rather than on the oral surface. In nearly all sea cucumbers the skeleton is reduced to microscopic ossicles imbedded in the leathery skin. Sea cucumbers have no arms, but tube feet around the mouth have been modified to form a circle of 10 to 30 tentacles of varying lengths and shapes that function in gathering food particles from the ocean bottom. The gut of the sea cucumber terminates in a chamber called the cloaca that opens into the anus. Two unique structures called respiratory trees, found in most sea cucumbers, also terminate in the cloaca. These are systems of highly branched tubes, one on either side of the body. The animal pumps water into the respiratory trees by contracting the cloaca, and oxygen diffuses through from the walls of the trees into the fluid of the body cavity. The madreporite in most sea cucumbers opens into the body cavity rather than to the outside and receives its fluid from the cavity. In a few sea cucumber species there is a large mass of tubules at the base of the respiratory tree that can be shot out of the anus if the animal is irritated. The extruded tubules, which may engulf and incapacitate an intruder, break off; they are then regenerated by the sea cucumber. In other species the respiratory trees, gonads, and part of the digestive tract are shot out through the anus; this evisceration is followed by regeneration of the lost organs.

Class Crinoidea. The SEA LILIES and FEATHER STARS are the only surviving members of an ancient group of stalked, sessile, detritus-feeding echinoderms. Most of the sea lilies remain stalked throughout life; their movements are limited to bending the stalk and the arms. Feather stars break off the stalk and become free-living as adults. Crinoids, whether free or stalked, always have the oral side upward, and the ring of arms about the mouth gives them a flowerlike appearance. Most have 10 arms, but some sea lilies have up to 40 and some feather stars up to 200 arms. The stalk and the arms have a jointed appearance, and each arm has a row of projections, the pinnules, on either side, giving a feathery appearance. A ciliated ambulacral groove runs along each arm and branches into the pinnules; the groove contains feathery, three-branched tube feet. These react to the presence of minute food particles in the water by bending inward, sweeping the particles into the groove, where they are trapped in mucus and swept by the cilia toward the mouth. Feeding, rather than locomotion, was probably the original function of the tube feet and water-vascular system of echinoderms. Gametes develop in some of the pinnules, which rupture at spawning time. The free-swimming larva eventually settles and develops a stalk and a crown.

Echmiadzin (ĕchmēädzĕn′), town (1967 est. pop. 26,000), SE European USSR, in Armenia, in the Araks River valley. It has winemaking and plastics industries. Known since the 6th cent. B.C., Echmiadzin (which was called Vagarshapat until 1945) was the capital of the ancient kingdom of Armenia (A.D. 184–344). It also became the center of the Armenian Church after the adoption of Christianity in the 2d cent. A.D. The famous Echmiadzin monastery has been the residence since 1441 of the patriarch (catholicus) of the church; inside the monastery walls is the cathedral founded in 303 by St. Gregory the Illuminator. The Ripsin church and the Gayan cathedral (both 7th cent.) have been restored.

Echo, in Greek mythology, mountain nymph. She assisted Zeus in one of his amorous adventures by distracting Hera with her chatter. For this Hera made her unable to speak except to repeat another's last words. She fell in love with Narcissus, but when he repulsed her, she pined away until only her voice remained. In another myth, she was loved by Pan, who, because he could not win her, caused shepherds to tear her asunder, leaving only her voice.

echo, reflection of a sound wave back to its source in sufficient strength and with a sufficient time lag to be separately distinguished. If a sound wave returns within 1/10 sec, the human ear is incapable of detecting it. Thus, since the velocity of sound is c.344 m (1,130 ft) per sec at a normal room temperature of about 20°C (68°F), a reflecting wall must be more than 16.2 m (56½ ft) from the sound source at this temperature for an echo to be heard by a person at the source. In this case the sound requires 1/5 sec to reach the reflecting surface and the same time to return. Bats navigate by listening for the echo of their high-frequency cry. Sonar and depth sounders work by analyzing electronically the echo time lag of sound waves, generally between 10 and 50 kilohertz, produced by underwater transducers. Radar sets broadcast radio waves, usually between 100 and 10,000 megahertz, pick up the portion reflected back by objects, and electronically determine the distance and direction of the objects. A sound echo that is reflected again and again from different surfaces, as by parallel walls in a tunnel, is called reverberation. When a surface reflects sound it partially absorbs and partially reflects the energy. As the process is repeated the sound becomes weaker and weaker and eventually ceases.

echo sounder, instrumentation system for indirectly determining ocean depth. Echo sounding is based on the principle that water is an excellent medium for the transmission of sound waves and that a sound pulse will bounce off a reflecting layer, returning to its source as an echo. If the speed of sound in water is known, the time interval between the initiation of a sound pulse and echo return from the bottom can be used to determine the depth of the bottom. In practice, an echo-sounding system aboard a ship consists of a transmitter that is attached to the hull or towed behind the ship and emits a pulse of sound energy; a receiver that picks up the reflected echo; electronic timing and amplification equipment to calculate depth automatically and filter out acoustical noise; and an indicator or graphic recorder. The first patent for an echo-sounding device was granted in 1907. The Fathometer, a registered trademark often loosely applied to all depth-sounding gear, was developed (1914) as a result of research by the Canadian engineer R. A. Fessenden in the application of echo-sounding principles to iceberg detection. Research and development studies were carried on throughout the 1920s. By the start of World War II, a variety of continuous recording echo-sounding devices capable of measuring limited depths had been developed. Application of echo-sounding principles to submarine detection during World War II resulted in the development of equipment to sound all ocean depths. In 1954 an advanced, highly accurate echo sounder called the precision depth recorder (PDR) was developed.

Echternach (ĕkh'tərnäkh), town, E Grand Duchy of Luxembourg, on the Sûre (Sauer) River, at the West German border. It is an agricultural, industrial, and tourist center, with mineral springs that have been frequented since Roman times. Of note in Echternach are the Church of St. Peter and St. Paul (11th cent.), part of the Benedictine abbey (founded c.700) where St. Willibrord is buried, and the town hall (16th cent.). A colorful pilgrimage and procession is held annually on Whit-Tuesday.

Écija (ä'thēhä), city (1970 pop. 36,056), Seville prov., S Spain, in Andalusia, on a hill overlooking the Genil River. It is an agricultural center for an area that produces olives, cereal, and cotton. Of pre-Roman origin, Écija was recovered from the Moors by Ferdinand III in 1240. Its notable churches include the Moorish style Santa Cruz.

Eck, Johann Maier von (yō'hän mī'ər fən ĕk), 1486–1543, German Roman Catholic theologian. He was of peasant stock, the name von Eck being taken from his birthplace in Swabia. He was a brilliant student and became a professor at Freiburg in his youth. He was renowned in Germany for his dialectic skill in public disputation and for his deep knowledge of church history and canon law. He had been suspected of unsound theology because of some of his humanistic ideas, but he had no hesitation in condemning (1518) the new theses of Martin LUTHER, with whom he held a public discussion at Leipzig in 1519. Eager for the condemnation of the heresy he saw in Lutheranism, he went to Rome and returned with the papal bull condemning Luther (1520). From that time he was a leader in the struggle against the reforming party in Germany. He was one of the leading theologians at the Diet of Augsburg (1530). He also attacked the Swiss reforms of Zwingli. Eck is usually known as the first theologian who forced Luther into a position of definite, open opposition to the teachings and practice of the Roman Catholic Church.

Eckermann, Johann Peter (yōhän' pä'tər ĕk'ərmän), 1792–1854, German scholar and author. He assisted Goethe in various literary labors, was professor of English and German at the Univ. of Jena, and later was librarian at Weimar. His *Conversations with Goethe* (1836–48, tr. 1850), which quotes the poet at length, is an invaluable biographical document.

Eckersberg, Christoffer Vilhelm (krĭstôf'ər vĭl'hĕlm ĕk'ərsbĕrkh), 1783–1853, Danish painter. He studied with J. L. David in Paris and in Rome became a friend of Thorvaldsen. After his return to Denmark (1816) he taught at the Copenhagen Academy, becoming its director. His finest works are portraits and seascapes, executed with great clarity of outline. Among his best works are *Moses Dividing the Waters of the Red Sea,* the series of historical paintings in the Christiansborg palace, and a portrait of Thorvaldsen (all: Copenhagen).

Eckhart, Meister (mīs'tər ĕk'härt) (Johannes Eckhardt), c.1260–c.1328, German mystical theologian, b. Hochheim, near Gotha. He studied and taught in the chief Dominican schools, notably at Paris, Strasbourg, and Cologne, and held a series of offices in his order. Eckhart communicated in various ways his burning sense of God's nearness to men. He exhorted the Dominicans, wrote scholarly tracts, addressed the *Book of Divine Comfort* to the queen of Hungary, and preached everywhere to the humble and ignorant, urging them all to seek the divine spark in man. His evangelical activities among the undisciplined were deemed suspect, and his election (1309) to be provincial of the German province was not confirmed. Toward the end of his life he was wrongly accused of connection with the BEGHARDS and charged with heresy. He was upheld by his order, but the charge was pressed. Eckhart appealed to Rome. He died between 1327, when his appeal was denied, and 1329, when John XXII issued a bull condemning 17 of Eckhart's propositions as heretical. His disciples tried vainly to have this decree set aside. From Eckhart's influence there sprang up a popular mystical movement in 14th-century Germany, which included among its leaders TAULER, SUSO, and various Dominicans. These were all intellectual as well as practical preachers and did not show the tendency to separate holiness and learning that characterized the mystics of the popular school of Gerard GROOTE. Eckhart was perhaps the first writer of speculative prose in German, and from that time German, not Latin, was the language of popular tracts. See R. B. Blakney, *Meister Eckhart: A Modern Translation* (1941); J. M. Clark and J. V. Skinner, ed., *Meister Eckhart: Selected Treatises and Sermons* (1958); studies by Jeanne Ancelet-Hustache (tr. 1957) and J. M. Clark (1957).

eclampsia (ĭklămp'sēə), term applied to toxic complications that can occur late in pregnancy. TOXEMIA of pregnancy occurs in 10% to 20% of pregnant women; symptoms include headache, vertigo, visual disturbances, vomiting, hypertension, and edema. Only 5% of these cases progress to eclampsia, which is accompanied by convulsions and coma. To avoid renal and cardiovascular damage of the mother and to prevent fetal damage, the condition is treated by termination of pregnancy.

eclecticism (ĭklĕk'tĭsĭz"əm), art technique in which features are borrowed from various styles. Notable examples occur in the works of the CARRACCI, in which elements are incorporated from the Renaissance and classical traditions. Among the most influential advocates of eclecticism were Sir Joshua REYNOLDS and John RUSKIN. The technique is now generally discredited, but the term is still used to describe any work of art depending heavily on other styles for source material.

eclecticism (ĭklĕk'tĭsĭz"əm) [from Gr. *eklektikos*= to choose], in philosophy, the selection of elements from different systems of thought, without regard to possible contradictions between the systems. Eclecticism differs from syncretism, which tries to combine various systems while resolving conflicts. Many Roman philosophers, especially CICERO, and the Neoplatonists were known for eclecticism. Eclecticism among Renaissance humanists, who drew from Christian and classical doctrines, was followed by a 19th cent. revival, particularly with French philosopher Victor Cousin, who coined the term and applied it to his own system. Eclectics are frequently charged with being inconsistent, and the term is sometimes used pejoratively.

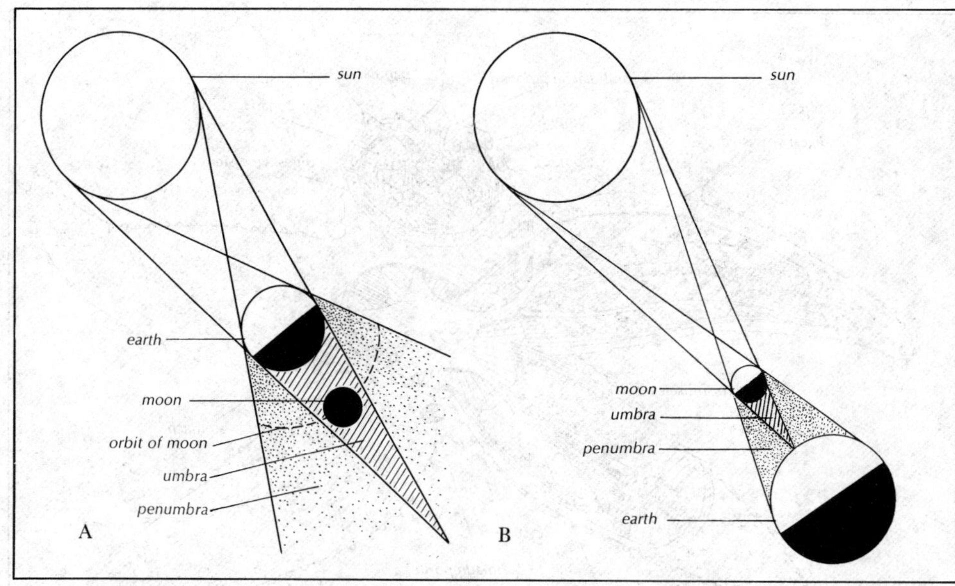

A. *Lunar eclipse* B. *Solar eclipse*

eclipse (ēklĭps', ĭ-) [Gr.,=failing], in astronomy, partial or total obscuring of one celestial body by the shadow of another. Best known are the lunar eclipses, which occur when the earth blocks the sun's light from the moon, and solar eclipses, occurring when the moon blocks the sun's light from the earth. Since the earth and moon shine only by the reflected light of the sun, each casts a shadow into space in the direction away from the sun. The shadow consists of a cone-shaped area of complete darkness called the umbra, where all light from the sun is cut off, and a larger area of partial darkness called the penumbra, which surrounds the umbra and receives light from a part of the sun's disk. Lunar eclipses can occur only when the moon is in its full phase, i.e., when the earth is between the sun and the moon. These eclipses may be total or partial, depending on whether the moon passes completely into the umbra of the earth's shadow or remains partly in the penumbra. Since the moon cuts the umbra close to the base, it can experience long periods of total eclipse ranging up to 1 hr, 42 min. A partial eclipse (when it passes through the penumbra) can last more than 2 hr, and the entire lunar eclipse may continue for as long as 4 hr. Some light is refracted, or bent, by the earth's atmosphere into the umbra, so that the moon at totality, instead of appearing black, is a dull coppery color. The longest possible duration of totality for a solar eclipse is 7 min, 40 sec at or near the equator when the sun is directly overhead; the duration decreases with increasing latitude. The eclipse of June 20, 1955, lasted 7 min, 8 sec, which was the longest duration of totality in 1,238 years. At apogee (when the moon is at its farthest point from the earth) the umbra of its shadow is too short to reach the earth's surface, causing the apparent diameter of the sun's disk to be larger than that of the moon. Where the moon would otherwise block the sun entirely, now the sun is seen as a bright ring completely surrounding the moon's disk; this eclipse is known as an annular, or ring, eclipse. A total solar eclipse can occur only when the moon is in its new phase. At this time the moon is between the sun and the earth and cannot be seen until it moves across the sun's disk. As it blocks out the light, the sky darkens to twilight, the brightest stars become visible, and there is a noticeable drop in temperature. At totality, parts of the sun may be seen shining brightly between the high points of the moon's irregular edge, a phenomenon known as Baily's beads; the disk of the moon appears black and is surrounded by the sun's CORONA, out of which shoot immense, flamelike spurts of gas called prominences. Baily's beads are seen again as the sun reappears and the sky grows lighter. Total solar eclipses have such importance to science that astronomers travel to distant parts of the world for a few minutes of viewing time. These eclipses provide information on the motions of the moon and on the surface phenomena of the sun, and they are of particular value in testing Einstein's general theory of relativity. If the plane of the moon's orbit about the earth coincided with that of the earth about the sun, a solar eclipse would be observed each month when the moon is new and a lunar eclipse when the moon is full. However, the moon's orbital plane is tilted at an angle of about 5°10′ to the earth's orbital plane, making eclipses possible only when the three bodies are aligned (at new or full moon) and when the moon is crossing the earth's orbital plane (at a point called the NODE). Within a given year, a maximum of seven eclipses can occur, either four solar and three lunar or five solar and two lunar. However, many more lunar eclipses are seen at any single location than solar eclipses, because a lunar eclipse can be seen from the entire half of the earth facing the moon at that time, while a solar eclipse is visible only along a narrow path on the earth's surface. From their observations of eclipses the Chaldeans (fl. 1000 B.C.–540 B.C.) discovered that similar eclipses of the sun recur in cycles of 18 years, 11⅓ days; this cycle, called the saros, is an interval in which the sun, earth, and moon return to nearly identical relative positions. Since the orbits of the earth and moon are quite accurately known, eclipses can be predicted far in advance, both in time and location. Similar calculations can determine the time and place of past eclipses; this information is useful for dating historical events that are known to have occurred at the same time as an eclipse. Also important to science have been the eclipses of Jupiter's satellites. In 1675 the Danish astronomer Ole Roemer used these eclipses to calculate the speed of light.

eclipsing binary star: see BINARY STAR; VARIABLE STAR.

ecliptic (ĕklĭp′tĭk, ĭ-), the great circle on the CELESTIAL SPHERE that lies in the plane of the earth's orbit (called the plane of the ecliptic). Because of the earth's yearly revolution around the sun, the sun appears to move in an annual journey through the heavens with the ecliptic as its path. The ecliptic is the principal axis in the ECLIPTIC COORDINATE SYSTEM. The two points at which the ecliptic crosses the celestial equator are the EQUINOXES. The obliquity of the ecliptic is the inclination of the plane of the ecliptic to the plane of the celestial equator, an angle of about 23½°. The constellations through which the ecliptic passes are the constellations of the ZODIAC.

ecliptic coordinate system or **celestial coordinate system,** an ASTRONOMICAL COORDINATE SYSTEM in which the principal coordinate axis is the ECLIPTIC, the apparent path of the sun through the heavens. The ecliptic poles are the two points at which a line perpendicular to the plane of the ecliptic through the center of the earth strikes the surface of the CELESTIAL SPHERE. The north ecliptic pole lies in the constellation Draco. In this system the coordinates of a star are its celestial longitude and celestial latitude.

Ecnomus, Cape: see LICATA, Italy.

École des Beaux-Arts (ākôl′ dā bōzär′)[Fr.,=school of fine arts], French national school of fine arts, on the Quai Malaquais, Paris, founded in 1648 by Charles LE BRUN with the consent of Cardinal Mazarin as the Académie de peinture et de sculpture; the title was changed in 1793, when it merged with the Académie d'architecture, founded in 1671 by Jean-Baptiste COLBERT. It includes three departments—painting and graphic arts, sculpture, and architecture—and is free to artists whose previous training enables them to pass the entrance examinations. Students are prepared in the various courses to compete for the PRIX DE ROME, which provides admission to the Académie de France à Rome. Besides its extensive collection of plaster casts of antiquities, the École is known for its superb collection of old-master drawings and for its exhibitions.

ecology, study of the relationships of organisms to their physical environment and to one another. The study of an individual organism or a single species is termed autecology; the study of groups of organisms is called synecology. Within the BIOSPHERE—the total expanse of water, land, and atmosphere able to sustain life—the basic ecological unit is the ecosystem. An ecosystem may be as small as a tidal pool or a rotting log or as large as an ocean or a continent-spanning forest. Each ecosystem consists of a community of plants and animals in an environment that supplies them with raw materials for life, i.e., chemical elements and water. The ecosystem is delimited by the climate, altitude, water and soil characteristics, and other physical conditions of the environment. The energy necessary for all life processes reaches the earth in the form of sunlight. By PHOTOSYNTHESIS green plants convert the light energy into chemical energy, and carbon dioxide and water are transformed into sugar and stored in the plant. Herbivorous animals acquire some of the stored energy by eating the plants; those animals in turn serve as food for, and so pass the energy to, predatory animals. Such sequences, called food chains, overlap at many points, forming so-called food webs. For example, insects are food for reptiles, which are food for hawks. But hawks also feed directly on insects and on other birds that feed on insects, while some reptiles prey on birds. Since a severe loss of the original energy occurs with each transfer from species to species, the ecologist views the food (energy) structure as a pyramid: Each level supports a smaller number and mass of organisms. Thus in a year's time it would take millions of plants weighing many tons to feed the several steers weighing a few tons that could support one or two men. The ecological conclusion is that if human beings would eat more plants and fewer animals, food resources would stretch much further. Once the energy for life is spent, it cannot be replenished except by the further exposure of green plants to sunlight. But the chemical materials extracted from the environment and elaborated into living tissue by plants and animals are continually recycled within the ecosystem by such processes as photosynthesis, RESPIRATION, nitrogen fixation and nitrification. These natural processes of withdrawing and returning materials are variously called the carbon cycle, the oxygen cycle, and the nitrogen cycle. Water is also cycled. Evaporation from lakes and oceans forms clouds; the clouds release rain that is taken up by the soil, absorbed by plants, and passed on to feeding animals—which also drink directly from pools and lakes that catch the rain. The water in plant and animal wastes and dead tissue then evaporates and can be recycled. Interference with these vital cycles by disturbance of the environment—for example, by POLLUTION of the air and water—may disrupt the workings of the entire ecosystem. The cycles are facilitated when an ecosystem has a sufficient diversity of species to fill its so-called ecological niches, the different functional sites in the environment where organisms can act as producers of energy, consumers of energy, or decomposers of wastes. Such diversity tends to make a community stable and self-perpetuating. A climax community is one that has reached the stable stage. When extensive and well defined, the climax community is called a biome. Examples are TUNDRA, grassland, DESERT, and the deciduous, coniferous, and tropical rain FORESTS. Stability is attained through a process known as succession, whereby relatively simple communities are replaced by those more complex. Thus, on a lakefront, grass may invade a build-up of sand. Humus formed by the grass then gives root to oaks and pines and lesser vegetation, which displaces the grass and forms a further altered humus. That soil eventually nourishes maple and beech trees, which gradually crowd out the pines and oaks and form a climax community. In addition to trees, each successive community harbors many other life forms, with the greatest diversity populating the climax community. The climax community thereafter tends to perpetuate itself unless the environment is severely altered by natural or man-made disturbances like prolonged drought or pollution. Stability is maintained by the complex interactions among the trees, the diverse lesser vegetation, and the many kinds of microscopic and larger plants and animals. All nourish one another while at the same time inhibiting the overgrowth of any one species. Similar ecological zonings occur among marine flora and fauna, dependent on such environmental factors as bottom composition, availability of light, and degree of salinity. In other respects, the capture by aquatic plants of solar energy and inorganic materials as well as their transfer through food chains and cycling by means of microorganisms, parallels those processes on land. See P. M. Dansereau, *Biogeography: An Ecological Perspective* (1957); E. J. Kormondy, ed., *Readings in Ecology* (1965); R. L. Smith, *Ecology and Field Biology* (1966); E. J. Kormondy, *Concepts of Ecology* (1969); E. P. Odum, *Fundamentals of Ecology* (3d ed. 1971); R. L. Smith, ed., *The Ecology of Man: An Ecosystem Approach* (1971); P. A. Colinvaux, *Introduction to Ecology* (1973); R. M. Darnell, *Ecology and Man* (1973); T. C. Emmel, *An Introduction to Ecology and Population Biology* (1973); D. B. Sutton and N. P. Harman, *Ecology: Selected Concepts* (1973); K. E. F. Watt, *Principles of Environmental Science* (1973).

econometrics, technique of economic analysis that combines economic theory with statistical and mathematical methods of analysis. It is an attempt to develop accurate economic forecasting and to make possible successful policy planning. In econometrics, economic theories are expressed as mathematical relationships and then tested empirically by statistical techniques. See Dennis Aigner, *Basic Econometrics* (1971); Michael Brennan, *Preface to Econometrics* (3d ed. 1973).

Economic and Social Council, constituent organ of the United Nations. It is established by Chapter 10 of the UN Charter and has 27 (18 before 1965) member nations elected for three-year terms by the General Assembly. The function of the council is to undertake investigations of international economic and social questions and to report its conclusions and suggestions to the General Assembly and other organs of the United Nations for action. The council also coordinates the activities of the specialized agencies of the United Nations and arranges for consultations with international nongovernmental organizations. The full council meets at least twice a year; decisions are taken by a majority of members present and voting. To facilitate its work the council has established a number of functional commissions, including the Statistical Commission, the Commission on Narcotic Drugs, the Commission for Social Development, the Commission on the Status of Women, the Population Commission, and the Commission on Human Rights; it also has regional commissions for Europe, for Asia and the Far East, for Latin America, and for Africa. The activities of the Commission on Human Rights have been particularly important. In Aug., 1948, a draft of a Universal Declaration of Human Rights, drawn up by the commission, was adopted by the General Assembly. The commission has drafted other covenants on human rights, passed by the General Assembly in 1966, which amplify and regularize many of the principles of the Universal Declaration; they still await ratification by individual nations. The council supervises the activities of the United Nations Children's Fund, the Office of the United Nations High Commissioner for Refugees, the United Nations Development Program, and the International Narcotics Control Board. It also undertakes special studies at the request of countries belonging to the United Nations. See bibliography under UNITED NATIONS.

Economic Cooperation Administration: see MARSHALL PLAN.

economic planning, control and direction of economic activity by a public authority, usually the state. The purpose of planning is to attain ends that are considered socially desirable. Economic planning is as old as government itself; wages and prices were controlled in ancient Egypt, Greece, and Rome. In the Middle Ages, wages and prices were regulated by merchant and craft guilds. In the 16th and 17th cent., nations attempted to acquire wealth and develop foreign trade and domestic industry by direct activity as well as by the encouragement and regulation of private activity (see MERCANTILISM). In the 18th cent. opposition to economic planning developed; proponents of LAISSEZ FAIRE believed that the economic system works best when there is no government interference. Even laissez-faire economists, however, recognized the need for some planning (e.g., in the construction and maintenance of public roads, canals, and port facilities). In the 20th cent. economic management played a major role in the heavily planned programs of SOCIALISM, COMMUNISM, and FASCISM and became an essential part of public policy in nations that did not adopt those doctrines. Most developing nations utilize economic plans—usually based on 5- or 10-year periods—in order to allocate resources and direct economic growth. The occurrence of war automatically subordinates all private activity to a unified national effort and thus increases national economic planning. Planning can involve the use of direct controls—such as rationing and price, rent, and wage limits—and indirect controls, such as monetary and fiscal policy. Since the 1930s the U.S. government has used a variety of direct and indirect controls. Trade and regional tariff arrangements such as the Common Market represent attempts to secure the benefits of economic planning on an international scale. See Rudolf Bicanic, *Problems of Planning, East and West* (1967); J. T. Dunlop and N. P. Fedorenko, *Planning and Markets* (1969); K. B. Griffin and J. L. Enos, *Planning Development* (1970).

economics, study of how human beings allocate scarce resources to produce various commodities and how those commodities are distributed for consumption among the people in society. In some respects, the first economic writings were the Oriental moral codes, which explained riches and physical well-being in terms of divine favor. The first attempts to analyze economic problems appear in the writings of the ancient Greeks. Plato recognized the economic basis of social life and in his *Republic* organized a model society on the basis of a careful division of labor. Aristotle, too, attributed great importance to economic security as the basis for social and political health and saw in the middle-sized landowner the ideal citizen. Roman writers made little advance over the Greeks, although Cicero, Vergil, and Varro gave advice about agriculture. The medieval period was marked by the disruption of the flourishing commerce of the ancient world, and its economic life was dominated by the manor, a self-sufficient economic unit (see FEUDALISM). Much of the writing on economics found in medieval literature centers about discussion of the just price for goods and criticism of usury. The revival of commerce after the Crusades led to the development of the two most important economic institutions of the later middle ages, the town and the GUILDS. In the transition to modern times (16th–18th cent.), with the European overseas expansion and the resultant growth of commerce, the economic policy called MERCANTILISM was developed to secure by tariffs and regulation of commerce as much bullion as possible to the economically successful state. In the late 17th and the 18th cent., protest against the governmental regulation characteristic of mercantilism was voiced, especially by the PHYSIOCRATS, who advocated LAISSEZ FAIRE—allowing business to follow freely the "natural laws" of economics. They regarded agriculture as the sole productive economic activity and encouraged the improvement of cultivation. Because they considered land to be the sole source of wealth, they urged the adoption of a tax on land as the only economically justifiable tax. In the 18th cent. important work in economics was done by the Scottish philosopher David HUME. His analysis of the natural advantages that some nations enjoy in the cultivation of certain products and his observations on the flow of commerce became the basis for the theory of international trade. The most important work of the 18th cent., however, was *An Inquiry into the Nature and Causes of the Wealth of Nations* (1776), by Adam SMITH. Smith identified self-interest as the basic economic force. More importantly, through his masterly analysis of the DIVISION OF LABOR and his comprehensive study of the development of economic institutions in the West, Smith established economics as a major area of study. Another Scotsman, John MILLAR, incorporated and developed Smith's ideas into a highly sophisticated economic interpretation of history. Smith's theories, especially his advocacy of FREE TRADE, played an important part in the INDUSTRIAL REVOLUTION then taking place in England. One of the most influential writers of the 19th cent. was Thomas MALTHUS, whose predictions that population would eventually outstrip the means of subsistence earned for economics the title "the dismal science." The most important economist to follow Smith was David RICARDO. His analysis of rent long remained the classic account, while his theory of labor value was later followed by socialists as well as classical economists. Ricardo's "iron law of wages" supplemented Malthus's pessimistic thesis by asserting that wages tend to stabilize at the subsistence level. John Stuart MILL was a follower of Ricardo and contributed to the study of international trade as well as to the study of the economics of industrial expansion. Among critics of free trade outside England were the German Friedrich List and the American Henry C. Carey. The early exponents of SOCIALISM, especially in France, attacked the idea of the necessity of private property and competition and were interested in revamping the economic and social order. Among those were C. H. Saint-Simon, Robert Owen, Charles Fourier, and Louis Blanc. In Germany the historical school arose under Wilhelm Roscher, Bruno Hildebrand, and Karl Knies, who doubted the existence of universal economic laws and emphasized the particular development of economic institutions in individual nations. The greatest challenge to classical economics came from the followers of Karl MARX. Marx's criticisms of CAPITALISM were moral and social, as well as economic; but in the exposition of the workings of the capitalist system he and his followers developed important insights into the structural weaknesses of the market economy, especially the recurrence of economic crises (see DEPRESSION). At the same time the principles of classical economics were being reformulated and refined—it was at that time that the term "economics" replaced the term "political economy," which had been used through the mid-19th cent. The most important refinement was the doctrine of marginal utility, which asserts that the VALUE of an item is determined by the need for it and by its relative scarcity or abundance at any given time—not by any intrinsic or inherent worth. The leading theorists in the development of the concept were William Stanley JEVONS of England, Leon Walras of France, and Eugen BÖHM-BAWERK of Austria. In America, some notable figures in the development of the marginal utility theory were John Bates Clark, Frank Fetter, and Irving Fisher. Classical economics reached its fullest expression at the end of the 19th cent. in the work of Alfred MARSHALL. Marshall used mathematics to perfect the application of classical techniques and introduced important modifications to the notions of competition, marginal utility, and rent. The most important modification of classical concepts of the free economy came from the work of John Maynard KEYNES. In his *General Theory of Employment, Interest, and Money* (1936), Keynes opened up a whole new range of investigation into business cycles. A principal result of Keynes's teaching has been reflected in governmental attempts to control the business cycle by putting money directly into the economy; such a "pump-priming" technique, often accompanied by an unbalanced budget, is now a major part of most capitalist economic systems. Following World War II, major emphasis was placed on the analysis of economic growth and development. Spurred by the competition between communism and capitalism to win the favor of the newly emerging nations, economists from all persuasions have contributed to the new field of growth economics. Western economists notable for their contributions to the economics of growth and development include Gunnar Myrdal of Sweden and Joseph Schumpeter, Walt W. Rostow, and neo-Marxist Paul Baran, all of the United States. The use of complex mathematical techniques and statistical data in economic forecasting has resulted in a new branch of economics known as ECONOMETRICS. Economists play a vital role in government (see ECONOMIC PLANNING) as well as in business and industry, and the President of the United States has his own council of economic advisers to assist him in policy decisions. Many subjects such as political science and sociology that were once regarded as part of the study of economics have today become separate disciplines. Other famous American economists, past and present, include John Rogers Commons, Herbert J. Davenport, Richard T. Ely, Milton Friedman, John Kenneth Galbraith, Wesley C. Mitchell, Paul Samuelson, Edwin R. A. Seligman, Frank W. Taussig, and Thorstein Veblen. See B. B. Seligman, *Main Currents in Modern Economics* (1962); L. C. Robbins, *The Evolution of Modern Economic Theory* (1970); R. L. Heilbroner, *The Worldly Philosophers* (rev. ed. 1971) and *The Making of Economic Society* (4th ed. 1972); Paul Samuelson, *Economics* (9th ed. 1973).

Ecorse (ē'kôrs), industrial city (1970 pop. 17,515), Wayne co., SE Mich., on the Detroit River; settled c.1815, inc. as a city 1941. Steel, automobile parts, furniture, and metal products are the principal manufactures.

ecosystem: see ECOLOGY.

ECSC: see EUROPEAN COAL AND STEEL COMMUNITY.

ectoderm, layer of cells that covers the surface of an animal embryo after the process of gastrulation has occurred. This outer layer, together with the ENDODERM, or inner layer, is present in all early embryos. In the development of animals of the phyla PORIFERA, CTENOPHORA, and CNIDARIA, these two primary layers give rise to all the tissues and organs of the animals, a process known as diploblastic development. In higher animals, such as those of the phyla ECHINODERMATA and CHORDATA, a third, middle layer, the MESODERM, is formed between the ectoderm and endoderm during gastrulation, and the process is termed triploblastic development. In most embryos, differentiation of ectodermal tissue gives rise to epidermis and its specialized structures (scales, feathers, nails, and hair); some exocrine glands (sweat and sebaceous glands); some endocrine glands (the pineal body and the pituitary gland); the nervous system; and the organs of special sense (ear and eye). In animals of some phyla, such as the MOLLUSCA and ANNELIDA, the fate of particular cells of the embryo is determined in the earliest stages of the fertilized egg and may even be fixed at or before fertilization.

Ectoprocta (ĕk"təprŏk'tə), phylum of inconspicuous, sessile, colonial aquatic animals. The zooids, or individual members of a colony, are microscopic, but colonies may grow up to 1 ft (30 cm) or more in diameter. Some colonies are erect and branching; others are thin, flat encrustations on rocks or water plants. The body wall of each zooid forms a rigid, boxlike case from which a U-shaped crown of ciliated tentacles, the lophophore, is extended for feeding. The cilia generate water currents that sweep small organisms and organic particles

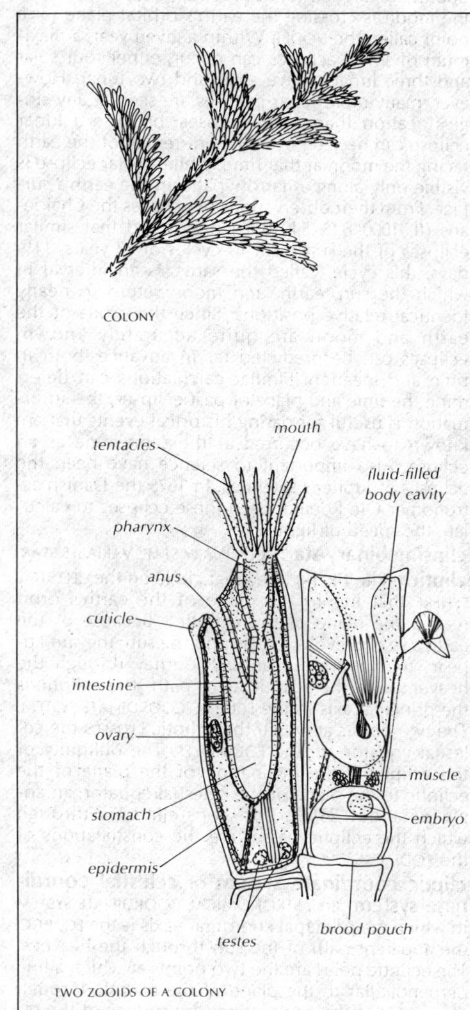

Bugula, *a moss animal, representative of the phylum Ectoprocta*

toward the mouth, located within the lophophore. The ectoprocts are divided into two classes, one predominantly marine, the other found in fresh water. They were formerly placed in the phylum Bryozoa along with the ENTOPROCTA, which they superficially resemble. The name bryozoan, or moss animal, is still commonly applied to the ectoprocts. Ectoprocts are a large and ancient group, and many fossil forms have been described. There are about 4,000 living species. *Bugula* is a common colonial marine ectoproct.

Ecuador (ĕk'wədôr) [Span.,=equator], republic (1973 est. pop. 6,600,000), 109,483 sq mi (283,561 sq km), W South America. The capital is QUITO. Ecuador is bounded on the N by Colombia, on the S and E by Peru, and on the W by the Pacific Ocean. The Andes, dominating the country, cut across Ecuador in two ranges and reach their greatest altitude in the snowcapped volcanic peaks of Chimborazo (20,577 ft/6,272 m) and Cotopaxi (19,347 ft/5,897 m). Within the mountains are high, often fertile valleys, where grains are cultivated, and the major urban centers, such as Quito, CUENCA, and RIOBAMBA, are located. Earthquakes are frequent and often disastrous; in 1949 the city of AMBATO was leveled. West of the Andes is a region of tropical jungle, through which run the tributaries of the Amazon River. The Pacific coast region, with hot, humid valleys N of the Gulf of Guayaquil, is the source of Ecuador's chief exports: oil, bananas, coffee, and cocoa. Large deposits of oil are located also in the northeast. Other exports include forest products, fish, sugar, rice, copper, and panama hats. The United States is the main trade partner; GUAYAQUIL and Esmeraldas are the chief ports. Two thirds of the work force engages in agriculture. Corn, barley, rice, and wheat are grown for subsistence. Manufacturing industries are few and small-scale. The per capita income at the start of the 1970s was only about $250. Roman Catholicism is the main religion, although there is no established church. Ecuador has 10 universities. About three fifths of the population live in the highlands. The majority is predominantly Indian or part

Indian, although there are many blacks and mulattoes, chiefly in the coastal region. Spanish is the official language, but many Indians speak Quechua or Jarvo. The few whites are mostly landholders and play a dominant role in Equador's unstable political life. In 1974, Ecuador was governed by the military under Gen. Guillermo RODRIQUEZ LARA. Despite the development of modern communications, the country is still rent by the personal and factional rivalry that began with the Spanish conquest. Francisco Pizarro's subordinate, BENALCÁZAR, entered the area in 1533. Not finding the wealth of the mythical El Dorado, he and other conquistadores, notably Gonzalo PIZARRO and ORELLANA, moved restlessly on. The region became a colonial backwater. Given an *audiencia* in 1563 and established politically as the presidency of Quito, it was at various times subject to Peru and to NEW GRANADA. After an abortive independence movement in 1809, the region remained under Spanish control. It was liberated by Antonio José de SUCRE in the battle of PICHINCHA (1822) and was joined by Simón BOLÍVAR to Greater Colombia. With the dissolution of the union in 1830, Ecuador, geographically isolated, became a separate state (four times its present size) under a constitution promulgated by its first president, Juan José FLORES. Ecuador unsuccessfully attempted to annex Popayán prov. from Colombia by war in 1832 and occupied the GALÁPAGOS ISLANDS that year. Boundary disputes led to frequent invasions by Peruvians in the 19th and 20th cent. The entire eastern frontier, known as Oriente, was in dispute. In 1942, Ecuador signed a treaty ceding a large area to Peru, but in 1960 it renounced the treaty. Bitter internecine struggles between Conservatives and Liberals marked the political history of Ecuador in the 19th cent. The Conservatives, led by Flores and GARCÍA MORENO (1821-75), supported entrenched privileges and the dominance of the Roman Catholic Church; the Liberals, led by ROCAFUERTE (1783-1847) and ALFARO (1867-1912) and championed by the writer MONTALVO (1832-89), sought social reforms. In the 20th cent. there have been a bewildering number of changes in government. In 1925 the army replaced the coastal banking interests, dominant since 1916, as the ultimate source of power. Military juntas supported various rival factions, and between 1931 and 1940, 12 presidents were in office. José María VELASCO IBARRA became president (for the second time) by a coup in 1944. He was ousted in 1947, and the next year Galo PLAZA LASSO was chosen in free elections. During Plaza's regime there was unprecedented political reform. Velasco Ibarra was elected again in 1952 and sponsored improvements in roads and schools. The first Conservative to rule in 60 years, Camilo Ponce Enríquez, followed (1956-60), but Velasco Ibarra was elected again in 1960. He was forced to resign the following year. His legal successor, Julio Arosemena Monroy, was deposed by a junta in 1963. Agitation for a return to civilian government led the military to remove the junta in 1966. A constitutional assembly installed Otto AROSEMENA GÓMEZ as provisional president and drafted the country's 17th constitution. Velasco Ibarra was elected for the fifth time in 1968. Two years later, faced with economic problems and protests by leftist students, he assumed absolute power. Velasco promised to hold elections in June, 1972. However, the military deposed him in Feb., 1972, and canceled the elections. Ecuador's relations with the United States deteriorated in the early 1970s after Ecuador claimed that its territorial waters extended 200 mi (322 km) out to sea. Several U.S. fishing boats were seized by Ecuadorians, and U.S. aid to the country was suspended. In the same period Ecuador became Latin America's second largest oil producer. Increased oil revenues and exploitation of the country's vast forests raised the prospect of rapid economic development. See Lilo Linke, *Ecuador: Country of Contrasts* (3d ed. 1960); G. I. Blanksten, *Ecuador: Constitutions and Caudillos* (1951, repr. 1964); E. E. Erickson et al., *Area Handbook for Ecuador* (1966); B. J. Meggers, *Ecuador* (1966); Pedro Cieza de León, *The War of Quito* (tr. and ed. by Sir Clements R. Markham, 1913; repr. 1967); Henri Michaux, *Ecuador* (tr. 1970); C. R. Gibson, *Foreign Trade in the Economic Development of Small Nations: The Case of Ecuador* (1971); P. H. Gore, *The Highland Campesino, Backward Peasant or Reluctant Pawn* (1971); J. D. Martz, *Ecuador: Conflicting Political Culture and the Quest for Progress* (1972).

ecumenical council: see COUNCIL, ECUMENICAL.

ecumenical movement (ĕk″yo͞omĕn′ĭkəl, ē″-), name given to the movement aimed at the unification of the Protestant churches of the world and ultimately of all Christians. Protestantism during and after the Reformation separated into numerous independent sects. An early attempt to reverse this tendency was the Evangelical Alliance founded in England in 1846; an American branch was formed by Philip Schaff in 1867. Other organizations that crossed denominational barriers were the Young Men's Christian Association (1844), the Young Women's Christian Association (1884), and the Christian Endeavor Society (1881). In 1908 the Federal Council of Churches of Christ, composed of the larger Protestant denominations in the United States, was organized and strove to represent Protestant opinion on religious and social questions. The movement known as Church Reunion in Great Britain and as Christian Unity (1910) in the United States was active in seeking a creed and polity behind which all Christians could unite. On an international scale the ecumenical movement really began with the World Missionary Conference at Edinburgh in 1910. This led to the establishment (1921) of the International Missionary Council, which fostered cooperation in mission activity and among the younger churches. Other landmarks in the development of the movement were the Universal Christian Conference on Life and Work (Stockholm, 1925), inspired by Nathan SÖDERBLOM of Sweden; the World Conference on Faith and Order (Lausanne, 1927); and the first assembly of the WORLD COUNCIL OF CHURCHES (Amsterdam, 1948). The World Council, bringing together more than 250 Protestant, Orthodox Eastern (including the Russian Orthodox Church), and Old Catholic bodies, is now the chief instrument of ecumenicity; in 1961 it united with the International Missionary Council. Progress has also been made in mergers between individual churches; notable examples include the Church of South India (see SOUTH INDIA, CHURCH OF), established in 1947, the first union between episcopal and nonepiscopal churches, and in the United States, where there have been many mergers, the UNITED CHURCH OF CHRIST. A proposal was made in 1960 to bring together the American Methodist, Protestant Episcopal, United Presbyterian, and United Church of Christ denominations; this led to the establishment (1962) of the Consultation on Church Union, whose discussions continued into the 1970s. A proposed merger between the English Methodists and the Church of England was rejected by the Methodists in 1969. The Anglicans did, however, reach several doctrinal accords with the Roman Catholic Church in the early 1970s. The Vatican did not give formal recognition to the existence of the ecumenical movement until 1960, when it established the Secretariat for Promoting Christian Unity. Protestant and Orthodox Eastern observers were invited to the Second Vatican Council (1962-65), and the Decree on Ecumenism (1964) promulgated by that council encouraged new dialogues with Protestant and Orthodox churches. In 1969, Pope Paul VI visited the headquarters of the World Council of Churches in Geneva. See Bernard Leeming, *The Churches and the Church* (1960); Matthew Spinka, *The Quest for Church Unity* (1960); Norman Goodall, *The Ecumenical Movement* (3d ed. 1966).

eczema (ĕk′səmə), acute or chronic skin disease characterized by redness, itching, serum-filled blisters, crusting, and scaling. Predisposing factors are familial history of allergic disorders (hay fever, asthma, or eczema) and sensitivity to contact allergens or certain foods. The condition is often irritated by excessive sweating, exposure to extreme heat or cold, and abnormal dryness or oiliness of the skin. Eczema may occur at any age and in both sexes. It is frequently chronic and difficult to treat, and it tends to disappear and recur. Itching can be extreme and severe, and it can often lead to an emotional disturbance. Treatment usually necessitates the avoidance of all unnecessary skin irritation; corticosteroid creams and lotions are sometimes helpful. Care should be taken to avoid secondary infections.

Ed, name of an altar raised on the left bank of the Jordan. Joshua 22.34.

Edam (ādäm′), town (1970 pop. 18,184), North Holland prov., N central Netherlands, on IJsselmeer lake; chartered 1357. It is a picturesque town that attracts many tourists. Edam is noted for its cheese; it also has fisheries.

Edar (ē′där), tower, near which Jacob pitched his tent. Gen. 35.21.

Edda (ĕd′ə), title applied to two distinct works in Old Icelandic. The *Poetic Edda,* or *Elder Edda,* is a collection (late 13th cent.) of 34 mythological and heroic lays, most of which were composed c.800-c.1200, probably in Iceland or W Norway. Despite uncritical arrangement and textual corruption, the *Poetic Edda* is the most valuable collection of texts in OLD NORSE LITERATURE. See English translations by L. M. Hollander (2d ed. 1962), P. B. Taylor and W. H. Auden (1969), and U. Dronke (Vol. I, 1969). The *Prose Edda,* or *Younger Edda,* was probably written c.1222 by SNORRI STURLUSON as a guide to the scaldic poetry of Iceland. The first two parts constitute an account of Scandinavian mythology and are the prime source on the subject; the third part is a compendium of the complex diction of scaldic poetry; the fourth, a treatise on the meters employed. Abridged translations of the *Prose Edda,* treating primarily the first mythical part, have been made by J. I. Young (new ed. 1966). For studies of both Eddas, see Stefan Einarsson, *A History of Icelandic Literature* (1957) and P. Hallberg, *The Icelandic Saga* (1962).

Eddington, Sir Arthur Stanley, 1882-1944, British astronomer and physicist. He was chief assistant (1906-13) at the Royal Observatory, Greenwich, and was from 1913 Plumian professor of astronomy at Cambridge, where he was director of the observatory from 1914. Eddington made important contributions to the study of the evolution, motion, and internal constitution of stars and was one of the first physicists to grasp the theory of relativity, of which he became a leading exponent. One of the foremost contemporary expositors of scientific subjects, he was also concerned with the relation of physics to philosophy. He was knighted in 1930. His writings include *Mathematical Theory of Relativity* (1923), *The Internal Constitution of the Stars* (1926), *Stars and Atoms* (1928), *New Pathways in Science* (1935), and *The Philosophy of Physical Science* (1939). See biographies by A. Vibert Douglas (1956) and C. W. Kilmister (1966); study by Sir Edmund Whittaker (1951).

Eddy, Mary Baker, 1821-1910, founder of the CHRISTIAN SCIENCE movement, b. Bow, near Concord, N.H. As her physical frailty prevented regular school attendance, she received much of her early instruction at home from her brother Albert Baker. She also attended Holmes Academy at Plymouth and Sanbornton Academy. At a young age she wrote poetry and prose, accepted for publication in periodicals. Widowed six months after her marriage to George W. Glover and left with her only child (also named George W. Glover), she spent nine years among relatives, teaching at times and often in ill health. Married in 1853 to Daniel Patterson, a dentist, she lived in the country for some time, going later to Lynn, Mass. Having heard of the success in mental healing of Phineas Parkhurst QUIMBY, she went in 1862 to Portland, Maine. She received benefit from his treatment and became his pupil, but later discarded his methods. In 1866 she separated from her husband; she later (1873) obtained a divorce. The year 1866 marks the actual beginning of Christian

Science as she apprehended it. Bible study, practice, and writing, in the ensuing years, brought steady development in the formulation of doctrine and plans for the new church. In 1875 the textbook of Christian Science, *Science and Health* (later *Science and Health with Key to the Scriptures*), was published. In 1877 she was married for the last time, to Asa Gilbert Eddy, an active Christian Scientist. She founded in 1883, and for a time edited, the *Journal of Christian Science.* As leader of the Christian Science movement Mary Baker Eddy herself planned the *Church Manual* for the conduct of the Church of Christ, Scientist, and directed every detail in its upbuilding. She lived in Boston for seven years, from 1882, then near Concord, N.H., until 1908, when she made her home in Chestnut Hill, near Boston. As pastor emeritus of the Mother Church in Boston and head of the whole church with all its branches, she exercised a strong influence, even in the retirement of her later years. In 1908 she founded the *Christian Science Monitor,* a daily newspaper. Her writings include *Retrospection and Introspection* (1891), *Miscellaneous Writings* (1896), and *Messages to the Mother Church* (1900, 1901, 1902). See the official biography by Sibyl Wilbur (1929 ed.) and a later one by J. M. Johnston (1946), impartial biographies by L. P. Powell (1930) and Robert Peel (1969, repr. 1972), and a critical one by E. F. Dakin (rev. ed. 1930).

Eddystone (ĕd'ĭstən), lighthouse, 135 ft (41 m) high, on dangerous rocks in the English Channel, S of Plymouth, SW England. It is the fourth lighthouse on the site (the first was begun in 1696) and was built between 1878 and 1882 by Sir James Douglass.

Edelinck, Gérard (zhărär' ādəlăNk'), 1640–1707, French engraver, b. Antwerp. He is known for his faithful interpretations of the work of Raphael, Le Brun, Champaigne, and other masters and for his portraits of celebrities of the time, including Louis XIV, Colbert, La Fontaine, John Dryden, and Descartes.

edelweiss (ā'dəlvĭs), perennial COMPOSITE plant (genus *Leontopodium*) found at high altitudes in the mountains of Europe, Asia, and South America. It is about 6 in. (15.2 cm) tall with woolly-white floral leaves and small heads of yellow disk flowers surrounded by silvery bracts. Despite its inconspicuous appearance it is esteemed (chiefly by the Swiss) as a symbol of purity and inaccessibility and is reputed to have brought death to many who have sought it. In Switzerland it is protected by law and has been reproduced on postage stamps. Probably because of its associations it has some popularity as a rock garden and pot plant. Edelweiss is classified in the division MAGNOLIOPHYTA, class Magnoliopsida, order Asterales, family Compositae.

edema (ĭdē'mə) or **dropsy,** abnormal accumulation of fluid in the body tissues or in the body cavities causing swelling or distention of the affected parts. Edema of the ankles and lower legs (in ambulatory patients) is characteristic of congestive heart failure, but it can accompany many other conditions, including obesity, diseased leg veins, kidney disease, cirrhosis of the liver, anemia, and severe malnutrition. The accumulation of fluid within the lungs is a serious complication of cardiac failure, pneumonia, and other disorders. The collection of fluid in the pleural space (within the two-layered membrane surrounding the lungs) can be the symptom of any of numerous infectious and circulatory disorders. The collection of water within the skull is a serious and usually incurable condition (see HYDROCEPHALUS). Since edema is a symptom, the underlying cause must be treated.

Eden. 1 Son of Joah. 2 Chron. 29.12. **2** Priest. 2 Chron. 31.15. Perhaps this is the same as **1. 3** See EDEN, GARDEN OF. **4** Unidentified trading center, possibly in Mesopotamia. 2 Kings 19.12; Isa. 37.12; Ezek. 27.23. **5** Place somewhere near Damascus. Amos 1.5.

Eden, Sir Anthony, 1897–, British statesman. After service in World War I he attended Oxford and entered (1923) Parliament as a Conservative. He soon made his mark as a champion of peace, internationalism, and the League of Nations and was made lord privy seal (1934–35) and "traveling ambassador." He served (1935) as British minister for League affairs and became foreign minister in 1935. He resigned in Feb., 1938, because of his opposition to Neville Chamberlain's policy of appeasement of the Axis powers, but at the beginning (1939) of World War II he was called back to the cabinet as secretary of state for dominion affairs. After Winston Churchill became (May, 1940) prime minister, Eden was briefly secretary of war before returning to the foreign office in Dec., 1940. He was instrumental in concluding the wartime Anglo-Soviet Alliance and in establishing the United Nations. He remained in Parliament under the Labour government of 1945–51, and with the Conservative victory of 1951 he returned once more to the foreign office. As chairman of the 1954 Geneva Conference, he helped to negotiate a temporary settlement of the conflict in Indochina. He was knighted in 1954 and became prime minister upon Churchill's resignation in 1955. Eden's decision to use armed intervention in the SUEZ CANAL crisis of 1956 provoked great controversy. His health collapsed, and he resigned in Jan., 1957. He was raised to the peerage as earl of Avon in 1961. See his memoirs, *Full Circle* (1960), *Facing the Dictators, 1923–1938* (1962), and *The Reckoning* (1965); study by Geoffrey McDermott (1969).

Eden, Emily, 1797–1869, English novelist. She went with her brother George, Lord Auckland, to India when he was governor general (1836–42). Her two novels, *The Semi-detached House* (1859) and *The Semi-attached Couple* (1860; with biographical introduction by Anthony Eden, 1947), give witty pictures of life in the early 19th cent. See her letters (ed. by Violet Dickinson, 1919).

Eden, town (1970 pop. 15,871), Rockingham co., N North Carolina.

Eden, name of several rivers in England and Scotland. The principal one rises in Westmorland, N England, and flows 65 mi (105 km) NW through Cumberland, past Carlisle, into Solway Firth. The Vale of Eden is a rich farming region.

Eden, Garden of, in the Bible, first home of man. God established the garden, with its trees of knowledge and of life, as a dwelling place for Adam and Eve, until, having eaten of the forbidden fruit, they were banished (Gen. 2; 3). Eden is often called Paradise. Eden has been located variously over the Old World, especially in lower Mesopotamia.

Edenvale, town (1970 pop. 24,843), Transvaal prov., NE Republic of South Africa, on the WITWATERSRAND. It is a residential and commercial suburb of JOHANNESBURG and GERMISTON.

Eder (ē'dər). **1** Levite. 1 Chron. 23.23; 24.30. **2** City of Judah, S Palestine. Joshua 15.21.

Eder (ā'dər), river, c.110 mi (180 km) long, rising near Siegen, central West Germany, and flowing E to the Fulda River. The Eder dam, at Hemfurth, impounds one of the largest reservoirs in West Germany; it has a hydroelectric power plant (51,000-kw capacity). The reservoir supplies water to the Ems-Weser Canal.

Ederle, Gertrude (ā'dərlē), 1906–, American swimmer, b. New York City. Ederle won many swimming championships, established numerous records, and represented the United States in the 1924 Olympic games. On Aug. 6, 1926, she became the first woman to swim the English Channel, which she crossed in 14 hr and 31 min, breaking previous men's records. She became a professional soon afterward, making several successful tours before her retirement.

Edessa (ĭdĕs'ə), ancient city of Mesopotamia, on the site of modern URFA, Turkey. It emerged into history in the 4th cent. B.C. as Orrhoe, or Arrhoe, and was later named Edessa by Seleucus I of Syria. From c.137 B.C. it was the capital of the independent kingdom of Osroene. It later became a Roman city. There in A.D. 260, Shapur I of Persia defeated Emperor Valerian and took him prisoner. Edessa was a center of Christianity by the 3d cent. A.D. and became one of the major religious centers of the Byzantine Empire. The city fell to the Arabs in 639 and remained in Muslim hands until captured by the Crusaders in 1097. Baldwin (later Baldwin I of Jerusalem) became the ruler of Edessa, and when he became king he turned it over to one of his cousins. The city, however, fell to the Muslims in 1144 and passed to the Turks in 1637.

Edfu: see IDFU, Egypt.

Edgar or **Eadgar** (both: ĕd'gər), 943?–975, king of the English (959–75), son of Edmund, king of Wessex. In 957 the Mercians and Northumbrians rebelled against Edgar's brother EDWY and chose Edgar as their king. In 959 he succeeded his brother as king of Wessex. His reign was one of orderly prosperity. He recalled (958) Saint DUNSTAN and with him initiated widespread monastic reforms. In 973 the king was crowned at Bath in an elaborate ceremony, the first of its kind in England, that stressed the analogy between kingship and priesthood. Shortly afterward he received homage from the other kings in Britain at Chester. He gave Lothian to the king of Scotland in return for his homage, and granted practical autonomy to the Danes in England (see DANELAW) in return for their loyalty. Edgar was succeeded by his son by his first wife, Edward the Martyr. His son by his second wife was Æthelred the Unready, who succeeded Edward.

Edgar Atheling (ăth'əlĭng) [O.E. *ætheling,*=son of the king], 1060?–1125?, English prince, grandson of Edmund Ironside. After the death of King HAROLD at the battle of Hastings in 1066, Edgar was chosen king, but he submitted to WILLIAM I in the same year. In 1068 he fled to the Scottish king MALCOLM III, who soon married Edgar's sister St. Margaret of Scotland. Edgar took part in the unsuccessful Northumbrian uprising (1069) in which the Danes also joined. After Malcolm made his peace with William in 1072, the Atheling probably lived in Flanders until he himself came to terms with William in 1074 and settled in France. After William's death Edgar joined Malcolm in raiding England in 1091, but after that he seems to have been at peace with William II of England. He led the English expedition that in 1097 dethroned Donald III and seated the Atheling's nephew Edgar (d. 1107) on the throne of Scotland. The Atheling went on the crusade of 1099 with Robert II, duke of Normandy, and later fought for Robert against Henry I of England. He was taken prisoner at the battle of Tinchebrai (1106) but was released.

Edgehill or **Edge Hill,** ridge on the border of Warwickshire and Oxfordshire, central England, NW of Banbury. A tower built in 1760 marks the scene of the first great battle of the English civil war, Oct. 23, 1642, between the royalists, under Charles I and Prince Rupert, and the parliamentarians, under the 3d earl of Essex. The outcome of the battle was indecisive.

Edge Island: see EDGEØYA.

Edgeøya (ĕd'yə-öyä) or **Edge Island,** island of the Svalbard group, 1,942 sq mi (5,030 sq km), Norway, in the Barents Sea, E of Spitsbergen Island. It rises to 2,349 ft (716 m). An ice field covers the southeastern portion of the island.

Edgeworth, Francis Ysidro, 1845–1926, British economist, grad. Trinity College, Dublin. He was professor of political economy at Oxford and first editor (1891–1926) of the *Economist.* His special contribution to economics was the application of mathematical measurements, as described in *Mathematical Psychics* (1881). Much of his writing was collected in *Papers Relating to Political Economy* (3 vol., 1925).

Edgeworth, Maria, 1767–1849, Irish novelist; daughter of Richard Lovell Edgeworth. She lived practically her entire life on her father's estate in Ireland. *Letters for Literary Ladies* (1795), her first publication, argued for the education of women. She is best known for her novels of Irish life—*Castle Rackrent* (1800), *Belinda* (1801), and *The Absentee* (1812). Although her works are marred somewhat by didacticism, they are notable for their realism, humor, and freshness of style. She also wrote a number of stories for children, including *Moral Tales* (1801). See selected letters ed. by Christina Colvin (1971); study by Marilyn Butler (1972).

Edgeworth, Richard Lovell, 1744–1817, Anglo-Irish educational theorist, b. Bath, England, educated at Trinity College, Dublin, and at Oxford; father of Maria Edgeworth. A member of the literary coterie of Lichfield, he was a close friend of Thomas Day and Erasmus Darwin. *Practical Education* (written with his daughter) and his other educational essays show the influence of Rousseau. He also did pioneering work in electricity and telegraphy. See Desmond Clarke, *The Ingenious Mr. Edgeworth* (1965).

Edhessa (ĕd'ĕsä) or **Vodena** (vôthänä'), city (1971 pop. 13,967), capital of Pella prefecture, N Greece, in Macedonia. It is a rail and road junction and an agricultural trading center. Textiles and rugs are manufactured. Known as Aegae in antiquity, it was the earliest seat of the Macedonian kings. After Philip II moved (4th cent. B.C.) the Macedonian capital to Pella, it continued to be the royal burial place.

Edina (ēdī'nə), village (1970 pop. 44,046), Hennepin co., E Minn., a suburb of Minneapolis. It is chiefly residential and is in an area with more than 60 lakes and much park land. Electronic and computer equipment are manufactured.

Edinburg, city (1970 pop. 17,163), seat of Hidalgo co., extreme S Texas; inc. 1919. It is a processing center in the irrigated portion of the lower Rio Grande valley. Agricultural products include packaged meats, dairy items, citrus fruits, vegetables, and cotton. Oil and gas are produced from surrounding fields, and oil field machinery, men's slacks, and paper, plastic, and metal products are manufactured.

Pan American Univ. is in Edinburg. In 1967 the city suffered extensive damage from a hurricane. A U.S. wildlife refuge and a state park are nearby.

Edinburgh, Philip Mountbatten, duke of (ĕd'ĭnbərə), 1921–, consort of Queen ELIZABETH II of Great Britain, b. Greece. He was the son of Prince Andrew of Greece and Princess Alice, daughter of Prince Louis of BATTENBERG, and a grandson of George I of Greece, great-grandson of Christian IX of Denmark, and great-great-grandson of Queen Victoria. He took his mother's name, Mountbatten, when he became a British citizen in 1947, at the same time renouncing his Greek and Danish titles. Philip served in the British navy during World War II. He was created duke of Edinburgh shortly before his marriage (Nov. 20, 1947) to Elizabeth. In 1957, Elizabeth conferred upon him the title of Prince.

Edinburgh, city (1971 pop. 453,422), royal burgh, capital of Scotland and formerly the county town of Midlothian, on the Firth of Forth. LEITH, part of the city since 1920, is Edinburgh's port. The city is famous in Scottish legend and literature as Dunedin or "Auld Reekie." It is divided into two sections. The Old Town, on the slope of Castle Rock, dates from the 11th cent. and contains most of the city's historic sites; the New Town spread to the north in the late 18th cent. Edinburgh is Scotland's banking and administrative center. The port exports coal, whiskey, and machinery. It imports grain, fertilizer, petroleum, minerals, woodpulp, cement, fruit, and vegetables. Edinburgh is a large brewing center, has a thriving publishing industry, and produces great quantities of high-grade paper. There are metalworks and rubber and engineering works. Other industries are distilling, the manufacture of glassware, drugs, and chemicals, and shipbuilding. The city has become an important center for nuclear and electronics research. The graduate faculty for electronic engineering at the Univ. of Edinburgh is one of the largest of its kind in Great Britain. Edinburgh's history may be said to have begun when Malcolm III of Scotland erected a castle there in the late 11th cent., and his wife built the Chapel of St. Margaret, the city's oldest surviving building. A town grew up around the castle and was chartered in 1329 by Robert I. It grew steadily despite repeated sacking and burning by the English in the border wars and became the capital city of Scotland in 1437. James IV was the first monarch to make Edinburgh his regular seat. The rooms of Mary Queen of Scots are preserved in HOLYROOD palace. The city lost importance when James VI became king of England in 1603 and commerce and society followed the court to London. After the Act of Union with England in 1707 dissolved the Scottish Parliament, Edinburgh retained the Supreme Courts of Law, which meet in Parliament House. Edinburgh blossomed as a cultural center in the 18th and 19th cent. around the figures of the philosophers David HUME and Adam SMITH and the writers Robert BURNS and Sir Walter SCOTT. The *Edinburgh Review*, founded in 1802, added to the city's literary reputation. In 1939 the offices of the Secretary of State for Scotland were moved from London to Edinburgh. The Edinburgh International Festival of Music and Drama, held every summer since 1947, is world famous. Other features of interest are the National War Memorial; the collections of the Royal Scottish Academy, the National Gallery of Scotland, and the Royal Scottish Museum; the National Library; Princes St.; the Royal Botanic Gardens; the house of the Protestant reformer John KNOX; the church of St. Giles's, dating from the 12th cent.; and the site of the famous prison, Old Tolbooth, which figures in Scott's novel, *The Heart of Midlothian*. The Univ. of Edinburgh, founded under James VI in 1583, has noted faculties of medicine, law, divinity, music, and the arts. Under the Local Government Act of 1973, Edinburgh became (1975) part of the Lothian region.

Edinburgh, University of, at Edinburgh, Scotland; founded 1583. It has faculties of divinity, law, medicine, arts, science, music, social sciences, and veterinary medicine. The Institute for Advanced Studies in the Humanities, the Centre of Rural Economy, and the Edinburgh School of Agriculture are associated with the university.

Edinburghshire: see MIDLOTHIAN, Scotland.

Edingen: see ENGHIEN, Belgium.

Edirne (ĕdĕr'nĕ), formerly **Adrianople** (ā"drēənō'pəl), city (1970 pop. 54,885), capital of Edirne prov., NW Turkey, in Thrace. It is the commercial center for a farm region where grains, fruits, and tobacco are grown and cattle and sheep are raised. Manufactures of Edirne include cheese and textiles. The city was founded (A.D. c.125) by Hadrian, the Roman emperor, on the site of Uscudama. Of great strategic importance and strongly fortified, the city has had a turbulent history. The defeat (378) of Emperor Valens by the Visigoths at Adrianople left Greece open to invasion by barbarian tribes. Later conquered by the Avars, the Bulgarians, and the Crusaders, the city passed to the Ottoman Turks in 1361 and was the residence of the Ottoman sultans until the conquest of Constantinople in 1453. Russia captured the city twice (1829 and 1878) during the Russo-Turkish Wars. It fell (1913) to Bulgaria in the First Balkan War but was restored to Turkey after the Second Balkan War. It passed to Greece by the Treaty of Sèvres (1920), but was again restored to Turkey by the Treaty of Lausanne (1923). The city's many mosques include the great mosque of Selim II (completed 1574). The city was also called Orestia by Byzantine writers.

Edison, Thomas Alva, 1847–1931, American inventor, b. Milan, Ohio. A genius in the practical application of scientific principles, Edison was one of the greatest and most productive inventors of his time. His schooling was limited to three months in Port Huron, Mich., in 1854. For several years he was a newsboy on the Grand Trunk RR, and it was during this period that he began to suffer from deafness, which was to increase throughout his life. Edison later worked as a telegraph operator in various cities. His first inventions were the transmitter and receiver for the automatic telegraph, the quadruplex system of transmitting four simultaneous messages, and an improved stock-ticker system. In 1877 he invented the carbon telephone transmitter (see MICROPHONE) for the Western Union Telegraph Company. His phonograph (patented 1878) was notable as the first successful instrument of its kind. Edison created the first commercially practical incandescent lamp (with a carbon filament) in 1879. Moreover, for use with it he developed a complete electrical distribution system for light and power, including generators, motors, light sockets with the Edison base, junction boxes, safety fuses, underground conductors, and other devices. The crowning achievement of his work in this field was the Pearl St. plant (1881–82) in New York City, the first central electric-light power plant in the world. He built and operated (1880) an experimental electric railroad. Edison produced a superior storage battery of iron and nickel with an alkaline electrolyte. He developed the Kinetoscope, or peep show machine, and later demonstrated experimentally the synchronization of motion pictures and sound; talking pictures were based on this work. Edison held over 1,300 U.S. and foreign patents. During World War I he helped to develop the manufacture in the United States of chemicals previously imported; he also served as head of the U.S. navy consulting board concerned with ship defenses against torpedoes and mines. He later worked on the production of rubber from American plants, notably goldenrod. His workshops at Menlo Park (1876) and West Orange, N.J. (1887) were significant as forerunners of the modern industrial research laboratory in which teams of workers, rather than a lone inventor, systematically investigate a given subject. An Edison memorial tower and light was erected (1938) in Menlo Park, N.J.; Edison's laboratory and other buildings associated with his career are preserved in GREENFIELD VILLAGE. His various companies were later consolidated to form the General Electric Company. See the autobiographical *Diary and Sundry Observations* (ed. by D. D. Runes, 1948, repr. 1968); biography by Robert Silverberg (1967); study by B. M. Vanderbilt (1971).

Edison National Historic Site: see NATIONAL PARKS AND MONUMENTS (table).

Edmer: see EADMER.

Edmond, city (1970 pop. 16,633), Oklahoma co., central Okla.; settled 1889. It is a trading center with small industries and a huge oil field. Central State Univ. is there.

Edmonds, Walter Dumaux, 1903–, American author, b. Boonville, N.Y., grad. Harvard, 1926. His popular historical novels about New York state include *Rome Haul* (1929; adapted for the stage as *The Farmer Takes a Wife*), *Erie Water* (1933), *Drums along the Mohawk* (1936), and *Chad Hanna* (1940). Later novels include *Cadmus Henry* (1949) and *The Boyds of Black River* (1953).

Edmonds, city (1970 pop. 23,998), Snohomish co., NW Wash., a suburb of Seattle, on Puget Sound; inc. 1890. Edmonds is primarily a residential city.

Edmonton (ĕd'məntən), city (1971 pop. 438,152), provincial capital, central Alta., on the North Saskatchewan River. Edmonton is in the center of the fertile northern park country and is also the gateway for the Peace River and Athabasca River country. It is a major market center for farm and petrochemical products and is the depot for the entire District of Mackenzie and an outfitting point for northern expeditions. In the vicinity are oil, gas, and coal fields. The city is on the site of Edmonton House, an important 19th-century trading post. The Univ. of Alberta is in the city.

Edmund, Saint, d. 869, king of East Anglia (855–869). He was supposedly martyred by the invading Danes for his adherence to Christianity. His shrine was at Bury St. Edmunds. Feast: Nov. 20.

Edmund, Saint (Edmund Rich), 1170?–1240, English churchman, archbishop of Canterbury, b. Abingdon. He taught at Oxford. A forceful preacher, he successfully preached (1227) the crusade against the Saracens. Edmund was made archbishop in 1234 and mediated the peace between Wales and England. His zeal for reform antagonized HENRY III who, to isolate St. Edmund, secured from Rome a papal legate sympathetic to himself, with jurisdiction over the archbishop. His episcopacy thus neutralized, St. Edmund retired reluctantly to Pontigny, a Cistercian abbey in France, where he died soon after. Feast: Nov. 16. See C. H. Lawrence, *St. Edmund of Abingdon* (1960).

Edmund, 921–46, king of Wessex (939–46), half brother and successor of Athelstan. Immediately after his accession he had to face an invasion of Irish vikings led by OLAF GUTHFRITHSON. He was forced to cede to them the territory between Watling Street and the Northumbrian border (already occupied partly by Danes), and he succeeded in recapturing it in 944 only because of the quarrels among the Norse leaders. In 945 he invaded Strathclyde, which he then turned over to the Scottish king Malcolm I. Edmund was killed in a brawl and was succeeded by his brother Edred.

Edmund Crouchback: see LANCASTER, HOUSE OF.

Edmund Ironside, d. 1016, king of the English (1016), son of Æthelred the Unready. Contrary to the wishes of his father, he married (1015) the widow of Siferth, a Danish thane, and was accepted as ruler of the Five Boroughs of the DANELAW. When CANUTE invaded England in 1015, Emund led the fighting against him. However, the people apparently felt that he was a rebel against his father, for he found it hard to gain a following without his father's aid. At Æthelred's death (April, 1016) Edmund was proclaimed king in London, but most of the nobles gave their support to Canute. Edmund continued the struggle with great courage (which earned him the appellation Ironside) and considerable success until he was defeated in the disastrous battle of Assandun (Oct. 18, 1016). He and Canute agreed to partition the country, but Edmund died the following month.

Edmundston (ĕd'mənstən), city (1971 pop. 12,365), NW N.B., Canada, at the confluence of the St. John and Madawaska rivers, at the U.S. border. It has a large pulp mill and is a railroad center and hunting and fishing base. Settled c.1785 by Acadians, it was known as Petit Sault to the French and Little Falls to the English before being named in 1850 for Sir Edmund Head, later governor general of Canada.

Edo: see TOKYO, Japan.

Edom (ē'dŏm), **Idumaea,** or **Idumea** (both: īdyōōmē'ə), mountainous country, called also Mt. Seir, given to ESAU, also called Edom, and his descendants. It extended along the eastern border of the Arabah valley from the Dead Sea to Elath on the Gulf of Aqaba. The history of the Edomites was one of continuous hostility and warfare with their neighbors—Jews, Assyrians, and Syrians—until finally they were subdued by the Maccabees and merged with the Jews. At one period they occupied S Judah. (Gen. 32.3; 36; Num. 20.14–23; Deut. 2.12; 1 Kings 9.26; 11.14–17; 22.47; 2 Kings 8.20–22; Isa. 34.5; Jer. 49.7–17; Ezek. 25.12–14; 35; 36.5; Mark 3.8.) The Romans grouped Idumaea with Judaea, Samaria, and Galilee in one procuratorship. After the destruction of Jerusalem, Idumaea was included in Arabia Petraea.

Edred or **Eadred** (both: ĕd'rĕd), d. 955, king of the English (946–55), son of Edward the Elder. He succeeded his brother Edmund and was faced with invasions of Danish Northumbria by Norsemen from Ireland and by Eric Bloodaxe of Norway. He finally reestablished control over Northumbria in 954, thus bringing to an end the last independent Scandinavian kingdom in England. Edred, being sickly, left affairs to his friend Saint DUNSTAN, who allowed the Danes of England to live under their own laws.

Edrei (ĕd'rēī). 1 Capital of Og, king of Bashan, not identified with certainty. Num. 21.33; Deut. 1.4; 3.1,10; Joshua 12.4; 13.12, 31. 2 Unidentified town of Naphtali. Joshua 19.37.

Edrisi: see IDRISI.

EDTA: see CHELATING AGENTS.

education, any process, either formal or informal, that shapes the potentialities of the maturing organism. Informal education results from the constant effect of environment, and its strength in shaping values and habits can hardly be overestimated. Formal education is a conscious effort by society to impart the skills and modes of thought considered essential for social functioning. Techniques of instruction reflect the attitudes of society, i.e., authoritarian groups sponsor dogmatic methods, while democratic systems emphasize freedom of thought. In ancient Greece education for freemen was a matter of studying Homer, mathematics, music, and GYMNASTICS. Higher education was carried on by the Sophists and philosophers before the rise of the ACADEMY and the philosophical schools. Most education in medieval Western Europe was a charge of the church: the monastic schools and universities were the chief centers, and virtually all students took orders. Lay education consisted of apprentice training for a small group of the common people and education in the usages of chivalry for the more privileged. With the Renaissance, education of boys, and of some girls, in classics and mathematics became widespread. After the Reformation both Protestant and Roman Catholic groups began to offer formal education to more people and there was a great increase in the number of private and public schools. Although the classical-mathematical curriculum became the substance of lay teaching, the development of scientific inquiry brought new methods and materials. As elementary and secondary schools were established and as larger proportions of the population attended, curriculums became differentiated (see PROGRESSIVE EDUCATION; GUIDANCE) and included aspects of VOCATIONAL EDUCATION. Opportunities for higher education were more widely provided in the 19th and 20th cent., especially in the United States in the LAND-GRANT COLLEGES. A large increase in college and vocational training resulted from the various veterans' assistance acts that have been passed since World War II. These measures have provided financial assistance to veterans seeking higher education or job training. Most modern political systems recognize the importance of universal education. The Soviet Union has a comprehensive national school system. In the United States education has traditionally been under state and local control, although the Federal government has been playing a larger role during the latter half of the 20th cent. Various religious groups, notably the Roman Catholic Church, have PAROCHIAL SCHOOLS that parallel public schools. Private schools and colleges have frequently been leaders in educational experiment. Education today is generally considered as important for girls as for boys (see COEDUCATION); equality of educational opportunity in the United States is an accepted principle, although not always observed in practice. Throughout history theories of education have reflected the dominant psychologies of learning and systems of ethics. An ancient idea, held by Socrates, is that the rightly trained mind would turn toward virtue. This idea has actually never been abandoned, although varying criteria of truth and authority have influenced both the content and the techniques of education. It was reflected in the classical curriculum of the Renaissance, the theorists of which included ERASMUS, Sir Thomas MORE, and George BUCHANAN. Since the 17th cent. the idea has grown that education should be directed to individual development for social living. John COMENIUS, Jean Jacques ROUSSEAU, Johann PESTALOZZI, Friedrich FROEBEL, Maria MONTESSORI, and Horace MANN were outstanding figures in this development. In the 20th cent. John DEWEY declared that young people should be taught to use the experimental method in meeting problems of the changing environment. Later in the century the psychologist B. F. SKINNER developed a theory of learning based on his animal experimentation that came to have a strong effect on modern theories of education, especially through the methods of PROGRAMMED INSTRUCTION. See ADULT EDUCATION; KINDERGARTEN; NURSERY SCHOOLS; SCHOOL. See John Dewey, *Democracy and Education* (1916, repr. 1966); Robert F. Butts and Lawrence A. Cremin, *A History of Education in American Culture* (1953, repr. 1961); Martin Mayer, *The Schools* (1961, repr. 1962); Rush Welter, *Popular Education and Democratic Thought in America* (1963); Robert Ulich, *The Education of Nations* (rev. ed. 1967); Lawrence A. Cremin, ed., *American Education: Its Men, Ideas, and Institutions* (46 vol., 1972); James A. Bowen, *A History of Western Education* (Vol. I, 1972).

Education, United States Office of, Federal agency in the Dept. of Health, Education and Welfare created to collect and disseminate information on education and to promote a higher standard of U.S. education. It was established (1867) as an independent government agency and transferred (1869) to the Dept. of the Interior as the Bureau of Education. In 1939 the bureau, by executive order, was transferred to the Federal Security Agency (which in 1953 became the Dept. of Health, Education and Welfare) and was renamed the Office of Education. The office's functions have been greatly expanded, and it is now empowered to administer funds appropriated as aids to education and to conduct special studies. The office publishes many reports and periodicals. Henry BARNARD was (1867–70) the first commissioner of education.

educational television: see AUDIO-VISUAL EDUCATION.

Edward I, 1239–1307, king of England (1272–1307), son of and successor of HENRY III. By his marriage (1254) to ELEANOR OF CASTILE he gained new claims in France and strengthened the English rights to Gascony. He received from his father the huge appanage of all outlying English dependencies, including Wales, Ireland, and the lands in France. After a brief alliance with Simon de MONTFORT, earl of Leicester, Edward supported his father in the BARONS' WAR (1263–67) and, by revitalizing the royal party and its forces, was responsible for the crown's triumph. From this time on the young heir was the real ruler of the realm. He joined (1270) the Ninth Crusade and was on his return journey when he learned of his father's death. He did not reach England until 1274, when he was crowned. Edward's vigorous reign was characterized by constant warfare. Trouble with LLEWELYN AP GRUFFYDD led to his successful conquest (1277–82) of Wales beyond the Welsh Marches, and in 1284 he extended the English administration to Wales. In France from 1286 to 1289 he improved the administration of Gascony. After the death in 1290 of Margaret Maid of Norway, Edward asserted his claim to overlordship of Scotland. John de BALIOL (1249–1315), his choice for the throne, soon entered an alliance with Philip IV of France, with whom Edward was already on bad terms. Edward's long struggle to conquer Scotland began in 1296. His first campaign was successful; he deposed Baliol and humiliated Scotland by removing the Coronation Stone from Scone to Westminster. But while he was heading an expedition against France in 1297 the Scots found a new leader in Sir William WALLACE, who defeated the English at Stirling Bridge. Edward immediately concluded a truce with Philip IV, and the English claims to Gascony were finally settled favorably in the treaty of 1303. In the meantime Edward invaded Scotland again and won a brilliant but inconclusive victory at Falkirk (1298). Campaigns in the following years led to Wallace's defeat (1305) and execution, but a new leader, ROBERT I, arose as king of a still defiant Scotland. Edward commenced an expedition against him in 1307 but died before reaching the border. Even more important than Edward's military exploits were the legal and constitutional developments of his reign; Edward has been called the English Justinian. He asserted the judicial supremacy of the crown by his quo warranto proceedings (inquiries to determine "by what warrant" private jurisdictions were held), which culminated in the statutes of Gloucester (1278) and of *Quo Warranto* (1290). By his law of 1285, *Circumspecte agatis,* he forced church courts to confine themselves to ecclesiastical cases. His three statutes of Westminster (1275, 1285, 1290; see WESTMINSTER, STATUTES OF) formulated the advances of a century of common law and supplemented them. By his Statute of Mortmain (1279), Edward prohibited grants of land to the church without the king's permission. In turn the English clergy, backed by Pope Boniface VIII's bull *Clericis laicos* (1296), refused in 1297 to contribute to Edward's campaign against the French until the king boldly denied protection to them and their goods and even threatened to confiscate all church property. This action was mainly prompted by his need for funds, as was his expulsion (1290) of the Jews from England (which enabled him to seize their property). His expensive wars also necessitated the frequent summoning of PARLIAMENT to grant taxes. The so-called Model Parliament of 1295 included representatives of the shires, boroughs, and lesser clergy, but the composition of Edward's parliaments varied. The increasing resistance of the country to heavy taxation and the refusal of many barons to fight in France in 1297 forced Edward to issue a confirmation of the charters of liberties, including the Magna Carta and those signed by Henry III. The king also promised that he would collect the nonfeudal forms of taxation only with the consent of Parliament. He did not keep this promise, however, and the last years of his reign were marked by increasing baronial opposition to the crown. This opposition and the war with Scotland proved to be a disastrous legacy for his son and successor, Edward II. See biographies by T. F. Tout (1903) and E. L. Stones (1968); Edward Jenks, *Edward Plantagenet, the English Justinian* (1902, repr. 1969); F. M. Powicke, *King Henry III and the Lord Edward* (1947); T. F. T. Plucknett, *Edward I and Criminal Law* (1960).

Edward II, 1284–1327, king of England (1307–27), son of Edward I and Eleanor of Castile, called Edward of Carnarvon for his birthplace in Wales. He became the first prince of Wales in 1301 and served in the Scottish campaigns from 1301 to 1306. The prince's dissipation caused his father to banish young Edward's friend Piers GAVESTON, who, however, returned to England immediately on Edward II's succession (1307) to the throne. Edward married ISABELLA of France in 1308. Edward was a weak and self-indulgent man, and his reliance on Gaveston's advice, to the exclusion of the baronial council, provoked a crisis almost immediately. The barons forced Edward to banish (1308) Gaveston, but the favorite soon returned again (1309). In 1310, therefore, a baronial coalition compelled Edward to consent to the appointment of a committee of 21 lords ordainers to share his ruling powers. The committee drafted the Ordinances of 1311, which, in addition to banishing Gaveston again, placed serious restrictions on the royal power. Gaveston was recalled (1311) once again, however, and the barons resorted to arms, capturing and killing Gaveston in 1312. Meanwhile Edward tried to renew his father's campaigns against Scotland, but his forces were routed by ROBERT I at Bannockburn in 1314. General disorder followed in England, and for a while the most powerful man in the country was Edward's cousin, Thomas, earl of Lancaster (see LANCASTER, HOUSE OF). Lancaster was supplanted (1318) by a moderate group of barons under Aymer de Valence, earl of PEMBROKE, who conciliated the king and maintained a relatively stable government until 1321. In that year, Lancaster led a rebellion against the king's new favorites, Hugh le DESPENSER (1262–1326) and his son. Lancaster was defeated and executed (1322). A Parliament at York (1322) revoked the Ordinances, and Edward, now dominated by the Despensers, regained control of the government. A truce was made (1323) with Robert I that virtually recognized him as king of the Scots. The Despensers carried through some notable administrative reforms, but their avarice caused them to make many enemies. Queen Isabella was finally disaffected by Edward's neglect and by mistreatment from his favorites. When trouble threatened with the new king of France (her brother, Charles IV), she went as envoy to France in 1325, taking her son (later Edward III). Refusing to return home while the Despensers ruled, Isabella, with her son and Roger de MORTIMER, 1st earl of March, gathered a force and in 1326 invaded England. Edward II found no one to support him and fled westward. The Despensers were executed and Edward himself was captured and forced to abdicate (1327). He was imprisoned in Berkeley Castle and almost certainly murdered there. See biography by H. F. Hutchison (1971); J. C. Davies, *Baronial Opposition to Edward II* (1918, repr. 1967); T. F. Tout, *The Place of the Reign of Edward II in English History* (2d ed. rev. by Hilda Johnstone, 1937); Hilda Johnstone, *Edward of Carnarvon, 1284–1307* (1947).

Edward III, 1312–77, king of England (1327–77), son of Edward II and ISABELLA. He was made earl of Chester in 1320 and duke of Aquitaine in 1325 and accompanied his mother to France in 1325. He returned to England with Isabella and Roger de MORTIMER, 1st earl of March, on their expedition of 1326. In 1327, on his father's deposition, he was made king, although the real power was in fact exercised by Isabella and Mortimer. In 1328 he married Philippa of Hainault, and in 1330 his first son, EDWARD THE BLACK PRINCE, was born. In this year the king executed a coup and seized the reins of government, putting Mortimer to death and forcing his mother into retirement. Edward, who had gone to Scotland on an unsuccessful expedition in 1327, resented the terms of the Treaty of Northampton (1328) by which he had renounced the Scottish throne and decided to support Edward de BALIOL against the young Scottish king David II. King Edward's victory at Halidon Hill in 1333 did not settle the Scottish question, but trouble with France arose to divide his attention. The series of wars known as the HUNDRED YEARS WAR, which was to dominate Edward's reign, began in 1337. Disputes over English holdings in France, trouble between the great Flemish weaving cities (allies of the English) and their French overlords, and French aid to the Scots were the chief causes of the war. Edward's assumption of the title of king of France in 1340, based on a claim through his mother, which was first advanced in 1328, was an immediate provocation. Edward took an active part in the war, fighting in the naval victory of Sluis (1340), in the famous battle of Crécy (1346), and in the successful siege of Calais (1346–47). His son, the Black Prince, achieved a popular reputation for his exploits, such as his victory at Poitiers (1356), where he captured the French king, John II. The fighting continued sporadically even after the Treaty of BRÉTIGNY (1360), by which Edward was awarded a large ransom for the French king and large concessions of French territory. In 1369, Charles V of France renewed the war, but Edward now took less interest in it. Various factors, among them the poor health of the Black Prince, led to a truce in 1375. Wars with the Scots, who had been receiving French aid, continued in a desultory manner. In 1346 the English had won a victory at Neville's Cross in England and made a prisoner of David II; in 1356, Edward had gone into Scotland on a harrying expedition known as Burnt Candlemas. Like the French wars, however, the Scottish wars were inconclusive in Edward's reign.

Domestic Affairs. Edward's long reign saw many constitutional developments. Most important of these was the emergence of the Commons as a distinct and increasingly powerful group within PARLIAMENT. The king's constant need for money for his wars enabled the Commons to assert their right to consent to all lay taxation and gain other substantial concessions. Considerable social change was also brought about by the decimation of England's population by visitations of the Black Death (see PLAGUE), which struck first in 1348–49 and again in 1362 and 1369. The resulting labor shortage allowed the lower classes to demand higher wages and social advancement and accelerated the breakdown of the system of serfdom. Parliament attempted to curb this development with the Statute of Labourers (1351), which froze wages, but it proved impossible to enforce. Edward's initially good relations with the church were damaged by the Statute of Provisors (1351) and the Statutes of Praemunire (first issued 1353), which were aimed at reducing papal influence on the English church, and by the king's attempts to get more money from the church. In 1371 the king's clerical councilors were dismissed. By this time Edward was under the influence of his greedy mistress, Alice PERRERS, and the political scene became one of rivalry between the court party headed by JOHN OF GAUNT and the clerical party led by the Black Prince. Supported by Alice Perrers, John of Gaunt gained control of the government, but the so-called Good Parliament of 1376 forced the expulsion of Alice Perrers from court, and several of John's supporters were impeached. John once again seized power after the death of the Black Prince. Edward III died soon afterward, and the son of the Black Prince came to the throne as Richard II. Of Edward's seven sons, five figured importantly in history: Edward the Black Prince; Lionel, duke of Clarence; John of Gaunt, duke of Lancaster; Edmund of Langley, duke of York; Thomas of Woodstock, duke of Gloucester. See William Longman, *The History of the Life and Times of Edward the Third* (2 vol., 1869; repr. 1969); T. F. Tout, *History of England, 1216–1377* (1905, repr. 1969); G. M. Trevelyan, *England in the Age of Wycliffe* (1909); May McKisack, *The Fourteenth Century* (1959).

Edward IV, 1442–83, king of England (1461–70, 1471–83), son of Richard, duke of YORK. He succeeded to the leadership of the Yorkist party (see ROSES, WARS OF THE) after the death of his father in Wakefield in 1460. Edward defeated the Lancastrians at Mortimer's Cross in 1461, entered London shortly thereafter, and was proclaimed king. Later in the year he won another victory over the Lancastrians at Towton Field, after which the deposed HENRY VI fled the country. Edward's secret marriage (1464) to Elizabeth WOODVILLE and subsequent favoritism to his wife's family angered his cousin, the able and ambitious Richard Neville, earl of WARWICK. At the same time severe reprisals taken by Edward's constable, John Tiptoft, earl of Worcester, against the Lancastrian party alienated many nobles. Warwick married his daughter to Edward's rebellious brother, George, duke of Clarence, and openly revolted in 1469. Although Warwick defeated Edward's forces at Edgecote, the king soon regained his strength, and Warwick fled (1470) to France. There he formed an alliance with Margaret of Anjou, wife of Henry VI. He returned to England with an army, and Edward, who lacked the forces to fight, fled to Holland. Warwick then restored Henry VI to the throne. Edward, however, gathered an army and returned in 1471 to defeat and kill Warwick at Barnet and rout the Lancastrians at Tewkesbury. In the latter battle Margaret was captured and her son, Edward, prince of Wales, killed. After the death of Henry in the Tower of London later in the year, Edward's position was secure. The remainder of his reign was a peaceful one. Edward invaded France in 1475 but allowed himself to be bought off without actual fighting. He reorganized the revenues of the crown lands (now greatly expanded by the addition of the Yorkist estates) and promoted trade, benefitting from the increased customs revenues. His resulting wealth allowed him to be largely independent of Parliament, and he developed many of the absolutist precedents inherited and utilized by the Tudor monarchs. See C. L. Scofield, *The Life and Reign of Edward IV* (2 vol., 1923; repr. 1967); E. F. Jacob, *The Fifteenth Century* (1961); Percival Hunt, *Fifteenth Century England* (1962).

Edward V, 1470–83?, king of England (1483), elder son of Edward IV and Elizabeth Woodville. His father's death (1483) left the boy king the pawn of the conflicting ambitions of his paternal uncle, the duke of Gloucester (later RICHARD III) and his maternal uncle, Earl Rivers. Gloucester had Rivers arrested and confined the king and the king's younger brother, Richard, duke of York, to the Tower of London. The young princes were declared illegitimate, and Gloucester, with a show of reluctance, took the throne. The two children disappeared from the English scene, and it is presumed that they were murdered. However, conclusive proof of their exact fate has never been found. One of the oldest and most prevalent theories—that they were smothered in their sleep by order of Richard III—is now believed to have been at least partially the result of anti-York propaganda spread by the victorious Tudors after 1485, and it has been suggested that either Henry STAFFORD, 2d duke of Buckingham, or Henry VII may have been responsible for the death of the princes. Skeletons, presumed to be those of the princes, were unearthed in the Tower in 1674. The skeletons appear to be those of boys aged 12–13 and 10, the ages of the princes in 1483. For a thorough discussion of this problem, see Paul Kendall, *Richard the Third* (1955).

Edward VI, 1537–53, king of England (1547–53), son of HENRY VIII and Jane Seymour. Edward succeeded his father to the throne at the age of nine. Henry had made arrangements for a council of regents, but the council immediately appointed Edward's uncle, Edward Seymour, earl of Hertford (later duke of SOMERSET), as lord protector. Henry's absolutism was relaxed by a liberalization of the treason and heresy laws. Tempering the reforming zeal of Thomas CRANMER, archbishop of Canterbury, the government moved slowly toward Protestantism. The Act of Uniformity (1549), which required use of the first Book of Common Prayer, increased contention between Roman Catholics and reformers, and an unsuccessful rebellion occurred in the west. The dissolution of chantries and the destruction of relics, both begun under Henry, proceeded apace. Somerset won a victory over the Scots at PINKIE (1547) but failed to persuade them to agree to a marriage between Edward and Mary Queen of Scots. The Scots instead strengthened their alliance with France, the power that increasingly threatened England's safety. War between France and England broke out in 1549 over the possession of Boulogne. Meanwhile there had arisen at home the pressing agrarian problem of INCLOSURE of common lands. By espousing the cause of the disgruntled peasantry, even after the rebellion of Robert KETT, Somerset aroused the opposition of the gentry and the council, thus affording his rival, John Dudley, earl of Warwick (later duke of NORTHUMBERLAND), an opportunity to secure his overthrow (1549). Dudley, after confining Somerset in the Tower of London, won complete ascendancy over Edward. With the prorogation (1550) of Parliament and the expulsion of Catholics from the council, the reformers triumphed, and Dudley gained control of the government. He secured peace with France by an ignominious treaty. The confiscation of chantry lands and church treasures brought needed revenue. A second Act of Uniformity and a second Book of Common Prayer, both more strongly Protestant, were adopted. After Somerset's execution (1552), Northumberland's government became increasingly unpopular. Fearing the accession of the Catholic princess, Mary (later MARY I), the duke inveigled Edward into settling the crown on Lady Jane GREY, granddaughter of Henry VIII's sister and wife of Northumberland's son, who was to receive the crown matrimonial. The young king, now dying of tuberculosis, secured the reluctant consent of the council, and Northumberland made hurried preparations for the coming unsuccessful struggle against Mary. Edward, who was only 15 when he died, had given indications that he might have matured into a strong-willed but intelligent and pious king, but his domination by Northumberland prevents accurate assessment. See A. F. Pollard, *England under Protector Somerset* (1900) and *Political History of England, 1547–1603* (1910); G. R. Elton, *England under the Tudors* (1953); H. W. Chapman, *The Last Tudor King* (1958); J. D. Mackie, *The Earlier Tudors, 1485–1558* (1952, 2d ed. 1959); studies by W. K. Jordan (1968 and 1970).

Edward VII, 1841–1910, king of Great Britain and Ireland (1901–10). The eldest son of Queen Victoria and Prince Albert, he was created prince of Wales almost immediately after his birth. As a youth he traveled widely on the Continent and visited the United States and Canada and the Middle East. In 1863 he married Alexandra, daughter of Christian IX of Denmark. They had six children. Victoria lived largely in seclusion for some years after the death (1861) of the prince consort, and the duty of representing the crown at public functions devolved upon Edward. A liberal patron of the arts and sciences, he became a leader of fashionable society and an enthusiastic sportsman. His love affairs and extravagant living, however, often offended his mother, who steadfastly denied him any political responsibilities. Edward succeeded to the throne on Jan. 22, 1901, at the age of 59 and was crowned on Aug. 9, 1902. As king, he took a deep interest in foreign policy and by his travels helped to promote better international understanding. The popularity he acquired in France smoothed the way for the Anglo-French entente of 1904. The end of his reign was marked by the constitutional crisis over the attempt to limit the veto power of the House of Lords. Edward cooperated somewhat reluctantly with the Liberal ministry of Herbert Asquith, but the issue was still unresolved at the time of his death. He was succeeded by his eldest surviving son, George V. See biographies by Sidney Lee (2 vol., 1925–27), E. F. Benson (1933), Philip Magnus (1964), and Keith Middlemas (1972); Philippe Julian, *Edward and the Edwardians* (1962, tr. 1967).

Edward VIII, 1894–1972, king of Great Britain and Ireland (1936), known in later years as the duke of Windsor; eldest son of George V. He attended the naval colleges at Osborne and Dartmouth and Magdalen College, Oxford. In 1911 he was made prince of Wales. During World War I he served as a staff officer in France, Italy, and Egypt. Between 1919 and 1936 he made state trips to the United States, Japan, South America, and the dominions. On the death of his father (Jan., 1936), Edward succeeded to the throne. He enjoyed immense popularity with his subjects until the crisis precipitated by the announcement of his intention to marry Wallis Warfield Simpson (see WINDSOR, WALLIS WARFIELD, DUCHESS OF), an American then suing her second husband for divorce. The government, headed by Stanley BALDWIN, opposed the marriage, and the issue developed into a struggle between monarch and cabinet. Edward insisted on his right to marry the woman of his choice, even though her marital background made her unacceptable to the public and the government. The government saw in his challenge to its wishes a threat to constitutional procedure. A proposal that there should be some kind of morganatic marriage came to nothing. Since no resolution seemed possible, the king executed a deed of abdication, ending a 325-day reign as the first English monarch to relinquish his throne voluntarily. On Dec. 11, 1936, Parliament passed a bill of abdication, and Edward's brother became King George V. The ex-king was granted the title of duke of Windsor. On June 3, 1937, he married Wallis Warfield in France. In 1937, on a trip to Germany, he visited

Adolf Hitler and other Nazi officials. In World War II the duke went to France as a major general, serving briefly as a liaison officer between British and French headquarters. From 1940 to 1945 he was governor of the Bahamas. After that time he lived in France but traveled a great deal. He died in Paris but was buried at Windsor. See his memoirs, *A King's Story* (1951); Brian Inglis, *Abdication* (1966).

Edward Nyanza (nīăn'zə, nē-) or **Lake Edward,** 830 sq mi (2,150 sq km), in the Great Rift Valley, central Africa, on the Zaïre-Uganda border. It lies at an altitude of c.3,000 ft (910 m), is c.47 mi (76 km) long, and has a maximum width of c.32 mi (52 km). Edward Nyanza is connected with the Nile system by the Semliki River, which drains the lake in the north and flows into Albert Nyanza. Edward Nyanza has many fish, and hippopotamuses abound on its southern shores. The lake was discovered in 1889 by Henry Morton Stanley, who named it after Albert Edward, then the prince of Wales (later Edward VII). In 1973 it was renamed Lake Idi Amin Dada after the president of Uganda.

Edwards, Edward, 1812-86, English library pioneer. As assistant from 1839 in the British Museum, he helped Sir Anthony Panizzi draw up the rules for the catalog. Edwards collected library statistics and advised William Ewart on the free-library legislation for the United Kingdom (1850). He was first librarian of the Manchester Free Library from 1850 to 1858. Edwards wrote a biography of Sir Walter Raleigh (1865), *Memoirs of Libraries* (1859), and *Lives of the Founders of the British Museum* (1870).

Edwards, Haden: see FREDONIAN REBELLION.

Edwards, Jonathan, 1703-58, American theologian and metaphysician, b. East Windsor (then in Windsor), Conn. He was a precocious child, early interested in things scientific, intellectual, and spiritual. After graduating from Yale at 17, he studied theology, preached (1722-23) in New York City, tutored (1724-26) at Yale, and in 1727 became the colleague of his grandfather, Solomon Stoddard, in the ministry at Northampton, Mass. In 1729, on his grandfather's death, Edwards took sole charge of the congregation. The young minister was not long in gaining a wide following by his forceful preaching and powerful logic. These abilities were in the best Calvinist tradition and were enriched by his reading in philosophy, notably Berkeley and Locke. His favorite themes were predestination and the absolute dependence of humble man upon God and upon divine grace, which alone could save man. He rejected with fire the Arminian (see REMONSTRANTS) modification of these Calvinist doctrines. He exhorted his hearers with great effect and held in 1734-35 a religious revival in Northampton that in effect brought the GREAT AWAKENING to New England. Edwards was stern in demanding strict orthodoxy and fervent zeal from his congregation. He was unbending in a controversy over tests for church membership, and in 1750 his congregation dismissed him from Northampton. At Stockbridge, Mass., where he went to care for the Indian mission and to minister to a small white congregation, he completed his theological masterpiece, *The Freedom of the Will* (1754), which sets forth metaphysical and ethical arguments for determinism. In 1757 he was called to be president of the College of New Jersey (now Princeton), but he died a few months later. Edwards's influence on American Christian thought was immense for a time, and he is often regarded as the last of the great New England Calvinists. However, his emphasis on personal religious experience and his use of the revival, leading to the Great Awakening, were partially responsible for the advent of evangelical revivalism, which was based on a belief contrary to Calvinist doctrine—that salvation was possible without predestined election. His theological writings are perhaps less read today than his more casual writings and some of his burning and poetic sermons, such as *Sinners in the Hands of an Angry God* and *God Glorified in the Work of Redemption by the Greatness of Man's Dependence on Him in the Whole of It.* A short selection of Edwards's works (ed. by Clarence H. Faust and Thomas H. Johnson) appeared in 1935. See his works, edited by Perry Miller (4 vol., 1957-72); bibliography, *Printed Works of Jonathan Edwards* (ed. by Thomas H. Johnson, 1940, repr. 1970); biographies by H. S. Parkes (1930), A. C. McGiffert (1932), O. E. Winslow (1940, repr. 1973), Perry Miller (1949), David Levin (1969), and E. M. Griffin (1971); Douglas Elwood, *Philosophical Theology of Jonathan Edwards* (1960); E. H. Davidson, *Jonathan Edwards: The Narrative of a Puritan Mind* (1966); John Opie, *Jonathan Edwards and the Enlightenment* (1969).

Edwards, Jonathan, the younger, 1745-1801, American theologian, b. Northampton, Mass., grad. College of New Jersey (now Princeton), 1765; son of Jonathan Edwards (1703-58). His career in some ways paralleled that of his famous father. After serving as pastor of a New Haven church from 1769 to 1795, he was dismissed for opposing the HALF-WAY COVENANT. Until 1799 he was pastor at Colebrook, Conn. Edwards was then made president of Union College at Schenectady, N.Y., but he died before he could make much impression on the college. He edited some of his father's works and generally held to his doctrines, although in *On the Necessity of the Atonement* the younger Edwards expounded a theory of the Atonement that was more liberal and more popular than his father's theory. See his works (2 vol., 1842) ed. by his grandson, Tryon Edwards.

Edwards, Ninian, 1775-1833, governor of Illinois, b. Maryland. A Kentucky lawyer and jurist, he was appointed (1809) governor of Illinois Territory and served in the formative years until 1818. He served (1818-24) as one of the first U.S. Senators from the new state and, despite growing political opposition, was elected governor in 1826.

Edwards Air Force Base, U.S. military installation, 301,000 acres (121,805 hectares), S Calif., NE of Lancaster; est. 1933. It is one of the largest air force bases in the United States and has the world's longest runway. The base houses the Air Force Flight Test Center, which researches and develops aerospace weapons and rocket-propulsion systems, and the National Aeronautical and Space Administration's Flight Research Center. The base is also the proving ground for military aircraft.

Edwardsville, city (1970 pop. 11,070), seat of Madison co., SW Ill.; inc. 1819. It is mainly residential, with many citizens commuting to St. Louis. A campus of Southern Illinois Univ. is there.

Edward the Black Prince, 1330-76, eldest son of EDWARD III of England. He was created duke of Cornwall in 1337, the first duke to be created in England, and prince of Wales in 1343. Joining his father in the campaigns of the Hundred Years War, he established his reputation for valor at the battle of Crécy (1346). It was apparently the French who called him the Black Prince, perhaps because he wore black armor; the name was not recorded in England until the 16th cent. In 1355 the prince led an expedition into Aquitaine, and in 1356 he defeated and captured John II of France in the battle of POITIERS. Edward became ruler of the newly created English principality of Aquitaine in 1363 and, with his wife JOAN OF KENT, maintained a brilliant court at Bordeaux. In 1367 he went to the support of PETER THE CRUEL of Castile and temporarily restored him to his throne by the victory of Nájera. However, the expenses of the war compelled Edward to levy a tax in Aquitaine that was protested by his nobles and by Charles V of France on their behalf. War with Charles resulted, and the prince, though ill, directed the capture and burning of Limoges (1370) with needless massacre of the citizens. By 1372 his bad health forced him to resign his principalities, leaving his brother, JOHN OF GAUNT, to attempt the impossible task of holding them for England. The aging Edward III had relaxed his hold on the government, and the Black Prince, aware that he would not live to succeed his father, tried to strengthen the hand of the clerical party against John of Gaunt so that the accession of his son (later Richard II) would be assured. To that end he supported (and possibly directed) the proceedings of the so-called Good Parliament of 1376, which, among other things, impeached two followers of John of Gaunt and removed Alice Perrers, the king's mistress, from court. The Black Prince died shortly thereafter. See biography by H. D. Sedgwick (1932), and May McKisack, *The Fourteenth Century* (1959).

Edward the Confessor, d. 1066, king of the English (1042-66), son of Æthelred the Unready and his Norman wife, Emma. After the Danish conquest (1013-16) of England, Edward grew up at the Norman court, although his mother returned to England and married the Danish king Canute. In 1041, Edward was brought to England by his half brother HARTHACANUTE, whom he succeeded as king in 1042. Edward was an able but not very energetic ruler, and he was unable to assert his authority over the great earls of the kingdom. Most powerful of these was GODWIN, whose daughter Edith married (1045) the king. Edward's natural inclination to favor the Normans in England—notably ROBERT OF JUMIÈGES, whom he made archbishop of Canterbury in 1051—led to a breach with Godwin. In 1051, after a fracas between the king's brother-in-law, EUSTACE II, count of Boulogne, and the citizens of Dover, Godwin refused to obey Edward's order to punish the men of Dover and tried to raise a revolt. Edward, however, was supported by Leofric of Mercia and SIWARD of Northumbria, and he outlawed and banished Godwin and his family. In their absence Edward received William, duke of Normandy (later WILLIAM I), and apparently made him his heir. In 1052, Godwin and his sons returned and demonstrated their power by forcing Edward to accept STIGAND as archbishop of Canterbury instead of Robert. Thenceforth the king took less interest in his realm, becoming absorbed in his religion and in supervising the rebuilding of Westminster Abbey. Shortly before his death, Edward named HAROLD, son of Godwin, as his successor, possibly in the hope of averting the threat of war posed by the rival claims to the throne of William of Normandy and HAROLD III of Norway. Edward's piety was responsible for his name the Confessor. He was canonized in the 12th cent. Feast: Oct. 13. See biography by Frank Barlow (1970).

Edward the Elder, d. 924, king of Wessex (899-924), son and successor of Alfred. He fought with his father against the Danes and was apparently joint king with him. At Alfred's death (899) Edward's succession was disputed by his cousin Æthelwold, who allied himself with the Danes of Northumbria and East Anglia. The death of Æthelwold in battle (902) put an end to that war, but later fighting with the Danes recommenced. Aided by his sister Æthelflœd, Lady of the Mercians, Edward undertook a series of advances against the Danes, systematically building fortresses to cover his positions. At the same time he repelled Viking attacks on the shore of England. After Æthelflœd's death (918) he asserted his full authority over Mercia and thus became ruler of all England S of the Humber River. He was also accepted as overlord by several Welsh rulers and by English Northumbria, and he is supposed to have received the submission of Constantine II of Scotland, although there is much dispute as to the reality of the submission. The right of the overlordship of Scotland, based on Edward's position, was asserted by later English kings. Edward was succeeded by his son Athelstan. Two other sons, Edmund and Eldred, also ascended the throne.

Edward the Martyr, c.962-978, king of the English (975-78), son of Edgar by his first wife. Despite the opposition of some of the nobles, Edward succeeded his father to the throne and was crowned. However, he could not control the kingdom and was murdered at Corfe by retainers in the service of his stepmother, Queen Ælfthryth or Ælfrida, and of her son ÆTHELRED. There is no proof that Ælfthryth or Æthelred planned his death, as later tradition said. Edward's body was moved to Shaftesbury, where miracles were reported, and he was regarded as a saint and martyr by the people. Feast: March 18.

Edwin or **Eadwin** (both: ĕd'wĭn), 585?-632, king of Northumbria (616-32). The son and heir of Ælla, king of Deira, he was kept from his inheritance by ÆTHELFRITH. Edwin sought refuge with Rædwald, king of East Anglia, who in 616 defeated and killed Æthelfrith and gave Edwin the rule of all Northumbria. In a few years Edwin succeeded or superseded Rædwald as overlord of all the English kingdoms except Kent. The king was converted to Christianity by St. PAULINUS, who accompanied the king's bride (a daughter of King Æthelbert of Kent) to Northumbria in 625. In 627, Edwin and many of his court were baptized at York, and he seems to have assisted Paulinus in the conversion of his people thereafter. Edwin in one of his raids attacked Cadwallon, king of North Wales. Later Cadwallon and PENDA of Mercia defeated and killed Edwin and his son in 632.

Edwy (ĕd'wē) or **Eadwig** (ĕd'wĭg), d. 959, king of the English (955-57) and king of Wessex (955-59), son of Edmund. He succeeded his uncle, Edred as king of the English, but in 957, Mercia and Northumbria shifted their allegiance to his brother EDGAR. Little is known of his short reign, except that he quarreled with and exiled St. DUNSTAN. Edwy was succeeded in Wessex by Edgar.

Eeckhout, Gerbrand van den (gĕr'bränt vän dĕn āk'hout), 1621-74, Dutch painter and etcher. He was a pupil and close follower of Rembrandt, especially in his religious works. A fine draftsman, he easily assimilated the styles of artists around him, including those of Flinck and Fabritius. His *Isaac Blessing Jacob* is in the Metropolitan Museum.

Eeden, Frederik van (frā'dərĭk vän ā'dən), 1860-1932, Dutch novelist and poet, a practicing physician. He founded a cooperative farm colony (1898). His work is pervaded by deep mysticism; best known is the novel trilogy *De kleine Johannes* (1885–1906, tr. *The Quest,* 1907). His dramas include the tragicomedy *Ijsbrand* (1908, tr. *Ysbrand,* 1910).

EEG: see ELECTROENCEPHALOGRAPHY.

eel, common name for any fish of the 10 families constituting the order Anguilliformes, and characterized by a long snakelike body covered with minute scales embedded in the skin. Eels lack the hind pair of fins, adapting them for wriggling in the mud and through the crevices of reefs and rocky shores. Most species are marine; the largest and most diverse group are the morays, family Muraenidae, sharp-toothed and vicious. The common freshwater eel, *Anguilla rostrata,* of the family Anguillidae, is found in the Atlantic coastal regions of Europe, in the Mediterranean area, and in North America E of the Rockies. Several other freshwater species are native to Asia. The mature European eel migrates 3,000 to 4,000 mi (4,828–6,437 km) to its spawning ground in the deep sea SW of Bermuda, a journey lasting several months. There it reproduces and then dies. The young hatch as transparent ribbonlike larvae that drift north and east on ocean currents for three years before entering a river; they then develop into elvers, tiny versions of the adult eel. The American eel follows the same pattern, except that the young require only one year to return to fresh water. Once there, the developing elvers feed voraciously on dead and living animals, even traveling over short stretches of land in search of frogs and lizards. They hunt at night and rest by day. The male, which attains a length of 2 ft (61 cm), remains at the river's mouth, while the female (4 ft/122 cm) swims upstream, staying there for from 5 to 20 years. When the eels are sexually mature their enormous appetite wanes, and they do not eat during migration to the spawning ground. The oily flesh is regarded by some as a delicacy; the skin was formerly used as leather. Eels are classified in the phylum CHORDATA, subphylum Vertebrata, class Osteichthyes, order Anguilliformes.

eel, electric: see ELECTRIC FISH.

Efate (ĕfä'tē), Fr. *Vaté* (vätā'), volcanic island (1967 pop. 10,008), c.300 sq mi (780 sq km), South Pacific, most important island of the NEW HEBRIDES and seat of Vila (1967 pop. 3,100), the administrative center. Efate produces copra, coffee, and sandalwood. Havannah Harbour was developed during World War II.

efficiency: see INDUSTRIAL MANAGEMENT; MACHINE; WORK.

Effigy Mounds National Monument: see NATIONAL PARKS AND MONUMENTS (table).

efflorescence: see HYDRATE.

eft: see NEWT.

EFTA: see INTERNATIONAL GOVERNMENTAL ORGANIZATIONS.

Egadi Islands (ĕ'gädē) or **Aegadian Isles** (ēgā'dēən), Lat. *Aegates,* archipelago (1968 est. pop. 5,800), c.15 sq mi (40 sq km), W Sicily, Italy, in the Mediterranean Sea. The chief islands are Favignana, Marettimo, and Levanzo. Fishing is the main occupation, and the most important tuna fisheries of Sicily are there. A Roman naval victory over the Carthaginians in the battle of the Aegates, fought near the islands in 241 B.C., ended the first of the PUNIC WARS.

Égalité, Philippe: see ORLÉANS, LOUIS PHILIPPE JOSEPH, DUC D'.

Egan, Patrick, 1841–1919, Irish and American political leader, b. Co. Longford, Ireland. Fervently devoted to the cause of Irish home rule and land reform, he was a member of the Irish Land League from the year of its founding (1879) and was an able lieutenant of Michael Davitt and Charles Stewart Parnell. One of the defendants in the ineffective "state trials" of 1880–81, he later fled to the United States to escape sterner British measures, settling in Lincoln, Nebr. He continued to work strenuously for the Irish Land League and Irish home rule but also took up American politics and was a minor power in the Republican party until he deserted it for William Jennings Bryan and the Democrats in 1896. As minister to Chile (1889–93), he ably represented the United States when relations were strained during the revolt against President José Balmaceda.

Egan, Pierce, 1772–1849, English sports writer. He was the author of *Life in London,* a lively account of the adventures of sporting gallants of the Regency. With its rough humor and colloquial style, it was exceedingly popular from its first installment in 1820.

Egbert, d. 839, king of Wessex (802–39). His name also appears as Ecgberht. He was descended from CERDIC and was apparently an unsuccessful aspirant for the crown of Wessex against Beohtric (reigned 786–802). He took refuge at the court of Offa of Mercia, but the alliance of Offa and Beohtric drove him to the Frankish court, where he may have spent three years. At Beohtric's death he became king of Wessex, apparently without opposition. In 815 he harried Cornwall, returning to defeat the Britons there again in 825. He also defeated King Beornwulf of Mercia at Ellandune (or Ellendun) in 825. He sent his son Æthelwulf and an army to Kent, which was then made a dependency of Wessex. East Anglia sought Egbert's protection and revolted against Mercia. Beornwulf was killed in battle, and Mercia submitted (828?) to Egbert. He then (829?) secured the nominal submission of Northumbria without a battle. Later historians called him the first king of England, an anachronistic title, for there was no conception of a kingdom of England in his day. The extent of his power varied from kingdom to kingdom and from year to year. After 834 he had to defend his realm against the Danes, and in his last battle (838) he again defeated the Britons of Cornwall, who had allied themselves with the Danes. Egbert was succeeded by his son, Æthelwulf.

Egede, Hans (häns ā'gədə), 1686–1758, Norwegian Lutheran missionary, called the Apostle of Greenland. He went to Greenland in 1721 and, with the support of the Danish government, founded a mission for the Eskimo. He also helped to initiate trade between Denmark and Greenland. He returned to Copenhagen in 1736 to become principal of a seminary that trained missionaries for Greenland. His son, **Paul Egede,** 1708–89, also a missionary to Greenland, completed a translation of the New Testament for use by the Eskimo.

Egedesminde (ā'gəthəsmĭn"ə), town (1969 pop. 3,215), in Egedesminde district (1969 pop. 3,572), W Greenland, at the mouth of Disko Bay. It is the third largest town in Greenland. It was founded in 1759 and named for Hans Egede, a Norwegian missionary. A large shrimp-canning factory is there.

Eger: see CHEB, Czechoslovakia.

Eger (ĕ'gĕr), Ger. *Erlau,* city (1970 pop. 45,229), NE Hungary, on the Eger River. It is the commercial center of a wine-producing region and has food- and tobacco-processing plants and a mechanical engineering industry. There are mineral springs nearby. One of the first Magyar settlements in E central Europe, Eger was made (11th cent.) a bishopric by St. Stephen. It was destroyed (13th cent.) by the Tatars, rebuilt and fortified, and captured in 1596 by the Turks, who held it for nearly 150 years. Francis II Rakoczy used the fortress in his fight against the Hapsburgs, who had it razed. In 1814, Eger became an archiepiscopal see; the many churches subsequently built have earned it the name "Rome of Hungary." The city's notable structures include a 16th-century minaret, an 18th-century archiepiscopal palace, a 19th-century cathedral, and the ruins of a medieval fortress.

Egeria (ējēr'ēə), in Roman religion, goddess or nymph of fountains. Consort and advisor of King Numa, she was also identified with Diana and worshiped as a goddess of childbirth. The name is used as an epithet for a female advisor or companion.

Egersund (ā'gərso͞on), town (1970 est. pop. 10,000), Rogaland co., S Norway, a modern fishing port on the North Sea. Often mentioned in the Norwegian sagas, Egersund was a busy port as early as the Middle Ages.

Egerton, Thomas: see ELLESMERE, THOMAS EGERTON, BARON.

egg: see OVUM.

Eggan, Fred Russell, 1906–, American anthropologist, b. Seattle, grad. Univ. of Chicago (Ph.B., 1927; A.M., 1928; Ph.D., 1933). A member of the faculty of the Univ. of Chicago from 1935, he was chairman of the department of anthropology there from 1948 to 1952 and from 1961 to 1963. His fields of study are social anthropology, ethnology, and acculturation. Among his writings are *Social Organization of the Western Pueblos* (1950) and *The American Indian* (1966).

Eggleston, Edward, 1837–1902, American author, a Methodist clergyman, b. Vevay, Ind., educated in the elementary schools of the frontier. Before 1866 he was a Bible agent, a farm worker, and a circuit rider in Minnesota and Indiana. After a few years of journalism in Chicago, he went to New York in 1870 to join the editorial staff of the *Independent.* His literary reputation was established with *The Hoosier Schoolmaster* (1871) and *The Circuit Rider* (1874), and he followed them with other novels and short stories of the Western frontier, including *Roxy* (1878) and *The Graysons* (1887). He was pastor of the Church of Christian Endeavor, Brooklyn, from 1874 until 1879, when he retired from all work but writing and historical research. Besides writing juvenile stories and historical essays and articles, he planned a history of American life, two volumes of which he completed as *The Beginners of a Nation* (1896) and *The Transit of Civilization* (1901). See *The First of the Hoosiers* (1903) by his brother, G. C. Eggleston; biography by W. P. Randel (1963).

eggnog, beverage made of well-beaten eggs combined with cream or milk, to which may be added sugar, wine, spirits, or fruit juices and usually nutmeg to flavor. A rich eggnog based on bourbon whiskey, brandy, or other spirits is a traditional Yuletide drink.

eggplant, name for *Solanum melongena,* a large-leaved woody perennial shrub (often grown as an annual herb) of the family Solanaceae (NIGHTSHADE family), and also cultivated for its ovoid fruit. Native to SE Asia, the eggplant is raised in tropical and (as an annual) in warm climates as a garden vegetable. The fruit (a berry, like its relative the tomato) varies in size and may be purple, white, or striped; it is usually eaten stuffed and baked or sliced and fried. Eggplants are classified in the division MAGNOLIOPHYTA, class Magnoliopsida, order Polemoniales, family Solanaceae.

Egham (ĕg'əm), urban district (1971 pop. 30,510), Surrey, SE England. Light engineering and gravel working are the main industries. RUNNYMEDE and part of Windsor Great Park, the royal estate, are in the district. Nearby is Cooper's Hill, celebrated in poems by John Denham and Alexander Pope. The Royal Holloway College of the Univ. of London is in Egham.

Eginhard: see EINHARD.

Eglah (ĕg'lə), one of David's wives. 2 Sam. 3.5.

Eglaim (ĕg'lāĭm, ēglā'ĭm), place E of the Dead Sea. Isa. 15.8. See also EN-EGLAIM.

eglantine (ĕg'ləntīn), name for various kinds of ROSE (family Rosaceae), chiefly SWEETBRIER, and for a HONEYSUCKLE (family Caprifoliaceae). The name eglantine has been much used in English poetry.

Eglevsky, André (äNdrā' ĕg'lĕvskē), 1917–, American ballet dancer, b. the Soviet Union. Trained in France, he made his debut in London in 1931 and thereafter became known for his classic style and virtuosity. Among the companies with which he has danced are the Ballet Russe de Monte Carlo (1939–42) and the Ballet Theatre in New York (1942–46). After 1951 he became premier danseur of the New York City Ballet. Eglevsky retired in 1958 to form his own company and school.

Eglon (ĕg'lŏn). **1** King of Moab. He was murdered by Ehud, who became judge of Israel. Judges 3.12. **2** Ancient city, Palestine, near Lachish. It was one of the cities allied against Joshua, who destroyed it after the battle of Ajalon. Joshua 10; 12.12; 15.39. It was excavated in 1890 by W. M. F. PETRIE, who there devised a system of pottery dating used in BIBLICAL ARCHAEOLOGY. Eglon is the present-day Tel Hasi (Israel).

Egmont, John Perceval, 1st **earl of,** 1683–1748, Irish peer, associate of James E. OGLETHORPE in founding Georgia. Elected (1727) to the British House of Commons, he served on Oglethorpe's committee investigating penal conditions. He was first president of the trustees of Georgia and kept a journal of their transactions, most of which has been published.

Egmont, Lamoral, count of (lä'mōräl), 1522–68, Flemish general and statesman, member of one of the noblest families of the Netherlands. In the service of Philip II of Spain he helped defeat the French at Saint-Quentin (1557) and Gravelines (1558) and was governor of Brabant and Artois. Although a devout Catholic, Egmont protested against the persecution inflicted on the Protestants of the Low Countries, and he helped force the removal of Cardinal GRANVELLE. In 1565 he journeyed to Madrid to persuade Philip II to change his policy but he failed. When the duke of Alba arrived (1567) at Brussels, he quickly had Egmont and Count HOORN arrested. Although they had sympathized with WILLIAM THE SILENT, they had actually never entertained the thought of treason against their king. Egmont held that Philip was the rightful ruler of the Netherlands and believed he would agree to a compromise with his subjects. Nevertheless, Alba meant to spread terror among the population by securing a death sentence. Egmont and Hoorn, both knights of the Golden Fleece, vainly sought to be tried by a court of their order or even to obtain a fair trial by the judges Alba had appointed. In 1568, Egmont and Hoorn were publicly beheaded in Brussels. Their deaths plunged the Low Countries into a state of unrest and upheaval and are generally considered the immediate cause of the outbreak of open rebellion against Spanish rule. Egmont is the central figure of Goethe's tragedy, *Egmont,* for which Beethoven composed an overture and incidental music.

Egmont, Mount, dormant volcanic cone, 8,260 ft (2,517 m) high, on North Island, New Zealand. Symmetrical and snow-capped, it dominates the island's west side.

ego: see PSYCHOANALYSIS.

egoism (ē'gōĭzəm), in ethics, the doctrine that the ends and motives of human conduct are the good of the individual. It is opposed to ALTRUISM, which holds the criterion of morality to be the welfare of others. The term has been variously used, from the broad interpretation of the self and all its concerns and interests (the benevolent self-interest of the utilitarians) to the egoism sentiment of Friedrich Nietzsche in which all altruistic sentiment is cowardice. Although egoism is most frequently associated with the ethics of the early Greek hedonists and the modern utilitarians, it may be associated with intuitionism, which is by nature ego-centered. Herbert Spencer attempted to reconcile egoism and altruism through social discipline, and some modern philosophers attempt this reconciliation through the concept of the growing self who invests his interests in an ever-widening social field.

Egorevsk: see YEGOREVSK, USSR.

egret (ēgrĕt'), common name for several species of herons of the Old and New Worlds, belonging to the family Ardeidae. Before they were protected by law the birds were nearly exterminated by hunters seeking their beautiful, white, silky plumage called aigrettes, used in millinery. These feathers develop during the breeding season. In the American egret the plumes are straight, about 21 in. (52.5 cm) long, growing on the back. The smaller snowy egret, or snowy heron (*Leucophoyx thula*), the most beautiful and most hunted, has curved plumes on the back, head, and breast. The reddish egret (*Dichromanassa rufa*) is white part of the year, changing to grayish with brown head and neck. The greater and lesser egrets are European species. Egrets are classified in the phylum CHORDATA, subphylum Vertebrata, class Aves, order Herodiones, family Ardeidae.

Eguren, José María (hōsā' mārē'ä ĕgōō'rän), 1882–1942, Peruvian poet. Originally devoted to MODERNISMO, Eguren avoided its excesses and wrote terse, musical, and sometimes obscure poems. His strange images, symbols, and dreamlike visions were wrought into a framework of formal perfection. *Simbólicas* (1911), *La canción de las figuras* (1916), and *Poesías* (1929) are his best-known collections.

Egypt (ē'jĭpt), Arab. *Misr,* biblical *Mizraim,* officially Arab Republic of Egypt, republic (1973 est. pop. 35,330,000), 386,659 sq mi (1,001,449 sq km), NE Africa and SW Asia, bordering on the Mediterranean Sea in the north, on Israel and the Red Sea in the east, on Sudan in the south, and on Libya in the west. The great mass of Egypt is located in Africa; the SINAI peninsula is situated in Asia and is separated from the rest of the country by the SUEZ CANAL. Egypt's capital and largest city is CAIRO; other major cities include ALEXANDRIA, PORT SAID, SUEZ, and TANTA. Egypt N of Cairo is often called Lower Egypt and S of Cairo, Upper Egypt. The principal physiographic feature of the country is the Nile River, which flows from south to north through E Egypt for c.900 mi (1,450 km). In the far south is Lake Nasser, a vast artificial lake impounded by the Aswan High Dam (built 1960-70), and in the north, below Cairo, is the great Nile delta (c.8,500 sq mi/22,000 sq km). Bordering the Nile between Aswan and Cairo are narrow strips (on the average 5 mi/8 km wide) of cultivated land; there are broad regions of tilled land in the delta. The vast majority of Egypt's inhabitants live in the Nile valley and delta, and the rest of the country (about 96% of Egypt's total land area) is sparsely populated. West of the Nile is the extremely arid Libyan (or Western) Desert, a generally low-lying region (maximum alt. c.1,000 ft/300 m), largely covered with sand dunes or barren rocky plains. The desert contains a few oases, notably Siwa, Farafirah, and Kharijah. In SW Egypt the desert rises to the Jilf al Kabir plateau. East of the Nile is the Arabian (or Eastern) Desert, a dissected highland area (rising to c.7,150 ft/2,180 m) that is mostly barren and virtually uninhabited except for a few settlements along the Red Sea coast. The Sinai peninsula is a plateau broken by deep valleys; Mount Catherine, or Jabal Katrinah (8,652 ft/2,637 m), Egypt's loftiest point, and Mount Sinai, or Jabal Musa (7,497 ft/2,285 m), are located in the south. Northern Sinai, largely a sandy desert, contains most of the peninsula's small population, which lives mainly in towns built around wells. The great majority of Egypt's inhabitants are of a complex racial mixture, being descended from the ancient Egyptians, Berbers, black Africans, Arabs, Greeks, and Turks. Arabic is the country's official language. About 92% of the people are Sunni Muslims, and most of the rest belong to the Egyptian Coptic Orthodox Church (see under COPT). Although the country's industrial base has been increased considerably in the 20th cent. (especially since 1952), Egypt in the early 1970s remained predominately an agricultural country. Farming generally contributed about 28% of the annual national product (compared to industry's contribution of about 23%), and about 60% of Egypt's workers were employed in agriculture. The state owns much of the economy and plays a decisive role in economic planning. Economic growth was hindered somewhat after 1945 by the large proportion of funds and energy devoted to preparing the country for warfare with Israel and by the destruction incurred in the Arab-Israeli wars. Development was also held back by the combination of a severely limited amount of arable land and a large and rapidly growing population (increasing about 2.6% per year). The country's farmland is intensively cultivated (usually two, and sometimes three, crops are produced annually) and yields-per-acre are extremely high, so that only by the opening of new cropland can production be increased significantly. Additional control of the Nile waters, made possible by the construction of the Aswan High Dam, has made considerable amounts of new land cultivable, but the needs of the growing population have prevented the accumulation of significant agricultural surpluses. Most farms in Egypt are small and labor-intensive; in the mid-1960s about 94% of the farms (constituting about 55% of the total arable land) were made up of 5 acres (2 hectares) or less. The principal crops produced are cotton (mostly of the long-staple variety), rice, maize, wheat, millet, onions, beans, barley, tomatoes, sugarcane, citrus fruit, and dates. Most agricultural produce is marketed, and cotton is by far the leading cash crop. Large numbers of poultry, cattle, sheep, buffalo, donkeys, and goats are raised. Cairo and Alexandria are the main industrial centers; major manufacturing plants are also located in the other cities of the Nile valley and delta and at Port Said and Suez. The leading manufactures are refined petroleum, chemicals (including fertilizer), textiles, clothing, processed food, construction materials (especially cement), iron and steel, and metal products. The principal minerals produced are petroleum, natural gas, phosphates, salt, iron ore, manganese, coal, and gold. The annual cost of Egypt's imports usually slightly exceeds the earnings from its exports. The leading imports are foodstuffs, chemicals, machinery, and transport equipment. The principal exports are raw cotton, cotton textiles, rice, and petroleum. The chief trade partners are the USSR, France, India, West Germany, and East Germany. Considerable foreign exchange is derived from the country's growing tourist industry. The Suez Canal, a more important source of foreign exchange, was closed during the 1967 Arab-Israeli war and remained closed through the mid-1970s, although it had been cleared of obstacles and dredged to a navigable depth. The country's rail and road networks are largely found along the Mediterranean coast and in the Nile valley. Egypt is governed under the constitution of 1971. The president is the head of state and the prime minister is the head of government. There is a 360-seat national assembly whose members serve five-year terms. The Arab Socialist Union (ASU) is the only legal political party.

The Ancient Empire of the Nile. The valley of the "long river between the deserts," with the annual floods and deposits of life-giving silt and with its equable climate, was the seat of one of the earliest civilizations built by man. The antiquity of this civilization is almost staggering, and whereas the history of other lands is measured in centuries, that of ancient Egypt is measured in millenniums. Thanks to the work of W. M. Flinders PETRIE and other archaeologists, much is known of even the period before the actual historic records began. Those records are abundant and, because of Egypt's dry climate, have been well preserved. Inscriptions have unlocked a wealth of information; for example, the existing fragments of the PALERMO STONE are engraved with the records of the kings of the first five dynasties. The hieroglyphic inscriptions have been deciphered by such experts as the French scholar Jean François CHAMPOLLION, who is considered the founder of scientific Egyptology. Later historical writings, especially those of MANETHO and, to a lesser extent, those of Greek historians (notably HERODOTUS), illuminate the meaning of the inscriptions. Finally, the great papyrus dumps, preserved for the most part in the dry climate of Upper Egypt, offer an enormous (and not infrequently confusing) amount of information, especially on the later periods of ancient Egyptian history. Among the many problems encountered in Egyptology, one of the most prominent and controversial is that of dating events. The system used in *The New Columbia Encyclopedia* has a margin of plus or minus 100 years for the time prior to 3000 B.C. Fairly precise dates are possible beginning with the Persian conquest (525 B.C.) of Egypt. The division of Egyptian history into 30 dynasties up to the

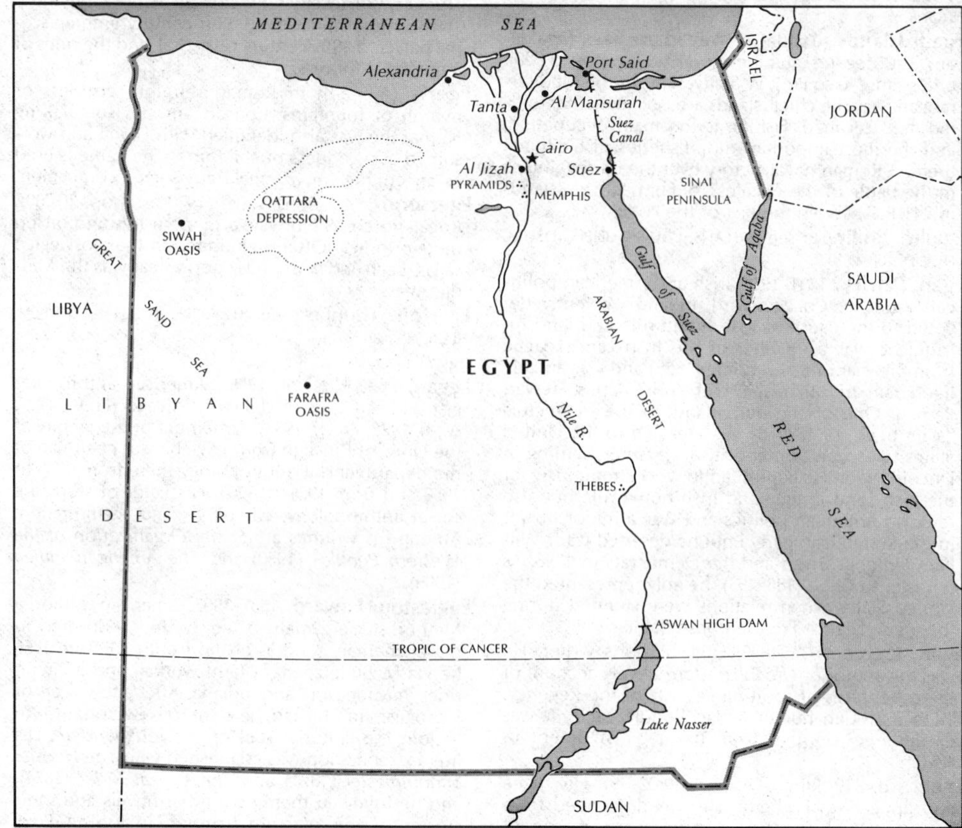

time of Alexander the Great (a system worked out by Manetho) is a convenient frame upon which to hang the succession of the kings and a record of events. In the accompanying table the numbers of the dynasties are given in Roman numbers, and the number is followed by the dates of the dynasty and a notation of famous monarchs of the era (each of whom has a separate article in *The New Columbia Encyclopedia*). Since there are many gaps and periods without well-known rulers (occasionally without known rulers at all), those are given simply with dates or are combined with better-recorded periods.

The Old Kingdom. A high culture developed early, and the Old Kingdom is notable for artistic and intellectual achievements (see EGYPTIAN ARCHITECTURE; EGYPTIAN ART; EGYPTIAN RELIGION). From the beginning there was a concept of the divinity or quasi-divinity of the king (pharaoh), which lasted from the time that Egypt was first united (c.3200 B.C.) under one ruler until the ultimate fall of Egypt to the Romans. According to tradition, it was MENES (or Narmer) who as king of Upper Egypt conquered the rival kingdom of Lower Egypt in the Nile delta, thus forming the single kingdom of Egypt. In the unified and centralized state created by Menes, the memory of the two ancient kingdoms was preserved in formalities of administration. Trade flourished, and the kings of the I dynasty appear to have sent trading expeditions under military escort to Sinai to obtain copper. There are indications that under the II dynasty there was trade with areas as far north as the Black Sea. The III dynasty was one of the landmarks of Egyptian history, the time during which sun-worship, a new form of religion that later became the religion of the upper classes, was introduced. At the same time mummification and the building of stone monuments were begun. The kings of the IV dynasty (which may be said to begin the Old Kingdom proper) were the builders of the great pyramids at Al JIZAH. The great pyramid of Khufu is a monument not only to the king but also to the unified organization of ancient Egyptian society. The V to the VII dynasties are remarkable for their records of trading expeditions with armed escorts. Although Egypt flourished culturally and commercially during this period, it started to become less centralized and weaker politically. The priests of the sun-god at Hierapolis gained increasing power; the office of provincial rulers became hereditary, and their local influence was thereafter always a threat to the state. In the 23d cent. B.C. the Old Kingdom, after a long and flourishing existence, fell apart. The local rulers became dominant, and the records, kept by the central government, tended to disappear. Some order was restored by the IX dynasty, but it was not until 2134 that power was again centralized, this time at THEBES. That city was to be the capital for most of the next millennium. The Middle Kingdom, founded at the end of the XI dynasty, reached its zenith under the XII. The Pharaoh, however, was not now an absolute monarch but rather a feudal lord, and his vassals held their land in their own power. The XII dynasty advanced the border up the Nile to the Second Cataract. Order was preserved, the draining of Al Fayyum was begun (adding a new and fertile province), a uniform system of writing was adopted, and civilization reached a new peak. After 214 years the XII dynasty came to an end in 1786 B.C. In the dimly known period that followed, Egypt passed for more than a century under the HYKSOS (the so-called shepherd kings), who were apparently Semites from Syria. They were expelled from Egypt by Amasis I (Ahmose I), founder of the XVIII dynasty, and the New Kingdom was established.

The New Kingdom. The XVIII dynasty is the most important and the best-recorded period in Egyptian history. The local governors generally opposed both the Hyksos and the new dynasty; those who survived were now made mere administrators, their lands passing to the crown. Ancient Egypt reached its height. Its boundaries were extended into Asia, with a foreign province reaching the Euphrates (see THUTMOSE I). Letters known as the TEL EL AMARNA tablets are dated to this dynasty and furnish the details of the reigns of Amenhotep III and his son, Ikhnaton. As Ikhnaton neglected his rule in the pursuit of religion, letters from local rulers became increasingly urgent in begging help, especially against the HITTITES. Of the rulers following Ikhnaton in this dynasty, Tutankhamen is important for his law code and his enforcement of those laws through the courts. Architecture was at its zenith with the enormous and impressive buildings at and around Thebes. Egyptian civilization seems to have worn out rapidly after conflicts with the Hittites under the XIX dynasty and with sea raiders under the XX dynasty. With a succession of weak kings, the Theban priesthood practically ruled the country and continued to maintain a sort of theocracy for 450 years. In the delta the Libyan element had been growing, and with the disappearance of the weak XXI dynasty, which had governed from Tanis, a Libyan dynasty came to power. This was succeeded by the alien rule of Nubians, Negroes who advanced from the south to the delta under Piankhi and later conquered the land. The rising power of Assyria threatened Egypt by absorbing the petty states of Syria and Palestine, and Assyrian kings had reached the borders of Egypt several times before ESAR-HADDON actually invaded (673 B.C.) the land of the Nile. Assyrian rule was, however, short-lived; by 650 B.C., under Psamtik, Egypt was once more independent and orderly. Greek traders became important, and their city of Naucratis, founded by Amasis II, throve. Attempts to reestablish Egyptian power in Asia were turned back (605 B.C.) by the Babylonian king Nebuchadnezzar, and Egypt fell easy prey (525 B.C.) to the armies of CAMBYSES of Persia. Despite occasional troubles, the Persians maintained their hegemony until 405 B.C. New dynasties were then established, but they did not regain any of the old splendor. The Persians again became dominant in 341 B.C. Egypt, rich and ill-defended, fell to Alexander the Great with no resistance in 332 B.C. When his brief empire faded, Egypt in the wars of his successors (the Diadochi) fell to his general Ptolemy, who became king as Ptolemy I. All the succeeding kings of the dynasty were also named Ptolemy. The great city of Alexandria became the intellectual center and fountainhead of the Hellenistic world. The Ptolemies maintained a formidable empire for more than two centuries and exercised great power in the E Mediterranean. The priesthood remained in native hands, but the splendor of the Ptolemaic government weighed heavily upon the overtaxed and hard-working peasantry. The Jewish population was large—perhaps as much as a seventh of the total population—and even the Palestinian Jews looked to the Alexandrian Jews for guidance. The rising power of Rome soon overshadowed Egypt, but it was not until Ptolemy XI sought Roman aid through POMPEY to regain his throne that Rome actually obtained (58 B.C.) a foothold in Egypt itself. CLEOPATRA, the daughter of Ptolemy XI, tried to win back power for Egypt, especially through Julius CAESAR and Marc ANTONY. Octavian (later Emperor Augustus) actually annexed Egypt to Rome, putting to death Cleopatra's son, Ptolemy XIV, who was the last of the Ptolemies. Egypt became a granary for Rome; the emperors from Augustus to Hadrian raised the irrigation system to great efficiency, and Trajan reopened the ancient Nile-Red Sea canal. In the 2d cent. A.D., strife between Jews and Greeks in Alexandria brought massacres, and a mutiny of the soldiers did irreparable damage. The taxes rose steadily to meet increasingly severe and frequent emergencies. Would-be conquerors looked longingly at Egypt, and Zenobia of Palmyra actually took the province, which was, however, soon recovered. Christianity was welcomed in Egypt, and several of the most celebrated Doctors of the Church, notably St. ATHANASIUS, St. CYRIL of Alexandria, and ORIGEN, were Egyptians. Egypt gave rise to the Arian and Nestorian heresies, and GNOSTICISM flourished there for a time. The patriarch of Alexandria was probably the most important figure in Egypt. After St. Cyril, MONOPHYSITISM became the national faith; out of this arose the Coptic Church. The hostility of the people to the Orthodox Byzantine emperors and officials probably helped Khosru II of Persia to gain Egypt in 616. It was recovered (c.628) by Heraclius I, but the Persian invasion proved to be only a forerunner of the more serious Arabian invasion. See E. R. Bevan, *History of Egypt under the Ptolemaic Dynasty* (1928); Georg Steindorff and K. C. Steele, *When Egypt Ruled the East* (rev. ed. 1957); W. S. Smith, *Art and Architecture of Ancient Egypt* (1958); A. C. Johnson, *Egypt and the Roman Empire* (1951, repr. 1961); J. H. Breasted, *A History of Egypt from the Earliest Times to the Persian Conquest* (2d ed. 1909, repr. 1965); H. I. Bell, *Egypt from Alexander the Great to the Arab Conquest* (1949, repr. 1966); Pierre Montet, *Lives of the Pharaohs* (1968); Barbara Sewell, *Egypt under the Pharaohs* (1968); A. H. Gardiner, *Egypt of the Pharaohs* (1961, repr. 1969); W. M. F. Petrie, *History of Egypt* (6 vol., 1898–1905, repr. 1972).

Islamic Egypt. The Arab conquest of Egypt (639–42), only some 20 years after the rise of Islam, made the country an integral part of the Muslim world. Until the 19th cent., Egyptian history was intimately involved with the general political development of ISLAM, whether unified or divided into warring states. Under the UMAYYAD caliphate many of the people continued their adherence to Coptic Christianity despite the special tax exacted from infidels. However, the settling of colonists from Arabia and the financial advantages of adopting Islam eventually reduced the Christian population to a small minority. With Arab dominance, the Greek and Coptic languages went out of use and Arabic alone was spoken. The ABBASID caliphate (founded 749) at first held Egypt under complete subjection, but the unwieldiness of its vast domain encouraged provincial governors to revolt and to assert their own rule. In the 10th cent. Egypt fell to the FATIMID claimants to the caliphate, who invaded from the west. The Fatimids founded (969) Cairo as their capital, and with the establishment (972) there of the Mosque of Al Azhar as a great (and still active) Muslim university they further emphasized the change of Egypt from an outpost of Islam to one of its centers. The strain of the CRUSADES may have been responsible for the fall of the Fatimids, which led to the founding by SALADIN of the Ayyubid dynasty. The strategic posi-

DYNASTIES OF ANCIENT EGYPT

DYNASTY	YEARS	FAMOUS RULERS
Old Kingdom (or Old Empire)		
I	3110–2884 B.C.	MENES
II	2884–2780 B.C.	
III	2780–2680 B.C.	SNEFRU
IV	2680–2565 B.C.	KHUFU (Cheops), KHAFRE, MENKAURE. Age of the great pyramids.
V	2565–2420 B.C.	
VI	2420–2258 B.C.	PEPI I, PEPI II
First Intermediate Period		
VII, VIII	2258–2225 B.C.	An obscure period.
IX, X	2225–2134 B.C.	Capital at Heracleopolis.
XI	2134–c.2000 B.C.	Capital at Thebes.
Middle Kingdom (or Middle Empire)		
XII	2000–1786 B.C.	AMENEMHET I, SESOSTRIS I, AMENEMHET II, SESOSTRIS II, SESOSTRIS III, AMENEMHET III, AMENEMHET IV
Second Intermediate Period		
XIII–XVII	1786–1570 B.C.	The HYKSOS. An obscure period.
New Kingdom (or New Empire)		
XVIII	1570–c.1342 B.C.	AMENHOTEP I, THUTMOSE I, THUTMOSE II with Hatshepshut, THUTMOSE III, AMENHOTEP II, THUTMOSE IV, AMENHOTEP III, Amenhotep IV (IKHNATON), TUTANKHAMEN
XIX	c.1342–1200 B.C.	HOREMHEB, RAMSES I, SETI I, RAMSES II, MERNEPTAH, SETI II
XX	1200–1085 B.C.	RAMSES III with TIY. New Kingdom declines.
XXI	1085–945 B.C.	Tanite dynasty (capital at Tanis).
XXII	945–745 B.C.	SHESHONK I. Libyan dynasty (capital at Bubastis).
XXIII	745–718 B.C.	Nubian dynasty with invasion of PIANKHI (capital at Bubastis).
XXIV	718–712 B.C.	Saïte dynasty (capital at Saïs).
XXV	712–663 B.C.	TAHARKA. Assyrian invasions begin foreign domination.
XXVI	663–525 B.C.	PSAMTIK, NECHO, APRIES, AMASIS II (capital at Saïs).
XXVII	525–405 B.C.	The ACHAEMENIDS of Persia in control. CAMBYSES II to DARIUS II. Egypt revolts.
XXVIII, XXIX, XXX	405–332 B.C.	NEKHTNEBF I, NEKHTNEBF II. Last native dynasties, ending with conquest of Alexander the Great. Capital at Saïs, then at Mendes, then at Sebennytos.

tion of Egypt made it a logical target of the Crusaders, who twice (1219–21, 1249–50) held Damietta, then the chief Mediterranean port, but could advance no farther. The later Ayyubid rulers came excessively under the control of their soldiers and advisers, the MAMELUKES, who in 1250 seized the country. Until 1517, when Egypt was conquered by the Ottoman Turks, the Mamelukes maintained their turbulent rule, with frequent revolts and extremely short tenure for most of the sultans. Nevertheless, they built many great architectural monuments. Their importance by no means disappeared with the establishment of Ottoman power, for the Egyptian pasha (governor) was compelled to consult the Mameluke beys (princes), who continued in control of the provinces. Ottoman control had become almost nominal by the administration (1768–73) of Ali Bey, who termed himself sultan. The Turks, however, by no means gave up attempts to assert power over the unruly beys. It was on the pretext of establishing order and restoring Turkish rule that Napoleon Bonaparte (NAPOLEON I) undertook the French occupation of Egypt (1798–1801), although his real object was to cut off British trade lines and, ultimately, to detach India from the British Empire. All efforts were bent to establishing French power in the region, and the Turks ultimately joined the British in forcing the French out. The French withdrawal was followed by the rise of MUHAMMAD ALI, a former common soldier, who was appointed (1805) Egyptian pasha by the Ottoman emperor. He permanently destroyed (1811) the Mamelukes' power by massacring their leaders. Using Europe as a model, Muhammad Ali laid the foundations of the modern Egyptian state. He introduced political, social, and educational reforms and developed an effective bureaucracy; he also undertook massive economic development by expanding and modernizing agriculture and by starting large-scale industry. Under his rule the empire eventually extended from the Sudan in the south to Arabia in the east and Syria in the northeast. Abbas I (reigned 1848–54), Muhammad Ali's successor, undid some of his reforms and was followed by Muhammad Said Pasha, who lacked an understanding of economics.

European Domination and Independence. In 1856, Said granted Ferdinand de Lesseps a concession for the construction of the Suez Canal, a project that put Egypt into deep financial debt and robbed it of its thriving transit-trade on the Alexandria-Cairo railroad. In addition, the strategic nature of the canal shifted Great Britain's focus in the Middle East from Constantinople to Cairo and opened the door to British intervention in Egyptian affairs. Said was followed by Khedive (viceroy) ISMAIL PASHA, whose rule was characterized by accelerated economic development, westernization, and the establishment of Egyptian autonomy. However, the cost of Said's reforms, of the construction of the Suez Canal, and of his conquests in Africa put Egypt deep into debt and forced Ismail to sell (1875) his Suez Canal shares to the British. Egypt's financial problems led to further subordination of the country to great power interests. Ismail was forced to accept the establishment of a French-British Debt Commission. In 1879, Ismail was compelled to abdicate in favor of his son TEWFIK PASHA, who was confronted with financial and political chaos; his situation was complicated by the outbreak of a nationalist and military revolt (1881–82) under Arabi Pasha. The British reacted to the revolt with a naval bombardment of Alexandria in July, 1882, and by landing British troops, who defeated Arabi Pasha at the battle of Tel al Kabir and went on to occupy Cairo. The British consolidated their control during the period (1883–1907) when Lord CROMER was consul general and de facto ruler. By 1904 the governments of France, Austria, and Italy agreed not to obstruct Britain in its intention to stay in Egypt indefinitely. During World War I, after Turkey joined the Central Powers, Great Britain declared Egypt a British protectorate and deposed ABBAS II, the allegedly pro-German khedive, substituting Husein Kamil (1914–17), a member of his family. After the war Egyptian nationalists of the WAFD party, led by ZAGHLUL PASHA, were especially vigorous in their demands for freedom. Under the rule of Ahmad Fuad (who later became FUAD I), a treaty providing for Egypt's independence was concluded (1922). It went into effect in 1923 following the proclamation of a constitution that made Egypt a kingdom under Fuad and established a parliament. Great Britain, however, retained the right to station troops in Egypt and refused to consider Egyptian claims to the Anglo-Egyptian Sudan. The British protectorate was maintained until the promulgation of a new treaty in 1936, which made the two countries allies and promised the eventual withdrawal of British troops. Fuad was succeeded by his son FAROUK. In 1937 a further step toward sovereignty was accomplished by an agreement (which went into effect in 1949) to end EXTRATERRITORIALITY in Egypt. In the postindependence years, Egypt's internal political life was largely a struggle for power between the Wafd party and the throne. The constitution was suspended in 1930, and Egypt was under a virtual royal dictatorship until the Wafdists forced its readoption in 1935. During World War II, Egypt remained officially neutral. However, all Egyptian facilities were put at the disposal of the British and several battles were fought on Egyptian soil (for details of the military engagements, see NORTH AFRICA, CAMPAIGNS IN). After the war, demands were made for a revision of the treaty of 1936. Repeated talks failed because of Egyptian insistence that Great Britain allow incorporation of the Anglo-Egyptian Sudan into Egypt. An Egyptian appeal (1947) on this subject to the Security Council of the United Nations was also in vain. Additional difficulties were occasioned by the British announcement that not all military forces in areas other than the Suez Canal Zone would be withdrawn. Egypt bitterly opposed the UN partition of Palestine in 1948 and, joining its forces with the other members of the ARAB LEAGUE, sent troops into the S Negev. Israeli forces, however, held the Egyptians to slight gains (see ARAB-ISRAELI WARS). In domestic politics the failure of any party to win a majority in the chamber of deputies resulted in frequent ministerial upsets. Early in 1950, however, the Wafd acquired a majority and formed a one-party cabinet. The struggle between King Farouk and the Wafdist government intensified in 1952. Several political uprisings led to violence. On July 23, 1952, the military headed by Gen. Muhammad Naguib took power by coup d'etat. Farouk abdicated in favor of his infant son, Ahmad Fuad II, but in 1953 the monarchy was abolished and a republic was set up. Naguib assumed the presidency, but, in his attempts to move toward a parliamentary republic, he met with opposition from other members of the Revolutionary Command Committee (RCC). Increasing difficulties led to extension of martial law. Col. Gamal Abdal NASSER emerged as a rival to Naguib, and in Feb., 1954, Naguib resigned.

Egypt under Nasser. Nasser took full power in Nov., 1954. Under the new constitution, he was elected president for a six-year term. The long-standing dispute over the Sudan was ended on Jan. 1, 1956, when Sudan announced its independence, recognized by both Egypt and Great Britain. British troops, by previous agreement (July, 1954), completed their evacuation of the Suez Canal Zone in June, 1956. Continued troubles with Israel over Gaza caused the United Nations to offer conciliation measures, but the situation remained taut. Tension increased in July, 1956, when, after the United States and Great Britain withdrew their pledges of financial aid for the building of the Aswan High Dam, Nasser nationalized the Suez Canal and expelled British oil and embassy officials from Egypt. On Oct. 29, Israel, barred from the canal and angered by border incursions, invaded Gaza and the Sinai peninsula; Great Britain and France, after demanding evacuation of all Egyptian and Israeli troops to 10 mi (16 km) beyond the Canal Zone, attacked Egypt on Oct. 31. Within a week Great Britain, France, and Israel yielded to worldwide pressure to halt the hostilities. A UN emergency force then occupied the Canal Zone in Dec., 1956. Both Israeli and UN troops evacuated Egyptian territory in the spring of 1957. On Feb. 1, 1958, Syria and Egypt merged as the UNITED ARAB REPUBLIC. In March, 1958, Yemen joined the UAR, creating the United Arab States. The union was soon torn by personal and political differences and a Syrian revolt (1961) led to its virtual dissolution. Egypt embarked on a program of industrialization, chiefly through Soviet technical and economic aid. Both industry and agriculture were almost completely nationalized by 1962. In the early 1960s Nasser strove to make Egypt the undisputed leader of a united Arab world, attacking, in intense propaganda campaigns, other Arab governments that resisted Egypt's leadership. Nasser's chief and most effective rallying cry for Arab unity remained his denunciation of Israel and his call for its extinction. From 1962 to 1967 Egyptian forces provided the chief strength of the republican government in YEMEN, where the royalists were backed by Saudi Arabia. Egyptian military might continued to increase with the acquisition of powerful modern weapons, many of which were supplied by the USSR. In domestic affairs Nasser faced formidable obstacles to his goals of continued social and economic progress. In 1964 a new provisional constitution was promulgated, and Nasser was elected (1965) president under it. The Egyptian economy continued to suffer a trade deficit, and there were a serious food shortage and an exploding population to contend with. In 1965 and 1966 two anti-Nasser plots were discovered and crushed. Nasser assumed near absolute control in 1967 by taking over the premiership and the leadership of the Arab Socialist Union (ASU), the country's sole political party. In the spring of 1967, Syria, which was involved in a series of border skirmishes with Israel, appealed to Egypt for aid under the 1966 mutual defense pact. Accordingly, Egyptian troops were ordered to positions on the Israeli border, and Nasser demanded that the UN peacekeeping force stationed on the Egyptian side of the border since 1956 be withdrawn. Following the UN evacuation, Arab troops massed on the frontier, and Nasser announced (May 22) that the Gulf of Aqaba was closed to Israeli shipping. The other Arab states rallied to Egypt's support. International diplomacy failed to resolve the crisis. On June 5 Israel launched air and ground attacks against Arab positions and after six days achieved a rapid and decisive victory despite the Arab superiority in numbers and armaments. When the UN cease-fire went into effect, Israel held the Sinai peninsula and the east bank of the Suez Canal. After the war Egypt received a massive infusion of Soviet military and economic aid in a program designed to rebuild its armed forces and economy, both shattered by the war. Egypt's postwar policy was based on two principles: no direct negotiations with Israel and the implementation of UN Security Council Resolution 242, which, in part, called for the withdrawal of Israeli armed forces from occupied territories. After Nasser's sudden death in Sept., 1970, Vice President Anwar al-SADAT succeeded him as president. There was an abortive coup in May, 1971, but Sadat emerged in full control. A permanent constitution was ratified in Sept., 1971. Although Sadat followed a modified version of Nasser's hard line toward Israel, he continued to demand Israeli withdrawal from the occupied territories and threatened to renew the war in order to regain the lands. In July, 1972, Sadat suddenly ousted all Soviet military personnel stationed in Egypt and placed Soviet bases and equipment under Egyptian control. This represented a reversal of a 20-year trend of increasing dependence on the USSR. Unrest in 1973 led to the forced resignation of the cabinet and to Sadat's assumption of the premiership. Sadat relinquished the premiership in Sept., 1974, turning the office over to Abdel Azziz Heqazi.

The 1973 war and after. Another war with Israel broke out on Oct. 6, 1973, when Egyptian forces crossed the Suez Canal and established footholds in the Israeli-occupied Sinai peninsula. At the same time fighting broke out between Israel and Syria on the Golan Heights. The fighting escalated both on the ground and in the air. Port Said, the suburbs of Cairo, and Damascus in Syria were bombed by the Israeli air force. After Israel had stabilized the Syrian front, its troops crossed (Oct. 15) the Suez Canal and by Oct. 24 were in control of some 475 sq mi (1,230 sq km) on the west bank of the canal between Ismailia and Adabiya, surrounding the city of Suez and trapping Egypt's Third Army on the east side of the canal. On Oct. 17, Sadat declared that the aim of the war was to liberate Arab territories occupied by Israel since 1967 and called for a cease-fire coupled with the withdrawal of Israel from those territories. At the same time Arab countries, by reducing—and later stopping—oil exports, put pressure on the United States to get Israel to pull back from the occupied lands. On Oct. 22, the United States and the USSR submitted a joint resolution to the UN Security Council calling for an immediate cease-fire with both forces remaining in their positions, immediate implementation of Security Council Resolution 242 of 1967, and the beginning of peace negotiations. On Oct. 26, the UN Security Council voted to establish a UN emergency force made up of troops from the smaller nations to supervise the cease-fire. By the time the 7,000-man emergency force reached the Middle East, the military situation had become very complex, with Israeli and Egyptian troops in positions on both sides of the Suez Canal and the Egyptian Third Army cut off from supplies of food. Through the mediation efforts of U.S. Secretary of State Henry A. KISSINGER, Egypt and Israel agreed (Oct. 28) to face-to-face negotiations on implementing the cease-fire. It was agreed that the Egyptian Third Army would receive supplies through the UN and the Red Cross. On Nov. 9, Israel accepted a proposal, worked out by Kissinger and Sadat, which called for a cease-fire, a prisoner exchange, the establishment of a UN-supervised nonmilitary supply corridor from Cairo to Suez city and to the trapped Third Army in the Sinai, an end to the Egyptian blockade of Bab el Mandeb at the southern end of the Red Sea, talks between military representatives of both sides to fix a cease-fire line, and peace negotiations. A result of the intense U.S. effort to secure a settlement was the resumption of diplomatic relations between the United States and Egypt, which had been severed since the 1967 war. This marked the beginning of a change in Egyptian foreign policy away from dependence on the USSR toward closer relations with the West. Face-to-face negotiations between Israeli and Egyptian representatives began in Geneva in late Dec., 1973, but remained deadlocked into Jan., 1974. In mid-January, Kissinger successfully negotiated an agreement providing for a disengagement of military forces on the Suez front. The pact was signed Jan. 18 and by March 4 Israel had withdrawn its forces from the west bank of the canal to a point on the east side behind an Egyptian zone adjacent to the canal (5–7.5 mi/8–12 km wide) and a UN-patrolled buffer zone (3.5–5 mi/5.8–8 km wide). After regaining both banks of the Suez Canal, Egypt, with U.S. assistance, began to clear the canal of the mines and sunken ships left from the 1967 war. In June, 1974, U.S. President Richard Nixon visited Egypt during his tour of the Middle East. At the conclusion of the visit, a treaty was signed providing U.S. aid to Egypt of nuclear technology for peaceful purposes. See Charles Issawi, *Egypt: An Economic and Social Analysis* (1947), *Egypt at Mid-Century* (1954), and *Egypt in Revolution* (1963); M. A. Rifaat, *Awakening of Modern Egypt* (1948, repr. 1964); Mahmoud Zayid, *Egypt's Struggle for Independence* (1965); P. M. Holt, *Egypt and the Fertile Crescent, 1566–1922* (1966); Tom Little, *Modern Egypt* (1967); Lord Cromer, *Modern Egypt* (2 vol., 1908, repr. 1968); Stanley Lane Poole, *History of Egypt in the Middle Ages* (1901, repr. 1969); P. J. Vatikiotis, *The Modern History of Egypt* (1969); Donald Wilbur, *United Arab Republic of Egypt: Its People, its Society, its Culture* (1969); G. A. Lloyd, *Egypt Since Cromer* (2 vol., 1933–34, repr. 1970); Peter Mansfield, *The British in Egypt* (1970); Jacques Berque, *Egypt: Imperialism and Revolution* (1972); Z. N. Mahmoud, *Land and People of Egypt* (rev. ed. 1972).

Egyptian architecture was formulated prior to 3000 B.C. Scant tree growth prevented the extensive use of wood as a building material, but because fine clay was deposited by the flood waters of the Nile, the ceramic arts developed early. Both sun-dried and kiln-dried bricks were used extensively. Fine sandstone, limestone, and granite were available for obelisks, sculpture, and decorative uses. A massive, static, and serene architecture emerged from primitive structures of clay and reeds. The incised and flatly modeled surface adornment of the granite buildings was apparently derived from mud wall ornamentation, and the slope given to the masonry walls suggests a method employed originally to obtain stability in the mud walls. The Egyptians developed post-and-lintel construction—the type exclusively used in their monumental buildings—even though the use of the arch was developed during the dynasty of Snefru. Walls were immensely thick. Columns were confined to the halls and inner courts. The massive sloping exterior walls, containing only a few small openings, as well as the columns and piers that they concealed, were covered with hieroglyphic and pictorial carvings in brilliant colors. Many motifs of Egyptian ornament are symbolic, such as the scarab, or sacred beetle, the solar disk, and the vulture. Hieroglyphics were decoration as well as records of historic events. Egyptian sculptors possessed the highest capacity for integrating ornamentation and the essential forms of their buildings. From natural objects, such as palm leaves, the papyrus plant, and the buds and flowers of the lotus, they developed conventionalized motifs. Roofs, invariably flat, suited to the lack of rain, were of huge stone blocks supported by the external walls and the closely spaced columns. All dwelling houses, built of timber or of sun-baked bricks, have disappeared; only temples and tombs, constructed in durable materials, have survived. The belief in existence beyond death resulted in sepulchral architecture of maximum impressiveness and permanence. Egyptian architectural development parallels the chronology (see EGYPT): Old Kingdom, 2680–2258 B.C.; Middle Kingdom, 2134–1786 B.C.; New Kingdom, 1570–1085 B.C. Old Kingdom remains are almost entirely sepulchral, chiefly the tombs of monarchs and nobles. The MASTABA is the oldest remaining form of sepulcher; it is a rectangular, flat-roofed structure with sloping walls containing chambers built over the mummy pit. The PYRAMID of a sovereign was begun as soon as he ascended the throne. Groups of pyramids remain; those at Gizeh, which include the Great Pyramid of Cheops (KHUFU), are among the best known. Many Middle Kingdom tombs were tunneled out of the rock cliffs on the west bank of the Nile, among them the remarkable group (c.1991–1786 B.C.) at Bani Hasan. New Kingdom temples in the environs of Thebes, such as those of Medinet Habu and the Ramesseum, derived their form from the funerary chapels of previous ages. The New Kingdom years cover the great period of temple construction, those temples extant conforming to a distinct type. The doorway in the massive facade is flanked on each side by great sloping towers, or pylons, in front of which obelisks and colossal statues were often placed. The more important temples were approached between rows of sculptured rams and sphinxes. A high enclosing wall screened the building from the common people, who had no share in the temple rituals practiced solely by the king, the officials, and the priesthood. Beyond the open colonnaded courtyard was the great hypostyle hall with immense columns arranged in a central nave and side aisles. The shorter columns of the latter permitted a clerestory for the admission of light. Behind the hypostyle hall were small sanctuaries, where only the king and priests might enter, and behind these were small service chambers. The Great Temple of Amon at Karnak is a product of many successive additions; the central columns of its hypostyle hall are the largest known. In the temples that resulted from many additions, unity of design was often sacrificed to sheer size. New Kingdom temples were also excavated from rock. The temples of ABU SIMBEL begun by Seti I, have four colossal figures, sculptured from solid rock, of Ramses II, who completed the temples. (The temples were cut apart and removed from their position by the Nile previous to the completion of the Aswan dam and reassembled in 1966 at a point higher and farther inland.) The temple at IDFU, (237 B.C.) by Ptolemy III, is the best preserved of the Ptolemaic period. Even during periods of foreign rule Egyptian architecture clung to its native characteristics, adopting almost no elements from other cultures. See W. M. Flinders Petrie, *Egyptian Architecture* (1938); W. Stevenson Smith, *Art and Architecture of Ancient Egypt* (1958, repr. 1965); A. Badawy, *Architecture in Ancient Egypt and the Near East* (1966), *A History of Egyptian Architecture* (Vol. I-III, 1954–68).

Egyptian art. The art of predynastic Egypt (c.4000–3200 B.C.), known from funerary offerings, consisted largely of painted pottery and figurines, ivory carvings, slate cosmetic palettes, and finely worked flint weapons. In painting, a monumental treatment was given to designs like those drawn in red on buff-colored pottery from Hieraconpolis, a palace city of upper Egypt. Toward the end of the predynastic period, sculptors began to carve monolithic figures of the gods from limestone, such as the Min at Coptos. In the protodynastic and early dynasitc periods (3200–2780 B.C.) some Mesopotamian motifs began to appear. The craftsmanship of the finely worked stone bowls and vases of these periods is particularly remarkable. With the beginning of the Old Kingdom, centered at Memphis (2680–2258 B.C.), there was a rapid development of the stylistic conventions that characterize Egyptian art throughout its history. In relief sculpture and painting, the human figure was usually represented with the head in profile, the eye and shoulders in front view, and the pelvis, legs, and feet in profile (the law of frontality). There was little attempt at plastic or spatial illusionism. The reliefs were very low; relief and shallow intaglio are often found in the same piece. Color was applied in flat tones, and there was no attempt at linear perspective. A relief masterpiece from the I dynasty is the palette of Namer (Cairo). It represents animal and human forms in scenes of battle with the ground divided into registers, and with emphasis on silhouette in the carving. In statuary in the round various standing and seated types were developed, but there was strict adherence to the law of frontality and a tendency to emphasize symmetry and to minimize suggestion of movement. Religious beliefs of the period held that the happy posthumous existence of the dead depended on the continuation of all phases of their earthly life. The artist's task was therefore to produce a statement of reality in the most durable materials at his command. Tombs were decorated with domestic, military, hunting, and ceremonial scenes. Entombed with the deceased were statues of him and of his servants and attendants, often shown at characteristic occupations. Outstanding Old Kingdom examples of sculpture in the round are the *Great Chephren*, in diorite, the *Prince Ra-hetep and Princess Neferet*, in painted limestone, the *Sheik-el-Beled* (mayor of the village), in painted wood (all: Cairo), and the *Seated Scribe*, in painted limestone (Louvre). Probably because of its relative impermanence, painting was little used as a medium of representation; it appears to have served principally as accessory to sculpture. A rare example is the painting of geese from a tomb at Medum (Cairo). The Middle Kingdom, with its capital at Thebes (2000–1786 B.C.), was a new age of experiment and invention that grew out of the turbulence of the First Intermediate Period (2134–c.2000 B.C.). The forms of the Old Kingdom were retained, but the unity of style was broken. Increasing formalism was combined with a meticulous delicacy of craftsmanship. The paintings of the rock-cut tombs at Bani Hasan (e.g., *Slaves Feeding Oryxes* and *Cat Stalking Prey*, Tomb of Khnemu-hetep) are outstanding for freedom of draftsmanship. In sculpture the sensitive portraits of Sesostris III and Amenemhet III (both: Cairo) are exceptional in Egyptian art, which at all other times showed a reluctance to portray inner feeling. The art of the New Kingdom (1570–1342 B.C.) can be viewed as the final development of the classic Egyptian style of the Middle Kingdom, a combination of the monumental forms of the Old Kingdom and the drive and inspiration of the Middle Kingdom. The paintings of this period are noted for boldness of design and controlled vitality. In sculpture the emphasis is on bulk, solidity, and impersonality. During the Amarna period (1372–1350 B.C.) a free and delicate style developed with many naturalistic tendencies and a new sense of life and movement. In sculpture the new style was carried to the point of caricature, e.g., in the colossal statue of Ikhnaton (Cairo). The outstanding masterpiece of this period is the painted limestone bust of Queen Nefertiti (Berlin Mus.). The delicacy, sophistication, and extreme richness of this style in its late period is best exemplified by the furnishings from the tomb of Tutankhamen. The Ramesside period (1314–1085 B.C.) saw an attempt to return to the classic formalism of the earlier New Kingdom, but the vitality that characterized that period could not be recovered. The sculpture, both in relief and in the round, became monotonous and even overbearing except in the numerous battle scenes. The period of decline (1085–730 B.C.) is characterized by mechanical repetition of earlier forms in the major arts and by the introduction of satirical and often cynical drawings in the papyri. In the Saïte period (730–663 B.C.) there was an attempt to return to the austerity of the Old Kingdom style, but for the simplicity of the earlier forms a coarse brutality was substituted. After the conquest of Egypt by the Assyrians in 663 B.C., all the arts declined with the exception of metalworking, in which a high standard of skill was maintained. Neither the Assyrian nor the subsequent Persian invasions left a mark on Egyptian art, and even under the Ptolemaic dynasty (332–30 B.C.) Egypt proved extraordinarily resistant to Hellenic conceptions of art. The ancient architectural tradition retained its vitality, as in the temples of Horus at Idfu and Isis at Philae, but painting and sculpture continued to decline. Native naturalism may have influenced the painted Fayum panels and orant (praying) portraits on mummy shrouds, but neither their subjects nor their style is essentially Egyptian. The minor arts continued to flourish; alabaster vases, faïence pottery and figurines, glassware, ivories, and metalwork were produced with the ancient skill and in the traditional Egyptian style. Among the outstanding collections of Egyptian art in the United States are those at the Brooklyn Museum and the Metropolitan Museum in New York City. See W. S. Smith, *History of Egyptian Sculpture and Painting in the Old Kingdom* (2d ed. 1950) and *Art and Architecture of Ancient Egypt* (1958); W. C. Hayes, *The Scepter of Egypt* (2 vol., 1959–60); Kurt Lange and Max Hirmer, *Egypt: Architecture, Sculpture, Painting in Three Thousand Years* (4th ed., tr. 1968).

Egyptian language, extinct language of ancient Egypt that is generally classified as a member of the Hamitic subfamily of the Hamito-Semitic family of languages (see HAMITIC LANGUAGES; HAMITO-SEMITIC). The development of ancient Egyptian is usually divided into four periods: (1) Old Egyptian, spoken and written in Egypt during the IV to VI dynasties of the Old Kingdom (3d millennium B.C.); (2) Middle Egyptian, a form of the language noted for its great literature and current from the XI dynasty (beginning 2134 B.C.) to the reign of Ikhnaton (c.1372–1354 B.C.) in the XVIII dynasty; (3) Late Egyptian, which was used from the time of Ikhnaton through the XX dynasty of the 12th cent. B.C.; and (4) demotic, dating from the late 8th cent. B.C. to the 5th cent. A.D. The ancient Egyptian language first used a HIEROGLYPHIC form of writing that underwent several stages of development in the course of the centuries. From hieroglyphics evolved an Egyptian cursive handwriting known as hieratic; and from hieratic, a simplified script called demotic, in which was recorded the form of the Egyptian language also called demotic. Egyptian hieroglyphics and the styles of writing derived from them are associated with pagan civilization. Their extinction followed the victory of Christianity over the pagan religions. Some scholars regard COPTIC as a fifth period of ancient Egyptian, although others classify it as a different language descended from the ancient tongue. If Coptic, which is written in a modified version of the Greek alphabet, is considered a continuation of the Egyptian language, a written record of the latter may be said to cover an unbroken span of at least 40 centuries, the longest such record known for a language. See Rosetta stone under ROSETTA. See A. H. Gardiner, *Egyptian Grammar* (3d ed. 1957); N. M. Davies, *Picture Writing in Ancient Egypt* (1958); E. W. Budge, *Egyptian Language* (8th ed. 1966).

Egyptian religion. Information concerning ancient Egyptian religion is abundant but unsatisfactory. Only certain parts of Egyptian religious life and thought are known; whole periods remain in the dark. What we do know is that the religious beliefs of the Egyptians were riddled with inconsistencies and confusions. Many gods and goddesses seem more or less identical, and yet they existed together. Contradictory myths explaining the creation of the world, natural phenomena, and the like were accepted without argument. Attributes of deities were freely and indiscriminately adopted from one group or locality to another, and combinations and fusions of gods were frequent. It is impossible to discern an orderly and consistent picture of Egyptian religion, and much scholarship remains hypothesis and conjecture. Probably the oldest form of religious worship in Egypt was animal worship. Early predynastic tribes venerated their own particular gods, who were usually embodied in a particular animal. Sometimes a whole species of animal was sacred, as cats at Bubastis; at other times only individual animals of certain types were worshiped, as the Apis bull at Memphis. As Egyptian civilization advanced, deities were gradually humanized. Many were represented with human bodies (although they retained animal heads) and other human characteristics and attributes. The wolf Ophois became a god of war, and the ibis Thoth became a patron of learning and the arts. We do not know precisely how or why certain animals became associated with certain gods. Moreover, the relationship between a god and his animal varied greatly. The god Thoth was not only identified with the ibis, but with the baboon and with the moon. Occasionally a god was a composite of various animals, such as Taurt, who had the head of a hippopotamus, the back and tail of a crocodile, and the claws of a lion. Similarly, just as a god could represent various natural phenomena, so could a single phenomenon be given different explanations. The ancient Egyptian conceived of the earth as a disk, with the flat plains of Egypt as the center and the mountainous foreign lands as the rim surrounding and supporting the disk. Below were the deep waters of the underworld, and above was the plain of the sky. Several systems of cosmic deities arose to explain this natural phenomenon. Some attributed the creation of the world to the ram-god Khnum, who styled the universe on his potter's wheel. Others said that creation was a spiritual and not a physical act, and that the divine thought of Ptah shaped the universe. Perhaps the most widely accepted explanation of the creation was that the sun-god, called either Ra or Atum, appeared out of primeval chaos and created the air-god Shu and his wife Tefnut, to whom were born the sky-goddess Nut and the earth-god Geb, who in turn bore Osiris, Isis, Set, and Nephthys. Some early cosmological myths represented the heavens as a great, star-studded cow, sometimes called Hathor or Athor, curving above the earth. Regardless of the different creation myths and ranking of gods, it is clear that the ancient Egyptian venerated many deities, that those gods were inherent in nature, and that they enabled the Egyptian to correlate human, natural, and divine life. At the end of the predynastic period (c.3200 B.C.), when a combined state was created, a national religion apparently grew out of the various primitive tribal and local religions, but still there were great inconsistencies and variations as various priesthoods attempted to systematize the gods and their myths. Changes in the political power of various localities also changed the status of the gods. In that way Amon became Egypt's most prominent deity, and by similar shifts of power Suchos, Bast, and Neith rose to importance. Some scholars have believed that the history of Egyptian religion was a sort of war of the gods, with the dominance of a god following directly the political dominance of a city or region. Others have pointed out that the national prominence of gods often centered in obscure cities or regions that never had political power. Nevertheless, shifts and changes did occur, making for new identifications and associations. Egyptian religion was remarkable for its reconciliation and union of conflicting beliefs. Some scholars have held, in fact, that the syncretism of Egyptian religion reveals a basic trend toward monotheism. But only during the reign of IKHNATON, who based his theology on the solar-god Aton and denied recognition to all but that god, was a monotheistic cult actually established. That unique cult apparently proved unsatisfactory to the ancient Egyptians; after Ikhnaton's death, polytheism was restored. The most important of the many forms of Egyptian worship were the cults of OSIRIS and of RA. Osiris was especially important as king and judge of the dead, but he was identified as well with the waters of the Nile, with the grain yield of the earth, with the moon, and even with the sun. A bountiful and loving king, Osiris was the protector of all, the poor and the rich. His myth, portraying the highest ideals of family devotion, expressed aspirations that were close to the people. His murder by his brother, SET, and his restoration to life by his wife, ISIS, made him the great symbol of the eternal persistence of life. The revenge exacted by his son and successor, HORUS, showed the triumph of good over evil. The worship of Ra, the great sun-god, chief of the cosmic deities, was perhaps more closely related to the fate of the royal house than to that of the people, but his cult was nevertheless one of the most important in ancient Egypt. His symbol, the PYRAMID, became the design of the monumental tombs of the Egyptian kings. Ra was said, in fact, to be the direct ancestor of the kings of Egypt, and in certain hymns was even addressed as a dead king. But he was more specifically thought of as a living power, whose daily cycle of birth, journey, and death was a fundamental theme in Egyptian life. Besides Osiris and Ra the other most prominent Egyptian god was AMON. By the XIX dynasty he was Egypt's greatest god, united with Ra as Amon Ra. Most scholars have concluded that, in later times at least, there was no close personal tie between the individual Egyptian and his gods, that the gods remained aloof, that their relationship to man was indirect, communicated to him by means of the king. There was no established book or set of teachings, as the Bible or the Koran, and few prescribed conditions of behavior or conduct. Man was guided essentially by human wisdom and trusted in his belief in the goodness of the gods and of their divine son, the king. An important concept in Egyptian life was the idea of *maat* [justice]. Although the Egyptian was entirely subservient to the state, the king had the duty of translating the will of the gods. The universe had been created by bringing order and justice to replace primeval chaos, and only through the continuance of order and justice could the universe survive. The law of nature, of society, and of the gods was an organic whole, and it was the duty of the king to administer that law, which was guided by the concept of *maat*. As Egypt flourished, so did the state cult. As the pharaohs grew more powerful, they poured riches into the state cult and built huge and splendid temples to their gods. The priesthoods thus grew very powerful. The populace found its expression of religious feeling in the funerary cults. The great body of mortuary texts has, in fact, provided us with much that we know of ancient Egypt, particularly of belief in the afterlife (see BOOK OF THE DEAD). The dead were provided with food and drink, weapons, and articles of toilet. Tombs were often visited by the family, who brought new offerings. Although the ancient Egyptian strongly believed in life after death, his idea of passing from his life on earth to life in the hereafter is somewhat obscure, and the concepts concerning the afterlife were complex. Proper precautions and care for the dead were mandatory to insure immortality (see MUMMY). The ancient Egyptian, however, hoped not only to extend his life beyond the grave, but to become part of the perennial life of nature. The two most important concepts concerning the afterlife were the *ka* and the *ba*. The *ka* was a kind of double or other self, not an element of the personality, but a detached part of the self which was sometimes said to guide the fortunes of the individual in life, like the Roman genius, but was clearly most associated with his fortunes in the hereafter. When a man died he was said to join with his *ka*. More important perhaps than the *ka* was the concept of the *ba*. The *ba* is perhaps loosely identifiable as the soul of a man. More specifically the *ba* was the manifestation of an individual after his death, usually thought to be represented in the form of a bird. The Egyptians also believed in the concept of *akh*, which was the transformation of some of the noble dead into eternal objects. The noblest were often conceived of as being transformed into stars, thus joining in the changeless rhythm of the universe. See J. H. Breasted, *Development of Religion in Ancient Egypt* (1912, repr. 1970); E. A. T. W. Budge, *From Fetish to God in Ancient Egypt* (1934, repr. 1972); Henri Frankfort, *Ancient Egyptian Religion* (1948, repr. 1961); Jaroslav Cerny, *Ancient Egyptian Religion* (1952, repr. 1957); Siegfried Morenz, *Egyptian Religion* (tr. 1973).

Egyptians, Gospel of the: see PSEUDEPIGRAPHA.

Eha Amufu (ähä' ämōō'fōō), city (1963 pop. 29,434), SE Nigeria. It is a farming and market city. Eha Amufu was a minor administrative center under the British, who established a court for black Africans in the city in 1917.

Ehi (ē'hī), the same as AHIRAM.

Ehime (ähē'mä), prefecture (1970 pop. 1,418,074), 2,188 sq mi (5,667 sq km), NE Shikoku, Japan. MATSUYAMA is the capital and chief port. The region is bounded on the N by the Inland Sea and on the W by Hoyo Strait. Mountainous, it rises to 6,497 ft (1,980 m) in Mt. Ishizuchi, the highest point on Shikoku. The region has extensive coniferous forests and orchards; rice and sweet potatoes are grown, and livestock is raised. Copper mining and paper making are important. Imabari, Saijo, Uwajima, and Yawatahama are the major manufacturing centers.

Ehrenbreitstein (ā''rənbrīt'shtīn), fortress at Koblenz, W West Germany, on a cliff (387 ft/118 m high) over the Rhine River. Built c.1000, it was later enlarged and strengthened. The fortress was held by France during the French Revolutionary Wars. In 1937 it was incorporated into Koblenz.

Ehrenburg, Ilya Grigoryevich (ēlyä' grĭgôr'yəvĭch ā'rənbŏŏrk), 1891–1967, Russian journalist and novelist, whose name is also spelled Erenburg. He wandered throughout Western Europe as a youth. He was noted for his articles about the two world wars. Some of these are translated in *The Tempering of Russia* (1944). Because of long residence abroad (1921–40), Ehrenburg was the most cosmopolitan of the Soviet writers. Among his satiric novels are *The Extraordinary Adventures of Julio Jurenito and His Disciples* (1921, tr. 1930) and *The Stormy Life of Lasik Roitschwantz* (1928, tr. 1960). He won Stalin Prizes for *The Fall of Paris* (1941, tr. 1942), a novel dealing with the decay of French society from 1935 to 1940, and *The Storm* (1948, tr. 1949), a panoramic war novel. The title of his postwar novel *The Thaw* (1954, tr. 1955) has been used in Russia to describe the general lessening of tension after Stalin's death. A lesser work, it was important because it dealt for the first time with the repressions under Stalin's rule. Much of his later journalism is severely critical of the United States. See his memoirs (tr., 6 vol., 1962–1967).

Ehrenfest, Paul (poul ā'rənfĕst), 1880–1933, Austrian physicist. In 1904, Ehrenfest received his doctorate in theoretical physics in Vienna and married the Russian mathematician Tatyana Alexeyevna Afanassyewa. Together they wrote what has become a classical exposition of statistical mechanics. He was one of the first to take German physicist Max Planck's quantum theory seriously and to try to define its relation to the older physics. In 1912 he succeeded Dutch physicist H. A. Lorentz in the chair of theoretical physics at the Univ. of Leiden. He proved an energetic, lucid, and inspiring teacher. His acute criticisms and his formulation of the adiabatic principle—which Niels Bohr placed among the foundations of quantum theory—were important contributions to advancing modern physics.

Ehrlich, Paul (poul ār'lĭkh), 1854–1915, German bacteriologist. He directed (1896) an institute for serum research at Steglitz, near Berlin, that was transferred (1899) to Frankfurt-am-Main as the Institute for Experimental Therapy. For his work in immunology he shared with Élie Metchnikoff the 1908 Nobel Prize in Physiology and Medicine. He made valuable contributions also in hematology, in cellular pathology, in the use of dyes in microscopy and in the treatment of disease, in the study of cancer, and in his discovery of salvarsan (or "606," so called from its numerical order in his experimental series) and of neosalvarsan (less toxic than salvarsan) for the treatment of syphilis.

Ehud (ē'həd). **1** Judge of Israel. He delivered Israel from Moab. Judges 3.12–30. **2** Benjamite. 1 Chron. 7.10; 8.6.

Eichendorff, Joseph, Freiherr von (yō'zĕf frī'hĕr fən ī'khəndôrf), 1788–1857, German poet, a leader of the late romantics. He studied law, volunteered in Lützow's corps in the Napoleonic Wars, and, as a civil servant in Berlin, associated with Schlegel, Arnim, Brentano, and other romantic poets. Eichendorff's lyric verse, in folk-song style, is notable for its highly personal expression of love of home and worship of nature. Much of it was set to music by Schumann, Franz, Mendelssohn, Brahms, Wolf, and many others. His prose is lyrical as well; *Aus dem Leben eines Taugenichts* (1826, tr. *Memoirs of a Good-for-Nothing,* 1866) is filled with his romantic yearnings and poetic dreams. There are many translations of his poems, among them *The Happy Wanderer and Other Poems* (1925).

Eichholtz, Jacob (īkh'hôlts), 1776–1842, American portrait painter, b. Lancaster, Pa.; pupil of Gilbert Stuart in Boston but mainly self-taught. He painted portraits of some of the most prominent men of the day, and he also painted family groups. He was especially successful in handling textures. Among his portraits are those of Chief Justices John Marshall (Historical Society of Penn., Philadelphia) and John Bannister Gibson (Philadelphia Law Association); James Buchanan (Smithsonian Institution); Col. James Gibson (capitol, Dover, Del.); and Nicholas Biddle.

Eichler, August Wilhelm (ou'go͝ost vĭl'hĕlm īkh'lər), 1839–87, German botanist. He worked out the symmetry of the parts of a flower and developed a system of plant classification which, after later work on it by Adolf Engler, was widely adopted by European botanists. He wrote a syllabus of pharmaceutical botany.

Eichmann, Adolf (īkh'män), 1906–62, German National Socialist official. A member of the Austrian Nazi party, he headed the Austrian office for Jewish emigration (1938). His zeal in deporting Jews brought him promotion (1939) to chief of the Gestapo's Jewish section. Eichmann promoted the use of gas chambers for the mass extermination of Jews in concentration camps, and he oversaw the maltreatment, deportation, and murder of millions of Jews in World War II. Arrested by the Allies in 1945, he escaped and settled in Argentina. He was located by Israeli agents in 1960 and abducted to Israel, where he was tried and hanged for crimes against the Jewish people and against humanity.

Eider (ī'dər), river, 117 mi (188 km) long, rising S of Kiel, N West Germany, and flowing N to the Kiel Canal before turning west and meandering to the North Sea at Tönning. It is navigable for most of its length. The Eider's lower course is regulated by locks; part of its upper course is followed by the Kiel Canal. The river separates Schleswig from Holstein.

eider: see DUCK.

Eidsvoll or **Eidsvold** (both: āts'vôl), town (1970 pop. 13,883), Akershus co., SE Norway, near Lake Mjøsa. Forest products are manufactured there. One of Norway's oldest confederacies, the *Eidsivalag,* held its assemblies there from the 1st cent. The present constitution of Norway was proclaimed (1814) at Eidsvoll manor by an assembly of Norwegian patriots.

Eielsen, Elling (āĕl'sən), 1804–83, Norwegian-American preacher. After itinerant missionary work in Scandinavia he came to the United States in 1839, preached in Chicago the first Norwegian sermon heard in America, and for many years exercised strong religious influence among Norwegian pioneers in the Middle West. In 1846 he organized the Norwegian Evangelical Lutheran Church. See J. M. Rohne, *Norwegian American Lutheranism* (1926).

Eifel (ī'fəl), undulating plateau, W West Germany, N of the Moselle River and E of the Ardennes. The Eifel forms the northwestern part of the Rhenish Slate Mts. and is a barren area characterized by deep valleys, extinct volcanoes, and crater lakes; it is a tourist attraction. The highest point (2,447 ft/746 m) is the Hohe Acht. Iron and lead deposits, now exhausted, were mined there in the 19th cent.

Eiffel, Alexandre Gustave (ī'fəl, Fr. äläksäN'drə güstäv' āfĕl'), 1832–1923, French engineer. A noted constructor of bridges and viaducts, he also contributed to the science of aerodynamics and wrote *The Resistance of the Air* (1913, tr. 1913). He designed the EIFFEL TOWER.

Eiffel Tower, structure designed by A. G. Eiffel and erected in the Champ-de-Mars for the Paris exposition of 1889. The tower is 984 ft (400 m) high and consists of an iron framework supported on four masonry piers, from which rise four columns uniting to form one shaft. Three platforms at different heights (the intermediate platform just above the junction of the columns is 644 ft/196 m high) are reached by stairs and elevators. On the top of the tower are a meteorological station, a wireless station, and a television transmission antenna.

Eigenmann, Carl H. (ī'gənmən), 1863–1927, American ichthyologist, b. Germany, grad. Indiana Univ., 1886. From 1891 he taught at Indiana Univ., founding and directing the biological station at Winona Lake. With his wife, Rosa Smith Eigenmann (1859–1947), he studied and published much on the fishes of South America. His greatest work was "The American Characinidae" (1917–29 in five parts in the *Memoirs of the Museum of Comparative Zoology*). He also studied degenerate evolution (in which characteristics that seem to be biologically regressive are inherited when they better enable the organism to survive its environment) in cave-dwelling vertebrates and wrote *Cave Vertebrates of North America* (1909).

Eight, the, group of American artists in New York City, formed in 1908 to exhibit paintings. They were men of widely different tendencies, held together mainly by their common opposition to academism. They were stigmatized as the "ashcan" school because they abandoned decorous subject matter and portrayed the more common aspects of American life. The group comprised Arthur B. Davies, a romanticist; Maurice Prendergast, Ernest Lawson, and William Glackens, impressionists; Everett Shinn, an illustrator; Robert Henri, a singularly honest virtuoso; and John Sloan and George Luks, at that time followers of Henri. These men, and above all Davies, were responsible for the Armory Show of 1913, which introduced modern European art to a shocked, recalcitrant, but curious America. In 1917, together with George Bellows and other adherents, they organized the Society of Independent Artists. Modern American painting owes much to their efforts and their example.

eight-hour day: see LABOR, HOURS OF.

Eijkman, Christian (krĭs'tyän īk'män), 1858–1930, Dutch physician. He was head of the Pathological Institute of Batavia and later (1898–1928) professor of hygiene at the Univ. of Utrecht. His work at Batavia on the cause of BERIBERI led to the isolation of the antineuritic vitamins. For this he shared with F. G. Hopkins the 1929 Nobel Prize in Physiology and Medicine.

Eikon Basilike (ī'kŏn bəsĭl'ĭkē) [Gr.,=royal image], subtitled "the Portraiture of His Sacred Majesty in His Solitudes and Sufferings," a work published soon after the execution of Charles I of England in 1649. It purports to be the king's spiritual autobiography. Written in simple, direct, and moving language, it ran into many editions and was translated into several languages. After the Restoration, John Gauden claimed authorship of the book, and this claim is still a subject of scholarly controversy. Because of the favorable image it created of the king, John Milton was assigned by the regicides to reply to it, which he did in his *Eikonoklastes* (1649). The name is also spelled *Icon Basilike* and *Ikon Basilike.* See edition by P. A. Knachel (1966); bibliography by F. F. Madan (1950).

Eilat: see ELAT, Israel.

Eilshemius, Louis Michel (īlshē'mēəs), 1864–1941, American painter, b. near Newark, N.J. The son of a wealthy Dutch importer, he spent much of his youth abroad. After two years at Cornell Univ. he studied art at the Art Students League and the National Academy of Design in New York City and at Julian's in Paris, where he worked under Bouguereau. He returned to New York c.1887, when two of his works were shown at the National Academy. Aside from this early notice he received no real recognition for more than 30 years. Although he continued to paint, he also tried his hand at inventing, composing, and writing witty letters to the editor of the New York *Sun.* His imaginative, atmospheric landscapes of the American scene are housed in many leading galleries. *Approaching Storm* (Phillips Memorial Gall., Washington, D.C.) is an excellent example of his work.

Einaudi, Luigi (lwē'jē änou'dē), 1874–1961, president of Italy (1948–55). A noted economist, a senator for life from 1919, and an opponent of Fascism after 1924, Einaudi taught at the Univ. of Turin until 1943, when he fled to Switzerland. After his return he was governor of the Bank of Italy (1945–48) and vice premier and minister of the budget under Alcide De Gasperi (1947). His drastic measures helped to curb inflation. In 1948 he was elected president under the new constitution. He was succeeded (1955) by Giovanni Gronchi.

Eindhoven (īnt'hō''fən), city (1971 pop. 189,613), North Brabant prov., S Netherlands, on the Dommel River. It is an industrial center and rail junction. Chartered in 1232, Eindhoven was for centuries a small town. However, after the founding (1891) of the Philips electrical works there, the city rapidly expanded. In World War II, Eindhoven was taken (Sept., 1944) by Allied troops in a major airborne operation; a simultaneous landing at Arnhem failed. Eindhoven has a technical university.

Einhard (īn'härt) or **Eginhard** (ā'gĭnhärt), c.770–840, Frankish historian. Educated in the monastery of Fulda, he continued his studies at Charlemagne's palace school in Aachen and rose to high favor with the emperor. Emperor Louis I made Einhard tutor or adviser to his son Lothair. In 830 he sought to reconcile Louis and the rebellious Lothair. Einhard's *Life of Charlemagne* (many translations) is an eminently readable book. Other writings include a history of the transferral from Rome to Germany of the relics of SS. Marcellinus and Peter (4th-century martyrs). His works and correspondence are prime sources on contemporary society. However, the annals that bear his name were almost certainly not written by him.

Einhorn, David (īn'hôrn), 1809–79, Jewish theological writer and leader of the Reform movement in Judaism in the United States. Born in Bavaria, he studied philosophy at Munich and was influenced by the ideas of Friedrich Schelling. After a stormy career as rabbi of several Reform congregations in central Europe, he accepted (1855) a position as rabbi in Baltimore. He was forced to flee (1861) when his vigorous antislavery campaign aroused the anger of Southern sympathizers. He then accepted positions in Philadelphia and in New York City (1866). Einhorn was a staunch supporter of Abraham Geiger's liberal views on the practice of Judaism. Some of his ideas found expression in the Pittsburgh Platform (adopted by a rabbinical conference in Pittsburgh, 1855), which remained the basis of American Reform Judaism for a generation, and in the original *Union Prayer Book,* which was modeled in part after his own prayer book, *Olat Tamid* (1856).

Einsiedeln (īn'zē''dəln), town (1970 pop. 10,020), Schwyz canton, E central Switzerland. Einsiedeln is the most famous pilgrimage center in Switzerland and one of the most noted in Europe. Its important Benedictine abbey, founded in the 10th cent., was built on the supposed site of the cell of St. Meinrad, a 9th-century martyr. The monastery (rebuilt in the early 18th cent.) is one of the largest and finest examples of Swiss baroque architecture. Its church contains the sacred image of the "Black Virgin." The townspeople annually perform *The Great World Theater,* a religious play by Calderón. Paracelsus is said to have been born in the town; Zwingli was (1516–18) a priest there.

Einstein, Albert (īn'stīn), 1879–1955, American theoretical physicist, known for the formulation of the relativity theory, b. Ulm, Germany, of Jewish parents. He is recognized as one of the greatest physicists of all time. He lived as a boy in Munich and Milan, continued his studies at the cantonal school at Aarau, Switzerland, and was graduated (1900) from the Federal Institute of Technology, Zürich. Later he became a Swiss citizen. He was examiner (1902–9) at the patent office, Bern. During this period he obtained his doctorate (1905) at the Univ. of Zürich, evolved the special theory of RELATIVITY, explained the PHOTOELECTRIC EFFECT, and studied the motion of atoms, on which he based his explanation of BROWNIAN MOVEMENT. In 1909 his work had already attracted attention among scientists, and he was offered an adjunct professorship at the Univ. of Zürich. He resigned that position in 1910 to become full professor at the German Univ., Prague, and in 1912 he accepted the chair of theoretical physics at the Federal Institute of Technology, Zürich. By 1913 Einstein had won international fame and was invited by the Prussian Academy of Sciences to come to Berlin as titular professor of physics and as director of theoretical physics at the Kaiser Wilhelm Institute. He assumed these posts in 1914 and subsequently resumed his German citizenship. For his work in theoretical physics, notably on the photoelectric effect, he received the 1921 Nobel Prize in Physics. His property was confiscated (1934) by the Nazi government, and he was deprived of his German citizenship. He had previously accepted (1933) a post at the Institute for Advanced Study, Princeton, which he held until 1945. In 1940 he became an American citizen. In 1939 at the request of a group of scientists, including Niels Bohr, he wrote to President Franklin Delano Roosevelt to stress the urgency of investigating the possible use of atomic energy in bombs. An ardent pacifist, however, Einstein was active in the cause of world peace. Einstein's early work on the theory of relativity (1905) dealt only with systems or observers in uniform (unaccelerated) motion with respect to one another and is referred to as the special theory of relativity; among other results, it demonstrated that two observers moving at great speed with respect to each other will disagree about measurements of length and time intervals made in each other's systems, that the speed of light is the limiting speed of all bodies having mass, and that mass and energy are equivalent. In 1911 he asserted the equivalence of GRAVITATION and INERTIA, and c.1916 he completed his mathematical formulation of a general theory of relativity that included gravitation as a determiner of the curvature of a space-time continuum. He then began work on his unified field theory, which attempts to explain gravitation, electromagnetism, and subatomic phenomena in one set of laws. He announced in 1929 that he had found a key to the formulation of this theory; its mathematical expression appeared in 1950 as an appendix (which he revised in 1953 and 1954) to *The Meaning of Relativity* (1921; tr., 5th ed. 1955). Einstein is known also for his contributions to the development of the QUANTUM THEORY; he postulated (1905) light quanta (photons) and on them based his explanation of the photoelectric effect, and he developed the quantum theory of specific heat. Although he was one of the leading figures in the development of quantum theory, Einstein regarded it as only a temporarily useful structure. He reserved his main efforts for his unified field theory, feeling that when it was completed the quantization of energy and charge would be found to be a consequence of it. Einstein wished his theories to have that simplicity and beauty which he thought fitting for an interpretation of the universe and which he did not find in quantum theory. His writings include *Relativity: The Special and the General Theory* (1918; tr., 1920, reissued 1947) and excerpts (most of them translated) from letters, articles, and addresses collected in *About Zionism* (1930), *The World as I See It* (1934), *Out of My Later Years* (1950), *Ideas and Opinions* (1954), and *Einstein on Peace* (ed. by Otto Nathan and Heinz Norden, 1960). Einstein's manuscripts and correspondence are presently at the Institute for Advanced Study, Princeton. See the Born-Einstein letters, ed. by Max Born (tr. 1971); biographies by Philipp Frank (rev. ed. 1957), R. W. Clark (1971), Banesh Hoffmann (with Helen Dukas, 1972), and Jeremy Bernstein (1973); studies by Max Born (rev. ed. 1962), Cornelius Lanczos (1965), and P. A. Schilpp, ed. (1949, repr. 1973).

einsteinium [for Albert Einstein], a radioactive chemical element; symbol Es; at. no. 99; mass no. of most stable isotope 254; m.p., b.p., and sp. gr. unknown; valence +3. Einsteinium is a member of group IIIb of the PERIODIC TABLE; its chemical properties are believed to be similar to those of the other members of the ACTINIDE SERIES. It was discovered in Dec., 1952, by Albert Ghiorso and his co-workers at the Univ. of California at Berkeley in residue from a thermonuclear explosion. They identified einsteinium-253, which has a half-life of 20 days. It was not until 1961 that a weighable quantity (about 0.01 microgram) of the element was separated; it was used to prepare the element MENDELEVIUM. Weighable quantities of einsteinium have since been prepared by neutron bombardment of plutonium. Twelve isotopes are known. Einsteinium-254, the most stable isotope, has a half-life of 276 days.

Einthoven, Willem (vĭl'əm īnt'hōvən), 1860-1927, Dutch physiologist, b. Java, M.D. Univ. of Utrecht, 1885. He was professor at the Univ. of Leiden from 1886. To measure the electric currents developed by the heart, he invented a string galvanometer and with its aid produced the electrocardiogram (EKG), a graphic record of the action of the heart. For this he received the 1924 Nobel Prize in Physiology and Medicine.

Eire: see IRELAND; IRELAND, REPUBLIC OF.

Eirene: see HORAE.

Eisenach (ī'zənäkh), city (1970 pop. 50,906), Erfurt district, SW East Germany. It is an industrial center and rail junction. Manufactures include machine tools, processed food, textiles, electrical supplies, agricultural machinery, and motor vehicles. There are salt mines and saline springs in the region. Eisenach was founded c.1150 and was chartered in 1283. The city passed to the house of Wettin in 1440, to Saxony in 1485, and to SAXE-WEIMAR (later Saxe-Weimar-Eisenach) in 1741. It often served as a residence of the electors of Saxony and the dukes of Saxe-Weimar. The German Social Democratic party was founded there (1869) at the Congress of Eisenach. The city's noteworthy buildings include the Church of St. Nicholas (12th cent.) and an 18th-century castle. Nearby is the famous Wartburg castle. Johann Sebastian Bach was born (1685) in Eisenach and Martin Luther studied there (1498-1501).

Eisenerz (ī'zənĕrts), town (1971 pop. 11,600), in Styria prov., central Austria, at the northern foot of the ERZBERG. There are large ironworks based on iron ore deposits that have been mined there for more than 1,000 years.

Eisenhower, Dwight David (ī'zənhou"ər), 1890-1969, American general and 34th President of the United States, b. Denison, Texas; his nickname was "Ike." When he was two years old, his family moved to Abilene, Kansas, where he was reared. He entered (1911) West Point and graduated in 1915. In 1916 he married Mamie Geneva Doud. In World War I, Eisenhower was commanding officer at Camp Colt, Gettysburg, Pa., a training camp for the new U.S. army tank corps. After the war he was stationed (1922-24) in the Panama Canal Zone, was a member of the American Battle Monuments Commission, and was assistant executive (1929-33) in the office of the Assistant Secretary of War. From 1935 to 1940 he was in the Philippines. His impressive performance in the 1941 army maneuvers led to his assignment in Washington, D.C., as chief of operations (1942) and preceded his meteoric rise as military commander in World War II. In June, 1942, General Eisenhower was named U.S. commander of the European theater of operations. He commanded U.S. forces in the North African landings (Nov., 1942) and in Feb., 1943, became chief of all Allied forces in North Africa. After successfully directing the invasions of Sicily (July, 1943) and Italy (September), he was called (December) to England to be supreme commander of the Allied Expeditionary Force. He was largely responsible for the cooperation between the British, American, and other forces and for the integration of land, sea, and air forces in the great battle for the European continent. His own account of the Allied defeat of Germany was published in book form as *Crusade in Europe* (1948). In Dec., 1944, he was made general of the army (five-star general), and in 1945 he commanded the U.S. occupation forces in Germany. In Nov., 1945, he became chief of staff of the U.S. army and advocated the unification of the U.S. armed forces and universal military training. He resigned (Feb., 1948) as chief of staff to become (June) president of Columbia. He was sought for the U.S. presidential candidacy in 1948 but rejected the offers made him. In Dec., 1950, he obtained a leave of absence as president of Columbia to become the supreme commander of the Allied Powers in Europe. After completing organization of the defense forces in the NORTH ATLANTIC TREATY ORGANIZATION, he resigned (1952) from the army to campaign for the Republican presidential nomination. With the support of Republican liberals and internationalists, he defeated his chief rival, Senator Robert A. Taft, for the nomination. His popularity as a World War II hero and his promise to end the Korean War brought Eisenhower an easy victory over his Democratic opponent, Adlai E. Stevenson, and he took office on Jan. 20, 1953. He soon fulfilled his campaign pledge when an armistice was signed (July, 1953) in Korea. Eisenhower and his secretary of state John Foster Dulles, continued the Truman administration policy of containing Communism. Defense treaties were signed with South Korea (1953) and Formosa (1954), the Southeast Asia Treaty Organization was formed in 1954 to halt Communist expansion in Asia, and military aid was sent to South Vietnam. Eisenhower also tried, however, to ease cold war tensions. His "atoms for peace" plan and his statements at the summit conference (see GENEVA CONFERENCE 2) in July, 1955, were widely heralded. At home, Eisenhower's record was less distinguished; in general, he remained aloof from the legislative process. The predominance of businessmen in his cabinet lent a conservative tone to his administration, while his concern for a balanced budget at a time when defense expenditures were rising rapidly, as well as his commitment to limiting the role of the government in the economy, kept Eisenhower from expanding the social welfare programs begun by his Democratic predecessors. Despite an attack of coronary thrombosis in Sept., 1955, he was reelected over Adlai Stevenson by an even wider margin than in 1952. During his second term Eisenhower took the initiative in the growing civil rights movement. In Sept., 1957, he sent Federal troops to Little Rock, Ark., to enforce a court-ordered school desegregation decision; he successfully pressed Congress to enact (1957, 1960) civil rights legislation; and he prohibited discriminatory practices in the District of Columbia and in Federal facilities such as navy yards and hospitals. International tensions increased, however, during his second term. In 1957 he promulgated the so-called Eisenhower Doctrine, in which he proposed to send military and economic aid to any Middle Eastern nation requesting it in order to bolster that region against Communist aggression. Under the doctrine, U.S. marines were sent to Lebanon in July, 1958. Although Eisenhower was host to Nikita Khrushchev during the latter's visit to the United States in 1959, at the Paris summit conference in the following year Khrushchev denounced Eisenhower for permitting espionage flights over the Soviet Union. Fidel Castro's Communist regime in Cuba brought further worries, and in Jan., 1961, Eisenhower broke diplomatic relations with Cuba. Eisenhower campaigned for the Republican candidate, Richard M. Nixon (his Vice President for both terms), in 1960. After leaving the White House, he remained generally aloof from politics, although he did occasionally comment on national issues and campaign for Republican candidates. In 1962 the Eisenhower presidential library was dedicated at Abilene, Kansas. See Eisenhower's memoirs of his years in the White House, *Mandate for Change* (1963) and *Waging Peace* (1965); his papers, ed. by A. D. Chandler, Jr., and S. E. Ambrose (5 vol., 1970); biographies by Arthur Larson (1968), H. S. Parmet (1972), and Peter Lyon (1974); Sherman Adams, *Firsthand Report: The Story of the Eisenhower Administration* (1961); S. E. Ambrose, *The Supreme Commander* (1970) and *Ike: Abilene to Berlin* (1973); E. K. G. Sixsmith, *Eisenhower as Military Commander* (1973).

Eisenhower, Milton Stover, 1899-, American educator and public official, b. Abilene, Kansas, grad. Kansas State College of Agriculture and Applied Science, 1924; brother of Dwight David Eisenhower. After a brief teaching career, he served in various government posts. In 1943 he became president of his alma mater. He was later president of Pennsylvania State Univ. (1950-56) and of Johns Hopkins Univ. (1956-67). During the administrations of Harry S. Truman and of Dwight Eisenhower, Milton Eisenhower frequently served the government in diplomatic positions, most notably as special ambassador for Latin American affairs (1957-60). In 1968-69 he was chairman of the National Commission on the Causes and Prevention of Violence. His book *The Wine Is Bitter* (1963) describes his experiences in Latin America.

Eisenhower National Historic Site: see NATIONAL PARKS AND MONUMENTS (table).

Eisenhüttenstadt (ī"zənhüt'ənshtät), city (1970 pop. 45,194), Frankfurt dist., E East Germany. Manufactures include iron and steel. It was founded by the state in 1951 as a residential town and until 1961 was known as Stalinstadt.

Eisenstadt (ī'zənshtät), town (1971 pop. 10,100), capital of Burgenland, E Austria, at the foot of the Leitha mts. The composer Joseph Haydn (1732-1809), who lived in Eisenstadt for many years under the patronage of the Esterházy family, is buried in the noted Bergkirche, an 18th-century church. The fine Esterházy palace (14th cent.; redone 17th cent. in baroque style) still stands.

Eisenstein, Sergei Mikhailovich (syĭrgā' mēkhī'ləvĭch ī'zənshtīn), 1898-1948, Russian film director. An architect and engineer, he became interested in a theatrical career and worked as a scene designer and stage director (1920). He began his film career in 1924 with *Strike,* followed by his silent film classic *Potemkin* (1925), which brought him world fame. His stature increased with such films as *October* ("Ten Days That Shook the World"; 1927) and *The Old and the New.* Footage that he shot in Mexico for his film *Que Viva Mexico!* was later edited and released by others. *Alexander Nevsky* (1938), his first sound film, was an international success. *Ivan the Terrible* (1942-46), his last film, was planned as a trilogy. Part II, arousing government disfavor, was withheld by the Soviet Film Trust, and released later. Part III was never completed. Eisenstein pioneered the development of film aesthetics and techniques. He wrote *The Film Sense* (tr. 1942, rev. ed. 1947), *The Film Form* (tr. 1949), and *Notes of a Film Director* (tr. 1959). See biography by Yon Barna (1974).

Eisleben (īs'lābən), city (1970 pop. 30,386), Halle district, central East Germany, at the foot of the Harz mts. It is an industrial city and has been a copper-mining center since the 14th cent. Manufactures include processed food, clothing, and wood products. Eisleben was first mentioned c.1000 as a market settlement. It passed to Prussia in 1815. In Eisleben are the house in which Luther was born (1483), the church where he was baptized, and the house in which he died (1546).

Eisler, Hanns (häns īs'lər), 1898–1962, German composer. Eisler was a pupil of Arnold Schoenberg. He went to the United States in 1933 and was musical assistant to Charlie Chaplin (1942–47) in Hollywood. Castigated as a Communist in 1947, he left the United States in 1948 to live in Vienna. Eisler believed music should serve the political needs of the masses. His didactic choral works are popular in Communist Europe. His opera *Johannes Faust* (1953) was less successful. Eisler wrote *Composing for the Films* (1947).

Eisner, Kurt (ko͝ort' īs'nər), 1867–1919, German socialist. He studied at the Friedrich Wilhelm Univ. in Berlin and edited several leading socialist newspapers. In 1917 he joined the newly formed Independent Social Democratic party. Eisner was convicted (1918) of treason for inciting a strike among munitions workers. Released, he organized the revolution that overthrew the Bavarian monarchy (Nov. 7, 1918), and he became the first republican premier of Bavaria. He opposed Prussian domination in German affairs and advocated a more genuinely federal German state to give Bavaria a leading role. Seeking to pacify the Allied powers, Eisner published documents from the Bavarian archives reputing to prove German responsibility for World War I. An idealist with little political ability, he rapidly lost support and was assassinated (Feb. 21, 1919) on his way to present his resignation to the Bavarian parliament. Eisner's collected writings were published in 1919. See study by Allan Mitchell (1965).

eisteddfod (āstĕth'vōd) [Welsh, =session], Welsh competitive festival. Contests are held in all the arts and crafts, with special emphasis on music and poetry. The National Eisteddfod is held annually for one week in August, alternately in the north and the south, but local eisteddfods are held throughout Wales during the year. An historical institution (12th cent.), it is important in maintaining national feeling and preserving the Welsh language and culture and is enthusiastically supported by all the Welsh. Its outstanding ceremony is the "chairing" of the winning bard. The bardic assembly (gorsedd) has been a part of the National Eisteddfod since 1819.

ejido (āhē'thō) [Span.,=common land], in Mexico, agricultural land expropriated from large private holdings and redistributed to communal farms. Communal ownership of land had been widely practiced by the Aztecs, but the institution was in decline before the Spanish arrived. The conquistadors instituted the ENCOMIENDA, which was superseded by the REPARTIMIENTO and finally, after independence (1821), by debt peonage. Although legally abolished by the constitution of 1917, which provided for the restoration of the ejido, peonage remained a general practice until the presidency of Lázaro CÁRDENAS. In the LAGUNA DISTRICT in 1936, the ejido became fact on a large scale. The intent of the ejido system is to remedy the social injustice of the past and to increase production of subsistence foods. The land is owned by the government, and the ejido is financed by a special national bank which supplies the necessary capital for reclamation, improvement, initial seeding, and so forth. In effect, the bank has replaced the colonial encomendero, with this difference—the laborer is paid on the basis of unit work accomplished. See David Ronfeldt, *Atencingo; The Politics of Agrarian Struggle in a Mexican Ejido* (1973).

ekaaluminum (ĕk'ə-əlo͞om'ĭnəm): see GALLIUM.

ekaboron (ĕk"əbôr'ŏn): see SCANDIUM.

ekasilicon (ĕk"əsĭl'ĭkŏn): see GERMANIUM.

Ekaterinburg: see SVERDLOVSK, USSR.

Ekaterinodar: see KRASNODAR, USSR.

Ekelund, Vilhelm (vĭl'əlm ā'kəlŭnd"), 1880–1949, Swedish essayist and poet. Ekelund's writings were influenced by the works of Nietzsche, Hölderlin, and Swedenborg. After publication of his poetic work *Havets stjärna* [the star of the sea] (1906), aphoristic prose writing became his primary concern. *Antikt ideal* [the antique ideal] (1909) was the first of his long series of essays. Ekelund's works were not widely read generally, but influenced other Scandinavian writers.

Eker (ē'kər), descendant of Judah through the family of Hezron. 1 Chron. 2.27.

EKG: see ELECTROCARDIOGRAPHY.

Ekholm, Gordon Frederick, 1909-, American archaeologist, b. St. Paul, Minn., grad. Univ. of Minnesota, 1933, Ph.D. Harvard, 1941. With the American Museum of Natural History in New York City after 1937, he gained a reputation by studies of the archaeological and ethnographic relations between the early civilizations of Asia and those of the New World, with focus on Mexico and Central America.

Ekibastuz (ĕkēbästo͞os'), city (1970 pop. 44,000), Central Asian USSR, in Kazakhstan. It is the industrial center of a bituminous coal-mining basin, which has coal reserves estimated at 8 billion tons. Although coal mining began in the late 19th cent., the city became industrialized only in the 1950s, when the railroad reached it.

Ekkehard (ĕk'əhärt), name of several medieval German authors, monks of the monastery of St. Gall, which is in present-day Switzerland. **Ekkehard I** wrote the famous Latin epic *Waltharius* (c.930), celebrating the deeds of the Alemannic prince Walter. **Ekkehard II,** fl. 10th cent., was the tutor of Hedwig of Swabia. He is the hero of Scheffel's novel *Ekkehard* (1856). Best known is **Ekkehard IV,** whose chronicle (c.1100) of St. Gall is an important, if historically inaccurate, account of medieval life. Another Ekkehard (fl. 1100) was an abbot of Aura who also wrote historical works.

Ekron (ĕk'rŏn), important Philistine city, SE of Jaffa, not far from the sea. It was on the border of Judah and was the last resting place of the Ark before its restoration to the Jews. Judges 1.18; Joshua 13.3; 15.45,46; 19.43; 1 Sam. 5.10; 6.16,17; 7.14; 17.52; Jer. 25.20; Amos 1.8; Zeph. 2.4; Zech. 9.5,7. Accaron: 1 Mac. 10.89.

Eladah (ĕl'ədə, ĕlā'də), Ephraimite. 1 Chron. 7.20.

Elagabalus: see HELIOGABALUS.

Elah (ē'lə). **1** King of Israel, son and successor of Baasha. He was murdered, and succeeded, by Zimri. 1 Kings 16.8–14. **2** Father of Hoshea, last king of Israel. 2 Kings 15.30; 17.1. **3** Duke of Edom. Gen. 36.41; 1 Chron. 1.52. **4** Father of one of Solomon's stewards. 1 Kings 4.18. **5** Son of Caleb the spy. 1 Chron. 4.15. **6** Benjamite. 1 Chron. 9.8. **7** Valley in which David slew Goliath. 1 Sam. 17.2, 19; 21.9.

Elaine, in Arthurian legend: see LAUNCELOT, SIR.

El Alamein: see ALAMEIN, EL, Egypt.

Elam (ē'ləm), ancient country of Asia, N of the Persian Gulf and E of the Tigris, now in W Iran. A civilization seems to have been established there very early, probably in the late 4th millennium B.C. The capital was SUSA, and the country is sometimes called Susiana. The land included a hot, rich plain and hill country to the east. In historical times the Elamites were known as a warlike people who rivaled and threatened Babylonia. The population was neither Sumerian nor Semitic. Their language survives in a copious cuneiform literature. The Elamites seem to have maintained their independence steadily, despite invasions and counterinvasions. At the beginning of the 2d millennium the Elamites invaded Babylonia and founded a dynasty at Larsa. Shortly thereafter they became masters of Erech, Babylon, and Isin. In the 18th cent. B.C., Hammurabi was able to keep the Elamites from expanding. A century later an Elamite king, Kutir-Nahunte, revived a kingdom that flourished. However, the golden age of Elam came in the 13th and 12th cent. B.C. The Elamite civilization grew strong; there was a literary renaissance and great development of architecture and sculpture. Elam drew much of its artistic inspiration from Mesopotamia and carried back to Susa such important monuments as the stele of Naram-Sin and the code of Hammurabi. Tchoga-Zanbil, excavated in 1952, was the Elamite religious center with its great ziggurat. By the 7th cent. B.C., however, the rising power of Assyria threatened Elam. SARGON of Assyria, SENNACHERIB, and ESAR-HADDON all attacked the Elamites, but Susa fell only to ASSURBANIPAL, who sacked the city. Possibly the house that in the person of Cyrus the Great took over the rule from the Medes and created the Achaemenid empire was originally Elamite. At any rate Susa became a favored provincial capital of Persia as is revealed by its great palace of the Achaemenid kings. Mention is made of Elam in Isa. 22.6; Jer. 49.34–39. See Walther Hinz, *The Lost World of Elam* (1964, tr. 1973).

Elamite (ē'ləmīt"), extinct language of uncertain relationship that was once spoken in the ancient kingdom of ELAM, located in SW Asia. It appears to be unrelated to any other languages, although some scholars see a kinship between Elamite and Brahui, one of the modern DRAVIDIAN LANGUAGES. Elamite is an agglutinative language in that different linguistic elements, each of which exists separately and has a fixed meaning, are often joined to form one word. A number of stone inscriptions and clay tablets that have Elamite texts written in CUNEIFORM survive. These texts cover a period of about 2,000 years that began at the end of the third millennium B.C.

eland (ē'lənd), large, spiral-horned African ANTELOPE, genus *Taurotragus,* found in brush country or open forest at the edge of grasslands. Elands live in small herds and are primarily browsers rather than grazers. The two species of eland are the largest of all living antelopes. The common eland, *Taurotragus oryx,* of S and E Africa, stands almost 6 ft (1.8 m) high at the shoulder and may weight up to 2,000 lb (910 kg). Its oxlike body is light brown, with a few narrow white stripes running across the back and down the sides. It has a hump between the shoulders, a short, erect, black mane, and a long tail with a short, black tuft. Both sexes have spiral horns about 2 ft (60 cm) long, stretching straight back from the head. The common eland is easily tamed, and some attempts have been made at domestication. The giant eland, *T. derbianus,* of W and central Africa, is slightly larger than the common eland and has horns up to 4 ft (1.2 m) long. Its numbers have been greatly reduced by hunting for meat and hides and by recurrent epidemics of rinderpest, a bovine disease to which elands are particularly susceptible. By 1968 the giant eland was nearly extinct in W Africa. A third species of *Taurotragus* is known as the BONGO. Elands are classified in the phylum CHORDATA, subphylum Vertebrata, class Mammalia, order Artiodactyla, family Bovidae.

Elasah (ĕl'əsə, ĕlā'sə). **1** One of Zedekiah's messengers to Babylon. Jer. 29.3–4. **2** Priest who married a foreign wife. Ezra 10.22.

elasmobranch (ĭlăs'məbrăngk), cartilaginous fish, member of the subclass Elasmobranchii of the vertebrate class Chondrichthyes (see CHORDATA). This group includes the SHARK and the RAY.

El Asnam (ĕl äsnäm'), formerly **Orléansville** (ôrlāävēl'), city (1966 pop. 49,109), capital of El Asnam dept., N Algeria, on the Chéliff River. It is the center of an important cereal and citrus fruit region. The city was founded in 1843 as a French military camp; it was rebuilt after a severe earthquake in 1954. A large Christian basilica dating from A.D. 324 has been discovered at El Asnam.

elasticity, the ability of a body to resist a distorting influence or stress and to return to its original size and shape when the stress is removed. All solids are elastic for small enough deformations or strains, but if the stress exceeds a certain amount known as the elastic limit, a permanent deformation is produced. Both the resistance to stress and the elastic limit depend on the composition of the solid. Some different kinds of stresses are tension, compression, torsion, and shearing (see STRENGTH OF MATERIALS). For each kind of stress and the corresponding strain there is a modulus, i.e., the ratio of the stress to the strain; the ratio of tensile stress to strain for a given material is called its YOUNG'S MODULUS. **Hooke's law** [for Robert Hooke] states that, within the elastic limit, strain is proportional to stress.

elastomer (ĭlăs'təmər), substance having to some extent the elastic properties of natural RUBBER. The term is sometimes used technically to distinguish synthetic rubbers and rubberlike plastics from natural rubber.

Elat or **Eilat** (both: ā'lät) [Heb.,=trees], city (1972 pop. 12,800), S Israel, a port on the Gulf of Aqaba, an arm of the Red Sea. It is strategically located near the Sinai peninsula, Jordan, and Saudi Arabia and is Israel's gateway to Africa and the Far East. A tourist center with small industries, the city is located near copper mines and is the terminus of an oil pipeline to Haifa. Elat was perhaps identical with, or near, EZION-GEBER, a port in Solomon's time (10th cent. B.C.). It was built up or rebuilt by King Uzziah of Judah and lost to the Syrians (8th cent. B.C.) by King Ahaz. The Roman port succeeding Elat was called Aelana or Elana. Elat was resettled in 1949, and its deepwater harbor was opened in 1965. The name is also spelled Elath.

Elba (ĕl'bä), island, 86 sq mi (223 sq km), Tuscany, central Italy, in the Tyrrhenian Sea, 6 mi (9.7 km) from the Italian mainland, part of the Tuscan Archipelago. Iron ore has been mined there since Etruscan and Roman times, and there are ironworks at PORTOFERRAIO, the island's main town. Wine, olive oil, and fruit are also produced, and there is a large tourist industry. Elba has come under numerous foreign powers, including Syracuse (mid-5th cent. B.C.), Pisa (11th cent. A.D.-A.D. 1399), Spain, and Naples. It was briefly (May, 1814-Feb., 1815) a sovereign principality under the exiled Napoleon I, who improved the island's roads and agriculture. After Napoleon's dramatic escape from Elba and his subsequent exile to Saint Helena Island, Elba passed to Tuscany.

Elbasan (ĕlbäsän') or **Elbasani** (ĕlbäsä'nē), town (1970 pop. 41,700), capital of Elbasan prov., central Albania, on the Shkumbin River. It is located in a fertile agriculture region where tobacco, olives, and fruit are raised. The city is also a commercial center producing foodstuffs, textiles, and tobacco, petroleum, wood, and metal products. Coal, chrome, and iron ore are mined nearby. Elbasan is linked by railroad with the port of Durrës. Known as Scampa in ancient times, it is sometimes identified with Albanopolis, the ancient capital (A.D. c.130) of the Albanians.

El Bayadh (ĕl bäyäd'), formerly **Géryville** (zhārēvēl'), town (1966 pop. 15,592), N Algeria. It is an important market for sheep. The town developed around a French military post established in 1852.

Elbe (ĕl'bə), Czech *Labe*, a major river of central Europe, c.725 mi (1,170 km) long, rising in the Krknoše mts., NW Czechoslovakia, and traversing NW Czechoslovakia in a wide arc. It then cuts through steep sandstone cliffs, enters East Germany, and flows generally NW through central East Germany (past Dresden, Wittenberg, and Magdeburg) and onto the North German plain. The Elbe forms part of the East German-West German border before flowing across N West Germany (past Hamburg) and into the North Sea at Cuxhaven. In Hamburg, the river divides into two arms before forming a 60-milong (97-km) estuary. The chief tributaries of the Elbe are the Vltava, Mulde, Saale, and Havel rivers. One of the chief waterways of Europe, the Elbe is navigable for c.525 mi (845 km); freight-laden barges move on the river. A canal system connects the Elbe with Berlin and the Oder River (to the east); with the Ruhr region and the Weser and Rhine rivers (to the west); and with the Baltic Sea (to the north). There are numerous dams in the Elbe River basin. Known as the Albis to the Romans, the river marked the farthest Roman advance into Germany (9 B.C.) and was later the eastern limit of Charlemagne's conquests. The Treaty of Versailles (1919) internationalized its course from the Vltava River to the sea, but Germany repudiated its internationalization after the Munich Pact (1938). In 1945 the river was made part of the demarcation line between East and West Germany.

Elbert, Mount, peak, 14,433 ft (4,399 m) high, central Colo.; highest point in the state and tallest peak in the U.S. Rocky Mts.

El-beth-el [Heb.,= God of the house of God], name given by Jacob to a place in Canaan where God appeared to him. Gen. 35.7.

Elbeuf (ĕlbŏf'), town (1968 pop. 19,827), Seine-Maritime dept., NW France, in Normandy, on the Seine River. It is the center of an industrial complex and is a river port for the shipping of coal. The town has been famous as a woolen center since the 16th cent. but was heavily industrialized only after World War II. Automobiles and chemicals are among the manufactures. Elbeuf's history dates back to Roman times. The town has numerous churches dating from the 15th to the 17th cent.

Elbing: see ELBLĄG, Poland.

Elbląg (ĕl'blôNk) or **Elbing** (ĕl'bĭng), city (1970 pop. 89,835), N Poland. A seaport near the Vistula Lagoon, it has shipyards, machinery plants, and an important metallurgical industry. In 1237 the Teutonic Knights built a castle, around which developed a settlement. Elbląg joined the Hanseatic League in the late 13th cent. Along with other Prussian towns, it revolted against the Teutonic Knights c.1450 and submitted to the rule of Poland. It gained increasing importance in the 16th and 17th cent. as a commercial port. The city was ceded to Prussia in 1772. It suffered heavy damage in World War II, after which it passed to Poland.

Elbrus, Mount (ĕlbro͝os', älbro͝os'), highest mountain of the Caucasus, SE European USSR, in Georgia, formed by two extinct volcanic cones, respectively 18,481 ft (5,633 m) and 18,356 ft (5,595 m) high. Its glaciers give rise to several rivers, notably the Kuban. The snow line is at c.11,000 ft (3,350 m).

Elburz (ĕlbo͝orz'), mountain range, N Iran, between the Caspian Sea and the central Iranian plateau; rises to 18,934 ft (5,771 m) in Mt. Damavand, the highest peak in Iran. The range consists of steep, narrow, parallel ridges crossed only by the Safid Rud, whose valley forms the main trans-Elburz route. The northern slopes of the Elburz are rainy and forested; the southern slope is semi-arid.

El Cajon (ĕl kähōn'), city (1970 pop. 52,273), San Diego co., S Calif.; inc. 1912. Electronic equipment, missile parts, and metal products are among the manufactures of this rapidly growing city. El Cajon has a junior college.

El Centro (ĕl sĕn'trō), city (1970 pop. 19,272), seat of Imperial co., SE Calif., near the Mexican border; inc. 1908. It is a processing and shipping center for a heavily irrigated agricultural region. A junior college is in the city and a U.S. naval air station is nearby.

El Cerrito (ĕl sərē'tō), residential city (1970 pop. 25,190), Contra Costa co., W Calif., on San Francisco Bay; inc. 1917.

Elche (ĕl'chā), city (1970 pop. 122,663), Alicante prov., SE Spain, in Valencia. It is surrounded by an extensive grove of date palms, the only grove of its kind in Europe. The city's industries produce leather, soap, oil, and palm products. The city preserves a North African atmosphere. Many Iberian, Greek, Roman, and Arabic artifacts have been found in the area; most important is the stone bust of a woman, La Dama de Elche, found in 1897.

El Cordobés (ĕl kōrdōvās'), 1936?-, Spanish bullfighter. His real name is Manuel Benítez Pérez. The highest paid matador in history, he rose to national fame in the early 1960s because of his extraordinary bravery and personal magnetism. An unorthodox and daring bullfighter who worked very close to the bull's horns, he became a great popular hero in Spain. He retired in 1971. See biography by Larry Collins and Dominique Lapierre, *Or I'll Dress you in Mourning* (1968).

Eldaah (ĕl'dāə, ĕldā'ə), son of Midian. Gen. 25.4; 1 Chron. 1.33.

Eldad (ĕl'dăd), one of the elders who with Moses received the gift of prophecy. Num. 11.26.

elder or **elderberry:** see HONEYSUCKLE.

Eldjárn, Kristján (krĭstyoun' ĕldyourn'), 1916-, Icelandic statesman and archaeologist. Educated at the universities of Copenhagen and Iceland, he was an assistant at the National Museum of Iceland (1945-47) and then its curator (1947-68). A prolific scholar, he belonged to numerous archaeological and literary societies. He was elected president of Iceland in 1968 and reelected in 1972.

Eldon, John Scott, 1st **earl of,** 1751-1838, British statesman and jurist. From a successful law practice he entered Parliament (1783) and became solicitor general in 1788 and attorney general in 1793. He prosecuted John Horne TOOKE and other sympathizers with the French Revolution, and he guided William PITT in drawing up the repressive laws of 1793-98 against radical agitation. Made chief justice of common pleas and Baron Eldon in 1799, he advanced in 1801 to the lord chancellorship, remaining in that office almost continuously until 1827. His influence in government during the period was great, and during the weak ministries of the 3d duke of Portland (1807-9) and Spencer PERCEVAL (1809-12), he was virtual prime minister. Eldon was a Tory politician of the most reactionary cast. He was an unrelenting opponent of Catholic Emancipation and liberal reform. Though he had a brilliant and influential legal mind, he was extremely dilatory, and chancery delays became notorious in his time. He was created earl in 1821.

El Dorado (ĕl'dərä'dō, -rā'-) [Span.,= the gilded man], mythical country of the Golden Man sought by adventurers in South America. The legend supposedly originated in a custom of the CHIBCHA Indians of Colombia who each year anointed a chieftain and rolled him in gold, which he then ceremonially washed off in a sacred lake, casting offerings of emeralds and gold into the waters at the same time. This custom had apparently disappeared long before the coming of the conquistadors, but the tales lived on and grew into a legend of a land of gold and plenty. Gonzalo PIZARRO and Francisco de Orellana set out in quest for it, the latter drifting down the length of the Amazon River in the process. From the middle of the 16th cent. a series of adventurers searched for El Dorado and its fabulous variants—Omagua, the Land of Cinnamon, or the golden land of Manoa. El Dorado passed into European literature and found its way to the maps. The conquistadors of Venezuela and New Granada—FEDERMANN, BENALCÁZAR, and JIMÉNEZ DE QUESADA—all searched for El Dorado. Perhaps best known to English-speaking peoples is the expedition of Sir Walter RALEIGH in 1595. The location of the mythical land shifted as new regions were explored, and similar legends appeared in W United States. Cabeza de Vaca told of the Seven Cities of Cibola; interest in these treasure-laden cities reached a peak with the stories of Fray MARCOS DE NIZA and culminated in a tremendous but fruitless expedition under Francisco Vásquez de CORONADO. El Dorado is used figuratively to mean any place of fabulous wealth, a utopian dream, or the land of desire. See A. F. Bandelier, *The Gilded Man* (1893, repr. 1962); Germán Arciniegas, *The Knight of El Dorado* (tr. 1942); Robert Silverberg, *The Golden Dream* (1967); V. S. Naipaul, *The Loss of El Dorado* (1970).

El Dorado (ĕl dərā'də). **1** City (1970 pop. 25,283), seat of Union co., S central Ark.; inc. 1845. The discovery of oil in 1921 made it the oil center of the state. The city has oil refineries, chemical plants, and poultry-packing houses. **2** City (1970 pop. 12,308), seat of Butler co., SE Kansas, on the Walnut River, on the edge of the Flint Hills, in a grain and livestock area; inc. 1871. Since the discovery (1915) of oil in the region, El Dorado has been a refining and shipping point for petroleum. Oil field equipment and aluminum and plastic products are made. A junior college is in the city.

Elead (ē'lēăd, ēlē'-), Ephraimite. 1 Chron. 7.21.

Elealeh (ē''lēā'lē), ancient city of Reuben. Num. 32.3,37; Isa. 15.4; 16.9; Jer. 48.34.

Eleanor Crosses: see ELEANOR OF CASTILE.

Eleanor of Aquitaine (ăkwĭtān', ăk'wĭtān), 1122?-1204, queen consort first of LOUIS VII of France and then of HENRY II of England. Daughter and heiress of William X, duke of Aquitaine, she married Louis in 1137 shortly before his accession to the throne. She accompanied him on the Second Crusade (1147-49). Eleanor bore Louis two daughters, but in 1152 their marriage was annulled. Soon afterward Eleanor married Henry, duke of Normandy and count of Anjou, uniting her vast possessions with those of her husband. Louis VII feared this powerful combination, and when Henry ascended the English throne in 1154, the stage was set for a long struggle between the English and French kings. Eleanor bore Henry three daughters and five sons, and two of the latter, RICHARD I and JOHN, became kings of England. Because of Henry's infidelities, especially his relationship with ROSAMOND, Eleanor's relations with her husband grew strained, and in 1170 she established a court of her own at Poitiers. She supported her sons in their unsuccessful revolt against Henry in 1173 and was held in confinement by Henry until 1185. Her efforts helped Richard secure the throne in 1189. While Richard was on the Third Crusade and later held captive in Europe (1190-94), Eleanor was active in forestalling the plots against him by his brother John and in collecting the ransom for his release. She brought about a reconciliation between the two brothers, and on Richard's death in 1199 she supported John's claims to the throne over those of ARTHUR I of Brittany. Eleanor's court at Poitiers was the scene of much artistic activity and was noted for its cultivation of courtly manners and the concept of courtly love. She was the patroness of such literary figures as Wace, Benoît de Sainte-More, and Chrestien de Troyes. In literature Eleanor has appeared as the jealous murderess of the "fair Rosamond," but she was apparently innocent of this crime. She was an able and strong-minded woman. See biographies by A. R. Kelly (1950, new ed. 1957), and Régine Pernoud (1968).

Eleanor of Castile (kăstēl'), d.1290, queen consort of EDWARD I of England and daughter of Ferdinand III of Castile. At her marriage (1254) she brought to Prince Edward the territories of Ponthieu and Montreuil and claims to Gascony. She went with Edward on the crusade of 1270-72 to the Holy Land where she supposedly saved his life after he had been wounded. On their return they were both crowned (1274), Henry III having died in 1272. After her death Edward had crosses erected to mark the stages of her funeral procession from Nottinghamshire to London. Of the 12 so-called Eleanor Crosses—at Lincoln, Grantham, Stamford, Geddington, Northampton, Stony Stratford, Woburn, Dunstable, St. Albans, Waltham, Westcheap, and Charing—those at Geddington, Northampton, and Waltham are extant, though partially restored.

Eleanor of Provence (prôvăNs'), d. 1291, queen consort of HENRY III of England. The daughter of Raymond Berengar, count of Provence, she was married to Henry in 1236. She was a vigorous and incisive woman and had much influence on her husband, as did her unpopular relatives and other foreign courtiers who followed her to England. During the ascendancy of Simon de MONTFORT in 1264–65, Eleanor raised mercenaries in France for her husband's cause. She retired to a convent in 1286 but was sometimes consulted by her son, Edward I.

Eleasah (ēlē'əsə, -lēā'). **1** Judahite. 1 Chron. 2.39. **2** Benjamite. 1 Chron. 8.37.

Eleatic school (ēlēăt'ĭk), Greek pre-Socratic philosophical school at Elea, a Greek colony in Lucania, Italy. The group was founded in the early 5th cent. B.C. by PARMENIDES, its greatest thinker. He denied the reality of change on the ground that things either exist or do not. Hence, there are no in-between stages, as the concept of change, or "becoming," ordinarily implies. His disciples were ZENO OF ELEA, who used a series of paradoxes to show the indefensibility of common-sense notions of reality, and Melissus of Samos, who systematized Eleatic views. The ultimate reality for the Eleatics was an undifferentiated "being," in contrast to the illusory testimony of the senses. See J. E. Raven, *Pythagoreans and Eleatics* (1966).

Eleazar (ĕlēā'zər). **1** Son of Aaron. Ex. 6.23,25; Num. 3.32; Deut. 10.6; Joshua 24.33. **2** Keeper of the Ark of the Covenant. 1 Sam. 7.1. **3** Mighty man of David. 2 Sam. 23.9; 1 Chron. 11.12. **4** Priest. Ezra 8.33; Neh. 12.42. **5** Jew who had married a foreign wife. Ezra 10.25. **6** Merarite Levite. 1 Chron. 23.21,22; 24.28. **7** Man in the Gospel genealogy. Mat. 1.15. **8** One of the chief martyrs in the Maccabean period. An old man, he refused to eat swine's flesh. 2 Mac. 6.18–31.

elecampane (ĕl"əkămpān'), hardy Old World herb, *Inula helenium*, of the family Compositae (COMPOSITE family), naturalized in America and sometimes cultivated in gardens. It has showy yellow-rayed flowers and a thick root which was formerly regarded as a tonic and remedy for coughs and diseases of the chest. It was used in horse medicine, whence its popular name horse-heal. It was formerly classed in the genus *Helenium* (sneezeweeds), whose name derives from several traditions: one that Helen carried the flower when Paris took her to Troy; another that it sprang from Helen's tears; and a third that it was named for Helenus, a son of Priam. Elecampane is classified in the division MAGNOLIOPHYTA, class Magnoliopsida, order Asterales, family Compositae.

election, choosing a candidate for office in an organization by the vote of those enfranchised or privileged to cast a BALLOT. In ancient Greek democracies (e.g., Athens) public officials were occasionally elected but more often were chosen by lot. In Rome the popular assemblies elected the tribunes and voted on certain laws. The Middle Ages saw the practical abandonment of popular suffrage and of elections, but the concept was kept alive by such processes as the elections to the papacy and, in an even more limited sense, of the Holy Roman emperor by a small and, in part, hereditary body of electors. In the modern period, elections have been an inseparable part of the growth of democratic forms of government. Elections were associated with the parliamentary process in England from the 13th cent. and were gradually regularized by acts prescribing the frequency of elections (the Triennial Act of 1694, and the Septennial Act of 1716), by successive reform bills widening the franchise in the 19th cent., and by the adoption of the secret ballot in 1872. In colonial America the election of church and public officials dates almost from the founding of the Plymouth Colony, and the paper ballot was instituted in elections to the Massachusetts governorship in 1634. Under the U.S. Constitution the right to hold elections is specified, but the method and place are left to the states, with Congress having the power to alter their regulations. The Constitution originally specified that elections to the House of Representatives should be direct, or popular, and that the election of the Senate and of the President and Vice President be indirect, Senators being chosen by the state legislatures and the President and Vice President by electors selected by the people. The Seventeenth Amendment (1913) provided for popular election of Senators. Qualifications for voters have varied. The Fourteenth Amendment (1868) and the Fifteenth Amendment (1870) were designed to forbid the disenfranchisement of the Negro, and the Nineteenth (1920) in effect conferred the vote on women. The Twenty-third Amendment (1961) permitted residents of the District of Columbia to vote in the presidential elections, while the Twenty-fourth Amendment (1964) outlawed payment of poll or other taxes as a condition for voting. The Twenty-sixth Amendment (1971) lowered the voting age from 21 to 18. Certain classes of felons and some others are deprived of the suffrage by law. All states have some residency requirements, and some impose literacy tests as a condition for suffrage. Voting frauds and disorder at the polls were common after the rise of political machines, and the enactment of registration laws after 1865 did little to ameliorate conditions. CORRUPT PRACTICES acts, poll watching, the institution of PRIMARY elections, and the introduction of the VOTING MACHINES after 1892 have been more effective in ensuring honest elections. Candidates are usually chosen by delegate convention, direct primary, nonpartisan primaries, or petition. The candidate who receives the most votes is usually elected, but an absolute majority of at least 50% of the vote cast may be required; it has not been required in the U.S. federal elections since 1850 except in the electoral vote cast for the President and Vice President. In presidential nominating conventions an absolute majority is required; the Democrats required a two-thirds vote of the delegates from 1832 to 1936. The existence of the electoral college has on occasion permitted a President to be chosen without a majority (1824, 1860, 1876, 1888, 1912, 1960, and 1968); in 1824 and in 1888 candidates without even a plurality succeeded in winning office. In some European countries and in some local elections in the United States, proportional representation or some other method of preferential voting is used to represent more adequately the minority groups within the electorate. Most nongovernmental organizations choose officers through some form of election. See Enid Lakeman, *How Democracies Vote* (1970); E. H. Rosebloom, *A History of Presidential Elections* (3d ed. 1970); H. A. Bone, *American Politics and the Party System* (4th ed. 1971) and *Politics and Voters* (3d ed. 1971); J. M. Clubb, ed., *Electoral Change and Stability in American Political History* (1971).

electoral college, in U.S. government, the body of electors that chooses the President and Vice President. The Constitution, in Article 2, Section 1, provides: "Each State shall appoint, in such Manner as the Legislature thereof may direct, a Number of Electors, equal to the whole Number of Senators and Representatives to which the State may be entitled in the Congress." However, no Senator, Representative, or officer of the U.S. government may be an elector. The electors are directed by the Constitution to vote in their respective states, and Congress is authorized to count their votes. To win, a presidential candidate must have a majority in the electoral college. Before adoption of the Twelfth Amendment (1804), in the event that no candidate had a majority, the House of Representatives (voting by states, with one vote for each state) was to choose the President from among the five candidates highest on the electoral list. Then, "after the choice of the President, the Person having the greatest Number of Votes of the Electors shall be the Vice President"; in case of a tie the Senate would choose the Vice President. The Twelfth Amendment, however, resulting from the confused election of 1800 (see JEFFERSON, THOMAS, and BURR, AARON) provided that electors vote for President and Vice President separately. It also reduced from five to three the number of candidates from among whom the House was to choose—in case no candidate had a majority (only two Presidents, Jefferson and John Quincy ADAMS, have been elected by the House). In the early days electors were most often chosen by the state legislatures, but with the growth of democratic sentiment popular election became the rule. After 1832 (and until the Civil War) only in South Carolina did the legislature continue to choose electors. In some of the states at first the people voted for electors by congressional districts, with two being elected at large from the whole state, but with the growth of political parties this plan was discarded (by 1832 only four states retained it and only for a brief time) in favor of the general-ticket system (the one now prevailing), whereby a party needs only a plurality to carry the whole state. Thus in every state a voter casts his ballot for as many electors as his state is entitled to. However, there is nothing in the Constitution that requires either that the electors be chosen by popular vote or that the general-ticket system be employed. Electors must be elected on the Tuesday following the first Monday in November, as required by a Federal law dating from 1845. As a belated result of the disputed election of 1876 involving Samuel J. TILDEN and Rutherford B. HAYES, the Electoral Count Act of 1887 placed the responsibility of deciding electoral disputes mainly on the states themselves. Congress now counts the votes (a mere formality) on Jan. 6. Only at the very outset did the electoral college function as planned, and there is widespread dissatisfaction with the institution. The outstanding objection is that it has given the nation nine so-called minority Presidents, i.e., Presidents who had a majority in the electoral college but lacked it in the total national popular vote—James Buchanan (1856), Abraham Lincoln (1860, but not 1864), Rutherford B. Hayes (1876), James A. Garfield (1880), Grover Cleveland (1884 and 1892), Benjamin Harrison (1888), Woodrow Wilson (1912 and 1916), Harry S. Truman (1948), John F. Kennedy (1960), and Richard M. Nixon (1968, but not 1972). Since the ratification of the Twelfth Amendment, numerous attempts have been made to alter the electoral college and to change the method of presidential election, but none has succeeded. See Lucius Wilmerding, Jr., *The Electoral College* (1958); N. R. Pierce, *The People's President* (1968); J. H. Parris and W. S. Sayre, *Voting for President: The Electoral College and the American Political System* (1970); L. P. Longley and A. G. Braun, *The Politics of Electoral College Reform* (1972).

electors, in the history of the HOLY ROMAN EMPIRE, the princes who had the right to elect the German kings or, more exactly, the kings of the Romans (Holy Roman emperors). Until the reign (1493–1519) of MAXIMILIAN I, however, an elected king was traditionally crowned by the pope before he was called emperor. Initially the electors merely confirmed hereditary succession. After the death of HENRY V in 1125 without direct heirs, the electors set aside the principle of hereditary monarchy, thus strengthening their elective rights. In succeeding years, particularly after the death of FREDERICK II in 1250, contests between rival claimants further enhanced the electoral principle. Originally all the princes served as electors, but gradually the right devolved upon a few preeminent princes. After 1257 the number of electors was narrowed to seven, but there was no agreement as to who they were. The frequency of contested elections led CHARLES IV to issue (1356) the Golden Bull (so called because of its golden seal), which regulated the procedure of elections and coronations and confirmed the electoral rights of the archbishops of Mainz, Trier, and Cologne, the king of Bohemia, the count palatine of the Rhine, the duke of Saxony, and the margrave of Brandenburg. The Golden Bull also imposed the laws of primogeniture and entail on the electoral territories. The electors, who became almost sovereign rulers, formed one of the three colleges of the imperial DIET. They served as a counterforce to imperial absolutism, even though after 1438 only members of the house of HAPSBURG were chosen emperor. The composition of the electors was changed in 1623 when FERDINAND II transferred the vote of the count palatine to the duke of Bavaria in order to punish FREDERICK THE WINTER KING; however, at the Peace of Westphalia (1648) an eighth vote was created for the count palatine. In 1692 a ninth vote (formally recognized, 1708) was created for Hanover; thus the kings of England became (1714) electors. In 1803 Emperor Napoleon I of France radically altered the list of electors. The electoral function disappeared with the end of the Holy Roman Empire in 1806.

Electra (ĭlĕk'trə), in Greek mythology. **1** Daughter of Agamemnon and Clytemnestra. After her mother and Aegisthus murdered Agamemnon, Electra, eager for revenge, longed only for the return of her brother, ORESTES. The reunion and vengeance of the brother and sister were dramatized by the three great tragedians Aeschylus, Sophocles, and Euripides. However, only in the work of Euripides did Electra take an active part in the killing of Clytemnestra. It is said that she later married Pylades, Orestes' friend, and bore him two sons. **2** One of the Pleiades. She was the daughter of Atlas and Pleione and mother by Zeus of Dardanus, the founder of Troy. According to one legend she was the lost Pleiad, disappearing in grief after the destruction of Troy. **3** A sea nymph, daughter of Oceanus and Tethys and mother by Thaumus of Iris, the rainbow, and the Harpies.

electret, solid electrically insulating, or dielectric, material that has acquired a long-lasting electrostatic polarization. Electrets are produced by heating certain dielectric materials to a high temperature and then letting them cool while immersed in a strong electric field. An electret is an analog of a permanent magnet.

electrical engineering: see ENGINEERING.

electric and magnetic units, units used to express the magnitudes of various quantities in electricity and magnetism. Three systems of such units, all based on the METRIC SYSTEM, are commonly used. One of these, the mksa-practical system, is defined in terms of the units of the MKS SYSTEM and has the AMPERE of electric current as its basic unit. The units of this system—the volt, ohm, watt, and farad—are those commonly used by scientists and engineers to make practical measurements. The two other systems are both based on the CGS SYSTEM. Electrostatic units (cgs-esu) are defined in a way that simplifies the description of interactions between static electric charges; there are no corresponding magnetic units in this system. Electromagnetic units (cgs-emu), on the other hand, are defined especially for the description of phenomena associated with moving electric charges, i.e., electric currents and magnetic poles. The two cgs systems have been widely used in the past and are still found in many texts and papers. However, there is a basic theoretical difference between the cgs-emu system and the mksa-practical system. In the cgs-emu system, the two quantities magnetic flux density (*B*) and magnetic intensity, or magnetic field strength (*H*), are related by a dimensionless constant (see DIMENSION, in physics), implying that they represent physically similar entities; in the mksa-practical system, this constant, the magnetic permeability, is not dimensionless and the two quantities are considered distinct. The latter interpretation in now agreed upon by most physicists as correct, and this fact, combined with the widespread use of mksa units in engineering and practical applications, has led to the gradual abandonment of the cgs-emu and cgs-esu systems. See F. B. Silsbee, *Systems of Electrical Units,* (U.S. National Bureau of Standards, 1962).

electric charge: see CHARGE.

electric circuit, unbroken path along which an electric current exists. A simple circuit, for example, can be set up with an electric cell, two conducting wires (one end of each being attached to each terminal of the cell), and a small lamp and socket to which are attached the free ends of the wires leading from the cell. When the wires are made fast, the circuit is said to be "closed," and the lamp will light. The current flow is from the cell along one wire to the lamp, through the lamp, and along the other wire back to the cell. This part of the circuit is called the external circuit to distinguish it from that part of the circuit within the cell itself, the internal circuit, where the current flows from one terminal to the other through the electrolyte inside the cell. When the wires are disconnected, the circuit is said to be "open" or "broken." In practice, this is accomplished by such devices as switches, fuses, and circuit breakers (see FUSE, ELECTRIC; CIRCUIT BREAKER; SHORT CIRCUIT). When a circuit is so arranged that the same current flows through its parts one after another, it is called a series circuit; when the current flows through all its parts at the same time and is divided among them, it is called a parallel circuit. When two cells are connected in series, the negative terminal of one cell is connected to the positive terminal of the other. The remaining two terminals are connected to the external circuit. The effective voltage is then the sum of the voltages of the individual cells. When two circuit elements are connected in series, their effective RESISTANCE (IMPEDANCE if the circuit is being fed alternating current) is equal to the sum of the separate resistances, and the current is the same throughout the circuit. When two cells are connected in parallel, the two positive terminals are connected together to one end of the external circuit, and the two negative terminals are connected together to the other end. (This connection is practical only if both cells have the same output voltage; otherwise the cell with the higher voltage discharges into the other.) The voltage resulting from the parallel connection of two cells is equal to the voltage of a single cell, but the resulting current capability is twice that of a single cell. When circuit elements are connected in parallel, the total resistance is less than that of the element having the least resistance, and the total current is equal to the sum of the currents in the individual branches. Series connections are impractical for many purposes since devices so connected must all operate at the same time; disconnecting one breaks the circuit for all. For this reason, the parallel circuit is most commonly used, e.g., in lighting and heating equipment and other electrical devices.

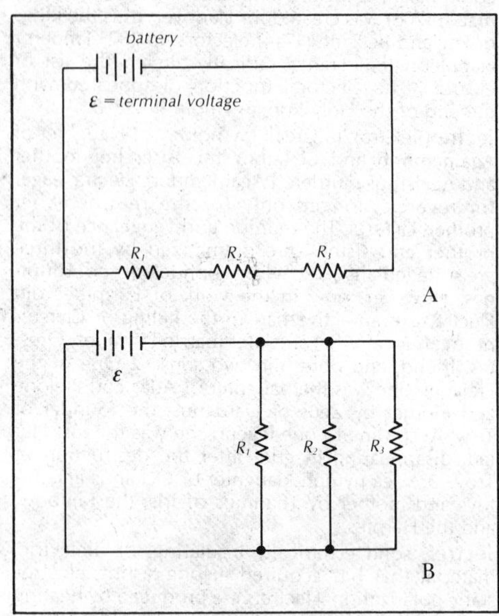

A. *Series circuit: Current is the same through each resistance; voltage divides in direct proportion to each resistance.*

B. *Parallel circuit: Voltage drop is the same over each resistance; current divides in inverse proportion to each resistance.*

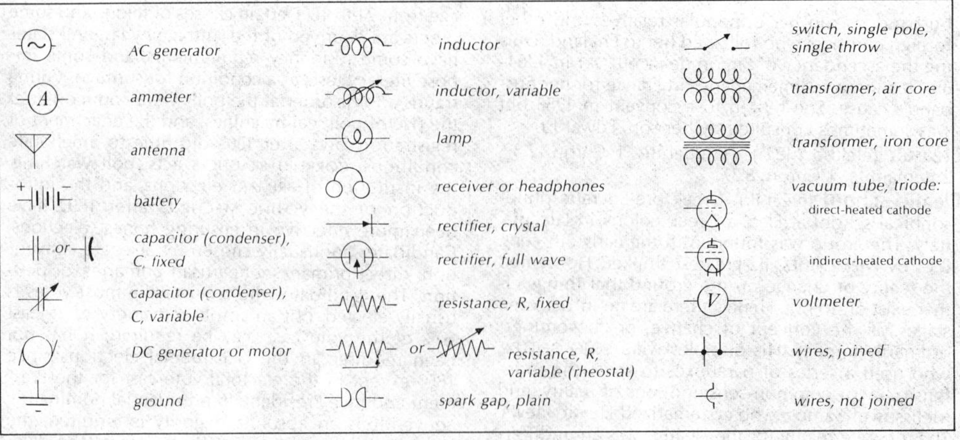

Electrical and radio symbols

electric current: see ELECTRICITY.

electric eel: see ELECTRIC FISH.

electric eye: see PHOTOELECTRIC CELL.

electric fish, name for various fish that produce electricity by means of organs usually developed from modified muscle tissue. The electric eel *(Electrophorus electricus),* a South American freshwater fish related to the carp, has organs along the ventral surface capable of producing from 450 to 600 volts of electricity—enough to light a neon bulb. Other electric fish include the electric RAY, or torpedo; a freshwater electric CATFISH with a jellylike subcutaneous electric organ (probably of epidermal origin) that extends over the whole body; and various species of STARGAZER. All these fish produce electricity at will to paralyze or kill their prey, to repel their enemies, and to aid in navigation. Recent experiments have shown that when an electric eel is in motion it generates pulses of low-energy electricity which serve to detect the presence of nearby objects. Scientists believe that electric organs in fishes may function also in communication between individuals. Electric eels are classified in the phylum CHORDATA, subphylum Vertebrata, class Osteichthyes, order Cypriniformes, family Electrophoridae.

electric furnace: see FURNACE.

electricity, class of phenomena arising from the existence of CHARGE. According to modern theory, most ELEMENTARY PARTICLES of matter possess charge, either positive or negative. Two particles with like charges, both positive or both negative, repel each other, while two particles with unlike charges are attracted (see COULOMB'S LAW). The electric FORCE between two charged particles is much greater than the gravitational force between the particles. The negatively charged ELECTRONS in an ATOM are held near the nucleus because of their attraction for the positively charged PROTONS in the nucleus. If the numbers of electrons and protons are equal, the atom is electrically neutral; if there is an excess of electrons, it is a negative ION; and if there is a deficiency of electrons, it is a positive ion. Under various circumstances, the number of electrons associated with a given atom may change; chemical bonding results from such changes, with electrons being shared by more than one atom in covalent bonds or being transferred from one atom to another in ionic bonds (see CHEMICAL BOND). Thus, many of the bulk properties of matter ultimately are due to the electric forces among the particles of which the substance is composed. Materials differ in their ability to allow charge to flow through them (see CONDUCTION; INSULATION); materials that allow charge to pass easily are called conductors, while those that do not are called insulators, or DIELECTRICS. A third class of materials, called SEMICONDUCTORS, conduct charge under some conditions but not under others. ELECTROSTATICS is the study of charges, or charged bodies, at rest. When positive or negative charge builds up in fixed positions on objects, certain phenomena can be observed that are collectively referred to as static electricity. The charge can be built up by rubbing certain objects together, such as silk and glass or rubber and fur; the friction between the objects causes electrons to be transferred from one to the other—from a glass rod to a silk cloth or from fur to a rubber rod—with the result that the object that has lost the electrons has a positive charge and the object that has gained them has an equal negative charge. An electrically neutral object can be charged by bringing it in contact with a charged object; if the charged object is positive, the neutral object gains a positive charge when some of its electrons are attracted onto the positive object; if the charged object is negative, the neutral object gains a negative charge when some electrons are attracted onto it from the negative object. A neutral conductor may be charged by induction using the following procedure. A charged object is placed near but not in contact with the conductor. If the object is positively charged, electrons in the conductor are drawn to the side of the conductor near the object. If the object is negatively charged, electrons are drawn to the side of the conductor away from the object. If the conductor is then connected to a reservoir of electrons, such as the ground, electrons will flow onto or off of the conductor with the result that it acquires a charge opposite to that of the charged object brought near it. ELECTRODYNAMICS is the study of charges in motion. A flow of electric charge constitutes an electric current. In order for a current to exist in a conductor, there must be an ELECTROMOTIVE FORCE (emf), or POTENTIAL difference, between the conductor's ends. An electric CELL, a BATTERY of cells, and a GENERATOR are all sources of electromotive force; any such source with an external conductor connected from one of the source's two terminals to the other constitutes an ELECTRIC CIRCUIT. If the source is a battery, the current is in one direction only and is called direct current (DC). If the source is a generator without a commutator, the current direction reverses twice during each rotation of the armature, passing first in one direction and then in the other; such current is called alternating current (AC). The number of times alternating current makes a double reversal of direction each second is called the frequency of the current; the frequency of ordinary household current in the U.S. is 60 cycles per sec (60 Hz) and electric devices must be designed to operate at this frequency. In a solid, the current consists not of a few electrons moving rapidly but of many electrons moving slowly; although this drift of electrons is slow, the impulse that causes it when the circuit is completed moves through the circuit at nearly the speed of light. The movement of electrons in a current is not steady; each electron moves in a series of stops and starts. In a direct current, the electrons are spread evenly through the conductor; in an alternating current, the electrons tend to congregate along the surface of the conductor. In liquids and gases, the current carriers are not only electrons but also positive and negative ions. Historically, the direction of current was described in terms of the motion of imaginary positive charges; this convention is still used by many scientists, although it is directly opposite to the direction of electron flow, which is now known to be the basis of electric current in solids. Current considered as composed of imaginary positive charges is often called conventional current. Another aspect of current electricity is its intimate connection with MAGNETISM. Any current-carrying conductor is surrounded by a magnetic FIELD of force, the lines of force of the field forming concentric closed circles with the conductor at the center; this effect finds practical application in the ELECTROMAGNET and many other devices. The reverse effect—the creation of an electric field from magnetism—also occurs; in electromagnetic induction, a changing magnetic field induces an electromotive force in a conductor in the field and a current as well if the conductor is part of a closed circuit. A changing magnetic field is caused by the motion of either the conductor or the magnet producing the field, or by variation in the strength of the magnet itself, which can be produced in the case of an electromagnet. These effects are used in the generation of ELECTROMAGNETIC RADIATION; an alternating current is fed to an ANTENNA, creating a changing magnetic field around the antenna that in turn produces a changing electric field, the two fields propagating outward through space at right angles to each other and also to the direction of motion of the electromagnetic wave. RADIO is one of many practical applications of electromagnetic radiation. There are three basic systems of units used to measure electrical quantities, the most common being that in which the AMPERE is the unit of current, the COULOMB is the unit of charge, the VOLT is the unit of electromotive force, and the OHM is the unit of resistance, reactance, or impedance (see ELECTRIC AND MAGNETIC UNITS). From the writings of Thales of Miletus it appears that Western man knew as long ago as 600 B.C. that amber becomes charged by rubbing. There was little real progress until the English scientist William Gilbert in 1600 described the electrification of many substances and coined the term *electricity* from the Greek word for *amber*. As a result, Gilbert is called the father of modern electricity. In 1660, Otto von Guericke invented a crude machine for producing static electricity. It was a ball of sulfur, rotated by a crank with one hand and rubbed with the other. Successors, such as Francis Hauksbee, made improvements that provided experimenters with a ready source of static electricity. Today's highly developed descendant of these early machines is the Van de Graaf generator, which is sometimes used as a PARTICLE ACCELERATOR. Robert Boyle realized that attraction and repulsion were mutual and that electric force was transmitted through a vacuum (c.1675). Stephen Gray distinguished between conductors and nonconductors (1729). C. F. Du Fay recognized two kinds of electricity, which Benjamin Franklin and Ebenezer Kinnersley of Philadelphia later named positive and negative. Progress quickened again after the Leyden jar was invented in 1745 by Pieter van Musschenbroek. The Leyden jar stored static electricity, which could be discharged all at once. In 1747, William Watson discharged a Leyden jar through a circuit, and comprehension of the current and circuit started a new field of experimentation. Henry Cavendish, by measuring the conductivity of materials (he compared the simultaneous shocks he received by discharging Leyden jars through the materials), and Charles A. Coulomb, by expressing mathematically the attraction of electrified bodies, began the quantitative study of electricity. A new interest in current began with the invention of the battery. Luigi Galvani had noticed (1786) that a discharge of static electricity made a frog's leg jerk. Consequent experimentation produced what was a simple electron cell using the fluids of the leg as an electrolyte and the muscle as a circuit and indicator. Galvani thought the leg supplied electricity, but Alessandro Volta thought otherwise, and he built the voltaic pile, an early type of battery, as proof. Continuous current from batteries smoothed the way for the discovery of G. S. Ohm's law (pub. 1827), relating current, voltage (electromotive force), and resistance (see OHM'S LAW), and of J. P. Joule's law of electrical heating (pub. 1841). Ohm's law and the rules discovered later by G. R. Kirchhoff regarding the sum of the currents and the sum of the voltages in a circuit (see KIRCHHOFF'S LAWS) are the basic means of making circuit calculations. In 1819, Hans Christian Oersted discovered that a magnetic field surrounds a current-carrying wire. Within two years André Marie Ampère had put several electromagnetic laws into mathematical form, D. F. Arago had invented the electromagnet, and Michael Faraday had devised a crude form of electric MOTOR. Practical application of a motor had to wait 10 years; however, until Faraday (and earlier, independently, Joseph Henry) invented the electric generator with which to power the motor. A year after Faraday's laboratory approximation of the generator, Hippolyte Pixii constructed a hand-driven model. From then on engineers took over from the scientists, and a slow development followed; the first power stations were built 50 years later (see POWER, ELECTRIC). In 1873, James Clerk Maxwell had started a different path of development with equations that described the electromagnetic field, and he predicted the existence of electromagnetic waves traveling with the speed of light. Heinrich R. Hertz confirmed this prediction experimentally, and Marconi first made use of these waves in developing radio (1895). John Ambrose Fleming invented (1904) the diode rectifier vacuum tube as a detector for the Marconi radio. Three years later Lee De Forest made the diode into an amplifier by adding a third electrode, and ELECTRONICS had begun. Theoretical understanding became more complete in 1897 with the discovery of the electron by J. J. Thomson. In 1910–11, Ernest R. Rutherford and his assistants learned the distribution of charge within the atom. Robert Millikan measured the charge on a single electron by 1913. See POLE, in electricity and magnetism. See Wolfgang Panofsky and Melba Phillips, *Classical Electricity and Magnetism* (2d ed. 1962); D. L. Anderson, *Discovery of the Electron: The Development of the Atomic Concept of Electricity* (1964); W. T. Scott, *The Physics of Electricity and Magnetism* (2d ed. 1966); Norman Feather, *Electricity and Matter* (1968); Milton Kaufman and J. A. Wilson, *Basic Electricity* (1973).

electric-light bug: see WATER BUG.

electric shock, effect of the passage of a current of electricity through the body. Fatality may result from shocks of from 1 to 2 amperes and 500 to 1,000 volts. However, the effect of electric shock on the body depends not only on the strength of the current, but on such factors as wetness of the skin, area of contact, duration of contact, constitution of the victim, and whether or not the victim is well grounded. The general range of disturbances include a mild tingling (usually produced by common static electricity), spasm of the muscles, loss of consciousness, and sometimes death. In addition, burns occur where the current enters and leaves the body. A lethal dose of electricity may paralyze the respiratory organs and damage the central nervous system; the immediate cause of death, however, is usually an interruption of heart action. Shock therapy is the use of electric shock to treat certain mental illnesses.

electrocardiography (ĭlĕk″trōkärdēŏg′rəfē), science of recording and interpreting the electrical activity that precedes and is a measure of the action of HEART muscles. Since 1887, when Augustus Waller demonstrated the possibility of measuring such action, physicians and physiologists have recorded it in order to study the heart's normal behavior and to provide a method for diagnosing abnormalities. Electrical current associated with contraction of the heart muscles passes through the various tissues and reaches the surface of the body. What is actually recorded is the change in electrical potential on the body surface. The first practical device for recording the activity of the heart was the string galvanometer developed by William Einthoven in 1903. In this device a fine quartz string is suspended vertically between the poles of a magnet. The string is deflected in response to changes in electrical potential and its movement can be optically enlarged and photographed, or, if an immediately visible record is desired, the string's movement can be recorded on a sheet of paper. A more sophisticated form of the electrocardiograph employs a vacuum-tube amplifier. The greatly amplified current from the body deflects a mirror galvanometer that causes a beam of light to move across a light-sensitive film. When an electrocardiograph is taken, electrodes (leads) are attached to the extremities and to the left chest. The recordings obtained in this manner are called electrocardiograms, or more simply EKG's or ECG's. A normal EKG shows a sequence of three waves arbitrarily labeled P, QRS, and T. The P wave is a small, low-amplitude wave produced by the excitation of the atria of the heart. It is followed by a resting interval that marks the passage of electrical impulses into the ventricles. Following this interval comes the QRS wave, a rapid, high-amplitude wave marking ventricular excitation, and then a slow-building T wave denoting ventricular recovery. Abnormalities may be noted from deviation in wave form, height, direction, or duration. The type of abnormal wave may sometimes indicate the type of heart disorder. Usually the physician must associate the EKG with other clinical observations to determine the cause of the abnormality.

electrochemical equivalent: see ELECTROLYSIS.

electrochemistry, science dealing with the relationship between electricity and chemical changes. Of principal interest are the reactions that take place between ELECTRODES and the ELECTROLYTES in electric and electrolytic cells (see ELECTROLYSIS), as well as the reactions that take place in an electrolyte as electricity passes through it. The principles of electrochemistry are applied in a variety of ways, e.g., in electroplating and in the generation of electricity by MAGNETOHYDRODYNAMICS. See BATTERY; VOLTAIC CELL.

electrode, terminal through which electric current passes between metallic and nonmetallic parts of an electric circuit. In most familiar circuits current is carried by metallic conductors, but in some circuits the current passes for some distance through a nonmetallic conductor. For example, in ELECTROLYSIS current passes through a liquid electrolyte; in a fluorescent lamp current passes through a gas. An electrode is usually in the form of a wire, rod, or plate. It may be made of a metal, e.g., copper, lead, platinum, silver, or zinc, or of a nonmetal, commonly carbon. The electrode through which current passes from the metallic to the nonmetallic conductor is called the anode, and that through which current passes from the nonmetallic to the metallic conductor, the cathode. (Electron flow is in a direction opposite that of conventional current.) In most familiar electric devices, current flows from the terminal at higher electric potential (the positive electrode) to the terminal at lower electric potential (the negative electrode); therefore, the anode is usually the positive electrode and the cathode the negative electrode. In some electric devices, e.g., an electric battery, nonelectric energy is converted to electric energy, causing current to flow within the device from the negative electrode to the positive electrode, so that the anode is the negative electrode and the cathode is the positive electrode.

electrode potentials: see ELECTROCHEMISTRY.

electrodynamics, study of phenomena associated with charged bodies in motion (see CHARGE; ELECTRICITY); since a moving charge produces a magnetic FIELD, electrodynamics is concerned with effects such as MAGNETISM, ELECTROMAGNETIC RADIATION, and electromagnetic INDUCTION, including such practical applications as the electric generator and the electric motor. This area of electrodynamics, often known as classical electrodynamics, was first systematically explained by the physicist James Clerk Maxwell. Maxwell's equations, a set of differential equations, describe the phenomena of this area with great generality. A more recent development is quantum electrodynamics, which was formulated to explain the interaction of electromagnetic radiation with matter, to which the laws of the QUANTUM THEORY apply. The physicists P. A. M. Dirac, W. Heisenberg, and W. Pauli were the pioneers in the formulation of quantum electrodynamics. When the velocities of the charged particles under consideration become comparable with the speed of light, corrections involving the theory of RELATIVITY must be made; this branch of the theory is called relativistic electrodynamics. It is applied to phenomena involved with particle accelerators and with electron tubes that are subject to high voltages and carry heavy currents.

electroencephalography (əlĕk″trōĕnsĕf″əlŏg′rəfē), science of recording and analyzing the electrical activity of the BRAIN. Electrodes, placed on or just under the scalp, are channeled to an electroencephalograph, which is an amplifier connected to a mechanism that converts electrical impulses into the vertical movement of a pen over a sheet of paper. The recording traced by the pen is called an electroencephalogram, or EEG. Readings may be obtained for a particular brain site by coupling a single electrode with an indifferent, or neutral, lead (monopolar technique) or between two areas of the brain through two independent electrodes (bipolar technique). The combination of impulses that are being recorded at any one time is called a montage. The electrical activity of the brain was first demonstrated in 1929 by the German psychiatrist Hans Berger. The scientific professions were slow in giving proper attention to Berger's discovery of the brain rhythms he named alpha waves, but since then at least three other standard brainwave patterns have been isolated and identified. Alpha waves are fast, medium-amplitude oscillations, now known to represent the background activity of the brain in the physically and psychologically healthy adult. They are most characteristically visible during dream-sleep or when a subject is relaxing with eyes closed. Delta waves are large, slow-moving, regular waves, typically associated with the deepest levels of sleep. In children up to the age of puberty the appearance of high-amplitude theta waves, having a velocity between those of alpha and delta rhythms, usually signals the onset of emotional stimulation. The presence of theta waves in adults may be a sign of brain damage or of an immature personality. Beta rhythms are small, very fast wave patterns, which indicate intense physiological stress, like that resulting from barbiturate intoxification. By observing abnormalities in recordings and determining the area of the brain from which they originate, the physician's ability to diagnose and treat such conditions as epilepsy, cerebral tumor, encephalitis, and stroke, is greatly enhanced. Electroencephalograms have also proven valuable in the general study of brain physiology and in the particular study of sleep. Various types of Eastern meditation, e.g., YOGA, use techniques that increase alpha and theta wave activity. Because of concomitant physiological changes during meditation, e.g., lessened anxiety, the techniques have recently become popular in the West. In brain wave feedback, a subject can be taught to monitor and regulate his own brain waves; the technique has been used experimentally in control of epilepsy.

electrolysis, passage of an electric current through a conducting solution or molten salt (either is a type of ELECTROLYTE) that is decomposed in the process. For example, when a cathode, or negative (−) electrode, and an anode, or positive (+) electrode, are dipped into a solution of hydrogen chloride (a compound of hydrogen and chlorine) and a current is passed through it, hydrogen gas bubbles off at the cathode and chlorine at the anode. Dissolved in water, hydrogen chloride dissociates (see DISSOCIATION) into hydrogen ions (hydrogen atoms that have lost an electron) and chloride ions (chlorine atoms that have gained an electron). When the electrodes are connected to a source of direct current, the hydrogen ions are attracted to the cathode, where they each gain an electron, becoming hydrogen atoms again. Hydrogen atoms pair off into hydrogen molecules that bubble off as hydrogen gas. Similarly, chlorine ions are attracted to the anode, where they each give up an electron, become chlorine atoms, join in pairs, and bubble off as chlorine gas. The migration of ions through the electrolyte constitutes the electric current in that part of the circuit. The migration of electrons into the anode, through the wiring and an electric generator, and then back to the cathode constitutes the current in the external circuit. Various substances are prepared commercially by electrolysis, e.g., chlorine by the electrolysis of a solution of common salt; hydrogen by the electrolysis of water; heavy water (deuterium oxide) for use in nuclear reactors, also by electrolysis of water. A metal such as aluminum is refined by electrolysis. A solution of aluminum oxide in a molten mineral decomposes into pure aluminum at the cathode and into oxygen at the anode. In the above examples the electrodes are inert. For plating, the plating metal is generally the anode, and the object to be plated is the cathode. A solution of a salt of the plating metal is the electrolyte. The plating metal is deposited on the cathode, and the anode replenishes the supply of positive ions, thus gradually being dissolved. An electric cell is an electrolytic system in which a chemical reaction causes a current to flow in an external circuit; it essentially reverses electrolysis. Metal corrosion can take place by electrolysis in an unintentionally created cell. The English scientist Michael Faraday discovered that the amount of a material deposited on an electrode is proportional to the amount of electricity used. The ratio of the amount of material deposited in grams to the amount of electricity used is the electrochemical equivalent of the material. Actual electric consumption may be as high as four times the theoretical consumption because of such factors as heat loss and undesirable side reactions. Electrotype printing plates, silverware, and chrome automobile trim are plated by electrolysis. Within a few weeks after the Italian physicist Alessandro VOLTA produced his electric cell (see VOLTAIC CELL) in 1800, William Nicholson and Sir Anthony Carlisle, English scientists, performed the first electrolysis, breaking water down into oxygen and hydrogen.

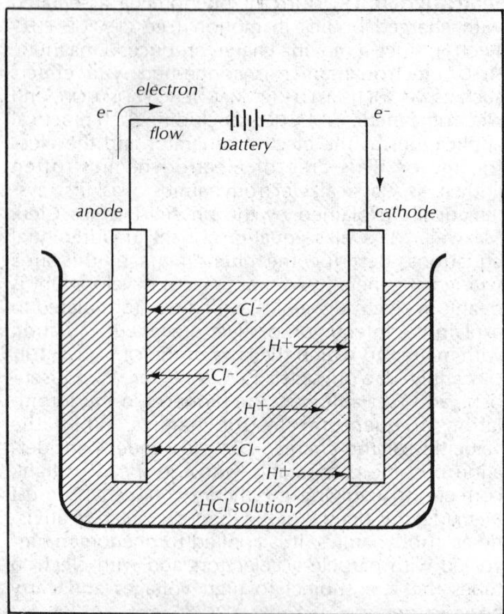

Electrolysis: In a typical reaction electrodes are placed in a solution of hydrogen chloride, HCl, which contains both hydrogen and chlorine ions. The battery removes electrons from the anode, making it positive and causing it to attract chlorine ions, Cl^-, which combine and are liberated as chlorine gas, Cl_2. The battery supplies electrons to the cathode, making it negative and causing it to attract hydrogen ions, H^+, which evolve as hydrogen gas, H_2, at the cathode.

electrolysis, cosmetic, method of permanently removing superfluous or unwanted hair. A fine needle is inserted into the hair follicle; the application of an electric current through the needle destroys the hair root, or papilla, and the hair is removed.

electrolyte (ĭlĕk'trəlīt''), electrical conductor in which current is carried by IONS rather than by free electrons (as in a metal). Electrolytes include water solutions of acids, bases, or salts; certain pure liquids; and molten salts. Gases may act as electrolytes under conditions of high temperature or low pressure. All inorganic acids, bases, and salts are electrolytes. Electrolytic substances are classified as strong or weak according to how readily they dissociate into conducting ions. Potassium chloride and sodium hydroxide are strong electrolytes; they are almost completely dissociated when in solution or fused. Acetic acid is a weak electrolyte. An electrolyte is decomposed when a current passes through it (see ELECTROLYSIS).

electromagnet, device in which MAGNETISM is produced by an electric current. Any electric current produces a magnetic field, but the field near an ordinary straight conductor is rarely strong enough to be of practical use. A strong field can be produced if an insulated wire is wrapped around a soft iron core and a current passed through it. The strength of the magnetic field produced by such an electromagnet depends on the number of coils of wire, the size of the current, and the magnetic permeability of the core material; a strong field can be produced from a small current if a large number of turns of wire are used. Unlike the materials from which permanent magnets are made, the soft iron in the core of an electromagnet retains little of the magnetism induced in it by the current after the current has been turned off. This property makes it more useful than a permanent magnet in many applications. Electromagnets are used to lift large masses of magnetic materials, such as scrap iron. They are essential to the design of the electric generator and electric motor and are also employed in doorbells, circuit breakers, television receivers, loudspeakers, and atomic particle accelerators. A special kind of electromagnet makes use of superconductivity, its coil being made of a superconducting metal; this type requires much less power to operate than does an ordinary electromagnet, but it must be kept at an extremely low temperature. The north pole of a bar electromagnet can be identified by means of the "right-hand rule": If the magnet is grasped by the right hand with the fingertips pointing in the direction of current (from positive to negative), the thumb will point in the direction of the electromagnet's north pole. The first practical electromagnet was invented early in the 19th cent. by William Sturgeon.

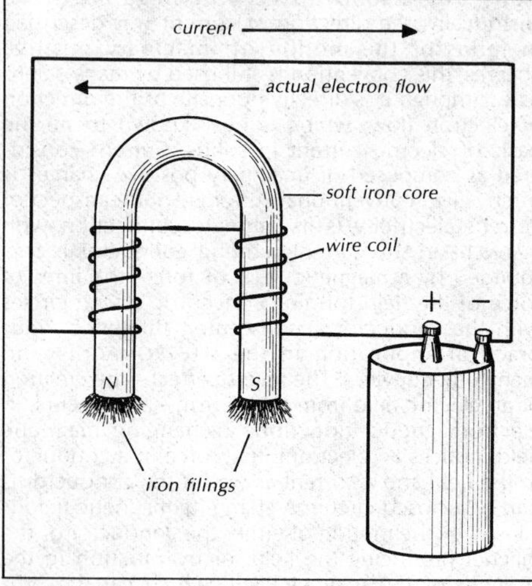

Electromagnet

electromagnetic induction: see INDUCTION.

electromagnetic radiation, ENERGY radiated in the form of a WAVE as a result of the motion of electric charges. A moving charge gives rise to a magnetic field, and if the motion is changing (accelerated), then the magnetic field varies and in turn produces an electric field. These interacting electric and magnetic fields are at right angles to one another and also to the direction of propagation of the energy. Thus, an electromagnetic wave is a transverse wave. Electromagnetic radiation does not require a material medium and can travel through a vacuum. The theory of electromagnetic radiation was developed by James Clerk Maxwell and published in 1865. He showed that the speed of propagation of electromagnetic radiation should be identical with that of LIGHT, about 186,000 mi (300,000 km) per sec. Subsequent experiments by Heinrich Hertz verified Maxwell's prediction through the discovery of radio waves, also known as hertzian waves. Light is a type of electromagnetic radiation, occupying only a small portion of the possible SPECTRUM of this energy. The various types of electromagnetic radiation differ only in wavelength and frequency; they are alike in all other respects. The possible sources of electromagnetic radiation are directly related to

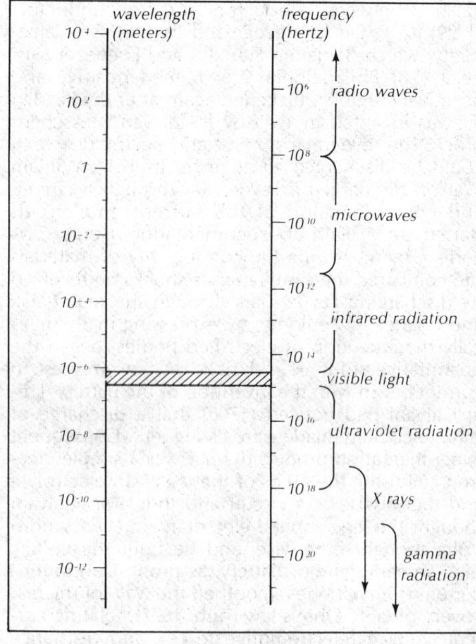

Electromagnetic spectrum

wavelength: long radio waves are produced by large antennas such as those used by broadcasting stations; much shorter visible light waves are produced by the motions of charges within ATOMS; the shortest waves, those of GAMMA RADIATION, result from changes within the NUCLEUS of the atom. In order of decreasing wavelength and increasing frequency, various types of electromagnetic radiation include: electric waves, RADIO waves (including AM, FM, TV, and shortwaves), microwaves, INFRARED RADIATION, visible light, ULTRAVIOLET RADIATION, X RAYS, and gamma radiation. According to the QUANTUM THEORY, light and other forms of electromagnetic radiation may at times exhibit properties like those of particles in their interaction with matter. (Conversely, particles sometimes exhibit wavelike properties.) The individual quantum of electromagnetic radiation is known as the PHOTON and is symbolized as γ, the Greek letter gamma. Quantum effects are most pronounced for the higher frequencies, such as gamma rays, and are usually negligible for radio waves at the long-wavelength, low-frequency end of the spectrum.

electromotive force, abbr. emf, difference in electric potential, or voltage, between the terminals of a source of electricity, e.g., a battery from which no current is being drawn. When current is drawn, the potential difference drops below the emf value. Electromotive force is usually measured in VOLTS.

electromotive series, list of METALS whose order indicates the relative tendency to be oxidized, or to give up electrons (see OXIDATION AND REDUCTION); the list also includes the gas hydrogen. The electromotive series begins with the metal most easily oxidized and ends with the metal least easily oxidized, i.e., the metal with the greatest electron-accepting tendency, or the metal most easily reduced. The tendency to be oxidized is not an absolute quantity; it can only be compared with the tendency of some other substance to be oxidized. In practice, the tendency to be oxidized, called the oxidation potential and expressed in volts, is measured relative to a standard hydrogen electrode, which is arbitrarily assigned an oxidation potential of zero. The oxidation potential measures the tendency of the half reaction $M \rightarrow M^{+n} + ne^-$ to occur, in which some metal M loses n electrons, e^-, and acquires a positive charge of ^+n. The more positive the oxidation potential, the more readily oxidation takes place. The electromotive series is thus a list of the metals in the order of their tendency to undergo the half reaction. The series is also called the replacement series, since it indicates which metals replace, or are replaced by, other metals (or hydrogen) in compounds. In general, a metal will replace any other metal lower in the series and will be replaced by any metal higher in the series. The order of some common metals in the electromotive series, starting with the most easily oxidized, is: lithium, potassium, radium, calcium, sodium, magnesium, uranium, aluminum, zinc, chromium, sulfur, iron, cobalt, nickel, lead, hydrogen, copper, mercury, silver, platinum, and gold. A list arranged according to oxidation potential and including not only metals but also all other elements and ions is called the electrochemical series.

electron, ELEMENTARY PARTICLE carrying a unit charge of negative electricity. Ordinary electric current is the flow of electrons through a wire conductor (see ELECTRICITY). The electron is one of the basic constituents of matter. An ATOM consists of a small, dense, positively charged nucleus surrounded by electrons that whirl about it in orbits, forming a cloud of charge. Ordinarily there are just enough negative electrons to balance the positive charge of the nucleus, and the atom is neutral. If electrons are added or removed, a net charge results, and the atom is said to be ionized (see ION). Atomic electrons are responsible for the chemical properties of matter (see VALENCE). The name *electron* was first used for a unit of negative electricity by the English physicist G. J. Stoney in the late 19th cent. The actual discovery of the particle, however, was made in 1897 by J. J. Thomson, who showed that cathode rays are composed of electrons and who measured the ratio of charge to mass for the electron. In 1909, R. A. Millikan measured the charge of the electron. Combining these two results gives the mass of the electron (about 1/1,840 of the mass of the proton). Ernest Rutherford, in 1903, showed that beta rays (see RADIOACTIVITY) are high-energy electrons. In 1927, Davisson and Germer, working with high-speed electron beams, discovered that electrons sometimes exhibit the wave property of diffraction. This confirmed L. V. de Broglie's hypothesis that electrons, which had previously been thought of as particles, also possess certain wave properties (see QUANTUM THEORY). The wavelike properties of electrons are utilized in the electron MICROSCOPE and other devices. The electron is the lightest particle having a non-zero rest mass. It belongs to the LEPTON class of particles and, together with its ANTIPARTICLE, the positron, and its associated NEUTRINO and antineutrino, constitutes a subfamily of the leptons. In any particle reaction involving any of the four members of the electron family, the total electron family number (+1 for ordinary particles, −1 for antiparticles) must be conserved (see CONSERVATION LAWS, in physics). As a consequence, an electron and a positron (total electron family number equals zero) can annihilate each other to yield two or more photons or a neutrino-antineutrino pair, but not two neutrinos (total electron family number equals two).

electronegativity (ĭlĕk"trōnĕgətĭv'ətē), in chemistry, tendency for an atom to attract a pair of electrons that it shares with another atom (see CHEMICAL BOND). For example, the molecule hydrogen chloride, HCl, consists of a hydrogen atom, H, and a chlorine atom, Cl, sharing a pair of electrons. If the pair of electrons are not shared equally, i.e., if they spend more time with one atom than with the other, the favored atom is said to be more electronegative. In the case of HCl, measurements indicate that the molecule has a dipole moment, that is, the chlorine end is relatively negative and the hydrogen end is relatively positive. This means that the electron pair spends more time with the chlorine atom than with the hydrogen atom and thus chlorine is more electronegative than hydrogen. Nonmetals have much higher electronegativities than metals; of the nonmetals, fluorine is the most electronegative, followed by oxygen, nitrogen, and chlorine. The larger the difference in electronegativity between two atoms, the more polar the bond between them. In the extreme case of a bond between a metal and a nonmetal, a complete transfer of electrons takes place.

electronic engineering: see ENGINEERING.

electronic music, term applied to compositions whose sonic components are either produced or modified electronically. Initially, a distinction must be made between the technological development of electronic instruments and the music conceived for the inherent advantages of these instruments. Experiments in electronic tone production began soon after the invention of the vacuum tube. The first important instrument, the Theremin, invented by the Russian Leon Theremin in 1924, used interference beats of two oscillators to produce sine-wave tones. The Ondes Martinot, invented in 1928, and the Trautonium, invented in 1930, were of similar design. Tone generators in current use are synthetic—producing desired frequencies from frequency bands (white noise) with electroacoustical filters. Complementary to sound generation is sound modification, accomplished by filters, frequency and amplitude modulators, and electronic reverberators. The perfection of the tape recorder in the 1940s was historically crucial to the development of electronic music. In permitting the combination and reproduction of sonic raw material, it made practical a degree of complexity comparable to that of conventional musical media and thus provided a new resource for composers. The first electronic compositions were taped montages of electronically altered sound obtained by microphone from non-electronic sources, such as voice and street noises. This genre, dubbed *musique concrète*, was introduced in Paris c.1924 by Pierre Schaeffer in the work *Études aux chemins de fer* [railroad study]. Subsequent experiments were begun in the early 1950s by Herbert Eimert and Karlheinz STOCKHAUSEN at the West German Radio Studio in Cologne, by Luciano BERIO and Bruno MADERNA at the Italian Radio Studio in Milan, and by Vladimir USSACHEVSKY and Otto Leuning at the Columbia-Princeton Electronic Music Center in New York City. In contrast with Schaeffer's work, these experiments were aimed at composing music with tones that were not only electronically manipulated but electronically produced as well. Early compositions of this group include Stockhausen's Electronic Composition No. 1 (1952) and Leuning's *12-tone Theme* (1952). Compositional needs directed further technical developments. In 1955 the synthesizer was developed, a single unit with numerous generating and modifying capacities. Work is still progressing to facilitate the computerized interconnection between sound producers, modifiers, and recorders. Computer programs automatically translate, produce, and record sound data supplied in digital form by composers. The present electronic music repertoire consists of "pure" electronic works such as Charles Wuorinen's *Time's Encomium* (1969) and pieces for various combinations of taped electronic sounds, concrete sounds, and conventional instruments, such as Stockhausen's *Hymnen* (1967) for electronic and concrete sounds and Milton BABBITT'S *Vision and Prayer* (1961) for voice and synthesized sound. The Greek composer Iannis XENAKIS has experimented with computer-generated music (see COMPUTER MUSIC). The complex counterpoint of recent works suggests that the advantages of electronic media include both their ability to generate new sounds and the absolute precision with which these sounds may be combined. One result of this complexity is the inadequacy of conventional musical notation. In response, the Index to Musical Notation has been established in the Library of Performing Arts of the New York Public Library. See Allen Strange, *Electronic Music* (1972); E. S. Schwartz, *Electronic Music* (1973); bibliography by L. M. Cross (1967).

electronics, science and technology based on and concerned with the controlled flow of ELECTRONS or other carriers of electric charge, especially in ELECTRON TUBES and SEMICONDUCTOR devices. It is one of the principal branches of electrical engineering. The invention of the transistor, announced in 1948, and the subsequent development of INTEGRATED CIRCUITS have brought about revolutionary changes in electronics, which was previously based on the technology of electron tubes. The miniaturization and savings in power brought about by these developments have allowed electronic circuits to be packaged more densely, making possible compact computers, advanced radar and navigation systems, and other devices that use very large numbers of components. It has also brought to the consumer such items as smaller and more reliable RADIO and TELEVISION receivers, advanced sound-reproducing systems, microwave-cooking ovens (see under STOVE), and electronic automotive accessories.

electron microscope: see MICROSCOPE.

electron paramagnetic resonance: see MAGNETIC RESONANCE.

electron tube, device consisting of a sealed enclosure in which electrons flow between electrodes separated either by a vacuum (in a vacuum tube) or by an ionized gas at low pressure (in a gas tube). The two principal electrodes of an electron tube are called the cathode and the anode. The simplest vacuum tube, the diode, has only those two electrodes.

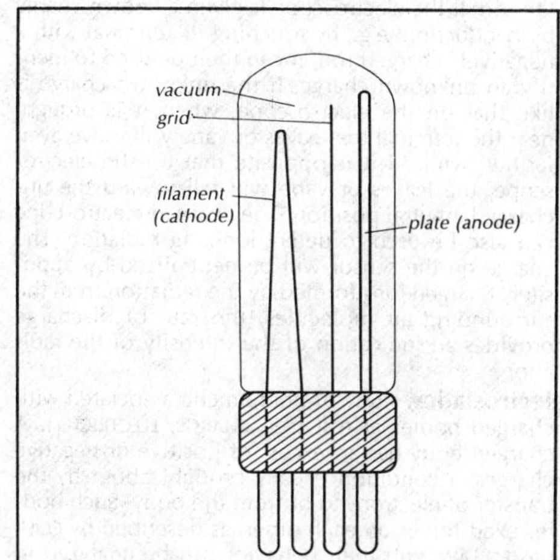

Triode electron tube

When the cathode is heated, it emits a cloud of electrons, which are attracted by the positive electric polarity of the anode and constitute the current through the tube. If the cathode is charged positively with respect to the anode, the electrons are drawn back to the cathode. However, the anode is not capable of emitting electrons and therefore no current can exist; thus the diode acts as a rectifier, i.e., it allows current to flow in only one direction. In the vacuum triode a third electrode called a GRID is placed between the cathode and the anode. Small voltage fluctuations, or signals, applied to the grid can result in large fluctuations in the current between the cathode and the anode. Thus the triode can act as a signal amplifier. X-ray tubes maintain a high voltage between a cathode and an anode. This enables electrons from the cathode to strike the anode at velocities high enough to produce X rays. A

CATHODE-RAY TUBE can produce electron beams that strike a screen to produce pictures of electrical phenomena. Gas tubes behave similarly to vacuum tubes but are designed to handle larger currents or to produce luminous discharges. In some gas tubes the cathode is not designed as an electron emitter; conduction occurs when a voltage sufficient to ionize the gas exists between the anode and the cathode. In these cases the ions and electrons formed from the gas molecules constitute the current. Many special-purpose tubes have multiple anodes, cathodes, or grids, or combinations of multiple electrodes often arranged in particular configurations. See PHOTOELECTRIC CELL.

electron-volt, abbr. EV, unit of energy used in atomic and nuclear physics; 1 electron-volt is the energy transferred in moving a unit CHARGE, positive or negative and equal to that charge on the electron, through a POTENTIAL difference of 1 volt. The maximum energy of a PARTICLE ACCELERATOR is usually expressed in multiples of the electron-volt, either million electron-volts (MEV) or billion electron-volts (BEV or GEV). Because mass is a form of energy (see RELATIVITY), the masses of ELEMENTARY PARTICLES are sometimes expressed in electron-volts; e.g., the mass of the electron, the lightest particle with measurable rest mass, is 0.51 MEV.

electrophoresis (ĭlĕk"trōfərē'sĭs): see COLLOID.

electrophorus, device used to generate static electric charges. It has two parts: a nonconducting plate (e.g., of hard rubber) that is negatively charged and a metal plate with an insulated handle. A positive charge is induced on the metal plate by placing it on the charged plate and then grounding the metal plate momentarily. This positive charge can then be used for experimentation. See ELECTROSTATICS.

electroplating: see PLATING.

electroscope, device for detecting electric CHARGE. There are various types of electroscopes. The most common has a cylindrical metal case closed by two round, flat, glass faces. A charge sensor is mounted within the case and electrically insulated from it and is joined to an external terminal by a conductor, e.g., a metal rod. The sensor consists of two leaves of metal foil (usually gold) or a metal vane mounted so that it can freely rotate about a metal rod. If a negatively charged body is brought near the terminal of the electroscope, it will cause electrons to be repelled into the sensor; a positively charged body attracts electrons out of the sensor. In either case a net charge is induced in the sensor, and the two leaves will fly apart or the vane will swing away from the rod. It the electroscope is given a known charge by conduction, e.g., by touching its terminal with a negatively charged rod, it can then be used to identify an unknown charge. If the unknown charge is like that on the electroscope, when it is brought near the terminal the leaves or vane will move even farther; while if it is opposite that on the electroscope, the leaves or vane will fall toward the uncharged, neutral position. The charged electroscope can also be used to detect ionizing radiation. The charge on the sensor will be neutralized by oppositely charged ions formed by the radiation from the surrounding air molecules; the rate of discharge provides an indication of the intensity of the radiation.

electrostatics, study of phenomena associated with charged bodies at rest (see CHARGE; ELECTRICITY). A charged body has an excess of positive or negative charges, a condition usually brought about by the transfer of electrons to or from the body. Such bodies exert forces on each other, as described by COULOMB'S LAW, and their behavior can be analyzed in terms of the concept of an electric FIELD surrounding any charged body such that another charged body located at any point in the field is subject to a force proportional to the magnitude of its charge and is attractive or repulsive, depending on the polarity of the charge. The combined electric field in a given region depends on the location, magnitude, and polarity of the charges in that region. Electric fields need not be constant with time. Time-varying electric fields are used in some devices that accelerate charged atomic particles. Electrostatics has many other applications, ranging from the analysis of phenomena such as thunderstorms to the study of the behavior of electron tubes.

electrotype, in printing, a plate made by electrically coating with copper or nickel a wax, lead, or plastic mold of type or relief engraving and then pouring melted type metal over this coating. Copper or nickel, instead of type metal, thus becomes the printing surface. Copper is better than type metal, and nickel is better than copper. The electrotype has largely superseded the STEREOTYPE except in the printing of newspapers.

electrovalent bond: see CHEMICAL BOND.

elegy, in Greek and Roman poetry, a poem written in elegiac verse (i.e., couplets consisting of a hexameter line followed by a pentameter line). The form dates back to the 7th cent. B.C. in Greece and was widely used by Catullus, Ovid, and other Latin poets. In English poetry, since the 16th cent., the term *elegy* has designated a reflective poem of lamentation or regret, with no set metrical form, generally of melancholy tone, often on death. The elegy can mourn one person, such as Walt Whitman's "When Lilacs Last in the Dooryard Bloom'd" on the death of Abraham Lincoln, or it can mourn mankind in general, like Thomas Gray's "Elegy Written in a Country Churchyard." In the pastoral elegy, modeled on Theocritus and Bion, the subject and his friends are depicted as nymphs and shepherds inhabiting a pastoral world in classical times. Famous pastoral elegies are Milton's "Lycidas," on Edward King; Shelley's "Adonais," on John Keats; and Matthew Arnold's "Thyrsis," on Arthur Hugh Clough.

El-elohe-Israel (ĕl-ĕlō'hē-ĭz'rēəl), name of an altar erected by Jacob in Shechem. Gen. 33.20.

element, in chemistry, substance composed of ATOMS all having the same number of protons in their nuclei. This number, called the atomic number, defines the element. For example, the element carbon consists of atoms all with atomic number 6, i.e., all having 6 protons in the nucleus; any atom with atomic number 6 is a carbon atom. Each element is assigned an official symbol by the International Union of Pure and Applied Chemistry (IUPAC). For example, the symbol for carbon is C, and the symbol for silver is Ag [Lat. *argentum* = silver]. In 1974, 105 elements were known, ranging from hydrogen with an at. no. of 1 to an as yet unnamed element with an at. no. of 105. The nuclei of most atoms also contain neutrons. The total number of protons and neutrons in the nucleus of an atom is called the mass number. For example, the mass number of a carbon atom with 6 protons and 6 neutrons in its nucleus is 12. Although all atoms of an element have the same number of protons in their nuclei, they may not all have the same number of neutrons. Atoms of an element with the same mass number make up an ISOTOPE of the element. All elements have isotopes; some have more than others. Hydrogen, for example, has only 3 isotopes, while xenon has 30. Over 1,000 isotopes of the elements are known. There are 7 isotopes of carbon, having from 4 to 10 neutrons in the nucleus and therefore mass numbers from 10 to 16. Not all of the elements have stable isotopes. Some have only radioactive isotopes, which decay to form other isotopes, usually of other elements (see RADIOACTIVITY). In some cases all the isotopes of an element are very unstable, and the element is therefore not found in nature. Only 92 of the elements are known to occur naturally on earth. Of these, 4 occur in minute amounts produced by the decay of other elements. These 4 extremely scarce elements and those that do not occur at all naturally were discovered when they were produced in the laboratory; they are often called the man-made, artificially produced, or SYNTHETIC ELEMENTS. There are several ways of designating an isotope. One designation consists of the name or symbol of the element followed by a hyphen and the mass number of the isotope; thus, the isotope of carbon with mass number 12 can be designated carbon-12 or C-12. The mass number is often written as a superscript, e.g., C^{12}; sometimes the atomic number is written as a subscript preceding the symbol, e.g., ${}_6C^{12}$. The IUPAC rules for nomenclature of inorganic chemistry state that the subscript atomic number and superscript mass number should both precede the symbol, e.g., ${}^{12}_{6}C$. Many isotopes were given special names and symbols when they were first discovered in natural radioactive decay series, e.g., uranium-235 was called actinouranium and represented by the symbol AcU. This practice is discouraged in the modern nomenclature except in the case of hydrogen. The isotopes hydrogen-2 and hydrogen-3 are usually called deuterium and tritium, respectively. Hydrogen-1, the most abundant isotope, has the name protium but is usually simply called hydrogen. Atoms are not very massive; a carbon atom weighs about 2×10^{-23} grams. Because atoms have so little mass, a unit much smaller than the gram is used. In the current system (adopted in 1960–61) the unit of atomic mass, called atomic mass unit (amu), is defined as exactly $1/12$ the mass of an atom of carbon-12. The ATOMIC WEIGHT of an element is the mean (weighted average) of the atomic masses of all the naturally occurring isotopes. Carbon has two principal naturally occurring isotopes, carbon-12 and carbon-13. Carbon-12, whose mass is defined as exactly 12 amu, constitutes 98.89% of naturally occurring carbon; carbon-13, whose mass is 13.00335 amu, constitutes 1.11%. (There are also small traces of the radioactive isotope carbon-14). The atomic weight of the element is determined by multiplying the percent abundance of each isotope by the atomic mass of the isotope, adding these products, and dividing by 100. Thus, for carbon, $[(98.89 \times 12.000) + (1.11 \times 13.00335)]\ /100 = 12.01115$, which is the atomic weight of the element carbon in amu. Certain synthetic elements exist only momentarily in the form of a few short-lived isotopes; in such cases the concept of atomic weight cannot be applied. Many elements (e.g., helium) occur as single atoms. Other elements occur as molecules made up of more than one atom. Elements that ordinarily occur as diatomic molecules include hydrogen, nitrogen, oxygen, and the halogens. Oxygen also occurs as a triatomic form called ozone. Phosphorus usually occurs as a tetratomic molecule, and crystalline sulfur occurs as molecules containing eight atoms. The chemical properties of an element are due to the distribution of electrons around the nucleus, particularly the outer, or valence, electrons; it is these electrons that are involved in chemical reactions. Chemical reaction does not affect the nucleus; the atomic number therefore remains unchanged in a chemical reaction. For this reason an element is often defined as a substance that cannot be decomposed into simpler substances by chemical means. (By chemical means a substance can be decomposed into its constituent elements, but no further simplification can be achieved.) An element can, however, be decomposed into simpler substances (such as protons and neutrons or various combinations of them) by the methods of nuclear physics, e.g., by bombardment of the nucleus. Some properties of an element can be observed only in a collection of atoms or molecules of the element. These properties include color, density, melting point, boiling point, and thermal and electrical conductivity. While some of these properties are due chiefly to the electronic structure of the element, others are more closely related to properties of the nucleus, e.g., mass number. Properties of an element are sometimes classed as either chemical or physical. Chemical properties are usually observed in the course of a chemical reaction, while physical properties are observed by examining a sample of the pure element. The elements are sometimes grouped according to their properties. One major classification of the elements is as METALS, NONMETALS, and metalloids. Elements with very similar chemical properties are often referred to as families; some families of elements include the halogens, the inert gases, and the alkali metals. In the PERIODIC TABLE the elements are arranged in order of increasing atomic weight in such a way that the elements in any column have similar properties.

History. Some elements have been known since antiquity. Gold ornaments from the Neolithic period have been discovered. Gold, iron, copper, lead, silver, and tin were used in Egypt and Mesopotamia before 3000 B.C. However, recognition of these metals as chemical elements did not occur until modern times. The Greek philosophers proposed that there are basic substances from which all things are made. Empedocles proposed four basic "roots," earth, air, fire, and water, and two forces, harmony and discord, joining and separating them. Plato called the roots *stoicheia* (elements). He thought that they assume geometric forms and are made up of some more basic but undefined matter. A different theory, that of Leucippus and his followers, held that all matter is made up of tiny indivisible particles (*atomos*). This theory was rejected by Aristotle, who expanded on Plato's theory. Aristotle believed that different forms (*eidos*) were assumed by a basic material, which he called *hulê*. The *hulê* had four basic properties, hotness, coldness, dryness, and moistness. The four elements differ in their embodiment of these properties; fire is hot and dry, earth cold and dry, water cold and moist, and air hot and moist. Although Aristotle proposed that an element is "one of those simple bodies into which other bodies can be decomposed and which itself is not capable of being divided into others," he thought the metals to be made of water, and called mercury "silver water" (*chutos arguros*). His idea that matter was a single basic substance that assumed different forms led to attempts by the alchemists to transmute other metals into gold. Although much early work was done in chemistry, especially with metals, and many recipes were recorded, there were few developments in the conception of the elements. In the 16th cent. Paracelsus proposed salt, mercury, and sulfur as three "principles" of which bodies were made, although he apparently also believed in the four "elements." Van Helmont (c.1600) rejected the four elements and three principles, substituting two elements, air and water. Robert Boyle rejected these early theories and proposed a definition of chemical elements that led to the currently accepted definition. His definition is strikingly similar to Aristotle's earlier definition. In *The Sceptical Chymist* (1661) Boyle wrote, "I now mean by elements . . . certain primitive and simple, or perfectly unmingled bodies; which not being made of any other bodies, or of one another, are the ingredients of which all those called perfectly mixed bodies [chemical compounds] are immediately compounded, and into which they are ultimately resolved." Whereas Aristotle and other early philosophers tried to determine the identity of the elements solely by reason, Boyle and later scientists used the results of numerous experiments to identify the elements. In 1789, Antoine Lavoisier published a list of chemical elements based on Boyle's definition; this encouraged adoption of standard names for the elements. Although some of his elements are now known to be compounds, they were accepted as elements since they could not be decomposed by any method then known. In 1803, John Dalton proposed (as part of his ATOMIC THEORY) that all atoms of an element have identical properties (including mass), that these atoms are unchanged by chemical action, and that atoms of different elements react with one another in simple proportions. Although symbols for some of the elements already existed, they were by no means universally accepted, and each compound also had a unique symbol that was unrelated to its chemical composition. Dalton devised a new set of circular symbols for the elements and used a combination of elemental symbols to represent a compound. For example, his symbol for oxygen was O, and for hydrogen ⊙. Since he thought water contained one atom of hydrogen for every atom of oxygen, he formed the symbol for water by writing the symbols for hydrogen and oxygen touching one another, ⊙O. J. J. Berzelius was the first to use the modern method, letting one or two letters of the element's name serve as its symbol. He also published an early table of atomic weights of 24 elements with most values very close to those now in use. As noted above, some of the elements were discovered in prehistoric times but were not recognized as elements. Arsenic was discovered around 1250 by Albertus Magnus, and phosphorus was discovered about 1674 by Hennig Brand, an alchemist, who prepared it by distilling human urine. Only 12 elements were known before 1700, and only about twice that many by 1800, but by 1900 over 80 elements had been identified. In 1919, Ernest Rutherford found that hydrogen was given off when nitrogen was bombarded with alpha particles. This first transmutation encouraged further study of nuclear reactions, and eventually led to the discovery in 1937 of technetium, the first synthetic element. Neptunium (atomic number 93) was the first TRANSURANIUM ELEMENT to be synthesized (1940). Its discovery prompted the search that led to the discovery of other transuranium elements.

ELEMENTS*

Element	Symbol	At. No.	Element	Symbol	At. No.
actinium	Ac	89	mercury	Hg	80
aluminum	Al	13	molybdenum	Mo	42
americium	Am	95	neodymium	Nd	60
antimony	Sb	51	neon	Ne	10
argon	Ar	18	neptunium	Np	93
arsenic	As	33	nickel	Ni	28
astatine	At	85	niobium	Nb	41
barium	Ba	56	nitrogen	N	7
berkelium	Bk	97	nobelium	No	102
beryllium	Be	4	osmium	Os	76
bismuth	Bi	83	oxygen	O	8
boron	B	5	palladium	Pd	46
bromine	Br	35	phosphorus	P	15
cadmium	Cd	48	platinum	Pt	78
calcium	Ca	20	plutonium	Pu	94
californium	Cf	98	polonium	Po	84
carbon	C	6	potassium	K	19
cerium	Ce	58	praseodymium	Pr	59
cesium	Cs	55	promethium	Pm	61
chlorine	Cl	17	protactinium	Pa	91
chromium	Cr	24	radium	Ra	88
cobalt	Co	27	radon	Rn	86
copper	Cu	29	rhenium	Re	75
curium	Cm	96	rhodium	Rh	45
dysprosium	Dy	66	rubidium	Rb	37
einsteinium	Es	99	ruthenium	Ru	44
erbium	Er	68	samarium	Sm	62
europium	Eu	63	scandium	Sc	21
fermium	Fm	100	selenium	Se	34
fluorine	F	9	silicon	Si	14
francium	Fr	87	silver	Ag	47
gadolinium	Gd	64	sodium	Na	11
gallium	Ga	31	strontium	Sr	38
germanium	Ge	32	sulfur	S	16
gold	Au	79	tantalum	Ta	73
hafnium	Hf	72	technetium	Tc	43
helium	He	2	tellurium	Te	52
holmium	Ho	67	terbium	Tb	65
hydrogen	H	1	thallium	Tl	81
indium	In	49	thorium	Th	90
iodine	I	53	thulium	Tm	69
iridium	Ir	77	tin	Sn	50
iron	Fe	26	titanium	Ti	22
krypton	Kr	36	tungsten	W	74
lanthanum	La	57	uranium	U	92
lawrencium	Lr	103	vanadium	V	23
lead	Pb	82	xenon	Xe	54
lithium	Li	3	ytterbium	Yb	70
lutetium	Lu	71	yttrium	Y	39
magnesium	Mg	12	zinc	Zn	30
manganese	Mn	25	zirconium	Zr	40
mendelevium	Md	101			

* Each element is discussed in a separate article. See also PERIODIC TABLE.

elementary particles, tiny bits of MATTER assumed to be the most basic constituents of the universe. Certain elementary particles combine to form an ATOM, which is the basic unit of any chemical ELEMENT and from which all forms of matter are built up. An elementary particle is distinguished from other particles, such as an alpha particle or a deuteron, in that the latter particles can be understood as combinations of two or more elementary particles (the alpha particle, for example, is formed from four elementary particles—two protons and two neutrons). The first elementary particle to be discovered was the ELECTRON, identified in 1897 by J. J. Thomson. After the NUCLEUS of the atom was discovered in 1911 by Ernest Rutherford, the nucleus of ordinary hydrogen was recognized as the second elementary particle and was named the PROTON. In 1932 the third basic particle in an atom, the NEUTRON, was discovered. An atom was seen to consist of a central nucleus—containing protons and, except for ordinary hydrogen, neutrons—surrounded by orbiting electrons. However, other elementary particles not found in ordinary atoms immediately began to appear. In 1928 the relativistic QUANTUM THEORY of P. A. M. Dirac hypothesized the existence of a positively charged electron, or positron, which is the ANTIPARTICLE of the electron; it was first detected in 1932. Difficulties in explaining beta decay (see RADIOACTIVITY) led to the prediction of the NEUTRINO in 1930, and by 1934 the existence of the neutrino was firmly established in theory (although it was not actually detected until 1956). With the discovery of the positron and the neutrino, it became apparent that material particles could be created and destroyed. As a result, another particle was added to the list: the PHOTON, which had been first suggested by Einstein in 1905 as part of his quantum theory of the PHOTOELECTRIC EFFECT. The photon is the basic particle composing light and other ELECTROMAGNETIC RADIATION. Although the photon has no mass, always travels at the speed of light, and is easily created or destroyed, it became apparent that it must be considered an elementary particle. The next particles discovered were related to attempts to explain the strong FORCE binding nucleons (protons and neutrons) together in an atomic nucleus. In 1935, Hideki Yukawa suggested that a MESON (a charged particle with a mass intermediate between those of the electron and the proton) might be exchanged between nucleons. The meson emitted by one nucleon would be absorbed by another nucleon; this would produce a strong force between the nucleons, analogous to the force produced by the exchange of photons between charged particles interacting through the electromagnetic force. The following year a particle of approximately the required mass (about 200 times that of the electron) was discovered and named the mu meson (see MUON). However, its behavior did not conform to that of the theoretical particle. In 1947 the particle predicted by Yukawa was finally discovered and named the pi meson, or PION. Both the muon and the pion were first observed in COSMIC RAYS. Further studies of cosmic rays turned up more particles: another meson, named the K meson, or kaon; neutral particles called V particles because a V-shaped track is left in a CLOUD CHAMBER when they decay into two oppositely charged particles (the V particles themselves leave no tracks because they are uncharged); and an assortment of other particles known as "strange" particles. By the 1950s these particles were also being observed in the laboratory as a result of particle collisions produced by a PARTICLE ACCELERATOR. As the list of particles and antiparticles grew, four basic categories of particles were distinguished according to their behavior. These classes correspond roughly to different ranges of mass as well, but there is some overlap in the mass ranges, and mass is not the basic criterion. The behavior associated with each class of particles can be described with reference to the interactions or forces experienced by those particles and the type of quantum STATISTICS that apply to the particles. Four distinct types of forces or interactions exist in nature: gravitational, electromagnetic, strong nuclear, and weak nuclear; a given particle experiences certain of these forces, while it may be immune to others. The gravitational force is experienced by all particles. The electromagnetic force is experienced only by charged particles, although it is transmitted by the photon, which has no charge. The strong nuclear force is responsible for the structure of the nucleus. Particles that participate in the strong nuclear interaction or force are called hadrons and include the proton and neutron and the pion that binds them together in nuclei; the new J, or ψ (psi), particles, discovered in 1974; and also many other particles of higher mass. Other particles, including the electron, muon, and neutrino, do not participate in the strong nuclear interactions but only in the weak nuclear interactions associated with particle decay; the charged electron and muon also experience the electromagnetic force. Two types of statistics are used to describe particles. The Fermi-Dirac statistics apply to those particles restricted by the Pauli EXCLUSION PRINCIPLE, which applies not only to the electron energy levels in an atom but also to the nucleon energy levels in a nucleus; particles obeying the Fermi-Dirac statistics are known as fermions. Two fermions are not allowed to occupy the same quantum state. The Bose-Einstein statistics describe all particles not covered by the exclusion principle, and such particles are known as bosons. The number of bosons in a given quantum state is not restricted. In general, fermions compose nuclear and atomic structure, while bosons act to transmit forces between fermions. A given particle is placed in one of the four basic classes by considering first whether or not it experiences the strong force and second whether or not it is restricted by the exclusion principle (i.e., whether it is a fermion or a boson). Of the four classes of particles, the smallest is that of the massless bosons, which are not strongly interacting. This class includes the photon and one hypothetical particle, the graviton, suggested as the carrier of the gravitational force (see GRAVITATION). The LEPTON class includes the fermions that are not strongly interacting: the electron, positron, negative and positive muons, and the neutrino or antineutrino associated with each of these particles—a total of eight particles. The meson class comprises bosons that do interact strongly; they are more massive than the leptons but generally less massive than the proton and neutron, although some mesons are heavier than these particles. The mesons are the "glue" that holds nuclei together. By far the largest class of particles is the BARYON class, which contains fermions that interact strongly; the lightest members of the baryon class are the proton and neutron, and the heavier members are known as hyperons. In the meson and baryon classes are included a number of particles that cannot be detected directly because their lifetimes are so short that they leave no tracks in a cloud chamber or BUBBLE CHAMBER. These particles are known as resonances, or resonance states, because of an analogy between their manner of creation and the resonance of an electrical circuit. In addition to the four categories based on behavior, further order in particle interactions can be seen by application of various CONSERVATION LAWS. Some of these apply both to elementary particles and to large-scale objects, such as the laws governing the conservation of mass-energy, linear momentum, angular momentum, and charge. Other conservation laws have meaning only on the level of particle physics, including the two conservation laws for leptons, which govern members of the electron family and the muon family, respectively, and the law governing members of the baryon class. New quantities have been invented to explain certain aspects of particle behavior. For example, the relatively slow decay of kaons, lambda hyperons, and some other particles led physicists to the conclusion that some conservation law prevented these particles from decaying rapidly through the strong interaction; instead they decayed through the weak interaction. This new quantity was named "strangeness" and is conserved in both strong and electromagnetic interactions, but not in weak interactions. Thus, the decay of a strange particle into nonstrange particles, e.g., the lambda baryon into a proton and pion, can proceed only by the slow weak interaction and not by the strong interaction. Another quantity explaining particle behavior is related to the fact that many particles occur in groups, called multiplets, in which the particles are of almost the same mass but differ in charge. The proton and neutron form such a multiplet. The new quantity describes mathematically the effect of changing a proton into a neutron, or vice versa, and was given the name *isotopic spin*. This name was chosen because the total number of protons and neutrons in a nucleus determines what ISOTOPE the atom represents and because the mathematics describing this quantity are identical to those used to describe ordinary spin (the intrinsic angular momentum of elementary particles). Isotopic spin actually has nothing to do with spin, but is represented by a VECTOR that can have various orientations in an imaginary space known as isotopic spin space. Isotopic spin is conserved only in the strong interactions. Closely related to conservation laws are three SYMMETRY principles that apply to changing the total circumstances of an event rather than changing a particular quantity. The three symmetry operations associated with these principles are: charge conjugation (C), which is equivalent to exchanging particles and antiparticles; parity (P), which is a kind of mirror-image symmetry involving the exchange of left and right; and time-reversal (T), which reverses the order in which events occur. According to the symmetry principles (or invariance principles), performing one of these symmetry operations on a possible particle reaction should result in a second reaction that is also possible. However, it was found in 1956 that parity is not conserved in the weak interactions, i.e., there are some possible particle decays whose mirror-image counterparts do not occur. Although not conserved individually, the combination of all three operations performed successively does result in a particle reaction that is possible; this law is known as the CPT theorem. One successful theory of elementary particles uses the various conservation laws to group particles into supermultiplets, containing up to 10 different particles in some cases. This theory has been called the "eight-fold way" because the baryon supermultiplet containing the nucleons and the meson supermultiplet containing the pion both have eight members. The theory is based on a specialized type of modern algebra that deals with objects known as special unitary (SU) groups, the different applications to particle theory being known as SU-3 symmetry, SU-6 symmetry, and so on. One theory has proposed that the particles now known are combinations of a still more fundamental particle called the quark. Unlike the particles now studied, quarks have fractional charges of one third or two thirds of the basic charge of the electron or proton. A rival theory holds that efforts to find ever more basic components of matter are not truly fruitful. Known as the bootstrap theory, it is geared toward the development of a self-consistent, self-contained description of all possible particle interactions without regard to questions about the fundamental nature of the particles. See C. N. Yang, *Elementary Particles* (1962); K. W. Ford, *The World of Elementary Particles* (1963).

elementary school: see SCHOOL.

Eleph (ē'lĕf), town, near Jerusalem. Joshua 18.28.

elephant, largest living land mammal, found in tropical regions of Africa and Asia. Elephants have massive bodies and heads, thick, pillarlike legs, and broad, short padded feet, with toes bearing heavy, hooflike nails. The gray skin is loose, tough, thick, and nearly hairless. The slender tail ends in a tuft of hair. The upper lip and nose are prolonged into a flexible trunk, or proboscis, reaching nearly to the ground; this sensitive appendage is used for picking up food and other objects and for drawing up water. Elephants drink by sucking water into the trunk and squirting it into the mouth; they also use the trunk to spray themselves with water and with dust. The trunk produces a variety of noises, including a loud trumpeting. The large, thin, floppy ears provide an extensive cooling surface; the animal flaps its ears vigorously when it is overheated. The upper incisor teeth are elongated into tusks—highly valued for their IVORY—which the animal uses for digging up roots and tubers. A gland between the eye and the ear periodically produces an oily substance called musth; during these periods the animal is in an excitable, dangerous condition, also called musth, meaning madness. Such a condition occurs more often in males than in females and is thought to be a state of sexual excitement. Elephants are browsing animals, feeding on fruits, leaves, shoots, and tall grasses; they consume hundreds of pounds of food a day and drink up to 50 gal (190 liters) of water. They have no fixed living place, but travel about in herds of up to 100 animals, led by a young, strong male and including young bulls (males), cows (females), and calves. Old males are generally solitary or live in small groups. A rogue elephant is a solitary old male that has become violent and dangerous. During the mating season, elephant pairs may live away from the herd for a few weeks. A single calf is born after a gestation of 18 to 22 months and is nursed for 5 years. Elephants reach maturity at between 15 and 25 years of age; their lifespan is usually 60 or 70 years. Elephants walk at a pace of about 4 mi (6.4 km) per hr, but can charge at speeds of 30 mi (48 km) per hr. They cannot jump and so cannot pass barriers too wide or too high to step over; they swim well, however. There are two species: the Indian elephant, *Elephas maximus,* found in India and SE Asia, and the African elephant, *Loxodonta africana,* found in Africa S of the Sahara. African bull elephants may reach a shoulder height of 13 ft (4 m) and weigh 6 to 8 tons (5400–7200 kg). Their tusks are more than 10 ft (3 m) long and weigh up to 200 lbs (90 kg) each. Females are somewhat smaller and have more slender tusks. African elephants have enormous ears, measuring up to 42 in. (107 cm) in diameter. The long, conspicuously wrinkled trunk terminates in two fleshy, fingerlike protuberances, used for handling objects. The Indian bull elephant reaches about 9 ft (2.7 m) in shoulder height and weighs about 3.5 tons (3200 kg); its tusks are up to 6 ft (180 cm) long. The female of this species has no tusks. The ears of the Indian elephant are much smaller than in the African species, and the trunk somewhat shorter and smoother, ending in a single protuberance. Elephants are regarded as among the most intelligent of mammals and can be trained to work and to perform. Indian elephants are extensively used as beasts of burden, especially in teak forests, where they carry logs with their trunks. They are not considered truly domesticated as they do not breed well in captivity; young animals are captured from the wild. Training and handling take skill, as elephants have complex emotions and vary individually in temperament. African elephants are often said to be less tractable, but they too were formerly used for work, as well as for warfare. Hannibal's army crossed the Alps using African elephants, which were at that time probably found in the Atlas Mts. Elephants seen in zoos and circuses are usually of the Indian species, although the famous Jumbo, who toured the United States in the late 19th cent. giving rides to children, was an African elephant. In Thailand and Burma, albino elephants have long been held sacred. Elephants have been extensively hunted for food and for ivory, and their numbers are now greatly reduced; however, they are now afforded protection in certain areas. They are the only living representatives of their order, which was once widespread over most of the world; it included the MAMMOTH and the MASTODON. Elephants are classified in the phylum CHORDATA, subphylum Vertebrata, class Mammalia, order Proboscidae, family Elephantidae. See S. K. Sikes, *The Natural History of the African Elephant* (1971); V. J. Maglio, *Origin and Evolution of the Elephantidae* (1973).

Elephanta (ĕlĭfăn'tə), island, c.2 sq mi (5.2 sq km), in Bombay harbor, Maharashtra state, W India. It is noted for six Brahmanic caves, carved (8th cent.) from solid rock some 250 ft (76 m) above sea level. The Great Cave, the largest (130 ft/40 m long), contains gigantic pillars supporting its roof and colossal statuary, especially the famous three-headed bust of the Hindu god Siva. The caves are much visited by Hindu pilgrims. The statue of an elephant, now removed to Bombay city, gives the island its English name. The Indian name is Gharapuri.

elephant bird, extinct, flightless bird of the family Aepyornithidae. Once native to the island of Madagascar, these gigantic birds may have survived until as late as 1649. Today, they are known only from bone specimens and a few well-preserved eggs. In appearance they are thought to have resembled monstrous ostriches, with the largest reaching heights of up to 10 ft (305 cm) and weighing perhaps as much as 1,000 lb (455 kg). Their eggs, the largest single cells in the animal kingdom, measured up to 13 in. (33 cm) in length and held a liquid content estimated at two gallons (7.5 liters). It is quite possible that the creation of the legendary roc of the Arabian nights was based on discoveries of such eggs or even on distant memories of the elephant bird, for, if the roc legend did not originate in Madagascar, it has long been localized there by tradition. The largest of the elephant birds, *Aepyornis maximus,* was also the heaviest of all known birds. Elephant birds probably became extinct at the same time as the moas. Elephant birds are classified in the phylum CHORDATA, subphylum Vertebrata, class Aves, order Aepyornithiformes, family Aepyornithidae.

Elephant Butte Dam, main unit of the Rio Grande project of the U.S. Bureau of Reclamation on the Rio Grande, SW N.Mex.; completed 1916. The dam, with its large reservoir, is used for flood control, power production (24,300-kw capacity), and irrigation. The project was involved in a water-rights dispute between the United States and Mexico that was settled by a treaty in 1906.

elephantiasis (ĕl'əfăntī'əsĭs), abnormal enlargement of any part of the body due to obstruction of the lymphatic channels in the area (see LYMPHATIC SYSTEM). In tropical countries the most common cause is a disease called filariasis, which results from infestation with *Filaria,* a small roundworm introduced into the body by many species of mosquitoes. The adult worms live in the lymphatic system or the connective tissues, causing local inflammation and hardening of the tissues, usually in the legs, arms, scrotum, or breast. Recovery from filariasis is possible, although any elephantiasis that develops during the disease cannot be cured; surgery sometimes helps. Mosquito control is instrumental in holding down its incidence. Blocking of the lymph channels and elephantiasis can also result from lymphogranuloma venereum, a venereal disease.

Elephantine (ĕl″əfăntī′nē), island, SE Egypt, in the Nile below the First Cataract, near Aswan. In ancient times it was a military post guarding the southern frontier of Egypt. The Elephantine papyruses, which date from the 5th cent. B.C. and describe a colony of Jewish mercenaries, were found there. Surviving ruins are extensive. The ancient nilometer, built to gauge the water level of the Nile, was restored in 1870.

elephant seal or **sea elephant,** a true SEAL of the genus *Mirounga.* It is the largest of the fin-footed mammals, or pinnipeds, exceeding even the walrus in size. Males commonly reach a length of 18 ft (5.5 m) and a weight of 5,000 lb (2,270 kg); the female may reach a length of 10 ft (3 m). The male is distinguished by a flabby snout about 18 in. (45 cm) long. The snout is normally pendant but becomes inflated with air when the animal is excited or angry; release of the air produces a deep roar. Elephant seals sleep on ocean beaches by day and feed at night; their diet consists of small fish, shellfish, squid, and some seaweed. On land they move clumsily, but they are swift and graceful in the water, where they descend to great depths in search of food. There is a northern species, *Mirounga angustirostris,* and a southern species, *M. leonina.* The northern species formerly inhabited the Pacific coast of California and Mexico, but because its blubber was highly valued it was hunted almost to extinction in the 19th century. In 1911 the Mexican government extended protection to the single remaining *M. angustirostris* colony on Guadalupe Island off Baja California; in recent years the species has returned to the Santa Barbara Islands off California, where it is protected by the U.S. government and is increasing in numbers. The southern species is circumglobal in range and is fairly widespread on subantarctic islands. Elephant seals are classified in the phylum CHORDATA, subphylum Vertebrata, class Mammalia, order Carnivora, suborder Pinnipedia, family Phocidae.

elephant's-ear: see ARUM.

elephant's-foot: see YAM.

Elets: see YELETS, USSR.

Eleusinian Mysteries (ĕlyo͞osĭn′ēən), principal religious MYSTERIES of ancient Greece. The mysteries may have originated as part of an early agrarian festival peculiar to certain families in Eleusis. The Athenians later (c.600 B.C.) took over the ceremonies. Because the mysteries were secret, little is known of them. Presumably fasting and ritual purification in the sea took place before the large procession from Athens to Eleusis. The rites, which fundamentally celebrated the abduction and return of Persephone, symbolized the annual cycle of death and rebirth in nature as well as the immortality of the soul. It was believed that they had originally been instituted in Eleusis by Persephone's mother, Demeter. Dionysus was also much honored. The festival at Eleusis, known as the Greater Mysteries, was celebrated in the early fall, at sowing time. Another festival, the Lesser Mysteries, was held in the early spring at Agrae. See G. E. Myloras, *Eleusis and the Eleusinian Mysteries* (1962, repr. 1969).

Eleusis (ĭlo͞o′sĭs), ancient city of Attica, Greece, 12 mi (20 km) NW of Athens. Through ancient times it was the seat of the ELEUSINIAN MYSTERIES. There was a large temple to Demeter. The Eleusinian games, also held there, were not connected with the mysteries. Excavation of the cemetery began in 1952; graves were found that date from the 7th and 8th cent. B.C. The temple and a type of theater with rock-cut seats for about 3,000 spectators were uncovered near the modern village of Eleusis.

Eleuthera: see BAHAMA ISLANDS.

elevation, height of a point on the earth above a datum plane, usually mean SEA LEVEL. The elevation of a feature is calculated through such surveying techniques as trigonometric triangulation, aerial photogrammetry, or, less accurately, barometric leveling. Elevation is represented on maps by different colors, by pictures, by printing the map on a piece of plastic, molded to show the shapes of hills and valleys in three dimensions, or, most precisely, by drawing CONTOURS of equal elevation, whose pattern delineates the landforms.

elevator, in aviation: see AIRPLANE.

elevator, in machinery, device for transporting people or goods from one level to another. The term is applied to the enclosed structures as well as the open platforms used to provide vertical transportation in buildings, large ships, and mines; it is also applied to devices consisting of a continuous belt or chain with attached buckets for handling bulk materials. Simple hoists were used from ancient times. From about the middle of the 19th cent., power elevators, often steam-operated, were used for conveying materials in factories, mines, and warehouses. In 1853 the American inventor Elisha G. Otis demonstrated a freight elevator equipped with a safety device to prevent falling in case a supporting cable should break. This increased public confidence in such devices and served as an impetus to the industry. Otis established a company for manufacturing elevators and patented (1861) a steam elevator. After the introduction by Sir William Armstrong of the hydraulic crane (1846), the hydraulic principle was applied to the elevator, and in the early 1870s hydraulic machines began to replace the steam-powered elevator. The hydraulic elevator is supported by a heavy piston, moving in a cylinder and operated by the water (or oil) pressure produced by pumps. As improvement of design made increased speed of movement possible, various safety devices, such as speed governors, were developed. Toward the end of the 19th cent., electric elevators came into use, and operation by electric motor gradually became the chief method. Later improved safety devices were added, and automatic and partly automatic elevators were introduced. Increase in speed of operation and improvement in general design also characterize the more modern elevators.

elf, in Germanic mythology, a type of fairy. Usually represented as tiny people, elves are said to dwell in forests, in the sea, and in the air. Although they can be friendly to man, they are more frequently vengeful and mischievous.

Elgar, Sir Edward William, 1857–1934, English composer. He received his early training from his father who was an organist, music seller, and amateur violinist. In 1885 he succeeded his father as organist of St. George's Church, Worcester. Music composed in 1897 for Queen Victoria's diamond jubilee brought him public recognition. Among his outstanding compositions are *Variations on an Original Theme* (1899; known as *Enigma Variations*); *The Dream of Gerontius* (1900), a cantata using Cardinal Newman's poem as a text; and the Violin Concerto in B minor. His most popular works are his five *Pomp and Circumstance* marches (1901–30), the first of which is the famous *Land of Hope and Glory.* Elgar's style, influenced by German romanticism, is marked by a majestic grandeur and sure musical craftsmanship. He was knighted in 1904 and became Master of the King's Music in 1924. See selected letters ed. by P. M. Young (1965); biographies by P. M Young (1955), Michael Kennedy (1968); J. F. Porte, (1921, repr. 1970), and Rosa Burley and F. C. Carruthers (1972).

Elgin, James Bruce, 8th **earl of** (ĕl′gĭn), 1811–63, British statesman, son of the 7th earl. He served as governor of Jamaica (1842–46) and in 1847 was appointed governor general of Canada. There he put into operation the proposals for responsible government outlined by his father-in-law, the earl of DURHAM. Elgin improved education and helped the Canadian economy, which was depressed by the new British policy of free trade. After personally negotiating the reciprocity treaty of 1854 with the United States, he returned to England. He later negotiated (1857–60) British trade agreements with China and Japan. Shortly before his death he was appointed governor general of India. See biographies by W. P. Kennedy (1926) and J. L. Morrison (1928, repr. 1970). His son, **Victor Alexander Bruce,** 9th **earl of Elgin,** 1849–1917, was viceroy of India (1894–99) during an extremely troubled period in that country's history and served as colonial secretary from 1905 to 1908.

Elgin, Thomas Bruce, 7th **earl of,** 1766–1841, British diplomat. He served on diplomatic missions to Vienna, Brussels, Berlin, and Constantinople. While in Constantinople (1799–1803), he arranged for the so-called ELGIN MARBLES to be brought to England. He was succeeded by his son James Bruce, who became the 8th earl.

Elgin, royal burgh (1971 pop. 16,401), county town of Morayshire, NE Scotland, on the Lossie River. Lossiemouth is its port. Elgin is the market town for Morayshire's farm belt. Whiskey and woolen textiles are manufactured. It became the cathedral town for the see of Moray in 1224, when Elgin Cathedral was founded. Called "the Lantern of the North," the cathedral was reputedly Scotland's finest piece of early Gothic architecture. Its ruins still stand. The ruins of Spynie Palace, seat of the bishops of Moray until the 17th cent., are nearby. Gordonstoun School, N of Elgin, was attended by Philip, Duke of Edinburgh, and Charles, Prince of Wales. In 1975, Elgin became part of the new Grampian region.

Elgin (ĕl′jĭn), city (1970 pop. 55,691), Cook and Kane counties, NE Ill., on the Fox River; inc. 1854. Elgin is a railroad, trade, and industrial city and the home of the Elgin watch factories. Among other manufactures are household appliances, gaskets, electrical and electronic equipment, paper products, precision instruments, and machinery. Judson College and a junior college are there.

Elgin Marbles (ĕl′gĭn), ancient sculptures taken from Athens to England in 1806 by Thomas Bruce, 7th earl of Elgin. The PARTHENON frieze by Phidias, a CARYATID, and a column from the ERECHTHEUM were sold to the British government in 1816 and are now on view in the British Museum, in a gallery donated by Lord Duveen.

Elginshire, Scotland: see MORAYSHIRE.

Elgon, Mount (ĕl′gŏn), extinct volcano, central Africa, on the Kenya-Uganda border. Its highest peak is Wagagai (14,178 ft/4,321 m). The inhabitants of Mt. Elgon's lower slopes cultivate arabica coffee, tea, bananas, and millet.

El Greco: see GRECO, EL.

Elhanan (ĕlhā′nən). **1** One of David's mighty men. 2 Sam. 23.24; 1 Chron. 11.26. **2** Israelite. 2 Sam. 21.19; 1 Chron. 20.5.

Eli (ē′lī), high priest and judge of Israel, teacher of the boy Samuel. 1 Sam. 1–4; 1 Kings 2.27; 1 Chron. 24.3.

Eli, Eli, lama sabachthani? (ē′lī, lā′mə săbăk′thənī; ā′lē, lä′mä säbäkh′thänē) or **Eloi, Eloi, lama sabach-thani?** (ē′loi; ā′loi) [*Eli, Eloi:* Heb. or Aramaic,=Lord; *lama sabachthani?:* Aramaic,=why hast thou forsaken me?], in the Gospel (Mat. 27.46; Mark 15.34), words of Jesus on the cross. The Greek text retains and translates the original, which is seemingly a quotation of Ps. 22.1.

Eliab (ēlī′ăb). **1** Chief of the tribe of Zebulun. Num. 1.9; 2.7; 7.24,29; 10.16. **2** Father of DATHAN. **3** Brother of David. 1 Sam. 16.6; 17.13,28; 1 Chron. 2.13. Elihu: 1 Chron. 27.18. **4** Musician of David. 1 Chron. 15.18,20; 16.5. **5** A follower of David. 1 Chron. 12.9. **6** The same as ELIHU **1.**

Eliada (ēlī′ədə). **1** Son of David. 2 Sam. 5.16; 1 Chron. 3.8. Beeliada: 1 Chron. 14.7. **2** Officer under Jehoshaphat. 2 Chron. 17.17.

Eliadah (ēlī′ədə), father of Rezon. 1 Kings. 11.23.

Eliah (ēlī′ə). **1** Benjamite. 1 Chron. 8.27. **2** Jew who had a foreign wife. Ezra 10.26.

Eliahba (ēlī′əbə), one of David's guard. 2 Sam. 23.32; 1 Chron. 11.33.

Eliakim (ēlī′əkĭm). **1** King of Judah: see JEHOIAKIM. **2** Important officer of state under King Hezekiah. 2 Kings 18.17–37; 19.1–5; Isa. 22.20–25; 36; 37.1–5. **3** Priest at the dedication of the new wall at Jerusalem. Neh. 12.41. **4, 5** Names appearing in the Gospel genealogies. Mat. 1.13; Luke 3.30.

Eliam (ēlī′ăm). **1** Father of Bath-sheba. 2 Sam. 11.3. Ammiel: 1 Chron. 3.5. **2** One of David's warriors. 2 Sam. 23.34.

Elias (ēlī′əs), Greek form of ELIJAH.

Eliasaph (ēlī′əsăf). **1** Tribal chief of Gad. Num. 10.20. **2** Head Gershonite. Num. 3.24.

Eliashib (ĭlī′əshĭb). **1** High priest. Neh. 3.1,20,21; 12.10,22,23; 13.4,7; Ezra 10.6. **2** Priest under David. 1 Chron. 24.12. **3** Descendant of David. 1 Chron. 3.24. **4, 5, 6** Men who had foreign wives. Ezra 10.24,27,36.

Eliathah (ēlī′əthə), temple musician. 1 Chron. 25.4,27.

Elidad (ēlī′dăd), Benjamite. Num. 34.21.

Eliel (ē′lĭēl). **1** Manassite chief. 1 Chron. 5.24. **2** The same as ELIHU **1. 3, 4** Benjamites. 1 Chron. 8.20,22. **5, 6, 7** Mighty men of David. 1 Chron. 11.46,47; 12.11. **8, 9** Levites. 1 Chron. 15.9,11; 2 Chron. 31.13.

Elienai (ē″lĭē′nāī), Benjamite chief. 1 Chron. 8.20.

Eliezer (ĕlĭē′zər, ĕlĭē′-). **1** Servant of Abraham. Gen. 15.2. **2** Son of Moses. Ex. 8.4; 1 Chron. 23.15,27; 26.25. **3** Prophet who rebuked King Jehoshaphat. 2 Chron. 20.37. **4** Benjamite. 1 Chron. 7.8. **5** Priest under David. 1 Chron. 15.24. **6** Chief Reubenite. 1 Chron. 27.16. **7** Messenger of Ezra. Ezra 8.16. **8, 9, 10** Men who had taken foreign wives. Ezra 10.18,23,31. **11** Man in the Gospel genealogy. Luke 3.29.

Elihoenai (ĕl″ĭhōē′nāī). **1** Korahite doorkeeper. 1 Chron. 26.3. **2** Leader in the return with Ezra. Ezra 8.4.

Elihoreph (ĕl″īhō′rĕf), scribe of Solomon. 1 Kings 4.3.

Elihu (ĕlī′hyo͞o). **1** Ancestor of Samuel. 1 Sam. 1.1. Eliab: 1 Chron. 6.27. Eliel: 1 Chron. 6.34. **2** One of Job's comforters. Job 32.2–37.24. **3** The same as ELIAB **3**. **4** Manassite captain of David. 1 Chron. 12.20. **5** Korahite doorkeeper. 1 Chron. 26.7.

Elijah (ĕlī′jə) or **Elias** (ēlī′əs) [both: Heb., = Jahweh is God], fl. c.875 B.C., Hebrew prophet in the reign of King AHAB. He is one of the outstanding figures of the Old Testament. Elijah's mission was to destroy the worship of foreign gods and to restore justice. His zeal brought about a temporary banishment of idolatry (see JEZEBEL). His story has many incidents—his raising the widow's son from the dead; his contest of faith with the priests of Baal, resulting in his triumph and their death; his being fed by ravens; his experience of the still, small voice on Mt. Horeb; and his departure from earth in a chariot of fire enveloped in a whirlwind. His disciple was ELISHA. Unlike the other great prophets, Elijah and Elisha left no written records. In Jewish tradition, Elijah is the herald of the Messiah. John the Baptist and Jesus were asked if they were the incarnation of the prophet. He appeared in the Transfiguration. He is prominent in the Koran. Mendelssohn composed an oratorio, *Elijah*. 1 Kings 17–19; 21.17–29; 2 Kings 1–2; Mal. 4.5; Mat. 11.14; 16.14; 17.3; Luke 4.25; John 1.21; James 5.17. An Elijah is mentioned among the Jews who came back after the Exile. Ezra 10.21.

Elijah ben Solomon, 1720–97, Jewish scholar, called the Gaon of Vilna, b. Lithuania. Although he was a student of the cabala, he fought the spread of Hasidism among the Jews of Lithuania and Poland because he feared that the creation of these new groups would weaken the Jewish community. His many influential works include commentaries on the Old Testament, the Mishnah, the Talmud, the Midrash, the cabala, and particularly upon the halakah, which he held as being of supreme importance for Jewish life. See study by Louis Ginzberg (1920).

Elika (ĕlī′kə), one of David's men. 2 Sam. 23.25.

Elikón: see HELICON, mountains, Greece.

Elim (ē′lĭm), oasis where the Israelites halted. Ex. 15.27; Num. 33.9.

Elimelech (ēlĭm′ēlĕk), Naomi's husband. Ruth 1.2,3; 2.1,3; 4.3,9.

Elioenai (ĕl″īōē′nāī). **1** One of the house of David. 1 Chron. 3.23,24. **2** Simeonite. 1 Chron. 4.36. **3** Benjamite. 1 Chron. 7.8. **4,5** Men who had taken foreign wives. Ezra 10.22,27. **6** Priest. Neh. 12.41.

Eliot, Charles William, 1834–1926, American educator and president of Harvard Univ., b. Boston, grad. Harvard, 1853. In 1854 he was appointed tutor in mathematics at Harvard and in 1858 became assistant professor of mathematics and chemistry. In 1863, Eliot went abroad for two years' study, returning to become professor of chemistry at the new Massachusetts Institute of Technology. Two articles on "The New Education: Its Organization," published in the *Atlantic Monthly*, were in part responsible for Eliot's election in 1869 to the presidency of Harvard. The corporation's choice of a layman and a scientist, coupled with the fact of Eliot's youth, aroused some opposition. Under Eliot's 40-year administration, Harvard developed from a small college with attached professional schools into a great modern university. Several notable reforms were introduced in the college: the elective system was extended, the curriculum was enriched through the addition of new courses, written examinations were required, the faculty was enlarged, and strict student discipline was relaxed in favor of flexible regulations. Increased entrance requirements prevailed both in the college and in the professional schools, which Eliot reformed and revitalized. The courses of study were radically revised, and the standards for professional degrees were raised with the able cooperation of such men as Christopher C. Langdell, dean of the law school. New schools were established, including the Bussey Institution (agriculture), schools of applied science, the graduate school of arts and sciences, and the school of business administration. Eliot also supported Elizabeth Cary Agassiz in her project to establish a women's college and then fostered the development of Radcliffe College, which was affiliated with Harvard. He was greatly interested in secondary education, and as chairman of the Committee of Ten, appointed in 1892 by the National Education Association, he was influential in securing a greater degree of uniformity in high school curriculums and college entrance requirements. After Eliot's resignation in 1909 he turned to public affairs. He had been a strong advocate of civil service reform for many years and was a member of the General Education Board and a trustee of the Carnegie Foundation for the Advancement of Teaching. Among his published works are *The Durable Satisfactions of Life* (1910, repr. 1969), which presents his religious and ethical views, and *The Conflict between Individualism and Collectivism in a Democracy* (1910, repr. 1967). His most important papers written before 1914 are reprinted in two volumes, edited by W. A. Neilson, under the title *Charles W. Eliot, the Man and His Beliefs* (1926), and those since 1914 in *A Late Harvest* (1924), edited by M. A. De Wolfe Howe. See biography by Henry James (1930); S. E. Morison, *The Development of Harvard University, 1869–1929* (1930); Hugh Hawkins, *Between Harvard and America: The Educational Leadership of Charles W. Eliot* (1972). In 1901 he wrote a biography of his son **Charles Eliot,** 1859–97, a landscape architect, who established a reputation through his work in planning the park system of Greater Boston.

Eliot, George, pseud. of **Mary Ann** or **Marian Evans,** 1819–80, English novelist, b. near Nuneaton, Warwickshire. She is considered one of the great English novelists. Reared in a strict evangelical atmosphere, she eventually rebelled and renounced religion totally. Her early schooling was supplemented by assiduous reading, and the study of languages led to her first literary work, *Life of Jesus* (1846), a translation from the German of D. F. Strauss. After her father's death she became subeditor (1851) of the *Westminster Review*, contributed articles, and came to know many of the literary people of the day. In 1854 she began a long and happy union with G. H. LEWES, which she regarded as marriage, though it involved social ostracism and could have no legal sanction because Lewes's estranged wife was living. Throughout his life Lewes encouraged Mary Ann Evans in her literary career; indeed, it is possible that without him Mary Ann, subject to periods of depression and in constant need of reassurance, would not have written a word. In 1856, Mary Ann began *Scenes of Clerical Life*, a series of realistic sketches first appearing in *Blackwood's Magazine* under the pseudonym Lewes chose for her, George Eliot. Although not a popular success, *Scenes of Clerical Life* was well received by literary critics, particularly Dickens and Thackeray. Three novels of provincial life followed—*Adam Bede* (1859), *The Mill on the Floss* (1860), and *Silas Marner* (1861). She visited Italy in 1860 and again in 1861 before she brought out in the *Cornhill Magazine* (1862–63) her historical romance *Romola*, a story of Savonarola. *Felix Holt* (1866), a political novel, was followed by *The Spanish Gypsy* (1868), a dramatic poem. *Middlemarch* (1871–72), a portrait of life in a provincial town, is considered her masterpiece. She wrote one more novel, *Daniel Deronda* (1876); the satirical *Impressions of Theophrastus Such* (1879); and verse, which was never popular and is now seldom read. Lewes died in 1878, and in 1880 she married a close friend of both Lewes and herself, John W. Cross, who later edited *George Eliot's Life as Related in Her Letters and Journals* (3 vol., 1885–86). Writing about life in small rural towns, George Eliot was primarily concerned with the responsibility that people assume for their lives and with the moral choices they must inevitably make. Although highly serious, her novels are marked by compassion and humor. See her letters (ed. by G. S. Haight, 7 vol., 1954–56); her collected essays (ed. by Thomas Pinney, 1964); biographies by Lawrence Hanson and Elizabeth Hanson (1952) and G. S. Haight (1968); studies by E. S. Haldane (1927), Jerome Thale (1959), Barbara Hardy (1967), David Carroll, ed. (1971), and T. S.Pearce (1973).

Eliot, Sir John, 1592–1632, English parliamentary leader. He was a staunch defender of parliamentary liberties. Eliot instituted (1626) the impeachment proceedings against Charles I's favorite, the 1st duke of BUCKINGHAM, and joined Sir Edward COKE and others in promoting the PETITION OF RIGHT, which was presented to the king in 1628. In 1629 he read a protest in the House of Commons against arbitrary taxation and the advance of "popery," while the speaker was held in the chair by force in defiance of the king's order of adjournment. Eliot was committed to the Tower of London and, refusing to submit to the authority of the king, was left to die in prison. See biography by Harold Hulme (1957).

Eliot, John, 1604–90, English missionary in colonial Massachusetts, called the Apostle to the Indians. Educated at Cambridge, he was influenced by Thomas Hooker, became a staunch Puritan, and emigrated from England. Arriving in Boston in 1631, he became teacher at the church in Roxbury in 1632 and held that position the rest of his life. He studied the Indian language spoken around Roxbury and was soon preaching in it. His determination to Christianize the Indians led him to establish villages for the converts—the "praying Indians"—with simple civic and religious organization. He won the aid of the colonial authorities and achieved the founding in England of the Society for the Propagation of the Gospel in New England under the auspices of Parliament. Funds and workers came to him, and he and his helpers founded some 14 communities on lands granted for the purpose. The most prominent and successful was at Natick. King Philip's War (1675–76) caught the "praying Indians" between the hostile tribes and the Indian-hating whites and all but wiped them out. White settlements took over most of the villages. The pamphlets by Eliot and, even more, his translation of the Bible into an Algonquian Indian language usually called Natick (1661–63; the first Bible printed in the United States) and his *Indian Primer* (1669) are prime sources of later knowledge of the peoples of Massachusetts. Eliot also helped to write the *Bay Psalm Book*. See biographies by Convers Francis (1849), repr. 1969), Carleton Beals (1957), and O. E. Winslow (1968).

Eliot, Thomas Stearns, 1888–1965, English poet and critic, b. St. Louis, Mo. One of the most distinguished literary figures of the 20th cent., T. S. Eliot won the 1948 Nobel Prize in Literature. He studied at Harvard, the Sorbonne, and Oxford. In 1914 he established residence in London and in 1927 became a British subject. After working as a teacher and a bank clerk he began a publishing career; he was assistant editor of the *Egoist* (1917–19) and edited his own quarterly, the *Criterion* (1922–39). In 1925 he was employed by the publishing house of Faber and Faber, eventually becoming one of its directors. His early poetical works—*Prufrock and Other Observations* (1917), *Poems* (1920), and *The Waste Land* (1922)—express the anguish and barrenness of modern life and the isolation of the individual, particularly as reflected in the failure of love. These early works, particularly *The Waste Land*, compelled immediate critical attention. Unique, complex, employing myths, religious symbolism, and literary allusion, they signified a complete break with the poetic tradition of the 19th century. Their models were the METAPHYSICAL POETS, Dante, the Jacobean dramatists, and the French symbolists, and their meter ranged from the sublimely lyrical to the conversational. In Eliot's later poetry, notably *Ash Wednesday* (1930) and the *Four Quartets* (1935–42), he turned from spiritual desolation to hope for man's salvation. Acceptance of religious faith as a solution to man's dilemma was expressed in the poet's espousal of Anglo-Catholicism in 1927. Eliot was an influential critic, combining literary and social criticism in a fashion that earned him comparison with Matthew Arnold. His outstanding critical works are contained in such volumes as *The Sacred Wood* (1920), *For Lancelot Andrewes* (1928), *The Use of Poetry and the Use of Criticism* (1933), *Elizabethan Essays* (1934), *Essays Ancient and Modern* (1936), and *Notes towards a Definition of Culture* (1948). Eliot's plays attempt to revitalize verse drama and usually treat the themes of his poetry within the framework of a conventional West End drama. They include *Murder in the Cathedral* (1935), dealing with the final hours of Thomas à Becket; *The Family Reunion* (1939); *The Cocktail Party* (1950); *The Confidential Clerk* (1954); and *The Elder Statesman* (1959). His complete poems and plays appeared in 1969. See biographies by Bernard Bergonzi (1971) and Robert Sencourt (1971, repr. 1973); studies by D. E. Jones (1960), Carol Smith (1963), E. M. Browne (1969), J. D. Margolis (1972), A. W. Litz (1973), and Linda Wagner (1974); bibliography by Donald Gallup (rev. ed. 1969).

Eliott, George Augustus, 1st **Baron Heathfield of Gibraltar,** 1717–90, British general. Appointed (1775) governor of Gibraltar, he was forced to defend it against a combined Spanish and French siege that lasted three and a half years (1779–83). For this memorable defense he was raised to the peerage in 1787. His name also appears as Elliott.

Eliphal (ĕl′ĭfăl, ēlī′fəl), the same as ELIPHELET **4.**

Eliphalet (ēlĭf′əlĕt), name of two sons of David. 2 Sam. 5.16; 1 Chron. 14.7. Eliphelet: 1 Chron. 3.6,8. Elpalet: 1 Chron. 14.5.

Eliphaz (ĕl′ĭfăz, ēlī′-). **1** Son of Esau and father of Teman. Gen. 36.4,10–16; 1 Chron. 1.35,36. **2** Temanite, a comforter of Job. Job 2.11; 4; 15; 22; 42.9.

Elipheleh (ēlĭf′ĕlē), harpist before the Ark. 1 Chron. 15.18,21.

Eliphelet (ēlĭf'əlĕt). **1, 2** The same as ELIPHALET. **3** Companion of Ezra. Ezra 8.13. **4** One of David's mighty men. 2 Sam. 23.34. Eliphal: 1 Chron. 11.35. **5** Benjamite. 1 Chron. 8.39. **6** One who had married a foreign wife. Ezra 10.33.

Elis (ē'lĭs), region of ancient Greece, in W Peloponnesus, W of Arcadia. It was divided into three parts—Elis proper, Pisatis, and Triphylia. A plain watered by the Alpheus and the Peneus rivers, Elis was notable as a place for breeding horses and growing flax. The Olympic games were held at OLYMPIA. Other important cities were Pisa and Elis. The Elians were early allied with the Spartans but fell out with them in 420 B.C. As a result, Elis lost (399 B.C.) Triphylia. Elis declined after the Olympic games were suppressed in the 4th cent. A.D.

Elisabeth: see ELIZABETH.

Elisabethville, Zaïre: see LUBUMBASHI.

Elisha (ēlī'shə) or **Eliseus** (ĕlĭsē'əs), Hebrew prophet. He continued the work of ELIJAH. Where Elijah had been aggressive, Elisha gained his objectives through a diplomatic use of his powers. With few exceptions his miracles show a milder nature—the raising of the dead boy, the healing of the Syrian captain Naaman, the timely aid to the poor widow in debt. Unlike Elijah, he had many disciples and probably had a fixed residence (Gilgal, Samaria). Far more is recorded of him than of Elijah. 1 Kings 19.16–21; 2 Kings 2; 13.14–21; Luke 4.27.

Elishah (ēlī'shə), unidentified geographical name in the Bible. Gen. 10.4; Ezek. 27.7.

Elishama (ēlĭsh'əmə). **1** Chief Ephraimite. Num. 1.10; 1 Chron. 7.26. **2, 3** Sons of David. 1 Chron. 3.6,8; 14.7; 2 Sam. 5.16. One is called Elishua twice. 2 Sam. 5.15; 1 Chron. 14.5. **4** Judahite. 1 Chron. 2.41. **5** Grandfather of ISHMAEL **6.** **6** Scribe. Jer. 36.11–21. **7** Priest under Jehoshaphat. 2 Chron. 17.8.

Elishaphat (ēlĭsh'əfăt), one of the leaders who aided Jehoiada to place Joash on the throne. 2 Chron. 23.1.

Elisheba (ēlĭsh'əbə) [Heb.,=worshiper of God; Elizabeth is a Greek form], Aaron's wife. Ex. 6.23.

Elishua (ēlī'shōōə, ĕl''ĭshōō'ə), son of David: see ELISHAMA **2.**

Eliud (ēlī'əd), in the Gospel genealogy. Mat. 1.14.

Elizabeth, Saint, mother of John the Baptist and kinswoman of the Virgin Mary. Luke I. Feast: Nov. 5.

Elizabeth, Saint, 1207–31, daughter of King Andrew II of Hungary and wife of Landgrave Louis II of Thuringia. She is called St. Elizabeth of Hungary. She led a simple life, personally tended the sick and the poor, and spent long hours at prayer. After the death of her husband (1227) she saw to it that her children's welfare was taken care of and retired to a small cottage near Marburg. There, under the spiritual direction of CONRAD OF MARBURG, she led an austere life. St. Elizabeth died at the age of 23. Feast: Nov. 19.

Elizabeth, 1837–98, empress of Austria and queen of Hungary. A Bavarian princess, she was married (1854) to her cousin, Emperor Francis Joseph. Despite her exceptional beauty, intelligence, and kindness she led an unhappy domestic life, which was marred, moreover, by family tragedies (notably the death of her only son, Archduke RUDOLF, and the death of one of her sisters in the charity bazaar fire in Paris, 1897). Independent and unconventional, she avoided the stiff etiquette of the Viennese court and spent much of her time abroad, chiefly on Corfu. She was assassinated by the Italian anarchist Luccheni in Geneva, Switzerland. See biographies by E. C. Corti (tr. 1936) and Joan Haslip (1965).

Elizabeth, 1709–62, czarina of Russia (1741–62), daughter of Peter I and Catherine I. She gained the throne by overthrowing the young czar, IVAN VI, and the regency of his mother, ANNA LEOPOLDOVNA. Her coup d'etat was made possible by her popularity with the imperial guards, who hated the German favorites of Anna Leopoldovna. Elizabeth herself, armed, led the bloodless revolution. Violently anti-German and guided in her foreign policy by her chancellor, A. P. BESTUZHEV-RYUMIN, Elizabeth rid Russia of German influence. She victoriously sided against Frederick II of Prussia in the SEVEN YEARS WAR, but her death and the accession of her nephew, Peter III, took Russia out of the war and made Frederick's ultimate victory possible. During her reign the nobles acquired more power over their serfs and gained a dominant position in local government, while the terms of service they owed the state were shortened. The Univ. of Moscow and the Academy of Fine Arts in St. Petersburg were founded during her reign.

Elizabeth, 1596–1662, queen of Bohemia, daughter of James I of England. Her beauty attracted most of the royal suitors of Europe (she was nicknamed the "Queen of Hearts"), but she was married (1613) to Frederick V, elector palatine (see FREDERICK THE WINTER KING) in order to cement an alliance between English and German Protestantism. She became queen of Bohemia in 1619, when her husband accepted the crown offered by the Bohemian diet. After Frederick was defeated (1620) in the battle of the White Mt., Elizabeth took up her residence in Holland, where she courageously endured privation and misfortune. She received little support from abroad, even from her son Charles Louis, who was restored to the Palatinate in 1648. In 1661 she returned to England against the wishes of King Charles II, who, however, pensioned her. Among her children were Prince RUPERT; Princess Elizabeth, who was the patroness of Descartes; and SOPHIA, who was electress of Hanover and mother of George I of England.

Elizabeth I, 1533–1603, queen of England (1558–1603). The daughter of HENRY VIII and Anne BOLEYN, she was declared illegitimate just before the execution of her mother in 1536, but in 1544 Parliament reestablished her in the succession after her half brother, Edward (later Edward VI), and her half sister, Mary (later MARY I). Elizabeth was well educated by a series of tutors, most notably Roger ASCHAM. In 1553 she supported the claims of Mary I over Lady Jane Grey. After Mary was crowned, Elizabeth was careful to avoid implication in the plot of the younger Sir Thomas WYATT (1554). Nevertheless, since Elizabeth's potential succession to the throne inevitably furnished a rallying point for discontented Protestants, she was imprisoned. She later regained a measure of freedom through outward conformity to Roman Catholicism.

Politics. When Elizabeth succeeded her sister to the throne in 1558, religious strife, a huge government debt, and failures in the war with France had brought England's fortunes to a low ebb. At her death 45 years later, England had passed through one of the greatest periods of its history—a period that produced William SHAKESPEARE, Edmund SPENSER, Francis BACON, Walter RALEIGH, Martin FROBISHER, Francis DRAKE, and other notable figures in literature and exploration; a period that saw England, united as a nation, become a major European power with a great navy; a period in which English commerce and industry prospered and English colonization was begun. Elizabeth came to the throne with the Tudor concept of strong rule and the realization that effective rule depended upon popular support. She was able to select and work well with the most competent of counselors. Sir William Cecil (Lord BURGHLEY) was appointed immediately, and Sir Francis WALSINGHAM in 1573. One of her first acts was to reestablish Protestantism (see ENGLAND, CHURCH OF) through the acts of Supremacy and Uniformity (1559). The measures against Roman Catholics (see PENAL LAWS) grew harsher over the course of her reign, particularly after the rebellion of the Catholic earls of NORTHUMBERLAND and WESTMORLAND (1569), Elizabeth's excommunication by the pope (1570), and the coming of the Jesuit missionaries (1580). But the persecution of the Catholics was due, at least in part, to a series of plots to murder Elizabeth and seat the Catholic MARY QUEEN OF SCOTS on the throne. English Puritans, like the Catholics, objected to the Established Church, and a severe law against conventicles in 1593 kept the separatist movement underground for the time. At the beginning of her reign, Elizabeth's government enacted needed currency reforms and took steps to mend English credit abroad. Other legislation of the reign dealt with new social and economic developments—the Statute of Apprentices (1563) to stabilize labor conditions; the poor laws (1563–1601) to attempt some remedy of widespread poverty; and various acts to encourage agriculture, commerce, and manufacturing.

Foreign Affairs and the Spanish War. Elizabeth had many suitors, including King PHILIP II of Spain; FRANCIS, duke of Alençon and Anjou; and her own favorite, Robert Dudley, earl of LEICESTER. For a combination of personal and political reasons, she was reluctant to choose a husband and remained unmarried, although she often used the lure of marriage as a weapon of diplomacy. Elizabeth engaged in a long series of diplomatic maneuvers against England's old enemy, France, and the new enemy, Spain, but for 30 years she managed to keep the country at peace. In 1559 she concluded a treaty ending her sister's unfortunate war with France and refused the marriage offer of Philip of Spain. The next year the Treaty of Edinburgh initiated a policy toward Scotland, successful in the long run, of supporting the Protestant lords against the Catholic party. By lending unofficial aid to French HUGUENOTS she managed for some time to harass France and Spain without involving England in an actual war. As part of her marriage negotiations she later supported the duke of Alençon's participation in the Dutch war against Spain. The major problem posed by Elizabeth's refusal to marry was that of the succession. The chief claimant was Mary Queen of Scots, but her Catholicism made her a threat to Elizabeth. In 1568 after Mary's forced abdication from the Scottish throne, Elizabeth gave her refuge, but then kept her prisoner for nearly 19 years. Despite the numerous plots, both real and alleged, on Mary's behalf, Elizabeth resisted until 1587 her counselors' advice that Mary be executed. By that time Spain had emerged as England's main enemy. English seamen had been unofficially encouraged to encroach on Spanish monopolies and raid Spanish shipping. In 1588, Philip launched the long-planned expedition of the Spanish ARMADA as a great Catholic crusade against Protestant England. The Armada was defeated by the skill of such leaders as John Hawkins and Francis Drake and by storms, rather than planning on Elizabeth's part, but the victory strengthened English national pride and lowered the prestige of Spain. An indecisive war with Spain dragged on until Elizabeth's death. From the beginning of the reign Ireland had been the scene of civil wars and severe rebellions, culminating with that of the earl of TYRONE, which was suppressed by the campaigns of Lord Mountjoy from 1600 to 1603.

Declining Years. After the Armada, Elizabeth's popularity began to wane. Parliament became less tractable and began to object to the abuse of royally granted monopolies. The rash uprising of Elizabeth's favorite, Robert Devereux, 2d earl of ESSEX, darkened her last years. She refused until on her deathbed to name her successor—the son of Mary Queen of Scots, James VI of Scotland, who became James I of England. Although Elizabeth has been accused, with some justice, of being vain, fickle, vacillating, prejudiced, and miserly, she was nonetheless exceedingly successful as a queen. Endowed with immense personal courage and a keen awareness of her responsibility as a ruler, she commanded throughout her reign the unwavering respect and allegiance of her subjects. See biographies by J. E. Neale (1934, repr. 1957), Theodore Maynard (1940), Elizabeth Jenkins (1958) and Paul Johnson (1974); J. B. Black, *The Reign of Elizabeth* (1936); A. L. Rowse, *The England of Elizabeth* (1950) and *The Expansion of Elizabethan England* (1955); J. E. Neale, *Elizabeth I and Her Parliaments* (2 vol., 1953 and 1957); Joel Hurstfield, *Elizabeth I and the Unity of England* (1960); Neville Williams, *The Life and Times of Elizabeth I* (1972) and *All the Queen's Men* (1972); Alison Plowden, *The Catholics under Elizabeth I* (1973).

Elizabeth II, 1926–, queen of Great Britain and Northern Ireland (1952–), elder daughter and successor of George VI. During World War II she was trained as a junior subaltern (second lieutenant) in the women's services and was a skilled truck driver and mechanic. On Nov. 20, 1947, she married Philip Mountbatten, duke of EDINBURGH. In 1951 they visited Canada and the United States, and they were in Kenya (en route for a tour of Australia and New Zealand) when the king died (Feb. 6, 1952) and Elizabeth succeeded to the throne. Her coronation took place on June 2, 1953. Later in the year (Nov., 1953–May, 1954) the queen made a 173-day tour of the Commonwealth. Other state visits have included return trips to Canada and the United States in 1957 and in 1959, when she joined President Eisenhower in opening the Saint Lawrence Seaway, and numerous trips to the Commonwealth nations and many European countries. Elizabeth has four children: Prince CHARLES, Princess ANNE, Prince Andrew (b. 1960), and Prince Edward (b. 1964).

Elizabeth, 1843–1916, queen of Rumania, consort of King Carol I, whom she married in 1869. Of German birth, she was the daughter of Hermann, prince of Wied. She completely identified herself with her adopted people and devoted herself to their cultural development. Under the pseudonym Carmen Sylva the queen wrote extensively and with almost equal facility in German, French, English, and Rumanian. She collaborated on several books with her lady-in-waiting, Mite Kremnitz. Among her chief works are *Pensées d'une reine* [a queen's thoughts] (1882) and an English collection of Rumanian folk tales, *The Bard of Dimbovitza* (1891).

Elizabeth, 1900–, queen consort of George VI of Great Britain, mother of Elizabeth II. The daughter of the 14th earl of Strathmore, she was known as

Lady Elizabeth Bowes-Lyon until her marriage (1923) to George, then duke of York.

Elizabeth, 1764–94, sister of King Louis XVI of France, known as Madame Elizabeth. Deeply loyal to her brother, she remained in France during the French Revolution, suffered imprisonment, and was guillotined.

Elizabeth: see RUSSELL, MARY ANNETTE.

Elizabeth, city (1970 pop. 112,654), seat of Union co., NE N.J., on Newark Bay; inc. 1855. It is an important shipping and transportation area, with some of the world's largest containerized dock facilities. Elizabeth's manufactures include sewing machines, foundry products, cord, office supplies, chemicals, biscuits, toys, cans, swimming-pool equipment, and industrial valves. The area, purchased from Indians in 1664 and called Elizabethtown, included all of present-day Union co. It was the home and provincial capital of Gov. Philip Carteret and from 1668 to 1682, the meeting place of the province's assembly. Chartered as the town of Elizabeth in 1740, it was the scene of several Revolutionary clashes; many buildings were burned (1780). Among the old buildings that have survived are the 18th-century Elias Boudinot House and Belcher Mansion and the 17th-century Nathaniel Bonnell House. Early industries were tanning and brewing. In the 19th cent., Elizabeth's proximity to New York City and the coming of the railroad stimulated great industrial expansion, especially in machine production, oil refining, and shipbuilding. Goethals Bridge (1928) links Elizabeth with Staten Island. Alexander Hamilton and Aaron Burr lived for a while in Elizabeth, which was also the birthplace of Nicholas Murray Butler and Matthias W. Baldwin. A campus of Union College is in the city.

Elizabethan style (ĭlĭz"əbē'thən), in architecture and the decorative arts, a transitional style of the English Renaissance, which took its name from Queen Elizabeth's reign (1558–1603). During this period many large manor houses were erected by the court nobility. The plans and facades tended more toward symmetry, although there remained many of the characteristics of the TUDOR STYLE. The great hall of medieval manors was retained, and features were added that increased the occupants' comfort—a broad staircase, a long gallery connecting the wings of the house on the upper floors, withdrawing rooms, and bedrooms of greater size and importance. Examples of the great manors of the period are Longleat, Wiltshire; Wollaton Hall, Nottinghamshire; Kirby Hall, Northamptonshire; Montacute House, Somerset; and Hardwick Hall, Derbyshire. The houses were often designed by the owners themselves, who furnished ideas that were amplified by their mason or carpenter. The freemason Robert SMYTHSON is one of the earliest names associated with English architecture. From Flemish and Italian books the planners haphazardly adapted Renaissance, mannerist, and Flemish motifs, including columns, pilasters, lozenges, festoons, scrolls, and grotesque figures. No attempt was made to achieve the unified classical style of architecture that had already appeared in Italy and France. A greater unity was achieved in the subsequent JACOBEAN STYLE. In landscape design, formal gardens were developed with clipped boxwood and yews along balustraded terraces, which formed a finished setting for the great manors. In the houses of lesser gentry and yeomen, construction in the Gothic style continued, with the use of half-timber construction, leaded windows, and hammer-beam roofs. See J. Buxton, *Elizabethan Taste* (1963).

Elizabeth Charlotte of Bavaria, 1652–1722, German princess, called the Princess Palatine and also known as Charlotte Elizabeth; wife of Philippe I d'ORLÉANS, brother of King Louis XIV. She abjured the Protestant faith before her marriage (1671). The death of her brother, Elector Charles, provided Louis XIV with an opportunity to use her tenuous claims to part of the Palatinate as a pretext to expand French influence in that area, eventually contributing to the outbreak (1689) of the War of the Grand Alliance. Her frank and vigorous letters are a valuable source for the social history of her time. She was a friend and patron of Gottfried Wilhelm von Leibniz and mother of Philippe II d'Orléans, regent to King LOUIS XV. See her letters ed. by Maria Kroll (tr. 1970).

Elizabeth City, city (1970 pop. 14,069), seat of Pasquotank co., NE N.C., a port of entry on the Pasquotank River (which, with the Dismal Swamp Canal, forms part of the Intracoastal Waterway); settled mid-1600s, inc. 1793. It is the largest city in the Albemarle Sound area, and a trade and shipping center for the region's diversified farm products. Cabinets, textiles, wearing apparel, and lumber are manufactured. The major source of employment, however, is the large U.S. coast guard air station nearby. The area was first visited (1584) and mapped by a scouting expedition from Roanoke Island. The first General Assembly of Carolina met there in 1665. In the Civil War, Elizabeth City was occupied (1862) by Federal troops and burned. It is the seat of Elizabeth City State Univ., a junior college, and a Bible college.

Elizabeth Farnese (färnā'sā), 1692–1766, queen of Spain, second consort of PHILIP V; niece of Antonio Farnese, duke of Parma. Soon after her marriage (1714), arranged by Cardinal ALBERONI and the princesse des URSINS, she gained a strong influence over her weak husband and for some time, at first with Alberoni, virtually ruled Spain, though after 1743, Ensenada was the chief power in government. Her ambition to recoup Spanish losses incurred at the Peace of Utrecht and to secure Italian thrones for her children plunged Spain into several wars. As a result of a Spanish attack on Naples during the War of the POLISH SUCCESSION, her son Carlos (later Charles III of Spain) became king of Naples and Sicily in 1734. Though Carlos was obliged to give up Parma and Piacenza, which he had inherited (1731), this duchy passed (1748) to his brother Philip. Elizabeth retired from court upon the accession (1746) of her stepson, Ferdinand VI.

Elizabeth Islands, chain forming the southern boundary of Buzzards Bay; off SE Mass. Naushon is the largest island. Cuttyhunk Island was settled in 1641 and has a U.S. coast guard station. The islands are a popular resort.

Elizabeth of Valois (văl'wä, Fr. välwä'), 1545–68, queen of Spain, daughter of Henry II of France. Originally intended to wed Don CARLOS, son of Philip II of Spain, she was married (1559) to Philip himself. The unfounded legend of a tragic love between Elizabeth and Carlos is often found in literature, notably in Schiller's *Don Carlos.*

Elizabethton, city (1970 pop. 12,269), seat of Carter co., NE Tenn., on the Watauga River; inc. 1799. It is an industrial center where rayon is produced. There are manganese deposits in the area. The region was one of the earliest settled in Tennessee. In 1772 the WATAUGA ASSOCIATION was organized there; Sycamore Shoals Monument commemorates this event, the treaty Richard Henderson made with the Cherokee Indians in 1775, and the formation of a Revolutionary force that later took part in the battle of Kings Mountain.

Elizabethtown, city (1970 pop. 11,748), seat of Hardin co., central Ky.; inc. 1797. Among its manufactures are steel magnets, automobile hoses, and men's slacks. Points of interest include an old church (1789); the Lincoln Heritage House, built by Abraham Lincoln's father; and many antebellum homes. Fort Knox is nearby.

Elizabeth Woodville: see WOODVILLE, ELIZABETH.

Elizaphan (ēlĭz'əfăn, ĕlĭzā'-). **1** Aaron's cousin. Num. 3.30; 1 Chron. 15.8; 2 Chron. 29.13. Elzaphan: Ex. 6.22; Lev. 10.4. **2** Zebulunite. Num. 34.25.

Elizur (ēlī'zər), Reubenite prince. Num. 1.5; 2.10; 7.30–35; 10.18.

elk, name applied to several large members of the deer family. It most properly designates the largest member of the family, *Alces alces,* found in the northern regions of Eurasia and North America. In North America this animal is called MOOSE. The name elk is used in North America to designate a different animal, the WAPITI, closely related to the red deer of Europe. The prehistoric Irish elk, *Megaceros giganteus,* is still another species, related to the fallow deer. It was found in Europe and W Asia in Pleistocene times and had an 11-ft (3.3-m) antler span, the largest of any deer. All animals called elk are classified in the phylum CHORDATA, subphylum Vertebrata, class Mammalia, order Artiodactyla, family Cervidae.

Elkanah (ĕl'kānə, ĕlkā'nə). **1** Husband of Hannah and father of Samuel. 1 Chron. 6.27,34; 1 Sam. 1; 2.11,20,21. **2** Head of a Levitical family. Ex. 6.24. **3** One of David's mighty men. 1 Chron. 12.6. **4** Officer of Ahaz's household. 2 Chron. 28.7. **5** Doorkeeper of the Ark of the Covenant. 1 Chron. 15.23. **6, 7, 8** Levites. 1 Chron. 6.23,25,26,35; 9.16.

Elk Grove Village, village (1970 pop. 24,516), Cook and Du Page counties, NE Ill., a suburb of Chicago; inc. 1956. With a population of c.100 at the time of its establishment on open farmland, Elk Grove Village has grown dramatically, largely because of its industrial park. Its manufactures include electronic components, electrical equipment, and rubber products.

Elkhart, city (1970 pop. 43,152), Elkhart co., N Ind., at the confluence of the Elkhart and St. Joseph rivers; settled 1824, inc. 1877. Its manufactures include musical instruments, electrical equipment, and pharmaceuticals.

Elkhorn Tavern: see PEA RIDGE.

elkhound: see NORWEGIAN ELKHOUND.

Elkins, Stephen Benton, 1841–1911, American statesman, b. Perry co., Ohio. He grew up in Missouri and after the outbreak of the Civil War enlisted in the Union army, although his father and brother were Confederates. Admitted to the bar in 1864, he moved to New Mexico, where he practiced law, engaged in banking, and had a political career capped by service (1873–77) as territorial delegate to Congress. In 1890 he moved to Elkins, W. Va., where he and H. G. Davis founded Davis and Elkins College. Prominent in Republican politics, he was (1891–93) Secretary of War under Benjamin Harrison. As Senator from West Virginia (1895–1911), Elkins, who had extensive railroad holdings, was author of the Elkins Act of 1903 against the system of the REBATE, and co-author of the 1910 Mann-Elkins Act, extending the power of the Interstate Commerce Commission although he did not support the more drastic Hepburn Act of 1906. His son, **Davis Elkins,** 1876–1959, b. Washington, D.C., was also Senator (1911, 1919–25) from West Virginia. See biography of Stephen Elkins by O. D. Lambert (1955).

Elk Island National Park, 75 sq mi (194 sq km), central Alta., Canada, near Edmonton; est. 1913. It occupies a wooded rolling region in the midst of level farmland. The park is Canada's major fenced preserve for buffalo and other prairie animals. Numerous small lakes offer summertime recreation.

Elkoshite (ĕl'kəshīt), surname of Nahum, of unknown meaning. Nahum 1.1.

Elks, Benevolent and Protective Order of, fraternal and charitable society founded (1868) in New York City. Through the Elks National Foundation, located in Chicago, the group carries on a broad-ranging program of charity and welfare, helping to support such organizations as the Salvation Army, the Red Cross, and the Boy and Girl Scouts. The Elks also sponsors health, veterans, and college scholarship programs, as well as various local community service activities. The organization has about 1.5 million members in more than 2,000 local lodges. Its official organ, known as the *Elks Magazine,* is published monthly. Membership in the society, originally limited to whites, was opened to all male U.S. citizens in 1973.

Ellasar: see LARSA.

Ellenborough, Edward Law, 1st **earl of,** 1790–1871, British statesman; son of the 1st Baron Ellenborough. He served as president of the Board of Control of the East India Company (1828–30, 1834–35, 1841) and as governor general of India (1841–44). His main achievement was the annexation of Sind (1843). After his return to England he was created (1844) earl, was first lord of the admiralty (1846), and served again as president of the Board of Control (1858). See biography by A. H. Imlah (1939).

Ellenborough, Edward Law, 1st **Baron,** 1750–1818, British jurist and statesman. He achieved fame by his successful defense of Warren HASTINGS in the impeachment trial (1788–95), but his principal influence on England lay in his lifelong conservatism. As attorney general (1801) and lord chief justice (1802–18), he opposed CATHOLIC EMANCIPATION and supported the repressive measures against radicals.

Ellensburg, city (1970 pop. 13,568), seat of Kittitas co., central Wash., on the Yakima River; inc. 1886. It is the trade and processing center for a region in which cattle raising, logging, and diversified farming are carried on. Central Washington State College is there, and Ginkgo Petrified Forest, Wanapum Dam, a state game farm, and two state parks are nearby. An annual rodeo is held in Ellensburg.

Ellery, William, 1727–1820, political leader in the American Revolution, signer of the Declaration of Independence, b. Newport, R.I. While a member of the Continental Congress (1776–81, 1783–85), Ellery distinguished himself in committee work pertaining to naval and commercial affairs. See biography by W. M. Fowler, Jr. (1973).

Ellesmere, Francis Egerton, 1st **earl of** (ĕlz'mēr), 1800–1857, British politician, author, and philanthropist. His family name was originally Leveson-Gower, but he changed it on inheriting (1833) the estates of his great uncle, Francis Egerton, 3d duke of Bridgewater. In Parliament (1822–46) he supported the liberal Tory policies, becoming an early exponent of free trade. He served as secretary for Ireland (1828–30) and secretary for war (1830). He lent his influence and wealth to the support of many intellectual societies, and he enlarged the Bridgewater Collection of paintings and opened it to the public. His many writings include essays, translations, poems, and plays. He was created an earl in 1846.

Ellesmere, Thomas Egerton, Baron, 1540?–1617, jurist and statesman. A distinguished early career at law brought him appointment (1581) as solicitor general, and he became a favorite and adviser of Queen Elizabeth I. In 1592 he was appointed attorney general and in 1596 lord keeper of the great seal. A friend of Robert Devereux, 2d earl of ESSEX, he tried to curb the earl's impetuosity, was lenient to him at the time of his first trial (1600), but abandoned him after his rebellion (1601) and was a witness against him in the trial that resulted in his execution. On his accession in 1603, James I made Egerton Baron Ellesmere and lord chancellor. A staunch supporter of royal prerogative, he championed the courts of chancery and high commission against those of common law and helped to secure the dismissal (1616) of Sir Edward COKE. As a man of learning and an incorruptible judge, he was highly regarded by such contemporaries as Francis Bacon and Ben Jonson. John Donne was Egerton's secretary (1597–1601) and married his niece. Ellesmere was created Viscount Brackley in 1616.

Ellesmere Island, 82,119 sq mi (212,688 sq km), c.500 mi (800 km) long, in the Arctic Ocean, N Northwest Territories, Canada; second-largest and northernmost island of the Arctic Archipelago. It is separated from NW Greenland by a narrow passage. The island's coast is indented by deep fjords. The interior plateau rises more than 2,000 ft (610 m) above sea level; the United States Ranges, in the north, are c.11,000 ft (3,350 m) high. An ice cap covers most of the island's east side. In snow-free areas vegetation supports large herds of musk oxen. There are scientific stations and some Eskimo settlements on the island. First sighted by the British explorer William Baffin in 1616, Ellesmere Island was explored in the latter half of the 19th cent. Since the 1950s the island has been the site of many glaciological, geological, and geographical expeditions.

Ellesmere Port, municipal borough (1971 pop. 61,556), Cheshire, W central England, on the Manchester Ship Canal near its junction with the Shropshire Union Canal and the entrance into the Mersey estuary. It is an important oil-refining center and the distribution center for imported commodities such as iron ore and grain. The town also has dye works and various light industries.

Ellice Islands (ĕl'ĭs) or **Lagoon Islands,** group of atolls (1968 pop. 6,332), 9.5 sq mi (25 sq km), South Pacific, part of the British colony of the GILBERT AND ELLICE ISLANDS. The group includes nine islands: FUNAFUTI, Nanumea, Nanumanga, Nui, Niutao, Vaitupu, Nukufetau, Nukulaelae, and Niulakita. All are low coral atolls with pandanus and coconut groves. Copra is the chief export. The Polynesian natives engage mainly in farming and fishing; their language is called Ellice. Discovered in 1764 by Capt. John BYRON and made a British protectorate in 1892, the group was included in the Gilbert and Ellice Island colony in 1915. The United States claims sovereignty over Funafuti, Nukufetau, Nukulaelae, and Niulakita.

Ellington, Duke (Edward Kennedy Ellington), 1899–1974, American jazz musician and composer, b. Washington, D.C. Ellington made his first professional appearance as a jazz pianist in 1916. By 1918 he had formed a band, and after appearances in nightclubs in Harlem he became one of the most famous figures in American jazz. Ellington's orchestra, playing his own compositions and arrangements, achieved a fine unity of style and made many innovations in the jazz idiom. Many instrumental virtuosos worked closely with Ellington for long periods of time. His best-known short works are *Mood Indigo, Solitude,* and *Sophisticated Lady.* He also wrote jazz works of complex orchestration and ambitious scope for concert presentation, notably *Creole Rhapsody* (1932), *Black, Brown and Beige* (1943), *Liberian Suite* (1947), *Harlem* (1951), and *Night Creatures* (1955). Ellington made many tours of Europe, appeared in numerous jazz festivals and several films, and made hundreds of recordings. See his memoirs, *Music is My Mistress* (1973); biographies by Barry Ulanov (1946) and Stanley Dance (1970).

Elliott, Charles Loring, 1812–68, American painter, b. Scipio, Cayuga co., N.Y.; pupil of John Trumbull and John Quidor. His portraits number over 700. His principal works include the portraits of Matthew Vassar (Vassar); A. B. Durand (Corcoran Gall.); several governors of New York (City Hall, New York City); Fletcher Harper; Erastus Corning (state lib., Albany, N.Y.); James E. Freeman (National Acad. of Design, New York City); Caleb Gasper, Mrs. James C. Griswold, M. B. Brady, and a self-portrait (Metropolitan Mus.).

Elliott, George Augustus: see ELIOTT, GEORGE AUGUSTUS, 1ST BARON HEATHFIELD OF GIBRALTAR.

Elliott, Herbert James, 1938–, Australian athlete. After setting world junior records in the mile (1,605-m), 2-mile (3,211-m) and 3-mile (4,816-m) runs in 1957, Elliott became (1958) the world's leading miler, breaking the 4-minute barrier 10 times during that year. On Aug. 6, 1958, at Dublin, he set a new world record for the mile—3 min 54.5 sec. In a race held in Goteborg, Sweden, on Aug. 28, 1958, he also set the world record for the 1,500 meters (3 min 36 sec), which he lowered to 3 min 35.6 sec in the 1960 Olympic games at Rome. Shortly afterward he retired. See his *Golden Mile* (1960).

Elliott, Jesse Duncan, 1782–1845, American naval officer, b. Hagerstown, Md. In the War of 1812, he helped capture two British vessels on Lake Erie and was made commander of the lake. He began building the fleet that O. H. Perry was to use after he succeeded (1813) Elliott. In the battle of Lake Erie (1813), Elliott was second in command. His conduct in the battle brought about a brisk argument with Perry—giving rise to a controversy that was continued long after the death of both and is still not completely settled.

Elliott Lake, district (1971 pop. 9,093), S central Ont., Canada, W of Sudbury. It is the center of a large uranium-mining area.

ellipse, closed plane curve consisting of all points for which the sum of the distances between a point on the curve and two fixed points (foci) is the same. It is the CONIC SECTION formed by a plane cutting all the elements of the cone in the same nappe. The center of an ellipse is the point halfway between its foci. The major axis is the chord that passes through the foci. The minor axis is the chord that passes through the center perpendicular to the major axis. The *latus rectum* is the chord through either focus perpendicular to the major axis. The vertices are the two points of intersection of the major axis with the curve. The eccentricity of an ellipse, a ratio of two lengths, is a measure of its flatness; it is the distance from the center to either focus divided by the distance from the center to either vertex. The CIRCLE may be considered an ellipse of eccentricity zero, i.e., one in which the center and the two foci all coincide.

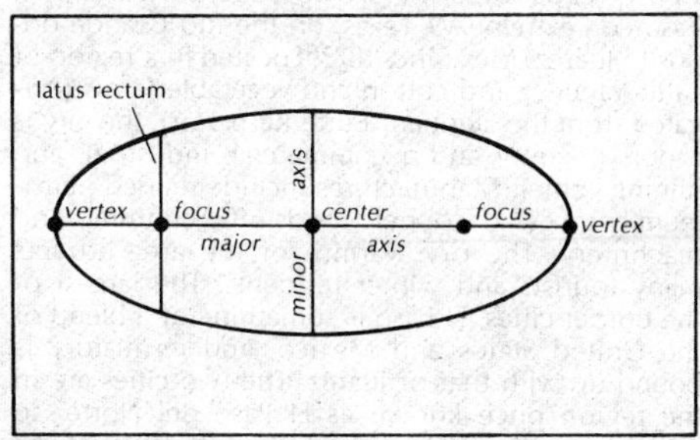

Ellipse

Ellis, Havelock (Henry Havelock Ellis), 1859–1939, English psychologist and author. He became a qualified physician but devoted himself to scientific study and writing. Although the first volume of the *Studies in the Psychology of Sex* (7 vol., 1897–1928; completed ed. 4 vol., 1936) was banned on charges of obscenity, the series—Ellis's major work—constituted a valuable contribution to the study of sex problems and had an important influence in changing the public attitude toward them. In 1891, Ellis married Edith Lees. The story of their marriage is the chief theme of his *My Life* (1940). His other works include, besides poems and essays, *A Study of British Genius* (1904), *The Dance of Life* (1923), and *Man and Woman* (rev. ed. 1934). See biographies by Isaac Goldberg (1926), Houston Peterson (1928), J. S. Collis (1959), and Arthur Calder-Marshall (1960).

Ellis, William, 1794–1872, English missionary, pioneer of printing in the Pacific. Sent in 1816 to Polynesia as a nonconformist missionary, he set up at Tahiti the first printing press in the South Seas. He developed a form of writing for the Hawaiian language, and included in his works valuable antiquarian materials on Polynesia. He also worked in Madagascar and wrote a history of that land.

Ellis Island, c.27 acres (10.9 hectares), in Upper New York Bay, SW of Manhattan island. Government property since 1808, it was long the site of an arsenal and a fort, but its most famous years were from 1892 until 1943, when it served as the chief immigration station of the country. Ellis Island is part of the Statue of Liberty National Monument (see NATIONAL PARKS AND MONUMENTS, table).

Ellison, Ralph, 1914–, American novelist, b. Oklahoma City, Okla. His literary reputation is based on one novel, *The Invisible Man* (1952), which is considered a classic of American literature. Drawing on the author's experiences, it details the harrowing progress of a nameless young black man trying to find a place for himself in a hostile society. Ellison has also published *Shadow and Act* (1964), essays on race, the artist, and society. Since 1970 he has been the Albert Schweitzer Professor in the Humanities at New York Univ. See John Hersey, ed., *Ralph Ellison: A Collection of Critical Essays* (1974).

Ellora (ĕlō'rə), village, E central Maharashtra state, India. Extending more than 1 mi (1.6 km) on a hill are 34 rock and cave temples (5th–13th cent.), most of them Hindu but some Buddhist and Jain. The most remarkable building is the great Kailasa temple, excavated on the instructions of the king Krishna I (reigned c.756–773). Dedicated to the god Shiva, who is enshrined as a giant lingam in the innermost sanctuary, the temple is a free-standing structure, carved like a statue from the surrounding hillside. The rear wall of its excavated courtyard (276 ft x 154 ft/84 m x 47 m) is 100 ft (30 m) high. The temple proper (164 ft x 109 ft/50 m x 33 m) was carved from a single mass of rock. The roof of its central hall is supported by 16 square columns. Mythological and animal figures are profusely carved on nearly all the surfaces. The temple is one of India's greatest architectural treasures.

Ellore, India: see ELURU.

Ellsworth, Elmer Ephraim, 1837–61, American Civil War hero, b. near Mechanicville, N.Y. Just before the Civil War he became famous for his Zouave company, which toured the North giving exhibition drills. A friend and law student of Lincoln, Ellsworth accompanied him to Washington in 1861. When war began, he recruited a regiment from the volunteer firemen in New York City. At Alexandria, Va., in May, 1861, he removed a Confederate flag from atop the Marshall House and was shot and killed by the proprietor. His sensational death was the first officer casualty on the Virginia front. See biography by R. P. Randall (1960).

Ellsworth, Henry Leavitt, 1791–1858, American agriculturist, b. Windsor, Conn., grad. Yale, 1810. His interests were varied. He was a lawyer, a businessman, and a farming enthusiast. In 1832 he made a trip west as one of the commissioners appointed to superintend the removal of the Indians to what is now Oklahoma. He was accompanied by Washington Irving, who recorded his impressions in *A Tour on the Prairies;* by C. J. Latrobe, an Englishman; and by the young comte de Pourtalès. Ellsworth's own account appears in *Washington Irving on the Prairie; or, A Narrative of a Tour of the Southwest in the Year 1832* (ed. by S. T. Williams and Barbara Simison, 1937). He served (1835–45) as commissioner of patents and worked to promote agricultural research and aid to farmers.

Ellsworth, Lincoln, 1880–1951, American explorer, b. Chicago, Ill. He was a surveyor and engineer in railroad building and later a prospector and mining engineer in NW Canada. Aided by the fortune left him by his father, he became the financial supporter and associate of Roald AMUNDSEN in his arctic aviation ventures. In 1925 they flew in the dirigible *Norge* N from Spitsbergen over the North Pole to Alaska, where Ellsworth distinguished himself by saving the lives of two companions. He was an observer in the 1931 flight of the *Graf Zeppelin* to Franz Josef Land and Northern Land. In 1936 he accomplished the first flight over Antarctica from the Weddell Sea to the Ross Sea, claiming 300,000 sq mi (777,000 sq km), named James W. Ellsworth Land, for the United States. In 1939 he flew into interior Antarctica from the Indian Ocean side, viewing and claiming for the United States 81,000 sq mi (209,790 sq km) of previously unseen land. It was named American Highland. With Amundsen he wrote *Our Polar Flight* (1925) and *First Crossing of the Polar Sea* (1927). His later books were *Search* (1932), *Exploring Today* (1935), and *Beyond Horizons* (1938).

Ellsworth, Oliver, 1745–1807, American political leader, third Chief Justice of the United States

(1796–99), b. Windsor, Conn. A Hartford lawyer, he was (1778–83) a member of the Continental Congress during the American Revolution. His great service was at the FEDERAL CONSTITUTIONAL CONVENTION, where he and Roger Sherman advanced the "Connecticut compromise," ending the struggle between large and small states over representation. He was also responsible for the term "United States" in the Constitution. As U.S. Senator (1789–96) from Connecticut, he framed the bill that set up the Federal judiciary. Ellsworth later served (1799–1800) as a commissioner to negotiate with the French government concerning the restrictions put on American vessels. See biography by W. G. Brown (1905, repr. 1970).

Ellwood City, industrial borough (1970 pop. 10,857), Beaver and Lawrence counties, W central Pa., near the Ohio line; inc. 1892. It has many metal products plants. Coal mines are in the area.

elm, common name for the Ulmaceae, a family of trees and shrubs chiefly of the Northern Hemisphere. Elm trees (genus *Ulmus*) have a limited use as hardwoods for timber, especially the rock or cork elm (*U. thomasi*). Tall and graceful, with fan-shaped crowns of finely subdividing branches and twigs, elms are widely planted as ornamental and shade trees, chiefly the American, or white, elm (*U. americana*) and the English, or Wych, elm (*U. campestris*) of N and central Europe and W Asia. Both species are among those plants attacked by the fungus known as Dutch elm disease (see DISEASES OF PLANTS). The mucilaginous inner bark of the slippery elm (*U. fulva*) is used medicinally in cough drops. Some species of the genus *Celtis* (the hackberries of America and the nettle trees of the Old World) are cultivated for their edible fruit. False sandalwood (*Planera abelica*) is a member of the elm family; its fragrant wood is used in cabinetmaking. The elm family is classified in the division MAGNOLIOPHYTA, class Magnoliopsida, order Urticales.

Elman, Mischa (mĭsh'ə ĕl'mən), 1891–1967, Russian-American violinist, b. Kiev. He studied in St. Petersburg with Leopold Auer, and first gained prominence in Berlin at the age of 13. After his American debut in New York City (1908) he toured throughout the world, receiving great acclaim everywhere. He became a U.S. citizen in 1923.

Elmer, John: see AYLMER, JOHN.

Elmhurst, city (1970 pop. 50,547), Du Page co., NE Ill., a suburb of Chicago; settled 1843, inc. 1910. A residential city in a truck-farming area, it also has three industrial parks. Elmhurst College is there.

Elmina (ĕlmē'nə), town (1970 pop. 11,612), S Ghana, on the Gulf of Guinea. It is a fishing center located in a region where corn and cassava are grown. Elmina was founded in 1471 by the Portuguese, who later (1482) built St. George's castle, which still stands. It was the first important European settlement on the Gold Coast.

Elmira, city (1970 pop. 39,945), seat of Chemung co., extreme S central N.Y., on the Chemung River; settled 1788, inc. 1864. It is a distributing and manufacturing center with plants making food items, electronic equipment, fire engines, automobile parts, and iron and steel products. The Treaty of Painted Post, ending warfare between settlers and the Iroquois confederation, was signed there in 1791. The city was the site of a Confederate prison camp in 1864–5; 3,000 Confederate prisoners are buried there. The well-known Elmira State Reformatory (est. 1876) was first supervised by Z. R. Brockway. Mark Twain spent many summers in Elmira and is buried there. Places of interest include his study, built in the shape of a riverboat pilot's house; the Arnot Art Gallery; and the Chemung County Historical Center, an Indian museum. Elmira College is in the city. Nearby are Harris Hill, site of an annual national glider contest, and Newtown Battlefield State Park, with the John Sullivan Monument.

El Misti, volcano, Peru: see MISTI, EL.

Elmo, Saint: see PETER GONZALEZ, SAINT.

Elmodam (ĕlmō'dăm), in the Gospel genealogy. Luke 3.28.

Elmont, uninc. city (1970 pop. 29,363), Nassau co., SE N. Y., on Long Island. Although chiefly residential, it has some light industry. Belmont Park racetrack is nearby.

El Monte, city (1970 pop. 69,837), Los Angeles co., S Calif.; inc. 1912. An industrial and commercial city in the San Gabriel Valley, El Monte manufactures such diverse items as aerospace products, electronic equipment, and plastic and metal products. The city is also known for its walnut groves. El Monte was founded in 1852 by westward-bound pioneers on the SANTA FE TRAIL.

El Morro National Monument: see NATIONAL PARKS AND MONUMENTS (table).

Elmwood Park, village (1970 pop. 26,160), Cook co., NE Ill., a residential suburb of Chicago; inc. 1914.

Elnaam (ĕl'nāăm, ĕlnā'-), father of two of David's guard. 1 Chron. 11.46.

Elnathan (ĕlnā'thăn). **1** Grandfather of Jehoiachin. 2 Kings 24.8. **2** Leader in Jerusalem in the time of Jehoiakim. Jer. 26.22; 36.12,25. This may be the same person as **1.** **3, 4, 5** Three emissaries of Ezra. Ezra 8.16.

Elohim (ĕlōhēm', ēlō'hĭm, ĕl'ōhēm), common Hebrew name of GOD.

Eloi, Eloi, lama sabachthani?: see ELI, ELI, LAMA SABACHTHANI?.

Elon (ē'lŏn). **1** Hittite father-in-law of Esau. Gen. 26.34. **2** Ancestor of the Elonites. Num. 26.26. **3** Judge of Israel. Judges 12.11. **4** Danite town. Joshua 19.43.

Elon-beth-hanan (ē'lŏn-bĕth-hā'nən), city in Solomon's 2d district. 1 Kings 4.9.

elongation, in astronomy, the angular distance between two points in the sky as measured from a third point. The elongation of a planet is usually measured as the angular distance from the sun to the planet as measured from the earth. When a planet lies on the line drawn from the earth to the sun, its elongation is 0° and is said to be in CONJUNCTION. When a planet's elongation is 90°, it is in QUADRATURE. When its elongation is 180°, it is in OPPOSITION. Elongation is measured east (eastern quadrature) or west (western quadrature) from the sun. The SUPERIOR PLANETS can have elongations between 0° and 180°; the elongations of the INFERIOR PLANETS are limited by their proximity to the sun. The greatest elongation of Mercury is 28°, and of Venus, 47°.

Eloth (ē'lŏth), the same as ELATH.

Elpaal (ĕl'pāăl, ĕlpā'ăl), founder of a Benjamite family. 1 Chron. 8.11,12,18.

Elpalet (ĕlpā'lĕt), son of David: see ELIPHALET.

El-paran (ĕlpā'răn), the same as PARAN.

El Paso (ĕl pă'sō), city (1970 pop. 322, 261), seat of El Paso co., extreme W Texas, on the Rio Grande opposite Juárez, Mex.; inc. 1873. Located in a region of cattle ranches and cotton and vegetable farms (irrigated from the Elephant Butte Reservoir), the city is a port of entry and a commercial, industrial, and mining center. Manufactures include refined petroleum, processed copper, foodstuffs, clothing, and machinery. The dry warmth of the area attracts many tourists and winter residents. The largest of the border cities, El Paso is something of a blend of the United States and Mexico, and its history is bound up with that of Juárez. The two cities are in the region once known as El Paso del Norte, so called because of the route through the mountains to the north. In the 16th and 17th cent. missionaries, soldiers, and traders came to the region. Although missions were founded at Ysleta and elsewhere north of the river, the major settlement was on the south (Juárez) bank. Not until 1827 was the first house built on the site of present-day El Paso. After the U.S.-Mexican border was set, settlement increased, and the coming of the railroad in 1881 prefaced the growth of a rendezvous of cowboys, exiles, border traders, and adventurers into a great commercial city. As a result of the settlement in 1963 of the Chamizal border dispute, a small area of El Paso was transferred to Mexico. The city is the seat of the Univ. of Texas at El Paso; Fort Bliss, a large U.S. military installation, is nearby.

Elphinstone, Arthur, 6th **Baron Balmerino:** see BALMERINO, ARTHUR ELPHINSTONE, 6TH BARON.

Elphinstone, William, 1431–1514, Scottish prelate, founder of the Univ. of Aberdeen. He was trained in the law and was employed on many political missions before becoming bishop of Aberdeen in 1483. For his loyalty in the struggle with the nobles, James III made him lord high chancellor in 1488. In 1494 he procured a papal bull founding King's College (part of the present-day Univ. of Aberdeen). Bishop Elphinstone introduced the printing press into Scotland.

El Reno, city (1970 pop. 14,510), seat of Canadian co., central Okla.; inc. 1889. It is a rail and marketing center, with railroad shops and grain mills. It is the seat of a junior college, an Indian agency, and the county historical museum.

El Salvador (sälväthōr'), republic (1970 est. pop. 3,533,628), 8,260 sq mi (21,393 sq km), Central America. The capital is SAN SALVADOR. The country is bounded on the S by the Pacific Ocean, on the W by Guatemala, and on the N and E by Honduras. Two volcanic ranges, running roughly west to east, segment the country, but in between are broad, fertile valleys, such as that of the Lampa, the principal

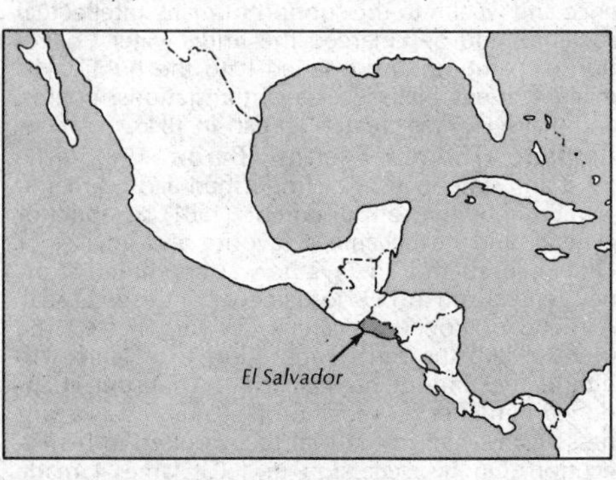

river. There are several fairly large lakes. El Salvador is the smallest Latin American republic and the most densely populated; overpopulation is a critical problem. The population is about 80% mestizo and there are small numbers of unmixed Indians, whites, and blacks. Spanish is the official language and Roman Catholicism the prevailing religion. The country has two universities. El Salvador is governed under the 1962 constitution. The president is popularly elected for a five-year term and may not succeed himself. The members of the unicameral legislature are elected for two-year terms under a system of proportional representation. The principal parties are the National Conciliation party, in power since 1961, and the National Opposition Union. The Inter-American Highway crosses El Salvador and forms the heart of an excellent transportation system that links San Salvador with the ports of ACAJUTLA and La LIBERTAD and the inland cities of SAN MIGUEL, SANTA ANA, and La UNIÓN. El Salvador's economy is primarily agricultural, although it is more highly industrialized than its neighbors. Two thirds of the land is used for either crops or pasturage. Rice is the chief subsistence crop; coffee is grown for export. Other exports are cotton and sugar. The leading imports are foodstuffs, petroleum, and manufactured goods. Textiles, processed foods, and footwear are among El Salvador's leading manufactures. Pedro de ALVARADO led the Spanish conquest (1524) of El Salvador. The region was governed under the captaincy general of Guatemala. With independence from Spain in 1821, it became briefly a part of the Mexican Empire of Augustín de Iturbide, and after the empire collapsed (1823) El Salvador joined the CENTRAL AMERICAN FEDERATION. El Salvador protested the dominance of Guatemala and under Francisco MORAZÁN succeeded in having the federal capital transferred (1831) to San Salvador. After the dissolution of the federation (1839), the republic was plagued by frequent interference from the dictators of neighboring countries, notably Rafael CARRERA and Justo Rufino BARRIOS of Guatemala and José Santos ZELAYA of Nicaragua. The primacy of coffee cultivation in the economy began in the second half of the 19th cent. Intense cultivation led to the predominance of landed proprietors. The economy became vulnerable to fluctuations in the world market price for coffee. In 1931, Maximiliano HERNANDEZ MARTÍNEZ, capitalizing on discontent caused by the collapse of coffee prices, led a coup d'etat. His dictatorship lasted until 1944, after which there was chronic political unrest. Under the authoritarian rule of Major Oscar Osorio (1950–56) and Lt. Col. José María LEMUS (1956–60) considerable economic progress was made. Lemus was overthrown by a coup, and after a confused period a junta composed of leaders of the National Conciliation party came to power in June, 1961. The junta's candidate, Lt. Col. Julio Adalberto RIVERA, was elected president in 1962. He was succeeded in 1967 by Col. Fidel SÁNCHEZ HERNANDEZ. Relations with Honduras deteriorated in the late 1960s. There was a border clash in 1967, and in 1969 Honduras passed land laws discriminating against immigrants from El Salvador. War broke out following a tension-filled soccer match between the two nations in July, 1969. After four days the Organization of American States imposed a cease-fire. The Salvadoran forces that had invaded Honduras were withdrawn. In the 1972 presidential election no candidate won a majority; as constitutionally prescribed the legislature acted and chose Col. Arturo Armando Molina, the government candidate. His leading opponent, José Napoeón Duarte, claimed that the election was fraudulent. A coup attempt was foiled in March, 1972. In the early 1970s there were several instances of leftist terrorism, notably before the March, 1974, legislative elections, handily won by the National Conciliation party. See D. R. Raynolds, *Rapid Development in Small Economies: The Example of El Salvador* (1967); E. G. Squier, *Notes on Central America* (1855, repr. 1969); T. P. Anderson, *Matanza: El Salvador's Communist Revolt of 1932* (1971); H. I. Blutstein et al., *Area Handbook for El Salvador* (1971); David Browning, *El Salvador: Landscape and Society* (1971); P. F. Flemion, *Historical Dictionary of El Salvador* (1972); Alastair White, *El Salvador* (1973).

El Segundo (ĕl sēgŭn'dō), industrial city (1970 pop. 15,620), Los Angeles co., S Calif., on Santa Monica Bay; inc. 1917. Its products include electronic equipment, aircraft and space vehicles, and petroleum. It was founded (1911) as an oil town. A U.S. air force missile station is there, and the Los Angeles international airport is adjacent to the city.

Elsene: see IXELLES, Belgium.

Elsheimer, Adam (ä'däm ĕls'hīmər), 1578–1610?, German painter. After studying in Frankfurt, Munich, and Venice, he settled in Rome and worked for Pope Paul V. He painted small pictures on copper. They were chiefly of biblical and mythological subjects with landscape backgrounds, which he executed with minute precision. He had numerous students (including Pieter Lastman, who was the teacher of Rembrandt) and is thought to have had a considerable influence on Dutch landscape painting. Elsheimer was particularly successful in rendering light effects. His *Good Samaritan* is in the Louvre. *Tobias* and *Coronis* are both in the National Gallery in London.

ELSI: see INTEGRATED CIRCUIT.

Elsinore: see HELSINGØR, Denmark.

Elssler, Fanny (fä'nē ĕl'slər), 1810–84, Austrian dancer. The youngest daughter of Johann Elssler, copyist and valet of Haydn, she made her debut (1833) in London. She danced at the Paris Opéra (1834–39) and in London (1838–40) and became a favorite in both cities. Her forte was folk dancing, especially of the cachucha, the cracovienne, and the tarantella. She toured (1841) the United States and after appearances throughout Europe retired in 1851. Her dancing was sensuous, earthy, and fired by great energy. Her sister, Thérèse, often supported her as partner. See biography by Ivor Guest (1970).

Eltekeh (ĕl'tĕkĕ), city of Dan. Near there Sennacherib of Assyria put down the western nations. Joshua 19.44; 21.23.

Eltekon (ĕl'tĕkŏn, ĕltē'-), unidentified town, S Palestine. Joshua 15.59.

Eltolad (ĕl'tōlăd, ĕltō'-), unidentified town, Negev, S Palestine. Joshua 19.4. Tolad: 1 Chron. 4.29.

Elton, Geoffrey Rudolph, 1921–, English historian, b. Germany. He was educated at the Univ. of London and began teaching at Cambridge in 1949, becoming professor of English constitutional history there in 1967. As a scholar of Tudor administrative history, Elton reassessed historical conceptions of the Tudor era. In *The Tudor Revolution in Government* (1953) he showed the Tudor monarchy and administration developing in response to new problems, notably those created by the English Reformation. Other works include *England under the Tudors* (1955), *The Tudor Constitution* (1960), *Reformation Europe* (1963), and *Reform and Renewal* (1973).

Éluard, Paul (pōl ālüär'), 1895–1952, French poet. He was a leading exponent of SURREALISM. Among his volumes of verse are *Mourir de ne pas mourir* [to die of not dying] (1924) and *L'Immaculée Conception* (with André Breton, 1930). A member of the French resistance in World War II, Éluard is revealed as poet and man of action in the verse of *Poésie et vérité* (1942) and *Au rendez-vous allemand* (1945).

Eluru (ĕl'o͞oro͞o) or **Ellore** (ĕlōr'), town (1971 pop. 127,047), Andhra Pradesh state, E central India. It is a district administrative center. Carpet making and tanning are important. Extensive ruins 8 mi (12.9 km) N of Eluru are thought to be the site of the capital of the Buddhist kingdom of Vengi (c.600–1000 A.D.).

Eluzai (ĕlyo͞o'zāī, ĕl"yo͞ozā'ī), Benjamite with David at Ziklag. 1 Chron. 12.5.

Elvas (ĕl'vəsh), town (1970 municipal pop. 24,510), E central Portugal, in Alto Alentejo, near the Spanish border. Jewelry is made there. A heavily fortified town, it was important in all the Portuguese wars but particularly in the wars against Spain after Portugal revolted (1640) against Spanish control and in the Peninsular War. The town retains a Moorish castle and aqueduct and a late Gothic cathedral.

Elvehjem, Conrad Arnold (ĕlvā'əm), 1901–62, American biochemist, b. McFarland, Wis., grad. Univ. of Wisconsin (B.A., 1923; Ph.D., 1927). Affiliated with the department of biochemistry at the Univ. of Wisconsin from 1923, he was professor from 1936. In 1946 he became dean of the graduate school, and in 1958 president of the university, a position that he held until his death. The discovery by Elvehjem and his associates that niacin (or nicotinic acid), part of the vitamin B complex, can cure blacktongue in dogs, a disease corresponding to pellagra in humans, led to the adoption of niacin in treating pellagra patients. His many other activities included productive research on various other components of the vitamin B complex, the discovery that copper is essential to the formation of hemoglobin, and work on respiration in tissues. With H. A. Waisman he wrote *The Vitamin Content of Meat* (1941).

Elvend: see ALVEND.

Elverum (ĕl'vəro͝om), town (1970 est. pop. 14,000), Hedmark co., SE Norway, on the Glåma River. A rail junction and an important military training center, it was badly damaged in World War II during the German invasion (1940). The Norwegian parliament held its last meeting there (April, 1940) before going into exile in England.

Elwood, city (1970 pop. 11,196), Madison co., central Ind.; inc. 1872. It has large canneries and plants making cans, wire and cables, electronic controls, machine tools, and aerospace components. Wendell L. Willkie was born there.

Ely, Richard Theodore (ē'lē), 1854–1943, American economist, b. Ripley, N.Y., grad. Columbia, 1876, Ph.D. Heidelberg, 1879. He taught at Johns Hopkins Univ. (1881–92), the Univ. of Wisconsin (1892–1925), and Northwestern Univ. (1925–33). One of the most influential teachers of his time, he was instrumental in popularizing the study of economics, and his *Outlines of Economics* (with R. H. Hess, 1889; 6th ed. 1937) was a standard text. He was a founder of the American Economic Association. An early leader of CHRISTIAN SOCIALISM in America, he advocated public control of resources, prohibition of child labor, and the development of labor unions. His many books include *Monopolies and Trusts* (1900), *Studies in the Evolution of Industrial Society* (1905), and *Land Economics* (with G. S. Wehrwein, 1940). See his autobiography, *Ground under Our Feet* (1938); J. R. Everett, *Religion in Economics* (1946); B. G. Rader, *The Academic Mind and Reform* (1966).

Ely, urban district (1971 pop. 9,969), Cambridgeshire and Isle of Ely, E central England. It is a market town for the surrounding rich farming area and has food-processing industries. Secluded in the Fens, it was the site of the last serious resistance to William I in 1071. Ely Cathedral, one of the largest in England, is on the site of an abbey founded by St. Ætheldreda in 673 and destroyed by Danes in 870.

Ely, Isle of, region, and until 1965 an administrative county, in the northern section of Cambridgeshire and Isle of Ely, E central England. Ely is the chief town; March was formerly the administrative center. The region has extensive fens, now drained and devoted to the cultivation of sugar beets and vegetables. Pigs and poultry are raised. The name *Isle* comes from the high ground amid the fens; *Ely* supposedly refers to the eels formerly in the waters. In 1974, Isle of Ely became part of the new nonmetropolitan county of Cambridgeshire.

Elymas (ĕl'ĭmăs), the same as BAR-JESUS.

Elyot, Sir Thomas, c.1490–1546, English author. He wrote the earliest Latin-English dictionary (1538) and is remembered especially for his sensible and well-written treatise on the education of statesmen, *The Book Named the Governour* (1531).

Elyria (ĕlēr'ēə), city (1970 pop. 53,427), seat of Lorain co., N Ohio, on the Black River; inc. 1833. It is a farm trade and industrial center. Cascade Park, with waterfalls, caves, nature trails, and a zoo, is in the heart of the city. Also in Elyria are a junior college and a Kent State Univ. extension center.

Élysée (ālēzā'), palace in Paris, on the Rue du Faubourg Saint-Honoré. Built in 1718 and once the property of Mme de Pompadour, it has been since 1873 the official residence of the presidents of France.

Elysian fields (ĭlĭzh'ən) or **Elysium** (ĭlĭzh'ēəm), in Greek religion, happy otherworld for heroes favored by the gods. Identified with the FORTUNATE ISLES or ISLES OF THE BLEST, Elysium was situated in the distant west, at the edge of the world. In later tradition and in Vergil, Elysium is a part of the underworld and a pleasant abode for the righteous dead.

Elzabad (ĕl'zəbăd, ĕlzā'-). **1** Gadite who came to David in Judah. 1 Chron. 12.12. **2** Levitical doorkeeper. 1 Chron. 26.7.

Elzaphan (ĕl'zəfăn, ĕlzā'-), the same as ELIZAPHAN **1**.

Elzevir, Louis (ĕl'zəvər, -vēr), 1540–1617, Dutch publisher, whose name also appeared as Elsevier or Elzevier. He produced his first book at Leiden in 1583. Under him and his descendants, the business was continued until the death of the second Abraham Elzevir at Leiden in 1712. In its best years it was easily the greatest publishing business in the world. The Elzevirs were typically neither printers nor scholars but businessmen. They owned presses and type and employed good editors and printers. Their books were good textually, legible, and inexpensive. Many of the Elzevir books were printed in the establishments of members of the family at Leiden, Amsterdam, Utrecht, and The Hague, but many books were printed for the Elzevirs by other printers. Agencies of the family, conducted by members of it, were established in numerous cities, from Denmark to Italy. The Elzevir types are typically legible and sturdy, rather than elegant, and the books tended to be of small size with narrow margins. The texts were usually in Latin, though the family printed and published books in Greek, French, and other languages. The most noted of the successors of Louis were his son **Bonaventure Elzevir,** 1583–1652, and his grandson **Abraham Elzevir,** 1592–1652. A famous designer of types employed by the Elzevirs was Christopher van DYCK. Roman type such as he designed, known in England and America as "old style" type, is known on the continent of Europe as "Elzevir" type.

emanation: see RADON.

emanation (ĕmənā'shən) [Latin,=flowing from], cosmological concept that explains the creation of the world by a series of radiations, or emanations, originating in the godhead. It is characteristic of NEOPLATONISM and of GNOSTICISM and is frequently encountered in Indian metaphysics. In the history of Western thought it has been to some extent, as in Neoplatonism, opposed to the Judeo-Christian conception of creation, in which the eternal God makes all from nothing. To explain the relation of a totally transcendent God to a finite and imperfect world, the belief in emanation denies that God directly created the world but maintains rather that the world is the result of a chain of emergence through emanations. From God (the One, or the Absolute), the one prime principle, flows the divine substance; his own substance never lessens. As the flow proceeds farther from God, however, its divinity steadily decreases. When a stone is dropped into water, the circles ever widening from the point (God) where the stone fell are emanations, becoming fainter and fainter. Emanation never ceases, the whole process moving continuously outward from God. In the 3d cent. A.D., PLOTINUS and other Neoplatonists developed a clear system of emanation. The Neoplatonists ascribed to Plato an emanative concept in his Idea of the Good as being supreme, the lesser ideas being in some way related to the Idea of the Good. The concept, in modified form, influenced the development of medieval Christian theology through the writings of Dionysius the Areopagite.

Emancipation, Edict of, 1861, the mechanism by which Czar Alexander II freed all Russian SERFS (one third of the total population). All personal serfdom was abolished, and the peasants were to receive land from the landlords and pay them for it. The state advanced the money to the landlords and recovered it from the peasants in 49 annual sums known as redemption payments. Until redemption began, the law provided for a period of "temporary obligation," during which the peasants held the land but paid for it in money or in labor. That initial stage dragged on for nearly 20 years in some regions. In many areas the peasants had to pay more than the land was worth, while in other areas they were given small plots, and many chose to accept "beggarly allotments"—i.e., one fourth of the prescribed amount of land without any monetary obligations. The peasants' landholdings were controlled by the *mir,* or village commune. The *mir* was responsible for redemption payments and periodically redistributed the land to meet the changing needs of the various households. The provisions concerning land redistribution produced the peasant discontent that eventually helped the Russian Revolution to succeed, despite the later reforms of P. A. STOLYPIN.

Emancipation Proclamation, in U.S. history, the executive order abolishing slavery in the Confederate States of America. In the early part of the Civil War, President Lincoln refrained from issuing an edict freeing the slaves despite the insistent urgings of abolitionists. Believing that the war was being fought solely to preserve the Union, he sought to avoid alienating the slaveholding border states that had remained in the Union. "If I could save the Union without freeing *any* slave, I would do it; and if I could save it by freeing *all* the slaves, I would do it; and if I could do it by freeing some and leaving others alone, I would also do that." He wrote these words to Horace Greeley on Aug. 22, 1862, in answer to criticism from that administration gadfly; he had, however, long since decided, after much reflection, to adopt the third course. Lincoln kept the plan to himself until July 13, 1862, when, according to the cabinet diarist Gideon Welles, he first mentioned it to Welles and Secretary of State William H. Seward. On July 22 he read a preliminary draft to the cabinet and acquiesced in Seward's suggestion to wait until after a Union victory before issuing the proclamation. The Antietam campaign presented that opportunity, and on Sept. 22, 1862, after reading a second draft to the cabinet, he issued a preliminary proclamation which announced that emancipation would become effective on Jan. 1, 1863, in those states "in rebellion" that had not meanwhile laid down their arms. On Jan. 1, 1863, the formal and definite Emancipation Proclamation was issued. The President, by virtue of his powers as commander in chief, declared free all those slaves residing in territory in rebellion against the Federal government "as a fit and necessary war measure for suppressing said rebellion." Congress, in effect, had done as much in its confiscation acts of Aug., 1861, and July, 1862, but its legislation did not have the popular appeal of the Emancipation Proclamation—despite the great limitations of the proclamation, which did not affect bondsmen in those slave states that had remained loyal to the Union or in territory of the Confederacy that had been reconquered. These were freed in other ways (see SLAVERY). Nor did the proclamation have any immediate effect in the vast area over which the Confederacy retained control. Confederate leaders, however, feared that it would serve as an incitement to servile insurrection and denounced it. The proclamation did not even reflect Lincoln's desired solution for the slavery problem. He continued to favor gradual emancipation, to be undertaken voluntarily by the states, with Federal compensation to slaveholders, a plan he considered eminently just in view of the common responsibility of North and South for the existence of slavery. The Emancipation Proclamation was chiefly a declaration of policy, which, it was hoped, would serve as an opening wedge in depleting the South's great man-power reserve in slaves and, equally important, would enhance the Union cause in the eyes of Europeans, especially the British. At home it was duly hailed by the radical abolitionists, but it cost Lincoln the support of many conservatives and undoubtedly figured in the Republican setback in the congressional elections of 1862. This was more than offset by the boost it gave the Union abroad, where, on the whole, it was warmly received; in combination with subsequent Union victories, it ended all hopes of the Confederacy for recognition from Britain and France. Doubts as to its constitutionality were later removed by the adoption of the Thirteenth Amendment. See J. H. Franklin, *The Emancipation Proclamation* (1963).

Emba (ĕm'bə), river, c.400 mi (640 km) long, SW Central Asian USSR, in Kazakhstan. It rises in the Mugodzhar mts. and flows SW into the Caspian Sea. The lower course traverses a region of flat salt domes, characteristic of the petroleum-rich Emba fields.

embalming (ĕmbä'mĭng, ĭm-), practice of preserving the body after death by artificial means. The custom was prevalent among many ancient peoples and still survives in many cultures. It was highly developed in dynastic Egypt, where it was used for some 30 cent. Although the embalming methods of the Egyptians varied according to the wealth and rank of the deceased, bodies were usually immersed for several weeks in a soda solution after the body cavities had been filled with resins and spices. Viscera were sometimes embalmed separately and either replaced in the body or preserved in canopic jars. Traditional embalming methods were largely abandoned with the spread of Christianity, but preservation of bodies continued in Egypt for several centuries. The corpse was no longer eviscerated but was packed in salts and spices and then wrapped in linen sheets. Modern methods originated in the 17th cent. in attempts to preserve anatomical specimens. Although practiced in Europe, the custom of routinely embalming corpses before burial is most widespread in North America. Formaldehyde, the essential element in embalming fluids today, is injected into the vascular system as the blood is drained out. In some cases embalming fluid is also pumped into the body cavities. See FUNERAL CUSTOMS; MUMMY. See C. G. Strub and L. G. Frederick, *Principles and Practice of Embalming* (4th ed. 1967).

Embalse del Río Negro: see NEGRO, RÍO, Uruguay.

embargo (ĕmbär'gō), prohibition by a country of the departure of ships or certain types of goods from its ports. Instances of confining all domestic ships to port are rare, and the EMBARGO ACT of 1807 is the sole example of this in American history. The detention of foreign vessels, on the other hand, has often occurred in the past, either as an act of REPRISAL designed to coerce diplomatic redress or in contemplation of war with the country to which the vessels belonged. Embargoes on goods, however, are far more common. The United States has used embargoes for both economic and strategic purposes. An example of the former was the prohibition of gold bullion exports in 1933, while the latter is seen in the embargo placed on certain war materials in 1940. An embargo may also be used as a political device. Thus, in 1912 the President was empowered to forbid the export of munitions to Latin America. The NEUTRALITY ACT of 1936 gave the President a similar power with regard to warring nations anywhere and was used during the Spanish civil war (1936-39) to ensure neutrality. Embargoes were authorized as a form of SANCTION by the Covenant of the League of Nations and were applied against Paraguay in 1934 in the CHACO dispute with Bolivia, and with less success against Italy in the Italian war with Ethiopia (1935-36). Article 41 of the United Nations Charter permits embargoes in case of military aggression, and during the Korean War the UN called upon its members to refrain from sending arms and strategic materials to territory controlled by the North Koreans and Chinese. In 1960 the United States imposed an embargo of all goods, excluding food and medicine, on Cuba, and in 1962 the ORGANIZATION OF AMERICAN STATES, amid great controversy, established its own Cuban trade embargo. Later in the 1960s the UN called for an arms embargo against South Africa and an arms and oil embargo against Rhodesia.

Embargo Act of 1807, passed Dec. 22, 1807, by the U.S. Congress in answer to the British ORDERS IN COUNCIL restricting neutral shipping and to Napoleon's restrictive CONTINENTAL SYSTEM. The U.S. merchant marine suffered from both the British and French, and Thomas Jefferson undertook to answer both nations with measures that by restricting neutral trade would show the importance of that trade. The first attempt was the Nonimportation Act, passed April 18, 1806, forbidding the importation of specified British goods in order to force Great Britain to relax its rigorous rulings on cargoes and sailors (see IMPRESSMENT). The act was suspended, but the Embargo Act of 1807 was a bolder statement of the same idea. It forbade all international trade to and from American ports, and Jefferson hoped that Britain and France would be persuaded of the value and the rights of a neutral commerce. In Jan., 1808, the prohibition was extended to inland waters and land commerce to halt the skyrocketing trade with Canada. Merchants, sea captains, and sailors were naturally dismayed to find themselves without income and to see the ships rotting at the wharves. All sorts of dodges were used to circumvent the law. The daring attempt to use economic pressure in a world at war was not successful. Britain and France stood firm, and not enough pressure could be brought to bear. Enforcement was difficult, especially in New England, where merchants looked on the scheme as an attempt to defraud them of a livelihood. When in Jan., 1809, Congress, against much opposition, passed an act to make enforcement more rigid, resistance approached the point of rebellion—again especially in New England—and the scheme had to be abandoned. On March 1, 1809, the embargo was superseded by the Nonintercourse Act. This allowed resumption of all commercial intercourse except with Britain and France. Jefferson reluctantly accepted it. Not unexpectedly, it failed to bring pressure on Britain and France. In 1810 it was replaced by Macon's Bill No. 2 (named after Nathaniel Macon), which virtually ended the experiment. It provided for trade with both Britain and France unless one of those powers revoked its restrictions; in that case, the President was authorized to forbid commerce with the country that had not also revoked its offensive measures. See L. M. Sears, *Jefferson and the Embargo* (1927, repr. 1967).

embassy: see DIPLOMATIC SERVICE; EXTRATERRITORIALITY.

ember days, in the Western Church, traditionally the Wednesday, Friday, and Saturday following the first Sunday in Lent; Whitsunday; Sept. 14 (Exaltation of the Cross); and Dec. 13 (St. Lucy's Day). They were days of fasting to sanctify the season, and the ember Saturdays were considered especially appropriate for ordinations. The ember days are of very ancient and uncertain origin. The dates of their celebration are now determined by national hierarchies rather than by the universal Roman liturgical calendar, and they are frequently called "days of prayer for peace."

embezzlement, wrongful use, for one's own selfish ends, of the property of another when that property has been legally entrusted to one. Such an act was not LARCENY at common law because larceny was committed only when property was acquired by a "felonious taking," i.e., when the act was committed with respect to property that was at the time in the legal possession of the owner. Consequently, unfaithful servants, employees, agents, trustees, or guardians who misappropriated another's property could be sued only in the civil courts, on the grounds that although the defendant had legally come into possession of the property, he had breached his trust by wrongfully misappropriating it to his own use. To remedy this situation statutes were passed in England and the United States that either made embezzlement a distinct crime or enlarged the definition of larceny in such a way as to include all cases of misappropriation of property in the lawful possession of the wrongdoer. In most states of the United States embezzlement is a FELONY. Under acts of Congress, stealing of letters by postmasters, clerks, and letter carriers is considered embezzlement.

embolus (ĕm'bələs), foreign matter circulating in and obstructing a blood vessel. It may be a portion of a clot that has separated from the wall of a vessel (see THROMBOSIS), a bubble of gas or air (known as an air embolus), a globule of fat, a clump of bacterial matter, or a clump of tumor cells. It circulates freely through the vessels until it reaches one so small that it cannot go further. An embolus in one of the vessels leading to the lungs, brain, or heart, if large enough, can be fatal; in an arm or leg it may lead to gangrene and, ultimately, the need for amputation. Emergency surgical removal is usually the treatment of choice for a solid embolus. Otherwise, drugs that dilate the vessels and anticoagulants are indicated.

embossing, process of producing upon various materials designs or patterns in relief by mechanical means. The material is pressed between a pair of dies especially adapted to its hardness and the depth of the design needed. A felt counter or female die is employed for embossing fabrics, while metal, millboard, or cardboard is used for embossing metal, cardboard, or paper. Leather for bookbinding and wood for furniture ornamentation are die stamped while wet. Embossing differs from other relief design processes, such as repoussé, chasing, carving, and leather tooling, in being machine wrought.

embroidery, ornamental NEEDLEWORK applied to all varieties of fabrics and worked with many sorts of thread—linen, cotton, wool, silk, gold, and even hair. Decorative objects, such as shells, feathers, beads, and jewels, are often sewn to the embroidered piece. The BAYEUX TAPESTRY is among the most famous examples of embroidery. The art probably antedates that of weaving. Needlework is mentioned in the Vedas and in Exodus in the Bible. In ancient Egypt, gold was used for the decorative stitches, which often covered the entire garment; such work has been found on mummy wrappings. The borders of Greek and Roman garments were often finely embroidered. In the Orient, sumptuous designs of gold and silver thread were produced from remotest times; the intricate embroidery of China became stylized and remained unchanged for centuries. From the richly decorative art of Byzantium (4th cent.) embroidery was introduced into Europe and thereafter followed the great period (12th-14th cent.) of church embroidery. The famous opus Anglicanum, or English work (e.g., the Syon cope, Victoria and Albert Mus.), dates from this time. Monasteries and convents were kept busy adorning vestments and altarpieces, and embroidery ateliers were founded. Secular needlework was far simpler, confined to embroidered bands around the edges of hems, sleeves, necks, and mantles in coarse and dull-colored threads. When Crusaders returned with examples of the superb fabrics of the East, interest in embroidery for nonecclesiastical uses was stimulated, and the technique of appliqué was developed. By 1389 pearls and spangles were being set in the embroidery. After the Renaissance, peasant embroidery flourished in Greece, Scandinavia, the Balkans, and many other areas. Embroidery as folk art was far less varied, complex, and imaginative than the masterworks produced by professional church and court embroiderers. The Elizabethan period was famous for its household and costume embroidery. Gold and silver thread was used on velvet, brocade, and silk, and the allover design was often enhanced with pearls and gems. "Spanish blackwork," black silk on white linen with touches of gold, became enormously popular, while the use of drawnwork and cutwork led to the development of fine LACE. In the 18th cent., French influence refined embroidery techniques; QUILTING was developed using backstitch embroidery, especially popular in making petticoats and coattails. By the 19th cent. embroidery for male attire had declined except for occasional decorative vests and ties. Modern embroidery is most frequently used on lingerie and linens, but with the introduction of machine-made embroidery, the quality has deteriorated. See U. C. Bath, *Embroidery Masterworks* (1972); L. F. Day and Mary Buckle, *Art in Needlework* (1900, repr. 1972); *Erica Wilson's Embroidery Book* (1972).

embryo (ĕm'brēō), name for the developing young of an animal or plant. In its widest definition, the embryo is the young from the moment of fertilization until it has become structurally complete and able to survive as a separate organism. Embryology, the scientific study of embryonic development, deals with the period from fertilization until the hatching or birth of an animal or the GERMINATION of a plant. However, since the young animal may undergo metamorphosis or may remain wholly dependent on the mother for some time after birth, and since the seedling derives nourishment from food stored in its fleshy cotyledons even after it has sprouted, the exact limit of the time during which an organism is an embryo is not well defined. In organisms that reproduce sexually, the union of the sperm with the ovum results in a zygote, or fertilized egg, which begins a rapid series of cell divisions called cleavage, or segmentation (see MITOSIS). Each kind of organism has its own characteristic sequence of development, and related species usually have similar developmental patterns. Development is most complex in higher forms. In a typical animal, cleavage (a continuous process arbitrarily divided into stages) proceeds in the following pattern. Early divisions produce a hollow ball one cell thick, called a blastula, which encloses the blastocoel, or cleavage cavity. The cells divide more rapidly in the area where the nucleus of the ovum was located; this results in an invagination (inpushing) of these cells to form a ball two cells thick (the gastrula). The new cavity thus formed is the gastrocoel, or primitive gut, also called the archenteron, and its opening is the blastopore. The outer layer of cells is the ectoderm, the inner the endoderm. Among the coelenterates (e.g., sponges and jellyfish) these two layers become the chief functional tissues of the adult. In higher forms a third layer of cells, the mesoderm, develops from one or both of the first two layers and fills the blastocoel, and invagination forms a digestive tract with, at this stage, only a single opening. The flatworms (e.g., the tapeworm and the fluke) stop developing at this stage. In most organisms, however, a later invagination of the ectoderm results in a gut that is open at both ends. The mesoderm then divides into two layers, the space between them being called the coelom, or body cavity. The embryo now roughly resembles a tube within a tube. From the three primary germ layers the organs and tissues develop. In general, the ectoderm gives rise to the skin, or integument, the skin appendages (e.g., scales, feathers, hair, and nails), and the nervous system. The endoderm forms the digestive glands and the lining of the alimentary tract and lungs. From the mesoderm develop the major internal organs: the skeletal, muscular, and connective tissue and the circulatory, excretory, and reproductive systems. Sense organs and endocrine glands arise from combinations of all three layers. In lower animals, which lay their eggs in water, the developing embryo is nourished by yolk and absorbs oxygen from and discharges wastes directly into the water. In terrestrial oviparous forms the egg contains the yolk and also a surrounding fluid (e.g., the albumen of bird eggs). In mammals, accessory membranes, comprising both embryonic and uterine tissue, develop around the embryo—the amnion, filled with liquid, and the chorion and allantois, which form the placenta, through which nourishment and oxygen in the blood of the mother diffuse into the fetus and wastes diffuse back. In the higher plants, the divisions of the fertilized ovum and the differentiation of the tissues to form the embryonic root (hypocotyl), stem (epicotyl), and leaves (cotyledons) occur inside the ovule within the ovary at the base of the pistil. The matured ovule is the SEED; the fruit, when it is produced, is the developed ovary.

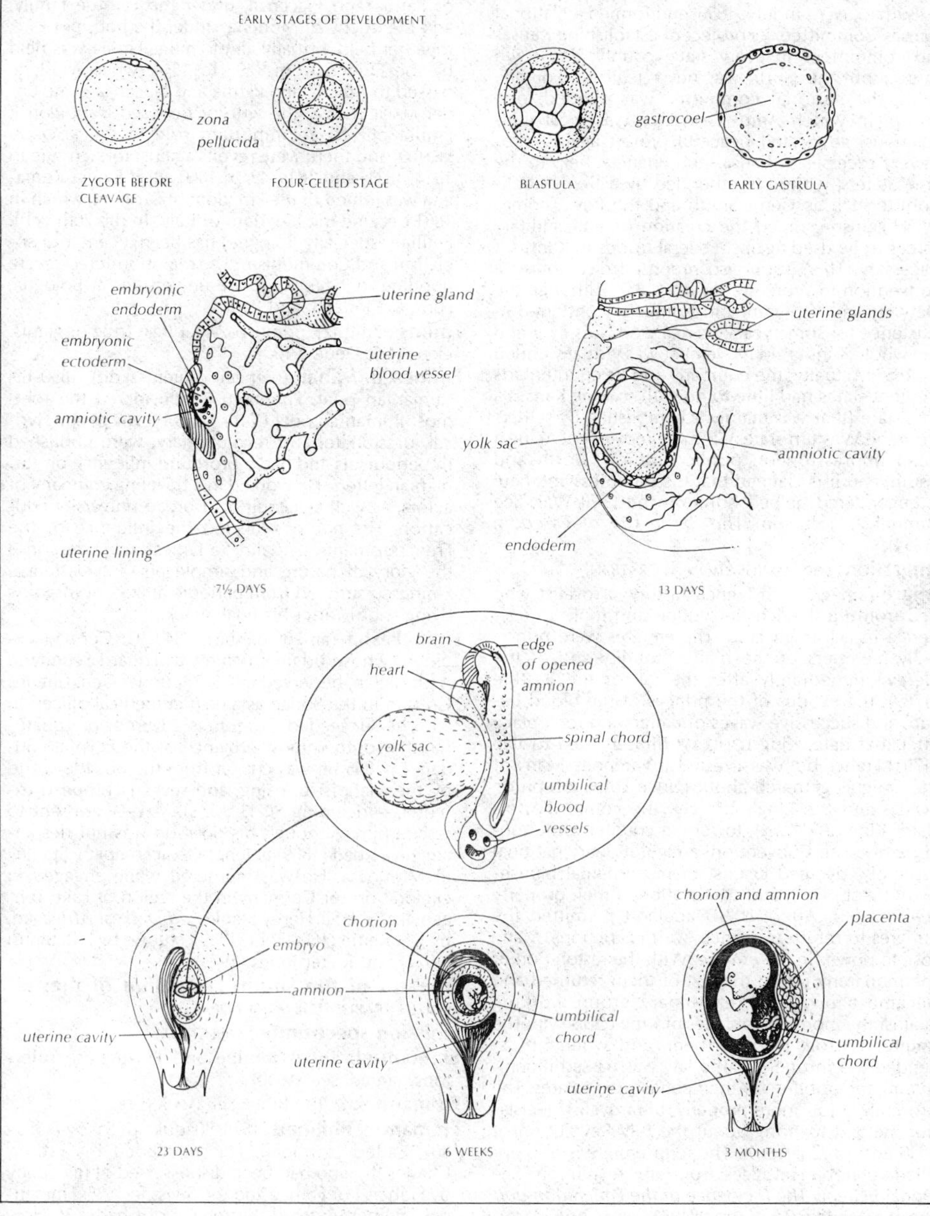

Development of the human embryo

embryophyte (ĕm'brēəfīt''), common name for members of the Embryophyta (or Embryobionta), a taxonomic group composed of the various divisions of the higher plants, i.e., the mosses, ferns, fern allies, gymnosperms, and angiosperms, as well as some smaller divisions. Embryophytes show a well-marked alternation of generations, that is, an alternation between a spore-producing diploid phase and a gamete-producing haploid phase. In the lower embryophytes (such as mosses and ferns) the male and female gametes (eggs and sperms) are produced in special structures within the haploid plant, or GAMETOPHYTE. In higher embryophytes (such as gymnosperms and angiosperms) the gametophyte phase is reduced in size and complexity. The specialized tissues of embryophytes—conducting tissue, for example—are an evolutionary adaptation for life on dry land. In contrast, the lower plants, or THALLOPHYTES, (such as bacteria, algae, and fungi) lack specialized tissues and alternation of generations of the type found in higher plants, and have mostly remained aquatic. See REPRODUCTION.

Emden (ĕm'dən), city (1970 pop. 48,525), Lower Saxony, NW West Germany, at the mouth of the Ems River, the terminus of the Dortmund-Ems and Ems-Jade canals. A major North Sea port, it has extensive shipyards and herring fisheries. Manufactures include chemicals, machinery, and motor vehicles. It was known in the 10th cent. and passed to East Friesland in 1453. The city reached a peak in the 16th cent., when it had one of Europe's largest merchant fleets. It went to Prussia in 1744, passed to Hanover in 1815, and was regained by Prussia in 1866. Its modern development dates largely from the late 19th cent., when the Dortmund-Ems Canal was constructed and the industrialization of the Ruhr district accelerated.

emerald, the green variety of BERYL, of which aquamarine is the blue variety. Chemically, it is a beryllium-aluminum silicate whose color is due to small quantities of chromium compounds. The emerald was highly esteemed in antiquity; both genuine and imitation emeralds were used in early Egypt. The finest emeralds are found in South America in Colombia, where they have been mined for over 400 years. The gem was a favorite in pre-Columbian Mexico and Peru, where it was cut in intricate designs with great skill. The treasure taken to Spain by the conquerors included emeralds. Good emeralds are the most highly valued of gem stones. There is some manufacture of emeralds, by a secret process, in Germany, France, and the United States. India, Rhodesia, and Australia are minor sources of the natural stones. The Oriental emerald, a different gem, is the transparent green variety of CORUNDUM.

Emerson, Ralph Waldo, 1803–82, American poet and essayist, b. Boston. Through his essays, poems, and lectures, Emerson established himself as a leading spokesman of TRANSCENDENTALISM and as a major figure in American literature. His father, William Emerson, descendant of New England clergymen, was minister of the First Unitarian Church in Boston. Emerson's early years were filled with books and a daily routine of studious and frugal homelife. After his father's death in 1811, his eccentric but brilliant aunt, Mary Moody Emerson, became his confidante and stimulated his independent thinking. At Harvard (1817–21) he began recording his thoughts in the famous *Journal.* Poor health hindered his studies at the Harvard divinity school in 1825, and in 1826, after being licensed to preach, he was forced to go South because of incipient tuberculosis. In 1829 he became pastor of the Old North Church in Boston (Second Unitarian). In the same year he married Ellen Tucker, whose death from tuberculosis in 1831 caused him great sorrow. Emerson's personal religious scruples and, in particular, his conviction that the Lord's Supper was not intended by Christ to be a permanent sacrament led him into conflict with his congregation. In 1832 he retired from his only pastorate. On a trip to Europe at this time he met Carlyle (who became a close friend), Coleridge, and Wordsworth. Through these notable English writers, Emerson's interest in transcendental thought began to blossom. Other strong influences on his philosophical thought, besides his own Unitarian background, were Plato and the Neoplatonists, the sacred books of the East, and the mystical writings of Swedenborg. He returned home in 1834, settled in Concord, Mass., married (1835) his second wife, Lydia Jackson, and began an active career as writer and lecturer. In 1836 he published anonymously his essay *Nature,* based on his early lectures. It is in that piece that he first set forth the main principles of transcendentalism, expressing a firm belief in the mystical unity of nature. He attracted wide attention with "The American Scholar," his Phi Beta Kappa oration at Harvard in 1837, in which he called for independence from European cultural leadership. In his lecture at the Harvard divinity school in 1838, his admonition that one could find redemption only in one's own soul was taken to mean that he repudiated Christianity. This caused such indignation that he was not invited to Harvard again until 1866, when the college granted him an LL.D. degree. In 1840 he joined with others in publishing *The Dial,* a magazine intended to promulgate transcendental thought. One of the younger contributors to *The Dial* was Thoreau, who lived in the Emerson household from 1841 to 1843 and became Emerson's most famous disciple. The first collection of Emerson's poems appeared in 1847. In spite of his difficulty in writing structurally correct verse, he always regarded himself essentially as a poet. Among his best-known poems are "Threnody," "Brahma," "The Problem," "The Rhodora," and "The Concord Hymn." It was his winter lecture tours, however, which first made him famous among his contemporaries. These lectures received their final form in his series of *Essays* (1841; second series, 1844). The most notable among them are "The Over-Soul," "Compensation," and "Self-Reliance." From 1845–47 he delivered a series of lectures published as *Representative Men* (1850). After a second trip to England, in 1847, he gave another series of lectures later published as *English Traits* (1856). During the 1850s he became strongly interested in abolitionism and was an active sympathizer with the North in the Civil War. His late lecture tours are contained in *The Conduct of Life* (1860) and *Society and Solitude* (1870). Though his last years were marked by a decline in his mental powers, his literary reputation rapidly continued to spread. Probably no writer has so profoundly influenced American thought as Emerson. See his letters (ed. by R. L. Rusk, 6 vol., 1939); biographies by Van Wyck Brooks (1932), R. L. Rusk (1957), Oliver Wendell Holmes (1885, repr. 1967), and Edward Wagenknecht (1974); studies by Jonathan Bishop (1964), Joel Porte (1966), K. W. Cameron, ed. (1967), and S. E. Whicher (2d ed. 1971). Emerson's son, **Edward Waldo Emerson,** 1844–1930, was a graduate of Harvard medical school. After his father's death he devoted himself to editing and to writing about the literary men of his father's generation. He was the editor of the Centenary edition (12 vol., 1903–4) of Emerson's works, and, with W. E. Forbes, of the *Journals of Ralph Waldo Emerson* (10 vol., 1909–14).

emery: see CORUNDUM.

Emesa: see HIMS, Syria.

emetic (əmĕt'ĭk), substance that produces vomiting. Direct, or gastric, emetics, which act directly on the stomach, include syrup of IPECAC, sulfate of zinc or copper, ALUM, ammonium carbonate, mustard in water, or copious quantities of warm salt water. Indirect, or systemic, emetics, such as apomorphine, induce vomiting by acting indirectly through the blood on the brain center that controls vomiting. Emetics are not used to treat poisoning by strong acids or alkalis, petroleum distillates such as kerosene, or substances causing convulsions.

emeu: see EMU.

emf: see ELECTROMOTIVE FORCE.

Emigrant Aid Company, organization formed in 1854 to promote organized antislavery immigration to the Kansas territory from the Northeast. Eli Thayer conceived the plan as early as Feb., 1854, even before the Kansas-Nebraska Act became law, and in April, Massachusetts chartered the Massachusetts Emigrant Aid Company. This organization, however, proved defective and was soon superseded by the New England Emigrant Aid Company. Many other Kansas aid societies were subsequently formed throughout the North (e.g., the Kansas Emigrant Aid Society of Northern Ohio and the New York Kansas League), but the New England group was preeminent in the field and the name Emigrant Aid Company is associated exclusively with it. Amos A. Lawrence served as treasurer of the company, which, despite its earnest soliciting of the support of clergymen throughout New England, remained in bad financial condition until Nov., 1855, when a notably successful campaign to raise money was launched. For Thayer, who was vice president of the company, the venture was not only philanthropic but profitable. As stock subscription agent he received 10% of all the money he collected, provided he gathered $20,000 or more. Thayer easily exceeded that figure, for by May, 1856, the company had received over $100,000. The company sent out an aggregate of 1,240 settlers under agents such as Charles Robinson, who founded Lawrence and other towns in Kansas. Southerners, at first confident that Kansas was safe for slavery, were moved to organize similar, though proslavery, societies of their own. However, such ill-advised actions by the proslavery societies as the sacking (May 21, 1856) of the town of Lawrence only stimulated the Kansas aid movement further. Delegates from 12 states and Kansas convened at Buffalo, N.Y., in July, 1856, and formed a National Kansas Committee. Its project of establishing Kansas aid committees in every state, county, and town throughout the North was never realized. For one thing the national committee was divided; one group, in which Amos Lawrence was most conspicuous, advocated peaceful protest against proslavery excesses in Kansas and financial help to the Free Staters, while the other, led by extreme abolitionists such as Gerrit Smith and the Rev. Thomas W. Higginson, urged the creation of state military forces to be used against Federal troops in Kansas if necessary. This group also proposed disunion at a convention in Worcester in Jan., 1857. Although the New England Emigrant Aid Company continued in existence for some years, its real work was over and the whole Kansas aid movement was virtually ended by 1857. Actually, the company and its counterparts in other states had little to do with making Kansas a free state (that was mainly accomplished by settlers from the Western states), but the movement made a deep impression on public opinion, North and South, and it is claimed that the bitterness and hate it engendered helped bring on the Civil War. See Samuel A. Johnson, *The Battle Cry of Freedom* (1954).

emigration: see IMMIGRATION; MIGRATION.

émigré (āmēgrā'), in French history, a royalist who fled from the French Revolution and took up residence in a foreign land. The émigrés were principally members of the higher nobility and of the clergy. Immediately after the fall of the Bastille (1789), the exodus of the princes of the blood began, and successive waves of emigration took place after that date. King LOUIS XVI himself tried to flee (1791) France but was arrested at Varennes. Many of the émigrés gathered about Prince Louis Joseph de CONDÉ and the king's brother, the comte d'Artois (later King CHARLES X), to form a counterrevolutionary army. The Convention, a revolutionary national assembly, decreed against them perpetual banishment (Sept., 1792) and confiscation of their property (Oct., 1792). After 1802, Napoleon permitted the émigrés to return to France, with restrictions. Many rose to power in the empire. With the restoration of the monarchy (1814) the rest of them returned and became a powerful reactionary group working against the moderate policies of King LOUIS XVIII. The comte d'Artois favored them, and when he ascended the throne (1824) a law was passed indemnifying the nobility for their confiscated estates. The pro-émigré (or, more properly, ultraroyalist) legislation helped to bring about the July Revolution of 1830 against Charles X. The term *émigré* is also applied to noble refugees from any revolution. See Donald Greer, *The Incidence of the Emigration during the French Revolution* (1951, repr. 1966); Margery Weiner, *The French Exiles, 1789–1815* (1960).

Emilia-Romagna (āmē'lyä-rōmä'nyä), region pop. 3,853,434), 8,542 sq mi (22,124 sq km), N c Italy, bordering on the Adriatic Sea in the ea LOGNA is the capital of the region, which is d into eight provinces named for their capitals. gna, Ferrara, Modena, Parma, Piacenza, and R nell' Emilia provs. are in Emilia, and Forlì ar venna provs. are in Romagna. The region fal two geographic zones, a fertile, low-lying pl the north and east, which is watered by the Po chia, Panaro, and Reno rivers, and the Ape mts. in the south and west. Agriculture is the occupation, and farming is particularly prod in the irrigated Po valley and in the reclaime along the Adriatic coast. Cereals, rice, vege and dairy goods are the chief farm products. E Romagna also has extensive industry, aided production of considerable hydroelectric and by a good transportation network. Ma tures include processed food, motor vehicles machinery, electrical equipment, refined petro and chemicals. There are large deposits of leum (near Piacenza) and natural gas (near Pia and near Ravenna). Fishing is pursued alor coast, which also has a number of popular resorts (including Marina di Romeo and Ri Emilia takes its name from the Aemilian Way, man road (laid out 187 B.C.) that crossed the from Piacenza to Rimini. After the fall of Rom region was conquered (5th cent. A.D.) by the bards. Bologna and most of present-day RO fell under Byzantine rule in the 6th cent. and then to the 19th cent. had histories separate Emilia. Divided into several duchies and co Emilia was conquered by the Franks in the 8th However, its subsequent history is that of its vidual cities, many of which became free munes in the 12th cent. By the 17th cent. the of Parma and Piacenza, under the Farnese f and the duchy of Modena, under the house o together held virtually all of Emilia. Emilia wa by the French from 1797 to 1814, when M passed to Austria and Parma and Piacenza ca der MARIE LOUISE, the wife of deposed Napo Emilia played an important role in the RI MENTO, and there were revolts against foreign 1821, 1831, and 1848–49. In 1860 all of Emilia- gna was joined to the kingdom of Sardinia, wh 1861 became the kingdom of Italy. In the 20th Emilia (especially Bologna) has been a center cialism and Communism. The region suffered flooding in 1966. There are universities at Bo Ferrara, Modena, and Parma.

Emims (ē'mĭmz), primitive Moabitish tribe of Gen. 14.5; Deut. 2.10.

Eminescu, Mihail (mēhäēl' yĕmēnĕ'skŏŏ), 18 Rumanian poet. Eminescu is considered the most Rumanian poet of his century. His poem cal, passionate, and revolutionary, were pub in periodicals and had a profound influence manian letters. He worked in a traveling comp actors, as well as acquiring a broad universit cation. His poetry reflected the influence French romantics. "Calin," a typical work, des the glory of nature and simple peasant exis Eminescu suffered from periodic attacks of in dying shortly after his final attack.

Emin Pasha (āmēn' pä'shä), 1840–92, Germa plorer, whose original name was Eduard Sch A physician, he served (1876–78) under Gen. C Gordon in the Sudan as a district medical offi 1878 he succeeded Gordon as governor of E ria, the southernmost province of the Egypti dan. In 1885 he was cut off from the outside by the Mahdist uprising, and several Europe plorers—including Sir H. M. STANLEY—were s rescue him. Although his position was not d ate, he agreed (1889) at length to accompany S to Mombasa. He was murdered while enga exploration for Germany in the region of Lak ganyika. See Sir Henry Stanley, *In Darkest Afr* by J. S. Keltie (1890, repr. 1969); studies by I. R. (1972) and Roger Jones (1973).

Emirates of the South, Federation of th SOUTH ARABIA, FEDERATION OF.

emission spectrum: see SPECTRUM.

Emmanuel. For Byzantine and Portuguese thus named, see MANUEL.

Emmanuel, in the Bible: see IMMANUEL.

Emmanuel Philibert, 1528–80, duke of Savoy 80), called Ironhead. He succeeded his Charles III, who had been dispossessed of his by Francis I of France and the Swiss in 1536. E uel Philibert entered the service of Charles V Roman emperor and king of Spain, and later

Philip II of Spain. As Philip's lieutenant general in Flanders he won a brilliant victory over the French at Saint-Quentin (1557) and captured the French commander, Anne de Montmorency. The Treaty of Cateau-Cambrésis (1559) restored most of Savoy (except Vaud and Geneva, which remained Swiss) to Emmanuel Philibert, who in the same year married Margaret of Valois, sister of Henry II of France. Savoy was in deplorable condition. The duke, with great energy and wisdom, reorganized its courts, finances, educational system, industry, and commerce. He also reformed the army, substituting local militias for mercenaries. His skillful diplomacy rid Savoy of the French and Spanish garrisons and secured peaceful relations with the Swiss. Toward the WALDENSES he displayed tolerance. By making Turin his capital, he shifted the center of his duchy from Savoy proper to Piedmont, thus making it an Italian rather than a French state. He was succeeded by his son, Charles Emmanuel I.

Emmaus (ĕmā'əs). **1** Place, outside of Jerusalem, where Cleopas and another disciple met the risen Christ. Luke 24.13. **2** Place, where Judas Maccabeus defeated Gorgias. 1 Mac. 3.40, 57; 4.3–27; 9.50. It is now called Imwas (Jordan) and lies halfway between Jerusalem and Jaffa, (Israel).

Emmaus, borough (1970 pop. 11,511), Lehigh co., E Pa., a suburb adjoining Allentown; inc. 1859. It is chiefly residential, with some light manufacturing industry. Emmaus was founded in 1740 by Moravians, and German customs are preserved there. An old house (1734) in Emmaus is of interest.

Emmen (ĕm'ən), city (1971 pop. 80,713), Drenthe prov., NE Netherlands. Manufactures include textiles and electronic equipment. Peat is produced in the region.

Emmen, town (1970 pop. 22,040), Lucerne canton, central Switzerland, on the Reuss River. Textiles, electrical and iron goods, and airplanes are made in the town.

Emmental (ĕm'əntäl), valley of the Emme River, W central Switzerland. In a region devoted to farming, cattle raising, and dairying, it produces some of the finest cheese in Switzerland.

emmer wheat: see WHEAT.

Emmet, Robert, 1778–1803, Irish nationalist and revolutionary. He studied at Trinity College, Dublin, but left in 1798 because of his nationalist sympathies. In 1800 he went to France, where with exiled United Irishmen he planned a French-aided uprising in Ireland. Returning (1802) to Ireland, he scheduled the uprising for the summer of 1803. The insurrection, which took place in July, 1803, ended in utter confusion. Emmet himself, who had attempted a march on Dublin Castle with about 100 disorderly men, fled. However, he returned to Dublin soon after, partly to be near Sarah Curran, daughter of John Philpot Curran. He was captured, tried, and hanged. Leonard MACNALLY, his attorney, was in the pay of the crown, and many of Emmet's associates were informers for the British government. Emmet became a great hero of Irish nationalists, largely on the basis of his stirring speech from the scaffold. See biography by León O'Broin (1958); study by Helen Landreth (1964).

Emmet, Thomas Addis, 1764–1827, Irish-American lawyer, b. Cork, Ireland, grad. Trinity College, Dublin, 1782; brother of Robert Emmet. He was trained in medicine at the Univ. of Edinburgh but abandoned that field for law and gained a brilliant reputation as a barrister in Ireland, particularly in defending members of the Society of United Irishmen. Imprisoned in 1798 for his activities in the Irish cause, he was later released on condition of perpetual exile and emigrated to the United States in 1804. He established a practice in New York and became one of the most notable American lawyers. His interest in the Irish cause continued, and he was of invaluable assistance to many of the early Irish immigrants who came to America.

Emmor (ĕm'ôr), the same as HAMOR.

Emory University, near Atlanta, Ga.; coeducational; United Methodist; chartered as Emory College 1836, opened 1837 at Oxford. It became Emory University in 1915 and in 1919 moved to Atlanta. In 1929, Emory-at-Oxford, a two-year junior college, was opened at the original site of the university; the junior college was renamed Oxford College in 1964. The university's additional facilities include a computer center, the Yerkes Regional Primate Research Center, and a cooperative program with the National Laboratories in Oak Ridge, Tennessee.

emotion, term commonly and loosely used as synonymous with feeling. In psychology, however, emotion is considered as a response (to stimuli) that involves characteristic physiological changes (such as increase in pulse rate, rise in body temperature, greater or less activity of certain glands, change in rate of breathing, and various other activities) and tends in itself to stimulate the individual to further activity. Fear, love, and anger are usually considered the three primary responses of this kind. They are apparently aroused either directly by some external environmental stimulus or indirectly by some internal one through memory. As individuals mature, specific stimuli no longer provoke the same emotion in every person, nor does there seem to be any universal manner of expressing a given emotion. Since emotional expression varies between cultures, it must be at least partly learned. The development of PSYCHOSOMATIC MEDICINE has emphasized the physiological role of emotions, demonstrating that tension from unrelieved emotions may be implicated in the development of certain physical disorders.

Empedocles (ĕmpĕd'əklēz), c.495–c.435 B.C., Greek philosopher, b. Acragas (present Agrigento), Sicily. Leader of the democratic faction in his native city, he was offered the crown, which he refused. A turn in political fortunes drove him and his followers into exile. Empedocles taught that everything in existence is composed of four underived and indestructible roots, material particles identified as fire, water, earth, and air. He declared the atmosphere to be a corporeal substance, not a mere void; and in the absence of the void or empty space he explained motion as the interpenetration of particles, under the alternating action of two forces, harmony and discord. Believing that motion, or change of place, is the only sort of change possible, he explained all apparent changes in quality or quantity as changes of position of the basic particles underlying the observable object. He was thereby the first to state a principle that is now central to physics. See Denis O'Brien, *Empedocles' Cosmic Cycle* (1969).

empennage: see AIRPLANE.

emperor [Lat. *imperator*=one holding supreme power, especially applied to generals], the sovereign head of an empire. In the Roman republic the term *imperator* referred to the chief military commander and was used only on the battlefield. It was first used continuously by Julius Caesar and was retained by his successor Augustus. It was then adopted by all succeeding Roman rulers as an official title. An emperor continuously ruled over the eastern segment of the Roman Empire, which became known as the Byzantine Empire, until the 15th cent. In the West, after the fall of the empire, the title was revived with the crowning of Charlemagne (800). Eventually the territory reigned over by the successors of Charlemagne became known as the Holy Roman Empire, which lasted until 1806. In 1721 the Russian czar Peter I adopted the title emperor, and his example was followed in the 19th cent. by the monarchs in Austria, France, Germany, and Great Britain (Indian Empire, 1877–1947). The title was also used by several rulers in the Americas—in Brazil from 1822 to 1889; in Mexico by Agustín de Iturbide and Maximilian; and in Haiti by Jean Jacques Dessalines and Henri Christophe. In a general sense the title has been used to describe a non-European ruler of considerable territory, e.g., the emperor of Japan and the emperor of Ethiopia. See also IMPERIALISM.

emphysema (ĕmfĭsē'mə), pathological or physiological enlargement or overdistention of the air sacs of the lungs. The condition is usually chronic and either localized, i.e., restricted to certain areas of the lungs, or diffuse. Localized areas of emphysema are usually of no importance. Emphysema can occur with advanced age, or as the result of long-standing respiratory ailments such as chronic bronchitis or asthma. It occurs predominantly in men over 45; evidence has increasingly linked the disease to both hereditary factors and cigarette smoking. Symptoms are difficulty in breathing, cough with thick sticky sputum, and a bluish tinge of the skin. Emphysema is a progressive disorder, and treatment is aimed at increasing the functional capacity of the lung through the use of bronchodilating aerosol sprays, aminophylline, and ammonium chloride or other sputum liquefiers. Infections that frequently complicate the condition may be controlled by antibiotics.

Empire State Building, in central Manhattan, New York City, on Fifth Ave. between 33d St. and 34th St. It was designed by the firm of Shreve, Lamb, and Harmon and built in 1930–31. For many years it was the tallest building in the world, having 102 stories. In 1951 a television mast was added, bringing its height to 1,472 ft (449 m); it had previously measured 1,250 ft (381 m). An office building, it accommodates some 25,000 tenants. On a very clear day the view from its highest observation tower embraces an area with a circumference of nearly 200 mi (320 km).

Empire style, manner of French interior decoration and costume which evolved from the DIRECTOIRE STYLE. Designated *Empire* because of its identification with the reign of Napoleon I, it was largely created for him by his architects PERCIER and FONTAINE and by the artist J. L. DAVID. Traditional classical motifs, already seen in the reign of Louis XVI, were supplemented by symbols of imperial grandeur—the emperor's monogram and his emblem, the bee; representations of military trophies; and after the successful campaigns in Egypt, Egyptian motifs. Furniture was characterized by clear-cut silhouettes and symmetry in decoration. Pedestal tables with claw feet and gondola, or sleigh, beds were in vogue. The staple wood was mahogany, solid or veneer; brass and ORMOLU mounts were the chief embellishment. Stucco decoration or painted classical motifs often enriched the walls; the ceilings were plain. The style continued in fashion until c.1830. A simplified form was adopted in England and the United States; a German bourgeois adaptation is known as Biedermeier. The empress Josephine introduced the court dress with train. Men began to wear full-length trousers and polished top hats. The style of the first Empire is to be distinguished from that of the second (1852–70), which was gaudy and ostentatious. See Serge Grandjean, *Empire Furniture: 1800–1825* (1966) and P. E. W. Cunnington, *Costumes of the Nineteenth Century* (1971).

empirical formula: see FORMULA.

empiricism (ĕmpĭr'ĭsĭzəm) [Gr.,=experience], philosophical doctrine that all knowledge is derived from experience. For most empiricists experience includes inner experience—reflection upon the mind and its operations—as well as sense perception. This position is opposed to rationalism in that it denies the existence of innate ideas. According to the empiricist, all ideas are derived from experience; therefore, knowledge of the physical world can be nothing more than a generalization from particular instances and can never reach more than a high degree of probability. Most empiricists recognize the existence of at least some a priori truths, e.g., those of mathematics and logic. John Stuart MILL was the first to treat even these as generalizations from experience. Empiricism has been the dominant but not the only tradition in British philosophy. Among its other leading advocates were John LOCKE, George BERKELEY, and David HUME. See James K. Feibleman, *Foundations of Empiricism* (1965); Fraser Crowley, *A Critique of British Empiricism* (1968).

employers' liability: see WORKMEN'S COMPENSATION.

employment bureau, establishment for bringing together the employer offering work and the employee seeking it. In Europe the public labor exchange is most common; in the United States, although a Federal-state system operates free agencies, the private agency, charging a fee, is perhaps more characteristic. In Great Britain the first public employment bureau was opened in 1885 at Egham. A national system was established in 1909, and when the Ministry of Labour was later founded, both unemployment insurance and the labor exchanges were transferred to it. The exchanges charge no fees. In Germany local public exchanges were founded in the late 1800s. France has had public employment agencies since 1916. The International Labor Conference of the League of Nations in 1919 included in the convention on unemployment an article providing that ratifying states would establish free public labor exchanges. In the United States the first state regulation of private employment agencies was in 1848, and Wisconsin and Minnesota required licensing by 1885. Other states enacted similar licensing laws. The first state agency was established in 1890 in Ohio. The Federal government in 1907 opened employment offices under the Bureau of Immigration and Naturalization. In 1918 the Employment Service was established as a unit in the Dept. of Labor. By the time World War I ended, decreasing appropriations and considerable opposition rendered it practically ineffective. With the passage of the Wagner-Peyser Act in 1933, the United States Employment Service (USES) was reestablished as part of the Dept. of Labor. Its functions as defined in the bill were to develop a national system of public employment offices, furnish information as to the opportunities of employment, and maintain a system for clearing labor among the states. In 1941 the states gained strong regulatory power over the privately owned agencies when the Supreme Court ruled (*Olsen* vs. *State of Nebraska*) that states would have the right to control the fees. During World War II the state employment services were brought directly under Federal operation, and later USES was incorporated into the War Manpower Commission. In 1945, USES was transferred back to the Dept. of Labor. The following year Congress turned the public offices back to the states. Today USES is under the Dept. of Labor and maintains over 2,300 employment offices in the states and territories. During the 1960s several acts were passed to expand the scope of services offered by USES. Some of these were the Area Redevelopment Act (1961), the Manpower Development and Training Act (1962), The Vocational and Educational Act (1963), and the Economic Opportunity Act (1964). See A. L. Green, *Manpower and the Public Employment Service in Europe* (1966); S. H. Ruttenberg, *The Federal-State Employment Service* (1970).

Empoli (ĕm'pōlē), town (1971 pop. 44,105), Tuscany, central Italy, on the Arno River. It is a commercial and industrial center. Manufactures include textiles, glass, and chemicals. Its principal church, the Collegiata, dates from 1093.

Emporia (ĕmpôr'ēə), city (1970 pop. 23,327), seat of Lyon co., E central Kansas, in the Flint Hills between the Neosho and Cottonwood rivers; inc. 1857. It is a commercial and shipping (railroad and highway) center for a large cattle and farm area. It has grain elevators, stockyards, industries processing beef and soybeans, and plants making printing equipment, baked goods, and steel tanks. William Allen White made the Emporia *Gazette* nationally known. The College of Emporia and Kansas State Teachers College are there.

Empson, William, 1906–, English critic and poet. His *Seven Types of Ambiguity* (1930), a study of the meanings of poetry, has become a classic of modern literary criticism. It was followed by *Some Versions of Pastoral* (1935), *The Structure of Complex Words* (1951), and *Milton's God* (1961). His poetry—*Poems* (1935) and *The Gathering Storm* (1940)—is noted for its wit and metaphysical conceits. A collected edition of his poems appeared in 1955. See study ed. by Roma Gill (1974).

empyema (ĕmpē-ē'mə), persistent purulent discharge into a cavity such as the pleural space or the gallbladder. Empyema results as a complication of bacterial infections such as pneumonia and lung abscess. It is now relatively rare because of the widespread availability of therapy for the infections that precipitate the disease.

Ems or **Bad Ems** (bät ĕms), town (1966 pop. 10,800), Rhineland-Palatinate, W West Germany, on the Lahn River. Chartered in 1324 as an important lead and silver mining center, it has been one of Europe's most famous spas since the late 17th cent. It was the site of the Congress of Ems (1786), which acted to reduce papal influence in the German Catholic Church. Bismarck drew up (1870) the EMS DISPATCH there.

Ems, river, 208 mi (335 km) long, rising in the Teutoburger Wald, NW West Germany, and flowing NW into the North Sea near Emden. Its wide mouth is called the Dollart. The Ems is paralleled for much of its course by the DORTMUND-EMS CANAL. The **Emsland** is a swampy region between the lower course of the Ems and the Dutch border. Extensive drainage projects (begun 1928) have reduced the moors and swamps. Oil and natural-gas fields were developed in the region after 1940.

Ems dispatch, 1870, communication between King William of Prussia (later German Emperor William I) and his premier, Otto von Bismarck. In June, 1870, the throne of Spain was offered to Prince Leopold of Hohenzollern-Sigmaringen, a relative of King William. Leopold at first accepted the candidacy, but withdrew it in July after the French government had protested. During these transactions William and Bismarck were taking the waters at Ems, Germany. There the French ambassador Comte Benedetti, in an interview with the king, requested William's guarantee that the candidacy of Leopold to the Spanish throne would never be renewed. William rejected the request. Bismarck, intent on provoking war with France, made the king's report of the conversation public (July 13) in his celebrated Ems dispatch, which he edited in a manner certain to provoke the French. France declared war on July 19, and the Franco-Prussian War began.

Emser, Hieronymus (hē"ĕrō'nümōōs ĕm'zər), 1477–1527, German Roman Catholic theologian. He was secretary to the elector of Saxony and urged reform of clerical abuse. In 1519 his enmity with Luther began; he and Luther indulged in the most violent invective, mainly on the subject of Luther's translation of the New Testament. Emser published his own translation in 1527.

Emsland: see under EMS, river.

emu or **emeu** (both: ē'myōō), common name for a large flightless bird of Australia, related to the CASSOWARY and the OSTRICH. It is 5 to 6 ft (150–180 cm) tall and a very swift runner. The head and neck are feathered. The six or seven dark green eggs, laid in a sandy pit, are sometimes incubated by the male and require 56 days to hatch. The emu is easily tamed. There is only one living species, *Dromiceius novaehollandiae.* Emus are classified in the phylum CHORDATA, subphylum Vertebrata, class Aves, order Casuariiformes, family Dromiceidae.

emulsion: see COLLOID.

Enam (ē'năm), city, SW Palestine. Joshua 15.34.

Énambuc, Pierre Belain d': see ESNAMBUC.

enamel, a siliceous substance fusible upon metal. It may be so compounded as to be transparent or opaque and with or without color, but it is usually employed to add decorative color. It was used to decorate jewelry in ancient Egypt, Greece, and Rome. Specimens of enamel-work found in Belgium and England date from as early as the 3d or 2d cent. B.C. Perfected in the Byzantine world, enamel, often in the CLOISONNÉ technique, was used to adorn screens and tabernacles. In the 12th cent. the Spanish excelled in the CHAMPLEVÉ technique. In France at that time brilliant coloristic effects were achieved in the Meuse valley. Concurrently, Limoges became a long-time center of superb enamelwork production. From Limoges in the 16th cent. emerged the most famous artist to work in enamel, Léonard LIMOUSIN. In England, from the 17th cent. on, enamel provided the surface for miniature portraits. It was also used for the florid decoration of vanity cases and snuffboxes. In the 19th cent. there was a decline in craftsmanship and a general loss of interest in the enamel medium. The mid-1960s produced an extensive craft revival and reborn interest in enamel techniques. See K. F. Bates, *The Enamelist* (1967); Therle and Bernard Hughes, *English Painted Enamels* (1967); Geoffrey Franklin, *Simple Enamelling* (1971).

enamelware, utensils having a metal foundation and a coating of special glass, called porcelain enamel, applied by fusion. The porcelain enamel, or vitreous enamel, is applied to make the utensils corrosion resistant, more attractive, and easy to clean. It is designed to withstand the heat encountered in cooking. However, it will crack if the metal it covers is bent out of shape or if it is subjected to a severe jolt. A ground coat, e.g., a mixture consisting chiefly of borax, feldspar, and quartz, and one or more cover coats, e.g., one consisting of quartz, dehydrated borax, and titanium dioxide, are generally applied to a piece of enamelware.

Enan (ē'năn), prince of Naphtali. Num. 1.15.

Enare, lake: see INARI, lake, Finland.

Encarnación (ĕngkärnäsyōn'), city (1972 pop. 24,211), capital of Itapúa dept., SE Paraguay, a port on the Paraná River. It is the commercial center for a rich agricultural region. Industries in the city produce textiles, food products, timber, and hides. Encarnación was founded as a Jesuit mission in 1632. It was almost completely destroyed by a tornado in 1926. Upstream from Encarnación are the picturesque waterfalls at Iguassú.

encaustic, painting medium in which the binder for the pigment is wax or wax and resin. Examples of encaustic tomb portraits from Roman Egypt bear witness to the durability of the medium, which is thought to have been widely used in ancient times. Pliny describes the process in which hot liquid colors were applied to the wall by means of heated irons. The technique was briefly revived in the 19th cent.

Enceladus (ĕnsĕl'ədəs), in astronomy, one of the 10 known moons, or natural satellites, of SATURN.

encephalitis (ĕnsĕf"əlī'təs), general term used to describe a diffuse viral inflammation of the brain and spinal cord, in contrast to a bacterial infection of the meninges (membrane surrounding the brain and spinal cord), known as meningitis. Diagnostic symptoms include capillary congestion, small hemorrhages into perivascular spaces, accumulation of plasma cells and lymphocytes, and increased pressure and protein content of cerebrospinal fluid. Among the several forms of viral brain inflammation are rabies, polio, and two types transmitted by the mosquito: EQUINE ENCEPHALITIS in its various forms and St. Louis encephalitis. The latter two have appeared in epidemic form in the United States and are characterized by high fever, prolonged coma (which is responsible for the disease being known as a sleeping sickness), and convulsions sometimes followed by death. Encephalitis that results as a complication of another systemic infection is known as parainfectious encephalitis and can follow such diseases as measles (rubeola), influenza, and scarlet fever. Although no specific treatment can destroy the virus once the disease has become established, many types of encephalitis can be prevented by immunization with appropriate vaccines.

Enchanted Mesa, sandstone butte, 430 ft (131 m) high, central N. Mex., near the pueblo of Acoma; called *Mesa Encantada* in Spanish and *Katzimo* by the Indians. According to one Pueblo Indian legend, the mesa was the home of their people until an earthquake destroyed the only approach; investigation does not support the legend.

enchantment: see MAGIC.

Encina or **Enzina, Juan del** (both: hwän dĕl änthē'nä), 1469?–c.1530, Spanish dramatist, musician, and poet, b. Encino. He served as court musician to the duke of Alba in Italy, and in 1513 his play *Plácida y Victoriano* was presented in Rome. His *Cancionero* (1496) contains several plays as well as musical compositions and a treatise on poetry. His best-known works, the *Églogas,* are pastoral religious plays in imitation of Vergil. Encina was ordained a priest in 1519. His works followed Italian influence in combining humanist culture with popular drama.

Enciso, Martín Fernández de (märtēn' fĕrnän'dāth dā ĕnthē'sō), fl. 1509–19, Spanish conquistador and geographer. Commanding the supply ship for the colony planted (1509) near Cartagena by OJEDA, he met the discouraged men who had abandoned the settlement and persuaded them to found a new one in Darien. There Diego de Nicuesa had earlier tried to settle a colony. Enciso, an ineffective administrator, was deposed by Vasco Núñez de BALBOA and sent to Spain. Enciso's complaints led to the appointment of Pedro ARIAS DE ÁVILA as governor, and with him Enciso returned (1514). His *Suma de geografía,* an excellent commentary on the flora and fauna he had observed in the New World, appeared in 1519.

Encke, Johann Franz (yō'hän fränts ĕng'kə), 1791–1865, German astronomer. He was assistant (1816–22) and director (1822–25) of the observatory at Seeberg (near Gotha) and director (from 1825) of the Berlin Observatory. He is known for his study of records of the orbit of the comet of 1680 and for calculations, based on transits of Venus, of the earth's distance from the sun. Encke's comet (discovered by J. L. Pons in 1818) was named for him because he calculated its orbit, finding the period of recurrence to be 3.3 years, and accurately predicted the date of its return.

enclosure of land: see INCLOSURE.

encomienda (ānkōmyān'dä) [from Span. *encomendar*=to entrust], system of tributory labor established in Spanish America. Developed as a means of securing an adequate and cheap labor supply, the encomienda was first used over the conquered Moors of Spain. Transplanted to the New World, it gave the conquistador control over the Indians by requiring them to pay tribute from their lands, which were "granted" to deserving subjects of the Spanish crown. The Indians often rendered personal services as well. In return the grantee was theoretically obligated to protect his wards, to instruct them in the Christian faith, and to defend their right to use the land for their own subsistence. When first applied in the West Indies, the system wrought such hardship that the Indian population was soon decimated. This resulted in efforts by the Spanish king and the Dominican order to suppress encomiendas, but the need of the conquerors to reward their supporters led to de facto recognition of the practice. The crown prevented the encomienda from becoming hereditary, and with the New Laws (1542) promulgated by LAS CASAS, the system gradually died out, to be replaced by the REPARTIMIENTO and finally debt PEONAGE. Similar systems of land and labor apportionment were adopted by other colonial powers, notably the Portuguese, the Dutch, and the French. See L. B. Simpson, *The Encomienda in New Spain* (rev. ed. 1966); J. F. Bannon, *Indian Labor in the Spanish Indies* (1966).

encounter group: see GROUP PSYCHOTHERAPY.

encounter theory, in astronomy, see SOLAR SYSTEM.

encyclical, originally, a pastoral letter sent out by a bishop, now a solemn papal letter, meant to inform the whole church on some particular matter of importance. Unlike those in the weightier papal BULL, doctrinal statements in an encyclical are not necessarily regarded as infallible; the faithful, however, are bound to give assent. Encyclicals became more numerous after the 18th cent. Leo XIII issued a whole series of encyclicals reorienting Roman Catholic life in the modern world; among these are *Aeterni Patris,* 1879, on Thomistic philosophy, and *Rerum novarum,* 1891, concerning the social order. Other noteworthy encyclicals include *Pascendi,* 1907, by Pius X, on MODERNISM; *Quadragesimo anno* [in the 40th year, i.e., since *Rerum novarum*], 1931, by Pius XI, dealing further with social questions; and two by Pius XI not written in Latin—*Non abbiamo bisogno,* 1931, against Italian Fascism, and *Mit brennender Sorge,* 1937, against the National Socialist regime in Germany. Among the numerous encyclicals of Pius XII are *Mystici corporis Christi,* 1943, on the nature of the church, and *Sacra virgintas,* 1954, on evangelical chastity. The encyclical *Mater et Magistra,* 1961, by John XXIII, makes current the church's teachings on social matters. Paul VI's *Humanae Vitae,* 1968, which reaffirms the church's traditional prohibition of contraception, caused considerable controversy. All papal edicts are normally known by their first word or words. See A. J. Fremantle, *The Papal Encyclicals in Their Historical Context* (1963).

encyclopedia, compendium of knowledge, either general (attempting to cover all fields) or special (aiming to be comprehensive in a particular field). Basically an encyclopedia differs from a DICTIONARY in that a dictionary is fundamentally devoted to words, an encyclopedia to information on various subjects, with data on and discussion of each subject identified. The terms are used confusingly in the titles of many modern reference books, and many special encyclopedias may be called dictionaries, manuals, handbooks, guides, companions, or the like. Distinction between an encyclopedia and an ALMANAC is somewhat clearer, for an almanac normally is issued periodically and includes ephemeral data applicable only at the time of issue, while an encyclopedia is assembled from accumulated knowledge within a broader scope. Attempts at encompassing universal knowledge began with the brilliantly comprehensive works of Aristotle. Other classical writers tried to follow his example, and the *Natural History* of Pliny the Elder is sometimes called the first encyclopedia. Alexandrian scholars did some work of an encyclopedic nature in compiling their lengthy anthologies and summations of knowledge. The Oriental encyclopedias, particularly the voluminous Chinese collections, were actually more in the nature of anthologies than reference works. In the Middle Ages various scholars drew up compendiums of knowledge; notable were the *Etymologiae* of Isidore of Seville, a curious mixture of fact and legend, and three 13th-century works by Vincent of Beauvais, Roger Bacon, and Brunetto Latini. In 1481, William Caxton printed an English translation of the encyclopedia of Vincent of Beauvais as *Mirror of the World,* and Caxton's successor, Wynkyn de Worde, printed an English translation by John of Trevisa of the encyclopedia of natural science written in Latin (c.1250) by Bartholomew de Glanville. The modern type of encyclopedia—with alphabetical arrangement and frequently with bibliographies—is usually said to have been definitively established by John Harris in his *Lexicon technicum,* published in 1704. Ephraim Chambers in 1728 published his notable *Cyclopedia,* a product of collaboration. In Germany, Johann Zedler published (1732–50) a *Universal-Lexikon.* In France was compiled the most renowned of all encyclopedias, the *Encyclopédie,* which was completed in 1772 by Diderot and others. The first edition of the *Encyclopaedia Britannica* was published in three volumes in 1771. It grew in size and reputation over the years; despite its name, it is now published in the United States. The oldest German encyclopedia still being published is *Brockhaus' Konversations-Lexikon,* first issued from 1796 to 1808. On this, rather than on the work of Ephraim Chambers, was based the British *Chambers's Encyclopedia* (1st ed. 1859–68). The famous Larousse *Grand Dictionnaire universel du XIXème siècle français* in 17 volumes was published from 1865 to 1888. The first noteworthy American encyclopedia was *The Encyclopedia Americana,* edited by Francis Lieber (13 vol., 1829–33). As knowledge in the 19th and 20th cent. became more and more specialized, encyclopedias tended to be more numerous and more massive; they also increased in value as tools because the terms used in a particular field steadily became more unintelligible to scholars outside that field. Several new German and French encyclopedias appeared, as did the Spanish *Enciclopedia universal ilustrada europeo-americana* (70 vol., 1905–33), the *Enciclopedia Italiana* (36 vol., 1929–39), and the Japanese *Sekai dai hyakka jiten* (32 vol., 1958–61). Notable was the large and valuable *Bolshaya Sovetskaya Entsiklopediya* [great Soviet encyclopedia] (1st ed., 65 vol., 1926–47). Important American encyclopedias include *Collier's Encyclopedia* (24 vol., 1949–51) and *Encyclopedia International* (20 vol., 1963). Notable multivolume juvenile encyclopedias are *The Book of Knowledge* (1910), *World Book Encyclopedia* (1917), *Britannica Junior* (1934), *Compton's Pictured Encyclopedia* (1922), and *Merit Students Encyclopedia* (1967). The *Encyclopaedia Britannica* completely revised its format and in 1974 published a 30-volume edition divided into three parts: the Propaedia, a 1-volume outline of the whole; the Micropaedia, a 10-volume short-entry set; and the Macropaedia, a19-volume long-entry set with articles by noted authors and scholars. Some special encyclopedias—all in alphabetical style—are in many volumes; examples are the *Encyclopedia of Philosophy; International Encyclopedia of the Social Sciences; Schaff-Herzog Encyclopedia of Religious Knowledge; The Encyclopedia of Islam; Encyclopedia of Science and Technology;* and *Encyclopedia of World Art.* Most special encyclopedias are, however, smaller, usually in one volume or two. The one-volume general encyclopedia became popular in Europe early in the 20th cent., but the first comprehensive one-volume general encyclopedia in English was *The Columbia Encyclopedia* (1935), of which *The New Columbia Encyclopedia* is the fourth edition. See *Guide to Reference Books* (latest edition); R. L. Collison, *Encyclopaedias: Their History throughout the Ages* (2d ed. 1966).

Encyclopédie (äNsěklôpādē′), the work of the French Encyclopedists, or philosophes. The full title was *Encyclopédie; ou, Dictionnaire raisonné des sciences, des arts, et des métiers.* This work was originally planned as a translation of the Chambers *Cyclopedia,* and the first editor was the Abbé Gua de Malves. The project was abandoned because of disagreements, and Le Breton, the publisher, agreed to let Denis DIDEROT and Jean le Rond d'ALEMBERT edit an entirely new work. With the aid of QUESNAY, MONTESQUIEU, VOLTAIRE, J. J. ROUSSEAU, TURGOT, and others, the two editors produced the first volume in 1751, with a famous "preliminary discourse" signed by Alembert. The discourse indicated the aims of the project and then presented definitions and histories of science and the arts. The rational, secular emphasis of the whole volume infuriated the Jesuits, who attacked the work as irreligious and used their influence to convince the government to withdraw (1759) the official permit. Alembert resigned as editor. The project was able to continue, however, as a result of Diderot's perseverance and the support he received from the statesman Malesherbes. With the help of the chevalier de Jaucourt, Diderot brought the clandestine printing of the work to completion in 1772. Of the 28 volumes, 11 were devoted to plates illustrating the industrial arts; Diderot compiled this information and made the drawings. When the work was in page proof, Diderot discovered that deletions made by the printer had mutilated many articles containing liberal opinions. Despite this unofficial censorship the *Encyclopédie* championed the skepticism and rationalism of the ENLIGHTENMENT. By 1780 a five-volume supplement and a two-volume index were added, compiled under other editors. The success of the *Encyclopédie* was immediate, and its influence was incalculable. Through its stress on scientific determinism and its attacks on legal, juridical, and clerical abuses, the *Encyclopédie* was a major factor in the intellectual preparation for the French Revolution. See selections ed. by N. S. Hoyt and Thomas Cassirer (tr. 1965); R. N. Schwab et al., *Inventory of Diderot's Encyclopédie* (1971); John Lough, *The Encyclopédie* (1971).

endangered species, any species of animal (or plant) whose ability to survive and reproduce has been jeopardized by man's activities; for example, by purposeful extermination to protect livestock or to obtain hides, feathers, food, or other animal products, or as a consequence of habitat destruction. In the United States today more than 100 species of animals are threatened with extinction, among them the Florida panther, eastern cougar, and other mountain lions; several species of wolves; the glacier and grizzly bears; the bald eagle, several species of hawks, the California condor, the whooping crane, and many smaller birds; the alligator and several other reptiles; and more than 30 species of fish. Hunting, TRAPPING, and poisoning to protect sheep and cattle have taken the greatest toll among predatory mammals and birds. Bird populations have also suffered great losses because of INSECTICIDES. The chemicals they contain, such as DDT, accumulate in birds' bodies and interfere with calcium metabolism. As a result, the females lay eggs with extremely thin shells or no shells at all, so that the embryos do not survive to hatching. Perhaps most serious of all, the destruction of habitat by strip mining, oil spills, and water pollution and by the drainage and filling of swamps and the leveling of forests for residential and industrial development has left many creatures with literally no room in which to live and breed. As a consequence, conservationists have been pressing for habitat preservation by the establishment of new WILDLIFE REFUGES and WILDERNESS areas and for LAND USE planning that would provide for development without habitat destruction. Recent legislation affecting endangered species includes the various federal antipollution laws, the banning of DDT, the National Environmental Policy Act (NEPA) of 1969, and the Endangered Species Acts of 1966, 1969, and 1973. This last prohibits any trade in endangered species or their products and requires that federal agencies henceforth assess the impact on wildlife habitat of proposed projects—much as NEPA requires a statement of environmental impact (see ENVIRONMENTALISM). On the international scene, efforts have been made to halt the trade in spotted cats and crocodiles and to curtail whaling and the taking of porpoises in tuna seines. A conference in Washington, D.C., in 1973, attended by 80 nations, drew up a Convention on International Trade in Endangered Species of Wild Fauna and Flora that, when ratified, would protect more than 500 species of animals and more than 20,000 plants, both land and marine. See CONSERVATION OF NATURAL RESOURCES. See James Fisher et al., *Wildlife in Danger* (1969), T. B. Allen, *Vanishing Wildlife of North America* (1974), and the *Red Data Books* published continuously by the International Union for the Conservation of Nature.

Endecott or **Endicott, John,** c.1588–1665, one of the founders of Massachusetts Bay colony, b. England. He led the first group of Puritan colonists to Massachusetts Bay in 1628 and was the first governor (1629–30) of the colony at Salem. Endecott remained important in public affairs after John Winthrop established the colony's center at Boston, serving as governor again a number of times (1644, 1649, 1651–53, 1655–64). As a military leader, he so mismanaged an expedition (1636) against the Indians that he helped bring on the Pequot War. One of the sternest of the Puritan fathers, he was zealous in persecuting the Quakers. See biography by L. S. Mayo (1936, repr. 1971).

Enderbury Island: see PHOENIX ISLANDS.

Enders, John Franklin, 1897–, American bacteriologist, b. West Hartford, Conn., grad. Yale, 1920, Ph.D. Harvard, 1930. He began teaching at Harvard in 1929, became associate professor in 1942, and joined the research staff of Children's Hospital, Boston. The 1954 Nobel Prize in Physiology and Medicine was awarded jointly to Enders, T. H. Weller, and F. C. Robbins for their success in growing polio viruses in cultures of various tissues.

Endicott, John: see ENDECOTT, JOHN.

Endicott, village (1970 pop. 16,556), Broome co., S central N.Y., on the Susquehanna River; settled c.1795, inc. 1906. Shoes and business machines are the chief manufactures.

endive: see CHICORY.

endless screw, screw fixed so that it cannot move longitudinally as it rotates. Thus, instead of the usual action in which a screw advances itself through a medium as it turns, the screw remains stationary and forces the medium or a mechanical part to advance. When a screw of this type is arranged to drive a cogwheel whose teeth mesh with its thread, the screw is called a worm GEAR. See ARCHIMEDES' SCREW.

endocarditis (ĕn″dōkärdī′tĭs), bacterial infection of the endocardium (inner lining of the heart) that can be either acute or subacute. In the acute form the symptoms (fever, malaise, fatigue, weight loss, anemia) are directly related to the presence of an active infection that runs its course within a few weeks. Acute endocarditis may follow respiratory infection, surgery, or other trauma; but in some cases the source of infection is unknown. Subacute bacterial endocarditis is an insidious, often progressive, disease that can lead to kidney failure and congestive heart failure. The causative agent in almost all cases is *Streptococcus viridans.* A previously damaged valve increases the risk of infection tenfold. The most common diseases causing these predisposing valvular deformities are RHEUMATIC FEVER and CONGENITAL HEART DISEASE. Thrombi associated with the infection on the valve often dislodge and spread septic emboli throughout the body that may damage the kidney. Primary diagnostic symptoms are fever and a changing heart murmur. Treatment with high doses of antibiotics often kills the bacteria, but the damage to the valve may put an additional strain on the heart that eventually can lead to cardiac failure. However, it is sometimes possible through follow-up corrective surgery to repair valves damaged by endocarditis.

endocrine system (ĕn'dəkrĭn), body control system composed of a group of glands that maintain the stable internal environment by producing chemical regulatory substances called HORMONES. The endocrine system includes the PITUITARY GLAND, THYROID GLAND, PARATHYROID GLANDS, ADRENAL GLAND, PANCREAS, OVARIES, and TESTES; the THYMUS GLAND, PINEAL BODY, and kidney (see URINARY SYSTEM) are also sometimes considered endocrine organs. The endocrine, or ductless, glands are unique in that the hormones they produce do not pass through tubes or ducts but are secreted directly into the internal environment where they are transmitted via the bloodstream or by diffusion and act at distant points in the body. In contrast, other glands such as sweat glands, salivary glands, or glands of the gastrointestinal system secrete the substances they produce through ducts and the substances are used in the vicinity of the gland. The regulation of body functions by the endocrine system depends on the existence of specific receptor cells in target organs that respond in specialized ways to the minute quantities of the hormonal messengers. Some endocrine hormones, such as THYROXINE from the thyroid gland, affect nearly all body cells; others, such as PROGESTERONE from the female ovary, which regulates the uterine lining, affect only a single organ. The quantities of hormones are maintained by feedback mechanisms that depend on interactions between the endocrine glands, the blood levels of the various hormones, and activities of the target organ. The hormones act by regulating cell metabolism; by accelerating, slowing, or maintaining enzyme activity in receptor cells, they control growth and development, metabolic rate, sexual rhythms, and reproduction. The master gland, i.e., the gland that regulates many of the other endocrine glands, is the pituitary, situated at the base of the brain. Also called the hypophysis, it secretes at least five hormones that directly affect the other endocrine glands. The pituitary secretes THYROTROPIC HORMONE, which regulates thyroid gland activity, ADRENOCORTICOTROPIC HORMONE (ACTH), which regulates activity of the adrenal cortex, and three GONADOTROPIC HORMONES, follicle-stimulating hormone (FSH), luteinizing hormone (LH), and luteotropic hormone (LTH), which control the growth and reproductive activities of the sex glands. The pituitary also produces substances that do not act directly on other endocrine glands: somatotropic hormone, or GROWTH HORMONE, which controls growth in all tissues, ANTIDIURETIC HORMONE (ADH), which controls the rate of water excretion in the urine, oxytocin, which stimulates uterine contraction and helps regulate milk production by the breasts, and melanocyte-stimulating hormone, which regulates the activity of the melanocytes, or pigment-producing cells. Of the endocrine glands regulated by the pituitary, the adrenal cortex, the outer part of each of the two adrenal glands, produces ALDOSTERONE, CORTISOL, and other STEROIDS. These substances regulate salt concentration in body fluids and glucose, fat, and protein metabolism. The inner portion of the gland, the adrenal medulla, secretes EPINEPHRINE (adrenaline) and norepinephrine, substances connected with the autonomic nervous system that help the body to respond to danger or stress. The thyroid, located below the larynx and partially surrounding the trachea, produces thyroxine, which controls the metabolic rate of most body cells. The testes produce the male sex hormone TESTOSTERONE, which controls the development of the male sex organs as well as secondary sex characteristics. The pituitary hormone LH regulates testosterone production, and FSH initiates sperm formation in the testes. In females, FSH, LH, and LTH are integrated into the complex monthly cycles of ovulation, production of the hormones ESTROGEN and progesterone by the ovaries and corpus luteum, and menstruation; LTH also contributes to lactation. Estrogen controls growth of the sex organs and breasts and regulates secondary sex characteristics. The most important function of progesterone is to prepare the uterine lining for implantation of a fertilized egg. The other endocrine glands are not directly controlled by the pituitary. The four parathyroid glands, located behind the thyroid, secrete a hormone that regulates calcium and phosphate metabolism. The endocrine portion of the pancreas, called the islets of Langerhans, secretes INSULIN, which regulates the level of sugar in the blood. The thymus, sometimes considered another endocrine gland, processes lymphocytes in newborn animals, seeding the lymph nodes and other lymph tissues; it is partly responsible for the development of the organism's immune system (see IMMUNITY). The kidney is sometimes considered an endocrine gland because it secretes the hormone renin which, with other substances, regulates blood pressure. The pineal body produces a substance called melatonin, which influences the development of the sex glands. Physiological processes are under nervous system as well as endocrine control and a gland adjacent to the pituitary, called the HYPOTHALAMUS, mediates between the two systems; the hypothalamus secretes pituitary-regulating substances in response to nervous system stimuli including smell, taste, pain, and emotions. Thus, stress, cold, heat, and other stimuli release CRF, or adrenocorticotropic hormone-releasing factor, from the hypothalamus, causing ACTH to be produced by the pituitary, which in turn stimulates the production of the adrenal hormone cortisol. Similar chemical regulatory mechanisms operate in the regulation of the sex and thyroid hormones. Hypothalamic activity is also regulated by body substances, e.g., cortisol inhibits the production of hypothalamic CRF.

endoderm, in biology, inner layer of tissue formed in the gastrula stage of the developing embryo. At the end of the blastula stage, cells of the embryo are arranged in the form of a hollow ball. Cell movement results in an invagination of the bottom region, or vegetal hemisphere, of the embryo so that it resembles a double-walled cup. The inner layer of the cup is the endoderm; the outer layer is the ECTODERM; a middle layer, the MESODERM, forms from a marginal zone. The endoderm is the germ layer from which are formed the digestive system, many glands, and part of the respiratory system. See EMBRYO.

endodontics: see DENTISTRY.

endogamy (ĕndŏg'əmē): see MARRIAGE.

En-dor, village, Palestine, S of Mt. Tabor, where lived a celebrated witch consulted by King Saul. 1 Sam. 28.7; Ps. 83.10.

endrin (ĕn'drĭn): see INSECTICIDE.

Endymion (ĕndĭm'ēən), in Greek mythology, young shepherd, loved by Selene (the moon). In one version of his legend, he asked Zeus for immortality and perpetual youth. Zeus consented on the condition that Endymion remain eternally asleep. The English poets Lyly, Drayton, and Keats all wrote poems based on the legend.

En-eglaim (ĕn-ĕg'lāĭm, ĕn-ēglā'ĭm), unidentified place, probably on the Dead Sea. Ezek. 47.10. It may be the same as EGLAIM.

enemy alien: see ALIEN.

energy, in physics, the ability or capacity to do work or to produce change. Forms of energy include HEAT, LIGHT, SOUND, ELECTRICITY, chemical energy, and, according to the theory of RELATIVITY, MASS. Energy and work are measured in the same units—foot-pounds, joules, ergs, or some other, depending on the system of measurement being used. When a FORCE acts on a body, the work performed (and the energy expended) is the product of the force and the distance over which it is exerted. Potential energy is the capacity for doing work that a body possesses because of its position or condition. For example, a stone resting on the edge of a cliff has potential energy due to its position in the earth's gravitational field. If it falls, the force of gravity (which is equal to the stone's weight) will act on it until it strikes the ground; the stone's potential energy is equal to its weight times the distance it can fall. A charge in an electric field also has potential energy because of its position. A stretched spring also has potential energy because of its condition. The energy associated with the different STATES OF MATTER is another form of potential energy. Kinetic energy is energy a body possesses because it is in motion. The kinetic energy of a body with mass *m* moving at a velocity *v* is one half the product of the mass of the body and the square of its velocity, i.e., $KE = \frac{1}{2}mv^2$. Even when a body appears to be at rest, its atoms and molecules are in constant motion and thus have kinetic energy. The average kinetic energy of the atoms or molecules is measured by the TEMPERATURE of the body. The difference between kinetic energy and potential energy, and the conversion of one to the other, is demonstrated by the falling of a rock from a cliff, when its energy of position is changed to energy of motion. Another example is provided in the movements of a simple pendulum (see HARMONIC MOTION). As the suspended body moves upward in its swing, its kinetic energy is continuously being changed into potential energy; the higher it goes the greater becomes the energy that it owes to its position. At the top of the swing the change from kinetic to potential energy is complete, and in the course of the downward motion that follows the potential energy is in turn converted to kinetic energy. It is common for energy to be converted from one form to another; however, the law of conservation of energy, a fundamental law of physics, states that although energy can be changed in form it can be neither created nor destroyed (see CONSERVATION LAWS). The theory of relativity shows, however, that mass and energy are equivalent and thus that one can be converted into the other. As a result, the law of conservation of energy includes both mass and energy. Chemical energy is a special kind of potential energy; it is the form of energy involved in chemical reactions. The chemical energy of a substance is due to the condition of the atoms of which it is made; it resides in the chemical bonds that join the atoms in compound substances (see CHEMICAL BOND). Many transformations of energy are of practical importance. COMBUSTION of fuels results in the conversion of chemical energy into heat and light. In the electric storage BATTERY chemical energy is converted to electrical energy and conversely. In the PHOTOSYNTHESIS of starch green plants convert light energy from the sun into chemical energy. Hydroelectric plants convert the kinetic energy of falling water into electrical energy, which can be conveniently carried by wires to its place of use (see POWER, ELECTRIC). The force of a nuclear explosion results from the partial conversion of matter to energy (see NUCLEAR ENERGY).

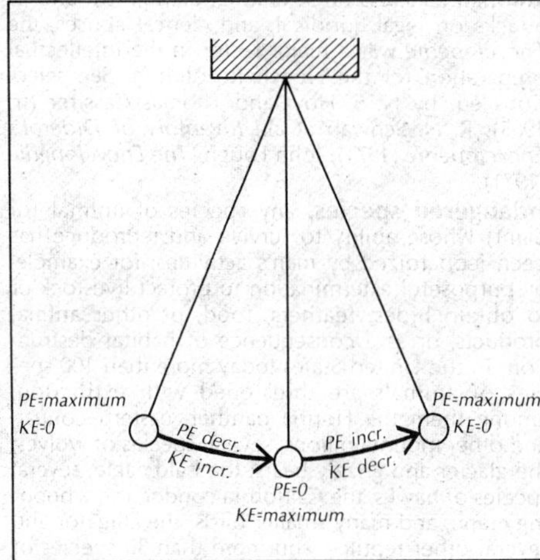

Relations between potential energy (PE) and kinetic energy (KE) for a swinging pendulum

energy, sources of. The development of science and civilization is closely linked to the availability of ENERGY in useful forms. Energy sources are used for transportation, for heat and light for dwelling and working areas, and for the manufacture of goods of all kinds, among other applications. Modern society consumes vast amounts of energy in all forms: light, heat, electrical, mechanical, chemical, and nuclear. The rate at which energy is produced or consumed is called POWER, although this term is sometimes used in common speech synonymously with *energy.* The source of energy, or prime mover, first used by man was animal power, i.e., the energy he himself could supply or obtain from animals he had tamed. Later, as civilization developed, he learned to use wind and water power as a prime mover, harnessing the wind to drive his ships and turn his WINDMILLS and the water of streams and rivers to turn his WATER WHEELS. The rotating shaft of a windmill or water wheel could then be used to crush grain, to raise water from a well, or to serve any number of other uses. The motion of the wind and water, as well as the motion of the wheel or shaft, represents a form of kinetic energy, which is one kind of mechanical energy. The source of animal power is ultimately the chemical energy contained in foods eaten by man or animal. The chemical energy contained in wood and other combustible FUELS has served since the beginning of history as a source of heat for cooking and warmth. At the start of the Industrial Revolution, water power was used to provide energy for factories through systems of belts and pulleys that transmitted the energy to many different machines. The invention of the STEAM ENGINE, which converts the chemical energy of fuels into heat energy and the heat into mechanical energy, provided another source of energy. The steam engine is an external-combustion engine, since fuel is burned outside the engine to create the steam used inside it. During the 19th cent. the INTERNAL-COMBUSTION ENGINE was developed; a variety of fuels, depending on the type of internal-combustion engine, are burned directly in the engine's chambers to provide a source of mechanical energy. Both steam engines and internal-combustion engines found application as stationary sources of power for different purposes and as mobile sources for transportation, as in the steamship, the railroad locomotive (both steam and diesel), and the automobile. All these sources of energy ultimately depend on the combustion of fuels for their operation. Early in the 19th cent. another source of energy was developed that did not necessarily need the combustion of fuels—the electric GENERATOR, or dynamo. The generator converts the mechanical energy of a conductor moving in a magnetic field into electrical energy, using the principle of electromagnetic INDUCTION. The great advantage of electrical energy, or electric power, as it is commonly called, is that it can be transmitted easily over great distances (see POWER, ELECTRIC). As a result, it is the most widely used form of energy in modern civilization; it is readily converted to light, to heat, or, through the electric MOTOR, to mechanical energy again. The large-scale production of electrical energy was made possible by the invention of the TURBINE, which efficiently converts the straight-line motion of falling water or expanding steam into the rotary motion needed to turn the rotor of a large generator. The development of NUCLEAR ENERGY made available another source of energy. The heat of a NUCLEAR REACTOR can be used to produce steam, which then can be directed through a turbine to drive an electric generator, the propellers of a large ship, or some other machine. The demand for energy has increased steadily, not only because of growing population but also because of the greater number of technological goods available and the increased affluence that has brought these goods within the reach of a larger proportion of the population. Many families in the United States in the 1970s owned more than one automobile, and many of these were equipped with power brakes, power steering, air conditioning, and other accessories requiring energy. Electrical devices, such as clothes washers and dryers, dishwashers, freezers, stereo phonographs, and even electric can openers and electric toothbrushes, also became more widely used. As a result of this huge increase in the demand for and consumption of energy, there was also a growing energy crisis by the 1970s, brought on mainly by two factors. First, most of the energy consumed is ultimately generated by the combustion of fossil fuels, such as coal, petroleum, and natural gas, and the world has only a finite supply of these fuels, which are rapidly being used up (see under CONSERVATION OF NATURAL RESOURCES). Second, there has been increasing concern for the effect on the environment of the waste products of various energy consumers (see POLLUTION). These wastes include heat dumped into rivers and streams by electric generating plants using steam turbines; harmful pollutants dumped into the atmosphere by these same plants, by factories, and by automobiles, trucks, and other vehicles; and radioactive wastes disposed of by nuclear-fueled electric plants. One solution to the second problem has been development of devices to treat wastes before they are disposed of, but these devices themselves require more energy, thus adding to the first problem. The result is that, unless man reduces his energy consumption, he must find new sources of energy. The search for conventional fossil fuels has been extended to the Arctic and Antarctic and under the oceans, but the discovery of new deposits will only alleviate the two basic problems, not solve them. Present nuclear-energy plants use nuclear fission, which requires scarce and expensive fuels and produces potentially dangerous wastes. The fuel problem has been partly helped by the development of breeder reactors, which produce more nuclear fuel than they consume, but the long-term hopes for nuclear energy center on the development of controlled sources using nuclear fusion rather than fission. The basic fuels for fusion are extremely plentiful (e.g., hydrogen, from water) and the end products are harmless. The basic problem is containing the fuels at the extremely high temperatures necessary to initiate and sustain nuclear fusion. Another possible source of energy is solar energy. The earth receives huge amounts of energy every day from the sun, but the problem has been harnessing this energy so that it is available at the appropriate time and in the appropriate form. For example, solar energy is received only during the daylight hours, but more heat and electricity for lighting are needed at night. Experimental solar-energy systems store this energy during the day, either by heating fluids or by charging storage batteries. Some scientists have suggested using the earth's internal heat as a source of energy. This geothermal energy is released naturally in geysers and volcanoes. Geothermal power has been used since 1904 in the Larderello area of Italy. As of 1971 the operation there had a capacity of 370 megawatts. The two other principal areas that utilize geothermal energy are the Geysers in N California and Wairakei in New Zealand. Still another possible energy source is tidal energy. Experimental systems have been set up to harness the energy released in the twice-daily ebb and flow of the ocean's tides. However, the tidal-electric plant on the Rance estuary on the Channel Island coast of France is the only full-scale operation of its kind. When it was started in 1966, its capacity was 240 megawatts. See C. R. Russell, *Elements of Energy Conversion* (1967); G. R. Harrison, *The Conquest of Energy* (1968); Frank Barnaby, *Man and the Atom: The Uses of Nuclear Energy* (1971).

Enesco, Georges (zhôrzh ĕnĕs'kō), 1881–1955, Rumanian violinist, composer, and conductor, studied at the Vienna Conservatory and in Paris with Massenet, Fauré, and others. Enesco made many concert tours as both violinist and conductor in Europe and the United States, including appearances with the New York Philharmonic-Symphony Orchestra (1936–39). He composed three symphonies; chamber music; an opera, *Oedipe* (Paris, 1936); and other orchestral music, notably two popular Rumanian Rhapsodies. Yehudi Menuhin was one of his pupils.

Enfantin, Barthélemy Prosper (bärtälmē' prôspĕr' äNfäNtăN'), 1796–1864, French socialist, sometimes called Père Enfantin. He became a leader of the movement started by the comte de SAINT-SIMON. Under his guidance the Saint-Simonian school put increasing emphasis upon religious and moral regeneration and less upon political reform. Following a schism developing out of Enfantin's disagreement with Saint-Amand BAZARD over marriage reform, Enfantin established (1832) a monastic settlement for the remnants of the movement at Ménilmontant. It disintegrated with the imprisonment of Enfantin for a year on charges of incitement to immorality and financial fraud. After his release he devoted himself mainly to business enterprises. His writings include *Religion Saint-Simonienne* (1831) and *Life Eternal* (1861, tr. 1920). See his complete works (16 vol., 1868–78).

Enfield, borough (1971 pop. 266,788) of Greater London, SE England. The borough was created in 1965 by the merger of the municipal boroughs of Enfield, Edmonton, and Southgate. It is residential, with important concentrations of industry. Rifles, electrical products, boilers, chemicals, cables, textiles, and cement are the leading manufactures. The poets John Keats and William Cowper lived in Edmonton. Southgate is noted for its parks.

Enfield, town (1970 pop. 46,189), Hartford co., N Conn., on the Connecticut River at the Mass. line, in a tobacco-growing area; settled c.1680. Among its many manufactures are carpets and plastic products. Originally part of Massachusetts, it became part of Connecticut in 1749. The site of a Shaker settlement (c.1780–1915) was bought for a state prison farm. The town hall was built in 1775.

Engadine (ĕng'gədēn), Romansh *Engiadina* (ĕnjädē'nä), valley of the upper Inn River, Grisons canton, E Switzerland, in the Rhaetian Alps. It extends for c.60 mi (100 km) NE from Maloja Pass to the Austrian border and consists of the Upper and the Lower Engadine. The valley, which is forested and partially cultivated, is dominated in the south by the Bernina Alps. The population is largely Romansh-speaking and Protestant. Noted for its majestic scenery and excellent climate, the Engadine is famous as a tourist and health center. Its many resorts include St. Moritz, Pontresina, Silvaplana, and Schuls, as well as Samaden, chief town of the Upper Engadine. The Swiss National Park (53 sq mi/137 sq km; est. 1909), in the Lower Engadine, is a wildlife sanctuary.

En-gannim (ĕn-găn'ĭm). **1** Town of Judah. Joshua 15.34. **2** Levitical city, the modern Janin (Jordan), at the southeastern end of the plain of Esdraelon. Joshua 19.21; 21.29. Anem: 1 Chron. 6.73.

En-gedi (ĕn-gē'dī, ĕn'-gēdī), oasis on the W shore of the Dead Sea, famed for its vineyards. David hid there from Saul. Joshua 15.62; 1 Sam. 24.1-4; Cant. 1.14; Ezek. 47.10; 2 Chron. 20.2.

Engelberg (ĕng'əlbĕrkh), town (1970 pop. 2,841), Obwalden half canton, central Switzerland. It is a winter and summer resort and has an early 12th-century Benedictine abbey.

Engelholm: see ÄNGELHOLM, Sweden.

Engelmann, George (ĕng'əlmən), 1809–84, American physician and botanist, b. Frankfurt-am-Main, Germany, educated at the universities of Heidelberg and Würzburg (M.D., 1831). Emigrating to America in 1832, he settled in St. Louis, Mo., and built up a large medical practice. His interest in general science led him also to do research in biology and botany and to conduct systematic meteorological observations from 1836 until his death. He was the first to call attention to the immunity of the American grape to the attack of the plant lice phylloxera. His large plant collection and botanical library and some 60 volumes of botanical notes and drawings are in the Missouri Botanical Gardens, St. Louis. Some of his more important papers were collected in *Botanical Works of the Late George Engelmann* (1877). Three plant genera and a number of species bear his name.

Engels, Friedrich (frē'drĭkh ĕng'əls), 1820–95, German socialist; with Karl MARX, one of the founders of modern Communism. The son of a wealthy Rhenish textile manufacturer, Engels went in 1842 to take a position in a factory near Manchester, England, in which his father had an interest. In 1844, while passing through Paris, he met Marx, and their lifelong association began. Engels's first major book was *The Condition of the Working Class in England in 1844* (1845, tr. 1887), which attracted wide attention. From 1845 to 1850 he was active in Germany, France, and Belgium, organizing revolutionary movements and collaborating with Marx on several works, notably the *Communist Manifesto* (1848). The failure of the revolutions of 1848 caused his return (1850) to England, where he lived the rest of his life. He was a successful businessman, and from his income he enabled Marx to devote his life to research and writing. Engels played a leading role in the First INTERNATIONAL and the Second International. After Marx's death, Engels edited the second and third volumes of *Das Kapital* from Marx's drafts and notes. The intimate intellectual relationship between Marx and Engels leaves little doubt that there was complete harmony of thought between them, although critics have sometimes questioned their full agreement. Marx's personality has overshadowed that of Engels, but the influence of Engels on the theories of MARXISM, and particularly on the elaboration of DIALECTICAL MATERIALISM, can scarcely be overestimated. Engels's *Anti-Dühring* (1878, tr. 1934) and *The Origin of the Family, Private Property, and the State* (1884, tr. 1902) rank among the fundamental books in Communist literature and profoundly influenced Vladimir Ilyich Lenin. Among his other works is *The Peasant War in Germany* (tr. 1926). See selected correspondence with Marx, ed. by Dona Torr (1942); his *Socialism, Utopian and Scientific* (1883, tr. 1892) and *Dialectics of Nature* (1925, tr. 1940); biography by Gustav Mayer (1936, repr. 1969); *The Marx-Engels Reader*, ed. by R. C. Tucker (1972); Steven Marcus, *Engels, Manchester and the Working Class* (1974).

Engels (ĕn'gĭls), city (1970 pop. 130,000), E European USSR, a port on the Volga River. It has a large chemical fiber complex. Founded by Ukrainian settlers, the city was called Pokrovsk until 1931. It was the capital (1924–41) of the former German Volga Autonomous SSR.

Enghien, Louis Antoine Henri de Bourbon-Condé, duc d' (lwē äNtwän' äNrē' də bo͝orbôN'-kôNdā' dük däNgyăN'), 1772–1804, French émigré; son of Louis Henri Joseph de CONDÉ. He was unjustly accused by Napoleon Bonaparte, then first consul of France, of participating in the conspiracy of Georges CADOUDAL against Napoleon. On Napoleon's orders, the duke was kidnapped from his residence in Ettenheim, Baden, and within the space of a few hours, was court-martialed and shot at Vincennes (March 21, 1804). Napoleon's brutal procedure provoked a revulsion of feeling against him throughout Europe.

Enghien, Flemish *Edingen,* town (1970 pop. 4,115), Hainaut prov., W central Belgium. It is a tourist center and has industries that manufacture linen, cotton textiles, and lace. Enghien was founded in the 11th cent. and became a trade center. It passed to the Bourbon family in the 15th cent. but was sold (1606) by Henry IV of France to the house of Liège.

The title of duke of Enghien remained with the Condé branch of the house of Bourbon.

engine: see DIESEL ENGINE; INTERNAL-COMBUSTION ENGINE; STEAM ENGINE; ROTARY ENGINE; AUTOMOBILE.

engineering, profession devoted to designing, constructing, and operating the structures, machines, and other devices of industry and everyday life. Until the Industrial Revolution there were only two kinds of engineers. The military engineer built such things as fortifications, catapults, and, later, cannons. The civil engineer built bridges, harbors, aqueducts, buildings, and other structures. During the early 19th cent. in England mechanical engineering developed as a separate field to provide manufacturing machines and the engines to power them. The first British professional society of civil engineers was formed in 1818; that for mechanical engineers followed in 1847. In the United States, the order of growth of the different branches of engineering, measured by the date a professional society was formed, is civil engineering (1852), mining and metallurgical engineering (1871), mechanical engineering (1880), electrical engineering (1884), and chemical engineering (1908). Aeronautical engineering and industrial engineering, the other major branches, are more modern developments. Civil engineering includes the planning, designing, construction, and maintenance of structures and altering geography to suit man's needs. Some of the numerous subdivisions are transportation (e.g., railroad facilities and highways); hydraulics (e.g., river control, irrigation, swamp draining, water supply, and sewage disposal); and structures (e.g., buildings, bridges, and tunnels). Mineral engineering includes the closely allied pursuits of mining, metallurgical, and petroleum engineering. Together these are concerned with extracting minerals from the ground and converting them to pure forms. Mechanical engineering is concerned with the design, construction, and operation of power plants, engines, and machines. It deals mostly with things that move. One common way of dividing mechanical engineering is into heat utilization and machine design. The generation, distribution, and use of heat is applied in boilers, heat engines, air conditioning, and refrigeration. Machine design is concerned with hardware, including that making use of heat processes. There are many more subspecialties, since mechanical engineering is the broadest engineering field. Electrical engineering encompasses the generation and transmission of electrical power and all the devices that use it. This complex and expanding field includes among its specialties power, electrical machinery, and illumination. Although in the past it also included electronics, this specialty, which deals mainly with computers and communication equipment, has been recognized as a separate branch known as electronic engineering. Chemical engineering deals with the design, construction, and operation of plants and machinery for making such products as acids, dyes, drugs, plastics, and synthetic rubber. The chemical engineer strives to adapt the chemical reactions discovered by the laboratory chemist to large-scale production. He must be familiar with both chemistry and mechanical engineering. Aeronautical engineering is applied in the designing of aircraft and missiles and in directing the technical phases of their manufacture and operation. Industrial engineering, or management engineering, is concerned with efficient production. The industrial engineer designs methods, not machinery. His jobs include plant layout, analysis and planning of workers' jobs, economical handling of raw materials, their flow through the production process, and the efficient control of the inventory of finished products. The more important of the many smaller branches of engineering are agricultural engineering, naval architecture and marine engineering, engineering physics, nuclear engineering, and geological engineering. Another way of dividing engineering is by function. Among the top functional divisions are design, operation, management, development, and construction; development engineering is concerned with converting an idea into a practical product. The first schools in the United States to offer an engineering education were the United States Military Academy (West Point) in 1817, an institution now known as Norwich Univ. in 1819, and Rensselaer Polytechnic Institute in 1825. An engineering education is based on a strong foundation in mathematics and science; this is followed by courses emphasizing the application of this knowledge to a specific field and studies in the social sciences and humanities to give the engineer a broader education. See SANITARY SCIENCE.

England, John, 1786–1842, Irish Roman Catholic churchman in America, b. Cork. He studied, was ordained, and ministered to several parishes in Co. Cork. His parishes were poor ones, but he became well known for his zeal for Catholic Emancipation and for advocating equality of his church with the Anglicans in Ireland. England was consecrated bishop of the new see of Charleston, S.C., in 1820 and moved to America. His diocese included the Carolinas and Georgia. Notable from the beginning for his intense interest in all things American, he traveled throughout his diocese continually, going many miles if necessary to visit even one of his coreligionists. He was especially devoted to the needs of the Negroes in his diocese. See P. K. Guilday, *Life and Times of John England, 1786–1842* (2 vol., 1927, repr. 1969).

England, part of the United Kingdom of Great Britain and Northern Ireland (1971 pop. of England, 45,870,062), 50,334 sq mi (130,365 sq km). It is bounded by Wales and the Irish Sea on the west and Scotland on the north. The English Channel, the Strait of Dover, and the North Sea separate it from the continent of Europe. The Isle of Wight, off the southern mainland in the English Channel, and the Scilly Islands, in the Atlantic Ocean off the southwestern tip of the mainland, are considered part of England. The Thames and the Severn are the longest rivers. Behind the white chalk cliffs of the southern coast lie the gently rolling downs and wide plains stretching to the CHILTERN HILLS and the COTSWOLD HILLS. Along the east coast are the lowlands of Norfolk, reaching up to the FENS, formerly marshy country that has been drained, lining The WASH, an inlet of the North Sea. In the east and southeast, river estuaries lead to some of England's great commercial and industrial centers: LONDON, on the Thames; Hull, on the Humber; TEESIDE, on the Tees; and NEWCASTLE UPON TYNE, on the Tyne. The north of England, above the Humber, is mountainous; the chief highlands are the Cumbrian Mts. in the northwest and the Pennines, which run north-south in N central England. The famous LAKE DISTRICT, in the Cumbrians, has England's highest points. The center of England, the MIDLANDS, is a large plain, interrupted and bordered by hills. In the Midlands are the industrial centers of BIRMINGHAM and the BLACK COUNTRY. The Midlands, especially its northern edge, was formerly a great coal-mining region. On the Lancashire plain is the great city of MANCHESTER, the center of the English textile industry. Durham and W Yorkshire are also highly industrialized, but E Yorkshire is an area of bleak moors and wolds, and the upper reaches of Northumberland are sparsely populated. In the west and southwest the border with Wales and the peninsula of Devonshire and Cornwall have a hilly, upland terrain. The main ports in the west are BRISTOL, on the Avon (which flows into Bristol Channel), and LIVERPOOL, on the Mersey. Despite its northerly latitudes (London is on the same parallel as the easterly tip of Labrador), England has a mild climate, attributable to warm currents in the surrounding seas. Most of the region is subject to much wet weather, some of it experiences severe cold, but in general the climate is favorable to a wide variety of agricultural and industrial pursuits. Prior to 1974, England had 45 administrative counties: BEDFORDSHIRE, BERKSHIRE, BUCKINGHAMSHIRE, CAMBRIDGESHIRE AND ISLE OF ELY, CHESHIRE, CORNWALL, CUMBERLAND, DERBYSHIRE, DEVONSHIRE, DORSETSHIRE, DURHAM, ESSEX, GLOUCESTERSHIRE, HAMPSHIRE, HEREFORDSHIRE, HERTFORDSHIRE, HUNTINGDON AND PETERBOROUGH, Isle of Wight (see WIGHT, ISLE OF), KENT, LANCASHIRE, LEICESTERSHIRE, LINCOLNSHIRE (which was divided into three administrative divisions), NORFOLK, NORTHAMPTONSHIRE, NORTHUMBERLAND, NOTTINGHAMSHIRE, OXFORDSHIRE, RUTLAND, SHROPSHIRE, SOMERSET, STAFFORDSHIRE, SUFFOLK (East and West), SURREY, SUSSEX (East and West), WARWICKSHIRE, WESTMORLAND, WILTSHIRE, WORCESTERSHIRE, and the three administrative divisions (called ridings) of YORKSHIRE. In addition there were 79 county boroughs, which governed themselves independently of the counties in which they were located. The Local Government Act of 1972 reorganized local government throughout Great Britain. As of 1974, the 45 English counties were abolished. In their place were created 6 metropolitan counties: Greater Manchester, Merseyside, South Yorkshire, West Yorkshire, Tyne and Wear, and West Midlands; and 39 nonmetropolitan counties: Avon, Bedfordshire, Berkshire, Buckinghamshire, Cambridgeshire, Cheshire, Cleveland, Cornwall, Cumbria, Derbyshire, Devon, Dorset, Durham, East Sussex, Essex, Gloucestershire, Hampshire, Hereford and Worcester, Hertfordshire, Humberside, Isle of Wight, Kent, Lancashire, Leicestershire, Lincolnshire, Norfolk, North Yorkshire, Northamptonshire, Northumberland, Nottinghamshire, Oxfordshire, Salop, Somerset, Staffordshire, Suffolk, Surrey, Warwickshire, West Sussex, and Wiltshire. The counties are divided into districts and parishes. London and its metropolitan area were organized into Greater London in 1965. For the history of England as well as more information on government and economy, see GREAT BRITAIN.

England, Church of, the established church of England and the mother church of the ANGLICAN COMMUNION. Christianity, introduced by the Romans, was fairly well established in Britain by the 4th cent. However, the young church was cut off from the Continent and almost destroyed by the Anglo-Saxon invasions beginning in the 5th cent. Surviving in isolation, the CELTIC CHURCH developed rituals and organization at variance with those on the Continent. This led to conflict when St. AUGUSTINE OF CANTERBURY arrived (597) to reconvert England. Roman usages were eventually adopted in preference to Celtic ones (see WHITBY, SYNOD OF), but the English Church remained somewhat isolated until the Norman Conquest, when Continental churchmen such as LANFRANC and St. ANSELM undertook its reform. During the Middle Ages the church in England was affected by the same clashes with the crown that bedevilled the relationship between CHURCH AND STATE elsewhere in Europe. A modus vivendi was finally achieved in the matter of INVESTITURE, but quarrels over the taxes demanded by Rome and appeals going from English courts to Rome were not resolved until HENRY VIII broke the union of the English church with Rome. This action, which created the Church of England, was occasioned by Henry's request for an annulment of his marriage to KATHARINE OF ARAGÓN and the pope's refusal to grant it. The Act of Supremacy (1534) acknowledged the king as "the only supreme head on earth of the Church of England." Thus the Reformation in England under Henry was at first a matter of policy, not doctrine. The theology of the new national church as shown in the Six Articles (1539) and the King's Book (1543) was largely unchanged, although some Lutheran influence may be detected. Henry authorized the Great Bible (1539), a revision of the English translations of William Tyndale and Miles Coverdale, and some slight alterations in service. The monasteries were suppressed, chiefly at the hands of Thomas CROMWELL. Under Edward VI changes came rapidly, and Protestantism gained ground. The first and second BOOK OF COMMON PRAYER, produced by Thomas CRANMER, were adopted in 1549 and 1552, respectively, and a statement of doctrine, the Forty-two Articles, was drawn up. Under Mary I all the measures that had separated the Church of England from Rome were reversed; the Roman ritual was brought back, and the nation was received again into the communion of Rome. ELIZABETH I restored independence. The Elizabethan Settlement steered the English church upon a middle course between Roman Catholicism and Calvinism. The prayer book of 1552 was restored, and the Forty-two Articles, revised toward a more Catholic position and reduced to Thirty-nine, were adopted as a doctrinal standard. The national church maintained the historical episcopate and retained its continuity with the early church of Britain and much of the ritualism sanctioned by the older rubrics. By the Act of Supremacy (1559) ecclesiastical jurisdiction was restored to the crown to be exercised by a court of high commission. The classical statement of the peculiar Anglican position was made by Richard HOOKER. Under JAMES I the steadily rising tide of Puritanism made necessary the Hampton Court Conference (1604), at which the king gave his decision for the existing doctrine. The great achievement of the conference was the King James, or Authorized, Version of the English Bible (1611). Under CHARLES I the extreme measures of the party headed by Archbishop William LAUD, in maintaining the discipline and worship of the church against the Calvinists, had much to do with bringing on (1642) the ENGLISH CIVIL WAR. The Long Parliament, after excluding the bishops, substituted Presbyterianism for the episcopacy in 1646, in accordance with the Solemn League and Covenant (see COVENANTERS). Under Oliver Cromwell, Independent rather than Presbyterian doctrines triumphed; it was a penal offense to use the Book of Common Prayer. Many bishops were imprisoned, and many churches were pillaged. With the Restoration (1660) the episcopacy was reestablished. After failure of the Savoy Conference (1661) to create a compromise with the Puritans, the prayer book was revised in a Catholic direction (1662) and made the only legal service book by an Act of Uniformity, which required the episcopal ordination of all ministers. About 2,000 nonconformist clergymen, instead of complying, resigned and, with their adherents, established their own worship in Protestant nonconformist chapels, in spite of severe acts passed against them by Parliament (see NONCONFORMISTS). The Roman Catholic JAMES II attempted to move the church toward Rome, but in 1688, William SANCROFT, archbishop of Canterbury, and six other bishops refused the king's order to read his declaration of toleration in all churches. They were imprisoned but acquitted by trial. After the overthrow of James in the Glorious Revolution (1688), the Bill of Rights (1689) declared that the monarch must be Protestant and the Act of Settlement (1701) required that he or she be a member of the Church of England. Some of the clergy, however, including Sancroft, refused to swear allegiance to William and Mary and therefore lost their positions (see NONJURORS). In the 18th cent. latitudinarians held control in the church; dogma, liturgy, and ecclesiastical organization were subordinated to the appeal to reason, abhorrence of religious enthusiasm, and Erastianism. In 1701 the first Anglican missionary society, the Society for the Propagation of the Gospel (SPG), was founded for work overseas, and much of its early work was done in America. In George I's reign the BANGORIAN CONTROVERSY led to the prorogation of convocation in 1717; the next council of the church was not reconvened until 1852. The revival of religious fervor in the late 18th cent. resulted both in the rise of the evangelical movement within the Church of England and in the Methodist schism. The Church Missionary Society, founded in 1799, grew out of the evangelical movement. In the first half of the 19th cent., the Catholic and apostolic character of the Church of England was strongly reaffirmed by the OXFORD MOVEMENT, which was led by John KEBLE and Edward Bouverie PUSEY and also by John Henry NEWMAN until he converted to Roman Catholicism. The Oxford movement—with its emphasis on ritual and its belief in the doctrines of apostolic succession and the Real Presence—gave new life and direction to the High Church tradition, which became known also as Anglo-Catholicism. At the same time the Broad Church movement was developing. It advocated liberal views in theology and biblical studies. Both of these movements challenged the position of the Evangelical, or Low Church, party, which emphasized the Bible and preaching and was the leading party of the church through the 19th cent. In the 20th cent. the Church of England became involved in revision of canon law and the prayer book (which has been impeded because of the need for approval of proposed revisions by Parliament), in church building, in attempts to minister to the world of industry (e.g., the Sheffield Industrial Mission), and in the ECUMENICAL MOVEMENT. The traditional divisions within the church remain, but the lines are less sharply drawn. The clergy of the church are of three ancient orders: deacons, priests, and bishops. Only the bishop can ordain, confirm, and consecrate churches. A bishop is given consecration at the hands of other bishops. The archbishop of Canterbury is the primate of all England, while the archbishop of York is the primate of England. The church is established, and all episcopal appointments are still made by the crown; however, the clergy are not paid by the state. Since 1919 an important force in church life has been the Church Assembly. This consists of three houses, formed by the upper and lower house of convocation (i.e., the bishops and other clergy) and an elected house of laity, which has the power to prepare measures for enactment by Parliament. Worship is liturgical and is regulated by the Book of Common Prayer, but it varies in degree of ritual between parishes. The creeds in use are the Apostles', the Nicene, and the Athanasian. General standards of doctrine are found in the Thirty-nine Articles, the Book of Common Prayer, the Catechism, and two 16th-century books of homilies. Authority rests in Scripture as interpreted by tradition. See W. R. W. Stephens et al., ed., *A History of the English Church* (8 vol., 1899–1910; repr. 1973); Norman Sykes, *Church and State in England in the Eighteenth Century* (1934, repr. 1962); Gordon Crosse, *A Short History of the English Church* (1947); E. W. Watson, *The Church of England* (3d ed. 1961); Guy Mayfield, *The Church of England* (2d ed. 1963); S. C. Neill, *Anglicanism* (3d ed. 1965); R. B. Lloyd, *The Church of England, 1900–1965* (1966); W. P. Haugaard, *Elizabeth and the English Reformation* (1968); M. A. Crowther, *Church Embattled* (1970); S. L. Ollard et al. ed., *A Dictionary of English Church History* (9th ed. rev. 1970); Anthony Armstrong, *The Church of England, the Methodists, and Society, 1700–1850* (1973).

Engleheart, George, 1752–1829, English miniature painter. He studied with Sir Joshua Reynolds and made copies in miniature of Reynolds's paintings. Court miniaturist under George III, he competed successfully with the famous Richard Cosway. His nephew **John Cox Dillman Engleheart,** 1784–1862, was also a noted miniaturist. Examples of both painters' work may be seen in the Metropolitan Museum.

Engler, Adolf (ä'dôlf ĕng'lər), 1844–1930, German botanist. He emphasized the importance of geological history in the study of plant geography and worked out an influential system of plant classification. He was professor at the Univ. of Berlin and director of the botanical gardens (1889–1921) and was founder and editor (from 1881) of the periodical *Botanische Jahrbücher*. He wrote several works on plant geography and taxonomy and collaborated with Karl Prantl on the early volumes of *Die natürlichen Pflanzenfamilien* (32 vol. in 17, 1887–1909).

Englewood (ĕng'gəlwo͝od). **1** City (1970 pop. 33,695), Arapahoe co., N central Colo., on the South Platte River, a residential and industrial suburb of Denver; inc. 1903. It has iron works, plant nurseries, dairy-processing plants, and factories producing precision instruments. **2** City (1970 pop. 24,985), Bergen co., NE N.J., a residential suburb of the New York City–N New Jersey area; inc. as a city 1899. It was originally settled by the Dutch in the 17th cent.

English, Thomas Dunn, 1819–1902, American ballad writer and playwright, b. Philadelphia. His poem "Ben Bolt" was made into a popular song during the Civil War. Of his several plays only *The Mormons* (1858) had any success.

English, William Hayden, 1822–96, U.S. Congressman (1853–61), b. Scott co., Ind. A lawyer, he entered politics and served in the House of Representatives (1853–1861). In 1858, when the terms under which Kansas would be admitted to the Union were a crucial question, he proposed a compromise; Kansas was offered a land grant if it would accept the proslavery Lecompton Constitution. Southern votes passed the "English compromise," but the Kansans—as English is said to have foreseen—refused it. He was vice-presidential running mate to Gen. W. S. Hancock on the unsuccessful Democratic ticket in 1880.

English art and architecture. English architecture as a distinctive national art may be said to have evolved in the 12th cent. with the Norman style. Building before that time was in what is commonly called the Saxon or Anglo-Saxon style, which combined Roman and Celtic features; it is represented by sparse remains of monasteries, churches, and cathedral crypts, notable for the use of long-and-short ashlar stonework. These churches were small, relatively simple structures, having one or more towers and one or three aisles, with wooden or stone roofing. The great impact of the Norman Conquest was manifested in the 12th-century Anglo-Norman churches, closely related to the Romanesque. They were built with extremely long naves, often with a rectangular east end, in contrast with the Gallic surge toward lofty, aspiring structures with a curved chevet. The cathedral at Durham (begun 1093) employs a complete system of ribbed vaulting, together with the pointed arch and concealed flying buttresses, which are thought to antedate these Gothic features in France. In Gothic decorative styles, England made a significant contribution. In phases known as the Decorated style (14th cent.; e.g., the cathedrals of Lincoln and Wells) and the Perpendicular style (late 14th–middle 16th cent.; e.g., Sherbourne Abbey and York Minster), exuberant and complicated networks of bar tracery and multiple ribbed vaults were devised, influencing the FLAMBOYANT STYLE in France. A flourishing religious art of painting, sculpture, monumental BRASSES, STAINED GLASS, and EMBROIDERY enriched the medieval church in England. The splendid and unique Anglo-Saxon embroidery, known as the BAYEUX TAPESTRY (c.1066–77), attests to the English interest in dramatic narrative. It is thought to be one of the rare secular works of the period. Enough architectural and memorial sculpture has survived to provide evidence of centuries of achievement, from the Anglican crosses of Cumberland (7th cent.) to the 15th-century figures of Henry V's chantry in Westminster Abbey. A similar long tradition can be traced in stained-glass windows still adorning many churches. Very little church painting has survived, but there are many superb examples of illuminated manuscripts, which by the 10th cent. show a considerable skill in the French Carolingian fashion (see ILLUMINATION). The high development of this art form influenced the growth of English sculpture, which abounds in fantasies and grotesqueries of the medieval period. Early reliefs at Chichester (c.1140), Lincoln (c.1145), and Malmesbury (c.1160–70) are particularly noteworthy sculptural works. The transition from Gothic to a classic Renaissance style was slow. Religious art of every kind had declined drastically by 1540, with the dissolution of the monasteries and the break with Rome. John Thynne and Robert Smythson were major builders of the 16th cent. at a time when secular art and architecture began to assume greater importance. Manor houses and palaces were designed for greater comfort than in previous eras and were often arranged according to a symmetrical plan, facing outward toward a splendid garden. Attention was paid to the paneling and stucco adornment of interiors. English builders inconsistently adapted Italian designs, particularly the published works of Sebastiano Serlio. Numerous foreign artists were imported by the nobility, largely for portraiture. From Holbein to Rubens and Van Dyck, these men found few worthy followers in England and no rivals; such painters as William Dobson and Robert Walker could hardly compete with the Dutch Lely or the German Kneller. However, with the Elizabethan portrait miniaturists Nicholas Hilliard and Isaac and Peter Oliver, an English art of exquisite delicacy came into being. They were followed by Samuel Cooper and Richard Cosway, and, late in the 17th cent., by the celebrated sculptor Grinling Gibbons, who decorated parts of Westminster Abbey and other churches and palaces. From the first quarter of the 17th cent., masterly interpretations of classical architecture were being produced in England. Initiated by Inigo Jones, who modeled his buildings directly after antique structures and designs by Andrea Palladio, the Palladian style spread throughout England. After the great fire of 1666 much of London had to be rebuilt. Influenced by Italian Renaissance architecture, Sir Christopher Wren, drawing upon diverse sources, created an English baroque through his original and grandiose plans for the rebuilding of St. Paul's Cathedral and through the variety and ingenuity of his designs for 51 of the City churches. His successors were Nicholas Hawksmoor and Sir John Vanbrugh, whose massive country houses were the crowning expression of the English baroque. During the 18th cent. a more restrained architectural style was determined and made popular in the works of Lord Burlington, Colin Campbell, James Gibbs, and William Kent. The GEORGIAN STYLE in architecture, decoration, furniture, silver, and the minor arts was developed during the reigns of the Hanoverian kings (1714–1820). An outstanding architectural fantasy employing Chinese decor was manifested in the REGENCY STYLE, of which George IV's Royal Pavilion at Brighton (1815–22) is an example. Early in the 18th cent., after two centuries of foreign domination in the arts, the English school of painting was revitalized by William Hogarth's brilliant and biting pictorial satires. The graphic art of social commentary which he began has flourished in England ever since. It was superbly expressed in Rowlandson's drawings at the close of the century, a time when an opposite trend, toward the poetic and mystical in the graphic arts, also reached its height in the work of William Blake and his followers, notably Samuel Palmer and Edward Calvert. In PORTRAITURE the 18th cent. produced a number of outstanding artists. Sir Joshua Reynolds, who helped found the ROYAL ACADEMY OF ARTS in 1768 and was the first Englishman to assert successfully the dignity of his profession, shares with Thomas Gainsborough the place of honor in English portraiture. Other major artists in this field include George Romney, Sir Henry Raeburn, and Sir Thomas Lawrence. Gainsborough is distinguished, too, for his landscape painting, a genre in which England has made contributions of the first order (see LANDSCAPE PAINTING). Notable 18th-century landscape painters were Richard Wilson, George Morland, John Robert Cozens, and Thomas Girtin. A type of painting that enjoyed great popularity in the 18th and 19th cent. was the sporting picture depicting hunting and racing scenes, a particularly English form of art. George Stubbs was the outstanding painter and engraver of this genre. From the 18th cent. on, considerable advances were made in city planning, with the schemes of John Wood I and John Wood II at Bath, and, in the 19th cent., with the efforts of John Nash in London. In the latter half of the 18th cent. England was engulfed by a wave of neoclassicism, characterized by the greater availability of, and greater stress on archaeological finds than during the Palladian trend. The principal exponents of neoclassicism were Robert Adam, Sir William Chambers, George Dance II, and Sir John Soane, all of whom developed tasteful variations of the style. In the late 18th cent. a search for the picturesque led to the resurgence of earlier modes, including Gothic, Renaissance, and Greek styles. Among the architects who exploited several styles were Robert Smirke and Sir Charles Barry. By the Victorian period, the Gothic revival predominated and was developed to great effect by A. W. N. Pugin, who worked under Barry in the design of the Houses of Parliament. Other imaginative variations of the Gothic style were conceived by William Butterfield, W. A. Nesfield, and R. N. Shaw. The latter two and Philip Webb also created remarkable plans for domestic architecture, as did C. F. A. Voysey and Sir Edwin Lutyens toward the end of the 19th cent. Coinciding with the mid-19th century Gothic revival, new structural and spatial possibilities were being explored with the use of such materials as iron and glass. Sir Joseph Paxton's Crystal Palace for the exposition of 1851 was a landmark in the direction of modern architecture. Among the most gifted landscape painters of the early 19th cent. were R. P. Bonington and the leaders of the Norwich school, John Crome and J. S. Cotman, who also excelled in the medium of watercolor. Their achievement was dwarfed by the two great landscape artists John Constable and J. M. W. Turner; developing totally different styles, they both created rich coloristic effects and worked with a spontaneity that had a strong influence on subsequent French painting. The English romantic period, of which they were the greatest exponents in painting, was followed by the rise of the Pre-Raphaelite school of D. G. Rossetti, William Holman Hunt, and Sir Edward Burne-Jones. William Morris did much to raise English standards in the applied arts, particularly in book design and interior decoration. Sculpture did not parallel the development of English painting, although John Flaxman, Sir Richard Westmacott, Sir Francis Chantrey, John Bacon, and Alfred Stevens worked effectively in a classicizing manner. In the 20th cent., England played a minor part in initiating experimental and intellectual movements in art and architecture but was profoundly affected by them. In 1933, 11 painters, sculptors, and architects formed a short-lived group known as Unit One, to further the contemporary spirit in the arts; among those who attained international fame were the sculptors Henry Moore and Dame Barbara Hepworth and the painters Ben Nicholson and Paul Nash. A touch of macabre fantasy can be seen in the works of three noted 20th-century painters, Sir Stanley Spencer, Graham Sutherland, and Francis Bacon. Other well-known painters include Victor Pasmore, William Scott, Alan Davie, John Bratby, and John Smith. In 1954 the POP ART movement originated in England in response to commercial culture and to establish criteria of art. Notable contemporary sculptors include Reginald Butler, Lynn Chadwick, and Kenneth Armitage. Since World War II, there has been an attempt to rebuild England in the modern spirit. Architects of the school dubbed "new brutalism" have been inspired by Le Corbusier to search for new forms and textures. The cathedral at Coventry (consecrated 1962) is the setting for a synthesis of the arts, with a sculpture of St. Michael by Sir Jacob Epstein, a tapestry designed by Sutherland, and engraved glass walls; the new cathedral, designed by Sir Basil Spence, provides an effective contrast to the adjacent ruins of its Gothic predecessor. In the minor arts, English pottery is justly famous, and such wares as Chelsea, Derby, Doulton, Staffordshire, and Wedgwood are highly prized. The same can be said of furniture prior to the Victorian era and of the work of such famous designers and craftsmen as Chippendale, Sheraton, Hepplewhite, and the Adam brothers. (See articles on individual artists and architects, e.g., J. M. W. TURNER; and styles, e.g., DECORATED STYLE; and the minor arts, e.g., DOULTON WARE.) See T. S. Boase, ed., *The Oxford History of English Art* (Vol. II–V, VII, VIII, X, 1949–62); Ellis Waterhouse, *Painting in Britain: 1530–1790* (1953); William Gaunt, *A Concise History of English Painting* (1964); John Summerson, *Architecture in Britain: 1530–1830* (3d ed. 1958, repr. 1969); Michael Foss, *The Age of Patronage* (1972); J. S. Curl, *Victorian Architecture* (1974).

English Bazar, town (1971 pop. 61,713), West Bengal state, E central India, on the Mahananda River. The British East India Company established factories for the production of silk and cotton fabrics, for which English Bazar is still known. The town is also the administrative center for a district where jute is the chief crop and mulberries and mangoes are grown.

English Channel, Fr. *La Manche* [the sleeve], arm of the Atlantic Ocean, c.350 (560 km) long, between France and Great Britain. It is 112 mi (180 km) wide at its west entrance, between Land's End, England, and Ushant, France. Its greatest width, c.150 mi (240 km) is between Lyme Bay and the Gulf of St.-Malo; between Dover and Cape Gris-Nez it is 21 mi (34 km) wide. At the east end the Strait of Dover connects the Channel with the North Sea. Principal islands are the Isle of WIGHT and the CHANNEL ISLANDS. A train-ferry service to carry passengers and freight without change between Paris and London was opened between Dover and Dunkirk in 1936. In 1785, J. P. Blanchard and Dr. John Jeffries crossed the Channel by balloon; the first to swim across was Matthew Webb (1875); and the first airplane crossing was made by Blériot in 1909. The construction of a Channel railroad tunnel, long under discussion, was begun in 1974; however, shortly thereafter the project was postponed indefinitely because of a shortage of funds. The French coast is a popular resort area. Channel fisheries are also important. The principal Channel ports are Plymouth, Southampton, Portsmouth, and Dover (in England) and Cherbourg, Le Havre, and Calais (in France).

English civil war, 1642–48, the conflict between King CHARLES I of England and a large body of his subjects, generally called the "parliamentarians," that culminated in the defeat and execution of the king and the establishment of a republican COMMONWEALTH. The struggle has also been called the Puritan Revolution because the religious complexion of the king's opponents was prevailingly Puritan, and because the defeat of the king was accompanied by the abolition of episcopacy. That name, however, overemphasizes the religious element at the expense of the constitutional issues and the underlying social and economic factors. Most simply stated, the constitutional issue was one between a king who claimed to rule by divine right and a Parliament that professed itself to have rights and privileges independent of the crown and that ultimately, by its actions, claimed real sovereignty. Parliament in this period did not represent the full body of the English people; it was composed of and represented the nobility, country gentry, and merchants and artisans. The 16th cent. had seen a decline in the influence of the nobility and a striking rise in the numbers, wealth, and influence of the gentry and merchants, the beneficiaries of a tremendous expansion of markets and trade in Tudor times. It was from this middle class of gentry and merchants that the opposition to the crown drew most of its members. Their ambition to do away with financial and commercial restrictions and their desire to have a say in such matters as religious and foreign policies had been severely restrained by the Tudors, but on the accession (1603) of a Scottish king to the English throne the popular party began to organize its strength.

The Rise of the Opposition. JAMES I was not long in gaining a personal unpopularity that helped to strengthen Parliament's hand. At the Hampton Court Conference (1604) he resolutely refused to compromise with Puritans on religious questions. The Parliament that met in 1604 soon clashed with the king on questions of finance and supply. James was forced to temporize because of his urgent need of money, but the dissolution of the Parliament in 1610 left feelings of bitterness on both sides. A new Parliament met in 1614, and the Commons engaged in quarrels not only with the king but also with the House of Lords. Because it passed not a single statute, this was called the Addled Parliament. James had little understanding of the popular unrest and aroused deeper opposition by his continued collection of impositions and benevolences, his dependence on favorites, and his scheme of a Spanish marriage for his son Charles. Meanwhile a legal battle was being waged in the courts, with Sir Francis BACON zealously upholding the royal prerogative and Sir Edward COKE defending the supremacy of common law. The king dismissed Coke from the bench in 1616, but the Parliament of 1621 impeached Bacon. The last Parliament (1624) of the reign accompanied its grant of money with specific directions for its use. James's reign had raised certain fundamental questions concerning the privileges of Parliament, claimed by that body as their legal right and regarded by James as a special grant from the crown. Charles I, married to a French Roman Catholic princess, Henrietta Maria, proved more intractable and even less acceptable to the Puritan taste than his father, and Parliament became even more uncompromising in the new reign. The leaders of the parliamentary party—Coke, John PYM, Sir John ELIOT, and John SELDEN—sought ways to limit the powers of the king. The Parliament of 1625 granted him the right to collect tonnage and poundage (customs duties) only for a year and not, as was customary, for his entire reign. The Parliament of 1626 went further and impeached the king's favorite, George Villiers, 1st duke of BUCKINGHAM. Charles dissolved it in anger. Failing to raise money without Parliament, he was forced to call a new one in 1628. The new Parliament drew up the PETITION OF RIGHT, and Charles accepted it in order to get his subsidy. He continued to levy customs duties, an act that the parliamentarians declared illegal under the Petition of Right. Parliament in 1629 vigorously protested Charles's collection of tonnage and poundage and the prosecution of his opponents in the STAR CHAMBER. The religious issue also came up, and Commons resisted the king's order to adjourn by forcing the speaker to remain in his chair while Eliot presented resolutions against "popery" and unauthorized taxation. In the succeeding 11 years Charles attempted to rule without a Parliament, resorting to such expedients as ship money (a tax levied originally on seaports but extended by Charles to the entire country) to raise revenue. The reprisals against Eliot and the prosecution of William PRYNNE and John HAMPDEN aroused widespread indignation. Charles's chief advisers, Archbishop William LAUD and Thomas Wentworth, later 1st earl of STRAFFORD, were cordially detested. The ominous peace was broken by troubles in Scotland, where efforts to enforce Anglican episcopal policy led to the violent opposition of the COVENANTERS and to war in 1639 (see BISHOPS' WARS) and compelled Charles to seek the financial aid of Parliament. The resulting Short Parliament (1640) once more met the king's request for supply by a demand for redress of grievance. Charles offered to abandon ship money exactions, but the opposition wished to discuss more fundamental issues, and the king dissolved the Parliament in just three weeks. The disasters of the second Scottish war compelled a virtual surrender by the king to the opposition, and the Long Parliament was summoned (Nov., 1640).

The Long Parliament. The parliamentarians quickly enacted a series of measures designed to sweep away what they regarded as the encroachments of despotic monarchy. Those imprisoned by the Star Chamber were freed. A Triennial Act provided that no more than three years should elapse between sessions of Parliament, while another act prohibited the dissolution of Parliament without its own consent. Ship money and tonnage and poundage without parliamentary authorization were abolished. Strafford was impeached, then attainted and executed (1641) for treason; Laud was impeached and imprisoned. Star Chamber and other prerogative and episcopal courts were swept away. However, discussions on church reform along Puritan lines produced considerable disagreement, especially between the Commons and Lords. Despite the king's compliance to the will of the opposition thus far, he was not trusted by the parliamentary party. This distrust was given sharp focus by the outbreak (Oct., 1641) of a rebellion against English rule in Ireland; an army was needed to suppress the rebellion, but the parliamentarians feared that the king might use it against them. Led by John Pym, Parliament adopted the Grand Remonstrance, reciting the evils of Charles's reign and demanding church reform and parliamentary control over the army and over the appointment of royal ministers. The radicalism of these demands split the parliamentary party and drove many of the moderates to the royalist side. This encouraged Charles to assert himself, and in Jan., 1642, he attempted to arrest in person Pym and four other leaders of the opposition in Commons. His action made civil war inevitable. In the lull that followed, both Parliament and the king sought to secure fortresses, arsenals, and popular support. In June, 1642, Parliament sent to the king a statement reiterating the demands of the Grand Remonstrance, but since the proposals amounted to a complete surrender of sovereignty by the crown to Parliament, the king did not even consider them as a basis for discussion. Armed forces (including many peers from the House of Lords and a sizable minority of Commons) gathered about him in the north. Parliament organized its own army and appointed Robert Devereux, 3d earl of ESSEX, to head it. On Aug. 22, 1642, Charles raised his standard at Nottingham.

The First Civil War. The followers of king and Parliament did not represent two absolutely distinct social groups as the popular conception of the royalist

Cavaliers and the parliamentary Roundheads would indicate. However, it is true that the parliamentary, or Puritan, group drew much of its strength from the gentry and from the merchant classes and artisans of London, Norwich, Hull, Plymouth, and Gloucester; it centered in the southeastern counties and had control of the fleet. The majority of the great nobles followed the king, who had the support of most Anglicans and Roman Catholics; geographically the royalist strength centered in the north and west. The first major engagement of the armies at Edgehill (Oct. 23, 1642) was a drawn battle. Charles then established himself at Oxford. The royalist forces gained ground in the north and west, although repeated attempts by the king to advance on London proved abortive. The indecisive engagements of 1643 were remarkable mainly for the emergence of Oliver CROMWELL, an inconspicuous member of the Long Parliament, to military prominence with his own regiment of "godly" men, soon to become famous as the Ironsides. Futile negotiations for peace had been conducted at Oxford early in 1643, and in Sept., 1643, Parliament took a decisive step by securing the alliance of the Presbyterian Scots in accepting the Solemn League and Covenant. Scottish aid was obtained only by a promise to submit England to Presbyterianism, which was soon to produce a reaction from the Independents and other sectarians (particularly in the army) who opposed the idea of any centralized national church. The war now entered a new phase. A Scottish army, under Alexander Leslie, 1st earl of LEVEN, advanced into Yorkshire early in 1644 and gave aid to the parliamentary army in the north. Charles's nephew, the brilliant and dashing Prince RUPERT, did something to stem royalist losses by retaking Newark, but his gains were temporary. His campaign to relieve the besieged York led to the battle of Marston Moor (July 2, 1644), in which Cromwell and Leslie inflicted a crushing defeat on the royalists. Charles managed to cut off Essex in the southwest but shortly thereafter met parliamentary troops from the north in an indecisive engagement at Newbury. To stem the rising dissension among parliamentary leaders, Cromwell sponsored in Parliament the Self-Denying Ordinance, by which all members of Parliament were compelled to resign their commands, and the parliamentary army was reorganized (1644-45) into the New Model Army. Thomas Fairfax (later 3d Baron FAIRFAX OF CAMERON) became the commander in chief. After further futile peace negotiations at Uxbridge, Charles, hoping to join the forces under James Graham, marquess of MONTROSE, moved north and stormed Leicester. He met Cromwell in a sharp battle at Naseby (June 14, 1645). This battle cost the king a large part of his army and rendered the royalist cause hopeless. Unable to join Montrose (who was defeated by Leslie in Scotland) and thwarted in his attempts to secure aid from Ireland or the Continent, the king was unable to halt the steady losses of his party and finally was compelled to surrender himself to the Scots, who made him reassuring but vague promises. The first civil war came to an end when Oxford surrendered in June, 1646.

The Second Civil War and the Republic. The king was delivered (1647) by the Scots into the hands of Parliament, but the Presbyterian rule in that body had thoroughly alienated the army. The army resisted Parliament's proposal to disband it by capturing the king from the parliamentary party and marching on London. Army discontent gradually became more radical (see LEVELERS), and the desire grew to dispose of the king altogether. Refusing to accept the army council's proposals for peace (the Heads of the Proposals), Charles escaped in Nov., 1647, and took refuge on the Isle of Wight, where he negotiated simultaneously with Parliament and the Scots. In Dec., 1647, he concluded an agreement with the Scots known as the Engagement, by which he agreed to accept Presbyterianism in return for military support. In the spring of 1648, the second civil war began. Uprisings in Wales, Kent, and Essex were all suppressed by the parliamentary forces, and Cromwell defeated the Scots at Preston (Aug. 17, 1648). Charles's hopes of aid from France or Ireland proved vain, and the war was quickly over. Parliament again tried to reach some agreement with the king, but the army, now completely under Cromwell's domination, disposed of its enemies in Parliament by Pride's Purge (Dec., 1648; see under PRIDE, THOMAS). The legislative remnant known as the Rump Parliament erected a high court of justice, which tried the king for treason and found him guilty. Charles was beheaded on Jan. 30, 1649, and the republic known as the Commonwealth was set up, governed by the Rump Parliament (without the House of Lords) and by an executive council of state. Charles I's son CHARLES II was recognized as king in parts of Ireland and in Scotland but was forced to flee to the Continent after his defeat at Worcester (1651). The years of the interregnum, under the Commonwealth to 1653 and the PROTECTORATE after that, are largely the story of Oliver Cromwell's personal rule, which was marked by strict military administration and enforcement of the Puritan moral code. After his death and the short-lived rule of his son, Richard CROMWELL, the Commonwealth was revived for a brief and chaotic period. It ended in 1660 with the RESTORATION of Charles II. Although some of the changes brought about by the war were swept away (e.g., in the restoration of Anglicanism as the state church), the settlement of the contest between the king and Parliament was permanently assured in the GLORIOUS REVOLUTION of 1688. The standard works on the period of the war are by Samuel Rawson GARDINER. See C. V. Wedgwood, *The King's Peace, 1637-1641* (1955) and *The King's War, 1641-1647* (1958); A. H. Burne and Peter Young, *The Great Civil War, a Military History* (1959); Godfrey Davies, *The Early Stuarts* (2d ed. 1959); J. E. Christopher Hill, *Puritanism and Revolution* (1958) and *The Intellectual Origins of the English Revolution* (1965); I. A. Roots, *The Great Rebellion, 1642-1660* (1968).

English cocker spaniel, breed of compact SPORTING DOG perfected in England, whose development may be traced back to the original spaniels of Spain. It stands about 16 in. (40.6 cm) high at the shoulder and weighs about 30 lb (13.6 kg). Its medium-length coat is silky and slightly wavy and forms fringes of longer hair, or feathers, on the dog's underside, ears, chest, and legs. It may be any of various colors or parti-colored. The tail is docked. Until its official recognition by the Kennel Club of England in 1892 as a separate breed, it and the larger springer spaniel were distinguished by size only. Thus, the same litter could produce both dogs, the cocker being used to hunt smaller game, such as woodcocks. It is still trained for that purpose today and is also widely kept as a house pet. The smaller cocker spaniel of America, derived from it, has been established as a separate breed. See DOG.

English foxhound, breed of medium-sized, swift HOUND perfected in England in the 17th and 18th cent. It stands from 21 to 25 in. (53.3-63.5 cm) high at the shoulder and weighs from 60 to 70 lb (27.2-31.8 kg). Its short, dense coat is glossy and usually black, tan, and white in color. The English foxhound, whose origins probably go back to French hounds of the 14th cent., was first used in packs to hunt foxes in the mid-17th cent. This sport, a favorite of the aristocracy, whose practice it was to follow the hounds on horseback, encouraged the careful breeding of the foxhound. By 1800 stud books had been published recording the lineages of all English foxhounds. The slightly smaller American foxhound was developed from it, as were many present-day varieties of coonhound. Still used in foxhunting, the English foxhound can be trained to hunt almost any ground game. See DOG.

English horn, musical instrument, the alto of the OBOE family, pitched a fifth lower than the oboe and treated as a TRANSPOSING INSTRUMENT. It has a pear-shaped bell, giving it a soft, melancholy tone. The first important parts for it were written by Rossini in *William Tell* (1829) and by Meyerbeer in *Robert le diable* (1831). Other composers, notably Wagner, have used it in opera and orchestral music. The 18th-century form of the instrument was curved, whence, possibly, its misleading designation as a horn. In Britain and Europe it is often termed *cor anglais.*

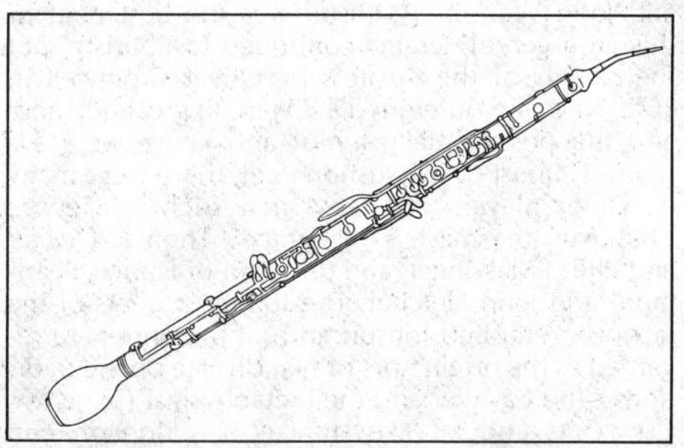

English horn

English language, member of the West Germanic group of the Germanic subfamily of the Indo-European family of languages (see GERMANIC LANGUAGES). Spoken by about 265 million people throughout the world, English is the native language of more people than any other except Mandarin Chinese. It is also used extensively as an auxiliary language, probably by another 200 million persons. Thus it serves about one out of every six people in the world. English is the mother tongue of about 56 million persons in the British Isles, from where it spread to many other parts of the world owing to British exploring, colonizing, and empire-building during the 18th and 19th centuries. It is now also the first language of an additional 165 million people in the United States; 13 million in Canada; more than 1 million in the Republic of South Africa; 11 million in Australia; 3 million in New Zealand and a number of Pacific islands; and approximately 15 million others in different parts of the Western Hemisphere, Africa, and Asia. As a result of such expansion, English is the most widely scattered of the great speech communities. The importance of English is shown by the fact that the United Nations uses English not only as one of its five official languages, but also as one of its two working languages. There are many dialect areas; in England and S Scotland these are of long standing, and the variations are striking; the Scottish dialect especially has been cultivated literarily. There are newer dialect differences also, such as in the United States. Standard forms of English differ also; thus, the standard British ("the king's English") is dissimilar to the several standard varieties of American and to Australian, Canadian, and New Zealand English. Today's English is the continuation of the language of the 5th-century Germanic invaders of Britain. No records exist of preinvasion forms of the language. The language most closely related to English is the West Germanic language FRISIAN. The history of English is an aspect of the history of the English people and their development. Thus in the 9th cent. the standard English was the dialect of dominant Wessex (see ANGLO-SAXON LITERATURE). The NORMAN CONQUEST (11th cent.) brought in foreign rulers, whose native language was Norman French; and English was eclipsed by French as the official language. When English became again (14th cent.) the language of the upper class, the capital was London, and the new standard (continued in Modern Standard English) was a London dialect. It is convenient to divide English into periods—Old English (or Anglo-Saxon; to c.1150), Middle English (to c.1500; see MIDDLE ENGLISH LITERATURE), and Modern English; this division implies no discontinuity, for even the hegemony of French affected only a small percent of the population. The English-speaking areas have expanded at all periods. Before the Normans the language was spoken in England and S Scotland, but not in Cornwall, Wales, or, at first, in Strathclyde. English has not yet quite ousted the Celtic languages from the British Isles, but it has spread vastly overseas. Like other languages, English has changed greatly, albeit imperceptibly, so that an Englishman of 1300 would not have understood the English of 500, nor would he understand that of today. Changes of every sort have taken place concomitantly in the sounds (phonetics), in their distribution (phonemics), and in the grammar (morphology and syntax). The following familiar words show changes of 1,000 years:

	home	*stones*	*name*	*tongue*
Old	hääm	stää'näs	nä'mä	to͝ong'gə
Middle	hôm	stô'nəz	nä'mə	to͝ong'gə
Modern	hōm	stōnz	nām	tŭng

The changes are more radical than they appear, for Modern English ō and ā are diphthongs. The words *home, stones,* and *name* exemplify the fate of unaccented vowels, which became ə, then ə disappeared. In Old English important inflectional contrasts depended upon the difference between unaccented vowels; so, as these vowels coalesced into ə and this disappeared, much of the case system disappeared too. In Modern English a different technique, word order (subject + predicate + object), is used to show what a case contrast once did, namely, which is the actor and which the goal of the action. There are other critical changes also. The vocabulary has naturally expanded, but many common modern words are derived from the lexicon of the earliest English; e.g., *bread, good,* and *shower.* From words acquired with Latin Christianity come *priest, bishop,* and others; and from words adopted from Scandinavian settlers come *root, egg, take, window,* and many more. French words, such as *castle*, began to come into English shortly before the Norman Conquest. After the Conquest, Norman French became the language of the court and of official life, and it remained so until the end of the 14th cent. During these 300 or more years English remained the language of the common people, but an increasingly large number of French words found their way into the language, so that when the 14th-century vernacular revival, dominated by Chaucer and Wyclif, restored English to its old place as the speech of all classes, the French element in the English vocabulary was very considerable. To this phase of French influence belong most legal terms (such as *judge, jury, tort,* and *assault*) and words denoting social ranks and institutions (such as *duke, baron, peer, countess,* and *parliament*), together with a great number of other words that cannot be classified—e.g., *honor, courage, season, manner, study, feeble,* and *poor.* Since nearly all of these French words are ultimately derived from Late Latin, they may be regarded as an indirect influence of the classical languages upon the English vocabulary. The direct influence of the classical languages began with the Renaissance and has continued ever since; even today Latin and Greek roots are the chief source for English words in science and technology, such as *conifer, cyclotron, intravenous, isotope, polymeric,* and *telephone.* During the last 300 years the borrowing of words from foreign languages has continued unchecked, so that now most of the languages of the world are represented to some extent in the vocabulary. English is written in the Roman alphabet. Although the spelling of English today has not been altered very much since the 15th cent., its pronunciation has changed greatly in the same period. As a result, English spelling is not a reliable guide to the pronunciation of the language. See G. P. Krapp, *The English Language in America* (2 vol., 1960); H. L. Mencken, *The American Language* (rev. 4th ed. 1963); Wilson Follett, *Modern American Usage* (1966); M. M. Mathews, *Americanisms: A Dictionary of Selected Americanisms on Historical Principles* (1966); G. W. Turner, *The English Language in Australia and New Zealand* (1966); R. A. Jacobs and P. S. Rosenbaum, *English Transformational Grammar* (1968); Mario Pei, *The Story of the English Language* (new ed. 1968); Paul Roberts, *Modern Grammar* (1968); M. M. Orkin, *Speaking Canadian English* (1971); Thomas Pyles, *The Origins and Development of the English Language* (2d ed. 1971); *The Oxford English Dictionary* (reissued 1971); *Webster's Third New International Dictionary of the English Language* (1971).

English literature. During the 15th cent. the English language developed into its modern form. The literature of previous linguistic periods is discussed in the articles on ANGLO-SAXON LITERATURE and MIDDLE ENGLISH LITERATURE (see also ANGLO-NORMAN LITERATURE). The beginning of the Tudor dynasty coincided with the first wide dissemination of printed matter (William Caxton's press was established in 1476; Henry VII's reign began in 1485). Caxton's achievement encouraged writing of all kinds and also led to the standardization of the English language.

The Elizabethan Age. The early Tudor period, particularly the reign of Henry VIII, was marked by the break with the Roman Catholic Church and the weakening of feudal ties, which brought about a vast increase in the power of the monarchy. Stronger political relationships with the Continent were also developed, exposing England to Renaissance culture. Humanism became the most important force in English literary and intellectual life, both in its narrow sense—the study and imitation of the Latin classics—and in its broad sense—the affirmation of the secular, rather than otherworldly, concerns of man. All these forces produced during the reign (1558-1603) of Elizabeth I one of the most fruitful eras in literary history. The energy of writers matched that of mariners and merchants. Accounts by men such as Richard Hakluyt, Samuel Purchas, and Sir Walter Raleigh were eagerly read. The activities and literature of the Elizabethans represented a new nationalism, which expressed itself also in the works of chroniclers (John Stow, Raphael Holinshed, and others), historians, and translators and even in political and religious tracts. A myriad of new genres, themes, and ideas became part of English literature. Italian poetic forms, especially the SONNET, became models for English poets. Sir Thomas Wyatt was the most successful sonneteer among early Tudor poets, and was, with Henry Howard, earl of Surrey, a seminal influence. *Tottel's Miscellany* (1557) was the first and most popular of many collections of experimental poetry by different, often anonymous, hands. The goal of all these poets was to make English as flexible a poetic instrument as Italian. Among the more prominent were Thomas Churchyard, George Gascoigne, and Edward de Vere, earl of Oxford. An ambitious and influential work was *A Mirror for Magistrates* (1559), a historical verse narrative by several poets, which presented the medieval view of history and the morals to be drawn from it. Though early Tudor drama owed much to medieval morality plays, classical models also were used. *Ralph Roister Doister* (c.1545) by Nicholas Udall, and *Gammer Gurton's Needle* (c.1552) were the first English comedies to combine elements of classical Roman comedy with native burlesque. The poet who best synthesized the ideas and tendencies of the English Renaissance was Edmund Spenser. His unfinished epic poem *The Faerie Queen* (1596) is a treasure-house of allegory, adventure, Neoplatonic ideas, patriotism, and Protestant morality, all presented in a variety of literary styles. The ideal English Renaissance man was Sir Philip Sidney—scholar, poet, critic, courtier, diplomat, and soldier—who died in battle at the age of 32. His best poetry is contained in the sonnet sequence *Astrophel and Stella* (1591). Other important late Tudor sonneteers were Spenser and Shakespeare, Michael Drayton, Samuel Daniel, and Fulke Greville. More versatile even than Sidney was Sir Walter Raleigh—poet, historian, courtier, explorer, and soldier—who wrote strong, spare poetry. During the late 16th and early 17th cent., drama flourished in England as never before or since. It came of age with the work of the University Wits, whose sophisticated plays set the course of Renaissance drama and paved the way for Shakespeare. The Wits included John Lyly, famed for the highly artificial and much imitated prose work *Euphues* (1578); Robert Greene, the first to write romantic comedy; the versatile Thomas Lodge and Thomas Nashe; Thomas Kyd, who popularized neo-Senecan tragedy; and Christopher Marlowe, probably the greatest dramatist of the group. Delineating heroes whose very greatness leads to their downfall, Marlowe wrote in blank verse of a rhetorical brilliance and eloquence superbly equal to the demands of high drama. William Shakespeare, of course, fulfilled the promise of the Elizabethan age. His history plays, comedies, and tragedies set a standard never again equalled, and he is universally regarded as one of the greatest poets of all time.

The Jacobean Era, Cromwell, and the Restoration. Elizabethan literature generally reflects the exuberant self-confidence of a nation expanding its powers, increasing its wealth, and thus keeping at bay its serious social and religious problems. Disillusion and pessimism, however, followed, during the unstable reign of James I (1603-25). The 17th cent. was to be one of great upheaval—revolution and regicide, restoration of the monarchy, and, finally, the victory of Parliament, Protestantism, and the middle class. Jacobean literature includes some of Shakespeare's greatest, and darkest, plays. The dominant literary figure of James's reign was Ben Jonson, whose varied and dramatic works followed classical models and were enriched by his worldly, peculiarly English wit. His satiric dramas, notably the great *Volpone* (1606), all take a cynical view of human nature. Also cynical were the horrific revenge tragedies of Cyril Tourneur, Thomas Middleton, John Ford, and John Webster (Webster was the best poet of this grim genre). Drama continued to flourish until the closing of the theaters by Oliver Cromwell in 1642. New and different plays were in great demand, and the possibilities of plot and genre were exploited almost to exhaustion. Still, there were many excellent plays written by men such as George Chapman, the masters of comedy Thomas Dekker and Philip Massinger, and the team of Francis Beaumont and John Fletcher. The foremost poets of the Jacobean era, Ben Jonson and John Donne, are regarded as the originators of two diverse poetic traditions—the Cavalier and the metaphysical (see CAVALIER POETS and METAPHYSICAL POETS). Jonson and Donne shared not only a common fund of literary resources, but also a dryness of wit and precision of expression. Donne's poetry is distinctive for its passionate intellection, Jonson's for its classicism and urbane guidance of passion. Although George Herbert and Robert Herrick were the principal metaphysical poets, the meditative religious poets Henry Vaughan and Thomas Traherne were also influenced by Donne, as were Abraham Cowley and Richard Crashaw. The Cavalier poets Thomas Carew, Sir John Suckling, and Richard Lovelace were lyricists in the elegant Jonsonian tradition. The highly individual Andrew Marvell partook of the traditions of both Donne and Jonson. Among the leading prose writers of the Jacobean period were the translators who produced the classic King James Version of the Bible and the divines Lancelot Andrewes, Jeremy Taylor, and John Donne. The work of Francis Bacon helped shape philosophical and scientific method. Robert Burton's *Anatomy of Melancholy* (1621) offers a varied, virtually encyclopedic view of the moral and intellectual preoccupations of the 17th cent. Like Burton, Sir Thomas Browne sought to reconcile the mysteries of religion with the newer mysteries of science. Izaak Walton (author of *The Compleat Angler,* 1653) wrote a number of graceful biographies of prominent writers. The most fiery and eloquent author of political tracts (many in defense of Cromwell's government, of which he was a member) was also one of the greatest of all English poets, John Milton. His *Paradise Lost* (1667) is a Christian epic of Homeric scope. In Milton the literary and philosophical heritage of the Renaissance merged with Protestant political and moral conviction. With the restoration of the English monarchy in the person of Charles II, literary tastes sweetened. The lifting of Puritan restrictions and the reassembling of the court produced a national outbreak of frivolity. Restoration comedy reveals both the influence of French FARCE (the English court spent its exile in France) and of Jacobean COMEDY. It generously fed the public's appetite for satire (broad), high style, and a licentiousness that justified the worst Puritan imaginings. Such dramatists as Sir George Etherege, William Wycherley, and William Congreve created superbly polished high comedy. Not quite as brilliant were the plays of George Farquhar, Sir Charles Sedley, and Sir John Vanbrugh. John Dryden, who wrote many undistinguished plays, became the foremost poet and critic of his time. His greatest works are satirical narrative poems, notably *Absalom and Achitophel* (1681), in which prominent contemporary figures are unmistakably and devastatingly portrayed. Another satiric poet of the period was Samuel Butler, whose *Hudibras* (1663) satirizes Puritanism together with all the intellectual pretensions of the time. Puritanism, however, remained vital, the Restoration notwithstanding. The most important Puritan literary work was John Bunyan's *Pilgrim's Progress* (1675), an allegorical prose narrative that is considered a forerunner of the novel. A lively and illuminating glimpse of Restoration manners and mores is provided by the diaries of Samuel Pepys and John Evelyn.

The Eighteenth Century. The Glorious Revolution of 1688 firmly established a Protestant monarchy together with effective rule by Parliament. The new science of the time, Newtonian physics, was thought to corroborate a deistic interpretation of the universe and reinforced the belief that everything, including human conduct, is guided by a rational order. Moderation and common sense thus became intellectual values as well as standards of behavior. These values achieved their highest expression in the poetry of Alexander Pope and the brilliant prose satire of Jonathan Swift. Pope—neoclassicist, wit, and master of the heroic couplet—was critical of human foibles but generally confident that order and happiness in human affairs were attainable if excesses were eschewed and rational dictates heeded. Swift was not so sanguine. His "savage indignation" prompted him to "hate mankind" though he "loved Tom, Dick, and Harry." Middle-class tastes were reflected in the growth of periodicals and newspapers, the best of which were the *Tatler* and the *Spectator* of Joseph Addison and Sir Richard Steele. The novels of Daniel Defoe, the first modern novels in English, owe much to the techniques of journalism. They also illustrate the virtues of enterprise vital to the rising middle class. Indeed, the novel was to become the literary form most responsive to middle-class needs and interests. The 18th cent. was the age of town life with its coffee houses and clubs. One of the most famous of the latter was the Scriblerus Club, whose members included Pope, Swift, and John Gay (author of *The Beggar's Opera*). Its purpose was to defend and uphold high literary standards. Letters were a popular form of polite literature. Pope, Swift, Horace Walpole, and Thomas Gray were masters of the form, and letters make up the chief literary output of Lady Mary Wortley Montagu and Lord Chesterfield. The novels of Samuel Richardson, including the influential *Clarissa* (1747), were written in epistolary form. With the work of Richardson, Henry Fielding, Tobias Smollett, and Laurence Sterne the English novel came of age. Probably the most celebrated literary circle in history was the one dominated by Samuel Johnson. It included Joshua Reynolds, David Garrick, Edmund Burke, Oliver Goldsmith, and James Boswell, whose biography of Johnson is a classic of the genre. Another master prose writer of the period was the historian Edward Gibbon. Dr. Johnson, who carried the arts of criticism and conversation to new heights, both typified and helped to form mid-18th-century views of life, literature, and conduct. The drama of the 18th cent. failed to match that of the Restoration. But Oliver Goldsmith and Richard Brinsley Sheridan rejected the prevalent "weeping comedy"—whose sentimentalism infected every literary genre of the period—for polished comedy in the Restoration tradition. Among the prominent poets of the late 18th cent. were James Thomson, who wrote in *The Seasons* (1726) of nature as it reflected the Newtonian concept of order and beauty, and Edward Young, whose *Night Thoughts* (1742) combined melancholy and Christian apologetics. Anticipations of ROMANTICISM can be seen in the odes of William Collins, the poems of Thomas Gray, and the lyrics of Robert Burns. The work of William Blake, the first great romantic poet, began late in the 18th cent. Blake is unique: poet, artist, artisan, revolutionist, and visionary prophet. In prose fiction, departures from social realism are evident in the Gothic romances of Horace Walpole, Anne Radcliffe, "Monk" Lewis, and others. These works catered to a growing interest in medievalism, northern antiquities, ballads, folklore, chivalry, and romance, also exploited in two masterpieces of forgery—the Ossian poems of James Macpherson and the "medieval" Rowley poems of Thomas Chatterton.

The Romantic Period. At the turn of the century, fired by ideas of personal and political liberty and of the purity of the natural world, artists and intellectuals sought to break the bonds of 18th-century convention. Although the works of Jean Jacques Rousseau and William Godwin had great influence, the French Revolution and its aftermath had the strongest impact of all. In England initial support for the Revolution was primarily utopian and idealist, and when the French failed to live up to expectations, most English intellectuals renounced the Revolution. However, the romantic vision had taken forms other than political, and these developed apace. In *Lyrical Ballads* (1798 and 1800), a watershed in literary history, William Wordsworth and Samuel Taylor Coleridge presented and illustrated a liberating aesthetic: poetry was to express, in simple language, experience as interpreted through personal emotion and imagination; and the fountainhead of truth was nature. Wordsworth's literary principles were probably most fully realized in his great autobiographical poem, "The Prelude" (1805). Among the favorite themes of the romantic poets were the marvelous and supernatural, the exotic, the medieval, the lives of simple rural people, and aspects of the natural world. The second generation of romantic poets included John Keats, Percy Bysshe Shelley, and George Gordon, Lord Byron. In Keats's great odes, aesthetic and emotional sensibility merge exquisitely. Shelley, a less restrained, sometimes self-indulgent poet, combined soaring lyricism with an apocalyptic political vision. Lord Byron was the prototype romantic hero, the envy and scandal of the age. He has been continually identified with his own characters, particularly the rebellious, irreverent, erotically inclined Don Juan. Byron's lyric gift was perhaps surpassed by his gift for satire and irony. Minor romantic poets include Robert Southey—best-remembered for the merciless satires of his work by Byron, Lewis Carroll, and others and for the story "Goldilocks and the Three Bears"—Leigh Hunt, Thomas Moore, and Walter Savage Landor. The romantic era was also rich in literary criticism and other nonfictional prose. Coleridge proposed an entire theory of literature in his *Biographia Literaria* (1817). William Hazlitt, who never forsook political radicalism, was also an important critic. The master of the personal essay was Charles Lamb, whereas Thomas De Quincey was master of the personal confession. The periodicals *Edinburgh Review* and *Blackwood's Magazine*, in which leading writers were published throughout the century, were major forums of controversy, political as well as literary. Although the great novelist Jane Austen wrote during the first decades of the romantic era, her work defies classification. With insight, grace, and irony she delineated human relationships within the context of English country life. Sir Walter Scott, Scottish nationalist and romantic, made the genre of the historical novel widely popular. However, his work was not a critical success until the 20th cent. Other novelists of the period were Maria Edgeworth, E. G. E. L. Bulwer-Lytton, and Thomas Love Peacock, the latter noted for his eccentric novels satirizing the romantics.

The Victorian Age. The Reform Bill of 1832 gave the middle class the political power it needed to consolidate—and to hold—the economic power it had already achieved. Industry and commerce burgeoned. While the affluence of the middle class increased, the lower classes, thrown off their land and into the cities to form the great urban working class, lived ever more wretchedly. The social changes were so swift and brutal that Godwinian utopianism had to be replaced by attempts to explain and change conditions, while those who profited offered justifications. The intellectuals and artists of the age had to deal in some way with the upheavals in society, the obvious inequities of abundance for a few and squalor for many, and, emanating from the throne of Queen Victoria (1837–1901), an aura of the greatest rectitude and moral propriety. The Victorian era was the great age of the English novel—realistic, thickly plotted, crowded with characters, and long. It was the ideal form to describe and entertain the middle class. The novels of Charles Dickens, full to overflowing with drama, humor, and an endless variety of vivid characters and plot complications, nonetheless spare nothing in their portrayal of what urban life was like for all classes. William Makepeace Thackeray is best known for *Vanity Fair* (1848), which wickedly satirizes hypocrisy and greed. Emily Brontë's single novel, *Wuthering Heights* (1847), is a unique masterpiece propelled by a vision of elemental passions but controlled by an uncompromising artistic sense. The fine novels of Emily's sister Charlotte Brontë are more conventionally romantic. During the 1860s and 70s appeared the novels of George Eliot (Mary Ann Evans). A woman of great erudition and moral fervor, Eliot was concerned with ethical conflicts and social problems. George Meredith produced comic novels noted for their psychological perception and their difficulty. Another novelist of the late 19th cent. was Anthony Trollope, famous for the Barchester novels, which examine life in an ecclesiastical town. Thomas Hardy's profoundly pessimistic novels are all set in the harsh, punishing midland county he called Wessex. Samuel Butler produced novels satirizing the Victorian ethos, and Robert Louis Stevenson, a master of his craft, wrote arresting adventure fiction and children's verse. The mathematician Charles Lutwidge Dodgson, writing under the name Lewis Carroll, produced the complex and sophisticated children's classics *Alice in Wonderland* (1865) and *Through the Looking Glass* (1871). Lesser novelists of considerable merit include Benjamin Disraeli, George Gissing, Elizabeth Gaskell, and Wilkie Collins. Among the Victorian masters of nonfiction were the great Whig historian Thomas Macaulay and Thomas Carlyle, the historian, social critic, and prophet whose rhetoric thundered through the age. Influential thinkers included John Stuart Mill, the great liberal scholar and philosopher; Thomas Henry Huxley, a scientist and popularizer of Darwinian theory; and John Henry, Cardinal Newman, who wrote earnestly of religion, philosophy, and education. The great art historian and critic John Ruskin also concerned himself with social and economic problems. Matthew Arnold's theories of literature and culture laid the foundations for modern literary criticism, and his poetry is also notable. The preeminent poet of the Victorian age was Alfred, Lord Tennyson. Although romantic, his poetry was transformed and tempered by personal melancholy and religious doubt. The poetry of Robert Browning was considered inferior to that of his wife, Elizabeth Barrett Browning, while she lived. Later, however, Browning was acknowledged the greater poet, best remembered for his superb dramatic monologues. Rudyard Kipling, the poet of the empire triumphant, truly captured the quality of the life of the soldiers of British expansion. Some fine religious poetry was produced by Francis Thompson, Alice Meynell, Christina Rossetti, and Lionel Johnson. Near the end of the 19th cent., the so-called PRE-RAPHAELITES, led by the painter-poet Dante Gabriel Rossetti, sought to revive what they judged to be the simple, natural values and techniques of medieval life and art. In their gropings for richer symbolic meanings, however, they embraced a vague neoromanticism. William Morris—designer, inventor, printer, poet, and social philosopher—was the most versatile of the group, which included the poets Christina Rossetti and Coventry Patmore. Algernon Charles Swinburne began as a Pre-Raphaelite, but soon developed his own classically influenced, sometimes florid style. A. E. Housman and Thomas Hardy, both essentially Victorian figures who also lived and worked in the 20th cent., share a pessimist view in their poetry, but Housman's well-constructed verse is rather more superficial. The great innovator among the late Victorian poets was the Jesuit priest Gerard Manley Hopkins. The concentration and originality of his imagery, as well as his jolting meter ("sprung rhythm"), had a profound effect on 20th-century poetry. During the 1890s the most conspicuous figures on the English literary scene were the DECADENTS. The principal figures in the group were Arthur Symons, Ernest Dowson, and, first among them in both notoriety and talent, Oscar Wilde. The decadents' disgust with bourgeois complacency led them to extremes of behavior and expression. However limited their accomplishments, they pointed out actual decay in Victorian certainties and institutions.

The Twentieth Century. The sparkling, witty comedies of Oscar Wilde and the comic operettas of W. S. Gilbert and Sir Arthur Sullivan were perhaps the brightest achievements of 19th-century British drama. But the early 20th cent. witnessed a flowering of Irish drama, largely under the aegis of the ABBEY THEATRE in Dublin (see IRISH LITERARY RENAISSANCE). John Millington Synge, William Butler Yeats, and Sean O'Casey all wrote on Irish themes—mythical in Yeats's poetic drama, political in O'Casey's realistic plays. Also Irish, George Bernard Shaw wrote biting dramas that satirize all aspects of British society. It is, perhaps, important to note that many of the towering figures of 20th-century English literature were not English; Shaw, Yeats, Joyce, O'Casey, and Beckett were Irish, Dylan Thomas was Welsh, T. S. Eliot was born an American, and Conrad was born a Pole. Poetry in the early 20th cent. was typified by the conventional romanticism of such poets as John Masefield, Alfred Noyes, and Walter De La Mare and by the experiments of the IMAGISTS, notably Hilda Doolittle, Richard Aldington, Herbert Read, and D. H. Lawrence. Splendidly untypical was the work of Yeats, whose visionary poetry was regarded as the best yet produced during the 20th cent. Arnold Bennett, William Henry Hudson, and John Galsworthy were novelists in the 19th-century tradition, while H. G. Wells wrote popular science fiction. Joseph Conrad, the finest novelist at the turn of the century, expressed the skepticism and alienation that were to become features of post-Victorian sensibility. World War I meant sudden death to British stability, which went the way of the imperial hegemony. As social mores were shaken, so too were artistic conventions. The work of war poets like Siegfried Sassoon and Wilfred Owen, the latter killed in the war (as were Rupert Brooke and Isaac Rosenberg), was particularly influential. So were the works of Gerard Manley Hopkins (first published in 1918) and the rediscovered metaphysical poets. *The Waste Land* (1922) by poet T. S. Eliot was a watershed in both American and English literary history. Its difficulty, formal invention, and bleak antiromanticism were to influence poets for decades. Equally important was the novel *Ulysses*, also published in 1922, by the expatriate Irishman James Joyce. The first serious novelist to deal freely with sexuality, Joyce revolutionized narrative form, the treatment of time, and nearly all other techniques of the novel. Also controversial and sexually liberated were the novels of D. H. Lawrence, which celebrated the primitive urges of man. Sensitivity and psychological subtlety mark the superb novels of Virginia Woolf, who, like Dorothy Richardson, experimented with the STREAM OF CONSCIOUSNESS technique. Woolf was the center of the brilliant BLOOMSBURY GROUP, which included the novelist E. M. Forster, the biographer Lytton Strachey, and many important English intellectuals of the early 20th cent. Aldous Huxley and Evelyn Waugh satirized the group and the period, and Katharine Mansfield and Elizabeth Bowen captured their flavor in fiction. Moved by the Great Depression, the rise of fascism, and English policies of appeasement, many writers and intellectuals sought solutions in the politics of the left. George Orwell fought with the Communists in the Spanish Civil War. His disillusion with the political left is eloquently expressed in such works as *The Road to Wigan Pier* (1937) and *Animal Farm* (1946). The poets W. H. Auden, Stephen Spender, and C. Day Lewis were also among those who for a while believed that artists had political responsibilities and could be effective. After World War II, however, with England's further decline in influence, wealth, and stature and with the onset of the Cold War, most writers steered clear of politics. The novelists Henry Green, Ivy Compton-Burnett, and W. Somerset Maugham, and the poets Robert Graves, Edwin Muir, Louis MacNeice, and Edith Sitwell at all times cultivated their own distinctive voices. Most novelists and playwrights of the 1950s reflected, in their separate ways, deep dissatisfaction with British society and despair that anything could be done about it. Many of these were designated part of the group called the ANGRY YOUNG MEN. While the postwar era has not been a great period of English literature, it has produced excellent critics, such as David Daiches, William Empsom, and F. R. Leavis, and a number of highly individual novelists, including Anthony Burgess, Kingsley Amis, John Fowles, Iris Murdoch, William Golding, Lawrence Durrell, Muriel Spark, and Doris Lessing. In the great 19th-century tradition, C. P. Snow, Anthony Powell, and Richard Hughes produced series of realistic novels chronicling life in England during the 20th cent. Important playwrights, many of them influenced by the theater of the absurd, include John Osborne, David Storey, Arnold Wesker, and Harold Pinter. Probably the two greatest postwar British authors are the Welsh poet Dylan Thomas and the Irish expatriate novelist and playwright Samuel Beckett. Thomas's lyricism and rich imagery reaffirmed the romantic spirit, and he was eventually appreciated for his technical mastery as well. Beckett, who wrote many of his works in French and translated them into English, is considered the greatest exponent of the theater of the absurd. His uncompromisingly bleak, difficult plays (and novels) depict the lonely, alienated human condition with compassion and humor. Also deserving of special note is Hugh McDiarmid, the outstanding figure of the Scottish literary renaissance. The poet Ted Hughes perhaps best articulates the British spirit of the 1970s. In his harsh, post-apocalyptic poetry, mere survival appears as something of a triumph. For further information see separate entries on the authors mentioned in this article. See also AMERICAN LITERATURE; CANADIAN LITERATURE, ENGLISH; SOUTH AFRICAN LITERATURE; NEW ZEALAND LITERATURE; AUSTRALIAN LITERATURE. See *The Cambridge History of English Literature*, ed. by A. W. Ward and A. R. Waller (15 vol., 1960–62); *Oxford History of English Literature*, ed. by F. P. Wilson and Bonamy Dobrée (multivolume, 2d ed., 1962–); *A Literary History of England*, ed. by A. C. Baugh et al. (2d ed., 4 vol., 1967); *The New Cambridge Bibliography of English Literature*, ed. by George Watson (4 vol., 1969–72); Emile Legouis et al., *A History of English Literature* (rev. ed. 1972); *The Penguin Companion to English Literature*, ed. by David Daiches (1972); *The New Oxford Book of English Verse*, ed. by Helen Gardner (1972); *The Oxford Book of Twentieth-Century English Verse*, ed. by Philip Larkin (1973); *The Oxford Anthology of English Literature*, ed. by Frank Kermode and John Hollander (2 vol., 1973).

English running horse: see THOROUGHBRED HORSE.

English setter, breed of large SPORTING DOG developed over hundreds of years in England. It stands about 25 in. (63.5 cm) high at the shoulder and weighs about 60 lb (27.2 kg). Its flat or slightly wavy coat of medium-length, silky hair forms fringes of longer hair, or feathers, on the dog's underside, ears, chest, legs, and tail. Its coat may be colored black, tan, and white; combinations of lemon, liver, orange, blue, or black with white; and solid white. A coloration composed of white flecked with another color is called belton. Although setters were originally trained to crouch down, or set, in front of game to allow the hunter to capture it with a net, the increasing popularity of shooting game birds on the wing led to the training of setters to point. They are so trained today. See DOG.

English sheepdog: see OLD ENGLISH SHEEPDOG.

English sparrow or **house sparrow,** small bird, *Passer domesticus,* common throughout most of the world. English sparrows are 4 to 7 in. (10–18 cm) long, with short, stout bills. The male is brown with black streaks above, grayish white below; it has white cheek patches and a black bib from bill to chest. The female is dull brown above and brownish white below. English sparrows are highly gregarious birds found in cities and settled rural areas; they are rarely seen away from human habitation. Chiefly seedeaters, they are agricultural pests, but they also eat insects that are harmful to crops. The house sparrow builds messy nests of grass and debris almost anywhere—under eaves, in drains, and in ventilator holes—and this has contributed to its reputation as an undesirable bird. It is extremely prolific, raising at least two broods a year; the clutch consists of four to seven olive-speckled white eggs. Native to the Old World, the bird was first introduced into the United States about 1850 to combat cankerworms, and it rapidly became widespread. Aggressive as well as prolific, it has largely replaced many native birds in urban areas. Unlike the native North American species called SPARROWS, which belong to the finch family, the English sparrow is a member of the Old World WEAVER BIRD family. It is classified in the phylum CHORDATA, subphylum Vertebrata, class Aves, order Passeriformes, family Ploceidae.

English springer spaniel, breed of medium-sized SPORTING DOG developed in England from the broader and very old category of "springing spaniels" that produced many of the present-day land spaniels. It stands about 18 in. (46 cm) high at the shoulder and weighs about 45 lb (20 kg). Its medium-length coat is flat or wavy with a fringe of longer hair, or feathers, on the ears, chest, legs, and belly. Its coat is usually either liver and white, tan and white, or black and white. Trained as a field dog, the springer flushes game and will retrieve on both land and water. It also has enjoyed great popularity as a house pet. See DOG.

English toy spaniel, breed of TOY DOG perfected in England over many centuries. It stands about 10 in. (25 cm) high at the shoulder and weighs from 9 to 12 lb (4–5 kg). Its long, silky coat is soft and wavy and forms a fringe of longer hair on the ears, chest, back of legs, and tail. English toy spaniels are divided into four groups corresponding to different color combinations: the King Charles is black with rich mahogany markings; the Prince Charles is white, black, and tan; the ruby is chestnut red; and the Blenheim is red and white. The English toy spaniel originated in the Orient thousands of years ago and became very popular as a pet in England during the 17th cent. See DOG.

English units of measurement, principal system of WEIGHTS AND MEASURES used in a few nations, the only major industrial one being the United States. It actually consists of two related systems—the U.S. Customary System of units, used in the United States and dependencies, and the British Imperial System. Great Britain, the originator of the latter system, announced plans in 1965 for a 10-year program of conversion to the METRIC SYSTEM. The names of the units and the relationships between them are generally the same in both systems, but the sizes of the units differ, sometimes considerably. The basic unit of length is the YARD (yd); fractions of the yard are the inch (1/36 yd) and the foot (1/3 yd), and commonly used multiples are the rod (5½ yd), the furlong (220 yd), and the mile (1,760 yd). The acre, equal to 4,840 square yards or 160 square rods, is used for measuring land area. The pound (lb) is the basic unit of mass (weight). Within the English units of measurement there are three different systems of weights. In the avoirdupois system, the most widely used of the three, the pound is divided into 16 ounces (oz) and the ounce into 16 drams. The ton, used to measure large masses, is equal to 2,000 lb (short ton) or 2,240 lb (long ton). In Great Britain the stone, equal to 14 lb, is also used. The troy system (named for Troyes, France, where it is said to have originated) is used only for precious metals. The troy pound is divided into 12 ounces and the troy ounce into 20 pennyweights or 480 grains; the troy pound is thus 5,760 grains. The grain is also a unit in the avoirdupois system, 1 avoirdupois pound being 7,000 grains, so that the troy pound is 5,760/7,000 of an avoirdupois pound. Apothecaries' weights are based on troy weights; in addition to the pound, ounce, and grain, which are equal to the troy units of the same name, other units are the dram (1/8 oz) and the scruple (1/24 oz or 1/3 dram). For liquid measure, or liquid capacity, the basic unit is the gallon, which is divided into 4 quarts, 8 pints, or 32 gills. The U.S. gallon, or wine gallon, is 231 cubic inches (cu in.); the British imperial gallon is the volume of 10 lb of pure water at 62°F and is equal to 277.42 cu in. The British units of liquid capacity are thus about 20% larger than the corresponding American units. The U.S. fluid ounce is 1/16 of a U.S. pint; the British unit of the same name is 1/20 of an imperial pint and is thus slightly smaller than the U.S. fluid ounce. For dry measure, or dry capacity, the basic unit is the bushel, which is divided into 4 pecks, 32 dry quarts, or 64 dry pints. The U.S. bushel, or Winchester bushel, is 2,150.42 cu in. and is about 3% smaller than the British imperial bushel of 2,219.36 cu in., with a similar difference existing between U.S. and British subdivisions. The barrel is a unit for measuring the capacity of larger quantities and has various legal definitions depending on the quantity being measured, the most common value being 105 dry quarts. Many American units of weights and measures are based on British units in use in Great Britain before 1824, when the British Imperial System was established. Since the Mendenhall Order of 1893, the U.S. yard and pound and all other units derived from them have been defined in terms of the metric units of length and mass, the METER and the KILOGRAM; thus, there is no longer any direct relationship between American units and British units of the same name. In 1959 an international agreement was reached among English-speaking nations to use the same metric equivalents for the yard and pound for purposes of science and technology; these values are 1 yd=0.9144 meter (m) and 1 lb=0.45359237 kilogram (kg). In the United States, the older definition of the yard as 3,600/3,937 m is still used for surveying, the corresponding foot (1,200/3,937 m) being known as the survey foot. The English units of measurement have many drawbacks: the complexity of converting from one unit to another, the differences between American and British units, the use of the same name for different units (e.g., *ounce* for both weight and liquid capacity, *quart* and *pint* for both liquid and dry capacity), and the existence of three different systems of weights (avoirdupois, troy, and apothecaries'). Because of these disadvantages and because of the wide use of the much simpler metric system in most other parts of the world, there have been proposals to do away with the U.S. Customary System and replace it with the metric system. See L. J. Chisholm, *Units of Weights and Measure: International and U.S. Customary* (U.S. National Bureau of Standards, 1967).

engraving, in its broadest sense, the art of cutting lines in metal, wood, or other material either for decoration or for reproduction through PRINTING. In its narrowest sense, it is an INTAGLIO printing process in which the lines are cut in a metal plate with a graver, or burin. Furrows are cleanly cut out, raising no burr, and then filled with ink which is transferred under high pressure to the printing surface of the press. The earliest known engravings printed on paper date from about the middle of the 15th cent. Among the early master engravers were Dürer, Schongauer, and Lucas van Leyden. Wood engraving differs from true engraving in that it is a relief process. During the 19th cent., steel engraving enjoyed a short popularity as a reproduction process because it made possible a large number of proofs, but it was superseded by photomechanical processes (see PHOTOENGRAVING). See also DRYPOINT, ETCHING, and MEZZOTINT. See A. M. Hind, *History of Engraving and Etching* (1923, repr. 1963); A. Gross, *Etching, Engraving, and Intaglio Printing* (1970).

engrossing, in English law, practice of acquiring a monopoly of goods in order to sell them at an inflated price. The offense was ordinarily limited to monopolies of foods. Related practices were forestalling, i.e., buying up food on the way to its normal markets, and regrating, i.e., gaining control of a commodity once it reaches the market. All these practices were declared criminal in 1844 in England. See MONOPOLY.

En-haddah (ĕn-hăd'ə), unidentified city of Issachar. Joshua 19.21.

En-hakkore (ĕn-hăk'ōrē), spring in Lehi that burst forth when Samson called upon the Lord. Judges 15.18,19.

En-hazor (ĕn-hā'zôr), place on Naphtali. Joshua 19.37.

Enid (ē'nĭd), city (1970 pop. 44,986), seat of Garfield co., N central Okla.; inc. 1893. It is an important trade and processing center for an area rich in wheat, dairy cattle, and poultry. Oil fields are nearby, and there are oil refineries as well as foundries and machine shops in the city. Phillips Univ., a state hospital, and Vance Air Force Base are there.

Enisei: see YENISEI, river, USSR.

Eniwetok (ĕnĭwē'tŏk, ĕnē'wĕtôk), uninhabited circular atoll, central Pacific, one of the Ralik Chain in the MARSHALL ISLANDS. Eniwetok is c.50 mi (80 km) in circumference and comprises about 40 islets surrounding a large lagoon. Mandated to Japan by the League of Nations in 1920, Eniwetok was captured in World War II by U.S. forces. Designated an atomic proving station, it was the site of atomic tests in 1948, 1951, 1952 (first thermonuclear tests), and 1954.

Enkhuizen (ĕngk'hoi"zən), town (1970 pop. 11,502), North Holland prov., N central Netherlands, a port on IJsselmeer lake. It is a commercial and industrial center and has shipyards. The town played an important part in the Dutch struggle for independence, was a prosperous fishing and trading center in the 17th cent., and has retained numerous buildings of the 16th and 17th cent.

Enki: see EA.

Enköping (ăn'chö"pĭng), city (1970 pop. 19,066), Uppsala co., E Sweden, near Stockholm. It is an industrial center whose manufactures include machinery and vehicles. Enköping was founded c.1300 and is one of Sweden's oldest cities.

Enlightenment, term applied to the mainstream of thought of 18th-century Europe. The scientific and intellectual developments of the 17th cent.—the discoveries of Isaac NEWTON, the rationalism of Réné DESCARTES and Pierre BAYLE, the pantheism of Benedict de SPINOZA, and the empiricism of Francis BACON and John LOCKE—fostered the belief in natural law and universal order and the confidence in human reason that spread to influence all of 18th-century society. Currents of thought were many and varied, but certain ideas may be characterized as pervading and dominant. A rational and scientific approach to religious, social, political, and economic issues promoted a secular view of the world and a general sense of progress and perfectibility. The major champions of these concepts were the philosophes, who popularized and promulgated the new ideas for the general reading public. These proponents of the Enlightenment agreed on several basic attitudes. With supreme faith in rational man, they sought to discover and to act upon universally valid principles governing humanity, nature, and society. They variously attacked spiritual and scientific authority, dogmatism, intolerance, censorship, and economic and social restraints. They considered the state the proper and rational instrument of progress. The extreme rationalism and skepticism of the age led naturally to deism; the same qualities played a part in bringing the later reaction of romanticism. The ENCYCLOPÉDIE of Denis DIDEROT epitomized the spirit of the Age of Enlightenment, or Age of Reason, as it is also called. Centered in Paris, the movement gained international character at cosmopolitan salons. Masonic lodges played an important role in disseminating the new ideas in Europe. Foremost in France among proponents of the Enlightenment were baron de MONTESQUIEU, VOLTAIRE, and comte de BUFFON; Baron TURGOT and other PHYSIOCRATS; and Jean Jacques ROUSSEAU, who greatly influenced romanticism. Many opposed the extreme materialism of Julien de LA METTRIE, baron d' HOLBACH, and Claude HELVÉTIUS. In England the coffeehouses and the newly flourishing press stimulated social and political criticism, such as the urbane commentary of Joseph ADDISON and Sir Richard STEELE. Jonathan SWIFT and Alexander POPE were influential Tory satirists. Lockean theories of learning by sense perception were further developed by David HUME. The philosophical view of rational man in harmony with the universe set the climate for the laissez-faire economics of Adam SMITH and for the utilitarianism of Jeremy BENTHAM. Historical writing gained secular detachment in the work of Edward GIBBON. In Germany the universities became centers of the Enlightenment (Ger. *Aufklärung*). Moses MENDELSSOHN set forth a doctrine of rational progress; G. E. LESSING advanced a natural religion of morality; Johann HERDER developed a philosophy of cultural nationalism. The supreme importance of the individual formed the basis of the ethics of Immanuel KANT. Italian representatives of the age included Cesare BECCARIA and Giambattista VICO. From America, Thomas PAINE, Thomas JEFFERSON and Benjamin FRANKLIN exerted vast international influence. The movement received its strongest support from the rising bourgeoisie and its most vigorous opposition from the high clergy and nobility. Some philosophes at first proposed that their theories be implemented by "enlightened despots"—rulers who would impose reform by authoritarian means. Czar Peter I of Russia anticipated the trend. Holy Roman Emperor JOSEPH II was the prototype of the enlightened despot; others were FREDERICK II of Prussia, CATHERINE II of Russia, and CHARLES III of Spain. The proponents of the Enlightenment have often been held responsible for the French Revolution. Certainly the Age of Enlightenment can be seen as a major demarcation in the emergence of the modern world. See Ernst Cassirer, *The Philosophy of the Enlightenment* (tr. 1951, repr. 1955); Paul Hazard, *The European Mind: The Critical Years, 1690–1715* (tr. 1953, repr. 1963) and *European Thought in* the Eighteenth Century (tr. 1954, repr. 1963); F. E. Manuel, *The Eighteenth Century Confronts the Gods* (1959, repr. 1967); Peter Gay, *The Enlightenment: An Interpretation* (2 vol., 1966–69); Alfred Cobban, ed., *Europe in the Age of the Enlightenment* (1969); L. G. Crocker, ed., *The Age of Enlightenment* (1969); Norman Hampson, *The Enlightenment* (1970); Franco Venturi, *Utopia and Reform in the Enlightenment* (1971).

Enlil (ĕnlĭl'), ancient earth god of Sumerian origin, worshiped in Babylonian religion. With the sky god Anu and the water god Ea, he formed the great divine triad. Enlil, also referred to as Bel, could be hostile or beneficent. He was responsible for the order and harmony in the universe, but as a god of storms and winds he brought terrible destruction.

En-mishpat (ĕn-mĭsh'păt), the same as KADESH (Kadesh-barnea).

Enna (ăn'nä), town (1971 pop. 28,220), capital of Enna prov., central Sicily, Italy. It is an agricultural market, resort, and sulfur-mining center. In ancient times Enna was devoted to the cult of Ceres. It was taken by Syracuse (396 B.C.) and by Rome (258 B.C.) and played a major part in the Sicilian slave rebellion that occurred from 135 B.C. to 132 B.C. The town was later captured by the Arabs (9th cent.) and then by the Normans (11th cent.). An imposing citadel (14th cent.) dominates Enna. Until 1927 the town was called Castrogiovanni.

Ennis, city (1970 pop. 11,046), Ellis co., N Texas; inc. 1872. It is a trading, financial, rail, and processing center in a rich blackland area that produces cotton and grain. Ennis also has plants that manufacture clothing, office supplies, and beds. Many residents commute to Dallas. The city, which was settled by Czechs, sponsors a national polka festival each May. Nearby Lake Bardwell offers recreational activities.

Enniskillen (ĕnĭskĭl'ən), municipal borough (1971 pop. 6,553), county town of Co. Fermanagh, SW Northern Ireland, on an island in the Erne River between Upper and Lower Loughs Erne. Farm produce is traded and hosiery is manufactured there. In 1689 the forces of William III defeated those of James II at Enniskillen.

Ennius, Quintus (kwĭn'təs ĕn'ēəs), 239–169? B.C., Latin poet, regarded by the Romans as the father of Latin poetry, b. Calabria. His birthplace was the meeting point of three civilizations—Oscan, Greek, and Latin—and Ennius learned to speak the languages of these cultures. He served (204) as a centurion in Sardinia under Cato the Elder, who took him to Rome. Ennius lived there most of his life, teaching and writing. In 184 B.C. he was made a Roman citizen. His ambition was to be a Latin Homer, and his innovations proved important in the development of Latin poetry. He introduced the Latin quantitative hexameter and the elegiac couplet, smoothed the current roughness of Latin diction, and gave to Latin poetry a definitive artistic base. A successful tragedian, he also wrote comedies, satires, and epigrams. Fragments amounting to some 400 lines survive from his tragedies, and about 600 lines remain from his masterpiece, the epic *Annales,* a literary history of Rome. Vergil, Lucretius, and Ovid borrowed freely from Ennius. See H. D. Jocelyn, *The Tragedies of Ennius* (1967).

Enns (ĕns), town (1964 est. pop. 9,300), Upper Austria prov., N central Austria, on the Enns River near its confluence with the Danube. One of Austria's oldest towns, Enns was established as a fortress in the 10th cent. and was chartered in 1212. The picturesque town retains part of its medieval walls, a 16th-century fortress, and a Gothic parish church (13th–15th cent.). The former town hall (16th cent.) now houses a museum that includes Roman relics. Lorch, incorporated into Enns in 1938, is on the site of a Roman camp established (A.D. c.170) by Marcus Aurelius. Near Enns is the Augustinian monastery of St. Florian.

Enoch (ē'nək). **1** Son for whom Cain named the city he built. Gen. 4.17. **2** Father of Methuselah. It was said of him that he walked with God—a phrase used also of Noah—and also that like Elijah he was translated to heaven. Gen. 5.18–24; Luke 3.37; Heb. 11.5; Jude 14. Henoch: 1 Chron. 1.3. For the Ethiopic Book of Enoch and the Secrets of Enoch, see PSEUDEPIGRAPHA.

Enos (ē'nŏs), son of Seth. Gen. 4.26; Luke 3.38. Enosh: 1 Chron. 1.1.

Enosh (ē'nŏsh), the same as ENOS.

enragés (äNrăzhā') [French, = madmen], term applied to the extremist Parisian workingmen in the FRENCH REVOLUTION. Rising prices and food shortages provoked them in Feb.–March, 1793, to pillage the city's food stores. Led by Jacques ROUX, they demanded strict economic controls and successfully agitated for the overthrow of the GIRONDISTS. To maintain popular support in a time of crisis, the government granted many of their demands in the early months of the REIGN OF TERROR. After Roux's arrest (Aug., 1793) Jacques René HÉBERT supported them.

En-rimmon (ĕn-rĭm'ən), place, reoccupied after the Exile. The same is meant by "Ain and Rimmon" in Joshua 15.32, by "Ain, Remmon" in Joshua 19.7, by "Ain, Rimmon" in 1 Chron. 4.32, and by "Rimmon" in Zech. 14.10. It was near the border of Simeon.

En-rogel (ĕn-rō'gĕl), spring, near Jerusalem. Joshua 15.7; 18.16; 2 Sam. 17.17; 1 Kings 1.9.

Enschede (ĕnskhədā'), city (1971 pop. 141,204), Overijssel prov., E Netherlands, near the West German border. It is a textile and machinery manufacturing center and a rail junction. Enschede was largely destroyed by fire in 1862, but was later rebuilt. A technical university is there.

Ensenada, Zenón de Somodevilla, marqués de la (thānōn' dā sōmōthāvē'lyä märkās' dā lä ānsänä'thä), 1702–81, Spanish statesman. He was created (1736) marquess for his part in the expedition to Naples that placed King Philip V's son, Carlos (later Charles III of Spain), on the Neapolitan throne. After 1743, when Philip appointed him chief minister, Ensenada virtually ruled Spain. He sought to maintain peace and to regain Spanish independence by avoiding subordination to either French or British policies. He was energetic and able, and his economic and fiscal reforms benefited the country. Court intrigues of the British ambassador led to Ensenada's downfall in 1754, when FERDINAND VI arrested and banished him. Ensenada returned (1760) to the court after the accession of Charles III, but he was banished again in 1766 because of his friendly attitude toward the Jesuits, who were expelled from Spain the following year.

Ensenada, city (1970 pop. 113,320), Baja California state, NW Mexico. Cereal growing, cattle raising, and fishing are the chief occupations. Tourism is also economically important.

En-shemesh (ĕn-shē'mĕsh), place, E of Jerusalem, on the border of Judah. Joshua 15.7; 18.17.

ensilage: see SILAGE.

Enskog, David, 1884–1947, Swedish physicist. In 1912, even before earning his doctorate, Enskog discovered a method of using heat to separate the different isotopes of a gas. In 1917, Uppsala Univ. awarded him the Ph.D. for a general solution to the Maxwell-Boltzmann equations on the flow of molecules, momentum, and energy in a gas. In 1922 he proposed a generalization of the Maxwell-Boltzmann equations for denser gases that remained the only experimentally verifiable theory for four decades. He taught in secondary schools until 1930, when he was named professor at Stockholm's Technical Institute.

Ensor, James Ensor, Baron, 1860–1949, Belgian painter and etcher. Ensor's imagery reflected one of the most bizarre and powerful visions of his era. He left his native Ostend to study painting (1877–80) at the Académie de Bruxelles. In Brussels he became one of the original members of "Les XX," a group of avant-garde artists, writers, and musicians. Ensor exhibited with them regularly until 1888, when his pictures, particularly the garish, nightmarish *Entry of Christ into Brussels,* were rejected as scandalous. While the public and press were at first hostile to his work, his paintings continued to be exhibited, and he gradually won worldwide acclaim. In 1929, Ensor was made a baron by King Albert. His home in Ostend became a museum after his death. His early style of painting is characterized by somber color, thick impasto, and an earthy realism with occasional hints of the fantastic. Toward 1883 his palette lightened, and by 1887 his paintings were flooded with intense light and strong color. From 1887 to 1900 he produced his most inventive and original work. His weird, often gruesome, compositions emphasized the macabre. Ensor's sources included the grotesque fantasies of Bosch, Bruegel, and Callot. Among his masterpieces is *The Temptation of St. Anthony* (Mus. of Modern Art, New York City). By 1900 the significant part of his work was finished; during the last 50 years of his life his paintings show hesitant draftsmanship and an absence of internal structure. Ensor ranks as one of the great innovators of the late 19th cent.; his art transformed reality, opening the way for SURREALISM. See studies by Paul Haesaerts (tr. 1959) and Libby Tannenbaum (1951, repr. 1967).

entablature (ĕntăb'ləchoor), the entire unit of horizontal members above the columns or pilasters in classical architecture—Greek, Roman or Renaissance. The height of the entablature in relation to the column supporting it varies with the three orders, Doric, Ionic, and Corinthian, but in Roman and Renaissance interpretations it is generally about one fourth the column height. The entablature's

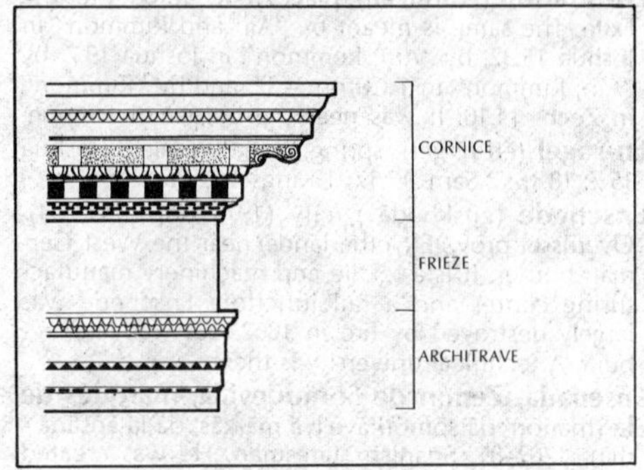

Corinthian entablature showing the parts of the architrave, frieze, and cornice

component members are the ARCHITRAVE, which rests directly upon the abacus, or top member of the column cap; the FRIEZE; and the CORNICE, or topmost member. Essentially the entablature is a development from the primitive lintel, which spans two posts and supports the ends of the roof rafters. In Renaissance and modern designs the entablature is also used upon a wall as the crowning member or as a horizontal band, irrespective of columns.

entail, in law, restriction of inheritance to a limited class of descendants for at least several generations. The object of entail is to preserve large estates in land from the disintegration that is caused by equal inheritance by all the heirs and by the ordinary right of free alienation (disposal) of property interests. Legal devices similar to entail were known in Roman law and in all the countries of Europe. In England the entail became common in the early 13th cent., and in its most usual form was a conveyance by a grantor (owner) of real property to a grantee and the "heirs of his body," i.e., his lawful offspring, in successive generations. In the inheritance the rule of PRIMOGENITURE was observed. The subsequent development of the entail reflects a continuing struggle between the effort to preserve large estates and the need for free alienation. By the mid-13th cent. the courts interpreted the birth of a live baby as the satisfaction of a condition that vested the grantee with the power of alienation. This result was overcome by the statute *De donis conditionalibus* [conditional gifts] (1285), which gave effect to the grantor's intent. In time the grantee was able to get control of the property despite the statutory prohibition by use of the FINE and other technical legal devices. Current English law permits the holder of entailed property (either real or personal) to dispose of it by DEED; otherwise the entail persists. In the United States for the most part entails are either altogether prohibited or limited to a single generation.

En-tappuah (ĕn-tăpyo͞o'ə), the same as TAPPUAH **2.**

entasis (ĕn'təsĭs) [Gr.,=stretching], the slight convex curvature of a classical COLUMN that diminishes in diameter as it rises. This device, as used by Greek builders, was of extreme subtlety, the freehand curvature being merely sufficient to guard the contours of the column from any appearance of inward sagging. In the Doric columns of the Parthenon, 34 ft (10.3 m) high and 6 ft 3 in. (1.9 m) in diameter at the bottom, the total convexity amounts to only ¾ in. (1.91 cm). In Greek Doric columns the entasis began at the foot, but in the Roman orders it was confined to the upper two thirds of the column.

Entebbe (ĕntĕb'ə), town (1969 pop. 10,900) S Uganda, on Victoria Nyanza (Lake Victoria), near Kampala. Located in a region producing cotton, coffee, and plantains, it is the site of a major international airport. Entebbe was founded in 1893, and from 1894 to 1962 it was the administrative capital of the British Uganda Protectorate. It has noteworthy botanical gardens.

Entente: see TRIPLE ALLIANCE AND TRIPLE ENTENTE; BALKAN ENTENTE; LITTLE ENTENTE.

Entente Cordiale: see TRIPLE ALLIANCE AND TRIPLE ENTENTE.

enteritis (ĕn"tərī'tĭs), inflammation of the gastrointestinal tract. Acute enteritis is not usually serious except in infants and older people, in whom the accompanying diarrhea can cause dehydration through the loss of fluids. The condition known as regional enteritis is a chronic disease that occurs most frequently in young adults, producing a segmented thickening of the bowel wall and narrowing of the bowel opening (lumen). The lower portion of the small intestine is usually affected, but the infection can extend up to the duodenum and down into the colon. Clinical symptoms include mild, intermittent diarrhea, abdominal pain, weight loss, and fever. In prolonged cases there may be anemia and nutritional deficiency. The term enteritis is sometimes applied to the conditions of gastroenteritis (inflammation of the stomach commonly caused by food poisoning) and ulcerative colitis (a granulomatous infection of the lower bowel). Surgery may be necessary to treat severe complications such as abscesses and obstructions.

Enterprise. 1 City (1970 pop. 15,591), Coffee co., SE Ala.; inc. 1896. It is a peanut-shipping center with many peanut-processing establishments. There are also lumber and textile mills and plants making concrete. The region's diversified farming began after the boll weevil destroyed (1910–15) the cotton; in gratitude for the resulting prosperity, the city erected (1919) a monument to the boll weevil. A state junior college is in Enterprise. **2** Uninc. town (1970 pop. 11,486), Shasta co., N central Calif. A state park is nearby.

enthalpy (ĕn'thălpē), measure of the HEAT content of a chemical or physical system; it is a quantity derived from the heat and work relations studied in THERMODYNAMICS. There is no absolute measure of the heat content of a given system; what is important is the change in heat content as the system changes from one state to another. The enthalpy change, ΔH, is equal to the enthalpy of the products minus the enthalpy of the reactants. If heat is given off during a transformation from one state to another, then the final state will have a lower heat content than the initial state, the enthalpy change ΔH will be negative, and the process is said to be exothermic. If heat is absorbed during the transformation, then the final state will have a higher heat content, ΔH will be positive, and the process is said to be endothermic. The enthalpy change accompanying a chemical reaction is called the heat of the reaction. For a reaction in which a compound is formed from its composite elements, the enthalpy increase or decrease is called the heat of formation of the compound. Changes of state, or phase, of matter are also accompanied by enthalpy changes; the change associated with the solid-liquid transition is called the heat of fusion and the change associated with the liquid-gas transition is called the heat of vaporization (see LATENT HEAT). The enthalpy change for a given reaction often may be used to tell how favorable the reaction is; an exothermic reaction involves a loss of heat and a consequent lower final energy and thus tends to be favorable, while an endothermic reaction tends to be unfavorable because it involves an increase in energy. However, there are other factors, such as ENTROPY changes, which must also be taken into account in determining whether or not a given process can occur; the FREE ENERGY of the system, which includes both enthalpy and entropy as factors, is important in such determinations.

entomology, study of INSECTS, an arthropod class that comprises about 675,000 known species, representing about nine tenths of all the classified animal species. Insects are studied because of their importance as pollinators for fruit crops, as carriers of bacterial, viral, and fungal diseases, as parasites of man or livestock, as destroyers of economically important plants, or as predators of other destructive insects. The role of insects in ecosystems, and their control by insecticides or by biological methods are studied in ECOLOGY. Some insects such as the FRUIT FLY, *Drosophila,* are used as laboratory tools in GENETICS; others are used to study behavior and physiology. The ability to increase productivity of insect populations that supply commercially important products such as dyes, silk, and honey, and the deliberate introduction of insect diseases into populations of insect pests, involves knowledge of microbiology and biochemistry as well as entomology.

Entoprocta, animal phylum consisting of small marine organisms living in shallow coastal waters. The entoprocts are either colonial or solitary. The body is vase-shaped, with the upper edge covered by ciliated tentacles that direct microscopic animals and debris into the U-shaped digestive tract. A stalk with an enlarged base attaches the organism to seaweed, other marine organisms, shells, or other material. Of the 60 or more known species, only one is found in fresh water. While in some species the sexes are separate, other species are hermaphroditic. Eggs and

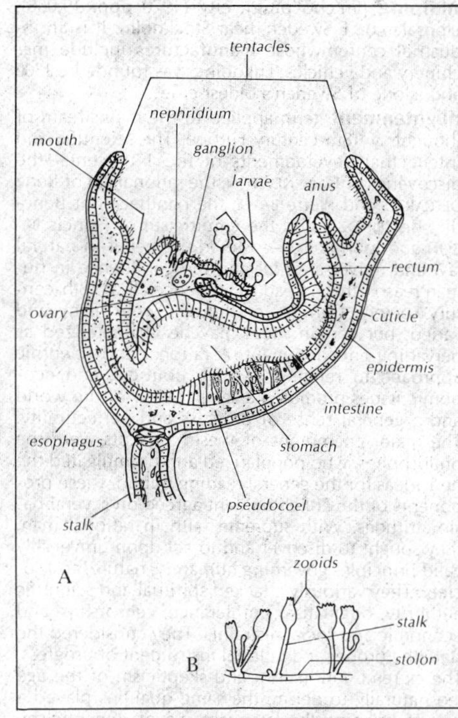

A. *Internal anatomy of a single animal in a* Pedicellina *colony*

B. *Part of a colony of* Pedicellina, *representative of the phylum Entoprocta*

larvae develop in the ovary, and larvae are free-swimming before growing stalks and attaching. *Pedicellina* is a common marine colonial entoproct.

Entragues, Henriette de Balzac d' (äNrĕēt' də bälzäk' däNträg'), 1579–1633, marquise of Verneuil, mistress of King Henry IV of France after the death (1599) of Gabrielle d'Estrées. She violently resented his marriage (1600) to Marie de' Medici and joined the plot of Marshal Biron against his life.

Entrecasteaux, Joseph Antoine Bruni d' (zhôzĕf' äNtwän' bro͞onē' däNtrəkästō'), 1739–93, French navigator. He entered the French navy in 1754, fought (1756) at Minorca, commanded (1786) the French fleet of the East Indies, and was appointed governor of Mauritius and the Isle of Bourbon in 1787. While in command of an expedition to search for LA PÉROUSE (1791–92) he determined the position of Amsterdam island, explored the coastlines of New Caledonia, Tasmania, and New Holland, and located several groups of islands. Many of the charts made by the expedition (particularly those of South Australia produced by Beautemps-Beaupré) were of unusually high standards. An archipelago, a point on the coast of Australia, and a channel are named for him. The journal of the voyage was published in Paris in 1807.

Entrecasteaux Islands, D': see D'ENTRECASTEAUX ISLANDS.

entrepreneur (än"trəpənûr') [Fr.,=one who undertakes], person who assumes the organization, management, and risks of a business enterprise. It was first used as a technical economic term by the 18th-century French economist Richard Cantillon. To the classical economist of the late 18th cent. the term meant an employer in the character of one who assumes the risk and management of business; an undertaker of economic enterprises, in contrast to the ordinary capitalist, who, strictly speaking, merely owns an enterprise and may choose to take no part in its day-to-day operation. In practice, the entrepreneur was not differentiated from the regular capitalist until the 19th cent., when his function developed into that of coordinator of processes necessary to large-scale industry and trade. Joseph Schumpeter and other 20th-century economists considered the entrepreneur's competitive drive for innovation and improvement to have been the motive force behind capitalist development. Richard Arkwright in England and William Cockerill on the Continent were prominent examples of the rising class of entrepreneurial manufacturers during the

Industrial Revolution. Henry Ford was a 20th-century American example. The entrepreneur's functions and importance have declined with the growth of the CORPORATION. See Joseph Schumpeter, *The Theory of Economic Development* (1934); J. W. Gough, *The Rise of the Entrepreneur* (1969); O. F. Collins, *The Organization Makers* (1970).

Entre Ríos (ĕn'trä rē'ōs), province (1970 pop. 812,000), 29,428 sq mi (76,219 sq km), E Argentina. Paraná is the capital.

entropy (ĕn'trəpē), quantity specifying the amount of disorder or randomness in a system bearing ENERGY or information. Originally defined in THERMODYNAMICS in terms of heat and temperature, entropy indicates the degree to which a given quantity of thermal energy is available for doing useful work—the greater the entropy, the less available the energy. Energy can be extracted only when a system changes from a more ordered state to a less ordered state. For example, consider a system composed of a hot body and a cold body; this system is ordered because the faster, more energetic molecules of the hot body are separated from the less energetic molecules of the cold body. If the bodies are placed in contact, heat will flow from the hot body to the cold one. This heat flow can be utilized by a heat engine (device which turns thermal energy into mechanical energy, or work), but once the two bodies have reached the same temperature, no more work can be done. Furthermore, the combined lukewarm bodies cannot unmix themselves into hot and cold parts in order to repeat the process. Although no energy has been lost by the heat transfer, the energy can no longer be used to do work. Thus the entropy of the system has increased. According to the second law of thermodynamics, during any process the change in entropy of a system and its surroundings is either zero or positive. In other words the entropy of the universe as a whole tends towards a maximum. This means that although energy cannot vanish because of the law of conservation of energy (see CONSERVATION LAWS), it tends to be degraded from useful forms to useless ones. When the universe as a whole reaches maximum entropy, the temperature will be the same everywhere and no energy will be able to be converted into work. This is known as the "heat death" of the universe. It should be noted that the second law of thermodynamics is statistical rather than exact; thus there is nothing to prevent the faster molecules from separating from the slow ones. However, such an occurrence is so improbable as to be impossible from a practical point of view. In INFORMATION THEORY entropy represents the "noise" or random errors that occur in the transmission of signals or messages.

Enugu (ĕno͞o'go͞o), city (1969 est. pop. 161,000), SE Nigeria. It is an industrial center and a road and rail hub. Furniture, ceramics, textiles, shoes, asbestos, cement, and steel are the chief products. Enugu developed as a mining town after the discovery of coal in 1909. In 1916 the railroad from Port Harcourt reached Enugu. The city served as capital of Nigeria's Southern Region (1929-39) and Eastern Region (1939-67), and of the short-lived secessionist state of Biafra (1967-70). Coal mining in the area has now been sharply curtailed because of Nigeria's increasing petroleum production. A campus of the Univ. of Nigeria that includes an economic development institute is in Enugu.

Enver Pasha (ĕnvĕr' päshä'), 1881-1922, Turkish general and political leader. He took a prominent part in the Young Turk revolution of 1908, which reestablished the liberal constitution of 1876. By a coup d'etat (1913) he became the virtual dictator. He fought in the Turco-Italian War (1911-12) in LIBYA and in the Balkan Wars (1912-13). Dissatisfied with the loss of Turkish territory in the Balkan Wars, he helped bring Turkey into World War I as a German ally. When Turkey signed an armistice, Enver fled to Berlin. He was killed while leading an anti-Soviet expedition in Bukhara.

environmentalism, movement to protect the quality and continuity of life through CONSERVATION OF NATURAL RESOURCES, prevention of POLLUTION, and control of LAND USE. The philosophical foundations for environmentalism in the United States were established in the works of Thomas Jefferson, Ralph Waldo Emerson, and Henry David Thoreau. In 1864, George Perkins Marsh published *Man & Nature*, in which he anticipated many concepts of modern ECOLOGY, such as the interrelationship of all living things, and questioned the idea that natural resources are inexhaustible. Organized environmentalism began with the efforts of conservationists in the late 19th cent. and thereafter to establish state and national parks and forests, wildlife refuges, and national monuments intended to preserve noteworthy natural features. Early conservationists included President Theodore Roosevelt; Gifford Pinchot, the director of the Forest Service under Roosevelt; and John Muir, the founder of the Sierra Club. Conservationists also organized the National Parks and Conservation Association, the Audubon Society, the Isaak Walton League, and other groups still active. In the years following World War II increasing encroachment on wilderness land evoked the continued resistance of conservationists. By undertaking economic and engineering studies and by marshaling public support, conservation organizations were able to block a number of projects in the 1950s and 1960s, including the proposed Bridge Canyon Dam that would have backed up the waters of the Colorado River into the Grand Canyon National Monument. Meanwhile, the public was becoming aware that conservation of wilderness and wildlife was but one aspect of defending an environment threatened by burgeoning population and industry, indiscriminate land use, and pollution of all sorts. Concern about AIR POLLUTION, WATER POLLUTION, SOLID WASTE disposal, dwindling energy resources, radiation, pesticide poisoning, NOISE POLLUTION, and other environmental problems engaged a broadening number of sympathizers and gave rise to what became known as the "new environmentalism." Public support for these issues culminated in the Earth Day demonstrations of 1970. The environmental movement generated extensive legislation, notably the National Environmental Protection Act (NEPA), signed into law in 1970, which established an Environmental Protection Agency and a Council on Environmental Quality; the Clean Air Act of 1970; the Water Pollution Control Act, as amended in 1972; other laws regulating noise, pesticides, toxic substances, and ocean dumping; and laws to protect endangered species, wilderness, and wild and scenic rivers. NEPA requires all federal agencies to file impact statements assessing the environmental consequences of proposed projects such as highways, jet runways, bridges, dams, and nuclear power plants. Moreover, the new laws provide for pollution research, standard setting, monitoring, and enforcement. Citizens are empowered to sue both private industry and government agencies for violating antipollution standards. Several environmental organizations, among them the National Resources Defense Council and the Environmental Defense Fund, specialize in bringing such lawsuits. Many other environmentalist groups, such as the National Wildlife Federation, Friends of the Earth, and the Wilderness Society, disseminate information, participate in public hearings, lobby, stage demonstrations, and purchase land for preservation. On an international level, concern for the environment was the subject of a UN conference in Stockholm in 1972. Adopted by the 114 nations represented were declarations to safeguard wildlife and its habitat, conserve natural resources, halt the discharge of toxic substances, prevent pollution of the sea, develop international law regarding liability and compensation for the victims of environmental damage, and promote environmental education, scientific research, and development. See Paul Shepard and Daniel McKinley, *The Subversive Science* (1969); Garett De Bell, comp., *The Environmental Handbook* (1970); R. J. Dubos, *So Human an Animal* (1970); Richard Saltonstall, *Your Environment and What You Can Do About It* (1970); R. M. Chute, *Environmental Insight* (1971); Environmental Action Association, *Earth Tool Kit*, ed. by Sam Love (1971); P. R. Ehrlich, comp., *Man and the Ecosphere* (1971) and, with A. H. Ehrlich, *Population, Resources, Environment* (2d ed. 1972); J. L. Sax, *Defending the Environment* (1972); P. R. Ehrlich et al., *Human Ecology* (1973).

envoy: see DIPLOMATIC SERVICE.

Enzeli: see BANDAR-E PAHLAVI, Iran.

Enzina, Juan del: see ENCINA, JUAN DEL.

Enzio (än'tsēō) or **Enzo** (än'tsō), c.1220-72, king of Sardinia, illegitimate son of Holy Roman Emperor FREDERICK II. He married a Sardinian heiress and was made king of Sardinia by his father. In the wars between Frederick and the pope he fought gallantly in Italy. Helping Modena against BOLOGNA, he was defeated and captured (1249) at Fossalta. Until his death he was kept prisoner in Bologna, in the palace that came to bear his name.

enzyme, biological CATALYST. The term enzyme comes from *zymosis*, the Greek word for FERMENTATION, a process accomplished by yeast cells and long known to the brewing industry, which occupied the attention of many 19th-century chemists. Louis Pasteur recognized in 1860 that enzymes were essential to fermentation but assumed that their catalytic action was inextricably linked with the structure and life of the yeast cell. Not until 1897 was it shown by German chemist Edward Büchner that cell-free extracts of yeast could ferment sugars to alcohol and carbon dioxide; Büchner denoted his preparation *zymase*. This important achievement was the first indication that enzymes could function independently of the cell. The first enzyme molecule to be isolated in pure crystalline form was urease, prepared from the jack bean in 1926 by American biochemist J. B. Sumner who suggested, contrary to prevailing opinion, that the molecule was a PROTEIN. In the period from 1930 to 1936, PEPSIN, CHYMOTRYPSIN, and TRYPSIN were successfully crystallized, it was confirmed that the crystals were protein, and the protein nature of enzymes was thereby firmly established. Over a thousand different enzymes have now been identified. Many of these have been isolated in pure form, and more than two hundred have been crystallized. Determination of the AMINO ACID sequence of the protein structure of enzymes has been of central concern to enzymologists over the last two decades and is now known, at least in part, for a great many of the purified enzymes. The 124-amino acid structure of ribonuclease was determined in 1967, and two years later the enzyme was synthesized independently at two laboratories in the United States. The technique of X-ray crystallography has developed in recent years as a powerful tool for analysis of crystal structure and has been employed successfully to elucidate the three-dimensional structure of several crystalline enzymes. Like all catalysts, enzymes serve to accelerate the rates of reactions while experiencing no permanent chemical modification as a result of their participation. The most remarkable feature of enzymes, which distinguishes them from simpler organic or inorganic catalysts, is the ability to accelerate, often by several orders of magnitude, reactions which under the mild conditions of cellular concentrations, temperature, pH, and pressure would proceed imperceptibly (or not at all) in the absence of the enzyme. Most enzymic reactions occur within a relatively narrow temperature range (usually from about 30°C to 40°C), a feature which reflects their complexity as biological molecules. Each enzyme would also appear to have an optimal range of pH for activity; for example, pepsin in the stomach has maximal reactivity under the extremely acid conditions of pH 1-3. Effective catalysis is also known to depend crucially upon maintenance of the molecule's elaborate three-dimensional structure. Loss of structural integrity, which may result from such factors as changes in pH or high temperatures, almost always leads to a loss of enzymic activity. An enzyme which has been so altered is said to be denatured (see DENATURATION). Consonant with their role as biological catalysts, enzymes show restricted selectivity for the molecules upon which they act (called substrates). Most enzymes will react with only a small group of closely related chemical compounds; many demonstrate absolute specificity, having only one substrate molecule which is appropriate for reaction. Numerous enzymes require for efficient catalytic function the presence of a small non-protein PROSTHETIC GROUP that is more or less tightly associated with the enzyme molecule. Some prosthetic groups are known to form chemical bonds with the protein during the course of reaction. Those groups only weakly associated with the enzyme, yet no less essential for catalysis, are generally termed COENZYMES. The region on the enzyme molecule in close proximity to where the catalytic event takes place is known as the active site. Prosthetic groups necessary for catalysis are usually located there, and it is the place where the substrate (and co-enzymes, if any) bind just before reaction takes place. Often it has been suggested that the side-chain groups of amino acid residues making up the enzyme molecule at or near the active site participate in the catalytic event. For example, the amino acids HISTIDINE and SERINE appear to be necessary for the action of the enzymes trypsin and chymotrypsin; CYSTEINE has been implicated in the workings of papain (an enzyme added to commercial meat tenderizer); and ASPARTIC ACID appears to be involved in pepsin activity. Among the hundreds of enzymes found in living cells are proteinases, e.g. pepsin, which degrade protein molecules; lipases, which break down fats and lipids; and AMYLASE, which is secreted by the salivary glands and aids in the digestion of starch in the mouth. Enzyme nomenclature, as indicated by the above examples, often adds the suffix *-ase* to the name of the substrate molecule upon which the enzyme acts. A variety of metabolic diseases are now known to be caused by deficiencies or malfunctions of enzymes. Albinism, for example, is often caused by the absence of tyrosinase, an enzyme essential for the production of cellular pigments. The hereditary lack of phenylalanine hydroxylase results in the disease phenylketonuria (PKU) which, if untreated, leads to severe mental retardation in children. See D. M. Locke, *Enzymes—The Agents of Life* (1969); G. R. Stark, *Enzymes: Function and Regulation* (1974).

Eocene epoch (ē'əsēn''), second epoch of the TERTIARY PERIOD in the CENOZOIC ERA of geologic time. The Eocene in North America was marked by the submergence of the Great Valley of California and a portion of the Atlantic and Gulf coastal plain extending from New Jersey to Texas and into the present Mississippi River valley as far north as S Illinois. There was also extensive sediment deposition in the Rocky Mt. region. Eocene sedimentary formations along the Atlantic-Gulf coast are chiefly sands, clays, and marls, with some limestone and lignite; in California, Oregon, and Washington they consist of shale and sandstone, with oil and coal. The Badlands of the West are partly cut into Eocene rock formations, e.g., the Wasatch, Green River, Bridger, and Uinta formations, which contain great quantities of volcanic ash and, in some districts, oil-producing shale. The Green River formation of SW Wyoming is noted for its freshwater fossil fish. The brightly colored Wasatch formation makes up the spectacular pillars of Bryce Canyon National Park. Interpretation of Eocene rock strata is based on the succession of beds in Belgian, French, and English basins, which became type areas. A great inundation from the Mediterranean covered most of S Europe, N Africa, and SW Asia, depositing nummulitic limestone, which is prominent in the Alps and Carpathians and from which the stones of the Pyramids were quarried. Australia and Antarctica began to separate during this epoch, Australia moving northward and Antarctica shifting toward the South Pole. Mammals became the dominant animals, and the ancestors of the common animals of Europe and North America made their appearance, possibly as immigrants from another region where they had developed. Eocene mammals included ancestral rhinoceroses, tapirs, camels, pigs, rodents, monkeys, whales, and the ancestral horse, eohippus, as well as animals such as the titanothere, which have since become extinct. The vegetation of the Eocene was fairly modern; the climate was warm.

eohippus: see HORSE.

Éon de Beaumont, Charles Geneviève Louis Auguste André Timothée, chevalier d' (shärl zhənəvyĕv' lwē ōgüst' äNdrā' tēmōtā' shəvälyā' dāōN' də bōmôN'), 1728–1810, French secret agent. His first exploit (1755) was a secret mission to the Russian court, where he was reputed to have appeared disguised as a woman in order to gain the confidence of the empress. The next year he reappeared in disguise, but this time as a man. He was attached to the French embassy in Russia from 1756 to 1760, served (1761) in the army, and went (1762) to England as secretary to the special ambassador. As minister plenipotentiary (1762–63) in London, he became involved in a public quarrel with the new ambassador and refused to accept his own recall or to surrender his papers. After the death of King Louis XV, he was given permission to return to France. However, the story of his Russian disguise had been revived, and the French government insisted on his wearing female dress after his return; he was thenceforth known as the Chevalière d'Éon. He returned to England in 1785. In later years he earned his living by giving fencing exhibitions. After his death, an examination of the body proved him a man. See his memoirs (tr. 1970); biographies by Edna Nixon (1965) and Cynthia Cox (1966).

Eos (ē'ŏs), in Greek religion, goddess of dawn; daughter of the Titans Hyperion and Theia. Every morning she arose early and preceded her brother Helios into the heavens. Her husband was Astraeus, by whom she bore the stars and the winds—Notus, the south wind; Boreas, the north wind; and Zephyr or Zephyrus, the west wind. Because Eos made love to Ares, Aphrodite cursed her with an insatiable desire for young men. Among her many lovers were TITHONUS and CEPHALUS. The Romans called her Aurora.

Eötvös, József, Baron (yō'zhĕf öt'vösh), 1813–71, Hungarian writer and statesman. A vigorous reformer and a Christian Liberal, he was minister of public instruction and religious affairs in 1848 and again in 1867. His novel *The Village Notary* (1844–46, tr. 1850) exposed the corrupt practices of county governments.

Epaenetus (ĭpē'nətəs), convert living at Rome. Rom. 16.5.

Epaminondas (ĭpămĭnŏn'dəs), d. 362 B.C., Greek general of Thebes. He was a pupil of Lysias the Pythagorean, but his early life is otherwise obscure. As the Theban delegate to the peace conference of 371 B.C. he refused to surrender his claim to represent all Boeotia. Agesilaus II of Sparta therefore excluded Thebes from the peace. In the resulting war Epaminondas commanded the Boeotian troops. His thorough victory over the Spartans at Leuctra (371 B.C.) proved the effectiveness of his military innovations and earned him a reputation as one of the greatest tacticians of ancient times. Later he bolstered Boeotian power by building up Messenian independence from Sparta. In 367 B.C. he forced Alexander of Pherae to release the Theban general Pelopidas. In 362 B.C. he again commanded the Boeotians against the Spartans and was victorious at Mantinea, but he died in battle. His brilliant tactics in war were studied by both Philip II and Alexander the Great.

Epaphras (ĕp'əfrăs), fellow worker of Paul. Col. 1.7; 4.12; Philemon 23.

Epaphroditus (ēpăfrōdī'təs), messenger from the Philippians to Paul in Rome. Philip. 2.25–30; 4.18.

Epée, Charles Michel, Abbé de l' (shärl mēshĕl' äbā' də lāpā'), 1712–89, French pioneer teacher of deaf-mutes. A Jansenist priest, he developed a manual system of communication for deaf-mutes and founded a school for their instruction in 1755. In 1776 he published a treatise on his educational method, which he later (1784) expanded as *La Véritable Manière d'instruire les sourds et muets* [the right way to teach deaf-mutes]. His dictionary of manual signs was completed after his death by Abbé Sicard, and in 1791 his school was taken over by the Institution nationale des Sourds-Muets à Paris.

Épernay (āpĕrnā'), town (1968 pop. 27,767), Marne dept., NE France, on the Marne River. It is, next to Rheims, the largest manufacturing center for CHAMPAGNE wine and the headquarters of some of the oldest firms, notably Moët. The wine is stored in caves (open to tourists) which form a labyrinth some 30 mi (48 km) long in the surrounding hills. Heavy fighting there during World War I destroyed many old buildings.

Épernon, Jean Louis de Nogaret, duc d' (zhäN lwē də nōgärā' dük dāpĕrnôN'), 1554–1642, French nobleman. He distinguished himself during the civil wars at the beginning of the reign of Henry III, and became a favorite of the king. He served Henry III in his dealings with Henry of Navarre (later King Henry IV of France). He was made governor of Provence and admiral of France. After the assassination of Henry III, he tried to set up an independent government in Provence but was forced to submit to Henry IV in 1596. He was involved in the conspiracy that resulted in the assassination of Henry IV (1610), and was largely responsible for the acceptance of MARIE DE' MEDICI as regent. He was conspicuous in the government until 1618; in 1619 and 1620 he supported Marie against the duc de LUYNES. He was governor of Guienne from 1622 until dismissed (1641) by Cardinal Richelieu.

Ephah (ē'fə). **1** Midianite. Gen. 24.4; 1 Chron. 1.33. **2** Concubine of Caleb. 1 Chron. 2.46. **3** Judahite. 1 Chron. 2.47.

Ephai (ē'fāī), man whose sons were massacred in Babylon by Ishmael. Jer. 40.8; 41.3.

ephedrine (ĭfĕd'rĭn, ĕf'ĭdrēn''), drug most commonly used to prevent mild or moderate attacks of bronchial asthma. Unlike EPINEPHRINE, to which it is chemically similar, ephedrine is slow to take effect and of mild potency and long duration. A bronchodilator and decongestant, ephedrine is used to relieve nasal congestion originating from allergic conditions, e.g., hay fever, or from bacterial or viral infection of the upper respiratory tract. Nonaddictive, it may cause side effects in the central nervous system such as insomnia, restlessness, and feelings of tension and anxiety. Ephedrine is the active constituent of a desert herb used medically in China for thousands of years.

ephemeris (ĭfĕm'ərĭs) (pl., ephemerides), table listing the position of one or more celestial bodies for each day of the year. The French publication *Connaissance de Temps* is the oldest of the national astronomical ephemerides, founded in 1679. The *Nautical Almanac and Astronomical Ephemeris* (usually abbreviated to the *Nautical Almanac*), an annual publication by the British Royal Observatory at Greenwich since 1767, has been a leading compilation of ephemerides since its inception. Its original purpose was to provide the astronomical information necessary to derive longitude at sea. In 1852 the U.S. Naval Observatory began publishing a book called the *American Ephemeris and Nautical Almanac*, which contained similar information to that published at Greenwich but adjusted for the meridian at Washington, D.C. Beginning with the edition for 1958, Great Britain and the U.S., as a joint effort, have issued ephemerides which are identical in content, although they remain separate publications with different names (the British volume has been renamed *The Astronomical Ephemeris*). These ephemerides (adapted to the Greenwich meridian) are issued four years in advance of the dates covered and contain such information as the daily right ascension and declination of the sun, moon, planets, and other celestial bodies, and daily data on the sunrise, sunset, moonrise, and moonset. Among other publications issued are *The Ephemeris* (U.S.) and *The Star Almanac for Land Surveyors* (Brit.), which are star ephemerides used by surveyors, and the *Air Almanac* (Brit./U.S.), used in air navigation. By international agreement the basic calculations of astronomical ephemerides are shared among a number of countries including France, Germany, Spain, and the Soviet Union.

ephemeris time (E.T.), astronomical TIME defined by the orbital motions of the earth, moon, and planets. The earth does not rotate with uniform speed, so the solar day is an imprecise unit of time. Ephemeris time is calculated from the positions of the sun and moon relative to the earth, assuming that Newton's laws are perfectly obeyed. By convention, the standard seasonal year is taken to be 1900 A.D. and to contain 31,556,925.9747 sec of ephemeris time. In 1960, when ephemeris time was adopted, it was 30 sec ahead of Greenwich mean time.

Epher (ē'fər). **1** Son of Midian. Gen. 25.4; 1 Chron. 1.33. **2** Judahite. 1 Chron. 4.17. **3** Head of a Manassite family. 1 Chron. 5.24.

Ephes-dammim (ē'fĭz-dăm'ĭm), bivouac of the Philistines when David killed Goliath. 1 Sam. 17.1. Pasdammim: 1 Chron. 11.13.

Ephesians (ĭfē'zhənz), epistle of the New Testament, the 10th book in the usual order. According to tradition it was written by St. PAUL to the Christians of Ephesus from his captivity at Rome (A.D. c.60). Scholars have doubted, without great agreement, each of these points; there is ground for believing the letter was intended as an encyclical. Ephesians is the most profound of the Pauline Epistles. No one subject is treated, but the whole epistle is pervaded with the doctrine of the mystical body of Christ, St. Paul's analogy of the perfect union of Christians (1.20–23; 2.19–22; 4.1–13). Ephesians contains a famous metaphor of the Christian as a soldier (6.10–17). The epistles to Colossians and Philemon were probably written at the same time as Ephesians, though some critics believe that Ephesians was written later in the 1st cent. by an unknown Christian. See G. H. Thompson, *The Letters of Paul to the Ephesians* (1967); M. G. Gutzke, *Plain Talk on Ephesians* (1973).

Ephesus (ĕf'əsəs), ancient Greek city of Asia Minor, near the mouth of the Caÿster River (modern Küçük Menderes), in what is today W Turkey, S of Smyrna (now İzmir). One of the greatest of the Ionian cities, it became the leading seaport of the region. Its wealth was proverbial. The Greek city was near an old center of worship of a native nature goddess, who was equated with the Greek Artemis, and c.550 B.C. a large temple was built. To this Croesus, who captured the city, contributed. From Lydian control Ephesus passed to the Persian Empire. The temple was burned down in the 4th cent. B.C., but rebuilding was begun before Alexander the Great took Ephesus in 334. The city continued to thrive during the wars of his successors, and after it passed (133) to the Romans it kept its hegemony and was the leading city of the province of Asia. Its great temple of Artemis, called by the Romans the temple of Diana, was considered one of the Seven Wonders of the World. Ephesus became a center of Christianity and was visited by St. Paul, who addressed one of his epistles to the congregation there. The city was sacked by the Goths in A.D. 262, and the temple was destroyed. The seat of a church council in 431, Ephesus was abandoned after the harbor silted up. Excavations (1869–74) of the ruins of the temple brought to light many artifacts. Later excavations uncovered important Roman and Byzantine remains.

Ephesus, Council of, 431, 3d ecumenical council, convened by Theodosius II, emperor of the East, and Valentinian III, emperor of the West, to deal with the controversy over NESTORIANISM. Adherents of both parties attended; St. CYRIL, patriarch of Alexandria, had the support of Pope CELESTINE I and most of Christendom; Nestorius was backed by Theodosius and the Antiochene hierarchy. The council, late in starting, was opened by St. Cyril before the Antiochene bishops arrived. It anathematized Nestorius and his views. The Antiochenes arrived and, accusing Cyril of deliberately rushing the vote, deposed him. Soon afterward the papal legates arrived and the council reconvened, reaffirmed its position, and excommunicated the Antiochenes. The controversy continued until Theodosius held a hearing at Chalcedon between the disputants. He exiled Nestorius and ordered the consecration of a new patriarch of Constantinople; the council then broke up. Its chief dogmatic pronouncement was that from the very words of the Nicene Creed it follows that Mary may be called Mother of God, for the perfect coherence of godhead and manhood in Christ prevents any separation of natures such as Nestorius implied. This doctrine was later defined further (see CHALCEDON, COUNCIL OF). For the Robber Synod (Latrocinium) of Ephesus, see EUTYCHES.

Ephialtes (ĕf″ēăl′tēz): see ALOADAE.

Ephlal (ĕf′lăl), descendant of Judah. 1 Chron. 2.37.

Ephod (ē′fŏd, ĕf′ŏd), Manassite. Num. 34.23.

ephod, sacred linen garment worn by the high priests of Israel. It was in two parts—one covering the back, one the front of the body to the hips—and was fastened at the shoulders by two clasps of onyx on which were engraved the 12 tribal names, six on each. The vestment was held in at the waist by a twined linen girdle of gold, blue, purple and scarlet, and upon it, hung by golden chains and rings, was the breastplate with the URIM AND THUMMIM. It was somehow used for divination. Ex. 28; Judges 8.27; 17.5; 18.14; 1 Sam. 2.28; 14.3; 22.18; 23.6,9; 30.7; Hosea 3.4.

ephors (ĕf′ərz) [Gr.,=overseers], in ancient Greece, magistrates in several Dorian states. In Sparta they comprised an executive, legislative, and judicial board of five Spartan citizens. This annually elected board functioned from at least the 8th cent. B.C. until the 3d cent. B.C. It was abolished (c.227 B.C.) by Cleomenes III, was revived, and lasted until A.D. 200. In the period of its greatest authority the board of ephors was the organ of citizen control over the dual kingship of Sparta. Its members were elected in various ways at different times, but for the most part, apparently, by drawing lots. Their relation to the two kings was curious. The kings were recognized as the only authorized military commanders, but the ephors had full discretion in levying troops, and some of them accompanied the armies. During campaigns they had no voice in command, but they might bring the royal leaders to trial for alleged errors in conducting war. The ephors cast the deciding voice when the kings disagreed. While one member of the board of ephors was its chairman and gave his name to the year of his office tenure, the authority of the five members was equal, and their decisions were the result of a simple majority vote. A particularly famous prerogative was that of control over the education of Spartan youth.

Ephorus (ĕf′ərəs), c.405–330 B.C., Greek historian, b. Cyme in Aeolis; pupil of Isocrates. His chief work is a universal history, in 30 books, of which only fragments survive, arranged by subjects. He was widely quoted by the ancients, notably by Diodorus Siculus.

Ephphatha (ĕf′əthə) [Aramaic,=be opened], words addressed by Jesus to a deaf-mute as Jesus made him hear and speak. Mark 7.34. As elsewhere in Mark, the Greek text retains and translates the Aramaic words: cf. 5.41; 14.36; 15.34.

Ephraem, Saint, 308?–373, Syrian theologian, Doctor of the Church. He taught at Nisibis and Edessa and composed biblical exegeses (now almost all lost) and numerous sacred verses. Ephraem converted Syria with his psalms, vehicles of orthodox doctrine, which soon supplanted those of BARDESANES. He is venerated by all the Eastern churches and by Rome. Feast: June 18. See his *Prose Refutations of Mani, Marcion, and Bardaisan* (tr. 1912–21, repr. 1969) and *An Exposition of the Gospel* (tr. 1968); study ed. by Arthur Vööbus (1958).

Ephraim (ē′frēəm). **1** Younger son of Joseph and Asenath and ancestor of one of the 12 tribes of Israel. The tribe occupied the rough country around Shiloh that later came to be called Mt. Ephraim. Ephraim was also a name for the Northern Kingdom. Gen. 41.52; 46.20; 48.14–20; Joshua 16; 1 Chron. 7.20. **2** City, N of Jerusalem, modern at Tayyibah (Jordan). 2 Sam. 13.23. **3** Place, to which Jesus retired after raising Lazarus from the dead. It is in the same region as **2.** John 11.54. **4** Forest of Ephraim, near Mahanaim. 2 Sam. 18.6.

Ephrain (ē′frāĭn), unidentified city, N of Jerusalem, where Abijah defeated Jeroboam. 2 Chron. 13.19.

Ephrata (ĕf′rətə), industrial borough (1970 pop. 9,662), Lancaster co., SE Pa., in a prosperous farm area; inc. 1891. A noted semimonastic religious community was founded (c.1732) there by Seventh-Day Baptists under the leadership of Johann Conrad Beissel. This austere colony, the Ephrata Cloisters, was famous for its music and established (1745) one of the earliest printing presses in the country. The well-preserved buildings are now maintained as a monument by the state.

Ephratah (ĕf′rətə) or **Ephrath** (ĕf′răth). **1** See BETHLEHEM. **2** Wife of CALEB. 1 Chron. 2.19,50; 4.4. At Ps. 132.6 Ephraim may be intended instead of Ephratah.

Ephron (ē′frŏn). **1** Owner of the cave of Machpelah. Gen. 23.8,9. **2** City, E of the Jordan, captured by Judas Maccabeus. 1 Mac. 5.46; 2 Mac. 12.27. **3** Mount, near Kiryat-jearim. Joshua 15.9.

epic, long, exalted narrative poem, usually on a serious subject, centered on a heroic figure. The earliest epics, known as primary, or original, epics, were shaped from the legends of an age when a nation was conquering and expanding; such is the foundation of the Babylonian epic of Gilgamesh, of the *Iliad* and the *Odyssey* of the Greek Homer, and of the Anglo-Saxon *Beowulf.* Literary, or secondary, epics, written in conscious imitation of earlier forms, are most notably represented by Vergil's *Aeneid* and Milton's *Paradise Lost.* The epic, which makes great demands on a poet's knowledge and skill, has been deemed the most ambitious of poetic forms. Some of its conventions, followed by epic writers in varying degrees, include a hero who embodies national, cultural, or religious ideals and upon whose actions depends to some degree the fate of his people; a course of action in which the hero performs great and difficult deeds; a whole era in the history of civilization; the intervention and recognition of divine or supernatural powers; the concern with eternal human problems; and a dignified and elaborate poetic style. Other works classified as epics are the Indian *Mahabharata* and *Ramayana,* the French *Song of Roland,* the Spanish *Song of the Cid,* the Germanic *Niebelungenlied,* Dante's *Divine Comedy,* Tasso's *Gerusaleme Liberta,* Ariosto's *Orlando Furioso,* Spenser's *Faerie Queene,* and Camões's *Lusiads.* A mock epic is a form of satire in which trivial characters and events are treated with all the exalted epic conventions and are made to look ridiculous by the incongruity. The plot of Pope's *Rape of the Lock,* one of the most famous mock epics, is based on a quarrel over the theft of a lady's curl. See studies by Sir C. M. Bowra (1961), A. S. Cook (1966), A. B. Giamatti (1966), H. V. Routh (2 vol., 1927; repr. 1968), and C. A. Yu (1973).

Epicharmus (ĕpĭkär′məs), d. c.450 B.C., Sicilian Greek comic poet. He was the first to write a coherent artistic comedy, and he dealt with forms other than personal satire such as mythological burlesque. His role as a Pythagorean philosopher and his connection with that school are debatable. See A. W. Pickard-Cambridge, *Dithyramb, Tragedy, and Comedy* (1927, repr. 1962).

Epictetus (ĕpĭktē′təs), A.D. c.50–c.138, Phrygian Stoic philosopher. He wrote nothing, but his teachings were set down by his disciple Arrian in the *Discourses* and the *Encheiridion.* Epictetus emphasized indifference to external goods and taught that the true good is within oneself. His Stoicism was outstanding in its insistence on the doctrine of the brotherhood of man. See study by Iason Xenakis (1969); bibliography by W. A. Oldfather (1927; supplemented by Marian Harman, 1952).

epic theater: see BRECHT, BERTOLT; PISCATOR, ERWIN.

epicureanism (ĕp″ĭkyo͝orē′ənĭz″əm), philosophy that follows the teachings of EPICURUS, who held that pleasure is the end of all morality and that real pleasure is attained through a life of prudence, honor, and justice. The philosophy was popular throughout the ancient world; it was spread by the successors of Epicurus, who included Polystratus, Zeno of Sidon, and Philodemus of Gadara. Only in later times did epicureanism come to mean devotion to extravagant pleasure.

Epicurus (ĕpĭkyo͝or′əs), 341–270 B.C., Greek philosopher, b. Samos; son of an Athenian colonist. He claimed to be self-taught, although tradition states that he was schooled in the systems of Plato and Democritus by his father and various philosophers. He taught in several towns in Asia Minor before going to Athens c.306 B.C. There Epicurus purchased the famous garden that has become linked in the annals of philosophy with the Academy of Plato and the Lyceum of Aristotle. He was a generous and genial man who lived on the warmest terms with his followers. Although his writings were voluminous, only fragments remain. Epicurus defined philosophy as the art of making life happy and strictly subordinated metaphysics to ethics, naming pleasure as the highest and only good. However, for Epicurus pleasure was not heedless indulgence but the opposite, *ataraxia* [serenity], manifesting itself in the avoidance of pain. His hedonism differed from the cruder variety of Aristippus and the Cyrenaics in the emphasis that it placed on *ataraxia* and on the superiority of intellectual pleasures over bodily pleasures. He also prescribed a code of social conduct, which advocated honesty, prudence, and justice in dealing with others, not because these virtues were good in themselves, but because they saved the individual from society's retribution. While Epicurus appropriated much of the mechanics of Democritus' metaphysics, he deviated from its deterministic implications by the introduction of an element of spontaneity, which allowed atoms to form the objects of the world by chance. The element of freedom in his metaphysics supported and paralleled his notion of man's freedom of will. He held blind destiny to be more dangerous to man's *ataraxia* than belief in fables about the gods; men could hope to propitiate the gods, but mechanical determinism was inexorable. He denied that the gods had supernatural powers that allowed them to interfere with man or nature. The system of Epicurus deemphasized the traditional power of religious and physical forces on man's life and emphasized man's freedom of action. The work of the Roman poet Lucretius *De rerum natura* (*On the Nature of Things*), contains the finest exposition of Epicurus' ideas. See studies by Cyril Bailey (1928, repr. 1964), N. W. De-Witt (1954), Benjamin Farrington (1967), and J. W. Rist (1972).

epicycle: see PTOLEMAIC SYSTEM.

Epidaurus (ĕpĭdôr′əs), ancient city of Greece, on an inlet of the Saronic Gulf, NE Peloponnesus. It was celebrated as the site of the temple of ASCLEPIUS, which dates from the 4th cent. B.C. and is renowned for its beautiful sculpture. Other relics of the city include a theater and a *tholos* [rotunda]. Though in the region of Argolis, Epidaurus was semi-independent until Roman times.

epidemic, outbreak of disease that affects a much greater number of people than is usual for the locality or that spreads to regions where it is ordinarily not present. A disease that tends to be restricted to a particular region (endemic disease) can become epidemic if nonimmune persons are present in large numbers (as in time of war or during pilgrimages), if the infectious agent is more virulent than usual, or if distribution of the disease is more easily effected. CHOLERA and PLAGUE, endemic in parts of Asia, can become epidemic under the above conditions, as can dysentery and many other infections. A worldwide epidemic is known as a pandemic, e.g., the influenza pandemic of 1918. Epidemic disease is controlled by various measures, depending on whether transmission is through respiratory droplets, food and water contaminated with intestinal wastes, insect vectors, or other means. A disease is said to be sporadic when a few cases occur here and there in a given region.

epidermis: see SKIN.

epiglottis (ĕp″əglŏt′ĭs): see LARYNX.

Epigoni (ĕpĭg′ənī), in Greek legend, the sons of the SEVEN AGAINST THEBES, who avenged the death of their fathers. Under the leadership of Adrastus and Alcmaeon, the Epigoni conquered Thebes 10 years after the Seven had fought alongside Polynices for the throne of Thebes. The Epigoni gave the kingdom to Thersander, son of Polynices.

epigram, a short, polished, pithy saying, usually in verse, often with a satiric or paradoxical twist at the end. The term was originally applied by the Greeks to the inscriptions on stones. The epigrams of the Latin poet Martial established the form for many later writers. In England the epigram flourished in the work of innumerable poets including Donne, Herrick, Ben Jonson, Pope, Byron, Coleridge, and Walter Savage Landor. Great German epigrammatists include Logau, Lessing, and Herder. In 18th-century France, Boileau-Despréaux, Lebrun, and Voltaire excelled in the form. Poets of the 20th cent. who are noted for their epigrams include Yeats, Pound, Roy Campbell, and Ogden Nash. One of the most brilliant of prose epigrammatists was Oscar Wilde. His works are studded with epigrams—stunningly brief ones like "I can resist everything except temptation," and longer, more subtle ones such as "Nothing is as dangerous as being too modern; one is apt to grow old-fashioned so suddenly." The epigram is a characteristic feature of Chinese speech and literature.

epigraphy: see INSCRIPTION.

epilepsy, a chronic disorder of cerebral function characterized by periodic convulsive seizures. Epileptic seizures are classified as (1) grand mal, in which there is loss of consciousness and involuntary contraction of all the muscles of the body, lasting a few minutes; (2) petit mal, in which there is clouding of the consciousness for about 1 to 30 sec and no falling, with as many as 100 attacks occurring daily; (3) various other forms, including Jacksonian epilepsy and psychomotor seizures, in which there may be localized convulsion with no loss of consciousness, as well as incoherent speech and various involuntary movements of the body. Although familial history of the disturbance is often present, no organic cause for the disorder can be found in most patients. However, seizures can result from injuries, infections (such as meningitis), and abnormalities (such as tumors) of the brain. The recording of brain waves with an electroencephalograph is an important diagnostic test. Treatment of epilepsy is with sedatives and anticonvulsive drugs. When a convulsive seizure does occur, there is little that can be done except to prevent the person from injuring himself, e.g., by cushioning the head.

Epimenides (ĕpĭmĕn'ĭdēz), fl. 6th cent.? B.C., Cretan prophet. According to one story, he was called to Athens to purify the city after the murder of Cylon on the Acropolis. Many poems, oracles, and sayings were attributed to him (Titus 1.12 is supposed to contain one of these).

Epimetheus (ĕp"əmē'thēəs): see PANDORA.

Épinal (āpēnäl'), town (1968 pop. 39,991), capital of Vosges dept., E France, in Lorraine, on the Moselle. Although considerably damaged during World War II, the city today is an active industrial center, with textile and metal industries and plants making morocco leather, precision instruments, and bicycles. It is famous for the *images d'Épinal,* popular illustrations printed there since the 16th cent. Of interest are the remains of a château containing the St. Maurice Basilica with its 11th-century nave. A school of textile weaving is in Épinal.

Épinay, Louise Florence Pétronille (de Tardieu d'Esclavelles) La Live d' (lwēz flôräNs' pātrōnē'yə də tärdyö' dāklävĕl' lä lēv dāpēnā'), 1726–83, French woman of letters. Influential in the ENLIGHTENMENT, she was the friend of many of its leaders, especially Grimm, her literary heir, and Diderot. She was Rousseau's benefactress until 1757, when they quarreled, and subsequently they attacked each other in their writings. She wrote a treatise on the education of girls, *Les Conversations d'Émilie* (pub. 1775 though volume bears date 1774). Her memoirs and correspondence (1818, tr. 1897, 1930) give a vivid account of her circle.

epinephrine (ĕp"ənĕf'rĭn), colorless crystalline HORMONE composed of carbon, hydrogen, and nitrogen, also known as adrenaline. Epinephrine, together with NOREPINEPHRINE, is a secretion of the medulla of the ADRENAL GLAND. Strong emotions such as fear and anger initiate an immediate acceleration of bodily functions. This heightened activity is prolonged by the subsequent effects of epinephrine, e.g., increase in heart rate and the hydrolysis of glycogen to glucose. The hormone was first extracted (1901) from the adrenal glands of animals by Jokichi Takamine; it was synthesized (1904) by Friedrich Stolz. Epinephrine is used medicinally as a stimulant in cardiac arrest, as a vasoconstrictor in shock, as a bronchodilator and antispasmodic in bronchial asthma, and to lower intra-ocular pressure in the treatment of glaucoma. Adrenaline is the English common name for epinephrine.

Epiphania: see HAMAH, Syria.

Epiphany (ĭpĭf'ənē) [Gr.,=showing], a prime Christian feast, celebrated Jan. 6, called also Twelfth Day or Little Christmas. Its eve is Twelfth Night. It commemorates three events—the baptism of Jesus (Mark 1), the visit of the Wise Men to Bethlehem (Mat. 2), and the miracle at Cana (John 2). In his baptism Jesus' sonship to God was manifested to the world; in the visit of the Wise Men he was manifested as king to the Gentiles; and at the marriage feast at Cana his power to perform miracles (a divine prerogative) was shown. In popular celebration the feast is far more ancient than Christmas. Technically it is more important than Christmas, ranking after Easter and Pentecost. It is a day of gifts in many countries. In the Eastern Church the waters are blessed on this day. The word *epiphany* means a manifestation, usually of divine power. Thus the actual appearance of God (as in the burning bush) or a moment of divine revelation may be called an epiphany.

epiphyte (ĕp'əfīt") or **air plant,** any plant that does not normally root in the soil but grows upon another living plant while remaining independent of it except for support (thus differing from a PARASITE). An epiphyte manufactures its own food (see PHOTOSYNTHESIS) in the same way that other green plants do, but obtains its moisture from the air or from moisture-laden pockets of the host plant, rather than from the soil. Some epiphytes are found in every group of the plant kingdom but particularly among the algae, lichens, mosses, and ferns. Of the flowering plants, the best-known epiphytes are orchids and bromeliads, such as Spanish moss. Epiphytes may grow upon the trunk, branches, or leaves of the host plant, sometimes so thickly as to damage the original plant by crowding out its leaves. They are most abundant in the moist tropics. Other plants not strictly epiphytes are popularly known as air plants. Such plants are usually capable of producing plantlets from the leaves without direct contact with the soil, as in *Bryophyllum.*

Epirus (ĕpī'rəs), ancient country of Greece, on the Ionian Sea and W of Macedon and Thessaly, a region now occupied by NW Greece and S Albania. At the time of Homer, Epirus was known as the home of the oracle of Dodona. It was inhabited from very early times by Epirote tribes, barely known to the Greeks. The tribes were molded into a state under the hegemony of one of them (the Molossi), whose chiefs became the paramount rulers in the 4th cent. B.C. A Molossian ruler, Neoptolemus, married his daughter to Philip II of Macedon, who placed Neoptolemus' son Alexander on the throne of Molossia (most of Epirus). Alexander died on an invasion of Italy, but the kingdom persisted and grew. It reached its height in the 3d cent. B.C. under PYRRHUS, who achieved great renown. However, Pyrrhus' exploits and the unsuccessful attempts of his successor, Alexander II (d. 240 B.C.), to take Macedon ruined the state. A republic was set up with its capital at Phoenice. The Epirotes sided with Macedon in the wars against Rome, and Epirus was sacked (167) by Aemilius Paullus, who took away many thousands of captives. The country passed under Roman dominion. Octavian (later Augustus) built (31 B.C.) a new capital at Nicopolis. Epirus was a more-or-less-neglected portion of the Byzantine Empire. After the Crusaders had conquered Constantinople, the despotate of Epirus, larger than ancient Epirus, was set up. At the end of the 18th cent. Ali Pasha, the pasha of Yannina, set up an independent state in Epirus and Albania. See studies by G. N. Cross (1932) of its constitutional organization, by S. I. Oost (1954) of Roman policy in Epirus, and by N. G. L. Hammond (1967) of the geography and ancient remains of the area.

Epirus, despotate of. When, in 1204, the army of the Fourth Crusade set up the Latin Empire of Constantinople on the ruins of the Byzantine Empire, an independent Greek state emerged in Epirus under Michael I, a member of the Angelus family. It stretched from Durazzo in the north to the Gulf of Patras in the south. In 1222 the despot of Epirus took Salonica from the Latins and claimed the title despot of Thessalonica. For a time the despotate of Epirus was a rival of the Greek empire of Nicaea (see NICAEA, EMPIRE OF) in the struggle for the restoration of the Byzantine Empire. It accepted, however, a status of semivassalage to Nicaea (c.1246) and was united (1336–49) with the restored Byzantine Empire. The Serbs and Albanians then assumed control of the vassal state. In the 15th cent. the Ottoman Turks took over, and the state disappeared. The despotate of Epirus played an important role in the preservation of Hellenism in W Greece. See study by D. M. Nicol (1957).

Episcopal Church, Protestant, in the United States of America, a part of the ANGLICAN COMMUNION. Its separate existence as an American ecclesiastical body with its own episcopate began in 1789. Anglican Church services in America were first held in 1607 in Jamestown, Va. Except in Maryland and Virginia, there were few clergymen of the Established Church in the colonies. The New England Puritans, although they had not actually seceded from the Church of England, proscribed all that was Anglican. However, in 1686, when the colonial charter of Massachusetts was revoked, Church of England clergymen were appointed in that colony. In 1689, King's Chapel, Boston, was opened, and Trinity Church in New York City was consecrated. Anglicans were active in establishing institutions of higher learning in the colonies. In 1693, James BLAIR, an Anglican missionary to colonial Virginia, secured the charter for the College of William and Mary. King's College (now Columbia Univ.) was founded in 1754. During the American Revolution the personal loyalties of the church's clergy and laymen were seriously split, and American independence brought about the disestablishment of the Anglican Church. After the Revolution the first objective of American Anglicans was to organize a native episcopacy and a national church. The new ecclesiastical body was called the Protestant Episcopal Church, a name approved in 1789 by the first General Convention of the denomination, which also adopted a constitution and a revised version of the BOOK OF COMMON PRAYER. Meanwhile, Dr. Samuel SEABURY of Connecticut was consecrated bishop in 1784 by bishops of Scotland, and William White of Pennsylvania and Samuel PROVOOST of New York were consecrated bishops in England in 1787. In 1817, General Theological Seminary was organized, and in 1820 the Domestic and Foreign Missionary Society was established. Episcopal churches were founded by settlers in the newly opened regions of the West. During the Civil War the church was necessarily disunited, but at the General Conference of 1865 there was a full reunion. In 1873 a group of clergy and laity withdrew from the main body, in disagreement over certain ritualistic practices and other matters, and formed the Reformed Episcopal Church. The Protestant Episcopal Church maintains that the Holy Scriptures are the ultimate rule of faith. Its symbols of doctrine are the Apostles' and the Nicene Creed and the Thirty-nine Articles of the Church of England, with certain modifications to fit American conditions. The ministry is of three orders: deacons, priests, and bishops. The system of organization includes the parish, the diocese, the province, and the General Convention. The General Convention, the highest ecclesiastical authority in the church, consists of the House of Bishops and the House of Deputies and meets in session every three years. The ecclesiastical head of the church is the presiding bishop, elected by the General Convention. The National Council, set up in 1919, is delegated by the General Convention to administer all the organized missionary, educational, and social work. Among the organizations within the church are the Brotherhood of St. Andrew, the Girls' Friendly Society, the Guild of St. Barnabas, and the Woman's Auxiliary. Church publications include the *Living Church* and the *Witness.* The church is represented in the National Council of Churches of Christ in the United States of America and the World Council of Churches. In 1974 the church had a membership of some 3.3 million. See E. C. Chorley, *Men and Movements in the American Episcopal Church* (1946, repr. 1961); J. T. Addison, *The Episcopal Church in the United States, 1789–1931* (1951, repr. 1969); W. W. Manross, *A History of the American Episcopal Church* (3d ed. rev. 1959); C. B. Moss, *A Summary of the Faith* (1961); R. W. Albright, *A History of the Protestant Episcopal Church* (1964).

Episcopal Church, Reformed: see REFORMED EPISCOPAL CHURCH.

Episcopius, Simon (ĕpĭskō'pēəs), 1583–1643, Dutch Protestant theologian, whose original name was Biscop, Bischop, or Bisschop. Episcopius accepted the teachings of Jacobus ARMINIUS and was a leader of the Arminians, or REMONSTRANTS, who opposed the Calvinist conception of predestination. Episcopius represented the Remonstrants at conclaves at The Hague (1611), at Delft (1613), and at the Synod of Dort (1618), where he presented a detailed defense of his position. However, the Calvinist views prevailed, Remonstrant church services were banned, and Episcopius and some other leaders were banished. In exile in the Spanish Netherlands he wrote an Arminian creed (1622). In 1625, upon the death of Prince MAURICE OF NASSAU, the ban was removed, and Episcopius returned (1626) to the Netherlands. Episcopius, in the *Institutiones theologicae* (1650), established the doctrine of the Remonstrants upon a consistent theological basis. His avowed aim was to present Christianity in a practical aspect and to liberate theology from too rigid limitations of theory and ecclesiasticism.

episome (ĕp'ĭsōm), unit of genetic material composed of a series of GENES that sometimes has an independent existence in a host cell and at other times is integrated into a CHROMOSOME of the cell, replicating itself along with the chromosome. Episomes have been studied in bacteria. One group of episomes are actually VIRUSES that infect bacteria. As autonomous units they destroy host cells, and as segments integrated into a chromosome they multiply in cell division and are transferred to daughter cells. Episomes called sex factors determine whether chromosome material will be transferred from one bacterium to another. Other episomes carry genes that make bacteria resistant to the inhibitory action of antibiotics. See RECOMBINATION.

epistemology (ĭpĭs″təmŏl′əjē) [Gr.,=knowledge or science], the branch of philosophy that is directed toward theories of the origin, sources, and grounds of knowledge. It is conventionally distinguished from logic, which is concerned with methods of treating data and with processes and operations of the mind in establishing knowledge. Since the 17th cent. epistemology has been one of the fundamental themes of philosophers, who were necessarily obliged to coordinate the theory of knowledge with developing scientific thought. Réné DESCARTES and other philosophers (e.g., Benedict de Spinoza, G. W. Leibniz, and Blaise Pascal) sought to retain the belief in the existence of innate (a priori) ideas together with an acceptance of the values of data and ideas derived from experience (a posteriori). This position was basically that of RATIONALISM. Opposed to it later was EMPIRICISM, notably as expounded by David Hume, John Locke, and John Stuart Mill, which denied the existence of innate ideas altogether. The impressive critical philosophy of Immanuel KANT had immense effects in an attempt to combine the two views. In later theories the split was reflected in idealism and materialism. The methods of perceiving, obtaining, and validating data derived from sense experience has been central to PRAGMATISM, with the teachings of C. S. Peirce, William James, and John Dewey. A prevalent view in the 20th cent., shared by several philosophic groups, is that knowledge arises in the functional relationship of a perceiving organism and a perceived universe within the framework of scientific method. See A. D. Woozley, *Theory of Knowledge* (1949, repr. 1966); A. J. Ayer, *The Problem of Knowledge* (1956, repr. 1962); L. M. Régis, *Epistemology* (tr. 1959); Michael Polyani, *Knowing and Being* (1968).

epistle (ĭpĭs′əl), in the Bible, a letter of the New Testament. The Pauline Epistles (ascribed to St. Paul) are ROMANS, First and Second CORINTHIANS, GALATIANS, EPHESIANS, PHILIPPIANS, COLOSSIANS, First and Second THESSALONIANS, First and Second TIMOTHY, TITUS, PHILEMON, and HEBREWS. The Catholic, or General, Epistles are JAMES; First and Second PETER; First, Second, and Third JOHN; and JUDE. This classification is traditional. There is an Epistle of Jeremiah in BARUCH. The reading of the Epistle of the day is a feature of the liturgy in many churches.

epitaph, strictly, an inscription on a tomb; by extension, a statement, usually in verse, commemorating the dead. The earliest such inscriptions are those found on Egyptian sarcophagi. In England epitaphs did not begin to assume a literary character until the time of Elizabeth I. Ben Jonson, John Milton, Alexander Pope, and Samuel Johnson were considered masters of the art. The epitaph on Ben Jonson's own tomb in Westminster Abbey was splendidly brief: "O rare Ben Jonson!" Epitaphs are often humorous; it is not known whether the epitaph printed below is amusing by design or by accident:

> Here lie I Martin Elginbrodde:
> Have mercy on my soul, Lord God,
> As I wad do, were I Lord God,
> And ye were Martin Elginbrodde.

epithalamium (ĕp″ĭthəlā′mēəm), song or poem written to celebrate a marriage. An elaborate form of PASTORAL, the epithalamium usually tells of the happenings of the wedding day. Nymphs, shepherds, and appropriate mythological figures are present to share the poet's joy. Epithalamiums were written in ancient times by Pindar, Sappho, and Catullus. The biblical *Song of Solomon* is a classic of the genre as is Edmund Spenser's "Epithalamium" (1595), written to celebrate his own marriage.

epithelium (ĕp″əthē′lēəm), sheet of tissue that covers or lines the external and internal body surfaces. The epithelium is closely packed, has little intercellular material, and is lacking in blood vessels. There are three characteristic types of epithelial cells: squamous, cuboidal, and columnar. Squamous epithelial cells are flat and often overlapping; they compose the outer layer of skin (epidermis) and line certain internal cavities, e.g., the mouth. Cuboidal epithelial cells are rounded and elastic and line such structures as the urinary bladder, where, by stretching and becoming flatter, they increase the organ's capacity to hold fluid. The cells of the columnar epithelium are long and thin; they are found as a single layer of secretory and absorptive cells in the gastrointestinal tract, and they form the ciliated lining of the respiratory tract. Embryologically, epithelium may be derived from any of the three germ layers, i.e., ectoderm, mesoderm, and endoderm, and may be classified accordingly as epithelium proper, mesothelium, and endothelium.

epitope: see IMMUNITY.

E Pluribus Unum (ē plŏŏr′ĭbəs yōō′nəm) [Lat.,= one made out of many], motto on the Great Seal of the United States and on many U.S. coins. Although selected in 1776 by Benjamin Franklin, John Adams, and Thomas Jefferson for the Continental Congress, it was not officially adopted as a national motto until six years later.

epoch, unit of geologic time that is a subdivision of a period, such as the Pleistocene epoch of the Quaternary period. See GEOLOGY; GEOLOGIC ERAS (table).

epoxy group (ĕpŏk′sē), in chemistry, FUNCTIONAL GROUP that consists of an oxygen atom joined by single bonds to two adjacent carbon atoms, thus forming the three-membered epoxide ring. It is the functional group of epoxides.

epoxy resins, group of synthetic resins used to make PLASTICS and adhesives. These materials are noted for their versatility, but their relatively high cost has limited their use. High resistance to chemicals and outstanding adhesion, durability, and toughness have made them valuable as coatings. Because of their high electrical resistance, durability at high and low temperatures, and the ease with which they can be poured or cast without forming bubbles, epoxy resin plastics are especially useful for encapsulating electrical and electronic components. Epoxy resin adhesives can be used on metals, construction materials, and most other synthetic resins. They are strong enough to be used in place of rivets and welds in certain industrial applications.

Epsom and Ewell (yōō′əl), municipal borough (1971 pop. 72,054), Surrey, SE England. Epsom salts were first prepared from the town's mineral waters in 1618. Epsom was a popular spa in the 17th and 18th cent. The town is now famous for horse racing at Epsom Downs. Epsom College, a public school, was founded in 1853.

Epsom salts, common name for magnesium sulfate heptahydrate, $MgSO_4 \cdot 7H_2O$, a water-soluble bitter-tasting compound that occurs as white or colorless needle-shaped crystals. It was first prepared from the waters of mineral springs at Epsom, England; it also occurs as the mineral epsomite. Epsom salts is used medicinally as a purgative; it is also used in leather tanning, mordant dyeing, and as a filler in cotton goods and paper.

Epstein, Sir Jacob (ĕp′stīn), 1880–1959, sculptor, b. New York City. He studied with Rodin in Paris and later worked chiefly in England. In revolt against the ornate and the pretty in art, Epstein produced bold, often harsh and massive forms in stone or bronze that were the subjects of frequent controversy. His 18 large figures on the British Medical Association Building (1907–8) were removed in 1937 as offensive and structurally dangerous. Epstein's major pieces include the Oscar Wilde Memorial (1911; Père-Lachaise, Paris); a marble *Venus* (1917; Yale Univ., New Haven, Conn.); a bronze *Christ* (1919; Wheathamstead, England); the "Rima" figure that forms the W.H. Hudson Memorial (1925; Hyde Park, London); an enormous *Adam* in alabaster (1939; Blackpool, England); figures for Fairmount Park, Philadelphia; and a *Madonna and Child* (Convent of the Holy Child Jesus, London). Some of Epstein's best-known work is in bronze portraiture, executed with roughly textured surfaces. His perceptive portraits include those of the duke of Marlborough, Joseph Conrad, Albert Einstein, and Jawaharlal Nehru. Epstein was knighted in 1954. See his autobiography (2d ed. 1963); drawings ed. by Kathleen Epstein (1962); study by Robert Black (1942).

Equal Employment Opportunities Commission (EEOC), U.S. agency created in 1964 to end discrimination based on race, color, religion, sex, or national origin in employment and to promote programs to make equal employment opportunity a reality. The commission receives charges of discrimination. After an investigation, if there is reasonable cause to believe the charge is true, the commission attempts to remedy the alleged unlawful practice through conciliation, conference, and persuasion. If an acceptable conciliation agreement is not secured, the commission may bring suit in Federal district court.

equal temperament: see TUNING SYSTEMS.

equation, in mathematics, a statement, usually written in symbols, that states the equality of two quantities or algebraic expressions, e.g., $x+3=5$. The quantity $x+3$, to the left of the equals sign (=), is called the left-hand, or first, member of the equation, that to the right (5) the right-hand, or second, member. A numerical equation is one containing only numbers, e.g., $2+3=5$. A literal equation is one that, like the first example, contains some letters (representing unknowns or variables). An identical equation is a literal equation that is true for every value of the variable, e.g., the equation $(x+1)^2=x^2+2x+1$. A conditional equation (usually referred to simply as an equation) is a literal equation that is not true for all values of the variable, e.g., only the value 2 for x makes true the equation $x+3=5$. To solve an equation is to find the value or values of the variable that satisfy it. POLYNOMIAL equations, containing more than one term, are classified according to the highest degree of the variable they contain. Thus the first example is a first degree (also called linear) equation. The equation $ax^2+bx+c=0$ is a second degree, or QUADRATIC, equation in the unknown x if the letters a, b, and c are assumed to represent constants. In algebra, methods are evolved for solving various types of equations. To be valid the solution must satisfy the equation. Whether it does can be ascertained by substituting the supposed solution for the variable in the equation. The simultaneous solution of two or more equations is a set of values of the variables that satisfies each of the equations. In order that a solution may exist, the number of equations (i.e., conditions) must generally be no greater than the number of variables. In chemistry an equation (see CHEMICAL EQUATION) is used to represent a reaction.

equation, chemical: see CHEMICAL EQUATION.

equation of time: see SOLAR TIME.

equator, imaginary great circle around the earth, everywhere equidistant from the two geographical poles and forming the base line from which latitude is reckoned. The equator, which measures c.24,000 mi (38,600 km), is designated as lat. 0°. It intersects N South America, central Africa, and Indonesia. The celestial equator is the projection of the plane of the earth's equator on the celestial sphere (see EQUATORIAL COORDINATE SYSTEM).

equatorial belt of calms: see DOLDRUMS.

equatorial coordinate system or **equator coordinate system,** the most commonly used ASTRONOMICAL COORDINATE SYSTEM for indicating the positions of stars or other celestial objects on the CELESTIAL SPHERE. The celestial sphere is an imaginary sphere with the observer at its center. It represents the entire sky; all celestial objects other than the earth are imagined as being located on its inside surface. If the earth's axis is extended, the points where it intersects the celestial sphere are called the

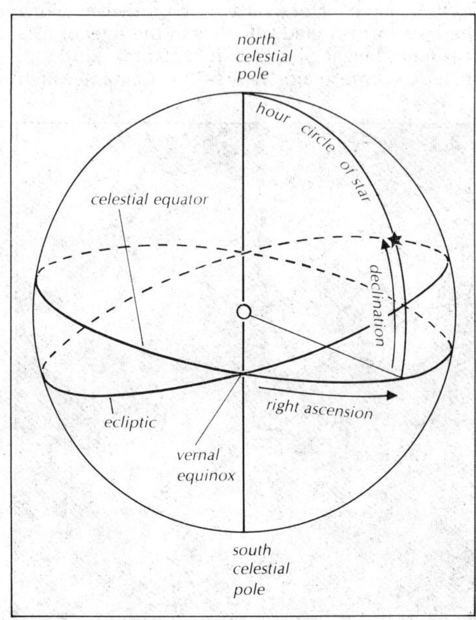

Equatorial coordinate system

celestial poles; the north celestial pole is directly above the earth's North Pole, and the south celestial pole directly above the earth's South Pole. The great circle on the celestial sphere half way between the celestial poles is called the celestial equator; it can be thought of as the earth's equator projected onto the celestial sphere. It divides the celestial sphere into the northern and southern skies. An important reference point on the celestial equator is the vernal EQUINOX, the point at which the sun crosses the celestial equator in March. To designate the position of a star, the astronomer considers an imaginary great circle passing through the celestial poles and through the star in question. This is the star's HOUR CIRCLE, analogous to a meridian of longitude on earth. He then measures the angle between the vernal equinox and the point where the hour circle intersects the celestial equator. This angle is called the star's right ascension and is measured in hours, minutes, and seconds rather than in the more familiar degrees, minutes, and seconds. (There are 360 degrees or 24 hours in a full circle.) The right ascension is always measured eastward from the vernal equinox. Next the observer measures along the star's hour circle the angle between the celestial equator and the position of the star. This angle is called the declination of the star and is measured in degrees, minutes, and seconds north or south of the celestial equator, analogous to latitude on the earth. Right ascension and declination together determine the location of a star on the celestial sphere. The right ascensions and declinations of many stars are listed in various reference tables published for astronomers and navigators. Because a star's position may change slightly (see PROPER MOTION), such tables must be revised at regular intervals. By definition, the vernal equinox is located at right ascension 0^h and declination 0°. Another useful reference point is the sigma point, the point where the observer's CELESTIAL MERIDIAN intersects the celestial equator. The right ascension of the sigma point is equal to the observer's local SIDEREAL TIME. The angular distance from the sigma point to a star's hour circle is called its HOUR ANGLE; it is equal to the star's right ascension minus the local sidereal time. Because the vernal equinox is not always visible in the night sky (especially in the spring), whereas the sigma point is always visible, the hour angle is used in actually locating a body in the sky.

Equatorial Guinea (gĭn'ē), formerly Spanish Guinea, republic (1973 est. pop. 300,000), 10,830 sq mi (28,051 sq km), W central Africa, including the islands of Fernando Po, Annobón, Corisco, Elobey Grande, and Elobey Chico in the Gulf of Guinea, and Río Muni on the African mainland. Río Muni, which includes about 93% of the nation's land area, is bordered by Cameroon in the north, by Gabon in the east and south, and by the Gulf of Guinea in the west. MALABO (formerly Santa Isabel), situated on Fernando Po, is the capital and largest city; other cities include San Carlos (also on Fernando Po) and Bata and San Benito (in Río Muni). Fernando Po is made up of three extinct volcanoes, the loftiest of which is c.9,870 ft (3,010 m) high. The island has abundant fertile volcanic soil. Río Muni, located just north of the equator, is made up of lowland along the coast, which gradually rises in the interior to a maximum height of c.3,600 ft (1,100 m). Río Muni includes three major rivers—the Campo, which forms part of the northern boundary; the Benito, located in the center; and Río Muni, which forms part of the southern boundary. There are forests of okoume, mahogany, and walnut along the coast and the rivers. Corisco and the Elobey islands are located near the Río Muni estuary. The inhabitants of Equatorial Guinea are black Africans, the great majority of whom speak a Bantu language. About 75% of the population lives in Río Muni, and the main ethnic group there is the Fang. The population of Fernando Po is made of the Bubi (the original inhabitants), descendants of slaves from W Africa liberated by the British in the 19th cent., and Nigerians and Fangs who migrated there in the 20th cent. Spanish is the official language. Many persons are Roman Catholic. Equatorial Guinea is almost exclusively agricultural. The money economy is based on the production of cacao (mostly on Fernando Po) and coffee and timber (in Río Muni). Other agricultural products include plantains, cassava, and palm oil. Manufactures are limited to basic consumer items and processed cacao and timber. There is a small fishing industry. Fernando Po has a good road network, but Río Muni lacks an adequate transportation system; there are no railroads. Malabo is the main port. Equatorial Guinea carries on a small foreign trade, principally with Spain; the annual value of its exports is usually somewhat higher than the cost of its imports. The main exports are cacao and coffee; the chief imports are food (especially rice) and petroleum products. Fernando Po was discovered and claimed by Fernão do Po, a Portuguese navigator, in 1472, and Annobón was also claimed. However, the Portuguese did little with the islands. In 1778, Portugal ceded them, and also the commercial rights to a part of the African coast that included present-day Río Muni, to the Spanish. Hoping to export black Africans as slaves to their American possessions, the Spanish sent settlers to the islands, but they died of yellow fever, and by 1781 the region was abandoned by the Europeans. From 1827 to 1843 the British leased bases at Malabo (then called Port Clarence) and San Carlos from Spain for use by their antislavery patrols, and some freed slaves were settled on Fernando Po. In 1844 the Spanish reacquired Fernando Po.and began to occupy it. In 1879, a Cuban penal settlement was established there, and some of the convicts remained on the island after being released from prison. The general region of Río Muni was awarded to Spain at the Conference of Berlin in 1885, and its boundaries were defined precisely in a treaty with France in 1900. The islands and Río Muni were grouped together as the colony of Spanish Guinea. Under the Spanish, economic development was largely confined to Fernando Po, although some measures were taken in Río Muni beginning in the 1940s. By 1960, about 6,000 Europeans (mostly Spanish) were living in the colony, and they controlled the production of cacao and timber. In 1959 the colony was reorganized into two overseas provinces of Spain, each under a governor. In a further move to assimilate the region to Spain, three Hispano-Guineans were elected to the Spanish Cortes in 1960. However, nationalists demanded independence and were not satisfied with assimilation. In 1963, Spain granted the country (renamed Equatorial Guinea) a limited amount of autonomy and on Oct. 12, 1968, granted it complete independence. The first president was Francisco Macías Nguema, a Fang from Río Muni, and in 1972 he was appointed president for life by the country's unicameral parliament. In 1969, there were violent anti-European demonstrations in Río Muni and most whites left the country, thus for a time severely dislocating the economy. In 1970 all political parties were merged into the Partido Unico Nacional, headed by Macías. In 1972, Equatorial Guinea became involved in a dispute with Gabon over the ownership of Elobey Grande and Elobey Chico, as well as Corisco, Mbanie, and Cocotiers, uninhabited islands in the Bay of Corisco. In 1973 a new constitution was adopted that abolished the nation's two semiautonomous provinces and created a unitary state. See René Pélissier, *Les Territoires espagnols d'Afrique* (1963) and *Études Hispano-Guinéennes* (1969).

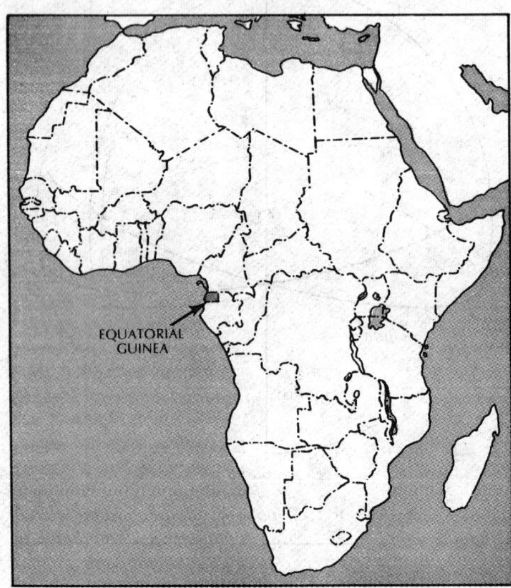

Equatorial Islands: see LINE ISLANDS.

equatorial mounting: see TELESCOPE.

equestrian: see HORSEMANSHIP.

equestrian sculpture: see PORTRAITURE.

equilibrium, state of balance. When a body or a system is in equilibrium, there is no net tendency to change. In mechanics, equilibrium has to do with the forces acting on a body. When no force is acting to make a body move in a line, the body is in translational equilibrium; when no force is acting to make the body turn (see MOMENT), the body is in rotational equilibrium. A body in equilibrium at rest is said to be in static equilibrium. However, a state

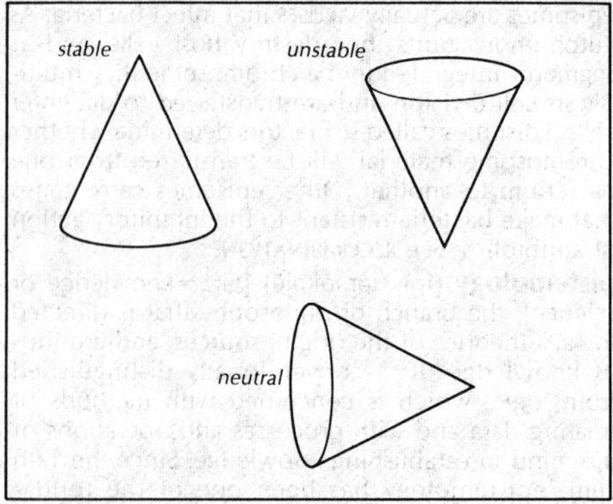

Equilibrium

of equilibrium does not mean that no forces act on the body, but only that the forces are balanced; thus a body in motion can also be in equilibrium, provided the state of its motion remains steady. For example, when a LEVER is being used to hold up a raised object, forces are being exerted downward on each end of the lever and upward on its fulcrum, but the upward and downward forces balance to maintain translational equilibrium, and the clockwise and counterclockwise moments of the forces on either end balance to maintain rotational equilibrium. The stability of a body is a measure of its ability to return to a position of equilibrium after being disturbed. It depends on the shape of the body and the location of its center of gravity (see CENTER OF MASS). A body with a large flat base and a low center of gravity will be very stable, returning quickly to its position of equilibrium after being tipped. However, a body with a small base and high center of gravity will tend to topple if tipped and is thus less stable than the first body. A body balanced precariously on a point is in unstable equilibrium. Some bodies, such as a ball or a cone lying on its side, do not return to their original position of equilibrium when pushed, assuming instead a new position of equilibrium; these are said to be in neutral equilibrium. In THERMODYNAMICS, equilibrium refers to a system in which all the variables, such as pressure and temperature, have the same values throughout the system. CHEMICAL EQUILIBRIUM refers to reversible chemical reactions in which the reactions involved are occurring in opposite directions at equal rates, so that no net change is observed.

equilibrium, chemical: see CHEMICAL EQUILIBRIUM.

equine encephalitis (ē'kwīn ĕnsĕf"əlī'tĭs), infectious disease of horses caused by one of several types of viruses. The three types that represent a serious public health problem in N South America and potentially threaten horses in the United States are the Eastern, Western, and Venezuelan viruses. A fourth, the St. Louis virus, does not produce a serious disease in horses; however, all four types can be contracted by humans. The virus begins its life cycle as a parasite of wild birds and is transferred to the salivary gland of a mosquito. The bird-arthropod host makes up a natural reservoir for the disease. It is transmitted to horses when they are bitten by the mosquito. The symptoms of equine encephalitis include fever, drowsiness, and incoordination, often followed by paralysis and death. The mortality rate is 90% in the Eastern type and about 20% to 50% in the Western type. There is no specific treatment for the disease once it is contracted, but prevention is possible through annual vaccination of herds.

equinox (ē'kwĭnŏks), either of two points on the CELESTIAL SPHERE where the ECLIPTIC and the celestial equator intersect. The vernal equinox, also known as "the first point of Aries," is the point at which the sun appears to cross the celestial equator from south to north. This occurs about March 21, marking the beginning of spring in the Northern Hemisphere. At the autumnal equinox, about Sept. 23, the sun again appears to cross the celestial equator, this time from north to south; this marks the beginning of autumn in the Northern Hemisphere. On the date of either equinox, night and day are of equal length (12 hr each) in all parts of the world; the word *equinox* is often used to refer to either of these dates. The equinoxes are not fixed points on the celestial sphere but move westward along the ecliptic, passing through all the constellations of the

ZODIAC; this motion is called the PRECESSION OF THE EQUINOXES. The vernal equinox is a reference point in the EQUATORIAL COORDINATE SYSTEM.

Equisetophyta (ĕk"wəsətŏf'ətə), small division of the plant kingdom consisting of the plants commonly called HORSETAILS and scouring rushes. *Equisetum,* the only living genus in this division, is descended evolutionarily from tree-sized fossil plants. There are about 20 species, distributed in every continent except Australia and Antarctica and in every climate from the tropics to the arctic. The plants, which generally grow in moist places, have roots and ribbed green stems, the surface of which is impregnated with silica crystals. Their abrasive texture made them useful in former times for scouring, hence their common name. Most species have numerous whorled branches that lend the plant a plumed or feathery appearance, thus giving rise to their other common name, horsetail. The nonphotosynthetic leaves are joined together to form a fringed whorl that encircles the stem at regular intervals; the green stems and branches are the photosynthetic organs. The stem has no CAMBIUM and no secondary growth. It consists of a silica-impregnated epidermis, a cortex, and a central structure called a stele that contains the vascular bundles consisting of xylem and phloem. The conspicuous plant form of *Equisetum,* which may be more than 3 ft (1 m) high in some species, represents the sporophyte generation. A cone, or strobilus, at the apex of the sporophyte stem bears spore-producing structures. Upon germination, the spores produce a green, frilled, thumbnail-sized plant form, the gametophyte; specialized structures on the mature gametophyte, the archegonia and antheridia, produce, respectively, eggs and sperms. As in mosses, the sperm swims to the egg through a film of water, attracted by specific chemical substances. A zygote, formed as the result of fertilization, develops into young green sporophytes to complete the life cycle. The order Calamitales contains plants known only from fossil remains so abundant in coals and associated shales from the Carboniferous period that it is assumed that they formed a major part of the vegetation that later became compressed into coal. The plants of the genus *Calamites* may have reached a height of 100 ft (30 m).

equites (ĕk'wĭtēz) [Lat.,=horsemen], the original cavalry of the Roman army, chosen, according to legend, by Romulus from the three ancient Roman tribes; the equites were selected from the patricians and plebeians on the basis of wealth. During the late republic they numbered 1,800, but during the empire their number more than doubled. A law passed by Caius Sempronius Gracchus in 123 B.C. transferred judicial functions from the senate to the body of equites, who, though later deprived of these powers by Sulla, attained much influence in the state. In the 1st cent. B.C. the equites were in actuality the capitalist class, and they allied themselves alternately with the popular and the senatorial parties. Under the emperors the equites gradually fell into disrepute; they disappeared in the reign of Constantine. It is conventional in English to call them knights, but their resemblance to any aspect of knighthood is neither apparent nor real.

equity, principles of justice originally developed by the English chancellor. In Anglo-American jurisprudence equitable principles and remedies are distinguished from the older system that the COMMON LAW courts evolved. One of the earliest functions of the king's chaplain (the chancellor) and of the chancery (the office that he headed) was to govern access to the royal courts by issuing on application the appropriate original WRIT. At first the chancellor had great discretion in framing writs, but in time he was limited to a few rigidly circumscribed forms, and in certain cases worthy claims could not be satisfied. From this inadequacy arose the practice of appealing directly for aid to the chancellor as the "keeper of the king's conscience." By the early 16th cent. a fairly well-defined jurisdiction was exercised by the court of chancery in rivalry with the common law. In the 17th cent. it was definitely established that the court of chancery would decide any claim to jurisdiction that the courts of common law disputed. The early chancellors purported to dispense equity in its original sense of fair dealing, and they cut through the technicalities of common law to give just treatment. Some of their principles were derived from ROMAN LAW and from CANON LAW. Soon, however, equity amassed its own body of precedents and tended to rigidity. Equity, even in its more limited modern sense, is still distinguished by its original and animating principle that no wrong should be without an adequate remedy. Among the most notable achievements of equity were the TRUST and the INJUNCTION. Because the DECREE (final order) of an equity court operated as an order of the king to the defendant, disobedience might be punished as CONTEMPT; in legal remedies, on the contrary, the plaintiff was limited to enforcing his JUDGMENT. The fact that equity trials were decided without a jury was thought advantageous in complex cases. The coexistence of different systems of justice and the delays of the courts of chancery presented such great procedural difficulties that in England, in 1873, the Judicature Act was adopted to amalgamate law and equity. In the United States only a few of the states have separate equity courts. Of the remaining states some divide actions and (to a lesser extent) remedies into legal and equitable, while the others have almost entirely abolished the distinction. Even in those states where law and equity remain unmerged, they are often handled by two sides of the same court, with relatively simple provisions for the transfer of a case which is brought on the wrong side. See F. W. Maitland, *Equity* (1909, repr. 1969); R. A. Newman, *Equity in Law* (1961); H. G. Hanbury, *Modern Equity* (9th ed., ed. by R. H. Maudsley, 1969); G. H. Webb and T. C. Bianco, *Equity* (1970).

equivalent weight. The equivalent weight of an element or radical is equal to its ATOMIC WEIGHT or FORMULA WEIGHT divided by the VALENCE it assumes in compounds. The unit of equivalent weight is the ATOMIC MASS UNIT; the amount of a substance in grams numerically equal to the equivalent weight is called a gram equivalent. Hydrogen has atomic weight 1.008 and always assumes valence 1 in compounds, so its equivalent weight is 1.008. Oxygen has an atomic weight of 15.9994 and always assumes valence 2 in compounds, so its equivalent weight is 7.9997. The sulfate radical (SO_4) has formula weight 106.062 and always has valence 2 in compounds, so its equivalent weight is 53.031. Some elements exhibit more than one valence in forming compounds and thus have more than one equivalent weight. Iron (atomic weight 55.847) has an equivalent weight of 27.924 in ferrous compounds (valence 2) and 18.616 in ferric compounds (valence 3). The weight proportion in which elements or radicals combine to form compounds can be determined from their equivalent weights. For example, hydrogen can combine with oxygen to form water; the weight proportion of oxygen to hydrogen in water is the same as the proportion of their equivalent weights, 7.9997 to 1.008 or 7.946 to 1; there is 1 weight of hydrogen for every 7.946 weights of oxygen, or water is about 11.2% hydrogen (by weight). Iron forms two oxides: ferrous oxide (FeO), in which there are 27.924 weights of iron for each 7.9997 weights of oxygen, and ferric oxide (Fe_2O_3), in which there are 18.616 weights of iron for every 7.9997 weights of oxygen.

Er (ûr). **1** In the Gospel genealogy. Luke 3.28. **2** Judah's first son. Gen. 38.1-7. **3** Judahite. 1 Chron. 4.21.

Er, chemical symbol of the element ERBIUM.

era, period of historic time. In geology, it is the name applied to large divisions of geological process, e.g., Paleozoic era (see GEOLOGY). In chronology an era is a period reckoned from a fixed point in time, as before or after the birth of Christ—before Christ, B.C.; *Anno Domini* [year of the Lord], A.D. The points best known for Western history are the creation of the world (Jewish, equivalent to 3761 B.C.; Byzantine, 5508 B.C.); the founding of the city of Rome [753 B.C.; year marked A.U.C. for *ab urbe condita* (from the founding of the city)]; the HEGIRA, the flight of Muhammad from Mecca (A.D. 622; abbreviation A.H.); and the founding of the Olympic games in ancient Greece (776 B.C.; time in Olympiads). In several non-Christian countries C.E. (originally, Christian era, now common era) and B.C.E. (before common era) are used in place of A.D. and B.C., respectively. Since in different calendars, years are of different lengths and do not begin on the same day (see CALENDAR), several factors have to be used in changing the year of one era to that of another, and even with conversion charts there are still difficulties. Because of poor time calculation in earlier times, there may be anomalies in dating. Thus, the beginning of the Christian era, originally fixed probably by Dionysius Exiguus, was set a little too late. Therefore the actual birth of Christ must be dated a little earlier, probably in 4 B.C. The term EPOCH is often confused with era in writing.

Eran (ĭr'ăn), grandson of Ephraim. Num. 26.36.

era of good feelings, period in U.S. history (1817–23) when, the Federalist party having declined, there was little open party feeling. After the War of 1812 all sections were anxious to return to a normal life and to forget political issues. The phrase was coined at the time of President Monroe's good-will tour through the North, including New England, where a President had not been seen since the Virginia "dynasty" came into power. Under the surface, however, vast sectional issues were shaping themselves, and personal rivalries also were gathering strength to break loose in the campaign of 1824. See George Dangerfield, *The Era of Good Feelings* (1952, repr. 1963).

Erasistratus (ĕrəsĭs'trətəs), *fl.* 3d cent. B.C., Greek physician, b. Chios. He was the leader of a school of medicine in Alexandria, and his works were influential until the 4th cent. A.D. He considered plethora (hyperemia) to be the primary cause of disease. As opposed to the then current belief in the HUMORS, he suggested that air carried from the lungs to the heart is converted into a vital spirit distributed by the arteries. He developed a reverse theory of circulation (veins to arteries). Studying from dissections, he observed the convolutions of the brain, named the trachea, and distinguished (as did his contemporary Herophilus) between motor and sensory nerves. He also devised a catheter and a calorimeter.

Erasmus (ĭrăz'məs) or **Desiderius Erasmus** (dĕsĭdĕr'ēəs) [Gr. *Erasmus,* his given name, and Lat. *Desiderius*=beloved; both are regarded as the equivalent of Dutch *Gerard,* Erasmus' father's name], 1466?–1536, Dutch humanist, b. Rotterdam. He was ordained priest of the Roman Catholic Church and studied at the Univ. of Paris. Erasmus' influence began to be felt in Europe after 1500. It was exercised through his personal contacts, his editions of classical authors, and his own writings. He was intimate with most of the scholars of Europe, and his circle of friends was especially large in England; it included Thomas More, John Colet, and Henry VIII. His editions of Greek and Latin classics and of the Fathers of the Church (especially of Jerome and Athanasius) were his chief occupation for years. His Latin edition of the New Testament was based on the original Greek text. For many years he was editor for the printer Johannes FROBEN in Basel. Erasmus' original works are mainly satirical and critical. Written in Latin, the language of the 16th-century scholar, the most important works are *Adagia* (1500, tr. *Adages* or *Proverbs*), a collection of quotations; *Enchiridion militis christiani* (1503, tr. *Manual of the Christian Knight*); *Moriae encomium* (1509, tr. *The Praise of Folly*); *Institutio principis christiani* (1515, tr. *The Education of a Christian Prince*); and *Colloquia* (1516, tr. *Colloquies*). His collected letters (tr., ed. by F. M. Nichols, 1904–18; repr. 1962) are perhaps more important still. Erasmus combined vast learning with a fine style, a keen and sometimes sharp humor, moderation, and tolerance. His position on the Reformation was widely denounced, especially by Martin Luther, who had first looked on Erasmus as an ally because of Erasmus' attacks on clerical abuse and lay ignorance. Though eager for church reform, Erasmus remained all his life within the Roman Catholic Church. As a humanist he deplored the religious warfare of the time because of the rancorous, intolerant atmosphere and cultural decline that it induced. Erasmus was finally brought into open conflict with Luther and attacked his position on predestination in *On the Freedom of the Will.* See studies by Preserved Smith (1923, repr. 1960), Margaret Mann Phillips (1949, repr. 1965), Johan Huizinga (tr. 1952, repr. 1957), R. H. Bainton (1969), T. A. Dorey, ed. (1970), and Geraldine Thompson (1974).

Erastus (ĭrăs'təs). **1** Companion of Paul. Acts 19.22. **2** Early Christian, probably the same as **1.** 2 Tim. 4.20. **3** Chamberlain of Corinth. Rom. 16.23.

Erastus, Thomas, 1524–83, Swiss Protestant theologian, a physician, whose original name was Lüber, Lieber, or Liebler. As a follower of Huldreich ZWINGLI, he supported the Swiss leader's view of the LORD'S SUPPER at the conferences of Heidelberg (1560) and Maulbronn (1564) and in a book (1565). In spite of his vigorous opposition to the Calvinist doctrine, Presbyterian church discipline and government were introduced in Heidelberg in 1570. In 1574, Erastus was excommunicated by the Heidelberg consistory, but a year later the edict was removed. Much controversy has arisen over his treatise, *Explicatio,* written in 1568 and posthumously published in 1589. It declares that excommunication is not a divine ordinance and that punishment of sins should be left to civil authorities. Erastus was motivated by his fear of the usurpation of temporal powers by the church. The term **Erastianism** has come to represent approval of the dominance of civil authority in all punitive measures and, by extension, complete dominance of the state over the church, though Erastus himself never held such an extreme view. Erastianism achieved its definitive expression in the *Leviathan* of Thomas HOBBES. See Erastus Evans, *Erastianism* (1931).

Erato (ĕr'ətō): see MUSES.

Eratosthenes (ĕrətŏs'thənēz), c.275–c.195 B.C., Greek scholar, b. Cyrene. A pupil of Callimachus in Athens, he became (c.240 B.C.) head of the library at Alexandria. Known for his versatility, he wrote poetry and works (most of them lost) on literature, the theater (notably on ancient comedy), mathematics, astronomy, geography, and philosophy; he also drew a map of the known world and evolved a system of chronology. Especially noted as an astronomer, he is credited with measuring the circumference and tilt of the earth and the size and distance from the earth of the sun and the moon.

Erbil: see IRBIL, Iraq.

erbium (ûr'bēəm) [from *Ytterby,* a town in Sweden], metallic chemical element; symbol Er; at. no. 68; at. wt. 167.26; m.p. 1522°C; b.p. 2510°C; sp. gr. 9.05 at 25°C; valence +3. Erbium is a soft, malleable, lustrous, silvery metal. It is a member of the LANTHANIDE SERIES in group IIIb of the PERIODIC TABLE. With other rare earths its oxide occurs in the mineral gadolinite, found in Sweden. Natural erbium is a mixture of 6 stable isotopes; in addition, 10 radioactive isotopes are known. Erbium does not oxidize in air as rapidly as some of the other RARE-EARTH METALS. Erbia is a rose-colored oxide of erbium; it has been used to a very limited extent in glazes and glass as a coloring agent. The discovery of erbium is generally credited to Carl G. Mosander, although he did not succeed in isolating the element. In 1843 he separated from gadolinite three oxide fractions that he called yttria, erbia, and terbia. Later, what he had called terbia became known as erbia and was shown to contain five distinct rare earths, now called erbia, scandia, holmia, thulia, and ytterbia. Fairly pure erbium oxide was first isolated in 1905; fairly pure erbium was isolated in 1934.

Ercilla y Zúñiga, Alonso de (älōn'sō thā ärthē'lyä ē thōō'nyĕgä), 1533–94, Spanish poet. In Chile (1556–63) he fought against the Araucanian Indians, and while there he began the epic poem *La Araucana,* considered the finest Spanish historical poem. This heroic work in 37 cantos is divided into three parts, published in 1569, 1578, and 1589. It tells of the courageous insurrection of the Araucanians and also relates the history of Chile and of contemporary Spain. See translations by Walter Owen (1945) and C. M. Lancaster and P. T. Manchester (1945).

Ercole de' Roberti (ärkō'lā dā rōbĕr'tē), 1456?–1496, Italian painter of the Ferrarese school. He probably began his career by assisting Francesco Cossa in the decoration of the Schifanoia Palace, Ferrara. A large altarpiece in the Brera, Milan, is the most certain work by Ercole. Other paintings ascribed to him reveal a style ranging from a nervous sensitivity to a dynamic intensity. Paintings by him are in the Cook Collection, Richmond, Va.; the Johnson Collection, Philadelphia; the National Gallery of Art, Washington, D.C.; the National Gallery, London; and at Liverpool, Berlin, and Dresden.

Erebus (ĕr'ĭbəs), in Greek religion, personification of darkness. According to Hesiod, Erebus sprang from Chaos and was the father of Day. His name was sometimes used for Hades.

Erebus, Mount, volcanic peak, 12,280 ft (3,743 m) high, on Ross Island, in the Ross Sea, E Antarctica. One of the loftiest volcanoes of the world, it was discovered in 1841 by the British explorer James C. Ross and named for one of his two ships. It was climbed in 1908 by a party under a British geologist, T. W. E. David.

Erech (ē'rĕk) or **Uruk** (ōō'rōōk), ancient Sumerian city of MESOPOTAMIA, on the Euphrates and NW of Ur (in present-day S Iraq). It is the modern Tall al Warka. Erech, dating from the 5th millennium B.C., was the largest city in S Mesopotamia and an important religious center. The sanctuaries of the goddess Inanna (who corresponds to the Babylonian Ishtar and is also called Nana or Eanna) and Anu, the sky god, date from the early 4th millennium B.C. The temple of Anu, known as the white temple, stood on a terrace and seems to have been a primitive form of ziggurat. Erech was the home of GILGAMESH and is mentioned in the Bible (Gen. 10.10). There have been excavations at the site since 1912.

Erechtheum (ĭrĕk'thēəm) [for Erechtheus], Gr. *Erechtheion,* temple in Pentelic marble, on the Acropolis at Athens. One of the masterpieces of Greek architecture, it was constructed between c.421 B.C. and 405 B.C. to replace an earlier temple to Athena destroyed by the Persians. Its design is sometimes ascribed to the architect Mnesicles. The Erechtheum contained sanctuaries to Athena Polias, Poseidon, and Erechtheus. The temple displays the finest extant examples of the Greek IONIC ORDER. The requirements of the several shrines and the location upon a sloping site produced an unusual plan. From the body of the building porticoes project on east, north, and south sides. The eastern portico, hexastyle Ionic, gave access to the shrine of Athena, which was separated by a partition from the western cella. The northern portico, tetrastyle Ionic, stands at a lower level and gives access to the western cella through a fine doorway. The southern portico, known as the Porch of the Caryatids (see CARYATID) from the six sculptured draped female figures that support its entablature, is the temple's most striking feature; it forms a gallery or tribune. The west end of the building, with windows and engaged Ionic columns, is a modification of the original, built by the Romans when they restored the building. In Justinian's reign the Erechtheum was made into a church, but it was used as a harem when the Turks captured (1458) Athens. One of the east columns and one of the caryatids were removed to London by Lord Elgin, replicas being installed in their places. The building was much damaged in 1827 during the Greek revolution. Partial reconstructions have taken place since 1838; in recent years the fragments on the site have been used for restoration.

Erechtheus (ĕrĕk'thēəs), in Greek mythology, king of Athens. He was said to have founded the worship of Athena, to have built the ERECHTHEUM, and to have established the PANATHENAEA. On the advice of an oracle he sacrificed one of his daughters during the battle between the Athenians and the Eleusinians. This enabled him to win the battle, but Poseidon later destroyed him and all his house. Erechtheus is often confused with Erichthonius.

Erenburg, Ilya Grigoryevich: see EHRENBURG.

Eretria (ĕrē'trēə), ancient city of Greece, in Euboea (now Évvoia), SE of Chalcis (now Khalkís), its rival. In the 7th and 6th cent. B.C., Eretria sent out many colonists to islands and coasts of the N Aegean. It supported (499 B.C.) the Ionian cities in the revolt against Persian control. In retaliation Darius I destroyed (490 B.C.) the city. Athens planted (c.445 B.C.) a colony there, which revolted in 411 with the rest of Euboea. Much later, after the second Delian League had been created, Eretria again revolted (349 B.C.). Excavations have uncovered the city walls, temple of Apollo, theater, and some public buildings.

Erfurt (ĕr'fōōrt), city (1970 pop. 195,994), capital of Erfurt district, SW East Germany, on the Gera River. It is an industrial and horticultural center and a rail junction. Manufactures include machinery, chemicals, precision and optical instruments, clothing, processed food, and electrical equipment. Erfurt is one of the oldest cities of Germany. It was mentioned by St. Boniface in the 8th cent., and Charlemagne later made it a center for trade with the Slavs. Martin Luther studied (1501–5) at its university (opened 1392, closed 1816), and he took his vows as an Augustinian friar at its monastery. Erfurt was a free imperial city and a member of the Hanseatic League. It passed (1664) to the electors of Mainz and (1802) to Prussia. In 1808, Napoleon I and Czar Alexander I met there at the Congress of Erfurt, and the Franco-Russian alliance concluded at Tilsit in 1807 was renewed. At a congress held at Erfurt in 1891 the German Social Democratic party adopted the Erfurt Program (see SOCIALIST PARTIES), which closely followed Marxist theories. Noteworthy buildings of the city include the cathedral (12th–15th cent.) and the 13th-century Church of St. Severus.

erg (ûrg), unit of WORK or ENERGY in the CGS SYSTEM of units, which is based on the METRIC SYSTEM; it is the work done or energy expended by a force of 1 dyne acting through a distance of 1 centimeter. In terms of the JOULE, the unit of work or energy in the mks system, 1 erg equals 0.0000001 joule.

Ergasteria, Greece: see LÁVRION.

ergot (ûr'gət), disease of rye and other cereals caused by the fungus *Claviceps purpurea.* The cottony, matlike body, or mycelium, of the fungus develops in the ovaries of the host plant; it eventually turns into a hard pink or purple body, the sclerotium, or ergot, that resembles a grain of rye in shape. The sclerotium contains certain active substances, or alkaloids, that are poisonous to men and livestock. Ergot poisoning, or ergotism, epidemic in the Middle Ages, results from eating bread made of rye contaminated with ergot. Ergot poisoning is characterized by constriction of blood vessels, resulting in numbness and the development of gangrene in extremities; it may also affect the nervous system. The ergot also contains several alkaloids, e.g., ergotamine and ergonovine, that are used as drugs; these alkaloids are chemical derivatives of lysergic acid, which is used in the synthesis of the hallucinogen LYSERGIC ACID DIETHYLAMIDE. Ergotamine alleviates migraine headaches. Ergonovine is used medicinally to stop hemorrhage and cause contraction of the uterus; during the 17th cent. midwives used ergot to stop postpartum uterine bleeding.

Erhard, Ludwig (lōōt'vĭkh ĕr'härt), 1897–, German political leader and economist. In Nuremberg he rose to be director of the institute for economic research. Dismissed (1942) by the Nazi regime, he then headed the institute for industrial research. He introduced (1948) the currency reform that paved the way for West German economic recovery. A member of the Christian Democratic Union (CDU), he became West German economics minister in 1949. In 1957 he was named vice chancellor, and in 1963 he succeeded Konrad Adenauer as chancellor. In late 1966, Erhard's government fell after the four Free Democratic party ministers in his cabinet resigned and left him without a ruling majority in the federal parliament. He headed the CDU in 1966–67. His writings include *Prosperity through Competition* (1957, tr. 1958).

Eri (ē'rī), son of Gad. Gen. 46.16; Num. 26.16.

Eric IX (Eric the Saint), d. 1160, king of Sweden. He led (1157?) a Christian crusade to Finland, where he left the bishop of Uppsala in charge of missionary work. While attending mass he was killed by a Danish prince. Soon afterward the people began to revere him as a saint, and c.1290 he became the patron saint of Sweden. Feast: May 18.

Eric XIV, 1533–77, king of Sweden (1560–68), son and successor of Gustavus I. To strengthen the power of the crown, he limited (1561) the privileges of the royal dukes. He forbade the marriage of his half brother John, duke of Finland, to the sister of the king of Poland. When John disobeyed he was accused of treason, lost his estates, and was imprisoned (1563) with his wife. Eric feared conspiracies among the nobles, many of whom were not reconciled to a strong hereditary monarchy. He had many nobles assassinated, including Nils Sture, of the powerful STURE family. Having unsuccessfully sought the hand of Elizabeth I of England, Eric married his peasant mistress in 1568 and had her crowned queen. Reverses in Sweden's war (1563–70) with Denmark, the unpopularity of his adviser, Goran Persson, and Eric's evident insanity enabled John, who had been released, to lead an insurrection against him. Eric was deposed (1568) and died in prison. He was succeeded by John, who ruled from 1568 to 1592 as John III, and then by John's son SIGISMUND III of Poland. Eric, a patron of arts and letters, was himself a writer.

Ericht, Loch (lŏkh ĕr'ĭkht), lake, 15 mi (24 km) long and 1 mi (1.6 km) wide, Inverness-shire and Perthshire, central Scotland. It is drained by the River Ericht. Part of a hydroelectric project, the lake is dammed and the river has been enlarged. The lake is famous for trout.

Erichthonius (ĕrĕkthō'nēəs), in Greek mythology, primeval creature, half man and half serpent. After his birth he was entrusted to Athena, who concealed him in a chest that she gave to the daughters of Cecrops to keep. They opened it and were so frightened by Erichthonius' shape that they killed themselves. Athena then reared him among the gods. He is often confused with Erechtheus.

Ericsson, Leif: see LEIF ERICSSON.

Eric the Red, fl. 10th cent., Norse chieftain, discoverer and colonizer of Greenland. He left (c.950) Norway with his exiled father and settled in Iceland. A feud resulting in manslaughter led to his banishment (c.981) from Iceland for three years. He sailed c.982 to seek land reputed to lie W of Iceland. The discovery of Greenland followed, and Eric and his Viking followers spent three years exploring the south and west coasts. On his return to Iceland he promoted a colonizing venture and is said to have given Greenland its attractive name to encourage settlers. He led (c.986) to the new land a group of 25 ships, of which 14 arrived, carrying about 500 people. Eric established a farmstead, Brattahlid, near present Julianehaab and was a leader of a southern settlement at Osterbygd. He resisted in vain the introduction (c.1000) of Christianity by his son LEIF ERICSSON. The Greenland colony may have survived for four or five centuries.

Eridanus (ĭrĭd'ənəs), large southern CONSTELLATION stretching SW from Orion for about 60°. Because of its long, winding shape it was identified with a river by many ancient civilizations; e.g., the Egyptians called it the Nile and the Babylonians called it the Euphrates. The brightest star in the constellation, ACHERNAR, marks the southern end of the river. Eridanus reaches its highest point in the evening sky in December.

Eridu (ā'rĭdo͞o), ancient city of SUMER, Mesopotamia, near the Euphrates, S of Ur (in present-day S Iraq). Excavations conducted from 1946 to 1949 revealed that Eridu was the earliest known settlement in S Mesopotamia and dated from c.5000 B.C. A temple discovered there was probably dedicated to the water god Ea.

Erie, city (1970 pop. 129,231), seat of Erie co., NW Pa., on Lake Erie; inc. as a city 1851. Pennsylvania's only port on the Great Lakes, Erie is a busy shipping point for coal, iron, grain, petroleum, heavy machinery, and lumber. Its manufactures include boilers, engines, power shovels, meters, foundry products, plastics, and paper. Fort Presque Isle was built in 1753 by the French, occupied and rebuilt in 1760 by the English, and destroyed during PONTIAC'S REBELLION in 1763. A peace conference between the British and Indians was held in 1764, but the town was not laid out until 1795. Oliver Hazard Perry's fleet was launched at Crystal Point before his victory over the British during the battle of Lake Erie in 1813. Gannon College, Mercyhurst College, Villa Maria College, and a branch of Pennsylvania State Univ. are in the city. Presque Isle State Park, located on the long peninsula that helps form Erie's superb harbor, is the area's leading tourist attraction.

Erie, Lake, 9,940 sq mi (25,745 sq km), 241 mi (388 km) long and from 30 to 57 mi (48–92 km) wide, bordered on the N by S Ont., Canada, on the E by W N.Y., on the S by NW Pa. and N Ohio, and on the W by SE Mich.; fourth largest of the GREAT LAKES. It is 572 ft (174 m) above sea level with a maximum depth of 210 ft (64 m), making it the shallowest of the Great Lakes and the only one with a floor above sea level. It is part of the Great Lakes–St. Lawrence Seaway system and is linked to Lake Huron by the Detroit River, Lake St. Clair, and St. Clair River, and with Lake Ontario by the Niagara River (Lake Erie's only natural outlet) and the Welland Canal. The New York State Barge Canal links the lake with the Hudson River. Several small rivers, including the Maumee, Sandusky, and Cuyahoga, flow into the lake from the south; the Grand River enters from Ontario. Lake Erie is partially icebound in winter and is usually closed to navigation from mid-December to the end of March. Rich agricultural lands border the Canadian shore, where the chief towns are Port Colbourne and Port Stanley. The principal U.S. cities on the lake are Buffalo, Erie, Cleveland, and Toledo; all are busy ports and are heavily industrialized. Untreated industrial and municipal wastes from lakeshore cities—and from Detroit, whose wastes enter the western end of the lake—have polluted the waters and rendered large areas foul smelling and devoid of oxygen in hot summers; a U.S.-Canadian pact (1972) agreed to end the discharge of all contaminating materials into the water. Commercial fishing is important in the summer months, but pollution and lamprey infestation have reduced the value of the catch. Numerous recreation facilities are provided at national (Point Pelee and Fort Malden in Canada), provincial, and state parks located on the lake's islands and shores. The lake was first seen by Louis Jolliet, the French explorer, in 1669. The British and the French, and later the British and the Americans, fought for its control. The battle of Lake Erie (Sept. 10, 1813), a naval engagement in the War of 1812, led successfully by the U.S. leader Oliver H. Perry against the British, was fought at Put-in Bay. See H. H. Hatcher, *Lake Erie* (1945, repr. 1971).

Erie Canal, former artificial waterway, c.360 mi (580 km) long; it extended across central N.Y. from Albany to Buffalo and connected the Hudson River with Lake Erie. Locks overcame the 571-ft (174-m) difference between the level of the river and that of the lake. The NEW YORK STATE BARGE CANAL now follows part of the Erie Canal's course. After the American Revolution, the need for an all-American water route between the Great Lakes and the Atlantic coast became evident. Political unity, easy and inexpensive transportation, and increased trade (free from Canadian competition) were the anticipated benefits of such a route. Several land surveys for a canal followed, and by 1810 the issue was paramount in the New York state legislature, where De Witt CLINTON lent his political support. A canal commission, including Clinton, Gouverneur Morris, Stephen Van Rensselaer, and Thomas Eddy, among others, formed (1810) by the legislature, recommended (1811) an Erie rather than an Ontario canal. The canal bill, drawn up by Clinton in 1815, was debated in the legislature (1816–17), with New York City and the Lake Ontario interests opposing it vigorously. Although a presidential veto of a national waterways project forced the proposed canal's financial burden on New York state, the canal bill passed the state legislature in April, 1817. Work on the canal was carried on by gangs of workers, many of whom were European immigrants. The canal's course was entirely enclosed; streams and lakes were not incorporated into the waterway. The Erie Canal's middle section (Utica to Salina) was completed in 1820; its eastern section was finished in 1823. Elaborate celebrations opened the canal in 1825; Clinton and other notables sailed from Buffalo to New York City, where Clinton emptied a barrel of Lake Erie water into the Atlantic Ocean. The canal was enlarged beginning in 1835; its most important branches, the Champlain (opened 1819), the Oswego (1828), and the Cayuga and Seneca (1829), were also enlarged. Railroad competition, beginning in the 1850s, eventually destroyed the canal's long-haul advantages; however, for many years the Erie Canal was a profitable route, and large profits were amassed from tolls. The tolls were abolished in 1882 because of the canal's state of disrepair and in order to lure more traffic. Although some improvements in the canal were made (1884–94), its inadequate navigability, the competition of Canadian routes, and the disclosure of fraudulent canal administration (the "Canal Ring"), brought about plans for its complete renovation and subsequent conversion (1904–18) into a large, modern barge canal. The Erie Canal contributed to New York City's financial development, opened the eastern markets to the farm products of the Midwest and encouraged immigration into that region, and helped to create numerous large cities. Its initial success started a wave of canal building in the United States. See F. P. Kimball, *New York: The Canal State* (1937); G. E. Condon, *Stars in the Water: The Story of the Erie Canal* (1973); bibliography by the Water Resources Scientific Information Center (1972).

Erie Indians, North American Indians of the Iroquoian branch of the Hokan-Siouan linguistic stock (see AMERICAN INDIAN LANGUAGES). In the Iroquoian language the word *erie* means "long tail" (i.e., cat), and, therefore, the Erie were referred to as the Cat Nation. In the 17th cent. they inhabited the region E and SE of Lake Erie in the present states of New York, Pennsylvania, and Ohio. They then numbered some 14,000. Although they were sedentary farmers of the Eastern Woodlands area, they exhibited some Southeastern cultural traits, such as the use of poisoned arrows and the building of palisaded villages. They were traditional enemies of the Iroquois Confederacy, and in 1656, after one of the most relentless and destructive Indian wars, the Erie were almost exterminated by the Iroquois. The surviving captives were either adopted or enslaved by the confederacy.

Erie Railroad, rail transportation line designed to connect the mouth of the Hudson River with the Great Lakes region. The New York and Erie RR Company was enfranchised and incorporated in 1832, and construction was begun in 1835 near Deposit, N.Y. The year 1851 saw 446 mi (718 km) of trunkline across New York state completed to Dunkirk, N.Y., on Lake Erie at a huge cost. The railroad was extended to Jersey City, N.J., and to Buffalo, N.Y., but in 1861 the company failed and was reorganized as the Erie Railway Company. The company gained sound financial footing during the Civil War before it became the subject of a tremendous financial battle. Daniel DREW, Jay GOULD, and James FISK allied themselves and from 1866 to 1868 outmaneuvered—with the aid of unauthorized stock issues, political chicanery, and incessant litigation—Cornelius Vanderbilt to keep control of the Erie Railway Company. Drew lost his control to Gould, who during his presidency (1868–72) further wrecked the Erie Railway Company. After further financial trickery, the Erie Railway Company went bankrupt and was reorganized (1878) as the New York, Lake Erie and Western Railway Company. By 1880 branch lines were built to Chicago. The New York, Lake Erie and Western went into receivership after the Panic of 1893 and was reorganized (1895) as the Erie RR Company. Under the presidency (1901–27) of Frederick D. Underwood, the Erie continued to suffer losses, and after a major reorganization (1941) it yielded (1942) a dividend for the first time in 69 years. On Oct. 15, 1960, the Erie merged with the Delaware, Lackawanna, and Western RR to form the Erie-Lackawanna RR Company, but in 1972 the merged organization filed for reorganization under the Federal bankruptcy act. See C. F. Adams, Jr., and Henry Adams, *Chapters of Erie* (1886, repr. 1967); F. C. Hicks, ed., *High Finance in the Sixties* (1929, repr. 1966).

Erigena, John Scotus (skō'təs ĕrĭj'ĭnə) [Lat. *Scotus*=Irish, *Erigena*=born in Ireland], c.810–c.877, scholastic philosopher, born in Ireland. About 847 he was invited by Charles II, king of the West Franks (later Holy Roman emperor), to take charge of the court school at Paris. At Charles's request he translated the writings of Pseudo-Dionysius and his commentator Maximus the Confessor. His own philosophical speculation is contained in the *De divisione naturae* and the fragmentary *De egressu et regressu animae ad Deum.* Erigena was perhaps the most learned man of his time and a remarkable thinker. His thought, based on that of Pseudo-Dionysius, Maximus the Confessor, the Greek Fathers, and St. Augustine, is Neoplatonic. Philosophy and theology are identified; all thinking and being begin and end with God, who is above all being and thought. Erigena makes a fourfold division of the things that are, or nature—that which creates and is not created; that which is created and creates; that which is created and does not create; that which neither creates nor is created. The first is God, the source of all things. The second is the Logos, existent in, and coeternal with, God, in whom are the primordial causes and types of things. The third is the world of space, time, and generation, which came into being from the primordial causes by emanation through the successive genera and species. The fourth is again God, but regarded now as the end of all things; for just as creatures have emanated from God, so they will return to Him. See study by Henry Bett (1925, repr. 1964).

Eriha: see JERICHO.

Erim, Nihat (nĕhät' ĕrĭm'), 1912–, Turkish political leader. A law professor, he served (1945–50) in parliament and was minister of public works and deputy prime minister from 1948 to 1950. After suffering a political setback in 1950, he returned to teaching. In 1961 he was reelected to parliament and became deputy chairman of the Republican People's party in the national assembly. Appointed prime minister in March, 1971, he hoped to halt extremist activity and unrest in the armed forces, but was forced to resign the following year due to lack of parliamentary support.

Erin (ĕr'ĭn, ĕr'-), ancient and poetic name of Ireland.

Erinyes (ĕrĭn'ē-ēz): see FURIES.

eriogonum: see BUCKWHEAT.

Eriphyle (ĕr"ĭfī'lē), in Greek legend, wife of Amphiaraüs and sister of Adrastus. She forced her husband into the battle of the SEVEN AGAINST THEBES when Polynices bribed her with the magic necklace of Harmonia. She later forced her son Alcmaeon into the war of the EPIGONI when Thersander, son of Polynices, bribed her with Harmonia's magic robe. When Alcmaeon learned the full truth of his mother's treachery, he killed her.

Eris (ē'rĭs), in Greek religion, goddess of strife. Angered at not being invited to the wedding of Peleus and Thetis, she threw down the apple of discord (see PARIS, in Greek mythology).

Eritrea (ĕrĭtrē'ə), province (1970 est. pop. 1,836,800), c.48,000 sq mi (124,320 sq km), N Ethiopia, on the Red Sea. ASMARA is the capital; other cities include Assab and Massawa, Ethiopia's chief ports. The southern part of the province is made up of a largely desert coastal strip c.30 mi (50 km) wide; in N Eritrea there is a narrower, level coastal zone adjoining a rugged inland plateau (3,000–8,000 ft/914–2,438 m high). Most of the province supports only a sparse population of pastoral nomads. The central plateau, however, has many fertile valleys where settled agriculture is pursued. Products of the province include citrus fruits, cereals, cotton, hides, and salt. There are pearl fisheries in the DAHLAK ARCHIPELAGO, located in the Red Sea. The province has little industry beyond food processing. Eritrea formed part of the ancient Ethiopian kingdom of Aksum until the 7th cent. Thereafter Ethiopia maintained an intermittent presence in the area until the mid-16th cent., when the Ottoman Empire gained control of much of the coastal region. Beginning in the mid-19th cent. Ethiopia struggled against Egypt and Italy for control of Eritrea. In the 1880s, Italy occupied the coastal areas around Assab and Massawa, and by 1890 had extended its territory enough to proclaim the colony of Eritrea (named after the Roman term for the Red Sea, *Mare erythraeum*). The colony was later the main base for Italy's conquest (1935–36) of Ethiopia. In World War II, Eritrea was captured (1941) by the British. Ethiopia had long demanded control of Eritrea on the ground of ethnic affinity, but Britain occupied Eritrea after the war and, beginning in 1949, administered it as a UN trust territory. In 1950 the United Nations decided that Eritrea was to be made independent as a federated part of Ethiopia, and in late 1952 this decision became effective. In late 1962 the Eritrean assembly voted to end the federal status and to unify Eritrea with Ethiopia. After 1962, Eritreans who opposed union carried on sporadic guerrilla warfare against Ethiopia. See S. H. Longrigg, *A Short History of Eritrea* (1945); G. K. Trevaskis, *Eritrea: A Colony in Transition* (1960); Ambaye Zekarias, *Land Tenure in Eritrea* (1966).

Erivan: see YEREVAN, USSR.

Erlach, Johann Bernhard Fischer von: see FISCHER VON ERLACH, JOHANN BERNHARD.

Erlander, Tage Fritiof (tä'gə frĭt'yəf ĕr'ländər), 1901–, Swedish socialist leader, prime minister of Sweden (1946–69). On the editorial staff of the encyclopedia *Svensk Upplagsbok* from 1929 to 1938, he was first elected to the Riksdag in 1933. He held several ministerial positions before 1946 and became a leading expert on education and social welfare. A Social Democrat, Erlander helped further the development of the Swedish socialist state. Although sympathetic to the West, Erlander preserved formal Swedish neutrality in the cold war. At his retirement he was succeeded as party leader and prime minister by Olaf Palme.

Erlangen (ĕr'läng-ən), city (1970 pop. 84,110), Bavaria, S West Germany, at the confluence of the Schwabach and Regnitz rivers. It is an industrial and transportation center. Manufactures include medical equipment, textiles, leather goods, and beer. Erlangen belonged to the bishopric of Bamberg from 1017 to 1361, when it was sold to Emperor Charles IV. Chartered in 1398, it passed (1402) to the Franconian branch of the house of Hohenzollern, under which it shared the history of Bayreuth. Industry began in Erlangen in the late 17th cent. with the settlement of Huguenot refugees from France. The city passed to Bavaria in 1810. Rebuilt after a devastating fire in 1706, the present city center has a predominantly baroque character; there are also modern industrial and residential sections. Erlangen is well known for its university (founded 1742 at Bayreuth and transferred to Erlangen in 1743). The philosopher Schelling and the theologian Schleiermacher taught at the university in the 19th cent.

Erlangen program: see GEOMETRY.

Erlanger, Joseph (ûr'lăng-ər), 1874–1965, American scientist, b. San Francisco, grad. Univ. of California (B.S., 1895), M.D. Johns Hopkins, 1899. For his contributions to physiology, especially his work on nerve action, he shared with Herbert Spencer Gasser the 1944 Nobel Prize in Physiology and Medicine. He was professor (1910–46) and (from 1946) professor emeritus of physiology at the medical school of Washington Univ., St. Louis. With H. S. Gasser he wrote *Electrical Signs of Nervous Activity* (1937).

Erlanger, city (1970 pop. 12,676), Kenton co., N central Ky.; inc. 1897. Its industries include metal fabrication and the manufacture of clothing, truck bodies, and electrical fixtures and supplies.

Erlau: see EGER, Hungary.

Erlenmeyer, Richard A. C. E. (ĕr'lənmī"ər), 1825–1909, German chemist. He studied at Giessen under Justus von Liebig and at Heidelberg under Friedrich Kekulé, both German chemists. Erlenmeyer was professor of chemistry at the Munich Polytechnic School from 1868 to 1883. His experimental work included the discovery and synthesis of several organic compounds, e.g., isobutyric acid (1865); in 1861 he invented the conical flask that bears his name. Among the first to adopt structural formulas based on valence, he proposed the modern naphthalene formula of two benzene rings sharing two carbon atoms. In 1880 he formulated the Erlenmeyer rule: All alcohols in which the hydroxyl group is attached directly to a double-bonded carbon atom become aldehydes or ketones.

Ermak: see YERMAK.

Ermanaric (ûrmăn'ərĭk), d. c.375, king of the Ostrogoths. He extended his power over other barbarian tribes and thus built up in eastern Europe an empire stretching from the Dneister River north to the Don and east to the head-waters of the Volga. He committed suicide as his empire was being overrun by the Huns. He was a legendary figure in medieval European literature, where his name appears variously as Ermenrichus and Hermeneric; in old Norse literature he was known as Jörmunrekkr.

Ermeland (ĕr'məlänt), **Ermland** (ĕrm'länt), or **Warmia** (wôr'mēə), historic region of East Prussia, extending far inland from the Baltic Sea. It was ceded to Poland in 1466 by the Teutonic Knights, passed to Prussia in 1772, and reverted to Poland after World War II.

ermine, name for a number of northern species of WEASEL having white coats in winter, and highly prized for their white fur. It most commonly refers to the white phase of *Mustela erminea,* called short-tailed weasel in North America and stoat in the Old World. The white pelts are made into wraps, coats, and trimmings. The black-tipped tails are used in the United States as ornament, and in Europe they were used with the ermine of royal robes.

Ermine Street, Saxon name for the Roman road in Britain that ran from London to Lincoln and York. It was one of the four main highways of Saxon England. The name is derived from the Earningas, a group of people who inhabited an area in Cambridgeshire through which the road passed. The road from Silchester to Gloucester was also called Ermine Street. See I. D. Margary, *Roman Roads in Britain* (3d ed. 1973).

Ermland: see ERMELAND.

Ernakulam (ĕrnä'ko͝oləm), city, Kerala state, SW India, near Cochin. Manufactures include mats, rope, glycerin, perfume, and soap. Ernakulam was the capital of the former Cochin state and has a Jewish community thought to have been founded in the 2d or 3d cent. A.D. Mattancheri Palace, on the city's outskirts, was built by the Portuguese. The Dutch established a trading post at Ernakulam in 1774.

Erne (ûrn), river, 72 mi (116 km) long, rising in Lough Gowna, Co. Longford, N Republic of Ireland. It flows NW through SW Northern Ireland, then back through the Republic before entering the Atlantic Ocean at Donegal Bay. Grazing predominates in the Erne basin; Enniskillen is the chief town. In Northern Ireland the river expands to form two large lakes—Upper Lough Erne (10 mi/16.1 km long) and Lower Lough Erne (18 mi/29 km long). An international flood-control scheme (completed 1959) controls the water level in the lakes. Hydroelectricity is produced along the 150-ft (46-m) drop in the river's course between Belleek and Ballyshannon; the lakes are a natural reservoir.

Ernest I, 1784–1844, duke of Saxe-Coburg-Gotha (see under SAXE-COBURG); brother of Leopold I of Belgium, uncle of Queen Victoria of England, and father of Victoria's consort, Prince Albert. He succeeded to the duchy of Coburg in 1806 and acquired Gotha in 1826.

Ernest Augustus, 1771–1851, king of Hanover (1837–51) and duke of Cumberland, fifth son of George III of England. At the accession of his niece Queen Victoria, the crowns of England and Hanover were separated, since succession in Hanover was only through the male line. Ernest Augustus had been associated with the reactionary Tories in England, and his reign in Hanover was ultraconservative. He rescinded the liberal constitution of 1833 and evoked the famous protest of seven GÖTTINGEN professors. The revolutionary outbreaks of 1848 forced him to allow revision of his constitution of 1840, but he returned to reactionary policies that were continued by his successor and son, George V.

Ernle, Rowland Edmund Prothero, 1st **Baron,** (prŏth'ərō, ûr'nəl), 1851–1937, British agriculturist, editor, and writer. He edited the *Quarterly Review* (1894–99) and was president of the Board of Agriculture (1916–19). Among his books are *Pioneers and Progress of English Farming* (1887), *Life and Correspondence of Dean Stanley* (1893), and *The Land and Its People* (1925). See his autobiography (1938).

Ernst, Max (mäks ĕrnst) 1891–, German painter. After World War I, Ernst joined the DADA movement in Paris and then became a founder of SURREALISM. Apart from the medium of COLLAGE, Ernst developed other devices to express his fantastic vision. In *frottage* he rubbed black chalk on paper held against various materials such as leaves, wood, and fabrics to achieve bizarre effects. A note of whimsy often characterizes his dreamlike landscapes. Other works reveal a satanic, allegorical imagination. *Two Children Are Threatened by a Nightingale* and several other works are in the Museum of Modern Art in New York City. See his *Beyond Painting* (1948); studies by John Russell (1967) and U. M. Schneede (1973).

Erode (ĕrōd'), city (1971 pop. 103,704), Tamil Nadu state, S India, on the Cauvery River. The city is located in a cotton-growing region, and its chief industry is cotton ginning. Erode was the site of much fighting during the British wars with the MAHRATTAS.

Eros, in astronomy: see ASTEROID.

Eros (ĕr'ŏs, ĕr'-), in Greek religion, god of love. He was the personification of love in all its manifestations, including physical passion at its strongest, tender, romantic love, and playful, sportive love. According to some legends he was one of the oldest of the gods, born from Chaos and personifying creative power and harmony. In most legends he was the son of Aphrodite and Ares and was represented as a winged youth armed with bow and arrows. In Greek poetry Eros was often a willful and unsympathetic god, carelessly dispensing the frenzies and agonies of love. At Thespiae and at Athens he was worshiped as a god of fertility. In Roman myth, where he was called Cupid or Amor, he was represented as a naked, winged child, the son and companion of Venus. Eros was sometimes attended by his brother, Anteros, who was said to be the avenger of unrequited love or the opposer of love. See also PSYCHE.

erosion (ĭrō'zhən), general term for the processes by which the surface of the earth is constantly being worn away, in which the principal agents are running water, waves, glaciers, and wind. Streams have the power to wear away their own channels. The nature of stream erosion depends in part on the materials making up the channel. One form of erosion is by hydraulic action, in which the shearing force of the current is directly exerted on the channel bed. While hydraulic action can erode uncemented river sediment or weakly cemented sedimentary rock, it is ineffective on hard rock. However, all running water gathers and transports particles of soil or fragments of rock, formed by WEATHERING, and every stream carries in suspension or rolls along its bottom material received from its tributaries or detached from its own banks. These particles in transport strike against the bedrock of the stream channel, literally grinding it away. Erosion by running water frequently enlarges slight depressions to form gullies, ravines, and ultimately valleys, widens and alters the courses of rivers, and reduces hilly areas to peneplains, or nearly level surfaces. Eroded materials either find their way to the deep sea or are deposited as alluvium. It has been established that the basin of the Mississippi River is being reduced by erosion at the rate of 1 ft (30 cm) in about 9,000 years. Seacoasts are eroded by ocean waves, which detach loose or nonresistant material and wear the rock by both the force of their own impact and the abrasive action of the detritus they carry. A GLACIER erodes by plucking off loose rocks and by its abrasive action on the surface over which it passes. The wind can drive sand and other particles against rocks, abrading them. In arid regions the wind may transport sand in the form of a DUNE. The continuous washing away of the fine rich topsoil of farmland is a problem in many parts of the United States, particularly in the Mississippi and other regions of the South and in California, Oregon, Washington, and Montana. Erosion is becoming increasingly more common in suburban areas, where careless developers strip vast areas of trees and plant cover before building. Strip mining is another major cause of erosion, especially in hilly country, often making land unsuitable for replanting for many years. Among the methods of preventing soil erosion are reforestation, maintenance of fallow strips, terracing, underdraining, ditching, deep plowing, and plowing across slopes rather than up and down. See CONSERVATION OF NATURAL RESOURCES.

Erpenius, Thomas (ûrpē'nēəs), 1584–1624, Dutch Orientalist, whose name in Dutch was Van Erpe. Erpenius was one of the most celebrated scholars of his day and wrote several grammars of Near Eastern languages, notably one of Arabic.

Errett, Isaac (ĕr'ĭt), 1820–88, American minister of the Disciples of Christ, b. New York City. After years of pastoral and evangelistic work in pioneer towns of Ohio and Michigan, he became (1866) the first editor of the *Christian Standard* and made it the denomination's foremost periodical. See biography by J. S. Lamar (1893).

error, in law: see APPEAL.

Ersch, Johann Samuel (yō'hän zä'mo͞oēl ĕrsh), 1766–1828, German encyclopedist, first editor of the great encyclopedia known as Ersch and Gruber's. At his death, 17 volumes had been completed. As editor he was succeeded by Johann Gottfried Gruber, his associate. Ersch is considered the father of German bibliography. He held professorships in the universities of Jena and Halle and was librarian of each.

Erse (ûrs), synonym for Irish and sometimes also for Scottish Gaelic. See CELTIC LANGUAGES.

Erskine, Ebenezer (ûr'skĭn), 1680–1754, founder of the Secession Church in Scotland, minister of Portmoak, Kinross-shire (1703) and of Stirling (1731). He upheld the right of the people to make their own choice of pastors, for which he was censured, suspended, and deposed (1733). With three other ministers he set up an Associate Synod, which was the origin of the Secession Church. In 1736 they reaffirmed their separation, but they were not ejected from their churches until 1740. After the split within the Associate Synod over the religious oaths required of burgesses of Scottish cities, Erskine became a leader of the BURGHERS.

Erskine, John, 1509–91, Scottish reformer, called Erskine of Dun. After several years on the Continent he returned to Scotland, where he introduced the study of Greek in Scottish schools. He was the friend and firm supporter of John KNOX and George WISHART. Erskine was a witness at the marriage (1557) of Mary Queen of Scots to Francis II of France and a participant in the coronation (1567) of James VI at Stirling. As a member of a noble family and a person of gracious manner, he was a valuable intermediary between the reforming party and Mary and, later, James. Although a layman, he was several times moderator of the general assembly of the Scottish Reformed Church. In 1578 he took part in compiling the *Second Book of Discipline* and in 1579 became a member of the king's council.

Erskine, John, 1695–1768, Scottish jurist and professor (1737–65) of Scots law in the Univ. of Edinburgh. He is best known for his authoritative *Institutes of the Law of Scotland* (1754). His *Principles of the Law of Scotland* was published posthumously in 1773.

Erskine, John, 1721?–1803, Scottish theologian. A leader of the evangelical party in the Church of Scotland, he was minister successively at Kirkintilloch, Culross, and New Greyfriars Church, Edinburgh, until, in 1767, he became the colleague of Dr. William Robertson at Old Greyfriars. He corresponded with many representatives of foreign churches, including Jonathan Edwards, whose works he edited and published in Great Britain.

Erskine, John, 1879–1951, American educator, author, and musician, b. New York City, grad. Columbia (B.A., 1900; Ph.D., 1903). He taught first at Amherst (1903–9) and then at Columbia, becoming professor of English in 1916. Among his many works on literature and music are *The Literary Discipline* (1923), *The Delight of Great Books* (1928), and *What is Music?* (1944); he also edited scholarly works and served as coeditor of *The Cambridge History of American Literature.* He is best known for his delightful, satiric novels based on legend, including *The Private Life of Helen of Troy* (1925) and *Galahad* (1926). In his late 40s he began appearing as a concert pianist and from 1928 to 1937 was president of the Juilliard School of Music. See his autobiographical *The Memory of Certain Persons* (1947), *My Life as a Writer* (1951), and *My Life in Music* (1950, repr. 1973).

Erskine, Robert, 1735–80, geographer and surveyor general to the American Revolutionary army, b. Dunfermline, Scotland. His several hundred detailed maps of the region W of the Hudson River, showing roads, buildings, and other details, were of much use to Gen. George Washington and are of great value to local historians. See biography by A. H. Heusser (1928, repr. 1966).

Erskine, Thomas, 1st **Baron Erskine,** 1750–1823, British jurist, b. Edinburgh. He was admitted to the bar in 1778. His eloquence and forensic skill won Erskine an enormous practice, during which he made notable contributions to commercial law. He is chiefly remembered for his defense of radicals at the time of the French Revolution, when prosecutions for sedition and libel were numerous. He defended Thomas Paine's publication of *The Rights of Man* against a charge of sedition, and his defense of the dean of St. Asaph led to a liberal revision (1792) of the laws of libel. Erskine served (1783–84, 1790–1806) in Parliament and was (1806–7) lord chancellor, but his service in office was undistinguished in comparison to his success as a trial lawyer. He was elevated to the peerage in 1806.

Eruli: see GERMANS.

Ervin, Samuel James, 1896–, U.S. Senator (1954–74), b. Morganton, N.C. Admitted to the bar in 1919, he became a distinguished jurist, serving as a judge on a county criminal court (1935–37), the North Carolina superior court (1937–43), and the state supreme court (1948–54), before being appointed (1954) to the U.S. Senate. Elected for a full term in 1956, Ervin joined the coalition of Southern Democrats and conservative Republicans who supported a large defense establishment while opposing civil rights and social welfare legislation. Becoming (1961) chairman of the subcommittee on constitutional rights of the Senate Judiciary Committee, he won a reputation as a civil libertarian. Ervin received (1973) national attention as chairman of the Senate Select Committee to Investigate Presidential Campaign Practices, which held televised hearings on the WATERGATE AFFAIR and the financing of the 1972 presidential election. See biography by P. R. Clancy (1974).

Erymanthian boar (ĕrĭmăn'thēən), in Greek mythology, a huge boar that ravaged the environs of Mt. Erymanthos. As his third labor, Hercules captured it by chasing it into deep snow and binding it with heavy chains.

Erymanthos, Erímanthos, or **Erymanthus** (ĕrĭmăn'thəs), mountain group, S Greece, in NW Peloponnesus, on the border of Achaea, Arcadia, and Elis. The highest peak (c.7,295 ft/2,220 m) is Mt. Erymanthos, also known as Mt. Olonos. In mythology the mountains were the haunt of the Erymanthian boar that Hercules captured.

Eryri, Wales: see SNOWDON.

erysipelas (ĕrəsĭp'ələs), acute infection of the skin characterized by a sharply demarcated, shiny red swelling, accompanied by high fever and a feeling of general illness. The causative agent is the hemolytic streptococcus, which often enters the body through a break in the skin. Erysipelas affects the skin of the face so frequently that when it strikes other parts of the body, it may often be misdiagnosed. Bacteremia (blood poisoning) and pneumonia are the most common complications. Erysipelas is a highly contagious disease that was formerly dangerous to life; however, it can now be quickly controlled by antibiotic therapy.

erythema (ĕr"əthē'mə), more or less diffuse redness of the skin due to concentration of an abnormally large amount of blood within the small vessels of the skin (hyperemia), as in burns. Erythema nodosum is often associated with systemic diseases such as tuberculosis and rheumatic fever. Tender, bright red, slightly elevated nodules develop along the shins. Erythema multiforme can have a number of causes, including viral and bacterial infection, chronic disease of the visceral organs, or allergic reactions to drugs.

Erythraean Sea (ĕrĭthrē'ən), name of unclear origin anciently applied to the Indian Ocean, later to the Arabian Gulf, and finally to the Red Sea.

erythroblastosis fetalis (ərĭth"rəblăstō'sĭs), hemolytic disease of a newborn infant caused by BLOOD GROUP incompatibility between mother and child. Although the RH FACTOR is responsible for the most severe cases of erythroblastosis fetalis, the disease may be produced by any of the other blood group antigens, such as those of the AOB system. With an Rh-negative mother and an Rh-positive father, the possibility exists that the fetus will be Rh positive. Microhemorrhages during gestation permit fetal red blood cells to enter the maternal circulation, causing an immunologic reaction that leads to sensitization of the mother against the Rh factor. Maternal antibodies against fetal red blood cell antigens pass through the placenta into the fetus, where an excessive destruction of fetal red blood cells occurs. When such hemolysis begins during pregnancy, stillbirth may result. While there is little danger of damage to the fetus during the first pregnancy, by the second pregnancy sufficient antibodies will have accumulated in the mother's bloodstream to cause increasing danger of hemolytic disease. The formation of maternal anti-Rh antibodies has been largely prevented in the United States by the injection of human immune globulin into the mother within 72 hours after delivery. This globulin contains antibodies against the Rh-positive fetal red blood cells, destroying them before the maternal blood stream reacts by producing its own anti-Rh antibodies. Thus during the next pregnancy there will be few, if any, antibodies in the maternal bloodstream to destroy the fetal Rh-positive blood cells.

erythrocyte (ĭrĭth'rəsīt"): see BLOOD.

erythromycin (ĭrĭth"rōmī'sĭn), any of several related antibiotic drugs produced by bacteria of the genus *Streptomyces* (see ANTIBIOTIC). Erythromycin is most effective against gram-positive bacteria such as pneumococci, streptococci, and some staphylococci (see GRAM'S STAIN). The antibiotic also has some effect on gram-negative bacteria and some fungi. Erythromycin inhibits protein synthesis in susceptible microorganisms. It is used to treat such diseases as pneumonia caused by fungi, and streptococcus and syphilis infections, especially where the patient is allergic to penicillin.

Eryx (ĕr'ĭks), ancient city, W Sicily, Italy. Long a source of conflict between Carthage and Syracuse, it was destroyed (c.260 B.C.) by the Carthaginians in the First Punic War. Its temple of Venus Erycina was an important religious shrine; the temple area was excavated in 1936. The most notable remains are Cyclopean walls, some with Phoenician inscriptions. The site is now occupied by the village of Erice.

Erzberg (ĕrts'bĕrkh), peak, 3,531 ft (1,076 m) high, in Styria, central Austria. Rising above the town of Eisenerz, the Erzberg is almost literally a mountain of iron. Its rich iron ore (about 35% pure iron) is mined on the surface in the summer. Some of the mines have been worked for more than 1,000 years.

Erzberger, Matthias (mätē'äs ĕrts'bĕrgər), 1875–1921, German public official. He was a leader of the left wing of the Catholic Center party in the Reichstag from 1903. Early in World War I, he supported an annexationist policy, but in 1917 he led the fight for the Reichstag peace resolution. He helped build the democratic coalition that pressed for more parliamentary government. He joined (Oct., 1918) the cabinet of MAXIMILIAN, PRINCE OF BADEN and headed the German delegation that signed the armistice. A member of the first republican cabinet under Philipp Scheidemann, he pressed for acceptance of the Treaty of Versailles. When Scheidemann resigned (June, 1919) rather than sign the treaty, Erzberger joined the new cabinet as vice chancellor and finance minister. He introduced drastic reforms, centralizing tax collection and bringing all railroads under national control. His policies were opposed by conservatives and reactionaries, who also despised him for his signing of the humiliating 1918 armistice. When an old rival, former finance minister Karl Helfferich, ruthlessly attacked Erzberger in a pamphlet questioning his competence and veracity, Erzberger sued. When the court found some of the charges libelous but—probably unwarrantedly—sustained others, Erzberger resigned. See Klaus Epstein, *Matthias Erzberger and the Dilemma of German Democracy* (1971).

Erzerum, Turkey: see ERZURUM.

Erzgebirge (ĕrts'gəbĭr"gə) [Ger.,=ore mountains], Czech *Krušné Hory,* mountain range, along the Czechoslovakian-East German border, extending c.95 mi (150 km) from the Fichtelgebirge in the southwest to the Elbe River in the northeast. It reaches its highest point (4,080 ft/1,244 m) in Klínovec (Ger. *Keilberg*) in Czechoslovakia. The Ohře and Bílina rivers drain most of the range. From the 14th cent. to the 19th cent. silver and iron were mined extensively in the Erzgebirge, notably at Jáchymov. At present, the chief ores mined are uranium, lead, zinc, wolframite, tin, copper, bismuth, sulfur, arsenic, and antimony. Coal and lignite mines are also exploited. The Erzgebirge has many famous mineral springs (notably at Karlovy Vary and Teplice-Šanov, both in Czechoslovakia) and is an important industrial area, particularly in the manufacture of machinery and textiles. Embroidering and toy making have long been traditional home industries. In 1938 the Czech part of the Erzgebirge was transferred to Germany by the Munich Pact. It was restored to Czechoslovakia in 1945.

Erzurum (ĕr'zo͝oro͞om") or **Erzerum** (-'zə-), city (1970 pop. 134,655), capital of Erzurum prov., E Turkey. It is an agricultural trade center and a railroad center. Manufactures include processed foods, cement, and metal goods. Although its origins are obscure, the city was known in the 5th cent. A.D. as Theodosiopolis, an important Byzantine frontier fortress. It was later held by various peoples, including the Armenians, Persians, and Seljuk Turks, before being captured by the Ottoman Turks in the early 16th cent. The first Turkish Nationalist congress was held there in 1919. It is the site of Atatürk Univ.

Es, chemical symbol of the element EINSTEINIUM.

Esaias (ēzā'yəs), variant of ISAIAH.

Esalin Institute: see GROUP PSYCHOTHERAPY.

Esar-Haddon (ē"sär-hăd'ən), king of ancient Assyria (681–668 B.C.), son of SENNACHERIB. Immediately upon ascending the throne he had to put down serious revolts and defeat the Chaldaeans. He was successful in both enterprises. One of the most powerful of the Assyrian kings, Esar-Haddon greatly extended Assyrian conquests. Most important was his conquest (673-670 B.C.) of Egypt, where, after initial difficulties, he took Memphis. He deposed the defeated Tirhakah and put Necho in power. Esar-Haddon fought against Elam and was still warring when he died on the way to subdue an Egyptian revolt. He was succeeded by Assurbanipal.

Esau (ē'sô) [Heb.,=hairy], son of Isaac, who sold his birthright to his younger twin, JACOB, for pottage and who was tricked by Jacob out of his father's blessing. Also known as EDOM [Heb.,=ruddy], the disinherited Esau settled on Mt. Seir, which became the home of his descendants, the Edomites, a tribe consistently hostile to the Jews. Esau in tradition is represented as a rough man, and he was deemed unworthy to inherit the mission of Abraham. The New Testament calls Esau profane. Yet he was beloved of God and his descendants were highly regarded. Gen. 25-28; 32; 33; 36; Deut. 2.4,5; Joshua 24.4; Jer. 49.8-22; Heb. 12.15-17.

Esbjerg (ĕs'byĕr), city (1970 com. pop. 76,428), Ribe co., SW Denmark, a port on the North Sea. It is a commercial and industrial center, with major fisheries. Esbjerg's main development came after the construction (late 19th cent.) of its port.

Escalante, Silvestre Vélez de (sĕlvā'strā vā'lāth dā āskālän'tā), fl. 1769-79, Spanish explorer in the American Southwest and Far West, a Franciscan missionary. He was in charge of Pueblo missions in present New Mexico and led the expedition that hoped to establish overland communications with Monterey in Alta California. A preliminary journey in 1775 took him to the Hopi towns in N Arizona, and in 1776 he led an expedition from Santa Fe that crossed land that is now Colorado and part of Utah, reaching Utah Lake—the first white men known to have seen the Utah country. Mountain snows in the Sierra Nevada prevented him from going on to California, and with great hardship the party returned to Santa Fe. Escalante kept a singularly accurate journal, which was signed also by his associate and superior, Francisco Atanasio Domínguez. See Herbert Bolton, ed., *Pageant in the Wilderness* (1951).

Escanaba (ĕskənä'bə), resort city (1970 pop. 15,368), seat of Delta co., W Upper Peninsula, N Mich., on Little Bay de Noc; settled 1852, inc. 1883. It is a railroad and manufacturing center, and from its fine harbor large amounts of ore are shipped. Among its varied manufactures are cranes, paper, wood, and plastics. The Upper Peninsula State Fair is held there annually. A junior college is in Escanaba.

escape velocity, the velocity a body must be given in order to escape the gravitational hold of some other larger body, e.g., the earth, moon, or sun. A body given less than the escape velocity will fall back toward the surface of the larger body; a body given a velocity equal to or greater than the escape velocity will still be attracted by the larger body, but this force will not be sufficient to cause it to return. Escape velocity depends on the mass of the larger body and the distance of the smaller body from its center, being proportional to the square root of the ratio of these two quantities. The velocity of escape from the earth at its surface is about 7 mi (11.3 km) per sec, or 25,000 mi per hr; from the moon's surface it is 1.5 mi (2.4 km) per sec; and for a body at the earth's distance from the sun to escape from the sun's gravitation, the velocity must be 26 mi (41 km) per sec.

escarole (ĕs"kərōl'): see CHICORY.

escarpment or **scarp,** long cliff, bluff, or steep slope, caused usually by geologic faulting (see FAULT) or by erosion of tilted rock layers. An example of a fault scarp is the north face of the San Jacinto Mts. in California. Examples of erosional escarpments include the Palisades along the Hudson River and the long break separating the coastal region from the inland area in Texas, roughly paralleling the coast.

Escaut, river: see SCHELDT.

Esch, John Jacob (ĕsh), 1861-1941, U.S. Congressman and Federal administrator, b. Norwalk, Wis. A lawyer in La Crosse, he became a member of the House of Representatives in 1899 and served until 1921, distinguishing himself as co-author of the Transportation Act (Esch-Cummins Act) of 1920. He was a member of the Interstate Commerce Commission from 1921 to 1928, when his renomination was rejected by the Senate because he allegedly was responsible for rates favoring Pennsylvania coal mines and discriminating against Southern mines. Esch was president of the American Peace Society from 1930 to 1938.

Eschenbach, Wolfram von: see WOLFRAM VON ESCHENBACH.

Escher, Maurits Corneille (môr'ĭts kôrnā'yə ĕsh'ər), 1898-1970, Dutch artist. Primarily a graphic artist, Escher composed works notable for their irony, often with impossible perspectives rendered with mechanical verisimilitude. He created visual riddles, playing with the pictorially logical and the visually impossible.

Escholtz Islands: see BIKINI.

eschscholtzia (ĕshōlts'ēə): see POPPY.

Esch-sur-Alzette (ĕsh-sür-älzĕt') or **Esch,** city (1970 est. pop. 27,600), SW Grand Duchy of Luxembourg, on the Alzette River. It is an industrial center and a rail junction. Manufactures include iron and steel, cement, tar products, and fertilizer.

Eschweiler (ĕsh'vīlər), city (1970 pop. 38,660), North Rhine-Westphalia, W West Germany, near Aachen. The center of a coal basin, it has iron and steel mills. Other manufactures include bricks, chemicals, and textiles. Known in the 9th cent., Eschweiler passed to the duchy of Jülich in 1420 and to Prussia in 1815. Noteworthy structures include the Church of Saints Peter and Paul (dating partly from the 12th cent.) and a 15th-century castle.

Escobedo, Juan de (hwän dā āskōbā'thō), d. 1578, Spanish politician, secretary to John of Austria in the Netherlands. He was murdered while on a mission in Madrid. According to one theory the murderer was Antonio PÉREZ.

Escoffier, Georges Auguste (zhôrzh ôgüst' ĕskôfyā'), 1846-1935, French authority on cooking. Regarded by some as the greatest chef in history, he went to work at the age of 13 in his uncle's kitchen in Nice. Six years later he became chef at the Reine Blanche in Paris, which was to become the Moulin Rouge. He was later chef at the Grand Hotel in Monte Carlo and finally at the Ritz Hotel in London, where he created some of his most famous dishes. In 1920, the "king of cooks," as Escoffier was known, was awarded the French Legion of Honor.

Escondido (ĕskəndē'dō), city (1970 pop. 36,792), San Diego co., S Calif.; inc. 1888. Located in a citrus-fruit- and grape-growing valley, Escondido has fruit-packing houses and one of the world's largest avocado processing plants. Textiles and ball point ink are among its chief manufactures. A huge wild animal park is under construction just south of the city. To the east is San Pasqual Battlefield State Monument, commemorating the battle fought in Dec., 1846, between U.S. forces under Gen. Stephen W. Kearny and Californians under Andrés Pico.

Escorial (ĕskôr'ēəl, Span. āskōrēäl') or **Escurial** (ĕskyŏŏr'ēəl), monastery and palace, in New Castile, central Spain, near Madrid. One of the finest edifices in Europe, it was built (1563-84) as the monastery of San Lorenzo del Escorial by Philip II to commemorate the Spanish victory over the French at Saint-Quentin (1557). The somber and massive pile of granite buildings, including monastery, church, royal palace, mausoleum, college, and library, form a quadrangle with towers rising from the corners. The Escorial was begun by the architect Juan Bautista de Toledo and finished by his pupil Juan de Herrera; it was decorated by Claudio Coello, Luca Giordano, and other noted artists. The Escorial has an art collection that includes paintings by Velázquez, Ribera, El Greco, and Tintoretto.

Escudero, Vicente (vĕthān'tā ās"kōōthā'rō), 1892?-, Spanish dancer. Escudero ran away from home at 15 to live with the gypsies in Granada, where he learned the native FLAMENCO dances. After a vagabond tour through Europe, he toured the United States in 1932. Returning to Spain, he formed his own company, which ultimately failed. Escudero, often considered the greatest of the flamenco dancers, was noted for his fiery execution; his farrucca (gypsy dance) was especially well received.

Escurial: see ESCORIAL.

Esdraelon (ĕs"drəē'lən) [Gr. for Jezreel], fertile plain, c.200 sq mi (520 sq km), extending southeast c.25 mi (40 km) between the coastal plain, near Mt. Carmel, and the Jordan River valley, N Israel; separates the hills of Galilee on the north from those of Samaria to the south. The plain is drained in the west by the Kishon River and in the east by the Harod. Once a swampy, malarial lowland, Esdraelon has been drained and turned into one of Israel's most fertile and densely populated regions; a great variety of crops are produced there in abundance. Afula is the economic center of the region. Since ancient times the plain has been a battleground, especially around Megiddo. Esdraelon is also called the plain of Jezreel or of Megiddo.

Esdras (ĕz'drəs) [Gr. from Heb. EZRA], name of two pseudepigraphic texts, included in the Western canon and the canon of the Septuagint, but placed in the Apocrypha in the Authorized Version, where they are called First and Second Esdras. The Western canon calls Ezra and Nehemiah First and Second Esdras respectively, and the terms Third and Fourth Esdras are then used for the pseudepigraphic books. Greek Bibles use the name First Esdras for Ezra and Nehemiah (taken as one book as in the original Hebrew canon) and Second and Third Esdras for the pseudepigraphic books. Below the pseudepigrapha are called Third and Fourth Esdras. Third Esdras is mainly a Greek translation of several parts of the Bible (3 Esdras 1=2 Chron. 35.1-36.21; 3 Esdras 2.1-15=Ezra 1; 3 Esdras 2.16-30=Ezra 4.7-24; 3 Esdras 3-5.6 not found elsewhere; 3 Esdras 5.7-73=Ezra 2-4.5; 3 Esdras 6-9.36=Ezra 5-10; 3 Esdras 9.37-55=Neh. 7.73-8.12). Third Esdras antedates 100 B.C. Third and Fourth Esdras is a Jewish apocalyptic work of which the bulk is a series of visions and revelations to Ezra in the style of the book of Revelation. This is considered by many the best Jewish apocalypse. The original language must have been Hebrew or Aramaic, from which a Greek translation was made, but none of these versions is extant. Most critics date Fourth Esdras as a whole after A.D. 100. Third Esdras has enjoyed a relatively greater prestige in Christendom than Fourth Esdras. See also APOCRYPHA. For Fourth Esdras, see W. O. E. Oesterley, *II Esdras* (1933).

Esek (ē'sĕk), one of Isaac's wells. Gen. 26.20.

Esenin, Sergei Aleksandrovich: see YESENIN.

Esfahan (ĕsfähän') or **Isfahan** (ĭs'fəhän), anc. *Aspadana,* city (1966 pop. 424,045), capital of Esfahan prov., central Iran, on the Zayandeh River. An ancient and picturesque city, rich in history, Esfahan has long been known for its fine carpets, hand-printed textiles, and metalwork, chiefly silver filigree. It has modern textile and steel mills. A noteworthy city in Sassanid times, Esfahan passed to the Arabs in the mid-7th cent. and served as a provincial capital. In the 11th cent. it was captured by the Seljuk Turks, who made it (1051) the capital of their empire. In the early 13th cent. Esfahan was taken by the Mongols. Tamerlane conquered the city in 1388 and, after its inhabitants rebelled, slaughtered c.70,000 persons in revenge; it is said that he built a large hill with the skulls of the dead. Under Shah Abbas I, who made (1598) Esfahan his capital, the city was embellished with many fine buildings—notably the beautiful imperial mosque, one of the masterpieces of world architecture; the lovely Lutfullah mosque; and a great royal palace. Shah Abbas founded the Julfa quarter, located across the Zayandeh River, by transferring Armenians from N Persia to that section. At its zenith, under the Safavid dynasty in the 17th cent., Esfahan had a population of c.600,000, making it one of the world's great cities of the time. However, the city declined rapidly after it was captured (1723) by the Afghans, who massacred most of its inhabitants. Russian troops occupied Esfahan in 1916. The city is the site of the Univ. of Esfahan. The name also appears as Ispahan.

Esh-baal (ĕsh-bā'əl, ĕsh'-bāəl): see ISH-BOSHETH.

Eshban (ĕsh'băn), Horite. Gen. 36.26; 1 Chron. 1.41.

Eshcol (ĕsh'kŏl), Amorite ally of Abraham. Gen. 14.13, 24.

Eshean (ē'shēən, ĕsh'-, ĕshē'-), unidentified city, near Hebron. Joshua 15.52.

Eshek (ē'shĕk), Benjamite. 1 Chron. 8.39.

Esher, Reginald Baliol Brett, 2d **Viscount** (bāl'yəl, ē'shər), 1852-1930, English historian and government official. After sitting in Parliament (1880-85) as a Liberal, he thereafter preferred to exercise his influence from behind the scenes and withdrew from active politics. He succeeded to the peerage in 1899. As deputy governor (later governor) of Windsor Castle (1901-30), he managed the royal household for 30 years. He was given access to Queen Victoria's papers, from which he edited, with A. C. Benson, *The Correspondence of Queen Victoria* (1907). He was offered many public offices, among them the viceroyalty of India and the secretaryship for war, but refused them all. His most important service was in the furtherance of army reforms before World War I. He wrote works on King Edward VII (1914) and Lord Kitchener (1921). See his journals and letters (ed. by his sons, M. V. Brett and Oliver Brett, Viscount Esher, 4 vol., 1934-38).

Esher, urban district (1971 pop. 64,186), Surrey, SE England. It is a largely residential suburb of London. Wolsey's Tower (a gatehouse), is in the district; it is the remnant of Esher Place, which was founded by William Waynflete and occupied by Cardinal Wolsey.

Eshkalon (ĕsh'kələn), variant of ASHKELON.

Eshkol, Levi (lā'vē ĕsh'kôl), 1895-1969, Israeli statesman, third prime minister of Israel, b. Ukraine; originally named Levi Shkolnik. In World War I he served in the Jewish Legion, which supported the British forces in Palestine. A leader in the Histradrut (General Federation of Jewish Labor) and the Mapai party, he served as Israel's minister of finance from 1952 to 1963, when he became prime minister. In 1965 he was challenged from within the Mapai party by David BEN-GURION in a dispute over government policy. The party supported Eshkol, at which time Ben-Gurion and his followers, including Moshe Dayan, split from Mapai to form the Rafi party. Just prior to the Six-Day War (June, 1967), amid pressure for a more militant posture toward the Arab countries, Eshkol expanded the base of his coalition cabinet by including two new parties, Rafi and the right-wing Gahal; Rafi was represented by Moshe Dayan, who took over the ministry of defense. Eshkol died in office in 1969. See his state papers, ed. by H. M. Christman (1969); biography by T. C. F. Prittie (1969).

Eshtaol (ĕsh'tāōl), unidentified city of SW Palestine. Joshua 15.33; 19.41; Judges 13.25; 16.31; 18.2,8,11.

Eshtemoa (ĕsh'tēmō'ə). **1** Judahite. 1 Chron. 4.19. **2** City, S Palestine, near Hebron in the mountains. Joshua 21.14; 1 Sam. 30.28; 1 Chron. 4.17; 6.57. It is called **Eshtemoh** (-mō') in Joshua 15.50. Ancient ruins mark the site.

Eshton (ĕsh'tən), Judahite. 1 Chron. 4.11,12.

esker, long, narrow, winding ridge of stratified sand-and-gravel DRIFT. Eskers, many miles long and resembling abandoned railway embankments, occur in Scandinavia, Ireland, Scotland, and New England; they arose from deposition of sediment in the beds of streams flowing through or beneath glaciers.

Eskilstuna (ĕ'skĭlstü"nä), city (1970 pop. 85,341), Södermanland co., SE Sweden, between lakes Hjälmaren and Mälaren. Named after Eskil, an 11th-century English missionary who was martyred, the city was chartered (1659) by Charles X, who founded a gun factory there. This factory became the nucleus of an expanding steel and tool industry, which has made Eskilstuna the rival of Sheffield, England, and Solingen, West Germany, in the production of cutlery. Diesel engines and heavy machinery are also manufactured. There is a technical college in the city. The statesman Axel Oxenstierna (1583-1654) is buried at the nearby Jader church.

Eskimo (ĕs'kəmō) [Algonquian,=eaters of raw meat], native inhabitant of the coastline from the Bering Sea to Greenland and of the Chukchi Peninsula in NE Siberia. The present Eskimo population is approximately 70,000, with about 30,000 in Greenland, 22,000 in Alaska, 16,000 in Canada, and 1,100 in Siberia. The decline of blood feuds and INFANTICIDE, formerly common among the Eskimo, may account, in part, for a recent population increase. Most of the Greenland Eskimo have mixed with the white population, but elsewhere the Eskimo have tended to remain of pure stock. Despite their wide dispersal, the Eskimo are surprisingly uniform in language, physical type, and culture, and, as a group, they are distinct in these traits from all neighbors. They speak dialects of the same language, Eskimo, which is a major branch of the Eskimo-Aleut family of languages (see ALEUT). Their Mongoloid features—unusual facial breadth and head height—suggest an Asian origin. Their eastern distribution is relatively recent—the first Eskimo known to the Norse settlers in Greenland appeared in the 13th cent. Their adjustment to a severe environment has perhaps been equaled by no other group. Sea mammals provide them with food, clothing, illuminating and cooking oil, tools, and weapons; the skill required to secure these necessities places the Eskimo among the foremost hunters of the world. Fish and caribou are next in importance in their economy. The practice of eating raw meat, disapproved of by their Indian neighbors, provides their limited diet with essential nutritional elements that cooking would destroy. Except for a small group of Caribou Eskimo living in central Canada, they are a littoral people who rove inland in the summer for freshwater fishing and game hunting. Tents of caribou skins or sealskins provide adequate summer dwellings; in colder seasons, shelter is constructed of sod, driftwood, or sometimes stone, placed over excavated floors. The snow hut, or IGLOO, is seldom used. The dogsled is used for the hauling of heavy loads over long distances, made necessary by the Eskimo's nomadic hunting life. Their skin canoe, known as a kayak, in experienced hands is one of the most highly maneuverable small craft ever invented. Their innumerable hunting devices and their clothing show an ingenuity essential to survival in such a cold climate. The Eskimo possess a well-developed art and are skilled artisans in bone, ivory, antler, and stone. They live in small bands, in voluntary association under a leader recognized for his superior ability to provide for the group. Only the most personal property is considered private; any equipment reverts through disuse to those who have need for it. In the traditional Eskimo economy the division of labor between the sexes was severe; men constructed homes and hunted, while the women took care of the homes. Their religion has a rich mythology, and shamanism has also been practiced. The native food supply has been reduced through the use of firearms, but, as a result of increased contact with other cultures, the Eskimo are no longer solely dependent on that source. See Peter Freuchen, *Book of the Eskimos* (1961); R. K. Nelson, *Hunters of the Northern Ice* (1969); Kai Birket-Smith, *The Eskimos* (rev. ed. 1971); Duncan Pryde, *Nunaga* (1972).

Eskimo-Aleut, family of American Indian languages consisting of Aleut (spoken on the Aleutian Islands and the Kodiak Peninsula) and Eskimo (spoken in Alaska, Canada, Greenland, and Siberia). Aleut is the tongue of several thousand people, and Eskimo is native to about 50,000. There are a few varieties of the Eskimo language. Eskimo and Aleut have enough similarities to justify the theory that they are descendants of a single ancestor language. A striking and important feature of both tongues is polysynthesism (see AMERICAN INDIAN LANGUAGES). In a polysynthetic language, a one-word unit composed of a number of word elements can convey the meaning of an entire sentence in an Indo-European language. Eskimo and Aleut make great use of suffixes, but almost never of prefixes. Internal vowel changes are rare. Both languages are highly inflected. The difference between transitive and intransitive verbs is clearly shown. Three numbers are found—singular, dual, and plural. Phonetically, there are three main vowels in Eskimo, and from 13 to 20 consonants, the number varying according to the dialect. In earlier times the Eskimos had only pictographic writing. Since the 18th cent., however, the Eskimos of Greenland, Labrador, and Alaska have used an adaptation of the Roman alphabet, introduced by missionaries. The Eskimos of modern Siberia and the Aleut-speaking groups employ the Cyrillic alphabet. See R. H. Geoghegan, *The Aleut Language* (1944); Knut Bergslund, *A Grammatical Outline of the Eskimo Language of West Greenland* (1955) and *Aleut Dialects of Atha and Attu* (1959); L. L. Hammerich, *The Eskimo Language* (1970).

Eskişehir (ĕskē'shĕhĕr"), city (1970 pop. 216,330), capital of Eskişehir prov., W central Turkey. An industrial center, its manufactures include refined sugar, cement, railroad equipment, textiles, and meerschaum products. It is noted for its hot mineral springs. Godfrey of Bouillon defeated the Seljuk Turks there in 1097. The city's modern development dates from the coming of the railroad (1894). Eskişehir is on or near the site of ancient DORYLAEUM.

Esli (ĕs'lī), in the Gospel genealogy. Luke 3.25.

Esna: see ISNA, Egypt.

Esnambuc or **Énambuc, Pierre Belain d'** (both: pyĕr bəlăN dānäNbük'), 1585-1636, French pioneer in the West Indies. Seeking to recoup his family fortune by privateering in the West Indies, Esnambuc instead became the founder of French colonial possessions in that area. In 1625 he established a settlement on St. Kitts in the Leeward Islands. Although St. Kitts had already been settled by the British, the island was divided between France and England. Firmly and justly he managed the colony's affairs through difficult times and explored and settled other islands. In 1635 he founded a colony at SAINT-PIERRE on Martinique.

esophagus (ĭsŏf'əgəs), portion of the digestive tube that conducts food from the mouth to the stomach. When food is swallowed it passes from the PHARYNX into the esophagus, initiating rhythmic contractions (peristalsis) of the esophageal wall, which propels the food along toward the stomach. The walls of the esophagus are lined with mucous glands that continue the lubrication of the food as it is conducted to the stomach. The human esophagus is about 10 in. (25 cm) long and 1 in. (2.5 cm) in diameter. See DIGESTIVE SYSTEM.

espalier (ĕspăl'yər), trellis or lattice used in horticulture for training a tree or vine flat against a wall, either for ornament or to fit it into a small space, allowing it to get a maximum of air and sun and bringing the fruit within easy reach for gathering. The plant, often an apple or pear tree, may be trained into various shapes, such as a fan or a fork. The term is more commonly used for the tree or vine so trained.

Espanola (ĕs"pənyōl'ə), city (1970 pop. 4,528), Rio Arriba and Santa Fe counties., N central N.Mex., on the Rio Grande, in the heart of the Indian pueblo country; founded 1880, inc. 1964. A shipping point for sheep and cattle, it has lumber mills and a candle factory. A three-day fiesta every July commemorates the establishment nearby of a settlement by Juan de Oñate on July 11, 1598. There are many scenic, historic, archaeological, and Indian attractions in the area.

esparcet (ĕspärsā'): see SAINFOIN.

Espartero, Baldomero, duque de la Victoria, conde de Luchana (bäldōmā'rō äspärtā'rō do͞o'kā dā lä vēktō'rēä kōn'dā dā lo͞ochä'nä), 1793-1879, Spanish general and statesman. He fought against the French in the Peninsular War (1808-14) and later against the revolutionists in South America. After Ferdinand VII's death (1833), he supported ISABELLA II against the CARLISTS and won important victories in the Carlist War of 1834-39. His agreement at Vergara (1839) with the Carlist general Rafael Maroto virtually ended the war, and he was rewarded (1840) with the title duque de la Victoria [duke of victory]. A member of the Progressive party in the Cortes from 1837, Espartero played an important political role. His opposition to the queen regent, MARIA CHRISTINA, helped force her to leave (1840) the country. In 1841, Espartero was made regent by the Cortes and became virtual dictator. His ruthless suppression of rebellions—notably at Barcelona—soon made him highly unpopular. In 1843 a general uprising drove him from office, and he fled to England. He returned (1848) to Spain but lived in retirement until 1854, when Isabella, whose throne was threatened by a revolt led by Gen. Leopoldo O'Donnell, recalled him to power. O'Donnell, who became his war minister, displaced him in 1856. Espartero later supported King Amadeus, then adhered to the republic, but he recognized Alfonso XII upon his accession in 1875.

Espejo, Antonio de (äntō'nyō thā äspā'hō), fl. 1582-83, Spanish explorer in the Southwest. In 1582 he was sent out from San Bartolomé, Mexico, to rescue missionaries said to be menaced by the Pueblo Indians. He went down the Conchos River and then up the Rio Grande, exploring much of the present New Mexico and going far into the present Arizona before returning in 1583. He found traces of gold that led the Spanish to support the expedition under Juan de OÑATE a few years later. His narrative is translated in H. E. Bolton, *Spanish Explorations in the Southwest* (1916). See study by Diego Pérez de Luxán (1929, repr. 1967).

Esperanto (ĕspərän'tō), an artificial language introduced in the late 19th cent. and intended by its inventor, Dr. Ludwig L. Zamenhof of Poland, to be of some help in breaking down the barriers separating people speaking different languages. See INTERNATIONAL LANGUAGE.

Espinel, Vicente Martínez (vēthān'tā märtē'nāth äspēnĕl'), 1550-1624, Spanish writer, musician, and adventurer. Espinel was notorious for his dissolute life, which his holy vows, taken in 1589, did little to change. An accomplished guitarist, he helped make the instrument popular and is sometimes credited with adding its fifth string. Espinel's *Rimas* (1591) introduced the *decima*, or *espinela*, a new poetic form of 10 eight-syllable lines rhyming *abbaaccddc*. Espinel is best known for his picaresque, semiautobiographical novel *Vida del escudero Marcos de Obregón* [the life of Squire Marcos de Obregón] (1618), from which Le Sage adapted episodes and characters for *Gil Blas*. See study by George Haley (1959).

espionage (ĕs'pēənäzh"), clandestine securing of information. The term applies particularly to the act of seeking military, industrial, and political data about one nation for the benefit of another. Espionage is a part of intelligence activity, which is also concerned with analysis of diplomatic reports, newspapers, periodicals, technical publications, commercial statistics, and radio and television broadcasts. The defensive side of intelligence activity, i.e., preventing another nation from gaining such information, is known as counterespionage. Under international law, intelligence activities are not illegal; however, all nations have laws against espionage. The importance of espionage in military affairs has been recognized since the beginning of recorded history. The Egyptians had a well-developed secret service, and spying and subversion are mentioned in the *Iliad* and in the Bible. Sun Tzu's treatise (c.500 B.C.) on the art of war in China devotes a chapter to espionage. In the Middle Ages political espionage became important. Joan of Arc was betrayed by Bishop Pierre Cauchon of Beauvais, a spy in the pay of the English, and Sir Francis Walsingham developed an efficient political spy system for Elizabeth I. With the growth of the modern national state, systematized espionage became a fundamental part of government in most countries. Joseph FOUCHÉ is credited with developing the first modern political espionage system, and Frederick II of Prussia is regarded as the founder of modern military espionage. In the United States, Nathan HALE achieved fame as a spy during the Revolutionary War, and there was considerable use of spies on both sides during the Civil War. By World War I all the great powers except the United States had elaborate espionage systems. To protect the country against foreign agents, the U.S. Congress passed the Espionage Statute of 1917. MATA HARI, who obtained information for Germany by seducing French officials, was the most noted spy of World War I. Germany and Japan established elaborate espionage nets in the years preceding World War II; German military and naval intelligence, headed by Wilhelm CANARIS, was especially efficient. Under the code name *Cicero,* the valet to the British ambassador to Turkey provided much valuable information to Germany throughout the war. German espionage activity in the United States was relatively ineffective because of the successful counterintelligence activities of the Federal Bureau of Investigation. In 1942 the Office of Strategic Services, under Gen. William J. Donovan, was formed as the first modern U.S. espionage agency. However, the efficient British system was the keystone of Allied intelligence. Since World War II, espionage activity has enlarged considerably, much of it growing out of the COLD WAR confrontation between the United States and the Soviet Union and their allies. The defection in 1945 of Igor Gouzenko, a Soviet code clerk, uncovered a vast Soviet ring in Canada that included the atomic scientist Alan Nunn May. The testimony of ex-Communists Elizabeth Bentley, Whittaker Chambers, and Louis Budenz led to the discovery of a ring that had operated in Washington since the early 1930s and implicated Alger Hiss, William W. Remington, Harry Dexter White, and many others. In 1949, Judith Coplon, a Justice Dept. employee, and Valentin Gubitchev, a member of the United Nations Secretariat who was her Soviet contact, were arrested. These revelations led to enactment of the National Security Act of 1947, which created the CENTRAL INTELLIGENCE AGENCY (CIA) to coordinate intelligence and the National Security Agency for research into codes and electronic communication. In addition to these, the United States has seven other intelligence gathering agencies. The arrest of the British atomic scientist Klaus Fuchs in 1949 led to the discovery of the espionage ring of Julius and Ethel Rosenberg (see ROSENBERG CASE). Other espionage cases have involved the Soviet spy Jack Soble and his brother Robert Soblen (1961) and Rudolf Abel (1961), an important Soviet agent. The CIA itself has operatives throughout the world. In 1952 the Communist Chinese captured two CIA agents, and in 1960 Francis Gary Powers, flying a U-2 reconnaissance mission over the Soviet Union for the CIA, was forced down and captured. Many Soviet intelligence officials have defected to the West and have provided valuable information about Soviet activities; among them are Gen. Walter Krivitsky, Victor Kravchenko, Vladimir Petrov, Peter Deriabin, and Pawel Monat. Another famed episode involved Oleg Penkovsky, of the GRU (Chief Intelligence Directorate, Soviet Union). Charged with supplying British and U.S. intelligence teams with invaluable information about Soviet espionage, he was executed in 1963. Among Western officials who defected to the Soviet Union are Guy F. Burgess and Donald D. Maclean of Great Britain in 1951, Otto John of West Germany in 1954, William H. Martin and Bernon F. Mitchell, U.S. cryptographers, in 1960, and Harold (Kim) Philby of Great Britain in 1962. The U.S. acknowledgment of its U-2 flights and the exchange of Francis Gary Powers for Rudolf Abel in 1962 implied the legitimacy of some espionage as an arm of foreign policy. In 1962 the United States carried out extensive aerial reconnaissance of Cuba with excellent intelligence results; surveillance from high-altitude planes and satellites became an important espionage technique. In an extraordinary feat, Soviet agents successfully stole (1967) a Sidewinder missile from a NATO base in West Germany. A major innovation in espionage operations has been the increasing use of diplomatic officials and others as intelligence gatherers. In 1967 it was disclosed that the CIA had subsidized the National Students Association, and in 1971 the British, in a single action, expelled 105 Soviet diplomatic and trade officials as spies. Industrial espionage—the theft of patents and processes from business firms—is not properly espionage at all. See Allison Ind, *A Short History of Espionage* (1963); R. W. Rowan and R. G. Deindorfer, *Secret Service: Thirty-Three Centuries of Espionage* (rev. ed. 1967); Ladislas Farago, *The Game of Foxes* (1971); J. C. Masterman, *The Double-Cross System* (1972); Miles Copeland, *Without Cloak or Dagger* (1974).

Espírito Santo (əspē'rētōō sän'tōō), state (1970 pop. 1,600,305), 15,200 sq mi (39,368 sq km), E Brazil, on the Atlantic Ocean. VITÓRIA is the capital.

Espiritu Santo (ĕspē'rētōō sän'tō) or **Santo,** volcanic island (1967 pop. 8,909), 1,485 sq mi (3,846 sq km), South Pacific, largest and westernmost island of the NEW HEBRIDES. It is jointly administered by Britain and France; British headquarters is at Hog Harbour, French headquarters at Segond Canal. Generally mountainous and fertile, the island produces copra, coffee, and cocoa. Its indigenous population is mainly Melanesian. Espiritu Santo was discovered in 1606 by the Portuguese navigator Pedro Fernandez de Queiros. It was the site of a large U.S. air base during World War II.

Espronceda, José de (hōsā' dā äsprōnthā'thä), 1808–42, Spanish romantic poet. Involved in radical intrigue from the age of 14, he suffered imprisonment and was twice exiled. His wide travels took him to Lisbon (1820), to London (1824), and to Paris, where he fought in the July Revolution of 1830. His *Poesías* (1840) brought him lasting fame. Of Espronceda's other major works, the long poem *El estudiante de Salamanca* is based on the Don Juan theme. The celebrated *El diablo mundo* (1841) contains the passionate "Canto a Teresa." Espronceda's sonorous and emotional verse and passionate nature labeled him as the Spanish Byron.

Espy, James Pollard (ĕs'pē), 1785–1860, American meteorologist. He developed a convection theory of storms, explaining it in 1836 before the American Philosophical Society and in 1840 before French and British scientific societies; his *Philosophy of Storms* was published in 1841. He became meteorologist to the War (1842) and Navy (1848) departments and developed the use of the telegraph in assembling weather observation data by which he studied the progress of storms and laid the basis for scientific weather forecasting.

Esquiline, hill: see *Rome before Augustus* and *Roman Empire* under ROME.

Esquimalt (skwī'môlt, -mălt, ĕskwī'-), regional district (1971 pop. 12,922), on Vancouver Island, SW British Columbia, Canada, just SW of Victoria. It has the chief naval station and naval dockyard of W Canada. The station was established by the British government in 1855 and taken over by Canada in 1906.

Esquipulas (äskēpōō'läs), town (1964 pop. 19,164), SE Guatemala, near the Honduran and Salvadoran borders. Believed to be a center of Mayan religious ceremonies, Esquipulas was chosen by the Spanish conquerors as a church site. They commissioned (1594) the carving of a figure of Christ from balsam, which became known as the Black Christ of Esquipulas. A series of reputed miracles led to the commissioning of a sanctuary in 1737. Completed in 1758, it is one of the most grandiose colonial churches in Latin America. It is still a center for pilgrims from all Central America.

Esrom (ĕs'rŏm), the same as HEZRON **1.**

Essad Pasha (ĕs-sät' päshä'), 1863–1920, Albanian dictator. Of a prominent Albanian family, he supported the bloodless and reformist Young Turk revolution (1908) in the Ottoman Empire. He was a member of the resulting Turkish parliament. In the First Balkan War he was entrusted (1912) with the defense of Scutari against the Montenegrins, to whom he surrendered the city in 1913. Early in 1914 he welcomed William, prince of Wied, as ruler of the newly independent Albania. Friction soon developed, however, and William was forced to leave in September. Essad Pasha then governed Albania dictatorially and maintained himself, with Italian aid, until defeated (1916) during World War I by the Austrians. He fled abroad and headed an Albanian commission in Paris, where he was assassinated by a fellow countryman.

Essaouira (ĕswēr'ə), city (1960 pop. 26,392), W Morocco, on the Atlantic Ocean. It was founded in 1760 by Sultan Muhammad ibn-Abdullah. In 1844 the French bombarded the city to force Morocco to stop supporting Abd al-Kadir, leader of an Algerian resistance movement. The city declined when AGADIR was opened to foreign trade in the 20th cent. Essaouira was formerly called Mogador.

essay, relatively short literary composition in prose, in which a writer discusses a topic, usually restricted in scope, or tries to persuade the reader to accept a particular point of view. Although such classical authors as Theophrastus, Cicero, Marcus Aurelius, and Plutarch wrote essays, the term *essai* was first applied to the form in 1580 by Montaigne, one of the greatest essayists of all time, to his pieces on friendship, love, death, and morality. In England the term was inaugurated in 1597 by Francis Bacon, who wrote shrewd meditations on civil and moral wisdom. Montaigne and Bacon, in fact, illustrate the two distinct kinds of essay—the informal and the formal. The informal essay is personal, intimate, relaxed, conversational, and frequently humorous. Some of the greatest exponents of the informal essay are Jonathan Swift, Charles Lamb, William Hazlitt, Thomas De Quincey, Mark Twain, James Thurber, and E. B. White. The formal essay is dogmatic, impersonal, systematic, and expository. Significant writers of this type include Joseph Addison, Samuel Johnson, Matthew Arnold, John Stuart Mill, J. H. Newman, Walter Pater, Ralph Waldo Emerson, and Henry David Thoreau. In the latter half of the 20th cent. the formal essay has become more diversified in subject and less stately in tone and language, and the sharp division between the two forms has tended to disappear. See studies by Leslie Fiedler, ed. (2d ed. 1969), and C. Sanders et al. (1970).

Essen (ĕs'ən), city (1970 pop. 693,434), North Rhine-Westphalia, W West Germany, on the Ruhr River. A major industrial center of the RUHR district, it is the seat of the KRUPP steel works and the chief site for producing electricity in West Germany. In addition to steel, glass, chemicals, textiles, and machinery are also produced, and coal is mined nearby. Essen grew up around a Benedictine convent (founded in the mid-9th cent.). It was a small imperial state, ruled by the abbess of the convent, from the 13th cent. until 1802, when it passed to Prussia. The city's main industrial growth dates from the second half of the 19th cent. Essen was heavily bombed during World War II, but was rebuilt in modern style after 1945. The city has a number of large parks. There is a noteworthy cathedral (9th–14th cent.).

essence, in philosophy, the nature of a thing. Aristotle maintained that there is a distinction between the form of a thing—its intelligible, verbally formulable character—and the essence of a thing, i.e., what it is in itself, which is not common to anything else. The essence of a thing is what is formulated as a universal in the mind and in language. St. Thomas Aquinas distinguished between the essence of a thing and the fact of its being, or its existence. In modern existentialist thought Jean Paul Sartre made use of Aquinas's distinction between essence and existence but reversed them by insisting that existence precedes essence. By this he asserted that men do not have predetermined natures; what a man is follows from the choices he makes.

Essenes (ĕs'ēnz), members of a small Jewish religious order, originating in the 2d cent. B.C. Very little historical information about the Essenes is available: our chief sources of information are Pliny the Elder, Philo's *Quod omnius probus liber,* and Josephus' *Jewish War* and *Antiquities of the Jews.* A feature of the Essenes' organization was the doctrine of communal possession. Ceremonial purity was another outstanding characteristic; this called for abstinence from conjugal relations (although some married), scrupulous cleanliness, the wearing of only white garments, and the most strict observance of the Sabbath. The Essenes believed in purification through baptism and in immortality, but not in resurrection. They condemned slavery and prohibited trading because it led to covetousness and cheating; they abhorred untruthfulness and forbade oaths. They subsisted by pastoral and agricultural activities and handicrafts. All these features, besides indicating that the sect was an outgrowth of extreme Pharisaism, also show Oriental and Hellenistic influences. The claim sometimes advanced that Jesus Christ or John the Baptist came from this sect has never been substantiated. The DEAD SEA SCROLLS have thrown new light on the origins and nature of the Essenes. The sect ceased to exist some time in the 2d cent. A.D. See C. D. Ginsburg, *The Essenes* (1955); Duncan Howlett, *The Essenes and Christianity* (1957); André Dupont-Sommer, *The Essene Writings from Qumran* (tr. 1961, repr. 1967); M. A. Larson, *The Essene Heritage* (1967).

essential oils, volatile OILS that occur in plants and in general give to the plants their characteristic odors, flavors, or other such properties. Essential oils are found in various parts of the plant body (in the seeds, flowers, bark, or leaves) and are also concentrated in certain special cells or groups of cells (glands). Because of their properties, they are widely used in perfumes, flavorings, and medicines. Their chemical composition differs: A great many, for example, are principally terpenes, compounds of carbon and hydrogen. Others contain aldehydes, ketones, or phenols. Oxygen, sulfur, and nitrogen are present in compounds in others. In general, they are complex mixtures. They are obtained from the plant in various ways, depending upon the nature of the part in which they occur—by compression, by distillation with steam, by dissolving the oils out (extraction) or absorbing them, and by pressure and maceration. Among the plants notable for their essential oils are members of the following plant families: CARROT (e.g., anise, dill, angelica), GINGER (cardamon), HEATH (wintergreen), LAUREL (cinnamon and camphor), MINT (pennyroyal, peppermint, spearmint, thyme), MYRTLE (clove and eucalyptus), OLIVE (jasmine and lilac), ORCHID (vanilla), PULSE (acacia and sweet pea), ROSE (attar of roses and almond), and RUE (lemon and other citrus plants).

Essequibo (ĕsăkē'bō), longest river of Guyana, c.600 mi (970 km) long, rising in the Guiana Highlands, S Guyana, and flowing generally N to the Atlantic Ocean. Most of the river's course is broken by rapids and waterfalls. There are many islands in its wide estuary. Bartica, the chief town on the river, is at the head of oceangoing navigation; gold, diamonds, and timber are moved on the river. With its tributaries the Essequibo drains more than half of Guyana.

Essex, Robert Devereux, 2d **earl of** (dĕv'ərōō), 1567-1601, English courtier and favorite of Queen ELIZABETH I. Succeeding to the earldom on the death (1576) of his father, he came under the guardianship of Lord BURGHLEY and soon won favor at court. He distinguished himself in action while serving (1585-86) as a cavalry officer in the Netherlands under his stepfather, Robert Dudley, earl of Leicester. When he returned to England he soon became a marked favorite of the queen, a position that involved him in a quarrelsome rivalry with Sir Walter RALEIGH. Pressed for money and hungering for adventure, Essex joined the expedition of Sir John Norris and Sir Francis Drake to Portugal but was ordered home by Elizabeth (1589). In 1590 he angered the queen by secretly marrying the widow of Sir Philip Sidney. The following year he commanded a flamboyant but unsuccessful expedition to Normandy to help Henry of Navarre (Henry IV of France). He returned home and, advised by Francis BACON, entered politics in an effort to seize power from the aging Burghley. But Essex was too obvious and impetuous in his demands on the queen; Elizabeth was wary, and gradually she conferred the power he sought on Burghley's son, Robert Cecil (later earl of SALISBURY). Essex became a national hero when he shared command of the expedition that captured Cádiz in 1596, but he failed the next year in an expedition to intercept the Spanish treasure fleet off the Azores. When Elizabeth created him earl marshal in 1597, Essex plunged again into a quest for power. In 1599, at his own demand, he was made lord lieutenant of Ireland and sent there with a large force to quell the rebellion of the earl of TYRONE. Failing completely to accomplish his mission, he made an unauthorized truce with Tyrone and returned to England, against the express orders of the queen, to try to justify his actions to her privately. He was confined by the council, and it was eight months before he was tried for disobedience by a special council and deprived of his offices (1600). He was soon released but was banned from the court. Still popular, Essex planned a coup that would oust the enemy party and establish his own about the queen. To this end he sought support from the army in Ireland and opened negotiations with James VI of Scotland, but these efforts failed. Desperately, Essex made his attempt with a small body of personal followers on Feb. 8, 1601. The Londoners failed to respond, the queen's government was thoroughly prepared, and he was arrested. At the trial Bacon contributed heavily to his former patron's conviction. Elizabeth, after some hesitation, signed the death warrant, and Essex was executed. See biographies by G. B. Harrison (1937) and R. Lacey (1971); Lytton Strachey, *Elizabeth and Essex* (1928).

Essex, Robert Devereux, 3d **earl of,** 1591-1646, English parliamentary general; son of the 2d earl. James I restored him (1604) to the estates of his father and arranged his marriage (1606) with Frances Howard, daughter of Thomas Howard, earl of Suffolk. The marriage ended in a famous trial when the countess, who had fallen in love with Robert Carr, earl of Somerset, sued for and obtained (1613) an annulment. After 1620, Essex followed a military and naval career, and from 1626 he was associated with the parliamentary opposition to CHARLES I. He was second in command of the royal army in the first of the BISHOPS' WARS in Scotland (1639) and was made privy councilor (1641), but Charles could not keep his allegiance thereafter. Essex commanded the parliamentary forces at the battle of Edgehill (1642). In 1643 he took Reading, relieved Gloucester, and took part in the first battle of Newbury. The next year, however, he quarreled bitterly with Sir William WALLER and, disobeying orders, pursued the royalists into the southwest. He was cut off in Cornwall and forced to escape with as many of his men as he could by sea. He opposed the formation of the New Model Army and reluctantly relinquished his command in 1645. See biographies by G. B. Harrison (1937, repr. 1973) and V. F. Snow (1970).

Essex, Walter Devereux, 1st **earl of,** 1541?-1576, English soldier. He helped in the suppression of the Northern Rebellion of 1569 and was created earl of Essex in 1572. In 1573 he volunteered to colonize a part of Ulster, then controlled by the O'Neill clan, and bring it under English rule. Famine, desertion of his troops, and the vacillation of Queen Elizabeth I negated his ruthless efforts to subdue the Irish. He was recalled (1575) and died soon afterward. His son, Robert, became the 2d earl of Essex.

Essex, one of the early kingdoms of Anglo-Saxon England. It was settled probably in the early 6th cent. by Saxons who traced their royal line back to a continental Saxon god instead of to Woden, as did the rulers of other early kingdoms. Essex eventually included the modern counties of Essex and Middlesex, most of Hertfordshire, and London. Under the influence of his uncle, Æthelbert of Kent, King Sæbert of Essex accepted (c.604) Christianity, but the kingdom lapsed into heathenism when his successors expelled (617) Mellitus, bishop of London. In c.653, however, at the request of King Sigbert, Oswy of Northumbria sent Cedd to convert the East Saxons and to build churches. The submission of Essex to the overlordship of Wulfhere of MERCIA marked the beginning of a long domination by the larger state. In 825, Essex joined other eastern kingdoms in submitting to Egbert of Wessex and became an earldom. Heavily settled by the Danes, it became part of the DANELAW by the treaty of 886, but was retaken by Edward the Elder of Wessex in 917. Its most famous later earl was BYRHTNOTH, who was killed in the battle of Maldon in 991.

Essex, county (1971 pop. 1,353,564), 1,528 sq mi (3,958 sq km) SE England, on the Thames River and the North Sea, one of the "Home Counties" of London. CHELMSFORD is the county town. The land rises from the low, irregular coastline to undulating pastoral country. There are numerous streams and salt marshes. The chief crops of Essex are wheat, barley, sugar beets, potatoes, fruits, and vegetables. There is market gardening for London and some dairy and sheep farming. Oyster fisheries are also important. The county has important industries that produce chemicals, machinery, textiles, cement, processed foods, and electrical goods. Essex was once part of the kingdom of the East Saxons, whence its name, and there are Roman and Saxon remains at Colchester and Maldon. Popular resorts line the coast.

Essex. 1 Uninc. city (1970 pop. 38,193), Baltimore co., NE Md., a suburb of Baltimore. A junior college is there. **2** Town (1970 pop. 10,951), Chittenden co., NW Vt., on the Winooski River; settled 1783. There is some light industry. The Champlain Valley Exposition is held in Essex. Fort Ethan Allen is nearby.

Essex Junto, group of New England merchants and lawyers, so called because many of them came from Essex co., Mass. They opposed the radicals in Massachusetts in the American Revolution and supported the Federalist faction of Alexander Hamilton. They later encouraged the disaffection of the Hartford Convention. Prominent among them were Timothy PICKERING, George Cabot, and Theophilus PARSONS.

Esslingen am Neckar (ĕs'lĭng-ən äm nĕk'är) or **Esslingen,** city (1970 pop. 87,418), Baden-Württemberg, SW West Germany, on the Neckar River. Manufactures include textiles, metal goods, furniture, and transportation equipment. It is noted for its wines. Founded in the 8th cent., Esslingen was a free imperial city from the 13th cent. to 1802, when it passed to Württemberg. It was (1488) the scene of the founding of the Great Swabian League. Noteworthy structures include a castle (13th-16th cent.) and a Gothic church, the *Frauenkirche* (14th-16th cent.).

Essonne (ĕsôn'), department (1968 pop. 674,157), N central France. EVRY is the capital.

Estaing, Charles Hector, comte d' (shärl ĕktôr' kôNt dĕstăN'), 1729-94, French admiral. After serving in India he was given (1778) command of a French fleet sent to aid the colonists in the American Revolution. Planning to attack Newport, R.I., he was undone by a storm and had to put in at Boston for repairs. In 1779 he cooperated with Gen. Benjamin LINCOLN in the unsuccessful attack on Savannah. In 1780 he returned to France. Estaing commanded the National Guard at Versailles during the invasion (Oct. 5-6, 1789) of the palace by a Parisian mob, but he took no action. Sympathetic to some of the aims of the French Revolution, yet personally close to the royal family, he testified (1793) in favor of Marie Antoinette during her trial. He was later guillotined as a royalist.

estate. 1 In property law, see PROPERTY; TENURE. **2** In constitutional law, an estate denotes an organized class of society with a separate voice in government. Representation by estate arose in Europe in the 13th cent. when the feudal system was being broken up as a result of the growth of the towns. The term generally designates three classes—the nobility, the clergy, and the commons. The commons were the knights and the townspeople of substance—the burgesses or bourgeoisie. The sovereign would occasionally consult the three estates and consider their grievances. Often voting was by an estate as a whole rather than by individual vote. In many cases the estates might merely advise the sovereign, and their decisions were not binding. From these practices modern parliamentary institutions gradually evolved in several countries. Much of the constitutional development of the later Middle Ages is a record of the emergence of the commons—sometimes called the third estate—into a position of equality with the other two estates. The process is clearly shown in the history of the STATES-GENERAL in France. The next step was the transition from representation by estates to popular representation. A crucial moment in the French Revolution was the rejection of voting according to estates and the merger of the States-General into the NATIONAL ASSEMBLY. The English PARLIAMENT may be viewed historically as a representative body of the estates; the nobility and the Church of England are represented by the House of Lords, and the commons—the remaining adult citizens—by the House of Commons. In fact, however, the term *estate* is not applicable to a country with democratic institutions and is probably not appropriate in any modern state.

Estates-General: see STATES-GENERAL.

estate tax: see INHERITANCE TAX.

Este (ĕs'tā), Italian noble family, rulers of FERRARA (1240-1597) and of MODENA (1288-1796) and celebrated patrons of the arts during the Renaissance. Probably of Lombard origin, they took their name from the castle of Este, near Padua. They succeeded to the house of the Guelphs when the original Guelph line died out. **Azzo d'Este II,** 996-1097, lord of Este and the founder of his family's greatness, was invested with Milan by the emperor. His son, **Guelph d'Este IV** or **Welf IV,** d. 1101, was adopted by his maternal uncle, Guelph III, whom he succeeded as duke of Carinthia. In 1070 he was made duke of Bavaria. The grandfather of Henry the Proud of Bavaria and Saxony, Guelph IV was the founder of the German line of the Guelphs, from whom the British royal family is descended. He died on Cyprus while crusading. Azzo d'Este II had another son, who continued the Italian line of the house; among that son's successors was **Obizzo d'Este I,** d. 1193. Obizzo and his grandson played an important part in the struggle of the Guelphs against Holy Roman Emperor Frederick I (see GUELPHS AND GHIBELLINES). He married the heiress of one of the two families contending for supremacy in Ferrara. His grandson, **Azzo d'Este VI,** 1170-1212, was podesta [chief magistrate] of Mantua and Verona and fought to obtain Ferrara, but it was left for his son, **Azzo d'Este VII,** 1205-64, to succeed in becoming (1240) podesta of that city at the head of the triumphant Guelph party. **Obizzo d'Este II,** d. 1293, was made perpetual lord of Ferrara in 1264, lord of Modena in 1288, and lord of Reggio (now REGGIO NELL' EMILIA) in 1289. Since Ferrara was held as a fief from the pope, the Este became papal vicars in 1332. **Niccolò d'Este III,** 1384-1441, made Ferrara a center of arts and letters and increased the power of his house by playing his more powerful neighbors against each other. Under his successors the court of the Este became one of the most brilliant in Europe. Among them were his illegitimate sons **Leonello d'Este,** 1407–50, an accomplished prince, and **Borso d'Este,** 1413–71, who received the title duke of Modena and Reggio from Holy Roman Emperor Frederick III in 1452 and that of duke of Ferrara from Pope Paul II in 1471. Niccolò's legitimate son **Ercole d'Este I,** 1431–1505, lost some territory in wars against Venice. Ercole's beautiful and brilliant daughter, **Beatrice d'Este,** 1475–97, married Ludovico SFORZA, duke of Milan, one of the most lavish of all Renaissance princes. Her sister, **Isabella d'Este,** 1474–1539, married Francesco GONZAGA, marquis of Mantua. Ariosto, Boiardo, and Berni were her friends, and Leonardo da Vinci and Titian painted portraits of her. Ercole I was succeeded by his son, **Alfonso d'Este I,** 1476–1534, second husband of Lucrezia BORGIA. In the ITALIAN WARS he entered the League of Cambrai against Venice and remained an ally of Louis XII of France even after Pope Julius II had made peace with Venice. The pope declared Alfonso's fiefs forfeited and excommunicated him (1510); Modena and Reggio were lost. However, in 1526–27 Alfonso participated in the expedition of Charles V, Holy Roman emperor and king of Spain, against Pope Clement VII, and in 1530 the pope again recognized him as possessor of those duchies. Ariosto lived at his court in Ferrara after a long employment by Alfonso's brother, **Ippolito I, Cardinal d'Este,** 1479–1520, to whom Ariosto's *Orlando Furioso* is dedicated. Alfonso's son and successor, **Ercole d'Este II,** 1508–59, married Renée, daughter of Louis XII of France. He joined the pope and France against Spain in 1556, but made a separate peace in 1558. He also was a patron of the arts, as was his brother, **Ippolito II, Cardinal d'Este,** 1509–72, an able diplomat who led the pro-French party at the papal court. Ippolito built the celebrated VILLA D'ESTE at Tivoli. With Ercole II's son, **Alfonso d'Este II,** 1533–97, the direct male line of the house ended. He willed his titles to his cousin, **Cesare d'Este,** 1533–1628, but Pope Clement VIII refused to recognize Cesare's rights, and Ferrara was incorporated into the Papal States in 1598. Holy Roman Emperor Rudolf II recognized Cesare's rights to Modena and Reggio, but without Ferrara the duchy lost political importance. The last duke, Ercole d'Este III, was deposed in 1796 by the French and died in 1803. His daughter, Maria Beatrice, married Archduke Ferdinand of Austria, a son of Austrian Emperor Francis I, who founded the house of Austria-Este. After the restoration (1815) of the duchy of Modena their son and grandson, Francis IV and Francis V, ruled as dukes of Modena, Massa, and Carrara. Francis V was expelled in 1859, and his territories were annexed (1806) to the kingdom of Sardinia. See W. L. Gundersheimer, *Ferrara: The Style of a Renaissance Despotism* (1973).

Este, town (1971 pop. 17,060), in Venetia, NE Italy. Manufactures include ceramics, chemicals, and metal goods. The ancient Ateste, it was a center of civilization (10th–2d cent. B.C.) of which many important remains have been found. It was later a Roman military colony. The Este family originated in the town. In 1275 it passed to Padua and in 1405 to Venice. Este has a castle (11th–14th cent.), several fine villas, and an excellent archaeological museum.

ester, any one of a group of organic compounds with general formula RCO_2R' (where R and R′ are alkyl groups or aryl groups) that are formed by the reaction between an alcohol and an acid. For example, when ethanol and acetic acid react, ethyl acetate (an ester) and water are formed; the reaction is called esterification. Ethyl acetate is used as a solvent. Methyl acetate, formed by the reaction between methanol and acetic acid, is a sweet-smelling liquid used in making perfumes, extracts, and lacquers. Esters react with water (HYDROLYSIS) under certain conditions to form an alcohol and an acid. When heated with a hydroxide certain esters decompose to yield soap and glycerin; the process is called saponification. Common FATS AND OILS are mixtures of various esters, such as STEARIN, PALMITIN, and linolein, formed from the alcohol GLYCEROL and FATTY ACIDS. Naturally occurring esters of organic acids in fruits and flowers give them their distinctive odors. Esters perform important functions in the animal body; e.g., the ester acetylcholine is a chemical transmitter of nerve stimuli.

```
        O
        ||
   R—C—OR′
general formula

   H   O        H   H
   |   ||       |   |
H—C—C—O—C—C—H
   |            |   |
   H            H   H
ethyl acetate
```

Esters

Esterházy (ĕs'tĕrhä"zē), princely Hungarian family. **Paul, Fürst Esterházy von Galantha,** 1635–1713, was elected palatine (regent) of Hungary in 1681 and distinguished himself in the defense of Vienna (1683) and the reconquest of Hungary from the Turks. A staunch supporter of Hapsburg rule, he was created prince of the Holy Roman Empire in 1687. His grandson, **Paul Anton, Fürst Esterházy von Galantha,** d. 1762, appointed Franz Joseph HAYDN assistant musical director at his seat at Eisenstadt, now in Austria. Paul Anton's brother, **Nikolaus Joseph, Fürst Esterházy von Galantha,** 1714–90, who succeeded him in 1762, made Haydn chief musical director in 1766. For Nikolaus Joseph, Haydn composed most of his chamber music, and numerous symphonies and operas for a vastly increased orchestra and a newly established private opera. Nikolaus Joseph, one of the most lavish art patrons of all time and immensely wealthy, built the celebrated Esterházy palace in Eisenstadt, on the southern end of the Neusiedler Lake. At his death he left Haydn a handsome pension. His nephew, **Nikolaus, Fürst Esterházy von Galantha,** 1765–1833, was offered (1809) the crown of Hungary by Napoleon I but refused it.

Esterhazy, Ferdinand Walsin (ĕs'tərhä"zē, Fr. fĕrdēnäN' välsăN' ĕstĕrăzē'), 1847–1923, French army officer, member of a French family possibly related to the Hungarian family of Esterhazy. A veteran of the papal army and the French Foreign Legion, he entered the regular French army and rose to be a major. Deep in debt, he sold French military secrets to the Germans. When treason became evident in 1894, the guilt was pinned on Captain Dreyfus (see DREYFUS AFFAIR). The suspicions of Col. Georges Picquart helped to bring about a court-martial for Esterhazy in 1898, but his fellow officers quickly acquitted him. He subsequently fled to England, where he later confessed.

Estevan (ĕs'təvăn), city (1971 pop. 9,150), S Sask., Canada, on the Souris River near the N.Dak. border. Lignite is mined there, and clay and plastic products are manufactured.

Esther (ĕs'tər), book of the Old Testament, 17th in the order of the Authorized Version (AV). It is the story of the beautiful Jewish woman Esther (named originally Hadassah), who is chosen as queen by the Persian king Ahasuerus after he has repudiated his previous wife, Vashti. It tells how the wicked courtier Haman attempted to bring about the massacre of the Jews and how Esther and her cousin Mordecai thwarted him. Haman was hanged, and Mordecai became the king's chief minister. The feast of PURIM commemorates the deliverance of the Jews. Extant Hebrew versions are different from those surviving in Greek. These latter are longer by several chapters, translations of which are treated as apocryphal in AV; in Roman Catholic translations, where they are canonical, they are appended, out of order, as 10.4–13 and 11–16. They contain a conclusion and supplementary material, including prayers of Esther and Mordecai. The Hebrew version contains no mention of God. Scholars are divided on the historicity of the book. Some critics date the book as late as 150 B.C. The French dramatic poet Racine wrote a play *Esther* (1689). See study by C. R. Anderson (1970); see also bibliography under OLD TESTAMENT.

esthetics: see AESTHETICS.

Estienne, Étienne (ātyĕn'), or, Latinized, **Stephanus** (stĕf'ənəs), family of Parisian and Genevan printers of the 16th and 17th cent., distinguished through five generations in scholarship as well as in their craft. The first of the line was **Henri Estienne,** d. 1520, who was by 1502 established as a printer in Paris. Before his death more than 100 books, some of them of great typographic beauty, had issued from his press. His foreman, Simon de COLINES, succeeded him and married his widow. Some years later, probably in 1526, Henri's son, **Robert Estienne,** b. 1498 or 1503, d. 1559, took over his father's shop, and Colines then founded a new establishment. Robert, a capable scholar, devoted himself to printing only scholarly works, many of which he himself edited. He put out editions of classical authors, dictionaries and lexicons, and, more especially, critical editions of the Bible. He enjoyed the favor of Francis I and became king's printer for Latin, Hebrew, and Greek. The printer's mark used by him, the Olive Tree, was apparently designed by Geofroy TORY, who is said to have been a proofreader for the elder Estienne; some of the Estienne types were designed by Claude GARAMOND. Robert Estienne, a thorough humanist, upheld the cause of the Reformation. Long-continued attacks upon him by the faculty of the Univ. of Paris and by political opponents of the king caused him to move to Geneva in 1550. He set up a press there and continued to print books until his death. His own Latin dictionary, *Thesaurus linguae Latinae* (1531), probably compiled with the aid of other scholars, is a monumental work. His grammatical treatises on French are also of great importance. His brother, **François Estienne,** d. 1553, was of minor importance as a bookseller, but another brother, **Charles Estienne,** c.1504–1564, succeeded Robert in the management of the Paris establishment in 1551. Educated in medicine and skilled in classical learning, Charles wrote many works on medicine, agriculture, and other subjects. A number of his books were printed by his brother, Robert, and by his stepfather, Colines. Among his best-known works are an encyclopedia, one of the earliest appearing in France, a treatise on dissection, and *Praedium rusticum,* which appeared later in English editions. The second **Henri Estienne,** 1531?–1598, the greatest scholar of the family, was one of Robert's sons. He inherited his father's press on the express condition that it should not be moved from Geneva. He was a well-trained scholar and devoted years to searching for manuscripts. Although humanism was far advanced, he, nevertheless, discovered numerous works of classical authors of which he issued first editions. His editions of Greek and Latin works are remarkable for their accuracy and textual criticism. The greatest monument to his scholarship is, perhaps, his *Thesaurus Graecae linguae* (1572). He also championed the use of the French language and wrote valuable treatises on the French tongue and on French grammar; the most important is *La Precellence du langage françois* (1579), in spite of its gross errors in philology. His satirical *Apologie pour Herodote* (1566) brought him trouble with the Consistory of Geneva, and after the publication of *Deux Dialogues du nouveau langage françois italianizé* (1578) he went to France to escape censure in Geneva. He was imprisoned for a short time on his return and afterward became a wandering scholar. The books he printed did not equal those of his father in typographic beauty. He marks, however, the highest point of the family's career, although the Estiennes continued prominent as printers until late in the 17th cent. See Mark Pattison, *The Estiennes* (1949).

Estonia (ĕstō'nēə), Estonian *Eesti,* Rus. *Estoniya,* Ger. *Estland,* constituent republic (1970 pop. 1,357,000), 17,413 sq mi (45,100 sq km), W European USSR. It borders on the Baltic Sea in the west; the gulfs of Riga and Finland (both arms of the Baltic) in the southwest and north, respectively; Latvia in the south; and the Russian Soviet Federated Socialist Republic in the east. TALLINN is the capital; other important cities are TARTU, NARVA, PARNU, and VILJANDI. Despite its northerly location, Estonia enjoys a mild climate because of marine influences. Mainly a lowland, the republic has numerous lakes, frequently of glacial origin; Lake Chudskoye (Peipus), the largest, is important for both shipping and fishing. Along Estonia's Baltic coast are more than 800 islands, of which Sarema is the most notable. The republic's rivers include the Narva, Parnu, Ema, and Kasari. Estonia ranks first among Soviet republics in the extraction of shale and the production of shale oil and gas. Peat, limestone, dolomite, marl, clays (for cement and earthenware), sand (for the glass industry), phosphorite (for fertilizer), and timber are other important natural resources. Estonia is a leading Soviet supplier of various wood products (cellulose, paper, plywood), cotton, linen, and wool textiles, oil industry equipment, chemical fertilizer, electrical and radio apparatus, building materials (notably cement, reinforced concrete, and bricks), window glass, leather footwear, and processed fish. Other industries include shipbuilding and repair, metalworking, and food processing. Fishing, dairy farming, and pig raising are important occupations. The main crops are flax, potatoes, and sugar beets. Estonians make up about 75% of the population, Russians constitute about 20%, and there are Finnish, Ukrainian, Belorussian, and Jewish minorities. The republic has a university (est. 1632), a branch of the

Soviet Academy of Sciences, and numerous other educational and cultural institutions. The Estonians, who are ethnically and linguistically close to the Finns, settled in their present territory before the Christian era. They were mentioned (1st cent. A.D.) by Tacitus, who called them Aesti. In the 13th cent. the Danes and the German order of the LIVONIAN BROTHERS OF THE SWORD formed an alliance to conquer the pagan Estonian tribes. The Danes founded Reval (now Tallinn) in 1219 and introduced Christianity and Western civilization to Estonia. While Denmark took the northern part of Estonia, the Knights occupied the southern portion. In 1346 the Danes sold their territory to the order, and Estonia remained under the rule of the knights and the Hanseatic merchants until the order's dissolution in 1561. Northern Estonia then passed to Sweden; the rest was briefly held by Poland but was transferred to the Swedes by the Treaty of Altmark (1629) that ended the first Polish-Swedish war. The lot of the Estonian peasants, who had been reduced to virtual serfdom under German landowners, improved somewhat under Swedish rule; but Peter I of Russia conquered Livonia in 1710, and Russian possession was confirmed by the Treaty of Nystad in 1721. Despite some land reforms, the German nobility—the Baltic barons—retained its sway over the Estonian peasantry until the eve of the 1917 Russian Revolution, and German burghers controlled most of the urban wealth. Meanwhile, industrialization proceeded apace during the 19th cent.; shipbuilding and the manufacture of railroad cars, agricultural machinery, electric motors, and textiles were major branches of industry. The republic became heavily interlaced with railroads, and the port of Tallinn ranked just after St. Petersburg, Odessa, and Riga in freight turnover. Estonian national consciousness began to stir in the mid-19th cent. but was countered by russification, which in turn spurred rebellion and considerable emigration (notably to the United States and Canada). Estonia suffered bloody reprisals for its important role in the Russian Revolution of 1905. In the aftermath of the 1917 Russian Revolution, Moscow appointed a puppet Communist regime under Jaan Anvelt to rule Estonia; its authority, however, failed to extend beyond Tallinn. An Estonian proclamation of independence in Feb., 1918, was followed shortly by German occupation. After Germany surrendered to the Allies in Nov. 1918, Estonia declared itself an independent democratic republic and repulsed the invading Red Army. In 1920, by the Peace of Tartu, Soviet Russia recognized Estonia's independence. Political stability, however, eluded the republic, which had 20 short-lived coalition regimes before 1933, when a new constitution gave the president sweeping authority. Political parties were abolished in 1934, and President Konstantin Päts instituted an authoritarian regime. A more democratic constitution came into force in 1938; but the Nazi-Soviet Pact of Aug., 1939, placed the Baltic countries under Soviet control, and the following month the USSR secured military bases in Estonia. Complete Soviet military occupation came in June, 1940. Following elections in July, Estonia was incorporated into the USSR as a constituent republic. Occupied by German troops during much of World War II, Estonia was retaken by Soviet forces in 1944. Collectivization of agriculture and nationalization of industry began in the late 1940s, and the Estonian economy was steadily integrated with that of the USSR.

Estournelles de Constant, Paul Henri Benjamin, baron d' (pōl äNrē' bäNzhămăN' bärôN' dātōōrnĕl' də kôNstäN'), 1852–1924, French diplomat and pacifist. He wrote and spoke tirelessly in favor of disarmament and international conciliation, was a delegate to the Hague peace conferences (1899 and 1907), and was awarded the 1909 Nobel Peace Prize jointly with Auguste Beernaert.

Estrada Cabrera, Manuel (mänwĕl' esträ'thä käbrä'rä), 1857–1924, president of Guatemala (1898–1920). He ruled as an absolute dictator, and there were several revolutionary movements and attempts on his life. Under his rule, Guatemala achieved material progress through advances in agriculture, construction, and public health. Estrada Cabrera gave strong support to education, although teachers were forbidden to criticize his administration. In spite of a ruinous currency system, the country experienced an increase in wealth. A revolution in 1920 forced Estrada Cabrera to leave office and flee the country.

Estrada Palma, Tomás (tōmäs', päl'mä), 1835–1908, Cuban revolutionist and first president (1902–6) of Cuba. An active participant in the Ten Years War (1868–78), he became a general (1876) and was captured by the Spanish (1877). Released and exiled, he spent some time in the United States, where he helped win support for the Cuban cause. As president he strove to balance the republic's economy and set Cuba on the road to material progress, but he was unable to stop the excessive graft and spoils sought by the revolution's military and political participants. He was reelected (1906) by the conservatives; the liberals charged fraud, and a revolt broke out under José Miguel GOMEZ. Estrada Palma sought aid from the United States but, refusing the American compromise, resigned.

Estrades, Godefroy, comte d' (gōdfrwä' kôNt dĕsträd'), 1607–86, French diplomat, marshal of France. An accomplished soldier, he negotiated (1662) the purchase of Dunkirk from the English. He served with King Louis XIV in the third of the Dutch Wars and was made marshal in recognition of his successes at Limbourg and Liège. He later negotiated the Treaty of Nijmegen (1678).

Estrées, Gabrielle d' (gäbrēĕl' dĕstrā'), 1573–99, famous beauty, mistress (1592–99) of Henry IV of France, who made her marquise of Monceaux and duchess of Beaufort. She divorced her husband, and Henry was preparing to divorce Margaret of Valois, with the object of marrying Gabrielle, when Gabrielle died. Her three children by Henry were legitimized. One of them was César, duc de Vendôme.

Estrela, Serra da (sĕr'ə thə əshträ'lə), mountain range, central Portugal. It rises to 6,532 ft (1,991 m) in Malhão da Estrela, Portugal's highest peak. The range is an important pastoral region. Its streams are used to generate hydroelectricity. Tungsten and tin are mined there. Notable for their beauty and their winter snows, the mountains are a year-round resort area.

Estremadura (əshtrəmədōō'rə), region, W Portugal, formerly a province, now divided between the provinces of Estremadura (2,064 sq mi/5,346 sq km) and Ribatejo, with a small part in Beira Litoral. Estremadura province consists of S Leira, N Setúbal, and most of Lisboa districts. The capital of the province is Lisbon. Wide plains flank the fertile and heavily wooded Tagus River valley. There are grainfields, orchards, and vineyards; copper, iron, marble, coal, and salt are found in the province. Fishing is important along the coast.

Estremadura (ĕstrəmədōō'rə), Span. *Extremadura,* region (1970 pop. 1,145,376), W central Spain, on the border with Portugal. A tableland crossed by mountains and by the Tagus (Tajo) and Guadiana rivers, it comprises the provinces of Badajoz and Cáceres. Much of it is poverty-ridden, with poor communications, absentee landlordism, and steady emigration. Wine, oil, and cereals are produced in valleys made fertile by extensive irrigation. Elsewhere, the more rugged terrain serves as winter grazing land for sheep from Castile and León; hogs are also raised in large numbers. Reconquered from the Moors in the 12th and 13th cent., the region was frequently a battlefield in the Spanish wars with Portugal and again in the Peninsular War. Most of Estremadura fell to the Nationalists early in the Spanish civil war. The conquistadors Pizarro and Cortés were born there.

Estremoz (ĕshtrəmôsh'), town (1970 municipal pop. 18,907), Évora dist., S central Portugal, in Altro Alentejo. It is famous for its white, almost translucent marble and also for its pottery. The castle, with its stately tower built in the 13th cent., is much admired. Some of the expeditions of Nun'Álvares Pereira were based at Estremoz, and in the 17th cent. it was important in the wars with Spain.

estrogen (ĕs'trəjən), any one of a group of HORMONES synthesized by the reproductive organs and ADRENAL GLANDS in females, and, in lesser quantities, in males. The estrogens cause the thickening of the lining of the uterus and vagina in the early phase of the ovulatory, or menstrual, cycle; in lower animals cyclical estrogen secretion also induces estrus, or "heat." The estrogens are also responsible for female secondary sex characteristics such as, in humans, pubic hair and breasts. The major estrogen secreted by the ovary is 17β-estradiol; this is converted to estrone in the blood. Estriol is the principal estrogen formed by the placenta during pregnancy. These three compounds, 17β-estradiol, estrone, and estriol, account for most of the estrogenic activity in humans. The ability of estrogens to suppress secretion of follicle stimulating hormone (FSH) by the PITUITARY GLAND and thereby inhibit ovulation makes estrogen and estrogenlike compounds major components in oral contraceptives. Estrogens have also been successful in treatment of carcinoma (cancer) of the prostate.

OH CH_3 HO

17β-estradiol

estuary (ĕs'chōōĕr"ē), partially enclosed coastal body of water, having an open connection with the ocean, where fresh water from inland is mixed with salt water from the sea. One type of estuary, called a drowned river valley, is caused by crustal subsidence associated with the general rise in sea level following the melting of the Pleistocene ice sheets (see PLEISTOCENE EPOCH). Chesapeake Bay is one of the largest estuaries of this type in the United States. FJORDS, or drowned glacial troughs, form similar types of estuaries, particularly in Norway, Alaska, New Zealand, and other glaciated, mountainous coastal regions. Salt marshes and lagoons found behind barrier beaches, such as along the south shore of Long Island, and down faulted sections of the earth's crust, such as San Francisco Bay, are additional types of estuaries. The shape of an estuary affects the height of the tide; some estuaries (such as the Severn and the Bay of Fundy) are characterized by a wavelike tidal BORE. Estuaries represent one of the most sensitive and ecologically important habitats on earth. They provide sanctuary for many species of waterfowl, store nutrients for larval and juvenile marine life, and serve as breeding grounds for many desirable species of ocean fish. Since estuaries commonly provide excellent harbors, most of the large ports in the United States (New York, Philadelphia, Baltimore, Mobile, Galveston, Seattle, and San Francisco) are located in estuaries. However, the development of high-density population centers causes deleterious effects that can destroy the very properties of the estuary that made development of the region possible. Man's impact on estuaries includes reclamation of tidal land by filling; pollution from sewage, solid waste, industrial effluent, and hot water; increased sedimentation filling the estuary; and alteration of the salinity of estuarine waters by withdrawal or increased influx of fresh water. Increasingly, federal and state governments are passing legislation to protect estuarine environments.

Esztergom (ĕ'stĕrgôm), Ger. *Gran,* city (1970 pop. 26,955), N Hungary, on the Danube River and the border of Czechoslovakia. It is a county administrative center, a river port, and a railroad terminus. There are industries producing iron products, machinery, machine tools, textiles, and alcoholic beverages. Situated in an extensive vineyard region, Esztergom carries on trade in wine and grain. Coal and lignite are mined nearby. Its mineral springs make the city popular with tourists. Esztergom is one of Hungary's oldest towns. The Roman Strigonium was the first royal residence and the capital of Hungary until the 13th cent. King Stephen I, later canonized as Hungary's patron saint, was crowned at Esztergom (his birthplace) in 1001. The city has been the seat of the archprimate of Hungary since 1198. Mongols sacked Esztergom in 1241, and the Turks occupied it during much of the 16th and 17th cent. Overlooking the Danube is the city's 19th-century dome-topped cathedral, thought to be the most beautiful church in Hungary. The palace of the primates contains a museum of antiquities and a library rich in old manuscripts and incunabula.

Etah (ē'tə), village, NW Greenland, on Smith Sound, opposite Ellesmere Island. The Eskimo tribe discovered there by John Ross in 1818 is known as the Polar Eskimo and has been studied by R. E. Peary, D. B. MacMillan, and Knud Rasmussen. Etah was frequently used as a base for arctic expeditions. See D. B. MacMillan, *Etah and Beyond* (1927).

Etam (ē'təm). **1** Village, S Palestine. 1 Chron. 4.32. **2** Town of Judah, SW of Bethlehem. 2 Chron. 11.6. **3** Cleft rock, where Samson hid. Judges 15.8,11. These may be the same.

Étampes, Anne de Pisseleu, duchesse d' (äN də pĕslö' düshĕs' dätäNp'), 1508–1580?, official mistress of Francis I of France from 1526. Intelligent as well as beautiful, she patronized men of letters and used her increasing influence over the king to procure the downfall of Anne, duc de Montmorency, and the reinstatement to royal favor in 1541 of Philippe de CHABOT, who had been previously banished and fined for peculation. In 1533, Francis married her to Jean de Brosses, whom he created duke and made governor of Brittany. Upon the death of Francis I (1547), Henry II exiled her from court.

Etawah (ĭtä'wə), town (1971 pop. 85,900), Uttar Pradesh state, N central India, on the Jumna River and the Delhi-Kanipur railroad. It is a district administrative center and a market for grain, oilseed, handloom fabrics, and leather. The town was held by the RAJPUTS from the 12th to the 16th cent., when it became the seat of a Muslim governor. In the 17th cent. it was a banking and commercial center. Etawah was occupied by rebels during the 1857 INDIAN MUTINY against the British.

etched circuit: see PRINTED CIRCUIT.

etching, the art of ENGRAVING with acid on metal; also the print taken from the metal plate so engraved. In hard-ground etching the plate, usually of copper or zinc, is given a thin coating or ground of acid-resistant resin. This is sometimes smoked so that lines scratched through the resin will be clearly visible. The needle exposes the metal without penetrating it. When the design is completed, the plate is submerged in an acid solution that attacks the exposed lines. During the bath the plate is frequently removed, and such lines as are bitten to sufficient depth are coated with stopping-out varnish. The lines receiving the longest exposure to the acid will be the heaviest and darkest in the print. It is also possible to apply the acid locally to the plate. In printing, all varnish is removed, the plate is warmed, coated with etcher's ink, and then carefully wiped so that the ink remains in the depressions but is largely or wholly removed from the surface. It is then covered with a soft, moist paper and run through an etching press. The best etchers have usually done their own wiping and printing. There are many variations in the technique of etching. Etchers often remove undesired lines by burnishing and otherwise change the first state of the plate from which they make their trial print. Certain etchings appear in many and widely differing states. Only a limited number of first-rate proofs can be made from a plate, and some etchers destroy their plates after making a given number of prints. Soft-ground etching gives effects similar to those obtained in pencil or crayon drawing, while AQUATINT approximates the effects of a wash drawing. Aquatint is often combined with hard-ground etching, as is also DRYPOINT. This latter technique is not true etching, as no acid is employed, but resembles it closely in the effect produced. Pictorial etching evolved gradually from the earlier burin engraving. Both seem to have originated in Germany, where Dürer's etchings on iron, made between 1515 and 1518, were probably the earliest important examples of an art that in the following centuries was practiced by many of the greatest draftsmen and painters. Among the foremost in the history of etching are the works of Dürer, Callot, Rembrandt, the Tiepoli, the Piranesi, Goya, and Whistler. See A. M. Hind, *A History of Engraving and Etching* (rev. ed. 1963); Joseph Pennell, *Etchers and Etching* (1919); A. Gross, *Etching, Engraving, and Intaglio Printing* (1970).

Eteocles (ētē'ōklēz): see SEVEN AGAINST THEBES.

Étex, Antoine (äNtwän' ātĕks'), 1808–88, French sculptor, painter, and architect. A pupil of Ingres, he is best known as a sculptor. Among his works are two large groups, *Resistance* and *Peace*, on the Arc de Triomphe de l'Étoile, Paris; Géricault's tomb; and the monument to Ingres at Montauban.

Etham (ē'thəm), encampment of the Jews. Num. 33.6,8.

Ethan (ē'thăn). **1** Ezrahite. 1 Kings 4.31; title of Ps. 89. He is probably the same as Ethan, son of Zerah. 1 Chron. 2.6. **2, 3** Two temple singers. 1 Chron. 6.42,44.

ethanal (ĕth'ənăl), IUPAC name for ACETALDEHYDE.

ethane (ĕth'ān), CH_3CH_3, gaseous hydrocarbon. It is a continuous-chain ALKANE. As a constituent of natural gas, it is used for fuel. It can be prepared by cracking and fractional distillation of petroleum.

ethanedioic acid (ĕth"āndīō'ĭk), IUPAC name for OXALIC ACID.

ethanediol, 1,2- (ĕth"āndī'ōl), IUPAC name for ethylene GLYCOL.

ethanol (ĕth'ənōl") or **ethyl alcohol,** CH_3CH_2OH, a colorless liquid with characteristic odor and taste; commonly called grain alcohol or, simply, ALCOHOL. It is a monohydric primary alcohol. It melts at −117.3°C and boils at 78.5°C. It is miscible with water in all proportions and is separated from water only with difficulty; ethanol that is completely free of water is called absolute ethanol. Ethanol forms a constant-boiling mixture, or azeotrope, with water that contains 95% ethanol and 5% water and that boils at 78.15°C; since the boiling point of this binary azeotrope is below that of pure ethanol, absolute ethanol cannot be obtained by simple distillation. However, if benzene is added to 95% ethanol, a ternary azeotrope of benzene, ethanol, and water, with boiling point 64.9°C, can form; since the proportion of water to ethanol in this azeotrope is greater than that in 95% ethanol, the water can be removed from 95% ethanol by adding benzene and distilling off this azeotrope. Because small amounts of benzene may remain, absolute ethanol should be considered poisonous. Ethanol burns in air with a blue flame, forming carbon dioxide and water. It reacts with active metals to form the metal ethoxide and hydrogen, e.g., with sodium it forms sodium ethoxide. It reacts with certain acids to form esters, e.g., with acetic acid it forms ethyl acetate. It can be oxidized to form acetic acid and acetaldehyde. It can be dehydrated to form diethyl ether or, at higher temperatures, ethylene. Ethanol is the alcohol of beer, wines, and liquors. It can be prepared by the fermentation of sugar (e.g., from molasses), which requires an enzyme catalyst that is present in yeast; or it can be prepared by the fermentation of starch (e.g., from corn, rice, rye, or potatoes), which requires, in addition to the yeast enzyme, an enzyme present in an extract of malt. The concentration of ethanol obtained by fermentation is limited to about 10% (20 proof) since at higher concentrations ethanol inhibits the catalytic effect of the yeast enzyme. (The proof concentration of an alcoholic beverage is numerically double the percentage concentration.) For nonbeverage uses ethanol is more commonly prepared by passing ethylene gas at high pressure into concentrated sulfuric or phosphoric acid to form the corresponding ester; the acid-ester mixture is diluted with water and heated, forming ethanol by hydrolysis, and the alcohol is then removed from the mixture by distillation, usually with steam. Ethanol is used extensively as a solvent in the manufacture of varnishes and perfumes; as a preservative for biological specimens; in the preparation of essences and flavorings; in many medicines and drugs; as a disinfectant and in tinctures (e.g., tincture of iodine); and as a fuel. Denatured, or industrial, alcohol is ethanol to which poisonous or nauseating substances have been added to prevent its use as a beverage; a beverage tax is not charged on such alcohol, so its cost is quite low. Medically, ethanol is a soporific, i.e., sleep-producing; although it is less toxic than the other alcohols, death usually occurs if the concentration of ethanol in the bloodstream exceeds about 5%. Behavioral changes, impairment of vision, or unconsciousness occur at lower concentrations. See ALCOHOLISM.

Ethbaal (ĕthbā'əl, ĕth'bāəl), king of the Zidonians, Jezebel's father. 1 Kings 16.31.

Ethel-. For Anglo-Saxon names beginning thus, see ÆTHEL-; e.g., for Ethelbald, see ÆTHELBALD.

ethene: see ETHYLENE.

Ether (ē'thər). **1** Unidentified location, SW Palestine. Joshua 15.42. **2** Unidentified place, SW Palestine. Joshua 19.7.

ether, any of a number of organic compounds whose molecules contain two hydrocarbon groups joined by single bonds to an oxygen atom. The most common of these compounds is ethyl ether, $CH_3CH_2OCH_2CH_3$, often called simply ether, a colorless, volatile liquid with a distinctive odor; its IUPAC name is ethoxyethane. Ethyl ether boils at 34.5°C and is extremely flammable. It is insoluble in water but mixes with many organic solvents and is widely used as a solvent itself, e.g., for fats and oils. Its most familiar application is as an anesthetic. An ether such as ethyl ether in which both hydrocarbon groups are identical is said to be a simple, or symmetrical, ether. An ether in which the two groups differ (e.g., methyl ethyl ether, $CH_3OCH_2CH_3$) is said to be a mixed, or unsymmetrical, ether. Ethers are often prepared commercially by heating an alcohol with sulfuric acid; the reaction is one of dehydration. In the laboratory ethers are often prepared by reaction of an alkyl halide with a sodium alkoxide (a method called the Williamson synthesis). Ethers are usually chemically unreactive but can be cleaved (broken apart) at high temperatures by concentrated hydrogen halides; initially an alkyl halide and an alcohol are formed. Epoxides are a special class of ethers.

$$R—O—R'$$

general formula

$$CH_3CH_2—O—CH_2CH_3$$

diethyl ether

$$C_6H_5—O—CH_3$$

phenyl methyl ether

Ethers

ether or **aether,** in physics and astronomy, a hypothetical medium for transmitting light and heat (radiation), filling all unoccupied space; it is also called luminiferous ether. In Newtonian physics all waves are propagated through a medium, e.g., water waves through water, sound waves through air. When James Clerk Maxwell developed his electromagnetic theory of light, Newtonian physicists postulated ether as the medium that transmitted electromagnetic waves. Ether was held to be invisible, without odor, and of such a nature that it did not interfere with the motions of bodies through space. The concept was intended to connect the Newtonian mechanistic wave theory with Maxwell's field theory; it was, however, inconsistent with Newtonian mechanics and with the fact that the velocity of light is a constant. Moreover, all attempts to demonstrate its existence, most notably the Michelson-Morley experiment of 1887, produced negative results and stimulated a vigorous debate among physicists that was not ended until the special theory of RELATIVITY, proposed by Albert Einstein in 1905, became accepted. The theory of relativity eliminated the need for a light-transmitting medium, so that today the term *ether* is used only in a historical context.

Etherege, Sir George (ĕth'ərĭj), 1634?–1691, English dramatist. His witty, licentious comedies—*The Comical Revenge; or, Love in a Tub* (1664), *She Wou'd If She Cou'd* (1668), and *The Man of Mode; or, Sir Fopling Flutter* (1676)—set the tone of the Restoration comedy of manners that Congreve was to perfect. His years spent as English minister to Ratisbon (1685–89) are recorded in his *Letterbook* (ed. by Sybil Rosenfeld, 1928). See his works (2 vol., ed. by H. F. B. Brett-Smith, 1927; repr. 1971).

Ethical Culture movement, originating in the Society for Ethical Culture, founded in New York City in 1876, by Felix ADLER. Its aim is "to assert the supreme importance of the ethical factor in all relations of life, personal, social, national, and international, apart from any theological or metaphysical considerations." No definite ethical system is insisted upon, although Adler's own ethical thought has naturally had much influence. The society holds its own religious services, but members may have other religious affiliations if they wish. Societies were organized in Chicago (1882), Philadelphia (1885), St. Louis (1886), Brooklyn, N.Y. (1906), and later in other cities. In England, Stanton Coit founded the South Place Ethical Society, London, in 1887; other societies have since been founded there. In 1896 the International Union of Ethical Societies was organized, uniting the movement, which had become worldwide. Although its membership is not large, the movement has enlisted a number of intellectual leaders. See David S. Muzzey, *Ethics as a Religion* (1951, repr. 1967); H. B. Radest, *Toward Common Ground* (1969).

ethics, in philosophy, the study and evaluation of human conduct in the light of moral principles. Moral principles may be viewed either as the standard of conduct that the individual has constructed for himself or as the body of obligations and duties that a particular society requires of its members. Ethics has developed as man has reflected on the intentions and consequences of his acts. From this reflection on the nature of human behavior, theories of CONSCIENCE have developed, giving direction to much ethical thinking. The intuitionists (Ralph Cudworth, J. J. Rousseau, the 3d earl of SHAFTESBURY, and Francis HUTCHESON) postulated an innate moral sense, which serves as the ground of ethical decision. The empiricists (Auguste Comte, John LOCKE, Claude HELVÉTIUS, John Stuart MILL) deny any such innate principle and consider conscience a power of discrimination acquired by experience. In the one case conscience is the originator of moral behavior, and in the other it is the result of moralizing. Between these extremes there have been many compromises. Another major difference in the approach to ethical problems revolves about the question of absolute good as opposed to relative good. Throughout the history of philosophy men have sought an absolute criterion of ethics. Frequently moral codes have been based on religious absolutes. Immanuel Kant, in his categorical imperative, attempted to establish an ethical criterion independent of theological considerations. Rationalists (PLATO, Baruch SPINOZA, Josiah ROYCE) founded their ethics on a metaphysics. All varying methods of building an ethical system pose the question of the degree to which morality is authoritarian (i.e., imposed by a power outside the individual). If the criterion of morality is the welfare of the state (G. W. HEGEL), the state is supreme arbiter. If the authority is a religion, then that religion is the ethical teacher. HEDONISM, which equates the good with pleasure in its various forms, finds its ethical criterion either in the good of the individual or the good of the group. An egoistic hedonism (ARISTIPPUS, EPICURUS, Julien de LA METTRIE, Thomas Hobbes) views the good of the individual as the ultimate consideration. A universalistic hedonism, such as utilitarianism (Jeremy BENTHAM, James MILL), finds the ethical criterion in the greatest good for the greatest number. Among modern ethical theories are instrumentalism (John DEWEY), for which morality lies within the individual and is relative to his experience; emotivism (Sir Alfred J. AYER), wherein ethical considerations are merely expressions of the subjective desires of the individual; and intuitionalism (G. E. MOORE), which postulates an immediate awareness of the morally good. See Albert Schweitzer, *Civilization and Ethics* (3d ed. 1946, repr. 1961); A. C. Ewing, *Ethics* (1953, repr. 1962); V. J. Bourke, *Ethics* (2nd ed. 1966); A. C. MacIntyre, *A Short History of Ethics* (1966); Frederick Olafson, *Ethics and Twentieth-Century Thought* (1973).

Ethiopia (ēthēō'pēə), country (1970 est. pop. 24,315,400), 471,776 sq mi (1,221,900 sq km), NE Africa, formerly widely called Abyssinia, bordering on the Red Sea in the north, on the French Territory of the Afars and Issas in the northeast, on Somalia in the east and southeast, on Kenya in the south, and on Sudan in the west. ADDIS ABABA is the capital and largest city of the country, which is divided into 14 provinces. Ethiopia falls into four main geographic regions from west to east—the Ethiopian Plateau, the Great Rift Valley, the Somali Plateau, and the Ogaden Plateau. The Ethiopian Plateau, which is fringed in the west by the Sudan lowlands (made up of savanna and forests), includes more than half the country. It is generally 5,000 to 6,000 ft (1,524–1,829 m) high, but reaches much loftier heights, including Ras Dashan (15,158 ft/4,620 m), the highest point in Ethiopia. The plateau slopes gently from east to west and is cut by numerous deep valleys. The Blue Nile River (in Ethiopia called the Abbai) flows through the center of the plateau from its source, Lake Tana, Ethiopia's largest lake. The Great Rift Valley (which in its entirety runs from SW Asia to E central Africa) traverses the country from northeast to southwest and contains the Danakil Desert in the north and several large lakes in the south. The Somali Plateau is generally not as high as the Ethiopian Plateau, but in the Urgoma Mts. it attains heights of more than 14,000 ft (4,267 m). The Awash, Ethiopia's only navigable river, drains the central part of the plateau. The Ogaden Plateau (1,500–3,000 ft/457–914 m high) is mostly desert but includes the Wabi-Shabale, Ganale-Dorya (Juba), and Dawa rivers. About 70% of Ethiopia's population (which is about 90% rural) lives in highlands above 5,900 ft (1,800 m), which receive plentiful rainfall and are free of malaria-carrying mosquitoes. The country's inhabitants are equally divided among adherents of Christianity (the great majority of whom belong to the Coptic Ethiopian Orthodox Church), Islam, and traditional religions. There are several distinct ethnic groups. The Amhara and Tigrinya, who together comprise about 33% of the population, live mostly in the central and northern Ethiopian Plateau; they are Copts and hold most of the higher positions in the government. AMHARIC is the country's official language. The GALLA, who make up about 40% of the country's population, live in S Ethiopia; about 40% of them are Muslim, and about 20% are Christian. The pastoral Somali, who are mostly Muslim, live in E and SE Ethiopia. The FALASHAS, a small group of Jews, live north of Lake Tana. There are also groups of Greeks, Italians, Armenians, Arabs, and Indians, totaling about 60,000, who play an important role in the country's commerce. Ethiopia is an overwhelmingly agricultural country, with the great majority of its economically active population engaged in inefficient subsistence farming. Modern commercial agriculture accounts for less than 10% of annual farm output. The chief farm products are teff and other millets, sorghum, barley, wheat, maize, plantains, peas, potatoes, coffee, groundnuts, cotton, sugarcane, and tobacco. Large numbers of poultry, cattle, sheep, and goats are raised. Industry is related mostly to basic consumer needs; the main industrial centers are Addis Ababa, ASMARA, DIREDAWA, and HARAR. The leading manufactures include processed food, beverages, textiles and clothing, leather goods, cement, and refined petroleum. No large-scale mineral deposits have been found in Ethiopia; salt, limestone, gold, platinum, iron ore, and sulfur are extracted in small quantities. Economic development in the country has been hindered by the poor transportation network; there are only two rail lines, and most roads are not usable year round. The chief ports serving Ethiopia are Djibouti (in the French Territory of the Afars and Issas), ASSAB, and MASSAWA. The annual value of imports into Ethiopia is usually considerably higher than the value of its exports. The principal imports are machinery, motor vehicles, petroleum products, chemicals, and manufactured consumer goods; the main exports are coffee, oilseeds, hides and skins, and grain. The leading trade partners are the United States, West Germany, Italy, and Japan. Educational facilities in Ethiopia are very limited, and in the early 1970s only about 10% of the inhabitants above nine years of age were literate. There are universities at Addis Ababa and Asmara.

History. According to tradition, the Ethiopian kingdom was founded (10th cent. B.C.) by Solomon's first son, Menelik I, whom the queen of Sheba is supposed to have borne. However, the first kingdom for which there is documentary evidence is that of AKSUM (Axum), probably founded in the 1st cent. A.D. by immigrants (mainly traders) from S Arabia who had been settling in N Ethiopia since about 500 B.C. Aksum controlled much of the Red Sea coast and had links with the Mediterranean world. Under King Ezana, Aksum was converted (4th cent.) to Christianity by Frumentius of Tyre, who was subsequently made the first bishop of Ethiopia by the patriarch of Alexandria. Closely tied to the Egyptian Coptic Church, the established Ethiopian church accepted MONOPHYSITISM following the Council of Chalcedon (451). In the 5th–6th cent. the rulers of Aksum sponsored vigorous missionary work, and in the mid-6th cent. King Kaleb invaded Yemen to aid Christians who were being persecuted there. Also in the 6th cent., Jewish influence penetrated Aksum, and some Ethiopians (of whom the modern Falashas are descendants) were converted to Judaism. With the rise of Islam in the 7th cent. Aksum declined, mainly because its land contacts with the Byzantine Empire were severed and its control of the Red Sea trade routes was ended. Thereafter, the focus of Aksum was directed inward toward the center of the Ethiopian Plateau (mainly the regions of Amhara and Shoa), and it was largely cut off from the outside world. Aksum soon lost its cohesion, and Ethiopia lapsed into a period of competition among small political units. The traditional Solomonian line was broken by the Zagwe dynasty (1137–1270), which temporarily moved the capital away from Aksum. A literary and artistic revival followed the restoration of Solomonian rule in 1270; many works were written in the fields of hagiology, biblical exegesis (based on the GEEZ translation of the Septuagint), and history, and book illumination and church architecture flourished. The close ties between Christianity and the government helped to strengthen central authority. At the same time, there were several wars (13–16th cent.) between Muslim states and the Solomonians, and Islam gained adherents in S and NE Ethiopia. The attendance of some Ethiopian monks at an ecumenical council at Florence in 1441 aroused European interest in Ethiopia, which, it was thought, might be the land of the fabulous PRESTER JOHN. A Portuguese embassy reached the Ethiopian court in 1520. In 1530–31, Ahmad Gran, a Muslim Somali leader, conquered much of Ethiopia. The Ethiopian negus (emperor) Lebna Dengel (reigned 1508–40) appealed to Portugal for help against the Somalis, and Portuguese troops were instrumental in defeating them (1543). However, the Somali war exhausted Ethiopia, end-

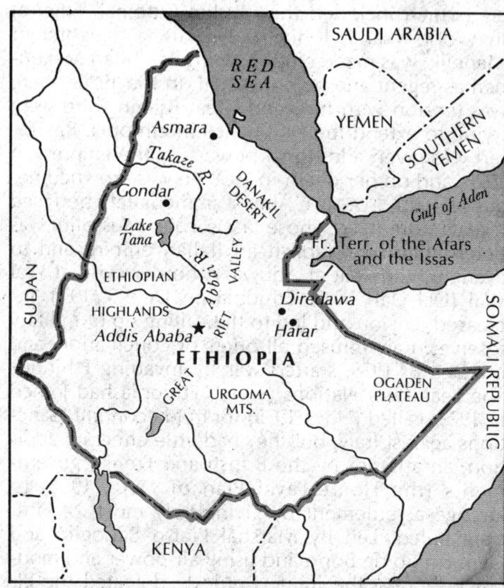

ing the cultural revival and exposing the empire to incursions by the Galla. In 1622, through the efforts of Pedro PAEZ, Negus Susenyos was converted to Roman Catholicism. The Ethiopian nobility and the Coptic clergy resisted Susenyos's efforts to impose Catholicism and forced him to abdicate in 1632. His son Fasilidas reestablished the Ethiopian church, expelled the Catholic clergy, and closed the country to foreigners. For the next two centuries the Ethiopian kingdom, centered at GONDAR near Lake Tana, was beset by ruinous civil wars among princes (especially those of Tigre and Amhara), was menaced by the Galla, and was again isolated from the outside world. In 1769–70, the Scots explorer James BRUCE, one of the few foreigners to visit Ethiopia, traveled through much of the country. The reunification of Ethiopia was begun in the 19th cent. by Kasa (Lij Kasa; c.1818–68), who, starting as a petty chieftain in NW Ethiopia, conquered Amhara, Gojjam, Tigre, and Shoa, and in 1855 had himself crowned negus as THEODORE (Tewodros) II. He began to modernize and centralize the legal and administrative systems, despite the opposition of local governors. Toward the end of his reign Theodore became mentally unbalanced. Feeling slighted because Queen Victoria of Great Britain had not replied to a letter he had sent her, he imprisoned (1867) several Britons, including the British consul. A British military expedition under Robert (later Lord) NAPIER was sent out, and the negus's forces were easily defeated near MAGDALA in 1868. To avoid capture, Theodore committed suicide. A brief civil war followed, and in 1872 a chieftain of Tigre became negus as John (Yohannes) IV. John's attempts to further centralize the government led to revolts by local leaders; in addition, his regime was threatened during 1875–76 by Egyptian incursions and, after 1881, by raids of the followers of the MAHDI in Sudan. The opening (1869) of the Suez Canal increased the strategic importance of Ethiopia, and several European powers (particularly Italy, France, and Great Britain) sought influence in the area. John was killed (1889) fighting the Mahdists, and, following a short succession crisis, the king of Shoa (who had Italian support) was crowned negus as MENELIK II. Also in 1889, Menelik signed a treaty of friendship and cooperation with Italy at Ucciali. A dispute promptly broke out over the meaning of article 17 of the treaty. Italy, citing the Italian version of the treaty, claimed that it had been given a protectorate over Ethiopia; Menelik, referring to the Amharic version, denied the claim. Italy invaded Ethiopia in 1895, and in the war that followed Menelik decisively defeated the Italians at ADUWA (Adowa) on March 1, 1896. By the subsequent Treaty of Addis Ababa (Oct., 1896), the Treaty of Ucciali was annulled, and Italy recognized the independence of Ethiopia. During his reign, Menelik also greatly expanded the size of Ethiopia, adding the provinces of Harar (in the east), Sidamo (in the south), and Kaffa (in the southwest). In addition, he further modernized the military and the government, made (1889) Addis Ababa the capital of the country, developed the economy, started a postal system, and promoted the building of the country's first railroad (financed by French capital). Menelik died in 1913 and was succeeded by his grandson Lij Iyasu, who was deposed in 1916. Lij

Iyasu had alienated his fellow countrymen by favoring Muslims and antagonizing the British, French, and Italians through his support of the Central Powers (which included the Muslim Ottoman Empire) in World War I. Judith (Zawditu), a daughter of Menelik, was made empress with Ras Tafari Makonnen as regent and heir apparent. In the 1920s, there was tension with Italy and Great Britain, who were trying to extend their influence in Ethiopia. Ras Tafari was given additional powers by the empress in 1928, and on her death in 1930 he was crowned negus as HAILE SELASSIE I. Almost immediately he faced threats from Italy, whose fascist ruler Mussolini was determined to establish an Italian empire and to avenge the defeat at Aduwa. A border clash at Wal Wal (Ual Ual) in SE Ethiopia on Dec. 5, 1934, increased tension and led to the calling up of military reserves. Italy refused all offers of conciliation, and on Oct. 3, 1935, started war by invading Ethiopia. The League of Nations (which Ethiopia had joined in 1923) called (Nov., 1935) for mild economic sanctions against Italy, but they had little effect. In addition, an attempt by the British and French governments (the Hoare-Laval Plan of Dec., 1935) to arrange a settlement by giving Italy much of Ethiopia failed. Led by Marshal Pietro Badoglio and Gen. Emilio de Bono and using air power and modern weapons, the Italians quickly defeated the ill-equipped Ethiopians. In May, 1936, Addis Ababa was captured, and Haile Selassie fled the country. On June 1, 1936, the king of Italy was also made emperor of Ethiopia, and the country was combined with Eritrea (already held by Italy) and Italian Somaliland to form ITALIAN EAST AFRICA. In the late 1930s, Italy greatly expanded the road system in Ethiopia. In 1941, during World War II, British and South African forces easily conquered Ethiopia, and Haile Selassie regained his throne. Britain had considerable influence in Ethiopian affairs until the end of the war and administered the small Haud region in the southeast (adjacent to present-day Somalia) until 1955. In 1945, Ethiopia became a charter member of the United Nations. Eritrea was federated with Ethiopia in 1952, and in 1962 it was made an integral part of the country; Ethiopia thus gained direct access to the sea. In 1955 a new Ethiopian constitution came into force, and in 1958 the Ethiopian church became independent of the Coptic patriarch in Egypt. Despite considerable aid from the United States and other countries, Ethiopia remained economically underdeveloped, with its wealth concentrated in the hands of a small number of large landlords and the Ethiopian church. On Dec. 14, 1960, while Haile Selassie was in Brazil, a coup d'etat was carried out by persons (especially members of the imperial bodyguard) seeking a more equitable distribution of wealth and power in the country. However, the negus was restored to power by the army and air force when he returned to Ethiopia a few days later. Between 1961 and 1967 there were border skirmishes between Ethiopia and Somalia, and in the late 1960s and early 70s there was considerable fighting between the central government and a guerrilla secessionist movement in Eritrea. In 1966, Haile Selassie instituted several reforms, including the granting of more power to the cabinet (led by prime minister Aklilou Habte-Wold). Nevertheless, unrest continued among groups (particularly high school and university students) seeking more far-reaching reforms. In a gradual coup d'etat that began in Feb., 1974, and culminated in September with the ouster of Haile Selassie, a group of military officers seized control of the government. After the deposition of the negus, the constitution was suspended, parliament was dissolved, and Lt. Gen. Aman Michael Andom became head of a newly formed cabinet. Crown Prince ASFA WOSSEN, who had suffered a stroke in 1972, was invited to return to Ethiopia from Europe to become negus with very little power, but it seemed unlikely that he would accept the offer. Northern Ethiopia in 1973–74 was ravaged by a long-term drought; Haile Selassie's failure to deal adequately with the widespread starvation there was reportedly a major reason for his downfall. Ethiopia has played a leading role in African affairs in the era of independence, as has been demonstrated by the establishment at Addis Ababa of the UN Economic Commission for Africa in 1958 and the Organization of African Unity in 1963. See Nathen Marein, *The Ethiopian Empire* (1955); E. S. Pankhurst, *Ethiopia: A Cultural History* (1955); D. R. Buxton, *Travels in Ethiopia* (1957); E. W. Luther, *Ethiopia Today* (1958); A. H. M. Jones and Elizabeth Monroe, *History of Ethiopia* (rev. ed. 1960); Richard Greenfield, *Ethiopia: A New Political History* (1967); Richard Pankhurst, *Economic History of Ethiopia, 1880–1935* (1968); Christopher Clapham, *Haile Selassie's Government* (1969); Assefa Bequele and Eshutu Chole, *A Profile of the Ethiopian Economy* (1969); R. L. Hess, *Ethiopia: The Modernization of Autocracy* (1970); Peter Schwab, *Decision-Making in Ethiopia: A Study of the Political Process* (1972); Edward Ullendorff, *The Ethiopians* (3d. ed. 1973); John Markakis, *Ethiopia: Anatomy of a Traditional Polity* (1974).

Ethiopian Highlands, rugged plateau region of E Africa, covering about two thirds of Ethiopia. It is divided into two massifs by the Great Rift Valley; the Amhara, or Ethiopian Plateau, is the larger of the two. The region, which slopes away from either side of the Great Rift Valley, is composed of a series of mountains and valleys; Ras Dashan (15,158 ft/4,620 m), Ethiopia's highest peak, is there.

Ethiopic (ēthēŏp'ĭk), extinct language of Ethiopia belonging to the North Ethiopic group of the Ethiopian Semitic languages, which, in turn, belong to the Southeast Semitic subdivision of the Semitic subfamily of the Hamito-Semitic family of languages (see HAMITO-SEMITIC LANGUAGES). Ethiopic (also called Geez or classical Ethiopic) ceased to be a spoken tongue in Ethiopia some time before the 14th cent. A.D., but it long remained the medium for Ethiopian literature and is still in use in the liturgy of the Abyssinian Church. Modern languages of some importance now spoken in Ethiopia that represent the extinct Ethiopic are Tigre, Tigrinya, and AMHARIC. Because Semitic Ethiopic is close to ancient South Arabic lexically and grammatically, it has been suggested that its speakers originally came from S Arabia, whence they apparently began to migrate to Ethiopia in the first millennium B.C. The native Cushitic tongues of Ethiopia (which were of the Hamitic subfamily of Hamito-Semitic languages) exerted a degree of influence on the newly arrived Semitic language or languages with respect to grammar, vocabulary, and phonology. Although the script used for Ethiopic and other Semitic tongues of Ethiopia is syllabic rather than alphabetic, it seems to be derived from the alphabetic South Semitic writing of the South Arabic inscriptions, to which it shows many similarities. The reason for the syllabic development of the Ethiopic script is not known. Since the 4th cent. A.D., when Ethiopia was Christianized, the Ethiopic script has been written from left to right, though previously the direction of writing was from right to left. See August Dillmann, *Ethiopic Grammar* (tr. 1907); A. B. Mercer, *Ethiopic Grammar with Chrestomathy and Glossary* (rev. ed. 1961).

Ethnan (ĕth'nən), son of Ashur. 1 Chron. 4.7.

Ethni (ĕth'nī), ancestor of Asaph the singer, perhaps the same as JEATERAI. 1 Chron. 6.41.

ethnic group, distinct category in the population of a larger society, whose culture is usually different from that of the majority of the society. The members of an ethnic group are bound together by common ties of race, nationality, or culture, or may feel themselves to be, or are thought to be. The existence of distinct ethnic groups is widespread and ancient and is found at most levels of culture. Early historians noted that ethnic groups might be found in a society as a result of the gradual migration of whole populations or segments; that military conquest brought in its wake soldiers and civilians who either settled permanently or administered the territory for a time; that the altering of political boundaries has incorporated some ethnic groups into a society. However they came to be there, the types of society in which ethnic groups are found vary as widely as the processes that gave rise to them.

ethnic studies, in American education, programs offering courses in the history and culture of minority groups in the United States. Ethnic studies arose as a result of the black protest movement of the 1960s, which, among other things, deplored the lack of cultural relevance for blacks in the curricula of the U.S. educational establishment. The contention was seconded by other non-European ethnic minorities. In the late 1960s, black history, literature, and interdisciplinary humanities courses were instituted at some universities to promote understanding of cultural heritage, analysis of political problems and solutions, and encouragement of artistic endeavors. To a lesser extent, other minorities, especially Chicano (Mexican-American) and Hispanic, have obtained similar course offerings.

ethnocentrism, the feeling that one's group has a mode of living, values, and patterns of adaptation that are superior to other groups. It is coupled with a generalized contempt for members of other groups. Ethnocentrism may manifest itself in attitudes of superiority or sometimes hostility. Violence, discrimination, proselytizing, and verbal aggressiveness are other means whereby ethnocentrism may be expressed.

ethnography: see ANTHROPOLOGY; ETHNOLOGY.

ethnology (ĕthnŏl'əjē), scientific study of the origin and functioning of humans and their cultures. It is usually considered one of the major branches of cultural ANTHROPOLOGY, the other two being anthropological archaeology and anthropological linguistics. In the 19th cent. ethnology was historically oriented and offered explanations for extant cultures, languages, and races in terms of diffusion, migration, and other historical processes. In the 20th cent. ethnology has focused on the comparative study of past and contemporary cultures. Since cultural phenomena can seldom be studied under conditions of experiment or control, comparative data from the total range of human behavior helps the ethnologist to avoid those assumptions about human nature that may be implicit in the dictates of any single culture. See R. H. Lowie, *The History of Ethnological Theory* (1938); E. A. Hoebel, *Man in the Primitive World* (1949, 2d ed. 1958); Margaret Mead, *People and Places* (1959); Barton Schwartz, *Culture and Society* (1968); Clifford Geertz, *The Interpretation of Culture* (1973); Elvin Hatch, *Theories of Man and Culture* (1973).

ethology, study of animal behavior, especially its physiological, ecological, and evolutionary aspects. Originally, an organism's actions were classified as either instinctive behavior or learned behavior; the former included those actions, such as common reflexes, that are not influenced by the animal's previous experience, and the latter comprised those actions, such as problem solving, that are dependent on earlier experiences. Current thinking emphasizes the interaction of environment and genetically determined responses, especially during early development. Among the early ethologists were Herbert Spencer, Charles Darwin, G. J. Romanes, and William James. In 1973 the Nobel Prize in Medicine and Physiology was awarded to Karl von Frisch, Konrad Lorenz, and Nikolaas Tinbergen for their work in animal behavior. See INSTINCT; IMPRINTING.

ethyl (ĕth'əl), CH_3CH_2, organic FREE RADICAL or ALKYL GROUP derived from ETHANE by removing one hydrogen atom.

ethyl alcohol: see ETHANOL.

ethylene (ĕth'əlēn") or **ethene** (ĕth'ēn), $H_2C=CH_2$, a gaseous unsaturated hydrocarbon. It is the simplest ALKENE. Ethylene is colorless, has a faint odor, and has a slightly sweet taste; it melts at −169.4°C and boils at −103.8°C. Because of the presence of the double bond in its molecule, ethylene is very reactive. It burns in air with a luminous flame and forms explosive mixtures with pure oxygen. It combines directly with the halogens, e.g., with chlorine to form 1,2-dichloroethane. With hydrogen it forms ethane. Ethylene may be prepared by the dehydration of ethanol with sulfuric acid at about 180°C. It is prepared commercially from natural gas and petroleum, e.g., by cracking and fractional distillation. Ethylene has many uses. It is important in the synthesis of many chemicals. It is used in making polyethylene and saran, in the manufacture of ethanol and ethylene oxide, and as an anesthetic. Ethylene was called olefiant gas by early chemists.

ethylene glycol: see GLYCOL.

ethylene series: see ALKENE.

ethyne (ĕth'īn), IUPAC name for ACETYLENE.

Étienne, family of printers: see ESTIENNE.

etiquette, name for the codes of rules governing social or diplomatic intercourse. These codes vary from the more or less flexible laws of social usage (differing according to local customs or taboos) to the rigid conventions of court, naval, and military circles, and they extend to the legal, medical, and other professions. Some system of etiquette has prevailed in all stages of culture; the variations that occur serve as a partial index to differing societal attitudes toward morals and conduct. See Emily Post, *Etiquette* (12th ed. 1968); *Amy Vanderbilt's Etiquette* (rev. ed. 1972).

Etna or **Aetna** (both: ĕt'nə), volcano, 10,958 ft (3,340 m) high, on the east coast of Sicily, S Italy. It is the highest active volcano in Europe. The shape and height of its central cone have often been changed by eruptions. There are more than 260 lesser craters on the slopes, formed by lateral eruptions. The southeastern slope is cut by a deep (2,000–4,000-ft/610–1219-m), precipitous cleft, the Valle del Bove. The first known eruption occurred in 475 B.C. and was described by Pindar and Aeschylus. Of the numerous later eruptions, often accompanied by earthquakes, those of 1169 and 1669 were the most destructive; the most recent occurred in 1971. The wide base of Mt. Etna, c.93 mi (150 km) in circumference, is encircled by a railroad. Up to 1,600 ft (488 m) the vegetation is subtropical, yielding citrus fruit, bananas, and figs; between 1,600 and 4,300 ft (488–1,311 m) is a temperate zone, with vineyards and various fruit trees; from there to c.7,000 ft (2,130 m) are chestnut, birch, and pine woods; above, there is a desolate waste of lava and ashes. Near the top there is snow most of the year. The fertile lower slopes are densely populated agricultural areas. There is an observatory at 9,650 ft (2,941 m). A motor road from Nicolosi, NW of Catania, to the 6,170-ft (1,881-m) level was completed in 1935.

Étoile, Place de l', Paris: see ARC DE TRIOMPHE DE L'ÉTOILE.

Eton, urban district (1971 pop. 3,954), Buckinghamshire, central England, on the Thames River. It is known chiefly for **Eton College,** largest and most famous of the English public schools, founded with King's College, Cambridge Univ., by King Henry VI in 1440. Some of the buildings (chapel, lower school, cloisters) date back to the 15th cent. Eton is unlike other English public schools in that it does not have a prefect system. At Eton senior students have a larger voice in the selection of student leaders. Another distinctive feature at Eton is the tutorial system, by which each student has a personal tutor. Many of England's outstanding men were schooled at Eton. It has had a close alliance with King's College, Cambridge, since their founding. Originally 70 Eton scholars were to go on to King's College. Today 24 King's College scholarships are reserved for Etonians; Eton grants 70 scholarships on the basis of competitive examinations. The annual cricket match between Eton and Harrow attracts much attention.

Etosha Game Park (ātō'shä), c.26,000 sq mi (67,300 sq km), NW South West Africa, SW Africa; est. 1928. It is Africa's largest game reserve and extends inland from the coast to Etosha Pan on the plains. The Moçâmedes Reserve (3,475 sq mi/9,000 sq km; est. 1957), in SW Angola, borders it on the north.

Etowah, river, 141 mi (227 km) long, rising in the Blue Ridge Mts., N Ga., and flowing SW to Rome, Ga., where it joins the Oostanaula River to form the Coosa. Allatoona Dam, built for flood control and hydroelectric power (110,000-kw capacity), is important in the development and growth of manufacturing in N Georgia and N Alabama. **Etowah Mounds,** a national historic landmark, is a group of prehistoric Indian earthworks 60 ft (18 m) high, located on the river near Cartersville, Ga.

Etruria (ĭtrŏŏr'ēə), ancient country, W central Italy, now forming Tuscany and part of Umbria. It was the territory of the Etruscans, who in the 6th cent. B.C. spread ETRUSCAN CIVILIZATION throughout much of Italy. They were later forced back into Etruria and ultimately dispersed.

Etruscan art, the art of the inhabitants of Etruria, which, by the 8th cent. B.C., incorporated the area in Italy from Salerno to the Tiber River. Archaeologists have been unable to trace the precise development of Etruscan art. Although clearly much is owed to Greek sources, Etruscan works have a definite character of their own. The principal centers of art were Caere (Cerveteri), Tarquinii, Vulci, and Veii (Veio). As a consequence of abundant ore deposits, bronze statuary was common, as were large-scale carvings. Most Etruscan sculpture, however, was executed in clay. The Etruscan cult of the dead, similar to contemporaneous Egyptian practices, produced a highly developed sepulchral art. Clay sarcophagi and urns were modeled with great skill. The sculptured lids of sarcophagi often represented a single figure or a couple reclining on a couch. These figures wore the haunting archaic smile evident in early Greek sculpture. The amazingly naturalistic Etruscan portrait busts were probably a source for later Roman portrait sculpture. Fresco paintings were common in the underground funerary vaults; they depict banquets, festivals, and scenes of daily life. Executed in a strictly two-dimensional style, they are decorated with foliage motifs. ROMAN ART absorbed the Etruscan by the 1st cent. B.C. See studies by Emeline Richardson (1964), Raymond Bloch (1966), Mario Moretti (1966, tr. 1972), Axel Boethius and J. B. Ward-Perkins (1970).

Etruscan civilization, highest civilization in Italy before the rise of Rome. The core of the territory of the Etruscans, known as Etruria to the Latins, was NW of the Tiber River, now in modern TUSCANY and part of UMBRIA. The Latins called the people Etrusci, and the Greeks called them Tyrrhenoi [whence Tyrrhenian Sea]. The fact that their language and culture differed markedly from that of other ancient peoples of the Italian peninsula at the time—Villanovans, Umbrians, and Picenes—indicates that they were of foreign origin. Some scholars consider them as indigenous to Italy, but evidence does not generally uphold this belief. The theory that they came down from the north has been largely abandoned, and modern research tends to uphold the tradition of Herodotus that the Etruscans migrated to Italy from Lydia in Asia Minor in the 12th cent. B.C. At any rate, a distinctive Etruscan culture evolved about the 8th cent. B.C., developed rapidly during the 7th cent., achieved its peak of power and wealth during the 6th cent., and declined during the 5th and 4th cent. Etruria had no centralized government, but rather comprised a loose confederation of city-states, based primarily on religious rather than political ties. Important centers were: Clusium (modern Chiusi), Tarquinii (modern Tarquinia), Caere (modern Cervetri), Veii (modern Veio), Volterra, Vetulonia, Perusia (modern Perugia), and Volsinii (modern Bolsena). The political domination of the Etruscans was at its height c.500 B.C., when they had consolidated the Umbrian cities and had occupied a large part of Latium. During this period the Etruscans were a great maritime power and established colonies on Corsica, Elba, Sardinia, the Balearic Islands, and on the coast of Spain. Etruscan wealth and power was in part based upon their knowledge of ironworking and their exploitation of iron deposits that were abundant in Etruria. They brought the older art of bronze working to a new level of achievement, and Etruscan goldwork was among the finest anywhere in the ancient world. Extant examples of their craftsmanship are the large bronze portraits *Brutus* (Palazzo dei Conservatori, Rome) and *Orator* (Museo Archeologico, Florence) as well as many fine tomb paintings. The Etruscans were also noted for their black *bucchero* pottery and were experts with the wheel. Much of the actual work in Etruria was done by the native population, who were subject to, though probably not slaves of, their conquerors; the nobility of Etruscan birth formed an exclusive caste. Fond of music, games, and racing, the Etruscans introduced the chariot into Italy. They kept up a large commerce with the East, and many of their art motifs are from the East. In the late 6th cent. a mutual agreement between Etruria and Carthage, with whom Etruria had allied itself against the Greeks c.535 B.C., restricted Etruscan trade, and by the late 5th cent. their sea power had come to an end. Meanwhile the Romans, whose culture had been greatly influenced by the Etruscans (the TARQUIN rulers of Rome were Etruscans), were distrustful of Etruscan power. In the early 4th cent., after Etruria had been weakened by Gallic invasions, the Romans attempted to beat the Etruscans back. Beginning with Veii (c.396 B.C.) one Etruscan city after another fell to the Romans, and civil war further weakened Etruscan power. During the Social War (90 B.C.–88 B.C.) of Sulla and Marius the remaining Etruscan families allied themselves with Marius and in 88 B.C. Sulla eradicated the last traces of Etruscan independence. The Etruscan language presents difficulties to the scholar. It can be easily read (the alphabet is of Greek extraction, and the sound value of the signs is known), but, with the exception of only a few words, the vocabulary is not understood. Although the language seems to contain both Indo-European and non-Indo-European elements as well as traces of ancient Mediterranean tongues, it cannot be classified into any known group of languages. Inscriptions in Etruscan are few and short and seem to refer entirely to funeral practices. While religion is perhaps the best-known aspect of Etruscan civilization, even it remains quite enigmatic. Etruscan art, formally dependent upon Greek art, is equally complex for, while the forms are recognizably Hellenized, the underlying spirit still retains a barbaric energy quite opposed to the Greek search for perfection in harmony. See Raymond Bloch, *The Etruscans* (tr. 1958); H. Harrel-Courtès, *Etruscan Italy* (tr. 1964); O. W. von Vacano, *The Etruscans in the Ancient World* (tr. 1960, repr. 1965); Leonard von Malt, *Art of the Etruscans* (1970); Werner Keller, *The Etruscans* (1974).

Ettwein, John (ĕt'vīn), 1721–1802, German-American churchman, leader and bishop of the MORAVIAN CHURCH in the United States. He came to America from Germany in 1754 as a missionary. In his mission work he traveled as far south as Georgia and made several trips to New England. He preached to many Indian tribes and established missions among those in Pennsylvania. In 1772 he led a band of Christian Indians to a new settlement established in Ohio by the Moravian missionary David ZEISBERGER, and after the Revolution he prevailed upon Congress to set aside reservations for the converted Indians. He represented the Moravians in negotiations with the Continental Congress over their refusal to bear arms or subscribe to the Test Act. From 1784 to 1801 he was bishop and head of the church in America. See study by K. G. Hamilton (1940).

Etty, William, 1787–1849, English painter. He studied with Sir Thomas Lawrence and later in Italy, where Venetian painting made a lasting impression on him. Etty is best known for his spirited figure compositions and his large and complex mythological scenes. He achieved fame in 1825 with his *Combat* (Edinburgh). Characteristic are his three Judith pictures (Edinburgh), *The Three Graces* (Metropolitan Mus.), and *Youth at the Prow and Pleasure at the Helm* (Tate Gall., London). See study by Dennis Farr (1958).

étude (ā'tōōd), a brief musical composition, usually for piano, fashioned to instruct an instrumentalist in a particular technical problem, such as scales or trills. Succeeding the toccata, popular in the baroque period, the étude was developed into a compactly crafted musical form by Frédéric Chopin and Franz Liszt.

etymology (ĕtĭmŏl'əjē), branch of linguistics that investigates the history, development and origin of words. It was this study that chiefly revealed the regular relations of sounds in the Indo-European languages (as described in GRIMM'S LAW) and led to the historical investigation of language in the 19th cent. In the 20th cent. linguists continued to use etymology to learn how meanings change, but they came to consider that the meaning of a form at a given time must be understood without reference to its history if it is to be understood at all. The term *etymology* has been replaced by *derivation* for the creation of combinations in a language, such as new nouns formed with the ending *-ness.* See GRAMMAR; DICTIONARY.

Etzel (ĕt'səl), in Germanic mythology, king who corresponds to the historic ATTILA. In the *Nibelungenlied* he appears as Etzel and in the *Volsungasaga* as Atli.

Eu, chemical symbol of the element EUROPIUM.

Euboea, Greece: see ÉVVOIA.

Eubulides (yōōbyōō'lĭdēz), 4th cent. B.C., Greek philosopher, native of Miletus. He was a contemporary and adversary of Aristotle and was the successor of Euclid of Megara as head of the Megarian school.

Eubulus (yōōbyōō'ləs), Christian at Rome. 2 Tim. 4.21.

eucalyptus (yōō"kəlĭp'təs): see MYRTLE.

Eucharist (yōō'kərĭst) [Gr.,=thanksgiving], Christian SACRAMENT that repeats the action of Jesus at his last supper with his disciples, when he gave them bread, saying, "This is my body," and wine, saying, "This is my blood." Mat. 26; Mark 14; Luke 22;1 Cor. 11. Partaking is called communion. The sacrament is a bloodless reenactment of the crucifixion and therefore an act of sacrifice. The performance is called the LITURGY; the Roman and Anglo-Catholic liturgy is the MASS. The official Roman Catholic explanation of the change taking place in the sacrament, called transubstantiation, is that the substances of bread and wine are turned miraculously into the substance of Christ himself, the elements changed retaining only the appearance, taste, etc. (the accidents) of bread and wine. John 6.47–57. Since the Godhead is indivisible, every particle or drop thus changed is wholly identical in substance with the divinity, body, and blood of the Crucified Savior. The views of the Orthodox Eastern Church are basically similar. The Anglican Church has not formally defined the sacrament. In receiving communion the Christian attains union with Jesus, and all who partake are mystically united. Traditionally in the Mass (but not in Eastern liturgies of the Roman Catholic Church) others than the celebrant received the HOST only, a practice that arose from the difficulty of transport and storage of wine. In this communion in one kind the believer was held to receive the same divine whole as the celebrant, who receives both kinds at the altar. Communion in two kinds was restored in the Roman Catholic Church in the liturgical renewal proclaimed at the Second Vatican Council. The Roman Catholic and Orthodox churches set conditions for the reception of communion, which is a sign of membership; to be "in communion with" means mutual recognition of membership in the true church. Devotion to the Eucharist (the Blessed Sacrament) is important in the

Roman Catholic Church. The object of the cult of the Blessed Sacrament is the Host reserved in churches (see BENEDICTION and CORPUS CHRISTI). Every leader of the Protestant Reformation attacked the traditional teaching of the Eucharist. For the communion services in many Protestant churches, see LORD'S SUPPER.

euchre (yo͞o'kər), card game, played usually by four persons (two sets of partners). The pack has 32 cards, from 7 up to ace in each suit. The jack of trumps, called the right bower, ranks highest, and the jack of the other suit of the same color, called the left bower, ranks next. The dealer gives five cards to each player, in two rounds, first three cards and then two or vice versa, as he chooses, and turns up the next card for trumps. The player to the left of the dealer (eldest hand) may accept the turn-up for trumps ("I order it up") or may pass, in which case the option goes to the next player and so on. If all four pass, then the eldest hand may name trumps or pass. A second round of passing calls for a new deal. A trick is won by the highest trump or by the highest card of the suit led. Five points make a game. By making all five tricks (march), the combination that has made trumps scores two points (four if the trump maker plays alone). They score only one point by making either three or four tricks, while if they fail to make three tricks they are euchred and the opponents score two points. Variations of the game are cutthroat, or three-hand euchre; two-hand euchre; and auction euchre. The game is similar to ÉCARTÉ and FIVE HUNDRED.

Eucken, Rudolf Christoph (ro͝o'dôlf krĭs'tôf oik'-ən), 1846–1926, German philosopher, studied at Göttingen and Berlin. He taught philosophy at Basel and became professor of philosophy at Jena (1874). His work attained wide popularity, and he won the 1908 Nobel Prize in Literature. In 1912 he lectured at Harvard. His philosophy, known as activism, stressed personal ethical effort rather than intellectual idealism. English translations of his work include *The Truth of Religion* (1901), *The Life of the Spirit* (1909), and *Knowledge and Life* (1913). See study by W. T. Jones (1914); E. E. Slosson, *Six Major Prophets* (1917, repr. 1972).

Euclid (yo͞o'klĭd), fl. 300 B.C., Greek mathematician. Little is known of his life other than the fact that he taught at Alexandria, being associated with the school that grew up there in the late 4th cent. B.C. He is famous for his *Elements*, a presentation in thirteen books of the geometry and other mathematics known in his day. The first six books cover elementary plane geometry and have served since as the basis for most beginning courses on this subject. The other books of the *Elements* treat the theory of numbers and certain problems in arithmetic (on a geometric basis) and solid geometry, including the five regular polyhedra, or Platonic solids. The great contribution of Euclid was his use of a deductive system for the presentation of mathematics. Primary terms, such as point and line, are defined; unproved assumptions, or postulates, regarding these terms are stated; and a series of statements are then deduced logically from the definitions and postulates. Although Euclid's system no longer satisfies modern requirements of logical rigor, its importance in influencing the direction and method of the development of mathematics is undisputed. One consequence of the critical examination of Euclid's system was the discovery in the early 19th cent. that his fifth postulate, equivalent to the statement that one and only one line parallel to a given line can be drawn through a point external to the line, can not be proved from the other postulates; on the contrary, by substituting a different postulate for this parallel postulate two different self-consistent forms of NON-EUCLIDEAN GEOMETRY were deduced, one by Nikolai I. Lobatchevsky (1826) and independently by János Bolyai (1832) and another by Bernhard Riemann (1854). A few modern historians have questioned Euclid's authorship of the *Elements*, but he is definitely known to have written other works, most notably the *Optics*.

Euclid, city (1970 pop. 71,552), Cuyahoga co., NE Ohio, a suburb adjoining Cleveland, on Lake Erie; settled 1798, inc. 1848. Its many manufactures include airplane and automobile parts, machinery, and machine shop products. The National American Shrine of Our Lady of Lourdes is there.

Euclid of Megara (mĕg'ərə), c.450–c.375 B.C., Greek philosopher, a disciple of Socrates and traditional founder of the Megarian school. He combined the Eleatic doctrine of the unity of being with the Socratic teaching that virtue is knowledge. He held that the idea of the good is the sole reality.

Eudes (yo͞odz, Fr. öd) or **Odo** (ō'dō), c.860–898, count of Paris, French king (888–898). The son of ROBERT THE STRONG, he was an antecedent of the Capetian royal house in France. He defended Paris against the Norsemen (885), and after the deposition of Emperor of the West CHARLES III (Charles the Fat), he was elected by the nobles to succeed Charles in the West Frankish kingdom (France). He continued to battle the Norsemen, but his energies were increasingly diverted by the rising tide of sentiment favorable to the legitimate Carolingian heir, CHARLES III (Charles the Simple), who in 893 was elected king by a party of nobles. The resulting warfare between the two rival kings, neither of whom controlled much territory, continued intermittently. When Eudes died, Charles was recognized as king.

Eudocia (yo͞odō'shə), d. 460, Roman empress of the East; daughter of an Athenian Sophist. She was selected by PULCHERIA as the wife of THEODOSIUS II, whom she married (421) after being baptized and changing her name from Athenaïs to Eudocia. She became powerful at court, but the victim of intrigues, she retired to Jerusalem, where she devoted herself to literary and charitable work. She embraced Eutychianism (see EUTYCHES) but finally returned to orthodoxy. See Charles Diehl, *Byzantine Portraits* (1906, tr. 1927).

Eudocia Macrembolitissa (măk"rəmbŏl"ĭtĭs'ə), fl. 11th cent., Byzantine empress. At the death of her husband, Constantine X, she married ROMANUS IV.

Eudoxia (yo͞odŏk'sēə), d. 404, Roman empress of the East (395–404), daughter of a Frankish general and wife of ARCADIUS. She had a great influence upon her weak husband. She helped bring about the downfall of EUTROPIUS, to whose intrigues she owed her marriage, and the exile of St. JOHN CHRYSOSTOM, who had criticized her.

Eudoxus of Cnidus (yo͞odŏk'səs, nī'dəs), 408?–355? B.C., Greek astronomer, mathematician, and physician. From the accounts of various ancient writers, he appears to have studied with Plato in Athens, spent some time in Heliopolis, Egypt, founded a school in Cyzicus, and spent his later years in Cnidus, where he had an observatory. It is claimed that he calculated the length of the solar year, indicating a calendar reform like that made later by Julius Caesar, and that he was the discoverer of some parts of geometry included in the work of Euclid. He was the first Greek astronomer to explain the movements of the planets in a scientific manner. His system involved a number of concentric spheres supporting the planets in their paths. Some scientists still held this belief at the time of Copernicus.

Eudoxus of Cyzicus (sĭz'ĭkəs), fl. 130 B.C., Greek navigator in the service of the Ptolemies. He explored the Arabian sea for Ptolemy VII. After being blown from his course to the east coast of Africa, he decided that Africa could be circumnavigated. Setting out from Gades (Cádiz), he was driven ashore at Morocco on a first voyage. He undertook a second voyage down the west coast of Africa and was never heard from.

Eugene III, d. 1153, pope (1145–53), a Pisan named Bernard (probably in full Bernardo dei Paganelli di Montemagno); successor of Lucius II. Before his election he was called Bernard of Pisa. He was prominent among the Cistercians, then in their first flower, and was the friend of St. BERNARD OF CLAIRVAUX, who wrote *De consideratione* for him when he became pope. Eugene's pontificate was disturbed from the beginning by ARNOLD OF BRESCIA, whom he ordered to return to Rome in penitence. In 1146 the agitation of Arnold and the republicans drove the pope from Rome. Eugene and St. Bernard led in promoting the disastrous Second Crusade. While in exile (1146–49, 1150–52) the pope busied himself with reforming the clerical discipline of Western Europe. He was succeeded by Anastasius IV. Eugene was beatified in 1872.

Eugene IV, 1383–1447, pope (1431–47), a Venetian named Gabriele Condulmer; successor of Martin V. He was of exemplary character and ascetic habits. Gregory XII, his uncle, made him cardinal (1408). The first part of Eugene's reign was beset with the difficulties created by the Council of Basel (see BASEL, COUNCIL OF), which began just after his election. Eugene at first opposed the council in its antipapal acts, but after he had been driven by rebellion from Rome into exile at Florence (1434) he was disposed to conciliate. Finally in 1437 he removed the council to Ferrara. Antipapal leaders refused to move, and the council, now in heresy, continued at Basel. It declared Eugene deposed and elected AMADEUS VIII of Savoy antipope (as Felix V). It attracted little support, however. Meanwhile the Council of FERRARA-FLORENCE met and proclaimed (1439) the reunion of Eastern and Western churches. Abortive as this union proved to be, it greatly enhanced the papal prestige, and in 1443 Eugene returned to Rome from Florence. Eugene was succeeded by Nicholas V. See biography by Joseph Gill (1961).

Eugene, city (1970 pop. 78,389), seat of Lane co., W Oregon, on the Willamette River; inc. 1862. A processing and shipping center in a farming area, it has huge lumbering and food-processing industries. Eugene is the seat of the Univ. of Oregon, Northwest Christian College, and a junior college. It is the headquarters of Willamette National Forest.

Eugene of Savoy, 1663–1736, prince of the house of Savoy, general in the service of the Holy Roman Empire. Born in Paris, he was the son of Eugène, comte de Soissons of the line of Savoy-Carignano, and Olympe Mancini, niece of Cardinal MAZARIN. After being refused a commission in the French army by King Louis XIV, Eugene entered (1683) the service of Holy Roman Emperor Leopold I against the Ottoman Turks. He fought bravely in the relief of Vienna and then in Hungary, where he helped in the capture of Belgrade (1688). By 1697, Eugene had been appointed imperial commander in Hungary, and at Zenta he annihilated the Turkish army. Faced with opposition in Vienna, he began to take a more active part in political affairs. He became (1700) a member of the emperor's privy council and (1703) president of the imperial war council. He was the principal imperial commander in the War of the Spanish Succession (1701–14; see SPANISH SUCCESSION, WAR OF THE). In N Italy, Eugene was victorious over the French forces under Nicolas CATINAT and the duke of VILLEROI. In 1704 he joined the duke of MARLBOROUGH in Bavaria, and together they won the signal victory of BLENHEIM. Returning to Italy, Eugene fought (1705) an inconclusive battle at Cassano against his cousin, Louis Joseph de VENDÔME. His invasion of Provence (1707) was a failure, owing to the inadequacy of his forces. In 1708, Eugene again cooperated with Marlborough in Flanders; the victories of Oudenarde (1708) and Malplaquet (1709) resulted. After the conclusion (1713) of the Peace of Utrecht (see UTRECHT, PEACE OF) by England and France, Eugene continued to campaign on the Rhine against the French under Marshal Villars. Holy Roman Emperor Charles VI empowered him late in the year to negotiate with the war-weary French at Rastatt. The Peace of Rastatt (1714) complemented that of Utrecht. Eugene was made governor of the Austrian Netherlands (1715) and later imperial vicar in Italy. He again fought (1716–18) the Turks successfully, defeating them at Petrovaradin (1716) and at Belgrade (1717) and making possible the Austrian triumph marked by the Treaty of Passarowitz (1719). In the War of the Polish Succession, Eugene was made commander despite his advanced age. One of the greatest commanders in modern history, Prince Eugene was noted for his severe character and his hatred of Louis XIV as well as for his patronage of the arts. See biography by Nicholas Henderson (1965).

eugenics (yo͞ojĕn'ĭks), study of human GENETICS and of methods to improve the inherited characteristics, physical and mental, of the race. Francis Galton, who introduced the term *eugenics*, is usually regarded as the founder of the modern science of eugenics; his emphasis was on the role of factors under social control that could either improve or impair the qualities of future generations. Modern eugenics is directed chiefly toward the discouragement of propagation among the unfit (negative eugenics) and encouragement of propagation among those who are healthy, intelligent, and of high moral character (positive eugenics). Such a program involves many difficulties, especially that of defining which traits are most desirable. One scientific problem is that most of the diseases and harmful abnormalities that are inheritable can be transmitted to subsequent generations in a hidden form and manifest themselves in only a few individuals. Preventing reproduction of the latter would insignificantly reduce the potential appearance of defects in a population of any size. In addition, determining whether negative traits (e.g., skeletal weakness or antisocial behavior) are caused by environment rather than heredity is often impossible among humans. Efforts to improve the human race through bettering housing facilities and other environmental conditions are known as euthenic measures. Eugenics has recently become of increased concern; many fear that the achievements of modern medicine will allow the survival of defective individuals who previously could not have lived to a reproductive age. The greatest hope for eugenics probably lies in education; much remains unknown about the inheritability among humans of many traits, but such knowledge is constantly increasing. Studies in heredity have revealed the frequency with which defective offspring result from marriages in which both families have a history of such weaknesses; inbreeding increases the chances of producing defectives. It is known that hemophilia, albinism, and a number of structural abnormalities are inheritable. See C. P. Blacker, *Eugenics: Galton and After* (1952); L. C. Dunn and T. G. Dobzhansky, *Heredity, Race, and Society* (rev. ed. 1952); F. Osborn, *The Future of Human Heredity* (1968).

Eugenie (yo͞ojĕ'nē, Fr. özhānē'), 1826–1920, empress of the French (1853–70), consort of NAPOLEON III. Born in Spain, she was christened Eugenia María de Montijo de Guzmán and was the daughter of the Spanish conde de Teba and of a woman of Scottish descent. Exceptionally beautiful and charming, she was presented (1851) to Prince Louis Napoleon, who fell in love with her and married her in 1853. She took an active part in the politics of the Second Empire, acting as regent when Napoleon was at war. In 1870 she strongly supported the measures that led to war with Prussia (see FRANCO-PRUSSIAN WAR). Deposed (Sept., 1870) after Napoleon's capture at Sedan, she fled to England, and with the death (1879) of her only child, the prince imperial, she retired to Farnborough, Hampshire, where she and her husband and son are buried. In later life she made numerous trips abroad. See biographies by Maurice Paléologue (tr. 1928), R. E. Sencourt (1931), Rita Wellman (1941), and Harold Kurtz (1964); N. N. Barker, *Distaff Diplomacy* (1967).

Euglenophyta (yo͞o"glənŏf'ətə), small division of the plant kingdom consisting of photosynthetic, aquatic organisms. Most are unicellular; many have flagella and are motile. The outer part of the cell consists of a firm but flexible layer called a pellicle, or periplast, which cannot properly be considered a cell wall. The organisms resemble plants in that they contain CHLOROPLASTS; however, like animals they have gullets for the ingestion of food and lack cell walls. The chloroplasts, which may be absent in some forms, contain the photosynthetic pigments chlorophyll *a* and *b*, as in the division CHLOROPHYTA. Reproduction occurs by the division of a single-celled organism following a unique form of MITOSIS in which the nucleus has no spindle. Sexual reproduction is rare and not fully understood. The most characteristic genus of the single class, Euglenophyceae, is *Euglena*, common in ponds and pools, especially those rich in the chemicals used in fertilizers. *Euglena* is frequently studied in biology classes.

Euhemerus (yo͞ohĕm'ərəs), fl. c.300 B.C., Cyrenaic philosopher. He is famous for a theory of mythology embodied in his philosophical romance, *Sacred History*, a work of which only fragments remain. Euhemerus' theory, called after him euhemerism, was that the gods originated from the elaboration of traditions of distinguished historical persons. His theory was consistent with the attempts of his period to explain religious beliefs in terms of naturalism.

Eulenburg, Philipp, Fürst zu (fĕ'lĭp fürst tso͞o oi'lən-bo͝orkh), 1847–1921, German diplomat, friend and confidential adviser of Emperor William II. He served (1894–1902) as ambassador to Austria-Hungary, but it was his role as intermediary between the emperor and his government that made him important. Because of his failing health Eulenburg's influence declined. In 1906 a scandal, which was ultimately (1908) dragged into the courts of law, seriously damaged his reputation and indirectly weakened respect for the government. A famous raconteur and a dilettante composer, Eulenburg also left memoirs. See biography by Johannes Haller (2 vol., tr. 1930, repr. 1971).

Eulenspiegel, Till (tĭl oi'lən-shpē"gəl) [Ger.,=owl-mirror, hence English Owlglass], a north German peasant clown of the 14th cent. who was immortalized in chapbooks describing his practical jokes on clerics and townsfolk. The first Till chapbook (c.1500) was probably in Saxon, but the story it told spread all over Europe and North Britain. Till is the hero of a tone poem by Richard Strauss and of many novels, poems, and stories. Tyll Ulenspiegel is one of the variant spellings. See K. R. H. MacKenzie's adaptation in English, *Master Tyll Owlglass* (1890).

Euler, Leonhard (lā'ônhärt oi'lər), 1707–83, Swiss mathematician. Born and educated at Basel, where he knew the Bernoullis, he went to St. Petersburg (1727) at the invitation of Catherine I, becoming professor of mathematics there on the departure of Daniel Bernoulli (1733). He was invited to Berlin (1741) by Frederick the Great and remained there until 1766, when he returned to St. Petersburg. Euler was the most prolific mathematician who ever lived; his collected works run to more than seventy volumes. He contributed to numerous areas of both pure and applied mathematics, including the calculus of variations, analysis, number theory, algebra, geometry, trigonometry, analytical mechanics, hydrodynamics, and the lunar theory (calculation of the motion of the moon). Euler was one of the first to develop the methods of the CALCULUS on a wide scale. Though half-blind for much of his life and totally blind for the last seventeen years, he retained to the end a near-legendary skill at calculation. Among his results are the differential equation named for him, the formula relating the number of faces, edges, and vertices of a polyhedron ($F+V=E+2$), and the famous equation $e^{i\pi}+1=0$ connecting five fundamental numbers in mathematics.

Euless, village (1970 pop. 19,316), Tarrant co., N Texas, a suburb of Fort Worth.

Eumenes (yo͞o'mĭnēz), c.361–316 B.C., secretary to Philip II of Macedon and to Alexander the Great. A Thracian Greek, he was capable, diplomatic, and eloquent and proved himself able as a general as well as a secretary. After Alexander's death he was given control of Cappadocia and Paphlagonia. In the wars of the DIADOCHI he threw in his lot with PERDICCAS and thus was opposed by ANTIPATER, ANTIGONUS I, PTOLEMY I, and Craterus. However, the death of Perdiccas (321 B.C.) deprived Eumenes of all dependable support. He was defeated in 316 B.C. by Antigonus, deserted by his troops, and killed.

Eumenides (yo͞omĕn'ĭdēz): see FURIES.

Eunapius (yo͞onā'pēəs), b. c.347, Greek Neoplatonic philosopher, whose *Lives of the Philosophers and Sophists* is a most valuable primary source. His continuation of Dexippus' history is lost. Like many Neoplatonists he opposed Christianity.

Eunice (yo͞onī'sē, yo͞o'nĭs), Timothy's mother, a Christian. 2 Tim. 1.5; Acts 16.1.

Eunice (yo͞o'nĭs), city (1970 pop. 11,390), St. Landry parish, S central Louisiana; inc. 1895. It lies in an oil and agricultural region in which rice, cotton, and soybeans are produced. Its manufactures include oil-field equipment and clothing.

Eunomia (yo͞onō'mēə): see HORAE.

Eunomius, c.333–393?, bishop of Cyzicus (c.361), founder of the Eunomian heresy. He was a disciple and secretary of AETIUS whose extreme ARIANISM he adopted. His followers were called Eunomians or Anomoeans [from Gr.,=unlike], from their denial of any substantial similarity between God the Father and God the Son. Using Platonic arguments, Eunomius taught that by definition God was unbegotten and that the Son, begotten of the Father, could not therefore be equal to the Father. His learning and sophistication won many admirers. St. Basil the Great refuted him in his doctrinal work *Against Eunomius* (364). The Eunomians were condemned at the First Council of Constantinople.

eunuch (yo͞o'nĭk) [Gr.,=keeper of the couch], castrated human male, particularly a chamberlain of a harem in the Orient. The custom of employing eunuchs as servants in wealthy or royal households is very ancient; it reached its epitome at the court of Constantinople under the Byzantine emperors, from whom the Ottoman sultans adopted it. Eunuchs often rose to high position, the Byzantine general NARSES being the most celebrated example. In the Muslim world the use of eunuchs was far less common than is generally believed; however, the sale of young males to be eunuchs was formerly an important element in African trade. The castrating operation, which retards the development of normal male characteristics, including the deepening of the voice, was performed with varying thoroughness and with varying success. From Constantinople spread the custom of using eunuchs in choirs. In the *opera seria* (see OPERA) of the 18th cent. the male heroes' roles were sung by *castrati*, and the papal choir used *castrati* until the beginning of the 19th cent. A famous CASTRATO was Carlo Broschi FARINELLI.

Euodias (yo͞ō'dēəs), Philippian Christian urged by Paul to be reconciled with Syntyche. Philip. 4.2.

euonymus (yo͞oŏn'ĭməs): see STAFF TREE.

Eupatoria: see YEVPATORIYA, USSR.

Eupen (oi'pən), town (1970 pop. 14,879), Liège prov., E Belgium, on the Vesdre River, near the West German border. It is an industrial and commercial center. Nearby is a major hydroelectric station. The districts of Eupen and MALMÉDY (c.380 sq mi/980 sq km) were awarded (1815) to Prussia by the Congress of Vienna. Strategically important for the defense of Belgium, the districts were transferred (1919) to Belgium under the terms of the Treaty of Versailles. Their population is predominantly German-speaking, and during World War II the districts were temporarily annexed (1940–44) by Germany.

euphorbia (yo͞ofôr'bēə): see SPURGE.

Euphorion (yo͞ofôr'ēən), 276?–187? B.C., Greek poet, b. Chalcis. He was made (c.223 B.C.) librarian at Antioch by Antiochus the Great and held the position until his death. The few remaining fragments of Euphorion's work show his indebtedness, which borders on plagiarism, to such poets as CALLIMACHUS.

euphotic zone: see OCEAN.

Euphranor (yo͞ofrā'nər), fl. 364 B.C., Greek painter and sculptor from Corinth. His most famous paintings were in the Stoa of Zeus at Athens—*A Cavalry Charge between the Athenians and Boeotians at Mantinea* and *Theseus* on one wall and the 12 great gods on the opposite. His statues, executed in metal or marble, were praised by Pliny for symmetry and dignity. Among them were *Paris* and *Leto with Apollo and Artemis*. A nude male statue in bronze, found in a sunken ship off Antikythera, has been identified by some scholars as his *Paris* (Athens).

Euphrates (yo͞ofrā'tēz), Turkish *Frat*, Arabic *Al Furat*, river of SW Asia, c.1,700 mi (2,740 km) long, formed by the confluence of the Kara and the Murad rivers, E central Turkey, and flowing generally S through Turkey into Syria, then SE through Iraq, joining with the Tigris River in SE Iraq to form the Shatt al Arab; the united river flows into the Persian Gulf. In its upper course, the Euphrates flows rapidly through deep canyons and narrow gorges. The middle Euphrates traverses a wide flood plain in Syria, where it is used extensively for irrigation. Euphrates Dam, 230 ft (70 m) high, constructed with Soviet aid at Tabqa, N Syria, is the main unit of the Tabqa Barrage Scheme. The huge reservoir impounded by the dam irrigates c.1.5 million acres (607,000 hectares) and has transformed the region into one of Syria's most productive agricultural areas. Below the dam the Euphrates receives the Belikh and Khabur rivers, its only major tributaries. Entering the Syrian Desert and the plains of Iraq, the river loses velocity and becomes a sluggish stream with shifting channels. In N Iraq it is studded with islands, some with remains of old castles. The river's lower course supplies water to Iraq's great date plantations through a system of dams and canals. Before merging with the Tigris at Al Basra, Iraq, the Euphrates divides into many channels, forming a marshland and Lake Hammar. The Euphrates is unnavigable except for very shallow draft vessels; dams have been built on its lower course to control flooding, improve navigation, and supply water for irrigation. The modern waterworks along the Euphrates do not equal in scope those of ancient times when Sippar, Erech, Ur, and Babylon flourished on the banks of the lower Euphrates. Mesopotamia, birthplace of many great civilizations, depended on the waters of the Euphrates and the Tigris for survival; however, water spread over the fields by irrigation evaporated quickly in this arid region, leaving a salt and silt residue that eventually made the land unsuitable for agriculture.

Euphrosyne (yo͞ofrŏs'ənē"): see GRACES.

euphuism (yo͞o'fyo͞oĭzəm), in English literature, a highly elaborate and artificial style that derived from the *Euphues* (1578) of John LYLY and that flourished in England in the 1580s. It was characterized by extensive use of simile and illustration, balanced construction, alliteration, and antithesis. Euphuism played an important role in English literary history by demonstrating the capabilities of English prose. The term has come to mean an artificial, precious, high-flown style of writing.

Eupolis (yo͞o'pəlĭs), fl. 430–411 B.C., Athenian comic poet. He seems to have collaborated with Aristophanes, whom he also attacked; another of his victims was Alcibiades. His plays, satirical and malicious, were greatly admired by the ancients. Fragments of his work survive.

Eupompus (yo͞opŏm'pəs), fl. 4th cent. B.C., Greek painter, founder of the Sicyonic school. The only one of his works of which there is record is *A Victor in the Olympic Games*.

Eurasia (yo͞orā'zhə, -shə), land mass comprising the continents of EUROPE and ASIA, in which Europe is geographically a western peninsula of Asia, rather than a separate continent.

Euratom: see EUROPEAN ATOMIC ENERGY COMMUNITY.

Eure (ör), department (1968 pop. 383,385), N France, in Normandy. ÉVREUX is the capital.

Eure-et-Loir (ör-ā-lwär), department (1968 pop. 302,207), N France. CHARTRES is the capital.

Eureka (yo͞orē'kə), city (1970 pop. 24,337), seat of Humboldt co., NW Calif., on Humboldt Bay; inc. 1856. It is a port of entry. Lumbering and fishing are the chief industries; tourism is also important. A 40-acre (16-hectare) redwood park lies within the city limits. Many of the early settlers came from Canada. Eureka has a junior college.

eurhythmics: see EURYTHMICS.

Euric (yo͞or'ĭk), d c.484, king of the Visigoths (466-c.484), brother and successor of Theodoric II. He made Toulouse his capital and under him the Visigothic kingdom reached its greatest extent, including the Iberian peninsula and southern Gaul. In 475 he made his first codification of Visigothic law. He was succeeded by his son Alaric II.

Euripides (yo͞orĭp'ĭdēz), b. 480 or 485 B.C., d. 406 B.C., Greek tragic poet, ranking with AESCHYLUS and SOPHOCLES. Born in Attica of a middle-class family, he lived in Athens most of his life, though he spent much time on Salamis. He wrote perhaps 92 plays (the first produced in 455); during his lifetime he won only four first prizes (the first in 441) at the competition for tragedy held at the annual spring festival of Dionysus in Athens. There are 19 of his plays extant (including one that is doubtful): *Cyclops* (date unknown), the only complete extant Greek satyr play; *Alcestis* (438); *Medea* (431); *Hippolytus* (428); the *Heraclidae* (perhaps c.428), a patriotic play inspired by the Peloponnesian War; *Andromache* (426?); *Hecuba* (425?); the *Suppliants* and *Hercules Furens* (both c.420); *Ion* (c.417); the *Trojan Women* (415), an indictment of war; *Electra* (413); *Helena* (412); *Iphigenia in Tauris* (date uncertain); the *Phoenician Women* (c.409), on the story of the SEVEN AGAINST THEBES; *Orestes* (408); *Iphigenia in Aulis* and the *Bacchae*, on the PENTHEUS story, both posthumously produced (405); and *Rhesus*, doubtfully attributed to Euripides. Provocative, concerned with problems and conflicts sometimes disturbing to his audiences, Euripides displayed a rationalistic and iconoclastic attitude toward the gods and an interest in less heroic, even homely, characters. He brings the mythical stories down to the immediate contemporary and human level. His plays are more realistic than those of Aeschylus or Sophocles, and they may lack in grandeur what they make up in penetration. Characteristic of Euripides' tragic form are the prologue, used as means for direct exposition of previous action, and the *deus ex machina* [god from a machine], used, in many cases, to resolve the play's problem. Though the *deus ex machina* often seems a forced addition to the play and though its presence often strains the play's meaning, Euripides used it probably because the Athenian audience considered it desirable. One theory has been that for Euripides the play ends before the *deus ex machina* and that the device simply is a yielding to convention. Choral passages (interludes in, rather than parts of, the action) have remarkable lyric power. Among the many translations of Euripides is *The Complete Greek Tragedies*, ed. by Richmond Lattimore and David Grene (1956-59). See studies by G. Murray (1918, repr. 1965), T. B. L. Webster (1967), and A. P. Burnett (1972).

Euroclydon (yûr''əklī'dŏn), east or northeast storm wind that caused Paul's shipwreck on Malta. Acts. 27.14.

Europa (yo͞orō'pə), in astronomy, one of the 12 known moons, or natural satellites, of JUPITER.

Europa, in Greek mythology, daughter of Agenor or Phoenix. Zeus, enamored of her, appeared as a white bull, enticed her to climb on his back, and swam off with her to Crete. There she bore him Minos, Rhadamanthus, and Sarpedon. She married the king of Crete, who adopted her sons. After her death she was worshiped as a goddess in the festival of the Hellotia.

Europe, 6th largest continent, c.4,000,000 sq mi (10,360,000 sq km) including adjacent islands (1973 est. pop. 640,000,000). It is actually a vast peninsula of the great Eurasian land mass. It is separated from Asia by the Urals and the Ural River in the east; by the Caspian Sea and the Caucasus in the southeast; and by the Black Sea, the Bosporus, the Sea of Marmara, and the Dardanelles in the south. The Mediterranean Sea and the Strait of Gibraltar separate it from Africa. Europe is washed in the north by the

Arctic Ocean, and in the west by the Atlantic Ocean, with which the North Sea and the Baltic Sea are connected. The huge Alpine mountain chain, of which the Pyrenees, the Alps, the Carpathians, the Balkans, and the Caucasus are the principal links, traverses the continent from west to east. The highest points are Mt. Elbrus (18,481 ft/5,633 m) in the Caucasus and Mont Blanc (15,771 ft/4,807 m) in the Alps. Europe's lowest point (92 ft/28 m below sea level) is the surface of the Caspian Sea. Between the mountainous Scandinavian peninsula in the north and the Alpine chain in the south extends the great European plain, stretching from the Atlantic coast of France to the Urals. A large part of this plain (which is interrupted by minor mountain groups and hills) is fertile agricultural soil; in the east and north there are vast steppe, forest, lake, and tundra regions. South of the Alpine chain extend the Iberian, Italian, and Balkan peninsulas, which are largely mountainous. The Po plain, between the Alps and the Apennines, and the Danubian plain, between the Carpathians and the Alps, are fertile and much-developed regions. Among the chief river systems of Europe are, from east to west, those of the Volga, the Don, the Dnepr, the Danube, the Oder, the Elbe, the Rhine, the Rhône, the Loire, the Garonne, and the Tagus. The climate of Europe varies from subtropical to polar. The Mediterranean climate of the south is dry and warm. The western and northwestern parts have a mild, generally humid climate, influenced by the North Atlantic Drift. In central and eastern Europe the climate is of the humid continental-type with cool summers. In the northeast subarctic and tundra climates are found. All of Europe is subject to the moderating influence of prevailing westerly winds from the Atlantic Ocean and, consequently, its climates are found at higher latitudes than similar climates on other continents. Europe can be divided into five geographic regions: Scandinavia (Denmark, Norway, Sweden, Finland, and Iceland); the British Isles (United Kingdom and Ireland); W Europe (the Netherlands, Belgium, Luxembourg, France, and Monaco); S Europe (Spain, Portugal, Italy, Malta, Andorra, San Marino, and Vatican City); Central Europe (Switzerland, Liechtenstein, Austria, Hungary, Poland, Czechoslovakia, East Germany, and West Germany); SE Europe (Greece, Albania, Yugoslavia, Rumania, Bulgaria, and the European part of Turkey); and E Europe (the European portion of the USSR). Indo-European languages (see LANGUAGE, table) predominate in Europe; others spoken include Basque, Maltese, and the languages classified as Finno-Ugric, Samoyedic, Bulgaric, and Turkic. Roman Catholicism is the chief religion of S and W Europe and the southern part of central Europe; Protestantism is dominant in the United Kingdom, Scandinavia, and the northern part of Europe, and the Orthodox Eastern Church predominates in E and SE Europe. With the exception of the northern third of the continent, Europe is densely populated. Nine cities have populations exceeding 2 million inhabitants; London, Moscow, and Paris are the largest cities. Europe is highly industrialized, and manufacturing employs most of the work force. Of the many industrial areas, the largest are found in W central Europe, England, N Italy, and central European USSR. Agriculture (especially in S Europe), forestry (in N Europe), and fishing (along the Atlantic coast) are also important. Europe has a large variety of minerals; coal, iron ore, bauxite, and salt are abundant. Oil and gas are found in E Europe and beneath the North Sea. Coal is used to produce most of Europe's electricity; in Norway and Sweden and in the Alps there are many hydroelectric power plants. The transportation system in Europe is highly developed; interconnecting rivers and canals provide excellent inland water transportation. The countries of Europe engage heavily in foreign trade, and some of the world's greatest ports are found there. Rotterdam with the huge new Europoort complex, London, Le Havre, Hamburg, Genoa, and Marseilles are the chief ports. The beginnings of civilization in Europe can be traced to very ancient times, but they are not as old as the civilizations of Mesopotamia and Egypt. The Roman and Greek cultures flourished in Europe, and European civilization—language, technology, political concepts, and the Christian religion—have been spread throughout the world by European colonists and immigrants. Throughout history, Europe has been the scene of many great and destructive wars that have ravaged both rural and urban areas. Once embraced by vast and powerful empires and kingdoms, successful nationalistic uprisings (especially in the 19th cent.) divided the continent into many sovereign states. The political fragmentation led to economic competition and political strife among the states. After World War II, Europe became divided into two ideological blocs (Eastern Europe, dominated by the USSR, and Western Europe, dominated by the United States) and became engaged in the Cold War. NATO was formed as a military deterrent to the spread of Communism, and a number of economic organizations, including the European Economic Community or Common Market, the European Free Trade Association, and the European Coal and Steel Community, strove for economic unification. The Eastern European counterparts are the Soviet-sponsored Council for Mutual Economic Assistance and the Warsaw Treaty Organization, a military pact. Cold War tensions eased in the 1960s, and signs of normalization of East-West relations appeared in the 1970s. The expanded Common Market, which also has the goal of political unification of member states, is now a strong economic rival to the United States and the USSR. See S. B. Clough et al., ed., *The European Past* (2 vol., 1964); Denis de Rougemont, *The Idea of Europe* (tr. 1966); John Bowle, *The Unity of European History: A Political and Cultural Survey* (rev. and enl. ed. 1970); Maurice Crouzet, *The European Renaissance since 1945* (tr. 1970); *Eastern Europe in the 1970's*, ed. by Sylva Sinanian et al. (1972); Walter Hallstein, *Europe in the Making* (tr. 1972); Richard Mayne, *The Europeans: Who Are We?* (1972); René Albrecht-Carrié, *A Diplomatic History of Europe since the Congress of Vienna* (rev. ed. 1973); S. H. Beer et al., *Patterns of Government: The Major Political Systems of Europe* (3d ed. 1973); *European Security and the Atlantic System*, ed. by W. T. Fox and W. R. Schilling (1973); A. H. Robertson, *European Institutions: Co-operation, Integration, Unification* (3d ed. 1973); Stephen Usherwood, *Europe, Century by Century* (1973); Roy Pryce, *The Politics of the European Community* (1974).

Europe, Council of: see INTERNATIONAL GOVERNMENTAL ORGANIZATIONS.

European Atomic Energy Community (Euratom), economic organization that came into being in 1958 as the 3d member of the EUROPEAN COMMUNITY. The members pledged themselves to the common development of Europe's nuclear energy resources by coordinating their nuclear research and development programs and by permitting the free movement of nuclear raw materials, equipment, investment capital, and specialists within the community. Euratom is vested with wide powers, including the right to conclude contracts, obtain raw materials, and establish standards to protect workers and the general population against the dangers of radiation. It is administered by the Commission of European Communities, which is advised by the Scientific and Technical Committee and the Economic and Social Committee. Euratom operates nuclear reactors and research centers at Ispra (Italy), Geel (Belgium), Petten (Netherlands), and Karlsruhe (West Germany). It has entered into agreements for joint projects with the United States, Canada, and Brazil.

European Coal and Steel Community (ECSC), 1st member of the EUROPEAN COMMUNITY; founded 1952. It is also known as the Schuman Plan, after the French foreign minister, Robert Schuman, who proposed it in 1950. Member nations of ECSC pledged to pool their coal and steel resources by providing a unified market for their coal and steel products, lifting restrictions on imports and exports, and creating a unified labor market. Economically, the Coal and Steel Community achieved early success; between 1952 and 1960 iron and steel production rose by 75% in the ECSC nations and industrial production rose 58%. When overproduction of coal became a problem after 1959, especially in Belgium, the ECSC demonstrated its flexibility by reducing Belgium's coal-producing capacity by 30% and by making available large sums of money to aid in retraining miners and developing new industries. The ECSC had, by 1970, granted about $150 million in aid to retrain over 400,000 coal miners. The executive machinery of the ECSC provided an important precedent for the future growth of a united Europe: The nine-member high authority, which became a part of the Commission of European Communities in 1967, was chosen by the member governments and made independent of those governments. Its independence was guaranteed by providing the authority with its own source of income.

European Community. After World War II there developed in Europe a strong revulsion against national rivalries and parochial loyalties. While postwar recovery was stimulated by the MARSHALL PLAN, statesmen like Jean Monnet and Robert Schuman of France and Paul Henri Spaak of Belgium looked ahead to a united Europe as the essential basis for European strength and security and the best way of preventing another European holocaust. Thus, three communities were created with the goal of unifying Western Europe, both economically and politically: the EUROPEAN COAL AND STEEL COMMUNITY, the European Economic Community (see COMMON MARKET), and the EUROPEAN ATOMIC ENERGY COMMUNITY. The original members were Belgium, France, West Germany, Italy, Luxembourg, and the Netherlands. In 1973, Denmark, Great Britain, and the Republic of Ireland joined. The three communities moved toward further unification when, in 1967, they consolidated their separate executives into one commission of the European Communities. The commission, which represents the interests of the European Community, is the executive operating branch, responsible for executing the different treaties and proposing ways to do this to the Council of Ministers. The council, which represents the interests of member nations, is the body with the final authority for decisions in the community. The legislative function of the community is fulfilled by the European Parliament. The parliament is consulted about a broad range of matters, including the budget, and has the power to dismiss members of the commission by a two-thirds majority vote. Parliament members are selected by and from their national parliaments, but plans for direct election are under consideration. The judicial branch of the community is the Court of Justice, composed of seven judges and responsible for settling conflicts among member countries in the application of the treaties. See William Diebold, *The Schuman Plan: A Study in Economic Cooperation, 1950–59* (1959); R. L. Heilbroner, *Forging a United Europe; the Story of the European Community* (Public Affairs Pamphlet, 1961); Walter Lippman, *Western Unity and the Common Market* (1962); Gordon Weil, *A Foreign Policy for Europe?* (1970); Max Kohnstamm and Wolfgang Hager, ed., *A Nation Writ Large?* (1973).

European corn borer: see CORN BORER.

European Court of Human Rights: see INTERNATIONAL GOVERNMENTAL ORGANIZATIONS.

European Economic Community: see COMMON MARKET.

European Free Trade Association (EFTA): see INTERNATIONAL GOVERNMENTAL ORGANIZATIONS.

European Monetary Agreement (EMA), international governmental organization to facilitate settlement of BALANCE OF PAYMENTS accounts between member states. The EMA existed from 1958 until 1972, replacing the European Payments Union, which had been formed in 1950 under the Organization for Economic Cooperation. The EMA was administered by the Organization for Economic Cooperation and Development (OECD) (see INTERNATIONAL GOVERNMENTAL ORGANIZATIONS). The EMA provided for the convertibility of the currencies of member states; that meant that the currency of one state could be exchanged directly for the currency of any other member state by nonresidents. Such an arrangement made settlement of balance of payments accounts between nations simpler than it was under the European Payments Union. The EMA provided for short-term credit facilities to be made available to states with temporary balance of payments difficulties. In view of the facilities available for balance of payments assistance in the International Monetary Fund, the OECD announced (1972) that there was no longer any need for short-term credits to members, and that the EMA would, therefore, be terminated.

European Organization for Nuclear Research or **CERN,** nuclear research center straddling the Franco-Swiss border W of Geneva, Switzerland. Founded in 1954, CERN is an intergovernmental organization whose activities are sponsored by 12 European countries. It is the principal European center for research in particle physics.

European Parliament: see EUROPEAN COMMUNITY.

European Payments Union: see EUROPEAN MONETARY AGREEMENT.

European Recovery Program: see MARSHALL PLAN.

European Southern Observatory, astronomical OBSERVATORY located on Cerro La Silla peak, Chile, at an altitude of about 8,000 ft (2,400 m), with headquarters in Santiago. It is operated jointly by several European countries. The principal instrument is a 3.6-m (142-in.) reflecting telescope, one of the largest in the world. Other instruments include a 50-cm (20-in.) reflector, a 1-m (39.4-in.) Schmidt camera telescope, twin 40-cm (15.7-in.) astrographic telescopes, a 1.52-m (60-in.) spectrographic reflector, and a 1-m (39.4-in.) photometric reflector. Also located at Cerro La Silla are a 50-cm (20-in.) reflector belonging to Denmark and a 62-cm (24.4-in.) reflector belonging to the Univ. of Bochum, West Germany. Among the programs of the observatory is the completion of the photographic Sky Survey for the Southern Hemisphere, in cooperation with the Siding Spring Observatory in Australia. This project is a continuation of the work begun in the Northern Hemisphere with the Schmidt telescope at Palomar Observatory.

European Space Research Organization (ESRO), organization consisting mainly of European countries, created to promote cooperative ventures in space research for nonmilitary purposes. It was founded in 1962 and formally organized in 1965 when 10 European countries agreed to pay for its operations. Australia was included as a nonpaying member because it placed its rocket-firing range at Woomera at the organization's disposal. One of its current projects, in cooperation with the European Conference of Postal and Telecommunications Administrations, is to create a European communications satellite system by the end of the 1970s.

europium (yŏŏrō'pēəm) [from *Europe*], metallic chemical element; symbol Eu; at. no. 63; at. wt. 151.96; m.p. about 820°C; b.p. about 1600°C; sp. gr. 5.25 at 25°C; valence +2 or +3. Europium is a ductile silvery-white metal; it is both rare and expensive. It is a member of group IIIb of the PERIODIC TABLE. Its oxides are found in minerals with the other RARE EARTHS. Europium has been identified in the sun and some stars by spectroscopy. Its physical properties are like those of the other members of the LANTHANIDE SERIES, but many of its chemical properties are more like those of calcium. The most reactive of the RARE-EARTH METALS, it tarnishes quickly in air at room temperature and ignites and burns above 150°C. It reacts readily with water. Twenty-one isotopes of europium are known, most of them unstable. Since it is a good neutron absorber, europium metal is used in nuclear reactor control rods. Europium oxide, a pinkish powder, is used to activate red phosphors in the manufacture of color television picture tubes. The discovery of europium is credited to Eugène Demarcay, who isolated fairly pure europium oxide in 1901.

Europus or **Europos,** Syria: see DURA.

Eurydice (yŏŏrĭd'ĭsē): see ORPHEUS.

Eurynome (yŏŏrĭn'əmē), in Greek mythology, daughter of Oceanus and Tethys and mother, by Zeus, of the Graces. In the mythology of the Pelasgians, an aboriginal non-Greek people living in Greece before the Mycenaean period, she rose alone out of chaos and separated the earth from the sky. She created the great serpent Ophion and mated with him. Thus she gave birth to all existing things.

eurythmics or **eurhythmics** (both: yŏŏrĭth'mĭks), harmonious bodily movement, especially as expressed according to the system of Émile JAQUES-DALCROZE, who developed eurythmics (1903) at the Geneva Conservatory of Music in an effort to overcome the rhythmic difficulties of his students. His aim was to bring the body under control of the mind through a system of gymnastics correlated with music. First, an unconscious technique of bodily response to the rhythm of music is developed, with the student eventually able to improvise an interpretation, through gesture language, of an entire composition. The system has influenced not only musical instruction but also the ballet and even fields outside of musical study. The first demonstrations of it were given in 1905, and the first Jaques-Dalcroze Institute in the United States was established ten years later. For a history of the Dalcroze method of eurythmics, see Nicolas Slonimsky, *Music since 1900* (4th ed., 1971). See Elsa Findlay, *Rhythm and Movement: Applications of Dalcroze Eurhythmics* (1971).

Eusebius of Caesarea (yŏŏsē'bēəs, sĕzərē'ə) or **Eusebius Pamphili** (păm'fĭlī), c.263–339?, Greek apologist and church historian, b. Palestine. He was bishop of Caesarea, Palestine (314?–339). In the controversy over ARIANISM, Eusebius seemed to favor the semi-Arian views of his relative Eusebius of Nicomedia, and he once gave refuge to Arius. A simple baptismal creed submitted by Eusebius at the First Council of Nicaea (325) was amended with the Greek word *homoousios* [consubstantial, of the same substance] to define the Son's relationship with the Father. Eusebius considered this addition to the creed as reflecting the ideas of SABELLIUS, which he opposed. Although he signed the formulary, he later did not support it. His works include the valuable histories *Chronicle* and *Ecclesiastical History* and the apologetic works *Praeparatio Evangelica* and *Demonstratio Evangelica.* See study by D. S. Wallace-Hadrill (1960).

Eusebius of Nicomedia (nĭkōmē'dēə), d. 342, Christian churchman and theologian, leader of the heresy of ARIANISM. He was bishop of Nicomedia (330–39) and patriarch of Constantinople (339–42); Eusebius was powerful because of his influence with Roman Emperor Constantine I and particularly with his son, Constantius II. He sheltered Arius in 321 and fought his condemnation at Nicaea (see NICAEA, FIRST COUNCIL OF). Eusebius signed the Nicene formulary but was exiled by Constantine shortly afterward. Eusebius' influence on the emperor's sister Constantia, however, soon won him his reprieve (328). As advisor to Constantius, a confirmed Arian, he systematically advanced a moderate Arianism throughout the empire.

Eustace II (yŏŏ'stĭs), d. 1093, count of Boulogne. He was the brother-in-law of EDWARD THE CONFESSOR of England. Visiting England in 1051, he and his followers became involved in a brawl with the citizens of Dover. Earl GODWIN refused to obey Edward's order to punish the people of the town and broke with the king as a result. Eustace took part in the Norman invasion of England in 1066, but the following year led an unsuccessful revolt against William I. They were subsequently reconciled. Eustace was the father of Eustace III, who was in turn father of Matilda, wife of King STEPHEN of England. Stephen and Matilda's son, **Eustace IV,** d. 1153, count of Boulogne, fought unsuccessfully against GEOFFREY IV of Anjou, husband of Henry I's daughter MATILDA, in Normandy. In 1152 Eustace was recognized as Stephen's successor by some of the English barons, but Theobald, archbishop of Canterbury, fled the country rather than crown him. Eustace's death cleared the way for the accession of HENRY II to the English throne.

Eustachi, Bartolomeo (bär"tōlōmĕ'ō ä"ŏŏstä'kē), d. 1574, Italian anatomist. He lived in Rome from 1549 and taught at the Collegia della Sapienza (later the Univ. of Rome). He described many structures in the human body, including the Eustachian tube of the ear, the adrenal glands, the thoracic duct, the uterus, and the kidneys, and studied the structure and development of the teeth. His *Tabulae anatomicae* (1552), a remarkable set of anatomical drawings, was published in 1714.

Eustachian tube (yŏŏstā'shən) [for Bartolomeo Eustachi], a hollow structure of bone and cartilage extending from the middle EAR to the rear of the throat, or pharynx. In humans the Eustachian tube is about 1½ in. (3.8 cm) long. By permitting air to leave or enter the middle ear, the tube equalizes air pressure on either side of the eardrum. The tube can become blocked, as by enlarged adenoids or the mucous secretions of a cold, so that external and internal pressure become imbalanced. Earache and diminution of hearing may result. The tube may also serve as a pathway to the ear for infections of the throat.

Eustathius, Saint (yŏŏstā'thēəs), c.280–c.335, patriarch of Antioch (324?–330?), leader at the First Council of Nicaea. He was deposed and exiled by a faction led by Eusebius of Nicomedia during the Arian reaction. His followers refused to acknowledge MELETIUS as bishop. Feast: July 16.

Eustathius, d. c.1194, Byzantine scholar, archbishop of Salonica (from 1175). He became renowned as master of the orators at Hagia Sophia, Constantinople, then a center of learning. He lectured on Homer and Pindar. As bishop Eustathius was active in the affairs of Salonica and secured religious freedom for its inhabitants when the Normans captured it. He attempted to reform the monasteries but failed and was temporarily obliged to leave the city. Works of interest include commentaries (especially on Homer), which are valuable for extracts from lost Greek works, also a history (1185) of the Norman conquest of Sicily and S Italy, funeral orations, and *The Reform of Monastic Life.* Michael ACOMINATUS was his student and friend.

Eustatius Island: see SAINT EUSTATIUS.

Eustis, William (yŏŏ'stĭs), 1753–1825, U.S. government official, b. Cambridge, Mass. A surgeon in the patriot forces during the American Revolution, he later served (1801–5) in Congress as a Jeffersonian. Eustis was appointed (1807) Secretary of War by Jefferson, but he was forced to resign in 1812 because of charges of incompetence in dealing with the problems of the War of 1812. He was later minister (1814–18) to the Netherlands, again a member (1820–23) of the House of Representatives, and governor (1823–25) of Massachusetts.

Euterpe (yŏŏtûr'pē): see MUSES.

euthanasia, either painlessly putting to death or failing to prevent death from natural causes in cases of terminal illness. The term formerly referred only to the act of painlessly putting incurably ill persons to death. However, technological advances in the field of medicine, which have made it possible to prolong the life of patients who have no hope of recovery, have led to the use of the term *negative euthanasia,* i.e., the withdrawing of extraordinary means used to preserve life. Accordingly, the term *positive euthanasia* has come to refer to actions that actively cause death. Positive euthanasia is illegal in the United States, but physicians may lawfully refuse to prolong life when there is extreme suffering. Much debate has arisen among physicians, religious leaders, lawyers, and the general public over the question of what constitutes actively causing death and what constitutes merely allowing death to occur naturally. The Roman Catholic Church and most other religious bodies, in general agreement with the government, support the view that a physician is not required to use extraordinary means to preserve life in patients having no hope of recovery. The physician is faced with deciding whether the measures used to keep patients alive are extraordinary in individual situations, e.g., whether a procedure such as intravenous feeding that is considered routine in the case of a younger patient should be prescribed for an elderly patient who has no hope of improvement, or whether a respirator or artificial kidney machine should be withdrawn from a terminally ill patient. Popular movements to gain support for legalization of positive euthanasia often assert that the patient has the right to make decisions concerning the circumstances surrounding his own death and that he should be allowed to refuse treatment if he chooses. The problem of incapacitation of the patient at the time of death can be solved, it is held, by the writing of a communication, popularly called a living will, which expresses the patient's wishes concerning his own death. Societies supporting the cause of positive euthanasia were founded in 1935 in England and in 1938 in the United States; thus far they have been unsuccessful in obtaining legislative approval for their proposals.

euthenics (yŏŏthĕn'ĭks): see EUGENICS.

eutrophication (yŏŏtrō"fĭkā'shən), aging of a lake by biological enrichment of its water. In a young lake the water is cold and clear, supporting little life. With time, streams draining into the lake introduce nutrients such as nitrogen and phosphorus, which encourage the growth of aquatic organisms. As the lake's fertility increases, plant and animal life burgeons, and organic remains begin to be deposited on the lake bottom. Over the centuries, as silt and organic debris pile up, the lake grows shallower and warmer, with warm-water organisms supplanting those that thrive in a cold environment. Marsh plants take root in the shallows and begin to fill in the original lake basin. Eventually the lake gives way to BOG, finally disappearing into land. Depending on climate, size of the lake, and other factors, the natural aging of a lake may span thousands of years. However, pollutants from man's activities can radically accelerate the aging process. During the past century, lakes in many parts of the earth have been severely eutrophied by sewage and agricultural and industrial wastes (see WATER POLLUTION). The prime contaminants are nitrates and phosphates, which act as plant nutrients. They overstimulate the growth of algae, causing unsightly scum and unpleasant odors, and robbing the water of dissolved oxygen vital to other aquatic life. At the same time, other pollutants flowing into a lake may poison whole populations of fish, whose decomposing remains further deplete the water's dissolved oxygen content. In such fashion, a lake can literally choke to death.

Eutropius (yŏŏtrō'pēəs), fl. 4th cent. A.D., Roman historian, a protégé of the emperors Julian and Valens. His *Breviarium ab urbe condita* (10 books) is a summary of Roman history.

Eutropius, d. 399, consul of East Roman Emperor ARCADIUS. A eunuch of the palace, he brought about the marriage (395) of Arcadius and EUDOXIA and succeeded RUFINUS as chief minister. He repelled (398) an invasion of Huns and was the first eunuch to be appointed (399) consul. He was hated for his cruelty and avarice; his fall, however, was caused by the enmity of Gaïnas, the leader of the Gothic mercenaries, and Eudoxia. Although at first his life was spared through the influence of St. John Chrysostom, he was later executed.

Eutyches (yo͞o'tĭkēs), c.378–c.452, archimandrite in Constantinople, sponsor of Eutychianism, the first phase of MONOPHYSITISM. He was the leader in Constantinople of the most violent opponents of NESTORIANISM, among whom was Dioscurus, successor to St. CYRIL (d. 444) as patriarch of Alexandria. Whereas Cyril had agreed with the Antiochenes in 433 that Christ had two natures, Eutyches and Dioscurus insisted that Christ's humanity was absorbed in his divinity and that to accept two natures at all was Nestorian. When THEODORET attacked Eutychianism (447), Dioscurus retaliated by anathematizing him, and Emperor THEODOSIUS II, who was friendly to Eutychianism, confined Theodoret to his diocese (448). But Eutyches was accused of heresy and deposed by a local synod called by St. Flavian, patriarch of Constantinople (Nov., 448). Eutyches appealed to his friends, and Theodosius called a general council to meet at Ephesus, Aug. 1, 449. This, the famous Robber Synod (Latrocinium), was disgraceful from the beginning. Dioscurus presided and disenfranchised most of the clergy inimical to Eutyches. The so-called council reinstated Eutyches, declared him orthodox, and deposed Flavian and Eutyches' accuser, Eusebius of Dorylaeum. Flavian denied the council's authority; the papal legates denounced the council's proceedings. The soldiery, called in by Dioscurus, compelled an affirmative vote; Flavian was severely beaten by members of the so-called synod and died shortly thereafter. The legates barely escaped. Theodoret was deposed. After the death of Theodosius (450) his orthodox successors convened the Council of Chalcedon (see CHALCEDON, COUNCIL OF) to right the wrongs of the Robber Synod, and Eutychianism was ended. Eutyches was deposed and exiled.

Eutychides (yo͞otĭk'ĭdēz), fl. early 3d cent. B.C., Greek sculptor from Sicyon; pupil of Lysippos. Records exist of several of his works, among which the best known is *Tyche* or *Fortune*, personifying the city of Antioch. The allegory is carried out in detail, as may be seen in a marble copy in the Vatican and in numerous statuettes. The identity of the statue was established through copies on coins issued by Tigranes, king of Armenia.

Eutychus (yo͞o'tĭkəs), young man whom Paul raised from the dead. Acts 20.9–12.

Evagoras (ĭvăg'ərəs), d. c.374 B.C., despot of Cyprus. Exiled in his youth, he returned (411 B.C.) and made good his claim as ruler of Salamis. By 410 B.C. he had spread his control over the whole island. Friendly to Athens, he sought to bring Athenian culture to Cyprus, partly by giving refuge to exiled Athenians (notably Conon). Evagoras built a powerful fleet and with it harried the mainland (under Persian control). After the Peace of ANTALCIDAS (386 B.C.), he lost all Greek support and found himself alone in war with Persia. ARTAXERXES II defeated him in 381 B.C. and destroyed his fleet. Given easy peace terms, Evagoras kept at least nominal rule of the island. Isocrates wrote an encomium of him.

Evagrius Scholasticus (ēvā'grēəs), c.536–c.600, Syrian ecclesiastical historian, a prominent, honored lawyer in Antioch and Constantinople. His *Ecclesiastical History* (431–594), written in excellent Greek, is an authentic source for the history of Nestorianism and Monophysitism.

Evald, Johannes: see EWALD, JOHANNES.

Evander (ĭvăn'dər), in Greek religion, a minor deity worshiped in Arcadia in connection with Pan. In Roman religion, he was said to have introduced the worship of FAUNUS and to have founded the festival of LUPERCALIA. In Vergil's *Aeneid*, Evander sends his son Pallas to help Aeneas.

Evangelical Alliance (ēvănjĕl'ĭkəl), an association of Evangelical Christians in a union, not of churches, but of individuals belonging to different denominations and different countries. It was formed to give evidence of the unity existing among Evangelical believers and to advance such unity. The Alliance was founded in 1846 in London, at a conference in which some 50 denominations were represented by several hundred clergymen and laymen, gathered from many parts of the world. Branches have been organized in various countries. An American branch was established in 1867. In 1908 the American Alliance was replaced by the Federal Council of Churches, which was superseded in 1950 by the NATIONAL COUNCIL OF CHURCHES OF CHRIST IN THE UNITED STATES OF AMERICA. The largest association is the one first formed in Great Britain, which in 1923 became known as the World's Evangelical Alliance. See A. J. Arnold, *History of the Evangelical Alliance* (1897); J. W. Ewing, *Goodly Fellowship: A Centenary Tribute to the Life and Work of the World's Evangelical Alliance, 1846–1946* (1946).

Evangelical and Reformed Church, Protestant denomination formed by the merger (1934) of the Reformed Church in the United States and the Evangelical Synod of North America. Both of these bodies had originated in the Reformation in Europe. Their churches in America were established by immigrants from Germany and Switzerland. The Reformed Church in the United States, long known as the German Reformed Church, organized its first synod in 1747 and adopted a constitution in 1793. The Evangelical Synod of North America (not to be confused with the Evangelical Church, which merged in 1946 with the United Brethren in Christ to form the Evangelical United Brethren Church) was founded in 1840 at Gravois Settlement, Mo., by a union of Reformed and Lutheran Christians. In its early years it was known as the German Evangelical Church Association of the West. The Evangelical and Reformed Church is presbyterian in organization, and its creed is the Heidelberg and Luther's catechisms and the Augsburg Confession; great latitude in interpretation is allowed, however, with greater emphasis leaning toward deed rather than creed. The church maintains educational institutions and foreign missions. In 1957 the Evangelical and Reformed Church united with the Congregational Christian Churches to form the UNITED CHURCH OF CHRIST.

Evangelical Church: see EVANGELICAL UNITED BRETHREN CHURCH.

Evangelical League: see PROTESTANT UNION.

Evangelical United Brethren Church, Protestant denomination created (1946) by the union of the Evangelical Church and the United Brethren in Christ. Both denominations originated early in the 19th cent. and had similarities in organization and polity. The Evangelical Church was begun by the evangelical, pietistic efforts of Jacob ALBRIGHT, a Lutheran convert to Methodism, who preached among his fellow Pennsylvania Germans. The United Brethren in Christ came into being as a result of the evangelistic preaching of Philip William OTTERBEIN of the German Reformed Church and Martin BOEHM, a Mennonite bishop. These two ministers conducted revivals among the German-speaking people of Pennsylvania, Maryland, and Virginia. The methods of Albright, Otterbein, and Boehm were similar: after evangelistic meetings, converts were encouraged to form classes or societies for strengthening their spiritual life. The groups formed under Albright held a general conference in 1807 at which he was elected bishop; in 1816 the name Evangelical Association was adopted. In 1891 a group that became the United Evangelical Church seceded from the Evangelical Association, but in 1922 the two bodies reunited as the Evangelical Church. The societies formed under Otterbein and Boehm took shape as a distinct ecclesiastical body, to be known as the United Brethren in Christ, at a conference in 1800, at which the two ministers were elected bishops. The United Brethren in Christ (Old Constitution) parted from the main body in 1889; from that time they have maintained a separate church. Members of the MORAVIAN CHURCH are also sometimes called the United Brethren. In earlier years the membership of the Evangelical Church and of the United Brethren in Christ included few who were not German in speech, but later the German-speaking element formed only a small proportion. Extension W of the Alleghenies was rapid. The newly combined church supported publishing houses in the United States and abroad, four theological seminaries, a number of colleges, and foreign missions. It had an episcopal form of government. In doctrine it was Arminian. Particular emphasis was laid on prayer, a life of devotion to Christ, and the responsibility of the individual. Having long maintained a close relationship with the Methodist Church, it merged with it to found (1968) the UNITED METHODIST CHURCH, U.S.A. See R. W. Albright, *History of the Evangelical Church* (1942, repr. 1956); J. W. Owen, *A Short History of the Church of the United Brethren in Christ* (1944).

evangelist (ĭvăn'jəlĭst) [from Gr., = Gospel], title given to saints Matthew, Mark, Luke, and John. The four evangelists are often symbolized respectively by a man, a lion, an ox, and an eagle, on the basis of Rev. 4.6–10. In modern times the term is applied to Protestant preachers who go about preaching personal conversion. The greatest effort of evangelism was undoubtedly the GREAT AWAKENING. METHODISM is essentially evangelical in its origins; John WESLEY and George WHITEFIELD were the great Methodist evangelists. George Fox, founder of the Quakers (see FRIENDS, RELIGIOUS SOCIETY OF), was also an evangelist. Dwight MOODY was a prominent 19th-century American evangelist. Billy GRAHAM is a notable modern example. See also CAMP MEETING and REVIVAL, RELIGIOUS.

Evans, Sir Arthur John, 1851–1941, English archaeologist. He was (1884–1908) keeper of the Ashmolean Museum at Oxford. From 1898 to 1935 he conducted excavations in Crete, principally at Cnossus, and there uncovered the remains of an ancient civilization, which he named Minoan. His writings include *Cretan Pictographs and Prae-Phoenician Script* (1895); *The Mycenaean Tree and Pillar Cult* (1901); and *The Palace of Minos* (4 vol., 1921–35). See biography by Joan Evans (1943).

Evans, Augusta Jane, 1835–1909, American novelist, b. Columbus, Ga. Of her sentimental, moralistic novels, *St. Elmo* (1866) achieved greatest popularity.

Evans, Caradoc, 1883–1945, Anglo-Welsh novelist and short-story writer. His chief works are his short-story collections, *My People* (1915), *Capel Sion* (1916), and *My Neighbors* (1919), and his novel *Nothing to Pay* (1930). His writings express a harsh and bitter criticism of his people. See biographies by his wife, Oliver Sandys, (1946) and by T. L. Williams (1970).

Evans, Charles, 1850–1935, American librarian and bibliographer, b. Boston. He organized many major American libraries including the Indianapolis public library, the Enoch Pratt Free Library in Baltimore, Md., and the Omaha public library. He also classified the Newberry Library in Chicago. An authority on American literature, Evans published *American Bibliography* (1903–55), a chronological directory of all material published in the United Staes from 1639 to 1820.

Evans, Dame Edith, 1888–, English actress. After her stage debut in 1912, Evans toured with Ellen Terry. She worked with the Old Vic (1925–26) and has had a distinguished career on the stage and in films. She was celebrated for her performances in Elizabethan, Restoration, and 18th-century drama, as well as in modern works. Evans was made Dame of the British Empire in 1946. Her notable films include *The Importance of Being Earnest* (1953), *Tom Jones* (1963), *The Whisperers* (1967), and *A Doll's House* (I973). See study by J. C. Trewin (1954).

Evans, Frederick H., 1853–1943, English photographer. Evans retired from bookselling in 1898 when he began his photographic career. He became internationally famous for his exquisite platinotype images of architectural subjects, principally English cathedrals, manors, and cloisters. Refusing to manipulate his prints in any way, Evans rendered the cool, massive stone buildings with an unsurpassed grandeur in straightforward contact prints from his plates. He exhibited and wrote extensively and was widely, if unsuccessfully, imitated. He ceased making prints in 1915 when platinum was no longer commercially available.

Evans, George Henry, 1805–56, American labor and agrarian reformer, b. England. After emigrating (1820) to New York City, he edited several newspapers, among them the *Workingman's Advocate.* He also led a number of workingman's parties from 1827 to 1837. His agrarian reform programs included the right of free homesteads for all.

Evans, John, 1814–97, American founder of educational institutions, b. Waynesville, Ohio, grad. Lynn Medical College, Cincinnati, 1838. He practiced medicine in Indiana and was the first superintendent (1845) of the state hospital for the insane, which he had helped establish. In 1848 he went to Chicago as professor of obstetrics at Rush Medical School. He invested in real estate and helped found Northwestern Univ. in Evanston, Ill., a city named for him. Evans served (1862–65) as governor of Colorado Territory and later worked for the promotion of what is now the Univ. of Denver. See biography by H. E. Kelsey, Jr. (1969).

Evans, Sir John, 1823–1908, English archaeologist, geologist, and numismatist. A president of the Royal Numismatic Society and of the Society of Antiquaries, he was active also in public welfare and was an authority on water supply. His works include *Coins of the Ancient Britons* (1864), *The Ancient Stone Implements, Weapons, and Ornaments of Great Britain* (1872), and *Ancient Bronze Implements . . . Great Britain and Ireland* (1881). Part of his coin collection is in the Ashmolean Museum, Oxford.

Evans, Lewis, c.1700–1756, colonial surveyor and geographer, b. Wales. Evans carried out several assignments for Benjamin Franklin. His travels and studies of the colonies nearest him bore fruit in two maps, *A Map of Pennsylvania, New Jersey, New York, and the Three Delaware Counties* (1749, rev. ed. 1752) and *A General Map of the Middle British Colonies in America* published together with an *Analysis* (1755). The first of these was used by migrating colonists for the excellent detail of the roads. The second was used by General Braddock during the French and Indian War, and was published many times over by London firms. In the *Analysis* he drew particular attention to the Ohio River and suggested ways and means of acquiring it by force from the French. His *Brief Account of Pennsylvania* (1753) was reprinted in the biography by L. H. Gipson (1939).

Evans, Luther Harris, 1902–, American librarian and political scientist, b. Bastrop co., Texas. After teaching political science at several universities, he became director of the Historical Records Survey under the Work Projects Administration (1935). In 1939 he was appointed director of the legislative reference service of the Library of Congress. Evans was chief assistant librarian of Congress from 1940 to 1945, when he was appointed librarian. From 1953 to 1958 he was director general of the United Nations Educational, Scientific and Cultural Organization. Evans was Director of International and Legal Collections, Columbia Univ. Libraries, from 1962 to 1967.

Evans, Mary Ann or **Marian:** see ELIOT, GEORGE.

Evans, Maurice, 1901–, Welsh-American actor. Evans came into prominence in 1928 and in 1934 was a leading man with the Old Vic. He first appeared on Broadway in 1936 in *Romeo and Juliet* with Katharine Cornell. Evans gained acclaim as a Shakespearean actor in such roles as King Richard II (1937), Hamlet (1938), and Macbeth (1941). He was also noted for his productions of Shaw's works. Evans's films include *Androcles and the Lion* (1952), *Macbeth* (1959), and *Planet of the Apes* (1967). He has performed in many classic dramas on television.

Evans, Oliver, 1755–1819, American inventor, b. near Newport, Del. He joined his brothers in a flour-milling business in Wilmington, and after studying similar earlier devices, he developed, installed, and patented a number of grain-handling machines. These inventions included an elevator, a conveyor, a descender, and a hopper boy; a generation later they were standard equipment in U.S. mills. His *Young Mill-Wright & Miller's Guide* (1795) went through many editions. After experimenting with a steam carriage to run on ordinary roads, Evans turned his attention to stationary steam engines. He was a pioneer in the building of high-pressure engines, and after establishing the Mars Iron Works in 1807 built about 50 engines, most of them used in pumping. He built the first steam river dredge to be used in the United States and brought it to the river under its own power. See biography by Greville Bathe and Dorothy Bathe (1935).

Evans, Walker, 1903–, American photographer, b. St. Louis. Evans began his photographic career in 1928. His studies of Victorian architecture and his photographs of the rural South during the depression, made for the Farm Security Administration, are among his best-known works. Many of Evans's photographs of tenant farmers appeared in the book *Let Us Now Praise Famous Men* (1941; coauthored with James Agee). Evans's other books include *American Photographs* (1938) and *Message from the Interior* (1966). His work is characterized by a spare precision that emphasizes the dignity of his subjects. See *Walker Evans* (Mus. of Modern Art, 1971).

Evans, Mount, peak, 14,260 ft. (4,346 m) high, N central Colo., in the Front Range of the Rocky Mts. At its summit is the Inter-University High Altitude Laboratory.

Evans-Pritchard, Edward Evan, 1902–, English social anthropologist. He made several expeditions to Africa. His major contributions lie in the fields of social anthropology and comparative religion. His writings include *Essays in Social Anthropology* (1962), *Theories of Primitive Religion* (1965), and *The Azande* (1971).

Evanston, residential city (1970 pop. 79,808), Cook co., NE Ill., on Lake Michigan; settled 1826, inc. 1892. It has a publishing industry, and photocopying machines, food products, and rust preventatives are among its manufactures. It is the seat of Northwestern Univ., the National College of Education, two theological seminaries, and a junior college. Evanston is also the national headquarters of many companies and organizations, including the Woman's Christian Temperance Union. Frances E. Willard once lived there.

Evansville, city (1970 pop. 138,764), seat of Vanderburgh co., extreme SW Ind., a port on the Ohio River; inc. 1819. It is the shipping and commercial center for a coal, oil, and farm region. Refrigeration and air-conditioning equipment, aluminum, pharmaceuticals, excavating machinery, and fabricated-metal items are among its manufactures. The Univ. of Evansville, an Indiana State Univ. campus, several technical colleges, and a state mental hospital are there. The city has a museum of arts and sciences, a zoo, a philharmonic orchestra, and an aviary. An Indian mound village site is a state memorial. In an extensive urban renewal program during the 1960s the main street was converted into a seven-block winding walkway shopping plaza.

evaporation, change of a liquid into vapor at any temperature below its BOILING POINT. For example, water, when placed in a shallow open container exposed to air, gradually disappears, evaporating at a rate that depends on the amount of surface exposed, the HUMIDITY of the air, and the temperature. Evaporation occurs because among the molecules near the surface of the liquid there are always some with enough heat energy to overcome the cohesion of their neighbors and escape (see ADHESION AND COHESION; MATTER). At higher temperatures the number of energetic molecules is greater, and evaporation is more rapid. Evaporation is also increased by increasing the surface area of the liquid or by increasing the air circulation, thus carrying away the energetic molecules leaving the liquid before they can be slowed enough by collisions with air molecules to be reabsorbed into the liquid. If the air is humid some water molecules from the air will pass back into the liquid, thus reducing the rate of evaporation. An increase in atmospheric pressure also reduces evaporation. The process of evaporation is always accompanied by a cooling effect. For example, when a liquid evaporates from the skin, a cooling sensation results. The reason for this is that only the most energetic molecules of liquid are lost by evaporation, so that the average energy of the remaining molecules decreases; the surface temperature, which is a measure of this average energy, decreases also. Many REFRIGERATION processes are based on this principle.

evaporimeter, instrument that measures the rate of evaporation of water into the atmosphere, sometimes called an atmometer. Evaporimeters are of two types, those that measure the evaporation rate from a free water surface and those that measure it from a continuously wet porous surface. In the first type, the level of water in a tank or pan, often sunk into the ground so that the water surface is at ground level, is measured by a micrometer gauge. After accounting for increases due to rain and decreases due to deliberate draining, the day-to-day decrease in the water level can be attributed to evaporation. In one evaporimeter of the second type, the evaporation rate is computed according to the rate of weight loss of a wet pack of absorbent material. The Piché evaporimeter uses an inverted graduated cylinder of water with a filter-paper seal at the mouth. Evaporation takes place from the wet filter paper and thus depletes the water in the cylinder, so that the rate of evaporation can be read directly from the graduations marking the water level. The Livingston sphere, another evaporimeter of the second type, uses a wet ceramic sphere as the evaporating surface to simulate evaporation rates from vegetation. Because evaporation rates are so sensitive to the water supply, to the nature of the evaporating surface, and to the surface's exposure to the atmosphere, the data collected by such instruments are often not representative of the natural evapotranspiration from the soil, vegetation, and the oceans; evaporimeters are therefore not in widespread use by environmental scientists.

Evarts, William Maxwell, 1818–1901, American lawyer and statesman, b. Boston; grandson of Roger Sherman. After attending Harvard Law School he began (1841) to practice law in New York City, where, with Charles E. Butler, he formed (1843) a firm that became one of the best known in the country. Evarts was government counsel in the abortive trial of Jefferson Davis for treason and later eloquently defended President Andrew Johnson in the impeachment proceedings. He was one of the counsel for the United States in the Geneva arbitration proceedings (1871–72) on the *Alabama* claims, and in 1877, as Republican counsel before the electoral commission, he argued the claims of Rutherford B. Hayes to the presidency. He was U.S. Attorney General under Johnson (1868–69) and Secretary of State under Hayes (1877–81). Confronted in the latter capacity with the activity of French interests in constructing an isthmian canal, he stated forcefully that any canal must remain under American control, thus formulating a policy subsequently maintained in American foreign relations. He was U.S. Senator from New York from 1885 to 1891, a period marked by failing eyesight, which resulted in total blindness for the last 11 years of his life. See Brainerd Dyer, *The Public Career of William M. Evarts* (1933, repr. 1969); biography by C. L. Barrows (1941).

Evatt, Herbert Vere (vēr ĕv'ət), 1894–1965, Australian statesman. After achieving prominence as a labor lawyer, Evatt became justice of the high court of Australia in 1930 and in 1940 became a Labour member of the House of Representatives. In 1941 he was appointed attorney general and minister of foreign affairs. During World War II, Evatt was the Australian member of the Pacific War Council, and he was a delegate to the UN Conference in 1945. He gained note for championing the rights of the smaller nations and opposing the veto power of the big nations. Evatt also urged international control of atomic energy. In 1948–49 he was president of the UN General Assembly. He later led the Labour opposition in Parliament. Among his many books is *The Task of Nations* (1949). See biography by Kylie Tennant (1971).

Eve [Heb.,=life], in the Bible, the first woman, wife of ADAM and the mother of Cain, Abel, and Seth. Fashioned from Adam's rib, she was beguiled by the serpent into eating the forbidden fruit of the tree of knowledge. Eve then tempted Adam to eat, whereupon they were banished from the Garden of Eden. Gen. 2–4; 2 Cor. 11.3; 1 Tim. 2.13. See also LILITH.

Evelyn, John (ēv'əlĭn, ĕv'lĭn), 1620–1706, English diarist and miscellaneous writer. Although of royalist sympathies, he took little active part in the civil war. After 1652 he lived as a wealthy country gentleman at Sayes Court, Deptford, where he cultivated his garden and wrote on various subjects, including reforestation, natural science, the history of art, and numismatics. After the Restoration he became a public servant and was one of the founders of the Royal Society. His best-known work is his lifelong diary, less intimate than that of Pepys, but full of historical information about 17th-century England. It was first published in 1818 (modern ed. by E. S. de Beer, 6 vol., 1955). He is also famous for his *Life of Mrs. Godolphin* (ed. by Harriet Sampson, 1939). See biographies by Walter Hiscock (1955), Arthur Ponsonby (1933, repr. 1969), and Beatrice Saunders (1970).

evening primrose, common name for the Onagraceae, a family of plants of worldwide distribution, most species of which grow as herbs in the temperate New World, and specifically for members of the genus *Oenothera*. Species of *Oenothera*, *Epilobium*, and *Godetia*, among others, are native to America; some are cultivated. Evening primroses (species of *Oenothera* and some other similar species) range from North America to Patagonia. Most are yellow, evening-flowering annuals or biennials. The common evening primrose (*O. biennis*) is naturalized in the Old World, where the roots are sometimes used for food. The hybrid *O. lamarckiana* was

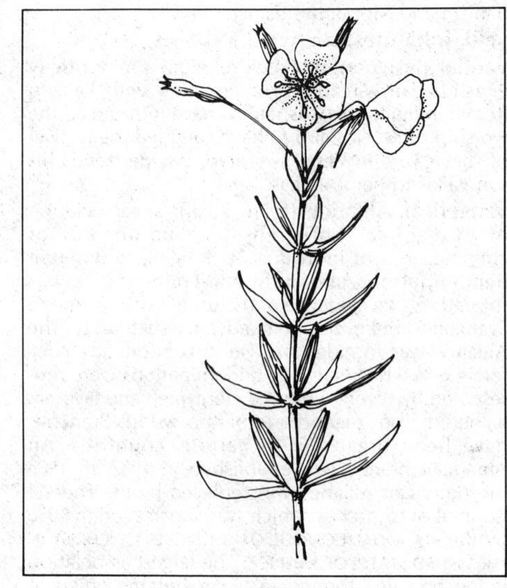

Evening primrose, Oenothera biennis

used by Hugo de Vries in formulating his mutation theory of heredity. *Godetia,* abundant in California, includes farewell-to-spring, or summer's-darling (*G. amoena*). The branching, bushy great willow herb (*E. angustifolium*) is a widespread FIREWEED and a good bee plant. Most species of the genus *Fuchsia* are tropical American shrubs cultivated elsewhere as ornamentals for their pendulous, brilliant red to purple and white flowers. Most garden fuchsias are hybrids. The evening primrose family is classified in the division MAGNOLIOPHYTA, class Magnoliopsida, order Myrtales.

evening schools: see VOCATIONAL EDUCATION.

evening star or **morning star,** planet that becomes visible in the western sky shortly after sunset or in the eastern sky shortly before sunrise. It can usually be seen in twilight, when it is too light for the true stars to be seen. Venus and Mercury are often seen as evening or morning stars. Other planets, especially Mars and Jupiter, may appear as evening or morning stars at certain points in their orbits.

Evenki National Okrug (ĕvyĕn'kē), administrative division (1970 pop. 13,000), 287,645 sq mi (745,000 sq km), N central Siberian USSR, in the Central Siberian Uplands. The village of Tura is the capital. The okrug occupies the entire central section of Krasnoyarsk Kray and is crossed by the Lower (Nizhnaya) Tunguska and the Stony (Pokmannaya) Tunguska rivers. The okrug lies in the forested taiga zone, with tundra vegetation in the north. Iron ore, graphite, zinc, lead, and nickel are mined; however, coal, salt, and timber resources remain largely untapped. Reindeer raising, fur trapping and breeding, and fishing are the chief occupations of the native Evenki. Some potatoes, vegetables, and dairy cattle are raised. Transportation is mainly by water and air; reindeer are often used for overland travel. Russians, Evenki, and Yakuts make up the bulk of the population, which is of a very low density. The Evenki are a Tungus-Manchurian-speaking people of Mongol origin; they are scattered throughout Siberia and number about 24,000. The Russian Orthodox and Lamaistic religions of the Evenki are permeated by shamanism. In prehistoric times, the Evenki lived around Lake Baykal. They were mostly conquered by Russia in the 17th cent. Under the Soviet government, the Evenki have largely abandoned their nomadic existence for a more sedentary life. The national okrug was formed in 1930.

Everdingen, Allart van (äl'ärt vän ä'fərdĭngən), 1621–75, Dutch painter and etcher. He worked primarily in Haarlem and Amsterdam. The scenery of Sweden and Norway forms the subject of some of his finest pictures. In color, atmosphere, and composition his paintings have been compared to those of Ruisdael. Everdingen executed over 150 etchings, treated in a broad and vigorous manner. Outstanding among them were his etchings for *Reynard the Fox.* His brother **Caesar Everdingen,** 1617–87, was a portrait and historical painter in the Italian academic style.

Everest, Sir George, 1790–1866, British surveyor, b. Brecknockshire, Wales. He worked on the trigonometrical survey of India from 1806 to 1843. He became superintendent of the survey in 1823 and surveyor general of India in 1830; Mt. Everest is named for him. He was knighted in 1861.

Everest, Mount, peak, 29,028 ft (8,848 m) high, on the border of Tibet and Nepal, in the central Himalayas. It is the highest elevation in the world. Called Chomo-Lungma [Mother Goddess of the Land] by the Tibetans, it is named in English for Sir George Everest, surveyor of the Himalayas. The first eight attempts to scale the peak were unsuccessful, but on May 28, 1953, Sir Edmund Hillary and Tenzing Norkay of Nepal reached the summit.

Everett, Edward (ĕv'rĭt, ĕv'ərĭt), 1794–1865, American orator and statesman, b. Dorchester, Mass., grad. Harvard (B.A., 1811; M.A., 1814). In 1814 he became a Unitarian minister in Boston, but, appointed (1815) professor of Greek literature at Harvard, he went abroad to study at the Univ. of Göttingen (Ph.D., 1817) and to travel. During his professorship (1819–25) he also edited (1820–23) the *North American Review.* He was a U.S. Representative (1825–35), governor of Massachusetts (1836–39), minister to England (1841–45), president of Harvard (1846–49), and Secretary of State in the last four months of President Fillmore's administration (1852–53). Massachusetts elected him U.S. Senator, but he resigned in the second year of the term (1854), embarrassed by his old-line Whig attitude of compromise on slavery. In the Civil War he traveled throughout the North speaking for the Union cause and drawing immense audiences. His most famous address, now almost forgotten, was the principal oration delivered at Gettysburg on the same occasion that called forth Abraham Lincoln's enduring Gettysburg Address. See biography by P. R. Frothingham (1925).

Everett, 1 City (1970 pop. 42,485), Middlesex co., E Mass., an industrial suburb of Boston, on the Mystic River; settled c.1643, set off from Malden 1870, inc. as a city 1892. A deepwater port, Everett has coal and petroleum storage facilities, chemical plants, foundries, and a great variety of manufactures. **2** City (1970 pop. 53,622), seat of Snohomish co., NW Wash., on Puget Sound at the mouth of the Snohomish River; inc. 1893. A port of entry with a fine natural harbor, it is an important lumber-shipping center, with pulp and paper mills. Other industries include commercial fishing and aircraft manufacturing; the huge Boeing 747 airplane is manufactured there. Tourism is also significant; the city is a gateway to both the Cascade Mts. and the offshore islands. A state junior college is in Everett, and an Indian reservation is nearby.

Everglades, marshy, low-lying tropical area, c.5,000 sq mi (12,950 sq km), S Fla., extending from Lake Okeechobee S to Florida Bay; highest point is 7 ft (2.1 m) above sea level. Characterized by water, saw grass, hammocks (islandlike masses of vegetation), coastal mangrove forests, and solidly packed black muck (resulting from millions of years of vegetable decay in near-stagnant, warm water), the Everglades receives an annual average rainfall of more than 60 in. (152 cm), mainly in the summer. Big Cypress Swamp, to the northwest, and Lake Okeechobee are the chief sources of water for the Everglades. Limestone rims the area, acting as a natural retaining wall against the sea. Colonial expeditions in the 1500s found Indians living in the Everglades. In the late 1830s the Everglades was the site of military operations against the Seminole Indians. Large tracts of land were drained in the late 19th and early 20th cent., when the Everglades was considered a potentially rich agricultural region, but only the area immediately bordering Lake Okeechobee was farmed. Winter vegetables and sugarcane are now the main crops. After the great fires of 1939 (caused by overdrainage), the first thorough studies of the Everglades concluded that most of the southern part was unfit for cultivation. Construction of retaining walls in the 1960s on the south shore of Lake Okeechobee and land development in Big Cypress Swamp have disrupted the natural flow of water into the Everglades, thus posing the threat of water shortages that can affect its plant and animal life. At the southwestern tip of Florida is **Everglades National Park,** 1,400,533 acres (566,796 hectares), the third largest national park; est. 1947. Florida Bay, with its many islets and the Ten Thousand Islands, is part of the park. A great variety of flora and fauna are found in the park, which is also a haven for such endangered species as the crocodile, alligator, egret, and bald eagle. The Tamiami Trail (completed 1928), a highway north of the park, links Miami with the west coast of Florida.

Evergood, Philip, 1901–73, American painter and etcher, b. New York City. His original name was Philip Blashki. He was educated at Eton and Cambridge and studied art in New York City and Paris. Evergood was famed for his murals, including *The Story of Richmond Hill* (1936–37; Public Library branch, Queens, N.Y.) and *Cotton from Field to Mill* (1938; U.S. Post Office, Jackson, Ga.). His work combines realism with fantasy, as in *Lily and the Sparrows* (1939; Whitney Mus., New York City). In the 1950s Evergood concentrated on symbolism, both biblical and mythological. A characteristic work is *The New Lazarus* (1954; Whitney Mus.). See his graphic work, selected by L. R. Lippard (1966); study by John Baur (1960).

evergreen, term commonly used as synonymous with CONIFER and applied also to all those broad-leaved plants that bear green leaves throughout the year. Of the latter, most are plants of the tropics, subtropics, and other areas where the growing season is prolonged (e.g., Australia and the Pacific Northwest of the United States). In colder climates various broad-leaved shrubs (e.g., box, holly, and members of the heath family) are evergreen. Some broadleaf evergreens shed all their leaves for a brief period; the rest lose them continually, producing new leaves as the old ones fall. The term "half-evergreen" is used for deciduous plants with persistent leaves.

Evergreen Park, village (1970 pop. 25,487), Cook co., NE Ill., a suburb of Chicago; inc. 1893. It is mostly residential and has a junior college.

everlasting or **immortelle** (ĭm"ôrtĕl'), names for numerous plants characterized by papery or chaffy flowers that retain their form and often their color when dried and are used for winter bouquets and decorations. Everlastings are usually cut before fully mature and hung head downward to dry in an area away from direct light (to prevent bleaching). Many of the more popular everlastings are of the family Compositae (COMPOSITE family), e.g., the STRAWFLOWER, pearly everlasting *(Anaphalis),* winged everlasting *(Ammobium),* pussy toes *(Antennaria),* common immortelle *(Xeranthemum),* and species of *Helipterum;* the cockscomb and globe AMARANTH and the thrift (see LEADWORT) are also used. Several grasses, the BITTERSWEET, and other plants are used as everlastings for their ornamental dried fruits.

Everyman, late-15th-century English morality play. It is the counterpart of the Dutch play *Elckerlijk;* which of these anonymous plays is the original has been the subject of controversy. When Everyman is summoned by Death, he can persuade none of his friends—Beauty, Kindred, Worldly Goods—to go with him, except Good Deeds. This allegory has been used as the basis of plays by later writers and has remained popular in modern times.

Evesham (ĕv'shəm, ē'shəm, ē'səm), municipal borough (1971 pop. 13,847), Worcestershire, W central England, on the Avon River. Evesham is the center of the Vale of Evesham, known for its fine market gardens. It is also a popular summer resort. Simon de Montfort, leader of the revolt against Henry III, was killed in 1265 during the battle of Evesham. In 1974, Evesham became part of the new non-metropolitan county of Hereford and Worcester.

Evi (ē'vī), Midianite king. Num. 31.8; Joshua 13.21.

Évian-les-Bains (āvyäN'-lā-băN) or **Évian,** town (1968 pop. 6,052), Haute-Savoie dept., E France, on Lake Geneva. It is a fashionable spa at the foot of the Alps. Évian-les-Bains's mineral water is bottled and exported to all parts of the world. Liqueur and precision instruments are also produced. A cease-fire agreement between the French government and the provisional government of Algeria was signed at Évian in 1962.

evidence, in law, means by which a judicial body resolves disputed questions of fact. The rules discussed in this article were developed in England for use in JURY trials. Today they are generally observed in all countries having the COMMON LAW, although they have been extensively modified by statute in some jurisdictions. The first juries were not triers of fact; rather they were convened because of their immediate knowledge of the dispute before the court. Later the practice developed of having witnesses testify before the jury. This was a relatively late development, however, and the groundwork of the rules of evidence was laid between 1500 and 1700. Because evidence is often presented in a tense, emotional atmosphere in a courtroom long after the event in question took place, the object of the law of evidence is to assure a high probability that the questions of fact in suits are resolved correctly. To that end the proof at the trial is ordinarily restricted to items of great probative value, and material that may arouse unreasoning passion is ordinarily excluded. The nature of the legal controversy and the written pleadings determine what assertions of fact each party must prove or disprove to win his case, and an item of evidence that at best has a remote bearing on the factual issues must be excluded as irrelevant (an alternative legal term is *immaterial*). A judge prefers direct evidence (such as an official document or a witness's assertion of his immediate knowledge of the question at issue) to indirect or circumstantial evidence that merely tends to establish the issue by proving surrounding circumstances from which the principal fact may be inferred. The type of controversy also determines the burden of proof, i.e., the obligation that a party bring forward some admissible proof of a factual contention on pain of having it decided against him. In criminal trials the prosecution has to prove every element of its case beyond a reasonable doubt. In civil trials, on the other hand, each party has the burden only of proving his affirmative contentions by a preponderance of the evidence. Thus the plaintiff must offer some proof of each of the elements that combine to constitute the defendant's alleged wrong (see PROCEDURE), while the defendant must prove his affirmative defenses, e.g., in a suit for NEGLIGENCE, that the plaintiff's own negligence contributed to the injury. Carrying the burden of proof requires the prosecutor or, in most civil cases, the plaintiff to present his evidence first. At the close of this presentation the criminal or civil defendant may move for a non-suit if admissible evidence supporting such necessary contention has not been offered. Proof may be dispensed with when an adversary formally admits the fact either in the pleadings or in court, or when the court may take judicial notice of the fact, i.e., when the fact is universally known or is easily ascertainable by the judge beyond possibility of reasonable dispute (e.g., the time that the sun rose on a particular day). Evidence at the trial, in addition to being relevant, must be competent, i.e., it must not fall under an exclusionary rule. Obviously if the evidence is documentary (e.g., a birth certificate introduced to prove a person's age) or if it is "real" (e.g., a bloody garment exhibited to prove that the victim suffered injury), there can be a question only whether the proffered evidence is itself incompetent. Most evidence, however, is testimonial, i.e., offered by the witnesses who testify before the court. Here the question of the witness's personal competency must be resolved; it must be shown that he was able to know, understand, and remember the matters on which he is to be examined. Thus a witness must possess the sensory faculties needed to apprehend the facts on which he reports, and he must not be feeble-minded or insane. Children offered as witnesses are examined by the judge to determine their intelligence and their understanding of the OATH usually required of witnesses. Children may be permitted to testify without an oath if the jury is cautioned that their statements then possess slight probative value. The witness is first directly examined by the party who offers him. The adversary party is then allowed to cross-examine the witness and attempt to disprove his testimony by eliciting additional facts or showing inconsistencies or lies. Testimonial evidence is limited both by exclusionary rules—chiefly concerning opinion evidence and hearsay evidence—and by rules respecting personal privilege. No witness may express his opinion on any matter when the jury can draw its own conclusions from the facts; but on technical questions an expert witness (e.g., a physician) may state his opinion. Hearsay declarations, i.e., testimony concerning a statement made out of court by persons who are not before the court when the statement is being offered, usually are excluded on the grounds that the person who made the statement may not be cross-examined, and only when the circumstances of the statement afford a high probability of its truth may it be admitted. Thus, if the victim of an attack, believing himself near death and so likely to speak the truth, identifies his assailant, the identification may be introduced in a trial for murder. Most jurisdictions have passed "dead man's statutes," which provide that when one of the participants in a contract or other transaction has died and a civil lawsuit arises between the survivor and the estate, the surviving party may not testify about any transaction or communication that he had with the deceased. This rule has been greatly criticized in recent years as being unfair to the survivor. Under the common law, parties to a civil suit and the defendant in a criminal action were not permitted to testify, but these rules have been abandoned. A witness may be excused from testifying about certain matters if he pleads personal privilege. In general, information confided in the course of the relations of attorney and client, priest and penitent, physician and patient, and husband and wife is subject to this privilege. Some jurisdictions hold such witnesses incompetent to testify. Witnesses are further protected by the privilege of withholding self-incriminating evidence. Criminal defendants have the privilege of refusing to take the witness stand, and in most situations evidence of previous criminal convictions is inadmissible. When an attorney believes that offered evidence should be excluded, he first makes the general objection that the item is "irrelevant, immaterial, and incompetent." If this is overruled, he may offer a specific objection on any grounds. Allegedly damaging errors in the admission of evidence are reviewable on appeal if an objection was made during the trial. In their final summing up, the attorneys may make any assertion that is supported to some degree by evidence. British judges, U.S. Federal judges, and, in some jurisdictions, state judges are permitted to comment on the credibility of the witnesses and the weight of the evidence. However, the judge must tell the jury that they are not bound by his remarks. In recent years the problems of procuring evidence have been eased somewhat by the introduction of broader discovery (i.e., disclosure) rules. In civil cases these rules compel each party to a suit to allow the other to have access to its witnesses and to certain types of evidence before the trial. In criminal cases the judge has the discretionary power to order discovery; however, on request the prosecutor must release all exculpatory evidence he has. Among the many modern treatises on the law of evidence those of J. H. WIGMORE are often accorded the highest authority. See also VERDICT. See T. G. Roady and R. N. Covington, ed., *Essays on Procedure and Evidence* (1961); E. W. Cleary, *Evidence* (1969).

evil, antithesis of good. The philosophical problem of evil is most simply stated in the question, why does evil exist in the world? Death, disease, and SIN are often included in the problem. Traditional Christian belief ascribes evil to the misdeeds of men, to whom God has granted FREE WILL. The Christian systems that believe in PREDESTINATION and justification by faith claim, like their Christian opponents, that God is still not the author of the evil men do. One explanation of evil is DUALISM, as in ZOROASTRIANISM and MANICHAEISM. In optimism evil is treated often as more apparent than real. The book of Job is a literary treatment of the problem. See Richard Taylor, *Good and Evil* (1970); Frederick Sontag, *The God of Evil* (1970).

evil eye, principally Sicilian and Mesoamerican Indian superstition, although it is known in other cultures. According to the Indian version, a person who stares fixedly at a pregnant woman or a child or who is too admiring or physically affectionate with children may produce a malicious effect on their lives, whether or not by intent. In Sicily any person or animal is considered vulnerable to the evil eye, and many individuals wear protective amulets or charms to nullify its effects.

evolution, concept which embodies the belief that existing animals and plants developed by a process of gradual, continuous change from previously existing forms. This theory, also known as descent with modification, constitutes organic evolution. Inorganic evolution, on the other hand, is concerned with the development of the physical universe from unorganized matter. Organic evolution, as opposed to belief in the special creation of each individual species as an immutable form, conceives of life as having had its beginnings in a simple primordial protoplasmic mass (probably originating in the sea) from which, through the long eras of time, arose all subsequent living forms. Evolutionary concepts appeared in some early Greek writings, e.g., in the works of Thales, Empedocles, Anaximander, and Aristotle. Under the restraining influence of the Church, no evolutionary theories developed during some 15 centuries of the Christian era to challenge the belief in special creation and the literal interpretation of the first part of Genesis; however, much data was accumulated that was to be utilized by later theorists. With the growth of scientific observation and experimentation, there began to appear from about the middle of the 16th cent. glimpses of the theory of evolution that emerged in the mid-19th cent. The invention of the microscope, making possible the study of reproductive cells and the growth of the science of embryology, was a factor in overthrowing hampering theories founded in false ideas of the reproductive process; studies in classification (taxonomy or systematics) and anatomy, based on dissection, were also influential. Linnaeus, in his later years, showed an inclination toward belief in the mutability of species as a result of his observations of the many variations among species.

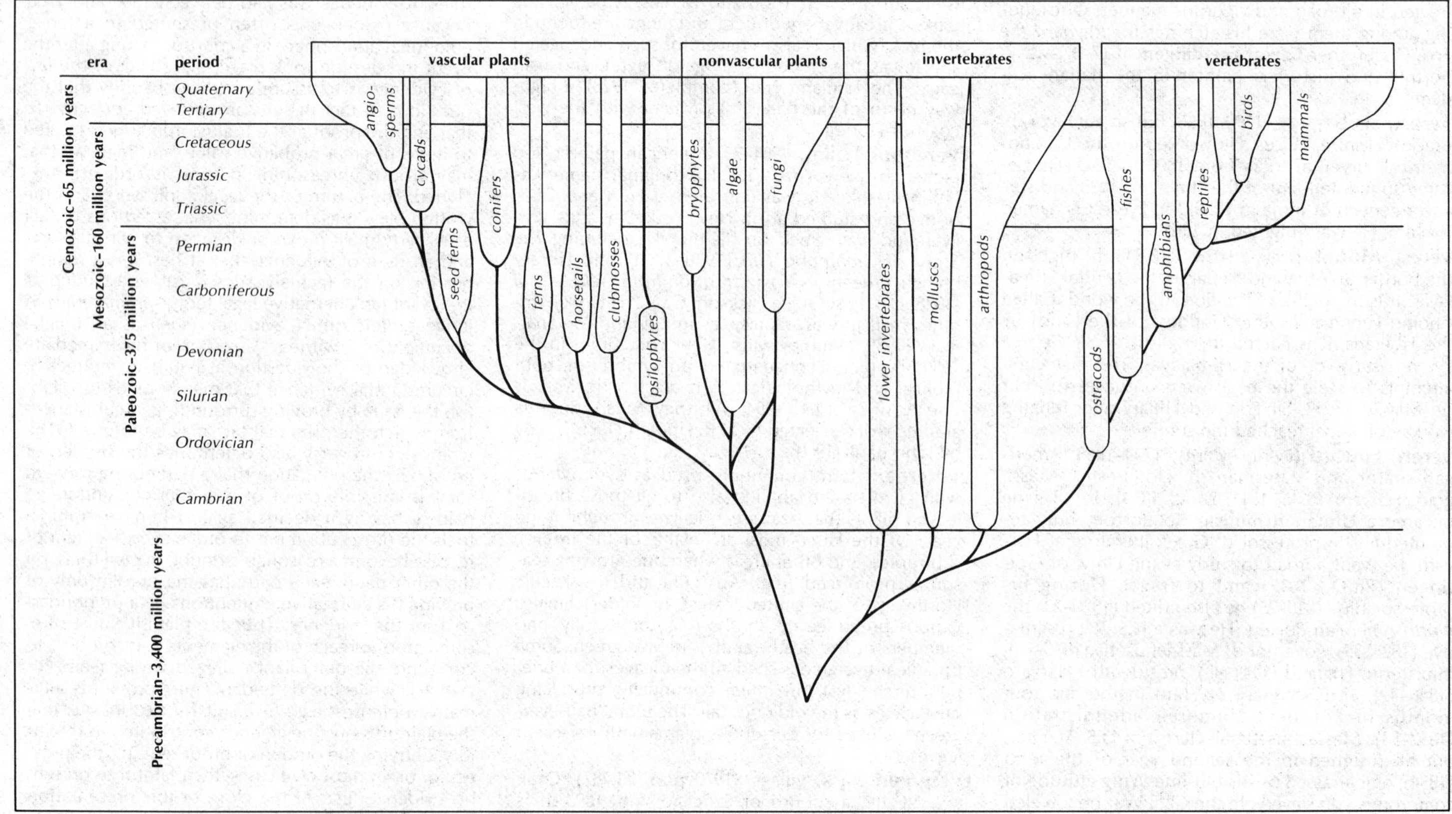

Plant and animal evolution [Modified from Alfred Gunderson in *Brooklyn Botanic Garden Leaflets*, Ser. 18, No. 4 (1930); used by permission.]

Buffon, on the basis of his work in comparative anatomy, suggested the influence of use and disuse in molding the organs of vertebrate animals. Lamarck was the first to present a clearly stated evolutionary theory, but because it included the inheritance of ACQUIRED CHARACTERISTICS as the operative force of evolution, his whole theory was ridiculed and discredited for many years. Although special creation of each species was the prevalent belief even among scientists in the first half of the 19th cent., the evidence in favor of evolution had by that time been uncovered. It remained for someone to assemble and interpret the evidence and to formulate a scientifically credible theory. This was accomplished simultaneously by A. R. WALLACE and Charles Robert DARWIN, who set forth the concepts that came to be known as DARWINISM. In 1859 appeared the first edition of Darwin's *Origin of Species.* The influence of this evolutionary theory upon scientific thought and experimentation cannot be overestimated. In the years following the promulgation of Darwin's theory of evolution, many accepted and many denied its validity. The theory found an opposing force in some religious creeds that declared it incompatible with their basic tenets. For a time evolution, sometimes falsely interpreted as meaning man's descent from monkeys rather than his descent from an ancient and extinct ancestor, became a target for attack by both church and educational authorities. Feeling ran high even as late as the time of the SCOPES TRIAL. Nevertheless, the theory of evolution became firmly entrenched as a scientific principle, and in most creeds it has been reconciled with religious teachings. It has, however, undergone modification in the light of later scientific developments. Evidence that evolution has occurred still rests on essentially the same grounds that Darwin emphasized: comparative anatomy, embryology, geographical distribution, and paleontology. Additional recent evidence from biochemistry demonstrates similarities in the chemical systems (e.g., of blood groups) and the metabolisms of related organisms. There is also evidence of biochemical RECAPITULATION in embryonic development. It can now be shown that, in general, the more closely related the groups of organisms, the greater the number of like structures and functions and the closer their similarity. Gradation, a step-by-step development of new forms, exists in fact as well as in theory (as evidenced by, for instance, the discovery of ARCHAEOPTERYX, the fossil missing link between reptiles and birds). Most significant is the fact that as more and more information accumulates, each fact corroborates the evidence furnished by every other field of investigation. The chief weakness of Darwinian evolution lay in its inability to explain satisfactorily the mechanism of evolution and of the origin of species. Natural SELECTION could explain why certain variations survived and others were lost, but not how these variations initially arose or were transmitted to offspring, and hence to subsequent generations. The science of GENETICS, originating at the beginning of the 20th cent. with the recognition of the importance of the earlier work of MENDEL, provided factual and systematic explanation for the mechanical basis of evolution. In 1901, De Vries presented his theory that MUTATION, or suddenly appearing and well-defined inheritable variation (as opposed to the slight, cumulative changes stressed by Darwin), is a force in the origin and evolution of species. Mutation in genes is now accepted by most biologists as a fundamental concept in evolutionary theory. The GENE is the carrier of heredity and determines the attributes of the individual; thus changes in the genes can be transmitted to the offspring and produce new or altered attributes in the new individual. A still prevalent misunderstanding of evolution is the belief that an animal or plant changes in order to better adapt to its environment; for example, that it develops an eye for the purpose of seeing. Since mutation is a random process and since most mutations are harmful rather than neutral or beneficial to the organism, it is evident that the occurrence of a variation is itself a matter of chance, and that one cannot speak of a will or purpose on the part of the individual to develop a new structure or trait that might prove helpful. However, a new characteristic that is not detrimental may sometimes better enable the organism to survive in its environment, especially if that environment is changing, or to penetrate a new environment—such as the development of a lunglike structure that enables an aquatic animal to survive on land, where there may be more food and fewer predators. Clearly, a variation which produces or occurs (often by chance) in conjunction with a higher rate of reproduction will be the most influential in the continuing survival of those individuals carrying the trait—and hence of the species. It is now understood that the success of the species—that is, its ability to maintain a constant or increased rate of reproduction—is at least as important in evolution as the success of the individual; the notion that the struggle for existence means actual physical competition among individuals is erroneous. Evolution is a continuing process in which chance variations are constantly interacting with environmental conditions to determine the success of the individual and of the species. For the evolution of man, see MAN, PREHISTORIC. See H. H. Ross, *Understanding Evolution* (1966); William Howells, *Mankind in the Making* (rev. ed. 1967); T. G. Dobzhansky, *Genetics of the Evolutionary Process* (1970); C. D. Darlington, *The Evolution of Man and Society* (1970); Ernst Mayr, *Population, Species, and Evolution* (1971); B. G. Campbell, *Human Evolution* (1974); P. R. Ehrlich, *Evolution* (1974).

Évora (ĕ'vôrə), town (1970 municipal pop. 47,806), capital of Évora dist. and of Altro Alentejo, S central Portugal. It is the commercial center of a fertile agricultural area. Called Ebora and Liberalitas Julia (after Julius Caesar) in Roman times, the temple of Diana there is an impressive ruin. Évora was an episcopal see early in the Christian era and later a center of trade under the Moors. It was recovered by the Portuguese under Gerald the Fearless (Geraldo Sem-Pavor) in 1166. After 1385 it was for many years the favorite seat of the Portuguese court. The old cathedral (12th-13th cent.) is a fine example of Romanesque style. The former Jesuit university (1559-1759) now houses a high school.

Evpatoriya: see YEVPATORIYA, USSR.

Évreux (āvrö'), town (1968 pop. 45,441), capital of Eure dept., N France, in Normandy. It is an industrial town where metals, textiles, rubber, radio and television parts, and pharmaceuticals are manufactured. Founded in Roman times and known as Mediolanum, the town became (10th cent.) the seat of a county that frequently changed hands throughout the Middle Ages. From 1349 to 1425 the counts of Évreux were also kings of NAVARRE. The French crown, which had held the county in the 12th cent. and again from 1404 to 1569, acquired it permanently in 1584. In 1642, Louis XIV exchanged Évreux for SEDAN with Frédéric Maurice, duc de Bouillon, who kept it until the county was abolished during the French Revolution. Devastated many times during the course of its history, the town was extensively rebuilt following World War II. Several monuments remain, the most famous of which are the Notre Dame Cathedral (14th-17th cent.), noted for its magnificent stained-glass windows, and St. Taurin Church, with its remarkable 13th-century shrine.

Évripos (ĕv'rĭpôs), strait, c.5 mi (8 km) long and from 120 ft to 1 mi (37 m-1.6 km) wide, forming the central and narrowest part of the channel separating the island of Évvoia from the Greek mainland. Khalkís, on Évvoia, is connected with the mainland by a drawbridge (built 1894).

Évros: see MARITSA, river.

Évry (āvrē'), town (1968 pop. 7,248), capital of Essonne dept., N central France. The major industry is the manufacture of aeronautic equipment.

Evtushenko, Evgeny: see YEVTUSHENKO, YEVGENY.

Évvoia (ĕv'ēä) or **Euboea** (yo͞obē'ə), island (1971 pop. 162,986), 1,467 sq mi (3,800 sq km), SE Greece, separated from Boeotia and Attica on the Greek mainland by the ÉVRIPOS strait. KHALKÍS is the main city and the administrative center. Évvoia is the largest of the Greek islands after Crete. The island is generally mountainous with fertile valleys; the highest points are Mt. Delphi (c.5,725 ft/1,745 m) and Mt. Oche (c.4,590 ft/1,400 m). Sheep, goats, and cattle are raised, and olives, grapes, and wheat are grown. Magnesite and lignite are mined, and marble is quarried. The island was settled by Ionian and Thracian colonists and was divided among seven independent cities, of which Khalkís and ERETRIA were the most important. Powerful and prosperous by the 8th cent. B.C., these cities established colonies in Macedonia, S Italy, and Sicily. The island was under the hegemony of Athens from 506 to 411 B.C. and was taken (c.338 B.C.) by Philip II of Macedon. It was annexed by Rome in 194 B.C. and later passed under Byzantine rule. As a result of the Fourth Crusade, it became (early 13th cent.) a colony of Venice. It was ceded to the Ottoman Turks in 1470. The island rebelled against the Turks in 1821 and in 1830 was incorporated into Greece. Its name in the Middle Ages was Negropont [black bridge], for the bridge connecting Khalkís with the mainland.

Ewald, Johannes (yōhän'əs ā'väl), 1743-81, Danish poet. Ewald's elegant verse made him the leading poet of his time. He studied for the ministry but soon turned to writing. His lyrical tragic drama *Adam and Eve* (1769) showed the influence of Klopstock. A prose work, *Rolf Krage* (1770), was based on a Danish legend from Saxo Grammaticus. The verse tragedy *Balder's Death* (1774) was a landmark in the revival of interest in Scandinavian mythology. His operetta *The Fishermen* (1779) contains the Danish national anthem, *King Christian Stood by the Lofty Mast.* The central figure of the Danish Literary Society, Ewald exerted marked influence on later writers. His name also appears as Evald.

Ewe (ā'vā,-wā), Negro tribe, numbering over one million, who live in SE Ghana, S Togo, and S Dahomey. When German Togoland was partitioned after World War I, the Ewe in that colony were divided between France and Britain. The question of reunion was constantly before the United Nations after World War II, but no satisfactory terms of reunification could be found. Part of the Ewe passed (1957) with British Togoland to Ghana by referendum. The Ewe are the largest political group in Togo. See Alfred Ellis, *The Ewe-speaking Peoples of the Slave Coast of West Africa* (1966).

Ewell, Benjamin Stoddert (yo͞o'əl), 1810-94, American educator, b. Georgetown, D.C., grad. West Point, 1832; brother of Gen. R. S. Ewell. He taught mathematics at West Point, Hampden-Sidney College, and Washington College (now Washington and Lee Univ.) before being elected (1848) professor of mathematics and acting president of William and Mary. In 1854 he became president. The college was closed during the Civil War, and Ewell, who had at first opposed secession, joined the Confederate army and was chief of staff to Gen. J. E. Johnston through most of the war. After the war he prevailed on Congress to reimburse the college for buildings burned by Federal troops and was thus able to reopen William and Mary in 1869, only to be forced to close it again in 1881 because of diminished income. Ewell spent his own money in keeping up the institution, until in 1888 it was reopened with state aid. He then became president emeritus until his death.

Ewell, Richard Stoddert, 1817-72, Confederate general, b. Georgetown, D.C., grad. West Point, 1840. Ewell rose rapidly in the Confederate army, becoming a major general by Oct., 1861. In 1862 he fought under T. J. (Stonewall) JACKSON in the Shenandoah Valley campaign, playing a decisive role at Winchester, Cross Keys, and PORT REPUBLIC. He continued in Stonewall's command through the Seven Days battles and Lee's subsequent advance on Pope but lost his leg in the second battle of Bull Run (Aug., 1862). Upon his return to duty, Ewell succeeded the late Stonewall Jackson as commander of the 2d Corps and led Lee's advance in the GETTYSBURG CAMPAIGN. During the WILDERNESS CAMPAIGN (1864) he sustained further injury and was forced to retire from the field but commanded the defenses of Richmond until the city fell in April, 1865. See D. S. Freeman, *Lee's Lieutenants* (3 vol., 1942-44).

Ewing, Sir James Alfred, 1855-1935, Scottish engineer and physicist. As professor at Tokyo (1878-83), Dundee (1883-90), and Cambridge (1890-1903), he helped establish programs in engineering. Ewing was director of naval education in the United Kingdom (1903-16) and was knighted in 1911. He was principal and vice chancellor of the Univ. of Edinburgh from 1916 to 1929. Ewing's researches in magnetism led him to observe the phenomenon of hysteresis (a term that he coined), and he investigated the crystalline structure of several important metals. He was one of the first Europeans to study earthquakes in Japan. His works include *Treatise on Earthquake Measurement* (1883), *The Strength of Materials* (1899), and *Thermodynamics for Engineers* (1920). See biography by L. F. Bates (1946).

Ewing, Thomas, 1789-1871, American statesman, b. Ohio co., Va. (now W. Va.). He represented Ohio in the U.S. Senate (1831-37) and supported Henry Clay in the Whig fight against the Jackson administration. Ewing was Secretary of the Treasury under President William Henry Harrison and his successor, President Tyler, from March to Sept., 1841, when all the cabinet except Daniel Webster resigned. President Taylor made him the first Secretary of the Interior (March, 1849) but in July, 1850, he resigned to fill a senatorial vacancy from Ohio until March, 1851. Defeated for reelection, Ewing resumed his law practice and subsequently won renown for his work before the U.S. Supreme Court.

Ewing, William Maurice, 1906-74, American oceanographer and geologist, b. Lackney, Texas, grad. Rice Institute, now Rice Univ. (B.S., 1926; M.A.,

1927; Ph.D., 1931). He taught physics and geology at the Univ. of Pittsburgh and Lehigh Univ. and was a research associate at Woods Hole Oceanographic Institution in Massachusetts. In 1944 he joined the faculty of Columbia Univ. and in 1949 became director of research at Columbia's Lamont Geological Observatory (now Lamont-Doherty Observatory) at Palisades, N.Y. While associated with Columbia, he collected evidence to support his theory that the sea floors were spreading from central ridges and that the continents were in motion with respect to one another. Ewing introduced the use of seismic waves to explore the ocean floor and with a former student developed a seismograph that has become standard throughout the world. In 1972 he joined the Marine Biomedical Institute of the Univ. of Texas at Galveston. In 1960, Ewing became the first recipient of the Vetlesen Prize, an award given by the Vetlesen Foundation to honor leaders in the earth sciences.

examination system: see CHINESE EXAMINATION SYSTEM.

Excalibur, in ARTHURIAN LEGEND, sword given to King Arthur by the LADY OF THE LAKE. At Arthur's death Sir Bedivere threw Excalibur into the lake; a hand rose from the water, caught the sword, and disappeared. Another sword, sometimes mistakenly identified with Excalibur, was drawn from a stone by Arthur to prove his royalty.

excess profits tax, levy on any profit above a standard level. Chiefly a wartime phenomenon, it is intended to increase revenue during periods of distress and to prevent businessmen from taking unfair advantage of the increased government spending and consumer demand that normally accompany wars. In 1917 the U.S. Federal government adopted such a tax, which continued in various forms and at increasing rates until 1921. It was revived by Federal legislation during World War II and during the Korean War. The tax was imposed on the excess over a firm's peacetime earnings or over an arbitrarily decreed earning rate. Great Britain levied an excess profits tax from 1915 to 1921, with a rate varying from 40% to 80%. During the era of World War II, Britain's excess profits tax was revived, with tax rates increased to 100%. Critics contend that such levies discourage productive enterprise by eliminating the profit motive.

exchange, mutual transfer of goods, money, services, or their equivalents; also the marketplace where such transfer occurs. In primitive society, exchange of unessential articles, such as jewelry, was common, but no primitive group could afford to rely on another group for the necessities of life. Gradually, division of labor led to the barter economy, in which articles were produced for exchange, each group producing what best it could. Modern capitalistic society, although an outgrowth of the exchange economy, is not, strictly speaking, based on exchange. Strict exchange depends on barter, and in modern society the money and price system, in which goods and services are produced in exchange for specified amounts of a standard currency, has replaced barter. Broadly, the term is used to signify exchange of goods and services for money. The price of the various factors in exchange is determined by their supply and the market demand for them. In commerce, an exchange is a place where trading goes on, especially a STOCK EXCHANGE or a commodity exchange. Conversion of one country's currency into that of another by means of still others is called arbitrage or arbitration of exchange. The term *exchange* also refers to the amount of money necessary to buy a given amount in a foreign country, usually for the FOREIGN EXCHANGE of goods. See J. A. Todd, *The Mechanism of Exchange* (5th ed. 1946); H. E. Evitt, *Exchange and Trade Control in Theory and Practice* (4th ed. 1960) and *A Manual of Foreign Exchange* (7th ed. 1971); Egan Sohmen, *Flexible Exchange Rates* (1961, rev. ed. 1969).

Exchequer, Court of (ĕkschĕk′ər, ĕks′chĕk″ər), in English history, governmental agency. It originated after the Norman Conquest as a financial committee of the Curia Regis. By the reign of Henry II it had a separate organization and was responsible for the collection of the king's revenue as well as for exercising jurisdiction in cases affecting the revenue. By the latter part of the 13th cent. a separation became discernible between the court proper and the exchequer or treasury, especially with the appointment of lawyers as barons (judges) of the exchequer. Its jurisdiction over common pleas now steadily increased, to include, for example, money disputes between private litigants on the assumption that the plaintiff was indebted to the crown and needed payment from the defendant to enable him to pay the king. A second Court of Exchequer Chamber was set up in 1585 to amend errors of the Court of the King's Bench. From an amalgamation in 1830, a single Court of Exchequer emerged as a court of appeal intermediate between the common-law courts and the House of Lords. In 1875 the Court of Exchequer became, by the Judicature Act of 1873, the exchequer division of the high court of justice.

excise taxes, governmental levies on specific goods produced and consumed inside a country. They differ from TARIFFS, which usually apply only to foreign-made goods, and from SALES TAXES, which typically apply to all commodities other than those specifically exempted. In their modern form, excise taxes were first developed by Holland in the 17th cent. and established by law in England in 1643. Introduced into the Dutch colonies in America, the system spread to other colonies. Such taxes were first used by the Federal government in 1791 and aroused great opposition. They were repealed (1802) in Thomas Jefferson's administration. During the War of 1812 comprehensive excise taxes were levied again but were repealed in 1817. The taxes imposed during the Civil War included an excise tax on all manufactured goods. Most of those were gradually repealed, and by 1883 only liquor and tobacco were taxed. The Spanish-American War saw a temporary expansion of excise taxes. In both World Wars such taxes were greatly increased; in World War II they were levied on furs, jewelry, and leather as well as on liquor, tobacco, and amusements. Excise taxes, which account for less than 10% of all Federal receipts, are far less important than the income tax. Nearly all the states and many municipalities levy excise taxes. The INTERNAL REVENUE SERVICE collects Federal excise taxes in the United States.

exclamation point: see PUNCTUATION.

exclusion principle, physical principle enunciated by Wolfgang Pauli in 1925 stating that no two electrons in an ATOM can occupy the same energy state simultaneously. The energy states, or levels, in an atom are described in the QUANTUM THEORY by various values of four different quantum numbers; the exclusion principle holds that no two electrons can have the same four quantum numbers in an atom. One of these quantum numbers describes one of the two possible directions for the electron's intrinsic spin. As a result of the exclusion principle, two electrons that are in the same general energy level as described by the other three quantum numbers are differentiated from each other because they have opposite spins. This principle applies not only to atoms but to other systems containing particles as well, and it applies not only to electrons but also to a large class of particles collectively known as fermions (see ELEMENTARY PARTICLES).

excommunication, formal expulsion from a religious body, the most grave of all ecclesiastical censures. Where religious and social communities are nearly identical it is attended by social ostracism, as in the case of Benedict Spinoza, excommunicated by the Jews. In Christianity the Roman Catholic Church especially retains excommunication; the church maintains that the spiritual separation of the offender from the body of the faithful takes place by the nature of the act when the offense is committed, and the decree of excommunication (or ANATHEMA) is a warning and formal proclamation of exclusion from Christian society. Those who die excommunicate are not publicly prayed for; but excommunication is not equivalent to damnation. Excommunications vary in gravity, and in grave cases readmission may be possible only by action of the Holy See. Excommunicates are always free to return to the church on repentance. Protestant churches have generally abandoned excommunication.

excretion, process of eliminating from an organism waste products of metabolism and other materials that are of no use. It is an essential process in all forms of life. In one-celled organisms wastes are discharged through the surface of the cell. The higher plants eliminate gases through the stomata, or pores, on the leaf surface. Multicellular animals have special excretory organs. In humans the main organs of excretion are the kidneys and accessory urinary organs, through which urine is eliminated (see URINARY SYSTEM), and the large INTESTINES, from which solid wastes are expelled. The skin and lungs also have excretory functions: The skin eliminates water and salt in SWEAT, and the lungs expel water vapor and carbon dioxide.

Exe (ĕks), river, c.55 mi (90 km) long, rising in the Exmoor, Somerset, SW England, and flowing S across the Cornwall peninsula, past Exeter to the English Channel at Exmouth. Salmon and shellfish are taken from the river; many waterfowl are found along its narrow estuary.

executive, one who carries out the will or plan of another person or of a group. In GOVERNMENT, the term refers not only to the chief administrative officer but to all others who execute the laws and to them as a group. In modern government, the executive also formulates and carries out governmental policies, directs relations with foreign governments, commands the armed forces, approves or disapproves legislative acts, recommends legislation, and in some countries summons and opens the legislature, appoints and dismisses some executive officials, and pardons any but those impeached. Usually the executive may also issue ordinances, often supplementing legislative acts, and may interpret statutes for the guidance of officials. These broad powers depend upon the theory that the state has a juristic personality whose will the government, in its various departments, must perform. The separation of the legislative, executive, and judicial powers of government was not only modified in the U.S. Constitution (see CONSTITUTION) but has been further modified in practice, for the President performs many judicial and legislative functions. State and municipal executives have likewise assumed larger powers. Distinction is sometimes made between executives who decide policies and the administration that carries out the laws and executive orders. In business, executives are those who manage, decide policies, and control the business. See C. A. Beard, *American Government and Politics* (1931); H. J. Laski, *The American Presidency* (1940, repr. 1972); J. M. Burns, *Presidential Government* (1965); D. B. James, *The Contemporary Presidency* (1970).

executors and administrators. An executor is the person designated in the WILL of a deceased person to carry out the provisions of the will. An administrator is the person appointed by a probate court to perform the identical functions if the will does not name any executors or if those who were named executors are not capable of performing the function or are dead. An administrator is also appointed in the case of the death without a will (intestate) of any person who owns property. Those chosen representatives collect the assets and pay the debts of the estate and then distribute what remains to those who are entitled by provisions of the will or by law. To allow performance of these duties the title to the personal property passes to the executor or administrator, rather than to the beneficiaries. The administrator derives his title from the court through his letters of administration. The executor's source of title is the will itself. Besides being the defendants in any suits brought against the estate, the representatives are also authorized to bring actions to compensate the estate for damage suffered before or after death. Administration is not necessary if the heirs, the creditors of the estate, and all others interested in the estate agree to the settlement of debts and the distribution of the property. Under modern statutes, priority of right to be administrator depends largely on nearness of relation to the deceased. Where no relative applies for papers of administration, creditors, public administrators, or suitable strangers may be appointed administrator. One is ineligible to act as an administrator by reason of being an infant, insane, or lacking ordinary integrity. Illiteracy, lack of business experience, immorality, or adverse interests are not disqualifications. The executor or administrator must, in some states, post a bond for honest and faithful discharge of his duties. After he has paid the legacies and otherwise followed the directions of the will so far as legally possible, the court will discharge him if his accounting is correct and he has shown himself to have acted honestly and in good faith; otherwise his bond may be forfeited, and he is made liable to suit.

exercise: see PHYSICAL FITNESS.

Exeter, county borough (1971 pop. 95,568), county town of Devonshire, SW England, on the Exe River. It is the market, transportation, and distribution center for SW England. There is small-scale manufacturing, with metal and leather goods, paper, and farm implements as the chief products. The fort town Isca Dumnoniorum occupied the site in Roman times. Because of its strategic location, Exeter was besieged by the Danes in the 9th and 11th cent., by William the Conqueror in 1068, by Yorkists in the 15th cent., and by religious factions in the middle of the 16th cent. From the 10th to the 18th cent. it was an important center for the production and export of woolen goods. The cathedral, with its massive Norman towers, is a classic example of DECORATED STYLE architecture. In the cathedral library is the famous EXETER BOOK. There are ruins of the Roman walls and of Rougemont Castle (11th cent.), built by

William the Conqueror. Severely damaged by bombing in World War II, the greater part of the city has since been rebuilt.

Exeter Book, manuscript volume of Old English religious and secular poetry, of various dates of composition, compiled c.975 and given to Exeter Cathedral by Bishop Leofric (d. 1072). See edition by George Philip Krapp and Elliott V. K. Dobbie (1936).

exhibition: see EXPOSITION.

Exile: see BABYLONIAN CAPTIVITY.

exile, removal of a national from his country for a long period of time or for life. Exile may be a forceful expulsion by the government or a voluntary removal by the citizen, sometimes in order to escape punishment. In ancient Greece, exile was often the penalty for homicide, while OSTRACISM was a common punishment for those accused of political crimes. In early Rome a citizen under sentence of death had a choice between exile and death. In this case, exile was a means of escaping a greater punishment. During the Roman Empire, deportation to certain islands became a general punishment for serious crimes. The ancient Hebrews allowed those who committed homicide to take refuge in designated cities of sanctuary. Until 1776, certain types of English criminals were transported to the American colonies, and later, until 1853, they were sent to penal settlements in Australia. Both the Russian czarist and Communist regimes have transported prisoners to Siberia. With the growth of nation-states and the acceptance of the doctrine that ties between state and citizen are indissoluble, exile for criminal reasons has become infrequent. However, modern civil wars and revolutions have produced many political exiles, including large numbers of refugees who have been victims of the upheavals in some manner. Such exiles are not subject to EXTRADITION and may demand protection from the country receiving them. The concept of "government in exile"—one person or a group of persons living outside their state and claiming to be the rightful government—has become accepted in international law during the 20th cent. This situation usually arises when a warring state is occupied by the enemy and its government is forced to seek ASYLUM in another state. The government is recognized as lawful it if attempts to regain control and if it has armed forces integrated in a large alliance. During World War II, the monarchs and governments of Norway, the Netherlands, Luxembourg, Belgium (without the king), Greece, and Yugoslavia were exiled in London, while the governments of Charles de Gaulle of France and Eduard Beneš of Czechoslovakia were formed in exile. See DEPORTATION; REFUGEE.

existential group therapy: see GROUP PSYCHOTHERAPY.

existentialism (ĕgzĭstĕn'shəlĭzəm, ĕksĭ-), any of several philosophic systems, all centered on the individual and his relationship to the universe or to God. Important existentialists of varying and conflicting thought are Søren Kierkegaard, Karl Jaspers, Martin Heidegger, Gabriel Marcel, and Jean-Paul Sartre. All revolt against the traditional metaphysical approaches to man and his place in the universe. Thinkers such as St. Thomas Aquinas, Blaise Pascal, and Friedrich Nietzsche have been called existentialists, but it is more accurate to place the beginnings of the movement with Kierkegaard. In his concern with the problem of the individual's relationship to God, Kierkegaard bitterly attacked the abstract metaphysics of the Hegelians and the worldly complacency of the Danish church. Kierkegaard's fundamental insight was the recognition of the concrete ethical and religious demands confronting the individual. He saw that these demands could not be met by a merely intellectual decision but required the subjective commitment of the individual. The necessity and seriousness of these ethical decisions facing man was for Kierkegaard the source of his dread and despair. Kierkegaard's analysis of the human situation provides the central theme of contemporary existentialism. Following him, Heidegger and Sartre were the major thinkers connected with this movement. Both men were students of Edmund Husserl, and through his influence each developed a phenomenological method that they used in developing their own existential analyses. Heidegger rejects the label of "existentialist" and describes his own philosophy as an investigation of the nature of being in which the analysis of human existence is only the first step. Sartre is the only self-declared existentialist among the major thinkers. For him the central idea of all existential thought is that existence precedes essence. For Sartre there is no God and therefore no fixed human nature that forces one to act. Man is totally free and entirely responsible for what he makes of himself. It is this freedom and responsibility that, as for Kierkegaard, is the source of man's dread. Sartre's thought, as expressed in his novels and plays as well as in his more formal philosophical writings, strongly influenced a current in French literature, best represented by Albert Camus and Simone de Beauvoir. In France the most prominent exponent of a Christian existentialism was Gabriel MARCEL, who developed his philosophy within the framework of the Roman Catholic Church. Aside from Heidegger, the leading German existentialist was Karl Jaspers, who developed the central Kierkegaardian insight along less theological lines. Various other theologians and religious thinkers such as Karl Barth, Martin Buber, Paul Tillich, and Reinhold Niebuhr are often included within the orbit of existentialism. See J. P. Sartre, *Existentialism* (1947); W. A. Kaufmann, ed., *Existentialism from Dostoevsky to Sartre* (1956, repr. 1969); Ronald Grimsley, *Existentialist Thought* (2d ed. 1960); John Macquarrie, *Studies in Christian Existentialism* (1966) and *Existentialism* (1972); F. R. Molena, *Sources of Existentialism as Philosophy* (1969); Ralph Harper, *The Existential Experience* (1972); R. C. Solomon, ed., *Existentialism* (1974).

Exmoor, high moorland of the Cornwall peninsula, SW England, comprising much of Exmoor National Park (265 sq mi/686 sq km; est. 1954). Underlaid by slate and sandstone, the rugged region with wooded glens rises to 1,707 ft (520 m) in Dunkery Beacon; the River Exe rises there. The region is sparsely populated. Sheep and the small Exmoor ponies are grazed on the moorland. Exmoor is a popular vacationland and contains many interesting prehistoric earthworks. It was the home of a legendary nomadic group of brigands called the Doones; Doone Valley became more famous after R. D. Blackmore incorporated the legend in his novel *Lorna Doone*.

Exmouth, Edward Pellew (pəlyo͞o' eks'məth), **1st Viscount,** 1757–1833, English admiral. He entered the navy in 1770 and served in both the American Revolutionary War and the subsequent British conflicts with Revolutionary and Napoleonic France. In 1793 he captured the *Cléopâtre*, the first French frigate to be taken in the war with France. He was given command of the Mediterranean fleet in 1811 and was created Baron Exmouth in 1814. In 1816 under his command a combined force of British and Dutch ships bombarded Algiers and thereby compelled its Turkish ruler to abolish Christian slavery. As a reward for his achievement at Algiers, he was created Viscount Exmouth. See biography by C. Northcote Parkinson (1934).

Exmouth (ĕks'mouth), urban district (1971 pop. 25,815), Devonshire, SW England, at the mouth of the Exe River. It is a port and a popular summer resort. In 1347, Exmouth provided 10 ships for the siege of Calais.

exobiology, search for extraterrestrial LIFE within the solar system and throughout the universe. Philosophical speculation that there might be other worlds similar to ours dates back to the ancient Chinese and Greeks. However until the advent of space exploration and molecular biology, some scientists stood aloof from the subject of extraterrestrial life. They feared professional ridicule because so many amateur speculations and hoaxes had been associated with the subject. Current biochemical theories hold that where conditions are favorable, life is virtually certain to arise. There are six basic parameters that determine whether an environment is suitable for life as we know it: temperature, pressure, salinity, acidity, water availability, and oxygen content. Advanced life is restricted to a narrow range of these parameters, but primitive microorganisms exist over a much wider range. Data already collected by space probes essentially rule out advanced life on other planets of our solar system. However, participants at a conference held in 1961 at the National Radio Observatory in Green Bank, W.Va., estimated that as many as 50,000 planets in our galaxy have earthlike conditions and that a substantial fraction of these are likely to have cultures as technologically advanced as our own. This conclusion prompted project Ozma, in which the radio emissions from several nearby stars were monitored for intelligent signals. When after one year no positive results were obtained, the project was abandoned, largely because success depended on many uncertainties, including whether or not another advanced civilization would want to communicate. However, a continuing effort is being made to detect primitive life within our solar system. This search is intimately connected with the question of how life arose on earth. According to the theory of the Russian biologist A. I. Oparin, life appeared on earth as the result of progressive development of organic matter from nonorganic under the changing ambient conditions. The principal constituents of organic matter, hydrogen, carbon, nitrogen, and oxygen, are among the most abundant atomic elements in the universe. Oparin assumed that these elements combined to form simple hydrocarbons and that the hydrocarbons combined to form the precursors of life, such as amino and nucleic acids. Once these precursor molecules existed in the earth's primitive seas, they spontaneously interacted to form increasingly complex structures, until self-replicating molecules like deoxyribonucleic acid (DNA) were created, leading the way to protein synthesis. Experimental support for the conjecture that the creation of hydrocarbons and precursor molecules can occur by nongenetic means was supplied by the work of the American chemists Stanley L. Miller and Harold C. Urey. They discovered that when a mixture of methane, ammonia, water, and hydrogen is exposed to an electric discharge, amino acids are formed. The composition of this gas mixture is similar to the atmosphere of Jupiter. It was later demonstrated that the same result can be obtained by exposing the gas mixture to ultraviolet radiation, which exists in outer space. Further support for Oparin's theory came with the discovery of organic molecules like ammonia and formaldehyde in the interstellar medium. There has also been evidence of organic material in certain carbonaceous chondrite meteorites, most notably the Orgeuil meteorite, which fell in France in 1864. Some scientists claim to have found traces of hydrocarbons, amino acids, and even "extraterrestrial fossils" of life forms resembling earthly algae. However, other scientists reject these claims, saying that the organic traces result from terrestrial contamination and that the "fossils" are merely nonorganic crystalline forms. Contamination of the moon and planets by earth life forms could lead to the erroneous conclusion that extraterrestrial life exists. Although efforts are made to sterilize all spacecraft components that land on alien worlds, absolute sterility is an impossibility. Some scientists believe that the moon and Venus have already been contaminated by microorganisms carried on space probes. Conversely, biologists warn that introduction into the earth's biosphere of destructive alien organisms could be disastrous. Therefore, returning Apollo astronauts were quarantined as long as two weeks, and lunar rock samples were kept carefully isolated. In 1975, an unmanned probe is scheduled to land on Mars to analyze the soil for the existence of microorganisms. Experiments on earth have shown that certain anaerobic bacteria can survive in the martian environment. See Gregg Mamikunian, ed., *Current Aspects of Exobiology* (1965); E. A. Shneour, ed., *Extraterrestrial Life* (1966).

exocrine gland (ĕk'səkrən): see GLAND.

Exodus (ĕk'sədəs), book of the Old Testament, 2d of the 5 books of the Law (the Pentateuch or Torah) ascribed by tradition to Moses. It is a religious history of the Jews during their flight from Egypt, the period when they began to receive the Law. The events may be outlined as follows: first, the bondage in Egypt, from which God prepares liberation through the agency of Moses (1–11), including Moses' early career and divine vocation (1.15–7.13), and the first nine plagues of Egypt (7.14–25; 8–11); second, the exodus proper (12–18), with the plague of the first-born and the institution of the Passover (12–13) and the dry crossing through the Red Sea (14); third, the first divine legislation at Mt. Sinai (19–40). The last portion includes the Ten Commandments (20), a law code (20.22–23.33), directions for a tabernacle and worship (25–27; 29–31), the designation of Aaron as high priest (28), the first national apostasy in worshipping the golden calf (32), a brief restatement of the code (34), and the institution of the tabernacle (35–40). A most solemn moment of biblical history occurs early in Exodus: the appearance of God to Moses in the burning bush revealing His name as I Am (3.11–15). The Mosaic law has parallels in other ancient codes but is more humane. See Walter Beyerlin, *Origins and History of the Oldest Sinaitic Traditions* (tr. 1966); Judah Goldin, *The Song at the Sea* (1971). For critical views on the composition of Exodus, see OLD TESTAMENT.

exogamy (ĕksŏg'əmē): see MARRIAGE.

exorcism (ĕk'sôrsĭz"əm), ritual act of driving out evil demons or spirits from places, persons, or things in which they are thought to dwell. It occurs both in primitive societies and in the religions of sophisticated cultures. The term is applied to all those acts that seek to dispel or frighten away demons or spirits, as distinguished from those rites that aim at propitiating or evoking their assistance (see MAGIC and SHAMAN). Exorcism may be applied to a particular person or thing or may be used in a more general way. In central Europe during Walburga's night (May 1), the traditional witches' sabbath, witches and demons are exorcised from the town by use of holy water, incense, and loud noises of all kinds. The scriptural justification for exorcism is found throughout the New Testament, and many instances of Christ's ability to cast out devils are recorded (Mat. 12.22-27; Acts 16.16-18; 19.13-17). The Roman Catholic Church still officially recognizes the existence of devils (or fallen angels) who are able to use the material universe to further their own aims. Exorcism of persons possessed by devils is, however, carefully regulated by the canon law of the church.

exosphere: see ATMOSPHERE.

expanding universe: see UNIVERSE.

expansion, in physics, increase in volume resulting from an increase in temperature. Contraction is the reverse process. When heat is applied to a body, the rate of vibration and the distances between the molecules composing it are increased and, hence, the space occupied by the body, i.e., its volume, increases. This increase in volume is not constant for all substances for any given rise in temperature, but is a specific property of each kind of matter. For example, zinc and lead undergo greater expansion in a one-degree rise in temperature than do silver or brass. Since SOLIDS have a definite shape, each linear dimension of the solid increases by a proportional amount for a given temperature increase. The amount that a unit length along any direction of a substance increases for a temperature increase of one degree is called the coefficient of linear expansion of the substance. Most liquids also expand when heated. However, since liquids do not have a definite shape, it is the expansion of their volume as a whole that is relevant rather than the increase in a linear dimension. The amount of expansion that a unit volume (e.g., a cubic centimeter or a cubic foot) of any substance undergoes per one-degree rise in temperature is called its volume coefficient or coefficient of cubical expansion and is listed as a property of that substance. The coefficient of linear expansion can be calculated by dividing the coefficient of cubical expansion of the substance by three. When the amount of expansion of a given length of a substance has been determined experimentally, the linear coefficient is calculated by dividing the total amount of expansion by the product of the original number of length units and the number of degrees of rise in temperature. Gases also exhibit thermal expansion. The coefficient of expansion is about the same for all the common gases at ordinary temperatures; it is $1/273$ of the volume at 0°C per degree rise in temperature. The Kelvin, or absolute, scale is based upon this behavior (see KELVIN TEMPERATURE SCALE). Charles's law concerning the expansion of gases states that the volume of a gas is directly proportional to its absolute temperature (see GAS LAWS). Liquids differ from each other as do solids in their expansion coefficients. Water, unlike most substances, contracts rather than expands as its temperature is increased from 0°C to 4°C; above 4°C it exhibits normal behavior, expanding as the temperature increases.

expatriation, loss of NATIONALITY. Such loss is usually, although not necessarily, voluntary. Generally it applies to those persons who have renounced nationality and citizenship in one country to become citizens or subjects of another. According to U.S. law, for example, a citizen who becomes naturalized in a foreign state is automatically expatriated. In addition, expatriation occurs when a naturalized citizen resides in his native land for two years or elsewhere outside the United States for five years, or when any citizen serves in the public employment or military of a foreign state. Prior to 1922 an American woman who married an alien was expatriated, but in that year the Cable Act nullified that provision and stipulated that a woman may retain her citizenship when marrying an alien "unless she makes a formal renunciation of her citizenship." The United States, in common with other countries, forbids voluntary expatriation in time of war. Expatriation may also occur involuntarily, as when a government chooses to renounce its obligations to individuals who desert in wartime. Such persons are stateless until NATURALIZATION under some other government takes place. A more general type of involuntary expatriation is the loss of nationality that occurs with the cession or conquest of a territory. The common law view that one's ALLEGIANCE cannot be renounced without the state's permission prevailed until 1868 when the United States challenged this doctrine in order to protect her naturalized immigrants against the claims of their native states, which did not recognize the right of subjects to expatriate themselves. Congress declared voluntary expatriation to be "a natural and inherent right of all people," and announced that the United States would protect her naturalized citizens abroad, even in their native countries. Great Britain abandoned the common-law interpretation in 1870. Many other nations, however, including France and the USSR, do not recognize expatriation. The United States at present has treaties operating with most European nations concerning that and other conflicting interpretations of citizenship.

experience, living through events and the impression on a person or animal of events. In epistemology, a distinction is made between things known inductively, from experience, and those known deductively or theoretically, from universal principles. The ancients, under the influence of Plato and of Euclidean geometry, tended to prize deductive or theoretical knowledge above that gained through experience. Their influence was dominant through the Renaissance. With the rise of modern empirical science the preference was reversed. Immanuel Kant's critical epistemology, however, emphasized the dependence of all experience on the mediation of the intelligence. Modern thought has tended to agree with Kant; accordingly, discussion has centered on what, if anything, can be said to be "naive" experience, and how this experience may be conditioned by social factors affecting the social milieu or by perceptual processes themselves.

experiential-existential group therapy: see GROUP PSYCHOTHERAPY.

Exploits, river, c.150 mi (240 km) long, rising in the Long Range, SW N.F., Canada, and flowing NE to Exploits Bay, an arm of Notre Dame Bay. On the river are Grand Falls and Bishop's Falls, the sites of large hydroelectric power plants.

exploration of the earth has from earliest times been motivated by a desire for trade, conquest, or colonization. Early Egyptian expeditions penetrated into Nubia and Mesopotamia; the Phoenicians and the Greeks explored the Mediterranean and the Black Sea regions earlier than 600 B.C.; and a Phoenician expedition (c.600 B.C.) is said to have sailed around Africa. After 500 B.C. the Carthaginians explored beyond the Strait of Gibraltar to trade along the coasts of Spain and Africa. A Greek navigator, Pytheas, probably sailed beyond Britain c.330 B.C. The conquests of Alexander the Great brought the West in closer relationship with the Orient, and the Roman legions extended the limits of geographical knowledge, especially in N Europe. Trade with the East was stimulated by the discovery (A.D. c.15) of a sea captain, Hippalus, that by using monsoon winds it was possible to sail across the Indian Ocean instead of hugging the coast. Roman trade was early established with India and Ceylon and later (A.D. c.100) with China. After the dissolution of the Roman Empire, the Arabs expanded their relationships with the East. The Chinese also made many explorations in this period. One of the best-known Chinese travelers is Hsüan-tsang, who traveled (A.D. 629-646) to India and farther west. Exploration by Europeans was carried on during the Middle Ages by the Norsemen who crossed the Atlantic to Iceland, Greenland, and North America. However, these Norse journeys did not have much influence on the rest of Europe. During the Crusades, Europe emerged from isolation and regained some knowledge of the Orient. This was extended by the remarkable journeys across Asia made by the missionaries Piano Carpini and William Rubruquis and by Marco Polo. By about 1400 the breakup of the Mongol empire and the growth of the Ottoman Empire had blocked Europe's overland trade routes to the East. The search for new trade routes initiated the great European age of discovery. Henry the Navigator promoted voyages along the coast of Africa that helped dispel the superstition and misinformation that had impeded previous attempts to sail through the torrid zone. The extent of the globe was revealed by Bartholomew Diaz's rounding of the Cape of Good Hope (1486-87), Vasco da Gama's voyage to India (1497-98), Christopher Columbus's discovery of America (1492), and the circumnavigation of the globe by the expedition of Ferdinand Magellan (1519-22). In the 16th cent. Spanish explorers, notably Vasco de Balboa, Hernán Cortés, Francisco Pizarro, Cabeza de Vaca, Hernán De Soto, and Francisco de Coronado, explored large areas of the Americas. Much of the interior of North America was revealed in the 17th cent. by Samuel de Champlain, Sieur de La Salle, Louis Jolliet, Jacques Marquette, and other French explorers. A Spanish and Portuguese monopoly of the new trade routes stimulated attempts to find other passages to the East (see NORTHEAST PASSAGE and NORTHWEST PASSAGE) and was soon challenged by English and Dutch voyages in the Pacific and Indian oceans. Most of the major islands of the Pacific and the coastline of Australia became known through the voyages of Francis Drake, Abel Tasman, William Dampier, James Cook, Vitus Bering, George Vancouver, and others. The interior of Australia was explored in the mid-19th cent., and by the end of the century most of Africa, the "dark continent," had been explored by David Livingstone, H. M. Stanley, and Richard Burton. In the late 19th and early 20th cent. the arctic regions were explored by Nils Nordenskjöld, Roald Amundsen, Donald MacMillan, Richard Byrd, and others. In 1909, Robert E. Peary reached the North Pole. The continent of Antarctica was explored in the first half of the 20th cent. by William Bruce, Jean Charcot, Douglas Mawson, Ernest Shackleton, and others. The South Pole was reached first by Amundsen (Dec. 14, 1911) and almost immediately thereafter (Jan. 18, 1912) by Robert Scott. The airplane provided a new method of antarctic exploration, with George Wilkins and Byrd as the pioneers. Since World War II there have been many well-equipped expeditions, notably those during the International Geophysical Year (1957-58), to the Antarctic. Once the far reaches of the globe had been attained, explorers concentrated on a detailed examination of the world's remote territories and on the challenges of space. For man's explorations beyond the earth see SPACE EXPLORATION. See also GEOGRAPHY; articles on localities, e.g., AFRICA, ARCTIC REGIONS, AUSTRALIA. See J. N. L. Baker, *A History of Geographical Discovery and Exploration* (6th ed. 1931, repr. 1967); Edgar Prestage, *Portuguese Pioneers* (1933, repr. 1967); L. P. Kirwan, *The White Road* (1959); J. B. Brebner, *The Explorers of North America, 1492-1806* (1964); C. S. Davies, *Exploring the World* (1965); J. H. Parry, *Age of Reconnaissance: Discovery, Exploration, and Settlement, 1450-1650* (1970); Louis B. Wright, *Gold, Glory, and the Gospel* (1970) and *West and by North* (1971); J. R. Hale, *Renaissance Explorers* (1972); Timothy Severin, *The African Adventure* (1973).

explosive, substance that undergoes decomposition or combustion with great rapidity, evolving much heat and producing a large volume of gas. The gas formed fills a volume many times greater than that filled by the original explosive substance. It expands because of the heat evolved in the explosion. The enormous pressure exerted by the gas is responsible for the action of explosives, such as the blasting of rocks or other materials and the propelling of bullets from guns. Important explosives include TRINITROTOLUENE (TNT), DYNAMITE, NITROCELLULOSE, NITROGLYCERIN, and PICRIC ACID. Cyclonite (RDX) was an important explosive in World War II. AMMONIUM NITRATE is of major importance in blasting. Chemical explosives are of two general kinds. Some, e.g., GUNPOWDER, are mixtures of readily combustible but not necessarily explosive substances, which, when set off (by ignition), undergo very rapid combustion. Others, e.g., TNT, are compounds whose molecules are unstable and can undergo explosive decomposition (detonation) without burning. These explosives, which decompose with the greatest rapidity, are called high explosives. High explosives are usually set off by means of DETONATORS. Nuclear explosives release energy by transformation of the atomic nucleus (see NUCLEAR ENERGY; ATOMIC BOMB; HYDROGEN BOMB). One important use of explosives is to break rocks in mining. A hole is drilled in the rock and filled with any of a variety of high explosives; the high explosive is then detonated, either electrically or with a special high-explosive cord. One important explosive used in mining, called ANFO, is a mixture of ammonium nitrate and fuel oil. Its use has revolutionized certain aspects of open-pit and underground mining due to its low cost and relative safety. Special explosives, called permissible explosives, must be used in coal mines. These explosives produce little or no flame and explode at low temperatures to prevent secondary explosions of mine gases (see DAMP) and dust. Dust explosions are a hazard in other places as well, e.g., flour mills, woodworking plants, and chemical factories. The major use of explosives has been in warfare. High explosives have been used in bombs, explosive shells, torpedoes, and missile warheads. Nondetonating explosives, e.g., gunpowder and the smokeless powders, have found extensive use as propellants. Until the 19th cent. gunpowder was widely used in most types of firearms. The invention of various smokeless powders led to the ultimate replacement of gunpowder as a propellant in rifles and guns. Probably the first successful smokeless powder was made by Edward Schultze, a Prussian artillery captain, c.1864. After 1870 it was known as Schultze powder. Its rate of burning was less than that of guncotton because of the partial gelatinization of the powder by a mixture of ether and alcohol; however, it still burned too rapidly for use in rifles. Schultze powder is used in shotguns, blank cartridges, and hand grenades and in igniting the dense, propellant powder used in artillery. The main constituent of Schultze powder is nitrocellulose. About 1885 a smokeless powder suitable for rifled guns appeared. Invented by Paul Vieille, it was called *poudre* B and was made from nitrocotton and ether-alcohol. Subsequently, Alfred NOBEL added to the growing list of smokeless powders a substance called Ballistite. It is made from nitrocotton (with a low nitrogen content) gelatinized by nitroglycerin. In Ballistite two of the most powerful explosives known at the time were united. Another smokeless powder, cordite, was invented by Sir Frederick Augustus Abel and Sir James Dewar in 1889; it contained a highly nitrated guncotton and nitroglycerin blended by means of acetone. Mineral jelly (vaseline) was added to act as a lubricant. Indurite, invented by Charles E. Monroe in 1891, is made from guncotton and is colloided with nitrobenzine; washing with methyl alcohol frees the lower nitrates from the guncotton. See T. C. Davis, *The Chemistry of Powder and Explosives* (2 vol., repr. 1972); J. F. Stoffel, *Explosives and Homemade Bombs* (2d ed. 1972).

exponent, in mathematics, a number, letter, or algebraic expression written above and to the right of another number, letter, or expression called the base. In the expressions x^2 and x^n, the number 2 and the letter *n* are the exponents respectively of the base *x*. The exponent indicates the power to which the base is to be raised. When exponents were first introduced, only positive whole numbers were used, and the exponent indicated how many times the base was to be taken as a factor; e.g., $2^5=32$, or $2\cdot2\cdot2\cdot2\cdot2=32$. In advanced algebra, fractions, zero, and negative numbers are also used as exponents. Particular meanings have been assigned to these types of exponents so that they obey the same algebraic rules as does the simpler type of exponent. A fractional exponent such as $\frac{1}{4}$ or $1/n$ indicates the fourth or *n*th ROOT, respectively, of the base. Any quantity raised to the zero power equals one; e.g., $x^0=5^0=(a^2+b^2)^0=1$. A negative exponent indicates the reciprocal of the quantity; e.g., x^{-2} means $1/x^2$. When quantities of the same base are multiplied together, their exponents are added; e.g., $x^2\cdot x^3=x^5$. Note that the base must be the same. When a quantity already containing an exponent is raised to a power, the exponents are multiplied; e.g., $(x^2)^3=x^6$.

exposition or **exhibition,** term frequently applied to an organized public fair or display of industrial and artistic productions, designed usually to promote trade and to reflect cultural progress. Expositions have also been important for their emphasis on scientific and technological innovations; when they are international in scope they have done much to promote understanding among participating countries. Although expositions grew out of the traditional medieval cloth fairs (see FAIR), organized exhibitions of fine and industrial arts date back to 18th-century France and England. The international exposition as we know it today began with the Crystal Palace exhibition in London in 1851; its huge success inspired a series of international expositions throughout the world. Among the most famous expositions and world's fairs are the following: Paris international expositions of 1867, 1889 (the Eiffel Tower was built for this occasion), and 1900; Centennial Exposition at Philadelphia (1876); World's Columbian Exposition at Chicago (1893); Louisiana Purchase Exposition at St. Louis (1904); British Empire Exhibition at Wembley (1924–25); Century of Progress Exposition at Chicago (1933–34); Golden Gate International Exposition at San Francisco (1939–40); two New York world's fairs (1939–40, 1964–65); Brussels World's Fair (1958); Century 21 Exposition at Seattle (1962); Expo 67 (1967 world's fair in Montreal, Canada); Expo 70 (1970 world's fair in Osaka, Japan, the first world's fair to be sponsored by an Asian country); and Expo 74 (1974 world's fair held in Spokane, Wash., which had the environment as its theme). The Bureau of International Expositions in Paris regulates and sanctions world's fairs and international expositions.

expressionism, term used to describe works of art and literature in which the representation of reality is distorted to communicate an inner vision. The expressionist transforms nature rather than imitating it. **1** In painting and the graphic arts, certain movements such as the BRÜCKE (1905), BLAUE REITER (1911), and NEW OBJECTIVITY (1920s) are described as expressionist. In a broader sense the term also applies to certain artists who worked independent of recognized schools or movements, e.g., Rouault, Soutine, and Vlaminck in France and Kokoschka and Schiele in Austria—all of whom made aggressively executed, personal, and often visionary paintings. Gauguin, Ensor, Van Gogh, and Munch were the spiritual fathers of the 20th-century expressionist movements, and certain earlier artists, notably El Greco, Grünewald, and Goya exhibit striking parallels to modern expressionistic sensibility. See articles on individuals, e.g., ENSOR. See Carl Zigrosser, *The Expressionists* (1957); Frank Whitford, *Expressionism* (1970); John Willett, *Expressionism* (1970); Wolfgang Pehnt, *Expressionist Architecture* (1973). **2** In literature, expressionism is often considered a revolt against realism and naturalism, seeking to achieve a psychological or spiritual reality rather than record external events in logical sequence. In the novel, the term is closely allied to the writing of Franz Kafka and James Joyce (see STREAM OF CONSCIOUSNESS). In the drama, Strindberg is considered the forefather of the expressionists, though the term is specifically applied to a group of early 20th-century German dramatists, including Kaiser, Toller, and Wedekind. Their work was often characterized by a bizarre distortion of reality. Playwrights not closely associated with the expressionists occasionally wrote expressionist drama, e.g., Karel Čapek's *R.U.R.* (1921) and Eugene O'Neill's *The Emperor Jones* (1921). The movement, though short-lived, gave impetus to a free form of writing and of production in modern theater. See Egbert Krispyn, *Style and Society in German Literary Expressionism* (1964).

exterritoriality: see EXTRATERRITORIALITY.

extinction, in biology, disappearance of species of living organisms. Extinction occurs as a result of changed conditions to which the species is not suited. If no member of the affected species survives and reproduces, the entire line dies out, leaving no descendants. This was the case with the saber-toothed tiger (*Smilodon*) of North America, which is not ancestral to any living species. However, a species may also become extinct through its gradual EVOLUTION into a new species, as a result of natural selection for characteristics suited to new conditions. An example of the latter situation is the evolution of HORSES from the eohippus (*Hyracotherium*) to *Miohippus* to *Merychippus* to the present-day *Equus*. There has been an unbroken line of descent, yet horses of the earlier types no longer exist.

extortion, in law, unlawful demanding or receiving by an officer, in his official capacity, of any property or money not legally due to him. Examples include requesting and accepting fees in excess of those allowed to him by statute or arresting a man and, with corrupt motives, demanding money or property unlawfully under pretense of duty. The taking of money or property is generally an essential element of the crime. In most states of the United States, extortion is more widely defined to include the obtaining of money or property of another by inducing his consent through wrongful use of fear, force, or authority of office; BLACKMAIL, RANSOM, and THREAT of force are included under this definition.

extradition (ĕkstrədĭsh'ən), delivery of a person, suspected or convicted of a crime, by the state where he has taken refuge to the state that asserts jurisdiction over him. Its purpose is to prevent criminals who flee a country from escaping punishment. Extradition first became a common policy in the 19th cent. International law does not recognize extradition as an obligation in the absence of a treaty, and although a state may, as a matter of courtesy, refuse ASYLUM to a fugitive and honor a request for extradition, virtually all extradition takes place under the authority of bilateral treaties. The provisions of each nation's treaties may differ greatly from those of another, and it should be noted that some treaties are formulated so that a nation is not obligated to extradite. Extradition treaties agreed to by the United States require evidence that would show the accused to have violated the laws of both the United States and the demanding country. Moreover extradition can occur only for an offense that has been named in the treaty. In common with many other nations, the United States will not surrender a fugitive wanted for a political crime. American treaties generally provide that U.S. nationals will be surrendered for trial in a foreign country. In contrast to the United States and Great Britain, most nations of the European Continent will surrender a fugitive upon simple demand and will try their own nationals domestically for crimes committed abroad. The U.S. Congress, pursuant to Article 4, Section 2, of the U.S. Constitution, has established a uniform law of extradition between the states, known as interstate rendition. This law provides that any person properly charged is subject to extradition regardless of the nature of the crime. Although the states normally comply with extradition demands, the Supreme Court has held that they have the right to refuse compliance.

extrasensory perception: see PARAPSYCHOLOGY.

extraterritoriality or **exterritoriality,** privilege of immunity from local law enforcement enjoyed by certain aliens. Although physically present upon the territory of a foreign nation, those aliens possessing extraterritoriality are considered by customary international law or treaty to be under the legal jurisdiction of their home country. This immunity from law enforcement is reciprocal between countries and is generally provided for visiting heads of state, those in the diplomatic services of foreign nations and their families, and officials of the United Nations. Generally such persons are exempt from both civil and criminal action; they may not be sued or arrested. Their property and residences are inviolable, and they are usually exempt from both personal and property taxes. While extraterritoriality insures that a diplomat will not be prosecuted for illegal behavior, it is emphasized that he is expected to adhere to the laws of the land in which he is serving. Any major transgressions may result not only in a formal complaint to his government but possibly in a demand for his expulsion. Extraterritoriality also extends to public (i.e., state-owned) vessels in foreign territorial waterways and ports. With the exception of the right of a state to regulate navigation within its own waters, a foreign public ship is entirely exempt from local jurisdiction. A private ship, on the other hand, is subject to local laws. With the growth of air transportation, air space over national territory has also become a question of extraterritoriality. There is little agreement, however, concerning the adoption of uniform standards of jurisdiction. Consequently all air agreements are currently bilateral. Extraterritoriality was in the past often granted to aliens not occupying diplomatic positions. After the conquest (1453) of Constantinople by the Turks, for example, extraterritoriality was bestowed as a courtesy upon several European states, notably Venice and Genoa. In the 19th cent. Western powers, often through coercion, secured unilateral extraterritorial rights for their citizens in China, Egypt, Japan, Morocco, Persia, Siam, and Turkey in the belief that these "uncivilized" states were incapable of establishing justice. Consequently the Western consul was assigned to handle all civil and criminal cases involving his countrymen. Extraterritoriality of this type was strongly resented as an infringement of sovereignty and was abolished in Japan in 1899, in Turkey in 1923, and in Egypt in 1949. In China opposition to extraterritoriality was but one phase of resistance to foreign control, which included the TREATY PORT system and territorial concessions in the major cities. In 1924 the USSR voluntarily abandoned its privileges in China, as did the United States and Great Britain in 1943. Italy and Japan lost their special status during World War II because they were enemies of China. In 1946, when France abandoned its privileges, nondiplomatic extraterritoriality in China came to an end. See Méir Ydit, *Internationalized Territories* (1961).

Extremadura: see ESTREMADURA, Spain.

extreme unction: see ANOINTING OF THE SICK.

extroversion and **introversion,** terms introduced into psychology by Carl Gustav Jung to identify two opposite psychological types. Jung saw the activity of the extrovert directed toward the external world and that of the introvert inward upon himself. This general activity or drive of the individual was called the LIBIDO by Jung, who removed from it the sexual character ascribed to it by Sigmund Freud. The extrovert is characteristically the active man who is most content when surrounded by people; carried to the neurotic extreme his behavior appears to constitute an irrational flight from himself into society, where his feelings are acted out. Jung called

HYSTERIA the neurosis of the extrovert. The introvert, on the other hand, is normally a contemplative individual who enjoys solitude and the inner life of ideas and the imagination. The extreme introvert's fantasies give him libidinal satisfactions and tend to become more meaningful to him than objective reality. Introversion is distinguished from extreme self-absorption, or NARCISSISM, although the turning inward of the libido can be narcissistic in character. Jung saw SCHIZOPHRENIA as the psychotic extreme of introversion. He did not suggest, however, strict classifications of individuals as extrovert or introvert since everyone has tendencies in both directions, although one direction generally predominates. See C. G. Jung, *Psychological Types* (tr. 1923, repr. 1970).

Exuma and Cays: see BAHAMA ISLANDS.

Eyadema, Ghansimbge (nyäsēm'bā āyädā'mə), 1937–, president of Togo (1967–). His original given name was Étienne, which he africanized in 1974. He served in the French army (1953–61) before entering the armed forces of Togo, where he became (1965) chief of the general staff. He seized power in 1967 and assumed the offices of president and minister of national defense.

Eyck, Hubert van (văn īk), c.1370–1426, and **Jan van Eyck,** c.1390–1441, Flemish painters, brothers. Very little is known of Hubert, the older of the two brothers. He is said to have worked (1414–17) for Duke William of Bavaria and is known to have settled in Ghent early in the 15th cent. Among the few works tentatively attributed to Hubert are an *Annunciation* and a remarkable miniaturistic diptych of the *Crucifixion and Last Judgment* (both: Metropolitan Mus.). Jan van Eyck was active at the courts of Count John of Holland (1422–25) and Philip of Burgundy. In the service of Duke Philip, he made several secret diplomatic journeys. A trip in 1428 took him to Portugal, and while there he painted a portrait of Philip's fiancée, Isabella. Eyckian style was based on a strong undercurrent of realism that constituted an important aspect of the development of late medieval art. Outstanding achievements of this realistic trend that may be cited as forerunners of the art of Jan van Eyck include the frescoes of Tommaso da Modena in Treviso and the paintings of Melchior Broederlam and of the Master of Flémalle. At the hands of Van Eyck, descriptive realism resulted in an astounding minuteness of detail and an unusually fine differentiation between qualities of texture and of atmospheric light. It is thought that his careful delineation of every detail of life was intended to reflect the glory of God's creation. Some writers have erroneously credited him with the discovery of the oil technique, but there can be no doubt that he played a crucial role in the perfection of this medium, achieving through its use an unprecedented richness and intensity of color. Of the Van Eycks' works that have survived, the most impressive is the altarpiece in the Church of Saint Bavon in Ghent, a collaborative effort of the two brothers, which Jan completed in 1432. On the panels of the exterior are shown the *Annunciation* and representations of St. John the Baptist, St. John the Evangelist, and the donors of the work, Jodocus Vijdt and his wife. The interior of the altar consists of an *Adoration of the Lamb* set in a magnificent landscape, and an upper row of panels showing God the Father flanked by the Virgin, John the Baptist, music-making angels, and Adam and Eve. Various parts of an illuminated manuscript, the *Heures de Turin,* have been credited to one or both brothers. Jan van Eyck has further left us a number of fine portraits, which are distinguished by a crystalline objectivity and precision of draftsmanship. Among these may be cited the *Portrait of an Unknown Man* (1432), thought to be the composer Gilles Binchois, and the *Man with the Red Turban,* possibly a self-portrait, both in London; the portrait of Jan de Leeuw (1436) in Vienna; and that of the painter's wife, Margarethe van Eyck, (1439) in Bruges. The wedding picture of *Giovanni Arnolfini and his Bride* (1434; National Gall., London) shows the couple in a remarkable interior. Van Eyck's interest in the texture and specific quality of material substances and his superb technical gifts are especially well demonstrated in two devotional panels, the *Madonna with Chancellor Rolin* in the Louvre, and the *Madonna with Canon Van der Paele* (1436) in Bruges. The National Gallery of Art, Washington, D.C., has a beautiful *Annunciation* that is generally accepted as his work. Some of his uncompleted paintings are thought to have been finished by Petrus Christus. The influence of Jan van Eyck upon the succeeding generation of artists, both in the North and in S Europe, cannot be overestimated, and the entire development of Flemish painting in the 15th cent. bears the direct imprint of his style. See studies by Ludwig Baldass (1952), L. B. Philip (1972), and Elizabeth Dhanens (1973).

eye, organ of VISION. In humans the eye is of the camera type, with an iris diaphragm and variable focusing, or accommodation. The human eye is a spheroid structure that rests in a bony cavity (socket, or orbit) on the frontal surface of the skull. The thick wall of the eyeball contains three covering layers: the sclera, the choroid, and the retina. The sclera is the outermost layer of eye tissue; part of it is visible as the "white" of the eye. In the center of the visible sclera and projecting slightly, in the manner of a crystal raised above the surface of a watch, is the cornea, a transparent membrane that acts as the window of the eye. A delicate membrane, the conjunctiva, covers the visible portion of the sclera. Underneath the sclera is the second layer of tissue, the choroid, composed of a dense pigment and blood vessels that nourish the tissues. Near the center of the visible portion of the eye, the choroid layer forms the ciliary body, which contains the muscles used to change the shape of the lens (that is, to focus). The ciliary body in turn merges with the iris, a diaphragm that regulates the size of the pupil. The iris is the area of the eye where the pigmentation of the choroid layer, usually brown or blue, is visible, because it is not covered by the sclera. The pupil is the round opening in the center of the iris; it is dilated and contracted by muscular action of the iris, thus regulating the amount of light that enters the eye. Behind the iris is the lens, a transparent, elastic, but solid ellipsoid body that focuses the light on the retina, the third and innermost layer of tissue. The retina is a network of nerve cells, notably the rods and cones, and nerve fibers that fan out over the choroid from the optic nerve as it enters the rear of the eyeball from the brain. Unlike the two outer layers of the eye, the retina does not extend to the front of the eyeball. Between the cornea and iris and between the iris and lens are small spaces filled with aqueous humor, a thin, watery fluid. The large spheroid space in back of the lens (the center of the eyeball) is filled with vitreous humor, a jellylike substance. Accessory structures of the eye are the LACRIMAL GLAND and its ducts in the upper lid, which bathe the eye with tears, keeping the cornea moist, clean, and brilliant, and drainage ducts that carry the excess moisture to the interior of the nose. The eye is protected from dust and dirt by the eyelashes, eyelid, and eyebrows. Six muscles extend from the eyesocket to the eyeball, enabling it to move in various directions. In addition to errors of refraction (ASTIGMATISM; FARSIGHTEDNESS; NEARSIGHTEDNESS) the human eye is subject to various types of injury, infection, and changes due to systemic disease. Strabismus is a condition in which the eye turns in or out because of an imbalance in the eye musculature. A cornea damaged by accident or illness can sometimes be surgically replaced with a healthy one from a deceased person. Eyes that are used in various ways for surgical repairs are supplied by eye banks. People can arrange to have their eyes donated to such organizations after their death. The camera type of eye, which forms excellent images, is found in all vertebrates, in cephalopods (such as the squid and octopus), and in some spiders. In each of those groups the camera type of eye evolved independently. Simple eyes, or ocelli, are found in a great variety of invertebrate animals, including flatworms, annelid worms (such as the earthworm), mollusks, crustaceans, and insects. An ocellus has a layer of photosensitive cells that can set up impulses in nerve fibers; the more advanced types also have a rigid lens for concentrating light on this layer. Simple eyes can perceive light and dark, enabling the animal to perceive the location and movement of objects. They form no image, or a very poor one. The compound eye is found in a large number of arthropods, including various species of insects, crustaceans, centipedes, and millipedes. A compound eye consists of from 12 to over 1,000 tubular units, called ommatidia, each with a rigid lens and photosensitive cells; each omnatidium is surrounded by pigment cells and receives only the light from its own lens. The lenses fit together on the surface of the eye, forming the large, many-faceted structure that can be seen, for example, in the fly. Each ommatidium supplies a small piece of the image perceived by the animal. The compound eye creates a poor image and cannot perceive small or distant objects; however, it is superior to the camera eye in its ability to discriminate brief flashes of light and movement, and in some insects (e.g., bees) it can detect the polarization of light. Because arthropods are so numerous, the compound eye is the commonest type of animal eye.

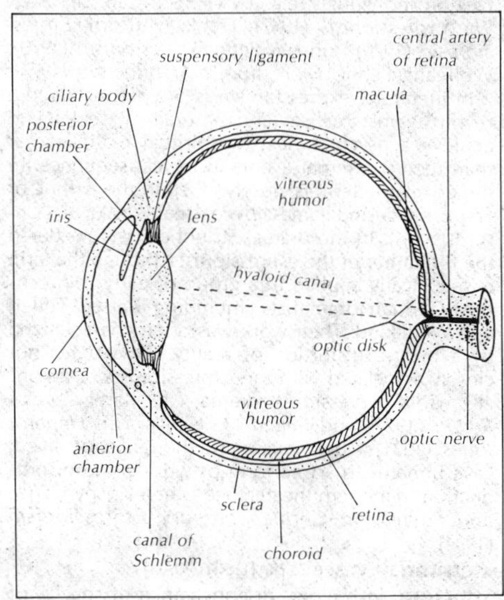

Cross section of human eye

eye bank, site for the collection, processing, and assignment of donated EYES. A donor's eyes are removed as soon as possible after death, sealed in a sterile container, and sent to the eye bank. There they are microscopically examined for corneal damage and then shipped to surgeons who have requested them. The intact eyes, if kept at a temperature of 4°C, may be preserved up to 48 hours. Subsequently, the corneas (the clear coverings of the eye) can be removed, preserved in glycerin, and stored at room temperature for six to eight months. Corneal transplants may restore vision to persons whose own corneas have become scarred through illness or injury. If free of bacteria, the vitreous humor, the fluid filling at the back of the eye, can be refrigerated and kept up to six months; it is used in the treatment of detached retina. The first eye bank in the United States, Eye-Bank for Sight Restoration, Inc., was founded in New York City in 1945.

eye fly, common name for a group of small FLIES of the family Chloropidae. Eye flies are common in parts of California and in the S United States. They inhabit grasslands and meadows and breed mainly on decaying matter and excrement. Eye flies are attracted to animal secretions such as are found in the eyes, mouth, and open wounds. Some are thought to carry diseases such as CONJUNCTIVITIS; West Indian species may transmit YAWS, a disease caused by a spirochete. Eye flies are classified in the phylum ARTHROPODA, class Insecta, order Diptera, family Chloropidae.

eyeglasses or **spectacles,** instrument or device for aiding and correcting defective sight. Eyeglasses usually consist of a pair of LENSES mounted in a frame to hold them in position before the eyes. The first device of this kind was probably invented by Roger Bacon in the 13th cent. although similar devices are believed to have existed in ancient times in China and in the Mediterranean civilizations. Early forms were crude and clumsy and were not improved until the 18th cent. when the grinding of lenses was first based upon the principles of light refraction. Lenses are made of clear or rock crystal glass or plastic ground to suit the defect of the eye. Concave glass is used for NEARSIGHTEDNESS, so that the rays of light are diverged. Convex lenses are used for FARSIGHTEDNESS, so that the light rays are converged. ASTIGMATISM is remedied by cylindrical lenses. Bifocal lenses, with a lower part for viewing objects near at hand (as in reading), were first devised by Benjamin Franklin. Telescopic lenses are used by the near-blind. A CONTACT LENS is shaped to fit the eye and is worn under the eyelid. Incorrect eyeglasses may do harm, and lenses should be prescribed by an ophthalmologist or optometrist and fitted by a skilled optician. Eyeglasses to protect the eyes from glare or from foreign bodies are made of tinted or polarized glass and of wire mesh. The Eskimo make and use wooden eyeglasses that have only narrow slits for eyepieces to protect the eyes from glare reflected by ice and snow.

Eyjafjördur (āʹyäfyör″thür), inlet of the Greenland Sea, longest (37 mi/60 km) and most scenic fjord in N Iceland. Akureyri is at its head.

Eylau: see BAGRATIONOVSK, USSR.

Eyre, Edward John (âr), 1815-1901, British colonial administrator. In Australia (1833-45) he was a magistrate, friend to the aborigines, explorer, and writer on Australian geography. After terms as lieutenant governor of New Zealand (1846-53) and governor of St. Vincent (1854-60), he became (1864) governor of Jamaica. A serious Negro uprising was suppressed (1865) with vigor by the military; Eyre was accused of brutality and illegal acts, especially in the execution of George Gordon, a mulatto member of the Jamaican legislature who had contravened the martial law imposed during the emergency. He was recalled in 1866. Several attempts, promoted by John Stuart Mill, Goldwin Smith, and Herbert Spencer, to try him for murder were forestalled by a committee of admirers, which included John Ruskin, Alfred Tennyson, Thomas Carlyle, and Charles Kingsley. The episode contributed to the fall of the government of Lord John Russell in 1866. See W. L. Mathieson, *Sugar Colonies and Governor Eyre* (1936).

Eyre, Sir James, 1734-99, English jurist. As a young lawyer he was counsel (1763) for John WILKES in the suit against the government that established the illegality of general warrants (warrants for the arrest of any or all persons, no names being specified, involved in an offense). He later became president of the Court of Exchequer (1787) and chief justice of common pleas (1793). He presided (1794) over the famous state trials of John Horne TOOKE and others for alleged subversion of the government.

Eyre, Lake, shallow salt lake, 3,430 sq mi (8,884 sq km), central South Australia state, Australia; largest lake in Australia. The lake, 39 ft (12 m) below sea level, is the continent's lowest point. Located in the arid interior of Australia, the lake is frequently dry. During the winter rainy season, numerous stream beds carry floodwaters into the lake.

Eyre Peninsula, 200 mi (322 km) long, southern South Australia state, Australia, between Spencer Gulf and the Great Australian Bight. There are large iron ore deposits in the Middleback Range near Whyalla, at the northeastern base of the peninsula.

Eyskens, Gaston (gästôNʹ īʹskəns), 1905-, Belgian political leader. He studied economics and political science and in 1931 became a professor at the Univ. of Louvain. A Christian Socialist member of parliament (1939-73), he headed the ministry of finance (1945, 1947-49, and 1965-66), served as governor of the International Bank for Reconstruction and Development (1947-49), and was minister of economic affairs (1950). He was three times prime minister (1949, 1958-61, and 1968-72). In his last term of office, he sought in vain to settle the long-standing friction between Belgium's French-speaking and Flemish-speaking communities and finally retired from politics.

Ezar (ēʹzər), the same as EZER **1.**

Ezbai (ĕzʹbāī, ĕzbāʹī), father of NAARAI.

Ezbon (ĕzʹbŏn). **1** Son of Gad. Gen. 46.16. Ozni: Num. 26.16. **2** Benjamin's grandson. 1 Chron. 7.7.

Ezechiel: see EZEKIEL.

Ezekias (ĕzəkīʹəs): see HEZEKIAH.

Ezekiel or **Ezechiel** (both: ēzēʹkēēl), book of the Old Testament, 26th in the order of the Authorized Version, 3d of the books of the Major Prophets. It is the account of the prophetic career of the priest Ezekiel, who preached to Jews of the Babylonian captivity from 592 B.C. to 570 B.C. (according to the chronology given in the book itself). This dual role of prophet and priest makes his position unique among the prophets of Israel. The central point of the work is the fall of Jerusalem (586 B.C.), what goes before (1-32) being prophetic of doom, the rest (33-48) inspired by the hope of restoration, ending with a vision of the ideal Temple (40-48). Ezekiel's work consisted not only of narration of his powerful visions but also of symbolic actions, e.g., eating a book (3), sleeping on one side (4), and not mourning his wife (24). Eloquent and famous passages are on the sword of God's wrath (21), on the greatness of Tyre (26-28), lament over Egypt (31-32), and on the field of dried bones (37). Ezekiel contains an explicit revocation of the principle of sins of the fathers visited on the children (18) and stresses the idea of individual responsibility. See Ecclus. 49.10-11. See Walther Eichrodt, *Ezekiel: A Commentary* (tr. 1970).

Ezel: see SAREMA, USSR.

Ezel (ēʹzəl), in the Bible, rock where David said farewell to Jonathan. 1 Sam. 20.19.

Ezem (ĕzʹĕm), the same as AZEM.

Ezer (ēʹzər). **1** Edomite chief. Gen. 36.21,27,30. Ezar: 1 Chron. 1.38,42. **2** One of Ephraim's sons. 1 Chron. 7.21. **3** Priest at the dedication of the wall. Neh. 12.42. **4** Son of Hur the Judahite. 1 Chron. 4.4. **5** Gadite ally of David. 1 Chron. 12.9. **6** Repairer of the wall. Neh. 3.19.

Ezion-geber (ēʹzēŏn-gēʹbər) or **Ezion-gaber** (-gāʹ-) [both: Heb., = giant's backbone], ancient port, on the Gulf of Aqaba. The site, near AQABA, is now some distance from the shore, which is advancing. The Bible reveals the existence of a port there from the reign of Solomon to at least that of Uzziah in the 8th cent. B.C. (Num. 33.35,36; Deut. 2.8; 1 Kings 9.26; 22.48; 2 Chron. 8.17). Excavations were carried out (1938-40) under American auspices. The largest copper refineries ever found to have existed in the ancient world were unearthed at the level of the oldest of the five periods of settlement. Trade relations existed with Phoenicia, Arabia, Egypt, Sinai, and Greece (5th cent. B.C.). Nearby was the ancient port of ELAT.

Eznite (ĕzʹnīt), ostensibly an epithet of ADINO in 2 Sam. 23.8. The name with its qualifier is translated in the parallel passage in 1 Chron. 11.11 as "he lifted up his spear." That translation has been added to the passage in 2 Sam. in AV.

Ezra. 1 Central figure of the book of EZRA. **2** Priest who returned with Zerubbabel. Neh. 12.1. **3** Judahite. 1 Chron. 4.17.

Ezra or **Esdras** (ĕzʹdrəs) and **Nehemiah** (nēəmīʹə), two books of the Old Testament, originally a single work in the Hebrew canon, occupying the 15th and the 16th place in the Authorized Version; they are usually called First and Second Esdras in the Greek versions and the Western canon (Roman Catholic Bible). The books narrate the history of the Jews from 538 B.C. to 432 B.C. as follows: the decree of the Persian king Cyrus permitting the Jews to return to Palestine from captivity (Ezra 1); the return of Zerubbabel with a certain number to Jerusalem, where they rebuild the Temple despite opposition (Ezra 2-6); the return of Ezra, "the priest, the scribe," to Jerusalem with orders from King Artaxerxes to restore Jewish Law (Ezra 7-10); the return (445 B.C.) of Nehemiah, cupbearer to Artaxerxes I and the rebuilding of Jerusalem's walls in spite of rich, powerful enemies (Neh. 1-7); the solemn reading of the Law and signing of a covenant (Neh. 8-10); the dedication of the walls (Neh. 11-12); and an addendum telling of some reforms of Nehemiah (13). The order of events is not chronological; although the traditional date for Ezra's return to Jerusalem is 458 B.C., it seems probable that he actually returned after Nehemiah, in 398 B.C. under Artaxerxes II. Much of the books consists of documents and lists, some of these not in Hebrew but in Western Aramaic. The work was probably originally combined with Chronicles as one book. The Ezra of Neh. 12.1, 13, 33, and the persons named Nehemiah in Ezra 2.2, Neh. 3.16, 7.7 are not the famous leaders. See bibliography for OLD TESTAMENT. See also C. C. Torrey, *Ezra Studies* (1970).

Ezrahite (ĕzʹrəhīt″), a patronymic: see ZERAH **1.**

Ezri (ĕzʹrī), officer under David. 1 Chron. 27.26.

Ezzelino da Romano (ĕt″sälēʹnō dä rōmäʹnō), 1194-1259, Italian Ghibelline leader (see GUELPHS AND GHIBELLINES) and soldier. After 1232 a faithful supporter of Holy Roman Emperor Frederick II against the pope, he held Verona, Vicenza, Padua, and other cities. When Frederick defeated (1237) the LOMBARD LEAGUE at Cortenuova, Ezzelino became the greatest power in N Italy. He married (1238) an illegitimate daughter of Frederick. Continuously at war with the Guelphs, he was excommunicated (1254) by Pope Innocent IV, and a strong alliance was formed against him. Ezzelino lost (1256) Padua, but in 1258 he took Brescia. After an attempt to conquer Milan he was defeated and wounded at Cassano and died in prison. Placed by Dante in the *Inferno,* he is remembered as a cruel tyrant.

F

F, sixth letter of the ALPHABET. The Greek letter corresponding to it, digamma, which probably represented a sound like *w,* disappeared before the classical period. In Western alphabets *f* has usually represented the voiceless labiodental fricative, as in the English *fast.* In MUSICAL NOTATION F stands for a note in the scale. In chemistry F is the symbol of the element FLUORINE.

Faber, Frederick William (fā'bər), 1814–63, English theologian and hymn writer. A friend of John Henry Newman and an adherent of the OXFORD MOVEMENT, he became (1843) rector of Eton. In 1845 he entered the Roman Catholic Church and with some of his friends and parishioners founded a religious community in Birmingham, which merged in 1848 into the Oratory of St. Philip Neri. Ordained a Roman Catholic priest in 1847, he helped found in 1849 the oratory in London, of which he was superior for the rest of his life. His poetical works include "The Cherwell Water-Lily" (1840); his many well-known hymns were collected in *Hymns* (1848). Other writings include nine contributions to *Lives of the Canonized Saints* (1844–45), *The Blessed Sacrament* (1855), and *The Foot of the Cross* (1853–60). See biography by Ronald Chapman (1961).

Faber, Johannes (yōhä'nəs fä'bər), 1478–1541, German churchman. His German surname was Heigerlin. He was a Dominican. After 1531 he was bishop of Vienna. He was friendly at first (until 1521) with Martin Luther and Huldreich Zwingli, but later he became their untiring opponent in polemics. He was, nevertheless, an ardent advocate of reform of clerical discipline and of preaching, especially with respect to indulgences.

Faber Stapulensis, Jacobus: see LEFÈVRE D'ÉTAPLES, JACQUES.

Fabian, Saint (fā'bēən), pope (236–50), a Roman; successor of St. Anterus and predecessor of St. Cornelius. He recast the ecclesiastical organization in Rome. Fabian was martyred under Decius. Feast: Jan. 20.

Fabian Society, British socialist society. An outgrowth of the Fellowship of the New Life (founded 1883 under the influence of Thomas DAVIDSON), the society was developed the following year by Frank Podmore and Edward Pease. George Bernard Shaw and Sidney Webb joined soon after this and became its outstanding exponents. The group achieved recognition with the publication of *Fabian Essays* (1889), with contributions by Shaw, Webb, Annie Besant, and Graham Wallas. The Fabians were opposed to the revolutionary theory of Marxism, holding that social reforms and socialistic "permeation" of existing political institutions would bring about the natural development of socialism. Repudiating the necessity of violent class struggle, they took little notice of trade unionism and other labor movements until Beatrice Potter (who later married Sidney Webb) joined the group. They subsequently helped create (1900) the unified Labour Representation Committee, which evolved into the Labour party. The Labour party adopted their main tenets, and the Fabian Society remains as an affiliated research and publicity agency. See studies by E. R. Pease (rev. ed. 1925), G. D. H. Cole (1942), and Margaret Cole (1961); Anne Fremantle, *This Little Band of Prophets* (1960).

Fabius (fā'bēəs), ancient Roman gens. The family was most distinguished from the 5th cent. B.C. onward. However, little is known of the early members. **Quintus Fabius Vibulanus,** fl. 450 B.C., was consul three times (467, 465, 459) and a member of the decemvirate. Although he had served Rome well in battle, he was exiled with the other decemvirs. His descendant, **Quintus Fabius Maximus Rullianus** or **Rullus,** d. c.291 B.C., was consul five times (322, 310, 308, 297, 295) and dictator (315). He attacked the Samnites in 325 and was victorious, but his disobedience of orders brought his condemnation by Lucius Papirius Cursor, who was dictator at the time. Rullianus was renowned as a general, especially for his victory over the Etruscans, the Samnites, and their allies at Sentinum (295). His descendant, **Quintus Fabius Maximus Verrucosus,** d. 203 B.C., the opponent of HANNIBAL, was called Cunctator [Lat.,= delayer] because of his tactics, from which the term *Fabian,* referring to a waiting policy, is derived. He was consul five times (233, 228, 215, 214, 209) and dictator (217). Fabius kept his army always near Hannibal's but never attacked, harassing Hannibal continually, but never joining battle. The Romans tired of Fabius' policy, and he was supplanted (216); the rout at Cannae was the result. In his last consulship Fabius took Tarentum (now Taranto) from Hannibal, a signal victory. Another branch of the family was represented by **Caius Fabius Pictor** [Lat.,= the painter], fl. 302 B.C., who painted the temple of Salus at Rome, the first recorded Roman painting. His grandson was **Quintus Fabius Pictor,** fl. 225 B.C., the first Roman annalist; his history covered Rome from Aeneas to the Second Punic War. His work is lost. **Quintus Fabius Labeo,** fl. 180 B.C., praetor (189), was commander of the fleet in an eastern campaign. He seems to have used his power largely for his own aggrandizement. An adoptive member of the gens was **Quintus Fabius Maximus,** fl. 121 B.C., consul (121), called *Allobrogicus,* because of his victory over the Allobroges in Gaul.

fable, brief allegorical narrative, in verse or prose, illustrating a moral thesis or satirizing human beings. The characters of a fable are usually animals who talk and act like people while retaining their animal traits. The oldest known fables are those in the *Panchatantra,* a collection of fables in Sanskrit, and those attributed to the Greek Aesop, perhaps the most famous of all fabulists. Other important writers of fables include Jean de La Fontaine, whose fables are noted for their sophistication and wit, and the German dramatist and critic Gotthold Lessing, who also wrote a critical essay on the fable. In England the tradition of the fable was continued in the 17th and 18th cent. by John Dryden and John Gay. The use of the fable in the 20th cent. can be seen in James Thurber's *Fables for Our Time* (1940) and in George Orwell's political allegory, *Animal Farm* (1945). The American poet Marianne Moore wrote poems quite similar to fables in their use of animals and animal traits to comment on human experience; she also published an excellent translation of *The Fables of La Fontaine* (1954). See Louis Auchincloss, ed., *Fables of Wit and Elegance* (1972) and bibliography comp. by Barbara Quinnam (1966).

fabliau, plural **fabliaux** (both: fäblēō'), short comic, often bawdy tale in verse that deals realistically and satirically with middle-class or lower-class characters. Fabliaux were often directed against marriage and against members of the clergy. The form was extremely popular in France during the Middle Ages. Excellent examples of fabliaux can be found in pre-Christian Oriental literature, in Chaucer's *Canterbury Tales,* and in Boccaccio's *Decameron.*

Fabre, Jean Henri (zhäN äNrē' fä'brə), 1823–1915, French entomologist and author. He is known for his observations on insects and his study of their behavior. Fabre demonstrated the importance of instinct among insects. He taught until 1870 at Carpentras, Ajaccio, and Avignon, wrote works on popular science at Orange (1870–79), then retired to nearby Sérignan, where he devoted himself to entomological studies. Fabre worked almost exclusively from nature, and his exquisite literary style brought him as much renown as his observations. His principal work is *Souvenirs entomologiques* (10 vol., 1879–1907); English translations of selections from this work include *The Life of the Spider* (1912), *The Marvels of the Insect World* (1938), and *The Insect World of J. Henri Fabre* (ed. with commentary and biographical notes by E. W. Teale, 1949). See studies on Fabre by Augustin Fabre (tr., 2d ed. 1921), P. F. Bicknell (1923), and G. V. Legros (1971).

Fabre d'Églantine, Philippe François Nazaire (fēlēp' fräNswä' näzĕr' fä'brə dägläNtēn'), 1755–94, French dramatist and revolutionist. His chief work, *Le Philinte de Molière* (1790), was a sequel to Molière's *Misanthrope.* A member of the Convention, he was selected to devise the names for the months and days of the French Revolutionary calendar. He was guillotined during the Terror.

Fabriano, Gentile da: see GENTILE DA FABRIANO.

Fabriano (fäbrēä'nō), town (1971 pop. 27,276), in the Marche, central Italy, in the Apennines. It is an agricultural and industrial center. Paper has been made there since the 13th cent. The local school of painting, founded by Allegretto Nuzi in the 14th cent., had Gentile da Fabriano as its best-known figure.

fabric: see TEXTILES.

Fabricius (Caius Fabricius Luscinus) (fəbrĭsh'əs), d. 250 B.C., Roman general and statesman, distinguished for simplicity of habit and probity in public life. He persuaded the Tarentines to abstain from war with Rome and, as consul (282 B.C.), defeated the Boii and the Etruscans. While negotiating with PYRRHUS for the ransom of prisoners captured at Heraclea (281) he rejected a bribe. When consul again (278), he negotiated terms of peace with Pyrrhus and subsequently defeated the Samnites, Lucani, and Bruttii.

Fabricius, Hieronymus (hīərŏn'əməs), 1537–1619, Italian anatomist; pupil and successor of Fallopius and teacher of William Harvey at Padua. He was a surgeon, an embryologist, and an anatomist; he described the venous valves but did not fully understand their function. See his *De venarum ostiolis* (1603; facsimile ed., with introduction by K. J. Franklin, 1933).

Fabricius, Johan Christian (yōhăn' krĭs'tyän fäbrē'syōōs), 1745–1808, Danish entomologist. Influenced by the methods of Linnaeus, under whom he studied, he devised a system of classification of insects based on mouth structure. He taught at the Univ. of Kiel from 1775.

Fabricius, Johan Wigmore (yōhän' vĭgmôr'ə fäbrē'sēōōs), 1899–, Dutch novelist and journalist, b. Indonesia. A correspondent in Europe in World War I, Fabricius later wrote from South America, Africa, and Asia. During World War II he made broadcasts from England to the occupied countries. His many novels include *Komedianten trokken voorbij* (1933, tr. *The Son of Marietta,* 1936), *Schimmenspel* (1958), and *Mijn Rosalia* (1961). Later works include *Met klein orkest* (1971). A volume of his memoirs appeared in 1951.

Fabritius, Carel (kä'rəl fäbrēt'sēōōs), 1622–54, Dutch painter; pupil and outstanding follower of Rembrandt. His early death in the explosion of a powder magazine at Delft cut short a career of the greatest promise. Among his few but remarkable works that remain are *Portrait of a Man* (Rotterdam); *The Goldfinch* (The Hague); and *View of Delft* (National Gall., London). He is thought to have had a strong influence on Vermeer. His brother **Barent Fabritius** (1624–73) worked in a similar though less accomplished manner, influenced by Maes as well as Rembrandt. His portrait of the Van der Helm family (1655) is in the Rijks Museum.

facade (fəsäd'), exterior face or wall of a building. The term implies ordered placement of its openings and other features and thus seems inapplicable to a wall without design. Any freestanding structure may have four or more facades, designated by their orientation (e.g., north facade); a building flanked by other buildings on either side generally has only a front and a rear facade. In medieval churches the chief facade is that of the building's west end, which contains the principal entrance portals. The facade has usually taken no more than a two-dimensional design whose purpose has been to give the viewer an impression of a building not necessarily revealing its internal structure. Most contemporary theorists demand that the facade be an uncompromising revelation of internal structure that strictly avoids architectural "effects."

Fackenthal, Frank Diehl (făk'ənthôl), 1883–1968, American educator, b. Hellertown, Pa., grad. Columbia, 1906. He served Columbia as chief clerk (1906–10), secretary (1910–37), and provost (1937–48). Between the retirement of Nicholas Murray Butler (1945) and the installation of General Eisenhower as president (1948), Dr. Fackenthal was acting president of the university, retaining his post as provost. After his retirement (1948) from the university he served as educational consultant to the Carnegie Corp. (1948–52) and then as president of the Columbia University Press (1953–58). His principal speeches as acting president were published as *The Greater Power and Other Addresses* (1949).

facsimile (făksĭm'əlē), in communications, system for transmitting pictures or other graphic matter by wire or radio. The surface of the material to be sent is traversed by a light-beam and a photosensor that translates the light and dark areas of the material thus scanned into electric signals for transmission by radio or wire. A receiving station reproduces the transmitted material by a variety of means. In one recording process the electric signals activate a variable lamp that is used to scan a photographic film. Newspapers and television stations utilize this method for recording news photographs. In another method the material is recorded by sending the electric signals through paper that is sensitive to electric current. Facsimile is used to transmit such materials as telegrams, drawings, pictures taken from satellites, and even entire newspapers.

factor, in arithmetic, any number that divides a given number evenly, i.e., without any remainder. The factors of 12 are 1, 2, 3, 4, 6, and 12. Similarly in algebra, any one of the algebraic expressions multiplied by another to form a product is a factor of that product, e.g., $a+b$ and $a-b$ are factors of a^2-b^2, since $(a+b)(a-b)=a^2-b^2$. In general, if r is a ROOT of a POLYNOMIAL equation $f(x)=0$, then $(x-r)$ is a factor of the polynomial $f(x)$.

factory, place of production characterized by wage labor, the use of machinery, and the division of labor. The large-scale use of machinery differentiates factory production from simple manufacture, and the division of labor sets it apart from even the most elaborate handicraft establishments. Standardized goods are produced and sometimes sold more cheaply by the factory system, and occasionally the goods are better than those made by craftsmen. The factory system makes possible huge increases in output per man-hour though at the same time division of labor deprives the individual worker of much of his sense of creativity. The factory system gave rise to serious social problems, both inside and outside the factory, some of which remain unsolved. The tedious routine of assembly line work can result in boredom and frustration among the workers. It may also lead to a sense of alienation and hostility toward both employer and product. The concentration of large plants and factories creates problems of urban congestion and slum dwellings and places a strain on transportation and communications systems. See AUTOMATION and DIVISION OF LABOR. For bibliography, see INDUSTRIAL REVOLUTION. See also R. C. Davis, *The Principles of Factory Organization and Management* (3d ed. 1957); C. R. Walker, *Toward the Automatic Factory* (1957); Elton Mayo, *Human Problems of an Industrial Civilization* (1960); F. C. Mann and L. R. Hoffman, *Automation and the Worker* (1960); B. B. Gardner and D. O. Moore, *Human Relations in Industry* (4th ed. 1964).

factory acts: see LABOR LAW.

faculae: see PHOTOSPHERE.

Facundo Quiroga, Juan: see QUIROGA, JUAN FACUNDO.

Fadeyev, Aleksandr Aleksandrovich (əlyĭksän'dər əlyĭksän'drəvĭch fūdyā'əf), 1901–56, Russian author. An active Communist, he fought in the Revolution of 1917. His first novel, *Razgrom* (1926, new tr., *The Rout,* 1957), concerns a group of partisans fighting in Siberia. Fadeyev continued this theme in the lengthy *Last of the Udegs* (1929–35), an unfinished epic. His novel *The Young Guard* (1945) describes the underground activities of a group of young Communists during World War II. Criticized, Fadeyev revised it in 1951 to give more prominence to the Communist party. In 1953 he lost his position as secretary of the Union of Soviet Writers. Diminished in status and emotionally and physically impaired by alcoholism, he committed suicide.

Faenza (fäān'tsä), city (1971 pop. 54,733), in Emilia-Romagna, N central Italy, on the Lamone River. A special kind of richly colored ceramic, called faïence or majolica, has been made there since the 12th cent.; ceramic art flourished from 1450 to 1550 and was revived in the 18th cent. The Manfredi family, which ruled Faenza in the 14th and 15th cent., enriched it with works of art. Noteworthy buildings include the Renaissance-style cathedral (15th cent.), the governor's palace (12th cent.), and the city hall (13th–15th cent.). The International Museum of Ceramics is there.

Faeroe Islands or **Faröe Islands** (both: fâr'ō), Dan. *Færøerne,* Faeroese *Føroyar,* group of volcanic islands (1970 pop. 36,681), 540 sq mi (1,399 sq km), Denmark, in the N Atlantic, between Iceland and the Shetland Islands. There are 18 main islands (one of which is not inhabited) and 4 small, uninhabited islands. The largest islands are STEYMOY, on which the group's capital, TÓRSHAVN, is situated, and Østerø. The Faeroes are high and rugged and have only sparse vegetation. Their inhabitants depend mainly on fishing and to a lesser extent on farming (including sheep raising), whaling, and fowling. Fish and wool are exported. The chief fishing ports are Vágur, Tórshavn, and Klaksvíg. The climate of the Faeroes is relatively mild, because of the influence of the North Atlantic Drift; there are frequent storms and much fog. The earliest known inhabitants were Celtic. In the 8th cent. A.D. the islands were settled by Norsemen. In the early 11th cent. they became part of the kingdom of Norway and were Christianized. The population was nearly wiped out by an outbreak of black plague in the 14th cent. and was soon after replaced by Norwegian settlers. With Norway, the Faeroes passed under Danish rule in 1380, and they remained Danish after the Treaty of Kiel (1814) transferred Norway from the Danish to the Swedish crown. A nationalist movement in the 19th cent. led to the revival of Faeroese, a language akin to Icelandic, and there is an extensive native literature. In World War II, Great Britain established (1940) a protectorate over the islands after the German occupation of Denmark. After the war there was considerable sentiment for full independence, and following a plebiscite in 1946, the islands' parliament, the Lagting, proclaimed independence. The Danish king dissolved the Lagting, and after a new parliament was elected, the proclamation was reversed. However, in 1948 the Faeroese obtained home rule. Since 1953 they have sent two representatives to the Danish parliament.

Faes, Pieter van der: see LELY, SIR PETER.

Fagersta (fä'gərstä"), city (1970 pop. 15,584), Västmanland co., S central Sweden. It is an industrial and winter sports center. Manufactures include iron and steel and forest products.

Fages, Pedro (pä'thrō fä'hās), fl. 1767–96, Spanish governor of Alta California (1782–91). In Mexico in 1767, he was ordered to accompany the expedition of Gaspar de Portolá, which established (1770) the mission at Monterey, where he became commandant. Later that year he led a small party to explore the east coast of San Francisco Bay. Friction developed at Monterey between Fages and Father Junípero Serra, and Fages was recalled (1774), but he returned in 1782 as governor. His administration was notable for its encouragement of colonization, agriculture, and missionary work. His diaries, *The Colorado River Campaign* (tr. 1913), *The Expedition to San Francisco Bay in 1770* (tr. 1911) and *A Historical, Political and Natural Description of California* (tr. 1937), are valuable source materials for the history of the period.

Faguet, Émile (āmēl' fāgā'), 1847–1916, French literary critic and historian. His prolific studies stimulated interest in French intellectual history of the 17th, 18th, and 19th cent. His major work, *Jean-Jacques Rousseau* (5 vol., 1911–13), reveals the energy and fertility of his mind.

Fahrenheit temperature scale, TEMPERATURE scale in which the temperature difference between two reference temperatures, the melting and boiling points of water, is divided into 180 equal intervals called degrees. The freezing point is taken as 32°F and the boiling point as 212°F. The scale was devised by G. D. Fahrenheit. Although the Fahrenheit scale was formerly used widely in English-speaking countries, many of these countries began changing to the more convenient CELSIUS TEMPERATURE SCALE in the late 1960s and early 1970s; a notable exception is the United States, where the Fahrenheit scale is still in common use together with other English units of measurement. Temperatures on the Fahrenheit scale can be converted to equivalent temperatures on the Celsius scale by first subtracting 32° from the Fahrenheit temperature, then multiplying the result by 5/9, according to the formula $(F-32)5/9=C$.

Faial: see FAYAL, Azores, Portugal.

Faidherbe, Louis Léon César (lwē lāôN' sāzär' fādĕrb'), 1818–89, French colonial administrator. As governor of Senegal (1854–61, 1863–65) he fought HAJJ OMAR and established an orderly and greatly expanded colony. In the FRANCO-PRUSSIAN WAR he assumed command of the army of the north in the dark days after the fall of Sedan (Sept., 1870) and gained some success. Faidherbe wrote numerous works on geography, ethnography, and ethnology.

faïence (fāĕns', -äns', fī-) [for FAENZA, Italy], any of several kinds of pottery, especially earthenware made of coarse clay and covered with an opaque tin-oxide glaze. The term is particularly applied to the ceramic ornaments and figurines of the ancient Egyptians. See also MAJOLICA.

Failly, Pierre Louis Charles de (pyĕr lwē shärl də fāyē'), 1810–92, French general. He fought in Algeria, in the Crimean War, and at Magenta and Solferino (1859) in the Italian War. Heading the French expeditionary forces to protect the Papal States, he defeated Giuseppe Garibaldi at Mentana (1867). In this campaign the Chassepot rifle was first used. In the Franco-Prussian War, Failly commanded the right wing of General MacMahon's army at Sedan (1870). The disastrous outcome of that battle is largely ascribed to Failly's tactics.

fainting or **syncope** (sĭng'kəpē), temporary loss of consciousness caused by an insufficient supply of oxygen to the brain. It can be concurrent with any serious disease or condition, such as heart failure, high blood pressure, hemorrhage, injury to the brain or other organs, or poisoning. Less serious conditions can also cause fainting, e.g., fatigue, prolonged standing, getting up after long confinement to bed, pain, hunger, dehydration, anemia, or fright or other emotional disturbance. A person aware of an oncoming fainting spell should sit down and lower his head between his knees for a moment or two to increase the flow of oxygen to the brain. The already unconscious person should be placed in a supine position, preferably with the feet raised. If unconsciousness persists, cold water on the face or the inhalation of aromatic spirits of ammonia may be tried. Under no circumstances should any liquid or medication be forced down the throat of an unconscious person. Fainting for more than a few minutes requires medical attention. After regaining consciousness, the patient should remain recumbent for at least 10 minutes and arise gradually.

Fair, James Graham, 1831–94, American financier, b. near Belfast, Ireland. He emigrated to America as a child, grew up on an Illinois farm, and went to the West in 1851 in search of gold. In partnership with J. W. Mackay, J. C. Flood, and William S. O'Brien, he made a large fortune from the silver of the Comstock Lode. He was U.S. Senator from Nevada from 1881 to 1887. See O. Lewis, *Silver Kings* (1947).

fair, market exhibition at which producers, traders, and consumers meet either to barter or to buy and sell goods and services. Before the development of transportation and marketing, fairs furnished the primary opportunity for the exchange of merchandise, and served as centers of community social life. Among the ancient Greeks and Romans the days of the public market were also used to announce new public laws. In early Christian times special occasions for marketing were frequently attached to religious gatherings, notably those of pilgrims coming to a town to celebrate a special feast. In the Middle Ages fairs flourished with the manorial system. They were the major means of exchanging commodities not produced for subsistence. Fairs were incorporated by royal charter and had their own officials, laws, and courts. Major trade routes affected the growth of individual fairs; among the most prominent were those of Geneva, Antwerp, Leipzig, Madrid, Lyons, Bordeaux, Novgorod, and Sturbridge and Bartholomew Fair in England. Of the variety of goods traded at such fairs, cloth was probably the most important. The volume of trade was so great that by the 15th cent. some fair towns became banking centers and were subjected to the regulations of emerging mercantilism. With the breaking of the manorial system, commerce became an expanding and regular part of economic life. Trade fairs declined and to a large extent were replaced by outdoor and indoor general markets. In the 17th cent. pleasure fairs, dominated by entertainments such as plays, became popular. The EXPOSITION, combining entertainment and commerce, flourishes today. A variety of advanced industrial wares are exhibited, and important technological innovations are displayed. International trade fairs, devoted solely to commercial display and directed toward businessmen, have also become popular since World War II. Agricultural fairs—held to improve farming methods, stocks, and crops—have been particularly important in the history of the United States. Many states and counties still maintain annual fairs, although their popularity has decreased in recent years and many have been discontinued. See Helen Augur, *The Book of Fairs* (1939); William Addison, *English Fairs and Markets* (1953).

Fairbanks, Charles Warren, 1852–1918, Vice President of the United States (1905–9), b. Union co.,

Ohio. He became wealthy as a railroad lawyer in Indianapolis, rose in Republican politics, and served in the U.S. Senate from 1897 to 1905. Fairbanks was recognized as the spokesman of President McKinley and of the conservatives and was chosen as vice presidential candidate with Theodore Roosevelt primarily to attract the conservative vote. He continued to dominate his party in Indiana and was in 1916 again vice presidential candidate, this time on the unsuccessful ticket with Charles Evans Hughes.

Fairbanks, Douglas, 1883–1939, American movie actor, b. Denver. From 1901 to 1914, Fairbanks appeared on stage in light comedies. In 1915 he began making movies, becoming the swashbuckling hero of his day in such films as *The Mark of Zorro* (1921), *The Three Musketeers* (1921), *Robin Hood* (1922), and *The Thief of Bagdad* (1924). He was married (1920–35) to Mary PICKFORD, and together with Charlie CHAPLIN and D. W. GRIFFITH they formed United Artists studio. See biographies by Ralph Hancock and Letitia Fairbanks (1935) and Richard Schickel (1974). His son, Douglas Fairbanks, Jr. (1907–), is also an actor.

Fairbanks, city (pop. 14,771), Fairbanks census division, central Alaska, on the Chena River near its confluence with the Tanana; inc. 1903. The Univ. of Alaska and the U.S. government are the principal employers. Private firms in the retail, wholesale, and construction industries depend heavily on government contracts. Gold was discovered there in 1902, and Fairbanks grew rapidly as a mining camp. It declined somewhat after placer mining reached its limits, but flumes were built and hydraulic methods used to continue mining. The building of the Alaska RR increased the importance of Fairbanks. The Richardson Highway from Valdez, on the Pacific coast, reaches Fairbanks, which, during World War II, became the terminus of the Alaska Highway. Points of interest include "Alaskaland," a 40-acre (16-hectare) site in the city, which includes a Gold Rush town, an Eskimo village, an art gallery, and a zoo. Fort Wainwright is adjacent to the city, and Eielson Air Force Base is to the south.

Fairborn, city (1970 pop. 32,267), Greene co., SW Ohio; settled 1799, inc. 1950 with the merging of Osborn and Fairborn. Major employers are Wright State Univ. in nearby Dayton and the huge Wright-Patterson Air Force Base. Cement is produced in Fairborn, and there are limestone quarries adjacent to the city.

Fairchild, David Grandison, 1869–1954, American botanist and agricultural explorer, b. East Lansing, Mich. He entered the service of the U.S. Dept. of Agriculture, where he organized (1895) and later (1906–28) was in charge of a division of plant exploration and introduction now part of the Bureau of Plant Industry. He had charge also of the foreign research expeditions, in many of which he participated. Fairchild wrote *Exploring for Plants, 1925–27* (1930) and *The World Grows Round My Door* (1947). He married the daughter of Alexander Graham Bell.

Fair Employment Practices Committee (FEPC), established (1941) within the Office of Production Management by executive order of President Franklin Delano Roosevelt. It was created to promote the fullest utilization of all available manpower and to eliminate discriminatory employment practices. President Truman advocated a permanent peacetime FEPC, but the Senate terminated the program in 1946. In 1964 the EQUAL EMPLOYMENT OPPORTUNITY COMMISSION was created to fight discrimination in employment. See Louis Ruchames, *Race, Jobs, & Politics: The Story of FEPC* (1953); Jacob K. Javits, *Discrimination: U.S.A.* (1960).

Fairfax, Edward, 1580?–1635, English translator. His excellent translation of Tasso's *Gerusalemme liberta* was published in 1600 under the title *Godfrey of Buloigne*. He also wrote a *Discourse on Witchcraft* (1621), in which he interpreted the seizures of his two young daughters as the result of witchcraft.

Fairfax of Cameron, Thomas Fairfax, 3d **Baron,** 1612–71, English general. He was the son of Ferdinando Fairfax, 2d Baron Fairfax of Cameron (1584–1648), whose title he inherited and under whom he fought in the early stages of the English civil war. In 1645 he was given command of the New Model Army, which he organized and trained and led to victory against Charles I at Naseby. Fairfax was conservative by nature, and when the quarrel developed between the army and Parliament he exercised little influence over army policies. Nominated as a judge of Charles I, he resigned when he realized the king's execution was predetermined. He resigned (1650) his command rather than invade Scotland, withdrew from public life during the Protectorate, and played some part in securing the Restoration (1660) of the monarchy.

Fairfax of Cameron, Thomas Fairfax, 6th **Baron,** 1693–1781, proprietor of the Northern Neck of Virginia, b. England. He inherited the Northern Neck, comprising the land between the Rappahannock and Potomac rivers, through his mother from his grandfather, the 2d Baron CULPEPER, colonial governor of Virginia. Virginia disputed the extent of his grant, and both parties had surveys made, Fairfax journeying (1735–37) to the colony for that purpose. In 1745 the British privy council, in return for certain concessions made by Fairfax, confirmed his claim in full (a minimum of 5,282,000 acres/2,137,500 hectares), and two years later he returned to Virginia to live permanently. He spent several years with his cousin and former agent, Col. William Fairfax, the patron of the youthful George WASHINGTON, at "Belvoir" on the Potomac before moving (1752) to the Shenandoah valley, where he built "Greenway Court," near Winchester. Although a Loyalist in sentiment (he was the only resident peer in the colonies), he went unharmed during the American Revolution. The state of Virginia canceled the proprietorship in 1785. See biography by S. E. Brown (1965).

Fairfax, city (1970 pop. 21,970), historic seat of Fairfax co., NE Va., a residential suburb of Washington, D.C.; inc. 1892, as a city 1961 (at which time it became independent and no longer included in a county). In its old courthouse (built 1799; restored 1967) are the wills of George and Martha Washington. The county was settled before 1700. During the Civil War it was in Federal hands. Both the county and the city have many historic structures, notably Gunston Hall (1755–58), Pohick Church (1774), and Sully Plantation (1794). George Mason Univ. is in the city, and Dulles International Airport is nearby.

Fairfield, city (1971 pop. 112,862), New South Wales, SE Australia. It is a suburb of Sydney.

Fairfield. 1 City (1970 pop. 14,369), Jefferson co., N central Ala., an industrial suburb of Birmingham; inc. 1919. Founded (1910) by the United States Steel Corp., it has steel and chemical industries. **2** City (1970 pop. 44,146), seat of Solano co., W Calif.; founded 1859, inc. 1903. Among the products of its industries are aluminum cans and sleeping bags. Nearby is Travis Air Force Base. **3** Town (1970 pop. 56,487), Fairfield co., SW Conn., on Long Island Sound; settled 1639, chartered 1947. It is chiefly residential, but there are diverse light industries. The town was settled on the site of the last battle (1637) in the Pequot War. It was a port of entry and a shipping center until 1890. During the Revolution much of it was burned (1777) by the British. Three colonial historical districts are maintained today. The town has many sandy beaches and a large municipal marina. Fairfield Univ. is there. **4** City (1970 pop. 14,680), Butler co., SW Ohio, in the fertile Miami River valley; inc. 1954. Auto body stampings, sulfates, metal products, and construction equipment are manufactured in the city.

Fairhaven, residential and resort town (1970 pop. 16, 332), Bristol co., SE Mass., at the mouth of the Acushnet River on Buzzards Bay, opposite New Bedford; settled 1670, set off from New Bedford and inc. 1812. A former whaling center, it now has commercial fishing industries, boatyards, and plants making machinery and nails.

Fair Havens, Crete: see LASEA.

Fair Isle, island, c.3 sq mi (7.8 sq km), off N Scotland, southernmost of the Shetland Islands. It is known for its knitted hosiery of bright, many-colored design and for its bird sanctuary.

Fair Labor Standards Act: see WAGES AND HOURS ACT.

Fair Lawn, borough (1970 pop. 37,975), Bergen co., NE N.J., across the Passaic River from Paterson; inc. 1924.

Fairleigh Dickinson University, at Rutherford, Teaneck, and Madison, N.J.; coeducational; incorporated and opened 1942 as a junior college, became a four-year college 1948 and a university in 1956. An overseas campus, Wroxton College, offering undergraduate and graduate programs, opened in Wroxton, England, in 1965.

Fairmont. 1 City (1970 pop. 10,751), seat of Martin co., S central Minn.; inc. 1878. It is the trade and manufacturing center for an agricultural area. The courthouse, on the site of a stockade built during the Sioux outbreak of 1862, has pioneer relics. **2** City (1970 pop. 26,093), seat of Marion co., N central W. Va., where the West Fork and the Tygart rivers form the Monongahela, in a rich bituminous coal area; settled 1793 around Prickett's Fort (1774), inc. as Fairmont 1843 with the merger of Palatine (inc. 1838) and Middleton (inc. 1819). Among the city's manufactures are glassware, electric light bulbs, and aluminum products. A Union supply depot in the Civil War, Fairmont was raided by Confederate cavalry in 1863. Fairmont State College and a state hospital are in the city.

Fair Oaks, uninc. residential village (1970 pop. 11,256), Sacramento co., N central Calif., on the American River, in a citrus fruit and farm area.

Fair Oaks: see PENINSULAR CAMPAIGN.

fair-trade laws, in the United States, group of statutes in most states that permit manufacturers to specify the minimum retail price of a commodity. The first fair-trade law was adopted (1931) by California. Intended to protect independent retailers from the price-cutting competition of large chain stores, such statutes were originally nullified by the courts, which found most fair-trade rules in violation of the Sherman Antitrust Act. As a result Congress passed (1937) the Miller-Tydings Act in order to exempt fair trade from antitrust legislation. Although a large majority of states have passed fair-trade laws, in the late 1950's many manufacturers began to abandon the practice of setting minimum retail prices, largely because of the difficulties involved in enforcing such agreements.

Fairview, borough (1970 pop. 10,698), Bergen co., NE N.J.; settled 1860, inc. 1894. Embroideries and apparel are the chief manufactures.

Fairview Park, city (1970 pop. 21,681), Cuyahoga co., NE Ohio; inc. 1950. It is a residential suburb of Cleveland.

fairy, in folklore, one of a variety of supernatural beings endowed with the powers of magic and enchantment. Belief in fairies has existed from earliest times, and literatures all over the world have tales of fairies and their relations with humans. Some Christians have said that fairies were the ancestors of the ancient pagan gods, who, having been replaced by newer deities, were therefore hostile. Others thought that fairies were nature deities, similar to the Greek nymphs. Still others identified fairies with the souls of the dead, particularly the unbaptized, or with fallen angels. Among their many guises, fairies have been described as tiny, wizen-faced old men, like the Irish leprechaun; as beautiful enchantresses who wooed men to their deaths, like Morgan le Fay and the Lorelei; and as hideous, man-eating giants, like the ogre. Fairies were frequently supposed to reside in a kingdom of their own—which might be underground, as with gnomes; in the sea, as with mermaids; in an enchanted part of the forest; or in some far land. Sometimes they were ruled by a king or queen, as were the trolls in Ibsen's *Peer Gynt* and the fairies in Shakespeare's *A Midsummer Night's Dream*. Although fairies were usually represented as mischievous, capricious, and, at times, even demonic, they could also be loving and bountiful, as the fairy godmother in Cinderella. Sometimes fairies entered into love affairs with mortals, but usually such liaisons involved some restriction or compact and frequently ended in calamity, as did those of Melusine and Undine. Various peoples have emphasized particular kinds of fairies in their folklore, as the Arabic jinn, the Scandinavian troll, the Germanic elf, and the English pixie. Among the great adapters of fairy lore into popular fairy tales were Charles Perrault, the brothers Grimm, and Hans Christian Andersen. Other notable contributors were Andrew Lang and James Stephens. See K. M. Briggs, *The Fairies in English Tradition and Literature* (1967).

fairy shrimp: see SHRIMP.

Faisal I or **Feisal I** (both: fī'səl), 1885–1933, king of Iraq (1921–33). The third son of Husein ibn Ali, sherif of Mecca, he is also called Faisal ibn Husein or Faisal al Husein. Faisal was educated in Constantinople and later sat in the Ottoman parliament as deputy for Jidda. In World War I he served with the Turkish army in Syria until 1916, when, escaping to Arabia, he joined with T. E. LAWRENCE in revolt. Faisal was disappointed in his hope to rule as king over all Arab territory in the Ottoman Empire. His aspirations were partly satisfied in 1920, when a Syrian nationalist congress proclaimed him king, but France, the mandatory power, forced him to abdicate later that year. Largely at the urging of Gertrude M. L. BELL, the British, who held the mandate of Iraq, nominated Faisal as king, and he was confirmed by a plebiscite. As king, he generally cooperated with the British and actively participated in the affairs of government. He was succeeded by his son, Ghazi.

Faisal II or **Feisal II,** 1935–58, king of Iraq (1939–58). He ascended to the throne on the death of his father, King Ghazi. After a long regency, Faisal attained his majority in 1953. Regarded as pro-Western in his sympathies, he was killed on July 14, 1958, when a revolution led by Abdul Karim Kassem overthrew the Iraqi monarchy.

Faisal, Ibn al Saud (ĭ'bən äl säōōd' fī'säl), 1905–, king of Saudi Arabia (1964–). Son of Ibn Saud, Faisal led several military campaigns in the making of Saudi Arabia. In 1958 he became premier and foreign minister in the cabinet of his brother, King Saud. Faisal was removed from office in 1961, but early in 1962 he was reinstated as premier. In Nov., 1964, King Saud was forced to abdicate in favor of Faisal. After becoming king, Faisal effected far-reaching economic and administrative reforms.

faith: see CREED.

faith healing, relief or cure of bodily ills through some religious attitude on the part of the sufferer. In the Jewish and Christian traditions prayers for cures and miracles are usual; thus the apostles developed a ritual of healing (James 5.14–16; see also MIRACLE). In the Catholic churches healing has centered about the sacraments of the Eucharist and ANOINTING OF THE SICK and around shrines (e.g., LOURDES and SAINTE ANNE DE BEAUPRÉ) and RELICS. Since 1800 there have appeared a number of Protestant faith-healing groups, e.g., that of John Alexander DOWIE, the Emmanuel movement, and the PECULIAR PEOPLE. The followers of CHRISTIAN SCIENCE, approaching the problem differently, do not consider their system one of faith healing. They consider man as like God and therefore not subject to material ills. Faith healing is of interest in the fields of psychosomatic medicine and psychotherapy. See J. E. Large, *The Ministry of Healing* (1959); M. T. Kelsey, *Healing and Christianity* (1973); Sybil Leek, *The Story of Faith Healing* (1973).

Faiyum: see FAYYUM, AL, Egypt.

Faizabad (fī'zəbăd, fīzäbäd'), city (1969 est. pop. 63,000), capital of Badakhshan prov., NE Afghanistan, on the Kokcha River. The chief commercial and administrative center of NE Afghanistan and the Pamir region, Faizabad also has rice and flour mills. Most of its people are Tadzhiks. In winter the city is sometimes isolated from the rest of Afghanistan by deep snow.

Faizabad or **Fyzabad** (both: fī'zəbăd), town, Uttar Pradesh state, N central India, on the Gogra River. It is a joint municipality with Ajodhya (total 1971 pop. 102,794). A district administrative center and market town, Faizabad trades in local produce and has sugar refineries. A government college is in the city and a military cantonment on the outskirts. Faizabad was the capital (1724–75) of the kingdom of Oudh (1724–1856). The mausoleum (c.1816) of a royal consort is in the city.

Fajardo (fähär'dō), town (1970 pop. 18,249), NE Puerto Rico. It is the center of an important sugar-producing region. Its port, Playa de Fajardo, is a sailing and fishing resort.

fakir (fākēr', fā'kər) [Arabic,=poor], Muslim monk. The term has been extended to Hindu India where it includes a variety of monks and wandering mendicants. Because of their skill at magical tricks and awe-inspiring feats, fakirs are commonly considered wonder-working magicians. In general, the word has come to mean an ascetic man who lives off charity, by begging and working miracles. In Islam, the terms *fakir* and DERVISH are used interchangeably.

Falaise (fälĕz'), town (1968 pop. 7,599), Calvados dept., N France, in Normandy. Once an important textile center, the town is now an agricultural marketplace and manufactures cheeses and household appliances. William I of England (William the Conqueror) was born in Falaise at the castle of the first dukes of Normandy. The town also has a château (12th–13th cent.) built on a promontory and housing a dungeon. Falaise was a key point in the NORMANDY CAMPAIGN of World War II and was heavily damaged.

Falange (fälän'hā) [Span.,=phalanx], Spanish political party, founded in 1933 as Falange Española by José Antônio Primo de Rivera, son of the former Spanish dictator. Professing generally the principles of FASCISM, the Falange distinguished itself from other fascist groups by its great emphasis on national tradition, particularly the imperial and Renaissance Christian traditions of Spain. The Falange militia joined the Insurgents in the Spanish civil war of 1936–39. Merged with the Carlist militia by Francisco FRANCO in 1937, the organization was renamed Falange Española Tradicionalista and was made the official party of the Nationalist state. Unlike Italian fascism, however, it was not an independent force, being exploited and manipulated by Franco. From the middle of World War II on, the party grew steadily weaker, and Franco sought to make it a kind of Roman Catholic nationalist front. By the early 1970s it had virtually no influence. See study by S. G. Payne (1961).

Falashas (fälä'shəz) [Ethiopic,=emigrant], group of approximately 30,000 Ethiopians who practice a form of Judaism. They believe in the Old Testament, certain apocryphal books, and some traditions that correspond to those found in the Midrash and the Talmud. They claim descent from those who migrated from Jerusalem with Menelik, the son of Solomon and the Queen of Sheba, but scholars believe they learned Judaism from Jews who migrated from S Arabia or from those living in Egypt. Pagan and Christian influences have affected their Judaism. In ancient times the Falashas probably ruled their own state. See W. Leslau, ed., *Falasha Anthology: Black Jews of Ethiopia* (1951, repr. 1969).

falcon, common name for members of the Falconidae, a heterogeneous family of long-winged birds of prey closely related to the HAWK. Falcons (genus *Falco*) range in size from the 6½-in. (16.5-cm) falconet to the 24-in. (60-cm) gyrfalcon, and in habits from the swift merlin to the sluggish caracara. True falcons, distinguished by their notched beaks, are widely distributed. In flight their wingbeats are rapid and powerful, and they sweep hundreds of feet at speeds of up to 175 mi (280 km) per hr to capture their prey—chiefly birds and small mammals. They kill cleanly, usually breaking the back of their victim. Some falcons eat insects; the long-legged caracaras (found in South America, with one species, the Audubon's caracara, or Mexican buzzard, ranging to the extreme S United States) feed also on carrion and sometimes rob other birds of their prey. The cosmopolitan peregrine falcon (called duck hawk in the United States) and the gyrfalcon of the arctic tundra have been much used in FALCONRY. The commonest and smallest American falcon is the sparrow hawk, *F. sparverius* (related to the European kestrel). Others are the pigeon hawk (related to the European merlin) and the prairie falcon. Falcons build no nests but lay their eggs on the ground, on cliff ledges, or in the abandoned nests of hawks and crows. Falcons are classified in the phylum CHORDATA, subphylum Vertebrata, class Aves, order Falconiformes, family Falconidae.

Falcone, Aniello (änyĕl'lō fälkô'nā), 1607–56, Italian baroque painter of the Neapolitan school. He is known primarily for his battle pieces. There are examples in the National Museum, Naples; the Prado; and the Louvre.

Falconer, William (fôk'nər), 1732–69, Scottish poet. The victim of a shipwreck off Greece, he described his ordeal in a long, didactic poem, *The Shipwreck* (1762). He also wrote (1769) a source book on shipping and naval practices.

Falconet, Étienne Maurice (ātyĕn' môrēs' fälkōnā'), 1716–91, French sculptor; pupil of Lemoyne. Under Louis XV he became director of sculpture at the Sèvres porcelain factory, where many small reproductions of his work were made. Versatile in his expression, he combined baroque and classical elements. His consummate skill is revealed in his equestrian statue of Peter the Great (1769) for St. Petersburg (now Leningrad). Six volumes of his urbane and erudite writings were published in 1781.

falconry (fôl'kənrē, fô'-, făl'-), sport of hunting birds or small animals with falcons or other types of hawks. It was known to the ancient Chinese, Persians, and Egyptians. Falconry probably spread from Asia to Eastern Europe and then to Western Europe. It became one of the chief sports of royalty and the nobility and attained its greatest popularity in late medieval and early modern Europe. After the 17th cent., falconry declined, and subsequent revivals never brought it into the favor it once enjoyed. It has limited popularity in W Europe, S Asia, Japan, and the United States. Falconry has never been very popular in the United States, largely because the laws of many states prohibit the employment of hawks to kill game. The birds, usually peregrine falcons, employed by falconers are taken when young from their nests. They are subjected to a rigorous course of training, in which they learn to fly, when released, at the quarry; to leave the prey untouched after killing it; and to sit quietly, when hooded, on the falconer's wrist. See W. F. Russell, Jr., *Falconry* (1940); Frank Illingworth, *Falcons and Falconry* (2d ed. 1964).

Falerii (fəlēr'ēī), ancient city of Etruria, Italy, W of the Tiber River. It was the capital of the Faliscans, a tribe who fought with the Etruscans against Rome. Falerii fell to Rome in 241 B.C. Modern Civita Castellana is on the site.

Faliero or **Falier, Marino** (mārē'nō fälyā'rō, fälyār'), 1274–1355, doge of Venice (1354–55). As commander of Venetian forces he defeated (1346) Louis I of Hungary at Zara, and later he held high diplomatic posts. Soon after his election as doge, the Genoese triumphed over the Venetians. The new doge, at odds with patricians who had insulted his family, joined dissatisfied plebeians in a conspiracy to assassinate the nobles, overthrow the oligarchy, and make Faliero dictator. The plot was discovered; Faliero and his accomplices, tried by the Council of Ten (see TEN, COUNCIL OF), were executed. Faliero's life has inspired works by Byron, Swinburne, Delavigne, Delacroix, and Donizetti.

Faliscan (fəlĭs'kən), extinct language belonging to the Italic subfamily of the Indo-European family of languages. See ITALIC LANGUAGES.

Falkberget, Johan (yō'hän fälk'bĕrgə), 1879–1967, Norwegian novelist. Falkberget's early poverty and toil in the mines colored all his works. The trilogies *Christianus Sextus* (1927–35) and *Bread of Night* (1940–50) concern mining life in the 17th and 18th cent. They emphasize the virtues of hard work and Christian love. Falkberget's other works include *Lisbeth of Jarnfjeld* (1915, tr. 1930), *Fourth Night Watch* (tr. 1968), poems, and memoirs.

Falkenhayn, Erich von (ā'rĭkh fən fäl'kənhīn), 1861–1922, German military officer. Minister of war from 1906 to 1915, he succeeded (1914) MOLTKE as chief of the German general staff. He was successful on the Eastern front during World War I, but after the disaster at Verdun (1916) he was replaced (Aug., 1916) by HINDENBURG. Falkenhayn later commanded (1916) the invasion of Rumania, and in 1917 led German reinforcements in Palestine.

Falkirk (fôl'kûrk), burgh (1971 pop. 37,587), Stirlingshire, central Scotland. The local coal and iron mines have been exhausted, but fireclay is still mined and the metal products industry (aluminium and metal casting) remains important. Concrete, chemicals, and hosiery are also produced. Livestock fairs (including the "trysts of Falkirk") have been held for centuries. Carron, c.2 mi (3 km) to the north, is well known for its ironworks. GRANGEMOUTH is Falkirk's port. In the first battle of Falkirk (1298), said to be the first battle in which the longbow was decisive, Edward I and the English defeated the Scots led by Sir William WALLACE. In 1746, during the Jacobite uprising, Gen. Henry Hawley was defeated there by Prince Charles Edward and his Highlanders (see SCOTLAND). In 1975, Falkirk became part of the Central region.

Falkland, Lucius Cary, 2d Viscount (fôk'lənd), 1610?–1643, English statesman and literary figure. He entered Parliament in 1640, where he opposed the exaction of ship money and spoke in favor of the attainder of the earl of STRAFFORD. However, he objected to the abolition of the episcopacy and in 1642 became an adviser to Charles I. He represented the king in attempts to make peace with Parliament in Sept., 1642, and was with Charles at Edgehill and the siege of Gloucester. In despair at the prospect of the civil war continuing, he is supposed to have deliberately allowed himself to be killed at the battle of Newbury. A poet in his own right, Falkland was also a liberal patron of many of his literary contemporaries. See biography by J. A. R. Marriott (1907); study by Kurt Weber (1940).

Falkland Islands (fôk'lənd), Span. *Islas Malvinas,* group of islands (1970 est. pop. 2,045), 4,618 sq mi (11,961 sq km), S Atlantic, c.300 mi (480 km) E of the Strait of Magellan. The islands are administered as a British crown colony with the capital at Stanley. There are two large islands (East Falkland and West Falkland) and some 200 small ones. Dependencies of the colony, scattered down into Antarctica, include SOUTH GEORGIA, the South Orkney Islands, the South Sandwich Islands, the South Shetland Islands, and Graham Land. The Falklands proper are rather bleak, rocky moorlands, swept by wind and drenched by chill rain. They are, however, flourishing sheep-raising centers. Whales and seals abound in the littoral waters and are hunted for oil and skins; guano is also exported. The British claim is based on probable discovery by the navigator John DAVIS in 1592; but the islands were claimed and occupied at various times by England, Spain, France, and Argentina. When the seizure of an American sealing vessel in 1832 led to a U.S. punitive expedition, the British, claiming sovereignty, occupied the islands. However, Argentina and Chile still claim them. Near the Falklands, in one of the most stirring naval engagements of World War I, the British under Sir Frederick Sturdee destroyed (Dec. 8, 1914) a German squadron under Graf von SPEE.

Falkner, William: see FAULKNER, WILLIAM.

Falköping (fäl'chö"pĭng), city (1970 pop. 14,780), Skaraborg co., S Sweden, between lakes Vänern and Vättern. It is a commercial and industrial center. Manufactures include textiles and cement. There are numerous prehistoric remains, including burial mounds and stone monuments. Nearby, in 1389, Margaret of Denmark defeated and captured Albert of Mecklenburg, the king of Sweden.

Fall, Albert Bacon, 1861–1944, American cabinet official, b. Frankfort, Ky. He became a rancher in New Mexico and a political leader in that state. Elected to the U.S. Senate in 1912, he served there until President Harding made him Secretary of the Interior in 1921. Fall was one of the chief figures in the scandal concerning oil lands that rocked the Republican administration (see TEAPOT DOME). He resigned in 1923 and was later tried and found guilty (1931) of conspiracy to defraud the government.

fall, the, i.e., the fall of man, in Christian thought: see ORIGINAL SIN; GRACE.

Falla, Manuel de (mänwĕl' dā fä'lyä), 1876–1946, Spanish composer; pupil of Felipe Pedrell. In Paris from 1907 to 1914, he met Debussy, Dukas, and Ravel, and was to some extent influenced by their impressionism. His music, however, remained distinctively Spanish, rooted both in Andalusian folk music and the classical tradition of Spain. Falla was an authority on flamenco music and made use of it in his compositions, keeping the vitality of flamenco but imposing upon it rigorous musical structure. Notable among his compositions are an opera, *La vida breve* (*Life is Short,* 1913); a suite for piano and orchestra, *Noches en los jardines de España* (*Nights in the Gardens of Spain,* 1916); and the celebrated ballets *El Amor Brujo* (*Wedded by Witchcraft,* 1915) and *El sombrero de tres picos* (*The Three-Cornered Hat,* 1917). From 1921 to 1939 Falla lived in Granada, organizing festivals of native folk songs and touring Europe to conduct his own works. He moved to Argentina in 1939, where he directed the first performance of his guitar solo, *Homenajes* (1920–39). His ambitious choral work *La Atlántida* occupied his later years; it was finished after his death by Ernesto Halffter and presented in Madrid in 1961. See Gilbert Chase, *The Music of Spain* (1960) and Susanne Demarquez, *Manuel de Falla* (tr. 1968).

fallacy, in logic, a term used to characterize an invalid argument. Strictly speaking, it refers only to the transition from a set of premises to a conclusion, and is distinguished from falsity, a value attributed to a single statement. The laws of syllogism were systematically elaborated by Aristotle, and for an argument to be valid, it must adhere to all the laws; to be fallacious, it need only break one (see SYLLOGISM). The term *fallacy* has come to be used in a somewhat wider sense than the purely formal one. Informal fallacies are said to occur when statements are ambiguous or vague as to the logical form they represent, or when a multiplicity of meaning is present and the validity of the argument depends on switching meanings of a word or a phrase in midstream.

Fallada, Hans (häns fä'lädä), pseud. of **Rudolf Ditzen** (ro͞o'dôlf dĭt'sən), 1893–1947, German novelist. *Little Man, What Now?* (1932, tr. 1933), his story of a young couple in Germany after World War I, was an immediate international success. It was followed by *The World Outside* (1934, tr. 1934), *Once We Had a Child* (1934, tr. 1935), and *Jeder stirbt für sich allein* [each man dies his own death] (1947). Fallada's work belongs to the 20th-century school of fiction that expressed its intellectual detachment from man's fate in words and a style intended to suppress emotional connotations.

fallen arches: see FLAT FOOT.

Fallen Timbers, battle fought in 1794 between Indian tribes of the Northwest Territory and the U.S. army commanded by Anthony WAYNE; it took place in NW Ohio at the rapids of the Maumee River just southwest of present-day Toledo. The Indian defeat hastened the collapse of Indian resistance in the area, secured the northwest frontier, and demonstrated the strength of the new national government. The battleground is now the site of a state historical monument.

Fallières, Armand (ärmäN' fälyĕr'), 1841–1931, president of the French republic (1906–13). A lawyer, he became a member of the chamber of deputies in 1876. He was a member of various cabinets from 1882 to 1892, served briefly as premier, and was also president of the senate. He succeeded Émile Loubet as president.

falling star: see METEOR.

fall line, boundary between an upland region and a coastal plain across which rivers from the upland region drop to the plain in falls or rapids. A fall line is formed in an area where the rivers from the upland region drop to the plain in falls or rapids. A fall line is formed in an area where the rivers have eroded away the soft rocks of a coastal plain more quickly than the older harder rocks of an upland region. Seagoing vessels cannot travel beyond a fall line and their cargoes must be unloaded there. The falls also supply water power for the development of industry. For these reasons a fall line is marked in developed areas, such as the eastern piedmont of the United States, by a band of commercial and industrial cities of an importance rivaling that of the ports. Typical fall-line cities on the Atlantic coast of the United States are Lowell, Mass.; Pawtucket, R.I.; Troy, N.Y.; Trenton, N.J.; Georgetown, now part of Washington, D.C.; Richmond, Va.; Raleigh, N.C.; Columbia, S.C.; and Augusta, Ga. Louisville, Ky., and Minneapolis, Minn., are among the fall-line cities of the Mississippi valley.

fallopian tube (fəlō'pēən), either of a pair of tubes extending from the uterus to the paired ovaries in the human female, also called oviducts. At one end the long, slender fallopian tube opens into the uterus; the other end expands into a funnel shape near the ovary. The epithelium that lines the tube is covered with cilia that beat continuously toward the uterus. When an ovum is expelled into the peritoneal cavity from the ovary during ovulation, it is propelled into the wide-mouthed opening of the fallopian tube, through the tube, and into the uterus by the wavelike motion of the cilia. If the ovum is fertilized, an event that normally takes place in the fallopian tube, and the embryo (fertilized ovum) implants in the tube, or another area outside the uterus, an ectopic pregnancy occurs. About 98% of ectopic implantations occur in the tubes, but other sites include the abdomen, ovary, and cervix. Immediate surgical removal of the products of conception is necessary to prevent hemorrhage and other complications resulting from ectopic pregnancy. The fallopian tubes are also the site of the most common surgical procedures used to prevent conception or cause sterility in women. Usually the tubes are tied off in a procedure known as tubal ligation, although they are also sometimes excised or occluded by other methods. See REPRODUCTIVE SYSTEM.

Fallopius (fəlō'pēəs), Ital. *Gabriello* or *Gabriele Fallopio* (gäbrĕĕl'lō, gäbrĕä'lä fäl-lō'pyō), 1523–62, Italian anatomist; pupil and successor of Andreas Vesalius and teacher of Hieronymous Fabricius at Padua. His important discoveries include the fallopian tubes, leading from uterus to ovaries. His collected works were published at Venice in 1584.

fallout, minute particles of radioactive material produced by nuclear explosions (see ATOMIC BOMB; HYDROGEN BOMB) and scattered throughout the earth's atmosphere by winds and convection currents. Heavier fallout particles tend to settle to earth around the explosion site and downwind from it soon after the explosion. Lighter particles may stay in the atmosphere for years. Radioactive decay products in fallout include strontium-90, potassium-40, carbon-14, and iodine-131. They may contaminate food supplies if taken up by plants and animals or contaminate water supplies by falling into streams. If they accumulate in the human system, they can form concentrated internal sources of dangerous radiation. Fallout may thus be a cause of leukemia, bone cancer, and other diseases. It can also cause genetic damage.

fallow land, cropland that is not seeded for a season; it may or may not be plowed. The land may be cultivated or chemically treated for control of weeds and other pests or may be left unaltered. Allowing land to lie fallow serves to accumulate moisture in dry regions (see DRY FARMING) or to check weeds and plant diseases. As a method of restoring productivity, ROTATION OF CROPS is now preferred to fallowing, which is considered wasteful of humus and nitrogen.

Fallows, Samuel, 1835–1922, American clergyman, bishop of the Reformed Episcopal Church, b. England, grad. Univ. of Wisconsin, 1859. He served with the Union army in the Civil War and afterward held Methodist pastorates in Milwaukee. In 1875 he joined the Reformed Episcopal Church, a dissident sect that had broken away from the Protestant Episcopal Church. He became a bishop in 1876. He was known as a leader who directed public improvement in education, in prison reform, and in the fight for temperance. See biography by A. K. Fallows, *Everybody's Bishop* (1927).

Fall River, industrial city (1970 pop. 96,898), Bristol co., SE Mass., a port of entry on Mt. Hope Bay, at the mouth of the Taunton River; settled 1656, set off from Freetown 1803, inc. as a city 1854. It was once the foremost cotton textile center in the United States, and textiles and clothing are still leading manufactures. The city's industries have greatly diversified, however, and a wide variety of products are made. In the American Revolution, Fall River was the scene (1778) of a skirmish between British and American forces. The first cotton mill there was built in 1811; Fall River's climate, excellent harbor, and access to water power contributed to its growth as a great textile center. The Bradford Durfee College of Technology (state supported) is in Fall River. The U.S.S. *Massachusetts,* the state's official World War II memorial, is berthed in the harbor. The city was the scene (1892) of the famous murder trial of Lizzie Borden, who was born and lived in Fall River.

Falls Church, independent city (1970 pop. 10,772), NE Va., a residential suburb of Washington, D.C.; inc. as a town 1875, as a city 1948. George Washington and George Mason (author of the Virginia Bill of Rights) were members of the vestry of the Falls Church (built 1767–69).

Falmouth (făl'məth), municipal borough (1971 pop. 17,883), Cornwall, SW England, on a small peninsula between Falmouth Bay and Carrick Roads estuary. Falmouth is a port, a resort, and the headquarters of the Royal Cornwall Yacht Club. China clay is exported from the excellent port. There are oyster fisheries and engineering and ship repairing industries. The climate is unusually warm; subtropical plants thrive. The harbor entrance is guarded by Pendennis Castle on the west and St. Mawes Castle on the east (both 16th cent.). Baron Fairfax of Cameron took the town in 1646 after a five-month siege of Pendennis Castle in the ENGLISH CIVIL WAR. The fall of the castle signaled the defeat of the royalists in Cornwall and the end of the civil war there.

Falmouth, town (1970 pop. 15,942), Barnstable co., SE Mass., on Cape Cod; settled c.1660, inc. 1686. Once a whaling and boatbuilding center, it is now a popular boating and summer resort. Falmouth was attacked by the British in the Revolutionary War and again in the War of 1812. Historic structures include the Ship's Bottom Roof House (1678); the Congregational church on the town green (1756; restored), with a bell cast by Paul Revere; and the Julia Wood House (1790), with a historical museum. The town includes the community of Woods Hole, seat of the Oceanographic Institution and Marine Biological Laboratories.

False Cross, in astronomy: see CARINA.

False Decretals (dĭkrē'təlz), collection of documents, partly spurious, treating of CANON LAW. It was published between 847 and 852 probably in France, either at Rheims or in the province of Tours (specifically at Le Mans), and composed by a man who called himself Isidore Mercator (hence the term Pseudo-Isidorian Decretals); the date is based on external evidence, the place chiefly on internal evidence. The collection was made to reform canon law and to support bishops in their perennial struggle against secular interference by conferring ancient legal sanction on episcopal demands for freedom from secular courts and from usurpation of diocesan properties on bare accusation. It gave sanction instead to the direct dependence of bishops on the Holy See without mediation of metropolitans and archbishops. The effect of the False Decretals was great in the Middle Ages, especially in their application to individual cases in France. In general they were accepted to some extent by the Holy See in support of its age-old claims. By incorporation and quotation in the *Decretum* of GRATIAN the False Decretals received a definite authority in textbooks of canon law in the Middle Ages. The False Decretals have gained their chief fame because they were one of the great forgeries of history. Included in the collection are 60 letters or decrees of popes from Clement I to Melchiades (d. 314), of which 58 are forged; an original essay on the early church and the Council of Nicaea, with canons of 54 councils, of which all canons but one are authentic or were accepted as authentic long before the author's time; and a collection of papal letters from the 4th to 8th cent., of which the majority are authentic. The forgeries are supported by liberal interlarding with quotations from authentic letters and by attribution to popes whose letters were known to be lost. The False Decretals were criticized almost from their inception until their complete exposure in the 16th cent.; among the many critics were Cardinal Nicholas of Cusa and Juan de Torquemada. The interpretation of the collection according to proper historical methods was not really begun until the 19th cent. See study by E. H. Davenport (1916).

false imprisonment, complete restraint upon a person's liberty of movement without legal justification. Actual physical contact is not necessary; a show of authority or a threat of force is sufficient. The person falsely imprisoned may sue the offender for damages. The suit would be brought against officials improperly issuing warrants for arrest and against private persons for any illegal total restraint of liberty. Release from such illegal restraint may be had through a HABEAS CORPUS proceeding. See KIDNAPPING.

false Solomon's-seal: see SOLOMON'S-SEAL.

false sunbird: see SUNBIRD.

falsetto (fôlsĕt'tō) [Ital.,=diminutive of *false*], high-pitched, unnatural tones above the normal register of the male VOICE, produced, according to some theories, by the vibration of only the edges of the larynx. Some male altos are tenors skilled in the use of falsetto. Falsetto tone is usually thin and expressionless, but can be used with good effect.

Falster (fäl'stər), island (1965 pop. 45,906), 198 sq mi (513 sq km), Storstrøm co., SE Denmark, in the Baltic Sea. Nykøbing is the chief city. The island's southern tip, Gedser Odde, is the southernmost point in Denmark. Falster has much fertile soil; sugar beets, fruit, and grain are the main crops. The island's east coast is a summer resort area.

Falun (fä'lŭn"), city (1970 pop. 38,358), capital of Kopparberg co., S central Sweden; chartered 1614. It is the headquarters of Sweden's oldest company, the Stora Kopparbergs Bergslags Aktiebolag, founded (1347) to operate the copper mines of Falun (now largely exhausted). The company, which helped considerably to finance Gustav II's campaigns during the Thirty Years War (1618–48), is still one of Sweden's largest, holding wide interests in iron, steel, lumber, paper, and mining industries as well as in hydroelectric power. Of note in Falun is a 17th-century church, the Kristine Kyrka.

Famagusta (fämägōō'stä), Gr. *Ammochostos,* city (1968 est. pop. 124,500), E Cyprus, on Famagusta Bay. It is the center of an administrative district and the chief port of the island. The main export is citrus fruit. About two thirds of the population is Greek. Famagusta occupies the site of ancient Arsinoë, built (3d cent. B.C.) by Ptolemy II. After the fall (1291) of Acre to the Saracens, Christian refugees greatly increased the city's wealth. The seat (15th-16th cent.) of the Venetian governors of Cyprus, it was strongly fortified by the Venetians; the governor's palace, the Cathedral of St. Nicholas, and many churches testify to its medieval splendor. As a British naval base the city was heavily bombed in World War II, and from 1946 to 1948 a British internment camp for illegal Jewish immigrants to Palestine was maintained near the city. Famagusta is thought to be the scene of Acts II through V of Shakespeare's *Othello.*

Familists (făm'ĭlĭsts), religious community founded in Friesland in the 16th cent. by Hendrik Niclaes. Niclaes, a merchant of Münster and originally a Roman Catholic, claimed to have been chosen prophet and prepared by special outpouring of the "spirit of the true love of Jesus Christ." His teachings combined elements of German mysticism with Anabaptist doctrines and the ethic of religious perfection. Making Emden his headquarters, he spread his beliefs, travelling much, particularly in Flanders and England. At Emden was first established (c.1540) the Family of Love, as his community was called. It held that the divine spirit of love within it placed it above Bible, creeds, liturgy, and law. However, since no specific form of worship was prescribed, many of its members remained in the Roman communion. They were, however, bound together into a hierarchical communistic organization. In 1560, Niclaes had to leave Emden, and he escaped to England. There his movement gained adherents although its emotionalism was frowned upon by the orthodox. There was some government procedure against them under Elizabeth I and James I. Although the sect died out in the 17th cent., it strongly influenced similar radical groups.

family, in taxonomy: see CLASSIFICATION.

family, in its narrowest sense, social group consisting of parents and their children. This is the nuclear, or conjugal, family, which has been found in most societies either as the sole existing form or as the basic unit in a broader system. Anthropological hypotheses of the 19th cent. asserting a primitive stage of group marriage or promiscuity have been largely discredited. The primary functions of the family are reproductive, economic, and educational; it is through his immediate kin that the child first absorbs the culture of his group. In preindustrial societies, the ties of kinship are strong; they bind the individual both to the family of orientation, into which one is born, and to the family of procreation, which one founds at marriage and which includes one's spouse's relatives. The nuclear family may be extended through the acquisition of more than one spouse (polygamy), or through the common residence of two or more married couples and their children or of several generations connected in the male or female line. This is called the extended family; it is widespread in many parts of the world, especially in pastoral and agricultural economies. The patriarchal family, which prevailed among the ancient Hebrews, Greeks, and Romans, is often associated with polygyny (see MARRIAGE). In Rome, the paterfamilias was the only person recognized as an independent individual under the law. He possessed all religious rights as priest of the family ancestor cult and all economic rights as sole owner of the family property, real and personal. In his power of life and death over the members of the family, including slaves, he exercised the functions of a monarch. At his death, his name, property, and authority descended to his male heirs. The Roman system was transferred in many of its details into both the canon and secular law of Western Europe and was little modified until the 19th cent., when the Western nations began to grant women equal rights with men with respect to the ownership of property (see HUSBAND AND WIFE), the control of children (see PARENT AND CHILD), divorce, and the like. The state has also intervened to modify the authority of parents over their children. At the same time, education has shifted increasingly from the household to the school. The effect has been to loosen traditional family ties. Another factor affecting the modern European-American family was the Industrial Revolution, which has removed from the home to the factory many economic tasks, such as baking, spinning, and weaving, that once made for family cooperation. Economic and social conditions have discouraged the presence of the husband and father in the home; in industrial communities the wife and mother is often employed outside the home, leaving the children to be cared for by others. Sociologists and psychologists find in these changed relations of the members of the family to each other and of the family to the community at large the germ of maladjustments that need to be resolved and are thought to have a bearing on many problems connected with education, divorce, mental health, and juvenile delinquency. See also DIVORCE. See W. J. Goode, *The Family* (1964); Bernard Farber, ed., *Kinship and Family Organization* (1966); W. F. Kenkel *The Family in Perspective* (2d ed. 1966); Ruth Cavan, *The American Family* (4th ed. 1969); R. H. Klemer, *Marriage and Family Relationships* (1970); S. A. Queen and J. B. Adams, *The Family in Various Cultures* (3d ed. 1970); Peter Laslett, *Household and Family in Past Time* (1972); E. B. Sheldon, *Family Economic Behavior* (1973).

Family Compact, several alliances between France and Spain in the form of agreements between the French and Spanish branches of the Bourbon family. The first of the three compacts, the Treaty of the Escorial (1733), was continued and extended by the second agreement (1743). The third, and most important, of the treaties was that of 1761. Both England and France sought Spanish support in the SEVEN YEARS WAR, but England's attack on Spanish colonies and shipping alienated Charles III of Spain and the king rejected the English offer in favor of the proposal made by the French minister the duc de Choiseul. The pact, which dealt with political and commercial relations and with the entry of Spain into the war, also included the Bourbon ruler of the Two Sicilies and the Infante Philip, duke of Parma. Spain entered the war (1762) but was of small use to France; the economic and political provisions of the pact proved more enduring than the military ones.

Family Compact, name popularly applied to a small, powerful group of men who dominated the government of Upper Canada (Ontario) from the closing years of the 18th cent. to the beginnings of responsible government under the Baldwin-LaFontaine Reform ministry (1848–51). The group, some of whose members belonged to the same family and most of whom were men of wealth, controlled the legislative and executive councils, had a virtual monopoly of political office, and strongly influenced banking, education, the issuing of land grants, the affairs of the Anglican church in Canada, and the courts. New settlers from Great Britain and the United States, finding themselves denied political opportunity, were drawn into an opposition movement, which in time became the Reform party. Religious differences embittered the struggle, since the Family Compact (the term first appeared c.1828) was composed almost entirely of members of the Church of England. The Chateau Clique was the name given to a similar powerful group in French Lower Canada. See G. M. Craig, *Upper Canada: The Formative Years, 1784–1841* (1963).

fan, device for agitating air or gases or moving them from one location to another. Mechanical fans with revolving blades are used for ventilation, in manufacturing, in winnowing grain, to remove dust, cuttings, or other waste, or to provide draft for a fire. They are also used to move air for cooling purposes, as in automotive engines and air-conditioning systems, and are driven by belts or by direct motor. The axial-flow fan (e.g., an electric table fan) has blades that force air to move parallel to the shaft about which the blades rotate. The centrifugal fan has a moving component, called an impeller, that consists of a central shaft about which a set of blades form a spiral pattern. When the impeller rotates, air that enters the fan near the shaft is moved away perpendicularly from the shaft and out of an opening in the scroll-shaped fan casing. As a light, flat instrument manipulated by hand to cool the body or ward off insects, the fan is of tropical origin and probably stems from the primitive use of palm or other leaves. The long-handled, disk-shaped fan carried by attendants was from ancient times associated with regal and religious ceremonies. In China an early form of the hand fan was a row of feathers mounted in the end of a handle; in Greece linen was often stretched over a leaf-shaped frame; and in Rome wooden fans, gilded and painted, were used. In Europe during the Middle Ages the fan virtually disappeared until the 13th and 14th cent., when Oriental fans were brought back by Crusaders and became fashionable for the wealthy. After 1500 the fan became generally popular; flag fans, disk-shaped fans, and tuft fans of ostrich plumes or peacock feathers, with handles of carved ivory or gold set with jewels, were common in women's wardrobes. In c.1600 the folding fan, developed in medieval Japan and introduced into Europe by way of China, became popular. The slats, of ivory, bone, mica, mother-of-pearl, or tortoise shell, were delicately carved and covered with paper or fabric. The fan reached a high degree of artistry, especially in France, in the 17th and 18th cent. Delicately folded fans of lace, silk, or parchment were decorated with original designs and paintings by contemporary artists. The management of the fan became a highly regarded feminine art. The function and employment of the fan reached its high point of social significance in Japan.

Fanar and **Fanariots:** see PHANAR.

fandango (făndăng'gō), ancient Spanish dance, probably of Moorish origin, that came into Europe in the 17th cent. It is in triple time and is danced by a single couple to the accompaniment of castanets, guitar, and songs sung by the dancers. At the end of certain measures, the music halts abruptly and the dancers remain rigid until it is resumed.

Faneuil Hall (făn'əl, făn'yəl), public market and hall in Boston, Mass. Given to the city by the merchant Peter Faneuil in 1742, the building burned in 1761 but was rebuilt. The scene of Revolutionary meetings, it became known as "the cradle of liberty." Charles Bulfinch enlarged the hall in 1806. The building is still in use as market, meeting hall, and museum.

Fanfani, Amintore (äměntô'rä fänfän'ē), 1908–, Italian political leader, a Christian Democrat. A noted scholar, he held several cabinet posts after World War II and was premier briefly in 1954 and in 1958–59. He was secretary of the Christian Democratic party from 1954 to 1959 and became premier again in 1960; in 1962 he succeeded in reorganizing his cabinet to include the Social Democrats, with the parliamentary support of the Socialist party headed by Pietro Nenni. His cabinet fell in April, 1963. A strong supporter of the European Economic Community, Fanfani was foreign minister in 1965 and in 1966–68. He entered the senate in 1968 and served as its president. In 1973, he resigned from that post to again become secretary of the Christian Democratic party.

Fannin, James Walker, 1804?-1836, hero in the Texas revolution, b. Georgia. Having been adopted by his maternal grandfather, he attended West Point (1819-21) under the name of James F. Walker but did not graduate. In 1834 he settled in Texas. An influential agitator in the preliminaries of the revolution, he eagerly advocated an expedition into Mexican territory, but the idea met with much opposition, particularly that of Gen. Sam Houston. With Houston occupied elsewhere and the governor removed, Fannin was left without orders or support. His force never got beyond Goliad, and in the delays there he realized the precariousness of his position in the face of the rapid Mexican advance. He retreated, but too late to prevent the capture of his small force after a hopeless battle (March, 1836). Soon after the surrender most of Fannin's men, including Fannin himself, were shot at the order of Santa Anna.

Fanning, David, c.1755-1825, American Loyalist in the American Revolution, b. Amelia co., Va. He led raids on the colonials in the Carolinas and wrote (1790) an account of his adventures in *The Narrative of Colonel David Fanning,* first published in 1861. He later served (1791-1801) in the provincial parliament of New Brunswick, Canada.

Fanning, Edmund, 1739-1818, American Loyalist in the American Revolution, b. Suffolk co., Long Island, N.Y. He moved to North Carolina, practiced law, held minor political posts, and supported the royal governor, William Tryon. Fanning was the special object of contempt for the rebels of the REGULATOR MOVEMENT. He went as Tryon's secretary to New York where he held offices. In 1775 he raised a Loyalist regiment that fought in partisan actions in the New York area throughout the war. After the Revolution he was lieutenant governor of Nova Scotia (1783-86) and lieutenant governor of Prince Edward Island (1786-1805). Fanning spent his last years in England.

Fanning, Edmund, 1769-1841, American trader, explorer, and promoter of trade and exploration in the South Seas, b. Stonington, Conn. At the age of 14 he went to sea. In command of a trading vessel, he realized a large profit from an expedition in 1797-98. In the course of the voyage he traded a cargo of trinkets for seal skins in the islands off the coast of Chile and exchanged them for valuable Chinese goods at Canton, returning around the Cape of Good Hope. During the expedition he discovered Fanning Island, Washington Island, and other islands. Convinced of the profits to be made from trade in the South Seas, he became the agent for a group of New York City merchants, supervising over 70 expeditions and participating in some of them. His *Voyages around the World* (1833), which shed light on some of the little-known parts of the globe, passed through several editions.

Fanning Island, atoll (1968 pop. 376), c.15 sq mi (40 sq km), central Pacific, one of the LINE ISLANDS and part of the British colony of the GILBERT AND ELLICE ISLANDS. Discovered by the American explorer Edmund FANNING in 1798, it was annexed by Great Britain in 1889, and became a part of the colony in 1916. Copra is the only export.

Fano (fä'nō), city (1971 pop. 47,871), in the Marche, central Italy, on the Adriatic Sea. It is a fishing port, a seaside resort, and an agricultural and silk-manufacturing center. An important town in Roman times, it was the scene of a victory by Rome over Carthage (207 B.C.). Fano was destroyed by the Goths in the 6th cent. A.D. but later flourished under the Malatesta family of Rimini. It was under papal control from the mid-15th cent. to 1860. The first printing press in Italy to use Arabic type was set up (1514) in Fano. Noteworthy structures include the Arch of Augustus (1st cent. A.D.), the Malatesta palace, and the Church of Santa Maria Nuova (16th-18th cent.).

Fanon, Frantz Omar (fräNts ômär' fänôN'), 1925-61, French West Indian psychiatrist, author, and leader of the Algerian National Front, b. Martinique. Educated in France, he went to Algeria (1953) to practice psychiatry. Sympathetic to the Algerian revolution from its inception (1954), Fanon resigned his medical post (1956) to become editor of the Algerian National Front's newspaper. His first book, *Black Skin, White Masks* (1952, tr. 1967), is a psychoanalytic study of black life in the white-dominated world. In the *Wretched of the Earth* (1961, tr. 1963), considered to be his most important work, Fanon calls for an anticolonial revolution led by the peasants, rather than the proletariat, of the Third World. According to Fanon, a new breed of man, modern yet proud of his nonwhite heritage, will emerge from this struggle. See biographies by David Caute (1970) and I. L. Gendzier (1973).

Fanshawe, Sir Richard, 1608-66, English diplomat and man of letters. He was secretary to the ambassador to Spain (1635-38) and chargé d'affaires there (1638). During the English civil war he served Prince Charles (after 1649 Charles II) in England, Ireland, and on the Continent until his own capture (1651) at Worcester. In subsequent retirement Fanshawe made the best-known of his many translations, *The Luciad* (1655), an English verse translation of Luis de Camões's masterpiece. After the Restoration he was sent (1661) on a mission to Portugal and served as ambassador to Portugal (1662-63), privy councilor, and ambassador to Spain (1664-66). See his translation of *The Luciad* (ed. by J. D. M. Ford, 1940).

Fan Si Pan (fäN sē päN), peak, 10,312 ft (3,143 m) high, on the divide between the Red and Black rivers, NW North Vietnam, near the Chinese border. It is the highest point in North Vietnam.

fan tan, card game for three to eight players using a regular deck. All cards are dealt after each player antes (pays) one chip into a pool. Play rotates to the left and if a player cannot play a card he must ante into the pool. Sevens must be played first. These are set (or foundation) cards, and sequences up to the king or down to the ace are formed. Play ends when any player gets rid of the last card in his hand.

fantasia (făntä'zhə) [Ital.,=fancy], musical composition not restricted to a formal design, but constructed freely in the manner of an improvisation. In the 16th and 17th cent., however, the term designated a contrapuntal piece employing IMITATION and thus was one of the forerunners of the FUGUE. The term is also applied to improvisatory pieces based on earlier works, e.g., Vaughan Williams's *Fantasia on "Greensleeves."*

Fanti (făn'tē, fän'-), black African ethnic group, S Ghana, living around Cape Coast and Elmina, one of the Akan peoples. The Fanti speak a Twi language, which is part of the Kwa group, and number about 250,000. Inheritance and succession to public office are determined mostly by matrilineal descent. According to their oral traditions, the Fanti arrived in their present habitat from the north by the 17th cent. They served as middlemen in the commerce between the interior and British and Dutch traders on the coast. In the early 18th cent. the Fanti formed a confederation, primarily as a means of protection against ASHANTI incursions from the interior. Several Fanti-Ashanti wars followed. The Fanti were aided by the British, who, however, destroyed the strong Fanti confederation established between 1868 and 1872, believing it a threat to their hegemony on the coast. In 1874 a joint Fanti-British army defeated Ashanti, and in the same year the Fanti became part of the British Gold Coast colony.

Fantin-Latour, Ignace Henri Jean Théodore (ēgnäs' äNrē' zhäN' tēōdôr' făNtăN'-lätōōr'), 1836-1904, French painter and lithographer. He is best known for his portrait groups of famous contemporaries. Notable examples are *The Studio at Batignolles, Hommage à Delacroix,* and *Around the Piano* (all: Louvre). His famous portrait of Manet is in the Chicago Art Institute. Influenced by Courbet, he depicted his friends with an almost photographic technique. He is also admired for still-life paintings of flowers in which the transitory aspect of their beauty is revealed.

Farabi, al- (äl-färä'bē), d. 950, Arab philosopher. He studied in Baghdad and later flourished in Aleppo as a sufi mystic (see SUFISM). He died in Damascus. Al-Farabi was the author of an encyclopedic work drawn largely from Aristotle; he was one of the earliest Islamic thinkers to develop a philosophical method reconciling Aristotle and Islam. In his own philosophy he is clearly influenced by NEOPLATONISM, especially that of the Greek school of Alexandria. A renowned musician, he is considered the greatest Arab music theorist. He is known in the West by the name Alfarabius. See Nicholas Rescher, *Al-Farabi: An Annotated Bibliography* (1962).

farad (făr'əd) [for Michael Faraday], unit of electrical CAPACITANCE, equivalent to 1 coulomb of stored charge per volt of applied potential difference.

Faraday, Michael (făr'ədē, -dā''), 1791-1867, English scientist. Apprenticed to a bookbinder at the age of 14, he had little formal education, but acquired a store of scientific knowledge through reading and by attending lectures by Sir Humphry Davy. In 1813 he became assistant to Davy at the Royal Institution in London. He was made a member of the institution in 1823 and a fellow of the Royal Society in 1824. In 1825 he became director of the laboratory, and from 1833 he was Fullerian professor of chemistry at the Royal Institution. He declined knighthood and the presidency of the Royal Society. His experiments yielded some of the most significant principles and inventions in scientific history. He developed the first dynamo (in the form of a copper disk rotated between the poles of a permanent magnet), the precursor of modern dynamos and generators. From his discovery of electromagnetic INDUCTION (1831) stemmed a vast development of electrical machinery for industry. In 1825, Faraday discovered the compound benzene. In addition to other contributions he did research on ELECTROLYSIS, formulating FARADAY'S LAW. He laid the foundations of the classical field theory, later fully developed by J. C. Maxwell. Some of his works were collected as *Experimental Researches in Electricity* (3 vol., 1839-55) and *Experimental Researches in Chemistry and Physics* (1859). See his diary (ed. by Thomas Martin, 7 vol., 1932-36); his correspondence (ed. by L. P. Williams, 2 vol., 1971); biographies by Thomas Martin (1934) and L. P. Williams (1965).

Faraday's law, physical law stating that the number of MOLES of substance produced at an electrode during ELECTROLYSIS is directly proportional to the number of moles of electrons transferred at that electrode; the law is named for Michael Faraday, who formulated it in 1834. The amount of electric CHARGE carried by one mole of electrons (6.02×10^{23} electrons) is called the faraday and is equal to 96,500 COULOMBS. The number of faradays required to produce one mole of substance at an electrode depends upon the way in which the substance is oxidized or reduced (see OXIDATION AND REDUCTION). For example, in the electrolysis of molten sodium chloride, NaCl, one faraday, or one mole, of electrons is transferred at the cathode to one mole of sodium ions, Na^+, to form one mole of sodium atoms, Na, while in the electrolysis of molten magnesium chloride, $MgCl_2$, two faradays of electrons must be transferred at the cathode to reduce one mole of magnesium ions, Mg^{+2}, to one mole of magnesium atoms, Mg.

Farah (färä'), town (1969 est. pop. 29,000), capital of Farah and Chakhansur prov., W Afghanistan, on the Farah River. Surrounded by a solid earth rampart, it is strategically located at the river crossing that controls the road from Herat to the Seistan region and the Indian subcontinent. The town also lies on the Herat-Kandahar trade route and is a market for the products of the surrounding agricultural region. Farah is inhabited mostly by Tadzhiks. Generally identified with ancient Phra, it flourished until Mongols destroyed it in 1221. It revived but suffered renewed devastation by the Persian ruler Nadir Shah in 1737.

farce, light, comic theatrical piece in which the characters and events are greatly exaggerated to produce broad, simple humor. Early examples of farce can be found in the comedies of Aristophanes, Plautus, and Terence. During the Middle Ages the term farce designated interpolations made in the church litany by the clergy. Later it came to mean comic scenes inserted into church plays. The farce emerged as a separate genre in 15th-century France with such plays as the anonymous *La farce de Maître Pierre Pathelin* (c.1470). In England two of the earliest and best-known farces are *Ralph Roister Doister* (1566) and Shakespeare's *Comedy of Errors* (c.1593). Broad, ribald humor, physical buffoonery, and absurd situations can be found in many plays that are not termed farces, such as the comedies of Molière. In the 19th and early 20th cent. plays called "bedroom farces" were popular. Usually French or modeled on the French, they had suggestive dialogue, and they usually concerned erring husbands and wives, silly servants, and mistaken identity.

farcy: see GLANDERS.

Far East, in the most restricted sense, region comprising the countries of E Asia, namely China, Japan, North Korea, South Korea, and Mongolia, and the easternmost portion of Soviet Siberia (see SOVIET FAR EAST). In a more extended sense, the term includes the countries of SOUTHEAST ASIA, including the Philippines, North Vietnam, South Vietnam, Cambodia, Laos, Thailand, Malaysia, Singapore, Burma, and Indonesia. Historically, it denotes those portions of the Asian continent and archipelagoes farthest from the 19th cent. W European maritime powers.

Far Eastern Republic: see SOVIET FAR EAST.

Far Eastern Territory: see SOVIET FAR EAST.

Farel, Guillaume (gēyōm' färĕl'), 1489-1565, French religious reformer, associate of John CALVIN. In 1520, Farel joined Jacques LEFÈVRE D'ÉTAPLES at Meaux to aid in church reform and to establish an evangelical school for students and preachers. Soon his iconoclastic ideas made him suspect, and he left for Switzerland, where he did most of his work. His fearless and eloquent evangelism aroused both support and opposition. He received permission to spread the reform doctrine throughout the canton of Bern. The opposition of the bishop forced him to leave Geneva in 1532, but he returned in 1533 to lead a public disputation in favor of the Reformation. The people declared in favor of Farel and his colleagues, and in 1535 the town council formally proclaimed the adoption of the Reformation. Farel entreated Calvin to assist in the organization of the new Protestant republic. The two men drew up a statement of doctrine and immediately instituted widespread reform of church practices. These measures were too sudden and too strict to be generally accepted, and Calvin and Farel were forced to leave Geneva in 1538. Farel went to Basel and then to Neuchâtel, where he worked unceasingly for the return of Calvin to Geneva, which he achieved in 1541. Throughout his life he remained a confidant and consultant of Calvin.

Farewell, Cape, southernmost point of Greenland, on Egger Island, at lat. 59°46'N. Egger Island and the surrounding islands are called the Cape Farewell Archipelago.

Fargo, William George, 1818–81, American pioneer expressman, b. Pompey, N.Y. He had been successively a postrider, freight agent, messenger, and resident agent (1843) for an express company in Buffalo, N.Y., when in 1844, with Henry Wells and another partner, he organized Wells & Company, the first express company operating W from Buffalo. The following year the firm became Livingston, Fargo & Company, and in 1850 it merged with others to form the American Express Company, with Fargo as secretary. By 1852 he and Wells had organized Wells, Fargo & Company to handle the express service between New York and San Francisco for which the gold rush had created a need, and they established stage and banking business on the Pacific coast, American Express Company serving as eastern representative. In 1868, Fargo became president of the American Express Company, making his home in Buffalo, where he served (1862–66) as mayor. See N. C. Wilson, *Treasure Express: Epic Days of the Wells Fargo* (1936); Lucius Beebe and Charles Clegg, *U.S. West: the Saga of Wells Fargo* (1949).

Fargo, city (1970 pop. 53,365), seat of Cass co., E N.Dak., at the head of navigation on the Red River, opposite Moorhead, Minn.; inc. 1875. A railroad hub and river port, it is the largest city in the state and the trade and distribution center of a great spring wheat and livestock region. It was founded (1871) with the coming of the Northern Pacific RR and named for William G. Fargo of the Wells-Fargo Express Company. In the city are North Dakota State Univ., Concordia Conservatory of Music, a veterans hospital, and a school for crippled children.

Faribault (fâr'ĭbō), city (1970 pop. 16,595), seat of Rice co., SE Minn.; inc. 1872. Its manufactures include hand trucks, electrical equipment, metal products, blankets, and food products. Faribault is noted for its peony farms. The city was founded in 1826 by Alexander Faribault, a French fur trader. It is located in "Hiawathaland," a year-round outdoor recreation area.

Farid ad-Din Attar (färēd' äd-dēn ät-tär') [Arab.= pearl of the faith, the druggist-perfumer], d. c.1229, Persian poet, one of the greatest mystic poets of Islam. Because he was converted to SUFISM and became an expounder of the faith, he was called Farid ad-Din. Of his many and varied works his masterpiece is the *Mantiq ut-Tair* [language of birds], a long allegory surveying the philosophy and practices of the Sufis. He also wrote *Tadkhirat al-Awliya,* which contains biographies of many Sufi mystics. He lived in and near Nishapur. His name also appears as Ferid Eddin Attar, Farid ud-Din Attar, and Faridun.

Faridpur (fərēd'poŏr), town (1961 est. pop. 28,300), S Bangladesh. It is a district administrative center, a railway terminus, and a market town for jute and rice. There are two colleges affiliated with Dacca Univ. The town is named for Farid Shah, a Muslim saint whose shrine is there.

Faridun: see FARID AD-DIN ATTAR.

Farinelli, Carlo Broschi (kär'lō brô'skē färēnĕl'lē), 1705–82, Italian male soprano, greatest of the castrati (see CASTRATO), pupil of Niccolò Porpora, in whose operas he sang (1734) in London. Farinelli's real name was Carlo Broschi. Having won fame in France and Italy, he became (1737) official singer to Philip V of Spain and renounced his public career. His sole duty was to sing the same four songs each night to the king, from whom he received an astronomical fee. He enjoyed a highly favored position in Spain until 1759, when he retired to a castle near Bologna.

Farley, James Aloysius, 1888–, American political leader, U.S. Postmaster General (1933–40), b. Rockland co., N.Y. He rose steadily in Democratic party politics in New York state and became (1930) chairman of the New York state Democratic committee. In 1932 he successfully pushed the presidential nomination of Franklin D. Roosevelt. Made chairman of the Democratic National Committee, Farley managed (1932) the presidential campaign with great success. He became U.S. Postmaster General and in 1936 directed Roosevelt's second presidential campaign, which resulted in another overwhelming Democratic victory. Opposed to Roosevelt's third-term candidacy, he was an unsuccessful Democratic presidential aspirant in 1940 and resigned (1940) his cabinet post and his national party chairmanship. He remained powerful in New York state politics until 1944, when he resigned as chairman of the state Democratic committee. See his autobiographical *Behind the Ballots* (1938) and *Jim Farley's Story* (1948).

Farlow, William Gilson, 1844–1919, American botanist, b. Boston, grad. Harvard, 1866. His chief contributions were made in the study of cryptogamic and parasitic plants. Many eminent botanists received their training in his Harvard laboratory.

Farm Credit Administration (FCA), an independent agency of the executive branch of the Federal government that supervises and coordinates the Farm Credit System for American agriculture. The FCA provides long-term and short-term credit to farmers and their cooperatives. Farmers need long-term mortgage loans to help them acquire property and to refinance existing debts; short-term loans are needed to finance the production and marketing of crops and livestock. Agricultural cooperatives also need credit to supplement their operating capital. Farmers have traditionally favored liberal credit facilities and low interest rates, and have complained that private institutions have not made funds available as cheaply and conveniently as possible. They asked for a banking system adapted to the peculiar needs of agriculture, and in answer to this demand the Federal Farm Loan Act of 1916 established a system for mortgage credit: 12 regional farm land banks were set up, with most of the original capital supplied by the government. Their function was to act as credit wholesalers, raising funds in the investment markets through the sale of bonds and lending the money to farmers at low interest rates. It was intended that the farmer-borrowers should ultimately own the banks. In 1923 new legislation was adopted to extend further Federal aid to farmers by the establishment of 12 intermediate credit banks (one in the district of each land bank), with capital supplied by the government. These banks make loans to agricultural cooperatives for periods ranging from six months to three years. The loans are secured by warehouse receipts for crops or by LIENS of livestock. Six years later, the whole structure of the land banks was severely hit by the great depression of 1929, with falling prices of farm products, increased debt delinquencies, and decline in the value of farms. To bolster the land banks, the government in 1932 invested $125 million in the bonds of the land banks and thus again became the majority stockholder. The Reconstruction Finance Corporation made some of its funds available to farm enterprise. All then existing Federal agricultural-credit organizations were unified into one agency, the FCA. Congress authorized that agency to extend the system of farm-mortgage credit. Funds were made available for loans for first or second mortgages—the so-called land bank commissioner loans—to debtors whose collateral was so low in value or so encumbered by debt as to make refinancing by the land banks unfeasible. Such loans were made on easier terms than the regular advances. In 1933 the FCA was also authorized to establish 12 production credit corporations, which finance short-term credit associations, and banks for cooperatives, which finance farmers' cooperative marketing. Those steps resulted in a centralized source of major types of farm credit. In addition to that more permanent work, the FCA makes emergency crop and feed loans to farmers who cannot obtain funds from other sources. A part of the Dept. of Agriculture after 1939, the FCA again became an independent agency in 1953. It operates under the authority of the Farm Credit Act of 1971, which superseded all other legislation.

Farmer, Fannie Merritt, 1857–1915, American cookbook author and teacher and writer on cookery, b. Boston. A paralytic stroke prevented her from attending college, and she turned to cooking, at home and at the Boston Cooking School, from which she graduated in 1889. She was director of the school from 1891 until 1902, when she opened Miss Farmer's School of Cookery, established to train housewives and nurses, rather than teachers, in cookery. One of her contributions was accurate measurement in recipes. For 10 years she contributed a popular page on cookery for the *Woman's Home Companion.* She edited *The Boston Cooking School Cook Book* (1896), one of the best-known and most popular of American cookbooks. See Wilma L. Perkins, *The Fannie Farmer Cookbook* (11th rev. ed. 1965).

Farmer, Moses Gerrish, 1820–93, American inventor, b. Boscawen, N.H. He helped build and maintain some of the pioneer telegraph lines of Massachusetts and experimented in multiple telegraphy. He exhibited (1847) an electric train that carried children, invented a process for electroplating aluminum, and installed (1851) in Boston the first electric fire-alarm service in any city. His later years were spent chiefly in developing the incandescent electric light. Twenty years before Edison's success he produced (1858–59) electric lamps, and in 1868, with a dynamo of his own invention, he illuminated a house in Cambridge, Mass., but was never able to perfect a marketable light.

Farmer-Labor party, in U.S. history, political organization composed of agrarian and organized labor interests. Formed in 1919 as the National Labor party, it changed its name at its 1920 presidential nominating convention in order to appeal to farmers. The party's platform called for the public ownership of railroads, utilities, and natural resources; an end to private banking; and the nationalization of unused land. The convention resisted the efforts of former Progressives to nominate Robert La Follette and instead chose as its candidate Parley P. Christensen. The party made a poor showing in the 1920 election; its main strength lay in the states of Washington, Montana, and South Dakota. In 1923, Communists gained control of the party, and in the following year it joined other dissident groups in the Conference for Progressive Political Action, which supported the presidential candidacy of La Follette. After the 1924 election, the party passed out of existence. Meanwhile, representatives of the Nonpartisan League in Minnesota, along with various labor unions, had entered a slate of candidates for state elections in 1918 and 1920 under the name of Farmer-Labor party. Remaining aloof from the national party of the same name, it established a permanent party structure in 1922. It quickly became a powerful political force in Minnesota, electing Henrik Shipstead and Magnus Johnson to the U.S. Senate and Floyd B. OLSON to the governorship. It also won many local elections. At first the party agitated for government ownership of industry, but in the 1930s it came to support Franklin Delano Roosevelt's New Deal programs. In 1944 it merged with the Minnesota Democratic party. See S. A. Rice, *Farmers and Workers in American Politics* (1924, repr. 1969).

Farmers Branch, city (1970 pop. 27,492), Dallas co., N Texas, a suburb adjacent to Dallas; settled 1841, inc. 1946. Insecticides, processed foods, brooms, and metal products are made there.

farming, in TAXATION, collection of taxes through private contractors. Usually, the tax farmer paid a lump sum to the public treasury; the difference between that sum and the sum actually collected represented his profit or loss. Although tax farming is no longer practiced, it was common in the cities of ancient Greece and in republican Rome, where the collection of direct taxes was farmed out to publicans; in the Roman Empire only indirect taxes were farmed. In the past, tax farming was practiced in most countries of Europe and Asia. In England the system was tried briefly but played no important part. It was most fully applied in France after 1681, when Jean Baptiste Colbert founded the general farms as an agency of royal administration. The collection of certain indirect taxes was leased by the king to the company of farmers general, a chartered body of 40 financiers (at one time they numbered 60) that guaranteed a fixed sum of revenue in advance. Popular hatred soon developed against the huge profits and extortionist practices of the farmers general, whose organization was abolished (1791) in the French Revolution; some 30 former members of the farm—Antoine Lavoisier among them—were guillotined in the Reign of Terror. See George T. Matthews, *The Royal General Farms in Eighteenth-Century France* (1958).

farming the taxes: see FARMING, in taxation.

Farmington. 1 Town (1970 pop. 14,390), Hartford co., central Conn., on the Farmington River; inc. 1645. It has light tool industries. Points of interest include Miss Porter's School and the Hillstead Museum. A junior college and the Univ. of Connecticut dental school are also there. 2 City (1970 pop. 10,329), Oakland co., SE Mich., a suburb of Detroit; settled 1824 by Quakers; inc. as a city 1925. Automotive parts, tools and dies, building supplies, and computer equipment are among its manufactures. 3 City (1970 pop. 21,979), San Juan co., NW N.Mex., at the confluence of the San Juan, Animas, and La Plata rivers; inc. 1901. A distribution point for the Navajo Indian Reservation, it is the trade center of an oil, natural gas, and irrigated farm area. A junior college is in Farmington. Aztec Ruins National Monument and Chaco Canyon National Monument are nearby.

Farnborough, Thomas Erskine May, 1st Baron: see MAY, THOMAS ERSKINE.

Farnborough, urban district (1971 pop. 41,233), Hampshire, S England. It is the site of the Royal Aircraft Establishment, which does experimental work in aeronautics. A civil and military air show is held by the Society of British Aerospace Companies biennially in Farnborough. "Farnborough Hill" was the home (1881–1920) of Empress Eugénie, wife of Napoleon III. With her husband and son she is buried in the crypt of a church she built.

Farnese (färnā'zā), Italian noble family that ruled PARMA and PIACENZA from 1545 to 1731. In the 12th cent. the Farnese held several fiefs in Latium. They became one of the most prominent families in Rome and were Guelph supporters of the papacy. In 1534, Alessandro Farnese became pope as PAUL III. He used his office to aggrandize his family and in 1545 he detached lands from the papal dominions to create the duchy of Parma and Piacenza for his illegitimate son, **Pier Luigi Farnese,** 1503–47. Pier Luigi attacked fiscal and judicial abuses; he thereby gained the hatred of the nobility and was assassinated. His son, **Ottavio Farnese,** 1520–86, who succeeded him, married Margaret of Austria (see MARGARET OF PARMA), illegitimate daughter of Holy Roman Emperor CHARLES V. Ottavio's brother, Alessandro Farnese, 1520–89, was a cardinal of the Roman Catholic Church. A patron of men of letters such as Pietro Bembo and of artists such as Giorgio Vasari, he oversaw the completion of the FARNESE PALACE in Rome. Ottavio's son and successor was Alessandro Farnese (1545–92), one of the great generals of his time (see separate article). Alessandro's son, **Ranuccio I,** 1569–1622, reformed the duchy's administration and judicial system and was a benefactor of education and the arts. The four dukes who succeeded Ranuccio I were less distinguished rulers, although they continued the family's patronage of the arts despite increasing economic and political troubles. The last duke of the line, Antonio, died in 1731. His niece, ELIZABETH FARNESE, queen of Philip V of Spain, secured (1748) the succession to the duchy for her son Philip, founder of the line of Bourbon-Parma.

Farnese, Alessandro (älĕs-sän'drō), 1545–92, duke of Parma and Piacenza (1586–92), general and diplomat in the service of Philip II of Spain. He was the son of Duke Ottavio Farnese and Margaret of Parma and thus a nephew of Philip II and of John of Austria, under whom he distinguished himself at the battle of Lepanto (1571). In 1577, Farnese joined John in the Low Countries to fight the rebels against Spain. Appointed (1578) governor of the Netherlands, he took Tournai, Maastricht, Breda, Bruges, Ghent, and Antwerp from the rebels and secured continued possession of the southern part of the Netherlands for Spain (see NETHERLANDS, AUSTRIAN AND SPANISH). In 1590 he was sent to France at the head of a Spanish army to assist the Catholic LEAGUE against Henry IV of France. He relieved the siege of Paris (1590) and the siege of Rouen (1592), but was wounded soon afterward and retired to Arras, where he died. Farnese showed exceptional skill in military art and diplomacy. See R. Solari, *The House of Farnese* (1968).

Farnese, Elizabeth: see ELIZABETH FARNESE.

Farnese Bull, sculptured group representing Zethus and Amphion, sons of Antiope, tying Dirce (who had ill-treated their mother) to an enraged bull. The sculpture is generally considered to have been executed by Apollonius of Tralles and his brother Tauriscus in the 1st or 2d cent. B.C. A copy made in the early 3d cent. A.D. decorated the Baths of Caracalla. This copy, with incorrect restorations, was later in the Farnese Palace and is now in the National Museum, Naples.

Farnese Palace, in Rome, designed by Antonio da Sangallo (see under SANGALLO) for Cardinal Alessandro Farnese (Pope Paul III). It was begun before 1514 and, after the architect's death, was continued by Michelangelo and completed by Giacomo della Porta. Built of huge blocks plundered from ancient monuments, it is one of the most magnificent palaces of Rome. The great halls were decorated by Annibale Carracci and his pupils. After the extinction of the Farnese family it passed by inheritance to the king of Naples. Since 1874 it has housed the French embassy and the French school of archaeology of Rome; in 1937 it was leased to France for 99 years.

Farnesina (färnāzē'nä), villa in Rome, Italy, built (1508–11) by PERUZZI for the banker Agostino Chigi at the foot of the Janiculum on the right bank of the Tiber. One of the finest examples of Italian Renaissance architecture, it is famous for its frescoes by Raphael and his pupils. It was long the residence of the Farnese family. See Paolo d'Ancona, *The Farnesina Frescoes at Rome* (1955).

Farnham, urban district (1971 pop. 31,175), Surrey, SE England, on the Wey River. It is a market town but is no longer the important grain and wool center it was in the 17th and early 18th cent. A castle, the residence of the bishops of Winchester from 1160 to 1926, now houses the Overseas Service College. The castle was built in the late 17th cent. on the site of a Norman castle that was destroyed in 1648. Aldershot, site of a military camp, is nearby. William Cobbett, the reformer, was born in Farnham.

Farnsworth, Philo Taylor, 1906–71, American inventor, b. Beaver, Utah, grad. Brigham Young Univ., 1925. He demonstrated (1927) a working model of a television system. His "dissector tube" (called the orthicon), like V. K. Zworykin's iconoscope, is a means of dividing an image into particles whose light values, when transmitted, are capable of being restored to form a replica of the original image. In 1938 he became research director of the Farnsworth Television and Radio Corp. In 1956, Farnsworth was granted a patent for a cathode-ray tube of the "storage" type intended for television sets of the future.

Farnworth, municipal borough (1971 pop. 26,841), Lancashire, NW England. It has cotton and rayon mills and produces finished textiles, hosiery, knitted goods, machinery, paper, and wood products. In 1974, Farnworth became part of the new metropolitan county of Greater Manchester.

Faro (fä'rō), town (1970 municipal pop. 30,289), capital of Faro dist. and of Algarve, S Portugal. The southernmost town in Portugal, it is a seaport from which fish, fruit (especially dried figs), wine, and cork are exported. Important under the Moors, it was retaken in 1249.

faro (fâr'ō) [for *Pharaoh,* from an old French card design], gambling game played with a pack of 52 cards. First played in France and England, faro was especially popular in U.S. gambling houses in the 19th cent. Players indicate on the table, which is marked with representations of the 13 cards of the spade suit, the card they believe will win or lose. The dealer then takes one card, called the soda, from the dealing box. This card is not used. The second card drawn loses, and the third card wins.

Faröe Islands: see FAEROE ISLANDS, Denmark.

Fårön (fôr'ən), island, 40 sq mi (104 sq km), Gotland co., E. Sweden, separated from Gotland Island by the Fårösund, an arm of the Baltic Sea. It has a lighthouse, fine beaches, and prehistoric and medieval ruins. It is also known as Fårö.

Farouk (färo͝ok'), 1920–65, king of Egypt (1936–52), son and successor of Fuad I. After a short regency he acceded (1937) to the throne. A constitutional monarch, Farouk was frequently at odds with the WAFD, the largest Egyptian party. Because of his pro-Axis sympathies during World War II, the British imposed upon him a pro-British premier in 1942. General corruption and his defeat in the Arab-Israeli conflict (1948) led to the military coup of 1952, headed by Muhammad Naguib and Gamal Abdal Nasser, which forced him to abdicate and go abroad. He was succeeded by his infant son Fuad II, who was officially deposed in 1953. Farouk became a citizen of Monaco in 1959.

Farquhar, George (fär'kər, -kwər), 1678–1707, English dramatist, b. Londonderry, Ireland. After a short career as an actor, he produced (1698) his first comedy, *Love and a Bottle.* His next play, *The Constant Couple* (1699), established him as one of the outstanding dramatists of his day. His experiences as an army officer are reflected in *The Recruiting Officer* (1706). In 1707 he produced his masterpiece, *The Beaux' Stratagem.* His plays, written in an atmosphere of genial merriment, represent the transition between the licentiousness and artificiality of the Restoration drama and the sentimentality and morality of the 18th cent. See his complete works (ed. by C. A. Stonehill, 1930); biography by W. C. Connely (1949); study by Eric Rothstein (1967).

Farragut, David Glasgow (făr'əgət), 1801–70, American admiral, b. near Knoxville, Tenn. Appointed a midshipman in 1810, he first served on the frigate *Essex,* commanded by David PORTER, his self-appointed guardian, and participated in that ship's famous cruise in the Pacific in the War of 1812. Farragut commanded his first vessel in Porter's Mosquito Fleet, which operated (1823–24) against the pirates in Gulf and Caribbean waters. In the Mexican War he had minor commands on blockade duty. The navy yard at Mare Island, Calif., was established by Farragut in 1854, and he was commandant there till 1858. On Virginia's secession Farragut, a Union sympathizer, moved from Norfolk, where he had made his home ashore, to Hastings-on-Hudson, N.Y. Yet his Southern connections placed him under suspicion, and he did not receive an important assignment until Jan., 1862. Then the Dept. of the Navy gave him command of the West Gulf Blockading Squadron, with orders to ascend the Mississippi River and reduce New Orleans. By April 18, 1862, Farragut's fleet, consisting of 17 vessels and a mortar flotilla under David Dixon PORTER, had reached forts Jackson and St. Philip, situated on opposite sides of the Mississippi just below New Orleans. When the mortars failed to reduce the forts, Farragut decided to try to get by them in the dark. This action was accomplished on April 24, with the loss of only three vessels. The Confederate flotilla was then defeated in a hot engagement, and on April 25, Farragut anchored at New Orleans. The forts surrendered on April 28, and on May 1, Union troops under Gen. Benjamin F. BUTLER entered the city. Farragut's attempt to reduce Vicksburg in May–June, 1862, failed. But in March, 1863, he successfully ran two ships past the batteries at Port Hudson and by thus controlling the Mississippi between that point and Vicksburg contributed to Ulysses S. Grant's ultimate success in the VICKSBURG CAMPAIGN. Farragut had succeeded in stifling Confederate blockade-running in the Gulf of Mexico, except at its chief source, Mobile, and he moved on that port in 1864. Mobile Bay was strongly defended by forts Gaines and Morgan, a double row of torpedoes (mines), and a Confederate flotilla commanded by Franklin BUCHANAN. Farragut, disregarding the torpedoes (with the famous cry "Damn the torpedoes"), forced these defenses and defeated Buchanan for his crowning victory on Aug. 5, 1864. The forts surrendered shortly afterward, and though the city itself did not fall until April, 1865, blockade-running was effectively ended there. Farragut was easily the outstanding naval commander of the war. He was the first officer in the U.S. navy to receive the ranks of vice admiral (1864) and admiral (1866). See biographies by his son Loyall Farragut (1879), A. T. Mahan (1892, repr. 1970), C. L. Lewis (2 vol., 1941–43), and Christopher Martin (1970).

Farrar, Edgar Howard (făr'ər), 1849–1922, American lawyer, b. Concordia, La. He made his home in New Orleans, where he had a large corporation practice. He was active in municipal reform movements and in the founding of Tulane. Among his writings two of the best known are *Legal Remedy for Plutocracy* (1902) and *State and Federal Quarantine Powers* (1905). In 1912–13 he assisted Arsène PUJO in a Congressional investigation of the money trust.

Farrar, Frederic William, 1831–1903, English clergyman and author, dean of Canterbury (1895–1903), b. Bombay, India, educated in England. He was assistant master at Harrow from 1855 to 1870 and headmaster of Marlborough College from 1871 to 1876. In 1876 he was installed canon of Westminster and rector of St. Margaret's. He became archdeacon of Westminster in 1883 and dean of Canterbury in 1895. He was influential in the spread of the Broad Church movement. His writings cover a wide range, from school stories to Scripture commentaries and theological studies. His *Life of Christ* (1874) and *Eternal Hope* (1878) have passed through several editions. See biography by his son (1904).

Farrar, Geraldine (fərär'), 1882–1967, American operatic soprano, b. Melrose, Mass.; pupil of Lilli Lehmann. She made her debut in Europe (1901) and sang at the Metropolitan Opera, New York City, from 1906 to 1922. Her most famous roles were in *La Bohème, Madame Butterfly,* and *Carmen.* See her autobiography, *Such Sweet Compulsion* (1938).

Farrell, Eileen, 1920–, American dramatic soprano, b. Willimantic, Conn. Farrell received her early musical training from her mother. Having begun her career in radio, she made concert tours in the United States in 1947–48 and in South America in 1949. She first appeared in New York City in 1950 at Carnegie Hall; in that season her 61 programs included the American premiere of Milhaud's *Les Choëphores.* Engagements with the San Francisco Opera Company and the Lyric Opera of Chicago followed. In 1953 Farrell joined the Bach Aria Society in New York. She made her debut at the Metropolitan Opera in 1960 in the title role of Gluck's *Alcestis.* She was celebrated for her performances in *Medea, Ariadne auf Naxos,* and *La Gioconda.* Farrell sang at the Metropolitan until 1966. Since then she has taught, and toured in concert extensively. Her voice has been characterized by its enormous power and beauty of tone.

Farrell, James Thomas, 1904–, American novelist, b. Chicago. In his fiction Farrell expressed anger against the brutal economic and social conditions that produce emotional and material poverty. His work, noted for the frankness of its language and its detailed realism, is in the tradition of NATURALISM. Farrell's first series of novels about life among the Irish Catholic population of Chicago's South Side was the Studs Lonigan trilogy: *Young Lonigan* (1932), *The Young Manhood of Studs Lonigan* (1934), and *Judgment Day* (1935). Another of his series was the Danny O'Neill pentalogy: *A World I Never Made* (1936), *No Star Is Lost* (1938), *Father and Son* (1940), *My Days of Anger* (1943), and *The Face of Time* (1953). Farrell's other works include numerous collections of short stories; several volumes of essays, including *Reflections at Fifty* (1954); and innumerable novels, among them *Ellen Rogers* (1941), *Boarding House Blues* (1961), and *Invisible Swords* (1971).

Farrell, city (1970 pop. 11,022), Mercer co., W central Pa., on the Shenango River at the Ohio line and adjoining Sharon; inc. 1901. It is a railroad and industrial center, with large steel and iron works.

Farrukhabad (fəro͝okh'äbäd"), joint municipality with Fategarh (total 1971 pop. 103,282), Uttar Pradesh state, N central India, on the Ganges River. It is a district administrative center and a market for grain, fruit, and potatoes. Leather and metal goods are manufactured. A fort was founded (c.1714) on the site of the present-day town by the Afghan ruler Nawab Muhammad Khan. Farrukhabad was captured by the MAHRATTAS in 1751 and ceded to the British in 1802. The town's British garrison was attacked during the INDIAN MUTINY of 1857.

Fars (färs) or **Farsistan** (färsĭstän'), province (1966 pop. 1,429,804), c.51,500 sq mi (133,400 sq km), SW Iran. SHIRAZ is the capital and chief city. The province is largely mountainous. Grain, cotton, tobacco, opium, fruit, and wine are produced, and sheep are raised there. Synthetic fertilizers and cement are among the few manufactures. The population is mostly organized by tribe; the leading tribes are the Qashqai and the Khamseh. One of the most historic regions of Iran, Fars is more or less identical with the ancient province of Pars, which was the nucleus of the Persian Empire. The ruins of PASARGADAE and PERSEPOLIS, early Persian capitals, are in Fars. The Arabs changed the name Pars to Fars after they conquered the region in the 7th cent.

farsightedness (hyperopia), condition in which far objects can be seen easily but there is difficulty in near vision. It is caused by a defect of refraction in which the image is focused behind the retina of the EYE rather than upon it, either because the eyeball is too short or because the refractive power of the lens is too weak. Presbyopia, a similarly faulty vision, is attributable to physiological changes in the lens brought on by age. Corrective EYEGLASSES with convex lenses compensate for the refractive errors.

Farsistan, Iran: see FARS.

Fas: see FEZ, Morocco.

Fasano, Renato (rānä'tō fäsä'nō), 1902–, Italian conductor and composer, b. Naples. He studied at the Conservatory of San Pietro in Naples. Fasano was the founder of the Italian Collegium Musicum and leads its chamber orchestra, I Virtuosi di Roma. He has composed chamber and orchestral music.

fasces (făs'ēz) [Lat.,=bundles], ancient Roman symbol of the regal and later the magisterial authority. The fasces were cylindrical bundles of wooden rods, tied tightly together, from which an axe projected; they were borne by guards, called lictors, before praetors, consuls, proconsuls, dictators, and emperors. The fasces, which symbolize unity as well as power, have often been used as emblems, e.g., on the arms of the French republic and on American coins. Italian Fascism derived its name and its emblem from the fasces.

fascia (făsh'ēə), fibrous tissue network located between the skin and the underlying structure of muscle and bone. Fascia is composed of two layers, a superficial layer and a deep layer. Superficial fascia is attached to the skin and is composed of connective tissue containing varying quantities of fat. It is especially dense in the scalp, the back of the neck, and the palms of the hands, where it serves to anchor the skin firmly to underlying tissues. In other areas of the body it is loose and the skin may be moved freely back and forth. Deep fascia underlies the superficial layers, to which it is loosely joined by fibrous strands. It is thin but strong and densely packed, and serves to cover the muscles and to partition them into groups.

fascism (făsh'ĭzəm), totalitarian philosophy of government that glorifies state and nation and assigns to the state control over every aspect of national life. The name was first used by the party started by Benito MUSSOLINI, who ruled Italy from 1922 until the Italian defeat in World War II. However, it has also been applied to similar ideologies in other countries, e.g., to NATIONAL SOCIALISM in Germany and to the regime of Francisco FRANCO in Spain. The term is derived from the Latin FASCES.

Origins of Fascist Philosophy. While socialism (particularly Marxism) came into existence as a clearly formulated theory or program based on a specific interpretation of history, fascism introduced no systematic exposition of its ideology or purpose other than a negative reaction against socialist and democratic egalitarianism. The growth of democratic ideology and popular participation in politics in the 19th cent. was terrifying to some conservative elements in European society, and fascism grew out of the attempt to counter it by forming mass parties based largely on the middle classes and the petty bourgeoisie, exploiting their fear of political domination by the lower classes. Forerunners of fascism, such as Georges Boulanger in France and Adolf Stöker and Karl Lueger in Germany and Austria, in their efforts to gain political power played on people's fears of revolution with its subsequent chaos, anarchy, and general insecurity. They appealed to nationalist sentiments and prejudices, exploited ANTI-SEMITISM, and portrayed themselves as champions of law, order, Christian morality, and the sanctity of private property. Fascism, especially in its early stages, is obliged to be antitheoretical and frankly opportunistic in order to appeal to many diverse groups. Nevertheless, a few key concepts are basic to it. First and most important is the glorification of the state and the total subordination of the individual to it. The state is defined as an organic whole into which the individual must be absorbed for his own and the state's benefit. This "total state" is absolute in its methods and unlimited by law in its control and direction of its citizens. A second ruling concept of fascism is embodied in the theory of social Darwinism. The doctrine of survival of the fittest and the necessity of struggle for life is applied by fascists to the life of a nation-state. Peaceful, complacent nations are seen as doomed to fall before more dynamic ones, making struggle and aggressive militarism a leading characteristic of the fascist state. Imperialism is the logical outcome of this dogma. Another element of fascism is its elitism. Salvation from rule by the mob and the destruction of the existing social order can be effected only by an authoritarian leader who embodies in his person the highest ideals of the nation. This concept of the leader as hero or superman, borrowed in part from the romanticism of Friedrich NIETZSCHE, Thomas CARLYLE, and Richard WAGNER, is closely linked with fascism's rejection of reason and intelligence and its emphasis on vision, creativeness, and "the will."

Emergence after World War I. The Russian Revolution of 1917, the collapse of the Central Powers in 1918, and the disorders caused by Communist attempts to seize power in Germany, Italy, Hungary, and other countries greatly strengthened fascism's appeal to many sections of the European populace. In Italy, particularly, social unrest was combined with nationalist dissatisfaction over the government's failure to reap the promised fruits of victory after World War I. The action of Gabriele D'ANNUNZIO in seizing Fiume was one manifestation of the discontent existing in Italy. Appealing to the masses and especially to the lower middle class through demagogic promises of order and social justice, the fascists could depend upon support, financial and otherwise, from vested interests, who could not muster such popularity themselves. Governmental paralysis enabled Mussolini in 1922 to obtain the premiership by a show of force. As leader of his National Fascist party, he presented himself as the strong-armed savior of Italy from anarchy and Communism. Borrowing from Russian Communism a system of party organization based on a strict hierarchy and cells, which became typical of fascism everywhere, he made use of an elite party militia—the Black Shirts—to crush opposition and to maintain his power. In Germany at about the same time a fascist movement similar to that in Italy steadily gathered strength; it called itself the National Socialist German Workers' party (Nazi party). Its leader, Adolf HITLER, won support from a middle class ruined by inflation, from certain elements of the working class, especially the unemployed, and from discontented war veterans; he also gained the backing of powerful financial interests, to whom he symbolized stability and order. However, it was not until 1933 that Hitler could carry through his plans for making Germany a fascist state and the National Socialists the sole legal party in the country.

The Fascist State. In its dictatorial methods and in its use of brutal intimidation of the opposition by the militia and the secret police, fascism does not greatly distinguish itself from other despotic and totalitarian regimes. There are particular similarities with the Communist regime in the Soviet Union under Joseph Stalin. However, unlike Communism, fascism abhors the idea of a classless society and sees desirable order only in a state in which each class has its distinct place and function. Representation by classes (i.e., capital, labor, farmers, and professionals) is substituted for representation by parties, and the CORPORATIVE STATE is a part of fascist dogma. Although Mussolini's and Hitler's governments tended to interfere considerably in economic life and to regulate its process, there can be no doubt that despite all restrictions imposed on them, the capitalist and landowning classes were protected by the fascist system, and many favored it as an obstacle to socialization. On the other hand, the state adopted a paternalistic attitude toward labor, improving its conditions in some respects, reducing unemployment through large-scale public works and armament programs, and controlling its leisure time through organized activities. Many of these features were adopted by the Franco regime in Spain and by quasi-fascist dictators in Latin America (e.g., Juan PERÓN) and elsewhere. A variation of fascism was the so-called clerico-fascist system set up in Austria under Engelbert DOLLFUSS. This purported to be based on the social and economic doctrines enunciated by Pope Leo XIII and Pope Pius XI, which, however, were never put into operation. The military aggression so inherent in fascist philosophy exploded in the Italian invasion (1935) of Ethiopia, the attack (1936) of the Spanish fascists (Falangists) on their republican government, and Nazi Germany's systematic aggression in Central and Eastern Europe, which finally precipitated (1939) World War II. Fascism has found adherents in all countries. Its essentially vague and emotional nature facilitates the development of unique national varieties, whose leaders often deny indignantly that they are fascists at all. See TOTALITARIANISM. See Herman Finer, *Mussolini's Italy* (1935, repr. 1965); E. B. Ashton, *The Fascist: His State and His Mind* (1937); René Albrecht-Carrié, *Italy from Napoleon to Mussolini* (1961); Hannah Arendt, *Origins of Totalitarianism* (rev. ed. 1966); Walter Laqueur and George Mosse, ed., *International Fascism* (1966); A. J. Gregor, *The Ideology of Fascism* (1969); William Ebenstein, *Today's Isms* (7th ed. 1973); Heinz Lubasz, ed., *Fascism: Three Major Regimes* (1973); O. E. Schuddekopf, *Fascism* (1973).

fashion, in dress, the prevailing mode affecting modifications in costume. Styles in the Orient have been characterized by freedom from change, and Greek and Roman dress preserved the same flowing lines for centuries. Fashion in dress and interior decoration may be said to have originated in Europe about the 14th cent. New styles were set by monarchs and prominent personages and were spread by travelers, by descriptions in letters, and, in COSTUME, by the exchange of the fashion DOLL. The first fashion magazine is thought to have originated c.1586 in Frankfurt, Germany; it was widely imitated, gradually superseding fashion dolls. *Godey's Lady's Book,* established in the United States in 1830, remained popular for decades. In interior decoration the influence of designers, such as Chippendale, Sheraton, and Robert and James Adam, was apparent in the 18th cent., but in costume the only influential designer at that period was Rose Bertin, milliner and dressmaker to Marie Antoinette. In Paris—the leading arbiter of fashion since the Renaissance—the fading influence of celebrities was coincident with the rise of designer-dressmakers in the mid-19th cent. Paris *haute couture* has remained preeminent in setting fashions for women's dress. Designers such as Charles Frederick Worth, Gabrielle Chanel, Lucien Lelong, Elsa Schiaparelli, Cristóbal Balenciaga, Christian Dior, and Yves Saint-Laurent have had fashion houses in Paris. In recent years such American designers as Norman Norell, Mainbocher, James Galanos, Bill Blass, and Pauline Trigère have competed successfully with Parisian designers. London, in the early 19th cent., became the center for men's fashions under the leadership of Regency dandies such as Beau BRUMMELL. In the mid-1960s, London was again for a time the center of fashion influence. Fashions are adapted for mass production by the garment industries of New York, Los Angeles, and other cities. See accompanying table of fashion designers. See E. B. Hurlock, *The Psychology of Dress* (1929); F. C. C. Boucher, *20,000 Years of Fashion* (tr. 1967); James Laver, *A Concise History of Costume and Fashion* (1969); Ruth Lynam, *An Illustrated History of the Great Paris Designers and Their Creations* (1972); Geoffrey Squire, *Dress and Society* (1974).

SOME MAJOR FASHION DESIGNERS

Adrian, Gilbert, 1903–59, worked in Hollywood, Calif. A vital influence in haute couture of the 1930s and 40s through private couturier work and costume designs for films, especially for the stars of C. B. DeMille and M-G-M movies, including Greta Garbo, Norma Shearer, Katharine Hepburn, and Joan Crawford. Created extravagant, draped evening gowns; hooded dresses; snoods; embroidered, padded evening jackets. Garbo dressed by him exclusively. Opened own house in 1940s.

Balenciaga, Cristóbal, 1895–1972, established houses of couture in Spain and in Paris (1937–68). Couturier to Europe's royalty and aristocracy. Major success achieved after World War II. Noted for his huge evening coats with dolman sleeves; long, full skirts; tunic and chemise dresses; fitted dressmaker suits; pillbox hats; perfumes; scarves; the seven-eighths coat.

Chanel, Gabrielle (Coco), 1883–1970, established house of couture in Paris. An enormously influential designer from the mid-1920s. Noted for simple jersey dresses and suits; perfumes (Chanel No. 5); black or gray pullovers with white piqué collar and cuffs; box-jacket suits; costume jewelry; knit suits; trousers for women; textiles; clothes designed for comfort. Among the most imitated of all designers; had major resurgence of popularity beginning in 1954. See Pierre Galante, *Mademoiselle Chanel* (tr. 1973); Claude Baillén, *Chanel Solitaire* (tr. 1974).

Courrèges, André, 1923–, established house of couture in Paris. Known for dresses and trouser suits with straight, flat line. Created the space age, unisex look that had a major success in mid-1960s.

Dior, Christian, 1905–57, established his main house of couture in Paris (1946). By 1958 had salons in 15 countries employing more than 2,000 people. Known particularly for the "New Look" of 1947 (narrow shoulders, constricted waist, emphasized bust, and long, wide skirt), nonfunctional but enormously popular in postwar era. Created short, waistless sack dress (early 1950s) and introduced the A-line dress (1956). Designs represented consistent classic elegance, stressing the feminine line. Succeeded by Yves Saint-Laurent as chief designer. See Dior's autobiography (1957).

Galanos, James, 1925–, working in California. Known as a master of ready-to-wear fashions; full, loose dresses and chiffon coats over simple sheaths. Noted for use of silk fabrics.

Gernreich, Rudi, 1922–, working in California. Noted for ready-to-wear sportswear. Created a short-lived sensation with topless bathing suits and nightgowns. Makes popular and inexpensive knitwear, long, straight halter dresses. Often uses fabrics with geometric patterns and narrow stripes. Introduced plastic fabrics in futuristic modes.

Givenchy, Hubert de, 1927–, established house of couture in Paris. A disciple of Balenciaga and assistant designer to Schiaparelli, opened his own house in 1952. Noted for separate skirts and tops; unusual embroidered and printed fabrics; tubular evening dresses; sumptuous ball gowns; jeweled headbands; shawls; the princess silhouette; sleeveless coats; funnel necklines; perfumes. Designer of Audrey Hepburn's clothes and film costumes.

Head, Edith, 1907–, working in Hollywood, Calif. Designed costumes for the movies beginning in the early 1930s. Received many Academy Awards: *The Heiress* (1949), *All About Eve* (1950), *Samson and Delilah* (1951), *A Place in the Sun* (1952), *Roman Holiday* (1954), *The Sting* (1973). Important influence on American haute couture. See her autobiography, *Fashion As a Career* (1966).

Lelong, Lucien, 1889–1958, operated Parisian house of couture from 1919 to 1948. Achieved major success in the 1930s and 40s. Noted for his perfumes N and Indiscret; hobble skirts; bared shoulders; tailored suits with cutaway bodices; flared skirts; dresses with pleats, tiers, and diagonal draping; décolletage in back.

Mainbocher (Main Rousseau Bocher), 1891–, working in United States. Known for his very expensive, elegant evening clothes; cardigan sweaters with jeweled buttons; high-waisted, long, and lacy or transparent ball gowns. Opened his Paris house of couture in 1929 and his New York house in 1939. Designed war uniforms for the WAVES and SPARS and made costume designs for a few stage productions.

Norell, Norman, 1900–1972, worked in California and New York. Noted for inexpensive casual wear as well as haute couture; lounging costumes; cloth coats; sequined cocktail dresses; chemise dresses; sweaters with evening skirts. Started his own firm making ready-to-wear clothing in 1960.

Poiret, Paul, 1879–1943, opened Parisian house of couture in 1904. Dominated French fashions from 1909 to 1914. Noted for his culottes; hobble-skirted day dresses and suits with light corsetting; walking coat and dress ensembles in novelty fabrics, often with touches of lace; short, printed hoop skirts over long sheath skirts. Made boyishness the vogue. Strongly influenced by art nouveau and Oriental designs. Refused to submit to changing tastes and died in poverty at 64. See Palmer White, *Poiret* (1973).

Pucci, Emilio (Marchese Emilio Pucci di Barsento), 1914–, established showrooms in Florence, Capri, and Rome. Began to design elegant sportswear, especially ski outfits, in 1947. Creates his own multicolored printed fabric with geometric and organic patterns. Uses brilliant colors in silk blouses, bulky knit sweaters, underclothes, scarves, towels. Designs accessories including perfumes, belts, jewelry; objects such as table tops and car roofs.

Quant, Mary, 1934–, opened boutique in London. One of the originators of the "mod" or "Chelsea" look of the 1960s that made London the new center of fashion. Noted for miniskirts; vinyl boots; dresses with striking geometric patterns and strong colors; the "wet" look. First to design for a youthful clientele. See her *Quant on Quant* (1966).

Saint-Laurent, Yves, 1936–, established houses of couture and boutiques in Paris and New York. Dior's foremost assistant and successor to him as head of the House of Dior at 21. Early collections were noted for their extreme, maverick quality. Opened his own Paris house in 1961, featuring "chic beatnik" look; knitted turtlenecks; thigh-length boots; skin-tight trousers; short jackets. Later designs include sophisticated tweed suits, pleated skirts, heavy costume jewelry. Designed for the Ballets de Roland Petit.

Schiaparelli, Elsa, 1890–1973, established house of couture in Paris (late 1920s to 1954) and New York showroom since 1949. A daring, flamboyant fashion innovator. Popularized brilliant colors, especially shocking pink. First to use synthetic fabrics and zipper fastenings and first to open own boutique. Noted for her perfume Shocking; small hats; angular, wide-shouldered suits and dresses; turbans; walking coats; evening sweaters; halter necklines; cocktail dresses with matching jackets; scarves. Created extravagant, daring, amusing designs (e.g., bouffant gloves ballooning to the shoulders). Known as an outspoken rebel. See her *Shocking Life* (1954).

Vionnet, Madeleine, 1878–, operated Parisian house of couture from 1918 to 1939. Known for her graceful, sensuous use of pure silks, organdies, chiffons, velvets, and clinging lamés. Created swirling evening gowns with remarkable use of bias cutting, transforming medieval and Greek-inspired styles into a look of sleek modernity. Diaphanous evening wear was antifunctional in the extreme. Made wide-sleeved coats and toques. Designed directly on half-scale mannequin dolls; collection of these is in the Union des arts de costume in Paris.

Worth, Charles Frederick, 1825–95, founder of the Maison Worth in Paris and London, arbiter of women's fashions for more than a century. First designed silks and then became court dressmaker to Empress Eugénie of France and Empress Elizabeth of Austria. Created the ancestor of the tailor-made suit; invented the puffed tunic called the Polonaise. His descendants continued business after his death. House of Worth in London still in operation. See Edith Saunders, *The Age of Worth* (1955).

Fashoda Incident (fəshōˈdə), 1898, diplomatic dispute between France and Great Britain. Toward the end of the 19th cent., while Britain was seeking to establish a continuous strip of territory from Cape Town to Cairo, France desired to establish an overland route from the Red Sea to the Atlantic Ocean. To make good their claim the French dispatched (May 1, 1897) Major J. B. MARCHAND with a small force from Brazzaville, in the face of a British warning. After crossing over 2,000 mi (3,200 km) of almost unexplored wilderness, Marchand reached (July 10, 1898) the village of Fashoda (now KODOK) on the Nile in the S Sudan. Beating off a Mahdist attack, he stopped there to await an expected Franco-Ethiopian expedition from the east. Meanwhile, Lord Kitchener's Anglo-Egyptian army had defeated (Sept. 2) the Mahdists in the N Sudan. When he heard of the French activities, Kitchener led forces upriver to Fashoda and, despite Marchand's presence, claimed (Sept. 19) the town for Egypt. The French government resisted for a time, but, fearing war, ordered its mission to withdraw on Nov. 3. In March, 1899, France yielded its claim to the upper Nile region and accepted part of the Sahara as compensation.

Fast, Howard, 1914–, American author, b. New York City. An extremely prolific writer, Fast is best known for his historical novels, most of which treat the themes of freedom and social justice. They include *Citizen Tom Payne* (1943), *My Glorious Brothers* (1948), *April Morning* (1961), and *Torquemada* (1966). From 1943 to 1956, Fast was a member of the Communist party. He served a prison term in 1950 for refusing to cooperate with the House Un-American Activities Committee; in 1953 he was awarded the Stalin Peace Prize. *The Naked God* (1957) is an account of his political experiences.

fasti (făsˈtī), in ancient Rome, days on which public business could be transacted without impiety. The word also came to be used for the calendars and almanacs that contained such information as holy days, festivals, and historical events. The first known fasti was published in 304 B.C.

fasting, partial or temporary abstinence from food, a widely used form of ASCETICISM. Among the stricter Jews the principal fast is the Day of Atonement, or Yom Kippur (see ATONEMENT, DAY OF); in Islam the faithful fast all the daytime hours of the month of RAMADAN. Fasting is general in Christianity. The most widely observed fasts are LENT and ADVENT. Both of these are preliminary to seasons of great rejoicing, and traditionally the VIGILS of several feasts were also kept as fasts, e.g. (in the West), those of Christmas, Easter, Whitsunday, the Assumption, and All Saints. EMBER DAYS were also fasts in the West. Protestants have generally abandoned fasting, but in New England an annual Fast Day was proclaimed (in Massachusetts until the 20th cent.). The Roman Catholic Church differentiates between fasting (eating only one full meal and little else in a day) and abstinence (eating no flesh meat). In 1966, Pope Paul VI issued *Poenitemini,* an apostolic constitution reorganizing the discipline of the Catholic Church. Ash Wednesday and Good Friday are now the only required days of fast. The observance of Fridays as days of abstinence is now urged rather than, as formerly, made a matter of obligation. Roman Catholics are asked to abstain from food and drink for one hour prior to receiving communion.

Fastnet Rock (făstˈnĭt), islet, Co. Cork, S Republic of Ireland. Its 160-ft (49-m) lighthouse is near the most southerly point of Ireland.

Fastolf, Sir John (făsˈtŏlf), 1378?–1459, English soldier. He won distinction for his long service in the latter part of the Hundred Years War. He was knighted some time prior to 1418 for service at Agincourt (1415) and in other engagements, acted as governor of Anjou and Maine (1423–26), and was made (1426) a Knight of the Garter. While convoying supplies in 1429, Fastolf repelled a French attack by using herring barrels as protection (see HERRINGS, BATTLE OF THE). His conduct at the defeat of the English by Joan of Arc at Patay (1429), where he retreated after a panic of his men, has been variously described as common sense or cowardice. Fastolf continued, however, to exercise responsible commands until his final return to England in 1440. He amassed a considerable fortune by somewhat sharp methods, and he spent his last years on his huge Norfolk estate. A neighbor to John Paston, the principal beneficiary of his will, he features prominently in the PASTON LETTERS. See James Gairdner, ed., *The Paston Letters* (1904); D. W. Duthie, *The Case of Sir John Fastolf* (1907).

fat: see OBESITY; FATS AND OILS.

fata morgana: see MIRAGE.

Fategarh, India: see FARRUKHABAD.

Fatehpur Sikri or **Fathpur Sikri** (both: fətəpo͞or' sĭk'rē), historic city (1971 pop. 13,998), Uttar Pradesh state, N India. It was founded (1569) by the Mogul emperor Akbar to honor the Muslim saint Shaikh Salim Chishti, who had foretold the birth of Akbar's son and heir, Jahangir. The city was Akbar's capital until 1584. By 1605 it was largely deserted because of the inadequate water supply. A masterpiece of Muslim architecture, the city is unique in India as a nearly intact Mogul city. The Buland Darwaza [gate of victory], flanked by colossal statues of elephants, was the principal entrance. Carvings and murals cover many of the buildings. Among the most notable are the Jami Masjid (the Great Mosque), with its ornate marble mausoleum of Salim Chishti; the palaces of Jodh Bai and Birbal; and the Panch Mahal, the royal audience hall.

Fates, in Greek religion, three goddesses who controlled the lives of men; also called the Moerae or Moirai. They were: Clotho, who spun the web of life; Lachesis, who measured its length; and Atropos, who cut it. Although the extent of their influence was uncertain, some legends state that the Fates' power was superior even to that of Zeus. The Roman Fates were the Parcae—Nona, Decuma, and Morta. In Germanic mythology, the three NORNS wove the web of life.

Fath Ali Shah (făth älē' shä', fät), 1762–1834, shah of Persia (1797–1834), nephew and successor of Aga Muhammad Shah, of the Kajar, or Qajar, dynasty. Most of his reign was spent in both internal and external warfare. An avaricious ruler, he managed to maintain himself against other claimants to the throne, but he was not so fortunate in his wars with Russia. He sought to enlist aid from Napoleon, who was then contemplating an attack on India, but the shah's hopes were dashed when Napoleon signed the Treaty of Tilsit (1807) with Russia. Fath Ali subsequently turned to England, but English influence failed to protect Persia from Russian encroachments. The shah's attempt to reconquer Georgia proved disastrous, and the Treaty of Gulistan (1813) and the Treaty of Turkamanchai (1828) deprived Persia of the Caucasus and marked a downward trend in Persian power. The name appears also as Feth Ali Shah.

Fathers of the Church, collective name for the Christian writers of early times whose work is considered generally orthodox. A convenient definition includes all such writers up to and including St. GREGORY I (St. Gregory the Great) in the West and St. JOHN OF DAMASCUS in the East (see PATRISTIC LITERATURE). There are several conventional groupings of the Fathers of the Church. One of these is the Apostolic Fathers, usually considered to include the authors of the *Didache*, of the Epistles of Clement, of the Epistles of Ignatius of Antioch, and of the Shepherd of Hermas. In an ancient category of honor eight **Doctors of the Church** are set apart; the Four Doctors of the Greek Church are St. Basil the Great, St. Gregory Nazianzen, St. John Chrysostom, and St. Athanasius; the Four Doctors of the Latin Church are St. Ambrose, St. Jerome, St. Augustine, and St. Gregory the Great. Since the 16th cent., the title Doctor of the Church has also been given by the Roman Catholic Church to later doctrinal writers, including St. Thomas Aquinas, St. Bonaventura, St. Anselm, St. Bernard of Clairvaux, St. John of the Cross, St. Theresa of Avila, and St. Catherine of Siena.

Fathpur Sikri: see FATEHPUR SIKRI.

fatigue, in engineering, microscopic cracking of materials, especially metals, after repeated applications of stress. Fissures may be formed within pieces of metal during their manufacture when, while cooling from the molten state, they shrink and tensile stresses arise. Once a crack has started it spreads under repeated stress until the metal ruptures. Examples of fatigue are found in steel rails, beams, and girders. Metallic fatigue resulted in the catastrophes encountered by many of the Liberty ships built during World Wars I and II and the crashes of a number of the earliest jet aircraft constructed. Materials used in construction are tested for fatigue strength, or endurance limit, by being subjected mechanically to cyclic applications of stress. Steel parts are sometimes treated by shot blasting to increase their fatigue resistance.

fatigue, in physiology, inability to perform reasonable and necessary physical or mental activity. When the metabolic reserves of the body are exhausted and the waste products increased, as for example after prolonged exertion, the body finds it difficult to continue its function and activity. The accumulation of LACTIC ACID in muscle tissue and the depletion of GLYCOGEN (stored glucose) results in muscle fatigue. The contractile properties of muscle are reduced and continued exertion is impossible unless the muscle is allowed to rest. In the normal body a period of rest permits a redistribution of nutritive elements to the muscles and tissues and the elimination of the accumulated waste products; the body is then ready to resume activity. There are some persons, however, in whom fatigue is a chronic state that does not necessarily result from activity or exertion. In some instances this abnormal fatigue may be associated with systemic disorders such as anemia, a deficiency of protein or oxygen in the blood, addiction to drugs, increased or decreased function of the endocrine glands, or kidney disease in which there is a large accumulation of waste products. If excessive fatigue occurs over a prolonged period, exhaustion (marked loss of vital and nervous power) may result. In most persons with chronic fatigue, however, the condition seems to be associated with nervous instability or psychic disorders. Thorough medical and psychiatric examination may be required.

Fatima (făt'ĭmə, fä'tĭmə, fətē'mə), 606?–632, daughter of MUHAMMAD by his first wife, Khadija. Fatima was the wife of ALI, the mother of Hasan and Husayn, and reputedly the ancestress of the Fatimids. She is revered by all branches of the Islamic faith and is the subject of many mysteries and legends.

Fátima (fä'təmə), hamlet, W central Portugal, in Beira Litoral. At the nearby Cova da Iria is the national shrine of Our Lady of the Rosary of Fátima. This became a great Roman Catholic center of pilgrimage after the six reported apparitions of the Virgin Mary to three shepherd children, May 13–Oct. 13, 1917. The oldest of these children was named Lucia de Jesus Santos. An impressive basilica was built in 1944.

Fatimid (făt'ĭmĭd) or **Fatimite** (-ĭmīt), dynasty claiming to hold the CALIPHATE on the basis of descent from FATIMA, a daughter of Muhammad the Prophet. In doctrine the Fatimids were related to other Shiite sects, including the Karmathians, the Assassins, and most closely, the Druses. The dynasty's founder, Said ibn Husayn of NE Syria, was long engaged in religious activity. A follower, Al-Shii, went (c.893) to NW Africa and inspired the Berbers to rebel against their Sunni Aghlabid rulers. Said ibn Husayn attempted (c.903) to join Al-Shii in NE Algeria, but he was arrested at Tripoli by the Aghlabid governor. He was rescued (909) by Al-Shii who in the meantime had overthrown the Aghlabids and won Tunisia, Sicily, NE Algeria and NW Libya for the Fatimids. Said ibn Husayn was then hailed as the MAHDI. He took the name Ubaidallah and set up a caliphate in opposition to the Abbasid Caliphate of Baghdad. His execution of Al-Shii caused (911) a short-lived rebellion among the tribes who had first supported the Fatimid claims. From their fortress capital of Mahdia (see AL MAHDIYAH), the Fatimids dominated most of NW Africa. Their fleets continually ravaged the W Mediterranean. After Ubaidallah's death in 934, Malta, Sardinia, Corsica, and the Balearics, and, for a time, Genoa were taken and held. In the reign (953–75) of the 4th caliph, Moizz, Fatimid fortunes reached their height. Moizz's great general, Jauhr, easily took Egypt in 969. Subsequently, Jauhr conquered Palestine, parts of Syria, and W Arabia. In 973, Moizz moved his capital to Egypt and the new city of Cairo. The policy of employing mercenary troops begun by the 5th caliph, Aziz, was to prove fatal to the dynasty. Hakim (996–1021), the 6th caliph, abandoned the religious toleration of his ancestors. He persecuted the Jews and Christians and destroyed (1010) the Church of the Holy Sepulcher in Jerusalem. In 1020, Hakim proclaimed himself the reincarnation of God. This claim was accepted only in Syria, where it is still espoused by the DRUSES. After Hakim's assassination, Fatimid power rapidly declined. Factious mercenary soldiers thereafter constantly threatened to destroy the state. The caliphs lost power to a series of viziers who eventually even took the title of king. Syria, Algeria, and Tunisia fell away (1043–48). By 1071 the Normans had conquered Sicily. Palestine was taken (1099) by the Crusaders, and the Fatimids were left with little more than Egypt. When the Assassins killed (1130) Amir, the last caliph of any ability, the country lapsed into anarchy. In 1169, Nur ad-Din of Damascus conquered Egypt, and his general, SALADIN, reluctantly ordered (1171) the name of the Abbasid Sunni caliph to be used in prayers throughout the land. In the same year the feeble Adid, the 14th and last of the Fatimid rulers, died. See De Lacey O'Leary, *Short History of the Fatimid Khalifate* (1923).

fats and oils, group of organic substances that form an important part of the diet and also are useful in many industries. The fats are usually solid, the oils generally liquid at ordinary room temperatures. Some tropical products, liquids in their sites of origin, become solids in cooler climates; in commerce these often retain the name originally given, e.g., palm oil and coconut oil. Chemically fats and oils are either simple or mixed glyceryl ESTERS of organic acids belonging to the fatty-acid series (see TRIGLYCERIDES; FATTY ACIDS). Fats and oils are derived from both plant and animal sources. Among the vegetable oils of greatest commercial importance are cottonseed, linseed, olive, palm, corn, peanut, soybean, and castor oils. The method of obtaining the oils is similar for all: the fruits or seeds after being cleaned are crushed and pressed cold to obtain the highest grade of oil and then pressed warm, yielding a grade suitable for industrial use. Sometimes solvents are used to remove the remaining oil from the crushed mass. Edible oils are those used in foods, and for these the highest grade is utilized; these must be pale in color, free from disagreeable odor and taste, and wholesome. The lower grades are suitable for making soap and for other industrial purposes. The chemical property that makes fats solid and oils liquid is the amount of saturation in the ester (see SATURATED FATS). Animal fats are esters of saturated fatty acids; vegetable oils are esters of unsaturated fatty acids. Conversion of liquid vegetable oils into solid fats is an important chemical industry. This process, sometimes called hardening, involves hydrogenation of the unsaturated fatty-acid portion of the oil molecule by heating the oil with hydrogen in the presence of a metal catalyst; by controlling the extent of hydrogenation, various products can be obtained. For example, controlled hydrogenation of cottonseed oil produces a solid vegetable cooking fat. Most fats become rancid upon standing; since a major factor leading to rancidity is air oxidation of double bonds (to form foul-smelling ALDEHYDES), saturated fats are much more resistant to rancidity than unsaturated fats. Animal fats used in foods include butter, lard, chicken fat, and suet. Cod-liver oil and some other fish oils are used therapeutically as sources of vitamins A and D. Nutritionally fats and oils are valued as a source of energy. Because they contain less oxygen than other nutrients they oxidize more readily and release more energy. Fats are digested in the human body chiefly by the enzyme lipase (in the pancreatic juice), aided by the bile. There are several theories to explain the method of absorption of fats; favored by many is the view that they are absorbed by the epithelial cells of the lining of the small intestine in the form of the fatty acids and glycerol into which they are split by digestion and that a recombination to reform the fat occurs within the cells. Most of the fat then enters the lymphatic system through the villi in the lining of the small intestine, although some is probably absorbed directly by the blood vessels of the villi. Medical research indicates the possibility that saturated fats in the diet contribute to the incidence of ARTERIOSCLEROSIS; such fats may raise the blood's level of cholesterol, which is deposited in the arteries. See OILS; PETROLEUM.

Fatshan: see FO-SHAN, China.

fatty acid, any of the organic carboxylic acids present in FATS AND OILS as esters of GLYCEROL. Molecular weights of fatty acids vary over a wide range. The carbon skeleton of any fatty acid is unbranched. Some fatty acids are saturated, i.e., each carbon atom is connected to its carbon atom neighbors by single bonds; and some fatty acids are unsaturated, i.e., contain at least one carbon-carbon double bond (see CHEMICAL BOND). When fats and oils are hydrolyzed with an alkali, the fatty acids are liberated as their metal salts; these salts are soaps. BUTYRIC ACID is a fatty acid found in butter.

Faubus, Orval, 1910–, governor of Arkansas (1955–67), b. Combs, Ark. A school teacher, he served in World War II and after the war became state highway commissioner. He won the governorship in a runoff election. In 1957, Faubus created a turmoil by calling out the Arkansas National Guard to prevent the integration of Central High School in Little Rock. He was eventually forced to withdraw the National Guard. Rioting broke out, and President Dwight D. Eisenhower sent U.S. troops to Little Rock and put the National Guard under Federal command in order to ensure the integration of the school. In 1974 he attempted a political comeback but lost the Democratic primary election for governor.

Fauchard, Pierre (pyĕr fōshăr'), 1678–1761, French dentist, a founder of modern dentistry. He practiced in Paris from c.1715 and was influential in raising dentistry from a trade to a profession. He advocated the sharing of dental knowledge and wrote *The Surgeon Dentist* (1728, tr. of 2d ed. 1946), long a standard work on dentistry. See study by B. W. Weinberger (1941).

Fauchet, Claude (klōd fōshā'), 1744–93, French clergyman and revolutionary, constitutional bishop of Calvados. A leader in the attack (1789) on the Bastille, Fauchet was a member of the Commune of Paris, of the Legislative Assembly, and of the Convention. Self-styled the Attorney General of the Truth, he sided with the GIRONDISTS; after their fall he was executed.

Faulkner, Brian, 1921–, Northern Irish politician. A businessman, he was elected to the Northern Ireland Parliament as a Unionist in 1949. As minister of home affairs (1959–63) he earned a reputation as a hard liner in his efforts to end the terrorism of the illegal Irish Republican Army (IRA). He served (1963–69) as commerce minister under Terence (later Lord) O'NEILL. Having lost a contest for the premiership to James Chichester-Clarke in 1969, Faulkner became minister of development and steered through Parliament reforms to end discrimination against Roman Catholics in housing and local government. He was increasingly identified as a moderate, and it was in this new image that he was chosen to succeed Chichester-Clarke as prime minister in March, 1971. By that time the British army, which had been sent to Northern Ireland in 1969 to act as a buffer between the warring Protestants and Catholics, had alienated much of the Catholic community and was the object of increasing IRA terrorist attacks. In Aug., 1971, Faulkner began a policy of interning suspected IRA members, but this move led to an intensification of the violence. Further polarization between Catholics and Protestants resulted from the so-called "Derry massacre" of Jan., 1972, when British troops fired on an illegal Catholic demonstration in Londonderry and killed 13 people. Two months later (March 30, 1972) the British cabinet suspended the Northern Ireland government, and Faulkner and his ministry resigned. Faulkner cooperated with the British in the establishment (1973) of a new provincial legislature and executive board. He became head of the board—a coalition of Protestants and Catholics—in Jan., 1974, but was forced to resign leadership of his party. When a general strike of Protestant workers crippled the province in May, 1974, Faulkner resigned from the board, bringing the collapse of the new executive and the reimposition of direct British rule.

Faulkner, William, 1897–1962, American novelist, b. New Albany, Miss., one of the great American writers of the 20th cent. Born into an old Southern family named Falkner, he changed the spelling of his last name to Faulkner when he published his first book, a collection of poems entitled *The Marble Faun*, in 1924. Faulkner trained in Canada as a cadet pilot in the Royal Air Force in 1918, attended the University of Mississippi in 1919–20, and lived in Paris briefly in 1925. In 1931 he bought a pre-Civil War mansion, "Rowanoak," in Oxford, Miss., where he lived, a virtual recluse, for the rest of his life. As a writer Faulkner's primary concern was to probe his own region, the deep South. Most of his novels are set in Yoknapatawpha county, an imaginary area in Mississippi with a colorful history and a richly varied population. The county is a microcosm of the South as a whole, and Faulkner's novels examine the effects of the dissolution of traditional values and authority on all levels of Southern society. One of his primary themes is the abuse of blacks by the Southern whites. Because Faulkner's novels treat the decay and anguish of the South since the Civil War, they abound in violent and sordid events. But they are grounded in a profound and compassionate humanism that celebrates the tragedy, energy, and humor of ordinary human life. The master of a rhetorical, highly symbolic style, Faulkner was also a brilliant literary technician, making frequent use of convoluted time sequences and of the STREAM OF CONSCIOUSNESS technique. He was awarded the 1949 Nobel Prize in literature. His best-known novels are *The Sound and the Fury* (1929), *As I Lay Dying* (1930), *Sanctuary* (1931), *Light in August* (1932), *Absalom, Absalom!* (1936), *The Unvanquished* (1938), *The Hamlet* (1940), *Intruder in the Dust* (1948), *Requiem for a Nun* (1951), *A Fable* (1954; Pulitzer Prize), *The Town* (1957), *The Mansion* (1959), and *The Reivers* (1962; Pulitzer Prize). In addition to novels Faulkner published several volumes of short stories including *These 13* (1931), *Go Down, Moses* (1942), *Knight's Gambit* (1949), and *Big Woods* (1955); and collections of essays and poems. See the reminiscences of his brother, John (1963); biographies by H. H. Waggoner (1959) and Joseph Blotner (2 vol., 1974); studies by R. P. Adams (1968), L. G. Leary (1973), and J. W. Reed, Jr. (1973); F. J. Hoffman and O. W. Vickery, ed., *William Faulkner: Three Decades of Criticism* (1960).

fault, in geology, fracture in the earth's crust in which the rock on one side of the fracture moves in relation to the rock on the other side. Faults are most evident in sedimentary formations where they result in conspicuous offsetting of previously continuous strata. The fracture (fault plane or fault surface) along which a fault takes place may be vertical, inclined, or nearly horizontal. Movement along a fault plane may be vertical, horizontal, or oblique in direction, or it may consist in the rotation of one or both of the fault blocks. The side of a fault that has been raised relative to the other is commonly called the upthrown side, and the other the downthrown side. These terms, however, are purely relative and not necessarily descriptive of the absolute movement, for the same effect is produced whether the two sides are moving in opposite directions, or one is stationary while the other moves, or both move in the same direction but not to the same extent. In inclined faults (which make up the great majority of all faults) the term "hanging wall" is used for the side that lies vertically above the other, called the "footwall." A fault in which the footwall is the upthrown side is called a normal, or gravity, fault; a fault in which the hanging wall is the upthrown side is called a reverse, or thrust, fault because the hanging wall appears to have been pushed up over the footwall. Faults are classified also as high-angle and low-angle, and these classes are generally considered to correspond, respectively, to gravity faults and thrust faults. Faults displaying horizontal movement, resulting in the lateral displacement of points originally opposite one another across the fault plane, are called strike-slip, lateral, or transcurrent faults. The SAN ANDREAS FAULT of California is of this type. Another type of fault with horizontal displacement, the transform fault, has been recognized on the ocean floor between offset portions of the mid ocean ridge. Movement of rock on each side of the fault is directed away from the center of the ridge, which is not further offset by the fault movement. Faults create interpretation problems for the geologist by altering the relations of strata (see STRATIFICATION), in some cases making the same bed, or rock layer, appear twice in a vertical cross section of a formation and in others making beds disappear altogether. Faults commonly recur along the same fault plane, so that the sum of the movements, although each movement is comparatively small, often produces a very great effect. A sudden movement of rock masses along the fault plane is the most frequent cause of earthquakes.

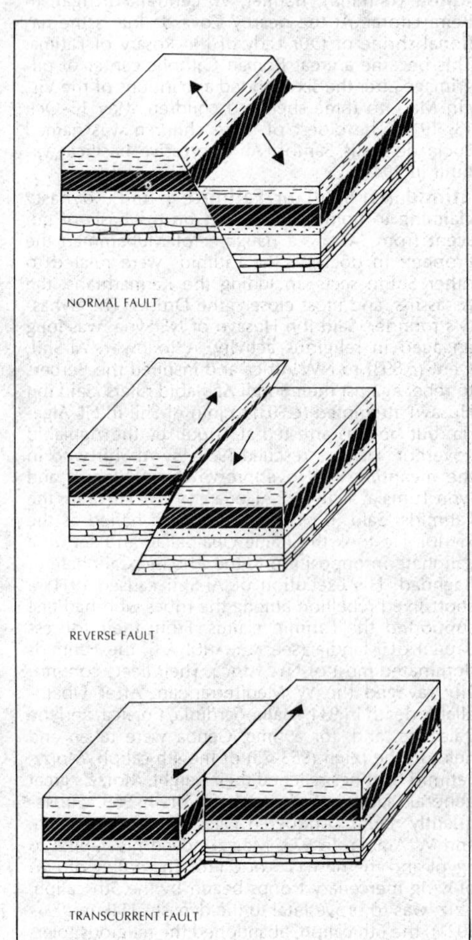

Types of faults

faun: see FAUNUS.

Faunus (fôn'əs), in Roman religion, woodland deity, protector of herds and crops. He was identified with the Greek Pan. His festival was observed on Dec. 5 with dancing and merrymaking. Another festival, the LUPERCALIA, held in February, is also generally believed to have been in honor of him. He was attended by fauns—mischievous and sportive creatures, half man and half goat, similar to satyrs. The female counterpart of Faunus was Bona Dea, also called Fauna.

Fauquier, Francis (fôkēr'), c.1704–1768, acting royal governor of Virginia (1758–68). He came to the colony as lieutenant governor in 1758, and in the absence of the governors—the earl of Loudon (1756–63) and Jeffrey Amherst (1763–68)—he was the chief administrative officer. Instructions sent with him demanded that the office of treasurer of the colony be taken from the speaker of the house of burgesses, but he disobeyed these instructions and gained and maintained the friendship of the house. In 1760 he informed the government of the trend toward opposition to British policies in the colony and proposed that British tax policy be changed. In 1765, however, he dissolved the house of burgesses when it passed a resolution against the Stamp Act.

Faure, Élie (ālē' fôr), 1873–1937, French art historian. Trained in medicine, he brought his scientific knowledge to bear in his study of the history of art, relating it to the progress of human culture. Of his long list of critical and historical works, the best known is his *History of Art* (5 vol., 1909–21; tr. by Walter Pach, 1937).

Faure, Félix (fālěks'), 1841–99, president of the French republic (1895–99). A leather merchant, he served in the Franco-Prussian War and became an undersecretary for commerce and colonies in the cabinet of Léon Gambetta (1881–82). He later (1882–85, 1888) occupied the post again and was vice president of the chamber of deputies and naval minister before becoming president. The DREYFUS AFFAIR was a notable development in his administration, and Faure marred his reputation by opposing a new trial. The Franco-Russian alliance was concluded, and the FASHODA INCIDENT occurred while he held office. Émile Loubet succeeded him as president.

Fauré, Gabriel Urbain (gäbrēĕl' ürbăN' fōrā'), 1845–1924, French composer; pupil of Saint-Saëns. In 1896 he succeeded Massenet as professor of composition at the Paris Conservatory, and was its director from 1905 to 1920. Among his many pupils were Ravel and Enesco. His works, largely of a refined, intimate quality, include nocturnes and barcarolles for piano, chamber music, and three operas. He is best known for his Requiem (1888) and many exquisite songs, including "Clair de Lune." See studies by Norman Suckling (1952) and E. Vuillermoz (1969).

Faust (foust), **Faustus,** or **Johann Faust** (yō'hän), fl. 16th cent., learned German doctor who traveled widely, performed magical feats, and died under mysterious circumstances. According to legend he had sold his soul to the devil (personified by Mephistopheles in many literary versions) in exchange for youth, knowledge, and magical power. Innumerable folk tales and invented stories were attached to his name. The first printed version is the *Volksbuch* (1587) of Johann Spiess, which, in English translation, was the basis of Christopher Marlowe's play *Dr. Faustus* (1593). Many versions followed, ranging from popular buffoonery to highly developed art forms. Spiess and Marlowe represent Faust as a scoundrel justly punished with eternal damnation, but Lessing instead saw in him the symbol of man's heroic striving for knowledge and power and therefore as worthy of praise and salvation. This view of Faust as seeker was continued by GOETHE in one of the greatest dramatic poems ever written. He enlarged upon the old legend, adding the element of love and the saving power of woman and presenting the story in a philosophical setting. Goethe first came to grips with the theme in 1774 (in what is called the *Urfaust*). The first part of *Faust* appeared in 1808; it is more suitable for the theater than the more profound and philosophic second part (1833). The many subsequent Faust novels and dramas, among them those of Klinger, Chamisso, Grabbe, and Lenau, could not rival the power and fame of Goethe's work. A recent variant of the Faust legend is Thomas Mann's novel *Doctor Faustus* (1947, tr. 1948). Goethe's *Faust* inspired innumerable composers of operas, oratorios, stage music, and symphonic works, including Berlioz, Gounod, Schumann, Liszt, and Boito. Spohr's and Busoni's Faust operas (respectively 1818 and 1925) are based on other literary models. See H. G. Meek, *Johann Faust* (1930); P. M. Palmer and R. P. More, *Sources of the Faust Tradition* (1936).

Fausta (Flavia Maximiana Fausta) (fôs'tə), d. c.326, Roman princess. She was the wife of CONSTANTINE I, the daughter of MAXIMIAN, and the mother of Constantine II, Constantius II, and Constans I. It is said that she was put to death by Constantine I when she falsely accused Crispus, Constantine's son by his first wife, of attempting to seduce her.

Faustina (fôstī'nə), name of two women, wives of Roman emperors. **1** The elder (c.104–141) was the wife of ANTONINUS PIUS, who founded a school for orphan girls in her honor. **2** The younger (c.125–176), daughter of Antoninus Pius and the elder Faustina, was the wife of MARCUS AURELIUS. She accompanied her husband on most of his campaigns, and she was called Mater Castrorum [mother of the camps] on the coinage.

Faustus: see FAUST.

fauvism (fō'vĭzəm) [Fr. *fauve*=wild beast], name derisively hurled at and cheerfully adopted by a group of French painters, including Matisse, Rouault, Derain, Vlaminck, Friesz, Marquet, van Dongen, Braque, and Dufy. Although fauvism was a short-lived movement (1905–8), its influence was international and basic to the evolution of 20th-century art. It was essentially an expressionist style, characterized by bold distortion of forms and exuberant color. Only Matisse continued to explore its possibilities after 1908. Most of the others contributed to the development of new styles, such as CUBISM, which immediately followed the fauvist movement. See J. P. Crespelle, *The Fauves* (tr. 1962); J. É. Muller, *Fauvism* (1967).

Favart, Charles Simon (shärl sēmôN' fävär'), 1710–92, French dramatist and theatrical manager, for a time director of the Opéra-Comique. He was the originator of the modern light opera and wrote, largely in collaboration with his wife, about 150 comedies and operettas, including *La Chercheuse d'esprit* (1741), *Les Amours de Bastien et de Bastiene* (1753), and *Les Trois Sultanes; ou, Soliman second* (1761). His wife, **Marie Justine Benoîte Duronceray Favart,** 1727–72, was a brilliant light-opera star.

Faversham (făv'ərshəm), municipal borough (1971 pop. 14,807), Kent, SE England, a port on a tributary of the Swale River. It is situated in a region where fruit and hops are grown. Timber, oil, fodder, apples, and cherries are shipped to London. Faversham has shipyards and light industries including brick-making, food processing, oyster fishing, and brewing. There are many Roman and Saxon remains. Faversham was an early member of the federation of the CINQUE PORTS. King Stephen, who founded the Cluniac abbey (now in ruins), was buried there in the 12th cent. with his queen, Matilda. In 1781 a powder mill blew up and destroyed half of the town.

Favras, Thomas de Mahy, marquis de (tômä' də mäē' märkē' də fävräs'), 1744–90, French royalist. After the outbreak of the French Revolution, he plotted (1789) with the comte de La Châtre to steal Louis XVI away to Metz and to proclaim the comte de Provence (later Louis XVIII) regent. The plan allegedly also called for the assassination of Jean Bailly, mayor of Paris, and the marquis de Lafayette, commander of the national guard. Denounced by some of his agents, Favras was arrested, but he divulged none of the details of the plot. He was hanged in 1790 despite lack of incriminating evidence.

Favre, Jules (zhül fä'vrə), 1809–80, French statesman. At first a partisan of the July Monarchy, he joined the republican opposition to King Louis Philippe. After the February Revolution of 1848 he was one of the leaders of the provisional government. Under Emperor Napoleon III he was a leader of the constitutional opposition. In 1858 he courageously defended Felice ORSINI. At the end of the Franco-Prussian War, Favre served briefly as foreign minister of the provisional government (1871); he negotiated the final peace with Germany, but was forced to withdraw from the government because of the rigorous conditions imposed by Germany on France.

Fawcett, Henry, 1833–84, English economist and statesman. A follower of John Stuart Mill, he was professor of political economy at Cambridge, and his *Manual of Political Economy* (1863) was widely read. As member of Parliament and later postmaster general under William Gladstone he achieved several important improvements in the postal system. His wife, **Dame Millicent Garrett Fawcett,** 1847–1929, noted English feminist, became the leader of the nonmilitant suffragists. She was made Dame of the British Empire in 1924. See biography by Ray Strachey (1931).

Fawkes, Guy: see GUNPOWDER PLOT.

Faxaflói (fäk'säflō"ē) or **Faxa Bay,** inlet, c.40 mi (60 km) long and c.55 mi (90 km) wide, W Iceland, between the Snaefellsnes and Reykjanes peninsulas. Most of Iceland's population live around the bay; Reykjavík is on the southeast shore. Two narrow arms, Hvalfjörður and Borgarfjörður, extend inland. The inlet is rich in fish.

Fay, Frank, 1870–1931, and **W. G. Fay,** 1872–1947, brothers, both Irish actors. The Fay brothers formed the Irish National Theatre, an amateur group founded on the conviction that only Irish actors could perform in Irish plays. Around the nucleus of this company Dublin's ABBEY THEATRE was formed in 1904 with W. G. Fay as its guiding force. The Fays emigrated to the United States in 1908, where they appeared in a repertory of Irish plays. See W. G. Fay and Catherine Carswell, *The Fays of the Abbey Theatre* (1935, repr. 1971).

Fay, Sidney Bradshaw, 1876–1967, American historian, b. Washington, D.C. Fay, professor of history at Dartmouth College (1902–14), Smith (1914–29), and Harvard (1929–46), earned his name as an authority on European diplomatic history. In *The Origins of the World War* (1928, 2d ed., rev. 1930, repr. 1967), Fay asserted that the responsibility for World War I was shared by all the powers involved, but that Austria, Serbia, and Russia were primarily to blame. His other works include *The Rise of Brandenburg-Prussia to 1786* (1937).

Fayal (fäyäl'), Port. *Faial,* island (1960 pop. 20,343), 66 sq mi (171 sq km), in the N Atlantic, one of the central AZORES, Portugal. It is in Horta dist., named for the island's chief town and port, Horta. Fruit and wine are exported.

Fayetteville (fā'ĕtvĭl). **1** City (1970 pop. 30,729), seat of Washington co., NW Ark., in the Ozarks; inc. 1836. It is a farm trade center with canneries and woodworking plants. The Univ. of Arkansas is there and maintains an agricultural experiment station nearby. Also in the vicinity are a state park and a U.S. veterans hospital. Because of its strategic location during the Civil War, the city was captured by troops of both sides; several battles occurred in the area, including the battle of Pea Ridge. **2** City (1970 pop. 53,510), seat of Cumberland co., S central N.C., at the head of navigation on the Cape Fear River; inc. 1783. An inland port (it is connected by a channel to the Intracoastal Waterway), Fayetteville is a marketing and shipping center in a farm and timber area. It has large textile and lumber industries and plants making power tools, plastics, tires, and automotive filters. Settled as two towns (1739) by Highland Scots, it became a Tory center during the American Revolution. The two towns were merged during the war, and in 1783 they were renamed for the Marquis de Lafayette. The city was state capital from 1789 to 1793 and the scene (1789) of the state convention that ratified the U.S. Constitution. A great fire in 1831 destroyed c.600 buildings. During the Civil War, Sherman occupied the town and razed its arsenal (1865). The city is the seat of Fayetteville State Univ., Methodist College, and a technical institute. It has a symphony orchestra. Nearby are U.S. Fort Bragg, Pope Air Force Base, and a veterans hospital.

Fayyum, Al (äl fīyōōm') or **Faiyum, El** (ĕl–), region, coextensive with Al Fayyum governorate, N Egypt, W of the Nile River, a depression (entirely below sea level) in the Libyan (or Western) Desert. It is an irrigated agricultural area made fertile by Nile water and silt, which are carried there by the canalized Bahr Yusuf River. The irrigation system in Al Fayyum makes use of canals originally dug under King Amenemhet III (d.1801 B.C.). Cereals, fruit, and cotton are produced. Lake Karun (known in ancient times as Lake MOERIS), located in the western part of the region, is used for fishing. Al Fayyum is rich in archaeological finds. These include the remains of a Neolithic farm settlement and many papyri written both in ancient Egyptian and in Arabic. The city of **Al Fayyum** (1970 est. pop. 151,000), located in the southeastern part of the governorate and its capital, is the region's trade, distribution, manufacturing, and transport center. Industries include cotton ginning; wool and cotton spinning and weaving; dyeing; tanning; and cigarette manufacturing.

Fazzan (fäz-zän') or **Fezzan** (fĕz–), historic region, SW Libya. MARZUQ, Sabhah, Brach, and Zawilah, all situated in oases, are the chief settlements. Located on caravan routes connecting the Mediterranean Sea with the Sudan, Fazzan was long important in the trans-Saharan trade. Herodotus, the 5th-century B.C. Greek historian, wrote that the region was part of the realm of the Garamantes, a people who have not been precisely identified. In 19 B.C., Rome conquered the region, calling it Phazania, and many of its inhabitants were converted to Christianity. After the Vandal invasion of North Africa in the 5th cent. A.D., Fazzan regained its independence. However, in 666 the Arabs conquered the region, and the people were soon converted to Islam. The Arabs held the area until the 10th cent., when it regained its independence. During the following centuries, Fazzan was at times ruled by foreign powers, and at times was independent. From the early 16th to the early 19th cent., it was the center of the Bani Muhammad dynasty, which originated in Morocco. Fazzan was annexed by the Ottoman Empire in 1842. Although Italian troops entered the region shortly after their landing in Libya in 1911, the area was not fully pacified by Italy until 1930. For later history, see LIBYA.

Fe, chemical symbol of the element IRON.

fealty: see FEUDALISM.

Fear, Cape, promontory on Smith Island, off SE N.C., at the mouth of the Cape Fear River. A lighthouse (built 1903) is on the cape, and a lightship is stationed off the dangerous Frying-Pan Shoals, which extend c.20 mi (32 km) to sea.

feast, commemorative banquet symbolizing communal unity. Generally associated with primitive rituals and later with religious practices, feasts may also commemorate such events as births, marriages, harvests, and deaths. The principal Christian feasts of the Western Church are EASTER, PENTECOST, EPIPHANY, and CHRISTMAS. The greater number of feasts (excluding Sunday, the weekly feast) fall on the same day of the month each year (e.g., Christmas) and constitute the temporal cycle. Some of the more important liturgical observances are movable (e.g., Easter) and are part of the sanctoral system. Among the Jews the chief feasts are ROSH HA-SHANAH, the Feast of TABERNACLES, PURIM, PASSOVER, HANUKKAH, and SHAVUOT. In the Muslim world the Islamic feasts vary according to country and locale, although there are several feast days of universal importance. The most widely celebrated are the little and great feasts following the fast of Ramadan and the feast commemorating the birth of Muhammad. In Buddhist countries festive celebrations are usually associated with the birthday of Buddha, his attainment of Nirvana, or enlightenment, and his death. In India there are many national and regional Hindu feasts. One of the most important is the feast of Holi. See also VIGIL and FASTING.

Feast of Fools: see FOOLS, FEAST OF.

Feather, Victor, 1908–, British labor leader. Born into extreme poverty, he went to work at age 14 filling flour sacks. In 1937 he joined the Trades Union Congress (TUC) as an organizer, becoming assistant secretary in 1947 and assistant general secretary in 1960. In 1969 he succeeded George Woodcock as general secretary, a post he held until 1973. He was made a life peer in 1974. Feather was the author of *Trade Unions, True Or False* (1951), *How Do the Communists Work?* (1953), and *The Essence of Trade Unionism* (1963). See Eric Silver, *Victor Feather, TUC* (1973).

Feather, river, 80 mi (129 km) long, rising in three forks in the Sierra Nevada, uniting N of Oroville, Calif., and flowing S into the Sacramento River, N of Sacramento, Calif. The Feather River basin was a rich source of gold in the mid-1800s. The Feather River project (1957–68), which includes Oroville Dam, is designed to furnish central and S California with water and to provide flood control, recreation, and hydroelectricity in the river basin.

feathers, outgrowths of the skin, constituting the plumage of birds. Feathers are believed to have evolved from reptilian scales in Mesozoic times. They grow only along certain definite tracts (pterylae), which vary in different groups of birds. Feathers develop from tiny projections of tissue (papillae) embedded in follicles and nourished by blood vessels in the dermis. When the feather is full grown, the blood supply is discontinued and the central shaft becomes hollow. Typically, barbs extend outward from the distal portion of the shaft, or rachis; smaller crosslinking barbules and hooks interlock neighboring barbs, forming a web that gives the feather both strength and flexibility. Down feathers, or plumulae, the first plumage of young birds and the protective undercoat of aquatic birds, lack these interlocking projections. A secretion of the thyroid gland stimulates the papilla to develop a new feather when one has been molted or pulled. Specialized feather forms are found in crests, top-knots, ruffs, and tail feathers. Bristles are modified feathers. The colors red, yellow, brown, and black are caused by pigment in the feathers. There are no blue pigments, and green and violet are rare; however, these colors, as well as iridescent effects, are caused by the reflection and diffraction of light. Feathers are lightweight, durable, and in some cases waterproof. They have protective and decorative functions, but, aside from their role in bird FLIGHT, their most important capacity is heat retention. Feathers have been used from ancient times for millinery and other ornamental purposes. The indiscriminate hunting of certain birds for their feathers has resulted in their near extinction; it is now prohibited by law in the United States.

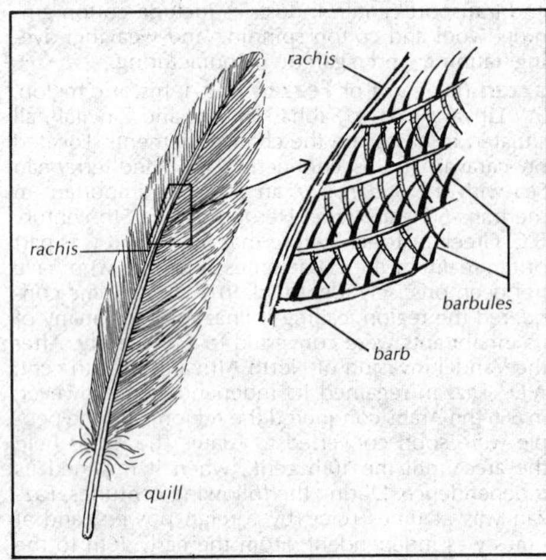

Structure of a bird feather

feather star, common name of a class of echinoderms that, as juveniles, are attached to the sea bottom by a stalk with rootlike branches; the mouth side faces upward. In the adult stage they break away from the stalk and move about freely. Feather stars have water-vascular (ambulacral) systems, similar to those in other echinoderms, that extend into the branched arms on the body, or crown. Some can swim by undulating movements of the arms. Feather stars creep about by means of projections at the base of the crown, called cirri, which can grasp bottom objects. They are marine animals, like all echinoderms, and are widely distributed. They are most common in relatively shallow, warm waters, but some live in cold water and a number of species occur in the ocean depths. Like other members of this class, feather stars may form extremely abundant local aggregations. Feather stars are classified in the phylum ECHINODERMATA, class Crinoidea.

February: see MONTH.

February Revolution, 1848, French revolution that overthrew the monarchy of LOUIS PHILIPPE and established the Second Republic. General dissatisfaction resulted partly from the king's increasingly reactionary policy, carried out after 1840 by François GUIZOT, and partly from the poor conditions of the working class, which were intensified by the economic crisis of 1846–47. A banquet campaign, organized to promote political opposition to the regime, led directly to the revolution when a huge banquet scheduled for Feb. 22, 1848, in Paris was forbidden by the government. On Feb. 22 street fighting began in Paris; on Feb. 23, in an incident that set off the revolution, government troops fired on the demonstrators. Louis Philippe abdicated the following day. The discrepancy of aims between bourgeois revolutionaries such as Alphonse de LAMARTINE and A. T. MARIE and the radicals, led by Louis BLANC, contributed to the eventual failure of the revolution. The chamber of deputies appointed a provisional government, including Lamartine, Alexandre LEDRU-ROLLIN, and L. A. GARNIER-PAGÈS, and, under popular pressure, proclaimed a republic. To appease the workers, the government guaranteed the right to work and established the national workshops. The workshops took their name from Louis Blanc's social workshops. The plan was deliberately mishandled, however, and amounted to nothing more than a dole. Radical demonstrations erupted (March), but these were turned into peaceful channels by Blanc himself. Many conservatives feared the "specter of communism." Elections in April gave a majority to the moderates, whose strength was greater in the provinces than in Paris. The provisional government was replaced by an executive commission (again including Lamartine and Ledru-Rollin). In the middle of May the workers attempted to overthrow the newly elected national assembly, but the revolt was quickly put down. The assembly determined to dissolve the national workshops. The resulting workers' rebellion, known as the JUNE DAYS, was crushed. After the completion of a republican constitution Prince Louis Napoleon (later NAPOLEON III) was elected president. The February revolution set off revolutions in most European nations, but, as in France, the movement failed virtually everywhere (see REVOLUTIONS OF 1848). See Alexis de Tocqueville, *Recollections* (new tr. 1970); studies by D. C. McKay (1933, repr. 1965) and Georges Duveau (1965, tr. 1968).

February Revolution, 1917, in Russian history: see *The February Revolution* under RUSSIAN REVOLUTION.

Fécamp (fākäN'), town (1968 pop. 21,745), Seine-Maritime dept., N France. A major port from the 12th to 17th cent., when Le Havre superseded it, Fécamp is now an important fishing port and a resort on the English Channel. The town also has shipyards, and food, textile, and machine-building industries. Fécamp dates back to Roman times. A monastery founded there c.660 became a pilgrimage site. Destroyed by Norsemen, it was rebuilt at the end of the 10th cent. and became the Benedictine Abbey of the Trinity. The abbey church, a magnificent example of 12th-century Norman architecture, has numerous additions from the 14th cent. Fécamp is famous for BENEDICTINE liqueur, which was first made by the monks in the 16th cent. and which is now made by a private company on the grounds of the old abbey.

Fechner, Gustav Theodor (go͝os'täf tā'ōdōr fĕkh'-nər), 1801–87, German philosopher and physicist, founder of psychophysics, educated at Dresden and Leipzig. He became professor of physics at Leipzig in 1834 but was forced by ill health to leave in 1839. Thereafter he devoted himself largely to the study of the relationship between body and mind, although under the name "Dr. Mises" he also wrote humorous satire. In philosophy he was an animist, maintaining that life is manifest in all objects of the universe. His greatest achievement was in the investigation of exact relationships in psychology and aesthetics. He formulated the rule known as Fechner's, or Weber's, law, that, within limits, the intensity of a sensation increases as the logarithm of the stimulus. Two of Fechner's most important works were *Zendavesta* (1851) and *Elementen der Psychophysik* (1860). See selections tr. by Charles Hartshorne and W. L. Reese, *Philosophers Speak of God* (1953); G. S. Hall, *Founders of Modern Psychology* (1912).

Feckenham, John de (fĕk'ənəm), 1518?–1585, English abbot. He became a Benedictine monk at Evesham, studied at Oxford, and later served as chaplain to the bishop of Worcester and to Edmund Bonner, bishop of London. Feckenham's sympathies were Roman Catholic, and his fortunes varied under the successive Tudor monarchs. He was confined to the Tower of London by Edward VI and kept there, except for brief periods, until Mary I became queen. He became chaplain and confessor to Mary and abbot of the reconstituted abbey of Westminster. After Elizabeth I's accession (1558), although his previous relations with her had been friendly, Feckenham spent most of the rest of his life in confinement for his refusal to recant his Roman Catholic beliefs.

Federal Art Project: see WORK PROJECTS ADMINISTRATION.

Federal Aviation Administration (FAA), U.S. Federal agency established in 1958 to regulate air commerce for the promotion of its safety and development. The agency combined the Civil Aeronautics Administration, the Airways Modernization Board, and the safety-regulating power of the Civil Aeronautics Board into one independent authority. In 1967 it was made a division of the newly formed Transportation Dept. Its responsibilities are: control of navigable airspace, including the regulation of both civilian and military air traffic under a common system; the development and promulgation of safety regulations and devices; and the promotion of the development of a national system of airports. The act that created the administration stipulates that its administrator be a civilian.

Federal Bureau of Investigation (FBI), division of the U.S. Dept. of Justice charged with investigating all violations of Federal laws except those assigned to some other Federal agency. The FBI has jurisdiction over some 185 investigative matters, among them espionage, sabotage, and other subversive activities; kidnapping; extortion; bank robbery; interstate transportation of stolen property; civil rights matters; interstate gambling violations; and fraud against the government. Created (1908) as the Bureau of Investigation, it originally conducted investigations only for the Justice Dept. After J. Edgar HOOVER became (1924) director of the Bureau of Investigation, Congress gradually added one duty after another to the jurisdiction of the bureau and reorganized (1933) it with wider powers as the Division of Investigation in the Dept. of Justice. Under Hoover's direction, it undertook a dramatic battle against the organized crime of the prohibition era. In 1935 it was designated the Federal Bureau of Investigation. The FBI played an important role in raising the standards of local police units through the FBI Academy. During Hoover's final years as director, the bureau became highly controversial and was the frequent target of attack from a wide variety of liberal groups. During the WATERGATE AFFAIR it was revealed that the FBI had yielded to pressure from top White House officials acting for President Richard M. Nixon to halt their investigation of the Watergate break-in. The FBI subsequently cooperated with the White House inquiry into the Watergate break-in and acting FBI director L. Patrick Gray destroyed files belonging to one of the convicted Watergate conspirators, E. Howard Hunt. Gray resigned (April, 1973) after his role became public. In June, 1973, Clarence Kelley was named director. See H. A. Overstreet, *The FBI in Our Open Society* (1969); W. W. Turner, *Hoover's FBI* (1970); R. O. Wright, ed., *Whose FBI?* (1974).

Federal Capital Territory: see AUSTRALIAN CAPITAL TERRITORY.

Federal Communications Commission (FCC), independent executive agency of the U.S. government established in 1934 to regulate interstate and foreign communications in the public interest. The FCC replaced the Federal Radio Commission—set up in 1927 to regulate radio communications. The FCC is composed of seven members, not more than four of whom may be members of the same political party, appointed by the President with the consent of the U.S. Senate for seven-year terms. The commissioners are authorized to classify television and radio stations, to prescribe the nature of their service, to assign broadcasting frequencies, and to carry out the regulations prescribed in the Federal Communications Act of 1934. The FCC has jurisdiction over standard, high-frequency, relay, international, television, and facsimile broadcasting stations and also has authority over experimental, amateur, coastal, aviation, strip, and emergency radio services and telegraph, telephone, and cable companies. The commission is empowered to grant, revoke, renew, and modify broadcasting licenses. The FCC is responsible for creating and implementing the policies and rules that will govern the development of cable television.

Federal Constitutional Convention, in U.S. history, the 1787 meeting in which the CONSTITUTION OF THE UNITED STATES was drawn up. The government adopted by the Thirteen Colonies in America (see CONFEDERATION, ARTICLES OF, and CONTINENTAL CON-

GRESS) soon showed serious faults. Congress, powerless to enforce its legislation, was unable to obtain adequate financial support. Although its achievements were not so inconsiderable as has been commonly thought, Congress was, on the whole, impotent, and Federal authority was too weak to be of consequence. The central government was unable to enforce any obligations it entered into with foreign nations. Severe economic troubles produced radical economic and political movements, such as SHAYS'S REBELLION. The monetary schemes of the states brought floods of paper money, which some of the states, notably Rhode Island, attempted to force creditors to accept. The threat to economic stability alarmed the wealthy conservative class; the merchants, who found the state tariffs not to their liking, were also harassed by the impossibility of making stable agreements with the English merchants. They were anxious to have a stronger Federal government to guarantee order and property rights. The men who had money invested in Western territories also favored a stronger Federal government controlling the territories. Therefore, agitation for the adoption of a stronger union grew steadily in force. Its advocates were zealous. James MADISON and George WASHINGTON in Virginia, Alexander HAMILTON in New York, and James WILSON (1742–98) and Benjamin FRANKLIN in Pennsylvania all favored some new scheme. The pamphlet of Pelatiah WEBSTER was important, although it has been, perhaps, overemphasized by enthusiasts; feeling for union was general. It was chiefly through the efforts of Madison that Virginia and Maryland agreed to a conference concerning navigation on the Potomac. The conference met in 1785 at Alexandria and at Mt. Vernon, but it was discovered that no agreements could be reached without the concurrence of Pennsylvania and Delaware. The upshot was the calling of a general convention of the states to discuss commercial problems. This met at Annapolis in Sept., 1786, but delegates from only five states—Virginia, Pennsylvania, New York, New Jersey and Delaware—arrived. The delegates therefore announced the calling of a general convention to revise the Articles of Confederation, to meet at Philadelphia in May, 1787. Notice was sent to Congress, but the new convention was launched as an extralegal body; cautious Congressional endorsement came only after five states had already selected their delegates. *The Constitution Emerges.* This convention drew up one of the most influential documents of Western world history, the Constitution of the United States. All the states except Rhode Island sent representatives. The delegates mainly came from the wealthier and more conservative ranks of society and included, besides Washington and the other proponents already mentioned, such leaders as Edmund RANDOLPH, Gouverneur MORRIS, Robert Morris, William PATERSON, Charles PINCKNEY, Charles Cotesworth PINCKNEY, Abraham BALDWIN, Luther MARTIN, and Roger SHERMAN. Washington was elected to preside, and the convention immediately set about drawing up a new scheme of government. However, it found itself faced with a rift: The smaller states wanted to retain their power, and the larger states wanted to have power determined by population. It was agreed that the new Congress should be made an effective body, but as to its composition there was great difference of opinion. The fundamental question was the apportionment of power in the new government. Edmund Randolph offered a plan known as the Randolph, the Virginia, or the Large-State Plan; it provided for a bicameral legislature, with the lower house elected according to population and the upper house elected by the lower. William Paterson offered the New Jersey, or the Small-State, Plan; it provided for equal representation of states in Congress. Neither the large states nor the small states would yield, and for a time it seemed that the convention would founder. Oliver Ellsworth and Roger Sherman put forward a compromise measure that gradually won approval; this provided for a lower house to be elected according to population (the House of Representatives) and an upper house to be chosen by the states (the Senate). This initial compromise eliminated the threat of a walkout by the small states, and the convention settled down to complete its task. It was agreed that Congress should have the power to levy direct but not indirect taxes, and the matter of counting slaves in the population for figuring representation was settled by a compromise agreement that three fifths of the slaves should be counted in apportioning representation and should also be counted as property in assessing taxes. Controversy over abolishing the importation of slaves ended with agreement that the importation should not be forbidden before 1808. There were, naturally, many other points of argument, and some of the delegates were so disgusted that they went home and later led the fight in their states against the ratification of the Constitution. James Madison was responsible for much of the substance of the Constitution, but the style was the work of Gouverneur Morris. The convention was in session until Sept. 17, 1787, and the document was then sent to the states for ratification. Delaware ratified it on Dec. 7 of that year. There were serious struggles in most of the states (see FEDERALIST, THE; FEDERALIST PARTY), especially since the convention had obviously gone beyond its mandate merely to amend the Articles of Confederation. North Carolina and Rhode Island rejected the Constitution, but the majority clause brought the Constitution into force without them by the end of June, 1788, and they were later forced to accept it. The thesis, associated with the name of Charles Austin BEARD, that the Constitution was framed solely to further the economic interest of special groups, notably creditors, land speculators, and holders of public securities, has not been generally accepted by historians. See C. A. Beard, *An Economic Interpretation of the Constitution* (1913, repr. 1960); Max Farrand, *The Framing of the Constitution* (1913, repr. 1962) and *Fathers of the Constitution* (1921); Carl Van Doren, *The Great Rehearsal* (1948); M. Jensen, *The New Nation* (1950, repr. 1962); Forrest McDonald, *We the People: The Economic Origins of the Constitution* (1958, repr. 1962) and *The Formation of the American Republic* (1967).

Federal Deposit Insurance Corporation (FDIC), an independent U.S. Federal executive agency designed to promote public confidence in banks and to provide insurance coverage for bank deposits up to $20,000. The corporation was established in 1933 to prevent a repetition of the losses incurred in the Great Depression when bankrupt banks could not return the money deposited in them. It is managed by a three-member board of directors. The FDIC provides coverage for deposits in national banks, state banks that are members of the Federal Reserve System, and in other qualified state banks. It may also make loans to insured banks in the interest of protecting the depositors. The corporation derives its income from assessments on insured banks and interest on government securities.

federal government or **federation,** government of a union of states in which sovereignty is divided between a central authority and component state authorities. A federation differs from a confederation in that the central power acts directly upon individuals as well as upon states, thus creating the problem of dual allegiance. Substantial power over matters affecting the people as a whole, such as external affairs, commerce, coinage, and the maintenance of military forces, are usually granted to the central government. Nevertheless, retention of jurisdiction over local affairs by states is compatible with the federal system and makes allowance for local feelings. The chief political problem of a federal system of government is likely to be the allocation of sovereignty, because the need for unity among the federating states may conflict with their desire for autonomy. The Greek city-states failed to solve this problem, although religious and political federations were often attempted and the Aetolian and Achaean leagues had many of the institutions of federal government. The primacy of the central over the state governments was not resolved in the United States until after the Civil War. The distribution of powers between the federal and state governments is usually accomplished by means of a written constitution, for a federation does not exist if authority can be allocated by ordinary legislation. A fairly uniform legal system, as well as cultural and geographic affinities, is usually necessary for the success of a federation. Varieties of federation include the Swiss, where the federative principle is carried into the executive branch of government; the Australian, which closely reflects American states' rights and judicial doctrines; and the Canadian, which reverses common federative practice and allots residuary rights to the dominion government. Other examples of federal governments are the German Empire of 1871 and the present state of West Germany, the USSR, Mexico, South Africa, and India. See James Bryce, *The American Commonwealth* (rev. ed. 1959); Kenneth Wheare, *Federal Government* (4th ed. 1964); W. H. Riker, *Federalism: Origin, Operation, Significance* (1964); I. D. Duchacek, *Comparative Federalism* (1970); D. J. Elazar, *American Federalism* (2d ed. 1972).

Federal Hall National Memorial: see NATIONAL PARKS AND MONUMENTS (table).

Federalist, The, series of 85 political essays, sometimes called *The Federalist Papers,* written 1787–88 under the pseudonym "Publius." Alexander Hamilton initiated the series with the immediate intention of persuading New York to approve the Federalist Constitution. He had as collaborators James Madison and John Jay. Hamilton certainly wrote 51 of the essays, Madison wrote 14, Jay 5; the authorship of 15 is in dispute (as between Hamilton and Madison). The essays were widely read as they appeared, and all except the last 8 were first printed in New York newspapers; the last 8 were first included in a two-volume edition of all the essays in 1788 and were then reprinted in the newspapers. Although the essays had little impact on the debate to ratify the Constitution, they are widely considered a classic work of political theory. The authors expounded at length upon the fundamental problems of republican government, and argued that federalism offered a means of both preserving state sovereignty and safeguarding the individual's freedom from tyrannical rule. There have been many editions of the papers and much literature about them, a great deal of it devoted to determining authorship. For one edition of the papers see J. E. Cooke, ed., *The Federalist* (1961). See study by Gottfried Dietze (1960).

Federalist party, in U.S. history, the political faction that favored a strong Federal government. In the later years of the Articles of Confederation there was much agitation for a strong federal union, which was crowned with success when the Federal Constitutional Convention drew up the Constitution of the United States. The men who favored the strong union and who fought for the adoption of the Constitution by the various states were called Federalists, a term made famous in that meaning by the *Federalist Papers (see* FEDERALIST, THE) of Alexander Hamilton, James Madison, and John Jay. After the Constitution was adopted and the new government was established under the presidency of George Washington, political division appeared within the cabinet, the opposing groups being headed by Alexander HAMILTON and by Thomas JEFFERSON. The party that emerged to champion Hamilton's views was the Federalist party. Its opponents, at first called Anti-Federalists, drew together into a Jeffersonian party; first called the Republicans and later the Democratic Republicans, they eventually became known as the Democratic party. The issue had not yet been joined when John ADAMS was elected President, but the choice of Adams was, nevertheless, a modest Federalist victory. The Federalists were conservatives; they favored a strong centralized government, encouragement of industries, attention to the needs of the great merchants and landowners, and establishment of a well-ordered society. In foreign affairs they were pro-British, while the Jeffersonians were pro-French. The members of the Federalist party were drawn largely from the ranks of the wealthy merchants, the big property owners of the North, and the conservative small farmers and businessmen. Geographically, they were concentrated in New England, with a strong element in the Middle Atlantic states. During Washington's second administration, and under that of John Adams, Federalist domestic policies were given a chance to prove themselves. The young nation's economy was established on a sound basis, while the governmental structure was expanded and an honest and efficient administrative system was developed. In foreign affairs, however, trouble with France led to virtual warfare in 1798. It led also to the ALIEN AND SEDITION ACTS, passed by the Federalist-controlled Congress ostensibly in response to hostile actions of the French Revolutionary government but actually designed to destroy the Jeffersonians. John Adams, who was a moderate and honest man, followed the course he considered wise, and by rejecting Hamilton's extreme desires, he caused something of a division in the Federalist ranks. The Jeffersonians were meanwhile winning popular support not only among Southern landowners but also among the mechanics, workers, and generally the less privileged everywhere. Jefferson showed skill in building his party, and the Jeffersonians were much better at publicity than were the Federalists. The election of 1800 was, therefore, a Federalist debacle. The Jeffersonians came to power and stayed there, establishing the so-called Virginia dynasty, with James Madison succeeding Jefferson and James Monroe succeeding Madison. The Federalist party remained powerful locally, but increasingly the leadership passed to the reactionaries rather than to the moderates. It tended to become a New England party. This trend was accentuated in the troubled period before the War of 1812. Merchants and shipowners were opposed to the EMBARGO ACT OF 1807, which caused considerable economic loss to the seaboard cities, and their feelings were expressed through the Federalist party. The Federalists, however, failed to enlist De Witt CLINTON and his followers in New York in their cause, and their challenge in the elections of 1808 was easily overridden by the Jeffersonians. Opposition to war brought the Federalists the support of Clinton and many others, and the party made a good showing in the election of 1812, winning New England (except for radical Vermont), New York, New Jersey, Delaware, and part of Maryland. They failed, however, in Pennsylvania and lost the election. While the country was at war, the disgruntled merchants of New England, represented by the ESSEX JUNTO, contemplated secession and called the HARTFORD CONVENTION. Thus, paradoxically the Federalists became the champions of STATES' RIGHTS. The successful issue of the war ruined the party, which became firmly and solely the party of New England conservatives. The so-called era of good feelings followed, and politics became a matter of internal strife within the Democratic party. The Federalist party did not even offer a presidential candidate in 1820, and by the election of 1824 it was virtually dead. See Claude G. Bowers, *Jefferson and Hamilton* (1925); W. O. Lynch, *Fifty Years of Party Warfare* (1931); L. D. White, *The Federalists* (1948); S. G. Kurtz, *The Presidency of John Adams: The Collapse of Federalism, 1795-1800* (1957, repr. 1961); J. C. Miller, *The Federalist Era, 1789-1801* (1960, repr. 1963); Shaw Livermore, *The Twilight of Federalism* (1962); D. H. Fischer, *The Revolution of American Conservatism* (1965); L. K. Kerber, *Federalists in Dissent* (1970).

Federal Power Commission (FPC), independent executive agency of the U.S. government established in 1920; it is charged with regulating interstate aspects of the electric power and natural gas industries. At first an interdepartmental agency of the departments of War, the Interior, and Agriculture, the commission was reorganized as an independent agency in 1930. The FPC operates under the control of five commissioners who are appointed by the President with the consent of the Senate. The FPC licenses non-Federal power sites and reviews Federal power sites; it passes on the location, design, and operation of hydroelectric projects on such sites. An investigation of each proposed project is made by the commission to determine if it is in the public interest, taking into consideration such matters as navigation, irrigation, flood control, and water supply; the agency considers both environmental protection and the nation's power needs. The FPC has the duty of determining the rental for power sites and of regulating wholesale rates and services. It regulates financial aspects of electrical utility companies. General surveys of power resources are also made by this agency. The FPC may help set up a voluntary coordination of a region's electrical energy. The FPC was given (1938) similar jurisdiction over natural gas projects, facilities, and rates.

Federal Reserve System, central banking system of the United States. Established in 1913, it began to operate in Nov., 1914. Its setup, although somewhat altered since its establishment, particularly by the Banking Act of 1935, has remained substantially the same.The Federal Reserve Act created 12 regional Federal reserve banks, supervised by a Federal Reserve Board. Each reserve bank is the central bank for its district. The boundary lines of the districts were drawn in accordance with broad geographic patterns of business, and the banks were placed in Boston, New York City, Philadelphia, Cleveland, Richmond, Atlanta, Chicago, St. Louis, Minneapolis, Kansas City, Dallas, and San Francisco. In addition some of the regional banks have one or more branch banks attached to them. All national banks must belong to the system, and state banks may if they meet certain requirements. Member banks hold the bulk of the deposits of all commercial banks in the country. Each member bank is required to own stock in the Federal reserve bank of its district and must maintain legal reserves on deposit with the district reserve bank. The required reserves are proportionate to the member bank's own deposits, the proportion varying according to the location of the member bank and the character of its deposits. Each reserve bank is managed by a board of nine directors (three appointed by the Federal Reserve Board, six by the local member banks). The Federal Reserve System's Board of Governors designates one of the federally appointed directors as chairman and Federal reserve agent; it is his duty to report to the Board. The board of directors appoints the bank's president and other officers and employees. The operations of the Federal reserve banks, although not conducted primarily for profit, yield an income that is ordinarily sufficient to cover expenses, to pay a 6% cumulative dividend annually on the stock held by member banks, to make additions to surplus, and to provide the U.S. Treasury with over $1 billion a year in revenue. The Board of Governors of the Federal Reserve System—the national supervisory agency—is composed of seven members appointed for 14-year terms by the President. Its offices are in Washington, D.C. The Federal Open Market Committee, created later (1923) than the system's other divisions, comprises the seven members of the Board of Governors and five representatives of the Federal reserve banks; it directs the purchases and sales by the reserve banks of Federal government securities and other obligations in the open market. The Federal Advisory Council consists of 12 members, one appointed annually by the board of directors of each reserve bank; it confers from time to time with the Board of Governors on general business conditions and makes recommendations with respect to Federal reserve affairs. The most important duties of the Federal reserve authorities relate primarily to the maintenance of monetary and credit conditions favorable to sound business activity in all fields—agricultural, industrial, and commercial. Among those duties are lending to member banks, open-market operations, fixing reserve requirements, establishing discount rates, and issuing regulations concerning those and other functions. In a sense, each Federal reserve bank is best understood as a bankers' bank. Member banks use their reserve accounts with the reserve banks in much the same way that a bank depositor uses his checking account. They may deposit in the reserve accounts the checks on other banks and surplus currency received from their customers, and they may draw on the reserve for various purposes, especially to obtain currency and to pay checks drawn upon them (see CLEARING). More importantly, the required reserves also enable the Federal reserve authorities to influence the lending activities of banks. So long as a bank has reserves in excess of requirements, it can enlarge its extensions of credit; otherwise it cannot increase its extensions of credit and may be impelled to borrow additional funds. Inasmuch as the Federal reserve authorities have power to increase or decrease the supply of excess funds, they are able to exercise considerable influence over the amount of credit that banks may extend. By controlling the credit market, the Federal Reserve System exerts a powerful influence on the nation's economic life. Federal reserve activities designed to expand bank credit may lead to an upswing in the business cycle, which tends to lead toward inflation; conversely, a restriction of credit generally results in decreased business growth and deflation. The principal means through which the Federal reserve authorities influence bank reserves are open-market operations, discounts, and control over reserve requirements. Open-market purchases of securities by Federal reserve authorities supply banks with additional reserve funds, and sales of securities diminish such funds. Through the power to discount and make advances, the Federal reserve authorities are able to supply individual banks with additional reserve funds. They may make the funds more or less expensive for member banks by raising or lowering the discount rate. Discounts usually expand only when member banks need to borrow. Raising or lowering requirements—within the limits imposed by law on the Board of Governors—concerning the reserves that member banks maintain on deposit with the reserve banks has the effect of diminishing or enlarging the volume of funds that member banks have available for lending. Such powers directly affect the volume of member bank funds but have no immediate effect in the use of those funds. However, in the field of stock market speculation the Federal reserve authorities have a direct means of control over the use of funds, namely, through the establishment of MARGIN REQUIREMENTS. Another of the important functions of the Federal Reserve System is furnishing Federal reserve notes (now the chief element in the nation's currency) for circulation. Most economists and bankers agree that the Federal Reserve System has achieved marked improvements in American monetary and banking institutions. See W. R. Burgess, *The Reserve Banks and the Money Market* (rev. ed. 1946); E. W. Kemmerer, *The ABC of the Federal Reserve System* (12th ed. 1950, repr. 1971); G. L. Bach, *Federal Reserve Policy-Making* (1950); H. V. Prochnow, ed., *The Federal Reserve System* (1960); U.S. Board of Governors of the Federal Reserve System, *The Federal Reserve System* (5th ed. 1963); D. S. Ahearn, *The Federal Reserve Policy Reappraised 1951-1959* (1963).

Federal Theatre (1935-39), branch of the WORK PROJECTS ADMINISTRATION designed to provide employment for actors, directors, writers, and scene designers. As well as providing a nationwide audience with inexpensive, high-quality productions, it gave impetus to experimental theaters, such as the Group Theatre, the Mercury Theatre of Orson Welles, the topical "Living Newspaper" (dramatizations of news stories), and the music-dramas of Marc Blitzstein. See study by J. D. Mathews (1967, repr. 1971).

Federal Trade Commission (FTC), independent agency of the U.S. government established in 1915 and charged with keeping American business competition free and fair. The FTC has no jurisdiction over banks and common carriers, which are under the supervision of other governmental agencies. It has five members, not more than three of whom may be members of the same political party, appointed by the President, with the consent of the Senate, for seven-year terms. The act was part of the program of President Wilson to check the growth of monopoly and preserve competition as an effective regulator of business. The duties of the FTC are, in general, to promote fair competition through the enforcement of certain antitrust laws; to prevent the dissemination of false and deceptive advertising of goods, drugs, curative devices, and cosmetics; and to investigate the workings of business and keep Congress and the public informed of the efficiency of such antitrust legislation as exists, as well as of practices and situations that may call for further legislation. The commission's law-enforcement activities have to do with the prevention of unfair methods of competition and false advertising (in accordance with the Federal Trade Commission Act of 1914 and the Wheeler-Lea Act of 1938); with administration of provisions restricting tying and exclusive dealing contracts, acquisition of capital stock, interlocking directorates, and price discriminations (in accordance with the CLAYTON ANTITRUST ACT of 1914 and the ROBINSON-PATMAN ACT of 1936); and with administration of the Webb-Pomerene Act of 1918, which permits associations to engage in export trade without incurring the penalties of the Sherman Antitrust Act. In 1946 the FTC was given the right to cancel faulty trademarks. The commission may undertake special investigations at the order of Congress, the President, or upon its own initiative. To enforce antitrust legislation, the commission is empowered to issue cease-and-desist orders upon ascertaining to its satisfaction that the laws are being violated. These orders, to be effective, usually must have court sanction, and the commission must, therefore, in various instances prove its case in court. In deciding such cases the courts have interpreted and applied the phrase "unfair methods of competition." Many of the judicial decisions have frustrated the work of the commission in restricting the growth of monopoly and also, to some degree, the intent of the antitrust laws. Yet the commission has done much toward ridding the business world of vicious competitive practices. In its investigatory work, the commission was delegated the power to require information from any corporation in interstate commerce. Many companies, however, gave only partial access to their records, and others gave none. A decision by the Supreme Court declared that access to records of private business, except where substantial proof is submitted as to a specific breach of the law, is a violation of the Fourth Amendment. Despite the fact that the commission's investigatory power was thus greatly limited, it has made and published a notable series of investigations. After the checks rendered by the courts, the commission tended more and more to carry out its recommendations through trade-practice conferences, at which representatives of an industry might voluntarily adopt regulations to control competition in that industry. The FTC enforces the provisions of the Truth in Lending Act of 1968 over creditors (e.g., finance companies, retailers, and non-Federal credit unions) not specifically regulated by another government agency. The act was designed to insure meaningful information about the actual cost of consumer credit to a potential borrower.

Federal Writers' Project: see WORK PROJECTS ADMINISTRATION.

federation: see FEDERAL GOVERNMENT.

Federation of Malaysia: see MALAYSIA, FEDERATION OF.

Federation of South Arabia: see SOUTH ARABIA, FEDERATION OF.

Federation of the Emirates of the South: see SOUTH ARABIA, FEDERATION OF.

Federmann, Nikolaus (nē'kōlous fā'dərmän), 1501–42, German adventurer in Venezuela and Colombia. In the service of the Welser brothers, Augsburg bankers to whom Charles V had granted rights in Venezuela, Federmann first landed at CORO in 1530. Contrary to the orders of his commander, Federmann launched an expedition in search of EL DORADO in 1535, going south to explore the Colombian llanos. Hearing of JIMÉNEZ DE QUESADA, Federmann and his men climbed the Andes, met Quesada, and in return for a large payment agreed not to dispute the latter's claims. An attempt by BENALCÁZAR to join with Federmann against Quesada failed. Entering Bogotá, the commanders settled their differences and returned (1539) to Europe to confirm their claims. Federmann, involved in a suit in which he accused the Welsers of defrauding the emperor, died in Madrid after confessing his accusation to have been false.

Fedin, Konstantin Aleksandrovich (kənstəntyēn' əlyĭksän'drəvĭch fyĕdyĕn'), 1892–, Russian novelist. Fedin was interned in Germany during World War I and returned to Russia in 1918. His first novels, *Cities and Years* (1924) and *The Brothers* (1928), concern the intellectual's problems in adjusting to Soviet society. Fedin traveled in Europe during the 1930s and based his novel *The Rape of Europe* (1934–35) on his observations. The three realistic novels of his postwar cycle—*Early Joys* (1945–46, tr. 1960), *No Ordinary Summer* (1948, tr. 1950), and *The Bonfire* (1962)—are among his best work, and the first two were awarded Stalin Prizes. They describe life in a small Russian town in the early 20th cent. Fedin also wrote reminiscences of Gorky (1943–44). See E. J. Simmons, *Russian Fiction and Soviet Ideology: Fedin, Leonov, and Sholokhov* (1958).

Fedor. For Russian rulers thus named, see FEODOR.

Fee, John Gregg, 1816–1901, American abolitionist clergyman, b. Bracken co., Ky. After two years (1842–44) at Lane Theological Seminary in Cincinnati, he devoted himself to the abolitionist cause in Kentucky; for this he was disinherited by his slaveholding parents. He founded antislavery churches, notably one at Berea, where he also established (1857) an abolitionist school that became Berea College. Driven from Kentucky in 1859, Fee was not able to return until 1863. He spent the rest of his life in Berea as pastor of the church and a trustee of the college. See his autobiography (1891).

fee, in property law: see PROPERTY; TENURE.

feeblemindedness: see MENTAL RETARDATION.

feedback, arrangement for the automatic self-regulation of an electrical, mechanical, or biological system by returning part of its output as input. A simple example of feedback is provided by a governor on an engine; if the speed of the engine exceeds a

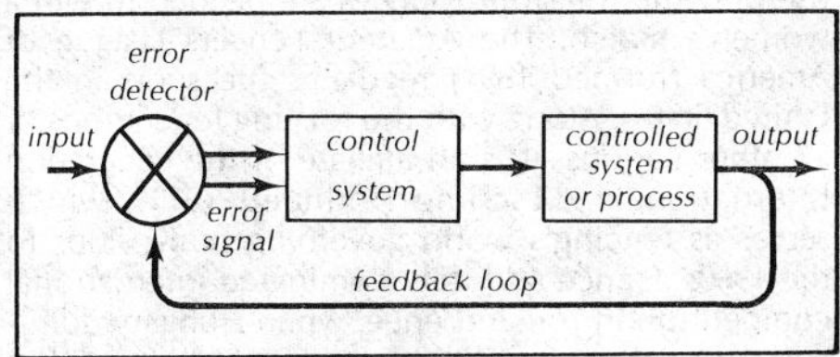

Basic feedback control system

preset limit, the governor reduces the supply of fuel, thus decreasing the speed. Electronic control systems employ feedback extensively. In voltage and current regulators, part of the output is used as a control input, providing self-regulation. For example, if the output becomes too great, it acts through the feedback loop to reduce itself. The use of feedback as the fundamental control mechanism for machinery occurs in AUTOMATION. Living organisms possess feedback control systems of great complexity. For example, when the hand reaches for an object, information about its position is continuously fed back to the brain, both by the eyes and by position-sensing nerves in the arm; the brain uses the position information to guide the hand to the object. Such feedback can be termed voluntary, since it is to some extent under conscious control. Automatic, involuntary feedback is constantly taking place as well, controlling processes such as respiration, circulation, digestion, and maintenance of body temperature. Feedback is one of the main concerns of CYBERNETICS. See SERVOMECHANISM.

Fehling's solution (fā'lĭngz), deep-blue, alkaline solution used to test for the presence of ALDEHYDES (e.g., formaldehyde, HCHO) or other compounds that contain the aldehyde functional group, —CHO. The substance to be tested is heated with Fehling's solution; formation of a brick-red precipitate indicates the presence of the aldehyde group. Simple sugars (e.g., glucose) give a positive test, so the solution has been used to test for the presence of glucose in urine, a symptom of diabetes; BENEDICT'S SOLUTION, which gives the same test, is now more widely used. Fehling's solution is prepared just before use by mixing equal volumes of two previously prepared solutions, one containing about 70 grams cupric sulfate pentahydrate per liter of solution and the other containing about 350 grams Rochelle salt (potassium sodium tartrate tetrahydrate) and 100 grams sodium hydroxide per liter of solution. The cupric ion (complexed with tartrate ion) is reduced to cuprous ion by the aldehyde (which is oxidized) and precipitates as cuprous oxide (Cu_2O); for this reason, sugars that react with Fehling's solution are called reducing sugars.

Fehmgericht: see VEHMGERICHT.

Fehrbellin, battle of, 1675. Allied with France in the third Dutch War, King Charles XI of Sweden invaded Brandenburg but was defeated near the town of Fehrbellin, 35 mi (56 km) NW of Berlin, by the forces of Frederick William the Great Elector. The defeat ended the Swedish reputation for military invincibility.

Feiffer, Jules (fī'fər), 1927–, American cartoonist and writer, b. Bronx, N.Y. He began submitting cartoons to the *Village Voice* in 1956, and they became nationally syndicated. Satirizing a world dominated by the atom bomb and psychoanalysis, Feiffer's cartoons have little physical but much mental activity. He is especially concerned with the breakdown of communication between government and citizen, black and white, man and woman. His best-known play is the black comedy *Little Murders* (1965). He has also written a novel, *Harry: The Rat With Women* (1963), and the screenplay for the film *Carnal Knowledge* (1971).

Feijóo y Montenegro, Benito Gerónimo: see FEYJÓO Y MONTENEGRO, BENITO GERÓNIMO.

Feininger, Lyonel (fī'nĭngər), 1871–1956, American painter and illustrator, b. New York City. Feininger studied painting in Berlin, Hamburg, and Paris. He was an illustrator and caricaturist for several periodicals in Paris and in Germany and had a weekly comic page (1906–7) in the Chicago *Tribune* before he turned to easel painting in 1907. He exhibited with the BLAUE REITER group and taught at the BAUHAUS in Germany (1919–32). His canvases appeared in the so-called degenerate art exhibition of 1933. He returned permanently to the United States in 1937, taught at Mills College, and exhibited extensively. Feininger was fascinated by sailboats and skyscrapers, themes that appear in many of his oils and watercolors. He developed a delicate geometric style with interlocking translucent planes, suggestive of both light rays and architectural forms. Feininger is represented in New York City in the Metropolitan Museum, the Museum of Modern Art, and the Whitney Museum, and in other leading collections. See his reminiscences, ed. by J. L. Ness (1974); definitive catalog of his graphic work by L. E. Prasse (1972); biographies by Hans Hess (1961) and E. Schuyer (1964); study by T. L. Feininger (1965).

Feira de Santana (fā'rə dĭ səntä'nə), city (1970 pop. 187,460), Bahia state, E Brazil, between the Jacuípe and Pojuca rivers. It is a distribution center for the products of Bahia's interior and is one of the state's leading producers of dried beef. Tobacco, manioc, beans, and maize are grown, and ceramics and resin oils are produced. Cattle breeding is also important. The city is a major highway nexus.

Feisal: see FAISAL.

Feith, Rhijnvis (rīn'vĭs fīt), 1753–1824, Dutch romantic poet, novelist, and dramatist. His principal works are the long poem on eternity *Het Graf* (1792) and the sentimental novel *Julia* (1783), which resembles Goethe's *Werther*.

Feke, Robert, c.1705–c.1750, early American portrait painter, b. Oyster Bay, N.Y. He practiced in Newport, R.I., New York City, Philadelphia, and Boston. He probably studied in Europe for a time, but soon developed a very personal painting style. His best-known portrait of Isaac Royall and his family (Harvard Univ.) shows the influence of John Smibert. His masterpiece of characterization is the portrait of Reverend Thomas Hiscox (1745; The Breakers, Newport, R.I.). His works are noted for their charm and elegance of costume. There are portraits by him at the Rhode Island Historical Society, Providence; Bowdoin College, Brunswick, Maine; and the Redwood Library, Newport, R.I. Feke disappeared at sea in 1750. See study by H. W. Foote (1930).

Feldberg: see BLACK FOREST.

Feldkirch (fĕlt'kĭrkh''), town (1971 pop. 21,200), in Voralberg, extreme W Austria, near the Rhine River and the Swiss and Liechtenstein borders; founded c.1190. There are textile mills and breweries in the town. Noteworthy buildings include the town hall and the Gothic Church of St. Nicholas (both 15th cent.).

feldspar (fĕl'spär, fĕld'-) or **felspar** (fĕl'spär), mineral of which there are many widely distributed varieties. As constituents of granite, gneiss, basalt, and other crystalline rocks the feldspars form a large part of the earth's crust. Clay is the chief substance formed when weathering decomposes feldspars. Feldspar crystals are either monoclinic or triclinic (see CRYSTAL), and all show clean cleavage planes in two directions. Orthoclase feldspars, which have cleavage planes intersecting at right angles, are monoclinic. The triclinic feldspars include the plagioclase feldspars (e.g., albite, anorthite, and labradorite) and microcline, and their cleavage planes form slightly oblique angles. Chemically the feldspars are silicates of aluminum, containing sodium, potassium, calcium, or barium or combinations of these elements. Pure feldspar is colorless and transparent but the mineral is commonly opaque and found in a variety of colors. Orthoclase and microcline are called potassium feldspars or potash feldspars, and usually they range from flesh color to brick red, although white, gray, and other colors are found. They are used in the making of porcelain and as a source of aluminum in making glass. A green variety of microcline known as amazonite, or Amazon stone, is used for ornament when cut and polished. The plagioclase feldspars are most commonly gray and occasionally red. Some labradorite exhibits a play of colors, which makes it useful for decorative purposes.

Felix, Roman deacon, antipope (355–56). Emperor Constantius, an Arian, set him up to replace LIBERIUS. He is wrongly known as Felix II.

Felix V, antipope: see AMADEUS VIII.

Felix, Antonius, fl. A.D. 60, Roman procurator of Judaea, Samaria, Galilee, and Peraea (A.D. c.52–A.D. 60), a freedman of Claudius I. The apostle Paul addressed him at Caesarea (Acts 23; 24). He married Drusilla, a Herodian princess. He was succeeded by Porcius FESTUS, and when recalled to Rome, he escaped being sentenced to death by Nero only through the intercession of his brother, Pallas. His oppressive rule had caused deep resentment among the Jews and strengthened the anti-Roman party.

Fell, John, 1625–86, English clergyman. He was dean of Christ Church, Oxford, and bishop of Oxford. While at Oxford, he initiated an extensive building program and promoted the development of the Oxford Univ. Press. His chief literary work was his critical edition (1682) of St. Cyprian. He is probably best remembered today as the subject of Tom Brown's jingle "I do not love thee, Dr. Fell, The reason why I cannot tell; But this alone I know full well, I do not love thee, Dr. Fell."

Fellenberg, Philipp Emanuel von (fĕ'lĭp āmä'nōōĕl fən fĕl'ənbĕrkh), 1771–1844, Swiss educator and agriculturist. He purchased (1799) an estate, Hofwyl (near Bern), where he put into practice his theory of combining farm training with a well-rounded education, encouraging productive labor, and bringing pupils from different social levels into contact. His school attracted students from all parts of Europe and was influential in the development of educational theories and especially of manual training in education. Fellenberg also founded an orphan asylum (1804), a colony for poor boys (1816), and other schools, including a vocational school.

Feller, Robert William Andrew (Bob Feller), 1918–, American baseball player, b. Van Meter, near Des Moines, Iowa. Famous for his extraordinary fast ball, Feller began pitching with the Cleveland Indians (American League) in 1936. He won 266 games in his career. In 18 seasons of major-league play the right-hander pitched 3 no-hit and 12 one-hit games. He was elected to the Baseball Hall of Fame in 1962. See his autobiography (1947).

Fellin: see VILJANDI, USSR.

Felling, urban district (1971 pop. 38,595), Durham, NE England. Felling is an industrial suburb of Gateshead and part of the Tyneside industrial concentration. There are coal mines nearby. Felling has engineering works and produces paint and radar equipment. In 1974, Felling became part of the new metropolitan county of Tyne and Wear.

Fellini, Federico (fādārē'kō fāl-lē'nē), 1920–, Italian film director. Fellini began his career in 1942 as a rewrite man. After World War II he was one of the first to write screenplays for neorealist films, such as Rossellini's *Open City* and *Paisan.* He then began directing his own scripts, noted for their montage of poetic lyricism and irony. *I Vitelloni* (1953), *Nights of Cabiria* (1957), *La Strada* (1956), and *La Dolce Vita* (1959) gained him international acclaim. His later major films include *8½* (1963), *Juliet of the Spirits* (1965), *Satyricon* (1969), *Roma* (1972), and *Amarcord* (1974). See his *Three Screenplays* (tr. 1970); study by Gilbert Salachas (tr. 1969).

felony (fĕl'ənē), any grave crime, in contrast to a MISDEMEANOR, that is so declared in statute or was so considered in COMMON LAW. In early English law a felony was a heinous act that canceled the perpetrator's feudal rights and forfeited his lands and goods to the king, thus depriving his prospective heirs of their inheritance. The accused might be tried by an appeal of felony, i.e., personal combat with his accuser, the losing party to be adjudged a felon (see ORDEAL). The appeal of felony was gradually replaced by rational modes of trial and was altogether abolished in England in 1819. In addition to the forfeiture of his property, the convicted felon usually suffered death, long imprisonment, or banishment. Death was an especially common English penalty in the 18th and the early 19th cent. To the list of common-law felonies—including murder, rape, theft, arson, and suicide—many were added by statute. With the abolition of forfeitures in England in 1870 the felony acquired essentially its modern character. Felony is used in various senses in the United States. In Federal law, any crime punishable by death or more than one year's imprisonment is a felony. This definition is followed in some states; in others the common-law definition is retained, or else statutes specifically label certain crimes as felonies. Other possible consequences of committing a felony are loss of the rights of citizenship, DEPORTATION if the felon is an alien, and liability to a more severe SENTENCE for successive offenses. Felonies are usually tried by jury, and in some states the accused must first have been indicted by a GRAND JURY.

felspar: see FELDSPAR.

felt, fabric made by matting or felting together WOOL, hair, or fur, most of which have a natural tendency to snarl or cling together owing to their notched or scaly surfaces. Processes of manufacture vary according to fibers used and purpose intended. Woven felt is first made into coarse cloth, given a heavy nap by teaseling, then ironed down. True felt is made by placing the cleaned fibers in the shape or mass desired, then beating, steaming, pressing, fulling, or otherwise compacting them to the required thickness. Impregnated felts, designed for industrial uses such as roofing and sheathing, are made from waste and sometimes from paper treated with a stiffening or waterproofing substance. As an art felt making probably preceded spinning. Felt was used in N Asia for clothing and tents, and the felt hat was known in ancient Greece and Rome. The invention (1846) of a machine for making felt first brought about the great popularity of the felt hat for men.

Felton, William Harrell, 1823–1909, American political leader, b. Oglethorpe co., Ga. After studying medicine he practiced for awhile, but gave it up for farming in 1847. Ordained a Methodist minister in 1848, he served occasionally in that capacity for the rest of his life. He was a surgeon in the Civil War. After the war he became the leading independent Democrat of Georgia, opposing reactionary machine politics. He fought corruption and advocated legislation for elementary schools, higher education, penal reform, and better charitable institutions. In 1874 he was elected to Congress as an independent in a bitter campaign against the party organization and served three terms before he was defeated. Later, in the state legislature, he worked effectively for improved returns from the state-owned railroad. In his long political struggle, his chief aid was his second wife, **Rebecca Latimer Felton,** 1835–1930. Born near Atlanta, she wrote for the *Atlanta Journal* for nearly 30 years and was a champion of clean government, penal reform, temperance, and woman suffrage. She was the first woman to enter the U.S. Senate, where she served briefly in 1922 by appointment. Her writings include *My Memoirs of Georgia Politics* (1911).

Femgericht: see VEHMGERICHT.

feminism, movement for the political, social, and educational equality of women with men; the movement occurred mainly in Great Britain and the United States. It had its roots in the humanism of the 18th cent. and in the Industrial Revolution, both of which contributed to the emergence of society from a feudal aristocracy to an industrial democracy. Women had been regarded as inferior to men physically and intellectually. Both law and theology had ordered their subjection. Women could not in their own names possess property, engage in business, or control the disposal of their children or even of their own persons. Although Mary ASTELL and others had pleaded earlier for larger opportunities for women, the first great feminist document was Mary Wollstonecraft's *Vindication of the Rights of Women* (1792). In the French Revolution, women's republican clubs demanded that liberty, equality, and fraternity be applied regardless of sex, but this movement was extinguished for the time by the Code Napoléon. In North America, although Abigail Adams and Mercy Otis Warren had pressed George Washington and Thomas Jefferson for the inclusion of women's emancipation in the Constitution, the feminist movement really dates from 1848, when Elizabeth Cady STANTON, Lucretia Coffin MOTT, and a few others, in a women's convention at Seneca Falls, N.Y., issued a declaration of independence for women, demanding full legal equality, full educational and commercial opportunity, equal compensation and the right to collect wages, and the right to vote. Led by Elizabeth Cady Stanton and Susan Brownell ANTHONY, the movement spread rapidly and soon extended to Europe. Little by little, women's demands for higher education, entrance into all trades and professions, married women's property and other rights, and the right to vote were conceded. In the United States after woman suffrage was won in 1920, women were divided on the question of equal standing with men (advocated by the National Woman's party) versus some protective legislation; various forms of protective legislation had been enacted in the 19th cent., e.g., limiting the number of hours women could work per week and excluding women from certain high-risk occupations. In 1946 the UN Commission on the Status of Women was established to secure equal political rights, economic rights, and educational opportunities for women throughout the world. In the 1960s feminism, or the Women's Liberation movement as it became known, experienced a rebirth, especially in the United States. The National Organization for Women (NOW), formed in 1966, had over 400 local chapters by the early 1970s. NOW, the National Women's Political Caucus, and other groups pressed for such changes as abortion reform, federally supported child care centers, equal pay for women, the occupational upgrading of women, and generally removing all legal and social barriers to education, political influence, and economic power for women. With the leadership of Bella Abzug, Shirley Chisolm, Betty Friedan, Gloria Steinem, and others, the movement successfully influenced Congress to pass the Equal Rights Amendment bill in 1972; the Amendment, requiring ratification by 38 states, would bar sex discrimination at the national level. For the political aspects of feminism, see WOMAN SUFFRAGE. See John Stuart Mill, *The Subjection of Women* (1867); Simone de Beauvoir, *The Second Sex* (tr. 1952, repr. 1968); Betty Friedan, *The Feminine Mystique* (1963); Germaine Greer, *The Female Eunuch* (1970); Kate Millett, *Sexual Politics* (1970); Robin Morgan, ed., *Sisterhood is Powerful* (1970); Jessie Bernard, *Women and the Public Interest* (1971); Vivian Gornick and B. K. Moran, ed., *Woman in a Sexist Society* (1971); Judith Hole and Ellen Levine, *Rebirth of Feminism* (1971); Elizabeth Janeway, *Man's World, Woman's Place* (1971); Evelyne Sullerot, *Woman, Society and Change* (1971); Miriam Schneir, ed., *Feminism* (1972); Helen Wortis, ed., *The Women's Movement* (1972); J. S. Lemons, *The Woman Citizen* (1973); Alice Rossi, ed., *The Feminist Papers* (1973).

femur (fē'mər): see LEG.

Fen (fŭn), river, 375 mi (604 km) long, rising in the Wu-t'ai Shan and flowing southwest, through a narrow valley, to the Huang Ho, Shansi prov., N central China; navigable for small junks only in its lower course. The wide and fertile lower Fen valley has been irrigated since ancient times; wheat, millet, and cotton are grown.

fence [short for defense], humanly erected barrier between two divisions of land, used to mark a legal or other boundary, to keep animals or people in or out, and sometimes as an ornament. In newly settled lands fences are usually made of materials at hand, e.g., stone, earth, or wood. A fence built of loose stones is called a dry-stone wall. Wooden fences may be built of boards, posts and rails, or pickets. Hardwoods such as oak and chestnut are preferred for fence posts, although softwoods treated with preservatives such as creosote may be used. Other fence materials are concrete, bricks, iron rails, woven wire, and BARBED WIRE. Electric wire fences that deliver slight, intermittent shocks of electricity are sometimes used for animal enclosures. Storm, or snow, fences are erected to prevent drifts from forming across roadways or against buildings. Rows of trees or shrubs (see HEDGE) are sometimes planted as windbreaks. See also WALL.

fence, in law: see STOLEN GOODS.

fencing, sport of dueling with foil, épée, and saber. Fencing with swords was a method of deadly combat long before the Christian era, but it was first developed as a sport by the Germans in the 14th cent. Not until the 16th cent., however, when the light Italian rapier replaced the heavy German sword, did the sport become widespread. Fencing schools, or *salles,* frequented by young aristocrats, soon sprang up all over Europe, and points of personal honor often came to be settled by a fencing DUEL. In the late 19th cent., after many countries had outlawed the duel, fencing became an organized sport, and in 1896 it was included in the first modern Olympic games. The weapons and rules of modern fencing evolved from combat weapons and their usage. The foil—a light, flexible thrusting weapon with a blunted point—was originally a practice weapon. The épée, or dueling sword, is a straight, narrow, and stiff thrusting weapon without cutting edges. The saber is a light version of the old cavalry broadsword and has a flexible, triangular blade with theoretical cutting edges along the entire front and one third of the back edge. Fencing matches may be conducted among individuals or between teams; a team is generally composed of nine players, three for each weapon. International rules stipulate that fencers must attack and parry on a strip that is 14 m (c.46 ft) long and 2 m (c.6½ ft) wide. The strip, or "piste," is marked off by two parallel lines, beyond which the fencer may not step without receiving a warning or a penalty. In foil the warning lines are 1 m (c.3¼ ft) from each end, and in saber and épée they are 2 m from the ends. Protective clothing includes heavy canvas jackets, wire-mesh masks (introduced in the 18th cent.), and gloves. A button blunts the weapon's tip, and points are made by touching the opponent. Foil and épée touches are made with the point; in foil the torso is the target area, in épée it is the whole body. Winning touches are five in foil, three in épée. Saber touches are made both by the point and the cutting edges. The saber target is any part of the body above the waist, and five touches win. All fencing bouts are ruled by a jury of which one man is the director and two or four others are judges. Because of the high speed of action, foil and épée contests are now scored electrically—an electrical circuit is closed when a valid touch is scored. Women, too, engage in fencing, but use only the foil; four touches are needed to win a women's match. The Amateur Fencers League of America (formed 1891) regulates the sport in the United States. Along with the fencing federations of 27 other nations, it is an affiliate of the Fédération Internationale d'Escrime (founded 1913), which serves as fencing's world governing body. Prior to the 1960s, France and Italy dominated international competition in foil and épée, while Hungary dominated in saber. Since then the Soviet Union has dominated all three classes. See Joseph Vince, *Fencing* (2d ed. 1962); Egerton Castle, *Schools and Masters of Fence from the Middle Ages to the Eighteenth Century* (3d ed. 1969); Maxwell R. Garret and Mary F. Heinicke, *Fencing* (1971).

Fénelon, François de Salignac de la Mothe (fräNswä' də sälēnyäk' də lä môt fānəlôN'), 1651–1715, French theologian and writer, a leader of the QUIETISM heresy, archbishop of Cambrai. As tutor to the duke of Burgundy, he wrote *Télémaque* (1699), holding up Ulysses as an example for the young prince. Other writings include a treatise (1687) on female education, and *Explications des maximes des saints* (1697), mystical instructions in faith for which Fénelon was banished to Cambrai, where he devoted himself to pastoral duties. His *Lettre à l'Académie* (1716) recommended literary activities for the French Academy. His quietism brought a long quarrel with his former patron BOSSUET, which was settled in 1699 when Pope Innocent XII condemned Fénelon's writings.

Feng-chieh (fŭng-jĕ) or **Fengkieh,** city, E Szechwan prov., China. The city is on the Yangtze River at the beginning of the series of gorges that extends to I-ch'ang, Hupeh prov. There are sulfur and coal mines nearby.

Fengkieh: see FENG-CHIEH, China.

Feng Yü-hsiang (fŭng yü-shyäng), 1882–1948, Chinese general. He held various military positions under the Ch'ing dynasty. Feng's conversion to Methodism in 1914 gained him the sobriquet the Christian General. From 1920 to 1926 he struggled with Wu Pei-fu and Chang Tso-lin for the control of N China and Manchuria. He then threw his support to the Nationalists, and he became minister of war and vice chairman of the Executive Yüan at Nanking in 1928. By 1930 he had broken with Chiang Kai-shek and had launched an unsuccessful military campaign against him. From 1931 he held office in the Nationalist government, but he never again wielded power. In 1947, while in the United States on an official mission, he denounced the government of Chiang Kai-shek. Feng died in a fire aboard a Russian ship, apparently while en route to Odessa. See James Sheridan, *Chinese Warlord: The Career of Feng Yü-hsiang* (1966).

Fenian Cycle: see GAELIC LITERATURE.

Fenian movement (fē'nēən), a secret revolutionary society, organized c.1858 in Ireland and the United States to achieve Irish independence from England by force. It was known variously as the Fenian Brotherhood, Fenian Society, Irish Republican Brotherhood, and Irish-American Brotherhood. The famine of the 1840s brought to a crisis Irish discontent with English rule, culminating in the abortive Young Ireland uprising of 1848, led by William Smith O'BRIEN. Vast numbers of embittered Irishmen emigrated to the United States, Australia, South America, and Canada, where they redoubled their agitation against England. John O'MAHONY, one of those revolutionists driven abroad in 1848, was the organizer of the movement in the United States, and it was he who gave the society its name, which was derived from the ancient Irish military corps of FENIANS. In Ireland the movement was led by James Stephens (1825–1901), who founded the party organ, the *Irish People,* in Dublin in 1863. The movement made its chief appeal to artisans and shop assistants rather than to the agrarian population. The opposition of the Roman Catholic Church to the society doubtless kept many potential members from joining its ranks. As the movement became stronger and rumors of actual plots arose, the British government took steps to crush it. In 1865 the *Irish People* was suppressed and Stephens was arrested, although he escaped to America. In 1866 the Habeus Corpus Act was suspended in Ireland, and many Fenians were imprisoned. Initiative shifted to America, where a huge store of arms and money had been accumulated by the Fenians, and where many Irish-American Civil War veterans were eager to strike a blow against England. In 1867 a ship, renamed *Erin's Hope,* was outfitted and sailed to Ireland, but the Fenians aboard were captured in their attempt to land. In the same year there were several small-scale risings in Ireland. Repeated attempts by the revolutionists to free their imprisoned comrades by force resulted in the execution of several Fenians. Agitation continued and terrorism was condoned by many as a result of the anger aroused by the executions. The long-range effect of the Fenian movement was to draw the attention of the English Parliament to Irish problems. The Fenian movement in America had a career of its own. In 1865 a convention at Cincinnati determined upon an invasion of Canada. In June, 1866, Gen. John O'Neill (1834–78) with about 800 men crossed the Niagara River and captured Fort Erie. His force was soon cut off by U.S. troops, and he was obliged to retreat toward Buffalo. Some 700 men were arrested. An attack on Campobello island (off Maine) was also frustrated. O'Neill became president of the society and prepared raids from Vermont in 1870. These, too, were unsuccessful, and O'Neill and many other participants were arrested. The Fenian movement continued until World War I, but its influence was largely drawn off into new organizations, notably SINN FEIN, founded by Arthur Griffith, a former Fenian. See studies by John O'Leary (1896, repr. 1969), William D'Arcy (1947, repr. 1971), and Brian Jenkins (1969).

Fenians (fē'nēənz), a professional military corps that roamed over ancient Ireland (c.3d cent.) in the service of the high kings. They figure in the legends that developed around FINN MAC CUMHAIL and OSSIAN.

fennec: see FOX.

fennel, common name for several perennial herbs, particularly those of the genus *Foeniculum* of the family Umbelliferae (CARROT family), related to dill. The strawlike foliage and the seeds are licorice-scented and are used (especially in Italian cooking) for flavoring. Sweet fennel, or finochio, has a thick, bulb-based stalk eaten like celery. In literature and legend fennel is a symbol of flattery, a remedy for failing eyesight, and an aphrodisiac. Its inflorescence is a flat-topped umbel of yellow florets. Fennel-flower, a member of the buttercup family, also produces aromatic seeds. The dog fennels are members of the family Compositae (COMPOSITE family). Fennel is classified in the division MAGNOLIOPHYTA, class Magnoliopsida, order Magnoliopsida, family Umbelliferae.

Fenneman, Nevin M., 1865–1945, American geologist, geographer, and teacher, b. Lima, Ohio; B.A. (1883) Heidelberg College, Ohio; M.A. (1900); Ph.D. (1901) Univ. of Chicago. He founded and was chairman (1907–37) of the department of geology and geography at the Univ. of Cincinnati. Fenneman was associated (1901–24) with the U.S. Geological Survey and also with three state geological surveys. He is noted for his work on the physiography of the United States; his physiographic map of the United States (1915–16) was adopted by the U.S. Geological Survey. He is the author of *Physiography of Western United States* (1931) and *Physiography of Eastern United States* (1938), both of which remain as standard reference works. Fenneman served as president of the Association of American Geographers (1918) and of the Geological Society of America (1935).

Fennoscandia, region: see BALTIC SHIELD.

Fenollosa, Ernest Francisco (fĕnəlō'sə), 1853–1908, American Orientalist, educator, and poet, b. Salem, Mass., grad. Harvard, 1874. A pioneer in the study of Oriental art, he lived much of his life in Japan. Besides teaching at Tokyo Univ., the Tokyo Academy of Fine Arts, and the Imperial Normal School, he was manager of the fine arts department of the Imperial Museum in Tokyo. His works include *East and West: the Discovery of America and Other Poems* (1893); *Epochs of Chinese and Japanese Art* (2d ed. 1912), compiled by his widow, Mary McNeil Fenollosa; and two works on Japanese drama (ed. by Ezra Pound, 1916).

Fenris: see LOKI.

Fens, the, district, E England, a flat lowland, W and S of The Wash. Extending c.70 mi (110 km) from north to south and c.35 mi (60 km) from east to west, it is traversed by numerous streams. The area was originally the largest swampland in England, formed by the silting up of a bay of the North Sea. The higher places were sites of Roman stations. The Romans attempted drainage and built a few roads across the Fens; however, the area had become marshy by Anglo-Saxon times, either from natural causes or from allowing Roman work to decay. The first effective drainage systems were developed in the 17th cent. by Cornelius Vermuyden, a Dutch engineer. Drainage and construction of dikes and channels in the various sections or "levels" continued through the 19th cent., but problems of land sinkage, water accumulation, and periodic flooding existed throughout the period. As a result of flooding in the 20th cent., a drainage-improvement project (completed in the mid-1960s) was undertaken. The district is now largely under intensive cultivation. Yields are high on the fertile alluvial soils, with vegetables, fruit, and wheat the principal crops. Wildlife sanctuaries have been preserved. The district is also called Fenland. See Henry C. Darby, *The Draining of the Fens* (2d ed. 1956, repr. 1968).

Fenton, Elijah, 1683–1730, English poet. A graduate of Cambridge, he was a schoolmaster for a time and later was a tutor in several noble families. He is chiefly remembered for his share in Pope's translation of the *Odyssey* (1725). Besides writing a volume of *Poems* (1708) and a tragedy, *Marianne* (1723), he edited the works of Milton (1725) and Waller (1729).

Fenton, Reuben Eaton, 1819–85, U.S. politician, b. Carroll, N.Y. He was elected to the New York assembly in 1849 and to Congress in 1852. Although he was elected as a Democrat, his position on slavery led him to become a founder of the Republican party in New York. He presided over the first Republican state convention, was a Republican member of Congress (1857–64), and in 1864 was elected governor, defeating Horatio Seymour. He was reelected in 1866. His administration was marked by progress in education, particularly in the establishment of normal schools; Cornell Univ. was established during his governorship. When Fenton entered the U.S. Senate (1869), he immediately entered into dispute with Senator Roscoe Conkling over control of the distribution of patronage. Conkling, having the support of President Grant, won, and in 1874 he prevented Fenton's renomination. Fenton spent his later years as a banker, and in 1878 he went to Paris as chairman of the U.S. commission to the International Monetary Conference.

Fenton, Roger, 1819–69, English pioneer photographer. Originally a barrister, Fenton worked until 1862 as a fashionable architectural, still-life, portrait, and landscape photographer. Sponsored by the royal family, he was commissioned in 1855 to document the Crimean War. Working under appalling conditions, he made 360 photographs emphasizing the romantic aspects of an unpopular war. His few combat pictures are among the earliest photographs of battle. See biography by Helmut and Alison Gernsheim (1954).

Fenwick, Edward Dominic, 1768–1832, American Roman Catholic prelate, first bishop of Cincinnati (1822–32), b. St. Marys co., Md. He was educated in Belgium, joined the Dominicans (1790), and was ordained (1793). After a short imprisonment by the French republicans he went to England and taught at a new Dominican college in Surrey. In 1804 he returned to the United States and set out for a Western mission. He set up the convent of St. Rose of Lima, the first Dominican house in the United States, near Springfield, Ky. He was an itinerant missionary in Kentucky and Ohio. His chief center became Cincinnati, of which he was made bishop (1822). In 1831 he founded there the Athenaeum, now Xavier Univ.

Fenwick, John, 1618–83, Quaker colonist in America, b. England. Planning to found a Quaker refuge in America, Fenwick obtained (1674) Lord Berkeley's share of NEW JERSEY in trust for the Quaker merchant Edward Byllynge. In 1675 he and other Quakers founded at Salem the first permanent English settlement in New Jersey. Conflict with Sir Edmund Andros over the administration of West Jersey led (1678) to Fenwick's imprisonment. After his release Fenwick became involved in an acrimonious dispute with the other proprietors. The dispute was not settled until 1682, when he gave up his proprietary rights to William Penn in exchange for 150,000 acres (60,703 hectares) of land.

Fenwick, Sir John, 1645?–1697, English conspirator. A persistent Jacobite plotter, he was arrested in 1696 for conspiring to murder William III. In his confession he tried to implicate leading Whigs in treasonable relations with the exiled James II. He was attainted and executed.

Feodor I (Feodor Ivanovich) (fyô'dər, ēvä'nəvĭch), 1557–98, czar of Russia (1584–98), son of Ivan IV (Ivan the Terrible). Weak and incompetent, he left the government in the hands of his brother-in-law, Boris GODUNOV, who became czar after Feodor's death.

Feodor II, 1589–1605, czar of Russia (1605). He succeeded his father, Boris GODUNOV, but was assassinated when the first false DMITRI was proclaimed czar.

Feodor III, 1661–82, czar of Russia (1676–82), son and successor of Alexis. Although an invalid, Feodor strove to carry out reforms. In 1681 he abolished the system of precedence among the boyar families, whereby appointments in civil and military service were based on social rank rather than on merit. He was succeeded jointly by his brother Ivan V and his half brother Peter I under the regency of his sister SOPHIA ALEKSEYEVNA.

Feodosiya (fā"ədô'sēə), city (1969 est. pop. 64,000), SE European USSR, in the Ukraine, on the Crimean peninsula. It is a major Black Sea port at the western end of the Feodosiya Gulf. Grain is exported, and oyster and sturgeon fishing and the production of caviar are important occupations. Feodosiya is also a rail terminus. Industries include printing, steel rolling, and tobacco processing. A popular Crimean sea and health resort, Feodosiya has beaches, mineral springs, and mud baths. The city occupies the site of ancient Theodosia, which was founded in the 6th cent. B.C. by Greek colonists from Miletus. Theodosia, noted for its grain exports, was destroyed by the Huns in the 4th cent. A.D.; it existed thereafter as an insignificant village until the Genoese arrived in the 13th cent., established a flourishing trade colony, and virtually monopolized Black Sea commerce. Under their rule, the city was called Caffa or Kaffa and served as the chief port and administrative center of Genoese possessions along the Black Sea coast. The khan of Crimea, an ally of the Turks, conquered the city in 1475; it remained under Turko-Tatar control until Russia's annexation of the Crimea in 1783. In 1802 it was named Feodosiya. German forces captured it twice during World War II. There are ruins of the Genoese fortifications.

Ferber, Edna, 1887–1968, American author, b. Kalamazoo, Mich. Her novels portray the lives of a wide variety of Americans in a vigorous, colorful, and panoramic fashion. Among her best-known novels are *So Big* (1924, Pulitzer Prize), *Show Boat* (1926, musical version 1927), *Cimarron* (1929), *Saratoga Trunk* (1941), *Giant* (1952), and *Ice Palace* (1958). Ferber also collaborated with George S. KAUFMAN on such plays as *The Royal Family* (1927), *Dinner at Eight* (1932), and *Stage Door* (1936).

Ferber, Herbert, 1906–, American sculptor, b. New York City, grad. Columbia (D.D.S., 1930). His original name was Herbert Ferber Silvers. Turning from early massive figures in wood and stone, he has developed large, spatially inventive abstractions in brazed metal called environmental sculpture. Among his works are *Green Sculpture II* (Albright-Knox Art Gallery, Buffalo), *Sunwheel* (Whitney Mus., New York City), and *Covenant II* and *Flood II* (Temple Anshe Chesed, Cleveland). See catalog by Wayne Andersen (1962).

fer-de-lance (fĕr″-də-lăns′), highly poisonous snake, *Bothrops atrox,* found in tropical South America and the West Indies. A PIT VIPER, related to the bushmaster and the rattlesnake, it has heat-sensitive organs on the head for detecting its warm-blooded prey. Usually about 5 to 6 ft (150–180 cm) long, the fer-de-lance may reach a maximum length of about 9 ft (3 m). It is gray or brown with light stripes and dark diamond markings and has a yellow throat. Common throughout most of its range, it causes many human fatalities. It is classified in the phylum CHORDATA, subphylum Vertebrata, class Reptilia, order Squamata, family Crotalidae.

Ferdinand I, 1503–64, Holy Roman emperor (1558–64), king of Bohemia (1526–64) and of Hungary (1526–64), younger brother of Holy Roman Emperor CHARLES V. Brought up in Spain, he was expected to succeed his grandfather, Ferdinand II of Aragón, who, instead, made Charles his heir. In 1521, Charles gave him the Austrian duchies of the Hapsburgs. In the same year Ferdinand married Anna, daughter of ULADISLAUS II, king of Hungary and Bohemia, in fulfillment of a treaty (1515) between his grandfather, Holy Roman Emperor Maximilian I, and Uladislaus II. When Anna's brother Louis II, who succeeded to the thrones of Bohemia and Hungary on his father's death (1516), was killed at the battle of Mohacs (1526), Ferdinand claimed the succession. He was elected king of Bohemia, but in Hungary he met the rival claim of JOHN I (John Zapolya), supported by Sultan SULAYMAN I. John's claims were inherited by his son John Sigismund (king as JOHN II). The sporadic warfare in Hungary was indecisive, except that Ferdinand had to pay tribute to the sultan for the strip of NW Hungary that he was allowed to keep with the royal title. In Bohemia, Ferdinand laid the groundwork for Hapsburg absolutism by virtually abrogating (1547) the prerogatives of the diet and the towns; he also began the reconversion of the kingdom to Catholicism by calling in the Jesuits. In Germany, Ferdinand increasingly acted as agent of Charles V, who in 1531 had him elected king of the Romans, which insured Ferdinand's succession as Holy Roman emperor. He had to deal with the PEASANTS' WAR and with the rebellions stirred up by Ulrich I, dispossessed duke of WÜRTTEMBERG, where Ferdinand was unpopular as governor. Ulrich secured the aid of PHILIP OF HESSE and defeated Ferdinand at Lauffen (1534). Ferdinand was obliged to restore the duchy to Ulrich. In the war against the Protestant SCHMALKALDIC LEAGUE (1546–47), Ferdinand was an important figure. Though a devout Catholic, Ferdinand was less committed against the Reformation than Charles V. When Charles's triumph against the league was turned to defeat by the betrayal of Maurice, elector of Saxony, Ferdinand acted as mediator in making the Treaty of Passau (1552), and in 1555 he negotiated a religious truce at Augsburg (see AUGSBURG, PEACE OF). Charles had practically surrendered the government of the empire to Ferdinand by 1556, although formal abdication was not complete until 1558. At the end of his reign, Ferdinand still hoped that the reconvened Council of Trent would bring about a union of the churches. He was succeeded by his son, MAXIMILIAN II, who had been crowned king of Bohemia (1562) and king of Hungary (1563) and had been elected king of the Romans (1562) before Ferdinand's death.

Ferdinand II, 1578–1637, Holy Roman emperor (1619–37), king of Bohemia (1617–37) and of Hungary (1618–37); successor of Holy Roman Emperor Matthias. Grandson of FERDINAND I, son of Archduke Charles of Styria, Ferdinand was educated by the Jesuits and supported the Catholic Reformation. He was chosen successor to Matthias and became, before the emperor's death, king of Bohemia and Hungary. His Catholicism, however, alienated the Bohemian nobles, who rebelled (1618) and chose (1619) Frederick V (FREDERICK THE WINTER KING), elector palatine, as their ruler. This began the THIRTY YEARS WAR. The Bohemians at first were successful and pressed upon Vienna, but Ferdinand, allied with MAXIMILIAN I of Bavaria and the Catholic League, won back Bohemia in 1620 in the battle of the White Mt. War continued in the Palatinate. In Hungary, Gabriel BETHLEN was successful in opposing Ferdinand in 1619 and 1620, but after the defeat of the Bohemians a peace was signed (1621). During the Danish phase (1625–29) of the Thirty Years War, TILLY, commander of the Catholic League, and WALLENSTEIN, head of the imperial army, defeated the Danes, and a favorable peace was made with Denmark. Ferdinand, then at the height of his power, issued (1629) the Edict of Restitution, ordering the restoration of ecclesiastical property secularized after 1552. That further antagonized the Protestant princes, but they did not take up arms. At that time, however, GUSTAVUS II (Gustavus Adolphus) of Sweden, a Protestant, came into the war. Ferdinand in 1630 had dismissed Wallenstein under pressure from the princes of the empire, who felt the general was becoming too powerful. In 1632, however, after a series of defeats, Wallenstein was restored. He was later suspected of treason and dismissed. In 1634, Wallenstein was assassinated, almost certainly at the instigation of Ferdinand. The battle of Nördlingen marked the resurgence of the imperialists, but the war was wrecking Germany and the house of Hapsburg. The Peace of Prague (1635), the last important act of the irresolute Ferdinand, did not end the fighting. The war reached its unhappy conclusion in the reign of his son, FERDINAND III.

Ferdinand III, 1608–57, Holy Roman emperor (1637–57), king of Hungary (1626–57) and of Bohemia (1627–57), son and successor of Holy Roman Emperor Ferdinand II. After the dismissal and assassination (1634) of the imperial commander WALLENSTEIN, Ferdinand became nominal leader of the imperial forces in the THIRTY YEARS WAR, but it was the imperial general GALLAS who was responsible for the successes that culminated in the victory of Nördlingen (1634). After Ferdinand's accession, however, the war took a disastrous turn. Although anxious for peace, Ferdinand rejected the early peace proposals, but in 1648 he had to assent to the treaties negotiated at Münster and Osnabrück (see WESTPHALIA, PEACE OF), which virtually ended the central power of the HOLY ROMAN EMPIRE. The emperor and his successors were left only the shadow of the imperial dignity, and their power was restricted to the hereditary Hapsburg dominions. In these dominions—a vast enough empire in themselves—Ferdinand devoted the rest of his reign to healing the wounds of war and to continuing administrative reforms. He was succeeded by his son, LEOPOLD I.

Ferdinand, 1793–1875, emperor of Austria (1835–48), son and successor of Emperor Francis I (who also, as Francis II, had been the last Holy Roman emperor). A well-meaning monarch in his lucid moments, he was subject to fits of insanity. A council of state that included Metternich governed in his name. After revolution broke out in Vienna in 1848 the emperor promulgated (April) a constitution, but it failed to satisfy the revolutionists. He fled from Vienna in May and—after the recapture of Vienna by Windischgrätz—was persuaded by Felix zu SCHWARZENBERG to abdicate (Dec. 2, 1848) in favor of his nephew, Francis Joseph.

Ferdinand, 1861–1948, czar of Bulgaria (1908–18), after being ruling prince (1887–1908). A grandnephew of Ernest I of Saxe-Coburg-Gotha, he was chosen prince of Bulgaria after the enforced abdication of Prince ALEXANDER. He was, however, opposed by Russia, and it was not until 1896 that he was recognized by the European powers. In 1908, taking advantage of the Young Turk revolution in Constantinople and the annexation of nominally Turkish Bosnia and Hercegovina by Austria, Ferdinand proclaimed the full independence of Bulgaria from the Ottoman Empire (Turkey) and proclaimed himself czar. Having then gained Russia's favor, Ferdinand concluded (1912) an alliance with Serbia, later joined by Greece and Montenegro. The four allies, attacking Turkey, were victorious in the first of the BALKAN WARS (1912–13), but in the second Balkan War (1913) Bulgaria suffered a humiliating defeat by Serbia, Greece, Rumania, and Turkey. In the hope of recovering most of Macedonia, lost to Serbia Greece by the Treaty of Bucharest (1913), Ferdir in 1915 joined the Central Powers in World War 1917 the tide of war turned against Bulgaria, ar 1918, Ferdinand was forced to abdicate in fav his son, Boris III. Ferdinand left Bulgaria to s most of the rest of his life at Coburg, Germany death was erroneously announced in April, See biography by John Macdonald (repr. 1971).

Ferdinand I, 1379?–1416, king of Aragón and S and count of Barcelona (1412–16), second so John I of Castile; nephew and successor of Mart Aragón. In 1406, Ferdinand became regent of Ca during the minority of his nephew, John II. He tured (1410) Antequera from the Moors and cla the vacant throne of Aragón in the same yea nally chosen king in 1412, he defeated (1413 chief rival for the throne and suppressed revo Sicily and Sardinia. In 1415 he met Holy Roman peror Sigismund at Perpignan and was oblige agree to the deposition of Antipope Benedict (see LUNA, PEDRO DE). Ferdinand was succeede his son, Alfonso V.

Ferdinand II or **Ferdinand the Catholic,** 1 1516, king of Aragón (1479–1516), king of Castile León (as Ferdinand V, 1474–1504), king of S (1468–1516), and king of Naples (1504–16). Hi ther, John II of Aragón, gave him Sicily during lifetime and left him Aragón when he died. In Ferdinand married ISABELLA I of Castile, and in they assumed joint rule of Castile. Thus, all of S except for the Moorish kingdom of Granada came united. The royal couple, known as the Ca lic kings, set out with energetic determinatio complete the unification, and Granada fell to at last in 1492. In the same year Ferdinand and bella took the fateful step of expelling from kingdoms all Jews who refused to accept Chris ity. One of the effects of this measure was to prive Spain of a valuable cultural and econ community. The expulsion of the Moors (1502) less impact, for many more Moors than Jews c to pretend to accept Christianity and remai Spain. The Catholic kings also instituted the INC TION in Spain to bolster religious and political u Their reign was crucial in the history of the wor well as that of Spain. In 1492, Christopher COLUN sailing under their auspices, discovered the World, and in 1494, by the Treaty of Tordesillas TORDESILLAS, TREATY OF), Spain and Portugal div the non-Christian world between them. Ferdi personally was more interested in Mediterranea fairs. He began Spain's struggle with France for trol of Italy in the ITALIAN WARS. His general Go FERNÁNDEZ DE CÓRDOBA conquered Naples in Ferdinand joined the League of Cambrai (1 against Venice and the Holy League (1511) ag France. In 1512 he annexed most of Navarre, b his claim on his marriage (1506) to Germain Foix. After Isabella's death (1504) he retained trol over Castile as regent for his daughter JOA Joanna's husband, PHILIP I, became king of Casti 1506 but died the same year. For the rest of hi Ferdinand continued his regency over Castile, in the name of Joanna, who became insane, then for his grandson, later Holy Roman Em Charles V. When Ferdinand died, he left his gr son a united Spain, as well as Naples, Sicily, dinia, and an overseas empire. During the rei the Catholic kings the power of the throne The nobles and the Cortes (parliament) curbed, and the church was used as an instru of political policy. Many of Ferdinand's policies long-lasting effects, especially the expulsion o Jews, the search for American gold, and the co sion of large agricultural areas into grazing land the benefit of the wool industry. Spain becam Atlantic power and revolutionized the commer Europe. See W. H. Prescott, *History of the Rei Ferdinand and Isabella* (4 vol., 1838; abridged ed. by C. H. Gardiner, 1963); J. H. Mariéjol, *Spain of Ferdinand and Isabella* (1892, tr. 1961); Merriman, *The Rise of the Spanish Empire* (V *The Catholic Kings,* 1918); J. H. Elliott, *Imp Spain: 1469–1716* (1963).

Ferdinand I or **Ferrante** (fār-rän′tā), 1423–94, of Naples (1458–94), illegitimate son and succ (in Naples) of ALFONSO V of Aragón. His succe was challenged by Pope Calixtus III, but Pope P made peace with him. Ferdinand promoted merce, industry, and education, but exercised royal control. The great barons, provoked b ruthless authoritarian policies, called in (1459) of Anjou, son of RENÉ, the rival king of Naples barons were defeated (1462) at Troja, and John departed. Another conspiracy in 1485 was crushed. Ferdinand's son Alfonso (later Alfonso II), reconquered (1481) the port of Otranto from the Turks. Ferdinand was succeeded by Alfonso II (1494–95), Ferdinand II (1495–96), and Frederick (1496–1501), none of whom was able to defend the kingdom of NAPLES against France and Spain in the ITALIAN WARS.

Ferdinand IV, king of Naples: see FERDINAND I, king of the Two Sicilies.

Ferdinand I, 1345–83, king of Portugal (1367–83), son and successor of Peter I. His ambitions and his private life plunged the realm into disaster, although during his reign agricultural reform was achieved and Portuguese commercial power grew. Ferdinand's desire for the throne of Castile involved him in three wars with Castile. The first (1369–71) ended with Ferdinand's promise to marry Leonor, daughter of HENRY II of Castile. Instead he fell in love with a Portuguese noblewoman, Leonor Teles, and after securing a dubious annulment of her earlier marriage, made her his queen. Ferdinand then allied (1372) himself with JOHN OF GAUNT and waged new war against Henry II, which led to a Castilian siege of Lisbon (1373) and a humiliating peace. After John I succeeded to the throne of Castile, Ferdinand, under the influence of his wife and her lover (the conde de Ourém), resumed the English alliance and engaged (1381–82) in a third humiliating war with Castile. It was concluded by the marriage of John with Ferdinand's daughter and heiress, Beatrice. Portugal would thus have gone to Castile on Ferdinand's death, but a national revolution gave the throne to Ferdinand's half brother, John I.

Ferdinand II, 1816–85, king consort of Portugal (1837–53). The eldest son of Ferdinand, duke of Saxe-Coburg-Gotha, he married Maria II (Maria da Glória) of Portugal in 1836. After her death (1853), he was regent for his son, Peter V, until the latter's majority (1855). However, he left the actual government to ministers, while he occupied himself with his art collection. In 1862 he was offered and refused the Greek crown, and in 1869 he declined the Spanish crown because the Spanish leader Juan Prim could not guarantee future Portuguese independence.

Ferdinand, 1865–1927, king of Rumania (1914–27), nephew of Carol I. The second son of the Prussian prince, Leopold of Hohenzollern-Sigmaringen, he was designated successor to the heirless Carol I in 1880. In 1893 he married MARIE, daughter of Alfred, duke of Edinburgh and of Saxe-Coburg-Gotha (and granddaughter of Queen Victoria and Czar Alexander II.) Although related to the German imperial family, Ferdinand took Rumania (1916) into World War I on the Allied side, and in 1922 he was crowned king of the enlarged Rumania established by the peace treaties. Ferdinand annexed (1918) Bessarabia from Russia and in 1919 ordered the Rumanian military intervention in Hungary that broke up the Communist government of Bela Kun. During his reign, universal male suffrage and agrarian reforms were introduced. Ferdinand's son, Carol (see CAROL II), renounced his succession in 1925, and Carol's son Michael succeeded in 1927.

Ferdinand I or **Ferdinand the Great,** d. 1065, Spanish king of Castile (1035–65) and León (1037–65). He inherited Castile from his father, Sancho III of Navarre, conquered León, and took parts of Navarre from his brother García. Ferdinand fought successfully against the Moors and reduced to vassalage the Moorish kings of Zaragoza, Badajoz, Seville, and Toledo. At the Council of Coyanza (1050) he confirmed the laws of Alfonso V and introduced church reforms. He divided his kingdom among his sons: Castile went to Sancho II, León to Alfonso VI, and Galicia to García.

Ferdinand II, d. 1188, Spanish king of León (1157–88), son and successor of Alfonso VII. He invaded Castile and set up a protectorate during the minority (1158–66) of his nephew ALFONSO VIII. He also fought the Moors in Estremadura. His son Alfonso IX succeeded him.

Ferdinand III, 1199–1252, Spanish king of Castile (1217–52) and León (1230–52), son of Alfonso IX of León and Berenguela of Castile. At the death (1217) of her brother, HENRY I of Castile, Berenguela renounced her right of succession in Ferdinand's favor. Having inherited (1230) León from his father, Ferdinand permanently united the kingdoms of Castile and León. Ferdinand spent most of his reign crusading against the Moors. He took Córdoba (1236), Jaén (1246), and Seville (1248) and occupied Murcia (1243). He thus completed the reconquest of Spain, except for the kingdom of Granada, which became a vassal state. Ferdinand was planning an expedition to Morocco when he died and was succeeded by his son, Alfonso X. In 1671, Ferdinand was canonized by the Roman Catholic Church. Feast: May 30.

Ferdinand IV, 1285–1312, Spanish king of Castile and León (1295–1312), son and successor of Sancho IV. His mother, MARIA DE MOLINA, was regent during his turbulent minority. He tried unsuccessfully to take Algeciras from the Moors but conquered (1309) Gibraltar with the help of Aragón. He was succeeded by his son, Alfonso XI.

Ferdinand V, Spanish king of Castile: see FERDINAND II, king of Aragón.

Ferdinand VI, b. 1712 or 1713, d. 1759, king of Spain (1746–59), son of Philip V by his first queen, Marie Louise of Savoy. When Ferdinand succeeded his father, his stepmother, ELIZABETH FARNESE, lost her power at court and went into retirement. Ferdinand's chief ministers were José de Carvajal y Lancaster, who was pro-British, and ENSENADA, who had for many years directed the affairs of Spain and strongly favored France. In the years preceding the Seven Years War (1756–63), both France and England sought a Spanish alliance. Carvajal died in 1754, and Ferdinand, desiring Spain to remain at peace, dismissed Ensenada, fearing that he might trap Spain in a French alliance. Richard Wall, an Irishman, succeeded Carvajal, and with his help Ferdinand kept Spain out of the war during his lifetime. In 1758, Ferdinand's queen, Maria Barbara de Braganza, died. Ferdinand did not recover from his grief and died soon afterward. He was succeeded by his half brother, Charles III.

Ferdinand VII, 1784–1833, king of Spain (1808–33), son of CHARLES IV and MARÍA LUISA. Excluded from a role in the government, he became the center of intrigues against the chief minister GODOY and attempted to win the support of Napoleon I. In 1807 he was arrested by his father, who accused him of plotting his overthrow and the murder of his mother and Godoy. He was soon forgiven, but the prestige of the family was shaken, and this facilitated Napoleon's invasion of Spain (see PENINSULAR WAR). A palace revolution at Aranjuez (March, 1808) caused the dismissal of Godoy and the abdication of Charles in favor of Ferdinand, who was enthusiastically acclaimed by the people. Ferdinand was soon persuaded to cross the French border and meet Napoleon at Bayonne. There he was forced to renounce his throne in favor of Charles IV, who in turn resigned his rights to Napoleon. The emperor gave the Spanish throne to Joseph Bonaparte. During the Peninsular War (1808–14) Ferdinand was imprisoned in France. In his name the nationalist and liberal elements of Spain resisted the French invaders, and a liberal constitution was proclaimed (1812) by the Cortes at Cádiz. Throughout the Spanish Empire his name was the rallying cry of revolutionary elements. When Ferdinand was restored (1814) to his throne, however, he promptly abolished the liberal constitution and revealed himself a thorough reactionary. After several unsuccessful uprisings, the Spanish liberals (who had organized in secret societies, e.g., the CARBONARI) staged a successful revolution in 1820 and forced the king to reinstate the constitution of 1812. The Holy Alliance became alarmed, and the Congress of TROPPAU was summoned to deal with the Spanish situation. The powers reached no decision, but in 1822 at Verona (see VERONA, CONGRESS OF) France was delegated by the Holy Alliance to undertake military intervention in Spain and to restore Ferdinand to absolute power. Ferdinand, backed by French arms, revoked the constitution in 1823, and ruthless repression followed. Ferdinand's death caused no less trouble than his reign. His fourth wife, MARIA CHRISTINA (1806–78), had persuaded him to set aside the SALIC LAW so that their only child, Isabella, might succeed to the throne, thus excluding Ferdinand's brother, DON CARLOS, from the succession. When Ferdinand died, the liberals supported ISABELLA II, while the reactionaries rallied around Don Carlos. The Carlist Wars were the result. During Ferdinand's reign, the Spanish colonies on the mainland of North and South America were lost through the very rebellions that had begun as risings in his favor and against Napoleon.

Ferdinand I, 1751–1825, king of the Two Sicilies (1816–25). He had previously been king of Naples (1759–99, 1799–1805, 1815–16) as Ferdinand IV and king of Sicily (1759–1816) as Ferdinand III. A Spanish Bourbon, Ferdinand succeeded (1759) to the two kingdoms when his father and predecessor became king of Spain as CHARLES III. His father's reforms were continued during Ferdinand's minority by the regent, Bernardo Tanucci, but after Ferdinand's marriage (1768) to MARIE CAROLINE a reactionary regime was instituted under her influence. Sir John ACTON was appointed prime minister. The execution (1793) of the queen's sister, Marie Antoinette of France, helped turn Ferdinand against France, and in 1798 he joined the Second Coalition. In Jan., 1799, the French took Naples shortly after the royal couple had fled to Sicily. The French-sponsored PARTHENOPEAN REPUBLIC was short-lived, and terror accompanied Ferdinand's return (June, 1799). Peace was made with France in 1801, but in 1805 Ferdinand joined the Third Coalition against Napoleon. The French reconquered Naples, and early in 1806 the royal couple again fled to Sicily, where Ferdinand ruled under English protection. In 1812 he made his son regent and had him grant a constitution. After Naples was restored to him (1815), Ferdinand abolished Sicilian autonomy and proclaimed (1816) himself king of the Two Sicilies. His reactionary government provoked an insurrection in 1820, and he was forced to grant a constitution, which he soon repudiated. He persecuted the CARBONARI and reestablished his despotism with Austrian aid. He was succeeded by his son Francis I.

Ferdinand II, 1810–59, king of the Two Sicilies (1830–59), son and successor of Francis I. Although initially he sought to improve the wretched conditions of his kingdom, he soon relapsed into the repressive policies of his predecessors and became an absolute despot. Fear of revolution made him grant a constitution in 1848, but when disorders broke out in Sicily he ordered the bombardment of Messina (1848) and Palermo (1849)—an act that earned him the nickname "King Bomba." He soon revoked the constitution, becoming even more reactionary. Great Britain and France, in protest against his inhuman treatment of at least 15,000 political prisoners, withdrew their envoys (1856). He was opposed by conservatives as well as liberals. The political isolation brought about by Ferdinand facilitated the fall of the dynasty under his son and successor, Francis II. See H. M. Acton, *The Last Bourbons of Naples* (1961).

Ferdinand, 1721–92, Prussian field marshal, a prince of the house of Brunswick, known as Ferdinand, duke of Brunswick. He served King Frederick II of Prussia brilliantly in the SEVEN YEARS WAR, notably by his victories at Krefeld (1758) and Minden (1759).

Fergana or **Ferghana** (both: fyĕrgänä'), city (1970 pop. 111,000), capital of Fergana oblast, Central Asian USSR, in Uzbekistan, in the Fergana Valley. It has silk and cotton industries. Oil, coal, and uranium ore lie in the area. Founded in 1876 by the Russians as Novy Margelan, the city was renamed (1907) Skobelev and later (1924) Fergana.

Fergana Valley or **Ferghana Valley,** region, 8,494 sq mi (22,000 sq km), Central Asian USSR. Politically, it is divided among the Uzbek, Tadzhik, and Kirghiz Soviet Socialist Republics. The Fergana Range (part of the Tien Shan system) rises in the northeast and the Pamir in the south. The narrow Khodzhent or Leninabad pass in the west has historically served as an invasion route into the valley. Chinese Turkistan (Sinkiang) borders the valley in the southeast. The Fergana Valley, consisting partly of the very fertile Kara-Kalpak steppe and partly of desert land, is drained by the Syr Darya River and by numerous mountain streams, which are fed by snowfields and glaciers in the mountains. A dense irrigation network is linked by the Great Fergana and South Fergana canals. Major cities of the valley include Fergana, Kokand, Andizhan, and Namangan, in Uzbekistan; Leninabad, in Tadzhikistan; and Osh, in Kirghizistan; many of them are connected by a circular rail line, which also has spurs serving the mining settlements on the valley's periphery. The Fergana Valley is one of Central Asia's most densely populated agricultural and industrial areas. Cotton fields, orchards, vineyards, walnut groves, and mulberry tree plantations (for silk) cover the region, which is one of the world's oldest cultivated areas. Along the fringes of the valley are deposits of oil, coal, natural gas, and iron ore. The region's natural resources have contributed heavily to the industrialization of all Soviet Central Asia. Cotton and silk milling and the manufacture of chemicals and cement are among the valley's important industries. According to ancient Chinese sources, the Fergana Valley was a major center of Central Asia as early as the 4th cent. B.C. The introduction of silk raising from China, the development of cotton cultivation, and its favorable location astride the silk route between China and the Mediterranean stimulated the valley's growth. The Arabs, following the path of earlier invaders, occupied the valley in the 8th cent. and introduced Islam. The region was held in the

9th and 10th cent. by the Persian Samanid dynasty, in the 12th cent. by the Seljuk Turks of Khorezm, and in the 14th cent. by the Mongols under Jenghiz Khan. The valley later belonged to the empire of Tamerlane and his successors, the Timurids. Early in the 16th cent., it was overrun by the Uzbeks, who established the khanate of Kokand. The opening of the sea route to the Orient around that time led to the decline of the prosperous caravan trade through the valley. Russian conquest of the Fergana Valley was completed in 1876 with the fall of Kokand; the region was then made part of a much larger unit called Fergana, which was a province of Russian Turkistan. During the Russian civil war, the valley was the center of the anti-Bolshevik Autonomous Turkistan Government, with Kokand as its capital.

Fergus Falls, city (1970 pop. 12,443), seat of Otter Tail co., W central Minn., on the Otter Tail River; inc. 1872. The chief manufactures are dairy products, packaged meats, clothing, and cabinets. Fergus Falls State Junior College, a Bible school and seminary, and a state mental hospital are in the city.

Ferguson, Adam, 1723-1816, Scottish philosopher and historian. He was professor of philosophy at the Univ. of Edinburgh (1759-85). His interest in ethics led to the writing of *Principles of Moral and Political Science* (1792), in which he advanced the principle of perfection and attempted to reconcile self-interest and universal benevolence. See studies by W. C. Lehmann (1930) and David Kettler (1965).

Ferguson, James Edward, 1871-1944, governor of Texas (1915-17), b. Bell co., Texas. After an adventurous youth he rose from poverty to become a lawyer, large landowner, and banker. Although unknown in state politics, he successfully ran for the governorship in 1914 as the champion of tenant farmers and poor independent farmers. He promised many radical agrarian reforms, some of which became law. He was not, however, favored by the reformers in Texas, because of his demagogic methods and the accusations of widespread corruption in his administration. In 1917, Ferguson was impeached, found guilty on several charges, and removed from office. He devoted himself to clearing his name. He was himself debarred from running for office, but in 1924 his wife, Miriam A. Wallace Ferguson (1875-1961), ran in his place and was triumphantly elected by the small farmers. A general amnesty was issued to vindicate her husband, but it was declared unconstitutional. Nevertheless in the midst of the depression Ma Ferguson (so called from her initials) once more was elected and served from 1933 to 1935, with a policy of extreme retrenchment. Although his wife held the office, it was Ferguson who wielded the power.

Ferguson, Miriam A. Wallace (Ma Ferguson): see FERGUSON, JAMES EDWARD.

Ferguson, Patrick, 1744-80, British army officer in the American Revolution. He invented an early breech-loading rifle in 1776. Ferguson fought at Brandywine and Charleston before he was assigned to organize and train Loyalist militia in South Carolina. He was defeated and killed in the battle of Kings Mt. in the CAROLINA CAMPAIGN.

Ferguson, Sir Samuel, 1810-86, Irish poet and antiquary. *Ogham Inscriptions in Ireland, Wales, and Scotland* (1887) is his best-known work on Irish antiquities. His major poetic works, which deal with Irish history, include the epic *Congal* (1872).

Ferguson, city (1970 pop. 28,759), St. Louis co., E Mo., a suburb of St. Louis; inc. 1894.

Fergusson, Robert, 1750-74, Scottish poet, b. Edinburgh. He was a precursor of Robert Burns, who proclaimed his debt to Fergusson's *Poems* (1773). After careers in the clergy and in medicine, he worked as a public official and periodical contributor. Graphic and amusing pictures of life among the Edinburgh poor are found in his best poems—"The Farmer's Ingle," "Leith Races," and "Auld Reekie." See his works (ed. by M. P. McDiarmid, 1954-56); study by A. H. MacLaine (1965).

Ferishtah: see FIRISHTA.

Ferland, Jean Baptiste Antoine (zhäN bätēst' äNtwän' fĕrläN'), 1805-65, French Canadian priest and historian, b. Kingston, Ont. He was educated at Nicolet College in Quebec prov. His lectures delivered while he was professor of history (1855-65) at Laval Univ. were published as *Cours d'histoire du Canada* (2 vol., 1861-65). They cover only the French history of Canada.

Ferlinghetti, Lawrence (fûr'lĭng-gĕt'ē), 1919-, American author and publisher, b. Yonkers, N.Y. In 1951 he moved to San Francisco and helped found the City Lights Bookshop, which became a center for writers of the BEAT GENERATION. He has written volumes of colloquial verse such as *A Coney Island of the Mind* (1958), *Starting from San Francisco* (1967), and *Open Eye, Open Heart* (1974), as well as essays, broadsides, and the surrealist novel *Her* (1960). He encouraged and published many Beat writers, notably Allen GINSBERG.

Fermanagh (fərmăn'ə), county (1971 pop. 49,960), 715 sq mi (1,852 sq km), SW Northern Ireland. Enniskillen is the county town, but the county council meets at Ardhowen. The Erne River, which widens into the extensive and beautiful Lough Erne, divides Fermanagh into two roughly equal parts. A hilly terrain, rising to more than 2,000 ft (610 m) in the south, is devoted largely to grazing. Potatoes are the chief crop. Pottery (see BELLEEK WARE) and linen are made, and some limestone and sandstone are quarried. The county's population has declined since the potato famine in the 19th cent.

Fermat, Pierre de (pyĕr də fĕrmä'), 1601-65, French mathematician. A magistrate whose avocation was mathematics, Fermat is known as a founder of the modern theory of numbers and probability theory. He also did much to establish coordinate geometry (see CARTESIAN COORDINATES) and invented a number of methods for determining maxima and minima that were later of use to Newton in founding the calculus. He presented without proof, although he claimed to have discovered one, the theorem now known as Fermat's Last Theorem, which states that the equation $X^n + Y^n = Z^n$, where X, Y, and Z are nonzero integers, has no solutions for n greater than 2. Prizes have been offered for a proof of this theorem, and attempted proofs have resulted in many developments in the theory of numbers. Fermat also recognized a principle in optics known as Fermat's law. M.S. Mahoney, *The Mathematical Career of Pierre de Fermat* (1973).

fermentation, process by which the living cell is able to accomplish the anaerobic degradation of GLUCOSE and other simple sugar molecules. Fermentation is achieved by a variety of different metabolic processes, with different chemical sequences that are characteristic of different species. Of the many different kinds of glucose fermentation, two closely related types predominate. In homolactic fermentation the six-carbon glucose molecule is degraded to two molecules of the three-carbon sugar called LACTIC ACID, which is the sole end product. This type of breakdown occurs in many microorganisms and in the cells of most higher animals. In alcoholic fermentation, such as occurs in brewer's yeast and some bacteria, the production of lactic acid is bypassed, and the glucose molecule is degraded to two molecules of the two-carbon ALCOHOL, ethanol, and to two molecules of carbon dioxide. Many of the enzymes of homolactic and alcoholic fermentation are identical to the enzymes that catalyze the metabolic conversion known as GLYCOLYSIS. Alcoholic fermentation is a process that was known to antiquity. Before 2000 B.C. the Egyptians apparently knew that crushed fruits stored in a warm place would produce a substance with a pleasant intoxicating power. By 1500 B.C. the production of beer from germinating cereals (malt) and the preparation of wines from crushed grapes were established technical arts in most of the Middle East. The Greek natural philosophers speculated extensively upon the mechanism by which fermentation might occur. Aristotle believed that grape juice was an infantile form of wine and that fermentation was, therefore, the maturation of the grape extract. Interest in the process of fermentation has continued through the ages, and much of the history of modern biochemistry is also the history of scientific research into this age-old phenomenon. One of the earliest laboratories established for the study of biological chemistry was that founded in Copenhagen in 1875 and financed by the brewing family of Jacob Christian Jacobsen. The modern science dealing with the chemistry of enzymes emerged directly from early studies on the fermentation process.

fermented milk, whole or skim milk curdled to beverage or custardlike consistency by lactic-acid-producing microorganisms. Many forms of fermented milk were used by early nomadic herdsmen, especially in Asia and S and E Europe, Scandinavia, Africa, and South America. Such milks are believed to have medicinal value in the control of intestinal fermentation by contributing bacteria that, establishing themselves in the lower intestine, predominate over putrefactive types. Fermented milks include acidophilus milk; cultured buttermilk; kumiss (koumiss), probably originated from mare's milk by western Mongols, effervescent and of acrid flavor and containing alcohol produced by yeasts; the similar kefir of SE USSR; yoghurt, similar to the Armenian matzoon; and the Scandinavian beverages, *kaeldermaelk* and *filbunke*.

Fermi, Enrico (ĕnrē'kō fĕr'mē), 1901-54, American physicist, b. Italy. He studied at Pisa, Göttingen, and Leiden, and taught physics at the universities of Florence and Rome. He contributed to the early theory of beta decay and the neutrino and to quantum statistics and discovered element 93, now called neptunium. For his experiments with radioactivity he was awarded the 1938 Nobel Prize in Physics. Fermi's wife, Laura, was Jewish, and the family did not return to Fascist Italy after the journey to Stockholm to receive the Nobel award, but continued on to the United States. Fermi was professor of physics at Columbia Univ. (1939-45) and at the Univ. of Chicago (1946-54). He created the first self-sustaining chain reaction in uranium at Chicago in 1942 and worked on the atomic bomb at Los Alamos. Later he contributed to the development of the hydrogen bomb and served on the General Advisory Committee of the Atomic Energy Commission, which named him to receive its first special award ($25,000) shortly before his death. Fermi was outstanding as an experimenter, theorist, and teacher. He wrote *Elementary Particles* (1951). In 1954 the chemical element FERMIUM of atomic number 100 was named for him. Publication of his *Collected Papers* (ed. by Edoardo Amaldi et al.) was begun in 1962. See Laura Fermi, *Atoms in the Family* (1954); biography by Emilio Segrè (1970).

fermion (fûr'mēŏn"): see ELEMENTARY PARTICLES; EXCLUSION PRINCIPLE.

fermium (fûr'mēəm) [for Enrico Fermi], a radioactive chemical element; symbol Fm; at. no. 100; mass no. of most stable isotope 257; m.p., b.p. and sp. gr. unknown; valence +3. Fermium is a member of group IIIb of the PERIODIC TABLE. The physical properties of fermium are largely unknown; its chemical properties are believed to be similar to those of the other members of the ACTINIDE SERIES. The element was first identified (1952) as fermium-255 (half-life about 20 hours) by Albert Ghiorso and his co-workers, who discovered it in residue from a thermonuclear explosion. Ten isotopes are known; the most stable is fermium-257, with a half-life of about 80 days. Isotopes of fermium have been produced by neutron bombardment of plutonium.

Fermo (fĕr'mō), town (1971 pop. 34,219), in the Marche, central Italy, on a hill in the Apennines, near the Adriatic Sea. Leather and cotton goods are manufactured, and silkworms are raised. An ancient town founded by the Sabines, Fermo was held by the papacy from the mid-16th cent. to 1860. Of note are pre-Roman walls, Roman ruins, and a 13th-century Gothic cathedral.

fern, any plant of the division Polypodiophyta. Fern species, numbering several thousand, are found throughout the world but are especially abundant in tropical rain forests. During the Carboniferous era, ancestors to modern ferns were the dominant vegetation of the earth; they contributed to the coal deposits then being formed. Ancient ferns were probably similar to the tree ferns, a declining race found today only in a few tropical areas. Their fronds are clustered at the top of a treelike trunk, sometimes 30 or 40 ft (9-12 m) in height, rather than growing directly from the rootstalk as do those of most temperate ferns. The ferns and their relatives (e.g., the CLUB MOSS and HORSETAIL) are the most primitive plants to have developed a true vascular system (see PLANT). Ferns reproduce by an alternation of generations (see REPRODUCTION), the fern itself being the sporophyte, which produces asexual spores. In most ferns the sporangia (SPORE-bearing sacs) are borne in clusters (called sori), which appear as brown dots or streaks on the underside of the leaves. Although no present-day ferns reproduce by seeds, there are fossils of some fernlike plants that were seed-producing, and it is believed that the seed plants (e.g., the conifers and true flowering plants) evolved from fernlike ancestors. The majority of the common living ferns are members of the polypody family (Polypodiaceae), characterized by the familiar triangular fronds subdivided into many leaflets (pinnae) and smaller pinnules. A popular house fern, a drooping-leaved variety of *Nephrolepis exaltata,* a tropical sword fern, is called the Boston fern (var. *bostoniensis*) because it was first found in a shipment of sword ferns received in Boston. The maidenhair ferns (*Adiantum*), with a few species (especially *A. pedatum*) native to North America, were formerly used as a cure for respiratory ailments. The Brazilian

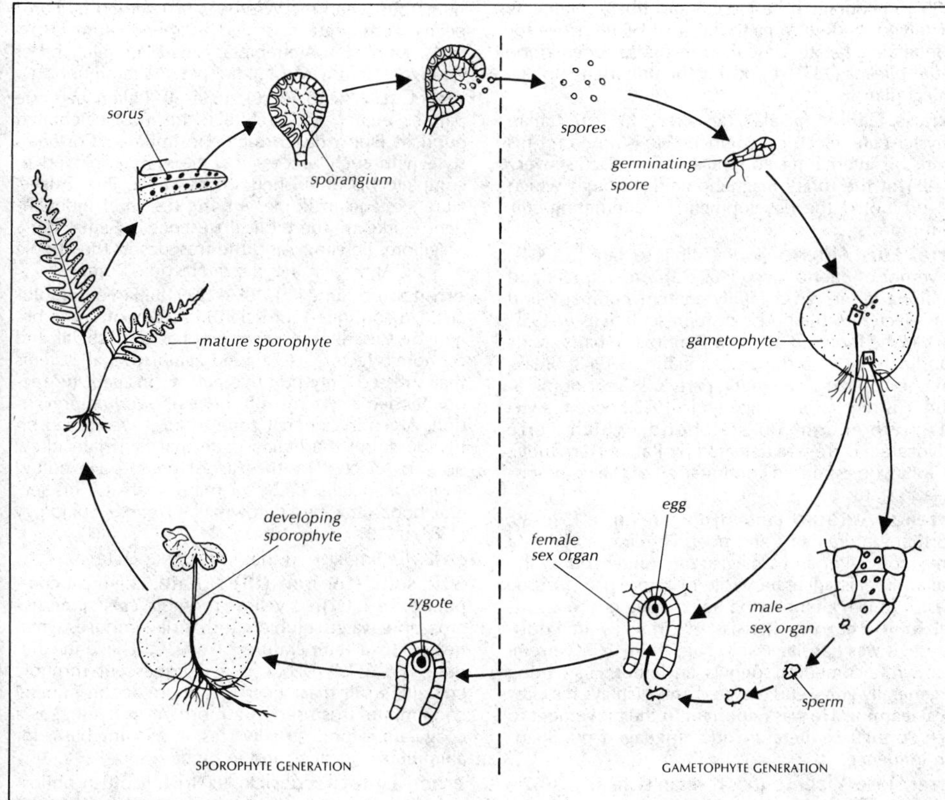

Life cycle of a fern

A. cuneatum and its numerous varieties are now the major greenhouse ferns in North America. The most familiar of all woodland ferns, found the world over, is *Pteridium aquilinum,* the common BRACKEN, or brake (names also applied to other similar ferns, especially species of *Pteris*). Other North American woodland ferns include the Christmas fern (*Polystichum acrostichoides*), a dark-green evergreen plant; the walking fern (*Camptosorus rhizophyllus*), native to limestone areas and named for its characteristic vegetative reproduction, in which new plantlets root from the tips of the elongated fronds; and the common polypody (*Polypodium vulgare*), called also wall, or boulder, fern, a low, matted plant that is the most common of the rock-inhabiting ferns. Also included in the polypody family are many of the fern epiphytes (see AIR PLANT), mostly tropical. Some ferns of other families are aquatic; among the better known genera are *Marsilea* and *Salvinia,* cultivated in aquariums. The adder's-tongue ferns (*Ophioglossum*) and rattlesnake ferns (*Botrychium*) belong to the most primitive fern family (*Ophioglossaceae*) and bear sporangia not in sori but in spikes arising from the leaves. The tree ferns (families Dicksoniaceae and Cyatheaceae) are the only living ferns of any commercial importance other than as ornamentals. In the tropics the trunks are employed in construction, and the starchy pith, formerly eaten by the Maoris and other native groups, is still widely used as stock feed. Dense golden hair covers the base of the leaf stalks and buds in many species and is exported as "pulu" for mattress and pillow stuffing and for packing material. *Dicksonia, Cibotium,* and *Cyathea* are the tree fern genera most frequently seen in greenhouses and conservatories. Numerous superstitions have arisen about ferns. The mythical "fern seeds," believed to be produced by the male fern (*Dryopteris filix-mas*) and by the lady fern (formerly a name for the common bracken but now applied to *Athyrium filix-femina*), were reputed to create invisibility if eaten by a member of the appropriate sex. The bracken was also considered protection against goblins and witches because the broken stem and root appear to be marked with a C, symbolizing Christ. The ASPARAGUS fern and shrub sweet fern (see BAYBERRY) of florists are not true ferns. Ferns are classified in the division POLYPODIOPHYTA, class Polypodiopsida. See G. M. Smith, *Cryptogamic Botany,* Vol. II (2d ed., 1955); Boughton Cobb, *A Field Guide to the Ferns* (1956); F. S. Shuttleworth and H. S. Zim, *Non-flowering Plants* (1967); F. E. Round, *Introduction to the Lower Plants* (1969).

Fernald, Merritt Lyndon (fûr'nəld), 1873–1950, American botanist, b. Orono, Maine, grad. Harvard, 1897. He taught at Harvard (1902–49) and was director of the Gray Herbarium there from 1937. Fernald was the editor (with Benjamin L. Robinson) of the seventh edition (1908) of Asa Gray's manual of botany and of *Rhodora,* the journal of the New England Botanical Club. Besides numerous botanical papers and monographs, he wrote (with A. C. Kinsey) *Edible Wild Plants of Eastern North America* (1943).

Fernández or **Hernández, Gregório** (grāgō'rēō fārnän'dāth, ārnän'dāth), c.1576–1636, Spanish baroque sculptor. By 1605 he was established in Valladolid and was working for Philip IV. His sculptures, often realistically polychromed, are dramatic in expression. His *Pietà* (1617), *Baptism* (1630), and *Mater Dolorosa* are famous examples of his work. He is best represented in the churches and the museum of Valladolid.

Fernández de Avellaneda, Alonso: see AVELLANEDA, ALONSO FERNÁNDEZ DE.

Fernández de Córdoba, Francisco (frānthēs'kō fārnän'dāth dā kōr'dōbä), d. 1518?, Spanish explorer in Mexico. Sailing from Cuba on a slave hunt, he discovered Yucatán in 1517. He died from wounds received in a battle with the Maya. His explorations were furthered by Juan de Grijalva.

Fernández de Córdoba, Francisco, d. 1526?, Spanish conquistador. Sent in 1523 by Pedro ARIAS DE ÁVILA to deprive Gil GONZÁLEZ DE ÁVILA (d. 1543) of his claims to Nicaragua, Fernández de Córdoba founded LEÓN and GRANADA (Nicaragua). In an attempt to seize Nicaragua for himself, he was surprised by his commander and put to death. The Nicaraguan unit of currency (córdoba) is named after him.

Fernández de Córdoba, Gonzalo (gōnthä'lō), 1453–1515, Spanish general, called the Great Captain. He fought in the civil wars preceding and following the accession of ISABELLA I and in the conquest of Granada. He commanded (1495–98) the army aiding Naples against Charles VIII of France. After expeditions against the rebellious MORISCOS of Granada and the Turks, he returned to Italy as an ally of Louis XII of France, who had joined with Ferdinand II of Aragón to partition Naples (see ITALIAN WARS). When Naples had been conquered, he expelled (1502–4) the French and was governor until 1507. He greatly improved the Spanish infantry by specializing the use of weapons. See biography by Mary Purcell (1962).

Fernández de Lizardi, José Joaquín (hōsā' hwäkēn' fārnän'dās dā lēsär'dē), 1776–1827, Mexican journalist, novelist, and dramatist, known by his pseudonym El Pensador Mexicano. His early liberalism, revealed in satiric poetry, put him at odds with the censors. His most revered fiction is the picaresque novel *El Periquillo Sarniento* (1816–30, tr. *The Itching Parrot,* 1942), considered by many to be the first Hispano-American novel. It is a sardonic account of the decadent court of the Mexican viceroys.

Fernández de Moratín, Leandro (lāän'drō fārnän'dāth dā mōrātēn'), 1760–1828, Spanish dramatist and poet. A supporter of Joseph Bonaparte, he lived in exile in France after Bonaparte fell. Molière, whose works he translated, was his literary model. His plays, satiric and psychologically acute, include *El sí de las niñas* [the maidens' consent] (1806), for which he was denounced to the Inquisition. He was subsequently compelled to give up playwriting.

Fernández Navarrete, Juan: see NAVARRETE, JUAN FERNÁNDEZ.

Fernando de Noronha (fərnän'dōō dĭ nōōrô'nyə), group of 20 islands (1970 pop. 1,239), c.10 sq mi (26 sq km), in the Atlantic Ocean, c.225 mi (360 km) off the northeast coast of Brazil. A federal territory of Brazil since 1942, the islands are governed by the army and used as a military base and (since the 18th cent.) as a penal colony. The population consists largely of military personnel and their families. The main resource of the islands are the guano deposits (c.1 million tons). The islands, discovered in 1503, were the first hereditary captaincy granted in Brazil by the Portuguese crown. A U.S. missile-tracking base was there from 1957 to 1962.

Fernando Po or **Fernando Póo:** see EQUATORIAL GUINEA.

Fernán González (fārnän' gōnthä'läth), d. 970, first count of Castile. As count of Burgos from c.930 he took advantage of Leonese divisions and the war against the Moors to establish the virtual independence of Castile from León. After c.950 he styled himself count of Castile. His feats are celebrated in an epic poem of the 13th cent., one of the chief works of popular Castilian poetry.

Ferndale, city (1970 pop. 30,850), Oakland co., SE Mich., a suburb of Detroit; inc. as a city 1927. Its numerous manufactures include automobile and aircraft parts, machinery, and tools.

Ferney-Voltaire (fĕrnā'-vôltĕr'), town (1968 pop. 3,064), Ain dept., E France, on the French-Swiss frontier near Geneva. The town grew after Voltaire bought the seigniory of Ferney in 1758 to escape harassment from both the Genevese and the French. Called the "patriarch of Ferney," Voltaire lived there until 1778, during which time he built the local church and founded a pottery industry that produced some of the finest craftsmen of modern France. Voltaire's handsome residence still stands.

Fernow, Bernhard Eduard (fûr'nō), 1851–1923, American forester, b. Germany. In 1876 he emigrated to the United States and became a leader in the movement to protect forests against fire and exploitation. In 1886 he was appointed chief of the Division of Forestry, U.S. Dept. of Agriculture. He organized several of the schools of forestry in the United States and Canada. Among his publications are *Economics of Forestry* (1902), *A Brief History of Forestry* (1907, 3d ed. 1913), and *The Care of Trees in Lawn, Street, and Park* (1910). See biography by A. D. Rogers (1951).

Ferozepore (fərōz'pôr), city (1971 pop. 51,187), Punjab state, NW India, on the Sutlej River. It is a transportation hub and district administrative center. Cotton and grain are traded, and there is some light manufacturing. The city, which also has several colleges, was founded by Firoz Shah Tughluk (reigned 1351–88), sultan of Delhi.

Ferrante: see FERDINAND I, king of Naples.

Ferrar, Nicholas (fĕr'ər), 1592–1637, English theologian. He was associated (1618–23) with the Virginia Company and, with his brother John, played a notable role in its affairs. He retired from Parliament and founded (1625) an austere religious community at Little Gidding in Huntingdonshire; the community consisted of 30 persons engaged in charitable works and intense study of the Scriptures. It was visited and approved (1633) by Charles I, but it was later attacked as an "Arminian nunnery" because of its monastic tendencies and disbanded by Parliament in 1647. See biography by H. P. Skipton (1907); J. E. Acland, *Little Gidding and Its Inmates in the Time of King Charles I* (1903); Bernard Blackstone, ed., *The Ferrar Papers* (1938); A. M. William, ed., *Conversations at Little Gidding* (1970).

Ferrara (fār-rä'rä), city (1971 pop. 153,119), capital of Ferrara prov., in Emilia-Romagna, N Italy. It is an industrial and agricultural center, located on a low-lying, marshy plain that has much reclaimed land. Manufactures include chemicals, food products, and refined petroleum. In the early 13th cent. the ESTE family founded in Ferrara a powerful principality, and during the Renaissance commerce, learning, printing, and the arts flourished about the brilliant court. The 15th-century painters Cossa and Tura and the 16th-century writers Tosso and Ariosto lived in Ferrara, and the religious reformer Savonarola was born there (1452). The city was incorporated into the Papal States in 1558. Among Ferrara's many noteworthy buildings are Este castle (14th cent.), the cathedral (begun 1135), Schifanoia palace (14th-15th cent.), and the Palazzo del Diamanti (15th-16th cent.). The city has a university (founded 1391).

Ferrara-Florence, Council of, 1438-45, second part of the 17th ecumenical council of the Roman Catholic Church; the first part was the Council of Basel, canonically convened but after 1437 schismatic (see BASEL, COUNCIL OF). The chief goal at Ferrara was to end the schism of East and West; it was vigorously promoted by John VIII, Byzantine emperor, who, hard pressed by the Turks, hoped Christian union might save his empire. The council, consummation of years of negotiations, was opened by the papal legate at Ferrara as the legitimate successor of the Council of Basel. The representatives of the East arrived soon after the council's beginning (Jan., 1438); they included the emperor, the patriarch of Constantinople, canonical representatives of the other Orthodox patriarchs, and the metropolitan of Kiev, head of the Russian church. The points at issue between East and West were the *Filioque* clause of the CREED, the use of unleavened bread in the EUCHARIST, the definition of purgatory, and the nature of the papal jurisdiction. The discussions were generally conducted without acerbity, the leading figure being BESSARION, archbishop of Nicaea, leader of the moderates among the Orthodox. About a year after its commencement the council moved to Florence (Jan., 1439) because of the plague at Ferrara and the financial inducements of the Florentines. In July, 1439, the pope issued the bull *Laetentur coeli*, announcing the religious union of East and West, which had been ratified by both sides, except for a few Orthodox. On the questions at issue the Orthodox conceded that the Western Church might use the *Filioque* in the creed and unleavened bread at Mass without danger to faith or right custom; the Orthodox also accepted the Western definition of purgatory and the papal supremacy over the patriarchs, without prejudice to patriarchal jurisdiction in the patriarchates. With the departure of the Orthodox from Italy, the party opposed to union on the council's terms gained power, and, before any lasting strength could be given the union, Constantinople fell to the Turks, who controlled the patriarchate of Constantinople thereafter. After the union was announced, the council continued to sit until 1445, moving to the Lateran in 1443. Its principal business was then to bring back into union with the Holy See the smaller non-Orthodox churches, i.e., Armenian, Jacobite, Nestorian, and Maronite. Of these, as of the Orthodox, small groups entered the Roman communion, but there was no great reunion. The chief result of the council was probably the increase of prestige it lent to the Holy See. It was also important in bringing Bessarion and other Greeks to Italy, strengthening the cultural connection between East and West. See studies by Joseph Gill (1959 and 1964).

Ferrari, Gaudenzio (goudän'tsēō fär-rä'rē), c.1480-1546, Italian painter, one of the leading representatives of the Lombard school. He worked chiefly in the churches of Varallo (N Piedmont), Vercelli, and Milan and produced many paintings, most of them now in the galleries of Lombardy and Piedmont. At its best his art is characterized by inventiveness, fine feeling for the dramatic and decorative, and bright and pleasing color. Notable examples include the frescoes in Santa Maria delle Grazie, Varallo; incidents in the lives of Mary Magdalene and the Virgin, in the Church of San Cristoforo, Vercelli; *Choir of Singing Angels*, in Santa Maria dei Miracoli, at Saronno; and the *Scourging of Christ*, in Santa Maria delle Grazie, Milan. See study by Ethel Halsey (1904).

Ferrari, Giuseppe (jōōzĕp'pā), 1812-76, Italian philosopher and politician. A thorough skeptic in metaphysics, he devoted himself to the more active aspects of social, political, and historical philosophy. From his self-imposed exile in France (1837-59), he exerted influence on the RISORGIMENTO. His development of a philosophy of revolution in *La filosofia della rivoluzione* (1851) and *Histoire des révolutions* (1858) encouraged the radical and liberal elements in Italy to act. Returning to Italy in 1859 he strove for a federalized state, described in his *La federazione repubblicana* (1851), opposing the unitarian, monarchical plan of Cavour.

Ferraris, Galileo (gälēlā'ō fär-rä'rēs), 1847-97, Italian physicist and electrical engineer. He is noted for his work on alternating current and for his discovery (1885) of the rotary magnetic field, through which he promoted the development of alternating-current motors.

Ferré, Luis Alberto (lōōēs' älbār'tō färā'), 1904-, governor of Puerto Rico (1969-73). An engineer and millionaire, he ran a family cement company and was elected to the house of representatives in 1952. In 1967 he founded the New Progressive party; as its candidate he won the governorship in 1968, breaking the Popular Democratic party's 28-year domination. His reelection campaign in 1972 became a virtual referendum on statehood, which Ferré advocated. Ferré was defeated by Rafael Hernández Colón, who espoused continuation of the commonwealth status.

Ferreira, António (äntô'nyōō fərē'rə), c.1528-69, Portuguese dramatist and poet. Ferreira served as a privy councillor and a magistrate. Influenced by the Italian Renaissance, he wrote his great play *Inés de Castro* (c.1557), employing Italian meters and classical form. The only Renaissance tragedy in Portuguese, it was translated into English in 1697. Ferreira also wrote comedies, sonnets, and odes. His writing is generally grave and elevated and displays his classical learning. He was important in the movement to free Portuguese literature and language from Spanish influence.

Ferrer, Jose Vicente (hōsā' vēsān'tā fərâr'), 1912-, American actor, director, and producer, b. Santurce, Puerto Rico. Ferrer made his debut in 1935 and in 1940 gained acclaim in *Charley's Aunt*. A versatile actor, he has appeared in many films, including *The Caine Mutiny* (1954) and *Ship of Fools* (1965). In 1950 he won an Academy Award for his performance in *Cyrano de Bergerac*.

Ferrer, Vincent: see VINCENT FERRER, SAINT.

Ferrer Guardia, Francisco (fränthēs'kō färär' gwär'dyä), 1859-1909, Spanish political theorist and educator. An ardent liberal, anticlerical, and republican, he took refuge in France (1886), where he was further influenced by radical thought. He returned to Spain to found (1901) a progressive, anticlerical, and antimilitarist school at Barcelona. Accused of complicity in the attempt (1906) to murder King Alfonso XIII, he was released and continued his educational work until 1909, when he was convicted of taking part in the uprising in Barcelona. He was executed. His death, viewed by liberals everywhere as a judicial murder, provoked demonstrations in W Europe.

Ferrero, Guglielmo (gōōlyĕl'mō fär-rĕ'rō), 1871-1942, Italian man of letters and historian. With his father-in-law, the criminologist Cesare LOMBROSO, he collaborated in the writing of *La donna delinquente* (1893, tr. *The Female Offender*, 1895). His interest in psychology and sociology permeates his writings. An outspoken critic of Fascism, Ferrero was exiled by Benito Mussolini and became (1930) professor of history at the Univ. of Geneva, Switzerland, where he died. Among his numerous works the best-known deal with Roman history, notably *The Greatness and Decline of Rome* (5 vol., 1902-7, tr. 1907-9), a challenging work treating Roman history in terms of economic problems. It was criticized by many professional historians on the grounds that it lacked objectivity. In his last years he wrote extensively on the French Revolutionary and Napoleonic periods, attempting to point out, by historical parallels, a solution of the modern political world crisis. Ferrero also wrote several novels. Most of his later works were written in French.

ferret, name for a domesticated POLECAT, *Mustela putorius*, common in the Old World. It has been used for centuries to hunt rats, mice, and rabbits. Most domestic ferrets are albinos, but some are brown and black, like wild polecats. The name is also applied to a related wild species, the North American, or black-footed, ferret, *M. nigripes*, which inhabits the Great Plains and is now extremely rare. Its range nearly coincides with that of the prairie dogs, which constitute most of its diet; it is often found in prairie dog burrows. The severe reduction of the prairie dog population by ranchers is probably partially responsible for the rarity of the black-footed ferret, although it was apparently not numerous when the West was first settled by Europeans. Ferrets are classified in the phylum CHORDATA, subphylum Vertebrata, class Mammalia, order Carnivora, family Mustelidae (WEASEL family).

Ferri, Ciro (chē'rō fĕr'rē), 1634-89, Italian baroque painter, etcher, and architect, the most celebrated pupil of Pietro da Cortona. He imitated Cortona's style with such success that he was employed to complete his unfinished works in the Pitti Palace, Florence, and in Rome. Among his chief independent works are the biblical frescoes in Santa Maria Maggiore, Bergamo, and the frescoes in the cupola of Sant' Agnese in the Piazza Navona, Rome.

Ferri, Enrico (ānrē'kō), 1856-1929, Italian criminologist. He continued the scientific study of crime begun by Cesare Lombroso, emphasizing social and economic factors. He argued against penal systems that stressed only punitive action. Instead, he recommended a system with the goal of crime prevention. Argentina's penal code of 1921 was based on his ideas, but the Italian code that Ferri later drew up was rejected by the Fascist regime. He edited *Avanti*, a Socialist daily, for many years. Of his several books the best known is *Criminal Sociology* (1884, tr. 1917, repr. 1967).

ferric (fĕr'ĭk), IRON in the +3 VALENCE state.

ferric sulfate or **iron (III) sulfate,** chemical compound, $Fe_2(SO_4)_3$, a yellow rhombic crystalline hygroscopic water-soluble salt that decomposes when heated to a temperature of 480°C. The enneahydrate, $Fe_2(SO_4)_3 \cdot 9H_2O$, is a deliquescent rhombic crystalline salt that occurs in nature as the mineral coquimbite. It is used as a mordant in dyeing, as a coagulant for industrial wastes, in pickling baths for aluminum and steel, and in pigments.

Ferrier, James Frederick, 1808-64, Scottish philosopher. He was a professor at Edinburgh (1842-45) and at St. Andrews from 1845 until his death. His major work, the *Institutes of Metaphysic* (1854), denied the absolute existence of matter and maintained instead that mind and matter necessarily coexist in all experience. See biography by E. S. Haldane (1899).

Ferrier, Kathleen, 1912-1953, British contralto, b. Higher Walton, Lancashire. Ferrier studied and taught piano, later working as a telephone operator. She began voice lessons at 25. Her celebrated performances include the title role in the premiere of Benjamin Britten's *Rape of Lucretia* (1946). Ferrier's interpretations of Gluck's *Orfeo* and works of Mahler and Brahms were greatly acclaimed. She died at 41 of cancer.

Ferris, Woodbridge Nathan, 1853-1928, American educator and public official, b. Tioga co., N.Y. After study (1873-74) at the Univ. of Michigan, he taught in country schools, and became a successful school superintendent in Illinois. In 1884 he founded a college at Big Rapids, Mich., the Ferris Institute, of which he remained head until his death. Active in Democratic party politics, he was governor (1913-16) of Michigan, gaining the title "Good Gray Governor." In 1922 he won a notable victory when he was elected to the U.S. Senate, the first Democrat to gain this office in Michigan since 1863; he served from 1923 until his death.

Ferris wheel, amusement park ride. It consists of a power-operated wheel that is about 50 ft (15 m) in diameter. It has two rims that are parallel to and equidistant from the shaft about which the wheel rotates. Between the rims there are a number of seats that carry passengers. George W. G. Ferris, a U.S. engineer from Galesburg, Ill., designed and built the first such wheel for the World's Columbian Exposition held in Chicago in 1892. This wheel was 250 ft (76 m) in diameter and carried 36 cars with a seating capacity of 40 passengers each; its total weight was 220 tons. Ferris wheels may be found at many exhibitions, fairs, and carnivals.

Ferrol, El (ĕl fārôl'), officially (since 1939) **El Ferrol del Caudillo** (dĕl kouthē'lyō), city (1970 pop. 87,736), La Coruña prov., NW Spain, in Galicia. The naval base on the Atlantic was built in the 18th cent. and is one of the most important in Spain. Shipbuilding and ironworks are the main industries. Francisco Franco, *El Caudillo*, was born there.

ferromagnetism: see MAGNETISM.

ferrous (fĕr'əs), IRON in the +2 VALENCE state.

ferrous sulfate or **iron (II) sulfate,** chemical compound, $FeSO_4$. It is known as the monohydrate, $FeSO_4 \cdot H_2O$; the tetrahydrate, $FeSO_4 \cdot 4H_2O$; the pentahydrate, $FeSO_4 \cdot 5H_2O$; and the heptahydrate, $FeSO_4 \cdot 7H_2O$. The heptahydrate is also called green vitriol, copperas, or melanterite (a mineral that commonly occurs with pyrite). It is a blue-green monoclinic crystalline water-soluble salt. It is prepared commercially by oxidation of pyrite (iron sulfide) or by treating iron with sulfuric acid. It is used in the manufacture of inks, in wool dyeing as a mordant, and in water purification as a substitute for aluminum sulfate. It melts at 64°C, and at 90°C it loses water of hydration to form the monohydrate, a white, monoclinic, crystalline powder that occurs naturally as the mineral szomolnokite. The mineral siderotil is iron sulfate pentahydrate.

Ferry, Jules (zhül fĕrē'), 1832–93, French statesman. A member of the government of national defense established after the defeat of Emperor NAPOLEON III in the Franco-Prussian War (1870–71), he later rose to prominence as minister of public instruction (1879–80, 1882). He was twice premier (1880–81, 1883–85). Ferry established the modern French educational system with universal, free, and compulsory education in the primary schools. He secularized the public schools, abolishing religious education in them, and barring members of Roman Catholic orders as public school teachers. Ferry is best known, however, as the builder of the French colonial empire. An exponent of imperialism, he was willing to cooperate with the German chancellor Otto von Bismarck in order to secure French expansion overseas. During his premiership the French occupied Tunis, entered Tonkin and Madagascar, and penetrated the regions of the Niger and the Congo. Ferry was overthrown after a temporary French defeat in Indochina. He was assassinated by a religious fanatic. See study by T. F. Power (1944, repr. 1966).

ferry, boat providing passage over a river, lake, or other body of water for passengers, vehicles, or freight; the term is also applied to the place where the crossing is made and, by extension, to overwater train or airplane transit. Ferries have a long history and were especially important in the days before engineers learned to construct permanent bridges and tunnels traversing large bodies of water. At first most ferries were small boats propelled by oars or poles. Large flatboats came later; they made use of a form of long oar, sometimes assisted by sails. Some large ferries today still make short passages by pulling on a chain fastened to the shore on both sides; on board such a ferry the chain passes around a hand-powered or engine-powered drum. On other ferries a cable or rope is extended from the ferry to a buoy anchored upstream and amidstream, and the force of the current against the side of the boat serves to push the ferry across. Modern ferries for heavier traffic and longer passages are usually powered by diesel or diesel-electric engines. Steam drives the very largest ferries, e.g., the Staten Island ferry in New York City and those across the English Channel, although the channel ferries have to some extent been replaced by hovercraft. Where railroad bridges are impracticable there are train ferries; these may use paddle wheels for maneuverability or may simply be barges pushed by tugs. Since 1936 a train ferry across the channel between Dunkirk and Dover has made through service possible between London and Paris. An extremely fast type of passenger ferry runs on HYDROFOILS, which are underwater wings or plates that rise to plane the vessel across the surface of the water.

Fersen, Count Fredrik Axel (frā'drĭk äk'səl fĕr'sən), 1719–94, Swedish politician and soldier. He served (1743–48) in the French army and retired as brigadier general. As lieutenant general in the Swedish army (1750–57), he distinguished himself in the Seven Years War. Fersen was a leader of the noble faction called the Hats. After the coup d'état of GUSTAVUS III, he became the king's adviser. At the diet of 1789 he opposed the king's war policy and was arrested. He was soon released, and he retired from politics. His history of 18th-century Sweden (largely autobiographical) is more interesting than accurate.

Fersen, Count Hans Axel, 1755–1810, Swedish soldier and diplomat; son of Count Fredrik Axel Fersen. He entered (1779) the French service, was aide-de-camp of comte de Rochambeau in the American Revolution, and later at the court of Versailles became a favorite of Marie Antoinette. He was recalled (1784) to Sweden, but returned to Paris on the eve of the French Revolution. In 1791 he helped the marquis de Bouillé plan the flight of Louis XVI and Marie Antionette, and he himself drove their coach outside the city limits, but the king and queen were arrested at Varennes. Fersen later held diplomatic posts at Vienna and Brussels and in 1801 was made marshal of Sweden by Gustavus IV, whom he accompanied to Germany in the Napoleonic Wars. After the Swedish revolution of 1809 that forced Gustavus IV to abdicate, Fersen was accused by popular rumor of reactionary intrigues and was killed by a mob. See his diaries (tr. 1902); biography by Stanley Loomis (1972); Marjorie Coryn, *Marie Antoinette and Axel de Fersen* (1938); Evan John (pseud. of E. V. Simpson), *Kings' Masque* (1941).

Fertile Crescent, historic region of the Middle East. A well-watered and fertile area, it arcs across the northern part of the Syrian desert. It is flanked on the W by the Nile and on the E by the Euphrates and Tigris rivers, and includes parts of Israel, Lebanon, Syria, Jordan, and Iraq. From earliest times this region was the site of ancient settlements and the scene of bloody raids and sudden invasions, especially from the Arabian peninsula. It changed hands many times.

fertility drug, any of a variety of substances used to increase the possibility of conception and successful pregnancy. Different methods are used to correct the many different functional disorders of both males and females that can interfere with conception and childbearing. In the male inadequate sperm resulting from hormonal imbalances or generally debilitated condition can often be corrected by controlling the diet and administering thyroid hormone and, sometimes, pituitary hormones. In women some sterility caused by sex organ dysfunction can be treated chemotherapeutically. The most common cause of female sterility, failure to ovulate, when caused by insufficient secretion of pituitary GONADOTROPIC HORMONES, can be treated by administering human chorionic gonadotropin, a hormone secreted by the placenta during pregnancy and obtained from the urine of pregnant women. In certain cases failure to ovulate can also be corrected with the drug clomiphene citrate (Clomid). A frequent result of ovulation induced by this drug is the production of more than one ovum in a month, and subsequent MULTIPLE BIRTHS. PROGESTERONE is often given in cases where fertilization of the ovum does occur but where there is evidence that the uterine lining is unable to support the developing fetus, as in repeated miscarriages or bleeding during pregnancy. Drugs are unable to correct many cases of infertility, such as the occasional case of chemical or immunological incompatibility between male and female, and various anatomical obstructions to successful fertilization, such as blocked Fallopian tubes in the female or blocked sperm ducts in the male, which conditions may be surgically corrected.

fertility rites, magico-religious ceremonies to insure an abundance of food and the birth of children. The rites, expressed through dances, prayers, incantations, and sacred dramas, seek to control the otherwise unpredictable forces of nature. In primitive agricultural societies natural phenomena, such as rainfall, the fecundity of the earth, and the regeneration of nature were frequently personified. One of the most important pagan myths was the search of the earth goddess for her lost (or dead) child or lover (e.g., Isis and Osiris, Ishtar and Tammuz, Demeter and Persephone). This myth, symbolizing the birth, death, and reappearance of vegetation, when acted out in a sacred drama, was the fertility rite par excellence. Other rites concerned with productivity include acts of sympathetic MAGIC, such as kindling of fires (symbolizing the sun) and scattering the reproductive organs of animals on the fields, displays of phallic symbols, and ritual prostitution. In India it was once believed that a fertile marriage would result if virgins were first deflowered by means of the lingam, a stone phallus symbolizing the god Shiva. Sacrifices of both humans and animals were believed to release the powers embodied within them and so make the fields or forests productive where the sacrifices had taken place. Many ancient fertility rites have persisted in modified forms into modern times. The Maypole dance derives from spring rituals glorifying the phallus.

fertilization, in biology, process in the REPRODUCTION of both plants and animals, involving the union of two unlike sex cells (gametes), the SPERM and the OVUM, followed by the joining of their nuclei. In the flowers of higher plants, the process occurs after POLLINATION has enabled the sperm to contact the egg cell in the plant's ovary. In lower plants and in animals the sperm is actively motile and swims to the egg through an external aqueous medium or through a fluid environment within the reproductive tract of the female. The fundamental principle of fertilization is the same in all organisms. The first sperm to establish successful contact is absorbed by the ovum and the two nuclei unite, thus combining the hereditary material of both parents (see GENETICS). In higher forms, the sperm contact initiates cell division in the fertilized egg (zygote), and the subsequent EMBRYO develops into a new individual. **Cross-fertilization** indicates fusion of a sperm of one hermaphroditic plant or animal with an ovum of another, as distinguished from self-fertilization, in which ovum and sperm of the same individual are fused.

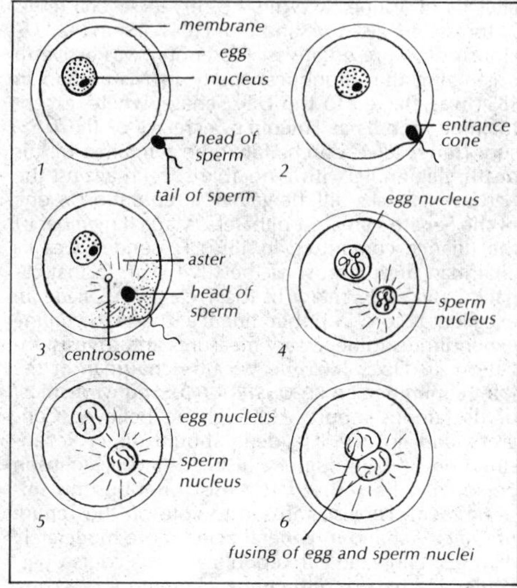

Fertilization of an egg cell

fertilizer, organic or inorganic material added to the soil in order to replace or to increase the amount of one or more plant nutrients. Plants require nitrogen, phosphorus, potassium, and other chemical elements in varying amounts. When the soil lacks sufficient quantities of these elements to support the growth of a crop—either as a result of the removal of crops (and thus of nutrients) by harvesting or grazing, or because of leaching or erosion—the insufficiency may be remedied by the application of fertilizers. Organic fertilizers include animal and green MANURE, fish and bone meal, and COMPOST (see also HUMUS). Microorganisms in the soil decompose organic material and free its elements for plant use. Inorganic or artificial fertilizers (also called chemical or mineral fertilizers) contain one or more of the necessary nutrients in the specific proportions required by the soil and the crop. They are applied in various ways: they may be spread over the surface or plowed under, drilled into deep or shallow layers of the soil, applied in bands under the rows where the seeds are to be sown, drilled into the bands at the time of planting, or side-dressed between planted rows. Properly used, fertilizers increase crop yields; they do not affect the chemical composition or the nutritive properties of the crop unless specifically intended to do so, as in the case of iodine added to the iodine-poor soils. See NITROGEN CYCLE. See publications of the U.S. Dept. of Agriculture.

Fertő tó, lake: see NEUSIEDLER LAKE, Austria and Hungary.

Fescennine verses (fĕs'ənīn, -nĭn), ancient Italian doggerel lines, bantering and scurrilous, originally chanted at rustic festivals—perhaps to avert the evil eye. As used in Rome, they were shouted extemporaneously (in dialogue form) by onlookers at weddings and triumphs and may have been forerunners of Latin drama.

fescue (fĕs'kyōō), any of some 100 species of introduced Old World grasses of the genus *Festuca.* Meadow fescue and tall, or reed, fescue are excellent forage crops and the Chewing's, red, and sheep fescues are planted for turf. Fescue is classified in the division MAGNOLIOPHYTA, class Liliatae, order Cyperales, family Gramineae. See GRASS; LAWN.

Fessenden, Thomas Green, 1771–1837, American journalist and satirical poet, b. Walpole, N.H. Throughout his life he practiced law and edited various newspapers. Under the pseudonym Christopher Caustic he wrote satirical poems, of which *Democracy Unveiled* (1805), a scurrilous attack on Jefferson and other Democratic leaders, was the most famous. In 1822 he established in Boston the *New England Farmer,* which he edited until his death. He also wrote various agricultural handbooks including the widely used *Complete Farmer and Rural Economist* (1834). In 1836 he was elected to the Massachusetts General Court. See study by P. G. Perrin (1925).

Fessenden, William Pitt (fĕs'əndən), 1806–69, American politician, b. Boscawen, N.H. Admitted (1827) to the bar, he began practice in Portland in 1829 and by 1835 was regarded as one of the leading lawyers of Maine. A Whig, he served several terms in the state legislature and one (1841–43) in the U.S. House of Representatives. Fessenden was active in organizing the Republican party in Maine and in 1854 was elected to the U.S. Senate, where, except for nine months as Lincoln's Secretary of the Treasury (June, 1864–March, 1865), he remained till his death. Beginning with a notable speech against the Kansas-Nebraska bill, he gained a reputation as one of the Senate's greatest debaters. Made a member of the finance committee in 1857, Fessenden was its chairman during most of the Civil War. In that capacity and as Secretary of the Treasury he made an excellent record in public finance, trying to confine expenditures to necessary measures and to resist inflation. In Dec., 1865, he became chairman of the joint committee on RECONSTRUCTION and wrote most of its famous report. Although he believed Congress, and not the President, should direct Reconstruction, and although he disliked Andrew Johnson personally, he refused to vote for Johnson's impeachment. He also refused to vote on the Tenure of Office Act and in general acted more moderately than his fellow radical Republicans. His course, particularly in regard to the impeachment proceedings, was contrary to the expressed wishes of his constituency, and for a time he was unpopular. See biography by his son, Francis Fessenden (1907, repr. 1970); B. J. Hendrick, *Lincoln's War Cabinet* (1946, repr. 1965); C. A. Jellison, *Fessenden of Maine: Civil War Senator* (1962).

Festa, Costanzo (kōstän'tsō fĕs'tä), c.1490–1545, Italian composer. An early madrigalist, Festa combined Flemish and Italian influences in his works and in turn influenced Palestrina. His *Te Deum* (1516) is still sung by the pontifical choir at the election of a new pope.

Festival of Lights: see HANUKKAH.

Festival of Two Worlds: see SPOLETO FESTIVAL.

festoon, sculptured or painted architectural or interior ornament consisting of a garland of leaves, flowers, or fruit, or some combination of these, held by ribbons or folds and draped at the ends. When a festoon hangs down from only one end, it is called a drop, but when it hangs from both ends it is termed a swag. The festoon reproduces the actual garland used on Greek and Roman festal altars and was much used as a decorative feature in Roman and Renaissance art. It was often represented as carried by putti, or infant figures.

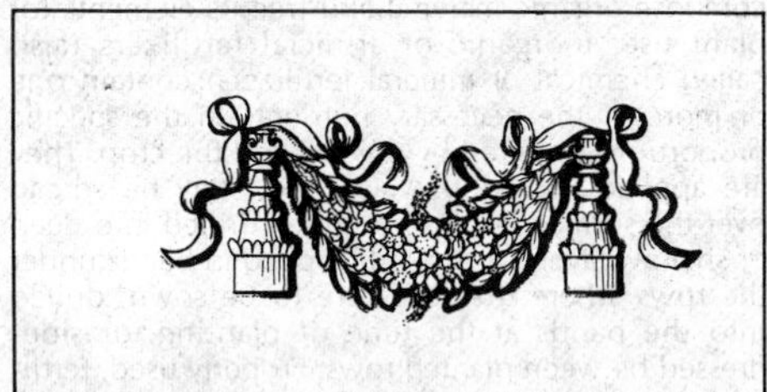

Festoon

Festus (Sextus Pompeius Festus), fl. at some time between 100 and 400 A.D., Roman lexicographer; his surviving work, *On the Meaning of Words,* is an abridgment of the lost glossary of Marcus Verrius Flaccus. It is important as a primary source for Roman scholarship and Roman antiquities. PAUL THE DEACON abridged Pompeius Festus' work.

Festus, Porcius (pôr'shəs), fl A.D. 60, Roman procurator of Judaea (A.D. 60–A.D. 62). He succeeded Antonius Felix. He was just in his administration of the province. Finding Paul in prison, he gave him a fair hearing before King Agrippa and then sent him to Rome (Acts 24.27–26.32).

FET: see TRANSISTOR.

fetch: see WAVE, in oceanography.

feterita (fĕtərē'tə): see SORGHUM.

Feth Ali Shah: see FATH ALI SHAH.

Feti or **Fetti, Domenico** (dōmā'nēcō fĕ'tē, fĕt'tē), c.1589–1624, Italian painter. Court painter to the Gonzaga family in Mantua, Feti was influenced by the chiaroscuro technique of CARAVAGGIO. His later works, such as *Melancholia* (Louvre), belong in color to the Venetian tradition. Feti painted biblical themes as detailed GENRE scenes, using illumination from several sources, as in works by ELSHEIMER.

Fétis, François Joseph (fräNswä' zhôzĕf' fātēs'), 1784–1871, Belgian music theorist, historian, and composer. A teacher and librarian at the Paris Conservatory, he became (1833) director of the conservatory at Brussels. He wrote two theoretical works (1824, 1844) based on the harmonic theories of Rameau. His *Biographie universelle des musiciens* (8 vol., 1835–44) and *Histoire général de la musique* (1837), despite inaccuracies, are of great value to music historians. In Paris in 1827 he founded *Revue musicale.* He wrote biographies of Paganini and Stradivarius and composed two symphonies, four operas, piano music, chamber music, and some church music.

fetish (fĕt'ĭsh), inanimate object believed to possess some magical power. The fetish may be a natural thing, such as a stone, a feather, a shell, or the claw of an animal, or it may be artificial, such as carvings in wood. The power of the fetish is thought to derive its efficacy from one of two sources. In some cases the object is said to have a will of its own; in others the source of power comes from the belief that a god dwells within the object and has transformed it into an instrument of his desires. Closely related to the idea of the power of a fetish is the notion of TABOO. Here the power within the fetish is thought to be so strong that it is extremely dangerous and may be handled only by special individuals, if at all. Any object of irrational or superstitious devotion may be called a fetish.

fetishism, in psychiatry, a sexual perversion, usually found in males, in which erotic interest and satisfaction are centered on an inanimate object. The presence of the fetish—frequently a garment (e.g., underclothing or high-heeled shoes) or even a part of the body (e.g., the foot) of a desired woman—may be a prerequisite or prelude to excitation and sexual intercourse, or it may displace any sexual interest in the woman herself. In psychoanalysis a fetish is believed to represent a substitute for the male genitalia, which women are imagined to have lost through castration. The fetish object may have a phallic quality, as in the bound and deformed feet of Chinese upper-class women from the Sung dynasty until the 20th cent.

Fetterman, William Judd, 1833?–1866, American army officer. In 1861 he enlisted in the Union army from Delaware; he served throughout the Civil War and was twice brevetted for gallant conduct. After the war he remained in the army and was sent, in Nov., 1866, to Fort Phil Kearney in Wyoming. The **Fetterman massacre** occurred when, despite his unfamiliarity with frontier conditions and methods of Indian fighting, he volunteered to lead a party of 80 men on supply escort duty. Fetterman ignored orders not to leave the trail and was ambushed by Indians under Red Cloud. He and his entire party were killed in the attack.

Fetti, Domenico: see FETI, DOMENICO.

Feuchtwanger, Lion (lē'ōn foikht'väng-ər), 1884–1958, German historical novelist. After writing several successful plays, he achieved fame with the novels *The Ugly Duchess* (1923, tr. 1928) and *Power* (1925, tr. 1926). Among his other well-known novels are the trilogy *Josephus* (1923, tr. 1932), *The Jew of Rome* (1935, tr. 1935), and *Josephus and the Emperor* (1942, English only); *Success* (1930, tr. 1930); *Proud Destiny* (1947, English only); and *Jephta and His Daughter* (tr. 1958). His works are noted for their imaginative historical reconstruction and their individualized characters. Feuchtwanger, of Jewish birth, left Germany for France in 1933; he was later arrested but dramatically escaped to the United States in 1940.

feud, formalized private warfare, especially between family groups. The blood feud (see VENDETTA) is characteristic of those societies in which central government either has not arisen or has decayed. In modern times the feud, outlawed in most countries, has persisted where public justice cannot be easily enforced and private means are a simpler recourse. A famous example is the 19th-century feud of the Hatfields and McCoys in the mountain regions of the southern United States. The frontier in U.S. history was also characterized by private justice and the feud.

feudalism (fyŏŏ'dəlĭzəm), form of political and social organization typical of Western Europe from the dissolution of Charlemagne's empire to the rise of the absolute monarchies. The term *feudalism* is derived from the Latin *feodum,* for "fief," and ultimately from a Germanic word meaning "cow," generalized to denote valuable movable property. Although analogous social systems have appeared in other civilizations, the feudalism of Europe in the Middle Ages remains the common model of feudal society.

The Model Feudal System. The evolution of highly diverse forms, customs, and institutions makes it almost impossible to accurately depict feudalism as a whole, but certain components of the system may be regarded as characteristic: strict division into social classes, i.e., nobility, clergy, peasantry, and, in the later Middle Ages, burgesses; private jurisdiction based on local custom; and the landholding system dependent upon the fief or fee. Feudalism was based on contracts made among nobles, and although it was intricately connected with the MANORIAL SYSTEM, it must be considered as distinct from it. Although some men held their land in ALOD, without obligation to any person, they were exceptions to the rule in the Middle Ages. In an ideal feudal society (a legal fiction, most nearly realized in the Crusaders' Latin Kingdom of Jerusalem), the ownership of all land was vested in the king. Beneath him was a hierarchy of nobles, the most important nobles holding land directly from the king, and the lesser from them, down to the seigneur who held a single manor. The political economy of the system was local and agricultural, and at its base was the manorial system. Under the manorial system the peasants, laborers, or SERFS, held the land they worked from the seigneur, who granted them use of the land and his protection in return for personal services (especially on the demesne, the land he retained for his own use) and for dues (especially payment in kind). The feudal method of holding land was by fief; the grantor of the fief was the suzerain, or overlord, and the recipient was the vassal. The fief was formally acquired following the ceremony of homage, in which the vassal, kneeling before the overlord, put his hands in those of the lord and declared himself his man, and the overlord bound himself by kissing the vassal and raising him to his feet. The vassal then swore an oath of fealty, vowing to be faithful to the overlord and to perform the acts and services due him. This formal procedure served to cement the personal relationship between lord and vassal; after the ceremony the lord invested the vassal with the fief, usually by giving him some symbol of the transferred land. Honors or rights, as well as land, could be granted as fiefs. Gradually the system of subinfeudation evolved, by which the vassal might in his turn become an overlord, granting part of his fief to one who then became vassal to him. Thus very complex relationships, based on fiefs, developed among the nobles, and the personal ties between overlords and vassals were weakened. Originally the fief had to be renewed on the death of either party. With the advent of hereditary succession and PRIMOGENITURE, renewal of the fief by the heir of the deceased became customary, and little by little the fief became hereditary. The system rested on the unsettled conditions of the times and thus on the need of the lord for armed warriors and the need of the vassal for protection. The nobility was essentially a military class, with the KNIGHT as the typical warrior. Since equipping mounted fighters was expensive, the lord could not create his armed force without the obligation of the vassal to supply a stipulated number of armed men, a number that varied from the service of the vassal himself to the service of hundreds in private armies. The gradations of nobility were, therefore, based on both military service and landholding. At the bottom of the social scale was the squire, originally the servant of the knight. Above the knight were classes that varied in different countries—counts, dukes, earls, barons, and other nobles. The vassal owed, in addition to military service, other dues and services that varied with local custom and tended to become fixed, as in the case of AIDS. The obligation of the overlord in the feudal contract was always the protection of the vassal.

Rise and Spread. The feudal system first appears in definite form in the Frankish lands in the 9th and 10th cent. A long dispute between scholars as to whether its institutional basis was Roman or Germanic remains somewhat inconclusive; it can safely be said that feudalism emerged from the condition of society arising from the disintegration of Roman institutions and the further disruption of Germanic inroads and settlements. Of course, the rise of feudalism in areas formerly dominated by Roman institutions meant the breakdown of central government; but in regions untouched by Roman customs the feudal system was a further step toward organization and centralization. The system used and altered institutions then in existence. Important in an economic sense was the Roman villa, with the peculiar form of rental, the precarium, a temporary grant of land that the grantor could revoke at any time. Increasingly, the poor landholder transferred his land to a protector and received it back as a precarium, thus giving rise to the manorial system. It was also possible for the manorial system to develop from the Germanic village, as in England. The development of fiefs was also influenced by the Roman institution of *patricinium* and the German institution of *mundium*, by which the powerful surrounded themselves with men who rendered them service, especially military service, in exchange for protection. More and more, this service-and-protection contract came to involve the granting of a beneficium, the use of land, which tended to become hereditary. Local royal officers and great landholders increased their power and forced the king to grant them rights of private justice and immunity from royal interference. By these processes feudalism became fixed in Frankish lands by the end of the 10th cent. The church also had great influence in shaping feudalism; although the organization of the church was not feudal in character, its hierarchy somewhat paralleled the feudal hierarchy. The church owned much land, held by monasteries, by church dignitaries, and by the churches themselves. Most of this land, given by nobles as a bequest or gift, carried feudal obligations; thus clerical land, like lay land, assumed a feudal aspect, and the clergy became participants in the temporal feudal system. Many bishops and abbots were much like lay seigneurs. This feudal connection between church and state gave rise to the controversy over lay INVESTITURE. Feudalism spread from France to Spain, Italy, and later Germany and Eastern Europe. In England the Frankish form was imposed by William I (William the Conqueror) after 1066, although most of the elements of feudalism were already present. It was extended eastward into Slavic lands to the marches (frontier provinces), which were continually battered by new invasions, and it was adopted partially in Scandinavian countries. The important features of feudalism were similar throughout, but there existed definite national differences. Feudalism continued in all parts of Europe until the end of the 14th cent.

Decline. A great disruptive force was always present in the system itself, which provided for the concentration of power in the hands of a few. The rise of powerful monarchs in France, Spain, and England broke down the local system. Another disruptive force was the increase of communication, which broke down the isolated manor, assisted the rise of towns, and facilitated the emergence of the burgess class. This process was greatly accelerated in the 14th cent. and did much to destroy the feudal classifications of society. The system broke down gradually. It was not completely destroyed in France until the French Revolution (1789), and it persisted in Germany until 1848 and in Russia until 1917. Many relics of feudalism still persist, and its influence remains on the institutions of Western Europe.

Other Feudal Systems. Other ages and other lands have seen the development of feudal institutions. In Japan the feudal system was well ordered before the 10th cent., and it persisted with modifications until the 19th cent. (see BUSHIDO; DAIMYO). In other areas, as in China, where feudal practices were in existence by 1100 B.C., society became feudalistic but not precisely feudal. Feudalism in India and in the Saracen and Ottoman civilizations was in many ways analogous to Western feudalism, but it proved less durable than its European counterpart. The existence of feudalism in several civilizations has given rise to theories of feudalism as a necessary and inevitable stage of political development. Some scholars, however, consider the European feudal system a unique phenomenon. See Sir Frederick Pollock and F. W. Maitland, *The History of English Law* (2d ed. 1898, repr. 1968); R. W. Carlyle and A. J. Carlyle, *A History of Medieval Political Theory in the West* (6 vol., 1903–36; repr. 1962); Henri Pirenne, *Medieval Cities* (tr. 1925, repr. 1969); J. W. Thompson, *Feudal Germany* (1927; repr., 2 vol., 1962); Carl Stephenson, *Mediaeval Feudalism* (1942, repr. 1956); A. L. Poole, *Obligations of Society in the XII and XIII Centuries* (1946, repr. 1960); Rushton Coulborn, ed., *Feudalism in History* (1956, repr. 1965); M. L. B. Bloch, *Feudal Society* (tr. 1961, repr. 1964); F. M. Stenton, *The First Century of English Feudalism, 1066–1166* (2d ed. 1961); F. L. Ganshof, *Feudalism* (3d Eng. ed. 1964); David Herlihy, ed., *The History of Feudalism* (1970).

Feuerbach, Anselm von (än'zĕlm fən foi'ərbäkh), 1829–80, German painter. He studied in Germany, Paris, and Rome, spending much of his life in Italy. He sought to produce works of pure classicism that were both didactic and idealistic. To his Roman period (1856–73) belong most of his famous works, including *Battle of the Amazons* (Nuremberg), *Iphigenia* (Stuttgart), and *Medea* (Munich). His portraits have withstood critical opinion better than his history paintings. His autobiography (1882) emphasizes his misunderstood genius.

Feuerbach, Ludwig Andreas (lo͝ot'vĭkh ändrā'äs), 1804–72, German philosopher, educated at Heidelberg and Berlin; son of Paul Johann Anselm von Feuerbach. At first a Hegelian, he abandoned absolute idealism for naturalistic materialism. He asserted that religious feeling is simply a product of man's yearnings and maintained that the proper study of philosophy is not what transcends experience but man himself and nature, on which humanity rests. Although Feuerbach approaches materialism in his later works, man for him is not to be regarded as simply a product of matter. Feuerbach's most important works were *Das Wesen des Christentums* (1841, tr. by George Eliot, *The Essence of Christianity*, 1957 ed.); *Geschichte der neueren Philosophie* (2 vol., 1833–37); and *Gottheit, Freiheit und Unsterblichkeit* (1866). See W. B. Chamberlain, *Heaven Wasn't His Destination* (1941); Eugene Kamenka, *The Philosophy of Ludwig Feuerbach* (1970).

Feuerbach, Paul Johann Anselm von (poul yō'hän än'zĕlm), 1775–1883, German jurist; father of Ludwig Feuerbach. His work was in the field of criminal law. In *Kritik des natürlichen Rechts* [critique of natural law] (1796) he argued that law was the positive mandate of the state and was not to be confused with natural morality. His *Revision der Grundsätze und Grundbegriffe des positiven peinlichen Rechts* [revision of the principles and rules of positive criminal law] (1799) ascribed a dual role to the penal law: It should protect society by deterring crime through the threat of finely adjusted penalties and should protect individual liberties by punishing only those crimes that had been exactly defined by statute. Feuerbach's writings earned him teaching positions at the universities of Jena (1799), Kiel (1802), and Landshut (1804), and in 1805 he joined the ministry of justice of Bavaria with the task of preparing a criminal code. He secured the abolition of torture in Bavaria in 1806. The liberal criminal code that he drafted (1813) had an important influence throughout Germany and was adopted by several German states and Swiss cantons. Feuerbach served as an appellate judge from 1814 to his death. Besides his systematic treatises he wrote vivid psychological studies, including *Narratives of Remarkable Criminal Trials* (1828–29, tr. 1846). See his *Wolf Children and Feral Man* tr. by J. A. Singh (1942, repr. 1966).

Feuermann, Emanuel (āmä'no͞oĕl foi'ərmän), 1902–42, Polish virtuoso cellist. He appeared with the Vienna Philharmonic Orchestra at the age of 11 and later (1917–23) taught at the Cologne Conservatory. From 1929 until 1933, when he fled to Switzerland, he taught at the Berlin Hochschule. His concerts in Europe and the United States established him as one of the world's greatest cellists. In 1938 he emigrated to the United States, and he joined the faculty of the Curtis Institute of Music, Philadelphia, in 1941.

Feuillants (föyäN'), political club of the French Revolution. It emerged in July, 1791, when those JACOBINS who opposed a petition for the dethronement of the king split off and began to meet at the former Feuillant convent. Its chief member was Antoine BARNAVE. The Feuillants advocated a constitutional monarchy. In March, 1792, GIRONDISTS overthrew the Feuillant ministry, which opposed war against Austria. From then on, the Feuillants were identified with the royalists and aristocrats and, after the fall (Sept., 1792) of the monarchy, were suppressed by the Jacobins.

Feuillet, Octave (ôktäv' föyā'), 1821–90, French novelist and dramatist. He wrote many plays and novels that were widely read throughout Europe, but his popularity has not survived. His best-known work was the *Roman d'un Jeune Homme Pauvre* (1858), a sentimental novel marked by Feuillet's typical moralism.

fever, elevation of body temperature above the normal level, which in humans is about 98°F (37°C) when measured orally. Fever is considered to be a symptom of a disorder rather than a disease in itself. Under normal conditions the heat that is generated by the burning of food by the body is dissipated through such processes as perspiration and breathing. It is believed that infectious disease, injury to the body tissues, and other conditions that cause fever somehow trigger a disturbance in the functioning of the hypothalamus, the center of temperature control in the body. The rise in temperature is thought to be one of the body's defenses against infection: It may kill bacteria that cause disease or it may increase the rate at which the body's defenses fight infection. The effects of fever on the body are weakness, exhaustion, and sometimes a depletion of body fluids through excessive perspiration. Extremely high fevers may cause convulsive reactions and eventual death. In addition to infectious diseases (such as pneumonia and tonsillitis), disorders of the brain, certain types of cancer, and severe heatstroke may cause fever. There are also cases of fever where the cause cannot be detected. Treatment includes increasing the intake of fluids and administering aspirin and other fever-reducing medications. However, primary treatment is directed at the underlying cause unless the fever is very high (above 104°F/40°C). Persons with such dangerously high fevers are sometimes sponged with cold water or immersed in cold baths.

fever blister: see HERPES SIMPLEX.

feverfew: see CHRYSANTHEMUM.

Few, William, 1748–1828, political leader in the American Revolution, b. near Baltimore. He was raised in North Carolina and was involved in the REGULATOR MOVEMENT there. He later moved to Georgia. Few participated in partisan activities in the American Revolution, served in the Continental Congress (1780–82, 1785–88), signed the Constitution, and was one of Georgia's first U.S. Senators (1789–93).

Feyjóo y Montenegro, Benito Gerónimo (bānē'tō hārō'nēmō fāēhō'ō ē mōntānā'grō), 1676–1764, Spanish Benedictine scholar and critic, abbot at Oviedo, Asturias. Feyjóo led in bringing the Enlightenment to Spain. In his social and political ideas, in philosophy, science, and literature, he represents the most advanced European thought of his time. His essays were collected in his *Teatro critico universal* (8 vol., 1726–39) and *Cartas eruditas y curiosas* (5 vol., 1742–60). Feijóo is a variant spelling of his name.

Feynman, Richard Phillips, 1918–, American physicist, b. New York City, B.S. Massachusetts Institute of Technology, 1939, Ph.D. Princeton, 1942. From 1942 to 1945 he worked on the development of the atomic bomb. He taught (1945–50) at Cornell Univ. and became professor of theoretical physics at the California Institute of Technology in 1950. In 1957 he and Murray Gell-Mann proposed the theory of weak nuclear FORCE. Also with Gell-Mann, he hypothesized the existence of the quark, a more fundamental type of ELEMENTARY PARTICLE than those then known. The Feynman diagram, proposed by him in 1949, shows the track of a particle in space and time and provides a clear means of describing particle interactions. Feynman shared the 1965 Nobel Prize in Physics with Shinichiro Tomonaga and J. S. Schwinger for work leading to the establishment of the modern theory of quantum electrodynamics.

Fez, Arab. *Fas,* Fr. *Fès,* city (1970 est. pop. 290,000), N central Morocco. It is located in a rich agricultural region and is connected by rail to Casablanca, Tangier, and Algeria. The city is noted for its Muslim art and its handicraft industries. It has given its name to the brimless felt caps that were formerly characteristic items of Muslim dress in the Middle East. Fez was the capital of several dynasties and reached its zenith under the Marinid sultans in the mid-14th cent. It declined under the Sa'adi and Filali dynasties, who chose Marrakesh as their capital. Fez consists of the old city (founded 808) and the new city (founded 1276), connected by walls; there is also a European suburb. The city has more than 100 mosques. The one containing the shrine of Idris II, founder of the old city, is one of the holiest places in Morocco. The Qarawiyin mosque is the center of a Muslim university that was especially influential in the Middle Ages. The ulama, or religious council, of the city has often played a role in the selection of the sultans of Morocco.

Fezzan: see FAZZAN, historic region, Libya.

Fianarantsoa (fyänäräntso͞o'ə, -tsō'ə), town (1968 est. pop. 45,800), S central Malagasy Republic, in the central highlands. It is the chief commercial center of a fertile agricultural region producing rice, coffee, potatoes, and tobacco. Food processing is the town's chief industry. A railroad connects Fianarantsoa with Manakara, a small port on the Indian Ocean.

Fianna Fáil (fē'ənə fäl), Irish political party, organized in 1926 by opponents of the Anglo-Irish treaty of 1921 establishing the Irish Free State. Led by Eamon DE VALERA, the party gained control of the government in 1932 and pursued a policy of complete political separation from Great Britain. Except for the years 1948–51 and 1954–57, it held power continuously until 1973 when it lost to an alliance of the FINE GAEL and Labour party.

fiat money (fī'ət, fī'ăt), inconvertible money that is made legal tender by the decree, or fiat, of the government but that is not covered by a specie reserve. It is commonly understood to be of paper, although it may also consist of overvalued metal coins. The circulation of fiat money may lead to inflation, whereas money redeemable in gold or other securities is held much less likely to do so. Under conditions of proper monetary management, however, fiat paper money can be a stable currency. In fact, contemporary American money is essentially fiat money. All Federal reserve notes and most circulating coins are money because the government says they are, not because they are backed by precious metals. Earlier, less stable examples of fiat paper money were the continentals issued by the American government during the Revolutionary War, the assignats issued during the French Revolution, and the greenbacks issued by the U.S. government during the Civil War. Most such issues were accompanied by severe price rises. See W. C. Mitchell, *History of the Greenbacks* (1903, repr. 1960); Fred Reinfeld, *Story of Paper Money* (rev. ed. 1960).

fiber, threadlike strand, usually pliable and capable of being spun into a yarn. Many different fibers are known to be usable; some 40 of these are of commercial importance, and others are of local or specialized use. Most commercial fibers are put to varied and interchangeable uses. Fibers may be classified as either natural or manmade. The natural fibers may be further classed according to origin as animal, vegetable, or inorganic fibers. Animal fibers are composed chiefly of proteins; they include SILK, WOOL, and hair of the goat (known as MOHAIR), llama and ALPACA, vicuña, camel, horse, rabbit, beaver, hog, badger, sable, and other animals. Vegetable fibers are composed chiefly of cellulose and may be classed as short fibers, e.g., COTTON and KAPOK; or long fibers, including FLAX, HEMP, MANILA HEMP, istle, ramie, SISAL HEMP, and SPANISH MOSS. The chief natural inorganic fiber is ASBESTOS. Fibers are also derived from other inorganic substances that can be drawn into threads, e.g., glass and metals (especially gold and silver). Artificial fibers are produced either by the synthesis of polymers (NYLON) or by the alteration of natural fibers (RAYON). Fibers are classified according to use as textile, cordage, brush, felt, filling, and plaiting fibers. The largest volume is used for textiles and cordage. The chief textile fibers used for clothing and domestic goods are cotton, wool, rayon, nylon, flax, and silk. Coarse-textured fibers (principally jute) are used for burlap, floor covering, sacks, and bagging materials. Cordage fibers include most of the long vegetable fibers and cotton. Brush fibers include istle, sisal, broomcorn, palmyra, and animal hairs. The chief felt fibers are rabbit and beaver hair. Filling fibers include horsehair, wool flock, kapok, cotton, and Spanish moss. Plaiting fibers are used for braided articles (e.g., hats, mats, and baskets) and include Manila hemp, sisal, rushes, and grasses. Flax, hemp, and wool have been used extensively from remote times; cotton, however, became the leading commercial fiber c.1800, and the artificial fibers are rapidly gaining in diversity and extent of use. The demand for fibers was greatly increased by the invention of spinning and weaving machinery during the Industrial Revolution.

fiber glass, thread made from glass. It is made by forcing molten glass through a kind of sieve, thereby spinning it into threads. Fiber glass is strong, durable, and impervious to many caustics and to extreme temperatures. For those qualities, fabrics woven from the glass threads are widely used for industrial purposes. Fiber glass fabrics can also be made to resemble silks and cotton and are used for curtains and drapery. A wide variety of materials are made by combining fiber glass with plastic. These materials, which are rust proof, are molded into the shape required or pressed into flat sheets. Boat hulls, automobile bodies, and roofing and ceiling compositions are some of the uses to which such material is put.

Fibiger, Johannes (yōhä'nəs fē'bēgər), 1867–1928, Danish pathologist and physician. He served as professor of pathological anatomy at the Univ. of Copenhagen. For his experimental studies of cancer, in which he was the first to produce tumors in the stomachs of rats, he received the 1926 Nobel Prize in Physiology and Medicine.

Fibonacci, Leonardo (lāōnär'dō fēbōnät'chē), b. c.1170, d. after 1240, Italian mathematician, known also as Leonardo da Pisa. In *Liber abaci* (1202, 2d ed. 1228), for centuries a standard work on algebra and arithmetic, he advocated the adoption of Arabic notation. In *Practica geometriae* (1220) he organized and extended the material then known in geometry and trigonometry. The sequence of numbers 0, 1, 1, 2, 3, 5, 8, 13, 21, . . . , formed by adding consecutive members, is named for him; it occurs in higher mathematics in various connections. Baldassare Boncompagni edited his works (2 vol., 1857–62). See study by Joseph and Frances Gies (1969).

fibrin: see BLOOD CLOTTING.

fibula (fĭb'yələ): see LEG.

Fichte, Johann Gottlieb (yō'hän gôt'lēp fĭkh'tə), 1762–1814, German philosopher. After studying theology at Jena and working as a tutor in Zurich and Leipzig, he became interested in Kantian philosophy. He received public recognition for his *Versuch einer Kritik aller Offenbarung* [critique of all revelation] (1792), which was at first attributed to Kant himself, who highly commended the work. As professor of philosophy at Jena (1793–99), Fichte produced a number of works, including the *Wissenschaftslehre* [science of knowledge] (1794). Charges of atheism forced him to leave Jena for Berlin where he restated his views in *Die Bestimmung des Menschen* (1800, tr. *The Vocation of Man*, rev. ed. 1956). His *Reden an die deutsche Nation* (1808, tr., *Addresses to the German People*, 1923) established him as a leader of liberal nationalism. After several brief professorships, he served (1810–12) as rector of the new Univ. of Berlin. Fichte's dialectic idealism attempted unification of the theoretical and practical aspects of cognition that had been set apart by Kant. He did this by rejecting the noumenal realm of Kant and by making the active indivisible ego the source of the structure of experience. From there his dialectical logic led to the postulation of a moral will of the universe, a God or absolute ego from which all eventually derives and which therefore unites all knowing. Fichte's philosophy had considerable influence in his day, but later he was remembered more as a patriot and liberal. Although he was in political disrepute in his own day and after the reaction of 1815, he became a hero not only to the revolutionaries of 1848 but also to the conservatives of 1871. His political theory had socialistic aspects that influenced Ferdinand Lassalle. See biography by H. E. Engelbrecht (1933, repr. 1968). His son, **Immanuel Hermann von Fichte,** 1797–1879, edited Fichte's works, wrote a biography of him, and also did original philosophical work.

Fichtelgebirge (fĭkh'təlgəbĭr"gə), mountain knot, in SE West Germany, between Bayreuth and the Czechoslovakian border; rises to 3,447 ft (1,051 m) in Schneeberg peak. The rugged mountains, composed mainly of metamorphic rock, have a complete geologic structure; the Erzgebirge, Bohemian Forest, Thuringian Forest, and Franconian Jura radiate from them. The Saale and Main rivers originate there. The Fichtelgebirge have dense pine forests and are dotted with resorts. The mountains were once rich in a variety of minerals, but now only lignite and iron are found in large quantities. Selb is the chief town of the region. Mining, forestry, porcelain production, glassmaking, grazing, granite quarrying, and tourism are major industries.

Ficino, Marsilio (märsē'lyō fēchē'nō), 1433–99, Italian philosopher. Under the patronage of Cosimo de' Medici, Ficino became the most influential exponent of Platonism in Italy in the 15th cent. He translated many of the Greek classics into Latin, among them Plato's dialogues and the writings of Plotinus. Chosen by Cosimo to head a new Platonic academy at Florence, he was important in the development of Renaissance humanism. His chief original work was *Theologica Platonica* (1482), in which he combined Christian theology and Neoplatonic elements. See study by P. O. Kristeller (tr. 1943); Sears R. Jayne, *John Colet and Marsilio Ficino* (1963).

Fick, August (ou'gŏŏst fĭk), 1833–1916, German philologist. Fick compiled the first comparative etymological dictionary of the Indo-European languages (1868).

fiction: see NOVEL; SHORT STORY.

fiddler crab, common name for small, amphibious CRABS belonging to the genus *Uca*. They are characterized by a rectangular carapace (shell) and a narrow abdomen, which is flexed under the body. They are called fiddler crabs because the males have one enormous claw, held in front of the body like a fiddle. This claw often contrasts in color with the rest of the body, and is used by the male at certain times of the year to attract females in a complicated courtship display procedure, characteristically different in each species of *Uca*. The claw also functions to warn off intruders and to establish territories. The female *Uca* has two small claws on the first appendages. Some species of fiddler crabs live on sandy beaches that are somewhat protected from extreme wave action. Others live in muddy marshes and estuaries. The *Uca* species living on sandy beaches, such as the common Atlantic fiddler, *U. pugilator*, make burrows about 1 ft (30 cm) deep, just below the high tide line. The sand is carried to the surface by specialized legs of the crab, and pushed away from the entrance. Fiddler crabs are poor swimmers and rarely enter the water during their adult lives. During the spring and summer, the fiddlers remain in their burrows only during high tide periods. The entrances of the burrows are covered with sand, and the burrows contain a bubble of air, which the crabs use for respiration. When the tide ebbs, the fiddlers emerge and scurry about, collecting food in the drift lines left by the ebbing water. Both claws of the female and the smaller claw of the male are used to scoop up sand and pass the grains to the mouthparts. Certain specialized appendages (the first and second maxillipeds) have spoon-shaped setae, used to scour organic matter from the sand grains and pass it to the mouth. The sand grains are then rejected in the form of small sand balls. After mating, the female fiddler crab carries the fertilized eggs under her flexed abdomen. Certain cyclic changes occur in *Uca* (as well as in some other crustaceans), such as changes in pigmentation. During the day the crabs are dark; at night they are pale. Fiddler crabs are classified in the phylum ARTHROPODA, class Crustacea, order Decapoda.

fiduciary (fĭdyōō'shēē"rē), in law, a person who is legally obliged to discharge faithfully a responsibility of trust toward another. Among the common relations in which fiduciary duties figure are guardian and ward, parent and child, lawyer and client, and partnership. In dealings with one who is entitled to repose trust in him, the fiduciary must be absolutely open and fair. Thus certain business methods that would be acceptable between independent parties dealing with one another "at arm's length" might expose a fiduciary to legal liability for having abused his position of trust. In an ordinary business transaction the prospective purchaser of land need not inform the seller of an imminent rise in realty values, but a man buying land from his partner must disclose such information. In many cases the courts will treat an unexplained profit derived from a fiduciary relationship as an instance of constructive FRAUD.

Fiedler, Leslie, 1917–, American critic, b. Newark, N.J., grad. Univ. of Wisconsin (Ph.D., 1941). A vital and controversial figure, Fiedler adapts Freudian analysis to literary criticism. In *Love and Death in the American Novel* (1960), he found that, due to personal confusion and public prudery, American writers have never been able to deal realistically with racial and sexual themes. His other works include *An End to Innocence: Essays on Culture and Politics* (1955); *Nude Croquet* (1969), a volume of short stories; *Being Busted* (1969), an account of a marijuana raid at his home; *The Stranger in Shakespeare* (1972); and *The Messengers Will Come No More* (1974), a novel.

fief: see FEUDALISM.

Field, Cyrus West, 1819–92, American merchant, promoter of the first Atlantic cable, b. Stockbridge, Mass.; brother of David Dudley Field and Stephen J. Field. As head of a paper business, he accumulated a modest fortune, and in 1853 he retired. In 1854 he conceived the idea of the cable. He secured a charter, organized the English and American companies, and obtained the British and American naval ships *Agamemnon* and *Niagara* to lay the cable. Five attempts were made in 1857–58 and the first message came over Aug. 16, 1858, but the cable ceased working three weeks later. It was necessary for Field to raise new funds and make new arrangements. The *Great Eastern* succeeded in laying a cable in 1866. Field was the object of much admiration and praise on both sides of the Atlantic for his persistence in accomplishing what many thought to be an absurd undertaking. He promoted other oceanic cables, notably that via Hawaii to Asia and Australia. In 1877 he resuscitated the New York City elevated system. See biography by S. Carter (1968).

Field, David Dudley, 1805–94, American lawyer and law reformer, b. Haddam, Conn.; brother of Cyrus W. Field and Stephen J. Field. He was graduated from Williams (1825), studied law in Albany and

New York City, was admitted to the bar in 1828, and soon had a large practice in New York City. After the Civil War he argued before the U.S. Supreme Court several cases involving significant constitutional issues. He was also counsel for Jay Gould and James Fisk in the Erie RR litigation in 1869 and later defended "Boss" Tweed. However, it was his work in behalf of law reform rather than his famous practice that established Field's legal reputation. He was responsible for the New York legislature's appointment in 1847 of one commission to reduce the laws of the state to a systematic code and another to prepare codes of court practice and procedure. Serving on the second commission, Field prepared a code of civil procedure that was adopted (1848-50). This Field code became the basis for the reform of civil law procedure throughout the United States. His reforms—notable among them abolition of the distinction between law and equity proceedings—strongly influenced the English Judicature Acts of 1873 and 1875, which were subsequently adopted by many British colonies. Field's code of criminal procedure eventually became law as well. His commission for the codification of the laws of New York, however, met with failure; consequently, Field became head of a new commission for the same purpose in 1857. He prepared complete civil, political, and penal codes, but only the penal code, in 1881, became law. The civil code several times passed the legislature but was killed by gubernatorial veto. See biography by his brother, H. M. Field (1898); study by F. C. Hicks (1929, repr. 1966).

Field, Erastus Salisbury, 1805-1900, American painter, b. Leverett, Mass. Field's paintings, executed in a primitive manner, included biblical and classical themes and portraits. His famous *Historical Monument of the American Republic* (c.1875) is in the Springfield Museum of Fine Arts, Massachusetts. Field's portrait of Ellen Tuttle Bangs is owned by the Metropolitan Museum.

Field, Eugene, 1850-95, American poet and journalist, b. St. Louis. For brief periods he attended Williams and Knox colleges and the Univ. of Missouri. After working on the editorial staffs of several Midwestern newspapers, including the St. Louis *Journal* and the Denver *Tribune*, he joined (1883) the staff of the Chicago *Daily News* (later the *Record*) as a columnist. His column, "Sharps and Flats," was a potpourri of whimsical humor, commentary on politics and personalities of the day, and children's verse. Appearing until Field's death, it helped set a vogue for urbane and witty columns in American newspapers. Among his books are *A Little Book of Western Verse* (1889), *With Trumpets and Drums* (1892), and *Echoes from the Sabine Farm* (with his brother Roswell Martin Field, 1892). His best-known poems for children include "Little Boy Blue" and "Wynken, Blynken, and Nod." See biographies by Slason Thompson (2 vol., 1927, repr. 1973) and Robert Conrow (1974).

Field, John, 1782-1837, Irish composer and pianist. In London he studied with Clementi, with whom he later toured Europe. In 1804 he settled in Russia. Field was a successful pianist and his style of composition was influential. Chopin's nocturnes were modeled after those of Field. See study by Patrick Piggott (1973).

Field, Marshall, 1834-1906, American merchant, b. Conway, Mass. In 1856, after five years' apprenticeship in a general store in Pittsfield, Mass., he went to Chicago and became a clerk for Cooley, Wadsworth & Co., a leading dry-goods house there, of which he became a junior partner in 1862. In 1865 he became a partner in the firm of Field, Palmer, and Leiter, the company that became Field, Leiter, and Co. in 1881. He amassed one of the largest private fortunes in the United States and pioneered in establishing many modern retailing practices. He made the first of his major philanthropies when he was a charter member of the corporation formed (1878) to found the institution which became the Art Institute of Chicago. In 1890 he gave the original tract of land for the Univ. of Chicago, ultimately becoming one of the largest donors to the school, and in 1893 he gave $1,000,000 to the fund for the museum at the World's Columbian Exposition. Its collections were the nucleus of the Field Museum of Natural History, now the Chicago Museum of Natural History, housed in a magnificent building on the Chicago lake front that was provided by a bequest of $8,000,000 from Field. See Lloyd Wendt and Herman Kogan, *Give the Lady What She Wants: The Story of Marshall Field and Co.* (1952). His son, **Marshall Field II,** 1868-1905, never made any move to follow his father into business. His early death from a gun wound was officially held to have been accidental. **Marshall Field III,** 1893-1956, son of Marshall Field II, was educated at Eton and at Cambridge Univ., then served in World War I. He engaged in numerous business activities until 1936, when he gave up all of them to devote himself to his various social projects. In June, 1940, Field helped found the New York City liberal newspaper *PM*. He was the publication's largest stockholder and, from Oct., 1940, its owner. He took no part in its editorial direction, but offered it financial support until April, 1948, when the paper was sold; soon afterward it went out of business. In 1941, Field started the Chicago *Sun*, and in Jan., 1948, he bought the Chicago *Times* and merged the two papers. In that journalistic enterprise Field took a more active part, ultimately becoming the paper's dominant personality. Through Field Enterprises, Inc. (est. 1944) he also published the *World Book Encyclopedia*. His charities included many child welfare organizations. Field's political and social beliefs are expressed in his book *Freedom Is More than a Word* (1945). See biography by S. D. Becker (1964) and John Tebbel, *The Marshall Fields: A Study in Wealth* (1947).

Field, Michael, pseud. used by two English authors, Katherine Harris Bradley (1846-1914) and her niece Edith Emma Cooper (1862-1913). They collaborated on numerous literary works, including lyrics and poetic tragedies. Although their work was praised by such contemporaries as Robert Browning and George Moore, it is almost forgotten today. See selected poems (1923); *Works and Days* (1933), a selection from their journal.

Field, Rachel, 1894-1942, American writer, b. New York City, educated at Radcliffe. Her books for children include *The Cross-Stitch Heart and Other One-Act Plays* (1927), *Hitty: Her First Hundred Years* (1929), and *Calico Bush* (1931). She also wrote several adult novels of which *All This and Heaven Too* (1938) and *And Now Tomorrow* (1942) were made into successful motion pictures.

Field, Stephen Johnson, 1816-99, American jurist, Associate Justice of the U.S. Supreme Court (1863-97), b. Haddam, Conn. After practicing law for several years in New York City with his brother David Dudley Field, he went to California in 1849, settled at Marysville, and in 1850 was elected to the legislature. He secured the passage of an act reorganizing the state judiciary and drafted codes of civil and criminal procedure based on his brother's codes for New York but adapted to certain local needs, such as established Spanish customs and miners' practices. His recommendations became the basis of mining law in all of the Western states and territories. In 1857, Field was elected as a Democrat to the California supreme court, becoming chief justice two years later. President Lincoln appointed him to the U.S. Supreme Court in 1863. A staunch conservative, he opposed government regulation of business activities and played a major role in the Supreme Court's extension of the due process clause of the Fourteenth Amendment to include corporations. See his *Personal Reminiscences of Early Days in California* (1880, repr. 1968); biography by C. B. Swisher (1930, repr. 1963).

field, in mathematics, set of elements (usually numbers) that may be combined under the operations of addition and multiplication and that satisfy the following axioms: (1) closure exists under both operations; i.e., if two elements are members of the set, their sum and product are also in the set; (2) the ASSOCIATIVE LAW and the COMMUTATIVE LAW hold for both operations and the DISTRIBUTIVE LAW holds for multiplication over addition; (3) there exists a zero element, 0, under addition and a unity element, 1, under multiplication such that $a+0 = a$ and $a \cdot 1 = a$ for every element a in the set; and (4) there exists an additive inverse $-a$ and a multiplicative inverse a^{-1} for every a in the set such that $a+(-a) = 0$ and $a \cdot a^{-1} = 1$. The set of real numbers (see NUMBER) and the set of complex numbers are both examples of fields.

field, in physics, region throughout which a force may be exerted; examples are the gravitational, electric, and magnetic fields that surround, respectively, masses, electric charges, and magnets. The field concept was developed by M. Faraday based on his investigation of the lines of force that appear to leave and return to a magnet at its poles (see FLUX, MAGNETIC). Fields are used to describe all cases where two bodies separated in space exert a FORCE on each other. The alternative to postulating a field is to assume that physical influences can be transmitted through empty space without any material or physical agency. Such action-at-a-distance, especially if it occurs instantaneously, violates both common sense and certain modern theories, notably RELATIVITY, which posits that nothing can travel faster than light. In a field description, rather than body A directly exerting a force on body B, body A (the source) creates a field in every direction around it and body B (the detector) experiences the field that exists at its position. If a change occurs at the source, its effect propagates outward through the field at a constant speed and is felt at the detector only after a certain delay in time. The field is thus a kind of "middleman" for transmitting forces. Each type of force (electric, magnetic, nuclear, or gravitational) has its own appropriate field; a body experiences the force due to a given field only if the body itself it also a source of that kind of field. The reciprocity implied by Newton's third law of MOTION (equal action and reaction) is thus preserved. If two bodies exert a mutual force, they possess potential ENERGY that depends on their relative positions; it is natural to regard this energy as residing in the field the bodies create.

field-effect transistor: see TRANSISTOR.

field-emission microscope: see MICROSCOPE.

field glass: see BINOCULAR.

field hockey: see HOCKEY, FIELD.

Fielding, Antony Vandyke Copley, 1787-1855, English landscape painter in watercolor. For the last 24 years of his life he was president of the Water Colour Society, where he exhibited yearly. Fielding is best represented in the Victoria and Albert Museum. His landscapes show a dexterity in the rendering of atmospheric effects.

Fielding, Henry, 1707-54, English novelist and dramatist. Born of a distinguished family, he was educated at Eton and studied law at Leiden. Settling in London in 1729, he began writing comedies, farces, and burlesques, the most notable being *Tom Thumb* (1730), and two satires, *Pasquin* (1736) and *The Historical Register for 1736* (1737), which attacked the Walpole government and provoked the Licensing Act of 1737. This act, setting up a censorship of the stage, ended Fielding's dramatic career and turned him to the less inhibited form of the novel. In that genre he achieved his greatest success, beginning with his first novel, *Joseph Andrews* (1742), which started simply as a burlesque of Samuel Richardson's sentimental novel *Pamela* but developed into a great comic creation. He followed with *Jonathan Wild* (1743), the history of a superman of crime, which has been called the most sustained piece of irony in English. His masterpiece is *Tom Jones*, a novel recounting the wild comic adventures of the good-hearted though highly fallible foundling, Tom Jones. In Tom and his guardian, Squire Allworthy, Fielding presents his concept of the ideal man, one in whom goodness and charity are combined with common sense. Because of its memorable characters and episodes, the brilliance of its plotting, and the generosity of its moral vision, *Tom Jones* is considered one of the greatest of English novels. *Amelia* (1751), his last novel, is a somewhat sentimental story about a young wife's devotion to her feckless husband, in which Fielding exposes numerous social evils of his day. Fielding had begun his serious study of law in 1737 and in 1740 was called to the bar. After spending several years as a political journalist, he was appointed justice of the peace for Westminster in 1748 and for Middlesex in 1749. A fearless and honest magistrate, he worked arduously in the administration of justice and the prevention of crime. Broken in health, he resigned his office in 1753 and the following year sailed for Portugal, where he died. His last work was the amusing journal *Voyage to Lisbon* (1755). See biographies by W. L. Cross (3 vol., 1918, repr. 1963) and F. H. Dudden (1952, repr. 1966); studies by M. Johnson (1961), R. Alter (1969), and R. Paulson, ed., (1962 and 1971).

Fielding, William Stevens, 1848-1929, Canadian statesman, b. Halifax, N.S. A newspaper editor in Halifax, he entered the provincial legislature in 1882 and was provincial prime minister (1884-96). He then entered the House of Commons, and for 15 years (1896-1911) he was Wilfrid Laurier's minister of finance. As a tariff expert, Fielding helped to negotiate the reciprocal trade treaty with the United States in 1911 that resulted in the fall of Laurier's government. Favoring military conscription for Canada in World War I, he parted with Laurier on the issue and supported Sir Robert Borden's Union government. After the war he returned to the Liberal party, and in Mackenzie King's cabinet he again served (1921-25) as minister of finance.

field-ion microscope: see MICROSCOPE.

field mouse: see MOUSE; VOLE.

Field Museum of Natural History, at Chicago, Ill. Founded in 1893 through the gifts of Marshall Field and others, it was first known as the Columbian Museum of Chicago and later as the Chicago Natural History Museum. It is especially noted for its lifelike exhibits of animals in their natural settings, displays of plant life, and anthropological and geological collections. The many expeditions sponsored by the museum have contributed much to its collections. The museum also conducts research and maintains a publishing plant. Many educational opportunities are offered by its library, school-service department, and special programs.

Field of the Cloth of Gold, locality between Guines and Ardres, not far from Calais, in France, where in 1520 HENRY VIII of England and FRANCIS I of France met for the purpose of arranging an alliance. Both kings brought large retinues, and the name given the meeting place reflects the unexampled splendor of the pageantry. The political result was negligible, because Henry, who had been undecided whether to support Francis or Holy Roman Emperor CHARLES V, had already turned toward the emperor and shortly afterward made an alliance with him.

Fields, Annie Adams: see FIELDS, JAMES THOMAS.

Fields, James Thomas, 1817–81, American author and publisher, b. Portsmouth, N.H. He was the junior partner of Ticknor and Fields, noted Boston publishing house in the mid-19th cent. He edited (1861–70) the *Atlantic Monthly* with notable success. His books, largely reminiscences of literary friendships, include *Yesterdays with Authors* (1872), *Hawthorne* (1876), and *In and Out of Doors with Charles Dickens* (1876). He was aided in his work by his wife, **Annie Adams Fields,** 1834–1915, a native of Boston, who also became a well-known author. Besides writing volumes of verse and biographies of Whittier (1893) and Harriet Beecher Stowe (1897), she was famous for her literary salon in Boston. See her journals, *Memories of a Hostess* (ed. by M. A. De Wolfe Howe, 1922).

Fields, Lew: see WEBER AND FIELDS.

Fields, W. C. (William Claude Fields), 1880–1946, American comic actor, b. Philadelphia. His original name was Claude William Dukenfield. He began his career at the age of 11 as an itinerant juggler. Much later he appeared in the *Ziegfeld Follies* and in Earl Carroll's *Vanities*. In 1925 he began his famed film work with D. W. Griffith. With his rasping voice and bulbous nose, he was an able satiric comedian; his portrayals of drunken, swaggering, and down-at-the-heels rascals blended hilarity with wistfulness. See his autobiography (1973); Donald Deschner, *The Films of W. C. Fields* (1966); W. K. Everson, *The Art of W. C. Fields* (1967).

field spaniel, breed of medium-sized SPORTING DOG developed in England from crosses between cocker spaniels and Sussex spaniels. It stands about 18 in. (45.7 cm) high at the shoulder and weighs about 40 lb (18.1 kg). Its medium-length, silky coat is flat or wavy and usually solid black in color, although it may be liver, golden liver, or mahogany red. Its tail is docked. Although the field spaniel is relatively slow, it has great endurance and can be trained as a bird hunter. It is not a common breed in the United States. See DOG.

Fieschi, Giuseppe (jo͞ozĕp'pä fyä'skē), 1790–1836, French conspirator, b. Corsica. He was a soldier in the Napoleonic army. A radical, he attempted in July, 1835, to assassinate King Louis Philippe. He rigged up an arrangement of several guns that fired together, killing approximately 18 people. He was executed. His attempted assassination resulted in increased repression by the government.

Fiesole, Mino da: see MINO DA FIESOLE.

Fiesole (fyä'zōlä), town (1971 pop. 14,138), Tuscany, central Italy. The villas and gardens of this tourist center are beautifully situated on a hill overlooking the Arno valley and the city of Florence. An ancient Etruscan town called Faesulae, it was enriched with fine buildings by the Romans. In 63 B.C the town served as the headquarters of Catiline, the Roman statesman and conspirator. Of note in Fiesole are a well-preserved Roman theater (c.80 B.C.); the ruins of Roman baths; a Romanesque cathedral (11th cent.), with works by the sculptor Mino da Fiesole; and a Franciscan church and convent (on the site of the Roman acropolis). On the lower slopes of the hill is the Church of San Domenico di Fiesole, which has paintings by Fra Angelico.

Fife, county (1971 pop. 326,989), 505 sq mi (1,308 sq km), E Scotland, between the Firth of Forth and the Firth of Tay. CUPAR is the county town. The land rises to 1,500 ft (457 m) in the Lomond Hills. Fishing villages of great antiquity dot the eastern coast. One of Scotland's most prosperous counties, Fife has pastures and productive farmland in the central valleys of the Leven and Eden and rich coal fields in the west and east. The new town of Glenrothes was opened in 1959 to accommodate the influx of miners into the growing coal industry. KIRKCALDY is a center of linoleum manufacture. Other industries are linen weaving, brewing, and shipbuilding. Fife was once a Pictish kingdom. SAINT ANDREWS, seat of Scotland's oldest university, was the ecclesiastical capital of Scotland until the Reformation, and DUNFERMLINE was once a royal seat. Under the Local Government Act of 1973, Fife was reorganized (1975) as a region.

fife, small transverse flute with six to eight finger holes adopted for military music by Swiss regiments

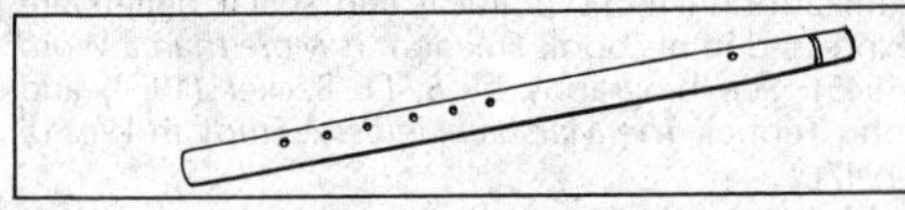

Fife

serving in France in the late 15th cent. The fife was used in the British army until the end of the 19th cent. The PICCOLO has largely replaced the fife in modern use.

Fifth Avenue, famous street of the borough of Manhattan, New York City. It begins at Washington Square and ends at the Harlem River. Between 34th and 59th streets, Fifth Ave. is lined with fashionable department stores and specialty shops. Fronting the avenue are the Empire State Building, the New York Public Library, Rockefeller Center, St. Patrick's Cathedral, and the Guggenheim Museum. From 59th to 110th streets it borders Central Park; on its east side are tall apartment houses (interspersed with private homes), built on the site of the elegant mansions of 50 years ago. On the west side of the avenue between 80th and 84th streets is the Metropolitan Museum of Art. North of the park Fifth Ave. runs through Harlem.

Fifth Monarchy Men, religious group active during the time of the Commonwealth and Protectorate in England. They were millenarians expecting the imminent coming of Jesus to rule the earth. His monarchy was to be the fifth kingdom described in Dan. 2.36–45; according to their intepretation, the first four were the Assyrian, Persian, Greek, and Roman empires. The Fifth Monarchy Men objected to the Established Church and believed it their duty to establish Christ's reign by force, if necessary. They attempted an uprising in 1657 and again, after the Restoration of the monarchy, in 1661. Their leaders were seized and executed for treason, and the group dissolved. See studies by L. F. Brown (1912, repr. 1964), P. G. Rogers (1966), and B. S. Capp (1972).

Fifth Republic: see FRANCE.

Fifty-four forty or fight, in U.S. history, phrase commonly used by extremists in the controversy with Great Britain over the OREGON country. The rights of the United States, they maintained, extended to the whole region, i.e., to lat. 54°40'N, the recognized southern boundary of Russian America. It was used as a Democratic campaign slogan in the presidential election of 1844 by James K. Polk, who was elected.

fig, name for members of the genus *Ficus* of the family Moraceae (MULBERRY family). This large genus contains some 600 species of widely varied tropical vines (some of which are epiphytic); shrubs; and trees, including the banyan, the peepul, or bo tree, and the India-rubber tree. It differs from other genera of the family in that the hundreds of tiny female flowers are borne on the inside of a fleshy fruitlike receptacle with a small opening at the apex. The common fig (*F. carica*), a native of the Mediterranean area, has been bred and cultivated from early times for its commercially valuable fruit and has been naturalized in other parts of the world that have a mild, semiarid climate; in the United States, figs are grown in California, Texas, Utah, Oregon, and Washington. Some edible varieties (e.g., the Smyrna, among the best) can be pollinated only by the fig wasp (*Blastophaga*), which passes its larval stage inside the inedible fruit of a wild variety called the caprifig. In order to produce mature fruit, the cultivated variety is subjected to a process called caprification; flowering branches of caprifig are hung in the tree so that the emerging wasps will transfer caprifig pollen to the edible fig. After entering the receptacle and laying its eggs, the wasp dies and its body and eggs are absorbed by the developing fruit; only the eggs laid inside the caprifig fruit survive. Other edible varieties (e.g., the Adriatic or mission fig) bear larger fruits when caprificated. Fig trees may also be propagated from cuttings and by grafting or layering. The ripe fruit (called a syconium) contains masses of tiny seeds and is soft and pear-shaped; it may be greenish, yellow to orange, or purple in color. The name *fig* is also applied to various unrelated plants that either resemble the fig tree or bear figlike fruits. Figs are classified in the division MAGNOLIOPHYTA, class Magnoliopsida, order Magnoliales, family Moraceae.

fighting fish: see BETTA.

Figueras, Estanislao (ästä"nēslä'ō fēgä'räs), 1819–82, Spanish politician. After the overthrow (1868) of Isabella II, he became leader of the Republican party. He opposed King Amadeus and, after the latter's abdication (1873), was briefly president of Spain's short-lived first republic. He retired to private life when the monarchy was restored (1875).

Figueras, town (1970 pop. 22,087), Gerona prov., NE Spain, in Catalonia, near the French border. Traditionally a fortified city because of its strategic location, it is now an important communications center. Its manufactures include chemicals, textiles, cement, and bicycles. In the Spanish civil war Figueras served briefly as the seat of the Loyalist government. Its 18th-century fortress is now a prison.

Figueres Ferrer, José (hōsā' fēgā'rās fār-rār'), 1906–, president of Costa Rica (1948–49, 1953–58, 1970–74). A planter, he rose to prominence as an outspoken critic of President Calderón in 1942 and was exiled to Mexico (1942–44). In 1948 he led a revolution to ensure the presidency of newly elected Otilio Ulate. He served as provisional president (1948–49), abolishing the army and nationalizing financial and communication services before turning the government over to Ulate. He was overwhelmingly elected president in 1953. Despite bitter opposition, he instituted a sweeping program of welfare legislation, public works, and educational reform. As president from 1970 to 1974, he pushed social and economic reform and established ties with the Soviet Union.

figure, in music, short melodic or rhythmic pattern, the smallest grouping of notes that will produce a single distinct impression. In this sense figure is synonymous with MOTIVE. In music before the 18th cent., a figure had an additional meaning of symbolic significance; it was an illustration in sound of textual details, e.g., a descending group of notes for any word expressing descent.

figured bass, in music, a system of shorthand notation in which figures are written below the notes of the bass part to indicate the chords to be played. Called also thorough bass and basso continuo, it arose in the early 17th cent. in Italy as a means of notating an accompaniment. It soon became so widespread that the baroque era is sometimes called the age of basso continuo. The harpsichord's part in sonatas was indicated by a figured bass, and the harpsichord and the organ are usually played from a figured bass in the vocal works of Bach and Handel. The realization of the basso continuo involves considerable improvisation, varying in style according to composer and period. Both Bach and Mozart wrote out rules for playing the figured bass. After the time of Bach, with the development of the symphony, the figured bass disappeared except for limited use in opera and as a device for teaching harmony. See F. T. Arnold, *The Art of Accompaniment from a Thorough-Bass* (1931, repr. 1965); Hermann Keller, *Thoroughbass Method* (tr. by Carl Parrish, 1965).

figurehead, carved decoration usually representing a head or figure placed under the bowsprit of a ship. The art is of extreme antiquity. Ancient galleys and triremes carried rostrums, or beaks, on the bow to ram enemy vessels. These beaks were often surmounted by figureheads representing national or religious emblems. Roman vessels were sometimes embellished with large heads of the gods in bronze. Viking ships had lofty and extended prows which were elaborately carved. Dragons and lions vied with the human form in the figureheads of the Renaissance. During the 18th and 19th cent. a highly developed and original art of figurehead wood carving flourished in the United States at a time when little other sculpture was practiced. Few examples survive. With the disappearance of the sailing vessel figurehead art became practically extinct. A fine collection of American figureheads is in the Mariners'

Museum, Newport News, Va. See Pauline Pinckney, *American Figureheads and Their Carvers* (1940).

figure of speech, intentional departure from straight-forward, literal use of language for the purpose of clarity, emphasis, or freshness of expression. See separate articles on ANTITHESIS; APOSTROPHE; CONCEIT; HYPERBOLE; IRONY; LITOTES; METAPHOR; METONYMY; PARADOX; PERSONIFICATION; SIMILE; and SYNECDOCHE.

figwort, common name for some members of the Scrophulariaceae, a family comprising chiefly herbs and small shrubs and distributed widely over all continents. The family includes a few climbing types and some parasitic and saprophytic forms. Among its many wild flowers are several European species that have been introduced to America and become thoroughly naturalized, e.g., the mulleins (genus *Verbascum*), the common speedwell (*Veronica officinalis*), and the butter-and-eggs (*Linaria vulgaris*). The common mullein (*V. thapsus*), also called flannel plant and torches, was formerly a favorite multipurpose medicinal plant; it is still occasionally used for domestic remedies, e.g., as a tea for coughs. Its large stalks are said to have been oiled and used for funeral torches in early times. The speedwells, of which several species are native to the United States, are also called veronica, supposedly because of a resemblance of the flower to the relic. Culver's root (*V. virginica*) has been used as a cathartic. Butter-and-eggs, or yellow toadflax, has small snapdragonlike flowers of yellow and orange and is consequently known also as wild snapdragon. Among the other toadflaxes (genus *Linaria*) is the well-known American species, blue toadflax. Other indigenous wild flowers of the family include species of beardtongue, or pentstemon (genus *Pentstemon*); gerardia, or false purple foxglove (*Gerardia*) [for John Gerard]; painted cup, or Indian paintbrush (*Castilleja*); and figwort (*Scrophularia*). The beardtongues, herbs or shrubs, are named for the flower's single sterile stamen that is bearded at its flattened extremity. The roots of the painted cups, chiefly a Western genus, are partially parasitic on the roots of other green plants. Their true flowers are inconspicuous but are commonly enveloped by bright red flowerlike bracts. *C. linariaefolia* is the state flower of Wyoming. The name *Scrophularia* derives from the early belief that because the figworts are characterized by deep-throated flowers, they should be medicinally valuable in treating throat ailments (e.g., scrofula). Many plants of the family are used medicinally; however, only the purple foxglove (*Digitalis purpurea*) of W Europe is economically important. Its leaves are the source of the drug digitalis, a powerful heart stimulant. The foxglove's tall spire of flowers, typical of many members of the family, makes it popular also as an ornamental. Each blossom, likened to the finger of a glove or to an elongated bell, points downward from the stalk. In England, where it grows wild, the plant has long been associated with fairies—as evidenced by many of its common names, e.g., fairy thimbles. Numerous other plants of the family also have curious names derived from their unusual flower shapes—e.g., the turtle heads (*Chelone*) and monkey flowers (*Mimulus*) of North America and the little red elephants (*Pedicularis groenlandica*) of arctic and alpine regions. A favorite cultivated plant is the snapdragon (*Antirrhinum majus*), native to the Mediterranean area. Its showy blossoms, likened to a dragon's snout, display a wide range of colors in the many varieties. Other ornamentals of the family include the Kenilworth ivy (*Cymbalaria muralis*), introduced into North America, and the calceolaria, or slipperwort (genus *Calceolaria*), herbs and shrubby plants of South America valued for their profusion of pouch-shaped, often spotted blossoms. Figworts are classified in the division MAGNOLIOPHYTA, class Magnoliopsida, order Magnoliales.

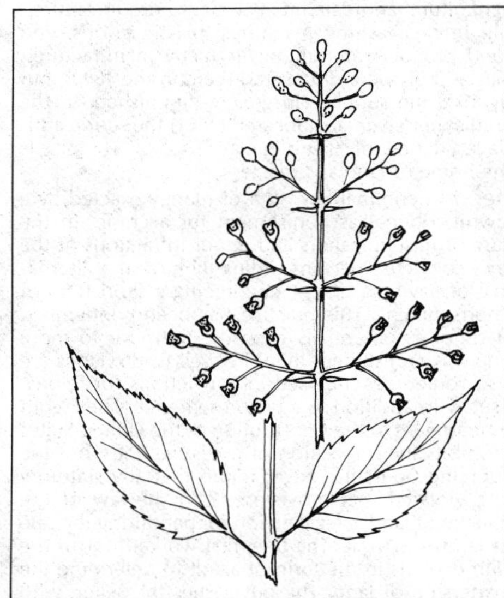

Figwort, Scrophularia lanceolata

Fiji (fē'jē) or **Viti** (vē'tē), Melanesian island group (1970 est. pop. 524,000), c.7,000 sq mi (18,130 sq km), South Pacific. An independent republic since 1970, Fiji comprises c.320 islands of which some 105 are inhabited. VITI LEVU, the largest, constitutes half the land area and is the seat of SUVA, the capital of the country. The other important islands are VANUA LEVU (the second largest), Taveuni, Kandavu, Koro, Ngau, and Ovalau. In the center of the group is the Koro Sea, east of which is the Lau group. The Yasawa and Mamanutha groups are W of Viti Levu. The larger islands are volcanic and mountainous; the highest peak, Mt. Victoria (4,341 ft/1,323 m), is on Viti Levu, which also has the longest river, the Rewa. Fiji's climate is warm and humid. There are dense tropical forests on the windward sides of the islands and grassy plains and clumps of casuarina and pandanus on the leeward sides; mangrove forests are abundant, and hot springs are common in the mountain regions. The fertile soil yields sugarcane, tropical fruits, taro, cotton, pineapples, bananas, and coconuts. Sugar, coconuts, and gold are the main exports, most of which go to Great Britain. Imports, principally from Australia, consist largely of foodstuffs, manufactures, and machinery. Tourism is also important to the economy. Fiji's chief towns are generally seaports: Suva and Lautoka on Viti Levu; and Levuka, on a small island E of Viti Levu. The islands were discovered by the Dutch navigator Abel TASMAN in 1643 and were visited by Capt. James COOK in 1774. In 1804 the first European settlement was established on the islands at Levuka. Missionaries arriving in 1835 helped abolish cannibalism. The Fijians, a dark-skinned people of Melanesian origin, constitute less than half of the population and predominate mainly in the western islands. The people of the eastern islands are largely Polynesian. Indians, imported (1879–1916) under the indenture system, are engaged chiefly in the sugar industry and in commerce. There are also small groups of Europeans, Chinese, and Micronesians. In 1874, after repeated requests by the tribal chiefs of Fiji, Great Britain annexed the islands. During World War II the islands were an important supply point of the South Pacific. Executive power is vested in a governor-general, who is appointed by the crown and who in turn appoints a prime minister. The cabinet is responsible to the legislature, which consists of a senate and a house of representatives. Eight senators are appointed by the council of chiefs, seven by the prime minister, six by the opposition party, and one by the island of Rotuma. The seats in the house of representatives are apportioned on a racial basis, and are filled by elections. In the elections of 1970, the multi-racial Alliance party won a majority over the National Federation party, an Indian-based party. The Univ. of the South Pacific (founded 1968) is located at Suva.

filament, in astronomy: see CHROMOSPHERE.

Filaret, Vasily Drosdov: see PHILARET, VASILY DROSDOV.

Filarete (fē'lärē'tā), c.1400–c.1465, Italian architect and sculptor, whose real name was Antonio Averlino, b. Florence. In the 1430s he went to Rome, where he studied the monuments of antiquity. His most famous project was the bronze doors for St. Peter's. In the panels he represented the *Madonna Enthroned, Christ Enthroned,* and saints Peter and Paul, filling in the border decoration with antique motifs. Although somewhat original in style, he was not a highly skillful artist. In 1451 he was summoned to Milan by Francesco Sforza to design parts of buildings. He wrote a treatise, *Trattato di architettura,* defending the principles of ancient architecture.

filariasis: see ELEPHANTIASIS.

filbert: see HAZEL.

Filchner, Wilhelm (vĭl'hĕlm fĭlkh'nər), 1877–1957, German explorer, geophysicist, and travel writer. He led several expeditions to China and Tibet, where he established magnetic stations, and also led the second German antarctic expedition (1910–12), which discovered Luitpold Land on the southeast coast of Weddell Sea.

Fildes, Sir Luke (fīldz), 1844–1927, English genre and portrait painter, b. Liverpool. He made drawings for the *Graphic* and other periodicals and illustrated Dickens's *Edwin Drood.* As a painter he excelled in depicting the life of the London poor. Later he specialized in portraiture and painted the coronation portraits of Edward VII and Queen Alexandra and a state portrait of George V. His *Doctor* (Tate Gall., London) is a well-known work.

Filene, Edward Albert (fīlēn', fĭl-), 1860–1937, American merchant, b. Salem, Mass. As president of the Boston firm of William Filene's Sons he pioneered in scientific and ingenious methods of retail distribution—the "bargain basement" was one of his innovations. He planned and helped organize the Boston Chamber of Commerce and the Chamber of Commerce of the United States and served in World War I as chairman of the War Shipping Committee. He was active in civic reform movements and was the founder (1919) of the Cooperative League, which became the Twentieth Century Fund. He wrote several books on business methods and on economics. His liberal economic and political views made him a controversial figure. See G. W. Johnson, *Liberal's Progress* (1948). His brother, **Lincoln Filene,** 1865–1957, b. Boston, also directed William Filene's Sons and served as business counsel to the Federal government after 1933. He played a prominent role in business associations and wrote a number of books and articles on economic problems.

filibuster, term used to designate obstructionist tactics in legislative assemblies. It has particular reference to the U.S. Senate, where the tradition of unlimited debate is very strong. It was not until 1917 that the Senate provided for cloture (i.e., the ending of the debate) by a vote of two thirds of the Senators present. Yet, despite many attempts, cloture was applied successfully only nine times between 1917 and 1974. The filibuster has been used by various blocs of Senators for different purposes, but in recent years it has been an effective weapon mainly on occasions when a minority of conservative Southern Senators were determined to prevent the enactment of civil rights legislation. Attempts to reduce the cloture requirement have not been successful, partly because of the reluctance of the Senate to interfere with the tradition of free debate. In the 17th cent. the term was applied to buccaneers who plundered the Spanish colonies in the New World. In the 19th cent. the word was used more in reference to adventurers who organized and led, under private initiative, armed expeditions into countries with which the country from which they set out was at peace. Complications between the governments involved were likely to result. There was a series of filibustering expeditions from the United States against Cuba, Mexico, and Central and South American countries in the 19th cent., some of them led by citizens of the United States, as those of John A. QUITMAN and William WALKER, and some by rebellious citizens of the government they sought to overthrow, as those of Narciso LÓPEZ against Cuba. Texas, when it was still part of Mexico, was the scene of many such filibustering activities. See J. J. Roche, *By-Ways of War: The Story of the Filibusters* (1901); F. L. Burdette, *Filibustering in the Senate* (1940, repr. 1965); H. G. Warren, *The Sword Was Their Passport* (1943); J. A. Stout, *The Liberators* (1973).

filigree (fĭl'ĭgrē), ornamental work of fine gold or silver wire, often wrought into an openwork design and joined with matching solder and borax under the flame of the blowpipe. Filigree is used as a decorative treatment for jewelry or other fine metalwork. It was made in ancient Egypt, China, and India. From the 6th to the 3d cent. B.C. the Greeks practiced the art, and the Etruscans were noted for fine granular work. Saxons, Britons, and especially the Celts in Ireland were skilled at devising intricate and ingenious designs in the Middle Ages. The Moors in Spain did much exquisite work in silver. Filigree is employed today in Mediterranean areas, as well as in Mexico, India, and Scandinavian countries. Antique examples are to be seen in the Vatican, the Louvre, the British Museum, and the Metropolitan Museum.

Filipepi, Alessandro di Mariano: see BOTTICELLI, SANDRO.

Fillmore, Millard, 1800–1874, 13th President of the United States (July, 1850–March, 1853), b. Locke (now Summerhill), N.Y. Because he was compelled to work at odd jobs at an early age to earn a living his education was irregular and incomplete. He read law in his spare time and was admitted (1823) to the bar. After practicing law in East Aurora, N.Y., until 1830, he settled in Buffalo. Thurlow Weed made Fillmore a lieutenant in the Anti-Masonic party, and with Weed's support he served in the New York state assembly (1829-31) and in the U.S. House of Representatives (1833-35). In 1834 he joined the WHIG PARTY and was reelected three times (1836, 1838, 1840) to the House. When the Whigs came into national power in 1840, Fillmore became prominent in his party. As chairman of the Ways and Means Committee, he promoted the high tariff of 1842. He was considered (1844) for the vice presidential candidacy, but instead became Whig candidate for the governorship of New York. His defeat by Silas WRIGHT in a close contest was caused by the split between proslavery and antislavery Whigs. With Henry Clay's backing, Fillmore was nominated (1848) for Vice President on the Whig ticket with Zachary TAYLOR. As Vice President, Fillmore presided with notable fairness over the Senate during the turbulent debates of 1850. Succeeding to the presidency upon Taylor's death, he encouraged and then signed the Compromise of 1850, which included the Fugitive Slave Act. He tried to enforce the measures despite the criticism his course evoked from the North. Cheaper postal rates were introduced during his administration. He appointed Daniel WEBSTER Secretary of State, emphasized nonintervention in foreign disputes, and approved the treaty that opened Japan to Western commerce. He unsuccessfully tried to make of the Whigs a national party that, by occupying middle ground on the issue of slavery, could conciliate North and South and prevent extremists from gaining power. Neither he nor Webster could win the support of the Whig convention in 1852, and the nomination went to Gen. Winfield SCOTT, representative of the more radical antislavery element. With the division of the Whigs over the slavery issue and the party's consequent rapid decline, Fillmore's political career came to an end. He joined the KNOW-NOTHING MOVEMENT in the vain hope that it might unite North and South, and he accepted (1856) the nomination of that group for the presidency, being endorsed also by the small remnant of the Whigs. He opposed Lincoln's election and his Civil War administration and supported Andrew Johnson's stand against radical Reconstruction measures, but he took no active part in the controversies over these issues. See biographies by R. J. Rayback (1959), Robert Scarry (1965, repr. 1970), and W. L. Barre (1856, repr. 1971).

Filmer, Sir Robert, d. 1653, English royalist political writer, author of *Patriarcha; or, The Natural Power of Kings* (pub. posthumously in 1680), a defense of the divine right of monarchs by an exposition of the patriarchal theory of the origin of government. He attacked Hobbes's contractual theory. Filmer's work was highly influential among Tory political leaders, and it was to refute Filmer that John Locke wrote his two *Treatises on Civil Government.* See J. N. Figgis, *The Divine Right of Kings* (1914); G. H. Sabine, *A History of Political Theory* (3d ed. 1961).

Filson, John, c.1753-1788, Kentucky pioneer, b. Chester co., Pa. In 1783 he acquired land in Kentucky, taught school, and wrote *Discovery, Settlement, and Present State of Kentucke* (1784). This first history, or traveler's description, of the state contained a very good map that was also published separately in several editions. Perhaps its most popular feature, however, was an appendix, "The Adventures of Col. Daniel Boon," which purported to be Daniel Boone's autobiography. Filson obviously wrote out, in the first person, material he garnered from Daniel BOONE, as the studiedly literary style of the alleged autobiography was hardly that of the simple, vigorous, and unlettered frontiersman. Filson's book is not completely reliable historically, but it went through a number of editions, including several in London and Paris. Boone, however, delighted with his ghostwritten "autobiography," pronounced every word true, and *Kentucke* was mainly responsible for his subsequent high reputation in American history. See W. R. Jillson, ed., *Filson's Kentucke* (1929), a facsimile reproduction with full bibliography; biography by John Walton (1956).

filtration: see SEWERAGE; WATER SUPPLY.

fin, organ of locomotion characteristic of fish and consisting of thin tissue supported by cartilaginous or bony rays. In some fish, e.g., the eel, a single fin extends from the back, around the tail, and along the ventral surface. In the majority of fishes, however, there are one, two, or three dorsal fins, a distinct tail fin, and an anal fin. These are called median, or unpaired, fins. In addition to these unpaired fins, most fish also have paired fins. These are the pectoral fins, placed just back of the gills, and the pelvic, or ventral, fins, variable in position and sometimes lacking entirely. The tail is an important organ of locomotion and the paired fins are used for steering, checking speed, balancing, and for slow movements. An adipose fin (fatty tissue without support) is found behind the dorsal fin in some fish, e.g., the salmon and the catfish. See CLIMBING PERCH; FLYING FISH.

finance, theory and practice of conducting large public and private dealings in money. Important institutions of private finance include those that deal with INSURANCE, BANKING, stocks (see STOCK), bonds, and other securities. With the development of the national state, public finance—the management of the revenues, expenditures, and debts of the state—has been of great political, as well as economic, importance. The financial policy of the U.S. government since 1921 has been embodied in an annual BUDGET, which shows how revenue is to be spent and how it is to be raised. The most important source of government revenue is taxes, but sale of public properties and franchises, as well as the sale of interest-bearing bonds, also contribute. Since the Korean War, a large part of governmental expenditures has gone for various military and defense needs. Other important areas of governmental expenditure are public works; health, education, and welfare; and interest on the national debt. Important institutions of international finance are the INTERNATIONAL BANK FOR RECONSTRUCTION AND DEVELOPMENT and the INTERNATIONAL MONETARY FUND. See C. N. Henning, *International Finance* (1958); W. J. Shultz and C. L. Harriss, *American Public Finance* (8th ed. 1965); Fred Hirsch, *Money International* (1968); Carl Dauten and Merle Welshans, *Principles of Finance* (3d ed. 1970).

Finch, Heneage: see NOTTINGHAM, HENEAGE FINCH, 1ST EARL OF.

finch, common name for members of the Fringillidae, the largest family of birds (including over half the known species), found in most parts of the world except Australia. Finches are characterized by their stout, conical bills, used to crack open the seeds that form the bulk of their diet. They are valued as destroyers of weed seeds; many also eat harmful insects. The finches, which are considered the most highly developed of the birds, are widely diversified; they are classified into three groups: those with small, triangular bills, such as the CANARY, SPARROW, BUNTING, TOWHEE, JUNCO, and those birds specifically named finch (e.g., chaffinch, bullfinch, and goldfinch); those with thick, rounded bills, as the GROSBEAK and CARDINAL; and the crossbills, rose-colored northern birds whose mandibles, as their name implies, cross over at the tips—an adaptation suited to their diet of conifer seeds. Since seeds, unlike insects, are not influenced by weather, many finches are year-round residents in colder areas. The sparrows, genus *Passer,* which are field and hedge birds, are inconspicuously colored in dull grays and browns, but among the other, tree-perching finches, the male is often brightly plumaged (although the female is usually duller and sparrowlike). Most finches (except the meticulous goldfinch) build sloppy cup-shaped nests for their four to six speckled eggs. Goldfinches, genus *Astragalinus,* named for the bright yellow markings of the male, are found in Europe and North America. The common American goldfinch, *A. tristis* (thistle bird, wild canary, or yellow bird), is a year-round resident everywhere on the North American continent except in the far north. There are several Western species. The British goldfinch is cinnamon brown with black and yellow wings and a red face. Goldfinches are cheerful, musical birds, although the so-called goldfinches commonly kept as cage birds are finchlike members of the WEAVER BIRD family. The European bullfinch, with blue-gray plumage above and terra-cotta below, is often caged; it can be taught to mimic tunes. The chaffinch, *Fringilla coelebs,* also popular in Europe as a cage bird, is similarly marked but with a chestnut back and wings and tail. In North America the sparrowlike eastern purple finch, *Carpodacus purpureus* (actually rose-brown), has been largely driven out by the house sparrow. There are several purple finches in the West, where the house finch, or linnet, is common. The rosy finches are western mountain dwellers. In the Midwest the dickcissel, which winters in Central and South America, is valued as a destroyer of grasshoppers. Several longspurs, genus *Centrophanes,* are found from the Great Plains northward; the Lapland longspur is a European finch that ranges to the NE United States. The redpolls, genus *Aegiothus,* are northern finches that winter in the N United States; with the pine siskins, goldfinches, and various other seedeaters they wander around the country in small flocks, often congregating at feeding stations. The grassquits, genus *Phonipara,* are native to the Bahamas and Cuba; the brambling, or mountain, finch is a N Eurasian bird that winters in the British Isles. Finches are classified in the phylum CHORDATA, subphylum Vertebrata, class Aves, order Passeriformes, family Fringillidae.

finder, in law. Ordinarily the finder of lost property is entitled to retain it against anyone except the owner. It is LARCENY, however, for the finder to keep the property if he knows or can easily determine who owns it. In some places the finder must deliver the lost object to the police; if it is unclaimed within a prescribed period it becomes his property. Lost objects that are embedded in the soil, e.g., a deeply buried ring, belong to the landowner even if another finds them. On the other hand, objects found in a privately owned place to which the public has the right of access, e.g., a hotel, belong to the finder and not to the owner of the realty. The purchaser of an article that, without his knowledge, has something of value concealed in it, e.g., money in a desk, is legally the finder, not the owner, of the valuable. See TREASURE-TROVE.

Findlay (fĭn'lē, fĭnd'lē), city (1970 pop. 35,800), seat of Hancock co., NW Ohio, on the Blanchard River; inc. 1887. Its economy is based upon manufacturing, agriculture, and dairying. Petroleum products, tires, tile brick, washing machines, plastic goods, and food products are among its many manufactures. Gas and oil were discovered there in the 1880s, but by 1900 the supply had greatly diminished. In the Findlay *Jeffersonian* appeared (1861) the satiric antislavery letters of "Petroleum V. Nasby." The city is the home of Findlay College.

fine. 1 In criminal law, sum of money exacted by a lawful tribunal as punishment for a crime. In the case of misdemeanors and minor infractions of the law, convicted persons ordinarily have the alternative of paying a fine or undergoing a short term of imprisonment. This practice has been condemned at times as potentially exposing the poor to more onerous punishment than the well-to-do. Fines are also sometimes imposed in convictions for felony, usually in addition to a prison sentence. The Eighth Amendment to the Constitution of the United States prohibits the imposition of excessive fines, but the Supreme Court has never found that any statutory fine violated that provision. **2** In the law of the transfer of land, a legal fiction for permitting the sale of lands in ENTAIL. The fine, first worked out in the 15th cent., is in the form of a suit to determine the ownership of land. The buyer sues the seller, who accedes to the buyer's claim that his right of ownership is superior. The judgment of the court to this effect constitutes the buyer's title. The fine was formerly widely used in England and the United States, but simplified methods of defeating the entail have made it obsolete. **3** In feudal law, payment to the lord for rights relating to tenancy, e.g., for the privilege of releasing to another or acquiring for oneself the tenancy of land.

Fine Gael (fēn gāl), Irish political party. Formed in 1933, it was the successor of the party founded by William COSGRAVE that held power from the creation of the Irish Free State in 1922 until ousted by the republican FIANNA FÁIL in 1932. Under John A. Costello, Fine Gael formed coalition governments with the Labour party from 1948 to 1951 and from 1954 to 1957. After a long period in opposition it regained power, again with the Labour party, in 1973; and William Cosgrave's son Liam Cosgrave became prime minister.

Finelli, Giuliano (jo͞olyä'nō fēnĕl'lē), 1605-57, Italian sculptor. Working as assistant to Bernini, Finelli rejected the baroque aesthetic and adopted a mannered style of expression influenced by Cortona. Finelli spent his last years in Naples, where he made bronze sculptures of saints Peter and Paul for the cathedral.

finfoot, bird: see SUN GREBE.

finfooted mammal: see SEAL.

Fingal: see FINN MAC CUMHAIL.

Fingal's Cave, cavern, 227 ft (69 m) long, celebrated for its unusual beauty, on Staffa island, one of the Inner Hebrides, W Scotland. The entrance is an archway supported by basaltic columns 20 to 40 ft (6.1-12.2 m) high. The cave is inundated by the sea. Felix Mendelssohn composed an overture called *The Hebrides* or *Fingal's Cave.*

Finger Lakes, group of 11 long, narrow, glacial lakes in north to south valleys, W central N.Y. CAYUGA and

Seneca, both more than 35 mi (56 km) long, are the largest and deepest lakes. KEUKA Lake is the center of the New York state wine industry. Fertile soil and hillside locations receiving a maximum amount of sunshine, make the Finger Lakes an important grape and truck-farming region. Skaneateles and Hemlock lakes are the source of water for Syracuse and Rochester, respectively. The Finger Lakes region is a major recreation area with many resorts and state parks.

fingerprint, an impression of the underside of the end of a finger or thumb, used for identification because the arrangement of ridges in any fingerprint is thought to be unique and permanent with each person. As an identification device, fingerprinting dates from antiquity, but modern systems began essentially with the work of Henry Faulds, William James Herschel, and Sir Francis Galton in the late 19th cent. The Galton method, elaborated by E. R. Henry, is still used in Great Britain and the United States. Juan Vucetich in Argentina, also using Galton as a guide, developed (1904) an alternate system that gained wide acceptance in Spanish-speaking countries. Fingerprinting for identification of criminals was first used in connection with the BERTILLON SYSTEM. Most countries now require that all criminals be fingerprinted. Methods have also been devised for developing fingerprint impressions left by criminals at the scene of a crime. In the United States, prints are also taken of civilian government employees and members of the armed forces and by some banks and other agencies. Palm prints and footprints are also used, especially for identification of infants. See Douglas Browne and Allan Brock, *Fingerprints: Fifty Years of Scientific Crime Detection* (1954); Eugene E. Block, *Fingerprinting* (1969).

Finiguerra, Maso or **Tommaso** (mä'zō, tōm-mä'zō fēnēgwĕr'rä), 1426–64, Florentine goldsmith and engraver during the Renaissance. In the 1450s he joined with Antonio Pollaiuolo. It is said that Pollaiuolo worked on original designs that Finiguerra translated into different media. An example of such collaboration is the pax of the *Crucifixion* for the baptistery, Florence, executed in niello engraving by Finiguerra. Others include the *Triumph of Bacchus and Ariadne* and *Crucifixion* (both: British Mus.). For the latter works he used the new process of copperplate engraving. Of his own design were the wood panels for the sacristy of the cathedral in Florence (1463) and some niello plaques now in the Metropolitan Museum. See Sir Sidney Colvin, *A Florentine Picture Chronicle* (1898).

Finistère (fēnēstĕr') [from Lat. *finis terrae*=land's end], department (1968 pop. 768,929), NW France, in Brittany. QUIMPER is the capital.

Finisterre, Cape (fĭnĭstâr') [from Lat. *finis terrae*= land's end], rocky promontory, extreme NW Spain, on the Atlantic coast of Galicia. Off the cape, the English won two naval battles against the French (1747, in the War of the Austrian Succession; 1805, in the Napoleonic Wars).

Fink, Mike, 1770?–1823?, American border hero, whose exploits have been so elaborated in legend that the actual facts of his life are difficult to discover. He was born probably at the frontier post of Pittsburgh, took part in the wars against the Ohio Indians, and subsequently became a keelboatman on the flatboats of the Ohio and Mississippi rivers. He later turned to trapping. He accompanied the first Ashley expedition (1822) up the Missouri and was killed in a shooting scrape somewhere near the mouth of the Yellowstone River. He was noted as a marksman, fighter, and teller of tall stories of his exploits. Stories of flatboat life are associated with his name in a manner similar to the Paul Bunyan stories of the lumber camps. See Walter Blair and F. J. Meine, *Mike Fink* (1933) and *Half Horse, Half Alligator* (1956).

Finland, Finnish *Suomi* (swô' mē), republic (1970 pop. 4,596,958), 130,119 sq mi (337,009 sq km), N Europe, bordering on the Gulf of Bothnia and Sweden in the west, on Norway in the north, on the USSR in the east, and on the Gulf of Finland and the Baltic Sea in the south. The country includes the Ahvenanmaa Islands, located at the mouth of the Gulf of Bothnia. HELSINKI is Finland's capital and its largest city; other cities include Espoo, HAMEENLINNA, Imatra, JOENSUU, JYVÄSKYLÄ, KEMI, KOTKA, KUOPIO, LAHTI, LAPPEENRANTA, OULU, PORI, TAMPERE, TURKU, and VAASA. The country is divided into 12 provinces. Finland falls into three main geographical zones. In the south and west is a low-lying coastal strip (20–80 mi/30–130 km wide) that includes most of the country's major cities and much of its arable land. The coastal strip rises slightly to a vast forested interior plateau (average elevation: 300–600 ft/90–180 m) that includes about 60,000 lakes, many of which are linked by short rivers, sounds, or canals to form busy commercial waterways. The largest lakes are Saimaa, Inari, and Päijänne. The Kemijoki and Oulujoki are the longest rivers of the region and, with the Torniojoki, are important logging waterways. The country's third zone lies north of the Arctic Circle and is part of Lapland (Finnish, *Lappi*). The region is thinly wooded or barren and has an average elevation of about 1,100 ft (340 m); it is somewhat higher in the northwest, where Haltiatunturi (4,344 ft/1,324 m), Finland's loftiest point, is located. Altogether, Finland is made up of about 70% forest, 11% nonarable land, 10% water surface, and 9% arable land. Finnish and Swedish are both official languages, and about 7.5% of the population speaks Swedish as its first language. In addition, there are about 2,500 Lapps living in Finnish Lapland. About 93% of Finland's inhabitants belong to the established Evangelical Lutheran Church. Traditionally an agricultural country, Finland accelerated the pace of its industrialization after 1945. By the end of the 1960s, manufacturing (plus construction and mining) accounted for about 25% of the annual national product and about 30% of employment; agriculture (plus forestry and fishing) accounted for about 15% of output and about 24% of employment; and services accounted for about 14% of putput and 20% of employment. The leading agricultural commodities produced are hay, oats, barley, potatoes, wheat, rye, sugar beets, and dairy products. Large numbers of poultry, cattle, hogs, reïndeer, and sheep are raised. The principal minerals extracted are iron ore, copper, zinc, nickel, titanium, and vanadium. The country's chief manufactures are forest products, processed food, metals, metal products, machinery, chemicals, transportation equipment, textiles, and clothing. Finland also produces fine glassware and porcelain. About half of the country's rapidly growing output of electricity is generated by hydroelectric plants. Finland's road and rail networks and its waterways system are largely limited to the southern half of the country. The annual cost of Finland's imports is usually slightly higher than the value of its exports. The chief imports are machinery, transportation equipment, refined petroleum, chemicals, iron and steel, and foodstuffs. The leading exports are forest products (which account for about 50% of exports), machinery, transportation equipment, and foodstuffs. The principal trade partners are Great Britain, Sweden, the USSR, West Germany, and the United States. In 1961, Finland became an associate member of the European Free Trade Association (EFTA).

History. Beginning in the 1st cent. A.D., Finnish-speaking persons, who were mostly nomadic hunters and fishers, migrated into Finland from the south. By the 8th cent. they had displaced the small number of Lapps who lived in central and S Finland and who were forced to move to the far north of the country, where they live today. The Finns were organized in small-scale political units, with only loose ties beyond the clan level. From the 11th cent. Christian missionaries were active in Finland. In the 13th cent. Sweden conquered the country. Under the Swedes, Finland enjoyed considerable independence, its political sophistication grew, commerce increased, and the Swedish language and culture were spread. In the mid-16th cent. Lutheranism was established in Finland, and in 1581 the country was raised to the rank of grand duchy. Finland suffered severely in the recurring wars between Sweden and Russia. In 1696 famine wiped out almost a third of the population. By the Treaty of Nystad (1721), which ended the NORTHERN WAR, Peter I of Russia acquired the province of VYBORG (Viipuri), and additional areas were lost to Russia in 1743. During the Napoleonic Wars, Finland was invaded (1808) by Russia, at the time an ally of Napoleon I, in an attempt to pressure Sweden into altering its pro-British stance. Despite considerable Finnish resistance, Russia conquered the country and annexed it in 1809. In the 19th cent., the czars, who were also grand dukes of Finland, allowed the country wide-ranging autonomy, and as a result Finland was able to develop its own democratic system with little interference from St. Petersburg. In 1811, Russia returned to Finland the territory it had taken in 1721 and 1743. In 1812, Finland's capital was moved from Turku to Helsinki. Government in the country was headed by a Russian governor general (the personal representative of the czar) in conjunction with the Finnish senate; in addition, there was a Finnish minister of state in St. Petersburg who dealt directly with the czar. Finnish nationalism became a powerful movement early in the 19th cent.; it was inspired by such leaders as the poet J. L. RUNEBERG; the statesman and philosopher J. V. Snellman, whose promotion of the Finnish language helped it to achieve

official status in 1863; and the philologist Elias LÖNNROT, who compiled the monumental epic KALEVALA. The intensive russification campaign (begun in 1899) of Czar Nicholas II brought determined resistance in Finland, including the assassination (1904) of Nikolai Bobrikov, the governor general, and a general strike (1905). Under terms obtained in 1906, a unicameral parliament (whose members were elected by universal suffrage) was established, but it was given little authority by the czar. Following the Bolshevik success in the Russian Revolution (1917), the parliament proclaimed (Dec. 6, 1917) the independence of Finland. In the ensuing civil war (Jan.–May, 1918) between the leftist Red Guard (supported by some 40,000 Soviet troops and favoring close ties with the USSR) and the conservative Finnish-nationalist White Guard, led by Marshal Carl Gustav Emil MANNERHEIM and aided by German troops, the White Guard emerged victorious. After brief periods of rule under Pehr Ervind SVINHUFVUD (1918) and Mannerheim (1918–19), a republic was established and its first president, Kaarlo Juho STAHLBERG, elected (1919). By the Treaty of Tartu in 1920, the USSR recognized Finland's independence. Stahlberg was succeeded as president by Lauri Kristian Relander (in office 1925–31), Svinhufvud (1931–37), Kyösti Kallio (1937–40), Risto Heikki Ryti (1940–44), Mannerheim (1944–46), Juho Kusti PAASIKIVI (1946–56), and Urho Kaleva KEKKONEN (1956–). Agrarian and social reforms enacted after 1918 did much to heal the wounds of civil war, but deep scars remained, and they contributed to the rise of extreme rightist and leftist movements. As a result, there was considerable political instability in the 1920s and early 1930s; there were several government crises, and most ministries were based on coalitions. The Communist party, suppressed in 1923, remained active until it was effectively removed from the scene by discriminatory laws in 1930, and the rightist Lapua movement, originating in anti-Communist disturbances in 1929, was itself suppressed after an unsuccessful coup d'etat in 1932. Finland was active in the League of Nations, which it joined in 1920, and it was the only European country to continue to honor its World War I debts to the United States after the advent of the economic depression at the start of the 1930s. During the 1930s, Finland followed a neutralist foreign policy, and in 1932 it signed a nonaggression treaty with the USSR. In late

Nov., 1939, shortly after the start of World War II, Finland was attacked by Soviet troops, and despite spirited Finnish resistance organized by Mannerheim, the USSR easily emerged victorious by early 1940 (see FINNISH-RUSSIAN WAR). By the treaty of Moscow (March 12, 1940), Finland ceded the Rybachi Peninsula, its part of the Karelian Isthmus (including Vyborg), and land bordering on Lake Ladoga; in addition, the USSR gained a 30-year lease of the port of HANGÖ. When Germany attacked the USSR in June, 1941, Finland allied itself with Germany, hoping thereby to regain territory from the USSR. Great Britain, but not the United States, declared war on Finland. After some initial Finnish successes, Soviet troops invaded Finland in 1944 and forced it to sign an armistice in Sept., 1944. This agreement confirmed the cessions of territory Finland had made in 1940; however, instead of Hangö, the USSR was given a lease on the PORKKALA peninsula near Helsinki. In addition, Finland was required to pay an indemnity to the USSR and to force the Germans to evacuate the country. In the ensuing warfare with Germany, N Finland was devastated. After the war, by a peace treaty signed in Paris in 1947, the 1944 armistice was largely confirmed; Finland was obliged to pay the USSR $300 million in reparations and to cede the Karelian Isthmus (with Vyborg), PECHENGA (Petsamo) in the far north, and additional border districts in the east. The USSR was given a 50-year lease to the Prokkala region. About 420,000 Finns left the territory ceded to the USSR and were resettled in Finland. Despite great difficulties, Finland completed its reparations payments by 1952; in 1948, the USSR had reduced the amount by about $74 million. A Finnish-Soviet treaty of cooperation was signed in 1948 (it was extended in 1955 and again in 1970), and a trade pact was negotiated in 1950 (another similar agreement was signed in 1969). In 1956 the Soviet Union returned Porkkala to Finland. In the immediate postwar period, Communists (working through the Finnish People's Democratic League) won a substantial number of seats in parliament and held several high-level cabinet posts, including for a short time that of prime minister. However, beginning in 1948, the Communists' power began to wane, and the Social Democrats and the Agrarian Union (in 1965 renamed the Center party) dominated politics from then on. These parties almost invariably had to form coalition governments either with each other or with other, smaller, parties. In 1955, Finland joined the United Nations. Economic problems (notably unemployment and inflation) led to a three-week general strike in 1956. In the late 1950s and early 1960s the USSR exercised some influence over internal Finnish politics, forcing, for example, the withdrawal of a candidate for president in 1962. In 1966, Communists were included in a coalition cabinet for the first time since 1948. In 1968 a five-party coalition government was established under Ahti Karjalainen. The Communists left the coalition in early 1971 (following major strikes that were ended by government arbitration), and in late 1971 Karjalainen resigned. A caretaker government led by Teuvo Aura was formed, and in Feb., 1972, a minority Social Democratic government headed by Rafael Paasio was established. Paasio resigned in July, 1972, and in Sept., 1972, a four-party coalition (including the Social Democratic, Center, Liberal, and Swedish People's parties) was set up under Kalevi Sorsa, a Social Democrat. In 1973 parliament passed an extraordinary law extending Kekkonen's third term as president (he had been elected in 1956 and reelected in 1962 and 1968) for four years to 1978; he had earlier expressed unwillingness to run for a fourth term. In the early 1970s, Finland was on good terms with the USSR and was extending its economic contacts with the nations of East Europe.

Government. Under the 1919 constitution as amended, Finland's head of state is the president, who is elected to a six-year term by a 300-member electoral college that is chosen by direct popular vote. The president is commander in chief of the armed forces, plays an important role in foreign affairs, and can have considerable influence over legislative matters. Legislation is handled by the unicameral parliament (*Eduskunta*), whose 200 members are elected to four-year terms by a system of proportional representation. All Finns who are at least 20 years old may vote. The country's main administrative body is the cabinet (headed by a prime minister), which is responsible to parliament. See J. H. Wuorinen, *A History of Finland* (1965); E. M. Kivikoski, *Finland* (tr. 1967); Wendy Hall, *The Finns and their Country* (1968); Hillar Kallas and Sylvie Nickels, *Finland: Creation and Construction* (1968); W. R. Mead, *Finland* (1968); Max Jacobson, *Finnish Neutrality: A Study of Finnish Foreign Policy since the Second World War* (1969); Jaakko Nousiainen, *The Finnish Political System* (tr. 1971); Sylvie Nickels et al., ed., *Finland: An Introduction* (1973).

Finland, Gulf of, eastern arm of the Baltic Sea, c.285 mi (460 km) long and from c.10 to c.75 mi (15-120 km) wide, between Finland and the USSR. The shallow gulf receives the Narva River and water from Lake Lagoda and the Saimaa lakes; it is frozen from December to March. The gulf, an important corridor for Soviet shipping, contains many islands. Leningrad and Tallinn (USSR) and Helsinki (Finland) are the chief ports.

Finlay, Carlos Juan, or **Charles John Finlay,** 1833-1915, Cuban physician of Scottish and French descent; studied in France; M.D. Jefferson Medical College, Philadelphia, 1855. Settling in Havana, he began his life work on yellow fever, suggesting in 1881 the mosquito as carrier and in 1882 specifying the genus *Stegomyia.* The Reed Commission of 1900 inaugurated experiments that conclusively proved his theories. Finlay served as chief health officer of Cuba from 1902 to 1909.

Finley, James Bradley, 1781-1856, Methodist preacher and frontier missionary, b. North Carolina. He was long a circuit rider and for 21 years was district superintendent of a backwoods circuit of the Western Conference of the Methodist Church. His autobiography (1854) and his other books are valuable sources on frontier life in Ohio.

Finley, Robert, 1772-1817, American clergyman, a founder of the AMERICAN COLONIZATION SOCIETY, b. Princeton, N.J. In 1787 he graduated from the College of New Jersey (now Princeton), where he later studied theology. Ordained in 1795, he served for over 20 years at Basking Ridge, N.J., both as pastor and as headmaster of a school for boys. His interest in the condition of American Negroes led him to lobby for the establishment of an organization that would help freed slaves return to Africa. His goal was realized (1816) with the establishment of the American Colonization Society. At his death he was president of the Univ. of Georgia. Finley wrote *Thoughts on the Colonization of Free Blacks* (1816). See biography by Isaac V. Brown (1857, repr. 1969).

Finley, Samuel, 1715-66, Presbyterian minister, president of the College of New Jersey (now Princeton Univ.), b. Ireland. He went to North America in 1734 and is believed to have studied under William Tennent. He preached in the series of religious revivals known as the Great Awakening, mainly in New Jersey and Pennsylvania. In the early 1740s, Finley founded a school in Nottingham on the Pennsylvania-Maryland border (now the West Nottingham Academy). He became president of the College of New Jersey in 1761.

Finnan, Scotland: see FINDON.

finnan haddie: see COD.

Finney, Charles Grandison, 1792-1875, American evangelist, theologian, and educator, b. Warren, Conn. Licensed to the Presbyterian ministry in 1824, he had phenomenal success as a revivalist in the Eastern states, converting many who became noted ABOLITIONISTS. In 1834 the Broadway Tabernacle, New York City, was organized for him. Under his leadership this church withdrew from its presbytery and adopted the Congregational form of government. In 1837, Finney went to Oberlin College, where he was professor of theology until 1875 and president of the college from 1851 to 1865. At the same time he was pastor of the Oberlin Congregational Church and continued his evangelistic tours until his death, twice visiting England to conduct revivals. His theological writings, published chiefly in the *Oberlin Evangelist,* which he founded and edited, were of great influence and set the tone of "Oberlin theology," one of the forms of New School Calvinism. His *Lectures on Revivals of Religion* (1835) became the classic book for generations of revivalists. See his memoirs (1876, repr. 1973); study by V. R. Edman (1951); W. G. McLoughlin, *Modern Revivalism* (1959).

Finnish language, also called Suomi, member of the Finnic group of the FINNO-UGRIC LANGUAGES. These languages form a subdivision of the Uralic subfamily of the Ural-Altaic family of languages (see URALIC AND ALTAIC LANGUAGES). Finnish is spoken by about 4 million people in Finland. Additional speakers totaling close to a million live in neighboring areas of Sweden and the USSR and also in the United States. There are several dialects. In Finnish the first syllable of a word is stressed. The language has 15 cases for nouns, personal pronouns, and adjectives. It lacks grammatical gender and the article. There is a negative conjugation for the verb. Like the other Uralic and Altaic languages, Finnish has vowel harmony and agglutination. Postpositions are employed instead of prepositions. Suffixation is used to form derived nouns and verbs. The Finnish vocabulary has been enriched by words borrowed from the Germanic, Slavic, and Baltic languages. A modified Roman alphabet is used for writing Finnish, which has been recorded since the 16th cent. See Lauri Hakulinen, *The Structure and Development of the Finnish Language;* M. K. T. Lehtinen, *Basic Course in Finnish* (1967).

Finnish literature. The first printed work in Finnish was the ABC book published c.1542 by Bishop Michael Agricola (1508-57). In 1642 the first complete translation of the Bible in Finnish appeared in Stockholm. Until the 19th cent. most of the writing done by Finns was in Swedish, since from the 13th cent. to 1809 Finland was in political vassalage to Sweden. The linguistic researches of Alexander Castrén (1813-53), as well as the historical writings of Henry Gabriel Porthan (1739-1804) and the publication (1835) by Elias Lönnrot of the KALEVALA, helped to feed interest in Finnish as a literary vehicle. Still many continued to write in Swedish, among them J. L. RUNEBERG, the national poet of Finland. Others who preferred Swedish were the romantic novelist Topelius; Arvid Mörne (1876-1946), poet, novelist, and playwright; Jarl HEMMER, poet; and the prose writer Runar Schildt (1888-1925). To the first generation of those writing in Finnish belong the novelist Pietari Päivärinta (1827-1913) and Alexis Stenvall (pseud. Kivi, 1834-72), who originated Finnish tragic and comic drama. He is known abroad for *The Seven Brothers* (1870, tr. 1929), a masterpiece combining elements of romanticism and realism. Eino Leino (1878-1926), Finland's most original lyricist, produced some 30 collections of poetry reflecting the influence of folklore. The poet Edith Södergran (1892-1923), inspired by the European symbolists and by her Russian childhood, had great influence on modern Finnish and Swedish poetry. The first Finnish writer to express modern realism was the playwright and champion of women's rights, Minna Canth (1844-97). Also influenced by realistic as well as radical literary currents in the 1880s was Juhani Aho (1861-1921), a novelist who gave literary Finnish a new maturity and artistic standard. The novelist and poet Ilmari Kianto depicted the bitter struggle for existence among the poor peasantry in N Finland. Also concerned with rural life were the novelists Joel Lehtonen (1881-1934) and Pentti Haanpää (1905-55). A champion of social reform was the Swedish-language poet Arvid Mörne. The conflicts rising from the civil war (1918) inspired the playwright and short-story writer Runar Schildt. The tensions of 20th-century industrial society are reflected in the novels of Toivo Pekkanen (1902-57). Frans SILLANPÄÄ, who won the 1939 Nobel Prize for Literature, gained fame for his lyrical impressionist novels. Dominating Finnish literature in the mid-20th cent. were the novelist Väinö Linna and the prolific novelist, poet, and playwright Mika Waltari. See P. I. Ravila, ed., *Finnish Literary Reader* (1965); Aleksis Rubulis, *Baltic Literature* (1970); Jaakko Ahokas, *A History of Finnish Literature* (1972).

Finnish-Russian War, 1939-40, war between Finland and the Soviet Union. After World War II broke out in Sept., 1939, the USSR, never on cordial terms with Finland, took advantage of its nonaggression pact (Aug., 1939) with Germany to make several far-reaching demands on Finland. These demands included the demilitarization of the Mannerheim Line (the Finnish fortification line across the Karelian Isthmus just N of Leningrad), a 30-year lease on Hanko as a naval base, and the cession of several islands in the Gulf of Finland. In return, Russia offered extensive but valueless districts along the eastern border of Finland. Finland balked; negotiations broke down in November. After alleging (Nov. 26) that Finnish artillery had fired on Russian troops, the USSR, denouncing (Nov. 28) the Russo-Finnish nonaggression pact of 1932 and breaking off (Nov. 28) diplomatic relations, attacked on Nov. 30. The Russians first concentrated their efforts on the eastern border of Finland, but the Finns, superior in winter warfare and ably commanded by Field Marshall MANNERHEIM, repulsed attacks at Lake Ladoga, Suomussalmi, Salla, and Ivalo. World sympathy was with Finland. Sweden and Norway sent volunteers and supplies, and some supplies came from France and Great Britain. Finally, however, small Finland was no match for the USSR. Air bombardments and well-prepared frontal attacks (Feb., 1940) on the Karelian Isthmus brought Finnish resistance to the verge of collapse. In the peace treaty signed on March 12, Finland ceded part of the Karelian Isthmus, Viborg (Viipuri), and several border territories to the USSR. In June, 1941, warfare was resumed between Finland and Russia and became part of the general world conflagration (see FINLAND). See Max Jakobson, *The Diplomacy of the Winter War* (1961), and A. L. Paley, *The Russo-Finnish War* (1973).

Finn mac Cumhail, Fionn mac Cumhail, or **Finn MacCool** (all: fĭn məko͞ol'), semimythical Irish hero. His exploits are recorded in long narrative poems by OSSIAN and in many ballads, called Fenian ballads after the Fenians, or Fianna, professional fighters whom Finn was said to have headed in the 3d cent. Certain tales involve such events as Finn's pursuit of the lovers Diarmuid and Grania, who was Finn's wife. The stories of Finn inspired the *Fingal* of James MACPHERSON and played an important part in the IRISH LITERARY RENAISSANCE. See *Duanaire Finn: The Book of the Lays of Fionn,* ed. and tr. by Eoin MacNeill (3 vol., 1908–53).

Finnmark (fĭn'märk), county (1972 est. pop. 77,000), 18,783 sq mi (46,648 sq km), N Norway, bordering on the Arctic Ocean in the north, on the Barents Sea in the east, on the Soviet Union in the southeast, and on Finland in the south. It forms the northernmost part of the Scandinavian peninsula and is the largest—but least populated—county of Norway. The main towns are Vadsø (the capital) and Hammerfest. Its coast is deeply indented by large fjords, notably the Tanafjord and the Varangerfjord. There are numerous islands off the coast; on one of them is North Cape. The population consists largely of Lapps and Finns. Fishing, reindeer raising, farming, and mining are the chief occupations. There are large iron mines near Kirkenes and rich mineral deposits in the Kautokeino region. Finnmark was severely damaged (1944) by the Germans in World War II.

Finno-Ugric languages (fĭn'ō-o͞o'grĭk), also called Finno-Ugrian languages, group of languages forming a subdivision of the Uralic subfamily of the Ural-Altaic family of languages (see URALIC AND ALTAIC LANGUAGES). The Finno-Ugric group of languages can be divided into two subgroups, Finnic and Ugric. These languages have about 20 million speakers distributed in enclaves scattered in a territory that stretches from Norway to the Ob River of Siberia and down to the Carpathian Mts. About 8 million of these people speak the Finnic tongues, which include FINNISH, native to about 4 million in Finland and close to 1 million elsewhere; Karelian, used by about 175,000 in Karelia; Estonian, the mother tongue of more than 1 million in Estonia; Lapp, native to 40,000 mainly nomadic people living in Norway, Sweden, and Finland; Mordvinian, spoken by more than 1 million in the Soviet Union in the neighborhood of the Volga River below its bend; Cheremiss, the mother tongue of 500,000 in the area where the Volga and Kama rivers join (W of the Ural Mountains); and the Permian languages Votyak, native to 700,000 between the Kama and Vyatka rivers of European Russia, and Zyrian, spoken by 500,000 living between the Pechora, Mezen, and Kama rivers (W of the Ural Mountains). The principal member of the Ugric subgroup is HUNGARIAN, with 12 million speakers, 9 million of whom reside in Hungary and 3 million elsewhere. Ostyak is spoken by more than 20,000 in the area of the Ob River of W Siberia, and Vogul is the language of some 6,000 in the neighborhood of the Ob and Irtysh rivers of W Siberia. The Finno-Ugric languages are agglutinative in that they add large numbers of suffixes to an unchanging root (one suffix following the other) to indicate such features as case, number, person, tense, and mood. Derivatives are also frequently formed by suffixes. See Björn Collinder, *An Introduction to the Uralic Languages* (1965) and *Survey of the Uralic Languages* (2d ed. 1969); Alo Raun, *Essays in Finno-Ugric and Finnic Linguistics* (1971).

finochio: see FENNEL.

Finsen, Niels Ryberg (nēls rü'bĕr fĭn'sən), 1860–1904, Danish physician. He established in Copenhagen an institute of light therapy and wrote several books on his work. He received the 1903 Nobel Prize in Physiology and Medicine for his method of treating disease, especially lupus vulgaris, with ultraviolet light.

Finsteraarhorn (fĭn"stərär'hôrn"), peak, 14,032 ft (4,277 m) high, S central Switzerland; highest of the Bernese Alps.

fiord: see FJORD.

fir, any tree of the genus *Abies* of the family Pinaceae (PINE family), tall pyramidal evergreen conifers characterized by short, flat, stemless needles and erect cylindrical cones that shed their scales rather than dropping off the tree whole. Firs, valued and cultivated for their fragrance and beauty, are found chiefly in alpine regions of the Northern Hemisphere. In North America the balsam fir, or balsam, popular as a Christmas tree and the source of CANADA BALSAM, is native to the Northeast; the southern fir, or she-balsam, grows in the South; and the noble, alpine, and red firs are found at high altitudes and the grand, silver, and white firs on lower mountain slopes in the Northwest. Fir wood is usually light and soft but is sometimes used for interior finishing and for crates and boxes. The Douglas fir is not a true fir. Firs are classified in the division PINOPHYTA, class Pinopsida, order Coniferales.

Firbank, Ronald, 1886–1926, English author, whose original name was Arthur Annesley Ronald Firbank. Of a delicate and eccentric nature, Firbank lived the life of a leisured aesthete. His novels, which have appealed to a small but appreciative audience, include *Vainglory* (1915), *Valmouth* (1919), *Prancing Nigger* (1924), and *Concerning the Eccentricities of Cardinal Pirelli* (1926). Written in a highly personal, satiric style with no conventional plots, his books are disciplined journeys into a world inhabited by bizarre characters. His writings have had an influence on the novels of such writers as Evelyn Waugh, Ivy Compton-Burnett, and Aldous Huxley. See his complete works (with a preface by Anthony Powell, 1961); biographies by M. J. Benkovitz (1969) and Brigid Brophy (1973).

Firbolgs (fĭr'bōlgz), in Irish mythology, early settlers of ancient Ireland. They were said to be a short, dark people. After their defeat by the invading Fomors, many fled to Greece.

Firdausi (fərdou'sē), c.940–1020, principal Persian poet, author of the *Shah Namah* [the book of kings], the great Persian epic. His original name was Abul Kasim Mansur; he is thought to have been born of a yeoman family of Khurasan. He received a thorough education in Muslim learning and in the Persian language and antiquities. The course of his life is not certain because of the immense accretion of legend about it. He lived at the court of Mahmud of Ghazni, with a group of antiquarians. Firdausi undertook his epic history of Persia dealing with the period from the arrival of the Persians to that of the Arabs to glorify Persia's past. He dedicated the work to the king, who paid him less than Firdausi expected. The poet wrote a savage satire on the king (usually prefaced to editions of the *Shah Namah*) and fled. He wandered from court to court and arrived in his old age at his home. His poem, in 60,000 verses, is the first great work of modern Persian literature. In it Firdausi set the mark for Persian poetry with his even rhyme, stately cadences, and continuous flow. The poem has taken a singular place in Persia, and long sections of it are recited by illiterate tribesmen. The version of the *Shah Namah* illustrated for the Shah Tahmasp in the early 16th cent., now known as the Houghton *Shah-Nameh* (facsimile ed., 1972), is one of the masterpieces of world art. Firdausi's *Yusuf and Zuleikha* (18,000 lines) is a version of the story of Potiphar's wife.

fire, the phenomenon of COMBUSTION as seen in light, FLAME, and heat; it is one of the basic tools of human culture. In ancient Greece and later, fire was considered one of the four basic elements, a substance from which all things were composed. Its great importance to humans, the mystery of its powers, and its seeming capriciousness have made fire divine or sacred to many peoples. Fire as a god is a characteristic feature of Zoroastrianism, in which, as in many sun-worshiping religions, fire is considered the earthly representative or type of the sun. The belief that fire is sacred is universal in mythology, and such beliefs have survived in some highly developed cultures. The connection between the Greek colony and the metropolis was the fire kindled in the colony from a brand brought from the mother city's fire. The most carefully preserved cult in Rome was that of Vesta, goddess of the hearth, and her virgins guarded the holy fire. One of the greatest Greek myths is the story of Prometheus, the fire bringer. The ramifications of the human ideas about fire are tremendously complex, extending as they do into the concepts about light and the heavens. See J. G. Frazer, *Myths of the Origins of Fire* (1930, repr. 1971); Gaston Bachelard, *Psychoanalysis of Fire* (tr. 1964).

fire, forest: see FORESTRY.

fire apparatus, devices and appliances, both portable and mobile, used to extinguish, to confine, or to escape from fire. Oxygen, fuel, and enough heat to kindle the fuel are necessary for burning; fires are fought by removing one of the three. There are three kinds of fires: those in solids, e.g., wood, paper, and cloth; those in flammable liquids, e.g., gasoline, alcohol, oils, lacquers, and paints; and those in electrical apparatus. These are called, respectively, class A, B, and C fires. Water, although supplanted somewhat by other materials, is still the most common substance used for quenching class A fires; water both cools and helps smother the fuel. Buckets of water are the simplest equipment for fighting small fires in solids. To form a stream of water there are special pumps. The commonly seen metal cylinder with short hose attached is the soda-and-acid extinguisher; inside it, above a solution of soda and water, is a container of acid. When the extinguisher is inverted, the acid mixes with the solution and reacts with the soda to generate carbon dioxide; gas pressure then forces the solution out of the hose. Wetting agents called detergents make water more penetrating, especially for such objects as cotton bales and mattresses. However, water spreads class B fires unless sprayed in a fine mist, for flammable liquids will usually float on water. Therefore foam is used to blanket the surface in such cases, particularly in oil fires. Foam can also be used on solids, but is untidy. A foam extinguisher is a metal cylinder containing water, sodium bicarbonate, an agent (often licorice powder) for strengthening the foam, and an inner container of aluminum sulfate powder. Mixed together, these ingredients form a foam of carbon dioxide bubbles. As both water and foam conduct electricity, they cannot be used against class C fires unless the power is shut off. Instead, vaporizing liquids or carbon dioxide are used. These are also used against flammable liquids and small fires in solids. When a vaporizing liquid such as carbon tetrachloride is pumped or forced by gas pressure out of an extinguisher, it turns into a vapor that is heavier than air and thus settles over the fire, smothering it. Unfortunately, the vapor is both toxic and corrosive. A carbon dioxide extinguisher consists of a tank of liquid carbon dioxide under pressure. When released, the carbon dioxide forms flakes that vaporize and blanket the fire. An example of a dry-chemical extinguishing agent is fine sodium bicarbonate, which is used on class B and C fires and is especially effective against class B fires. Certain dry materials that melt and coat the burning material, thus excluding air, are useful against all classes of fire. In certain cases inert gases such as argon or nitrogen are used to fight fires in materials that would react dangerously with water or with other extinguishing agents; sodium and water, for example, is a dangerous combination. Many buildings have protective sprinkler systems in which overhead pipes have outlets that are normally closed but that open at high temperatures to spray water on any fire causing such heat. Most large buildings provide water for firefighting through a standpipe system with hose connections on each floor. Forest and brush fires are fought by making a firebreak and by covering the fire with extinguishing substances. A narrow strip is cut and cleared in front of the fire down to mineral soil. As the fire approaches, embers flying into the strip are put out. The equipment to carry out this procedure includes axes and power saws to cut, bulldozers and special fire plows to clear, torches to burn, and flailers to smother embers. Water and other fire-extinguishing substances are spread from land-based vehicles or are dropped on the fire from the air. The inventor Ctesibius of Alexandria devised the first known fire pump c.200 B.C. His development was so little known to Europeans that when they began reinventing the fire pump about A.D. 1500 they thought the idea entirely new. At the time of the London fire in 1666 there were only two-quart hand syringes and a similar, slightly larger syringe. In the American colonies the ordinary fire-fighting equipment included a leather bucket, ladders, hooks for pulling down burning buildings, and a long swab for smothering small fires on roofs. The London fire stimulated the development of a two-man piston pump on wheels. Boston imported (1679) the first fire engine to reach America. For a long time the ten-man pump devised by the English inventor Richard Newsham in 1725 was the most widely used. The inventor Thomas Lote of New York built (1743) the first fire engine made in America. About 1672 leather hose and couplings for joining lengths together were produced. Leather hose was expensively sewn together like a fine boot. Fabric and rubber-treated hose did not come into general use until 1870. A steam fire engine was built in London in 1829, but the volunteer fire companies of the day were very slow to accept it. When a group of insurance companies in New York had a self-propelled engine built in 1841, the firemen so hindered its use that the insurance companies gave up the project. Finally, in Cincinnati, Ohio, the public forced a steam engine on the firemen. The aerial ladder wagon appeared in 1870; the hose elevator, about 1871. Gasoline engines were at first used either as pumping engines or as tractors to pull apparatus. In 1910 the two functions were combined, one engine both propelling the truck and driving the pump. The modern diesel pump developed later delivers about 2,000 gal per min (8,000 liters per min) through lightweight hose reinforced with artificial fibers. Each nozzle on a fireboat can deliver 6,500 gal per min (25,000 liters per min), and there are usually several nozzles on a boat. On a ladder truck, push-button controls raise tubular steel ladders over 100 ft (30 m). In addition, modern fire apparatus includes rescue trucks, mobile laboratories, searchlight cars, double-ended tunnel engines, smoke ejectors, high-pressure spray trucks, foam trucks, and even coffee wagons. For fires of long duration there are tank trucks to bring extra fuel to the pumpers. Some of the smaller equipment includes explosion meters, battering rams, resuscitators, guns to shoot lifelines, two-way lifelines, two-way radios, pike poles, and a full complement of tools such as welding torches, saws, and drills. Special salvage crews may go into a burning building and put covers over machinery to protect it from water damage. Mobile laboratories have apparatus for testing noxious fumes given off in a fire in order to find the right antidote. Airports have specially equipped crash trucks, and refineries have chemical applicators. See C. F. Haywood, *General Alarm* (1967); L. W. Erven, *Fire Company Apparatus and Procedure* (1969).

firearm, device consisting essentially of a straight tube, to propel shot, shell, or bullets by the explosion of GUNPOWDER. Firearms came into general use in Europe early in the 14th cent. in the form of heavy cannon; from the 15th cent., when the matchlock appeared, to the end of the U.S. Civil War, they became increasingly important in battle, and military tactics had to adapt constantly to successive improvements in their design. In the 15th cent. firearms also came into use in hunting. Although the Chinese discovered gunpowder as early as the 9th cent., they did not develop firearms until the mid-14th cent. Firearms are generally classified either as large firearms, i.e., ARTILLERY, or as SMALL ARMS; however, some firearms, notably the MORTAR, ROCKET, and RECOILLESS RIFLE, are generally classified in neither group.

fireball, very bright METEOR leaving a trail in the sky that can remain visible for several minutes; often a distinct sound is associated with it. A bolide is a fireball that explodes in the air because of thermal stresses created when it passes through the earth's atmosphere.

firebrat: see SILVERFISH.

firebrick, brick that can withstand high temperatures, used to line flues, stacks, furnaces, and fireplaces. In general, such bricks have high melting points that range from about 2800°F (1540°C) for fireclay to 4000°F (2200°C) for silicon carbide. They also should resist the chemicals in slags and not spall, i.e., flake under wide temperature changes. Clay bricks of fireclay or kaolin are common. Silica has good strength at high temperatures, but since it spalls, it is used in furnaces that remain hot continuously. High alumina bricks can stand high temperatures and high loads. To withstand alkalis there are magnesite bricks. Firebricks are not good insulators. A special insulating firebrick of highly porous fireclay or kaolin has low conductivity and low heat content but a melting point of only about 1600°F to 2800°F (870°C–1540°C). It makes a thin, light wall that saves fuel because it heats quickly. A separate layer of insulating material backs up other kinds of firebrick. Refractory mortar binds firebricks together. Additional support comes from metal anchors projecting from the metal casing. Special coatings give bricks extra protection from slags and dust-laden gases. Plastic or castable mixes are used for repairs or special shapes.

fire clay, CLAY that has a high degree of resistance to heat. By the best standards it should have a fusion point higher than 1600°C. The term "fire clay" is commonly held to exclude kaolin and other refractory potter's clays. Fire clay should contain high percentages of silica and alumina, with as little as possible of such impurities as lime, magnesia, soda, and potash, which lower the fusion point of the clay. Fire clay often forms the bed layer of earth under seams of coal. Two types are recognized—flint clay, exceedingly hard, nonplastic, and resembling flint in appearance, occurring in the United States; and plastic fire clay. The principal uses of fire clay are in the manufacture of firebrick and of various accessory utensils, such as crucibles, saggers, retorts, and glass pots, used in the metalworking industries.

firedamp: see DAMP.

fire-eaters, in U.S. history, term applied by Northerners to proslavery extremists in the South in the two decades before the Civil War. Edmund RUFFIN, Robert B. RHETT, and William L. YANCEY were the most notable of the group. As early as 1850, at a convention held in Nashville, Tenn., the "fire-eaters" urged secession upon the South, but the Compromise of 1850 and more moderate counsel combined to postpone that event for another 10 years. Although the "fire-eaters" were in large measure responsible for the movement to organize a separate Southern government, they filled minor offices under the Confederacy.

fire engine: see FIRE APPARATUS.

fire escape, in architecture, device, either fixed or movable, to facilitate escape from a burning building. In the United States the term usually is applied to the common exterior iron balconies and stairways or ladders that give egress from each floor to the ground; this type, although of doubtful value in time of panic and usually a disfigurement architecturally, is still in general use on multi-family dwellings and other buildings. The fire stair, enclosed in an independent fireproof wall and accessible at each floor level through a self-closing fireproof door, is a more dependable device now widely used (often required by ordinance) in apartment and commercial buildings and in places of public assemblage. Even more desirable is the smokeproof fire tower, which contains a fireproof stair entered from each floor across an open-air balcony. Other varieties of fire escape in more or less general use range from the simple knotted rope to elaborate systems of spiral chutes. In England the term refers to a portable extension ladder that may be wheeled up to a burning building to enable occupants to escape when ordinary exits are cut off.

fire extinguisher: see FIRE APPARATUS.

firefly or **lightning bug,** small, luminescent, carnivorous BEETLE of the family Lampyridae. Fireflies are well represented in temperate regions, although the majority of species are tropical and subtropical. They are nocturnal in their behavior, and males commonly fly about in the evening during early summer. In many species the females are wingless. Males, females, and larvae emit a heatless, greenish-yellow to reddish-orange light; in some species even the eggs glow. The light, believed to play a role in sexual attraction between the adults, is produced by light organs located on the underside of the abdomen. These consist of several layers of small reflector cells and a layer of light-producing cells. The light-producing cells are permeated by nerves and air tubes; oxygen supplied by the air tubes converts the cell product luciferin to oxyluciferin. This oxidation, catalyzed by the enzyme luciferase, releases energy in the form of light. The insect controls the emission of light by regulating the amount of air supplied to the cells. The intensity and frequency of the flashes vary with the species and probably serve to identify males and females to each other. Synchronized flashing is characteristic of some tropical species. Adult fireflies of many species do not feed. The larvae, which hatch from eggs laid on or in wet soil, feed on snails and earthworms, injecting their prey with a paralyzing fluid. Pupation (see INSECT) occurs after one or two years. Both larvae and wingless females are called glowworms. The common European glowworm is the female of the *Lampyris noctiluca*. Oriental glowworms are considered beneficial controllers of crop-damaging snails and slugs. There are other luminescent insects, including members of other beetle families; the most spectacular are found in the CLICK BEETLE family. Fireflies are classified in the phylum ARTHROPODA, class Insecta, order Coleoptera, family Lampyridae.

fire insurance: see INSURANCE.

Fire Island, narrow barrier beach, 32 mi (52 km) long, off the south shore of Long Island, SE N.Y., separating Great South Bay from the Atlantic Ocean; part of the Outer Barrier. Robert Moses State Park and several resort colonies dot the island. Formerly accessible only by boat or ferry, Fire Island enjoyed a rare privacy until the construction in 1959 of a bridge linking the eastern end of the island with Long Island. There are now two bridges. **Fire Island National Seashore** (est. 1964) covers part of the island and includes wooded areas, marshes, and Sunken Forest, an area of unusual plant and animal life (see NATIONAL PARKS AND MONUMENTS, table).

Firenze, Italy: see FLORENCE.

fireproofing, method of making normally combustible materials as nearly noncombustible as possible. In most cases it is possible only to treat them with a solution or coating of some substance that will tend to retard their ignition. Wood is protected by being impregnated with such substances as ammonium phosphate solution or by being covered with special paints, mastics, or glazes. Textiles for use indoors are soaked in solutions made up mostly of boric acid and borax. Textiles for outdoors are soaked with chlorinated paraffin, chlorinated synthetic resins, or chlorinated rubber. The standard for effectiveness of these treatments is the weight of chemicals remaining after the materials dry. Large areas of textiles are brushed or sprayed, but they gain little resistance against severe fire exposure; the treatment is mainly a guard against lit cigarettes and short exposure to flame. Rain, washing, or dry cleaning leaches the chemicals from the fabric, necessitating reprocessing; for this reason, treatment for the outdoor fabrics combines fireproofing with waterproofing. Glass and glass-and-asbestos textiles are noncombustible. Mixing cotton with asbestos to make a fabric pliable renders it less fireproof; if the percentage of cotton is high enough, protection by the asbestos becomes nil. Wood construction can resist fire for a long time if the timbers are much heavier than necessary for structural strength; fire will burn very slowly inward from the surface, leaving enough sound timber in the center to prevent collapse. Stucco or other incombustible facing gives a wood frame some protection from fire. Buildings classed as fire resistive are made of reinforced concrete or protected steel that will stand considerable fire with minor damage. The noncombustible class of building has no combustibles, but a building made of unprotected steel may be damaged. While steel retains its strength up to a very high temperature, it fails rapidly at temperatures over 1,000°F (540°C). Brick, concrete, and tile were at first the major fireproofing materials. A protective layer of concrete over all surfaces of a beam or over the steel bars in reinforced concrete had to be at least 2½ in. (6.4 cm) thick to be effective; hollow clay tile used to cover beams and girders had to be at least 4 in. (10 cm) thick. Construction with these materials was very heavy, so that much of the weight carried by the steel frame was fireproofing material. Later buildings have had a light frame made possible by light curtain exterior walls and lightweight fireproofing throughout. Modern materials have included gypsum, perlite, and vermiculite mixed in plaster, concrete, and mineral fiber. Concrete is still used, but mostly as a thin slab on floors. Membrane fireproofing consisting of a thin, light fireproof ceiling below a bare metal roof or floor or contact fireproofing sprayed directly on metal floor and roof supports minimizes weight inside the building. However, the use of asbestos spray has been banned in certain areas because the asbestos particles have been found to induce lung disease in persons regularly exposed to them. Fireproof board made from a mixture of asbestos and cement is used extensively; for all practical purposes it is noncombustible, and it is also a good insulator. The layout of a building can contribute to its safety, as with horizontal and vertical cutoffs to keep fire from spreading within the building. Fireproof doors are often entirely of steel, but some have a wooden core encased in sheet metal. Protection against fire in neighboring buildings can be provided by exterior walls—preferably windowless, since windows are fire openings. Standards for fireproofing are set by organizations such as the American Insurance Association and the International Conference of Building Officials.

Firestone, Harvey Samuel, 1868–1938, American industrialist, manufacturer of rubber products, b. Columbiana co., Ohio. The son of a prosperous farmer, Harvey Firestone began to manufacture rubber tires in 1896. He organized (1900) the Firestone Tire & Rubber Company and rapidly became a leader of the rubber industry, with various properties over the world. By 1926 he leased a 1,000,000-acre (404,686-hectare) rubber plantation in Liberia to control the output of raw rubber needed in his factories. See biography by Alfred Lief (1951).

firethorn: see PYRACANTHA.

fireweed, any of several plants that spring up in fire-swept regions, especially the great willow herb *Epilobium,* which is classified in the family Onagraceae (EVENING-PRIMROSE family).

fireworks: see PYROTECHNICS.

firing, process of treating clay or other plastic ceramic materials with heat to produce a hard, durable but brittle material such as pottery. Primitive potters baked their clay in an open fire, but for firing at higher temperatures and for the use of glaze, a KILN is needed. In general, pottery is fired once to harden it into biscuit ware, then a glaze is applied and fused with the clay by a second firing. China painting, enamel work, and STAINED GLASS also require firing. Temperatures of firing vary from about 1100°F (590°C) for fixing paint on glass to about 2800°F (1540°C) for producing hard porcelain. Certain ceramic materials, such as those used for rocket nose cones, are fired at still higher temperatures.

Firishta or **Ferishtah** (both: fĭrĭshtä'), c.1570–c.1620, Indian Muslim historian. His given name was Muhammad Kasim Hindu Shah. Under the patronage of the shah of Bijapur, he wrote a history of the Muslims in India from the 10th cent. His work, *History of the Rise of the Muhammadan Power in India* (tr. 1829), is a landmark in Indian historiography; without it the medieval period in India would be largely unknown. Although Firishta is considered uncritical and occasionally erroneous, he has preserved writings otherwise lost, and his history remains an important source.

Firozabad (fĭrō'zäbäd''), town (1971 pop. 133,945), Uttar Pradesh state, N central India. It is India's chief producer of glass bangles. Electrical, leather, and cotton goods are also manufactured. Firozabad is the administrative center of a district that grows cotton and grain. An ancient city on the site was destroyed by Muslims in the 16th cent. and rebuilt by Mogul emperor AKBAR (reigned 1556–1605).

first aid, immediate and temporary treatment of a victim of sudden illness or injury while awaiting the arrival of medical aid. Proper early measures may be instrumental in saving life and ensuring a better and more rapid recovery. The avoidance of unnecessary movement and overexcitation of the victim often prevents further injury. Conditions that require immediate attention to avert death include cessation of breathing (ASPHYXIA), severe bleeding, poisoning, and HEATSTROKE. The essentials of first aid treatment also include the correct bandaging of a wound; the application of splints for FRACTURES and dislocations; the effective methods of ARTIFICIAL RESPIRATION; and treatment of SHOCK, FROSTBITE, FAINTING, bites and stings, BURNS, and HEAT EXHAUSTION. See Red Cross literature for a complete description of first aid techniques.

Asphyxia and obstruction of air passages. Symptoms: Blue discoloration of face, tongue, lips; gasping; inability to speak; unconsciousness. Treatment: Encourage victim to cough up foreign objects in throat; as a last resort, rap victim between shoulder blades to dislodge object. For asphyxia caused by gas or fumes, remove victim to a clear atmosphere; use artificial respiration.

Bites and stings. Symptoms: Wound (animal or human bite) or swelling and pain (insect sting). Treatment: For animal and human bites, cleanse wound with water and cover; submit animal for rabies test. For poisonous snakebite apply constricting band 2 to 4 in. (5–10 cm) above the bite (between wound and victim's heart). Band should not be tight enough to stop pulsing of blood, i.e., it should be loose enough for index finger to be slipped between band and skin. Keep affected part lower than rest of body if possible. Prevent exertion and taking of stimulants by victim. For insect stings apply soothing lotions or cool compress; for severe reactions use artificial respiration; apply constricting band between site of sting and heart.

Bleeding (severe). Symptoms: External wound. Treatment: Apply pressure over wound with wad of sterile gauze or other clean material. If bleeding continues and no fracture is present, elevate wound. If bleeding still continues, apply pressure to blood vessels leading to area—in arm, press just below armpit; in leg, press against groin where thigh and trunk join. Use a TOURNIQUET (tight band that cuts off circulation) only when it has been decided that the sacrifice of a limb is necessary to save life.

Burns. Symptoms: Redness (first-degree burns), blistering (second-degree burns), charring of skin (third-degree burns). Treatment: Immerse burned part in cold water. For third-degree burns, do not immerse; cover with thick sterile dressing or clean cloths and keep burned part elevated. For chemical burns, wash with large quantity of water.

Drowning. Treatment: Immediate artificial respiration.

Fainting. Symptoms: Unconsciousness, paleness, rapid pulse, coldness of the skin, sweating. Treatment: Leave victim lying down, loosen clothing, if victim vomits, roll him to the side and wipe out mouth with fingers wrapped in cloth. Seek medical attention if recovery is not prompt.

Foreign body in eye. Symptoms: Pain, redness, burning, tears. Treatment: Pull down lower lid and remove unembedded object with clean tissue if it lies on the inner surface of lower lid. If object has not been located, pull upper lid forward and down over lower lid. Object can be removed from surface of upper eyelid by turning lid back over a swabstick or similar object and lifting off the foreign body with a clean tissue. Finally, flush the eye with water. If object is suspected to be embedded, apply a dry, protective dressing over eye and call physician. Keep victim from rubbing his eye. For chemical burns, flood eyes with water.

Fractures and joint injuries. Symptoms: Pain or tenderness, deformity of bones, swelling, discoloration. Treatment: Prevent movement of injured parts until splint is applied; treat for shock; if ambulance service is not available, splint entire limb before moving. For sprains, elevate affected part and apply cold compresses.

Frostbite. Symptoms: Numbness, pale, glossy skin, possible blistering. Treatment: Warm by placing victim indoors, remove covering, bathe frozen part in warm water; do not massage. For cold exposure, give artificial respiration. Warm victim by placing in blankets or warm water; if conscious give hot liquids by mouth.

Heat exhaustion. Symptoms: Pale, clammy skin, profuse perspiration, weakness, headache, possibly cramps. Treatment: Rest, cool atmosphere, cool salt water by mouth if conscious. In case of heat cramp, exert firm pressure on cramped muscle (usually abdomen or legs) to help relieve spasms.

Heatstroke. Symptoms: High temperature (as high as 108°F–112°F/42°C–44°C), hot dry skin, rapid pulse, possibly unconsciousness. Treatment: Undress victim and sponge with or immerse in cool water. Use fan or air conditioner.

Poisoning. Symptoms and signs: Information from victim or observer, stains about mouth, presence of poison container, breath odor, pupils contracted to pinpoint size from morphine or narcotics. Treatment: Dilute ingested poison by administering water or milk, administer specific antidote if described on label of commercial product. In most cases, induce vomiting. Do not induce vomiting if poison is strong acid, strong alkali, or petroleum product, or if victim is unconscious or convulsive.

Shock. Symptoms: Pale (or bluish) skin (in victim with dark skin examine inside of mouth and nailbeds for bluish coloration); cool skin, weakness, weak pulse; unresponsiveness and dilated pupils in later stages. Treatment: Keep victim lying down and covered enough to prevent loss of body heat. The body position should be adjusted according to the victim's injuries. Victims in shock may improve if the feet are raised 8 to 12 in. (20–30 cm). For ELECTRIC SHOCK, cut off current or separate victim from contact with electricity by using dry wood, rope, or cloth; administer artificial respiration.

Wound. Treatment: Stop severe bleeding. If bleeding is not severe cleanse wound, remove foreign objects from surface only, and cover with sterile or clean cloth.

Firth, Sir Charles Harding (fûrth), 1857–1936, English historian. He was educated at Oxford, and in 1883 he began a long career of teaching there. Under the influence of S. R. Gardiner, he edited texts and wrote works on 17th-century England; he became one of the greatest authorities on the English civil war. His *Oliver Cromwell* (1900) is still widely read. *Cromwell's Army* (1902), *The Last Years of the Protectorate* (1909; a continuation of Gardiner's great work), and *The House of Lords during the Civil War* (1910) complete the list of his major works. He was remarkable for his high standards of research in original materials and was a renowned editor. Although his writing tends to be somewhat dry, his powers of narration are considerable.

Firth, Raymond William, 1901–, British social anthropologist, b. Auckland, New Zealand. He was educated at Auckland Univ. and received his Ph.D. from the London School of Economics in 1927. He did much research in the Pacific and in West Africa, focusing chiefly on social organization and economic systems. He was professor of anthropology at the Univ. of London from 1944 to 1968. His works include *Economics of the New Zealand Maori* (1929, 2d ed. 1959), *We, the Tikopia* (1936, 2d ed. 1957), *Human Types* (1938, rev. ed. 1957), *Social Change in Tikopia* (1959), and *Symbols: Public and Private* (1973).

firth or **frith,** Scottish term applied to an arm of the sea, usually an estuary or strait. For Firth of Clyde, see CLYDE; for Firth of Forth, see FORTH.

Firuzabad (fĭrōō'zəbäd''), town (1966 pop. 8,718), Fars prov., S Iran, near Shiraz. The town has a noteworthy palace built (3rd cent.) by Ardashir I; it is a large rectangular building, 180 ft (55 m) wide and 300 ft (91 m) long. Firuzabad is said to be the birthplace of Firuzabadi (1329–1414), compiler of a great Arabic dictionary.

Fischart, Johann (yō'hän fĭsh'ärt), b. 1548, d. 1590 or 1591, German satirist and moralist. He lived in Strasbourg. He translated and paraphrased works by Rabelais called *Geschichtsklitterung* (1572, 1575, and 1590); by the Dutch writer Philip van Marnix, *Bienenkorb* [the beehive] (1579); and from a French source, *Jesuiterhütlein* [Jesuit's hat] (1580). Among his many works his versification of Till EULENSPIEGEL stories and his narrative poem *Das Glückhafft Schiff von Zürich* [the lucky boat of Zurich] (1576) are noteworthy. Fischart's writings are largely political and anti-Catholic polemics, witty and original.

Fischer, Bobby (Robert James Fischer), 1943–, American chess player, b. Chicago. He began to play chess as a child, and soon made a name for himself, becoming the U.S. chess champion in Jan., 1958; that year he also became the youngest international grand master in the history of the game. In late 1971 he qualified to challenge Boris SPASSKY for the world championship. Initially holding out for better playing conditions and more money, he finally arrived (July, 1972) for the match in Reykjavík, Iceland. Although he lost the first game to Spassky, he soon pulled ahead, defeating his opponent. He was the first American to win the world championship since the International Federation of Chess began running the matches in 1948. In June, 1974, Fischer resigned his title as the result of a dispute on international match rules with the International Federation of Chess.

Fischer, Emil (ā'mēl fĭsh'ər), 1852–1919, German organic chemist. He is especially noted for his researches on the structure and synthesis of sugars and of purines and purine base derivatives, e.g., caffeine; for this work he received the 1902 Nobel Prize in Chemistry. His many other valuable discoveries include a method of synthesizing polypeptides. He was an assistant of Adolf von Baeyer and was professor at the universities of Erlangen (1882–85), Würzburg (1885–92), and Berlin (from 1892).

Fischer, Fritz, 1908–, German historian. Appointed professor at the Univ. of Hamburg in 1948, he became famous as the result of his book *Griff nach der Weltmacht* (1961; tr. *Germany's Aims in the First World War,* 1967). His controversial thesis held that Germany's bid for world power before and during World War I was the main cause of the conflict in 1914. Fischer's unflattering picture of imperial Germany led to sharp criticism by German conservatives. In 1969 he published *Krieg der Illusionen,* a reinforcement of his earlier work that covered in greater detail the period before 1914.

Fischer-Dieskau, Dietrich (dē'trĭkh fĭsh'ər-dēs'-kou), 1925–, German baritone. He served in the German army during World War II and was an American prisoner of war in Italy for two years. He made his debut at the State Opera in Berlin in 1948 singing Rodrigo in Verdi's *Don Carlo.* Possessed of a sensitive voice capable of a wide variety of range and expression, Fischer-Dieskau is regarded as one of the foremost singers of German lieder. He is particularly noted for his interpretations of the songs and song cycles of Brahms, Schubert, Schumann, and Wolf. He has also performed many roles in German and Italian opera. During the early 1970s, Fischer-Dieskau began to appear as a conductor.

Fischer-Tropsch process (fĭsh'ər-trōpsh), method for the synthesis of hydrocarbons and other aliphatic compounds. Synthesis gas, a mixture of hydrogen and carbon monoxide, is reacted in the presence of an iron or cobalt catalyst; much heat is evolved, and such products as methane, synthetic gasoline and waxes, and alcohols are made, with water or carbon dioxide produced as a by-product. An important source of the hydrogen-carbon monoxide gas mixture is the gasification of coal (see WATER GAS). The process is named after F. Fischer and H. Tropsch, the German coal researchers who discovered it in 1923.

Fischer von Erlach, Johann Bernhard (yō'hän bĕrn'härt fĭsh'ər fən ĕr'läkh), 1656–1723, Austrian architect and decorator. After studying in Rome he returned to Vienna. In 1705 he was appointed imperial court architect. His early works, exuberant examples of the high baroque, include his redecoration of the mausoleum of Ferdinand II at Graz and the Hercules fountain in Brünn. In the Dreifaltigkeitssäule monument in Vienna he designed masses of stone to give the appearance of billows of cloud and smoke. Among his major buildings in Salzburg are the Church of the Trinity (1694–1710) and the University Church (1694–1707) and in Vienna the royal library (1722) and the Karlskirche or Church of San Carlo Borromeo (1715–37). They are characterized by a richness of wall surface, achieved by the ingenious use of curves and ovals. He wrote *A Plan of Civil and Historical Architecture* (tr. 1973). See biography by Hans Aurenhammer (tr. 1974).

Fish, family long prominent in New York politics. **Nicholas Fish,** 1758–1833, b. New York City. He studied law before serving ably as a major in a New York regiment throughout the American Revolution. A New York City alderman (1806–17), he was a leading Federalist and a close friend of Alexander Hamilton. He also served (1824–32) as chairman of the board of trustees of Columbia College, a post later held by his son, Hamilton Fish (1808–93), the most illustrious member of the clan (see separate articles for Hamilton Fish, 1808–93, and for his youngest son, Stuyvesant Fish). **Nicholas Fish**, 1848–1902, b. New York City, was Hamilton's eldest son. He entered (1871) the U.S. diplomatic service and was minister to Belgium (1882–86). A third son, **Hamilton Fish**, 1849–1936, b. Albany, N.Y., studied law and was admitted to the bar in 1873. He was a member of the New York state assembly (1874–96), serving as speaker in 1895–96, and was long Republican boss of Putnam co. On appointment by President Theodore Roosevelt, he was Assistant Treasurer of the United States in New York City (1903–8). He also served (1909–11) as a U.S. Representative. The family's third **Hamilton Fish**, 1888–, son of the foregoing, b. Garrison, N.Y., was a famous football player at Harvard. A lawyer, Fish served in the New York state assembly (1914–16), distinguished himself in World War I as a captain of Negro infantry, and from 1920 to 1945 was a U.S. Representative. A leading isolationist and vigorous anti-Communist, once accused of having connections with the Bundists and with other Axis supporters, he was opposed for renomination in 1944 by Gov. Thomas E. Dewey and other Republican leaders. Fish, nevertheless won the primary but was defeated for reelection in November. His son **Hamilton Fish**, 1926–, b. Washington, D.C., continued the family's involvement in Republican politics. Admitted to the bar in 1957, he was elected to the U.S. House of Representatives from New York in 1968.

Fish, Carl Russell, 1876–1932, American historian, b. Central Falls, R.I. From 1900 to his death he taught history at the Univ. of Wisconsin. Fish considered the Univ. of Wisconsin the "most democratic institution in America," and he was extremely popular there among both students and colleagues. He wrote *The Civil Service and the Patronage* (1904, repr. 1963); *The Development of American Nationality* (1913, rev. ed. 1940), a useful and popular textbook; *American Diplomacy* (1915, 5th ed. 1929); *The Path of Empire* ("Chronicles of America" series, 1919); *The Rise of the Common Man, 1830–1850* ("History of American Life" Vol. VI, 1927, repr. 1971); and *The American Civil War: an Interpretation* (ed. by William E. Smith, 1937).

Fish, Hamilton, 1808–93, American statesman, b. New York City, grad. Columbia, 1827; son of Nicholas Fish (1758–1833). He studied law and was admitted to the bar in 1830. Named for his father's friend Alexander Hamilton, and heir to the Federalist tradition, Fish naturally gravitated to politics as a Whig. He served as U.S. Representative (1843–45), and was elected lieutenant governor of New York in 1847 and governor, for a two-year term, in 1848. From 1851 to 1857, Fish was a U.S. Senator, serving on the foreign relations committee in 1855–57. A moderate antislavery man, he opposed both abolitionist and proslavery excesses and deplored the breakup of the Whigs as a national party. Slow to join the new Republican party, he lost his national political standing but became prominent in civic activities in New York. Fish was one of many to lionize the victorious Civil War general Ulysses S. GRANT, but his appointment (March, 1869) as Grant's Secretary of State, to succeed the grossly miscast Elihu B. Washburne, came as a surprise. He accepted reluctantly and expected to hold the office for only a few months, but actually remained in the cabinet longer than any other member, serving through both of Grant's administrations. He was one of the ablest of U.S. Secretaries of State. His greatest achievement as Secretary was bringing about the treaty (see WASHINGTON, TREATY OF) that paved the way for settlement of the Alabama claims and other long-standing disputes with Great Britain. This was accomplished amid great difficulties, especially those offered by the vigorously anti-British chairman of the Senate foreign relations committee, Charles SUMNER. The period was one of constant trouble with Spain, arising out of the Ten Years War, and Fish was hard pressed to persuade Grant not to recognize the belligerency of Cuba. Under Fish's vigilant eye filibustering expeditions from the United States to Cuba were kept to a minimum, but the VIRGINIUS affair in 1873 nearly brought the nation, long sympathetic to the Cuban cause, to war with Spain. To secure Grant's support of other policies Fish supported without enthusiasm the President's unsuccessful project to annex Santo Domingo. Grant was much impressed with Fish's character and ability, and he called upon Fish's aid in the administration of domestic affairs as well. See Allan Nevins, *Hamilton Fish: the Inner History of the Grant Administration* (1936, repr. 1957).

Fish, Hamilton, 1849–1936, 1888–, and 1926–: see FISH, family.

Fish, Nicholas, 1758–1833, and 1848–1902: see FISH, family.

Fish, Stuyvesant (stī'vəsənt), 1851–1923, American railroad executive, b. New York City; son of Hamilton Fish (1808–93). He became (1877) a director of the Illinois Central RR, and as its president (1887–1907) he built the railroad into a large system. Fish was ousted from the presidency by E. H. Harriman after Fish's participation in the state committee that investigated (1906) the Mutual Life Insurance Company of New York.

fish, limbless aquatic vertebrate animal with fins and internal gills. There are three living classes of fish: the primitive jawless fishes, or Agnatha; the cartilaginous (sharklike) fishes, or Chondrichthyes; and the bony fishes, or Osteichthyes. These groups, although quite different from one another anatomically, have certain common features related to their common evolutionary origins or to their aquatic way of life. A typical fish is torpedo-shaped, with a head containing a brain and sensory organs, a trunk with a muscular wall surrounding a cavity containing the internal organs, and a muscular post-anal tail. Most fish propel themselves through the water by weaving movements of their bodies and control their direction by means of the FINS. All have skins covered with slimy glandular secretions that decrease friction with the water; in addition, nearly all have SCALES, which together with the secretions form a nearly waterproof coating. All fishes have a lateral line system of sensory organs for detecting pressure changes in the water. All have water-breathing organs called GILLS located in passages leading from the throat, or pharynx, to the exterior; a few fishes also have air-breathing lungs as an additional means of respiration. In all but the most primitive class, the gill passages are supported by skeletal structures called gill arches. Fish breathe by taking water into the mouth and forcing it out through the gill passages; as the water passes over the thin-walled gills, dissolved oxygen diffuses into the gill capillaries and carbon dioxide diffuses out. The circulatory system is closed, and the heart is two-chambered; the blood is red. With few exceptions, fish are cold-blooded; that is, they cannot regulate their body temperature, which is the same as that of the environment. A number of aquatic invertebrate animals and groups have common names that include the term *fish* (for example, crayfish and shellfish), but these do not resemble and and are not related to true fishes. Furthermore, there are members of the terrestrial vertebrate classes, such as whales and sea snakes, that have adopted an aquatic way of life; these may superficially resemble fishes and are sometimes erroneously called fishes, but they are air-breathers, and their anatomical structure reveals their relationship to land animals. Fish were the earliest vertebrates and presumably evolved from a group of aquatic lower chordates (see CHORDATA); the terrestrial vertebrates evolved from fishes. The primitive fishes of the class Agnatha lack jaws and the paired pelvic and pectoral fins characteristic of more advanced fishes. This largely extinct class includes two living groups, the blood-sucking lampreys and the scavenging HAGFISHES. Fishes of the extinct class Placodermi were the first vertebrates to develop jaws and paired fins. These fish had bony skeletons and were covered with bony armor. A branch of this group probably gave rise to the two main modern classes of fish, the cartilaginous fish and the bony fish. The cartilaginous fish (SHARKS, RAYS, and CHIMAERAS) are distinguished from the bony fish by their cartilage skeletons, by the absence of either a SWIM BLADDER or lungs, by the construction of their tail fins, and by the absence in most of a gill covering, or operculum. The skin of members of this group is covered with imbedded toothlike structures called denticles, giving it a rough, sandpapery quality. Sharks are almost exclusively marine in distribution. The bony fishes are distinguished from other living fishes by their bone skeletons and by the presence of either a swim bladder (which functions as a float) or, in a few fishes, lungs. The bony fishes are divided into two subclasses, the fleshy-finned fish and the ray-finned fish. The latter group includes over 95% of all living fish species. The earliest bony fishes were fleshy-finned. They evolved during a period of widespread draught and stagnation and gave rise to the amphibians (the first terrestrial vertebrates) on the one hand and to the ray-finned fish on the other. The only surviving fleshy-finned fishes are the LUNGFISHES and one species of coelacanth (see LOBEFIN). These fishes retain some of the traits of ancestral bony fishes: fleshy fins with supporting bones (precursors of the limbs of land vertebrates), internal nostrils, and lungs. Ray-finned fishes, now predominant in both fresh and marine waters, represent an advanced adaptation of the bony fishes to strictly aquatic conditions; they are the most highly successful and diverse of the fishes. In nearly all of these fishes the lung has evolved into a hydrostatic organ, the swim bladder. The fins in this group consist of a web of skin supported by horny rays. Each ray is moved by

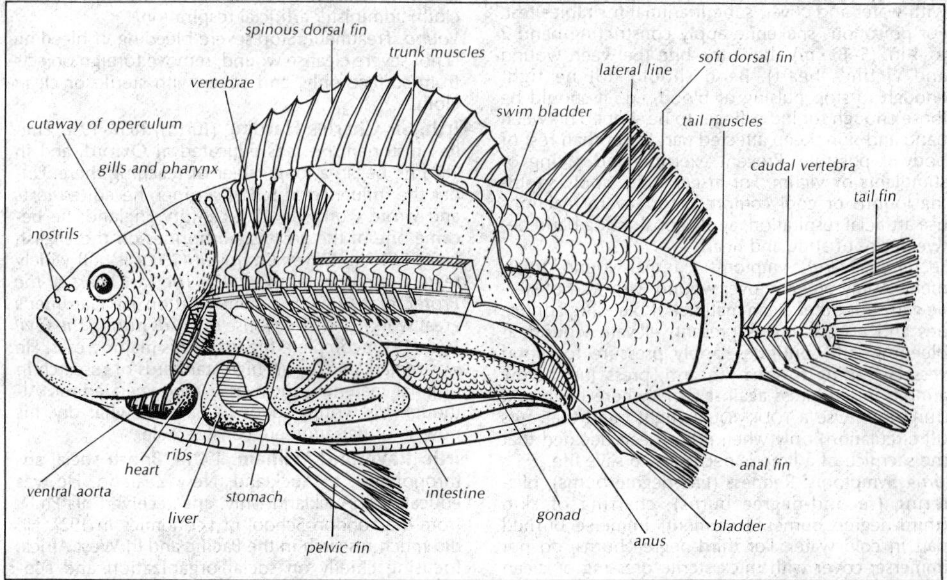

Anatomy of a ray-finned fish

a set of muscles, giving the fin great flexibility. Most ray-finned fish have overlapping scales made of very thin layers of bone. Their skeletal structure is light but strong. Their brains are complex, and most have excellent vision. There are over 20,000 living species of fish. They range in size from the ½-in. (1.3-cm) goby of the Philippines to the 45-ft (14-m) whale shark. Many are brightly colored, and many have shapes and patterns that serve as camouflage. They are found in all marine, fresh, and brackish waters throughout the world and at all depths. Members of different species of fish tolerate water temperatures ranging from freezing to over 100°F (38°C). Most are confined either to salt water or to fresh water, but some are physiologically adapted to moving from one to the other. A number of fishes that are born in fresh water spend their adult lives in the ocean, returning to their birthplace to spawn; the reverse of this migration occurs in some fishes born in the ocean. Many fishes stay in tightly organized groups, called schools; others are solitary, and congregate only for feeding and spawning. Fish may be carnivorous, herbivorous, or omnivorous. Plankton-feeding fish have structures called gill rakers attached to the gill arches; these strain minute organisms from the water as it passes out of the pharynx. Some fish are scavengers on lake or ocean bottoms. Methods of reproduction are varied. Sharks have internal fertilization, and most give birth to live young. Those that lay eggs produce large ones with tough shells. Since embryonic development is well-protected in these fish, they produce a relatively small number of young, only seven or eight at a time in some species. A few of the bony fishes, including some aquarium species, are live bearers, but most lay small, unprotected eggs that are fertilized after deposition in water. In most marine species the eggs float freely in the currents, where they are eaten by other animals. An enormous number of eggs is therefore necessary to ensure the maturation of a few; in many species a female produces as many as 5 million eggs in one spawn. The eggs of most marine fishes contain oil droplets that buoy them up, while those of most freshwater fishes are heavy, with sticky surfaces that adhere to objects in the water. Most freshwater species build nests for the protection of the eggs, and in some the adults guard the nests. Fish are a major source of human food as well as of oil, fertilizer, and feed for domestic animals (see FISHING). See U. N. Lanham, *The Fishes* (1967); W. S. Hoar and D. J. Randall, *Fish Physiology* (6 vol., 1969–71); E. S. Herald, *Living Fishes of the World* (1961) and *Fishes of North America* (1972).

fish curing. Methods of curing fish by drying, salting, smoking, and pickling, or by combinations of these processes have been employed since ancient times. On sailing vessels fish were usually salted down immediately to prevent spoilage; the swifter boats of today commonly bring in unsalted fish. Modern freezing and canning methods have largely supplanted older methods of preservation. Fish to be cured are usually first cleaned, scaled, and eviscerated. Fish are salted by packing them between layers of salt or by immersion in brine. The fish most extensively salted are cod, herring, mackerel, and haddock. Smoking preserves fish by drying, by deposition of creosote ingredients, and, when the fish are near the source of heat, by heat penetration. Herring and haddock (finnan haddie) are commonly smoked. Kippers are split herring, and bloaters are whole herring, salted and smoked. Sardines, pilchards, and anchovies are small fish of the herring family, often salted and smoked and then preserved in oil. Fish are dried under controlled conditions of temperature, humidity, and air velocity. Since the dried product is relatively unappetizing and rehydration slow, other preservation methods are more common.

Fisher, Andrew, 1862–1928, Australian statesman. He emigrated from Scotland to Australia in 1885, helped organize the Australian Labour party, and served three times as Labour prime minister of Australia (1908–9, 1910–13, and 1914–15). He guided the passage of much social legislation in the fields of taxation, banking, and land policy. After his last ministry he served as high commissioner in London.

Fisher, Dorothy Canfield, 1879–1958, American novelist and juvenile writer, b. Lawrence, Kansas, grad. Ohio State, 1899, Ph.D. Columbia, 1904. Her novels include *The Bent Twig* (1915), *The Deepening Stream* (1930), *Seasoned Timber* (1939) and *Four-square* (1949). She also wrote short stories; *Vermont Tradition* (1953), personal views of Vermont life; and several notable juvenile books, including *Understood Betsy* (1916) and *Something Old, Something New* (1949).

Fisher, Geoffrey Francis, 1887–1972, archbishop of Canterbury (1945–61). He was educated at Oxford and ordained priest in 1913. For 21 years he was an educator, serving as assistant master of Marlborough College (1911–14) and as headmaster of Repton School (1914–32). In 1932 he became bishop of Chester; from 1939 to 1945 he was bishop of London. As archbishop of Canterbury (1945–61) he traveled widely in the interest of church unity. His visit to the pope in 1960 was the first by the archbishop of Canterbury since the Reformation. He was president of the World Council of Churches from 1946 to 1954. Upon his retirement in 1961 he was raised to the peerage.

Fisher, Herbert Albert Laurens, 1865–1940, English historian. In addition to his academic career at New College, Oxford, and at the Univ. of Sheffield, he led a distinguished public life. A member of Parliament (1916–26) and president of the Board of Education (1916–22), he was responsible for the law of 1918 that broadened and liberalized public education. As a historian, Fisher stressed political and religious elements over economic ones. He was an expert on the Napoleonic era, and his studies of the period include a biography of Napoleon (1913). His other works include an impressive *History of Europe* (3 vol., 1935–36) and lives of the historians F. W. Maitland (1910), Lord Bryce (1927), and Sir Paul Vinogradoff (1927). See his *Unfinished Autobiography* (1941); biography by David Ogg (1947).

Fisher, Irving, 1867–1947, American economist, b. Saugerties, N.Y., Ph.D. Yale, 1891. He began teaching at Yale in 1890 and was active there until 1935. His earliest work was in mathematics, and he made a distinguished contribution to mathematical economic theory. He was noted chiefly for his studies in managed currency, in which he set forth the theory of the "compensated dollar" whereby purchasing power might be stabilized. He was also one of the first to work out a numbered index system for filing. Fisher's interests were wide; they included activities in academic, business, welfare, and public organizations, especially public health societies. Important among his many books are *Mathematical Investigations in the Theory of Value and Prices* (1892), *Appreciation and Interest* (1896), *The Nature of Capital and Income* (1906), *The Rate of Interest* (1907), *The Making of Index Numbers* (1922), and *Theory of Interest* (1930). See biography by his son, I. N. Fisher (1956).

Fisher, John (Saint John Fisher), c.1469–1535, English prelate, cardinal, bishop of Rochester (1504–34). Known for his scholarship at Cambridge, he was chosen confessor to Margaret Beaufort, mother of Henry VII. As vice chancellor of the university (1501–4) and chancellor thereafter, he helped carry out her plans for establishing St. John's College and Christ's College. As bishop he was firm in his denunciation of abuses by the clergy; however, he resisted reforms, like those of Martin Luther, that affected doctrines of the church. Giving his support to the new learning, he brought Erasmus to lecture at the university. Fisher, who was confessor to Katharine of Aragón, was the only English bishop to oppose the invalidation of the marriage of Henry VIII and Katharine. He refused to acknowledge the king as supreme head of the church and to accede to the Act of Succession, which declared Katharine's child (Mary I) illegitimate. In 1534 he was imprisoned in the Tower and deprived of his bishopric. Pope Paul III, to show his support, created Fisher a cardinal in May, 1535. Henry, infuriated, pushed the trial forward. A fortnight before Sir Thomas More was executed, Fisher was beheaded on Tower Hill. He was canonized as a martyr in 1935. Most of the Latin writings that he left were published in 1597. Some of his English works still remain in manuscript. Feast: July 9. See Thomas Bayly, *The Life and Death of That Renowned John Fisher, Bishop of Rochester* (1635, new ed. 1893); biography by E. E. Reynolds (1955); study by E. L. Surtz (1967).

Fisher, John Arbuthnot Fisher, 1st Baron (ärbŭth'nət), 1841–1920, British admiral. Entering the navy in 1854, he specialized in gunnery and in 1872 was responsible for instituting the developmental work that perfected the torpedo. He was director of ordnance and torpedoes at the admiralty (1886–90), third sea lord and controller of the navy (1892–97), and commander in chief of the Mediterranean fleet (1899–1902). As second sea lord (1902–3) he reorganized and improved the method of training naval officers. Returning to the admiralty as first sea lord (1904), Fisher redistributed British naval forces to meet the newly recognized threat from Germany. In 1905 he began construction of the *Dreadnought* (see BATTLESHIP) and thereafter pressed hard for an expanded program of naval construction. He encouraged the development of submarines and supervised the conversion of the navy from steam to oil power. Created a baron in 1909, Fisher resigned as first sea lord in 1910 but returned to that position after the outbreak (1914) of World War I. He advocated an amphibious strike against Germany in the Baltic but opposed the Dardanelles expedition and resigned (1915) because of it. His reforms proved crucial to Britain's wartime naval supremacy. See his correspondence, ed. A. J. Marder (3 vol., 1952–59); biographies by R. H. Bacon (1929), R. A. Hough (1969), and R. F. Mackay (1973); A. J. Marder, *From the Dreadnought to Scapa Flow* (5 vol., 1961–70).

fisher, name of a large North American MARTEN, *Martes pennanti*. This carnivorous, largely arboreal mammal is found in hardwood forests of Canada, the extreme N United States, and mountain ranges of the W United States. Fishers have dark brown fur shading to black and frosted with white-tipped hairs. Males are over 3 ft (90 cm) long, including the bushy tail, which may reach 15 in. (38 cm), and weigh 6 to 12 lb (1.8–3.6 kg); females weigh about half as much. Active both by night and by day, on the ground and in trees, the fisher makes its den in a hollow tree or a hole in the ground. It feeds on small mammals, birds, carrion, and fruits. Despite its name, it does not catch fish, although it will eat them. It is one of the few animals that eats porcupines, which it attacks by striking at the unprotected underparts. The fisher is not abundant and is difficult to trap; its beautiful fur brings high prices. Once considered threatened with extinction, fishers are now increasing in numbers. They are classified in the phylum CHORDATA, subphylum Vertebrata, class Mammalia, order Carnivora, family Mustelidae.

Fisher, Fort: see FORT FISHER.

fisheries. From earliest times and in practically all countries, fisheries have been of industrial and commercial importance. In the large N Atlantic fishing grounds off Newfoundland and Labrador, European and American fishing fleets have been taking cod, herring, haddock, and mackerel for centuries. Today the largest and most valuable U.S. catch—mainly shrimp—is made in the Gulf of Mexico. Other valuable U.S. catches are tuna, salmon, crab, oyster, and lobster. Peru is the world's leading fishing nation, followed by Japan, the USSR, and China. The United States and Norway vie for fifth place. In 1971 more than 76.5 million tons of fish were taken by all fishing nations. The commercial methods chiefly in use today—each with a great variety of modifications—employ encircling nets (purse seine, haul seine, trawl seine), entangling nets (gill and trammel), line, and trap (for lobster and crab). Trawlers and purse boats take most commercial catches. Since World War II, Japan and the USSR have been operating factory ships that freeze or can fish shortly after they are caught. The drying, canning, salting, and preserving of fish comprise a vast industry with, in addition, the manufacture of numerous by-products, including glue, fertilizer, and in the Orient, fish sauces. In the United States, since all waters within a state are subject to state jurisdiction, domestic fisheries are governed by state regulations, except when national control results from the treaty-making power and except for the regulation of navigation, customs, and interstate commerce, which are granted to the Federal government by the Constitution. Agreements between states concerning fishing in boundary waters (such as that between Washington and Oregon concerning the Columbia River salmon fisheries) require the ratification of Congress. State fishery legislation is generally both restrictive and protective. Fish may be protected by imposing closed seasons during the spawning season or for the period necessary for the increase of depleted species; certain waters may be entirely closed to commercial fishing; and the taking of fish below a certain size may be forbidden. Undesirable types of fishing gear are prohibited and the use of other apparatus restricted. State statutes forbidding the pollution or the obstruction of nonnavigable streams are general. National governments generally restrict fishing rights within territorial waters to citizens and may establish jurisdiction over portions of the open sea, often for the purpose of protecting shore fisheries (Chesapeake Bay and Delaware Bay thus constitute closed seas). While a national government may regulate the high-seas fisheries of its own citizens, the right to take products from the high seas is a subject for international agreements. Fisheries have occupied an important place in the economic structure of many countries throughout history. The

Black Sea fisheries formed an important source of Phoenician and Greek income; Spanish and Sicilian waters yielded fish for Rome; the economy of the Hanseatic League was partly based on the North Sea herring fisheries; cod fishing was a chief industry of New England; and fisheries in the Pacific are vital to Japan. For that reason fishing rights have long been the basis of controversy. In the modern age such disputes have generally been settled by arbitration or by treaties. Fishing rights, which had been enjoyed by the American colonists on the entire Atlantic coast, were confirmed in the Treaty of Paris (1783), but the right to dry fish on the Newfoundland coast and on the settled parts of the Labrador and Nova Scotian coasts (except by agreement with the inhabitants) was expressly denied. That treaty was abrogated by the British upon the outbreak of the War of 1812, and the Treaty of Ghent (1814) contained no provisions relating to the controversial issue of fishing rights. Friction developed, and, after prolonged parleying, another treaty further restricting American rights was negotiated (1818). This convention was replaced by the reciprocity treaty of 1854, which abolished all restrictions except for shellfish. The United States abrogated the treaty in 1866, but a new treaty (1871, with a protocol in 1873) revived the provisions of the agreement of 1854 (to lat. 39°N). Since the Canadians declared their waters more valuable than those of the United States, the question was arbitrated, and Canada received an award of $5,500,000 (1877). When the United States denounced the treaty (1885), American vessels were again seized and strained relations resulted. In 1910, however, the North Atlantic Coast Fisheries Arbitration at The Hague ended the prolonged controversy. Canada and the United States in 1923 and 1930 signed agreements regulating the halibut fisheries of the N Pacific. In 1882, Great Britain, Germany, France, Denmark, and Belgium signed the North Sea Fisheries Convention, which ended lawlessness in that area by granting a mutual right of visit, search, and arrest to the public vessels of the treaty powers. A similar treaty, regulating the fishing banks off Iceland and the Faeroe Islands, was signed by Great Britain and Denmark in 1901, and three years later Anglo-French rights in the N Atlantic were set forth in a convention. The fisheries of the Pacific have also been the subject of many international agreements, such as the Japanese right to fish in specified sections of Siberian waters, first granted by the Treaty of Portsmouth in 1905 and continued by later agreements. One of the most celebrated contentions about territorial rights in waters concerned not fishing proper but the hunting of fur seals (see BERING SEA). New international problems raised in recent years involve territorial limits and marine pollution. Current international practice recognizes a 12-mi exclusive fisheries zone, but some nations—among them Peru, Ecuador, Argentina, and Brazil—claim territorial jurisdiction up to 200 mi. To stabilize international rules governing national rights in the oceans, the United Nations began an ongoing Conference on the Law of the Sea in the summer of 1974. A prime concern of the conference is pollution. The oceans have long been used as a dumping ground, but in recent years levels of pollutants in the open seas as well as in coastal areas have risen sharply. Nuclear wastes, heavy metals, dredge spoils, pesticides and other persistent petrochemicals, plastics, accidentally spilled oil, deliberately discharged ship bilge, and sewage—all threaten marine ecology and resources and thus global food supplies (see WATER POLLUTION). The FOOD AND AGRICULTURE ORGANIZATION of the United Nations has done important work in developing fisheries by transmitting information on fishing techniques to underdeveloped nations. See Robert Morgan, *World Sea Fisheries* (1956); M. E. Stansby, *Industrial Fishery Technology* (1963); W. D. Russel-Hunter, *Aquatic Productivity* (1970).

Fishers Hill, bluff, near Strasburg, Va., in the Shenandoah Valley; site of Union Gen. Philip Sheridan's defeat of Gen. Jubal Early on Sept. 22, 1864, during the Civil War. After routing Early's army, Sheridan destroyed the valley's farms and crops, an important Confederate food source.

Fishes, The, English name for PISCES, a CONSTELLATION.

fish hawk: see OSPREY.

fishing, act of catching fish for consumption or display. Fishing—usually by hand, club, spear, or net, and possibly by hook—was known to prehistoric man. It was practiced by the ancient Persians, Egyptians, and Chinese, and it is mentioned in the *Odyssey* and in the Bible. It is a major means of subsistence and livelihood today, not only in simple societies such as those in the South Pacific but also in most nations of the world (see FISHERIES). The development of fishing as a sport or pastime is comparatively recent, although books on angling have been published since the early 16th cent.; the most famous work is Izaak Walton's *The Compleat Angler* (1653). The basic equipment of the modern sport fisherman consists of a barbed metal hook at the end of a nylon or Dacron line, and a wood, fiberglass, or metal rod, or pole, that usually has some type of spool, or reel, near the handle, around which the line is wound. Recreational fishing, which is practiced throughout the world, may be done in either fresh or salt water. There are two basic types of freshwater tackle, those for fly casting and those for bait casting. Fly rods and reels are light and require that a hooked fish be "played" rather than reeled in by force; they are used to catch fish that inhabit running streams, such as trout and salmon. Live bait (worms, insects, minnows, or frogs) or artificial flies and lures are cast into or on the stream as an enticement for the fish to bite. A sturdier rod and reel are used for bait casting, which is done mainly in lakes and large rivers. Live bait or a variety of plugs, spoons, and other artificial lures can be cast and pulled in, "popped" along the surface, trolled from a moving boat, or allowed to rest near the bottom. Spinning tackle, which greatly simplifies bait casting by allowing the line to unwind more evenly, has become very popular. The familiar bamboo pole, without reel, can be used for still fishing. Heavier rods and reels of the bait-casting type are used in saltwater fishing; trolling and casting from the surf are the usual methods. Big game fishing is a type of saltwater recreation in which sportsmen troll at great depths for large fish such as tuna, swordfish, and shark. The most popular game fish are salmon, trout, bass, and pike in fresh water, and sailfish, tuna, marlin, tarpon, and bonefish in salt water. However, fishermen generally are pleased with anything that bites, other than turtles. Fishing with handlines through holes in the ice, and spearfishing under water are other popular ways of taking game fish. There are many annual tournaments both for catching fish and for accuracy and distance in casting; records are kept for the largest catch in each species. The largest known catch of any type was a 2,664-lb (1208-kg) white shark that was caught off the Australian coast (1959). In the United States each state issues fishing licenses and sets regulations as to the season in which a certain species of fish may be caught, the minimum permissible size, and the number that may be taken per day. The International Game Fish Association (founded 1939) standardizes rules for saltwater fishing throughout the world. See William Radcliffe, *Fishing from Earliest Times* (1921); Ira N. Gabrielson, *The New Fisherman's Encyclopedia* (1963); Andres von Brandt, *Fish Catching Methods of the World* (2d ed. 1972).

Fisk, James, 1834–72, American financial speculator, b. Pownal, Vt. In his youth he worked for a circus and as a wagon peddler of merchandise. During the Civil War he became wealthy purchasing cotton in occupied areas of the South for Northern firms and selling Confederate bonds in England. In 1866 he established a brokerage house in New York City with the aid of Daniel Drew, whom he had formerly served as agent. He audaciously helped Drew and Jay Gould conduct the famous struggle with Cornelius Vanderbilt for control of the Erie RR. Afterward he and Gould unscrupulously manipulated Erie stock so as to gain millions for themselves but wreck the road. They also engineered the attempt to corner the gold market in 1869, causing the famous BLACK FRIDAY scandal. Other raids by Fisk and his associates upset markets and aroused public indignation. Fisk controlled the Fall River and Bristol steamboat lines on Long Island Sound, operated ferries on the Hudson, and bought an opera house in New York City, producing drama and light opera there. He was killed by Edward S. Stokes, a former business associate who was a rival for the attentions of the well-known actress Josie Mansfield. See C. F. Adams and Henry Adams, *Chapters of Erie* (1871); W. A. Swanberg, *Jim Fisk* (1959).

Fisk, Willbur, 1792–1839, American clergyman and educator, b. Brattleboro, Vt. Ordained a Methodist minister in 1818, he rapidly became a leader of that denomination in New England. In 1825, Fisk helped to reestablish Wesleyan Academy at Wilbraham, Mass., and became its principal. He was a founder (1831) and first president of Wesleyan Univ., Middletown, Conn. See biographies by Joseph Holditch (1842) and George Prentice (1890).

Fiske, Bradley Allen (fĭsk), 1854–1942, American naval officer and inventor, b. Lyons, N.Y., grad. Annapolis, 1874. In the U.S. navy he devoted himself to the invention of instruments for shipboard use. His numerous inventions include an electrically powered gun turret, the torpedo plane, a naval telescopic sight, an electromagnetic system for detonating torpedos under ships, and an electric range finder—a device that brought him many citations when, as navigating officer of the gunboat *Petrel,* he successfully employed it in the battle of Manila Bay. He was promoted to rear admiral in 1911, but he was forced to retire in 1916 when his agitation for a stronger navy clashed with the policies of Secretary of the Navy Josephus Daniels. See his autobiography, *From Midshipman to Admiral* (1919).

Fiske, John, 1842–1901, American philosopher and historian, b. Hartford, Conn. Born Edmund Fisk Green, he changed his name in 1855 to John Fisk, adding the final *e* in 1860. He opened a law practice in Boston but soon turned to writing. A wide reader, he had been an enthusiastic follower of Herbert Spencer while in college, and the first part of his life was given mainly to popularizing Spencerian evolution. He tried to reconcile orthodox religious beliefs with science, both on the lecture platform and in such books as *Outlines of Cosmic Philosophy* (1874, repr. 1969), *Darwinism and Other Essays* (1879, repr. 1913), *Excursions of an Evolutionist* (1884), *The Idea of God as Affected by Modern Knowledge* (1886), and *Through Nature to God* (1899). Early in his career Fiske also achieved popularity as a lecturer on history and in his later life was occupied mostly with that field. His historical writings include *The Critical Period of American History, 1783–1789* (1888), *The Beginnings of New England* (1889), *The American Revolution* (1891), *The Discovery of America* (1892), *Old Virginia and Her Neighbors* (1897), *Dutch and Quaker Colonies in America* (1899), *The Mississippi Valley in the Civil War* (1900), and *New France and New England* (1902). These books were popular accounts based largely on secondary authorities and noted for an easy, lucid, and dramatic style. See *The Letters of John Fiske* (ed. by his daughter, Ethel F. Fisk, 1940); biographies by Milton Berman (1961) and G. P. Winston (1972); H. B. Pannill, *The Religious Faith of John Fiske* (1957).

Fiske, Minnie Maddern, 1865–1932, American actress, b. New Orleans. For more than a generation she was a leading figure in the theatrical world. Born of a family of actors, she spent her childhood on the stage, retiring in 1890 to marry Harrison Grey Fiske, the editor of the New York *Dramatic Mirror.* She returned to the stage in 1893 to star in his *Hester Crewe,* appearing thereafter under his management. *A Doll's House* (1894) and later *Ghosts* and *Hedda Gabler* established Fiske as one of the greatest interpreters of the intellectual drama of her time. Her Becky Sharp and Tess of the D'Urbervilles were particularly admired, although she was best loved as a comedienne. Fiske's revival of Sheridan's *Rivals* toured the country almost to the time of her death. In 1901 she opened the Manhattan Theatre in New York City, and was influential in combating the powerful and destructive monopoly of the 1890s: the Theatrical Syndicate. A director of great talents, she encouraged young playwrights; her company was noted for their fine productions. See biography by Archie Binns and Olive Kooken (1955); *Mrs. Fiske: Her Views on the Stage,* ed. by Alexander Woollcott (1917, repr. 1968).

Fisk University, at Nashville, Tenn.; coeducational; founded 1865, opened 1866, and chartered 1867. It is divided into the Basic College (a general education program for freshman and sophomore years) and the College of Higher Studies, which offers specialized instruction and research leading to undergraduate and graduate degrees. Fisk, long an outstanding Negro school, is now open to all qualified students. The Cravath Memorial Library is especially noted for its Negro Collection.

fission, in physics: see NUCLEAR ENERGY; NUCLEUS.

fistula (fĭs'cho͝olə), abnormal, usually ulcerous channel-like formation between two internal organs or between an internal organ and the skin. It may follow a surgical procedure with improper healing, or it may be caused by injury, abscess, or infection with penetration deep enough to reach another organ or the skin. When open at only one end it is called an incomplete fistula or sinus. The most common sites of fistula are the rectum and the urinary organs, but almost any part of the body may be affected. Rectal fistulas are often associated with colitis, cancer, venereal disease, and other disorders. Usually a fistula requires surgery. In horses an abscess on the withers from chafing and infection is termed a fistula.

Fitch, Clyde (William Clyde Fitch), 1865-1909, American dramatist, b. Elmira, N.Y. An extremely prolific and versatile playwright, he wrote over 36 original plays, including melodramas, farces, social comedies, and historical dramas. Much of his best work reflects American social life of the period. Among his most notable plays are *Nathan Hale* (1898), *The Climbers* (1901), *The Girl with the Green Eyes* (1902), *The Truth* (1907), and *The City* (1909). His works were popular both in the United States and in Europe.

Fitch, John, 1743-98, American inventor, b. Windsor, Conn. Fitch began (1785) work on the invention of the steam engine and steamboat and secured soon afterward the exclusive right to build and operate steamboats on the waters of New Jersey, Pennsylvania, New York, Delaware, and Virginia. A trial run of his first steamer (1786) was only a partial success. His next vessel, launched and operated on the Delaware River in 1787, was followed by two others. Although Fitch was not alone in developing the steam engine and steamboat, there is good evidence that he invented the first American steamboat. Nevertheless, he failed to receive either the opportunity to commercialize his invention or the recognition he justly deserved. Frustrated by endless disappointments, Fitch committed suicide in Bardstown, Ky.

Fitch, Thomas, c.1700-1774, colonial governor of Connecticut, b. Norwalk, Conn. A lawyer, Fitch was an assistant in the colony (1734-35, 1740-50). The assembly elected him deputy governor in 1750, and for the next three years he was returned to that office by the qualified voters. Elected governor in 1754, he remained chief executive until 1766, when he was turned out by the Whigs. Although he had been the chief author of the colony's protest against the Stamp Act, he felt duty-bound to take the oath of office required of governors by the act and was, as a result, consistently defeated for reelection thereafter. See A. C. Bates, ed., *The Fitch Papers* (2 vol., 1918-20).

fitch: see POLECAT.

Fitchburg, industrial city (1970 pop. 43,343), seat of Worcester co., N Mass., on the north branch of the Nashua River; settled c.1730, inc. as a city 1872. Its important paper industry dates approximately from 1805. Fitchburg State College is there.

Fitzgerald, Lord Edward, 1763-98, Irish revolutionary; son of James Fitzgerald, 20th earl of Kildare and 1st duke of Leinster. After an early career in the army and the Irish House of Commons, Lord Edward, attracted by the French Revolution, went (1792) to Paris and was expelled from the British army for his avowed republicanism. Returning home, he joined the UNITED IRISHMEN, whom he pledged to assist as commander in chief of their rebel army. In 1796 he went to Basel to negotiate French aid for the planned Irish uprising. On the eve of the rebellion in 1798 Lord Edward was betrayed by an informer, and he was arrested. He died of wounds sustained at his arrest.

FitzGerald, Edward, 1809-83, English man of letters. A dilettante and scholar, FitzGerald spent most of his life living in seclusion in Suffolk. His masterpiece, a translation of *The Rubaiyat of Omar Khayyam,* appeared anonymously in 1859 and passed unnoticed until Dante Gabriel Rossetti made it famous. Revised editions followed in 1868, 1872, and 1879. FitzGerald's *Rubaiyat* has long been one of the most popular English poems. Although actually a paraphrase rather than a translation of a poem by the 11th-century Persian poet OMAR KHAYYAM, it retains the spirit of the original in its poignant expression of a philosophy counseling man to live life to the fullest while he can. Among FitzGerald's other works are *Euphranor* (1851), a Platonic dialogue, and *Polonius* (1852), a collection of aphorisms. See his letters (ed. by J. M. Cohen, 1960); biographies by A. M. Terhune (1947) and Thomas Wright (2 vol., 1904; repr. 1971).

Fitzgerald, Ella, 1918-, American jazz singer, b. Newport News, Va. Reared in an orphanage in Yonkers, N.Y., Fitzgerald won an amateur contest at Harlem's Apollo Theater in 1934. Thereafter she performed with Chick Webb's band. When he died in 1939 she managed the band herself until 1942, when she began to make solo appearances in supper clubs and theaters. Principally a jazz and blues singer of remarkably sweet and effortless style, Fitzgerald was noted for her sophisticated interpretation of songs by George Gershwin and Cole Porter. She also wrote a number of songs and made numerous recordings and concert tours of Europe and Asia. In 1955 she appeared in the film *Pete Kelly's Blues.*

Fitzgerald, F. Scott (Francis Scott Key Fitzgerald), 1896-1940, American novelist and short-story writer, b. St. Paul, Minn. Ranked among the great American writers of the 20th cent., Fitzgerald is considered the literary spokesman of the "jazz age"—the decade of the 1920s. Part of the interest of his work derives from the fact that the gay, mad, gin-drinking, morally and spiritually bankrupt men and girls he wrote about led lives that closely resembled his own. Born of middle-class parents, Fitzgerald attended private schools, entering Princeton in 1913. He was placed on academic probation in his junior year, and in 1917 he left Princeton to join the army. While stationed in Montgomery, Ala., he met and fell in love with Zelda Sayre, the daughter of a local judge. He also began working on his first novel, *This Side of Paradise,* which describes life at Princeton among the glittering, bored, disillusioned, postwar generation. Published in 1920, the novel was an instant success and brought Fitzgerald enough money to marry Zelda that same year. The young couple moved to New York City, where they became notorious for their madcap life style. Fitzgerald made money by writing stories for various magazines. In 1922 he published his second novel, *The Beautiful and Damned,* about an artist and his wife who are ruined by their dissipated way of life. After the birth of their daughter, Frances Scott, in 1921, the Fitzgeralds spent much time in Paris and on the French Riviera, becoming part of a celebrated circle of American expatriots. Fitzgerald's masterpiece, *The Great Gatsby,* appeared in 1925. It is the story of a bootlegger, Jay Gatsby, whose obsessive dream of wealth and lost love is destroyed by a corrupt reality. Cynical yet poignant, the novel is a devastating portrait of the so-called American Dream, which measures success and love in terms of money. Fitzgerald's later years were plagued by financial worries and his wife's progressive insanity. His long-awaited novel *Tender is the Night* (1934), a complex study of the spiritual depletion of a psychiatrist who marries a wealthy former patient, although later regarded highly, was received coolly. The author spent his last years as a scriptwriter in Hollywood, Calif. He died of a heart attack in 1940 at the age of 44. *The Last Tycoon,* a promising unfinished novel about the motion picture industry, was published in 1941. Fitzgerald published four excellent short story collections: *Flappers and Philosophers* (1920), *Tales of the Jazz Age* (1922), *All the Sad Young Men* (1926), and *Taps at Reveille* (1935). See *The Crack-up,* ed. by Edmund Wilson (1945), a miscellaneous collection of notes, essays, and letters; Fitzgerald's letters, ed. by Andrew Turnbull (1963); biographies by Arthur Mizener (1951), Andrew Turnbull (1962) and H. D. Piper (1965); study by J. F. Callahan (1972).

Zelda Sayre Fitzgerald, 1900-47, b. Montgomery, Ala., was also a writer. She was intermittently confined to sanatoriums after 1930, a hopeless schizophrenic, but still managed to publish short stories and a novel, *Save Me the Waltz* (1932). Although incoherent, the novel reveals a genuine, if unformed, writing talent. She was also a ballet dancer and painter. See biography by Nancy Milford (1970); Sara Mayfield, *Exiles from Paradise: Zelda and Scott Fitzgerald* (1971).

Fitzgerald, George Francis, 1851-1901, Irish physicist. Fitzgerald was born in Dublin and studied and taught at Trinity College there. He is best known for suggesting how the ETHER, by causing the contraction of bodies moving through it, could account for the null results of the Michelson-Morley experiment (see RELATIVITY). His main research effort, however, was to work out the consequences of Maxwell's electromagnetic theory for phenomena not considered by Maxwell, such as the reflection and refraction of light.

Fitzgerald, Gerald: see DESMOND, GERALD FITZGERALD, 15TH EARL OF.

Fitzgerald, James: see KILDARE, JAMES FITZGERALD, 20TH EARL OF.

Fitzgerald, Maurice, d. 1176, Anglo-Norman soldier. He was the son of Gerald, steward of Pembroke castle, and Nesta, daughter of the prince of South Wales. Fitzgerald crossed to Ireland in 1169 to aid DERMOT MCMURROUGH, king of Leinster. He served in expeditions against Dublin and Waterford. He acquired vast landholdings in Ireland and increased them by advantageous marriages of his children. From his sons, Gerald and Thomas the Great, descend the two branches of the Fitzgeralds who became earls of Kildare (through Gerald) and earls of Desmond (through Thomas).

Fitzgerald, Thomas: see KILDARE, THOMAS FITZGERALD, 10TH EARL OF.

Fitzgerald contraction: see LORENTZ CONTRACTION.

Fitzgibbon, John: see CLARE, JOHN FITZGIBBON, 1ST EARL OF.

Fitzherbert, Maria Anne, 1756-1837, wife of George, Prince of Wales (later GEORGE IV). He was her third husband. The marriage (1785) was illegal by the terms of the Royal Marriage Act (1772) and the Act of Settlement (1701), since the prince was under age and Mrs. Fitzherbert was a Roman Catholic. It was therefore ignored in 1795 when the prince, for purposes of state, married Caroline of Brunswick, but the relationship continued fitfully for many years. See biography by Anita Leslie (1960).

Fitzmaurice, Henry Charles Petty: see LANSDOWNE, HENRY CHARLES KEITH PETTY, 5TH MARQUESS OF.

Fitzmaurice, William Petty: see SHELBURNE, WILLIAM PETTY FITZMAURICE, 2D EARL OF.

Fitzpatrick, Benjamin, 1802-69, governor of Alabama (1841-45), b. Greene co., Ga. As a youth, he moved to Alabama (then still part of Mississippi Territory), where he became a successful lawyer and developed a large plantation near Montgomery. After two terms as governor he served in the U.S. Senate (1848-49, 1853-61). A conservative, Fitzpatrick opposed secession but later supported the Confederacy. He was prominent in the early days of the Reconstruction period in Alabama and presided over the constitutional convention of 1865, but was soon afterwards disfranchised.

Fitzpatrick, Sir Charles, 1853-1942, Canadian jurist, b. Quebec. He won renown as defense counsel for Louis RIEL. In Wilfrid Laurier's government he became solicitor general (1896) and minister of justice (1902), resigning to accept appointment as chief justice of the Supreme Court of Canada in 1906. After his retirement from the bench in 1918, he was lieutenant governor of Quebec prov. until his retirement in 1923. He was knighted in 1907.

Fitzpatrick, Thomas, c.1799-1854, American trapper, fur trader, and guide, one of the greatest of the MOUNTAIN MEN, b. Co. Cavan, Ireland. He emigrated early to the United States, and by 1823 he was engaged in St. Louis for a trading expedition of William Henry ASHLEY up the Missouri. Like others of the mountain men, he spent many of the succeeding years opening up the West. He went with Jedediah S. Smith into the Green River country through the SOUTH PASS in 1824. Fitzpatrick worked for the Ashley interests until Ashley withdrew (1826) from the trade; then he was a trader for Smith, Jackson, and Sublette until 1830, when the Rocky Mountain Fur Company was formed with Fitzpatrick as senior partner. After that company was dissolved (1834), Fitzpatrick became a guide. He piloted the John Bidwell party, the first emigrant train bound for California, as far as Fort Hall in 1841, and the next year he performed the same service for the first train to Oregon. He gained some celebrity as guide to John C. Frémont on his second expedition and in 1846 was guide to Stephen W. KEARNY on the march to Santa Fe. In Nov., 1846, he was appointed Indian agent for a large part of the present Colorado and was successful in negotiating treaties. See L. R. Hafen and W. J. Ghent, *Broken Hand: the Life Story of Thomas Fitzpatrick* (1931); Bernard De Voto, *Across the Wide Missouri* (1948).

Fitzroy, city (1971 pop. 29,300), Victoria, SE Australia, part of the Melbourne urban agglomeration.

Fitzroy, rivers in Australia. **1** River, 174 mi (280 km) long, formed by the junction of the Dawson and the Mackenzie rivers, E Queensland, Australia, and flowing past Rockhampton to Keppel Bay of the Coral Sea. **2** River, c.325 mi (525 km) long, rising in the King Leopold Range, N Western Australia state, Australia, and flowing generally west to King Sound of the Indian Ocean.

Fitzsimmons, Robert L., 1863-1918, British boxer, b. Cornwall, England. Fitzsimmons began fighting professionally in Australia and New Zealand before going to the United States in 1890. He won the world's middleweight championship in 1891. In 1897 he defeated James J. Corbett at Carson City, Nev., for the heavyweight crown but lost it in 1899 to James J. Jeffries at Coney Island, N.Y. He won the light heavyweight title in 1903 and held it for two years. Fitzsimmons retired from boxing at the age of 52.

Fitzwilliam, William Wentworth Fitzwilliam, 2d **Earl,** 1748-1833, British administrator. Sent to Ireland as lord lieutenant in 1795, he expressed sympathy for the cause of CATHOLIC EMANCIPATION and was almost immediately recalled by William Pitt's ministry for allegedly exceeding his instructions. The "Fitzwilliam affair," as much as any other single factor, contributed to the Irish rebellion of 1798.

Fitzwilliam, Sir William, 1526-99, lord deputy of Ireland. He acquired (1547) land in Ireland by a grant of Edward VI. Although a Protestant, he was loyal to Queen Mary I, and she appointed him keeper of the great seal in Ireland (1555). Under Elizabeth I he was vice treasurer (1550-73) and several times lord justice of Ireland in the absence of the 3d earl of SUSSEX. His terms as lord deputy (1572-75, 1588-94) were marked by insufficient funds, his own lack of military skills, ineffective communication between him and the English court, and vague charges of maladministration. He did, however, successfully defend Ireland against the Spanish (1588) and establish order in Monaghan. He was governor of Fotheringhay Castle when Mary Queen of Scots was executed there (1588).

Fitzwilliam Museum, building erected to house the art collection and library bequeathed in 1816 to Cambridge Univ. by Richard, Viscount Fitzwilliam. Both the collection and the building have been enlarged by later bequests, notably that of Charles Brinsley Marlay in 1912. The collection, which is particularly strong in Italian, Spanish, Dutch, and English paintings and in 17th-century prints, especially of the Dutch school, also includes antiquities, medieval manuscripts, ancient coins, porcelains, furniture, and armor. The music collection is one of the best in England.

Fiume: see RIJEKA, Yugoslavia.

Five, The, name of a group of late 19th-century Russian composers. They were Balakirev, the leader, Cui, Moussorgsky, Borodin, and Rimsky-Korsakov. These men, united by a nationalistic fervor, tried to write music of distinctively Russian character, drawing on the history, literature, and folklore of their country. See V. I. Seroff, *The Mighty Five* (1948); M. O. Zetlin, *The Five* (tr. 1959).

Five Civilized Tribes, inclusive term used since mid-19th cent. for the CHEROKEE, CHICKASAW, CHOCTAW, CREEK, and SEMINOLE tribes of E Oklahoma. By 1850 some 60,000 members of these tribes were settled in Indian Territory under the Removal Act of 1830, which provided that this territory was to be held communally on the condition that the tribes surrendered certain land rights E of the Mississippi River. These tribes never lived on a reservation and were officially recognized as domestic dependent nations. Before crossing the Mississippi River, the Cherokee and the Creek had evolved a highly developed agricultural civilization in the SE United States. Each tribe had a written constitution, a judiciary system, a bicameral legislature, an executive branch, and a public school system. After the American Civil War, the majority of the Indians having aided the Confederacy, all treaties were put aside, their lands were restricted to E Oklahoma, and their Negro slaves, who had numbered several thousands, were freed. Later a Federal policy of detribalization resulted in loss of the governmental functions of the Five Tribes and the division of all land into individual holdings. Although the tribal governments have continued to function, they have little authority and serve mainly in an advisory capacity. See Grant Foreman, *The Five Civilized Tribes* (1934, repr. 1966) and *Indian Removal: The Emigration of the Five Civilized Tribes* (new ed. 1953, repr. 1966); Angie Debo, *And Still the Waters Run* (1940, repr. 1966); R. S. Cotterill, *Southern Indians* (1954, repr. 1963); M. T. Bailey, *Reconstruction in Indian Territory* (1972).

Five Dynasties and Ten Kingdoms, period of Chinese history between the fall of the T'ang dynasty (A.D. 907) and the establishment of the Sung dynasty (A.D. 960). It is named for the five successive short-lived dynasties and the ten dominant kingdoms that existed during this period. Characterized by anarchy and national disunity, the period is one of the bleakest in Chinese history. Warfare and official corruption were endemic, and barter replaced the monetary system in many parts of the country. Northern China was particularly affected; its canal and dam system fell into disrepair, causing extensive flooding and famine. The period, however, was marked by one major accomplishment—the widespread development of printing. Many Confucian, Buddhist, and Taoist classics were printed, including the first complete set (130 vol.) of the Confucian writings.

Five Forks, crossroads near Dinwiddie Courthouse, SW of Petersburg, Va. The last important battle of the Civil War was fought there on April 1, 1865. Philip H. SHERIDAN, leading his own and Gouverneur K. Warren's corps, decisively defeated the Confederates under Pickett. The victory led to the fall of PETERSBURG, the capture of Richmond, and the surrender of Lee's army at Appomattox Court House.

five hundred, card game, similar in principle to EUCHRE, usually played by three persons with a pack of 32 cards and a joker. Each player receives 10 cards, and highest bidder for the widow (the three cards left over) names trump. The two other players play in temporary combination against the bidder, and 500 points wins the game. In the early 20th cent. five hundred was very popular in the United States.

Five Nations: see IROQUOIS CONFEDERACY.

Five-Power Treaty: see NAVAL CONFERENCES.

Five-Year Plan, Soviet economic practice of planning to augment agricultural and industrial output by designated quotas for a limited period of usually five years. Nations other than the USSR and the Soviet bloc members, especially developing countries, have adopted such plans for four, five, or more years. Joseph Stalin, in 1928, launched the first Five-Year Plan; it was designed to industrialize the USSR in the shortest possible time and, in the process, to expedite the collectivization of farms. The plan, put into action ruthlessly, aimed at making the USSR self-sufficient and emphasized heavy industry at the expense of consumer goods. It covered the period from 1928 to 1933, but was officially considered completed in 1932. The second Five-Year Plan (1933-37) continued and expanded the first. The third plan (1938-42) was interrupted by World War II. The fourth covered the years 1946-50, the fifth 1951-55. The sixth plan (1956-60) was discarded in 1957, primarily because it overcommitted available resources and could not be fulfilled. It was replaced by a Seven-Year Plan (1959-65), which fell far short of estimated increases in agricultural (especially wheat) production. The Seven-Year Plan was considered the start of a longer period (20 years) devoted to the establishment of the material and technical basis of a Communist society. The late 1960s and early 1970s saw increased emphasis placed on consumer goods, and the 9th Five-Year Plan (1971-75) for the first time gave priority to light industry rather than heavy industry.

fixation: see PSYCHOANALYSIS.

Fizeau, Armand Hippolyte Louis (ärmäN' ēpôlēt' lwē fēzō'), 1819-96, French physicist. The first to measure (1849) the velocity of light in air, he also determined its speed in water. He made valuable discoveries on the polarization of light and the expansion of crystals, explained the Doppler effect, and devised a method of increasing the permanency of daguerreotypes. With Léon Foucault he took the first clear photograph of the surface of the sun.

fjord or **fiord** (fyôrd), steep-sided inlet of the sea characteristic of glaciated regions. Fjords probably resulted from the scouring by glaciers of valleys formed by any of several processes, including faulting and erosion by running water. When the regions occupied by these valleys subsided, the valleys were drowned by the sea. The fjord coast lines of Norway, Scotland, Greenland, Alaska, British Columbia, S Chile, S New Zealand, and Antarctica are examples. A fjord differs from most estuaries in its sheer, parallel walls, often extending far below the water surface, and in its many branches of similar form. Often shallow at the mouth, fjords are frequently very deep farther inland. Sognafjord (Norway) is 4,000 ft (1,220 m) deep and over 100 mi (160 km) long. Loch Moran, Scotland (1,017 ft/310 m), is a typical fjord but is separated from the sea. Norwegian fjords are noted for their grandeur.

Flaccus, Quintus Fulvius (kwĭn'təs fŭl'vēəs flă'kəs), Roman consul four times (237, 224, 212, 209 B.C.), censor (231), pontifex maximus (216), and urban praetor (215). In the Second Punic War he defeated (211) the Carthaginians near Beneventum, captured (211) Capua, and overcame (209) Hannibal's garrisons in Lucania and Bruttium.

Flacius Illyricus, Matthias (məthī'əs flā'shəs ĭlĭr'ĭkəs), 1520-75, German Lutheran reformer, whose original name was Matthias Vlachich or Francowich, b. Istria. After studying for the priesthood, he went (1541) to Wittenberg, where he became (1544) professor of Hebrew. Greatly influenced by Martin Luther, Flacius became the acknowledged leader of the strict Lutherans. His rigid position led to many theological controversies. He was the chief opponent of Melanchton, objecting to his compromising with the Roman Catholic Church on nonessentials. In 1557, Flacius became professor of the New Testament at the Univ. of Jena. His conception of original sin, which excluded the notion of free will, made him the subject of attack. After leaving Jena in 1562, he wandered about until he found refuge at Frankfurt. Chief among his writings are *Catalogus testium veritatis* (1556), *Clavis scripturae* (1567), and *Glossa compendiaria in Novum Testamentum* (1570).

flag, common name for several plants belonging to the families Iridaceae and Araceae. See IRIS; ARUM.

flag, piece of cloth, usually bunting or similar light material, plain, colored, or bearing a device, varying in size and shape, but often oblong or square, used as an ensign, standard, or signal or for display and decorative purposes, and generally attached at one edge to a staff or to a halyard by which it may be hoisted. The part of the flag attached to the staff or halyard is the hoist; the portion from the attached part to the free end is the fly; the top quarter of the flag next to the staff is the canton. Symbolical standards were used by the ancient Egyptians, Assyrians, and Jews. Biblical references to standards, ensigns, and banners are numerous. Early flags usually had a religious significance. The Dannebrog of Denmark, a red ensign that is swallow-tailed and bears a white cross, is no doubt the oldest flag design still in use. In France the Cape de St. Martin, originally kept in Marmoutier abbey, was borne upon the standards of the early kings, but this was succeeded by the oriflamme, the ancient banner of the abbey of St. Denis. William the Conqueror received his banner from the pope, and the ensign of Great Britain, the Union Jack, is formed by the crosses of St. George, St. Andrew, and St. Patrick, the national saints, respectively, of England, Scotland, and Ireland. In medieval times there were numerous flags in use—banners, banderoles, gonfalons, gonfanons, pennons, pennoncells, standards, streamers, and guidons. The banner, usually quadrangular in shape, was a battle flag bearing the arms of the person entitled to carry it. The banderole was smaller in size than the banner. The gonfalon and the gonfanon, also battle flags, were hung from a crosspiece attached to a staff or spear. The pennon was a long triangular flag, generally swallow-tailed, used as a knight bachelor's ensign. The pennoncell was a small pennon used for ceremonial purposes. The standard, used by nobles on ceremonial occasions, was a long, narrow flag, tapering toward the free end and richly decorated. The royal standard of today is derived from the medieval banner; it bears the royal arms and is smaller than the national flag, or ensign. The streamer was a long, narrow flag, tapering toward the fly, and generally carried at the masthead of a vessel. It has been replaced by the present-day pennant (or pendant, as it was earlier called and is still called in the British navy). The guidon was carried by horsemen; today it is used by the U.S. army for practically all units in dress parade and as a distinguishing flag. In France the oriflamme was replaced by the Bourbon white flag sprinkled with fleurs-de-lis, which in turn was succeeded by the tricolor at the time of the Revolution. In the British colonies of North America before the Revolution, each of the 13 colonies had its flag. On Jan. 2, 1776, the first flag of the United States was raised at Cambridge, Mass., by George Washington. Known as the Grand Union flag, it consisted of 13 stripes, alternate red and white, with a blue canton bearing the crosses of St. George and St. Andrew. Congress, on June 14, 1777, enacted a resolution "that the Flag of the United States be 13 stripes alternate red and white, that the Union be 13 stars white in a blue field representing a new constellation." The story of Betsy Ross and the first flag is now somewhat discredited; official records have not confirmed that she was responsible for the design and making of the first flag. On Jan. 13, 1794, Vermont and Kentucky having been admitted to the Union, Congress added a stripe and a star for each state. Congress in 1818 enacted that the 13 stripes, denoting the 13 original colonies, be restored and a star added to the blue canton for each state after its admission to the Union. All of the states and territories of the United States have their own flags. The International Code flags and pennants enable mariners to communicate regardless of differences of language. In the armies and navies of the various nations of the world, flags are used for signaling. The white flag is used universally for truce; the black in early times was a symbol for piracy; the red symbolizes mutiny or revolution; the yellow is a sign of infectious diseases. Shipping lines have their own flags. Striking a flag signifies surrender, and the flag of a victor is hoisted above that of the vanquished. A flag flown at half-mast is the symbol of mourning. The inverted national ensign is a signal of distress. In 1942 a law was passed by the U.S. Congress establishing specific rules for the display of the U.S. flag by civilians or groups previously not subject to U.S. governmental regulations. The intent of the law was to ensure that the U.S. flag be given a position of honor. In a procession the U.S. flag is carried on the military right of the column; in procession with other flags it is carried in front; with another flag on a wall, both flags with staffs, the U.S. flag is to the right with the U.S. flagstaff in front of the other; with other flags on the same halyard, the U.S. flag is on top, although an exception is made when the church pennant of the services is flown from the same staff; with two or more flags in line, the U.S. flag is at right; with a group of other flags on display where the bottoms of the staffs touch in fanlike fashion, the U.S. flag is displayed in the center. Although the U.S. flag is usually displayed from sunrise to sunset, through law or presidential proclamation it is flown both day and night at the following patriotic sites: Fort McHenry National Monument and Historical Shrine, Md.; Flag House Square, Baltimore, Md.; United States Marine Corps (Iwo Jima) Memorial, Va.; and Battle Green, Lexington, Mass. See M. M. Quaife, *The Flag of the United States* (1942); E. M. C. Barraclough, *Flags of the World* (rev. ed. 1965); Gordon Campbell and I. O. Evans, *The Book of Flags* (5th ed. 1965).

Flag Day, anniversary of the adoption of the American flag in 1777. It is celebrated on June 14 but is not a legal holiday.

flagellants (flăj'ələnts, fləjĕl'ənts), term applied to the groups of Christians who practiced public flagellation as a penance. The practice supposedly grew out of the floggings administered as punishment to erring monks, although flagellation as a form of religious expression is an ancient usage. Among the flagellants it was an extreme expression of the ascetic ideal. Self-flagellation as a penance was approved by the early Christian church. However, the flagellant movement itself did not appear until the 13th cent., and it was not until c.1260 that the flagellants grew into large, organized bodies. Arising in the towns of N Italy, the movement spread across the Alps to Germany, Bohemia, and even to Poland. Bands of flagellants marched from town to town and in public places bared their backs and beat each other and themselves, all the while exhorting the people to repent. The disorderly and morbid nature of these exhibitions led civil and ecclesiastical authorities to suppress them. The movement died down, although it occasionally reappeared, especially in Germany in 1296 and in Italy under the leadership of Venturino of Bergamo. During the general societal confusion that accompanied the Black Death (1348-49) it flared up again. From the East bands of flagellants spread across Hungary and Germany, to S Europe and even to England, where no converts were gained. In 1349, Pope Clement VI prohibited the practice. Heretical flagellant sects as the Bianchi of Italy and France (c.1399) and the followers of Karl Schmidt (c.1414) were suppressed; milder forms of flagellation were tolerated, however, and even encouraged by such leaders as St. Vincent Ferrer. There was a reappearance of public flagellation within the church after the Reformation. Catherine de' Medici and King Henry III of France encouraged flagellant orders, but Henry IV forbade them. The Jesuits after a time abandoned this public penance and the practice died out again, although tertiaries from time to time degenerated into flagellant groups. In Spanish America flagellant orders persisted, usually in defiance of the ecclesiastical disapproval; in New Mexico the Hermanos Penitentes, a flagellant order, is said to practice secret rites today.

flageolet (flăjəlĕt'), small straight flute of conical bore, with a whistle mouthpiece. The number of finger holes varies, as does the length, which may be from 4 to 12 in (10.2-30.5 cm). The flageolet, related

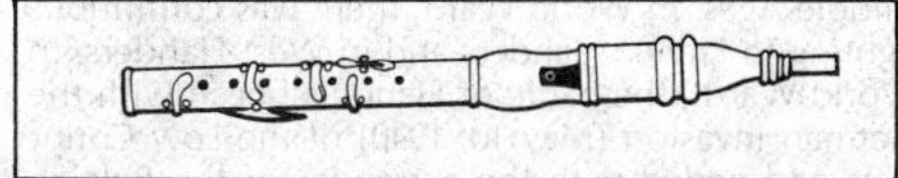

Flageolet

to the RECORDER, was known as early as the 16th cent., its invention in 1581 being ascribed to Juvigny, a Parisian. It was in use until the end of the 19th cent.

Flagg, Azariah Cutting, 1790-1873, American political leader, b. Orwell, Vt. He fought in the War of 1812, was editor of the Plattsburgh (N.Y.) *Republican* until 1825, and was elected (1823) to the New York state assembly. Flagg, a relentless Jeffersonian Democrat, was a leader of the ALBANY REGENCY and helped sustain its drive for political reforms. He served in New York as secretary of state (1826-32) and twice as state comptroller (1834-39, 1842-46). He opposed any form of Federal banks and advocated reform of the New York state banking system. After 1846 he helped organize the BARNBURNERS and was (1852-59) comptroller of New York City.

Flagg, Ernest, 1857-1947, American architect, b. Brooklyn, N.Y., studied at the École des Beaux-Arts, Paris. The 45-story Singer Building in New York City, which he built in 1908, marked a revolutionary height. Flagg's other works include the Scribner Building, New York City, the Corcoran Gallery of Art, Washington, D.C., and numerous residences. In magazine articles and in his book *Small Houses: Their Economic Design and Construction* (1922), Flagg advocated various structural economies and innovations. These include a method of house planning on a module basis and a thin metal and plaster partition eliminating supporting studs. He wrote also *Le Naos du Parthenon* (1928, in French and English), a study in Greek units of proportion.

Flagg, James Montgomery, 1877-1960, American painter, illustrator, and author, b. Pelham Manor, N.Y. He studied in New York City, in England, and in Paris. Returning to New York, he rapidly won a reputation as an illustrator of versatility, vivacity, and technical skill, contributing to *St. Nicholas, Judge, Life,* and other magazines. As official artist for New York state during World War I, he designed 45 military posters. See his autobiography, *Roses and Buckshot* (1946).

Flagler, Henry Morrison, 1830-1913, American financier, b. Hopewell, near Canandaigua, N.Y. As a youth he struck out for himself in Ohio. After trying the grain and salt business, he joined John D. Rockefeller in oil refining. The firm of Rockefeller, Andrews & Flagler became the Standard Oil Company in 1870, and Flagler was connected with it until 1911, resigning as vice president, however, in 1908. He had been Rockefeller's closest associate in the early development of the company. Flagler visited Florida in 1883, and, annoyed at the inadequate transportation and hotel facilities, he undertook to improve them. He bought up and consolidated several local railroads and organized the Florida East Coast Railway, which he extended S from Daytona through Palm Beach to Miami (1896) and thence 150 mi (241 km) to Key West (1912). He established steamship lines, dredged the Miami harbor, and built palatial hotels, all to encourage the development of Florida as a winter playground. He also made anonymous gifts to build schools, churches, and hospitals. Altogether Flagler invested over $40 million in the peninsula and, more than any other, was responsible for Florida's growth. See S. W. Martin, *Florida's Flagler* (1949).

Flagstad, Kirsten (kyĭrsh'tən fläg'stät), 1895-1962, Norwegian soprano. She made her debut in 1913 but sang only in Scandinavia until 1934, when she appeared at the Bayreuth Festivals. In 1935 she made her debut at the Metropolitan Opera, New York, as Sieglinde in Wagner's *Die Walküre* and was soon acclaimed as the greatest living Wagnerian soprano. In 1941 she returned to Norway. From 1947 until 1953, when she retired, she sang in the United States and Europe.

Flagstaff, city (1970 pop. 26,117), seat of Coconino co., N Ariz., near the San Francisco Peaks; inc. 1894. Lumbering, ranching, and a lively tourist trade thrive in the region, where many ruined Indian pueblos (as in Walnut Canyon), numerous state parks, several lakes, and large pine forests are found. Sunset Crater National Monument, Lowell Observatory (est. 1894 by Percival Lowell), and Northern Arizona Univ. are there. A powwow of southwestern Indians is held each July.

flagstone: see SILT.

Flahaut de La Billarderie, Auguste Charles Joseph, comte de (ōgüst' shärl zhōzĕf' kôNt də flăō' də lä bēyärdərē'), 1785-1870, French general and statesman; illegitimate son of Charles Maurice de Talleyrand and Adèle de Flahaut. He fought under Napoleon I and served as ambassador to Berlin, London, and Vienna under Louis Philippe. He supported the coup d'etat (1851) of Louis Napoleon (later Napoleon III) and served again (1860-62) as ambassador to London. The lover of Hortense de BEAUHARNAIS, Flahaut was the father of Napoleon III's half brother, the duc de MORNY.

Flaherty, Robert Joseph (flă'ərtē), 1884-1951, American explorer and film producer. He was born in Michigan and grew up in Canada. He explored (1910-16) subarctic E Canada and in 1922 completed the first full-length documentary film, *Nanook of the North.* His films include *Moana of the South Seas* (1925), *Tabu* (1931), *Man of Aran* (1934), *Elephant Boy* (1936), *The Land* (1941), and *Louisiana Story* (1949). See biographies by Arthur Calder-Marshall (1963, repr. 1970), Frances Flaherty (1960, repr. 1972), and Richard Griffith (1953, repr. 1973).

Flamborough Head, chalk promontory, Humberside, E England, N of Bridlington Bay. There is a lighthouse at the tip. Danes' Dyke (an ancient earthwork fortification) crosses the peninsula. The chalk cliffs are wave-carved into caves and stacks and are inhabited by flocks of seafowl.

flamboyant style, the final development in French GOTHIC ARCHITECTURE that reached its height in the 15th cent. It is characterized chiefly by ornate tracery forms that, by their suggestion of flames, gave the style its name. Although these free-flowing patterns in lines of double curvature originated in the English Decorated Gothic (early 14th cent.), the French adopted them as the basis of a lavish style quite different from the English original. Flamboyant works exhibit pronounced freedom and exuberance, created by high, attenuated proportions, accumulated and elaborate traceries, and many crockets, pinnacles, and canopied niches. It is believed that the style first appeared in the west facade of the cathedral at Rouen (1370); its culmination is in the Church of St. Maclou, Rouen (1437-50). Other conspicuous examples are the Palais de Justice at Rouen, begun 1482; the west chapels of Amiens Cathedral; the northern spire of Chartres; and the south transept of the cathedral at Beauvais.

flame, phenomenon associated with the chemical reaction of a gas that has been heated above its kindling temperature with some other gas, usually atmospheric oxygen (see COMBUSTION). The heat and light given off are characteristic of the specific chemical reaction (or reactions) going on; the luminosity of the flame is usually caused by solid particles of foreign matter present (naturally or artificially) in the burning gas and heated to incandescence; and the shape of the flame is commonly that of a hollow cone. The simple flame occurring when a single gas, such as hydrogen, burns in another gas, such as air, shows two areas, or zones: an inner, cone-shaped area consisting of unburned gas; and an outer area in which the chemical reaction (the combination of hydrogen and oxygen to form water) is taking place. Furthermore, the flame is nonluminous and therefore very hot, since the chemical energy is nearly all transformed into heat energy. This reaction is illustrated in the flame of the oxyhydrogen BLOWPIPE. The flame of the OXYACETYLENE TORCH is also extremely hot. A decrease in light with an increase in heat is brought about in the BUNSEN BURNER flame (a more complex flame) by mixing the combustible gas with air before it is ignited. Flames become more complex as the combustible gas increases in complexity, since an increasing number of chemical reactions are involved. Three zones, for example, are apparent in the Bunsen burner flame, which is commonly caused by the combustion of ordinary illuminating gas: an inner zone of unburned gas; a middle zone called the reduction zone or reducing flame, since there the supply of oxygen is deficient and the oxygen is therefore removed from an oxide placed in it; and an outer, or oxidizing, zone. The candle flame is extremely complex. Several zones can be observed: a nonluminous inner portion where the melted wax produces gases; a middle area where the gases are decomposed to hydrogen, which burns, and carbon, which is heated to incandescence; and an outer, hardly visible region in which combustion is complete (carbon dioxide and water being formed). Flames are colored by the introduction of various substances, a fact utilized in the FLAME TEST for the identification of certain metals.

flamen (flā'mĕn), in Roman religion, one of 15 priests, each concerned with the cult of a particular deity. The most honored were those dedicated to Jupiter, Mars, and Quirinus.

flamenco, in Spanish music and dance, typical of the GYPSY, or gitano. Flamenco dancing is characterized by colorful costumes, alluring and erotic movements, stamping of the feet (*zapateado*), and clapping of the hands (*palmada*); its execution is brilliant, noisy, and passionate. Flamenco music is believed to have originated in the early 19th cent. from the *cante hondo* [Sp.,=deep song] of Andalusia, a highly emotional and tragic type of song accompanied by a guitar. By the mid-19th cent. flamenco had become a generally popular entertainment form. The most notable flamenco dancers have been La Argentina (d. 1936), Vicente ESCUDERO, La Argentinita (1898-1945), Antonio, and José GRECO.

flame test, test used in the identification of certain metals. It is based on the observation that light emitted by any element gives a unique SPECTRUM when passed through a spectroscope. When a salt of the metal is introduced into a Bunsen burner flame, the metallic ion produces characteristic color in the flame. Some metals and the colors they produce are: barium, yellow-green; calcium, red-orange; copper salts (except halides), emerald green; copper halides or other copper salts moistened with hydrochloric acid, blue-green; lithium, crimson; potassium, violet; sodium, yellow; and strontium, scarlet. The value of this simple flame test is limited by interferences (e.g., the barium flame masks calcium, lithium, or strontium) and by ambiguities (e.g., rubidium and cesium produce the same color as potassium). A colored glass is sometimes used to filter out light from one metal; for instance, blue cobalt glass filters out the yellow of sodium.

flamethrower, mechanism for shooting a burning stream of liquid or semiliquid fuel at enemy troops or positions. Primitive types of flamethrowers, consisting of hollow tubes filled with burning coals, sulfur, or other materials, came into use as early as the 5th cent. B.C. Modern flamethrowers were introduced by the Germans in 1915 during World War I. They were not widely used, however, until World War II, when the Americans found them especially useful, either hand-carried or mounted on tanks, in attacking Japanese fortifications in the Pacific Islands. After World War II improved flamethrowers, lighter in weight and with greater range, were developed and used in combat.

Flaming Gorge Dam, in a deep canyon of the Green River, NE Utah; built 1958–63 by the U.S. Bureau of RECLAMATION as a major unit in the COLORADO RIVER STORAGE PROJECT. The dam regulates the flow of the upper river and produces hydroelectricity (108,000-kw capacity). Flaming Gorge Lake, extending 91 mi (146 km) upstream, is part of Flaming Gorge National Recreation Area, administered by the U.S. Forest Service. The canyon was named in 1869 by the U.S. explorer John Powell because the brilliant red gorge, from a distance, looked as if it were afire.

flamingo, common name for a large pink or red wading bird, similar to the related heron, stork, and spoonbill but with a longer neck, webbed feet, and a unique down-bent bill. Flamingos are tropical birds, although large colonies have been observed high in the Andes. The American, or greater, flamingo, *Phoenicopterus ruber,* is now rarely seen in Florida, nesting chiefly in the West Indies. Its plumage is vermilion with black-edged wings; a common S Asian and African flamingo is scarlet with black wing feathers. The flamingo scoops its large bill backward through shallow water in marshes and lagoons. When closed, the serrated edges of the bill strain from the muddy water the aquatic plants, shellfish, and frogs on which the bird feeds. The nest is a cone of mud 1 to 2 ft (30–61 cm) high and about 1 ft (30 cm) across with a depression on top. The mates take turns incubating the one or two eggs, sitting astride the nest with their legs folded flat on either side. Flamingos are classified in the phylum CHORDATA, subphylum Vertebrata, class Aves, order Ciconiiformes, family Phoenicopteridae.

Flaminian Way, one of the principal ROMAN ROADS, the greatest artery from Rome to Cisalpine Gaul. Construction was begun (220 B.C.) by Caius Flaminius. The road ran N from Rome to Narnia (modern Narni), to Mevania (Bevagna), NE to Nuceria (Nocera Umbria), thence N to the Burano River at Cales (Cagli), thence to the Metauro River, thence NE to Fanum Fortunae (Fano) on the Adriatic, thence along the coast NW to Ariminum (Rimini). The Aemilian Way was an extension of it. The original length was 209 mi (336 km), but it was increased to 215 mi (346 km) when the course was changed after A.D. 69 between Narnia and Nuceria to run an alternate route via Interamna (Terni), Spoletium (Spoleto), and Fulginium (Foligno).

Flamininus, Titus Quinctius (tī'təs kwĭngk'shəs flămĭnī'nəs), c.230–175 B.C., Roman general and statesman, known as the Liberator of Greece. He was consul in 198 B.C. Flamininus defeated (197) Philip V of Macedon at Cynoscephalae and, at the Isthmian games (196), declared the independence of the Greek cities. When Nabis, tyrant of Sparta, failed to abide by the Roman terms, he was crushed (195) by Flamininus and forced to surrender Argos. In 183, Flamininus sought to induce Prusias, king of Bithynia, to deliver up Hannibal, who committed suicide rather than be surrendered to the Romans.

Flaminius, Caius (kā'əs fləmĭn'ēəs, kī'əs), d. 217 B.C., Roman statesman and general. In his tribuneship (232) he sponsored an agrarian law for the benefit of the plebeians and, as praetor (227), governed Sicily successfully. While consul (223) he campaigned against the Insubres and although chosen master of the horse (221) was barred from office by the occurrence of a bad omen. As censor (220) he constructed the Circus Flaminius and the Flaminian Way. In 218 he was the only senator to support the tribune Claudius in prohibiting senators and senators' sons from possession of seagoing vessels except for the transportation of the produce of their own estates. As consul again (217) he was a leader against HANNIBAL in the invasion of Italy, and he was killed in battle at Trasimene. See PUNIC WARS.

Flammarion, Camille (kămē'yə flămäryôN'), 1842–1925, French astronomer and author. He served for some years at the Paris Observatory and the Bureau of Longitudes, and in 1883 he set up a private observatory at Juvisy (near Paris) and continued his studies, especially of double and multiple stars and of the moon and Mars. He is noted chiefly as the author of popular books on astronomy, including *Popular Astronomy* (1880, tr. 1907) and *The Atmosphere* (1871, tr. 1873). His later studies were on psychical research, on which he wrote many works, among them *Death and Its Mystery* (3 vol., 1920–21; tr. 1921–23).

Flamsteed, John (flăm'stēd), 1646–1719, English astronomer. He was appointed (1675) astronomer royal by King Charles II and carried on his researches at Greenwich Observatory. Over his protests—he did not consider it ready for publication—the *Historia Coelestis,* which included the first of the Greenwich star catalogues, was published in 1712. His complete work, *Historia Coelestis Britannica,* finished after his death by his assistants, did not appear until 1725. See E. F. McPike, *Hevelius, Flamsteed and Halley* (1937).

Flanagan, John, 1865–1952, American sculptor and medalist. In 1932 he designed the George Washington silver quarter. In addition to medals and plaquettes, he produced larger works, including a clock for the Library of Congress; and the Bulkeley Memorial, Aetna Life Insurance Building, Hartford, Conn.

Flanders (flăn'dərz), former county in the Low Countries, extending along the North Sea and W of the Scheldt (Escaut) River. It is now divided among EAST FLANDERS and WEST FLANDERS provs., Belgium; Nord and Pas-de-Calais depts., France; and (to a small extent) Zeeland prov., the Netherlands. Flanders varied considerably in size in the course of its history and at one time also included Artois and parts of Picardy. In Belgian Flanders, the Flemish language, a Low German dialect akin to Dutch, is spoken by the majority of the inhabitants; all the Flemish-speaking persons of Belgium and France are, by extension, known as Flemings. In 862, Baldwin Bras-de-Fer [Iron Arm], a son-in-law of Emperor Charles II, became the first count of Flanders. In the divisions (9th cent.) of the Carolingian empire, Flanders became a fief of the French crown, but its powerful counts enjoyed virtual independence. They extended (11th cent.) their domains to the east; these additions, being held in fief to the Holy Roman Empire, became known as Imperial Flanders, in contrast to Crown Flanders, held from the French kings. In the 12th cent. the direct line of counts died out, and in 1191 the counts of HAINAUT (with which Flanders previously had been briefly united) also became counts of Flanders. The struggle for the succession to Flanders in the 12th cent. resulted in the loss of Artois and other districts and towns in W and S Flanders to the French crown. At the same time, the Flemish cities—among which Ghent, Bruges, Ypres, and Kortrijk were foremost—gained vast privileges and liberties (see COMMUNE). Their prosperity and the prosperity of Flanders as a whole depended on the growing cloth industry, which had been introduced in the 10th cent., and on the transit trade at such major ports as Bruges (later superseded by Antwerp) and Ghent. By the 13th cent., the Flemish cloth industry was the foremost in Europe, and it has retained much of its importance to the present day. Flanders had a turbulent history in the 13th and 14th cent., because of social and economic as well as political tensions. One result of the intensive industrialization of the cities was a struggle between the guild workers and the patricians. This struggle was reflected in the political rivalry of the Leliaerts (supporters of the French kings, so named for the fleur-de-lis on the French arms), who were backed by the patricians, and the Clauwaerts (supporters of the counts of Flanders, so named for the lion's claws in the counts' shield), who represented the lower classes. In addition, there was a long-standing rivalry among the cities, which often led to open warfare. Flanders was weakened by the departure of its count, Baldwin IX, on the Fourth Crusade, during which he was proclaimed (1204) emperor of Constantinople as BALDWIN I. Baldwin's absence was exploited by Philip II of France to strengthen his influence in Flanders; the Flemings were aided by John of England and Emperor Otto IV, but nevertheless were defeated by Philip at Bouvines (1214). In 1297, Guy of Dampierre, count of Flanders, allied himself with Edward I of England against Philip IV of France, but Philip, with the help of the Leliaerts, overran Flanders and imprisoned Guy (1300). Yet only two years later the Clauwaerts seized power; the French were massacred in the Matins of Bruges and were thoroughly routed in the BATTLE OF THE SPURS (1302). The accession (1322) of the pro-French Louis of Nevers as count of Flanders threw the country into a civil war in which Bruges and Ypres sided against, and Ghent sided with, the count. The pro-French party emerged victorious, and Flanders became little more than a French province. When Edward III of England, about to embark on what was to become the Hundred Years War with France, stopped wool exports from England to Flanders, the Flemish cloth industry faced ruin. Aware of the danger, the Flemings united under the leadership of Ghent, where Jacob van ARTEVELDE was given dictatorial powers in 1337, and allied themselves with England, taking part in Edward's great naval victory at Sluis (1340). After Artevelde's death (1345), Louis de Maële, son of Louis of Nevers, regained control over Flanders and sought to balance the influences of England and France; in 1381, however, the weavers of Ghent rebelled once more, this time under Philip van ARTEVELDE. The weavers captured Bruges but were defeated (1382) by a French army at Rozebeke. Louis de Maële's son-in-law, Duke PHILIP THE BOLD of Burgundy, succeeded to Flanders on Louis's death (1384) and in 1385 subdued Ghent. Under the Burgundian dynasty (see BURGUNDY), Flemish commerce and Flemish art flourished, but Flanders lost its independence; the Burgundians and (after 1477) the Hapsburgs kept a firm grip on Flanders, which was a major source of their income. The cloth industry was in decline, and the political rights of the cities, although asserted in many revolts, were curtailed. On the death (1477) of Charles the Bold, duke of Burgundy, his heir, MARY OF BURGUNDY, restored the Flemish liberties in the Great Privilege. Her son by Archduke Maximilian (later Emperor Maximilian I), Philip of Burgundy (later PHILIP I of Castile), succeeded on Mary's death in 1482, but the burghers kept him a virtual prisoner in Ghent until 1485. In 1506, Flanders came under the Spanish line of the house of Hapsburg through Philip's wife Joanna. Flanders joined (1576) in the revolt of the NETHERLANDS against Philip II of Spain, but by 1584 the Spanish under Alessandro Farnese had recovered the county. It continued under Spanish rule until 1714, when the Peace of Utrecht awarded it to Austria (see NETHERLANDS, AUSTRIAN AND SPANISH). Parts of W Flanders, including Lille, were annexed (1668–78) to France by Louis XIV and became known as French Flanders. Austria ceded the remainder of Flanders to France in the Treaty of Campo Formio (1797), but the Congress of Vienna awarded (1815) the former Austrian Flanders to the Netherlands. When Belgium gained (1830) independence, its part of Flanders was divided into the provinces of East Flanders and West Flanders. The second oldest son of the king of the Belgians bears the title of count of Flanders. Flanders's strategic location has made it a major battleground since the Middle Ages. In World War I, there was continuous fighting in French Flanders and in West Flanders. In World War II, the battle of Flanders began with the German invasion (May 10, 1940) of the Low Countries and ended with the surrender of the Belgian army and the evacuation of the British at Dunkirk (May 26–June 4, 1940). For bibliography, see BELGIUM.

Flanders, French, region of N France, on the North Sea and along the Belgian border. It is coextensive with Nord dept. The area is studded with important industrial cities and historic towns, and is a rich coal-mining region. It was incorporated into France in 1678 by Louis XIV and was a province until the French Revolution. LILLE was the provincial capital, DOUAI the seat of the parlement. The area has been a battleground in several major European conflicts.

Flandrin, Hippolyte Jean (ēpôlēt' zhäN fläNdrăN'), 1809–64, French painter; student and follower of Ingres. Influenced by the primitivism of Giotto, he is best known for his religious paintings, such as *St. Clair Curing the Blind* (1837; cathedral, Nantes); his decorations for the Church of St. Séverin, Paris; and his frescoes for Saint-Germain-des-Prés, Paris. He was also a fine portraitist.

Flannagan, John Bernard, 1895–1942, American sculptor, b. Fargo, N.Dak., studied at the Minneapolis Institute of Arts. His early life was a bitter struggle against poverty. Too poor to buy quarried stone, he picked up field stones for carving. His sculptures, often of animals, range from profound to humorous in conception and are simple and direct in execution. In 1930 and again in 1932 he lived for a year in Ireland. He is well represented in the museums of various colleges including Vassar, Oberlin, Harvard, and the Univ. of Nebraska. A mountain goat, *Figure of Dignity,* is in the Metropolitan Museum. He committed suicide in 1942. See his letters (with an introduction by W. R. Valentiner, 1942).

flannel, large group of napped plain-weave or twill-weave fabrics made of cotton, wool, or man-made fibers. Flannel fabrics vary in closeness or firmness of weave, and degree of napping. A French flannel, for example, is a very fine twill-weave fabric, slightly napped on the right side only, whereas a suede flannel is napped on both sides and sheared, with the fibers pressed into the fabric.

flare, solar: see CHROMOSPHERE.

flash spectrum: see CHROMOSPHERE.

flat-coated retriever, breed of large SPORTING DOG developed in England in the mid-19th cent. It stands about 23 in. (58 cm) high at the shoulder and weighs about 65 lb (30 kg). Its dense, flat coat of long, shiny hair may be liver or black in color. Counting the Labrador retriever as one of its ancestors, the flat-coated retriever is a natural water dog. Today it is trained to retrieve from both land and water and is used on a wide variety of game birds. See DOG.

flatfish, common name for any member of the unique and widespread order Pleuronectiformes containing over 500 species (including the flounder, halibut, plaice, sole, and turbot), 130 of which are American. Flatfishes are common in both the Atlantic and Pacific; many are important food and game fishes. All flatfishes have an unusual flattened body form well suited to life on the bottom. The development of the young flatfish recapitulates to some degree the probable evolutionary process. The newly hatched transparent larvae are bilaterally symmetrical, but soon the characteristic compression of the body develops and one eye "migrates" to the other side of the head—either the left or the right, depending on the species. Changes occur also in the skeletal and digestive systems; adults have only one dorsal and one anal fin, both without spines. The underside of the flatfish is pale and the top is colored to match the environment; some species, especially the flounders, are able to change their PIGMENTATION. Flatfishes are divided into two groups, the soles, families Soleidae, Cynoglossidae, and Achiridae, and the flounders, families Bothidae and Pleuronectidae. The American soles, of which there are several Atlantic and one Pacific species, have small, close-set eyes and small, twisted mouths with few or no teeth. They prefer warm, shallow water with a sandy or muddy bottom and are generally too small and bony for food. The hogchoker, or broad sole, and the tonguefish, family Cynoglossidae, are most common. The European species *Solea solea,* a 2-ft (61-cm) flatfish found from the Mediterranean to the North Sea, is a valuable food fish, the source of filet of sole (in the United States filet of sole is usually flounder). The flounders are much larger fishes, including the fluke (*Paralichthys*), the halibut (*Hippoglossus*), the dab (*Limanda*), and the plaice (*Pleuronectes*). The smooth flounder is found on muddy bottoms in cold, shallow northern waters. The Southern, or winter, flounder (*Pseudopleuronectes americanus*) is an important food and game fish, taken in large numbers by trawlers. Like other flounders it migrates in winter to deeper waters to breed. It belongs to the righteye flounder family, Pleuronectidae. Similar is the summer flounder (*Paralichthys dentatus*), of the lefteye flounder family, Bothidae, called fluke by fishermen, common from Maine to the Carolinas. The starry flounder, more brightly colored than its drab relatives, is a common Pacific species found from mid-California N to Alaska and W to Asia. Flounders feed on worms, crustaceans, and other small bottom invertebrates. The European plaice is an important food fish, as is the American plaice, or sand dab, of which 3,000 tons are taken annually. The American plaice is common at depths of from 20 to 100 fathoms on muddy or sandy bottoms, where it feeds on sea urchins, sand dollars, and other bottom life and grows to 30 in. (76.2 cm) and 14 lb (6.4 kg). The halibuts are the largest flatfishes and are of great commercial importance. The Atlantic and the Pacific halibuts, *Hippoglossus hippoglossus* and *H. stenolepis,* respectively, are very similar, with large mouths and sharp, strong teeth. They feed voraciously on other fish and are found in colder waters. The maximum weight of a halibut is 600 lb (270 kg), but the usual specimens caught offshore at 100 to 400 fathoms weigh from 20 to 100 lb (9–45 kg); the male is generally much smaller than the female. The California halibut, a smaller species (up to 60 lb/27 kg), is found S of San Francisco. The commercially valuable tribe of European flatfishes called turbots is represented in American waters by a single species, *Psetta maxima,* commonly called the window pane, found on the Atlantic coast from Maine to the Carolinas. It is much smaller than its European cousins, rarely weighing over 2 lb (.9 kg), whereas the European turbots may reach 30 lb (13.5 kg). Flatfishes are classified in the phylum CHORDATA, subphylum Vertebrata, class Osteichthyes, order Pleuronectiformes.

flat foot, condition of the human FOOT in which the entire sole rests on the ground when the person is standing. When the foot muscles are weakened or the ligaments are strained and stretched, the arch lowers, so that instead of the natural curved contour, there is flattening of the entire sole. Sometimes no discomfort accompanies flat foot. However, fallen arches may cause disalignment of other foot structures so that there is pain not only in the arch area but also in the calf muscles and sometimes as far up as the lower back; the discomfort is increased by prolonged standing. Flat foot may be inherited or may be caused by rickets, obesity, metabolic disorder, debilitating disease, or faulty footwear. Treatment and exercise directed by an orthopedic physician are sometimes advisable. Arch supports or other devices to be worn inside the shoe are often prescribed.

Flathead, river, c.240 mi (390 km) long, rising as the North Fork, in SE British Columbia, Canada, and flowing generally SE through NW Montana, to Coram, where it is joined by the Middle Fork (c.85 mi/140 km long) and the South Fork (c.80 mi/130 km long). It continues S through Flathead Lake, then W and S to Clark Fork River. Hungry Horse Dam and Kerr Dam are the centers of hydroelectric, irrigation, and flood control projects in the river's basin.

Flathead Indians, North American Indians, also known as the Salish Indians, who in the early 19th cent. inhabited the Bitterroot River valley of W Montana. Their language belongs to the Salishan branch of the Algonquian-Wakashan linguistic stock (see AMERICAN INDIAN LANGUAGES). These people never practiced head flattening, but the Columbia River tribes who shaped the front of the head to create a pointed appearance spoke of their neighbors, the Salish, as "flatheads" in contrast. After the introduction of the horse the Flathead adopted a Plains culture, including the hunting of buffalo and the use of the tepee. They fought a series of wars with the Blackfoot Indians over hunting land. The Jesuit missionary Pierre Jean DE SMET, who in 1841 founded the mission of St. Mary in Bitterroot valley among the Flathead, persuaded the Blackfoot to make peace. By the Garfield Treaty (1872) the Flathead agreed to move north to the valley of the lake and river now bearing their name, where, with a band of the Kootenai Indians, they dwell and together number some 2,800. The city of Seattle is named after one of their great chiefs. See O. W. Johnson, *Flathead and Kootenay* (1969); J. G. Jorgensen, *Salish Language and Culture* (1969).

Flathead Lake, 197 sq mi (510 sq km), 30 mi (48 km) long, NW Mont.; largest natural lake in Montana. Formed by the glacial damming of the Flathead River, which flows through it from north to south, Flathead Lake has an irregular shoreline and many small islands. Surrounded by mountains, the lake is a noted recreation area. Kerr Dam, at the southern end of the lake, provides hydroelectricity (168,000-kw capacity) and water for irrigation.

Flatman, Thomas, 1637–88, English poet and miniature painter. There were several editions of his *Poems and Songs* (1674). One of his self-portraits is in the Victoria and Albert Museum. A portrait of Charles II is in the Wallace Collection, London. His miniatures are noted for their vitality.

Flattery, Cape, NW Wash., at the rocky entrance to Juan de Fuca Strait; discovered in 1778 by Capt. James Cook. A lighthouse and an Indian reservation are on the cape, whose cliffs rise 120 ft (37 m) above the Pacific Ocean.

flatworm: see PLATYHELMINTHES; WORM.

Flaubert, Gustave (güstäv' flōbĕr'), 1821–80, French novelist. Flaubert is regarded as one of the supreme masters of the realistic novel. He was a scrupulous, slow writer, intent on the exact word (*le mot juste*) and complete objectivity. The son of a surgeon, he studied law unsuccessfully in Paris and returned home to devote himself to writing. Because of a severe nervous malady he spent most of his life at Croisset, near Rouen, with his mother and niece. In 1856, after five years of work, Flaubert published his masterpiece, *Madame Bovary,* in a Paris journal. Portraying the frustrations and love affairs of a romantic young woman married to a dull provincial doctor, the novel is written in a superbly controlled style. The book resulted in his being prosecuted on moral grounds, but he won the case. This was followed by *Salammbô* (1863), a meticulously documented novel of ancient Carthage; a revision of an earlier novel, *L'Éducation sentimentale* (1870); the final version of *The Temptation of St. Anthony* (1874), which had been written three times; and the volume *Three Tales* (1877), which contained the great short story "A Simple Heart." After his death his unfinished satire *Bouvard and Pécuchet* was published (1881). His correspondence, including that with George Sand and the letters to his niece Caroline, appeared in nine volumes (1926–33). See *The Selected Letters of Flaubert* (ed. and tr. by Francis Steegmuller, 1954); studies by V. H. Brombert (1966) and Enid Starkie (Vol. I, 1967; Vol. II, 1971); Francis Steegmuller, *Flaubert and Madame Bovary* (1939, rev. ed. 1968), and Henry James, *Notes on Novelists* (1914, repr. 1969).

Flavian (flā'vēən), ancient Roman gens. The name was applied especially to three Roman emperors, VESPASIAN and his sons TITUS and DOMITIAN.

Flavian of Antioch (ăn'tēŏk), d. 404, Catholic patriarch of Antioch. He succeeded St. MELETIUS. A rival claimant to the patriarchate, Evagrius, was illegally consecrated, but when Evagrius died Flavian was recognized (c.398), ending the Antioch schism.

Flavin, Dan (flā'vĭn), 1933–, American sculptor, b. New York City. In the early 1960s, Flavin experimented with fluorescent lights, bending them into complex, angular shapes and testing the effects they have on their immediate environment. His sculptures, which incorporate installations of commercially made fixtures, diffuse colored light so as to break down the space around them. Flavin's work is represented in the Solomon R. Guggenheim and Los Angeles County museums.

flavin: see COENZYME.

flavin adenine dinucleotide (FAD): see COENZYME.

flax, common name for members of the Linaceae, a family of annual herbs, especially members of the genus *Linum,* and for the fiber obtained from such plants. The flax of commerce (several varieties of *L. usitatissimum*) has been cultivated since prehistoric times (see LINEN). It was the major source of cloth fiber until the growth of the cotton industry (c.1800) and the competitive use of other fibers, such as jute. Flax has been transplanted from its native locales in Eurasia to all temperate zones of the world that provide a suitable habitat (a cool, damp climate) for its cultivation as a fiber plant; it is also grown in many tropical countries for its oil-bearing seeds. Flax plants grow to 4 ft (120 cm) in height and bear blue or white flowers that mature into bolls containing 10 seeds each. When grown for fiber, flax is sown densely to prevent branching and is gathered before maturity; for seed, it is sown sparsely and allowed to branch and fruit. To obtain the fiber, the stems, stripped of leaves, may be tied in bunches and immersed in warm water for a few days or in cool water for one or two weeks, or they may be spread out on grass and exposed to the dew and sun for several weeks. This process, called retting, permits bacteria to break down the woody tissues by fermentation and to dissolve by enzyme action the substances binding the fiber cells. After retting, the stems are washed and allowed to dry and then are scutched (beaten) to separate the fibers from other material and to crush the pith. A combing process (called hackling) removes any remaining nonfibrous matter. The fiber cells range in length from ½ to 2 in. (1.3–5.1 cm); the cell bundles (fibers) range from 12 to 36 in. (30–90 cm). Short, broken fibers are called tow and are used to make coarse fabrics and cordage; the long fibers are used for strong threads and fine linens. Flax fiber is also used for such products as insulating material and writing and cigarette paper. The seeds are crushed to make LINSEED OIL, and the remaining LINSEED CAKE is used for fodder; dried flaxseed is used in various medicinal preparations. Flax is classified in the division MAGNOLIOPHYTA, class Magnoliopsida, order Linales, family Linaceae.

Flaxman, John, 1755–1826, English sculptor and draftsman. At 20 he went to work for Josiah Wedgwood, designing the cameo-like decorations for Wedgwood's pottery. Later, in Rome, he devoted himself to sculpture and produced outline figure drawings from Greek vases as illustrations for works of Homer, Dante, Aeschylus, and Hesiod. These were engraved by his friend William Blake. He is well known for his neoclassical memorial sculpture of Sir Joshua Reynolds, Admiral Earl Howe, and Lord Nelson (all: St. Paul's Cathedral). See study by W. G. Constable (1927).

flea, common name for any of the small, wingless INSECTS of the order Siphonaptera. The adults of both sexes eat only blood and are all external parasites of mammals and birds. Fleas have hard bodies flattened from side to side, and piercing and sucking mouthparts. Their legs are powerful and adapted for fast movement and jumping, enabling them to find new hosts as well as to escape quickly the attempts of the hosts to remove them. The adults can survive away from a host for several weeks without eating. Flea eggs are usually laid in dirt or in the nest of the host; the larvae feed on organic material and the feces of adult fleas. METAMORPHOSIS is complete; the larvae spin silken cocoons when ready to pupate. Many species are not specific to a particular host species, and cat and dog fleas, as well as the human flea of the warmer parts of Europe and Asia, attack man. Certain rat fleas transmit TYPHUS and bubonic PLAGUE to man, and another species transmits TULAREMIA from rabbits. Fleas also transmit several species of TAPEWORMS that sometimes infest man. The CHIGOE is a flea. Water fleas and beach fleas are CRUSTACEANS and not closely related to the insects. Fleas are classified in the phylum ARTHROPODA, class Insecta, order Siphonaptera.

fleabane, any plant of the genus *Erigeron,* widely distributed herbs of the family Compositae (COMPOSITE family), especially abundant in temperate and mountainous regions of North America. The flowers, ranging from white to pink and purple, resemble daisies or asters, hence many of the common names, e.g., the daisy fleabanes (*E. ramosus, strigosus,* and sometimes other species), widespread weeds, and the beach aster, or seaside daisy (*E. glaucus*), of the Pacific coast. The eastern *E. pulchellus* is called robin's-plantain. Other similar composites are sometimes also called fleabane. Fleabane is classified in the division MAGNOLIOPHYTA, class Magnoliopsida, order Asterales, family Compositae.

Flèche, La (lä flĕsh), town (1968 pop. 15,951), Sarthe dept., on the Loir River. Tanning and the manufacture of clothing and paper are the chief industries. The town is famous for its college, the Prytanée, founded by Henry IV in the 16th cent., where René Descartes was a pupil. In 1808, Napoleon I transformed the school into a military academy open only to the sons of officers and members of the Legion of Honor. La Flèche has a 15th-century château that houses the town hall.

flèche: see SPIRE.

Fléchier, Esprit (ĕsprē' flāshyā'), 1632–1710, French writer. He was a famous pulpit orator and became bishop of Nîmes. His principal work is an account of special assizes held at Clermont (1665) for the repression of crime, in which most of the local nobility was involved. Fléchier's manner is witty and detached; he attended the proceedings only as an onlooker. See W. W. Comfort, *The Clermont Assizes of 1665: Translated from Abbé Fléchier's Mémoires sur les Grands Jours d'Auvergne* (1938).

Flecker, James Elroy, 1884–1915, English poet and playwright. From 1910–13 he served in the diplomatic corps. A preoccupation with the exotic is revealed in his verse, particularly in *The Golden Journey to Samarkand* (1913). His two plays, *Hassan* (pub. 1922) and *Don Juan* (pub. 1925), were written in verse. In 1923–24, *Hassan* was lavishly and successfully produced in London.

fleece, mat of WOOL formed by shearing a sheep in one continuous operation. The average fleece weighs from 5 to 10 lb (2.3–4.5 kg); in highbred wool sheep such as the American Merinos a ram's fleece may reach 30 lb (13.6 kg). The weight lost in cleansing the fleece of grease before sorting the wool is called shrinkage. On large sheep ranches hand shearing, once a competition skill, has largely been replaced by machine shearing. In heraldry a fleece is a whole, stuffed ram's fleece, complete with head and feet, suspended by a band around its middle. See also GOLDEN FLEECE and SHEEP.

Fleet, Thomas, 1685–1758, American colonial printer, b. Shropshire, England. He arrived in Boston c.1712, a refugee because of his opposition to the High Church, and became a prominent printer and publisher of the colony. From 1731 until his death he published a weekly paper first called *Weekly Rehearsal* and changed in 1735 to the Boston *Evening Post.*

Fleet Prison, former jail in London, England. Rebuilt after it was destroyed in the Peasants' Revolt of 1381, again after the great fire of 1666, and once more after the Gordon riots of 1780, it was finally demolished in 1845–46. After the 17th cent. it was notable as a debtors' prison. Fleet marriages were clandestine and irregular ceremonies performed at Fleet Prison by debtor clergymen. Although not illegal, the system was so abused that it was abolished in the reign of George II.

Fleet Street, street in the City of London, England. It is the center of English journalism.

Fleetwood, Charles, 1618?–1692, English parliamentary general. He fought under Oliver Cromwell in many battles of the English civil war and later (1650) in Scotland. He became (1651) a member of the council of state and married (1652) Bridget, daughter of Cromwell and widow of Henry IRETON. He succeeded Ireton as commander in chief in Ireland (1652–55) and continued Ireton's work in directing the settlement of English soldiers on lands confiscated from Irish landholders. As ranking military officer under Richard CROMWELL, he led (1659) the army coup that forced the protector to dissolve Parliament. At the Restoration (1660) he was barred from holding further public office.

Fleetwood, municipal borough (1971 pop. 28,584), Lancashire, NW England, on Morecambe Bay at the mouth of the Wyre estuary. Fleetwood, a port, trades with the Isle of Man and Belfast. Fishing is the major industry. Sir Peter Hesketh Fleetwood founded the town in 1836 and developed it into a trading port and seaside resort. Industries include radio-valve assembly and shoe manufacture. Rossall public school, founded in 1844, is in Fleetwood.

Flémal, Bertholet (bĕrtōlĕ' flāmäl'), 1614–75, Flemish painter of mythological and religious subjects. He went to Italy in 1638 and worked in Florence for the Grand Duke Ferdinand III. Returning to Paris, he was commissioned to decorate one of the galleries at Versailles. He did paintings in a classical style for many churches in his native Liège. Among his few surviving works are *Death of Lucretia* (Kassel) and *Mysteries of the Old and New Testaments* (Louvre). His name is also spelled Flémalle and Flamaël.

Flémalle, Master of: see CAMPIN, ROBERT.

Fleming, Sir Alexander, 1881–1955, Scottish bacteriologist, discoverer of penicillin (1928) and lysozyme (1922), an antibacterial substance found in saliva and other body secretions. Educated at St. Mary's Hospital Medical School, Univ. of London, where he later became professor of bacteriology, he published many articles on bacteriology, immunology, and chemotherapy. He shared the 1945 Nobel Prize in Physiology and Medicine with Ernst B. Chain and Sir Howard W. Florey for work on penicillin. Fleming was knighted in 1944. See biography by André Maurois (tr. 1959).

Fleming, Sir John Ambrose, 1849–1945, English electrical engineer. He was a leader in the development of electric lighting, the telephone, and wireless telegraphy in England and the inventor of a thermionic valve (the first electron tube). Fleming was a professor at the Univ. of London and at University College and was knighted in 1929. Among his many publications are *Fifty Years of Electricity* (1921) and *The Propagation of Electric Currents in Telephone and Telegraph Conductors* (1911). See his *Memories of a Scientific Life* (1934); biography by J. T. MacGregor-Morris (1954).

Fleming, Peggy, 1948–, U.S. ice skater, b. San Jose, Calif. She began skating at age 9, and after distinguished accomplishments as a juvenile and novice skater, she was U.S. Ladies Champion from 1963 to 1968, Olympic champion in 1968, and World Champion in 1966, 1967, and 1968. In 1968 she became a professional ice skater. Her style is marked not only by superb technical control but also by an exceptional sense of music and dance.

Fleming, Walter Lynwood, 1874–1932, American historian, b. near Brundidge, Ala. He taught at West Virginia Univ. (1904–7) and at Louisiana State Univ. (1907–17) before becoming professor of history at Vanderbilt. From 1923 to his retirement in 1928 because of ill health, Fleming was dean of the college of arts and sciences and director of the graduate school at Vanderbilt. His scholarly reputation is based chiefly upon his studies of the Reconstruction period. He edited *Documents Relating to Reconstruction* (1904) and wrote *Civil War and Reconstruction in Alabama* (1905), *Documentary History of Reconstruction* (2 vol., 1906–7), *The Sequel of Appomattox* ("Chronicles of America" series, 1919), and *The Freedmen's Savings Bank* (1927). He also edited *General W. T. Sherman as College President* (1912), wrote *Louisiana State University, 1860–1896* (1936), and contributed widely to periodicals. From 1914 to 1922 he was a member of the board of editors of the *Mississippi Valley Historical Review* and was also an editor of the series "The South in the Building of the Nation."

Flemish art and architecture. Flanders achieved special eminence in art c.1200 and in the 15th and 17th cent. and was among the most culturally productive regions at other times. During the Middle Ages, Flemish art followed the contemporary early Christian, Carolingian, and Romanesque styles. In the 12th cent. Rainer of Huy, Godefroid de Claire, and Nicholas of Verdun, among others, were noted for their work in metal and enamel. In the same century an important late Romanesque cathedral was built at Tournai (see ROMANESQUE ARCHITECTURE AND ART). In succeeding centuries, the metalworks of Dinant lent their name to the French word *dinanderie*, for *metalwork*, and Flemish brass workers and copper workers produced sophisticated pieces. Flanders followed the French in their adaptation of Gothic styles until the late 14th cent., when Flemish artists contributed vigorously realistic figures to the elegant, more fragile French manner of painting and manuscript ILLUMINATION (see GOTHIC ARCHITECTURE AND ART). Jean de Cambrai introduced similarly powerful and realistic forms into French sculpture, along with André Beauneveu and Jacques de Baerze. Jean Bondol of Bruges was a leading illuminator and TAPESTRY designer. The marriage in 1369 of the daughter of the count of Flanders to the duke of Burgundy led to a concentration of artists around the wealthy Burgundian court. It was the center of activity for such painters and manuscript illuminators as Melchior Broederlam, the Limbourg brothers, the Boucicaut master, Jean Malouel, and Jan van Eyck. Claus Sluter executed the famous sculpture at the court-sponsored Carthusian monastery of Champmol. Splendid examples of secular architecture were executed in the 14th and 15th cent., including the Ypres cloth hall and the city halls of Brussels and Louvain. Robert Campin, identified with the Master of Flémalle, painted at Tournai, where sculpture and tapestry-making also flourished. The masterpieces of 15th-century Flemish painting are remarkable for acute observation of nature, symbolism in realistic disguise, depiction of spatial depth and landscape backgrounds, and delicate precision of brushwork. The achievements in symbolism (see ICONOGRAPHY) and REALISM of Campin and the Van Eycks, who mastered the technique of oil PAINTING in the first third of the century, were continued in the second third by Roger van der Weyden, Dieric Bouts, and Petrus Christus. These artists refined the depiction of psychological expression, landscape, and space. In the last third of the 15th cent. Hugo van der Goes and Hieronymus Bosch were especially sensitive to complex emotional expression and fantastic subject matter, while Hans Memling, Gerard David, Joachim Patinir, Quentin Massys, Justus of Ghent, and Joos van Cleef produced paintings in a calmer mood, based on the achievements of earlier Flemings with occasional influences from Italian art. Italy attracted many 16th-century artists. Jan Gossaert and Jan van Scorel were among those who imported Italian Renaissance forms and motifs into the North. The center of Flemish artistic activity moved at this time to Antwerp, where a school of mannerist artists arose, more clearly influenced by Southern European aesthetic development (see MANNERISM). Frans Floris was a leading representative of this trend. In general, with the exception of the brilliantly original Pieter Bruegel, the elder, late 15th-century Flemish art followed Italian models, although it preserved interest in GENRE realism and LANDSCAPE PAINTING as seen in the works of Paul Brill, Gillis van Coninxloo, and others. With Rubens, Flemish art again became preeminent in Europe, and his influence dominated painting throughout much of the 17th cent. The greatest patron of Flemish art remained the church, and Rubens's greatest influence was exerted through his religious paintings rather than his portraiture or his apotheoses of European rulers. Elements of his energetic line, brushwork, and understanding of form, his rich, warm color, and his ideal of robust beauty were emulated in the work of his pupil Jacob Jordaens and in that of his more consciously elegant and more highly individual follower Sir Anthony Van Dyck. The 16th-century landscape style, emphasizing exquisite detail and brilliant color, persisted in the works of Jan Bruegel, the elder; Roelandt Savery; Joost de Momper; and Gilles de Hondecoeter, who worked in Holland. Outstanding 17th-century painters of STILL LIFE include Jan Bruegel and Frans Snyders; genre painters included David Teniers and Adriaen Brouwer. The principal exponent of CLASSICISM, the painter Abraham Janssens, brought elements of Caravaggesque painting to the Flemish school (see CARAVAGGIO, MICHELANGELO MERISI DA). The graphic arts also flourished in Flanders at this time. The principal Flemish sculptor was François Duquesnoy, who practiced in Italy. Architecture in the later 16th and 17th cent. blended heavy northern decorative taste and steeply pitched roofs with Italian mannerist and BAROQUE forms; the Antwerp town hall (1561-65) and Rubens's house (c.1610) are characteristic buildings. In the 18th cent. French ROCOCO taste predominated in Flanders, but in the 19th cent. a flourishing Belgian school of romantic painters arose (see ROMANTICISM), including Gustave Wappers, Hendrik Leys, and the genre painter Henri de Braekeleer (1840-88). Two other noted Belgians, Alfred Stevens and Henri Evenepoel, worked chiefly in Paris. The principal figures in 20th-century Belgian art include James Ensor, an individualistic painter of grotesque personal visions whose major works were created by 1900; the founders of Belgian EXPRESSIONISM, Jakob Smits and Eugene Laermans; the sculptor and painter Rik Wouters; the later expressionist painters Frits van den Berghe and Constant Permeke; the internationally recognized exponents of SURREALISM Paul Delvaux and René Margritte; and later painters of the abstract school Anne Bonnet and Louis van Lint. The architects Victor Horta and Henri van de Velde stand alone as the major 20th-century Belgians in their field. See articles on individual artists, e.g., Claus SLUTER. See M. D. Whinney, *Early Flemish Painting* (1968); William Gaunt, *Flemish Cities* (1970); Leo and Thierry van Puyvelde, *Flemish Painting* (2 vol., tr. 1970 and 1972); Max Friedländer, *Early Netherlandish Painting* (9 vol. in 10, tr. 1967-72).

Flemish language, member of the West Germanic group of the Germanic subfamily of the Indo-European family of languages (see GERMANIC LANGUAGES). Generally regarded as the Belgian variant of Dutch (see DUTCH LANGUAGE) rather than as a separate tongue, Flemish is spoken by approximately 5 million people in Belgium, where it is one of the official languages, and by another 200,000 persons in France. So closely are Flemish and Dutch related that the difference between them has been compared to the difference between American and British English; however, some scholars hold that they have diverged sufficiently since the 16th cent. to be described as separate languages.

Flemish literature: see DUTCH AND FLEMISH LITERATURE.

Flensburg (flĕns'bŏŏrkh), city (1970 pop. 95,476), Schleswig-Holstein, N West Germany, on the Flensburg Fjord, an arm of the Baltic Sea, at the Danish border. An active Baltic port and commercial center, it has shipyards, rum distilleries, smoked-fish plants, and paper factories. Flensburg was chartered in 1284 and acquired commercial importance in the 16th cent. In 1867 it passed from the Danish crown to Prussia. During World War II it was heavily bombed and lost its large merchant fleet. There is a municipal museum in the city.

Fleta (flē'tə), treatise of unknown authorship on the English common law, written in the late 13th cent. Its name is derived from the belief that it was written in the old Fleet Prison. The book is almost entirely based upon the work of Henry de BRACTON. The name is sometimes spelled Fleda.

Fletcher, Andrew, 1655-1716, Scottish politician, known as Fletcher of Saltoun. An opponent of the policies of the duke of Lauderdale and the duke of York (later James II) in Scotland, he fled to Holland in 1682. He joined the rebellion (1685) of the duke of MONMOUTH but abandoned it as a result of a private quarrel. Returning to Scotland at the time of the Glorious Revolution (1688), Fletcher and others formed a party to work for greater independence for Scotland. They were responsible for the Act of Security (1704), which provided that at the death of Queen Anne the Scottish Parliament would nominate a separate monarch unless Scotland's civil and religious liberties were guaranteed. After the passage of the Act of Union (1707), which he vehemently opposed, Fletcher devoted himself to agricultural experiments and to writing on Scottish affairs. See biography by W. C. Mackenzie (1935).

Fletcher, Giles, the elder, 1548?-1611, English writer and diplomat. He became a member of Parliament and later treasurer of St. Paul's. An envoy to Russia in 1588, he published an account of his experiences, *Of the Russe Common Wealth* (1591). His principal poetic work is a sonnet sequence, *Licia* (1593). See *The English Works of Giles Fletcher, the Elder,* ed. by L. E. Berry (1963). His oldest son, **Giles Fletcher,** the younger, b. 1585 or 1586, d. 1623, was also a poet. Educated at Trinity College, Cambridge, he served as a reader in Greek until 1618, when he took holy orders; he became rector at Alderton, Suffolk, in 1619. His best poem, *Christ's Victory and Triumph* (1610), an example of baroque devotional poetry, owed much to Spenser. Giles Fletcher the elder's second son, **Phineas Fletcher** (1582-1650), was a poet also. Educated at Eton and Cambridge, he was ordained in 1611. Although he was called the Spenser of his age and had an influence on the writing of Milton, he is chiefly remembered for *The Purple Island* (1633), a belabored allegorical poem on the human body and mind. His other works include *The Locusts or Apollyonists* (1627), *Britain's Ida* (1628), and *A Father's Testament* (1670). See study by A. B. Langdale (1937, repr. 1968).

Fletcher, John, 1579-1625, English dramatist, b. Rye, Sussex, educated at Cambridge. A member of a prominent literary family, he began writing for the stage about 1606, first with Francis BEAUMONT, with whom his name is inseparably linked, later with Massinger and others. It is thought that Fletcher collaborated with Shakespeare on *Henry VIII* and *Two Noble Kinsmen.* Though there is great uncertainty in dating the plays of Beaumont and Fletcher, their chief works appeared between 1607 and 1613. In *Philaster, A Maid's Tragedy, A King and No King,* and *The Scornful Lady,* they developed the form of the romance tragicomedy, which came to characterize a whole generation of later plays. In these plays a potentially tragic situation is developed until, at the end, through a twist of plot a happy solution is effected. Though Beaumont and Fletcher proved very popular in their own time as well as in the 18th cent., today critics generally agree that they relied on contrivance and extravagance in place of moral insight and intellectual honesty. See edition of the works of Beaumont and Fletcher by F. Bowers (Vol. I, 1966-); studies by E. Waith (1952), A. E. Thorndike (1965), and J. H. Wilson (1968).

Fletcher, John Gould, 1886-1950, American poet, b. Little Rock, Ark., educated (1903-7) at Harvard. As a young man he traveled throughout Europe, finally settling in England, where he became a leader of the imagist school of poetry. The influence of the IMAGISTS appears in his early collections *Irradiations: Sand and Spray* (1915) and *Goblins and Pagodas* (1916). In his later, more mature work Fletcher turned from free verse to more exacting and traditional forms. *The Black Rock* (1928), *XXIV Elegies* (1935), *Selected Poems* (1938, Pulitzer Prize), *South Star* (1941), and *The Burning Mountain* (1946) reveal his growth as a poet. Many of his poems reflect his childhood and youth in the Southwest. See his autobiography, *Life Is My Song* (1937).

Fletcher, Thomas Clement, 1827-99, governor of Missouri (1865-69), b. Herculaneum, Mo. A Democrat opposed to slavery, he became a Republican in 1856 and supported Lincoln for the presidential nomination in 1860. In the Civil War, Fletcher commanded a Missouri regiment and served in the Vicksburg, Chattanooga, and Atlanta campaigns. He was brevetted brigadier general of volunteers for his service in repulsing Sterling Price at Pilot Knob, Mo. (Oct., 1864). As governor in the difficult postwar period, he proved an exceptionally able administrator.

Fletcher vs. Peck, case decided by the U.S. Supreme Court in 1810, involving the YAZOO LAND FRAUD. The court ruled that an act of the Georgia legislature rescinding a land grant was unconstitutional because it revoked rights previously granted by contract. The decision was the first to declare a state legislative act unconstitutional.

Flettner, Peter: see FLÖTNER, PETER.

Fleurus (flörüs'), town (1970 pop. 8,523), Hainaut prov., S Belgium. It is a manufacturing center. At Fleurus, Mansfield and Christian of Brunswick defeated (1622) the Spanish in the Thirty Years War, the French under Marshal Luxembourg defeated (1690) the Dutch and their allies in the War of the Grand Alliance, and the French under Jourdan defeated the Austrians in a decisive battle (1794) of the French Revolutionary Wars.

Fleury, André Hercule de (äNdrā' ĕrkül' də flörē'), 1653-1743, French statesman, cardinal of the Roman Catholic Church. Tutor of the young LOUIS XV, he became, at the age of 73, chief adviser to the king and virtual ruler of France (1726-43). Fleury restored order to the national finances, disorganized by the speculative schemes of John LAW. The currency was stabilized, roads were built, the merchant marine expanded, and a growth in commerce resulted. By his attempts to suppress the Jansenists (see JANSEN, CORNELIS) Fleury provoked opposition, particularly from the parlements [courts]. He strove for peace abroad but became involved in the War of the POLISH SUCCESSION; through it, however, he assured the eventual reversion of Lorraine to France and established a Spanish Bourbon on the throne of Naples. He was also drawn into the War of the Austrian Succession. See A. McC. Wilson, *French Foreign Policy during the Administration of Cardinal Fleury* (1936, repr. 1972).

Fleury, Claude (klōd), 1640-1723?, French ecclesiastical historian, a Roman Catholic priest, confessor to Louis XV, and author of the learned and unbiased *Histoire ecclésiastique.* This great work, in 20 volumes, occupied him for 30 years. It was the first systematic history of the Church, its organization, doctrines, and rites.

Flexner, Abraham, 1866-1959, American educator, b. Louisville, Ky., grad. Johns Hopkins Univ., 1886. After 19 years as a secondary school teacher and principal, he took graduate work at Harvard and at the Univ. of Berlin. In 1908 he joined the research staff of the Carnegie Foundation for the Advancement of Teaching and in 1910 wrote a report, *Medical Education in the United States and Canada,* which is generally called the Flexner Report. It hastened much-needed reforms in the standards, organization, and curriculums of American medical schools. From 1912 to 1925, Flexner was a member of the General Education Board, serving as secretary after 1917. He was director of the newly organized Institute for Advanced Study at Princeton from 1930 to 1939. His influential works on education range from *A Modern School* (1916) and *The Gary Schools* (with F. B. Bachman, 1918) to *The Burden of Humanism* (the Taylorian Lecture at Oxford Univ., 1928) and his widely known study, *Universities: American, English, German* (1930). His biography of H. S. Pritchett was published in 1943. See his autobiography (rev. ed. 1960).

Flexner, Simon, 1863-1946, American pathologist, b. Louisville, Ky., M.D. Univ. of Louisville, 1889; brother of Abraham Flexner. He served with the Rockefeller Institute (now Rockfeller University) from 1903 to 1935 (as its first director, 1920-35) and was Eastman professor at Oxford from 1937 to 1938. He worked on experimental epidemiology and venoms and is known especially for his serum treatment of cerebrospinal meningitis and for his studies of poliomyelitis. He also isolated a bacillus of dysentery.

flicker: see WOODPECKER.

Fliedner, Theodor (tā'ōdôr flēt'nər), 1800-1864, German Protestant minister and philanthropist. In 1826 he organized the first prison society of Germany. Ten years later at Kaiserswerth he founded the pioneer deaconess house and hospital for the indigent sick. Here Florence Nightingale worked and gained many ideas. Fliedner established schools and orphanages in Europe and from 1849 to 1851 stimulated the organization of mother houses for deaconesses in Europe, America, and Asia. See biography by Catherine Winkworth (1867).

flight, sustained, self-powered motion through the air, as accomplished by an animal, aircraft, or rocket. Adaptation for flight is highly developed in birds and insects. The bat is the only mammal that accomplishes true flight; flying squirrels, flying fish, and flying lizards glide rather than fly. Birds fly by means of the predominantly up-and-down motion of their wings. The flapping motion is not, however, straight up and down but semicircular, the wings generally moving backward on the upstroke and forward on the downstroke. That motion pushes air downward and to the rear, creating a lift and forward thrust. The leading edge of the slightly concave wings is rather sharp, and the feathers are small and close-fitting, so that a streamlined surface meets the air. On the trailing edge of each wing the interlocking of the larger feathers forms a surface that acts somewhat like the ailerons, or movable airfoils, of an airplane. In wing motion, the leading edge is

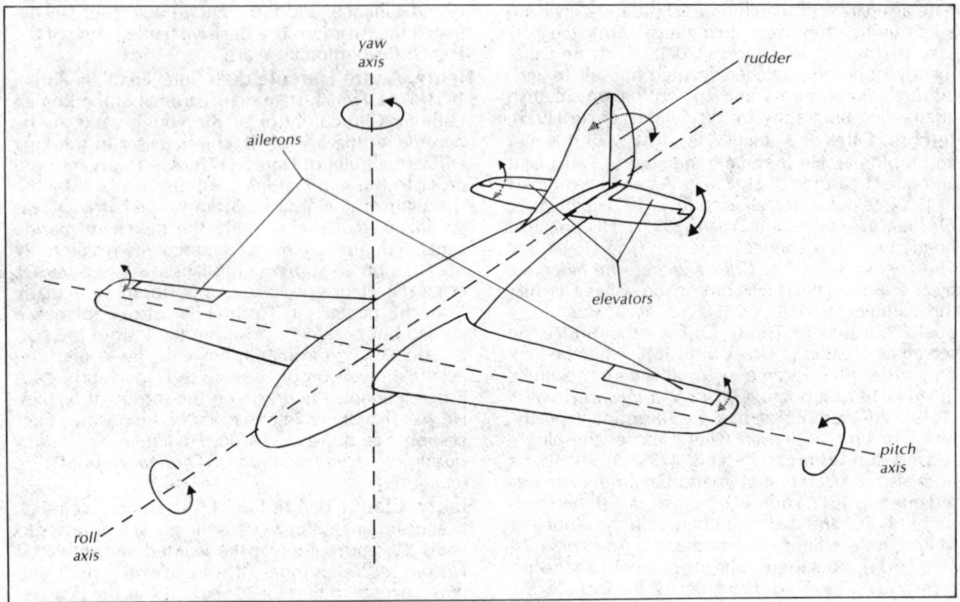

Aircraft motions and control surfaces: Yaw, or motion to the left or right, is controlled by the rudder. Pitch, or climbing or dropping, is controlled by the elevators, which move in the same direction, both up or both down. Roll, or lifting of one wing and dropping of the other, is controlled by the ailerons, which move in opposite directions, one up and the other down.

twisted so as to be lower than the trailing edge in the downward stroke and above the trailing edge in the upward stroke. Besides flapping, some birds also use gliding and soaring techniques in flight. In gliding, a bird holds its outstretched wings relatively still and relies on its momentum to keep it aloft for short distances. In soaring, a bird uses rising warm air currents to give it lift. The form and size of wings vary in different birds. In woodland birds the wings are somewhat rounded and have a relatively broad surface area. Birds with well-developed gliding ability, such as gannets and gulls, usually have narrow, pointed wings. Especially noted for their soaring power are eagles, vultures, crows, and some hawks. In soaring flight the feathers on the wings of these birds separate at the tips, resembling opened fingers against the sky. It is thought that this movement diverts the airstream over the wing and aids the bird in turning, banking, and wheeling. There is disagreement as to the maximum speeds achieved by birds in flight. While the flight speeds of most birds range from 10 to 60 mi (16–100 km) per hr, some have been recorded at speeds reaching 70 mi (110 km) per hr, for long distances and near 100 mi (160 km) per hr, for short flights. Man's first attempts at flight were made with flapping wings strapped to his arms in imitation of birds, but these had no success. Machines designed to fly in this way, called ornithopters, date to antiquity (c.400 B.C.) and models that are capable of flight have been known for more than 100 years. However, there are no practical aircraft based on ornithopter designs, even though an ornithopter—which has no theoretical top speed limit—should be capable at least of efficient low-speed flight. In the 1930s an Italian model weighing approximately 50 lb (110 kg) and powered by a 0.5-hp motor was successfully flown. Airships and balloons owe their ability to ascend and remain aloft to their inflation with a gas lighter than air; this is an application of Archimedes' principle of flotation, i.e., that a body immersed in a fluid (liquid or gas) is buoyed up by a force equal to the weight of the fluid that it displaces. Aircraft, which are heavier than air, are able to remain aloft because of forces developed by the movement of the craft through the air. Propulsion of most aircraft derives from the rearward acceleration of the air. It is an application of Newton's third law, i.e., that for every action there is an equal and opposite reaction. In propeller aircraft the forward motion is obtained through conversion of engine power to thrust by means of acceleration of air to the rear by the propeller. Lift is obtained largely from the upward pressure of the air against the airfoils (e.g., wings, tail fins, and ailerons), on whose upper surface the pressure becomes lower than that of the atmosphere. In jet-propelled aircraft, propulsion is achieved by heating air that passes through the engine and accelerating the resultant hot exhaust gases rearward at high velocities. Rockets are propelled by the rapid expulsion of gas through vents at the rear of the craft. The high speeds that are produced by jet and rocket engines have brought about substantial changes in the science of flight. See AERODYNAMICS; AIRPLANE; JET PROPULSION; ROCKET. See Bernard Ethin, *Dynamics of Atmospheric Flight* (1972); C. H. Gibbs-Smith, *History of Flying* (1957) and *Aviation* (1972); Roger Caras, ed., *Birds and Flight* (1971). See also bibliography under AVIATION.

flight simulator, device providing a controlled environment in which a flight trainee can experience conditions approximating those of actual flight. A simulator generally consists of an enclosure housing a working replica of the interior of the cockpit of an aircraft. This replica has all the usual instruments and is mounted in such a way that it can be moved to simulate the rolling, pitching, and yawing motions of an aircraft. The instrument readings, the student's control inputs, the position of the simulator, information about the characteristics of the aircraft being simulated, and information about the terrain over which it is supposed to be flying are coordinated by a computer so that the student experiences everything but the accelerations of actual flight. In early simulators, all visual information was provided by the instruments. Thus the student received practice in flying blind. The recent use of sophisticated computers has made it possible to provide video displays suggestive of conditions outside the cockpit.

Flinck, Govert (gō'värt flĭngk), 1615–1660, Dutch painter. A student of Rembrandt, Flinck is remembered mainly for his numerous portraits. There is a large and representative collection of Flinck's works in the Rijks Museum, one example from which, his *Blessing of Jacob,* illustrates his competent handling of religious subjects.

Flinders, Matthew, 1774–1814, English naval captain and hydrographer, noted for his charting and coast surveys of Australia and Tasmania. From 1795 to 1799 and again from 1801 to 1803 he made valuable maps and charts of the water and coasts, circumnavigating both Australia and Tasmania. He is said to have been the first to perceive and correct compass errors caused by iron ships. He wrote *A Voyage to Terra Australis* (1814). Sir William Matthew Flinders Petrie was his grandson. See biography by J. D. Mack (1966); study by Max Colwell (1970).

Flinders Island, Australia: see FURNEAUX GROUP.

Flinders Petrie, Sir William Matthew: see PETRIE, SIR WILLIAM MATTHEW FLINDERS.

Flinders Ranges, mountain chain, extending 260 mi (418 km) between Lake Torrens and Lake Frome, South Australia state, Australia; rises to 3,900 ft (1,189 m) at St. Mary's Peak. Uranium and copper are mined there.

Flin Flon (flĭn flŏn), city (1971 pop. in Manitoba, 8,873; in Saskatchewan, 471), on the Man.-Sask. border, Canada. It is a mining and smelting center in a region producing copper, zinc, silver, gold, and cadmium; it also serves a lumbering and fishing area.

Flint, Timothy, 1780–1840, American author, b. North Reading, Mass., grad. Harvard, 1800, and entered the ministry. As a missionary he traveled up and down the Mississippi valley from 1815 until 1825 and recorded in *Recollections of the Last Ten Years* (1826) the frontier life he experienced. He also wrote several romantic novels of frontier life, notably *Francis Berrian* (1826) and *George Mason, the Young Backwoodsman* (1829). His vivid *Biographical Memoir of Daniel Boone* (1833) did much to develop the Boone legend. See biography by J. E. Kirkpatrick (1911, repr. 1968); study by J. K. Folsom (1965).

Flint, city (1970 pop. 193,317), seat of Genessee co., S Mich., on the Flint River; inc. 1855. Since 1902 it has been one of the chief automobile-manufacturing centers of the world. The huge General Motors Corp. had its beginnings there in 1908, and many other major automobile makers (Chrysler, Chevrolet, Nash, Champion, Buick) also started in Flint. A fur-trading post was established there in 1819. Fur trading was succeeded by lumbering and then by cart and carriage making as Flint's major industry. The city was extensively damaged by a tornado in June, 1953. In the city are a branch of the Univ. of Michigan, a junior college, the General Motors Institute, an art institute, a state school for the deaf, a historical museum, a planetarium, and a nature preserve.

Flint, municipal borough (1971 pop. 14,660), Flintshire, NE Wales, on the Dee estuary. Flint has industries that produce rayon, nylon, paper, and clothing. The castle, built c.1300, was the scene of Richard II's submission to Bolingbroke in 1399. In 1974, Flint became part of the new nonmetropolitan county of Clwyd.

Flint, river: see CHATTAHOOCHEE, river.

flint, variety of QUARTZ that commonly occurs in rounded nodules and whose crystal structure is not visible to the naked eye. Flint is dark gray, smoky brown, or black in color; pale gray flint is called chert. When found in chalk or in other rocks containing lime, the nodules frequently have a white coating. Flint is translucent to opaque. It was early used by primitive peoples for making knives and spearheads because, although it is very hard, it is more readily shaped than stone; edges can be flaked off with comparative ease, especially those of freshly dug pieces, by pressure exerted with a piece of stone or bone. Since it is not chipped by pounding, as stone is, sharper edges are obtained. Use of flint tools defines the Stone Age cultures of the Pleistocene epoch. It was long used with steel for lighting fires and later for setting off the powder in flintlock firearms.

flint clay: see FIRE CLAY.

Flintshire, county (1971 pop. 175,396), 256 sq mi (663 sq km), NE Wales, bounded on the NE by the Dee estuary. The smallest county in Wales, it includes a small detached portion to the southeast. The county town is Mold; the chief industrial center is FLINT. The county lies in the North Wales coal field. The upland country of the Clwydian Hills is devoted to pasturage, while the fertile Clwyd and Dee valleys are given over to farming. Coal mining and the manufacture of iron and steel, rayon, bricks, textiles, paper, and chemicals are the chief industries. After the Norman conquest the region was heavily fortified by the border lords against the partially conquered Welsh. In 1974, Flintshire became part of the new nonmetropolitan county of Clwyd.

floatplane: see SEAPLANE.

flocculi (flŏk'yəlī"): see CHROMOSPHERE.

Flodden, field, Northumberland, N England, just across the border from Coldstream, Scotland. It was the scene of the battle of Flodden Field (1513), in which the English under Thomas Howard, 2d duke of Norfolk, defeated the Scots under James IV, who was killed.

Flood, Henry, 1732–91, Irish statesman. He entered the Irish House of Commons in 1759 and joined the fight to gain independence for the Irish Parliament. He lost favor with the nationalists, however, when he accepted (1775) a position in the government, and the leadership of the nationalists passed to Henry GRATTAN. Flood recaptured popularity when, following the repeal (1782) of Poynings's Law (see under POYNINGS, SIR EDWARD), he went beyond Grattan in demanding positive assurance of Irish legislative independence. But his opposition to CATHOLIC EMANCIPATION, which Grattan favored, once more reduced his following. Flood served (1783–90) in both the English and the Irish House of Commons, but he never regained his leadership of the Irish nationalists.

Flood, in the Bible: see DELUGE.

flood, inundation of land by the rise and overflow of a body of water. Floods occur most commonly when water from heavy rainfall, from melting ice and snow, or from a combination of these exceeds the carrying capacity of the river system or the lake into which it runs. Usually the combined flow of several tributaries causes flooding along the river bank or the shoreline. The rise and fall of the water level in a river is called the flood wave. Its highest point, or crest, travels progressively downstream. In the upstream portions of a river, the flood crest passes quickly. Further downstream the greater volume of water causes slower passage of the flood crest, resulting in floods of longer duration. In many regions, annual floods follow the thaws and rains of spring; in the arctic regions, especially in the basins of northward flowing rivers, the floods are caused by the thawing of the southern portion of the basin before the ice blocking the lower course of the river melts. Less predictable are floods resulting from waves, called storm surges, pushed onshore by an advancing hurricane, and from sudden torrential flows, called flash floods, following a brief, intense rainstorm or the bursting of a natural or man-made dam or levee. In addition to the duration and quantity of rainfall, the nature of the soil (permeability; state of saturation) composing the drainage area around a body of water affects the frequency of floods. Generally, flood control measures along a river are attempted at both its headwaters and its low-lying floodplains. Runoff can be detained in the headwaters by planting ground cover on the slopes, by building terraces to increase soil infiltration and prevent soil erosion, and by building small check dams to reduce the flow of water. Flood control on the lower floodplains involves building levees to contain the flow and straightening or dredging the channel to improve flow characteristics. Among the chief flood-control projects in the United States are the flood control works along the Mississippi River, the installations of the Tennessee Valley Authority, the Glen Canyon and Hoover dams on the Colorado River, and the systems of dams in the Columbia River basin (including Grand Coulee Dam) and in the Missouri River basin. Since early times continuous records of flood heights of the Nile have been kept at Cairo. The annual floodwaters of the Nile deposit fertile soil and are used for irrigation. A flood of the Tiber was recorded in 413 B.C. Records of floods on the Danube date from A.D. 1000. In China some of the world's most disastrous floods have been caused by the unstable Huang Ho. The river, which flows at or above the level of the bordering land, is contained in part by levees; however, because its channel has gradually become filled with deposited sediment, any appreciable increase in its volume causes the river to overflow and flood the surrounding area. The Netherlands, dependent on its dikes for protection from inundation, has suffered many disastrous floods from the sea and from the Rhine and Meuse rivers. In 1970 hundreds of thousands of people and livestock in Bangladesh were killed when the combination of astronomically high tides and a hurricane storm surge caused extremely widespread and sudden flooding of the low-lying delta of the Ganges and Brahmaputra rivers at the head of the Bay of Bengal. In the United States the Johnstown, Pa., flood of 1889, in which thousands of lives were lost, was caused by the breaking of a mud dam above the city. Even greater loss of life occurred (1900) in Galveston, Texas, when tide and storm surges engulfed the city after a hurricane. The hurricanes of 1938 on the New England and Long Island coasts and Hurricane Donna in 1960 along the Atlantic coast from Florida to the Long Island Sound were also followed by storm surges. In June, 1972, extremely heavy rainfall associated with a hurricane inundated the basins of the Chemung and Susquehanna rivers of New York and Pennsylvania, causing severely damaging floods in Corning and Elmira, N.Y., and Wilkes-Barre and Harrisburg, Pa. The worst floods in the United States from river overflow were in 1913 on the Miami River (a tributary of the Ohio), in 1927 and 1973 on the Mississippi River, and in 1935-36 on the Connecticut and other New England rivers. Accounts of floods that destroyed nearly all life are found in the mythology of many peoples. For the flood described in the Old Testament, see DELUGE. See W. G. Hoyt and W. B. Langbein, *Floods* (1955); Peter Briggs, *Rampage* (1973).

flood plain, level land along the course of a river formed by the deposition of sediment during periodic floods. Flood plains are sometimes of great extent. Below the conflux of the Ohio and the Mississippi, for example, the flood plains have a width of 80 mi (130 km) in some places. Among the rivers with extensive flood plains are the Nile, Ganges, Danube, Po, and most of the rivers of China. Flood plains are generally very fertile. In the United States in recent years there has been extensive house construction on flood plains, necessitating the construction of new dams to control annual small floods. Some scientists feel that this has greatly increased the danger to life and property from the major, uncontrollable floods that occur once or twice in a century.

Flor, Roger de, d. c.1306, German commander of Spanish mercenaries, b. Italy. He entered the order of the KNIGHTS TEMPLARS and fought (1291) at ACRE, but he was obliged to leave the order when accused of theft. He subsequently served as vice admiral under Frederick II of Sicily and after 1302 became the leader of a band of Spanish adventurers who entered the service of the Byzantine emperor ANDRONICUS II against the Turks. This Catalan company won several victories, but its oppression of the native population led to Roger's assassination by imperial order. His followers ravaged the countryside in revenge. They later migrated into Greece and established (1311) the duchy of Athens.

Flora, in Roman religion, goddess of flowers and fertility. Her festival, the Floralia, April 28–May 1, was celebrated with great gaiety and licentiousness.

Floral Park, village (1970 pop. 18,422), Nassau co., SE N.Y., on Long Island, a residential suburb of New York City; inc. 1908. It has a commercial flower industry.

Florence, Ital. *Firenze,* city (1971 pop. 461,602), capital of Tuscany and of Firenze prov., central Italy, on the Arno River, at the foot of the Apennines. Florence, the jewel of the Italian Renaissance, is one of the world's great historic cities. It is a commercial, industrial, and tourist center, and a rail junction. Manufactures include machinery, chemicals, furniture, and pharmaceuticals. The city is noted for its handicraft industry (producing ceramics, mosaics, and metal and leather goods) and is a leading center of women's fashions. Florence was the site of an Etruscan settlement. It later became a Roman town on the Cassian Way (the modern Piazza della Repubblica is on the site of the Roman Forum). In the 5th and 6th cent. A.D. the city was controlled, in turn, by the Goths, Byzantines, and Lombards. It became an autonomous commune in the 12th cent. In the 13th cent. the Guelphs (who were propapal) and the Ghibellines (who were proimperial) fought for control of the city. By the end of the 13th cent. the Guelphs held control, but they then split into warring factions, the Blacks and the Whites, best remembered because Dante, a Florentine, was banished (1302) as a White Guelph. Warfare raged, too, with other cities, notably Pisa, as the merchants and bankers of Florence made their own fortunes and that of the city; the sale of Florentine silks, tapestries, and jewelry brought great wealth. Florence grew as a result of war, absorbing Arezzo, Pistoia, Volterra, and Pisa. Growth was temporarily halted in 1348, when the Black Death killed approximately 60% of the city's population. Florence became a city-state and in the 15th cent. came under the control of Cosimo de' Medici, a wealthy merchant and patron of the arts. Although republican forms were kept until the 16th cent., the MEDICI family ruled, and Lorenzo de' Medici, who held power from 1469 to 1492, was able to put down the PAZZI CONSPIRACY (1478), instigated by Pope Sixtus IV. Under Lorenzo and his successors, Florence was for two centuries the golden city, with an incredible flowering of intellectual and artistic life. The list of artists working in the city was headed by Michelangelo, Leonardo da Vinci, Raphael, and Donatello. There were also numerous poets and scholars active in Florence, and the Accademia della Crusca was established (1582). Political life continued to be turbulent. The Medici were expelled by a revolution in 1494, the fiery religious reformer SAVONAROLA briefly held power (1494–98), and MACHIAVELLI was a diplomatic representative of the republic. The revolt against the Medici was over by 1512, but another revolution (1527-30) established a new republic, which, however, was forced to surrender to Emperor Charles V after a heroic defense. Under the restored Medici, Florence went on expanding and controlled most of Tuscany. In 1569, Cosimo I de' Medici was made grand duke, and Florence became the capital of the grand duchy of TUSCANY. The grand duchy, ruled by the house of Hapsburg-Lorraine after the extinction (1737) of the Medici line, was annexed to the kingdom of Sardinia in 1860. Florence was the capital of the newly founded kingdom of Italy from 1865 to 1871. Relatively few of the art treasures of Florence were harmed in World War II; the flooding of the Arno in Nov., 1966, however, caused considerable damage, which art experts sought, with considerable success, to repair. Only one bridge, the Ponte Vecchio (14th cent.), survived World War II, and now several modern bridges span the Arno. It is impossible to mention here all of the city's monuments, most of which date from the 13th to 15th cent. The Gothic cathedral of Santa Maria del Fiore (begun 1296) has a dome (1420–34) by BRUNELLESCHI; nearby are the slim campanile (269 ft/82 m high) designed by GIOTTO and the baptistery with famous bronze doors by Andrea Pisano and Lorenzo GHIBERTI. The large Franciscan Church of Santa Croce is the Florentine pantheon and has frescoes by Giotto, a crucifix by Donatello, and fine works by the DELLA ROBBIA family, ROSSELLINO, and others. The Church of Santa Maria Novella (1278–1350) has frescoes by Masaccio, Orcagna, and Ghirlandaio; fine cloisters; and a facade (1470) by Alberti. Some of the best works of Fra ANGELICO are in the museum of the Monastery of St. Mark. Important frescoes by Masolino, Masaccio, and Filippino LIPPI adorn the Church of Santa Maria del Carmine. The Church of San Lorenzo contains Michelangelo's tombs of the Medici; many works by Donatello; and the Laurentian Library, which holds approximately 10,000 manuscripts. On the Piazza della Signoria are the Palazzo Vecchio, which contains frescoes by Vasari and sculptures by Michelangelo; the Loggia dei Lanzi (later 14th cent.), which has the *Perseus* (1533) of CELLINI; and Ammanati's *Fountain of Neptune* (1576). The Uffizi Museum, housed in a Renaissance palace designed by Vasari, contains great collections of paintings, especially by Botticelli, Masaccio, and Piero della Francesca. The Pitti Palace (15th–17th cent.) also houses fine paintings, particularly by Raphael, Andrea del Sarto, and Titian. Behind the Pitti Palace are the terraced Boboli Gardens (1550), a good example of Italian landscaping architecture. Other important art museums include the Academy, with works by Michelangelo; the gallery in the BARGELLO palace, with works by Donatello; and the archaeological museum, with Etruscan, Egyptian, and Greco-Roman art. Among the numerous medieval and Renaissance palaces, the Medici-Riccardi, Strozzi, and Rucellai deserve special mention. The oratory of Orsanmichele (originally a wheat granary; rebuilt 1337–1404) has a tabernacle (14th cent.) by Orcagna. On a hill overlooking the city is the Romanesque basilica of San Miniato al Monte. The Univ. of Florence is an international cultural center. The National Library is in Florence. A school of music flourished in the city during the Renaissance, and the earliest operas, Peri's *Dafne* (1594) and *Euridice* (1600), were performed there.

Florence. 1 City (1970 pop. 34,031), seat of Lauderdale co., NW Ala., on the Tennessee River near MUSCLE SHOALS and adjacent to Wilson Dam (a national historic landmark); inc. 1818. It is in a cotton and mineral area, and power from Muscle Shoals has stimulated the growth of diversified industries. Aluminum and aluminum products, ceramic tile, textiles, stoves, chemicals, boats, and corrugated boxes are made. The mountain lakes in the area attract many tourists. Florence State Univ. is in the city. Of interest are the birthplace of W. C. Handy, now a museum; Pope's Tavern (1811), once a stagecoach stop and later a Civil War hospital; and an Indian mound, with a museum. **2** City (1970 pop. 11,661), Boone co., N central Ky., in a bluegrass farm region; inc. 1830. The city has a race course. Big Bone Lick State Park is nearby. **3** City (1970 pop. 25,997), seat of Florence co., NE S.C., in a farm and timber area; inc. 1871. It is an important focal point for railroads (with extensive repair shops and yards) and an industrial and trade center. During the Civil War it was a transportation and supply point and served as the site of a prison camp. It is the seat of Francis Marion College and a branch of the Univ. of South Carolina. Nearby are a national military cemetery and an agricultural experiment station.

Florence, Council of: see FERRARA-FLORENCE, COUNCIL OF.

florentium: see PROMETHIUM.

Flores, Juan José (hwän hōsā' flō'rās), 1800–1864, president of Ecuador (1830–34, 1839–45), b. Puerto Cabello, Venezuela. A commander under Bolívar in the War of Independence, Flores led (1830) the secession of Ecuador from the Colombian union and became its first president. A conservative who supported entrenched privileges, especially those of the Church, he was soon opposed by a liberal opposition under ROCAFUERTE, who succeeded him as president. Flores was twice reelected but, accused of dictatorial ambitions, he was exiled. Returning in 1860 with Gabriel García Moreno, he served as army chief until his death.

Flores (flôr'ĕs), island (1961 pop. 803,000), 6,627 sq mi (17,164 sq km), E Indonesia, one of the Lesser Sunda Islands. Flores is heavily wooded, rugged, and mountainous, rising to 7,872 ft (2,399 m). The inhabitants are predominantly Christian; those in the west are chiefly Malayans, and those in the east are Papuans. Copra is exported; rice, maize, and coffee are also grown, and cattle are raised. Ende is the chief town and port. Originally under the rule of the princes of Celebes, Flores came under Dutch influence c.1618. The Dutch gradually gained control of the island, although Portugal held the eastern end until 1851 and the natives were not completely subjugated until 1907. The Flores Sea is north of the island and S of Celebes.

Flores (flô'rĭz, Port. flô'rəsh), island (1960 pop. 6,556), 58 sq mi (150 sq km), Horta dist., in the N Atlantic, the most westerly of the AZORES, Portugal. Santa Cruz is its chief town.

Florey, Howard Walter (Baron Florey of Adelaide), 1898–1968, British pathologist, b. Australia. He was educated at Adelaide Univ. and at Cambridge and Oxford and returned to Oxford as professor of pathology in 1935. Florey shared the 1945 Nobel Prize in Physiology and Medicine with Sir Alexander Fleming and Ernst B. Chain for work on penicillin. In 1939, under a Rockefeller grant, Florey and his associates began work on penicillin and proved its effectiveness against many harmful bacteria. See biography by Lennard Bickel (1973).

Florianópolis (flo͝orēənô'po͞olēs), city (1970 pop. 138,566), capital of Santa Catarina state, SE Brazil, on Santa Catarina Island. An administrative and cultural center and a port city, it is linked with the mainland by a huge suspension bridge (built 1926). The city was founded as Destêrro in 1673 by colonists from São Paulo and became the capital of the captaincy of Santa Catarina in 1739. It was renamed (1893) for Floriano Peixoto, a president of Brazil. Its commercial importance began to decrease in the late 19th cent. as the interior of the state was developed. The Univ. of Santa Catarina is in Florianópolis.

Florida (flŏr'ĭdə), state (1970 pop., 6,789,443), 58,560 sq mi (151,670 sq km), extreme SE United States, admitted 1845 as the 27th state of the Union. TALLAHASSEE is the capital, and JACKSONVILLE, MIAMI, TAMPA, and SAINT PETERSBURG are the largest cities. A long, low peninsula, Florida is bounded on the E by the Atlantic Ocean, on the W by the Gulf of Mexico, and on the N by Georgia and Alabama (where the St. Marys River in the northeast and the Perdido River in the northwest form part of the boundary). Florida is separated from Cuba to the S by the Straits of Florida. Much of the east coast is shielded from the Atlantic by narrow sandbars and islands that protect the shallow lagoons, rivers, and bays. Immediately inland, pine and palmetto flatlands stretch from the Georgia border almost to the southern tip of the state. The NW of Florida is a gently rolling panhandle area, cut into by deep swamps along the coast. Central Florida abounds in lakes, with Lake Okeechobee being the largest. The Everglades, which includes Big Cypress Swamp, is a unique wilderness region of subtropical plant growth and animal life and extends over almost the entire southern part of the peninsula. Florida's lower Gulf coast is dotted with tiny islands, and the Florida Keys, extending south and west from the southern tip of the state, are linked to the mainland by a causeway. The Saint Johns River is the principal waterway of the state. Warmed by the surrounding subtropical waters and cooled by the trade winds, Florida is famous for its pleasant climate, abundant sunshine, and beautiful scenery. Tourism plays a primary role in the state's economy. Beautiful beaches, such as those at Miami Beach, Daytona Beach, Sarasota, and Fort Lauderdale, attract thousands of vacationers annually, and abundant recreational facilities have made tourism a year-round enterprise. With more than 4,000 sq mi (10,360 sq km) of inland water and with the sea readily accessible from almost any point in the state, Florida is a fisherman's paradise. Other attractions include Everglades National Park, with its unusual plant and animal life; Cypress Gardens, near Winter Haven; Palm Beach, with its palatial estates and fine resort facilities; Walt Disney World, an entertainment park near Orlando; and many other picturesque resort areas. Famous also for its citrus fruits, Florida leads the nation in the production of oranges, grapefruits, and tangerines. Other important crops raised in the state are tomatoes, sugarcane, and tobacco. Florida also supplies much of the country with many varieties of winter

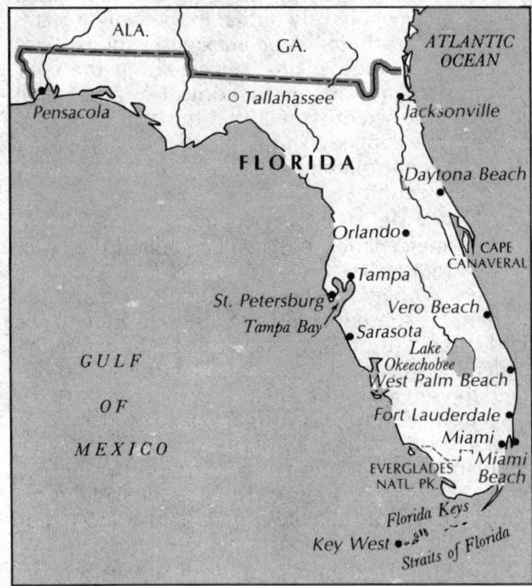

vegetables, and cattle and dairy products are important. Florida's leading manufactured items are food products, chemicals, paper products, electrical equipment, and transportation equipment. Lumber and wood products are also important. Most of the state's timber is yellow pine. Florida's mineral resources include phosphate rock, stone, cement, and sand and gravel. Commercial fishing is important, and the species caught include crabs, lobsters, and shrimps. Although the Florida peninsula was probably sighted by earlier navigators, the Spanish explorer Juan Ponce de León is credited with the discovery of the area. Seeking the fabled Fountain of Youth, Ponce de León landed near the site of St. Augustine in 1513. He claimed the area, which he thought was an island, for Spain and named it Florida, probably because it was then the Easter season (*Pascua Florida*). Other Spanish adventurers, notably Pánfilo de Narváez and Hernando De Soto, later explored the region and established the fact that Florida was not an island. The vast region that now comprises most of the SE United States was claimed for Spain, the whole being known as Florida. It was the activity of the French in the area, however, that led to actual Spanish settlement of the Florida peninsula. In May, 1562, Jean Ribaut had discovered the St. Johns River, and two years later René de Laudonnière built Fort Caroline at its mouth. Alarmed at this encroachment by the French, Philip II of Spain commissioned Pedro Menéndez de Aviles to drive the French out of the area; this he did ruthlessly. Spanish colonization began when Menéndez founded St. Augustine in 1565. Florida had no precious metals to spur conquest (as in Mexico and Peru), its soil seemed infertile (Spanish Florida was never self-sufficient agriculturally), and the native Indians were not peaceful. However, the Spanish were compelled to hold Florida because of its strategic location along the Straits of Florida, through which rich treasure ships from the south sailed for Spain. In the 1600s the English, who were trying to expand their American colonial holdings after 1607, began to threaten Florida. St. Augustine was attacked several times by English corsairs and in 1702–3 was besieged by a force from the English colony in South Carolina. In 1742, English colonists from Georgia under James E. Oglethorpe, Georgia's founder, defeated the Spanish in the battle of Bloody Marsh on St. Simons Island, making Florida's northern boundary the St. Marys River. Spain's last-minute entry (1762) into the Seven Years War cost her Florida, which the British acquired through the Treaty of Paris (1763). Under the British (1763–83), Florida was divided into two provinces, and St. Augustine and Pensacola were made the respective capitals of East Florida and West Florida. The Floridas prospered under British rule and remained loyal to the mother country during the American Revolution. The influx of English settlers reached a peak during the Revolution when Tories flocked to the region from the north. Patriot forces twice attempted invasion, but on the whole the Floridas were little touched by the war. Under the Treaty of Paris (1783), Florida was returned to Spain. Many colonists in Florida abandoned the region and moved to British possessions in the West Indies. Spain's hold over Florida, however, was extremely tenuous. Boundary disputes developed with the United States (see WEST FLORIDA CONTROVERSY). Incoming American settlers resisted Spanish authority and looked to the United States for support, and British traders and agents still wielded powerful influence. In the War of 1812, Pensacola served as a British base until captured (1814) by U.S. General Andrew Jackson. In 1818, Jackson again defied Spanish authority and invaded Florida in a punitive attack against the Indians. In 1819, after years of diplomatic wrangling, Spain reluctantly signed the Adams-Onis treaty ceding Florida to the United States in return for U.S. assumption of $5 million in damage claims by U.S. citizens against Spain. Official U.S. occupation took place in 1821, and Andrew Jackson was appointed military governor. Florida, with its present boundaries, was organized as a territory in 1822, and William P. Duval became its first territorial governor. Settlers poured in from neighboring states, settling especially in the area around the newly founded capital of Tallahassee. A plantation economy flourished there, with cotton and tobacco the chief crops. Settlement expanded southward and displaced the SEMINOLE INDIANS, and wars with the Seminoles seriously impeded Florida's development. A group of Seminoles, under Osceola, resisted attempts to move them to the West, but eventually most of them were transported out of the region at the end of the Second Seminole War (1835–42). However, a small band fled to the wilderness of the Everglades and today their descendants live on reservations in the Lake Okeechobee area. Florida was admitted to the Union in 1845 as a slaveholding state. After Abraham Lincoln was elected president in 1860 proslavery sentiment in Florida led the state to secede from the Union in 1861 and join the Confederacy. State troops seized the navy yard at Pensacola, but the Federals held Fort Pickens and in 1862–63 captured the coastal cities of Fernandina, Jacksonville, St. Augustine, and Tampa. Florida furnished vital supplies (particularly salt and cattle) to the Confederacy. The most important Civil War engagement fought in Florida was the battle of Olustee (Feb. 20, 1864), a Confederate victory. After the war Florida was placed under military rule by Congress. A constitution was drafted providing for Negro suffrage, and the state was readmitted to the Union in 1868. The constitution had been drafted by moderate Republicans, some of whom were from the North, and these same Republicans held most political offices until 1876, when the Democrats were returned to power and Negroes were once again relegated to an inferior position. In 1885 a new constitution replaced the Reconstruction charter of 1868. Meanwhile, the state sold (1881) 4,000,000 acres (1,618,800 hectares) of land to real-estate promoters. Northern capitalists such as Henry M. Flagler built railroads and hotels, and Florida began to develop. Close to Cuba, Florida has often been involved in the affairs of that island. During the latter half of the 19th cent., Cubans rebelling against Spain received sanctuary and aid in Florida, and the state enthusiastically supported and profited economically from the Spanish-American War (1898), in which Tampa was the chief U.S. base. In the 20th cent. there was another large influx of Cubans, as political refugees from the Cuban revolution of 1958–59 poured into Florida by the thousands, creating acute resettlement problems. The drainage of the Everglades, begun in 1906, precipitated one of the state's periodic land booms. The most famous of Florida's land booms started after World War I and reached its peak in 1925 when land values achieved fantastic heights, only to collapse completely the following year. Florida weathered the depression of the 1930s with the help of the Federal government, and during World War II prospered from army, navy, and air force installations. After the war the state enjoyed phenomenal growth. Manufacturing, particularly industries related to aeronautics, developed at an extraordinary rate. Cape Canaveral became famous as the site of the John F. Kennedy Space Center, a missile-testing and space-research center, and many defense and scientific-research companies were drawn to the area. Many space flights, including some to the moon, have been launched from Cape Canaveral. Virtually unlimited water resources, as well as the pleasant climate, were important factors in attracting new industries. After a 1954 U.S. Supreme Court decision, Florida began to desegregate its public schools. Cutbacks in the nation's space program in the late 1960s caused the elimination of many jobs in and around Cape Canaveral. Despite this setback, Florida is one of the fastest growing states in the country and thousands of retired persons have settled in the state, particularly in St. Petersburg. In 1968, Florida adopted a new state constitution. The governor of the state is elected for a term of four years, and the legislature has a house of representatives of 120 members elected to serve for two years and a senate of 40 members elected to terms of four years. The state also elects 15 Representatives and 2 Senators to the U.S. Congress. Florida has 17 electoral votes. Since Reconstruction the Democratic party has been the most influential political party in Florida. Republicans have been gaining in the state, however, and in the presidential elections from 1952 to 1972, Florida voters supported Republicans more often than Democrats. In 1966 a Republican was elected governor for the first time since the 1870s. However, Reubin Askew, a Democrat, was elected governor in 1970 and was reelected in 1974. Florida's institutions of higher education include the Univ. of Florida, at Gainesville; the Univ. of Miami, at Coral Gables; Florida State Univ. and Florida Agricultural and Mechanical Univ., at Tallahassee; Rollins College, at Winter Park; the Univ. of Tampa and the Univ. of South Florida, at Tampa; Florida Southern College, at Lakeland; Stetson Univ., at De Land; Barry College, at Miami; and Bethune-Cookman College, at Daytona Beach. See Federal Writers' Project, *Florida: a Guide to the Southernmost State* (1946); R. W. Patrick, *Florida under Five Flags* (rev. ed. 1967); M. Douglas, *Florida: The Long Frontier* (1967); C. W. Tebeau, *A History of Florida* (1971).

Florida (flōrē'thä), city (1970 pop. 32,679), Camagüey prov., E central Cuba. It has good road and rail communications and an economy based on the raising of cattle, citrus fruits, and sugarcane. Florida was founded in 1907.

Florida: see CONFEDERATE CRUISERS.

Florida, Straits of, passage, c.90 mi (145 km) wide, between the Florida Keys in the north and Cuba and the Bahamas in the south and southeast. It connects the Gulf of Mexico with the Atlantic Ocean.

Florida, University of, at Gainesville; land-grant and state supported; coeducational; chartered and opened 1853 at Ocala, moved to Gainesville in 1906. The Center for Latin American Studies and the Division of Nuclear Sciences are among its programs. The Florida State Museum is also located there.

Florida Agricultural and Mechanical University, at Tallahassee; land-grant and state supported; coeducational; chartered and opened 1887.

Floridablanca or **Florida Blanca, José Moñino, conde de** (hōsā' mōnyē'nō kōn'dā dā flōrē'thä bläng'kä), 1728–1808, Spanish statesman. After the expulsion of the Jesuits from Spain (1767), he was sent to Rome as ambassador to obtain the papal suppression of the Society of Jesus. He was ennobled (1773) for the success of his mission. In 1776 Charles III appointed him chief minister. Under Floridablanca, Spanish absolutism reached its peak, but his internal reforms, notably in finance, were beneficial, and the economic life of the country was improved. He made peace and concluded economic treaties with the Turks and with Morocco and reached agreement with Portugal, but was reluctantly drawn into war with England during the American Revolution. Floridablanca remained in power after the accession of Charles IV (1788), but his intransigent opposition to the French Revolution (which, it was feared, would provoke war) and the intrigues of the new queen led to his dismissal in 1792. During the French invasion (see PENINSULAR WAR), Floridablanca became (1808) president of the Central Junta, but he died shortly after.

Florida Keys, chain of small coral and limestone islands and reefs, c.150 mi (240 km) long, extending from Virginia Key, S of Miami Beach, to Key West, and forming the southern tip of Florida. Between the keys and the mainland lies Florida Bay; they are separated from Cuba by the Straits of Florida. Many of the islands are habitable and are generally covered by dense growths of low trees and shrubs, with mangrove swamps on the landward side. The best known islands are Key Largo and Key West, on which is the city of Key West. The Florida Keys are noted for their commercial fisheries, resort areas, and tropical vegetation. Most of the islands are joined to the mainland by a causeway.

Florida Southern College, at Lakeland; United Methodist; coeducational; founded and opened 1885.

Florida State University, at Tallahassee; coeducational; chartered 1851, opened 1857. Present name was adopted in 1947. Special research facilities include those in nuclear science and oceanography.

Flórina or **Phlorina** (both: flôr'ĭnə), city (1971 pop. 11,164), capital of Flórina prefecture, N Greece, in Macedonia, near the Yugoslavian border. It is connected with Bitola, Yugoslavia, by a road that runs through the Monastir gap.

Florio, John (flô'rēō), 1553?–1625, English author, b. London of Italian parentage. Educated at Oxford, Florio served in various capacities at the court of James I. He is chiefly remembered for his free translation (1603) of the essays of Montaigne. He wrote works on Italian grammar and compiled an Italian-English dictionary, *A World of Words* (1598).

Floris, Frans (fräns flō'rĭs), c.1517–70, Flemish painter, originally named Frans de Vriendt; son of an Antwerp stonecutter. He studied in Liège and Rome. Returning to Antwerp in 1540, he opened a large school and enjoyed the patronage of William of Orange and of many Flemish and Spanish notables. Floris exemplifies the overpowering influence of Italian mannerists on many Flemish painters of his period. Characteristic are his *Last Judgment* (Brussels), *Adoration of the Shepherds* (Dresden), and *Fall of the Rebellious Angels* (Antwerp). In addition to such ambitious figure compositions, Floris produced several excellent portraits and etchings.

Florissant, city (1970 pop. 65,908), St. Louis co., E Mo., a residential suburb of St. Louis, on the Missouri River; inc. 1829. It was settled by French farmers and fur trappers c.1769, and the first civil government was established in 1786 by the Spanish, who named it San Ferdinand. The village was predominantly French until the mid-19th cent. Its present name, from the French *fleurissant* [flowering or flourishing], was adopted in 1939. Points of interest include Old St. Ferdinand's Shrine and Convent (founded 1789; rebuilt 1820), where the first U.S. Indian school for girls was established; and historic French and Spanish homes, some dating from 1790. Jesuit Father Pierre Jean De Smet was ordained in Old St. Ferdinand's Church in 1827.

Florissant Fossil Beds National Monument: see NATIONAL PARKS AND MONUMENTS (table).

Florit, Eugenio (ā͞oohā'nyō flōrĕt'), 1903–, Cuban poet, diplomat, and scholar, b. Madrid. Florit's early poems (*Trópico*, 1930; *Doble acento*, 1937) reveal a mastery of classical forms. His moving *El Martirio de San Sebastián* was acclaimed by the poet Juan Ramón Jiménez, who later met Florit and exercised a profound influence on his work. Florit was a member of the Cuban State department (1927–40). After 1941 he was professor of Spanish at Columbia Univ. Florit is a refined and introspective poet, whose work reflects an intense preoccupation with mystical values. Collections of his poems include *Poema mío* (1946), *Antología poética: 1930–1955* (1956), *Siete poemas* (1960), and *Hábito de esperanza: 1936–1964* (1965). He has also written religious playlets, *Tres autos religiosos* (1960), and edited several anthologies of Spanish poetry.

flotation process, in mineral treatment, process for concentrating the metal-bearing mineral in an ORE. Crude ore is ground to a fine powder and mixed with water, chemical-conditioning reagents, and collecting reagents. When air is blown through the mixture, mineral particles cling to the bubbles, which rise to form a froth on the surface. The waste material (gangue) settles to the bottom. The froth is skimmed off, and the water and chemicals are distilled or otherwise removed, leaving a clean concentrate. Among the minerals effectively concentrated by this method are sulfide and phosphate ores. The method is also called the froth-flotation process.

Flötner or **Flettner, Peter** (pā'tər flöt'nər, flĕt'nər), c.1485–1546, German medalist and craftsman, possibly Swiss by birth. He was active in decorative sculpture, wood carving, and other crafts, making medals and plaques and furnishing designs of classical motifs for silversmiths. He was in Nuremberg by 1522 and did most of his work there, although he made two trips to Italy. Flötner is now regarded as a pioneer of the German Renaissance. His *Kunstbuch* was published in 1549. In the Metropolitan Museum are five of his bronze plaques illustrating biblical episodes.

Flotow, Friedrich von (frē'drĭkh fən flō'tō), 1812–83, German operatic composer. Flotow's operas show the influence of French opéra comique, which set the tone for light opera in the 19th cent. Many of his 29 operas were translated into English, French, or Italian for performances throughout Europe. The most successful were *Alessandro Stradella* (1844) and *Martha* (1847), which incorporates the Irish tune "The Last Rose of Summer."

flotsam, jetsam, and ligan (flŏt'səm, jĕt'səm, lī'gən) [O.Fr.], in maritime law, goods lost at sea as distinguished from goods washed ashore, i.e., WRECK. The goods that remain floating on the surface are called flotsam (or floatsam or flotsan), while jetsam refers to goods thrown overboard, or jettisoned, that sink and remain under water. Ligan (or lagan) designates those goods that go down with a vessel or that are sunk in the sea and have a buoy or floating object attached to them as a mark of ownership or in order that they may be found again. Such goods found by other persons must be returned to the owner, while flotsam and jetsam must be returned only if the owner makes a proper claim. The rules of SALVAGE apply to all three types of goods. See JETTISON.

flounder: see FLATFISH.

flour, finely ground, usually sifted, meal of GRAIN, such as wheat, rye, corn, rice, or buckwheat. Flour is also made from potatoes, peas, beans, peanuts, etc. Usually it refers to the finely ground and bolted (i.e., sifted through a fine sieve) flour of WHEAT, which forms the largest proportion of all flour milled in the United States, Canada, and W Europe. MILLET is ground in India, the Soviet Union, and China. Rye is much used for bread in N Europe, buckwheat in the Netherlands and the Soviet Union, and corn in the United States. Rice may be used for bread in combination with other grains richer in GLUTEN. Wheat and rye flour can be used in baking leavened bread, as they contain gluten in sufficient amount to retain the gas formed by the action of yeast. Corn flour, rich in fats and starches, is a favorite for making quick breads. Graham, or whole-wheat, flour contains the whole grain, unbolted. This flour will not keep long, as the germ contains fats and ferments that cause deterioration when exposed to the air. Wheat flour is separated into grades by milling. In the United States, patent flour, freed of the bran and most of the germ, is the highest grade; clear flour is the second grade; and red dog, a low-grade residue, is used mainly for animal feed. The composition of flour depends on the type of wheat and the milling processes; gluten is the chief protein, and starch the principal carbohydrate, although some sucrose, invert sugar, and dextrin may be present. On the market are prepared flours, such as the self-rising, which contains a leavening agent, and numerous cake, pancake, and pastry mixes requiring only the addition of water. Flour improves if stored from six to nine months under conditions permitting the enzyme action that gives better baking qualities. Good flour, rich in gluten, has a creamy color and adhesive quality. Bleaching, which is accomplished by the addition of chemicals to flour to improve its appearance and baking qualities, was begun about 1900. The bleaching of flour has been a controversial issue since its beginning, with charges that it destroys valuable nutrients or is injurious to health; some bleaching agents have been banned (e.g., nitrogen trichloride), but new ones have been introduced. Bleached flours must be so labeled.

Flourens, Pierre (Marie Jean Pierre Flourens) (pyĕr flōōräNs'), 1794–1867, French physiologist. He demonstrated the respiratory center in the medulla and the function of the cerebellum in muscular coordination and studied bone formation. He was long a professor at the Collège de France.

flower, name for the specialized part of a plant containing the reproductive organs, commonly applied to seed plants only. A flower may be thought of as a modified, short, compact branch bearing lateral appendages. Like twigs, flowers develop from buds, and the basic floral parts (sepal, petal, stamen, and pistil) are in actual fact greatly modified leaves. A typical flower is a concentric arrangement of these parts attached at their base to the receptacle, the tip of the stem. Outermost is a whorl of leaflike green sepals (the calyx) encircling a whorl of usually showy, colored petals (the corolla). Within the corolla the stamens, bearing anther sacs full of POLLEN, surround the central pistil. Inside the ovary at the base of the pistil are the ovules, containing the female sex cells; after fertilization of the egg, the ovule becomes the SEED and the ovary becomes the FRUIT. The pistils and stamens are termed essential flower parts, the petals and sepals accessory parts. The number and arrangement of the floral organs vary considerably among the many families and orders of plants and are used in the classification of plants; they also indicate the degree of evolution of the plant. In general, the higher a plant is on the evolutionary scale, the greater is the flower's complexity and efficiency for REPRODUCTION. The basic number of parts differs from class to class and from family to family; in monocotyledonous plants the parts generally occur in groups of three or in multiples of three, and in dicotyledons in groups of two, four, and five. Flowers may be staminate (lack pistils), pistillate, or both; staminate and pistillate flowers may appear on the same plant, on separate plants, or in the same inflorescence, as in the COMPOSITE flowers, where what appears to be a single

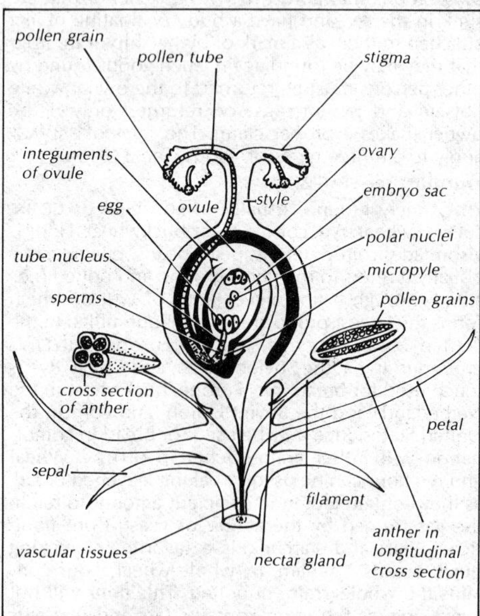

Longitudinal cross section of a flower at the time of fertilization, showing a pollen grain and a pollen tube

blossom is actually a head of many small individual flowers. Another type of inflorescence, characteristic of the parsley family, is the umbel, in which the tiny florets are borne on separate stalks radiating out from the stem tip. Sometimes the parts serve unusual purposes: the true flowers of the dogwood and the poinsettia are inconspicuous, and the showy "petals" are really modified leaves called bracts. In the jack-in-the-pulpit the florets are clustered on a spike canopied by a large bract, the spathe; the hood of the lady's-slipper, on the other hand, is a modified sterile stamen. Grass inflorescences are tiny spikelets sheathed by protective scales called glumes (the chaff or grain). Flowers have been cultivated and bred for their beauty, their perfume, and their products (e.g., poppy, sunflower seed, and saffron) from earliest times and have accumulated a vast and intricate treasury of symbolic associations derived from legend and folklore. Individual flowers have been celebrated in heraldry (ROSE), in religion (lotus), and in politics (VIOLET) and have become state emblems for many countries, including Switzerland (edelweiss), France (fleur-de-lis), Scotland (thistle), Holland (tulip), and the United States (see STATE FLOWERS).

flowering almond, name for several species of ornamental shrubs of the family Rosaceae (ROSE family), chiefly those of the genus *Prunus,* which also includes the plum, cherry, and apricot. The pink or white blossoms (often double) usually appear before the leaves. Showy, double-flowered varieties of the genus *Amygdalus* (including the true almond and the peach) also are called flowering almond. These species are classified in the division MAGNOLIOPHYTA, class Magnoliopsida, order Rosales, family Rosaceae.

flowering maple: see MALLOW.

flowering quince: see QUINCE.

Floyd, Carlisle, 1926–, American composer, b. Latta, S.C. He attended Syracuse Univ. and later studied with Ernst Bacon. Since 1947 he has taught at Florida State Univ. Floyd gained national recognition for his folk opera *Susannah,* which has been performed at the New York City Opera. Floyd writes his own texts as well as music and has a basically conservative style. His other operas include *Wuthering Heights* (1958), adapted from the Emily Brontë novel; *The Passion of Jonathan Wade* (1962), about the Reconstruction period in the South; and *Of Mice and Men* (1970), adapted from the Steinbeck novel.

Floyd, John Buchanan, 1807–63, U.S. Secretary of War (1857–60) and Confederate general, b. Smithfield, Va. After failing as a lawyer and cotton planter in Arkansas, he returned to Virginia and practiced law at Abingdon. He served (1847–48, 1855) in the state assembly and was governor (1849–52). His cabinet post was a reward for aiding in James Buchanan's successful campaign for the presidency. Though a states' rights man, Floyd opposed secession. He maintained that Major Robert Anderson's removal from Fort Moultrie to FORT SUMTER in Charleston harbor was contrary to his orders. When President Buchanan refused to allow him to order Anderson back, Floyd resigned and became an ardent secessionist. The President, meanwhile, had requested his resignation because of irregular and unauthorized practices in the War Dept., which involved an apparent loss of $870,000. Feeling was bitter against Floyd in the North, although the belief that before he resigned he had conveniently transferred large quantities of arms to Southern arsenals has since been discounted. However, his inefficient administration of the War Dept. certainly was no help to the Union later. As a Confederate brigadier general in the Civil War, serving first under Lee in the western section of Virginia, Floyd was equally incompetent. After his defeat at FORT DONELSON, Jefferson Davis, who nursed an old quarrel with Floyd, removed him from command.

Floyd, William, 1734–1821, a signer of the Declaration of Independence, b. Brookhaven, N.Y. His career in the Continental Congress (1774–77, 1778–83) was marked by conscientious service on the admiralty and treasury committees. As New York state senator (1784–88), he strongly advocated a practical and conservative financial policy. He was elected to Congress for one term, 1789–91.

Fludd or **Flud, Robert,** 1574–1637, English mystic philosopher. Educated at Oxford and on the Continent, he became a London physician. Strongly influenced by the mystical doctrines of PARACELSUS, he attempted to reconcile these speculations with the new science of the 17th cent. From his study of Paracelsus he arrived at the theory that spiritual and physical truth are identical. His mystical pantheism centered in God as the all-pervading form of which the world and man are manifestations. He held that the dualism of light and darkness is inherent in all things. The best-known English representative of the Rosicrucians, he spread their ideas in a number of medico-theosophical books. His major works include *Utriusque cosmi, maioris scilicet et minoris, metaphysica, physica atque technica historia* (1617–21) and *Philosophia Moysaica* (1638; tr. *Mosaicall Philosophy,* 1659). See J. B. Craven, *Robert Fludd, the English Rosicrucian* (1902); F. A. Yates, *Theatre of the World* (1969).

Flüe, Nicholas von der (fən dĕr flü'ə), 1417–87, Swiss patriot. Leader of the cantonal forces fighting Austria, and counselor for many years to the duke of Saxony, he retired to Obwalden in 1467 to become a hermit. When dissension arose among the federated cantons, his influence at the Diet of Stans (1481) brought about the preservation of peace. A covenant, drawn up to regulate federal relations, made the urban cantons a majority; it remained in effect until 1798.

flügelhorn (flü'gəlhôrn"), three-valved brass instrument similar in size and shape to the TRUMPET but having a conical rather than a cylindrical bore and

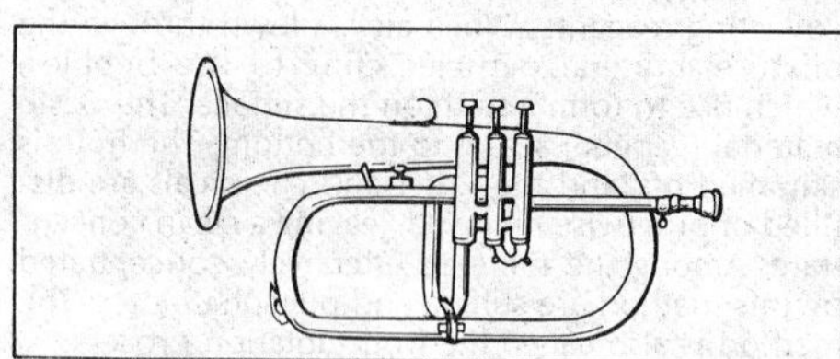

Flügelhorn

possessing a larger bell. Because of these differences the tone of the flügelhorn is mellower than that of the trumpet. It is used traditionally in concert bands and has recently been used in jazz ensembles.

fluid, any substance that is able to flow. Of the four STATES OF MATTER, only a SOLID is not a fluid, since it has a definite shape that is not readily changed. Any LIQUID, GAS, or PLASMA is classed as a fluid.

fluidics, branch of engineering and technology concerned with the development of equivalents of various electronic circuits using movements of fluid rather than movements of electric charge. The basic devices used in fluidics are specially designed valves that, like transistors, can be arranged to act as amplifiers and logic circuits. The principal advantage of fluidic systems is that they can be designed to tolerate conditions under which electronic systems could not possibly operate. For example, a fluidic system could operate in the exhaust of a rocket, using the exhaust as its working fluid. Fluidic systems are also advantageous where the system output is to be a flow of fluid, as in an automobile carburetor.

fluid mechanics, branch of MECHANICS dealing with the properties and behavior of fluids, i.e., liquids and gases. Because of their ability to flow, liquids and gases have many properties in common not shared by solids. The special study of fluids in motion, or fluid dynamics, makes up the larger part of fluid mechanics. Branches of fluid dynamics include hydrodynamics (study of liquids in motion) and aerodynamics (study of gases in motion). Hydrodynamics is often used synonymously with fluid dynamics, since most of the results from the study of liquids also apply to gases. A PLASMA is also a fluid (see STATES OF MATTER) and can be described by many of the principles of fluid mechanics, but its electromagnetic properties must also be taken into account. The study of plasmas in motion is known as MAGNETOHYDRODYNAMICS and includes principles from several fields.

fluke, parasitic flatworm of the trematode class, related to the TAPEWORM. Instead of the cilia, external sense organs, and epidermis of the free-living flatworms, adult flukes have sucking disks with which they cling to their hosts, and an external cuticle that resists digestion by the host. In most species the adult worms absorb nutriment through the digestive system; in a few whose digestive system is reduced or completely absent, food is absorbed through the cuticle. Adult flukes are commonly hermaphroditic, that is, each individual possesses both male and female reproductive organs; however, they reproduce sexually. One worm may produce over 500,000 embryos. Species of the order Monogenea are external parasites on the skin and gills of fish; their simple life cycle is completed in a single host. The order Digenea includes the internal parasites, many of which have complicated life cycles, the various asexual stages living in mollusks and the sexual stages invading the internal organs of vertebrates; more than 35 species are known to inhabit humans. The human liver fluke, *Clonorchis sinensis,* has a life cycle that requires two intermediate hosts, snails and fish. The eggs pass out of humans via the feces. They survive if they are deposited in water and eaten by snails. The larvae invade the soft tissues of the snail from the digestive tract where they pass through several stages and reproduce asexually; they emerge from the snail as free-swimming larvae. If they manage to encounter fish, they penetrate into the flesh and encyst; if the raw fish is eaten by humans, the young flukes are released in the intestines. They then crawl up the bile duct, attach by their suckers, mature, reproduce sexually, and begin to shed eggs. In addition to the infestation of the liver by *Clonorchis,* which is prevalent in the Far East, many other disorders are caused by flukes. The Asian and African blood fluke disease, SCHISTOSOMIASIS, is caused by adults of the genus *Schistosoma* that burrow into the skin of humans and animals and lodge in the blood vessels. Lung flukes, common in the Orient, infest uncooked crab meat and encapsulate as adults in the lungs of humans. Liver rot, fatal to sheep and other herbivorous animals, is caused by a liver fluke, *Fasciola hepatica,* whose larvae encyst in grasses after leaving the snail host. A species of fluke prevalent in lakes of the N central United States causes a rash called "swimmer's itch." The name fluke is also applied to species of FLATFISH. Flukes are classified in the phylum PLATYHELMINTHES, class Trematoda, orders Monogenea and Digenea.

fluorescence, LUMINESCENCE in which light of a visible color is emitted from a substance under stimulation or excitation by light or other forms of electromagnetic radiation or by certain other means. The light is given off only while the stimulation continues; in this the phenomenon differs from PHOSPHORESCENCE, in which light continues to be emitted after the excitation by other radiation has ceased. Fluorescence of certain rocks and other substances had been observed for hundreds of years before its nature was understood. Probably the first to explain it was the British scientist Sir George G. Stokes, who named the phenomenon after fluorite, a strongly fluorescent mineral. Stokes is credited with the discovery (1852) that fluorescence can be induced in certain substances by stimulation with ultraviolet light. He formulated Stokes's law, which states that the wavelength of the fluorescent light is always greater than that of the exciting radiation, but exceptions to this law have been found. Later it was discovered that certain organic and inorganic substances can be made to fluoresce by activation not only with ultraviolet light but also with visible light, infrared radiation, X rays, radio waves, cathode rays, friction, heat, pressure, and some other excitants. Fluorescent substances, sometimes also known as phosphors, are used in paints and coatings, but their chief use is in fluorescent LIGHTING.

fluoridation (flo͝or″ĭdā′shən), process of adding a fluoride to the water supply of a community to preserve the teeth of the inhabitants. Tooth enamel ordinarily contains small amounts of fluorides and when the amount is augmented through the intake of fluoridated water, especially during the first eight years of childhood, tooth decay in children can be greatly reduced. In the early 1900s, Frederick S. McKay, a Colorado dentist, discovered that an unknown substance in the local drinking water caused a mottling or staining of the teeth and that these teeth also showed fewer cavities. In 1931 the substance was identified as a fluoride. Later, in the 1930s, it was found that a fluoride level in drinking water of about one part per million was high enough to reduce tooth decay but low enough to prevent teeth from becoming mottled. In some communities fluorides are a natural constituent of the water supply; other communities have added fluorides to their reservoirs. Such action has the support of the American Dental Association, the American Medical Association, and other scientific organizations. Although studies have proved that fluoridation at levels of one part per million is safe, attempts at fluoridation have met with resistance and controversy. Its opponents say that it constitutes compulsory medication, that the amount of fluorine taken into the body cannot be controlled, and that those who wish to prevent tooth decay through fluorides can do so individually by adding the compound to their beverages or by using toothpaste and other dental substances to which fluorides have been added. Despite such resistance, many Americans drink artificially fluoridated water, and fluoridation programs have been started in several other countries as well.

fluorine (flo͞o′ərēn, -rĭn), gaseous chemical element; symbol F; at. no. 9; at. wt. 18.998; m.p. −219.6°C; b.p. −188.14°C; density 1.696 grams per liter at STP; valence −1. Fluorine is a yellowish, poisonous, highly corrosive gas. It is the most chemically active nonmetallic element and is the most electronegative of all the elements. Fluorine is a member of group VIIa of the PERIODIC TABLE. It readily displaces the other HALOGENS from their salts. It combines spontaneously with most other elements—exceptions are chlorine, nitrogen, oxygen, and the so-called inert gases (helium, neon, argon, krypton, xenon, and radon), but it even combines with most of these when heated. Fluorine reacts with most inorganic and organic compounds. With hydrogen it forms hydrogen fluoride gas, whose water solution is called hydrofluoric acid. Because of its extreme reactivity, fluorine does not occur uncombined in nature. Fluorine gas is produced commercially by electrolysis of a solution of hydrogen fluoride containing potassium hydrogen fluoride. The mineral FLUORITE, or fluorspar (calcium fluoride), is the chief commercial source. CRYOLITE and APATITE are other important natural compounds. Although there was no commercial production of fluorine before World War II, the use of the gas in a process for refining uranium ores prompted its manufacture. The importance of fluorine lies largely in its compounds. Fluorite is used as a flux in refining iron; cryolite serves as the electrolyte in the production of aluminum. Compounds of fluorine are also used in the ceramic and glass industries; hydrofluoric acid is used to etch glass and in the manufacture of light bulbs. The addition of one part per million of soluble fluorides to public water supplies has reduced the incidence of tooth decay in many communities; however, in larger amounts fluorine and fluoride compounds are poisonous. Sodium fluoride is employed as an insecticide. Halocarbons (compounds of carbon, fluorine, chlorine, and hydrogen) are used extensively in refrigeration and air-conditioning systems and as aerosol propellants (Freon and Genetron are familiar examples). One of the most important advances in fluorine chemistry was the discovery in the late 1930s of fluorocarbons. The linking of fluorine and carbon has created some of the most chemically inert compounds known. Fluorocarbons such as Teflon have found extensive use as lubricants and bearing materials because of their low friction. Because of their inertness and heat resistance they may be used, for example, as a coating on cooking ware. Because they are not wetted by water or oils, they are sometimes used to add antisoil properties to textiles. The use of fluorite as a flux was described in 1529 by Georgius Agricola. Many early chemists experimented with hydrogen fluoride gas, among them Scheele, Davy, Lavoisier, and Gay-Lussac. Fluorine gas was first prepared in 1886 by Henri Moissan after nearly three quarters of a century of effort.

fluorine dating: see DATING.

fluorite (flo͞o′ərīt) or **fluorspar** (flo͞o′ərspär), mineral appearing in various colors, e.g., green, yellow-brown, rose, and red. Chemically, it is calcium fluoride, CaF_2. Its crystals, commonly cubic, are transparent or translucent and under certain conditions exhibit fluorescence. The mineral also occurs in granular and massive forms. Fluorite is found in various parts of the world, especially in England, Germany, Mexico, and in Kentucky and Illinois in the United States. Its chief use is as a flux in metallurgy, but it is also employed in the preparation of hydrofluoric acid and in the manufacture of opal glass and enamel; some of its colorless crystals are used for making lenses and prisms.

fluorodeoxyuridine: see METABOLITE.

fluoroscope (flo͝or′əskōp), instrument consisting of an X-ray machine (see X RAY) and a fluorescent screen that may be used by physicians to view the internal organs of the body. During medical diagnosis the patient stands between the X-ray machine, or other radiation source, and the fluorescent screen. Radiation passes through the body, producing varying degrees of light and shadow on the screen. Although the regular X-ray photograph shows more detail, fluoroscopy is preferable when the physician wants to see the live image, i.e., observe the size, shape, and movement of the patient's internal organs. In industry the fluoroscope is used for the examination of materials, manufactured objects, welds, castings, and other objects, principally for flaws.

fluorouracil: see METABOLITE.

fluorspar: see FLUORITE.

Flushing, Netherlands: see VLISSINGEN.

Flushing, former village, now in N Queens borough of New York City, SE N.Y.; chartered 1645, inc. into Greater New York City with Queens in 1898. Although chiefly residential, Flushing has gained importance as a trading and manufacturing center. It was chartered (as Vlissingen) by the Dutch West India Company to English settlers, who anglicized the name. It is the seat of Queens College, York College, and the Queens Botanical Gardens. The Bowne House (1661) and the Quaker meetinghouse (c.1696) are landmarks of the colonial period. Flushing Meadow (now a park) was the site of two New York World's Fairs (1939–40 and 1964–65) and temporary headquarters of the United Nations (1946–49). Shea Stadium, home of the New York Mets (baseball) and Jets (football) is there. See Haynes Trebor, *Colonial Flushing* (1945).

flute, in music, generic term for such wind instruments as the FIFE, the FLAGEOLET, the PANPIPES, the PICCOLO, and the RECORDER. The tone of all flutes is produced by an air stream directed against an edge, producing eddies that set up vibrations in the air enclosed in the attached tube. In the transverse flute, the principal orchestral flute today, the edge is on the mouth hole on the side of the instrument, over which the player blows. The transverse flute is an extremely old instrument, universal in ancient and primitive cultures. It was known in Europe by the 9th cent. During the baroque period both the recorder and the transverse flute were used in the orchestra, the latter by Lully in 1672. In the classical period the transverse flute displaced the less-powerful recorder, which could not match its dynamic range. In the 19th cent. the transverse flute assumed substantially its present form after the improvements of Theobald Boehm (1794–1881), who ascertained the acoustically correct size and placement of the holes and devised an ingenious system of keys to cover them. The flute was originally made of wood but is now most often of silver. It is the most brilliant and agile of the orchestral woodwinds, and it also has a considerable solo and chamber-music literature. The transverse flute has been made in several keys, but the C flute has long been standard. The alto flute in G, a fourth below the regular flute, is notated as a TRANSPOSING INSTRUMENT.

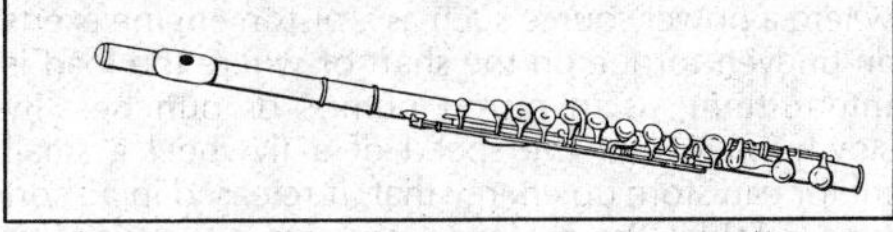

Flute

flux, magnetic, in physics, term used to describe the total amount of MAGNETISM in a given region. The term *flux* was chosen because the power of a magnet seems to "flow" out of the magnet at one pole and return at the other pole in a circulating pattern, as suggested by the patterns formed by iron filings sprinkled on a paper placed over a magnet or a conductor carrying an electric current. These patterns are called lines of induction. Although there is no actual physical flow, the lines of induction suggest the correct mathematical description of magnetism in terms of a FIELD of force. The lines of induction originate on the north pole of the magnet and end on the south pole; their direction at any point is the direction of the magnetic field, and their density (the number of lines passing through a unit area) gives the strength of the field. Near the poles where the lines converge, the field and the force it produces are large; away from the poles where the lines diverge, the field and force are progressively weaker.

Fly, largest river of the island of New Guinea, c.650 mi (1,050 km) long, rising in the Victor Emmanuel Range and flowing generally SE through Papua New Guinea to the Gulf of Papua. The Fly is navigable for steamers c.500 mi (800 km) upstream.

fly, name commonly used for any of a variety of winged INSECTS, but properly restricted to members of the order Diptera, the true flies, which includes the HOUSEFLY, GNAT, MIDGE, MOSQUITO, and TSETSE FLY. All have sucking or piercing-and-sucking mouthparts and, except for a few wingless species, bear one pair of wings. The hind wings are reduced to knobbed balancing organs called halteres. All flies undergo complete METAMORPHOSIS, i.e., a four-stage development. The larvae, which occupy a wide variety of ecological niches, typically require a moist environment such as rotting flesh, decaying fruit, or the internal organs of other animals (see BLOWFLY; BOTFLY; FRUIT FLY; TACHINID FLY). Adults often feed on nectar and plant sap, but some, such as the female HORSEFLY and female mosquito, feed on blood; the adults of some species do not feed at all. A few species are found worldwide, often dispersed by humans; more than 15,000 species are found in North America. Many flies are harmful either as carriers of disease or as destroyers of crops. Some parasitize harmful insects. Some, such as the fruit fly, are important in laboratory studies. Flies are classified in the phylum ARTHROPODA, class Insecta, order Diptera.

flycatcher, common name for various members of the Old World family Muscicapidae, insectivorous songbirds including the kingbirds, phoebes, and pewees. Flycatchers vary in color from drab to brilliant, as in the crested monarch and paradise flycatchers of Asia and Africa. The New World family Tyrannidae (tyrant flycatchers), includes 365 species distributed over the Americas from the Canadian tree limit to Patagonia. Most are arboreal and inconspicuously colored in olive-green, brown, or gray, the species grading into one another almost imperceptibly. They range in length from 3½ in. to 16 in. (8.7–40 cm), the majority being under 10 in. (25 cm). Flycatchers have large heads, broad shoulders, flattish bills, pointed wings, and small, weak legs and feet. The tails are rounded or shallowly forked, except for that of the scissor-tailed flycatcher of the SW United States, a gray bird with black wings and tail and reddish patches at the wing base, whose long (7–10 in./17.5–25 cm), deeply-forked tail enables it to perform aerial acrobatics. Flycatchers characteristically feed by darting after insects from an advantageous perch; the name tyrant reflects their pugnacity toward crows, hawks, and other large birds, which they harass with great determination. Their crown feathers are more or less erectile; in the royal flycatcher of Mexico and Brazil, *Pyrocephalus rubineus Mexicanus,* also called vermilion flycatcher, they are developed into a flaming crest. Many flycatchers are found near water, e.g., the eastern phoebe, or water pewee (*Sayiornis fusca*), a gray bird named for its plaintive, repetitive call and identifiable by its habit of flicking or bobbing its tail while perched. The wood pewee, genus *Contopus,* is a shy forest bird. The Say's, black, and San Jose phoebes are Western species. The 9-in. (22.5 cm) eastern kingbird is typical of the kingbird group; it has a dark back, white breast, and white-tipped tail. Kingbirds are also called bee martins, though they actually prefer other insects. The small (under 6 in./15 cm) empidonax flycatchers are all olive-green and are difficult to distinguish; they include the least, Acadian, and alder (or Traill's) flycatchers of the East and the western, Hammond's, Wright's, and vermilion flycatchers of the West. The South American kiskadee dives for fish like a kingfisher. The nesting habits of flycatchers vary; the typical nest is an open cup in a tree, but some nest on buildings and in concealed places, and the great crested flycatcher of E North America is a cavity-nester which habitually lines its nest with cast snake skins. Certain fly-catching warblers, belonging to a different family, are sometimes called flycatchers. Flycatchers are classified in the phylum CHORDATA, subphylum Vertebrata, class Aves, order Passeres, families Muscicapidae and Tyrannidae.

Flygare-Carlén, Emilie (flü'gärĕ"-kärlān'), 1807–92, Swedish novelist. In *The Rose of Thistle Island* (1842, tr. 1844) and *A Merchant's House on the Skerry* (1860–61), she wrote of sea life on the Bohuslan skerries where she spent her childhood. Her 26 multivolume novels were written with the aid of a large staff of relatives and friends and throughout Europe were the most popular Swedish works of the 19th cent.

flying boat: see SEAPLANE.

flying buttress: see BUTTRESS.

flying dragon, gliding lizard of the genus *Draco,* found in tropical forests of SE Asia. There are about 15 species. Most are about 8 in. (20 cm) long. On either side of the lizard's body are thin, winglike folds of skin supported by five to seven ribs that extend from the body. With its "wings" extended the lizard is capable of gliding for distances of up to 30 ft (9 m). The wings are often brightly colored, sometimes with stripes or spots, but when they are folded the body, greenish with a pale yellow belly, blends with the foliage. Flying dragons have slender legs, tapering tails, and brilliantly colored throat sacs, typically blue in the female and yellow-orange with a blue spot in the male. They live in trees, rarely descending to the ground, and feed on arboreal ants. They are classified in the phylum CHORDATA, subphylum Vertebrata, class Reptilia, order Squamata, family Agamidae.

Flying Dutchman, in legend, a phantom ship seen near the Cape of Good Hope. Its captain is said to be doomed to sail forever because of a blasphemous oath he made. The ship's crew is composed of dead men. A form of the story is used in Wagner's opera *Der fliegende Holländer.*

flying fish, common name for members of the Exocoetidae, a family of carnivorous or herbivorous fish of warmer seas. Flying fishes usually swim in schools. They average 7 to 12 in. (17.5–30 cm) in length and have pectoral fins that compare in size with the wings of birds; in some species the pelvic fins also are enlarged. Of the latter type, best known in Atlantic waters are the four-winged flying fish and the bearded flying fish, named for the long barbels around the mouths of the young. The young of many species of flying fishes resemble blossoms of the plant *Baringtonia,* and are thus protected from predators. The California flying fish (*Cypselurus californicus*), the largest (up to 18 in./45 cm) of the family, is common in the Pacific; the black-winged flying fish is found in both oceans. Flying fishes generally do not actually fly, but glide on their outstretched fins for distances of up to 1/4 mi (0.4 km). Their velocity (up to 30 mi/48 km per hour) builds as they approach the water's surface until they launch themselves into the air, vibrating their specially adapted tail fins in order to taxi along the surface. The flying gurnard of the South Atlantic has enormous pectorals and makes short leaps clear of the water. A 3-in. (7.5 cm) CHARACIN of the Amazon basin actually flies short distances by buzzing its winglike fins. Flying fishes are excellent food; their aerial talents help them to avoid the tuna, mackerel, and dolphins that prey on them. Flying fishes are classified in the phylum CHORDATA, subphylum Vertebrata, class Osteichthyes, order Beloniformes, family Exocoetidae.

flying fox: see FRUIT BAT.

flying lemur, gliding mammal native to the tropical lowland forests of S Asia, Malaya, and the Philippines. Also called the colugo, the flying lemur is brownish or grayish above and paler below. It ranges in length from 14 to 17 in. (36–43 cm), plus a 12-in. (30-cm) tail. A membrane stretching from forelimbs to tail resembles that of the bat (but unlike the bat membrane it is not supported by fingers) and allows the animal to glide from tree to tree; the flying lemur does not truly fly. Although its teeth resemble those of carnivores, the flying lemur's diet consists of fruit and leaves. It sleeps by day and forages at dusk. Females give birth to one or two young following a gestation period of 60 days. Flying lemurs are not related to true lemurs, but belong to an order of their own. There are two species, classified in the phylum CHORDATA, subphylum Vertebrata, class Mammalia, order Dermoptera, family Cynocephalidae, genus *Cynocephalus.*

flying saucer: see UNIDENTIFIED FLYING OBJECTS.

flying squirrel, name for certain nocturnal tree SQUIRRELS adapted for gliding; they do not actually fly. Most are found in Asia, but one species of the genus *Pteromys* extends into SE Europe and the two species of *Glaucomys* are found in North America. The gliding mechanism is a fold of furry skin extending along each side of the body from the wrist to the ankle and, in some species, to the tail. When the animal is at rest the flaps are folded; when it stretches its limbs for leaping, as do all tree squirrels, the flaps are stretched out taut like a parachute. The tail in many species is broad and flat, with a flat row of hairs on either side. The animal uses movements of the flaps, limbs, and tail to control direction. The glide always starts from a high tree branch; if it is a long glide the animal comes to rest near the ground and must climb up again. The small North American flying squirrels leap from heights of 50 ft (15 m) or more and may travel a horizontal distance of over 100 ft (30 m). Flying squirrels are seldom seen because of their nocturnal habits and high dwelling places. They nest, often many together, in holes in trees. They feed on a variety of plant matter, as well as on insects. The North American flying squirrels, found in forested regions over much of the continent, have soft, thick, brownish fur. The northern species, *Glaucomys sabrinus,* of Canada and the NE and W United States, is up to 12 in. (30 cm) long including the tail, which is nearly as long as the head and body; it weighs 4 to 6½ oz (110–180 grams). The southern species, *G. volans,* of the eastern half of the United States and parts of Mexico and Guatemala, is slightly shorter and weighs about a third as much. Most Old World species are similar, but the giant flying squirrels, genus *Pteromys,* of S Asia, are up to 4 ft (120 cm) long and may be observed sleeping on branches during the day. The scaly-tailed squirrels, or African flying squirrels, are not true squirrels, but members of a separate rodent family (Anomaluridae). Found only in tropical Africa, they are anatomically quite different from the true flying squirrels and include both gliding and nongliding species. Flying squirrels are classified in the phylum CHORDATA, subphylum Vertebrata, class Mammalia, order Rodentia, family Sciuridae.

Flynn, Edward Joseph, 1892–1953, American political leader, b. New York City. He practiced law in New York City and served (1917–21) in the New York state legislature. Flynn became leader of the Democratic party in Bronx co. and a power in New York and national politics. He succeeded (1940) James A. FARLEY as national chairman of the Democratic party and successfully directed Franklin Delano Roosevelt's third-term presidential campaign. Named (1943) envoy to Australia by President Roosevelt, Flynn quit as Democratic national chairman, but when his appointment was not confirmed by the U.S. Senate, he returned to the Democratic National Committee. He described his political experiences in *You're the Boss* (1947, repr. 1970).

flyway: see MIGRATION OF ANIMALS.

flywheel, heavy metal wheel attached to a drive shaft, having most of its weight concentrated at the circumference. Such a wheel resists changes in speed and helps steady the rotation of the shaft where a power source such as a piston engine exerts an uneven torque on the shaft or where the load is intermittent, as in piston pumps or punches. By slowly increasing the speed of a flywheel a small motor can store up energy that, if released in a short time, enables the motor to perform a function for which it is ordinarily too small. The flywheel was developed by James Watt in his work on the steam engine.

Fm, chemical symbol of the element FERMIUM.

FM: see MODULATION; RADIO.

Foakes-Jackson, Frederick John, 1855–1941, English theologian and church historian. A fellow of Jesus College, Cambridge, from 1886, he was lecturer there from 1882 and dean from 1895 to 1916. From 1916 to 1934 Foakes-Jackson was Briggs professor of Christian institutions at Union Theological Seminary, New York City. His many books include *Introduction to the History of Christianity, A.D. 590–1314* (1921), *Biblical History of the Hebrews to the Christian Era* (4th ed. 1921), *History of the Christian Church from the Earliest Times to A.D. 461* (7th ed. 1924), *Studies in the Life of the Early Church* (1924), *St. Paul, the Man and the Apostle* (1926), *Peter, Prince of Apostles* (1927), and *A History of Church History: Studies of Some Historians of the Christian Church* (1939).

foam: see COLLOID.

foamflower: see SAXIFRAGE.

Foch, Ferdinand (fĕrdēnäN' fôsh), 1851–1929, marshal of France. A professor at the École de Guerre, he later served (1908–11) as director of that institute. In World War I, he was responsible, with General Joffre and General Gallieni, for halting the German advance at the Marne (1914). He participated in the first battle of Ypres (1915) and that of the Somme (1916); and, after a brief eclipse, he was appointed (1917) chief of the French general staff. In April, 1918, Foch assumed the unified command of the British, French, and American armies. In this capacity, he was perhaps more responsible than any other one man for the victory in 1918. See B. H. Liddell Hart, *Foch, the Man of Orléans* (1932); Charles Bugnet, *Foch Speaks* (tr. 1929).

Focillon, Henri (äNrē' fôsēyôN'), 1881–1943, French art historian. Focillon, who was professor of art history at the Collège de France, was an authority on medieval art, the subject of his two-volume treatise *Art of the West in the Middle Ages* (2d ed. 1969). His book *Life Forms in Art* (1934) outlines his formal, organic conception of the art historical method, stressing analysis of style and technique over subjective interpretation.

Fock, Jenő (yĕ'nö fōk), 1916–, Hungarian Communist politician. He joined the Communist party in 1932, and from 1940 to 1943 he was imprisoned for his Communist activities. An economist, Fock held several offices, including that of deputy premier (1961–67). In 1967 he was appointed premier.

Focşani (fōk-shän', -shä'nē), town (1970 est. pop. 40,000), E central Rumania, at the foot of the Transylvanian Alps. The administrative center of a district famed for its vineyards, Focşani is an industrial town and a market for wine and grain. It was founded in the 15th cent. The German-Rumanian armistice in World War I was signed (1917) there.

focus, in optics, the point at which rays converge after reflection by a concave MIRROR or refraction by a convex LENS, also known as a real focus. The point from which rays appear to diverge after reflection by a convex mirror or refraction by a concave lens is known as a virtual focus. See IMAGE.

foehn (fān, Ger. fön), warm, dry wind that occurs on the leeward slopes of a ridge of mountains. The term was originally applied to a wind of the Alps but is now used as a generic term for all winds of this type. In other parts of the world the various foehn winds have often been given local names, e.g., the CHINOOK over the eastern slopes of the Rocky Mts., the "sky sweeper" over Majorca, and the *aspre* over the Garonne plain of France. A foehn originates as follows: Air is first forced upward over the windward mountain slopes, cooling as it encounters the lower pressures of higher altitudes. If, however, it reaches its condensation temperature, the cooling is somewhat reduced owing to the release of LATENT HEAT that results from water vapor condensing into liquid water. As the air flows downward over the leeward slopes, it is warmed as it encounters the greater pressures of lower altitudes. This warming, however, is greater than the cooling that occurred during the ascent if heat was added to the air as a result of condensation, so that the air is both warmer and drier than originally. The foehn occurs when the circulation is strong enough to force air over the mountains in a relatively short period of time. The nature of the foehn in a particular locale depends on the topography, the strength and direction of circulation, and the moisture supply on the windward side of the mountains. The chinook, for example, generally blows from the southwest and sometimes raises temperatures by as much as 20°F (7°C) in 15 min.

fog, aggregation of water droplets immediately above the surface of the earth, i.e., a cloud near the ground. A light or thin fog is usually called a mist. Fog may occur either when the moisture content of the air is increased beyond the saturation point or when the air is cooled below a critical temperature called the dew point; in either case condensation of the excess moisture takes place on the microscopic dust particles (condensation nuclei) in the atmosphere. An example of the first case is fog resulting from the evaporation of warm water into cold air, occurring either when cold air streams over a warm water surface (steam fog) or when a warm rain falls through a layer of cold air near the ground (frontal fog). Examples of the second case include fog caused by radiation of heat from the ground during a calm, cloudless night, with subsequent cooling, by conduction, of the air adjacent to the ground (radiation fog); by the flow of warm air over a cold land or water surface (advection fog); or by air ascending a slope and cooling by expansion (upslope fog). Fog commonly found in valleys and depressions in the morning, especially during autumn, is of the radiation type, which because of its shallow nature is dissipated by the sun's heat as the day progresses. On the other hand, the extensive fog banks occurring frequently along the coasts of Newfoundland and Labrador are of the advective type and, being generally quite deep, often persist for days at a time, greatly hindering shipping and aviation activity.

Fogazzaro, Antonio (äntô'nyō fōgät-tsä'rō), 1842–1911, Italian novelist and poet. His first work was a verse romance, *Miranda* (1847). Primarily concerned with moral issues, he was particularly adept at depicting character. His famous novel *Malombra* (1881, tr. *The Woman,* 1907) reveals the conflict between the spiritual and the sensual. *Piccolo mondo antico* (1896, tr. *The Patriot,* 1906) explores the synthesis of an agnostic wife's moral sense and her husband's deep religious faith; it is considered one of the great Italian novels of the 19th cent. Its sequels were *Piccolo mondo moderno* (1901, tr. *The Sinner,* 1907), *Il santo* (1905, tr. *The Saint,* 1906), and *Leila* (1911). Because of their sharp comments on religion and ethics, the last two novels were placed on the Vatican Index, a list of works forbidden to Roman Catholics.

Fogelberg, Bengt Erland (bĕngt ĕr'länd fo͞o'gəlbĕr"yə), 1786–1854, Swedish sculptor. He studied in Stockholm, in Paris, and in Rome, where he lived for many years. His statues of Greek and Norse mythological figures, such as *Venus Victrix, Odin,* and *Thor,* are in the Stockholm Museum. He also made portrait statues of Swedish heroes including Gustavus Adolphus and Birger Jarl.

Foggia (fôd'jä), city (1971 pop. 141,667), capital of Foggia prov., in Apulia, S Italy. It is a transportation and industrial center and the main wheat market of S Italy. Manufactures include food products, paper, and chemicals. It has long been the custom to store grain in huge holes dug in the squares of the city. An earthquake in 1731 destroyed much of Foggia. The city was a favorite residence of Emperor Frederick II, who built (13th cent.) a fortified castle there (since greatly reconstructed).

Foggini, Giovanni Batista (jōvän'nē bätēs'tä fōdjē'nē), 1652–1725, Italian sculptor and architect. An important exponent of the Florentine baroque style, Foggini followed Roman models in his architecture (e.g., the Feroni Chapel, Santi Annunziata, Florence). He was influenced by Bernini and Cortona in his sculpture. His relief *The Ascent to Heaven of St. Andrew Corsini* (1675; Santa Maria del Carmine, Florence) reveals remarkable baroque vigor.

Fogo Island (fō'gō), c.100 sq mi (260 sq km), at the entrance to Notre Dame Bay, E N.F., Canada. It rises to 382 ft (116 m). The town of Fogo (1971 pop. 1,155) is a fishing port with fish canneries and fox and mink farms.

Föhr (fŏr), island (1966 est. pop. 8,400), 32 sq mi (83 sq km), Schleswig-Holstein, N West Germany, in the North Sea, one of the North Frisian Islands. Wyk (1966 est. pop. 4,500), the principal town, is a bathing resort. The island has farms, fisheries, and oyster beds. Until 1864, Föhr was included in the Danish duchy of Schleswig.

foie gras (fwä grä) [Fr.,=fat liver], livers of artificially fattened geese. Ducks and chickens are also sometimes used in the making of foie gras. The birds, kept in close coops to prevent exercise, are systematically fed to the limit of their capacity. Under this treatment the livers are brought to weigh 2 or 3 lb (1.0–1.5 kg) or more. Foie gras was prized by epicures in Egypt, Greece, and Rome, but the fattening of geese for their livers became a lost art during the Middle Ages except in Strasbourg. The industry was revived in the 18th cent. following the creation of pâté de foie gras by Jean Joseph Close (or Clause), a chef brought to Alsace by a French governor of the province. The pâté is made by cooking fresh livers, reducing them to a paste delicately seasoned with wine and aromatics and combining it with truffles and finely chopped veal. The making of foie gras has become a famous industry of Strasbourg and of Toulouse, France. The product is exported to all parts of the world in several forms—the esteemed pâté; foie gras au naturel, the plain cooked livers; a sausage; and a purée.

Foix, Gaston de (gästôN' də fwä), 1489–1512, duc de Nemours, French general in the ITALIAN WARS; nephew of King Louis XII. As commander of the French army in Italy in 1512, he proved his outstanding ability, making his small army highly effective by the use of surprise and forced marches. He relieved Bologna, defeated the Venetians at Isola della Scala and Brescia, and successfully laid siege to Ravenna, where he was killed.

Foix (fwä), town (1968 pop. 10,110), capital of Ariège dept., S France, on the Ariège River at the foot of the Pyrenees. It is an administrative and tourist center with some small industry. It grew around an oratory founded by Charlemagne and became the capital of the countship of Foix. The most famous of the many powerful Foix counts was Gaston III. Foix was united with the crownland in 1607. Of interest are an imposing château (12th and 14th cent.; restored), which now houses a museum of prehistoric, Gallo-Roman, and medieval art; and the ancient St. Volusieu Church (reconstructed in the 14th and 17th cent.).

Fokine, Michel (mēshĕl' fōkēn', Rus. fô'kyĭn), 1880–1942, American choreographer and ballet dancer, b. Russia. He studied at the Imperial Ballet School (1889–98) and danced at the Marinsky Theatre, St. Petersburg. Here his choreographical reforms won Nijinsky and Pavlova as followers. In 1905 he created *Le Cygne (The Dying Swan)* for Pavlova to music of Saint-Saëns. He accompanied Sergei DIAGHILEV to Paris in 1909 and was choreographer for his company until 1914. Fokine, considered the founder of modern ballet, based his choreography on the old system of training but eliminated rigid traditions, thus paving the way for the new freedom to come with expressionism. He emigrated in 1919 to the United States, where he formed several companies and conducted a ballet school. In 1932 he became a U.S. citizen. Among the approximately 70 ballets created by Fokine are *Les Sylphides* (1909), *Prince Igor* (1909), *The Firebird* (1910), *Scheherazade* (1910), *The Spectre of the Rose* (1916), and *Petrouchka* (1916). See his memoirs (ed. by Anatole Chujoy, tr. 1961); study by C. W. Beaumont (2d ed. 1945).

Fokker, Anton Herman Gerard (än'tōn hĕr'män gä'rärt fôk'ər), 1890–1939, American aircraft manufacturer, b. Kediri, Java. He established aircraft factories in Germany before World War I and became famous as the builder of the Fokker triplanes and biplanes, which were employed by the Germans. He also developed an apparatus that allowed machine guns to fire through moving aircraft propellers. After the war he turned to the development of commercial aircraft. In 1922 he came to the United States and was later naturalized. He was for a time president of the Fokker Aircraft Corporation of America. See his autobiography, *The Flying Dutchman* (1931, repr. 1972).

folacin: see VITAMIN.

fold, in geology, bent or deformed arrangement of stratified rocks. These rocks may be of sedimentary or volcanic origin. Although stratified rocks are normally deposited on the earth's surface in horizontal layers (see STRATIFICATION), they are often found inclined or curved upward or downward. Arches, or upfolds, in stratified rock are called anticlines; depressions or downfolds, synclines. A third type of fold, the monocline, is a steplike structure sloping in one direction only. It is more correctly called a flexure and generally passes at depth into a fracture called a fault. An imaginary line drawn along the crest of an anticline or the trough of a syncline is its axis; the two sides curving away from the axis are the limbs. If both limbs, dipping in opposite directions, make the same angle with the horizontal, and if an imaginary axial plane passed through the axis and the center of the fold is vertical and divides the fold into two equal halves, the fold is symmetrical; if the limbs make unequal angles, and if the axial plane is inclined and does not bisect the fold, the fold is asymmetric. If one limb lies partly under the other, and the axial plane is inclined, the fold is overturned; if one limb lies almost completely under the other, and the axial plane is almost horizontal, the fold is recumbent. The axis of a fold cannot be indefinitely extended parallel to the horizontal, but plunges or emerges as the fold tapers off to a plane. Certain domes are very short anticlines with axes plunging at both ends, while some basins, similarly, are synclinal structures. Folds are commonly formed at some distance below the surface, but complete folds or portions of folds are exposed by erosion. Anticlines frequently have their crests eroded, till only the worn-down stumps of the two limbs remain. In a similar manner synclines may be eroded so that only the edges of the limbs project above the surface. The ridge crests of the Appalachian Mts. are eroded limbs of folds. The nature of the original fold can generally be determined from the arrangement of the outcrops, or exposed portions; thus, two outcrops dipping toward each other mark a syncline, and two outcrops dipping away from each other, an anticline. Folds on a grand scale, extending, for example, most of the length of a continent, are known as geosynclines and geanticlines. The immediate cause of folding is generally conceded to be the horizontal compression of the earth's surface, anticlines being squeezed up by this compression and synclines formed between anticlines. The problem of the ultimate cause of fold formation is similar to that of fault formation, both being earth movements involved in MOUNTAIN building and PLATE TECTONICS. Porous and permeable rocks of anticlines often contain oil and gas reservoirs. Organic remains of late Paleozoic tree fern swamps were converted to anthracite coal during the folding of the Appalachian Mts.

Folengo, Teofilo (tāô'fēlō fōlĕng'gō), 1496–1544, Italian burlesque poet, who used the pseudonym Merlinus Cocaius or Merlino Cocajo. A Benedictine monk, he left (c.1515) his monastery to become a wandering poet, returning in 1534. Folengo was outstanding among the macaronic poets (who wrote mixing Latin grammatical forms with vernacular vocabulary). His *Baldus,* which antedates *Don Quixote,* is a burlesque of the chivalric romance and is considered the great epic of the macaronic type.

Folger, Charles James (fōl'jər), 1818–84, U.S. Secretary of the Treasury (1881–84), b. Nantucket, Mass. A lawyer of Geneva, N.Y., he held judicial posts and was (1861–69) a state senator. Opposition to slavery caused him to turn from the Democratic to the Republican party, but in 1870 he was the candidate of both parties for the post of associate justice of the state court of appeals—a post he held (except when chief justice briefly in 1880) until he entered President Arthur's cabinet. He reduced the public dept and initiated civil service administration in the Treasury Department.

Folger, Henry Clay, 1857–1930, American industrialist and collector of Shakespeareana. His connection with Standard Oil companies, beginning in 1879, continued until his retirement 49 years later as chairman of the board of the New York company. He was an enthusiastic student of Shakespeare during his college days, and became a discerning collector. His wife, **Emily Jordan Folger** (d. 1936), was his associate in this work. Their collection, quietly acquired, became one of the largest and most valuable of its sort in the world. The **Folger Shakespeare Library,** east of the Library of Congress, Washington, D.C., was dedicated in 1932. Its major collections contain more than 250,000 volumes, primarily 16th- and 17th-century works of literature, drama, and history of the English Renaissance. It is administered by Amherst College trustees.

Folger, Peter, 1617–90, British settler on Nantucket. He was associated with Thomas Mayhew on Martha's Vineyard, becoming missionary, schoolmaster, and surveyor. He moved to Nantucket in 1663, added other duties to those he possessed in Martha's Vineyard, and became a leader in the community. Folger was a Baptist and was opposed to the intolerance of the Massachusetts leaders. He wrote *A Looking Glass for the Times* (1676), which his grandson, Benjamin Franklin, described as a defense of liberty of conscience in "homespun verse—written with a good deal of decent plainness and manly freedom." See F. M. Anderson, *A Grandfather for Benjamin Franklin* (1940).

Folger Shakespeare Library: see FOLGER, HENRY CLAY.

Folgore da San Geminiano (fôl'gōrā dä sän jāmēnyä'nō), fl. 1308–16, Italian poet. *Mesi,* his cycle of sonnets on the seasons and their appropriate pleasures, is interspersed with zestful descriptions of the manners of his day.

folic acid: see COENZYME; VITAMIN.

Foligno (fōlē'nyō), city (1971 pop. 49,818), in Umbria, central Italy. It is a commercial and industrial center and a railroad junction. Manufactures include chemicals, machinery, paper, and textiles. Foligno was under papal control from the mid-15th cent. until 1860. Of note in the city are the Romanesque cathedral (12th cent., frequently restored) and the Palazzo Trinci (15th cent., with a 19th-century neoclassical facade). A local school of art flourished in the 15th cent.

folk art, the art works of a culturally homogeneous people produced by artists without formal training. The forms of such works are generally developed into a tradition that is either cut off from or tenuously connected to the contemporary cultural mainstream. Folk art often involves craft processes, e.g., in America, QUILTING and sculpture of ships' FIGUREHEADS, cigar-store figures, and carousel animals. Paintings in the tradition of PRIMITIVISM also reflect the folk idiom. Folk art is generally nationalistic in character and expresses the values and aspirations of a culturally united group. Much folk art possesses a rough-hewn, awkward quality frequently admired and imitated by sophisticated artists. In works of the American regionalist school of the 20th cent., folk and mainstream traditions merged to form a hybrid art.

folk dance, primitive, tribal, or ethnic form of the DANCE, sometimes the survival of some ancient ceremony or festival. The term is used also to include characteristic national dances, country dances, and figure dances in costume to folk tunes. Many children's games, such as "London Bridge" and "The Farmer in the Dell," are traditional folk dances. More elaborate examples are the Spanish FANDANGO, the Bohemian POLKA, the Hungarian czardas, the Irish JIG, the Scottish HIGHLAND FLING, and the English MORRIS DANCE, sword dance, and Maypole dance. American barn dances, such as the Virginia reel, are largely derived from European sources. Early in the 20th cent. Cecil James SHARP, founder of the English Folk Dance Society, made a notable collection of English folk songs and dances. The American Folk Dance Society has done much to preserve the knowledge of old American country dances, and a similar interest has developed in other countries. A popular form of recreation, folk dancing is often taught in schools. See A. S. Duggan and others, *Folk Dance Library* (5 vol., 1948); S. F. Damon, *The History of Square Dancing* (1957); M. D. Lidster and D. H. Tamburini, *Folk Dance Progressions* (1965).

folk drama, noncommercial, generally rural theater and pageantry based on folk traditions and local history. This form of drama, common throughout the world, declined in popularity in the West (although not in the Orient) with the advent of printing, general literacy, and with the increasing emphasis on the individual contribution to the drama of playwright, director and actors. The mid-19th cent. witnessed a revival of folk drama in the United States and parts of Western Europe. Some of the major figures responsible for this resurgent interest are the Americans Percy McKaye and Paul Green, the Englishman Louis N. Parker, and the French actor-manager and poet Maurice Pottecher. American universities, including the State Agricultural College at Fargo, N.Dak., and the universities of North Carolina and Wisconsin, have sponsored much experimental work in producing regional history plays. One yearly drama presented outside the university environment is the "Trail of Tears" history play performed by the Indians of Cherokee, N.C.

Folkestone (fōk'stən), municipal borough (1971 pop. 43,760), Kent, SE England. Folkestone is a summer resort and an active port. The Leas promenade runs along the chalk cliffs overlooking the English Channel. There are vestiges of Roman occupation in the vicinity, and a 13th-century parish church has been restored. Folkestone was a prosperous port in the Middle Ages and early modern period.

Folketing (fôl'kətĭng), national parliament of Denmark. Formerly the lower house of the bicameral Rigsdag, it became the sole parliamentary body in 1953. It shares legislative power with the monarch, who can dissolve the body but cannot assume major international obligations without its consent. It is elected by universal suffrage, and its term is four years. Ministers can vote in the Folketing only if they are members.

folk high school, type of adult education that in its most widely known form originated in Denmark in the middle of the 19th cent. The idea as originally conceived by Bishop Nikolai GRUNDTVIG was to stimulate the intellectual life of young adults (generally from 18 to 25 years of age) of rural Denmark, to foster patriotism and strengthen religious conviction, and to provide agricultural and vocational training. The first school, established in Schleswig (1844), was moved across the Danish border after Schleswig passed to Prussia. The movement then gained momentum, and numerous schools were established, with national history and literature emphasized in the curriculum. The folk high schools had a great influence on the civic life of rural Denmark and helped to improve the condition of the small farmer whose products were marketed through cooperative societies. The folk school idea spread throughout Europe with local adaptations, but by the early 20th cent. the movement had abated. Since then the number of folk high schools in Denmark has remained stable at about 70. In the United States notable experiments in this type of adult education were instituted at Rome, Ga., and at Brasstown, N.C., where the John C. Campbell Folk School was founded (1925). Most attempts to found folk high schools in the United States, however, have been unsuccessful. See Thomas Rordam, *The Danish Folk High Schools* (1965); David C. Davis, *Model for a Humanistic Education: The Danish Folk High School* (1971).

folklore, the body of customs, legends, beliefs, and superstitions passed on by oral tradition. It includes FOLK DANCES, FOLK SONGS, FOLK MEDICINE (the use of magical charms and herbs), and FOLK TALES (myths, rhymes, and proverbs). The study of folklore emerged significantly in the 19th cent., partly out of the rise of European romanticism, with its interest in the past, and partly out of nationalism, with its stress on the indigenous. Today most folklorists and anthropologists regard folk customs, legends, and beliefs as an imaginative expression by a people of its desires, attitudes, and cultural values. Folk heroes (e.g., Frederick Barbarossa in Germany, the Cid in Spain, Robin Hood in England, Cuchulain in Ireland, Paul Bunyan in the United States, and Yü in China) have been said to reflect the civilization from which they sprang. Many theories have arisen to explain folk tales—Max Müller, a philologist, interpreted the legends as linguistic corruptions; Jakob Grimm saw them as corrupted cosmic allegories; the German school considered them as personified elements of nature; Edward Tylor and Andrew Lang held them to be survivals from a savage society; Freud and the psychoanalytical school found them fraught with sexual symbolism. Folklore has become increasingly important in the study of primitive societies and in understanding the history of mankind. Almost every country has a folklore society which collects, analyzes, and publishes folk material (e.g., in the United States the American Folklore Society publishes the *Journal of American Folklore*). For further information, see GAMES, CHILDREN'S; MONSTERS AND IMAGINARY BEASTS IN FOLKLORE; MYTHOLOGY. See C. L. Daniels and C. M. Stevens, ed., *Encyclopedia of Superstitions, Folklore, and the Occult Sciences of the World* (1971); Duncan Emrich, *Folklore on the American Land* (1972); R. M. Dorson, ed., *Folklore and Folklife: An Introduction* (1972); T. P. Coffin and Hennig Cohen, *Folklore from the Working Folk of America* (1973); R. M. Dorson, *America in Legend* (1974).

folk medicine, methods of curing by means of magic; healing objects, herbs, or animal parts; ceremony; conjuring; witchcraft; and other means apart from the formalized practice of medical science. In nearly all ancient and preliterate societies disease and death were and are attributed to the workings of malevolent beings, spirits, or forces. Extremely complex rituals and medicinal applications were devised to heal these ills. Many such cures coincide with what modern research has proved to be effective: The taking of castor oil has been advocated by sailors for centuries and is known today to be the source of essential vitamins; the age-old successful application of bread mold and soil fungi to infected areas corresponds to the antibiotic practice of modern medicine. There remains a widespread belief in the efficacy of certain plants or animal parts that are shaped or colored like the diseased part of the body: hence, red poppies for blood disorder, spotted plants for skin eruptions, trefoil plants for heart trouble. Preventive medicine and ritual to produce sickness in one's enemies have also been popular in addition to curative methods. The Indians of South and Central America, among others, perform purification ceremonies and hold festivals for cleansing and to ward off the EVIL EYE. Medicine men, shamans, and other doctors credited with magical powers generally massage, draw liquid off by suction, or blow upon the diseased area. They recite ancient formulas and incantations to cure or banish illness, both physical and mental. In all cultures most medicinal lore of this nature is handed down by word of mouth from one generation to the next. That which was written by the ancients formed the beginnings of medical science. In the United States in the 1960s and 70s, there occurred an enormous expanding interest in folk remedies, herbal medicines, vitamins, and so-called health foods and organic foods that are free of insecticides and other pollutants. As a result the production of such foods became a growing business enterprise. See D. C. Jarvis, *Folk Medicine* (1969); D. T. Atkinson, *Magic, Myth and Medicine* (1956, repr. 1972); Clarence Meyer, *American Folk Medicine* (1973).

folk song, music of anonymous composition, transmitted orally. The theory that folk songs were originally group compositions has been modified in recent studies. These assume that the germ of a folk melody is produced by an individual and altered in transmission into a group-fashioned expression. National and ethnic individuality can be seen in folk music, even in the case of songs transplanted from one country to another. There is scarcely any people whose folk song is wholly indigenous, and among notable cases of transplanting is the English ballad found in various parts of the United States. Interest in folk music grew during the 19th cent., although there were earlier scholars in the field, such as Thomas Percy whose *Reliques*, a collection of English ballad texts, appeared in 1765. Sir Walter Scott's *Minstrelsy of the Scottish Border* (3 vol., 1803) is a major source on Scottish ballads. Béla Bartók did outstanding work in notating the folk music of central Europe early in the 20th cent., and before him the Russian nationalist composers made use of their country's folk music. Conversely, folk song often shows the influence of formally composed music; this is particularly true of 17th- and 18th-century European folk song. Americans occasionally consider as folk songs certain songs of traceable authorship, e.g., "Dixie." The collection and transcription of folk music was greatly facilitated by the invention of the phonograph and tape-recorder. Since the early 1950s folk music has become a significant influence and source for much popular vocal and instrumental music. Folksingers such as Woody Guthrie and Pete Seeger performed traditional songs and wrote their own songs in the folk idiom. See CHANTEY; AMERICAN NEGRO SPIRITUALS; bibliography under BALLAD. See J. A. Lomax and Alan Lomax, *Folk Songs, U.S.A.* (1948); Bruno Nettl, *Folk and Traditional Music of the Western Continents* (1965); C. Haywood, ed., *Folk Songs of the World* (1966); A. L. Lloyd, *Folk Song in England* (1967); W. R. Trask, ed., *The Unwritten Song* (1966); and H. H. Glassie, *Folk Songs and Their Makers* (1970).

folktale, general term for any of numerous varieties of traditional narrative. The telling of stories appears to be a cultural universal, common to primitive and complex societies alike. Even the forms folktales take are demonstrably similar from culture to culture, and comparative studies of themes and narrative techniques have been successful in showing these relationships. Among the foremost folklorists of the 19th cent. were Oskar Dähnhardt in Germany, S. O. Addy in England, Paul Sébillot in France, and Y. M. Sokolov in Russia. Major 20th-century scholars in the field include Franz Boas, Richard Chase, Marie Campbell, and Stith Thompson. Folklorists make distinctions among the categories of folktales. Legends and traditions are narratives of an explanatory nature concerning creation and tribal beginnings, supernatural beings, and quasi-historical figures (e.g., King Arthur, Lady Godiva). These stories are related as fact and concern a specific time and place. Fairy tales are entirely fictional and often begin with such formulas as "Once upon a time. . ." and "In a certain country there lived. . . ." Popular examples recount the supernatural adventures and mishaps of youngest daughters, transformed princes, MERMAIDS, and wood fairies and elves (e.g., CINDERELLA, Rumplestiltskin, Snow White, Sleeping Beauty, and Hansel and Gretel). Animal tales abound in every culture; most of them are clearly anthropomorphic, the animals assuming human personalities. Such tales are classified according to three subdivisions: the etiological tale, or tale concerning origins (e.g., Great Hare of the North American Indians); the fable pointing to a moral (Aesop's fables); and the beast epic (e.g., REYNARD THE FOX; see BESTIARY). Myths, which are more difficult to define satisfactorily, treat happenings of a long-ago time; they generally concern the adventures of gods, GIANTS, HEROES, NYMPHS, SATYRS, and villains, as well as etiological themes. See also MYTHOLOGY; MONSTERS AND IMAGINARY BEASTS IN FOLKLORE; ELF; FAIRY; GOBLIN; GREMLIN; TROLL. See Stith Thompson, *The Folktale* (1946); V.O. Binner, *American Folktales* (1966) and *International Folktales* (1967); R. M. Dorson, *America in Legend* (1974).

folkways, term coined by William Graham SUMNER in his treatise *Folkways* (1906) to denote those group habits that are common to a society or culture and are usually called CUSTOMS. The word provided a useful contribution to the development of the concept of CULTURE and is still used in its technical sense in sociological literature. Fashions in clothing or modes of recreation exemplify folkways. The term has failed to maintain the currency it once enjoyed among the other social sciences but has gained acceptance as a colloquial term. See MORES.

follicle-stimulating hormone (FSH): see GONADOTROPIC HORMONE.

Folline, Miriam: see LESLIE, FRANK.

Folquet de Marseille (fôlkā' də märsā'yə), 1150–1231, Provençal troubadour. He took orders, rose to be archbishop of Toulouse, and became notorious as the chief prosecutor in Provence of the Albigensian Crusade. Dante awarded him a place in Paradise.

Folsom culture (fōl'səm, fŭl'-), early North American culture known through artifacts first excavated (1926) near Folsom, E of Raton, N. Mex. The artifacts, including chipped flint points known as Folsom points and a variety of stone implements, were found in association with remains of extinct mammals including the mastodon. The Folsom points are shaped somewhat like a laurel leaf and show a distinct lengthwise groove on each face. Other sites in Canada and W and SW United States have yielded evidences of Folsom culture. The Folsom findings are significant in furnishing evidence that indicates, according to some scientists, the existence of man in North America from 15,000 to 25,000 years ago. Others hold to the view that man reached North America between 7,000 and 10,000 years ago.

Fomalhaut (fō'məlhôt"), brightest star in the constellation Piscis Austrinus (southern fish); Bayer designation Alpha Piscis Austrini; 1970 position R.A. $22^h56.0^m$, Dec. $-29°47'$. A white, main-sequence star of SPECTRAL CLASS A3 V, its apparent MAGNITUDE of 1.16 makes it one of the 20 brightest stars in the sky. Fomalhaut is one of the nearer bright stars, lying at a distance of 23 light-years. Its name is from the Arabic meaning "mouth of the southern fish."

Fomors (fō'môrz), in Irish mythology, a seafaring people who defeated the Firbolgs and ruled ancient Ireland. They were themselves defeated by the TUATHA DE DANANN.

Fonda, Henry, 1905–, American actor, b. Grand Island, Nebr. He has had considerable stage experience, appearing in such plays as *Mr. Roberts* (1948), *The Caine Mutiny Court Martial* (1958), and *Two for the Seesaw* (1959). Fonda played honest, homespun young men in such films as *The Trail of the Lonesome Pine* (1936) and *The Grapes of Wrath* (1940). With maturity his acting range increased. His later films include *The Wrong Man* (1956), *Twelve Angry Men* (1957), *The Best Man* (1964), *Firecreek* (1967), and *Sometimes a Great Notion* (1972). His daughter, **Jane Fonda,** 1937–, b. New York City, is a movie actress. She was pert and sexy in such films as *Tall Story* (1960), *Cat Ballou* (1965), and *Barefoot in the Park* (1967), but her strong performances as tough, disillusioned women in *They Shoot Horses Don't They?* (1969) and *Klute* (1971) established her reputation as a formidable dramatic actress. See biography by Thomas Kiernan (1973). Henry Fonda's son, **Peter Fonda,** 1939–, b. New York City, is a film actor, director, and producer. He is best known for the film *Easy Rider* (1969), a critical study of American life, which he starred in and produced. His other movies include *Lillith* (1964) and *The Hired Hand* (1971; also produced by him).

Fond du Lac (fŏn də lăk, -jo͞o-), city (1970 pop. 35,515), seat of Fond du Lac co., E central Wis., in a resort region at the south end of Lake Winnebago; inc. 1852. Industries include dairy processing and the manufacture of machine tools, leather goods, engines, and snowmobiles. It was a French fur-trading post in the late 18th cent. and grew into a lumbering town in the 19th cent. After the arrival of the railroad, it became an industrial city. Marian College of Fond du Lac and a junior college are there.

Fong, Hiram Leong, 1907–, U.S. Senator from Hawaii (1959–), b. Honolulu. His parents came to Oahu from China to work as indentured laborers on a sugar plantation. Hiram Fong went into law practice in Honolulu and was later successful in real estate and insurance. He served 14 years in the territorial house of representatives, including three terms as speaker. In 1959, when Hawaii elected state officials for the first time, Fong, a Republican, was chosen as senior Senator. He was twice reelected.

Fonseca, Juan Rodríguez de (hwän rōdrē'gāth dā fōnsā'kä), 1451–1524, Spanish prelate. He was bishop successively of Badajoz, Córdoba, Palencia, and Burgos and later archbishop of Rosana. As head of the department of affairs of the Indies, he closely supervised the explorations of Columbus and of Hernán Cortés.

Fonseca, Manuel Deodoro da (mänwĕl' dēo͞othô'ro͞o dä fo͞onsĕ'kə), 1827–92, first president of Brazil (1891). A leader of the discontented militarists who helped overturn the empire (Nov., 1889), he headed the provisional government that established the republic. In 1891, Fonseca was elected president by the constituent assembly. Faced with growing opposition, he dissolved Congress (Nov., 1891) and was forced to resign. He was succeeded by vice president Floriano PEIXOTO. See study by C. W. Simmons (1966).

Fonseca, Golfo de (gôl'fō thā fōnsä'kä), inlet of the Pacific Ocean, c.700 sq mi (1,810 sq km), c.50 mi (80 km) long and c.30 mi (50 km) wide, W Central America. In a volcanic area, it is a natural but shallow harbor shared by Nicaragua, Honduras, and El Salvador. It receives the Choluteca River. La Unión, in El Salvador, and Ampala, in Honduras, are the chief ports. Nicaragua leased (1916) a site for a naval base on the gulf to the United States as an adjunct of the Nicaragua Canal, causing serious protests from El Salvador. Upheld by the Central American Court of Justice, the protests were ignored by the United States and Nicaragua. The gulf was discovered (1522) by Gil González de Ávila, the Spanish explorer.

Fontaine, Pierre François Léonard (pyĕr fräNswä' lāōnär' fôNtĕn'), 1762–1853, French architect. He was known chiefly for the work which, beginning in 1794, he did jointly with Charles PERCIER; the development of the Empire style in France was almost exclusively an expression of their talents. After Napoleon's fall the partnership dissolved (1814), and Fontaine thereafter practiced as court architect during the reigns of Louis XVIII, Charles X, and Louis Philippe. He laid out the Rue de Rivoli in Paris, enlarged the Palais Royal, of which he also wrote a history, and wrote a number of books on architecture.

Fontainebleau (fôNtĕnblō'), town (1968 pop. 19,803), Seine-et-Marne dept., N France, SE of Paris. It is a favorite spring and autumn resort and was long a royal residence, chiefly because of the excellent hunting in the vast Forest of Fontainebleau. Louis IV resided in Fontainebleau, and Philip IV and Louis XIII were born there. Francis I built the magnificent palace, the chief glory of French Renaissance architecture and the scene of many historic events. Francesco Primaticcio and Sebastiano Serlio were the principal artists of the palace. In the palace Louis XIV signed (1685) the revocation of the Edict of NANTES, Pope Pius VII was imprisoned (1812–14), and Napoleon signed his first abdication (1814). Fontainebleau also has a military museum. The town was headquarters of the military branch of the North Atlantic Treaty Organization (NATO) from 1945 to 1967.

Fontainebleau, school of, group of 16th-century artists who decorated the royal palace at Fontainebleau. The major figures in this group were Italian painters invited to France by Francis I. Il Rosso, a Florentine and the most important member of the school, arrived at Fontainebleau in 1530; he was followed in 1532 by Francesco Primaticcio, a disciple of Raphael, and Sebastiano Serlio. Niccolò dell'Abbate appeared at the court in 1552 during the reign of Henry II. The art of Fontainebleau, today represented chiefly by the Gallery of Francis I, was an offshoot of the mannerist style developed in N Italy. It was characterized by a refined elegance often verging on artificiality, with crowded figural compositions in which painting and elaborate stucco work were closely integrated. The work of the Fontainebleau artists incorporated allegory in accordance with the courtly liking for symbolism.

Fontana, Carlo (kär'lō fōntä'nä), 1634–1714, Italian architect. During his early years he worked for three of the most important architects of the high baroque period—Rainaldi, Cortona, and Bernini. His works include various palaces, fountains, tombs, and the Church of San Marcello al Corso (1682–83) in Rome and plans for the Jesuit church and college in Loyola, Spain. His style was more academic than original. Nevertheless, he influenced important architects, such as James Gibbs and Filippo Juvarra. He published his projects for the completion of St. Peter's, along with an erudite history of its origins, in *Templum Vaticanum* (1694).

Fontana, Domenico (dōmĕ'nēkō), 1543–1607, Italian architect. He went to Rome, where he built (c.1580) the Sistine Chapel in the Church of Santa Maria Maggiore for Cardinal Peretti. When his patron was made pope (Sixtus V), Fontana played a leading part in the great rebuilding of Rome. He designed the Lateran palace (1588) and portions of the Vatican, notably the library (1588). An engineer as well as an architect, he built, with his brother Giovanni, the great aqueduct and fountain known as the Acqua Felice (1587) and in 1586 erected the obelisk in front of St. Peter's, a feat that won him wide renown. With Giacomo della Porta, he completed the dome of St. Peter's. On the death of Sixtus V, Fontana's Roman career collapsed; he withdrew to Naples, where he built the imposing royal palace (1600) and where he died before the execution of his magnificent designs for the improvement of the harbor.

Fontana, Prospero (prô'spärō), 1512–97, Italian mannerist painter. He aided Primaticcio in the decoration of Fontainebleau but was active chiefly in Bologna, where most of his work remains. His *Entombment* (Bologna) is characteristic. His daughter **Lavinia Fontana,** 1552–1614, was a fashionable portrait painter in Bologna and Rome. Her self-portraits (two, Pitti Gall., Florence; another, St. Luke's Acad., Rome) and a portrait of Pope Gregory XIII show a fine decorative sense in the treatment of costume.

Fontana, city (1970 pop. 20,673), San Bernardino co., S Calif., at the foot of the San Bernardino Mts.; inc. 1952. Local industries produce steel (at the huge Kaiser plant) and gases for industrial and military uses. There is also a large steam plant for the production of electricity. Mormons farmed on the site in the 1850s; in the early 1900s extensive orchards were planted. During World War II the Kaiser mill was built and the city began its transformation from an agricultural to an industrial community.

Fontana Dam, N.C.: see LITTLE TENNESSEE, river.

Fontane, Theodor (tā'ōdôr fôntä'nə), 1819–98, German writer. Although he is primarily important as a novelist, he did not begin to write fiction until he was almost 60 years old. Earlier he had written two volumes of poetry, *Gedichte* (1851) and *Balladen* (1861), as well as accounts of his travels and his experiences as a war correspondent and prisoner during the Franco-Prussian War. He was also a drama critic for many years. The first master of the realistic novel in Germany, he wrote perceptive novels revealing the decay of contemporary Berlin society. They include *L'Adultera* (1882), *Irrungen, Wirrungen* (1888, tr. *Trials and Tribulations,* 1917), and his masterpiece, *Effi Briest* (1895, tr. 1913–15). He also wrote short novels and the autobiographical *Meine Kinderjahre* (1894, tr. of extracts, *My Childhood Days,* 1913–15).

fontanel (fŏn'tənĕl"): see SKULL.

Fontanne, Lynn: see LUNT, ALFRED, AND LYNN FONTANNE.

Fontenelle, Bernard le Bovier de (bĕrnär' lə bōvyā' də fôNtənĕl), 1657–1757, French writer; nephew of Corneille. His forte was the interpretation of science. His works include *Dialogues des morts* (1683), observations on man; *Histoire des oracles* (1687), attacking superstition; *L'Origine des fables* (1724), on the origin of religions; and *Entretiens sur la pluralité des mondes* (1686), an exposition of the Copernican system. As secretary (1699–1741) of the Académie royale des Sciences, Fontenelle paved the way for the ideas of the Enlightenment. See *The Achievement of Bernard le Bovier de Fontenelle* (selected works, tr. and introd. by L. M. Marsak, 1970).

Fontenoy (fôNtənwä'), village, Hainaut prov., SW Belgium, near Tournai. There, in 1745, Count Maurice de Saxe, in his most celebrated victory, led the French against the British and their allies under the duke of Cumberland in the War of the Austrian Succession.

Fonteyn, Dame Margot (fŏntān'), 1919–, English ballerina. Fonteyn was for many years *prima ballerina assoluta* of the Royal Ballet. Her original name was Margaret Hookham. In 1934 she joined the Sadler's Wells Ballet School, and in the same year she made her debut as a soloist. She became prima ballerina of the Vic-Wells Ballet in 1935. Fonteyn gained a reputation for expressive acting and versatility, creating such roles as Aurora in *The Sleeping Beauty* and Agathe in *Les Demoiselles de la Nuit.* Her performances in *Cinderella, Giselle, Sylvia,* and *The Firebird* were also outstanding. Sir Frederick Ashton created a number of major ballets especially for Fonteyn, among them *Symphonic Variations* (1946), *Ondine* (1958), and *La Fille Mal Gardée* (1960). She was made a Dame of the British Empire in 1956. Fonteyn's international reputation reached an unprecedented height after 1962, when she began her partnership with the Russian dancer Rudolf Nureyev. See biographies by Keith Money (1965 and 1974).

Foochow: see FU-CHOU, China.

food: see FROZEN FOODS; NUTRITION; VITAMIN.

food adulteration, act of intentionally debasing the quality of food offered for sale either by the admixture or substitution of inferior substances or by the removal of some valuable ingredient. The Greek and Roman classics contain allusions to wine makers and dealers who colored and flavored their wine. In

England as early as the 13th cent., bakers cheapened their wares or scanted the weight and lawmakers for the first time made an effort to prevent fraudulent dealings on the part of butchers and brewers. In Great Britain in the 18th and early 19th cent., coffee, tea, and cocoa were placed under protection laws by Parliament, passed not so much in the interest of the consumer as to keep up internal revenues. About the middle of the 19th cent. chemical and microscopal knowledge had reached the stage that food substances could be analyzed, and the subject of food adulteration began to be studied from the standpoint of the rights and welfare of the consumer. In 1860 the first food law framed in the interest of the purchaser was passed. That law, lacking sufficient means of enforcement, remained largely ineffective until 1872, when administrative officials were appointed and penalties for violation provided. In the United States the Federal Food and Drug Act of 1906 was the result of a long and stormy campaign led by Dr. Harvey Washington WILEY. This law defined food adulteration and the misbranding of products; it provided regulations covering the interstate movement of food and penalties for violations. The act was superseded in 1938 by the more rigorous Food, Drug, and Cosmetic Act administered since 1940 by the Food and Drug Administration (now within the Dept. of Health, Education, and Welfare). It is charged with enforcing truthful and informative labeling of essential commodities, maintaining staff laboratories, and formulating definitions and standards promoting fair dealing in the interests of the consumer. The 1938 act broadened the definitions of adulteration, misbranding, and lack of informative labeling; it provided for factory inspections; and it increased the penalties for violations. It was amended in 1958 and 1962 to define and regulate food additives and food coloring. Imported goods that violate the provisions of the act may be denied admittance to the United States and if not exported within a given time may be destroyed. The Federal law controls traffic from one state to another and is supplemented by local regulations that require food handlers to be licensed, thereby discouraging the spread of disease; it provides for the inspection by health officers of meat and other foods, of restaurants, and of dairies and cold storage methods. Food may be poisonous for reasons other than deliberate adulteration; see BOTULISM, FOOD POISONING. See J. C. Ayres et al., ed., *Chemical and Biological Hazards in Food* (1962, repr. 1969); B. T. Hunter, *Consumer Beware* (1971).

Food and Agriculture Organization (FAO), specialized agency of the United Nations, established in 1945. It developed out of the conference on food and agriculture held at Hot Springs, Va., in May, 1943. The organization is governed by a conference composed of the entire membership, which meets at least once biennially, and by a council of 27 members. Operations of the staff are managed by a director general. The objective of the FAO is to contribute toward an expanding world economy by bettering the conditions of rural life, improving agricultural production and distribution, and raising the level of nutrition. The FAO has no mandatory powers but seeks to accomplish its purposes by making investigations, publishing reports, and organizing conferences. The program operations are conducted by standing committees, such as those on agriculture, fisheries, and rural welfare. The FAO, among other activities, devises plans for food allocation, offers technical aid to members, increases forestry yield, improves seeds, and develops serums and vaccines. The FAO also has charge of part of the UN technical assistance program. In the early 1970s the FAO supervised over 250 UN projects for economic development; a major concern was alleviating the famine in stricken areas of Africa. In 1973 the agency had 127 members.

Food and Drug Administration (FDA), agency of the Public Health Service division of the U.S. Department of Health, Education, and Welfare. Its purpose is to protect the health of the nation by ensuring that foods are safe and pure, drugs effective, cosmetics harmless, and products honestly labeled and packaged. The Food, Drug, and Cosmetic Act of 1938 and various bills since have strengthened government control by requiring prior-evidence-of-safety tests and procedures for new drugs, pesticides, and additives and colorings in foods and cosmetics. The FDA was first established by the Agricultural Appropriation Act of 1931, although similar functions had been performed by other agencies since the Food and Drug Act of 1906. In 1940 the FDA was transferred from the Agriculture Department to the Federal Security Agency and in 1953 to Health, Education, and Welfare. The FDA consists of bureaus of Food, Product Safety, Drugs, and Veterinary Medicine.

food chain: see ECOLOGY.

Food, Drug, and Cosmetic Act: see FOOD ADULTERATION.

food poisoning, acute illness following the eating of foods contaminated by bacteria, bacterial toxins, or harmful chemical substances. The symptoms, in varying degree and combination, include abdominal pain, vomiting, diarrhea, headache, and prostration. It was once customary to classify all such illnesses as "ptomaine poisoning," but it was later discovered that ptomaines, the products of decayed protein, do not cause disease. In general, the bacteria that cause food poisoning do not affect the appearance, aroma, or flavor of food. In gastrointestinal disturbances due to bacteria the most frequent cause is an organism of the *Salmonella* group. The symptoms of bacterial food poisoning, which appear about 12 hr after ingestion of the contaminated food and last one or two days, are usually headache, chills, fever, muscle aches, prostration, nausea, vomiting, abdominal cramps, and diarrhea. In severe cases there may be dehydration, acid-base imbalance, and shock. Bacterial food poisoning is rarely fatal. Treatment includes rest, sedation, and replacement of fluid loss if necessary. The most common type of food poisoning is caused not by bacteria per se but by their toxins (staphylococcus toxins). Custards, mayonnaise, cream-filled pastry, milk, processed meat, and fish are the foods most often contaminated. Carriers and food handlers with staphylococcic skin infections are mainly responsible for the spread of staphylococcus toxin poisoning. The onset of symptoms from such poisoning (similar to those of *Salmonella* infection) occurs abruptly 2 to 4 hr after ingestion of the polluted food. The illness rarely lasts more than 6 hr, and fatalities are rare. Treatment is the same as for *Salmonella* infection. The most serious type of food poisoning caused by bacterial toxins is due to improper preservation or canning of food (see BOTULISM). Nonbacterial food poisoning may occur after eating foods that contain a naturally occurring or acquired deleterious substance. Ingestion of poisonous mushrooms or toadstools (muscarine poisoning) may be followed in a matter of several minutes to 2 hr by severe thirst, abdominal cramps, diarrhea, vomiting, sweating, dizziness, confusion, collapse, coma, and, occasionally, convulsions. Poisoning may occur also after the ingestion of immature or sprouting potatoes because of the presence of solanine, an alkaloid. Mussels and clams that have fed on a poisonous plankton are a cause of food poisoning, since the poisonous substance is not destroyed by cooking. Ergot poisoning, caused by ingestion of rye grain infected with that fungus, causes damage to the blood vessels and gangrene, as well as gastrointestinal and neurologic symptoms. It is also possible to take into the body gross poisons such as arsenic and lead with foods that have been accidentally contaminated or sprayed with preservatives and not properly cleansed before ingestion. Food from containers lined with cadmium has been known to cause poisoning. See G. M. Dack, *Food Poisoning* (3d ed. 1956); E. B. Dewberry, *Food Poisoning* (4th ed. 1959); B. C. Hobbs, *Food Poisoning and Food Hygiene* (2d ed. 1968).

food preservation. Because most foods remain edible for only a brief period of time, people since the earliest ages have experimented with methods for successful food preservation. Among the products of early food conservation were cheese and butter, raisins, pemmican, sausage, bacon, and grain. As scientific investigations regarding the causes of food spoilage were undertaken, they pointed the way to a wider application of methods already in use and to the discovery of new ones. Before 1860, changes in food were explained on the theory of spontaneous generation. Pasteur demonstrated that ferments, molds, and some forms of putrefaction were caused by the presence of microorganisms widely distributed in the environment. Since these microorganisms are the main cause of food spoilage, food preservation depends on rendering conditions unfavorable for their growth. Processes of preservation may be generally classified as drying, heating, refrigeration, and the use of chemicals or other particular agencies. The most ancient method is drying, and it was employed early for fruits, grains, vegetables, fish, and meat. It was sometimes combined with parching, as in the oatmeal of Scotland or the corn of the American Indian. Modern applications of this ancient device are seen in dried or dehydrated fruits and vegetables, milk, meat, and eggs. A more recent variation, known as freeze-drying, is now being used on such foods as coffee, meat, orange juice, and soup. The early method of drying was by direct exposure to the sun's rays; in modern industry the process is hastened by complex apparatus and by chemical agencies. The use of sugar was early combined with drying. Smoking, a method used mainly for fish and meat, combines the drying action with chemicals produced from the smoke, which form a protective coating. The process of heating was used centuries before its action was understood (see CANNING.) One of the most important modern applications of the heat principle is the PASTEURIZATION of milk. Food may be preserved in its original state for a great length of time by REFRIGERATION (see also FROZEN FOODS). In modern food preservation, preservatives function in two ways. One is by delaying the spoilage of the food, while the other is by ensuring that the food retains, as nearly as possible, its original quality. The first method includes the use of sugar (see JELLY AND JAMS), vinegar for pickling meats and vegetables, salt (one of the oldest preservatives), and alcohol. Good wine will keep almost indefinitely, and fruit placed in a 15% to 20% alcohol solution (brandying) is well preserved. The second method includes the use of ascorbic acid (which prevents color deterioration in canned fruits), benzoic acid, sulfur dioxide, and a variety of neutralizers, firming agents, and bleaching agents. The excessive or unacknowledged use of these chemical agencies has been legislated against by most governments. The exclusion of air, nowadays accomplished by hermetic sealing, is an old device, formerly practiced by pouring hot oil over potted meat or fish, by coating or mixing food with melted fat, as in pemmican, or by burying vegetables in the earth or in sand. The use of melted paraffin achieves the same result. Eggs may be preserved by preventing air from penetrating their porous shells, usually by coating them with an impervious substance. Atomic radiation has also been used successfully to destroy many of the microorganisms that might cause spoilage in food. See Georg Borgstrom, *Principles of Food Science* (2 vol., 1968); N. W. Desrosier, *The Technology of Food Preservation* (3d ed. 1970).

fool, absurd person. In all countries from ancient times and extending into the 18th cent., mental and physical deformity provided amusement. Attached to noble and royal courts were dwarfs, cripples, idiots, albinos, and freaks. The medieval court fool was seldom mentally deficient. For the freedom to indulge in satire, tricks, and repartee, many men of keen insight and caustic wit obtained powerful patronage by assuming the role of fool. This role was played in the courts of the East, in ancient Greece and Rome, and in the court of Montezuma. The clown or jester was common in Elizabethan drama (e.g., the Fool in *King Lear*), and by donning the fool's garb the actor gained the freedom of the fool. His costume, which was hung with bells, usually consisted of a varicolored coat, tight breeches with legs of different colors—occasionally a long petticoat was worn—and a cap which fitted close to the head or fell over the shoulders in the form of asses' ears. Till Eulenspiegel and Robin Goodfellow are mythical fools. See Barbara Swain, *Fools and Folly* (1932); Enid Welsford, *The Fool* (1936, repr. 1961).

Fools, Feast of, burlesque religious festival of the Middle Ages. It occurred during the Christmas and New Year's revels, on or near New Year's Day. In many places a Lord of Misrule ruled over the revels. In France and England the ceremonies were under the charge of the Boy-Bishop, a young man fitted out as a high clergyman. During the feast, lower clergymen and minor officials parodied the sacred rites and customs of the Church. A similar burlesque, the Feast of the Ass, celebrating the donkey on which Mary and the Christ Child rode, was widespread in France. Such burlesques were generally put down by the 15th cent.

fool's gold: see PYRITE.

Foot, Michael, 1913–, British politician and journalist. The son of a Liberal party politician, he joined the Labour party in 1935 and was first elected to Parliament in 1945. An articulate member of the more radical left wing of the party, he joined Aneurin Bevan and other dissidents in opposing the foreign and economic policies of Clement Attlee as being insufficiently socialist, and he has remained a frequent critic of the party's policies. Joining the staff of the left-wing Labour organ *Tribune* as columnist and assistant editor (1937–38), he later served as editor (1948–52, 1955–60) and became managing director in 1961. He was (1944–64) also a columnist for the *Daily Herald*, and has at various times written for the Beaverbrook press. A consistent opponent of British membership in the European Common Market, he became secretary of state for employment in the Labour government of 1974. He is the author of a biography of Aneurin Bevan (2 vol., 1962–73) among other works.

Foot, Samuel Augustus, 1780–1846, American politician, b. Cheshire, Conn. He served as a Democratic Republican in the Connecticut legislature (1817–18, 1821–23, 1825–26) and in the U.S. House of Representatives (1819–21, 1823–25) before he was U.S. Senator (1827–33). In the Senate he became prominent by offering (1829) the FOOT RESOLUTION. He was again (1833) elected—this time a Whig—to the House of Representatives, but he resigned to become governor of Connecticut. His name appears sometimes as Foote.

Foot, Solomon, 1802–66, U.S. Senator from Vermont (1851–66), b. Cornwall, Vt. He taught school, studied law, and was admitted to the bar in 1831. Foot served several terms in the state legislature and was in the U.S. House of Representatives (1843–47). His antislavery convictions carried him into the new Republican party. In the Senate he was recognized as a master of parliamentary law (he was often president pro tempore) and established many customs in the Senate's procedure.

foot: see ENGLISH UNITS OF MEASUREMENT.

foot, in anatomy, terminal part of the vertebrate leg. The term *foot* is also applied to any invertebrate appendage used for locomotion or attachment, e.g., the legs of insects and crustacea, and the single locomotive appendage of the clam. In vertebrates the foot is the area from the ankle to the toes. In some animals, including man, the weight is supported on the entire surface of the foot. Such animals are

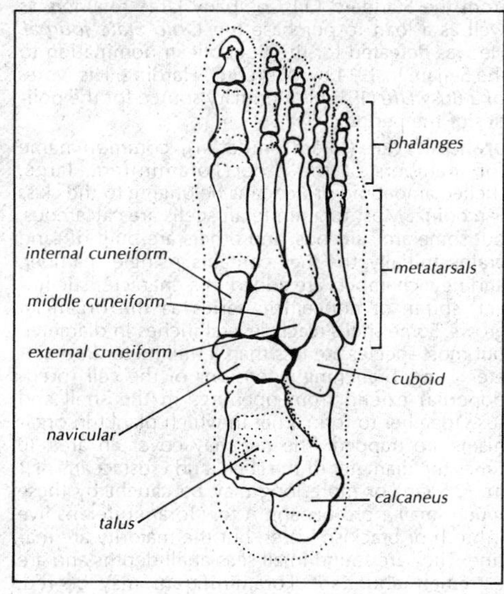

Foot

known as plantigrades. In digitigrade animals, e.g., the dog and cat, the weight is supported on a pad behind the toes. Animals, such as horses and cows, that walk on a nail-like structure, or hoof, at the end of one or more toes are called unguligrades. Like the HAND, the human foot has five digits; however, it is less flexible and lacks an opposable digit, or thumb. It consists of 26 bones connected by tough bands of ligaments. Seven rounded tarsal bones (the internal, middle, and external cuneiform bones, navicular, cuboid, talus, and calcaneus) lie below the ankle joint and form the instep. Five metatarsal bones form the ball of the foot. There are 14 phalanges in the toes (two in the great toe and three in each of the others). The foot bones form an arch that normally meets the ground only at the heel and ball of the foot (see FLAT FOOT).

foot-and-mouth disease, highly contagious disease of cattle, sheep, swine, goats, and other cloven-hoofed animals. It is caused by a virus (discovered by Friedrich Löffler), and its symptoms are fever, loss of appetite and weight, and the eruption of blisters on the mucous membranes—especially those of the mouth, feet, and udder. The discharge of the blisters is heavily infected with the virus, which is present also in the saliva, milk, urine, and other secretions. Thus the disease is spread not only by direct contact but indirectly by way of contaminated food, water, soil and other materials—even by the wind. Human beings, who seldom contract the disease, may be carriers, as may rats, dogs, birds, wild animals, and frozen meats. No vaccine has yet been perfected, though many have been devised and tested. The only certain method of control is strict quarantine, the slaughter and complete disposal of infected animals, and the thorough disinfection of their quarters and of any possibly contaminated material. Epidemics are much feared and cause enormous losses to the livestock industry. Outbreaks are more frequent in Europe and South America than in the United States. In 1946 a serious epidemic in Mexico was brought under control only after mass slaughter of cattle. Other outbreaks occurred in Canada in 1950 and in England in 1960. See publications of the U.S. Dept. of Agriculture.

football, any of a number of games in which two opposing teams attempt to score points by moving an inflated rubber ball past a goal line or into a goal area. The games, differing greatly in their rules, include SOCCER (association football) and RUGBY, in addition to the games covered in this article: American football, Canadian football, Gaelic football, and Australian football. In the United States, the word *football* generally refers only to the American game; in other parts of the world it usually means soccer. Most of the modern forms of football are derived from many ancient games, especially *harpaston* and *harpastrum,* played in Greece and Rome. These games were carried over through the Middle Ages down to present times in Tuscany and Florence under the name *calcio.* Meanwhile a rugged, undisciplined type of football took root in England in the Middle Ages, and despite several royal edicts banning the game from time to time, football remained popular among the masses until the early 19th cent. Different forms of the game were soon developed at the various English public schools—Rugby, Eton, Harrow, and others. Eventually, two main games emerged. One was primarily a kicking game, which later became association football, or soccer; the other (dating from 1823) was football as played at Rugby, in which carrying the ball and tackling were permitted. It was from the two English games, especially rugby, that **American football** developed. The American game is played by two opposing teams of 11 men each. The football field is level, measures 100 by 53⅓ yd (91.4 by 48.8 m), is marked off by latitudinal stripes every 5 yd (4.57 m) and is flanked on each end by an end zone 10 yd (9.14 m) deep. In each end zone stand H-shaped goal posts not exceeding 20 ft (6.10 m) in height, with the crossbar 10 ft (3.05 m) from the ground and with the vertical posts 24 ft (73.2 m) apart. Play is directed toward gaining possession of the football—an inflated, egg-shaped leather ball, often called the "pigskin"—and moving it across the opponent's goal line, thereby scoring a touchdown, worth six points. In advancing the ball a team may run or pass (forward or laterally), but it must gain 10 yd in four tries (or downs), or else yield possession of the ball to the opponent. The defending team tries to stop the ball carrier from advancing by tackling him, i.e., forcing him to the ground—thus causing the team with the ball to use up one of its downs. The defending team can gain possession of the ball before the end of four downs by recovering a dropped ball, or fumble, or by intercepting a pass. Because the strategies and skills required on offense and on defense differ so greatly, most organized football clubs have offensive and defensive squads that alternate on the field as possession of the ball changes. The offensive team is traditionally composed of a quarterback (the field leader), a fullback, two halfbacks, a center, two guards, two tackles, and two ends. A typical defensive unit has two tackles, two ends, three linebackers, two cornerbacks, and two safeties. The game is divided into two halves, each consisting of two periods, or quarters, of 15 minutes playing time. At the end of each of the first three quarters, the teams exchange goals. Each half is begun by a kickoff, which also initiates play after every score (except a safety). In addition to the touchdown, points are scored by kicking the ball over the crossbar between the goal posts (a field goal), counting three points; and by downing a man in possession of the ball behind his own goal line (a safety), counting two points. Additional points, known as conversions, may be scored in football after the completion of a touchdown. In professional play the conversion is worth one point and is earned by kicking the ball over the crossbar of the goal post or by running or passing the ball over the goal line from 2 yd (1.83 m) away. In amateur (high school and college) football, where the conversion play is begun 3 yd (2.74 m) from the end zone, the kick is worth one point and the running or passing conversion two points. When a team is not likely to gain 10 yd in four downs, it often kicks, or punts, the ball downfield, usually on the fourth down. After each down, before resuming play, the opposing teams face each other along an imaginary line, called the line of scrimmage, determined by the position of the ball relative to the goals. Standard scrimmage formations on offense are the T formation, the double wing, and the single wing. The basic T formation (a balanced line with the quarterback behind the center and the other backs behind the quarterback) is, along with modern variations, the most popular setup in both amateur and professional football. Blocking and tackling make football one of the most rugged sports played; thus football players wear heavy protective gear. Five men—the referee, umpire, field judge, linesman, and electric clock operator—officiate in a game, and penalties, in the form of moving the ball away from a team's object goal, are meted out for violations of the rules. The first intercollegiate football match in America (actually a 50-man soccer game) was played (1869) at New Brunswick, N.J. The Intercollegiate (Soccer) Football Association, composed of Columbia, Princeton, Rutgers, and Yale, was created (1873) to standardize rules. Harvard, meanwhile, refused to join the group and, looking for other opponents, accepted a challenge from McGill Univ. of Canada to play a series of games (1874–75) under Rugby rules. The Rugby-type game soon caught on at the other schools also, and within the next 10 years the distinctive game of American football evolved. College football coaching became professionalized in the 1890s, and from the beginning of the 20th cent. football has enjoyed tremendous popularity as a collegiate sport. Rules concerning the field, scoring, playing time, downs, scrimmage, substitution, officials, and equipment have undergone several changes, and the general trend has been toward making the game safer. In 1902 the first Rose Bowl football game was played at Pasadena, Calif., and that postseason tournament has been conducted annually since 1916. Other annual, postseason, collegiate football games include the Sugar Bowl, Orange Bowl, Sun Bowl, and Cotton Bowl games. Selection of All-America teams, begun (1889) by Walter Camp and Caspar Whitney, also contributed to football's popularity. The Heisman trophy, originated (1935) by the Downtown Athletic Club of New York City, is awarded annually to the nation's outstanding college football player. Most collegiate teams play in athletic conferences. Among the more famous are the Ivy League, Western (Big Ten), and Pacific Coast conferences. Many intense collegiate rivalries have developed, including Army-Navy and Yale-Harvard. With the added color provided by bands, cheering sections, and other devices, college football is not only the most popular collegiate sport of the fall season, but also a big business. Revenues from football often finance other sports at a college, and some games are played before crowds of 100,000 people in university-owned stadiums. Despite the strict amateur code of the National Collegiate Athletic Association and its member conferences in various sections of the country, illegal subsidization of football players still exists. Six-man football and touch football, both usually played as participant sports, are other forms of the amateur game. Although professional football was played as early as 1895 in Pennsylvania, it was not until 1920 that the organized game began with the formation of the American Professional Football Association at Canton, Ohio. Originally consisting of five teams, the association was reorganized a number of times and in 1922 was renamed the National Football League (NFL). The professional game received a tremendous boost when Red Grange, a star halfback at the Univ. of Illinois, signed a professional contract (1925) with the Chicago Bears. Other college stars soon followed, and the public, attracted by their former collegiate heroes, began to show interest in NFL teams. In the period immediately following World War II professional football's popularity grew tremendously. A new league, the All-America Conference (established 1944), competed with the NFL until the two groups agreed to a merger (1949). The American Football League (AFL; formed 1959) competed with the NFL during the early 1960s. A merger between the two leagues was negotiated in 1966 and the first Super Bowl championship game was held that same year between the NFL and AFL champions. Four years later the two leagues were merged completely into the present NFL, consisting of two conferences of 13 teams each. The National Conference includes the following teams: Atlanta Falcons,

Chicago Bears, Dallas Cowboys, Detroit Lions, Green Bay Packers, Los Angeles Rams, Minnesota Vikings, New Orleans Saints, New York Giants, Philadelphia Eagles, St. Louis Cardinals, San Francisco 49ers, and Washington Redskins. The American Conference consists of the following clubs: Baltimore Colts, Buffalo Bills, Cincinnati Bengals, Cleveland Browns, Denver Broncos, Houston Oilers, Kansas City Chiefs, Miami Dolphins, New England Patriots, New York Jets, Oakland Raiders, Pittsburgh Steelers, and San Diego Chargers. The winners of the professional world championship have been: 1933, Chicago; 1934, New York; 1935, Detroit; 1936, Green Bay; 1937, Washington; 1938, New York; 1939, Green Bay; 1940, 1941, Chicago; 1942, Washington; 1943, Chicago; 1944, Green Bay; 1945, Cleveland; 1946, Chicago; 1947, Chicago; 1948, 1949, Philadelphia; 1950, Cleveland; 1951, Los Angeles; 1952, 1953, Detroit; 1954, 1955, Cleveland; 1956, New York; 1957, Detroit; 1958, 1959, Baltimore; 1960, Philadelphia; 1961, 1962, Green Bay; 1963, Chicago; 1964, Cleveland; 1965, 1966, 1967, Green Bay; 1968, New York; 1969, Kansas City; 1970, Baltimore; 1971, Dallas; 1972, 1973, Miami; 1974, Pittsburgh. Another professional football league, the World Football League, began play in Aug., 1974. The rules of professional football differ somewhat from those of the college game. Both games, however, are highly complex in terms of plays and strategy. All professional and most collegiate teams employ a number of special teams for various game situations (e.g., offense, defense, kickoffs, punt returns) and coaches that specialize in various aspects of the game. Football, amateur and professional, is the second most popular spectator sport in the United States, attracting a total attendance of more than 43 million people a year. Famous personalities in American football, past and present, include Sam Baugh, Earl Blaik, Jim Brown, Paul Brown, Walter C. Camp, George Gipp, Otto Graham, Red Grange, Lou Groza, George Halas, Tom Harmon, Woody Hayes, Mel Hein, John Heisman, Paul Hornung, Sonny Jurgenson, Vince Lombardi, Sid Luckman, Johnny Lujack, Tim Mara, Bronko Nagurski, Joe Namath, Knute K. Rockne, O. J. Simpson, Fran Tarkenton, Jim Thorpe, Y. A. Tittle, John Unitas, Glenn S. Warner, Byron White, Bud Wilkinson, Norm Van Brocklin, and Fielding Yost. See Robert Riger, *The Pros: A Documentary of Professional Football in America* (1960); Harold Claasen and Steve Boda, *Ronald Encyclopedia of Football* (3d ed. 1963); Harold Claasen, *The History of American Football* (1963); Allison Danzig, *Oh, How They Played the Game* (1971); Roger Treat, ed., *Official Encyclopedia of Football* (10th rev. ed. 1972). **Canadian football** is similar to the U.S. game in that it is also a North American variant of soccer and rugby. In the Canadian game, however, the field and the end zone are larger, measuring 110 yd by 65 yd (100 m by 59 m) and 25 yd by 65 yd (23 m by 59 m), respectively. Canadian teams have 12 players on the field rather than 11 and are allowed only three downs to advance the ball 10 yd. The present game developed from rules established (1891) by the Canadian Rugby Union, the first organizing body for Canadian football. In 1959 the two professional leagues in the union broke away to form the Canadian Football League (CFL). The professional game grew quickly and is now the second most popular spectator sport in Canada. Divided into a western and eastern conference, the CFL holds an annual championship game known as the Grey Cup. See Gordon Currie, *100 Years of Canadian Football* (1968). **Gaelic football,** played almost exclusively in Ireland, is perhaps the roughest of the football-type games. It is played by two teams of 15 men each on a field that measures 84 to 100 yd (76.81-91.44 m) in width and 140 to 160 yd (128.02-146.3 m) in length. The object of the game is to punch, dribble, or kick the ball into (3 points) or directly over (1 point) the rectangular goal-net. As with soccer and rugby, Gaelic football probably developed from the rough-and-tumble football games played in medieval England. Originally a sort of melee between as many as 200 representatives of rival parishes, the game was given a set of standard rules by Dan and Maurice Gavin, who founded (1884) the Gaelic Athletic Association after witnessing a particularly brutal game. The association sponsors the annual all-Ireland championship match, an elimination tournament between teams from Ireland's 32 counties. The only major football-type sport that does not appear to have developed from the medieval game is **Australian football.** Probably an outgrowth of earlier native games, it is played on an oval field that is about 200 yd (183 m) long and 150 yd (137 m) wide across the middle. Each team, composed of 19 players, attempts to kick the egg-shaped ball past a set of goal posts. The ball may be advanced by punches, kicks, or dribbles. The game, played only in Australia, is especially popular in the southern and western parts of the continent. See Jack Pollard, *High Mark: The Complete Book on Australian Football* (1964).

foot-candle: see PHOTOMETRY.

Foote, Andrew Hull, 1806–63, American naval officer, b. New Haven, Conn.; son of Samuel Augustus Foot. He became a midshipman in 1822. As executive officer of the *Cumberland* (1843–45), Foote made her the first temperance ship of the navy. He was largely responsible for ending the alcohol ration in the navy in 1862. From 1849 to 1851 he was active against the slave trade on the African coast and later wrote *Africa and the American Problem* (1854). In 1856, while commanding the *Portsmouth* at Canton, China, he led a small naval force that captured the four barrier forts in reprisal for acts against the American flag. In the Civil War, Foote was given (1861) command of Union naval operations on the upper Mississippi River. His flotilla of gunboats cooperated brilliantly with the army in the victories at FORT HENRY, FORT DONELSON, and ISLAND NO. 10. He was promoted to rear admiral for his work, but wounds received at Fort Donelson forced him to retire from combat service. See biography by J. M. Hoppin (1874).

Foote, Arthur William, 1853–1937, American organist, teacher, and composer, b. Salem, Mass.; pupil of J. K. Paine at Harvard. He was organist (1878–1910) at the First Unitarian Church in Boston, where he taught for many years. Among his compositions, romantic and lyrical, are orchestral works, songs, choral and chamber music. His Suite for Strings in E major is his best-remembered work.

Foote, Henry Stuart, 1804–80, U.S. Senator (1847–52) and governor of Mississippi (1852–54), b. Fauquier co., Va. An able criminal lawyer, he practiced in several different states. In the U.S. Senate, Foote's aversion to states' rights doctrines emphasized his antagonism to his Mississippi colleague, Jefferson Davis, with whom he actually traded blows (Foote also fought several duels in his day). He defeated Davis for the governorship in 1851, the last Union Whig victory in antebellum Mississippi. Rejected for the Senate, he resigned the governorship just before the end of his term and moved to California, where he was narrowly defeated (1856) for the Senate. Foote moved eastward again in 1858, and he settled in Tennessee. In the Confederate congress his consistent opposition both to Davis and to the continuation of the Civil War caused him to participate in peace schemes. His *War of the Rebellion* (1866) tells his story. After the war Foote supported the national Republican administrations, and in 1878 he was appointed superintendent of the U.S. mint at New Orleans. His *Casket of Reminiscences* (1874) and *The Bench and Bar of the South and Southwest* (1876) contain contemporary and personal history of the time.

Foote, Samuel Augustus: see FOOT, SAMUEL A.

foot-pound, abbr. ft-lb, unit of WORK or ENERGY in the customary English gravitational system; it is the work done or energy expended by a force of 1 pound acting through a distance of 1 foot. It is equal to 1.356 JOULES. The term *foot-pound* is also used to designate a unit of TORQUE that is sometimes called the pound-foot to distinguish it from the energy unit. A force of 1 pound applied 1 foot from and perpendicular to the direction to an axis of rotation produces a 1 foot-pound (or pound-foot) torque at the axis.

Foot Resolution, offered in 1829 by Samuel Augustus FOOT in the U.S. Senate. This resolution instructed the committee on public lands to inquire into the limiting of public land sale. The Jacksonian Democrats, who wished to encourage migration to the West, opposed the resolution; the New England manufacturing interests, who demanded a ready labor supply, backed it. When the Foot Resolution was introduced, the advocates of states' rights saw an opportunity to coalesce with the interests of the West. This touched off (1830) the dramatic debates between Robert HAYNE and Daniel WEBSTER.

Footscray (fo͝ots'krā), city (1971 pop. 51,710), Victoria, SE Australia, part of the Melbourne urban agglomeration. It has factories producing munitions, household appliances, and chemicals.

Foppa, Vincenzo (vēnchĕn'tsō fôp'pä), c.1427–c.1515, Italian painter. Giving new life to the art of the Lombard school, he exercised a great influence upon northern Italian art until the advent of Leonardo da Vinci. He settled (c.1456) in Pavia. There and in Milan he executed many important frescoes, most of which have been destroyed. He painted religious subjects exclusively, ranging from powerful renditions of the *Crucifixion* (Bergamo) to poignant depictions of the *Madonna* (Milan; Johnson Coll., Philadelphia; Davis Coll., Newport, R.I.; National Gall. of Art, Washington, D.C.). His large altarpiece of the *Madonna and Child with Saints* (Brera, Milan) is a notable example of his technical skill and variety of characterization.

Forain, Jean Louis (zhäN lwē fôräN'), 1852–1931, French painter, etcher, and lithographer. One of the foremost etchers of his day, Forain is best known for his political cartoons and social satires, particularly of the worlds of theater and courtroom. His work enlivened a large number of publications, including *Vie moderne, Cravache, Parisien, Figaro,* and the New York *Herald.* In 1898 he founded with Caran d'Ache the short-lived *Psst.* His work was generally of a somber range of color similar to Daumier's. See study by Campbell Dodgson (1936).

Foraker, Joseph Benson (fŏr'əkər), 1846–1917, American politician, b. Highland co., Ohio. After service in the Civil War, he practiced law in Cincinnati and was a judge of the superior court (1879–82), governor of Ohio (1886–90), and U.S. Senator (1897–1909). He supported President McKinley's policies. When Mark Hanna died, Foraker became the undisputed Republican boss of Ohio. His second term in the Senate was marked by notable clashes with Theodore Roosevelt. Foraker, in many ways a progressive governor, became an able Old Guard Senator. He led the opposition to the Hepburn bill on railroad rebates in 1906 and opposed the direct election of U.S. Senators. His political career was ended when, in the election campaign of 1908, William Randolph Hearst revealed that Foraker had accepted from the Standard Oil Company large retainers as well as a loan to purchase the *Ohio State Journal.* He was defeated for the Republican nomination to the Senate in 1914 by Warren G. Harding. His *Notes of a Busy Life* (1916) is a primary source for the politics of the period.

foraminiferan (fərăm"ənĭf'ərən), common name for members of the order Foraminifera, large, shelled amoeboid protozoans belonging to the class Sarcodina. Most foraminiferan shells are calcareous, but some are siliceous, and others are built of sand grains. Initially, the shell contains a single chamber, and new chambers are added in a characteristic linear, spiral, or concentric series as the organism grows. Some shells reach several inches in diameter, but most species are less than a millimeter in diameter. Long, branching extensions of the cell (pseudopodia) extend from openings in the shell and fuse together to form a net in which plankton organisms are trapped. The net may cover an area 10 times the diameter of the shell, and crustaceans of 1 in. (2.5 cm) or more long may be caught by these much smaller protozoans. A few foraminiferans live in fresh or brackish water, but the majority are marine. They are found in all seas at all depths and are extremely abundant. Foraminiferans may be red, brown, or white in color. About 30 pelagic species live in the open sea, the most important belonging to the genus *Globigerina.* Foraminiferans live near the water surface when young, but gravitate downward with age. When the animals die, the shells drop to the bottom, forming "globigerina ooze." Nearly 50 million sq mi (1,295 million sq km) of the ocean bottom in warm and tropical seas are covered with sediment; 50% of this sediment is composed of globigerina ooze. Similar deposits in the past have contributed heavily to the formation of sedimentary rock, and the study of fossil Foraminifera has been extremely important in recognizing geological strata and for dating deposits. Layers of limestone or chalk, such as are found in Dover, England, and in Alabama and Mississippi, solidified from similar deposits of ooze in ancient seas. Limestone used in some Egyptian pyramids contains skeletons of foraminiferans, especially of nummulites, which have coin-shaped skeletons. These fossil remains have been particularly useful in locating domes where petroleum deposits occur. Foraminiferans are classified in the phylum PROTOZOA, class Sarcodina, order Foraminifera.

Forbes, Duncan, 1685–1747, Scottish statesman, known as Forbes of Culloden. As lord advocate of Scotland (1725–37) and lord president of the court of session (1737–47), his influence and diplomacy did much to consolidate the union of England and Scotland, but his plan to create royal highland regiments to prevent clan uprisings was not adopted until 1739 when the famous regiment, the BLACK

WATCH, was founded. He actively opposed the Jacobite rebels in 1715 and 1745 and urged lenient treatment in pacifying the country after the defeat of the rebels at the battle of CULLODEN MOOR (1746). See biography by George Menary (1936).

Forbes, John, 1710–59, British general in the French and Indian Wars, b. Scotland. He entered the British army in 1735, won distinction and promotion in the War of the Austrian Succession, and in 1757 was made a colonel and was sent to reinforce the expedition against Louisburg, Nova Scotia. Courageous, thorough, and particularly able as a quartermaster, he was promoted (Dec., 1757) to brigadier general (in America only) and assigned to command an expedition to take Fort Duquesne, the French stronghold at the forks of the Ohio River. Forbes decided not to use the road that Gen. Edward BRADDOCK had taken to his disastrous defeat on the same mission in 1755. Instead he moved (1758) his force of nearly 7,000 men in short stages through W Pennsylvania, establishing successive depots as he went. West of Raytown (now Bedford) he cut a wagon road over the Alleghenies, which, later known as Forbes Road, became a chief highway of Western migration. An advance column under Major James Grant was severely repulsed by the French on the night of Sept. 13–14 while making a reconnaissance in force. However, French and Indian prisoners captured in a subsequent skirmish (Nov. 12) revealed that the French were weak. George Washington was given command of one of the three brigades into which Forbes then divided his army to assure fullest mobility in a quick thrust at Duquesne. But the French garrison decamped (Nov. 24), and Forbes occupied the burned fort on Nov. 25 without further fighting, promptly renaming it Fort Pitt (whence Pittsburgh). See A. P. James, ed., *Writings of General John Forbes Relating to His Service in North America* (1938, repr. 1971).

Forbes, William Cameron, 1870–1959, American business executive and diplomat, b. Milton, Mass. He entered the mercantile house of his grandfather, John Murray Forbes, in Boston and was a partner in the firm after 1899. Appointed (1904) to the Philippine Commission by President Theodore Roosevelt, he held several administrative posts there before he served (1909–13) as governor general of the islands. He was a member of the Wood-Forbes Commission, which was sent (1921) by President Harding to the Philippines. He was later (1930) chairman of a commission to study conditions in Haiti, served (1931–32) as ambassador to Japan at the time of the Manchurian crisis, and led (1935) an economic mission to the Far East.

Forbes-Robertson, Sir Johnston, 1853–1937, English actor-manager. He was trained by Samuel Phelps, made his first appearance in 1874, and thereafter performed with the Bancrofts (1878), John Hare, and Henry Irving (1882). His portrayal of Hamlet was said to be the greatest of his time. In 1900 he married Gertrude Elliott, an American actress, with whom he often starred. Forbes-Robertson was ascetic in appearance and possessed a magnificent speaking voice. He was knighted in 1913 and retired in the same year. See his autobiographical *Player under Three Reigns* (1925).

Forbidden City: see PEKING and CHINESE ARCHITECTURE.

Forbin, Claude, comte de (klōd kôNt də fôrbăN'), 1656–1733, French naval commander. He fought in the Antilles (1680) and in Abraham Duquesne's Algerian campaign (1682–83) and from 1685 to 1687 was grand admiral and generalissimo of the king of Siam. Forbin distinguished himself in the War of the Grand Alliance and the War of the Spanish Succession. He failed (1708) in an attempt to land James Francis Edward Stuart, the Old Pretender, in Scotland. His memoirs were published in 1729–30.

Force, Peter, 1790–1868, American journalist and historian, b. near Paterson, N.J. He served in the War of 1812 and afterwards established himself in Washington, D.C., as a printer. Entering local politics, he was at different times president of both the city council and the board of aldermen and was mayor of Washington (1836–40). His *National Journal,* established in 1823 to support John Quincy Adams for the presidency, continued as a daily from 1824 to 1831. He issued for many years the *National Calendar,* a yearbook of historical and statistical information, and edited four volumes of rare documents, *Tracts and Other Papers Relating Principally to the Origin, Settlement, and Progress of the Colonies in North America* (1836–46). His project for publishing early American documents, national, state, and private, dealing with colonial and American history down to 1789, was authorized by Congress but was discontinued before completion. The resulting *American Archives* (9 vol., 1837–53), the work by which Force is chiefly known, covers only the years 1774–76 but has proved indispensable to students of the American Revolution. Force's large collections were purchased by the Library of Congress.

force, commonly, a "push" or "pull," more properly defined in physics as a quantity that changes the motion, size, or shape of a body. Force is a VECTOR quantity, having both magnitude and direction. The magnitude of a force is measured in units such as the pound, DYNE, and NEWTON, depending upon the system of measurement being used. An unbalanced force acting on a body free to move will change the MOTION of the body. The quantity of motion of a body is measured by its MOMENTUM, the product of its MASS and its VELOCITY. According to NEWTON'S second law of motion, the change in momentum is directly proportional to the applied force. Since mass is constant at ordinary velocities, the result of the force is a change in velocity, or an ACCELERATION, which may be a change either in the SPEED or in the direction of the velocity. Two or more forces acting on a body in different directions may balance, producing a state of EQUILIBRIUM. For example, the downward force of gravity (see GRAVITATION) on a man weighing 200 lb (91 km) when standing on the ground is balanced by an equivalent upward force exerted by the earth on the man's feet. If the man were to fall into a deep hole, then the upward force would no longer be acting and the man would be accelerated downward by the unbalanced force of gravity. If a body is not completely rigid, then a force acting on it may change its size or shape. Scientists study the STRENGTH OF MATERIALS to anticipate how a given material may behave under the influence of various types of force. There are four basic types of force in nature. Two of these are easily observed; the other two are detectable only at the atomic level. Although the weakest of the four forces is the gravitational force, it is the most easily observed because it affects all matter and because its range is theoretically infinite, i.e., the force decreases with distance but remains measurable at the largest separations. Thus, a very large mass, such as the sun, can exert over a distance of many millions of miles a force sufficient to keep a planet in orbit. The electromagnetic force, which can be observed between electric charges or between magnetic poles, is stronger than the gravitational force and also has infinite range. Both electric and magnetic forces are ultimately based on the electrical properties of matter; they are propagated together through space as an electromagnetic FIELD of force (see ELECTROMAGNETIC RADIATION). At the atomic level, two additional types of force exist, both having extremely short range. The strong nuclear force, or strong interaction, is associated with certain reactions between ELEMENTARY PARTICLES and is responsible for holding the atomic NUCLEUS together. The weak nuclear force, or weak interaction, is associated with RADIOACTIVITY and particle decay; it is weaker than the electromagnetic force but stronger than the gravitational force. The strong nuclear force is the strongest force in nature.

force bill, popular name for several laws in U.S. history, notably the act of March 2, 1833, and the Reconstruction acts of May 31, 1870; Feb. 28, 1871; and April 20, 1871. The first force bill, passed in response to South Carolina's ordinance of NULLIFICATION, empowered President Jackson to use the army and navy, if necessary, to enforce the laws of Congress, specifically the tariff measures to which South Carolina had objected so violently. In the second set of force bills, or enforcement acts, as they were also called, the radical Republicans controlling Congress strengthened their Reconstruction program for the South by imposing severe penalties on those Southerners who tried to obstruct it. The act of May 31, 1870, designed to enforce the Fifteenth Amendment, provided heavy penalties of fine and imprisonment for anyone preventing qualified citizens (in this case Negroes) from voting. Such cases were to come under the jurisdiction of the Federal courts. Congressional elections were placed exclusively under Federal control, and the President was authorized to use the armed forces. In a similar vein but even more drastic was the act of Feb. 28, 1871. The act of April 20, 1871, inspired by the activities of the Ku Klux Klan, declared the acts of armed combinations tantamount to rebellion and empowered the President to suspend the privilege of habeas corpus in lawless areas. President Grant did this in certain counties of South Carolina. Hundreds were indicted, fined, and imprisoned, and the act was partially responsible for the subsequent decline of the Klan.

Ford, Edsel Bryant: see under FORD, HENRY.

Ford, Ford Madox, 1873–1939, English author; grandson of Ford Madox Brown. He changed his name legally from Ford Madox Hueffer in 1919. The author of over 60 works including novels, poems, criticism, travel essays, and reminiscences, Ford also edited the *English Review* (1908–11) and the *Transatlantic Review* (1924, Paris); among his contributors were Thomas Hardy, James Joyce, and D. H. Lawrence. Ford's most important fictional works are *The Good Soldier* (1915), a subtle and complex novel about the relationship of two married couples, and a tetralogy (1924–28): *Some Do Not, No More Parades, A Man Could Stand Up,* and *The Last Post* (pub. together as *Parade's End,* 1950). These works reveal the collapse of the Tory-Christian virtues under the violence and social hypocrisy that culminated in World War I. Ford collaborated with Joseph Conrad on *The Inheritors* (1901), *Romance* (1903), and other works. His memoir of Conrad (1924) discusses the narrative techniques that the two writers evolved. Toward the end of his life, Ford lived in France and the United States and was a member of the faculty of Olivet College in Michigan. See his letters (ed. by R. M. Ludwig, 1965); biography by Arthur Mizener (1971); studies by P. L. Wiley (1962), Frank MacShane (1965), and H. R. Huntley (1970).

Ford, Gerald Rudolph, 1913–, 38th President of the United States (1974–), b. Omaha, Nebr. He was originally named Leslie Lynch King, Jr., but his parents were divorced when he was two, and when his mother remarried he assumed the name of his stepfather. Admitted to the Michigan bar in 1941, he was a member (1949–73) of the U.S. House of Representatives, where he served as the Republican minority leader (1965–73). Ford gained a reputation as a loyal Republican who supported his party on virtually all issues. A consistent proponent of a large defense budget, he led the Republican opposition to the Great Society programs of President Lyndon B. Johnson. He was permanent chairman of the Republican National Convention in 1968 and 1972. In Oct., 1973, Ford was nominated by Richard NIXON to succeed Spiro T. AGNEW as Vice President of the United States; on Dec. 6, 1973, he became Vice President, the first to be appointed under the procedures specified by the 25th Amendment. As Vice President, Ford traveled widely around the country, attempting to rally for the Nixon administration the support that had eroded as a result of the WATERGATE AFFAIR. His tenure as Vice President was short, however; when Nixon resigned on Aug. 9, 1974, Ford became President. He pledged to continue Nixon's foreign policy and to work to curb inflation. One month later he issued a complete pardon to Nixon for all criminal acts perpetrated by Nixon while he was President. In the 1974 election the Republicans suffered substantial losses, attributable both to Watergate and to the economy. To deal with the economic recession, Ford proposed (1975) tax cuts, limited social spending (with continued high defense expenditure), and heavy taxation on imported oil. The Democratic Congress opposed many elements of the program. See Ford's *Selected Speeches,* ed. by M. V. Doyle (1973); J. F. terHorst, *Gerald Ford and the Future of the Presidency* (1974).

Ford, Henry, 1863–1947, American industrialist, pioneer automobile manufacturer, b. Dearborn, Mich. He showed mechanical aptitude at an early age and left (1879) his father's farm to work as an apprentice in a Detroit machine shop. He soon returned to his home, but after considerable experimentation with power-driven vehicles, he went (1890) to Detroit again and worked as a machinist and engineer with the Edison Company. Ford continued working in his spare time as well, and in 1892 he completed his first automobile. Resigning (1899) from the Edison Company he launched the Detroit Automobile Company, but a disagreement with his associates led him to organize (1903), in partnership with James COUZENS, the Dodge brothers, and others, the Ford Motor Company. In 1907 he purchased the stock of most of his associates, and thereafter the Ford family remained in control of the company. By cutting the costs of production, by gaining control of raw materials and the means of distribution, by adapting the conveyor belt and assembly line to automobile production, and by featuring an inexpensive, standardized car, Henry Ford was soon able to outdistance all his competitors and become the largest automobile producer in the world. He came to be regarded as the apostle of mass production. In 1908 he designed the Model T; over 15,000,000 cars were sold before the model was discontinued (1928) and a new design—the Model A—was created to meet growing competition. Highly publicized for paying wages considerably above the average, Ford began in 1914—the year he created a sensation by announcing that in future his workers would receive $5 for an 8-hr day—a profit-sharing plan that would distribute up to $30 million annually among his employees. In 1915, in an effort to end World War I, he headed a privately sponsored peace expedition to Europe that failed dismally, but after the American entry into the war he was a leading producer of ambulances, airplanes, munitions, tanks, and submarine chasers. In 1918 he ran unsuccessfully for U.S. Senator on the Democratic ticket. After weathering a severe financial crisis in 1921, he began producing high-priced motor cars along with other vehicles and founded branch firms in England and in other European countries. Strongly opposed to trade unionism, Ford—who incurred considerable antagonism because of his paternalistic attitude toward his employees and his statements on political and social questions—stubbornly resisted union organization in his factories by the United Automobile Workers until 1941. Although a staunch isolationist before World War II, Ford again converted his factories to the production of war material after 1941. In 1945 he retired. His numerous philanthropies, in addition to the FORD FOUNDATION, included $7.5 million for the Henry Ford Hospital in Detroit and $5 million for a museum in Dearborn, where in 1933 he established Greenfield Village—a reproduction of an early American village. His international reputation made him a natural object for journalists. His libel suit against the Chicago *Tribune* in 1919 led to an examination by the *Tribune* attorney, intended to show Ford's lack of education. Anti-Semitic articles in Ford's *Dearborn Independent* brought further legal controversy; he was forced to apologize for the articles. Ford's relations with others in the business community were frequently strained; he was hostile to bankers and financiers, and all his life he refused to allow outside investment in Ford holdings. He wrote, in collaboration with Samuel Crowther, *My Life and Work* (1923), *Today and Tomorrow* (1926), *Moving Forward* (1931), and *Edison as I Knew Him* (1930). See biographies by W. C. Richards (1948), Allan Nevins and F. E. Hill (3 vol., 1954-62), and Booton Herndon (1969); R. M. Wik, *Henry Ford and Grass-roots America* (1970). His son, **Edsel Bryant Ford,** 1893-1943, b. Detroit, shared in the control of the vast Ford industrial interests. He was president of the Ford Motor Company from 1919 until his death, when his father once more became (1943) president of the company. The eldest Ford soon retired again when his grandson, **Henry Ford II,** 1917-, b. Detroit, succeeded him in 1945. Upon his appointment, the younger Henry Ford moved quickly to restructure and modernize the company, which had been losing ground to Chrysler and General Motors. He removed a number of long-time Ford executives and, for the first time in company history, recruited outsiders for positions of responsibility. In 1960 he became chairman and chief executive officer of the corporation.

Ford, John, 1586-c.1640, English dramatist, b. Devonshire. He went to London to study law but was never called to the bar. The early part of his playwriting career was taken up with collaborations, primarily with Dekker. His three major tragedies, *'Tis Pity She's a Whore, The Broken Heart,* and *Love's Sacrifice,* appeared between 1627 and 1633. Ford was the most important playwright during the reign of Charles I. His plays are characterized by a sympathetic treatment of thwarted love, and they stress the conflict between the power of human passion and the laws of conscience and society. They are intense, melancholy, and violent, often treating abnormal characters and taboo subjects—*'Tis Pity She's a Whore* deals with incest. See biography by D. K. Anderson (1972); study by Mark Stavig (1968).

Ford, John, 1895-1973, American film director, b. Cape Elizabeth, Maine. The director of nearly 200 feature films, he won Academy Awards for *The Informer* (1935), *The Grapes of Wrath* (1940), *How Green Was My Valley* (1941), and *The Quiet Man* (1952). Known especially for the spectacular scope of his Westerns, such as *Rio Grande* (1951) and *The Horse Soldiers* (1959), Ford often worked in association with Dudley Nichols, a well-known screen writer. See study by Peter Bogdanovich (1968).

Ford, Paul Leicester, 1865-1902, American historian and novelist, b. Brooklyn, N.Y. His father, Gordon L. Ford, then possessed probably the best library of Americana in the country; Paul edited, with his brother Worthington Chauncey Ford, rare material from this library in *Winnowings in American History* (15 vol., 1890-91) and made valuable bibliographies, including ones on Hamilton (1886) and Franklin (1889). He was the editor of many documents of the early Republic, such as *Pamphlets on the Constitution of the United States* (1888) and the *Writings of Thomas Jefferson* (10 vol., 1892-99). His *True George Washington* (1896, repr. 1970) was the first to present Washington as human and fallible. Ford also wrote several novels, two of which were extremely popular, *Janice Meredith: a Story of the American Revolution* (1899) and *The Honorable Peter Stirling* (1894, repr. 1969).

Ford, Worthington Chauncey, 1858-1941, American historian and editor, b. Brooklyn, N.Y. He was joint editor, with his brother Paul Leicester Ford, of *Winnowings in American History* (15 vol., 1890-91). While chief of the manuscripts division of the Library of Congress (1902-9), Ford edited the first 15 volumes of the new edition of the *Journals of the Continental Congress.* From 1909 until his retirement in 1929 he was editor of the Massachusetts Historical Society and lectured on historical manuscripts at Harvard. Ford edited *The Writings of George Washington* (14 vol., 1889-93) and wrote a standard biography of Washington (1899). He also edited *The Writings of John Quincy Adams* (7 vol., 1913-17), *A Cycle of Adams Letters, 1861-1865* (1920, repr. 1968), and *Letters of Henry Adams* (2 vol., 1930-38), and other volumes of correspondence and documents. In addition, Ford contributed many articles and monographs on historical and literary subjects.

ford, shallow place in a body of water, especially a river, that may be crossed by wading. Around the crossings habitually forded, cities sprang up; hence fords came to be the sites of numerous river towns. They have been of particular importance in migrations and in the deployment of armies in campaigns and have therefore been frequently fortified.

Ford Foundation, philanthropic institution, established (1936) in Michigan by Henry FORD and his son, Edsel, for the general purpose of advancing human welfare. Until 1950 the foundation was involved in local philanthropic activities, mainly aiding the Henry Ford Hospital in Detroit and the Edison Institute of Dearborn. Since 1950, after receiving the bulk of the estates of Henry Ford, his wife, and Edsel, the foundation from its New York City headquarters has engaged in broad philanthropic work. By the early 1960s its multibillion-dollar endowment made the foundation the largest philanthropic trust in the world. By 1974 it had assets of about $2 billion. The foundation is committed to acting in support of five broad areas: world peace, democratic government, economic well-being, education, and the scientific study of man. In addition, the Ford Foundation has developed programs in the humanities and fine arts; science and engineering; population growth and the world food supply; and public affairs, particularly problems of the young, the elderly, and those living in urban ghetto areas. Especially active in international affairs, the foundation is one of the most innovative in the United States. The Ford Foundation's involvement in controversial programs, such as its establishment (1951) of the civil rights oriented Fund for the Republic, has drawn criticism from conservative elements. In attempting to maintain flexibility in its operations, the foundation concentrates on aiding efforts for the initial attack on problems, leaving the follow-up action to other institutions. The foundation has also established funds to work in areas closely allied to its primary activities. See Dwight Macdonald, *The Ford Foundation* (1956).

Fordham University (fôr'dəm), in New York City; Jesuit; coeducational (except Fordham College for men and Thomas More College for women); founded as St. John's College 1841, chartered as a university 1846; renamed 1907. Fordham also operates Bensalem College (est. 1967), which has an experimental program in which faculty and students work and live together.

Ford's Theatre National Historic Site: see NATIONAL PARKS AND MONUMENTS (table).

forebrain: see BRAIN.

foreign agent: see ESPIONAGE.

foreign aid, economic, military, technical, and financial assistance given on an international, and usually intergovernmental level. U.S. foreign aid programs have included at least three totally different major objectives: rehabilitating and reconstructing the economies of war-devastated countries, strengthening and subsidizing the military defenses of the non-Communist world, and promoting economic growth in underdeveloped areas. Aid may be given as a grant, with no obligation concerning repayment, or it may be loaned, i.e., furnished on the understanding that it will in due course be repaid. Foreign aid, as an integral part of U.S. foreign policy, began during World War II with LEND-LEASE. The Lend-Lease Act (1941), which provided the Allies with more than $8 billion of military equipment, foodstuffs, and industrial materials, is generally regarded as the prototype of U.S. foreign aid legislation. During the period of wartime planning for the postwar world, the hope of the United States was that after a brief period of relief aid the international balance would gradually be restored, and long-term reconstruction projects would be financed by loans from two newly established agencies, the INTERNATIONAL BANK FOR RECONSTRUCTION AND DEVELOPMENT (IBRD; also known as the World Bank) and the INTERNATIONAL MONETARY FUND. Consequently U.S. foreign aid in the immediate postwar years was chiefly in the form of emergency grants without any kind of central organization. Initially the United States provided a large proportion of the funds of the international cost-sharing organization, the UNITED NATIONS RELIEF AND REHABILITATION ADMINISTRATION (UNRRA), established in 1943 by the Allied governments to provide a broad range of services to the war-devastated Allies. UNRRA spent $4 billion (70% contributed by the United States). The actual dimensions of postwar reconstruction had been greatly underestimated, and conditions in Western Europe, which, unlike Southern and Eastern Europe, had received little UNRRA aid, became desperate. In 1947, the Truman Doctrine was announced, which provided aid to Greece in its struggle against Communist guerrilla forces, and to Turkey, which was under pressure from the Soviet Union. In June, 1947, the plan that became known as the MARSHALL PLAN was announced by Secretary of State George C. Marshall. Known formally as the European Recovery Program, it distributed (1948-51) over $12 billion through the Organization for European Economic Cooperation. In the next phase of U.S. foreign aid to Western Europe, emphasis was shifted from economic to military assistance as the United States and the Soviet Union became involved in the cold war. In 1949 the first major postwar program of military assistance, the Mutual Defense Assistance Act, was passed by Congress to provide military aid to the Western European nations that had become members of the NORTH ATLANTIC TREATY ORGANIZATION. Under this act such aid could also be made available to nonmember nations. Concurrently, the increasingly apparent needs of the underdeveloped nations led to the proposal by President Truman of the POINT FOUR PROGRAM. From the time of the KOREAN WAR, the lines between different kinds of aid were blurred, and defense became the umbrella for most forms of U.S. foreign assistance. The Mutual Security Act of 1951 was the first measure that covered, in a single act of Congress, the continuation on a worldwide basis of military aid, economic aid, and technical assistance. The administration of aid was centralized under the Mutual Security Agency, an executive agency in the office of the President. During the early 1950s the increase of surplus agricultural commodities accumulated under domestic price-support programs, became available as an additional source of aid. The Food for Peace program of 1954 made available grants of such commodities where needs were urgent, and also permitted their sale for local currencies and the lending or granting of the currencies for purposes of military and economic assistance. In 1955 responsibility for administering foreign aid was returned to the Dept. of State when the International Cooperation Administration was established within the State Dept. Military aid was to be administered by the Dept. of Defense. While military aid continues to be provided, with few exceptions, on a grant basis, U.S. aid for economic development has increasingly taken the form of loans. The principal U.S. lending agencies are the AGENCY FOR INTERNATIONAL DEVELOPMENT, which provides investment capital on flexible terms to the less developed economies, and the Export-Import Bank, which makes loans primarily to finance the export of U.S. capital goods and agricultural products. The geography of U.S. aid distribution has also changed. From the end of World War II until the middle 1950s, Europe received 75% of all U.S. aid. When the success of the Marshall Plan eliminated the need for aid to Europe, the United States began to channel an increasing share of foreign aid to the underdeveloped nations of Africa, Asia, and Latin America. Although the

United States continues to provide various forms of foreign aid (over $100 billion between 1946 and 1968), the level has gradually declined. The share of the gross national product (GNP) for foreign aid dropped from 2.75% in 1949 to less than 0.5% by 1968. In the early 1950s the Soviet Union, followed by other Soviet-bloc countries, began a program of technical and economic aid to the underdeveloped nations as a means of extending the bloc's political and economic influence, and to strengthen the neutralist tendencies in those countries. Soviet aid generally is given in the form of low-interest loans, industrial equipment on a credit basis accompanied by technical assistance, or long-term agreements for the purchase of raw materials from the countries in question. Starting in earnest c.1955, Soviet offers of aid built up from year to year until the total was over $6 billion by 1966. France has contributed over $9 billion in grants and loans to her colonial possessions and former colonies. Great Britain, although on a much smaller scale than France, has also provided aid to her former colonies, administered by the ministry of overseas development (over $4 billion between 1960 and 1968). Besides these countries other donor nations include Australia, Canada, the People's Republic of China, Japan, New Zealand, and most of the countries of Eastern and Western Europe. Aid is also provided by international bodies, although it constitutes only about 15% of total development assistance. Included among these are: the IBRD and its affiliates, the International Development Association and the International Finance Corporation; the Inter-American Development Bank; the European Development Fund; the United Nations Development Program; and the specialized agencies of the United Nations, e.g., the Food and Agriculture Organization, the United Nations Educational, Scientific, and Cultural Organization, and the World Health Organization. See F. C. Benham, *Economic Aid to Underdeveloped Countries* (1961); Barbara Ward, *The Rich Nations and the Poor Nations* (1962); Lloyd D. Black, *The Strategy of Foreign Aid* (1968); W. L. Thorp, *The Reality of Foreign Aid* (1971); Steve Weissman et al., *The Trojan Horse: a Radical Look at Foreign Aid* (1974).

foreign exchange, methods and instruments used to adjust the payment of debts between two nations that employ different currency systems. A nation's BALANCE OF PAYMENTS has an important effect on the exchange rate of its currency. Bills of exchange, drafts, checks, and telegraphic orders are the principal means of payment in international transactions. The rate of exchange is the price in local currency of one unit of foreign currency and is determined by the relative supply and demand of the currencies in the foreign exchange market. Buying or selling foreign currency in order to profit from sudden changes in the rate of exchange is known as arbitrage. The chief demand for foreign exchange within a country comes from importers of foreign goods, purchasers of foreign securities, government agencies purchasing goods and services abroad, and travelers. See W. M. Clarke and George Pulay, *The World's Money: How it Works* (1970); Paul Einzig, *History of Foreign Exchange* (2d ed. 1970); Immanuel Wexler, *Fundamentals of International Economics* (2d ed. 1972).

Foreign Legion, French volunteer armed force composed chiefly, in its enlisted ranks, of foreigners. Its international character and the tradition of not revealing enlistees' backgrounds have helped to surround the Foreign Legion with an aura of mystery and romance. Although foreigners had served in French armies previously, King Louis Philippe created (1831) this specific foreign legion. Originally intended to pacify Algeria, the legion also was active in the pacification of Morocco and fought in other areas of the French colonial empire and in both world wars. It was later active in the French campaigns in Indochina and Algeria. The legion was normally stationed in Algeria until 1962, when its headquarters were transferred to S France, near Marseilles, and its regiments scattered throughout the world. There have been many other foreign legions; e.g., a British legion participated in the Carlist Wars in Spain, and in the Spanish civil war (1936–39) the International Brigade fought on the Loyalist side. See Edgar O'Ballance, *The Story of the French Foreign Legion* (1961); Patrick Turnbull, *The Foreign Legion* (1966); Hugh McLeave, *The Damned Die Hard* (1973); Martin Windrow, *The French Foreign Legion* (1973).

Foreign Ministers, Council of, organization of the foreign ministers of the World War II Allies—the United States, Great Britain, France, and the USSR—that, in a long series of meetings, attempted to reach political settlements after the war. In accordance with the agreements reached at the POTSDAM CONFERENCE, the ministers of Great Britain, the USSR, and the United States met in London and then at Moscow in 1945 in efforts to conclude peace treaties with those countries that had aided Germany's aggression. In the first meeting at London there was a great deal of conflict between the Soviet Union and the United States over the latter's role in the occupation of Japan, and little was accomplished. At the Moscow Conference it was decided to draft peace treaties with Italy, Hungary, Rumania, Bulgaria, and Finland and to establish an 11-power Far Eastern Commission and a 4-power Allied Council for Japan. Despite difficulties and protracted quarrels over procedure, the council (to which France was admitted in 1946) reached agreement at the next conference in Paris (1946). The final peace treaties with Italy, Rumania, Hungary, Bulgaria, and Finland were drafted, and the remaining difficulties concerning the Free Territory of Trieste were resolved at another meeting in New York (Nov.–Dec., 1946). In March–April, 1947, the foreign ministers met again in Moscow to discuss peace treaties with Germany and Austria, but the only agreement reached was on the formal dissolution of the Land [state] of Prussia (a large part of which had already been annexed by the Soviet Union and Poland). Another attempt to reach agreement on Germany and Austria failed when the foreign ministers met at London (Nov.–Dec., 1947); at this meeting there was a marked deterioration in the relations between the USSR and the other three powers. A new meeting (Sept., 1948) at Paris, regarding the disposition of the former Italian colonies, also reached no conclusions. The council was revived in May–June, 1949, when the foreign ministers, meeting at Paris, reached an agreement ending the Soviet blockade of Berlin but again failed to agree on German reunification. In Jan.–Feb., 1954, the foreign ministers met in Berlin to discuss German reunification and an Austrian peace treaty. Although this conference ended in deadlock, the ministers agreed to the calling of the Geneva Conference of 1954 to discuss "peaceful settlement of the Korean question" (see GENEVA CONFERENCE **1**). They agreed on an Austrian peace treaty the following year in Vienna. The foreign ministers met during the Geneva Summit Conference of July, 1955, and again in Geneva later in the year. On neither occasion, however, could they reach agreement on the principal topics for discussion—German reunification, European security, and disarmament. In 1959 tension over Berlin led to another foreign ministers' conference in Geneva. The Western powers insisted that a German peace treaty be signed only after Germany was united through free elections; that the 4-power occupation of Berlin be maintained until Berlin again became the capital of a united Germany; and that any European security plan be linked to progress in German reunification. The Soviet Union proposed that West Berlin be transformed into a demilitarized free city; that separate peace treaties be signed with the two German regimes; and that a zone be established in Central Europe within which arms and troops would be limited or banned. After failing to reach any agreement the conference recessed for an indefinite period. In June, 1972, however, the foreign ministers of the four powers did sign a comprehensive agreement on Berlin, worked out over the previous two years. It regularized West Berlin's status and its relationships with East and West Germany and paved the way for East and West German entry into the United Nations and the normalization of relations between the two German states.

foreign missions: see MISSIONS.

foreign service: see DIPLOMATIC SERVICE; CONSULAR SERVICE.

Foreland, North, and **South Foreland,** headlands of Kent, SE England, forming parts of the boundary of The Downs (a roadstead). South Foreland is 4 mi (6.4 km) NE of Dover, and North Foreland is near Margate. Both are chalk cliff formations, and both have lighthouses. The defeat (1666) of the Dutch under De Ruyter off the Forelands was an important battle in the history of British seapower.

Foreman, George, 1949–, American boxer, b. Marshall, Texas. A high school dropout, Foreman learned how to box in the Job Corps in 1967. In 1968 he was the Olympic heavyweight gold medalist, and in 1969 he turned professional. Foreman became world heavyweight champion in 1973 when he defeated Joe Frazier. He successfully defended his title twice but lost to Muhammad Ali in 1974.

forensic medicine: see MEDICAL JURISPRUDENCE.

foreshore: see BEACH.

forest, a dense growth of trees, together with other plants, covering a large area of land. A forest is an ecosystem—a community of plants and animals interacting with one another and with the physical environment (see ECOLOGY). The forests of the world are classified in three general types, or formations, which are primarily expressions of the climate in which the vegetation grows. The tropical hardwood forests, or rainforests, occur throughout the lowland areas of the tropics—especially along the routes of rivers in Central and South America and in central and W Africa—and in the East Indies, the Malay Peninsula, and parts of India, Indochina, and Australia. They are characterized by year-round high humidity and temperature and support a great diversity of plant life. The foliage is a luxuriant and interlaced community from ground level to the tree canopies, and the trees support the omnipresent woody vines (see LIANA) and air plants (see EPIPHYTE). Most tropical trees are considered evergreen because their leaves are not shed simultaneously at a certain season; however, they are believed to drop and renew their leaves sporadically each year. The temperate hardwood forests of North America, Europe, and the USSR are marked by a climate with a seasonal rainfall distribution. The trees, typically species of beech, maple, ash, oak, elm, and basswood, are deciduous but are often mixed with CONIFERS, especially in areas of poorer soil. These hardwood forests overlap the boreal, or northern, conifer forest belts, which encircle the earth in the subarctic and cool temperate regions south of the treeless TUNDRA. The vegetation is typically fir and spruce in northern regions and at higher altitudes, and pine, larch, and hemlock in southern regions and at lower altitudes. In transitional areas, especially where there is a pronounced season without rain (e.g., the CHAPARRAL and tropical mountain slopes), scrub forests are frequently found in which the trees are more widely spaced and grasses intervene. In the United States east of the prairies are the northern (boreal) forest belt, in which sugar maple, beech, and birch mix with the conifers; the hardwood forest belt, a typical temperate forest; and the warmer southern forest belt, encompassing many stands of smaller pines and cypress thickets. In the chiefly coniferous Rocky Mt. forest belt, the Ponderosa pine is most common. The Pacific forest belt has the heaviest stands of trees in America and probably in the world. The characteristic redwood and giant sequoia mingle with Douglas fir and other species. In early times the only nonforested areas of the earth were those where the land was either excessively dry (e.g., the plains and deserts) or excessively wet (e.g., the swamps). Where the environment was favorable, virgin forests extended from the equator to the timber line, i.e., as far as those regions in the extreme north or at high altitudes where there is generally perpetual snow. As the ice cap continues to recede and the timber line to withdraw, the forests, with their mammal and bird inhabitants, continue to expand; scrub willows are often found as the first tree life to reclaim land from the glaciers. The major agent in reducing the extent of the earth's forests has been man, primarily through clearing—for fuel, lumber, and agricultural space—and through fire. About 30% of the world is forested today, but the ratio between forest and population varies immensely. More than one half of the world's softwood timber (the major forest product) comes from North America and Europe—an area with only a fourth of the world's population. Yet the Mediterranean countries have been cleared of most of their forests for centuries, and the forested area of the United States has shrunk in 300 years from about one half to one third of the total land acreage. India and China together have less than 3% of the world's forests; sparsely populated Latin America has 22%. The chief economic product of forests is timber. The forest is also vital as a WATERSHED. Because of the thick humus layer and loose soil typical of the forest floor, and because of the soil-retaining powers of the trees' long roots, preventing the runoff of surface water, forests are vitally important even to distant areas as the chief agent for preserving adequate water supplies. Almost all water ultimately feeds from forest rivers and lakes and from forest-derived water tables. In addition, the forest provides shelter for wildlife, recreation and aesthetic renewal for man, and irreplaceable supplies of oxygen and soil nutrients. The science concerned with the study, preservation, and management of forests is FORESTRY. A highly informative account of the aboriginal North American forest is R. G. Lillard's *The*

Great Forest (1947, repr. 1973). See R. H. Platt, *The Great American Forest* (1965); Jack McCormick, *The Life of the Forest* (1966); P. W. Richards, *The Tropical Rain Forest* (1952, repr. 1966) and *The Life of the Jungle* (1970).

forestalling: see ENGROSSING.

Forester, Cecil Scott, 1899–1966, English novelist, b. Cairo, Egypt, educated in England. A prolific and popular author, C. S. Forester is best known for his novels of the royal navy in the days of sail, especially the series about Capt. Horatio Hornblower, naval officer during the Napoleonic Wars. Included among his other well-known works are *Payment Deferred* (1926), *The African Queen* (1935), and *The Good Shepherd* (1955). See his *Hornblower Companion* (1964).

forest fire: see FORESTRY.

Forest Hill, part of metropolitan TORONTO, S. Ont., Canada.

Forest Park. **1** City (1970 pop. 19,994), Clayton co., NW Ga., a suburb of Atlanta; inc. 1908. An army depot and a large state farmers' market are there. **2** Village (1970 pop. 15,472), Cook co., NE Ill., a suburb of Chicago, on the Des Plaines River; inc. 1884 as Harlem, name changed 1907. Its manufactures include packaged meats and office supplies.

forestry, the management of forest lands for WOOD, water, wildlife, forage, and recreation. Because the major economic importance of the forest lies in wood and wood products, forestry has been chiefly concerned with timber management, especially reforestation, maintenance of the extant forest stands at prime condition, and fire control. Silviculture is the name usually given to this manipulation of the forest for man's own purposes. Forests are vast and valuable expanses; the necessity for government supervision has long been recognized and is today employed virtually throughout the world. The earliest known instance of organized reforestation was in Germany in 1368, and by the mid-18th cent. the practice was well established also in neighboring Austria, Switzerland, and France. German immigrants to the United States (notably Carl Schurz, the first Secretary of the Interior) were instrumental in conserving the new forest lands. After the Timber Culture Act (1873), extensive planting began, although at first mostly in an attempt to forest the plains and prairies. Under President Theodore Roosevelt the first public forests were set aside (see NATIONAL FOREST SYSTEM). The Civilian Conservation Corps, instituted by President Franklin D. Roosevelt, planted about 2.25 billion trees in the decade from 1933 to 1942, and efforts in forestry have increased significantly in recent years. Today about 27% of U.S. forest is under public ownership, 17% as national forests administered by the Forest Service of the Dept. of Agriculture. It is the chief goal of forestry to devise methods for felling trees that provide for the growth of a new forest crop, and to ensure that adequate seed of desirable species is shed onto the ground and that conditions are optimal for seed germination and the survival of saplings. The basic rule of timber management is sustained yield; that is, to cut each year a volume of timber no greater than the volume of wood that grew during that year on standing trees. Desirable timber species are usually those of the native climax vegetation (see ECOLOGY) that can perpetuate themselves by natural succession, although at times (intentionally or unintentionally) a forest may not represent the climax vegetation—such as the pine of the SE United States, which grows faster than, and has replaced, the hardwoods destroyed by fire and logging. The Douglas fir of Western forests is encouraged because it is more valuable than the climax vegetation of mixed conifers that tends to establish itself if man does not intervene. Planting trees of different sizes (either because of species or of age) prevents crowding and insures maximal growth for the given area. Extermination of diseases and insect pests is standard forestry practice. The control of forest fires has developed into an independent and complex science costing approximately $100 million annually in the United States. Because of the extremely rapid spreading and customary inaccessibility of fires once started, the chief aim of this work is prevention. However, despite the use of modern techniques (e.g., radio communications, rapid helicopter transport, and new types of chemical fire-fighting apparatus) more than 10 million acres of forest are still burned annually. Of these fires, about two thirds are started accidentally by man, almost one quarter are of incendiary origin, and more than 10% are due to lightning. However, modern fire-fighting practice now recognizes that fires caused by lightning are an important tool of nature. Such fires do away with dead underbrush and diseased areas of growth, leaving clear areas for new growth of grass and new generations of trees. Some trees, it has been found, cannot grow without the aid of fire. The cones of the jack pine, for example, need exposure to intense heat to release seed. Other species, such as the Douglas fir and the sequoia, cannot flourish in shaded areas but need the open sunlit space cleared by fire. For such reasons lightning-caused fires in many cases—especially in wilderness areas far from habitation—are now permitted to burn but are carefully monitored and kept under control. The potential commercial value of the land lost to man-caused fire cannot be calculated: aside from the loss of timber, the damage is inestimable in terms of land rendered useless by ensuing soil erosion, elimination of wildlife cover and forage, and the loss of water reserves collected by a healthy forest. The increasing demand for water to supply growing metropolitan areas and for agricultural irrigation has stimulated the study of the essential role of forests in water conservation. In 1960 the Forest Service was charged by law with management of the national forests according to a philosophy of sustained yield and multiple use: production of timber, preservation of fish and wildlife habitat, watershed maintenance, mining, grazing, and recreation. In 1964, however, demand for timber led the Forest Service to adopt the practice of clearcutting used also by the commercial timber industry: Vast forest tracts are stripped of all trees, leaving an unsightly bald area. Environmentalists claim that clearcut areas are liable to insect infestation, landslides, and erosion, and that runoff causes siltation of neighboring streams and spoils fish spawning grounds. Environmentalists have also decried the ecologically disruptive effects of strip-mining and overgrazing in the national forests and have urged restoration of blighted areas and more equitable multiple-use management in future. In particular, emphasis has been placed on managing the forests in terms of broad concepts of LAND USE and environmental quality. Like other Federal agencies, the Forest Service must now assess the environmental impact of proposed actions, such as building new roads through the forests or granting rights to drill for oil or mine for coal and other minerals (see ENVIRONMENTALISM). See F. S. Baker, *Principles of Silviculture* (1950); S. W. Allen, *An Introduction to American Forestry* (3d ed. 1960); D. M. Smith, *The Practice of Silviculture* (7th ed. 1962); H. L. Shirley, *Forestry and its Career Opportunities* (2d ed. 1964); C. H. Stoddard, *Essentials of Forestry Practice* (2d ed. 1968).

Forez (fôrā'), hilly agricultural region, E central France, in the MASSIF CENTRAL, mostly in Loire dept. and partially in Puy-de-Dôme dept. ROANNE is the chief town. The region was known as Pagus Forensis under the Carolingians. In the 10th cent. it was an earldom dependent on Burgundy. Annexed to the French crown lands in 1527, it was incorporated into Lyonnais prov.

Forfar (fôr'fər), burgh (1971 pop. 10,500), county town of Angus, E Scotland. Jute, linen, processed foods, iron goods, and farm tools are produced. Royalist in the civil wars, Forfar had its charter destroyed by Oliver Cromwell in 1651. It was reissued in 1665 by Charles II, who gave the burgh a tower that still stands. In 1974, Forfar became part of the new Tayside region.

forgery, in art, the false claim to authenticity for a work of art. Because the provenance of works of art is seldom clear and because their origin is often judged by means of subtle factors, art forgery has always been commonplace. The sorts of deception involved include the complete production of a work that is passed off as being of a particular period, false claims regarding materials or workmanship, the piecing together of old fragments to simulate antiquity, the selling as originals of faithful copies that were not intended to be taken as anything but copies, and the false attribution of minor works to great masters. Forgeries are distinguished from falsifications, which include copies or even mechanical reproductions not initially meant to pass for the original, in that they are intended to defraud. These sorts of deceptions, made for financial gain, reflect prevailing taste and fashion, conventions in collecting, and current modes of art criticism. A forger often unconsciously produces a confusion of styles or subtly accents elements reflecting contemporary bias. A major example is the work passed off as Lucas Cranach's by the brilliant German forger F. W. Rohrich (1787–1834). These paintings he imbued with a touch of the Biedermeyer aesthetic, prevalent in his own day, that betrayed their falsity. The 19th-century Russian creator of the famous tiara of Saïtapharnes (Louvre), an engraved headdress in gold, supposedly a Scythian work of the 3d cent. B.C., borrowed freely from motifs displayed in 19th-century publications concerning recent excavations. Art falsification and forgery are ancient endeavors, but they were not so widely practiced before the collection of antiques came into vogue (see ANTIQUE COLLECTING) or before the cult of artistic personalities developed. Still, many minor Greek sculptors carved Phidias' and Praxiteles' signatures into their works for export to Roman collectors. During the Renaissance, Michelangelo himself, according to Vasari, carved a marble cupid, buried it for a time to give it an antique look, and sold it as an ancient sculpture. Ghiberti produced ancient-looking Greek and Roman medals in imitation of aesthetic styles he admired. Large numbers of forgeries of antique works have invariably followed directly after great archaeological discoveries, e.g., the 18th-century unearthing of Pompeii and Herculaneum resulted in quantities of forged Roman paintings. Museums are the principal victims of such handiwork: Pietro Pennelli's fake antique terracotta pottery found its way into the Louvre in 1873. Copies of Parthenon sculpture in England were determined as forgeries by Bernard Ashmole in 1954. A bronze horse, purportedly an antique Greek work, and an Etruscan warrior are two famous cases of forged sculpture brought to light at the Metropolitan Museum of Art. Thousands of lesser faked objects are displayed in private and public collections. Museum authorities, in an effort to avoid being duped, are sometimes overzealous in their rejection of works that are difficult to integrate within accepted concepts of stylistic development. The Fayum portraits of early Christian Egypt were just such a case. There is, of course, some opposition to revealing known frauds; an object's reputation may stand in an uneasy limbo of doubted authenticity for years. The 20th cent., with its ever-increasing emphasis on the financial value of works of art, has witnessed the discovery of two master forgers. Alceo Dossena of Cremona (1878–1936) was a sculptor expert in the carving techniques of antiquity, the Middle Ages, and the Renaissance. His work was of the highest quality and not made in deliberate imitation of the styles he admired; rather he was inspired by them to the creation of his own, similar works. His *Virgin and Child* in the 15th-century Florentine manner is at the Victoria and Albert Museum. Hans van Meergeren (1884–1947), a mediocre Dutch painter, claimed to have discovered several lost paintings by Vermeer. He sold them to Hermann Goering and was put on trial after World War II for selling national treasures. Van Meergeren proved himself innocent by painting another "Vermeer" in his jail cell. Controversy has often raged over the authenticity of the *Mona Lisa* in the Louvre; each of five other versions has been credited with being the original. The number of forgeries of the works of Corot and of the American painters A. P. RYDER and R. A. BLAKELOCK greatly exceeds these artists' actual productions. Despite modern technological advances, much forgery remains impervious to detection by other than empirical means. Critical expertise in the styles and aesthetics of various periods is still the principal tool of the authenticator; artistic clumsiness, a jumble of styles or motifs, and a discernible emphasis on the aesthetic values of the forger's own day more consistently reveals fakery than does technical analysis. X-ray, infrared, and ultraviolet photography are employed to reveal PENTIMENTO and overpainting. CRAQUELURE may be microscopically examined. Chemical analysis and carbon-14 dating may provide only inconclusive testimony when ancient materials have been used. As scientific techniques grow more sophisticated, so do the techniques of forgers. The discovery of forgery results in a curious phenomenon: A work of art may be considered a priceless masterpiece one day and worthless the next. Without proof of origin its valuation as false or authentic is at best a matter of subjective human judgment. See COUNTERFEITING. See Max Friedländer, *Genuine and Counterfeit* (tr. 1930); P. B. Coremans, *Van Meegeren's Faked Vermeers and De Hooghs* (tr. 1949); Bernard Ashmole, *Forgeries of Ancient Sculpture* (1961); Heinrich Schmitt, *The Art of the Faker* (tr. 1961); Otto Kurz, *Fakes* (2d ed. 1967); Adolf Rieth, *Archaeological Fakes* (1967, tr. 1970).

forgery, in criminal law, willful fabrication or alteration of a written document with the intent to injure the interests of another in a fraudulent manner.

The crime may be committed even though the fraudulent scheme fails. The forgery of government obligations—e.g., money, bonds, postage stamps—constitutes the separate offense of COUNTERFEITING. Typical examples of forgery are making insertions or alterations in otherwise valid documents and appending another's signature to a document without permission. It is, of course, lawful to sign another's signature as his attorney or representative so long as there is no plan to commit fraud. Most instances of forgery occur in connection with instruments for the payment of money. The crime may also concern documents of title, e.g., deeds, or public documents, including birth and marriage certificates. In the United States forgery ordinarily is a state crime; but to send forged documents through the post office may constitute the Federal crime of mail fraud.

forget-me-not: see BORAGE.

forging, shaping metal by heating it and then hammering or rolling it. Forging is the method by which metal was first worked when it came into use about 4000 B.C. in Egypt and Asia. Modern forging is done with a power-driven hammer; DIES are usually used. These are steel blocks hollowed out or carved in relief in the shape of the desired part. One die is stationary, the other is attached to the underside of a hammer or press ram. A piece of metal is then hammered or squeezed until it takes on the shape of the die cavity. Sometimes there are several sets of dies that form the metal in stages into the final shape. Smaller parts may be forged cold; larger parts, hot. Maximum pressure exerted is about 100 tons per square inch. Variations of the forging process are called sizing, heading, and coining. Some industrial machines for forging are the drop hammer, steam hammer, and hydraulic press. Forging toughens iron and steel, while casting makes them brittle.

Forillon National Park, 92 sq mi (238 sq km), at the tip of Forillon Peninsula, SE Que., Canada, near Gaspé; est. 1970. On the Gulf of St. Lawrence, the park has a scenic coastal landscape.

Forlì, Melozzo da: see MELOZZO DA FORLÌ.

Forlì (fōrlē'), city (1971 pop. 104,892), capital of Forlì prov., Emilia-Romagna, N central Italy. It is an agricultural and industrial center. Manufactures include silk, rayon, clothing, and household appliances. A Roman trade center (Forum Livii) on the Aemilian Way, Forlì became a free commune in the 11th cent. After much strife between rival families, the Ordelaffi held power there for nearly two centuries. In 1504, Forlì became part of the Papal States. Of note are the citadel (14th–15th cent.), the clock tower (12th cent.), and the Basilica di San Mercuriale.

formaldehyde (fôrmăl'dəhīd") or **methanal** (mĕth'ənôl"), HCHO, the simplest ALDEHYDE. It melts at −92°C, boils at −21°C, and is soluble in water, alcohol, and ether; at STP (see separate article), it is a flammable, poisonous, colorless gas with a suffocating odor. Formaldehyde is used in the preparation of dyes, in the production of BAKELITE and other plastics and synthetic resins, and for several other purposes. Pure gaseous formaldehyde is uncommon, since it readily polymerizes into paraformaldehyde, a white crystalline solid. Paraformaldehyde in the form of candles has been used for fumigating rooms, since it yields formaldehyde when heated. Formalin is a 40% by volume solution of formaldehyde in water, usually with a small amount of methanol added to prevent polymerization; it is used as an antiseptic, disinfectant, and preservative for biological materials. Formaldehyde is prepared commercially by passing methanol vapor mixed with air over a catalyst, e.g., hot copper, to cause oxidation of the methanol; it is also prepared by the oxidation of natural gas. It forms formic acid when it is oxidized.

formality, in chemistry: see CONCENTRATION.

formic acid or **methanoic acid,** HCO_2H, a colorless, corrosive liquid with a sharp odor; it boils at 100.7°C and solidifies at 8.4°C. It has the lowest molecular weight and is the simplest of the carboxylic acids. Functionally, it is both an acid and an aldehyde. Like other acids, it reacts with most alcohols to form esters and decomposes when heated; like other aldehydes, it is easily oxidized. Formic acid occurs in the bodies of red ants and in the stingers of bees. It can be made by the oxidation of FORMALDEHYDE; it is prepared commercially by heating carbon monoxide and sodium hydroxide to form sodium formate which, when carefully treated with sulfuric acid, yields formic acid. Formic acid is used industrially in textile dyeing, in leather tanning, and in coagulating latex rubber.

Formosa: see TAIWAN.

Formosa, province (1970 pop. 234,000), 27,825 sq mi (72,067 sq km), N Argentina. The city of Formosa is the capital.

Formosa Strait, Chinese *T'ai-wan Hai-hsia,* arm of the Pacific Ocean, between China's Fukien coast and Taiwan, linking the East and South China seas. It contains the PESCADORES. It is also called the Strait of Formosa.

Formosus (fôrmō'səs), c.816–896, pope (891–96), probably a Roman; successor of Stephen VI. Under Pope NICHOLAS I he had been bishop in Bulgaria, where he pursued a rigorous Romanizing campaign. Recalled to his diocese of Porto, he became influential in the church. He was excommunicated by Pope JOHN VIII for leading the party that opposed John's coronation of Charles the Bald. Later, he was restored and was subsequently elected pope. Involved in the dispute over the imperial power, he sided against the dukes of Spoleto, whose growing power was menacing the papacy. However, he was forced to crown Guido, duke of Spoleto, and his son Lambert. Formosus encouraged the German claimant, ARNULF, to invade Italy and crowned (896) him emperor. After Formosus' death, the Spoletos came into power. He was succeeded by Boniface VI. Formosus' grave was desecrated, and his pontificate declared invalid. In 897 he was reinterred, and John XI validated his acts.

formula, in chemistry, an expression showing the chemical composition of a COMPOUND. Compounds are combinations in fixed proportions of the chemical ELEMENTS. The smallest unit of an element is the ATOM. A well-known formula is that of water, H_2O. Water is made up of molecules, and the formula shows that each molecule consists of two atoms of hydrogen, H, bonded to an atom of oxygen, O. The subscript 2 indicates that there are two atoms of hydrogen in the molecule; where no subscript appears, as after the O, the subscript 1 is implied. It should be kept in mind that not all compounds are molecular. For example, sodium chloride, NaCl, is an ionic rather than a molecular compound. Solid sodium chloride consists of a collection of sodium ions and chloride ions arranged in a regular, three-dimensional pattern called a crystalline structure. One cannot say that a certain sodium ion and a certain chloride ion are grouped together into a unit, since each sodium ion is equally associated with all its neighboring chloride ions and each chloride ion is equally associated with all its neighboring sodium ions. The formula NaCl, therefore, cannot be taken as showing the composition of some particular unit, such as a molecule. Rather, it shows the proportion of the atoms of each element making up the compound—in this case, one atom of sodium to every atom of chlorine. Such a formula is called an empirical formula, whereas a formula such as H_2O, which shows not only the proportion of the atoms of each element making up the compound (two atoms of hydrogen to every atom of oxygen), but also the actual number of atoms of each element in a molecule (two atoms of hydrogen and one atom of oxygen), is called a molecular formula. If a compound is molecular, the molecular formula is preferred to the empirical formula since it gives more information. A molecule of glucose, for example, consists of 6 carbon atoms, 12 hydrogen atoms, and 6 oxygen atoms. Its molecular formula, $C_6H_{12}O_6$, displays this information explicitly. From the formula one can also deduce the proportion of the atoms of each element making up the compound: one atom of carbon to every two atoms of hydrogen to every one atom of oxygen (6:12:6=1:2:1). The empirical formula of glucose, CH_2O, shows only the proportion, not the actual number of atoms. Many compounds may have the same empirical formula. For example, formaldehyde, each molecule of which consists of one carbon atom, two hydrogen atoms, and one oxygen atom, has the molecular formula CH_2O, which is identical to the empirical formula of glucose. Another example is furnished by ethyne (acetylene), whose molecular formula is C_2H_2, and benzene, whose molecular formula is C_6H_6. Both have the same empirical formula, CH. Molecular formulas are also more useful than empirical formulas in that they explicitly show RADICALS. For example, the molecular formula for aluminum sulfate, $Al_2(SO_4)_3$, shows that the molecule contains three sulfate radicals (SO_4). The empirical formula, $Al_2S_3O_{12}$, does not show this. When only one radical is present in the molecule, the parentheses and subscript are omitted, e.g., $CuSO_4$ for cupric sulfate. Other groups are also shown in molecular formulas, e.g., the water molecules in the mineral chalcanthite (blue vitriol), which consists of cupric sulfate atoms to each of which are attached five water molecules. Its molecular formula is $CuSO_4 \cdot 5H_2O$, its empirical formula $CuSO_9H_{10}$. In many cases, especially with organic compounds, even the molecular formula does not provide enough information to identify a compound, so that structural formulas are needed. For example, both ethanol (ethyl alcohol) and dimethyl ether have the molecular formula C_2H_6O (see ISOMER). Their structural formulas are:

```
    H   H              H         H
    |   |              |         |
H — C — C — OH     H — C — O — C — H
    |   |              |         |
    H   H              H         H
   ethanol          dimethyl ether
```

In these formulas each line represents a single covalent CHEMICAL BOND. A double bond is represented by a double line and a triple bond by a triple line. In ethene (ethylene), C_2H_4, the carbon atoms are joined by a double bond. The structural formula of ethene is:

```
H       H
 \     /
  C = C
 /     \
H       H
```

(In most representations of structural formulas, the angles of the lines indicating bonds do not have meaning.) In ethyne (acetylene), C_2H_2, the carbon atoms are joined by a triple bond. The structural formula of ethyne is:

```
H — C ≡ C — H
```

Structural formulas are often simplified so that they can be written on a single line; the simplified formulas are often called semistructural formulas. The semistructural formula for ethanol is CH_3CH_2OH, or more simply C_2H_5OH. In such a semistructural formula the OH is written explicitly to indicate that the oxygen has a hydrogen bonded to it. The C_2H_5 indicates that the two carbon atoms are bonded to one another. The semistructural formula for dimethyl ether may be written CH_3OCH_3. Here the O is placed between the two Cs to show that the carbons are bonded to the oxygen. A carbon often has three hydrogens bonded to it, and the H_3 is written after the C. In some cases the H_3 is written before the C for clarity; thus the formula for dimethyl ether might be written H_3COCH_3. The double or triple lines in the structural formula that represent the double or triple bond are sometimes replaced in the semistructural formula by dots; sometimes they are simply omitted. For example, the semistructural formula of ethene can be written $CH_2{:}CH_2$ or $H_2C{:}CH_2$, and that of ethyne can be written CH⋮CH or HC:CH. Dots are also used in a type of formula called the electron dot diagram, but with a different meaning. Here each pair of dots represents a pair of shared electrons in a covalent bond. The diagrams for ethane (CH_3CH_3), ethene, and ethyne are:

```
  H H        H  H
  ¨ ¨        ¨  ¨
H:C:C:H      C::C       H:C:::C:H
  ¨ ¨        ¨  ¨
  H H        H  H
 ethane     ethene        ethyne
```

Formulas of compounds are used in writing the EQUATIONS that represent chemical reactions.

formula, in mathematics and physics, EQUATION expressing a definite fixed relationship between certain quantities. The quantities are usually expressed by letters, and their relationship is indicated by algebraic symbols. For example, $A=\pi r^2$ is the formula for the area *A* of a circle of radius *r*, and $s=\frac{1}{2}at^2$ is the formula for the distance *s* traveled by a body experiencing an acceleration *a* during a time interval *t*.

formula weight, in chemistry, a quantity computed by multiplying the ATOMIC WEIGHT (in atomic mass units) of each ELEMENT in a FORMULA by the number of atoms of that element present in the formula, and then adding all of these products together. For example, the formula weight of water (H_2O) is two times the atomic weight of hydrogen plus one times the atomic weight of oxygen. Numerically, this is

$(2\times1.00797)+(1\times15.9994)=2.01594+15.9994=18.01534$. If the formula used in computing the formula weight is the molecular formula, the formula weight computed is the MOLECULAR WEIGHT. The percentage by weight of any atom or group of atoms in a compound can be computed by dividing the total weight of the atom (or group of atoms) in the formula by the formula weight and multiplying by 100. For example, the weight percentage of hydrogen in water is determined by taking two times the atomic weight of hydrogen, dividing it by the formula weight of water, and multiplying by 100. Numerically, this is $100\times(2\times1.00797)/18.01534=11.19\%$ hydrogen in water by weight. Formula weights are especially useful in determining the relative weights of reagents and products in a chemical reaction. For example, it is known that two molecules of hydrogen gas, H_2, react with one molecule of oxygen gas, O_2, to form two molecules of water, H_2O. This reaction may be represented by the chemical EQUATION $2H_2+O_2\rightarrow2H_2O$. The formula weight of hydrogen gas is 2.01594, that of oxygen gas 31.9998, and that of water 18.01534. Our chemical equation is numerically equivalent to $2\times2.01594+31.9998=2\times18.01534$ or $4.03188+31.9998=36.03068$ if the formula weight of each reactant is substituted for the formula of that reactant. From this equation we know, for example, that 4.03188 grams of hydrogen gas will react with 31.9998 grams of oxygen gas to yield 36.03068 grams of water. The relative proportions by weight of these reactants is the same in any reaction of hydrogen and oxygen to form water. These relative weights computed from the chemical equation are sometimes called equation weights.

formyl group (fôr'mĭl), in chemistry, FUNCTIONAL GROUP that consists of a CARBONYL GROUP joined by a single bond to a hydrogen atom. ALDEHYDES are compounds that contain a formyl group joined by a single bond to a hydrogen atom, an ALKYL GROUP, or an ARYL GROUP.

Forrest, Edwin, 1806–72, American actor, b. Philadelphia. He was the first national idol of the American theater. He appeared at 14 as Young Norval in Home's *Douglas* and gained experience supporting Edmund Kean in Shakespearean roles. In 1826 with his New York debut as Othello, Forrest established himself as one of the great tragedians of the century. His acting was bold and forceful, and he was often criticized for ranting. In England in 1845, his Macbeth was received with hostility by those who favored William Charles Macready. Their rivalry brought about the Astor Place riot of 1849, a demonstration against Macready at New York by partisans of Forrest in which many were killed. His violent temper did not injure his reputation as an actor, and his last appearance as Richelieu in Boston (1871) was greeted with acclaim. Throughout his career Forrest championed native dramas and performers. He bequeathed a large share of his fortune to found the Edwin Forrest Home for Retired Actors in Philadelphia. See biographies by Richard Moody (1960) and W. R. Alger (1877, repr. 1972).

Forrest, John Forrest, 1st **Baron,** 1847–1918, Australian explorer and statesman. In 1869 he led an expedition to the west of Lake Barlee in search of the missing Friedrich LEICHHARDT, and the following year he returned from Perth along the Great Bight to Adelaide. After other explorations he became surveyor general of Western Australia (1883) and its first premier (1890–1901). In 1901 he became postmaster general of the commonwealth. Successively he was commonwealth minister of defense (1901–3), minister of home affairs (1903–4), and treasurer (1905–7, 1909–10, 1913–14, and 1917–18). His writings include *Explorations in Australia* (1875) and *Western Australia* (1884–87). See biography by F. K. Crowley (1971).

Forrest, Nathan Bedford, 1821–77, Confederate general, b. Bedford co., Tenn. (his birthplace is now in Marshall co.). At the beginning of the Civil War, Forrest, a wealthy citizen of Memphis, organized a cavalry force, which he led at Fort Donelson (Feb., 1862) and Shiloh (April). He assumed command of a cavalry brigade in the Army of Tennessee (June) and in July captured a large Union garrison at Murfreesboro. He was made a brigadier general. With a newly recruited command he effectively cut Grant's communications in a raid through W Tennessee (Dec., 1862). After foiling a Union attempt to cut the railroad between Chattanooga and Atlanta (May, 1863), Forrest participated in the Chattanooga campaign until trouble with Braxton Bragg led him to accept a command in N Mississippi. He was promoted to major general (Dec., 1863); captured FORT PILLOW (April, 1864); defeated a superior force at Brices Cross Roads, Miss. (June); and held Gen. Andrew Jackson Smith to a drawn battle at Tupelo, Miss. (July). These Union failures against Forrest caused Sherman, then advancing on Atlanta, much concern for his communications. Forrest commanded all the cavalry under John Bell HOOD in that general's Tennessee campaign (Nov.–Dec., 1864) and was promoted to lieutenant general (Feb., 1865). He surrendered shortly after his defeat at Selma, Ala., in April. After the war he engaged for a time in railroading and also was important in the activities of the KU KLUX KLAN. Forrest, probably the greatest Confederate cavalryman, is one of the most interesting figures of the war. See biographies by J. A. Wyeth (1899, repr. 1959), E. W. Sheppard (1930), R. S. Henry (1944), and A. N. Lytle (rev. ed. 1960).

Forrestal, James Vincent (fŏr'ĭstäl), 1892–1949, U.S. Secretary of the Navy (1944–47) and Secretary of Defense (1947–49), b. Beacon, N.Y. He was a naval aviator in World War I and later began (1923) a career as an investment banker. He was appointed administrative assistant to President Franklin Delano Roosevelt (June, 1940), Under Secretary of the Navy (Aug., 1940), and Secretary of the Navy (1944) as successor to Frank Knox. With the reorganization of the War and the Navy departments, he became the first Secretary of Defense (see DEFENSE, U.S. DEPARTMENT OF). Illness forced his resignation, and he later committed suicide. See studies by A. A. Rogow (1963 and 1966) and Cornell Simpson (1967).

Forrest City, city (1970 pop. 12,521), seat of St. Francis co., E central Ark., at the foot of Crowley's Ridge; inc. 1871. It is a rail and trade center in an area producing timber, peaches, and cotton. The city was named for the Confederate general N. B. Forrest.

Forssmann, Werner (vĕr'nər fôrs'män), 1904–, German physician and physiologist, M.D. Univ. of Berlin, 1929. He developed (c.1929) the technique of cardiac catheterization, whereby a long tube (catheter) is inserted into a vein in the arm and pushed through the vein until it reaches the heart. Forssmann first performed this technique on himself. His work was not recognized until after World War II, when André F. Cournand and Dickinson W. Richards in the United States demonstrated the importance of catheterization to the diagnosis of heart and lung diseases. Forssmann and the two Americans shared the 1956 Nobel Prize in Physiology and Medicine for their work.

Forster, Edward Morgan, 1879–1970, English author, one of the most important British novelists of the 20th cent. After graduating from Cambridge, Forster lived in Italy and Greece. During World War I he served with the International Red Cross in Egypt. In 1946, Forster became an honorary fellow of King's College, Cambridge, where he lived until his death. He received the Order of Merit in 1968. Forster's fiction, conservative in form, is in the English tradition of the novel of manners. He explores the emotional and sensual deficiencies of the English middle class, developing his themes by means of irony, wit, and symbolism. His first novel, *Where Angels Fear to Tread,* appeared in 1905 and was followed in quick succession by *The Longest Journey* (1907), *A Room with a View* (1908), and *Howard's End* (1910). His last novel, *A Passage to India* (1924), treats the relations between a group of British colonials and native Indians and considers the difficulty of forming human relationships, of "connecting"; the novel also explores the nature of external and internal reality. Forster's short stories are collected in *The Celestial Omnibus* (1911) and *The Eternal Moment* (1928). After 1928 he turned his attention increasingly to nonfictional prose. Notable collections of his essays and literary criticism are *Abinger Harvest* (1936) and *Two Cheers for Democracy* (1951). *Aspects of the Novel* (1927) is a major study of the novel and Forster's most important critical work. In 1971, *Maurice,* a novel Forster had written in 1913–14, was published posthumously. He had refrained from publishing it during his lifetime because of the work's sympathetic treatment of homosexuality. The story of a young man's self-awakening, *Maurice* treats a familiar Forster theme, the difficulty of human connection. In all his works Forster's style is impeccable. His unpublished short stories and essays were published posthumously in *Albergo Empedocle and Other Writings* (1972). See his selected writings ed. by G. B. Parker (1968); biography by D. Godfrey (1968); studies by F. C. Crews (1962), L. Trilling (rev. ed. 1964), G. H. Thomson (1967), O. Stallybrass (1969), and P. Gardner (1973).

Forster, Johann Reinhold, 1729–98, German naturalist and teacher. His *Philosophical Transactions of the Royal Society* (1772–73) on zoology, ornithology, and ichthyology established him as one of the earliest authorities on North American zoology. Forster accompanied Capt. James Cook on his second voyage around the world and published (1778) his observations on the trip. His son, **Georg Forster,** 1754–94, was a naturalist, traveler, and author. He also accompanied Cook on his second world voyage. Georg's account of the trip was published in 1777, and although not so scholarly as Johann's account, Georg's work established a new genre of travel books presenting scientific information in a fine literary style.

Forster, John, 1812–76, English biographer and critic. He was influential as literary and dramatic critic of the London *Examiner.* His *Lives of the Statesmen of the Commonwealth* (5 vol., 1836–39) established his reputation as a biographer. He is best known for his excellent *Life of Charles Dickens* (3 vol., 1872–74). In addition he wrote lives of Goldsmith (1848), Landor (1869), and Swift (Vol. I only, 1875).

Forster, William Edward, 1818–86, British statesman. He entered Parliament as a Liberal in 1861. As vice president of the council in William Gladstone's first ministry (1868–74), he introduced the Elementary Education Act (1870), which provided aid for existing schools, established supplementary nondenominational "board schools," and was the foundation for the English system of national compulsory education. In 1880 he went unwillingly to Ireland as chief secretary, but his opposition to Charles Parnell and his stern enforcement of the law made him so unpopular that attempts were made on his life. He resigned in 1882. See Frank Smith, *A History of English Elementary Education 1760–1902* (1931).

Forsyth, Alexander John (fôrsīth'), 1769–1843, Scottish inventor. He invented in 1807 the first workable percussion cap for the ignition of gunpowder in firearms. Forsyth refused an offer from Napoleon of £20,000 for the secret and was later pensioned by the British government.

Forsyth, John, 1780–1841, American cabinet member, b. Fredericksburg, Va. He began law practice in Augusta, Va., and was in the House of Representatives from 1813 until his election to the Senate in 1818. In Feb., 1819, he resigned to become minister to Spain. After serving again in the House of Representatives (1823–1827), as governor of Georgia (1827–1829), and for a second time as U.S. Senator (1829–34), he became Secretary of State under President Jackson and continued to hold the office during President Van Buren's administration. As Secretary of State he was concerned chiefly with gaining compensation from France for plundering U.S. ships during the Napoleonic Wars, with the question of the annexation of Texas, with the CAROLINE AFFAIR, and with the disputed boundary between Maine and New Brunswick, Canada. See biography by A. L. Duckett (1962).

forsythia (fôrsĭth'ēə), common name for any member of the small genus *Forsythia* of the family Oleaceae (OLIVE family), European and Asian shrubs with abundant bell-shaped yellow flowers that appear before the leaves. They are easily cultivated and are used in hedges and borders. In some species the branches droop and in others they grow erect. Forsythia branches are often cut in early spring and forced into bloom indoors. Forsythia are classified in the division MAGNOLIOPHYTA, class Magnoliopsida, order Scrophulariales, family Oleaceae.

Fort Abercrombie, U.S. army post on the west bank of the Red River, at Abercrombie, N.Dak.; est. 1858. Built to protect settlers in the Red River valley from attacks by the Dakota Indians, the fort played an important role in opening the Dakota Territory to settlement. It was twice attacked unsuccessfully by the Sioux in 1862. With the signing of a treaty with the Ojibwa and the Sioux there in 1870, the fear of Indians declined and the fort was abandoned in 1877. Part of the former installation is now a state park.

Fort Albany, Canadian fur-trading post, N Ont., at the mouth of the Albany River on James Bay. It was founded (before 1682) by the Hudson's Bay Company as one of its earliest forts. In the Anglo-French struggle for the Hudson Bay trade, Fort Albany was taken by the French in 1686. It was recaptured by the British in 1693 and from 1697 to 1713 was the only post of the region in the British company's possession. It has continued as an important fur-trading post.

Fortaleza (fōōrtəlĕ'zə), city (1970 pop. 859,135), capital of Ceará state, NE Brazil, a port on the Atlantic Ocean. The city, which is bisected by the Paejú River, is often called Ceará by foreigners. Fortaleza is a commercial and industrial city and a processing and shipping center for the products of Brazil's interior (cotton, coffee, hides, carnauba wax, and oiticica oil). Textiles are manufactured, and the city is also known for its traditional handicrafts, especially lace making and hammock weaving. Fortaleza [Port., = fortress] was founded in 1609 and became a center of the great sugar plantations of NE Brazil in colonial times. It was occupied by the Dutch from 1637 to 1654. The city grew after 1808, when the ports of NE Brazil were opened to international trade. Fortaleza has a state university.

Fort Anne National Historic Park: see ANNAPOLIS ROYAL, N.S., Canada.

Fortas, Abe, 1910–, Associate Justice of the U.S. Supreme Court (1965–69), b. Memphis, Tenn. After receiving his law degree from Yale in 1933, he taught there (1933–37) and also held a variety of government posts. He was (1942–46) Undersecretary of the Interior before entering private law practice. Among his notable contributions to criminal law were his arguments in the Durham Case (1954), which helped broaden the definition of legal insanity, and in *Gideon* vs. *Wainwright* (1962), in which the Supreme Court ruled unanimously that states must assure free legal counsel to the poor in every criminal trial. A close friend and adviser to President Lyndon B. Johnson, he was appointed by the President to succeed Arthur Goldberg on the Supreme Court. There he continued to support the expansion of criminal rights and joined with the other liberal justices in most civil liberties cases. In antimonopoly cases, he often sided with the minority in upholding business. In 1968, President Johnson nominated Fortas as Chief Justice of the United States; Republicans and Southern Democrats held a Senate filibuster against the nomination, causing President Johnson to withdraw Fortas's nomination. The following year, Fortas resigned from the court after it was revealed that he had, while on the bench, accepted $20,000 from a private foundation; the money was part of a life stipend to Fortas by the foundation. Although he returned the money, Fortas resigned from the court under public pressure, the first justice to do so. See Robert Shogan, *A Question of Judgment: The Fortas Case and the Struggle for the Supreme Court* (1972).

Fort-Bayard: see CHAN-CHIANG, China.

Fort Beauséjour (bōsäzho͞or'), N.B., Canada, near Amherst, N.S. Built by the French between 1751 and 1755 to command Chignecto isthmus between Nova Scotia and New Brunswick, it was captured (1755) by British and American troops under General Monckton and was renamed Fort Cumberland. Since 1926 it has been the site of Fort Beauséjour National Historic Park.

Fort Benning, U.S. army post, 189,000 acres (76,500 hectares), W Ga., S of Columbus; est. 1918. One of the largest army posts in the United States, it is the nation's largest infantry training center and the home of the Army Infantry School.

Fort Bliss, U.S. army post, 1,122,500 acres (454,300 hectares), W Texas, E of El Paso; est. 1849 and named for Col. William Bliss, Gen. Zachary Taylor's adjutant in the Mexican War. Originally strategically located near the only ice-free pass through the Rocky Mts., it guarded the U.S.-Mexican border and protected West-bound gold seekers from hostile Indians; task forces against COCHISE and GERONIMO were based there. The fort's location has changed several times as a result of flooding; its present site, on a mesa, was established in 1890. In 1916, post commander Gen. John J. Pershing led an unsuccessful expedition into Mexico to catch the bandit Francisco (Pancho) VILLA. Fort Bliss is now the Army Air Defense Center, training missilemen, artillerymen, and air-defense units.

Fort Bowie National Historic Site: see NATIONAL PARKS AND MONUMENTS (table).

Fort Bragg, U.S. army base, 11,136 acres (4,507 hectares), E N.C., N of Fayetteville; est. 1918. Originally an artillery post, it is now the principal U.S. army airborne-training center and the site of the Special Warfare School. Pope Air Force Base is located within the reservation.

Fort Bridger State Park, on Blacks Fork of the Green River, SW Wyo. The supply post, founded by U.S. fur trader James Bridger in 1843, was an important station on the OREGON TRAIL. The Mormons held Fort Bridger from 1853 until 1857 but fled into Utah with the approach of Federal troops sent against them. Bridger then leased the post to the U.S. army, which maintained it as a fort until 1890. Some of the original buildings still survive.

Fort Caroline, settlement near the mouth of the St. Johns River, NE Fla.; est. 1564 by French Huguenots under René de Laudonnière. Angered by the French presence in Florida, a Spanish force led by Pedro Menéndez de Avilés attacked the fort in 1565, killed most of the colonists, and renamed the fort San Mateo. This slaughter, and Menéndez's subsequent massacre of Jean Ribaut and his men, was avenged by a French force led by Dominique de Gourgues, who in 1568 wiped out the garrison at San Mateo. **Fort Caroline National Memorial** includes a replica of the original fort (see NATIONAL PARKS AND MONUMENTS, table).

Fort Chimo (shēmō'), village, N Que., Canada, on the Koksoak River near its mouth at Ungava Bay. It is a Hudson's Bay Company post, established in 1830.

Fort Chipewyan (chĭpəwī'ən), trading post, NE Alta., Canada, at the west end of Lake Athabasca. The old Fort Chipewyan, on the south shore, was built for the North West Company at the instigation of Alexander Mackenzie in 1788. It formed the base from which he set out on his expedition (1789) down the Mackenzie River to the Arctic Ocean and in 1792 across the mountains to the Pacific Ocean. The present post, built in 1804 on the north shore, was taken over by the Hudson's Bay Company in 1821.

Fort Clatsop National Memorial: see NATIONAL PARKS AND MONUMENTS (table).

Fort Collins, city (1970 pop. 43,337), seat of Larimer co., N Colo., on the Cache la Poudre River, at the foot of the Rocky Mts., inc. as a city 1883. The area was settled in 1864 around a fortification built to protect a strategic trading post from Indians. The city is a trading, shipping, and processing center of a rich agricultural area raising grain, sugar beets, and livestock. The principal manufactures are dental appliances, aircraft instruments, generators, pipe coatings, farm equipment, concrete, prefabricated homes, and engine governors. Colorado State Univ. is in Fort Collins; nearby are the Roosevelt National Forest, Rocky Mountain National Park, and several dams of the COLORADO-BIG THOMPSON PROJECT.

Fort Davis National Historic Site: see NATIONAL PARKS AND MONUMENTS (table).

Fort Dearborn, U.S. army post on the Chicago River, NE Ill.; est. 1803 and named for Secretary of War Henry Dearborn. Threatened by Indians at the start of the War of 1812, the little frontier post was ordered by Gen. William Hull to evacuate. On Aug. 15, 1812, as Capt. Nathan Heald, the commander, led the small contingent of troops, militia, women, and children from the fort, a large Indian force attacked. More than half of the people were killed and most of those remaining were taken prisoner; the fort was destroyed. Fort Dearborn was rebuilt in 1816–17. Around it and nearby trading posts, the city of Chicago grew.

Fort-de-France (fôr-də-fräNs), city (1967 est. pop. 99,000), capital of MARTINIQUE, French West Indies. It is a popular tourist resort and a free port, exporting mainly sugar, rum, and bananas. It was settled in 1762 by the French, who built Fort Royal by the strategically situated harbor. Yellow fever hampered its prosperity, however, and Fort-de-France did not gain importance until after 1902, when the city of St.-Pierre was destroyed by an eruption of Mont Pelée. Drainage of the swamps to control disease further stimulated Fort-de-France's growth. Empress Josephine, wife of Napoleon I, was born across the bay from the city.

Fort Dix, U.S. army training center, 32,000 acres (12,950 hectares), central N.J., SE of Trenton; est. 1917 as Camp Dix and named for U.S. statesman John A. Dix. In 1939 it was made a permanent garrison and renamed Fort Dix. During World War II, Fort Dix was the largest army training center in the country. It remains one of the main induction, discharge, and overseas-transfer points. **McGuire Air Force Base,** adjacent to the fort, is the main East Coast terminal for domestic and European military flights.

Fort Dodge, city (1970 pop. 31,263), seat of Webster co., central Iowa, on the Des Moines River; settled c.1846. Fort Clarke, built on the site in 1850, was renamed Fort Dodge the following year, but was abandoned in 1853. The town was laid out in 1854 and incorporated in 1869. Situated in a mining and agricultural area producing corn, poultry, and hogs, Fort Dodge is a rail, distributing, and industrial center. Agricultural processing plants and gypsum mills are in the city; the region has one of the largest gypsum beds in the country. The city houses Fort Dodge Community College and the Fort Dodge Historical Museum, which is located in a replica of the old Fort Dodge.

Fort Donelson, Confederate fortification in the Civil War, on the Cumberland River at Dover, Tenn., commanding the river approach to Nashville, Tenn. After capturing Fort Henry, on the Tennessee River (Feb. 6, 1862), Gen. Ulysses S. Grant, on Feb. 12, marched his men 12 mi (19 km) to Fort Donelson, which he proceeded to invest. Although assisted by gunboats, his army was repulsed by the Confederates. The Confederates were thrown back by the Union forces on the next day, after attempting to retreat. The fort fell on Feb. 16, opening the way for the advance on Nashville. Fort Donelson National Military Park and National Cemetery are there (see NATIONAL PARKS AND MONUMENTS, table).

Fort Duquesne (dəkān', do͞o-), at the junction of the Monongahela and Allegheny rivers, on the site of Pittsburgh, SW Pa. Because of its strategic location, it was a major objective in the last of the FRENCH AND INDIAN WARS. The fort was begun by a group of Virginians in 1754 at the insistence of Gov. Robert Dinwiddie. The French drove the Virginians away on April 17, 1754, and completed the fort; they named it after the Marquis de Duquesne, governor general of New France. George Washington's Virginia militia had failed to reach the fort before the arrival of the French (see FORT NECESSITY). Fort Duquesne was also the goal of an unsuccessful expedition under English Gen. Edward Braddock in 1755. On Nov. 24, 1758, the French abandoned their position without a fight to advancing British troops led by Gen. John Forbes and retreated north after burning Fort Duquesne. The English rebuilt it and renamed it Fort Pitt, around which Pittsburgh grew.

Fort Erie, town (1971 pop. 23,113), S Ont., Canada, on the Niagara River, opposite Buffalo, N.Y. A number of branch factories of U.S. firms are in the town. Fort Erie was built in 1764 by Captain Montressor and was taken from the British in the War of 1812 by American forces. In Aug., 1814, the Americans withstood successfully a siege by a superior British force but afterward blew up and abandoned the stronghold. The site was long desolate; the modern town developed in the 20th cent. The fort has been considerably restored.

Fortes, Meyer, 1906–, British anthropologist, b. Britstown, South Africa, grad. Univ. of Cape Town (M.A., 1926) and the Univ. of London (Ph.D., 1930). From 1946 to 1950 he was a reader in social anthropology at Oxford, and from 1950 to 1973 he was William Wyse professor of social anthropology at Cambridge. An ethnologist, he specialized in African social structures. Among his writings are *Oedipus and Job in West African Religion* (1959), *Kinship and the Social Order* (1969), and *Time and Social Structure and Other Essays* (1970).

Fortescue, Sir John (fôr'tĭskyo͞o), c.1394–1476, English jurist. A supporter of the Lancastrian king Henry VI, he was chief justice of the Court of King's Bench from 1442 until 1461, when Henry was deposed by the Yorkist Edward IV. Fortescue was attainted and fled to France with the royal family. It is likely that while there he was tutor to the crown prince, Edward, and that his *De laudibus legum Angliae* [in praise of English law] was written (c.1470) for the prince's instruction. An important work in the history of English law, it was not published until the reign of Henry VIII. He joined the abortive attempt at a Lancastrian restoration (1471), but he was pardoned by Edward IV and later admitted to the council. His *Difference between an Absolute and Limited Monarchy* (c.1471) was an early plea for limited monarchy and a perceptive analysis of the bases of the Lancastrian monarchy and the reasons for its failure. First published in 1714, it was later issued as *The Governance of England* (1885).

Fort Fisher, Confederate earthwork fortification, built by Gen. William Whiting in 1862 to guard the port of Wilmington, N.C.; scene of one of the last large battles of the Civil War. Because Wilmington was one of the few ports open to blockade-runners, a joint land-sea expedition under Gen. Benjamin Butler and Admiral David Porter was sent against Fort Fisher in Dec., 1864; the Union forces, however, failed to take it. A second attempt, with Gen. Alfred Terry replacing Butler, captured the fort on Jan. 15, 1865. The port was closed and Wilmington fell soon afterward. Fort Fisher is now a historic site.

Fort Frances, town (1971 pop. 9,947), SW Ont., Canada, on Rainy River, opposite International Falls, Minn. It is chiefly a lumbering center with sawmills and a pulp and paper factory. Formerly there was a Hudson's Bay Company post on the site, built (1820) near the ruins of an earlier (1731) French post, Fort St. Pierre.

Fort Frederica National Monument: see NATIONAL PARKS AND MONUMENTS (table).

Fort Frontenac: see KINGSTON, Ont., Canada.

Fort Garry, two trading posts of the Hudson's Bay Company, built on the present-day site of Winnipeg, Man., Canada, at the confluence of the Red and Assiniboine rivers. The first, Upper Fort Garry, was built in 1822 on the site of Fort Gibralter, a post of the North West Company from 1809 to 1816. It was named for Nicholas Garry, the deputy governor of the Hudson's Bay Company. Damaged by flood, it was replaced by Lower Fort Garry (1831–33) farther down on the Red River. Upper Fort Garry was rebuilt in 1835 and became the center of the Red River fur trade. Fort Garry National Historic Park contains a restoration of Lower Fort Garry.

Fort George, river, c.480 mi (770 km) long, rising in Lake Nichicun, E Que., Canada. It flows W into James Bay at Fort George, a Hudson's Bay Company trading post.

Fort George G. Meade, U.S. army post, 13,500 acres (5,460 hectares), central Md., between Baltimore and Washington, D.C.; est. 1917 as a World War I induction center. The fort is headquarters for the First Army and has missile units for the defense of Washington, D.C.

Forth, river, c.60 mi (100 km) long, formed by streams that join near Aberfoyle in Perthshire, S central Scotland. It meanders generally eastward past Stirling to the Firth of Forth at Alloa. Its chief tributaries are the Teith and Allan rivers. The **Firth of Forth** extends c.55 mi (90 km) E from Alloa to the North Sea, reaching widths up to 19 mi (31 km) across. Rosyth is an important naval base, and Leith is the port of Edinburgh. The port of Grangemouth is at the eastern end of the Forth and Clyde Canal (35 mi/56 km long; completed 1890), which links the Firth of Forth with the River Clyde. Rivers flowing into the firth include the Leven, Esk, Avon, and Carron. The Isle of May and Bass Rock, with lighthouses and ruins, are at the entrance to the firth; Inchkeith and Inchcolm islands are within the firth. At Queensferry three bridges cross the firth—the Forth Bridge (completed 1936); the Forth Road Bridge, one of the longest suspension bridges in Europe (3,300 ft/1,006 m long; completed 1964); and the Forth Railway Bridge (5,350 ft/1,631 m; completed 1890), the world's first cantilever bridge. Coal is mined from beds beneath the firth.

Fort Hall, trading post on the Snake River, near Pocatello, SE Idaho; est. 1934 by U.S. trader Nathaniel Wyeth. In 1836 he sold it to the HUDSON'S BAY COMPANY, which occupied the post until 1856. Fort Hall was the main stopping point on the OREGON TRAIL W of Fort Bridger. During the Indian wars of the 1850s and early 60s, soldiers were housed there. The ruins of Fort Hall were destroyed by floods in 1862 and 1864.

Fort Henry: see KINGSTON, Ont., Canada.

Fort Henry, Confederate fortification on the Tennessee River, S of the Ky.-Tenn. line; site of the first major Union victory of the Civil War (Feb. 6, 1862). The fort was attacked and reduced by Union gunboats commanded by Commodore Andrew Foote. Confederate commander Gen. Lloyd Tilghman, foreseeing capture, sent the bulk of his force to Fort Donelson before surrendering.

Fort Hood, U.S. army post, 209,000 acres (84,580 hectares), central Texas, near Killeen; est. 1942 on the site of old Fort Gates and named for Confederate Gen. John Hood. It is the army's main armor-training center.

Fortier, Alcée (älsā' fôrtyā'), 1856–1914, American educator and historian, b. St. James parish, La. His career was associated with the Univ. of Louisiana (later Tulane). He taught French at Tulane after 1880, becoming professor of Romance languages in 1894. His most important works are his *History of Louisiana* (4 vol., 1904) and his studies of the Creoles and of Louisiana folklore. He also wrote historical works and literary criticism in French. He was director of the Louisiana Historical Society for many years.

fortification, system of defense structures for protection from enemy attacks. Fortification developed along two general lines; permanent sites were fortified in peacetime, and fortifications and obstacles in the field were hastily constructed in time of war. As long as weapons remained relatively primitive, permanent fortifications predominated. The art developed in earliest times with the building of earthworks made up of layers of mud, sticks, rocks, and the like. These soon were developed into walls, then into palisades and elaborate wooden stockades. In the Middle East city walls appeared very early. The old cities of Mesopotamia had walls of mud or sun-dried brick to withstand invaders. The citadel, a fort or fortified section within the city, also appeared early. Phoenician cities were strongly walled and offered sturdy resistance to Assyrian, Persian, and Macedonian conquerors. Major developments in permanent fortification were made by the Romans, who constructed walls along the Danube and Rhine and in England (e.g., HADRIAN'S WALL). Some of these had elaborate systems of watchtowers, with provisions for garrisoning men along the walls. In the Far East the famous Great Wall of China (see CHINA, GREAT WALL OF) was an even more ambitious undertaking of the same type. The Romans, with their engineering skill, also developed field fortifications in their camps. To overcome advances in fortification, siegecraft (see SIEGE) was evolved, and devices such as battering rams, scaling ladders, catapults, and movable towers appeared. As siegecraft became more effective, walls were made higher and thicker—often 30 to 40 ft (9.1-12.2 m) thick. However, with the breakdown of Roman authority and the increase of raids and incursions of invading hordes from the North and the East, fortification on the grand scale was largely replaced by local fortifications. In the Middle Ages, when petty warfare was customary, the typical fortifications were town walls of masonry, great citadels in the cities, and CASTLES. Similar fortifications were used in the anarchic warfare of feudal China, India, and Japan. In the West many castles and citadels, notably those of the Moors in Spain, were defensible against all but a long siege. The development of ARTILLERY in the 15th cent. greatly diminished the value of castles; one of the great military problems of the Renaissance and the succeeding centuries was to develop fortifications able to withstand artillery. Moats were deepened to afford greater protection and widened to put artillery at a greater distance. Walls were slanted and rounded to make projectiles ricochet, and stone bulwarks were thrown up in front of towers and gates. New fortifications, set in ditches, were buttressed to withstand heavy shot, and defense guns were mounted behind earthen ramparts. In fortifications of towers (roundels) connected by walls (curtains), there were areas that could not be covered by defensive fire from the towers. Hence artillery positions, or bastions, were constructed at angles to the main wall. The proper distribution of bastions became the main preoccupation of military engineers. The science of military engineering reached a high point in the wars of Louis XIV. Sébastien le Prestre, marquis de Vauban, who worked out fortification and siege methods in the late 17th cent., has perhaps the most illustrious name in the history of fortification. His methods, supported by the work of others such as Menno van COEHOORN, were used for centuries. On the American frontier semipermanent forts and stockades were built in large numbers as garrisons for troops engaged in Indian wars and as refuges for settlers. In Europe the detached fort as a support for outer defense of the fortress chain was introduced to create an entrenched camp between the citadel of the fortress and the outer edges of the defended area. The trend toward spreading the chain of defense (the enceinte) was hastened in the 19th cent. by the development of explosive shells and more effective artillery. In the second half of the 19th cent., lines of smaller forts and entrenched camps, connected by belt-line railroads, were used to encircle cities and guard strategic points on frontiers. Batteries were dispersed, artillery was placed in revolving or disappearing cupolas with subterranean bases, and PILLBOXES, armed with machine guns, were introduced. This system was predominant in Europe at the beginning of World War I. However, the Belgian fortresses, which had been thought impregnable, fell with ease to the Germans in 1914, and the ring system of fortification was generally superseded during the war by trench warfare. The resistance of French concrete forts, even to the heaviest fire, seemed to offer a promise of permanent defensive fortification and inspired the construction of the MAGINOT LINE. That elaborate system of pillboxes, forts, and underground communications was constructed at great expense, but at the beginning of World War II it was quickly outflanked (May, 1940). The development of air power, heavy artillery, and mechanized warfare further proved the inefficacy of such defense systems and brought them to an end. Despite the value of the German Siegfried Line, which long withstood heavy assault in 1944, and despite the usefulness of the Stalin line in channeling the German attack on Russia, field fortifications predominated over fixed fortifications in World War II. Underground shelters were used for protection from air attack, and the Germans constructed large concrete shelters to protect submarines in harbor. The Japanese fortified Pacific islands with caves and with simply constructed pillboxes and bunkers. Similar fortifications were used in the Korean and Vietnam wars. During both those wars, with their emphasis on mobile and mechanized warfare, the theory of fortification seemed to return to the idea of the temporary and even improvised shelter, intended mainly to delay the enemy until a stronger force could be brought against him. In 1965 the U.S. Dept. of Defense proposed that an electronic barrier be constructed across the demilitarized zone that separated North Vietnam from South Vietnam. The plan was never put into effect, however. See Armin Tuulse, *Castles of the Western World* (1958); Sidney Toy, *A History of Fortification from 3000 B.C. to A.D. 1700* (2d ed. 1966).

Fort Île-aux-Noix: see ÎLE-AUX-NOIX, Canada.

Fort Jefferson National Monument: see NATIONAL PARKS AND MONUMENTS (table).

Fort Knox [for Henry Knox], U.S. military reservation, 110,000 acres (44,515 hectares), Hardin and Meade counties, N Ky.; est. 1917 as a training camp in World War I. It became a permanent post in 1932, and the Armored Center was located there in 1940. In the steel and concrete vaults of the U.S. Depository, built at Fort Knox in 1936 by the Dept. of the Treasury, the bulk of the nation's gold bullion is stored. Of interest is the Patton Museum of Cavalry and Armor. An extension of the Univ. of Kentucky is there.

Fort-Lamy: see NDJAMENA, Chad.

Fort Laramie National Historic Site, 563 acres (228 hectares), SE Wyo.; est. 1938. Founded in 1834 as a fur-trading post by William Sublette and Robert Campbell, it was bought by the American Fur Company in 1836. In 1849 it became a U.S. army post, which later served as a major stopping place on the OVERLAND TRAIL. The fort was garrisoned until 1890.

Fort Larned National Historic Site: see NATIONAL PARKS AND MONUMENTS (table).

Fort Lauderdale (lô'dərdāl), city (1970 pop. 139,590), seat of Broward co., SE Fla., on the Atlantic coast; settled around a fort built (c.1837) in the Seminole War, inc. 1911. The city, located on New River and a navigable canal to Lake Okeechobee, is interwoven with more than 270 mi (435 km) of natural and artificial waterways. It has one of the largest marinas in the world and one of the most popular beaches in the state. Manufactures include many electronic products, boats and yachts, and concrete, fiberglass, metal, and plastic items. Fort Lauderdale Univ., Nova Univ., and a junior college are in the city. Nearby are Port Everglades (a noted artificial port and a port of entry), a Seminole Indian reservation, and a state park.

Fort Leavenworth, U.S. military post, 6,000 acres (2,430 hectares), on the Missouri River, NE Kansas, NW of Leavenworth; est. 1827 by Col. Henry Leavenworth to protect travelers on the Santa Fe Trail. The oldest U.S. military prison (est. 1874), and the U.S. Army Command and General Staff College are at the fort.

Fort Lee, borough (1970 pop. 30,631), Bergen co., NE N.J., on the Palisades overlooking the Hudson River; settled c.1700, inc. 1904. The fort built there by the Americans to command the Hudson during the Revolution was abandoned on Nov. 20, 1776, by General Greene after Fort Washington, on the opposite shore, fell to the British. Fort Lee was an early center of the motion-picture industry. Today it is the western terminus of the George Washington Bridge.

Fort Lennox: see ÎLE-AUX-NOIX.

Fort Leonard Wood, U.S. army post, 71,000 acres (28,700 hectares), S central Mo.; est. 1940. It is one of the largest basic-training centers in the United States and also provides training for army engineers.

Fort McHenry, former U.S. military post in Baltimore harbor; built 1794–1805. In the War of 1812 it was bombarded (Sept. 13–14, 1814) by a British fleet under Sir Alexander Cochrane, but the fort, commanded by Maj. George Armistead, resisted the attack. Its defense inspired Francis Scott Key to write "The Star-spangled Banner." During the Civil War the fort was a Union prison camp. Restored in 1933, it became Fort McHenry National Monument and Historic Site (see NATIONAL PARKS AND MONUMENTS, table).

Fort Madison, city (1970 pop. 13,996), seat of Lee co., SE Iowa, on the Mississippi River; inc. 1838. Fort

Madison, a U.S. trading post, was established there in 1808 as the first fort west of the Mississippi; it was named for James Madison, then President. The fort was burned by Indians and abandoned in 1813, and the area was resettled in 1833. Fort Madison is a river port for barge traffic, and is a rail, commercial, and industrial center in a rich agricultural area. Its manufactures include pens, van trailers, decorating and protective finishes, chemicals, fertilizers, paper and paper products, paints, and ammunition containers. Iowa State Penitentiary (1839) and Lee County Courthouse (1841), the oldest courthouse in continuous use in Iowa, are in Fort Madison.

Fort Matanzas National Monument: see SAINT AUGUSTINE, Fla.

Fort Meigs (mĕgz), American fortification on the Maumee River, near Perrysburg, N central Ohio; est. Feb., 1813, by Gen. William Henry Harrison across the river from British Fort Miami (see MAUMEE, Ohio). Through the spring and summer of 1813, the Americans held out against British attacks. The defense of this "Gibraltar of the Northwest" helped to lift American morale.

Fort Mims, temporary stockade near the confluence of the Tombigbee and Alabama rivers. It was the scene of a massacre (Aug. 30, 1813). A large force of Indians, led by William WEATHERFORD, massacred over 500 whites.

Fort Monroe, SE Va., commanding the entrance to Chesapeake Bay and Hampton Roads; named for President James Monroe. The present fortress (80 acres/32 hectares) was built (1819-34) by the U.S. government on the site of English fortifications erected in 1609 and 1727. Negro slavery was introduced to the American colonies there in 1619. Completely surrounded by a moat, the six-sided fort is the only one of its kind left in the United States. Fort Monroe was held by Union forces throughout the Civil War; Jefferson Davis, president of the Confederacy, was imprisoned there from 1865 until 1867. Long a U.S. army coast-artillery post and school, the fort became headquarters of the U.S. Continental Army Command in 1946.

Fort Moultrie (mo͞ol'trē), on Sullivans Island at the entrance to the harbor of Charleston, S.C.; originally called Fort Sullivan. Constructed by Col. William Moultrie, the fort was renamed for him after he repulsed a British naval attack in June, 1776, in one of the most decisive battles of the American Revolution that kept the South free of British control. During the Seminole Wars (see SEMINOLE INDIANS), Osceola, a chief, and 200 Seminoles were imprisoned in the fort; Osceola's tomb is there. Fort Moultrie figured in the action that started the Civil War (see FORT SUMTER). The Confederates held the fort until the evacuation of Charleston in 1865. It was Charleston's chief harbor defense until 1947, when it was abandoned. Fort Moultrie is part of Fort Sumter National Monument (see NATIONAL PARKS AND MONUMENTS, table).

Fort Myers, city (1970 pop. 27,351), seat of Lee co., SW Fla., on the Caloosahatchee River, near the Gulf of Mexico; founded 1850, inc. 1905. It has a large tourist industry and is a shipping point for citrus fruits, winter vegetables, flowers (especially gladioli), fish, and cattle. Fort Harvie, built (c.1841) in the Seminole War, was held by Union troops in the Civil War. The city grew up around the fort in a region of tropical vegetation noted for its royal palms. Tourist attractions include boat trips up the Caloosahatchee to the Everglades. Thomas A. Edison's estate in the city is open to the public. A junior college and a fairgrounds are also in Fort Myers.

Fort Nassau. **1** Built (1614) by the Dutch explorer Hendrick Christiaensen on Castle Island, in the Hudson River, S of Albany, N.Y. The fort served as a trading post for the Dutch until 1617, when it was destroyed by flood, and a new fort, Fort Orange, was built on the western bank of the river on the site of Albany. **2** Built (1623) by the Dutch under Capt. Cornelius Jacobsen Mey on the eastern bank of the Delaware River near Gloucester City, N.J. The Dutch soon abandoned the fort, but after the Swedish colonization in that area, the Dutch reoccupied it and for a time united with the Swedes against the English. Fear of Swedish competition in the fur trade caused Dutch Gov. Peter Stuyvesant to take over (1655) the Swedish forts on the Delaware basin. After the Swedes evacuated Fort Elfsborg, the Dutch destroyed Fort Nassau.

Fort Necessity, entrenched camp built in July, 1754, by George Washington and his Virginia militia at Great Meadows (near the present Uniontown, Pa.). He retired there when he learned that the British fort at the forks of the Ohio (the site of Pittsburgh) had been captured (and renamed Fort Duquesne) by the French. In late May, 1754, a French patrol had been defeated and its leader killed in a surprise attack led by Washington near Great Meadows. A large French reprisal force attacked Fort Necessity and forced Washington to surrender on July 4. He secured easy terms from the French and departed for Virginia with all his surviving men and their baggage. These two skirmishes marked the opening of the last of the French and Indian Wars. Near Fort Necessity National Battlefield (see NATIONAL PARKS AND MONUMENTS, table) is the grave of the British general Edward Braddock.

Fort Niagara, post on the southern shore of Lake Ontario, at the mouth of the Niagara River, NW N.Y. It was strategically located on the water route to the fur lands. French explorer Robert LaSalle erected a blockhouse on the river in 1679; in 1726 a stone fort overlooking the river was completed. A British force, led by Sir William Johnson, captured Fort Niagara in 1759 during the French and Indian War (see under FRENCH AND INDIAN WARS). The British held the fort until 1796, when it was turned over to the United States by Jay's Treaty. During the War of 1812, the British captured Fort Niagara but returned it to the United States in 1815. The fort remained a U.S. military post until 1946. It is now a New York state park.

Fort Peck Dam, 21,026 ft (6,409 m) long and 250 ft (76 m) high, on the Missouri River, NE Mont.; largest earth-filled dam in the world. The dam was built (1933-40) by the U.S. Bureau of RECLAMATION as a flood-control and navigation-improvement project. In 1944 it became part of the MISSOURI RIVER BASIN PROJECT and is now also used for irrigation and generation of hydroelectricity (165,000-kw capacity). Fort Peck Reservoir, 189 mi (304 km) long, is one of the largest man-made lakes in the world and is an important recreation area of the N Great Plains.

Fort Pickens, fortification on the western end of Santa Rosa Island at the entrance to Pensacola Bay, NW Fla. When Florida joined the Confederacy in Jan., 1861, Fort Barrancas on the mainland was evacuated and its garrison sent to Fort Pickens. Refusing to surrender, the fort was reinforced and repulsed a Confederate attack in Oct., 1861; it remained in Union hands throughout the war. Fort Pickens is part of a Florida state park.

Fort Pierce, city (1970 pop. 29,721), seat of St. Lucie co., SE Fla., on Indian River (a lagoon; part of the Intracoastal Waterway); settled 1860s, inc. 1901. With a good harbor and rail facilities, it is a distributing center for a cattle and farm area yielding citrus fruits and vegetables. Other industries are fishing and tourism. Two bridges connect the city with its ocean beaches. Fort Pierce grew around a fort built in 1838 as protection against the Seminole Indians. It is the seat of a junior college, a state museum, and a county museum. To the west is Halpatiokee Swamp.

Fort Pillow, fortification on the Mississippi River, N of Memphis, Tenn.; built by Confederate Gen. Gideon Pillow in 1862. Evacuated by the Confederates after the fall of ISLAND NO. 10 to the north, the fort was occupied by Union troops on June 6, 1862. Confederate Gen. Nathan Forrest stormed and captured Fort Pillow on April 12, 1864, killing many Negro defenders. Often called the Fort Pillow Massacre, it became one of the greatest atrocity stories of the Civil War. Charged with ruthless killing, Forrest argued that the soldiers had been killed trying to escape; however, racial animosity on the part of his troops was undoubtedly a factor.

Fort Point National Historic Site: see NATIONAL PARKS AND MONUMENTS (table).

Fort Polk, U.S. army post, 147,856 acres (59,839 hectares), SW La.; est. 1941 and named for the Rev. Leonidas Polk, the "Fighting Bishop" of Louisiana. It is a major army warm-weather training center and was especially suited for Southeast Asian infantry assignments in the 1960s because of its similar climate and terrain.

Fort Pulaski (pəlăs'kē), brick fortification on Cockspur Island, SE Ga., at the mouth of the Savannah River; built 1829-47 by the U.S. government and named for Casimir Pulaski. The fort was seized by Georgia troops during the Civil War in Jan., 1861, but fell to a Union force under Q. A. Gillmore on April 11, 1862, after a two-day bombardment in which the Federals used rifled cannon for the first time in the war; the battle proved the superiority of rifled cannon over masonry forts. Fort Pulaski National Monument was established in 1924 (see NATIONAL PARKS AND MONUMENTS, table).

Fort Raleigh National Historic Site: see ROANOKE ISLAND.

FORTRAN [from FORmula TRANslation], science-oriented symbolic language used in programming a COMPUTER.

Fort Riley, U.S. military post, 5,760 acres (2,331 hectares), NE Kansas, on the Kansas River; est. 1852 to protect travelers on the Santa Fe Trail from Indian attacks. Located near the geographic center (though not the geodetic center) of the United States, it was first called Camp Center, but in 1853 it was renamed for Gen. Bennett Riley. It was a cavalry post and school until 1917, when it became a reserve-officer training center. Fort Riley is now a U.S. army staging and training area for transportation, supply, and service units.

Fort-Royal, Martinique: see FORT-DE-FRANCE.

Fort Saint John, town (1971 pop. 8,264), NE British Columbia, Canada, on the Peace River and the Alaska Highway. A North West Company post established in 1805 is still operated by the Hudson's Bay Company. The town is a supply point for nearby gas and oil fields.

Fort Sam Houston, U.S. army base, 3,300 acres (1,335 hectares), S Texas, in San Antonio; headquarters of the Fourth Army. San Antonio, long a military center, donated land in 1870 for the site of a permanent military post that was constructed from 1876 to 1890 and named for Gen. Sam Houston. The famous **Brooke Army Medical Center,** the major training center for army medics and the home of the Army Medical Service School, is located on the post.

Fort Schuyler (skī'lər). **1** Name given during the American Revolution to the rebuilt FORT STANWIX, on the site of Rome, N.Y. **2** Fort built on the site of Utica, N.Y., in 1758. **3** Fort built as part of the defenses of New York City in the Bronx.

Fort Scott Historic Area: see NATIONAL PARKS AND MONUMENTS (table).

Fort Sill, U.S. military reservation, Comanche co., SW Okla., 4 mi (6.4 km) N of Lawton; est. 1869 by Gen. Philip Sheridan. A 95,000-acre (38,445-hectare) field artillery and missile base, it is the home of the U.S. Army Artillery and Missile Center. Fort Sill was named in memory of Joshua W. Sill, a Civil War general. The fort underwent extensive construction in the early 1870s and became the base of operations for Indian campaigns and for the maintenance of law and order in SW Oklahoma. The Wichita, the Kiowa, the Comanche, and other Indian tribes were given homes on the reservation and trained in agriculture; occasionally, Indians, including Geronimo (who is buried in the Apache cemetery there), were imprisoned at the fort. The reservation was almost abandoned in 1904; it was revitalized by the establishment (1911) of a school that was to become the U.S. army's main field artillery training base. The 48 designated historic sites there include the Field Artillery Center Museum, several frontier buildings, and the Old Post Chapel (1876), the oldest house of worship in continuous use in Oklahoma. See W. S. Nye, *Carbine and Lance* (3d ed. 1969); M. T. Brown, *Letters from Fort Sill, 1886-1887,* ed. by C. R. King (1970).

Fort Smith, city (1970 pop. 62,802), seat of Sebastian co., NW Ark., at the Okla. line where the Arkansas and the Poteau rivers join; inc. 1842. It is the rail and trade center of a farm and livestock area and a major industrial hub. Its many manufactures include refrigerators and heating equipment, electric motors and appliances, baby foods, and glass, paper, metal, concrete, and plastic products. The city was founded as a military post in 1817 and was an important supply point during the 1848 gold rush. It was a lawless area until it was cleaned up by "Hanging Judge" Isaac Parker. Of interest are Fort Smith National Historic Site, which includes the Old Fort Museum and Judge Parker's court (see NATIONAL PARKS AND MONUMENTS, table); a national Civil War cemetery; and an annual rodeo. A junior college is there, and a U.S. forest reserve is to the south. In 1969 the city was linked by the Arkansas River project with the inland waterway to the Gulf of Mexico and the Great Lakes; the dam built E of Fort Smith has created a huge lake.

Fort Snelling, on a bluff above the junction of the Mississippi and Minnesota rivers, SE Minn.; est. 1819. It served as protection against Indians and as a nucleus for settlement. Minneapolis grew on the fort reservation in the mid-1800s.

Fort Stanwix, colonial outpost on the site of Rome, N.Y., controlling a principal route from the Hudson River to Lake Ontario. Originally a French trading center, it was rebuilt by the English general John Stanwix in 1758. The British colonial leader Sir William Johnson signed an important treaty with the Iroquois there in 1768. The fort fell into disrepair until early in the American Revolution, when it was rebuilt by the patriots and called Fort Schuyler. In 1777 (see SARATOGA CAMPAIGN) the fort, commanded by Peter Gansevoort and Marinus Willet, was held against British and Tory forces under Barry St. Leger. Reinforcements, led by the American general Nicholas Herkimer, were ambushed on their way to the besieged fort, but when new forces under Benedict Arnold approached, the siege was lifted. Fort Stanwix is now a national monument (see NATIONAL PARKS AND MONUMENTS, table).

Fort Sumter, fortification, built 1829–60, on a shoal at the entrance to the harbor of Charleston, S.C., and named for Gen. Thomas Sumter; scene of the opening engagement of the Civil War. Upon passing the Ordinance of Secession (Dec., 1860), South Carolina demanded all Federal property within the state, particularly the forts of Charleston harbor—Fort Sumter, Fort Moultrie, and Castle Pinckney. On Dec. 26, 1860, Major Robert Anderson removed his U.S. army command of about 100 men from Fort Moultrie to Fort Sumter, a stronger defensive site. Gov. F. W. Pickens of South Carolina had the other two forts, along with the Charleston arsenal, seized, and upon the refusal of President James Buchanan to order Anderson's evacuation, had guns trained on Fort Sumter. On Jan. 9, 1861, an unarmed merchant ship sent to reinforce the fort's garrison was driven back by the South Carolina forces. Pickens's subsequent formal demand for the fort's surrender was declined, and South Carolina prepared to reduce Anderson's stronghold. Pickens hoped to secure the fort before Abraham Lincoln took office, but in Feb., 1861, the newly organized Confederate government assumed the state's part in the controversy, sending Gen. P. G. T. Beauregard to command Charleston. On April 8, 1861, Pickens received Lincoln's notice that a naval expedition would be sent to provision the beleaguered garrison. On April 11, Beauregard called for Anderson's surrender, but the demand was again refused. After a 34-hour Confederate bombardment, begun at 4:30 A.M. on April 12, Anderson accepted terms, and on April 14 the garrison departed with the honors of war. Although no one was killed, the action made manifest the belligerent spirit in both the North and the South. In 1863, Union naval attacks on the fort were thoroughly repulsed. After Sherman forced the evacuation of Charleston, the U.S. flag was again raised over the fort by Anderson on April 14, 1865. Fort Sumter became a national monument in 1948; Fort Moultrie is part of the monument.

Fort Thomas, city (1970 pop. 16,338), Campbell co., N Ky., on the Ohio River, a residential suburb S of Cincinnati, Ohio; inc. 1867. The city was named after an Army post (est. 1890) that is now a veterans hospital.

Fortuna (fôrto͞o'nə), in Roman religion, goddess of fortune. Worshiped under several forms, she appears to have originally been a goddess of fertility. She was later identified with Tyche, the Greek goddess of chance, and like her was represented with a ship's rudder and a cornucopia.

Fortunate Isles or **Isles of the Blest,** in classical and Celtic legend, islands in the Western Ocean. There the souls of favored mortals were received by the gods and lived happily in a paradise. Belief in the islands long persisted, and the Canaries and the Madeira Islands were sometimes identified with them.

Fortunatus, Saint: see VENANTIUS FORTUNATUS, SAINT.

Fortunatus (fôr"chənā'təs), Christian, probably Corinthian. 1 Cor. 16.17,18.

Fortune, Robert, 1813–80, British botanist. He traveled in the Orient for the Royal Horticultural Society and later for the East India Company and brought back to England a number of chrysanthemums, the Japanese anemone, tree peonies, the kumquat, and other plants. Fortune introduced the tea plant into India.

Fortune Bay, arm of the Atlantic Ocean, c.80 mi (130 km) long, S N.F., Canada. Its shores are lined with many fishing villages. The French islands of Miquelon and St. Pierre are at its mouth.

fortunetelling: see DIVINATION.

Fort Union, trading post of the American Fur Company, erected in 1828 near the confluence of the Yellowstone and Missouri rivers, on the Mont.-N.Dak. line; it controlled converging routes of travel from the Rocky Mts. For c.40 years it was the most important post in the U.S. fur country and was under the control of American fur trader Kenneth McKenzie. When the U.S. army assumed control in 1867, Fort Union was torn down and Fort Buford, a military post, erected nearby. Fort Union Trading Post is a national historic site (see NATIONAL PARKS AND MONUMENTS, table).

Fort Union National Monument: see NATIONAL PARKS AND MONUMENTS (table).

Fortuny, Mariano (märēä'nō fōrto͞o'nē), 1838–74, Spanish genre painter, etcher, and watercolorist. Sent to Morocco in 1859 to paint war scenes, he made many brilliant sketches of Oriental life. His canvases demonstrate his facility and vivid sense of the exotic. The Walters Art Gallery, Baltimore, has his well-known *Snake-Charmers.* Fortuny is also represented in the Metropolitan Museum.

Fort Vancouver National Historic Site: see NATIONAL PARKS AND MONUMENTS (table).

Fort Walton Beach, city (1970 pop. 19,994), Okaloosa co., NW Fla., on the Gulf of Mexico; inc. 1941. It is a year-round resort, with beaches and freshwater and deep-sea fishing. Its manufactures include sophisticated electronic equipment and small boats. Eglin Air Force Base, on the city's outskirts, contributes significantly to the economy. The city grew around a fort constructed during the Seminole War (1835–42; see SEMINOLE INDIANS). Its main growth came after 1941, when it developed as a resort center and the air force base was expanded. Indian Temple Mound, a national historic landmark that includes a museum of Indian culture, is there.

Fort Washington, military post during the American Revolution, situated on the highest point of Manhattan island, New York City, overlooking the Hudson River opposite Fort Lee, N.J. It was a hastily built earthwork with no water supply within its walls and no fortifications able to withstand a strong attack. It was, however, strategically located, and its maintenance was a mark of American prestige. When Gen. George Washington was retreating before the British general William Howe, in 1776, he left a garrison under Gen. Nathanael Greene at Fort Washington. In spite of Washington's advice to abandon the fort, Greene chose to remain. Howe attacked and captured the fort on Nov. 16, 1776.

Fort Wayne, city (1970 pop. 178,021), seat of Allen co., NE Ind., where the St. Joseph and the St. Marys rivers join to form the Maumee River; inc. 1840. It is the second-largest city in the state, a major railroad and shipping point, a wholesale and distribution hub, and a manufacturing center, with large electronics and automotive industries. The Miami Indians had their chief town at this strategic water intersection before the French founded (shortly before 1680) a trading post there. In 1697 the elder sieur de Vincennes built a fort, which remained under French control until 1760, when it was surrendered to the British. The fort was held briefly by Indians in Pontiac's Rebellion. Later, the Miami Indians successfully opposed the Americans under Josiah Harmar, but they were subdued by Anthony Wayne, who built (1794) the fort that bore his name. There was further Indian fighting in the War of 1812, but afterward the peaceful fur-trading center began to grow. Industrialization was spurred by the development of the Wabash and Erie Canal and the coming of the railroad (both in the mid-1800s). Today the city is the seat of St. Francis College, Concordia Senior College, Fort Wayne Bible College, a Roman Catholic seminary, the Indiana Institute of Technology, and a branch of Purdue Univ. The city has its own philharmonic orchestra and numerous museums, including one devoted exclusively to Lincoln memorabilia. Also of interest are The Landing, the restored main street of the city's original frontier settlement; the sunken gardens at Lakeside Park; and the burial place of John Chapman (Johnny Appleseed). A veterans hospital is in the city.

Fort William: see THUNDER BAY, Ont., Canada.

Fort William Henry, at the southern end of Lake George, NE N.Y.; built in 1755 by British colonial leader Sir William Johnson. In 1757, during the FRENCH AND INDIAN WAR, it was captured and destroyed by French Gen. Louis Montcalm. Although Montcalm had promised safe-conduct from the fort, he was unable to control his Indian allies, who killed or carried off most of the garrison. Fort William Henry was rebuilt in 1953 and is now a museum.

Fort Worth, city (1970 pop. 393,476), seat of Tarrant co., N Texas, 30 mi (48 km) W of Dallas; settled 1843, inc. 1873. An army post was established on the site of Fort Worth in 1847, and after the Civil War the settlement became an Old West cow town. The first railroad (completed 1876) helped establish Fort Worth as a meat-packing and cattle-shipping point. Later in the 19th cent., wheat growing made the city an important center for milling and shipping grain. In 1919 oil was discovered W of Fort Worth, and large refineries and other oil and gas installations were built. Today Fort Worth is one of the focal points of the large N Texas industrial area. Oil, cattle, and grain are still important, but after World War II new industries were developed. The aircraft industry is the largest in the Dallas–Fort Worth area. General Dynamics and Bell Helicopter are in Fort Worth, as well as Carswell Air Force Base, a huge Strategic Air Command installation. A huge airport (the largest in the world when it was opened in early 1974) is situated midway between Dallas and Fort Worth. Fort Worth is the seat of Texas Christian Univ., Texas Wesleyan College, Tarrant County Junior College, and Southwestern Baptist Theological Seminary. Points of interest include Tarrant County Convention Center (1968), Tarrant County Courthouse (1895), Fort Worth Art Center, Amon Carter Museum of Western Art, a museum of science and history, the Health Museum, Greer Island Nature Center, a botanic garden, a zoo, an aquarium, a planetarium, and Heritage Hall.

forum, market and meeting place in ancient Roman towns in Italy and later in the provinces, corresponding to the Greek AGORA. By extension the word *forum* may indicate in modern usage the meeting itself. The forum was usually square or rectangular in shape and had, among other buildings, a basilica with shops, the public treasury, the curia, and a prison; under Greek influence colonnades were introduced. The old Roman Forum extended into a marshy valley from Capitoline Hill along the Palatine Hill. When, much later, the Basilica of Constantine was added it reached almost to the Colosseum. The valley between the hills was crossed by a small stream emptying into the Tiber, which drained the area and was canalized underground (probably in the 6th cent. B.C.) to become the great sewer, the Cloaca Maxima (a portion of which still exists). At the south end of the Forum was the house of the vestal virgins and nearby the temple of Vesta. West of the temple, as an entrance to the Forum proper, was the Arch of Augustus, having on one side the temple of deified Julius Caesar and on the other that of Castor and Pollux. Behind it was a building, now the Church of Santa Maria Antiqua, with fine 8th-century frescoes. Along the southwest side of the Forum was the Basilica Julia, along its northeast side were the Basilica Aemilia and the curia, where the senate met. The Forum was closed to the northwest by the Arch of Septimius Severus and by the rostra (platforms adorned with beaks of captured vessels), from which tribunes, consuls, and orators made their speeches. Beyond them, toward Capitoline Hill, were temples, among them the Temple of Concord and the temple of Saturn, housing the treasury. In imperial times the old Forum became inadequate; the emperors built new forums to the northeast, from the Basilica of Constantine to the valley between the Capitoline and Quirinal. On the southeast were the Forum of Vespasian with the Temple of Peace surrounded by a colonnade; next the Forum of Nerva; then that of Augustus with the temple of Mars. Southwest was the smaller Forum of Julius Caesar, a colonnade enclosing the temple of Venus. Beyond the Forum of Augustus was the Forum of Trajan, a vast colonnaded square; then the Basilica Ulpia; then the two libraries with, between them, the Column of Trajan, which is still standing. The temple of Trajan closed the Emperors' Forums to the northwest. In the 4th cent., the decay of the old Forum began; earthquakes, fires, and the barbarian invasions completed its destruction. In the Middle Ages materials from the forums were used to build new monuments throughout the city. Only in the 19th and 20th cent. were systematic excavations made to bring to light what was left. The forums are now, with the Palatine and Colosseum, an imposing complex of ruins, testifying to the magnificence of ancient Rome. See Michael Grant, *The Roman Forum* (1970).

Forum Appii (ăp'ēī): see APPII FORUM.

Foscolo, Ugo (o͞o'gō fôs'kōlō), 1778–1827, Italian poet and patriot. His name was originally Niccolò Foscolo. A devoted Venetian, he pinned his hope of a restored republic on Napoleon and fought under him against the Austrians, even after Napoleon's political untrustworthiness had become evident. Upon Napoleon's defeat and the annexation of Venice to Austria, Foscolo exiled himself to London, where at first he had great social success. Having spent his earnings, he was forced to give lessons and write articles and for several years before his death lived in extreme poverty. His novel, *The Last Letters of*

Jacopo Ortis (1798-1802, tr. 1818), an account of his political disillusionment, exerted a strong influence on Italian letters, as did also his critical essays, translations, and lyric poems, especially *Sepulchres* (1807).

Fosdick, Harry Emerson (fŏz'dĭk), 1878-1969, American clergyman, b. Buffalo, N.Y., grad. Colgate Univ., 1900, and Union Theological Seminary, 1904. Ordained a Baptist minister in 1903, he was pastor in Montclair, N.J., until 1915. From that year until 1946, Fosdick was professor of practical theology at Union Theological Seminary. He became pastor of the Park Ave. Baptist Church, New York City, in 1926; this was transformed into the Riverside Church in 1930, when the congregation and Fosdick moved to an impressive new structure on Riverside Drive. He served there until 1946, when he became pastor emeritus. His position as a Modernist leader in the Fundamentalist controversies of the 1920s and his forceful, practical sermons won wide recognition. His radio addresses were nationally broadcast. Among his writings are *The Meaning of Prayer* (1915), *Twelve Tests of Character* (1923), *A Guide to Understanding the Bible* (1938), *On Being a Real Person* (1943), *A Great Time to Be Alive* (1944), *The Man from Nazareth, as His Contemporaries Saw Him* (1949), and his autobiography, *The Living of These Days* (1956).

Fo-shan (fô-shän) or **Namhoi** (näm'hoi'), city (1958 est. pop. 120,000), E Kwangtung prov., SE China, in the Canton River delta. An industrial city c.10 mi (15 km) from Canton, it is known for its silk and porcelain manufactures. The Cantonese name for Fo-shan is Fatshan.

Foss, Lukas (fôs), 1922–, American composer, pianist, and conductor, b. Berlin as Lukas Fuchs. He came to the United States in his early teens and studied at the Curtis Institute in Philadelphia. His composition *Four Inventions*, for piano, was published when he was 15. In 1957, while professor of composition at the Univ. of California, he founded the Improvisation Chamber Ensemble, which performed many of his experimental works. From 1963 to 1971 he was music director and conductor of the Buffalo Philharmonic Orchestra, where he became noted for performing avant-garde compositions. In 1971 he was named music director of the Brooklyn Philharmonia. As a composer Foss was initially influenced by American composers, notably Aaron Copland, and produced traditional works such as *The Tempest* (1942), an orchestral suite; *The Prairie* (1944), a cantata based on Carl Sandburg's poem; and *Griffelkin* (1955), an opera. His later interest in improvisational techniques and ALEATORY MUSIC is reflected in such works as his chamber piece *Elytres* (1964).

Fosse Way (fŏs), Roman road in England. It apparently ran from Exeter (Isca Dumnoniorum) NE past Bath (Aquae Sulis), Cirencester (Corinium Dobunnorum), and Leicester (Ratae Coritanorum) to Lincoln (Lindum). It intersected Watling Street.

fossil, remains or imprints of plants or animals preserved from prehistoric times by natural methods. Fossils are found in sedimentary rock, asphalt deposits, and coal and sometimes in amber and certain other materials. Fossilization of skeletal structures or other hard parts is most common; only rarely are flesh and other soft parts preserved. Conditions that were conducive to the formation of fossils include quick burial in moist sediment or other material that tends to prevent weathering and exclude oxygen and bacteria, thereby preventing decay. Shells and bones embedded in sediment in past geologic time, under conditions suitable for preservation, left exact reproductions of both external and internal structures. Sometimes after such specimens were enclosed in the rock formed from the hardened sediments, water percolating through the ground dissolved out the shell and other structures, leaving a space within which only the form was preserved. This is known as a natural mold. When such molds are discovered by fossil hunters, casts can be made from them by pouring in plastic materials. If molds are filled with mineral matter by subsurface water, natural casts are formed. Molds of insects that lived many millions of years ago are sometimes found preserved in amber. These were formed by the enveloping and permeation of an insect by sticky pine tree resin which hardened to become amber. So perfectly formed are these molds that detailed microscopic studies can be made of the insect's minute structure. Molds of thin objects such as leaves are usually known as imprints. Impressions of dinosaur skin have aided scientists in making restorations of these animals. Imprints of footprints and trails left by both vertebrate and invertebrate animals are also valuable aids to studies of prehistoric life. Coprolites are fossilized excrement material; if it is possible to determine their sources they are useful in revealing the feeding habits of the animals. Entire animals of the late Pleistocene have sometimes been preserved. In Siberia some 50 specimens of woolly mammoths and a long-horned rhinoceros were found preserved in ice with even the skin and flesh intact. Several specimens of the woolly rhinoceros bearing some skin and flesh have been found in oil-saturated soils in Poland. Skeletal remains have been preserved as a result of the engulfment of an animal's body in ancient asphalt pits, bogs, and quicksand. At Rancho La Brea, near Los Angeles, Calif., asphalt deposits have yielded a rich variety of skeletons of birds and mammals. Some fossils have been found buried in volcanic ash; such fossil deposits exist in the Cenozoic rocks of the W United States. Petrifaction is another method of preservation of both plant and animal remains. This can occur in several ways. Mineral matter from underground water may be deposited in the interstices of porous materials, e.g., bones and some shells, making the material more compact and more stonelike and thus protecting it against disintegration. The original material may be entirely replaced with mineral matter, molecule by molecule, so that the original appearance and the microscopic structure are retained, as in petrified wood. Sometimes, on the other hand, all details of structure are lost in the replacement of organic matter by minerals, and only the form of the original is retained. In shales are sometimes found the silhouettes of plant tissues (more rarely of animals) formed by the carbon residue of the organism that remains after the volatile elements have been driven off. The scientific study of fossils is PALEONTOLOGY. Not until c.1800 were fossils generally recognized as the remains of living things of the past and accepted as an invaluable record of the past. See C. L. and M. A. Fenton, *The Fossil Book* (1958); C. D. Simak, *Trilobite, Dinosaur, and Man,* (1966); Marian Murray, *Hunting For Fossils* (1967).

Fossil Butte National Monument: see NATIONAL PARKS AND MONUMENTS, table.

fossil fuel: see ENERGY, SOURCES OF; FUEL.

Foster, Abigail Kelley, 1810-87, American abolitionist and advocate of women's rights, b. near Amherst, Mass. Abby Kelley, as she was known to her contemporaries, began her crusade against slavery in 1837 after teaching in several Quaker schools. In 1845 she married Stephen S. Foster, a radical abolitionist and reformer. As one of the first female lecturers before sexually mixed audiences, she was often greeted by listeners with extreme hostility. After suffering a great deal of abuse, even from fellow abolitionists, she began to devote more of her efforts toward women's rights. During the last 30 years of her active life, she was more prominent as a suffragist than as an abolitionist.

Foster, Charles, 1828-1904, U.S. Secretary of the Treasury (1891-93), b. Seneca co., Ohio. He was long identified with the business interests of Fostoria, Ohio—named for C. W. Foster, his father. A Republican, he served (1871-79) in the U.S. House of Representatives and as a member of the Committee on Ways and Means aided in exposing (1874) fraudulent contracts in connection with the U.S. Treasury Dept. He was twice (1879, 1881) elected governor of Ohio. On the death of William Windom, President Benjamin Harrison appointed Foster, a declared bimetallist, to the Treasury post.

Foster, Sir George Eulas, 1847-1931, Canadian statesman, b. New Brunswick. He first entered the Canadian House of Commons in 1882 and later held a number of cabinet positions, including minister of finance (1888-96). He was a Canadian delegate (1918-19) to the Paris Peace Conference and chairman (1920-21) of the Canadian delegation to the first assembly of the League of Nations, of which he was made vice president. In 1920, Foster was acting prime minister of Canada after the retirement of Sir Robert Borden because of illness. In 1921 he was appointed to the Senate. He was knighted in 1914. See his memoirs (ed. by W. S. Wallace, 1933).

Foster, Hannah Webster, 1759-1840, American novelist, b. Boston. Her didactic novel, *The Coquette* (1797), was one of the earliest American novels.

Foster, John Watson, 1836-1917, American diplomat, b. Pike co., Ind.; grandfather of John Foster Dulles. Foster practiced law (1857-61) at Evansville, Ind., and then served (1861-65) with the Union army in the Civil War. He later edited (1865-69) the Evansville *Daily Journal* and became a leader of the Indiana Republican party. The U.S. minister to Mexico (1873-80), to Russia (1880-81), and to Spain (1883-85), Foster was (1892-93) Secretary of State under President Benjamin Harrison. He represented (1893) the United States in the arbitration of the Bering Sea Fur-Seal Controversy and acted (1894) for China in negotiations for the treaty with Japan. His numerous books include *A Century of American Diplomacy, 1776-1876* (1900, repr. 1969), *The Practice of Diplomacy* (1906), and *Diplomatic Memoirs* (1909).

Foster, Stephen Collins, 1826-64, American song writer and composer, b. Lawrenceville, Pa. His pioneer family was aware of his talent for music, but not understanding it they provided him with little formal musical education. Foster's knowledge of the Negro was gained from minstrel shows, in particular the troupe of E. P. Christy, for which many of his songs were written. Because of their utter simplicity, his Negro dialect songs are often thought of as folk music. Feeling that prejudice against these "Ethiopian songs" existed, he was at first unwilling to risk his reputation by having his name appear on them. He had little aptitude for business, and his returns were never commensurate with the popularity of his songs. Excessive drinking and extreme poverty ruined his last years. He died in Bellevue Hospital, New York City. Although his work was occasionally banal, the songs that have remained popular, such as *Oh! Susannah* (1848), *Camptown Races* (1850), *Old Folks at Home* (1851), *My Old Kentucky Home* (1853), *Jeanie with the Light Brown Hair* (1854), and *Old Black Joe* (1860), are unpretentious and genuine. See biography by J. T. Howard (rev. ed. 1962); Morrison Foster, *My Brother Stephen* (1932); Evelyn Foster Morneweck, *Chronicles of Stephen Foster's Family* (2 vol., 1944, repr. 1973).

Foster, William Zebulon, 1881-1961, American Communist leader, b. Taunton, Mass. An itinerant worker in many different occupations, he was first affiliated with the Socialist party, next with the Industrial Workers of the World, and then with the American Federation of Labor. In his early years as a laborer he was profoundly influenced by Marxism. His activities among steelworkers were climaxed by his leadership of the famous steel strike of 1919. With the organization of the American COMMUNIST PARTY in 1920, he became a prominent leader and was its presidential candidate in 1924, 1928, and 1932. In 1930 he was displaced as party head by Earl BROWDER, but on Browder's fall he became (1945) national chairman. He held this position until 1957. In 1948, Foster was charged with advocating the overthrow of the U.S. government, but because of ill health he did not go on trial (1949) with 11 other top Communists. Many of his personal experiences are recounted in *From Bryan to Stalin* (1937) and *Pages from a Worker's Life* (1939, repr. 1970). His other writings include *Toward Soviet America* (1932) and *History of the Three Internationals* (1955).

Fostoria (fŏstôr'ēə), city (1970 pop. 16,037), Hancock, Seneca, and Wood counties, NW Ohio; inc. 1854. A trade and shipping center for a livestock and farm area, the city has grain elevators, livestock markets, and a soybean-processing industry. Its manufactures include carbon products and automotive and electrical equipment.

Fotheringhay (fŏth'ərĭng-gā), village, Northamptonshire, central England, on the Nene River. Fotheringhay Castle (12th cent.), now in ruins, was the birthplace of Richard III and the scene of the imprisonment and execution (1587) of Mary Queen of Scots.

Foucauld, Charles, vicomte de (shärl vĕkôNt' də fōōkō'), 1858-1916, French priest and missionary in the Sahara. After a career as an army officer and an explorer in Algeria and Morocco, he entered a Trappist monastery in 1890. In 1901 he was ordained and volunteered to go to the Sahara under the patronage of the White Fathers (the Society of Missionaries of Africa). In 1905 he went to Algeria and lived among the Tuareg. He settled near the small village of Tamanrasset, where he produced his studies of Tuareg language and literature. He was killed when the desert tribes revolted against France. Foucauld is revered for the sincerity of his vocation. See his *Spiritual Autobiography,* ed. and annotated by J. F. Six (tr. 1964); biography by M. L. Trouncer (1972).

Foucault, Jean Bernard Léon (zhäN bĕrnär' lāôN' fōōkō'), 1819-68, French physicist. Known especially for his research on the speed of light, he determined its velocity in air and found that its speed in water and other media diminished in proportion to the index of refraction. He originated the Foucault PENDULUM, with which he demonstrated the earth's rotation. He also improved astronomical instruments, especially the telescope; invented (1852) the gyroscope; and investigated the eddy current (known also as the Foucault current), an electric current induced in metal by a moving magnetic field. With Armand Fizeau he took the first clear photograph of the sun. From 1855 he was physicist at the Paris Observatory.

Foucault pendulum: see PENDULUM.

Fouché, Joseph (zhōzĕf' fo͞oshā'), b. 1759 or 1763, d. 1820, French revolutionary and minister of police. A teacher in the schools of the Oratorian order, he joined the French Revolution and was elected to the Convention (1792). There he sided at first with the GIRONDISTS, but then became a JACOBIN. As a Jacobin, he supported the Reign of Terror and assisted Jean Collot d'Herbois in the ruthless massacre (1793) of the counterrevolutionists in Lyons. He was instrumental in the overthrow of Maximilien ROBESPIERRE (1794), was envoy to Milan and The Hague (1798), and became minister of police (1799). Always an opportunist, he closed the Jacobin clubs and helped Napoleon Bonaparte's coup d'etat of 18 Brumaire (Nov. 9–10, 1799). As police minister under the CONSULATE, he organized a ruthlessly efficient spy system, but his opposition to Napoleon's being made first consul for life caused his dismissal (1802). He was, however, made a senator and continued to maintain an unofficial espionage system. He discovered the CADOUDAL plot (1804) and was reappointed police minister in the same year. One of the indispensable men of the Napoleonic empire, Fouché is sometimes considered the father of the modern police state; nevertheless, his reforms of the criminal police were a lasting achievement. In 1809 he was created duke of Otranto as reward for his defense of Antwerp during Napoleon's absence in Austria. Shortly afterward, he entered into an intrigue with the English against Napoleon. Dismissed again (1810), he fled to Italy but soon afterward returned. In 1813, Napoleon made him governor of Illyria, and in 1814–15 he served both Napoleon and King Louis XVIII. After the second Bourbon restoration he was forced out of office and was sent as ambassador to Saxony. Shortly afterward, he was proscribed as a regicide, was exiled, and died in obscurity in Trieste. See biographies by Nils Forssell (1928, repr. 1970), Stefan Zweig (tr. 1930), and Hubert Cole (1971); R. E. Cubberly, *The Role of Fouché during the Hundred Days* (1969).

Foucquet: see FOUQUET.

Fouillée, Alfred Jules Emile (älfrĕd' zhül āmēl' fo͞oyā'), 1838–1912, self-educated French philosopher and sociologist. Until 1875, when he retired, he was a teacher at various French universities. Fouillée regarded it as his particular work to "reconcile idealism and naturalism." To achieve this synthesis of Platonism and modern science he developed the conception of *idées-forces,* in which ideas are inseparable from action. This motor theory of consciousness makes ideas the agent of change and progress. Fouillée expanded this idea of self-consciousness into a metaphysics (*L'Avenir de la metaphysique,* 1889). In the sphere of sociology and ethics he stressed the interdependence of the individual and society. Chief among his works are *Critique des systemes de morale contemporaine* (1883), *L'Evolutionnisme des idées-forces* (1890), and *La Psychologie des idées-forces* (1893).

Fould, Achille (äshēl' fo͞old), 1800–67, French financier and politician. Fould gave financial backing to Louis Napoleon (later Emperor Napoleon III), whom he served four times as minister of finance and once (1852–60) as minister of state. In his tenure as finance minister the Bank of Algeria was founded and the floating debt was reduced (1863) by a loan.

Foulis, Andrew (foulz), 1712–75, and **Robert Foulis,** 1707–76, Scottish printers, brothers. They worked in partnership as printers to the Univ. of Glasgow. Their publications were famous both for beauty and accuracy; the 554 works they printed included outstanding editions of Horace, Homer, Milton, and Thomas Gray. Changes in taste impaired the prestige of their typography, which nonetheless represented high achievement in a style of the time. Their typefaces, the most enduring of which is Scotch roman, were designed by Alexander Wilson.

Foulques. For persons thus named, see FULK.

foundation, institution through which private wealth is contributed and distributed for public purpose. Foundations have existed since Greek and Roman times, when they honored deities. During the Middle Ages in Europe the church had many foundations, and in the Arab lands the waqf, or pious endowment, developed with the growth of Islam. In modern times European foundations, generally smaller than their U.S. counterparts, have been closely regulated by the state (e.g., the Nobel Prizes; see NOBEL, ALFRED BERNHARD). In the United States there were a few early foundations, notably those endowed by Benjamin Franklin in 1791 to provide funds for loans to "young married artificers of good character" and by James Smithson in 1846 for the establishment of the SMITHSONIAN INSTITUTION; however, it was not until after the Civil War that foundations developed rapidly. Social disintegration in the South and the establishment of early foundations such as the Peabody Education Fund and the John F. Slater Fund (both designed to provide educational opportunities for Southern blacks) promoted the movement. The rapid growth of Northern industrial enterprise in the postbellum years brought with it an accumulation of huge private fortunes. By the turn of the century, persuasive preachers of the "social gospel" urged the wealthy to meet their charitable obligations to society. Andrew CARNEGIE and John D. ROCKEFELLER, Sr., in the period 1896 to 1918, led the way in creating foundations that could distribute their enormous surplus wealth in the most efficient and socially beneficent manner. Favorable income tax laws in the 1940s further spurred philanthropic activity. During the early 1950s many American foundations were attacked by right-wing journalists and Congressmen; between 1950 and 1953 the House of Representatives conducted two separate investigations into "subversion and Communist penetration" of the nation's philanthropic foundations. Attacks on the foundations began to subside, however, with the passing of the so-called McCarthy era. Although a number of foundations have been restricted by their charters to specific philanthropic functions, the larger U.S. foundations have devoted themselves to broad areas. (See separate articles on LILLY ENDOWMENT, INC.; FORD FOUNDATION; ROCKEFELLER FOUNDATION; SLOAN FOUNDATION; and COMMONWEALTH FUND.) Since 1961 education has been the single largest recipient of foundation support, followed by international activities, health, welfare, the humanities, and religion. See Abraham Flexner and E. S. Bailey, *Funds and Foundations* (1952); Marianna O. Lewis, ed., *The Foundation Directory* (5th ed. 1975); Merrimon Cuninggim, *Private Money and Public Service* (1972); Waldemar A. Nielsen, *The Big Foundations* (1972).

founder: see LAMINITIS.

founding: see CASTING.

foundling hospital, institution for receiving and caring for abandoned children. In Athens and in Rome until the 4th cent., unwanted children were exposed, or left to die, in appointed places. The first modern foundling hospital was established by the archpriest of Milan in 787. Other cities throughout Europe followed this example. One of the best-known of such hospitals was founded in 1739 in London by Thomas CORAM. In the United States, the first foundling hospital, St. Vincent's Infant Asylum, was begun in 1856 by Roman Catholic nuns in Baltimore. It was followed shortly by the founding of other infant asylums supported by religious denominations or private philanthropies. In both Great Britain and the United States foundling hospitals have for the most part been replaced by foster care programs under the supervision of state welfare agencies. Other maternal and child care programs are financed by municipal agencies or under the social security program (see CHILDREN, DEPENDENT). See M. P. Hall, *The Social Services of Modern England* (6th ed., rev. 1963).

fountain, natural or artificially conveyed flow of water that either simply issues from an orifice and is received into a basin or is so disposed with architecture or sculpture as to form an effective decoration. In ancient Greece columnar shrines were built over springs and dedicated to deities or nymphs. In ancient Rome fountains fed by the great aqueduct system furnished water in the streets, in the villa gardens, and in town houses. Though there were few public fountains in the Middle Ages, a number of beautiful examples remain, especially in Italy, where splendid Renaissance fountains, showing the full artistic exuberance of the period, are also found even in the smallest village square or the least pretentious villa. A fine example of the early 15th cent. is that of the Fonte Gaia, Siena, by Jacopo della Quercia. The development of the great 16th- and 17th-century villas, with their hillside gardens and natural water sources, called forth amazing ingenuity in water decoration. In the Villa d'Este at Tivoli and the villas at Frascati, near Rome, the various disposals of water constituted an integral element of the garden composition. In France the gardens of the palace of Versailles, designed by Le Nôtre, embodied a vast scheme of water adornment, with elaborate sculptural treatment. The supply, held in a reservoir at Marly, was raised 500 ft (152 m) above the Seine by machinery. The theatrical trend of the baroque period found expression also in fountains. In keeping with the animated postures of the sculptured nymphs, sea horses, and dolphins, the water issued splashing over the rims of the uppermost bowls and down upon artificial rocks and shells. A colossal figure of Neptune was a favorite motif, as in famous examples at Florence, Bologna, and Rome. Bernini designed one such fountain in Rome. He also planned the superbly simple fountains in St. Peter's Square and the dramatic fountains in the Piazza Navona. In 1762 one of the most famous and elaborate examples was completed, the fountain of Trevi. In sharp contrast with these are the fountains of Moslem countries, which instead of gushing water often emit an inconspicuous trickle. In their gardens the water lies in quiet pools and long, narrow channels. Of the Moorish fountains employing basins and sculpture, the Fountain of the Lions in the Alhambra, Granada, is a noted specimen. Invariably a fountain for ablutions stands in the courtyard of a mosque. In Oriental cities the public fountains are entirely enclosed within structures richly finished in marbles and ceramics and with wide projecting roofs; the passer-by drinks through a metal grille. Examples are numerous in Istanbul, Cairo, and Damascus. The modern public drinking fountain is usually of strictly utilitarian design. American architects and landscape artists, however, are encouraging the use of the ornamental fountain with definite success. Two striking examples in New York City are the cotton boll fountains at the Burlington Mills Building and the fountain at Lincoln Center, the actions of which are regulated by a computer-programmed tape.

Fountains Abbey, ruined Cistercian abbey, West Riding of Yorkshire, N England, near Ripon. It was founded in 1132.

Fountain Valley, city (1970 pop. 31,826), Orange co., S Calif.; inc. 1957. Chiefly residential, Fountain Valley also has industries producing mobile homes, microelectronic components, aerospace fittings, and bathtubs. A U.S. marine corps helicopter facility is in the city.

Fouqué, Friedrich Heinrich Karl, Baron de La Motte- (frē'drĭkh hīn'rĭkh kärl bärōn' də lä môt-fo͞okā'), 1777–1843, German poet and novelist. He wrote many chivalric romances, tales, and plays based on Norse mythology. He is chiefly remembered, however, for his fairy tale of the nymph who had no soul, *Undine* (1811), of which there have been innumerable editions in English, and for the patriotic song *Frisch auf, zum fröhlichen Jagen* (1813).

Fouquet or **Foucquet, Jean** or **Jehan** (all: zhäN fo͞okā'), c.1420–c.1480, French painter and illuminator. He was summoned to Rome in the 1440s to paint the portrait (now lost) of Pope Eugenius IV. His work subsequently revealed the influence of contemporary Italian artists, particularly of Fra Angelico. Fouquet's style is marked by a delicacy of line combined with an amplitude of volume in his portrayal of the human figure. He was court painter to Charles VII and Louis XI and a protégé of Agnès Sorel and Étienne Chevalier, treasurer to Charles VII. His best-known paintings include a diptych, one wing of which represents Agnès Sorel as the Virgin (Antwerp) and the other a kneeling figure of Étienne Chevalier, and his portraits of Charles VII and of the chancellor Guillaume Juvénal (both: Louvre). He is also famous for his illuminations in the Book of Hours for Chevalier (Chantilly) and those for the French translations of Boccaccio and of Josephus' *Antiquities of the Jews* (Bibliothèque nationale). See studies by Trenchard Cox (1931) and Paul Wescher (tr. 1949).

Fouquet or **Foucquet, Nicolas** (nēkôlä'), 1615–80, superintendent of finance (1653–61) under King Louis XIV of France. His loyalty to Cardinal MAZARIN during the FRONDE helped to secure his position. By his transactions with financiers, to whom he allowed huge profits, he impoverished the treasury and accumulated a vast personal fortune. He spent large sums for his own purposes, notably on his mansion at Vaux, and was a patron of literary men, among them Jean Baptiste Molière and Jean de La Fontaine. He was created marquis of Belle-Isle. Aroused by Jean Baptiste COLBERT, who gave the king reports of Fouquet's mismanagement of funds, and made jealous by a magnificent fete he attended at

Vaux, Louis XIV ordered Fouquet's arrest in 1661. The trial took three years. Fouquet was sentenced (1664) to banishment, but the king, still resentful, changed the sentence to life imprisonment.

Fouquier-Tinville, Antoine Quentin (äNtwän' käNtăN' fōōkyä'-tăNvēl'), 1746–95, French revolutionary. A lawyer, he was public prosecutor (March, 1793–July, 1794) of the Revolutionary Tribunal; he personified the ruthlessness of the REIGN OF TERROR. Among his numerous victims were Marie Antoinette and Georges Danton. After the fall of Maximilien ROBESPIERRE, Fouquier-Tinville was tried and guillotined.

four-color process: see PRINTING.

Fourcroy, Antoine François, comte de (äNtwän' fräNswä' kôNt də fōōrkrwä'), 1755–1809, French chemist. He was a pioneer in animal and plant chemistry and collaborated with Lavoisier and others in reforming the system of chemical nomenclature. He was professor from 1784 at the Jardin du Roi (later the Jardin des Plantes), Paris, held public offices during the Revolution, and as director general of public instruction from 1801 instituted reforms in the French system of higher education. He was made a count in 1808. His writings include *The Philosophy of Chemistry* (1792, tr. 1795) and *A General System of Chemical Knowledge* (11 vol., 1801–2; tr. 1804).

Four Forest Cantons, the, Ger. *Die Vier Waldstätten*, in central Switzerland, the cantons of UNTERWALDEN, SCHWYZ, URI, and LUCERNE, the first Swiss communities to win their freedom. The Lake of the Four Forest Cantons (Vierwaldstättersee) is called in English the Lake of Lucerne.

Four Freedoms. In his message to Congress proposing lend-lease legislation (Jan. 6, 1941), President Franklin Delano Roosevelt stated that Four Freedoms should prevail everywhere in the world—freedom of speech and expression, freedom of worship, freedom from want, and freedom from fear. These were substantially incorporated (Aug., 1941) in the ATLANTIC CHARTER.

Four-H clubs or **4-H clubs,** organizations for boys and girls from 9 to 19 years of age. The group is part of an educational program designed to improve techniques of agriculture and home economics, promote high ideals of civic responsibility, provide training for community leadership, and foster international understanding. Founded (about 1905) to enable rural youth to "learn by doing," the American 4-H program is run by the Cooperative Extension Service of the U.S. Dept. of Agriculture, with the cooperation of the state land-grant colleges and universities. Local groups are guided by Extension Service workers and by volunteer leaders. Each group elects its officers and plans its activities and programs. The club motto is "To make the best better"; its pledge is "My Head to clearer thinking, my Heart to greater loyalty, my Hands to larger service, and my Health to better living, for my club, my community, and my country." The 4-H club movement has spread from the United States to more than 50 other countries. A National 4-H Club Congress is held annually in Chicago at the same time as the International Livestock Show; club members display their achievements in such fields as the breeding and raising of poultry and cattle; the cultivation of vegetables and fruits; the canning and preserving of foods; handicrafts; and needlework. In response to the steady decline in the U.S. agricultural population since World War II, 4-H has expanded its program to include groups for youngsters living in the nation's cities and suburbs. In 1972 it had 3.5 million members in the United States. See F. M. Reck, *The 4-H Club Story* (1951); T. A. Erickson, *My Sixty Years with Rural Youth* (1956).

Four Horsemen of the Apocalypse (əpŏk'əlĭps), allegorical figures in the Bible. Rev. 6.1–8. The rider on the white horse has many interpretations—one is that he represents Christ; the rider on the red horse is war; on the black horse is famine; and on the pale horse, death.

Fourier, Charles (shärl fōōryä'), 1772–1837, French social philosopher. From a bourgeois family, he condemned existing institutions and evolved a kind of utopian socialism. In *Théorie des quatre mouvements* (1808) and later works he developed his idea that the natural passions of man would, if properly channeled, result in social harmony. To achieve this goal, many of the artificial restraints of civilization were to be destroyed. The social organization for such development was to be based on the "phalanx," an economic unit composed of 1,620 people. Members would live in the *phalanstère* (or phalanstery), a community building, and work would be divided among people according to their natural inclinations. Fourier was not ready to discard capitalism completely; basically his ideal was an agricultural society, systematically arranged. His writings anticipated the 20th-century social problems resulting from mechanization and industrialization. **Fourierism** obtained a number of converts in France, and several newspapers spread the doctrines, but followers failed to establish any lasting colony there. After Fourier's death his principal disciple, Victor Prosper CONSIDÉRANT, tried to found a colony in Texas. Albert BRISBANE and Horace GREELEY were the principal figures in the sudden and wide development of colonies in the United States. BROOK FARM was for a time Fourierist. The most successful of the communities was the North American Phalanx at Red Bank, N.J. See studies by N. V. Riasanovsky (1969) and David Zeldin (1969).

Fourier, Jean Baptiste Joseph, Baron, 1768–1830, French mathematician and physicist. He was noted for his researches on heat and on numerical equations. He originated Fourier's theorem on vibratory motion and the Fourier series, which provided a method for representing discontinuous functions by a trigonometric series. Fourier was professor (1795–98) at the École polytechnique, Paris; accompanied Napoleon I to Egypt; and was prefect of Isère (1802–15). In 1808 he was made a baron. He wrote *Théorie analytique de la chaleur* (1822; tr. 1878, repr. 1955). His scientific writings were collected in two volumes (1888–90).

Four Lakes, chain of canalized lakes in S Wis.: Waubesa, Kegonsa, Mendota, and Monona. Between the last two lies Madison, the state capital. Largest of the four is Mendota, c.6 mi (9.7 km) long, on which the Univ. of Wisconsin campus is located. Indian mounds are nearby.

Fournier, Alain-: see ALAIN-FOURNIER.

Fournier, Pierre Simon (pyĕr sēmôN' fōōrnyā'), 1712–68, Parisian type founder. Fournier devised the first point system for measuring and naming sizes of type in 1737. He designed a number of typefaces and many typographic ornaments. He was the author of *Manuel typographique* (2 vol., 1764–66).

four-o'clock, common name for members of the Nyctaginaceae, a family of plants found in warm climates, especially in the Americas, chiefly as herbs but often in the tropics as shrubs or trees. Species native to the United States are mostly restricted to the southern and Pacific regions, e.g., the sand verbena of the deserts. The four-o'clock, or marvel of Peru (genus *Mirabilis*), of tropical Asia and America and the woody BOUGAINVILLEA vine with its showy bracts are widely cultivated as garden ornamentals in suitable climates and in greenhouses. Some members of the family are of minor importance medicinally. Four-o'clocks are classified in the division MAGNOLIOPHYTA, class Magnoliopsida, order Caryophyllales, family Nyctaginaceae.

Four-Power Treaty: see NAVAL CONFERENCES.

Foursquare Gospel, International Church of the, fundamentalist Christian Church and evangelistic missionary body organized in California by Aimee Semple MCPHERSON and Minnie Kennedy in 1927. It derived its name from the fourfold teaching of Christ as savior, healer, baptizer, and coming king. The parent church is Angelus Temple in Los Angeles. Ministers are trained at the Lighthouse of International Foursquare Evangelism (LIFE) Bible Training College, a coeducational institution in Los Angeles. In 1969, membership in the church was more than 193,000; there were 776 churches in the United States and Canada and more than 2,000 overseas mission stations and "meeting places."

Fourteen Points, formulation of a peace program, presented at the end of World War I by U.S. President Woodrow WILSON in an address before both houses of Congress on Jan. 8, 1918. The message, though intensely idealistic in tone and primarily a peace program, had certain very practical uses as an instrument for propaganda. It was intended to reach the people and the liberal leaders of the Central Powers as a seductive appeal for peace, in which purpose it was successful. It was intended also to make it plain to the Allies that the United States would not be a party to a selfish peace, and it was planned to appeal for the support of the liberal elements in Allied countries in achieving an unselfish settlement. It was intended to stimulate moral fervor at home. Finally it was hoped that the points would provide a framework for peace discussions. The message immediately gave Wilson the position of moral leadership of the Allies and furnished him with a tremendous diplomatic weapon as long as the war persisted. In this period few stopped to analyze the practical implications of its far-reaching principles or realized that it cut across the secret treaties of the Allies. After the armistice, opposition to the points quickly crystallized, and the actual treaty (see VERSAILLES, TREATY OF) represented a compromise or defeat of many of them. The first five points were general in nature and may be summarized as follows: (1) "open covenants openly arrived at"; (2) freedom of the seas in peace and war; (3) removal of economic barriers between nations as far as possible; (4) reduction of armaments to needs for domestic safety; (5) adjustment of colonial claims with concern for the wishes and interests of the inhabitants as well as for the titles of rival claimants. The next eight points referred to specific questions: (6) evacuation and general restoration of conquered territories in Russia; (7) preservation of Belgian sovereignty; (8) settlement of the Alsace-Lorraine question; (9) redrawing of Italian frontiers according to nationalities; (10) the division of Austria-Hungary in conformance to its nationalities; (11) the redrawing of Balkan boundaries with reference to historically established allegiance and nationalities; (12) Turkish control only of their own peoples and freedom of navigation through the Dardanelles; (13) the establishment of an independent Poland with access to the sea. The last point (14) was a provision for "a general association of nations . . . under specific covenants." The League of Nations grew out of the last point. See Ray Stannard Baker, *Woodrow Wilson and World Settlement* (1923, repr. 1960); Thomas A. Bailey, *Wilson and the Peacemakers* (2 vol., 1947, repr. 1963).

Fourteenth Amendment, to the U.S. Constitution, adopted 1868. The amendment comprises five sections. Section 1 will be discussed later in detail. Section 2 provides for apportionment of membership in the House of Representatives on the basis of the whole state population, excluding Indians not taxed. A supplemental provision, intended to protect Negro suffrage but never implemented, allows reduction of the congressional representation of a state if male citizens over 21 years old are forbidden to vote. The main effective constitutional guarantee of Negro suffrage has been the Fifteenth Amendment (adopted 1870), which forbids the United States or any state to abridge the right to vote on account of race, color, or previous condition of servitude. Section 3 of the Fourteenth Amendment excludes from political office persons who, having sworn to uphold the U.S. Constitution (e.g., army officers and members of Congress) violate this oath, as in the case of those who aided the Confederacy in the Civil War; Congress by a two-thirds vote of each house can remove this disability. Section 4 confirms the public debt but makes void all claims arising from credit extended to the Confederacy or from the loss of slaves. By Section 5, Congress is empowered to enact legislation enforcing the foregoing sections. Section 1 of the amendment declares substantially that all persons born or naturalized in the United States are American citizens and citizens of their state of residence; the citizenship of Negroes was thereby established and the effect of the DRED SCOTT CASE was overcome. The section forbids the states to abridge the privileges and immunities of U.S. citizens, to deprive any person of life, liberty, or property without due process of law (a similar provision restraining the Federal government is in the Fifth Amendment), and to deny any person the equal protection of the laws. Section 1 has been used extensively by the U.S. Supreme Court to test the validity of state legislation. The privileges and immunities of citizenship have never been defined by a majority of the court, but some justices have argued that among the activities envisaged are freedom to cross state boundaries and freedom to gather for peaceable discussion of legislation. The court has preferred to base its decisions on the due process and the equal protection clauses, which apply to all persons (the term *person* was soon applied to corporations as well as human beings) irrespective of citizenship. In the early view of the court any deprivation of life, liberty, or property simply meant the punishment for crime. The requirements of due process would be met by fair procedure, including notice to the defendant and an open trial with the right to counsel. In time, however, the court concluded that due process was not limited to procedural considerations but had a substantive aspect as well. Thus, even if proper legal procedure were observed, the ground on which a person was deprived of life, liberty, or property might in itself violate due process. The constitutionality of much state legislation was opened to question, and so many laws were attacked that at times about one third of the cases before the Supreme Court dealt with due process. The court did not stipulate limitations on traditional exercises of the POLICE POWER, such as the ordinary criminal law and the regulation of NUISANCE (see SLAUGHTERHOUSE CASES). However, it did severely restrain the power of the states to legislate on economic matters. The court held that only businesses "dedicated to the public interest" (defined to exclude virtually all businesses except utility companies) might be regulated by the states and that state laws that limited the hours of work of women were an unwarranted interference with liberty of contract. The equal protection clause, which was also brought to bear on the economic legislation of the states, was held to invalidate restraints on corporations from which other businesses were exempted. In several early cases this clause was used to foster individual economic rights, with the court striking down state laws that prevented aliens from pursuing certain occupations. However, Negroes who claimed that the discrimination they suffered at the hands of private persons (e.g., exclusion from hotels) denied them the equal protection of law were refused redress by the court, which held that the Fourteenth Amendment was concerned with official state action only. In 1896 in the PLESSY VS. FERGUSON case the court enunciated the view that the states might provide segregated facilities for Negroes (e.g., in education) so long as they were equal to those afforded white persons; this is the so-called "separate but equal" doctrine. Although state regulation of working conditions and hours of employment were permitted after a time, the court substantially maintained the views outlined above until the 1930s, when drastic reinterpretations were made. (For factors producing the change, see SUPREME COURT, UNITED STATES.) The court thereafter permitted state legislatures to make economic regulations without regard to the question whether the businesses concerned were dedicated to the public interest. The states, it was also held, might meet the requirements of equal protection even if distinctions based upon "reasonable classifications" were made. Thus, corporations, with their great potential power and size, might reasonably be subjected to severer restrictions than other types of business organizations. While the states were given greater freedom in enacting economic legislation, their power to limit personal liberties was brought under greater restraint. Gradually, the protection afforded by the Bill of Rights against Federal action was almost entirely extended to the states. In a number of decisions it was held that the provisions of the First Amendment to the Constitution of the United States were made applicable to the states by the substantive aspect of the due-process clause. Thus, the states, like the Federal government, were forbidden to favor or suppress any religious establishment or to deny freedom of speech, of the press, and of peaceable assembly. Only when the exercise of these rights created a "clear and present danger" of some grave evil might the states take repressive steps. The court has not found such danger in most cases of peaceable picketing (defined as a form of speech) or in the distribution of religious or political propaganda, despite objectionable littering of the streets. The court condemned all voluntary religious instruction in public schools as aid to establishments of religion. With the new attitude of the court, the equal-protection clause became one of the main weapons of those who were determined that blacks should enjoy the same rights as white persons. Although there had been decisions forbidding segregation on interstate transportation and ruling that state courts cannot enforce a restrictive covenant (agreement that a buyer will not resell to certain categories of persons, e.g., Negroes or Jews), it was not until 1954 that the "separate but equal" doctrine was firmly repudiated (see BROWN VS. BOARD OF EDUCATION OF TOPEKA, KANSAS). In recent years the Supreme Court has also used the equal-protection clause to invalidate legislation discriminating against women and to order the apportionment of state legislatures on the basis of population alone. See C. W. Collins, *The Fourteenth Amendment and the States* (1912); Jacobus Ten Broek, *Equal under Law* (1951, repr. 1965); J. B. James, *The Framing of the Fourteenth Amendment* (1956, repr. 1965); Bernard Schwartz, ed., *The Fourteenth Amendment* (1970); H. N. Meyer, *The Amendment that Refused to Die* (1973).

Fourth of July, Independence Day, or **July Fourth,** U.S. holiday, commemorating the adoption of the DECLARATION OF INDEPENDENCE. Celebration of it began during the American Revolution. It has been the most important patriotic holiday ever since. Traditionally it has been celebrated with the firing of guns and fireworks, parades, open-air meetings, and patriotic speeches. Today local ordinances prevent much of the former display of fireworks and use of firearms.

Fourth Republic: see FRANCE.

Fouta Djallon or **Futa Jallon** (both: fo͞o'tä jälôN'), highland region, c.30,000 sq mi (77,700 sq km), central Guinea, W Africa. Largely a rolling grassland (average alt. c.3,000 ft/910 m), the region is grazed by cattle of the Fulani. The Niger, Senegal, and Gambia rivers rise there. Since the 18th cent. it has been a stronghold of Islam.

Fowey, England: see SAINT AUSTELL WITH FOWEY.

Fowke, Gerard (fouk), 1855–1933, American archaeologist, whose name was originally Gerard Smith, b. Maysville, Ky. Known especially for his study of antiquities in the Ohio valley, he also investigated aboriginal remains in the E United States (1885–88, 1891–93) and alleged Norse remains near Boston (1894, 1896). Fowke also explored (1898) Vancouver Island and the Amur River region in Siberia, and made ethnological studies in the Hawaiian Islands (1920).

fowl: see POULTRY.

Fowler, Charles Henry, 1837–1908, American Methodist bishop and educator, b. Canada. For 11 years he held pastorates in Chicago churches. He was president of Northwestern Univ. from 1873 to 1876. After his election as bishop in 1884, he traveled in several mission fields and helped found the universities of Peking and Nanking in China, Nebraska Wesleyan Univ., and the Twentieth Century Forward Movement.

Fowler, Henry Hamill, 1908–, U.S. Secretary of the Treasury (1965–68), b. Roanoke, Va. From 1934 to 1939 he was a lawyer for the Tennessee Valley Authority, rising to become its assistant general counsel. He was (1939–40) chief counsel of the Senate subcommittee on education and labor and in 1941 became assistant general counsel of the Office of Production Management. He was appointed Undersecretary of the Treasury in 1961, and he held that office until April, 1964. In 1965, President Lyndon B. Johnson appointed him Secretary of the Treasury to succeed Douglas Dillon. He resigned in 1968 to enter private law practice.

Fowler, Henry Watson, 1858–1933, English lexicographer, educated at Oxford. Both he and his brother, Francis G. Fowler (1870–1918), had been teachers before they began their literary collaboration with a translation of Lucian (1905). They also worked together on *The King's English* (1906), a trenchant and witty book of modern English usage and misusage, and on *The Concise Oxford Dictionary of Current English* (1911) and *The Pocket Oxford Dictionary* (1924). After the death of his brother in 1918, H. W. Fowler completed alone *A Dictionary of Modern English Usage* (1926). These works became invaluable reference books for writers, editors, and all those interested in the usage of modern English.

Fowler, Sir John, 1817–98, English engineer. With Benjamin Baker, he designed and built the Forth Bridge (1882–90) in Scotland, the first major structure made of steel. He also designed much of the London Metropolitan Railway, forerunner of the underground railways, and later served as an engineer in the development of the London subway system. He was knighted in 1885.

Fowles, John, 1926–, English novelist, b. Leigh-on-Sea, Essex, grad. Oxford, 1950. He has taught in France and in Greece. Fowles is a complex, cerebral writer, interested in manipulating the novel as a form. His first novel, *The Collector* (1963), is a study of a clerk who is psychologically impelled to kidnap and murder—that is, "collect"—a girl to whom he is attracted. *The French Lieutenant's Woman* (1969) is a "Victorian" novel that has three endings and can be called a parody of Victorianism and of the novel itself. He has also written *The Aristos: A Self-Portrait in Ideas* (1964); *The Magus* (1966), a novel; and *The Ebony Tower* (1974), a collection of stories.

Fowliang: see CHING-TE-CHEN, China.

Fox, Charles James, 1749–1806, British statesman and orator, for many years the outstanding parliamentary proponent of liberal reform. He entered Parliament in 1768 and served as lord of the admiralty (1770–72) and as lord of the treasury (1772–74) under Frederick, Lord NORTH. Dismissed by George III, he went into bitter opposition, lending his remarkable oratorical genius to the attack on North's policy in North America. Despite the king's objection, he became foreign secretary in the marquess of Rockingham's Whig ministry (1782) and helped to secure the repeal of Poynings's Law (see under POYNINGS, SIR EDWARD), thus giving Ireland legislative independence. He quarreled with the earl of SHELBURNE over the negotiation of peace with the former American colonies, France, and Spain, and he resigned when Shelburne succeeded Rockingham. Fox then allied himself with his old enemy, Lord North, to insure Shelburne's defeat, and he became (1783) foreign secretary again, in a coalition with North. This ministry fell in the same year, when George III brought his influence to bear in the House of Lords to secure defeat of Fox's bill vesting the government of India in a commission nominated by Parliament. He was replaced in office by William Pitt, whom he bitterly opposed for the rest of his life. In 1788, when George III became temporarily insane, Fox wanted an unrestricted regency vested in the prince of Wales (later GEORGE IV). This position seemed to belie his strongly professed belief in the supremacy of Parliament and the need to restrict royal power, but the prince, who was Fox's close friend, would have brought Fox and the Whigs back to office. George III recovered, however, and Fox remained out of power. Fox favored the French Revolution and opposed British intervention in the French Revolutionary Wars. He objected to the suppression of civil liberties in wartime and was the parliamentary spokesman of several reform movements, urging such measures as enlargement of the franchise, parliamentary reform, and political rights for Roman Catholics and dissenters. At Pitt's death he became (1806) for a few months foreign secretary in the "ministry of all the talents." Abolition of the slave trade, which he proposed and urged, was passed in 1807, soon after his death. Fox combined dissolute habits with remarkable warmth of character and great courage and skill in debate. Although he could be opportunistic as well as idealistic, he is remembered as a great champion of liberty. See biographies by G. O. Trevelyan (1880, repr. 1971), J. L. Hammond (1903), John Drinkwater (1928), E. C. P. Lascelles (1936, repr. 1970), and J. W. Derry (1972); Erich Eyck, *Pitt versus Fox* (tr. by Eric Northcott, 1950); John Carswell, *The Old Cause* (1955); John Cannon, *The Fox-North Coalition* (1970); L. G. Mitchell, *Charles James Fox and the Disintegration of the Whig Party, 1782–1794* (1971).

Fox, Dixon Ryan, 1887–1945, American historian and educator, b. Potsdam, N.Y. He taught at Columbia from 1912 to 1934, becoming full professor in 1927. From 1934 until his death he was president of Union College and chancellor of Union Univ. His writings include *The Decline of Aristocracy in the Politics of New York* (1919, repr. 1971); biographies of the historian Herbert L. Osgood, his father-in-law (1924), and of Caleb Heathcote (1926); *Ideas in Motion* (1935); and *Yankees and Yorkers* (1940). Fox was a leader of research in social history and with Arthur M. Schlesinger, Sr., was editor of the excellent "A History of American Life" series. *The Completion of Independence, 1790–1830* (1944, repr. 1971) Vol. V in the series, was written by John A. Krout and Fox.

Fox, George, 1624–91, English religious leader, founder of the Society of FRIENDS, b. Fenny Drayton in Leicestershire. As a boy he was apprenticed to a shoemaker and wool dealer. By nature serious and contemplative, Fox at the age of 19 entered upon a wandering quest for spiritual enlightenment. In 1646 he underwent a mystical experience that convinced him that Christianity was not an outward profession but an inner light by which Christ directly illumines the believing soul. Revelation was for Fox not confined to the Scriptures. In 1647 he began to preach. Although often the victim of mob brutality and eight times imprisoned between 1649 and 1675, Fox won many followers, especially among groups of SEPARATISTS. In 1668 he prepared the first pattern of organization, which was for some years to serve as the discipline of the Society of Friends. The London Yearly Meeting was started in 1671. To confirm his followers in their beliefs and to spread the truths, Fox went in 1671 to the West Indies and to America, where he made arduous journeys to various colonies scattered between New England and North Carolina. Later he twice visited Holland. His sincerity, serenity, fearlessness, and powerful preaching are attested to by a number of his contemporaries. His journal (1694, with a preface by William Penn) has appeared in various editions. See *George Fox: An Autobiography* (ed. by R. M. Jones, 2 vol., 1903–4); his narrative papers (ed. by H. J. Cadbury, 1972); biography by H. E. Wildes (1965); studies by R. H. King (1940) and J. H. Yolen (1972).

Fox, Gustavus Vasa, 1821–83, American naval officer, b. Saugus, Mass. Appointed a midshipman in 1838, he resigned from the navy in 1856 but in April, 1861, at the beginning of the Civil War, commanded the expedition that attempted to relieve the garrison at Fort Sumter. Fox was chief clerk of the Dept. of the Navy from May to Aug., 1861, when the post of Assistant Secretary of the Navy was created for him. He held that office till May, 1866. His honesty, efficiency, and wide knowledge of naval affairs were of incalculable benefit to the Union cause. See his *Confidential Correspondence* (1918–19).

Fox, Henry Richard Vassall: see HOLLAND, HENRY RICHARD VASSALL FOX, 3D BARON.

Fox or **Foxe, Luke,** 1586–1635, English explorer. As a master mariner, he set forth in 1631 to hunt for the NORTHWEST PASSAGE. He explored the southern shore of Hudson Bay, satisfied himself that there was no passage through it, and when scurvy struck his crew returned that same year to England. His *Northwest Fox; or, Fox from the North-West Passage* was published in 1635 (ed. by R. M. Christy, 1894). He gave many names to geographical features that are still used today; Foxe Basin and Foxe Peninsula were named after him. At about the time that Fox was in Hudson Bay, Thomas JAMES was also conducting a search there for the Northwest Passage.

Fox, Margaret, 1836–93, American spiritualist, b. Bath, Ont. She claimed to have established communication with the spirit world by means of spirit rappings. Although she and her sisters, Katherine and Leah, gained much notice and notoriety in the United States and Europe, Margaret later admitted that the effects were fraudulent. See SPIRITISM.

Fox, river, 176 mi (283 km) long, rising in S central Wis. and flowing SW to within 1.5 mi (2.4 km) of Portage, Wis., on the Wisconsin River, then NE through Lake Winnebago into Green Bay, an arm of Lake Michigan, at Green Bay, Wis.; the Wolf River is its main tributary. Appleton and Oshkosh are important cities on the Fox. Above Lake Winnebago the river is called the Upper Fox, below it, the Lower Fox. Rapids at points along the river furnish water power. The river was a well-known route used by early explorers, missionaries, and fur traders to reach the Northwest and the Mississippi River system from the Great Lakes. In 1673, the French explorers Louis Jolliet and Father Marquette were the first Europeans to reach the Mississippi by way of the Fox-Wisconsin portage. A barge canal now links the Fox and Wisconsin rivers at Portage, forming a continuous waterway from Lake Michigan to the Mississippi River.

fox, carnivorous mammal of the DOG family, found throughout most of the Northern Hemisphere. It has a pointed face, short legs, long, thick fur, and a tail about one half to two thirds as long as the head and body, depending on the species. Foxes feed on insects, earthworms, small birds and mammals, eggs, carrion, and vegetable matter, especially fruits. Unlike other members of the dog family, which run down their prey, foxes usually hunt by stalking and pouncing. They are known for their raids on poultry but are nonetheless very beneficial to farmers as destroyers of rodents. Solitary most of the year, foxes do not live in dens except in the breeding season; they sleep concealed in grasses or thickets, their tails curled around them for warmth. During the breeding season a fox pair establishes a den, often in a ground burrow made by another animal, in which the young are raised; the male hunts for the family. The young are on their own after about five months; the adults probably find new mates each season. Foxes are preyed upon by larger carnivores, such as wolves and bobcats, as well as by humans and their dogs; birds of prey may capture the young. Most fox species belong to the red fox group, genus *Vulpes*. The common red fox, *Vulpes vulpes,* is found in Eurasia, N Africa, and North America. It is hunted for its valuable fur and, especially in England, for sport. An extremely wary animal, it is skilled at evading traps and dodging pursuers. There are many local varieties; European red foxes are larger than those of North America, which average about 23 in. (58 cm) in body length, stand about 16 in. (41 cm) at the shoulder, and weigh about 5 to 10 lb (2.3–4.6 kg). North American red foxes inhabit areas of forest mixed with open country, from the Arctic Ocean to the S United States. Although most active at night, they are also seen by day. There is great color variation among them, but the tail is always tipped with white, and the legs, feet, and tips of the ears are always black. The rest of the coat is commonly reddish; black, silver, and cross (reddish, with a dark, cross-shaped region on back and shoulders) are among the variations which may appear in any red fox litter. Silver fox pelts, black with white-tipped outer hairs, are much in demand; many are derived from animals raised on fox farms. From the silver fox, breeders have developed a platinum fox whose pale gray pelt is highly valued. The kit and swift foxes (*V. velox* and *V. macrotis,* respectively) are small, swift, pale gray or yellowish foxes, found on the deserts and plains of the W United States and N Mexico. Their numbers have been greatly diminished by trapping and poisoning, and they are now rare in many parts of their range. Other *Vulpes* species are found in Asia and Africa. The gray fox, *Urocyon cinereoargenteus,* is a New World species; it is the only fox that commonly climbs trees. Found from the N United States to N South America, this fox is slightly larger, on the average, than the North American red fox. Its coat is salt-and-pepper above and buff-colored below; the upper side of its tail is black. Gray foxes inhabit woods, swamps, and brushy areas that afford them cover; they are more retiring and more strictly nocturnal in their habits than red foxes. Their fur is of little value. The arctic fox, *Alopex lagopus,* is found on arctic coasts and islands; it has a circumpolar distribution. Characterized by short, rounded ears and heavily furred feet, all arctic foxes are brown to gray in summer; some turn pure white in winter, while others, called blue foxes, turn bluish gray. The blue fox, a natural variant that is more common in some areas than in others, is highly valued for its pelt, and breeders have developed all-blue strains. Although their diet includes small animals and plant matter, arctic foxes are chiefly scavengers, feeding especially on the remains of polar bears' kills. The smallest fox is the fennec, or desert fox (*Fennecus zerda*), of the Sahara and Arabian deserts. An excellent burrower, it has enormous ears and a fluffy pale cream coat. Other foxes (sometimes called zorros) are found in South America. Despite extensive killing of foxes, most species continue to flourish. In Europe this is due in part to the regulatory laws passed for the benefit of hunters. Mounted fox hunting, with dogs, became popular in the 14th cent. and was later introduced into the Americas; special hunting dogs, called foxhounds, have been bred for this sport. Foxes are classified in the phylum CHORDATA, subphylum Vertebrata, class Mammalia, order Carnivora, family Canidae. See Roger Burrows, *Wild Fox* (1968); L. L. Rue, *The World of the Red Fox* (1969).

Foxborough or **Foxboro,** town (1970 pop. 14,218), Norfolk co., SE Mass.; settled 1704, inc. 1778. The chief industrial product is precision instruments. In the town is Schaefer Stadium, home of the New England Patriots football team. During the Revolutionary War cannons and cannonballs were manufactured in Foxborough.

Foxe, John, 1516–87, English clergyman, author of the noted *Book of Martyrs.* He early became a Protestant and, when Mary Tudor became queen, he fled from England to Strasbourg. There was printed (1554), in Latin, the first part of his history of the persecution of Protestant reformers. Foxe moved to Basel and had published (1559) the first complete edition, in Latin, of his history. After Elizabeth's accession, an expanded English edition appeared (1563) entitled *The Actes and Monuments of These Latter and Perilous Dayes.* The work was commonly known as the *Book of Martyrs,* and its chief purpose was to praise the heroism and piety of the Protestant martyrs of Mary's reign. The book was widely read, and its influence was extensive, although as history it is highly prejudiced and not altogether trustworthy. See J. F. Mozley, *John Foxe and His Book* (1940).

Foxe, Luke: see FOX, LUKE.

Foxe Basin, a widening of the waterway between Baffin Island and the Melville Peninsula, c.340 mi (550 km) long and c.225 mi (360 km) wide, E Franklin dist., Northwest Territories, Canada. The basin is shallow and is ice-clogged most of the year. **Foxe Channel** (c.200 mi/320 km long and c.90 mi/140 km wide) connects it with Hudson Bay and Hudson Strait.

foxglove: see FIGWORT.

foxhound: see AMERICAN FOXHOUND; ENGLISH FOXHOUND.

Fox Indians: see SAC AND FOX INDIANS.

Fox Islands: see ALEUTIAN ISLANDS.

fox terrier, breed of long-legged TERRIER developed over several centuries in England. There are two varieties, the smooth and the wirehaired. The coat of the former is dense, short, and flat, while that of the latter is longer, harsh, and wiry. The color in both varieties is white with black or black-and-tan markings. The fox terrier stands about 15 in. (38.1 cm) high at the shoulder and weighs from 15 to 19 lb (6.8–8.6 kg). Although the wirehaired is the older variety—some authorities trace its ancestry to the mid-17th cent.—the smooth was the first to be exhibited in the show ring. Both were perfected in the 19th cent. Widely bred to hunt foxes, the fox terrier is a very popular family companion and pet. See DOG.

Foxx, James Emory (Jimmy Foxx), 1907–67, American baseball player, b. Sudlersville, Md. Foxx played for the Philadelphia Athletics (1926–35), the Boston Red Sox (1936–42), the Chicago Cubs (1942–44), and the Philadelphia Phillies (1945). He hit a career total of 534 home runs (seventh all-time high) and batted .325. Foxx led the American League in home runs four seasons, hitting 58 in 1932. He was elected to the Baseball Hall of Fame in 1951.

Foyle (foil), river, c.10 mi (16 km) long, formed by the junction of the Mourne and Finn rivers at Strabane, Co. Tyrone, W Northern Ireland. It flows northeast through the city of Londonderry to Lough Foyle, a navigable inlet of the Atlantic Ocean c.15 mi (25 km) long. With its tributaries, the Foyle drains c.1,100 sq mi (2,850 sq km). There are valuable freshwater fisheries on the Foyle.

F.P.A.: see ADAMS, FRANKLIN PIERCE.

Fr, chemical symbol of the element FRANCIUM.

Fra: see ANGELICO, FRA; BARTOLOMEO DI PAGHOLO DEL FATTORINO, FRA; LIPPI, FRA FILIPPO.

Fracastoro, Girolamo (jĕrô'lämō fräkästô'rō), 1483–1553, Italian physician and poet. He was born in Verona, where he practiced after studying at Padua. He studied epidemic diseases and attributed their spread to tiny particles, or spores, that could transmit infection by direct or indirect contact or even without contact over long distances. He wrote a long poem (1530) on syphilis, from the title of which the disease takes its name.

fraction [Lat.,=breaking], in arithmetic, an expression representing a part, or several equal parts, of a unit. In writing a fraction, e.g., $2/5$ or $\frac{2}{5}$, the number after or below the bar represents the total number of parts into which the unit has been divided. This number is called the denominator. The number before or above the bar, the numerator, denotes how many of the equal parts of the unit have been taken. The expression $2/5$, then, represents the fact that two of the five parts of the unit or quantity have been taken. When the numerator is less than the denominator, the fraction is proper, i.e., less than unity. When the reverse is true, e.g., $5/2$, the fraction is improper, i.e., greater than unity. A fraction has been reduced to its lowest terms when the numerator and denominator are not divisible by any common divisor except 1, e.g., when $4/6$ is reduced to $2/3$. When a fraction is written with a whole number, e.g., $3\frac{1}{2}$, the expression is called a mixed number. This may also be written as an improper fraction, as $7/2$, since three is equal to six halves, and by adding the one half, the total becomes seven halves, or $7/2$. When fractions having the same denominator, as $3/10$ and $4/10$, are added, only the numerators are added, and their sum is then written over the common denominator: $3/10+4/10=7/10$. Fractions having unlike denominators, e.g., $1/4$ and $1/6$, must first be converted into fractions having a common denominator, a denominator into which each denominator may be divided, before addition may be performed. In the case of $1/4$ and $1/6$, for example, the lowest number into which both 4 and 6 are divisible is 12. When both fractions are converted into fractions having this number as a denominator, then $1/4$ becomes $3/12$, and $1/6$ becomes $2/12$. The change is accomplished in the same way in both cases—the denominator is divided into the 12 and the numerator is multiplied by the result of this division. The addition then is performed as in the case of fractions having the same denominator: $1/4+1/6=3/12+2/12=5/12$. In subtraction, the numerator and the denominator are subjected to the same preliminary procedure, but then the numerators of the converted fractions are subtracted: $1/4-1/6=3/12-2/12=1/12$. In multiplication, the numerators of the fractions are multiplied together as are the denominators without needing change: $2/3\times 3/5=6/15$. It should be noted that the result, here $6/15$, may be reduced to $2/5$ by dividing both numerator and denominator by 3. The division of one fraction by another, e.g., $3/5\div 1/2$, is performed by inverting the divisor and multiplying: $3/5\div 1/2=3/5\times 2/1=6/5$. The same rules apply to the addition, subtraction, multiplication, and division of fractions in which the numerators and denominators are algebraic expressions. The present notation for fractions is of Hindu origin, but some types of fractions were used by the

Egyptians before 1600 B.C. Another way of representing fractions is by decimal notation (see DECIMAL SYSTEM).

fracture, breaking of a bone. A simple fracture is one in which there is no contact of the broken bone with the outer air, i.e., the overlying tissues are intact. In a comminuted fracture the bone is splintered. In greenstick fracture (common in children) one side of the bone is fractured and the other side bent. In multiple fracture there is more than one break. A compound fracture is one in which the broken bone is in contact with the air because there is a wound through the skin; the bone may project through the wound. The bones of the very old are especially liable to fracture, although no age is exempt. Fractures are caused most often by injury, although certain pathological conditions may predispose a bone to fracture. A person with a fracture should not be moved unless the broken bone has been splinted or otherwise immobilized (see FIRST AID). Proper setting of bones and the application of a cast should be performed by a doctor. X-ray aids in the repositioning of the bone as well as in determining the state of healing. Surgery that involves implanting metal pins or screws to join broken bones may be necessary; in certain cases traction devices are used to align bone fragments. Skull and jaw fractures require special treatment.

Fra Diavolo (frä dēä'vōlō) [Ital.,=friar devil], 1771–1806, Italian bandit and soldier, whose real name was Michele Pezza. He entered the service of the king of Naples in 1798 and with Cardinal Ruffo resisted the French invasion (1799) of the kingdom. He was captured (1806) and hanged by the French. The plot of Auber's opera *Fra Diavolo* (libretto by Scribe) is in no respect historical.

Fragonard, Jean-Honoré (zhäN-ōnôrā' frägônär'), 1732–1806, French painter. He studied with Chardin, Carle Van Loo, and intensively with Boucher, whose style he assimilated. He won the Prix de Rome and studied in Italy from 1756 to 1761; there he was particularly attentive to the works of Tiepolo. In 1765 he was admitted to the Académie royale for the historical *Coresus and Callirrhoë* (Louvre), but thereafter he devoted himself to painting polished and delicately erotic scenes of love and gallantry for the court. Characteristic examples are *Love's Vow, The Swing* (Wallace Coll., London), and the *Music Lesson* (Louvre). He married and his works became less sensual and more sentimental. Ruined by the Revolution, he retired to Grasse, where he decorated the house of a friend with the panels *Roman de l'amour et de la jeunesse* [tale of love and youth], originally intended for Mme Du Barry (Frick Coll., New York City). Fragonard is esteemed for the freedom of his brush technique, the strength and vitality of his portraiture and landscapes, and for his virtuosity in depicting the character of gaiety and charm in the age of Louis XV. Well represented in the Louvre, the Wallace Collection in London, and the Frick Collection and the Metropolitan Museum in New York City, his work can also be seen in the museums of Washington, D.C., Boston, Cleveland, Detroit, and St. Louis. See studies by G. Wildenstein (1960) and J. Thuillier (tr. 1967).

Frame, Janet (Janet Paterson Frame Clutha), 1924–, New Zealand novelist. Her complex, disturbing novels are marked by startling images and mastery of language. Frame's characters are often psychologically disturbed people who live on the edge of a terrifying, unknowable state such as madness or death. In the last part of her novel *Intensive Care* (1970), all of mankind has experienced a nightmarish apocalypse and human fate is decided by a computer. Frame's other works include a volume of poems, *The Pocket Mirror* (1967); the short-story collections *The Lagoon: Stories* (1951) and *The Reservoir and Other Stories* (1966); and the novels *Owls Do Cry* (1957), *Faces in the Water* (1961), *Scented Gardens for the Blind* (1963), and *The Rainbirds* (1968).

Framingham (frā'mĭnghăm"), town (1970 pop. 64,048), Middlesex co., E Mass., on the Sudbury River between Worcester and Boston; settled 1650, inc. 1700. It has varied manufacturing industries. Framingham State College is there.

Framingham State College, at Framingham, Mass.; chartered 1838, opened 1839 at Lexington, moved to Framingham 1853, a normal school until 1930. Formerly known as the Massachusetts State Teachers College, it adopted its present name in 1960. The college is the oldest existing U.S. school for teachers and was the first under state control. It was established by Horace MANN, and its early success influenced the development of other normal schools.

France, Anatole (änätôl' fräNs), pseud. of **Jacques Anatole Thibault** (zhäk, tēbō'), 1844–1924, French writer. He was probably the most prominent French man of letters of his time. Among his best-remembered works is *L'Île des pingouins* (1908, tr. *Penguin Island,* 1909), an allegorical novel satirizing French history. His early fiction was characterized by a somewhat sentimental charm—e.g., *Le Crime de Sylvestre Bonnard* (1881, tr. 1906), his first successful novel, and *Le Livre de mon ami* (1885, tr. *My Friend's Book,* 1913), the first of a series of autobiographical novels. Half his work appeared in periodicals and newspapers. After the Dreyfus Affair (in which he supported Zola) his work was slanted more to political satire. The elegance and subtle irony of his style are displayed in *Thaïs* (1890, tr. 1909), *La Rôtisserie de la reine Pédauque* (1893, tr. *At the Sign of the Reine Pédauque,* 1912), *Le Lys rouge* (1894, tr. *The Red Lily,* 1908), *Les Dieux ont soif* (1912, tr. *The Gods are Athirst,* 1913), and *La Révolte des anges* (1914, tr. *The Revolt of the Angels,* 1914). He also wrote a life of Joan of Arc (1908, tr. 1909). His liaison with Mme de Caillavet, lasting 27 years, had a profound influence on his work; she spurred his ambition and saved him from material concern. In 1896 he was elected to the French Academy, and he was awarded the 1921 Nobel Prize in Literature. See biographies by J. J. Brousson (tr. 1925) and David Tylden-Wright (1967); Barry Cerf, *Anatole France: the Degeneration of a Great Artist* (1926); Nicolas Ségur, *Conversations with Anatole France* (tr. 1926); J. M. Pouquet, *The Last Salon* (tr. 1927).

France, republic (1968 pop., excluding overseas departments and territories, 49,778,540), 211,207 sq mi (547,026 sq km), W Europe. The capital is PARIS. France is bordered by the English Channel in the north, the Atlantic Ocean and the Bay of Biscay in the west, and the Mediterranean Sea in the south. The natural land frontiers are the Pyrenees, along the border with Spain, in the southwest; the Jura Mts. and the Alps, along the border with Switzerland and Italy, in the east and southeast; and the Rhine River, which is part of the border with West Germany, in the northeast. Elsewhere in the northeast, the frontiers with West Germany, Luxembourg, and Belgium follow no natural line. Legally, the overseas departments and territories are part of the French Republic. The overseas departments are MARTINIQUE, GUADELOUPE, RÉUNION, and FRENCH GUIANA. The overseas territories are FRENCH POLYNESIA, NEW CALEDONIA, the French Territory of the AFARS AND THE ISSAS, the COMORO ISLANDS, SAINT PIERRE AND MIQUELON, the Southern and Antarctic Territories, and the WALLIS AND FUTUNA ISLANDS. Since the Revolution of 1789, France has had an extremely uniform and centralized administration. It is governed under the 1958 constitution, amended in 1962, which established the Fifth French Republic. The constitution reflected the views of Charles de Gaulle. It provides for a strong president, directly elected for a seven-year term. A premier and cabinet, appointed by the president, are responsible to the national assembly, but they are subordinate to the president. Parliament consists of the national assembly and the senate. Deputies to the assembly are elected for five-year terms from single-member districts. The president may dissolve the assembly. Senators are elected for nine-year terms from each department by an electoral college composed of the deputies, the district council members, and the municipal council members from that department. National politics in the Fifth Republic are dominated by the rightist-centrist Gaullist Union of Democrats for the Republic and its allies, and the leftist parties—Communists, Socialists, and left-wing Radicals—who sometimes form coalitions. There are small centrist and extreme right-wing parties. The central government appoints the prefects who administer the departments. There are 95 departments in metropolitan (European) France. The departments are subdivided into districts (arrondissements), municipalities (communes), and cantons. The municipalities are governed by mayors, who, although they are elected by municipal councils, are responsible to the prefects. The districts and cantons have little power. In 1964 the departments were grouped into 21 larger units to facilitate economic planning. These units, each of which has a prefect, approximately correspond to the old historic provinces of France, which were abolished by the Revolution but remain the basic cultural, economic, and geographic divisions of France. The historic provinces mirror the natural geographic regions and, despite administrative centralization, retain their striking diversity. The heart of France N of the Loire River is the province of ÎLE-DE-FRANCE, which occupies the greater part of the Paris basin, a fertile depression drained by the Seine and Marne rivers. The basin is surrounded by the provinces of CHAMPAGNE and LORRAINE in the east; ARTOIS, PICARDY, French Flanders (see NORD dept.), and NORMANDY in the northeast and north; BRITTANY, MAINE, and ANJOU in the west; and TOURAINE, ORLÉANAIS, NIVERNAIS, and BURGUNDY in the south. Further south are BERRY and BOURBONNAIS. Further east, between the Vosges Mts. and the Rhine, is ALSACE; S of Alsace, along the Jura, is FRANCHE-COMTÉ. S central France is occupied by the rugged mountains of the Massif Central. It comprises the provinces of MARCHE, LIMOUSIN, AUVERGNE, and LYONNAIS. To the E of the Rhône River, which divides the Massif Central from the Alps, are SAVOY, DAUPHINÉ, and PROVENCE. The French Alps have some of the highest peaks in Europe, including Mont Blanc. The Rhône valley widens into a plain near its delta on the Mediterranean; part of the coast of Provence forms the celebrated French RIVIERA. LANGUEDOC extends from the Cevennes Mts. to the Mediterranean coast W of the Rhône. CORSICA lies off the Mediterranean coast. The southwestern part of France comprises the small Pyrenean provinces of ROUSSILLON, FOIX, BÉARN, and French NAVARRE and the vast provinces of GASCONY and GUIENNE. The last two constitute the great Aquitanian plain, drained by the Garonne and Dordogne rivers, which flow into the Bay of Biscay. The central section of the west coast, between the Gironde estuary and the Loire, is occupied by the provinces of SAINTONGE, ANGOUMOIS, AUNIS, and POITOU. France is one of the world's major economic powers. Agriculture plays a larger role in its economy than in the economies of most other industrial countries. About two thirds of France's land is used for agricultural purposes. Three fifths of the value of total agricultural output derives from livestock (especially cattle, hogs, poultry, and sheep). The mountain areas and NW France are the livestock regions. The leading crops by yield are sugar beets, wheat, corn, potatoes, and barley. Wheat, barley, and corn are the most widely cultivated. Wheat and sugar beets are intensively cultivated N of the Loire. The soil in the Central Massif is less fertile. Fruit growing is important in the south. France is exceeded only by Italy in wine production. The best-known vineyards are in Burgundy, Champagne, the Rhône and Loire valleys, and the BORDEAUX region. France is among the world's largest producers of iron ore (Lorraine) and bauxite (S France), but it has inadequate supplies of coal and petroleum. France's leading industries produce metals, chemicals, foods, and textiles. Tourism is an important industry, and Paris is famous for its luxury goods. In addition to the Paris area, important industrial cities are, in the northeast, METZ, STRASBOURG, ROUBAIX, and LILLE; in the southeast, LYONS, SAINT-ÉTIENNE, CLERMONT-FERRAND, and GRENOBLE; in the south, MARSEILLES and NÎMES; and in the west, Bordeaux and NANTES. The centers of the wine trade are Bordeaux, RHEIMS, ÉPERNAY, DIJON, and COGNAC. Other important cities are ORLÉANS, TOURS, TROYES, TOULOUSE, ARLES, and NICE. More than half of France's trade is with other Common Market members. The franc area (French dependencies and former colonies) and the United States are also important trade partners. Leading exports are machinery, textiles, iron and steel, motor vehicles, chemicals, wheat, beet sugar, and wines. Leading imports are fuels, nonferrous metals, textile components, and manufactured goods that France does not make. The chief ports are ROUEN, LE HAVRE, CHERBOURG, BREST, SAINT-NAZAIRE, Nantes, Bordeaux, TOULON, and Marseilles. The railroads, utilities, large commercial banks, and aircraft, Renault motor vehicle, fertilizer, and coal industries are nationally owned. In 1968 there were 32 French cities that had more than 100,000 inhabitants, but only Paris exceeded the million mark. More than half of the population lives in urban areas of 10,000 or more inhabitants. Until the end of World War II the population increase in France was perhaps the lowest in Europe, but in postwar decades the rate has increased. The mingling of peoples over the centuries as well as immigration in the 20th cent. has given France great ethnic diversity. Alsatian, a German dialect, is spoken in Alsace and in parts of Lorraine. A small number speak Flemish in French Flanders. In Celtic Brittany, Breton is still spoken, as is Basque in the BAYONNE region and Catalan at the eastern end of the Pyrenees. Roman Catholicism is by far the largest religion in France. Separation of church and state was made final by the law of 1905. The educational level in France is high. Among the universities of France the largest are those of Paris, Lyons, Toulouse, Aix-Marseilles,

Bordeaux, Lille, Montpellier, Strasbourg, Rennes, Grenoble, and Nancy.

Ancient Gaul and the Birth of France. Some of the earliest anthropological and archaeological remains in Europe have been found in France, yet little is known of France before the Roman conquest (1st cent. B.C.). The country was known to the Romans as GAUL. It was inhabited largely by CELTS, or Gauls, who had mingled with still older populations, and by BASQUES in present Gascony. Some of the Gallic tribes undoubtedly were Germanic. Settlements on the Mediterranean coast, notably Marseilles, were established by Greek and Phoenician traders (c.600 B.C.), and Provence was colonized by Rome in the 2d cent. B.C. The conquest of Gaul by Julius Caesar (58–51 B.C.; see GALLIC WARS) became final with the defeat of VERCINGETORIX. Early in the course of the following five centuries of Roman rule Gaul accepted Latin speech and Roman law, developed a distinct Gallo-Roman civilization, and produced many large and prosperous cities. Lugdunum (Lyons) was the Roman capital. Christianity, introduced in the 1st cent. A.D., spread rapidly. From the 3d cent., however, the internal decline of the Roman Empire invited barbarian incursions. Among the Germanic tribes that descended upon fertile Gaul, the VISIGOTHS, FRANKS, and Burgundii were the most important. Rome and its governors in Gaul sought, by alliances, to play the barbarians off against each other. Thus Aetius defeated (A.D. 451) the Huns under Attila with the help of the Franks. But in 486 (10 years after the traditional date for the fall of Rome) the Franks, under CLOVIS I, routed Syagrius, last Roman governor of Gaul. Clovis, who had made himself ruler of all the Franks, then defeated the Visigoths and, after accepting Christianity (496), conquered the Alemanni. He extinguished the Arian heresy (see ARIANISM) and founded the dynasty of the MEROVINGIANS—but he failed to provide for the unity of Gaul when, as was customary, he divided his lands among his sons at his death. Throughout the 6th and 7th cent., Gaul was torn by fractricidal strife between the Merovingian kings of NEUSTRIA and of AUSTRASIA, the two realms that ultimately emerged from Clovis's division and were united only for brief periods under a sole ruler. Especially after DAGOBERT I (d. 639), Merovingian rule sank into indolence, cruelty, and dissipation. Gaul was depopulated, the cities were left in ruins, commerce was destroyed, and the arts and sciences were ignored. In the 8th cent. the only remnant of Roman civilization, the church, was threatened by extinction when the Saracens invaded Gaul. In the meantime a more rigorous dynasty, the CAROLINGIANS, had come to rule Austrasia as mayors of the palace in the name of the decadent Merovingian kings, and had united (687) Austrasia with Neustria. In 732, the Carolingian CHARLES MARTEL decisively defeated the Saracens between Poitiers and Tours. His son, PEPIN THE SHORT, dethroned the last Merovingian in 751 and proclaimed himself king with the sanction of the pope. Pepin's son was CHARLEMAGNE. Crowned emperor of the West in 800, Charlemagne expanded his lands by conquest. He gave his subjects an efficient administration, created an admirable legal system, and labored for the rebirth of learning, piety, and the arts. But his son, Emperor LOUIS I, could not maintain the empire he inherited. At Louis's death (840), his three sons were fighting each other. In 843 the brothers, CHARLES II (Charles the Bald), king of the West Franks, LOUIS THE GERMAN, and Emperor LOTHAIR I, redivided their territories (see VERDUN, TREATY OF). Charles was recognized as the ruler of the lands that are now France. The Carolingians had only superficially transcended the economic, social, and political fragmentation of the land. The weakness of central authority was a major reason for the development of FEUDALISM and the MANORIAL SYSTEM. Raids by NORSEMEN, beginning in the late 8th cent., contributed to the decline of royal authority; in 885-86, the Norsemen even besieged Paris. The authority of the kings was increasingly usurped by feudal lords. Among the most powerful of these were the dukes of AQUITAINE and of Burgundy and the counts of FLANDERS, of Toulouse, of BLOIS, and of Anjou. In 911 the Norse leader ROLLO was recognized as duke of Normandy. When the Carolingian dynasty died out in France, the nobles chose (987) HUGH CAPET as king. It is from this date that the history of France as a separate kingdom is generally reckoned. The early CAPETIANS were dukes of Francia, a small territory around Paris, and were without power in the rest of France. By unremitting effort they gradually extended their domain, razed the castles of robber barons, and held their own against the great feudatories. LOUIS VI (reigned 1108-37) brought this process into full force, and it was continued by LOUIS VII (1137-80). In the 11th cent. the towns had begun regaining population and wealth. Drawing together for their common defense (see COMMUNE), the townspeople won increasingly advantageous charters from the king and from their feudal lords. Commerce revived, and the great fairs of Champagne made France a meeting place for European merchants. The CLUNIAC ORDER and the revival of theological learning at Paris (which was to make the SORBONNE the fountainhead of SCHOLASTICISM) gave France tremendous prestige in Christendom. This rebirth reached its height in the 13th cent. and was aided by the leading role that France played in the CRUSADES. The crusaders established the French ideal of chivalry—personified in LOUIS IX (St. Louis)—in most of Europe. French courtly poetry and manners became European models. In England, French manners and culture also predominated among the nobles because of the Norman Conquest (1066). The fact that the Norman English kings were also French nobles, holding or claiming vast fiefs in France, brought the two nations into centuries of conflict. When HENRY II, king of England and duke of Normandy, married (1152) ELEANOR OF AQUITAINE, the divorced wife of Louis VII of France, Eleanor brought as her dowry extensive areas in France. Louis's successor, PHILIP II (Philip Augustus; 1180-1223), clashed repeatedly with Henry's sons, Richard I and John. Defeating John in 1204 and again, resoundingly, at BOUVINES (1214), Philip soundly established the military prestige of France. During Philip's reign a greater France emerged. The crusade against the ALBIGENSES (begun 1208) netted the crown the huge fiefs of the counts of Toulouse in S France, and the royal domain (directly subject to the king) now formed the larger part of the kingdom. Philip made the royal authority felt throughout the land. Paris was rebuilt. Louis IX (1226-70) organized an efficient and equitable civil and judicial system. Under PHILIP IV (1285-1314), the royal administration was improved even more. Philip failed to incorporate Flanders into his holdings, as the Flemish crushed the French at Courtrai (1302). To meet his revenue needs Philip taxed the clergy, summoning the first national STATES-GENERAL (1302) to support his policy. He also destroyed the wealthy KNIGHTS TEMPLARS. Papal objections to these moves led to the Babylonian Captivity (1309-77) of the popes (see PAPACY). Philip's son, LOUIS X, ruled briefly (1314-16); he was succeeded by two brothers, PHILIP V (1317-22) and CHARLES IV (1322-28). Within a few years after the death of Charles IV, who was also without a male heir, progress toward national unification was halted, and for more than a century France was rent by warfare and internal upheaval.

The Making of a Nation. In 1328, PHILIP VI (1328-50), of the house of VALOIS, a younger branch of the Capetians, succeeded to the throne. The succession was contested by Philip's remote cousin, EDWARD III of England (grandson of Philip IV), who in 1337 proclaimed himself king of France. Thus began the dynastic struggle known as the HUNDRED YEARS WAR (1337-1453), actually a series of wars and truces. It was complicated by many secondary issues, notably civil troubles in Flanders and the War of the BRETON SUCCESSION. The French defeats at CRÉCY (1346) and POITIERS (1356), the epidemic of the Black Death, the Parisian insurrection under Étienne MARCEL (1357-58), the JACQUERIE (peasant revolt) of 1358, and the pillaging bands of écorcheurs plunged France into anarchy and forced JOHN II (1350-64) to accept the humiliating Treaty of BRÉTIGNY (1360). Under CHARLES V (1364-80), however, Bertrand DU GUESCLIN recovered (1369-73) all lost territories except Calais and the Bordeaux region. CHARLES VI (1380-1422) went insane in 1392, although he had lucid intervals. Rivalry for power at court led to the terrible strife between ARMAGNACS AND BURGUNDIANS. In 1415, HENRY V of England revived the English claim, renewed the war, and crushed the French—unaided by the Burgundians—at AGINCOURT. In 1420, Charles VI made Henry V his heir, disinheriting his son, the dauphin, later CHARLES VII (see TROYES, TREATY OF). The dauphin nevertheless assumed the royal title in 1422, but his authority extended over only a small area. The English held most of France, including Paris. Powerful Burgundy, under PHILIP THE GOOD, was allied with England. In 1428 the English besieged the key city of Orléans. At this hour appeared JOAN OF ARC, who helped relieve Orléans, rallied the dauphin's followers, and in 1429 stood by the dauphin's side as he was crowned at Rheims. In 1435, Burgundy, although exacting exorbitant concessions, allied itself with France (see ARRAS, TREATY OF). In 1453 the English lost their last hold on French soil outside CALAIS. It was left for LOUIS XI (1461-83) to destroy the power of the last great feudal lords and to incorporate into the royal domain almost all of present France. He was aided by the downfall (1477) of CHARLES THE BOLD of Burgundy and by the extinction of the ANGEVIN dynasty. Brittany was united with France shortly afterward (see ANNE OF BRITTANY), and the larger part of the fiefs held by the BOURBON family was confiscated in 1527. Under the reigns (1483-1560) of CHARLES VIII, LOUIS XII, FRANCIS I, HENRY II, and FRANCIS II, France proved its amazing recuperative powers despite the heavy drain imposed on its resources by the ITALIAN WARS (1494-1559). The superficially brilliant reign of Francis I (1515-47) was taken up with almost constant warfare against the Hapsburg Charles V; however, this period also saw the spread of the Italian Renaissance into France (see FRENCH ART; FRENCH LITERATURE). The first phase of the struggle between France and the house of Hapsburg ended with the triumph of Hapsburg Spain in the Treaty of CATEAU-CAMBRÉSIS (1559). At the same time the Reformation was gaining many adherents in France (see HUGUENOTS). In 1560 religious conflict flared up in the first of the ferocious civil wars (see RELIGION, WARS OF) that tore France asunder during the reigns (1560-89) of the last Valois kings, CHARLES IX and HENRY III. The Catholics, led by the ambitious GUISE family, eventually formed the Catholic LEAGUE and obtained Spanish support against the Protestant Henry of Navarre, the legal heir of Henry III. Navarre was supported by some moderate Catholics as well as by the Protestants. He defeated the League but had to accept Catholicism before being allowed to enter (1594) Paris. Ruling as HENRY IV, he became the first Bourbon king of France. With his great minister, SULLY, he made France prosperous once again and encouraged French explorers in Canada. Religious freedom and political security for Protestants were promulgated in the Edict of Nantes (1598; see NANTES, EDICT OF), but after Henry's assassination (1610) by a Catholic fanatic the rights of the Huguenots were steadily reduced. Under his successor, LOUIS XIII (1610-43), and in the minority of Louis XIV, two great statesmen successively shaped the destiny of the kingdom—Cardinal RICHELIEU and Cardinal MAZARIN. They led France to victory in the THIRTY YEARS WAR (1618-48), which France entered openly in 1635, joining the Protestant allies against the Hapsburg powers, Austria and Spain. Austria was defeated in 1648 (see WESTPHALIA, PEACE OF), Spain in 1659 (see PYRENEES, PEACE OF THE). At home, Richelieu destroyed the political power of the Huguenots, and Mazarin overcame the nobles in the wars of the FRONDE. LOUIS XIV (1643-1715), aided by the genius of Jean Baptiste COLBERT (d. 1683) and François LOUVOIS, completed Richelieu's and Mazarin's work of centralization. Raising the position of the king to a dignity and prestige hitherto unknown in France, Louis XIV made France the first power in Europe and

RULERS OF FRANCE SINCE 987 *(including dates of reign)*

The Capetians

Hugh Capet, 987-96
Robert II (the Pious), son of Hugh Capet, 996-1031
Henry I, son of Robert II, 1031-60
Philip I, son of Henry I, 1060-1108
Louis VI (the Fat), son of Philip I, 1108-37
Louis VII (the Young), son of Louis VI, 1137-80
Philip II (Augustus), son of Louis VII, 1180-1223
Louis VIII, son of Philip II, 1223-26
Louis IX (Saint Louis), son of Louis VIII, 1226-70
Philip III (the Bold), son of Louis IX, 1270-85
Philip IV (the Fair), son of Philip III, 1285-1314
Louis X (the Quarrelsome), son of Philip IV, 1314-16
John I (the Posthumous), son of Louis X, 1316
Philip V (the Tall), son of Philip IV, 1317-22
Charles IV (the Fair), son of Philip IV, 1322-28

House of Valois

Philip VI, grandson of Philip III, 1328-50
John II (the Good), son of Philip VI, 1350-64
Charles V (the Wise), son of John II, 1364-80
Charles VI (the Mad or the Well Beloved), son of Charles V, 1380-1422
Charles VII (the Victorious or the Well Served), son of Charles VI, 1422-61
Louis XI, son of Charles VII, 1461-83
Charles VIII, son of Louis XI, 1483-98
Louis XII, descendant of Charles V, 1498-1515
Francis I, cousin and son-in-law of Louis XII, 1515-47
Henry II, son of Francis I, 1547-59
Francis II, son of Henry II, 1559-60
Charles IX, son of Henry II, 1560-74
Henry III, son of Henry II, 1574-89

House of Bourbon

Henry IV (of Navarre), descendant of Louis IX, 1589-1610
Louis XIII, son of Henry IV, 1610-43
Louis XIV, son of Louis XIII, 1643-1715
Louis XV, great-grandson of Louis XIV, 1715-74
Louis XVI, grandson of Louis XV, 1774-92

The First Republic

The National Convention, 1792-95
The Directory, 1795-99
The Consulate (Napoleon Bonaparte, First Consul, 1802-4), 1799-1804

The First Empire

Napoleon I (Napoleon Bonaparte), 1804-15

Bourbon Restoration

Louis XVIII, grandson of Louis XV, 1814-24
Charles X, grandson of Louis XV, 1824-30

House of Bourbon-Orléans

Louis Philippe, descendant of Louis XIII, 1830-48

The Second Republic

Louis Napoleon Bonaparte, nephew of Napoleon I, president, 1848-52

The Second Empire

Napoleon III (Louis Napoleon Bonaparte), 1852-70

The Third Republic (presidents)

Louis Jules Trochu (provisional), 1870-71
Adolphe Thiers, 1871-73
Marie Edmé Patrice de MacMahon, 1873-79
Jules Grévy, 1879-87
Sadi Carnot, 1887-94
Jean Paul Pierre Casimir-Périer, 1894-95
Félix Faure, 1895-99
Émile François Loubet, 1899-1906
Armand Fallières, 1906-13
Raymond Poincaré, 1913-20
Paul Eugène Louis Deschanel, 1920
Alexandre Millerand, 1920-24
Gaston Doumergue, 1924-31
Paul Doumer, 1931-32
Albert Lebrun, 1932-40

The Vichy Government

Henri Philippe Pétain, chief of state, 1940-44

The Provisional Government

Charles De Gaulle, president, 1944-46

The Fourth Republic (presidents)

Georges Bidault (provisional), 1946
Vincent Auriol, 1947-54
René Coty, 1954-58

The Fifth Republic (presidents)

Charles De Gaulle, 1958-69
Georges Pompidou, 1969-74
Valéry Giscard d'Estaing, 1974-

his court at VERSAILLES the cynosure of Europe. But his many wars undermined French finances, and his persecution of the Huguenots (the Edict of Nantes was revoked in 1685) caused serious harm to the economy as thousands of merchants and skilled workers left France. His successes in the War of DEVOLUTION (1667–68) against Spain and the Dutch War (see DUTCH WARS) of 1672–78 inspired all Europe with fear of French hegemony and resulted in the diplomatic isolation of France. The War of the GRAND ALLIANCE (1688–97) against Louis XIV began to turn the tide; the War of the SPANISH SUCCESSION (1701–14), although it did not end with a clear victory over France, marked the end of French expansion in Europe. The reign of Louis XIV saw the height of French power in America. France, at the end of Louis's reign, was exhausted from its attempt at primacy; yet its latent strength and wealth were so great that it recovered prosperity within a few years.

The Ancien Régime and the New France. LOUIS XV (1715–74) inherited a unified France, but a France still burdened by the remnants of feudalism. The "absolute" power of the king was hedged in by a stupendous multitude of dusty charters and special privileges—often granted to remove the recipients from national politics—held by families, guilds, monopolies, communes, and provinces, and by the clergy and nobles. Taxes, although onerous, were raised inefficiently and inequitably, partly by the farmers general (see FARMING, in taxation), partly by the state. Commerce, based on MERCANTILISM, was hampered by restrictive regulations, monopolies, and internal tariff barriers. Rural overpopulation outstripped the stagnant agricultural productivity. Colbert had reorganized the administration by curtailing the power of the provincial governors and by reestablishing the administrative units called intendancies, originated by Richelieu. The intendants were trusted civil servants who carried out the policies of the central government, but their capacity to break down local privilege was limited. In several provinces, notably Brittany, the local assemblies of the three estates retained the power to thwart reforms. A more significant stronghold of aristocratic privilege and vested interests was the PARLEMENT; the parlements skillfully related their special interests to the still popular ideal of local liberty. The ever-expanding bourgeoisie as well as the large body of landowning farmers, however, were finding the remnants of feudal dues, services, and other customs increasingly intolerable. Economic reform became the rallying cry of the PHYSIOCRATS and their disciples such as TURGOT. Many philosophers of the ENLIGHTENMENT, notably VOLTAIRE, looked hopefully to the monarchy for administrative rationalization, but the crown's sporadic attempts at reform, particularly of finances, were hindered by the parlements. Operating under a system of outworn privilege, the wealthiest country in Europe was ruled by a government perennially on the verge of bankruptcy. The honest administration (1726–43) of Cardinal FLEURY had barely extricated France from the disastrous failure of the MISSISSIPPI SCHEME (1720), when Louis XV plunged into the War of the AUSTRIAN SUCCESSION (1740–48) and the SEVEN YEARS WAR (1756–63). Not only was the treasury drained, but France lost its empire in India and North America. Turgot's reforms, instituted early in the reign of LOUIS XVI (1774–92), were cut short in 1776, when he was dismissed. Seeking to avenge its defeat by Britain in the Seven Years War, France supported the American Revolution (1775–83). Financially the war was a disaster for France. In 1788, after neither CALONNE nor LOMÉNIE DE BRIENNE could get the necessary financial measures enacted, NECKER was called back to office to attempt to repair the irreparable, and the States-General were convoked for the first time since 1614. Thus began the upheaval that shook Europe from 1789 to 1815 (see FRENCH REVOLUTION; FRENCH REVOLUTIONARY WARS; DIRECTORY; CONSULATE; NAPOLEON I). The States-General were transformed into the National Assembly (1789); a constitutional monarchy was created (1791); war with much of Europe began, accompanied by violence and the growth of radical factions in France (1792); the king and queen were beheaded (1793); ROBESPIERRE presided over the REIGN OF TERROR (1793–95) until his own execution; and a reaction ushered in the Directory (1795–99), terminated by Napoleon Bonaparte's coup d'etat. Napoleon made himself emperor (1804) and led his armies as far as Moscow. After his defeat at Waterloo (1815) virtually nothing remained for France from the Napoleonic conquests except the basis for a powerful legend. But Napoleonic administration and law (see CODE NAPOLÉON) left a permanent impact on France. From the ancien régime there reemerged the church (1801 Concordat with the Vatican) and an aristocracy less affluent and shorn of its feudal privileges but still influential.

Modern France. The French Revolution and Napoleon established a uniform, modern administrative system, gave land tenure to the peasants, and left to the bourgeoisie a political heritage that they quickly reclaimed. The Congress of Vienna (1814–15; see VIENNA, CONGRESS OF) restored the borders of 1790 and recognized LOUIS XVIII as France's legitimate sovereign. The king granted a moderately liberal charter but took France into the reactionary HOLY ALLIANCE. His successor, CHARLES X (1824–30), was the champion of the ultraroyalists. Charles's efforts to restore absolutism led to the JULY REVOLUTION of 1830, which enthroned LOUIS PHILIPPE. The July Monarchy was a frank plutocracy run by the upper bourgeoisie. Under the "citizen king," France conquered Algeria (1830–38). The regime became increasingly autocratic, disregarding the plight of the new urban proletariat. Brought low by the unpopularity of the ministry of GUIZOT and by economic depression (1846–47), it fell in the FEBRUARY REVOLUTION of 1848. The revolution was at first distinctly radical, but the bourgeoisie triumphed in the JUNE DAYS. In Dec., 1848, Louis Napoleon Bonaparte, nephew of Napoleon I, was elected president of the Second Republic. In 1852, by a coup d'etat, he extended his term and then proclaimed himself emperor as NAPOLEON III. He emulated his uncle's autocratic regime at home and carried on a confused foreign policy with unrewarding wars (in Russia, Italy, and Mexico). The Second Empire was, however, a period of colonial expansion (in Senegal and Indochina) and of material prosperity. In 1869, Napoleon instituted a more liberal regime with a parliamentary government. But the empire ended disastrously in the FRANCO-PRUSSIAN WAR (1870–71), in which Alsace and Lorraine were lost to Germany until 1918. The Third Republic (1870–1940) was proclaimed after Napoleon III was captured by the Prussians. After the bloody suppression of the COMMUNE OF PARIS (1871) by the right-wing provisional government under Adolphe THIERS, Marshal MACMAHON, a royalist sympathizer, was elected president (1873). But for the intransigence of Henri, comte de Chambord (the legitimist pretender), France might again have become a monarchy. A republican constitution was finally adopted in 1875. As the various parties combined, separated, and recombined into political blocs, new cabinets followed in quick succession. The 1880s witnessed the expansion of railroads and public education; the latter revived the age-old quarrel in France between church and state. In 1905, after other issues had been added to the dispute, church and state were separated by law. After the rapid rise and fall (1888–89) of General BOULANGER, the stability of France was once more shaken by the DREYFUS AFFAIR (begun 1894), which discredited monarchists and reactionaries and brought anticlerical, moderate leftists to power. Socialism, led by GUESDE and JAURÈS, was now a major political force but was weakened by internal dissensions. In foreign policy the years before 1914 were marked by continued colonial expansion in Africa (Morocco, Tunisia, West Africa, Madagascar) and Indochina, bringing conflict with Great Britain (see FASHODA INCIDENT) and with Germany (see MOROCCO). Eventually, France, England, and Russia allied themselves to balance the German-Austrian-Italian combination (see TRIPLE ALLIANCE AND TRIPLE ENTENTE). In World War I, France bore the brunt of the ground fighting in the west. CLEMENCEAU was France's outstanding leader. At the Paris Peace Conference (see VERSAILLES, TREATY OF) France obtained heavy German reparations and the right to occupy the left bank of the Rhine for 15 years. When reparations payments were defaulted, France occupied the RUHR (1923–25). Outstanding among French political figures of the 1920s were POINCARÉ, HERRIOT, and BRIAND. In the middle of the decade relations with Germany improved (see LOCARNO PACT). The depression of the 1930s was aggravated by the immobile economic policies of the government, and political complacency was rocked by the STAVISKY AFFAIR (1934). The Popular Front, a coalition, led by Léon BLUM, of Socialists, Radical Socialists, and Communists, won the elections of 1936; Popular Front governments (1936–38) enacted important social and labor reforms before being overturned by conservative opposition. After Blum's fall, Édouard DALADIER assented to the appeasement policy toward Nazi Germany, Fascist Italy, and Spain favored by Britain and made France a party to the MUNICH PACT (1938). After the outbreak (1939) of World War II he was replaced by Paul REYNAUD. In May–June, 1940, France was ignominiously defeated by Germany. Marshal PÉTAIN became head of the VICHY GOVERNMENT of unoccupied France (other Vichy leaders were LAVAL and DARLAN), which became a German tool, while Gen. Charles DE GAULLE proclaimed, from London, the continued resistance of the "Free French." The Allied invasion (Nov., 1942) of North Africa resulted (1943) in the establishment of a provisional Free French government at Algiers and in the complete German occupation of metropolitan France. De Gaulle's government moved to Paris after the city was liberated (Aug., 1944). By the end of 1944 the Allies, with heroic aid from the French resistance, had expelled the Germans from France. German occupation had been costly and oppressive. Thousands had been executed, and hundreds of thousands made slave laborers in Germany. The liberation campaign itself caused much destruction. Although reduced in power and prestige, France became one of the five great powers in the United Nations and shared in the occupation of Germany. De Gaulle became provisional president. The Fourth Republic was officially proclaimed in 1946; the new constitution reorganized the empire as the FRENCH UNION and was otherwise quite similar to that of the Third Republic. In the immediate postwar years the Communists, the moderate Mouvement Républicain Populaire, founded by Georges BIDAULT, and the Socialists were the strongest of the many political parties; the pattern of short-lived coalitions reappeared. Banks and major industries were nationalized. American aid (see MARSHALL PLAN) helped rebuild the shattered economy. To further economic recovery and begin the political integration of Europe, France participated in creating the institutions of the EUROPEAN COMMUNITY, most notably the COMMON MARKET. French military resources were committed to the West by adherence to the NORTH ATLANTIC TREATY ORGANIZATION (NATO). France sent thousands of soldiers to INDOCHINA in an attempt to defeat the nationalist-communist movement led by the Vietnamese Ho Chi Minh. The effort collapsed with the French defeat at DIENBIENPHU (May, 1954). Pierre MENDÈS-FRANCE came to power, determined to end French involvement. French withdrawal from Indochina was agreed upon at the GENEVA CONFERENCE. Subsequently Morocco and Tunisia also achieved independence. But the war for independence in ALGERIA destroyed the Fourth Republic. When a right-wing French military coup in Algeria (1958) threatened to spread to metropolitan France, De Gaulle was invited back to power. De Gaulle established the Fifth Republic and became its first president (Dec., 1958). The French Union was transformed into the FRENCH COMMUNITY, and most of France's African holdings became independent by 1960. Algerian independence was negotiated despite a terrorist campaign by the Secret Army Organization (OAS) of extremist French soldiers. De Gaulle aimed at restoring France's prestige in world affairs. France became a nuclear power (1960). France blocked Britain's entrance into the Common Market and for a time (1965) boycotted the Market's meetings. Diplomatic recognition was extended (1964) to Communist China. In 1966, De Gaulle withdrew French forces from the integrated command of NATO and forced all U.S. and NATO forces to leave France. In the spring of 1968 widespread student demonstrations against France's obsolete educational system were joined by striking workers and farmers. De Gaulle dissolved the national assembly, and, blaming the Communists for the disorders, won a great electoral victory (June, 1968). The Gaullist party won the first absolute majority in the assembly in French history. But De Gaulle resigned in April, 1969, after his proposals for regional reorganization and for revision of the senate were defeated in a referendum. Georges Pompidou was elected president in June. Later in the year the franc was devalued. In 1971, Pompidou reversed French policy and declared support for Britain's entrance into the Common Market. In the 1973 elections Pompidou retained a majority in the assembly, although it was greatly reduced. Pompidou died in April, 1974, and was succeeded as president by Valéry Giscard d'Estaing, his finance minister, who defeated Socialist leader François Mitterand in a close runoff election in May, 1974.

Bibliography. A fine geographic study is Jean Brunhes, *Géographie humaine de la France* (2 vol., 1920–26), and E. E. Evans, *France* (1966), is also useful. Jules MICHELET is still regarded by many as the greatest of French historians. Among recent general histories of France, those edited by Ernest LAVISSE and by Gabriel HANOTAUX are outstanding. A monumental multivolume work is Frantz Funck-Brentano, ed., *National History of France* (tr., 10 vol., 1916–36). A short general history is A. L. Guérard, *France, a Modern History* (rev. and enl. ed. 1969). The many authors of classic historical works on France include, for the medieval period, M. L. BLOCH, C. V. Langlois, Ferdinand Lot, Achille LUCHAIRE, and FUSTEL DE COULANGES; for the 17th cent., VOLTAIRE; for the French Revolution and Napoleon I, Hippolyte TAINE, Alphonse AULARD, Georges LEFEBVRE, Albert MATHIEZ, and Frédéric MASSON; for the history of the working class and of commerce, Émile LEVASSEUR; for cultural history, Alfred RAMBAUD. See Alfred Cobban, *A History of Modern France* (3d ed., 3 vol., 1966–67); D. M. Pickles, *The Fifth French Republic* (3d ed. 1966) and *France* (2d ed. 1971); J. P. Bury, *France, 1814–1940* (4th ed. 1969); J. M. Hughes, *To the Maginot Line* (1971); Philippe Alexandre, *The Duel: De Gaulle and Pompidou* (tr. 1972); H. D. Clout, *The Geography of Post-War France: A Social and Economic Approach* (1972); W. L. Kohl, *French Nuclear Diplomacy* (1972); Annie Kriegel, *The French Communists* (tr. 1972); Philip Ouston, *France in the Twentieth Century* (1972); P. M. Williams, *Crisis and Compromise: Politics in the Fourth Republic* (3d ed. 1972) and, with Martin Harrison, *Politics and Society in De Gaulle's Republic* (1972); R. O. Paxton, *Vichy France* (1972).

Francesca, Piero della: see PIERO DELLA FRANCESCA.

Francesca da Rimini (frănchĕs'kä dä rē'mēnē), fl. 13th cent., Italian beauty, daughter of Guido da Polenta of Ravenna. She was married by proxy to the hunchbacked lord of Rimini, Gianciotto Malatesta; the proxy, Gianciotto's young and handsome brother Paolo, became Francesca's lover. Gianciotto, discovering their guilt, killed them. The story is immortalized in Dante's *Divine Comedy* and is the subject of many other literary and artistic works and of Tchaikovsky's symphonic poem.

Franceschi, Piero de': see PIERO DELLA FRANCESCA.

Franceschini, Baldassare (bäldäs-sä'rä frănchăskē'nē), 1611–89, Florentine painter; pupil of his father, who was a sculptor. He was also called Volterrano. His works include the *Coronation of the Virgin,* a fresco in the dome of the Church of the Annunziata, Florence; paintings in the Niccolini Chapel, Church of Santa Croce, Florence; and *St. John the Evangelist* (Church of Santa Chiara, Volterra).

Franceschini, Marcantonio (märkäntô'nyō), 1648–1729, Italian painter of the Bolognese school. After working as Carlo Cignani's assistant for more than 10 years, Franceschini developed an independent style about 1680. For the next two decades he executed many large-scale decorations in northern Italy, among them the three large frescoes in the tribune of San Bartolomeo, Bologna (1691–92) and the ceiling decoration of the palace, Modena (1696).

Francesco di Stefano: see PESELLINO, IL.

Frances Xavier Cabrini, Saint: see CABRINI, SAINT FRANCES XAVIER.

Franche-Comté (fräNsh-kôNtā') or **Free County of Burgundy,** region and former province, E France. It is coextensive with Haute-Saône, Doubs, and Jura depts. Dôle was the capital until 1676; BESANÇON was the later capital and remains the chief city. Other important towns are MONTBÉLIARD, LONS-LE-SAUNIER, and SAINT-CLAUDE. The Jura mts. form the region's eastern border with Switzerland; the Vosges mts. are in the north. The chief rivers are the Doubs and the upper Saône. Franche-Comté is largely an agricultural region and has a large dairy industry. Livestock is raised in the Jura district, where there are dense pine forests and extensive grazing lands. Clocks, watches, machines, and plastics are the leading industrial products. The region was occupied by the Celtic tribe of the Sequani (4th cent. B.C.) and was conquered by Julius Caesar (52 B.C.). Overrun by the Burgundians (5th cent.), it was included in the First Kingdom of BURGUNDY and was annexed by the Franks in 534. The territory was united in the 9th cent. as the Free County of Burgundy, or Franche-Comté, a fief held from the kings of Transjurane Burgundy, who were later (933–1032) kings of ARLES. Franche-Comté passed to the Holy Roman Empire in 1034; but the allegiance was tenuous, and for six and a half centuries Franche-Comté was perpetually invaded and contested by France, Germany, Burgundy, Switzerland, and Spain. Philip the Bold, duke of Burgundy, acquired Franche-Comté through his marriage to Margaret of Flanders in 1369. After the defeat and death of Charles the Bold (1477), the region passed to Archduke Maximilian of Austria (later Emperor Maximilian I), who in turn gave it to his son Philip I of Spain. Governed by native officials and its PARLEMENT at Dôle, Franche-Comté enjoyed relative autonomy under the Spanish crown. At the end of Charles V's reign (1556), Franche-Comté became a possession of the Spanish Hapsburgs. Although some of the region's fortified towns were occupied by France during the Wars of Religion (16th cent.), peace and prosperity continued until the Thirty Years War (1618–48), when the region was ravaged by both Catholics and Protestants. Louis XIV conquered Franche-Comté in 1668 and again in 1674 and finally obtained its cession from Spain. Although the parlement continued to function after its transfer to Besançon (1676), the provincial assembly was abolished, and Franche-Comté became an integral part of France.

Franchet d'Esperey, Louis Félix Marie François (lwē fālĕks' mărē' fräNswä' fräNshā' dāpərā'), 1856–1942, marshal of France. He commanded the French 5th army in the battle of the Marne in 1914, the eastern army in 1916, and the northern army in 1917. In June, 1918, he took command at Thessaloníki, where the Allies were stalled. There, he brilliantly accomplished the defeat of the Bulgarian armies and led the Allies to victory in the Balkans. He was made a marshal of France in 1921 and was elected to the French Academy in 1934.

franchise, in government, a right specifically conferred on a group or individual by a government, especially the privilege conferred by a municipality on a corporation of operating public utilities, such as electricity, telephone, and bus services. Franchises may not be revoked without the consent of the grantee unless so stipulated in the contract. They may, however, be forfeited by the grantee's violation of terms, and the government may take back granted rights by eminent domain proceedings with tender of just compensation. Franchise provisions usually include tenure; compensation to the grantor; the services, rates, and extensions; labor and strike regulations; capitalization; and reversion to the grantor. In politics, the franchise is the right conferred on an individual to vote. In the United States, the states, with some restrictions by the Federal Constitution, govern the qualifications of voters. By the Fourteenth and Fifteenth amendments, states were forbidden to deny suffrage to male residents over 21 years of age "on account of race, color, or previous condition of servitude." The Nineteenth Amendment conferred suffrage upon women, and the Twenty-fifth Amendment lowered the voting age to 18. See VOTING. See Chilton Williamson, *American Suffrage from Property to Democracy, 1760–1860* (1960, repr. 1968); C. L. Vaughn, *Franchising* (1974).

Francia (frän'chä), c.1450–1517, Italian painter, goldsmith, and medalist of the early Bolognese school, whose real name was Francesco Raibolini. Until the age of 40 he was famous chiefly as a goldsmith and engraver of nielli and of dies for medals. His paintings reflect the influence of Perugino and Raphael. Among the most noted are *Crucifixion* (Louvre); *Pietà* (National Gall., London); and *Assumption* (Church of San Frediano, Lucca). Others include *Head of the Virgin* (Pa. Acad. of the Fine Arts); *Madonna* (Gardner Mus., Boston); a portrait of Federigo Gonzaga (Metropolitan Mus.); and *Madonna and Child* (National Gall. of Art, Washington, D.C.). See study by G. C. Williamson (1907).

Francia, José Gaspar Rodríguez (hōsā' gäspär' rōthrē'gās frän'syä), 1766–1840, dictator of Paraguay and creator of its national independence, known as El Supremo. Incorruptible and of superior cultural attainments for his epoch, he took part in the bloodless revolution against Spain (1811), was first consul, declared himself dictator in 1814, and ruled until his death. He limited the power of the church and kept the aristocracy in subjection. He was harsh with his enemies and intransigent with foreigners. Cutting off Paraguay from the rest of the world and limiting trade to his personal supervision, he gained international ill will but effectively stimulated the growth of local industry and agriculture. See contemporary study by J. R. Rengger and M. F. X. Longchamp (tr. 1827, repr. 1971); J. P. and W. P. R. Robertson, *Letters from Paraguay* (3 vol., 1839, repr. 1970).

Francis, Saint, or **Saint Francis of Assisi** (əsē'zē), 1182?–1226, founder of the Franciscans, one of the greatest Christian saints, b. Assisi, Umbria, Italy. His baptismal name was Giovanni (John), his father's name was Pietro de Bernardone; from his birth Giovanni di Bernardone was called Francesco (Francis) [Ital., =Frenchman], because his father was a frequent traveler in France. The name Francis (and its equivalents in other languages) owes its great popularity to St. Francis, for before him it was a name rarely given. Pietro de Bernardone was a wealthy merchant, and his son's early life was ordinary. At the age of 20, however, Francis was taken prisoner in a battle between Assisi and Perugia and spent a year in prison in Perugia. Two years after his return he set out for the wars in Apulia, but illness forced him home again. He then underwent a conversion that turned him from the worldly life he had been leading. He became markedly devout and ascetic, began dressing in rags, and went on a pilgrimage to Rome (1206). A series of events at that time revealed strikingly the characteristics that Francis was always to exemplify: humility, love of absolute poverty, singular devotion to other men, and joyous religious fervor. In 1209, as he was hearing Mass, the words of Jesus in the Gospel (Mat. 10.7-10) bidding his apostles to go forth on their mission struck Francis as a call. So he set out, still a layman, to preach; when a little group had gathered about him, they went to Rome to see Pope INNOCENT III, who gave them oral permission to live in the manner Francis had chosen. Thus began the Franciscan order of friars, an entirely new type of order in the church. They wandered about Umbria and through Italy preaching the Gospel, working to pay for their very simple needs. The expansion of the friars was amazing. In 1212 St. CLARE began to follow St. Francis, and the Poor Clares (Second Order of St. Francis) were established. Francis not only sent the brothers abroad but went himself—to Dalmatia, to France, to Spain, and in 1219–20 to the Holy Land. On his way to Palestine he stopped at Damietta and preached to the sultan. A growing dissension in his order recalled him from Palestine, and after his return (1221) a great assembly was held at the little chapel of the Porziuncola near Assisi, with which Francis's career was closely identified. There the saint gave up active leadership of the order, for he felt it had become too unwieldy to command. He continued his preaching and the composition of his rule and sponsored the Franciscan tertiaries (Third Order of St. Francis). Two years before his death (1224) the most famous event of his life occurred. He received the STIGMATA; as he prayed on the Monte della Verna, he had a vision and was afflicted with the wounds of the Crucifixion, from which he suffered for the rest of his life. It is the first known appearance of the stigmata, one of the best attested, and the only one that is celebrated liturgically (on Sept. 17) in the Western Church. Francis died Oct. 3, 1226, and was mourned throughout the country. Two years later Pope Gregory IX, who had been his patron and friend, canonized him; his feast is Oct. 4. The sources for the life of St. Francis are two lives by THOMAS OF CELANO and the biography by St. Bonaventure. Later medieval works are the *Legenda trium sociorum*, the *Sacrum commercium*, and the *Speculum perfectionis.* The Italian *Fioretti di San Francesco* [little flowers of St. Francis], a series of short anecdotes, has always been popular for its picture of St. Francis and his companions. It exemplifies in simplest form his love of nature and of man, a love so great that he preached one time to the sparrows at Alviano (he is often depicted in art preaching to the birds). His spirit also breathes in the *Cantico del sole* [hymn of the sun], which he may have written, and in the rules for his orders. Artistic and literary representations of St. Francis are innumerable; see Laurence Cunningham, comp., *Brother Francis* (1972); biography by J. H. Smith (1972); study by E. A. Armstrong (1973).

Francis I, 1708–65, Holy Roman emperor (1745–65), duke of Lorraine (1729–37) as Francis Stephen, grand duke of Tuscany (1737–65), husband of Archduchess MARIA THERESA. He succeeded his father in Lorraine, but agreed (1735) to cede his duchy to STANISLAUS I of Poland to end the War of the Polish Succession (see POLISH SUCCESSION, WAR OF THE); in exchange he received the right of succession to Tuscany. In 1736 he married Maria Theresa, heiress of all Hapsburg lands. Francis succeeded (1737) the last Medici ruler of Tuscany and carried out several long-needed reforms. In 1740, Maria Theresa acceded to her inheritance, which was immediately contested in the War of the Austrian Succession (see AUSTRIAN SUCCESSION, WAR OF THE; 1740–48) by an alliance under FREDERICK II of Prussia. The election (Sept., 1745) of Francis to succeed CHARLES VII as emperor was recognized by Frederick in the Treaty of Dresden (Dec., 1745) with Maria Theresa. Francis I governed little; the real rulers were Maria Theresa and chancellor KAUNITZ. Founder of the house of Hapsburg-Lorraine, Francis was succeeded as Holy Roman emperor by his eldest son, Joseph II, and as grand duke of Tuscany by his younger son, Leopold (later Holy Roman Emperor Leopold II).

Francis II, 1768–1835, last Holy Roman emperor (1792–1806), first emperor of Austria as Francis I (1804–35), king of Bohemia and of Hungary (1792–1835). He succeeded his father, Leopold II, shortly before the outbreak of war with France (see FRENCH

REVOLUTIONARY WARS). Francis's armies were eventually defeated by Napoleon Bonaparte; by the Treaty of CAMPO FORMIO (1797) Francis ceded the left bank of the Rhine to France but obtained Venetia and Dalmatia. In 1798 he joined the Second Coalition against France, was again defeated, and in the Treaty of Lunéville (1801) consented to the virtual dissolution of the HOLY ROMAN EMPIRE, which was formally ended (1806) after the Austrian rout at AUSTERLITZ (see also PRESSBURG, TREATY OF). Francis assumed the title emperor of Austria in 1804. In 1809 he again declared war on Napoleon, now Emperor NAPOLEON I, who was embroiled in difficulties in Spain. Francis's brother, Archduke CHARLES, defeated Napoleon at Aspern, but was crushed at Wagram. Napoleon entered Vienna and imposed on Francis the Peace of Schönbrunn, in which Austria was forced to give up Galicia, Istria, and part of Dalmatia, and to join Napoleon's CONTINENTAL SYSTEM. In 1810, Francis's daughter, MARIE LOUISE, married Napoleon. This marriage was engineered by METTERNICH, who from 1809 dominated Austrian politics. In Aug., 1813, Francis joined Russia, Prussia, and England in their war against Napoleon. He presided (1814-15) over the Congress of Vienna (see VIENNA, CONGRESS OF), in which Austria, through Metternich's diplomacy, emerged as the leading power in Europe. Francis was a chief architect of the HOLY ALLIANCE. The events of his early reign shaped his later reactionary views, and he instituted severe repressive measures throughout the empire. Francis was succeeded by his son FERDINAND. See biography by W. C. Langsam (1949).

Francis I, emperor of Austria: see FRANCIS II, Holy Roman emperor.

Francis I, 1494-1547, king of France (1515-47), known as Francis of Angoulême before he succeeded his cousin and father-in-law, King Louis XII. He resumed the ITALIAN WARS, beginning his reign with the recovery of Milan through the brilliant victory at Marignano (1515). A candidate for the Holy Roman emperor's crown (1519), he was defeated by CHARLES V, king of Spain, whose supremacy in Europe Francis was to contest in four wars. In 1520, Francis tried to secure the support of King Henry VIII of England against the emperor in the interview on the FIELD OF THE CLOTH OF GOLD. Although no agreement was reached, Francis began his first war against the emperor (1521-25). He was defeated at La Bicocca (1522) and at Pavia (1525), where he was captured. Francis regained his freedom by consenting to the Treaty of Madrid (1526); he renounced his claims in Italy, agreed to surrender Burgundy to Charles, and abandoned his suzerainty over Flanders and Artois. Resolved to violate a treaty signed under duress, Francis created the League of Cognac (1526) with Pope Clement VII, Henry VIII, Venice, and Florence, and commenced his second war (1527-29) against Charles. It ended, unfavorably for Francis, with the Treaty of Cambrai (see CAMBRAI, TREATY OF), which left Burgundy to France but otherwise duplicated the Treaty of Madrid. Francis fulfilled its terms until 1535, when the death of the duke of Milan, Francisco Sforza, opened the question of the Milanese succession. In a third attempt to regain Milan, Francis invaded (1536) Italy. Charles retaliated by invading Provence, and in 1538 a 10-year truce was arranged at Nice. In 1542, with the support of the Turkish sultan SULAYMAN I, Francis for the fourth time attacked the emperor, who allied himself (1543) with Henry VIII. Their invasion of France resulted (1544) in the Treaty of Crépy, in which Francis relinquished his claims to Naples, Flanders, and Artois. Peace with England (1546) confirmed the loss of Boulogne. Despite Francis's military failures, his reign had some notable achievements, including a CONCORDAT with the papacy and an alliance with Switzerland (both in 1516). Jacques Cartier, exploring the coast of North America for Francis, established French interest in Canada. In domestic affairs, Francis expanded the absolutism of the monarchy. Government affairs were dominated by successive personal favorites, including Anne, duc de MONTMORENCY, and Francis's mistresses. LOUISE OF SAVOY, the king's mother, was also influential. Francis's persecution of the WALDENSES (1545), his ruinous expenditures for foreign wars, and the prodigality of his court foreshadowed some aspects of the reign of King Louis XIV. In Francis's reign the French Renaissance saw its fullest development. Leonardo da Vinci, Benvenuto Cellini, and Andrea del Sarto worked at his court. Francis and his sister, MARGARET OF NAVARRE, were the patrons of François RABELAIS, Clément MAROT, and Guillaume BUDÉ; Francis also founded the COLLÈGE DE FRANCE. The most permanent monuments of Francis's reign are the châteaus of the Loire, notably Chambord, and the royal residence at FONTAINEBLEAU. He was succeeded by his son, Henry II. See biographies by Francis Hackett (1935, repr. 1968) and Desmond Seward (1973).

Francis II, 1544-60, king of France (1559-60), son of King Henry II and Catherine de' Medici. He married (1558) Mary Queen of Scots (Mary Stuart), and during his brief reign the government was in the hands of her uncles, François and Charles de GUISE. Their ruthless persecution of Protestantism led to the conspiracy of Amboise (1560; see AMBOISE, CONSPIRACY OF), an attempt to remove the Guises from power. During Francis's reign French Protestantism became a political force (see HUGUENOTS). Francis was succeeded by his brother, Charles IX.

Francis I, 1777-1830, king of the Two Sicilies (1825-30), son and successor of Ferdinand I. He continued the ruthless and reactionary policy of his father, and his court was notorious for waste and corruption. He was succeeded by his son Ferdinand II.

Francis II, 1836-94, last king of the Two Sicilies (1859-61), son and successor of Ferdinand II. A weak ruler, he let his ministers follow his father's reactionary policy. Faced with the growing movement for Italian unity (see RISORGIMENTO), he first sided with Austria. When he sought the alliance of Victor Emmanuel II of Sardinia, around whom the movement for Italian unification had coalesced, it was too late—GARIBALDI had conquered Sicily and was marching (1860) on Naples. Francis fled to Gaeta. There he and his queen, Maria of Bavaria (sister of Empress Elizabeth of Austria), resisted gallantly until 1861, when they surrendered to Victor Emmanuel. They went into exile, at first in Rome, then in Paris and the Tyrol.

Francis, 1554-84, French prince, duke of Alençon and Anjou; youngest son of King Henry II of France and Catherine de' Medici. Although ill-shapen, pockmarked, and endowed with a curiously formed nose, he was considered (1572-73) as a possible husband for Queen Elizabeth I of England. During the Wars of Religion (see RELIGION, WARS OF), he opposed the anti-Protestant policy of his mother and conspired with Huguenots and moderate Catholics against his mother and his brother, King Charles IX. By the peace of 1576, which ended the fifth war of religion, he obtained the appanages of Anjou, Touraine, and Berry. He led (1578) an expedition into the Netherlands, which was then in rebellion against Spain. In the same year, he was again prominent as Elizabeth's suitor. Offered (1580) the rule of the Low Countries by William the Silent, leader of the rebellious states, he led a new invasion and was for a time the ruler of several provinces, but in 1583 was compelled to withdraw. His death opened the French succession to Henry of Navarre (later King Henry IV).

Francis II, 1435-88, duke of Brittany. He succeeded (1458) his uncle Arthur III. In his struggle with the French crown for the independence of his duchy, Francis entered (1465) the League of the Public Weal against King LOUIS XI and invaded Normandy in 1467. Though forced to sign the Peace of Ancenis (1468), he continued to plot against Louis. In 1484 he joined in a rebellion against Louis's successor, King Charles VIII, but was decisively defeated in 1488. After Francis's death his daughter, ANNE OF BRITTANY, was married to Charles VIII.

Francis, David Rowland, 1850-1927, U.S. Secretary of the Interior (1896-97), b. Richmond, Ky. He established a large grain business in St. Louis, entered politics, and served (1885-89) as mayor in a reform administration and later (1889-93) as governor of Missouri. As a member of President Cleveland's cabinet, he obtained a presidential proclamation setting aside millions of acres as forest reserves. Francis was a leading promoter and official of the Louisiana Purchase Exposition of 1903-4. He became ambassador to Russia in 1916 and remained at his post after the Russian Revolution in efforts to keep Russia united with the Allies. He wrote *Russia from the American Embassy* (1921, repr. 1970); his memoirs and letters were published in 1928.

Francis, Sir Philip, 1740-1818, British statesman and pamphleteer. He may have been the author known as JUNIUS. He held several minor posts in government offices before being appointed to the council of Bengal in 1773. While in India he conducted a long, bitter feud with Warren HASTINGS, which culminated in a duel in 1780 in which Francis was wounded. He returned to England the following year, became a member of Parliament in 1784, and took an active part in the impeachment proceedings against Hastings. An advocate of various political reforms and the advancement of individual liberty, he contributed articles to periodicals and wrote numerous pamphlets.

Francis, Sam, 1923-, American painter, b. San Mateo, Calif. Educated in medicine, Francis began painting while recovering from an injury received in World War II. His mural-sized paintings are stained with brilliant, transparent oil color. Small areas of color are concentrated irregularly over a canvas that is largely white. In his later works the use of color is confined to the sides of the canvas.

Francis Borgia, Saint (bôr′jə), 1510-72, Spanish Roman Catholic reformer, third general of the Jesuits (see JESUS, SOCIETY OF). He was a member of the famous BORGIA family, a great-grandson of Pope Alexander VI, and cousin to Holy Roman Emperor Charles V. In 1528 he was received at the imperial court and at that time he witnessed St. Ignatius Loyola being taken to prison. This incident was to have great significance for him. He became duke of Gandia in 1543. After the death of his wife he resolved to become a Jesuit and went (1550) to St. Ignatius in Rome. He resigned his duchy by transferring his title and estates to his eldest son, and in 1551 became ordained. He provided the money to the Society for the building of the Roman College. He and St. Ignatius became close co-workers. The "duke turned Jesuit" became the talk of all Spain and he was called to preach in many cities. His example made a deep impression everywhere, and he was responsible for many high-born youths joining the order. In 1554 as commissary-general of the Society in Spain, he was given charge of all Jesuit missions. By 1566 he had founded missions in the New World. In 1565 he succeeded Lainez as master-general of the order. He published the rules for the order and established in Rome and elsewhere houses of study under his rule. Feast: Oct. 10. See Margaret Yeo, *The Greatest of the Borgias* (1936).

Franciscans (frănsĭs′kənz), members of several Roman Catholic religious orders following the rule of St. FRANCIS (approved by Honorius III, 1223). There are now three organizations of Franciscan friars: the Friars Minor (formerly called Observants), the second largest order in the church [Lat. abbr., O.F.M.]; the Friars Minor Capuchin (see CAPUCHINS), the third largest of the great religious orders; and the Friars Minor Conventual [Lat. abbr., O.M.C.]. Within 50 years of St. Francis's foundation, the order had a very strong wing of zealots—the Spirituals, who deplored the convents and any settled life. They allied themselves with the anarchical monks who were preaching the teachings of JOACHIM OF FLORIS. St. Bonaventure tried to reconcile the factions of the order, but the Spirituals grew stronger and saw one of their heroes made pope as St. CELESTINE V. His abdication made their agitation one of the major social and religious problems of Italy. So far as the order was concerned, John XXII settled (1322) the matter by putting the Franciscans on a level with every other order with respect to owning property corporately. He also put a stop (1323) to a Franciscan boast that their way was more nearly perfect than any other. However, within the order there still remained a desire for reform, and in the following years a movement developed toward restoring primitive practice. The friars of this tendency (Observants) gained recognition within the order and eventually were made independent (1517) by Leo X. Soon afterward a movement among the Observants established the Capuchins (1525) as a still stricter adherence to the rule. All the Franciscan orders have shared in home and foreign missions; the Franciscans were in many parts of America the dominant missionaries. They have had a continuous role in education and were leaders in medieval university life. They have had a major place in preaching among Catholics: from them come the Stations of the Cross and the Christmas Crib. Since the 15th cent. the Observants have been charged with the care of Roman Catholic interests in the Holy Places in Palestine. Besides the friars, the Franciscans include the Poor Clares, the order of nuns founded by St. CLARE, and countless members of the third order (see TERTIARY), an order consisting of both men and women, some of whom live in communities and many of whom live in the world. There are scores of religious communities of sisters of every sort of charitable mission who are regular Franciscan tertiaries. Of canonized and beatified saints, far more have been Franciscans than members of any other order. The best-known of them is perhaps St. Anthony of Padua. The Franciscans were called Gray Friars. Their habit is now typically brown. For the place of Franciscans among orders, see MONASTICISM. See studies by Alexandre Masseron (rev. ed. 1959), John Moorman (1968), and Kajetán Esser (tr. 1970).

Francis de Sales, Saint: see FRANCIS OF SALES, SAINT.

Francis Ferdinand, 1863–1914, Austrian archduke, heir apparent (after 1889) of his great-uncle, Emperor Francis Joseph. In 1900 he married a Czech, Sophie Chotek. She was made duchess of Hohenberg, but because she was of minor nobility their children were barred from succession. Laboring to transform the dual Austro-Hungarian Monarchy into a triple monarchy including a Slavic kingdom under Croatian leadership, he won the enmity of both the Pan-Serbians and the Pan-Germans, and his support of the Christian Socialist campaign for universal suffrage brought the hostility of the Hungarian magnates. In 1913 he became inspector general of the armies. On June 28, 1914, while at Sarajevo on an inspection tour, he and his wife were assassinated by Gavrilo PRINCIP, a Serbian nationalist. Francis Ferdinand's death was the occasion for the Austrian ultimatum, addressed to Serbia by Count BERCHTOLD, that led directly to World War I. See Sylvie Nickels, *Assassination at Sarajevo* (1969).

Francis Joseph or **Franz Joseph,** 1830–1916, emperor of Austria (1848–1916), king of Hungary (1867–1916), nephew of FERDINAND, who abdicated in his favor. His long reign began in the stormy days of the REVOLUTIONS OF 1848 and ended in the midst of World War I. In that troubled period of growing nationalism, he held the many peoples of his empire together. He subdued Hungary (1849) and in the same year defeated VICTOR EMMANUEL II of Sardinia. In the Italian War of 1859, in which he faced NAPOLEON III and Victor Emmanuel, he lost Lombardy to Sardinia by the Treaty of VILLAFRANCA DI VERONA. In the AUSTRO-PRUSSIAN WAR (1866) his only territorial loss was that of Venetia to Italy, but his crushing defeat resulted in the loss of Austrian influence over German affairs and in the ascendancy of Prussia. Constant pressure from Hungary led to the reorganization (1867) of the empire as a dual monarchy—the AUSTRO-HUNGARIAN MONARCHY. In 1879, Francis Joseph joined Germany in an alliance that later also included Italy (see TRIPLE ALLIANCE AND TRIPLE ENTENTE). His reign, although it brought material prosperity, was disturbed by the discontent of the national minorities, notably the Slavs. When Russian Pan-Slavism backed Serbia, particularly after the annexation of BOSNIA AND HERCEGOVINA (1908), a situation was created that helped bring on World War I. Francis Joseph's private life was beset by the tragedies falling on his wife, Empress ELIZABETH, his brother, MAXIMILIAN of Mexico, and his son, Archduke RUDOLF. In 1914 his great-nephew, the heir apparent, FRANCIS FERDINAND, was assassinated, and his death was the spark that set off World War I. Francis Joseph died before the empire actually fell apart under the impact of military defeat, as it did under his successor, CHARLES I. See biographies by Joseph Redlich (1928; tr. 1929, repr. 1965), Karl Tschuppik (1928, tr. 1930) and Anatol Murad (1968); C. W. Clark, *Franz Joseph and Bismarck* (1934, repr. 1968); Edward Crankshaw, *Fall of the House of Habsburg* (1963, repr. 1971); G. B. Marek, *The Eagles Die* (1974).

Francis of Assisi, Saint: see FRANCIS, SAINT.

Francis of Sales, Saint, 1567–1622, French Roman Catholic preacher, Doctor of the Church, and key figure in the Catholic Reformation in France. He was a member of an aristocratic family of Savoy and was trained for the law, but he entered (1593) the priesthood against his father's wishes. His first years in the priesthood were spent in the district of Chablais preaching to its Protestant inhabitants. Credited with many conversions, he was made coadjutor bishop of Geneva in 1599 and bishop in 1602; he resided at Annecy in nearby Savoy. His fame as a preacher spread abroad, and from 1600 until his death he delivered Lent and Advent sermons in many of the great cities of France. In his diocese he set up schools and paid special attention to the poorer parishes. He was instrumental in the important reform of the Cistercian abbey PORT-ROYAL. With St. Jane Frances de Chantal he founded the Order of the Visitation for women who could not undergo the austerities of the great established orders. His *Introduction to the Devout Life* is a widely read religious classic. His other major work is the *Treatise on the Love of God.* He is the patron saint of Roman Catholic writers. Feast: Jan. 29. See biographies by Jean Pierre Camus (1639; tr. by C. J. Kelly, 1952); Michael Muller (1937); Michael de La Bedoyère (1960).

Francistown, town (1971 pop. 11,936), E Botswana; founded 1870. It is the commercial and administrative center for a farming and ranching region. Gold is mined nearby.

Francis Xavier, Saint, 1506–52, Basque Jesuit missionary, called the Apostle to the Indies, b. Spanish Navarre, of noble parents. He studied in Paris (1525–34), where he became an associate of St. IGNATIUS OF LOYOLA, with whom he and five others took the vow in Montmartre that made them the nucleus of the Society of Jesus (see JESUS, SOCIETY OF). In 1536–37 he went to Venice, where he worked in the hospitals; he was ordained (1537) there with Ignatius. He worked at Rome with Ignatius for the new order until 1540, when he left for Portugal to join a mission the king was sending to Goa. St. Francis left Lisbon in 1541 with a brief as papal nuncio. At Goa he immediately began to preach and was very successful. After five months he went to the pearl fisheries of W India and spent 15 months on the coast from Ceylon northward. After a second stay in Goa he sailed to Malacca (1545), which he left in 1546 for the Moluccas; in 1547 he went back to Malacca. Meanwhile more Jesuits were coming to India, and St. Francis assigned them to missions he had started. In 1549 he set sail for Japan and landed at Kagoshima. He and his companions remained in Japan for more than two years and set up many Christian communities. He went back to Goa (1552) and set out for China with a Portuguese embassy. On his way he died on the island of Changchuen (St. John). He is buried at Goa. St. Francis was one of the greatest of Christian missionaries; his travels covered many thousands of miles in 11 years, and his successes in preaching and in personal conversion were tremendous. He possessed a singular combination of profound mysticism and common sense. Feast: Dec. 3. See biography by J. M. Langlois-Berthelot (tr. 1963); study by Georg Schurhammer (tr. 1973).

francium (frăn'sēəm) [from *France*], radioactive chemical element; symbol Fr; at. no. 87; mass no. of most stable isotope 223; m.p., b.p., and sp. gr. unknown; valence +1. Francium is extremely rare; its most stable isotope (half-life about 22 minutes) occurs naturally, to a very limited extent, in uranium minerals. Twenty other isotopes of francium are known; some are prepared by bombarding thorium with protons, deuterons, or alpha particles. Francium is one of the ALKALI METALS found in group Ia of the PERIODIC TABLE. Because it is so rare, its chemical and physical properties are not known, but it is believed to resemble cesium. The element was discovered in 1939 by Marguerite Perey at the Curie Institute in Paris as a product of the radioactive disintegration of actinium. In the United States it was at one time called virginium.

Franck, family of painters: see FRANCKEN.

Franck, César Auguste (săzär' ōgüst' fräNk), 1822–90, Belgian-French composer and organist. He studied at the conservatories of Liège and Paris, taking prizes in piano, composition, and organ. In 1858 he became organist of Ste Clotilde, Paris, where he demonstrated great skill in the art of improvisation. From 1872 until his death, he was professor of organ at the Paris Conservatory, where he exercised a strong influence on an entire generation of composers. His music is highly distinctive, rooted in the polyphonic and chromatic techniques of Bach. Among his most significant works are the Symphony in D minor (1886–88); *Variations symphoniques* (1885) for piano and orchestra; and *Trois Chorals* (1890) for organ. See biographies by Norman Demuth (1950) and L. Davies (1970).

Franck, Hans: see LÜTZELBURGER, HANS.

Franck, James, 1882–1964, German physicist. He was professor of physics at Göttingen and at Johns Hopkins (1935–38) and professor of physical chemistry at the Univ. of Chicago from 1938. He specialized in atomic structure and photosynthesis. With Gustav Hertz he shared the 1925 Nobel Prize in Physics for their discovery of the laws governing the effect of the impact of the electron on the atom.

Franck, Sebastian (sābäs'tyän frängk), 1499–1542, German religious writer. He was a Roman Catholic priest who came under the influence of the Reformation, but he shortly broke with the Lutherans and for his liberal views expressed in his *Chronica* (1531) was banished from Strasbourg. He founded printing presses at Ulm and Basel and wrote vigorously, mostly in defense of extremely liberal religious views.

Francke, August Hermann (ou'go͝ost hĕr'män fräng'kə), 1663–1727, German Protestant minister and philanthropist. In 1686, encouraged by Philipp Jakob Spener, he helped found the *Collegium philobiblicum* for systematic study of the Scriptures. He became a leading exponent of PIETISM c.1689 and from 1692 served as professor at the Univ. of Halle (now in East Germany) and as pastor in a nearby town. He found (1695) at Halle the Francke Institutes, which started with a paupers' school at his parsonage. It grew rapidly, and other institutions, such as a dispensary, were added until, by Francke's death, over 2,200 children were being served. The institutes exerted strong influence on the growth of Prussian education. See H. E. Guericke, *August Hermann Francke* (1827, tr. 1837).

Francken (fräng'kən) or **Franck** (frängk), family of Flemish painters in the 16th and 17th cent. Prominent members were **Hieronymus Francken,** c.1540–1610, student of Frans Floris, who worked mainly in Antwerp in a classicist style; his brother **Frans Francken,** c.1542–1616, also a student of Floris, whose altarpiece in the Antwerp cathedral is a typical work; **Frans Francken II,** 1581–1642, son of the first Frans, who studied in Italy and was influenced by Rubens and whose *Works of Mercy* (Antwerp) and *Prodigal Son* (Louvre) are well known; and his son, **Frans Francken III,** 1607–67, a follower of Rubens and the painter of *Moses Striking the Rock* (Augsburg).

Franco, Francisco (fränthēs'kō fräng'kō), 1892–, Spanish general and *caudillo* [leader]. He became a general at the age of 32 after commanding the Spanish Foreign Legion in Morocco. During the next 10 years he enhanced his military reputation in a variety of commands and became identified with the conservative nationalist position in politics. In 1934 he was appointed chief of the general staff by the rightist government then in power, and he suppressed the uprising of the miners in Asturias. When the Popular Front came to power (Feb., 1936), he was made military governor of the Canary Islands, a post that amounted to exile. In July, 1936, Franco joined the military uprising that precipitated the SPANISH CIVIL WAR. He flew to Morocco, took command of the most powerful segment of the Spanish army, and led it back to Spain. He became head of the Insurgent government in Oct., 1936. In 1937 he merged all the other Nationalist political parties with the FALANGE, assuming leadership of the new party. With German and Italian help he ended the civil war with victory for the Nationalists in March, 1939. Franco dealt ruthlessly with his opposition and established a firmly controlled corporative state. Although close to the AXIS powers and despite their pressure, Franco succeeded in keeping Spain a nonbelligerent in World War II. He dismissed (1942) his vigorously pro-Axis minister and principal collaborator, Ramón SERRANO SÚÑER. After the war Franco maneuvered to establish favorable relations with the United States and its allies. He further reduced the already limited power of the Falange and erected the façade of a liberalized regime. The law of succession (1947) promulgated by Franco declared Spain a kingdom, with himself as regent pending the choice of a king. Diplomatic relations were established with the United States and other members of the United Nations in 1950, and as the cold war continued Franco secured massive U.S. economic aid in return for military bases in Spain. In the 1960s there was growing vocal opposition to Franco's regime, even from the Falange, whose exclusion from power was increased after the appointment of Luis CARRERO BLANCO as vice president. Franco, however, firmly maintained his position of power, even after the assassination of Carrero Blanco in 1973. In 1969, Franco named as his successor the Bourbon prince, JUAN CARLOS. See biographies by Brian Crozier (1968) and J. W. Trythall (1970); Herbert Matthews, *The Yoke and the Arrows* (1957); George Hills, *Franco: The Man and His Nation* (1968).

Franco-German War, 1870–71: see FRANCO-PRUSSIAN WAR.

Franconia (frăngkō'nēə), Ger. *Franken,* historic region and one of the five basic or stem duchies of medieval Germany, S West Germany. The region was included in the Frankish kingdom of Austrasia, becoming in the 9th cent. a duchy and the center of the East Frankish (or East German) kingdom. It stretched from the western bank of the Rhine eastward along both banks of the Main and included the cities of Speyer, Worms, Mainz, Frankfurt, Würzburg, and Fulda. After the demise of the German Carolingian house with the death of Louis the Child, Duke Conrad of Franconia was elected (911) German king as Conrad I, but was unable to keep the royal crown in his family. As a result of the rebellion of Duke Eberhard, King Otto I seized the duchy in 939 and partitioned it; vast territories passed to the loyal clergy, notably to the bishops of Würzburg and Bamberg and to the abbot of Fulda. Two nominal duchies—that of Western or Rhenish Franconia and that of Eastern Franconia—emerged. Rhenish Franconia, which gave the empire the Franconian or Salian dynasty (1024–1125; Conrad II, Henry III, Henry IV, and Henry V), broke up into the free cities of Frankfurt and Worms, the ecclesiastical states of Mainz and Speyer, the Rhenish Palatinate, the landgraviate of Hesse, and other territories. Eastern Franconia, which Emperor Henry V had awarded to his nephew Conrad of Hohenstaufen in 1115, came increasingly under the control of the bishops of Würzburg, who were given legal title by Emperor Frederick I in 1168. The title of duke of Franconia fell into disuse until it was again assumed (15th cent.) by the bishops of Würzburg, who continued to use it until their bishopric was secularized at the beginning of the 19th cent. The margraviates of Ansbach and Bayreuth, under the Franconian branch of the house of Hohenzollern, were the main secular territories in Eastern Franconia. The division (16th cent.) of the Holy Roman Empire into circles resulted in the creation of the Franconian circle, which included the bishoprics of Würzburg and Bayreuth, the free imperial city of Nürnberg, and the margraviates of Ansbach and Bayreuth. Most of Eastern Franconia passed to Bavaria between 1803 and 1815, and in 1837 King Louis I of Bavaria revived the name Franconia by creating the administrative districts of Lower, Middle, and Upper Franconia. **Lower Franconia,** Ger. *Unterfranken* (1970 pop. 1,181,200), 3,277 sq mi (8,487 sq km), is a hilly region in NW Bavaria, famous for the forested Spessart hills. It is traversed by the Main River. Agriculture is widely pursued, and industry is centered at Würzburg (the region's capital), Schweinfurt, and Aschaffenburg. Bad Kissingen is a noted resort. **Middle Franconia,** Ger. *Mittelfranken* (1970 pop. 1,484,600), 2,941 sq mi (7,617 sq km), in N central Bavaria, is a hilly, fertile region located in the Franconian Jura mts. It is drained by the Altmühl, Rednitz, and Pegnitz rivers. Ansbach is the capital; Nürnberg, Fürth, and Erlangen are important industrial and cultural centers. **Upper Franconia,** Ger. *Oberfranken* (1970 pop. 1,116,300), 2,896 sq mi (7,501 sq km), in NE Bavaria, is a hilly, forested region, drained by the Main and Pegnitz rivers. It includes the FRANKENWALD and the FICHTELGEBIRGE near the Czech border. Bayreuth, the capital, and Bamberg, Coburg, and Hof are the chief cities and industrial centers.

Franconia Mountains (frăngkō'nēə), range in the White Mts., N N.H., rising to 5,249 ft (1,600 m) at Mt. Lafayette; part of White Mts. National Forest. **Franconia Notch,** a scenic, narrow pass (6 mi/10 km long), is west of the range. Echo and Profile lakes, and the Flume, a gorge with granite walls 70 ft (21 m) high, are in the notch. Overlooking the pass is the Old Man of the Mountain, or the Profile, jutting cliffs that form the "Great Stone Face," which inspired Nathaniel Hawthorne's story. Franconia, N.H., northwest of the notch, is a year-round resort.

Franco-Prussian War or **Franco-German War,** 1870–71. The emergence of Prussia as the leading German power and the increasing unification of the German states were viewed with apprehension by NAPOLEON III after the Prussian victory in the AUSTRO-PRUSSIAN WAR of 1866. BISMARCK, at the same time, deliberately encouraged the growing rift between Prussia and France in order to bring the states of S Germany into a national union. He made sure of Russian and Italian neutrality and counted—correctly—on British neutrality. War preparations were pushed on both sides, with remarkable inefficiency in France and with astounding thoroughness in Prussia. The immediate pretext for war presented itself when the throne of Spain was offered to a prince of the house of Hohenzollern-Sigmaringen, a branch of the ruling house of Prussia. The offer, at first accepted on Bismarck's advice, was rejected (July 12) after a strong French protest. But the aggressive French foreign minister, the duc de Gramont, insisted on further Prussian assurances, which King William I of Prussia (later Emperor WILLIAM I) refused. Bismarck, by publishing the famous EMS DISPATCH, inflamed French feeling, and on July 19, France declared war. Partly because they believed France the aggressor, the states of S Germany enthusiastically joined the North German Confederation—just as Bismarck had hoped. The military conduct of the war was, for the Germans, in the hands of Helmuth Karl Bernhard von MOLTKE, a military genius. On the French side, Napoleon III took active command, but it soon devolved on Marshal BAZAINE. On Aug. 4, 1870, the Germans crossed the border into Alsace. They defeated the French at Wissembourg, pushed the French under Marshal MACMAHON to Châlons-sur-Marne, and forced a wedge between MacMahon's forces and those of Bazaine, centered on Metz. Bazaine, attempting to join MacMahon, was defeated at Vionville (Aug. 16) and Gravelotte (Aug. 18) and returned to Metz. The Germans began their march on Paris. On Sept. 1 the attempt of Napoleon III and MacMahon to rescue Bazaine led to disaster at Sedan. The emperor and 100,000 of his men were captured. When the news of Sedan reached Paris a bloodless revolution occurred. Napoleon was deposed, and a provisional government of national defense was formed under General TROCHU, Léon GAMBETTA, and Jules FAVRE. Paris was surrounded by the Germans on Sept. 19, and a grueling siege began. Gambetta escaped from Paris in a balloon to organize resistance in the provinces. FAIDHERBE made a gallant stand on the Loire, CHANZY in the north, and BOURBAKI in the east, but the surrender (Oct. 27) of Bazaine, with a garrison of 180,000 men, made such resistance useless. Paris, however, held out until Jan. 28, 1871, suffering several months of famine. Though Bismarck and Adolphe THIERS signed an armistice on the same day, the fortress of BELFORT resisted until Feb. 16. Thiers was named chief of the executive power, and provision was made for the election of a French national assembly, which met at Bordeaux. The assembly accepted (March 1) the preliminary peace agreement, which was formalized in the Treaty of Frankfurt (ratified May 21, 1871). France agreed to pay an indemnity of $1 billion within three years—an indemnity fully paid before the term expired. ALSACE, except the Territory of Belfort, and a large part of LORRAINE were ceded to Germany, which on Jan. 18, 1871, had been proclaimed an empire under William I, in the Hall of Mirrors at Versailles. Paris refused to disarm and to submit to the Thiers regime, and the COMMUNE OF PARIS was formed. The French troops loyal to Thiers began the second siege of Paris (April–May, 1871). After the cruel suppression of the commune, peace returned to France. Besides establishing the Third French Republic and the German Empire, the Franco-Prussian War had other far-reaching results. Desire for revenge guided French policy for the following half century. Prussian militarism had triumphed and laid the groundwork for German imperialistic ventures. The Papal States, no longer protected by Napoleon III, were annexed by Italy, which thus completed its unification. These and other effects were among the chain of causes that helped to set off World War I. See R. H. Lord, *The Origins of the War of 1870* (1924, repr. 1966); David Clarke, ed., *Roger de Mauni: The Franco-Prussian War* (1970).

Francowich, Matthias: see FLACIUS ILLYRICUS, MATTHIAS.

francs-tireurs: see GUERRILLA WARFARE.

Frank, Bruno (brōō'nō frängk), 1887–1945, German novelist and dramatist. His popular works include the historical novels *The Days of the King* (1924, tr. 1927), *Trenck* (1926, tr. 1928), and *A Man Called Cervantes* (1934, tr. 1934) and the play *Twelve Thousand* (1927, tr. 1928). A Jew, he was exiled (1933) from Germany and came to the United States in 1937.

Frank, Glenn, 1887–1940, American editor and educator, b. Queen City, Mo., grad. Northwestern Univ., 1912. He was assistant to the president of Northwestern Univ. from 1912 to 1916. In 1919, Frank joined the staff of the *Century Magazine,* becoming editor in 1921. In 1925 he was appointed president of the Univ. of Wisconsin, where he initiated the university's famous Experimental College and instituted changes in the teaching of agriculture. Ousted from his position by Gov. Philip Fox Follette in 1937, Frank became editor of *Rural Progress.* He was also active in the Republican party and was campaigning for the position of Senator from Wisconsin when he died in an automobile accident. His works include *The Politics of Industry* (1919), *An American Looks at His World* (1923), and *America's Hour of Decision* (1934). See biography by L. H. Larsen (1965).

Frank, Jacob, c.1726–1791, Polish Jewish sectarian and adventurer, b. Podolia. His real name was Jacob Ben Judah Leib. He was founder of the Frankists, a heretical Jewish sect that was an anti-Talmudic outgrowth of the mysticism of the false Messiah, SABBATAI ZEVI. After traveling in Turkey, where he was called Frank and where he joined the Sabbatean sect, he returned (c.1755) to Podolia. Posing as a Messiah, Frank gathered a following, by whom he was addressed as "holy master." Professing to find in the Cabala the doctrine of Trinitarianism and feigning conversion to Roman Catholicism, he and the Frankists were baptized in 1759 in Lvov. The church, however, soon became suspicious of the sincerity of its new converts, and in 1760, Frank was arrested in Warsaw on a charge of heresy and imprisoned in the fortress of Czestochowa; he was released in 1773 after that section of Poland came into Russian possession. Moving to Moravia, he enjoyed for a time the favor of Empress Maria Theresa of Austria, who believed him a disseminator of Christianity. When she discovered his sectarianism, Frank fled to Offenbach, Germany, where he lived in luxury, supported by Polish and Moravian Frankists. Upon his death his daughter Eve became "holy mistress" of the Frankists. She died in 1816, and the sect eventually disappeared, most of its members having actually become true Catholics. Many of them later became prominent members of the Polish nobility.

Frank, Leonhard (lā'ônhärt frängk), 1882–1961, German expressionist writer. He gained acclaim with his first novel, *The Robber Band* (1914, tr. 1928), and it was followed by such works as *The Cause of the Crime* (1920, tr. 1928), *A Middle-Class Man* (1924, tr. 1930), and *Carl and Anna* (1927, tr. 1929), his best-known novel, which he dramatized in 1929. *In the Last Coach* (1925, tr. 1935) was a volume of short stories. His writing, much translated, is psychological in approach, anti-war, and shows a compassion for victims of an authoritarian society. Frank fled Germany in 1933 and did not return until after World War II.

Frank, Robert, 1924–, Swiss-American photographer and filmmaker. Frank is considered the pioneer of the "snapshot aesthetic," in which the documentary image is rendered bluntly and without conscious artistry. His best-known work is *The Americans* (1959), a composite portrait of U.S. culture made in terms of telling glimpses of clutter and trivia. These powerfully composed images were considered gross and shocking when they were first published; they soon became an intrinsic part of American iconography, greatly influencing other artists in many media. Frank's films, also documentary in style, include *Pull My Daisy* (1959–60, with Alfred Leslie), *OK, End Here* (1963), and *Me and My Brother* (1965–68). See his book of photographs *Lines of My Hand* (1972).

Frank, Tenney, 1876–1939, American historian, b. Clay Center, Kansas. After 1919 he was a professor at Johns Hopkins Univ. Among his best-known works are *A History of Rome* (1923), *Economic History of Rome* (1920, rev. ed. 1927), and *Catullus and Horace* (1928, repr. 1965).

Frankel, Charles, 1917–, American philosopher, b. New York City, grad. Columbia 1937, Ph.D., 1946. A teacher at Columbia since 1939, he became Old Dominion professor of philosophy and public affairs in 1970. His extensive writings are on social philosophy, the philosophy of history, and value theory, as well as on education and religion. His emphasis, like that of John Dewey, is on practical philosophy rather than metaphysical speculation. Between 1965 and 1967, Frankel was Assistant Secretary of State for Educational and Cultural Affairs. His works include *The Faith of Reason* (1948); *The Case for Modern Man* (1956, rev. ed. 1959); *The Democratic Prospect* (1962); and *Pleasures of Philosophy* (1972).

Frankel, Zecharias (zĕkərī'əs fräng'kəl), 1801–75, Jewish theologian, called the founder of historical Judaism, b. Prague. Frankel believed that only through an appreciation of the historical development of the Jewish tradition could reforms be made to meet contemporary needs without violating the spirit of Judaism. In 1854 he was elected head of the new Conservative rabbinical seminary of Breslau. The school's "positivist-historical" approach to tradition influenced American Conservative Judaism, and its curriculum was followed by many modern rabbinical schools. Frankel's many works on biblical-Talmudic law include the highly influential *Darkhei ha-Mishnah* [introduction to the Mishna] (1859; with suppl. and index, 1867). He also wrote numerous articles on Jewish cultural history. See J. L. Blau, *Modern Varieties of Judaism* (1966).

Franken, region, West Germany: see FRANCONIA.

Frankenthaler, Helen (frăngk'ənthōlər), 1928–, American painter, b. New York City. Frankenthaler studied with Jackson POLLOCK and subsequently developed a technique for staining canvases with color. Her abstract works evoke a lyrical and sensuous mood, as in *Blue Territory* (1955) and *Arden* (1961; both: Whitney Mus., New York City).

Frankenwald (fräng'kənvält), wooded plateau, in E West Germany, between the Fichtelgebirge and the Thuringian Forest. Döbraberg is the highest (2,608 ft/795 m) point. Barley growing and cattle raising are important there.

Frankfort, Henri, 1897–1954, American archaeologist, b. Netherlands. He directed the excavations of the Egypt Exploration Society (1925–29) and the Iraq expeditions (1929–37) of the Oriental Institute of the Univ. of Chicago at Tell Asmar and Khorsabad. From 1932 to 1949 he taught at the Oriental Institute and in 1949 was appointed director of the Warburg Institute of the Univ. of London. Frankfort became an American citizen in 1944. His writings include *Ancient Egyptian Religion* (1948), *The Birth of Civilization in the Near East* (1951), and *Art and Architecture of the Ancient Orient* (1954, rev. ed. 1958).

Frankfort. 1 City (1970 pop. 14,956), seat of Clinton co., W central Ind.; laid out in 1830. It is a trade and processing center for a rich farm and livestock region. It has railroad shops, a food-packing plant, and factories making electronic equipment, candy, and automotive parts. **2** City (1970 pop. 21,902), state capital and seat of Franklin co., N central Ky., on both sides of the Kentucky River, in the heart of the bluegrass country; inc. 1796. It is the trade and shipping center for an area yielding tobacco, livestock, and limestone. Among its products are whiskey, metal items, automobile parts, shoes, and wearing apparel. Daniel Boone reached the site in 1770. The city was organized (1786) by the Virginia legislature on lands owned by Gen. James Wilkinson and was selected as the capital in 1792. Many old homes and buildings have been preserved. Of interest are the present-day capitol (1909–10), with a giant floral clock in its plaza; the old state house (1827–30), which houses the state historical society; Liberty Hall (1796); the Corner of Celebrities, where the homes of 32 nationally prominent men are in close proximity; and the old cemetery with the graves of Daniel and Rebecca Boone. Kentucky State Univ. is there.

Frankfurt (frängk'fo͝ort) or **Frankfurt am Main** (äm mīn), city (1970 pop. 669,635), Hesse, central West Germany, a port on the Main River. It is also known, in English, as Frankfort. The city is an industrial, commercial, and financial center and a transportation hub. Manufactures include chemical and pharmaceutical products, machinery, electrical equipment, leather goods, clothing, printed materials, and motor vehicles. Chemical production is concentrated in the HÖCHST district. Frankfurt is the site of major international trade fairs, including an annual book fair. A Roman town founded in the 1st cent. A.D., Frankfurt became (8th cent.) a royal residence under Charlemagne. After the Treaty of Verdun (843) it was briefly the capital of the kingdom of the Eastern Franks (i.e., Germany). It prospered as a commercial center and held annual fairs (first mentioned 1240) that drew merchants from all of Europe. Frankfurt was designated in the Golden Bull (1356) of Emperor Charles IV as the seat of the imperial elections, which took place in the chapel of the Church of St. Bartholomew. It was made a free imperial city in 1372. After the emperors ceased to be crowned by the popes, the coronation ceremonies took place (1562–1792) at Frankfurt. The emperors-elect, after being crowned at St. Bartholomew's by the archbishop-elector of Mainz, proceeded with much pageantry to a banquet in the city hall, called *Römer* [Ger.,= Romans] because the emperors-elect were crowned kings of the Romans. The coronation (1764) of Joseph II has been described in the autobiography of the writer Goethe, a native of Frankfurt. Frankfurt accepted the Reformation in 1530, and was a member of the Schmalkaldic League. It was occupied many times in the wars of the 17th and 18th cent. After the dissolution (1806) of the Holy Roman Empire, Frankfurt was included in the ecclesiastic principality of Regensburg and Aschaffenburg, created by Napoleon I for Karl Theodor von Dalberg. The principality was converted in 1810 into the grand duchy of Frankfurt, also under Dalberg. The Congress of Vienna (1814–15) restored Frankfurt to the status of a free city and made it the seat of the diet of the GERMAN CONFEDERATION. The FRANKFURT PARLIAMENT, the first German national assembly, met there in 1848–49. Having sided with Austria in the Austro-Prussian War of 1866, Frankfurt was annexed by Prussia. In 1871 the Treaty of Frankfurt, which ended the Franco-Prussian War, was signed there. The city was heavily damaged in World War II, but after 1945 many of its historic landmarks were restored and numerous modern structures were built. Points of interest include the *Römer* (begun in the 15th cent.); the Gothic Church of St. Bartholomew (13th–15th cent.), also called the coronation cathedral, which has a high (312 ft/95 m) tower; the house (now a museum) in which Goethe was born (1749); the Lutheran Church of St. Paul, or *Paulskirche* (built 1789–1833), where the Frankfurt Parliament met; and the Städel art museum (founded 1816). Frankfurt was the original home of the Rothschilds, who, along with other Jewish merchants and bankers, played a leading role in the economic growth of the city (especially after 1700). Frankfurt is the seat of a university (opened 1914) and of the West German central bank and national library.

Frankfurt, Treaty of, 1871: see VERSAILLES, TREATY OF, 1871.

Frankfurt am Main, West Germany: see FRANKFURT.

Frankfurt-an-der-Oder (än-dĕr-ō'dər), city (1970 pop. 62,001), capital of Frankfurt district, E East Germany, a port on the Oder River, at the Polish border. It is an industrial center, agricultural market, and rail junction. Manufactures include machinery, wood products, shoes, transistors, chemicals, and food products (notably frankfurter sausages). Lignite is mined nearby. Frankfurt was chartered in 1253. It joined the Hanseatic League in the 14th cent. and became an important commercial center. Frankfurt was frequently besieged, notably in 1631 (during the Thirty Years War), when it was stormed and sacked by the Swedes under Gustavus II. The university founded there in 1506 was transferred to Breslau in 1811. The city was severely damaged in World War II. The suburb of Damm-Vorstadt on the east bank of the Oder was placed under Polish administration in 1945 and is called Słubice by the Poles. The dramatist and poet Heinrich von Kleist was born (1777) in Frankfurt.

Frankfurter, Felix, 1882–1965, American jurist, Associate Justice of the U.S. Supreme Court (1939–62), b. Vienna, Austria. He emigrated to the United States as a boy and later received (1906) his law degree from Harvard law school. He was assistant U.S. attorney (1906–10) in New York state and legal officer (1911–14) in the Bureau of Insular Affairs. A professor (1914–39) at Harvard law school, Frankfurter was also active during these years outside the academic world. A frequent appointee to special government posts, he fought for the release of Sacco and Vanzetti, helped found the American Civil Liberties Union, and played an important part in staffing the agencies of the New Deal. His appointment by President Franklin Delano Roosevelt to the U.S. Supreme Court brought a man of marked liberal tendencies to the high bench; but Frankfurter was also a firm adherent of judicial restraint. Although much concerned with fair legal procedure, he upheld legislation limiting civil liberties in the belief that the government has a right to protect itself through investigative committees and legislation, and that the court must exercise self-restraint in interfering with the popular will as expressed by its representatives. Among his works are *The Public and Its Government* (1930), *The Commerce Clause under Marshall, Taney, and Waite* (1937), and *Of Law and Men* (1956). His lectures appear in *Law and Politics*, ed. by Archibald MacLeish and E. F. Pritchard (1939, repr. 1962). See also his reminiscences, ed. by H. B. Phillips (1960, repr. 1962); his correspondence with Franklin D. Roosevelt, ed. by Max Freedman (1967); biography by Liva Baker (1969); studies by H. S. Thomas (1960) and P. B. Kurland (1971); Wallace Mendelson, ed., *Felix Frankfurter* (2 vol., 1964) and *Justices Black and Frankfurter* (2d ed. 1966).

Frankfurt Parliament, 1848–49, national assembly convened at Frankfurt on May 18, 1848, as a result of the liberal revolution that swept the German states early in 1848. The parliament was called by a preliminary assembly of German liberals in March, 1848, and its members were elected by direct manhood suffrage. They represented the entire political spectrum and included the foremost German figures of the time. The president of the parliament was Heinrich von GAGERN. Its purpose was to plan the unification of Germany. Having suspended (June, 1848) the diet of the GERMAN CONFEDERATION, the assembly appointed Archduke John of Austria regent of Germany and head of the provisional (and virtually nonexistent) executive power. While the parliament was lengthily debating various schemes of union, it was diverted from its purpose by the war with Denmark over the SCHLESWIG-HOLSTEIN question; the parliament commissioned Prussia to send troops to aid the duchies, but finally accepted (Sept., 1848) an armistice. It resumed deliberations on unification, but conflict among the traditionally separate German states, notably Austria and Prussia, made progress difficult. In the meantime the revolutionary movement was suppressed, and the very basis of the Frankfurt assembly destroyed. At last, in March, 1849, the parliament adopted a federal constitution of the German states, excluding Austria, with a parliamentary government and a hereditary emperor. FREDERICK WILLIAM IV of Prussia was chosen emperor but refused to accept the crown from a popularly elected assembly and the entire scheme foundered. Most of the representatives withdrew and the remainder were dispersed. Frederick William attempted to substitute a union scheme of his own, but his efforts were smothered by Austria through the Treaty of Olmütz (1850), which restored the German Confederation. The constitution drafted by the Frankfurt Parliament influenced that of the NORTH GERMAN CONFEDERATION in 1866, particularly in providing direct suffrage.

frankincense: see INCENSE-TREE.

Frankland, Sir Edward, 1825–99, English chemist. He studied under Bunsen and Liebig and taught at several English institutions. In working on the synthesis and isolation of compounds he evolved the theory of valence. He made studies of water purification; of flame and luminosity with John Tyndall; of gases with J. N. Lockyer, with whom he discovered helium; and of the chemistry of foods. His work on water purification was continued by his son, **Percy Faraday Frankland,** 1858–1946, also a chemist, who with his wife, Grace Toynbee Frankland, conducted bacteriological studies. He and his wife wrote *Micro-organisms in Water* (1894) and *Pasteur* (1898).

Franklin, Ann Smith, 1696–1763, American printer; sister-in-law of Benjamin Franklin. After the death in 1735 of her husband, James Franklin, she carried on his commercial printing business, in Newport, R.I., aided by two daughters and her son James. She printed a series of almanacs: the first numbers (1728–35) were written by Joseph Stafford and published by James Franklin. Those published from 1736 to 1741 she wrote herself. Franklin published the Newport *Mercury* and, as colony printer, printed its many legal documents and its paper money. In 1748 her son James became her partner.

Franklin, Benjamin, 1706–90, American statesman, printer, scientist, and writer, b. Boston. The son of a tallow chandler and soapmaker, he left school at 10 years of age to help his father. He then was apprenticed to his half brother James, a printer and publisher of the *New England Courant*, to which young Ben secretly contributed. After much disagreement he left his brother's employment and went (1723) to Philadelphia to work as a printer. Industry and thrift—qualities he was to praise much later—helped him to better himself. After a short stay in London (1724–26), he returned and in 1729 acquired an interest in the *Pennsylvania Gazette*. As owner and editor after 1730, he made the periodical popular. His common sense philosophy and his neatly turned phrases won public attention in the *Gazette*, in the later *General Magazine*, and especially in his *Poor Richard's Almanack*, which he published from 1732 to 1757. Many sayings of Poor Richard, praising prudence, common sense, and honesty, became standard American proverbs. Franklin also interested himself in selling books, established a circulating library, organized a debating club that developed into the American Philosophical Society, helped to establish (1751) an academy that eventually became the Univ. of Pennsylvania, and brought about civic reforms. Meanwhile he had steadily extended his own knowledge by study of foreign languages, philosophy, and science. He repeated the experiments of other scientists and showed his usual practical bent by inventing such diverse things as the Franklin stove, bifocal eyeglasses, and a glass harmonica (see HARMONICA **2**). The phenomenon of electricity interested him deeply, and in 1748 he turned his printing business over to his foreman, intending to devote his life to science. His spectacular experiment of flying a kite in a thunderstorm, which proved the identity of the electricity in lightning, and his invention of the lightning rod were among a series of investigations that won him recognition from the leading scientists in England and on the Continent. He took local public offices and served long (1753–74) as deputy postmaster general of the colonies. As such he reorganized the postal system, making it both efficient and profitable. His status as a public figure grew steadily. A Pennsylvania delegate to the ALBANY CONGRESS (1754), he proposed there a plan of union for the colonies, which was accepted by the delegates but later rejected by both the provincial assemblies and the British government. He worked for the British cause in the French and Indian War, especially by providing transportation for the ill-fated expedition led by Edward Braddock against Fort Duquesne. Franklin was a leader of the popular party in Pennsylvania against the Penn family, who were the proprietors, and in

1757 he was sent to England to present the case against the Penns. He won (1760) for the colony the right to tax the Penn estates but advised moderation in applying the right. He returned to America for two years (1762–64) but was in England when the Stamp Act caused a furor. Again he showed prudent moderation; he protested the act but asked the colonists to obey the law, thus losing some popularity in the colonies until he stoutly defended American rights at the time of the debates on repeal of the act. He was made agent for Georgia (1768), New Jersey (1769), and Massachusetts (1770) and seriously considered making his home in England, where his scientific attainments, his brilliant mind, and his social gifts of wit and urbanity had gained him a high place. However, as trouble between the British government and the colonies grew with the approach of the American Revolution, Franklin's deep love for his native land and his devotion to individual freedom brought (1775) him back to America. There, while his illegitimate son, William FRANKLIN, was becoming a leader of the Loyalists, Benjamin Franklin became one of the greatest statesmen of the American Revolution and of the newborn nation. He was a delegate to the Continental Congress, was appointed postmaster general, and was sent to Canada with Samuel Chase and Charles Carroll of Carrollton to persuade the people of Canada to join the patriot cause. He was appointed (1776) to the committee that drafted the Declaration of Independence, which he signed. Late in 1776 he sailed to France to join Arthur LEE and Silas DEANE in their diplomatic efforts for the new republic. Franklin, with a high reputation in France well supported by his winning presence, did much to gain French recognition of the new republic in 1778. Franklin helped to direct U.S. naval operations and was a successful agent for the United States in Europe—the sole one after suspicions and quarrels caused Congress to annul the powers of the other American commissioners. He was chosen (1781) as one of the American diplomats to negotiate peace with Great Britain and laid the groundwork for the treaty before John JAY and John ADAMS arrived. British naval victory in the West Indies made the final treaty less advantageous to the United States than Franklin's original draft. The Treaty of Paris was, in contradiction of the orders of Congress, concluded in 1783 without the concurrence of France, because Jay and Adams distrusted the French. Franklin returned in 1785 to the United States and was made president of the Pennsylvania executive council. The last great service rendered to his country by this "wisest American," as he is sometimes called, was his part in the Federal Constitutional Convention of 1787. Although his proposal of a single-chamber congress was rejected, he helped to direct the compromise that brought the Constitution of the United States into being. Though not completely satisfied with the finished product, he worked earnestly for its ratification. His writings are still widely known today, especially his autobiography (covering only his early years), which is generally considered one of the finest autobiographies in any language and has appeared in innumerable editions. See the definitive edition of his works, Vol. I-14 ed. by Leonard W. Labaree, Vol. 15–18 ed. by William B. Willcox (1959–1973), covering the period from Jan. 6, 1706, to Dec. 31, 1771. See biographies by James Parton (1864, repr. 1971), S. G. Fisher (1899), P. L. Ford (1899, repr. 1972), Bernard Faÿ (1933, repr. 1969), Carl Van Doren (1938, repr. 1973), P. W. Conner (1965), A. O. Aldridge (1965), and T. J. Fleming (1971).

Franklin, Christine Ladd-: see LADD-FRANKLIN, CHRISTINE.

Franklin, Sir John, 1786–1847, British explorer in N Canada whose disappearance caused a widespread search of the Arctic. Entering the navy in 1801, he fought in the battle of Trafalgar. On his first overland expedition (1819–22) in N Canada, his party crossed the barren grounds from Great Slave Lake to the Arctic coast at the mouth of the Coppermine River and explored eastward along the coast for c.175 mi (280 km). In his *Narrative of a Journey to the Shores of the Polar Sea* (1823, repr. 1969), Franklin describes this journey. On his next expedition (1825–27), the party descended the Mackenzie River and surveyed another long stretch of the Arctic shore line, westward to Return Reef (c.160 mi/260 km from Point Barrow, Alaska) and eastward to the mouth of the Coppermine. By way of the Coppermine he went to Great Bear Lake, where he built Fort Franklin. Franklin's *Narrative of a Second Expedition to the Shores of the Polar Sea* (1828, repr. 1968) is an account of these feats. On both of these expeditions he was accompanied by Sir George Back. After serving (1836–43) as governor of Van Diemen's Land (now Tasmania), Franklin set out in the *Erebus* and the *Terror* in 1845 to search for the NORTHWEST PASSAGE. When, three years later, no word from him had been received, there was dispatched the first of the more than 40 parties that in the following years were to search the arctic regions for traces of the expedition. Although the geographical knowledge gained by the searchers was immense, no certain clues as to Franklin's fate were revealed until John Rae, in 1853–54, and Sir Francis McClintock, between 1857 and 1859, found evidence of the great arctic tragedy. The latter expedition, fitted by Lady Franklin, found records at Point Victory that established that Franklin's ships had been frozen in the ice between Victoria Island and King William Island. After his death in 1847, the survivors had abandoned ship in 1848 and had undertaken a journey southward over the frozen wastes of Boothia Peninsula toward civilization. Of the entire expedition of some 129 men, not one is known to have survived. Relics and documents of the Franklin party and of later search expeditions have been found as recently as 1960, and the quest for Franklin's diaries is still being continued. See biographies of Franklin by A. H. Markham (1891) and H. D. Traill (1896); the life, diaries, and correspondence of his wife, Lady Franklin (ed. by W. F. Rawnsley, 1923); Paul Nantor, *Arctic Breakthrough* (1970); Leslie Neatby, *The Search for Franklin* (1970).

Franklin, William, c.1730–1813, last royal governor of New Jersey; illegitimate son of Benjamin Franklin. He grew up in Philadelphia, served in King George's War, and was (1754–56) comptroller of the general post office in Philadelphia. In 1757 he went with his father to England, where he studied law and through influential friends was appointed (1763) governor of New Jersey. Although well-liked at first, his strong attachment to England and British authority soon made him unpopular. After the American Revolution began, he sided with the Loyalists and quarreled bitterly with his father. The New Jersey congress ordered (1776) his arrest, and he was imprisoned in Connecticut until he was exchanged in 1778. Franklin went to England in 1782, never to return. In 1784 he was reconciled with his father.

Franklin, district (1971 pop. 7,747), 549,253 sq mi (1,422,565 sq km), Northwest Territories, N Canada. The district was created in 1895 and named for the British explorer Sir John Franklin. It comprises the Boothia and Melville peninsulas and the islands of the Canadian Arctic Archipelago, including Baffin, Victoria, and the Queen Elizabeth Islands. Baffin Island National Park (est. 1972) is there.

Franklin. 1 City (1970 pop. 11,477), seat of Johnson co., S central Ind., inc. 1823. It is a farm trade center. Manufactures include auto parts, electrical components, and copper panels. Franklin College of Indiana is there. **2** Town (1970 pop. 17,830), Norfolk co., SE Mass., near the R.I. line; settled 1660, set off from Wrentham and inc. 1778. Foundry products and rubber goods are manufactured. A memorial marks the birthplace of the educator Horace Mann. **3** City (1970 pop. 10,075), Warren co., SW Ohio, on the Great Miami River, in a farm area; inc. 1813. Paper products are manufactured in the city. It was a flourishing river port in the mid-19th cent. **4** City (1970 pop. 12,247), Milwaukee co., W central Wis., a residential suburb of Milwaukee; inc. 1956.

Franklin, State of, government (1784–88) formed by the inhabitants of present-day Washington, Sullivan, and Greene counties in present-day E Tennessee after North Carolina ceded (June, 1784) its western lands to the United States. Following preliminary conventions at Jonesboro (Aug. and Dec., 1784), the first assembly, meeting at Greeneville early in 1785, elected John SEVIER governor for a three-year term, established courts, appointed magistrates, levied taxes, and enacted laws. A permanent constitution was adopted in Nov., 1785. Unable to secure congressional recognition and pressed by North Carolina in its attempt to reestablish jurisdiction (in Dec., 1784, North Carolina repealed the act ceding the lands), Sevier's government passed out of existence when the terms of its officers expired. The region reverted temporarily to North Carolina. See S. C. Williams, *History of the Lost State of Franklin* (rev. ed. 1933).

Franklin and Marshall College, at Lancaster, Pa.; United Church of Christ (Evangelical-Reformed); coeducational; est. 1787 as Franklin College, reorganized 1853 when it merged with Marshall College (chartered 1836).

Franklin D. Roosevelt Lake: see under GRAND COULEE DAM.

Franklin Institute, in Philadelphia; chartered and opened 1824 "for the promotion of the mechanic arts," the first of its kind in the country. It was named for Benjamin Franklin. Since the 19th cent. it has been noted for its lecture series, trade exhibitions, investigations of new inventions, and work on governmental, industrial and scientific problems. *The Journal of the Franklin Institute* (published continuously since 1826) enjoys wide recognition, and its library is one of the outstanding technical collections in the country.

Franklin Park, village (1970 pop. 20,497), Cook co., NE Ill., a residential suburb of Chicago; inc. 1892.

Franklin Square, uninc. residential city (1970 pop. 32,156), Nassau co., SE N.Y., on Long Island.

Franko, Ivan (ē'vän frän'kō), 1856–1916, Ukrainian writer and nationalist. His realistic novels *Boryslav Laughs* (1881–82) and *Boa Constrictor* (1878, tr. 1961) portray the harsh existence of Ukrainian workers and peasants. Franko was an ardent political radical who sought to inspire Ukrainian nationalism in works such as *Zakhar Berkut* (1883, tr. 1944), which deals with Ukrainian history. He treated social and psychological problems in *Basis of Society* (1895) and the autobiographical *In the Sweat of the Brow* (1890). Franko's poetic works include poems on social themes as well as purely lyrical poetry (*Withered Leaves*, 1896) and philosophical contemplations (*Semper Tiro*, 1906). In *Death of Cain* (1889) and *Moses* (1905), Franko draws an analogy between the Israelite search for a homeland and the Ukrainian desire for independence. His dramatic masterpiece is *Stolen Happiness* (1893). Franko's works, numbering more than 1,000, include volumes of history, criticism, ethnography, politics, and translation. See his *Selected Poems* (tr. 1948).

Franks, group of Germanic tribes. By the 3d cent. A.D., they were settled along the lower and middle Rhine. The two major divisions were the Salian Franks in the north and the Ripuarian Franks in the south. The two groups expanded independently, although they sometimes united against a common enemy. The Salian Franks became allies of the Roman Empire late in the 4th cent. In the following century they moved southward into Gaul, and under their leader CLOVIS I they overthrew (486) the Romans. Clovis permanently united the Salian and Ripuarian Franks, accepted Roman Catholicism, and founded the Frankish empire. By the conquest of the First Kingdom of BURGUNDY, of BAVARIA, of the territories of the ALEMANNI, the Thuringians, and the Saxons, and of the kingdom of the LOMBARDS, the Frankish empire grew (6th–9th cent.) to include most of France, the Low Countries, Germany W of the Elbe, Austria, Switzerland, and N and central Italy. Under its first dynasty, the MEROVINGIANS, the empire was, for most of the time, divided into several kingdoms, notably NEUSTRIA in the west, AUSTRASIA in the east, and Burgundy in the south. Internal warfare among the kingdoms was almost constant. In contrast to the high degree of political organization, commerce, and culture under the Romans, the Merovingians represented a barbaric civilization. Only the Church kept alive the remnants of Gallo-Roman culture. The height of Frankish development and power occurred under the CAROLINGIANS, who first ruled as mayors of the palace, and then, from 751, as kings of the reunited Frankish domains. CHARLEMAGNE was the greatest Frankish ruler. His empire was partitioned in 843 (see VERDUN, TREATY OF) and again in 870 by the Treaty of MERSEN. From these partitions developed the kingdom of the West Franks, who merged with the far more numerous Gallo-Roman population of Gaul and became France; and the kingdom of the East Franks, who retained their Germanic speech and became Germany. Both France and the region of Franconia in Germany derive their names from the Franks. Throughout the Middle Ages the word *Frank* was identified with the word *free* (Fr. *franc*). See study by Peter Lasko (1971).

Františkovy Lázně (frän'tĭshkôvĭ läz'nyĕ), Ger. *Franzensbad*, town, NW Czechoslovakia, in Bohemia. It is a famous spa with numerous mineral springs. There are extensive peat deposits in the vicinity.

Franz, Robert (rō'bĕrt fränts), 1815–92, German composer of about 350 lieder, intimate songs, usually in strophic form. The first of them (pub. 1843) drew warm praise from Schumann. Franz championed a revival of the music of Bach and Handel.

Franzén, Frans Michael (fräns mē'kāĕl fränsän'), 1772–1847, Swedish poet, a bishop, b. Finland. He became professor of philosophy at Åbo in 1798. His *Ode to Gustaf Philip Creutz* (1797) marks the birth of romantic lyric poetry in Sweden.

Franzensbad: see FRANTIŠKOVY LÁZNĚ, Czechoslovakia.

Franz Josef Land (frăns jō'zəf, fränts yō'zĕf), Rus. *Zemlya Frantsa Iosifa,* archipelago, c.8,000 sq mi (20,720 sq km), in the Arctic Ocean N of Novaya Zemlya, USSR. It consists of 85 islands of volcanic origin, including Aleksandra Land, George Land, Wilczek Land, Graham Bell Island, Hooker Island, and Rudolf Island. Government observation stations (erected 1929) and settlements are on the latter two islands. Some 90% of Franz Josef Land is covered by ice interspersed with poor lichen vegetation; the average mean temperature is 6.5°F (−14.2°C). It was discovered in 1873 by Karl Weyprecht and Julius von Payer, leaders of an Austrian expedition, and was subsequently more fully explored by expeditions such as those led by Frederick George Jackson (1894–97), Fridtjof Nansen (who spent the winter of 1895–96 in Franz Josef Land), Walter Wellman (1898–99), the duke of the Abruzzi (1899–1900), Evelyn Baldwin (1902–3), and Anthony Fiala (1903–5). In 1926 the USSR claimed the archipelago as national territory.

Franz Joseph, emperor of Austria and king of Hungary: see FRANCIS JOSEPH.

Frascati (fräskä'tē), town (1971 pop. 18,670), in Latium, central Italy. Beautifully situated in the Alban Hills near the site of ancient Tusculum, it has been a popular summer resort since Roman times. It is famous for its white wine and its patrician villas, including the Villa Aldobrandini (1598–1603) and the Villa Mondragone (16th cent.).

Frasch process [for Herman Frasch], process for the extraction of SULFUR from subsurface deposits. Three pipes, one inside another, are sunk to the bottom of the sulfur bed. Water heated under pressure to a temperature well above the melting point of the sulfur is conducted down the outer pipe, and air under pressure down through the innermost pipe. The heated water melts the sulfur and the compressed air forces it through the middle pipe to the surface.

Frasconi, Antonio (äntō'nyō fräskō'nē), 1919–, American graphic artist, b. Montevideo, Uruguay. Frasconi emigrated to the United States in 1945, where he has had an influential and revitalizing effect on the art of woodblock printing. His gaily colored, forceful prints of everyday scenes and activities are in many public and private collections. He has designed covers for books, magazines, and records. Among his illustrated books are *See and Say* (1955), *Frasconi Woodcuts* (1958), *A Whitman Portrait* (1960), and *A Kaleidoscope in Woodcuts* (1968).

Fraser, James Earle, 1876–1953, American sculptor, b. Winona, Minn., studied at the Art Institute of Chicago and in Paris. The best known of his many works are *The End of the Trail* (Visalia, Calif.); the designs of Indian head and buffalo on a U.S. nickel; and a statue of Alexander Hamilton (Treasury Building, Washington, D.C.).

Fraser, Peter, 1884–1950, New Zealand political leader, b. Scotland. He emigrated to New Zealand in 1910. Previously active in Labour politics in London, he was elected to Parliament in 1918, becoming Labour party leader there. From 1935 to 1940 he held the posts of minister of education, health, and marine. He served as prime minister from 1940 to 1949, mobilizing his country for the war effort, and pushing forward its plan of socialization.

Fraser, Simon: see LOVAT, SIMON FRASER, 11TH BARON.

Fraser, Simon, 1776–1862, Canadian explorer and fur trader. Born in Bennington, Vt., he was taken to Canada as a child. He entered the service of the NORTH WEST COMPANY in 1792, and in 1801 he was made a partner. In 1805 he was chosen to inaugurate the company's operations beyond the Rocky Mts., and after exploring and establishing trading posts on the upper reaches of the Fraser River, he and John Stuart and 20 companions explored (1808) the same river to tidewater. From the point of view of danger it was one of the most difficult exploration trips on record in North America. He was disappointed to discover that the river he had explored was not the Columbia as he had hoped. In 1811, Fraser was placed in charge of the important Red River department of his company, where he came into conflict with the earl of SELKIRK over the Red River Settlement. Fraser's journals of the expedition were edited by W. K. Lamb (1960).

Fraser, city (1970 pop. 11,868), Macomb co., SE Mich., a suburb of Detroit; inc. as a village 1894, as a city 1957. Automated machine tools and steel products are manufactured there.

Fraser, chief river of British Columbia, Canada, c.850 mi (1,370 km) long. It rises in the Rocky Mts., at Yellowhead Pass, near the British Columbia–Alta. line and flows northwest through the Rocky Mt. Trench to Prince George, thence south and west to the Strait of Georgia at Vancouver. Its chief tributaries are the Nechako, Quesnel, Chilcotin, and Thompson rivers. It is navigable to Yale, c.80 mi (130 km) upstream. The Fraser River canyon, which begins at Yale, is noted for its scenery; its mountain walls rise more than 3,000 ft (914 m). The river contains the chief spawning grounds in North America for the Pacific salmon. Logging is important along the upper course. The Fraser delta is the most fertile agricultural region of British Columbia; dairying and truck farming are important. The delta has the largest concentration of people in W Canada. Sections of the river are followed by oil and gas pipelines as well as transcontinental rail and highway routes. The Fraser River was discovered by Sir Alexander Mackenzie, the Canadian explorer, who followed its upper course on his expedition (1793) to the Pacific Ocean and takes its name from Simon Fraser, the Canadian explorer and fur trader, who followed (1808) the river to its mouth, establishing fur-trading posts along the way. The river valley was the domain of the fur traders until the gold rush of 1858. With the discovery of gold (1859) in the Cariboo dist., on the river's upper reaches, the government built a road to serve the valley and settlement of the region followed.

Fraserburgh (frā'zərbərə), burgh (1971 pop. 10,605), Aberdeenshire, NE Scotland, on the North Sea. It is one of Scotland's leading fishing ports. Herring and whitefish are caught. It was founded in 1570 by Sir Alexander Fraser, and the remains of his castle are at Kinnairds Head below a lighthouse. In 1975, Fraserburgh became part of the new Grampian region.

fraternal orders, organizations whose members are usually bound by oath and who make extensive use of secret ritual in the conduct of their meetings. Most fraternal orders are limited to members of one sex, although some include both men and women. The best-known orders are the Freemasons (see FREEMASONRY) and the Odd Fellows, both of which originated in 18th-century England (although enthusiasts have placed the origin of the Freemasons at the time of the construction of Solomon's Temple). Most American fraternal orders were established in the 19th cent. and were formed for a special purpose or for the benefit of particular groups; e.g., the Patrons of Husbandry, or the Grange (see GRANGER MOVEMENT), was founded to improve the lot of the farmer and was for a time an important political force. The KNIGHTS OF COLUMBUS was formed (1882) to provide a fraternal order for Roman Catholics free of the oath-taking requirement to which they were opposed. Other orders, founded when commercial insurance companies did not extend coverage to workingmen, provided sickness and death benefits to members. That function of fraternal orders declined as insurance companies expanded their coverage, and today most fraternal orders serve mainly as charitable institutions and social centers. Other well-known fraternal orders and their years of founding in the United States are the Order of Hibernians (1836), Knights of Pythias (1864), and Order of Elks (1868).

fraternity, in American colleges, a student secret society formed for social purposes, into which members are initiated by invitation and occasionally by a period of trial known as hazing. Fraternities are usually named by two or three Greek letters and are also known as Greek-letter societies; women's Greek-letter societies are commonly called sororities. The oldest Greek-letter society is Phi Beta Kappa, founded (1776) at the College of William and Mary, Williamsburg, Va. It soon became a scholarship honor society. After 1830 the literary societies that existed in many colleges were slowly supplanted by fraternities modeled on the three established (1825–27) at Union College. After 1870 many professional and honorary fraternities were established to give recognition to scholarship in various fields. Most fraternities and sororities, however, serve mainly as social clubs. The typical Greek-letter society owns or rents a house that is used as a residence hall for members and as a center for social activities. Some Greek-letter societies have only one local organization or chapter; others are nationally organized with chapters in several institutions. The Interfraternity Conference (1909) and the National Panhellenic Congress (1929) were established to consult on the common interests of American fraternities and sororities. Because most fraternities only admit new members on the basis of a unanimous vote, many of the organizations have been able to maintain discriminatory entrance policies. For this reason, and because of reported incidents of violent or abusive hazing, fraternities are forbidden on some campuses. See William R. Baird, *Manual of American College Fraternities* (rev. ed. 1949); William A. Scott, *Values & Organizations: A Study of Fraternities and Sororities* (1965).

fraud, in law, willful misrepresentation intended to deprive another of some right. The offense, generally only a TORT, may also constitute the crime of false pretenses. Frauds are either actual or constructive. An actual fraud requires that the act be motivated by the desire to deceive another to his harm, while a constructive fraud is a presumption of overreaching conduct that arises when a profit is made from a relation of trust (see FIDUCIARY). The courts have found it undesirable to make a rigid definition of the type of misrepresentation that amounts to actual fraud and have preferred to consider individually the factors in each case. The misrepresentation may be a positive lie, a failure to disclose information, or even a statement made in reckless disregard of possible inaccuracy. Actual fraud can never be the result of accident or NEGLIGENCE, because of the requirement that the act be intended to deceive. The question of commission may depend upon the competence and commercial knowledge of the alleged victim. Thus dealings with a minor, a lunatic, a feeble-minded person, a drunkard, or (in former times) a married woman are scrutinized more closely than dealings with an experienced businessman. A lawsuit based upon actual or constructive fraud must specify the fraudulent act, the plaintiff's reliance on it, and the loss suffered. The remedy granted to the plaintiff in most cases is either compensatory (and possibly punitive) DAMAGES for the injury or cancellation of the contract or other agreement and the restoration of the parties to their former status. In a few states of the United States both damages and cancellation are available. In certain suits based upon a contract, fraud may be interposed as a defense.

Frauds, Statute of, basis of most modern laws requiring that certain promises must be in writing in order to be enforceable; it was passed by the English Parliament in 1677. In the United States, although state laws vary, most require written agreements in four types of contracts: contracts to assume the obligation of another; contracts that cannot be performed within one year; contracts for the sale of land; and contracts for the sale of goods.

Frauenfeld (frou'ənfĕlt), city (1970 pop. 30,701), capital of Thurgau canton, NE Switzerland, on the Murg River. Although it has aluminum, food, publishing, and textile industries, it is chiefly known for its 11th-century castle (now a museum), which was the seat (1712–98) of the federal diet.

Fraunces, Samuel (frôn'sĭs), c.1722–95, American innkeeper, proprietor of the historic **Fraunces Tavern** in New York City. This building at the corner of Broad and Pearl streets was the DE LANCEY mansion before Fraunces purchased it in 1762 and opened it as the Queen's Head Tavern. It became famous for its wines and food and was a gathering place for the Sons of Liberty and other organizations before the American Revolution and for British officers during their occupation of the city. Fraunces himself was a patriot, and his tavern was the center of the celebration on the occasion of the British evacuation of New York. In its Long Room, George Washington bade farewell (1783) to his officers. Fraunces sold the tavern in 1785. When Washington returned (1789) to New York as President, Fraunces became steward of his household, maintaining that position even after Philadelphia was made the capital. The tavern, extensively restored, is now owned by the Sons of the Revolution (not the Sons of the American Revolution); it is open to the public as a restaurant and houses many historical objects and documents.

Fraunhofer lines (froun'hôfər): see SUN.

Fray Bentos (frī'bān'tōs), city (1963 pop. 20,755), capital of Río Negro dept., SW Uruguay, a port on the Uruguay River. It was founded in 1859 as Independencia and renamed for an 18th-century religious hermit of the region. Meat-packing is the chief industry, and frozen and canned meats, hides, and wool are exported.

Frayser's Farm: see SEVEN DAYS BATTLES.

Frazee, John, 1790–1852, American pioneer sculptor, b. Rahway, N. J. Without formal instruction, he advanced from tombstone cutting to portrait busts, including those of Daniel Webster, John Marshall, and other notables. The portrait of John Wells (1824; St. Paul's Church, New York City) is said to be the first marble bust executed in this country by a native American. The Pennsylvania Academy of the Fine Arts owns the original cast of a self-portrait.

Frazer, Sir James George, 1854–1941, Scottish classicist and anthropologist, b. Glasgow, educated at the universities of Glasgow and Cambridge. He is known especially for his masterpiece, *The Golden Bough,* published originally in two volumes (1890); in later editions it was enlarged to 13 volumes. A monumental study in comparative folklore, magic, and religion, it showed parallels between the rites and beliefs of early cultures and those of Christianity. The work had a great impact on the early 20th cent., its influence extending to psychology and literature. An abridged one-volume edition was published by the author in 1923. A new one-volume version, cut and annotated by T. H. Gaster, appeared in 1959 as *The New Golden Bough.* Frazer's other writings include *Totemism and Exogamy* (1910) and its supplement, *Totemica* (1937); *The Belief in Immortality and the Worship of the Dead* (3 vol., 1913–24); *Folklore in the Old Testament* (1919, abr. ed. 1923); and *Anthologia Anthropologica,* ed. by R. A. Downie (4 vol., 1938–39). See studies by R. A. Downie (1940), Bronislaw Malinowski (in *A Scientific Theory of Culture,* 1944, repr. 1960), and J. B. Vickery (1973).

Fréchette, Louis Honoré (lwē ônôrā' frāshĕt'), 1839–1908, French Canadian poet and politician, b. Lévis, Que. He worked (1865–71) as a journalist in Chicago and while there wrote a volume of poetry entitled *La Voix d'un exilé* [the voice of an exile] (1866–68). Returning to Canada, he served in Parliament (1874–78), tried journalism again, and in 1889 received a government clerkship, which he held until his death. His volumes of poetry include *Les Oiseaux de neige* [snowbirds] (1879), on old Quebec, and *La Légende d'un peuple* [the story of a people] (1887), an epic of the French Canadians. He was the first Canadian poet to be honored by the French Academy. His collected poems appeared posthumously in 1908.

Fredegunde (frē"dəgŭn'də), c.545–597, Frankish queen. The mistress of King CHILPERIC I of Neustria, she became his wife after inducing him to murder his wife Galswintha (567). Fredegunde and BRUNHILDA, Galswintha's sister and wife of King SIGEBERT I of Austrasia, were among the leading figures in the long war (561–613) between the Frankish kingdoms of Neustria and Austrasia. Fredegunde procured the deaths of Sigebert I and of her own stepchildren. After Chilperic's murder (584) she acted as regent for her son CLOTAIRE II.

Fredericia (frĭthərē'tsyä), city (1970 com. pop. 43,869), Vejle co., central Denmark, on the Lille Baelt. It is a port, an industrial center, and an important rail junction. Manufactures include refined petroleum, chemicals, and textiles. Fredericia was built in 1650 by Frederick III as the principal fortress on Jylland and was not permitted to expand beyond its ramparts. In 1849 the Danes defeated the Prussians there. The fortress was closed in 1909, and the city's modern development began.

Frederick I or **Frederick Barbarossa** (bärbərôs'ə) [Ital.,=red beard], c.1125–90, Holy Roman emperor (1155–90) and German king (1152–90), son of Frederick of HOHENSTAUFEN, duke of Swabia, nephew and successor of Holy Roman Emperor Conrad III. His mother, Judith, was a Guelph (see GUELPHS), and Frederick frequently acted as a mediator between his Hohenstaufen uncle, Conrad, and his Guelph cousin, HENRY THE LION. Prior to his death Conrad III named Frederick as his successor hoping that Frederick's reign would end the discord between the rival houses of Hohenstaufen and Guelphs. Frederick's coronation as emperor in Rome was delayed by unrest in Germany and by the revolutionary commune of Rome (1143–55), headed by ARNOLD OF BRESCIA, which controlled the city. In 1152, Frederick pacified Germany by proclaiming a general land peace to end the anarchy, and in 1156 he satisfied Henry the Lion by restoring the duchy of Bavaria to him, at the same time making Austria into a new duchy as a counterweight to Henry's power. In Italy, Frederick's policy was to restore the imperial power, which had virtually disappeared as a result of neglect by previous emperors. It was thus necessary for him to conciliate the pope. In a treaty (1153) with Pope Eugene III, Frederick promised to assist him against Arnold of Brescia and against the powerful Normans in Sicily. Frederick entered Italy in 1154 and was crowned in Rome (June 18, 1155) amid hostile demonstrations. The reluctance of his troops to remain in Italy forced him to return to Germany without assisting the new pope, ADRIAN IV, against King William I of Sicily. Adrian, obliged to ally himself (1156) with William, turned against Frederick. At the Diet of Besançon (1157) the papal legate presented a letter that Frederick interpreted as a claim by the pope that the empire was a papal fief. Frederick replied in a manifesto that he held the throne "through the election of the princes from God alone" and prepared to invade Italy, where Milan had begun the conquest of Lombardy. Adrian explained that he had not intended that interpretation of his words, but Frederick entered Italy, seized Milan, and at the Diet of Roncaglia (1158) laid claim, as emperor and king of the Lombards, to all imperial rights, including the appointment of an imperial podesta, or governor, in every town. The rapacity of his German officials led to the revolt (1159) of Milan, Brescia, Crema, and their allies, secretly encouraged by Adrian IV. After a long siege, Frederick stormed and burned Milan (1162). Moreover he set up an antipope to Adrian's successor, ALEXANDER III, who excommunicated him. Frederick withdrew temporarily, but returned in 1166, captured Rome, and was preparing to attack the pope's Sicilian allies when his army was decimated by an epidemic. In 1167 the rebellious Italian communes united against Frederick in the LOMBARD LEAGUE, and Frederick retreated with difficulty to Germany, where he turned to increasing his territorial power and pacifying the constantly feuding German princes. In 1174 he returned to Italy. He was decisively defeated (1176) at Legnano by the Lombard League, partly because of lack of support from the German princes, notably Henry the Lion. After his defeat Frederick became reconciled with the pope; he agreed to recognize Alexander III as pope and was restored (1177) to communion. He made peace with the Lombard towns (confirmed by the Peace of Constance in 1183) and arranged a truce with the pope's Sicilian allies. After his return to Germany, Frederick brought about the downfall (1180) of Henry the Lion, whose large duchies were partitioned; Frederick's divisions of the German territories were of lasting consequence. At the Diet of Mainz (1184) the emperor celebrated his own glory in fabulous pomp. He arranged the marriage (1186) of his son and successor, Henry (later HENRY VI), to Constance, heiress-presumptive of Sicily, thus insuring peace with Sicily. In March, 1188, Frederick took the Cross, and he set out (1189) on the Third Crusade (see CRUSADES). He was drowned in Cilicia. Legend, however, has him asleep in the KYFFHÄUSER, waiting to restore the empire to its former greatness. Among the positive and lasting achievements of Frederick's reign are the foundations of new towns, the increase of trade, and the colonization and Christianization of Slavic lands in E Germany. In his administrative reforms the emperor was ably assisted by his chancellor, Rainald of Dassel. See study by Peter Munz (1969); Otto of Freising, *The Deeds of Frederick Barbarossa* (tr. 1953).

Frederick II, 1194–1250, Holy Roman emperor (1220–50) and German king (1212–20), king of Sicily (1197–1250), and king of Jerusalem (1229–50), son of Holy Roman Emperor Henry VI and of CONSTANCE, heiress of Sicily. In 1196, Henry VI secured the election as German king, or emperor-elect, for his infant son Frederick. When Henry died (1197), his brother, PHILIP OF SWABIA, was unable to hold the German magnates to this election, but in Sicily Constance secured Frederick's investiture as king from Pope INNOCENT III. Prior to her death (1198) Constance named the pope as Frederick's guardian; as a child, however, he passed from one Sicilian faction to another. Meanwhile, in Germany, Otto of Brunswick (OTTO IV) and Philip of Swabia were elected rival kings. Otto finally prevailed and was crowned emperor (1209) at Rome, but immediately alienated the pope by attempting to reassert imperial control in Italy. His invasion of Apulia (1210) led Innocent to promote Frederick's coronation (1212) at Mainz as German king even though this meant putting a HOHENSTAUFEN on the imperial throne. After Otto's defeat at Bouvines (1214) by Frederick's French ally King PHILIP II, Frederick was recrowned (1215) at Aachen and took the Cross (i.e., pledged to lead a Crusade). Despite his promises to Pope Innocent III that when crowned Holy Roman emperor he would separate Sicily from the empire by establishing a regency there for his infant son Henry, he reversed these arrangements in 1220. Promising Pope HONORIUS III to start on his crusade, he secured Henry's election as German king, and thus his position as imperial successor, shortly before his own imperial coronation (1220) at Rome. This action seemed to insure the union of Sicily and the empire. Under Frederick, however, no such union was effected; Henry governed, first under a regency, in Germany, and Frederick governed Italy and Sicily, which became the seat of his empire. After his coronation Frederick returned to Sicily. While in Germany, the success of Frederick's early rule (1212–20) was due largely to his lavishness with imperial lands and rights. In his Sicilian kingdom, which included S Italy, he pursued the reverse of his German policy; he suppressed the barons, transported the SARACENS to a colony on the mainland, recovered alienated lands, and began his legislative reforms. In 1224 he founded the university at Naples. Having married (1225) Yolande, daughter of JOHN OF BRIENNE, he claimed the crown of Jerusalem, but again postponed his departure on crusade. He further offended the pope by reasserting at the Diet of Cremona (1226) the imperial claim to Lombardy. The LOMBARD LEAGUE was immediately revived, but open conflict did not break out until 1236. On the insistent demand of the new pope, GREGORY IX, Frederick embarked on a crusade (Sept., 1227), but fell ill, turned back, and was excommunicated. In 1228 he finally embarked. His "crusade," actually a state visit, was a diplomatic victory. At Jaffa he made a treaty by which Jerusalem, Nazareth, and Bethlehem were surrendered to the Christians, with the Mosque of Omar being left to the Muslims. In 1229 he crowned himself king at Jerusalem. The pope denounced the treaty by Frederick, who was still under excommunication, and sent a papal army to invade Frederick's kingdom. Frederick returned in 1229 and signed (1230) the Treaty of San Germano, by which he was temporarily reconciled with the pope. He then turned to strengthening his Sicilian domains in preparation for the inevitable conflict with the Lombard League. Among his achievements in Sicily were his *Liber Augustalis* (1231), a new body of laws that were the most constructive of the era. In Germany, Frederick attempted to insure support for his Italian policy by granting the princes practically absolute authority within their territories. This policy led to a conflict with his son Henry, who objected to Frederick's virtual renunciation of his imperial rights in Germany. In 1234 Henry rebelled with the aid of the German towns, but Frederick easily deposed and imprisoned (1235) his son. At the Diet of Mainz (1235), Frederick issued a land peace establishing an imperial court of justice to try all cases except those involving the great vassals. This land peace is one of the monuments of imperial legislation. In 1236 he began a successful campaign against the Lombard cities, but in March, 1239, Pope Gregory IX joined the Lombards and excommunicated the emperor. Frederick issued a circular against the pope and seized most of the Papal States; in May, 1241, he captured a number of prelates en route from Genoa to a general council in Rome, and he was threatening Rome when Gregory died. While emperor and pope were thus at swords' points, Europe was threatened (1241) by a Mongol invasion under BATU KHAN. The Mongols withdrew in 1242. After the election (1243) of Pope INNOCENT IV, Frederick offered sweeping concessions to the pope and his allies, but the pope fled (1244) to Lyons, deposed Frederick at the Council of Lyons (1245), and gave the emperor's foes the privileges of Crusaders. The election (1246) of an anti-king to CONRAD IV, Frederick's younger son, plunged Germany into civil war. The war in Italy turned in Frederick's favor in 1250, but in December he died of dysentery. Frederick II was one of the most arresting figures of the Middle Ages. He called himself "lord of the world"; his contemporaries either praised him as *stupor mundi* [wonder of the world] or reviled him as anti-Christ. Norman and German in ancestry but essentially a Sicilian, Frederick always felt a stranger in Germany. He spent most of his time in Italy and Sicily, where his legal reforms set up an efficient administration. This system he tried, with some success, to transfer to Germany. Himself an expert trader engaging in far-flung business affairs, Frederick encouraged commerce and soon expanded it to Spain, Morocco, and Egypt. Agriculture and industry were likewise fostered. Towns, though at first somewhat curbed, enjoyed a more generous treatment in the later years of his reign, and many developed into important trade centers. Frederick was also a gifted artist and scientist. A poet himself, he was surrounded by Provençal troubadours and German minnesingers. He patronized science and philosophy and interested himself in medicine, mathematics, astronomy, and astrology. His *De arte venandi cum avibus,* on hawking as well as the anatomy and life of birds, was the first modern ornithology. Frederick's personality was a curious mixture of German-Christian and Byzantine-Muslim influences. Although Christian, he maintained a harem; though he was frequently at odds with the papacy, he ruthlessly persecuted heretics; though sensitive to art and poetry, he could be extremely cruel. The intense struggle between Frederick and the papacy led to the ruin of the house of Hohenstaufen and severely damaged papal prestige. With his rule the great days of the German empire ended and the rise of states in Italy began. The interregnum (see HOLY ROMAN EMPIRE) ended only with the election (1273) of Rudolf I of Hapsburg. See biographies by Ernst Kantorowicz (1927, in German; tr. 1931, repr. 1957) and T. C. Van Cleve (1972); study by Georgina Masson (1957, repr. 1973).

Frederick III, 1415–93, Holy Roman emperor (1452–93) and German king (1440–93). With his brother Albert VI he inherited the duchies of Styria, Carinthia, and Carniola. He became head of the house of HAPSBURG at the death (1439) of his distant cousin Albert II, whom he was elected (1440) to succeed as German king. Although Frederick was generally a weak ruler, he made considerable progress toward reuniting the Hapsburg family lands under his own branch. On Albert II's death Frederick became guardian for his young son Ladislaus Posthumus (see LADISLAUS V) and regent of Austria for Ladislaus. In Bohemia and Hungary, however, he was unable to establish himself as regent for Ladislaus. In 1453 he temporarily lost Austria when he was forced to give up the youth. After the death (1457) of Ladislaus, Frederick relinquished Bohemia to GEORGE OF PODEBRAD and Hungary to MATTHIAS CORVINUS. In Austria, his succession to Ladislaus as duke was challenged by his brother, but Albert's death (1463) left Frederick with an undisputed claim. In 1485, Matthias Corvinus, who had invaded Bohemia and Austria, occupied Vienna, and Frederick was forced to abandon his hereditary lands. However, longevity again proved an advantage; Matthias died in 1490, and Frederick recovered his possessions. In his relations with the Roman Catholic Church, Frederick was guided by his secretary, the brilliant Aeneas Silvius Piccolomini (later Pope PIUS II). In return for his support of Pope EUGENE IV against Antipope Felix V (see AMADEUS VIII), Frederick was promised an imperial coronation at Rome and various subsidies and revenues. He was the last emperor crowned at Rome. Frederick's greatest success was his acquisition of Burgundy, including the Netherlands and Belgium, for the house of Hapsburg. In 1473 at an interview at Trier with CHARLES THE BOLD of Burgundy, Frederick attempted to arrange the marriage of his son, later King MAXIMILIAN I, to Charles's daughter MARY OF BURGUNDY. However, he was not prepared to meet Charles's demands and the negotiations ended abruptly. In 1477, soon after the defeat and death of Charles at Nancy, the marriage of Maximilian and the Burgundian heiress nevertheless took place and netted Austria a huge and cheap prize. This alliance set the pattern for the subsequent marriages and successions through which the Hapsburgs came to dominate a large part of the globe. In 1486, Maximilian was elected king of the Romans, or German king, and after 1490, Frederick resigned most of his duties to his son. The anagram AEIOU, inscribed on Frederick's personal possessions, has traditionally been explained as signifying *Austria est imperare orbi universo* [Lat.,=it is Austria's destiny to rule the whole world] or *Alles Erdreich ist Österreich untertan* [Ger.,=all the earth is subject to Austria].

Frederick III, 1831–88, emperor of Germany and king of Prussia (March–June, 1888), son and successor of William I. In 1858 he married VICTORIA, the princess royal of England, who exerted considerable influence over him. Frederick was a liberal and a patron of art and learning. In the Franco-Prussian War he distinguished himself as a military commander. He was popular, and much good was expected of his reign, but he died of cancer of the throat soon after his accession and was succeeded by his son, William II. His war diary of 1870–71 has been translated into English.

Frederick III, 1609–70, king of Denmark and Norway (1648–70), son and successor of Christian IV. He at first made great concessions to the powerful nobles but later asserted his own power. In 1657 war with Sweden began anew. CHARLES X of Sweden forced Denmark to accept the humiliating Treaty of Roskilde (1658). Charles soon renewed the war, and it was only through the heroic defense of Copenhagen by Frederick, assisted by Dutch ships, that the Danish kingdom was saved from utter destruction. The Netherlands and Brandenburg, allies of Denmark, then assisted in repulsing the Swedes, and the peace of Copenhagen was made (1660). Denmark lost Skåne, Halland, and Blekinge to Sweden. Denmark was devastated and in debt. To help the country recover, the burghers and clergy united to end aristocratic power and privilege. The monarchy was declared hereditary, and the state administration was centralized and staffed by civil servants. A constitution granting absolute power to a hereditary monarch was published after Frederick's death (see GRIFFENFELD). Frederick was succeeded by his son, Christian V.

Frederick IV, 1671–1730, king of Denmark and Norway (1699–1730), son and successor of CHRISTIAN V. He allied himself (1699) with Augustus II of Poland and Saxony and with Peter I of Russia against CHARLES XII of Sweden in the NORTHERN WAR, but was forced to sign the humiliating Treaty of Travendal in 1700. Still hoping to recover S Sweden (lost in 1660) and to assure Danish rule in Schleswig, he again entered the war in 1709. In the peace treaties of 1720–21, Denmark renounced S Sweden but obtained Schleswig. Frederick was industrious and able. He systematized absolute monarchy, reduced corruption, built schools, attempted to repair the damage caused by the war, and reduced the national debt. He was succeeded by his son, Christian VI.

Frederick V, 1723–66, king of Denmark and Norway (1746–66), son and successor of Christian VI. Frederick's reign was one of commercial expansion and prosperity. Loans, subsidies, and treaties aided industry, and a strong system of PROTECTION was introduced. The conditions of the peasantry, however, remained poor. In 1757 a commission was appointed to study agricultural affairs. During Frederick's rule foreign affairs were conducted by J. H. E. BERNSTORFF. Frederick was succeeded by his son, Christian VII.

Frederick VI, 1768–1839, king of Denmark (1808–39) and Norway (1808–14), son and successor of CHRISTIAN VII. After the court party had executed Struensee, expelled Frederick's mother, Caroline Matilda, and imposed their will on the demented Christian (1772), Frederick grew up under the guardianship of the dowager queen. In 1784 by a peaceful coup d'etat he established himself as regent. He made Andreas Peter BERNSTORFF minister, and liberal reforms were instituted. Except for a short war with Sweden (1788), peace reigned in a prosperous Denmark until the close of the century. Denmark clung to its neutrality in the French Revolutionary Wars, but its opposition to the British ruling on neutral shipping resulted in an English attack on the Danish fleet (see COPENHAGEN, BATTLE OF, 1801). Again, in 1807, England attacked neutral DENMARK and bombarded COPENHAGEN. Frederick thereupon allied himself with Napoleon I and was punished at the Congress of Vienna (1814–15) by the loss of Norway to Sweden. As compensation he received the island of Rügen and Swedish Pomerania, which he exchanged with Prussia for the duchy of Lauenburg. Frederick had no male issue; his cousin Christian VIII succeeded him.

Frederick VII, 1808–63, king of Denmark, duke of Schleswig, Holstein, and Lauenburg (1848–63), son and successor of CHRISTIAN VIII. He accepted a liberal constitution in 1849 that ended the absolute monarchy. The vexed SCHLESWIG-HOLSTEIN question continued during his reign. Frederick's attempt (1848) to tie Schleswig more closely to Denmark than to Holstein was tentatively settled by the Berlin Treaty (1850) and the London Protocol (1852). Just before Frederick died Schleswig was incorporated into Denmark, which led to war with Prussia under his successor, CHRISTIAN IX. Numerous liberal reforms, such as emancipation of slaves in the colonies, freedom of the press, and civil marriage, were incorporated into Danish law in Frederick's reign.

Frederick VIII, 1843–1912, king of Denmark (1906–12), son and successor of Christian IX. He fought in the war with Prussia in 1864 and always retained an interest in military affairs. He was succeeded by his son Christian X. Another son became king of Norway as Haakon VII.

Frederick IX, 1899–1972, king of Denmark (1947–72), son and successor of Christian X. He married (1935) Princess Ingrid of Sweden. Because he did not have a son the constitution was amended in 1953 to allow for a female heir to the throne; Frederick was succeeded by his daughter, Queen Margaret II.

Frederick I, 1657–1713, first king of Prussia (1701–13), elector of Brandenburg (1688–1713) as Frederick III. He succeeded his father, Frederick William the Great Elector, in Brandenburg. Through a renewed alliance with Holy Roman Emperor Leopold I prior to the War of the SPANISH SUCCESSION, Frederick obtained the emperor's approval for the elevation of PRUSSIA to a kingdom. On Jan. 18, 1701, Frederick crowned himself at Königsberg. His extravagant expenses drained the finances of Prussia. Frederick was a patron of LEIBNIZ. He was succeeded by his son, Frederick William I.

Frederick II or **Frederick the Great,** 1712–86, king of Prussia (1740–86), son and successor of FREDERICK WILLIAM I. His coarse and tyrannical father despised Prince Frederick, who showed a taste for French art and literature and no interest in government and war. At the age of 18, Frederick, who had been repeatedly humiliated and ill-treated, planned to escape to England. He was arrested, imprisoned, and forced to witness the beheading of his friend and accomplice, Lieutenant Katte. Frederick submitted to his father and was released. In 1733, at his father's request, he married Elizabeth of Brunswick-Bevern, but he separated from her shortly afterward and for the rest of his life showed no interest in women. He spent the next few years at Rheinsberg, where he wrote his *Anti-Machiavel*, an idealistic refutation of Machiavelli, and began his long correspondence with VOLTAIRE. Immediately upon his accession Frederick showed the qualities of leadership and decision that characterized his reign. In the War of the AUSTRIAN SUCCESSION (1740–48) against MARIA THERESA, Frederick invaded Silesia without warning, simultaneously offering his aid to Maria Theresa if she ceded a portion of Silesia to him. A brilliant campaigner, Frederick acted with utter disregard of his allies, notably France, and twice concluded separate peace treaties with Maria Theresa (1742, 1745), both times securing Upper and Lower Silesia for Prussia. In the SEVEN YEARS WAR (1756–63) possession of Silesia was again in dispute; Maria Theresa wished to recover it, and Frederick faced a strong coalition including Austria, Russia, and France. England was his only strong ally. Victorious at Rossbach and Leuthen (1757), he was routed (1759) at Kunersdorf by the Austro-Russian forces, who in 1760 occupied Berlin. In that dark period, it is said, Frederick was on the verge of suicide. However, the accession (1762) of his admirer, Peter III of Russia, took Russia out of the war and opened Frederick's way to victory. The Peace of Hubertusburg (1763) left Frederick his previous conquests and made Prussia the foremost military power in Europe. Frederick was brilliantly assisted by his principal generals, SEYDLITZ, James KEITH, FERDINAND of Brunswick, Hans Joachim von Zieten, and others. His tactics were studied and admired by Napoleon Bonaparte and exerted great influence on the art of warfare. After the peace of 1763, Frederick promoted an alliance with Russia, which had nearly defeated him in the Seven Years War. The establishment of a Russo-Prussian alliance prepared the way for the eventual dismemberment of Poland. By the first partition of Poland (see POLAND, PARTITIONS OF) in 1772, Frederick vastly expanded the limits of Prussia. His rivalry with Austria persisted. He opposed any attempts by Austria to extend its power within the Holy Roman Empire and instigated the War of the BAVARIAN SUCCESSION (1778–79) to prevent Austrian annexation of Bavaria. He also created (1785) the Fürstenbund [league of princes] to check Austrian schemes. In internal affairs Frederick continued his father's fundamental policies. His first care was the strength and discipline of his army. An "enlightened despot," he instituted important legal and penal reforms, set up trade monopolies to create new industries, forwarded education, and accomplished internal improvements such as drainage projects, roads, and canals. Though he improved the lot of his own serfs, the nobility had more control over their peasants after his reign than before. He was tolerant in religious matters, personally professing atheism to his intimates. Cold and curt, he relaxed only during his famous midnight suppers at SANS SOUCI, his residence at Potsdam. There he was surrounded by a group of educated men, mostly French, that included, at times, Voltaire (who broke with him in 1753 but who later resumed his friendship from a safe distance), d'Alembert, La Mettrie, and Maupertuis. Frederick's wit was corrosive and icy. He wrote inconsequential poetry and remarkable prose on politics, history, military science, and philosophy. Nearly all his writings were in French. He failed to appreciate such men as Lessing and Goethe, who were among his most ardent admirers. A pupil of Quantz, he played the flute creditably, and he composed marches, concertos for the flute, and other pieces. Frederick's personal appearance in his later years—small, sharp-featured, untidy, and snuff-stained—has become part of the legend of "Old Fritz." He was succeeded by his nephew, Frederick

William II. See J. D. E. Preuss, ed., *Œuvres de Frédéric le Grand* (33 vol., 1846–57). See also biographies by Carlyle and Macaulay, both classics, and the more scholarly studies by Ernest Lavisse (tr. 1891), Gerhard Ritter (1936, tr. 1968), Pierre Gaxotte (tr. 1941), G. P. Gooch (1947), Ludwig Reiners (1952, tr. 1960), and Peter Paret, ed. (1972).

Frederick III, king of Prussia: see FREDERICK III, 1831–88, emperor of Germany and king of Prussia.

Frederick II, 1272–1337, king of Sicily (1296–1337), 3d son of Peter III of Aragón. When his brother, who was king of Sicily, became (1291) king of Aragón as JAMES II, Frederick was his regent in Sicily. In 1295 James renounced Sicily in favor of the Angevin king of Naples, CHARLES II, but the Sicilians rebelled and crowned Frederick. A war ensued in which Frederick fought his own brother, now Charles's ally. In the Peace of Caltabellotta (1302) Charles and Pope Boniface VIII recognized Frederick as king of Trinacria (an ancient name for Sicily) for his lifetime. At his death the kingdom was to revert to the Angevin dynasty of Naples. Although Frederick married a daughter of Charles, war with Naples resumed in 1312. Frederick, allied successively with Holy Roman Emperors HENRY VII and Louis IV, retook the title king of Sicily and, with his son Peter, was crowned in 1322. The war continued after Frederick's death.

Frederick III (Frederick the Pious), 1515–76, elector palatine (1559–76). The first German prince to accept Calvinism, he ordered the Heidelberg Catechism (1563) drawn up (see under HEIDELBERG). He aided the Calvinists in the Netherlands and in France.

Frederick V, elector palatine: see FREDERICK THE WINTER KING.

Frederick I, 1371–1440, elector of Brandenburg (1415–40), first of the Hohenzollerns (see HOHENZOLLERN, family) to rule Brandenburg. As Frederick VI, burgrave of Nuremburg, he served under King Sigismund of Hungary (later Holy Roman Emperor SIGISMUND) against the Turks in E Europe and took part in the battle of Nikopol (1396), in which the crusaders were defeated. As a reward for aiding Sigismund's election as emperor (1410), Sigismund granted (1411) Frederick a regency over Brandenburg and named him (1415) elector of Brandenburg; in 1417 he was formally invested with the electoral dignity. After subduing the recalcitrant nobles of Brandenburg, Frederick departed (1425) to command the imperial forces against the Hussites, but he later broke with Sigismund. His own ambition to be emperor was never fulfilled, but at his death the Hohenzollerns were well ensconced in Brandenburg.

Frederick I or **Frederick the Warlike,** 1370–1428, elector of Saxony (1423–28). As margrave of Meissen he was involved in disputes with his brothers and his uncles over the division of his father's territory. He founded (1409) the university at Leipzig for German students who were driven from Prague. A neighbor of the HUSSITES, he was one of the first to take the field against them (1420–22) and was rewarded by Holy Roman Emperor Sigismund with electoral Saxony. In 1426 he was defeated by the Hussites at Aussig.

Frederick III or **Frederick the Wise,** 1463–1525, elector of Saxony (1486–1525). At Wittenberg he founded (1502) the university where Martin LUTHER and MELANCHTHON taught. At a crucial period for the early Reformation, Frederick protected Luther from the pope and the emperor, and took him into custody at the Wartburg castle after the Diet of Worms (1521), which put Luther under the imperial ban. Frederick, however, had little personal contact with Luther and remained a Catholic, although he gradually inclined toward the doctrines of the Reformation.

Frederick, city (1970 pop. 23,641), seat of Frederick co., NW Md.; settled 1745, inc. 1817. The processing center of a rich farm area, it has canneries, milk-receiving stations, and plants manufacturing household utensils, aluminum, optical and glass products, leather goods, clothing, and electronic equipment. Frederick was a stop on the road to the Ohio valley and an important grain trading center. In the Civil War, Confederate troops passed through the city en route to the battle of Antietam. During the battle of Monocacy, General Jubal Early's Confederate forces extracted a $200,000 ransom from Frederick's citizens. Points of interest include the home of Chief Justice Roger Taney; the grave of Francis Scott Key, the author of "The Star-spangled Banner"; the house of Barbara Fritchie, a Civil War heroine; and many restored historic buildings. Hood College; a junior college; a school for the deaf; and Fort Detrick, a U.S. Army research center, are in Frederick. Several scenic state parks and the Monocacy National Battlefield are nearby.

Frederick Augustus I, 1750–1827, king (1806–27) and elector (1763–1806) of Saxony, grand duke of Warsaw (1807–14). He sided with the allies in the French Revolutionary Wars and joined Prussia in the campaign of 1806 against the French emperor Napoleon I. However, after the French victory at Jena he made a separate peace with Napoleon, with whose approval he took the title king of Saxony. Napoleon also made him nominal ruler of the grand duchy of Warsaw. Frederick Augustus did not abandon his alliance with Napoleon in time and as a result lost a large part of Saxony to Prussia at the Congress of Vienna (1815).

Frederick Augustus I, elector of Saxony: see AUGUSTUS II, king of Poland.

Frederick Augustus II, elector of Saxony: see AUGUSTUS III, king of Poland.

Frederick Barbarossa: see FREDERICK I, Holy Roman emperor.

Frederick Douglass Home National Memorial: see NATIONAL PARKS AND MONUMENTS (table).

Frederick Henry, 1584–1647, prince of Orange; son of William the Silent and Louise de Coligny. He became stadtholder of the United Provinces of the Netherlands upon the death (1625) of his brother MAURICE OF NASSAU. The Netherlands were still struggling to maintain their independence from Spain. An able diplomat, he maintained friendship with France and in 1635 concluded an alliance with France and Sweden against the Hapsburgs in the THIRTY YEARS WAR. By the capture of the frontier forts of 's Hertogenbosch (1629), Maastricht (1632), and Breda (1637), he became famous as a master of siegecraft. In 1631 the United Provinces showed their trust in his leadership by declaring the stadtholderate hereditary in his family. The period of his rule is known as "the Golden Age of Frederick Henry" because of the remarkable state of DUTCH ART (represented by such men as Rembrandt and Frans Hals), of the sciences, and of the commerce, prosperity, and prestige of the Netherlands. One year after his death the independence of the Netherlands was recognized in the Peace of Westphalia. His son, William II, succeeded him as stadtholder.

Frederick Louis, 1707–51, prince of Wales, eldest son of George II of England. By his wife, Princess Augusta of Saxe-Gotha, he had several children, the eldest of whom became George III. He quarreled with his parents over his financial allowance and in 1737 was expelled from court. Thereafter he maintained his own household, chiefly at Leicester House, which became a center of political opposition to George II and the ministries of Robert Walpole and later of Henry Pelham.

Frederick of Austria: see FREDERICK THE FAIR, German antiking.

Fredericksburg, independent city (1970 pop. 14,450), N Va., on the Rappahannock River, midway between Washington, D.C., and Richmond; settled 1671, laid out 1727, inc. as a town 1781, as a city 1879. A city of fine old houses and much historic interest, Fredericksburg attracts many tourists. It is also a farm trade center and an industrial city producing clothing, shoes, and veneers. Its historic buildings include the home of Mary Washington (1772–89), the mother of George Washington; "Kenmore," the home of George Washington's sister; the Rising Sun Tavern (c.1760), a rendezvous for American patriots in the Revolution; the law office of James MONROE; and the home of John Paul Jones. Fredericksburg is the seat of Mary Washington College of the Univ. of Virginia. Nearby are WAKEFIELD (Washington's birthplace) and Fredericksburg and Spotsylvania County Battlefields Memorial National Military Park (see NATIONAL PARKS AND MONUMENTS, table), commemorating the Civil War battles of Fredericksburg, CHANCELLORSVILLE, and Spotsylvania Courthouse (see WILDERNESS CAMPAIGN). See O. H. Darter, *Colonial Fredericksburg and Neighborhood in Perspective* (1957).

Fredericksburg, battle of, in the Civil War, fought Dec. 13, 1862, at Fredericksburg, Va. In Nov., 1862, the Union general Ambrose BURNSIDE moved his three "grand divisions" under W. B. Franklin, E. V. Sumner, and Joseph Hooker to the north side of the Rappahannock River opposite Fredericksburg; his objective was Richmond. Delay in bringing up pontoons prevented Burnside from seizing the heights on the south bank immediately. Robert E. Lee, having anticipated the move, soon confronted him from those heights with James Longstreet's 1st Corps, which soon was joined by Stonewall Jackson's 2d. The Federals crossed on Dec. 11–12 and attacked Lee on Dec. 13. After Jackson had repulsed Franklin's attack on the Confederate right, Burnside ordered Sumner to storm Longstreet's impregnable position on Marye's Heights. Successive charges brought death to droves of courageous Union troops. Burnside's subordinates protested against renewing the foolhardy assaults, and on Dec. 15 the Federals made an undisturbed withdrawal to the north bank. Union losses, more than twice the Confederate, were over 12,000. The defeat caused profound depression throughout the North. See E. J. Stackpole, *Drama on the Rappahannock* (1957); Vorin E. Whan, Jr., *Fiasco at Fredericksburg* (1961).

Frederick the Fair, c.1286–1330, German antiking (1314–26), duke of Austria, son of Albert I, German king. On the death of Henry VII, Holy Roman emperor and German king, the split between the supporters of the houses of Hapsburg and Luxemburg resulted in the dual election (1314) of Frederick and Louis of Bavaria (Holy Roman Emperor LOUIS IV). War ensued and Frederick and his supporters were defeated (1322) by Louis at Mühldorf. However, the pope refused to confirm Louis as Holy Roman emperor, and Frederick remained a possible rival until his death.

Frederick the Great: see FREDERICK II, king of Prussia.

Frederick the Warlike: see FREDERICK I, elector of Saxony.

Frederick the Winter King, 1596–1632, king of Bohemia (1619–20), elector palatine (1610–20) as Frederick V. The Protestant diet of Bohemia deposed the Roman Catholic King Ferdinand (Holy Roman Emperor FERDINAND II) and chose Frederick as king. Influenced by his minister CHRISTIAN OF ANHALT, Frederick accepted but did not receive the aid expected from his father-in-law, James I of England, and from the PROTESTANT UNION against Ferdinand. After initial success, his supporters were routed at White Mt. (1620). Frederick thus lost Bohemia; from his short tenure came the derisive name, the Winter King. He was put under imperial ban and was stripped of all his remaining territories. The electorate was transferred to Maximilian I of Bavaria (see ELECTORS). These struggles were the first campaigns of the THIRTY YEARS WAR. The Hanoverian kings of England were descended from Frederick and his wife, Elizabeth, through their daughter Sophia, who was the mother of George I of England.

Frederick the Wise: see FREDERICK III, elector of Saxony.

Frederick William I, 1688–1740, king of Prussia (1713–40), son and successor of Frederick I. He continued the administrative reforms and the process of centralization begun by Frederick William, the Great Elector, creating a strong, absolutist state. He practiced rigid economy, and at his death there was a large surplus in the treasury. The Prussian army was made an efficient instrument of war. Although Frederick William built up one of the most powerful armies in Europe, he was essentially a peaceful man. He intervened briefly in the NORTHERN WAR, but gained little territory. Later, he signed a treaty (1728) with Holy Roman Emperor Charles VI in the hope of acquiring the territories of Jülich and Berg, to which he had a hereditary claim. The emperor subsequently went back on this agreement. Frederick William was a coarse man, and he had contempt for his gifted heir, who was to succeed him as FREDERICK II (Frederick the Great). See studies by R. R. Ergang (1941) and R. A. Dorwart (1952, repr. 1971).

Frederick William II, 1744–97, king of Prussia (1786–97), nephew and successor of FREDERICK II (Frederick the Great). He had the power but lacked the ability of his distinguished predecessors. He joined the European coalition in support of Louis XVI and fought in the early campaigns of the French Revolutionary Wars. Financial difficulties and the revolt (1794) in Poland against the Prussian and Russian occupiers of that country following the second partition of Poland (see POLAND, PARTITIONS OF) led Frederick William II to make a separate peace with the French at Basel (1795). Frederick William's extravagance left a ruined exchequer. He was a patron of the arts and an amateur cellist; Mozart dedicated three string quartets to him. His son, Frederick William III, succeeded him.

Frederick William III, 1770–1840, king of Prussia (1797–1840), son and successor of Frederick William II. Well-intentioned but weak and vacillating, he endeavored to maintain neutrality in the Napoleonic Wars. In 1806, French troops were massed on Prussia's frontier and Frederick William was forced to take up arms against France. His crushing defeat by the French at Jena and the humiliating Treaty of Tilsit (1807), which virtually made Prussia a French vassal, served to waken the king to the need of reconstruction in Prussia. Unable to carry through the reforms himself, he was far-sighted enough to appoint capable ministers. The reforms of Karl vom und zum STEIN, Karl August von HARDENBERG, and SCHARNHORST laid the basis of the modern Prussian state and prepared for the eventual war against Napoleon. Forced to send an auxiliary force to aid Napoleon's Russian campaign, the king was finally persuaded to support the Convention of Tauroggen (see TAURAGE), concluded with the Russians by the commander of the Prussian auxiliary force, General YORCK VON WARTENBURG. A few weeks later a military alliance with Russia was signed, and in March, 1813, the king declared war on France. After Napoleon's defeat and the Congress of Vienna, which he attended, Frederick William grew more reactionary. Influenced by Czar Alexander I and by Metternich, he joined the HOLY ALLIANCE and refused to grant the constitution he had promised. His consort, Queen LOUISE, far more popular than the king, died in 1810. His elder son, Frederick William IV, succeeded him. His second son was to become Emperor William I.

Frederick William IV, 1795–1861, king of Prussia (1840–61), son and successor of Frederick William III. A romanticist and a mystic, he conceived vague schemes of reform based on a revival of the medieval structure, with the rule of estates and a patriarchal monarchy. During the revolution of 1848 in Prussia, which broke out in March, Frederick William was forced at first to accede to revolutionary demands. Later, however, he crushed the opposition, dissolved (Dec., 1848) the constituent assembly, and promulgated a conservative constitution, which, as modified in 1850, remained in force until 1918. Frederick William refused the crown of a united Germany offered him (1849) by the FRANKFURT PARLIAMENT on the grounds that a monarch by divine right could not receive authority from an elected assembly. Although unwilling to accept the crown from an elected assembly, Frederick William desired German unity under Prussian leadership and presented the Prussian Union plan for a confederation of Prussia and the smaller German states. Austrian opposition to the plan forced Frederick William to abandon it in the Treaty of Olmütz (1850). In 1848, Frederick William briefly supported the revolt in SCHLESWIG-HOLSTEIN against Denmark but yielded to British pressure for an armistice. In 1857 his mental condition necessitated a temporary (later permanent) regency of his brother, who succeeded him as William I.

Frederick William, crown prince of Germany: see WILLIAM.

Frederick William, known as the **Great Elector,** 1620–88, elector of Brandenburg (1640–88), son and successor of George William. At his accession the scattered lands of the Hohenzollern were devastated and depopulated by the THIRTY YEARS WAR and occupied by Swedish troops. Frederick William immediately negotiated an armistice with Sweden and then turned to building his military strength. Beginning with few resources and no dependable troops, he raised an efficient army. At the Peace of Westphalia, which ended the Thirty Years War, he received E Pomerania and several other territories. Frederick William subsequently joined Sweden in its war against Poland (1655–60) but deserted the Swedes after Russia and Denmark entered the war. In a treaty with Poland (1657) he obtained recognition of his sovereignty over Prussia, previously held as a fief of the Polish crown. Now allied against Sweden, he gained W Pomerania, but was deprived of it by the Peace of Oliva (1660). In succeeding years Frederick William continued in his attempt to consolidate his widely scattered lands, at the same time trying to avoid French or Hapsburg domination. In the Dutch War of 1672–78 he achieved his objective of uniting all of Pomerania, but was forced to give up his conquest as a result of the peace between France and the Holy Roman Empire. Nevertheless, his prestige was enormously enhanced by his brilliant victory at Fehrbellin (1675) over France's Swedish allies. Frederick William laid the foundation of the Prussian state by repressing the estates, strengthening central administration, husbanding the resources of his lands, improving communication, and building the army. His son became king of Prussia as Frederick I. See biography by F. Schevill (1947).

Frederick William, 1771–1815, duke of Brunswick, German military hero. On the death (1806) of his father, CHARLES WILLIAM FERDINAND, his duchy was seized by NAPOLEON I and added to the kingdom of Westphalia. He attempted to liberate his duchy from French control in 1809, when Austria reopened war against France. Frederick William formed a free corps, the "Black Brunswickers," and in a dashing foray advanced through Germany and captured Brunswick. He soon was driven out but succeeded in fleeing with his troops to England. Returning in 1813, he took possession of Brunswick but was killed at Quatre Bras in the Waterloo campaign.

Fredericton, city (1971 pop. 24,524), provincial capital, S central N.B., Canada, on the St. John River. It is a commercial and distribution center where shoes and wood products are manufactured. The city was founded by United Empire Loyalists in 1783 and was made the provincial capital in 1785. Of interest are the government buildings, the Beaverbrook Art Gallery, and the Playhouse Theatre. The Univ. of New Brunswick and St. Thomas Univ. are in the city. Nearby is a federal experimental farm.

Frederiksberg, Denmark: see COPENHAGEN.

Frederiksborg castle: see HILLERØD, Denmark.

Frederikshåb (frĭth'rĭkshôp"), town (1969 pop. 1,949), in Frederikshåb dist. (1969 pop. 2,496), SW Greenland; founded in 1792. It is an important fishing center.

Frederikshald: see HALDEN, Norway.

Frederikshavn (frĭth'rĭks-houn), city (1970 com. pop. 33,071), Nordjylland co., N Denmark, a port on the Kattegat; chartered 1818. It is a commercial and industrial center.

Frederiksted (frĕ'drĭkstĕd), town (1970 pop. 1,548), chief port and commercial center of St. Croix, U.S. Virgin Islands. Sugar is the principal export.

Fredonia, village (1970 pop. 10,326), Chautauqua co., SW N.Y., near Lake Erie; inc. 1829. Grape juice, wine, canned foods, and seeds are produced there. Fredonia was the site of the first gas well in the United States. The first local unit of the GRANGER MOVEMENT was also founded there. Fredonia has a state-university college.

Fredonian Rebellion, 1826–27, in Texas history, a premature attempt to make Texas independent from Mexico. Two Americans, Haden Edwards and his brother, had undertaken to make settlements on a land grant in E Texas around Nacogdoches, where there were already some Mexican settlers, some American squatters, and some Cherokee Indians. Haden Edwards tried to oust those settlers who could not show clear title, and the resultant trouble led the Mexican government to revoke his charter. The impetuous Edwards decided, against the advice of Stephen F. Austin, to take up arms. He expected some American support and attempted an alliance with the Indians, agreeing to divide Texas with them; but he could gather only a few men for the army of his hastily constituted state of Fredonia, and the whole scheme fell apart at the approach of a Mexican force. The incident served, however, to draw the attention of the Mexican and U.S. governments to the conflict of cultures in Texas.

Fredrikshald: see HALDEN, Norway.

Fredrikshamn, Finland: see HAMINA.

Fredriksten: see HALDEN, Norway.

Fredrikstad (frĕ'drĭkstä"), city (1970 pop. 30,009), Østfold co., SE Norway, a port on the Oslofjord (an arm of the Skagerrak) at the mouth of the Glåma River. Manufactures include forest products, processed food, and chemicals. Founded by Frederick II in 1567, it was fortified in the 17th cent. Its 17th-century fortress, once the strongest in Norway and the main depot for the fleet and army, was decommissioned in 1903.

Fredro, Alexander (ä"lĕksän'dĕr frĕ'drô), 1793–1876, Polish comic dramatist. From 1809 to 1814, Fredro served in the Polish regiments of Napoleon I's army, taking part in the invasion of Russia. He returned to the family estates in Poland, devoting himself to the life of a country gentleman and writing plays that were at first influenced by the Molière and Goldoni works he had seen in Paris. *Husband and Wife*, the best of his early dramas, was performed in 1822. Of his many facile plays, the best-known include *Ladies and Hussars* (1825), *Maidens' Vows* (1832), *Mister Joviality* (1832), *The Vengeance* (1833), and *The Life Annuity* (1835). His period of literary inactivity from 1835 to 1854 was in part the result of attacks from literary critics. Fredro's plays are notable for their brilliant characterization, complex plots, and idiomatic, colorful language. See *The Major Comedies of Alexander Fredro*, ed. by H. B. Segel (4 vol., tr. 1969).

free association: see ASSOCIATION; PSYCHOANALYSIS.

Free Church of Scotland: see SCOTLAND, FREE CHURCH OF.

Freedmen's Bureau, in U.S. history, a Federal agency, formed to aid and protect the newly freed Negroes in the South after the Civil War. Established by an act of March 3, 1865, under the name "bureau of refugees, freedmen, and abandoned lands," it was to function for one year after the close of the war. A bill extending its life indefinitely and greatly increasing its powers was vetoed (Feb. 19, 1866) by President Andrew Johnson, who viewed the legislation as an unwarranted (and unconstitutional) continuation of war powers in peacetime. The veto marked the beginning of the President's long and unsuccessful fight with the radical Republican Congress over RECONSTRUCTION. In slightly different form, the bill was passed over Johnson's veto on July 16, 1866. Organized under the War Dept., with Gen. Oliver O. HOWARD as its commissioner, and thus backed by military force, the bureau was one of the most powerful instruments of Reconstruction. Howard divided the ex-slave states, including the border slave states that had remained in the Union, into 10 districts, each headed by an assistant commissioner. The bureau's work consisted chiefly of five kinds of activity—relief work for both blacks and whites in war-stricken areas, regulation of Negro labor under the new conditions, administration of justice in cases concerning the Negro, management of abandoned and confiscated property, and support of education for Negroes. In its relief and educational activities the bureau compiled an excellent record, which, however, was too often marred by unprincipled agents, both military and civilian, in the local offices. Its efforts toward establishing the freed Negroes as landowners were nil. To a great degree the bureau operated as a political machine, organizing the black vote for the Republican party; its political activities made it thoroughly hated in the South. When, under the congressional plan of Reconstruction, new state governments based on Negro suffrage were organized in the South (with many agents holding various offices), the work of the Freedmen's Bureau was discontinued (July 1, 1869). Its educational activities, however, were carried on for another three years. See P. S. Peirce, *The Freedmen's Bureau* (1904); L. J. Webster, *The Operation of the Freedmen's Bureau in South Carolina* (1916, repr. 1970); G. R. Bentley, *A History of the Freedmen's Bureau* (1955, repr. 1970); Martin Abbott, *The Freedmen's Bureau in South Carolina* (1967).

freedom: see LIBERTY.

freedom of the press: see PRESS, FREEDOM OF.

freedom of the seas: see SEAS, FREEDOM OF.

free energy or **Gibbs free energy,** quantity derived from the relationships between heat and work studied in THERMODYNAMICS and used as a measure of the relative stability of a physical or chemical system, i.e., the tendency of the system to react or change. The absolute value of the free energy of a system is arbitrary, and it is the relative value as the system changes from one state to another that is significant. If the change in free energy, ΔG, is negative, the transformation of the system will occur spontaneously, since transitions in which the energy decreases are favored, whereas those in which it increases (ΔG positive) are not. The change in free energy for a given process at a particular temperature depends on three factors, as seen from the equation $\Delta G = \Delta H - T\Delta S$, where ΔH is the change in the ENTHALPY of the system, T is the temperature in degrees Kelvin, and ΔS is the change in ENTROPY. A negative value of the enthalpy change indicates a decrease in the heat content of the system and contributes to a favorable value of the free energy; a positive entropy change indicates a decrease in the orderliness of the system and also contributes to a favorable value of the free energy, since a system tends to go from more ordered to less ordered states. It may happen that the change in enthalpy for the reaction is favorable but that of the entropy is unfavorable, or vice versa; in such a case the temperature is the deciding factor since it determines how much weight is given to the entropy change. For example, in the transition of liquid water to ice, the enthalpy change is favorable because heat is released in the process but the entropy change is unfavorable because the transition is to the more ordered, crystalline state. Below a temperature of 32°F (273°K) the enthalpy term, ΔH, is larger and the process is spontaneous, but at higher temperatures the entropy term, $T\Delta S$, predominates, and the transition does not occur. Although the free energy indicates whether or not a given reaction will occur, it gives no information about the speed of such a reaction.

The reaction of hydrogen with oxygen to form water has a favorable, negative, free energy, but the reaction rate is so slow that without the presence of a catalyst it is not observable. Scientists use tables listing the standard free energy, $\Delta G°$, of various compounds; the standard free energy is the change in free energy when one mole of the compound is formed at 25°C and 1 atmospheric pressure.

free enterprise system: see CAPITALISM.

Freehold, borough (1970 pop. 10,545), seat of Monmouth co., E central N.J.; settled c.1650, called Monmouth Courthouse (1715-1801), inc. as a town 1867, as a borough 1919. Freehold is a farm trade center, with some industry. Points of interest include the Monmouth County Historical Association Museum and St. Peter's Episcopal Church (c.1683). The Revolutionary War battle of Monmouth (see MONMOUTH, BATTLE OF) took place nearby in 1778. Philip Freneau, the poet and journalist, lived in Freehold.

freehold: see TENURE.

Freeman, Douglas Southall, 1886-1953, American editor and historian, b. Lynchburg, Va. He was editor of the Richmond *News Leader* from 1915 to 1949, when he retired to devote most of his time to historical writing. An authority on military strategy and on the military history of the Civil War, Freeman wrote *R. E. Lee* (4 vol., 1934-35), which won the 1935 Pulitzer Prize for biography, and *Lee's Lieutenants* (3 vol., 1942-44). He edited *A Calendar of Confederate Papers* (1908) and also wrote *Virginia, a Gentle Dominion* (1924), *The South to Posterity* (1939), and *John Stewart Bryan* (1947). His biography of George Washington (7 vol., 1949-57), the last volume of which was written by his assistants John Alexander Carroll and Mary Wells, won a Pulitzer Prize in 1958.

Freeman, Edward Augustus, 1823-92, English historian, educated at Oxford. In 1884 he was made regius professor of modern history at Oxford. His major work is the monumental *History of the Norman Conquest* (6 vol., 1867-79), which minimized the results of the Norman Conquest and glorified Teutonic influences. His extreme views have since been generally conceded to be in error, but his care in his work and his deep understanding of politics gained him wide repute. His lectures, *Methods of Historical Study* (1886), were influential in historiography. Unfortunately his narrow understanding of the scope of sources and his overstatement of political views in his works also affected British history writing. His other works include *A History of Architecture* (1849), *The Growth of the English Constitution* (1872), *The Ottoman Power in Europe* (1877), *The Reign of William Rufus* (2 vol., 1882, repr. 1970), and *History of Sicily* (4 vol., 1891-94).

Freeman, Mary Eleanor Wilkins, 1852-1930, American short-story writer, b. Randolph, Mass. Her stories give realistic pictures of the severe rural New England life of her time. Among the best collections are *A Humble Romance and Other Stories* (1887) and *A New England Nun and Other Stories* (1891).

Freeman, Orville Lothrop, 1918-, U.S. Secretary of Agriculture (1961-69), b. Minneapolis. In World War II he served in the U.S. marine corps, was severely wounded, and was discharged with the rank of major in 1945. After the war he engaged in private law practice and became active in politics. Running on the Democratic-Farmer-Labor party ticket, Freeman was elected governor of Minnesota in 1954 (the first non-Republican governor in 17 years) and was reelected in 1956 and 1958. As governor he greatly expanded state aid to elementary and higher education and worked to improve the state's health institutions. Following his defeat for reelection as governor, he was appointed Secretary of Agriculture by President John F. Kennedy. He advocated substantial crop supports and controls, use of farm surpluses as an instrument of foreign policy, food gifts to depressed areas, and the food stamp program. He served throughout the Kennedy and Johnson administrations.

Freeman's Farm, battle of: see SARATOGA CAMPAIGN.

Freeman-Thomas, Freeman: see WILLINGDON, FREEMAN FREEMAN-THOMAS, 1ST MARQUESS OF.

Freemasonry, teachings and practices of the secret fraternal order officially known as the Free and Accepted Masons, or Ancient Free and Accepted Masons. With more than 6 million adherents representing almost every nation where Freemasonry is not officially banned, it forms the largest secret society in the world. There is no central Masonic authority; jurisdiction is divided among autonomous national authorities, called grand lodges, and many concordant organizations of higher degree Masons. Custom is the supreme authority of the order, and there are elaborate symbolic rites and ceremonies, most of which utilize the instruments of the stonemason—the plumb, square, level, and compasses—and apocryphal events concerning the building of King Solomon's Temple for allegorical purposes. The principles of Freemasonry have traditionally been liberal and democratic. *Anderson's Constitutions* (1723), the bylaws of the Grand Lodge of England, which is Freemasonry's oldest extant lodge, cites religious toleration, loyalty to local government, and political compromise as basic to the Masonic ideal. Masons are expected to believe in a Supreme Being, use a holy book appropriate to the religion of the lodge's members, and maintain a vow of secrecy concerning the order's ceremonies. The order is thought to have arisen from the English and Scottish fraternities of practicing stonemasons and cathedral builders in the early Middle Ages; traces of the society have been found as early as the 14th cent. Because, however, some documents of the order trace the sciences of masonry and geometry from Egypt, Babylon, and Palestine to England and France, some historians of Masonry claim that the order has roots in antiquity. The formation of the English Grand Lodge in London (1717) was the beginning of the widespread dissemination of speculative Freemasonry, the present-day fraternal order, whose membership is not limited to working stonemasons. The six lodges in England in 1700 grew to about 30 by 1723. There was a parallel development in Scotland and Ireland, although some lodges remained unaffiliated and open only to practicing masons. By the end of the 18th cent. there were Masonic lodges in all European countries and in many other parts of the world as well. The first lodge in the United States was founded in Philadelphia (1730); Benjamin Franklin was a member. Many of the leaders of the American Revolution, including John Hancock and Paul Revere, were members of St. Andrew's Lodge in Boston. George Washington became a Mason in 1752. At the time of the Revolution most of the American lodges broke away from their English and Scottish antecedents. Freemasonry has continued to be important in politics; 13 Presidents have been Masons, and at any given time quite a large number of the members of Congress have belonged to Masonic lodges. Notable European Masons included Voltaire, Giuseppe Mazzini, Giuseppe Garibaldi, Franz Joseph Haydn, Johann von Goethe, Johann von Schiller, and many leaders of Russia's Decembrist revolt (1825). Because of its identification with 19th-century bourgeois liberalism, there has been much opposition to Freemasonry. The most violent in the United States was that of the ANTI-MASONIC PARTY. Freemasonry's anticlerical attitude has also led to strong opposition from the Roman Catholic Church, which first expressed its anti-Masonic attitude in a bull of Pope Clement XII (1738). The Catholic Church still prohibits its members from joining the order. Totalitarian states have always suppressed Freemasonry; the lodges in Italy, Austria, and Germany were forcibly eradicated under Fascism and Nazism, and there are now no lodges in Hungary, Poland, the Soviet Union, Spain, Portugal, or Communist China. The basic unit of Freemasonry is the local Blue lodge, generally housed in a Masonic temple. The lodge consists of three Craft, Symbolic, or Blue Degrees: Entered Apprentice (First Degree), Fellow Craft (Second Degree), and Master Mason (Third Degree). These gradations are meant to correspond to the three levels—apprentice, journeyman, and master—of the medieval stonemasons' guilds. The average Mason does not rise above Master Mason. If he does, however, he has the choice of advancing through about 100 different rites, encompassing some 1,000 higher degrees, throughout the world. In the United States, the two most popular rites are the York, also known as the Holy Royal Arch, and the Scottish. The Scottish Rite awards 30 higher degrees, from Secret Master (Fourth Degree) to Sovereign Grand Inspector General (Thirty-third Degree). The York Rite awards ten degrees, from Mark Master to Order of Knights Templar, the latter being equivalent to a Thirty-third Degree Scottish Rite Mason. Other important Masonic groups are the Veiled Prophets of the Enchanted Realm (the "fraternal fun order for Blue Lodge Masons") and the Ancient Egyptian Arabic Order of Nobles of the Mystic Shrine (Thirty-second degree Masons who, as the Shriners, are noted for their colorful parades and support of children's hospitals). There are also many subsidiary Masonic groups, including the Order of the Eastern Star, limited to Master Masons and their female relatives; De Molay, an organization for boys; and Job's Daughters and Rainbow, two organizations for girls. Many of the orders maintain homes for aged members. See R. F. Gould, *History of Freemasonry throughout the World* (rev. ed., 6 vol., 1936); A. G. Mackey, *Encyclopedia of Freemasonry* (rev. ed., 3 vol., 1946); F. L. Pick and G. N. Knight, *The Pocket History of Freemasonry* (4th ed. 1963); Calvin Kephart, *Concise History of Freemasonry* (2d ed. 1964).

Freeport. **1** City (1970 pop. 27,736), seat of Stephenson co., NW Ill., on the Pecatonica River; inc. 1850. It is a trade and manufacturing center in a fertile farm and dairy region. Among its manufactures are farm machinery, plastics, and cosmetics. In 1832 a battle with Black Hawk's Indian forces occurred near there. Freeport was the scene of the second Lincoln-Douglas debate (1858), in which Douglas expounded his famous "Freeport doctrine." A junior college is in the city. **2** Village (1970 pop. 40,374), Nassau co., SE N.Y., on the south shore of Long Island, a residential suburb of New York City; settled c.1650, inc. 1892. It is a resort and a deep-sea fishing and oystering center, with access to the Atlantic Ocean through Jones Inlet. Jones Beach State Park is nearby. **3** City (1970 pop. 11,997), Brazoria co., SE Texas, on the Gulf of Mexico at the mouth of the Brazos River, on the Intracoastal Waterway; inc. 1913. The center of a thriving industrial area in a ranching, oil, and natural gas region known as Brazosport, Freeport has large chemical and shrimping industries. One plant extracts magnesium from seawater. The city's beaches and deep-sea fishing facilities attract tourists. Although a port from the 1820s, it became important only with the opening of sulfur mines a century later. Chemical and petrochemical industries developed there during World War II. New port facilities were opened in 1955. Historic Velasco was annexed in 1957. A Federal seawater purification plant was inaugurated in 1961.

free port, port, or section of a port, exempt from customs regulations. (See TARIFF.) Goods may be landed at a free port for storage and handling, and they may even be processed into manufactured goods. Duty is charged only if the goods are moved from the free port into the adjacent territory. Free ports originated in the late Middle Ages, when the burdensome tariffs charged by many petty states threatened the reemerging maritime commerce. The high tariffs later levied in the period of MERCANTILISM necessitated additional free ports. Cities of the Hanseatic League were among the earliest free ports. The system was extended to Leghorn and Genoa in the 16th cent. and to other Italian cities, as well as Marseilles, Bayonne, and Dunkirk, in the 18th cent. In the 19th cent. the danger of smuggling caused the closing of many free ports. In Europe, Copenhagen, Danzig, and Hamburg were free ports until 1939; in the Far East, Hong Kong and Singapore still are. In the United States, bonded warehouses serve some of the functions of the free port. That arrangement permits goods to be stored and processed in specially licensed warehouses if a bond exceeding the amount of the customs duties is first posted. In 1934 the Foreign Trade Zones Act authorized the establishment of free ports in the United States, but with a prohibition of manufacturing. The first American free port was opened in New York City in 1937, and others have since been added to serve major U.S. ports. Many international airports today have free ports. See R. S. Thomas, *Free Ports and Foreign Trade Zones* (1956).

Freer, Charles Lang (frēr), 1856-1919, American art collector, b. Kingston, N.Y. He gave to the Smithsonian Institution in Washington, D.C., his entire collection and the building (designed according to his direction) that houses it, called the Freer Gallery of Art. A railway and industrial capitalist, he retired from active business in 1900, devoting the rest of his life to art collecting. His taste for the works of Whistler and of Oriental masters, and discovery of a close kinship between the two, resulted in a warm friendship with Whistler and the development of an unrivaled collection of his works; this included the Peacock Room from the Leyland house, London, which had Whistler decorations. The gallery also contains a fine collection of Chinese and Japanese paintings and art objects and a remarkable collection of antique glazed pottery with examples from Egypt, Persia, India, China, Korea, and Japan. See Horace Gregory's *The World of James McNeill Whistler* (1959); *The World of Whistler* by Tom Prideaux and others (1970).

free radical, in chemistry, a molecule or atom that contains an unpaired electron but is neither positively nor negatively charged. Free radicals are usually highly reactive and unstable. They are produced by homolytic cleavage of a covalent bond (see

CHEMICAL BOND); i.e., each of the atoms connected by the bond retains one of the two electrons making up the bond. The homolytic cleavage of a hydrogen molecule, H_2, produces two hydrogen free radicals (hydrogen atoms). Similarly, two chlorine free radicals can be produced from a chlorine molecule. Homolytic cleavage of the carbon-bromine bond in methyl bromide, CH_3Br, would produce a methyl free radical and a bromine free radical. The term *free* is often dropped in referring to free radicals; this could lead to confusion if the term *radical* were used synonymously with *group* in organic chemistry, e.g., by calling an alkyl group an alkyl radical when free radical was not intended.

freesia: see IRIS.

free silver, in U.S. history, term designating the political movement for the free coinage of silver. Free silver became a popular issue soon after the Panic of 1873, and it was a major issue in the next quarter century. The hard times of 1873–78 stimulated advocacy of cheap money, and the GREENBACK PARTY nominated presidential candidates several times and flourished in local elections, especially in 1876 and 1878. The market price of silver fell rapidly after 1873, because of American and European demonetization of silver and because of increases in mine production. Inflationists failed to secure paper-money expansion and turned to silver, believing its free coinage would serve their purpose as well as greenbacks so long as a silver dollar was worth intrinsically less than a gold dollar. Silver-mining interests also wanted silver coinage to aid their business. The ensuing demands for unlimited silver coinage led to the passage of a compromise measure, the BLAND-ALLISON ACT, over President Hayes's veto in 1878. The act provided for definitely limited coinage at a ratio of 16 to 1 with gold. Its provisions were insufficient to halt the decline of silver prices, or to increase the circulation of money. Meanwhile, sectional lines over money were becoming sharply drawn. The financial interests in the East favored sound money and the gold standard. The indebted agrarian classes of the South and West demanded inflation, to ease debt burdens in the face of falling prices of farm products. Their silver demands were reinforced by Western silver-mining interests. As the prosperity of the early '80s vanished, demands arose again for free silver. By 1890 the political strength of the silver advocates, especially in the West, was so great that the SHERMAN SILVER PURCHASE ACT, another compromise, was passed, to replace the Bland-Allison Act and to provide for greater government purchase of silver. The West's discontent was further emphasized by the rise of the POPULIST PARTY, with demands including free silver. The silver advocates were no longer content with compromise measures and were displeased by the presidential candidacy of Grover Cleveland, a supporter of the gold standard, in 1892. Many silver Democrats deserted Cleveland to support James B. Weaver, the Populist candidate. This coalition of silverites and Populists was able to gain control of half a dozen Western states. Advocates of free silver were enraged when the Panic of 1893 brought repeal of the Sherman Silver Purchase Act. By the middle of his second term, Cleveland's Western and Southern opponents had captured the Democratic party. Publication of *Coin's Financial School*, by William Hope HARVEY (1894), made many converts to free silver by presenting the complicated money question in easily understood terms. In 1896 free silver became the major issue of a presidential campaign when William Jennings BRYAN made it the chief plank of his platform. McKinley's victory over Bryan then and again in 1900, coupled with increasing gold supplies and returning prosperity, minimized free silver as a political issue. Subsequent ideas for monetary expansion have largely taken other forms. Yet the silver bloc, partly inspired by Nevada silver interests, continued to be active and secured mandatory legislation for heavy Treasury purchases of silver under Franklin Delano Roosevelt. The decreasing supply of silver in the 1960s led the U.S. Treasury to end its use in coins and to sell its surplus stock of silver in 1970. See A. B. Hepburn, *History of Coinage and Currency in the United States* (1924, repr. 1967); D. R. Dewey, *Financial History of the United States* (12th ed. 1934, repr. 1968); Margaret Leech, *In the Days of McKinley* (1959).

Free-Soil party, in U.S. history, political party that came into existence in 1847–48 chiefly because of rising opposition to the extension of slavery into any of the territories newly acquired from Mexico. The struggle in Congress over the WILMOT PROVISO helped to consolidate the Free-Soil forces, which comprised those New York Democrats known as BARNBURNERS, the antislavery Whigs, and members of the former LIBERTY PARTY. These forces met in mass convention at Buffalo in Aug., 1848, where the party was formally organized and Martin Van Buren and Charles F. Adams (1807–86) were chosen as its candidates for President and Vice President. The platform also declared for a homestead law, internal improvements, and a tariff for revenue only. The party polled nearly 300,000 votes and, by giving New York state to the Whigs, was a decisive factor in making Zachary Taylor President. The party elected one Senator, Salmon P. CHASE of Ohio, and 13 Congressmen. The Compromise of 1850 supposedly settled the slavery issue, and the Barnburner element went back to its old allegiance. A few radical antislavery men kept the organization in existence and nominated John P. Hale for President in 1852; he received more than 150,000 votes. In 1854 the party was absorbed into the new Republican party. See T. C. Smith, *The Liberty and Free Soil Parties in the Northwest* (1897, repr. 1969); Eric Foner, *Free Soil, Free Labor, Free Men* (1970); J. G. Rayback, *Free Soil: The Election of 1848* (1970); F. J. Blue, *The Free Soilers* (1973).

freethinkers, those who arrive at conclusions, particularly in questions of religion, by employing the rules of reason while rejecting supernatural authority or ecclesiastical tradition. The freethinkers believe that independence of thought from such authority leads all men to essentially identical conclusions concerning morality and religion. The name came into general use in the 18th cent. after the publication (1713) of Anthony Collins's *Discourse of Freethinking Occasioned by the Rise and Growth of a Sect Called Freethinkers.* The movement took different forms in different countries. In England it was intimately connected with deism but did not break completely with traditional Christianity. It took a more radical form in France. Voltaire renounced all connection with Christianity, and the Encyclopedists broke with religion altogether. Freethinking also has an important social side and influenced the philosophies of the Freemasons and, in France, the Culte de l'Être Suprême. In the United States the organizations established to further freethinking include the American Rationalist Association, the American Secular Union, and the Freethinkers of America. The International Order for Ethics and Culture, organized at Bern in 1908, is designed to investigate the ethical factors in society without theological or metaphysical bias.

Freetown, city (1970 est. pop. 178,600), capital of Sierra Leone, W Sierra Leone, a port on the Atlantic Ocean. Located on the Sierra Leone peninsula, Freetown is the nation's administrative, communications, and economic center, as well as its main port. The city's economy revolves largely around its fine natural harbor, which is capable of receiving ocean-going vessels and which handles Sierra Leone's main exports. Industries include food and beverage processing, petroleum refining, and the manufacture of cigarettes, shoes, and beer. Lebanese play a major role in local trade, especially wholesaling. Roads and a railroad link Freetown with the interior of the country. The area was settled in 1787 by freed slaves sent from England by British abolitionists, including Granville Sharp and Thomas Clarkson, who started the Sierra Leone Company. In 1792, Freetown was founded by former slaves from Nova Scotia sent out by the company. Freetown was used by the British as the base for creating (1808) the Sierra Leone Crown Colony, and from 1808 to 1874 it served as the capital of British West Africa. In 1893 it was made the first British colonial municipality in Africa, with the right to elect a mayor. During World War II, Britain maintained a naval base at Freetown. Although they constitute only a minority today, descendants of the freed slaves, called Creoles, play a leading role in the city. Freetown is the site of the Univ. of Sierra Leone (1967), which incorporates Fourah Bay College (1827) and Njala Univ. College (1963), and also of a technical institute.

free trade, in modern usage, trade or commerce carried on without such restrictions as import duties, export bounties, domestic production subsidies, trade quotas, or import licenses. The basic argument for free trade is based on the economic theory of comparative advantage: each region should concentrate on what it can produce most cheaply and efficiently and should exchange its products for those it is less able to produce. Free trade within national borders is in some places a comparatively recent development. Jean Baptiste COLBERT tried to abolish internal trade barriers in France in the 17th cent., but that work was not completed until the French Revolution, a hundred years later. In the German states Prussia took the lead in organizing the ZOLLVEREIN movement after 1818. In England internal free trade is of long standing. In the United States the desire to assure freedom from internal trade barriers was a factor in calling the Constitutional Convention. In England, the classic home of the free trade movement, the term "free trade" was first used during the agitation for removal of the privileges of the chartered companies in the 17th cent. Later, free trade came to mean the desire for a moderate tariff policy in international trade, especially with France. The rapid growth of English industry in the late 18th cent. (see INDUSTRIAL REVOLUTION) gave added force to the attack on international trade restrictions (see MERCANTILISM). Adam Smith's *Wealth of Nations* (1776) provided a powerful intellectual basis for the free trade movement, and the later work of David Ricardo was important in developing the notion of comparative advantage as an argument in its favor. The most important practical blow in favor of the free trade movement came with the formation (1839) of the ANTI-CORN-LAW LEAGUE, and the repeal (1846) of the CORN LAWS. The Anglo-French commercial treaty of 1860 represented perhaps the high-water mark of free trade. After World War I, Britain reintroduced protection and a system of imperial preference in an attempt to establish a greater measure of economic autonomy. France, along with other European nations, historically followed a policy of PROTECTION. Throughout most of its history, the United States has followed high-tariff policies despite the strong protest of a large minority. In the period of international economic dislocation in the mid-1930s, the United States reversed earlier policy and signed reciprocal trade treaties with many foreign governments, embracing a policy of selective tariff reduction for economic and political reasons. At present the United States is a relatively low tariff nation, although it still maintains a fairly restrictive system of import quotas. Japan also has restrictive import quotas, as well as high tariffs and other trade restrictions. After World War II, strong sentiment developed throughout the world against protection and high tariffs and in favor of freer trade. The results were new organizations and agreements on international trade such as the GENERAL AGREEMENT ON TARIFFS AND TRADE (1948), the BENELUX ECONOMIC UNION (1948), the COMMON MARKET (1957), and the European Free Trade Association (1959; see INTERNATIONAL GOVERNMENTAL ORGANIZATIONS). See P. H. Douglas, *America in the Market Place* (1966); Norman McCord, *Free Trade: Theory and Practice from Adam Smith to Keynes* (1970); Bernard Semmel, *Rise of Free Trade Imperialism* (1970).

free verse, term loosely used for rhymed or unrhymed verse made free of conventional and traditional limitations and restrictions in regard to metrical structure. Cadence, especially that of common speech, is often substituted for regular metrical pattern. *Free verse* is a literal translation of the French *vers libre*, which originated in late 19th-century France among poets, such as Arthur Rimbaud and Jules Laforgue, who sought to free poetry from the metrical regularity of the ALEXANDRINE. The term has also been applied by modern literary critics to the King James translation of the Bible, particularly the Song of Solomon and the Psalms, to certain poems of Matthew Arnold, and to the irregular poetry of Walt Whitman's *Leaves of Grass.* The form is probably most closely associated with such English and American poets as Ezra Pound, Amy Lowell, and T. S. Eliot who sought greater liberty in verse structure. Other poets who used the free verse form were William Carlos Williams, Carl Sandburg, and Marianne Moore.

free will, in philosophy, the doctrine that the will of an individual can and does determine some of his acts. Determinists have challenged the doctrine for reasons philosophic and religious: Plato held that no one would knowingly choose evil; all vice was a matter of ignorance, and actions were determined by the extent of a person's understanding. Aristotle disagreed, holding that the nature of incontinence was to know that an action was wrong but to be unable to keep from doing it. The Christian ethical tradition, unlike the Greek, did not always identify goodness with practicality or understanding; virtue was often impractical and beyond the scrutiny of reason. The question became whether virtue was within the power of the individual or completely dependent on the power of God. St. Augustine, although he argued that God's foreknowledge of human actions (a consequence of his omniscience) did not cause them, did hold that God's omnipotent providence implied predestination: man was wholly dependent on divine grace. St. Thomas Aquinas maintained the freedom of man's will in spite of divine omnipotence, holding that God's omnipotence meant he could do all things possible or consistent with his goodness and reason, which did not include the predetermination of human will. William of Occam admitted that divine omnipotence and omniscience were logically incompatible with free will, but thought this showed not the limitations of man's will but the limitations of logic in matters of theology. Martin Luther and John Calvin both followed Augustine's doctrine of predestination, but later Protestant writers disputed their position. Advocates of free will have usually begun with the overwhelming testimony of common practice and common sense: Men do believe they in some way determine their actions, and hold each other accountable for doing so. Therefore advocates of free will have argued that the human will, unlike inanimate things, can initiate its own activity. Modern psychology has provided a new arena of discussion for many of these problems. Although it has introduced a new source of determination, the unconscious, it still faces the problems that have always accompanied discussions of free will: the possibility of human improvement and the question of personal responsibility.

freezing, change of a substance from the liquid to the solid state. The temperature at which freezing occurs for a pure crystalline solid is called the freezing point and is a characteristic of the particular substance. The reverse process, the change of a solid to a liquid, is called melting. See MELTING POINT; REFRIGERATION.

Frege, Gottlob (gôt'lōp frā'gə), 1848–1925, German philosopher and mathematician. He was professor of mathematics (1879–1918) at the Univ. of Jena. Frege was one of the founders of modern SYMBOLIC LOGIC, and his work profoundly influenced Bertrand Russell. He demonstrated that all mathematics could be derived from purely logical principles and definitions. He considered verbal concepts to be expressible as symbolic functions with one or more variables. His books include *Begriffsschrift* (1879); *Die Grundlagen der Arithmetik* (1884; tr. *The Foundations of Arithmetic,* 1950); *Grundgesetze der Arithmetik* (2 vol., 1893–1903). See Peter T. Geach and Max Black, ed., *Philosophical Writings of Gottlob Frege* (1952); studies by Reinhardt Grossman (1969) and Michael Dummett (1973).

Freiberg (frī'bĕrkh), city (1970 pop. 50, 272), Karl-Marx-Stadt district, S East Germany, at the foot of the Erzgebirge. It is an industrial center and a rail junction. Manufactures include precision and optical equipment, leather goods, and textiles. Lead and zinc are mined in the region. Freiberg was for centuries a silver-mining center and was settled by miners in the 12th cent. The city passed in 1485 to the house of Wettin, and it was the main commercial center of Saxony until the 16th cent. In the Thirty Years War it resisted a siege by the Swedes (1642–43), and in the Seven Years War the Prussians defeated (1762) the Austrians there. Noteworthy buildings include a late Gothic cathedral and numerous Renaissance style and baroque houses. There is a famous mining academy (founded 1765) in Freiberg.

Freiburg: see FRIBOURG, Switzerland.

Freiburg im Breisgau (frī'bŏŏrk ĭm brīs'gou), city (1970 pop. 162,222), Baden-Württemberg, SW West Germany, near the Rhine River and at the edge of the Black Forest. Manufactures include textiles, optical and musical instruments, paper, and chemicals; wine and timber are traded. The city is a tourist center. Freiburg was founded in 1120 and passed, with the rest of the Breisgau, to the Hapsburgs in 1368. In the Thirty Years War (1618–48) the Bavarians and Austrians were defeated there (1644) by the French under Turenne and Louis II de Condé. The French held Freiburg from 1677 to 1697 and again (1744–48) during the War of the Austrian Succession. In 1805 the city passed to Baden. Freiburg is famous as a cultural center and is the seat of a noted university (founded 1457) and of a number of museums. The city has been an archiepiscopal see since 1821 and has a splendid Gothic cathedral (begun in the 13th cent.), with a high (380 ft/116 m) tower.

Freiligrath, Ferdinand (fĕr'dēnänt frī'lĭkhrät), 1810–76, German poet. In 1844 he expressed radically liberal sentiments in his collection of political verse *Ein Glaubensbekenntnis* [a confession of faith] (1844) and was forced to flee from Germany. He returned in 1848 but fled again after the publication of his *Neuere politische und soziale Gedichte* (1850). His best-known poem, "O lieb'," was set to music by Liszt and served as the motto of the composer's piano arrangement of the third *Liebestraum.* Selections of Freiligrath's works appeared in translation in 1867.

Frei Montalva, Eduardo (ā"thwär'thō frā mōntäl'vä), 1911–, president of Chile (1964–70). A lawyer and editor, he was a founder (1938) of the National Falange, an independent party based on progressive Christian principles, which in 1957 became the core of the new Christian Democratic party. Frei served as minister of roads and public works (1945–49) and in the senate after 1949. On his second try for the presidency (1964), he won a decisive victory. A popular president, he introduced sweeping social and economic reforms within a democratic framework and secured Chilean control of the copper industry. After turning the presidency over to his elected successor, Salvador Allende Gossens, he remained active as head of the Christian Democratic party.

Freising (frī'zĭng), city (1970 pop. 29,325), Bavaria, S West Germany, on the Isar River. Manufactures include machinery and textiles. Freising was founded in 724 by St. Corbinian, and its bishops held temporal power until the see was secularized in 1802–3. The diocese was restored in 1817, the archbishop of Munich being also bishop of Freising. The city has a Romanesque cathedral (c.1160), with 18th-century baroque additions.

Freital (frī'täl), city (1970 pop. 42,159), Dresden dist., SE East Germany; founded 1921. Manufactures of this industrial city include high-quality steel, machinery, optical equipment, and paper.

Fréjus (frāzhüs'), town (1968 pop. 25,736), Var dept., SE France. With adjoining Fréjus-Plage, located on the Mediterranean, it is a well-known resort of the French Riviera. Corks are made, and masonry is done there. Founded by Julius Caesar in 49 B.C., it was an important Roman naval port. The Argens River has since silted up the harbor, pushing the sea about ¾ mi (1.2 km) from the city. Many Roman ruins are preserved, notably the oldest surviving arena of Gaul. Also of interest is a cathedral with a 5th-century baptistery. A French military school and army base are at Fréjus.

Frelinghuysen, Frederick Theodore (frē'lĭnghī"zən), 1817–85, U.S. Secretary of State (1881–85), b. Millstone, Somerset co., N.J. He studied law in the office of his uncle, Theodore Frelinghuysen, who had adopted him when he was three, and on admission to the bar in 1839 inherited his uncle's practice. Frelinghuysen, a Republican, was attorney general of New Jersey (1861–66) and U.S. Senator (1866–69, 1871–77). In the Senate he supported the radical Republican Reconstruction program and later was associated with the Stalwarts led by Roscoe Conkling. On the death of James A. Garfield and the accession of Chester A. Arthur to the presidency, James G. Blaine resigned as Secretary of State to be succeeded (Dec., 1881) by Frelinghuysen, who canceled Blaine's plans for a Pan-American Congress and urged reciprocity agreements with Latin American countries. Unable, like his predecessors, to persuade Great Britain to modify the terms of the Clayton-Bulwer Treaty, he negotiated (Dec., 1884) a treaty with Nicaragua allowing the United States the right to build a canal there under joint ownership of the two countries. However, Grover Cleveland, when he became President, withdrew the treaty from consideration by the Senate. Frelinghuysen generally carried on a patient, pacifistic policy throughout Arthur's term. See S. F. Bemis, ed., *The American Secretaries of State and Their Diplomacy,* Vol. VIII (1928).

Frelinghuysen, Theodore, 1787–1862, American politician and educator, b. Franklin, N.J. Admitted to the bar in 1808, he practiced law in Newark and soon gained political prominence. As U.S. Senator (1829–35), he won renown for his speech opposing the removal of the Cherokee and other southern Indians to lands W of the Mississippi. He was mayor of Newark (1836–39) until he became (1839) chancellor of New York Univ. In 1844 he was vice presidential candidate on the Whig ticket with Henry Clay. From 1850 until his death, Frelinghuysen was president of Rutgers College.

Fremantle (frē'măn"təl, frĭm'əntəl), city (1971 pop. 25,990), Western Australia, SW Australia, a suburb of Perth, on the Indian Ocean at the mouth of the Swan River. It is the terminus of the Trans-Australian RR and the chief commercial port of the state. The chief exports are wheat, wool, fruit, and flour; oil, steel, and phosphates are imported. Fremantle is also a fishing and passenger port.

Frémiet, Emmanuel (ĕmänüĕl' frāmyā'), 1824–1910, French sculptor; pupil and nephew of Rude. He was noted for his vigorous characterizations of animal and historical figures. His equestrian statue of Joan of Arc (Place des Pyramides, Paris) is a familiar landmark. Portrait statues include one of Colonel John Eager Howard (1903; Baltimore).

Frémont, Jessie Benton (frē'mŏnt), 1824–1902, American author, b. Lexington, Va.; daughter of Thomas H. BENTON and wife of John Charles Frémont. Her elopement with the dashing Frémont caused a temporary break with her father. She was very helpful to her husband, aiding him in writing his able reports and encouraging his exploits. When their fortune was lost, she helped to support the household by her writing, turning out chiefly books recounting her own experiences—*A Year of American Travel* (1878), *Souvenirs of My Time* (1887), *Far West Sketches* (1890), and *The Will and the Way Stories* (1891). She also helped her husband write his memoirs. See biography by C. C. Phillips (1935).

Frémont, John Charles, 1813–90, American explorer, soldier, and political leader, b. Savannah, Ga. He taught mathematics to U.S. naval cadets, then became an assistant on a surveying expedition (1838–39) between the upper Mississippi River and the Missouri. He eloped (1841) with Jessie, daughter of Senator Thomas H. BENTON, who, after he became reconciled to the match, helped his son-in-law secure command of an expedition to explore the Des Moines River. The next year (1842) Frémont headed an expedition to the Rocky Mts. with Kit Carson as guide, and in 1843–44, with first Thomas Fitzpatrick and then Carson as guide, he went to Oregon. He explored the Nevada country, crossed the Sierra Nevada to California, and returned home by a more southerly route. His enthusiastic reports created wide interest in Western scenery and Western concerns. In 1845 he again went to California. Under his influence American settlers there raised the standard of revolt against the Mexican authorities and set up (1846) the Bear Flag republic at Sonoma. The arrival of Stephen W. KEARNY and Commodore Robert STOCKTON resulted in a quarrel, as both had orders placing them in command. Frémont sided with Stockton and accepted from him an appointment as civil governor. When Kearny received orders indicating that Stockton was not his superior, Frémont was arrested, court-martialed, and found guilty. The penalty was remitted by President Polk, but Frémont, proud and injured, resigned from government service. In 1848 he led an ill-judged and disastrous effort to locate passes for a transcontinental railroad. His fortunes climbed after gold was discovered on his California estate, although he was deprived of some of his wealth by the sharp practice of others. He served briefly (1850–51) as one of the first U.S. Senators from California and the Republicans chose him as presidential candidate in 1856. In the Civil War he was given command of the Western Dept., but his radical policy toward slaveholders led to his removal. He was given a new command, but, when placed under the orders of John Pope, he resigned. Unsuccessful attempts (1870) to build a railroad to the Pacific—accompanied by actions of his agents that roused sharp criticism—cost him his fortune. Beggared, he struggled on, supported by his wife's earnings from writing and by his appointment as governor of Arizona Territory (1878–1883). In 1890 he was belatedly given a pension but did not live long to enjoy it. The Pathfinder, as he is sometimes called, is one of the most controversial figures of Western history. His critics call him braggart and charlatan; his supporters point to his courage, his handling of men, and his determination to open the West. Frémont's early reports were combined as *Report of the Exploring Expedition to the Rocky Mountains in the Year 1842, and to Oregon and North California in the Years 1843–44* (1845). His memoirs (1887) are disappointing and incomplete. See biographies by Allan Nevins (rev. ed. 1955); R. J. Bartlett, *John C. Frémont and the Republican Party* (1930, repr. 1970); William Brandon, *The Men and the Mountain* (1955); LeRoy and Ann W. Hafen, ed., *Fremont's Fourth Expedition* (1960).

Fremont (frē'mŏnt). **1** City (1970 pop. 100,869), Alameda co., W Calif., on San Francisco Bay; inc. 1956 with the merger of Irvington, Niles, Warm Springs, Centreville, and Mission San Jose. Long an agricultural center, with champagne vineyards founded (1870) by Leland Stanford, it still has brewing and canning industries and is a shipping point for fruits and vegetables. Its economy was transformed in 1963, however, when General Motors opened an automobile assembly plant there. As a result, the city's population almost doubled in four years. Mission San Jose de Guadalupe (1797) has been restored as a museum. The city has a junior college, a 420-acre

(170-hectare) park, and a 3,000-acre (1,210-hectare) aquatic park. **2** City (1970 pop. 22,962), seat of Dodge co., E central Nebr., on the Platte River; inc. 1858. It is a trade, shipping, and processing center for a grain-growing, dairying, and grazing prairie area. Midland Lutheran College is there. **3** City (1970 pop. 18,490), seat of Sandusky co., N Ohio, on the Sandusky River; inc. 1849. It is a trade and industrial center in a rich agricultural region. A government trading post was established on the site in 1795. The battle of Fort Stephenson was fought there (1813) during the War of 1812. After the war the two towns of Croghansville and Lower Sandusky were settled; in 1829 they were united as Lower Sandusky and in 1849 named for John C. Frémont. Shipbuilding was an early industry. The house and tomb of Rutherford B. Hayes (a state memorial) are in Spiegel Grove State Park.

Fremstad, Olive Nayan (frĕm'stăd), 1871–1951, Swedish-American soprano; pupil of Lilli Lehmann. She came to the United States as a child. After her European debut (Cologne, 1895), she sang contralto roles until she returned to the United States to sing dramatic soprano parts at the Metropolitan Opera, New York (1903–14). She retired in 1920.

French, Daniel Chester, 1850–1931, American sculptor, b. Exeter, N.H., studied in Florence and in Boston with William Rimmer. After executing his first large work, *The Minute Man* (1875), he received many important commissions, including his most famous achievement, the heroic Lincoln in the Lincoln Memorial, Washington, D.C. His style varies from a detailed realistic rendering, especially in portraiture, to a grand ideal in his allegorical works. Some of the best of his statues and memorials are John Harvard and the bust of Ralph Waldo Emerson (Harvard Univ.); *Death and the Young Sculptor*, Milmore Memorial (Boston); *Mourning Victory*, Melvin Memorial (Concord, Mass.); Lewis Cass (Capitol, Washington, D.C.); and *Alma Mater* (Columbia Univ.). In collaboration with Edward C. Potter he executed equestrian statues of General Grant (Philadelphia), General Washington (Paris), and General Joseph Hooker (Boston). See biography by his daughter, M. F. Cresson (1947).

French, John Denton Pinkstone, 1st **earl of Ypres** (ē'prə), 1852–1925, British field marshal. After a long career in the army, during which he served in the Sudan (1884–85) and in the South African War (1899–1902), he was chief of the imperial general staff (1912–14) and became a field marshal in 1913. His command of the British Expeditionary Force in France and Belgium from the outbreak of World War I (Aug., 1914) to Dec., 1915 was marked by failure to coordinate the movements of his forces and heavy casualties in the first and second battles of Ypres and the battle of Loos. On his return to England he reorganized the home defenses. He was lord lieutenant of Ireland (1918–21) and was created earl in 1922. He wrote *1914* (1919).

French Academy (*L'Académie française*), learned society of France. It is one of the five societies of the INSTITUT DE FRANCE. Its origins were in a coterie of literary men who met informally in Paris in the early 1630s to discuss rhetoric and criticism. Recognized by Cardinal Richelieu, the academy received the royal letters patent in 1635 (registered by the Parlement of Paris in 1637). Its aims included chiefly the governance of French literary effort, grammar, orthography, and rhetoric. The membership was soon fixed at 40 (called often, because of their former motto, "the forty immortals") and was established as self-perpetuating, with a veto of elections reserved to the official *protecteur* (or patron), later to the state. The first notable act of the society was the criticism of the *Cid* of Pierre CORNEILLE. After Richelieu's death (1642) the patronate went (1643) to Pierre Séguier, the chancellor; on his death (1672), King Louis XIV assumed the position of *protecteur*, which remained ever after a prerogative of the head of the French state. The suppression of the academies in 1793 ended the French Academy; it reappeared in the second class of Napoleon's Institut (1803), and the old name and organization were "restored" in the first division of the Institut of 1816. The work of the French Academy has chiefly consisted of the preparation and revision of a dictionary (1st ed. 1694, 8th ed. 1932–35) and of a grammar (1932). The very conservative attitude of these books toward orthography, new words, and grammatical development has led to much criticism. The academy, however, has never claimed to legislate, but simply to record forms; legislation on orthography and grammar under the Third Republic was made a function of the minister of public instruction. The awarding of literary prizes has been an important function of the French Academy, and in the 19th cent. its nonpartisanship encouraged the general recognition of the academy as a suitable trustee for the distribution of grants and prizes for courage and civic virtue. The academy has often been accused of literary conservatism, owing to the failure of certain writers to attain membership; the most prominent of these are perhaps Molière, Marquis de La Rochefoucauld, Duc de Saint-Simon, Jean Jacques Rousseau, Honoré de Balzac, Gustave Flaubert, Stendhal, Émile Zola, and Marcel Proust. But not all omissions from the academy roster are attributable to literary criteria, for personal respectability and loyalty to the existing state have always been conditions of membership. The membership of the academy has traditionally included eminent Frenchmen outside the field of literature.

French and Indian Wars, 1689–1763, the name given by American historians to the North American colonial wars between Great Britain and France in the late 17th and the 18th cent. They were really campaigns in the worldwide struggle for empire and were roughly linked to wars of the European coalitions. At the time they were viewed in Europe as only an unimportant aspect of the struggle, and, although the stakes were Canada, the American West, and the West Indies, the fortunes of war in Europe had more effect in determining the winner than the fighting in the disputed territory itself. To the settlers in America, however, the rivalry of the two powers was of immediate concern, for the fighting meant not only raids by the French or the British but also the horrors of Indian border warfare. The conflict may be looked on, from the American viewpoint, as a single war with interruptions. The ultimate aim—domination of the eastern part of the continent—was the same; and the methods—capture of the seaboard strongholds and the little Western forts and attacks on frontier settlements—were the same. The first of the wars, **King William's War** (1689–97), approximately corresponds to the European War of the GRAND ALLIANCE (1688–97). It was marked in America principally by frontier attacks on the British colonies and by the taking of Port Royal (now Annapolis Royal, N.S.) by British colonial forces under Sir William PHIPS in 1690. (The French recaptured it the next year.) The British were unable to take Quebec, and the French commander, the comte de Frontenac, attacked the British coast. The peace that followed the Treaty of Ryswick in 1697 was short-lived, and shortly the colonies were plunged into war again. **Queen Anne's War** (1702–13) corresponds to the War of the SPANISH SUCCESSION. The frontier was again the scene of many bloody battles; the French and Indian raid (1704) on Deerfield, Mass., was especially notable. Another British attempt to take Quebec, this time by naval attack, failed. Port Royal, and with it ACADIA, fell (1710) to an expedition under Francis Nicholson and was confirmed to the British in the Peace of Utrecht, as were Newfoundland and the fur-trading posts about Hudson Bay. Hostilities lapsed for years until trouble between England and Spain led to the so-called War of Jenkins's Ear, which merged into the War of the AUSTRIAN SUCCESSION. The American phase, **King George's War,** did not begin until 1744, when the French made an unsuccessful assault on Port Royal. The next year, a Massachusetts-planned expedition under William PEPPERRELL with a British fleet under Sir Peter Warren took LOUISBURG. Border warfare was severe but not conclusive. The Treaty of Aix-la-Chapelle (1748) returned Louisburg to France, but the hostile feelings that had been aroused did not die. Rivalry for the West, particularly for the valley of the upper Ohio, prepared the way for another war. In 1748 a group of Virginians interested in Western lands formed the OHIO COMPANY, and at the same time the French were investigating possibilities of occupying the upper Ohio region. The French were first to act, moving S from Canada and founding two forts. Robert DINWIDDIE, governor of Virginia, sent an emissary, young George WASHINGTON, to protest. The contest between the Ohio Company and the French was now joined and hinged on possession of the spot where the Monongahela and the Allegheny join to form the Ohio (the site of Pittsburgh). The English started a fort there but were expelled by the French, who built FORT DUQUESNE in 1754. Dinwiddie, after attempting to get aid from the other colonies, sent out an expedition under Washington. He defeated a small force of French and Indians but had to withdraw and, building FORT NECESSITY, held his ground until forced to surrender (July, 1754). The British colonies, alarmed by French activities at their back door, attempted to correlate their activities in the ALBANY CONGRESS. War had thus broken out before fighting began in Europe in the SEVEN YEARS WAR. The American conflict, the last and by far the most important of the series, is usually called simply the **French and Indian War**. The British undertook to capture the French forts in the West—not only Duquesne, but also Fort Frontenac (see KINGSTON, Ont., Canada), FORT NIAGARA, and the posts at TICONDEROGA and CROWN POINT. They also set out to take Louisburg and the French cities on the St. Lawrence, Quebec and Montreal. They at first failed in their attempts. The expedition led by Edward BRADDOCK against Duquesne in 1755 was a costly fiasco, and the attempt by Admiral Boscawen to blockade Canada and the first expeditions against Niagara and Crown Point were fruitless. After 1757, when the British ministry of the elder William Pitt was reconstituted, Pitt was able to supervise the war in America. Affairs then took a better turn for the British. Lord AMHERST in 1758 took Louisburg, where James WOLFE distinguished himself. In that year, Gen. John FORBES took Fort Duquesne (which became Fort Pitt). The French Louis Joseph de MONTCALM, one of the great commanders of his time, distinguished himself (1758) by repulsing the attack of James ABERCROMBY on Ticonderoga. The next year that fort fell to Amherst. In the West, too, the hold of Sir William JOHNSON over the Iroquois and the activities of border troops under his general command—most spectacular, perhaps, the rangers under Robert ROGERS—reduced French holdings and influence. The war became a climactic fight for the St. Lawrence, with Montcalm pitted against the brilliant Wolfe. The climax came in 1759 in the open battle on the Plains of Abraham (see ABRAHAM, PLAINS OF). Both Wolfe and Montcalm were killed, but Quebec fell to the British. In 1760, Montreal also fell, and the war was over. The Treaty of Paris in 1763 (see PARIS, TREATY OF) ended French control of Canada, which went to Great Britain. The wars had helped to bring about changes in the British colonies. In addition to the fact of their ocean-wide distance from the mother country, the colonies now felt themselves less dependent militarily on the British; they also tended to concentrate on their own problems and institutions. In other words, they began to think of themselves as American rather than British. The classic works in English on the conflict are those of Francis PARKMAN. See William Wood, *The Passing of New France* (1915); G. M. Wrong, *The Conquest of New France* (1918); L. H. Gipson, *The British Empire before the American Revolution,* Vol. IV–VIII (with individual titles, 1939–53); Brian Connell, *The Savage Years* (1959); E. P. Hamilton, *The French and Indian Wars* (1962); Harrison Bird, *Battle for a Continent* (1965); Guy Fregault, *Canada: The War of the Conquest* (1955, tr. 1969).

French architecture. Of the early developments of Gallic architecture, including early Christian, Merovingian, and Carolingian buildings, scant traces remain. The basilica form predominated and, during the Carolingian period, was greatly enriched by design innovations that gave rise to ROMANESQUE ARCHITECTURE AND ART. Many Romanesque and Gothic monuments are still extant (see GOTHIC ARCHITECTURE AND ART). In the 15th and 16th cent. the majority of the famous French Renaissance châteaux were erected, especially in the Loire valley. During the first half of the 16th cent., many Italian artists went to France and clustered around the court of Francis I at Fontainebleau (see FOUNTAINEBLEAU, SCHOOL OF). Those of special note who were involved in the construction and interior decoration of the palace were Il Rosso and Primaticcio. The great architect and theorist Sebastiano Serlio applied the classical aesthetic to French building tastes. At the same time native architects came into favor, such as Pierre Lescot, who built portions of the Louvre, and Philibert Delorme, who designed the château of Anet. The major architects of the succeeding generation include Jean Bullant, builder of the little château at Chantilly (c.1560), and Jacques Androuet du Cerceau, whose fame rests on his books of designs, which were widely circulated. The early 17th cent. introduced the BAROQUE, which was also largely derived from Italy, as is clearly shown in the facade of the Church of St. Gervais (1616), Paris, by Salomon de Brosse and in Jacques Lemercier's Church of the Sorbonne (begun 1635). A refined classicism is revealed in the château of Maisons (1642–46), Seine-et-Oise, by François Mansart, who added a steeply pitched roof of the form associated with his name. Another splendid château, Vaux-le-Vicomte, was completed (1657–61) under the supervision of Louis

Le Vau. A turning point in French architecture was reached when Louis XIV rejected the designs of the great Italian Bernini for the east front of the Louvre and employed instead Le Vau and Claude Perrault. They created a splendid scheme (1667–70), with a purity of classical detail that can best be seen in the celebrated colonnade. The grandeur of scale apparent in the Louvre is even more strongly stressed in the transformation of the château into the palace of Versailles. The project was initiated in 1669 by Le Vau, continued with the famous Galérie des Glaces by Jules Hardouin Mansart, and embellished by the gardens of André Le Nôtre. J. H. Mansart also worked on the opulent baroque Church of the Invalides, Paris (1680–1708). In 1699, Pierre Le Pautre, in his refurbishments at Marly, began the trend that culminated in the ROCOCO, a style that for most of the 18th cent. was to exert a profound influence on European architecture. A galaxy of architects and decorators continued Le Pautre's work, including Robert de Cotte and Juste-Aurèle Meissonier, whose published designs were instrumental in disseminating the rococo throughout the continent. The Petit Trianon (1762) by Jacques Ange Gabriel at Versailles, with its use of neoclassical detail, signaled the decline of the rococo style. One of the most famous examples of the classical revival was the Panthéon (1764–81) by J. G. Soufflot. Napoleon's favorite architects, Charles Percier and P. F. L. Fontaine, contributed to the development of the EMPIRE style. This era produced the Colonne Vendôme as well as the impressive Arc de Triomphe de l'Étoile, designed and executed primarily by J. F. Chalgrin. The Gothic revival was ardently championed in France by Viollet-le-Duc, whose writings are of major significance in the history of architecture. Following a different course, H. P. F. Labrouste designed buildings utilizing cast-iron construction, such as the Bibliothèque Ste Geneviève (1843–50), which were the forerunners of modern functional architecture. The sumptuous Paris Opéra (1861–75) by J. L. C. Garnier is a superb and grandiose monument of 19th-century building as the Eiffel Tower (1889; see under EIFFEL, Alexandre Gustave) is a remarkable example of 19th-century engineering design and construction. Auguste Perret, whose church, Le Raincy (1922–23), Seine-et-Oise, exemplifies the early application of modern aesthetic functionalism and modern materials, is a major 20th-century figure as is Tony Garnier, whose stadium at Lyons and plan for Cité Industrielle reveal bold, imaginative techniques in steel and concrete construction. Le Corbusier, who was born in Switzerland but lived and worked in France, is often considered to be the greatest of modern European architects. See articles on individual architects (e.g., MANSART) and works (e.g., LOUVRE). See Fiske Kimball, *The Creation of the Rococo* (1943); Pierre Lavedan, *French Architecture* (tr. 1956); Anthony Blunt, *Art and Architecture in France, 1500–1700* (2d ed. 1970).

French art. Artistic remains in France date back to the Paleolithic age (see CAVE ART; PALEOLITHIC ART), and abundant examples attest to the art of the periods of Roman and barbarian occupation as well as to the Christian art of the subsequent periods (see MEROVINGIAN ART AND ARCHITECTURE; CAROLINGIAN ART AND ARCHITECTURE). During the Middle Ages artistic production centered about the church and the feudal court. In the Romanesque period (11th–12th cent.) the church encouraged the development of manuscript ILLUMINATION and the minor arts at several monastic centers including Rheims, Tours, St. Gall, Paris, and Metz (see ROMANESQUE ARCHITECTURE AND ART). Important schools of sculpture centered in the regions of Languedoc and Burgundy. The hierarchic austerity characteristic of many Romanesque figures was modified in the period of GOTHIC ARCHITECTURE AND ART (12th–15th cent.) by tendencies toward idealization and naturalism. These tendencies are manifest in the sculpture of Rheims and Amiens cathedrals, where the figures show greater variety of pose and articulation and are less severely architectonic than those of the preceding Romanesque period. Cathedral architecture gave impetus in the 13th cent. to the development of the art of STAINED GLASS, which reached its height in such windows as those of the cathedral at Chartres. At the same time Paris became a center of MINIATURE painting in which Italian and Netherlandish innovations were adopted and the observation of natural detail highly developed. Great patrons of art emerged, and Charles V transformed the Louvre into a treasure house for the government art collections. Toward the end of the Gothic period these influences began to be harmonized in terms of a style marked by a taste for formal simplicity and elegance, such as is revealed in the works of Jean Fouquet. In the 16th cent. there was a strong new wave of Italian influence. Francis I employed Francesco Primaticcio of Bologna as artistic director, and a school of French painters worked in an Italianate manner at the palace of Fontainebleau (see FONTAINEBLEAU, SCHOOL OF). The French sculptors Jean Goujon and Germain Pilon contributed classical grace and expressiveness to the work of the time. Elegant portraits were painted by Jean Cousin and Jean and François Clouet. French engraving gained significance in the works of the mannerists Jacques Bellange and Jacques Callot. During the BAROQUE (17th and early 18th cent.) enthusiasm for classical antiquity, combined with a cult of rationalism, encouraged the development of a monumental and formalized art. The most important painters were the landscape artists Nicolas Poussin and Claude Lorrain, who worked in Italy. Other major painters of the period include Simon Vouet, Philippe de Champaigne, George de la Tour, and the Le Nain brothers. The movement toward political centralization, culminating in the absolute monarchy of Louis XIV, was attended by aesthetic authoritarianism marked by a consolidation and control of artistic production in the service of the state and the founding of art institutions. The French Academy was chartered in 1635, and the Gobelins tapestry factory was established in 1662. Typical of the decorative magnificence of the age was the painting of Charles Le Brun and Pierre Mignard and the sculpture of François Girardon, Pierre Puget, and Antoine Coysevox. After the ascension of Louis XV, baroque monumentality was replaced by the lighter, more animated spirit of the ROCOCO, which had early manifestation in the art of J. A. Watteau. François Boucher and J. H. Fragonard succeeded Le Brun as official painters; their decorative, sensuous style was favored by the court but not adopted generally. The GENRE painter J. B. Chardin and the sculptor J. A. Houdon exhibited independent tendencies. The 18th-century aesthetic styles were named after political periods; they include the RÉGENCE STYLE, the LOUIS PERIOD STYLES, and the DIRECTOIRE STYLE. Characteristic gracefulness and delicacy prevailed in the minor arts, exemplified in the bronze work of Jacques Caffieri and in Sèvres porcelains produced at the royal potteries established in 1745 at Vincennes and moved to Sèvres in 1753. A self-important manner in PORTRAITURE flourished in the work of Nicolas de Largillière and Jean-Marc Nattier. Toward the end of the century reaction against the frivolity of court art and interest in new archaeological excavations encouraged the rise of the neoclassical style, which found government favor under Directory, Consulate, and Empire. As its principal exponent J. L. David, Napoleon's official painter, wielded authoritarian influence over the national taste (see EMPIRE STYLE). After neoclassicism, no single style predominated. Rather, individual artists gave definition to a variety of movements. J. A. D. Ingres succeeded David as leading academician and favored an essentially linear and meticulously finished style in part inspired by a new enthusiasm for the art of the Italian Renaissance. Opposed to the academic discipline manifest in yearly SALON exhibitions were the romantic painters led by Delacroix and Géricault. At the same time that ROMANTICISM championed subjective emotion, the artist's independence from social purpose, and the taste for exotic subject matter, various currents of realism had notable exponents in Honoré Daumier, J. B. C. Corot, and Gustave Courbet. Revived interest in landscape painting was revealed in the works of the BARBIZON SCHOOL. After the middle of the century, interest in rendering purely visual effects and in expressing transient and accidental aspects of nature resulted in the emergence of IMPRESSIONISM, an enormously influential movement that was formally launched with the exposition of 1874. This movement drew allegiance from a variety of highly individual artists including Manet, Monet, Renoir, Degas, and Pissarro. Cézanne drew inspiration from the impressionist group, but he rejected their emphasis on transient effects and evolved an independent approach based on the expression of the fundamental characteristics of shapes and spatial effects. Toward the end of the 19th cent. a postimpressionist reaction arose in the work of Seurat, Van Gogh, Toulouse-Lautrec, and Gauguin. This reaction combined with the influence of Cézanne and a new current of interest in the art of Africa to give rise to the early 20th-century movements of FAUVISM, led by Matisse and Rouault, and CUBISM, created by Picasso and Braque. Picasso's work, spanning seven decades, provided in its enormous variety of styles a working vocabulary for many of the major art movements of the 20th cent. After World War I, a further reaction against the decorative and formal emphasis of prewar art resulted in the emergence of SURREALISM and DADA. Paris had become the artistic center of Europe in the 19th cent. and the SCHOOL OF PARIS continued as a source of aesthetic inspiration in the 20th cent. In comparison with painting, 19th-century sculpture on the whole maintained more conservative trends. In the first half of the century, François Rude infused his works with an animation that marked a break with the neoclassic conventions. A. L. Barye, notable for his animal sculptures, and J. B. Carpeaux, leading sculptor of the Second Empire, exemplify tendencies toward naturalism and an interest in rendering effects of movement that reached their culmination in the second half of the century in the sculpture of Auguste Rodin. A new emphasis on relatively static, simplified forms was shown in the works of Aristide Maillol and the Rumanian Constanin Brancusi, who worked in Paris and whose strong, exquisite style had a profound influence on 20th-century sculpture. Other major sculptors of the modern era include Charles Despiau, Henri Laurens, and Raymond Duchamp-Villon. The break with the 18th-century tradition effected by the Revolution, combined with increasing substitution of machine for hand labor, resulted in a marked decline in quality of design and craftsmanship in French 19th-century decorative arts. On the whole a heavy-handed eclecticism prevailed. Various elements from the styles of the Louis XIV and Louis XV periods were combined with surviving neoclassic forms. In the 20th cent. there was an attempt to revive the craft tradition and to introduce nonderivative designs. Leading artists such as Maillol and Matisse furnished tapestry and textile designs. New tendencies toward simplification and functionalism were manifest in the furniture of the modern style. Since 1945 the leading painters, including Nicholas de Staël, Jean Fautrier, Georges Mathieu, and Pierre Soulages have worked in the idiom of ABSTRACT EXPRESSIONISM, while Jean Dubuffet emerged as the initiator of *l'art brut,* with strikingly grotesque images constructed of almost any conceivable sort of material. See articles on individual artists, e.g., CLAUDE LORRAIN, and movements, e.g., CUBISM. See also FRENCH ARCHITECTURE. See Sir Anthony Blunt, *Art and Architecture in France, 1500–1700* (1953); Gerd Muehsam, ed., *French Painters and Paintings from the Fourteenth Century to Post-Impressionism* (1970); Sven Lövgren, *The Genesis of Modernism* (rev. ed. 1971).

French brier: see HEATH.

French Broad River, 210 mi (338 km) long, rising in the Blue Ridge, W N.C., and flowing N and then NW to Knoxville, E Tenn., where it joins with the Holston to form the Tennessee River. The French Broad River was an important route from the southeast coastal states into Tennessee during the colonial period. Douglas Dam, part of the TENNESSEE VALLEY AUTHORITY, forms Lake Douglas, which is used for flood control.

French bulldog, breed of small, alert NONSPORTING DOG with batlike ears, developed in France in the second half of the 19th cent. It stands about 12 in. (30.4 cm) high at the shoulder and weighs from 19 to 28 lb (8.6–12.7 kg). Its short, smooth coat may be brindle, fawn, white, or brindle and white in color. The French bulldog descends from a toy variety of the English bulldog. These toys were not popular in England, and in the mid-19th cent. many were shipped to France, where they were crossed with native breeds. The French bulldog was much desired as a pet in fashionable circles both in France and in the United States in the early 20th cent. In recent times it has become popular as a house pet and companion. See DOG.

French Cameroons: see CAMEROONS.

French Community, established in 1958 by the constitution of the Fifth French Republic to replace the FRENCH UNION. Its present members are the French Republic, including metropolitan France (continental France and Corsica), the overseas territories (Comoro Islands, French Polynesia, the Territory of Afars and Issas, New Caledonia, Saint Pierre and Miquelon, the French Southern and Antarctic territories, and the Wallis and Futuna Islands), the overseas departments (French Guiana, Guadeloupe, Martinique, and Réunion), and six independent African republics—the Central African Republic, Chad, Congo (Brazzaville), Gabon, Malagasy Republic, and Senegal. In 1958 all of the former French Union, with the exception of Guinea, ended ties with France and became member states of the Community. The member states were self-governing but were represented through the institutions of the Community in matters of common interest: foreign policy, defense, economic and financial policy, policy on strategic raw materials, supervision of courts, higher education, and communications. In 1960 all of the states of French West Africa and French Equatorial Africa became independent; while a 1962 constitutional amendment permitted sovereign states to be members of the Community, only the six current African members chose to join. In 1962 the metropolitan departments of Algeria and the Sahara became the sovereign state of Algeria and ceased to be part of the Community. Since 1962 the Community has operated primarily through bilateral agreements in the areas of military, economic, technical, and cultural affairs between the French Republic and the other members.

French Congo: see CONGO, PEOPLE'S REPUBLIC OF THE.

French East India Company: see EAST INDIA COMPANY, FRENCH.

French Equatorial Africa, former French federation in W central Africa. It consisted of four constituent territories: GABON, Middle Congo (see CONGO, PEOPLE'S REPUBLIC OF THE), CHAD, and Ubangi-Shari (now the CENTRAL AFRICAN REPUBLIC). The capital was Brazzaville. The federation was formed mainly through the efforts of Savorgnan de BRAZZA, who forged the link between French possessions in the Congo basin and those in W Africa. French Equatorial Africa (originally called French Congo) was officially established in 1910. Until 1920, Chad and Ubangi-Shari were a single territory. The federation was ruled by a governor general, resident in Brazzaville, who had a deputy in each of the four territories. About 100,000 sq mi (259,000 sq km) were ceded to Germany as a result of the Agadir crisis (1911) but were returned to France by the Treaty of Versailles. During World War II the federation supported the Free French. In the Fourth French Republic, French Equatorial Africa was given representation in the French parliament and in the assembly of the French Union. When the constituent territories voted (1958) to become autonomous republics within the French Community, the federation was dissolved. In 1959 the new republics formed a loose association called the Union of Central African Republics, and in 1960 they became fully independent republics within the French Community.

French Guiana (gēăn'ə, -än'-), Fr. *La Guyane française,* French overseas dept. (1972 est. pop. 50,400), 35,135 sq mi (91,000 sq km), NE South America, on the Atlantic Ocean. CAYENNE is the capital. It is the easternmost of the GUIANA territories. The Oiapoque River on the east and the Tumuc-Humac mts. on the south separate it from Brazil. The Maroni River on the west forms the border with SURINAM. The department has two districts (*arrondissements*): Cayenne, the coastal region, where more than 90% of the population is concentrated; and the larger interior district of Inini, which was administered separately

from 1930 to 1947. The population is largely Creole. French is the official language. The department is represented in the French national assembly and senate. It is governed by a prefect and an elected council. French Guiana is less prosperous than either GUYANA or Surinam. Timber, shrimp, and rum made from local sugarcane are the chief exports. Rice, corn, and bananas are grown for subsistence. There are gold (discovered in 1855) and bauxite deposits; exploitation, however, has been hindered by inadequate transportation and scarcity of labor. French settlement dates from 1604. In the Dutch wars of Louis XIV, Cayenne was captured (1676) by the Dutch but was later retaken. The Portuguese and British occupied it during the Napoleonic Wars, but the Congress of Vienna (1815) restored French authority. French Guiana was used as a penal colony and place of exile during the French Revolution, and under Napoleon III permanent penal camps were established. DEVILS ISLAND, one of the Îles du Salut, off the coast, became notorious. The penal colonies were evacuated after World War II. In 1947, French Guiana became an overseas department of the French Republic.

French Guinea: see GUINEA, republic, Africa.

French horn, brass wind musical instrument. Fundamentally a metal tube of narrow conical bore, it is curved into circles because of its great length. The horn ends in a wide flare. It is a development (c.1650) of the small hunting horn. Although sometimes used in a more grandiose manner, it is still

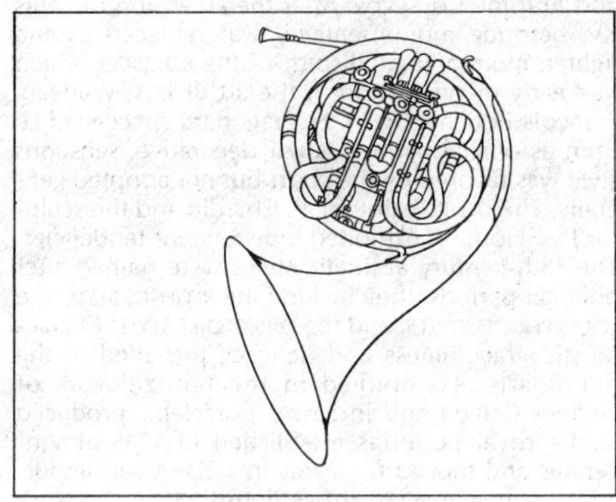

French horn

employed symphonically to produce the simple woodland sound. In modern orchestras it is usually in the key of F and is a TRANSPOSING INSTRUMENT. The present-day French horns normally have three valves, introduced in the 19th cent. The valves supplanted crooks that were used in the 18th cent. to reduce the horn to different keys. Hand stopping and modulation are still used to control the open tone, though mutes may also be used. The first important work to call for valved horns was Halévy's opera *La Juive.* See Morley-Peppe, *The French Horn* (2d ed. 1973).

French India, former overseas territory of France in India, composed of the coastal enclaves of Pondicherry (or Pondichéry), Karikal, Yanaon, and Mahé in the south and the inland trade settlement of Chandernagor near Calcutta. They were administered from the capital at Pondichéry. For the later history of the territory, see PONDICHERRY.

French Indochina: see INDOCHINA.

French language, member of the Romance group of the Italic subfamily of the Indo-European family of languages (see ROMANCE LANGUAGES). It is spoken as a first language by about 60 million people, chiefly in France (45 million speakers), Belgium (4 million), Switzerland (1,500,000), former French and Belgian colonies in Africa (5 million), and Canada (5 million). French probably ranks next after English as a second tongue. Having served as an international language in diplomacy and commerce as well as among educated people during the last few centuries, it still enjoys great prestige culturally and is one of the languages used officially by the United Nations. French is descended from Vulgar Latin, the vernacular Latin (as distinguished from literary Latin) of the Roman Empire (see LATIN LANGUAGE). When ancient Gaul (now modern France) was conquered by the Romans in the 2d and 1st cent. B.C., its inhabitants spoke Gaulish, a Celtic language, which was rapidly supplanted by the Latin of the Roman overlords. In the 5th cent. A.D. the Franks, a group of Germanic tribes, began their invasion of Gaul, but they too were Romanized. Although modern French thus inherited several hundred words of Celtic origin and several hundred more from Germanic, it owes its structure and the greater part of its vocabulary to Latin. By the 9th cent. the language spoken in what is now France was sufficiently different from Latin to be a distinct language. It is called Old French and was current from the 9th to the 13th cent. The earliest extant text in Old French is the *Oaths of Strasbourg,* dated 842. Of the various dialects of Old French, Francien (the north-central dialect spoken in Paris and the region around it) in time became the standard form of the language because of the increasing political and cultural importance of Paris. French from the 14th through 16th cent. is known as Middle French. During this period many words and expressions were borrowed from Latin, Greek, and Italian, and a group of French poets, the Pléiade (see under PLEIAD), encouraged Frenchmen to develop and improve their language and literature. The modern period of French began in the 17th cent. In 1635 the FRENCH ACADEMY was founded by Cardinal Richelieu to maintain the purity of the language and its literature and to serve as the ultimate judge of approved usage. While the vocabulary and style of Modern French have been influenced by movements such as ROMANTICISM and REALISM, structurally French has changed comparatively little since the Middle French period. Standardization of the French language has been aided in modern times by more widespread education and by the mass media. Phonetically distinctive French sounds are the nasal vowels and the uvular *r.* Written French uses the Roman alphabet. Three accents over vowels are employed: the acute (´) over *e,* the grave (`) over *a* and *e,* and the circumflex (ˆ) over *a, e, i, o,* and *u.* An accent may serve to indicate the pronunciation of a vowel, distinguish homonyms, or mark the discarding of the letter *s* from a word. A cedilla placed below the letter *c* (ç) signals that the *c* is to be pronounced as *s.* Ordinarily, *c* is pronounced as *k* before *a, o, u,* or a consonant and as *s* before *e* and *i.* French spelling, which has many silent letters, is not always a reliable guide to pronunciation. For example, final consonants are generally not sounded. An *s* or *x* added to the end of a noun to form the plural is also usually not pronounced. In such a case, the plural number is actually indicated in speech by the form of the article, as in *le garçon* (lə gärsôN') [the boy] and *les garçons* (lā gärsôN') [the boys]. French spelling, however, is closer to the pronunciation than is English spelling. See U. T. Holmes and A. H. Schutz, *A History of the French Language* (1938); M. K. Pope, *From Latin to Modern French* (2d ed. 1952, repr. 1961); John Fox and Robin Hood, *Concise History of the French Language* (1968).

French literature, writings in medieval French dialects and standard modern French. Writings in Provençal and Breton are considered separately, as are works in French produced abroad (such as CANADIAN LITERATURE, FRENCH). Until the 12th cent. A. D. most forms of writing in Gaul were in Latin. Old French emerged from the Latin vernacular of the south known as the langue d'oïl. Because of the French Crusades and military interests abroad (1050–1210), Old French became an international tongue, and a literature arose reflecting the attitudes and activities of the military, as in the *Chanson de Roland* (c.1100; see ROLAND). A tradition of epic poetry was developed by traveling minstrels, or jongleurs. Lengthy narratives were recited in groups of laisses, 10- to 12-syllable lines rhyming in groups of varied lengths (see CHANSONS DE GESTE). Another early literary strain developed in the 12th cent. from the stories of saints and heroes and the Celtic romances of Chrétien de Troyes. Later, more refined romances and allegories include the philosophical ROMAN DE LA ROSE and the witty *Reynard the Fox.* Marie de France and others created new forms, including the *lai,* animal fable, and *fabliau* (rhymed anecdotal piece). Many of these were based on themes from classical mythology. The works of Ovid and Aesop were especially popular sources, as was ARTHURIAN LEGEND. French lyric poetry developed with the songs of the TROUBADOURS and the TROUVÈRES and from the more personal works of the professional poet. Among the best-known lyric poets of the Middle Ages are Colin Muset, Rutebeuf, Christine de Pisan, Alain Chartier, Charles d'Orléans, and the outstanding poet of Old French, François Villon. The earliest French drama consisted of religious plays, most familiar of which are the anonymous *mystères* (such as the *Mystère d'Adam*) of the 12th cent. The MIRACLE PLAYS of the 13th cent. include Jean Bodel's *Jeu de St. Nicolas* (1200). By the end of the century, secular and didactic pieces, many of them comedies and fantasies, were being performed by nonclerics. French prose literature began with the writings of the chroniclers and historians, among them Geoffroi de Villehardouin, Jean de Joinville, Jean Froissart, and Philippe de Comines, last of the major medieval historians. The late 15th and early 16th cent. saw the flowering of the Renaissance in France. Three giants of world literature—François Rabelais, Pierre de Ronsard, and Michel Eyquem de Montaigne—towered over a host of brilliant but lesser figures in the 16th cent. Italian influence was strong in the poetry of Clément Marot and the dramas of Étienne Jodelle and Robert Garnier. The poet Ronsard and the six poets known collectively as the *Pléiade* (see PLEIAD) reacted against Italian influence to produce a body of French poetry to rival Italian achievement. The early 17th-century critic François de Malherbe attacked the excesses of the *Pléiade*; his zeal for the correct choice of words has marked French literature ever since. The civil and religious strife of the later 16th cent. was reflected clearly in the works of the period, particularly in the poetry of Théodore d'Aubigné, Guillaume de Bartas, and Jean de Sponde. The greatest prose of the period was produced in the fiction of the ebullient Rabelais and in the magnificent essays of Montaigne. Under the stable and prosperous Bourbon monarchy Paris became the glittering cultural center of Western civilization. The 17th cent. produced the great academies and coteries of French literature. The elegant, controlled aesthetic of French classicism was the hallmark of the age: in the brilliant dramas of Pierre Corneille, Jean Racine, and Molière; in the poetry and satire of Jean de La Fontaine and Nicolas Boileau-Despréaux; in the prose of Blaise Pascal, Marie, marquise de Sévigné, Jacques-Bénigne Bossuet, Marie-Madeleine, comtesse de La Fayette, and François, duc de La Rochefoucauld. The works of the ecclesiastic François de la Mothe Fénelon, the social philosopher Claude Henri, comte de Saint-Simon, and the satirist and classical scholar Jean de La Bruyère belong to this illustrious period as well as to the 18th cent. These great writers vary enormously in their attitudes and interests but share a style that is lucid, polished, and restrained. They are, as a group, chiefly concerned with observing the subtleties of human behavior. Their works display qualities that have become permanently identified with the best French writing: wit, sophistication, imagination, and delight in debate. From the mid-1680s French prose writers honed their critical facility as poetical and theatrical works waned in number and distinction. Ecclesiastical writing abounded and among the foremost figures in this field were Fénelon, Esprit Fléchier, Pasquier Quesnel, and Richard Simon. Major precursors of the ENLIGHTENMENT of the 18th cent. were the philosophers Bernard de Fontenelle and Pierre Bayle. The great French rationalists of the Age of Reason, François-Marie Voltaire, Jean Jacques Rousseau, and Charles de Secondat, baron de Montesquieu, produced some of the most powerful and influential political and philosophical writing in Western history. The political and religious opinions expressed by the compilers of the *Encyclopédie* (completed 1765), led by Denis Diderot and the mathematician Jean d'Alembert, had great impact upon French and foreign thought. The period was also notable for advances in drama and fiction. Successful writers of tragic drama, other than Voltaire, include Antoine Houdar de La Motte and Buyrette de Belloy; the great writers of comedy were Pierre de Marivaux and Pierre de Beaumarchais. The French novel, to which literary form Diderot and Marivaux contributed, gained popularity with the works of Alain René Le Sage, Abbé Prevost, and Jacques Henri Bernardin de Saint-Pierre, and by the end of the century was among the foremost of literary genres. Another significant form of literature was the memoir; among the many writers of the period who excelled at this sort of autobiography were Mathieu Marais, Edmond Barbier, and Jean François Marmontel. The upheavals of the French Revolution and the Napoleonic era were accompanied by new intellectual trends. ROMANTICISM, greatly influenced by the philosophy of Rousseau, was heralded in the writings of Germaine de Staël and François René, vicomte de Chateaubriand. The principal figures of the Romantic period include Victor Hugo, Alphonse de Lamartine, Alfred, comte de Vigny, Alfred de Musset, Gérard de Nerval, Prosper Mérimée, Alexandre Dumas, père, and Théophile Gautier. The period that saw the transformation from Romanticism to the realism of Gustave Flaubert was spanned by the writings of the great 19th-century novelists Stendhal, George Sand, and Honoré de Balzac. The Romantics and realists alike wrote of the painful discovery of self-awareness, the torments of the inner life, and in differing degrees concerned themselves with contemporary social mores. Hugo and Balzac both wrote much-imitated historical novels. Balzac's multivolume, panoramic description of French society, entitled *La Comédie Humaine*, stands as a unique literary monument to individual genius and a remarkable portrait of an era. The outstanding critic of the era was Charles Augustin Sainte-Beuve, whose literary essays were models of perceptive criticism. In the later part of the century major writers of fiction included Alphonse Daudet and Guy de Maupassant, renowned for his short stories. The movement toward NATURALISM had its foremost French representative in the prolific novelist Émile Zola. The plays of Eugène Labiche, Émile Augier, the younger Alexandre Dumas, and later of Edmond Rostand won popularity in France and abroad. In poetry the *Fleurs du mal* (1857) of Charles Baudelaire had enormous influence, both at the time it was published and for many decades thereafter. In the later 19th cent. several circles, or schools, of literary figures became a prominent feature of Parisian letters: the PARNASSIANS, led by Charles Marie Leconte de Lisle; the group around the Goncourt brothers; the SYMBOLISTS, who were followers of Stéphane Mallarmé; and the DECADENTS, who sought to glorify Baudelaire and Arthur Rimbaud. The great poets of the age, including Paul Verlaine, Rimbaud, Péguy, and later, Paul Valéry, worked for the most part outside such groups. Major 19th-century French writers of history include Augustin Thierry, Jules Michelet, and François Guizot. Hippolyte Taine and Ferdinand Brunetière were outstanding critics, and Anatole France is considered the leading satirist of the age. In the 20th cent., as in the 19th, the novel was the chief form of literary achievement. Although the impact on fiction writing of such factors as the vast changes in political climate, the new concentration on modern culture, the great wars, the development of major publishing houses, the introduction of the paperback, and the evolution of the movies has been very great, French writing has maintained a concern for moral questions, individual liberty and character, and, above all, respect for language and form. The novelists Paul Bourget, Maurice Barrès, and Pierre Loti explored the psychological explanation of human behavior. Colette, in her novels, stories, and journals, expressed penetrating insight into human nature. Marcel Proust, in his great novel cycle *À la recherche du temps perdu* (1913–27) made subtle use of subconscious memory. Psychological examination was continued in the works of André Gide. The cyclical novels of Jules Romains and Roger Martin Du Gard comment upon society and morality. The surge of writing with strong Catholic inspiration encompasses the works of François Mauriac and the novels of Georges Bernanos. Jean Giraudoux's dramas are distinguished for exquisite style and treatment, as are the varied works of Henri de Montherlant. The novels of André Malraux, Édouard Peisson, Roger Vercel, and Joseph Kessel treat man's commitment to action, while the extraordinary and complex works of Jean-Paul Sartre and Simone de Beauvoir developed a form of existentialist philosophy to express the pain of living. EXISTENTIALISM was also a primary aspect of the early writing of Albert Camus. The standard novel form was abandoned in the mid-20th cent. by many writers of fiction, including Antoine de Saint-Exupéry, Vercors, Nathalie Sarraute, Alain Robbe-Grillet, Marguerite Duras, Michel Butor, Roger Vailland, and Romain Gary. The post-World War II writers established a type of novel not greatly related to earlier works of fiction. The "new novel" or "antinovel" dispensed with previous notions of plot, character, style, theme, psychology, chronology, and message. By the 1970s it had created a tradition of its own and was widely considered to have diminished the stature of French fiction and to have forced a self-indulgent subjectivity onto the novel form. Among the authors who continued working in a more traditional and still popular vein are the detective-story writer Georges Simenon, Françoise Mallet-Joris, Jean Cau, Boris Vian, Marguerite Yourcenar, Gilbert Cesbron, Jean Louis Curtis, Pierre Daninos, Henri Queffelec, and Roger Peyrefitte. At the end of the 19th cent. the Théâtre Libre was founded, the first of a number of theatrical groups that invigorated the French stage. Alfred Jarry scandalized Paris with *Ubu Roi* (1896), a play now seen as ancestral to the theater of the mid-1900s. François de Curel, Georges de Porto-Riche, Jules Renard, and Eugène Brieux adapted the new social realism to drama. Symbolism was fitted to the drama by Maurice Maeterlinck, and later by Paul Claudel. Tristan Bernard and Henri-René Lenormand exploited psychoanalytical techniques. The experimental plays and films of Jean Cocteau reflect his astonishing versatility. Sartre and Camus brought to the stage a deep concern for man's predicament. The human situation is described as tragically absurd in the theater of Jean Anouilh, Samuel Beckett, Jean Genet, and Eugène Ionesco. The brilliant plays of Michel de Ghelderode were granted tardy recognition. The early years of the 20th cent. proved a fertile time for poetic writing. Among outstanding works are the powerful verses of Paul Claudel, the experimental poetry of Guillaume Apollinaire, and the elusive imagery of Paul Valéry. In the 1920s, André Breton issued a manifesto of SURREALISM, rallying around him Paul Éluard, Philippe Soupault, René Char, Tristan Tzara, Louis Aragon, and Elsa Triolet. Poets who reacted against the force of surrealism include Francis Carco, Léon Paul Fargue, Robert Desnos, and Pierre-Jean Jouve. The poetry of Alexis Saint-Léger Léger is distinguished for its imagery. Among the few outstanding poets of the decades after World War II are Jacques Prévert, Francis Ponge, Jules Supervielle, and Raymond Queneau, and among the younger poets, Patrice de la Tour du Pin, Pierre Emmanuel, Jean Tardieu, Jean Follain, Georges Clencier, Andrée Chédid, and Kateb Yacine. See articles on individual writers, e.g., SARTRE. See Sir Paul Harvey and J. E. Heseltine, *The Oxford Companion to French Literature* (1959); D. C. Cabeen et al., ed., *Critical Bibliography of French Literature* (4 vol., 1947–68); John Cruikshank, ed., *French Literature and Its Background* (6 vol., 1968–70); 17th and 18th cent.: A. A. Tilley, *The Decline of the Age of Louis XIV* (1968); Antoine Adams, *Grandeur and Illusion* (tr. 1972); 19th cent.: Albert Thibaudet, *French Literature from 1795 to Our Era* (1968); 20th cent.: Justin O'Brien, *The French Literary Horizon* (1967).

French Morocco: see MOROCCO.

French North Africa, originally general name for ALGERIA, former French MOROCCO, and TUNISIA.

French Polynesia, overseas territory of France (1971 est. pop. 114,000), consisting of 105 islands in the South Pacific. The capital is PAPEETE, on TAHITI. The territory comprises five main groups: the SOCIETY ISLANDS; MARQUESAS ISLANDS; AUSTRAL ISLANDS; TUAMOTU ISLANDS; and GAMBIER ISLANDS. Tropical fruits are grown, and vanilla and copra exported. Phosphate mining, once the major industry, ceased in 1966, and tourism is being encouraged in its place. The inhabitants of the territory are mainly Polynesians. French Polynesia is administered by a governor and council and an elected assembly. A territorial representative sits in the French national assembly and in the senate. The small, uninhabited atoll of Clipperton Island, c.3,400 mi (5,470 km) NE of Tahiti, is also part of the territory.

French Revolution, political upheaval of world importance that began in France in 1789. Historians disagree in evaluating the factors that brought about the cataclysm. Among the indirect causes, one of the most important certainly was the rise of capitalism and the commercial expansion of the 17th and 18th cent. To some extent at least, the Revolution came not because France was backward, but because its rapid economic and intellectual development was not matched by social and political change. In the fixed order of the ancien régime, the newly risen bourgeois class was unable to exercise the political and social influence to which its economic position entitled it. King Louis XIV, by consolidating absolute monarchy, had destroyed the roots of feudalism; yet outward feudal forms persisted and became increasingly irritating. France was still ruled by the privileged classes—the nobility and the clergy—who supplemented their diminishing funds in the 18th cent. by exacting more dues from the productive classes. Among the peasants, a few were still serfs in certain provinces in 1789; a larger minority were landowners. For the most part, however, the peasants were tenant farmers, subject to feudal dues, to the avarice of the royal agents who were FARMING the taxes, to the CORVÉE, and to military service, tithes, and other impositions. Backward agricultural methods and internal tariff barriers caused recurrent famines, which netted fortunes to grain speculators, and rural overpopulation created land hunger. The ancien régime, economically outdated, was undermined intellectually by the apostles of the ENLIGHTENMENT. VOLTAIRE attacked the church and absolutism; Denis DIDEROT and the ENCYCLOPÉDIE propagated scientific materialism; the baron de MONTESQUIEU made English constitutionalism fashionable; and the marquis de CONDORCET preached his faith in progress. Most direct in his influence on Revolutionary thought was J. J. ROUSSEAU, especially through his dogma of popular sovereignty. Economic reform, advocated by the PHYSIOCRATS and attempted (1774–76) by A. R. J. TURGOT, was thwarted by the unwillingness of the nobles and the clergy to sacrifice any privileges and by the king's failure to support strong measures.

Creation of a Constitutional Monarchy. The direct cause of the Revolution was the chaotic state of government finance. Jacques NECKER vainly sought to restore public confidence. French participation in the American Revolution had increased the huge debt, and Necker's successor, Charles Alexandre de CALONNE, called an Assembly of Notables (1787), hoping to avert bankruptcy by inducing the privileged classes to share in the financial burden; they refused. Étienne Charles LOMÉNIE DE BRIENNE succeeded Calonne. His attempts to procure money were thwarted by the Parlement of Paris (see PARLEMENT), and King LOUIS XVI was forced to agree to the calling of the STATES-GENERAL. Elections were ordered in 1788, and on May 5, 1789, for the first time since 1614, the States-General met at Versailles. The chief purpose of the king and of Necker, who had been recalled, was to obtain the assembly's consent to a general fiscal reform. Each of the three estates—clergy, nobility, and the third estate, or commons—presented its particular grievances to the crown. Innumerable cahiers (lists of grievances) came pouring in from the provinces, and it became clear that sweeping political and social reforms, far exceeding the object of its meeting, were expected from the States-General. The aspirations of the bourgeoisie were expressed by Abbé SIEYÈS in a widely circulated pamphlet that implied that the third estate and the nation were virtually identical. The question soon arose whether the estates should meet separately and vote by order or meet jointly and vote by head (thus assuring a majority for the third estate, whose membership had been doubled). As Louis XVI wavered, the deputies of the third estate defiantly proclaimed themselves the National Assembly (June 17); on their invitation, many members of the lower clergy and a few nobles joined them. When the king had their meeting place closed, they adjourned to an indoor tennis court, the *jeu de paume,* and there took an oath (June 20) not to disband until a constitution had been drawn up. On June 27 the king yielded and legalized the National Assembly. At the same time, however, he surrounded Versailles with troops and let himself be persuaded by a court faction, which included the queen, MARIE ANTOINETTE, to dismiss (July 11) Necker. A Paris mob revolted and on July 14 stormed the BASTILLE prison. Louis XVI meekly recalled Necker and went to the Hôtel de Ville in Paris, where he accepted the tricolor cockade of the Revolution from the newly formed municipal government, or commune. The national guard was organized under the marquis de LAFAYETTE. This first outbreak of violence marked the entry of the lower classes into the Revolution. Mobilized by alarm over food shortages and economic depression, by hopes aroused with the calling of the States-General, and by the fear of an aristocratic conspiracy, peasants pillaged and burned châteaus; this reaction is known as the *grande peur* [great fear]. In Paris and other cities, labor troubles erupted. On Aug. 4, the nobles and clergy in the Assembly, driven partly by terror and partly by a hysterical outburst of generosity, relinquished their privileges, abolishing in one night the feudal structure of France. Shortly afterward, the Assembly adopted the DECLARATION OF THE RIGHTS OF MAN AND CITIZEN. Radical political clubs were gaining strength in Paris. Rumors of counterrevolutionary court intrigues circulated, and on Oct. 5, 1789, a Parisian mob marched to Versailles. Lafayette was barely able to save the lives of the king and queen, who were taken to the Tuileries palace in Paris. The Assembly was also removed to Paris, where it drafted a constitution. Completed in 1791, the constitution created a limited monarchy with a unicameral legislature elected by voters who had the requisite property qualifications. Of gravest consequence were the Assembly's antireligious measures. Church lands were nationalized (1789), religious orders suppressed (1790), and the clergy required (July, 1790) to take oath to adhere to the state-controlled Civil Constitution of the Clergy. Few priests obeyed; disturbances broke out, especially in the pious rural districts; and Louis XVI, though forced to assent, was roused to action. Numerous princes and nobles had already fled abroad (see ÉMIGRÉ); Louis decided to join them and to obtain foreign aid to restore his authority. The flight (June 20–21, 1791) was halted at Varennes, and the king and queen were brought back in humiliation. Louis accepted the constitution. On Oct. 1, 1791, the Legislative Assembly convened. Its members represented the various political clubs of Paris, such as the FEUILLANTS, JACOBINS, and CORDELIERS. Most deputies were middle-of-the-roaders, whose indecision was exploited by the more radical clubs, and by the GIRONDISTS. Jacobinism was gaining; "Liberty, Equality, Fraternity" became a catch phrase. Meanwhile, abroad, early sympathy for the Revolution was turning to hatred. Émigrés incited the courts of Europe to intervene; in France, war was advocated by the royalists as a means to restore the old regime and also by many republicans, who either wished to spread the revolution abroad or hoped that the threat of invasion would rally the nation to their cause. The Feuillant, or right-wing, ministers fell and were succeeded by Girondists. On April 20, 1792, war was declared on Austria, and the FRENCH REVOLUTIONARY WARS began. Early reverses and rumors of treason by the king again brought the lower classes, especially those in Paris, into action.

Establishment of the Republic. An abortive insurrection of June 20, 1792, was followed by a decisive one on Aug. 10, when a mob stormed the Tuileries and an insurrectionary commune replaced the legally elected one (see COMMUNE OF PARIS). Under pressure from the commune, the Assembly suspended Louis XVI and ordered elections by universal manhood suffrage for a National Convention to draw up a new constitution. Mass arrests of royalist sympathizers were followed by the September massacres (Sept. 2–7), in which spontaneous mobs entered jails throughout France and killed hundreds of prisoners. On Sept. 21, 1792, the Convention held its first meeting. It immediately abolished the monarchy, set up the republic, and proceeded to try the king for treason. His conviction and execution (Jan., 1793) provoked royalist insurrections, notably in the VENDÉE, and, abroad, contributed to the forming of a coalition against France. The Convention undertook the foreign wars with vigor but was itself torn by the power struggle between the Girondists and the MOUNTAIN (Jacobins and extreme left). The Girondists were crushed in June, 1793. A republican constitution was adopted, but it never became active; instead the Convention established a war dictatorship operating through the Committee of Public Safety, the Committee of General Security, and numerous agencies such as the Revolutionary Tribunal. Known to history as the REIGN OF TERROR, this period represented the efforts of a few men to govern the country and wage war in a time of crisis. Georges DANTON and Maximilien ROBESPIERRE dominated the new government, with Robespierre gradually gaining over Danton and others. Prices and wages were fixed, and acceptance of the inflated paper currency, the ASSIGNATS, was severely enforced. A huge number of suspects were arrested; thousands were executed, including Marie Antoinette. A revolutionary calendar was adopted. The fanatic Jacques HÉBERT, who had introduced the worship of a goddess of Reason, was arrested and executed in March, 1794. The next month Danton and his followers, the "Indulgents," who advocated relaxation of emergency measures, were executed. To counter Hébertist influence, Robespierre proclaimed (June, 1794) the cult of the Supreme Being. France's military successes lessened the need for strong domestic measures; members of the Convention, fearing that the Terror would be turned against them, arrested Robespierre on July 27, 1794 (see THERMIDOR), and had him guillotined.

Government by a Directory. The Convention drew up a new constitution, setting up the DIRECTORY and a bicameral legislature. The constitution went into effect after the royalist insurrection of VENDÉMIAIRE (Oct., 1795) had been put down by armed force. The rule of the Directory was marked by corruption, bankruptcy, constant intrigues, and a fatal dependence on the army to maintain control. Conflict among the five directors led to the coup d'etat of 18 FRUCTIDOR (Sept. 4, 1797). Discontent with Directory rule was increased by military reverses. In 1799, Napoleon Bonaparte, the hero of the Italian campaign, returned from his Egyptian expedition and, with the support of the army and several government members, overthrew the Directory on 18 BRUMAIRE (Nov. 9) and established the CONSULATE. Until the RESTORATION of the Bourbons (1814), Napoleon (see NAPOLEON I) ruled France.

Effects of the Revolution. The French Revolution, though it seemed a failure in 1795 and appeared nullified by 1815, had far-reaching results. In France, the bourgeois and capitalist class was established as the dominant power; feudalism was dead; social justice was introduced by the CODE NAPOLÉON; and Paris became the center of European liberal thought. The Revolutionary and Napoleonic Wars tore down the ancient structure of Europe, hastened the advent of nationalism, and inaugurated the era of modern, total warfare. The unsuccessful attempts of the proletariat to gain economic, social, and political advancement from the Revolution foreshadowed the class conflicts of the 19th cent. Historical interpretations of the French Revolution differ greatly. See the older works by François MIGNET, Adolphe THIERS, Jules MICHELET, Thomas CARLYLE, Alphonse de LAMARTINE, Alexis de TOCQUEVILLE, Louis BLANC, Edgar QUINET, and H. A. TAINE; the great modern studies by Alphonse AULARD, Albert MATHIEZ, and Georges LEFEBVRE; the diplomatic history by Albert SOREL; the Socialist interpretation of Jean JAURÈS; Pierre Gaxotte, *La Révolution française* (1928, in French), a royalist account. See also L. R. Gottschalk, *The Era of the French Revolution* (1929); Crane Brinton, *A Decade of Revolution* (1934); J. H. Thompson, *The French Revolution* (1945); Albert Goodwin, *The French Revolution* (1953); Leo Gershoy, *The Era of the French Revolution, 1789–1799* (1957); Georges Lefebvre, *The French Revolution* (2 vol., tr. 1962–64); M. J. Sydenham, *The French Revolution* (1965). On the historiography of the French Revolution, see Paul Farmer, *France Reviews Its Revolutionary Origins* (1944, repr. 1963).

French Revolutionary calendar, the official CALENDAR of France, Nov. 24, 1793–Dec. 31, 1805. Its introduction was decreed by the Convention on Oct. 5, 1793, but it was computed from Sept. 22, 1792, the autumnal equinox and the day after the proclamation of the republic. Supposedly philosophical in its basis, it was divided into 12 months of 30 days (their names were invented by FABRE D'ÉGLANTINE): Vendémiaire (vintage month); Brumaire (fog); Frimaire (sleet); Nivôse (snow); Pluviôse (rain); Ventôse (wind); Germinal (seed); Floréal (blossom); Prairial (pasture); Messidor (harvest); Thermidor or Fervidor (heat); Fructidor (fruit). The remaining five days, called *sans-culottides,* were feast days; they were named for Virtue, Genius, Labor, Reason, and Rewards, respectively. In leap years (the years III, VII, and XI) the extra day, the last of the year, was Revolution Day. The first day of the year (1 Vendémiaire) of year I, II, III, V, VI, and VII fell on Sept. 22 of the corresponding year A.D.; in the years IV, VIII, IX, X, XI, XIII, and XIV, it fell on Sept. 23; in the year XII, it fell on Sept. 24. There was no week; the months were divided into three decades, with every 10th day *(décadi)* a day of rest. For the outstanding events known by the names of the revolutionary months in which they occurred, see VENDÉMIAIRE; BRUMAIRE; THERMIDOR; FRUCTIDOR.

French Revolutionary Wars, 1792–1802. The peace obtained in 1801–2 is generally considered to divide the French Revolutionary from the Napoleonic Wars, but the character of the conflict changed only gradually, beginning as an effort to spread the Revolution and developing into wars of conquest under the empire. The FRENCH REVOLUTION aroused in foreign lands the hostility of monarchs, nobles, and clergy, who feared the spread of republican ideas to the lower classes abroad. Ceaseless ÉMIGRÉ intrigues led the Austrian and Prussian rulers to make the declaration of Pillnitz (Aug., 1791), stating that, if all the powers would join them, they were willing to restore Louis XVI to his rightful authority. French public opinion was aroused. When the GIRONDISTS obtained control of the ministry (March, 1792) and Emperor Francis II acceded in Austria, war became almost inevitable. It was desired by many revolutionists who—with the notable exceptions of Robespierre and Marat—believed that war would insure the permanence of the new order and propagate revolution abroad, and by the royalists, who hoped that victory would restore the powers of Louis XVI. On April 20, 1792, Louis, still nominally king, declared war on Austria. The French armies lacked organization and discipline, and many noble officers had emigrated. The allied Austrian and Prussian forces under CHARLES WILLIAM FERDINAND, duke of Brunswick, quickly crossed the frontier and began to march on Paris. The duke issued a manifesto threatening to raze Paris should the royal family be harmed. This manifesto angered the French and thus contributed to the suspension of the king (Aug., 1792). The comte de ROCHAMBEAU, commanding the northern sector, and the marquis de LAFAYETTE, commanding the center, resigned. Their able successors, the generals DUMOURIEZ and KELLERMANN, turned the tide when they repulsed the invaders at

Valmy (Sept. 20). Dumouriez advanced on the Austrian Netherlands (Belgium), and he seized it after the battle of Jemappes (Nov. 6), while CUSTINE captured Mainz and advanced on Frankfurt. Late in 1792 the Convention issued a decree offering assistance to all peoples wishing to recover their liberty. This decree, the execution of Louis XVI (Jan., 1793), and the opening of the Scheldt estuary (contrary to the Peace of Westphalia) provoked Great Britain, Holland, and Spain to join Austria and Prussia in the First Coalition against France. Sardinia had already declared war after France had occupied Savoy and Nice (Sept., 1792). On Feb. 1, 1793, France declared war on Britain and Holland, and on March 7, on Spain. Things rapidly turned against France. Dumouriez, defeated at Neerwinden (March 18) by the Austrians, deserted to the enemy; revolt broke out in the VENDÉE; and Custine lost Mainz to the Prussians (July 23). In the emergency the first Committee of Public Safety was created (April 6), and a *levée en masse* (universal conscription) was decreed in August. The Committee, guided by the genius of Lazare CARNOT, raised 14 new armies; revolutionary commissioners were attached to the commands; defeated generals, like Custine, were executed "to encourage the others." By the end of 1793 the allies had been driven from France. In 1794 the new French commanders, JOURDAN and PICHEGRU, took the offensive. Jourdan, after defeating the Austrians at Fleurus (June 26, 1794), drove S along the Rhine as far as Mannheim; Pichegru seized the Low Countries. On May 16, 1795, Holland, transformed into the BATAVIAN REPUBLIC, made peace. Prussia on April 5, 1795, signed a separate peace (the first Treaty of Basel), ceding the left bank of the Rhine to France; Spain made peace on July 22 (second Treaty of Basel). Warfare against Austria and Sardinia continued under the newly established Directory. Carnot gradually evolved a plan calling for a three-pronged attack: Jourdan was to advance southeastward from the Low Countries; Jean Victor MOREAU was to strike at S Germany; and Napoleon Bonaparte was to conquer Piedmont and Lombardy, cross the Austrian Alps, and join with Moreau and Jourdan. During 1795 the French overran Baden, Württemberg, and Bavaria, but in 1796 the new Austrian commander, Archduke CHARLES, took the offensive, defeating first Jourdan, then Moreau, both of whom had retreated to the Rhine by Sept., 1796. On the Italian front, where a starving French army had been engaged in desultory and defensive operations until Bonaparte's arrival in 1796, one victory followed another (for details of the Italian campaign, see NAPOLEON I). Sardinia submitted in May, 1796, and in April, 1797, the preliminary peace of Leoben with Austria was signed by Bonaparte, just as Moreau had resumed his offensive in Germany. The armistice was confirmed by the Treaty of CAMPO FORMIO (Oct., 1797). Britain, however, remained in the war, retaining naval superiority under such able commanders as Samuel HOOD, Richard HOWE, John JERVIS, and Horatio NELSON. Bonaparte's plan to attack the British Empire by way of Egypt was doomed by Nelson's naval triumph at Aboukir in Aug., 1798. Meanwhile, France again aroused the anger of the European powers by creating the CISALPINE REPUBLIC and the Roman Republic and by invading Switzerland, which was transformed into the HELVETIC REPUBLIC. Under the leadership of Czar Paul I a Second Coalition was formed by Russia, Austria, Britain, Turkey, Portugal, and Naples. Naples was defeated and transformed into the PARTHENOPEAN REPUBLIC (Jan., 1799), but in N Italy the Austrians and the Russians drove out the French, and in Aug., 1799, General SUVOROV crossed the Alps into Switzerland, where Archduke Charles had already won (June 4-7) a victory at Zurich over MASSÉNA. However, disunity between the Austrians and the Russians resulted in disastrous defeats in Switzerland, and Suvorov, after a masterly retreat through the Alps, returned to Russia (Sept.-Oct., 1799). At this juncture, Bonaparte returned from Egypt and by the coup d'etat of 18 Brumaire became First Consul (Nov., 1799). The coalition was weakened by Russia's withdrawal, and Napoleon feverishly prepared a campaign to recoup French losses. The campaign of 1800 was decisive. In Italy, Napoleon, after crossing the St. Bernard Pass, crushed the Austrians at Marengo (June 14); in Germany, Moreau crossed the Rhine and demolished allied opposition at Hohenlinden (Dec. 3, 1800). With the Peace of Lunéville—a more severe version of the Treaty of Campo Formio—Austria was forced out of the war (Feb. 9, 1801). Great Britain, however, continued victorious, taking Malta (Sept., 1800) and compelling the French to surrender in Egypt (Aug., 1801). When Denmark, encouraged by France, defied British supremacy of the seas, Lord Nelson destroyed the Danish fleet in the battle of Copenhagen (April 2, 1801). Nevertheless, the British were warweary and, after Pitt's retirement, consented to the Treaty of Amiens (March 27, 1802), by which all conquests were restored to France. Malta was to be restored to the Knights Hospitalers (Britain's refusal to execute this stipulation was to lead to the resumption of warfare in 1803). Peace had already been made with Naples (March, 1801) and with Portugal (Sept., 1801), and in Oct., 1802, France signed a treaty restoring Egypt to Turkey. See Crane Brinton, *A Decade of Revolution, 1789-1799* (1935); Arthur Bryant, *Years of Endurance, 1793-1802* (1942); Leo Gershoy, *The Era of the French Revolution* (1957); John H. Rose, *William Pitt and the Great War* (1911, repr. 1971).

French Separatists: see FRONT DE LIBÉRATION DU QUÉBEC.

French Somaliland: see AFARS AND THE ISSAS, FRENCH TERRITORY OF THE.

French Sudan: see MALI.

French Union, 1946-58, political entity established by the French constitution of 1946. It comprised metropolitan France (the 90 departments of continental France and Corsica); French overseas departments, territories, settlements, and United Nations trusteeships; French colonies, which became overseas departments of France; and associate states (protectorates), which became autonomous. The union replaced the colonial system. In 1954, the associate states of Vietnam, Laos, and Cambodia withdrew from the union, and in 1956 Morocco and Tunisia, also associate states, became independent. The FRENCH COMMUNITY replaced the French Union in 1958.

French West Africa, former federation of eight French overseas territories. The constituent territories were Dahomey, French Guinea, French Sudan, Ivory Coast, Mauritania, Niger, Senegal, and Upper Volta. The federation was created in 1895 to consolidate the French holdings in W Africa. It was ruled by a governor general, who resided in Dakar. During World War II the federation supported the Vichy government until Nov., 1942, when it accepted the authority of the Free French. In 1958 the constituent territories became autonomous republics in the FRENCH COMMUNITY, except for Guinea, which became independent. The federation was dissolved in 1959.

French West Indies: see WEST INDIES.

Freneau, Philip (frĕnō'), 1752-1832, American poet and journalist, b. New York City, grad. Princeton, 1771. During the American Revolution he served as soldier and privateer. His experiences as a prisoner of war were recorded in his poem *The British Prison Ship* (1781). The first professional American journalist, he was a powerful propagandist and satirist for the American Revolution and for Jeffersonian democracy. Freneau edited various papers, including the partisan *National Gazette* (Philadelphia, 1791-93) for Jefferson. He was usually involved in editorial quarrels, and, influential though he was, none of his papers was profitable. His political and satirical poems have value mainly for historians, but his place as the earliest important American lyric poet is secured by such poems as "The Wild Honeysuckle," "The Indian Burying Ground," and "Eutaw Springs." See his *Poems* (ed. by F. L. Pattee, 3 vol., 1902-7) and *Last Poems* (ed. by Lewis Leary, 1946); biography by Lewis Leary (1941, repr. 1964); studies by P. M. Marsh (1968 and 1970).

Freon (frē'ŏn) [trade name], any one of a special class of chemical compounds that are used as refrigerants, aerosol propellants, and solvents. These compounds are haloalkanes, i.e., halogen derivatives of saturated hydrocarbons (see ALKANE). Every Freon contains at least some fluorine in its molecule, and most contain chlorine or bromine as well. Freons are generally colorless, odorless, nontoxic, noncorrosive, nonflammable, and chemically unreactive. The most commonly used is Freon-12, or dichlorodifluoromethane (CCl_2F_2), which boils at $-29.8°C$ and is thus a gas at ordinary temperatures and pressures. It is prepared by the reaction of carbon tetrachloride with hydrogen fluoride in the presence of a catalyst. There are a number of other Freons. Some of those containing bromine in their molecules are used in fire extinguishers.

frequency: see HARMONIC MOTION; WAVE.

frequency modulation: see MODULATION; RADIO.

Frere, Sir Henry Bartle Edward (frēr), 1815-84, British colonial administrator; nephew of John Hookham Frere. He served (1850-59) as chief commissioner of Sind, distinguishing himself during the Indian Mutiny (1857-58), and was (1862-67) governor of Bombay. In 1872 he negotiated a treaty with the sultan of Zanzibar for the suppression of the slave trade. Appointed (1877) governor of Cape Colony and high commissioner of British South Africa, Frere had to cope with Boer discontent in the newly annexed Transvaal and with Zulu unrest. Intent on breaking the military power of the Zulus, he precipitated (1878) the Zulu War. His action was disapproved in London, and although he was popular in the Cape he was recalled to England in 1880. See biography by W. B. Worsfold (1923).

Frere, John Hookham, 1769-1846, British writer and diplomat. He was a member of Parliament (1796-1802) and with his friend George CANNING wrote effective parodies and satires for the political newspaper, the *Anti-Jacobin*. He was undersecretary of state (1799-1800) and minister to Lisbon (1800-1802) and Madrid (1802-4, 1808-9). Thereafter he devoted himself to writing, living most of the time in Malta. Frere's best work is in his metrical translations from Aristophanes (*The Acharnians, the Knights, and the Birds,* 1840). See biography by Albert Eichler (1905, repr. 1965).

Fréron, Élie (ālē' frārôN'), 1718-76, French critic and journalist. His critical journal, *Année littéraire*, virulently attacked the philosophes of the Enlightenment. Voltaire made him a butt of his ridicule in several of his works.

Fréron, Louis Marie Stanislas (lwē mārē' stānēslās'), 1754-1802, French revolutionary; son of Élie Fréron. After the outbreak (1789) of the French Revolution, he founded a radical journal, *Orateur du peuple*. Fréron was a member of the Convention, took part in the Reign of Terror, and helped to bring about the downfall of Maximilien Robespierre in the Thermidorian reaction (July, 1794), of which he was a leader. He died as a member of the French expedition to Haiti.

fresco (frĕs'kō) [Ital.,=fresh], in its pure form the art of painting upon damp, fresh, lime plaster. In Renaissance Italy it was called *buon fresco* to distinguish it from *fresco secco,* which was executed upon dry plaster with pigments having a glue or casein base. In true fresco the binder is provided by the lime of the plaster; in drying this forms a calcium carbonate that incorporates the pure pigments, mixed only with water, with the material of the wall. During the Renaissance it was customary to prepare a CARTOON of the same dimensions as the contemplated fresco. To transfer the design to the wall, pounce, or dust, was applied through perforations in the cartoon to the wet coat of plaster (*intonaco*). The plaster was made of fine sand, lime, and marble dust that was applied in small sections daily. A large fresco therefore consists of many small sections, each painted in a day. The sections were planned in such a way as to make the joinings inconspicuous. As not all colors are lime-proof, fresco does not permit as large a palette or as delicate a manipulation of transitional tones as the oil medium. However, its clear, luminous color, fine surface, and permanence make it ideal for bold, monumental murals. The Minoans decorated the palace at Knossos and the Romans painted the villas at Pompeii in this fashion. The technique has not altered substantially since the 15th cent., when it was brought to perfection by the great masters of the Italian Renaissance. Only dry climates are hospitable to the medium, so fresco was used rarely in N Europe. The art of fresco painting declined until the 20th cent., when it was revived in Mexico by Diego Rivera and José Clemente Orozco. See Cennino Cennini, *Il libro dell' arte* (tr. 1932); Eve Borsook, *The Mural Painters of Tuscany* (1960); Millard Meiss, *The Great Age of Fresco* (1968).

Frescobaldi, Girolamo (jērō'lämō frāskōbäl'dē), 1583-1643, Italian organist and composer. He became organist at St. Peter's in Rome in 1608, where huge crowds came during most of his life to hear him play and improvise. From 1628 to 1634 he was organist at the court of the Medici in Florence. Through his pupil Johann FROBERGER, who carried his style to Germany, Frescobaldi's "noble" style and technique of improvisation influenced German organ style through the time of J. S. Bach. Besides numerous works for organ, he wrote some instrumental and vocal music.

Freshfield, Douglas William, 1845-1934, English explorer and mountaineer. A prominent member of the Royal Geographical Society, he did pioneer climbing in the Caucasus, the Himalayas, and the mountainous regions of many other countries. He edited (1872-80) the *Alpine Journal* and wrote *The*

Exploration of the Caucasus (1896), *Round Kangchenjunga* (1903), *Italian Alps* (1875; new ed. 1937), a biography of H. B. de Saussure (1921), and *Below the Snow Line* (1923).

Fresnel, Augustin Jean (ōgüstăN′ zhäN frānĕl′) 1788–1827, French physicist and engineer. He is known for his research on light, especially on conditions governing interference phenomena in polarized light and on double refraction. His work supported the wave theory of light and the concept of transverse vibrations in light waves, which he analyzed mathematically. He devised a method of producing circularly polarized light and promoted the replacement of mirrors with compound lenses in lighthouses. He served as a government engineer during most of his career.

Fresnillo (frăsnē′yō), city (1970 pop. 101,316), Zacatecas state, N central Mexico.

Fresno (frĕz′nō), city (1970 pop. 165,972), seat of Fresno co., S central Calif.; inc. 1885. It is the financial hub of the San Joaquin valley and an important railroad, processing, and marketing center. Grapes, figs, vegetables, and cotton are grown in the area. Among Fresno's manufactures are boxes, prefabricated buildings, carpets, and wines. The city is the seat of California State Univ. at Fresno; Pacific College; and Fresno City College (the oldest junior college in California; est. 1910). It has a veterans hospital, a large zoo, and its own philharmonic orchestra.

fretted instrument, in music, a stringed instrument that has frets set across its fingerboard. Frets are narrow strips of material, usually wood or metal, which mark the place on the fingerboard where the player's fingertips should be applied to stop the strings and produce the various notes. The frets also give the "stopped" string added resonance. The BALALAIKA, BANJO, CITTERN, GUITAR, LUTE, and UKULELE are all fretted instruments.

Fretum Herculeum: see GIBRALTAR.

Freud, Sigmund (froid), 1856–1939, Austrian psychiatrist, founder of PSYCHOANALYSIS. Born in Moravia, he lived most of his life in Vienna, receiving his medical degree from the university in 1881. With the National Socialist occupation of Austria, Freud fled (1938) to England, where he died. His medical career began with studies (1885–86) under J. M. Charcot in Paris, and soon after his return to Vienna he began his famous collaboration with Josef Breuer on the use of hypnosis in the treatment of hysteria. Their paper, *On the Psychical Mechanism of Hysterical Phenomena* (1893, tr. 1909), more fully developed in *Studien über Hysterie* (1895), marked the beginnings of psychoanalysis by the discovery that the symptoms of hysterical patients—directly traceable to psychic trauma in earlier life—represent undischarged emotional energy (conversion). The therapy, called the cathartic method, consisted of having the patient recall and reproduce the forgotten scenes while under hypnosis. The work was poorly received by the medical profession, and the two men soon separated over Freud's growing conviction that the undefined energy causing conversion was sexual in nature. Freud then rejected hypnosis and devised a technique called free association (see ASSOCIATION), which would allow emotionally charged material that the individual had repressed in his unconscious to emerge to conscious recognition. Further works, *The Interpretation of Dreams* (1900, tr. 1913), *The Psychopathology of Everyday Life* (1904, tr. 1914), and *Three Contributions to the Sexual Theory* (1905, tr. 1910), increased the bitter antagonism toward Freud, and he worked alone until 1906, when he was joined by the Swiss psychiatrists Eugen Bleuler and C. G. Jung, the Austrian Alfred Adler, and others. In 1908, Bleuler, Freud, and Jung founded the journal *Jahrbuch für psychoanalytische und psychopathologische Forschungen*, and in 1909 the movement first received public recognition when Freud and Jung were invited to give a series of lectures at Clark Univ. in Worcester, Mass. In 1910 the International Psychoanalytical Association was formed with Jung as president, but the harmony of the movement was short-lived; between 1911 and 1913 both Jung and Adler resigned, forming their own schools in protest against Freud's emphasis on infantile sexuality and the Oedipus complex. Although these men, and others who broke away later, objected to Freudian theories, the basic structure of analysis is still Freudian, and disagreement lies in the degree of emphasis placed on concepts largely originated by Freud. He considered his last contribution to psychoanalytic theory to be *The Ego and the Id* (1923, tr. 1927), after which he reverted to earlier cultural preoccupations. *Totem and Tabu* (1913, tr. 1918), an investigation of the origins of religion and morality, and *Moses and Monotheism* (1939, tr. 1939) are the result of his application of psychoanalytic theory to cultural problems. Freudian theory has had wide impact, influencing anthropology, education, art, and literature. Other works include *A General Introduction to Psychoanalysis* (1910, tr. 1920) and *New Introductory Lectures on Psycho-analysis* (1933). See his *Basic Writings* (tr. and ed. by A. A. Brill, 1938); *The Freud-Jung Letters*, ed. by William McGuire (1974); his autobiography (1925, tr. of rev. ed. 1935); biography by Ernest Jones (3 vol., 1953–57, abr. ed. 1961); studies by Norman Brown (1959), Reuben Fine (1962), Giovanni Costigan (1965), and B. B. Wolman (1968); Fritz Wittels, *Freud and His Time* (1931, repr. 1956).

Freundlich, Erwin Finlay (froind′lĭkh), 1885–1964, German astronomer. Freundlich obtained a doctorate in mathematics at Göttingen, then joined the Royal Observatory at Berlin, where he worked under the direction of Albert Einstein. His observations of the motion of Mercury, which differs slightly from the Newtonian prediction, were published in 1913 and helped convince the scientific community of the validity of Einstein's theory of relativity. In 1921, Freundlich joined the new Einstein Institute at Potsdam, and in 1929 he observed a solar eclipse that yielded data intriguingly different from the Einstein prediction. His speculations on these data and on astronomical red shifts, published and defended during the last half of his life, are still controversial.

Frey (frā), Norse god. He was a beneficent deity associated with the fertilizing powers of the sun and the rain and, like his sister FREYJA, with the return of spring. His worship, which extended throughout most of Scandinavia, had its chief seat at Uppsala.

Freycinet, Charles de (shärl də frāsēnā′), 1828–1923, French statesman. A mining engineer, he helped Léon GAMBETTA organize resistance to the Germans during the Franco-Prussian War (1870–71). Later he was elected (1876) to the senate. He repeatedly held cabinet posts—public works, foreign affairs, and war—and was four times premier.

Freycinet, Louis Claude Desaulses de (lwē klōd dəsōls′), 1779–1842, French marine officer. He was assigned (1800) to a French exploring expedition in Australian waters; after his return to Paris (1805) he edited the maps and reports of the journey. In 1817, accompanied by Arago and other scientists, he sailed in command of the *Uranie* and the *Physicienne* to make observations in geography, ethnology, astronomy, and meteorology and to collect specimens of flora and fauna. After visiting Australia and the Marianas, Hawaii, and other Pacific islands, Freycinet lost his ship off the Falkland Islands. The expedition records and collections were saved, and Freycinet returned to Paris in 1820. He edited the scientific findings and the narrative of the journey, which appeared as *Voyage autour du monde* (13 vol., 1824–44).

Freyja (frā′yä) or **Freya** (frā′ä), Norse goddess of love, marriage, and fertility. Her identity and attributes were often confused with those of the goddess Frigg. As a deity of the dead, Freyja was entitled to half the warriors killed in battle, the other half going to Odin. She was the sister of the god Frey and was frequently represented as riding in a chariot drawn by cats.

Freyre, Gilberto (jĕlbĕr′to͞o frā′rə), 1900–, Brazilian sociologist and anthropologist, grad. Baylor Univ., 1920, M.A. Columbia, 1922. He taught, traveled, and gave lectures in many countries, especially in the United States. For opposition to the government he was briefly imprisoned in 1934. He established a worldwide reputation as a social historian. His linked masterpieces, *Casa grande e senzala* (5th ed. 1946; tr. *The Masters and the Slaves*, rev. ed. 1956), and *Sobrados e mucambos* (tr. *The Mansions and the Shanties*, 1936), are an anthropological and psychological study of Brazilian society. Among his many other works are two books written in English, *Brazil: An Interpretation* (1945) and *New World in the Tropics* (1959).

Freyssinet, Eugène (özhĕn′ frāsēnā′), 1879–1962, French engineer. Freyssinet was noted as a designer of bridges and industrial buildings. He was the inventor of the internationally used prestressing technique devised to overcome difficulties in executing curved shapes in reinforced concrete. An austere, highly functional beauty characterizes his designs for airship hangars at Orly Airport, Paris, for harbor construction at Brest and Le Havre, and for runways, roads, and bridges on several continents.

Freytag, Gustav (go͞o′stäf frī′täkh), 1816–95, German novelist and playwright. He taught at the Univ. of Breslau and edited the *Grenzboten* (1848–70). His most successful play, *The Journalists* (1855, tr. 1888), is an adroit comedy of small-town life and politics. Best known today are his realistic novels *Soll und Haben* (1855, tr. *Debit and Credit*, 1856), *Die verlorene Handschrift* (1864, tr. *The Lost Manuscript*, 1865), and his ambitious series of German historical novels, *Die Ahnen* (1873–81, tr. of selections *Ingo and Ingraban*, 1873).

friar, member of certain Roman Catholic religious orders, notably, the DOMINICANS, FRANCISCANS, CARMELITES, and AUGUSTINIANS—called "mendicants" from the original prohibition against ownership of property, personal or corporate. This was a restriction lightened by the Council of Trent. Friars differ from cloistered monks by their widespread outside activity and by their highly centralized organization. See MONASTICISM.

friarbird: see HONEYEATER.

Fribourg (frī′bûrg, Fr. frēbo͞or′), Ger. *Freiburg*, canton (1970 pop. 180, 309), 645 sq mi (1,671 sq km), W Switzerland. Located on the Swiss Plateau and amid the foothills of the Alps, Fribourg is an agricultural region known for its cattle and cheese (notably Gruyère). Industries include the production of watches and chocolate. The canton is overwhelmingly Catholic, and the inhabitants are mainly French-speaking. It joined the Swiss Confederation in 1481 after being enlarged with land ceded from Vaud. A new constitution was adopted in 1857. The town of **Fribourg** (1970 pop. 39,695), the canton's original settlement and capital, is rich in medieval architecture and picturesquely situated on the Sarine River. It is famous for its chocolate, although other products are also made. Founded in 1178 by Berchtold IV, duke of Zähringen, it passed successively to the houses of Kyburg (1218), Hapsburg (1277), and Savoy (1452). Fribourg is an episcopal residence. It has many convents and churches, including the Cathedral of St. Nicholas (13th–14th cent.). The Catholic Univ. was founded in 1889.

Frick, Ford Christopher, 1894–, U.S. commissioner of baseball (1951–1965), b. Wawaka, Ind. After serving on the staff of the Colorado Springs *Telegraph* (1919–21) and the New York *Journal* (1921–34), he was elected (1934) commissioner of the National Baseball League. In 1951 he succeeded "Happy" Chandler as commissioner of major league baseball. During Frick's tenure as commissioner, each of the two major leagues expanded from 8 to 10 teams (the American League in 1961, the National League in 1962; see BASEBALL). In 1970 he was elected to the Baseball Hall of Fame.

Frick, Henry Clay, 1849–1919, American industrialist, b. Westmoreland co., Pa. He worked on his father's farm, was a store clerk, and did bookkeeping before he and several associates organized (1871) Frick & Company to operate coke ovens in the Connellsville coal district. He strengthened his position by buying out competitors during the Panic of 1873 and soon held a key place in the industry. Andrew CARNEGIE, in order to control a business so vital to steelmaking, acquired heavy interests in Frick's organization. Frick, in turn, was given large holdings in the Carnegie company, and because of his managerial ability, he was made (1889) chairman of the steel company. He played a key role in the organization (1892) of the Carnegie Steel Company, and as its acting head Frick engineered a large expansion of the company by buying out competing companies and acquiring many holdings in railroad securities and in Lake Superior iron ore lands. Frick, frequently over Carnegie's protest, dealt in strong-handed fashion with the company's workers, and his adamant stand resulted in a pitched battle in the strike (1892) at Homestead, Pa.—one of the bitterest strikes in U.S. history. He was largely responsible for the antiunion policy that characterized the steel industry for many decades. Disputes between Frick and Carnegie led to a struggle between them for control, and in 1899 Frick resigned. He became a director of the U.S. Steel Corp. and turned to other interests, chiefly railroads. His mansion in New York City, together with his art collection and endowment of $15 million, was willed to the public as a museum. Princeton Univ. and the city of Pittsburgh also benefited from his philanthropies. See biography by G. B. M. Harvey (1928).

friction, resistance offered to the movement of one body past another body with which it is in contact. It depends partly on the smoothness of the contacting surfaces, a greater force being needed to move two surfaces past one another if they are rough than if they are smooth. However, friction decreases with smoothness only to a degree; friction actually increases between two extremely smooth surfaces because of increased attractive electrostatic forces between their atoms. Friction does not depend on the amount of surface area in contact between the moving bodies or (within certain limits) on the relative speed of the bodies. It does, however, depend on the magnitude of the forces holding the bodies together. When a body is moving over a horizontal surface, it presses down against the surface with a force equal to its weight, i.e., to the pull of gravity upon it; an increase in the weight of the body causes an increase in the amount of resistance offered to the relative motion of the surfaces in contact. The **coefficient of friction** is the quotient obtained by dividing the value of the force necessary to move one body over another at a constant speed by the weight of the body. For example, if a force of 20 newtons is needed to move a body weighing 100 newtons over another horizontal body at a constant speed, the coefficient of friction between these two materials is 20/100 or 0.2. Different materials in contact yield different results; e.g., different resistances are felt if one pushes a block of wood over surfaces of wood, steel, and plastic. A different coefficient of friction must be calculated for each different pair of materials. There is more than one coefficient of friction for a given pair of materials. More force is needed to start a body moving across a surface than is needed to keep it in motion once started. Thus, the coefficient of static friction (describing the former case) for a pair of substances is greater than the coefficient of kinetic friction (describing the latter case) for the substances. Similarly, sliding friction is greater than rolling friction. The force of friction between two materials can be calculated by multiplying the coefficient of friction between these materials (determined experimentally and listed in engineering handbooks) by the force holding them together (e.g., the weight of the moving body). In certain situations friction is desired. Without friction the wheels of a locomotive could not "grip" the rails nor could power be transmitted by belts. On the other hand, in the moving parts of machines a minimum of friction is desired; an excess of friction produces heat, which in turn causes expansion, the locking of the moving parts, and a consequent breakdown of the machinery. LUBRICATION is important in minimizing friction as are also such devices as ball and roller BEARINGS. **Fluid friction** is observed in the flow of liquids and gases. Its causes are similar to those responsible for friction between solid surfaces, for it also depends upon the chemical nature of the fluid and the nature of the surface over which the fluid is flowing. The tendency of the liquid to resist flow, i.e., its degree of viscosity, is another important factor. Fluid friction is affected by increased velocities, and the modern streamline design of airplanes is the result of engineers' efforts to minimize fluid friction, while retaining speed and protecting structure.

Frida, Emil Bohuslav: see VRCHLICKY, JAROSLAV.

Friday: see SABBATH; WEEK.

Fridigern: see FRITIGERN.

Fridley, city (1970 pop. 29,233), Anoka co., SE Minn., a suburb of Minneapolis, on the Mississippi River; settled 1847, inc. as a city 1957. A distribution center with railroad yards and warehouses, Fridley produces naval ordnance, pumps, machine tools, transportation equipment, dies and parts, portable generators, electro-medical devices, cosmetics, and linseed oil. In 1965 three tornadoes destroyed substantial parts of the city.

Fried, Alfred Hermann (äl'frät hĕr'män frēt), 1864–1921, Austrian pacifist. He moved to Berlin, where he was a bookseller and a writer. Influenced by Bertha von Suttner, he devoted himself after 1891 to the international peace movement. Fried founded the Deutsche Friedengesellschaft [German league for peace], edited from 1899 the periodical *Friedenswarte*, contributed to other pacifist journals, and wrote books. He shared the 1911 Nobel Peace Prize with Tobias Asser. In World War I, Fried continued his work in Switzerland. His approach to international peace particularly stressed forming international juridical organizations.

Friedan, Betty Naomi, 1921–, American social reformer and feminist, b. Peoria, Ill., educated at Smith College (B.A., 1942) and the Univ. of California at Berkeley. In 1963 she published *The Feminine Mystique*, an attack on the popular notion that women could find fulfillment only through childbearing and housewifery. In 1966 she founded the NATIONAL ORGANIZATION FOR WOMEN (NOW) and served as its president until 1970. It was in that year that she organized a nationwide Women's Strike for Equality. In 1971 she helped to found the National Women's Political Caucus (NWPC).

friedcakes: see DOUGHNUTS.

Friedlaender, Walter (frēd'lĕndər), 1873–1966, American art historian, b. Germany. Friedlaender pursued a distinguished academic career in Germany until 1934 and afterward taught at New York Univ. His best-known works on 16th- and 17th-century art include *Caravaggio Studies* (1955), his edition of *The Drawings of Nicolas Poussin* (3 vol., 1939–55), and *Mannerism and Anti-Mannerism in Italian Painting* (1957), all basic works in their fields. Friedlaender's *David to Delacroix* (tr. 1952) is a broad and important survey in the study of 19th-century art. His publications in German include studies on 16th-century architecture at the Vatican (1912) and on Claude Lorrain (1921).

Friedland: see FRÝDLANT, Czechoslovakia.

Friedland: see PRAVDINSK, USSR.

Friedlander, Leo (frēd'lăndər), 1890–1966, American sculptor, b. New York City, studied in New York, Paris, Brussels, and at the American Academy in Rome. His many decorative works include sculptures on Washington Memorial Arch, Valley Forge, Pa.; reliefs for the National Chamber of Commerce, Washington, D.C.; the main central pediment of the Museum of the City of New York; facades for the Jefferson County (Ala.) Courthouse; groups for the RCA Building, Rockefeller Center, New York City; and statues for the Oregon state capitol.

Friedländer, Max J. (frēd'lĕndər), 1867–1958, German art historian. Educated in Munich, he became director of the Kaiser Friedrich Museum in Berlin. He left Germany in 1933 and settled in Holland. A specialist in Netherlandish painting of the 15th and 16th cent., he is best known for his monumental work on that subject, *Die Altniederländische Malerei* (14 vol., 1924–37). Friedländer was also the author of *On Art and Connoisseurship* (1942), *Landscape, Portrait, Still-Life: Their Origin and Development* (tr. 1949), and *From Van Eyck to Bruegel* (tr. 1956).

Friedman, Milton, 1912–, American economist, b. Brooklyn, N.Y., grad. Rutgers Univ. (B.A., 1932), Univ. of Chicago (M.A., 1933), Columbia (Ph.D., 1946). A staff member of the National Bureau of Economic Research (1937–46, 1948–), he has taught economics at the Univ. of Chicago since 1946. A leading conservative figure, Friedman is best known among economists for his theory that, contrary to Keynesian beliefs, changes in the monetary supply precede, rather than follow, changes in overall economic activity. He is a persuasive defender of the free market system, especially in his regular column in *Newsweek* magazine, to which he has been a contributing editor since 1971. Friedman is an unusually prolific writer. His publications include *A Theory of the Consumption Function* (1957), *Capitalism and Freedom* (1962), and, with Anna Schwartz, *Monetary History of the United States, 1867–1960* (1963).

Friedmann, Meir (mī'ər frĕt'män), 1831–1908, Hungarian Jewish scholar. He made important contributions in the field of scientific criticism of rabbinical texts. Friedmann's editions of the Midrash are standard.

Friedrich, Caspar David (käs'pär dä'fēt frē'drĭkh) 1774–1840, German romantic landscape painter. After studying painting in Copenhagen he visited various scenic spots in Germany and chose to live in Dresden, where he remained until his death. Friedrich's melancholy and symbolic compositions were singular expressions of the significance of landscape. His use of unusual, often eerie, light effects unified the mood of his works. His approach was a solitary one and his influence was not great, although he taught from 1816 until his death. *Capuchin Friar by the Sea* and *Man and Woman Gazing at the Moon* (both: Berlin) typically project his mystical and pantheistic attitude toward nature. See study by Helmut Börsch-Supan (1974).

Friedrichshafen (frē'drĭkhs-hä"fən), city (1970 pop. 43,140), Baden-Württemberg, S West Germany, a port on the Lake of Constance. Manufactures include textiles, leather goods, machinery, and electrical products. Friedrichshafen was formed in 1811 by the union of the towns of Buchhorn (founded by the 9th cent.) and Hafen (founded in the mid-11th cent.). In 1824 it became the summer residence of the kings of Württemberg. As the site of the Zeppelin aircraft works, Friedrichshafen suffered heavy damage in World War II. Of interest are the baroque ducal castle (originally a Benedictine abbey) and its church (both built in the late 17th cent.).

Friendly Islands: see TONGA.

Friends, Religious Society of, religious body originating in England in the middle of the 17th cent. under George Fox. The members are commonly called Quakers, originally a term of derision. Claiming that no theologically trained priest or outward rite is needed to establish communion between the soul and its God, Fox taught that everyone could receive whatever understanding and guidance in divine truth he might need from the "inward light," or "inner light," supplied in his own heart by the Holy Spirit. Many of his early converts were from among groups of SEPARATISTS. Calling themselves Children of Light, Friends in the Truth, and Friends, they eventually agreed upon the name Religious Society of Friends. The Friends regard the sacraments of the church as nonessential to Christian life. They refused to attend worship in the established church and to pay tithes. They also resisted the requirement to take oaths and opposed war, refusing to bear arms. Believing in the equality of all men and women, Friends would not remove their hats before alleged superiors. Consequently, they were subject to persecution until the passage at the Toleration Act of 1689. As religious freedom grew, the Friends sent representatives to the Continent and to America, Asia, and Africa. They found a wide field of activity in philanthropic movements, taking the lead in the effort to abolish slavery. Among noted American abolitionists were John WOOLMAN, Lucretia MOTT, and John Greenleaf WHITTIER. The Friends worked for prison reform (e.g. Elizabeth FRY), for improvement in insane asylums, for mitigation of the penal code (especially abolition of capital punishment), and for the betterment of common education. In colonial America they often met with severe condemnation and some persecution, except in Rhode Island and in Pennsylvania, where in 1682 William PENN settled his famous colony. Although for reasons of conscience Friends could not take an active part in the Revolutionary War, they were loyal in upholding the new national government. In 1827 questions arising in connection with the preaching of Elias HICKS divided the American Friends into two groups, the "Hicksites," who placed emphasis upon the individual's belief as guided by revelation to his own spirit, and the "Orthodox," who gave to the elders the duty of decision as to soundness of doctrine. At the same time, under Joseph J. Gurney, there was an evangelical revival among Friends in the Western states, with a tendency to discard many of the old forms and distinctions. Another break occurred in 1845 in New England, when the adherents of John Wilbur set up a new yearly meeting in protest against what they considered dangerous departure from the teachings and ways of the early Friends. Two superficial marks of the sect have been generally disappearing—the plain language, in which the Friends used "thee" to everyone as a mark of equality, and the plain gray dress, the broad-brimmed men's hats, and the women's bonnets. The Friends have long been workers in the cause of peace and international understanding. The accomplishments in overseas relief and reconstruction achieved by the American Friends Service Committee, organized in 1917, are widely recognized. This body and the Service Council of the British Society of Friends were jointly awarded the 1947 Nobel Peace Prize. Educational activity among the Friends has resulted in the establishment and support of a number of schools and colleges. Avoiding liturgies and all elaboration that they fear might interfere with the direct guidance of the Holy Spirit, the Friends meet for worship without set form and frequently without stated leaders. Any member is at liberty to follow the impulse of the spirit in prayer, praise, or exhortation. A meeting may be spent entirely in silent receptivity and communion. Ministers are not required to have special training; any man or woman who experiences the call to the work and gives evidence of his sincerity and ability may be recorded as a minister. In recent years, however, many of the Friends who seek the ministry have studied at theological schools. The organization of the Society includes meetings for worship and monthly, quarterly, and yearly meetings. In the United States, the old lines of division between Orthodox, Hicksite, and Conservative (or Wilburite) Friends have grown considerably less, and there have been many signs of interest in reunion. The Religious Society of Friends is a member of the World Council of Churches. The Friends World Committee for Consultation is valuable to the international community of Friends, and the organization of the Wider Quaker Fellowship offers to non-Quakers in sympathy with the Quaker spirit a chance to aid in the work of the Friends. See R. M. Jones, *The Later Periods of Quakerism* (1921, repr. 1971) and *The Faith and Practice of the Quakers* (1927); Elbert Russell, *The History of Quakerism* (1942); W. W. Comfort, *Quakers in the Modern World* (1949) and *The Quaker Persuasion: Yesterday, Today, Tomorrow* (1956); W. C. Braithwaite, *The Beginnings of Quakerism* (2d ed. 1955); Anna Brinton, *Then and Now* (1960, repr. 1970); Elfrida Vipont, *The Story of Quakers Through Three Centuries* (2d ed. 1960); M. H. Bacon, *The Quiet Rebels* (1969); J. W. Frost, *The Quaker Family in Colonial America* (1973); Hugh Barbour and A. O. Roberts, ed., *Early Quaker Writings* (1973).

Fries, Elias Magnus (ĕlē'äs mäng'nəs frēs), 1794–1878, Swedish botanist. He taught (1834–59) at the Univ. of Uppsala. Fries originated the modern classification of fungi and lichens. His works include *Systema mycologicum* (3 vol., 1821–32) and *Icones selectae Hymenomycetum* (2 vol., 1867–84).

Fries, John, c.1750–1818, American rebel, b. Montgomery co., Pa. After serving in the American Revolution, Fries became a traveling auctioneer. Strongly opposed to the Federal property taxes levied (1798) for a possible war with France, he stirred the Pennsylvania Germans into an uprising (called Fries's Rebellion) against assessors and collectors. He hid from Federal troops, but his hiding place was betrayed by his dog. He was arrested and sentenced to death, but President John Adams pardoned him.

Friesland (frēz'lənd, Du. frēs'länt) or **Frisia** (frĭzh'ə), province (1971 pop. 526,700), c.1,325 sq mi (3,430 sq km), N Netherlands. Leeuwarden is the capital. The province includes several of the West Frisian Islands along the North Sea coast and borders on the IJsselmeer in the west. A great dairying and cattle-raising region, Friesland has fertile land near the coast and sandy heath and fenland in the interior. It is drained by numerous canals and small rivers and has many picturesque lakes. The Frisians, a Germanic people, were conquered by the Franks in the 8th cent. Their language, which differs considerably from Dutch, is still spoken by a sizeable part of the population. In the early Middle Ages, Friesland extended from the Scheldt River in the south to the Weser in the east. Later it was partly conquered by the counts of HOLLAND. When Holland passed (1433) to the house of Burgundy, the authority of the Burgundian dukes was not recognized by the independence-minded Frisians. In 1498, Emperor Maximilian I bestowed all Friesland on Duke Albert of Saxony. Albert also was unable to establish his authority, and in 1515 his son, for a payment, restored Friesland to Maximilian. Maximilian's grandson, Emperor Charles V, reduced Friesland by force in 1523. (East Friesland, created a country in 1454, was not included in the transfer and its history became separate.) Friesland joined (1579) in the Union of Utrecht against Spanish domination, but it continued to appoint its own stadtholders until 1748, when its stadtholder, Prince William IV of Orange, became sole and hereditary stadtholder of all the United Provinces of the Netherlands.

Friesz, Othon (Achille Émile Othon Friesz) (ôtôN' frēēs, āshēl' āmēl'), 1879–1949, French painter. He studied under Bonnat at the École des Beaux-Arts, along with Matisse, Marquet, and Rouault. Early influenced by impressionism, he adopted the bold, colorful style of the painters involved in the development of FAUVISM. He exhibited with them until 1908 when his work changed to become less explosive. His *Miarka* (Art Inst., Chicago) is characteristic of his later period.

frieze, in architecture, the member of an entablature between the architrave and the cornice or any horizontal band used for decorative purposes. In the first type the Doric frieze alternates the metope and the triglyph; that of the other orders is plain or sculptured. The 5th-century B.C. treasury of the Cnidians at Delphi shows figures in the frieze. Roman and Renaissance examples, a notable one being on the 1st-century B.C. temple of Vesta at Tivoli, display acanthus leaves and other ornamentation; they are frequently pulvinated or convexly curved. The Panathenaic frieze on the cella wall of the PARTHENON is the best example of the second type of frieze.

frigate (frĭg'ĭt), originally a long, narrow nautical vessel used on the Mediterranean, propelled by either oars or sail or both. Later, during the 18th and early 19th cent., the term was applied to a very fast, square-rigged sailing vessel carrying 24 to 44 guns on a single flush gun deck. Frigates were employed by the European naval powers in large numbers as commerce raiders and for blockade duty. In the United States before the War of 1812, Joshua Humphreys designed a number of frigates superior to any other vessels of their class in speed and armament. With the introduction of steam and steel warships in the middle of the 19th cent., frigates as a class of warship passed out of use. However, during World War II frigates were reintroduced by the British as a form of antisubmarine escort larger than a corvette and smaller than a DESTROYER. Destroyer-type ships called frigates are important combat vessels today; however, there is no clearcut uniform distinction between a frigate and a destroyer. Modern frigates are often armed with antisubmarine weapons and guns; many are missile-armed and some are nuclear-powered. The nuclear-powered frigate U.S.S. *Truxtun*, launched in 1964, was the largest destroyer-type ship ever built. See Frank Dorovan, *The Tall Frigates* (1962); James Henderson, *The Frigates* (1970); *Jane's Fighting Ships* (pub. annually since 1897).

frigate-bird: see MAN-O'-WAR BIRD.

Frigg or **Frigga,** Norse mother goddess and the wife of Odin (Woden). One of the most important goddesses of Germanic religion, she was queen of the heavens, a deity of love and the household. She was often confused with Freyja. From her likeness to the Roman goddess Venus, the Latin day of Venus became in Germanic countries Frigg's day (Friday).

frigid zone: see ARCTIC REGIONS; ANTARCTICA; ZONE.

frijole (frēhō'lē) [from Span. *fríjol*], in Mexico and the Spanish American countries, any cultivated bean of the genus *Phaseolus*. The term *frijole* refers to the small, flat, black bean that ranks next to corn in importance in the diet of most Latin American countries. It is probably of South American origin and belongs to the same family as the bean introduced into Europe in the 16th cent., from which sprang many of the modern cultivated varieties.

Friml, Rudolf (Charles Rudolf Friml) (frĭm'əl), 1879–1972, American composer, b. Prague. Friml lived in the United States after 1906. The best-known of his 33 light operas are *The Firefly* (1912), *Rose Marie* (1924), and *The Vagabond King* (1925). Friml's operettas generally concerned gallants and princesses moving through fairy-tale complexities of plot. Presented on stage, on Broadway and in road companies and revived in film versions, his operettas succumbed to the change in musical tastes by the late 1940s.

Frimley and Camberley, urban district (1971 pop. 44,784), Surrey, S England. The district is in an area that has important military installations. The Royal Staff College and the Royal Military Academy at Sandhurst are in the district.

fringeflower: see BUTTERFLY FLOWER.

Frisch, Karl von (frĭsh), 1887–, Austrian zoologist, b. Vienna, Austria. He studied zoology with Richard von Hertwig, whom he later succeeded as professor of zoology at Munich Univ. For his pioneering work in comparative behavioral physiology, particularly his studies of the complex communication between insects, von Frisch was awarded the 1973 Nobel Prize for Physiology and Medicine. In his early work he showed that fish and honeybees can see colors, fish can hear, and bees can distinguish dozens of closely related floral scents. In 1923 he described as a simple language the round and waggle dances of honeybees. He found that round dances mean that food is nearby and waggle dances that there is food at a distance. The straight component of the waggle dance points the way to the food, and the duration of the dance indicates the distance. In some cases bees orient themselves by the direction of the sun or, if the sky is overcast, by the polarization of light from patches of blue sky. An important implication of von Frisch's work is that behavioral continuity exists between animal communication and human language.

Frisch, Max, 1911–, Swiss writer. He obtained a diploma in architecture in 1941, and his designs include the Zurich Recreation Park. After 1955 he devoted all his time to writing. Frisch is essentially concerned with man's search for personal identity in the novels *Stiller* (1954; tr. *I'm Not Stiller*, 1958), *Homo faber* (1957, tr. 1959), and *Mein Name sei Gantenbein* (1964; tr. *A Wilderness of Mirrors*, 1965). In the play *Die chinesische Mauer* (1946; tr. *The Chinese Wall*, 1961) he asks if atomic-era man will remember humanity. His best-known plays are *Biedermann und die Brandstifter* (1953; tr. *The Firebugs*, 1963), and *Andorra* (1961, tr. 1962), a study of mass psychology. Two collections of his dramas have appeared in English, each entitled *Three Plays* (1962 and 1967). His *Sketchbook 1966–71* was published in English in 1974. See biographies by U. W. Weisstein (1967) and Carol Petersen (tr. 1972).

Frisch, Ragnar (räng'när frĭsh), 1895–1973, Norwegian economist, corecipient with Jan TINBERGEN of the Ist Nobel Memorial Prize in economics (1969). Educated at the Univ. of Oslo (M.A., 1919; Ph.D., 1926), Frisch was briefly a visiting professor at Yale (1930). In 1931 he returned to the Univ. of Oslo as professor of economics, a post he held until his retirement (1965). While at the university, he helped to found (1931) the Econometric Society and was editor (1933–55) of the journal *Econometrica*. A major figure in the development of ECONOMETRICS, Frisch did much to facilitate the application of statistics to economic theory.

Frischlin, Nikodemus (nēkōdā'mo͞os frĭsh'lĭn), 1547–90, German satirist and philologist. His dramas, written in Latin and seemingly dealing with antique or biblical subjects, were in fact merciless anti-Catholic and political polemics. His *Julius redivivus* (1584), a comedy in the style of Aristophanes, brings Olympian gods onto German soil, where they discuss contemporary figures. He was imprisoned for his attacks on local aristocrats and died while attempting an escape.

Frisia: see FRIESLAND.

Frisian Islands (frĭzh'ən), chain of low-lying islands, off the coasts of the Netherlands, West Germany, and Denmark, in the North Sea. The West Frisian Islands, belonging to the Netherlands, are off the shores of North Holland, Friesland, and Groningen provs. and include the islands of Texel, Vlieland, Terschelling, Ameland, and Rottum. The East Frisian Islands, belonging to West Germany, are east of the mouth of the Ems and include Norderney and Borkum. The North Frisian Islands, off the coast of Schleswig-Holstein, West Germany, and S Jutland, Denmark, include SYLT, FÖHR, and RØMØ. Fishing and stock raising are pursued on most of the Frisian Islands. There are many bathing resorts there.

Frisian language, member of the West Germanic group of the Germanic subfamily of the INDO-EUROPEAN family of languages (see GERMANIC LANGUAGES). It has a number of dialects and is spoken by more than 300,000 people, most of whom live in Friesland, a province of the Netherlands. There are also some speakers of Frisian along the North Sea coast of Germany, on the Frisian Islands, and in the United States. An official language of the Netherlands, Frisian is a subject of instruction in the schools of Friesland and also has a literature of its own. Of all foreign languages, it is most like English.

Frissell, Mount, peak, 2,380 ft (725 m) high, NW Conn., in the Taconic Mts., near the Mass.-N.Y. line.

Frith or **Fryth, John** (both: frĭth), 1503–33, English Protestant martyr. He aided William Tyndale in translating the New Testament. After a short time in prison because of suspected heresy, Frith went to Germany in 1528 and was in Marburg, where he again assisted Tyndale. Upon his return to England in 1532, Frith was arrested and imprisoned. Firm in his denial of transubstantiation, purgatory, and infallibility of papal authority, he was burned at Smithfield as a heretic. His works were edited (1573) by John Foxe. See M. L. Loane, *Pioneers of the Reformation in England* (1964).

Frith, William Powell, 1819–1909, English anecdotal and genre painter. His early paintings were illustrations, such as his *Scene from a Sentimental Journey* (Victoria and Albert Mus.). Later he painted many enormously popular pictures of everyday English life, among them *Derby Day* (National Gall., London) and *The Railway Station* (Leicester Mus.). See his memoirs, *A Victorian Canvas* (1957).

Fritigern (frĭt'ĭgûrn), d. 380, Visigothic chieftain. An intermittent rival of ATHANARIC for leadership of the VISIGOTHS, he adopted Arian Christianity (see ARIANISM) and thus gained the support of Emperor VALENS. Fleeing the invading Huns, Fritigern was given permission (376) by Valens to cross the Danube and enter Roman territory. After being badly mistreated, the Goths rebelled and in 378 Fritigern defeated and killed Valens at the battle of Adrianople. The Goths subsequently ravaged the Balkan Peninsula until the Roman general Theodosius (later THEODOSIUS I) restored peace. Fritigern is also known as Fridigern.

Friuli (frēo͞o'lē), historic region, now divided between Friuli-Venezia Giulia, NE Italy, and Slovenia, NW Yugoslavia. It extends from the E Alps to the Adriatic and includes, in the east, a fertile plain and a section of the Karst region. The inhabitants are Italians in the west and Slovenes in the east. UDINE and GORIZIA, both in Italy, are the principal cities. Friuli derives its name from the Roman city of Forum Iulii (modern Cividale del Friuli). Occupied by the Romans (2d cent. B.C.), it became a Lombard duchy (6th–8th cent.) and a Frankish march (8th cent.). Before A.D. 1000 it was divided into the counties of Gorizia (east) and Friuli (west). The western county passed (11th cent.) to the patriarchs of AQUILEIA, who made Udine their capital. In 1420 it went to Venice, and the name *Friuli* lost its political connotation. After the counts of Gorizia became extinct (1500), Emperor Maximilian I incorporated the eastern county into the Hapsburg possessions; attempts by Venice to acquire it were unsuccessful. By the treaties of Campo Formio (1797) and Paris (1814, 1815) all Friuli became Austrian. After the Austro-Prussian War, Austria ceded (1866) W Friuli (i.e., Udine prov.) to Italy. During World War I, Friuli was a battlefield. In 1919, E Friuli was also awarded to Italy; with Istria and Trieste it formed the region of VENEZIA GIULIA. The Italian peace treaty of 1947 gave E Friuli (but not Gorizia) to Yugoslavia. The name *Friuli* was officially revived when Friuli-Venezia Giulia was formed as a region of Italy.

Friulian: see RHAETO-ROMANIC.

Friuli-Venezia Giulia (frēo͞oʹlē-vānĕʹtsyä jo͞oʹlyä), region (1971 pop. 1,209,810), 3,031 sq mi (7,850 sq km), NE Italy, bordering on Austria in the north and on Yugoslavia in the east. TRIESTE is the capital of the region, which is divided into Gorizia, Pordenone, Trieste, and Udine provs. (named for their capitals). It extends from the E Alps in the north to the Adriatic Sea in the south and is drained by the Tagliamento River. Farming is the chief occupation; cereals, potatoes, and grapes are the leading crops, and dairy cattle and hogs are raised. Industrialization has accelerated since 1945; manufactures include textiles, processed food, refined petroleum, chemicals, and machinery. The region was formed in 1947 by the merger of Udine prov. with that part of the former region of VENEZIA GIULIA not annexed by Yugoslavia. Trieste prov. was added in 1954. In 1963 Friuli-Venezia Giulia was given limited autonomy. It contains the western part of the historic region of FRIULI. There is a university at Trieste.

Fröbel, Friedrich Wilhelm August: see FROEBEL.

Froben, Johannes (yōhäʹnəs frōʹbən), 1460–1527, German printer. He established himself at Basel and there in 1516 printed the Greek New Testament, edited and translated into Latin by Erasmus. Erasmus edited many publications of Froben, contributing to the fame of Froben's press for printing scholarly texts. Froben also employed the then unknown Hans Holbein as designer.

Frobenius, Leo (läʹō frōbäʹnēo͝os), 1873–1938, German archaeologist and anthropologist. An authority on prehistoric art and culture, especially of Africa, he organized 12 expeditions to Africa between 1904 and 1935. In 1922 he founded the Institute for Cultural Morphology, Frankfurt, where he established a noted collection of facsimiles of prehistoric paintings and engravings. He also dealt with living African cultures and their folklore. He wrote *The Voice of Africa* (tr. 1913) and was coauthor (in English) of *Prehistoric Rock Pictures in Europe and Africa* (1937).

Froberger, Johann Jakob (yōʹhän yäʹkôp frōʹbĕrgər), 1616–67, German organist and composer; pupil of FRESCOBALDI. His style influenced German keyboard music during the baroque era. He is best known for his harpsichord and clavichord suites.

Frobisher, Sir Martin (frōʹbĭshər), 1535?–1594, English mariner. He went to sea as a boy, and spent much of his youth in the African trade. He later gained the friendship of Sir Humphrey GILBERT, through whom he became interested in the NORTHWEST PASSAGE. Licensed by Queen Elizabeth I and backed by a group of merchant adventurers, Frobisher made three voyages (1576, 1577, and 1578) to the ARCTIC REGIONS in search of the passage. On his first voyage he sailed into Frobisher Bay to S Baffin Island, and from its shores brought back some black ore thought to contain gold and an Eskimo to prove his belief that he had actually reached fabled Cathay. Returning to Baffin Island on his next two journeys, he explored Frobisher Bay to its head and penetrated a short distance up Hudson Strait. Since his geographical discovery was slight and no gold was revealed in his cargoes of ore, Frobisher's name was discredited for a time. However, he won new glory in 1585 as commander of a ship in Sir Francis Drake's expedition to the West Indies and was knighted for his services with Drake and Sir John Hawkins in the defeat of the Spanish Armada in 1588. He died as the result of wounds received at Brest during an English campaign against the Spanish. The narratives of his voyages, first published in 1578, have passed through several editions. *The Three Voyages of Martin Frobisher* by George Best was edited from the original 1578 text by Vilhjalmur Stefansson (1937). See biography by William McFee (1928).

Frobisher Bay, arm of the Atlantic Ocean, 150 mi (240 km) long and from 20 to 40 mi (32–64 km) wide, E Franklin dist., Northwest Territories, Canada. Cutting deeply into SE Baffin Island, it has steep, deeply indented shores and numerous islets. On its southwest side the Grinnell and Southeast icecaps rise to c.3,000 ft (910 m), extending tongues into the bay. At its head are Frobisher Bay trading post (est. 1914) and an air base. The bay was discovered (1576) by Sir Martin Frobisher; until 1860 it was believed to be a strait separating Baffin Island from another island.

Fröding, Gustaf (gŭsʹtäv frö'dĭng), 1860–1911, Swedish lyric poet. His first two volumes of poems, *Guitar and Concertina* (1891) and *New Poems* (1894), both translated into English in 1925, assured his popularity. They include songs, meditations, and poems in praise of nature. His complete works (1917–23) number 16 volumes. Fröding suffered from melancholia and mental instability for much of his life. His last collections were clearly marked by his derangement.

Froebel, Friedrich Wilhelm August (frāʹbəl, frōʹ-, Ger. frēʹdrĭkh vĭlʹhĕlm ouʹgo͝ost fröʹbəl), 1782–1852, German educator and founder of the KINDERGARTEN system. He had an unhappy childhood and very little formal schooling, learning what he could from wide reading and close observation of nature; he studied for a short time at the Univ. of Jena. He was studying architecture at Frankfurt (1805) when he was persuaded by the master of the model school at Frankfurt to become a teacher. He visited Johann Heinrich PESTALOZZI at Yverdon, Switzerland, and then returned to Germany to study at the universities of Göttingen and Berlin. In 1813 he joined Lützow's free corps and saw active service in the Napoleonic Wars. While serving in the army he met Heinrich Langethal and Wilhelm Middendorff, with whom he was associated throughout the rest of his career. He returned to the Univ. of Berlin in 1814 and was given a position in the school's mineralogical museum. In 1816 he founded at Griesheim a school (later moved to Keilhau) called the Universal German Educational Institute where other teachers came to study his methods. Early in 1837 he went to Bad Blankenburg (near Keilhau), where he opened the first kindergarten. In 1849 he founded a kindergarten training school at Liebenstein. However, Froebel was unable to control constant disputes among his subordinates, and after a group of former associates accused him of propagating treason, the government issued an edict (1851) forbidding the establishment of kindergartens. The measure was repealed in 1860. Froebel was influenced greatly by the philosophy of Johann Gottlieb Fichte and Friedrich Wilhelm Schelling. His theories of education are based on a belief in the divine unity of nature, so that spiritual training is a fundamental principle. Froebel stressed the importance of pleasant surroundings, self-activity, and physical training in the development of the child. His most important work is *Menschenerziehung* (1826; tr. *The Education of Man,* 1877). The translation by Susan Blow of his *Mutter-und Kose-Lieder* (1844) is called *Mother Play* (1895). Other works translated into English are *Letters on the Kindergarten* (1891), *Froebel's Chief Writings on Education* (1912), and his fragmentary autobiography. His name is also written Fröbel. See biographies by H. C. Bowen (1903, repr. 1970) and A. B. Hanschmann (tr. 1897); W. H. Kilpatrick, *Froebel's Kindergarten Principles* (1916).

frog, common name for an AMPHIBIAN of the order Anura. Frogs are found all over the world, except on the continent of Antarctica. They require moisture and usually live in quiet fresh water or in the woods. Some frogs are highly aquatic, while others are better adapted to terrestrial habitats. Among the latter type, those with stout bodies and thick skins are often called TOADS, although the name *toad* is sometimes restricted to members of the most terrestrial family of the Anura, the Bufonidae. Frogs lack tails in their adult stage. They have short, neckless bodies; long, muscular hind legs specialized for jumping; and webbed feet for swimming. The skin is smooth, usually some shade of green or brown, and often spotted. Frogs have no outer ears; their prominent eardrums are exposed on the sides of the head. The bulging eyes have lids that close when the eyeballs are pulled back into the sockets and nictitating membranes to keep the eyes moist. Adult frogs have lungs, but their breathing mechanism is poorly developed. At rest they breathe mainly through the lining of the mouth, filling the lungs only occasionally. When they are in wet places they also absorb much dissolved oxygen through their skins. Frogs have true voice boxes and are noted for their production of various noises. Most frogs hibernate in underwater mud and lay their eggs in early spring. With few exceptions fertilization is external. The eggs—up to 20,000 at one time—are fertilized as they are laid in the water and are given buoyancy and protection by a gelatinous covering secreted by the female. The gilled, aquatic larvae, or TADPOLES, hatch after 3 to 10 days; by the end of their first summer most frogs have completed their metamorphosis to the air-breathing, tailless, carnivorous adult. In some species, however, eggs are laid on land, and the young hatch as tiny frogs. Growth to full adult size usually takes several years. Frogs capture insects and worms by a thrust of the sticky, forked tongue attached at the front of the lower jaw. Some large tropical species eat small mammals and snakes. A few frogs have skin glands that can produce irritating or poisonous secretions. There are over a dozen families of frogs; the term "true frog" is often applied to members of the family Ranidae. The cosmopolitan genus *Rana* belongs to this family and includes many of the commonest frogs of North America, such as the bullfrog, *R. catesbeiana,* and the leopard frog, *R. pipiens.* Species of *Rana* are important laboratory animals, as they are readily available and easy to handle and maintain. Frogs are classified in the phylum CHORDATA, subphylum Vertebrata, class Amphibia, order Anura. See A. H. and Anna Wright, *Handbook of Frogs and Toads of the United States and Canada* (3d ed. 1949); M. C. Dickerson, *The Frog Book* (1906, repr. 1969).

froghopper or **spittlebug,** small, hopping INSECT of the order Homoptera. The adult, under ½-in. (1.2-cm) long in most species, is triangular in shape and usually gray or dull green to brown. Most froghoppers feed on plants and shrubs; a few feed on trees. They leap from plant to plant, seldom flying. Females insert their eggs in plant stems and sometimes cover them with a protective frothy material. When the nymphs, or larvae, emerge, they feed on the surface of the stem, sucking the plant juices. In many species the nymphs envelop themselves in a mass of foam (called spittle, frog spit, or cuckoo spit) made by blowing air through a viscid fluid expelled from the anus. The spittle, often conspicuous on grasses, protects the enclosed nymphs from desiccation and probably also from predators. Some froghopper species are injurious to pine trees and garden plants. Froghoppers are classified in the phylum ARTHROPODA, class Insecta, order Homoptera, family Cercopidae.

frogmouth, common name for small, owllike birds of the family Podargidae, ranging in size from 9 to 21 in. (22.5–52.5 cm). Their soft plumage is a mottled gray-brown in color with little distinction between sexes. Their eyes are wide and the tongue large and paperlike. A close relative of the nightjars (see GOATSUCKER), they share with them a wide, horny, flat, sharply hooked, boat-shaped bill, but unlike them, do not use it to capture insects on the wing. Rather, frogmouths feed on crawling animals, such as caterpillars, beetles, scorpions, and centipedes. They fly swiftly, but only over short distances, and the reduced tail feathers limit maneuverability. Nine species in the genus *Batrachostomus* are found from India to Malaysia. The remaining three species, in the genus *Podargus,* are found throughout Australia, New Guinea, and the Solomon Islands. All are nocturnal forest dwellers. *Podargus* species build flat, twig platform nests, while species of *Batrachostomus* make cushions of their own feathers and camouflage them with moss and spiderwebs. Frogmouths lay one or two whitish eggs, which the males incubate by day and the females at night. Frogmouths are classified in the phylum CHORDATA, subphylum Vertebrata, class Aves, order Caprimulgiformes, family Podargidae.

frog's-bit, common name for members of the Hydrocharitaceae, a family of aquatic herbs found in warm fresh and salt waters throughout the world. Most species grow partially or completely submerged, rarely floating. The family includes an eelgrass (genus *Vallisneria*), called also water celery and tape grass; the frog's-bit (*Hydrocharis morsus-ramae*); and the waterweeds (genus *Elodea*), often used in aquariums and in botanical experiments. Frog's-bit is classified in the division MAGNOLIOPHYTA, class Liliatae, order Heliobiae, family Hydrocharitaceae.

Frohman, Charles, 1860–1915, American theatrical manager and producer, b. Sandusky, Ohio. Starting his career as a box-office clerk in Brooklyn, N.Y., Frohman became a successful producer with Bronson Howard's *Shenandoah* (1889). In 1893 he organized the Empire Theatre Stock Company. Soon he acquired five other New York City theaters and later headed the Theatrical Syndicate. He was known for his ability to develop talent; his stars included John Drew, Ethel Barrymore, E. H. Sothern, Julia Marlowe, Maude Adams, and Henry Miller. In 1897 he leased the Duke of York's Theatre, London, introducing plays there as well as in the United States. Clyde Fitch, J. M. Barrie, and Edmond Rostand were among the playwrights he promoted. The system of exchange of successful plays between London and New York was largely a result of his efforts. He was known as an exceptionally fair man whose word was his only contract. Frohman died at sea on the *Lusitania*. See biography by I. F. Marcosson and Daniel Frohman (1916).

Froissart, Jean (zhäN frəwäsär'), c.1337–1410?, French chronicler, poet, and courtier, b. Valenciennes. Although ordained as a priest, he led a worldly life. He became a protégé of Queen Philippa of England, visited the court of David II of Scotland, and accompanied (1366) Edward the Black Prince on the campaign in Gascony. He also traveled widely in the Low Countries and in Italy. In the south of France he saw the brilliant court of Gaston III of Foix, and he later described it in a famous passage. Nothing is known of his life after 1404: his death date is traditionally 1410. His chronicle, continuing that of Jean le Bel, canon of Liège, covers the history of Western Europe from the early 14th cent. to 1400, roughly the first half of the Hundred Years War. In literary merit Froissart's chronicle far surpasses similar efforts in any European language. He described events with brilliance and gusto, and his sympathy was with the established order—or disorder—of his time. His highly partisan spirit and disregard for accuracy limit the value of his chronicle as pure history, yet few historians have so successfully brought an era to life. The chronicle remains a superb portrait of contemporary society. Apart from a tedious romance, *Méliador,* Froissart's poetry is charming and light; it somewhat influenced Chaucer, whom Froissart probably knew personally. The standard English translation (1523–25) of the chronicles by John Bourchier, Lord Berners, is available in many editions. See study by R. M. Smith (1965).

Froment, Nicolas (nēkôlä' frômäN'), fl. 2d half of 15th cent., French painter of the Provençal school. While in the service of René of Anjou at Avignon, he painted *The Resurrection of Lazarus* (Uffizi) and the triptych *The Burning Bush* (cathedral, Aix). He is credited also with the diptych of René and his wife, Jeanne Laval (Louvre).

Fromentin, Eugène (özhĕn' frômäNtăN'), 1820–76, French painter and art critic. After studying in Paris, he traveled in the Orient and painted Moorish subjects. His *Quarry* and *Fellah Women* (both: Louvre) and *Arabs Crossing a Ford* (Metropolitan Mus.) are typical of his work. Fromentin is known for his psychological and romantic novel *Dominique* (1863) and his book of art criticism, *The Masters of Past Time* (1876, tr. 1948).

Fromm, Erich, 1900–, psychoanalyst and author, b. Frankfurt, Germany, Ph.D. Univ. of Heidelberg, 1922. From 1929 to 1932 he lectured at the Psychoanalytic Institute, Frankfurt, and at the Univ. of Frankfurt. He came to the United States in 1934, where he practiced psychoanalysis and lectured at various institutions, including the International Institute for Social Research (1934–39), Columbia Univ. (1940–41), the American Institute for Psychoanalysis (1941–42), and Yale (1949–50). From 1941 to 1950 he was on the faculty of Bennington College. In 1951 he became professor at the National University of Mexico, in 1957 at Michigan State Univ., and in 1961 at New York Univ. Fromm held that man is a product of his culture and that in industrial society he has become estranged from himself. The principal problem with which Fromm dealt was how, specifically, Western man could come to terms with his sense of isolation, insignificance, and doubt about the meaning of life. Fromm's works include *Escape from Freedom* (1941), *Man for Himself* (1947), *Psychoanalysis and Religion* (1950), *The Sane Society* (1955), *The Art of Loving* (1956), *Sigmund Freud's Mission* (1958), *May Man Prevail?* (1961), *Beyond the Chains of Illusion* (1962), *The Revolution of Hope* (1968), and *The Anatomy of Human Destructiveness* (1973). See biographical studies by J. S. Glen (1966) and Don Hausdorff (1972); R. I. Evans, *Dialogue with Erich Fromm* (1966).

Fronde (frôNd), 1648–53, series of outbreaks during the minority of King Louis XIV, caused by the efforts of the Parlement of Paris (the chief judiciary body) to limit the growing authority of the crown; by the personal ambitions of discontented nobles; and by the grievances of the people against the financial burdens suffered under cardinals RICHELIEU and MAZARIN. The period of the **Fronde of the Parlement** (1648–49) began when the parlement rejected a new plan for raising money, proposed by ANNE OF AUSTRIA, regent for Louis XIV, and her adviser, Cardinal Mazarin. The scheme would have required that the magistrates of the high courts (except the parlement) give up four years' salary. The high courts, including the parlement, opposed the proposal and drafted a reform document limiting the royal prerogative. The government, in retaliation, arrested several members of the parlement, notably Pierre BROUSSEL, but the Parisian populace rose in protest and barricaded the streets (Aug., 1648). Anne and Mazarin were forced to yield and Broussel was released. Meanwhile, the Peace of Westphalia (Oct., 1648), which ended the Thirty Years War, freed the royal army to take action against the Fronde. Anne, the king, and Mazarin secretly left Paris (Jan., 1649), and the city was blockaded by royal troops under Louis II, prince de Condé (See CONDÉ, LOUIS II DE BOURBON, PRINCE DE). Louis's brother, Armand de Conti (See under CONTI, family) and his sister Mme de LONGUEVILLE were among the leaders of the Fronde. Other leaders were Frédéric Maurice de BOUILLON and Paul de Gondi (later Cardinal de RETZ). A compromise peace was arranged between the parlement and the regent at Rueil in March, 1649. Condé, having aided Mazarin and Anne, expected to control them. His overbearing attitude and intrigues caused his arrest in Jan., 1650, and precipitated a second outbreak, the **Fronde of the Princes,** or the **New Fronde.** Mme de Longueville called on Marshal TURENNE for aid in releasing her brother. Government troops defeated Turenne and his Spanish allies at Rethel (1650), but Mazarin was forced to yield when Retz, Mme de CHEVREUSE, Gaston d'ORLEANS, and François de BEAUFORT all united in demanding Condé's release. Mazarin fled to Germany in Feb., 1651, but the victorious nobles soon fell out among themselves and Condé left Paris to take up open warfare against the government. Although joined by Gaston d'Orléans, Beaufort, Conti, and the provincial parlements of S France, Condé lost the principal support of Turenne, who went over to the government's side after Louis XIV reached his majority. In Dec., 1651, Mazarin was recalled. Condé concluded an alliance with Spain, but was defeated by Turenne at the Faubourg Saint-Antoine beneath the walls of Paris; he was saved by Mlle de MONTPENSIER, who admitted him and his army into Paris. His arrogant conduct there alienated the people. As the Fronde disintegrated, Mazarin once more left France to clear the air for a reconciliation. In October the king returned to Paris; Mazarin followed in Feb., 1653. The princes soon made peace with the government, except for Condé, who commanded the Spanish forces against France until the Peace of the Pyrenees (1659; see PYRENEES, PEACE OF THE). The Fronde was the last attempt of the nobility to resist the king by arms. It resulted in the humiliation of the nobles, the strengthening of royal authority, and the further disruption of French economy. See P. R. Doolin, *The Fronde* (1935); A. L. Moote, *The Revolt of the Judges: The Parlement of Paris and the Fronde, 1643–1652* (1972).

Frondizi, Arturo (ärtōō'rō frôndē'sē), 1908–, president of Argentina (1958–62). A lawyer and economist, he opposed Juan PERÓN and rose to prominence after the latter was overthrown in 1955. A realist, he accepted Peronist support in his successful bid for the presidency in 1958. As president he attempted to revitalize the economy by imposing strict austerity measures and arranging for aid from the International Monetary Fund. Reversing a previous stand, he permitted the exploitation of Argentine petroleum by foreign countries, a move that aroused much opposition, He allowed the Peronists to participate in the 1962 elections; after they scored impressive victories, outraged anti-Perón elements in the army arrested Frondizi and annulled the elections. José Guido assumed the presidency.

front, in meteorology, zone of transition between adjacent AIR MASSES. If a cold air mass is advancing to replace a warmer one, their mutual boundary is termed a cold front; if the reverse, then the boundary is termed a warm front, whereas a stationary front indicates that no relative advance of either air mass is occurring. An occluded front is one in which a warm front has been completely undermined by cold air and is therefore positioned aloft. Since warmer air always overrides colder, denser air, the frontal boundary is sloped closer to the horizontal than the vertical. A mature CYCLONE usually involves all of the frontal types. The recognition of atmospheric fronts and their relative importance to weather forecasting came about only at the beginning of the 20th cent. as a result of publications by the meteorologists Vilhelm and Jakob BJERKNES.

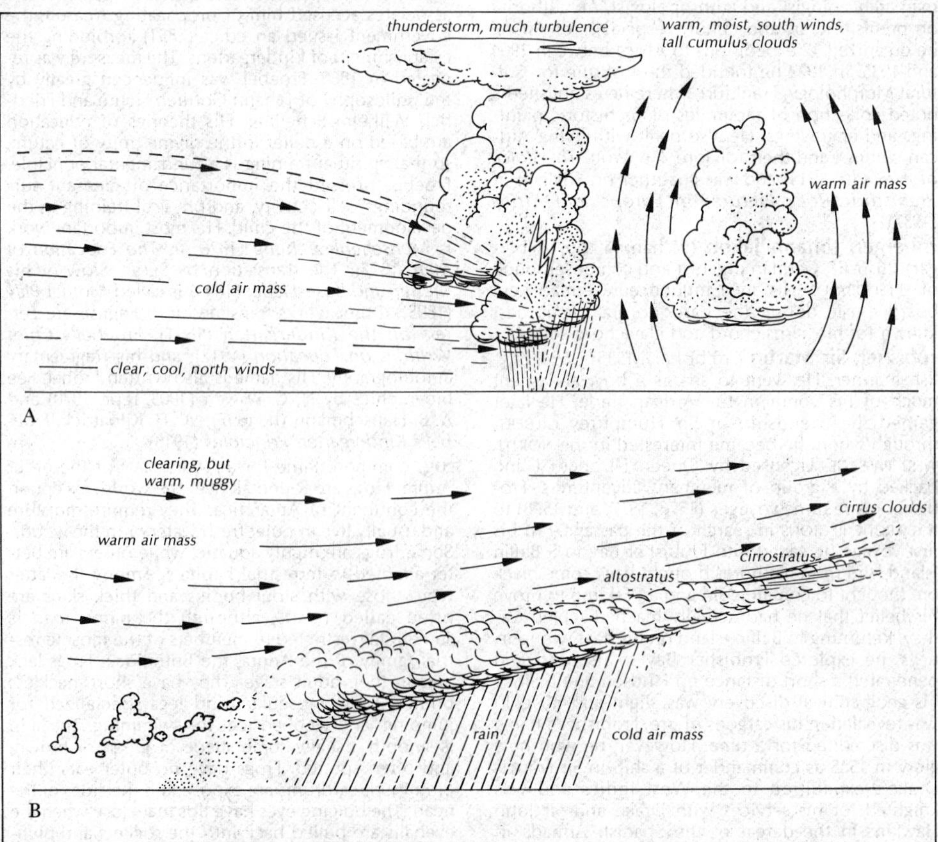

Fronts
A. *Advance of a cold front* B. *Advance of a warm front*

Front de Libération du Québec (FLQ)(frôN də lēbĕräsyôN' dü kābĕk'), Canadian separatist group formed in the 1960s to bring about the independence of Quebec, which has a French heritage, from the rest of Canada, which has a primarily British tradition. Using public demonstrations and terrorist activities, the FLQ attracted considerable attention. In 1970 members of the organization, demanding release of separatist prisoners, kidnapped a British official and the Canadian minister of labor; the latter was murdered. Their action persuaded Prime Minister Trudeau to institute martial law for six months.

Frontenac, Louis de Buade, comte de Palluau et de (frŏn'tĭnăk, Fr. lwē də büäd' koNt də pälüō' ā də frôNtənäk'), 1620–98, French governor of New France. His early military career was spent in service in the Low Countries, Italy, and Germany. Appointed in 1672 to the post in New France, he entered with vigor upon a course that would have resulted in considerable political independence for Canada. His policy was not acceptable to Louis XIV and to his minister Jean Colbert, and, adding to the power of the council in New France, they reduced that of the governor. Frontenac was embroiled in quarrels with the Jesuits, with the intendant, and with the governor of Montreal, but he tried to develop new policies toward the Indians, forwarded explorations by Louis Jolliet, Jacques Marquette, and the sieur de La Salle, and aided in the establishment of forts and posts in the new French territory. When disagreements among the heads of the colony caused division and confusion, Frontenac was recalled (1682) to France. During the following years, however, the Iroquois became increasingly aggressive, and his successors, Joseph de La Barre and the marquis de Denonville, failed to resolve New France's problems; Frontenac was therefore returned to Canada as governor in 1689. He energetically warred against the Iroquois until they were subdued in 1696, and he held Quebec against the British in the first French and Indian War. Under him French forces drove Sir William Phips's fleet from Quebec, Boston was attacked, and raids were made on the British coast as far south as New Jersey. His leadership during the war with the British enabled the French to maintain the status quo in New France until the signing of the Treaty of Ryswick (1697) ended the war. See biography by W. D. Le Sueur (1926, repr. 1964); study by Francis Parkman (1902, repr. 1969).

frontier, in U.S. history, the border area of settlement of Europeans and their descendants; it was vital in the conquest of the land between the Atlantic and the Pacific. The importance of the westward movement of the population and the lure of the frontier was clear even to colonial writers and early U.S. historians. The theory that the frontier was a governing factor (if not the governing factor) in developing a distinctive U.S. civilization, however, was not formulated until 1893, when Frederick Jackson TURNER presented his thesis. Basically, Turner held that American democracy was shaped by the frontier, namely by the contest of the settler with the wilderness of the frontier. There the settler learned self-reliance, judged others by their abilities, strove to improve his or her lot, and grew distrustful of external authority and formal institutions. In short, the frontier molded an American national character that was individualistic and egalitarian. Turner's work stimulated a tremendous amount of research and writing on the history and meaning of the frontier. There is no question that this process of peopling the West is a central theme in U.S. history, although not, perhaps, for the reasons Turner suggested. The cultivation of frontier lands provided food for the growing number of workers in Eastern cities; its mineral wealth and other natural resources aided industrialization; and the need to keep the East and West united led to a complex and efficient national system of transportation and communication. At the same time, the existence of barely settled lands helped preserve a rural tinge to America well into the 20th cent. Many studies have been devoted to the fur trade frontier, the mining frontier, the grazing frontier, and other types of frontier, but emphasis has been to a large extent on the solid achievements of the farming frontier and on the central United States. See F. J. Turner, *The Frontier in American History* (1920); F. L. Paxson, *History of the American Frontier* (1924); Walter Prescott Webb, *The Great Plains* (1931) and *The Great Frontier* (1952); R. A. Billington and J. B. Hedges, *Westward Expansion* (1949); Henry N. Smith, *Virgin Land* (1950); Louis B. Wright, *Culture on the Moving Frontier* (1955); G. R. Taylor, ed., *The Turner Thesis* (1966).

Frontinus (Sextus Julius Frontinus) (frŏntī'nəs), fl. A.D. 74, Roman administrator and writer. As governor of Britain from A.D. 74 or A.D. 75 to A.D. 78, he reduced the Silures, a rebellious tribe in SE Wales, and pacified Britain within its borders; it was this work, successfully done, that probably rendered possible the achievements of Frontinus' successor, AGRICOLA. From his experience as *curator aquarum,* or water commissioner, he wrote *De aquis urbis Romae,* which treats exhaustively of the water supply of Rome, with complete descriptions and history of the aqueducts. He also wrote *Strategematica,* which is important as a guide to Roman military tactics and strategy.

Fronto (Marcus Cornelius Fronto) (frŏn'tō), fl. 2d cent., Roman teacher and rhetorician, b. Numidia, Africa. He was the tutor of Marcus Aurelius, and Antoninus Pius made him consul in 143. A successful teacher and government official, Fronto was an admirer of the early Latin writers and tried unsuccessfully to bring about a renaissance. His extant letters (discovered by Angelo Mai and published in 1815–23) reveal a fondness for an archaic and recondite vocabulary.

Front Range, highest part of the U.S. Rocky Mts., bordering the Great Plains and extending c.300 mi (480 km) S from SE Wyo. to the Arkansas River, central Colo. Part of the Continental Divide, the range has several peaks, including Mt. Elbert and Pikes Peak, that are more than 14,000 ft (4,270 m) high. The Colorado and the South Platte rivers are the largest streams rising in the range. Most of Colorado's population is located along the range's eastern foothills. The Front Range was scouted by U.S. explorers Zebulon Pike, in 1806–7, and Stephen Long, in 1819–20. In 1858 gold was discovered at Cripple Creek, Colo., and goldseekers rushed into the S Front Range. Gold, silver, and beryllium are still mined there. Most of the range is in national forests; Rocky Mts. National Park is located in the north.

Frost, Arthur Burdett, 1851–1928, American illustrator and cartoonist, b. Philadelphia; pupil of Thomas Eakins at the Pennsylvania Academy of the Fine Arts. He worked chiefly in New York City and became one of the most popular illustrators of his time. His most characteristic drawings portrayed various aspects of American rural life, but he is best known for his illustrations of Joel Chandler Harris's "Uncle Remus" stories.

Frost, Robert, 1874–1963, American poet, b. San Francisco. Perhaps the most popular and beloved of 20th-century American poets, Frost wrote of the character, people, and landscape of New England. He was taken to Lawrence, Mass., his family's home for generations, at the age of 10. After studying briefly at Dartmouth, he worked as a bobbin boy in a cotton mill, as a cobbler, a schoolteacher, and a journalist; he later entered Harvard but left after two years to try farming. In 1912 he went to England, where he received his first acclaim as a poet. After the publication of *A Boy's Will* (1913) and *North of Boston* (1914), he returned to the United States, settling on a farm near Franconia, N.H. Frost taught and lectured at several universities, including Amherst, Harvard, and the Univ. of Michigan. In later life he was accorded many honors; he made several goodwill trips for the U.S. State Dept., and in 1961 he recited his poem "The Gift Outright" at the inauguration of President John F. Kennedy. Among his volumes of poetry are *New Hampshire* (1923), *West-running Brook* (1928), *Collected Poems* (1930), *A Further Range* (1936), *A Witness Tree* (1942), *Steeple Bush* (1947), and *In the Clearing* (1962). *A Masque of Reason* (1945) and *A Masque of Mercy* (1947) were blank verse plays. Although his work is rooted in the New England landscape, Frost was no mere regional poet. The careful local observations and homely details of his poems often have deep symbolic, even metaphysical, significance. His poems are concerned with man's tragedies and fears, his reaction to the complexities of life, and his ultimate acceptance of his burdens. Frost was awarded the Pulitzer Prize for poetry in 1924, 1931, 1937, and 1943. See his complete poems (1967); his letters, ed. by Arnold Grade (1972); biographies by M. L. Mertens (1965) and L. R. Thompson (2 vol., 1966–70); studies by L. R. Thompson (1942, repr. 1961), J. R. Doyle (1962), and Jean Gould (1964).

frost or **hoarfrost,** ice formed by the condensation of atmospheric water vapor on a surface when the temperature of the surface is below 32°F (0°C). In the formation of frost, a gas (water vapor) is changed directly to a solid (see DEW). Frost appears as a light feathery deposit of ice, often of a curious and delicate pattern. The dates on which killing frosts (frost destructive to vegetation and staple agricultural products) occur vary considerably. Maps showing the GROWING SEASON and the probable date of occurrence of frost may be obtained from the U.S. National Weather Service. The Weather Service stations issue warnings when frost is likely to occur; such warnings are broadcast by radio and are telegraphed or telephoned to farmers and fruitgrowers, who may protect their crops accordingly. Methods of protection vary: small flower beds and vegetable gardens are commonly protected by a screen or cloth that prevents excessive radiation from the earth and from the plants; in orchards, especially in California and Florida, simple oil-burning stoves or smudge pots placed at intervals throughout an orchard are used to heat and circulate the air sufficiently to prevent frost. Huge fans operated by gasoline engines have been used in lemon groves to circulate the air and so prevent freezing. Valleys are more subject to frosts than slopes, since cold air "slides" downhill and settles in depressions; topography is thus a factor in the occurrence of frost, as are altitude, latitude, location with reference to large bodies of water, and other factors determining temperature. Orchards and citrus fruit groves are usually planted on slopes. Frost, an element of climate, is an important agent of erosion. Frost heaving, an upthrust of ground caused by freezing, is a factor of consideration in engineering construction, especially in highway foundations. In England the word *frost* denotes freezing weather and *degrees of frost* means the number of degrees that the temperature falls below the freezing point. See W. J. Rogers and H. L. Swift, *Frost and the Prevention of Frost Damage* (1971).

frostbite (chilblains), injury to the tissue caused by exposure to cold, usually affecting the extremities of the body, such as the hands, feet, ears, or nose. Extreme cold causes the small blood vessels in the extremities to constrict. The blood circulates more slowly and stagnation results. Eventually the body fluids may freeze. The condition is aggravated by tight clothing, physical inactivity, and dampness. Severe frostbite that is not treated may result in gangrene; amputation of the affected part may be necessary. See FIRST AID.

frostweed or **frostwort,** North American woodland flowers (*Helianthemum canadense* and sometimes other related species) of the family Cistaceae (rock-rose family). In cold weather, crystals of ice shoot from the cracked bark at the base of the stem. The names frostweed and frostflower are also used for several other unrelated plants that have white flowers or bloom late (e.g., the asters). Frostweeds are classified in the division MAGNOLIOPHYTA, class Magnoliopsida, order Violales, family Cistaceae.

froth-flotation process: see FLOTATION PROCESS.

Frothingham, Octavius Brooks (frŏth'ĭnghəm), 1822–95, American clergyman and writer, b. Boston. While a Unitarian minister in Salem (1847–55) he came under the influence of Theodore PARKER. In 1859 he organized the Third Unitarian Church of New York City and soon achieved wide renown. In 1865 his followers, wishing to increase the sphere of his influence, organized the Independent Liberal Church, which was made up of people from all faiths. Frothingham was president of the Free Religious Association in Boston from 1867 until his health broke down in 1878. In addition to writing sermons and such religious books as *The Religion of Humanity* (1872), he was the author of *Transcendentalism in New England* (1876), *Boston Unitarianism, 1820–1850* (1890), and biographies of his friends—Theodore Parker (1874), Gerrit Smith (1877), and George Ripley (1882). See his *Recollections and Impressions, 1822–1890* (1891).

Froude, James Anthony (frōōd), 1818–94, English historian. Educated at Oxford, he was initially influenced by the Oxford movement. He later became a skeptic, however, and left Oxford for London. There he met Thomas Carlyle, who became his close friend and exercised considerable influence over him as a historian. The best known and most important of Froude's many works, *The History of England from the Fall of Wolsey to the Defeat of the Spanish Armada* (12 vol., 1856–70), was the first detailed account of this period in English history. He treated the English Reformation as a contest to decide whether England would be ruled by the pope or by the king, rather than as a struggle of opposing dogmas. He was the first to take a sympathetic and laudatory view of Henry VIII and to denigrate Elizabeth I by giving Lord Burghley and Sir Francis Walsingham full credit for the success of her reign. As a technician, Froude was careless in citing detail and in transcribing documents, but he never deliberately distorted documentary evidence to serve his point of view. His strong and ever-present Protestant bias is the main scholarly weakness of his books. As literature his works are outstanding; his style is graceful and fluent, and his opinions are competently and clearly expressed. See biography by W. H. Dunn (2 vol., 1961–63); studies by D. A. Wilson (1888, repr. 1970) and W. H. Dunn (1933, repr. 1969).

frozen foods, products of the FOOD PRESERVATION process of freezing. This process has been employed by people in arctic regions from prehistoric times. Eskimos throw fresh-caught fish on the ice to freeze, and naturally frozen fish have been a trade staple of the Great Lakes region of North America since the mid-19th cent. Brine and cold-room convection methods were in use in Europe and the United States from about 1860 for freezing meat, fish, poultry, and eggs. In the early part of the 20th cent. small fruits were frozen for manufacturers of preserves, bakery products, and ice cream. Freezing prevents food spoilage by inhibiting microorganic and enzyme action. Deterioration is rapid after thawing, since reactivated organisms attack cells injured by ice crystals. Earlier methods involved inserting the food into chilled brine or an ice and salt mixture. In quick freezing, commercially begun in Germany in the early 20th cent., rapid chilling gives less time for the diffusion of salts and water for microorganic action. Methods of quick freezing include direct contact with refrigeration, indirect cooling by contact of the product with refrigerated shelves, cold blasts, or a combination of these methods. The frozen food industry has expanded rapidly because of the labor-saving and space-saving advantages of frozen foods and because the freezing process generally involves less loss of taste, flavor, and appearance than do other methods; it has been paralleled by the development of suitable containers and of specialized methods of transportation, storage, and retailing. Preparation of foods for freezing in the home has become common since the establishment of community locker plants and the manufacture of small freezing units.

Fructidor (frŭk'tĭdôr, Fr. früktēdôr'), 12th month of the FRENCH REVOLUTIONARY CALENDAR. The coup d'etat of 18 Fructidor (Sept. 4, 1797), in which General Augereau was a key figure, annulled the previous elections and removed Lazare Carnot and François de Barthélemy from the DIRECTORY. The coup was directed against those who wished to restore a constitutional monarchy.

fructose (frŭk'tōs), **levulose** (lĕv'yəlōs"), or **fruit sugar,** simple sugar found in honey and in the fruit and other parts of plants. It is much sweeter than SUCROSE (cane sugar). It is best obtained by hydrolysis of inulin, a polysaccharide found in dahlia bulbs and the Jerusalem artichoke. Chemically it is a monosaccharide (see CARBOHYDRATE) with the empirical formula $C_6H_{12}O_6$. It has the same formula as glucose but differs from it in structure (see ISOMER). It is often found with glucose in nature. Glucose and fructose are formed in equal amounts when sucrose is hydrolyzed by the enzyme invertase or by heating with dilute acid; the resulting equimolar mixture of fructose and glucose, called invert sugar, is the major component of honey. Fructose reacts with FEHLING'S SOLUTION and can be differentiated from glucose by its reaction with lime water to form a water-insoluble precipitate, calcium fructosate. In solution fructose exists as a ring compound in equilibrium with a straight-chain form.

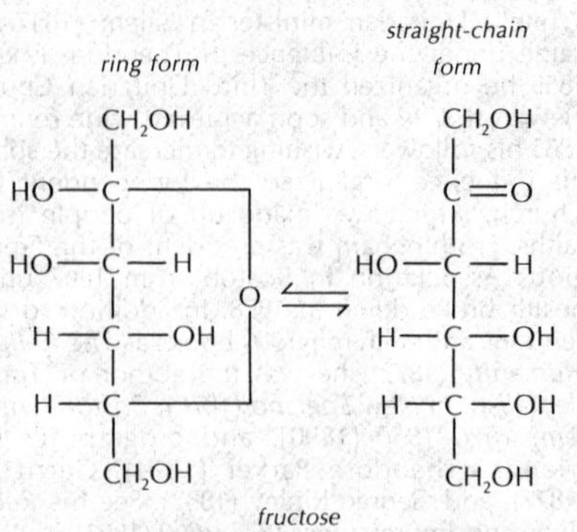

ring form | straight-chain form

CH_2OH | CH_2OH
HO—C— | C=O
HO—C—H | HO—C—H
O ⇌
H—C—OH | H—C—OH
H—C— | H—C—OH
CH_2OH | CH_2OH

fructose

Frug, Simeon Samuel (sĭmyôn' səmo͞oĕl' fro͝ok), 1860–1916, Russian-Jewish lyricist and writer. His poems, dealing mainly with Zionist themes, appeared in Russian and Jewish periodicals under various pseudonyms.

fruit, matured ovary of the pistil of a flower, containing the SEED. After the egg nucleus, or ovum, has been fertilized (see FERTILIZATION) and the embryo plantlet begins to form, the surrounding ovule (see PISTIL) develops into a seed and the ovary wall (pericarp) around the ovule becomes the fruit. The pericarp consists of three layers of tissue: the thin outer exocarp, which becomes the "skin"; the thicker mesocarp; and the inner endocarp, immediately surrounding the ovule. A flower may have one or more simple pistils or a compound pistil made up of two or more fused simple pistils (each called a carpel). Fruits are classified according to the arrangement from which they derive. There are four types—simple, aggregate, multiple, and accessory fruits. Simple fruits develop from a single ovary of a single flower and may be fleshy or dry. Fleshy fruits are the berry, in which the entire pericarp is soft and pulpy (e.g., the grape, tomato, banana, watermelon, orange, and blueberry) and the drupe, in which the outer layers may be pulpy, fibrous, or leathery and the endocarp hardens into a pit or stone enclosing one to three seeds (e.g., the peach, cherry, olive, coconut, and walnut). Dry fruits are divided into those whose hard or papery shells split open to release the mature seed (dehiscent fruits) and those that do not split (indehiscent fruits). Among the dehiscent fruits are the LEGUME (e.g., the pod of the pea and bean), which splits at both edges, and the follicle, which splits on only one side (e.g., milkweed and larkspur); others include the dry fruits of the poppy, snapdragon, lily, and mustard. Indehiscent fruits include the single-seeded achene of the buttercup and the composite flowers; the caryopsis (GRAIN); the NUT (e.g., acorn and hazelnut); and the fruits of the carrot and parsnip (not to be confused with their edible fleshy roots). An aggregate fruit (e.g., blackberry and raspberry) consists of a mass of small drupes (drupelets) each of which developed from a separate ovary of a single flower. A multiple fruit (e.g., pineapple and mulberry) develops from the ovaries of many flowers growing in a cluster. Accessory fruits contain tissue derived from plant parts other than the ovary; the strawberry is actually a number of tiny achenes (miscalled seeds) outside a central pulpy pith that is the enlarged receptacle or base of the flower. The core of the pineapple is also receptacle (stem) tissue. The best-known accessory fruit is the pome (e.g., apple and pear), in which the fleshy edible portion is swollen stem tissue and the true fruit is the central core. The skin of the banana is also stem tissue, as is the rind of the berrylike fruit of the squash, cucumber, and melon. The structure of a fruit often facilitates the dispersal of its seeds. The "wings" of the maple, elm, and ailanthus fruits and the "parachutes" of the dandelion and the thistle are blown by the wind; burdock, cocklebur, and carrot fruits have barbs or hooks that cling to fur and clothing; and the buoyant coconut may float thousands of miles from its parent tree. Some fruits (e.g., witch hazel and violet) explode at maturity, scattering their seeds. A common method of dispersion is through the feces of animals that eat fleshy fruits containing seeds covered by indigestible coats. The name *fruit* is often applied loosely to all edible plant products and specifically to the fleshy fruits, some of which (e.g., eggplant, tomatoes, and squash) are commonly called vegetables. A new variety of fruit is obtained as a HYBRID in plant BREEDING or may develop spontaneously by MUTATION.

fruit bat, fruit-eating BAT found in tropical regions of the Old World. It is relatively large and differs from other bats in the possession of an independent, clawed second digit; it also depends on sight rather than echo-location in maintaining orientation. The Pteropodidae, or flying foxes, are S Asian fruit bats whose short jaws and powerful teeth are specially adapted for piercing the rinds of tough fruit. They include the largest of all bats, the kalang (*Pteropus vampyrus*), which has a wingspan greater than 5 ft (1.5 m). The Macroglossidae, or long-tongued fruit bats, are widespread throughout S Asia, Africa, New Guinea, and Australia. Specialized for a diet of pollen and nectar, their snouts and tongues are greatly elongated. All fruit bats are highly mobile, traveling as much as 30 mi (48 km) in search of food. They nest in trees and all but a few species are completely nocturnal. Fruit bats are classified in the phylum CHORDATA, subphylum Vertebrata, class Mammalia, order Chiroptera.

fruit fly, common name for any of the FLIES of the families Tephritidae and Drosophilidae. All fruit flies are very small INSECTS that lay their eggs in various plant tissues. The Tephritidae contains about 1,200 species characterized by wide heads, black or steely green or blue bodies, iridescent greenish eyes, and wings that are usually mottled brown or black. The eggs of most species are laid directly in the pulp of the fruit on which the larvae feed; in North America, blueberries, cherries, and apples are much damaged by these insects. In warm regions, the Mediterranean fruit fly, *Ceratitis capitata,* was a serious pest of citrus fruits; it has now been eradicated from the S United States. Some species, e.g., the goldenrod gall fly, *Eurosta solidaginis,* which deposits its eggs in species of goldenrod, lay their eggs in plants of no economic importance. The Drosophilidae, or pomace flies, are yellowish and in the wild are largely found around decaying vegetation. The larvae living in fruit actually feed on the yeasts growing in the fruit. *Drosophila melanogaster,* also called vinegar fly, is a much used laboratory insect; its 10-day life cycle and large chromosomes, particularly those of the salivary glands of the larva, have made it invaluable in the study of GENETICS. Fruit flies are classified in the phylum ARTHROPODA, class Insecta, order Diptera, families Tephritidae and Drosophilidae.

fruit sugar: see FRUCTOSE.

Frundsberg, Georg von (gä'ôrkh fən fro͞onts'bĕrkh), 1473–1528, German commander in the service of Holy Roman emperors Maximilian I and CHARLES V. He was the principal organizer and commander of the imperial *Landsknechte,* a mercenary infantry. In the ITALIAN WARS, Frundsberg contributed to the victories of La Bicocca (1522) and Pavia (1525) over the French. He then helped to end the Peasants' War in Germany, but in 1526 returned to Italy to aid Charles de BOURBON against the anti-imperial League of Cognac. While trying to pacify a mutiny caused by rumors of a truce (the troops had not been paid), Frundsberg suffered a stroke and died. The troops continued their march on Rome under Charles de Bourbon and sacked the city.

Frunze, Mikhail Vasilyevich (mēkhəyēl' vəsē'lyəvĭch fro͞on'zĕ), 1885–1925, Russian general. A revolutionary, he was exiled (1914) to Siberia but returned to take part in the October Revolution of 1917. In the civil war that followed, he led the Soviet armies that forced A. V. Kolchak back into Siberia and drove P. N. Wrangel from the Crimea. He also helped establish Soviet control over Russian Turkistan. As people's commissar for the army and navy (1924–25), he reorganized the armed forces.

Frunze, city (1970 pop. 431,000), capital of the Kirghiz Soviet Socialist Republic, Central Asian USSR, on the Chu River and on a branch of the Turkistan-Siberia RR. It is a rail and highway hub and the industrial and cultural center of Kirghizia. Its meat-packing and agricultural machine plants are among the largest in the USSR. Other industries include metalworking, food processing, and the manufacture of motor vehicles, textiles, building materials, and clothing. Frunze has a powerful hydroelectric station. The Uzbek khans of Kokand built a fortress on the site in 1846; it was taken by Russian forces in 1862 and became the fort of Pishpek. The city, which grew up around the fort, was chartered in 1878. It was renamed in 1925 in honor of Gen. M. V. Frunze, who was born there. In 1926 the city became the administrative center of the Kirghiz Autonomous Soviet Socialist Republic, which was raised to the status of a union republic in 1936. Frunze has a university (est. 1951).

Fry, Christopher, 1907–, English dramatist, b. Bristol. He taught briefly, acted, and directed a repertory company before gaining acclaim as a playwright. Fry has been one of the few 20th-century dramatists to write successfully in verse. Among his plays are the comedies *The Lady's Not for Burning* (1949), *Venus Observed* (1950), *The Dark Is Light Enough* (1954), and *Yard of Sun* (1970); and the religious dramas *Thor, with Angels* (1949) and *A Sleep of Prisoners* (1951). He has also written English versions of plays by Giraudoux *(Tiger at the Gates,* 1955) and Anouilh *(Ring Round the Moon,* 1950; *The Lark,* 1955).

Fry, Sir Edward, 1827–1918, English lawyer. In 1877 he was made a judge of the high court of justice, and he served (1883–92) as judge of the court of appeal. Later he arbitrated several important international disputes at The Hague. Fry wrote *Specific Performance of Contracts* (1858). See memoir by his daughter Agnes Fry (1921).

Fry, Elizabeth (Gurney), 1780–1845, English prison reformer and philanthropist. Deeply religious, she was recognized as a minister by the Society of Friends (Quakers). From 1813 she worked untiringly to improve the conditions of women in Newgate prison, advocating separation of the sexes, employment, and religious training. The success of her methods at Newgate impressed the government and were tried in other prisons. For several years she traveled throughout Europe, visiting penal institutions. Her other philanthropies included the founding of soup kitchens in London. See her memoirs, ed. by her daughters (2 vol., rev. and enl. 1848, repr. 1972); biography by J. H. S. Kent (1963); studies by David Johnson (1969) and Janet Whitney (1937, repr. 1972).

Fry, Roger Eliot, 1866–1934, English art critic and painter. A champion of modern French schools of art, he introduced Cézanne and the postimpressionists to England. From 1905 to 1910 he was curator of paintings at the Metropolitan Museum. In 1933 he was made Slade Professor of Fine Arts at Cambridge. Interested in all eras, he consistently stressed the importance of analyzing the formal qualities within a work of art. His writings include *Vision and Design* (1920), *Transformations* (1926), *Cézanne* (1927), and an outstanding collection, posthumously published, *Last Lectures* (1939). See his letters, ed. by Denys Sutton (2 vol., (1973); biography by Virginia Woolf (1940).

Frýdlant (frĕd'länt), Ger. *Friedland,* town, N Czechoslovakia, in Bohemia, near the East German and Polish borders, at the foot of the Sudetes Mts. A railroad junction, Frýdlant has breweries and industries that manufacture textiles and metal products. Its castle, now a museum, was the seat (1625–34) of the duchy of Friedland, which was awarded to the German imperial general Wallenstein in 1625.

Frye, Northrop, 1912–, Canadian literary critic, b. Quebec. In 1948 he was appointed professor of English at Victoria College, of which he later became principal (1959–66). He is the author of *Fearful Symmetry* (1947), an authoritative study of William Blake's symbolism and religious mysticism, and of *Anatomy of Criticism* (1957), a synoptic view of the principles and techniques of literary criticism. His other major works include *The Well-Tempered Critic* (1963) and two collections of his lectures: *A Natural Perspective* (1965) and *The Modern Century* (1967). Frye edited *Romanticism Reconsidered* (1968), a collection of lectures. See study by Ronald Bates (1971).

Fryth, John: see FRITH, JOHN.

Fuad I (Ahmed Fuad Pasha) (fo͞oäd'), 1868–1936, first king of modern Egypt, son of the khedive Ismail Pasha. Fuad was educated in Europe. In 1880 he returned to Egypt and was concerned with military and cultural affairs, founding (1906) the Univ. of Cairo. He succeeded his brother Hussein as sultan in 1917. Fuad took the title king in 1922, although the final dissolution of the British dominion in Egypt was delayed until 1923. Fuad's difficulties with the WAFD party led him, in 1928, to abrogate the constitution of 1923 and substitute a new constitution providing for a parliament with advisory powers only. Great agitation compelled him, in 1935, to restore the earlier constitution. He was succeeded by his son Farouk.

Fu-chou (fo͞o-jō) or **Foochow** (fo͞o'chou'), city (1970 est. pop. 900,000), capital of Fukien prov., China, a port on the Min River delta c.25 mi (40 km) from the coast. A regional commercial and fishing center that used to trade chiefly with Taiwan, Fu-chou was linked with the central Chinese railway system in 1958, and its economic ties are now with the mainland. It has chemical plants, a small integrated iron and steel complex, textile mills, machine shops, food-processing establishments (tea and sugar), and paper mills. Fu-chou consists of an old walled city, which lies c.2 mi (3 km) from the river, and a modern riverside town. A bridge crosses to Nan-t'ai island, the former foreign settlement and business center. Large vessels dock 15 mi (24 km) downstream to transship their goods. The old city of Fu-chou dates from the T'ang dynasty (A.D. 618–906). Marco Polo, who called it Fugiu, visited the city on his return journey. After the OPIUM WAR (1839–42) Fu-chou was established as a TREATY PORT. By 1850 it was the principal Chinese port and the world's largest tea-exporting center. Its importance declined when the demand for tea decreased and when harbor silting barred large vessels. Fu-chou has several institutions of higher learning, including Fu-chou Univ. In the surrounding hills are beautiful pagodas and monasteries, and a summer resort.

Fu-chou or **Fuchow** (both: fo͞o-chou, fo͞o-jō), city, N central Kiangsi prov., China. It is an agricultural and commercial center and a road hub, known for its hot springs. Barite deposits are nearby. The city was formerly called Linchwan.

Fuchow: see FU-CHOU, China.

Fuchs, Klaus Emil, 1911–, British physicist and Communist spy, b. Germany. In 1933 he fled from Germany and went to England, where he completed his education. Interned (1940–41) in Canada as an enemy alien, he made no attempt to conceal his Communist sympathies and was soon released, becoming a naturalized British citizen. In 1943 he began work on the development of the atomic bomb in the United States; during this period he started transmitting information to the Soviet Union. He later became head of the theoretical physics division of the atomic research center at Harwell and continued his espionage activities, which were suspected only because of information gleaned by the U.S. Federal Bureau of Investigation from confessed Communist agents in the United States. Arrested in 1950, he pleaded guilty and was imprisoned. Fuchs was released in 1959 and went to East Germany, where he became director of the Institute for Nuclear Physics.

Fuchs, Sir Vivian Ernest, 1908–, English geologist and explorer, b. Kent, educated at Cambridge. He was a geologist on expeditions to Greenland (1929) and to Africa (1930–38). After service in World War II, Fuchs became connected (1947) with the Falkland Islands Dependencies Survey, which included Antarctica; he directed the survey after 1950. With Sir Edmund Hillary he led (1957–58) the Commonwealth Trans-Antarctic Expedition and accomplished the first completely overland crossing of Antarctica. Beginning at Shackleton base near the Weddell Sea, the expedition crossed the South Pole and then continued onward to Scott base on the Ross Sea. The trek of 2,158 mi (3,473 km) took 99 days. Fuchs was knighted in 1958 and in 1959 received the Hubbard Medal, the highest award of the National Geographic Society. See Vivian Fuchs and Edmund Hillary, *The Crossing of Antarctica* (1958).

fuchsia: see EVENING PRIMROSE.

fuchsin (fyo͝ok'sĭn) or **magenta** (məjĕn'tə), bright red dyestuff consisting of the mixed hydrochlorides or acetates of rosaniline and pararosaniline. It is composed of small crystals possessing a brilliant green sheen; when dissolved they produce a red solution, which dyes animal fibers directly and vegetable fibers after mordanting. The solution is used in the textile and leather industries and as a stain in biology.

Fuchu (fo͞o'cho͞o), city (1970 pop. 47,651), Hiroshima prefecture, W Honshu, Japan, on the Ashida River. It is an agricultural and livestock center.

Fuchu, city (1970 pop. 163,173), Tokyo Metropolis, E central Honshu, Japan. It is a residential suburb of Tokyo and the site of a racetrack. It was the ancient capital of Musashi prov. and is noted for the Okumitama (Shinto) Shrine.

Fuego, Tierra del: see TIERRA DEL FUEGO.

fuel, material that can be burned or otherwise consumed to produce heat. The common fuels used in industry, transportation, and the home are burned in air. The carbon and hydrogen in fuel rapidly combine with oxygen in the air in an exothermal reaction—one that liberates heat. Most of the fuels used by industrialized nations are in the form of incompletely oxidized and decayed animal and vegetable materials, or fossil fuels, specifically COAL, PEAT, LIGNITE, PETROLEUM, and NATURAL GAS. From these natural fuels other artificial ones can be derived. COAL GAS, COKE, WATER GAS, and PRODUCER GAS can be made using coal as the principal ingredient. GASOLINE, KEROSINE, and fuel oil are made from petroleum. Wood is also used as a fuel, but it is not as concentrated a form of energy as fossil fuels. From wood another fuel called CHARCOAL can be made. There is a growing concern about the environmental contamination caused by the burning of great amounts of fossil fuels and about the increasing expense of finding them and processing them into easily usable forms (see ENERGY, SOURCES OF). One proposed solution to these problems is to use hydrogen, now employed as a fuel only for a few special purposes, in place of fossil fuels. These fuels are rated according to the amount of heat (in calories or Btu) that a unit weight or volume can produce. Nuclear fuels are also possible substitutes for fossil fuels. Nuclear fuels are not burned; they undergo reactions in which the nuclei of their atoms either split apart, i.e., undergo fission, or combine with other nuclei, i.e., undergo fusion. In either case, a small part of the nuclear mass is converted to heat energy. All nuclear fuels currently employed in practical, nonweapons applications react by fission. Examples are the isotopes uranium 235 and plutonium 239. Nuclear fuel ratings are based on the same principle as fossil fuel ratings, but are stated in larger units, e.g., megawatt days per ton. High-energy fuels, usually with a self-contained supply of oxygen or some other oxidizer, are used in rockets. Fuels such as turpentine, alcohol, aniline, and ammonia use nitric acid, hydrogen peroxide, and liquid oxygen as oxidizers. More power can be obtained by oxidizing hydrazine, diborane, or hydrogen with oxygen, ozone, or fluorine. High energy fuels are rated by their specific impulse, or thrust per unit weight of fuel consumed per second. See OIL GAS; LIQUEFIED PETROLEUM GAS; GAS, FUEL; NUCLEAR ENERGY.

fuel cell, electric CELL in which the chemical energy from the oxidation of a gas fuel is converted directly to electrical energy in a continuous process (see OXIDATION AND REDUCTION). The efficiency of conversion from chemical to electrical energy in a fuel cell is between 65% and 80%, nearly twice that of the usual indirect method of conversion, in which fuels are used to heat steam to turn a turbine connected to an electric generator. The earliest fuel cell, in which hydrogen and oxygen were combined to form water, was constructed in 1829 by the Englishman William Grove. In the hydrogen and oxygen fuel cell, hydrogen and oxygen gas are bubbled into separate compartments connected by a porous disk through which an electrolyte such as aqueous potassium hydroxide (KOH) can move. Inert graphite electrodes, mixed with a catalyst such as platinum, are dipped into each compartment. When the two electrodes are connected by a wire, the combination of electrodes, wire, and electrolyte form a complete circuit, and an oxidation-reduction reaction takes place in the cell: hydrogen gas is oxidized to form water at the anode, or hydrogen electrode; electrons are liberated in this process and flow through the wire to the cathode, or oxygen electrode; and at the cathode the electrons combine with the oxygen gas and reduce it. The modern hydrogen-oxygen cell, operating at about 250°C and a pressure of 50 atmospheres, gives a maximum voltage of about 1 volt. Fuel cells have been used to generate electricity in space flights.

Fuente Obejuna or **Fuenteovejuna** (both: fwān'tā ōvāho͞o'nä), town (1970 pop. 9,247), Córdoba prov., S Spain, in Andalusia. An important farm center with livestock-raising and food-processing industries, the town is especially noted for its honey. Lumber, coal, and lead are exploited in the area. In 1430, Fuente Obejuna was given to the Knights of CALATRAVA. The revolt of the people against a tyrannical governor is the subject of a play by Lope de Vega Carpio. The palace of the Knights, formerly a Moorish castle, is now the parish church.

Fuentes, Carlos (kär'lōs fwān'tās), 1928–, Mexican writer, editor, and diplomat. From 1956 to 1959 he was head of the department of cultural relations in the Mexican ministry of foreign affairs. Much of his fiction is a synthesis of reality and fantasy; his writing transcends the limits of time and space. His works include *La región más transparente* (1958; tr. *Where the Air is Clear,* 1960), *La muerte de Artemio Cruz* (1962; tr. *The Death of Artemio Cruz,* 1964), *Cambio de piel* (1967; tr. *A Change of Skin,* 1968), and *Good Conscience* (tr. 1968). See study by Daniel de Guzmán (1972).

Fuentes de Oñoro (fwān'tās dā ōnyō'rō), village (1970 pop. 1,069), Salamanca prov., W Spain, in León, near the Portuguese border. It was the scene of two bloody engagements between the British under Wellington and the French under Masséna (May 3 and 5, 1811) in the Peninsular War.

Fuertes, Louis Agassiz (fo͞oĕr'tēs), 1874–1927, American artist and naturalist, b. Ithaca, N.Y., grad. Cornell Univ., 1897. His paintings of birds appear in most of the leading American ornithological works published in the latter half of his lifetime. He is also known for his murals and for his habitat groups at the American Museum of Natural History. With W. H. Osgood he made a scientific expedition to Ethiopia (1926–27); *Artist and Naturalist in Ethiopia* (1936) is a joint account. Fuertes was killed accidentally a few months after his return. See F. G. Marcham, ed., *Louis Agassiz Fuertes and the Singular Beauty of Birds* (1971).

Fuessli, Johann Heinrich: see FUSELI, HENRY.

Fuga, Ferdinando (fārdēnän'dō fo͞o'gä), 1699–1781, Italian architect. Fuga is best known for his rebuilding of Santa Maria Maggiore in Rome. He served as papal architect during the pontificate of Clement XII and worked later in Naples. He was considered a virtuoso in the synthesis of classical, baroque, and mannerist styles.

Fugger (fo͝og'ər), German family of merchant princes. The foundation of their wealth was laid by

Hans Fugger, allegedly a weaver, who moved to Augsburg in 1367. His descendants built up the family fortune by trade and banking. With Jacob Fugger II (1459–1525), called Jacob the Rich, the house entered its zenith. It owned extensive real estate, merchant fleets, and palatial establishments throughout Europe. Jacob's fortune was largely built on a virtual monopoly in the mining and trading of silver, copper, and mercury. He lent immense sums to Holy Roman Emperor Maximilian I and helped secure the election (1519) of Charles V as Holy Roman emperor by bribing the electors. Charles ennobled the family and granted them sovereign rights over their lands, including that of coining their own money. Then the richest family in Europe, the Fuggers were generous as patrons of the arts and learning and as philanthropists, notably at Augsburg, their residence. Under Raimund Fugger (1489–1535) and Anton Fugger (1493–1560) the house reached the limits of its power and fortune. Its decline paralleled that of the Hapsburgs, whose wars the Fuggers financed. Several descendants were prominent, but, except for some real estate, little is left of the once fabulous wealth. See Richard Ehrenberg, *Capital and Finance in the Age of the Renaissance* (tr. 1928); Jacob Strieder, *Jacob Fugger the Rich* (tr. 1931, repr. 1966); G. T. Matthews, ed., *News and Rumor in Renaissance Europe: The Fugger Newsletters* (1959).

fugitive slave laws, in U.S. history, the Federal acts of 1793 and 1850 providing for the return between states of escaped Negro slaves. Similar laws existing in both North and South in colonial days applied also to white indentured servants and to Indian slaves. As slavery was abolished in the Northern states, the 1793 law was loosely enforced, to the great irritation of the South, and as abolitionist sentiment developed, organized efforts to circumvent the law took form in the UNDERGROUND RAILROAD. Many Northern states also passed personal-liberty laws that allowed fugitives a jury trial, and others passed laws forbidding state officials to help capture alleged fugitive slaves or to lodge them in state jails. As a concession to the South a second and more rigorous fugitive slave law was passed as part of the COMPROMISE OF 1850. By it "all good citizens" were "commanded to aid and assist [Federal marshals and their deputies] in the prompt and efficient execution of this law," and heavy penalties were imposed upon anyone who assisted slaves to escape from bondage. When apprehended, an alleged fugitive was taken before a Federal court or commissioner. He was denied a jury trial and his testimony was not admitted, while the statement of the master claiming ownership, even though absent, was taken as the main evidence. The law was so weighted against the fugitives that many Northerners, formerly unconcerned, were now aroused to opposition. New personal-liberty laws contradicting the legislation of 1850 (and described, with some justice, by Southerners as equivalent to South Carolina's notorious ordinance of nullification) were passed in most of the Northern states. Abolitionists fearlessly defied the 1850 act, often mobbing Federal officials in attempts to rescue fugitives. In Boston, for instance, the "good citizens," including some of the foremost Brahmans, stormed the Federal courthouse, but failed to free the escaped Virginia slave Anthony Burns; moreover, it was thought expedient to have 1,100 soldiers guard him when he was marched aboard ship for his return to bondage. In Lancaster co., Pa., a riot broke out when a Federal official ordered Quaker bystanders to help catch a runaway; the Quakers were prosecuted, but not convicted. Other notable fugitive slave cases arose in Northern courts, and the trials further stirred up public opinion both North and South. The whole dispute, combined with the question of the extension of slavery into the territories, served to set the two sections at each other's throats. The actions of Northern states in nullifying the fugitive slave laws or rendering "useless any attempt to execute them" were cited (Dec. 24, 1860) by South Carolina as one cause for secession. Both acts were finally repealed by Congress on June 28, 1864.

fugue (fyo͞og) [from Ital.,=flight], in music, a form of composition, originally choral, in which the basic principle is imitative COUNTERPOINT of several voices. Its main elements are: (1) a theme, or subject, stated first in one voice alone and then successively in all voices; (2) the continuation of a voice after the subject, forming an accompaniment to the subject statements in the other voices and sometimes assuming sufficiently distinct character as to be called a countersubject; and (3) passages that are built on a MOTIVE or motives derived from the subject or the countersubject but in which these themselves do not appear. Those sections in which the subject appears at least once in all voices are called expositions; those in which it does not appear at all are called episodes. Expositions other than the opening one often modulate. The formal structure of any fugue is an alternation of exposition and episode, and an infinite variety of formal scheme is possible. The term *fugue* designates a contrapuntal texture which may be in any formal design. The principle was established by Flemish composers in the 15th cent. and was first systematically applied in the motets of Josquin Desprez c.1500. During the 16th cent. the technique was further developed in the instrumental ricercare and canzone. In Germany in the 17th cent. composers such as Sweelinck, Froberger, and Buxtehude developed contrapuntal pieces based on one subject, which led to the fugal style exemplified in the *Art of the Fugue*, the *Goldberg Variations*, and the *Well-tempered Clavier* of J. S. Bach, the master of fugue. After him fugue was adapted by Haydn, Mozart, and Beethoven to the classical style. Brahms was the chief composer to make use of the fugue in the romantic period. A contemporary volume of preludes and fugues is Paul Hindemith's *Ludus Tonalis* (1943). See Alfred Mann, *The Study of Fugue* (1958), Ebenezer Prout, *Fugue* (1891, repr. 1970).

Fujairah (fo͝ojī'rä), sheikhdom (1968 pop. 9,724), c.450 sq mi (1,170 sq km), part of the federation of UNITED ARAB EMIRATES, E Arabia, on the Gulf of Oman. Although oil has been produced since 1966, agriculture is the most important economic activity. Fujairah was a British protectorate until it joined the United Arab Emirates in 1971.

Fuji (fo͞o'jē), city (1970 pop. 180,939), Shizuoka prefecture, S central Honshu, Japan, on Suruga Bay. It is an important communications and industrial center producing paper and paper pulp, machinery, household appliances, and chemical fibers.

Fujinomiya (fo͞ojēnō'mēyä), city (1970 pop. 88,880), Shizuoka prefecture, central Honshu, Japan, at the foot of Mt. Fuji. It is an important railway junction and point of departure for the Mt. Fuji resort region. The city has a large paper pulp industry and is noted for its Sengen (Shinto) shrine.

Fujioka (fo͞ojē'ōkä), city (1970 pop. 44,311), Gumma prefecture, central Honshu, Japan, on the Tone River. It is a manufacturing center where silk and soy sauce are produced.

Fujisawa (fo͞ojē'säwä), city (1970 pop. 228,978), Kanagawa prefecture, central Honshu, Japan, on Sagami Bay. It is an industrial and residential suburb of Tokyo and a market for agricultural products from the Sagami plain. Fujisawa is also a resort town noted for its Shojokoji (Buddhist) temple.

Fujiyama, Fuji-yama (both: fo͞o"jēyä'mä, fo͞ojē'-yämä), **Mount Fuji,** or **Fuji-san** (fo͞o"jē-säN), volcanic peak, 12,389 ft (3,776 m) high, central Honshu, Japan, in Fuji-Hakone-Izu National Park (472 sq mi/1,222 sq km; est. 1936). The highest point on Honshu, it is a sacred mountain and the traditional goal of pilgrimage. According to legend, an earthquake created Fuji in 286 B.C. The beauty of the snow-capped symmetrical cone, ringed by lakes and virgin forests, has inspired Japanese poets and painters throughout the centuries. Its last major eruption was in 1707.

Fujiyoshida (fo͞ojē'yōshēdä), city (1970 pop. 50,046), Yamanashi prefecture, central Honshu, Japan, on the Katsura River. It is an important communications center for the Mt. Fuji region. The city has a large textile industry.

Fukaya (fo͞okä'yä), city (1970 pop. 60,609), Saitama prefecture, E central Honshu, Japan. It is an industrial and residential suburb of Tokyo with raw silk, tire, and textile industries.

Fukien (fo͞o'kyĕn'), Mandarin *Fu-chien,* province (1968 est. pop. 17,000,000), c.46,000 sq mi (119,100 sq km), SE China, on Formosa Strait. The capital is FU-CHOU (Foochow). The climate is warm and very moist, the terrain mostly hilly or mountainous. Of the many ports on the heavily indented coast, Amoy, the only one which can accommodate large vessels, handles most of the trade, although there is some at Fu-chou. Other harbors are undeveloped. About a tenth of the land is arable. Rice, sweet potatoes, wheat, and tea are grown in the uplands, and fruit, silk, and jute are produced in the lowlands. The coastal region from Amoy to Fu-chou is a major sugar-producing area. The chief oil-producing seed is rapeseed, but peanuts and soybeans are also grown. There is some tobacco, and the extensive forests on the mountains provide considerable lumber (fir, pine, bamboo), camphor, and wood oils. Fishing off the island-strewn coast is important. The mineral resources are iron ore, tungsten, and manganese; coal reserves are poor. The industries are light; most important are lumbering and woodworking, tea processing, sugar refining, salt panning, and the manufacturing of textiles, cement, ceramics, and processed foods, including preserved fruits, for which the province has long been famous. The rugged, mountainous terrain until recently retarded the building of roads or railroads; lines of communication from the hinterland were chiefly the narrow rivers, which rise in the mountains and flow eastward to the sea. The Min, the most important, flows southeast, emptying below Fu-chou. Chinese painters have often depicted its gorges and the surrounding hills. Because so many of its localities were long isolated, Fukien has perhaps the largest number of dialects of any province (over 100). The people are diverse. Most derive from local Chinese stocks, but many are descendants of ancient Hakka migrants from the northern provinces or of non-Chinese aborigines. The people of Fukien have long been faced with an inadequate food supply, aggravated by the continual immigration of N Chinese fleeing floods and droughts. Since the 17th cent., the people of Fukien have emigrated in large numbers, chiefly to SE Asia; together with Kwangtung prov., Fukien has provided the majority of overseas Chinese. Strategically located opposite the island of Taiwan, the location of the Nationalist Chinese government, Fukien has (since 1950) maintained large numbers of troops. Fukien's former economic base of trade with Taiwan has changed, prompting an improvement in internal communications by rail and road and new emphasis on agricultural production. A rail line now links Fukien with Kiangsi prov. and the Chinese transportation net.

Fukuchiyama (fo͞oko͞ochē'yämä), city (1970 pop. 57,174), Kyoto prefecture, W central Honshu, Japan, on the Yura River. Now an important railway junction and an agricultural market, it was a major castle town during the Edo era.

Fukui (fo͞oko͞o'ē), city (1970 pop. 200,506), capital of Fukui prefecture, central Honshu, Japan. A modern textile center, it is especially noted for rayon manufactures. It was an important silk weaving center in the 10th cent. and became a castle town in the 16th cent. The city suffered a disastrous earthquake in 1948. Fukui prefecture (1970 pop. 744,198), 1,647 sq mi (4,266 sq km), is bounded by Wakasa Bay and the Sea of Japan. It is mountainous, with a wide coastal plain and small streams. The manufacture of lacquer and raw silk, poultry raising, and fishing are major occupations. Tsuruga is the main port, and Takebu is an important town.

Fukuoka (fo͞oko͞o'ōkä), city (1970 pop. 853,271), capital of Fukuoka prefecture, N Kyushu, Japan, on Hakata Bay. A port and textile-producing center, it is one of the largest and most prosperous cities on Kyushu. Fukuoka is also the seat of five universities, including Kyushu Univ. The well-known Hakata dolls have been made there for centuries. The ancient port area, Hakata, was in medieval times one of the chief ports of Japan. The Mongols under Kublai Khan twice (1274, 1281) were defeated at Hakata. The city of Fukuoka has three noted shrines—the Buddhist temple of Kannonji, the Dazaifu Temmangu shrine, and a 16th-century Shinto temple. Fukuoka prefecture (1970 pop. 4,027,414), 1,907 sq mi (4,939 sq km), is bounded on the north by Shimonoseki Strait and on the east by the Inland Sea. The Chikuho River valley in the north is a rich agricultural district and contains Japan's largest coal mine.

Fukushima (fo͞oko͞o'shĭmä), city (1970 pop. 227,525), capital of Fukushima prefecture, N Honshu, Japan, on the Kiso plain. A silk-textile center, it is a major commercial city of NE Japan. Fukushima prefecture (1970 pop. 1,946,077), 5,321 sq mi (13,781 sq km), is partly mountainous. Its main agricultural area is watered by the Abukuma River. Rice and soybeans are the major crops, and fishing, horsebreeding, lumbering, and textile production are the principal occupations. Fukushima (the capital), Koriyama, Taira, and Wakamatsu are the chief cities.

Fukuyama (fo͞oko͞o'yämä), city (1970 pop. 255,086), Hiroshima prefecture, W Honshu, Japan, on the Ashida River. It is an important commercial, industrial, and communications center with a large electronics industry.

Fulani (fo͞olä'nē), people of W Africa, numbering approximately 7 million. They are of mixed black African and Berber origin. First recorded as living in the Senegambia region, they are now scattered throughout the area of the Sudan from Senegal to Cameroon. Both as a sedentary and as a nomadic people, they have played an important part in the history of W Africa. A number of African states, including ancient Ghana and Senegal, had Fulani rulers. The Fulani became zealous Muslims (11th cent.), and from 1750 to 1900 they engaged in many holy wars in the name of Islam. During the first part of the 19th cent. the Fulani carved out two important empires. One, based on Massina, for a time controlled Timbuktu; the other, centered at SOKOTO, included the Hausa States and parts of BORNU and W Cameroon. The Fulani emir of Sokoto continued to rule over part of N Nigeria until the British conquest in 1903. The Fulani of Massina were conquered (1861) by HAJJ OMAR, but their resistance ultimately resulted in his death. See D. J. Stenning, *Savannah Nomads* (1959, repr. 1964); H. A. S. Johnston, *The Fulani Empire of Sokoto* (1967).

Fulbright, James William, 1905–, U.S. Senator from Arkansas (1945–75), b. Sumner, Mo. A Rhodes scholar, he was admitted (1934) to the bar and served (1934–35) in the antitrust division of the U. S. Dept of Justice. He taught law at George Washington Univ. law school (1935–36) and at the Univ. of Arkansas (1936–39), becoming president of the university in 1939. In 1942, Fulbright was elected as a Democrat to the U.S. House of Representatives and in 1944 to the Senate. He gained international recognition from the Fulbright Act (1946), which provided for the exchange of students and teachers between the United States and many other countries. As chairman of the Senate Foreign Relations Committee from 1959 to 1974, Fulbright conducted frequent open hearings to educate the public and to reassert the Senate's influence in long-range policy formulation. An outspoken critic of U.S. military intervention abroad, Fulbright opposed the Bay of Pigs invasion (1961), the landing of marines in the Dominican Republic (1965), and the escalation of the war in Vietnam. In the 1974 Democratic primary in Arkansas, Fulbright was defeated for the senatorial nomination by Dale Bumpers. He wrote *Old Myths and New Realities* (1964); *The Arrogance of Power* (1966); *The Pentagon Propaganda Machine* (1970); and *The Crippled Giant* (1972). See biographies by Tristram Coffin (1966) and H. B. Johnson and B. M. Gwertzman (1968).

fulcrum: see LEVER.

Fulda (fo͝ol'dä), city (1970 pop. 45,539), Hesse, E central West Germany, on the Fulda River. It is an agricultural market and an industrial center. Manufactures include textiles, chemicals, rubber products, and carpets. Fulda grew around a Benedictine abbey founded in 744 by Sturmius, a pupil of St. Boniface, the missionary. From this abbey Christianity was spread throughout central Germany; numerous scholars were associated with the abbey school. From the 13th cent. the abbots of Fulda ruled the town and the surrounding area as princes of the Holy Roman Empire, and in 1752 they were raised to the rank of prince-bishops. Fulda was secularized in 1802, and most of it passed to Hesse-Kassel in 1816. Since 1829, Fulda has again been an episcopal see and is now the site of the annual conference of the Catholic bishops of West Germany. A theological seminary is in the city. Noteworthy buildings include the baroque cathedral (1704–12), in the crypt of which St. Boniface is buried; the Michaelskirche (c.820), a Carolingian-style church; and a castle (1720).

Fulk (fŭlk), 1092–1143, Latin king of Jerusalem (1131–43), count of Anjou (1109–29) as Fulk V, great-grandson of Fulk Nerra. He journeyed (1120) to the Holy Land as a pilgrim and returned there in 1129, making his son, Geoffrey Plantagenet, count of Anjou as GEOFFREY IV. Having taken as his new wife Melisende, daughter of King Baldwin II of Jerusalem, he succeeded his father-in-law in 1131. Fulk's reign was disturbed by dissensions among the Latin princes and by the raids of the Turks, whose prisoner he was for a time in 1137. He was succeeded as king of Jerusalem by his son by Melisende, Baldwin III.

Fulk Nerra (nĕrä'), 972–1040, count of Anjou (987–1040). Continuously at war with his neighbors (Brittany, Blois, Touraine, Normandy), he vastly increased his lands, notably by seizing Saumur. He built numerous castles on his borders and made several pilgrimages to the Holy Land. He was one of the early members of the Angevin dynasty.

Fulk of Neuilly, Fr. *Foulques de Neuilly* (fo͝olk də nöyē'), d. 1201, French preacher. His sermons and alleged miracles gave him a wide popular following in N France, and in 1199 Pope Innocent III appointed him to preach a new crusade (the Fourth Crusade). Tremendous crowds heard him, but he lost his following when the suspicion spread that he had misused some funds he had collected.

Fuller, George, 1822–84, American portrait, figure, and landscape painter, b. Deerfield, Mass.; pupil of Henry K. Brown at Albany. He first practiced portraiture in Boston and later in New York City, and then turned to farming. Acclaim for his painting came in the last decade of his life, when the originality of treatment, richness of tone, and pictorial qualities of his later works awakened widespread interest. Among Fuller's best canvases are *Nydia, And She Was a Witch, The Quadroon,* and *Head of a Boy* (all: Metropolitan Mus.); *Winifred Dysart* (Worcester, Mass., Art Mus.); *Turkey Pasture, Kentucky* and *Arethusa* (both: Mus. of Fine Arts, Boston). See J. B. Millet, *George Fuller: His Life and Works* (1886).

Fuller, John Frederick Charles, 1878–1966, British soldier. In World War I, he recognized the importance of mechanized warfare and, as general staff officer of the tank corps, planned the stunning tank attack at Cambrai in 1917 (see TANK, MILITARY). His ideas, expressed in *Tanks in the Great War* (1920), *On Future Warfare* (1928), and other works, had a great effect on military thinking on the Continent. His military analysis extended far beyond championship of armored warfare, and he established himself as one of the leading military commentators of the day. He retired from the army in 1933 but was active as an analyst in World War II. Among his other works are *Foundations of the Science of War* (1926), *The Generalship of Ulysses S. Grant* (2d ed. 1958), *The Dragon's Teeth* (1932), *War and Western Civilization* (1932), *The Second World War* (rev. ed. 1968), and *A Military History of the Western World* (3 vol., 1954–56).

Fuller, Margaret, 1810–50, American writer and lecturer, b. Cambridgeport (now part of Cambridge), Mass. She was one of the most influential personalities of her day in American literary circles. A precocious child, she was forced by her father through an education that impaired her health but nonetheless gave her a broad knowledge of literature and languages. Her first published work was *Conversations with Goethe* (1839), a translation of Johann Peter Eckermann. A stimulating talker, she conducted in Boston conversation classes for society women on social and literary topics. She was an ardent feminist, and her book *Woman in the Nineteenth Century* (1845) treated feminism in its economic, intellectual, political, and sexual aspects. She was a leader of the TRANSCENDENTALISM movement and edited its journal, the *Dial,* for its first two years (1840–42). Although she has been identified as Zenobia in Hawthorne's *Blithedale Romance,* she was never in sympathy with the Brook Farm experiment upon which the book is based. More recognizable is Lowell's caricature of her as Miranda in the *Fable for Critics.* Horace Greeley, attracted by her writings, including *Summer on the Lakes in 1843* (1844), called her to New York City as the first literary critic of the New York *Tribune,* from which her *Papers on Literature and Art* (1846) were republished. In 1847, Fuller went to Rome, where she married the Marchese Ossoli, a follower of Mazzini, and with him took part in the Revolution of 1848–49 and wrote letters home describing the situation for the *Tribune* readers. In 1850, while sailing to the United States, she was drowned with her husband and infant son when the ship was wrecked off Fire Island. Her works were republished incompletely by her brother, Arthur Fuller, and her love letters were edited by Julia Ward Howe. See her memoirs (ed. by R. W. Emerson et al., 1852; repr. 1972) and *The Writings of Margaret Fuller* (selected and ed. by Mason Wade, 1941, repr. 1970); biographies by Julia Ward Howe (1883), Mason Wade (1940, repr. 1973), and Faith Chipperfield (1957); studies by Perry Miller, ed. (1963) and J. J. Deiss (1969).

Fuller, Melville Weston, 1833–1910, American jurist, 8th Chief Justice of the United States (1888–1910), b. Augusta, Maine. He studied at Harvard law school, and after 1856 he became a prominent lawyer in Chicago and acquired a national reputation in Democratic politics. Fuller was appointed Chief Justice by President Cleveland. In his opinions he leaned toward strict construction of the Constitution. He also served as a commissioner to help settle the Venezuela Boundary Dispute and was a member (1900–1910) of the Permanent Court of Arbitration (The Hague Tribunal). See biography by W. L. King (1950, repr. 1967).

Fuller, (Richard) Buckminster, 1895–, American architect and engineer, b. Milton, Mass. Fuller devoted his life to the invention of revolutionary technological designs to solve problems of modern living. His developments include "energetic" geometry (1917); the "4-D" house (1928), a self-contained, dustless unit (transportable by air); the streamlined Dymaxion auto (1933); and the Dymaxion house (1944–45), Wichita, Kansas. *Dymaxion* is the term for Fuller's principle of deriving maximum output from a minimum input of material and energy, best realized in his GEODESIC DOMES. These are spherical structures of extremely light, enormously strong triangular members. In the 1950s these domes were widely used for military and industrial purposes. Fuller's many controversial books include *Nine Chains to the Moon* (1938), the autobiographical *Ideas and Integrities* (1963), *Operating Manual for Spaceship Earth* (1969), *Utopia or Oblivion* (1970), *Approaching the Benign Environment* (1970), and *Earth, Inc.* (1973). See biography by Alden Hatch (1974); studies by Sidney Rosen (1969) and Hugh Kenner (1973); *The Buckminster Fuller Reader,* ed. by James Meller (1970).

Fuller, Thomas, 1608–61, English clergyman and author. He was an able preacher and a noted wit. He adhered to the royalist cause during the civil war and the Commonwealth and served briefly as a royal chaplain. He is best known for his posthumously published *Worthies of England* (1662), an invaluable store of antiquarian information. His other works include a *History of the Holy War* (1639), *The Holy State and the Profane State* (1642), and *The Church History of Britain* (1655). See biography by William Addison (1951, repr. 1971); study by W. E. Houghton, Jr. (1938, repr. 1970).

fuller's earth, mineral substance characterized by the property of absorbing basic colors and removing them from oils. It is composed mainly of alumina, silica, iron oxides, lime, magnesia, and water, in extremely variable proportions, and is generally classified as a sedimentary CLAY. In color it may be whitish, buff, brown, green, olive, or blue. It is semiplastic or nonplastic and may or may not disintegrate easily in water. It was originally used in the fulling of wool to remove oil and grease, but is now used chiefly in bleaching and clarifying petroleum and secondarily in refining edible oils. Fuller's earth is mined in many parts of the United States, Georgia and Florida being the leading producers, and in England near Reigate, Nutfield, and Bath. Before it can be used, it has to be crushed and dried.

Fullerton, city (1970 pop. 85,987), Orange co., S Calif., SE of Los Angeles; founded 1887, inc. 1904. It is named for George H. Fullerton, head of a land company, who arranged to route the San Diego–Los Angeles–Sante Fe RR through the settlement in 1888. Oil was discovered near Fullerton in 1892, but the city's main growth came with the construction of the Santa Ana Freeway in the 1950s. Fullerton's manufactures include aerospace equipment, food products, electrical and electronic components, ordnance, paper products, musical instruments, and aluminum building products. Fullerton College and California State Univ. at Fullerton are in the city. Muckenthaler Center houses two symphony orchestras, a theater group, and other art associations.

fulmar (fŭl'mər): see SHEARWATER; PETREL.

fulminate (fŭl'mĭnāt), any salt of fulminic acid, HONC, a highly unstable compound known only in solution. The term is most commonly applied to the explosive mercury (II) fulminate, also called fulminate of mercury, $Hg(ONC)_2$. The pure compound forms white cubic crystals. It is made by the action of nitric acid on mercury metal in the presence of alcohol and is often collected as a gray or brown sandy powder. It is very sensitive to heat, shock, or friction and is used in primers, detonators, and blasting caps.

Fulton, Robert, 1765–1815, American inventor, engineer, and painter, b. near Lancaster, Pa. He was a man remarkable for his many talents and his mechanical genius. An expert gunsmith at the time of the American Revolution, he later turned to painting (1782–86) landscapes and portraits in Philadelphia. In England and France his painting gained some notice, but he became interested in canal engineering and the invention of machinery. He worked at making underwater torpedoes and submarines as well as other mechanical devices. In 1802 he contracted to build a steamboat for Robert R. Livingston, who held a monopoly on steamboat navigation on the Hudson. In 1807 the *Clermont,* equipped with an English engine, was launched. A number of men had built steamboats before Fulton (see STEAMSHIP), including John Fitch and William Symington. Fulton's steamship, however, was the first to be commercially successful in American waters, and Fulton was therefore popularly considered the inventor of the steamboat. He also designed other vessels, among them a steam warship. See H. W. Dickinson, *Robert Fulton* (1913, repr. 1971); W. B. Parsons, *Robert Fulton and the Submarine* (1922); Corinne Lowe, *Quicksilver Bob* (1946).

Fulton. **1** City (1970 pop. 12,248), seat of Callaway co., central Mo., in a farm area; inc. 1859. It has printing plants and factories making farm and industrial equipment. During the Civil War the county seceded from the United States and by treaty with the state militia formed the "Kingdom of Callaway." On March 5, 1946, Winston Churchill delivered his famous "iron curtain" speech at Westminster College there. The college now houses the Winston Churchill Memorial and Library, including a reconstruction of a Christopher Wren church destroyed in the bombing of London. William Woods College, a state mental hospital, and a state school for the deaf are also there. **2** City (1970 pop. 14,003), Oswego co., N central N.Y., on the Oswego River; inc. 1835. Machinery, corrugated boxes, thermometers, chocolate, and frozen foods are among its products.

Fulvia (fŭl'vēə), d. 40 B.C. Roman matron. She was wife, in turn, of Publius CLODIUS, Quintus Scribonius Curio, and (44) Marc ANTONY, to whom she remained completely loyal. She had been attacked (in the *Philippics*) by Cicero, and she pierced his tongue with a needle when his head was brought to Rome (43). She led a revolt in Antony's interest against Augustus. Her forces were defeated at Perusia (40), and she died at Sicyon.

fumaric acid (fyo͞omăr'ĭk) or ***trans*-butenedioic acid,** $HO_2CCH{=}CHCO_2H$, unsaturated dicarboxylic acid that melts at 287°C. Maleic acid, or *cis*-butenedioic acid, is a geometric ISOMER of fumaric acid; it melts at about 140°C. Of the two isomers fumaric acid is the more stable and can be prepared from maleic acid by heating it. Fumaric acid can be prepared by catalytic oxidation of benzene or by bacterial action on glucose. It is found in small amounts in a variety of plants and is essential to the respiration of animal and vegetable tissue. Fumaric acid is used as a substitute for TARTARIC ACID in beverages and baking powder. It is used as a mordant in dyeing and in the manufacture of synthetic resins and polyhydric alcohols.

fumigation: see DISINFECTANT.

fumitory, common name for some members of the Fumariaceae, a family of herbs native to much of the Old World, especially temperate Eurasia. The family is closely related to (and sometimes classified with) the poppies. The early spring wild flowers Dutchman's-breeches and squirrel corn, of the NE

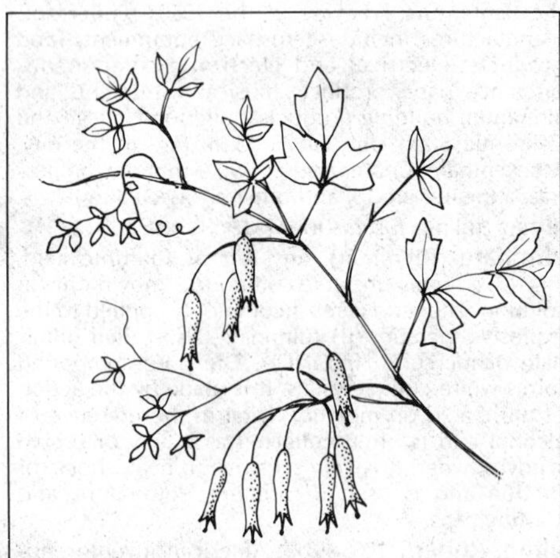

Climbing fumitory, Adlumia fungosa

United States, are of the same genus (*Dicentra*) as is the bleeding heart, a native of Japan naturalized and cultivated in the United States as a garden perennial. Fumitory is a predominantly Mediterranean genus (*Fumaria*) that was once used medicinally. The climbing fumitory, or Allegheny vine, is a North American plant of another genus (*Adlumia*). Several genera of the family are native to S Africa. Fumitory is classified in the division MAGNOLIOPHYTA, class Magnoliopsida, order Papaverales, family Fumariaceae.

Funabashi (fo͞onä'bäshē), city (1970 pop. 325,426), Chiba prefecture, E central Honshu, Japan, on Tokyo Bay. It is an industrial and residential suburb of Tokyo.

Funafuti (fo͞onäfo͞o'tē), chief atoll of the ELLICE ISLANDS, S Pacific, a part of the British colony of the GILBERT AND ELLICE ISLANDS. It comprises 30 islets of a reef 13 mi (21 km) long, with a land area of c.1 sq mi (2.6 sq km). The island was discovered in 1819 and became part of the colony in 1915. An expedition led by Sir Edgeworth David in 1897 proved the Darwinian theory of atoll formation by sinking a 1,100 ft (335 m) bore into the island.

Funchal (fo͞onshäl'), city (1970 municipal pop. 105,791), capital of Funchal dist., on Madeira island, Portugal. A busy port, it is best known for its beautiful setting and balmy climate, which make it a much-frequented resort. It has a late-15th-century cathedral and a convent church containing the tomb of João Gonçalves Zarco, who founded the city in 1421.

function, in mathematics, a relation f that assigns to each member x of some set X a corresponding member y of some set Y; y is said to be a function of x, usually denoted $f(x)$ (read "f of x"). In the equation $y=f(x)$, x is called the independent variable and y the dependent variable. In practice, X and Y will most often be sets of numbers, vectors, points of some geometric object, or the like. For example, X might be a solid body and $f(x)$ the temperature at the point x in X; in this case, Y will be a set of numbers. The formula $A=\pi r^2$ expresses the area of a circle as a function of its radius. A function f is often described in terms of its graph, which consists of all points (x,y) in the plane such that $y=f(x)$. Although a function f assigns a unique y to each x, several x's may yield the same y; e.g., if $y=f(x)=x^2$ (x is a number), then $f(2)=f(-2)$. If this never occurs, then f is called a one-to-one, or injective, function.

functional group, in organic chemistry, group of atoms within a molecule that is responsible for certain properties of the molecule and reactions in which it takes part. Organic compounds are frequently classified according to the functional group

FUNCTIONAL GROUPS

Group	*Formula*	*Compounds*
amino	$\mathrm{(H)(H)N-}$	*amines*
carbonyl	$\mathrm{O{=}C<}$	*ketones*
carboxyl	$\mathrm{(O{=})(HO)C-}$	*carboxylic acids*
chloro	$\mathrm{-Cl}$	*chlorides*
epoxy	$\mathrm{-C-C-}$ (bridged by O)	*epoxides*
ethynylene	$\mathrm{-C{\equiv}C-}$	*alkynes*
fluoro	$\mathrm{-F}$	*fluorides*
formyl	$\mathrm{(H)(O{=})C-}$	*aldehydes*
hydroxyl	$\mathrm{-O-H}$	*alcohols*
nitro	$\mathrm{NO_2-}$	*nitro compounds*
oxy	$\mathrm{-O-}$	*ethers*
vinylene	$\mathrm{>C{=}C<}$	*alkenes*

or groups they contain. For example, methanol, ethanol, and isopropanol are all classified as alcohols since each contains a functional hydroxyl group. The accompanying table shows important functional groups and the classes of compounds in which they occur.

functionalism, in art and architecture, an aesthetic concept developed in the early 20th cent. emphasizing unity of form and purpose. Functionalist architects and artists design utilitarian structures in which the unobscured purpose of individual elements is defined as their beauty. After World War I the BAUHAUS produced a number of influential architects and designers, notably LE CORBUSIER, who worked within this aesthetic.

fundamentalism, religious movement that arose among conservative members of various Protestant denominations early in the 20th cent., with the object of maintaining traditional interpretations of the Bible and of what adherents believe to be the fundamental doctrines of the Christian faith. The movement developed in reaction to the emergence of liberal theology, which attempted to recast Christian teachings in light of the scientific and historic thought of the time. In 1909 a group of those who felt that the orthodox truths of Christianity were in danger organized a protest against the liberals, or modernists; it was circulated in a 12-volume publication, *The Fundamentals* (1910–12). Five points of doctrine were set forth as fundamental. They are the Virgin birth, the physical resurrection of Christ, the infallibility of the Scriptures, the substitutional atonement, and the physical second coming of Christ. Among the denominations most affected by the controversy were the Baptists and the Presbyterians, but separations arose within various denominations, even within individual congregations. Two widely publicized events of the controversy were the case of Harry Emerson Fosdick and the SCOPES TRIAL. Fosdick, although a Baptist, became minister of the First Presbyterian Church, New York City. A leader and spokesman for the liberals, he aroused the enmity of the fundamentalists in the Presbyterian Church when he refused to accept the standards of doctrine required for the continuance of his ministry in that church. He resigned. The struggle to prohibit teaching in the schools of subjects considered a threat to orthodoxy was climaxed in a trial in Dayton, Tenn. There, in 1925, William Jennings BRYAN, a fundamentalist leader, won the state's case against J. T. Scopes, accused of teaching evolution in the public schools. Aggressive fundamentalism was particularly strong in the South and in agricultural districts in the late 1920s. By the 1930s the fundamentalists began to withdraw into independent churches and splinter denominations. Fundamentalism became stereotyped as narrow-minded and rigid. By the 1970s many fundamentalists had rejected that image and had begun a movement to present their position in a more scholarly and balanced way. See Norman Furniss, *The Fundamentalist Controversy, 1918–1931* (1954, repr. 1963); Louis Gasper, *The Fundamentalist Movement* (1963).

Fundamental Orders, in U.S. history, the basic law of Connecticut colony from 1639 to 1662, formally adopted (Jan. 14, 1639) by representatives from the towns of Hartford, Wethersfield, and Windsor, meeting at Hartford. Thomas HOOKER, John HAYNES, and Roger LUDLOW were most influential in framing the document. It was not "the first written constitution that shaped a government," as it has been popularly called; nor did it mark the beginning of a "commonwealth democracy"—another misconception fostered by 19th-century historians straining hard to mark the foundations of American democracy. Its provisions for voting in what is now Connecticut reveal how far from democratic it actually was. However, this deficiency is no reflection on the importance or soundness of the document, for political democracy as we know it today was virtually nonexistent in the 17th cent. except in such rare cases as the Rhode Island colony under Roger Williams. Indeed the Puritans regarded unconfined democracy as an aberration. To them only the most substantial, respectable, and reliable Christians were considered worthy to build up a community essentially religious in design. The Fundamental Orders consisted of a preamble and 11 orders or laws. The preamble bound the inhabitants of the three towns to be governed in all things by the orders that followed, and these were similar to the statute laws elsewhere in New England, differing only in that they were shaped into a brief, clear, compact frame of government (Ludlow, a lawyer, is believed chiefly responsible for the excellence of the final form). The government, or "combination," as Hooker called it, confirmed the system that had functioned in the three towns since 1636 and was very like the Massachusetts model. The main concern of the Fundamental Orders was the welfare of the community; the individual always had to give way if the needs of the community at large so required. The charter of Connecticut in 1662 superseded and was largely based on the Fundamental Orders. See C. M. Andrews, *The Beginnings of Connecticut, 1632-1662* (1934).

fund raising, large-scale soliciting of voluntary contributions, especially in the United States. Fund raising is widely undertaken by charitable organizations, educational institutions, and political groups to acquire sufficient funds to support their activities. Among the methods used are door-to-door appeals, direct mail campaigns, charity dinners and testimonials, charity balls, benefit entertainments, and, more recently, television appeals called telethons. These techniques are generally accompanied by advertising and public relations campaigns. Before World War I private social agencies conducted individual fund raising drives in their own communities, but with the war came the start of federated drives conducted by several agencies for purposes related to the war effort. The community chest movement had its origin in these federated efforts. These joint efforts were highly successful in that they raised more money at a considerably lower cost. The United Way of America is now the national association of all community chests and community welfare councils. In addition to federated drives, the period following World War I also saw the development of professional organizations that raise funds for a percentage of the total. Although the united fund movement spread rapidly, there were still many agencies that chose to conduct independent campaigns, notably the health-promoting organizations. After the American Red Cross reversed its position in the 1950s and allowed local chapters to join United Fund drives, most of the health groups did likewise. See S. M. Cutlip, *Fund Raising in the United States* (1965); H. J. Seymour, *Designs for Fund Raising* (1966).

Fundy, Bay of, large inlet of the Atlantic Ocean, c.170 mi (270 km) long and 30 to 50 mi (50-80 km) wide, between New Brunswick and SW Nova Scotia, Canada. It is famous for its tide and tidal BORE; in its upper arms, Chignecto Bay and the Minas Basin, tides reach 40 to 50 ft (12-15 m) in height and create the reversing falls of the Saint John River. At low tide, wide flats are laid bare, and the long estuaries of the rivers are drained. Many of the surrounding flats have been reclaimed and transformed into fertile farmland since Acadian settlers began to build dikes in the early 17th cent. Annapolis Royal, on the Nova Scotia side of the bay, is the oldest settlement in Canada. St. John, N.B., is the chief port on the bay.

Fundy National Park, 80 sq mi (207 sq km), S N. B., Canada, on the Bay of Fundy near St. John; est. 1947. It has a rugged terrain with a wooded interior and an irregular shoreline that is constantly being eroded by the bay's great tidal range.

funeral customs, rituals surrounding the death of a human being and the subsequent disposition of the corpse. Such rites may serve to mark the passage of a person from life into death, to secure the welfare of the dead, to comfort the living, and to protect the living from the dead. Disposal of the body may be by BURIAL, by conservation (see MUMMY), by CREMATION, by exposure (see PARSIS), or by other methods. Funeral ceremonies have certain common features: for example, the laying out of the corpse; the watching of the dead, of which the WAKE is a standard example; and the period of mourning with the accompanying ceremonies. Preparation of the corpse is usually most elaborate in the case of burial (see COFFIN; EMBALMING), but it is a general practice to wash and clothe the body. Many of the observances connected with death recall the rites of passage associated with other life crises such as birth and the initiation into adulthood. The watching period occasionally includes lamentation by hired mourners. The body is then taken to a resting place, sometimes only temporarily. It may be laid on a scaffold, to await later cremation, or it may be buried until the flesh has rotted away, after which the bones are exhumed for a second burial. Such practices derive from a belief that the soul remains in this world for a brief period before departing for the next. Final disposition of the corpse implies final disposition of the soul, and until this has been achieved the mourners have certain ritual obligations toward the deceased. In the past, the spirit of the deceased was regarded as potentially both harmful and helpful by certain peoples. Attempts to discourage it from returning and disturbing the living were made by placing near the corpse such foods and personal possessions as would help the spirit during its journey and equip it for the other world. Funeral customs have traditionally varied by religion. In Buddhism, death is prepared for through meditation, and death itself is viewed as a rebirth. Once dead, the body is washed, rituals are performed over it, a wake is held, and then it is cremated (the typical method of disposition). Christian custom has changed from an earlier period where a funeral was treated as a joyous occasion to one where it is a time for mourning. In the Roman Catholic Church, the body is prepared for burial, usually by embalming; this is followed by a REQUIEM Mass and burial; additional Masses may be conducted periodically over the next year. Protestant churches usually hold one ceremony, followed by either burial (the usual form) or cremation. Hindu ceremonies are closely tied to a belief in reincarnation. Thus an elaborate set of rituals is conducted, mostly by relatives, to ensure a proper rebirth. Islamic ceremonies include washing and preparing the body, prayers, reading from the Koran, and placing the body on the right side facing Mecca for burial (cremation is not practiced). Early Judaism, with perhaps the simplest of all ceremonies, included a prayer service, washing the body and wrapping it in linen, followed by a funeral banquet. See Effie Bendann, *Death Customs* (1930, repr. 1969); Robert Hertz, *Death and the Right Hand* (tr. 1960); R. W. Habenstein and W. M. Lamers, *The History of American Funeral Directing* (rev. ed. 1962) and *Funeral Customs the World Over* (rev. ed. 1963).

Fünfkirchen: see PÉCS, Hungary.

Fungi (fŭn'jī), a division of morphologically very simple plants lacking chlorophyll. Like algae, fungi lack the vascular tissues (phloem and xylem) that form the true roots, stems, and leaves of higher plants. All fungi are capable of asexual REPRODUCTION by cell division, fragmentation, or SPORE formation. Those that reproduce sexually have an alternation of generations between a GAMETOPHYTE that produces sex cells and a sporophyte that produces spores. There are no flowers or seeds. Unlike algae, fungi lack the chlorophyll necessary for photosynthesis and must therefore live as parasites or saprophytes (see PARASITE). The large number of organisms commonly classed together as fungi may be separated into two groups, the SLIME MOLDs and the true fungi (Eumycophyta). Most Eumycophyta (with the notable exception of the YEASTS) are multicellular. Their bodies usually consist of slender, cottony filaments called hyphae; a mass of hyphae is called a mycelium. The mycelium carries on all the processes necessary for the life of the organism, including, in most species, that of sexual reproduction. The true fungi are divided into four classes: the algalike fungi (Phycomycetes), the sac fungi (Ascomycetes), the basidium fungi (Basidiomycetes), and the imperfect fungi (Deuteromycetes). The algalike fungi include species that cause black bread MOLD, potato BLIGHT, water mold (found on dead leaves and sticks in water), and downy MILDEW. The sac fungi include the yeasts, the powdery mildews, the blue and green molds (e.g., *Penicillium* and others producing ANTIBIOTIC substances), edible types such as the morel and the TRUFFLE, and species that cause such DISEASES OF PLANTS as Dutch elm disease (so named because Dutch scientists discovered its cause), chestnut blight, and apple scab. The basidium fungi include types that cause SMUT and RUST in plants, the gill fungi (most MUSHROOMS), the pore fungi (e.g., the bracket fungi, which grow shelflike on trees, and an edible type called TUCKAHOE), and the PUFFBALL types. The imperfect fungi (which apparently do not reproduce sexually) include species that cause diseases of plants and of animals (e.g., athlete's foot and RINGWORM). Fungi are valuable economically as a source of antibiotics, of vitamins, and of various industrially important chemicals (e.g., alcohols, acetone, and enzymes) as well as for their role in fermentation processes (e.g., the production of alcoholic beverages, vinegar, cheese, and bread dough). They are extremely important in soil renewal, through the decomposition of organic matter (see HUMUS)—a function unwelcome when it results in the rotting of clothing and other goods and the spoilage of foods. See also LICHEN. See C. M. Christensen, *The Molds and Man* (3d. rev. ed., 1965); John Webster, *Introduction to Fungi* (1970).

fungicide (fŭn'jəsīd", fŭng'gə-), any substance used to destroy FUNGI. Sulfur compounds, long used to destroy fungi on plants, have been supplemented by other chemicals, especially by compounds of copper, such as BORDEAUX MIXTURE. Organic salts of iron, zinc, and mercury are also synthesized as fungicides. Fungicides, including formaldehyde, are applied also to seeds and soil for the destruction of vegetative spores. Plant fungicides are usually applied by spraying or dusting. Fungicides used on wood, including creosote, prevent dry rot, and certain compounds are used to make fabrics resistant to mildews. Antibiotic and sulfa drugs are used for human fungus diseases as well as for fungus DISEASES OF PLANTS. Most agricultural fungicides are preventive; those applied after infection are called eradicant, or contact, fungicides. In the United States, fungicides must be registered with the Food and Drug Administration and must conform to specifications; e.g., they must control the disease without injuring the plant and must leave no poisonous residue on edible crops. See PESTICIDE.

fungus infection, infection caused by a pathogenic fungus; also called a mycosis. Many fungal infections affect only the outer layers of skin, and although they are sometimes difficult to cure, they are not considered dangerous. Athlete's foot and RINGWORM are among the common superficial fungal infections. Fungal infections of the mucous membranes are caused primarily by *Candida albicans* (moniliasis). It usually affects the mouth (see THRUSH) and the vaginal and anal regions; it is rarely fatal. Treatment is with gentian violet, potassium permanganate, and ammoniated mercury. The fungi that affect the deeper layers of skin and internal organs are capable of causing serious, often fatal illness. ACTINOMYCOSIS, which is also a disease of cattle, causes deep-seated abscesses of the face and neck. Sporotrichosis is an infection of farmers, horticulturists, and others who come into contact with plants or mud. The disease affects the skin and lymphatic system and, in rare cases, becomes disseminated. Only in the latter form is it ever fatal. Treatment is with iodides. Blastomycosis is caused by a yeastlike fungus that reproduces by budding. Occurring more often in men, it seems to be limited to the central and E United States and Canada. Lesions appear most often on the skin, sometimes spreading to the bones and other organs. In the latter cases it is usually fatal. The South American variety of blastomycosis is almost always fatal. Among the fungi that infect the deeper tissues is *Coccidioides immitis,* which causes COCCIDIOIDOMYCOSIS, a lung infection that is prevalent in the SW United States. Cryptococcosis is another fungal disease that may be localized in the lung or disseminated, especially to the central nervous system. It has a worldwide distribution, affecting men twice as often as women. The causative agent (*Cryptococcus neoformans*) has been isolated in pigeon excretions. The symptoms of pulmonary cryptococcosis are cough, fever, and malaise. Gelatinous lesions are present in the lung, and they become granulomatous in later stages. Lesions may then spread to other tissues, especially those of the central nervous system. Diagnosis is made upon culturing the fungus from cerebrospinal fluid or other tissues. There is no specific treatment, and the disease is usually fatal. Nocardiosis is another pulmonary mycosis that spreads to other tissues, causing degenerative abscesses and lesions. The majority of cases accompany underlying malignancies such as leukemia and lymphoma. Histoplasmosis is a severe infection that shows varied symptoms. In acute cases ulcers of the pharynx and enlargement of the liver and spleen are present. In other forms tubercularlike lesions of the lung occur. In its benign form no symptoms are present, and the disease is usually discovered accidentally by lung X ray. Fungal infections sometimes follow the use of antibiotics since such drugs rid the body of nonpathogenic as well as pathogenic bacteria, thereby providing a free field for fungal invasion.

Funk, Casimir (kăz'ĭmēr fo͝ongk), 1884-1967, American biochemist, b. Poland, Ph.D. Univ. of Bern, 1904. He first came to the United States in 1915 and was naturalized in 1920. Credited with the discovery of vitamins, Funk stirred public interest with his paper (1912) on vitamin-deficiency diseases. He coined the term *vitamine* and later postulated the existence of four such materials (B_1, B_2, C, D), which he stated were necessary for normal health and for the prevention of deficiency diseases. Funk contributed to knowledge of the hormones of the pituitary gland and the sex glands and emphasized the importance of the balance between hormones and vitamins. He is the author of *Vitamines* (tr. 1922). See biography by Benjamin Harrow (1955).

funny bone, highly sensitive area at the back of the elbow where the ulnar nerve passes close to the surface of the skin in a groove between end prominences of the humerus (the upper arm bone) and the ulna (the large forearm bone). A blow to the area compresses the nerve against bone, producing a characteristic tingling in the forearm and the last two fingers.

Funston, Frederick, 1865–1917, U.S. general, b. New Carlisle, Ohio. He was a newspaper reporter and a field agent (1888–95) of the Dept. of Agriculture, exploring Death Valley and the Yukon. Love of adventure led him to enlist in the army of Máximo Gómez y Báez to help win Cuban independence from Spain. As a result of this experience, he was called to head a Kansas regiment in the Spanish-American War. Although his troops took no active part in the war itself, they were sent to the Philippine Islands to help put down the insurrection there. When his army discharge papers were already made out, Funston by a daring feat captured the insurgent leader, Emilio Aguinaldo. Instead of leaving the army he became a brigadier general. In 1914 when U.S. troops entered the city of VERACRUZ, he was given command of the occupying troops, and as major general he commanded later in wars on the Mexican border. He wrote *Memories of Two Wars* (1911).

fur, hairy covering of an animal, especially the skins of animals that have thick, soft, close-growing hair next to the skin itself and coarser protective hair above it. The underhair is frequently called the underfur or fur proper; the outer hairs are the guard hairs; the whole, when dried, is the pelt. The term *fur* is extended to dressed sheep and lamb skins when they are prepared for wearing with the hair retained, and usually to curled pelts such as Persian lamb, karakul, astrakhan, and mouton. Since prehistoric times man has used furs for clothing. Because many animals change the color of their coats from winter to summer, it is possible to have two different types of fur from the same species (e.g., Arctic hare, arctic fox). Some of the more prized furs are sable, marten, and fisher (all of the genus *Martes*), the related mink and ermine (of the genus *Mustela*), and the chinchilla, from South America. The staple fur of the great fur-trading days in North America was the beaver, though the fur seal was and is the object of highly lucrative fur hunts. During the 1960s, however, the clubbing of fur seals on the Pribilof Islands became the focus for considerable concern among the various humane societies of Canada and the United States. The humbler muskrat and otter have also been important. The coats of the ocelot, the wildcat, the common house cat, the marmot, the nutria, the raccoon, the hare, and the rabbit are less expensive because the animals are numerous and easy to trap. While beaver and seal are prized for their durability, such furs as squirrel and skunk are valued for their delicacy of texture. Fox furs have also been much esteemed, and the rare wild silver fox and Pribilof blue fox are sought after, although silver fox is now much bred on fur farms. Many other furs are also now grown extensively by fur farming, which has developed into a major industry in the United States and Canada in the 20th cent. The hunting of wild furs is still an important occupation in wilderness areas, notably in N Canada, Alaska, Mongolia, and Siberia. The finer wild furs come from northerly regions, where because of the climate the animals produce sleeker and better pelts. Good furs have, however, been produced and utilized in some regions of the S United States. In the more populated and temperate regions of the world, however, only small pockets of territory retain enough wild animal life to be good for fur hunting. Because of this condition furs have always been luxury goods and were associated early with royalty and nobility (e.g., sable and ermine). FUR TRADE has gone on since antiquity, but it reached its apogee in the organized exploitation of the wilderness of North America and Asia from the 17th to the early 19th cent. The depletion of fur-bearing animals was strikingly indicated in the fate of the sea OTTER on the Northwest Coast. The threat of similar extinction of the fur seal later led to the international quarrel called the Bering Sea Fur-Seal Controversy (see under BERING SEA). The preparation and sale of fur remains, however, a very considerable business. The dressing and dyeing and the matching and cutting of furs to make fine coats and other garments occupy the labors of a great many people concentrated in the few great fur markets of the world. Dressing and dyeing have produced such unnatural products as blue mink, which has become a market commonplace. Because some fur-bearing species are in danger of extinction, the U.S. government in 1969 enacted the Endangered Species Act, which bans the importation and sale of pelts of such animals as the polar bear, the jaguar, and the tiger. In 1970, New York state passed the Harris Act, which prohibits the importation, transportation, and sale of pelts of animals designated as endangered by the U.S. Dept. of the Interior; and the Mason Act, which extends such protection to cheetahs, vicuñas, red wolves, cougars, alligators, caimans, and crocodiles. (See ENDANGERED SPECIES.) After World War II **synthetic fur,** a deep-pile fabric closely resembling fur, became popular. George W. Borg was among the first to adapt circular knitting machines to make a pile fabric from synthetic fibers. The machines knit a double layer of fabric leaving free ends of yarn that form a pile as deep as 4 in. (10.2 cm). The pile is a loosely twisted rope of fibers representing an intermediate step in the making of yarn. In 1953 an improved form resembling sheared beaver or mouton was introduced. An electrification process like that used for furs gives the fabric sheen and furlike appearance. Dyeing and a treatment to prevent stretching further modify the fabric. Later types use different synthetics and are woven as well as knit; they also use cotton backing. Other synthetic furs imitate Persian lamb, seal, ermine, chinchilla, and mink. During the 1960s synthetic furs became increasingly popular as a result of their relatively low cost and realistic appearance, greater public awareness of endangered species, and the disappearance of certain furs from the market because of restrictive conservation laws.See Arthur Samet, *Pictorial Encyclopedia of Furs* (rev. ed. 1950); P. C. Phillips and J. W. Smurr, *The Fur Trade* (2 vol., 1961; repr. 1967); Elliott Coues, *The Fur Bearing Animals of North America* (1877, repr. 1970); L. R. Hafen, ed., *The Mountain Men and the Fur Trade of the Far West* (10 vol., 1965–72).

furan: see FURFURAL.

furfural (fûr'fərəl) or **furfuraldehyde** (fûr″fəräl'dəhīd) [Lat.,=bran], C_4H_3OCHO, viscous, colorless liquid that has a pleasant aromatic odor; upon exposure to air it turns dark brown or black. It boils at about 160°C. It is commonly used as a solvent; it is soluble in ethanol and ether and somewhat soluble in water. Furfural is the ALDEHYDE of pyromucic acid; it has properties similar to those of benzaldehyde. A derivative of furan, it is prepared commercially by dehydration of pentose sugars obtained from cornstalks and corncobs, husks of oat and peanut, and other waste products. It is used in the manufacture of pesticides, phenolfurfural resins, and tetrahydrofuran. Tetrahydrofuran is used as a commercial solvent and is converted in starting materials for the preparation of NYLON.

furfural furan tetrahydrofuran

furnace, enclosed space for the burning of fuel. There are many kinds of furnaces, the type depending upon the fuel and the use to which the heat produced within it is put. Most familiar are the furnaces used in the heating of buildings. In the hot-air furnace, fuel is burned within an inner wall and air, led into a space between the inner and the outer wall, is heated and is led away to the various rooms of the building. Hot-water furnaces, by which water is heated to be led through pipes to radiators, and furnaces that turn water to steam for heating purposes are common. The KILN is a kind of furnace. In metallurgy, the separation of many metals from their ores is accomplished by the use of various kinds of furnaces, e.g., the BLAST FURNACE and the REVERBERATORY FURNACE. The structure of these furnaces makes possible a good control of temperature. In the production of STEEL, however, the open-hearth furnace and the Bessemer converter are used in the treatment of cast iron. The electric furnace is extensively employed in the production of high-grade steels for use in making steel alloys and for the manufacture of high-speed tools. Heat may be generated in such a furnace by using an electric arc or by sending an electric current through resistive elements in the furnace. If the material to be processed is electrically conductive, heat may also be generated by creating an electric current in the material by induction or by inserting into it electrodes to which a voltage is applied. In the preparation of phosphorus from calcium phosphate, this compound of phosphorus is mixed with sand and coke and treated in an electric furnace. An electric current is sent from one electrode to another through the mass to create the extremely high temperature needed to bring about the chemical action that results in the production of free phosphorus. Graphite is produced from coal or coke in an electric furnace, and the extremely hard substance carborundum is made there by the combination of carbon and silicon (from sand). Nitrogen is obtained from the air (in the Birkeland-Eyde process) by passing a stream of air through an arc. The nitrogen and oxygen of the air combine to form nitric oxide.

Furnas Dam, c.390 ft (120 m) high, at the junction of the Rio Grande and Sapucaí rivers, SE Brazil, in Minas Gerais state; completed 1962. It has a 620-sq mi (1,606-sq km) reservoir. It includes large hydroelectric facilities and is the center of an extensive regional electrical grid serving the industrial centers of São Paulo, Rio de Janeiro, and Belo Horizonte.

Furneaux Group (fûr'nō), about 25 islands, c.900 sq mi (2,330 sq km), Tasmania, SE Australia, in Bass Strait between Tasmania and the Australian mainland. The largest is Flinders Island, and the group forms Flinders municipality (1971 pop. 967). The islands were discovered in 1773 by the British navigator Tobias Furneaux.

Furies or **Erinyes** (ĕrĭn'ē-ēz), in Greek religion, goddesses of vengeance. Born from the blood of Uranus, their function was to punish wrongs committed against kindred blood regardless of the motive. They were usually represented as three ugly crones with bat's wings, dog's heads, and snakes for hair. Their names were Megaera [envious], Tisiphone [blood avenger], and Alecto [unceasing, i.e., in pursuit]. When called upon to act, they hounded their victim until he died in torment. In the myth of Orestes they appear as Clytemnestra's agents of revenge. After Athena absolves Orestes of guilt in the murder of his mother, the Furies accept her decision and become known as the Eumenides [kindly ones].

Furka (fŏŏr'kä), road, S central Switzerland, linking Uri and Valais cantons. Built (1864–66) chiefly for military reasons, it crosses Furka Pass, 7,992 ft (2,436 m) high, in the Alps. A rail line goes through Furka Tunnel (1 mi/1.6 km long), under the pass, to Brig.

furlong: see ENGLISH UNITS OF MEASUREMENT.

Furman University, at Greenville, S.C.; Southern Baptist; coeducational; opened at Edgefield in 1827 as Furman Academy and Theological Institution. In 1851 it moved to Greenville and was rechartered under the present name. In 1933 the university merged with Greenville's Woman's College.

Furness, Horace Howard (fûr'nĭs), 1833–1912, American Shakespearean scholar, b. Philadelphia; son of William Henry Furness. He was the editor of the New Variorum edition of Shakespeare (plays published separately, 1871–1913). His son, **Horace Howard Furness, Jr.,** 1865–1930, succeeded him as editor and donated his father's Shakespearean library to the Univ. of Pennsylvania.

Furness, peninsula, 15 mi (24 km) long and 4 mi (6.4 km) wide, Cumbria, NW England, between the estuary of the River Duddon and Morecambe Bay. The term is also applied to areas N of Morecambe Bay that are part of the Lake District. In the southwest are iron mines, now virtually exhausted, and great steelworks which center at Barrow-in-Furness. Furness Abbey (now in ruins), near Barrow, was a wealthy institution founded by the Benedictines in 1127.

furniture, properly such movables as chairs, tables, and beds; it is extended to include draperies, rugs, mirrors, lamps, and other furnishings. In its gradual evolution from periods of earliest civilization, the history of furniture parallels the progress of culture. Furniture has been made in a great variety of materials and decorated by many methods, the most usual being INLAYING, painting or gilding, WOOD CARVING, veneering, and MARQUETRY. Western furniture has drawn motifs of ornament from four main sources: Egyptian, Asiatic (Persian and Chinese), Greek, and Gothic. Probably the first pieces to be in demand were the chest, the stool (prototype of the chair), the table, and the bed. From remote times Oriental furniture has exhibited carving and inlay on ebony and teak. Egyptian pieces 6,000 years old display an advanced form of woodworking, structure, and decoration and are characterized by inlays of gold and ivory and by carved supports representing animal forms. The Greeks favored the low couch, the tripod, and a chair with graceful, curved outlines. The Romans adopted Greek and Etruscan forms and during the imperial period developed many ornately decorated variations. The heavily carved Gothic furniture reflected styles in architecture. Under Italian influence, the Renaissance brought richly decorated pieces designed specifically for domestic interiors. Peasant pieces were generally solid, painted or rudely carved, and slow to change in style. Provincial pieces followed in simplified form and in native woods; the period styles developed in the centers of culture. France became a leading influence with the LOUIS PERIOD STYLES, DIRECTOIRE STYLE, and EMPIRE STYLE. English period styles include Elizabethan, in oak, with huge, bulbous supports; Jacobean, lighter and more comfortable, with spiral supports; William and Mary, introducing curved outlines, the trumpet leg, and the inverted-cup foot; Queen Anne, in walnut, characterized by cyma curves (double curves formed by joining a convex and a concave line), the rounded cabriole leg, and the broken pediment; Georgian, with its fine cabinetwork in a number of styles set by such designers as CHIPPENDALE, HEPPLEWHITE, Robert ADAM and his brother James, and SHERATON. Early American furniture adapted current English styles in utilitarian form and in native woods—pine, maple, cherry. Later PHYFE, SAVERY, John GODDARD, and other expert cabinetmakers added walnut and mahogany. The late 19th cent. brought mass production of machine-made furniture and saw an expression of flamboyant taste in golden oak of rococo design; this was followed by a reaction in the United States to the Mission style of rectilinear construction in weathered oak. Around the turn of the 20th cent., the organic forms of the art nouveau style achieved popularity. In the 1910s and '20s many attempts were made to develop a new and, at the same time, functional design. The efforts of the Dutch group *de Stijl* are notable, especially those of Gerrit RIETVELD. Modern materials were effectively employed by Miës van der Rohe in his famous Barcelona chair made of unadorned steel and leather, and contributions were also made by Saarinen and Bertoia. Other popular materials are welded metal and plastic. The use of fine woods in starkly simple design is the keynote of the elegant work that has been produced in the Scandinavian countries and won worldwide popularity since World War II. See Joseph Aronson, *The Encyclopedia of Furniture* (3d ed. 1965); J. Gloag, *A Social History of Furniture Design* (1966); O. Wanscher, *The Art of Furniture: 5000 years of Furniture and Interiors* (1967); K. McClinton, *An Outline of Period Furniture* (1972).

fur seal, fin-footed marine mammal of the eared seal family (Otaridae), highly valued for its fur. Like its close relative the SEA LION, the fur seal is distinguished from a true SEAL by its external ears and its ability to turn its hind flippers forward for walking on land. The northern, or Alaskan, fur seal, *Callorhinus ursinus,* has an outer coat of long coarse hair known as guard hair and an inner coat of thick soft fur; it is the inner coat that is valued in the fur trade. Males are dark brown and females and young are grayish. The male is about 6 ft (1.8 m) long and weighs about 600 lb (270 kg), while the much smaller female is up to 4 ft (1.2 m) long and weighs only about 100 lb (45 kg). Herds of northern fur seals, mostly females and young, winter in open ocean off the California coast, migrating in spring to their breeding grounds on the Pribilof Islands in the Bering Sea. Adult males winter along the coast of S Alaska and arrive at the islands several weeks ahead of the females. During the breeding season the stronger of the males control individual territories on the shore and have harems averaging 50 females; young and weak males remain unmated. Breeding occurs after the birth of the young conceived the previous summer; each female bears a single pup after a gestation period of almost a year. The pups are nursed for about four months before the start of the 3,000-mi (4,828-km) migration southward. Fur seals feed on squid and fish. By the beginning of the 20th cent. the northern fur seal population was reduced to about 100,000 as the result of wanton slaughter, but an international treaty signed in 1911 limited hunting to a fixed number of nonbreeding males each year and the population has since increased to over 3 million. Southern fur seals, species of the genus *Arctocephalus,* are similar to the northern fur seal in size and appearance, but their fur is not considered desirable. Nonetheless, they have been hunted almost to extinction. They were formerly found throughout the Southern Hemisphere and as far north in the Pacific as Guadalupe Island off Baja California. Most southern fur seal populations do not migrate, but remain near their breeding grounds all year. Fur seals are classified in the phylum CHORDATA, subphylum Vertebrata, class Mammalia, order Carnivora, suborder Pinnipedia, family Otariidae. See also Bering Sea Fur Seal Controversy, under BERING SEA.

Fürst, Julius (yo͞o'lyo͞os fürst), 1805–73, German Orientalist. Fürst was one of the most distinguished scholars of Semitic languages and literature of his time. During his years as chairman of the department of Oriental languages and literature at Leipzig Univ. (1864–73), he wrote several major works on literary history and linguistics.

Fürth (fürt), city (1970 pop. 94,774), Bavaria, S West Germany, at the confluence of the Rednitz and Pegnitz rivers. It is an industrial suburb of Nuremberg; manufactures include toys and glass. Reputedly founded by Charlemagne in the late 8th cent., Fürth rose to importance when the Jews who were denied entrance to Nuremberg settled there (14th cent.). During the Thirty Years War (1618–48), Gutavus II (Gustavus Adolphus) of Sweden made the city his headquarters and fought an indecisive battle there with Wallenstein in 1632. Fürth passed to Bavaria in 1806 and became part of Middle Franconia. It was a terminal of the first German railroad (Nuremberg-Fürth, opened 1835).

fur trade, in American history. Trade in animal skins and pelts had gone on since antiquity, but reached its heights in the wilderness of North America from the 17th to the early 19th cent. The demand for furs was an important factor in the commercial life of all the British and Dutch seaboard colonies, as well as of S Louisiana, Texas, and the far Southwest. But its effect in opening the wilderness was even more striking in Canada, where the rivers and lakes offered avenues to the heart of the continent. The speed with which fur traders traveled halfway across the continent was remarkable. The Great Lakes region was extensively exploited by men buying furs from the Indians before the end of the 17th cent. The effect on the Indians who received the white man's goods (including firearms and liquor, as well as the white man's diseases) in exchange for the furs was cataclysmic; native cultures were overturned. This process occurred also among the natives of far NE Siberia as Russian traders reached that remote region in the 18th cent. The *promyshlenniki* [fur traders] pushed even farther across the icy seas and prepared the way for the long Russian occupation of ALASKA. The greatest of the British companies, the HUDSON'S BAY COMPANY, contended after 1670 with the French traders in Canada, and after Canada became British in 1763, with French and Scottish traders based in Montreal. The NORTH WEST COMPANY was created, and rivalry was bitter until the two companies were combined in 1821, taking the name Hudson's Bay Company. The largest of the companies in the United States was John Jacob Astor's AMERICAN FUR COMPANY, which also came into conflict with the North West Company, notably in 1812–13 at the Pacific coast establishment of ASTORIA. By that time the Canadian traders had set up posts across the continent (first crossed in the north by Sir Alexander MACKENZIE) and had approached the Russian posts in Alaska. A U.S. law in 1816 excluded British traders from the United States, and many British fur traders who had helped to build the Old Northwest were compelled to become U.S. citizens and were reluctant in complying. The trade in the United States was now pushing west ahead of the advancing line of settlement, and the rich fur territories of the upper Missouri River, which had been tapped earlier by such traders as Manuel Lisa and Andrew Henry, attracted attention. After the first expedition of William Henry ASHLEY in 1823, the now celebrated MOUNTAIN MEN (chief among them Kit CARSON, Jedediah SMITH, James BRIDGER, and Thomas FITZPATRICK), who were trappers more than they were traders, made the Rocky Mt. West known. The popularity of the beaver hat had helped to create an enormous demand for beaver, which was the staple article of the American fur trade, but fashion changed, and the fur trade declined accordingly. An equally important factor in the decline of fur trade was the advance of settlement, for the trade in wild furs could not flourish on a large scale near farms. Finally, there was the depletion of the stock of beaver and other fur-bearing animals, hunted relentlessly for centuries; the square miles of beaver country were shrinking to acres. The era of the fur traders ended in the 1840s in the United States and S Canada, but only after the traders had contributed untold amounts of geographical knowledge and lore learned from the Indians to the development of both nations. There are innumerable studies of the history of the fur trade, many of them monographs on particular areas or particular traders. For a detailed bibliography see P. C. Phillips, *The Fur Trade* (2 vol., 1961). Other general works include H. M. Chittenden, *The American Fur Trade in the Far West* (1902, repr. 1954); K. Kelsey, *Young Men So Daring: Fur Traders Who Carried the Frontier West* (1956); M. Sandoz, *The Beaver Men* (1964); L. O. Saum, *The Fur Trader and the Indian* (1965); J. E. Sunder, *The Fur Trade on the Upper Missouri 1840–1865* (1965); E. E. Rich, *The Fur Trade and the Northwest to 1857* (1967); A. MacKenzie, *Exploring the Northwest Territory,* (ed. by T. H. McDonald, 1967); G. Simpson, *Fur Trade and Empire: George Simpson's Journal* (rev. ed. 1968).

Furtwängler, Adolf (ä'dôlf fo͝ort'vĕng-lər), 1853–1907, German archaeologist, authority on ancient vases and gems. He made important excavations at Olympia, Aegina, and Orchomenus and wrote the authoritative *Meisterwerke der griechischen Plastik* [masterpieces of Greek sculpture] (1893), of which a smaller edition was later translated into English; *Die antiken Gemmen* [antique gems] (1900); and, with Karl Reichhold, *Griechische Vasenmalerei* [Greek vase paintings] (1900–1904).

Furtwängler, Wilhelm (vĭl'hĕlm), 1886–1954, German conductor; son of Adolf Furtwängler. He began his career conducting opera in Lübeck (1911–15) and Mannheim (1915–19). In 1922 he succeeded Arthur Nikisch as conductor of the Berlin Philharmonic Orchestra. Furtwängler was a regular conductor of the New York Philharmonic from 1925 to 1927 and its permanent conductor in the season of 1937–38. In 1934 he resigned his important posts in Germany when the performance of Hindemith's music was prohibited. In 1935 he returned to conduct the Berlin orchestra. After World War II he was absolved of the charge of having collaborated with the Nazis and retained the position of conductor of the Berlin Philharmonic until his death. He was renowned for his interpretations of the music of Beethoven, Brahms, Bruckner, Wagner, and Schumann. See biography by Curt Riess (tr. 1955).

Furukawa (fo͞oro͞o'käwä), city (1970 pop. 52,515), Miyagi prefecture, NE Honshu, Japan, on the Eai River. It is an agricultural market that specializes in horse trading and in the processing and distribution of rice.

Fury and Hecla Strait (hĕk'lə), narrow channel, c.100 mi (160 km) long and from 10 to 15 mi (16–24 km) wide, N Canada, between Baffin Island and Melville Peninsula. It connects Foxe Basin with the Gulf of Boothia. It was discovered (1822) by Sir William E. Parry and named for his ships. The strait is nearly always ice-blocked.

furze, any plant of the genus *Ulex* of the family Leguminosae (PULSE family), low, densely branched shrubs with spiny leaves (when present) and fragrant yellow blossoms. *U. europaeus,* the common furze (also called gorse and whin), thrives in sandy soil; naturalized from Europe, it is used as a hedge plant, a sand binder, and sometimes as fodder. Furze is classified in the division MAGNOLIOPHYTA, class Magnoliopsida, order Rosales, family Leguminosae.

Fusan: see PUSAN, Korea.

fuse, electric, safety device used to protect an electric CIRCUIT against an excessive current. A fuse consists essentially of a strip of low-melting alloy enclosed in a suitable housing. It is connected in series with the circuit it is to protect. Because of its electrical resistance, the alloy strip in the fuse is heated by an electric current; if the current exceeds the safe value for which the fuse was designed, the strip melts, opening the circuit and stopping the current. The fuse housing is designed to resist the pressure generated if the overcurrent vaporizes the alloy strip, provided the voltage across the fuse does not exceed its rating. Some fuses, called slow-blow fuses, are designed to carry a small overload for a short time without opening the circuit, while others are designed to open very rapidly if the rated current is exceeded. The choice of one type or the other depends on the ruggedness of the equipment to be protected and whether large pulses of current often occur in the circuit; a slow-blow fuse is usually used to protect motors, and a fast-blow fuse to protect electronic equipment. A circuit can also be protected by a CIRCUIT BREAKER.

fuselage: see AIRPLANE.

Fuseli, Henry (fyo͞o'zĭlē), 1741–1825, Anglo-Swiss painter and draftsman, b. Zurich. He was known also as Johann Heinrich Fuessli or Füssli. He took holy orders but never practiced the priesthood. Fuseli went (c.1763) to England and studied in London, where Joshua Reynolds befriended him. He spent a few years in Italy, where he made the studies for his famous series of nine paintings for Boydell's Shakespeare Gallery. Returning to England, he exhibited a number of works of a grotesque and visionary type, including the celebrated *Nightmare* (1782). His own Milton Gallery housed a series of his paintings illustrating the poet's works. His drawings, of which he left over 800, further reveal his romantic fascination with the terrifying and weird. Fuseli admired and encouraged William Blake. Some of his lectures to the Royal Academy have been published. See studies by Frederick Antal (1956), P. A. Tomory (1972), and Gert Schiff (2 vol., 1974).

fusel oil (fyo͞o'zəl), oily, colorless liquid with a disagreeable odor and taste. It is a mixture of alcohols (largely amyl alcohols) and fatty acids, formed during the alcoholic fermentation of organic materials. After imperfect distillation of these fermentation products it becomes an impurity in the distilled liquor. Fusel oil is used as a solvent in the manufacture of certain lacquers and enamels (it dissolves nitrocellulose). It has a detrimental effect on the human system.

Fu-shun or **Fushun** (both: fo͞o-sho͞on), city (1970 est. pop. 1,700,000), NE Liaoning prov., China, in a highly industrialized area. It is connected by rail with nearby Shen-yang (Mukden) and with Lü-ta. Fu-shun has one of the largest opencut coal mines in the world (more than 4 mi/6.4 km long and almost 1 mi/1.6 km wide); in operation since about the 12th cent., it is now highly mechanized. Oil shale deposits, also mined there, are processed in the Fu-shun oil refineries, one of which is the largest in the country. Fu-shun also has a major aluminum reduction plant and factories making automobiles, machinery, chemicals, and synthetic fibers. The city was developed by Russia until 1905 and by Japan until 1945.

fusion, in physics. **1** The change of a substance from the liquid to the solid state, also known as FREEZING. The heat given up by a unit mass of a substance during fusion is called the LATENT HEAT of fusion. **2** The combining of two light atomic nuclei to form a single heavier NUCLEUS, with the release of energy (see NUCLEAR ENERGY; HYDROGEN BOMB).

Füssli, Johann Heinrich: see FUSELI, HENRY.

Fust or **Faust, Johann,** d. 1466?, printer at Mainz. Johann GUTENBERG borrowed substantial sums of money from Fust, a goldsmith, lawyer, and money lender. When Gutenberg was unable to repay these sums, his press and types became Fust's property. In partnership with his brother-in-law, Peter Schöffer, Fust carried on the work begun by Gutenberg. Fust and Schöffer were the first to print in colors (1457), using red and blue inks as well as black. They printed the first dated book, a great psalter (1457). Their Greek type was first used in 1465. After the death of Fust, Schöffer continued the work of the press.

Fustel de Coulanges, Numa Denis (nümä' dənē' füstĕl' də ko͞oläNzh'), 1830–89, French historian. His masterly study, *La Cité antique* (1864, tr. *The Ancient City*, 1874), stressed the influence of primitive religion on the development of Greek and Roman institutions. Losing (1870) his professorship in antiquities at the Univ. of Strasbourg after Strasbourg became German, he turned to medieval history. The result was a work of profound and original scholarship, *Histoire des institutions politiques de l'ancienne France* (6 vol., 1888–92; rev. ed. by Camille Jullian, 6 vol., 1905–14). In it Fustel, attacking belief in the Germanic origin of feudalism and the manorial system, traced these institutions to Roman influences. His theories were widely attacked, but they opened the way for new interpretations of early medieval history. See Jane Herrick, *The Historical Thought of Fustel de Coulanges* (1954).

fustic: see MULBERRY.

Futa Jallon: see FOUTA DJALLON, region, Guinea.

futurism, Italian school of painting, sculpture, and literature that flourished from 1909, when Filippo Tommaso Marinetti's first manifesto of futurism appeared, until the end of World War I. Carlo Carrà, Gino Severini, and Giacomo Balla were the leading painters and Umberto Boccioni the chief sculptor of the group. The architect Antonio Sant' Elia also belonged to this school. The futurists strove to portray the dynamic character of 20th-century life; their works glorified danger, war, and the machine age, attacked academies, museums, and other establishment bastions, and, in theory at least, favored the growth of fascism. The group had a major Paris exhibition in 1912 that showed the relationship of their work to CUBISM. Their approach to the rendering of movement by simultaneously representing several aspects of forms in motion influenced many painters, including Duchamp and Delaunay. Futurist principles and techniques strongly influenced Russian CONSTRUCTIVISM. See studies by M. W. Martin (1968), Jane Rye (1972), and Umbro Apollino (1973).

Fyn (fün), Ger. *Fünen,* island (1971 pop. 433,765), c.1,340 sq mi (3,471 sq km), Fyn co., S central Denmark. Odense, Svendborg, Nyborg, Assens, and Middelfart are the chief cities of Fyn, which is the second largest of the Danish islands. It is largely a fertile lowland; dairy goods, sugar beets, and cereals are the chief products. There are many summer residences along the island's coast.

Fyne, Loch (lŏkh fīn), arm of the Firth of Clyde, Argyllshire, W Scotland. It extends 40 mi (64 km) N and NE from the Sound of Bute. The loch has long been famous for its herring fisheries. The Crinan Canal (9 mi/14.5 km long) connects Loch Fyne with the Sound of Jura.

Fyt, Jan (yän fīt), 1611–61, Flemish animal and still-life painter and etcher. A pupil of Frans Snyders, Fyt spent 10 years in France and Italy. Returning to Antwerp in 1641, he enjoyed considerable success. He is admired for his realistic textural and lighting effects. The Metropolitan Museum has four of his studies of spoils of the hunt.

Fyzabad, India: see FAIZABAD.

G

G, 7th letter of the ALPHABET. It is a usual symbol for a voiced velar stop, as in the English *go.* It was originally a differentiated form of Greek gamma, which has *C* as its formal Roman correspondent. In MUSICAL NOTATION G represents a note on the scale. In physics, G stands for the gravitational constant (see GRAVITATION).

Ga (gä), black African ethnic group, SE Ghana. The Ga speak a Kwa language and together with the closely related Adangme number about 700,000. Inheritance and succession to public office are determined mostly by patrilineal descent. According to their oral traditions, the Ga came from the region of Lake Chad and migrated into present-day Ghana beginning in the 16th cent. They established Great Accra (near modern Accra) as their capital. The Ga were on friendly terms with Danish traders in the mid-17th cent. Between 1677 and 1681 they were conquered by the Akwamu state, and in 1742 the ASHANTI gained control over them. In 1874 the Ga were incorporated into the British Gold Coast colony.

Ga, chemical symbol of the element GALLIUM.

Gaal (gā'ăl), leader of the Shechemites in their uprising against Abimelech. Judges 9.26–57.

Gaash (gā'ăsh), hill in Mt. Ephraim. There Joshua was buried. Joshua 24.30; Judges 2.9; 2 Sam. 23.30; 1 Chron. 11.32.

Gaba (gā'bə), variant of GEBA.

Gabbai (găb'āī), Benjamite. Neh. 11.8.

Gabbatha (găb'əthə), yard or porch where Pilate sat in judgment on Jesus. John 19.13.

gabbro: see BASALT.

Gabelentz, Hans Conon von der (häns kō'nôn fən dĕr gä'bəlĕnts), 1807–74, German linguist. Gabelentz showed the broad relationships among Pacific languages. He spoke 30 languages well and knew some 50 others. His son, Hans Georg Canon von der Gabelentz (1840–93) was an authority on East Asiatic languages.

Gabelsberger, Franz Xaver (fränts ksävĕr' gä'bəlsbĕr"gər), 1780–1849, German stenographer. He invented a popular German shorthand system.

Gabès: see QABIS, Tunisia.

Gabii (gā'bēī), ancient town of Latium, 12 mi (19.3 km) E of Rome on the road to Praeneste (modern Palestrina). According to legend, Romulus was reared there. One of the most important of the Latin cities, it supposedly resisted a siege by Lucius Tarquinius Superbus but was early overshadowed by Rome and had lost all importance even in the days of the republic. The modern village of Castiglione is on the site.

Gabin, Jean (zhäN gābăN'), 1904–, French film actor, b. Paris; his original name was Alexis Moncourge. Gabin's work as a cabaret entertainer led to a career in films. He usually plays the tough yet sympathetic anti-hero. His films include *Pépé Le Moko* (1936), *La grande illusion* (1937), *Quai des brumes* (1938), *Le plaisir* (1951), *Un singe en hiver* (1962), and *Fin de journée* (1969).

Gabirol: see IBN GABIROL, SOLOMON BEN JUDAH.

Gable, Clark, 1901–1960, American film actor, b. Cadiz, Ohio. He began his career in films in 1930 and soon after became a star. He won an Academy Award in 1934 for his brilliant comic performance in *It Happened One Night.* His best-remembered role was that of Rhett Butler in *Gone with the Wind* (1940). For many years a leading box-office attraction, Gable was known to Hollywood as "the King" and was considered a symbol of the rugged and raffish American male. He made more than 65 films, the last of which was *The Misfits* (1960).

Gablonz: see JABLONEC NAD NISOU, Czechoslovakia.

Gabo, Naum (noum gä'bō), 1890–, Russian sculptor, architect, theorist, and teacher, brother of Antoine PEVSNER. Gabo lived in Munich and Norway until the end of the revolution, when he returned to Russia. With Pevsner he wrote the *Realist Manifesto* (1920), which proposed that new concepts of time and space be incorporated into works of art and that dynamic form replace static mass. His sculptural experiments with CONSTRUCTIVISM, a movement he helped to found, were often transparent, geometrical abstractions composed of plastics and other materials. Gabo's art conflicted with Soviet art directives. In 1922 he left Moscow for Berlin where he taught at the BAUHAUS, later moving to England and then emigrating to the United States. In 1957 he executed a huge public monument in Rotterdam. See his *Gabo* (1957) and *Of Divers Arts* (1962); study by Ruth Olson and Abraham Chanin (1948).

Gabon (gäbôN'), republic (1970 pop. 950,000), 103,346 sq mi (267,667 sq km) W central Africa, bordering on the Atlantic Ocean in the west, on Equatorial Guinea and Cameroon in the north, and on the Republic of the Congo in the east and south. LIBREVILLE (the capital) and PORT-GENTIL, both seaports, are the country's only large cities. Much of Gabon, which is situated astride the equator, is drained by the Ogooué River (and its tributaries, the Ngounie and the Ivindo), which flows into the Atlantic through a long and broad estuary. The rest of the coastline comprises a narrow low-lying strip, which, south of the Ogooué's mouth, includes a series of lagoons. The interior of the country is made up of mountain ranges and high-lying plateaus. To the N of the Ogooué are the Cristal Mts. and to the south is the Chaillu Massif, which includes Mt. Ibounzi (5,165 ft/1,574 m), Gabon's highest point. In the northeast is the Woleu-Ntem Plateau, which reaches c.2,500 ft (760 m), and in the southeast is the hot and arid Bateke Plateau (c.2,700 ft/820 m). The inhabitants of Gabon are black Africans, who belong to several ethnic groups including the Fang (who make up about one third of the population) in the north, the Omiéné along the coast, the Batoka in the northeast, and the Eshira in the southwest. French is the country's official language. Most of the people follow traditional beliefs, but Christianity has gained numerous adherents in the cities. The majority of the Gabonese workers are engaged in subsistence farming, cassava, plantains, taro, and rice being the chief crops. However, food must be imported to meet the country's needs. Cacao, coffee, and palm products are produced for export. Few animals are raised, partly because of the prevalence of the tsetse fly. Forestry and mining, both largely controlled by European-owned firms, form the backbone of the modern sector of the country's economy. The most important forest products are okoume (a softwood used in making plywood), mahogany, and ebony. The principal minerals extracted are petroleum (found near Port-Gentil), manganese and uranium ores, and gold. There are large deposits of iron ore in the east near Makambo; their exploitation awaits the construction of a railroad to the coast (planned for the late 1970s) since the country's transportation network is very limited. The chief manufactures of Gabon's small industrial sector include processed timber, refined petroleum, and agricultural goods. The country engages in a small foreign trade, but the annual revenue from exports is usually considerably higher than the cost of imports. The main exports are crude petroleum, forest products, manganese and uranium ores, and cacao; the principal imports are machinery, transport equipment, foodstuffs, and textiles. The leading trade partners are France, the United States, and West Germany.

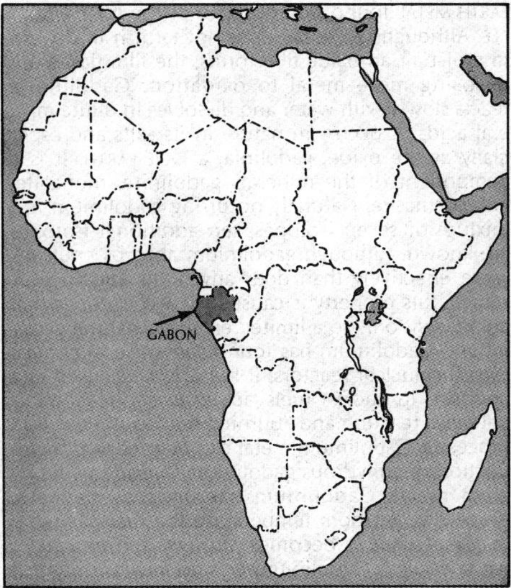

History. Discoveries by archaeologists indicate that present-day Gabon was inhabited in the late Paleolithic period and that it was later the site of Neolithic cultures. By the 16th cent. A.D. the Omiéné were living along the coast, and in the 18th cent. the Fang entered the region from the north. From the 16th to the 18th cent. Gabon was part of the decentralized Loango empire, which included most of the area between the Ogooué and Congo (Zaïre) rivers. In the 1470s Portuguese navigators discovered the Ogooué estuary, and shortly thereafter they began to trade with coastal merchants for black African slaves who had been acquired in the interior. The Portuguese were followed by Dutch, English, and French traders, and by the late 18th cent. the French had gained a dominant position. Although the slave trade was abolished (1815) by the Congress of Vienna, slaves continued to be exported from the Gabon coast until the 1880s. However, French naval patrols succeeded in reducing the number exported annually. In 1839 and 1841, Edouard Bouet-Willaumez, a French naval officer, signed treaties with the African rulers of the Ogooué estuary. Christian missions were established there between 1842 and 1844, and additional treaties were signed with nearby African leaders between 1842 and 1862. In 1849, Libreville was founded by the French as a settlement for freed slaves. Paul B. Du Chaillu (in the 1850s) and A. M. A. Aymes (in the 1860s) explored the lower Ogooué. In the late 1870s, Pierre Savorgnan de Brazza reached the source of the river, and in the 1880s he founded Franceville (near the present-day border with the Republic of the Congo). In 1885 the Conference of Berlin recognized French rights to the region N of the Congo River that included Gabon. In 1886 the French assigned a governor to Gabon, which from 1889 to 1904 was included in the French Congo. From 1910 to 1957, Gabon was a part of FRENCH EQUATORIAL AFRICA. The Fang and some other African peoples resisted the imposition of French rule until 1911. In 1913 Albert Schweitzer established a hospital at Lambaréné on the Ogooué. During World War II, Free French forces gained control (1940) of Gabon from the Vichy government. In 1946, Gabon became an overseas territory of France, with its own parliament and representation in the French National Assembly. In 1958 the country became internally self-governing within the FRENCH COMMUNITY, and on Aug. 17, 1960, it became an independent republic. Leon Mba, a Fang, was the first president of Gabon. In Feb., 1964, Mba was ousted by a military coup led by Jean-Hilaire Aubame, but he was restored to power within a day with the help of French troops. Mba died in 1967 and was succeeded by Omar Bongo, who established (1968) the *Parti démocratique* gabonais (Gabonese Democratic party) as the country's sole political organization. Bongo was elected to a new seven-year term as president in 1973. Gabon was one of the few countries to recognize the Republic of Biafra (1967–70), which seceded from the Federation of Nigeria, and supplies were flown from Gabon to Biafra. During its first decade of independence, Gabon retained close political and economic ties with France. However, in the early 1970s the government sought increased influence in the foreign (mainly French) companies active in Gabon, and it generally tried to loosen its ties with France and to replace French civil servants with Gabonese. See Herbert Deschamps, *Traditions orales et archives du Gabon* (1962); Brian Weinstein, *Gabon: Nation-Building on the Ogooué* (1967); Jacqueline Bouquerel, *Le Gabon* (1970).

Gaborone (gäbərō'nē), city (1971 pop. 18,436), capital of Botswana. Primarily an administrative center, it is located on the country's major railroad line and has a small international airport. The city was founded c.1890 by Gaborone Matlapin, a black African chief. In 1965 it replaced MAFEKING, South Africa, as capital of the Bechuanaland Protectorate; it remained the capital when Bechuanaland became independent as Botswana in 1966. Gaborone is the seat of the Botswana Training Center, which offers instruction in clerical, administrative, and technical skills.

Gabriel, archangel, the divine herald. In the Bible he appears to Daniel (twice), to Zacharias, and to the Virgin Mary in the Annunciation (Dan. 8.16; 9.21; Luke 1.19,26,27). Christian tradition makes Gabriel the archangel trumpeter of the Last Judgment (1 Thes. 4.16). In Islam, Gabriel revealed the Koran to Muhammad, becoming the angel of truth. In art and literature Gabriel is mainly treated as the angel of the Annunciation. In the Annunciation he often carries a lily, properly the symbol of the Virgin. He is often represented on churches with trumpet raised and facing east, ready to proclaim the second coming of Christ. Feast: Sept. 29 (jointly with other archangels).

Gabriel, Jacques Ange (zhäk äNzh gäbrēĕl'), 1698–1782, French architect of the rococo. Descendant of a long line of architects, he ranks as one of the most distinguished French architects of his century. His work is characterized by classical repose, purity of form, and restraint. In 1742 he succeeded his father, Jacques Gabriel (1667–1742), as first architect to the king. For 30 years he worked for Louis XV at Versailles, Compiègne, and other royal residences. In 1753 he designed Place Louis XV (now Place de la Concorde) in Paris. He designed also the twin palaces north of the square and (1748) the theater of the palace of Versailles. In 1751, Gabriel commenced the vast École militaire in Paris and in 1755 began work on the unfinished parts of the Louvre, which he later had to suspend. In 1768 he finished the Petit Trianon in the gardens of Versailles.

Gabrieli, Andrea (ändrē'ä gäbrēä'lē), c.1510–1586, Italian organist and composer; pupil of Adrian Willaert. In 1536 he was a chorister at St. Mark's Cathedral, Venice, where, in 1566, he became organist at the second organ. He composed madrigals, motets, masses, and *ricercari* and canzones for organ. He was important in the development of multiple-choir technique, and he was the teacher of Hans Leo Hassler and of his nephew **Giovanni Gabrieli** (jōvän'nē), c.1555–1612. Giovanni was for a time a singer in the court choir under Lasso in Munich and became (1585) second organist at St. Mark's, succeeding to first organ on the death of his uncle two years later. He brought the multiple-choir technique to its highest development, and he was most important in the development of the CONCERTO style, i.e., differentiation of choral and solo ensembles. His *Sonata pian'e forte* (pub. in *Sacrae symphoniae,* 1597), the first piece of printed instrumental music containing dynamic indications, and the indication of specific instrumentation in his late (posthumously published) works represent the beginnings of modern orchestration. See E. F. Kenton, *Life and Works of Giovanni Gabrieli* (1967).

Gabrilowitsch, Ossip (ô'sĭp gäbrĭlô'vĭch), 1878–1936, Russian-American pianist and conductor; pupil of Anton Rubinstein at the St. Petersburg Conservatory and of Leschetizky. His debut was made in Berlin in 1896. He was well-known both as a brilliant pianist and as conductor of the Munich Konzertverein Orchestra, 1910–14, and the Detroit Symphony Orchestra, 1918–36. He married Clara Clemens, concert singer, daughter of Mark Twain.

Gabrovo (gäbrô'vô), town (1968 est. pop. 68,000), N central Bulgaria, in the foothills of the Balkan Mts. It is Bulgaria's chief woolen textile center. The town developed as a strategic point on the northern approaches to Shipka Pass and now stands on a highway running through the pass.

Gad. 1 Son of Jacob and Zilpah and eponymous founder of one of the 12 tribes of Israel. Its allotment was half of GILEAD; this was the land best suited to the pastoral life, which Gad, like Reuben, continued after the years in Egypt. The "people of Gad" are mentioned on the Moabite stone. Gen. 30.11; 35.26; 49.19; Num. 2.14; 13.15; 32; Deut. 3.12; 33.20; Joshua 13.24; 1 Chron. 5.18,26; 12.8,14. **2** Seer of David's reign. He wrote one of the lost histories. 1 Sam. 22.5; 2 Sam. 24.11–19; 1 Chron. 21.9; 29.29; 2 Chron. 29.25.

Gadara (găd'ərə), ancient city of the Decapolis, the modern Umm Qays (Jordan), SE of the Sea of Galilee. Extensive ruins mark the site. This Gadara must be distinguished from Gadara, the capital of Perea, which was destroyed by Vespasian in 68 B.C. The terms *Gadarenes, Gergesenes,* and *Gerasenes* appear variously for the locale of the celebrated miracle of the possessed swine. They probably refer to an obscure town on the east shore of the lake. Mat. 8.28; Mark 5.1; Luke 8.26.

Gadda, Carlo Emilio (kär'lō āmē'lyō gäd'dä), 1893–1973, Italian novelist. Although trained as an electrical engineer, Gadda devoted his energies to writing. His difficult style, deliberately obscure, precludes a wide audience. A fascination with words led him to use phonetic tricks (e.g., deliberate misspellings, dialects) to distort and mock formal writing and produce a fresh realism. Gadda's early works are collected in *I sogni e la folgore* (1955). His best-known novel is *Quer pasticciaccio brutto de via Merulana* (1957, tr. *That Awful Mess on Via Merulana,* 1965). His *Acquainted with Grief* appeared in English in 1969.

Gaddi (găd'ī), Manassite sent by Moses into Canaan. Num. 13.11.

Gaddi (gäd'dē), celebrated family of Florentine artists. **Gaddo Gaddi,** c.1260–c.1333, painter and mosaicist, is said by Vasari to have been associated with Cimabue and Giotto. Among the mosaics attributed to him are those in the portico of Santa Maria Maggiore, Rome, and *Coronation of the Virgin,* over the portal in the Florentine cathedral. His son, **Taddeo Gaddi,** c.1300–c.1366, was a favorite pupil and godson of Giotto, whom he assisted for 24 years. He became the leader of Florentine painting after his master's death. His works include the ceiling painting and a series of frescoes representing scenes from the life of the Virgin in the Baroncelli Chapel in Santa Croce, Florence; the fine *Last Supper* in the refectory of the same church; remains of frescoes in San Francesco, Pisa; altarpieces (Naples; Berlin; and the Uffizi); and *Madonna with Saints* (Santa Felicita, Florence). Taddeo's son, **Agnolo Gaddi,** c.1350–1396, a pupil of his father and of Giovanni di Milano, was also a follower of Giotto. His works are somewhat rigid in design and lack imagination. Among them are frescoes of the *Story of the True Cross* (Santa Croce, Florence); *Life of the Virgin* (cathedral, Prato); and four paintings in the National Gallery of Art, Washington, D.C.

Gaddiel (găd'ēĕl, găd'īəl), leader of Zebulun sent by Moses to explore Canaan. Num. 13.10.

gadding machine: see QUARRYING.

Gade, Niels Vilhelm (nēls vĭl'hĕlm gä'thə), 1817–90, Danish composer. He studied (1843–48) in Leipzig, where he met Mendelssohn and Schumann. His eight symphonies, his chamber music, and his cantatas are essentially romantic.

Gades, Spain: see CÁDIZ.

gadfly, name for various biting flies, especially those that attack livestock, e.g., the BOTFLY and the HORSEFLY.

Gadi (gā'dī), father of Menahem, king of Israel. 2 Kings 15.14,17.

Gadir, Spain: see CÁDIZ.

gadolinium (gădəlĭn'ēəm), metallic chemical element; symbol Gd; at. no. 64; at. wt. 157.25; m.p. 1312°C; b.p. 3233°C; sp. gr. 7.898 at 25°C; valence +3. Gadolinium is a malleable, ductile, lustrous silver-white metal with a hexagonal close-packed crystalline structure at room temperature. It is a RARE-EARTH METAL found in group IIIb of the PERIODIC TABLE. Although the metal does not tarnish in dry air, in moist air an oxide film forms; the film flakes off, exposing more metal to oxidation. Gadolinium reacts slowly with water and dissolves in dilute mineral acids. It occurs in nature in its salts and especially as the oxide, gadolinia, a RARE EARTH. It is a component of the minerals gadolinite, monazite, and bastnasite. Naturally occurring gadolinium is a mixture of seven isotopes; ten additional isotopes are known. Although gadolinium absorbs neutrons more effectively than does any other known substance, this property is caused by two isotopes that are present only to a limited extent in natural gadolinium. Gadolinium has found some use in control rods for nuclear reactors; it has also been used as a "poison" in nuclear fuels, added to control the initial rapid reaction and "burning out" as the reaction proceeds. Gadolinium metal can be prepared by reduction of anhydrous gadolinium fluoride with calcium metal. Gadolinium has unusual magnetic properties. At room temperature the metal is paramagnetic, but it becomes strongly ferromagnetic when cooled. Gadolinium compounds are used as phosphors in the manufacture of color-television picture tubes. Gadolinia, the oxide, was extracted from the mineral gadolinite [for F. Gadolin] in 1880 by J. C. G. de Marignac; in 1886, P. E. Lecoq de Boisbaudran independently isolated the oxide from Mosander's "yttria."

Gadsden, Christopher, 1724–1805, American Revolutionary leader, b. Charleston, S.C., educated in England. He returned to Charleston (1746) and became a wealthy merchant. At the Stamp Act Congress (1765) he was one of the first to urge colonial union against England's policy of taxation. Gadsden served (1774–76) in the Continental Congress and favored independence. In the struggle over the South Carolina constitution in 1778 he was a radical, favoring separation of church and state and popular election of senators. He was captured when the British took Charleston (1780), and imprisonment by the British broke his health. He later helped to secure ratification of the Constitution and still later opposed the Jeffersonians. See Richard Walsh, ed., *The Writings of Christopher Gadsden, 1746–1805* (1966).

Gadsden, James, 1788–1858, American railroad promoter and diplomat, b. Charleston, S.C.; grandson of Christopher Gadsden. He served in the War of 1812, under Andrew Jackson against the Seminole Indians, and, later, as commissioner to remove the Seminole to their reservation in Florida. He was a promoter of railroads and advocated a Southern rail system, the purpose of which would be to control the trade of the South and the West, thereby freeing those regions from their dependency on the North. To further this end he promoted Southern commercial conventions, and at a convention in Memphis in 1845 he boldly urged the construction of a railroad to the Pacific. In 1853, when his friend Jefferson Davis was Secretary of War in Pierce's cabinet, Gadsden was appointed minister to Mexico to negotiate for territory along the border. The result was the GADSDEN PURCHASE. He was recalled (1856) for exceeding his instructions.

Gadsden, city (1970 pop. 53,928), seat of Etowah co., NE Ala., on the Coosa River; inc. 1871. Iron, coal, limestone, sand, clay, and timber are found in the area. Gadsden has metal and textile industries and a large tire and rubber plant. A junior college is in the city.

Gadsden Purchase, strip of land purchased (1853) by the United States from Mexico. The Treaty of Guadalupe Hidalgo (1848) had described the U.S.–Mexico boundary vaguely, and President Pierce wanted to insure U.S. possession of the Mesilla Valley near the Rio Grande—the most practicable route for a southern railroad to the Pacific. James GADSDEN negotiated the purchase, and the U.S. Senate ratified (1854) it by a narrow margin. The area of c.30,000 sq mi (77,700 sq km), purchased for $10 million, now forms extreme S New Mexico and Arizona S of the Gila. See P. N. Garber, *The Gadsden Treaty* (1923; repr. 1959); O. B. Faulk, *Too Far North, Too Far South* (1967).

Gaea (jē'ə), in Greek mythology, the earth, daughter of Chaos, both mother and wife of Uranus (the sky) and Pontus (the sea). Among Gaea's offspring by Uranus were the Cyclopes, the Hundred-handed Ones (the Hecatoncheires), and the Titans. To Pontus she bore five sea deities. Because Uranus had imprisoned her sons she helped bring about his overthrow by the Titans, who were led by Cronus. She was worshiped as the primal goddess, the mother and nourisher of all things. The Romans identified her with Tellus.

Gaelic (gā'lĭk), or Goidelic, group of languages belonging to the Celtic subfamily of the Indo-European family of languages. See CELTIC LANGUAGES; IRISH LANGUAGE.

Gaelic football: see under FOOTBALL.

Gaelic literature, literature in the native tongue of Ireland and Scotland. Since Scottish Gaelic became separate from Irish Gaelic only in the 17th cent., the literature is conventionally divided into Old Irish (before 900), Middle Irish (until 1350), Late Middle or Early Modern Irish (until 1650), and Modern Irish and Scottish Gaelic (from 1650). The early literature has survived in Middle and Late Middle Irish manuscripts that are, for the most part, miscellaneous collections of prose and verse in which legend, history, bardic and lyric poetry, and medical, legal, and religious writings of several periods are all preserved side by side. The chief works are the Book of the Dun Cow (before 1106), the Book of Leinster (before 1160), and the Yellow Book of Lecan, the Great Book of Lecan, the Lebor Brecc, and the Book of Lismore (late 14th or early 15th cent.); the first three are especially important because they contain the heroic sagas. The oldest writings are poems from the 6th cent.; Dallán Forgaill is the most famous of the *filid* or official poets. There are some fine anonymous nature poems from the 8th cent. With the 9th-century (Middle Irish) period begin the heroic tales in which epic and romance go hand in hand. These stories were classified by the medieval Irish according to type; in modern times they have been divided into two major cycles, the Ulster and the Fenian. The Ulster cycle deals with swaggering pagan heroes of the century before Christ. Its central hero and the hero of its longest story, *Táin Bó Cúalnge* [the cattle raid of Cooley], is CUCHULAIN, an Irish Achilles. The finest of all the Ulster stories is *Longes Mac Nusnig* [exile of the sons of Usnech], the tragedy of DEIRDRE. Early Celtic literature is characterized by a simplicity and terseness of style interspersed with richness of imagery, color, and detail. The Fenian tradition, which became prominent in the late Middle Irish period, is 300 years later than the Ulster. Paganism is modified; Christianity is represented as coming in the extreme old age of OSSIAN, the poet of the Fenians; the temper is more romantic than epic—the lyrics sing more of nature, love, and separation than of war and death. The characteristic form of this cycle is the ballad. Its ideal hero is Finn, the Irish counterpart of the Welsh Arthur. The Fenian cycle begins with the composition of the long *Acallam na Senórech* [colloquy of the old men], c.1200. The great prose story of the cycle is *Tóraigheacht Agus Ghráinne* [the pursuit of Diarmuid and Grainne], a variant of the Ulster story of Deirdre. Except for Deirdre, the Ulster tales have been forgotten; Fenian legends have survived to modern times, especially in Scotland. The variety of motifs encompassed by the cycles—the doomed lovers, the knights-errant, adventures in an earthly paradise, visions and voyages—influenced medieval romance. The privileged position held by the poet in ancient Ireland was continued after the advent of Christianity; the poets, who were the successors of the pagan priests, became guardians of the native tradition, and after the coming of the Norman English in the 12th and 13th cent., the spokesmen of Gaelic culture. The late medieval prose includes one of the most celebrated Gaelic narrative collections, *The Three Sorrows of Storytelling.* The 16th and 17th cent. saw a great poetic revival and the rise of modern Irish prose. Gaelic Ireland was now fighting a losing battle with England, and as the English conquered, Gaelic literature became more passionately patriotic and more militantly Catholic. The 16th-and 17th-century prose in Ireland is transitional; it begins with some delightful tales in Middle Irish and comes to its fruition with Geoffrey Keating, whose religious works and monumental historical study of Ireland are the foundation of modern Irish literature. The greatest Irish scholar of the time was Michael O'Clery; among other students of Gaelic culture were some English-speaking Protestants, notably Bedell, bishop of Kilmore and Ardagh, translator of the Old Testament. The penal age of Ireland may be dated from Cromwell's arrival (1649). During this time Gaelic literature served to keep alive the old culture of the submerged Catholics. From Paris and Louvain came a stream of religious books in Gaelic, probably published by the Franciscans, who at this time became the chief guardians of the Irish language. Even before Cromwell and the intense hardships suffered under English rule, however, bardic poetry had begun to decline. The early 17th cent. was an age of transition from the strict verse of the bardic schools to the less formal meters of untrained poets. Chief among the poets were Aodhagán Ó Raithille, Eóghan Ruadh Ó Súilleabháin, Brian Merriman, and Anthony Raftery. That period was hardly over before Irish Gaelic received another great blow, following the potato famine of 1847. With the terrible depopulation of Ireland, Gaelic literature began to fade, and the proportion of Gaelic speakers in Ireland dropped in three years from more than three fourths to one quarter. Later in the 19th cent., Irish scholarship came into its own again and resulted, through the efforts of John O'Donovan, Eugene O'Curry, Douglas Hyde, and Standish Hayes O'Grady, in a Gaelic literary revival. The principal figures in this new Gaelic literature were Canon Peter O'Leary, Patrick O'Connor, Patrick Henry Pearse, and Maurice O'Sullivan. The connections between Gaelic Scotland and Gaelic Ireland were close until the rise of Presbyterianism in Scotland; since the 16th cent., Scottish Gaelic has had a literature of its own. The great event of modern Scottish Gaelic culture is "the '45," when Bonnie Prince Charlie (Charles Edward Stuart) led the Jacobites in an ultimately unsuccessful uprising. There was a great burst of poetry that defied the repressive measures of Parliament and mourned the English triumph. The poet par excellence of the rebellion was Alexander Macdonald (MacMaster Alasdair); he was more original than Duncan Ban McIntyre, whose poems recall older forms and older themes. At the end of the century came James Macpherson's famous forgery *Ossian,* supposedly the work of a 3d-century Irish bard. A sharp decline in technique and content was evident in the 19th cent. Some excellent writers of prose, however, were Dr. Norman Macleod and Donald Mackechnie. In the 20th cent. the best-known poets are Somalirle Maclean, George Campbell Hay, and Derick Thomson. A popular satirist and newspaper columnist was Flann O'Brien (Myles Na Gopaleen), whose novels, particularly *At Swim Two Birds* (tr. 1956) were popular in translation. In general the Scottish Gaels have preserved their language and literary activity better abroad (for instance, in Nova Scotia) than the Irish; but at home Scottish Gaelic is disappearing faster than Irish. Most of the monuments of Gaelic literature have been translated into English, as by Lady Gregory, Eleanor Hull, Tom Peete Cross, and (for Scotland) James MacGregor. See Douglas Hyde, *A Literary History of Ireland* (1899); Myles Dillon, *Early Irish Literature* (1948); Alexander Carmichael, ed., *Carmina Gadelica* (6 vol., 1928–71); Derick Thomson, *An Introduction to Gaelic Poetry* (1974).

Gaeta (gäĕ'tä), town (1971 pop. 22,185), in Latium, central Italy, a seaport on a high promontory in the Tyrrhenian Sea. It was a favorite resort of the ancient Romans and was a prosperous duchy from the 9th to the 12th cent. Gaeta lost its independence to the Normans (mid-12th cent.) and thereafter shared the fortunes of the kingdom of Naples. The citadel (8th cent.) and the port were strongly fortified (15th–16th cent.). Pope Pius IX took refuge in Gaeta in 1848–49. The fall of the town to Victor Emmanuel II of Sardinia after a siege (1860–61) marked the end of the rule of Francis II of the kingdom of the Two Sicilies. Gaeta has a cathedral (12th cent.) with a fine campanile (13th cent.)

Gaffney, city (1970 pop. 13,253), seat of Cherokee co., NW S.C., near the N.C. line, in a cotton, grain, and peach region; settled in the early 1800s, inc. 1873. Textiles and garments are its major products; the city also has a large peach-packing plant and a variety of light manufactures. Gaffney is the seat of Limestone College. Cowpens National Battlefield and Kings Mountain National Military Park are nearby (see NATIONAL PARKS AND MONUMENTS, table).

Gafsa: see QAFSAH, Tunisia.

Gagarin, Yuri Alekseyevich (yo͞o'rē əlyĭksyä'yəvĭch gägä'rĭn), 1934–68, Russian astronaut (cosmonaut), b. near Gzhatsk, RSFSR. He was the first in history to be rocketed into orbital space flight. His flight on April 12, 1961, lasted 89.1 min. and circled the earth once. The vehicle in which he traveled, named the *Vostok* [East], weighed over five tons; it reached a maximum altitude of 188 mi (303 km). All control over the spacecraft was handled from the ground, the pilot's reactions being carefully recorded. The success of this flight may be said to have opened the modern era of man in space. Gagarin was killed when a plane he was testing crashed.

Gage, Lyman Judson, 1836–1927, American banker and cabinet member, b. Madison co., N.Y. He moved to Chicago in 1855 and from 1868 was associated with the First National Bank of Chicago, of which he became (1891) president. Gage supported William McKinley for President against William Jennings Bryan and became (1897) President McKinley's Secretary of the Treasury. He won public approval for his conduct of fiscal affairs during the Spanish-American War and helped secure passage of the act establishing the gold standard in 1900. He resigned in 1902 after serving briefly under President Theodore Roosevelt.

Gage, Matilda Joslyn, 1826–98, American woman suffrage leader, b. Cicero, N.Y. Joining the woman's rights movement in 1853, she edited in Syracuse, N.Y., the *National Citizen,* a feminist journal. She was president (1875–76) of the National Woman Suffrage Association. She collaborated with Elizabeth Cady Stanton and Susan B. Anthony in their *History of Woman Suffrage* (1881–86).

Gage, Thomas, d. 1656, English traveler. He went (1612) to Spain to study and became a Dominican. He lived and traveled among the Indians of Central America from 1625 to 1637, when he returned to Europe. Renouncing Roman Catholicism, he went to England in 1641 and became an Anglican clergyman. In 1654 he went as chaplain with an expedition to the West Indies and died in Jamaica. His chief claim to fame is his *English-American: His Travail by Sea and Land; or, A New Survey of the West Indies* (1648), an account of the wealth and defenseless condition of the Spanish possessions in America. See study by Norman Newton (1969).

Gage, Thomas, 1721–87, English general in North America. He came to America (1754) with Gen. Edward Braddock and took part in the ill-fated expedition against Fort Duquesne (1755). Later in the last of the French and Indian Wars he served under James Abercromby and Jeffrey Amherst. Gage was appointed (1760) governor at Montreal and later succeeded Amherst (1763) as commander in chief of British forces in North America. He thus had a highly significant post in the years when trouble between the colonists and the British government grew, and the British soldiers were receiving the brunt of the colonists' resentment. In the critical year of 1774, Gage was chosen to succeed Thomas HUTCHINSON as governor of Massachusetts, where affairs were most serious. He tried to put down the dissident forces in the colony and to enforce the Intolerable Acts. He ordered the arrest of Samuel Adams and John Hancock. In April, 1775, he sent soldiers to seize military stores at Concord, and the colonial militia resisted; the battles of Lexington and Concord on April 19 began the American Revolution. In Oct., 1775, he resigned and was succeeded by Gen. William Howe as commander in chief in the colonies, and by General Guy Carleton as commander in Canada. See biography by John Alden (1948); study by A. French (1932, repr. 1968).

Gagern, Heinrich, Freiherr von (hīn'rĭkh frī'hĕr fən gä'gərn), 1799–1880, German statesman. A Hessian parliamentary leader and leading advocate of German unity, he became (1848) president of the FRANKFURT PARLIAMENT. He at first favored Prussian leadership and the exclusion of Austria from German affairs but later reversed his stand.

Gagnoa (gänyō'ä), town (1964 est. pop. 18,000), S Ivory Coast. It is the commercial center for a fertile region producing coffee, cacao, kola nuts, rice, and timber. Gold is also extracted nearby.

Gagra (gä'grə) or **Gagry** (gä'grē), city (1970 pop. 23,000), SE European USSR, in Georgia, on the Black Sea and at the foot of the Greater Caucasus. It is a subtropical health resort.

gag rules, in parliamentary procedure, rules limiting or prohibiting free debate on a particular issue. In U.S. history, the term is applied especially to procedural rules in force in the House of Representatives from 1836 to 1844. With the growth of antislavery feeling after the founding of the American Anti-Slavery Society in 1833, the House was deluged with thousands of anti-slavery petitions, most of which requested the abolition of slavery in the District of Columbia. Southerners, with the aid of Northern Democrats, secured passage of the gag rules, which prevented the discussion of antislavery proposals in the House. The fight to secure the right of petition, waged virtually singlehandedly, and brilliantly, by John Quincy Adams, aroused the North, and the gag rules were repealed. They had the effect of strengthening the cause of the ABOLITIONISTS.

Gaham (gā'həm), nephew of Abraham. Gen. 22.24.

Gahanna (gəhăn'ə), city (1970 pop. 12,400), Franklin co., central Ohio, a residential suburb of Columbus; inc. 1881.

Gahar (gā'här), Nethinim family returning with Zerubbabel. Ezra 2.47; Neh. 7.49.

gaillardia (gālär'dēə), any plant of the genus *Gaillardia* of the Compositae family (COMPOSITE family), including annual, biennial, and perennial herbs with showy heads of red and/or yellow ray flowers and usually purple disk flowers. In the W United States they grow wild in large quantities (hence the name blanketflower); they are also popular garden flowers. Gaillardias are classified in the division MAGNOLIOPHYTA, class Magnoliopsida, order Asterales, family Compositae.

Gaines, Edmund Pendleton, 1777–1849, U.S. army officer, b. Culpeper co., Va.; brother of George Strother Gaines. He spent his boyhood in Tennessee and at the age of 22 joined the U.S. army. He surveyed (1801–4) Gaines Trace between Nashville and Natchez. In 1807 he arrested Aaron Burr and then testified at the Burr trial in Richmond. For his service in the War of 1812 he received many citations. Sent as a commissioner to negotiate with the Creek Indians, he served under Andrew Jackson in the Creek and Seminole campaigns. He later took part in the Black Hawk War and led an expedition against the Seminole in Florida. There he fell into dispute with Gen. Winfield Scott, and a court of inquiry censured them both. In command of the Western Dept. of the army at the opening of the Mexican War, Gaines faced a court of inquiry for calling for volunteers on his own authority. He defended himself so ably that the charges were dismissed. See biography by J. W. Silver (1949).

Gaines, George Strother, c.1784-1873, Alabama pioneer, b. Stokes co., N.C.; brother of Edmund Pendleton Gaines. From 1806 to 1819 he was U.S. factor and Indian agent at Saint Stephens, a strategic post on the Tombigbee River near the disputed West Florida boundary. Gaines's influence over the Choctaw Indians kept them from joining Tecumseh's confederation against the Americans. He opened Gaines Trace from the Tennessee River to the Tombigbee and aided the settlers who poured into the Alabama country after 1816. When the Choctaw Indians were to be removed beyond the Mississippi, they insisted that Gaines, whom they considered a friend, join their chiefs in selecting their lands, and Gaines later accompanied them on their migration. He served (1825-27) in the Alabama senate and later gained wealth as a merchant in Mobile, retiring in 1856 to his plantation at State Line, Miss.

Gaines's Mill: see SEVEN DAYS BATTLES.

Gainesville. 1 City (1970 pop. 64,510), seat of Alachua co., N central Fla.; inc. 1869. The Univ. of Florida is a major source of employment in the city. There are also industries manufacturing electronic equipment and wood products. Points of interest, in addition to the huge campus of the university, are Paynes Prairie State Park, Warrens Cave, and many natural sinkholes, including Devils Millhopper, said to be the largest in Florida. A state museum and a state school for the mentally retarded are there. **2** City (1970 pop. 15,459), seat of Hall co., N central Ga., on Lake Lanier, in the foothills of the Blue Ridge Mts.; inc. 1821. It is a trade center for NE Georgia, and has a textile industry. Brenau College and a junior college are there. Riverside Military Academy and Chattahoochee National Forest are nearby. **3** Town (1970 pop. 13,830), seat of Cooke co., N Texas, on the Elm Fork of the Trinity River; inc. 1873. It is the commercial and industrial hub of a farm and oil area. Dairy items, oil field equipment, fishing lures, mobile homes, and furniture are among the manufactures. Gainesville was founded (1850) on the California Trail and later was a riotous cow town, a stopping point on the Chisholm Trail just below a Red River crossing. Historical markers are on various houses, churches, and sites of early Indian raids. The city has a community circus, founded in 1930. A junior college is there.

Gainsborough, Thomas (gānz'bûr"ō), 1727-88, English portrait and landscape painter, b. Sudbury. In 1740 he went to London and became the assistant and pupil of the French engraver Hubert Gravelot. He was also influenced in his youth by the painter Francis Hayman. Gainsborough studied the landscapes of the 17th-century Dutch artists. In 1745 he returned to Sudbury, later moving to Ipswich and finally to Bath, where he gradually acquired a large and lucrative portrait practice rivaling that of Sir Joshua Reynolds. Gainsborough is celebrated for the elegance, vivacity, and refinement of his portraits, which were greatly influenced by the work of Van Dyck. He had little taste for the high society he painted, however, and spent much spare time painting his favorite subject, landscape, entirely for his own pleasure. These works were among the first great landscapes painted in England. As a colorist Gainsborough has had few rivals among English painters. In his last years he excelled in fancy pictures, a pastoral genre that featured idealized subjects (e.g., *The Mall,* 1783; Frick Coll., New York City). Gainsborough painted all parts of his pictures himself, an unusual practice for his day. He left a large collection of landscape drawings, which influenced the development of 19th-century landscape art. He is well represented in the national galleries of London, Ireland, and Scotland; in the Wallace Collection, London; and in many private collections. Examples of his work may be seen in the Metropolitan Museum and the museums of Cincinnati, Boston, Philadelphia, and St. Louis. Outstanding among his well-known works are *Perdita* (Wallace Coll., London), *The Blue Boy* (Huntington Art Gall., San Marino, Calif.), and *Lady Innes* (Frick Coll.). See his letters, ed. by M. Woodall, (rev. ed. 1963); his drawings, ed. by J. Hayes (2 vol., 1971); his prints, ed. by J. Hayes (1972); study by G. Williamson (1972).

Gaiseric (gī'sərĭk) or **Genseric** (gĕn'sərĭk, jĕn'-), c.390-477, king of the Vandals and Alani (428-77), one of the ablest of the barbarian invaders of the Roman Empire. He led (429) his people from Spain into Africa, possibly at the request of Pope BONIFACE, and quickly subdued a large territory, which was later (435) ceded to him by treaty. He took Carthage in 439, sent a fleet to raid Sicily in 440, and gained recognition of his independence in 442. He then dispossessed many Roman landowners and persecuted the Roman Catholic clergy, meanwhile gaining control of the Mediterranean through his pirate fleets. In 455 he sacked Rome. In 460 he caused the failure of an expedition sent against him by MAJORIAN, and in 468 he undermined a similar attempt by LEO I. By the time of his peace (476) with ZENO, his lands included Roman Africa, Sicily, Sardinia, Corsica, and the Balearic Islands.

Gaitskell, Hugh Todd Naylor, 1906-63, British statesman. Educated at Oxford, he taught economics at the Univ. of London. During World War II he was a civil servant in the new ministry of economic warfare (1940-42) and in the Board of Trade (1942-45). He entered Parliament as a Labour member in 1945 and served as minister of fuel and power (1947-50) and chancellor of the exchequer (1950-51). In 1955 he succeeded Clement Attlee as leader of the Labour party. After Labour's defeat in the 1959 general election, Gaitskell supported some moderation of party policies. At the party conference of 1960 the left wing of the party defeated him on the issue of unilateral nuclear disarmament, which he opposed, but he had recovered his authority in the party by the time of his premature death. See biography by Geoffrey McDermott (1971); Stephen Haseler, *The Gaitskellites* (1969).

Gaius (gā'yəs). **1** Corinthian Christian, Paul's host. Rom. 16.23. **2** Corinthian baptized by Paul. 1 Cor. 1.14. **3** Companion of Paul, native of Derbe. Acts 20.4. **4** Macedonian companion of Paul. Acts 19.29. **5** Christian to whom 3 John is addressed. It is not known which, if any, of these men are identical.

Gaius (gā'əs, gī'-), fl. 2d cent., Roman jurist. He is known for the *Institutes* (repr., 2 vol., 1967; Vol. I is a translation of the text, Vol. II consists of commentaries), a legal textbook that contributed materially to modern knowledge of early Roman law. It was much used in the compilation of the CORPUS JURIS CIVILIS. See study by A. M. Honore (1962).

galactic cluster: see STAR CLUSTER.

galactic coordinate system, ASTRONOMICAL COORDINATE SYSTEM in which the principal axis is the galactic equator (the intersection of the plane of the Milky Way with the CELESTIAL SPHERE) and the reference points are the north galactic pole and the zero point on the galactic equator; the coordinates of a celestial body are its galactic longitude and galactic latitude. In the IAU galactic coordinate system, introduced in 1958 by the International Astronomical Union, the zero point on the galactic equator has the equatorial coordinates R.A. $17^h39.3^m$ and Dec. −28°55'; this lies in the direction of the center of our galaxy, the Milky Way.

galactose: see LACTOSE.

galactosemia (gəlăk"təsē'mēə), inherited metabolic disorder caused by an enzyme deficiency and transmitted as a recessive trait; it results in the accumulation of the sugar galactose in the body. The disorder is manifested soon after birth by feeding problems and diarrhea. Galactose is accumulated principally in the liver of the newborn infant, where it may induce cirrhosis, and in the lens of the eye, where cataracts may develop. Low glucose levels cause sufficient hypoglycemia to affect the central nervous system with resulting mental retardation. These ill effects can be prevented by removing milk and all other foods containing galactose and lactose from the diet.

galago: see BUSH BABY.

Galahad, Sir, hero of ARTHURIAN LEGEND. He was the son of Launcelot and Elaine, the daughter of King Pelles. Because he was the noblest and purest of the knights of Christendom, he alone, according to Sir Thomas Malory, achieved the Holy Grail (see GRAIL, HOLY).

Galal (gā'lăl), two Levites, sons of Asaph and Jeduthun. 1 Chron. 9.15,16; Neh. 11.17.

Galanos, James: see under FASHION.

Galapagos finches: see DARWIN'S FINCHES.

Galápagos Islands (gəlăp'əgōs) [Span.,=tortoises], or **Archipiélago de Colón** (ärchēpyä'lägō thā kōlōn'), Pacific archipelago belonging to Ecuador (1970 est. pop. 3,000), 3,029 sq mi (7,845 sq km), c.650 mi (1,045 km) W of Ecuador, on the equator. They were discovered in 1535 by the Spanish navigator Tomás de Bertanga and named for the gigantic (up to 500 lb/227 kg.) land tortoises which are now facing extinction. Ecuador claimed the islands in 1832. There are 13 large islands and many smaller ones; Isabela (Albemarle) (c.2,250 sq mi/5,827 sq km) is the largest. Largely desolate lava piles, the islands have little vegetation or cultivable soil except on the upper slopes of high volcanic mountains that receive heavy rains from the prevailing trade winds and are mantled by dense vegetation. The climate is modified by the cool Humboldt Current. The islands are famous for their wild life. Besides tortoises, there are land and sea iguanas and hosts of unusual birds, such as the flightless cormorant, which exists nowhere else. Shore lagoons teem with marine life. Early travelers to this naturalist's paradise, now a wildlife sanctuary, were astonished by the tameness of the animals. The Galápagos were visited (1835) by Charles Darwin in the famous voyage of the *Beagle.* He gathered an impressive body of evidence there that was used later in support of his theory of natural selection. Although buccaneers, seeking food, made inroads on the fauna, real depredations did not begin until the arrival in the 19th cent. of the whalers and then the oilers, who killed the tortoises wholesale for food and oil. During World War II the United States maintained an air base there for the defense of the Panama Canal. Since 1967 a satellite tracking station has been manned on the islands. The Galápagos remain one of the few places in the world where naturalists can study living survivals of species arrested at various evolutionary stages. See Charles Darwin, *The Voyage of the H.M.S. Beagle* (1840); William Beebe, *Galapagos: World's End* (1924); Irenaeus Eibl-Eibesfeldt, *Galapagos: The Noah's Ark of the Pacific* (tr. 1960); Brian Nelson, *Galapagos: Islands of Birds* (1968); I. W. Thornton, *Darwin's Islands* (1971).

Galashiels (găl"əshēlz'), burgh (1971 pop. 12,605), Selkirkshire, SE Scotland, on the Gala Water. Famous for fine tweeds and woolens, Galashiels is the site of the Scottish College of Textiles. There is also a tanning industry. In 1975, Galashiels became part of the new Borders region.

Galata: see ISTANBUL.

Galatea (gălətē'ə), in Greek mythology. **1** Sea nymph, daughter of Nereus and Doris. She was loved by the brutish Polyphemus, a Cyclops who wooed her with love songs; but Galatea loved Acis, the handsome son of a river nymph. When Polyphemus discovered them together, he crushed the youth under a huge boulder. In response to his pitiful cries, Galatea turned Acis into a river. **2** See PYGMALION **1.**

Galaţi or **Galatz** (both: gäläts'), city (1970 est. pop. 179,000), E Rumania, on the lower Danube. It is a regional administrative and economic center and a major inland port, home of the Rumanian Danube flotilla. Grain and timber are the chief exports. The city is also an important rail junction and has a large iron and steel plant and shipyards. Of medieval origin, Galaţi became an international trading center in the 18th cent. and was a free port from 1834 to 1883. It was the seat (1856-1939) of the European Danube Navigation Commission. Galaţi is the see of an Orthodox bishop and is a cultural center. An agricultural college and a technical institute are in the city. The 17th-century Cathedral of St. George contains the tomb of Ivan Mazeppa.

Galatia (gəlā'shə) [from Gr.,=Gaul], ancient territory of central Asia Minor, in present Turkey (around modern Ankara). It was so called from its inhabitants, the Gauls, who invaded from the west and conquered it in the 3d cent. B.C. The name applies to the Gallic territory that was originally composed of parts of Phrygia and Cappadocia. Attalus I checked (230 B.C.) the advance of the Gauls and reduced the size of Galatia. The region was subjected (189 B.C.) by the Romans. The name was also used for the Roman province, formed in 25 B.C. At first the Roman province was much larger than old Galatia, but it was reduced (A.D. 72) to a smaller scope.

Galatians (gəlā'shənz), epistle of the New Testament, the 9th book in the usual order. It was written by St. PAUL to Christians of central Asia Minor, probably those of S Galatia. It may have been the earliest-written epistle (A.D. c.48); or, as many scholars hold, it may date after A.D. 52. The Galatians had apparently been influenced by Judaist Christians who asserted that circumcision was essential and that Christians were bound by the Law of Moses. This contradicted Paul's basic belief that salvation could be achieved by faith alone. To defend his position Paul gives a short account of his life (1.11-2.21), his intention being to show that his apostleship resulted from divine revelation. The central part of the book, on justification by faith (3.1–5.12), is of great importance in Christian theology.

Galatz, Rumania: see GALAŢI.

galax: see DIAPENSIA.

galaxy, large aggregation of STARS, gas, and dust, typically containing billions of stars; about a million galaxies are within the optical range of the largest telescopes. A galaxy is held together by the gravitational attraction between its constituent parts (see GRAVITATION), while its rotational motion prevents it from collapsing on itself. Just as gravitation binds individual stars into galaxies, it also acts to hold clusters of galaxies together. Many large galaxies have smaller galaxies, called satellites, in close proximity. The sun and its solar system, as well as the visible stars, are all in the MILKY WAY galaxy. The galaxies nearest the Milky Way form a cluster called the LOCAL GROUP. The local group includes the ANDROMEDA GALAXY, which is similar to the Milky Way, and the Magellanic Clouds, which are satellite galaxies of the Milky Way. The vast majority of observed galaxies are classified as either spiral or elliptical, with a small minority, e.g., the Magellanic Clouds, classified as irregular according to a scheme originated by E. P. Hubble. A typical spiral galaxy is shaped like a flat disk, about 100,000 LIGHT YEARS in diameter, with a central bulge, or nucleus, containing old stars; winding through the disk are the characteristic spiral arms of dust, gas, and young stars (see STELLAR POPULATIONS). This type of galaxy is further classified as being either a normal or a barred spiral. In the normal spiral, the arms, at least two in number, join smoothly with the nucleus; in the barred spiral, the arms project from a bank of stars that runs through the nucleus. The elliptical galaxies, lacking spiral arms entirely and containing little or no gas and dust, resemble the nuclei of spiral galaxies. Their shapes vary from nearly spherical to highly flattened ellipsoids. Elliptical galaxies have a much greater variation in size, mass, and luminosity than do spiral galaxies; their sizes range from the largest known galaxies of all, with luminosities about 10 times that of the Andromeda galaxy, to the small dwarf ellipticals, which can contain as few as a million stars. Irregular galaxies appear structureless and without any nucleus or rotational symmetry; they contain only young stars. Most astronomers believe that galaxies evolve; one theory suggests that irregulars evolve into spirals or ellipticals depending on the initial amount of rotational motion. Recognition that galaxies are independent star systems outside the Milky Way came from a study of the Andromeda galaxy that indicated the great distances at which this and other galaxies are located. Previously, the galaxies had been classified with the luminous gas clouds, or bright NEBULAS, within our own galaxy. Hence, galaxies are sometimes referred to as extragalactic nebulas, to distinguish them from the true nebulas. Some galaxies radiate a large fraction of their energy in forms other than visible light. With the development of RADIO ASTRONOMY, many radio galaxies were discovered. By looking with an optical telescope at the position of a radio source a faint visual galaxy would sometimes be found. Other galaxies radiate strongly in the infrared, ultraviolet, or X-ray part of the spectrum. See Walter Baade, *Evolution of Stars and Galaxies* (1963); Thornton Page and Lou Williams, ed., *Beyond the Milky Way* (1969); Harlow Shapley, *Galaxies* (3d ed. 1972).

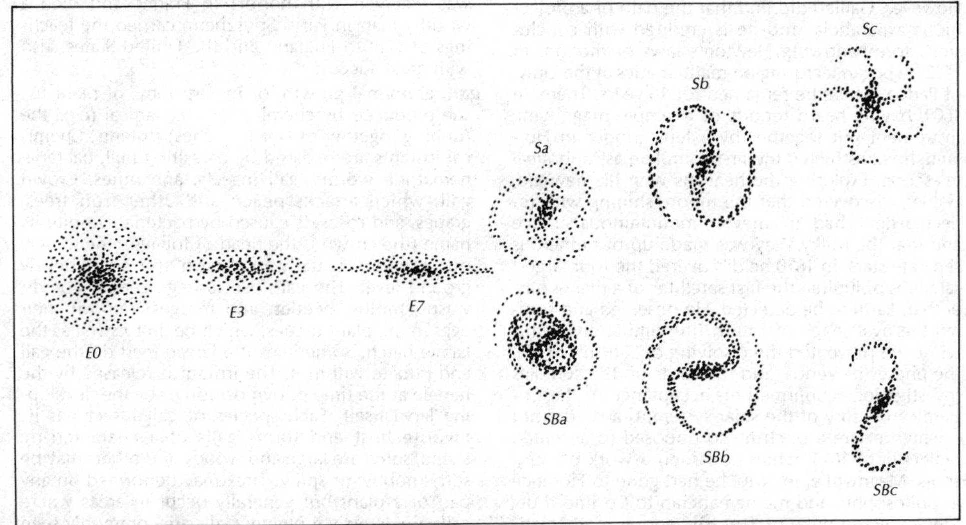

Hubble classification of galaxies: Elliptical galaxies (E) are classified according to the degree of flattening of the ellipse. Spiral galaxies (S) and barred spiral galaxies (SB) are classified according to how tightly the spiral arms are wound around the core. Galaxies that do not correspond to these classes are called irregular.

Galba (Servius Sulpicius Galba) (găl'bə), 3 B.C.–A.D. 69, Roman emperor (A.D. 68–A.D. 69). He distinguished himself in a political and military career as praetor (A.D. 20), governor of Aquitania, consul (A.D. 33), commander in Gaul, and governor of Hispania Tarraconensis (A.D. 60). In A.D. 68 an insurrection against NERO broke out, and Galba was proclaimed emperor by his soldiers. Nero committed suicide, and Galba succeeded him. A few months after his reign began, a rebellion led by OTHO took place. Galba was killed, and Otho succeeded him. Galba's brief reign was distinguished by an honest but parsimonious administration.

Galbraith, John Kenneth, 1908–, American economist and public official, b. Ontario, Canada, grad. Univ. of Toronto (B.S., 1931), Univ. of California (M.S., 1933; Ph.D., 1934). After teaching economics at Harvard (1934–39) and at Princeton (1939–40) he entered government service to work (1941–43) in the Office of Price Administration. He was an editor of *Fortune* magazine from 1943 to 1948, then returned (1949) to Harvard as professor of economics. An adviser to President John F. Kennedy, he served (1961–63) as U.S. ambassador to India. He rejoined the Harvard faculty in 1963, but continued his political activities, serving (1967–69) as national chairman of Americans for Democratic Action. A Keynesian economist, Galbraith advocates government spending to fight unemployment and using more of the nation's wealth for public services and less for private consumption. His works, influential with both economists and laymen, include *American Capitalism: The Concept of Countervailing Power* (1952); *The Great Crash: 1929* (1955); *The Affluent Society* (1958); *The Liberal Hour* (1960); *The New Industrial State* (2d rev. ed., 1971); *Economics and the Public Purpose* (1973). See studies by C. H. Hession (1972) and M. E. Sharpe (1973).

Galdhøpiggen, peak: see JOTUNHEIMEN, Norway.

Galdós, Benito Pérez: see PÉREZ GALDÓS, BENITO.

Gale, George Washington, 1789–1861, American educator and clergyman, b. Stanford, N.Y., grad. Union College, 1814, and Princeton Theological Seminary, 1819. In 1827 he founded Oneida Institute at Whitesboro, N.Y., where students paid for their instruction by doing manual labor. He planned a college in the West to be similarly maintained, and he organized a land company that founded Galesburg, Ill. From the proceeds he established Knox Manual Labor College in 1837; the manual labor feature was later dropped and the institution became KNOX COLLEGE. Gale served as trustee and taught literature and moral philosophy there until his retirement in 1857. See his autobiography (1964).

Gale, Zona, 1874–1938, American novelist and short-story writer, b. Portage, Wis., grad. Univ. of Wisconsin, 1895. After five years (1899–1904) of newspaper work in Milwaukee and New York City, she returned to her home town, determined to win success as a fiction writer. Of her bleak, realistic novels of life in the Middle West, *Birth* (1918), *Miss Lulu Bett* (1920), and *Papa La Fleur* (1933) won much attention in their time. Her dramatization of *Miss Lulu Bett* won the Pulitzer Prize in 1921. Among her other novels are *Faint Perfume* (1923) and *Light Woman* (1937).

Galeed (găl'ēĕd), **Jegar-sahadutha** (jē'gär-sā"hədyo͞o'thə), or **Mizpah** (mĭz'pə), cairn, raised by Jacob and Laban to mark their covenant. The so-called Mizpah benediction given here was a mutual warning, not a blessing. Gen. 31.44–55.

Galen (gā'lən), c.130–c.200, physician and writer, b. Pergamum, of Greek parents. After study in Greece and Asia Minor and at Alexandria, he returned to Pergamum, where he served as physician to the gladiatorial school. He resided chiefly in Rome from c.162. Noted for his lectures and writings, he established a large practice and became court physician to Marcus Aurelius. He is credited with some 500 treatises, most of them on medicine and philosophy; at least 83 of his medical works are extant. He correlated earlier medical knowledge in all fields with his own discoveries (based in part on experimentation and on dissection of animals) and systematized medicine in accordance with his theories, which emphasized purposive creation. His work in anatomy and physiology is especially notable. He demonstrated that arteries carry blood instead of air and added greatly to knowledge of the brain, nerves, spinal cord, and pulse. Until the 16th cent. his authority was virtually undisputed, thus discouraging original investigation and hampering medical progress. See study by Owsei Temkin (1973).

galena (gəlē'nə) or **lead glance,** lustrous, blue-gray mineral crystallizing usually in cubes, sometimes in octahedrons. It is the most important ore and the principal source of lead. It consists of lead sulfide, PbS, but frequently contains silver (it is mined for this metal in some localities) and other accessory metals. It is widely distributed throughout the world, occurring in veins and in bedded deposits, in Missouri, Idaho, Iowa, Wisconsin, and Utah in the United States (leading producer of lead) and in Australia, Canada, England, France, and Mexico. Galena crystals were once much used in radio "crystal" sets.

Galena Park, city (1970 pop. 10,479), Harris co., S Texas, a suburb of Houston.

Galerius (Caius Galerius Valerius Maximinianus) (gəlēr'ēəs), d. 310, Roman emperor (305–10). Diocletian appointed him caesar for the eastern part of the empire in 293 (Constantius I was caesar of the West). He had to conduct hard campaigns in Pannonia and Asia. Defeated by the Persians in 296, he retrieved his reputation by a resounding victory over them in 297. On the abdication of Diocletian and Maximian in 305, he and Constantius succeeded as emperors. Galerius tried to increase his power, and after Constantius died in 306 he recognized SEVERUS (d.307) as coemperor in the West. Severus and he attempted without success to put down the claims of MAXENTIUS. After they were defeated and Severus was captured, Galerius had Diocletian approve the appointment of Licinius as emperor of the West. Constantius' son Constantine (CONSTANTINE I) and MAXIMIN (d.313) then both claimed power. Galerius died before the confusion was eliminated by the victory of Constantine. Galerius had prompted the persecution of Christians under Diocletian but issued (309) an edict of toleration shortly before his death.

Galesburg, city (1970 pop. 36,290), seat of Knox co., W Ill., in a farm, livestock, and coal area; chartered 1841. A trade, rail, and industrial center, it has railroad shops and plants manufacturing power lawn mowers, refrigerators, air conditioners, plastics, containers, and automotive and steel products. Galesburg was founded by Presbyterians from the Mohawk valley, N.Y., under the leadership of George Washington Gale. They established Knox College, and in 1858 a debate between Abraham Lincoln and Stephen Douglas took place in Knox Old Main, now the oldest building on the campus. The birthplace of the poet Carl Sandburg has been preserved in Galesburg, which also has a junior college.

Galiani, Ferdinando (fārdēnän'dō gälyä'nē), 1728–87, Italian economist, educated for the church. As a very young man he wrote *Della moneta* [on money] (1750), which attacked the mercantilist theory that money has no intrinsic value. Sent (1759) to Paris as secretary of the Neapolitan embassy, he wrote his *Dialogues sur le commerce des blés* (1770). Galiani contributed greatly to the modern theory of value and to the relativistic, historical approach to economics. He opposed the physiocrat view that land is the source of all wealth. A noted wit, he was an intimate of the circle of Holbach and Mme d'Épinay.

Galicia (gəlĭsh'ēə, –ə), Pol. *Galicja,* Ukr. *Halychyna,* historic region (32,332 sq mi/83,740 sq km), SE Poland and W Ukraine, covering the slopes of the N Carpathians and plains to the north and bordering on Czechoslovakia in the south. It is drained by the upper Dnestr, the upper Vistula, and the San, which divides Galicia into the western (Polish) and the eastern (Ukrainian) parts. The Polish section (area 13,226 sq mi/34,255 sq km) covers Rzeszów and the larger part of Kraków provinces; the Ukrainian section (area 19,106 sq mi/49,485 sq km) includes Lvov, Ivano-Frankovsk and Tarnopol oblasts. Mainly agricultural, Galicia also has mineral resources, notably oil wells around Drogobych and Borislav, in Ukraine, and in Rzeszów prov., in Poland. Originally the duchy of Galich, it was united with the duchy of Vladimir (see VLADIMIR-VOLYNSKY) in 1188 and annexed by Casimir III of Poland in the 14th cent. With the first partition of Poland (1772) most of the region passed to Austria, which made it a crownland with the capital at Lvov (Lemberg) and named it Galicia. Austria enlarged its holdings with the third Polish partition (1795) and again in 1815. In 1846 an abortive Polish insurrection in Galicia served Austria as a pretext for annexing Kraków, an independent republic since 1815. In 1848 Kraków and Lvov were centers of revolution against Austria, and in 1861 Galicia won limited autonomy, including representation in the Austrian parliament, where Galician deputies formed a powerful bloc. Polish, spoken in W Galicia, and Ukrainian, spoken in E Galicia, became official languages along with German; the Jews, a substantial minority, were refused recognition by the Austrian government. The Austrians maintained an uncertain peace by playing off the three major ethnic groups. However, the growing Ukrainian nationalist movement resulted in demands for increased political and cultural rights, or even for independence, in E Galicia. The Polish independence movement also gained ground, but in World War I the Polish legions, organized in Galicia by Marshal Piłsudski, fought under Austrian command until 1917. In 1918 the Poles, having proclaimed national independence, wrested W Galicia from Austria and fought the troops of the newly established Ukraine republic in E Galicia, forcing them to withdraw. The Paris Peace Conference (1919) assigned E Galicia to Poland pending a plebiscite scheduled for 1944. However, in a treaty (1920) with the Ukrainians, upheld by the Polish-Soviet Treaty of Riga (1921), Poland obtained full title to E Galicia. In 1939 most of E Galicia was incorporated into Ukraine, an act upheld by the Polish-Soviet Treaty of 1945.

Galicia (gälē'thēä), region (1970 pop. 2,583,674), NW Spain, on the Atlantic Ocean, S of the Bay of Biscay and N of Portugal. It comprises the provinces of La Coruña, Lugo, Orense, and Pontevedra. The area is mostly mountainous, with several swift rivers, of which the Miño is the most important. Fishing and cattle and hog raising are the chief sources of livelihood. Food is processed in the few urban areas, and an important naval base is at El Ferrol. The region's mineral resources, chiefly iron and tin, were known to the Romans but are now little exploited. Galicia was (5th–6th cent. A.D.) the center of the kingdom of the German Suevi. It was liberated (8th–9th cent.) from the Moors by the king of Asturias. Its people's strong spirit of independence was shown in the Middle Ages by the frequent rebellions of the feudal lords against the crown and again in the 19th cent. by the popular resistance to Napoleon I. The shrine of Santiago de Compostela, a center of culture in medieval times, remains a great place of pilgrimage. In the 19th cent., Galicia was the scene of a remarkable cultural and literary revival. The Galician dialect is closely related to Portuguese.

Galigaï, Leonora: see CONCINI, CONCINO.

Galilee (găl'ĭlē), region, N Israel, roughly the portion north of the plain of Esdraelon. Galilee was the chief scene of the ministry of Jesus Christ. The Sea of Galilee, the countryside, and the towns—CANA, CAPERNAUM, TIBERIAS, NAZARETH—are repeatedly referred to in the Gospels. Jesus himself was called the Galilean, and his disciples were chosen from the local fishermen. (Joshua 20.7; 21.32; 1 Kings 9.11; 2 Kings 15.29; Isa. 9.1; Mat. 26.69–75; John 7.52) After the destruction of Jerusalem (A.D. 70), Galilee became the main center of Judaism in Palestine. Zionist colonization of the region began at the end of the 19th cent. The Beit Natufa Dam there is part of a national irrigation system, and olives and grains are the chief crops of Galilee's fertile farming areas. Nazareth is the chief urban center of Galilee. The main portion of the Israeli community of DRUSES lives in W Galilee.

Galilee, Sea of, or **Lake Tiberias** or **Lake Kinneret,** lake, 64 sq mi (166 sq km), 14 mi (23 km) long, and 3 to 7 mi (4.8–11.3 km) wide, NE Israel; its surface is c.700 ft (210 m) below sea level. The lake, occupying a downwarped basin, is fed and drained by the Jordan River. The Syria border follows part of the eastern shore. Mineral springs, some of them hot, discharge into the lake, giving it a saline character. Israel's National Water Carrier Project uses the Sea of Galilee as a reservoir for water pumped south, via the National Water Conduit, to the Negev desert for irrigation and to the coastal plain to recharge the overdrawn watertable. However, the project has been hindered by the lake's salinity and by the cost of pumping water. In the time of Christ there was a flourishing fishing industry in the lake; some fishing is still carried on. In the Old Testament the Sea of Galilee was called the Sea of Chinnereth or Chinneroth (Joshua 12.3; 13.27; Num. 34.11). In the New Testament it is named variously from nearby geographical features—Galilee, Gennesaret, or Tiberias.

Galilei, Vincenzo (vĕnchĕn'tsō gälēlĕ'ē), d. 1591, Italian lutanist, singer, writer, and composer; father of Galileo. As a member of the Florentine *camerata* (see OPERA), he was one of the first to compose recitatives. Thoroughly trained in the contrapuntal tradition of the Renaissance, he wrote the first literary treatise attacking counterpoint and advocating monody, *Dialogo della musica antica e della moderna* (1581).

Galileo (Galileo Galilei) (găl'ĭlē'ō; gälēlĕ'ō gälēlĕ'ē), 1564–1642, great Italian astronomer, mathematician, and physicist. By his persistent investigation of natural laws he laid foundations for modern experimental science, and by the construction of astronomical telescopes he greatly enlarged man's vision and conception of the universe. He gave a mathematical formulation to many physical laws. His early studies, at the Univ. of Pisa, were in medicine, but he was soon drawn to mathematics and physics. It is said that at the age of 19, in the cathedral of Pisa, he timed the oscillations of a swinging lamp by means of his pulse beats and found the time for each swing to be the same, no matter what the amplitude of the oscillation, thus discovering the isochronism of the pendulum, which he verified by experiment. Galileo soon became known through his invention of a hydrostatic balance and his treatise on the center of gravity of solid bodies. While professor (1589–92) at the Univ. of Pisa, he initiated his experiments concerning the laws of bodies in motion, which brought results so contradictory to the accepted teachings of Aristotle that strong antagonism was aroused. He found that bodies do not fall with velocities proportional to their weights, but he did not arrive at the correct conclusion (that the acceleration is proportional to time and independent of both weight and density) until perhaps 20 years later. The famous story in which Galileo is said to have dropped weights from the Leaning Tower of Pisa is false, the actual experiment having been performed by Simon Stevin several years before Galileo's work. However, Galileo did find that the path of a projectile is a parabola, and he is credited with conclusions foreshadowing Newton's laws of motion. In 1592 he began lecturing on mathematics at the Univ. of Padua, where he remained for 18 years. There, in 1609, having heard reports of a simple magnifying instrument put together by a lens-grinder in Holland, he constructed the first complete astronomical telescope. Exploring the heavens with his new aid, Galileo discovered that the moon, shining with reflected light, had an uneven, mountainous surface and that the Milky Way was made up of numerous separate stars. In 1610 he discovered the four largest satellites of Jupiter, the first satellites of a planet other than Earth to be detected. He observed and studied the oval shape of Saturn (the limitations of his telescope prevented the resolving of Saturn's rings), the phases of Venus, and the spots on the sun. His investigations confirmed his acceptance of the Copernican theory of the solar system; but he did not openly declare a doctrine so opposed to accepted beliefs until 1613, when he issued a work on sunspots. Meanwhile, in 1610, he had gone to Florence as philosopher and mathematician to Cosimo II de' Medici, grand duke of Tuscany, and as mathematician at the Univ. of Pisa. In 1611 he visited Rome to display the telescope to the papal court. In 1616 the system of Copernicus was denounced as dangerous to faith, and Galileo, summoned to Rome, was warned not to uphold it or teach it. But in 1632 he published a work written for the nonspecialist, *Dialogo . . . sopra i due massimi sistemi del mondo* [dialogue on the two chief systems of the world], (tr. 1661; rev. and ed. by Giorgio de Santillana, 1953; new tr. by Stillman Drake, 1953, rev. 1967); that work, which supported the Copernican system as opposed to the Ptolemaic, marked a turning point in scientific and philosophical thought. Again summoned to Rome, he was tried (1633) by the Inquisition and brought to the point of making an abjuration of all beliefs and writings that held the sun to be the central body and the earth a moving body revolving with the other planets about it. Since 1761, accounts of the trial have concluded with the statement that Galileo as he arose from his knees exclaimed sotto voce, *"E pur si muove"* [nevertheless it does move]. That statement was long considered legendary, but it was discovered written on a portrait of Galileo completed c.1640. After the Inquisition trial Galileo was sentenced to an enforced residence in Siena. He was later allowed to live in seclusion at Arcetri near Florence, and it is likely that Galileo's statement of defiance was made as he left Siena for Arcetri. In spite of infirmities and, at the last, blindness, Galileo continued the pursuit of scientific truth until his death. His last book, *Dialogues Concerning Two New Sciences* (tr., 3d ed. 1939, repr. 1952), which contains most of his contributions to physics, appeared in 1638. See biography by Ludovico Geymonat (tr. 1965); studies by Giorgio de Santillana (1955), Stillman Drake (1970), and W. R. Shea (1973).

Galion (găl'yən), city (1970 pop. 13,123), Crawford co., N central Ohio; inc. as a borough 1840, as a city 1878. Road-building equipment is the chief manufacture; other products include electric conversion equipment, burial vaults, truck bodies, and pollution-control facilities. Galion was settled in 1831.

Galitzin or **Galitsin:** see GALLITZIN.

Gall (gôl), c.1840–1894, war chief of the Sioux Indians, b. South Dakota. He refused to accept the treaty of 1868 (by which he would have been confined to a reservation), joined SITTING BULL and other dissident chiefs, and was the chief military lieutenant of Sitting Bull in the great defeat of George Armstrong Custer in the battle of Little Bighorn in 1876. He retreated to Canada but, after a quarrel with Sitting Bull about returning to their former lands, returned and surrendered at Poplar, Mont. He became a farmer on the reservation and with his friend James McLaughlin, the Indian agent, did much to improve relations between Indians and whites. See T. B. Marquis, *Sitting Bull and Gall* (1934).

Gall, Francis Joseph, 1758–1828, Austrian anatomist and founder of phrenology. He devoted most of his life to a minute study of the nervous system, especially the brain. With the collaboration of a favorite pupil, John Caspar Spurzheim (1776–1832), he incorporated his research into a four-volume work and atlas that appeared from 1810 to 1819. Gall demonstrated that the white matter of the brain consists of nerve fibers, and he launched the doctrine of localization in parts of the brain of various mental processes. Derided for his later involvement with the pseudoscience of PHRENOLOGY, he left Austria but was received with honors in France and died a wealthy man in Paris. Spurzheim carried the teachings of Gall to England and the United States, also with great success.

gall, abnormal growth, or hypertrophy, of plant tissue produced by chemical or mechanical (e.g., the rubbing together of two branches) irritants. Chemical irritants are released by parasitic fungi, bacteria, nematode worms, gall insects, and mites. Crown gall, which attacks peach and other fruit trees, grapes, and roses, is caused by bacteria. Despite its name (the crown is the head of foliage), the tumorous growths usually occur on the stem below ground level. The gall insects (e.g., certain aphids, wasps, moths, beetles, and midges) deposit their eggs in the plant tissues, which begin to swell as the larvae hatch. Sometimes the larvae feed on the gall and pupate within it. The irritant is released by the female at the time of oviposition or by the developing larva itself. Each species of gall insect has its favorite host and forms galls of a characteristic shape; some are large and woody and others may be soft, knobby, or spiny. They may be formed on any part of a plant but generally occur in areas where cells are actively growing. Galls are commonly seen on oak and willow trees and on rose bushes, goldenrod, and witch hazel. The Hessian fly, the wheat midge, and the mites and midges that attack fruit trees are the most damaging economically of the gall insects. Galls are rich in resins and tannic acid and are used in the manufacture of permanent inks and astringent ointments, in dyeing, and in tanning. A high-quality ink has long been made from the Aleppo gall, found on oaks in the Middle East; it is one of a number of galls resembling nuts and called gallnuts or nutgalls.

Galla (găl'ə), Hamitic pastoral tribes who live in W and S Ethiopia and part of Kenya. They number about 10 million and are either Muslim, Christian, or pagan. Originally from N Somalia, they later migrated to the region of Lake Rudolf. In the mid-16th cent. they began to move into the Ethiopian highlands. Never a united group, they were not a serious threat to the Ethiopian state. Their raids, however, were a considerable nuisance, and they were able to establish small states in many areas nominally controlled by the Ethiopian emperor. They were used as mercenary soldiers by the Ethiopians. See G. W. B. Huntingford, *The Galla of Ethiopia* (1955, repr. 1969); H. S. Lewis, *A Galla Monarchy* (1965).

Galla Placidia (găl'ə pləsĭd'ēə), c.388–450, Roman empress of the West, daughter of Theodosius I. Captured by Alaric I in the course of his Italian campaign, she was held by the Visigoths as a hostage and married (414) Alaric's successor ATAULF. After the murder (415) of Ataulf she was at first ill-treated but was returned in 416 to her brother HONORIUS. In 417 she married the general Constantius; shortly before his death he was made (421) coemperor as CONSTANTIUS III. In 423 she quarreled with Honorius and fled to the court of Theodosius II; after the death of Honorius she became regent for her son VALENTINIAN III, whom Theodosius placed on the throne after overthrowing (425) the usurper John. She had great personal influence over her son, but she was forced to leave the government largely in the hands of AETIUS.

Gallas, Matthias, Graf von (mätē'äs gräf fən gäl'äs), 1584–1647, imperial general in the THIRTY YEARS WAR. He served under TILLY, commander of the Catholic League, in Germany until 1629, and then entered Italy, helping to take Mantua (1630). He served as field marshal under WALLENSTEIN, chief of the imperial forces, but later participated in the conspiracy that brought about Wallenstein's removal by Holy Roman Emperor Ferdinand II and his subsequent assassination (1634). Gallas succeeded to a large part of Wallenstein's duchy of Friedland and to the actual command of the armies (nominally under the emperor's son). At Nördlingen (1634) he defeated the Swedes and BERNHARD OF SAXE-WEIMAR. After 1635 his drunkenness and total incompetence caused him several times to lose his command, but he regained it each time through influence at court.

Gallatin, Albert (găl'ətĭn), 1761–1849, American financier and public official, b. Geneva, Switzerland. Left an orphan at nine, Gallatin was reared by his patrician relatives and had an excellent education. He immigrated to the United States in 1780 and later settled (1784) in W Pennsylvania. A member of the Pennsylvania constitutional convention in 1789–90, he also served in the state legislature from 1790 to 1792. Although elected U.S. Senator in 1793, he was deprived (1794) of his office by the Federalist-controlled Senate, which claimed he had not been a citizen long enough to hold a seat. Returning to Pennsylvania, his statesmanlike efforts helped restrain the Western farmers in the WHISKEY REBELLION (1794), although Gallatin himself opposed the tax on whiskey. As a member of the U.S. House of Representatives (1795–1801), Gallatin became a recognized leader of the Republican (Jeffersonian) minority and was active in advocating financial reform and in opposing war with France. His demand that the Treasury Dept. be accountable to Congress led to the creation of a standing committee on finance in the House (later the Ways and Means Committee). As Secretary of the Treasury under President Jefferson, Gallatin undertook to change aspects of the country's financial policy from Federalist to Jeffersonian principles, and he reduced the country's debt despite the war against the Barbary States and the Louisiana Purchase. Continuing in office under President Madison, he helped to curtail appropriations for the armed forces and opposed the war hawks prior to the War of 1812 because he believed that Federal money should go toward realizing the democratic vision of a broadly expanding internal economy. His fiscal accomplishments were virtually destroyed by the Embargo Act of 1807 and the War of 1812. Gallatin left the Treasury Dept. to undertake a diplomatic mission in 1813. He was a key figure in negotiating the Treaty of Ghent, which ended the war with Great Britain. He later served as minister to France (1816–23) and to Great Britain (1826–27). Greatly interested in the Indians, Gallatin wrote papers on them and was responsible for founding the American Ethnological Society in 1842. Gallatin's eclectic financial policies—although a Jeffersonian he was a consistent supporter of the Bank of the United States—have been widely praised by conservatives and liberals alike; he was one of the most brilliant and successful of Jeffersonian statesmen. See biographies by Raymond Walters, Jr. (1957, repr. 1969), and F. E. Ewing (1959).

Gallatin, city (1970 pop. 13,271), seat of Sumner co., N central Tenn., near Nashville; inc. 1815. It is a livestock and agricultural center that produces tobacco. Shows of locally bred Tennessee walking horses are held there. Its manufactures include tobacco goods, cheese products, furniture, apparel, storm windows and doors, and locks. Nearby is Old Hickory Lake, a popular fishing and recreation area. The city is named for Albert Gallatin, Secretary of the Treasury under Presidents Jefferson and Madison. Andrew Jackson's home, the Hermitage, is nearby.

Gallatin, river, c.120 mi (190 km) long, rising in the Gallatin Range in the northwest corner of Yellowstone National Park, NW Wyo., and flowing generally northwest to join the Madison and Jefferson rivers at the Three Forks of the Missouri, SW Mont. The river is used for irrigation.

Gallaudet, Thomas Hopkins (gă"lôdĕt'), 1787–1851, American educator of the deaf, b. Philadelphia, grad. Andover Theological Seminary. In England and France he studied methods of education in schools for the deaf, and in Hartford, Conn., he founded (1817) the first such free school in the United States. He was interested also in many other philanthropies. See biography by his son, E. M. Gallaudet (1888). His oldest son, **Thomas Gallaudet,** 1822–1902, was ordained (1851) as an Episcopal priest. He devoted most of his time to missionary work among the deaf, founding St. Ann's Church for Deaf-Mutes in New York City and the Gallaudet Home for aged deaf-mutes at Poughkeepsie, N.Y. **Edward Miner Gallaudet,** 1837–1917, youngest son of Thomas Hopkins Gallaudet, opened a school for deaf-mutes in Washington, D.C.; the upper branch of this became Gallaudet College. One of the most progressive teachers in his field, he studied European methods and wrote many articles.

gall bladder, small pear-shaped sac that stores and concentrates BILE. It is attached to the liver (which produces the bile) by the hepatic duct. When food containing fat reaches the small intestine, the hormone cholecystokinin is produced by cells in the intestinal wall and carried to the gall bladder via the bloodstream. The hormone causes the gall bladder to contract, forcing bile into the common bile duct. A valve, which opens only when food is present in the intestine, allows bile to flow from the common bile duct into the duodenum where it functions in the process of fat digestion. Sometimes the substances contained in bile crystallize in the gall bladder, forming gallstones. These small, hard concretions are more common in persons over 40, especially in women and the obese. They can cause inflammation of the gall bladder, a disorder that produces symptoms similar to those of indigestion, especially after a fatty meal is consumed. If a stone becomes lodged in the bile duct, it produces severe pain. Gallstones may pass out of the body spontaneously; however, serious blockage is treated by removing the gall bladder surgically.

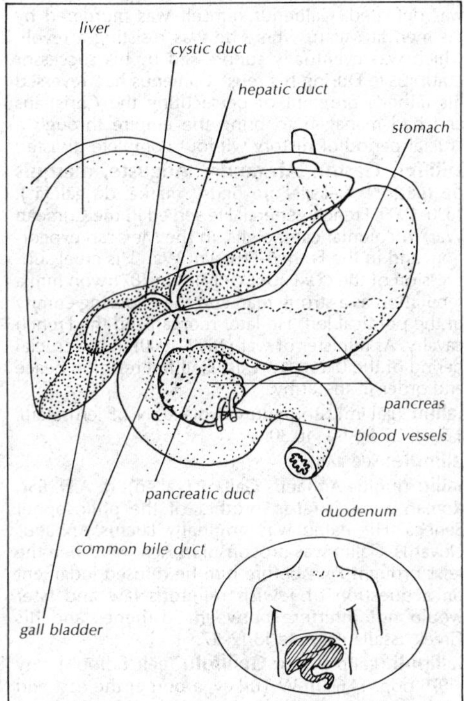

Gall bladder

Galle, Johann Gottfried (yō'hän gôt'frēt gä'lə), 1812–1910, German astronomer. He is noted for his discovery of the planet Neptune, Sept. 23, 1846, by following the guidance of calculations by LEVERRIER. Galle was then a member of the staff of the Berlin Observatory and had discovered three comets. In 1851 he became professor of astronomy at Breslau and director of the observatory there. His particular field of research was meteorology.

Galle (gäl), city (1963 pop. 64,942), capital of Southern prov., extreme S Sri Lanka (Ceylon), on the Indian Ocean. An agricultural market center, it exports tea, rubber, coconut oil, cloves, and other products of the surrounding region. Famous as a trade center for Chinese and Arabs by 100 B.C., Galle rose to prominence under Portuguese rule (1057–1640), when it became Sri Lanka's chief port. It was the capital of Sri Lanka under the Dutch (1640–56), whose original fort, built to guard the harbor, still stands. The city passed to the British in 1796. Its commercial importance continued until the opening of the Suez Canal in 1869 and the construction (1885) by the British of a modern harbor at Colombo. Since the 1960s congestion and labor problems at the port of Colombo have diverted some shipping to Galle.

Gallegos, Rómulo (rō'mo͞olō gäyä'gōs), 1884–1969, Venezuelan novelist and statesman. Gallegos lived in Spain in voluntary exile from the Venezuelan dictatorship from 1931 until 1935. He returned to his country and was appointed minister of education, being elected president in 1948. In office for only a few months, he was overthrown by a reactionary military coup. He lived in Mexico until his return to Venezuela in 1958. He is best known as the author of the novel *Doña Bárbara* (1929, tr. 1931), about the Venezuelan plains. The landscape is essentially the protagonist of the novel, in which primitive barbarism is overcome by civilizing influences. Gallegos's other important works are two episodic novels, *Cantaclaro* (1931) and *Canaíma* (1935), and *La Brizna de Paja en el Viento* (1952).

Gallen-Kallela, Akseli Valdemar (äk'sälē väl'dämär gälān'-käl'lälä), 1865–1931, Finnish painter. He was a student of Bouguereau. His series of stark, linear paintings of the *Kalevala* epic are among the finest Finnish works on national folk themes. Most of Gallen-Kallela's work is in Helsinki.

galleon, oceangoing warship used by the European naval powers in the 15th and 16th cent. A large, cumbersome vessel, the galleon was three-masted and square-rigged, usually with two decks, and with its main batteries in broadsides. Galleons were much used to transport treasure and other cargo from the Americas. The military disadvantage of the typical galleon was shown clearly in the defeat of the Spanish Armada (1588), when unwieldy Spanish galleons were outmaneuvered by the lighter, swifter English vessels constructed by John HAWKINS.

galley, long, narrow vessel widely used in ancient and medieval times, propelled principally by oars but also fitted with sails. The earliest type was sometimes 150 ft (46 m) long with 50 oars. Rowers were slaves, prisoners of war, or (later) convicts; they were usually chained to benches set along the sides, the center of the vessel being used for cargo. Galleys were decked at the bow and stern but were otherwise open. The typical galley was the trireme, with three banks of oars; smaller and more manageable galleys (biremes) had two banks. These vessels became very large, some reputedly having as many as 40 banks of oars, but smaller vessels were again common by the 1st cent. B.C. When galleys were employed in war, the sides were so designed that they could be raised to afford protection for the rowers. The Romans used hooks to fasten onto enemy vessels and carried bridges for boarding. Galleys were used in the Mediterranean by the French and Venetians until the 17th cent. In modern usage the galley is the kitchen of a ship.

gall fly: see FRUIT FLY.

gallic acid or **3,4,5-trihydroxybenzoic acid** (trī"hīdrŏk'sēbĕnzō'ĭk), $C_6H_2(OH)_3CO_2H$, colorless crystalline organic acid found in gallnuts, sumach, tea leaves, oak bark, and many other plants, both in its free state and as part of the tannin molecule (see TANNIN). Since gallic acid has hydroxyl groups and a carboxylic acid group in the same molecule, two molecules of it can react with one another to form an ester, digallic acid. Gallic acid is obtained by the hydrolysis of tannic acid with sulfuric acid. When heated above 220°C, gallic acid loses carbon dioxide to form pyrogallol, or 1,2,3-trihydroxybenzene, $C_6H_3(OH)_3$, which is used in the production of azo dyes and photographic developers and in laboratories for absorbing oxygen.

Gallicanism (găl'ĭkənĭz"əm), in French Roman Catholicism, tradition of resistance to papal authority. It was in opposition to ULTRAMONTANISM, the view that accorded the papacy complete authority over the universal church. Two aspects of Gallicanism are sometimes distinguished: royal Gallicanism, which defended the special rights of the French monarch in the French church; and ecclesiastical Gallicanism, which tried to preserve for the French clergy a certain administrative independence from Rome. Gallicanism in both senses received its theoretical formulation during the crisis of the Great SCHISM through the conciliar theory, which asserted the supremacy of general councils over the pope. The Council of Basel (see BASEL, COUNCIL OF) further extended the conciliar ideas and in 1438 the French king, Charles VII, legalized these antipapal measures in the Pragmatic Sanction of Bourges (see under PRAGMATIC SANCTION). For additional chapters in the long struggle between monarch and pope for control of the French church; see INVESTITURE; CHURCH AND STATE; PHILIP IV; BONIFACE VIII; CONCORDAT. The quarrel between Louis XIV and Innocent XI occasioned the famous "Four Gallican Articles," drawn up for Louis by the French bishops (see also INNOCENT XII). These declare that kings are not subject to the pope, that general councils supersede the pope's authority, that the pope must respect the customs of the local church, and that papal decrees do not bind unless accepted by the entire church. Gallicanism was much encouraged by Jansenism and remained fashionable at court. It was furthered by the followers of the Swiss theologian Thomas ERASTUS. No French king, however, sought to separate the French church from Rome, as did Henry VIII with the church in England; nor did any French king, despite the development of Gallican theory, ever manage to gain a hold over the church comparable to that exercised by the Spanish kings. The French clergy generally supported Gallicanism and during the French Revolution had little difficulty assenting to the Civil Constitution of the Clergy. The First Vatican Council in 1870 established the authority of the pope as a matter of dogma, and Gallicanism continued to live on only in the heretical OLD CATHOLICS. See W. H. Jervis, *The Gallican Church and the Revolution* (1882).

Galli-Curci, Amelita (āmālē'tä gäl'lē-ko͝or'chē), 1889–1963, Italian-American coloratura soprano. She studied piano at the Milan Conservatory and meanwhile trained her own voice. From the time she made her debut in the role of Gilda in *Rigoletto* at Rome in 1909 until goiter forced her retirement from opera in 1930, her full and golden voice won great praise; at her best she was not excelled by any coloratura of her day. After her American debut (Chicago, 1916) she sang with the Chicago Opera Company until 1924. At the Metropolitan Opera, New York City, she sang first in 1920 and regularly from 1926 to 1930, presenting all the standard coloratura roles. She then continued to sing for several more years in concert recitals. See biography by C. E. Le Massena (1945).

Gallic Wars (găl'ĭk), campaigns in GAUL led by Julius CAESAR in his two terms as proconsul of Cisalpine Gaul, Transalpine Gaul, and Illyricum (58 B.C.–51 B.C.). Caesar's first campaign was to prevent the Helvetii (who lived N of the Lake of Geneva) from crossing the Roman territory Provincia (Provence) on their way to a new home in SW Gaul. Inspired by Orgetorix, they had started from the Alps northwestward with Caesar in pursuit, but he split their forces as they crossed the Saône, and pursued them to BIBRACTE, where he defeated them. In the same year the Aedui asked Caesar's help against the German ARIOVISTUS, whom Caesar routed. In 57 B.C., Caesar pacified Belgica (roughly Belgium). In the winter of the same year an anti-Roman confederacy was formed, and in 56 B.C. Caesar attacked its leaders, the Veneti, who maintained a fleet in what is now the Gulf of Morbihan, Brittany. He defeated them after building ships of his own. In 55 B.C., Caesar went to the Low Countries to repel a group of invading Germans and, as a punitive measure, in turn invaded German territory, crossing the Rhine on a bridge he built near Cologne. He then went to Britain on a brief exploring expedition. In 54 B.C. he invaded Britain and defeated the Britons and their leader Cassivellaunus. The following winter the Roman legions were quartered separately because of the scarcity of food, and some Belgian tribes led by AMBIORIX raised a revolt. One legion was utterly defeated and another, under Quintus CICERO, was in dire straits when Caesar arrived and routed the rebels. In 53 B.C., Caesar put down another Belgian revolt and entered Germany again. But the real test came when, in the dead of winter, Caesar, in Italy, learned that all central Gaul had raised a revolt, organized by VERCINGETORIX. With incredible speed and brilliant tactics, Caesar crossed the Alps and suppressed the Gauls. After 51 B.C., Caesar moved around Gaul putting down the last signs of disorder. Caesar's Gallic Wars were the theater in which he displayed his abilities, and his organization of the new territory was the seed of modern France. When Caesar became proconsul, he received a wide strip along the Mediterranean beyond the Alps; when he gave up his command, his territory included everything from the Rhine to the Pyrenees, from the Alps to the Atlantic. The prime source of the Gallic Wars is Caesar's own commentaries, *De bello Gallico*. See also T. Rice Holmes, *Caesar's Conquest of Gaul* (2d ed. 1911).

Galli da Bibiena: see BIBIENA, GALLI DA.

Gallieni, Joseph Simon (zhôzĕf' sēmôN' gälyānē'), 1849–1916, French general and colonial administrator. He served well in the Sudan and Tonkin and, as governor general (1896–1905), solidly established French administration in Madagascar. Called from retirement in World War I, he served as military governor of Paris and was the crucial figure in the French victory of the Marne (1914). Although credit for the victory went to General Joffre as commander, it seems clear that it was Gallieni who saw the opportunity for counterattack and urged Joffre into action. Gallieni later became (1915) minister of war under Aristide Briand and demanded reorganization of the command and more complete preparation for war. The cabinet refused, and he resigned (1916) on a plea of ill health, dying within the year. His proposals were implemented after his death; in 1921 he was made a marshal posthumously. Gallieni wrote several books on colonial affairs.

Gallienus (Publius Licinius Valerianus Egnatius) (găl"ĭē'nəs), d. 268, Roman emperor. He ruled as the colleague (253–60) of his father, VALERIAN, and alone (260–68). When his father was in the East, Gallienus checked the Alemanni near Milan, and even after the capture of Valerian he was successful. Later, however, the provinces began to be too rebellious for his control. POSTUMUS had established his independence in Gaul, and in the East Odenathus, spreading the conquests of PALMYRA, was being recognized. A force sent by Gallienus against ZENOBIA was defeated. Gallienus himself was murdered by his men at Milan, where he was resisting a revolt, which was eventually suppressed by his successor CLAUDIUS II. During his reign Gallienus had reversed his father's program of persecuting the Christians and had managed to bring the empire through a crucial period of history without complete disaster.

Galliffet, Gaston Alexandre Auguste, marquis de (gästôN' älĕksäN'drə ōgüst' märkē' də gälĕfā'), 1830–1909, French general. He served in the Crimean War, in colonial campaigns, in the Mexican expedition, and in the Franco-Prussian War. His cruel suppression of the COMMUNE OF PARIS in 1871 won him a reputation as a strong man and the enduring enmity of the political left. He later reorganized the French cavalry. As minister of war (1899–1900) in the crucial period of the DREYFUS AFFAIR, Galliffet restored peace and order in the army.

Gallim (găl'ĭm), unidentified place, N of Jerusalem. 1 Sam. 25.44; Isa. 10.30.

gallinule: see RAIL.

Gallio (Junius Annaeus Gallio) (găl'ēō), d. A.D. 65?, Roman administrator; brother of the philosopher Seneca. His name was originally Lucius Annaeus Novatus. Gallio was proconsul in Achaea. When the Jews brought Paul before him he refused judgment on a question of Jewish religious law and later would not interfere between Sosthenes and his Greek assailants. Acts 18.12–17.

Gallipoli (gəlĭp'əlē) or **Gelibolu** (gĕlē'bōlo͞o"), city (1970 pop. 14,600), W Turkey, a port at the east end of the DARDANELLES, near the neck of the GALLIPOLI PENINSULA. It has long been a strategic point in the defense of İstanbul (Constantinople) and has numerous historic remains. It was captured by the Ottoman Turks in 1354.

Gallipoli campaign, 1915, Allied expedition in World War I for the purpose of gaining control of the DARDANELLES and Bosporus straits, capturing Constantinople, and opening a Black Sea supply route to Russia. The idea of forcing the straits was originally promoted by Winston Churchill, then first lord of the admiralty. After the failure (March, 1915) of a British naval force to open the straits, British, Australian, and New Zealand troops landed (April 25) at various points on the east coast of the Gallipoli Peninsula, while a French force landed on the Asiatic side of the straits. The Turks, under General LIMAN VON SANDERS, had been reinforced, and they put up stubborn resistance, preventing the Allies from making any important gains. Allied cooperation was poor, and there was lack of coordination between land and naval forces. A landing (Aug., 1915) at Suvla, on the west coast of the peninsula, was equally futile and resulted in severe casualties. After months of costly fighting the Allied commander, Sir Ian Hamilton, was replaced by Sir Charles Munro, and the Allies withdrew from the area on Jan. 9, 1916. The evacuation was brilliantly executed; it was the only successful operation of a disastrous campaign. See Sir Ian Hamilton, *Gallipoli Diary* (1920); R. R. James, *Gallipoli* (1965).

Gallipoli Peninsula, Lat. *Chersonesus Thracica*, narrow peninsula, c.50 mi (80 km) long, W Turkey, extending southwestward between the Aegean Sea and the DARDANELLES. The port of Gallipoli gives it its name. It was the scene of the GALLIPOLI CAMPAIGN of 1915 and was (1920–36) part of the demilitarized Zone of the Straits.

Gallitzin (gəlĭt'sĭn), Rus. *Golytsin* (gəlyē'tsĭn), Russian princely family. Among many alternate spellings are Galitzin, Galytzin, and Galitsin. **Vasily Vasilyevich Gallitzin,** d. 1619, helped to enthrone the first false DMITRI but later joined the Shuiski conspiracy against him. Sent to offer the Russian crown to Prince Ladislaus of Poland, he was thrown into prison by King Sigismund III of Poland after refusing to help Sigismund obtain the crown for himself. He died in prison. **Vasily Vasilyevich Gallitzin,** 1643–1714, was the lover and chief counselor of SOPHIA ALEKSEYEVNA, regent during the joint reign of Ivan V and Peter I. After Sophia's downfall (1689), he was exiled to Siberia by Peter I. **Boris Alekseyevich Gallitzin,** 1654–1714, was the tutor of Peter I and helped to depose Sophia Alekseyevna. He headed the government in Russia during Peter's first foreign tour. **Dmitri Mikhailovich Gallitzin,** 1665–1737, held administrative posts, was ambassador to Turkey and Poland, and fought with distinction against Sweden in the Northern War. After the death (1730) of Peter II, he persuaded the supreme privy council to offer the throne to ANNA, daughter of Ivan V, on the condition that she sign articles limiting her power. After Anna's ascension, however, she began to rule absolutely, and she had Gallitzin sentenced to death but later commuted his sentence to exile. **Mikhail Mikhailovich Gallitzin,** 1675–1730, commanded Russian operations in Finland (1714–21) during the Northern War with Sweden and was responsible for the Treaty of Nystad, concluded at the end of the war. As governor of Finland he was popular with the Finns. **Aleksandr Mikhailovich Gallitzin,** 1718–83, Russian field marshal, distinguished himself in the Seven Years War and in the Russo-Turkish Wars. **Dmitri Alekseyevich Gallitzin,** 1735–1803, was Russian ambassador at Paris (1765–73) and later at The Hague. He was the father of Demetrius Augustine Gallitzin (see separate article) and a friend of Diderot and Voltaire. **Aleksandr Nikolayevich Gallitzin,** 1773?–1844, a statesman of liberal tendencies, was an influential counselor of Alexander I. He was procurator of the holy synod and minister of education, but he lost his influence after the accession of Nicholas I. **Nikolai Borisovich Gallitzin,** 1794–1866, was an amateur cellist and a patron of Beethoven, who dedicated string quartets (Opus 127, Opus 130, and Opus 132) and his overture *The Consecration of the House* to him. **Nikolai Dmitreyevich Gallitzin,** 1856–1925, appointed head of Czar Nicholas II's council of ministers in 1916, was the last holder of that office prior to the Russian Revolution.

Gallitzin, Demetrius Augustine, 1770–1840, American frontier missionary; son of Dmitri Alekseyevich Gallitzin. The young prince followed his mother in joining the Roman Catholic Church and determined to devote himself to church work in the United States. He was trained in the seminary at Baltimore, was ordained a priest in 1795, and began itinerant missionary work among the frontiersmen and Indians of SW Pennsylvania, where he was known as Father Smith. At much expense to himself he founded (1799) the Catholic colony of Loretto near Gallitzin (which is named for him). There he lived out his life, refusing to return to claim his patrimony in Russia and declining ecclesiastical preferment.

gallium (găl'ēəm), metallic chemical element; symbol Ga; at. no. 31; at. wt. 69.72; m.p. 29.78°C; b.p. 2403°C; sp. gr. 5.904 at 29.6°C (solid), 6.095 at 29.8°C (liquid); valence +2 or +3. Solid gallium is a blue-gray metal with orthorhombic crystalline structure. The liquid metal has a beautiful silver color. Although gallium is solid at normal room temperatures, it becomes liquid when heated slightly. It is the only metal other than mercury, cesium, and rubidium that has this property. Gallium is a liquid over a wide temperature range and has a low vapor pressure even at high temperatures; it has found limited use in thermometers and manometers for high-temperature measurements. Gallium expands about 3% when solidified. The metal is relatively unreactive. It does not react with air or water at room temperature and is only slightly attacked by mineral acids; it is oxidized slowly when red-hot and reacts with water at high temperatures. Liquid gallium wets porcelain and glass surfaces; it forms a bright, highly reflective surface when coated on glass. It is used to form low-melting alloys. Gallium is chemically similar to aluminum, the element above it in group IIIa of the PERIODIC TABLE. It forms many compounds, among them oxides, hydroxides, halides, alums, and numerous organometallic compounds. Gallium arsenide and gallium phosphide are used in rectifiers and transistors as semiconductors and in lasers, light-emitting transistors, photocells, and electronic refrigeration. Although gallium is widely distributed in nature, it does not occur in appreciable concentrations even in germanite, the ore richest in gallium. Gallium is produced commercially as a by-product in the production of zinc and aluminum. In Europe and Great Britain it is recovered from flue dust, a residue from the burning of coal. D. I. MENDELEEV predicted the properties of gallium, which he called ekaaluminum, before it was discovered spectroscopically in 1875 by P. E. Lecoq de Boisbaudran.

gallon: see ENGLISH UNITS OF MEASUREMENT.

gallotannic acid (găl"ōtăn'ĭk): see TANNIN.

Galloway, Joseph, c.1731–1803, American Loyalist leader, b. West River, Md. Galloway was a prominent lawyer with an interest in commerce and in speculation in Western lands. He entered the Pennsylvania assembly in 1756 and soon joined Benjamin Franklin in petitioning the king to abolish the proprietary government of the Penns. As speaker of the Pennsylvania assembly (1766–75) he attempted to conciliate between the colonies and the British government; he believed that the growing conflict could be settled by legal means, especially by a written constitution for the empire. Galloway served as a delegate to the first Continental Congress and proposed a plan for union between the colonies and Great Britain. Unable to maintain neutrality in the American Revolution, he joined Sir William Howe after the British occupied Philadelphia and acted as civil administrator during the British occupation of the city. Later (1778) Galloway went to England and became the spokesman of American Loyalists there. See study by B. H. Newcomb (1972).

Galloway, region and parliamentary division of SW Scotland, comprising Wigtownshire and Kirkcudbrightshire. The Rhinns, or Rinns, of Galloway is a rocky peninsula of Wigtownshire; its southern extremity is called the Mull of Galloway and is the southernmost point in Scotland. The black, hornless Galloway cattle have long been bred in this region. Dairying is the principal industry.

gallstone: see GALL BLADDER.

Gallup, George Horace, 1901–, American public opinion statistician, originator of the Gallup POLL, b. Jefferson, Iowa. After teaching journalism at Drake Univ. (1929–31) and at Northwestern Univ. (1931–32), he founded the American Institute of Public Opinion (1935) and the Audience Research Institute (1939), both at Princeton, N.J. His *Guide to Public Opinion Polls* appeared in 1944. Gallup's polls are most famous for preelection surveys. The 1936 presidential elections brought public attention to his organization because of the accuracy of its predictions. Since then the Gallup poll has had a good record, except for its prediction in 1948 that Thomas Dewey would defeat President Truman.

Gallup, town (1970 pop. 14,596), alt. 6,515 ft (1,986 m), seat of McKinley co., NW N. Mex., on the Puerco River near the Ariz. line; inc. 1891. It is a rail and trade center in a large mining, timber, and ranching area. Located in a region heavily populated by Indians (chiefly Navajo, Zuñi, and Hopi), its economy is based upon Indian trade, and the city's major employer is the U.S. Bureau of Indian Affairs. Uranium, oil, natural gas, and coal are among the minerals found and processed. There is also some manufacturing, and tourism is important; nearby natural and archaeological wonders draw many visitors, as does the intertribal Indian ceremonial held every August. A U.S. public health service Indian hospital is in Gallup, and an army depot is at nearby old Fort Wingate.

Gallus (Caius Vibius Trebonianus Gallus) (găl'əs), d. 253 or 254, Roman emperor after 251. He fought in the eastern campaign that proved fatal to DECIUS. Gallus became emperor and accepted Hostilianus, Decius' son, as his colleague, or nominal coruler. In Gallus' reign the Persians overran Mesopotamia, and the Goths invaded Moesia and Thrace. In 252 or 253 a new invasion was repelled in the Danube valley by the general Aemilianus, whose troops proclaimed him emperor. Gallus sent VALERIAN to put down the sedition. Aemilianus entered Italy, and the army murdered Gallus. Aemilianus succeeded, and Valerian succeeded him soon afterward.

Galois, Évariste (āvārēst' gälwä'), 1811–32, French mathematician. At the age of 17 he had evolved original concepts on the theory of algebra. He made important contributions to the theory of equations, the theory of numbers, and the theory of functions and was a pioneer in establishing the theory of groups in algebraic substitutions. Galois was twice imprisoned for his republican sympathies. He was killed in a duel with a political opponent. See Ian Stewart, *Galois Theory* (1973).

Galsworthy, John (gôlz'wûrthē, gălz'–), 1867–1933, English novelist and dramatist. Winner of the 1932 Nobel Prize in Literature, he is best remembered for his series of novels tracing the history of the wealthy Forsyte family from the 1880s to the 1920s. Of an old and rich family, Galsworthy spent his youth in relative leisure, studied at Oxford, was called to the bar in 1890, and in 1894 began a period of extensive travel. After the publication of his first novel, *Jocelyn* (1898), he devoted himself entirely to writing. The bulk of his fiction deals with the fortunes of the Forsytes, an upper-middle-class family—complacent, acquisitive, snobbish, and ruled by money. His attitude towards them was not unsympathetic, and he created several memorable characters, notably Soames Forsyte, "the man of property," who treats even his wife as a possession. The Forsyte novels are grouped in three trilogies. The first of these, *The Forsyte Saga* (1922), includes *The Man of Property* (1906), *In Chancery* (1920), and *To Let* (1921). The second trilogy, *A Modern Comedy* (1928), includes *The White Monkey* (1924), *The Silver Spoon* (1926), and *Swan Song* (1928). The third group, *End of the Chapter* (1934), includes *Maid in Waiting* (1931), *Flowering Wilderness* (1932), and *One More River* (1933). Galsworthy also wrote a series of dramas concerned with various social problems. Although their impartiality makes them less than exciting, the plays were remarkably successful. They include *The Silver Box* (1906), *Strife* (1909), *Justice* (1910), *The Pigeon* (1912), *The Skin Game* (1920), *Loyalties* (1922), and *Escape* (1926). See his *Life and Letters* by H. V. Marrot (1935, repr. 1973); his letters to Edward Garnett (1934); biographies by R. H. Mottram (1956) and R. Sauter (1967); studies by Genji Takahashi (1954) and Dudley Barker (1963); bibliography by H. V. Marrot (1928, repr. 1973).

Galt, Sir Alexander Tilloch (tĭl'ək gôlt), 1817–93, Canadian statesman, b. England; son of John Galt. In 1835 he went to Canada in the service of the British American Land Company. He directed (1844–55) the affairs of this company and was also involved in promoting the building of railroads. He was a member of the Canadian Legislative Assembly (1849–50, 1853–67) and of the Canadian House of Commons (1867–72). Although Galt had in 1849 signed the manifesto favoring the annexation of Canada by the United States, he became one of the most persistent and influential leaders of the movement for confederation of the provinces, and when he accepted (1858) the ministry of finance in the Cartier-Macdonald administration, it was on the understanding that the government would work to achieve confederation. In 1859, in answer to Great Britain's protests against the protective tariff newly adopted by Canada, Galt declared that Canada must be allowed control of its financial policies. While serving (1858–62, 1864–66) as minister of finance he was an influential member of the two conferences (1864) on confederation and of the London Conference that resulted in the British North America Act. He became (1867) minister of finance in the first dominion government, but he resigned in 1868 because of disagreement with Prime Minister John A. Macdonald and in 1872 retired from Parliament. He was the dominant member of the Halifax Fisheries Commission, which won for Canada a large award from the United States. From 1880 to 1883 he served as Canadian high commissioner in London, the first to hold that position. In the last 10 years of his life he had economic interests in W Canada, among them the development of coal deposits in Alberta; in this connection he founded LETHBRIDGE. He was knighted in 1878. See biography by O. D. Skelton (rev. ed. 1966).

Galt, John, 1779–1839, Scottish novelist. He went to Canada as secretary for the Canada Company, founding there in 1827 the town of Guelph and encouraging Canadian immigration. He wrote poems, blank-verse tragedies, and travel books, but he is known chiefly for his novels of Scottish country life, notably *The Ayrshire Legatees* (1821), *Annals of the Parish* (1821), and *The Entail* (1823). While traveling on the Continent as a young man, he made the acquaintance of Lord Byron, of whom he wrote a biography that appeared in 1830. See his autobiography (1833); biography by I. A. Gordon (1973).

Galt, industrial city (1971 pop. 38,897), S Ont., Canada, on the Grand River, NW of Hamilton. Manufactures include textiles, chemicals, and plastics.

Galton, Sir Francis (gôl'tən), 1822–1911, English scientist, founder of eugenics; cousin of Charles Darwin. He turned from exploration and meteorology (where he introduced the theory of the anticyclone) to the study of heredity and EUGENICS (a term that he coined). Galton devised the correlation coefficient and brought other statistical methods into this work, which was carried on by his pupil Karl Pearson as the science of biometrics. In his *Hereditary Genius* (1869) he presented strong evidence that talent is an inherited characteristic. Galton established a system of classifying fingerprints that is still used today. He was knighted in 1909. The best known of his books is *Inquiries into Human Faculty* (1883). See his *Memories of My Life* (1908, repr. 1974); biography by Karl Pearson (3 vol. in 4, 1914–30); study by H. F. Crovitz (1970).

Galuppi, Baldassare (bäldäs-sä'rā gälo͞op'pē), 1706–85, Italian composer. A pupil of Lotti, he developed the opera buffa style in the period between Scarlatti and Mozart, and he also wrote oratorios and chamber music. He is immortalized in Robert Browning's poem "A Toccata of Galuppi's."

Galvani, Luigi (lo͞oē'jē gälvä'nē), 1737–98, Italian physician. He was professor of anatomy from 1775 at the Univ. of Bologna and was noted as a surgeon and for research in comparative anatomy. During experiments on muscle and nerve preparations of frogs, he noticed the contraction of a frog's leg touched with charged metal. He devised an arc of two metals with which contractions could be induced and in 1791 published his results, attributing the source of electricity to the animal tissue. The explanation was disputed by Volta, who correctly believed that the electricity originated in the metallic arc. The controversy focused attention on electricity in animals and stimulated research in electrotherapy and on electric currents. Many terms in electricity are derived from Galvani's name.

galvanizing, process of coating a metal, usually iron or steel, with a protective covering of zinc. Galvanized iron is prepared either by dipping iron, from which rust has been removed by the action of sulfuric acid, into molten zinc so that a thin layer of the zinc remains on the surface of the iron upon removal or by a method of electroplating. Iron is also coated with zinc by a method in which the iron is first covered with the zinc dust and then baked; an alloy is formed at the surface, the resulting product being known as sherardized iron. Sheets of pure iron, copper iron, and various steels, as well as wire and netting, are often galvanized, since the zinc coating resists oxidation and the action of moisture very successfully. When the coating is broken or pierced some protection is still afforded, since the zinc reacts with the corroding agent first.

galvanometer (găl"vənŏm'ətər), instrument used to determine the presence, direction, and strength of an electric current in a conductor. All galvanometers are based upon the discovery by Hans C. Oersted that a magnetic needle is deflected by the presence of an electric current in a nearby conductor. When an electric current is passing through the conductor, the magnetic needle tends to turn at right angles to the conductor so that its direction is parallel to the lines of induction around the conductor and its north pole points in the direction in which these lines of induction flow. In general, the extent to

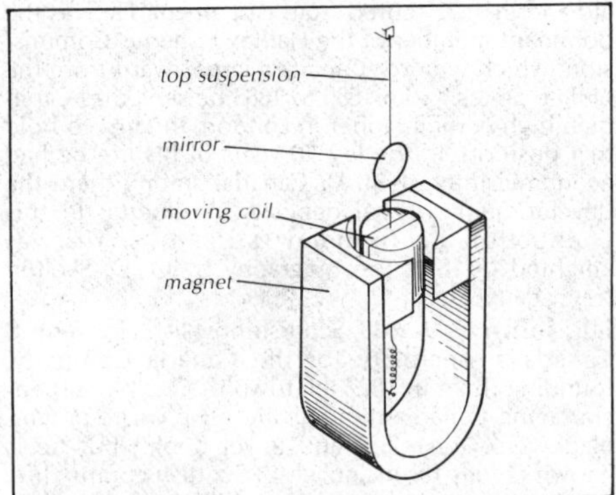

Galvanometer

which the needle turns is dependent upon the strength of the current. In the first galvanometers, a freely turning magnetic needle was hung in a coil of wire; in later versions the magnet was fixed and the coil made movable. Modern galvanometers are of this movable-coil type and are called d'Arsonval galvanometers (after Arsène d'Arsonval, a French physicist). If a pointer is attached to the moving coil so that it passes over a suitably calibrated scale, the galvanometer can be used to measure quantitatively the current passing through it. Such calibrated galvanometers are used in many electrical measuring devices. The DC AMMETER, an instrument for measuring direct current, often consists of a calibrated galvanometer through which the current to be measured is made to pass. Since heavy currents would damage the galvanometer, a bypass, or shunt, is provided so that only a certain known percentage of the current passes through the galvanometer. By measuring the known percentage of the current, one arrives at the total current. The DC VOLTMETER, which can measure direct voltage, consists of a calibrated galvanometer connected in series (see ELECTRIC CIRCUIT) with a high resistance. To measure the voltage between two points, one connects the voltmeter between them. The current through the galvanometer (and hence the pointer reading) is then proportional to the voltage (see OHM'S LAW).

Galveston (găl'vəstən), city (1970 pop. 61,809), seat of Galveston co., on Galveston Island, SE Texas; inc. 1839. The island lies across the entrance to Galveston Bay, an inlet of the Gulf of Mexico. Long causeways connect the city with the mainland and with Texas City. Trains and trucks bring cotton, sulfur, rice, flour, and other products to Galveston to be stored, processed, and shipped all over the world. Despite the ship channel to the larger port at Houston, Galveston remains a key port of entry. Oil refining and shipbuilding are major industries, and the city has grain elevators, machine shops, cotton compresses, chemical plants, and large fishing and shrimping fleets. It is also a beach and fishing resort, with its attractions enhanced by pink and white oleanders, rich bougainvillea, and other subtropical blooms. The Spanish knew the bay and the island early; it was probably there that Cabeza de Vaca was shipwrecked in 1528. For three hundred years it was visited and occupied by wandering Indian tribes, adventurers, revolutionists, and buccaneers, notably the crews of Jean Laffite. Settlement began in the 1830s, and Galveston was named for Bernardo de Gálvez. The good natural port came gradually into its own despite scourges of yellow fever, hurricanes, and occupation for a few months in 1862 by a small Union force. In 1900 hurricane winds struck Galveston, driving water across the low-lying island. Thousands were killed, and the city left in ruins. After the city was rebuilt, the municipal-commission form of government was adopted (1901); Galveston was the first city to have it. Against future storms an enormous 10-mi (16-km)-long protective seawall was built. However, in 1961 another hurricane caused much damage. Besides the great seawall, the Texas Heroes monument and several old homes are of interest today. Fort Crockett, once headquarters for the city's harbor defenses, is now used by the U.S. Army Corps of Engineers. A Coast Guard base and the Texas maritime academy are in Galveston, as are a junior college and the Univ. of Texas medical school, with a large group of hospitals. See E. W. Fornell, *The Galveston Era* (1962).

Gálvez, Bernardo de (bĕrnär'thō dā gäl'vāth), c.1746–1786, Spanish governor of Louisiana. He served in the Spanish army before going to Louisiana in 1776 as the young commandant of the troops stationed there. The favorite protégé of his powerful uncle José de Gálvez, he assumed the governorship on Jan. 1, 1777. In the American Revolution, Gálvez first played the role of benevolent neutral to the rebels. American frontiersmen were furnished with arms and supplies through the agency that he permitted Oliver Pollock to establish at New Orleans. After Spain declared war on England in 1779, he became a more active ally, capturing Baton Rouge and Natchez (1779), Mobile (1780), and Pensacola (1781). These victories were largely responsible for the British cession of both East and West Florida to Spain in the peace settlement of 1783. In Spain (1783–84) he was richly rewarded for his services, being made count of Gálvez, lieutenant general of the royal armies, and captain general of Louisiana and the Floridas. He became, in addition, captain general of Cuba in 1784, and in 1785 succeeded his father, Matías de Gálvez, as viceroy of New Spain (Mexico). The city of Galveston, Texas, was named for him. See J. W. Caughey, *Bernardo de Gálvez in Louisiana, 1776–1783* (1934).

Gálvez, José de (hōsā' dā), 1720–87, Spanish colonial administrator. Appointed as a governor in the Philippines in 1750, he later became visitor general to New Spain (1765–72). After a thorough inspection of the viceroyalty, he engineered the dismissal of the viceroy (1766). Under the successor in office, the marqués de CROIX, Gálvez held actual power. War against the northern Indians opened the way for expansion of the realm, and the development of defenses made it more secure against foreign enemies. After his return to Spain (1772), Gálvez became the leading spirit of the Council of the Indies, minister general of the Indies (1775), and councilor of state. He was responsible for two ordinances that profoundly affected the colonial policy of Spain—that of 1778, which established restricted free trade to replace the narrow mercantile policy of earlier days, and that of 1786, which made sweeping changes in colonial administration and set up a system of intendancies modeled on the French. He was rewarded for his services with the title marqués de la Sonora. His influence advanced the fortunes of his brother, Matías de Gálvez, and of his nephew, Bernardo de Gálvez. See H. I. Priestly, *José de Gálvez* (1916).

Gálvez, Matías de (mätē'äs), 1717–84, Spanish colonial administrator, captain general of Guatemala (1779), viceroy of New Spain (1783–84); brother of José de Gálvez. He was succeeded as viceroy by his son, Bernardo de Gálvez.

Galway (gôl'wā), county (1971 pop. 148,220), 2,293 sq mi (5,939 sq km), W Republic of Ireland. The county town is GALWAY. The county is divided into two sections by Lough Corrib. The mountains of the CONNEMARA region lie to the west; to the east stretches a rolling plain, partially covered with bogs. Principal rivers are the Clare, the Clarinbridge, the Dunkelin, and the Shannon (which forms part of the eastern boundary) and its tributary, the Suck. The shore line is extremely irregular, and there are numerous islands, the chief of which are the ARAN ISLANDS, lying off the mouth of Galway Bay. The main industries are agriculture (sheep, cattle, oats, and potatoes) and fishing (salmon). Marble is quarried, and there is some light manufacturing.

Galway, urban district (1971 pop. 26,896), county town of Co. Galway, W Republic of Ireland, on Galway Bay near the mouth of the Corrib River. Tourism, food processing, and the production of textiles and furniture, are the industries. Agricultural produce, salmon, herring, marble, and woolen goods are exported. Galway was first incorporated by Richard II of England in the late 14th cent. In 1651 the town was taken by parliamentary forces, and in 1691 it was taken by William III after the battle of Aughrim. For centuries Galway traded extensively with Spain, and Spanish influence may be seen in the architecture. The Church of St. Nicholas dates from 1320. The Lynch Stone behind the church commemorates the execution by the lord mayor, James Lynch Fitzstephen, of his own son for murder. Claddagh, once noted for its unique customs, is a quarter of the town said to be the oldest fishing village in Ireland. Noteworthy is the edifice (1849) of University College, a constituent of the National Univ. of Ireland.

Galway Bay, inlet of the Atlantic Ocean, 30 mi (48 km) long, W Republic of Ireland, in counties Galway and Clare. The Aran Islands protect its entrance, and there are many other islands in the bay itself, which receives water from Lough Corrib.

Galytsin or **Galytzin:** see GALLITZIN.

Gama, Vasco da (vă'skō də gă'mə, Port. väsh'kō dä gä'mə), c. 1469–1524, Portuguese navigator, the first European to journey by sea to India. His epochal voyage (1497–99) was made at the order of MANUEL I. With four vessels, he rounded the Cape of Good Hope, passed the easternmost point reached by Bartolomeo DIAS in 1488, continued up the east coast of Africa to Malindi, and sailed across the Indian Ocean to Calicut. This voyage opened up a way for Europe to reach the wealth of the Indies, and out of it grew the Portuguese Empire. Immediately Portugal gained great riches from the spice trade. Gama dictated the instructions for Cabral's voyage (1500–1502) to India, and in 1502 he himself led a fleet of 20 ships on his second India voyage. With this force he attempted to establish Portuguese power in Indian waters and sought to secure the submission of a number of chiefs on the African coast. He was harsh in his methods and was not as good an administrator as many of the Portuguese captains who later went to the East, but he was the first, and he was fittingly honored with many tributes and the title of count of Vidigueria. In 1524 he was sent back to India as viceroy, but he died soon after his arrival. Gama's voyage is the subject of Camoens's epic *The Lusiads.* See *A Journal of the First Voyage of Vasco da Gama* (1898), the journal of one of Gama's subordinates; G. Corrêa, *The Three Voyages of Vasco da Gama and His Viceroyalty* (1869, repr. 1964); K. G. Jayne, *Vasco da Gama and His Successors* (1910, repr. 1970); H. H. Hart, *Sea Route to the Indies* (1950, repr. 1971).

Gamaliel (gəmā'lēəl). **1** Manassite chief. Num. 1.10. **2** President of the Sanhedrin at Jerusalem and teacher of Paul. He was Hillel's grandson and disciple. He advocated leniency toward Christians. Acts 5.34; 22.3.

Gamaliel of Jabneh (jăb'nē), fl. A.D. 100, Jewish scholar; grandson of the Gamaliel who taught St. Paul the Law. He was recognized even by the Romans as a leader of his people. He strengthened the morale of the Jews and played a significant role in the formulation of two important innovations in Jewish ritual: the final version of the 18 benedictions, and the Passover seder, which substituted for the paschal sacrifice of the now destroyed Temple. His purpose was to retain the spirit of Judaism after the destruction of Jerusalem.

Gambarelli, surname of two Florentine painters: see ROSSELLINO.

Gambetta, Léon (lāôN' gäNbĕtä'), 1838–82, French republican leader. A lawyer who achieved some note as an opponent of the Second Empire of NAPOLEON III, he was elected deputy in 1869 and joined the parliamentary opposition. After the FRANCO-PRUSSIAN WAR precipitated the downfall of the empire (1870), he became prominent in the provisional government. His organization of a government of national defense to drive out the Germans, his spectacular escape from Paris in a balloon, and his gallant opposition to the Prussian forces won worldwide sympathy. Gambetta bitterly fought French capitulation and briefly retired from politics, but after 1871 he devoted himself to the creation of the Third Republic. After the resignation of Adolphe THIERS as president, Gambetta pursued a policy of moderation and compromise and opposed both the radical republicans with whom he had been identified earlier in his career, and the monarchists and conservatives. He was influential in shaping the republican constitution of 1875, and as the real leader of the republican forces, he strove for unity against President MACMAHON. Under President Grévy, Gambetta was briefly premier (1881–82), but his attempt to strengthen the executive power and to reconcile French political and social factions was unsuccessful, and his suggested electoral reform was widely denounced. He died soon after. A vigorous republican and patriot and a strong anticlerical, Gambetta was later highly revered. See studies by Paul Deschanel (1920), Harold Stannard (1921), and J. P. T. Bury (1936, repr. 1970).

Gambia (găm'bēə), officially **The Gambia,** republic (1973 est. pop. 400,000), 4,361 sq mi (11,295 sq km), W Africa, on the Atlantic Ocean. The capital is BANJUL. The smallest country in Africa, Gambia comprises Saint Mary's Island (site of Banjul) and, on the adjacent mainland, a narrow enclave, never more than 30 mi (48 km) wide, in Senegal; this territorial strip borders both banks of the Gambia River for c.200 mi (320 km) above its mouth. The river, which rises in Guinea and flows c.600 mi (970 km) to the Atlantic, is navigable throughout Gambia. Along Gambia's coast are fine sand beaches; inland is the

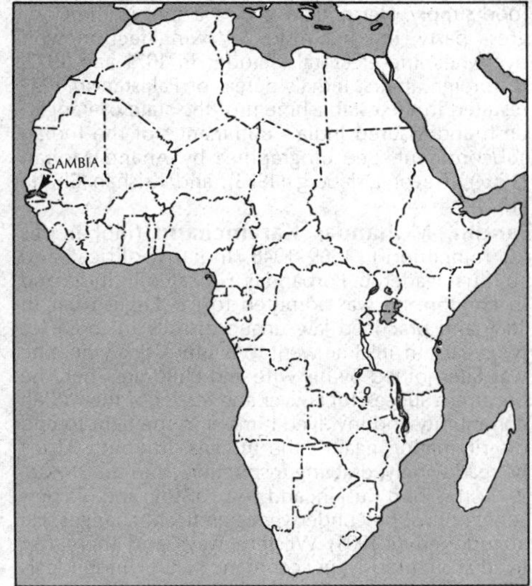

swampy river valley, whose fertile alluvial soils support rice cultivation. Peanuts, the country's chief cash crop, and some grains are raised on higher land. The climate is tropical and fairly dry. Gambia's population consists primarily of Muslim black African ethnic groups; the Mandingo is the largest, followed by the Fula, Wollof, Jola, and Serahuli. West Indians constitute an important minority. During the sowing and reaping seasons migrants from Senegal come to work in the country. Despite attempts at diversification, Gambia's economy remains overwhelmingly dependent on the export of peanuts and their by-products. Swamp rice, millet, sorghum, maize, cassava, and beans are grown for subsistence, and cattle are raised. Some dried and smoked fish (fishing follows agriculture as the chief occupation), palm kernels, and hides and skins are also exported. By far the most important trading partner is Great Britain, which also provides the bulk of Gambia's economic aid. Smuggling along the Gambia-Senegal border brings some additional revenue. Gambia has few all-weather roads, and most transportation is by river. There is an airport at Banjul. The country's official language is English. The only institution of higher education is a teacher-training college. Portuguese explorers reaching the Gambia region in the mid-15th cent. reported a group of small Mandingo and Wollof states that were tributary to the empire of Mali. Englishmen won trading rights from the Portuguese in 1588, but their hold was weak until the early 17th cent., when British merchant companies obtained trading charters and founded settlements along the Gambia River. In 1816 the British purchased Saint Mary's Island from a local chief and established Banjul (called Bathurst until 1973) as a base against the slave trade. The city remained a colonial backwater under the administration of Sierra Leone until 1843, when it became a separate crown colony. Between 1866 and 1888 it was again governed from Sierra Leone. As the French extended their rule over Senegal's interior, they sought control over Britain's Gambia River settlements but failed during negotiations to offer Britain acceptable territory in compensation. Meanwhile, the trading companies urged Britain to hold on to Gambia. In 1889, Gambia's boundaries were defined, and in 1894 the interior was declared a British protectorate. Gambia achieved full self-government in 1963 and independence in 1965 under Dauda Kairaba Jawara and the People's Progressive party (PPP). The PPP is mainly a party of the predominant Mandingo tribe; the major opposition group is the United party (UP), dominated by smaller tribes. Following a referendum in 1970, Gambia became a republic. The president and most members of the House of Representatives are popularly elected; a few representatives are chosen by tribal chiefs from among themselves. In contrast with many other new African states, Gambia preserved democracy and remarkable political stability in its early years of independence. The country belongs to the Commonwealth of Nations. Economic diversification and relations with Senegal continue to rank as the government's chief concerns. See H. A. Gailey, Jr., *A History of the Gambia* (1964); Berkeley Rice, *Enter Gambia: The Birth of an Improbable Nation* (1968).

Gambia, river, c.700 mi (1,130 km) long, rising on the Fouta Djallon, N Guinea, W Africa, and flowing generally NW through SE Senegal then west, bisecting Gambia, to the Atlantic Ocean at Banjul. It is navigable for the entire length of Gambia; ocean-going vessels can reach Georgetown, c.175 mi (280 km) upstream. The site of the first English trading stations in W Africa, the river is the chief transport artery of Gambia.

gambier: see CATECHU.

Gambier Islands (găm'bēr), coral group (6 sq mi/15.5 sq km), South Pacific, near the southeast end of the TUAMOTU ISLANDS. The group is a part of FRENCH POLYNESIA. It comprises a cluster of four inhabited islands known as Mangareva and many uninhabited atolls. The Mangareva cluster is within a barrier reef having a circumference of c.40 mi (60 km). The islands have copra and coffee plantations and pearl fisheries. Many of the uninhabited atolls are privately owned and are worked for copra. Mangareva (1967 est. pop. 500) is the seat of Rikitea, the capital. Discovered in 1797 by the British (who named the group), the Gambier Islands were annexed by France in 1881. Some of the atolls were used for French nuclear tests.

gambling or **gaming,** betting of money and valuables on, and often the participation in, games of chance and skill. In England and in the United States, before statutes were passed that made it unlawful, gambling was not a crime at common law if it was conducted privately. If it was public in nature and open to all comers, gambling became criminal as a public nuisance, and those who participated in such activities or who conducted gambling establishments were subject to prosecution. In the United States, the provisions of the common law have been limited in varying degrees by the statutes of the several states. Some prohibit certain games entirely, others prohibit wagering of money on them, and still others allow wagering up to a certain amount but not in excess, or forbid public wagers, or prohibit betting by minors. In some of the states parimutuel betting on horse races at the tracks has been legalized and provides both state and local governments with large revenues. In 1971 the first legalized offtrack betting system (OTB) in the United States opened in New York City. Connecticut became the second state (if Nevada is not counted) to approve offtrack betting. Nevada sanctions many types of gambling. The LOTTERY is a common form of gambling, and games involving playing cards or dice usually involve wagering. In recent years betting on popular sports such as baseball, basketball, boxing, and football, although illegal, has increased tremendously. Organized sport, however, has frowned on the practice ever since the "Black Sox" scandal of the 1919 world series in baseball and the 1951 collegiate basketball scandal in New York City. Nevertheless, instances of professional gamblers attempting to fix sporting events still occur. In contests that are sure to be closely contested, the gambling brokers, or bookies, as they are popularly called, usually establish two sets of odds, one for each side of the bet, so that no matter what the outcome of the contest they are bound to profit. In this and in many other ways easily demonstrated by mathematics the odds are so heavily stacked against a bettor that in the long run he is almost certain to lose. Yet illegal gambling flourishes in the United States, usually under the control of a criminal element and sometimes with the blessings of corrupt police officials. See Herbert Asbury, *Sucker's Progress* (1938, repr. 1969); Edmund Bergler, *Psychology of Gambling* (1957, repr. 1970); John Scarne, *Complete Guide to Gambling* (1961); H. C. Levinson, *Chance, Luck, and Statistics* (1963); J. P. Jones, *Gambling Yesterday and Today* (1973).

gamboge (gămbōj') [Fr.,=Cambodia], an intensely yellow PIGMENT obtained from the sap of *Garcinia morella,* a tree of SE Asia and Sri Lanka (Ceylon).

Gambrinus (gămbrī'nəs), mythical Flemish king, to whom the invention of beer is attributed. He is represented in modern folk art as straddling a keg.

game birds, a term used variously for all birds of the order Galliformes (gallinaceous, or chickenlike, birds), for certain quarry species within this order, and for a variety of quarry birds of several other orders. In Britain game bird refers particularly to partridge, grouse, and quail. In North America the term may include various gallinaceous birds such as quail and turkey, aquatic quarry birds such as duck and geese, and shorebirds such as woodcock, snipe, and plover. Game birds are hunted extensively, especially in the English-speaking world, and a number of dogs, including pointers, setters, and retrievers, have been specially bred for this purpose. Laws designating game birds and licensing their hunting were originally enacted in England to protect the privileges of nobility. Today, many countries enact licensing laws (see GAME LAWS), but these are generally for the protection of the animals rather than the hunters.

game laws, restrictions on the hunting or capture of wild game, whether bird, beast, or fish. After the Norman Conquest (1066) stringent game laws, known as the Forest Laws, which made hunting the sole privilege of the king and his nobles, were enacted in England. Other feudal states of Europe had similar laws. English laws were progressively softened after the 16th cent., and in the 19th cent. they were modified so that anyone who obtained a hunting license might hunt game. In the United States game laws have been directed at protecting wildlife from indiscriminate slaughter by trappers, hunters, and fishermen. The almost total extermination of the bison in the 19th cent. demonstrated the need for such conservation. Almost all states have game laws of this conservational type. Common protective devices include prohibition against lake and river pollution; designation of a closed season during which game may not be captured or killed; limitation of the age, size, or sex of the game hunted; the requirement of licenses before game can be hunted, even in the open season; and restrictions and prohibition of the sale or possession of game meat. See G. B. Grinnell and Charles Sheldon, ed., *Hunting and Conservation* (1925); R. H. Connery, *Governmental Problems in Wild Life Conservation* (1935, repr. 1970); S. S. Hayden, *International Protection of Wild Life* (1942, repr. 1970).

Gamelin, Maurice Gustave (môrēs' güstäv' gäməlăN'), 1872–1958, French army officer. During World War I he served on General Joffre's staff and as a division commander. He was made chief of the French general staff (1931) and chief of staff of national defense (1938). When World War II broke out, he commanded the Allied forces. Considering France ill prepared for war, he relied on the MAGINOT LINE and on passive warfare. In May, 1940, Germany began to overrun France; on May 19, Gamelin was replaced by Gen. Maxime Weygand. Arrested by the Vichy government, Gamelin was a defendant at the abortive trial at RIOM. He was freed from imprisonment in Germany in 1945.

Gamelyn, The Tale of, a romance in verse, written c.1350, containing about 900 lines. It tells of the tribulations of a young man abused by his older brothers. The story is included in several manuscripts of the *Canterbury Tales,* but not in the final version; it was evidently going to be called "The Cook's Tale." It served as a prototype for several later works, including Shakespeare's *As You Like It.*

games, children's. Games are amusements or pastimes involving more than one individual in which there is some sort of formalized dramatic element, contest, or plot. Games appear to be a cultural universal; for example, the string play called Cat's Cradle is common to cultures as varied as Eskimo, Australian, and African. Games differ from the serious pursuits of life in several ways: They are played according to tacit or explicit rules, and they are performed within a context that defines them as games (e.g., tin soldiers, house and marriage games, racing) although they may be clearly derived from and imitative of everyday living. Because the rules of the various sorts of games vary from place to place, comparable game types are often difficult to identify precisely. Most common are contest games, in which players vie, either as individuals or as team members, to see who is best at a given form of activity. Such dissimilar games as I Spy, Bombardment, Red Rover, baseball, rope-jumping, tag, charades, and "Last one to the corner is a rotten egg" are all in the contest category. Amusements with predictable outcomes such as the Farmer in the Dell, often classified as games, resemble games but are considered to be children's folk drama. Game classification has been the subject of frequent and profound investigation. Among the foremost researchers in this field are the Americans Iona and Peter Opie. Some of the many types defined are games of dexterity, games of chance, showdown games, tug-of-war games, and games requiring specialized materials (jacks, marbles, mumblety-peg, dice). However, no generally useful system of classification has yet been devised. In many—if not all—cultures, formalized child's play provides a training ground where the child learns skills useful to him in later life, a counterpart to the play-training of young animals. Considerable controversy exists as to whether children's games have been to a great extent influenced by adults or whether they are passed independently from one generation of children to another. The importance of related variants and how they are transmitted are further continuing puzzles. It seems likely that complex games are developed locally from simple basic elements that have been widely diffused. Games reflect the social, economic, religious, and artistic life of the culture from which they develop and have, themselves, become an intrinsic part of human existence. See Henry Bett, *Games of Children* (1929, repr. 1969); Iona and Peter Opie, *Children's Games in Street and Playground* (1969); Jean Belch, ed., *Contemporary Games: A Directory* (Vol. I, 1973).

games, theory of, group of mathematical theories first developed by John Von Neumann. A game consists of a set of rules governing a competitive situation in which from two to *n* individuals or groups of individuals choose strategies designed to maximize their own winnings or to minimize their opponent's winnings; the rules specify the possible actions for each player, the amount of information received by each as play progresses, and the amounts won or lost in various situations. A zero-sum game is one in which the sum of the winnings of all the players is zero at every stage of the game. The theory of games applies statistical logic to the choice of strategies. It is applicable to many fields, including military problems and economics. See John Von Neumann and Oskar Morgenstern, *Theory of Games and Economic Behavior* (3d ed. 1953).

gamete (găm'ēt): see REPRODUCTION.

gametophyte (gəmē'təfīt"), phase of plant life cycles in which the gametes, i.e., egg and sperm, are produced. The gametophyte is haploid, that is, each cell contains a single complete set of chromosomes, and arises from the germination of a haploid spore. In many plants, especially lower plants, the gametophyte phase is the dominant plant form; for example, the familiar mosses are the gametophyte form of the plants. The alternate phase of the plant life cycle is the sporophyte, the diploid plant form, with each cell containing two complete sets of chromosomes. For example, in mosses the sporophyte is a capsule atop a slender stalk that grows out of the top of the gametophyte. The sporophyte develops from the union of two gametes, such as an egg fertilized by a sperm; in turn, the sporophyte forms spores that develop into gametophytes. The alternation between haploid gametophyte and diploid sporophyte phases, known as alternation of generations, occurs in all multicellular plants. As plants have advanced in evolutionary development, the sporophyte has become the increasingly dominant plant form and the gametophyte form has been correspondingly reduced. In contrast to mosses, for example, in the advanced angiosperms the male and female gametophytes are reduced to three-celled and seven-celled structures, respectively, found within the reproductive organs of the familiar flowering plant (the sporophyte). See also FERTILIZATION; REPRODUCTION.

gaming: see GAMBLING.

Gammadims (găm'ədĭmz), obscure proper name. Ezek. 27.11.

gamma globulin, any of a group of globulin proteins in human blood plasma, including most ANTIBODIES. These antibody substances are produced as a protective reaction of the body's immune system to the invasion of disease-producing organisms (see IMMUNITY). Injections of gamma globulin are used to create a rapid but temporary immunity in patients who have been exposed to certain diseases. Children who have been exposed to but not immunized against measles and patients with hepatitis receive some protection from gamma globulin when it is administered during the incubation period of the infection. The plasma used for such purposes is drawn from large diverse groups of the adult population and pooled; the resulting mixture is likely to contain antibodies against most of the infections occurring in a given area.

gamma radiation, one of the three types of natural RADIOACTIVITY. It is the most energetic form of ELECTROMAGNETIC RADIATION, with very short wavelength (high frequency). Wavelengths of the longest gamma radiation are less than 10^{-10} m, with frequencies greater than 10^{18} hertz (cycles per sec). Gamma rays are essentially very energetic X rays; the distinction between the two is not based on their intrinsic nature, but rather on their origins. X rays are emitted during atomic processes involving energetic electrons. Gamma radiation is emitted by excited nuclei (see NUCLEUS); it often accompanies alpha or beta radiation, as a nucleus emitting those particles may be left in an excited (higher-energy) state. The applications of gamma radiation are much the same as those of X rays, both in medicine and in industry. In medicine, gamma ray sources are used for cancer treatment and for diagnostic purposes. Some gamma-emitting radioisotopes are also used as tracers (see RADIOACTIVE ISOTOPE). In industry, principal applications include inspection of castings and welds. Data from artificial satellites and high-altitude balloons have indicated that a flux of gamma radiation is reaching the earth from outer space, thus opening up the field of research known as gamma-ray astronomy. Gamma radiation appears to be coming from the plane of the Milky Way and possibly from various other isolated points in the sky.

gamma-ray astronomy, study of astronomical objects by analysis of the most energetic ELECTROMAGNETIC RADIATION they emit. Gamma rays are shorter in wavelength and hence even more energetic than X RAYS (see GAMMA RADIATION). However, X rays and gamma rays are produced throughout the universe by the same catastrophic astrophysical events, such as SUPERNOVAS and GRAVITATIONAL COLLAPSE. Hence, gamma-ray astronomy can be considered an extension of X-RAY ASTRONOMY to the extreme short-wave end of the SPECTRUM; experimental methods of the two fields are virtually the same, involving observations from orbiting satellites using techniques of nuclear physics.

Gamow, George (găm'ŏf), 1904-68, Russian-American theoretical physicist and author, b. Odessa. A nuclear physicist, Gamow is better known to the public for his excellent books popularizing abstract physical theories. He did his earlier research at the Univ. of Copenhagen, Cambridge Univ., and the Univ. of Leningrad, where he was professor (1931-33). He then came to the United States, where he taught at George Washington Univ. (1934-56) and the Univ. of Colorado (from 1956) and served with U.S. government agencies. He formulated (1928) a theory of radioactive decay and worked on the application of nuclear physics to problems of stellar evolution. In 1954 he proposed an important theory concerning the organization of genetic information in the living cell. His writings include *Constitution of Atomic Nuclei* (1931; 3d ed., with C. L. Critchfield, *Theory of Atomic Nucleus,* 1949), *Mr. Tompkins in Wonderland* (1939), *One, Two, Three . . . Infinity* (1947, rev. ed. 1961), *The Creation of the Universe* (1952, rev. ed. 1961), *Mr. Tompkins Learns the Facts of Life* (1953), *The Atom and its Nucleus* (1961), and *Gravity* (1962). See his autobiography, *My World Line* (1970).

Gamul (gā'məl), chief priest. 1 Chron. 24.17.

Gananoque (gănənŏk'wē, -wə), town (1971 pop. 5,212), SE Ont., Canada, on the St. Lawrence River. It has steelworks and copperworks. Gananoque is a summer resort, serving as a starting point for excursions to the Thousand Islands and the Rideau Lakes.

Gand: see GHENT, Belgium.

Gander, town (1971 pop. 7,748), NE N.F., Canada. Gander's airport was an important base in World War II.

Gandersheim, Hrotswith or **Roswitha von:** see HROTSWITH OR ROSWITHA VON GANDERSHEIM.

Gandhara (gəndä'rə), historic region of India, now in NW Pakistan. Situated astride the middle Indus River, the region had Taxila and Peshawar as its chief cities. It was originally a province of the Persian Empire and was reached (327 B.C.) by Alexander the Great. The region passed to Chandragupta, founder of the Maurya empire, in the late 4th cent. B.C., and under Asoka was converted (mid-3d cent.) to Buddhism. It was part of Bactria from the late 3d cent. to the 1st cent. B.C. Under the Kushan dynasty (1st cent.-3d cent. A.D.), and especially under KANISHKA, Gandhara developed a noted school of sculpture, consisting mainly of images of Buddha and reliefs representing scenes from Buddhist texts, but with marked Greco-Roman elements of style. The art form flourished in Gandhara until the 5th cent., when the region was conquered by the Huns.

Gandhi, Indira (ĭndē'rə găn'dē), 1917-, Indian political leader, daughter of Jawaharlal Nehru. Educated in India, in Switzerland, and at Oxford, she married (1942) Feroze Gandhi, who died in 1960. Her first years in Indian politics, especially after Indian independence in 1947, were served as an aide to her father, who was prime minister from 1947 until his death in 1964. She was president of the Indian National Congress party in 1959-60 and was minister of information in Lal Bahadur Shastri's government (1964-66). On Shastri's death in 1966, she succeeded him as prime minister. Her administration was marked, in domestic affairs, by increased stress on socialist programs and government planning, in the face of severe economic problems aggravated by the difficulty of producing an adequate food supply. Her policies led to a split in the Congress party, but her more left-wing faction won overwhelming electoral victories in 1971 and 1972. In foreign affairs, India's defeat of Pakistan in 1971 resulted in the establishment of the state of Bangladesh and assured India's dominance of the Indian subcontinent. See biographies by Anand Mohan (1967), Trevor Drieberg (1973), and Krishan Bhatia (1974).

Gandhi, Mohandas Karamchand (mōhän'dəs kŭ"rəmchŭnd'), 1869-1948, Indian political and spiritual leader, b. Porbandar. Educated in India and in London, he was admitted to the English bar in 1889 and practiced law unsuccessfully in India for two years. In 1893 he went to South Africa where he was later joined by his wife and children. There he became a successful lawyer and leader of the Indian community and involved himself in the fight to end discrimination against the Indians. In South Africa he read widely, drawing inspiration from the BHAGAVAD-GITA, John Ruskin, and Leo Tolstoy, and his personal philosophy underwent significant changes. He abandoned (c.1905) Western ways and thereafter lived abstemiously, in accordance with Hindu ideals of asceticism, including celibacy; this became symbolized in his eschewal of material possessions and his dress of loincloth and shawl. While in South Africa he organized (1907) his first satyagraha [holding to the truth], a campaign of civil disobedience expressed in nonviolent resistance to what he regarded as unjust laws. So successful were his activities that he secured (1914) an agreement from the South African government that promised the alleviation of anti-Indian discrimination. He returned (1915) to India with a stature equal to that of the nationalist leaders Gopal Krishna GOKHALE and Bal Gangadhar TILAK. Gandhi actively supported the British in World War I in the hope of hastening India's freedom, but he also led agrarian and labor reform demonstrations that embarrassed the British. The AMRITSAR massacre of 1919 stirred Indian nationalist consciousness, and Gandhi organized several satyagraha campaigns. He discontinued them when, against his wishes, violent disorder ensued. His program included a free, united India; the revival of cottage industries, especially of spinning and the production of handwoven cloth (khaddar); and the abolition of untouchability (see CASTE). These ideas were widely and vigorously espoused, although they also met considerable opposition from some Indians. The title Mahatma [great soul] reflected personal prestige so high that he could exact political concessions from the British by threatening "fasts unto death" and could unify the diverse elements of the organization of the nationalist movement, the Indian National Congress, which he dominated from the early 1920s. In 1930, in protest against the government's salt tax, he led the famous 200-mi (320-km) march to extract salt from the sea. For this he was imprisoned but was released in 1931 to attend the London Round Table Conference on India as the sole representative of the Indian National Congress. When the Congress refused to embrace his program in its entirety, Gandhi withdrew (1934), but his influence was such that Jawaharlal NEHRU, Gandhi's protégé, was named leader of the organization. In 1939, by fasting and satyagraha, he compelled several Indian princely states to grant democratic reforms. In 1942, after rejection of his offer to coöperate with Great Britain in World War II if the British made immediate concessions to Indian nationalism, Gandhi called for satyagraha and launched the Quit India movement. He was then interned until 1944. Gandhi was a major figure in the postwar conferences with the viceroy, Lord Mountbatten, and Muslim League leader Muhammad Ali Jinnah that led to India's independence and the carving out of a separate Muslim state (Pakistan), although Gandhi vigorously opposed the partition. When violence broke out between Hindus and Muslims, Gandhi resorted to fasts and tours of disturbed areas to check it. On Jan. 30, 1948, while holding a prayer and pacification meeting at New Delhi, he was fatally shot by a Hindu fanatic who was angered by Gandhi's solicitude for the Muslims. Asserting the unity of mankind under one God, Gandhi throughout his adult life preached Christian and Muslim ethics along with Hindu. After his death his methods of nonviolent civil disobedience were adopted by protagonists of civil rights in the United States and by many protest movements throughout the world. See his autobiography (tr. 1927, repr.

1966); his collected works (50 vol., 1958–72); selected writings, ed. by Ronald Duncan (1972); biographies by D. G. Tendulkar (8 vol., 1951–54), B. R. Nanda (1958), Louis Fisher (1959), and Geoffrey Ashe (1969); studies by J. V. Bondurant (rev. ed. 1965), Erik Erikson (1969), J. M. Brown (1972), and R. N. Iyer (1973).

Gandía (gändē'ä), town (1970 pop. 36,342), Valencia prov., E Spain, in a fertile garden region near the Mediterranean. Large quantities of oranges are exported through its port, El Grao de Gandía. Several members of a branch of the Borja, or Borgia, family were dukes of Gandía. The palace of the Borgias now houses a Jesuit college.

Gandzha: see KIROVABAD, USSR.

Ganesa (gənā'sə), b. 1507, d. after 1564, Indian astronomer. As a boy of 13 in a village N of Bombay, Ganesa wrote a treatise on astronomy, the *Grahalaghava,* which has often been reprinted and which has inspired many commentaries. In 1525 he composed a book of lunar tables that was also widely studied. His other works on astronomy, astrology, and Hindu law are less familiar.

Ganesha: see HINDUISM.

gang, group of people organized for a common purpose, often criminal. Gangs of outlaws were long known in frontier sections of the United States and wherever government was weak. Notorious were the Sydney Ducks of San Francisco (active in the 1850s) and the Hudson Dusters of turn-of-the-century New York City. Modern criminal gangs are largely urban and highly organized (see ORGANIZED CRIME). Adolescent gangs before World War II were generally poverty-area recreational groups that turned to crime under the influence of adult gangs. Often the groups were rehabilitated through recreational leadership and guidance in community centers. In the late 1940s fighting gangs arose in the poverty areas of most large cities, and they constitute a continuing problem. Uniting to seek security and status in a discouraging environment, the young members divide their neighborhoods into rival territories and amass homemade and stolen weapons. Boundary violations or other insults invite intergang fights in streets or parks. Most fighting gangs are organized intricately, with caste systems and with officers, including war counselors who arrange battles and prepare strategy; the gang may range in size from several members to over 100. Criminologists have investigated a number of factors related to the development of delinquent gangs. Among them are blighted communities, early school leaving, unemployment, family disorganization, neighborhood traditions of gang delinquency, and psychopathology. Another factor in gang development seems to be ethnic status. Most urban street gangs are composed of members of ethnic minorities; e.g., there are black gangs in Chicago, Mexican-American gangs in Los Angeles, Puerto Rican gangs in New York City, Arab gangs in Paris, Irish gangs in Liverpool, and Korean gangs in Tokyo. See also JUVENILE DELINQUENCY. For information on adult gangs, see Herbert Asbury, *Gangs of New York* (new ed. 1937, repr. 1970); Craig Thompson and Allen Raymond, *Gang Rule in New York* (1940). For material on youth gangs, see Lewis Yablonsky, *The Violent Gang* (1962, repr. 1970); Kitty Hanson, *Rebels in the Streets* (1964); Gilbert Geis, *Juvenile Gangs* (1965); M. W. Klein and B. G. Myerhoff, *Juvenile Gangs in Context* (1967); J. F. Short, ed., *Gang Delinquency and Delinquent Subcultures* (1968); R. W. Poston, *The Gang and the Establishment* (1971).

Ganganagar (gŭng'gänəgər), town (1971 pop. 90,053), Rajasthan state, NW India, on the Ganga Canal. It is a district administrative center and a market for grain, oilseed, vegetables, sheep, and cattle. Leather goods are made and sugar is refined in Ganganagar.

Ganges (găn'jēz) or **Ganga** (gŭng'gä), river, c.1,560 mi (2,510 km) long, rising in an ice cave in the Himalayas and flowing generally east through a vast plain to the Bay of Bengal; the most sacred river of Hindu India. The fertile Ganges plain is one of the world's most densely populated regions; rice, grains, oilseed, sugarcane, and cotton are the main crops. The upper Ganges supplies water to extensive irrigation works. The river passes the especially holy bathing sites at Hardwar, Allahabad (where the Jumna River enters the Ganges), and Varanasi. Below Allahabad the Ganges becomes a slow, meandering stream with shifting channels. The lower Ganges is joined by the Brahmaputra River W of Dacca, Bangladesh, to form the Padma, its main channel to the sea. The united rivers branch into many distributaries, forming the vast and fertile Ganges-Brahmaputra Delta, which stretches from the Hooghly River on the west to the Meghna on the east. Rice, sugarcane, and jute are the delta's main crops. The delta's southern fringe, a great wilderness of swamp, dense timber forest, small islands, and tidal creeks, is known as the Sundarbans; it has been the site of land reclamation projects. This low-lying area has repeatedly suffered great devastation from cyclones and tidal waves. Calcutta, India, and Chittagong, Bangladesh, are the delta's main ports.

ganglion: see NERVOUS SYSTEM.

gangrene, local death of body tissue. Dry gangrene, the most common form, follows a disturbance of the blood supply to the tissues, e.g., in diabetes, arteriosclerosis, thrombosis, or destruction of tissue by injury. A second type, moist gangrene, results from an invasion of toxin-producing bacteria that destroy tissue. Gangrene usually affects an arm or leg, but it may occur anywhere; e.g., pulmonary gangrene may follow an abscess of the lung. Treatment of gangrene includes rest and the administration of antibiotics if the gangrene is moist and bacterial invasion is present. Excision of the diseased portions of the body may be necessary and, in advanced involvement, amputation of the part. In gas gangrene, which results from the invasion of wounds by anaerobic bacteria, gas forms under the skin and a watery exudate is produced. Emergency treatment with penicillin and antitoxin is needed; without treatment, gas gangrene is invariably fatal.

Gangtok: see SIKKIM.

Ganja: see KIROVABAD, USSR.

gannet: see BOOBY.

Gannett, Henry, 1846–1914, American geographer, b. Bath, Maine, grad. Harvard (B.S., 1869; M.E., 1870). His first work as a topographer was on the Hayden Survey. After 1882 he was chief geographer of the U.S. Geological Survey. Through his work as geographer of the U.S. censuses of 1880, 1890, and 1900 and the Philippine, Cuban, and Puerto Rican censuses, he became interested in place names, and his efforts to resolve difficulties caused by confusion of names led to the establishment (1890) of the U.S. Board of Geographic Names; he served as the board's chairman until 1910. Gannett is distinguished as one of the founders of the National Geographic Society (president, 1910–14), the Geological Society of America, and the Association of American Geographers. His books include *Physiographic Types* (1898–1900) and *Topographic Maps of the United States Showing Physiographic Types* (1907).

Gannett Peak, Wyo.: see WIND RIVER RANGE.

Gansevoort, Peter (găns'vo͝ort), 1749–1812, soldier in the American Revolution, b. Albany, N.Y. He served in the Quebec campaign and in 1777 was in command of Fort Schuyler (former Fort Stanwix). In the Saratoga campaign he gallantly defended that post against British siege under Gen. Barry ST. LEGER until reports that Gen. Benedict Arnold was approaching frightened the British into retreat. He again won favorable notice for his part in the campaign (1779) of Gen. John Sullivan against the Iroquois and the Loyalists in W New York. See study by A. P. Kenney (1969).

Ganymede (găn'əmēd), in astronomy, largest of the 12 known moons, or natural satellites, of JUPITER and the largest and most massive satellite in the solar system, being larger than the planet Mercury.

Ganymede, in Greek mythology, a youth of great beauty. He was carried off by Zeus to be cupbearer to the gods.

Gaonim (gäō'nĭm) [Heb.,=excellencies], title given to the heads of the Jewish academies at Sura and Pumbedita in Babylonia immediately following the period of the SABORAIM until the middle of the 11th cent. Thereafter the title was adopted by the heads of the Palestinian academies; later it was used as an honorific title to indicate a great scholar. Although political power was nominally in the hands of the Jewish exilarch (who was appointed by the caliph at Baghdad), the Gaonim, as religious leaders, usually held true power in the Jewish community. The greatest Gaon at Sura was SAADIA BEN JOSEPH AL-FAYUMI. Of those who held office at Pumbedita, Sherira Gaon (968–98) and his son Hai Gaon (998–1038) are most notable. Under Sherira the already waning prestige of the Babylonian academies was restored, and it was maintained by Hai until his death. Thereafter European Jewry came to play an ever more dominant role in Jewish life. See Jacob Neusner, *There We Sat Down* (1972).

Gaon of Vilna: see ELIJAH BEN SOLOMON.

Gap (gäp), city (1968 pop. 25,417), capital of Hautes-Alpes dept., SE France, on the Luye River at the foot of the Dauphiné Alps. It has flour mills, creameries, printing plants, and factories making bricks, tile, clothing, and leather products. Founded by Augustus c.14 B.C., it was the capital of medieval Gapençais, which was annexed to the crown of France in 1512. The city was devastated during the Wars of Religion (16th cent.).

gar, member of the family Lepisosteidae, freshwater fishes found in the warmer rivers and lakes of the S United States, Central America, Mexico, and the West Indies. Gars are highly predacious and destroy many useful fish. They are cylindrical fishes with long jaws and formidable teeth; their peculiar armature of diamond-shaped platelike scales, composed of a hard inorganic salt, is often found also in fossil fish. The largest species is the 9-ft (275-cm) alligator gar of the Mississippi valley. Others are the long-nosed gar (*Lepisosteus osseus*), the spotted gar, and the short-nosed gar. The name garfish is sometimes used for the gar but is more correctly applied to the saltwater gar (see NEEDLEFISH). Gars are classified in the phylum CHORDATA, subphylum Vertebrata, class Osteichthyes, order Lepisosteiformes, family Lepisosteidae.

Garamond, Claude (klōd gärämôN'), 1480–1561, Parisian designer and maker of printing types. According to tradition he learned his art from Geofroy TORY. Types designed by Garamond were used in the printeries of the ESTIENNE family, COLINES, PLANTIN, and BODONI, and types used by the ELZEVIR family were based on his designs. His royal Greek type (*grecs du roi*), designed for Francis I, imitated the Greek writing of a scholar of his time (Angelos Vergetios). His roman and italic types, however, were innovations in being designed as metal types, not as imitations of handwriting. His roman letter forms won general acceptance in France and elsewhere and were a chief influence in establishing the roman letter as standard, in place of the gothic or black letter. Some modern type designs given his name are not closely related to his, but are based on types that were mistakenly attributed to him.

Garat, Dominique Joseph (dōmēnēk' zhōzĕf' gärä'), 1749–1833, French revolutionary. He was minister of justice (1792–93) during the trial of King Louis XVI and notified the king of the death verdict. Appointed (1793) minister of the interior, Garat proved inadequate in the post. He was twice imprisoned during the REIGN OF TERROR, and held high government posts after the terrorists were overthrown. He also served under the empire. After the Restoration he was forced to retire (1816). Garat wrote many works of political reminiscence and history, notably his *Mémoires historiques sur le XVIIIe siècle et sur M. Suard* (1820).

Garay, Juan de (hwän dā gärī'), c.1528–1583, Spanish conquistador in South America, refounder of Buenos Aires. He came to Peru (1544) in the train of the first viceroy, Blasco Núñez Vela, and was active against Gonzalo Pizarro in the civil war. From 1548 to 1568 his activity, as a soldier and colonizer, was centered in Upper Peru (present-day Bolivia). Moving to Asunción (Paraguay) in 1568, he quickly became prominent in the provincial government. He founded Santa Fé (in present-day Argentina) in 1573. Named lieutenant governor of the provinces of the Río de la Plata in 1574, he continued in this office until his death. With colonists from Asunción, he made a permanent settlement in 1580 at Buenos Aires, which, first founded in 1536, had been abandoned in 1541.

garbage: see SOLID WASTE.

Garbett, Cyril Forster (gär'bĭt), 1875–1955, English prelate, archbishop of York. Educated at Oxford, he was assistant curate of Portsea (1899–1909) and then vicar there (1909–19). As bishop of Southwark (1919–32) he advocated Anglican social consciousness by publicizing the district's impoverishment. He was archbishop of York from 1942 to 1955. His numerous publications include *The Claims of the Church of England* (1947), *Watchman, What of the Night?* (1948), *Church and State in England* (1950), and *In an Age of Revolution* (1952). See biography by Charles Smyth (1959).

Garbo, Greta, 1905–, American film actress, b. Stockholm, Sweden, as Greta Gustafson. Garbo's success in the Swedish film *The Atonement of Gösta Berling* (1923) brought her to Hollywood. An extraordinary classic beauty, she was known for her portrayals of sexual passion in early films, such as *Flesh and the Devil* (1927). Her image as a tragic heroine was established with her work in *Anna Christie* (1930), *Queen Christina* (1933), *Anna Karenina* (1935), and *Camille* (1936). Garbo retired from the screen and has lived in legendary seclusion since 1941. See biography by John Bainbridge (1971); Michael Conway, *The Films of Greta Garbo* (1968).

Garborg, Arne (är'nə gär'bŏŏrg), 1851-1924, Norwegian writer of the naturalistic school. He founded the weekly *Fedraheim* (1877), in which he urged reforms in many spheres—political, social, religious, agrarian, and linguistic. Garborg championed the use of Landsmaal (a rural dialect based on Old Norse) as a literary language. His verse cycle *The Hill Innocent* (1895) treats the triumph of human faith over the powers of darkness. Two outstanding novels, *Tired Men* (1891) and *Peace* (1892, tr. 1929), relate the tragic disintegration of morally bankrupt and guilt-ridden men. Garborg also translated the *Odyssey* into Landsmaal. He was married to the prominent author Karen Hulda Bergersen.

García, Manuel del Popolo Vicente (mänwĕl' dĕl pōpō'lō vēthān'tā gärthē'ä), 1775-1832, Spanish tenor, teacher, impresario, and composer of a number of operas very popular in their time. After several successful seasons in Paris, he created (1816) the role of Count Almaviva in Rossini's *Barber of Seville* in Rome. García founded a school of singing in London and organized an opera company that included his wife, his son, and his daughter Maria MALIBRAN. He was the first to produce opera in Italian in New York (1825-26) and in Mexico (1827-28). Pauline Viardot-García was also his daughter. His son, **Manuel Patricio Rodríguez García** (pätrē'thyō rōdrē'gāth), 1805-1906, left (1829) the operatic stage to teach at the Paris Conservatory (1830-48) and the Royal Academy, London (1848-95). Jenny Lind and Mathilde Marchesi were among his pupils. He invented (1854) the laryngoscope. See biography by M. S. MacKinlay (1908).

García Godoy, Héctor (ĕk'tōr gärsē'ä gō'thoi), 1921-70, president of the Dominican Republic (1965-66). A lawyer and diplomat, he served as foreign minister under President Juan Bosch and was named provisional president under the auspices of the Organization of American States after the 1965 civil war. He held the country together until elections could be conducted in 1966. He served as ambassador to the United States (1966-69) and ran for president in 1970 against President Balaguer, but died unexpectedly of a heart attack during the campaign.

García Gutiérrez, Antonio (äntō'nyō gärthē'ä gōōtyär'rĕth), 1813?-1884, Spanish romantic playwright. He was a soldier when his best-known play, *El trovador,* was staged in 1836. This play and his *Simón Bocanegra* (1843) were adapted by Verdi for the operas *Il Trovatore* (1852) and *Simon Boccanegra* (two versions: 1857 and 1881). His last major plays were *Venganze catalana* (1864) and his masterpiece *Juan Lorenzo* (1865).

García Icazbalceta, Joaquín (hwäkēn' gärsē'ä ēkäsbälsā'tä), 1824-94, Mexican philologist, bibliographer, and historian. He edited the works of many early Mexican writers, compiled the *Bibliografía mexicana del siglo XVI* (1880), wrote the masterly biography *Don Fray Juan de Zumárraga* (1881), and translated foreign historical works, notably W. H. Prescott's *Conquest of Mexico.*

García Lorca, Federico (fāthārē'kō gärthē'ä lôr'kä), 1898-1936, Spanish poet and dramatist, b. Fuente Vaqueros. The poetry, passion, and violence of his work and his own tragic and bloody death brought him enduring international acclaim. A joyous, versatile person, he was an accomplished musician and had an enormously original theatrical imagination. García Lorca's works combine the spirit and folklore of his native Andalusia with his very personal understanding of life. His first book, in prose, *Impresiones y paisajes* [impressions and landscapes] (1918), was followed by *Libro de poemas* (1921), written in the year he went to Madrid. *Romancero gitano* (1928; tr. *Gypsy Ballads,* 1953) made him the most popular Spanish poet of his generation. His celebrated *Llanto por Ignacio Sánchez Mejías* (1935; tr. *Lament for the Death of a Bullfighter,* 1937) and *Poeta en Nueva York* (1940; tr. *The Poet in New York,* 1955) are among his later poetry. Between 1927 and 1931 he wrote the plays *La zapatera prodigiosa* [the shoemaker's wonderful wife], *Amor de don Perlimplín con Belisa en su jardín* [love of Don Perlimplín and Belisa in his garden], and *Retablillo de don Cristóbal* [portrait of Don Cristóbal]. Under the Republic he directed and wrote for several theatrical groups. *Doña Rosita la soltera* [Doña Rosita the spinster] was staged in 1935. *Bodas de sangre* (1938; tr. *Blood Wedding,* 1939), *Yerma* (1934), and *La Casa de Bernardo Alba* (1936) are continually produced internationally. García Lorca was shot by Franco's soldiers at the outbreak of the Spanish civil war. His works have been widely translated. See biography by Edwin Honig (rev. ed. 1969); studies by Manuel Duren, ed. (1962), C. W. Cobb (1967), and R. C. Rupert (1972).

García Márquez, Gabriel (gäbrēĕl' gärsē'ä mär'käs), 1928-, Colombian novelist and short-story writer. His works chronicle the physical and moral collapse of Macondo, an imaginary town in Colombia. Rich and lucid, his style is a mixture of realism and fantasy. Among his works are *La hojarasca* (1955; tr. *Leaf Storm and Other Stories,* 1972), *El coronel no tiene quien le escriba* (1958; tr. *No One Writes to the Colonel, and Other Stories,* 1968), *Los funerales de la Mamá Grande* [the funeral of Mama Grande] (1962), and *Cien años de soledad* (1967; tr. *One Hundred Years of Solitude,* 1970).

García Moreno, Gabriel (gäbrēĕl' gärsē'ä mōrā'nō), 1821-75, president of Ecuador (1861-65, 1869-75), b. Guayaquil. A man of fervent religious convictions, he gradually became obsessed with the idea of government dominated by the Roman Catholic Church. As president he promulgated new constitutions (1861, 1869) and signed (1862) a concordat with the church by which the civil power became the guarantor and executor of the church's independence and granted to it control over education. With the end of state patronage, inquisitional methods were restored. A storm of liberal opposition was vigorously suppressed. Between terms as president he retained his hold by installing puppets. He was reelected in 1869 and granted additional extravagant privileges to the clerics; he also took extraordinary powers for himself. The fanaticism and despotism of the tall, severe caudillo are much more remembered than his ability as an administrator who put his country on a sound financial basis and introduced material reforms. He died when set upon near the capitol steps by liberal assassins.

García y Iñigues, Calixto (kälēk'stō gärsē'ä ē ēnyē'gäs), 1839-98, Cuban revolutionist, a leader in the Ten Years War (1868-78). Captured and imprisoned until 1878, he entered upon revolutionary activities immediately after his release and was again arrested. In 1895 he went to the United States and shortly afterward played an important part in the revolution in Cuba and in the Spanish-American War, particularly distinguishing himself at El Caney. Sent as a member of a committee to discuss Cuban affairs with President McKinley in 1898, he died in Washington, D.C. Elbert Hubbard's *A Message to Garcia* made his name a byword in the United States.

Garcilaso de la Vega (gärthēlä'sō thā lä vä'gä), 1503?-1536, lyric poet of the Spanish Golden Age, b. Toledo. A soldier of Emperor Charles V, he died in a reckless attack on a castle in Provence. Garcilaso, the embodiment of the cultured and gifted courtier, was chiefly responsible for the renovation of Spanish poetry. He was the first to adapt successfully the 11-syllable line, characteristic of Italian verse, to the mood and content of Spanish poetry—an innovation suggested by his friend BOSCÁN. Garcilaso's verse, noted for its delicacy, was published with that of Boscán in 1543. It includes sonnets, elegies, odes, and three eclogues.

Garcilaso de la Vega (gärsēlä'sō dā lä vä'gä), 1539-1616, Peruvian historian; son of the Spanish conquistador Sebastián Garcilaso de la Vega and an Incan princess and therefore called the Inca. He grew up in Peru during the turbulent post-Conquest period. He went (1560) to Spain, where he first served in the army and later began to write. His most important work, *The Royal Commentaries of Peru* (1609-1617; tr. 1871) is a valuable source of information about the conquest of Peru and the lives and legends of the Inca. See biography by J. G. Varner (1968).

Gard (gär), department (1968 pop. 478,544), S France, on the Rhône River and the Mediterranean Sea. NÎMES is the capital.

Garda, Lake (gär'dä), Ital. *Lago di Garda* or *Benaco,* largest lake of Italy, 143 sq mi (370 sq km), between Lombardy and Venetia, N Italy. It is c.32 mi (52 km) long, with a maximum width of c.11 mi (18 km). The northern tip, with Riva di Trento, is an Alpine resort. The Sarca River enters the lake at the northern end; the Mincio River drains the lake. Long celebrated for their beauty and mild climate, the shores are dotted with vineyards and such well-known resorts as Torbole, Maderno, and Gardone.

Garden, Mary, 1877-1967, Scottish-American operatic soprano, b. Aberdeen, Scotland, studied in Paris. Her debut (1900) occurred when she replaced, without rehearsal, the star of Charpentier's *Louise,* at the Opéra-Comique, Paris. In 1902 she created the role of Mélisande in Debussy's *Pelléas et Mélisande.* In the title role of Massenet's *Thaïs* she made her American debut (1907) with the Manhattan Opera Company, New York City. In 1909 she created a sensation in the American revival of Richard Strauss's *Salomé.* A member of the Chicago Opera Company (1910-31), she directed it for one season (1921-22). Garden was noted for her vivid portrayal of character. She retired in 1930.

garden, land set aside for the cultivation of flowers, herbs, vegetables, or small fruits, for either utility or ornament. Gardens range in size from window boxes and small dooryard plots to the public BOTANICAL GARDEN and commercial truck garden (see TRUCK FARMING). Garden types are also widely varied: a garden may be devoted entirely to one kind of plant—e.g., cactuses, aquatic plants, alpine plants (see ROCK GARDEN), or herbs—or may combine many types of plants to achieve maximum beauty and productivity. In landscape gardening an overall aesthetic effect is sought, usually to enhance dwellings, public buildings, and monuments and to integrate and beautify parks, playgrounds, and fairgrounds. Formal landscaping involves artificial modifications of the terrain and emphasizes balanced plantings and geometrical design; the naturalistic style incorporates plantings with the natural scenery. Ornamental gardening and landscape gardening are ancient arts. The Egyptians built formal walled gardens and the Mesopotamians constructed private parks and terraced gardens—usually on artificial mounds or supported by columns, as the Hanging Gardens of Babylon. The Persians were especially skilled in using water for decorative effects; the Moors carried Near Eastern styles to Spain. In the East the planting of sacred groves was spread by the Buddhists from India to China and set a style there for naturalistic gardens, in which the beauty of the natural scenery was accentuated by distributing plants so as to allow them free growth and set off their colors and fragrances to best advantage. The Japanese adopted this principle and elaborated it into a distinct style of highly disciplined arrangements of plants and their settings with the object of achieving subtle beauty based on economy and simplicity. The Japanese art of BONSAI gave rise to the unique miniature gardens and dish gardens. In Europe landscape gardening was highly developed under the Roman Empire; formal gardens, often terraced and adorned with statuary and fountains, were designed by architects. The Crusaders brought back from the East new gardening techniques that gave great impetus to horticulture in Western Europe. During the Renaissance the classical style was revived in Italy; the Italian gardens, planned by leading artists, sometimes went to extremes of formality and decor, among them those employing elaborate waterworks displays (see FOUNTAIN). The Italian style was widely imitated. In Spain the Italian influence was modified by Moorish features. In turn, the Spaniards and the Portuguese introduced their ideas in the Americas, where these techniques were combined with the already well-developed Aztec and Inca traditions. The Dutch, famous for the development of the NURSERY, were noted also for their TOPIARY WORK, an art practiced earlier by the Romans. France became the leader in formal landscaping; the work of André Lenôtre is exemplified in the gardens of Versailles. In the 18th cent. England inaugurated a revival of the naturalistic trend under such leaders as William Kent, Lancelot Brown, and Humphrey Repton. The 19th cent. brought a partial reversion to formal landscaping and an interest in HORTICULTURE as well as in design. American landscape artists generally followed the example of the English masters. Landscaping, especially of public parks and buildings, was stimulated by the work of A. J. Downing, Calvert Vaux, and F. L. Olmsted and his son. John Bartram established the first BOTANICAL GARDEN in the United States; his sons did much to advance horticulture as a science. Today landscape gardening stresses practical as well as aesthetic design, selecting from a wealth of gardening traditions and emphasizing casual, naturalistic effects. Vegetable, herb, and fruit growing (see ORCHARD and VINEYARD) have become more the province of large-scale agriculture as advanced marketing techniques have overcome the need for subsistence farming. However, home vegetable gardens provided a major source of food during the emergency conditions of both World Wars. See also GARDEN CITY. See M. L. Gothein, *A History of Garden Art* (tr. 1928); Montague Free, *Gardening* (rev. ed. 1947); Osvald Sirén, *Gardens of China* (1949); James Bush-Brown and Louise Bush-Brown, *America's Garden Book* (3d rev. ed. 1958); Sylvia Crowe, *Garden Design* (1958); *Tay-*

lor's Encyclopedia of Gardening (4th ed. 1961); M. M. Roberts, *Public Gardens and Arboretums of the United States* (1962); James Bush-Brown and Louise Bush-Brown, *America's Garden Book* (rev. ed. 1965); Edward Hyams, *A History of Gardens and Gardening* (1971).

Gardena (gärdē'nə), city (1970 pop. 41,021), Los Angeles co., SW Calif., an industrial suburb of Los Angeles; inc. 1930. Gardena is often called "Freeway City." Among its diverse manufactures are aircraft and missile components, electronic equipment, machinery, tools, chemicals, metal products, clothing, and food products. Gardena is also noted for its plant nurseries. About one fourth of the city's population is of Oriental descent; an annual Japanese cultural exhibit is held there. El Camino College and Harbor Junior College are in Gardena.

Gardena, Val (väl gärdä'nä), Alpine valley, c.15 mi (25 km) long, in the Dolomites, Trentino-Alto Adige, N Italy. Its scenery attracts many tourists. Ortisei is the best-known resort. Wood carving (mainly of toys) is a traditional home industry.

Garden City. **1** City (1970 pop. 14,790), seat of Finney co., SW Kansas, on the Arkansas River; inc. 1887. A trade center in an irrigated farm and dairy region producing grain, sugar beets, and alfalfa, it has a gas field, cattle feedlots, and hide-processing and meat-packing plants. Agricultural equipment and concrete and plastic pipes are manufactured there. The city has a junior college and an agricultural experiment station. **2** City (1970 pop. 41,864), Wayne co., SE Mich., a suburb of Detroit; inc. as a city 1934. Chiefly residential, the city also manufactures wire cloth, aluminum extrusions, and golf balls. **3** Village (1970 pop. 25,373), Nassau co., SE N.Y., on Long Island; inc. 1919. It is primarily a residential community, with printing and publishing as the major industries. Garden City was founded in 1869 and planned by the merchant Alexander T. Stewart. Adelphi College and two preparatory schools are there.

garden city, urban residential and industrial community surrounded by a rural belt, established with a predetermined maximum population and area and with land ownership vested in the community. The name, however, has been commonly applied to any community planned to secure the advantages of both city and country life and to encourage decentralization of industry. The idea originated as a method of preventing the overcrowding of metropolitan areas—with its resultant slums—that followed the Industrial Revolution. The garden city was foreshadowed in Robert Owen's proposal to create new communities in the country, in Charles Fourier's advocacy of communal "phalansteries," and in James Silk Buckingham's plan (1849) for an ideal city. It found partial expression, especially in England, in the building of workers' dwellings near factories already situated in rural areas and in new communities built to house workers in industries that were moved to the country to take advantage of lower land values. Notable among centers established in England by industrialists are Saltaire, founded 1851 by Sir Titus Salt; Bournville, founded 1879 by George Cadbury; and Port Sunlight, near Birkenhead, founded 1887 by Sir William Lever. The term *garden city* was introduced, and the ideal city presented, by Sir Ebenezer Howard in his book *To-morrow: A Peaceful Path to Real Reform* (1898); it was revised (1902) under the title *Garden Cities of To-morrow* (reedited by F. J. Osborn, 1946). Howard organized the Garden-City Association (1899) in England and secured backing for the establishment of Letchworth (1903) and Welwyn Garden City (1920). The garden-city idea spread rapidly in Europe and the United States but commonly resulted in residential suburbs of individually owned homes. The ideal was more fully realized in satellite communities in rural areas of a moderate distance from a large city, such as Radburn, N.J., and the greenbelt towns (organized between 1936 and 1938 by the Federal Resettlement Administration), such as Greenbelt, Md., Greendale, Wis., and Greenhills, Ohio. Most satellite towns, however, failed to attain Howard's ideal, since local industries were unable to provide employment for the inhabitants, many of whom commuted to work in larger centers. The congestion and destruction accompanying World War II greatly stimulated the garden-city movement, especially in England and on the Continent. The open layout of garden cities had much influence on the development of modern CITY PLANNING. See F. J. Osborn, *Green-Belt Cities: The British Contribution* (1946). M. H. Smith, *History of Garden City* (1963); W. L. Creese, *The Search for Environment* (1966).

Garden Grove, city (1970 pop. 121,371), Orange co., S Calif., a residential suburb of Long Beach and Los Angeles, in a citrus fruit area, on the Santa Ana River; founded 1877, inc. 1956. Many of its residents work in nearby space and defense installations.

gardenia: see MADDER.

Garden of the Gods, park, 770 acres (312 hectares), central Colo., near Colorado Springs; noted for its curious, multicolored rock formations. Narrow-crested sandstone hills and ridges have been eroded into grotesque groups with such fanciful names as Kissing Camels. Since 1921, Easter sunrise services have been held at Gray Rock, a natural amphitheater.

Garden Reach, city (1971 pop. 155,222), West Bengal state, NE India, on the Hooghly River. It is a suburb of Calcutta.

Gardez (gərdäz'), city (1967 pop. 33,000), capital of Paktia prov., E Afghanistan, on the Jilga River. It lies on the old trade routes between Afghanistan and the Peshawar region of Pakistan and is now a market for lumber.

Gardiner, Sir Christopher, fl. 1630–32, figure in the early history of the Massachusetts Bay colony. When the Puritans arrived in Massachusetts Bay in 1630, they found that Gardiner had preceded them. Although he was living with a woman who was not his wife, the colonists left him alone until it was discovered that he had deserted several wives in Europe and was an agent of Sir Ferdinando GORGES, who claimed title to the land the Puritans occupied. Forced to leave, Gardiner went to Maine and then to England, where, in 1632, he was one of the leading witnesses before the privy council in Gorges's attempt to have the Massachusetts charter revoked. His career has provided inspiration for a number of literary works, particularly for Henry Wadsworth Longfellow's "Rhyme of Sir Christopher" in *Tales of a Wayside Inn*.

Gardiner, Lion, 1599–1663, English colonist in America. Under contract with patentees of Connecticut, Gardiner designed and erected (1635–36) the blockhouse at Saybrook, which he defended in the Pequot War (1636–37). He purchased (1639) Gardiners Island from the Indians and founded there the first English colony in present-day New York.

Gardiner, Samuel Rawson, 1829–1902, English historian, educated at Oxford. His life work was a thorough, careful history of the English civil war, and it was based on researches into all the sources in England and in such foreign archives as those in Paris, Rome, and Simancas. His history appeared as several separate works, later regrouped into three—*The History of England from the Accession of James I to the Outbreak of the Great Civil War, 1603–1642* (10 vol., 1863–82; repr. 1883–84); *History of the Great Civil War 1642–1649* (3 vol., 1886–91; repr. in 4 vol., 1893); and *History of the Commonwealth and Protectorate, 1649–1660* (3 vol., 1895–1901), which was interrupted at the year 1656 by his death and was carried on by Sir Charles H. Firth in his *Last Years of the Protectorate* (1909). Gardiner also wrote many textbooks, edited the *Constitutional Documents of the Puritan Revolution* (1889, 2d ed. 1899), wrote a biography of Oliver Cromwell (1899), and was for 10 years after 1891 editor of the *English Historical Review*. See biography by H. B. Learned (1902); R. P. Usher, *A Critical Study of the Historical Method of Samuel Rawson Gardiner* (1916).

Gardiner, Silvester or **Sylvester,** 1708–86, American colonial physician and landowner, b. South Kingstown, R.I. He studied medicine in London and Paris, built up a large practice in Boston, and established a chain of apothecary shops. Gardiner was the chief promoter of the Kennebec Company, which obtained (1753) a large strip of land on either side of the Kennebec River in Maine. He built the towns of Pittston and Gardiner in the development of this holding. Because he was an ardent Loyalist, his land was confiscated at the beginning of the American Revolution, and he fled to Halifax and later (1778) to England. He returned to the United States in 1785 and recovered part of his land in Maine, but his Boston property had been destroyed.

Gardiner, Stephen, 1493?–1555, English prelate. He was educated at Cambridge. He became secretary to Thomas (later Cardinal) WOLSEY and later secured the favor of Henry VIII by a mission to Rome to further the king's plans for divorce from Katharine of Aragón. He was made bishop of Winchester (1531) and wrote *De vera obedientia* (1535), justifying the royal supremacy in ecclesiastical affairs. Thomas Cromwell's fall was in part due to him, and he was the probable author of the Six Articles, which reaffirmed the king's adherence to medieval church doctrines as against those of the Reformation. After the accession of Edward VI he was deprived of his bishopric and put in the Tower of London for five years. When Mary I came to the throne, he was restored to his see and made lord high chancellor. Gardiner was condemned by Catholics for his support of royal supremacy and by Protestants for his opposition to Reformation doctrines. See J. A. Muller, *Stephen Gardiner and the Tudor Reaction* (1926, repr. 1970).

Gardiners Island, c.3,000 acres (1,210 hectares), in Gardiners Bay between the two flukelike peninsulas of E Long Island, SE N.Y. It was settled by colonist Lion Gardiner in 1639 as the first permanent English settlement in what is now New York state and was owned for 300 years by his descendants; it is now a private game preserve.

Gardner, Erle Stanley, 1889–1970, American detective-story writer, b. Malden, Mass. He served as a trial lawyer for many years. About 1921 he began writing detective stories for magazines; after that time he produced an extraordinary number of novels and stories noted for their fast action and clever legal devices. His most famous character was the lawyer Perry Mason. Gardner often wrote under two pseudonyms, A. A. Fair and Carleton Kendrake.

Gardner, Ernest Arthur: see under GARDNER, PERCY.

Gardner, Isabella Stewart, 1840–1924, American art collector, b. New York City. She lived in Boston following her marriage to the financier Jack Gardner. After the Civil War her home became known for brilliant social affairs and as a center for gatherings of painters, literary people, musicians, and other celebrities. Her lifelong interest in art led her to sponsor various contemporary artists and the young connoisseur Bernard Berenson, who advised her in the collecting of many works. Her husband cooperated with her in her plan to create an art museum. Fenway Court was built after the Venetian manner to house their valuable collection and was willed to the city of Boston as a public museum to be preserved without change. See Arthur Pope and J. D. Hatch, Jr., ed., *The Isabella Stewart Gardner Museum: Reproductions of Paintings* (1935); Morris Carter, *Isabella Stewart Gardner and Fenway Court* (2d ed. 1940); Louise Hall Tharp, *Mrs. Jack* (1965).

Gardner, John William, 1912–, American public official, U.S. Secretary of Health, Education, and Welfare (1965–68), b. Los Angeles. After teaching psychology at Connecticut and Mt. Holyoke colleges and serving as an intelligence officer with the U.S. Marine Corps in World War II, he joined the Carnegie Corp. of New York in 1946, becoming its vice president in 1949 and its president in 1955. Also in 1955 he became president of the Carnegie Foundation for the Advancement of Teaching. A Republican, he was named by President Lyndon B. Johnson to succeed Anthony J. Celebrezze as Secretary of Health, Education, and Welfare in July, 1965, but resigned in Jan., 1968, to head the National Urban Coalition. In 1970 he became chairman of the newly formed nonpartisan citizens' lobby, COMMON CAUSE. He is the author of *Excellence: Can We Be Equal and Excellent Too?* (1961), *Self-Renewal: The Individual and the Innovative Society* (1964), and *No Easy Victories* (1968).

Gardner, Percy, 1846–1937, English classical archaeologist. From 1887 to 1925 he was professor of archaeology at Oxford, where he was instrumental in building up the archaeology department and its library and collections. His works include *The Types of Greek Coins* (1883), *New Chapters in Greek History* (1892), *A Manual of Greek Antiquities* (with F. B. Jevons, 1895), *Principles of Greek Art* (1913), *A History of Ancient Coinage* (1918), and *New Chapters in Greek Art* (1926). His brother **Ernest Arthur Gardner,** 1862–1939, was also a classical archaeologist. He served as director of the British School of Archaeology at Athens (1887–95) and as professor of archaeology (1896–1929) and vice chancellor at the Univ. of London. He took a prominent part in excavations in the Middle East, particularly at Megalopolis and Paphos. His principal work is *Handbook of Greek Sculpture* (1897, rev. ed. 1915). Other works include *Religion and Art in Ancient Greece* (1910), *The Art of Greece* (1925), and *Greece and the Aegean* (1933).

Gardner, city (1970 pop. 19,748), Worcester co., N central Mass.; settled 1764, inc. as a city 1921. Its furniture industry dates from c.1805.

Gárdonyi, Géza (gä'zə gär'dōnyē), 1863–1922, Hungarian writer. Gárdonyi first attracted attention with a cycle of satirical novels about peasant life. His works include the play *The Wine* (1901) and the novels *The Invisible Man* (1902) and *The Old Man*

(1905). Gárdonyi's meditative idealism combined elements from Schopenhauer, Indian philosophy, and Christian mysticism.

Gareb (gā'rĕb). **1** Member of David's guard of 30 men. 2 Sam. 23.38; 1 Chron. 11.40. **2** Unidentified hill, in the vicinity of Jerusalem. Jer. 31.39.

Garey, Thomas Andrew, 1830-1909, American pioneer in citrus culture, b. Cincinnati. He traveled from Iowa to California by ox team (1849-52). In 1865 he built a citrus nursery on land now a commercial street in Los Angeles. The market for young citrus trees grew, and Garey introduced new varieties, among them a lemon that he called Garey's Eureka. It became one of two main varieties of lemon grown in California. His *Orange Culture in California* (1882) was a valuable work.

Garfield, Harry Augustus, 1863-1942, American educator, b. Hiram, Ohio, grad. Williams 1885, studied law at Columbia; son of President James A. Garfield. From 1888 to 1903 he practiced law in Cleveland, Ohio, where he was active in civic affairs and also taught law at Western Reserve Univ. He was professor of politics at Princeton from 1903 to 1908 and president of Williams from 1908 until his retirement in 1934. He served as U.S. fuel administrator in 1917-19 and in 1921 founded the Institute of Politics at Williams. See biography and study by Lucretia Comer (1965 and 1959).

Garfield, James Abram, 1831-81, 20th President of the United States (March-Sept., 1881). Born on a frontier farm in Cuyahoga co., Ohio, he spent his early years in poverty. As a youth he worked as farmer, carpenter, and canal boatman. After graduation (1856) from Williams College, he became a teacher of ancient languages and literature at the Western Reserve Eclectic Institute at Hiram, Ohio (the name was later changed, largely through his influence, to Hiram Institute), and later (1857-61) was its principal. He was also a lay preacher of the Disciples of Christ, was admitted (1859) to the bar, and was elected an antislavery state senator. During the Civil War he served in the Union army and was a major general of volunteers when he resigned (1863) to take his seat as Representative in Congress. He was a regular Republican, unhesitatingly following his party's postwar program of radical Reconstruction and later of hard-money deflationism and opposition to civil service reform. On the tariff issue he was evasive. Garfield was prominent in the settlement of the disputed election of 1876 (in which Rutherford B. HAYES was finally adjudged the winner), but in 1880 he was still only moderately well known nationally. He was campaign manager for John Sherman in the Republican convention but on the 36th ballot was himself chosen as compromise candidate for President. Former President Grant, who had wanted the nomination, and his supporter, Roscoe CONKLING, gave Garfield only formal aid in the election—and allegedly even that was conditioned on a promise of a share in the President's political favors. After Garfield had defeated W. S. Hancock and was President, he passed over Conkling's "Stalwarts" in his appointments and appointed James G. Blaine, Conkling's political enemy, Secretary of State. War was thus declared between the President and the most important faction of the Republican party. Garfield won the first round of the fight, getting his appointee for the New York port collectorship approved over Conkling's objections. He began prosecution of the STAR ROUTE frauds. Constantly harassed by office seekers, President Garfield met his death through one of them. On July 2, 1881, he was shot by Charles J. Guiteau. On Sept. 19 he died, and Chester A. Arthur succeeded to the presidency. Garfield was a brilliant orator and an able, knowing, and charming man. He had shown little originality or force in his 17 years as Congressman, and his early death prevented him from showing whether or not he might have demonstrated statesmanship as President. See his diary, ed. by H. J. Brown and F. D. Williams (Vol. I-, 1967-); T. C. Smith, *Life and Letters of James A. Garfield* (1925, repr. 1968); biography by J. M. Taylor (1970).

Garfield, James Rudolph, 1865-1950, U.S. Secretary of the Interior (1907-9), b. Hiram, Ohio; son of President James A. Garfield. After being admitted to the Ohio bar in 1888, he became a lawyer in Cleveland. He was a member of the U.S. Civil Service Commission (1902-3) and commissioner of corporations in the Dept. of Commerce and Labor (1903-7) before being given a cabinet post under President Theodore Roosevelt. Garfield was a noted advocate of the conservation of natural resources. In the 1912 election he aided Roosevelt and the Progressive party in their unsuccessful bid for power.

Garfield, industrial city (1970 pop. 30,797), Bergen co., NE N.J., on the Passaic at its confluence with the Saddle River; settled 1679 by the Dutch, inc. 1898.

Garfield Heights, city (1970 pop. 41,417), Cuyahoga co., NE Ohio, a residential and industrial suburb adjacent to Cleveland; founded 1904, inc. 1932. It has oil refineries, chemical plants, and iron and steel works.

garfish: see GAR; NEEDLEFISH.

Gargarus, Mount: see KAZ DAĞI.

gargoyle (gär'goil), waterspout used in medieval Europe to draw rainwater from church and cathedral roofs. Gargoyles were fashioned imaginatively in the form of human grotesques, beasts, and demonic spirits. This form of sculpture reached its peak in the Gothic period and declined with the introduction of lead drainpipes in the 16th cent.

Gargoyle

Garian: see GHARYAN, Libya.

Garibaldi, Giuseppe (gărĭbôl'dē, Ital. jōōzĕp'pā gārēbäl'dē), 1807-82, Italian patriot and soldier, a leading figure in the RISORGIMENTO. He was born at Nice and as a youth entered the Sardinian navy (Nice was ceded to Sardinia in 1814). Under the influence of MAZZINI he became involved in an unsuccessful republican plot and fled (1835) to South America. There he gained his first experience in guerrilla warfare. He served (1836-42) the state of Rio Grande do Sul in its rebellion against Brazil and fought (1842-46) in the Uruguayan civil war, winning fame for his heroism. In Uruguay he met Anita Ribeiro da Silva, whom he married in 1842; she remained his faithful companion until her death in 1849. When revolution swept over Europe in 1848, Garibaldi found a new theater of action. Though a convinced republican, he joined the forces of King Charles Albert of Sardinia in the war against Austria. After the Sardinian defeat he went to Rome (1849) and, at the head of some improvised forces, fought for Mazzini's short-lived Roman republic against the French forces intervening for Pope Pius IX. During his spectacular retreat across central Italy, Anita died. He was refused asylum by the king of Sardinia and went to the United States. Soon he resumed his seafaring life, but in 1851 he returned to Italy and bought part of the island of Caprera, N of Sardinia. By then he had definitely renounced the dream of an Italian republic and gave his support to the realistic policy of CAVOUR, publicly declaring that the monarchy as represented by VICTOR EMMANUEL II should be the basis of Italian unity. Garibaldi's popularity won many of Mazzini's republican followers for the monarchist cause. Garibaldi took part in the war of 1859 against Austria. After the Treaty of VILLAFRANCA DI VERONA he violently attacked Cavour and denounced the cession of Savoy and his native Nice to France. In 1860, with Victor Emmanuel's connivance, Garibaldi embarked on the crowning enterprise of his life—the conquest of the kingdom of the Two Sicilies. With 1,000 volunteers, the Red Shirts, he landed (May, 1860) in Sicily, which had rebelled against FRANCIS II, king of the Two Sicilies, and conquered the island in a spectacularly daring campaign. He then crossed to the mainland, took Naples, and won a decisive battle on the Volturno River. Mazzini wanted to make liberated S Italy a republic while the populace acclaimed Garibaldi as ruler, but Garibaldi himself remained faithful to his pledge to Victor Emmanuel. After meeting the king at Teano, near Naples, he relinquished his conquests to Sardinia and retired to Caprera. Shortly afterward (1861) Victor Emmanuel was proclaimed king of a united Italy. Only part of the PAPAL STATES, including Rome, remained outside the new kingdom. In 1862, Garibaldi led a volunteer corps against Rome, but the king, fearing international intervention, sent an Italian army that defeated Garibaldi at Aspromonte. Garibaldi was given a pardon. In the Austro-Prussian War of 1866 he commanded a volunteer unit, and in 1867 he was defeated by French and papal forces at Mentana while attempting once again to capture Rome. In the Franco-Prussian War of 1870-71 he commanded a group of French and Italian volunteers and won a battle near Dijon (1871). Garibaldi was elected to the Italian parliament in 1874, but his political career was unimportant. He remained a popular hero of Italians the world over. See his autobiography (tr. 1889); biography by D. Mack Smith (1956, repr. 1969); G. M. Trevelyan, *Garibaldi's Defence of the Roman Republic* (1907, repr. 1971), *Garibaldi and the Thousand* (1909, repr. 1948), and *Garibaldi and the Making of Italy* (1911, repr. 1948).

Garigliano (gärēlyä'nō), lower part of the Liri River, S central Italy, below its junction with the Rapido, or Gari, River (hence Gari-Liriano) near Cassino. It separates Latium from Campania and empties into the Tyrrhenian Sea. A strategic battleground since antiquity, it was the scene (1503) of Gonzalo Fernández de Córdoba's victory over Louis XII of France in the Italian Wars. In World War II heavy fighting occurred (Nov., 1943-May, 1944) near the Garigliano during the Allied drive on Rome, which included the battle for Cassino.

Garland, Augustus Hill, 1832-99, American lawyer and politician, b. Tipton co., Tenn. He became a prominent lawyer in Arkansas and during the Civil War served in the Confederate House of Representatives (1861-64) and Senate (1864-65). After the war, he was pardoned by President Andrew Johnson. He could not practice law, however, because of a congressional act of Jan., 1865, that debarred former members of the Confederate government. This led to *Ex parte Garland* (1867), a Supreme Court case in which Garland successfully pleaded that since the act was an ex post facto law it was unconstitutional. He was elected to the U.S. Senate in 1867 but was refused his seat. As governor of Arkansas (1874-76), Garland was influential in restoring the soundness of the state's finances. He served in the U.S. Senate from 1877 to 1885 and as Attorney General from 1885 to 1889. He wrote *Experiences in the Supreme Court of the United States* (1898) and, with Robert Ralston, *A Treatise on the Constitution and Jurisdiction of the United States Courts* (1898).

Garland, Hamlin, 1860-1940, American author, b. near West Salem, Wis. He grew up in the Middle Western farmlands, the region he later wrote about in verse, stories, and autobiography. His tales, collected as *Main-travelled Roads* (1891), *Prairie Folks* (1893), and *Wayside Courtships* (1897), were bitter pictures of the futility of farm lives. Besides realistic novels of the prairies—*A Little Norsk* (1892) and *Rose of Dutcher's Coolly* (1895), he wrote several propagandist novels, including *Jason Edwards: an Average Man* (1892), urging the single tax doctrine, and *A Spoil of Office* (1892), supporting the Populist party. Garland is perhaps best remembered for his two autobiographical works, *A Son of the Middle Border* (1917) and *A Daughter of the Middle Border* (1921, Pulitzer Prize). He was also the author of essays, a biography of President Grant (1898), and several books on spiritualism. See biography by Jean Holloway (1960, repr. 1971).

Garland, Judy, 1922-69, American singer and film actress, b. Grand Rapids, Minn., originally named Frances Gumm. She sang in her father's theater from the age of four as one of The Gumm Sisters; she later toured in vaudeville. Beginning her film career in 1935, she endeared herself to the public in the Andy Hardy film series and in *The Wizard of Oz* (1939). Her later films include *Meet Me in St. Louis* (1944), *Easter Parade* (1948), *A Star is Born* (1954), and *Judgment at Nuremburg* (1960). She performed in concert internationally, radiating the spirit of vaudeville in spite of great personal unhappiness. Her first husband was the director Vincente Minnelli. See biographies by Mel Tormé (1970) and her husband Mickey Deans (1972). Garland's daughter, **Liza Minnelli,** 1946-, b. Hollywood, Calif., is a singer and actress hailed for her performance in the films *The Sterile Cuckoo* (1969) and *Cabaret* (1972).

Garland, city (1970 pop. 81,437), Dallas co., N Texas, a suburb of Dallas; inc. 1891. Since World War II, Garland has grown from an agricultural community into an important center for electronics research and for production of electronic equipment for airplanes and missiles. Other manufactures include cartons, cans, paint, oil-field equipment, hats, and processed foods.

garlic: see ONION.

Garmisch-Partenkirchen (gär'mĭsh-pär"tənkĭr'-khən), town (1970 pop. 26,586), Bavaria, S West Germany, in the Bavarian Alps, at the foot of the Zugspitze. It is an international winter resort and a regional commercial center. The 1936 Olympic winter games were held there. The picturesque town has two well-decorated 18th-century churches.

Garmite, obscure tribal name. 1 Chron. 4.19.

Garneau, François Xavier (fräNswä' zävyā' gär-nō'), 1809-66, French Canadian historian. He was educated at the Quebec seminary. He is remembered for his *Histoire du Canada* (3 vol., 1845-48; 2d ed., with added material, 1852), a work as captivating in its style as it is distinguished in its scholarship. Garneau is said to have undertaken his history under the sting of a remark made by Lord Durham that the French Canadians were a people "without a history and without a literature." The history covers the period from the exploration and settling of Canada by the French to the union of the two Canadas in 1841. It has appeared in abridged editions and in an English translation. There are several biographies of Garneau in French.

Garner, John Nance, 1868-1967, Vice President of the United States (1933-41), b. Red River co., Texas. A lawyer, he served (1898-1902) in the Texas legislature and then (1902) was elected to Congress. His senior standing made him (1921) the ranking minority member of the Committee on Ways and Means, and subsequently he became minority leader in Congress. With the shift to Democratic control in 1931 he was elected speaker of the House. After 30 years of service in Congress, Garner was in 1932 elected Vice President under President Franklin Delano Roosevelt. He was reelected in 1936 but opposed Roosevelt's third-term candidacy and retired (1941) from politics. See biography by B. N. Timmins (1948).

Garnet, Henry: see GARNETT, HENRY.

Garnet, Henry Highland (gär'nĭt), 1815-82, American Negro abolitionist clergyman, b. Kent co., Md. Born a slave, he escaped in 1824 and was educated at the Oneida Institute, Whitesboro, N.Y. He was an eloquent speaker, but his radicalism, particularly in a speech at Buffalo in 1843, in which he called upon slaves to rise and slay their masters, caused his influence to decline. He was opposed and superseded in leadership by the more moderate Frederick Douglass. Garnet served as a Presbyterian pastor in Troy, N.Y., in New York City, and in Washington, D.C. In 1881 he was appointed minister to Liberia, but he died two months after his arrival there. See study by Earl Ofari (1972).

garnet, name applied to a group of isomorphic minerals crystallizing in the cubic system. They are used chiefly as gems and as abrasives (as in garnet paper). The garnets are double silicates; one of the metallic elements is calcium, magnesium, ferrous iron, or manganese and the other aluminum, ferric iron, or chromium. Six varieties (of which there are also intermediate forms) are distinguished according to composition—grossularite (calcium-aluminum), pyrope (magnesium-aluminum), spessartite (manganese-aluminum), almandite (iron-aluminum), andradite (calcium-iron), and uvarovite (calcium-chromium). Grossularite occurs commonly in a red, green, yellow, or brown shade, depending on the impurities; if pure it would be colorless. The yellow and brown stones, coming chiefly from Ceylon, are used as gems under the names essonite (or hessonite) and cinnamon stone; sometimes they are miscalled hyacinth. Grossularite is found also in the Transvaal, in Mexico, and in Oregon. The most popular variety of garnet is the ruby-red pyrope from Bohemia, S Africa, and Arizona, sold as Cape ruby and Arizona ruby. Rhodolite, a mixture of pyrope and almandite from North Carolina, is rose-red or purple. Spessartite, a brown to brownish-red garnet from Bavaria, Ceylon, and parts of the United States, is seldom used for jewelry. Deep red, transparent almandite is the carbuncle; it was formerly a very popular gem. Almandites come chiefly from Brazil, India, and Ceylon; Australia and parts of the United States are also important sources. Andradite, a very common variety, is usually some shade of red, black, brown, yellow, or green. Gem varieties include topazolite, similar in color and transparency to TOPAZ; demantoid, a green variety with a high dispersion and adamantine luster, sometimes miscalled olivine and Uralian emerald; and black melanite. Demantoid is found in the Urals, and the other andradites come chiefly from Europe and the United States. Uvarovite, an emerald-green variety from the USSR and Finland, is rarely suitable for gem use. Garnet occurs in many different kinds of rocks—grossularite, in metamorphosed impure limestones; pyrope, in basic igneous rocks; spessartite, in granite rocks; almandite, in schists and other metamorphic rocks as well as in igneous rocks; andradite, in serpentine; and uvarovite, chiefly in serpentine.

Garnett, Constance (Beach): see GARNETT, RICHARD.

Garnett, David: see GARNETT, RICHARD.

Garnett, Edward: see GARNETT, RICHARD.

Garnett or **Garnet, Henry,** 1555?-1606, English Jesuit. He was converted to Roman Catholicism and in 1575 became a Jesuit. After some years on the Continent he returned as a missionary to England (1586) and became superior of the English Jesuits. He is principally remembered as one of the priests accused of taking part in the GUNPOWDER PLOT. Garnett admitted to knowledge of the plot as confessor to two of the conspirators, was convicted of treason on confusing evidence, and was executed.

Garnett, Richard, 1835-1906, English librarian and author. From 1851 until his retirement in 1899 he was connected with the British Museum, which he served with great distinction. Besides writing voluminous essays, biographies, and novels, he discovered hitherto unpublished poems by Shelley (*Relics of Shelley*, 1862). His works include the novel *Twilight of the Gods* (1888), *Essays in Librarianship and Bibliography* (1899), *Poems* (1893), and *The Age of Dryden* (1895). His son was **Edward Garnett,** 1868-1937, critic and author. Although his own work never achieved great distinction, Edward encouraged and guided many writers, including Conrad and Galsworthy, and published their letters to him. **Constance (Beach) Garnett,** 1862-1946, Edward's wife, was famous for her translations from the Russian, including the great novels of Dostoyevsky and Tolstoy. The son of Edward and Constance, **David Garnett,** 1892-, novelist, won acclaim for the imaginativeness of such works as *Lady into Fox* (1923) and *A Man in the Zoo* (1924). See C. G. Heilbrun, *The Garnett Family* (1961).

Garnier, Charles (Saint Charles Garnier) (shärl gär-nyā'), 1606-49, French missionary in North America, one of the Jesuit Martyrs of North America. He entered the Society of Jesus in 1624 and went as a missionary to the Huron Indians of Canada in 1636. He was killed by the Iroquois. Feast: Sept. 26 or (among the Jesuits) March 16.

Garnier, Jean Louis Charles (zhäN lwē shärl), 1825-98, French architect, studied at the École des Beaux-Arts and won the Grand Prix de Rome (1848). He was awarded the commission for the Opéra in Paris (1861-75), which is his principal work. It provided an impressive focus for the new boulevards of G. E. Haussmann's city planning. It is an ornate interpretation of Renaissance architecture, especially noted for the grand staircase. Garnier also built the casino at Monte Carlo.

Garnier, Marie Joseph François (märē' zhôzĕf' fräNswä'), 1839-73, French explorer and naval officer, usually known as Francis Garnier. He served (1860-62) against Annam and China, then in the administration of Cochin China. In 1866-68 he accompanied Doudart de Lagrée's expedition through Cambodia, Laos, and Yünnan. The route followed, largely unknown to European geographers, was accurately mapped. On the death of the leader en route, Garnier led the party down the Yangtze River to Shanghai. After taking part in the defense of Paris against the Prussians (1870-71), which he described in *Le Siège de Paris* (1871), he returned to the Far East. In the Tonkin expedition of 1873 he captured Hanoi but was killed there. He wrote *Voyage d'exploration en Indo-Chine* (1873).

Garnier, Robert (rōbĕr'), 1534?-1590, French dramatic poet. He wrote mainly closet dramas in the classical manner of Seneca. *Les Juives* [the Jewish women] (1583), based on the Bible, is perhaps the best of his tragedies. He is also credited with the first tragicomedy in French, *Bradamante* (1582).

Garnier, Tony, 1869-1948, French architect. His greatest achievement was in urban planning. After his study of sociological and architectural problems of an industrial city, he began in 1901 to formulate an elaborate solution, published as *Une cité industrielle* (1918). His proposals served as a stimulus to young architects of the 1920s. From 1905 to 1919 Garnier was architect to the city of Lyons. In this capacity he built the municipal slaughterhouse, a hospital, and a stadium, which are of interest for their use of reinforced concrete.

garnierite (gär'nēərīt"), pale apple-green mineral, chemically a hydrous silicate of nickel and magnesium. An important ore of nickel, it is found in New Caledonia, the USSR, and S Africa. In the United States it occurs in Oregon and North Carolina.

Garnier-Pagès, Étienne Joseph Louis (ātyĕn' zhôzĕf' lwē gärnyā'-päzhĕs'), 1801-41, French politician; brother of Louis Antoine Garnier-Pagès. He was a leading figure in the opposition to the restoration of the Bourbons in 1814. He also opposed the accession (1830) of Louis Philippe.

Garnier-Pagès, Louis Antoine (äNtwän'), 1803-78, French politician; brother of Étienne Joseph Louis Garnier-Pagès. Becoming active in politics after his brother's death, he was elected (1842) to the chamber of deputies. He opposed the government of King LOUIS PHILIPPE and was a leader of the banquet campaign (1847-48) that helped bring about its downfall in the FEBRUARY REVOLUTION of 1848. He was mayor of Paris and finance minister in the provisional government (1848). After 1864 he was a member of the parliamentary opposition to Emperor Napoleon III, and in 1870-71 he was a member of the government of national defense, formed after Napoleon's defeat at Sedan in the Franco-Prussian War.

garnishment, in law, means of requiring a third party who holds a DEBT (including wages) due a defendant to retain the property temporarily. The garnishment consists of a warning, in the form of a JUDGMENT, to the third party, called the garnishee, not to deliver the goods or money due to the defendant, but to hold them in TRUST pending the outcome of the plaintiff's suit. This provisional remedy guarantees the plaintiff at least some recovery if he wins the case.

Garofalo, Il (ēl gärô'fälō), 1481-1559, Italian painter of the Ferrarese school, whose real name was Benvenuto Tisi or Tisio. Influenced by Raphael, he painted in a competent though unoriginal style. He worked chiefly in the churches and palaces of Ferrara, Bologna, and Rome. Examples of his work in Ferrara are the *Nativity* and *Resurrection of Lazarus* in the museum; *The Kiss of Judas*, in the Church of San Francesco; and *Madonna Enthroned* and the beautiful frescoes of saints Peter and Paul in the cathedral. Other notable examples are two paintings of the miracles of St. Nicholas (Metropolitan Mus.) and *The Baptism of Christ* and *The Meditation of St. Jerome* (National Gall. of Art, Washington, D.C.). Garofalo went blind in 1550.

Garofalo, Raffaele (räf-fäē'lā), 1851-1934, Italian jurist and criminologist. He studied at the Univ. of Naples, where he later taught law and criminal procedure. Second only to Enrico Ferri, he is considered to be the most important follower of Cesare LOMBROSO. His major contribution was the formulation of a theory of "natural crime." The theory embraces crimes of two types: those of violence and those against property. His *Criminologia* (1885) was translated by R. W. Millar (1914).

Garonne (gärôn'), river, 402 mi (647 km) long, rising in the central Pyrenees just inside Spain, and flowing generally NE to Toulouse, in SW France, where it swings northwest to join the Dordogne River and forms the Gironde estuary. The Garonne receives nearly all of the smaller rivers of SW France but is navigable only in its lower course; Bordeaux is the head of oceangoing navigation. The river suffers from irregular flow, fluctuating channels, and steep gradients. The famed Bordeaux vineyards overlook the lower river. The Garonne Lateral Canal, 120 mi (193 km) long, parallels the river from Castets to Toulouse.

Garrastazú Médici, Emílio: see MÉDICI, EMÍLIO GARRASTAZÚ.

Garretson, James Edmund, 1828-95, American pioneer in oral surgery, b. Wilmington, Del., M.D. Univ. of Pennsylvania, 1859. From 1874 he taught at Philadelphia Dental College (now part of Temple Univ.), serving as dean from 1880. His textbook on oral surgery (1869) was the first and long the standard work in its field. Under the name John Darby he published many popular books.

Garrett, João Batista de Almeida: see ALMEIDA GARRETT, JOÃO BATISTA DE.

Garrett, Thomas, 1789-1871, American abolitionist, b. Upper Darby, Pa. A Quaker, he joined the Pennsylvania Abolition Society in 1818. At Wilmington, Del., where he became a hardware merchant and toolmaker, he made his home a station on the UNDERGROUND RAILROAD, helping numerous slaves to freedom. He was convicted in 1848 and used up all of his resources to pay a fine imposed on him. Friends helped him rebuild his position, and he continued to aid slaves.

Garrettson, Freeborn, 1752-1827, American Methodist preacher, b. Maryland. At the time of his conversion to Methodism (1775), he freed his slaves and began his journeys as a preacher. In 1784 he traveled through the South, summoning preachers to the conference at which the Methodist Episcopal

Church of the United States was organized (see METHODISM) and at which he was ordained. He organized congregations in Nova Scotia, New York, and New England. At the request of John Wesley, he wrote *The Experience and Travels of Mr. Freeborn Garrettson* (1791). His zeal and travels helped greatly in the spread of Methodism in the United States.

Garrick, David, 1717–79, English actor, manager, and dramatist. He was indisputably the greatest actor of the 18th-century English stage, and his friendships with Diderot and with Samuel Johnson, Oliver Goldsmith, and other notables who made up "The Club" resulted in detailed records of his life. He was sent to study at Dr. Johnson's academy at Lichfield and six months later went with Johnson to London, where he set up a wine shop. It was in the coffeehouses of London that he met the actors associated with Covent Garden, among them Charles Macklin and Margaret (Peg) Woffington, who became Garrick's mistress. The three of them lived together for some time but in later years became virtual enemies. After some work in the provinces, Garrick made his formal debut in 1742 as Richard III and was an immediate success, becoming the idol of London. He was noted for his versatility, playing the tragic heroes of contemporary drama as well as Shakespearean roles. His King Lear was especially praised. Although he was short in stature and had a mercurial nature, his straightforward manner and diction swept the declamatory school from the stage. From 1747 until his retirement in 1776, he was the manager of Drury Lane, where he initiated many reforms. Most important, he concealed (1765) stage lighting from the audience and discontinued the practice of having spectators sit on the stage. He freed Shakespeare's texts from 17th-century corruptions, but made drastic cuts and changes in several of the works. Besides training actors for his company and composing prologues and epilogues, he wrote many plays, the most successful being the farces *Bon Ton* (1775) and *Miss in Her Teens* (1747), and he collaborated with George Colman the elder in writing *The Clandestine Marriage* (1766). His portrait was painted by Reynolds, Hogarth, and Gainsborough, and he was buried in Westminster Abbey. The Garrick Club was established in London in 1831 for distinguished actors. See his diary, ed. by R. C. Alexander (1928, repr. 1971); his letters, ed. by D. M. Little and G. M. Kahrl (3 vol., 1963); biographies by C. M. A. Lenanton (1958), K. A. Burnim (1961, repr. 1973), and F. A. Hedgcock (1912, repr. 1969); studies by E. P. Stein (1938, repr. 1967) and F. M. Parsons (2d ed. 1969).

Garrido Canabal, Tomás (tōmäs' gärē'thō känäbäl'), 1891–1943, Mexican caudillo, governor of TABASCO (1921–35). A fierce and fanatical anticlericalist, he organized the Red Shirts, a Fascist organization that terrorized Roman Catholics during the regime of Plutarco Elías Calles. In 1935 the Red Shirts were disbanded, and Garrido Canabal was exiled.

Garrison, William Lloyd, 1805–79, American abolitionist, b. Newburyport, Mass. He supplemented his limited schooling with newspaper work and in 1829 went to Baltimore to aid Benjamin Lundy in publishing the *Genius of Universal Emancipation.* This episode ended (1830) in his imprisonment for seven weeks for libel. On Jan. 1, 1831, he published the first number of the *Liberator,* a paper that he continued for 35 years (the last number was dated Dec. 29, 1865), until after the Thirteenth Amendment had been adopted. In the *Liberator,* Garrison took an uncompromising stand for immediate and complete abolition of slavery. Though its circulation was never over 3,000, the paper became famous (notorious, to Southerners) because its editor wrote in startling and quotable language. Garrison relied wholly upon moral persuasion, believing in the use of neither force nor the ballot to gain his end. His intemperate language antagonized many. In 1835 he was physically attacked in Boston by a mob composed of seemingly respectable people and thereby won a valuable convert to his cause in Wendell PHILLIPS. Garrison opposed the work of the American Colonization Society in his *Thoughts on African Colonization* (1832). He was active in organizing (1831) the New England Anti-Slavery Society and (1833) the American Anti-Slavery Society, of which he was president (1843–65). Garrison crusaded for other reforms that he united with abolitionism, notably woman suffrage and prohibition. He went to the extreme of advocating Northern secession from the Union because the Constitution, which Garrison characterized as "a covenant with death and an agreement with Hell," permitted slavery. He burned the Constitution publicly at an abolitionist meeting in Framingham, Mass., on July 4, 1854, and opposed the Civil War until Lincoln issued the Emancipation Proclamation. That Garrison was the foremost leader of the antislavery cause, a view generally held in the 19th cent., has been characterized as a "New England myth." The weight of historical evidence seems to indicate strongly that, while Garrison attracted attention, the effective fight against slavery was carried on by less well-known men who, for all their idealism, tackled the problem in a realistic manner (see ABOLITIONISTS). Garrison, a difficult personality, was not a good organizer. Even so, his contribution to the cause, though it was not as mighty as many consider it, was important. See his letters, ed. by W. M. Merrill (1971); *William Lloyd Garrison . . . His Life Told by His Children* (4 vol., 1885–89, repr. 1969); biographies by W. M. Merrill (1963), J. L. Thomas (1963), A. H. Grimké (1891, repr. 1969); study by A. S. Kraditor (1969).

Garrison Dam, c.11,300 ft (3,400 m) long and 210 ft (64 m) high, on the Missouri River, near Riverdale, W central N.Dak.; one of the world's largest earth-filled dams. Built by the U.S. Army Corps of Engineers (completed 1956), it is a key unit in the Missouri River basin project. It impounds Lake Sakajawea.

Garry, Fort: see FORT GARRY, Canada.

Garshin, Vsevolod Mikhailovich (fəsyĕ'vələt mĕkhī'ləvĭch gär'shĭn), 1855–88, Russian short-story writer. "Four Days" (1877), his story of a wounded soldier's ordeal in battle, first won him fame. "The Scarlet Blossom" (1833), about a madman's efforts to destroy the evil he saw in a flower, is considered his masterpiece. These and others, translated in *The Signal and Other Stories* (1912), express a profound pity for mankind. Garshin suffered intermittently from a mental disorder that resulted in suicide. Chekov's story "The Fit" was suggested by Garshin's life.

Garstang, John, 1876–1956, English archaeologist. He was professor of archaeology at the Univ. of Liverpool from 1907 to 1941, when he became professor emeritus. In 1897 he began conducting archaeological research and directed expeditions in England, Africa, Asia Minor, and Palestine. Garstang was director of the British School of Archaeology at Jerusalem (1919–26). Among his writings are *Meroë, the City of the Ethiopians* (1911), *The Hittite Empire* (1929), *Foundations of Bible History: Joshua, Judges* (1931), and *Prehistoric Mersin* (1950).

garter snake, harmless SNAKE of the genus *Thamnophis,* abundant from Canada to Central America. There are many common species; members of most species are about 2 ft (60 cm) long. Most garter snakes are striped or banded lengthwise, and some are spotted between the stripes. Less aquatic as a group than the related water snakes, they are found near water in dry country and are widely distributed in moist regions. They prey on cold-blooded animals, chiefly frogs, toads, small fish, and earthworms. Females bear live young in large litters, sometimes numbering 50 or more. The common garter snake of the NE United States, *Thamnophis sirtalis,* varies in color and pattern but is usually blackish or brownish with three yellow stripes. The ribbon snake, *T. sauritus,* is a very slender garter snake that prefers wet places. Garter snakes are classified in the phylum CHORDATA, subphylum Vertebrata, class Reptilia, order Squamata, family Colubridae.

Garth, Sir Samuel, 1661–1719, English poet and physician, b. Yorkshire. He studied medicine at Leiden and Cambridge. His chief work is the satirical poem *The Dispensary* (1699), in which he advocates free dispensaries for the treatment of the poor and ridicules those who oppose them.

Garvan, Francis Patrick, 1875–1937, American lawyer, b. East Hartford, Conn., grad. New York Law School, 1899. He was dean (1919–23) of the Fordham law school. In 1919 he was appointed alien property custodian by the U.S. government. He organized the Chemical Foundation, Inc., to develop German patents seized by the United States and thus did much to establish the American chemical industry.

Garvey, Marcus, 1887–1940, American Negro leader, a proponent of black nationalism, b. Jamaica. At the age of 14, Garvey went to work as a printer's apprentice. After leading (1907) an unsuccessful printers' strike in Jamaica, he edited several newspapers in Costa Rica and Panama. During a period in London he became interested in African history and black nationalism. His concern for the problems of blacks led him to found (1914) the Universal Negro Improvement Association and in 1916 he moved to New York City and opened a branch in Harlem. The UNIA was an organization designed "to promote the spirit of race pride." Broadly, its goals were to foster worldwide unity among all Negroes and to establish the greatness of the African heritage. Garvey addressed himself to the lowest classes of blacks and rejected any notion of integration. Convinced that the Negro could not secure his rights in countries where he was a minority race, he urged a "back to Africa" movement. In Africa, an autonomous black state could be established, possessing its own culture and civilization, free from the domination of whites. Garvey was the most influential black leader of the early 1920s. His brilliant oratory and his newspaper, *Negro World,* brought him millions of followers. His importance declined, however, when his misuse of funds intended to establish a Negro steamship company, the Black Star Line, resulted in a mail fraud conviction. He entered jail in 1925 and was deported to Jamaica two years later. From this time on his influence decreased, and he died in relative obscurity. See *Philosophy and Opinions of Marcus Garvey,* compiled by A. J. Garvey (2d ed. 1967); biography by E. D. Cronon (1955, repr. 1969); studies by A. J. Garvey (1963), Theodore Vincent (1971), E. C. Fax (1972), E. D. Cronon, ed. (1973), and J. H. Clarke, ed. (1974).

Gary, Elbert Henry, 1846–1927, American lawyer and industrialist, b. near Wheaton, Ill., grad. Union College of Law, Chicago, 1868. Rising rapidly as a corporation lawyer, he became mayor of Wheaton and served two terms as county judge—afterward he was always known as Judge Gary. His able organization of the American Steel and Wire Company prepared the way for J. Pierpont Morgan to entrust him with the organization of the Federal Steel Company in 1898 and in 1901 with the organization of the enormous U.S. Steel Corp. As chairman of the board of directors, Gary was the dominant personality in the corporation until his death. He closely directed its physical expansion and aided in founding the steel town, Gary, Ind. (named for him). He adopted a policy of management cooperation in the industry, and out of his noted "Gary dinners," where policy was discussed and informal agreements were reached, grew the American Iron and Steel Institute. In 1919 the Supreme Court ended the efforts of the U.S. government to dissolve the corporation as a monopoly. Gary believed in high wages, promoted welfare and safety measures for employees, and introduced a scheme of employee stock ownership. He was, however, adamantly opposed to recognizing labor unions and insisted on the open shop. This policy and the notoriously long hours in the steel industry helped to bring on the bitter steel strike of 1919. It failed, but Gary later, under pressure of public opinion, shortened the working hours. See biography by Ida Tarbell (1925, repr. 1969).

Gary, Romain, 1914–, French novelist, b. Vilna, of Russian parentage. Gary's original name was Romain Kacev. In France after 1928, he fought in World War II and later entered the diplomatic service. He won acclaim for *L'Éducation européenne* (1945, tr. 1960), concerning the pain of war. His passion for wildlife conservation is reflected in *The Roots of Heaven* (1956, tr. 1958). His later works include *The Talent Scout* (1960, tr. 1961), the autobiographical *Promise at Dawn* (1960, tr. 1961), *White Dog* (1970, tr. 1972), and *The Gasp* (tr. 1973).

Gary, city (1970 pop. 175,415), Lake co., NW Ind., a port of entry on Lake Michigan; inc. 1906. One of the world's greatest steel centers, Gary was founded by the U.S. Steel Corporation, which bought the land in 1905. Its location midway between the iron-ore beds of the Northwest and the coal areas of the East and Southeast made it ideal for industry. Gary steelworkers were especially active in the nationwide steel strike of 1919, when federal troops occupied the city for several months. The Dunes National Lakeshore Park is adjacent to Gary.

Gary plan: see PROGRESSIVE EDUCATION.

gas, in physics, one of the three states of matter, the other two being solid and liquid. A substance in the gaseous state has neither definite shape nor definite volume. Like liquids, gases are fluids and assume the shape of their containers. Unlike liquids, they will expand to fill any container, regardless of its size. All gases condense into liquids or solids when sufficiently cooled or compressed (see COMPRESSION; CONDENSATION; LIQUEFACTION). Most gases first liquefy, but some pass directly into the solid state (see SUBLIMATION); carbon dioxide, for example, can condense into dry ice. Some gases are extremely soluble in certain liquids, the liquid absorbing many times its own volume of gas. Some solids, by a process called adsorption, can take up many times their own volume of certain gases. The behavior of gases under various conditions of pressure, temperature, and volume is described by the various GAS LAWS. Many of the properties of gases can be understood by considering the fact that only a small part of the volume of a gas is occupied by its atoms or molecules, which are in rapid, random motion. See KINETIC-MOLECULAR THEORY OF GASES.

gas, fuel, gaseous substance that burns in air and releases enough heat to be useful as a fuel, while also remaining sufficiently stable at ordinary temperatures to permit long-term storage without deterioration or undue hazard. It is advantageous if a fuel gas is readily transportable through pipes and is easily liquefied. Practically all fuel gases meet the first condition, and some meet the second as well. NATURAL GAS, which occurs alone and in conjunction with petroleum deposits, is an excellent fuel gas in wide commercial use. LIQUEFIED PETROLEUM GAS is a manufactured mixture of flammable gases that is easily stored in its liquefied condition. OIL GAS is a type of gas made by applying heat to various petroleum distillates. Its principal use is as a supplement to natural gas during periods of heavy demand. COAL GAS may be any of a variety of gases produced by heating coal in the absence of air and driving off the volatile constituents. It is not as high in fuel value as other gases and often contains tars, light oils, ammonia, and hydrogen sulfide. PRODUCER GAS is made by forcing a mixture of air and steam through burning coal or coke. WATER GAS, or blue gas, which burns with a bright blue flame, is made by passing steam over glowing coke.

Gasca, Pedro de la (pā'thrō thā lä gäs'kä), c.1485–1567?, Spanish colonial administrator. A priest as well as a lawyer, he was selected by Charles V to restore order in Peru, was given full discretionary and executive powers as president of the audiencia of Lima, and was ordered to repeal the hated New Laws of LAS CASAS. He arrived in 1547 after the death of the viceroy Blasco Núñez Vela. Tactful, judicious, but unyielding, he wisely offered pardon to all and repealed the New Laws before mustering his forces and entering the field against Gonzalo PIZARRO, whom he defeated in 1548 and ordered executed. He restored some semblance of order to Peru, but his methods were always strictly expedient. After his return to Spain in 1550 he was made bishop of Siguenza and Palencia.

Gascoigne, George (găskoin'), c.1539–1577, English author, a pioneer in various fields of English literature. A reckless, dissipated youth, he left Cambridge without a degree to study law, but he spent most of his time in debtors' prison and was never admitted to the bar. In spite of this, he served in Parliament from 1557 to 1559, and from 1572 to 1574 he served in the army of William of Orange. His "Certain Notes of Instruction" was the first English essay on prosody. It appeared in *The Posies of George Gascoigne* (1575), a revision of his earlier collected poems, *A Hundred Sundry Flowers* (1573). Gascoigne's *Supposes,* a translation of Ariosto's *I suppositi,* was the first English prose comedy, while his *Jocasta,* translated from an Italian version of Euripides' *Phoenician Women,* was the first Greek tragedy in English to be staged and one of the earliest English tragedies in blank verse. Both plays were performed at Gray's Inn in 1566. He also wrote *The Steel Glass* (1576), a nondramatic work in blank verse, noted as the first English satire. See his complete works ed. by John Cunliffe (1907–10; repr. 1969); studies by C. T. Prouty (1942), F. E. Schelling (1893, repr. 1967), and R. C. Johnson (1972).

Gascony (găs'kənē), Fr. *Gascogne,* region of SW France. It is now coextensive with the departments of Landes, Gers, and Hautes-Pyrénées and parts of Pyrénées-Atlantiques, Lot-et-Garonne, Tarn-et-Garonne, Haute-Garonne, Gironde, and Ariège. The sandy and swampy LANDES along the Atlantic coast, the majestic Pyrenees forming the border with Spain, and the hilly ARMAGNAC region between the Adour and Garonne rivers are the main geographic areas of Gascony. Fishing, stock raising, wine making, brandy distilling, and the tourist trade are the chief industries. The historical capital is AUCH; other important towns are BAYONNE, BIARRITZ, Luchon (see BAGNÈRES-DE-LUCHON), TARBES, DAX, and LOURDES. Under the Romans the region was known first as Aquitania Propria and later as Novempopulana or Aquitania Tertia and was inhabited by the Vascones, or BASQUES, who since prehistoric times had lived in the lands N and S of the Pyrenees. Except in the region SW of the Adour, where the Basque language and customs have persisted to the present, Latin soon became the tongue of Novempopulana. Conquered by the Visigoths (5th cent.) and by the Franks (6th cent.), Novempopulana was invaded in turn by the Basque-speaking peoples (the Vascones) from S of the Pyrenees, who in 601 set up the duchy of Vasconia or Gascony. The duchy's borders fluctuated as the Basques fought the Visigoths, the Franks, and the Arabs throughout the MEROVINGIAN period. The duchy kept an independent spirit throughout its history, even when Charlemagne forced the duke of Gascony to recognize Louis the Pious, king of Aquitaine, as his suzerain (9th cent.). Invaded by Norsemen early in the 9th cent., Gascony fell into anarchy and split up into small counties and seignories. In 1052, with the exception of lower NAVARRE and BÉARN, which continued separate, the remainder of Gascony passed to the duchy of AQUITAINE. Gascony shared the fate of Aquitaine, fell under English control in 1154, and was a major battleground in the Hundred Years War (1337–1453); it was completely recovered by France in 1453. Gascony was then not a political unit; most of its territory was held by the counts of Armagnac, the counts of FOIX, and the lords of ALBRET. All these lands passed, through marriage and inheritance, to Henry of Navarre, who became king of France as Henry IV in 1589. The lands were united with the royal domain in 1607. The resulting province of Guienne and Gascony was divided under the jurisdictions of the parlements of Bordeaux and of Toulouse. The province was divided into the present-day departments in 1790.

Gashmu (găsh'myo͞o), the same as GESHEM.

Gaskell, Elizabeth Cleghorn (Stevenson) (găs'kəl), 1810–65, English novelist. When she was still an infant her mother died, and she was brought up by an aunt in Knutsford, Cheshire, the background for several of her novels of provincial life. In 1832 she married William Gaskell, a Unitarian minister. They settled in Manchester, and she lived a quiet, small-town life, rearing a large family and writing her novels. In *Cranford* (1853) and *Wives and Daughters* (1866), Mrs. Gaskell describes the joys and sorrows common to middle-class village life. In *Mary Barton* (1848) and *North and South* (1855) she depicts the social conditions of early Victorian England, particularly of the working classes in the large industrial towns. Although often overly moralistic, her novels are distinguished by humor, perceptive characterization, and superb descriptive passages. Her excellent *Life of Charlotte Brontë* (1857) roused a furor because of its candid statements about the Brontë family, particularly concerning the excesses of Branwell. See her letters, ed. by J. A. V. Chapple and Arthur Pollard (1966); biographies by Arthur Pollard (1966), G. De W. Sanders (1929, repr. 1971), and A. B. Hopkins (1952, repr. 1971).

gas laws, physical laws describing the behavior of a GAS under various conditions of pressure, volume, and temperature. The simplest gas laws relate these quantities in pairs. Boyle's law states that the pressure and volume of a gas are inversely proportional to one another, or $PV = k$, where P is pressure, V is volume, and k is a constant of proportionality. Charles's law, sometimes known as Gay-Lussac's law, states that the volume of an enclosed gas is directly proportional to its temperature, or $V = kT$. This expression is strictly true only if the temperature is defined in such a way that zero degrees corresponds to zero volume. Experimental results indicate that all real gases behave in approximately the same manner, having their volume reduced by about the same proportion of the original volume for each drop of 1° on the CELSIUS TEMPERATURE SCALE. Graphs drawn to describe this behavior can be extrapolated and all converge to a point corresponding to about −273°C (−395°F). A temperature scale defined so that zero degrees corresponds to this zero-volume temperature coordinate is known as an absolute scale. The KELVIN TEMPERATURE SCALE begins at this absolute zero and has degrees the same size as those of the Celsius scale. Only if the temperature is measured on an absolute scale does Charles's law have the form $V = kT$. A third law states that the pressure is directly proportional to the absolute temperature, or $P = kT$. These three laws can be combined into a single law relating pressure, temperature, and volume, which states that the product of pressure and volume is directly proportional to the absolute temperature, or $PV = kT$. This law describes the behavior of real gases only with a certain range of values for the variables. At temperatures or pressures near those at which the gas condenses to a liquid, the behavior departs from this equation. Nevertheless, it is useful to consider an ideal gas, or perfect gas, an imaginary substance that conforms to this equation for all values of the variables. The behavior of an ideal gas can be described in terms of the KINETIC-MOLECULAR THEORY OF GASES and leads directly to the relationship $PV = kT$, which is therefore called the ideal gas law, or general gas law. The constant of proportionality k is usually expressed as the product of the number of MOLES, n, of the gas and a constant R, known as the universal gas constant. In MKS units, R has the value 8.3149×10^3 joules/kilogram-mole-degree. The ideal gas law can be further simplified by replacing the ordinary volume V by the specific volume v, which is equal to V/n. The law then has the form $Pv = RT$. This form has the advantage that all of the variables are intensive; that is, none of the variables depends on the mass of the gas. The van der Waals equation is another gas law involving pressure, temperature, and volume. It takes into account the variations in behavior of different real gases from that of an ideal gas. The van der Waals equation is usually given as $(P + a/v^2)\ (v - b) = RT$, where a and b are constants that have different particular values for different real gases. Other, more complicated equations exist that describe the behavior of real gases over an even wider range of values for pressure, temperature, and volume. See also THERMODYNAMICS.

gas mask, face covering or device used to protect the wearer from injurious gases and other noxious materials by filtering and purifying inhaled air. In addition to military use (see CHEMICAL WARFARE), gas masks are employed in mining, in industrial chemistry, and by firemen and rescue squads. The gas mask consists essentially of a face cover with two eyepieces and a mouthpiece that communicates with a canister containing a filter. The filter absorbs noxious gases as they pass through the canister to the mouth. The face cover also has a one-way outlet valve for exhaled air. See POISON GAS.

gasoline, light, volatile fuel oil, a mixture of hydrocarbons, obtained in the fractional distillation and "cracking" of petroleum and widely used as a fuel for INTERNAL-COMBUSTION ENGINES, for cooking, and as an organic solvent. It is obtained also from natural gas, and by the destructive distillation of oil shales and coal. In England it is called petrol. Gasoline intended for use in engines is rated by OCTANE NUMBER, an index of quality that reflects the ability of the fuel to resist detonation and burn evenly when subjected to high pressures and temperatures inside an engine. Premature detonation produces "knocking" and "pinging"; it wastes fuel and may cause engine damage. In the past tetramethyllead and tetraethyllead have been added to gasoline to raise the octane number. However, large amounts of lead in the atmosphere may be a health hazard, and lead has a deleterious effect on certain pollution control devices. As a result of these and other problems, it was decided in the United States to remove lead additives from gasoline in a gradual program during the 1970s. New AUTOMOBILES are being designed to run on low-octane gasolines having little or no lead content.

gasoline engine: see INTERNAL-COMBUSTION ENGINE.

Gaspar: see WISE MEN OF THE EAST.

Gasparri, Pietro (pyĕ'trō gäspär'rē), 1852–1934, Italian churchman, cardinal of the Roman Catholic Church. He taught canon law at the Catholic Institute in Paris (1879–98) and was apostolic delegate thereafter in South America. After his return he was asked by Pope Pius X to direct the great codification of the canon law, and he was created a cardinal in 1907. In 1914, just after the outbreak of World War I, Pope Benedict XV made Cardinal Gasparri papal secretary of state. Pius XI retained his services, which he brought to a culmination in the LATERAN TREATY of 1929, ending the Roman question, establishing an agreement between Italy and the papacy, and setting up Vatican City (see under VATICAN). He retired in 1930 and was succeeded by his pupil, Eugenio Pacelli, who later became pope as Pius XII. Gasparri is the author of a widely used catechism.

Gaspé, Philippe Aubert de (fēlēp' ōbĕr' də gäspā'), 1786–1871, French Canadian author. He was high sheriff of Quebec for several years. His *Les Anciens Canadiens* (1863, tr. 1864, 1890), a classic of French Canadian literature, is valuable for its picture of life and customs in Quebec at the end of the 18th cent. Gaspé's *Mémoires* (1866) also are of historical interest.

Gaspé (găspā', găs'pā, Fr. gäspā'), city (1971 pop. 17,211), E Que., Canada, on Gaspé Bay near the eastern extremity of the Gaspé Peninsula. It is a resort. Cartier landed there in 1534.

Gaspé Bay (găs'pā, gäspā'), deep inlet of the Gulf of St. Lawrence, 22 mi (35 km) long and 6 mi (9.7 km) wide, E Que., Canada, at the east end of the Gaspé Peninsula. The village of Gaspé is near its head.

Gaspee (găs'pē"), British revenue cutter, burned (June 10, 1772) at Namquit (now Gaspee) Point in the present-day city of Warwick on the western shore of Narragansett Bay, R.I. The vessel arrived in March, 1772, to enforce the revenue laws in an area where virtually the whole citizenry was engaged in smuggling, and her presence was decidedly unwelcome. Her commander, Lieutenant Dudingston, provoked the navigators of the bay further by the manner in which he carried out his duties. On June 9, 1772, the *Gaspee* was lured aground c.7 mi (11 km) S of Providence while giving chase to a suspect. A group of prominent Providence men, including John Brown and Joseph Bucklin, decided to burn the ship, and Capt. Abraham WHIPPLE led the raiders. They boarded the *Gaspee,* wounded the commander, captured the crew, and then burned the vessel at the water's edge. Gov. Joseph Wanton, in the difficult position of having to enforce British regulations without offending his constituents (Rhode Island elected its own governor), admirably solved the problem by issuing proclamations for the arrest of the officially unknown offenders and then doing virtually nothing about them. Despite a large reward offered by the British, the names of the men involved, though well known in Providence, were not revealed until after the outbreak of the American Revolution. The incident was one of the most famous colonial acts of defiance in the troubled years before independence.

Gaspé Peninsula or **Gaspésie** (gäspāzē'), tongue of land, E Que., Canada, between the estuary of the St. Lawrence River on the north and Chaleur Bay on the south, and extending eastward into the Gulf of St. Lawrence. It is c.150 mi (240 km) long and from 60 to 90 mi (97–145 km) broad. Its backbone is an extension of the Appalachian mountain system and is known in its highest part as the Shickshock Mts. Mt. Jacques Cartier, or Tabletop Mt. (4,160 ft/1,268 m), is the highest elevation in SE Canada. The interior of the peninsula is a mountain wilderness, completely forested, and with numerous mountain streams and lakes, offering excellent hunting and fishing. Copper is mined near Murdochville. Settlement is almost wholly confined to the coastal rim, where there is a succession of picturesque villages whose residents live by combining agriculture with fishing (chiefly cod) and lumbering. The inhabitants on the north and northeast are chiefly French Canadian, Acadian, Scottish, Irish, and English. The coast, with its combination of mountain and sea and its many bold headlands, is famed for its beauty. The chief towns are Gaspé, Matane, Percé, Chandler, and New Carlisle. Gaspesian Provincial Park is in the Shickshock Mts., and there are bird sanctuaries off the east coast. Jacques Cartier landed on the peninsula in 1534.

Gasperi, Alcide de: see DE GASPERI, ALCIDE.

Gasquet, Francis Aidan (găs'kĭt), 1846–1929, English prelate and scholar, cardinal of the Roman Catholic Church, a Benedictine. In historical studies of English religious and social life in the Middle Ages and the Reformation, Gasquet emphasized the purity in medieval Catholicism and criticized the English Reformation as harsh and unnecessary. Although his conclusions have been greatly modified by later scholars, his work had considerable influence on prevailing views of the period. Notable among his works are *Henry VIII and the English Monasteries* (2 vol., 1888–1889) and *The Eve of the Reformation* (1899). He was made a cardinal in 1914 and appointed prefect of the Vatican archives in 1918. See study by Sir Shane Leslie (1954).

Gass, Patrick, 1771–1870, American explorer, member of the LEWIS AND CLARK EXPEDITION, b. Perry co., Pa. His journal of the trip across the continent first appeared in 1807 and was widely read. Gass later fought under Andrew Jackson against the Creeks and in the War of 1812. See his journal ed. by J. K. Hosmer (1904).

Gass, William H., 1924–, American author, b. Fargo, N. Dak., grad. Kenyon College, 1947, Ph.D. Cornell, 1954. Since 1969 he has been professor of philosophy at Washington Univ., St. Louis. He is particularly interested in experimenting with the form of the novel. He has been compared to Sherwood Anderson in his treatment of his "grotesque" characters and to Joyce in his mastery of language. His works include the novels *Omensetter's Luck* (1966) and *Willie Master's Lonesome Wife* (1968); and *Fiction and Figures of Life* (1970), literary criticism.

Gassendi, Pierre (pyĕr gäsäNdē'), 1592–1655, French philosopher and scientist. A teacher and priest, Gassendi taught at Digne, Aix, and the Royal College at Paris and held several church offices. He ranked with the leading mathematicians of his day. He violently opposed the authoritarianism of Aristotle, especially in the *Exercitationes paradoxicae adversus Aristoteleos* (1624). He revived and interpreted the atomic theory of Democritus and Epicurus in terms of the new science, thereby opposing the Cartesian school, and also attempted to reconcile atomism and Epicurean ethics with the teachings of the church.

Gasser, Herbert Spencer (găs'ər), 1888–1963, American physiologist, b. Platteville, Wis., grad. Univ. of Wisconsin (B.A., 1910; M.A., 1911), M.D. Johns Hopkins, 1915. From 1931 to 1935 he was professor of physiology at the medical college of Cornell Univ. He was director of the Rockefeller Institute for Medical Research from 1935 to 1953. Gasser shared the 1944 Nobel Prize in Physiology and Medicine with Joseph Erlanger for their work on the electrophysiology of nerves, using a cathode-ray oscillograph.

Gastein (gä'stīn), valley, Salzburg prov., central Austria, in the N Hohe Tauern range. A popular and beautiful resort area, it has hot radioactive springs. Badgastein, one of the most fashionable spas in Europe, and Bad Hofgastein, also a resort, are found there. Gold and silver have been mined in the region since Roman times. Near Badgastein, the Gasteiner Ache River (c.25 mi/40 km long) forms two waterfalls. There is a hydroelectric plant near the mouth of the river, at Lend.

Gaster, Moses (găs'tər), 1856–1939, Rumanian Jewish scholar and writer, b. Bucharest. Expelled (1885) from Rumania for championing the Jewish cause, he went to England and was lecturer at Oxford (1886–91), principal of Judith Montefiore College (1890–96), and chief rabbi of the Sephardic communities in England (1887–1919). He was active in the Zionist movement. Among his works on theological, historical, and literary subjects are *History of Rumanian Popular Literature* (1883) and a new edition of the Sephardic prayer book (5 vol., 1901–6). He was also a noted folklorist; a selection of his essays appeared in *Studies and Texts in Folklore, Magic, Medieval Romance* (3 vol., 1925–28), which covered many other subjects with which he was concerned. His son **Theodore Herzl Gaster**, 1906–, b. London, went to the United States and taught at Columbia Univ., among other educational institutions. His works concerning Judaism, comparative religion, and folklore include *Passover: Its History and Traditions* (1949), *Purim and Hanukkah in Custom and Tradition* (1950), *Thespis: Ritual, Myth, and Drama in the Ancient Near East* (1950), *Holy and Profane: Evolution of Jewish Folkways* (1955), and *Myth, Legend, and Custom in the Old Testament* (1969).

Gaston, William, 1778–1844, American jurist, b. New Bern, N.C. He served a number of terms in each house of the state legislature. While in the U.S. Congress (1813–17) during the War of 1812, he was a sharp critic of the administration's war program. From 1833 until his death, Gaston, one of the few Roman Catholics in the state, was a justice of the North Carolina supreme court, winning respect for the clarity and liberality of his opinions. He declined several national positions to continue his work in North Carolina. See biography by J. H. Schauinger (1949).

Gaston de Foix: see FOIX, GASTON DE.

Gastonia, city (1970 pop. 47,142), seat of Gaston co., SW N.C.; inc. 1877. An important textile-mill center, Gastonia is a major producer of fine-combed cotton yarn. Sheeting, tire fabric, and textile machinery are also made. Nearby is Kings Mountain National Military Park.

gastric juice, thin, strongly acidic (*p*H varying from 1 to 3), almost colorless liquid secreted by the glands in the lining of the stomach. Its essential constituents are the digestive enzymes PEPSIN and rennin (see RENNET), hydrochloric acid, and mucus. Pepsin converts proteins into simpler, more easily absorbed substances; it is aided in this by hydrochloric acid, which provides the acid environment in which pepsin is most effective. Rennin aids the digestion of milk proteins. Mucus secreted by the gastric glands helps protect the stomach lining from the action of gastric juice; if this protection is insufficient or if an oversecretion of acid is present, a peptic ulcer in either the stomach or duodenum may result. Gastric secretion is stimulated by a number of hormones and chemical substances, by the presence of food in the stomach, and by a number of psychological factors, such as the smell of a favorite food. A decrease or total absence of gastric juice secretion may be a congenital abnormality or a concomitant of advanced age. Certain cells of the stomach lining secrete a substance known as intrinsic factor which is necessary for the absorption of vitamin B_{12}; absence of this substance results in pernicious anemia, or B_{12} deficiency (see VITAMIN).

gastroenteritis: see ENTERITIS.

gastrointestinal system: see DIGESTIVE SYSTEM.

gastropod, member of the class Gastropoda, the largest and most successful class of mollusks (phylum MOLLUSCA), containing over 35,000 living species and 15,000 fossil forms. The shell of gastropods is of one piece (called univalve) and usually coiled or spiraled as in SNAILS, PERIWINKLES, CONCHES, WHELKS, LIMPETS, and ABALONES; however, in some forms, as in SLUGS and SEA SLUGS, it is reduced or completely absent. There is usually a definite head, bearing one or two sensory tentacles and a mouth that is often equipped with a rasplike tongue called a radula. The lower surface of the animal is modified into a large, flattened foot, used by bottom-dwelling forms for creeping about. The foot and other soft parts of the body can usually be completely withdrawn into the shell and the opening covered by a permanent plate called the operculum. Ancient gastropods were probably bilaterally symmetrical, but living species undergo a process known as torsion in which most of the body behind the head rotates 180° so that the anal and urinary openings are relocated behind the head, and the digestive tract and nervous system become U-shaped. Most gastropod species are marine but many groups, notably the pulmonate (lung-bearing) snails, have successfully invaded freshwater and moist terrestrial habitats.

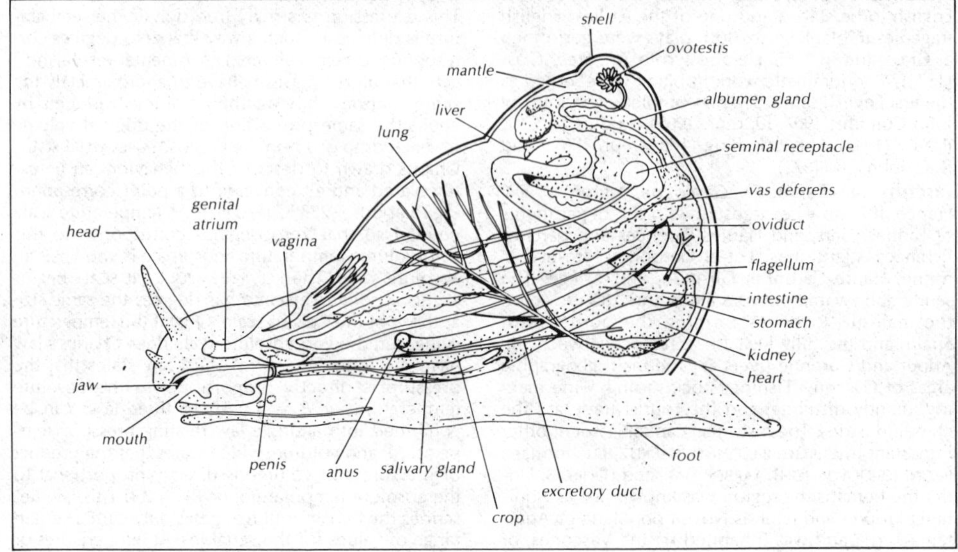

Internal anatomy of a snail, Helix aspersa, *representative mollusk of the class Gastropoda*

Gastrotricha: see ASCHELMINTHES.

gas tube: see ELECTRON TUBE.

Gat: see GHAT, Libya.

Gata, Sierra de (syăr'rä thā gä'tä), mountain range, W Spain. Between the valleys of the Douro and Tagus rivers, it separates León from Estremadura. Its highest point is the Jálama peak (5,577 ft/1,700 m).

Gatam (gā'təm), son of ELIPHAZ **1.**

Gatchina (gä'chēnə), city (1969 est. pop. 69,000), NW European USSR. Industries include ironworking, sawmilling, and the manufacture of papermaking equipment. The city developed around the imperial palace (built 1766–81), which was used as a summer residence by Paul I in the 18th cent. and was a favorite residence of the Russian czars during the 19th cent. The palace (now a museum) was looted and damaged by the Germans in World War II and has been partly restored.

Gates, Horatio, c.1727–1806, American Revolutionary general, b. Maldon, Essex, England. Entering the British army at an early age, he fought in America in the French and Indian War and served in the expedition against Martinique. Later he resigned from the army, and returned to America (1772) to settle in what is now West Virginia. At the start of the American Revolution, he joined the colonial cause as a general and played a part in training American troops outside Boston. In 1776, Gates was given a command in the north under the supreme command of Philip J. Schuyler, whom he replaced as commander in the SARATOGA CAMPAIGN (1777). His army overwhelmingly defeated the British under General Burgoyne, and the Continental Congress appointed Gates president of the board of war. His great victory was aided by the superb leadership of his generals Benedict Arnold and Daniel Morgan. At the time Gates was considered a serious rival of General Washington, and the aim of the so-called CONWAY CABAL was to make Gates commander in chief. Gates's part in this unsuccessful plan has never been fully determined. In June, 1780, he was ordered south to command in the Carolinas. In the CAROLINA CAMPAIGN poorly organized supply, badly trained troops, and hasty planning paved the way for a disgraceful defeat at Camden (1780). He was plunged into deep disgrace and was superseded by Nathanael Greene. An official investigation of the affair was ordered but never took place, and Gates rejoined (1782) the army. He returned home the following year. Gates later freed his slaves and moved to New York, where he spent the rest of his life. See biography by S. W. Patterson (1941, repr. 1966).

Gates, John Warne, 1855–1911, American financier and promoter, known as Bet-a-Million Gates, b. near Chicago. He discovered a market for wire fencing on the Western plains, began the manufacture of fencing in St. Louis, and, by a succession of consolidations and promotion schemes, organized (1898) the American Steel and Wire Company. He was a well-known figure on the grain and stock exchanges and later, interesting himself in oil, became prominent in the development of Port Arthur, Texas. See Stewart Holbrook, *Age of the Moguls* (1953).

Gates, Sir Thomas, fl. 1585–1621, English colonial governor of Virginia. He was knighted for his services under the 2d earl of Essex in the successful expedition against Cádiz in 1596. Gates, who had been a lieutenant in the expedition (1585–86) under Sir Francis Drake that removed Sir Walter Raleigh's first colony from Roanoke Island, was the first named of the grantees in the original charter (1606) of the LONDON COMPANY, which founded Virginia. In 1609 he commanded, as deputy governor, the "third supply" to the colony, a fleet of nine ships with over 500 colonists. Two of the ships, including Gates's, the *Sea Venture,* were wrecked in the Bermudas (the story of this wreck apparently inspired William Shakespeare's *Tempest*). The survivors supported themselves for 10 months in the Bermudas before they completed two pinnaces in which they finally reached Jamestown in May, 1610. Arriving to find that only about one tenth of the colonists had survived the rigorous winter, Gates resolved to abandon the colony. As he was departing for England in June, however, he was met by the governor, Lord DE LA WARR, heading a new relief. At De la Warr's orders the settlers turned back to Jamestown. That autumn Gates returned to England, and in Sept., 1611, he reappeared at Jamestown with a new expedition containing 300 persons (including his wife and daughters) and many cattle and swine. Since De la Warr had returned to England in March, Gates now served as governor until March, 1614, when he also went back to England. He planned further expeditions to Virginia, but they never materialized. He is thought to have died in the East Indies in 1621.

Gateshead (gāts'hĕd), county borough (1971 pop. 94,457), Durham, NE England, on the Tyne River opposite Newcastle upon Tyne. There are locomotive works and railroad shops. Flour milling, shipbuilding, light engineering, packaging, and the manufacture of clothing, glass, iron goods, cables, and chemicals are important. There are coal mines in the vicinity, and Gateshead Fell is noted for its grindstone quarries. Gateshead is a very old community, probably dating back to Saxon times. The iron and steel industry developed there in the 19th cent. The town was swept by fire in 1854, but several old churches survive. In 1974, Gateshead became part of the new metropolitan county of Tyne and Wear.

Gateway National Recreation Area, N.Y.-N.J.: see NATIONAL PARKS AND MONUMENTS, table.

Gath (găth), unidentified royal city of the Philistines, on the borders of Judah. It was the birthplace of Goliath, and it was a place of refuge for David in the outlaw years. Later he had a loyal bodyguard of Gittites, i.e., inhabitants of Gath. Joshua 11.22; 13.3; 1 Sam. 5.8; 6.17; 17.4,23,52; 21.10; 2 Sam. 6.10; 15.18; 21.19; 2 Kings 12.17; 1 Chron. 7.21; 18.1; 2 Chron. 11.8; 26.6; Amos 6.2.

Gathas (gā'täz): see ZOROASTRIANISM.

Gath-hepher (găth-hē'fər), town, Palestine, near Nazareth. It was the home of Jonah. 2 Kings 14.25. Gittah-hepher: Joshua 19.13.

Gath-rimmon (găth-rĭm'ən). **1** Town, W central Palestine. Joshua 19.45; 21.24; 1 Chron. 6.69. **2** Town, central Palestine. Joshua 21.25. It may also be an erroneous transcription of IBLEAM.

Gatineau (găt'ĭnō), river, c.240 mi (390 km) long, rising in the Laurentians, SW Que., Canada, and flowing S to the Ottawa River at Hull. There are several rapids with hydroelectric power plants on the river. Lumber is moved on the river.

Gatling, Richard Jordan, 1818–1903, American inventor, b. Winton, N.C. He invented agricultural implements, which he manufactured in St. Louis, and then studied medicine in Indiana and Ohio, but he is remembered as the creator of a rapid-firing gun that was the precursor of the modern machine gun. He offered the Gatling gun to the Union army in the Civil War and successfully demonstrated it in Dec., 1862, but it was not accepted by the Ordnance Dept. until 1866, after the war had ended. It was long used by the U.S. army until replaced by more modern types.

Gatschet, Albert Samuel (gä'chĭt), 1832–1907, American ethnologist, b. Switzerland. He was trained as a linguist in the universities of Bern and Berlin, and after his arrival in the United States he was a pioneer in the scientific study of American Indian languages. In 1877 he became ethnologist of the U.S. Geological Survey and in 1879 a member of the newly organized Bureau of American Ethnology. His many reports and records were valuable; a study of the Klamath Indians published in 1890 was particularly outstanding.

Gatti-Casazza, Giulio (jo͞o'lyō gät'tē-käzät'sä), 1869–1940, Italian operatic manager. In 1893 he succeeded his father as director of the municipal theater at Ferrara. After directing (1898–1908) the La Scala Opera Company in Milan, he became (1908) director of the Metropolitan Opera, New York City. In 1935 he retired to Italy. His first wife was the singer Frances Alda (1883–1952). See his autobiography, *Memories of the Opera* (1941).

Gattinara, Mercurino Arborio, marchese di (mĕrco͝orē'nō ärbô'rēō märkĕ'za dē gät''tēnä'rä), 1465–1530, Italian statesman and jurist, cardinal of the Roman Catholic Church. After a distinguished legal career in his native Piedmont, he served MARGARET OF AUSTRIA as counselor. In 1518 he was made chancellor by the king of Spain, later Holy Roman Emperor CHARLES V. A humanist and a scholar, Gattinara had much influence upon Charles, whom he urged to create a dynastic empire. Gattinara was made a cardinal in 1529.

Gatún Lake (gäto͞on'), artificial lake, 163 sq mi (422 sq km), Panama Canal Zone, formed by the impounding of the Chagres River. Gatún Dam (completed 1912), 1½ mi (2.4 km) long and 115 ft (35 m) high, controls the level of the lake (c.85 ft/26 m above sea level), which is part of the canal route. Barros Colorado Island, high ground to which animals fled as the basin slowly filled, is a wildlife sanctuary. The lower Chagres valley, now submerged, was first selected as a transisthmian route (for a railroad) in 1848 by John Lloyd Stephens, the American author and traveler.

gaucho (gou'chō), cowboy of the Argentine PAMPA, commonly a mestizo (i.e., a person of mixed European and Indian ancestry). The typical gaucho, a familiar figure from the early 18th cent., was a daring, skillful horseman and plainsman, with an independent nature and a love for adventure and for wandering. As an Indian fighter, revolutionary soldier, and campaigner in frequent internal struggles, he played a significant role in national life. He was an especially strong political force in the early years of the Argentine republic. Gaucho support of the federalists was instrumental in overthrowing the government of Juan Martín de Pueyrredón and in bringing to power such caudillos as Quiroga and Juan Manuel de ROSAS. The immigration of large numbers of European farmers to the Pampa in the late 19th cent. marked the beginning of the gaucho's gradual disappearance. The *payador,* a wandering minstrel of the plain, was a type of gaucho. An extensive gaucho literature was developed in Argentina, Uruguay, Paraguay, and Brazil. Argentine writers, however, have treated the theme more fully, most notably the epic poems *Martín Fierro* (1872) and *La Vuelta de Martín Fierro* (1879), by José HERNÁNDEZ, and the novel *Don Segundo Sombra* (1926), by Ricardo GÜIRALDES. See René Burri, *The Gaucho* (1968).

Gauden, John (gô'dən), 1605–62, English clergyman. He claimed to have written the EIKON BASILIKE (1649), a tract in defense of Charles I. After the Restoration, Gauden was bishop of Exeter (1660–62) and of Worcester (1662).

Gaudier-Brzeska, Henri (äNrē' gōdyā'-bərzĕskä'), 1891–1915, French sculptor. He was the chief exponent of VORTICISM in sculpture. Mainly self-taught in England and Germany, Gaudier showed exceptional precocity in his draftsmanship, animal figures, and abstract works such as *The Dancer.* Returning to France in 1910, he added the name of his Polish companion Sophie Brzeska to his own. Ezra Pound became his patron some time before Gaudier-Brzeska was killed in World War I at the age of 24. Several of his works are in the South Kensington Museum, London. See his drawings and sculpture, introd. by Mervyn Levey (1965); biography by H. S. Ede (1930); study by Ezra Pound (1916, repr. 1970).

Gaudí i Cornet, Antonio (äntô'nyō goudē' ē kōr'nĕt), 1852–1926, Spanish architect. Working mainly in Barcelona, he created startling new architectural forms that paralleled the stylistic development of ART NOUVEAU or *modernismo.* Many of his buildings resemble sculptural configurations; examples are the bizarre structures in the Park Güell (1900–14) and the undulating facades of the Casa Battló (1905–7) and the Casa Milá (1905–10). Gaudí also introduced color into his facades. Improvising designs from odd bits of material, such as rubble, bricks, and polychrome tiles, he achieved variegated effects, evoking comparisons to abstract expressionism and surrealism. Gaudí is as remarkable for his innovations in technology as for his aesthetic audacity. He ingeniously constructed various devices that enabled him to achieve his unusual building shapes; he is particularly admired for his use of the hyperbolic paraboloid form. The Expiatory Church of the Holy Family (1882–1930) represents the height of Gaudí's achievements. See studies by E. Casanelles (1967) and J. J. Sweeney and J. L. Sert (rev. ed. 1970).

Gauguin, Paul (pôl gōgăN'), 1848–1903, French painter and woodcut artist, b. Paris; son of a journalist and a French-Peruvian mother. He was first a sailor, then a successful stockbroker in Paris. In 1874 he began to paint on weekends. By the age of 35, with the encouragement of Camille Pissarro, he devoted himself completely to his art, having given up his position and separated (1885) from his wife and five children. Allying himself with the impressionists, he exhibited with them from 1879 to 1886. The next year he sailed for Panama and Martinique. In protest against the "disease" of civilization, he determined to live primitively, but illness forced him to return to France. The next years were spent in Paris and Brittany, with a brief but tragic stay with VAN GOGH at Arles. In 1888, Gauguin and Émile Bernard proposed a synthetist theory of art, emphasizing the use of flat planes and bright, nonnaturalistic color in conjunction with symbolic or primitive subjects. *The Yellow Christ* (Albright-Knox Art Gall., Buffalo) is characteristic of this period. In 1891, Gauguin sold 30 canvases and with the proceeds went to Tahiti. There he spent two years living poorly, painting some of his finest pictures and writing *Noa Noa* (tr. 1947), an autobiographical novel set in Tahiti. In 1893 he returned to France, collected a legacy, and exhibited his work, rousing some interest but making very little money. Disheartened and sick from syphilis, which had afflicted him for many years, he again set out for the South Seas in 1895. There his last years were spent in poverty, despair, and physical suffering. In 1897 he attempted suicide and failed, living to paint for five more years. He died on Hiva Oa in the Marquesas Islands. Today Gauguin is recognized as a highly influential founding father of modern art. He rejected the tradition of Western naturalism, using nature as a starting point from which to abstract figures and symbols. He stressed linear patterns and remarkable color harmonies, imbuing his paintings with a profound sense of mystery. He revived the art of woodcutting with his free and daring knife work and his expressive, irregular shapes and strong contrasts. He produced some fine lithographs and a number of pottery pieces. There are major examples of Gauguin's work in the United States, including *The Day of the God* (Art Inst., Chicago), *la Orana Maria* (1891; Metropolitan Mus.), *By the Sea* (1892; National Gall., Washington, D.C.), and his masterpiece *Where do we come from? What are we? Where are we going?* (1897; Mus. of Fine Arts, Boston). W. Somerset Maugham's *Moon and Sixpence* (1919), based loosely on the life of Gauguin, did much to promote the Gauguin legend that arose shortly after his death. See his letters ed. by M. Malingue (tr. 1949); his intimate journals tr. by V. W. Brooks (1958); Pola Gauguin, *My Father, Paul Gauguin* (tr. 1937); studies by R. J. Goldwater (1957), B. Danielsson (tr. 1965), and W. Andersen (1971).

Gauhati (gouhä'tē), town (1971 pop. 122,981), Assam state, NE India, on the Brahmaputra River. It is a district administrative center and a railroad and shipping point for tea, rice, jute, and cotton. The town has an oil refinery and is the site of Gauhati Univ. and Earle Law School. Gauhati is identified with Pragjyoushapura, capital of King Bhavadatta, who is mentioned in the great Sanskrit epic MAHABHARATA. The town was overrun by Muslims in the 17th cent.

Gaul, Alfred Robert, 1837-1913, English composer. He wrote numerous cantatas, of which *The Holy City* (1882) is most famous.

Gaul (gôl), Lat. *Gallia,* ancient designation for the land S and W of the Rhine, W of the Alps, and N of the Pyrenees. The name was extended by the Romans to include Italy from Lucca and Rimini northwards, excluding Liguria. This extension of the name is derived from its settlers of the 4th and 3d cent. B.C.—invading Celts, who were called Gauls by the Romans. Their cousins in Gaul proper (modern France) probably had been there since 600 B.C., for the Greeks of Massilia (Marseilles) knew them. The Gaul in Italy was called Cisalpine Gaul [Cisalpine, from Lat.=on this side the Alps], as opposed to Transalpine Gaul; Cisalpine Gaul was divided into Cispadane Gaul [on this side the Po] and Transpadane Gaul. By 121 B.C., Rome had acquired S Transalpine Gaul, and by the time of Julius CAESAR it had been pacified. It was usually called the Province (*Provincia,* hence modern Provence), and it included a strip 100 mi (160 km) wide along the sea from the E Pyrenees northeastward and up the Rhone valley nearly to Lyons. Julius Caesar conquered Gaul in the GALLIC WARS (58 B.C.-51 B.C.). He is the best ancient source on Gaul, and he has immortalized its three ethnic divisions, Aquitania (S of the Garonne), Celtic Gaul (modern central France), and Belgica (very roughly Belgium). Aquitania was probably inhabited by the ancestors of the Basques, and the Belgae were probably Celts, like the rest of the Gauls. On the basis of these distinctions, Augustus in 27 B.C. set up great administrative divisions: Narbonensis (the old Province), under the direct rule of the Roman senate; Aquitania, now extending from the Pyrenees to the Loire; Lugdunensis (Celtic Gaul), a central strip mainly between the Loire and the Seine; and Belgica, including most of the rest. The latter three provinces were administered from Lugdunum (now Lyons), capital of Lugdunensis. Upper and Lower Germany were taken from Gaul; these included the upper Rhine, Alsace, W Switzerland, and the Franche-Comté, and E Belgium, S Netherlands, and the Rhineland. The Romanization of Gaul was rapid; the only serious attempt to rebel against Rome was the uprising of POSTUMUS (A.D. 257), but Gallo-Roman civilization was too strong to fall before anything but the Germans of the 5th and 6th cent. In Roman Gaul it often became customary to call the chief center of a tribe or the country around it by some form of the tribe's name. Many of these names survive today. The principal tribes of Gaul (with the modern survivals or locations) were: Abrincati (Avranches); Aedui; Allobroges; Ambiani (Amiens); Andecavi (Angers, Anjou); Atrebates (Arras); Baiocassi (Bayeux); Bellovaci (Beauvais); Bituriges (Bourges, Berry); Cadurci (Cahors, Quercy); Carnutes (Chartres); Catalauni (Châlons); Cenomani (Le Mans, Maine); Eburovici (Évreux); Helvetii; Lemovices (Limoges, Limousin); Lingones (Langres); Lexovii (Lisieux); Meldae (Meaux); Namnetes (Nantes); Nervii; Parisii (Paris); Petrocorii (Périgueux, Périgord); Pictones or Pictavi (Poitiers, Poitou); Redones (Rennes, Breton *Roazon*); Remi (Rheims); Ruteni (Rodez); Santones (Saintes); Senones (Sens); Sequani, in the Franche-Comté; Silvanecti (Senlis); Suessiones (Soissons); Treveri (Trier, French *Trèves*); Tricassi (Troyes); Turones (Tours, Touraine); Veneti (Vannes, Breton *Gwened*). Gallo-Roman civilization was essentially the extension of the villa system (see FEUDALISM). A landed aristocracy grew up, employing the laborers, who made up the principal part of the population. The influence of Christianity and the ravages of Germanic invaders forwarded the local organization around the cities. The greatest testimony to the stability and thoroughness of the culture of Roman Gaul is the survival of the Latin language as French. For history see FRANCE. See Samuel Dill, *Roman Society in Gaul in the Merovingian Age* (1966); Robert Latouche, *Caesar to Charlemagne* (tr. 1968); Henri Pirenne, *Mohammed and Charlemagne* (tr. 1968); J. J. Hatt, *Celts and Gallo-Romans* (tr. 1970).

Gaulle, Charles de: see DE GAULLE, CHARLES.

Gaulli, Giovanni Battista (jōvän'nē bät-tēs'tä gäo͞ol'lē), 1639-1709, Italian painter, called Baciccia or Baciccio. He was noted for his airy, illusionistic frescoes, his figures of children, and his fine portraits. He was influenced by the style of Pietro da Cortona, Correggio, and the late works of Bernini. *Adoration of the Name of Jesus* (Il Gesù, Rome) is his most noted work. Others are *Four Cardinal Virtues* (Sant' Agnese, Rome) and a self-portrait (Uffizi).

Gault, in re, case decided in 1967 by the U.S. Supreme Court. Fifteen-year-old Gerald Gault had been found a delinquent by an Arizona juvenile court and sentenced to the state industrial school for up to six years for having made allegedly obscene telephone calls to a female neighbor. Under the juvenile code Gault had been denied notice of the charges, right to counsel, right to confront and cross-examine witnesses, and the privilege against self-incrimination. In overturning the juvenile court's decision the Supreme Court ruled that these rights were fundamental to a fair trial and could not be denied children. Justice Abe Fortas's opinion noted that although juvenile courts were originally set up to benefit children, the discrepancy between theory and reality required procedural safeguards.

Gaunt, John of: see JOHN OF GAUNT.

Gaur (gour), ruined city, West Bengal state, India. Known also as Lakhnauti, the city was an ancient Hindu capital of Bengal. It was captured (c.1200) by the Muslims and remained a center of their culture until its abandonment in the late 16th cent. In 1537-38 Gaur was besieged and burnt by the Afghan ruler Sher Khan. The Kadam Rasul Mosque (1530), erected over relics supposedly belonging to Muhammad, is still a place of worship. The best-preserved structures are the Bara Sona Mosjid and the finely carved Golden Mosque.

gaur, large wild ox of Southeast Asia, having a humplike ridge on the back. The gaur, *Bos garus,* is thought to be the largest of the wild cattle; the bulls may measure more than 6 ft (1.8 m) at the shoulder and weigh more than a ton. The coat in both sexes is generally dark brown, but the lower legs are white. The strongly curved horns sweep backward and inward. The gaur is native to hilly, forested districts of India, Burma, and the Malay Peninsula. It roams about in hilly country in small herds during the day, descending to the lowlands for fresh grass in the morning and evening. Another closely related animal, the semidomesticated gayal of Burma, is slightly smaller than the gaur. Some authorities believe that it is merely a domesticated version of the same animal. Another related species, the kouprey, was not discovered until 1936 in central Cambodia. The gaur is classified in the phylum CHORDATA, subphylum Vertebrata, class Mammalia, order Artiodactyla, family Bovidae.

Gauss, Carl Friedrich (kärl frē'drĭkh gous), born Johann Friederich Carl Gauss, 1777-1855, German mathematician, physicist, and astronomer. He was educated at the Caroline College, Brunswick, and the Univ. of Göttingen, his education and early research being financed by the Duke of Brunswick. Following the death of the duke in 1806, Gauss became director (1807) of the astronomical observatory at Göttingen, a post he held until his death. Considered as the greatest mathematician of his time and as the equal of Archimedes and Newton, Gauss showed his genius early and made many of his important discoveries before he was twenty. His greatest work was done in the area of higher arithmetic and NUMBER THEORY; his *Disquisitiones Arithmeticae* (completed in 1798 but not published until 1801) is one of the masterpieces of mathematical literature. Gauss was extremely careful and rigorous in all his work, insisting on a complete proof of any result before he would publish it. As a consequence, he made many discoveries that were not credited to him and had to be remade by others later; for example, he anticipated Bolyai and Lobachevsky in non-Euclidean geometry, Jacobi in the double periodicity of elliptic functions, Cauchy in the theory of functions of a complex variable, and Hamilton in quaternions. However, his published works were enough to establish his reputation as one of the greatest mathematicians of all time. Gauss early discovered the law of quadratic reciprocity and, independently of Legendre, the method of least squares. He showed that a regular polygon of n sides can be constructed using only compass and straight edge only if n is of the form $2^p(2^q+1)(2^r+1)\ldots$, where $2^q+1, 2^r+1, \ldots$ are prime numbers. In 1801, following the discovery of the asteroid Ceres by Piazzi, Gauss calculated its orbit on the basis of very few accurate observations, and it was rediscovered the following year in the precise location he had predicted for it. He tested his method again successfully on the orbits of other asteroids discovered over the next few years and finally presented in his *Theoria motus corporum celestium* (1809) a complete treatment of the calculation of the orbits of planets and comets from observational data. From 1821, Gauss was engaged by the governments of Hanover and Denmark in connection with geodetic survey work. This led to his extensive investigations in the theory of space curves and surfaces and his important contributions to DIFFERENTIAL GEOMETRY as well as to such practical results as his invention of the heliotrope, a device used to measure distances by means of reflected sunlight. Gauss was also interested in electric and magnetic phenomena and after about 1830 was involved in research in collaboration with Wilhelm Weber. In 1833 he invented the electric telegraph. He also made studies of terrestrial magnetism and electromagnetic theory. During the last years of his life Gauss was concerned with topics now falling under the general heading of TOPOLOGY, which had not yet been developed at that time, and he correctly predicted that this subject would become of great importance in mathematics. See biography by Tord Hall (tr. 1970).

gauss (gous) [for C. F. Gauss, German mathematician and astronomer], abbr. G, unit of magnetic flux density (see FLUX, MAGNETIC) equal to 0.0001 (10^{-4}) WEBER per square meter. Since this unit is derived from the CGS SYSTEM of units rather than the MKS SYSTEM; it is largely obsolete. See ELECTRIC AND MAGNETIC UNITS.

Gautama: see BUDDHA.

Gautier, Émile Félix (āmēl' fālĕks' gōtyā'), 1864-1940, French geographer, an authority on Algiers, the Sahara, and the French African possessions. He explored W Madagascar (1892-94) and traversed the Sahara in various directions. His books include *Madagascar* (1902), *Le Sahara* (1923: tr. *Sahara, the Great Desert,* 1935), *Un Siècle de colonisation* (1930), and *L'Afrique blanche* (1939).

Gautier, Théophile (tāôfēl'), 1811-72, French poet, novelist, and critic. He was a leading exponent of art for art's sake—the belief that formal, aesthetic beauty is the sole purpose of a work of art. An important manifesto of this theory appeared in the preface of his novel *Mademoiselle de Maupin* (1835). Gautier was a painter before he turned to writing. His theory of plasticity, that words should be used as the painter and sculptor use their tools, is illustrated in his volumes of poems *Voyage en Espagne* (1845) and *Emaux et camées* [enamels and cameos] (1852). His other works include the poem *La Comédie de la mort* (1838), the novel *Le Capitaine Fracasse* (1863), and *L'Histoire de l'art dramatique en France* (1858-59). He prepared the way for the Parnassians and symbolists in their reaction against romanticism. See biographies by Joanna Richardson (1959) and Midu Camp (1893, repr. 1971). His daughter, **Judith Gautier,** 1850-1918, was married to the poet Catulle Mendès and then to Pierre Loti, with whom she wrote the novel *La Fille du ciel* (1911; tr. *The Daughter of Heaven,* 1912). Her novels, poems, and essays were usually on Oriental subjects. She was the first woman to become a member of the Goncourt Academy.

Gavarni (gävärnē'), pseud. of **Sulpice Guillaume Chevalier** (sülpēs' gēyōm' shəvälyā'), 1804–66, French caricaturist and lithographer. He was first known for his amusing drawings of costumes, which appeared in the *Mode.* Later he contributed satirical drawings to *Charivari.* In his early delineation of society he appeared more capricious than his great contemporary Daumier. However, Gavarni's last work, published mostly in *L'Illustration,* reflects a bitter attitude. His trip to London in 1847 resulted in drawings strongly condemning working-class conditions there. Gavarni produced over 8,000 drawings, watercolors, and lithographs.

Gavarnie (gävärnē'), village (1968 pop. 167), Hautes-Pyrénées dept., SW France, in the central Pyrenees. Nearby are a celebrated waterfall, 1,385 ft (422 m) high, and a gigantic natural amphitheater, the **Cirque de Gavarnie.** The amphitheater rises in concentric levels from an altitude of c.5,740 ft (1,750 m) and is enclosed by crests reaching altitudes of more than 9,000 ft (2,743 m). The famous BRÈCHE DE ROLAND gorge is a cleft in one of the crests.

Gavazzi, Alessandro (älĕs-sän'drō gävät'tsē), 1809–89, Italian preacher and patriot. A Barnabite monk, he left the order in 1848. His liberal ideas and disillusionment with the social order in Italy led him to emigrate from the Papal States to London, where he joined the Italian Protestant community and led an antipapal campaign. Upon his return to Italy (1859) he was twice Giuseppe Garibaldi's army chaplain (1860, 1866). Later he organized in Rome the Free Christian Church in Italy, also known as the Evangelical Church in Italy.

Gávdhos (gäv'thôs), **Clauda** (klô'də), or **Cauda** (kô'də), small Mediterranean island, S Greece, near Crete. It was the refuge of St. Paul's ship during the tempest (Acts 27.16).

gavelkind (găv'əlkīnd) [M.E.,=family tenure], custom of inheritance of lands held in socage TENURE, whereby all the sons of a holder of an estate in land share equally in such lands upon the death of the father. Most of the lands in England were held in gavelkind tenure prior to the Norman Conquest in 1066, and the custom of dividing lands among the male heirs is still preserved in parts of England, notably the county of Kent. This system of inheritance of lands is to be contrasted with BOROUGH-ENGLISH and PRIMOGENITURE.

Gaveston, Piers (pērz găv'əstən), d. 1312, favorite of EDWARD II of England. Son of a Gascon knight at the court of Edward I, he was a boyhood playmate of the future Edward II and acquired great influence over him. Edward I exiled him (1307), but he returned on his friend's accession later in the year. He was made earl of Cornwall and married the new king's niece. When Edward was absent in France (1308), Gaveston was regent. His greed and arrogance and the king's reliance on his counsel aroused strong hostility among the barons, who forced (1308) Edward to banish him. He was made lieutenant of Ireland, but he returned to England the following year. In 1311 the lords ordainers, who temporarily controlled the government, exiled Gaveston again. When he returned within the same year, the barons rose in rebellion. He was captured and executed.

gavial (gā'vēəl), large reptile of the CROCODILE order, found in rivers from Pakistan to Burma. Also called gharial, the gavial (*Gavialis gangeticus*) is distinguished from the crocodiles and ALLIGATORS by its extremely long, slender, parallel-sided snout. It feeds chiefly on fish, which it catches with side-to-side sweeps of the head. The young are hatched from eggs buried in the riverbank. Gavials are not known to attack humans. They average 12 to 15 ft (3.7–4.6 m) in length, with some individuals over 20 ft (6.1 m) long. The so-called false gavial is actually a narrow-snouted crocodile. The true gavial is classified in the phylum CHORDATA, subphylum Vertebrata, class Reptilia, order Crocodilia, family Gavialidea.

Gävle (yĕv'lə), city (1970 pop. 79,112), capital of Gävleborg co., E Sweden, on the Gulf of Bothnia. Although icebound for three months of the year, the port of Gävle has a busy export trade, especially in iron ore and lumber. Manufactures of the city include chemicals, textiles, and beer. Chartered in 1446, Gävle is the oldest and largest city in Norrland. It was largely destroyed by a fire in 1869 and was rebuilt in a modern style.

gavotte (gəvŏt'), originally a peasant dance of the Gavots in upper Dauphiné, France. A type of circle dance characterized by lively, skipping steps, it was introduced at the court of Louis XIV and was used by Lully in his ballets and operas and by François Couperin and J. S. Bach in their keyboard suites.

Gawain, Sir (gä'wān, -wĭn), one of the most popular heroes of ARTHURIAN LEGEND; nephew of King Arthur. He was regarded, particularly in the early romances, as the model of chivalry—pure, brave, and courteous. In later romances, when spiritual purity was valued more than chivalrous deeds, his character deteriorated, becoming treacherous and brutal. Gawain is most famous as the hero of *Sir Gawain and the Green Knight* (see PEARL, THE).

Gay, Delphine: see GIRARDIN, DELPHINE GAY DE.

Gay, John, 1685–1732, English playwright and poet, b. Barnstaple, Devon. Educated at the local grammar school, he was apprenticed to a silk mercer for a brief time before commencing his literary career in London. The first of his writings to have any real merit were the mock pastoral, *The Shepherd's Week* (1714), and *Trivia* (1716), an amusing description of London life. He is remembered chiefly today for his ballad opera, *The Beggar's Opera* (1728), a lighthearted story of highwaymen and thieves, which satirizes both the corruption of contemporary society and the then current fashion for Italian opera. Its sequel, *Polly,* written the following year, was suppressed by Sir Robert Walpole since it (like *The Beggar's Opera*) ridiculed his government. Gay was also the author of two books of verse called *Fables* (1727, 1738), which were very popular in his generation. See his poetical works edited by G. C. Faber (1926, repr. 1969); study by P. A. Spacks (1965).

Gaya (gī'ə), city (1971 pop. 179,826), Bihar state, E central India. The region is sacred to Buddhist and Hindu pilgrims, who visit the temple of Vishnupad [Sanskrit,=Vishnu's footstep]. BODH GAYA, the site of the Buddha's enlightenment, is 6 mi (10 km) to the south. The city, a district administrative center, processes cotton, jute, sugar, and stones. Tobacco and betel leaves are traded.

gayal: see GAUR.

Gayarré, Charles Étienne Arthur (ātyĕn', găyärā'), 1805–95, American historian, b. New Orleans. After studying law in Philadelphia, he returned home and was elected to the state legislature. Rapid political advances were climaxed by his election at 30 years of age to the U.S. Senate, but ill health compelled him to resign his seat at once. He spent the next seven years in France, where he did much documentary research for his history of Louisiana. Upon his return he was again elected to the legislature, and from 1846 to 1853 he served efficiently as Louisiana secretary of state. Defeated for Congress in 1853, he helped found a branch of the Know-Nothing party in Louisiana, but when he was excluded as a Roman Catholic from the national council of the party (June, 1855), he retired from politics. However, he continued to be prominent in state affairs and a leader of Louisiana literary circles until his death. He wrote a number of novels and a study of Philip II of Spain (1866), but his chief work was his *History of Louisiana* (4 vol., 1851–66).

gay-feather: see BLAZING STAR.

Gay-Lussac, Joseph Louis (zhôzĕf' lwē gā-lüsäk'), 1778–1850, French chemist and physicist. He was professor in Paris at the Sorbonne, at the Polytechnic School, and at the Jardin des Plantes. Gay-Lussac made two balloon ascensions in 1804, attaining on the second a height of about 7,016 m (23,000 ft), to test the variation of the earth's magnetic field and the composition of the atmosphere at varying altitudes. He made advances in industrial chemistry; in the field of analytical chemistry he improved the methods of analyzing gas mixtures, studied prussic acid and iodine, and isolated cyanogen. With L. J. Thénard he improved Davy's method of isolating alkali metals, showed chlorine to be an element, and isolated boron. In physics he is known especially for his work on gases. In 1802 he discovered independently that a gas at constant pressure expands, for each degree of temperature, by a constant fraction of its volume at 0°C. This law, first discovered (1787) by J. A. C. Charles, is known as Charles's law or as Gay-Lussac's law (see GAS LAWS). However, Gay-Lussac's name is more commonly associated with another law of gases, the law of combining volumes, which Gay-Lussac was the first to formulate (c.1808). This law states that the volumes of gases that interact to give a gaseous product are in the ratio of small whole numbers to each other and that each bears a similar relation to the volume of the product.

Gay-Lussac's law: see GAS LAWS.

Gaynor, William Jay, 1849–1913, U.S. political leader, mayor of New York City, b. Oneida co., N.Y. He rose to prominence as a civic reformer in Brooklyn and, as justice of the New York supreme court (1893–1909), continued to oppose municipal graft. Tammany named him candidate; he won the 1909 election but soon lost Tammany support by his reform program, which was not highly successful. His strong and unconventional personality made him a spectacular figure of his time. See biographies by Mortimer Smith (1951) and R. V. P. Steele (1969).

Gayoso de Lemos, Manuel (mänwĕl' gīō'sō dā lā'mōs), c.1752–1799, governor of Louisiana (1797–99). In 1787 he was appointed governor of the newly organized District of Natchez, under the orders of the governor of Louisiana. He encouraged American settlement on Spanish soil and interested a number of Americans, notably Gen. James WILKINSON, in his intrigues to separate the American West from the United States. Spanish forts were built at Walnut Hills (Vicksburg) and Chickasaw Bluffs, and alliances were concluded with the Indian tribes of the Southwest. By the terms of a treaty negotiated in 1795, Spain agreed to relinquish the Natchez region to the United States, but Gayoso de Lemos, on secret orders, delayed evacuation until 1798. He succeeded CARONDELET as governor of Louisiana in 1797 and spent his last years in strengthening the province's defense against an expected American invasion. He was an able administrator and a man of much personal charm. See biography by J. D. L. Holmes (1965); A. P. Whitaker, *The Spanish-American Frontier* (1927, repr. 1969).

Gaza, Theodore (gä'zə, gä'-), c.1398–c.1478, Greek scholar, b. Salonica. When the Turks attacked Constantinople, he went to Italy, where he became one of the greatest classical scholars and humanists of the Renaissance. His patrons included the Este family, Pope Nicholas V, and Cardinal BESSARION. Gaza was responsible for spreading Greek learning from Ferrara, Rome, and Naples. His Greek grammar was printed by Aldus Manutius in 1495.

Gaza, Ghazzah (both: gäz'ə), or **Ghuzzeh** (gŭz'ə), town (1968 est. pop. 118,300), SW Asia, on the Philistia plain between the Mediterranean Sea and W Israel. Anciently it was an Egyptian garrison town (it is mentioned in the Tel el Amarna letters) and later was one of the chief cities of the Philistines. There Samson brought down the temple on his captors and himself. Gaza was besieged for five months by Alexander the Great and during the wars of the Maccabees and in the Crusades. The town has long been of commercial importance, the meeting place of caravans between Egypt and Syria. The site of modern Gaza dates from the building programs of Herod the Great. Opinions differ on the site of ancient Gaza. Gen. 10.19; Joshua 10.41; 11.22; 15.47; Judges 1.18; 16; 1 Sam. 6.17; Jer. 47.1; Amos 1.6,7; Zeph. 2.4; Zech. 9.5; 1 Mac. 11.61–62; Acts 8.26. Azzah: Deut. 2.23; 1 Kings 4.24. Present-day Gaza is the principal city and administrative center of the **Gaza Strip** (1971 est. pop. 365,000), a rectangular coastal area (c.140 sq mi/370 sq km), in what was formerly SW Palestine. It is a densely populated and impoverished region inhabited largely by Arab refugees from Israel. The number of inhabitants has fluctuated with tensions in the Middle East, increasing greatly during periods of armed conflicts; after the 1967 Arab-Israeli War the region had an estimated population of 650,000. The Gaza Strip has some farming, a modest citrus fruit industry, and livestock grazing. Between 1917 and 1948 the region was part of Great Britain's Palestine mandate from the League of Nations. After the armistice agreement of 1949 until the 1967 War (with the exception of the Israeli occupation from Nov., 1956, to March, 1957), the Gaza Strip was under Egyptian administration; after the 1967 War, Israel occupied the region. Since the late 1940s the Gaza Strip has been the scene of many clashes between Egyptian, Arab guerrilla, and Israeli forces. The United Nations has supported huge Arab refugee camps there.

Gazel, Al-: see GHAZALI, AL-.

gazelle, name for the many species of delicate, graceful ANTELOPES of the genus *Gazella,* inhabiting arid, open country. Most gazelles are found only in Africa, but several species range over N Africa and SW Asia; the Persian, or goitered, gazelle (*Gazella subgutterosa*) is found only in S and central Asia. Gazelles are rather small antelopes, most standing from 2 to 3 ft (60–90 cm) high at the shoulder, and are generally fawn colored. Some are strikingly marked with black and white. In most the horns are heavily ringed and curve backward and inward in the form of a lyre. Gazelles live in herds on grassy plains and in scrub country. They are very swift animals; members of some species can maintain a speed of 30 mi (48 km) per hr indefinitely, with bursts of 60 mi (96 km) per hour. They are also powerful jumpers. Largest of the gazelles is the addra, or dorcas gazelle (*G. dorcas*), of the Sahara Desert. It has very long legs and a long neck and is white over most of its body. Closely related to the true gazelles are the Tibetan and Mongolian gazelles (species of the genus *Procapra*), the BLACKBUCK of Asia, and the African IMPALA. Gazelles are classified in the phylum CHORDATA, subphylum Vertebrata, class Mammalia, order Artiodactyla, family Bovidae.

Gazer (gā'zər), the same as GEZER.

gazetteer (găz"ĭtēr'), dictionary or encyclopedia listing alphabetically the names of places, political divisions, and physical features of the earth and giving some information about each. The term *gazetteer* originally was applied to one who wrote a gazette. It was first used in its modern sense early in the 18th cent., after the publication (1703) by Lawrence Echard of the *Gazetteer's or Newsman's Interpreter,* a geographical index. But lists of place names, with descriptions, had been made as early as the 6th cent.; part of the gazetteer of Stephen of Byzantium, of this time, is extant. The 19th cent., when geographical knowledge and the need for having geographical facts readily available had both increased greatly, was the great period of development of gazetteer making. Attempts were made to produce complete gazeteers, necessitating several volumes. Famous gazetteers include Johnston's (Scotland, 1850), Blackie's (Scotland, 1850), Bouillet's (France, 1857), Ritter's (Germany, 1874), Longman's (England, 1895), Garollo's (Italy, 1898), and Lippincott's (United States, 1865); later editions of many of these have appeared. Many states of the United States and most countries of the world have separate gazetteers. The most important modern gazetteer is *The Columbia Lippincott Gazetteer of the World* (1952).

Gazez (gā'zĕz), name of a son and of a grandson of Caleb. 1 Chron. 2.46.

Gaziantep (gä"zēän'tĕp), formerly **Aintab** (īntäb'), city (1970 pop. 225,881), capital of Gaziantep prov., S Turkey. Gazientep is an important trading and manufacturing center known for its textiles and pistachio nuts. An ancient Hittite city, it was occupied (8th cent. B.C.) by Sargon of Assyria. It occupied a strategic position in the Crusades and was taken by Saladin in 1183. It was the center of Turkish resistance (1920–21) to the French occupation of the region. After a long siege it was captured by the French, but was returned to Turkey in 1921. For its heroic resistance the city was awarded the title of *Gazi,* or "Warrior for the Faith," and from that time has been known as Gaziantep.

Gazzam (găz'ăm), family returning with Zerubbabel. Ezra 2.48; Neh. 7.51.

GCA, ground-controlled approach: see INSTRUMENT-LANDING SYSTEM.

Gd, chemical symbol of the element GADOLINIUM.

Gdańsk (gədänsk') or **Danzig** (dăn'sĭg), city (1970 pop. 364,285), capital of Gdańsk prov., N Poland, on a branch of the Vistula and on the Gulf of Danzig. One of the chief Polish ports on the Baltic Sea, it is a leading industrial and communications center. Its shipyards are among the world's largest, and it has important mechanical-engineering, machine-building, chemical, and metallurgical industries. Sawmilling, food processing, brewing, distilling, and light manufacturing are also important. The actual port is located at Nowy Port (Neufahrwasser), a northern suburb. The port cities of Gdańsk and GDYNIA and the nearby resort of SOPOT are administered as a single city. An old Slavic settlement, Gdańsk was first mentioned in 997. It soon became the capital of Pomerelia (see POMERANIA). After its settlement by German merchants, it joined (13th cent.) the Hanseatic League and developed as an important Baltic trading port. In 1308 it was conquered by the Teutonic Knights and became an object of struggle between their order and Poland. Pomerelia and Gdańsk passed to Poland in 1466. Gdańsk was granted local autonomy under the Polish crown. In 1576, Gdańsk successfully withstood a siege by Stephen Báthory and thus preserved its established privileges against domination by the Polish crown. After the Thirty Years War the city began to decline. In the War of the Polish Succession, King Stanislaus I took refuge in Gdańsk until it fell (1734) after a heroic defense. The first partition of Poland in 1772 made Gdańsk a free city; the second partition (1793) gave it to Prussia. Napoleon I restored its status as a free city (1807). Reverting to Prussia in 1814, it was fortified and, as Danzig, was the provincial capital of West Prussia until 1919, when by the Treaty of Versailles it once more became a free city with its own legislature. In order to give Poland a seaport, it was included in the Polish customs territory and was placed under a high commissioner appointed by the League of Nations; as the League's authority waned after 1935, Gdańsk came under Nazi control. Hitler's demand (1939) for the city's return to Germany was the principal immediate cause of the German invasion of Poland and thus of World War II. Gdańsk was annexed to Germany from Sept. 1, 1939, until its fall to the Soviet army early in 1945. The Allies returned the city to Poland, which restored the name Gdańsk. In 1970 workers' grievances sparked riots in Gdańsk that spread to other cities and led to changes in Poland's national leadership. Gdańsk has numerous educational and cultural facilities. Historic landmarks include the Gothic Church of St. Mary (1343), one of the world's largest Protestant churches.

GDP (guanosine diphosphate): see GUANINE.

Gdynia (gədĭn'yə), Ger. *Gdingen,* city (1970 pop. 190,125), N Poland, a port on the Baltic Sea and the Gulf of Danzig. It is an important rail center with industries producing metals, machinery, and food products. Originally a small German fishing village, it was transferred to Poland after World War I. Gdynia as a port was built up after 1924 to end Poland's dependence on Danzig (Gdańsk). By 1934, Gdynia handled more freight than Danzig and was a leading Baltic port. It also became the main naval base and shipbuilding center of Poland. Although the harbor was heavily damaged in World War II, the city suffered relatively little destruction. By 1950 most of the harbor was rebuilt, and Gdynia was again an important commercial port.

Ge, chemical symbol of the element GERMANIUM.

gear, toothed wheel, cylinder, or cone that transmits motion from one part of a machine to another; it is one of the oldest means of transmitting motion. When the teeth of two gears are meshed, turning one gear will cause the other to rotate. In most cases both gears are mounted on shafts so that when one shaft turns, the other also rotates. By meshing two gears of different diameters, a variation in both speed and torque between the two shafts is obtained; the smaller gear in this case is called the pinion. A spur gear consists of a wheel with straight teeth mounted radially either on the inner circumference (internal spur gear) or outer circumference (external spur gear) of the wheel. Two meshed spur gears are used to transmit motion between parallel shafts. A rack and pinion consists of a pinion engaging and transferring motion to or from a special kind of spur gear, called a rack, consisting of a series of teeth in a straight line on a flat surface. The rack and pinion changes linear motion into rotary motion, or vice versa. A helical gear is similar to a spur gear, but its teeth are twisted instead of straight. Helical gears can be used to transmit motion between shafts that do not intersect and are at any angle with respect to each other. A bevel gear has straight or curved teeth on a conical surface near its rim. Bevel gears are used to transmit rotary motion between shafts that are not parallel and that would intersect at an angle if extended. Hypoid gears are special bevel gears used in the DIFFERENTIAL of an automobile to connect the drive shaft to the rear axle. A worm gear, meshed with a threaded cylinder, or worm, that resembles a screw, is used to transmit motion between perpendicular, nonintersecting shafts. See TRANSMISSION. See H. E. Merritt, *Gears* (3d ed. 1954); D. W. Dudley, ed., *Gear Handbook* (1962); H. J. Watson, *Modern Gear Production* (1970).

Geary, John White (gēr'ē), 1819–73, American politician and Union general in the Civil War, b. Mt. Pleasant, Pa. In San Francisco from 1849 to 1852, Geary was the first U.S. postmaster, the last alcalde, and the first mayor. President Pierce appointed him governor of "bleeding" KANSAS in July, 1856. His energy and firmness brought peace to the territory for the first time in many months, but the meeting of the determined proslavery legislature (Jan., 1857) and the discovery that little antislavery support could be expected from the incoming President Buchanan led Geary to resign (March). In the Civil War, Geary was made a brigadier general of volunteers in April, 1862. He was wounded at Cedar Mt. (1862), commanded a division of the Army of the Potomac at Chancellorsville and Gettysburg (1863), distinguished himself under Joseph Hooker in the Chattanooga campaign (1864), and fought in W. T. Sherman's campaigns (1864–65). He was made major general of volunteers in Jan., 1865. Geary, elected governor of Pennsylvania in 1866, held that office until shortly before his death. See biography by H. M. Tinkcom (1940); J. H. Gihon, *Geary and Kansas* (1971).

Geba (gē'bə), town, Palestine, c.5 mi (8 km) NW of Jerusalem, the modern Jaba (Jordan). There Jonathan slaughtered the Philistines. Joshua 21.17; 1 Sam. 13.3; 1 Kings 15.22; 2 Kings 23.8; 1 Chron. 6.60; Neh. 11.31; Isa. 10.29. Gaba: Joshua 18.24; Ezra 2.26; Neh. 7.30.

Gebal (gē'bəl), biblical name of BYBLOS.

Geber: see JABIR.

Geber (gē'bər). **1** Father of a steward of Solomon. 1 Kings 4.13. **2** Officer of Solomon. 1 Kings 4.19.

Gebim (gē'bĭm), unidentified place. Isa. 10.31.

gecko, (gĕk'ō), small or medium-sized lizard of the family Gekkonidae. The more than 300 species are distributed throughout the warm regions of the world, mostly in the Old World. Despite folklore to the contrary, their bite is not poisonous. Many species are arboreal, while others inhabit human dwellings. Most lack moveable eyelids and have characteristic pads on the undersides of their feet that enable them to cling to apparently smooth surfaces and to run upside down on ceilings. The pads contain microscopic backward-projecting hooks that cling to even the smallest surface irregularity. Geckos are unique among lizards in that they possess voices, and different species make characteristic sounds. They feed on small animals, chiefly insects. Nearly all lay eggs. The largest species is the 14-in. (35.5-cm) tokay, *Gekko gecko,* of SE Asia. The wall gecko, *Tarentola mauritanica,* of the Mediterranean region is commonly seen basking by day on walls and rocks; it hunts by night. There are two native species in the United States, the leaf-fingered gecko (*Phyllodactylus tuberculatus*) of extreme S California and Baja California, and the banded, or ground, gecko (*Coleonyx variegatus*) of the deserts of the SW United States and N Mexico. The latter is a ground-dwelling form and lacks foot pads. In Florida there are several introduced West Indian species as well as the widely distributed Turkish gecko, *Hemidactylus turcicus,* originally from Africa. Geckos are classified in the phylum CHORDATA, subphylum Vertebrata, class Reptilia, order Squamata, family Gekkonidae.

Gedaliah (gĕdəlī'ə). **1** Son of Jeremiah's protector Ahikam and guardian under Nebuchadnezzar of the Jews exempt from the Captivity. He was treacherously murdered, and the day of his death in the seventh month is still observed as a Jewish fast. Jer. 40–41. **2** Musician. 1 Chron. 25.3,9. **3** Ancestor of Zephaniah. Zeph. 1.1. **4** Opponent of Jeremiah. Jer. 38.1. **5** One who had a foreign wife. Ezra 10.18.

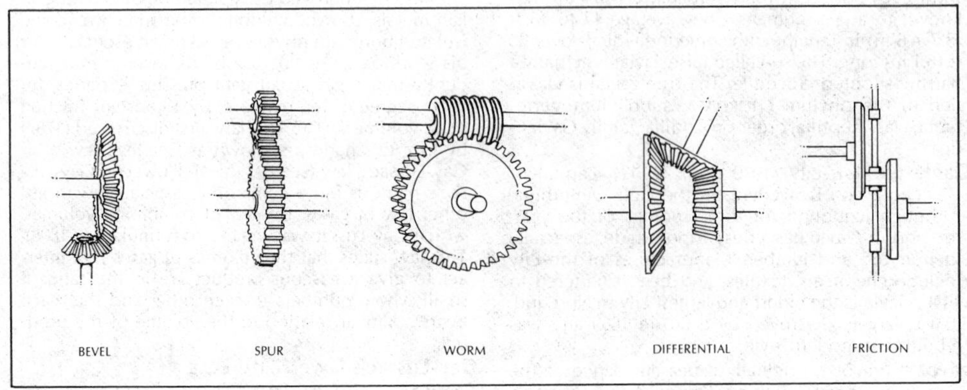

Types of gears

Geddes, Norman Bel, 1893-1958, American designer, b. Adrian, Mich. Geddes began his career in 1918 as scene designer for the Metropolitan Opera. He became known for imaginative designs both for the New York stage (most notably *The Miracle* in 1924) and for numerous industrial products. Geddes also designed several theaters and other buildings in the United States and abroad. See his *Miracle in the Evening* (1960). His daughter, **Barbara Bel Geddes,** 1922-, b. New York City, is a stage and film actress. She created the role of Maggie in *Cat on a Hot Tin Roof* (1955) and the title role in *Mary, Mary* (1961). Her films include *Vertigo* (1959).

Geddes, Sir Patrick, 1854-1932, Scottish biologist and sociologist, distinguished especially in town planning. He received his biological training in T. H. Huxley's laboratory; from the beginning he was interested in relating biological knowledge to civic welfare. His conviction of the importance of environment led to the organization of University Hall in Edinburgh as a center of student life and to his plan for the reconstruction of Edinburgh, with the eventual elimination of slums. He was selected by Zionist leaders to design the Hebrew Univ. building at Jerusalem and to plan the enlargement of the city. In biology, Geddes was an authority on the evolution of sex, collaborating with Sir J. Arthur Thomson in several works on the subject. Other books by Geddes include *City Development* (1904) and *Cities in Evolution* (1915). Geddes held professorships at Edinburgh, London, Aberdeen, St. Andrews, and Bombay and at his death was director of the Scots College, Montpellier, France. He was knighted in 1932. See biographies by P. L. Boardman (1944) and Philippe Mairet (1957).

Gedeon (gĕd'ēən), the same as GIDEON.

Geder (gē'dər): see BETH-GADER.

Gederah (gēdē'rə, gĕd'-), town, SW Palestine. Joshua 15.36. Modern Gederah (Israel) has been the site of a Zionist agricultural settlement since the late 19th cent. The name is also spelled Gedera.

Gederoth (gēdē'rŏth, gĕd'ə-), town, SW Palestine. Joshua 15.41; 2 Chron. 28.18.

Gederothaim (gĕd"ərəthā'ĭm), unidentified Judahite town, SW Palestine. Joshua 15.36.

Gedor (gē'dôr). **1** Ancestor of Saul. 1 Chron. 8.31; 9.37. **2** Unidentified Judahite town. 1 Chron. 4.18. **3** Judahite town, N of Hebron. Joshua 15.58. **4** Home of two of David's archers. 1 Chron. 12.7. **5** Unidentified town, Palestine, in the territory of Simeon. 1 Chron. 4.39.

Geel (khāl), city (1970 pop. 29,346), Antwerp prov., N Belgium. It is famous for its large colony of mentally disabled persons, who live with private families rather than in institutions. The tradition of the city centers on St. Dymphna, a 6th-century Irish virgin martyr at whose shrine demoniacs are said to have been cured. The colony dates from the 14th cent. The city's name is sometimes spelled Gheel.

Geelong (jēlông'), city (1971 pop. 17,775; urban agglomeration pop. 115,047), Victoria, SE Australia, on an inlet of Port Phillip Bay. It is a major port. Wool, wheat, meat, and hides are the principal exports; oil and phosphates are imported. Among the many industries are wool trading, meat-packing, oil refining, and the manufacture of fertilizers and automobiles.

Geertgen tot Sint Jans (gârt'gən tôt sĭnt yäns), fl. latter half of 15th cent., Dutch painter. Geertgen is the earliest painter of record in Haarlem. He may have gone to Ghent and had some contact with Hugo van der Goes, for there are analogies in their works. Geertgen developed a bold and original style. His figures often have haunting features, particularly the eyes. Examples of his paintings are *Man of Sorrows* (Utrecht) and *Adoration of the Kings* (Cleveland Mus. of Art). He created a lyrical landscape background in *St. John the Baptist in the Wilderness* (Berlin) and one of the first known full-scale nocturnal scenes, *The Nativity at Night* (National Gall., London). His striking use of monochrome detail can be seen in *Virgin and Child* (Mus. Boymans-van Beuningen, Rotterdam).

Geffrard, Nicholas Fabre (nēkôlä' fä'brə zhĕfrär'), 1806-79, president of Haiti (1859-67). He took part (1843) in the revolt against Jean Pierre Boyer and led the insurrection that overthrew Faustin Élie SOULOUQUE in 1859. Although he tried to reform the government, he was continually harassed by counterrevolutions and could accomplish little. He was exiled in 1867.

Gegenbaur, Karl (kärl gā'gənbour), 1826-1903, German anatomist. A professor at the universities of Jena (1855-73) and Heidelberg (1873-1901), he was influential as a teacher. He emphasized the value of comparative anatomy in the study of evolution and of homologies. He showed (1861) that the ovum of every vertebrate is a single cell.

gegenschein (gā'gənshīn") or **counterglow,** a brightening of the night sky in the region of the ZODIAC directly opposite the sun, i.e., 180° from the sun. It is caused by reflection of sunlight by small particles that lie in the plane of the solar system. The nature and origin of the particles are not known; they may include gas molecules blown from the earth's atmosphere by the solar wind or may be particles of the same sort that cause the ZODIACAL LIGHT.

Gehazi (gēhā'zī), Elisha's dishonest servant. 2 Kings 5; 8.

Gehenna (gĭhĕn'ə): see HELL.

Gehrig, Lou (Louis Gehrig) (gâr'ĭg), 1903-41, American baseball player, b. New York City. He studied at Columbia. As the first baseman (1925-39) for the New York Yankees of the American League, Gehrig established the record of playing 2,130 consecutive league games, batted .361 in seven world series, and broke many other major-league records. The "Iron Horse," as he was known to admirers, had a lifetime batting average of .340 and his 493 home runs rank among the game's best records. He four times won the most-valuable-player award. Stricken by a rare type of paralysis, Gehrig retired from baseball in 1939 and served (1940-41) as a parole commissioner in New York City. He was elected to the baseball Hall of Fame in 1939. See biographies by Richard Hubler (1941) and Frank Graham (1942).

Geibel, Emanuel von (āmä'nŏŏĕl fən gī'bəl), 1815-84, German poet. He taught German literature at Munich and became the center of an influential school of German poetry. Although at first a revolutionary poet, he gradually became more conservative, reflecting the growing German nationalistic spirit. His poems (1840, 1857, tr. of selections from both volumes 1864), which aimed at formal perfection rather than profundity of thought, were very popular, although not particularly original. His dramas include *Brunhild* (1858, tr. 1879) and *Sophonisba* (1869).

Geiger, Abraham (gī'gər), 1810-74, German rabbi, Semitic scholar and Orientalist, theologian, and foremost exponent of the Reform movement in Judaism. He sought to remove all elements of Jewish particularism (especially the "Chosen People" doctrine) and to establish a reworked Judaism based upon a rational examination of the tradition in both its doctrinal statements and its ritual. He was a prolific writer. His great work is *Urschrift und Übersetzungen der Bibel* [text and translations of the Bible] (1857). He helped found the Jewish theological review *Zeitschrift für jüdische Theologie* in 1835. In 1870 he became chief rabbi of the Berlin congregations and director of the newly established seminary for the scientific study of Judaism. See J. L. Blau, *Modern Varieties of Judaism* (1966).

Geiger, Johannes Wilhelm (Hans Geiger) (yōhän'əs vĭl'hĕlm), 1882-1945, German physicist. Geiger received a doctorate in physics at Erlangen in 1906, then went to Manchester, where he assisted British chemist Ernest Rutherford. They devised an alpha-particle counter that permitted great strides in research on radioactivity. In 1912, Geiger returned to Germany, directing radiation research first at the Physikalisch-Technische Reichsanstalt and later at the universities of Kiel and Tübingen and at the Technische Hochschule, Berlin. In 1928 he participated in the invention of the sensitive, portable radiation counter that bears his name.

Geiger counter or **Geiger-Müller (G-M) counter** (gī'gər-mŭl'ər, -myŏŏ'lər), instrument for the detection and quantitative determination of ionizing radiation such as the alpha and beta rays given off by radioactive minerals and cosmic rays. It was first developed by Hans Geiger and later improved by Geiger and A. Müller. Variously designed for different uses, it consists commonly of a gas-filled metal cylinder that acts as one electrode, and a needle or thin taut wire along the axis of the cylinder that acts as the other electrode. Glass caps used to seal the ends of the tube serve as insulators. A voltage applied to the device is so adjusted that it is almost strong enough to cause a current to pass through the gas from one electrode to the other. The gas becomes ionized whenever the counter is brought near radioactive substances, however little the quantity and however faint the emanations. The resulting ionized particles of gas are able to carry the current from one electrode to the other, thus completing a circuit. Once established, the current is amplified by an electronic device so that it can indicate by an audible click the presence of ionized particles. The gas quickly returns to its normal nonionized state, permitting each new particle or ray to register, making counting possible. The instrument can also register ionization by a pointer and scale called a rate meter. The Geiger counter is used in the detection of cosmic rays and for locating radioactive minerals. Counters enable radioactive TRACERS to be followed as they make their way through complex organisms such as the human body; in medicine Geiger counters have found several successful uses in the location of malignancies. They are used also to follow radioactive isotopes in chemical reactions. For a number of research applications the Geiger counter has been largely replaced by scintillometers and other more complex devices.

Geijer, Erik Gustav (ā'rĭk gŭs'täv yī'ər), 1783-1847, Swedish historian and poet. A leader in the revival of Swedish national literature, he also taught history at the Univ. of Uppsala. His *History of the Swedes* (tr. 1845), terminating with the reign of Queen Christina, is his best-known work. Geijer also wrote hymns, lyrics, and songs that enjoyed wide popularity. Previously known as a conservative, he created considerable stir in 1838 when he turned to liberalism and reform.

Geikie, Sir Archibald (gē'kē), 1835-1924, British geologist, educated at the Univ. of Edinburgh. He joined the Geological Survey of Scotland, becoming its director in 1867. He was professor of geology at the Univ. of Edinburgh (1871-82) and director general of the Geological Survey of the United Kingdom (1882-1901). He was knighted in 1891. His numerous publications include *Outlines of Field Geology* (1876, 5th ed. 1896), *Text-Book of Geology* (1882, 4th ed., 2 vol., 1903), *The Founders of Geology* (1897, 2d ed. 1905), and *Types of Scenery and Their Influence on Literature* (1898, repr. 1970). See his autobiography (1924). His brother, **James Geikie,** 1839-1915, also a geologist, was a specialist in glacial geology. He wrote *The Great Ice Age* (1874, 3d ed. rev. 1894), *Earth Sculpture* (1898), and *Structural and Field Geology* (1905, 6th ed. 1953).

Geissler tube (gīs'lər), gas discharge tube in which light is produced when an electric discharge passes through the rarefied gas in the tube. The color of the glow depends on the gas used. The tubes are made in a variety of shapes and are especially useful in spectroscopy. One later form of the tube is widely used in luminous signs ("neon" signs) and another in fluorescent lamps.

gel: see COLLOID.

Gela (jä'lä), city (1971 pop. 67,355), S Sicily, Italy, on the Mediterranean Sea. It is a port, industrial center, and seaside resort. Petroleum is produced nearby and is refined in the city. Much cotton is grown in Gela's hinterland. The city was founded c.688 B.C. by Greek colonists from Crete and Rhodes and soon flourished, founding (c.580 B.C.) Acragas (the later AGRIGENTO). It attained its greatest prosperity under the tyrants Hippocrates and GELON in the 5th cent. B.C. However, the city was sacked by Carthage in 405 B.C. and never fully recovered. In 282 B.C., Mamertine mercenaries (see MESSINA) destroyed the city, and Phintias, tyrant of Acragas, resettled the inhabitants in the new city of Phintias (now Licata). In a necropolis near Gela, Greek vases and other objects have been found; excavations (begun in 1901) have uncovered the ancient Greek wall of Gela (5th-4th cent. B.C.) and two temples. The modern city was founded by Emperor Frederick II in 1230; until 1927 it was known as Terranova di Sicilia. In World War II, Gela was a landing point (July, 1943) for the Allied invasion of Sicily.

Gelasius I, Saint (jĭlā'shēəs), d. 496, pope (492-96); successor of St. Felix III (also known as Felix II). He was a firm upholder of the papal supremacy in a dispute with Anastasius, the Byzantine emperor. This contest was an opening wedge in the struggle between Constantinople and Rome. The *Gelasian Sacramentary* has been erroneously attributed to him. Feast Day: Nov. 21. He was succeeded by Anastasius II.

gelatin or **animal jelly,** foodstuff obtained from connective tissue (found in hoofs, bones, tendons, ligaments, and cartilage) of vertebrate animals by the action of boiling water or dilute acid. It is largely composed of denatured COLLAGEN, a protein particularly rich in the amino acids proline and hydroxyproline. The process of manufacture is a complex one that involves removing foreign substances, boiling the material (usually in distilled water in aluminum vessels to prevent contamination), and purifying it of all chemicals used in freeing the gelatin from the connective tissues. The final product in its purest form is brittle, transparent, colorless, tasteless, and odorless and has the distinguishing property of dissolving in hot water and congealing when cold. In contact with cold water it takes up from 5 to 10 times its own weight and swells to an elastic, transparent mass. Gelatin, being readily digested and absorbed, is a good food for children and invalids. It is important in fine cookery as a vehicle for other materials, in the form of jellied soups, molded meats and salads, and frozen desserts. Preparations of it are used in the home manufacture of jam, jellies, and preserves to ensure jellification of fruit juices. It is used in the drying and preserving of fruits and meats, in the glazing of coffee, and in the preparation of powdered milk and other powdered foods. Bakeries use it in making meringues, eclairs, and other delicacies. In confectionery making it is used as the basis of taffy, nougat, marshmallows, and fondant. Ice cream manufacture employs it to maintain a permanent emulsion of other ingredients and thus to give body to the finished product. In scientific processes gelatin is widely employed, being used in electrotyping, photography, waterproofing, and dyeing, and in coating microscopic slides. It is used as a culture medium for bacteriological research and also to make coatings for pills and capsules, for court plaster, and for some surgical dressings. It affords a base for ointments and pastes, such as toothpaste; it is an emulsifying agent useful in making liquid combinations and various sprays. In its less pure forms gelatin is known as glue and size. Vegetable gelatin, or AGAR, is derived from East Indian seaweeds.

Gelderland, Guelderland (both: gĕl'dərlənd), or **Guelders** (gĕl'dərz), province (1971 pop. 1,533,700), c.1,940 sq mi (5,000 sq km), E central Netherlands. It borders on West Germany in the east. Arnhem, the capital, as well as Nijmegen and Apeldoorn are the chief cities. Largely an agricultural region, it is drained by the IJssel River and by the Lower Rhine and Waal rivers, which enclose the Betuwe, a fertile agricultural lowland, in the southwest. The Veluwe, west of the IJssel, is an unproductive, hilly heathland, which is popular as a resort area. The duchy of Gelderland was conquered (1473) by Charles the Bold of Burgundy, after whose death (1477) it regained its independence. It passed to the House of Hapsburg in 1543 and joined (1579) the Union of Utrecht of the Netherlands against Spain. Part of Gelderland, including Geldern, the ducal capital, was ceded (1715) by the Netherlands to Prussia.

Gelée, Claude: see CLAUDE LORRAIN.

Gelibolu, Turkey: see GALLIPOLI.

Geliloth (gĕl'ĭlŏth, gĕlī'–), boundary landmark, S Palestine, between Benjamin and Judah. Joshua 18.17. It is probably the same as the Gilgal of Joshua 15.7.

Gell, Sir William (gĕl), 1777–1836, English archaeologist. He served as chamberlain to Caroline, consort of the prince of Wales (later George IV), and accompanied her to Italy in 1814. His original drawings of classical ruins are in the British Museum. Among his works, which he illustrated, are *Topography of Troy* (1804), *Pompeiana* (1817–19), *Journey in the Morea* (1823), and *Topography of Rome* (1834).

Gellée, Claude: see CLAUDE LORRAIN.

Gellert, Christian Fürchtegott (krĭs'tyän fürkh'təgôt gĕl'ərt), 1715–69, German poet and moralist. His best-known works are *Fabeln und Erzählungen* (1746–48, tr. *Fables and Other Poems,* 1850), the novel *Leben der schwedischen Gräfin von G———* (1747–48, tr. *The History of the Swedish Countess of G———,* 1752), and the collection of hymns, *Geistliche Oden und Lieder* (1757). His emphasis on simplicity and heartfelt expression made him one of Germany's literary and spiritual arbiters. Lessing, Klopstock, and Goethe were his students. His poems were set to music by many composers, among them C. P. E. Bach, Haydn, and Beethoven.

Gelligaer (gĕlĭgär'), urban district (1971 pop. 33,670), Glamorganshire, S Wales. Three coal-mining valleys are in the district. Automobiles and rubber products are manufactured. In 1974, Gelligaer became part of the new nonmetropolitan county of Mid Glamorgan.

Gellius, Aulus (jĕl'yəs), fl. 2d cent., Roman writer. He was a lawyer who spent at least a year in Athens and wrote *Noctes Atticae* [Attic nights], a collection of discussions of law, antiquities, and sundry other subjects in 20 books (of which 19 and a fraction survive). The work is chiefly valuable as a storehouse of quotations from lost works.

Gelon (jē'lŏn), d. 478 B.C., Greek Sicilian ruler. As tyrant of Gela, his native city, he interfered in the struggle for power in Syracuse (485 B.C.) and made himself the leader of the popular party there. From that time he ruled Syracuse and dominated Greek Sicily. In 480 B.C., Hamilcar and his Carthaginians attacked Sicily in great force, landing at Panormus and advancing to besiege Gelon's father-in-law, Theron of Acragas, in Himera. Gelon came to his aid and crushed the Carthaginian army, which was the first great blow to Punic prestige. It is celebrated by Pindar in his great *First Pythian.* Gelon was succeeded by his brother HIERO I.

Gelsenkirchen (gĕl"zənkĭrkh'ən), city (1970 pop. 348,292), North Rhine-Westphalia, W West Germany, a port on the Rhine-Herne Canal. It is a major industrial and coal-mining center of the RUHR district. Manufactures include iron and steel, chemicals, glass, and clothing. Gelsenkirchen was a small village in 1850, but grew rapidly after the opening of the first coal mines in the 1850s. In 1928 the neighboring towns of Buer and Horst were absorbed by Gelsenkirchen. The city has a fine moated castle (16th–18th cent.), a municipal museum, and a zoological park.

GEM: see AIR-CUSHION VEHICLE.

gem, commonly, a mineral or organic substance, cut and polished and used as an ornament. The qualities sought in gems are beauty, rarity, and durability. The beauty of a gem depends primarily on its optical properties, which impart its luster, fire, and color; the durability depends on hardness and resistance to cleavage or fracture. The physical properties by which gems are distinguished from each other are form of the crystal, index of refraction of light, hardness, presence or absence of cleavage, type of fracture (conchoidal, even, or uneven) in stones without cleavage, specific gravity, color, streak (color of the powder as determined by rubbing it over white, unglazed porcelain), luster (appearance of the surface in reflected light—adamantine, vitreous, resinous, greasy, silky, or pearly), and transparency. Minor properties that serve to identify some stones are chatoyancy, opalescence, asterism, play of color, fluorescence, phosphorescence, iridescence, and electrical properties. The unit of weight used for gem stones is the metric carat; one carat equals 200 mg. Artificial and imitation gems are of various kinds. Synthetic stones are made in the laboratory of the same chemical elements as natural stones. Among the synthetic gems produced commercially are rubies, sapphires, emeralds, and spinels. Diamonds of gem quality have also been manufactured. Color changes are produced in diamonds by exposing them to radioactive bombardment. Synthetic stones may sometimes be detected by the presence of air bubbles, which, when numerous, cause a cloudy appearance; by having curved rather than straight striae; and by their unnatural color. Doublets are made by combining a crown or upper part, which is a thin slice of either the true stone or some inferior but hard gem, with a lower part of the true stone, a substitute stone, colored glass, or colored paste. Triplets generally consist of a layer of paste between two genuine stones of poor color. Paste (glass) gems usually contain lead and are consequently very soft; they soon lose their brilliance and color. Imitation pearls are glass or plastic beads coated with a preparation made from fish scales. A cultured pearl is made by inserting a small bead inside the oyster; the irritation causes the oyster to deposit pearly material upon the bead, leading to the formation of a pearl. Gems are generally cut to bring out their natural color and brilliancy and to remove flaws. In the cabochon cut, the upper surface of the stone is smoothed and rounded into a simple curve of any degree of convexity; the lower surface may be concave, convex, or flat. All the remaining cuts have flat facets. In the table cut, the facets of the natural octahedron of the diamond are ground to smoothness and polished; one facet, the table, is ground much larger than any other and made the top of the gem, while the opposite facet, the culet, is left quite small. The rose cut consists of a flat base and (usually) 24 triangular facets—resembling a cabochon with facets. The brilliant cut is scientifically designed to bring out the maximum brilliancy of the stone. The crown of a brilliant consists of a table and 32 smaller facets, of which 8 are quadrilaterals and 24 are triangles; the base, of a culet and 24 larger facets, of which 8 are quadrilaterals and 16 are triangles. The base and crown are separated by a girdle. The brilliant has certain proportions—in general, the depth of the crown is one third the depth of the stone and the width of the table one half the width of the stone. The trap, step, or emerald cut consists of a table and quadriangular facets above and below the girdle with parallel horizontal edges. Diamond cutting and the cutting of other precious stones are distinct trades. In diamond cutting the stone is first cleaved or sawed to remove excrescences or to break it into smaller stones. Cleaving is accomplished by making a groove in the surface in the direction of the grain, inserting a steel knife, and striking the back of the knife a sharp blow. The next process was formerly bruting, i.e., roughly shaping two stones by rubbing them against one another. In modern practice the stones are sawed with a revolving wheel coated on its rim with diamond powder, then shaped by inserting a holder, or dop, containing one diamond into a turning lathe that revolves it against a stationary diamond. The cutting of the facets and the polishing are done by a revolving iron wheel charged with diamond dust. After the facets are cut, the diamonds are cleaned and are ready for sale. Stones other than diamonds are cleaved or slit by a revolving diamond-dusted wheel, faceted by being pressed against a lap charged with diamond dust or a carborundum wheel, and polished with a softer abrasive. Most (and in the case of some gems all) of the work of faceting is done with only the eye of the workman as guide. The precious stones are DIAMOND; some forms of CORUNDUM (RUBY, SAPPHIRE, Oriental emerald, Oriental topaz, and Oriental amethyst); and EMERALD. The chief semiprecious stones are AQUAMARINE, AMETHYST, TOPAZ, GARNET, TOURMALINE, spinel, peridot, zircon, CHRYSOBERYL, QUARTZ, OPAL, TURQUOISE, MOONSTONE, and JADE. The organic gems are PEARL, AMBER, CORAL, and JET; of these, pearl is usually counted as a precious stone. Gems are used as seals and as talismans. For birthstones, see MONTH. See J. Sinkankas, *Gemstones of North America* (1959); F. J. Sperisen, *The Art of the Lapidary* (rev. ed. 1961); Robert Webster, *Gems* (2d ed. 1970); J. D. Dana, *Manual of Mineralogy* (18th ed., rev. by C. S. Hurlbut, Jr., 1971).

Gemalli (gĕmăl'ī), father of Ammiel the spy. Num. 13.12.

Gemara: see TALMUD.

Gemariah (gĕmərī'ə). **1** Jewish noble favorable to Jeremiah and Baruch. Jer. 36. **2** Envoy to Nebuchadnezzar. Jer. 29.3.

Gemini (jĕm'ənī, –nē) [Lat.,=the twins], northern CONSTELLATION lying on the ECLIPTIC (the sun's apparent path through the heavens) between Taurus and Cancer, N of Canis Minor; it is one of the constellations of the ZODIAC. Gemini is traditionally depicted as two men. The two brightest stars in Gemini, CASTOR and POLLUX (north of the bright star Procyon in Canis Minor), are two of the brightest stars in the sky and were identified by the Greeks with two children, in most accounts the twin sons of Zeus and Leda. The Egyptians identified the two stars with a pair of young goats. An annual METEOR SHOWER known as the Geminids appears to radiate from this constellation during the second week in December. Owing to the PRECESSION OF THE EQUINOXES, the summer solstice now lies in Gemini, rather than in Cancer as it did 2,000 years ago. Gemini reaches its highest point in the evening sky in February.

Geminiani, Francesco (fränchās'kō jāmēnyä'nē), c.1687–1762, Italian composer and violinist; pupil of Arcangelo Corelli and Alessandro Scarlatti. He migrated (c.1730) to the British Isles, settling in Ireland, where he gave concerts and taught. In addition he composed music and wrote several works on violin technique that preserve the style and technique of Corelli. His *Art of Playing the Violin* (1740) was the first work of its kind for the violin.

Geminids: see METEOR SHOWER.

Gemini space program: see SPACE EXPLORATION.

Gemistus Pletho, Georgius (jôr'jəs jĭmĭs'təs plē'thō), c.1355–1452, Byzantine scholar and philosopher, b. Constantinople. He represented the Orthodox Eastern Church at the Council of Florence in 1439, led Cosimo de' Medici to found the Florentine Academy, and inspired the enthusiastic study of Plato that characterized the Italian Renaissance. In his *Laws* he advocated a polytheism similar to that of the ancient Greeks. He rejected Aristotle's criticisms of Plato but did not always distinguish Plato's doctrine from the Neoplatonic.

Gemmi (gĕm'ē), pass, 7,620 ft (2,323 m) high, S Switzerland, connecting Bern and Valais cantons, in the Bernese Alps.

Gemniczer, Wenzel: see JAMNITZER.

gemsbok: see ORYX.

gender [from Lat. *genus*=kind], in grammar, subclassification of nouns or nouns or nonlike words in which the members of the subclass have characteristic features of agreement with other words. The term *gender* is not usually considered to include the classification of NUMBER. In French, *la viande* [the meat] and *le vin* [the wine] are marked as belonging to different genders by the form of the articles *la* and *le* [both: the]. The terms for these genders, feminine and masculine, respectively, indicate that most French nouns referring to males are masculine, and most referring to females are feminine thus conforming to the concept of natural gender. Other words are placed in either gender, e.g., *le jardin* [the garden] and *la table* [the table], being instances of grammatical gender. In German, Russian, and Latin there are three genders, called masculine, feminine, and neuter. Scandinavian and Dutch languages have in addition to these three a "common" gender, which combines, and often distinguishes between, masculine and feminine. A two-gender distinction between animate and inanimate is widespread, e.g., in Algonquian languages of North America and the Andamanese of the Bay of Bengal. Some Bantu languages have 20 genderlike noun classes. English nouns may be divided into gender classes according to the personal pronoun used to refer to them; these do not match sex classes, e.g., *she*, corresponding to *the ship*. The grammatical device of concord, or agreement, is bound up with gender distinctions. By it one word bears a formal signal to show its relationship to the word it accompanies or modifies; thus, in *la viande* the form of *la* shows that it is related to a word of the feminine gender class, and it may be said to agree with, or be in concord with, *viande*. While in Indo-European languages gender involves nouns, adjectives, and pronouns, in Semitic languages even verbal forms must agree with the gender of their subjects. Although gender is present in many languages, it is far from universal. In English a few words retain gender inflection (e.g., *actress, executrix, chorine*), but since the 12th to 15th cent. English has dropped most of the gender distinctions characteristic of the ancestor languages.

gene, ultimate unit by which inheritable characteristics are transmitted to succeeding generations in animals and plants. Genes are contained by and apparently linearly arranged along the length of the CHROMOSOME. The basic and universal chemical constituent of the gene is deoxyribonucleic acid, commonly called DNA (see NUCLEIC ACID). Chemically, the gene consists of a series of building blocks called nucleotides, each of which is comprised of three subunits: a nitrogen-containing compound, a sugar, and phosphoric acid. Geometrically, the gene is a double helix, formed by the nucleotides. It has been established that each chromosome of each species has a definite number and arrangement of genes and that each gene has a specific and constant locus, or position, in the chromosome. In the fruit fly *Drosophila*, for example, specific genes for eye color, size and shape of wings, and other characteristics have been identified and located. Alteration of either the number or the arrangement of the genes, as through exposure to radiation, can result in MUTATION, i.e., a change in the inheritable traits of that cell. There are many genes, called lethals or lethal genes, that in some way inhibit the development of the organism at some stage and cause it to die (usually before maturity). Genes govern both the morphological structure and the metabolic functions of the cell—and thus of the organism—through control of the synthesis of enzymes that stimulate specific biochemical processes. The scientific study of the method of inheritance is called GENETICS.

genealogy (jē″nēŏl′əjē, -ăl′-, jĕ-), the study of family lineage. Genealogies have existed since ancient times. Family lineage was originally transmitted through oral tradition and later, with the invention of writing, was passed on through written records. The genealogies in the Bible probably originated in oral tradition. Ancient Greeks and Romans traced their ancestry to gods and heroes, and primitive tribes often claim descent from bears, wolves, and other animals. Genealogies flourished in the Middle Ages because the development of feudalism made status and the transference of possessions dependent upon the tracing of family lines. In a lesser degree, this condition continues in some countries, as England, to the present day. In the United States pedigree has not been crucial in determining status or in transferring property, but interest in genealogy has received a certain emphasis; there are societies that limit membership to descendants of ancestors of a given group, such as soldiers in the American Revolution. Many libraries have departments of genealogy, where genealogies of families may be inspected. Examples of English genealogies are the books of Burke, Collins, and others on the peerage. Since the 18th cent. genealogy has developed into a subsidiary academic discipline, serving sociology, eugenics, history, and law. See G. H. Doane, *Searching for Your Ancestors* (3d ed. 1960); D. L. Jacobus, *Genealogy as Pastime and Profession* (2d ed. 1968); Theodore Bestermann, *Family History* (1971); V. D. Greenwood, *The Researcher's Guide to American Genealogy* (1974).

Genelli, Bonaventura (bōnävāntōō′rä jānĕl′lē), 1798–1868, German painter and illustrator. He studied at the Berlin Academy and in Rome. Genelli painted mythological and biblical subjects, such as *Triumph of Bacchus and Ariadne*, but his greatest success was in illustrating. Among his best designs are 48 outline illustrations for Homer, 36 for Dante, and copperplate illustrations for *Life of a Profligate*.

gene pool, the total of all GENES in a population of a particular species. See GENETICS.

genera, in taxonomy: see CLASSIFICATION.

General Agreement on Tariffs and Trade (GATT), specialized agency of the United Nations. It was established in 1948 as an interim measure pending the creation of the International Trade Organization. However, plans for the latter were abandoned, so GATT remained in existence. Members of GATT are pledged to work together to reduce tariffs and other barriers to international trade and to eliminate discriminatory treatment in international commerce. The most important service of GATT has been to negotiate multilateral extensions of tariff reductions through the application of the MOST-FAVORED-NATION CLAUSE. GATT also provides for regular meetings to consider other problems of international trade. An important GATT principle is that protection of domestic industries is to be done strictly through the customs tariff and not through other commercial measures, such as import quotas. The only exceptions permitted to GATT rules are those dealing with BALANCE OF PAYMENTS difficulties, and these exceptions are carefully supervised. In 1972 there were 81 full members of GATT; Czechoslovakia was the only member from the Soviet bloc. Most important tariff negotiations today, including those between the COMMON MARKET and outside nations, are carried out within the GATT framework. A major problem has been the different concerns of the developing and the developed nations.

General Grant National Memorial: see NATIONAL PARKS AND MONUMENTS (table).

General Land Office, established (1812) in the U.S. Treasury Dept. and transferred (1849) to the U.S. Dept. of the Interior. Empowered to survey, manage, and dispose of the public domain, the office administered the preemption acts, homestead laws, and all legislation affecting public lands. After 1900 it was more concerned with conservation of the remaining land. In 1946 it was consolidated with the Grazing Service into the Bureau of Land Management. See Milton Conover, *The General Land Office* (1923, repr. 1973); M. J. Rohrbough, *The Land Office Business* (1968).

general strike, sympathetic cessation of work by a majority of the workers in all industries of a locality or nation. Such a stoppage is economic if it is for the purpose of redressing some grievance or pressing upon the employer a series of economic demands. It is political if called for the purpose of wresting some concession from the government or if the goal is the overthrow of the existing government. The political strike has been advocated by the syndicalists and to a certain extent by anarchistic movements. Practically unknown in the United States and Canada, except for some local instances (e.g., Seattle, 1919; Winnipeg, 1919; San Francisco, 1934), the general strike has been a powerful weapon in the hands of European labor since the latter part of the 19th cent. General strikes in Belgium in 1893 and 1902 won suffrage concessions; in Italy, a general strike (1904) protested the use of troops as strikebreakers; a general strike (1905) in Russia resulted in the issuance of the October Manifesto, instituting reforms; a general strike (1909) in Sweden, called against the repeated use of the lockout by employers, encouraged the idea that economic reforms could be gained without resorting to violence; a general strike (1920) in Germany successfully warded off a rightist takeover. In 1926 a general strike in Great Britain was called in sympathetic protest against the national lockout of the coal miners, but the strikers were forced to capitulate when it became clear that the government was able to keep essential services running and when only about half of the workers answered the strike call. In France a general strike, which failed, was called (1938) to protest against a government decree lengthening hours and penalizing strikers. Since World War II, general strikes have occurred mostly on a local level. Notable exceptions are the Belgian workers' reaction (1961) against a government austerity program and the French unions' support (1962) of President Charles De Gaulle during a military insurrection in Algeria. In 1968 another general strike occurred in France when university students and workers joined together during May and June and closed the major industries and universities. The strike ended with an agreement to provide increases in wages for the workers and stronger representation in factory management. In the 1970s the general strike became an often-employed tactic of the Italian trade unions. See W. H. Crook, *The General Strike* (1931, repr. 1972); Julian Symons, *The General Strike* (1957).

Generation of '98, Spanish literary and cultural movement in the first two decades of the 20th cent. It was so named by Azorín (see MARTÍNEZ RUIZ, JOSÉ) in 1913 to designate a group of young writers who, in the face of defeat (1898) in the Spanish-American War, proclaimed a moral and cultural rebirth for Spain. Azorín's original list included VALLE INCLÁN, UNAMUNO, BENAVENTE Y MARTÍNEZ, BAROJA Y NESSI, Ramiro de Maeztu, DARÍO, and Azorín himself. It has since been emended to include Ganivet and Antonio MACHADO, as well as ORTEGA Y GASSET, PÉREZ DE AYALA, and Marañón. Darío is more often considered as the founder of MODERNISMO. The group was concerned with defining the essential quality of Spain, studying its history and culture. In the austere life of Castile many of them discovered the key to the essence of Hispanicism. While they attacked aestheticism and the current adulation of the Austrian satiric poet Karl KRAUS, they also represented cosmopolitan trends, including political liberalism. They greatly influenced the work of later Spanish writers.

generator, in electricity, machine used to change mechanical energy into electrical energy. It operates on the principle of electromagnetic INDUCTION, discovered (1831) by Michael Faraday. When a conductor passes through a magnetic field, a voltage is induced across the ends of the conductor. The generator is simply a mechanical arrangement for moving the conductor and leading the current produced by the voltage to an external circuit, where it actuates devices that require electricity. In the simplest form of generator the conductor is an open coil of

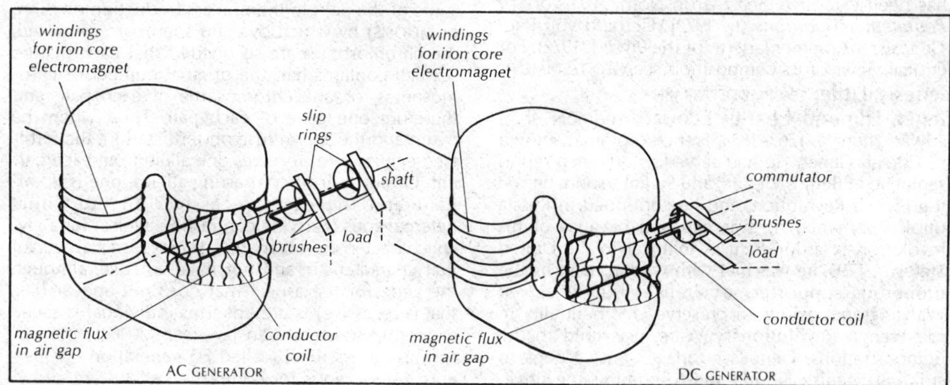

Generator: The rotation of the conducting coil of wire in a magnetic field causes a current to be induced in the coil. This current is alternating and is conducted from the coil by means of slip rings and brushes in the AC generator. In the DC generator, a split-ring commutator changes the direction of the current with each half rotation, resulting in a pulsing direct current.

wire rotating between the poles of a permanent magnet. During a single rotation, one side of the coil passes through the magnetic field first in one direction and then in the other, so that the induced current is alternating current (AC), moving first in one direction, then in the other. Each end of the coil is attached to a separate metal slip ring that rotates with the coil. Brushes that rest on the slip rings are attached to the external circuit. Thus the current flows from the coil to the slip rings, then through the brushes to the external circuit. In order to obtain direct current (DC), i.e., current that flows in only one direction, a commutator is used in place of slip rings. The commutator is a single slip ring split into left and right halves that are insulated from each other and are attached to opposite ends of the coil. It allows current to leave the generator through the brushes in only one direction. This current pulsates, going from no flow to maximum flow and back again to no flow. A practical DC generator, with many coils and with many segments in the commutator, gives a steadier current. There are also several magnets in a practical generator. In any generator, the whole assembly carrying the coils is called the ARMATURE, or rotor, while the stationary parts constitute the stator. Except in the case of the magneto, which uses permanent magnets, AC and DC generators use electromagnets. Field current for the electromagnets is most often DC from an external source. The term *dynamo* is often used for the DC generator; the generator in automotive applications is usually a dynamo. An AC generator is called an alternator. To ease various construction problems, alternators have a stationary armature and rotating electromagnets. Most alternators produce a polyphase AC, a complex type of current that provides a smoother power flow than does simple AC. By far the greatest amount of electricity for industrial and civilian use comes from large AC generators driven by steam turbines.

Genesee (jĕnəsē'), river, 158 mi (254 km) long, rising in the Allegheny Mts., N Pa., and flowing through W N.Y. to Lake Ontario at Rochester; it is crossed by the New York State Barge Canal. The Genesee valley is noted for its fertility and beauty. Along the middle Genesee is Letchworth State Park, with a gorge and several waterfalls. A dam and reservoir at Mt. Morris, N.Y., form part of a flood-control project. Rochester, on the lower Genesee, grew around two waterfalls that are used to produce hydroelectricity.

Genesis (jĕn'əsĭs), 1st book of the Old Testament, first of the five books of the Law (the Pentateuch or Torah) ascribed by tradition to Moses. It is a religious account of the origin of the Hebrew people. Its contents may be outlined as follows: first, the origin of the world and of man (1–11), including accounts of the creation and man's first disobedience (1–3), of Cain and Abel (4), and of Noah (9–10); second, the career of God's special servant Abraham (12–24), including the stories of Hagar and Ishmael (16; 21), of Lot (19), of the sacrifice of Isaac (22), and notably Abraham's journey to Canaan and God's promises to him (12; 13; 15; 17); third, the career of Isaac (25–26); and, fourth, the life of Jacob, who was called Israel (27–50), including his replacement of Esau (27), his vision of the ladder (28), his wrestling with an angel (32), and the extensive story of his son Joseph, with the migration of the family to Egypt (37–50). Several of the stories are taken from Babylonian and Egyptian folklore. Genesis is written with a straight narrative simplicity. Controversy over its interpretation and its literary history has been extensive. See Martin Noth, *A History of Pentateuch Traditions* (tr. 1972); Gerhard von Rad, *Genesis: A Commentary* (tr. of the 9th ed. 1972). For critical views of its composition see OLD TESTAMENT.

Genesis, Little: see PSEUDEPIGRAPHA.

Genêt, Edmond Charles Édouard (ĕdmôN' shärl ādwär' zhənā'), 1763–1834, French diplomat, known as Citizen Genêt. He had served as a French representative in Berlin, Vienna, and St. Petersburg before the French Revolution, and he continued in Russia until 1792, when he was expelled because of his revolutionary ardor. Sent as minister to the United States in 1793, he was met with wild acclaim by the numerous supporters of France, but President Washington, anxious to preserve U.S. neutrality in the French Revolutionary Wars, was cold to the demonstrations. Genêt's efforts to raise troops to strike at Spanish Florida and to commission privateers to prey on British commerce were not approved by Washington. The President, backed by pro-British Alexander Hamilton, forbade the French privateers to use U.S. ports as bases, despite the warm public approval and the provisions of a 1778 treaty with France. Genêt challenged Washington's authority by threatening to appeal to the American people, and the U.S. government demanded (1793) his recall. Before he could go back to France, his party, the Girondists, had fallen, and his return would have meant the guillotine. Washington therefore refused to allow his extradition. Genêt remained in the United States and married the daughter of Gov. George Clinton of New York. See study by Harry Ammon (1973).

Genet, Jean (zhäN), 1910–, French dramatist. Deserted by his parents as an infant, Genet spent much of his youth and early manhood in reformatories and prisons. Between 1940 and 1948 he wrote several autobiographical prose narratives dealing with homosexuality and crime, including *Our Lady of the Flowers* (tr. 1963), *Miracle of the Rose* (tr. 1965), and *The Thief's Journal* (tr. 1964). In 1948 he was pardoned from a sentence of life imprisonment, primarily through the efforts of important French literary figures including Gide, Sartre, and Cocteau. Genet's first two plays, *The Maids* (1948, tr. 1954) and *Deathwatch* (1949, tr. 1954), established his reputation as a dramatist concerned with theater as ritual and ceremony. Considered classic examples of the theater of the absurd, his dramas portray a world of outcasts in revolt against everything that renders man helpless, subservient, and alone. Among his later works are *The Balcony* (1957, tr. 1960), *The Blacks* (1959, tr. 1960), *The Screens* (1961, tr. 1962), *Funeral Rites* (tr. 1969), and *Querelle* (tr. 1974). See his *Reflections on the Theatre* (1972); Jean-Paul Sartre, *Saint Genet* (1952, tr. 1963); studies by T. F. Driver (1966), Bettina Knapp (1968), P. M. W. Thody (1969), and R. N. Coe (1970).

genet: see CIVET.

genetic drift: see GENETICS.

genetics, scientific study of heredity. The growth of the science dates from 1900, when Hugo de Vries, C. G. Correns, and Erich Tschermak-Seysenegg in the course of their own research independently rediscovered the work of Gregor Mendel on inheritance. These three scientists, working in different countries, arrived at a general concept of segregation of inheritable factors into units and of a random recombination of such units to explain the variations which they had observed; they then discovered that Mendel had presented similar conclusions in 1866. Under the stimulus of these discoveries a more widespread interest in the mechanism of heredity was aroused. With the discovery of the CHROMOSOME and the GENE scientists found the physical basis of the transmission of hereditary characteristics. A brief summary of the basic laws of heredity and the terms used follows. The gene is defined as the unit of inheritance; each gene transmits chemical information that is expressed as a trait, e.g., tall or dwarf size in the garden pea. Each species has a genome, or characteristic set of genes. Two genes for each trait are present in each individual, and these paired genes, both governing the same trait, are called alleles. The two allelic genes in any one individual may be alike (homozygous) or different (heterozygous). If genes may be compared roughly to beads, then chromosomes may be thought of as strings of these beads. The chromosomes of any plant or animal that reproduces sexually exist in pairs; the members of a chromosome pair are termed homologous (see REPRODUCTION). Thus in humans there are 46 chromosomes or 23 homologous pairs. Pairs of genes are borne on homologous chromosomes, one gene to each chromosome of the pair. In the process (reduction division, or MEIOSIS) by which ova and sperm are produced, the chromosomes are so divided that each mature sex cell contains half the original number of chromosomes, or one chromosome of each pair, and therefore one gene of each pair. Thus, when the ovum and the sperm fuse on fertilization, the fertilized egg (zygote) receives one allele from each parent. Of any pair of contrasting alleles, one is dominant and the other recessive: an individual heterozygous (carrying contrasting alleles) for a given characteristic invariably displays one aspect of that characteristic and not its alternative, although the gene for the aspect that does not appear (i.e., that is recessive) is present. This individual is called a HYBRID. By Mendelian law (see MENDEL) the offspring—or first filial (called F_1) generation—of parents homozygous for contrasting alleles are all hybrids heterozygous for the dominant characteristic and are said to be of the same phenotype, i.e., they are all similar in appearance to the homozygous dominant parent because the recessive characteristic is masked, although their gene composition (genotype) is different from either parent. A cross of members of the F_1 generation produces a second filial (F_2) generation of which approximately three fourths show the dominant characteristic and one fourth the recessive. However, since great numbers of characteristics are inherited simultaneously, the process is almost always much more complex than Mendelian law describes, and the expression "Mendelian heredity" is now restricted to transmission of characteristics by chromosomes. Modification of Mendel's principles developed as knowledge of the chromosomes increased; many discoveries have helped to account for apparent deviations from Mendelian ratios. Among them are the discoveries that there are many genes in the same chromosome, which sheds light on the tendency of certain characteristics to appear in combination with one another (linkage); that some characteristics are sex-linked, i.e., are transmitted by genes carried by the sex chromosomes (see SEX); and that homologous portions of paired chromosomes may be interchanged during meiosis (CROSSING OVER). Other research has shown that there may be multiple alleles (more than two alternative genes) for a given characteristic: the human blood groups A, B, AB, and O are determined by a combination of any two of three possible alleles (see BLOOD). It is therefore apparent that the interaction of many genes is responsible for determining a single recognizable trait in any individual (e.g., the shape of an insect's wing, the length of a mouse's tail, the pigmentation of human skin). Recent work on the role of DNA (see NUCLEIC ACID) is of major importance in explaining how genes direct the cell's metabolism—and hence all life processes—through the synthesis of enzymes that regulate the biochemical activities of the cell. It has also been found that the cytoplasm of cells contains genes, which determine specific traits of the organism. In addition, the cytoplasm of a differentiated cell (one having a specific function within an organ or an organism) has some effect on the chromosomes in its nucleus, so that while the chromosomes control the cell's activities the cytoplasm itself influences the chromosomes. It has also become clear that an individual organism's heredity and environment interact in the manifestation of many traits: a pea plant with a genetic tendency toward tallness will not achieve its full size if deprived of adequate water and minerals for growth. However, true alterations in gene and chromosome structure are the product of MUTATION and are not affected by environmental conditions, as was postulated by the theory of ACQUIRED CHARACTERISTICS. The discovery by H. J. Muller in 1927 of methods for artificially inducing mutations by means of ionizing radiations and other mutagens opened the way for much new genetics research, including the study of the genetic effects of atomic radiation and the resulting increase in the rate of mutation. The study of mutations, together with the analyses of population genetics, has been used to explain the mechanism of EVOLUTION. The elementary process of evolution is considered to be the changes in the frequency of occurrence of alleles in a population. Mutation, which causes the appearance of new alleles or changes the relative frequency of already existing alleles, is one important mechanism by which evolution occurs. Selection, often acting along with mutation, also affects gene frequencies. For example, if the presence of a particular allele makes a homozygous individual unable to mate, the allele may be eliminated from the population. Genetic drift—the random fluctuation in the frequency of an allele, resulting mainly from the vagaries of chance mating—is also an evolutionary mechanism. Although in large populations drift varies only a little above and below a statistical mean, in small breeding populations an entire generation might, by chance alone, be born with the same genotype with respect to a particular allelic pair of genes; genetic drift may eventually result in the elimination of one gene allele in a population. It may also make a population homozygous for a particular gene, i.e., all members of the population would have both genes of a pair identical. Because fluctuations in the proportions of alleles are more significant in the gene pools of small isolated breeding populations, genetic drift is a mechanism of species diversity and evolution in such groups. Genetic drift is most probably the cause of much of the diversity of human populations. It is likely that many modern populations originated from small, migratory hunting groups. Gene frequencies would change in different ways for each group after it became isolated from its original parental stock. Most of the knowledge of chromosome structure and the behavior of genes has come from studies of the vinegar, or fruit, fly *(Drosophila melanogaster),* which reproduces so rapidly that many generations can be studied over a short time. The work of T. H. Morgan and his associates on *Drosophila* was the basis of much of the progress of genetics in the United States. Certain other small laboratory animals and plants, especially microbes, are now used, also largely because of their ability to reproduce rapidly. For obvious reasons human beings are poor subjects for genetic studies; however, much that aids understanding heredity in humans has been learned from the lower forms of life. Also, by tracing the appearance of certain abnormal characteristics (e.g., hemophilia, color blindness, and certain mental disorders and anatomical defects) through a number of generations the hereditary pattern of these conditions has been established. The study of blood groups has also contributed to knowledge of human heredity. See Charlotte Auerbach, *Genetics in the Atomic Age* (2d ed. 1965); Amram Scheinfeld, *Your Heredity and Environment* (1965); Ernest Borek, *The Code of Life* (1965); George and Muriel Beadle, *The Language of Life* (1966); Theodosius Dobzhansky, *Genetics of the Evolutionary Process* (1970); G. W. Burns, *The Science of Genetics* (2d ed. 1972); Louis Levine, *Biology of the Gene* (2d ed. 1973); Hans Stubbe, *History of Genetics* (2d ed. tr. 1973); Amitai Etzioni, *Genetic Fix* (1973); Daniel Halacy, *Genetic Revolution* (1974).

Geneva (jənē'və), Fr. *Genève,* canton (1970 pop. 331,599), 109 sq mi (282 sq km), SW Switzerland, surrounding the southwest tip of the Lake of Geneva. Geneva is in the plain between the Jura and the Alps and is almost entirely surrounded by French territory. The population is French-speaking and divided between Protestants and Roman Catholics. Fruit, vegetables, cereals, and wine are produced in the rural areas, while industry—as well as population—is chiefly centered in the city of **Geneva** (1970 pop. 173,618), the capital of the canton. Situated on the Lake of Geneva and divided by the Rhône River, which emerges from the lake, it is a picturesque city joined by numerous bridges. Geneva is a cultural, financial, and administrative center and manufactures watches, jewelry, precision instruments, machinery, automobiles, aluminumware, chocolate, and clothes. It was an ancient settlement of the Celtic Allobroges and was later included in Roman Gaul. An episcopal see under the Roman Empire, Geneva passed successively to the Burgundians (5th cent.), to the Franks (6th cent.), to Transjurane Burgundy (9th–11th cent.), and to the Holy Roman Empire. The bishops of Geneva gradually absorbed the powers of the feudal counts of Geneva and in 1124 became rulers of the city. The rising merchant class soon grew antagonistic to episcopal authority. In 1285, the citizens of Geneva placed themselves under the protection of the counts (later dukes) of SAVOY, and by 1387 they had won extensive rights of self-rule. However, by gradually transforming the bishops into their tools, the dukes nearly succeeded in mastering the city by the beginning of the 16th cent. Incensed, the citizens allied themselves with two Swiss cantons—Fribourg and Bern—expelled the bishop (1533), and accepted (1535) the Reformation preached by Guillaume Farel. The arrival (1536) of John Calvin thrust upon Geneva a role of European importance as the focal point of the REFORMATION. With its population swelled by Protestant refugees, notably HUGUENOTS, Geneva became a cosmopolitan intellectual center. During the 18th cent., when the stern theocracy of Calvin had mellowed into patrician rule, the city's intellectual life reached its zenith. Voltaire settled there; J. J. Rousseau, H. B. de Saussure, Jacques Necker, Albert Gallatin, and P. E. Dumont were among the famous sons of Geneva in the 18th cent. The city, annexed to France from 1798 to 1813, joined Switzerland as a canton in 1815—the last canton to join the Confederation. In 1864, Geneva was made the seat of the International Red Cross; it was also the seat of the League of Nations (1920–46). Geneva is headquarters for the International Labor Organization, the World Health Organization, and other international bodies. Among its historic buildings are the Cathedral of St. Pierre (12th–14th cent.), where John KNOX preached, the 16th-century town hall, and the 18th-century palace of justice. The Univ. of Geneva (1473; founded as an academy by Calvin in 1559) faces the noted Reformation monument (1917). A very high fountain on the south shore of the lake has become a symbol of the city. Geneva has been the scene of the GENEVA CONFERENCES and other high-level international meetings.

Geneva, city (1970 pop. 16,793), Ontario co., W central N.Y., in the Finger Lakes region; inc. as a city 1897. Located in a farm area, Geneva's manufactures include cans and canning machinery, paper containers, metal products, and water purification systems. There are also printing plants. Hobart College, William Smith College, and a state agricultural experiment station are there.

Geneva, Lake, Fr. *Lac Léman* (läk lāmäN'), crescent-shaped lake, 224 sq mi (580 sq km), c.45 mi (70 km) long, on the Swiss-French border, between the Alps and the Jura mts. It has a maximum depth of 1,017 ft (310 m). The Rhône River traverses the lake, emerging at the western end at the city of Geneva. Noted for its deep blue and remarkably transparent waters, the lake is dotted with numerous resorts and villas. The northern (Swiss) shore is bounded by sloping vineyards and orchards. The lake is subject to seiches, tidal fluctuations that suddenly change the lake's level. A region of great scenic beauty, Lake Geneva has been the favorite theme of many writers (notably Rousseau and Byron). Lausanne and Montreux are large lakeside cities.

Geneva Arbitration: see ALABAMA CLAIMS.

Geneva Conference, any of various international meetings held at Geneva, Switzerland. Some of the more important ones are discussed here. **1** International conference held April–July, 1954, to restore peace in KOREA and INDOCHINA. The chief participants were the United States, the Soviet Union, Great Britain, France, the People's Republic of China, North Korea, South Korea, Vietnam, the Viet Minh party, Laos, and Cambodia. No agreement was reached on transforming the Korean armistice into a permanent peace, but three agreements were reached providing for an armistice and political settlement in Indochina. (For the main terms, see VIETNAM; CAMBODIA; LAOS.) **2** The so-called Summit Conference, held in July, 1955, to end the cold war and restore mutual trust between East and West. President Dwight D. Eisenhower (United States), Marshal Nikolai Bulganin and Chairman Nikita Khrushchev (Soviet Union), Prime Minister Anthony Eden (Great Britain), and Premier Edgar Faure (France) discussed German reunification, European security, disarmament, and cultural and economic interchange. Although no substantive agreements were reached, the meeting closed on a note of optimism. Directives were issued for a meeting of the foreign ministers of the four countries to be held later that year to reach agreement on German reunification, disarmament, and other issues. For the Geneva conferences of foreign ministers in 1955 and 1959, see FOREIGN MINISTERS, COUNCIL OF. **3** Conference beginning Oct., 1958, between Great Britain, the United States, and the Soviet Union, held in an attempt to reach an accord on banning tests of nuclear weapons. Since then, most international meetings held at Geneva have concerned the basic problems of the limitation of nuclear arms and provisions for international inspection and control. The UN Disarmament Commission, which began meeting in Geneva in 1960, has met there permanently since 1962. See DISARMAMENT, NUCLEAR.

Geneva Convention: see RED CROSS.

Geneva Protocol: see PROTOCOL.

Genevieve, Saint, d.512, patron saint of Paris. A nun renowned for good works, she is said to have averted, by fasting and prayer, an expected attack of Attila the Hun on Paris. Feast: Jan. 3.

Genghis Khan: see JENGHIZ KHAN.

Genichesk Strait: see AZOV, SEA OF.

genie: see JINNI.

Génissiat Dam (zhānēsyä'), 338 ft (103 m) high, on the Rhône River, Ain dept., E France, near Bellegarde and c.20 mi (32 km) S of Geneva, Switzerland; begun 1937, inaugurated 1948. The dam impounds a lake, c.14 mi (23 km) long. It is part of a project to develop and make navigable the entire Rhône valley from Geneva to Marseilles—a plan that somewhat resembles the Tennessee Valley Authority. The Génissiat hydroelectric plant is the largest in France and one of the largest in Europe. Power lines connect the dam and secondary plants with the Paris and Lyons industrial regions. The navigation project is related to a Swiss plan for connecting the Lake of Geneva with the Rhine, thus permitting direct traffic from Marseilles to Rotterdam via Geneva and Basel. Operated by a semiprivate company, the project is to a large extent under government control.

genista (jənĭs'tə): see BROOM.

genitive (jĕn'ĭtĭv) [Lat.,=genetic], in Latin grammar, the CASE typically used to refer to a possessor. The term is used in the grammar of other languages, but the phenomenon referred to may not resemble a Latin genitive closely; thus a Latin genitive will be translated by a number of different cases in Finnish. Such forms in English as *his* and *father's* are said to be genitive, or, more often, possessive.

genius, in Roman religion, guardian spirit of a man, a family, or a state. In some instances, a place, a city, or an institution had its genius. As the guardian spirit of an individual, the genius (corresponding to the Greek demon) was largely the force of one's natural desires. The genius was honored in familial worship as a household god and was thought to perpetuate a family through many generations. Notable achievements or high intellectual powers of an individual were attributed to his genius, and ultimately a man of achievements was said to have genius or to be a genius.

Genk (khĕngk), city (1970 pop. 57,913), Limburg prov., NE Belgium. It is a commercial and industrial center, a rail junction, and a resort.

Gennesaret (gĕnĕs'arĕt). **1** See GALILEE, SEA OF. **2** Fertile plain, NW of the Sea of Galilee. Mat. 14.34; Mark 6.53.

Gennevilliers (zhĕnvēyā'), town (1968 pop. 46,099), Hauts-de-Seine dept., N central France, on the right bank of the Seine River. It is mainly an industrial community; aircraft equipment, electrical products, radio tubes, ball bearings, and automobiles are manufactured there. The town has a large thermoelectric power plant.

Genoa (jĕn'ōwə), Ital. *Genova,* city (1971 pop. 812,206), capital of Genoa prov. and of Liguria, NW Italy, on the Ligurian Sea. Beautifully situated on the Italian RIVIERA, it is the chief seaport of Italy and rivals Marseilles, France, as the leading Mediterranean port. It is an outlet for central Europe and handles extensive passenger and freight traffic. Genoa's harbor facilities, badly damaged in World War II and by storms in 1954–55, have been rebuilt and greatly modernized. The city is also a commercial and industrial center; manufactures include iron and steel, chemicals, petroleum, airplanes, motor vehicles, and textiles. There are large shipyards in the city. An ancient town of the Ligures, Genoa flourished under Roman rule. Around the 10th cent. it became a free commune governed by consuls. Its maritime power increased steadily. Helped by Pisa, Genoa drove (11th cent.) the Arabs from Corsica and Sardinia. Rivalry over control of Sardinia resulted in long wars with Pisa; Genoa finally triumphed in the naval battle of Meloria (1284). The Crusades brought Genoa great wealth. The republic acquired possessions and trading privileges in areas from Spain to the Crimea. Genoa's expansion and its military defense were largely financed by a group of merchants who in 1408 organized a powerful bank, the Banco San Giorgio. Genoese policy in the Orient clashed with the ambitions of Venice, and long wars resulted, ending with the Peace of Turin (1381), which slightly favored Venice. Meanwhile, the Genoese republic was weakened by factional strife between Guelphs and Ghibellines, between nobles and the popular party. In 1339 the first doge (chief magistrate) for life was elected. As Genoa gradually gained control of the cities of Liguria, it lost its outlying possessions. Rival factions in the city resorted to foreign aid. From the late 14th to the 16th cent., France and Milan in turn controlled the city, although nominal independence was preserved. The power of Genoa was revived by the seaman and statesman Andrea DORIA, who wrote a new constitution in 1528; the conspiracy (1547) of the Fieschi family against his dictatorship failed. Later the city came under Spanish, French, and Austrian control. The Austrians were expelled by a popular uprising in 1746, but in 1768 Genoa had to cede Corsica, its last outlying possession, to France. In 1797, French military pressure resulted in the end of aristocratic rule and the formation of the Ligurian Republic, which Napoleon I formally annexed to France in 1805. The Congress of Vienna united (1814) Genoa and Liguria with the kingdom of Sardinia. In 1922 a major European economic conference (see GENOA, CONFERENCE OF) was held in the city. Among Genoa's notable buildings are the Cathedral of San Lorenzo (rebuilt in 1100 and frequently restored), the palace of the doges, the richly decorated churches of the Annunciation and of St. Ambrose (both 16th cent.), the medieval Church of San Donato, and many Renaissance palaces. The city is surrounded by old walls and forts, and the steep and narrow streets of the harbor section are very picturesque. Genoa has several museums and a university (founded 1243).

Genoa, Conference of, 1922, at Genoa, Italy. Representatives of 34 nations convened on April 10 to attempt the reconstruction of European finance and commerce. It was the first conference after World War I in which Germany and the Soviet Union were accepted on a par with other nations. The USSR, despite its repudiation of the czarist national debt, had offered to discuss the question at an international assembly. This offer marked the first Soviet attempt to enter the European diplomatic circle after the Russian Revolution. At Genoa the creditor nations—all represented except the United States—demanded recognition of the czarist debt, compensation for confiscated property, and guarantees for future contracts. The Russians, headed by Georgi CHICHERIN, offered to recognize the debt in return for cancellation of the Russian war debt, compensation for damages inflicted by Allied forces in their intervention after the revolution, and extensive credit for the Soviet government. The divergent purposes of the former Allies and the distrust caused by the announcement of the Treaty of Rapallo (see RAPALLO, TREATY OF, 1922) between Germany and the USSR made agreement impossible, and the conference adjourned on May 19.

genocide, in international law, the intentional and systematic destruction, wholly or in part, by a government of a racial, religious, or ethnic group. Although the word *genocide* was first coined in 1944, the crime itself has been committed often in history. A systematic campaign for the extermination of peoples was carried on by Nazi Germany in its attempts in the 1930s and 40s to destroy the entire European Jewish community and to eliminate other national groups in Eastern Europe. In 1945 the charter of the Nuremberg Tribunal listed persecution on racial or religious grounds as a crime for which the victorious Allies would try Nazi offenders. It established the principle of the individual accountability of government officials who carried out the extermination policies. The United Nations, by a convention concluded in 1949, defined in detail the crime of genocide and provided for its punishment by competent national courts of the state on whose territory the crime was committed or by international tribunal. Charging that the convention violated national SOVEREIGNTY, especially in its provision for an international tribunal and in the potential liability of an individual citizen, the United States never ratified it. See P. N. Drost, *Genocide* (1959); Nehemiah Robinson, *The Genocide Convention* (1960).

genome: see GENETICS.

genotype (jĕn'ətīp"): see GENETICS.

Genova: see GENOA, Italy.

Genovesi, Antonio (äntô'nyō jänōvĕ'zē), 1712-69, Italian philosopher and economist, a pioneer in writing philosophy in Italian instead of in Latin. Genovesi introduced new ideas, particularly those of Locke, Leibniz, and Hume into Italy, and this introduction was bitterly opposed by the scholastics. In his works he strove for a balancing of idealism and sensualism. His book *Lezioni di commercio* (1765), the first inclusive work on Italian economics, stressed human wants as the basis of economic theory. Other writings include *Disciplinarum metaphysicarum elementa* (1743).

genre (zhän'rə), in art-history terminology, a type of painting dealing with unidealized scenes and subjects of everyday life. Although practiced in ancient art, as shown by Pompeiian frescoes, and in the Middle Ages, genre was not recognized as worthy and independent subject matter until the 16th cent. in Flanders. There it was popularized by Pieter Bruegel, the elder. It flourished in Holland in the 17th cent. in the works of Ter Borch, Brouwer, Metsu, De Hooch, Vermeer, and many others, and extended to France and England, where in the 18th and 19th cent., its major practitioners were Watteau, Chardin, Greuze, Morland, and Wilkie. In Italy genre elements were present in Carpaccio's and Caravaggio's paintings, but not until the 18th cent. did genre become the specialty of an Italian artist, Pietro Longhi. The French impressionists often painted genre subjects as did members of the American ashcan school.

genro (gĕn'rō') [Jap.,=elder statesmen], a group that exercised collective leadership in Japan from the end of the MEIJI period until c.1932. After the Meiji Restoration (1868), westernizers from the former Choshu and Satsuma domains came to power, abolishing feudalism and modernizing society. Weakened in number by death and political disagreement, surviving members of this oligarchy (among them Hirobumi ITO, Aritomo YAMAGATA, Kaoru INOUYE, and Masayoshi MATSUKATA) consolidated power (1881) and established a cabinet form of government (1885). They drafted the Constitution of 1889, creating a diet (1890) to check the cabinet, but making selection of the prime ministers an imperial prerogative. In practice, the oligarchs selected the prime ministers and made many decisions that were constitutionally reserved for the emperor. The term *genro,* or elder statesmen, came into use in this period. For two decades this small group provided stable leadership, ruling actively as premiers and cabinet ministers until 1901, when they relinquished the premiership to protégés. The political crisis of 1912 over the selection of Taro KATSURA as premier was a severe challenge to their authority. Retiring further into the background, the remaining genro in 1918 asked Takashi HARA, the Seiyukai party leader, to form the first party cabinet. Kimmochi SAIONJI, who survived as the last genro from 1924 until his death in 1940, continued to select premiers until 1932 when this power passed to a new group consisting of former prime ministers and court officials.

gens (jĕnz), ancient Roman kinship group. It was the counterpart of what is known in other societies as a patrilineal CLAN or sib, and the word has been used in social science as a generic term for such groupings. The members of the Roman gens were descended (or assumed to be descended) from a common ancestor, whose name was used by all the members of the group. The second name was the gens name (e.g., *Tullius* in Marcus Tullius Cicero). The members were united in worship of the common ancestor, and marriage within the gens was discouraged. In early Rome the gens had economic, political, religious, and social functions; it later came to mean little more than a family name. The Greek gens (*genos*) was similar to the Roman.

Gensan: see WONSAN, North Korea.

Genseric: see GAISERIC.

gentian (jĕn'shən), common name for some members of the Gentianaceae, a family of widely distributed herbs, chiefly perennial and fall blooming. The family includes many types of gentians (genus *Gentiana* and similar species of other genera), most of which have blue flowers. Gentians flourish in north-temperate and alpine regions. Many are grown as ornamentals in rock gardens; the alpine blue gentian (usually *G. acaulis,* native to Europe) is most common. Indigenous North American species include the bottle, or closed, gentian of the East, the similar soapwort gentian of the West, and several fringed gentians (especially *G. crinita*), rare and beautiful wild flowers cultivated with difficulty in gardens. Some members of the family are aquatic or marsh plants, e.g., the marsh pinks (genus *Sabatia*) and the floating heart, or water snowflake (genus *Nymphoides*). Stomachics and bitter tonics have been made from ancient times from the rhizomes and roots of several species, especially the European yellow gentian (*G. lutea*), which is also used in the manufacture of liqueurs. Gentians are classified in the division MAGNOLIOPHYTA, class Magnoliopsida, order Gentianales, family Gentianaceae.

Gentile, Giovanni (jōvän'nē jäntē'lā), 1875-1944, Italian philosopher and educator. He taught philosophy in several Italian universities and for many years contributed to the magazine of Benedetto Croce. In 1920 he founded the *Giornale critico della filosofia italiana.* An early supporter of the Fascist movement, he has been called the philosopher of Fascism. In 1922 he was made a senator and until 1924 was minister of public instruction. While in this office he reformed the structure of public education. He also directed the work of the new *Enciclopedia italiana.* Gentile's philosophy, called actual idealism, is a form of neo-Hegelian idealism and was developed in *Teoria generale dello spirito come atto puro* (1916, tr. *The Theory of Mind as Pure Act,* 1922). See studies by H. S. Harris (2d ed. 1966), M. E. Brown (1966), and W. A. Smith (1970).

Gentile da Fabriano (dä fäbrēä'nō), c.1370-1427, Italian painter, one of the outstanding exponents of the elegant international Gothic style. In 1409 he was working in the Doge's Palace, Venice, painting historical frescoes that subsequently perished. In 1422 he was in Florence where he created his most celebrated painting, the resplendent Strozzi altarpiece (Uffizi). Gentile painted in the spirit and the manner of the older school, with glowing color and lavish use of gilt, thereby achieving a jewellike, courtly style. By 1425 he had responded to the new Florentine realism. His refined forms yielded to a sturdier rendering of figures in the Quaratesi altarpiece (panels are now in the Uffizi; Vatican; National Gall., London; and National Gall. of Art, Washington, D.C.). He later worked in Siena and Orvieto. Gentile died in Rome before the completion of the frescoes of *St. John the Baptist* in the Lateran Basilica. Other examples of his art are the *Madonna and Child with Angels* (Perugia); a polyptych (Brera, Milan); *Madonna of Humility* (Pisa); and *Madonna and Child* (Yale Univ.).

Gentileschi, Orazio (ōrä'tsēō jäntēlĕ'skē), c.1562-1647, Tuscan painter. His real surname was Lomi, but he adopted his uncle's name. He studied in Rome, where he was associated with Agostino Tassi in the decoration of palace interiors. Influenced at first by Caravaggio, Gentileschi developed a cooler, more lyrical style. He also painted frescoes in Santa Maria Maggiore and in the Lateran. After spending several years in Genoa and in France, he settled in England (1626) at the invitation of Charles I. Gentileschi's principal works include *The Annunciation* (San Siro, Genoa); *Flight into Egypt* (Louvre); *Sibyl* (Hampton Court, England); and *Moses Saved from the Waters* (Prado). He also painted numerous portraits. His daughter and pupil, **Artemisia Gentileschi,** c.1597-c.1651, studied under Tassi and achieved renown for her spirited execution and admirable chiaroscuro. About 1638 she visited England, where she was in great demand as a portraitist. Among her works are *Judith and Holofernes* (Uffizi); *Mary Magdalen* (Pitti Gall., Florence); *Christ among the Doctors* (N.Y. Historical Society); and a self-portrait (Hampton Court).

Gentili, Alberico (älbārē'kō jäntē'lē), 1552-1608, Italian writer on international law. Forced to leave Italy because of his Protestantism, he went to England (1580), where he became regius professor of civil law, Oxford, and in 1605 became advocate for the king of Spain in the British admiralty court. His *De legationibus* (1585) had a great influence in shaping modern diplomatic practice. In *De jure belli* [on the law of war] (1598), one of the earliest works on international law, he developed many ideas on the legal conduct of war to which Hugo Grotius later gave wider circulation.

gentlemen's agreement, in U.S. history, an agreement between the United States and Japan in 1907 that Japan should stop the emigration of its laborers to the United States and that the United States should stop discrimination against Japanese. This agreement was ended in 1924 by the act of Congress excluding immigration from Japan, as immigration from China had been previously excluded.

Gentofte, Denmark: see COPENHAGEN.

Gentz, Friedrich von (frē'drĭkh fən gĕnts), 1764-1832, German political theorist. A disciple of Kant and a lifelong admirer of the English political system of checks and balances, Gentz soon turned away from his early enthusiasm for the French Revolution. He translated (1793) Burke's *Reflections on the Revolution in France.* At first in Berlin and after 1802 in Vienna and Prague, he conducted a relentless polemical campaign against Napoleon I. In 1812 he became secretary to Metternich and was thus a powerful figure in Austrian and European politics. He was secretary of the congresses of Vienna, Aachen, Troppau, Laibach, and Verona. Some of his writings, all in exemplary style, were published as *Staatschriften und Briefe* (1921). See his *The French and American Revolutions Compared* (tr. by J. Q. Adams, 1803, new ed. 1955). See also biography by P. R. Sweet (1941, repr. 1970); Golo Mann, *Secretary of Europe* (tr. 1946, repr. 1970); study by P. F. Reiff (1912, repr. 1967).

Genubath (gĕnyo͝o'băth), son of the exile Hadad and an Egyptian princess. He was reared with Pharaoh's sons. 1 Kings 11.20.

genus, in taxonomy: see CLASSIFICATION.

geocentric system: see PTOLEMAIC SYSTEM.

geochemistry, study of the chemistry of the earth. More specifically, it is the study of the absolute and relative abundances of elements and their isotopes in the earth and of the distribution and movement of these elements from one place to another as a result of chemical processes. Geochemical studies have provided a theoretical basis for ore prospecting and have refined and improved the methods of determining the age of rocks. Chemical studies of ancient sedimentary rocks and the fluids contained in them have provided insights into the evolution of the oceans and the atmosphere. Experiments have been conducted with gases that recreate the primordial atmosphere. In one series of experiments, amino acids and proteins were synthesized from methane, ammonia, and water, thus providing some supportive evidence to theories concerning the chemical evolution of life. Today, some of the most important and practical work in geochemistry involves the study of geochemical cycles in the atmosphere, in marine and estuarine waters, and in the earth's crust. These studies are quantitatively assessing the effects of the massive introduction of pollutants into the environment. See B. H. Mason, *Principles of Geochemistry* (1966); K. B. Krauskopf, *Introduction to Geochemistry* (1967).

geode (jē'ōd), hollow, globular rock nodule ranging in diameter from 1 to 12 in. (2.54-30.5 cm) or more. Most geodes are partly filled with mineral matter; they have a thin layer of chalcedony ("wavy" quartz) covering an inner lining of inward-projecting crystals. These spectacular crystals, generally quartz or, less often, calcite, make geodes highly prized by collectors. Geodes are formed in a cavity such as might be found inside a fossil shell buried in sediment. At the beginning, this cavity is probably filled with a concentrated salt solution. The first step in the creation of a geode is the formation along the inner cavity wall of a layer of gelatinous silica, which will eventually be transformed into the chalcedony layer. As the water surrounding the layer becomes less salty, osmosis induces migration of fluids into the cavity. This results in a buildup of pressure, causing the cavity to expand until the water inside and outside are equally salty. When the silica gel dehydrates, crystallizes to form chalcedony, and cracks, mineral-bearing water enters to slowly deposit the inward-projecting crystals. See CONCRETION.

geodesic dome, structure that roughly approximates a hemisphere. Popular in recent years as economical, easily erected buildings, geodesic domes are geometrically determined from a model and

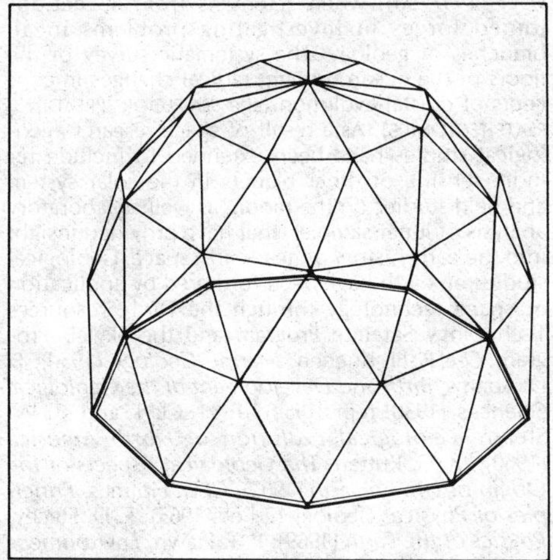

Geodesic dome

may be constructed from limited materials. The architect Buckminster FULLER was an early proponent of geodesics for housing and other functions. Among the best-known examples of geodesic domes is the United States Pavilion at Montreal's Expo 67.

geodesy (jēŏd'ĭsē), or **geodetic surveying,** theory and practice of determining the position of points on the earth's surface and the dimensions of areas so large that the curvature of the earth must be taken into account. It is distinguished from plane SURVEYING, the operations of which are executed without regard to the earth's curvature. In geodetic surveying, two points, called stations, many miles apart are selected, and the latitude and longitude of each is determined by astronomical means. The line between these two points, the base line, is measured with a high degree of accuracy. The position of a third station is determined by the angle it makes with each end of the base line. This process, called triangulation, is continued until the whole area to be surveyed is mapped. For indicating a triangulation station the U.S. Coast and Geodetic Survey uses a bronze disk suitably marked and having a projection on the bottom for anchoring it in concrete. Where the curvature of the earth is great or where there are hills or high trees between stations, towers are built so that one station may be seen from another. In recent years, artificial earth satellites have come into wide use as geodetic instruments. Shifts in the orbits of the satellites Explorer I and Vanguard I provided data by which geodesists corrected the value for the oblateness of the earth. This led to a program of geodetic satellites specifically designed to measure variations in the earth's gravitational field, and to determine the exact geographic position of points on the earth's surface. A triangulation station in space, the geodetic satellite is photographed against the background of stars in order to compare accurately the relative positions of points on the earth. Some geodetic satellites, such as Echo and Pageos, are passive, i.e., they shine by reflected sunlight. Others have high intensity lights that periodically blink on and off.

geodimeter (jēōdĭm'ətər): see SURVEYING.

geoduck (gōō'ēdŭk"), common name of a Pacific CLAM, *Panope generosa.* The largest intertidal burrowing BIVALVE in the world, the geoduck may weigh up to 12 lb (5.4 kg). The shell is thin, lacks teeth, and may attain a length of 8 in. (20 cm). The valves, or two parts of the shell, are always open in the adult, because the body and siphons are too large to be retracted. Geoducks are found from British Columbia to S California, with the largest population in Puget Sound. They inhabit mud flats, burrowing to a depth of 3 or 4 ft (90-120 cm), where they live in semipermanent burrows. Although they are edible, they are not widely marketed due to their inaccessibility: They are exposed for only a few hours a month during minus tides, at which time they can be obtained with a shovel. Digging geoducks is considered a sport in Washington, where there is a limit of three per day. Geoducks are classified in the phylum MOLLUSCA, class Pelecypoda, order Eulamellibranchia, family Saxicavidae.

Geoffrey, 1158-86, duke of Brittany (1171-86); fourth son of Henry II of England. Betrothed (1166) to Constance, heiress of Brittany, he was recognized as heir to the duchy in 1169 and succeeded to it on the death of her father. He married Constance in 1181. With his brothers he rebelled (1173-74) against Henry II and was subsequently involved (1182-84) in territorial disputes with his brother Richard (later Richard I). Geoffrey died in Paris while forming an alliance with Philip II of France against Henry II.

Geoffrey IV, known as **Geoffrey Plantagenet** [O.Fr.,=sprig of broom; he usually wore a sprig in his helmet], 1113-51, count of Anjou (1129-51); son of FULK, count of Anjou and king of Jerusalem. In 1128 he married MATILDA, daughter of King Henry I of England and widow of Holy Roman Emperor Henry V. After Henry I's death (1135) Geoffrey, hitherto occupied in complex feuds with Angevin barons and rival nobles, undertook to conquer Normandy, to which he laid claim through his wife. After 1139, Matilda attempted the conquest of England from her cousin King Stephen, who had gained the crown after Henry I's death. Geoffrey did not accompany her, being still engaged in the conquest of Normandy, which he completed in 1144. In 1147 he undertook a crusade with King Louis VII of France. In 1150, Geoffrey and Matilda ceded Normandy to their son Henry (later King Henry II of England), who founded the English ANGEVIN dynasty. Geoffrey is also known as Geoffrey the Fair.

Geoffrey of Monmouth (mŏn'məth), c.1100-1154, English author. He was probably born at Monmouth and was of either Breton or Welsh descent. In 1152 he was named bishop of St. Asaph. His *Historia regum Britanniae* (written c.1135), supposedly a chronicle of the kings of Britain, is one of the chief sources of the ARTHURIAN LEGEND. Geoffrey was the first to write a coherent account of Arthur, establishing the great warrior as a national hero, the conqueror of Western Europe. He drew information from the writings of Bede, Gildas, Nennius, the Welsh chronicles, and folklore, and imaginatively wove the whole into a fictional narrative in the form of a history. His work had great influence on Wace, Layamon, and many chroniclers of the Middle Ages. Another work attributed to him, the *Vita Merlini* (1148), also influenced later stories of Arthur and Merlin. See his *History of the Kings of Britain,* tr. by Lewis Thorpe (1966); study by J. S. P. Tatlock (1950).

Geoffrey Plantagenet: see GEOFFREY IV.

Geoffroy, Étienne François (ātyĕn' fräNswä' zhôfrwä'), 1672-1731, French physician and chemist, also known as Geoffroy the Elder. He became a pharmacist in 1694 and received an M.D. at Paris in 1704. He was professor of medicine at the Collège Royal from 1709 until his death and dean of the Paris Faculty of Medicine from 1726 to 1729. In 1718 he advanced the general proposition that if two substances in combination encounter a third with which one of the two has a greater affinity, that one will leave the original combination and unite with the third substance to form a new compound. He gave a 16-column table showing the order of many such displacements, the first of many "Tables of Affinity." Geoffroy was also largely responsible for a pharmacopoeia published by the Paris Faculty of Medicine in 1732.

Geoffroy Saint-Hilaire, Étienne (ātyĕn' zhôfrwä' săNtēlĕr'), 1772-1844, French zoologist. He was professor at the Museum of Natural History (1793-1840) and also at the Faculty of Sciences (from 1809), both in Paris, and was a member (1798-1801) of Napoleon's scientific staff in Egypt. He expressed in his *Philosophie anatomique* (2 vol., 1818-22) and in other works the theory that all animals conform to a single plan of structure. This attracted many supporters but was strongly opposed by Cuvier, who had been his friend, and in 1830 a widely publicized debate between the two took place. His son, **Isidore Geoffroy Saint-Hilaire,** 1805-61, also a zoologist, was an authority on deviation from normal structure. He succeeded to his father's professorships.

Geoffroy the Elder: see GEOFFROY, ÉTIENNE FRANÇOIS.

geography, the science of place, i.e., the study of the surface of the earth, the location and distribution of its physical and cultural features, and the interrelation of these features, as they affect man. Geography is a synoptic science that uses the same elements as the other sciences but in a different context. It integrates data in a study of areal differentiation in the world, making elaborate use of MAPS as its special tool. Geography may be studied by way of several interrelated approaches, i.e., systematically, regionally, descriptively, and analytically. The systematic approach organizes geographical knowledge into individual categories that are studied on a worldwide basis; the regional approach integrates the results of the systematic method and studies the interrelationships of the different categories while focusing on a particular area of the earth; the descriptive approach depicts where geographical features and populations are located; the analytical approach seeks to find out why those features are located where they are. In the study of geography two main branches may be distinguished, physical geography and human (or cultural) geography, originally anthropogeography. The first, based on the physical sciences, studies the world's surface, the distribution, delineation, and nature of its land and water areas. CLIMATE, landforms (see GEOMORPHOLOGY), and SOIL are examined as to origin and are classified as to distribution. Drawing on the biological sciences, fauna and flora (biogeography) are brought into an areal pattern. Through the mathematical sciences the motion of the earth and its relationship to the sun (seasons), the moon (tides), and the planets are studied, as well as map making and navigation. Human geography places man in his physical setting; it studies his relationship with that environment as well as his conscious activities and continuous progress in adapting himself to it (and to other men) and in transforming his environment to his needs. Human geography may in turn be subdivided into a number of fields, such as economic geography, political geography (with its 20th-century offshoot, GEOPOLITICS), social geography (including urban geography, another 20th-century ramification), and military geography. Historical geography (which reconstructs geographies of the past and attempts to trace the evolution of physical and cultural features) and urban and regional planning are sometimes considered branches of geography.

History of Geography. Geography was first systematically studied by the ancient Greeks, who also developed a philosophy of geography; THALES of Miletus, HERODOTUS, ERATOSTHENES, ARISTOTLE, STRABO, and PTOLEMY made major contributions to geography. The Roman contribution to geography was in the exploration and mapping of previously unknown lands. Greek geographic learning was maintained and enhanced by the Arabs during the Middle Ages. Arab geographers, among whom IDRISI, Ibn Battata, and Ibn Khaldun are prominent, traveled extensively for the purpose of increasing their knowledge of the world. The journeys of Marco POLO in the latter part of the Middle Ages began the revival of geographic interest outside of the Muslim world. With the Renaissance in Europe came the desire to explore unknown parts of the world that led to the voyages of EXPLORATION and to the great discoveries. However, it was mercantile interest rather than a genuine search for knowledge that spurred these endeavors. The 16th and 17th cent. reintroduced sound theoretical geography in the form of textbooks (the *Geographia generalis* of Bernhardus VARENIUS) and maps (Gerardus MERCATOR'S world map). In the 18th cent. geography began to achieve recognition as a discipline and was taught for the first time at the university level. The modern period of geography began toward the end of the 18th cent. with the works of Alexander von HUMBOLDT and Karl RITTER. Thenceforth two principal methods of approach to geography can be distinguished, the systematic, following Humboldt, and the regional, following Ritter. Of the national schools of geography that developed, the German and the French schools were the most in-

GEOLOGIC ERAS

Era	*Period*	*Epoch*	*Approximate duration (millions of years)*	*Approximate number of years ago (millions of years)*
Cenozoic	Quaternary	Holocene	10,000 years ago to the present	
		Pleistocene	2	2
	Tertiary	Pliocene	11	13
		Miocene	12	25
		Oligocene	11	36
		Eocene	22	58
		Paleocene	71	65
Mesozoic	Cretaceous		71	136
	Jurassic		54	190
	Triassic		35	225
Paleozoic	Permian		55	280
	Carboniferous		65	345
	Devonian		60	405
	Silurian		20	425
	Ordovician		75	500
	Cambrian		100	600
Precambrian			3,380	3,980

fluential. The German school, which dealt mainly with physical geography, developed a scientific and analytical style of writing. The French school became known for its descriptive regional monographs presented in a lucid and flowing manner; human and historical geography were its forte. Although emphasis has shifted several times between the approaches and viewpoints, their interdependence is recognized by all geographers. Since the end of World War II, geography, like other disciplines, has experienced the explosion of knowledge brought on by the new tools of modern technology for the acquisition and manipulation of data; these include aerial photography, remote sensors (including infrared and satellite photography), and the computer (for quantitative analysis and mapping). The quantitative method of geographical research has gained much ground since the 1950s, William Garrison of the United States and Peter Haggett of Great Britain being its leading exponents. Important contributions to the advancement of geography and to the development of geographic concepts have been made by Ferdinand von RICHTHOFEN, Albrecht PENCK, Friedrich RATZEL, Alfred HETTNER, Karl HAUSHOFER, and Walter Christaller in Germany; Paul VIDAL DE LA BLACHE, Jean Brunhes, Conrad MALTE-BRUN, Elisée RECLUS, and Emmanuel de Martonne in France; and William Morris DAVIS, Isaiah BOWMAN, Ellen Churchill SEMPLE, Albert BRIGHAM, and Richard Hartshorne in the United States. Today geography is studied by governmental agencies and in many of the world's universities. Research is stimulated by such noted geographic institutions as the Royal Geographical Society (1830, Great Britain), the American Geographical Society (1852, United States), and the Société de Geographie (1821, France). See R. E. Dickinson and O. J. Howarth, *The Making of Geography* (1933); Richard Hartshorne, *Perspective on the Nature of Geography* (1959); Nafis Ahmad, *Muslim Contribution to Geography* (rev. and enl. ed. 1965); J. O. Thomson, *History of Ancient Geography* (1965); J. O. Broeck, *Compass of Geography* (1966); G. H. Kimble, *Geography in the Middle Ages* (1938, repr. 1968); Eric Fischer et al., *A Question of Place* (2d ed. 1969); Rhoads Murphy, *The Scope of Geography* (1969).

Geological Survey, United States, bureau organized in 1879 under the Dept. of the Interior to unify and centralize the work already undertaken by separate surveys under Clarence KING, F. V. Hayden, George W. Wheeler, and J. W. POWELL. The functions of the bureau cover the exploration of the country to gather information as to geological structure; the preparation of geological maps and of topographical maps of all parts of the country showing surface features; the examination of natural resources with a view to their development; the study of problems of irrigation and water power; the classification of public lands; and the publication of papers, bulletins, and maps based upon surveys made. The work is divided among four branches: geologic, topographic, water resources, and conservation. In 1962 the bureau was authorized to conduct surveys outside the national domain.

geologic dating: see DATING.

geologic eras, major units of geologic time. For the purpose of dating rock formations and the fossils contained within them, the earth's history has been divided into four eras. These eras have been subdivided into briefer time spans, called periods. The periods of the present era, the Cenozoic, have been further broken down into epochs. For each era and its subdivisions, which are listed in the accompanying table, see separate articles.

geology, science of the earth's history, composition, and structure, and the associated processes. It draws upon chemistry, biology, physics, astronomy, and mathematics (notably statistics) for support of its formulations. Geology is divided into several fields. Physical geology includes mineralogy, the study of the chemical composition and structure of minerals; petrology, of the composition and origin of rocks; geomorphology, of the origin of landforms and their modification by dynamic processes; geochemistry, of the chemical composition of earth materials and the chemical changes that occur within the earth and on its surface; geophysics, of the behavior of rock material in response to stresses and according to the principles of physics; sedimentation, of the erosion and deposition of rock particles by wind, water, or ice; structural geology, of the forces that deform the earth's rocks and the description and mapping of deformed rock bodies; economic geology, of the exploration and recovery of natural resources, such as ores and petroleum; and engineering geology, of the interactions of the earth's crust with man-made structures such as tunnels, mines, dams, bridges, and building foundations. Historical geology deals with the historical development of the earth from the study of its rocks. They are analyzed to determine their structure, composition, and interrelationships and are examined for remains of past life. Historical geology includes PALEONTOLOGY, the systematic study of past life forms; STRATIGRAPHY, of layered rocks and their interrelationships; paleogeography, of the locations of ancient land masses and their boundaries; and geologic mapping, the superimposing of geologic information upon existing topographic maps. Historical geologists divide all time since the formation of the earliest known rocks (c.4 billion years ago) into four major divisions—the PRECAMBRIAN, PALEOZOIC, MESOZOIC, and CENOZOIC eras. Each, except the Cenozoic, ended with profound changes in the disposition of the earth's continents and mountains and was characterized by the emergence of new forms of life (see GEOLOGIC ERAS). Broad cyclical patterns, which run through all historical geology, include a period of mountain and continent building followed by one of erosion and, in turn, by a new period of elevation. Observations on earth structure and processes were made by a number of the ancients, including Herodotus, Aristotle, Lucretius, Strabo, and Seneca. Their individual efforts in the natural history of the earth, however, provided no sustained progress. Their major contribution is that they attributed the phenomena they observed to natural and not supernatural causes. Many of the ideas expressed by these men were not to resurface until the Renaissance. Later Leonardo da Vinci correctly speculated on the nature of fossils as remains of ancient organisms and on the role that rivers play in the erosion of land. Agricola made a systematic study of ore deposits in the early 16th cent. Robert Hooke and Nicolaus Steno both made penetrating observations on the nature of fossils and sediments. Modern geology began in the 18th cent. when field studies by the French mineralogist J. E. Guettard and others proved more fruitful than speculation. The German geologist Abraham Gottlob Werner, in spite of the many errors of his specific doctrines and the diversion of much of his energy into a fruitless controversy (in which he maintained that the origin of all rocks was aqueous), performed a great service for the science by demonstrating the chronological succession of rocks. In 1795 the Scottish geologist James Hutton laid the theoretical foundation for much of the modern science with his doctrine of UNIFORMITARIANISM, first popularized by the British geologist John Playfair; largely through the work of Sir Charles Lyell, this doctrine replaced the opposing one of CATASTROPHISM. Geology in the 19th cent. was influenced also by the work of Charles Darwin and enriched by the researches of the Swiss-American Louis Agassiz. In the 20th cent. geology has advanced at an ever-increasing pace. The unraveling of the mystery of atomic structure and the discovery of radioactivity allowed profound advances in many phases of geologic research. Important discoveries were made during the INTERNATIONAL GEOPHYSICAL YEAR (1957–58), when scientists from 67 nations joined forces in investigating problems in all branches of geology. The systematic survey of the floors of the ocean brought radical changes in concepts of crustal evolution (see SEA-FLOOR SPREADING; PLATE TECTONICS). As a result of space research, geological studies have been extended to include remote sensing of other planets in the solar system and field studies on the moon, as well as laboratory analysis of lunar samples, that have provided insight into the early history of near-earth space. Geological studies on earth have been furthered by application of space technology through the Earth Resources Technology Satellite Program and the Skylab Program. See P. H. Kuenen, *Marine Geology* (1950); F. D. Adams, *Birth and Development of the Geological Sciences* (1938, repr. 1954); T. H. Clark and C. W. Stearn, *Geological Evolution of North America* (1960); M. G. Rutten, *The Geological Aspects of the Origin of Life on Earth* (1962); C. D. Holmes, *Principles of Physical Geology* (2d ed. 1965); F. D. Stacey, *Physics of the Earth* (1969); P. T. Flawn, *Environmental Geology* (1970); R. H. Dott, Jr., and R. L. Batten, *Evolution of the Earth* (1971); W. H. Matthews III, *Invitation to Geology* (1971); W. C. Putnam, *Geology* (2d ed. 1971); J. H. Zumberge and A. N. Clemens, *Elements of Geology* (3d ed. 1972); W. L. Ramsey and R. E. Burckley, *Modern Earth Science* (3d ed. 1974).

geomagnetism: see MAGNETISM.

geometric problems of antiquity, three famous problems involving elementary geometric constructions with straight edge and compass, conjectured by the ancient Greeks to be impossible but not proved to be so until modern times. The three problems are: (1) the duplication of the cube, also known as the Delian problem because it is said to have originated with the task of constructing a cubical altar at Delos having twice the volume of the original cubical altar; (2) the trisection of an arbitrary angle; (3) the squaring, or quadrature, of the circle, i.e., the construction of a square whose area is equal to that of a given circle. These problems were solved in the 19th cent. by first transforming them into algebraic problems involving "constructible numbers." A constructible number is one that can be obtained from a whole number by means of addition, subtraction, multiplication, division, or extraction of square roots. The problems of antiquity correspond to the following algebraic problems: (1′) Is $\sqrt[3]{2}$ constructible? (2′) Given an angle A for which $\cos A$ is constructible, is $\cos (A/3)$ constructible? (3′) Is the area π of a unit circle constructible? The number $\sqrt[3]{2}$ is not constructible, since it involves a cube root. (Note, however, that roots that are powers of 2, e.g., 4th, 8th, 16th roots, are constructible because they can be expressed as combinations of square roots.) In problem (2′), certain special angles can be trisected, e.g., 90°, since both cos 90° and cos 30° are constructible, but for most angles this is easily shown to be impossible. Finally, the solution of problem (3′) did not come until 1882, when the German Ferdinand Lindemann showed that π is a transcendental number and thus cannot be expressed in terms of any roots of any rational numbers (see

NUMBER). Although these problems cannot be solved using only straight edge and compass, the Greeks developed methods of solving them using higher curves. See Felix Klein, *Famous Problems of Elementary Geometry* (1956).

geometric progression: see PROGRESSION.

Geometric style, in architecture: see DECORATED STYLE.

geometry [Gr.,=earth measuring], branch of MATHEMATICS concerned with the properties of and relationships between points, lines, planes, and figures and with generalizations of these concepts. Elementary geometry of two and three dimensions (plane and solid geometry) is based largely on the *Elements* of the Greek mathematician Euclid (fl. c.300 B.C.), who organized the geometry then known into a systematic presentation that is still used in many texts. Euclid first defined his basic terms, such as point and line, then stated without proof certain AXIOMS and postulates about them that seemed to be self-evident or obvious truths, and finally derived a number of statements (theorems) from the postulates by means of deductive LOGIC. This axiomatic method has since been adopted not only throughout mathematics but in many other fields as well. In 1637, René Descartes showed how numbers can be used to describe points in a plane or in space and to express geometric relations in algebraic form, thus founding ANALYTIC GEOMETRY, of which ALGEBRAIC GEOMETRY is a further development (see CARTESIAN COORDINATES). The problem of representing three-dimensional objects on a two-dimensional surface was solved by Gaspard Monge, who invented DESCRIPTIVE GEOMETRY for this purpose in the late 18th cent. DIFFERENTIAL GEOMETRY, in which the concepts of the CALCULUS are applied to curves, surfaces, and other geometrical objects, was founded by Monge and C. F. Gauss in the late 18th and early 19th cent. The modern period in geometry begins with the formulations of PROJECTIVE GEOMETRY by J. V. Poncelet (1822) and of NON-EUCLIDEAN GEOMETRY by N. I. Lobachevsky (1826) and János Bolyai (1832). Another type of non-Euclidean geometry was discovered by Georg Riemann (1854), who also showed how the various geometries could be generalized to any number of dimensions. These different geometries and others discovered during the 19th cent. were classified and related to one another in various ways. The non-Euclidean geometries are exactly analogous to the geometry of Euclid, except that Euclid's postulate regarding parallel lines is replaced and all theorems depending on this postulate are changed accordingly. Both Euclidean and non-Euclidean geometry are types of metric geometry, in which the lengths of line segments and the sizes of angles may be measured and compared. Projective geometry, on the other hand, is more general and includes the metric geometries as a special case; pure projective geometry makes no reference to lengths or angle measurements. The general metric geometry consisting of all of Euclidean geometry except that part dependent on the parallel postulate is called absolute geometry; its propositions are valid for both Euclidean and non-Euclidean geometry. Another type of geometry, called affine geometry, includes Euclid's parallel postulate but disregards two other postulates concerning circles and angle measurement; the propositions of affine geometry are also valid in the four-dimensional geometry of space-time used in the theory of RELATIVITY. Ordered geometry consists of all propositions common to both absolute geometry and affine geometry; this geometry includes the notion on intermediacy ("betweenness") but not that of measurement. An important step in recognizing the connections between the different types of geometry was the Erlangen program, proposed by the German Felix Klein in his inaugural address at the Univ. of Erlangen (1872), according to which geometries are classified with respect to the geometrical properties that are left unchanged (invariant) under a given GROUP of transformations. For example, Euclidean geometry is the study of properties unchanged by similarity transformations, affine geometry is concerned with properties invariant under the linear transformations (affine collineations) that preserve parallelism, and projective geometry studies invariants under the more general projective transformations (collineations and correlations). TOPOLOGY, perhaps the most general type of geometry although often considered a separate branch of mathematics, is concerned with properties invariant under continuous transformations, which carry neighborhoods of points into neighborhoods of their images. The close examination of the axioms and postulates of Euclidean geometry during the 19th cent. resulted in the realization that the logical basis of geometry was not as firm as had previously been supposed. New axiom and postulate systems were developed by various mathematicians, notably David Hilbert (1899). See H. G. Forder, *The Foundations of Euclidean Geometry* (1927); H. S. M. Coxeter, *Introduction to Geometry* (2d ed. 1969).

geomorphology, study of the origin and evolution of the earth's landforms, both on the continents and within the ocean basins. It is concerned with the internal geologic processes of the earth's crust, such as tectonic activity and vulcanism that constructs new landforms, as well as externally driven forces of wind, water, waves, and glacial ice that modify such landforms in orderly sequential patterns. Geomorphology originally developed from William Morris Davis's concept of the geomorphic cycle, set forth in his *Geographic Essays* (1909). His theory states that landforms pass through a series of well-organized stages in an inorganic evolution. Opposition to the theory by European geomorphologists, such as Austrian-born Walther Penck, and development of mathematical models of landform analysis have influenced the direction of modern geomorphic research.

Geophysical Year, International: see INTERNATIONAL GEOPHYSICAL YEAR.

geophysics, study of the structure, composition, and dynamic changes of the EARTH and its ATMOSPHERE based on the principles of PHYSICS. The term was probably first used in Germany, where it appeared in scientific writings of the mid-19th cent. Geophysics, which embraces the concepts, data, and methods of various other sciences, is very broad in scope. For example, GEOLOGY, meteorology, hydrology, OCEANOGRAPHY, and seismology all enter into geophysical studies. The location of petroleum, mineral deposits, and subsurface water supplies is the province of applied geophysics. The techniques used to locate these substances include seismic and electrical measurements at shallow depths. Gravimetric, magnetic, and radiometric surveys are performed both at ground stations and in airplanes. Where possible the information thus derived is correlated with visible surface features; subsurface conditons are then inferred, and boreholes are drilled to determine the extent and richness of promising areas.

geopolitics, method of political analysis, popular in Central Europe during the first half of the 20th cent., that emphasized the role played by geography in international relations. Geopolitical theorists stress that natural political boundaries and access to important waterways are vital to a nation's survival. The term was first used (1916) by Rudolf Kjeflen, a Swedish political scientist, and was later borrowed by Karl HAUSHOFER, a German geographer and follower of Friedrich RATZEL. Haushofer founded (1922) the Institute of Geopolitics in Munich, from which he proceeded to publicize geopolitical ideas, including Sir Walford J. Mackinder's theory of a European "heartland" central to world domination. Haushofer's writings found favor with the Nazi leadership, and his ideas were used to justify German expansion during the Nazi era. Many expansionist justifications, including the American "manifest destiny" as well as the German *Lebensraum*, are based on geopolitical considerations. Geopolitics is different from political geography, a branch of geography concerned with the relationship between politics and the environment. See Andreas Dorpalen, *The World of General Haushofer* (1942, repr. 1966); W. A. D. Jackson, ed., *Politics and Geographic Relationships* (2d ed., 1971); S. B. Cohen, *Geography and Politics in a World Divided* (2d ed. 1973).

George, Saint, 4th cent.?, patron of England. He was perhaps a soldier in the imperial army who died for the faith in Asia Minor. His life is cloaked in legends; Gibbon's identification of him with George of Cappadocia is false. One of the great saints of the Eastern Church, and the ancient patron of soldiers, he was adopted by England in the late Middle Ages. In old plays and in art St. George is the slayer of the dragon; *The Golden Legend* did much for the extension of the tale. The Red Cross Knight of Edmund Spenser's *Faërie Queene* is St. George and stands for the Church of England. St. George's Cross is red, and it appears in the Union Jack. Feast: April 23. See Alexander Barclay, *Life of St. George*, ed. by William Nelson (1955, repr. 1960).

George I (George Louis), 1660–1727, king of Great Britain and Ireland (1714–27); son of SOPHIA, electress of Hanover, and great-grandson of James I. He became (1698) elector of Hanover, fought in the War of the Spanish Succession, and in 1714 succeeded Queen Anne under the provisions of the Act of SETTLEMENT, becoming the first British sovereign of the house of HANOVER. He was personally unpopular in England because of his German manners, his German mistresses (see SCHULENBURG, EHRENGARD MELUSINA VON DER, DUCHESS OF KENDAL), his treatment of his divorced wife, SOPHIA DOROTHEA, and his inability to speak English. George's dual role as elector of Hanover and king of England also raised problems; he spent much of his time in Hanover and was widely (although unjustly) believed to be indifferent to English affairs. Yet, despite the uprising of the JACOBITES in 1715, his crown was never in danger, for he stood to Englishmen as the guarantee of the "revolution settlement" against a return of the Roman Catholic Stuarts. George's succession brought the Whigs to power, and the early years of his reign saw constant maneuvering for power among his ministers—the 1st Earl STANHOPE, the 3d earl of SUNDERLAND, Viscount TOWNSHEND, and Robert WALPOLE. The principal achievement of these years was the QUADRUPLE ALLIANCE of 1718, which provided an international guarantee of the Hanoverian succession and the status quo of the Peace of Utrecht (1713). Rising to power in the SOUTH SEA BUBBLE crisis, Walpole dominated the end of the reign, beginning his long tenure as virtual prime minister. George was succeeded by his son, George II. See biography by H. M. Imbert-Terry (1927, repr. 1972); J. H. Plumb, *The First Four Georges* (1956); Alvin Redman, *The House of Hanover* (1960, repr. 1968); Basil Williams, *The Whig Supremacy, 1714–60* (2d ed. 1962).

George II (George Augustus), 1683–1760, king of Great Britain and Ireland (1727–60), son and successor of George I. Though devoted to Hanover, of which he was elector, George was more active in the English government than his father had been. CAROLINE OF ANSBACH (whom he married in 1705), through the subtle influence she exerted over him, furthered the ascendancy of the great Whig minister, Sir Robert WALPOLE. The early part of his reign was peaceful and notably prosperous. However, just as George had quarreled with his father over personal matters, so FREDERICK LOUIS, prince of Wales, was strongly at odds with the king and became nominal head of the opposition group that ousted Walpole in 1742. In the War of the Austrian Succession, George led his troops in person at the battle of Dettingen (1743)—the last time a British monarch did so. In 1745–46 the last uprising of the JACOBITES was suppressed. England was expanding as a commercial and colonial power and clashed with France in India and in America (see FRENCH AND INDIAN WARS) as well as in Europe in the complex struggle known as the SEVEN YEARS WAR (1756–63). The principal ministers after the fall of Walpole were Henry PELHAM, his brother, Thomas Pelham-Holles, duke of NEWCASTLE, and William Pitt, later earl of CHATHAM, the architect of England's victory in the Seven Years War. George was succeeded by his grandson George III. See J. D. G. Davies, *A King in Toils* (1938); Basil Williams, *The Whig Supremacy, 1714–60* (2d ed. 1962); J. H. Plumb, *The First Four Georges* (1956).

George III, 1738–1820, king of Great Britain and Ireland (1760–1820); son of Frederick Louis, prince of Wales, and grandson of George II, whom he succeeded. He was also elector (and later king) of Hanover, but he never visited it. After his father's early death (1751), young George was educated for his future role as king by his domineering mother, Princess Augusta of Saxe-Gotha, and by John Stuart, earl of BUTE. He succeeded to the throne at the age of 22 and earnestly set himself to cleanse politics of corruption and to curb the arrogance of the aristocratic Whig leaders, who he believed had weakened the royal powers. George, for his part, was viewed with suspicion by those who resented Lord Bute's inordinate influence over the young king. This suspicion appeared justified when the successful and popular William Pitt, later earl of CHATHAM, was allowed to resign (1761) and was replaced by Bute. Bute, however, could not muster parliamentary support and resigned in 1763, and George, who matured rapidly in office, quickly outgrew his dependence on him. Political instability marked the first 10 years of the reign, for the king's lack of faith in most of the available ministers and increasing factionalism led to a rapid turnover of ministries and inconsistency of policy. The ministry of George GRENVILLE (1763–65) initiated prosecution of John WILKES and imposed the unpopular STAMP ACT on the American colonies; that of the marquess of ROCKINGHAM (1765–66) repealed the Stamp Act; that of Lord Chatham (1766–68) levied new duties in America with the TOWN-

SHEND ACTS; while that of the duke of GRAFTON (1768–70) renewed prosecution of Wilkes. Thwarted in his unrealistic attempts to break the system of patronage and connection by which political groupings were formed, George himself resorted to the lavish use of patronage to establish in Parliament a group of supporters known as the "king's friends." Only in 1770 did George find in Frederick, Lord NORTH, a chief minister who was able to manage Parliament and willing to follow royal leadership. Although North achieved financial consolidation at home and imposed closer government control over the East India Company by the Regulating Act (1772), his 12-year ministry is remembered chiefly for his policy of coercion against the American colonists that led finally to the AMERICAN REVOLUTION. This policy of course reflected the views of the king, whose refusal to accept the loss of the colonies prolonged the war. Opposition in Parliament to what was regarded as increasing royal influence finally forced George to accept the resignation (1782) of North and the formation of ministries first by Lord Rockingham and then by the earl of SHELBURNE, who concluded the Treaty of Paris (1783), granting independence to the United States. Shelburne's ministry was brought down (1783) by the surprising coalition of George's old friend Lord North and his leading Whig opponent Charles James FOX. This alliance so incensed the king that he exerted his influence in the House of Lords to secure defeat of Fox's East India Bill (1783) and thus forced the ministry out, replacing it with one formed by the younger William PITT. Despite the furious reaction to the king's action among Whigs, Pitt won control of Parliament in the 1784 election and was to retain power until 1801 and then hold it again from 1804 to 1806. After Pitt's appointment George retired from active participation in government, except for taking an interest in such major issues as CATHOLIC EMANCIPATION, which he defeated in 1801. Pitt was able to improve trade, reform the governments of Canada and India, and unite the kingdoms of Ireland and England (1800). He also managed the wars with France (see FRENCH REVOLUTIONARY WARS; NAPOLEON I). George, who had suffered a short nervous breakdown in 1765 and a more serious one in 1788–89 (which caused a fierce conflict between Pitt and Fox over the powers to be vested in the regency), became permanently insane in 1810. It has been suggested that he was a victim of the hereditary disease porphyria. He spent the rest of his life in the care of his devoted wife, Charlotte Sophia, whom he had married in 1761, and the prince of Wales (later GEORGE IV) was made regent (see REGENCY).

England in the Reign of George III. Before George died in 1820 the fabric of English life had been vastly altered from the stable society of 1760. Despite the loss of the American colonies there had been a great expansion of empire and trade, and the ground for further expansion had been laid by the explorations of James COOK. At home, the population almost doubled, improved agricultural methods increased productivity, and advances in technology and transportation marked the onset of the INDUSTRIAL REVOLUTION. Social reform, although much discussed, made little headway, and all attempts to effect an extension of the suffrage or a redistribution of parliamentary representation failed. The Church of England, fettered by apathy and patronage, failed to move into the new factory towns, but METHODISM spread rapidly to fill the gap. Science made great strides with the work of Henry CAVENDISH, Joseph PRIESTLEY, John DALTON, and Sir Humphrey DAVY. In ENGLISH LITERATURE 18th-century neoclassicism declined, and the romantic movement had its rise. A revolution in social and economic thinking, assisted by the spread of literacy and learning through a wider distribution of books and periodicals, promoted theories of UTILITARIANISM and LAISSEZ-FAIRE. Among important thinkers of the period were Adam SMITH, David RICARDO, Thomas MALTHUS, Jeremy BENTHAM, and Edmund BURKE. Through all these developments George himself patronized the arts, especially portraiture, and founded the ROYAL ACADEMY OF ARTS. He was a friend of Josiah WEDGWOOD and other industrialists. Unlike the first two Georges, George III had a tranquil domestic life, although scandal touched his brothers and sons. George was an honest and well-intentioned man, but his stubborness and limited intellectual power confounded his efforts to rule well and made him a somewhat tragic figure. See editions of George III's correspondence by John Fortescue (6 vol., 1927–28; additions and corrections by L. B. Namier, 1937) and by Arthur Aspinall (5 vol., 1962–70); biographies by J. C. Long (1961), S. E. Ayling (1972), John Brooke (1972), and J. C. Clarke (1972); studies by Herbert Butterfield (1949, repr. 1968; rev. ed. 1959), Richard Pares (1953, repr. 1967), and J. S. Watson (1960).

George IV, 1762–1830, king of Great Britain and Ireland (1820–30), eldest son and successor of George III. In 1785 he married Maria Anne FITZHERBERT, a Roman Catholic. The marriage was illegal, however; and in 1795, to secure parliamentary settlement of his enormous debts, he made a political marriage with CAROLINE OF BRUNSWICK. In constant and open opposition to his father, George associated closely with the Whigs, particularly Charles James FOX, whose friend he became in 1781. As a result, when George III had his first serious fit of insanity in 1788–89, the Tory William PITT proposed that the regency vested in the prince be closely restricted (to prevent George bringing his Whig friends to power), while Fox, usually the opponent of royal prerogative, wanted the prince to have unlimited powers as regent. In 1811, after the king had become permanently incapacitated, George became regent on terms very similar to those proposed by Pitt in 1788. However, when the limitations on his power to make appointments and spend crown revenues were removed in 1812, the prince regent retained most of his father's ministers, breaking his connection with the Whigs. The Tories, under the leadership of the 2d earl of LIVERPOOL for most of the period, remained entrenched in power throughout the regency and George's subsequent reign. As regent and as king, George was hated for his extravagance and dissolute habits, and he aroused particular hostility by an unsuccessful attempt, immediately after his accession (1820) to the throne, to divorce his long-estranged wife, Caroline. During his reign the monarchy lost a significant amount of power. George's only legitimate child, Charlotte Augusta, married (1816) Prince Leopold of Saxe-Coburg (later Leopold I, king of the Belgians) but died in childbirth in 1817. George was succeeded by his brother William IV. See REGENCY. See biographies by Roger Fulford (rev. ed. 1949, repr. 1963) and Christopher Hibbert (1974).

George V (George Frederick Ernest Albert), 1865–1936, king of Great Britain and Ireland (1910–36), second son and successor of Edward VII. At the age of 12 he commenced a naval career, but this ended with the death (1892) of his elder brother, the duke of Clarence, which made him the eventual heir to the throne. In 1893 he married Victoria Mary, daughter of the duke of Teck. While his father was king (1901–10), George visited many parts of the British empire, developing an interest in imperial affairs that he maintained throughout his own reign. After his coronation (1911) he went to India for a coronation durbar in Delhi. Within the limitations of his constitutional position, he occasionally played a decisive personal part in political controversies, acting as moderator in the debates over the Parliament Act of 1911 (see PARLIAMENT) and the Irish HOME RULE Bill of 1914 and later helping in the formation of the national government of 1931. In 1917, during World War I, he abandoned his German titles and changed the name of the royal house from Saxe-Coburg-Gotha to Windsor. The celebrations marking the 25th anniversary of his accession (May 6, 1935) showed the affection in which he was held by the British people. On his death (Jan. 20, 1936) George was succeeded by his eldest son, Edward VIII. His second son, on the abdication of Edward, took the throne as George VI. See biographies by John Gore (1941), Harold Nicolson (1952), and Denis Judd (1973).

George VI (Albert Frederick Arthur George), 1895–1952, king of Great Britain and Northern Ireland (1936–52), second son of George V; successor of his elder brother, EDWARD VIII. He attended the royal naval colleges at Osborne and Dartmouth and served in World War I. Later he served in the Royal Air Force. He studied at Cambridge for a time after the war, was created duke of York in 1920, and married (1923) Lady Elizabeth Bowes-Lyon. They had two daughters: Princess Elizabeth (later Queen ELIZABETH II) and Princess MARGARET. When Edward VIII abdicated on Dec. 11, 1936, George became king. He and his consort were crowned on May 12, 1937. They made a state visit to France in July, 1938, and an unprecedented royal voyage to Canada and the United States in 1939. During World War II the king worked to keep up British morale by visiting bombed areas, inspecting war plants, and touring theaters of war action. In 1947 the royal family made a state visit and tour of South Africa. A tour of Australia and New Zealand, scheduled for 1949, was postponed indefinitely because of the king's illness at the end of 1948. Like his father, George was held in deep affection by his people. He was succeeded by Elizabeth II. See biography by J. W. Wheeler-Bennet (1958).

George V, 1819–78, last king of Hanover (1851–66), son and successor of Ernest Augustus. He was blind after 1833. Fearing Hanover's absorption by Prussia, he sided with Austria in the Austro-Prussian War (1866). When Prussia was victorious, he lost his throne, and Hanover was annexed to Prussia. Thereafter he styled himself duke of Cumberland.

George I, 1845–1913, king of the Hellenes (1863–1913), second son of Christian IX of Denmark. After the deposition (1862) of OTTO I, he was elected to succeed on the throne of Greece. Shortly afterward, Britain returned the Ionian Islands to Greece. George introduced (1864) a democratic constitution, acquired (1881) Thessaly and part of Epirus from Turkey, and in 1896 declared war on Turkey in order to aid the insurrection in CRETE. Although badly defeated (1897), Greece eventually annexed (1908) Crete, which was officially incorporated with Greece in 1913. George saw Greece through the first of the BALKAN WARS but was assassinated before the outbreak of the second. Eleutherios VENIZELOS was the outstanding political figure in George's reign. George married Grand Duchess Olga, a niece of Alexander II of Russia. He was succeeded by his son Constantine I.

George II, 1890–1947, king of the Hellenes (1922–23, 1935–47), successor and eldest son of King CONSTANTINE I. He was married (1921–35) to Elizabeth of Rumania, sister of Prince Carol of Rumania (later CAROL II). When Constantine I was forced by the Allies to abdicate in 1917, George, also suspected of being pro-German, was passed over in favor of his younger brother Alexander, who succeeded to the Greek throne. Later, however, George succeeded Constantine I, who had been restored (1920) and again deposed (1922). Hostility to the dynasty was such, however, that George was compelled to leave Greece in 1923; a plebiscite shortly afterward established a republic. George spent his exile in Rumania and later in London. Restored to his throne in 1935, King George allowed his premier, John METAXAS, to set up (1936) a dictatorship. After the conquest of Greece by Germany and Italy in World War II, George fled (1941) his country. He spent most of his exile in London. When Greece was liberated (1944) the question of the king's return was a major issue in the Greek civil war that began in Dec., 1944. George returned only in 1946, after a plebiscite had decided in favor of the monarchy. Although strongly backed by Great Britain and the United States, King George's government and army failed to defeat the rebels, and civil war continued after George's death, when his brother Paul succeeded him.

George, David Lloyd: see LLOYD GEORGE, DAVID, 1ST EARL LLOYD-GEORGE OF DWYFOR.

George, Henry, 1839–97, American economist, founder of the SINGLE-TAX movement, b. Philadelphia. Of a poor family, his formal education was cut short at 14, and in 1857 he emigrated to California; there he worked at various occupations before turning to newspaper writing in San Francisco. George's experience in a number of trades, his desperate poverty while supporting a family, and the examples of financial rapacity that came to his attention as wage earner and newspaperman gave impetus to his reformist tendencies. George saw that an increase in poverty accompanied and even surpassed the increase in national wealth. He believed that the answer to this seeming paradox lay in the fact that the rental of land and the unearned increase in land values profited a few individuals rather than the community whose existence made the land valuable. He believed that a single tax on land would meet all the costs of government and even leave a surplus, besides unburdening labor and capital of taxes on their output. He first outlined the doctrine in the pamphlet *Our Land and Land Policy* (1871) and set himself to write a more elaborate treatise, which appeared under the title *Progress and Poverty* (1879); it sold millions of copies all over the world. In 1880 George moved to New York City and spent the remainder of his life writing and lecturing. He supported the Irish Land League and various economic and political reforms. In 1886 he ran for mayor of New York on a reform platform, and the incumbent Tammany machine was forced to go outside its ranks to find in Abram S. HEWITT a man strong enough to oppose him. Hewitt won, but George, without a party organization, polled a heavy vote, running ahead of the Republican candidate Theodore ROOSEVELT. In 1897 George ran again but died just before the election. Clear presentation and moral fervor rather than originality make George's ideas outstanding. His theories have influenced tax legislation in Australia, in parts of Canada, in the United States, and in certain nations of Western Europe. See biography by Henry George, Jr. (1900); studies by A. A. G. DeMille (1950, repr. 1972), S. B. Cord (1965), E. J. Cord (1965), and Jacob Oser (1973).

George, James Zachariah, 1826–97, American jurist and legislator, b. Monroe co., Ga. He moved to Mississippi in 1834 and, after serving in the Mexican War, became a prominent lawyer. He was long reporter and later (1879–81) chief justice of the state supreme court. A signer of Mississippi's secession ordinance and a Confederate brigadier general in the Civil War, he was a leader in the struggle for white supremacy in Mississippi during the Reconstruction period. George wrote the "grandfather clause," which effectively ended Negro suffrage, in the Mississippi constitution of 1890. He later defended his views on the floor of the U.S. Senate, where he served from 1881 until his death. Known in Mississippi as the Great Commoner, he played an important role in drafting the Sherman Antitrust Act (1890). His unfinished *Political History of Slavery in the United States* (1915) contains a biographical sketch by W. H. Leavell.

George, Stefan (shtā'fän gāôrg'ə), 1868–1933, German poet, leader of the revolt against realism in German literature. Widely traveled and well read, he was poetically influenced by Greek classical forms, by the Parnassians, and by the French symbolists. Intellectually he was a disciple of Nietzsche. George devoted himself to the purifying and ennobling of German language and culture. His lyrics, intended for an intellectual aristocracy, were esoteric and remote, but their fine classicism, their melodious words, and the austerity of George's pure art made him a major poet. His representative verse includes *Algabal* (1892), *Die Bücher der Hirten* [book of the shepherds] (1895), *Das Jahr der Seele* [the soul's year] (1897), *Der siebente Ring* [the seventh ring] (1907), *Der Stern des Bundes* [the star of the covenant] (1914), and *Das neue Reich* [the new kingdom] (1928). George formulated an aesthetic ideal of a controlled but harmonious "living" humanism. He was antagonistic to traditional humanism, to democracy, and to progress. He had great influence on younger poets, both through his verse and through *Blätter für die Kunst* (founded 1892), the literary organ of his circle. George made gifted translations of the works of many French and English poets and of Dante. In contemporary life George looked toward the rise of a "superman" who would unify state and culture. Realizing the divergence between his aesthetic ideal and its brutalized reality, he left Germany after the Nazis came to power. Nevertheless the Nazis adopted him as national poet after his death. See studies by G. R. Urban (1962), U. K. Goldsmith (1970), and M. M. and E. A. Metzger (1972).

George, river, c.345 mi (560 km) long, rising in a lake on the Quebec-Labrador boundary, E Canada. It flows N through Indian Lake (125 sq mi/324 sq km) to Ungava Bay (an arm of Hudson Strait).

George, Lake, glacial lake, 33 mi (53 km) long and 1 to 3 mi (1.6–5 km) wide, in the foothills of the Adirondack Mts., NE N.Y.; it drains N into Lake Champlain. The lake was discovered in 1646 by Isaac Jogues, a French Jesuit missionary, who named it Lac du St. Sacrement; the English colonial leader Sir William Johnson renamed it for the king of England in 1755. On the water route between the Hudson and St. Lawrence rivers, the lake was used for many years by the Indians and colonists to move north or south; it is still part of an important route between Canada and New York. During the French and Indian Wars and the American Revolution, the area around Lake George was the scene of many battles. The ruins of Fort George (built 1759) and Fort William Henry are at the southern end of the lake; historic Fort Ticonderoga, a national historic landmark, is at the northern end. Lake George, with numerous small islands, is noted for its scenery; it is the center of a large resort area.

George, Fort: see PRINCE GEORGE, British Columbia, Canada.

George-Brown, George Alfred George-Brown, Baron: see BROWN, GEORGE ALFRED.

George V Coast, region: see ANTARCTICA.

George Junior Republic, community at Freeville, N.Y., founded (1895) by the American philanthropist William Reuben George (1866–1936) for neglected and maladjusted adolescents. The community is a miniature republic modeled after adult society, which the members (13–18 years old) assist in running. All must work on the farm or in the community's industries. Schooling is provided. Similar junior republics have been established in other states and countries. See W. R. George, *The Junior Republic* (1910).

George of Podebrad (pôd'yĕbrät), 1420–71, king of Bohemia (1458–71). A Bohemian nobleman, he became leader of the Utraquists, or the moderate Hussites, in the wars between HUSSITES and Catholics. He seized Prague (1448) during the minority of King LADISLAUS V, was elected (1452) governor by the Bohemian diet, and continued to rule the country after the formal accession (1453) of Ladislaus. His relations with Ladislaus were friendly. In Ladislaus's reign, George ended the anarchy of the interregnum that had preceded Ladislaus's accession, restored the power of the courts, recovered lost crownlands, and secured the recognition of the central government at Prague in the Bohemian dependencies of Moravia, Silesia, and Lusatia. Ladislaus died in 1457 and George was elected king in 1458. Holy Roman Emperor FREDERICK III invested him with the kingdom in 1459. When in 1462, Pope Pius II abolished the Compactata, by which the Utraquists had been reconciled with the Roman Catholic Church, George promptly declared his loyalty to the Utraquists. An immediate break with Rome was averted through his alliance with France and Poland, and the emperor's intervention delayed papal action. In 1466, however, Pope PAUL II excommunicated George, declared him deposed, and enlisted the aid of the emperor and of MATTHIAS CORVINUS, king of Hungary, against him. Matthias won Moravia and most of Silesia and Lusatia; in 1469 the Catholic party in Bohemia proclaimed Matthias king. George, at the head of the Utraquists, expelled Matthias. To strengthen his position George had signed a treaty with Casimir IV of Poland, naming Casimir's son as his successor. As a result, Ladislaus II (later, as ULADISLAUS II, also king of Hungary) became king on George's death. George of Podebrad unsuccessfully proposed a European alliance against the Turks. Bohemia recovered peace and prosperity in his reign, which, however, was marked by the persecution of the Bohemian and the Moravian Brethren, descendants of the more radical Hussites. See studies by F. G. Heymann (1965) and Otakar Odlozilik (1965).

George of Trebizond (trĕb'ĭzŏnd), c.1396–1486, Greek scholar, b. Crete. Settling in Venice, he taught Greek, philosophy, and rhetoric there and in Vicenza before going to Rome in 1442. He became known as a translator of Aristotle and enjoyed the favor of popes Eugene IV, Nicholas V, and Paul II. He made translations of Plato and translated some Greek church writings into Latin.

George Rogers Clark National Historical Park: see NATIONAL PARKS AND MONUMENTS (table).

Georgetown, city (1970 pop. 66,070), capital and largest city of Guyana, on the Atlantic Ocean at the mouth of the Demerara River. It was known as Stabroek when the Dutch controlled the region and was renamed Georgetown in 1812, after the British had occupied the colony during the Napoleonic Wars. The city has wide, tree-lined streets, many with lily-covered canals reminiscent of the Dutch period. The tropical botantical gardens are among the finest in the world, and the markets operated by East Indians are curious transplants of Asian culture. Georgetown has a hot and humid climate partially relieved by year-round ocean winds. Below sea level at high tide, the city is protected by a mole. Sugar, bauxite, rice, and diamonds are brought to Georgetown by river and rail and are exported. The city has a university (founded 1963).

Georgetown. 1 Residential section (since 1895) of Washington, D.C., on the Potomac River near the confluence of Rock Creek; settled c.1665, inc. 1789. It was part of the land granted by Maryland in 1790 to the Federal government for a national capital. Its many picturesque old houses lend it charm. Georgetown Univ. is there. **2** City (1970 pop. 10,449), seat of Georgetown co., E S.C., on the Sampit River at its entrance into Winyah Bay, c.15 mi (24 km) from the ocean; inc. 1805. It is an historic port of entry, a resort, and a shipping center, with a steel industry and one of the world's largest paper mills. Rice and indigo plantations were established in the area in the early 1700s, and the city was founded c.1734 as a shipping point for their products. Great quantities of lumber and naval stores were also exported from its docks. The Church of Prince George (parish organized in 1721) dates from the 1740s.

Georgetown University, in the Georgetown section of Washington, D.C.; Jesuit; coeducational; founded 1789 by John Carroll, chartered 1815, inc. 1844. Its law and medical schools are noteworthy, and its archives are especially rich in letters and manuscripts by and about persons important in American and Roman Catholic history. The School of Foreign Service is the largest school of international relations in the world and the oldest in the United States. See study by J. T. Durkin (1964).

George Washington Birthplace National Monument: see WAKEFIELD.

George Washington Bridge, vehicular suspension bridge across the Hudson River, between Manhattan borough of New York City and Fort Lee, N.J.; constructed 1927–31. It is one of the longest suspension bridges in the world. Its main span is 3,500 ft (1,067 m) long and 250 ft (76 m) above the water. Cass Gilbert was the consulting architect, and O. H. Ammann was in general charge of the planning and construction. In 1962 a lower deck of six lanes was completed.

George Washington Carver National Monument: see NATIONAL PARKS AND MONUMENTS (table).

George Washington Memorial Parkway: see NATIONAL PARKS AND MONUMENTS (table).

George Washington University, at Washington, D.C.; coeducational; chartered 1821 as Columbian College (one of the first nonsectarian colleges), opened 1822, became a university in 1873, renamed 1904.

George William, 1597–1640, elector of Brandenburg (1619–40). Mild and irresolute, he was a Calvinist, yet he ruled a Lutheran people. He failed to turn the strategic position of Brandenburg to advantage in the THIRTY YEARS WAR, and his possessions were devastated by the armies of both sides. After a long neutrality, he was in 1631 forced into a Swedish alliance by his brother-in-law, Gustavus Adolphus. After the Swedish defeat at Nördlingen (1634), he changed sides and, influenced by his powerful Catholic minister, Adam von Schwarzenberg, allied himself with the Holy Roman emperor (Treaty of Prague, 1635). The Swedes ravaged N Brandenburg. Discouraged by the invasions and misfortunes of his realm, George William retired to Königsberg (1638), leaving the state to Schwarzenberg's management. He was succeeded by his son, Frederick William (the Great Elector).

Georgia, USSR: see GEORGIAN SOVIET SOCIALIST REPUBLIC.

Georgia, state (1970 pop. 4,589,575), 58,876 sq mi (152,489 sq km), SE United States, the last of the Thirteen Colonies to be founded (1733). The most important cities are ATLANTA (the capital and largest city), COLUMBUS, MACON, SAVANNAH, ALBANY, and AUGUSTA. Georgia is bounded on the N by Tennessee and North Carolina, on the E by South Carolina and the Atlantic Ocean, on the S by Florida, and on the W by Alabama. A number of islands, part of the Sea Islands chain, lie off Georgia's coastline. The state has three main topographical areas. Extending inland from the coast is a low coastal plain that covers the southern half of the state. In mountainous N Georgia are the Appalachian Plateau, the valley and ridge province (of the Appalachian Valley), and the Blue Ridge province. Bridging these two sections and embracing about one third of the state is the Piedmont plateau in middle Georgia. Georgia is well drained by many rivers, including the Savannah,

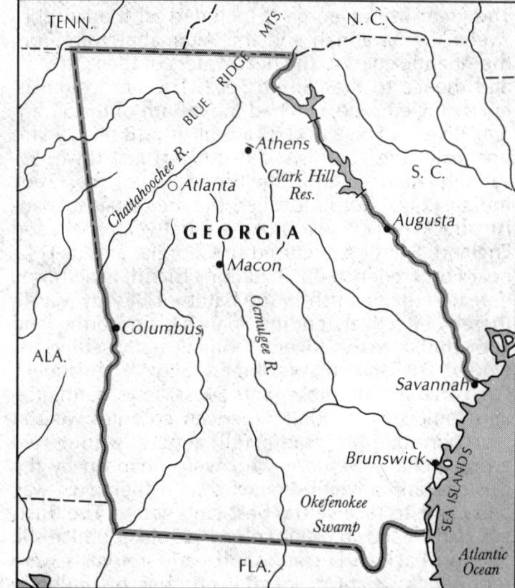

which forms the boundary with South Carolina; the Ocmulgee and the Oconee, which merge in the southeast to form the Altamaha; the Chattahoochee, which forms part of the Alabama boundary and joins with the Flint in the extreme southwest corner of the state to form the Apalachicola; and the Saint Marys, which rises in the large Okefenokee Swamp and forms part of the Georgia-Florida line. Although the climate of Georgia is temperate, it varies considerably throughout the state. Nowhere is the contrast between the brisk pace of modernization and the struggle to retain the traditional ways of the Old South more evident than in Georgia, where modern housing developments press against dignified old mansions and manufacturing outstrips agriculture in economic importance. Cotton, once Georgia's chief crop, has declined in importance; in the early 1970s it ranked in value behind peanuts, tobacco, and corn. Tobacco is the principal crop in the central and southern sections of the state, and peanuts rank first in the southwest. Livestock and poultry raising account for the largest share of farm income; broilers, eggs, and cattle are the most important products. The manufacture of textiles and textile products has long been Georgia's leading industry, centering mainly around Columbus, Augusta, Macon, and Rome. Other major manufactures include transportation equipment, food products, paper products, and chemicals. Much of Georgia is heavily forested with pine, and the state is a leading producer in the South of lumber and pulpwood. Georgia is also a major world supplier of naval stores, especially turpentine and resin. Although the state is rich in minerals, mining is not as important as manufacturing and agriculture. The most valuable minerals produced are clays, stone, kaolin, iron ore, and sand and gravel. Georgia is famous for its fine marble. With its ideal winter climate and its Southern charm and beauty, the state is a popular vacation area. The Sea Islands are especially noted for their picturesque resorts. Warm Springs, established with the help of President Franklin D. Roosevelt for the treatment of poliomyelitis, has long attracted health seekers. Georgia's other attractions include Okefenokee Swamp, a large wilderness area; Chattahoochee and Oconee national forests, with facilities for hunting and fishing; Chickamauga and Chattanooga National Military Park; Kennesaw Mountain National Battlefield Park (see NATIONAL PARKS AND MONUMENTS, table); and Stone Mountain, near Atlanta, on which is carved a Confederate memorial. Creek and Cherokee Indians inhabited the Georgia area when Hernando De Soto and his expedition passed through the region c.1540. The Spanish later established missions and garrisons on the Sea Islands. In 1663, Charles II of England made a grant of land that included Georgia to the eight proprietors of Carolina. However, Spain claimed the whole eastern half of the present United States and protested the grant. The English ignored the protest, and the English-Spanish contest for the territory between Charleston (S.C.) and St. Augustine (Fla.) continued intermittently for almost a century. England became interested in settling Georgia as a buffer colony to protect South Carolina from Spanish invasion from the south. In June, 1732, the English philanthropist James E. Oglethorpe, and 19 associates, chief of whom was the earl of Egmont, received a charter from George II (for whom the colony was named) to settle the colony of Georgia and form a board of trustees to manage it. Oglethorpe planned to settle Georgia as a refuge for debtors in England. The grant from George II included all the land between the Savannah and the Altamaha rivers from the Atlantic coast to the headwaters of these streams and thence to the "South Sea." The first colonists, led by Oglethorpe, reached the mouth of the Savannah River in Feb., 1733. On a bluff c.18 mi (29 km) upstream, the colonists laid out the first town, Savannah. After gaining the friendship of the Creek Indians, Oglethorpe fortified the area against Spanish attack. In 1739 war broke out between Spain and England. Fighting occurred in Georgia, and in 1742, near Fort Frederica on St. Simons Island, Oglethorpe defeated the Spanish in the battle of Bloody Marsh, thereby effectively ending Spain's claim to the land N of the St. Marys River. Georgia's early settlers included Englishmen, Welshmen, Scots Highlanders, Germans, Piedmontese, and Swiss. Jews, Catholics, and settlers from other American colonies were at first barred. Immigrants fell generally into two groups: charity settlers, who were financed by the trustees, and adventurers, who paid their own way and came to receive the best land grants. The trustees had hoped that the colony would produce silk to send back to England, and early colonists were required to plant a specific number of mulberry trees for the cultivation of silkworms. The scheme, however, came to nothing. At first Negro slavery was prohibited, but this and other restrictions impeded the colony's growth, and by the time Georgia became a royal colony in 1754, most of the restrictions had been abolished. Georgia flourished as a royal colony. It fitted well into the British mercantile system, exporting rice, indigo, deerskins, lumber, naval stores, beef, and pork to England and buying there the manufactured articles it needed. Georgia's citizens were slower to resent those acts of the crown that exasperated the other colonies, but by June, 1775, Georgian patriots had begun to organize, and the following month delegates were elected to the Second Continental Congress. Georgia's colonists were about equally divided into Loyalists and patriots during the American Revolution, but the patriots, exposed to Loyalist Florida on the south and the Indians on the west, fared badly. In Dec., 1778, the British captured Savannah, and by the end of 1779 they held every important town in Georgia. After American independence had been won, Georgia was the first Southern state to ratify (1788) the Constitution. Georgia came into conflict with the Federal government over states' rights when the U.S. Supreme Court ruled, in *Chisholm* vs. *Georgia* (1793), that an individual could sue a state, a decision equally as obnoxious to other states as to Georgia. (This decision was later nullified by the Eleventh Amendment to the U.S. Constitution.) Further difficulties with the Federal government stemmed from the related problems of Indian removal and land speculation centering around the YAZOO LAND FRAUD. In 1795 the Georgia legislature passed the Yazoo act authorizing the sale of large tracts of the state's western lands to speculators. In 1796 a newly elected legislature, detecting fraud in passage of the Yazoo act, repudiated it. However, the U.S. Supreme Court later ruled (1810) that the 1796 legislature had violated the right of contract in repudiating the Yazoo act, despite the fraud involved. In the midst of the Yazoo controversy Georgia ceded (1802) its western lands to the United States in return for $1,250,000 and a pledge that the Indians would be removed from Georgia lands. By 1826 the Creek Indians had yielded their lands, but in 1827 the CHEROKEE INDIANS set themselves up as an independent nation. The U.S. Supreme Court held (1832) that the state had no jurisdiction over the Cherokee, but President Jackson declined to support the Chief Justice, and in 1838 the state forced the Indian chief John Ross to lead his people west. With the invention of the cotton gin (1793) by Eli Whitney, Georgia began to prosper as a cotton-growing state. Cotton was grown under the plantation system with labor supplied by slaves. By the 1840s a textile industry was established in the state. Although Georgia was committed to slavery before the Civil War, state leaders such as Alexander H. Stephens, Robert Toombs, and Howell Cobb opposed secession. However, successive defeats on the national scene, culminating in the election of Lincoln as president, fostered separatist sentiment in the state. On Jan. 19, 1861, Georgia seceded from the Union and shortly afterward joined the CONFEDERACY. The coast was soon blockaded by the Union navy, and in April, 1862, Fort Pulaski (which had been seized by the state in Jan., 1861) was recaptured by Union forces. Georgia became a major Civil War battlefield when, in 1864, Union Gen. W. T. Sherman launched his successful ATLANTA CAMPAIGN. On Nov. 15, 1864, Sherman set fire to Atlanta, and his subsequent march through Georgia to the sea, culminating in the fall (Dec.) of Savannah, left in its path a scene of great destruction. During RECONSTRUCTION Georgia at first refused to ratify the Fourteenth Amendment and was consequently placed under military rule. During the period of military rule Rufus B. Bullock, a radical Republican, was elected governor. Corruption prevailed during Bullock's administration (1868–71), but after the legislature approved the Fifteenth Amendment (the Thirteenth and Fourteenth having been ratified earlier), Georgia was readmitted (1870) to the Union, and Bullock resigned. The textile industry recovered from the effects of the war and was expanding by the 1880s. Atlanta, which had succeeded Milledgeville as the capital in 1868, grew into a thriving industrial city. The effect of the war on agriculture—which had formerly been dependent on slave labor—was more serious. The breakup of large plantations resulted in the rise of tenant farming and sharecropping, systems often accompanied by poverty and abuse. After World War I agriculture suffered further setbacks as the boll weevil caused great destruction to cotton crops and the soil became exhausted through erosion and overuse. A farm depression began in Georgia long before the general depression of the 1930s. The state weathered the depression, but its subsequent history was marked by political and racial conflict. In 1941, Gov. Eugene Talmadge caused nationwide commotion by discharging three educators in the state university system alleged to have advocated racial equality in the schools. The state university system lost its accreditation for a time as a result of Talmadge's action. Talmadge was defeated in the 1942 Democratic primary by Ellis G. Arnall. Under Arnall's administration Georgia became the first state to grant the vote to 18-year-olds, and in 1946 (on the strength of a U.S. Supreme Court decision) Negroes voted for the first time in the Georgia Democratic primary. Among Arnall's other administrative acts was the adoption of a new constitution in Aug., 1945. The 1945 constitution, which, in amended form, is still in effect in the state today, contained a provision for Georgia's notorious county-unit system. This system for nominating state officials in Democratic primaries led to the political control of urban areas by sparsely populated rural areas. The integration of public schools, following the 1954 Supreme Court decision, was strenuously opposed by many Georgians. However, in 1961 the legislature abandoned a "massive resistance" policy, and Georgia became the first state in the deep South to proceed with integration without a major curtailment of its public school system. Racial tensions persisted, however, and in May, 1970, racial disorders broke out in Augusta. Georgia's county-unit system (held constitutional by the Supreme Court in April, 1950) was finally abolished by Federal court order in 1962. Georgia's constitution provides for an elected governor who serves for a term of four years and may not be reelected to a consecutive term. The legislature, called the general assembly, is made up of a senate with 56 members and a house of representatives with 180 members. Members of both houses are elected to terms of two years. Georgia sends 10 Representatives and 2 Senators to the U.S. Congress and has 12 electoral votes. The Democratic party in Georgia has dominated that state's politics since the end of Reconstruction. Jimmy Carter, a Democrat, was elected governor in 1970; his term was marred in part by conflicts with Lt. Gov. Lester Maddox, a former (1967–70) governor and also a Democrat. In 1974, George Busbee, a Democrat, was elected governor. Leading educational institutions include the Univ. of Georgia, at Athens; Georgia Institute of Technology, Emory Univ., Clark College, and Morris Brown College, at Atlanta; Agnes Scott College, at Decatur; Mercer Univ. and Wesleyan College, at Macon; and several state colleges. See Federal Writers' Project, *Georgia: A Guide to Its Towns and Countryside* (rev. ed. by G. G. Leckie, 1954); E. S. Sell, *Geography of Georgia* (2d ed. 1958); E. M. Coulter, *Georgia: A Short History* (rev. ed. 1960); S. B. King, *Georgia Voices* (1966); H. E. Bolton, *The Debatable Land* (1968); R. H. Shyrock, *Georgia and the Union in 1850* (1926, repr. 1968); R. M. Myers, ed., *The Children of Pride* (1972).

Georgia, Strait of, channel, c.150 mi (240 km) long, between the mainland of British Columbia and Vancouver Island, Canada, between Puget Sound and Queen Charlotte Sound. It forms part of the inland steamship passage to Alaska.

Georgia, University of, at Athens, Ga.; land-grant and state-supported; coeducational; chartered 1785 as the first state-supported university in the United States, opened 1801. The university's library contains the DeRenne and Moore collections of Georgiana and a large mathematics collection.

Georgia Institute of Technology, in Atlanta, Ga.; coeducational; state supported; chartered 1885, opened 1888. It is a member school in the university system of Georgia. Significant among its facilities and programs are the Frank H. Neely Nuclear Research Center and the School of Information and Computer Sciences.

Georgian Bay, large northeastern extension of Lake Huron, S Ont., Canada, separated from Lake Huron by Manitoulin Island and by the Bruce Peninsula; Lucas Channel is its chief connection with Lake Huron. Rivers draining the lake regions of S Ontario flow into it; they include the French River, which, with North Channel, the northern connection of Georgian Bay with Lake Huron, forms part of the old voyageur's trading route from Montreal to the northwest. Georgian Bay is connected with Lake Ontario by the Severn River and Trent Canal. Christian Island is the largest in the bay. Many of the well-timbered, rock-bound islands of Georgian Bay are summer resorts. The **Georgian Bay Islands Na-**

tional Park (5.4 sq mi/13.9 sq km; est. 1929) includes 40 of the islands and part of the mainland.

Georgian literature. The early literature of Georgia was influenced by two distinctive civilizations—medieval Orthodox Eastern Christianity and the civilization of Persia. From the 6th to the 10th cent. the literature, produced primarily in monasteries, was ecclesiastical. Translations of Holy Writ and other sacred writings were the principal works. From the end of the 11th cent. to the early 13th cent., classical old Georgian poetry enjoyed its greatest flowering. This was a secular literature, sparkling with the vibrance of the Persian epics of the time. The masterpiece of this period was the epic poem by Shota Rustaveli, *The Man in the Panther's Skin* (tr. 1912). Nationalistic in feeling, it is distinguished by a remarkable metrical pattern of fluent rhymes and subtle alliterations and is the best-known work in Georgian literature. In this golden age of Georgian civilization the poet Chakrudkhadze wrote 20 odes, titled *Tamariani,* and Ioane Shavteli completed *Abdul Messiah.* The Mongol invasion in the 13th cent. crushed the Georgian civilization and there was little writing of excellence until the 17th and 18th cent. In the 17th cent., King T'eimuraz I and King Archil Sulkhan wrote extensively, contributing to the evolution of Georgia's modern prose literature, and Saba Orbelian wrote the oustanding *Book of Wisdom and Lies.* In the 18th cent. the foremost writers were David Guramishvili, author of *The Woes of Kartli,* and the lyric poet Bessarion Gabashvili. Throughout these years troubadour literature also evolved. In the 19th cent., romanticism was the dominant style, as seen in the writings of Alexander Chavchavadze, Nikoloz Baratashvili, and Grigol Orbeliani. The outstanding representatives of classical Georgian poetry were Ilia Chavchavadze and Alaki Tsereteli. In the early 20th cent., A. Abashili and S. Shanshiashvili were the leading writers of the pre-Soviet period. Major Georgian literary figures, including the poets Paolo Iashvili and Titsian Tabidze and the novelist Mikheil Javakhishvili, were victims of the Stalin purge of 1937. Later Georgian writers, including the novelist Konstantine Gamsakhurdia, the playwright Shalva Dadiani, and the poet Ioseb Grishashvili, have in general reflected the literary trends, styles, and topics of writers in the USSR. See Mikhail Kvesselava, *Anthology of Georgian Poetry* (1958); A. G. Baramidze and D. M. Gamezardashvili, *Georgian Literature* (tr. 1968).

Georgian Military Road, highway, SE European USSR. It is c.135 mi (220 km) long and crosses the Greater Caucasus mts. Starting from its northern terminus at ORDZHONIKIDZE, the road winds upward through the Daryal gorge. Skirting Mt. Kazbek, it crosses the Caucasus at an altitude of 7,815 ft (2,382 m), descends through the Krestovy Pass, and cuts through rain forests and villages to its southern terminus at TBILISI. Following an ancient route used by traders and invaders, it was started by the Russians in 1799 and completed in 1863. The road was protected by military outposts in the 19th cent., during fighting between Russian troops and Caucasian mountaineers.

Georgian Soviet Socialist Republic or **Georgia,** Georgian *Sakartvelo,* Rus. *Gruziya,* constituent republic (1970 pop. 4,688,000), c.26,900 sq mi (69,700 sq km), SE European USSR, in W Transcaucasia. TBILISI is the capital; other important cities are GORI, RUSTAVI, KUTAISI, BATUMI, SUKHUMI, and POTI. Georgia borders on the Black Sea in the west, on Turkey and the Armenian Republic in the south, on the Azerbaijan Republic in the east, and on the Russian Soviet Federated Socialist Republic in the north. Included in Georgia are the ABKHAZ AUTONOMOUS SOVIET SOCIALIST REPUBLIC, the ADZHAR AUTONOMOUS SOVIET SOCIALIST REPUBLIC, and the South Ossetian Autonomous Oblast (see OSSETIA). Situated on the southern slopes of the Greater Caucasus and in the Lesser Caucasus, Georgia is largely mountainous. The Suram Mts. separate the Rion (Rioni) and Kura river valleys. The perpetually snowcapped Mt. Kazbek, the tallest peak within Georgia, rises to 16,541 ft (5,042 m). The climate is humid subtropical in the Black Sea lowland of MINGRELIA, alpine in the Greater and Lesser Caucasus, and dry in the Kura steppes in the east. Agriculture is the leading occupation in Georgia, whose warmer districts produce most of the USSR's tea and citrus fruits, as well as abundant tobacco, wine grapes, and mulberry trees (for silk). Sheep, pig, and poultry raising are widespread. Because the rugged terrain makes large-scale collective agriculture difficult, individual farming remains important. Georgia is rich in minerals, notably manganese (mined mostly at Chiatura and in IMERITIA); coal, lignite, barites, iron, molybdenum, oil, and peat are also found. There are sizable deposits of marble, dolomite, talc, and clays for use in construction. Georgia has abundant hydroelectric energy. The republic's chief manufactures are machinery, iron and steel, railroad and mining equipment, chemicals, machine tools, and building materials. The Black Sea shore is dotted with resorts and spas that attract numerous tourists. The Black Sea coast railway, the line from Batumi through Tbilisi to Baku, the GEORGIAN MILITARY ROAD, and the OSSETIAN MILITARY ROAD are the republic's main transportation arteries. About two thirds of the population are Georgians—a people of high and ancient culture who speak a language related to the Ibero-Caucasian family of languages. Armenians and Russians are the other major ethnic groups, with Ossetians, Abkhazians, and Azerbaijanians in much smaller numbers. The Georgian church is one of the oldest Eastern Orthodox congregations. There has been a standard Georgian literary language flourishing since about the 5th cent. (see GEORGIAN LITERATURE). Educational and cultural institutions include the university at Tbilisi (est. 1918) and the Georgian Academy of Sciences. Known to the ancients as COLCHIS (in the west) and as IBERIA (in the east), Georgia developed as a kingdom about the 4th cent. B.C. MTSKHET was its earliest capital. The Persian Sassanidae, who ruled the country from the 3d cent. A.D., were expelled c.400. In the 4th cent. Christianity was introduced in Georgia. In the 6th cent. began the rule of a branch of the Armenian Bagratid. Alp Arslan held the region in the 11th cent., but King David II expelled the Seljuk Turks, united the Georgians, and reestablished their independence. In the 12th and 13th cent. Georgia under Queen Thamar (1184–1213) reached its greatest expansion (it then included the whole of Transcaucasia) and cultural flowering. From that period dates the national poem, *The Man in the Panther's Skin,* by Shota Rustaveli. Ravaged (13th cent.) by the Mongols, Georgia revived but was again sacked by Tamerlane (c.1386–1403). In the 15th cent. King Alexander I divided Georgia into three kingdoms (Imertia, Kakhetia, and Karthlia) among his sons, and the period of decline set in. In the 16th cent. Georgia became an object of struggle between Turkey and Persia. In 1555, W Georgia passed under Turkish suzerainty and E Georgia (Kakhetia and Karthlia) under Persian rule. In the 18th cent. kings of Kakhetia tried to unite Georgia, but, hard pressed by the Turks and the Persians, accepted (1783) vassalage to Russia in exchange for assistance. The last king, George XIII, threatened by Persia, abdicated (1801) in favor of the czar and ceded Kakhetia and Karthlia to Russia. Between 1803 and 1829 Russia also acquired from Turkey the western parts of Georgia (Abkhazia, Mingrelia, Imeritia, and Guria). After the Russian Revolution of 1917, the Georgian Menshevik party (see BOLSHEVISM AND MENSHEVISM) proclaimed (May, 1918) Georgia's independence. The Soviet government in Moscow recognized (May, 1920) the independence, but in 1921 the Red Army invaded Georgia, and in Feb., 1921, it was proclaimed a soviet republic. It joined the USSR in 1922 as a member of the Transcaucasian Soviet Federated Socialist Republic, and in 1936 it became a separate union republic. See Z. D. Avalov, *The Independence of Georgia in International Politics, 1918–21* (1940); D. M. Lang, *The Last Years of the Georgian Monarchy, 1658–1832* (1957), *A Modern History of Soviet Georgia* (1962), and *The Georgians* (1966); W. E. Allen, *A History of the Georgian People* (new ed. 1971); C. A. Burney and D. M. Lang, *The Peoples of the Hills* (1972).

Georgian style. It includes several trends in English architecture that developed during the reigns (1714–1820) of George I, George II, and George III. The first half of the period (c.1710–c.1760) was dominated by Neo-Palladianism (see PALLADIO). Colin Campbell, with his first publication of the *Vitruvius Britannicus* in 1715, inspired the patron-architect Richard Boyle, earl of Burlington, and his protégé, William Kent, to return to a classicizing form of architecture, based on the works of Inigo Jones and Palladio. Campbell's Mereworth Castle, Kent (1723), is an outstanding example of this style. Other exponents of Palladian theory were Nicholas Dubois (1665–1735) and Giacomo Leoni (1688–1746), who published an edition of the *Architecture of A. Palladio in Four Books* (c.1716–c.1720). Toward the middle of the century these men were succeeded by a second generation who were loyal to the style, the most notable of whom were Sir Robert Taylor (1714–88) and James Paine (1716–89). The Palladian tradition exerted an obvious and powerful influence throughout the Georgian period both in England and America. During the first half of the 18th cent. there was a countercurrent of baroque architecture stemming from buildings by Sir Christopher Wren and carried on by Sir John Vanbrugh, Nicholas Hawksmoor, and James Gibbs. From the second half of the 18th cent. new archaeological discoveries in Greece and Italy led architects to draw freely from antiquity and other sources (see CLASSIC REVIVAL). Neoclassicism had for its principal exponents Sir William Chambers, Robert Adam, George Dance II, and Sir John Soane. A vast increase in population and the birth of industrialism brought an increasing demand for formal mansions for the aristocracy and for dwelling houses for the middle classes. A purely English type of dwelling, somewhat standardized as to plan and materials, was produced for the needs of town and country. The use of brick had become common under William of Orange (William III), as an element of Dutch influence, and was popularized by Wren. The red brick house, with courses and cornices of white stone and trimmings of white painted woodwork, is what is popularly termed the Georgian style. New types of public, commercial, civic, and governmental architecture arose, examples of which are Queensberry House by Giacomo Leoni; the Old Admiralty, Whitehall, by Thomas Ripley; the treasury and Horse Guards buildings, by William Kent; Somerset House, by Sir William Chambers; the Bank of England, by Sir John Soane; and monumental street groupings, such as those by John Wood and his son at Bath and by the Adam brothers in London. Among notable churches are St. Martin's-in-the-Fields and St. Mary-le-Strand, both by James Gibbs; other important architects of the period were James Gandon and Henry Holland. American buildings and arts of the period, which closely resemble their English prototypes, are usually designated as Georgian. See J. Gloag, *Georgian Grace* (new ed. 1967); J. Harris, *Georgian Country Houses* (1968); J. Summerson, *Architecture in Britain 1530–1830* (3d ed. 1958) and *Georgian London* (1962, repr. 1970).

Georgiyevsk (gēôr'gēĭfsk), city (1967 est. pop. 67,000), SE European USSR, in the northern foothills of the Caucasus. It is an agricultural center with some industry. It was founded (1777) as a Russian fortress. The agreement by which Georgia became a vassal of Russia was signed at Georgiyevsk in 1873.

geothermal energy: see ENERGY, SOURCES OF.

Gepidae: see GERMANS.

Gera (gē'rə), Benjamite. Gen. 46.21; 1 Chron. 8.3.

Gera (gā'rä), city (1970 pop. 111,099), capital of Gera district, S East Germany, on the White Elster River. It is an industrial center and a rail and road junction. Manufactures include textiles, metal products, and furniture. Gera was chartered in the early 13th cent. and was badly damaged by several fires in the 17th and 18th cent. It was the capital of the former principality of Reuss (Younger Line) from 1806 to 1918. Noteworthy buildings of the city include Osterstein Palace (built 1686–1735) and the city hall (18th cent.).

Geraardsbergen (khä'rärtsbĕr''khən), Fr. *Grammont,* town (1970 pop. 17,533), East Flanders prov., W central Belgium, on the Dender River. Manufactures include textiles, watches, and chemicals. Of note is the 15th-century Gothic town hall.

Gérando, Joseph Marie de (zhôzĕf' märē' də zhär-äNdō'), 1772–1842, French philosopher and political figure. Joining the insurrection in Lyons against the French Revolutionary government, he was captured and condemned to death (1793) but escaped abroad. Under the empire of Napoleon I, he held administrative offices in France, Italy, and Spain. A member of the Academy of Moral and Political Sciences from 1832, he was made a peer in 1837. He did much for the education of the working classes and of deaf-mutes. His philosophical writings are partly based on the system of Étienne Bonnot de Condillac.

geranium, common name for some members of the Geraniaceae, a family of herbs and small shrubs of temperate and subtropical regions. Their long, beak-shaped fruits give them the popular names crane's-bill (for species of the genus *Geranium,* the true geranium), heron's-bill (genus *Erodium*), and stork's-bill (genus *Pelargonium*). The American wild geranium, or wild crane's-bill, has rose-to-purple five-petaled flowers and handsome, deeply forked leaves; the woodland herb Robert is similar but smaller. Florists' geraniums are hybrid varieties of the S African genus *Pelargonium* in which the "petals" are actually highly modified stamens. Geraniums are cultivated not only as ornamentals but for the aromatic oils extracted from their foliage and flowers for use in flavorings and perfumes. Geraniums are classified in the division MAGNOLIOPHYTA, class Magnoliopsida, order Geraniales, family Geraniaceae.

Gerar (gē'rär), city-state of Canaan, SE of Gaza. Abraham and Isaac sojourned there. Its identification is controversial; the most likely site is Tel Haror, where remains from the appropriate biblical period have been found. Gen. 10.19; 20.1,2; 2 Chron. 14.13,14.

Gérard, Étienne Maurice (ātyĕN' môrēs' zhārär'), 1773–1852, French army officer. He fought with distinction in the French Revolutionary and Napoleonic Wars, and in the Waterloo campaign he served with gallantry at Ligny. Returning from exile in 1817, he became a deputy of the opposition and supported the July Revolution of 1830, which brought LOUIS PHILIPPE to the French throne. He was twice minister of war under Louis Philippe, who created him marshal. Gérard led the French expedition to Belgium, taking Antwerp in 1832.

Gérard, François Pascal Simon, Baron (fräNswä' päskäl' sēmôN' bärôN'), 1770–1837, French portrait and historical painter, b. Rome. In Paris, after brief study under Pajou and others, he became a favorite pupil of J. L. David, who influenced such works as *Psyche Receiving the Kiss of Cupid* and *Daphnis and Chloë*, both in the Louvre. As a leading portraitist, Gérard was patronized by the court during the Empire and the Bourbon restoration. His portrait of Mme Récamier, of this period, is in the Louvre. Louis XVIII appointed him court painter in 1814. Many examples of his historical paintings are in the Versailles Museum. His portrait of the Countess Regnault de Saint-Jean-d'Angély (1798; Louvre) exemplifies his style of studied elegance and meticulous finish.

Gerard, James Watson, 1867–1951, U.S. ambassador to Germany (1913–17), b. Geneseo, N.Y. As ambassador, he handled many delicate negotiations, including those concerning the German submarine campaigns in World War I. He earned warm praise for his skillful representation of American and Allied interests. His impressions of the period are found in *My Four Years in Germany* (1917) and *Face to Face with Kaiserism* (1918). See his memoirs (1951).

Gérard, Jean Ignace Isidore (zhäN ēnyäs' ēzēdôr' zhārär'), 1803–47, French caricaturist, illustrator, and lithographer, better known as Grandville. He is noted for his spirited caricatures of social and political life. Gérard contributed to many periodicals and published numerous collections of his drawings and lithographs, such as *Les Métamorphoses du jour, Le Convoi de la liberté* and *La Basse-Cour.* Among his illustrations are those for La Fontaine's *Fables.*

Gerard, John (jĕ'rärd), 1545–1612, English botanist and barber-surgeon. He compiled a catalog (1596) of the plants in his garden, the first of its kind to be published in England. He is best known for his *Herball* (1597), largely an adaptation of other works to which he added bits of folklore and some original observations.

gerardia (jərär'dēə): see FIGWORT.

Gerasa (jĕr'əsə), **Gerash,** or **Jerash** (both: jĕ'räsh, jəräsh'), ancient city of the Decapolis, 22 mi (35 km) N of Amman, in present-day Jordan. According to Josephus it was captured (83 B.C.) by Alexander Jannaeus, king of the Hasmonean dynasty, and rebuilt (A.D. 65) by the Romans. Though twice destroyed thereafter, it was a flourishing city in the 2d and 3d cent. The Graeco-Roman city was called Jerash and is probably the best-preserved Palestinian city of Roman times. The site is covered with interesting Roman ruins, including a long colonnaded street with more than a hundred columns still standing, a great theater and a smaller one, a triumphal arch, and many temples. It was also important in the development of early Christianity, and several churches of the period have been found there. Gerasa is not the biblical country of the Gerasenes. A colony of Circassians lives among the ruins. See C. H. Kraeling, ed., *Gerasa, City of the Decapolis* (1938).

Gerasenes: see GADARA.

Gerash, ancient city: see GERASA.

Gerbert: see SYLVESTER II.

gerbil (jûr'bĭl), small desert RODENT found throughout the hot arid regions of Africa and Asia. Also known as sand rats, gerbils have large eyes and powerful, elongated hind limbs upon which they can spring. Gerbils are 3 to 5 in. (7.6–12.7 cm) long, excluding the long tufted tail, and are sandy, gray, brown, or reddish in color with white underparts. Most species are nocturnal and all live in burrows. Their diet consists of seeds and grains; they also eat desert plants, from which they obtain almost all the water they need. With the exception of a few species, gerbils tend to hoard food. In recent years gerbils have become popular as house pets. They are odorless, easy to raise, and usually gentle. Females may bear as many as 15 litters in a lifetime; each litter may contain up to 10 young. Gerbils are classified in the phylum CHORDATA, subphylum Vertebrata, class Mammalia, order Rodentia, family Cricetidae.

gerenuk: see ANTELOPE.

Gergesenes: see GADARA.

Gerhardt, Charles Frédéric (shärl frādārēk' zhārär'), 1816–56, French chemist, b. Strasbourg. He revived the theory of acid radicals, which he called the theory of residues, and did valuable research in organic chemistry, especially on the anhydrides of organic acids. He contributed to the development of the atomic weight theory.

Gerhardt, Elena (ālā'nä gĕr'härt), 1883–1961, German mezzo-soprano and teacher of singing, studied at the Leipzig Conservatory. She made her debut in 1903. After a concert career in both the United States and Europe as an outstanding interpreter of German lieder, she taught in London from 1933 until her death. See her autobiography, *Recital* (1953).

Gerhardt, Paul, 1607–76, German hymn writer and clergyman. Some of his famous texts, such as *O Sacred Head Sore Wounded,* are much used in English translations.

Gerhart, Emanuel Vogel (gâr'härt), 1817–1904, American minister of the German Reformed Church and educator, b. Freeburg, Pa. Gerhart was president of Heidelberg College (1851–55), of Franklin and Marshall College (1855–66), and of the theological seminary at Mercersburg and later at Lancaster, Pa. (1868–1904). He influenced the doctrinal development of the German Reformed Church (see EVANGELICAL AND REFORMED CHURCH).

geriatrics (jĕrēă'trĭks), study of the medical problems of the aged. Many disabilities in old age are caused by or related to the deterioration of the circulatory system (see ARTERIOSCLEROSIS); e.g., mental deterioration and disturbances of motor and sensory function are often associated with an insufficient blood supply. Older persons are more prone to gastrointestinal disturbances, partly because of a reduced blood supply to the gastrointestinal tract and partly because of other reasons, such as poor dentition. Changes in bone tissue create susceptibility to fractures on slight injury or even for no apparent reason. There may also be diminished pulmonary function due to degenerative changes in the lungs. Elderly males may suffer from prostatic enlargement (see PROSTATE GLAND), often accompanied by urinary obstruction. Obesity, causing increased strain on the heart and blood vessels, is also a serious problem of the aged. Although the exact cause of aging is unknown, it is thought to be related to changes in the activities of body cells. Aging cells are more susceptible to malignant changes and to the accumulation of calcium, cholesterol, and other substances that may cause tissue deterioration. These factors have made geriatrics an important specialty, particularly since the proportion of elderly persons in the general population is increasing steadily. Geriatrics is one of the fields included in the general study of old age, or gerontology, which covers psychological, economic, and social factors as well. Both public and private institutions are expending steadily rising funds on research in geriatrics and gerontology. See R. W. Prehoda, *Extended Youth: The Promise of Gerontology* (1968); Simone de Beauvoir, *The Coming of Age* (tr. 1972); S. R. Curtin, *Nobody Ever Died of Old Age* (1973).

Géricault, Jean Louis André Théodore (zhäN lwē äNdrā' tāōdôr' zhārēkō'), 1791–1824, French painter. He studied with Antoine Vernet and with Pierre Guérin, in whose studio he met Delacroix. In 1812 he exhibited his *Cavalry Officer* and in 1814 the *Wounded Cuirassier* (both: Louvre). From 1816 to 1817 he studied in Rome. On his return to Paris he exhibited his famous *Raft of the Medusa* (Louvre), a large, turbulent painting of a group of shipwrecked men at sea. The work was based on an event of that period that had scandalous elements and political significance, thus exciting much public interest. The extraordinarily free conception and realistic handling of this theme awoke a storm of protest from the followers of the classical school and ushered in romanticism in French painting. In 1820, Géricault exhibited the picture in London and won general acclaim and a considerable fortune. His three years' stay in England resulted in fine paintings of horses, including *The Village Forge, Horse Fed by a Child,* and the celebrated *Epsom Derby* (Louvre). He also modeled small figures and made excellent lithographs. A fall from a horse in England caused his untimely death. His active life as an artist lasted little over 10 years, but it sufficed to place him among the finest painters of his century. His enlivening influence on French painting was immediate and lasting. See study by K. Berger (tr. 1955); Lorenz Eitner, *Géricault's Raft of the Medusa* (1973).

Gérin-Lajoie, Antoine (äNtwän' zhārăN'-läzhwä'), 1824–82, French Canadian author and journalist, b. Quebec prov. After serving as an editor (1845–52) on the *Minerve,* a Montreal newspaper, he entered government employment and spent the later part of his life as assistant librarian of Parliament. He also founded two short-lived literary magazines, *Les Soirées canadiennes* and *Le Foyer canadien.* His most popular works, the two novels *Jean Rivard le défricheur* (1874) and *Jean Rivard l'économiste* (1876), idealize the simple life of rural French Canadians. He also wrote *Dix Ans au Canada, de 1840 à 1850,* a history of the government in that crucial time.

Gerizim (gĕr'əzĭm, gērī'-), Arabic *Jabal at Tur,* mountain, 2,890 ft (881 m) high, in the Samaritan Hills, W Jordan. Nablus, near the ancient Shechem, lies in the valley between Gerizim and Mt. Ebal. Gerizim is sacred to the Samaritans, whose tradition holds that Abraham's offer to sacrifice Isaac occurred there. The 300-year-old Samaritan temple at Gerizim was destroyed by the Maccabean leader, John Hyrcanus, in 128 B.C. (Joshua 8.33; Judges 9.7; John 4.20,21).

Gerlachovka (gĕrläkh-ôf'kä), peak, 8,737 ft (2,663 m) high, in the Tatra mts.; highest peak of the Capathian mt. system and of Czechoslovakia.

Germain, George Sackville, 1st **Viscount Sackville** (jûr'mən, -mān), 1716–85, British soldier and statesman. He was known as Lord George Sackville until 1770, when under the terms of a will he took the name Germain. His early military career, in the War of the Austrian Succession and the Seven Years War, ended in court-martial and dismissal (1760) for insubordination at the battle of Minden (1759). A member of Parliament intermittently from 1741, he attached himself to Lord NORTH and was his secretary for the colonies (1775–82). With the 4th earl of SANDWICH, Germain has received much of the blame for the British reverses in the American Revolution. He and John BURGOYNE were the chief authors of a plan (see SARATOGA CAMPAIGN) to end the Revolution by splitting New England from the rest of the colonies. However, his vague orders to Sir William Howe to join Burgoyne may have cost Burgoyne the campaign of 1777, while the confusion in the plans of Lord Cornwallis and Sir Henry Clinton, arising partly from Germain's ignorance of American geography, contributed to the disaster of the YORKTOWN CAMPAIGN. He was created viscount in 1782. See biographies by A. C. Valentine (1962) and Louis Marlow (1974).

Germain, Sophie (sôfē' zhĕrmăN'), 1776–1831, French mathematician. Although self-taught, she mastered mathematics and corresponded with J. L. Lagrange and C. F. Gauss. She is known especially for her study of the vibrations of elastic surfaces.

German art and architecture. Artistic works produced within the region that became politically unified as Germany in 1871 generally followed the stylistic currents of Western Europe. CAROLINGIAN ARCHITECTURE AND ART are commonly considered to have been the earliest manifestations of discernibly Germanic art. As the center of Charlemagne's empire, the Rhineland was the home of the massive palace chapel at Aachen (c.800), decorated with mosaics, and contemporary churches such as the one at Fulda; many of these show the revival of early Christian plans (see EARLY CHRISTIAN ART AND ARCHITECTURE). Carolingian ivory book covers and diptychs were also notable. The first outstanding examples of German painting and sculpture were created (c.960–c.1060) during the Ottonian dynasty. Splendid manuscripts, enriched by ILLUMINATIONS remarkable for their force of linear expression, issued from the school of Reichenau (e.g., the *Gospels of Otto III,* State Library, Munich), while in Cologne MINIATURE PAINTING exhibited a brilliant use of color. Fine craftsmanship is apparent in the metalwork of this period, from the small objects produced by the goldsmiths of Mainz to more massive achievements, such as the bronze doors (1015) for the Church of St. Michael at Hildesheim. The architecture of St. Michael's exemplifies a tendency in Ottonian buildings toward the development of a complex ground plan. A highly rational system was devised of dividing the church into a series of separate units, a method that was to be of consequence in Romanesque design. ROMANESQUE ARCHITECTURE AND ART flourished in Germany, and the cathedrals in BASILICA form at Worms, Mainz, and Speyer typify the characteristic divisive style of the period. Little remains of Romanesque fresco painting, of which Regensburg and Salzburg were major Germanic centers. With the diffusion of the French Gothic style throughout Europe (see GOTHIC ARCHITECTURE AND ART), notable contributions were made by the Germans. The magnificent sculpture of the portals for the cathedrals at Bamberg, Strasbourg, and Naumburg was executed during the first half of the 13th cent. French influence is most strongly revealed in the cathedral of Cologne (c.1250). Modifying the French emphasis on decoration, however, the Germans built simpler, unadorned piers and evolved a more unified, spacious form of church. This style may be seen in the Church of St. Sebald (c.1370), Nuremberg, or in the cathedral (c.1470) at Munich. Outstanding sculpture was created in the late 15th cent. with the powerfully realistic works, particularly in wooden altarpieces, of Peter Vischer, the elder, Veit Stoss, Adam Kraft, and Tilman Riemenschneider. Active both as a sculptor and as a painter, Hans Multscher established the Swabian school. In the late 15th and early 16th cent., manuscript illumination and fresco painting declined as STAINED GLASS technique and panel painting became highly developed. The refined paintings of Stephan Lochner are among those that reflect Flemish influence, particularly of the van Eycks and of Rogier van der Weyden. Martin Schongauer, painting at the same time, developed a more individual style, characterized by delicate and curving lines. Hans Holbein, the elder, and Michael Pacher were among the other major 15th-century figures. But the artistic genius of the century was Albrecht Dürer. His paintings, woodcuts, and engravings were produced at an unprecedented level of perfection, influencing all European art of the time. He visited Venice and was chiefly responsible for bringing elements of the Italian Renaissance style to Germany. Painting in the 16th cent. was at its height in Germany and led all other arts. Hans Holbein, the younger, Mathias Grünewald (creator of the last major Gothic altarpiece), Albrecht Altdorfer (who brought pure LANDSCAPE PAINTING into vogue), Lucas Cranach, the elder, and Hans Baldung were the great masters of the age. Gothic architecture prevailed so long in Germany that when the Church of St. Michael's in Munich was built (c.1590), the Renaissance and mannerist periods had already ended, and early BAROQUE churches, heavily influenced by Italian design, were being constructed. Some of Germany's finest buildings date from the 17th and 18th cent.—exuberant baroque and ROCOCO churches and palaces that are marvels of lightness and spatial complexity. Among the best are the works of the Austrian Fischer von Erlach. Ceiling decoration was widely practiced. The rococo style came to the fore c.1730, with the Tischbein family and Angelica Kauffmann its chief exponents in painting. In this time, too, small Dresden china figures and groups became very popular, with the workshops at MEISSEN producing exquisite miniature statuettes of GENRE subjects. The monumental sculptures of J. G. Schadow were regarded as the model for a century of subsequent German plastic art. A. R. Mengs's work marked the widespread revival of classicism modeled on the theories of J. J. Winckelmann and on the art of Rome. J. F. Overbeck, Schadow-Godenhaus, Peter von Cornelius, and Schnorr von Carolsfeld banded together to form the group of NAZARENES active in Rome. Alfred Rethel became a leader of a school of German historical painting. He and the realist A. F. E. von Menzel executed woodcuts as well and were responsible for the 19th-century revival of the medium. The BIEDERMEIER period brought to the fore genre painters including Moritz von Schwind and Karl Spitzweg. In the late 19th cent. a new wave of romanticism emerged that had been foreshadowed by the desolate landscapes of C. D. Friedrich and the complex allegories of P. O. Runge. Romanticism was exemplified in architecture by K. F. Schinkel. Romantic painters who were influenced by Italian art included Anselm von Feuerbach and Hans von Marées. The sentimental genre scenes and derivative neoclassic artistic production of the 19th cent. were replaced in the 20th cent. by a fresh, more vital sensibility. In the early years of the century the influence of Gauguin was strong. English ART NOUVEAU design innovations were adopted in the applied arts in Germany and termed *jugendstil.* The wave of 20th-century masters that emerged from the Berlin SECESSION, led by Max Liebermann, created an art known as EXPRESSIONISM for its purposeful distortion of natural forms. The expressionist movement came in three waves: the first, the BRÜCKE (1905) included E. L. Kirchner and Emil Nolde; the BLAUE REITER (1911) attracted several foreign artists, such as Paul Klee, Lyonel Feininger, and Wassily Kandinsky; and in the 1920s Otto Dix and Max Beckmann were principal exponents of the disenchanted realism called the NEW OBJECTIVITY. Artists working in related styles included Oskar Kokoschka and Käthe Kollwitz. Several of these same artists also taught at the BAUHAUS, led by Walter Gropius and later by Miës van der Rohe. This establishment became the chief breeding place of FUNCTIONALISM and encouraged experimentation and abstraction with the ideal of combining artistic beauty with usefulness. The Nazi regime, however, regarding abstract and expressionist works as degenerate, discouraged and destroyed any but heroic, propagandistic art, and the Germany of the 1930s and early 40s produced nothing of artistic significance. The Bauhaus aesthetic was taught and practiced in the United States, while German architecture, massive and dull, glorified the Nazi style. In the period since World War II the dominant architectural designers have included Hans Scharoun, Helmut Striffler, Werner Duttmann, and Gottfried Bohm. The abstract movement has been led by Willi Baumeister, Theodore Werner, Fritz Winter, E. W. Nay, Winfred Gaul, and G. K. Pfaher. An excellent collection of German art is at the Busch-Reisinger Museum, Harvard Univ. See articles on individual artists, e.g., DÜRER. See Fritz Novotny, *Painting and Sculpture in Europe, 1780–1880* (1960); Franz Roh, *German Art in the 20th Century* (tr. 1968); Gottfried Lindemann, *History of German Art* (tr. 1971).

German Baptist Brethren: see BRETHREN.

German Catholics, religious groups founded in 1844 by dissidents from the Roman Catholic Church. They were led by two excommunicated priests, Johann Czerski of Schneidemühl, Posen, and Johann Ronge of Breslau. The church, organized by a council in Leipzig in 1845 under the name of Deutschekatholische Kirche was attractive to Roman Catholics because it retained the traditional practices of baptism and communion. In keeping with the rationalism and nationalism of the period, it rejected papal primacy, celibacy, indulgences, devotion to saints, veneration of relics, and all but the abovementioned sacraments. Following an early period of growth, with several hundred congregations consisting of some 80,000 members, a slow decline set in. Roman Catholics who had sought reform became disillusioned following the merger with the Protestant Free Congregations in 1850, and the later merger of many of these churches with the Friends of Light, an anti-Christian sect. Greatly reduced in membership, several German Catholic churches survived into the 20th cent.

German Confederation, 1815–66, union of German states provided for at the Congress of Vienna to replace the old Holy Roman Empire, which had been destroyed during the French Revolutionary and Napoleonic Wars. It comprised 39 states in all, 35 monarchies and 4 free cities. Its purpose was to guarantee the external and internal peace of Germany and the independence of the member states. In case of attack the members pledged mutual aid.

German Confederation (1815)

Certain princes, however, were exempt from this provision. These were the king of England, as king of Hanover; the king of the Netherlands, as duke of Luxembourg; and the King of Denmark, as duke of Holstein and Lauenburg. As it was constituted, the confederation was little more than a loose union for mutual defense. Its main organ, a central diet that met at Frankfurt under the presidency of Austria, functioned as a diplomatic conference. Unanimity or a two-thirds majority was required for most decisions, and, in voting, the delegates were bound to instructions from their respective governments. The diet thus was ineffective. The strong reactionary influence of the Austrian statesman METTERNICH, backed by Prussia, dominated the confederation until 1848, when the liberal revolutions that swept Germany resulted in the creation of the FRANKFURT PARLIAMENT. The diet was resumed in 1850. By the treaty agreed upon at OLMÜTZ, Austrian leadership was temporarily restored, but the AUSTRO-PRUSSIAN WAR (1866) led to the dissolution of the confederation and the establishment of the NORTH GERMAN CONFEDERATION under Prussian leadership.

German East Africa, former German colony, c.370,000 sq mi (958,300 sq km), E Africa. Dar es Salaam was the capital. German influence emerged in the area in 1884 when Carl Peters, the German explorer, obtained treaties over parts of the territory. The German government declared a protectorate over the area in 1885 and the German East Africa Company was organized to administer it. In 1888, the sultan of Zanzibar relinquished the coastal areas, but German control was hindered by the Abushiri revolt (1888–90). In Jan., 1891, the German government took over the administration of the colony and by 1898 had conquered all of the territory. Plantations were established and railroad and harbor systems were begun. Discontentment with the administration and with the plantation system, however, led to the widespread Maji Maji rebellion (1905–7). After the rebellion, the colony entered a period of reform and economic expansion. During World War I the Allies captured German East Africa; after the war it was divided into League of Nations mandates. Great Britain was given most of the area, renamed Tanganyika (now TANZANIA), while Belgium received Ruanda-Urundi (now RWANDA and BURUNDI), and Kionga, a village, was ceded to Portugal. See V. T. Harlow and E. M. Chilver, ed., *History of East Africa,* Vol. II (1965); Jon Bridgman and D. E. Clarke, *German Africa: A Selected Annotated Bibliography (1965).*

Germanic languages, subfamily of the Indo-European family of languages, spoken by about 420 million people in many parts of the world, but chiefly in Europe and the Western Hemisphere. All of the modern Germanic languages are closely related; moreover, they become progressively closer grammatically and lexically when traced back to the earliest records. This suggests that they all derive from a still earlier common ancestor, which is traditionally referred to as Proto-Germanic and which is believed to have broken from the other Indo-European languages before 500 B.C. Although no writing in Proto-Germanic has survived, the language has been substantially reconstructed by using the oldest records that exist of the Germanic tongue. The Germanic languages today are conventionally divided into three linguistic groups: East Germanic, North Germanic, and West Germanic. This division had begun by the 4th cent. A.D. The East Germanic group, to which such dead languages as Burgundian, Gothic, and Vandalic belong, is now extinct. However, the oldest surviving literary text of any Germanic language is in Gothic (see GOTHIC LANGUAGE). The North Germanic languages, also called Scandinavian languages or Norse, include Danish, Faeroese, Icelandic, Norwegian, and Swedish. They are spoken by about 20 million people, chiefly in Denmark, the Faeroe Islands, Iceland, Norway, and Sweden. These modern North Germanic languages are all descendants of Old Norse (see NORSE) and have several distinctive grammatical features in common. One is the adding of the definite article to the noun as a suffix. Thus "the book" in English is expressed in Swedish as *boken,* "book-the" (*bok* meaning "book" and *-en* meaning "the"). Also distinctive is a method of forming the passive voice by adding *-s* to the end of the verb or, in the case of the present tense, by changing the active ending *-r* to *-s* (*-st* in Icelandic). This is illustrated by the Swedish *jag kaller*="I call"; *jag kallas*="I am called"; *jag kallade*="I called"; *jag kallades*="I was called". The West Germanic languages are English, Frisian, Dutch, Flemish, Afrikaans, German, and Yiddish.

They are spoken by about 400 million people. Among the dead West Germanic languages are Old Franconian, Old High German, and Old English (or Anglo-Saxon) from which Dutch, German, and English respectively developed. Strong evidence for the unity of all the modern Germanic languages can be found in the phenomenon known as the first Germanic sound shift or consonant shift (also called GRIMM'S LAW), which set the Germanic subfamily apart from the other members of the Indo-European family. Consisting of a regular shifting of consonants in groups, the sound shift had already occurred by the time adequate records of the various Germanic languages began to be made in the 7th to 9th cent. According to Grimm's law, certain consonant sounds found in the ancient Indo-European languages (such as Latin, Greek, and Sanskrit) underwent a change in the Germanic tongue. For example, the sounds *p, d, t,* and *k* in the former became *f, t, th,* and *h* respectively in the latter, as in Latin *pater,* English *father;* Latin *dent,* English *tooth;* and Latin *cornu,* English *horn.* Before the 8th cent. a second shift of consonants took place in some of the West German dialects. For instance, under certain circumstances, *d* became *t,* and *t* became *ss* or *z,* as in English *bread,* Dutch *brood,* but German *Brot;* English *foot,* Dutch *voet,* but German *Fuss;* and English *ten,* Dutch *tien,* but German *zehn.* The dialects in which this second consonant shift took place were the High German dialects, so called because they were spoken in more mountainous areas. Standard modern German arose from these dialects. The West Germanic dialects not affected by the second shift were the Low German dialects of the lowlands, from which Dutch and English evolved. Also peculiar to the Germanic languages is the recessive accent, whereby the stress usually falls on the first or root syllable of a word, especially a word of Germanic origin. Another distinctive characteristic shared by the Germanic languages is the umlaut, which is a type of vowel change in the root of a word. It is demonstrated in the pairs *foot* (singular), *feet* (plural) in English; *fot* (singular), *fötter* (plural) in Swedish; and *Kampf* (singular), *Kämpfe* (plural) in German. All Germanic languages have strong and weak verbs; that is, they form the past tense and past participle either by changing the root vowel in the case of strong verbs (as in English *lie, lay, lain* or *ring, rang, rung;* German *ringen, rang, gerungen*) or by adding as an ending *-d* (or *-t*) or *-ed* in the case of weak verbs (as in English *care, cared, cared* or *look, looked, looked;* German *fragen, fragte, gefragt*). Also typically Germanic is the formation of the genitive singular by the addition of *-s* or *-es.* Examples are English *man, man's;* Swedish *hund, hunds;* German *Lehrer, Lehrers* or *Mann, Mannes.* Moreover, the comparison of adjectives in the Germanic languages follows a parallel pattern, as in English: *rich, richer, richest;* German *reich, reicher, reichst;* and Swedish *rik, rikare, rikast.* Lastly, vocabulary furnished evidence of a common origin for the Germanic languages in that a number of the basic words in these languages are similar in form; however, while word similarity may indicate the same original source for a group of languages, it can also be a sign of borrowing. See articles on the individual languages mentioned and on INDO-EUROPEAN. See A. L. Streadbeck, *A Short Introduction to Germanic Linguistics* (1966); R. K. Seymour, *A Bibliography of Word Formation in the Germanic Languages* (1968); Antoine Meillet, *General Characteristics of the Germanic Languages* (tr. 1970).

Germanic laws, customary law codes of the GERMANS before their contact with the Romans. They are unknown to us except through casual references of ancient authors and inferences from the codes compiled after the tribes had invaded the Roman Empire. These codes (called *leges barbarorum*), dating from the 5th to the 9th cent., are usually divided into four groups: the Gothic (Visigothic, Burgundian, and Ostrogothic), the Frankish (Salic, Ripuarian, Chamavian, and Thuringian), the Saxon (Saxon, Anglo-Saxon, and Frisian), and the Bavarian (Alemannic and Bavarian). The Langobardic, or Lombard, laws are sometimes classed with the Saxon. The Roman population under Germanic rule continued to live under Roman law, for law was regarded as personal, not territorial. Their law was codified (the *leges Romanae,* or *leges Romanorum*) in the Gothic and Burgundian kingdoms and was applied to Roman subjects and to the church. Another type of legislation distinct from these was the Frankish capitulary (see CAPITULARIES). A codification was sometimes called a *pactus* (e.g., *Pactus Alamannorum*), because people and ruler cooperated in enactment of the laws. It is now generally agreed that the laws were substantially Germanic, although the form in which they were cast was a more or less crude imitation of Roman codes. Roman influence was generally strong, since German customs had been thrown into a new pattern by Roman contacts when these compilations were drawn up; all except the Anglo-Saxon are in Latin, although interspersed with Germanic legal terms. For the most part, the *leges barbarorum* deal with penal law and legal procedure; some of the older ones are merely lists of COMPOSITIONS to be paid for specific personal injuries. Private and public law are scantily treated. Much material can, however, be found concerning landholding (one of these provisions became the basis for the SALIC LAW of succession) and the personal relationships that governed public law. Many of the codes are important. Probably the oldest is the *Codex Euricianus* by King Euric, the personal law of the Visigoths; a related code was adopted in 506 under ALARIC II, the *Lex Romana Visigothorum,* or BREVIARY OF ALARIC, for the Roman subjects. Both were later superseded (c.654) by the *Lex Visigothorum,* or *Liber iudiciorum,* compiled under CHINDASWINTH and RECESWINTH; this for the first time applied to Goths and Romans alike. In the 13th cent. it was translated into Spanish as the *Fuero juzgo.* The *Lex Gundobada* (*Loi Gombette*) was adopted (c.501) for Burgundians and for cases involving both Burgundians and Romans, while the *Lex Romana Burgundiorum* (c.506), also from the reign of Gundobad, applied only to the Romans in the Burgundian kingdom. Because of a mistake in copying, it has come to be known as *Papianus,* or Papian law; it was gradually replaced by the *Breviary of Alaric.* The most accomplished Germanic code was the *Edictum Rotharis,* promulgated in 643. Together with the Italian legislation of the Holy Roman emperors (the *Capitulare Langobardicum*), it became the basis for a renaissance of jurisprudence in Italy and maintained itself till the revival in the 13th cent. of Justinian's CORPUS JURIS CIVILIS, which subsequently spread over all of Western Europe. Its influence reaches to the threshold of modern times. As to the Franks and more northerly Germans, their codes were less elaborate and they had none for Romans. Most ancient and also most important was the law of the Salian Franks, *Lex Salica,* first compiled (c.508–11) under CLOVIS I, which exerted great influence, for it was the fundamental law of the Merovingian and Carolingian rulers and later of the Holy Roman emperors. The *Lex Saxonum* and the *Lex Angliorum et Verinorum* probably owe their compilation to the initiative of Charlemagne; the *Lex Ripuaria* of the Ripuarian Franks, the *Lex Baiuvariorum,* and the *Lex Alamannorum* are distinguished by inclusions of public law. The most important compilation of northern and central German laws was the *Sachsenspiegel.* This, originally written (c.1230) in Latin, was subsequently translated into the vernacular. It showed an earlier stage of development than contemporary treatises in England and N France. Our knowledge of the early German laws is much hampered by the faultiness of manuscripts; many are known only in fragments. See Edward Jenks, *Law and Politics in the Middle Ages* (1913, repr. 1970); Rudolph Hübner, *A History of Germanic Private Law* (1918, repr. 1968).

Germanic religion, pre-Christian religious practices among the tribes of Western Europe, Germany, and Scandinavia. The main sources for our knowledge are the *Germania* of Tacitus and the *Elder Edda* and the *Younger Edda.* Although it is possible to perceive certain basic concepts that were important to the pre-Christian Germans, there was no Germanic religion common to all the Scandinavian and Teutonic peoples; neither can we know whether a ritual or legend peculiar to one Germanic tribe was common to all Germanic tribes. Germanic religion, like most ancient religions, was polytheistic. In early times there were two groups of gods—the Aesir and the Vanir. However, after a war between the rival pantheons (which perhaps reflects a war between two rival tribes), the defeated Vanir were absorbed into the Aesir, and the gods of both were worshiped in a single pantheon. This pantheon, which according to some accounts consisted of 12 principal deities, had WODEN (Odin) as its chief god. Other important deities were TIW (Tyr), THOR (Donar), BALDER, FREY, FREYJA, and FRIGG. The gods dwelled in ASGARD, where each deity had his own particular abode. The most beautiful of the palaces was VALHALLA; there Woden, attended by the VALKYRIES, gave banquets to the dead heroes. The ancient Nordic gods, however, unlike the gods of most religions, were not immortal. They continually renewed their youth by eating the apples of IDUN, but they were doomed, like mortals, to eventual extinction. The gods were opposed by the giants and demons, representing the destructive and irrational forces of the universe. It was prophesied that at RAGNAROK, the doom of the gods, the forces of evil and darkness led by LOKI and his brood of monsters, would attack the gods of Asgard. After a ferocious battle, in which most of the gods and giants would be destroyed, the universe would end in a blaze of fire. However, it was also prophesied that from the ashes of the old world a new cosmos would emerge and a new generation of gods and men would dwell in harmony. In early Nordic belief, from the mixture of the glacial waters of Niflheim (the land of ice and mist) and the warm winds of Muspellsheim (the land of fire), came forth the first two creatures—the giant Ymir, who fathered a race of giants, and the cow Audhumla, who created the first god, Buri. Buri's son, Borr, fathered the gods Odin, Vili, and Ve, who together destroyed Ymir and from his body fashioned the heavens and the earth. From two trees the gods created the first man and woman—Ashr (Ask) and Embla. The universe was supported by the great ash tree YGGDRASILL, whose roots and branches extended into the heavens, the earth, and the underworld. Near one of the roots of the tree flowed the fountain of MIMIR, in whose sacred waters all the wisdom of the universe flowed. Near another root dwelled the Norns, who represented fate. (The concept of fate was one of the most important beliefs of Germanic religion; everything, even the gods, was subject to it.) In the tree's branches perched a sacred bird, who, with the god Heimdall, warned the gods when an attack from the giants was imminent. The temples of the gods were attended by priests who were responsible essentially for the reading of omens and other types of divination, for administering the propitiation of the gods, and for guarding the sacred groves and objects. Their duties were frequently performed by the political leader of a particular tribe. Festivals and religious ceremonies were held throughout the year, usually for celebration of the harvest or of victory in battle. At festivals, animal (or sometimes human) sacrifices and libations were offered to the gods, and the dead were commemorated. In Germanic religion the dead were believed to retain their faculties and to affect the fate of the living. Burial places were sacred, and sacrifices were made at them. Conversion of the Germans to Christianity began as early as the 4th cent. A.D., but it took many centuries for the new religion to spread throughout the northern lands of Europe. In Nazi Germany the spirit of the old religion and the heroic attributes of the Germanic gods were revived as part of the propaganda program of the Nazi party. See P. D. Chantepie de la Saussaye, *The Religion of the Teutons* (1902); P. A. Munch and Olsen Magnus, *Norse Mythology* (1926, repr. 1970); J. A. MacCulloch, *The Celtic and Scandinavian Religions* (1948).

Germanicus, A.D. 41?–A.D. 55: see BRITANNICUS.

Germanicus Caesar (jərmăn'ĭkəs), 15 B.C.–A.D. 19, Roman general, son of Drusus Senior. He was adopted (A.D. 4) by his uncle Emperor TIBERIUS. Germanicus fought (A.D. 8) in Pannonia and Dalmatia and in A.D. 14, when he was commander in Germany, put down the mutiny of the Roman legions after the death of Augustus. He took advantage (A.D. 15) of an opportunity to attack ARMINIUS, and though not at first successful he eventually defeated the German leader. In A.D. 16 he attacked and defeated the Germans at the Weser River. Tiberius recalled Germanicus and sent him to the East, where he reduced (A.D. 18) Cappadocia and Commagene to the status of provinces. After a visit to Egypt, Germanicus died suddenly, supposedly of poison at the hand of Cneius Calpurnius Piso, governor of Syria. Germanicus was the brother of the Emperor Claudius I, and the father of the Emperor Caligula and Agrippina II by his wife Agrippina I.

germanium (jərmā'nēəm) [from *Germany*], semimetallic chemical element; symbol Ge; at. no. 32; at. wt. 72.59; m.p. 937.4°C; b.p. 2830°C; sp. gr. 5.323 at 25°C; valence +2 or +4. Pure germanium is a lustrous, gray-white, brittle metalloid with a diamond-like crystalline structure. It is similar in chemical and physical properties to silicon, below which it appears in group IVa of the PERIODIC TABLE. Germanium is very important as a semiconductor. Transistors and integrated circuits provide the greatest use of the element; they are often made from germanium to which small amounts of arsenic, gallium, or other metals have been added. Numerous alloys containing germanium have been prepared. Germanium forms many compounds. Germanium oxide is added to glass to increase the index of refraction; such glass is used in wide-angle lenses. Since the oxide is transparent to infrared radiation, it has found use in optical instruments. Germanium tetrachloride is a liquid that boils at 84°C; it is an intermediate in the production of pure germanium. Other halides are known. Germane (germanium tetrahydride) is a gas that decomposes at about 300°C to hydrogen and germanium; it is sometimes used in the production of semiconductor devices. A sulfide and numerous organo-germanium compounds are known. Germanium occurs in a few minerals, e.g., argyrodite (with silver and sulfur), zinc blende (with zinc and sulfur), and tantalite (with iron, manganese, and columbium). The chief ore of germanium is germanite, which contains copper, sulfur, about 7% germanium, and 20 other elements. Germanium is produced as a by-product of the refining of other metals; there is considerable recovery from flue dusts and from ashes of certain coals with high germanium content. The element was called ekasilicon by D. I. MENDELEEV, who predicted its properties with striking accuracy from its position in his periodic table. It was first isolated from argyrodite in 1886 by Clemens Winkler, a German chemist, who gave it the name *germanium*.

German language, member of the West Germanic group of the Germanic subfamily of the Indo-European family of languages (see GERMANIC LANGUAGES). It is the official language of the Federal Republic of Germany, the German Democratic Republic, and Austria, and is one of the official languages of Switzerland. Altogether close to 100 million people speak German as their first language, among them 75 million in East and West Germany; 7 million in Austria; 4 million in Switzerland; 4,500,000 in the United States; 500,000 in Canada; about 2 million in Latin America; and several additional millions in such European countries as Czechoslovakia, France, Hungary, Poland, Rumania, Yugoslavia, and the Soviet Union. German is also important as a cultural and commercial second language for millions of people in Central, Northern, and Eastern Europe and in North and South America. There are two principal divisions of the German language: High German, or *Hochdeutsch*, and Low German, or *Plattdeutsch*. One of the most striking differences between them is the result of a consonant shift (usually referred to as the second, or High German, sound shift) that took place before the 8th cent. A.D. in certain West Germanic dialects. This sound shift affected the southern areas, which are more elevated and hence referred to as the High German region, whereas it left untouched the Low German prevalent in the lowland regions of the North. In a broader and purely linguistic sense, the term *Low German* can also be extended to cover all the West Germanic languages in which the second sound shift did not take place, such as Dutch, Flemish, Frisian, and English. Historically, German falls into three main periods: Old German (A.D. c.750–c.1050); Middle German (c.1050–c.1500); and Modern German (c.1500 to the present). The earliest existing records in German date back to about A.D. 750. In this first period, local dialects were used in writing, and there was no standard language. In the middle period a relatively uniform written language developed in government after the various chancelleries of the Holy Roman Empire began, in the 14th cent., to use a combination of certain dialects of Middle High German in place of the Latin that until then had dominated official writings. The German of the chancellery of Saxony was adapted by Martin LUTHER for his translation of the Bible. He chose it because at that time the language of the chancelleries alone stood out in a multitude of dialects as a norm, and Luther thought he could reach many more people through it. The modern period is usually said to begin with the German used by Luther, which became the basis of Modern High German, or modern standard German. The spread of a uniform written German was also helped by printers, who, like Luther, wanted to attract as many people as possible. During the 18th cent. a number of outstanding writers gave modern standard German essentially the form it has today. It is now the language of church and state, education and literature. A corresponding norm for spoken High German, influenced by the written standard, is used in education, the theater, and broadcasting. Dialectal differences exist within both the High German and Low German regions, but a trend toward uniformity in the direction of the written standard is expected partly as a result of widespread broadcasting, diminishing isolation, and increased socioeconomic mobility. Besides differences in word order, the German language is unlike English in that German makes extensive use of inflectional endings. The verb is inflected to show person, number, tense, and mood; and the subjunctive is frequently used. The declensional scheme has four cases: nominative, genitive, dative, and accusative. There are two ways of declining the adjective, and there are three grammatical genders: masculine, feminine, and neuter. A distinctive feature of German is its extensive use of lengthy compound words. For example, the English "history of antiquity" is translated into German as *Altertumswissenschaft*; the English "worthy of distinction" is translated as *auszeichnungswürdig*. The Gothic or Black Letter form (in German called Fraktur) of the Roman alphabet, which first appeared in Europe around the 12th cent., is now rarely used, although knowledge of Fraktur is needed in order to read many works printed before 1945. The Roman alphabet is now exclusively used in printing. To it have been added the symbol *ß*, representing a voiceless *s* (as in English *mouse*), and the umlauted vowels *ä*, *ö*, and *ü*. German is the only language in which all nouns are capitalized, common as well as proper. There is a closer relationship between German spelling and pronunciation than there is in English. See R. E. Keller, *German Dialects* (1961); Robert Priebsch and W. E. Collinson, *The German Language* (6th ed. 1966); J. T. Waterman, *A History of the German Language* (1966); J. Allen Pfeffer, *Basic Spoken German Grammar* (1974),

German literature, works in the German language by German, Austrian, and Swiss authors, as well as those by ethnic German writers in other countries. Heroic legends, among them the *Lay of Hildebrand*, date from the turn of the 8th cent. to the 9th cent. and are the earliest known works in Old High German (see GERMAN LANGUAGE). The *Waltherius* (10th cent.) is written in Latin. Low German and Saxon dialects are also used in these epics. Writings of the 9th to the 11th cent., largely inspired by the church, include the works of the monks Rabanus Maurus Magnentius, Otfried, and Notker Labeo. The succeeding period of Middle High German (12th–14th cent.) is characterized by chivalric poetry, such as the songs and lyrics of the MINNESINGERS on COURTLY LOVE and other subjects. Courtly epics, such as Gottfried von Strassburg's *Tristan* and Wolfram von Eschenbach's *Parzival* (see PARSIFAL), were often based on French troubadour and trouvère sources (see TROUBADOURS; TROUVÈRES), while epics like the *Nibelungenlied* (see under NIBELUNGEN) and GUDRUN use Germanic traditions. A gradual decline of chivalric poetry is evident in the works of Ulrich von Lichtenstein, and the rise of the middle classes is seen in such epics as Wernher der Gartenaere's *Meier Helmbrecht* (c.1250). After 1400 the citizenry took the lead in literature, and popular folk songs, fables, folktales, and short stage plays were written. The aristocratic heritage of the minnesingers was replaced by MEISTERSINGERS, notably Hans Sachs. The Reformation profoundly influenced the course of German literature, and Martin Luther's translation (1522–34) of the Bible propagated a unified High German language. Religious and scholarly writings were also affected by HUMANISM; German humanists included Ulrich von Hutten and Conradus Celtes. The Thirty Years War (1618–48) brought religious schism, widespread devastation, and, concomitantly, a consolidation of national consciousness resulting in a flowering of German literature with strong courtly and absolutistic tendencies. Literary academies, arising in Hamburg, Nuremberg, and other cities, worked for the purification and development of the German language. Most influential was the Silesian school, which included Martin Opitz, noted for his metrical reforms, and the poets Hofmann von Hofmannswaldau (1618–79), Paul Fleming (1609–40), Andreas Gryphius, and Daniel Casper von Lohenstein (1635–83). Leading writers of hymns were the Protestant Paul Gerhardt and the Catholic Angelus Silesius. Hans Jakob von Grimmelshausen's *Simplicissimus* (1669), based on war experience, may be considered the first German novel. The great age of German literature began in the 18th cent. The classicist theories of Johann Christoph Gottsched aroused violent critical reactions, indirectly paving the way for Friedrich Klopstock and especially for Gotthold Lessing, the greatest preclassical critic and dramatist. The period known as STURM UND DRANG embraced the works of Johann Hamann, Johann Gottfried von Herder, and Jakob Lenz, as well as the early works of Goethe and Schiller. The subsequent classical period, when all artistic forms were characterized by restraint, lucidity, and balance, produced Goethe and Schiller, widely considered the greatest figures in German literature (see CLASSICISM). During the classical period the idea of the aesthetic education of the populace was spread by C. M. Wieland, Goethe, Schiller, and Friedrich Hölderlin. At the beginning of the 19th cent., literary ROMANTICISM, initiated in Germany by the brothers Friedrich and H. W. von Schlegel and by Novalis, brought greater emphasis on subjective emotion. A new literary form appeared in the *novelle*, a prose tale often dealing with supernatural elements. Typical early Romantic poets were Ludwig Tieck, Clemens Brentano, and Achim von Arnim, who were also collectors and editors of folktales and folk songs. Freiherr von Eichendorff, Adelbert von Chamisso, and Ludwig Uhland were also notable Romantic poets. The historical tendencies of romanticism were supplemented by the philological and folkloristic researches of the brothers Grimm. The prose writer E. T. A. Hoffmann held a special position as social critic in the Romantic movement. Notable dramatists were Heinrich von Kleist, Franz Grillparzer, and C. F. Hebbel. The revolutionary literary movement known as Young Germany, which strove to arouse German political opinion, turned from romanticism to the more sober REALISM. Its great leaders were Karl Börne and Heinrich Heine. Realism was consolidated in the social novels of Gustav Freytag, Friedrich Spielhagen, Otto Ludwig, and Theodor Fontane, whereas Eduard Mörike and Adalbert Stifter adhered to an epigonic classicism. The theory of realism was further developed by the school of NATURALISM, represented by Arno Holz, Hermann Sudermann, and the young Gerhart Hauptmann. Antinaturalistic movements grew stronger in the German imperialistic period. They became evident as symbolism and impressionism in poetry (Stefan George, Rainer Maria Rilke, Hugo von Hofmannsthal) and in the novel (Thomas Mann, Alfred Döblin, Hermann Hesse, Franz Kafka, Robert Musil, Hermann Broch) and as EXPRESSIONISM in verse (Georg Trakl, Georg Heym, Gottfried Benn, J. R. Becher) and drama (Frank Wedekind, Carl Sternheim, Georg Kaiser, Bertolt Brecht). The literature of the Weimar Republic carried forward prewar traditions and excelled in formal experimentation and innovation. This activity was stifled by the rise of National Socialism, which forced leading writers like Heinrich and Thomas Mann and Arnold Zweig into emigration. Although the years after 1945 saw a gradual literary resurgence, it was not until the 1950s that the social and critical novels of authors like Heinrich Böll, Günter Grass, and Max Frisch brought German literature up to the level of the 1920s. In the 1960s formalistic tendencies abounded among the younger writers of Western Germany, whereas social realism (Anna Seghers) became the dominant style in East Germany. For further information see articles on individual authors mentioned in this entry, e.g., Franz KAFKA, except those with life dates. See general histories of German literature by E. A. Rose (1960), August Closs, ed. (4 vol., 1967–70), J. M. Ritchie, ed. (3 vol., 1967–70), Wilhelm Scherer (2 vol., tr. 1906, repr. 1970), Kuno Francke (1931, repr. 1970), Calvin Thomas (1909, repr. 1970), and J. G. Robertson (6th ed. 1971); W. T. H. Jackson, *The Literature of the Middle Ages* (1960); W. H. Bruford, *Germany in the 18th Century* (2d ed. 1965); H. T. Moore, *Twentieth-Century German Literature* (1967); A. K. Domandi, ed., *Modern German Literature* (2 vol., 1972).

German measles: see RUBELLA.

German Reformed Church: see EVANGELICAL AND REFORMED CHURCH.

Germans, great ethnic complex of ancient Europe, a basic stock in the composition of the modern peoples of Sweden, Norway, Denmark, Iceland, Germany, Austria, Switzerland, N Italy, the Netherlands, Belgium, Luxembourg, N and central France, Lowland Scotland, and England. From archaeology it is clear that the Germans retained little ethnic solidarity; by the 7th cent. B.C. they had begun a division into many peoples. They did not call themselves Germans; the origin of the name is uncertain. Their rise to significance (4th cent. B.C.) in the history of Europe began roughly with the general breakup of Celtic culture in central Europe. Before their expansion, the Germans inhabited N Germany, S Sweden and Denmark, and the shores of the Baltic. From these areas they spread out in great migrations southward, southeastward, and westward. Although the earliest mention of the Germans is by a Greek navigator who saw them in Norway and Jutland in the 4th cent. B.C., their real appearance in history began with their contact (1st cent. B.C.) with the

Romans. The chief historical sources for the culture and distribution of the Germans are Tacitus' *Germania* and *Agricola* and the remnants in later ages of early Germanic institutions. Apart from describing their barbarity and warlikeness, Caesar's *Commentaries* tell little. As the centuries passed, the Germans became increasingly troublesome to the Roman Empire. The VANDALS in the west and the OSTROGOTHS in the east were the first to attack the empire seriously. The Ostrogoths were a part of the Gothic people, often called the East Germanic, whose language (Gothic) was the first written Germanic language. The Goths apparently moved SE from the Vistula River to the Balkans, thence W across Europe. The chief German tribes included the ALEMANNI, the Angles (see ANGLO-SAXONS), the Burgundii (see BURGUNDY), the LOMBARDS, the SAXONS, and the VISIGOTHS. The many Scandinavians included the Icelanders, who produced the first Germanic literature (see OLD NORSE LITERATURE). Many other Germanic tribes appeared in various ancient periods. The Chamavi were in the 1st cent. N of the Rhine and SE of the Zuider Zee; by the 4th cent. they had moved southward and joined with the Frankish people. The Cimbri appeared in Transalpine Gaul late in the 2d cent. B.C. and fought Roman armies; c.103 B.C. they migrated to Italy with some Helvetii and Teutons and were crushed by MARIUS in 101 B.C. The Eruli, or Heruli, possibly stemming from Jutland, inhabited the shores of the Sea of Azov, E of the Don, in the 3d cent. A.D. They fought with the Goths against the Huns, joined ODOACER in his attack on the Roman emperor, and settled in N Lower Austria. In the 6th cent. their kingdom was destroyed by Lombards, and they disappeared as a group. The Gepidae, a Gothic people, moved southward from the Baltic at Vistula into the Hungarian plain W of the Danube. Overwhelmed by ATTILA, they survived only to be defeated in 489 by Theodoric the Great and in 566 by the Lombards and Avars. They disappeared soon after. The Marcomanni, probably originally part of the Suebi, lived N of the Danube in Germany in the 1st and 2d cent. A threat to the Roman border, they were defeated by Marcus Aurelius in the Marcomannic War (166–180). They moved into the country of the Celtic Boii and probably expanded into Bavaria, where they seem to be the Baiuoarii, or Boiarii, ancestors of the Bavarians. The Suebi, or Suevi, mentioned by Tacitus as a central German people, gave their name to SWABIA. They probably included a number of smaller tribes, of whom the Alemanni and the Marcomanni were two. Others were the Semoni, the Hermunduri, and the Quadi. The Suebi lived near the Elbe c.650 B.C.; thence they spread S into Germany. By 100 B.C. they no longer constituted a political unit, although Tacitus maintained that they retained cultural and religious unity. The Teutons, who were allied with the Cimbri in 103 B.C., were crushed (102 B.C.) by Marius at Aquae Sextiae (present-day Aix-en-Provence). By an extension of the name of that tribe the Germanic peoples are sometimes called Teutonic. See GERMANIC LAWS; GERMANIC RELIGION; GERMANY. See Francis Owen, *The Germanic People* (1960); Adolph Schalk, *The Germans* (1971).

German shepherd, breed of large, muscular WORKING DOG perfected in Germany at the turn of the 20th cent. It stands about 25 in. (64 cm) high at the shoulder and weighs from 60 to 85 lb (27.2–38.5 kg). Its double coat is composed of dense, woolly underhair and a medium-length, harsh, straight or slightly wavy outercoat. Although it may be any color except white, it is usually black and tan, black, or gray. Developed over centuries from sheepherding and farm-dog stock, the German shepherd has been trained in a variety of specialities other than herding, e.g., as a police dog, as a carrier of messages and a patrol dog in war, and as a leader of the blind. It is also very popular as a pet. See DOG.

German shorthaired pointer, breed of large SPORTING DOG developed in Germany in the mid-19th cent. It stands about 23 in. (58 cm) high at the shoulder and weighs about 60 lb (27 kg). Its dense coat of short hair is hard to the touch and is colored solid liver or liver spotted or ticked with white. Intended as a utility dog, the original stock was crossed with several breeds, such as the bloodhound and the English pointer, in order to insure this versatility. Thus, the German shorthaired pointer has been used to hunt both waterfowl and upland game birds, as a retriever on land and water, and to trail such small animals as rabbits and opossums. See DOG.

German silver, name for various alloys of copper, zinc, and nickel, sometimes also containing lead and tin. These alloys were named for their silver-white color, although use of the term *silver* is now prohibited for alloys not containing that metal. The composition of German silver varies, the percentage of the three elements ranging approximately as follows: copper, from 50% to 61.6%; zinc, from 19% to 17.2%; nickel, from 30% to 21.1%. The proportions are always specified in commercial alloys. German silver is extensively used because of its hardness, toughness, and resistance to corrosion for articles such as tableware (commonly silver plated), tea and coffee pots, jugs, marine fittings, and plumbing fixtures. Because of its high electrical resistance it is used also in heating coils. It was discovered (early 19th cent.) by a German industrial chemist, E. A. Geitner.

German South-West Africa: see SOUTH WEST AFRICA.

Germantown, residential section of Philadelphia, Pa., on Wissahickon Creek. Settled by Dutch and Germans in 1683, Germantown became one of the earliest printing and publishing centers in the country. When the British occupied Philadelphia during the American Revolution, the greater part of their army encamped at Germantown. George Washington's forces unsuccessfully attacked the camp on Oct. 4, 1777, in the last important engagement conducted by Washington before he took the army to Valley Forge for the winter. In 1854, Germantown was annexed to Philadelphia. The Howe House and several other colonial houses, inns, and churches are still standing. Germantown Ave. is a National Historic Landmark.

Germanus of Auxerre, Saint (jərmā'nəs, ōsĕr'), d. 448, Gaulish churchman, bishop of Auxerre (after c.418). St. Patrick was under his tutelage for 12 years. Popes Celestine I and Leo I sent him to England (429, 447) to combat Pelagianism; on the first occasion he was accompanied by the deacon Palladius, first recorded missionary to Ireland. On his second trip, Germanus led the Britons in the defeat, located by tradition near Mold, Wales, of an Irish and Pictish marauding party. As it was Easter, the war cry was Alleluia, and the battle is called the Alleluia Victory. Germanus was popular in Celtic Britain. Feast: July 31.

German Volga Republic, former autonomous state, c.18,000 sq mi (46,600 sq km), central European USSR, along the lower Volga. Its largely German population was descended from the German colonists whom Catherine II had invited to settle there in 1762. The autonomous republic was formed in 1924. As a result of the German invasion of the USSR, the republic was dissolved (1941), and the entire German population (about 440,000) was deported to Siberia.

German wirehaired pointer, breed of large SPORTING DOG developed in Germany in the mid-19th cent. It stands about 24 in. (61 cm) high at the shoulder and weighs about 60 lb (27 kg). Its harsh, wiry outercoat is flat-lying and approximately 1.5 in. (3.8 cm) long. The woolly undercoat is very dense in winter but thins out in the warmer months. Its color is usually liver and white or liver with white spotting or ticking, while the head and ears are brown. The tail is docked. The German wirehaired pointer is bred as an all-purpose retrieving pointer; its tough double coat allows it to hunt in the roughest underbrush and to withstand the iciest water. See DOG.

Germany, country of central Europe, divided since 1949 into the Federal Republic of Germany, or West Germany, Ger. *Bundesrepublik Deutschland* (bŏŏn'-dəsrāpōōblēk' doich'länt), and the German Democratic Republic, or East Germany, Ger. *Deutsche Demokratische Republik* (doich'ə dāmōkrät'ĭshə rā''pōōblēk'). Germany as a whole can be divided into three major geographic regions: the N German plain, the central German uplands, and, in the south, the ranges of the Central Alps and other uplands. West Germany includes parts of all three regions; East Germany is made up largely of the N German plain but includes a small part of the central German uplands.

Germany to 1871. Various aspects of the early, medieval, and early modern history of Germany are covered in the articles GERMANS; GERMANIC LAWS; GERMANIC RELIGION; HOLY ROMAN EMPIRE; AUSTRIA; and in the articles on the major historic German states (PRUSSIA, BAVARIA, SAXONY, WÜRTTEMBERG, BADEN, THURINGIA, HESSE, MECKLENBURG, OLDENBURG, BRUNSWICK, ANHALT, LIPPE, SCHAUMBURG-LIPPE) and on the free cities of HAMBURG, BREMEN, and LÜBECK. The survey that follows is a very general outline of the complex history of Germany. At the end of the 2d cent. B.C., the German tribes began to expand at the expense of the Celts to the west and south, but they were confined by Roman conquests (1st cent. B.C.–1st cent. A.D.) to the region E of the Rhine and N of the Danube. The Romans penetrated briefly (12 B.C.–A.D. 9) as far east as the Elbe River (see TEUTOBURG FOREST), and from the late 1st cent. A.D. to the 3d cent. they held the *Agri Decumates*, protected against Germanic inroads by a fortified line from Cologne to Regensburg. In a series of great migrations (4th–5th cent.) the German tribes (who did not all come from present-day Germany) overran most of the Roman Empire, while Slavic tribes occupied Germany E of the Elbe. By the 6th cent., the ANGLO-SAXONS had established themselves in Britain, and the FRANKS had taken over nearly all of present-day France, W and S Germany, and Thuringia. CLOVIS I, who first united the Franks late in the 5th cent., accepted Christianity, and St. BONIFACE in the 8th cent. spread the gospel in the areas acquired by Clovis's successors. In 751, Pepin the Short deposed the dynasty of the MEROVINGIANS and established his own, that of the CAROLINGIANS. His son CHARLEMAGNE conquered the SAXONS and extended the Frankish domain in Germany to the Elbe. He was crowned emperor at Rome in 800. In the first division (843) of Charlemagne's empire (see VERDUN, TREATY OF) the kingdom of the Eastern Franks, under LOUIS THE GERMAN, emerged as the nucleus of the German state. The Treaty of MERSEN (870) enlarged it by the addition of part of LOTHARINGIA (Lorraine), but after the death (876) of Louis it was divided among his sons CARLOMAN, LOUIS THE YOUNGER, and CHARLES III (Charles the Fat). Emperor ARNULF reunited the kingdom, but during his reign (887–99) and that of his son LOUIS THE CHILD (900–911), last of the Carolingian kings of Germany, the Norsemen, Slavs, and Magyars began to make devastating inroads. These contributed to economic breakdown and localization, manifest in the MANORIAL SYSTEM. Political localization was evident in the emergence of powerful duchies and in the growth of FEUDALISM. The dukes of Franconia, Swabia, Bavaria, Saxony, and Upper and Lower Lorraine emerged as the most powerful magnates of Germany. On the death (911) of Louis the Child, they elected the Franconian duke CONRAD I as king. Conrad's reign was spent in struggles against the Magyars and against the rebellious dukes, one of whom (Henry the Fowler of Saxony) succeeded him in 918 as HENRY I, beginning a century of Saxon rule. Henry restored some of the royal authority, took territory from the Slavs, and secured the election in 936 of his son, OTTO I, as his successor. The Holy Roman Empire came into existence with the imperial coronation (962) of Otto I. (A list of Otto's successors until 1806 is appended to the article on the HOLY ROMAN EMPIRE). As a result of their difficult dual role as emperors and German kings, and especially because of their interests in Italy, Otto's successors could not prevent the German dukes and their vassals from increasing their power at the expense of the central authority. Imperial power was further undermined by the conflict between emperors and popes, manifest in the struggle over INVESTITURE. Emperor FREDERICK I (reigned 1152–90; also known as Frederick Barbarossa) of the HOHENSTAUFEN line was one of the most energetic medieval German rulers. He unsuccessfully challenged the power of the pope (see GUELPHS AND GHIBELLINES), being defeated by the LOMBARD LEAGUE in 1176. However, Frederick did succeed in partitioning (1180) the domains of HENRY THE LION of Saxony and Bavaria, thus destroying the last great independent German duchy. Until the dissolution of the Holy Roman Empire in 1806, Germany remained a patchwork of numerous small temporal and ecclesiastical principalities and free cities. The campaigns of the 12th and 13th cent. against the Slavs (see WENDS) resulted in tremendous eastward expansion and the establishment of the margraviate of BRANDENBURG and the domain of the TEUTONIC KNIGHTS. The turbulent reign (1212–50) of Emperor FREDERICK II, who was active in Sicily, and who engaged in a major conflict with the papacy, left Germany in a state of anarchy. Several rival kings appeared, but none held wide authority, and lawlessness prevailed. The dark period of the Great Interregnum (1254–73) ended with the election of RUDOLF I, count of Hapsburg (see HAPSBURG), as German king, but neither he nor his successors could create a centralized monarchy. Germany thus diverged from the great kingdoms of Western Europe—France, England, and Spain—where the trend was toward increasing centralization. To offset the tendency toward independence of the nobles, the emperors relied chiefly on the prosperous cities, many of which formed into leagues for their common defense and interests—e.g., the HANSEATIC LEAGUE and the SWABIAN LEAGUE. German commerce and banking prospered in the late 15th and early 16th cent., the heyday of such merchant princes as those of the FUGGER and WELSER families of Augsburg. With the help of these capitalists, Emperor CHARLES V (reigned 1519–58) financed his many campaigns. The weakness of the imperial position was evident when, in the Protestant REFORMATION (16th cent.), the Catholic emperor was unable to enforce his religious policies or to prevent the conversion to Protestantism of many powerful princes. Links between religious and economic unrest were reflected in the PEASANTS' WAR (1524–26) and in the unsuccessful attempt of the Imperial Knights under Franz von SICKINGEN to secularize ecclesiastical domains. Continued unrest and Protestant gains helped stimulate the Catholic Reformation, which hardened the religious and political divisions in Germany. A religious settlement was reached only after the devastating THIRTY YEARS WAR (1618–48), which was a crushing setback to the cause of German unity. The chief theater of the war, Germany was reduced to misery and starvation, lost a large part of its population, and became, as a result of the Peace of Westphalia (1648; see WESTPHALIA, PEACE OF), a loose confederation of petty principalities under the nominal suzerainty of the emperor. Depopulation brought increased competition for peasant labor and helped to perpetuate the institution of serfdom, which was declining in other parts of Western Europe. The most powerful German state to emerge from the wars of the 17th and 18th cent. was PRUSSIA, which under FREDERICK II (reigned 1740–86) successfully challenged the military might of AUSTRIA and became a European power. The French Revolution and the wars of NAPOLEON I brought the demise (1806) of the moribund Holy Roman Empire and also forced the German states, notably Prussia, to accept long-needed social, political, and administrative reforms. Germany's military humiliation by Napoleon stimulated nationalist fervor for a strong and unified state. By the Congress of Vienna (see VIENNA, CONGRESS OF) the German map was redrawn in 1814–15, eliminating many petty states and expanding Prussia and Bavaria. The German states were loosely linked in the GERMAN CONFEDERATION, set up by the congress. Conservative Austria obtained control of the confederation, and METTERNICH, who also dominated the HOLY ALLIANCE, frustrated nationalist ambitions. In ensuing decades, nationalist sentiment was furthered by German romanticism, a noteworthy exponent of which was the poet Ernst Moritz ARNDT, and by persons like Friedrich JAHN, the educator and gymnast. German nationalism, linked with liberalism, emerged in the REVOLUTIONS OF 1848, which shook the German states. However, the revolutionists were soon defeated, and the FRANKFURT PARLIAMENT, having failed to obtain the unification of Germany under Frederick William IV, disbanded. Prussia was humiliated by Austria in the Treaty of OLOMOUC (1850) but used the ZOLLVEREIN, a customs union from which Austria was excluded, to consolidate Prussian hegemony in N Germany. Otto von BISMARCK, who in 1862 took charge of Prussian policy, resolved on the course of creating a "Little Germany" (a Germany without Austria) under Prussian leadership. In the AUSTRO-PRUSSIAN WAR of 1866, Prussia triumphed over its rival, and Austria was excluded from the newly created NORTH GERMAN CONFEDERATION. As a result of the FRANCO-PRUSSIAN WAR of 1870–71 Bismarck attained his goal: WILLIAM I of Prussia was proclaimed German emperor by the assembled German princes in the Palace of Versailles (1871). The peace treaty with France awarded ALSACE and LORRAINE to Germany and stamped it as the chief power of continental Europe.

The German Empire and the Weimar Republic. The new German empire continued under the rule of Bismarck's autocratic rule and a constitution that favored conservative interests. The Reichstag (the lower house of parliament) had some power over money bills but only slight influence in military matters or foreign policy; autocratic Prussia dominated the Bundesrat (the upper house of parliament). Bismarck's rule was complicated by far-reaching internal changes. The INDUSTRIAL REVOLUTION, which came late in Germany, transformed the country into Europe's foremost manufacturing nation and also accelerated the pace of urbanization. Economic factors in turn affected politics. The National Liberal party and the Progressives, both representing the middle class, became important, as did German SOCIALISM and the Social Democrats, guided by August BEBEL and Karl KAUTSKY. The strong Center party represented Roman Catholic interests. Bismarck's only certain ally was the Conservative party, a Protestant faction particularly strong in agrarian and semifeudal Prussia. Bismarck ruled chiefly through force of will, prestige, and the steadfast support of the emperor. He attempted to vitiate German Catholicism in the KULTURKAMPF (1872–79). Both paternalism and an effort to lessen the appeal of the Socialists and the Liberals motivated his SOCIAL SECURITY laws, which became models of welfare legislation throughout the world. A master of foreign policy, Bismarck secured Germany against France by maintaining alliances in the east. Reconciliation with Austria led to an alliance (1879), joined in 1882 by Italy (see TRIPLE ALLIANCE AND TRIPLE ENTENTE). Simultaneously, Bismarck kept alive the THREE EMPERORS' LEAGUE of Germany, Austria-Hungary, and Russia. He weathered the Liberal opposition and retained his chancellorship during the brief reign (1888) of FREDERICK III, but he was dismissed in 1890 by WILLIAM II. Bismarck was succeeded as chancellor by von CAPRIVI, HOHENLOHE-SCHILLINGSFÜRST (1894), and Bernhard von BÜLOW (1900). By the mid-1880s, Germans had acquired some African territories, but it was only under William II that German colonial expansion began to collide seriously with British and French interests. (For a list of former German colonies, see MANDATES.) Equally serious threats to peace were Germany's increasing commercial rivalry with England, heightened by the naval expansion under TIRPITZ, German influence in Ottoman affairs (e.g., in the construction of the BAGHDAD RAILWAY), and German support of Austria's Balkan policy, which clashed with Russian interests (see EASTERN QUESTION). Two crises (1905–6 and 1911) over MOROCCO helped to create and strengthen the Triple Entente of France, Russia, and England, which faced Germany and its allies (see CENTRAL POWERS) in WORLD WAR I (1914–18). In 1909, von BETHMANN-HOLLWEG had replaced von Bülow as chancellor of Germany; Bethmann was overthrown (1917) by Field Marshal Paul von HINDENBURG and Chief of Staff Erich LUDENDORFF, who together controlled Germany until late 1918. Exhausted to the point of collapse but with no enemy troops on its soil, Germany was obliged to accept the Allied armistice terms (Nov., 1918) and, in 1919, the harsh peace terms of Versailles (see VERSAILLES, TREATY OF). William abdicated and fled (Nov., 1918) after national and international demands for his abdication (led by Chancellor MAXIMILIAN, prince of Baden) and after the outbreak of a left-wing revolution, started at Kiel, which swept the rulers of the German states from their thrones. A democratic and more centralized federal constitution was adopted at Weimar in 1919, and Germany became known as the Weimar Republic. Friedrich EBERT, a Social Democrat, became the first president. His middle-of-the-road government suppressed attempts by the radical left (see SPARTACUS PARTY) and by the extreme right (see KAPP, WOLFGANG) to seize power. However, the economic crisis of the postwar years, marked by mass unemployment and rampant currency inflation, strengthened the extremist parties and wiped out a large portion of the middle class. The assassinations of Matthias ERZBERGER (1921) and of Walther RATHENAU (1922) were symptomatic of the terrorist tactics adopted by the extreme nationalists, many of whom later joined the National Socialist (Nazi) party of Adolf HITLER or the Nationalist (monarchist) party of Alfred HUGENBERG. The election (1925) of Hindenburg as president after the death of Ebert seemed a nationalist victory, but Hindenburg cooperated with the cabinets (1923–32) of Wilhelm MARX, Hans LUTHER, Hermann Müller, and Heinrich BRÜNING, in which coalitions drawn mainly from the Social Democrats, the Catholic Center party, and the conservative German People's party fulfilled moderate programs. Under Luther, Hjalmar SCHACHT helped stabilize the currency, and a remarkable return to economic prosperity began. Gustav STRESEMANN, as foreign minister from 1923 to 1929, secured an easing of the terms of the Treaty of Versailles, particularly with regard to German REPARATIONS payments, and the admission (1926) of Germany into the League of Nations. Germany had apparently recovered economically and politically by 1929, but soon afterward the world economic depression brought about mass unemployment and business failure, and political and social tensions mounted. As the Nazi and Communist parties gained strength in the Reichstag, Brüning and his successors, Franz von PAPEN and Kurt von SCHLEICHER, failed in their efforts to mold parliamentary majorities without Hitler's support. Government came to a standstill. Rather than accept Schleicher's alternative of a military dictatorship, Hindenburg, old and exhausted, accepted von Papen's assurance that Hitler could be held in check. In Jan., 1933, Hindenburg made Hitler chancellor. In the elections of March, 1933, Hitler played upon the electorate's fear of the Communists (especially after the REICHSTAG building was largely destroyed by fire in Feb., 1933) to win a bare majority of seats in the Reichstag for the National Socialists and the Nationalists. On March 23, the Enabling Act, opposed only by the Social Democrats and the disbarred Communist party, gave Hitler dictatorial powers.

The Third Reich. Hitler had promised to build a Third Reich, successor to the Holy Roman and Hohenzollern empires, which would last a thousand years. As chancellor, he began the "coordination" (*Gleichschaltung*) of every aspect of German life. Young persons were organized in semimilitary groups (the *Hitlerjugend*) and were indoctrinated with the Nazi creed. The powers of the state governments were abolished, and the adherents of NATIONAL SOCIALISM from 1934 made up the sole legal party. Hitler's opponents within the party (including Ernst ROEHM) were eliminated in the "Blood Purge" of June, 1934. The Gestapo (see SECRET POLICE) quashed open discontent among the German people. Many scientists, artists, educators, and scholars followed the Nazi doctrines without much protest, and some Germans welcomed what they considered the rebirth of German strength. After the death of Hindenburg (1934), the offices of president and chancellor were combined in the person of the *Führer* [leader] of the Nazi party. In 1935, the Nuremberg Laws deprived Jews of citizenship, forbade marriage between Jews and non-Jewish Germans, and barred Jews from the liberal professions. In order to coordinate cultural affairs, the radio, press, cinema, and theater came under the control of propaganda minister GOEBBELS, who raised Hitler to the status of a quasi-divinity. Jews and others (especially those holding liberal or leftist political beliefs) made outcasts by the Nazi regime were harassed, and some were placed in CONCENTRATION CAMPS. Labor unions were dissolved, and workers were organized in a state-controlled labor front. Hitler attempted to make Germany economically self-sufficient, and industry, commerce, and foreign trade were strictly supervised by the government. In order to ease unemployment and to prepare for war, Hitler expanded the armaments industry, increased the size of the armed forces, and sponsored large-scale public works (e.g., the construction of a network of superhighways, the *Autobahnen*). Hermann GOERING was a leading protagonist of German rearmament and preparations for war. Albert SPEER was at first Hitler's official architect; during World War II he assumed important posts as minister for armaments and later as chief planner of the war economy. Outside Germany, fifth columns were used to undermine the governments of nations that Hitler sought to annex in order to increase the *Lebensraum* [living space] of the Germans. In Oct., 1933, Hitler withdrew from the Geneva Disarmament Conference and from the League of Nations. In March, 1936, Germany remilitarized the Rhineland in violation of the Treaty of Versailles and the Locarno Pact. Hitler followed this by concluding an alliance with Fascist Italy (see AXIS), by interfering in the Spanish Civil War (1936–39) in support of the Insurgents led by Franco, and by annexing Austria (March, 1938). The MUNICH PACT (Sept., 1938) marked the culmination of British and French attempts to appease Germany in the hope that Hitler had limited aims. However, in March, 1939, Germany marched into Czechoslovakia, thus violating the Munich agreements, and also annexed Memel, on the Baltic coast. On Aug. 23, 1939, in a surprise move, Germany and the USSR signed a nonaggression pact and other agreements. On Sept. 1, 1939, cutting short negotiations on the status of Danzig (Gdańsk) and the POLISH CORRIDOR, Hitler invaded Poland, thus precipitating World War II. In the early years of the war Germany had great success; its conquests included Poland, Denmark, Norway, Belgium, the Netherlands, Luxembourg, France, the Balkan states, and Greece. Great Britain, particularly London and other industrial areas, was subjected to massive German air attacks (the "Battle of Britain"), as a prelude to invasion, but the island successfully withstood the onslaught and was not invaded. In June, 1941, Hitler launched a vast offensive against the USSR, his former ally. In Dec., 1941, shortly after the Japanese attack on Pearl Harbor, the United States declared war on Germany. In 1942, the tide of the war began to turn against Germany; the Allies scored successes in North Africa, the USSR stopped the German army at Stalingrad (now VOLGOGRAD), and British and U.S. airplanes began the massive terror bombing of German cities. As its fortunes waned, Germany treated its remaining conquered territories more harshly. Millions of Jews and many other civilians were sent to concentration camps and exterminated, vast slave-labor systems were organized, and many thousands were deported to Germany for forced labor. By early 1945, Germany was being invaded from the west and the east, and most of its cities lay in ruins. On April 30, 1945, with the total collapse of Germany imminent, Hitler committed suicide.

Postwar Germany. Hitler's successor, Admiral Karl DOENITZ, signed (May 7–8, 1945) an unconditional surrender to the Allies, whose military commanders assumed the functions of government in Germany. The agreements of the YALTA CONFERENCE (Feb., 1945) were implemented at the POTSDAM CONFERENCE (July–Aug., 1945). These agreements were to be tentative, pending a peace conference, but as no peace conference was held, they tended to shape the course of German history after 1945. A line formed mostly by the Oder and Neisse rivers was made the eastern boundary of Germany, as East Prussia and Upper and Lower Silesia were placed under Polish administration (except N East Prussia, which was awarded to the USSR). In the west, the Saarland was occupied by French military forces. What remained of Germany was divided into four zones, occupied separately by the armies of Great Britain, France, the United States, and the USSR. Berlin, similarly divided although situated well within the Soviet zone, was made the seat of the four-power Allied Control Council, authorized to take economic and administrative measures for Germany as a whole. However, the council failed to agree on how to implement the often imprecise Potsdam decisions, and separate governments were soon established in each of the four zones. The National Socialist party and affiliated organizations were outlawed, and many leading Nazis were tried, convicted, and executed for WAR CRIMES; other leaders, including von Papen and Schacht, were acquitted. Some Germans (including the philosopher Karl Jaspers and the historian Friedrich Meinecke) called for moral regeneration, but as Germany became a battleground of the COLD WAR, concern with the guilt for the past receded. During 1945–47 there was a serious shortage of food, caused by the crippled state of the German economy and by poor harvests; this situation was intensified in W Germany by the arrival of about 10 million ethnic German refugees from the Soviet zone and the former German territories of E central Europe. In the Soviet zone, a military administration under ZHUKOV was established in June, 1945. In 1946, politics there were brought under the control of the Communist-dominated Socialist Unity party (SED), led by Wilhelm Pieck, Otto Grotewohl, and Walter ULBRICHT. At the same time, a major program of nationalization and collectivization was carried out. As a kind of reparations, the Soviets took much of E Germany's industrial equipment for use in rebuilding their own industry. The Western Allies rejected a plan by Henry Morgenthau, Jr. (see under MORGENTHAU, HENRY), to center the German economy around agriculture. Industrial machinery was restored to use, restrictions against the German cartels went largely unenforced, and W Germany's remarkable recovery and reindustrialization soon began. By 1947, the Western occupation zones were increasingly coordinating their policies (especially in economics) whereas the Soviet zone followed an increasingly divergent policy. The split between the three Western Allies and the USSR became complete in 1948. After the Western powers had planned steps toward establishing a W German constitution and had instituted a currency reform, the Soviet authorities unsuccessfully blockaded (1948–49) West Berlin as part of the cold war. Since 1949, Germany has been divided for all practical purposes into two states, the Federal Republic of Germany (West Germany) and the German Democratic Republic (East Germany). The precise legal status of West Berlin has remained unclear; however, West Berlin is intimately tied to West Germany in many ways (see BERLIN). **West Germany,** a republic (1970 est. pop. 59,214,400), 95,742 sq mi (247,973 sq km), in central Europe, borders on Austria and Switzerland in the south, on France, Luxembourg, Belgium, and the Netherlands in the west, on the North Sea and Denmark in the north, on the Baltic Sea in the northeast, and on East Germany and Czechoslovakia in the east. BONN is the seat of government. The country is divided into 10 states (*Länder*): SCHLESWIG-HOLSTEIN, HAMBURG, LOWER SAXONY, BREMEN, NORTH RHINE-WESTPHALIA, HESSE, RHINELAND-PALATINATE, BADEN-WÜRTTEMBERG, BAVARIA, and SAARLAND. Virtually all citizens of the country speak German (including several dialects). About 49% of the population are Protestant, and about 45% are Roman Catholic, with the Protestants concentrated in the northern part of the country and the Catholics in the west and south. Despite the dislocation and destruction caused by World War II, West Germany recovered relatively quickly so that by the early 1950s the "economic miracle" of creating anew a great industrial power was well under way. The rebuilding process was facilitated by the MARSHALL PLAN. West Germany in the 1970s was one of the world's leading industrial countries. In the late 1960s, manufacturing contributed about 55% of the annual national product, commerce and transport 18%, services 15%, and agriculture 3%. In the early 1970s, about 2.5 million "guest workers" from other countries (notably Yugoslavia, Turkey, and Italy) were employed in West Germany. N West Germany, drained by the Weser and Elbe rivers, is largely agricultural, despite poor soil; crops include potatoes, sugar beets, oats, and rye. Dairy cattle are widely raised, especially in Schleswig-Holstein. The region also includes the major industrial and transportation centers of KIEL, Hamburg, Bremen, and HANOVER. The Rhine River runs through W West Germany. Along the northern rim of the Rhenish Slate Mts. lies West Germany's chief mining and industrial region, which includes the RUHR and Saar basins and takes in such industrial centers as DÜSSELDORF, DUISBURG, KREFELD, ESSEN, WUPPERTAL, BOCHUM, GELSENKIRCHEN, and DORTMUND. The southern section of the Rhineland, which contains the Eifel and Hunsrück mts., is largely agricultural and has famous vineyards. The southern part of West Germany extends roughly from the Rhine in the west to the Bohemian Forest in the east, and from the Rhine, the Lake of Constance, and the Bavarian Alps in the south to the Central German highlands in the north. The region is drained by the Danube, Iller, Lech, Isar, Inn, Neckar, and Main rivers. Rising to the Zugspitze (9,721 ft/2,963 m) in the Bavarian Alps, the highest point in West Germany, it consists of plateaus and forested mountains, e.g., the Black Forest and the highlands of Swabia. Notable agricultural products of the region are fruit, wheat, barley, and dairy goods. Important industrial centers include MUNICH, FRANKFURT, AUGSBURG, NUREMBERG, STUTTGART, and KARLSRUHE. Overall, the principal West German agricultural products are milk and eggs, potatoes, sugar beets, wheat, barley, rye, and oats. Large numbers of cattle, hogs, and poultry are raised. The chief minerals produced are coal, lignite, potash, petroleum, and iron ore. The leading industrial products include iron and steel, chemicals, motor vehicles, electric and electronic equipment, precision instruments, textiles, refined petroleum, and food products. The country has a dense road and rail network. West Germany carries on a very large foreign trade, and usually the value of its exports exceeds the value of its imports. The main exports are machinery, motor vehicles and other transport equipment, chemicals, and iron and steel; the leading imports are food (including animals for slaughter), machinery, petroleum and petroleum products, chemicals, and metals. The principal trade partners are France, the Netherlands, the United States, Italy, and Austria. West Germany is a leading member of the European Economic Community (Common Market) and other international economic organizations. The country has numerous universities, notably those at Bochum, Bonn, Frankfurt, Freiburg, Göttingen, Hamburg, Heidelberg, Cologne, Konstanz, Mainz, Marburg, Munich, and Münster. The states included in the U.S., British, and French occupation zones adopted a constitution in May, 1949, that established the Federal Republic of Germany. The new republic was similar in structure to the Weimar Republic, except that the individual states had somewhat more power, and the president's powers were much reduced. In the first elections (Aug., 1949), the Christian Democratic party (CDU), along with its close ally, the Bavarian-centered Christian Social Union (CSU), gained a small plurality of seats in the Bundestag (Federal Diet). The CDU leader Konrad ADENAUER formed a coalition government and became the first chancellor of West Germany; he remained in office until 1963. The Social Democratic party (SPD), led successively by Kurt Schumacher, Erich Ollenauer, and Willy BRANDT, was the main opposition party until 1969, when it came to power. The middle-class-oriented Free Democratic party (FDP) was influential, although small, and it participated in coalition governments with both the CDU (1949–53; 1961–66) and the SPD (from 1969). The first president of West Germany was Theodor Heuss; he was succeeded by Heinrich Lübke (1959), Gustav Heinemann (1969), and Walter Scheel (1974). The occupying powers allowed West Germany considerable autonomy from the start, except in foreign affairs. The three resident High Commissioners could review actions taken by the Bonn government, but in practice they rarely intervened. In 1951, West Germany was given the right to conduct its own foreign relations. In 1952, West Germany, the United States, France, and Great Britain signed the Bonn Convention, in effect a peace treaty, which granted West Germany most of the attributes of national sovereignty. The Paris agreements of 1954, which came into force in 1955, gave West Germany full independence, except that the former occupying powers reserved the right to negotiate with the USSR on matters relating to Berlin and to Germany as a whole. Also, the powers continued to maintain troops in the country. In 1955, West Germany was recognized as an independent country by numerous nations, including the USSR, and it became a member of the North Atlantic Treaty Organization, thus solidifying its ties with the West. In the same year, legislation was passed providing for the creation of West German armed forces. In postwar West Germany, there have been occasional, mostly minor, recurrences of anti-Semitism and extreme nationalism (e.g., the temporary growth of the nationalistic National Democratic Party in the mid-1960s); more importantly, however, the country has tried to make up in part for the Nazi atrocities by granting considerable aid to Israel and by paying reparations to individuals who suffered loss or injury at the hands of the Nazi regime. During the 1950s, the West German economy grew dramatically; in 1958, the country became a charter member of the Common Market. It also gave much economic and technical assistance to the developing nations of Asia and Africa. In 1957, the Saarland was assigned to West Germany by France, after a plebiscite. National politics in the 1950s and early 1960s were stable and were dominated by Adenauer. The CDU-CSU held firmly to the position that Germany should be reunited on the basis of democratic elections; it followed the "Hallstein doctrine" (named for Walter Hallstein, an official in the ministry of foreign affairs), under which West Germany refused to have diplomatic relations with any nation (except the USSR) that recognized East Germany. Also, Bonn was deemed to be only a provisional, de facto capital, and Berlin was held to be the proper capital. Until the 1970s, East and West Germany had virtually no contact on an official level, but there was considerable trade between them. In 1963, West Germany signed a treaty of friendship and cooperation with France. Later that year, Adenauer retired and was replaced as chancellor by Ludwig ERHARD, also a Christian Democrat and an expert on economics. Erhard's government was shaken by a downturn in the economic boom, by controversy over foreign policy, and by a poor showing in the 1965 general election. In 1966, Erhard resigned and was replaced by Kurt Georg Kiesinger, a Christian Democrat, who headed a "grand coalition" of the CDU-CSU and the SPD; SPD leader Willy Brandt assumed the posts of vice chancellor and foreign minister. Under Kiesinger, economic conditions improved, ties with France were strengthened, and talks with the nations of Eastern Europe (with whom West Germany did not have diplomatic relations) were initiated. In 1967, Rumania recognized West Germany. The general election of 1969 resulted in only a small plurality for the CDU-CSU; however, Brandt was able to become chancellor at the head of an SPD-FDP coalition government. In the 1972 general election the coalition was returned to power with a substantial majority. Largely because he depended on the support of the more conservative FDP, Brandt was unable to make significant departures in internal matters. However, in foreign affairs he launched a major program, called the *Ostpolitik* [eastern policy], to improve relations with Eastern Europe. Brandt, unlike Adenauer, was willing to accept the de facto settlements that followed World War II, including the division of Germany into two states and the loss of German territory east of the Oder-Neisse line. However, Brandt maintained that neither East nor West Germany were fully sovereign entities, and he upheld the idea of one German nation, of which the two existing German states were part. Important milestones in the *Ostpolitik* were the signing (1970) of treaties of nonaggression and cooperation with the Soviet Union and Poland (ratified in 1972); the signing (1972) of an agreement among the four former occupying powers improving access to West Berlin and permitting West Berliners to visit East Berlin and East Germany more often; a treaty (1973) between East and West Germany that called for increased cooperation between the two states and prepared the groundwork for the establishment of full diplomatic relations; and the initialing (1973) of a treaty between West Germany and Czechoslovakia. Under Brandt, the West German currency was revalued several times, thus taking into account the steady growth of the West German economy (especially its foreign trade) compared to other Western nations. West Germany was admitted to the United Nations in 1973, after having held permanent observer status since 1953. Brandt resigned in May, 1974, after it was revealed that an East German spy had been on his personal staff. He was succeeded by Helmut Schmidt, the finance minister. Under the 1949 constitution as amended, West Germany has a bicameral parliament made up of the Bundestag (Federal Diet) and the Bundesrat (Federal Council). The Bundestag consists of 496 members, of whom half are directly elected and half are chosen by a system of proportional representation. In addition, there are 22 nonvoting delegates from West Berlin. Political parties must gain 5% of the popular vote in order to be represented in the Bundestag. The normal term of the Bundestag is four years, but it may be dissolved earlier by the federal president. The Bundesrat consists of representatives of the governments of the 10 West German states (plus nonvoting delegates from Berlin), and it acts on legislation initiated in the Bundestag. The country's executive is the cabinet, which is led by the chancellor and must have the confidence of the Bundestag. The head of state is the federal president, chosen for a five-year term by an assembly consisting of members of the Bundestag plus an equal number of representatives of the parliaments of the states. **East Germany,** a republic (1970 est. pop. 17,056,983), 41,610 sq mi (107,771 sq km), in central Europe, borders on Czechoslovakia in the south, West Germany in the south and west, the Baltic Sea in the north, and Poland in the east. East Berlin is the capital of the country, which is divided into 15 districts (*Bezirke*). Other major cities include LEIPZIG, DRESDEN, KARL-MARX-STADT(formerly Chemnitz), MAGDEBURG, HALLE, ROSTOCK, and ERFURT. Virtually all citizens speak German (including several dialects). About 60% of the population are Protestant, and about 8% are Roman Catholic. East Germany is largely made up of a low-lying plain, but there are mountains in the west and south. The highest point is Fichtelberg Mt. (3,983 ft/1,214 m), located in the Erzgebirge in the south. The Thuringian Forest is in the southwest and the Harz mts. are in the west. The country's chief rivers are the Elbe (whose main tributaries are the Havel, the Saale, and the Mulde) and the Oder, which, with its tributary the Neisse, forms most of the eastern boundary. Before 1945, the territory that now constitutes East Germany was largely agricultural. Since then, however, industrialization has been greatly accelerated, so that by the late 1960s industry (including mining) contributed about 67% of the country's annual income and agriculture (including forestry) only about 9%. Among the nations of Eastern Europe, East Germany is the largest producer of industrial goods after the USSR. With very few exceptions, the economy is controlled by the state. The country is a member of the COUNCIL FOR MUTUAL ECONOMIC ASSISTANCE. The leading agricultural commodities produced in East Germany are wheat, rye, barley, potatoes, and sugar beets. Large numbers of cattle, hogs, sheep, and poultry are also raised. The main industrial centers are situated in the southeast along and near the Elbe River and its tributaries. The country's principal manufactures include iron and steel, chemicals, cement, textiles, machinery, precision instruments, footwear, motor vehicles, and electric and electronic equipment. East Germany is a major producer of lignite; coal, potash, uranium, and iron ore are also mined. The country carries on a large-scale foreign trade, the annual value of exports being usually roughly equal to the value of imports. The chief exports are lignite, chemicals, textiles, and watches and clocks; the main imports are coal, iron ore, crude petroleum, and grain. The leading trade partners are the USSR, Czechoslovakia, Poland, and West Germany. Universities are located at East Berlin, Dresden, Greifswald, Halle, Jena, Leipzig, and Rostock. To keep up with events in West Germany, a congress organized by the Socialist Unity party (SED) in May, 1949, adopted a constitution establishing the German Democratic Republic. The initial constitution, superseded by one adopted in 1968, provided for a president and a bicameral parliament. Wilhelm Pieck became the country's first president and Otto Grotewohl its first prime minister, with Walter Ulbricht as first deputy prime minister. The government was controlled by the SED and was much more centralized than that of West Germany. At first, East Germany was divided into 5 states, but in 1952 it was split into 15 districts. In 1950, a treaty was signed with Poland recognizing the Oder-Neisse line as East Germany's permanent eastern boundary. A drive to collectivize remaining privately held farmland was started in 1952. In the same year, a 3-mi-wide (4.8-km) zone, guarded by police, was established along the border with West Germany (but not with West Berlin) in order to reduce emigration to the West. Agitated by the forced changes in the country and by food shortages and other economic hardships, workers in East Berlin began on June 17, 1953, a rising that soon spread to much of the country; the revolt was suppressed only after the intervention of Soviet forces. Following the rising, the USSR attempted to improve East German economic conditions, especially the availability of consumer goods, and in 1954 it ceased to collect reparations for German actions in World War II. Also in 1954, the USSR recognized the sovereignty of East Germany, which in 1955 became a charter member of the Warsaw Treaty Organization. East German armed forces were established in 1956; Soviet troops, however, remained stationed in the country. During the 1950s, Ulbricht, who was first secretary of the SED from 1950, emerged as the leader of East Germany. Under Ulbricht, the country was closely aligned with the USSR, and the liberalizing policies introduced in some of the other East European Communist nations were avoided. After the death of Pieck in 1960, the office of president was abolished; it was replaced by a council of state, with Ulbricht as its chairman. In order to reduce the large flow of persons leaving East Germany (about 4 million during 1945–61), many of whom crossed from East to West Berlin, a wall was erected (Aug., 12–13, 1961) between the two parts of the city; it was later reinforced and enlarged. The wall drastically cut the number of emigrants, and gradually this had the effect of solidifying East Germany as an independent country. In 1963, a "New Economic System" (*Neue Ökonomische System*), calling for more efficient and decentralized economic planning, was adopted. Partly as a result of the new system, East Germany's economy expanded considerably in the 1960s. Also, large-scale building programs were undertaken in the cities. In 1964, a treaty of friendship and cooperation—in effect a peace treaty—was signed with the USSR; similar treaties with Poland, Czechoslovakia, Hungary, and Bulgaria followed in 1967. Grotewohl died in 1964 and was succeeded as prime minister by Willi STOPH, who had served as de facto prime minister since the onset (1960) of Grotewohl's terminal illness. In 1968, East German forces actively participated in the invasion of Czechoslovakia. In the late 1960s, diplomatic contacts with West Germany were initiated; these culminated in 1973 with the signing of a treaty between the two states. At the same time, East Germany for the first time was accorded diplomatic recognition by a number of non-Communist countries, including the United States (1974). In 1971, Ulbricht resigned as first secretary of the SED and was replaced by Erich HONECKER. Under Honecker, most of the few remaining private enterprises were taken over by the state. Checks on intellectual and cultural activities were relaxed somewhat. After being granted permanent observer status in 1972, East Germany was made a full member of the United Nations in 1973. Later in 1973, Stoph was elected chairman of the council of state and was replaced as prime minister by Horst Sindermann. Under the 1968 constitution, the Volkskammer [People's Chamber], consisting of 500 members elected to four-year terms, is the "supreme organ of state power" and is the country's legislative body. The Volkskammer selects the council of state, which is made up of 23 members led by a chairman; the council of state carries on the functions of the chamber when the latter is not in session. The country's executive is the council of ministers headed by a prime minister; it is chosen by, and is responsible to, the Volkskammer. Although there are several political parties in East Germany, by far the most important is the SED, which is headed by a first secretary in conjunction with a politburo of about 14 members. There is usually only one "National Front" candidate in an electoral district. Such candidates, and also most officials of the country, are chosen by the SED, which in practice is the most important organization in East Germany.

Bibliography. The chief source collection for medieval German history is the MONUMENTA GERMANIAE HISTORICA. Of the writings of the great German historians of the 19th cent., the monumental works of RANKE, SYBEL, and TREITSCHKE remain important. Among more recent works, see those of Geoffrey Barraclough, Veit Valentin, Erich Eyck, A. J. P. Taylor, G. P. Gooch, Hans Kohn, Fritz Fischer, Klaus Epstein, Eckart Kehr, and G. D. Feldman; Hajo Holborn, *History of Modern Germany, 1840–1945* (3 vol., 1959–69); Peter Gay, *Weimar Culture* (1968); Gerhard Ritter, *The Sword and the Scepter* (tr., 4 vol., 1969–73); P. C. Ludz, *The German Democratic Republic* (1970) and *The Changing Party Elite in East Germany* (1972); Alfred Grosser, *Germany in Our Time* (tr. 1971); A. J. Heidenheimer, *The Governments of Germany* (3d ed. 1971); John Strawson, *Hitler's Battles for Europe* (1971); E. K. Keefe et al., *Area Handbook for East Germany* (1972); John Midgley, *Germany* (2d ed. 1972); Anthony Nicholls and Erich Matthias, ed., *German Democracy and the Triumph of Hitler* (1972); Malcolm Pasley, ed., *Germany* (1972); F. R. Stern, *The Failure of* Illiberalism (1972); K. D. Bracher, *The German Dictatorship* (tr. 1973); F. T. Epstein, *Germany and the East* (1973); Dietrich Orlow, *The History of the Nazi Party: 1933–1945* (1973); A. J. Ryder, *Twentieth-Century Germany: From Bismarck to Brandt* (1973). The U.S. occupation is discussed in the study by Eugene Davidson (1959), the British in that by Raymond Ebsworth (1961), and the French in that by F. R. Willis (1962). Bibliographies will also be found under other related headings.

germicide (jûr'mĭsīd), chemical substance capable of killing many different types of microorganisms; also called DISINFECTANT.

germination, in a seed, process by which the plant embryo within the SEED resumes growth after a period of dormancy and the seedling emerges. The length of dormancy varies; the seed of some plants (e.g., most grasses) can sprout almost immediately, but many seeds require a resting stage before they are able to germinate. The viability of seeds (their capacity to sprout) ranges from a few weeks (orchids) to over 400 years (Indian lotus) and up to 10,000 years (Arctic lupine). The majority are viable for five or six years, the percentage of viable seed decreasing with age. Dormancy serves to enable the seed to survive poor growing conditions; a certain amount of embryonic development may also take place. Dormancy is prolonged by extremely tough seed coats that exclude the water necessary for germination. Internally, growth is regulated by hormones called auxins. When the temperature is suitable and there is an adequate supply of moisture, oxygen, and light—although some seeds require darkness and others are unaffected by either—the seed absorbs water and swells, rupturing the seed coat. The growing tip (radicle) of the rudimentary root (hypocotyl) emerges first and then the growing tip (plumule) of the rudimentary shoot (epicotyl). Food stored in the endosperm or in the cotyledons provides energy for the early stages of this process, until the seedling is able to manufacture its own food.

Germiston (jûr'mĭstən), city (1970 pop. 210,298), Transvaal, NE South Africa, on the WITWATERSRAND. The chief industries are gold mining and processing and the manufacture of liquid oxygen; other chemicals, machinery, textiles, and clothing are also produced. Germiston is an important railroad hub.

Gernreich, Rudi: see under FASHION.

Gérôme, Jean Léon (zhäN lāôN' zhārōm'), 1824–1904, French historical and genre painter. He enjoyed a successful career in his day. He studied with Delaroche and adhered to academic technique. A good draftsman and facile illustrator, he produced a large number of paintings, meticulous in execution. In his last years he gave up painting for sculpture. His painting *The Cock Fight* (1847) is in the Louvre.

Gerona (hārō'nä), city (1970 pop. 50,338), capital of Gerona prov., NE Spain, in Catalonia, on the Oñar River. There are food, textile, paper, chemical, and other industries in Gerona. The city dates from pre-Roman times, and the old town has preserved its medieval aspect. The Moors ruled Gerona, with two interruptions, from 714 to 797. In 1808–9, during the Peninsular War, townspeople heroically resisted the French. The Gothic cathedral (14th–16th cent.) has a nave 73 ft (22 m) wide and a Romanesque cloister.

Geronimo (jərŏn'əmō), c.1829–1909, leader of a Chiricahua group of APACHE INDIANS, b. Arizona. As a youth he participated in the forays of Cochise, Victorio, and other Apache leaders. When the Chiricahua Reservation was abolished (1876) and the Indians removed to the arid San Carlos Agency in New Mexico, Geronimo led a group of followers into Mexico. He was soon captured and returned to the new reservation, where he farmed for a while. In 1881 he escaped again with a group (including a son of Cochise) and led raids in Arizona and Sonora, Mexico. He surrendered (1883) to forces under Gen. George CROOK and was returned to the reservation. In 1885 he again left, and after almost a year of war he agreed to surrender to Crook, but at the last minute Geronimo fled. His escape led to censure of Crook's policy. Late in 1886, Geronimo and the remainder of his forces surrendered to Gen. Nelson Appleton MILES, Crook's successor. They were deported as prisoners of war to Florida; contary to an agreement, they were not allowed to take their families with them. After a further period in prison in Alabama, Geronimo was placed under military confinement at Fort Sill, Okla., where he settled down, adopted Christianity, and became a prosperous farmer. He became a national celebrity when he appeared at the St. Louis World's Fair and in Theodore Roosevelt's inaugural procession. He dictated his autobiography to S. M. Barrett (1906, repr. 1970). See biography by A. B. Adams (1971); studies by Britton Davis (1929, repr. 1963), John Bigelow (1958, repr. 1968), and O. B. Faulk (1969).

Gerontius (jərŏn'shəs), d. 411, Roman general, b. Britain. He at first supported the usurper CONSTANTINE (d. 411), and was left in charge of Spain. He set up (409) his own candidate, Maximus, as emperor, at the same time inviting or permitting the entrance of the Alani, Suevi, and Vandals. In 411 he besieged Constantine at Arles, but at the approach of Constantius (later Emperor Constantius III) his troops deserted; he escaped to Spain but was assassinated.

gerontology: see GERIATRICS.

Gerry, Elbridge (gĕr'ē), 1744–1814, American statesman, Vice President of the United States, b. Marblehead, Mass. He was elected (1772) to the Massachusetts General Court, where he became a follower of Samuel Adams, who enlisted him in the colonial activities preceding the American Revolution. Gerry was (1774–76) a member of the provincial congresses and of the committee of safety, and as chairman of the state committee of supply he worked energetically to procure supplies for the army gathering around Boston. In Jan., 1776, he left for Philadelphia to attend the Continental Congress, of which he was a member until 1785, although he absented himself in 1781–83. He voted for and signed both the Declaration of Independence and the Articles of Confederation. With his brothers at Marblehead, he carried on a large trade with Spain and other countries and procured articles needed by the Continental forces. After the war Gerry was an opponent of a large standing army and of a stronger central government. However, his views were modified by Shays's Rebellion, and he consented to be a delegate to the Federal Constitutional Convention of 1787. There he was one of the most frequent speakers, and while realizing the need for a stronger union, he opposed those leaders who were anxious to consolidate power in the proposed central government. He refused to sign the completed Constitution, for reasons stated in his published message to the Massachusetts legislature, entitled *Observations on the New Constitution . . . by a Columbian Patriot* (1788). Most of these objections were later met by the first 10 amendments (Bill of Rights). He served (1789–93) in the first two U.S. Congresses. In 1797, President John Adams chose him, together with C. C. Pinckney and John Marshall, for a mission to France in a new attempt to secure a recognition of U.S. rights from Talleyrand (see XYZ AFFAIR). He was elected governor of Massachusetts in 1810 and reelected in 1811. In his second term his party, the Jeffersonians, desiring to retain their control of the state, rearranged the election districts in their favor in a grotesque salamander-like shape, a political maneuver then named by his opponents and since known as a GERRYMANDER (from his name and salamander). Gerry was defeated for reelection in 1812, but he was immediately nominated by the Jeffersonians for Vice President on the ticket with James Madison, and he was elected. He loyally supported the War of 1812, though his Massachusetts constituency was opposed to it. Gerry died in office.

Gerry, Elbridge Thomas, 1837–1927, American reformer, b. New York City; grandson of Elbridge Gerry. Admitted (1860) to the New York bar, he came to be adviser to the American Society for the Prevention of Cruelty to Animals and soon afterward became interested in child welfare. In 1875 he founded, with the help of Henry Bergh, the New York Society for the Prevention of Cruelty to Children (called sometimes the Gerry Society). He ultimately devoted most of his attention to this cause, which became national in scope, though he retained his interest in other humanitarian movements.

gerrymander (jĕr'ēmăn"dər, gĕr–), in politics, rearrangement of voting districts so as to favor the party in power. The objective is to create as many districts as possible in areas of known support and to concentrate the opposition's strength into as few districts as possible. Extremely irregular boundary lines are sometimes necessary to obtain the results desired. The U.S. Supreme Court, however, has placed (1964) the vague limit of "compact districts of contiguous territory" on such apportionment schemes. The origin of the term, though by no means the origin of the practice, was in such an arrangement made by the Massachusetts Jeffersonians when Elbridge GERRY was governor. See E. C. Griffith, *The Rise and Development of the Gerrymander* (1907, repr. 1974).

Gers (zhĕr), department (1968 pop. 181,577), SW France. AUCH is the capital.

Gershom (gûr'shəm). **1** Moses' first son. Ex. 2.21,22; 18.2,3; 1 Chron. 23.15. **2** See GERSHON. **3** One of Ezra's companions. Ezra 8.2.

Gershom ben Judah (gûr'shəm bĕn jo͞o'də), b. 960, d. 1040 or 1028, rabbi, religious poet, and scholar, b. Metz. He was also called Me'or ha-Golah [light of the exile]. He died in Mayence, in Germany, where he had founded a Talmudic academy. He is famous for his edict against polygamy, which was highly influential among the Jews of Europe.

Gershon (gûr'shŏn), Levi's first son. Gen. 46.11; Num. 3.21; 1 Chron. 6.1. Gershom: 1 Chron. 6.16–20.

Gershon, Levi ben: see GERSONIDES.

Gershwin, George (gŭrsh'wĭn), 1898–1937, American composer, b. Brooklyn, N.Y. Gershwin wrote some of the most original and popular musical works produced in the United States. Although he studied harmony with Rubin Goldmark (see under GOLDMARK, KARL), he received most of his musical training in Tin Pan Alley, playing the piano for a publisher of popular music. He first achieved wide success with his song "Swanee." In addition to a great number of songs, he wrote the scores for several musicals, including George White's *Scandals* (1920), *Lady, Be Good!* (1924), *Oh, Kay!* (1926), *Funny Face* (1927), *Girl Crazy* (1930), and George S. Kaufman's *Of Thee I Sing* (1931; Pulitzer Prize). In his more serious compositions he combined traditional musical forms with jazz and folk themes and rhythms. They include *Rhapsody in Blue* (1923), a symphonic jazz composition for piano and orchestra; the Piano Concerto in F (1925); *An American in Paris* (1928), a tone poem incorporating elements of jazz as well as realistic sound effects; *Porgy and Bess* (1935; from the book by Dubose Heyward), a folk opera about American Negro life, from which comes the famous song "Summertime"; and Three Preludes (1936), for the piano. Gershwin also composed music for Hollywood films. His brother, Ira Gershwin (1896–), wrote the lyrics for many of his songs. See biographies by Edward Jablonski and L. D. Steward (1958), Isaac Goldberg (new ed. 1958), and David Ewen (rev. ed. 1970); Charles Schwartz, *Gershwin: His Life and Music* (1973); R. E. Kimball and A. E. Simon, *The Gershwins* (1973).

Gerson, John (Jean Charlier de Gerson) (gûr'sən; zhäN shärlyā' də zhârsôN'), 1363–1429, French ecclesiastical statesman and writer. He studied (1377–94) under Pierre d'AILLY at the Univ. of Paris, where he took his doctorate in theology and succeeded

Ailly as chancellor (1395). Both Ailly and Gerson were anxious to end the Great Schism (see SCHISM, GREAT). When they were unsuccessful in having both Benedict XIII (see LUNA, PEDRO DE) and Gregory XII resign, they began to urge that the schism be ended by action of a general council. The Council of Pisa resulted, and Gerson wrote a tract (1409) to defend it. The tract is a classic statement of theounciliar theory (later condemned)—that a council can supersede the pope when the good of the church requires it. Gerson was not at Pisa, but he did attend (1414) the Council of Constance (see CONSTANCE, COUNCIL OF) as head of the French delegation. There, he supported Ailly in ending the schism and led in the condemnation of John HUSS. But Gerson had made an enemy of John the Fearless, duke of Burgundy; from 1408 he had publicly demanded that John do penance for the murder of Louis, duc d'Orléans. Fearing John, Gerson did not return to France from Constance but went to Vienna to teach. From 1419 he lived in Lyons, where he wrote many works, chiefly theological, and a tract defending Joan of Arc. He strongly condemned as immoral the *Roman de la Rose* of Jean de Meun. Gerson opposed the nominalist philosophy of WILLIAM OF OCCAM, and as chancellor he began the change to realism as the official philosophy of the Univ. of Paris. See biography by J. L. Connolly (1928); J. B. Morrall, *Gerson and the Great Schism* (1960).

Gersonides (gərsŏn'ĭdēz) or **Levi ben Gershon** (lē'vī bĕn gûr'shən), 1288–1344, Jewish philosopher, astronomer, and mathematician, called also Ralbag, from the initials of his Hebrew name, b. Languedoc. He wrote commentaries on Averroës, the Pentateuch, and various scientific works. His chief work was the *Milchamoth Adonai* [the wars of the Lord], an elaborate treatise modeled after the *Moreh Nevukhim* of Maimonides. It is mainly a systematic criticism of the syncretism of Maimonides from an Averroistic point of view. He greatly influenced Spinoza. The camera obscura and other inventions are attributed to Gersonides.

Gersoppa, Falls of (gərsŏp'ə), cataract of the Sharavati River, Karnataka state, SW India. It is one of the most spectacular natural beauties of India. The river cuts through the Western Ghats to fall in four cascades, of which the highest is c.830 ft (250 m). The Mahatma Gandhi power station is at the falls.

Gervase of Canterbury, d. c.1210, English chronicler. A monk of Christ Church, Cambridge, he wrote an account of the reigns of Stephen, Henry II, and Richard I. His *Chronica* is an ecclesiastical history of Canterbury, the *Gesta regum* a history of the kings of England into the reign of John. Gervase was noted for his discriminating choice of facts.

Gervase of Tilbury, fl. 1200, medieval author, b. England. He became marshal of the kingdom of Arles under Emperor Otto IV and wrote the *Otia imperiala,* a miscellany of legend, history, and politics.

Geryon (jĕr'ēən, jərī'ən), in Greek mythology, three-bodied monster who, with his dog Orthrus, watched over a great herd of cattle. He and Orthrus were killed by Hercules when, as his 10th labor, he stole the cattle.

Géryville: see EL BAYADH, Algeria.

Gesenius, Wilhelm (vĭl'hĕlm gāzā'nyo͝os), 1786–1842, German Orientalist, one of the greatest Hebrew and biblical scholars. He is principally known for his *Hebrew Grammar,* which has been reedited so many times that it differs widely from his original. Perhaps his finest work was his biblical commentary. He was, in this, a moderate rationalist, and he aroused bitter opposition. He was one of the first to open Semitic to scientific study, because of his point of view that Hebrew and its sister languages were not sacrosanct, as most contemporary Christians thought them to be. See E. F. Miller, *The Influence of Gesenius on Hebrew Lexicography* (1927).

Gesham (gē'shəm), descendant of Caleb. 1 Chron. 2.47.

Geshem (gē'shĕm), Arabian leader who opposed Nehemiah in the rebuilding of Jerusalem. Neh. 2.19; 6.1,2. Gashmu: Neh. 6.6.

Geshur (gē'shər) or **Geshuri** (gĕsh'yo͝orī, gĕshyo͞o'rī). **1** Small Aramaic kingdom that remained in the territory allotted to Manasseh. It occupied barren land NE of the Sea of Galilee. After the division of Israel, it became a part of the Aramaic kingdom of Damascus. A daughter of one of its kings married David and was the mother of Absalom. Deut. 3.14; Joshua 12.5; 13.11; 2 Sam. 3.3; 15.8. See ARAM **1.** **2** Aboriginal people in Philistia. Joshua 13.2; 1 Sam. 27.8.

Gesner, Konrad von (kôn'rät fən gĕs'nər), 1516–65, Swiss scientist and bibliographer. Gesner was noted for his scholarship and erudition in almost every field of knowledge. He lived in Zürich and other European cities, teaching physics and natural history and practicing medicine and surgery. Among his works was a dictionary of plants, *Historia plantarum,* written in 1541; most of his botanical writings were collected and published (2 vol., 1751–71) as the *Opera botanica.* He is most important as a reviver of the classical school of zoological description that culminated in the work of Linnaeus. Gesner's beautifully illustrated compendium *Historia animalium* (5 vol., 1551–58, 1587) influenced both biology and the arts and is considered the foundation of zoology as a science. Other works include *Mithridates* (1555), a philological study of 130 languages, and *Bibliotheca universalis* (4 vol., 1545–49), an index in Greek, Latin, and Hebrew of writings in all languages.

gesneria (gĕsnĭr'ēə), common name for some members of the Gesneriaceae, a family of chiefly tropical and subtropical perennial herbs and shrubs with showy blossoms. The best-known members of the family are the African violets (most of which are hybrids of *Saintpaulia ionantha*), cultivated for their blossoms and for the purplish leaves often characteristic of this family. Other cultivated ornamentals include the African Cape primrose (genus *Streptocarpus*) and several rock garden and pot plants, e.g., *Ramonda* and *Haberlea* of Europe, and gloxinia (*Sinningia speciosa*) of Brazil—not to be confused with species of the genus *Gloxinia,* which are not cultivated. The *Gesneria* genus is native to tropical America and the West Indies. Gesneria is classified in the division MAGNOLIOPHYTA, class Magnoliopsida, order Scrophulariales, family Gesneriaceae.

Gestalt (gəshtält') [Ger.,=form], school of psychology that interprets phenomena as organized wholes rather than as aggregates of distinct parts and maintains that the whole is more than the sum of its parts. The term *Gestalt* was coined by Charles von Ehrenfels in 1890. In 1912 the movement was given impetus by the German-born psychologists Max Wertheimer, Wolfgang Köhler, and Kurt Koffka as a protest against the prevailing atomistic, analytical psychological thought; it was also a departure from the general intellectual climate, which emphasized a scientific approach characterized by a detachment from basic human concerns, i.e., value, order, and meaning. The Gestalt school was brought to the United States by refugee psychologists in the 1930s. According to the school, the characteristics of phenomena such as perceptual illusions and binocular depth perception cannot be derived from a summation of the constituents into which they might be analyzed, but instead depend upon the given whole. In addition, because the significance of structured wholes does not depend upon specific constituent elements, a drawn figure, for example, will still have meaning even when there are gaps in the drawing. Gestalt psychologists suggest that the events in the brain bear a structural correspondence to psychological events; indeed, it has been shown that steady electric currents in the brain correspond to structured perceptual events. The Gestalt school has made substantial contributions to the study of learning, recall, the nature of associations, thinking, and related problems. A related school headed by Kurt Lewin made important contributions to human motivation, personality, and social psychology. In its emphasis on structural wholes, Gestalt psychology has been thought of as analogous to field physics. See Kurt Lewin, *A Dynamic Theory of Personality* (tr. 1935); Wolfgang Köhler, *The Mentality of Apes* (2d ed. tr. 1931, repr. 1959) and *Gestalt Psychology* (new ed. 1970); Max Wertheimer, *Productive Thinking* (rev. ed. 1959, repr. 1971).

Gestalt group therapy: see GROUP PSYCHOTHERAPY.

Gestapo: see SECRET POLICE.

Gesta Romanorum (jĕs'tə rō"mənôr'əm), medieval collection of Latin stories. Although the title means "Deeds of the Romans," the tales have very little to do with actual Roman history. Each tale is characterized by a moral. The earliest manuscript dates from the 14th cent., but it had probably been first collected several centuries earlier. Many of the stories were used later by such authors as Chaucer and Shakespeare.

Gesualdo, Carlo (kär'lō jāzo͞oäl'dō), Prince of Venosa, c.1560–1613, Italian composer. Gesualdo's later madrigals are striking in their harmonic and dramatic boldness. They are contained in the last two (1611) of his six published books of madrigals. Gesualdo was a flamboyant personality: He had many love affairs, and his first wife and her lover were murdered at his order. See studies by Cecil Gray and Philip Heseltine (1926, repr. 1971) and Glenn Watkins (1974); Alfred Einstein, *The Italian Madrigal* (3 vol., 1949, repr. 1971).

Getae: see DACIA.

Getafe (hātä'fā), town (1970 pop. 69,424), Madrid prov., central Spain, in New Castile. An industrial and agricultural center S of Madrid, Getafe is located at the exact geographical center of Spain. It has electrical and chemical industries. Cereals, vegetables, grapes, and olives are grown in the surrounding area. The Spanish air force has its headquarters in Getafe.

Gether (gē'thər), descendant of Shem. Gen. 10.23; 1 Chron. 1.17.

Gethsemane (gĕthsĕm'ənē), olive grove or garden, E of Jerusalem, near the foot of the Mount of Olives. It was the scene of the agony and betrayal of Jesus. Mark 14.32; Mat. 26.36. Ruins of a 4th-century church and of a church as old as the Crusades were found here.

Getty, Jean Paul, 1892–, American business executive, considered one of the richest men in the world, b. Minneapolis, Minn. He inherited his father's oil business, George F. Getty, Inc., becoming its president and general manager in 1930. When it was reorganized (1956) as the Getty Oil Company, he became the firm's director and principal owner. Since the early 1950s Getty has resided in Great Britain. From his 16th-century Tudor estate, known as Sutton Place, Getty controls a vast business empire made up of almost 200 concerns. His personal worth is estimated to be approximately $3 billion.

Gettysburg (gĕt'ĕzbərg), borough (1970 pop. 7,275), seat of Adams co., S Pa.; inc. 1806. Electrical equipment, food products, and shoes are manufactured there. Gettysburg was settled c.1780 and is named for Gen. James Gettys, to whom its site was granted (17th cent.) by William Penn. The GETTYSBURG CAMPAIGN (1863) was a turning point in the Civil War, and President Abraham Lincoln made his famous GETTYSBURG ADDRESS there. Gettysburg National Military Park, Gettysburg National Cemetery, and the farm of President Dwight David Eisenhower are all national historic shrines and popular tourist attractions (see NATIONAL PARKS AND MONUMENTS, table). Gettysburg Lutheran Theological Seminary (1826) and Gettysburg College (1832) are in the borough.

Gettysburg Address, speech delivered by Abraham Lincoln on Nov. 19, 1863, at the dedication of the national cemetery on the Civil War battlefield of Gettysburg, Pa. It is one of the most famous and most quoted of modern speeches. The final version of the address prepared by Lincoln, differing in detail from the spoken address, reads: "Four score and seven years ago our fathers brought forth on this continent, a new nation, conceived in Liberty, and dedicated to the proposition that all men are created equal. Now we are engaged in a great civil war, testing whether that nation, or any nation so conceived and so dedicated, can long endure. We are met on a great battle-field of that war. We have come to dedicate a portion of that field, as a final resting place for those who here gave their lives that that nation might live. It is altogether fitting and proper that we should do this. But, in a larger sense, we can not dedicate—we can not consecrate—we can not hallow—this ground. The brave men, living and dead, who struggled here, have consecrated it, far above our poor power to add or detract. The world will little note, nor long remember what we say here, but it can never forget what they did here. It is for us the living, rather, to be dedicated here to the unfinished work which they who fought here have thus far so nobly advanced. It is rather for us to be here dedicated to the great task remaining before us—that from these honored dead we take increased devotion to that cause for which they gave the last full measure of devotion—that we here highly resolve that these dead shall not have died in vain—that this nation, under God, shall have a new birth of freedom—and that government of the people, by the people, for the people, shall not perish from the earth." See Allan Nevins, ed., *Lincoln and the Gettysburg Address* (1964); W. E. Barton, *Lincoln at Gettysburg* (1930, repr. 1971).

Gettysburg campaign, June–July, 1863, series of decisive battles of the U.S. Civil War. After his victory in the battle of CHANCELLORSVILLE, the Confederate general Robert E. LEE undertook a second invasion of the North. The reorganized Army of Northern Virginia crossed the Potomac (June 17) via the Shenandoah valley, which Richard S. EWELL (2d Corps), as leader of the advance, swept clear of Union forces.

By late June, Ewell was seriously threatening Harrisburg, Pa., while Lee, with James LONGSTREET (1st Corps) and A. P. HILL (3d Corps), was at Chambersburg, Pa. However, with the absence of his cavalry under J. E. B. STUART, which was raiding in the area between Washington and the position of the Union army, Lee was unable to determine the enemy's strength and movements. When he finally learned that George G. MEADE was concentrating N of the Potomac, he ordered the concentration of his own force. Meade, intending to make his stand at Pipe Creek in Maryland, sent ahead John F. Reynolds, commanding the left wing. But on July 1, John Buford's cavalry, covering Reynolds, came into contact with Harry Heth's division of Hill's corps on the Chambersburg pike just W of Gettysburg. The environs of Gettysburg thus became the unintended site of the greatest battle of the war (July 1–3, 1863). The Federals had the best of Hill until midafternoon, when, outflanked by Ewell, advancing from the north, they were driven to Cemetery Hill, south of the town. Meade on the recommendation of Winfield Scott HANCOCK abandoned his Pipe Creek plans and hurried up his whole force. On July 2, against the Union left, Longstreet led the main attack, which was not delivered until about 4 P.M.; the Army of the Potomac thus had time to consolidate its strong position. The Confederates took the Peach Orchard but were repulsed in attempting to seize Round Top and Little Round Top, commanding eminences at the south end of Cemetery Ridge. On the Union right, Ewell carried Culp's Hill but was beaten off at Cemetery Hill. Meade's counterattack on the morning of July 3 retook Culp's Hill. Lee ordered Longstreet to attack the Union center with George E. PICKETT's division, supported by part of Hill's corps (about 15,000 men in all). After a bombardment of the Union position by the massed Confederate artillery, Pickett moved forward in his famous charge. In the face of terrific artillery and musket fire, the gallant Southerners reached and momentarily held the first Union line. But Pickett's support gave way, and Hancock drove him back with tremendous losses. Meanwhile Stuart's cavalry, in an attempt to get at the Union right and rear, was defeated by David M. GREGG. Both armies, exhausted, held their positions until the night of July 4, when Lee withdrew. High water in the Potomac delayed his crossing back to Virginia, but Meade did not attack him in force. The Union army, which had been the more numerous, lost 23,000 men either killed, wounded, or missing; the Confederate army lost 25,000 (although that figure is questionable). Both commanding generals have been criticized for their conduct of the campaign—Lee for his unwarranted reliance on unseasoned commanders and his authorization of Pickett's charge; Meade for failing to organize his forces for a counterattack and pursuing the fleeing enemy. The campaign marked the high point of the Confederate activity during the war; thereafter the fortunes of the South went into a marked decline. See F. A. Haskell, *The Battle of Gettysburg* (1898); Cecil Battine, *The Crisis of the Confederacy* (1905); J. B. Young, *Battle of Gettysburg* (1913); D. S. Freeman, *R. E. Lee,* Vol. III (1935); F. D. Downey, *The Guns at Gettysburg* (1958); Edwin B. Coddington, *The Gettysburg Campaign* (1968); Bruce Catton, *Gettysburg: The Final Fury* (1974).

Geuel (gyo͞o'ĕl), tribal chief of Gad. Num. 13.15.

Geulincx, Arnold (gö'lĭngks), 1624–69, Flemish Cartesian philosopher, b. Antwerp. One of the founders of OCCASIONALISM, his philosophy is characterized by a curious blending of rationalism and mysticism. Arguing that God is the sole active power, he denied any real interaction between finite things, which serve merely as "occasional causes." He explained the relationship between mind and body by the analogy of two clocks that are synchronized by God at each instant. Although there is no interaction, there is a continual harmony between them. His principal works, which appeared posthumously, were *Ethica* (1675) and *Metaphysica vera* (1691). See H. J. de Vleeschauwer, *Three Centuries of Geulincx Research* (1957).

geyser (gī'zər) [Icel.], hot spring from which water and steam are ejected periodically to heights ranging from a few to several hundred feet. Notable geysers are found in Iceland, New Zealand and W United States, which are areas of recent volcanic activity. Geyser action in Iceland was studied by the German chemist R. W. Bunsen, whose explanation of it (1847) is generally accepted. Water, mainly from rainfall, is heated by absorbing hot gases or by contact with hot rocks. If it flows into a crooked tube or fissure in the ground, the heat fails to circulate by convection and is concentrated in one section of the tube, located well below the surface. Here the water may be superheated without boiling because of the pressure of the colder water above. When at last it does turn to steam it raises the upper part of the column of water, causing it to overflow This reduces the pressure on the water below, a great deal is abruptly converted into steam, and the whole column—steam and water—is forced to erupt. Geyser activity is influenced by earth tides, which are caused by the moon's gravitational pull on the earth. Geysers often build cones of opaline silica called geyserite around their vents. "Old Faithful" in Yellowstone Park usually erupts at intervals of about 66 min, but it has become less regular in recent years. Mud geysers or mud volcanoes are eruptive mud springs. Geothermal generating plants, notably in California and New Zealand, use geysers to produce electricity. See T. F. Barth, *Volcanic Geology, Hot Springs and Geysers of Iceland* (1950); G. A. Waring, *Thermal Springs of the United States and Other Countries of the World* (rev. ed. 1965).

Geysir (gā'sĭr), hot spring, SW Iceland, c.75 mi (120 km) W of Reykjavík. Although in medieval times it erupted three times daily, weeks now elapse between eruptions. The height and temperature of the jet are variable, reaching up to 200 ft (60 m) and 180°F (82°C). There are many other hot springs in the vicinity, but few have eruptions. Hot water is piped into Reykjavík and used for heating. The generic term *geyser* in English is derived from Geysir.

Gezelle, Guido (gē'dō khĕzĕl'ə), 1830–99, Flemish poet, b. Bruges, a Roman Catholic priest. A forerunner of the Flemish literary revival, he was the leading poet of the Flemings. In six volumes of lyrics, especially *Rijmsnoer* [necklace of rhymes] (1897), he combined a love of nature, a championing of the Flemish cause, and an intense feeling for religion. He wrote in the popular idiom of his region. See English translation of some of his work by Maude Swepstone (1937).

Gezer (gē'zər), ancient city of Canaan, on the coastal plain of Sharon, NW of Jerusalem. Its position guarding the road from Jerusalem to Jaffa has always given it importance, e.g., in the wars of Joshua, David, the Maccabees, and in the Crusades. Excavations there (1902–8, 1929, 1934) have made it possible to trace the history of Gezer from Chalcolithic times. It was an Egyptian outpost c.1900 B.C. Among the important findings were evidence of troglodyte dwellings, a Middle Bronze Age water tunnel, stone monoliths, and an agricultural calendar of the late 10th cent. B.C. In 1945 a communal settlement of the same name was founded there. Joshua 10.33; 12.12; 16.3; 21.21; Judges 1.29; 1 Kings 9.16,17; 1 Chron. 6.67; 7.28; 20.4. Gazer: 2 Sam. 5.25; 1 Chron. 14.16. See GOB.

Ghadames: see GHUDAMIS, Libya.

Ghana (gä'nə), ancient empire, W Africa, in the savanna region of what is now E Senegal, SW Mali, and S Mauritania. The empire was founded c.6th cent. by Soninke peoples and lay astride the trans-Saharan caravan routes. Its capital was Kumbi Salih (in present-day SE Mauritania). It prospered from trade—particularly in salt and gold—and tribute. Internal divisions and an Almoravid invasion (1076) contributed to Ghana's decline, and by the 13th cent. it had disintegrated. Modern Ghana takes its name from the former empire. See Nehemia Levtzion, *Ancient Ghana and Mali* (1973).

Ghana, republic (1973 est. pop. 9,200,000), 92,099 sq mi (238,536 sq km), W Africa, on the Gulf of Guinea, an arm of the Atlantic Ocean. The capital is ACCRA. Other important cities are KUMASI, SEKONDI-TAKORADI, CAPE COAST, and TAMALE. Modern Ghana comprises the former British colony of the Gold Coast and the former mandated territory of British Togoland. It is bordered by the Ivory Coast on the west, Upper Volta on the north, and Togo on the east. The coastal region and the far north of Ghana are savanna areas; in between is a forest zone. The country's largest river is the Volta; the damming of the river for a hydroelectric station at Akosombo (1964) created the enormous Lake Volta. Ghana's economy is predominantly agricultural. The biggest crop and major export is cacao; the country's economic health is in large measure determined by the often fluctuating world price of cacao. Coffee, oil palms, and coconuts are also widely grown. Minerals (gold, diamonds, manganese, and bauxite) are found in the north, south, and coastal regions and constitute the second largest export, followed by timber. The major industries in Ghana are aluminum smelting, the processing of cacao, and the production of lumber and foods and beverages. Manufacturing, however, produces a relatively small portion of the national income. Great Britain and the United States are Ghana's major trade partners. The country has a

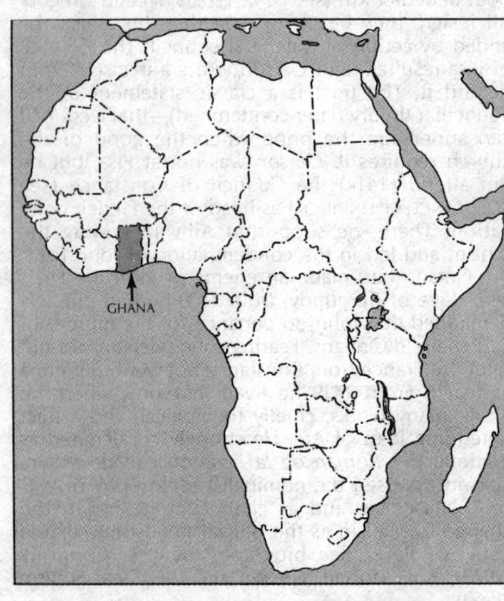

large but poorly maintained road system, and rail lines connect the major centers in the south. Ghana's population is composed of many linguistic groups, the principal of which are the Akan (Ashanti and Fanti), Mole-Dagbani, Ewe, and Ga-Adangme. English is the official language. About two fifths of the population is Christian and one tenth is Muslim (living mainly in the north); the remainder follow tribal religions. In precolonial times the area of present-day Ghana comprised a number of independent kingdoms, including Gonja and Dagomba in the north, ASHANTI in the interior, and the FANTI states along the coast. In 1482 the first European fort was established by the Portuguese at Elmina. Trade was begun, largely in gold and slaves, and intense competition developed among many European nations for trading advantages. With the decline of the slave trade by the 19th cent. only the British, Danes, and Dutch still maintained forts on the Gold Coast. The Danes (1850) and Dutch (1872) withdrew in the face of expansionist activities by the Ashanti kingdom; the British, however, remained and allied themselves with the Fanti states against Ashanti. In 1874 the British defeated Ashanti and organized the coastal region as the colony of the Gold Coast. There was fighting between British and Ashanti again in 1896, and in 1901 the British made the kingdom a colony. In the same year the Northern Territories, a region north of Ashanti, were declared a British protectorate. After World War I part of the German colony of Togoland was mandated to the British, who linked it administratively with the Gold Coast colony. In the Gold Coast, nationalist activity, which began in the interwar period, intensified after World War II. Kwame Nkrumah of the Convention People's Party (CPP) emerged as the leading nationalist figure. In 1951, Britain granted a new constitution, which had been drawn up by Africans, and general elections were held. The CPP won overwhelmingly and Nkrumah became premier. On March 6, 1957, the state of Ghana, named after the medieval W African empire, became an independent country within the Commonwealth of Nations. At the same time the people of British Togoland chose by plebiscite to become part of Ghana. In 1960, Nkrumah transformed Ghana into a republic, with himself as president for life. By a 1964 referendum all opposition parties were outlawed, and many critics of the government were subsequently imprisoned. Nkrumah followed an anticolonial, Pan-African policy and grew increasingly less friendly to the West. Falling cacao prices and poorly financed large development projects led to chaotic economic conditions, and in 1966 Nkrumah was overthrown by a military-police coup. A National Liberation Council (NLC) was set up to rule until the restoration of civilian government. Under the NLC relations with the Western powers were improved. In 1969 the NLC transferred power to a civilian government elected under a new constitution and headed by K. A. Busia. The Busia government was undermined by labor problems, an unpopular currency devaluation, and serious inflation, and in Jan., 1972, it too was overthrown in a bloodless coup led by Col. I. K. Acheampong. The constitution was suspended, and a National Redemption Council (NRC) set up to govern. The NRC pursued a more neutralist course in foreign affairs and concentrated on developing Ghana's economy. The country's large foreign debt (mainly contracted under Nkrumah) was partly repudiated and partly refinanced; imports were curtailed; and the state took controlling interest in foreign mining and timber firms operating in the country. See David Kimble, *A Political History of Ghana, 1850–1928* (1963); W. E. Ward, *History of Ghana* (3d ed. 1966); E. R. Forde, *The Population of Ghana* (1968); Dennis Austin, *Politics in Ghana, 1946–1960* (1970); E. A. Boateng, *A Geography of Ghana* (1970); Irving Kaplan et al., *Area Handbook for Ghana* (2d ed. 1971); David E. Apter, *Ghana in Transition* (2d rev. ed. 1972).

Gharapuri, India: see ELEPHANTA.

Ghardaïa (gärdäyä'), town (1966 pop. 30,167), N Algeria. It is the chief town of the Mzab, a stony, barren valley of the N Sahara. Ghardaïa is a center of date production and of the manufacture of rugs and cloth. The city was founded in the 11th cent. by Muslim Kharijite sectaries fleeing persecution by the orthodox Muslims of the north. First occupied by French troops in 1854, Ghardaïa was not officially annexed to France until 1882.

Gharyan (gäryän') or **Garian** (gärēän'), town, NW Libya, connected by rail and highway with nearby Tripoli. Many of the inhabitants live in a centuries-old subterranean town. A modern settlement was built (20th cent.) above ground by the Italians as a garrison.

Ghat or **Gat** (both: gät), walled town, SW Libya, in an oasis in the Sahara, near the Algerian border. It formerly was an important caravan center. Ghat was captured by the Ottoman Turks in 1875, by the Italians in 1930, and by the French in 1943, during World War II.

Ghats (gôts) [Hindi,=steps], two mountain ranges of S India, paralleling the coasts of the Arabian Sea and the Bay of Bengal and forming two sides of the Deccan plateau. Anai Mudi (8,841 ft/2,695 m) is the highest peak in the two ranges, which are joined by the Nilgiri Hills in the south. The **Western Ghats,** c.1,000 mi (1,600 km) long, extend SE from the Tapti valley, N of Bombay, to Cape Comorin at the southern tip of India; a formidable barrier, they have only one major break, the Palghat Gap. The western side of the range, which receives heavy rainfall from moist monsoon winds, has lush tropical vegetation and dense hardwood forests; the eastern side is relatively dry. Conchona, tea, and coffee are the main crops. The Western Ghats are the watershed for S India's main eastward-flowing rivers, the Godavari, Kistna, and Cauvery. Short, steep westward-flowing streams provide hydroelectricity to west-coast cities. The **Eastern Ghats,** a series of hills c.900 mi (1,450 km) long, extend SW from the Mahanadi valley to the Nilgiri Hills; the highest elevations are at the northern and southern ends. Numerous rivers cut across the Eastern Ghats and are used for hydroelectric-power generation and irrigation. The range has valuable hardwood trees.

Ghazali, al- (ăl-găză'lē), 1058–1111, Islamic theologian, philosopher, and mystic. He was born at Tus in Khurasan, of Persian origin. He is considered the greatest theologian in Islam. Al-Ghazali was appointed professor at Baghdad in 1091, but following a spiritual crisis in 1095 he abandoned his career to become a mystic (see SUFISM). After ten years of wandering he settled down to teach in accordance with his new mystical insights, which he formulated very closely to orthodox Islam. Al-Ghazali was the author of several important works; his *Destruction of the Philosophers,* written just prior to his spiritual crisis, opposes the philosophical method of approaching metaphysics when it contradicts orthodox theology. That position had a great influence on the future of speculative thought in Islam. Al-Ghazali's chief work, *The Revival of the Religious Sciences,* outlines a complete and orthodox system of the mystical attainment of unity with God. Al-Ghazali is most important for his attempt to reconcile mysticism with orthodox Islam. He was well known in medieval Europe by his Latin name, Algazel. See W. M. Watt, *Muslim Intellectual: A Study of al-Ghazali* (1963).

Ghaziabad (gä'zēäbäd''), city (1971 pop. 119,179), Uttar Pradesh state, N central India. Ghaziabad is an agricultural market. Diesel engines and other goods are made there. It is on the Delhi-Kanpur railroad. The city was the scene of fighting during the INDIAN MUTINY (1857).

Ghazipur (gä'zēpo͝or''), town (1971 pop. 45,636), Uttar Pradesh state, N central India, on the Ganges River. A district administrative center, Ghazipur is the headquarters of the Indian government's opium monopoly. There is also a perfume industry. Lord Cornwallis, governor-general of British India, died in Ghazipur and is buried there.

Ghazni (gŭz'nē), city (1967 pop. 39,900), capital of Ghazni prov., E central Afghanistan, on the Lora River. Located on the Kabul-Kandahar trade route, Ghazni is a market for sheep, wool, camel's hair cloth, corn, and fruit. The famed Afghan sheepskin coats are made in the city. Most of the inhabitants are Tadzhiks. Ghazni was flourishing by the 7th cent. but reached its peak (962–c.1155) under the Turkish Ghaznivid dynasty, when it was one of Asia's most glorious cities. Mahmud of Ghazni built a magnificent mosque, the Celestial Bride, there. The kings of Ghor sacked Ghazni in 1149 but later (1173) made it their secondary capital. Ogotai, a son of Jenghiz Khan, completed its downfall in 1221; Mahmud's tomb and two high columns outside the city escaped destruction. In 1737 the city became part of the new kingdom of Afghanistan. Ghazni's strong fortress was taken by the British in 1839 and 1842 during the Afghan Wars. The old city of Ghazni, with its numerous bazaars, retains its walls and is topped by a citadel used as a military fort.

Ghazzah: see GAZA.

ghee (gē) [from Skt.], the clarified BUTTER of India. Ghee is one of the most commonly used foods in India. It is also used medicinally and as one of the most ancient sacrificial materials in Hinduism. The best quality is made from cow's milk, though the milk of the buffalo is also used. The usual process is to melt butter until the separated water comes to a boil and to strain or skim off the solid residue. Only the oil of the butter is left, and this may be bottled or put in covered jars (sometimes with aromatic essences) and kept for long periods of time.

Ghelderode, Michel de (mēshĕl' də gĕldərōd'), 1898–1962, Belgian dramatist. He wrote in French and is considered one of the most original French playwrights of modern times. He lived in obscurity until 1949, when he gained prominence with the production of *Fastes d'enfer* (1929). He was influenced by Maeterlinck and Crommelynck, with whom he shared a love for the rich history of ancient Flanders. His vast and varied output reveals a utilization of many sources; *Barabbas* (1928), *Mademoiselle Jaïre* (1934), and *Marie la misérable* (1952) make use of biblical themes or medieval morality plays. The influences of Flemish painters (notably of Bosch and Bruegel), of puppet theater and commedia dell' arte, of Rabelais and the English Elizabethans, and of cultivators of the grotesque and the macabre, especially Poe, are evident in *Pantagleize* (1929), *Magie rouge* (1931), *La Balade du grand macabre* (1934), and *Hop Signor!* (1935). Complex dramatic techniques are used in *Christophe Colomb* (1927) and *Don Juan* (1928). A satirist as well as an exquisite poet, Ghelderode favored themes of death and the devil, gluttony, avarice, and lust, but he also explored the meaning of sacrifice and the heights of religious exaltation. Among his prose works *La Flandre est un songe* (1953) is well known. See his *Théâtre complet* (5 vol., 1950–52). *Les Entretiens d'Ostende* (1956) has been partly translated, together with some of his best plays, in *Seven Plays* (1960).

Ghent (gĕnt), Flemish *Gent,* Fr. *Gand,* city (1970 pop. 148,860), capital of East Flanders prov., W Belgium, at the confluence of the Scheldt and Leie rivers. Connected with the North Sea by the Ghent-Terneuzen Canal and by a network of other canals, Ghent is a major port and the chief textile, clothing, and steel-manufacturing center of Belgium. Other products of the city include plastics, chemicals, paper, processed food, and motor vehicles. It is also the trade center of a flower- and bulb-producing region. One of Belgium's oldest cities (first mentioned in the 7th cent.) and the historic capital of Flanders, Ghent developed around a fortress built (early 10th cent.) by the first count of Flanders on a small island. The town soon spread to nearby islets, still today connected by numerous bridges. By the 13th cent. Ghent had become a major wool-producing center, rivaled only by Bruges and Ypres. Medieval Ghent was an industrial city in the modern sense. Its four chief guilds—weavers, fullers, shearers, and dyers—comprised the majority of the working population. There was social conflict between the workers and the rich bourgeoisie; strikes and insurrections were frequent. After the BATTLE OF THE SPURS (1302), at Kortrijk, the guilds' role in communal government increased rapidly, although not without opposition. A turbulent period of oligarchic rule followed, but the guilds regained power at the beginning (1337) of the Hundred Years War under Jacob van ARTEVELDE and, later, Philip van ARTEVELDE. The guilds continued to rule even after the French defeated and killed (1382) Philip van Artevelde at Rozebeke, and in 1385 the weavers made a favorable peace with Philip the Bold of Burgundy, who had inherited Flanders in the previous year. Ghent retained all its liberties and privileges until 1453, when, as a result of an unsuccessful rebellion, they were drastically curtailed by Philip the Good of Burgundy. They were restored by the Great Privilege, promulgated (1477) by MARY OF BURGUNDY. Mary's marriage (1477) to Archduke Maximilian (later Emperor Maximilian I) took place at Ghent, and their children were kept virtual prisoners by the burghers after Mary's death (1482). It was only in 1485 that Maximilian was able to master the rebellious city and obtain the release of his son Philip (later Philip I of Castile). Philip's son, later Emperor Charles V, was born (1500) and reared at Ghent. In 1539, Ghent rose against Charles, who hastened to Flanders, suppressed (1540) the rebellion, abrogated Ghent's liberties, and established a garrison to prevent further outbreaks. Ghent later joined (1576) William the Silent in the revolt of the NETHERLANDS and Flanders against Spain; the Pacification of Ghent, signed there in November of the same year, was an alliance of the provinces of the Netherlands for the purpose of driving the Spanish from the country. For a time Ghent was a city-republic under Calvinist domination, but its capture (1584) by the Spanish under Alessandro Farnese restored it to Hapsburg rule, under which it remained until the French Revolution. The modern industrialization of Ghent began in the early 19th cent. with the development of its port and the establishment of textile factories. The city was occupied by the Germans in World Wars I and II. Ghent is noted for its many beautiful medieval and Renaissance structures, among which are the ruins of the Abbey of St. Bavon (founded 631) and of the imposing castle (begun 867) of the counts of Flanders, the Cathedral of St. Bavon (10th–16th cent.), the cloth weavers' hall (16th cent.), an unfinished 14th-century belfry (c.300 ft/91 m high) with a celebrated carillon, and the churches of St. Nicholas (13th cent.) and St. James (13th–16th cent.). Flemish painting flourished in Ghent under the Burgundian dynasty (15th cent.); Hugo van der Goes worked there most of his life, and the world famous masterpiece of the Van Eyck brothers, *The Adoration of the Lamb,* is the altarpiece of the Cathedral of St. Bavon. The cathedral also contains a noted Rubens painting. Ghent is an episcopal see and the seat of a university (founded 1816). The poet and dramatist Maurice Maeterlinck was born (1862) in the city.

Ghent, Treaty of, 1814, agreement ending the WAR OF 1812 between the United States and Great Britain. It was signed at Ghent, Belgium, on Dec. 24, 1814, and ratified by the U.S. Senate in Feb., 1815. The American commissioners were John Q. ADAMS, James A. BAYARD, Henry CLAY, Jonathan Russell, and Albert GALLATIN. Negotiations were begun in August, with the recent defeat of Napoleon I giving the British an advantage reinforced by the burning of the Capitol at Washington shortly afterward. Only the victory of Thomas Macdonough at Plattsburg and the threat of further hostilities in Europe induced the British to give up their demands to control the Great Lakes and erect an Indian state under British control in the country NW of the Ohio. Thus the agreement to restore territory and places taken by either party was a diplomatic victory for the United States. It was provided that commissions would be set up to determine the boundary from the St. Croix River west to Lake of the Woods. Both parties were to use their best endeavors to abolish the slave trade. No mention was made of the fisheries question, the impressment of American seamen, or the rights of neutral commerce. See F. L. Engelman, *The Peace of Christmas Eve* (1962).

Gheorghiu-Dej, Gheorghe (gāôr'gā gāôr'gyo͞odăzh), 1901–65, Rumanian Communist leader, b. Moldavia. He joined the Communist party in 1930 and while in prison (1933–44) was elected (1936) to the central committee. Escaping in 1944, he became a leading figure in Rumanian Communist politics. In 1945 he was elected secretary-general of the party, which became the Rumanian Workers' party in 1948. He became premier in 1952. In 1954 he relinquished his party post; in 1955 he resumed party leadership as first secretary of the central committee, yielding the premiership. Elected president of the newly created state council in 1961, he again served as head of both state and party until his death. He stressed a more rational economic policy, including emphasis on the manufacture of consumer goods and Rumanian independence within the socialist context.

Gherardesca, Ugolino della: see UGOLINO DELLA GHERARDESCA.

Gherardo delle Notti: see HONTHORST, GERRIT VAN.

gherkin (gûr'kĭn), species of GOURD of the cucumber genus.

ghetto (gĕt'ō), originally, a section of a city in which Jews lived; it has come to mean a section of a city where members of any racial group are segregated. In the early Middle Ages the segregation of Jews in separate streets or localities was voluntary. The first compulsory ghettos were in Spain and Portugal at the end of the 14th cent. The ghetto was typically walled, with gates that were closed at a certain hour each night, and all Jews had to be inside the gate at that hour or suffer penalties. The reason generally given for compulsory ghettos was that the faith of Christians would be weakened by the presence of Jews; the idea of Jewish segregation dates from the Lateran Councils of 1179 and 1215. Within the ghetto the inhabitants usually had autonomy, with their own courts of law, their own culture, and their own charitable, recreational, educational, and religious institutions. Economic activities, however, were restricted, and beyond the ghetto walls Jews were required to wear badges of identification. One of the most infamous ghettos was that of Frankfurt, to which Jews were compelled to move by a city ordinance of 1460. Crowded into a narrow section, the ghetto underwent several disastrous fires. The ghetto in Venice was established in 1516 after long negotiations between the city and the Jews. In 1870 the last ghetto in Western Europe, in Rome, was abolished. In Russia the Jewish PALE continued to exist until 1917. After the 18th cent. ghettos were also to be found in some Muslim countries. During World War II the Nazis set up ghettos in many towns in E Europe from which Jews were transported to CONCENTRATION CAMPS for liquidation; the WARSAW (Poland) ghetto was a prime example. In the United States blacks, Chicanos, and immigrant groups have been forced to live in ghettos through economic and social forces rather than being required to do so by law. See also ANTI-SEMITISM. See Louis Wirth, *The Ghetto* (rev. ed. 1956).

Ghibellines: see GUELPHS AND GHIBELLINES; HOHENSTAUFEN.

Ghiberti, Lorenzo (lōrĕn'tsō gēbĕr'tē), c.1378–1455, Florentine sculptor. He received his early training in the workshop of Bartoluccio. In 1401 he entered the competition for a bronze portal for the baptistery in Florence. He won the contest against his closest rival, Brunelleschi. Their trial panels, depicting *The Sacrifice of Isaac*, are now in the Bargello. From 1403 to 1424 Ghiberti worked on the north portal. The door was designed to match the earlier portal by Andrea Pisano. Consequently, Ghiberti had to work within the limits of the ornate quatrefoil framework of the Gothic period. The reliefs depicted scenes from the life of Christ and representations of the Evangelists and the Fathers of the Church. During these years Ghiberti also executed several imposing statues for the Church of Or San Michele: *St. John the Baptist, St. Matthew,* and *St. Stephen.* In 1424 he took a short trip to Venice. On his return to Florence he began to design the east portal of the baptistery. He devoted some 23 years to this project, during which time his workshop became one of the leading centers of Florentine activity. Ghiberti was allowed more freedom in the execution of this portal, and within ten square panels he adapted the recent innovations in art. He employed various grades of relief most effectively, from the round to the almost flat *schiacciato* technique. The new system of perspective was skillfully used in the architectural setting of three reliefs, *Isaac, Joseph,* and *Solomon.* The Florentines proudly named his portal the Gates of Paradise. Five of the ten panels were torn off the doors by the flood of 1966 and restored with the aid of exact replicas from San Francisco, Calif. Ghiberti was asked to supervise the building of the Cathedral dome, but he was unsuccessful in this endeavor. In his last years he wrote an important book, the *Commentarii* (tr. by Ludwig Goldscheider, 1949), which contains an analysis of earlier art and an account of his own life. This is the earliest surviving autobiography by an artist. See study by Richard Krautheimer (2d ed. 1970).

Ghilan, Iran: see GILAN.

Ghirlandaio or **Ghirlandajo, Domenico** (both: dōmĕ'nēkō gĕrländä'yō), 1449–94, Florentine painter, whose family name was Bigordi. He may have studied painting and mosaics under Alesso Baldovinetti. Though not a highly inventive artist, Ghirlandaio was an excellent technician. Keenly observant of the contemporary scene, he depicted many prominent Florentine personalities within his religious narrative paintings. Among his earliest frescoes are the *Madonna with the Vespucci Family* and the *Last Supper* (Church of the Ognissanti, Florence). He painted scenes from the life of Santa Fina (collegiate church in San Gimigniano) and frescoes in the Palazzo Vecchio, Florence. In 1481, Pope Sixtus IV called him to Rome, along with Botticelli, to decorate the Sistine Chapel. He painted the *Calling of the First Apostles,* a scene close in spirit to Masaccio. He returned to Florence to work on the frescoes in the Sassetti Chapel in Santa Trinita. He introduced Sassetti, Corsi, Politian, the Medici, and many other contemporaries as participants in the life of St. Francis. Ghirlandaio's most famous achievement is his fresco cycle of the life of Mary and St. John the Baptist for the choir of Santa Maria Novella. Michelangelo served an apprenticeship with him at this time and probably worked on these frescoes. Other examples of his art are the *Adoration of the Magi* (Uffizi); another *Adoration* (Hospital of the Innocents); a mosaic of the *Annunciation* for the Cathedral; a portrait of Francesco Sassetti and his son (Metropolitan Mus.); a portrait of Giovanna Tornabuoni (Morgan Lib., New York City); and the highly realistic portrayal of *Grandfather and Grandson* (Louvre).

Ghor (gôr) or **Ghur** (gŏŏr), mountainous region and province, W central Afghanistan, including a ruined medieval city of the same name. The powerful Muslim Ghorid dynasty was established there in the 12th cent. It was overthrown by Muhammad of Khorezm in 1215. Mongols under Jenghiz Khan took Ghor in 1221, after which the Karts (Mongol clients) ruled (c.1245–1379). The city then lapsed into obscurity.

Ghor, the, Arabic *Al Ghawr,* region of the Jordan Valley, c.70 mi (110 km) long, between the Sea of Galilee (Lake Tiberias) and the Dead Sea, on the Jordan-Israel border. Entirely below sea level and bordered by steep escarpments, it is part of the Great Rift Valley complex. The Jordan River meanders 160 ft (49 m) below the surface through the Ghor. Although the Ghor's flat terraces are fertile, agricultural development is impeded by aridity. In the northern half of the valley, on the Jordan side, is the **East Ghor irrigation project** (built 1958–66). The cement-lined East Ghor Canal parallels the Jordan River for 45 mi (72 km) from the Yarmuk River S to the Zarqa River and irrigates c.30,000 acres (12,100 hectares). The project makes year-round cultivation possible; two or more crops can be grown, with wheat, vegetables, and citrus fruit the main products. The southern extension of the project was halted by the 1967 Arab-Israeli War. In the southern part of the Ghor, oasis farming is practiced; in the nonirrigated parts, sheep and goat herding predominates.

ghor-khar: see ASS.

Ghose, Aurobindo (ôrōbĭn'dō gōsh), 1872–1950, Indian nationalist leader and mystic philosopher. Born in Bengal, he was sent to England and lived there for 14 years, completing his education at Cambridge. Returning to India in 1893, he plunged into the study of Indian languages and culture. The agitation against the partition (1905) of Bengal drew him into the nationalist movement, and for several years he acted as leader of a secret revolutionary organization, becoming well known through his eloquent patriotic writings. He was eventually jailed for subverting British rule and while in prison experienced visions that completely altered his outlook. On release from prison he announced his withdrawal from active political life and retired to Pondicherry in S India where he devoted himself to the practice of yoga and to writing. In his major works, all written in English, he formulates the metaphysics and system of spiritual discipline that he called Integral Yoga (*Purna Yoga*). Rejecting the traditional ideal of world-renunciation and negation of physical existence, he based his philosophy on the principle of the descent of divine force and consciousness into both the individual and the universal processes of nature and history. He described evolution as the effect of progressively higher forces, of which the highest is the "supramental" force that initiates man's final transformation into a state of perfection. In 1926, Sri Aurobindo, as he came to be called, retired into seclusion. He put in charge of his disciples his spiritual consort (SHAKTI), Mira Richard (1878–1973), a French-born woman of Egyptian descent who had joined him in Pondicherry in 1914. His seclusion marked the official establishment of his spiritual community, or ashram. The ashram, the largest in India, remains active. In 1968 construction was begun for a utopian city called Auroville to function on the principles of Aurobindo's philosophy. His writings include *The Life Divine* (1949), *The Synthesis of Yoga* (1948), and *Essays on the Gita* (1921–28, repr. 1950). See Sisirkumar Mitra, *The Liberator Sri Aurobindo, India, and the World* (1970); Beatrice Bruteau, *Worthy is the World* (1971); Kishore Gandhi, ed., *Contemporary Relevance of Sri Aurobindo* (1973); R. A. McDermott, ed., *The Essential Aurobindo* (1973).

Ghose, Chinmoy (gōs), 1931–, Indian mystic and poet. Orphaned at the age of 12, he went to live at the Sri Aurobindo Ashram in S India, where he stayed for the next 20 years, practicing spiritual disciplines. In 1964 he went to the United States, where he lectured and established meditation centers. In 1970 he was appointed director of the United Nations Meditation Group. His numerous writings describe his Yoga of "love, devotion, and surrender" as a swift and safe path to union with God or the Supreme. He stresses the development of the spiritual heart as a human faculty higher than mind and emphasizes the necessity for manifesting God in one's daily life rather than withdrawing from the world. See his *Yoga and the Spiritual Life* (1970), *Meditations: Food for the Soul* (1971), and *Songs of the Soul* (1971).

ghost: see APPARITION; POLTERGEIST.

ghost dance, central ritual of the messianic religion instituted in the late 19th cent. by a Paiute Indian named WOVOKA. The religion prophesied the end of the westward expansion of whites and a return of the land to the Indians. The ritual lasted five successive days, being danced each night and on the last night continued until morning. Hypnotic trances and shaking accompanied this ceremony, which was supposed to be repeated every six weeks. The dance originated among the Paiute c.1870; later, other Indians sent delegates to Wovoka to learn his teachings and ritual. In a remarkably short time the religion spread to most of the Western Indians. The ghost dance is chiefly significant because it was a central feature among the Sioux Indians just prior to the massacre of hundreds of Sioux at Wounded Knee, S. Dak., in 1890. The Sioux, wearing shirts called ghost shirts, believed they would be protected from the soldiers' bullets.

ghost town, term for any once flourishing American community that has been abandoned, generally for economic reasons. While most of the towns have little or no population, they usually contain old buildings, which often serve as tourist attractions. Many, such as Virginia City, Nev., were gold-mining towns hastily built during a boom. When the gold strike ended, the itinerant prospectors left. Ranking with the largest and most interesting Western ghost towns are Silver City, Idaho; Elkhorn, Mont.; Bodie, Calif.; and St. Elmo, Colo. Other ghost towns were former milling centers, railroad connections, or oil-well communities. In Texas several ghost towns were originally settled by European exiles who emigrated to the United States following the 1848 revolutions. Some, such as Burning Bush, Texas, were religious havens. Connecticut has Dudleytown, near Cornwall Bridge on the Housatonic River, a town that was supposedly doomed to extinction because of a hereditary curse on the Dudley family. On the south shore of Massachusetts Bay are deserted shipbuilding towns, where from 1640 to 1872 over 1,000 ships were built. Many deserted areas of towns have been restored to their original appearance; notable examples are Mystic, Conn., Williamsburg, Va., and Harpers Ferry, W. Va. See Dick King, *Ghost Towns of Texas* (1953); F. S. Blanchard, *Ghost Towns of New England* (1960); Lambert Florin, *Western Ghost Towns* (1961); Robert Silverberg, *Ghost Towns of the American West* (1968).

Ghudamis or **Ghadames** (both: gədä'mĕs), town, W Libya, in an oasis in the Sahara, near the borders with Algeria and Tunisia. It was long an important caravan center on the route from Tripoli to the Sudan. The town was held by the Romans and was captured (7th cent.) by the Arabs. In 1830, it submitted to the dey of Tripoli. The town was occupied by the Italians in 1924 and in 1943, during World War II, by the French.

Ghuzzeh: see GAZA.

Giacometti, Alberto (älbĕr'tō jäkōmĕt'tē), 1901–66, Swiss sculptor and painter; son of the impressionist painter Giovannia Giacometti. He settled in Paris in 1922, studying with Bourdelle and becoming associated first with the cubists and then the surrealists. His *Slaughtered Woman* (1932; Mus. of Modern Art, New York City) is a violent surrealist work. In the

1930s and after, he began creating highly original sculptures of elongated, emaciated human figures, usually in bronze. He made open cagelike structures (e.g., *The Palace at 4 A.M.*, 1933; Mus. of Modern Art, New York City) that were equally powerful. These haunting images, disturbing in their palpable isolation, have been described as a perfect expression of existentialist pessimism. In the early 1940s he created works on a reduced scale that nevertheless suggest monumentality. In his later years he again formed tall, nervous figures that are among his most impressive sculptures. Giacometti's tragic imagery and his plastic technique have had an extensive influence on modern sculpture. Many of his drawings and oil paintings are also works of distinction. See catalog by Museum of Modern Art, New York (1965); drawings ed. by J. Lord (1971); studies by J. Lord (1965) and R. Hohl (1971).

Giacosa, Giuseppe (jōōzĕp'pā jäkô'zä), 1847–1906, Italian dramatic poet. After *Una partita a scacchi* [a game of chess] (1873) won him his first success, he devoted himself to playwriting. His plays, which deal largely with life in Piedmont and reflect the bourgeois attitudes of his day, are notable for their simplicity and perceptiveness. Among them are *Tristi amori* (1888, tr. *Unhappy Love* in *Poet Lore*, Vol. XXVII, 1916); *La Dame de Challant*, written in French for Sarah Bernhardt and produced by her in New York in 1891; *Come le foglie* (1900, tr. *As the Leaves Fall*, 1911); and *Il più forte* (1904, tr. *The Stronger*, 1913). With Luigi Illica, Giacosa also wrote the librettos of Puccini's operas *La Bohème* (1896, tr. 1898), *Tosca* (1899, tr. 1900), and *Madame Butterfly* (1904, tr. 1905).

Giah (gī'ə), place, near Gibeon, or possibly a corruption of the text. 2 Sam. 2.24.

Giambologna: see BOLOGNA, GIOVANNI.

Giambono, Michele (mēkĕ'lā jämbō'nō), fl.1420–62, Venetian mosaicist and painter, whose original name was Michele Giovanni Boni. One of the last exponents of the international Gothic style, his work has close affinities with the paintings of Gentile da Fabriano and Jacobello del Fiore. Of his mosaics the most important are *Birth of the Virgin* and *Presentation in the Temple* (St. Mark's, Venice). Among his paintings are *Christ Rising from the Tomb* (Metropolitan Mus.) and *St. Peter* (National Gall. of Art, Washington, D.C.).

Giannotti, Donato (dōnä'tō jän-nôt'tē), 1492–1573, Italian political theorist, b. Florence. He studied at Pisa and in 1527 became secretary of the supreme council of the Florentine republic. After the Medici returned to power (1530), he lived in exile. Giannotti, whose precepts resemble those of Machiavelli, explained his political theory in several books. An ideal government, he believed, was a fusion of aristocratic, monarchical, and democratic institutions. He also wrote the comedy *Vecchio amoroso* [old man in love]. See Randolph Starn, ed., *Donato Giannotti and His Epistolae* (1968).

giant, in mythology, manlike being of great size and strength. The giant has been the symbol for the expression of certain recurring beliefs in the mythologies of all races. He is universally represented as being a brutish power of nature, lacking the stature of gods and the civilization and cunning of men. Among the myths of such different cultures as the Greeks, the Scandinavians, and the American Indian tribes of the Great Plains, giants were believed to be the first race of people that inhabited the earth. Two of the most familiar legends concerning giants are those of Jack the Giant Killer and David and Goliath.

giant clam, common name for the largest bivalve mollusk in the world, *Tridacna gigas*, also known as the bear's paw clam. The giant clam may weigh over 500 lb (225 kg) and attain a length of over 4 ft (120 cm). The heavy shell is coarsely fluted and toothed. Giant clams are found in the South Pacific and Indian oceans, especially in the Great Barrier Reef. They lie with the hinge downward in the coral reefs, usually in shallow water. The adductor muscles, which cause the shell to close, are a source of food for people of the South Pacific. The shell closes very slowly; stories of human beings trapped within giant clams have never been substantiated. Small giant clam shells have been used as birdbaths and baptismal fonts. An interesting symbiosis occurs between a unicellular green alga *(Zooanthella)* and the clam. The algae live in the tissues of the clam's siphon and mantle; they are able to obtain the sunlight needed for photosynthesis because the clam lies with its valves opening upward and part of the thick, purple mantle extruding over the shell. In addition, there are crystalloid vesicles on the mantle surface that let in sunlight, thus allowing the algae to live deep within the tissues. The clam uses the algae as a supplementary or perhaps even a major source of food. *Tridacna gigas* is classified in the phylum MOLLUSCA, class Pelecypoda, order Eulamellibranchia, family Tridacnidae.

giantism: see GIGANTISM.

giant orders: see ORDERS OF ARCHITECTURE.

Giant's Causeway, headland on the north coast of Co. Antrim, N Northern Ireland, NE of Coleraine; est. as a national trust territory in 1961. Extending 3 mi (4.8 km) along the coast, it consists of thousands of basaltic columns of volcanic origin, forming three natural platforms (Little, Middle, and Grand Causeway). There are several large caves and rock formations. According to legend, the Causeway was built for giants to travel across to Scotland. A ship of the Spanish Armada was wrecked in Port-na-Spania (Spanish Bay) nearby.

giant schnauzer: see SCHNAUZER.

giant star: see RED GIANT.

Giap, Vo Nguyen (vô nəwĭn' jäp), 1912–, soldier and government official of the Democratic Republic of (North) Vietnam. A nationalist, he joined the Vietnamese Communist party in the early 1930s. In 1939 he fled to China, where he joined Ho Chi Minh as a military aide. Giap helped to organize the Viet Minh forces, which fought to oust the Japanese in World War II and the French after the war; he became commander of the Viet Minh in 1946. Acclaimed as a master of guerrilla warfare, he was credited with the defeat of the French at Dien Bien Phu (1954) and later directed the strategy of the North in the VIETNAM WAR, with particular success in the Tet offensive of 1968. In addition to his position as commander in chief, Giap also held the posts of deputy prime minister and minister of defense. See his *Military Art of People's War: Selected Writings*, ed. by Russell Stetler (1970); R. J. O'Neill, *General Giap: Politician and Strategist* (1969).

Giauque, William Francis (jēōk'), 1895–, American chemist, b. Niagara Falls, Ont., Canada, grad. Univ. of California (B.S., 1920; Ph.D., 1922). A member of the faculty of the Univ. of California from 1922, he became professor in 1934. He was awarded the 1949 Nobel Prize in Chemistry for his studies of the properties of substances at temperatures approaching absolute zero. In addition to discovering the adiabatic demagnetization method of producing temperatures below 1°K, he was also the discoverer (with H. L. Johnston, 1929) of the second and third isotopes of oxygen.

Gibault, Pierre (pyĕr zhēbō'), 1737–1804, Roman Catholic missionary priest in America, patriot in the American Revolution, b. Montreal. He was sent (1768) to the Illinois country. When Kaskaskia (in his parish) was captured by George Rogers CLARK in 1778, the priest and the frontier soldier became friends, and Father Gibault swore allegiance to the commonwealth of Virginia. He was of tremendous assistance to Clark in winning the people of Vincennes to the patriot cause and in raising a force for the recapture of Vincennes in 1779. Gibault later resided in Vincennes (1785–89) and Cahokia (1789–90), then, after the government had refused to grant land for a seminary, moved to New Madrid (now in Missouri) in Spanish territory.

Gibbar (gĭb'är), family that returned with Zerubbabel. Ezra 2.20. In a similar list, Neh. 7.25, Gibeon appears instead; therefore, Gibbar may stand for Gibeon, and the children of Gibbar are then Gibeonites.

gibberellins (jĭb"ərĕl'ĭnz), a group of growth-regulating substances of plants, having complex chemical structure, of which the best known, gibberellic acid, is noted for its promotion of stem growth. In Japan it was long known that when rice seedlings were attacked by the fungus *Gibberella fujikuroi* they would grow to several times their normal height and then die, a phenomenon the Japanese called "the foolish seedling disease." A substance that caused these same effects was isolated from the fungus and named gibberellin. Other gibberellins exist rather widely in plants, and only an excess appears to cause abnormal effects. Gibberellins are used commercially in agriculture and horticulture to break dormancy, to speed up flowering and fruiting, and to stimulate the production of seedless fruits in the absence of pollination.

Gibbethon (gĭb'əthən), unidentified town, W Palestine. Joshua 19.44; 21.23; 1 Kings 15.27; 16.17.

Gibbon, Edward, 1737–94, English historian, author of *The History of the Decline and Fall of the Roman Empire*. His childhood was sickly, and he had little formal education but read enormously and omnivorously. He went at the age of 15 to Oxford, but was forced to leave because of his conversion to Roman Catholicism. His father sent him (1753) to Lausanne, where he was formally reconverted to Protestantism. Actually, he became a skeptic and later greatly offended the pious by his famous chapters of historical criticism of Christianity in his great work. In Lausanne he fell in love with the penniless daughter of a pastor, Suzanne Curchod (who was later to be the great intellectual, Mme Necker). The two were engaged to be married, but Gibbon's father refused consent. Gibbon "sighed as a lover" but "obeyed as a son" and gave up the match. He left Lausanne in 1758. It was on a visit to Rome that he conceived the idea of his magnificent and panoramic history. This appeared as *The History of the Decline and Fall of the Roman Empire* (6 vol., 1776–88) and won immediate acclaim, despite some harsh criticism. Gibbon himself was assured of the greatness of his work, which is, indeed, one of the most-read historical works of modern times. Gibbon himself was not, however, accorded much personal admiration. He moved in the high circles of society and was a member of the literary circle of Samuel JOHNSON, but he was personally unprepossessing. Short (under 5 ft/1.5 m), bulbously fat, always dressed in ornate and vivid clothes that flattered his vanity but not his appearance, and affected in manner and speech, he was a figure of ridicule. The salons buzzed with stories mocking him. He entered upon a short and highly inglorious political career, serving as a member of Parliament from 1774 to 1783. He violently opposed the American Revolution, although later he was to look with favor on the more radical French Revolution. In 1783 he withdrew to Lausanne, where he completed his masterpiece. One of the fascinating things about Gibbon is the disparity between his personal character and his work, a disparity not resolved by his own *Memoirs of His Life and Writings*, commonly called the *Autobiography*, which first appeared in the edition of his miscellaneous works by Lord Sheffield in 1796 (repr. 1959). The autobiography is, however, one of the most subtle and interesting works of its kind in English. An edition of Gibbon's original six drafts appeared as *The Autobiographies* in 1896. A new edition, edited by G. A. Bonnard, was published in 1969 (Am. ed.). Editions of the *Decline and Fall* are legion. The modern standard edition is that of J. B. Bury (7 vol., 1896–1900). See his collected letters (ed. by J. E. Norton, 3 vol., 1956); biographies by J. W. Swain (1966) and G. De Beer (1968); studies by D. P. Jordan (1971) and R. N. Parkinson (1974).

Gibbon, John, 1827–96, Union general in the Civil War, b. near Holmesburg (now part of Philadelphia), Pa., grad. West Point, 1847. Made a brigadier general of volunteers (1862), he fought in the second battle of Bull Run, at South Mt., at Antietam, and in the Wilderness campaign (1864). After the war he fought in the Indian campaigns in the West. He commanded one of the columns that moved against the Sioux in 1876. The next year he fought an inconclusive battle with the Nez Percés at Big Hole in W Montana. He wrote *Personal Recollections of the Civil War*, which was published posthumously in 1928.

gibbon, small APE, genus *Hyloblates*, found in the forests of SE Asia. The gibbons, including the siamang, are known as the small, or lesser, apes; they are the most highly adapted of the apes to arboreal life. Gibbons are about 3 ft (90 cm) tall and weigh about 15 lb (6.4 kg). Their arms are extremely long in proportion to their body length, and they swing through the trees with great speed and agility, clearing gaps up to 20 ft (6 m) wide. On the ground they walk on two feet, holding their arms up awkwardly; they can also run on all fours. Members of most gibbon species have black faces surrounded by a white ruff; their fur ranges in color from black to buff. Like Old World monkeys and unlike other apes, gibbons have callosities on their buttocks. Gibbons live in permanent families consisting of a male, a female, and their young; families occupy definite territories. They feed on fruits and other plant matter as well as insects and other small animals. Gibbons have powerful voices and at times engage in loud howling, which is answered by other gibbons in the vicinity. The largest gibbon is the siamang, sometimes classified in a separate genus, *Symphalangus*. Deep black, with a reddish brown face, the siamang may weigh up to 25 lb (11.3 kg). Siamangs are further distinguished by the presence in both sexes of a large vocal sac on the throat; this sac is inflated before the animal howls and probably functions to magnify the sound. Such a sac is also found in the male concolor gibbon (*Hyloblates concolor*). Siamangs are found in the high mountain forests of Sumatra and the Malay Peninsula. There are six gibbon species besides the siamang. Gibbons are classified in the phylum CHORDATA, subphylum Vertebrata, class Mammalia, order Primates, family Pongidae.

Gibbons, Grinling, 1648–1721, English wood carver and sculptor, b. Rotterdam. From the reign of Charles II to that of George I he was master wood carver to the crown. Sir Christopher Wren employed him for architectural decoration. Blenheim, Whitehall Palace, and the library of Trinity College, Cambridge, contain masterly carvings by Gibbons. Other works include a marble font in St. James's, Piccadilly, and a bronze statue of James II outside the National Gallery, London.

Gibbons, Orlando, 1583–1625, English organist and composer. He became organist of the Chapel Royal in 1605, court virginalist in 1619, and organist at Westminster Abbey in 1623. His compositions include English anthems and services, chamber music, and madrigals. His brothers, Edward Gibbons (1568–c.1650), who was his teacher, and Ellis Gibbons (1573–1603), were also composers. Only a few pieces of their works survive. His son Christopher Gibbons (1615–76) was organist of Westminster Abbey and left some anthems and string compositions. See E. H. Fellowes, *Orlando Gibbons and His Family* (2d ed. 1952).

Gibbons vs. Ogden, case decided in 1824 by the U.S. Supreme Court. Aaron Ogden, the plaintiff, had purchased an interest in the monopoly to operate steamboats that New York state had granted to Robert Fulton and Robert Livingston. Ogden brought suit in New York against Thomas Gibbons, the defendant, for operating a rival steamboat service between New York City and the New Jersey ports. Gibbons lost his case and appealed to the U.S. Supreme Court, which reversed the decision. At issue was the scope of the commerce clause of Article I, Section 8, of the Constitution; this provides that Congress shall have the power to "regulate Commerce with foreign Nations, and among the several States, and with the Indian Tribes." Chief Justice John Marshall held that the New York monopoly was an unconstitutional interference with the power of Congress over interstate commerce. He condemned the view that the states and the Federal government are equal sovereignties. Federal power is specifically enumerated, but within its sphere Congress is supreme. State legislation may be enacted in areas reserved to the Federal government only if concurrent jurisdiction is feasible (as in the case of taxation). The decision was highly influential in its explication of the Federal structure of the United States.

gibbous phase (gĭb'əs): see PHASE, in astronomy.

Gibbs, James, 1682–1754, English architect, b. Scotland, studied in Rome under Carlo Fontana. Returning to England in 1709, he was appointed a member of the commission authorized to build 50 churches in London. Only 10 of these were completed; they include two of Gibbs's most distinguished works, St. Mary-le-Strand (1714–17) and St. Martin's-in-the-Fields (1721–26); the latter formed a basic inspiration for many of the steepled churches of the colonial period in America. Gibbs did considerable work for the universities, including the circular Radcliffe Camera at Oxford (1739–49), considered his finest design, and the Senate House at Cambridge, where from 1722 onward he was constantly employed. He designed also many town and country houses. His works have the distinction characteristic of the Georgian period and of the work of Sir Christopher Wren, by whom he was chiefly influenced. He wrote a *Book of Architecture* (1728, repr. 1968) and *Rules for Drawing the Several Parts of Architecture* (1732). See study by Bryan Little (1955).

Gibbs, Josiah Willard, 1839–1903, American mathematical physicist, b. New Haven, Conn., grad. Yale, 1858. He studied abroad and was professor of mathematical physics at Yale from 1871. His great contributions to physical chemistry and thermodynamics have had a profound effect on industry, notably in the production of ammonia. He formulated the concept of chemical potential. In mathematics he wrote on quaternions and was influential in developing vector analysis. His work in statistical mechanics was especially important. Gibbs also contributed to crystallography, the determination of planetary and comet orbits, and electromagnetic theory. James Clerk Maxwell was one of the first European scientists to recognize Gibbs as a theoretical physicist of international stature. Gibbs was also interested in the practical side of science; his doctorate was the first granted by Yale for an engineering thesis, and he received a patent (1866) for an improved type of railroad brake. His *Scientific Papers* appeared in 1906 (repr. 1961) and his *Collected Works* in 1928.

Gibbs, Sir Philip, 1877–1962, English journalist and author. As a result of his distinguished service in World War I as a front-line correspondent for the *Daily Chronicle* (London) he was knighted in 1920. Among his many novels are *The Street of Adventure* (1909), *The Middle of the Road* (1922), and *This Nettle Danger* (1939). He also wrote historical studies, astute commentaries on world events, and several autobiographical works, including *The Pageant of the Years* (1946).

Gibbs free energy: see FREE ENERGY.

Gibea (gĭb'ēə), name of Caleb's grandson occurring in a list of Judahite towns. 1 Chron. 2.49. It is possibly the same as GIBEAH **2.**

Gibeah (gĭb'ēə). **1** Home town and capital of Saul, the present-day Tall al Ful (Jordan), 3 mi (4.8 km) N of Jerusalem. It was the first political center of Israel. Judges 19.12; 1 Sam. 10.26; 11.4; 13; 14; Isa. 10.29. A fortress that may have been Saul's residence was excavated there. See L. A. Sinclair, *An Archaeological Study of Gibeah* (1960). **2** Town, S. Palestine, somewhere S of Hebron. Joshua 15.57. The Gibeah of 2 Chron. 13.2 may be the same as either of these or a different place. See also GIBEA.

Gibeon (gĭb'ēən), ancient town, NNW of Jerusalem. Its alliance with Israel saved its inhabitants from destruction but not from slavery. Joshua 9; 10; 21.17. Modern excavations in the area have discovered an interesting water system, perhaps referred to in 2 Sam. 2.13; Jer. 41.12. See GIBBAR. See studies by J. B. Pritchard (1962 and 1964) and Joseph Blenkinsopp (1972).

Giblite, inhabitant of BYBLOS.

Gibraltar (jĭbrôl'tər), town (1970 pop. 27,965), 2.5 sq mi (6.5 sq km), a British crown colony. Gibraltar is located at the northwest end of the Rock of Gibraltar (Lat. *Calpe*), one of the PILLARS OF HERCULES. The rock itself forms a peninsula of S Spain at the eastern end of the Strait of Gibraltar, which joins the Mediterranean with the Atlantic. The peninsula is connected with the mainland by a low sandy area of neutral ground. West of the peninsula is the Bay of Gibraltar, an inlet of the strait. There is a safe enclosed harbor of 440 acres (178 hectares). The rock, of Jurassic limestone, contains caves in which valuable archaeological finds have been made. It is honeycombed by defense works and arsenals, which are largely concealed. A tunnel bisects the rock from east to west. The town is a free port, with some transit trade. The climate is mild and pleasant, and efforts have been made recently to attract more tourists. Since the colony is a fortress, most of the area is taken up by military installations, and the civilian population is kept small. Many of the laborers live in the Spanish border town of La Línea. The population is mostly of Spanish, Italian, or Portuguese descent. English is the official language. The name *Gibraltar* derives from the Arabic *Jabal-al-Tarik* [mount of Tarik], which dates from the capture (711) of the peninsula by the Moorish leader Tarik. The Spanish took the peninsula in 1309 and held it until 1333, but did not definitively recover it from the Moors until 1462. The English have maintained possession since 1704 despite continual Spanish claims to it. The British post was besieged unsuccessfully by the Spanish and French in 1704, by the Spanish in 1726, and again by the Spanish and French from 1779 to 1783. In World War I, Gibraltar served as a naval station. Many refugees fled there in the Spanish civil war (1936–39). In World War II its fortifications were strengthened, and most of the civilian population was evacuated. It was frequently bombed in 1940–41, but not seriously damaged. After the war Spain renewed claims to Gibraltar, which, as a British strategic air and naval base, continues to be a major source of friction between Great Britain and Spain. In the late 1960s, Spain closed its border with Gibraltar. The residents affirmed (1967) their ties with Britain in a UN-supervised referendum. See studies by J. D. Stewart (1967) and E. D. S. Bradford (1972).

Gibson, Althea, 1927–, U.S. tennis player, b. Silver, S.C. In 1948 she won the first of 10 straight national Negro women's singles championships. She was the first black to play in the U.S. grass court championships at Forest Hills, N.Y. (1950), and at Wimbledon, England (1951). In addition to many international tournament victories, she won both the U.S. and English women's singles championships in 1957 and 1958. She retired from competition in 1958. In 1971 she was named to the National Lawn Tennis Hall of Fame. See her autobiography, *I Always Wanted to Be Somebody* (1958).

Gibson, Charles Dana, 1867–1944, American illustrator, b. Roxbury, Mass., studied at the Art Students League and in Paris. His work for *Life, Century, Harper's, Scribner's, Collier's Weekly,* and other magazines established him as a leading illustrator and delineator of aristocratic social ideals, most notably that of the ideal woman who came to be known as the Gibson Girl. His incisive drawings of fashionable life often convey both humor and understanding. He illustrated numerous books, notably Anthony Hope's *Prisoner of Zenda* and R. H. Davis's *Soldiers of Fortune.* Among the books of his drawings are *The Education of Mr. Pipp* (1899), *The Americans* (1900), *A Widow and Her Friends* (1902), *The Social Ladder* (1902), and *The Gibson Book* (1906).

Gibson, John, 1740–1822, American frontiersman, b. Lancaster, Pa. After taking part in the capture (1758) of Fort Duquesne (renamed Fort Pitt) in the French and Indian War, he became an Indian trader there. He was captured by Indians in Pontiac's Rebellion and served in Lord Dunmore's War. In the American Revolution he was principally useful in dealing with the Western Indians. For a time (1781–82) he was commander at Fort Pitt. Later he was living in Pennsylvania at the time of the Whiskey Rebellion and earned much animosity from his neighbors by siding with the government. He served (1800–1816) as secretary of Indiana Territory and was of great aid to William Henry Harrison. See biography by C. W. Hanko (1955).

Gibson, John, 1790–1866, English sculptor of the classical school. His early promise gained him admirers, and in 1817 he was sent to Rome. There he worked successively in the studios of Canova and Thorvaldsen. He lived chiefly in Rome, although most of his commissions came from England. Gibson, invoking the precedent of the Greeks, endeavored to popularize tinted statues. See biography by Lady Eastlake (1870), containing his autobiography.

Gibson, John Bannister, 1780–1853, American jurist, b. Westover Mills, Pa.; nephew of John Gibson. He studied law, was unsuccessful in practice, and served (1810–12) with distinction in the state legislature before being appointed judge. In 1816 he became an associate justice and in 1827 the chief justice of the Pennsylvania supreme court. His diligent study made him an authority on the common law, and his many forceful, well-worded decisions, based on principles rather than precedents, showed great ability to adapt the law to a particular society and did much to mold Pennsylvania law. His decisions were widely quoted by his contemporaries in both England and the United States. See his memoirs (ed. by T. P. Roberts, 1890).

Gibson, Paris, 1830–1920, American pioneer and politician, b. Brownfield, Maine. After serving in the Maine legislature he moved to Minneapolis, where he built the first flour mill and started woolen mills. By 1879 he was in Fort Benton, Mont., where he became a sheep raiser. Realizing the industrial value of the great falls of the Missouri River, he promoted and planned the city of Great Falls, becoming its first mayor. He was a pioneer in power mining, railroading, and sheep raising in Montana. As U.S. Senator (1901–5) he urged progressive Western views on conservation, reclamation, and homestead legislation.

Gibson, Randall Lee, 1832–92, Confederate general and U.S. legislator, b. Woodford co., Ky. Gibson served in most of the Western campaigns of the Civil War, first as an artillery officer and later as commander of an infantry brigade. After the war he practiced law in New Orleans and later was a U.S. Representative (1875–83) and Senator (1883–92). He was Paul Tulane's agent in reorganizing the Univ. of Louisiana as Tulane; he became the first president of the board of administrators of the university.

Gibson, Robert, 1935–, U.S. baseball player, b. Omaha, Neb. A right-handed fastball pitcher with the St. Louis Cardinals since 1959, he won a total of 237 games through the 1973 season and was second to Walter Johnson in lifetime strikeouts (2,928). In 1968, Gibson was named the National League's most valuable player, and in 1970 he won the Cy Young Award for best pitcher.

Giddalti (gĭdăl'tī), temple musician. 1 Chron. 25.4, 29.

Giddel (gĭd'əl), name of a family that returned with Zerubbabel. Ezra 2.47, 56; Neh. 7.49, 58.

Giddings, Franklin Henry, 1855–1931, American sociologist, b. Fairfield co., Conn., grad. Union College, Schenectady, N. Y. His early experience was in journalism. In 1894 he became professor of sociology at Columbia, where he earned a reputation as a brilliant teacher. His explanation of social phenomena was based on the principle of "consciousness of kind." Giddings encouraged statistical studies in sociology. His most important works are *The Principles of Sociology* (1896), *Democracy and Empire* (1900), *Studies in the Theory of Human Society* (1922), and *The Scientific Study of Human Society* (1924).

Giddings, Joshua Reed, 1795–1864, American abolitionist, b. Tioga Point (now Athens), Pa. A successful lawyer in Jefferson, Ohio, he represented the Western Reserve in Congress (1838–59). For his militant antislavery tactics he was censured (1842) by Congress. He resigned, but was promptly reelected despite the opposition of his party (Whig). He became a Free-Soiler in 1848 and a Republican in 1855. After 1861 he was consul general to Canada. See biography by his son-in-law, George W. Julian (1892); J. B. Stewart, *Joshua R. Giddings and the Tactics of Radical Politics* (1970).

Gide, André (äNdrā′ zhēd), 1869–1951, French writer. He established a reputation as an unconventional novelist with *The Immoralist* (1902, tr. 1930), a partly autobiographical work in which he portrays a young man contravening ordinary moral standards in his search for self-fulfillment. In this and other major novels, including *Strait is the Gate* (1909, tr. 1924), *Lafcadio's Adventures* (1914, tr. 1927), and *The Counterfeiters* (1926, tr. 1927), Gide shows individuals seeking out their own natures, which may be at conflict with prevailing ethical concepts. Raised as a Protestant, Gide became a leader of French liberal thought and was one of the founders (1909) of the influential *Nouvelle Revue française*. He was controversial for his frank defense of homosexuality and for his espousal of Communism and his subsequent disavowal of it after a visit to the Soviet Union. His voluminous writings, which include plays, stories, and essays, show great diversity of subjects and literary techniques. His use of myth to embody his thought is evident in such early satirical tales as *Prometheus Misbound* (1899, tr. 1933). His *Travels in the Congo* (1927, tr. 1929) and *Retour du Tchad* (1928) helped bring about reform of French colonial policy in Africa. In 1947 he was awarded the Nobel Prize in Literature. See his autobiography, *If It Die* (tr. 1935, repr. 1957), and his journals (1889–1949), tr. and ed. by Justin O'Brien (4 vol., 1947–51); studies by Justin O'Brien (1953), Jean Hytier (tr., 1967), Vinio Rossi (1967), G. D. Painter (rev. ed. 1968), and A. J. Guérard (2d ed. 1969).

Gide, Charles (shärl), 1847–1932, French economist. A professor at the universities of Bordeaux, Montpellier, and Paris, Gide was an expert on international monetary problems. He also played an important part in the cooperative movement, and his *Consumers' Co-operative Societies* (1904; tr. from 3d French ed., 1921) is a classic in the field. His other works include *Principles of Political Economy* (1883; tr. from 23d ed., 1924) and, with Charles Rist, *History of Economic Doctrines* (1909; tr. from 2d ed., 1915). See Karl Walter, ed., *Co-operation and Charles Gide* (1933).

Gideon (gĭd′ēən), **Gedeon** (gĕ′dēən), **Jerubbaal** (jērŭb′āəl, -rəbā′əl), or **Jerubbesheth** (jē″rəbē′-shĕth, jērŭb′ə-), one of the greater judges of Israel, a strong opponent of the Baal cult. He defeated the Midianite oppressors and appeased the rival Ephramites. He refused the kingship because of his belief that God was the king of Israel. Judges 6–8; Heb. 11.32. Jerubbaal: Judges 6.30–32; 7.1. Jerubbesheth: 2 Sam. 11.21. For the relation between these names, see BAAL.

Gideoni (gĭdēō′nī), father of ABIDAN.

Gideons: see BIBLE SOCIETIES.

Gideon vs. Wainwright, case decided in 1963 by the U.S. Supreme Court. Clarence Earl Gideon was convicted of a felony in a Florida court. He had defended himself after being denied a request for free counsel. The Supreme Court, in overturning his conviction, held that the right to counsel, guaranteed in Federal trials by the Sixth Amendment to the Constitution, is fundamental to a fair trial. State failure to provide counsel for a defendant charged with a felony violated the due process clause of the FOURTEENTH AMENDMENT to the Constitution. The decision was one of many by the Supreme Court under Chief Justice Earl Warren that protected the rights of accused criminals and extended the guarantees in the Bill of Rights to state actions. The holding was expanded in 1972 to require counsel for any defendant who would spend even one day in jail if found guilty. See Anthony Lewis, *Gideon's Trumpet* (1964).

Gidom (gī′dŏm), place, Palestine. Judges 20.45.

Giedion, Sigfried (zēkh′frēd gē′dēôn), 1883–1968, Swiss historian of architecture. Giedion was a student of Heinrich WÖLFFLIN and close associate of Walter GROPIUS. He was a key figure of the International Congress of Modern Architecture (see CIAM) from its inception (1928), and taught at Massachusetts Institute of Technology and Harvard where he became chairman of the graduate school of design. Author of several major histories of architecture, Giedion presented lectures at Harvard in which he broke with the German materialist tradition of 19th-century art history and described history in terms of constancy and change. These lectures were collected in *Space, Time, and Architecture* (1941). Among Giedion's other works are *Gropius* (1931, tr. 1954) and the two volumes of lectures entitled *The Eternal Present* (1964).

Gielgud, Sir John (gĭl′gŏŏd), 1904–, English actor, director, and producer. A grandnephew of Ellen Terry, Gielgud made his debut at the Old Vic in 1921. He soon established himself as an actor of the first rank; his portrayal of Hamlet, which he first gave in 1929 and repeated more than 500 times, is considered the finest of his generation. Gielgud was widely applauded for his solo reading of excerpts from Shakespeare in *Ages of Man* (1956–59). He gave outstanding performances in revivals of works by Wilde and Congreve and in several films, notably *Secret Agent* (1936), *Julius Caesar* (1953), *Richard III* (1956), and *The Charge of the Light Brigade* (1968). He was acclaimed as Harry in David Storey's stage production *Home* (1970). He was knighted in 1953. See his autobiography, *Early Stages* (1939) and reminiscences, *Distinguished Company* (1973); study by Ronald Hayman (1971).

Gierek, Edward (gyĕ′rĕk), 1913–, Polish politician. His family immigrated to France, where he was raised. He joined the French Communist party in 1931 and was later deported to Poland for organizing a strike. He went to Belgium, joining the Communist party there. He returned to Poland in 1948 after the merger of Communists and Socialists into the Polish United Workers' party. Rising in the party hierarchy, he also became (1957) a deputy to the Polish parliament. In 1959 he regained the politburo seat that he had occupied briefly in 1956. As first secretary of the Katowice city party organization (1957–70), Gierek created a personal power base and became the recognized leader of the young technocrat faction of the party. When rioting over economic conditions broke out in late 1970, Gierek replaced Władysław Gomułka as party first secretary.

Giers, Nikolai Karlovich (nyĭkəlī′ kär′ləvĭch gē-yĕrs′), 1820–95, Russian statesman. Appointed deputy foreign minister in 1875, he increasingly took over the duties of the elderly foreign minister Aleksandr GORCHAKOV, whom he succeeded in 1882. He sought to preserve the THREE EMPERORS' LEAGUE with Germany and Austria-Hungary. This policy, however, conflicted with the expansionist desires of all three powers, particularly those of Austria-Hungary and Russia in the Balkans, and in 1887 Czar Alexander III refused to renew the league. Nevertheless, Giers was able to maintain a limited alliance with Germany through the Reinsurance treaty (1887). In 1890, however, Germany refused to renew the Reinsurance treaty and Giers reluctantly negotiated (1891–94) a Franco-Russian alliance, which became the nucleus of the Triple Entente (see TRIPLE ALLIANCE AND TRIPLE ENTENTE).

Gies, William John (gīz), 1872–1956, American biological chemist, b. Reisterstown, Md., grad. Gettysburg College (B.S. 1893; Ph.D. Yale, 1897). He began teaching at Columbia in 1898 and served as secretary of the faculty of the College of Physicians and Surgeons (1905–21). He was instrumental in establishing the School of Dentistry at Columbia, and his negotiations led to the formation of the American Association of Dental Schools. Gies wrote many textbooks, contributed articles to scientific journals, and edited the *Journal of Dental Research*.

Giesebrecht, Wilhelm von (vĭl′hĕlm fən gē′zə-brĕkht), 1814–89, German historian. A gifted student of Ranke, he later taught at the Univ. of Königsberg. His *Geschichte der deutschen Kaiserzeit* [history of the imperial period of Germany] (5 vol., 1855–88) remains a monument of scholarship as well as literature. It terminates with the reign of Emperor Frederick I.

Gieseking, Walter (väl′tər gē′zəkĭng), 1895–1956, German pianist, b. Lyons, France, grad. Hanover Municipal Conservatory, 1916. He began touring Europe in 1920 and made his American debut in 1926. A brilliant pianist with a wide repertoire, he especially excelled in performing the music of Debussy. In 1939 he returned to Germany. After World War II, political controversy prevented his performing in the United States, but after being cleared of the charge of Nazi collaboration he again gave concerts in both hemispheres.

Giessen (gē′sən), city (1970 pop. 75,555), Hesse, central West Germany, on the Lahn River. It is an industrial center and rail junction. Its manufactures include textiles, tobacco products, rubber goods, and machinery. Iron ore is mined nearby. Giessen was chartered by 1248 and became the chief town of Upper HESSE. The city was heavily damaged in World War II. It is the seat of a famous university (founded 1607), where the chemist Justus von Liebig taught (1824–52).

Gifford, Sanford R., 1823–80, American painter, b. Greenfield, N.Y. A major painter of the American movement known as LUMINISM, Gifford is celebrated for his atmospheric landscapes. Characteristic of his romantic panoramas is the shimmering *Ruins of the Parthenon* (1880; Corcoran Gall., Washington, D.C.).

Gifford, William, 1756–1826, English journalist and critic. He was editor (1797–98) of the *Anti-Jacobin* and first editor (1809–24) of the archconservative *Quarterly Review*. Although perceptive, his critical writings are frequently marred by harsh and short-sighted opposition to young and "radical" poets. His most famous poems are *The Baviad* (1794) and *The Maeviad* (1795), satirizing the English DELLA-CRUSCANS. He translated Juvenal (1802) and Persius (1821) and edited the works of Massinger, Jonson, and John Ford.

gift, in law, voluntary transfer of property from one person to another without any compensation for it and without any obligation of an agreement or contract. The one who gives is the donor; the one who receives the gift, the donee. There are two main classes of gifts, gifts *inter vivos* and gifts *causa mortis*. The former is an outright transfer of property, the ordinary type of gift. A gift *causa mortis*, on the other hand, resembles a LEGACY, or bequest made under a WILL. It is a gift made by a person in expectation of imminent death and is not complete until the donor dies. The donor in such a situation may make a gift by delivering the goods or note or whatever is the subject of the gift to the donee, but the donor retains full TITLE to the gift and may revoke it at any time before his death. The ordinary gift *inter vivos* is complete and unconditional as soon as the delivery of the gift is made. The nature of the gift is of considerable importance in taxation. In both types of gifts, it is essential that there be an actual and full delivery of the article given as well as donative intent on the part of the donor. The delivery may be by handing to the donee or by giving it to some other person for the donee, but in all cases the delivery must be such as to take the property given out of the hands and the control of the donor. Commonly gifts are spoken of as involving both real estate and personal PROPERTY. The law does not recognize a true gift of real estate, for real estate can be transferred only by deed or will. Gifts in law are only of personal property. A promise to deliver a gift in the future, or a promise to make a gift, unless under seal or made under very unusual circumstances, cannot be legally enforced. A gift should be distinguished from a barter or exchange, as the element of consideration (payment of some sort) necessary for the latter two is not present in a gift.

Gifu (gē′fōō), city (1970 pop. 385,614), capital of Gifu prefecture, central Honshu, Japan. A manufacturing and railway center, it has textile and paper industries. It is the seat of three universities and of the Nawa Entomology Institute (founded 1896). Strategically located between Kyoto and Tokyo, Gifu served as the headquarters (16th cent.) of Nobunaga. The city was reduced to ashes by fires following an earthquake in 1891. Gifu prefecture (1970 pop. 1,758,791), 4,052 sq mi (10,495 sq km), is mountainous and includes part of the Kiso plain. There are large zinc deposits in the region. Population is concentrated in Gifu (the capital), Ogaki, and Seki.

gigantism, condition in which an animal or plant is far greater than normal in size. Plants are often deliberately bred to increase their size. However, among animals, gigantism is usually the result of hereditary and glandular disturbance. Among humans, gigantism is produced by an oversecretion of growth hormones by the acidophilic cells in the anterior lobe of the pituitary, causing excessive growth of all the tissues of the body. The metabolic rate is usually at least 20% above normal, which could be caused by an excess of the growth hormone alone, or oversecretion of the thyroid hormone in addition. Usually hyperglycemia (overactivity of the insulin-producing cells of the pancreas) is present. This condition eventually leads to degeneration of the islet cells, causing diabetes. Because of these metabolic abnormalities, the life expectancy of a giant is considerably less than normal. The treatment for gigantism is usually irradiation of the pituitary. The excessive height of the pituitary giant, which is defined at various levels above 7 ft (213 cm) is caused by excessive growth of the long bones. However, if the pituitary becomes overactive after growth is complete (marked by closure of the epiphyses of the long bones), the condition known as ACROMEGALY results. GIANTS appear in the legends and folklore of many cultures.

Gigli, Beniamino (bānyämē'nō jē'lyē), 1890–1957, Italian tenor. He made his debut (1914) at Rovigo, Italy, as Enzo in *La Gioconda*. At the Metropolitan Opera, New York City, he was a leading tenor in French and Italian operas from 1920 to 1932. After guest appearances there in the season of 1938–39, he returned to Italy.

gigue: see JIG.

Gihon (gī'hŏn). **1** One of the four rivers of Eden. Gen. 2.13. **2** Spring, in the Qidron valley. 1 Kings 1.33; 2 Chron. 32.30.

Gijón (hēhōn'), city (1970 pop. 187,612), Oviedo prov., N Spain, in Asturias, on the Bay of Biscay. This major seaport, the largest city in Asturias, is an industrial and commercial center exporting large quantities of coal and iron. It has steel, iron, chemical, glass, and food and tobacco industries. Of pre-Roman origin, Gijón was one of the first places recaptured from the Moors early in the 8th cent. The city flourished under the first Asturian kings. In 1588 the defeated Spanish Armada took refuge there. Of interest are Roman baths; 14th-, 15th-, and 16th-century palaces; a 15th-century church; and several 17th-century mansions.

Gila (hē'lə), river, 630 mi (1,014 km) long, rising in the mountains of W N.Mex. and flowing W across Ariz. to the Colorado River at Yuma, Ariz.; the San Francisco River is its main tributary. The Gila valley was occupied by the ancestors of the Pima and Papago Indians, who farmed the region by irrigation; the ruins of their dwellings are preserved in Casa Grande Ruins and Gila Cliff Dwellings national monuments (see NATIONAL PARKS AND MONUMENTS, table). In the headwater region of the Gila are Gila National Forest and the government-preserved "unimproved" Gila Wilderness Area. The Gila and its tributaries have many dams to provide flood control, hydroelectricity, and water for irrigation in the arid Southwest (see SALT RIVER VALLEY). Coolidge and Painted Rock dams are the largest dams on the Gila River.

Gila Cliff Dwellings National Monument: see NATIONAL PARKS AND MONUMENTS (table).

Gilalai (gĭl'əlā, gĭlā'lāī, gĭləlā'ī), one of Ezra's musicians. Neh. 12.36.

gila monster (hē'lə), venomous lizard, *Heloderma suspectum*, found in the deserts of the SW United States and NW Mexico. It averages 18 in. (45 cm) in length, with a large head, stout body, thick tail that acts as a food reservoir, and short legs with strong claws. Its skin is covered with beadlike scales. Its coloring is marbled, a combination of brown or black with orange, pink, yellow, or dull white. The lizard's movements are slow and clumsy. It feeds on young birds and mammals and on eggs. Because the neurotoxic venom is produced by glands in the lower jaw and the grooved teeth through which it passes are set far back in the mouth, venom does not always enter the wound when a victim is bitten. The gila monster must fix its teeth deeply in a certain position to give a fatal bite. The only other member of the genus *Heloderma*, the beaded lizard, *H. horridum*, is a somewhat larger black and yellow lizard, found in W Mexico. These two species are the only known venomous lizards. They are classified in the phylum CHORDATA, subphylum Vertebrata, class Reptilia, order Squamata, family Helodermatidae.

Gilan or **Ghilan** (both: gēlän'), province (1966 pop. 1,752,504), c.15,700 sq mi (40,700 sq km), NW Iran, bounded in the N by the Caspian Sea and in the NE by the Elburz mts. RASHT is the capital and chief city; other cities include Zanjan and Bandar-e Pahlavi. Much of the province has a subtropical climate. Fish, caviar, and rice are important products; tobacco, fruit, tea, and peanuts are also produced. Textiles are manufactured. Gilan was ruled by the Mongols in the 13th and early 14th cent. and was incorporated into Persia by the Safavid dynasty in the late 16th cent. It was occupied by Russia from 1722 to 1732 and was (1920–21) a Soviet republic.

Gilbert, Cass, 1859–1934, American architect, b. Zanesville, Ohio, studied at the Massachusetts Institute of Technology and in Europe. In 1880 he entered the employ of McKim, Mead, and White, New York City, and three years later opened his own office in St. Paul, Minn. He returned in 1899 to New York, where he became widely known for the design of the Woolworth Building (1913). This 60-story office building, with its Gothic trim, exerted considerable influence in its time on the development of the SKYSCRAPER. Among Gilbert's other conspicuous works are the New York Life Insurance Company Building and the Federal Courts Building, New York City; the U.S. Treasury Annex, the U.S. Chamber of Commerce, and the Supreme Court Building, Washington, D.C.; and public libraries in Detroit, St. Louis, and New Haven, Conn. He was consulting architect for the George Washington Bridge.

Gilbert, Grove Karl, 1843–1918, American geologist, b. Rochester, N.Y., grad. Univ. of Rochester, 1862. When the U.S. Geological Survey was created in the Dept. of the Interior in 1879 (to replace four surveys in the Dept. of the Interior and the Dept. of War), Gilbert was appointed senior geologist. His *Report on the Geology of the Henry Mountains* (U.S. Geographical and Geological Survey of the Rocky Mountain Region, 1877, 2d ed. 1880) contains the first description of a laccolithic mountain group, a form of mountain structure that he was the first to recognize and explain. The report introduced concepts of erosion, river development, and glaciation that are incorporated in modern theories of physical geology. One of the publications of the Geological Survey is Gilbert's *Lake Bonneville* (1890), a study of the ancient lake of which Great Salt Lake is the remnant. He mapped the ancient shores and outlets of the Great Lakes and was the first to recognize that the successive levels of the lakes were caused by the barrier of the receding glacier, which cut off the natural drainage of the region. He also published notable studies on Niagara Falls and the Niagara River, the glaciation and morphology of the Sierra Nevada, and hydraulic mining debris in the Sierra Nevada. In 1899 he accompanied the Harriman Alaskan expedition and wrote the volume *Glaciers and Glaciation* in its reports. See biography by W. M. Davis in the *Memoirs* of the National Academy of Sciences, Vol. XXI (1926).

Gilbert, Henry Franklin Belknap, 1868–1928, American composer, b. Somerville, Mass.; pupil of Edward MacDowell. In much of his music he made use of Negro folk tunes. Outstanding among his orchestral works are his *Comedy Overture on Negro Themes* (1911), *Negro Rhapsody* (1913), and *Dance in the Place Congo* (1918).

Gilbert, Sir Humphrey, 1537?–1583, English soldier, navigator, and explorer; half brother of Sir Walter RALEIGH. Knighted (1570) for his service in the campaigns in Ireland, he later (1572) served in the Netherlands. Becoming convinced of the existence of a NORTHWEST PASSAGE, he set forth his theories in his famous *Discourse* (ed., with some additions, by George Gascoigne in 1576), which inspired the voyages of Martin FROBISHER and John DAVIS and for many years motivated English exploration in the northern regions. In 1578, Queen Elizabeth I granted Gilbert a patent authorizing him to explore and to found colonies in America or other lands of his finding. His first expedition, undertaken the same year, failed completely, but upon his second voyage (1583) he reached Newfoundland. Entering the harbor of present-day St. John's, he took possession of the region in the name of the queen and assumed authority as governor over the colony of fishermen he found there. Still in search of the Northwest Passage, he explored to the southwest, but the loss of one of his ships and other disasters led to his decision to return to England. The little vessel in which Gilbert insisted upon making his voyage was lost in a storm in the Azores. The narrative of Gilbert's voyage by Edward Hayes is included with other documents in *Sir Humfrey Gylberte and His Enterprise* (ed. by Carlos Slafter, 1903, repr. 1967). See also D. B. Quinn, ed., *The Voyages and Colonising Enterprises of Sir Humphrey Gilbert* (2 vol., 1940); biography by W. G. Gosling (1911, repr. 1970).

Gilbert, William, 1544–1603, English scientist and physician. He studied medicine at Cambridge Univ. (M.D., 1569), where he was elected a Fellow of St. John's College, and set up practice in London, becoming president of the College of Physicians (1599) and court physician to Queen Elizabeth I (1600) and later also to James I. He is best known, however, for his studies of electricity and magnetism. He coined the word *electricity* (from the Greek for "amber"), was the first to distinguish clearly between electric and magnetic phenomena, and published (1600) *De Magnete*, the most important work on MAGNETISM until the early 19th cent. In it he described his methods for strengthening natural magnets (loadstones) and for using them to magnetize steel rods by stroking; he also outlined his investigations of the earth's magnetic field, from which he concluded that the earth as a whole behaves like a giant magnet with its poles near the geographic poles. He found that an iron bar that is left in alignment with the earth's magnetic field will slowly become magnetized, and that sufficient heating will cause a magnet to lose its magnetism. See translations of his *De Magnete* by P. F. Mottelay (1893, repr. 1958) and S. P. Thompson (1901, repr. 1958).

Gilbert, Sir William Schwenck, 1836–1911, English playwright and poet. He won fame as the librettist of numerous popular operettas, written in collaboration with the composer Sir Arthur SULLIVAN. While on the staff of the magazine *Fun*, he first became known as the author of *Bab Ballads*, amusing but often bitter and cynical poems, published in that magazine and collected in 1869. His first play *Dulcamara* was produced in 1866. It was followed by several fairly successful comedies, dramas, and burlesques. In 1871, Gilbert began his collaboration with Arthur Sullivan, lasting about 20 years, which resulted in the popular operettas for which they are famous. The first of their joint works was *Thespis* (1871) and the last was *The Grand Duke* (1896). Their most famous operettas are *Trial by Jury* (1875), *H.M.S. Pinafore* (1878), *The Pirates of Penzance* (1879), *Patience* (1881), *Iolanthe* (1882), *Princess Ida* (1884), *The Mikado* (1885), *Ruddigore* (1887), *The Yeoman of the Guard* (1888), and *The Gondoliers* (1889). Gilbert's lyrics are those of a metrical craftsman. In his songs he satirized various aspects of Victorian life: aesthetes, the navy, the law, and women's education. The Savoy Theatre, built by Richard D'Oyly Carte in 1881 to house Gilbert and Sullivan operas, gave them the name Savoy operas. About 1896 a quarrel between Gilbert and Sullivan concerning a business arrangement with Carte terminated their collaboration. Thereafter neither of them produced anything to equal their joint works. See Gilbert's collected poems and plays (1947); his life and letters by Sidney Dark and Rowland Grey (1923, repr. 1972); study by Hesketh Pearson (1957); bibliography by Townley Searle (1931, repr. 1967); Leslie Ayre, *The Gilbert and Sullivan Companion* (1972).

Gilbert and Ellice Islands, British colony in the central and S Pacific (1968 pop. 53,517). The colony consists of the GILBERT ISLANDS, the ELLICE ISLANDS, some of the PHOENIX ISLANDS, some of the LINE ISLANDS (including FANNING ISLAND, WASHINGTON ISLAND, and CHRISTMAS ISLAND), and OCEAN ISLAND, and comprises 42 islands in all, with a total land area of c.375 sq mi (970 sq km). Except for Ocean Island, all are low-lying atolls offering little opportunity for agriculture. There are coconut and pandanus palms and breadfruit trees; pigs and fowl are raised. Copra and phosphates are the chief exports, but fishing and tourism are of increasing importance. The government, headquarters on TARAWA, is headed by a British governor, who presides over an executive council (10 members) and a legislative council (38 members), both of which are partially elected and partially appointed. In 1966 local governments were established on most of the islands. Proclaimed a protectorate in 1892, the islands were formed into a colony in 1915–16 at the request of the indigenous governments. The inhabitants of the Gilbert Islands are Micronesians; those of the Ellice Islands are Polynesians. Both the equator and the international dateline run through the colony.

Gilbert de la Porrée (zhēlbĕr' də lä pôrā'), 1076–1154, French scholastic philosopher, b. Poitiers. He taught for 20 years at Chartres, where he was for some time chancellor. He later lectured at Paris. In 1142 he was made bishop of Poitiers. He was twice accused of heresy. Gilbert's works—*De sex principiis*, an elucidation of Aristotle's last six categories, and his commentary on the *De trinitate* ascribed to Boethius—reveal his somewhat obscure position in scholastic realism, to which he adhered in a moderated form. See his *Commentaries on Boethius* ed. by N. M. Häring (1966); study by M. E. Williams (1951).

Gilbert Islands, group of 16 islands (1968 pop. 44,206), central Pacific, a part of the GILBERT AND ELLICE ISLANDS, a British colony. The group includes TARAWA (the capital of the colony), BUTARITARI (Makin), Little Makin, Marakei, Abaiang, Maiana, Abemama, Kuria, and Aranuka in the north; Nonouti and Tabiteuea in the central region; and Beru, Nukunau, Onotoa, Tamana, and Arorae in the south. The total land area is 102 sq mi (260 sq km). The equator runs through the center of the group. There are coconut and breadfruit trees on the islands; fishing and the export of copra are the main economic activities. Most of the inhabitants are Micronesians, but there are Polynesian, Chinese, and European minorities. Nukunau was discovered by British Commodore John BYRON in 1765; other islands were discovered by captains Thomas Gilbert and John Marshall in 1788, and the remainder were visited between 1799 and 1824. The American missionary Hiram BINGHAM visited the islands in 1856 and translated the Bible into Gilbertese. The British made the islands a protectorate in 1892 and a colony in 1915-16. Tarawa, Butaritari, Abaiang, Marakei, and Abemama were occupied by the Japanese in 1941 and liberated by U.S. forces in 1943.

Gilboa (gĭlbō'ə), Arabic *Jabal Faqquah,* range of hills, eastern spur of the Samarian Hills, located at the southeastern edge of the Esdraelon plain, NE Israel; rising to 1,630 ft (497 m) at Mt. Gilboa. Saul was defeated and severely wounded there by the Philistines and killed himself (1 Sam. 28.4; 31; 2 Sam. 1.21).

Gildas, Saint (gĭl'dəs), d. 570, British historian, possibly a Welsh monk. Shortly before 547 he wrote the *De excidio et conquestu Britanniae,* a Latin history of Britain dealing with the Roman invasion and the Anglo-Saxon conquest of England, the earliest authority for the period. Gildas is said to have gone to Brittany and to have founded the monastery named after him near Vannes.

Gilder, Richard Watson (gĭl'dər), 1844-1909, American editor and poet, b. Bordentown, N.J. In 1869 he became an editor of the magazine *Hours at Home,* which merged with *Scribner's Monthly* in 1870. Just before *Scribner's* became the *Century,* Gilder succeeded J. G. Holland as its editor (1881), a position he retained until his death. The *Century* was a leading publication during his life. In 1874 he married an artist, Helena de Kaye, and their home became a literary and artistic center; the Authors' Club was founded there in 1882. Gilder's volumes of poetry include *The New Day* (1875) and *The Fire Divine* (1907). See his letters (ed. by his daughter, Rosamund Gilder, 1916). His sister was **Jeannette Leonard Gilder,** 1849-1916, American editor and novelist, b. Flushing, N.Y. She was an assistant editor of *Scribner's Monthly.* With her brother Joseph Gilder, she was coeditor of the *Critic* from 1881 to 1885, after which she was sole editor until 1906. A keen dramatic and music critic, she wrote columns for various newspapers.

Gildersleeve, Virginia Crocheron, 1877-1965, American educator, b. New York City, grad. Columbia (B.A., Barnard, 1899; Ph.D., 1908). She was professor of English at Barnard from 1900 to 1911, when she was appointed dean, a position she held until her retirement in 1947. She was an early supporter of the League of Nations, a founder and twice president of the International Federation of University Women, chairman of the American Council on Education, the only woman member of the U.S. delegation to the San Francisco Conference in 1945, and a member of the advisory commission on education sent to Japan in 1946. Her works include *Many a Good Crusade* (1954) and *A Hoard for Winter* (1962).

Gil de Taboada y de Lemos, Francisco (fränthēs'kō hĕl dā täbōä'thä ē thā lā'mōs), d. 1809, Spanish colonial administrator. After serving as viceroy of New Granada (1789), he was viceroy of Peru (1790-96). In Peru he introduced administrative reforms, encouraged the arts, and sent out exploring expeditions. Returning to Spain, he became a member of the governing junta after Ferdinand VII fled before Napoleon.

gilding, process of applying a thin layer of real or imitation gold to a surface. The process is employed on wood, metal, ivory, leather, paper, glass, porcelain, and fabrics and is used to embellish the decorative elements, domes, and vaults of buildings. Gold, or a substitute, may be applied in leaf form to a surface prepared by a treatment of size, mercury, acid, or heat. The applied leaf is burnished or left matte. Mechanical and chemical gilding of metals has been largely superseded by electroplating (see PLATING). The art of gilding is of ancient origin. It was lavishly employed in Egypt, Greece, and Rome and during the Renaissance and has been used continuously in the Orient.

gilds: see GUILDS.

Gilead (gĭl'ēăd). **1** Eponym of the Gileadites, grandson of Manasseh. Num. 26.29; 27.1; Josh. 17.1. **2** Gadite. 1 Chron. 5.14. **3** Jephthah's father. Judges 11.1,2. **4** City near Mizpah, denounced by Hosea. Hosea 6.8. **5** Fertile, mountainous region, NE of the Dead Sea. It was allotted to Reuben, Gad, and Manasseh and was noted for its spices, myrrh, and balm. It was the home of Jair, Jephthah, and Elijah, and here Jacob met Laban; Ishbosheth was once its king, and in it David found refuge from Absalom. After the partition of Israel it became part of the northern kingdom. It was captured by Assyria. Hosea denounced it. It has been called variously Mt. Gilead, Land of Gilead, and Gilead. Gen. 31.21,25; 37.25; Deut. 3.12-17; Judges 5.17; 10.3; 11; 20.1; 1 Sam. 13.7; 2 Sam. 2.9; 19.31; 24.6; 1 Kings 4.13; 17.1; 2 Kings 15.25; Jer. 8.22; Hosea 6.8; 12.11; Amos 1.3,13.

Giles, William Branch (jīlz), 1762-1830, American statesman, b. Amelia co., Va. After practicing as a lawyer in Petersburg, Va., he entered the U.S. House of Representatives as an Anti-Federalist in 1790. There he opposed the establishment of the Bank of the United States and in 1793 brought charges of corruption against Alexander Hamilton; they were rejected. Resigning in 1798, he was a member of the Virginia legislature (1798-1800), but in 1801 was again elected to Congress. From 1804 to 1815 he was a U.S. Senator. He took a leading part in the impeachment of Justice Samuel Chase, was active in factional contests within the Jeffersonian party, and vigorously directed his hostility against Albert Gallatin and James Monroe. Giles was again a Virginia legislator for several terms, was governor of Virginia (1827-30), and took part in the state constitutional convention (1829-30). His career was marred by the intense personal animosities he held. *Political Miscellanies* (1829) contains a number of his speeches and letters. See biography by D. R. Anderson (1914, repr. 1965).

Gilgal (gĭl'găl). **1** First encampment of the Israelites W of the Jordan. Joshua 4.20; 5.9, 10; 1 Sam. 13.4; Hosea 4.15; Amos 4.4. **2** Place, N of Lod, scene of Elijah's translation to heaven in a fiery chariot. 2 Kings 2.1; 4.38. **3** Place near Shechem, sometimes identified with **2**. Deut. 11.30. **4** Place, mentioned in list of defeated Canaanite kings. Joshua 12.23. **5** Place on the northern boundary of Judah. Joshua 15.7.

Gilgamesh (gĭl'gəmĕsh), in Babylonian legend, king of Erech. He is the hero of the Gilgamesh epic, a work of some 3,000 lines, written on 12 tablets c.2000 B.C. and discovered among the ruins at Nineveh. It tells of the adventures of the warlike and imperious Gilgamesh and his friend Enkidu. When Enkidu suddenly sickened and died, Gilgamesh became obsessed by a fear of death. His ancestor Utnapishtim (who with his wife had been the only survivor of a great flood) told him of a plant that gave eternal life. After obtaining the plant, however, Gilgamesh left it unguarded and a serpent carried it off. The hero then turned to the ghost of Enkidu for consoling knowledge of the afterlife, only to be told by his friend that a gloomy future awaited the dead. See verse translation by Herbert Mason (1970); prose translation by N. K. Sandars (1960); Alexander Heidel, *Gilgamesh Epic and Old Testament Parallels* (2d ed. 1949).

gilia: see PHLOX.

Gill, Sir David (gĭl), 1843-1914, Scottish astronomer, educated at the Univ. of Aberdeen. He made observations of the transits of Venus and Mars and investigated the solar parallax. As astronomer royal (1879-1907) at the Cape of Good Hope, he carried out the geodetic survey of Natal and Cape Colony and organized the geodetic survey of Rhodesia. He was a leader in the use of photography in the preparation of star catalogs. His photographic survey of almost half a million stars in the Southern Hemisphere (with J. C. Kapteyn) is known as *The Cape Photographic Durchmusterung for the Equinox 1875* (1896-1900). This work extended Argelander's *Bonn Durchmusterung* to the South Pole. Gill was knighted in 1900. His writings include his *History and Description of the Royal Observatory, Cape of Good Hope* (1913).

Gill, Eric Rowland, 1882-1940, English sculptor, wood engraver, typographer, and writer. His sculpture includes *Stations of the Cross* (Westminster Cathedral, London); *Prospero and Ariel* (Broadcasting House, London); and the war memorial at the Univ. of Leeds. Gill illustrated many books for the Golden Cockerel Press after 1923. Among his books are *Essay on Typography* (1931) and *Work and Property* (1937). See his autobiography (1941); biography by Evan Gill (1953, repr. 1974); studies by Roy Brewer (1973) and E. A. Brady (rev. ed. 1974).

gill, external respiratory organ of most aquatic animals. In fishes the gills are located in gill chambers at the rear of the mouth (pharynx). Water is taken in through the mouth, is forced through openings called gill slits, and then passes through the gill clefts, spaces between the ranks of delicate gills, bathing them continuously. Each gill is composed of numerous threadlike gill filaments containing capillaries enclosed in a thin membrane; oxygen is absorbed from the passing water and carbon dioxide is discharged. The gills, which may be platelike or tufted, are attached to the outer edges of a series of paired cartilaginous or bony gill (or branchial) arches. Gill rakers, bony comblike projections on

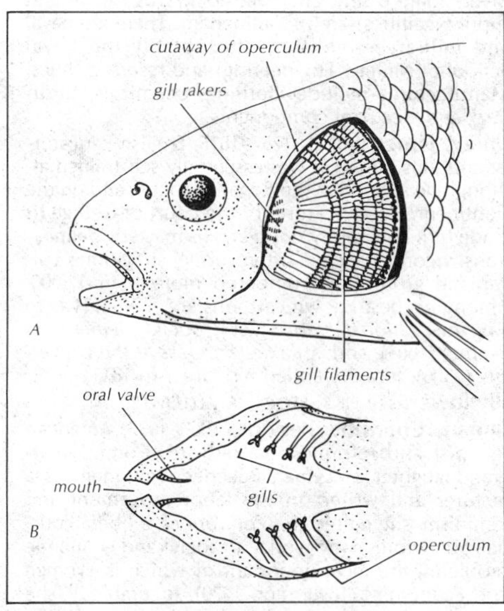

Gills of a fish: side view (A) and ventral view (B)

the inner edge of the arches, strain solid material from the water, preventing it from passing out through the gill slits and directing it down the esophagus. Gill rakers are present in all fishes except those that feed on large organisms. In primitive fishes (e.g., the shark) the gill slits are exposed; in the bony fishes they are protected by an operculum, or gill cover. In the higher aquatic invertebrates the gills protrude from the body surface and contain extensions of the vascular system. In the crustaceans these external gills are covered by a protective carapace, part of the shell; in the echinoderms they are branched appendages extending from various parts of the body. In the mollusks the gills (called ctenidia) are internal and are located inside the mantle cavity. Horseshoe crabs have gill books, which are membranous flaps like the pages of a book. Amphibians breathe by means of external gills in their aquatic larval stage; a few forms retain the gills after metamorphosing into terrestrial adults. Aquatic insect larvae accomplish the oxygen-carbon-dioxide exchange by means of tracheal gills, projections from the walls of the air tubes (tracheae); these gills disappear when the insect leaves the water. The embryos of all higher vertebrates pass through a stage in which rudimentary gill slits occur, but these never become functional and disappear as the embryo continues to develop.

gill, in weights and measures: see ENGLISH UNITS OF MEASUREMENT.

Gillespie, Dizzy (John Birks Gillespie), 1917-, American jazz musician and composer, b. Cheraw, S.C. He began to play the trumpet at 15, and later he studied harmony and theory at Laurinburg Institute, N.C. Gillespie and Charlie (Bird) Parker are considered the leaders of the bop (or bebop) movement in modern jazz. Gillespie's playing is characterized by intelligent musicianship and technical facility. See biography by Michael James (1961).

Gillett, Ezra Hall (jĭlĕt'), 1823-75, American Presbyterian clergyman and historian, b. Colchester, Conn. After serving (1845-70) as pastor in Harlem, New York City, he became professor of political science in the Univ. of the City of New York (now New York Univ.). He began the McAlpin Collection of British history and theology for the library of Union Theological Seminary. His books include *The Life and Times of John Huss* (1863).

Gillette, William, 1853-1937, American actor and dramatist, b. Hartford, Conn. His New York debut in Mark Twain's *Gilded Age* (1877) was shortly followed by his own first play, *The Professor* (1881). In the same year *Esmeralda,* written with Frances Hodgson Burnett, established his success. *Held by the Enemy* (1886) was the first of his popular Civil War plays, the second being *Secret Service* (1896). Both won him high personal praise. With *Sherlock Holmes* (1899), however, Gillette scored his lasting triumph, creating a play and a character with which he was permanently associated. He was one of the first to profess that an actor should build his characterization on the dominant qualities of his own personality.

Gillingham (jĭl'ĭng-əm), municipal borough (1971 pop. 86,714), Kent, SE England, on the Medway River. Some of the Chatham dockyards (repair and supply facilities) are in Gillingham. There are naval and military establishments (notably the Royal School of Military Engineering) and resort facilities. Manufactures include clothing, chemicals, furniture, and electrical components.

Gillray, James (gĭl'rā), 1757-1815, English caricaturist and illustrator. He was essentially self-trained although he studied at the Royal Academy and on the Continent. His caricatures of the court of George III made him immensely popular. His masterly delineations, vigorous, clever, often subtle, sometimes vulgar and grotesque, numbered more than 12,000. Among his best-known cartoons are *A New Way to Pay the National Debt* (1796), *Social Elements in Skating* (1805), and *A Rake's Progress at the University* (1806). Insanity ended his career in 1811.

gillyflower: see PINK; STOCK; WALLFLOWER.

Gilman, Charlotte Perkins, 1860-1935, American feminist and reformer, b. Hartford, Conn.; great-granddaughter of Lyman Beecher. Prominent as a lecturer and writer on the labor movement and feminism, she edited the *Forerunner,* a liberal journal. She wrote many works on social and economic problems, the most important of which is *Women and Economics* (1898, repr. 1970). Incurably ill, she committed suicide. See her autobiography (1935).

Gilman, Daniel Coit, 1831-1908, American educator, first president of Johns Hopkins Univ., b. Norwich, Conn., grad. Yale, 1852. After serving as attaché (1853-55) of the American legation at St. Petersburg, he returned to Yale and was active in planning and raising funds for the founding of Sheffield Scientific School. From 1856 to 1865 he was librarian of Yale College and was also concerned with improving the New Haven public school system. Appointed (1863) professor of geography at Sheffield Scientific School, he became secretary and librarian as well in 1866. He resigned these posts in 1872 to become president of the newly organized Univ. of California. His work there was hampered by the state legislature, and in 1875 Gilman accepted the offer to establish and become first president of Johns Hopkins Univ. at Baltimore. Before being formally installed as president in 1876, he spent a year studying university organization and selecting an outstanding staff of teachers and scholars. Gilman's primary interest was in fostering advanced instruction and research, and as president he developed the first great American graduate university in the German tradition. Gilman was also active in founding Johns Hopkins Hospital (1889) and Johns Hopkins Medical School (1893). He founded and was for many years president of the Charity Organization of Baltimore and served as a trustee of the John F. Slater and Peabody Education funds and as a member of the General Education Board. He retired from Johns Hopkins in 1901, but accepted the presidency (1902-4) of the newly founded Carnegie Institution of Washington. His books include biographies of James Monroe and James Dwight Dana, a collection of addresses entitled *University Problems* (1898), and *The Launching of a University* (1906). See biographies by Fabian Franklin (1910, repr. 1973) and Abraham Flexner (1946); Hugh Hawkins, *Pioneer: A History of the Johns Hopkins University, 1874-1899* (1960).

Gilman, Lawrence, 1878-1939, American music critic and author, b. Flushing, N.Y. He was music critic for *Harper's Weekly* (1901-13) and the *North American Review* (1913-23), and in 1923 he succeeded H. E. Krehbiel as music critic for the New York *Herald Tribune,* a post he held until his death. An able and highly respected critic, he wrote many books on music, and from 1921, the program notes for the New York Philharmonic Society and the Philadelphia Orchestra.

Gilmer, Thomas Walker, 1802-44, U.S. Secretary of the Navy (Feb., 1844), b. Albemarle co., Va. He practiced law, served in the Virginia legislature, and became (1840) governor of Virginia. Elected to Congress, he served (1841-44) as a spokesman for the Tyler administration. Appointed Secretary of the Navy, he, along with other government officials, was a victim of the gun explosion on the *Princeton* in 1844. This accident brought to the fore the question of succession to the presidency in the event of wholesale death of public officials.

Giloh (gī'lō), unidentified town, S central Palestine. Joshua 15.51. The adjective is Gilonite. 2 Sam. 15.12; 23.34. See PELONITE.

Gilpin, Henry Dilworth (gĭl'pĭn), 1801-60, American public official, U.S. Attorney General (1840-41), b. Lancaster, England. He practiced law in Pennsylvania and served as U.S. district attorney in that state. An ardent Jacksonian Democrat, Gilpin was solicitor of the Treasury Dept. (1837-40) and then was Attorney General. Interested in literary and historical work, he edited the papers of James Madison (3 vol., 1840).

Gil Robles, José María (hōsā' märē'ä hēl rō'blās), 1898-, Spanish politician. Son of a law professor, he worked as a journalist until 1931, when he became leader of the newly organized right-wing Catholic party, known as *Acción Popular.* Within two years several right-wing parties had joined under his direction to form the CEDA (*Confederación Española de Derechos Autónomos).* Although the group became the most powerful in the republic after the Nov., 1933, elections, Gil Robles was denied a role in the government until late 1934 because of pressure by left-wing parties that feared his monarchist leanings and desire to establish a Catholic corporative state; the issue of his participation in the government caused rioting and a cabinet crisis, but in 1935 Gil Robles served briefly as minister of war in the Alejandro Lerroux cabinet. By 1936 his nonviolent methods of obtaining power had alienated his radical supporters who joined Ramón Serrano Suñer's Falange. He was an intended victim of the conspiracy responsible for the murder of José Calvo Sotelo, an event that helped precipitate the Spanish civil war. After the outbreak of the war Gil Robles lived in Portugal as head of the Catholic émigrés and as a member of the privy council of Don Juan, pretender to the Spanish throne. He returned to Spain in 1950, only to go into exile once more from 1962 to 1969.

Gilroy, city (1970 pop. 12,665), Santa Clara co., W Calif.; inc. 1870. Located in the fertile Santa Clara valley, Gilroy supports diversified agriculture, including vineyards, orchards, dairy farms, and plant nurseries. The chief manufactures are farm equipment, processed spices and other foods, wines, paint, fabricated metals, fiber glass, and paper products. The city is the site of Gavilan College. Mt. Madonna County Park, with its redwood stands, is nearby.

Gilson, Étienne (ātyĕn' zhĕlsôN'), 1884-, French philosopher and historian, b. Paris. He taught the history of medieval philosophy at the Sorbonne (1921-32) and then took the chair of medieval philosophy at the Collège de France. In 1929 he helped found the Pontifical Institute of Medieval Studies at Toronto, Canada. Although primarily a historian of philosophy, he was also one of the leaders of the Roman Catholic neo-Thomist movement. He was elected to the French Academy in 1946. Among his works are *The Philosophy of St. Thomas Aquinas* (1919, tr. 1924); *The Christian Philosophy of Saint Augustine* (1929, tr. 1960); *The Spirit of Mediaeval Philosophy* (2 vol., 1932, tr. 1936); *God and Philosophy* (1941); *Being and Some Philosophers* (1949); and *The Philosopher and Theology* (1960, tr. 1962). See his *Gilson Reader*, ed. with an introd. by A. C. Pegis (1957).

Gil Vicente: see VICENTE, GIL.

Gimbel (gĭm'bəl), family of American merchants and philanthropists. **Adam Gimbel**, 1815-96, b. Bavaria, emigrated (1835) to the United States and traveled up and down the Mississippi River peddling notions. He set up (1842) a small business in Vincennes, Ind., and expanded it considerably over a period of 40 years. He sold his business to join his sons, **Jacob Gimbel**, 1850-1922, b. Vincennes, and **Isaac Gimbel**, 1857-1931, b. Vincennes, who had opened in the 1880s a successful department store in Milwaukee, Wis. In 1894 the Gimbels founded a large department store in Philadelphia, and in 1910 a store was opened in New York City under the direction of Jacob Gimbel. Other businesses were absorbed; Saks and Company was purchased in 1923. Branch stores were also opened in Pittsburgh, Chicago, Detroit, Beverly Hills, Calif., and other cities. During his lifetime, Jacob Gimbel gave generously to Jewish charities. **Charles Gimbel**, 1861-1932, b. Vincennes, for many years headed the Philadelphia establishment and was active in many philanthropies of the city. Another brother, **Ellis A. Gimbel**, 1865-1950, b. Vincennes, headed the department stores for several years and was the founder of the Gimbel Awards. The three other sons of Adam Gimbel, Louis S., Daniel, and Benedict, were also connected with the firm. **Bernard F. Gimbel**, 1885-1966, b. Vincennes, grad. Univ. of Pennsylvania (B.S., 1907), son of Isaac Gimbel, was president of Gimbel Bros., Inc. from 1927 until 1953, when he became chairman of the board. His son **Bruce Gimbel**, 1913-, b. New York City, grad. Yale (B.A., 1935), then succeeded to the presidency. In 1973 the company was absorbed by Brown and Williamson Tobacco Corp.

gimlet (gĭm'lĭt): see DRILL.

Gimzo (gĭm'zō), town, SW Palestine, N of Gezer. It was conquered by the Philistines in Ahaz's time. 2 Chron. 28.18.

gin [archaic *geneva*, from Du. from O.Fr. from Lat.,= juniper], spirituous liquor distilled chiefly from fermented cereals, malted and unmalted, and flavored with juniper berries. It originated in Holland (thus the name Hollands, or Holland, gin) but is now manufactured also in other countries, chiefly England and the United States. A type of gin developed in England is known as London gin; it is more highly distilled than Holland gin. Dry gin has been highly rectified. Old Tom gin is sweetened for use as a liqueur. Sloe gin is flavored with fresh sloes instead of juniper.

Ginastera, Alberto (älbär'tō hĕnästä'rä), 1916-, Argentinian composer, b. Buenos Aires. Ginastera is considered the most prominent comtemporary Latin American composer. His early works used Latin American folk material; later compositions have been less nationalistic and utilize serial techniques (see SERIAL MUSIC). Among Ginastera's best-known works are the ballets *Panambi* (1940) and *Estancia* (1941); a piano sonata (1952); the *Variations Concertantes* for orchestra (1953); piano, violin, harp, and cello concertos; and the operas *Don Rodrigo* (1964), *Bomarzo* (1967), and *Beatrix Cenci* (1971).

Ginath (gī'năth), father of Tibni. 1 Kings 16.21,22.

Giner de los Ríos, Francisco (fränthēs'kō hĕnār' dā lōs rē'ōs), 1839-1915, Spanish educator and philosopher. He founded the Institución Libre de Enseñanza, a school that sought to develop a spirit of inquiry in its students; it did much to reform teaching methods in Spain and to shape liberal politics there. In his work on the philosophy of law Giner attempted to reconcile positivist and rationalist trends. His collected works (1916-27) total 18 volumes.

ginger, common name for members of the Zingiberaceae, a family of tropical and subtropical perennial herbs, chiefly of Indomalaysia. The aromatic oils of many members of the family are used in medicines, especially as stimulants and carminatives; for condiments; and in the making of perfumes. Ginger (*Zingiber officinale*), cultivated since ancient times in many countries, no longer grows wild. Commercial ginger is made from the root, either preserved by candying or dried for medicines and spice. Zedoary (*Curcuma zedoaria*), turmeric (*C. longa*), and the seeds of cardamom (*Elettaria cardamomum*) are similarly used, the latter two often combined with ginger to make one kind of CURRY. Turmeric root yields a yellow dye and is also used as an indicator of acidity or alkalinity. *C. augustifolia* is an East Indian ARROWROOT. Ginger is classified in the division MAGNOLIOPHYTA, class Magnoliopsida, order Zingiberales, family Zingiberaceae.

ginger ale, a nonalcoholic sweetened beverage made of carbonated water flavored with ginger and other ingredients. Ginger beer is a similar beverage.

gingivitis (jĭn"jəvī'tĭs), inflammation of the gums. It may be acute, subacute, chronic, or recurrent. The gums usually become red, swollen, and spongy, and bleed easily. Chronic gingivitis is the usual form, resulting from irritating bacteria or debris, food impaction, or poor dental restoration. It can also accompany vitamin C deficiency or metabolic disturbances such as diabetes. If left untreated, it can lead to the more serious PYORRHEA, with gum destruction and loosening of teeth. TRENCH MOUTH, an ulcerative infection of the gums and mouth, is sometimes referred to as a form of gingivitis.

Ginkel, Godart van, 1st **earl of Athlone** (gō′därt vän gĭng′kəl), 1644–1703, Dutch general in the service of WILLIAM III of England. He accompanied (1688) William to England and took part in William's victory over James II in the battle of the BOYNE. He then (1690) became commander in chief of the army in Ireland, capturing Ballymore and Athlone, winning a decisive victory at Aughrim, and taking Limerick, where peace was made (1691). In the War of the Spanish Succession (1701–14) he commanded the Dutch wing of the forces under the duke of Marlborough.

ginkgo (gĭng′kō), or **maidenhair tree,** tall, slender, picturesque deciduous tree (*Ginkgo biloba*) with fan-shaped leaves. The ginkgo is native to China and Japan, where for centuries it has been revered as a sacred tree and planted near temples. A "living fossil," the ginkgo is the only remaining species of a large order (Ginkgoales) of gymnosperms that existed in the Triassic period. Its form has not changed in millions of years, as is shown by fossils widely scattered over Europe, North and South America, and Asia. The ginkgo is valued today in Europe and the United States as an avenue tree, being exceptionally tolerant of smoke, low temperatures, and minimal water supply. The male and female flowers are borne on separate trees. The "fruit," botanically a seed, is surrounded by a malodorous pulp, making the male trees more desirable as ornamentals; however, the seed kernel is highly esteemed in the Orient as a food. Ginkgo is classified in the division PINOPHYTA, class Ginkgoopsida, order Ginkgoales.

Ginner, Charles (jĭn′ər), 1878–1952, English painter. After study in Paris, Ginner settled in London, becoming a founder of the neorealist school. During both world wars he was an official government artist. Among his World War II paintings are several scenes of air raids.

Ginnetho (gĭn′ĕthō, gĭnē′-), priest who returned with Zerubbabel. Neh. 12.4. He is probably the same as **Ginnethon,** mentioned in Neh. 10.6 and 12.16.

gin rummy: see RUMMY.

Ginsberg, Allen, 1926–, American poet, b. Paterson, N.J., grad. Columbia, 1949. An outspoken member of the BEAT GENERATION, Ginsberg is best known for *Howl,* (1956) a long, rambling poem attacking American values, particularly materialism. Other volumes of his poetry, which resembles the verse of Walt Whitman in its romantic glorification of experience and its use of everyday speech, include *Kaddish and Other Poems, 1958–1960* (1961) and *The Fall of America* (1973). *Allen Verbatim* (1974) is a collection of lectures.

Ginsburg, Christian David (gĭnz′bərg), 1831–1914, English Hebrew scholar, b. Warsaw. He was converted to Christianity in 1846 and settled in England. He translated (1857) the Song of Songs, with a critical commentary, but he is best known for his Masoretic studies, including Hebrew and English editions of Jacob ben Hayyim's *Introduction to the Rabbinic Bible* (1865), Elias Levita's *The Massoreth ha Massoreth* (1867), and *The Massorah* (4 vol., 1880–1905).

ginseng (jĭn′sĕng), common name for the Araliaceae, a family of tropical herbs, shrubs, and trees that are often prickly and sometimes grow as climbing forms. The true ginseng (*Panax schinseng*), long prized by the Chinese for a panacea prepared from its root, was in such demand that a North American ginseng, *P. quinquefolius,* was imported in large quantities as a substitute; however, both species have been all but exterminated by commercial exploitation. The widely varied family includes also the dwarf ginseng (*P. trifolium*) of North America; the English ivy (*Hedera helix*), a popular ornamental evergreen vine; the Hercules'-club, devil's-club, or devil's-walking-stick (names applied to several related species) of North America and E Asia, used locally for medicinal purposes; and the rice-paper plant (*Tetrapanax papyriferus*) of China, the pith of which is used to make Chinese rice paper. Native American species of this family include the wild sarsaparilla (*Aralia nudicaulis*) and the American, or wild, spikenard (*A. racemosa*). The names SARSAPARILLA and SPIKENARD are applied also to plants of other families. Ginseng is classified in the division MAGNOLIOPHYTA, class Magnoliopsida, order Umbellales, family Araliaceae.

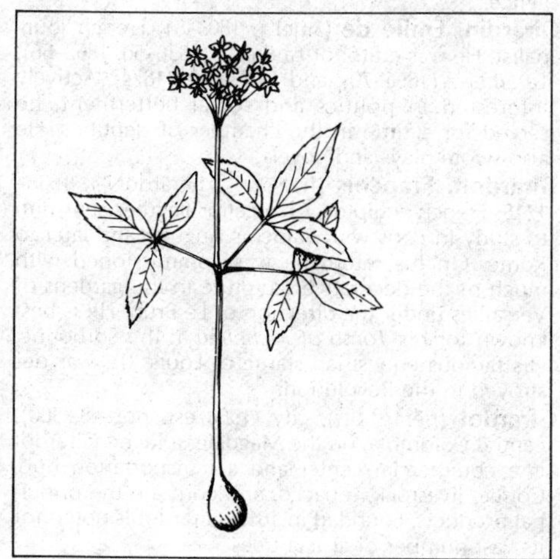

Dwarf ginseng, Panax trifolium

Ginzberg, Asher (Ahad Ha'am) (äkhäd′hä-äm′), 1856–1927, Russian essayist who wrote in Hebrew. An early champion of ZIONISM, he opposed immediate colonization of Palestine, recommending instead a strengthening of Jewish national consciousness through reexamination of the Jewish cultural heritage. He wrote under the Hebrew name Ahad Ha'am. Among his collections of essays is *Lo Zeh ha-Derekh* (1889; tr. *The Wrong Way,* 1962). Ginzberg debated Theodor HERZL at the First Zionist Conference.

Gioberti, Vincenzo (vĕnchän′tsō jōbĕr′tē), 1801–52, Italian philosopher and political writer, b. Turin. Ordained a priest in 1825, he went into exile (1833–48) in Paris and Brussels because of his liberal political ideas. His treatise *The Civil and Moral Primacy of the Italians* (1843), an influential exposition both of Italian nationalism and of the need for papal political leadership, brought Gioberti recognition as an advocate of the primacy of religion as a motivating force in civilization. In 1848 he became first deputy and then premier of the kingdom of Sardinia, but he resigned after the Austrian victory over the Sardinians at Novara (1849). He served briefly as minister to Paris, then retired to private life. At first a republican, favoring a federation of Italian states under papal arbitration, he later advocated the complete unification of Italy as a constitutional monarchy.

Giocondo, Fra Giovanni (frä jōvän′nē jōkôn′dō), c.1435–1515, Italian architect, engineer, and antiquary. A Franciscan friar, he was accomplished in philosophy, archaeology, and classical literature but is best known for his architectural and engineering works. He designed a drainage system for the lagoons of Venice, built the fortifications of Treviso, and is universally credited with the design of the Palazzo del Consiglio (1476) at Verona, an elegant, arcaded monument of the early Renaissance. He accompanied Charles VIII to France in 1495 as court architect.

Gioia or **Gioja, Melchiorre** (both: mālkyôr′rā jō′yä), 1767–1829, Italian economist and political theorist. An early advocate of the unification of Italy, he was several times imprisoned, once on charges of association with the Carbonari movement. He opposed the doctrines of Adam Smith, insisting on the economic duty of the state. He also conducted important statistical studies. His chief works are *Del merito e delle ricompense* [concerning merit and rewards] (1818–19) and *Filosofia della statistica* [philosophy of statistics] (1829–30).

Giolitti, Giovanni (jōvän′nē jōlēt′tē), 1842–1928, Italian public official, five times premier (1892–93, 1903–5, 1906–9, 1911–14, 1920–21). He entered parliament in 1882 and served (1889–90) as minister of finance before becoming premier. By controlling elections, especially in S Italy, and by regrouping coalitions, he was able to maintain his political supremacy, and the period 1901–14 is often called the Age of Giolitti. A progressive Liberal, he favored the organization of labor and was responsible for social and agrarian reforms and the introduction (1912) of universal male suffrage. Although he supported the Italian conquest of Libya during his fourth ministry, he opposed Italian participation in World War I. In the troubled period of his fifth premiership, Italy made a treaty with Yugoslavia to settle the dispute over Rijeka. In the 1921 elections he helped Benito Mussolini gain power by including Fascists among government-sponsored candidates, thus enabling them to win 35 seats in the chamber. Giolitti failed at first to condemn the increasing Fascist brutality, and only after Nov., 1924, did he openly oppose Mussolini. See his memoirs (tr. 1923, repr. 1973); study by F. J. Coppa (1971).

Giono, Jean (zhäN jônō′), 1895–1970, French novelist, b. Provence. His semiautobiographical novel, *Jean le bleu* (1932, tr. *Blue Boy,* 1946) concerns his childhood. His pastoral trilogy—*Colline* (1920, tr. *Hill of Destiny,* 1929), *Un de Baumugnes* (1929, tr. *Lovers Are Never Losers,* 1931), and *Regain* (1930, tr. *Harvest,* 1939)—describes Provençal life, emphasizing closeness to nature. Giono expressed his pacifism in *Refus d'obéissance* (1937). Among his later novels are *Le Bonheur fou* (1957, tr. *The Straw Man,* 1959), *Angelo* (1958), and *Ennemonde* (1968, tr. 1970). See study by N. L. Goodrich (1973).

Giordano, Luca (lōō′kä jōrdä′nō), 1632–1705, Italian decorative painter, b. Naples. He was the pupil of Ribera and Pietro da Cortona. He imitated the works of the great masters with amazing speed and facility and ultimately based his style upon those of Veronese and Cortona. Giordano decorated the cupola of the Corsini Chapel and a ceiling in the Palazzo Riccardi (1682–83), both in Florence. In 1692 he went to Madrid, where he remained ten years and produced numerous works in oil and in fresco, achieving fame and wealth. On the death of his patron Charles II, he accompanied Philip V to Naples. His pictures are in the leading European galleries, particularly those of Madrid, Vienna, and Naples. His best-known frescoes in Naples include *The Story of Judith* (San Martino) and *Christ Expelling the Traders from the Temple* (San Filippo Neri). In Spain he painted airy and luminous frescoes in the Chapel of San Lorenzo and in the ESCORIAL, Madrid, and in the churches and palaces of Madrid and Toledo.

Giordano, Umberto (ōōmbĕr′tō), 1867–1948, Italian operatic composer. His most famous work is the richly melodic *Andrea Chénier* (1896). *Fedora* (1898) and *Madame Sans-Gêne* (1915) are also well known. Other operas include *Siberia* (1903) and *Cena delle Beffe* (1924).

Giorgio, Francesco di (fränchās′kō dē jôr′jō), 1439–1502, Italian engineer, architect, painter, and sculptor, b. Siena. With Renaissance versatility he worked as military architect and engineer, first at Siena (1463–78) and later in the service of Lorenzo de' Medici and the duke of Urbino. He constructed parts of the ducal palace at Urbino and influenced architectural design in the Marches. In Milan he made a model for the dome of the cathedral. He invented the mines used in the siege of Naples in 1495. As a sculptor, he is remembered for his work in the choir of the Siena Cathedral. His paintings, which show the influence of the Botticelli circle, have great charm. They remain mostly in Siena; *The Rape of Europa* is in the Louvre and *The Chess Players* in the Metropolitan Museum. His treatise *Trattato di architettura civile e militare* was edited by Cesare Saluzzo in 1841. See study by A. S. Weller (1943).

Giorgione (jōrjô′nā), c.1478–1510, Venetian painter, b. Castelfranco Veneto; fellow student of Titian under Giovanni Bellini in Venice. Giorgione was known also as Zorgo or Zorgi da Castelfranco and as Giorgio Barbarelli. Almost nothing is known of his life except that he worked in Venice, undertook various important commissions in oil and fresco, and died of the plague in his early 30s. Legend concedes him great personal charm. A major innovator, he is credited with having been the formative influence in the lives of Titian, Pordenone, Sebastiano del Piombo, and Jacopo Palma il Vecchio. Thus, in a sense, 16th-century Venetian painting stems from him. So absolute was his domination that it is impossible to separate with certainty his work from that of his imitators. His frescoes are practically obliterated. The list of his extant works in oil is computed variously at from 4 to 70. But if Giorgione himself is an unknown quantity, his style is not. It was new to Venetian painting both in technique and in spirit. Technically it introduced a greater fusion of all forms and a subordination of local color to the pervading tone, used to emphasize forms in space. This revolution was accomplished simultaneously by Leonardo, but whereas Leonardo tended to suppress color in his opaque shadows, the colors of Giorgione are luminous and warm. The Giorgionesque style was liberating. The ostensible subject no longer limited the artist but became a pretext for self-expression. The specific works associated with Giorgione have the poetic quality of a bucolic dreamworld never recaptured by his famous followers. Among the best authenticated are *Madonna with SS. Francis and Liberale* (cathedral, Castelfranco Veneto); *The Three Philosophers* (Vienna); and the puzzling seminude woman with child set in a stormy landscape known as the *Tempesta* (Academy, Venice). Also celebrated, if more dubious are *Concert Champêtre* (Louvre); *Laura* (Vienna); *Judith* (Leningrad); *Adoration of the Shepherds* (National Gall. of Art, Washington, D.C.); the *Concert* (Pitti

Palace); *Judgment of Solomon* and *Trial of Moses* (Uffizi). His pastoral *Sleeping Venus* (Gemäldegalerie, Dresden) was finished by Titian. See complete ed. of his works by T. Pignatti (1971); studies by G. M. Richter (1937), Ludvig Baldass (1965), and Teresio Pignatti (1971).

Giottino (jōt-tē'nō), early Florentine painter of the school of Giotto. He is supposed to have lived in the first half of the 14th cent. and has been variously identified as Giotto di Stefano, Tommaso di Stefano, and Maso di Banco. It is possible that the work of more than one man has been associated with this name. He has been credited with frescoes in Santa Croce, Florence, and in the Lower Church of St. Francis in Assisi. Also attributed to him is a fine *Pietà* in the Uffizi.

Giotto (Giotto di Bondone) (jôt'tō dē bōndô'nā), c.1266–c.1337, Florentine painter and architect. More than any other artist he may be said to have determined the course of painting in Europe. He reputedly was born at Colle, near Florence. According to tradition, he was a pupil of Cimabue. Modern critics also see the influence of the Roman school (i.e., Pietro Cavallini) and of the sculptors Nicola and Giovanni Pisano. Whatever his training, it is certain that Giotto broke with the formulas of Byzantine painting and gave new life to the art of painting in Italy. He designed a great number of works, many of which have disappeared. It is thought that he first participated in the decoration of the Upper Church at Assisi. Scenes from the *Life of Christ, Legend of St. Francis,* and *Isaac and Esau* have all been credited to Giotto (and questioned). About 1300 he was in Rome, where he executed the mosaic of the *Navicella* now in St. Peter's. He also worked on frescoes in the Lateran Basilica (lost). About 1304 he began to design the series of 38 frescoes in the Scrovegni (Arena) Chapel in Padua. These frescoes are among the greatest works of Italian art. The cycle consists of scenes from the *Life of the Virgin, Life of Christ,* the *Last Judgment,* and *Virtues and Vices.* Compared with the gracefulness of Byzantine forms, Giotto's figures are monumental, even bulky. While he creates figures that are solemn and slow-moving, Giotto builds up a mounting rhythm into an incredibly forceful drama. His power of narration is exemplified by such episodes as the *Flight into Egypt, Betrayal of Judas, Raising of Lazarus,* and *Lamentation.* In Padua, Giotto also seems to have painted a fresco of the *Crucifixion* (Church of Sant' Antonio) and may have designed the astrological motifs for the Palazzo della Ragione (now repainted). Returning to Florence, he decorated two chapels in the Church of Santa Croce; in the Peruzzi Chapel he painted frescoes of *St. John the Baptist* and *St. John the Evangelist;* in the Bardi Chapel he worked on the magnificent cycle of scenes from the *Life of St. Francis.* His figures are imbued with a new compassion for the human being, probably inspired by the tenets of the Franciscan order. In his era, Giotto achieved a remarkably convincing representation of space, harmoniously allying figures and background. These effects were not obtained from a system of perspective, but through his own inherent clarity of conception, his ability to give strength and simplicity to his forms. About 1330 Giotto went to Naples. Working in the service of King Robert, he painted a series of famous men in the Castelnuovo and executed works in the palace chapel and monastery of Santa Chiara. Nothing remains of these works or of the *Vana Gloria* executed later in Milan for Azzo Visconti. Upon the death of Arnolfo di Cambio he became chief architect of the cathedral in Florence. During his last years he designed the campanile next to the cathedral, known as "Giotto's Tower." He is probably also responsible for the design of some of the relief decoration later completed by Andrea Pisano. His reforms in painting were carried throughout Italy by his many pupils and followers. Giotto's popularity as a great Florentine and artist is attested in literature by Dante, Petrarch, Boccaccio, Sacchetti, and Villani. Among the panel paintings attributed to Giotto are the *Madonna in Glory* (Uffizi); an altarpiece created for the Badia (now in the Church of Santa Croce, Florence); a crucifix (Church of Santa Maria Novella, Florence); altarpieces in the Vatican and Bologna galleries; *Death of the Virgin* and *Crucifixion* (Berlin); *Madonna and Child* (National Gall. of Art, Washington, D.C.); and *Presentation in the Temple* (Gardner Mus., Boston). His *Wedding of St. Catherine* in the Uffizi was badly damaged in the flood of 1966. See his paintings ed. by A. Martindale (1969); studies by Leonetto Tintori and Eve Borsook (1965), and J. H. Stubblebine, ed. (1969).

Giovanni, Bertoldo di: see BERTOLDO DI GIOVANNI.

Giovanni Bologna: see BOLOGNA, GIOVANNI.

Giovanni da Fiesole: see ANGELICO, FRA.

Giovanni delle Bande Nere: see MEDICI, GIOVANNI DE'.

Giovanni di Paolo (jōvän'nē dē pä'ōlō), c.1403–1483, major Italian painter of the Sienese school. Typical of the Sienese painters of his era, he paid scant attention to the artistic innovations made in nearby Florence, but often depended on the style established by the Sienese masters of the 14th cent. Fortunately, Giovanni di Paolo was endowed with great imagination. His first dated work (1426) was the Pecci altarpiece (major panels in Siena; predella panels in the Walters Art Gall., Baltimore). He produced a tremendous number of works during his long career. Many paintings have remained in Siena, but there are probably more examples of his art in the United States. The Metropolitan Museum has several of his paintings; among them is a delightful scene of *Paradise;* in the Philip Lehman collection is the exquisite *Creation of the World.* The *Madonna and Child in a Landscape* (Mus. of Fine Arts, Boston) exemplifies his inclination toward pure fantasy and disregard for the laws of perspective. Giovanni di Paolo is best represented by six highly expressive scenes from the life of St. John the Baptist (Art Inst., Chicago). Examples of his work are in the National Gallery of Art, Washington, D.C.; the Johnson Collection, Philadelphia; the Gardner Museum, Boston; the Fogg Museum, Cambridge; and at Yale Univ.

Giovanni di Pietro: see SPAGNA, LO.

Gippius, Zinaida Nikolayevna (zĕnĭē'də nyĭkəlī'-əvnə gē'pēo͞os), pseud. **Anton Krainy,** 1869–1945, Russian writer. Her St. Petersburg salon was a meeting place (1905–17) for young poets of the SYMBOLIST movement. Self-educated, she wrote Dostoyevskian novels, morbid and mystical poetry, and essays. Her best-known poetry appeared in *Sobraniye stikov* (1904–10). With her husband, the writer D. S. Merezhkovsky, she immigrated to France after the February Revolution. Her name is also spelled Hippius. See her selected works, ed. by Temira Pachmuss (1972); biography by Temira Pachmuss (1971).

Gippsland (gĭps'lănd), geographical area, 13,655 sq mi (35,366 sq km), Victoria, SE Australia, E of Melbourne. Dairy and beef cattle are raised, and corn, oats, and sugar beets are grown. The region also supports a timber industry. There are deposits of coal, oil and natural gas (offshore), and limestone. Gold was formerly mined.

Gipson, Lawrence Henry (gĭp'sən), 1880–1971, American historian, b. Greeley, Colo. A Rhodes scholar, he received his Ph.D. from Yale in 1918 and taught at several schools before becoming (1924) professor of history and head of the department of history and government at Lehigh Univ. In 1947 he became research professor of history at Lehigh. Gipson became an outstanding authority on the British Empire in the 18th cent., especially, although not exclusively, on its American colonies. His outstanding work, *The British Empire before the American Revolution* (15 vol., 1936–70), designed to be a comprehensive study, has earned a distinguished place in American historical writing. In 1962 he was awarded a Pulitzer Prize for one of these volumes, *The Triumphant Empire: Thunder-Clouds Gather in the West, 1733–66* (1961). Other of his works include *Jared Ingersoll* (1920); *Studies in Connecticut Colonial Taxation* (1931); *Some Reflections upon the American Revolution and Other Essays in American Colonial History* (1942); *The Coming of the Revolution, 1763–1775* (1954, in the "New American Nation" series).

gipsy: see GYPSY.

giraffe, African ruminant mammal, *Giraffa camelopardalis,* living in open savanna S of the Sahara. The tallest of animals, giraffes browse in treetops at heights inaccessible to other leaf-eaters. A male may be 18 ft (5.5 m) from hoof to crown. The neck, which is up to 7 ft (2.1 m) long, has only seven vertebrae, the usual number in mammals, but each is very elongated. The legs are also long and end in large hooves; the body is relatively short. The short horns are covered with skin and hair. Giraffes have large, sandy to chestnut, angular spots closely spaced on a lighter background. They feed chiefly on leaves of acacia and mimosa, using their extensible tongues and mobile lips to secure food. Giraffes travel in small herds led by a male. They can outrun most of their enemies and have been known to kill lions with a kick. They are most vulnerable when spreading their forelegs and lowering their heads to drink; however, they can do without water for long intervals. They are among the very few mammals that cannot swim at all. Females bear a single calf, which is about 6 ft (180 cm) tall at birth. The only other member of the giraffe family is the OKAPI. Giraffes are classified in the phylum CHORDATA, subphylum Vertebrata, class Mammalia, order Artiodactyla, family Giraffidae. See Dorcas MacClintock, *A Natural History of Giraffes* (1973).

Giralda (hĕräl'dä), tower adjoining the Cathedral of Seville, Spain. It was built (1163–84) to serve as minaret to the main mosque of Seville, on the site of which the cathedral now stands. In 1568 it was converted into a bell tower by the addition of an ornate Renaissance superstructure on the simple square Moorish tower; a weathervane, or *giraldillo,* in the shape of a crowning figure representing Faith, gave the tower its name. The original square minaret, with an interior ramp, is 197 ft (60 m) high; the superstructure adds 123 ft (37 m).

Giraldi, Giovanni Battista (jōvän'nē bät-tēs'tä jēräl'dē), 1504–73, Italian author, known also as Cinthio, Cintio, Cinzio, or Cynthus. He wrote tragedies, lyric verse, and tales. Some of the stories in his *Ecatommiti* [one hundred tales] (1565) were translated by Whetstone and other 16th-century English writers. Shakespeare derived from them the plots of *Othello* and *Measure for Measure.*

Giraldus Cambrensis (jĭrăl'dəs kămbrĕn'sĭs), c.1146–1223, Norman-Welsh churchman and historian, called also Gerald de Barri. He was associated (from 1184) with the king and court of England. His historical works include two descriptive works on Ireland (resulting from a visit) and *Descriptio Cambriae* [description of Wales]. They contain rare glimpses of medieval life and folklore. He also wrote autobiographical works, lives of churchmen, pastoral admonitions, Latin poetry, and treatises on the rights of the see of St. David's. See his autobiography (ed. and tr. by H. E. Butler, 1937).

Girard, Stephen (jĭrärd'), 1750–1831, American merchant, banker, and philanthropist, b. Bordeaux, France. Girard went to sea and at the age of 23 was a captain. In 1776 he settled in Philadelphia as a shipowner and merchant. He became wealthy and interested himself in the Bank of the United States. When its charter was not renewed, he set up his own bank in Philadelphia. He helped to finance the United States in the War of 1812, and in 1816 he put up a large amount of money for the Second Bank of the United States. Girard contributed much to the improvement of Philadelphia. He bequeathed several million dollars to found GIRARD COLLEGE. See biographies by J. B. McMaster (1918) and C. A. Herrick (1923); H. E. Wildes, *Lonely Midas* (1943); Meade Minnegarde, *Certain Rich Men* (1970).

Girard (jĭrärd'), city (1970 pop. 14,119), Trumbull co., NE Ohio, adjacent to Youngstown, on the Mahoning River; settled c.1800, inc. 1891. Its ironworks date from 1866.

Girard College, in Philadelphia; for fatherless boys (mainly from Pennsylvania), a free home and elementary and secondary school. It opened 1848 with a bequest, now grown to a huge endowment, from Stephen GIRARD.

Girardin, Delphine Gay de (dĕlfēn' gā də zhĕrär-dăN'), 1804–55, French writer; wife of Émile de Girardin. She wrote patriotic poems and, under the pseudonym Vicomte Charles de Launay, was the author of comedies, stories, and a series of sketches of Parisian life. Her literary salon was noted for its brilliance.

Girardin, Émile de (āmēl'), 1806–81, French journalist. He was editor of *La Presse* (1836–56, 1862–66), *La Liberté* (1866–70), and *La France* (1874). Actively interested in politics and social betterment, he served for a time in the chamber of deputies. He also wrote plays and novels.

Girardon, François (fräNswä' zhĕrärdôN'), 1628–1715, French sculptor. Chancellor Séguier sent him to study in Paris with François Anguier and later to Rome. On his return he was commissioned with much of the decorative sculpture in the gardens of Versailles under the direction of Le Brun. He is best known for his *Tomb of Richelieu* at the Sorbonne. His famous equestrian statue of Louis XIV was destroyed in the Revolution.

Girardot (hĕrärthōt'), city (1968 est. pop. 82,300), central Colombia, on the Magdalena River. Girardot is a commercial center and a transportation hub. Coffee, livestock, tobacco, and corn are the principal products. Founded in 1853, Girardot is noted for its vast number of acacia trees.

Giraud, Henri Honoré (äNrē' ônôrā' zhĕrō'), 1879–1949, French general. He served in World War I and in the campaign in Morocco (1925-26). A commander in World War II, he was captured by the Germans in May, 1940, but made a dramatic escape (1942) to unoccupied France and from there to Gibraltar. He took part in the Allied landing in North Africa, where he was given command of all French armed forces. On the assassination (Dec., 1942) of Admiral DARLAN, Giraud succeeded as high commissioner of French North and West Africa. His conservatism earned him the opposition of the Free French Committee of General DE GAULLE. He and De Gaulle met fruitlessly at the CASABLANCA CONFERENCE, but in June, 1943, a semblance of union was effected by the formation at Algiers of the French Committee of National Liberation, with the two generals as copresidents. Despite strong backing by the United States, Giraud was soon removed (November) from the co-presidency. In April, 1944, he was virtually forced by De Gaulle to retire as commander in chief.

Giraudoux, Jean (zhäN zhĕrōdōō'), 1882-1944, French novelist and dramatist. He was a prolific writer and combined his literary work with a long and successful diplomatic career. His early novels, which display his impressionistic, fanciful style, include *Les Provinciales* (1909) and *Suzanne and the Pacific* (1921, tr. 1923). *Amica America* (1919) relates a stay in the United States. In 1928, Giraudoux launched his dramatic career with *Siegfried* (tr. 1930), an adaptation of his novel *Siegfried et le Limousin* (1922, tr. *My Friend from Limousin*, 1923). Most of his subsequent plays, including *Amphitryon 38* (1929, tr. 1937), *La Guerre de Troie n'aura pas lieu* (1935, tr. *Tiger at the Gates*, 1955), and *Électre* (1937), are imaginative modern reinterpretations of Greek myths, satirizing selfishness, greed, and moral frailty. *The Madwoman of Chaillot* (1945, tr. 1947) is a bitter satire on 20th-century materialism. See studies by Robert Cohen (1968, repr. 1970) and Georges Lemaitre (1971).

Giresun (gĕrĕsōōn'), city (1970 pop. 30,692), capital of Giresun prov., NE Turkey, a port on the Black Sea. It is the trade center for a farm region in which maize, filberts, beans, and potatoes are produced. Known as Cerasus, the city was famous in ancient times for its cherry trees. From there the Roman general Lucullus is said to have introduced (1st cent. B.C.) the cherry tree into Italy. The English word *cherry* is derived from the name of the city, which formerly also appeared as Kerasun.

Girga: see JIRJA, Egypt.

Girgashite (gûr'gəshīt) or **Girgasite** (-sīt), Canaanite nation, whose land was occupied by Israel. Gen. 10.16; 15.21; Deut. 7.1; Joshua 3.10; 24.11; Neh. 9.8; 1 Chron. 1.14.

Girgenti: see AGRIGENTO, Italy.

Giri, Varahgiri Venkata (vərä'gərē vĕn'kətä gē'rē), 1894-, president of India (1969-74). He took a law degree in Ireland, where he practiced law and participated in the Easter Rebellion (1916), for which he was deported to India. He became active in the nationalist movement and was an influential trade union organizer. After independence he served as high commissioner in Ceylon (1947-51) and as governor successively of Uttar Pradesh, Kerala, and Mysore until 1967, when he was elected vice president. In 1969 he became acting president and later in the year, as a supporter of Indira Gandhi's policies, was elected to a five-year term. He was succeeded by Fakhruddin Ali Ahmed.

Girl Scouts, recreational and service organization founded (1912) in Savannah, Ga., by Mrs. Juliette Gordon Low (1860-1927). It was originally modeled after the Boy Scouts and Girl Guides, organizations created in Great Britain by Sir Robert BADEN-POWELL during the early 20th cent. The membership is divided into four age groups—Brownies (7 to 8), Junior Girl Scouts (9 to 11), Cadette Girl Scouts (12 to 14), and Senior Girl Scouts (14 to 17). Girls of every race, creed, color, national origin, and economic group are eligible. Good citizenship and service to others are stressed in their activities, which cover 11 different fields—agriculture, arts and crafts, community life, health and safety, homemaking, international friendship, literature and dramatics, music and dancing, nature, the outdoors, and sports and games. Camping is an important phase of Girl Scout training. Since 1917 the organization has published a monthly magazine, the *American Girl*. The World Association of Girl Guides and Girl Scouts (founded 1928) serves as the international federation for the Girl Scout organizations of some 68 countries.

Girnar (gĭrnär'), sacred mountain, 3,666 ft (1,117 m) high, Gujarat state, W India, on the Kathiawar Peninsula; a pilgrimage place for adherents of JAINISM. It has five peaks, the sides of which are dotted with ancient reservoirs and temple ruins bearing inscriptions that date from 250 B.C. The Neminath (restored, A.D. 1278) is the largest and possibly the oldest of the Jain temples on the mountain.

Girodet-Trioson, Anne-Louis (än-lwē zhĕrōdā'-trēôzôN'), 1767-1824, French painter. His name was originally Girodet de Roussy or Roucy. He was a student of J. L. David. He won the Prix de Rome and while in Italy painted the *Sleeping Endymion* (Louvre), which brought him recognition. His *Deluge* (Louvre) demonstrates his interest in unusual color and lighting problems. Much of his work, including a series for Malmaison, glorifies Napoleon. His *Atala at the Tomb* (1808; Louvre) was inspired by Chateaubriand. His classical training was sometimes at variance with his romantic expression.

Gironde (zhĕrôNd'), department (1968 pop. 1,009,-390), SW France, on the Bay of Biscay. BORDEAUX is the capital.

Gironde, estuary, c.45 mi (70 km) long and from 2 to 7 mi (3.2-11.3 km) wide, formed by the Garonne and Dordogne rivers, which join c.14 mi (23 km) N of Bordeaux. Sand banks and a high tidal range hamper navigation; oceangoing vessels ascend to Bordeaux and Libourne. The Bordeaux industrial region extends along the Gironde's southern coast. Located between the Médoc and the Cotes vineyards, the Gironde is the great artery of the Bordeaux wine region.

Girondists (jĭrŏn'dĭsts) or **Girondins** (zhĕrôNdăN'), political group of moderate republicans in the FRENCH REVOLUTION, so called because the central members of the original group were deputies of the Gironde dept. At first affiliated with the JACOBINS, they split with them over the issue of a continental war, which the Girondists advocated. Led at first by Jacques BRISSOT DE WARVILLE, the Girondists were known as Brissotins. Other notable members were Pierre VERGNIAUD, Charles DUMOURIEZ, and Jean Marie and Jeanne Manon ROLAND DE LA PLATIÈRE. Representative of the educated middle class of the provinces, they were mainly lawyers, journalists, and merchants, who desired a constitutional government. Early in 1792 the Girondists succeeded, against Jacobin opposition, in having war declared on Austria. In the Revolutionary assembly, the Convention, they engaged in personal rivalry against Maximilien Robespierre, Georges Danton, and Jean Paul Marat. The Girondists championed the provinces against Paris, in particular against the commune. They were unable to prevent the trial of King Louis XVI or the passing of the death sentence upon him. The leftist MOUNTAIN became dominant in the Convention. The treason of Dumouriez, who defected to the Austrians (March, 1793), further weakened the position of the Girondists, who also aroused popular hostility in Paris by opposing workers' demands for economic controls. On May 31 the insurrectionary Commune of Paris invaded the Convention and demanded the arrest of the Girondists. The Convention resisted, but a popular revolt forced it to order the arrest of 29 Girondists on June 2. Brissot, Vergniaud, and other leaders were executed. The fall of the Girondists assured complete control to the Mountain. See studies by R. M. Brace (1947, repr. 1968) and M. J. Sydenham (1961).

Girtin, Thomas, 1775-1802, English draftsman and watercolorist. He was apprenticed to an engraver but was employed, together with J. M. W. Turner, to make topographical drawings. Girtin was among the first to paint naturalistically in watercolor, abandoning the tinted drawing for a direct painting technique, using broad, strong areas of color. In this technique he radically influenced English landscape painting and anticipated the 19th-century watercolor. Characteristic among his drawings are *Tynemouth, View on the Wharf*, and *Kirkstall Abbey* (Victoria and Albert Mus.). See study by Thomas Girtin and David Loshak (1954).

Girty, Simon (gûr'tē), 1741-1818, American frontiersman, known as the Great Renegade, b. near Harrisburg, Pa. After three years of captivity with the Indians, he acted as an interpreter around Fort Pitt (1759-74). He served as a scout under Simon Kenton in Lord Dunmore's War and in the Revolution was in the pay of the Continentals until 1778, when he joined the British at Detroit. Girty led or participated in many savage Indian raids and was known for his cruelty. In the Indian wars in Ohio late in the 18th cent., he took part in General St. Clair's defeat (1791) and fought against Gen. Anthony Wayne at Fallen Timbers (1794). When the British surrendered Detroit (1796), Girty moved into Canada and afterward lived on a British pension. See biography by Thomas Boyd (1928).

Giry, Arthur (ärtür' zhĕrē'), 1848-99, French historian. His *Manuel de diplomatique* (new ed., 1925) remains a standard work on the scientific study of documents.

Gisborne (gĭz'bôrn), city (1971 pop. 26,726), E central North Island, New Zealand, on Poverty Bay. It is a resort and a port, exporting wool, frozen meat, and dairy goods. Captain Cook landed there in 1769.

Giscard d'Estaing, Valéry (välārē' zhĕskär' dĕstăN'), 1926-, French political leader, president of France (1974-). He received high academic honors and became a member of the national assembly at the age of 29. In 1959 he was appointed deputy finance minister in Charles De Gaulle's government, and in 1962 he was named minister of finance. Dismissed in 1966, he resumed the post in 1969 under President Pompidou. He supported European economic integration and closer ties with the United States. Leader of the Independent Republicans, a conservative group allied with the Gaullists, he ran for president after Pompidou's death in 1974, winning the office in a runoff election with the Socialist leader François Mitterand.

Gish, Lillian, 1896-, American stage and movie actress, b. Springfield, Ohio. In 1912 she began her film career with D. W. Griffith. *The Birth of a Nation* (1915) brought her worldwide fame. In such films as *Broken Blossoms* (1918), *Way Down East* (1920), and *The Scarlet Letter* (1926), her delicate heroines caught in cruel circumstances are powerfully portrayed. She returned to the stage (1930), after which she made occasional films including *Night of the Hunter* (1955) and *The Unforgiven* (1959). Gish's career again flourished in the 1960s and 70s; she appeared in many stage productions including *All the Way Home* (1960) and *Uncle Vanya* (1973). See her autobiography (1969) and biography by A. B. Paine (1932). Her sister, **Dorothy Gish**, 1898-1968, appeared with her in such films as *Hearts of the World* (1918), *Orphans of the Storm* (1922), and *Romola* (1924). The two sisters acted together again on the stage in *The Chalk Garden* (1956).

Gispa (gĭs'pə), one of the overseers of the Nethinim. Neh. 11.21.

Gissing, George (gĭs'ĭng), 1857-1903, English novelist. His promising future as a scholar was curtailed by his expulsion from Owens College at Manchester because of his association with a young prostitute whom he later married. Years of poverty and hard work followed. He visited America in 1876-77 and wrote several short stories for the Chicago *Tribune*. Gissing's novels, often grimly realistic studies of late 19th-century life, frequently reflect with bitterness his years of misery. His subjects are usually social issues—poverty, the exploitation of women, the effects of industrialization. *New Grub Street* (1891), his best-known work, depicts the dilemma of the poverty-stricken artist in an alien world. Other works include *Thyrza* (1887), *The Nether World* (1889), *Born in Exile* (1892), and *The Whirlpool* (1897). In *By the Ionian Sea* (1901) and in the somewhat autobiographic *Private Papers of Henry Ryecroft* (1903), Gissing reveals his love of books and the past. His excellent critical study (1898) of Charles Dickens, whose works greatly influenced him, is still read. See studies by Frank Swinnerton (3d ed. 1966) and Pierre Coustillas and Colin Partridge, eds. (1972); Gillian Tindall, *The Born Exile* (1974).

Gist, Christopher (gĭst), c.1706-1759, American frontiersman, b. Maryland. Commissioned by the OHIO COMPANY to explore their western lands, in 1750 he descended the Ohio River, explored E Kentucky, and crossed to Roanoke, N.C.; he thus penetrated the Kentucky region 18 years before the more celebrated Daniel Boone. The next season he more carefully traversed and mapped the Ohio watershed in western Virginia. He accompanied George Washington in 1753-54 on his historic trip to order the French out of the Ohio valley and on the journey twice saved Washington's life. On Gen. Edward Braddock's expedition (1755) against Fort Duquesne Gist served as a guide. He died of smallpox in the Cherokee country, where he had gone to enlist the Indians' aid against the French. An expert woodsman and surveyor, he was highly regarded by his contemporaries. See his journals ed. by W. M. Darlington (1893).

Gittah-hepher (gĭt'ə-hē'fər): see GATH-HEPHER.

Gittaim (gĭt'āĭm, gĭtā'-), unidentified town, S central Palestine. 2 Sam. 4.3; Neh. 11.33.

Gittite (gĭt'īt), inhabitant of GATH.

Gittith (gĭt'ĭth), in the titles of Pss. 8, 81, and 84, apparently the name of the tune to which the psalms were to be sung or instrument on which they were to be played.

Giulio Romano (jōō'lyō rōmä'nō), c.1492–1546, Italian painter, architect, and decorator, whose real name was Giulio Pippi. He was the favorite pupil of Raphael and while still a youth was entrusted with the painting of most of the frescoes in the loggias (from designs by Raphael) and a group of figures in the Stanza of the Incendio di Borgo in the Vatican and also, together with Gianfrancesco Penni, with the decoration of the ceiling of the Villa Farnesina, all in Rome. After the death of Raphael, he completed the frescoes of the life of Constantine in the Vatican as well as Raphael's *Coronation of the Virgin* and *Transfiguration* (both: Vatican Gall.). Forced to flee Rome in 1524 for having designed pornographic prints, he entered the service of the duke of Mantua, for whom he executed paintings and architectural and engineering projects. He reconstructed the cathedral, established a school of art, and designed the nearby Church of San Benedetto. He was the architect of the ducal palace and rebuilt the Palazzo del Te, decorating both of them with celebrated illusionistic and somewhat melodramatic frescoes. In 1546 he was appointed architect to St. Peter's, but he died in the same year. Well-known oils include *The Stoning of St. Stephen* (Church of Santo Stefano, Genoa) and *Adoration of the Kings* (Louvre). Romano was one of the creators of mannerism. See study by Frederick Hartt (1958).

Giunta Pisano (jōōn'tä pēzä'nō), fl. 1236–1255, Italian painter of Pisa. Among his signed works are three awesome depictions of the *Crucifixion* executed for the churches of San Ranierino, Pisa; Santa Maria degli Angeli, Assisi; and San Domenico, Bologna. He also painted a *Crucifixion with the Franciscan Father Elias* for the Church of St. Francis at Assisi, which has perished.

Giurgiu (jōōr'jōō), city (1970 est. pop. 44,000), S Rumania, in Walachia, on the Danube River opposite Ruse, Bulgaria, with which it is linked by a bridge. An important inland port, Giurgiu is connected by two oil pipelines with Ploieşti. There are shipyards and food and other light industries. The city was founded (10th cent.) on the site of a Roman settlement by Genoese merchants, who named it San Giorgio. Conquered by the Turks in 1417, it played an important role in the 16th-century wars between Walachia and Turkey and in the later Russo-Turkish Wars. Remains of the old town walls, the ruins of a medieval fortress, and an old clock tower still stand.

Giusti, Giuseppe (jōōzĕp'pä jōōs'tē), 1809–50, Italian satirical poet. He directed his original and ironic polemics against Austrian rule and also attacked demagoguery and graft. The idiomatic Tuscan of his verse and its contemporary character attracted a wide audience but have detracted from its lasting popularity.

Givatayim (gĭvätä'yĭm), town (1972 pop. 48,500), W central Israel, a residential suburb of Tel Aviv; founded 1942. Industries include printing and food processing.

Givenchy, Hubert de: see under FASHION.

Gizeh or **Giza:** see JIZAH, AL.

Gizikis, Phaidon (fĕī'thôn gēzē'kēs), 1917–, Greek general and politician. A career army officer, Gizikis served in World War II and in the civil war that followed. He advanced quickly through the ranks after the 1967 coup staged by George PAPADOPOULOS. He became commander of the third corps in 1970 and commander of the first army in the late summer of 1973. In Nov., 1973, Gizikis took office as president of the Greek republic, following a coup that he had helped to lead against the Papadopoulos government. After the government of the military junta collapsed in 1974, Gizikis resigned; he was succeeded by Michael Stassinopoulos.

Gizonite (gī'zōnīt): see JASHEN.

Gjellerup, Karl Adolf (kärl ä'dôlf yĕl'ərōōp), 1857–1919, Danish poet and novelist, b. Zealand. His early novels, naturalistic and partly autobiographical, include *The Young Denmark* (1879) and *The Disciple of the Teutons* (1882). Some of his later work shows the influence of Buddhism and Indian thought, as in *The Pilgrim Kamanita* (1906, tr. 1911). Gjellerup shared the 1917 Nobel Prize in Literature with Henrik Pontoppidan.

Gjinokastër (gyēnôkäs'tər), Gr. *Argyrokastron*, It. *Argirocastro*, town (1970 pop. 17,100), capital of Gjinokastër prov., S Albania. A commercial center, it produces foodstuffs, leather, and textiles. There are several 18th-century mosques and churches and an old citadel (rebuilt in the 19th cent.) in the town. Dating probably from the 4th cent., Gjinokastër passed to the Turks in the 15th cent. It was captured (1811) by Ali Pasha and was the center (late 1800s) of anti-Turkish resistance. In the early part of World War II it was occupied by Greece. Enver Hoxha, an Albanian political leader, was born there.

Gjuhëzës, cape: see CERAUNIAN MOUNTAINS, Albania.

Glace Bay (glās), coal-mining town (1971 pop. 22,440), E Cape Breton Island, N.S., Canada. Exploitation of the mines began toward the end of the 19th cent. The mines extend for several miles under the sea and are among the best equipped in the world. Glace Bay has a good harbor and a large deep-sea fishing fleet. The Marconi wireless tower at Table Head nearby was the transmitter in 1902 of the first transatlantic wireless message.

glacial period, time span during which large portions of the earth's surface were covered with the ice of glaciers. In the PLEISTOCENE EPOCH, in the CARBONIFEROUS and PERMIAN PERIODS of the Paleozoic era, and in Huronian time of the PRECAMBRIAN ERA, large areas of the earth's surface were subjected to an extremely cold climate, as a result of which great ice sheets spread over the land. More or less extensive continental glaciations, or glacial advances, may have occurred at other times. No satisfactory theory of the cause of glacial periods has yet been evolved. The earliest conception was that the earth's history is one of progressive cooling, resulting in glaciation during the Pleistocene epoch. This concept lost its validity when the existence of earlier glacial periods, after which the earth again became warm, was established. Possible explanations for glacial advances include the elevation of the glaciated regions into higher altitudes, changes in the direction of ocean currents, shifting of the earth's axis, shifting of the continents over the earth's surface, loss of heat from the earth's surface through reduction of the carbon dioxide content of the atmosphere, cutting off of solar heat by a blanket of volcanic dust, and variation in intensity of solar radiation. The Ewing-Donn theory, which was put forth recently, postulates a combination of plate tectonic movement of the earth's crust and circulation of Atlantic-Arctic ocean waters to explain glaciation during the Pleistocene epoch beginning about 2 million years ago. According to this theory, Pleistocene glaciation began when movement of the plates carrying the North American and Eurasian continents formed the present configuration of the Arctic Ocean. Since that time ice-free and ice-covered conditions have prevailed in the Arctic Ocean. The result has been continental glaciation in the northern hemisphere during ice-free conditions and waning of glaciers during times, such as the present, when the Arctic ocean is ice covered. The study of glacial periods owed its first impetus to the Swiss-American naturalist Louis Agassiz, whose conception of Pleistocene glaciation was presented in his address before the Helvetic Society (1837) and in his *Études sur les glaciers* (1840). See I. W. Cornwall, *Ice Ages* (1970), R. F. Flint, *Glacial and Quaternary Geology* (1971).

glacier, moving mass of ice, formed in high mountains and in the polar regions by the compacting of snow into névé and then into granular ice and set in motion outward and downward by the pressure of the accumulated mass. Glaciers are of four chief types. Valley, or mountain, glaciers are tongues of moving ice sent out by mountain snowfields into valleys originally formed by streams. They follow the courses of the valleys and are held in by the valley walls. In the Alps there are more than 1,200 valley glaciers. Piedmont glaciers, which occur only in high latitudes, are formed by the spreading of valley glaciers where they emerge from their valleys or by the confluence of several valley glaciers. Small ice sheets known as ice caps are flattened, somewhat dome-shaped glaciers spreading out horizontally in all directions and covering mountains and valleys alike. Continental glaciers are ice sheets of huge extent whose margins may break off to form icebergs (see ICEBERG). The only existing continental glaciers are the ice sheets of Greenland and Antarctica, but in the GLACIAL PERIOD of the world's geological history they were far more widespread. Glaciers may be classified as warm or cold depending on whether their temperatures are above or below −10°C (14°F). Glaciers are of considerable importance in the alteration of topography, and their work includes EROSION, transportation, and deposition. Mountain glaciers carve out amphitheaterlike vertical-walled valley heads, or cirques, at their sources. They transform V-shaped valleys into U-shaped valleys by grinding away the projecting bases of slopes and cliffs and leveling the floors of the valleys; in this process tributary valleys are frequently left "hanging," with their outlets high above the new valley floor. When the tributary valleys contain streams, waterfalls and cascades are formed, such as Bridal Veil Falls of Yosemite National Park. Elevations over which glaciers pass usually are left with gently sloping sides in the direction from which the glacier approached (stoss sides) and rougher lee sides. Humps and bosses of rock so shaped are known as roches moutonnées. The debris of glacial erosion is carried upon, within, and underneath the ice. The debris frozen into the underside of the glacier acts as a further erosive agent, polishing the underlying rock and leaving scratches, or striae, running in the direction of the movement of the glacier. Glacial deposits are known as DRIFT. The melting of the ice in summer forms glacial streams flowing under the ice, while the retreat of a large glacier sometimes leaves a temporary glacial lake, such as Lake AGASSIZ. FJORDS generally owe their origin to glaciers. A glacier moves as a solid rather than as a liquid, as is indicated by the formation of crevasses (see CREVASSE). The center of a glacier moves more rapidly than the sides and the surface more rapidly than the bottom, because the sides and bottom are held back by friction. The rate of flow depends largely on the volume of ice in movement, the slope of the ground over which it is moving, the slope of the upper surface of the ice, the amount of water the ice contains, the amount of debris it carries, the temperature, and the friction it encounters. Glaciers are always in movement, but the extent of the apparent movement depends on the rate of advance and the rate of melting. If the ice melts at its edge faster than it moves forward, the edge of the glacier retreats; if it moves more rapidly than it melts, the edge advances; it is stationary only if the rate of movement and the rate of melting are the same. The causes of glacial movement are exceedingly complex and doubtless are not all operative on the same glacier at the same time. Important elements in glacial movement are melting under pressure followed by refreezing, which tends to push the mass in the direction of least resistance; sliding or shearing of layers of ice one on top of the other; and rearrangement of the granules when pressure causes melting. Sudden, rapid movements of glaciers, called glacier surges, have recently been observed in Alaskan glaciers. The evidence for such abnormally fast movement by these glaciers is the crumpled lines of surface debris found on them.

Glacier Bay National Monument, 2,803,840 acres (1,134,714 hectares), SE Alaska, near Juneau; est. 1925. Glaciers descending from the towering snow-covered mountains into the bay create one of the world's most spectacular displays of ice. Among the bay's most famous glaciers is Muir Glacier, c.2 mi (3.2 km) wide and rising c.265 ft (80 m) above the water. Many of the glaciers flow into the Pacific. Wildlife includes bears, deer, mountain goats, porpoises, whales, and water fowl.

Glacier National Park, 521 sq mi (1,349 sq km), SE British Columbia, Canada, in the Selkirk Mts.; est. 1886. It contains extensive glaciated areas including Illecilliwaet Glacier. Snow-capped peaks, with densely forested lower slopes include Mt. Bonney, with the resort village of Glacier at its base. The rugged terrain of the park is crossed by the main line of the Canadian Pacific Railway. The park is administered from Revelstoke.

Glacier National Park, 1,013,100 acres (410,002 hectares), NW Mont.; est. 1910. Straddling the Continental Divide, the park contains some of the most beautiful primitive wilderness in the Rocky Mts. There are about 50 glaciers, more than 200 glacier-fed lakes (Lake McDonald and St. Mary Lake are the largest), high peaks, sheer precipices, large forests, waterfalls, much wildlife, and a great variety of wild flowers. Along with the adjacent WATERTON LAKES NATIONAL PARK (Canada), it forms Waterton-Glacier International Peace Park (est. 1932).

Glackens, William James, 1870–1938, American landscape and genre painter and illustrator, b. Philadelphia. An illustrator for Philadelphia and New York City newspapers and magazines for many years, Glackens first exhibited his paintings with the EIGHT and achieved fame as a brilliant painter of the contemporary scene. In his early works he used a dark palette. After staying in Paris, he adapted the technique of the French impressionist school and turned to a brighter range of colors. He was particularly influenced by Renoir. *Parade, Washington Square* (Whitney Mus., New York City), and *Nude with Apple* (Brooklyn Mus., New York) are characteristic of his later work. He is well represented in the Barnes Foundation, Merion, Pa., and other leading American collections. See Ira Glackens, *William Glackens and the Ashcan Group* (1957).

Gladbeck (glät'bĕk), city (1970 pop. 83,246), North Rhine-Westphalia, W West Germany, an industrial center of the Ruhr district. Its manufactures include chemicals, clothing, electrical equipment, and metal goods. Gladbeck's growth dates from the late 19th cent.

Gladden, Washington, 1836-1918, American clergyman, writer, and lecturer, b. Pottsgrove, Pa. He was pastor of the First Congregational Church, Columbus, Ohio, from 1882 until his death. He helped to popularize modernist views in such books as *Burning Questions* (1890) and *Who Wrote the Bible* (1891). An early proponent of the SOCIAL GOSPEL, he advocated application of Christian principles to social problems. Among his works are *Working People and Their Employers* (1876), *Social Salvation* (1902), and *Recollections* (1909).

gladiators [Lat.,=swordsmen], in ancient Rome, class of professional fighters, who performed for exhibition. Gladiatorial combats usually took place in amphitheaters. They probably were introduced from Etruria and originally were funeral games. The gladiators were paired off to fight each other, usually to the number of about 100 couples, although in the imperial shows there were sometimes as many as 5,000 pairs. There were various types of gladiators, armed and armored differently. Thus a heavily armored man, a Mirmillo or Samnite, might be opposed to a Retiarius, who fought almost naked, with a net and a trident as his only weapons. He also might be pitted against a Thracian, who fought with a dagger and a small round shield. Often gladiators were made to fight wild beasts. A defeated gladiator was usually killed by the victor unless the people expressed their desire that he be spared. At first, gladiators were invariably slaves or prisoners, including Christians. They normally underwent rigid training, and some gained immense popularity. Later, impoverished freedmen also sought a living as gladiators, and finally even members of the ruling classes took part in gladiatorial combats on an amateur basis. Constantine I forbade gladiatorial games, but they nonetheless continued until A.D. 405. Some gladiators, led by SPARTACUS, took part in the third of the SERVILE WARS (73 B.C.-71 B.C.). See study by Michael Grant (1968).

gladiolus: see IRIS.

Gladkov, Feodor Vasilyevich (fyô'dər vəsē'lyəvĭch glətkôf'), 1883-1958, Russian author. Born into poverty, Gladkov spent his youth wandering along the Volga and in the N Caucasus reading and teaching. He described this period in *Story of My Childhood* (1949), which reflects the influence of Gorky's tales of his own youth. This work was awarded a Stalin Prize. Gladkov's enormously popular novel *Cement* (1926, tr. 1929), was set in the period of industrialization after the end (1920) of the Russian revolution.

Gladstone, Herbert John Gladstone, 1st Viscount, 1854-1930, British statesman; son of William Gladstone. A member of Parliament from 1880 to 1910, he held various offices under his father, was chief whip of the Liberal party (1899-1905), and served as home secretary (1905-9). His influence in the advancement of welfare legislation was seen in bills providing workmen's compensation (1906) and an eight-hour day for miners (1908). Gladstone was created (1910) viscount and was the first governor general and high commissioner for South Africa (1910-14). His two books about his father are *W. E. Gladstone* (1918) and *After Thirty Years* (1928).

Gladstone, William Ewart, 1809-98, British statesman, the dominant personality of the LIBERAL PARTY from 1868 until 1894. A great orator and a master of finance, he was deeply religious and brought a highly moralistic tone to politics. To many he represented the best qualities of Victorian England, but he was also passionately disliked, most notably by his sovereign, Queen VICTORIA, and by his chief political rival, Benjamin DISRAELI. Entering Parliament (1833) as a Tory, he became a protégé of Sir Robert PEEL, who made him undersecretary for war and the colonies (1835). In Peel's second ministry, he became vice president (1841) and president (1843) of the Board of Trade, introducing the first government regulation of the railroads, and then (1845) colonial secretary. A supporter of free trade, he resigned (1846) with Peel in the party split that followed repeal of the corn laws and gradually aligned himself more and more with the Liberals. As chancellor of the exchequer (1852-55, 1859-66), he eloquently proposed and secured measures for economic retrenchment and free trade. He also espoused the cause of parliamentary reform (see REFORM BILLS). Gladstone served as prime minister four times (1868-74, 1880-85, 1886, and 1892-94). In his first ministry the Church of Ireland was disestablished (1869) to free Roman Catholics from the necessity of paying tithes to support the Anglican church, and an Irish land act was passed (see IRISH LAND QUESTION) to protect the peasantry. He achieved important reforms—competitive admission to the civil service, the vote by secret ballot, abolition of the sale of commissions in the army, educational expansion, and court reorganization. Conservative reaction to reforms and a weak foreign policy defeated him in 1874. In 1876, Gladstone published a pamphlet, *Bulgarian Horrors and the Questions of the East,* attacking the Disraeli government for its indifference to the brutal repression by the Turks of the Bulgarian rebellion. His renewed attack on Disraeli's pro-Turkish and generally aggressively imperialist policies in the Midlothian campaign of 1879-80 brought the Liberals back to power in 1880. During Gladstone's second ministry, a more effective Irish land act was passed (1881), and two parliamentary reform bills (1884, 1885) further extended the franchise and redistributed the seats in the House of Commons. The army's failure to relieve Charles George GORDON at Khartoum helped to bring this ministry to an end (1885). Gladstone's advocacy of HOME RULE for Ireland was a notable recognition of Irish demands, but wrecked his third ministry (1886) after a few months. Many anti-Home Rule Liberals allied themselves with the Conservatives, and the slow decline of the Liberal party may be traced from this date. Gladstone also split with the Irish leader, Charles Stewart PARNELL, because of the divorce case in which Parnell was involved. Gladstone's program in the election of 1892, which brought in his last ministry, committed the party more fully to social welfare. In office he struggled once more to obtain Home Rule and retired in 1894 after the House of Lords defeated (1893) his bill. Many of his speeches and letters have been collected. See biographies by John Morley (3 vol., 1903, repr. 1968), Philip Magnus (1954, repr. 1964), and E. G. Collieu (1968); study by J. L. Hammond and M. R. D. Foot (2d ed. 1967).

Gladstone, city (1970 pop. 23,422), Clay co., W Mo., a suburb surrounded by Kansas City; founded c.1878, inc. 1952. It has some manufacturing industries.

Gladwin, Henry, 1729-91, British army officer in colonial America, b. Derbyshire, England. He served in the disastrous campaign of Edward Braddock and in other actions in the French and Indian War but is best remembered for his defense of Detroit in PONTIAC'S REBELLION.

Glaisher, James (glā'shər), 1809-1903, English meteorologist and balloonist, b. London. He served as superintendent of the department of meteorology and magnetism at Greenwich Observatory from 1838 to 1874. He established the Meteorological Society in 1850 and later became one of the founders of the Aeronautical Society of Great Britain. Between 1862 and 1866 he made a series of balloon ascensions with Henry T. Coxwell. He wrote many scientific books and papers; his best-known work is *Travels in the Air* (1867, in French; tr. 1871).

Glåma or **Glomma** (both: glô'mä), longest river of Norway, c.365 mi (590 km) long, rising in the highlands of Sør-Trøndelag co., SE Norway. It flows generally S past Sarpsborg (the head of navigation), into the Skagerrak at Fredrikstad. The Vorma River, which drains Mjøsa Lake, is its chief tributary. The Glåma's numerous waterfalls are the sites of hydroelectric stations; the lower river furnishes power to the urban industrial complex between Sarpsborg and Fredrikstad. The Glåma, passing through a heavily forested region, is Norway's chief timber-floating river.

Glamis (glämz), village, Angus, E Scotland. King Malcolm II died (1034) nearby, and a sculptured cross in the village is known as King Malcolm's Gravestone. Macbeth was thane of Glamis, and the castle, seat of the earl of Strathmore, is erroneously claimed to be the scene of Duncan's murder in Shakespeare's play. Actually Duncan was slain in battle against Macbeth.

Glamorganshire (gləmôr'gənshĭr), county (1971 pop. 1,255,374), 818 sq mi (2,119 sq km), S Wales. The county town is CARDIFF. The mountainous northern region of the county is worked for its rich coal deposits. The fertile coastal plain is devoted to wheat and dairy farming and cattle grazing. In the southwest the Gower Peninsula is a beautiful fruit and vegetable region. The Taff, the Neath, and the Tawe are the principal rivers. The great mineral wealth of Glamorganshire has made it one of the chief industrial districts of the British Isles. There are notable tinplate, steel, and iron works. The county contains nearly half of the entire population of Wales. Before the Norman conquest there were several centers of Celtic Christianity in the region. The Normans organized the county as a marcher lordship (see WELSH MARCHES) with palatine powers. Great industrial development began in the latter half of the 18th cent. In the 1930s the area was stricken by a severe industrial depression, but since World War II conditions have been improved through government aid and planning. Cardiff and SWANSEA are important British ports. RHONDDA and MERTHYR TYDFIL are other important industrial centers. Richard Llewellyn's novel *How Green Was My Valley* (1939) gives a picture of the spread of industrialism in the 19th cent. typical of the area. In 1974, Glamorganshire was divided into the new nonmetropolitan counties of West Glamorgan, Mid Glamorgan, and South Glamorgan.

gland, organ that manufactures chemical substances. A gland may vary from a single cell to a complex system of tubes that unite and open onto a surface through a duct. The endocrine glands, e.g., the thyroid, adrenals, and pituitary, produce hormones that are secreted directly into the bloodstream (see ENDOCRINE SYSTEM). Exocrine glands secrete their substances onto an external or internal body surface. Most exocrine glands, e.g., the salivary and lacrimal glands, release their secretions through ducts. However, some open directly onto a body surface, as in the sebaceous glands of the skin and the digestive glands of the intestinal mucosa. A simple exocrine gland may consist only of a tube lined with secretory cells. In more complex types, clumps of cells produce the secretion and a duct or system of ducts discharges the secreted material. Some glands have dual functions, e.g., the liver, pancreas, ovary, and testis produce both a secretion that is emitted through a duct and a hormone that is taken up by the blood. Such structures are called mixed glands. Among the substances produced by exocrine glands in humans are sweat, lubricants like mucus and tears, and digestive juices. There are specialized exocrine glands in the animal world that produce such substances as the shells of bird eggs, spiderwebs, and the cocoons of the silkworm larvae. Simple glands are also common in the plant kingdom. The sweet nectar of flowers and the resinous pitch of pine trees are substances produced by plant glands.

glanders, highly contagious disease of horses, mules, and donkeys, caused by the bacterium *Actinobacillus mallei.* Although it can be transmitted to humans, it is limited almost exclusively to handlers of equine animals. The disease causes death in infected animals or humans. Glanders has been virtually eradicated in the United States, Canada, and Great Britain but still occurs in Asia and South America. There are three primary sites of infection: the nasal membranes and upper respiratory tract; the lungs; and the skin. The bacteria cause lumps or nodules to form in the affected area. The nodules enlarge, form ulcers, and release pus that spreads the germs to other parts of the body. In the cutaneous form of the disease, craterlike ulcers form on the skin along the course of the lymph vessels of the extremities; this form of glanders is commonly called farcy. There is no effective treatment for glanders and the infected animal must be destroyed to prevent the spread of the disease.

Glanvill or **Glanvil, Joseph** (glăn'vĭl), 1636-80, English clergyman and philosopher. He was chaplain in ordinary to Charles II and prebendary of Worcester Cathedral. An exponent of OCCASIONALISM and precursor to Hume, Glanvill sought to prove the inefficacy of all secondary causes, which he regarded as merely the occasion of the activity of the first cause, God. This idea was presented in *The Vanity of Dogmatizing* (1661), recast as *Scepsis scientifica* (1665). Although in later life Glanvill attested to a belief in witchcraft, his appreciation of the scientific method is evidenced by *Plus Ultra; or, The Progress and Advancement of Knowledge since the Days of Aristotle* (1668). See biographies by Ferris Greenslet (1900) and M. E. Price (1932).

Glanvill, Ranulf de (rā'nəlf), d. 1190, English jurist. He served Henry II in many offices, finally as chief justiciar after 1180. He commissioned one of the great works of English law, the *Tractatus de legibus et consuetudinibus regni Angliae* [treatise on the laws and customs of the realm of England], a compilation that bears his name. It is based on the COM-

MON LAW then evolving in the royal courts. See T. F. Plucknett, *Early English Legal Literature* (1958).

Glarus (glä'rəs), Fr. *Glaris,* canton (1970 pop. 38,155), 264 sq mi (684 sq km), E central Switzerland. Located in the basin of the Linth River, it is a mountainous and pastoral region, with forests and meadows in the valleys. It lies between the Walensee in the north and the Glarus Alps in the south. Cattle are raised in the canton, and there are industries producing electrical and metal goods, machinery, textiles, paper, and other goods. The inhabitants are mainly German-speaking Protestants. Sparsely settled by the Romans after 15 B.C., Glarus was permanently occupied c.500 A.D. by the Alemanni. Glarus joined the Swiss Confederation in 1352. The town of **Glarus** (1970 pop. 6,189), on the Linth, is the capital. Furniture and bleaches are made there. Zwingli was a parish priest in the town from 1506 to 1516.

Glas or **Glass, John,** 1695–1773, Scottish minister, founder of an independent Presbyterian sect whose members were often called Glasites or Glassites. He believed that national churches and civil interference in religious matters are not authorized in the Scriptures. These views found expression in his *Testimony of the King of Martyrs* (1727). Glas was deposed from the ministry in 1730; he formed an independent congregation at Dundee. The Glasite church moved to Perth in 1733, where it was joined by Robert Sandeman, who later took the lead in extending the movement to England and America. There the Glasites were known as Sandemanians.

Glasgow, Ellen (glăs'gō), 1873–1945, American novelist. She was born in Richmond, Va., where she lived all her life. In revolt against the romantic treatment of Southern life, Glasgow presented in fiction a social history of Virginia since 1850, stressing the changing social order and the emergence of a dominant middle class and rejecting the outworn code of Southern chivalry and masculine superiority. Her radicalism was apparent in her first novel, *The Descendant* (1897), and was sustained through her many subsequent books, including *Virginia* (1913), *Life and Gabriella* (1916), *Barren Ground* (1925), *The Romantic Comedians* (1926), *Vein of Iron* (1935), and *In This Our Life* (1941; Pulitzer Prize). See her critical prefaces, collected in *A Certain Measure* (1943); autobiography, *The Woman Within* (1954); letters (ed. by Blair Rouse, 1958); studies by Louis Auchincloss (1964), M. K. Richards (1971), and E. S. Godbold (1972).

Glasgow (glăs'gō, -kō, glăz'gō), city (1971 pop. 896,958), Lanarkshire, S central Scotland, on the river Clyde. Its suburbs spill over into Renfrewshire and Dumbartonshire. Glasgow is Scotland's leading seaport and largest city and is the center of the great Clydeside industrial belt. Known for its large shipyards, metalworks, and engineering works, Glasgow's manufactured products include electronic equipment, chemicals, carpets, textiles, tobacco, and machine tools. Plagued by wide-spread slums, the city began a rebuilding program in the late 1950s. Glasgow was founded in the late 6th cent. by St. Mungo (St. Kentigern), who is remembered in the city's arms and motto. The battle of LANGSIDE (1568) was fought in what is now a suburb of Glasgow. Glasgow's modern commercial growth began with the American tobacco trade in the 18th cent. and the cotton trade in the early 19th cent. Its proximity to the Lanarkshire coal fields and its location on the Clyde (first deepened at Glasgow in 1768) aided its development as a center of heavy industry during the mid-19th cent. Points of interest include St. Mungo's Cathedral (mostly 13th cent.), the Corporation Art Galleries, and the People's Palace museum. Glasgow was the center of a school of realistic art in the late 19th cent. Educational institutions include the Univ. of Glasgow (founded 1451), the Univ. of Strathclyde, and a 17th-century public school. Under the Local Government Act of 1973, Glasgow became part of the Strathclyde region.

Glasgow, city (1970 pop. 11,301), seat of Barren co., S central Ky.; inc. 1799. It is a trade and industrial center for a timber, oil, livestock, and farm area. The Spotswood home there, built in 1795 under the direction of George Washington for his niece, is still occupied. A state fish hatchery is nearby.

Glasgow, University of, at Glasgow, Scotland; founded 1451. Its charter provided for studies in theology, canon and civil law, arts, and "any other lawful faculty." Today it has faculties of arts, science, medicine, veterinary medicine, law, divinity, and engineering. In 1970 a marine biological station was established in association with the Univ. of London.

Glaspell, Susan (glăs'pĕl), 1882–1948, American author, b. Davenport, Iowa, grad. Drake Univ. She married George Cram Cook (1913) and with him organized (1915) the Provincetown Players. For this group she wrote several plays, including the one-acts *Suppressed Desires* (written with her husband, 1916) and *Trifles* (1916). She also served as actress and producer. Her longer plays include *The Inheritors* (1921) and *Alison's House* (1930; Pulitzer Prize, 1931). In addition she wrote several novels, short stories, and a biography of Cook, *The Road to the Temple* (1926).

Glass, Carter, 1858–1946, American politician, U.S. Secretary of the Treasury (1918–20), U.S. Senator from Virginia (1920–46), b. Lynchburg, Va. He learned the printer's trade and became owner of the Lynchburg *Daily News* and *Daily Advance.* Glass became prominent in local politics, then served (1902–18) in the House of Representatives. As chairman of the House Committee on Banking and Currency, he was active in the framing of the FEDERAL RESERVE SYSTEM. In 1918 he became Secretary of the Treasury under President Wilson, but in 1920 he resigned to become Senator from Virginia by appointment. Elected Senator for the balance of the term, he was reelected four times, serving until his death. He violently opposed President Franklin Delano Roosevelt's monetary and New Deal policies, but supported Roosevelt's foreign policy. See biography by Rixey Smith and Norman Beasely (1939, repr. 1972).

Glass, Hugh, fl. 1822–33, trapper in the American West. His experience while on an expedition in the Missouri River country of being mauled by a grizzly bear and left for dead and of dragging himself 100 mi (160 km) to Fort Kiowa is related in John G. Neihardt's *Song of Hugh Glass.* He was probably killed by Blackfoot Indians. See biography by J. M. Myers (1963).

Glass, Montague Marsden, 1877–1934, American humorist and playwright, b. England, educated at the College of the City of New York and at New York Univ. He won fame for his humorous delineations of American Jewish life and character, especially in the "cloak and suit trade." *Potash and Perlmutter* (1910) and *Abe and Mawruss* (1911) were both successful as magazine stories and later as plays.

glass, hard substance, usually brittle and transparent, composed chiefly of silicates and an alkali fused at high temperature. Most glass is a mixture of silica obtained from beds of fine sand or from pulverized sandstone; an alkali to lower the melting point, usually a form of soda or, for finer glass, potash; lime as a stabilizer; and cullet (waste glass) to assist in melting the mixture. The properties of glass are varied by adding other substances, commonly in the form of oxides, e.g., lead, for brilliance and weight; boron, for thermal and electrical resistance; barium, to increase the refractive index, as in optical glass; cerium, to absorb infrared rays; metallic oxides, to impart color; and manganese, for decolorizing. Man has used glass since prehistoric times, at first fashioning small objects from natural glass such as obsidian, a volcanic glass, or from rock crystal, a colorless, transparent quartz whose brilliance and clarity are emulated in manufactured glass. The term "crystal glass," derived from rock crystal, was at first applied to clear, highly refractive glass; it has come to denote in the trade a high-grade, colorless glass and is sometimes applied to any fine hand-blown glass. The processes of glassmaking have remained essentially the same since ancient times. The materials are fused at high temperatures in seasoned fireclay containers, boiled down, skimmed, and cooled several hundred degrees; then the molten glass (called metal) is ladled or poured into molds and pressed, or is blown (sometimes into molds), or is drawn. The shaped glass is annealed to relieve stresses caused by manipulation, then is slowly cooled. The glass, formerly annealed on shelves in a melting furnace, is now usually carried on rollers through annealing ovens (lehrs). Although today most hollow vessels such as light bulbs or containers are machine blown, fine ornamental hollow ware is still made by gathering a mass of glass at the end of a long, iron blowpipe, blowing it into a pear-shaped bulb, which is rolled on an oiled slab (marver), shaped with tools, and then reblown, often into a mold; the glass is reheated periodically in a small furnace (glory hole). It is finally transferred to an iron rod (punty) attached to the base of the vessel, and the lip is shaped and smoothed. Methods of decoration include cutting, copper-wheel engraving, etching with hydrofluoric acid, enameling, gilding, and painting. The place and date of origin of manufactured glass are not known. The oldest known specimens of glass are from Egypt (c.2000 B.C.), where the industry was well established c.1500 B.C. Many varieties of glass were known during Roman times, including cameo glass, such as the PORTLAND VASE, and millefiore glass, produced from fused and molded bundles of thin glass rods of many colors. Glass was also used for window panes, mirrors, prisms, and magnifying glasses. Except for the work done in Constantinople, little is now known of the methods of glassmaking used in Europe from the fall of Rome until the 10th cent., when STAINED GLASS came into use. Venice was the leader in making fine glassware for almost four centuries after the Crusades and attempted to monopolize the industry by strict control at Murano of glassworkers, who were severely penalized for betraying the secrets of the art. After the invention (c.1688) of a process for casting glass, France was for many years supreme in the manufacture of plate glass such as that used to line the Galerie des Glaces at Versailles. Late in the 17th cent. England began to make flint glass, whose lead oxide content imparted a brilliance and softness that made it suitable for cut glass. The first glass factory in America was built in 1608, and glass was carried in the first cargo exported to England. Although other glasshouses were operated in the colonies, especially in New Amsterdam, the first successful and enduring large-scale glasshouse was set up by the German-born manufacturer Caspar Wistar in New Jersey in 1739. Some of the finest colonial glassware was produced in the Pennsylvania glasshouses of the German-born manufacturer H. W. Stiegel. The invention of a glass-pressing machine (c.1827), used by the American manufacturer Deming Jarves in his Boston and Sandwich Glass Company (1825–88), permitted the manufacturing of inexpensive and mass-produced glass articles. Nevertheless, in the 19th and 20th cent., there has remained a sense of pride in individual craftsmanship. The American artist Louis C. Tiffany was responsible for the design and manufacture of an extraordinary iridescent glass used in a variety of objects in the late 1800s. Exceptionally fine blown glassware has been designed by such artists as René Lalique and Maurice Marinot in France, Edvard Hald and Simon Gate in Sweden, as well as Sidney Waugh in the United States. Glass has become invaluable in modern architecture, illumination, electrical transmission, instruments for scientific research, optical instruments, household utensils, and even fabrics. New forms of glass, new applications, and new methods of production have revolutionized the industry. Recently developed forms of glass include safety glass, which is usually constructed of two pieces of plate glass bonded together with a plastic that prevents the glass from scattering when broken; fiber glass, which is made from molten glass formed into continuous filaments and used for fabrics or for electrical insulation; and foam glass, which is made by trapping gas bubbles in glass to yield a spongy material for insulating purposes. Certain uses of glass are now being superseded by newly developed plastics. See WINDOW. See Frances Rogers and Alice Beard, *5000 Years of Glass* (1937); E. B. Haynes, *Glass Through the Ages* (1959); G. O. Jones, *Glass* (2d ed. 1971); L. D. Pyle et al., *Introduction to Glass Science* (1972).

Glassboro, borough (1970 pop. 12,938), Gloucester co., SW N.J.; settled 1775, inc. 1920. It is a trade and processing center for a fruit-growing (especially apples) region and has a large glass industry. Glassboro State College there was the site of a summit meeting (1967) between President Lyndon Johnson and Soviet Premier Aleksei Kosygin.

Glasse, Hannah, fl. 1747, writer of a popular English cookbook, *Art of Cookery* (1747). She is also credited with writing *The Compleat Confectioner* and *The Servant's Directory,* both published in 1770.

glass fiber: see FIBER GLASS.

Glassites: see GLAS, JOHN.

glass snake, common name for the snakelike legless lizards of the genus *Ophisaurus* found in the S and central United States and in Eurasia. The shiny, scaled body is gray or greenish brown, sometimes striped, above and whitish below. The American species, *Ophisaurus ventralis,* is 2 to 3 ft (60–90 cm) long; two thirds of the length is tail. The tail of a glass snake breaks easily from the body, either whole or in pieces, if struck; the lizard regenerates a new, usually shorter, tail without a real backbone. Like other lizards, and unlike snakes, the glass snake has eyelids and ear openings. Its tongue is broad. It feeds mostly on insects, worms, and slugs. A burrower, it lives in fields and meadows and seldom appears above ground in daylight. Glass snakes are classifed in the phylum CHORDATA, subphylum

Vertebrata, class Reptilia, order Squamata, family Anguidae.

Glastonbury, municipal borough (1971 pop. 6,571), Somerset, SW England. There is a leather industry, but the town is famous for its religious associations. It is a place of many legends. One tells that St. Joseph of Arimathea founded there the first Christian church in England. On Wearyall Hill he rested his staff, which rooted and became the Glastonbury thorn, blooming annually on Christmas Eve. Another story identifies Glastonbury as the Isle of Avalon of Arthurian legend. Glastonbury Abbey was a center of learning and an object of pilgrimages in the Middle Ages. Extensive remains of an Iron Age lake village have been found nearby.

Glastonbury, town (1970 pop. 20,651), Hartford co., central Conn., on the Connecticut River; inc. 1690. Its manufactures include aircraft engines, helicopters, typewriters, machine tools, electrical equipment, furniture and fixtures, leather, and meat products. Poultry, dairy products, fruit, and tobacco are also important to the city's economy. Gideon Welles was born in Glastonbury. Several 17th-century houses still stand.

Glatz: see KŁODZKO, Poland.

Glatzer Neisse, river: see under NEISSE.

Glauber, Johann Rudolf (yō'hän rōō'dôlf glou'-bər), 1604–70, German alchemist. A forerunner of scientific chemists, Glauber made many practical advances in analytical chemistry; he devised new procedures and was the first to prepare several compounds, including GLAUBER'S SALT. Little is known of his life.

Glauber's salt, common name for sodium sulfate decahydrate, $Na_2SO_4 \cdot 10H_2O$; it occurs as white or colorless monoclinic crystals. Upon exposure to fairly dry air it effloresces, forming powdery anhydrous SODIUM SULFATE. Johann Glauber was the first to produce the salt (from Hungarian spring waters). The naturally occurring salt is called mirabilite. Glauber's salt is water soluble, has a salty, bitter taste, and is sometimes used in medicine as a mild laxative; it is also used in dyeing.

glaucoma (glôkō'mə), ocular disorder characterized by pressure within the eyeball caused by an excessive amount of aqueous humor (the fluid substance filling the eyeball). This causes pressure against the retina, and the resulting impairment of vision ranges from slight abnormalities to total blindness. Chronic glaucoma begins gradually over a period of months or years, usually in patients over the age of 40. There are no symptoms in the early stages, and the condition can be detected only by a physical examination and measurement of the intraocular pressure. Such an examination is recommended every three years for all persons over the age of 20. As the disease progresses, often the only symptom is a gradual loss of peripheral vision. Chronic glaucoma can be controlled with drugs that increase the outflow or decrease the production of aqueous humor. If treatment is continued throughout life, useful vision will be preserved in most cases; untreated individuals will gradually become blind. Acute glaucoma, which accounts for only 10% of the incidence of the disease, begins abruptly with severe pain and blurred vision. It is a medical emergency that causes permanent blindness in two to five days if left untreated.

glaucophane (glô'kəfān"): see AMPHIBOLE.

Glaucus (glô'kəs), in Greek mythology. **1** Sea god who loved SCYLLA. **2** Trojan hero who, according to Homer, exchanged his golden armor for the bronze armor of Diomed. **3** Son of Sisyphus and father of Bellerophon. He was devoured by his own horses.

glaze, translucent layer that coats pottery to give the surface a finish or afford a ground for decorative painting. Glazes—transparent, white, or colored—are fired on the clay. Of the various artificial mixtures used for glazes, that for whiteware contains borax and lead, whereas a salt glaze is used for stoneware. No lead is used for porcelain. The coloring agents are oxides of different metals. In the 16th and 17th cent. glazes were also used in painting to enhance the luminosity of oil or tempera colors. Titian and Rembrandt were especially adept at glazing techniques.

glaze, in meteorology: see SLEET.

Glazunov, Aleksandr Konstantinovich (əlyĭksän'dər kənstəntyē'nəvĭch gläzōō'nôf), 1865–1936, Russian composer, director of the St. Petersburg Conservatory, 1906–17. He assisted his teacher, Rimsky-Korsakov, in completing Borodin's unfinished opera *Prince Igor.* Glazunov's early works reflect the spirit of Russian nationalism, but Western influences are discernible in his later works. He wrote eight symphonies, a piano concerto and a violin concerto, ballets, chamber music, and orchestral tone poems.

glee, in music, an unaccompanied song for three or more solo voices in harmony. The word *glee* [Anglo-Saxon, *gligge* or *gliw*=music] has been associated with vocal music from the time of the medieval gleeman or jongleur. The glee consisted of several short, individual pieces interpreting a poetic passage. The form is exclusively English and flourished mainly between 1750 and 1830, after which time it was displaced by the part songs of the Victorian composers. *Glorious Apollo* by Samuel Webbe (1740–1816) was the most famous glee. Gentlemen's glee societies were popular in England during the 18th cent., and women's glee societies had some vogue at the end of the century. In the United States glee clubs are simply choral organizations.

Gleiwitz: see GLIWICE, Poland.

Gleizes, Albert Léon (älbĕr' lāôN' glĕz), 1881–1953, French cubist painter, illustrator and writer. He was among the outstanding cubists in the Salon des Indépendants of 1911. Gleizes employed a rich palette in contrast to the essentially monochromatic effects of Braque and Picasso, and his work remained more representational than theirs. His painting is represented in the Museum of Modern Art, New York City. Gleizes was also well-known as an illustrator and as a writer on art. With Jean Metzinger, he wrote the first exposition of the principles of cubism in *Du Cubisme* (1912, tr. 1913).

Glenalmond (glĕnä'mənd), valley of the Almond River, Perthshire, central Scotland, N of Crieff. A huge flat stone marks the traditional grave of Ossian, the legendary Gaelic poet. There was a Roman camp at Fendoch. Trinity College (founded 1841), a public school for boys, is there.

Glen Canyon Dam, 710 ft (216 m) high, 1,560 ft (475 m) long, N Ariz., on the Colorado River. The key unit of the U.S. Bureau of Reclamation's COLORADO RIVER STORAGE PROJECT, it is one of the world's largest concrete dams (larger in bulk, though not in height, than Hoover Dam). The dam, completed in 1964, regulates the flow of the upper Colorado and its tributaries and produces 900,000 kw of electricity. Lake Powell, formed by the dam, will eventually extend 186 mi (299 km) upstream into S Utah. It was named after the American explorer J. W. Powell who mapped and named the canyon in 1870. This 252-sq mi (653-sq km) lake, having the second largest reservoir capacity in the United States, is the nucleus of the Glen Canyon National Recreation Area (see NATIONAL PARKS AND MONUMENTS, table). The Glen Canyon Bridge, 1,271 ft (387 m) long and 700 ft (213 m) high, is one of the world's longest and highest steel-arch bridges.

Glencoe (glĕn'kō), residential village (1970 pop. 10,675), Cook co., NE Ill., on Lake Michigan; inc. 1869. A Nike missile site is there.

Glencoe (glĕnkō'), valley of the Coe River, N Argyllshire, W Scotland. It was the scene of the massacre of the Macdonald clan (Feb., 1692) by the Campbells, under the direction of John Campbell, 1st earl of Breadalbane, and John Dalrymple, 1st earl of Stair.

Glen Cove, city (1970 pop. 25,770), Nassau co., SE N.Y., on the north shore of Long Island, at the entrance to Hempstead Harbor; settled 1668, inc. as a city 1918. Although chiefly residential, it has varied light industries. The Webb Institute of Naval Architecture is there.

Glendale. 1 City (1970 pop. 36,228), Maricopa co., S central Ariz., adjacent to Phoenix; inc. 1910. It is located in a rich agricultural region irrigated by the Salt River project. The city has food-processing plants and is a shipping point for fruits and vegetables. Luke Air Force Base, a large jet fighter training center, is in Glendale, and a junior college is also located there. **2** City (1970 pop. 132,752), Los Angeles co., S Calif., a suburb of Los Angeles; inc. 1906. It has aerospace supporting facilities and other defense-oriented plants, as well as a film industry. The city was founded on part of a ranch that had been the first Spanish land grant in California (1784). Forest Lawn Memorial Park, a large cemetery, is located there. The city also has a junior college and a chiropractic college. **3** City (1970 pop. 13,436), Milwaukee co., SE Wis., a suburb of Milwaukee, on the Milwaukee River; inc. 1950. It has a grain elevator and plants that make water purification equipment, electrical switches and appliances, batteries, cans, and plastic products. Part of Cardinal Stritch College is within the city limits.

Glendale, battle of: see SEVEN DAYS BATTLES.

Glendalough (glĕn'dəlō"), wooded valley, Co. Wicklow, E Republic of Ireland, W of Wicklow. It is noted for the ruins of several churches of the 11th and 12th cent. (part of the center of Irish Christianity that St. Kevin founded). Also of interest are a round tower and Kevin's Cross (a granite monolith). A ledge in the face of the rocky mountainside, above the lake that lies at the foot of the vale, is the legendary retreat of St. Kevin.

Glendora, city (1970 pop. 31,349), Los Angeles co., S Calif., a residential suburb of the Los Angeles metropolitan area, at the base of the San Gabriel Mts.; inc. 1911. Sprinklers and pumps are made in the city. The region was declared open government land in 1869 and a rush of homesteaders began. By the early 1900s it was covered with magnificent groves of orange and lemon trees. Glendora was an important citrus center, with large packinghouses. Although some citrus fruit is still grown in the area, the housing boom following World War II converted the city into a bedroom community.

Glendower: see OWEN GLENDOWER.

Glenelg (glĕnĕlg'), city (1971 pop. 15,383), a suburb of Adelaide, S Australia, on an inlet of Gulf St. Vincent. It is a residential area and summer resort. In 1836, South Australia's first colonists landed at the site.

Glen Ellyn, village (1970 pop. 21,909), Du Page co., NE Ill., a residential suburb of Chicago; inc. 1892. A junior college is there. Points of interest include Stacy Tavern, a 19th-century stagecoach stop on the Chicago-Galena route; a wildlife sanctuary; and an arboretum.

Glen More: see GREAT GLEN, valley, Scotland.

Glenn, John Herschel, Jr., 1921–, American astronaut, b. Cambridge, Ohio. He was the first American and the third man to be put into orbital space flight. On Feb. 20, 1962, he circled the earth three times in 4 hr 56 min in a space vehicle launched from a rocket at Cape Canaveral, Fla.; on descending he was recovered from the Atlantic Ocean off the Bahamas. His vehicle reached a maximum altitude of 187.75 mi (302.16 km), achieved a velocity of 17,545 mi (28,236 km) per hr, and covered a distance of about 81,000 mi (130,400 km). After leaving the space program, Glenn entered Ohio politics and was elected to the U.S. Senate as a Democrat in 1974.

Glen Rock, borough (1970 pop. 13,011), Bergen co., NE N.J.; settled c.1710, inc. 1896. A residential suburb of New York City, it has a small industrial park. George Washington's army used the area for camping grounds during the Revolutionary War.

Glenrothes, new town, Fifeshire, E Scotland, on the Leven River. Glenrothes was designated one of the NEW TOWNS in 1948 to provide housing, community services, and increased social and economic diversity for an expanding mining area. In 1961 the Glenrothes colliery closed. The town is now intended to relieve overpopulation in Glasgow. Its industries include light and electronic engineering, food processing, and plastics manufacturing.

Glen Roy, valley, Inverness-shire, W Scotland, E of Loch Lochy. The Parallel Roads, three terraces on each side of the valley at corresponding heights, are believed to mark receding levels of a lake that once filled the valley.

Glens Falls, city (1970 pop. 17,222), Warren co., E central N.Y., in the foothills of the Adirondack Mts. and on the Hudson River; settled 1762, inc. as a city 1908. Paper, clothing, chemicals, and cement are produced. A navy training center and a junior college are there. Charles Evans Hughes was born in Glens Falls.

Glenview, village (1970 pop. 24,880), Cook co., NE Ill., a suburb of Chicago; settled 1833, inc. 1899. It is chiefly residential. A dairy research center and a U.S. naval air station are there.

glial cells: see BRAIN.

glider, type of aircraft resembling an airplane but having at most a small auxiliary propulsion plant and often no means of propulsion at all. Modern gliders usually have very slender wings and a streamlined body. The unpowered variety is launched by an elastic shock cord, a rope, or a cable, attached to the front of the glider and pulled by a launching crew, a winch, a tow car, or a tow plane. Gliders have been towed behind airplanes over great distances. The powered variety can take off and climb on its own. An unpowered glider or one with its engine off uses gravity and updrafts of air to keep it flying. In soaring the glider is repeatedly maneuvered through updrafts to gain altitude. It can then glide down through air that is not rising.

In a powered glider the engine can be turned on to keep the glider aloft when there are no updrafts. The type of craft built especially for soaring and sustained flight is called a sailplane. The usual flight controls in a glider consist of a pedal to operate the rudders and a control stick to operate the elevators and ailerons. Otto and Gustav Lilienthal of Germany made the first successful piloted glider flight in 1891. The Lilienthals demonstrated the superiority of curved over flat surfaces in flight and encouraged others to make glider experiments. Early gliders were launched from elevated positions or by running forward. The machine maintained stability while in flight by the pilot's shifting body weight. At the beginning of the 20th cent. the Wright brothers constructed and flew many gliders. They introduced land skids, wing warping, and other improvements that characterize present-day gliders. In World War II troop-transport gliders were used for aerial invasions. The gliders were launched and towed by cargo aircraft to the invasion area, where they were released. See Norman Ellison, *British Gliders and Sailplanes, 1922–1970* (1971); Derek Piggott, *Gliding: A Handbook on Soaring Flight* (3d ed. 1971); W. T. Carter, *Soaring* (1973).

Glière, Reinhold Moritzovich (rīn'hōlt mōrētsô'-vĭch glēĕr'), 1875–1956, Russian composer. He studied in Moscow and Berlin, then became professor of composition (1913) and director (1914) at the Kiev Conservatory and a professor (1920) at the Moscow Conservatory. Among his pupils were Prokofiev, Miaskovsky, and Khachaturian. His compositions, generally nationalistic with romantic and impressionistic elements, show the influence of Russian folk melodies that he collected in Europe and Asia. His best-known works are the ballet *The Red Poppy* (1927) and his Third Symphony (*Ilya Mourometz*, 1909–11).

Glinka, Mikhail Ivanovich (mĕkhəyēl' ēvä'nəvĭch glēn'kä), 1804–57, first of the nationalist school of Russian composers. His two operas, *A Life for the Czar* (1836) and *Russlan and Ludmilla* (1842), marked the beginning of a characteristically Russian style of music. His best symphonic work was the incidental music to the play *Prince Kholmsky*. See study by David Brown (1973).

Glittertinden (glĭt'tərtĭn"ən), peak, 8,104 ft (2,470 m) high, S central Norway, in the Jotunheimen mts. It is the highest point in Scandinavia.

Gliwice (glĭvē'tsĕ), Ger. *Gleiwitz*, city (1970 pop. 170,900), SW Poland. A coal-mining and steel-making center of the Katowice region, it also has industries producing machinery and chemicals. Chartered in 1276, Gliwice was ceded by Austria to Prussia in 1742.

globe, spherical map of the earth (terrestrial globe) or the sky (celestial globe). The terrestrial globe provides the only graphic representation of the areas of the earth without significant distortion or inaccuracy in shape, direction, or relative size. However, the flattening of the earth at the poles and its slight bulge below the equator are normally disregarded in the construction of a globe. Probably the earliest globe was constructed by the Greek geographer Crates of Mallus in the 2d cent. B.C. Few attempts were made to construct globes in the Middle Ages, although Strabo and Ptolemy, at the beginning of the Christian era, had formulated precise and detailed instructions for doing so. The first globes of modern times were made in the late 15th cent. by Martin Behaim of Nuremberg and Leonardo da Vinci. One of the earliest globes constructed (1506) after the discovery of America is in the New York Public Library. A celestial globe is a model of the CELESTIAL SPHERE intended primarily to show the positions of the stars. See S. Carl Hirsch, *Globe for the Space Age* (1963).

globe amaranth: see AMARANTH.

globeflower, common name for any plant of the genus *Trollius* of the family Ranunculaceae (BUTTERCUP family), hardy perennials of north temperate meadows and swamps. Their blossoms are larger than those of the familiar yellow buttercup and may be white, yellow, orange, or purple. *T. europaeus*, with flower parts incurved in a globe shape, is most commonly cultivated. Globeflowers are classified in the division MAGNOLIOPHYTA, class Magnoliopsida, order Ranunculales, family Ranunculaceae.

Globe Theatre, London playhouse, built in 1598, where most of Shakespeare's plays were first presented by the CHAMBERLAIN'S MEN. It burned down in 1613, was rebuilt in 1614, and destroyed by the Puritans in 1644. See J. C. Adams, *The Globe Playhouse* (1945).

globular cluster: see STAR CLUSTER.

globulin, any of a very large family of PROTEINS widely distributed throughout the plant and animal kingdoms. Many of these substances have been prepared in pure crystalline form. The term globulin is a procedural one, used in classifying an otherwise diverse group of proteins that are soluble in dilute solutions. The globulins are distinguished from ALBUMINS on the basis of the greater solubility in ammonium sulfate solution of the latter group. The γ-globulins, isolated from mammalian blood serum, are the ANTIBODIES of the immune system (see IMMUNITY); some β-globulins are responsible for the transportation throughout the body of a variety of substances, including LIPIDS, HORMONES, and inorganic ions.

glockenspiel (glŏk'ənspēl) [Ger.,=bell-play], percussion instrument. The medieval glockenspiel was a sort of miniature carillon (see BELL), sometimes played mechanically by means of a rotating cylinder

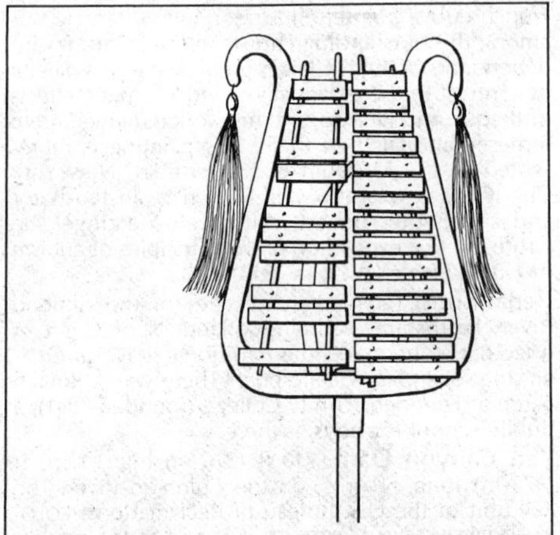

Glockenspiel

with protruding pins. In the 16th cent. it was given a keyboard. The 18th-century glockenspiel had metal bars instead of bells, and in the 19th cent. the keyboard disappeared and the bars were struck by hammers. It has been used in the orchestra since the 18th cent. Related modern instruments are the tubophone, which uses a keyboard with tubes instead of bars, and the vibraphone, which has resonating tubes beneath its bars that vibrate using electricity. See also XYLOPHONE.

glomerulonephritis: see NEPHRITIS.

Glomma, river: see GLÅMA, river, Norway.

Gloria Dei National Historic Site: see NATIONAL PARKS AND MONUMENTS (table).

Gloria in excelsis (ĕksĕl'sĭs) [Lat.,=glory in the highest], the *Angelic Hymn*, or greater DOXOLOGY, ancient Christian hymn beginning, according to the Authorized Version, "Glory be to God on high, and on earth, peace, good will towards men." An amplification of Luke 2.14, it was of Greek origin and took its place in the Roman Mass about the beginning of the 6th cent. In the Mass it follows the Kyrie, but in the Anglican Communion it is just before the benediction. In both services it is omitted at certain seasons.

Gloria Patri (pä'trē) [Lat.,=glory to the Father], the lesser DOXOLOGY, brief Christian hymn in praise of the Persons of the Trinity. The hymn is much used in the Roman Catholic liturgy, in the Anglican morning and evening prayers, and in Protestant services in general.

Glorious Revolution, in English history, the events of 1688–89 that resulted in the deposition of JAMES II and the accession of WILLIAM III and MARY II to the English throne. It is also called the Bloodless Revolution. The restoration of Charles II in 1660 was met with misgivings by many Englishmen who suspected the Stuarts of Roman Catholic and absolutist leanings. Charles II increased this distrust by not being responsive to Parliament, by his toleration of Catholic dissent, and by favoring alliances with Catholic powers in Europe. A parliamentary group, the WHIGS, tried to ensure a Protestant successor by excluding James, duke of York (later James II), from the throne, but they were unsuccessful. After James's accession (1685) his overt Catholicism and the birth of a Catholic prince who would succeed to the throne united the hitherto loyal Tories (see TORY) with the Whigs in common opposition to James. Seven Whig and Tory leaders sent an invitation to the Dutch prince William of Orange and his consort, Mary, Protestant daughter of James, to come to England. William landed at Torbay with an army. James's forces, under John Churchill (later duke of Marlborough), deserted him, and James fled to France (Dec., 1688). There was some debate in England on how to transfer power; whether to recall James on strict conditions or under a regency, whether to depose him outright, or whether to treat his flight as an abdication. The last course was decided upon, and early in 1689 William and Mary accepted the invitation of Parliament to rule as joint sovereigns. The Declaration of Rights and the BILL OF RIGHTS (1689) redefined the relationship between monarch and subjects and barred any future Catholic succession to the throne. The royal power to suspend and dispense with law was abolished, and the crown was forbidden to levy taxation or maintain a standing army in peacetime without parliamentary consent. The provisions of the Bill of Rights were the conditions upon which the throne was offered to and accepted by William and Mary. These events were a milestone in the gradual process by which practical power shifted from the monarch to Parliament. The final ascendancy of Parliament was never thereafter successfully challenged. See G. M. Trevelyan, *The English Revolution, 1688–1689* (1938); Lucile Pinkham, *William III and the Respectable Revolution* (1954).

glory lily: see LILY.

gloss [Gr.,=tongue], explanatory note on a word or words of a text, usually written between the lines or in a margin of a manuscript. In copying a manuscript, a copyist sometimes incorporated a gloss in the text, so that the copy departed from the original. The gloss may be in a language different from that of the text. Old glosses on the Bible have value as evidence of tradition, as have glosses in civil and canon law.

glossolalia [Gr.,=speaking with tongues], ecstatic utterances usually of unintelligible sounds made by individuals in a state of religious excitement. Religious revivals are often accompanied by manifestations of glossolalia, and various Pentecostal (see PENTECOSTALISM) movements cite for authority Acts 2, which records that on the day of Pentecost the Apostles "were all filled with the Holy Ghost and began to speak with other tongues as the Spirit gave them utterance." There are other New Testament references to the phenomenon (Acts 4.31; 10.44–48; 11.15–17; 19.1–7; 1 Cor. 12–14), showing that it was very important in the early church. Glossolalia usually consists of meaningless sounds, although several instances have been reported where a person began to speak a language previously unknown to him. See M. T. Kelsey, *Tongue Speaking* (1964, repr. 1968); J. C. Sherill, *They Speak with Other Tongues* (1964); F. D. Goodman, *Speaking in Tongues* (1972); J. P. Kildahl, *The Psychology of Speaking in Tongues* (1972).

Glossop (glŏs'əp), municipal borough (1971 pop. 24,147), Derbyshire, central England. A residential suburb of Manchester, Glossop is also the chief cotton-manufacturing city of Derbyshire. Other products are woolens, canned goods, and paper. The borough is adjacent to Peak District National Park.

Gloucester, Gilbert de Clare, 8th **earl of** (glŏs'tər), 1243–95, English nobleman, son of the 7th earl. He married (1253) Alice de Lusignan, niece of HENRY III, and succeeded to the earldom in 1262. In the BARONS' WAR he was at first a leader of the baronial party under Simon de MONTFORT, earl of Leicester, and was a member, with Montfort and the bishop of Chichester, of the three-man provisional administration set up after the royal defeat at Lewes (1264). In 1265, however, he defected to the royalist side and aided Prince Edward (later EDWARD I) in the defeat of Montfort at Evesham. He seized London in 1267 to force from the king a more lenient settlement for the rebels. After Edward's accession (1272), Gloucester engaged in much fighting in Wales. His first marriage was annulled, and in 1290 he married Edward's daughter Joan. He also held the titles of earl of Clare and earl of Hertford, as did his son by Joan, **Gilbert de Clare**, 9th **earl of Gloucester**, 1291–1314, who served Edward II faithfully and was killed at the battle of Bannockburn.

Gloucester, Henry William Federick Albert, duke of, 1900–1974, British prince; third son of George V, brother of Edward VIII and George VI, and uncle of Elizabeth II. He was created duke in 1928. He was educated at Sandhurst and made the army his career, serving as a major general in World War II. Governor general of Australia from 1945 to 1947, he was promoted to the rank of field marshal in 1955.

Gloucester, Humphrey, duke of, 1391–1447, English nobleman; youngest son of Henry IV and Mary de Bohun. He was well educated and had a great interest in humanist scholarship. After the accession of his eldest brother as Henry V, Humphrey was created (1414) duke of Gloucester and earl of Cambridge. He served in Henry's French campaigns and was wounded at the battle of Agincourt (1415). In 1420–21 he remained in England as regent during Henry's absence. When Henry was succeeded by his infant son, HENRY VI, Gloucester claimed the regency. However, the 1422 Parliament disregarded this claim, which was based on Henry V's will, and made Gloucester's older brother, John of Lancaster, duke of BEDFORD, protector of the realm. Since Bedford was occupied in France, Gloucester was given the title of protector during his absences, but he had to share his authority with a council of magnates. Gloucester's ensuing struggle for power against his uncle, Henry BEAUFORT, forced Bedford to return from France several times to reconcile them. Gloucester married (c.1422) JACQUELINE of Hainaut but abandoned (1425) her after their disastrous military expedition to Hainaut. A papal decree of 1428 invalidated that marriage and permitted him to marry his mistress, Eleanor Cobham, but he was severely criticized. Henry was crowned king of England in 1429 and king of France in 1431, and Beaufort's ascendancy henceforth increased. After the death of Bedford in 1435, Gloucester became heir presumptive, but his influence with the young king waned as he advocated continuing the unsuccessful war in France. When Eleanor, Gloucester's wife, was imprisoned in 1441 for sorcery against the king, Gloucester's political importance was practically ended. In 1447, William de la Pole, 4th earl of Suffolk (see under POLE, family), who had succeeded Beaufort as the king's chief adviser, had Gloucester arrested for treason. The duke fell sick and died in custody. He was known as "Good Duke Humphrey," probably because of his patronage of scholars and men of letters. He corresponded with the leaders of the new Italian humanism, had translations made from the Greek classics, and collected a considerable library. His gift of books to Oxford Univ. formed the nucleus later restored and developed by Sir Thomas BODLEY into the Bodleian Library. However, in matters of state he lacked determination, flitting from one project to another and following through with none. Unable to appear decisive, he thus antagonized all by his assertions of power. See biographies by K. H. Vickers (1907) and E. F. Jacob, *The Fifteenth Century* (1961).

Gloucester, Richard de Clare, 7th **earl of,** 1222–62, English nobleman. He succeeded his father as earl in 1230. For some years Gloucester vacillated in his allegiance to HENRY III; he served the king in diplomatic missions to Scotland and Germany, but in 1258 he became a leader of the baronial party that forced Henry to accept the PROVISIONS OF OXFORD. Gloucester and Simon de MONTFORT, earl of Leicester, were now the leading political figures in England. They soon quarreled, however, and in 1259 Gloucester was reconciled with the king. When Henry repudiated (1261) the provisions Gloucester briefly rejoined the opposition but made his peace with the king within the year. Gloucester also held the titles of earl of Clare and earl of Hertford.

Gloucester, Robert, earl of, d. 1147, English nobleman; illegitimate son of Henry I. Henry created (c.1121) the earldom of Gloucester for him. After his father's death (1135), Robert appeared to accept the seizure of the throne by Henry's nephew, STEPHEN, to whom he did conditional homage in 1136. They soon quarreled, however, and after Stephen had seized (1138) Robert's lands, Robert led a baronial rebellion in favor of his half sister, MATILDA. The earl captured Stephen at Lincoln in 1141, but later in the year he himself was captured, while covering Matilda's retreat from Winchester, and exchanged for the king. Robert then went to France to get aid from Matilda's husband, Geoffrey IV of Anjou, and returned to England with her son Henry (later Henry II). Robert held the Angevin party in England together and consistently labored for Matilda's cause.

Gloucester, Thomas of Woodstock, duke of, 1355–97, English nobleman; youngest son of Edward III. He was betrothed (1374) to Eleanor, heiress of Humphrey de Bohun, earl of Hereford, and became earl of Buckingham at the coronation of RICHARD II (1377). He was the king's lieutenant in France (1380), but returned to England after the failure of his siege of Nantes. In 1385 he was created duke of Gloucester and soon emerged as the head of the baronial party, which in 1386 forced Richard to dismiss Michael de la Pole, 1st earl of Suffolk (see under POLE, family), as chancellor. In 1388, Gloucester was one of the five "lords appellant" who secured conviction of the king's counselors for treason in the Merciless Parliament. When Richard regained power in 1389, Gloucester made his peace with him and accompanied the king to Ireland in 1394. In 1397, Gloucester was suddenly arrested and imprisoned at Calais. He was probably murdered there a few days before he was "appealed" and condemned for treason by the same procedure as that used in 1388.

Gloucester (glŏs'tər), county borough (1971 pop. 90,134), county town of Gloucestershire, W central England, on the Severn River. It is a market town. Manufactures include aircraft components, agricultural machinery, railroad equipment, and processed foods. The port is still active but has been eclipsed by Bristol since the 15th cent. Gloucester stands upon the site of the Roman city Glevum. In Saxon times it was the capital of MERCIA. There is a notable cathedral (begun 1089) in which Edward II is buried. The Three Choirs Festival is held in Gloucester every third year. A technical college and an old public school are there.

Gloucester, city (1970 pop. 27,941), Essex co., NE Mass., on Cape Ann; settled 1623, inc. as a city 1873. It is a port of entry at the head of the excellent Gloucester Harbor, which is protected by a breakwater built from Eastern Point. The harbor has been used by fishing ships for over three centuries, and Gloucester is still a great fishing port, with many fish-processing industries and related manufactures. It was once an important shipbuilding center, and the first schooner is said to have been built there in 1713. The picturesque old city is also the center of an extensive summer resort area. Gloucester's development as a resort and artists' colony began late in the 19th cent. Tourist attractions include the famous bronze *Fisherman,* a memorial to the thousands of Gloucestermen lost at sea; Hammond Castle, which houses collections of medieval art; and numerous pre-Revolutionary houses. The city has furnished material for authors (e.g., Rudyard Kipling in his *Captains Courageous*) as well as artists. See the works of James B. Connolly; J. E. Garland, *Eastern Point* (1971).

Gloucester City, city (1970 pop. 14,707), Camden co., SW N.J., on the Delaware River, a suburb adjoining Camden and opposite Philadelphia; site of Fort Nassau (built 1623 by the Dutch), settled c.1682 by Irish Quakers, inc. 1868.

Gloucestershire (glŏs'tərshĭr), county (1971 pop. 1,069,454), 1,258 sq mi (3,258 sq km), W central England. The county seat is GLOUCESTER. In the eastern part of the county are the Cotswold Hills, devoted largely to dairy and crop farming; in the center is the fertile valley of the Severn River, devoted to dairy farming (Gloucester cheese) and sheep raising; and in the west, on the Welsh border, are the Wye valley and the Forest of Dean, also with sheep raising. Manufacturing (aircraft, engineering, paper, and tobacco products) is centered in Bristol, Gloucester, and Cheltenham. Cirencester and Gloucester were centers of networks of Roman roads. The region became part of the Anglo-Saxon kingdom of MERCIA. In the Middle Ages the Cotswolds provided wool for an important wool trade in the county.

glove, hand covering with a separate sheath for each finger. The earliest gloves, relics of the cave dwellers, closely resembled bags. Reaching to the elbow, they were most probably worn solely for protection and warmth. Although there is some indication of the use of separate fingers in an Egyptian relic, most early gloves were much like mittens, usually of skin with the fur inside. The glove as we know it today dates from the 11th cent. In England after the Norman conquest, gloves, richly jeweled and ornamented, were worn as a badge of distinction by royalty and by church dignitaries. The glove became meaningful as a token; it became custom to fling a gauntlet, the symbol of honor, at the feet of an adversary, thereby challenging his integrity and inviting satisfaction by duel. In the 12th cent. gloves became a definite part of fashionable dress, and ladies began to wear them; the sport of falconry also increased their use. In the 13th cent. the metal gauntlet appeared as a part of armor. Gloves became accessible to the common people, and their popularity grew. Scented gloves, an innovation that was to last until the 18th cent., came into vogue. The 16th and 17th cent. saw extravagantly ornamented gloves; they were of leather, linen, silk, or lace and were jeweled, embroidered, or fringed. After the 17th cent. the emphasis was on proper fit, and gloves were less ornamental. The first known glove maker was in Perth, Scotland, after 1165; a guild of glove makers was incorporated in France in 1190, and one in London c.1600. In the United States, glove making began in 1760 when a settlement of Scottish glovers was established at Gloversville, N.Y.; New York state has since been the center of the glove industry in the United States. Modern gloves are made of fabric, plain or knitted; of leather from almost every variety of animal hide; and of rubber and plastic used in surgical, laboratory, and household work. See C. C. Collins, *Love of a Glove* (1945).

Glover, Jose (glŭv'ər), d. 1638, English nonconformist minister, generally considered the father of printing in the English colonies of North America. He visited New England c.1634 and on his return to England solicited support for what became Harvard College. He also bought a printing press and equipment and contracted for the services of Stephen DAYE and his household (including Matthew DAYE). Glover died on the voyage to America. His wife came into control of the printing equipment, and Stephen and Matthew Daye worked for her.

Gloversville (glŭv'ərzvĭl"), city (1970 pop. 19,677), Fulton co., E central N.Y.; inc. 1890. Glove making has been important since the late 18th cent. Other industries include tanning and the manufacture of records and toys. Gloversville has a noteworthy colonial church building.

glowworm, name for a larval or wingless female FIREFLY.

gloxinia: see GESNERIA.

Glubb, Sir John Bagot, 1897–, British soldier. He served in France during World War I and in 1920 was posted to Iraq, where he lived among the Bedouin tribes and studied their language and culture. After serving (1926–30) as administrative inspector for the Iraqi government, he was transferred to Jordan and attached to the Arab Legion, of which he assumed command in 1939. A trusted friend and personal adviser of King ABDULLAH of Jordan, he made the legion the best-trained force in the Arab world. Many Arabs saw in him a symbol of British influence in the Middle East, and during the Arab-Israeli War of 1956 public opinion forced his dismissal. Knighted after his return to England, he is often referred to as Glubb Pasha. His many writings include *The Story of the Arab Legion* (1948), *A Soldier with the Arabs* (1957), *Britain and the Arabs* (1959), and *Peace in the Holy Land* (1971). His most important work is his history of the Arab world: Vol. I, *The Great Arab Conquests* (1963), Vol. II, *The Empire of the Arabs* (1963), Vol. III, *The Course of Empire: The Arabs and Their Successors* (1965).

glucagon (glōō'kəgŏn), HORMONE secreted by the α cells of the islets of Langerhans, specific groups of cells in the PANCREAS. It tends to counteract the action of INSULIN, i.e., it raises the concentration of glucose in the blood. Glucagon was first purified and crystallized in 1955; the amino acid sequence of this 29-amino acid POLYPEPTIDE was published in 1956–57. One of the most important actions of glucagon is the promotion of glycogenolysis, i.e., the degradation of GLYCOGEN to glucose, in the liver. Glucagon stimulates adenyl cyclase, the enzyme that catalyzes the conversion of ADENOSINE TRIPHOSPHATE to 3'5'-cyclic ADENOSINE MONOPHOSPHATE (cyclic AMP). The resultant increased concentration of cyclic AMP in turn facilitates a series of reactions which finally results in the breakdown of glycogen to glucose. The mediation of the process by cyclic AMP is exactly analogous to the mediation of the action of EPINEPHRINE by the same compound in liver cells.

glucinum (glōōsī'nəm): see BERYLLIUM.

Gluck, Alma (glŏŏk), 1884–1938, American soprano, b. Bucharest, Rumania. Her real name was Reba Fiersohn. She sang (1909–12) at the Metropolitan Opera, New York City, and was one of the first singers to make phonograph records. In 1914 she married Efrem Zimbalist. Her daughter, by a previous marriage, was the writer Marcia Davenport.

Gluck, Christoph Willibald von (krĭs'tôf vĭl'ēbält fən glŏŏk), 1714–87, German-born operatic composer. Gluck revolutionized opera by establishing lyrical tragedy as a unified vital art form. He studied music at Prague and later in Italy with G. B. Sammartini. His first 10 operas, in the Italian style, were successfully performed in Italy in the years 1741–45. In 1752, after sojourns in England and Germany, Gluck became conductor of Prince Hildburghausen's private orchestra in Vienna, and for the next decade he directed musical productions at the Viennese court. With his opera *Orfeo ed Euridice* (1762), inspired by Greek legend, Gluck introduced an entirely new kind of opera, in which dramatic, emotional, and musical elements were artistically fused for the first time. To Ranieri Calzabigi, the librettist of *Orfeo* and also *Alceste* (1767), Gluck gave much of the credit for his new operatic style. In 1773, Gluck went to Paris, where his first serious opera with a French libretto, *Iphigénie en Aulide* (1774), was performed. That and subsequent productions created much controversy between supporters of Gluck and proponents of traditional Italian opera. His last important work, *Iphigénie en Tauride* (1779), is often considered his masterpiece, and it firmly established his reputation. Eventually, Gluck's emphasis on dramatic impact and musical simplicity became incorporated into the French operatic tradition, and his influence on later composers was considerable. See his collected correspondence and papers, ed. by Hedwig and E. H. Mueller von Asow (tr. 1962); biographies by Martin Cooper (1935) and Alfred Einstein (tr. 1936); study by Ernest Newman (1895, repr. 1964).

Gluckman, Herman Max, 1911–, British anthropologist, b. Johannesburg, South Africa, grad. Univ. of Witwatersrand (B.A., 1930) and Oxford (Ph.D., 1936). From 1947 to 1971 he was professor of social anthropology at the Univ. of Manchester; thereafter he was research professor there. His major contribution was in the area of primitive law. Among his writings are *Rituals of Rebellion in South-East Africa* (1954), *Order and Rebellion in Tribal Africa* (1963), *Politics, Law and Ritual in Tribal Society* (1965), and *The Allocation of Responsibility* (1972).

glucose, dextrose, or **grape sugar,** monosaccharide sugar with the empirical formula $C_6H_{12}O_6$. This CARBOHYDRATE occurs in the sap of most plants and in the juice of grapes and other fruits. Glucose is a normal component of animal blood; it thus requires no digestion prior to absorption into the bloodstream. Glucose can be obtained by HYDROLYSIS of a variety of carbohydrates, e.g., milk and cane sugars, maltose, cellulose, or glycogen, but it is usually manufactured by hydrolysis of CORN STARCH with steam and dilute acid; the corn syrup thus obtained contains also some dextrins and maltose. Glucose is used in the manufacture of candy, chewing gum, jams, jellies, table syrups, and other foods, and for many other purposes. It is the major source of energy in animal metabolism. Glucose tastes only about three fourths as sweet as table sugar (SUCROSE). The presence of glucose can be detected by use of FEHLING'S SOLUTION; various modifications of this test are used to detect glucose in urine, which may be a symptom of diabetes.

glue: see ADHESIVE.

Glueck, Nelson, 1900–1971, American archaeologist and educator, b. Cincinnati, grad. Univ. of Cincinnati, 1920, Ph.D. Univ. of Jena, Germany, 1926. Among the more than 1,000 sites in the Middle East that Glueck uncovered were the copper mines of King Solomon and the ancient Red Sea port of Ezion Geber. In 1947 he became president of Hebrew Union College in Cincinnati; from 1950 he served as president of the merged Hebrew Union College–Jewish Institute of Religion. He wrote several books on archaeology, including *Explorations in Eastern Palestine* (4 vol., 1934–51), *The Other Side of the Jordan* (1940), *The River Jordan* (1946), *Rivers in the Desert: A History of the Negev* (1959), *Deities and Dolphins* (1965), and *Hesed in the Bible* (1968).

glutamic acid (glo͞otăm′ĭk), organic compound, one of the 22 α-AMINO ACIDS commonly found in animal proteins. Only the L-stereoisomer occurs in mammalian proteins. Like ASPARTIC ACID, glutamic acid has an acidic carboxyl group on its side chain which can serve as both an acceptor and a donor of ammonia, a compound toxic to the body. Once glutamic acid has coupled with ammonia, it is called GLUTAMINE and can as such safely transport ammonia to the liver, where the ammonia is eventually converted to UREA for excretion by the kidneys. Free glutamic acid (that not incorporated into proteins) can also be converted reversibly to α-ketoglutaric acid, an intermediate in the Krebs cycle, and as such can be degraded to carbon dioxide and water, or transformed into sugars. The acidic side chain of glutamic acid confers one negative charge under most conditions to proteins in which this amino acid is found, thus increasing the water solubility of the protein; an especially reactive glutamic acid residue has been found at the active site of at least one enzyme, that of a type of ribonuclease. Monosodium glutamate (MSG), the monosodium salt of L-glutamic acid, is widely used as a condiment. The amino acid was isolated from wheat gluten in 1866 and chemically synthesized in 1890. It is not essential to the human diet, since it can be synthesized in the body from the common intermediate α-ketoglutaric acid.

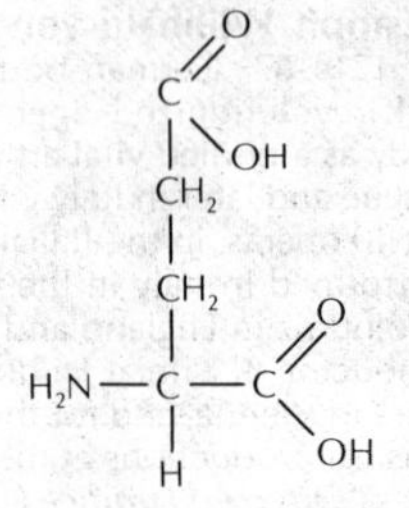

glutamic acid

glutamine (glo͞o′təmēn), organic compound, one of the 22 α-AMINO ACIDS commonly found in animal proteins. Only the L-stereoisomer occurs in mammalian protein. Its structure is identical to that of GLUTAMIC ACID, except that the acidic side-chain carboxyl group of glutamine has been coupled with ammonia, yielding an amide. The glutamic acid-glutamine interconversion is of central importance to the regulation of the levels of toxic ammonia in the body, and it is thus not surprising that when the concentrations of the amino acids of blood plasma are measured, glutamine is found to have the highest of all. Glutamine can donate the ammonia on its side chain to the formation of UREA (for eventual excretion by the kidneys) and to PURINES (necessary for the synthesis of genetic material). Once glutamine is incorporated into proteins, its relatively unreactive side-chain amide participates in very few reactions. Glutamine is not essential to the human diet, since it can be synthesized in the body from glutamic acid. Glutamine was isolated from beet juice in 1883, but was not isolated from a protein until 1932; it was chemically synthesized in 1933.

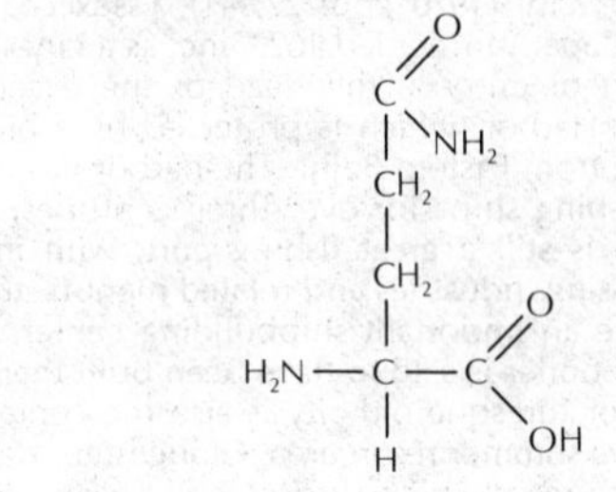

glutamine

glutathione: see COENZYME.

gluten, mixture of proteins obtained from cereal grains, particularly corn and wheat. Tough, elastic, almost tasteless, and insoluble in water, it is found in hard wheat and is the constituent that makes good flour for yeast bread. Its composition includes carbon (53%), hydrogen (7%), nitrogen (15%–18%) and sulfur (1%). It is obtained from wheat by washing in water and is used in particularly high concentrations in the manufacture of breadstuffs for a diabetic diet. It appears that the disease called nontropical SPRUE is associated with an abnormal sensitivity to partially digested gluten. In this disease polypeptides resulting from the cleavage of gluten by the enzymes PEPSIN and TRYPSIN not only cause severe intestinal distress, but also are absorbed into the circulation, eliciting the production of antibodies.

glutton: see WOLVERINE.

glycerol, glycerin, glycerine, or **1,2,3-propanetriol** (prō′păntrī″ōl), $CH_2OHCHOHCH_2OH$, colorless, odorless, sweet-tasting, syrupy liquid. Glycerol is a trihydric ALCOHOL. It melts at 17.8°C, boils with decomposition at 290°C, and is miscible with water and ethanol. It is hygroscopic; i.e., it absorbs water from the air; this property makes it valuable as a moistener in cosmetics. Glycerol is present in the form of its ESTERS (glycerides) in all animal and vegetable fats and oils. It is obtained commercially as a by-product when fats and oils are hydrolyzed to yield fatty acids or their metal salts (soaps). Glycerol is also synthesized on a commercial scale from propylene (obtained by cracking petroleum), since supplies of natural glycerol are inadequate. Glycerol can also be obtained during the fermentation of sugars if sodium bisulfite is added with the yeast. Glycerol is widely used as a solvent; as a sweetener; in the manufacture of dynamite, cosmetics, liquid soaps, candy, liqueurs, inks, and lubricants; to keep fabrics pliable; as a component of antifreeze mixtures; as a source of nutrients for fermentation cultures in the production of ANTIBIOTICS; and in medicine. It has many other uses as well.

glycine (glī′sēn), organic compound, one of the 22 α-AMINO ACIDS commonly found in animal proteins. Glycine is the only one of these amino acids that is not optically active, i.e., it does not have D-and L-stereoisomers. It is structurally the simplest of the α-amino acids, having merely a hydrogen atom for a side chain, and is thus very unreactive when incorporated into proteins. Nevertheless, in the free state glycine participates in several important reactions, including the biosynthesis of heme, an important constituent of HEMOGLOBIN, and the biosyntheses of SERINE (another amino acid), PURINES (constituents of genetic material), and glutathione (a COENZYME). Defects of glycine metabolism are very rare. The amino acid is not essential to the diet since it can be made from other substances in the body. Glycine was the first amino acid to be isolated from a protein, in this case gelatin.

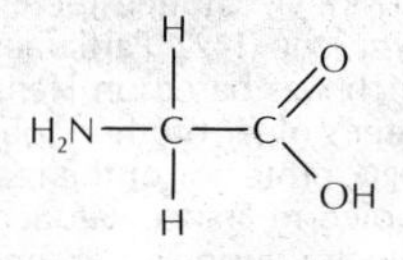

glycine

glycogen (glī′kəjən), starchlike polysaccharide (see CARBOHYDRATE) that is found in the liver and muscles of man and the higher animals and in the cells of the lower animals. Chemically it is a highly branched condensation polymer of GLUCOSE; it is readily hydrolyzed to glucose. Glycogen is formed by the LIVER from glucose in the bloodstream and is stored in the liver; conversion of glucose to glycogen (glycogenesis) and HYDROLYSIS of glycogen to glucose (glycogenolysis) together are the usual mechanism for maintenance of normal levels of blood sugar. Glycogen is also produced by and stored in muscle cells; during short periods of strenuous activity, energy is released in the muscles by direct conversion of glycogen to lactic acid. During normal activity, energy is released by metabolic oxidation of glucose to lactic acid.

glycol (glī′kōl), dihydric ALCOHOL in which the two hydroxyl groups are bonded to different carbon atoms; the general formula for a glycol is $(CH_2)_n(OH)_2$. The most important glycol is the simplest, ethylene glycol, or 1,2-ethanediol, CH_2OHCH_2OH, a slightly sweet-tasting, somewhat viscous liquid that is miscible with water. Because of its low volatility (b.p. 197°C) and low corrosive activity, it is widely used in mixtures of automobile ANTIFREEZE. Ethylene glycol can be esterified to form polyesters, e.g., DACRON, and can be nitrated to form an explosive used in mining. Cellosolves (e.g., methyl cellosolve, $CH_3OCH_2CH_2OH$) are monoether derivatives of ethylene glycol. They are excellent solvents, having solvent properties of both ethers and alcohols; they have other uses as well. Ethylene glycol is prepared commercially by oxidation of ethylene at high temperature over a silver oxide catalyst, followed by acid-catalyzed HYDROLYSIS of the ethylene oxide that is formed.

glycolysis (glīkŏl′ĭsĭs), term given to the central metabolic pathway utilized by most microorganisms (yeast and bacteria) and by all higher animals (including man) for the degradation of GLUCOSE. *Glycolysis* means, literally, the dissolution of sugar. The process is a series of consecutive chemical conversions that require the participation of eleven different ENZYMES, most of which have been crystallized and thoroughly studied. They are easily extracted from the cell in soluble form. Glycolysis begins with a single molecule of glucose and concludes with the production of two molecules of a simpler sugar called LACTIC ACID. The pathway is seen to be degradative, or catabolic, in that the six-carbon glucose is reduced to two molecules of a three-carbon compound. Much of the energy that is liberated upon degradation of glucose is conserved by the simultaneous formation of the so-called high-energy molecule ADENOSINE TRIPHOSPHATE (ATP). Since two reactions of the glycolytic sequence proceed with the concomitant production of ATP, ATP synthesis is said to be coupled to glycolysis. Hundreds of cellular reactions, particularly those involved in the synthesis of cellular components and those that allow the cell to perform mechanical work, require the participation of ATP as a source of chemical energy.

Thus glycolysis is a process extremely critical for fueling the cell. Glycolysis occurs in two major stages, the first of which serves as a concentration point for all the various sugars found in the cell that must be converted to a common intermediate, glucose-6-phosphate, before participation. The second major phase is the conversion of glucose-6-phosphate to lactic acid. The products of glycolysis are further metabolized to complete the total degradation of glucose. Their ultimate fate varies depending upon the organism. In certain microorganisms lactic acid is the final and single product of glycolysis, and the process is referred to as homolactic FERMENTATION. In certain bacteria and in brewer's yeast, lactic acid is not produced in large quantities. Instead, the penultimate product of glycolysis, pyruvic acid, which is also the precursor of lactic acid, is converted to ethanol and carbon dioxide by an enzyme-catalyzed two-step process, termed alcoholic fermentation. In the tissues of mammals, glycolysis is only a portion of the complex metabolic machinery that ultimately converts pyruvic acid to carbon dioxide and water. See CITRIC ACID CYCLE; RESPIRATION.

Glycon (glī'kən), fl. c.3d cent. A.D., Athenian sculptor and copyist. He executed the *Farnese Hercules* after the original by Lysippos.

glycoprotein (glī"kōprō'tēn), any organic compound composed of both a PROTEIN and a CARBOHYDRATE joined together in covalent chemical linkage. Although these structures occur in plants and bacteria, they are most prevalent and important in mammalian tissues. The carbohydrate portion of a glycoprotein is usually a small oligosaccharide of no more than 8 to 10 individual monosaccharide units. Only seven of the many different sugar molecules known to occur in nature comprise the saccharide portion of mammalian glycoproteins: GLUCOSE, glucosamine, galactose, galactosamine, mannose, fucose, and sialic acid (a derivative of glucosamine). The linkage between the oligosaccharide and the protein occurs by formation of a chemical bond to only one of four protein amino acids: ASPARAGINE, HYDROXYLYSINE, SERINE, or THREONINE. Solutions of glycoproteins usually exhibit high viscosity, an observation explaining the highly viscous character of egg white, which is composed largely of the glycoprotein ovalbumin. Salivary mucus contains the glycoprotein called mucin. Other tissues which are "mucusy" in character are usually rich in glycoproteins. The membranes of nervous tissue are abundant with glycoprotein, particularly with those that contain sialic acid in the terminal position of the oligosaccharide side-chain. Sialic acid binds the cations of sodium and calcium and is thought to function centrally in the transmission of the nerve impulse. One particularly interesting glycoprotein is isolated from certain antarctic fishes who survive near-freezing water temperatures as a result of freezing-point depression of their blood serum by a globular glycoprotein. This molecule is a remarkably effective freezing point depressant; it behaves as a compound with molecular weight about 15 grams per mole when, in fact, its molecular weight is near 10,000.

Glyndebourne Festivals (glĭn'dəbərn, glĭn'bôrn), operatic festivals given each summer since 1934 on the estate of John Christie at Glyndebourne, near Lewes, Sussex, England. The productions, under the directorship of Fritz Busch, were suspended in 1938 and resumed after the war in 1947. Vittorio Gui became musical director after Busch's death in 1951.

glyoxylate cycle: see CITRIC ACID CYCLE.

Glyptothek (glüp"tōtāk'), museum in Munich on the Königsplatz, founded by Louis I of Bavaria to house his collection of ancient and modern sculptures. Among these is the famous Barberini faun (c.200 B.C.). The neoclassical building, designed by Leo von Klenze, was constructed between 1816 and 1830. Its severe, imposing Ionic portico projects from a wall containing six large sculptures in niches. The interior is structured with domical vaulting.

GMP (guanosine monophosphate): see GUANINE.

Gmünd: see SCHWÄBISCH GMÜND, West Germany.

gnat, common name for any one of a number of small, fragile-looking two-winged flies of the suborder Nematocera, order Diptera, which includes the families Tipulidae (CRANE FLIES), Bibionidae (hairflies), Ceratopogonidae (biting MIDGES), Chironomidae (true midges), Cecidomyidae (gall midges), Simuliidae (BLACK FLIES), Culicidae (MOSQUITOES), and others. They often assemble together in large mating swarms. In England mosquitoes are called gnats; in the United States it is chiefly the smaller forms of Diptera, especially irritating because of their great numbers and their vicious biting habits, that are referred to as gnats. All gnats have long, hairlike antennae, which are particularly well-developed in the males. Gnat larvae are free-living, most feeding on plants. Larval plant feeders, e.g., the HESSIAN FLY larvae, cause root, stem, and leaf galls to be formed by the host plant. Some species of fungus gnats (families Mycetophilidae and Sciaridae) are very common pests of mushrooms and roots of potted plants in homes and greenhouses. One group of dipterans (family Chloropidae) of the suborder Cyclorrhapha are commonly called eye gnats, or eye flies. These annoying flies are attracted to and feed on animal secretions, such as mucous secretion, pus, and blood. Eye gnats are suspected of being the vectors of the organisms causing the highly contagious pinkeye and yaws. Gnats are classified in the phylum ARTHROPODA, class Insecta, order Diptera.

gnat-catcher or **gnatwren:** see KINGLET.

Gneisenau, August, Graf Neithardt von (ou'-gōost grăf nīt'härt fən gənī'zənou), 1760–1831, Prussian field marshal. In the Napoleonic Wars he fought at Jena (1806) and, as a major, won fame for his valiant defense of Kolberg. After Prussia's capitulation to Napoleon I (1807), he served with General von SCHARNHORST on the military reorganization commission and helped reform the defeated Prussian army. The army's leading strategist during Prussia's War of Liberation against the French (1813–15), he was chief of staff to the commander of the army, BLÜCHER. He retired from active service in 1816, when the need for military reform had passed, but returned to lead an expedition against the Polish insurrection, in which he was killed.

gneiss (nīs), coarse-grained, imperfectly foliated, or layered, metamorphic ROCK. Gneiss is characterized by alternating light and dark bands differing in mineral composition and having coarser grains than those of schist. The light bands of gneiss are generally composed of quartz and feldspar. Hornblende, biotite mica, garnet, or graphite commonly form the dark bands. Gneisses result from the metamorphism of many igneous or sedimentary rocks, and are the most common types of rocks found in Precambrian regions. Gneiss is found in New England, the Piedmont, the Adirondacks, and the Rocky Mts. Some gneisses are used as facing stone on buildings.

Gnesen, Poland: see GNIEZNO.

Gniezno (gənyĕz'nô), Ger. *Gnesen,* city (1970 pop. 50,643), central Poland. It is a railway junction with industries producing clothing, leather goods, and metals. The legendary cradle of the Polish nation, Gniezno was the first capital of Poland. At the Congress of Gniezno (1000), Emperor Otto III established the metropolitan see of Poland. The kings of Poland were crowned at Gniezno until 1320. From 1572 until the early 19th cent. the archbishops of Gniezno acted as protectors of Poland. The city passed to Prussia in 1793 and again in 1815. In 1821 the archiepiscopal see was transferred to Poznań. The city was restored to Poland in 1919. Gniezno has many medieval art objects. Its most notable buildings are a 10th-century rotunda and a 14th-century Gothic cathedral.

gnome (nōm), in folklore, tiny subterranean creature associated with mines and quarries. Usually represented as misshapen, frequently as hunchbacked, gnomes are said to be guardians of hidden treasures.

gnomon (nō'mŏn): see SUNDIAL.

Gnosticism (nŏs'tĭsĭzəm), dualistic religious and philosophical movement of the late Hellenistic and early Christian eras. The term designates a wide assortment of sects, numerous by the 2d cent. A.D.; they all promised salvation through an occult knowledge that they claimed was revealed to them alone. Scholars trace these salvation religions back to such diverse sources as the Jewish cabala, Hellenistic mystery cults, Iranian religious dualism (see ZOROASTRIANISM), and Babylonian and Egyptian mythology. The definition of *gnosis* [knowledge] as concern with the Eternal was already present in earlier Greek philosophy, but its connection with the later Gnostic movement is distant at best. Christian ideas were quickly incorporated into these syncretistic systems, and by the 2d cent. the largest of them, organized by Valentinus and BASILIDES, posed a serious threat to Christianity. Much of early Christian doctrine was formulated in reaction to this danger. Until the discovery in Egypt of key Manichaean (1930) and Coptic Gnostic (c.1945) papyri, our knowledge of Gnosticism depended on Christian sources, notably St. Irenaeus, St. Hippolytus, and Clement of Alexandria. Among principal Gnostic writings are the Valentinian documents *Pistis-Sophia* and the *Gospel of Truth* (perhaps by Valentinus himself). Important too is the literature of the MANDAEANS, who, in modern Iraq, are the only Gnostic sect extant. Gnostic elements are found in the *Acts of Thomas,* the *Odes of Solomon,* and other wisdom literature of the pseudepigrapha. Gnosticism taught that the world is ruled by evil archons, among them the deity of the Old Testament, who hold captive the spirit of man. The heavenly pleroma was the center of the divine life, and Jesus Christ is interpreted as an intermediary eternal being, or aeon, sent from pleroma to restore the lost knowledge of man's divine origin. Gnostics held secret formulas, which they believed would free them at death from the evil archons and restore them to their heavenly abode. See VALENTINUS for typical Gnostic teaching on the pleroma. Gnosticism held that man consists of flesh, soul, and spirit (the divine spark), and that mankind is divided into classes representing each of these elements. The purely corporeal man (hylic) lacked spirit and could never be saved; the Gnostics proper (pneumatic) bore knowingly the divine spark and their salvation was certain; those, like the Christians, who stood in between (psychic), might attain a lesser salvation through faith. Such a doctrine inspired extreme asceticism (as in the Valentinian school) or extreme licentiousness (as in the sect of Caprocrates and the OPHITES). Gnosticism merged with MANICHAEISM, which adopted many of its ideas. See Hans Jonas, *Gnostic Religion* (rev. ed. 1964); R. McQ. Grant, *Gnosticism and Early Christianity* (2d ed. 1966); Robert Haardt, *Gnosis: Character and Testimony* (1971); Werner Foerster, ed., *Gnosis* (tr. 1972).

gnu (nōō) or **wildebeest** (wĭl'dəbēst"), large African ANTELOPE, genus *Connochaetes.* Its heavy head and humped shoulders resemble those of a buffalo, while the compact hindquarters are like those of a horse. The gnu has a beard, a short, erect mane, and a long, flowing tail. Members of both sexes have large horns that curve down, outward, and up. Gnus are grazing animals and live in herds on open grassland. There are two species. The brindled gnu, or blue wildebeest (*Connochaetes taurinus*), is a large fierce-looking animal of S and E Africa. It stands 4½ ft (135 cm) high at the shoulder and weighs about 500 lb (225 kg); its coat is bluish gray mottled with brown on the sides. The tail, mane, and beard are black. In the northern variety of this species (called the white-bearded gnu), which ranges as far N as Kenya, the beard is white. The brindled gnu lives in herds of 20 to several thousand individuals, often led by one or several old females and often found grazing with herds of zebra. Gnus are swift runners and herds engage in elaborate evasive maneuvers when threatened; their chief predator is the lion. They graze in the morning and evening, resting during the heat of the day; they often travel long distances in search of water. The white-tailed gnu, or black wildebeest (*C. gnou*), is a somewhat smaller animal once abundant in S Africa. It is now probably extinct in the wild, but is protected in parks and reserves, where its numbers are increasing. *Gnu* is the San (Bushman) term for these animals; *wildebeest* is Afrikaans. Gnus are classified in the phylum CHORDATA, subphylum Vertebrata, class Mammalia, order Artiodactyla, family Bovidae.

Goa (gō'ə), **Daman** (dəmän'), and **Diu** (dē'ōō), union territory (1971 pop. 857,180), c.1,480 sq mi (3,800 sq km), W India, on the Arabian Sea. The union territory is composed of three noncontiguous former Portuguese colonies that were seized by India in 1961. It is administered by the home minister in the central Indian government. There is an elected local assembly. The capital is Panjim (Panaji) (1971 pop. 34,837), in Goa. Portuguese, Marathi, and Konkani, a dialect, are spoken. **Goa** (1971 pop. 794,530), c.1,430 sq mi (3,700 sq km), on the Malabar Coast, has three principal ports: Agoada, Marmagao, and Panjim. The chief products are rice, cashew nuts, and coconuts. Muslims conquered Goa in 1312. It became part of the Hindu kingdom of Vijayanagar in 1370 but was recaptured by the Muslims 100 years later. The Portuguese under Afonso de Albuquerque annexed it in 1510 from territory belonging to the sultan of Bijapur. Old Goa, the original capital, was a prosperous port city in the late 16th cent. A cathedral, churches, and several palaces survive from this period. The most notable structure is the Church of Bom Jesus, with its tomb of St. Francis Xavier, whose missionary work (1542–52) was so successful that today about 40% of the population of the region is Roman Catholic. In 1842, Panjim was built to replace Old Goa as capital. **Daman,** Port. *Damão* (1971 pop. 38,741), c.30 sq mi (80 sq km), at the mouth of the Daman River on the Gulf of Cambay, was acquired by the Portuguese in 1588. It consisted of a coastal section, Daman proper, and a detached inland section, Nagar-Haveli, which in 1961 became part of the Indian union territory of Dadra and Nagar-Haveli. Until the Indians took over, the capital was Daman city, which before the decline of Portuguese power in the 18th cent. enjoyed a large overseas trade, especially with E Africa. Rice, wheat, and tobacco are the chief crops, and fishing is important. **Diu** (1971 pop. 23,909), c.20 sq mi (50 sq km), consisting of Diu island and a small area on the coast of the nearby Kathiawar Peninsula, was acquired by Portugal in 1535. Diu town has several splendid Catholic churches built before the overseas trade of Diu declined in the late 18th cent. Fishing is the principal occupation, and salt is produced.

goat, ruminant mammal with hollow horns and coarse hair belonging to the genus *Capra* of the CATTLE family and closely related to the sheep. True wild goats, all of Old World origin, include the Persian bezoar goat, or pasan, possibly the ancestor of the domestic varieties; the several species of IBEX (including the tur), and the MARKHOR of Asia, with spirally twisted horns. The Rocky Mountain goat and the CHAMOIS are not true goats but are closely related. Goats are hardy cliff dwellers, preferring an arid climate. They live in herds and feed on grass, weeds, shrubs, and other vegetation. Goats were early domesticated; they are pictured in ancient Egyptian art and mentioned in the Bible. Domestic goats, varieties of *Capra hircus*, are found throughout the world, most abundantly in Asia. They are raised for milk, flesh, hair and wool, skins, and, in certain areas, to control scrub growth. Goat's milk is easily digested and has greater protein and fat content than that of cows. The chief dairy breeds in the United States are the Toggenburg and Saanen (both of Swiss origin), as well as the Nubian, French Alpine, and Rock Alpine goats. Many dairy goats are hornless. The Cashmere goat is raised in central Asia, N India, and Iran for the wool of its downy undercoat. Angora goats, whose clipped wool is known as mohair, are more numerous than other breeds in the United States; they are raised chiefly in Texas. The Spanish, or common, goat, familiar in the Southwest, was brought to Mexico by early Spanish settlers. Goats are classified in the phylum CHORDATA, subphylum Vertebrata, class Mammalia, order Artiodactyla, family Bovidae. See David Mackenzie, *Goat Husbandry* (3d ed. 1970).

Goat, The, English name for CAPRICORNUS, a CONSTELLATION.

Goath (gō'ăth), unidentified place, near Jerusalem. Jer. 31.39.

Goat Island. 1 Former name of YERBA BUENA ISLAND, Calif. **2** Island, W N.Y., in the Niagara River, dividing Niagara Falls into the American and the Canadian falls.

goatsbeard, common name for plants of the genus *Tragopogon* (see SALSIFY) of the family Compositae (COMPOSITE family) and of the genus *Aruncus* of the family Rosaceae (ROSE family), related to the spiraeas. False goatsbeard, a saxifrage, is named for its resemblance to *Aruncus*. The two families are classified in the orders Asterales and Rosales, respectively. These orders belong to the division MAGNOLIOPHYTA, class Magnoliopsida.

goatsucker, common name for nocturnal or crepuscular birds of the order Caprimulgiformes, which includes the frogmouth, the oilbird, potoos, and nightjars. Goatsuckers are medium in size and are found in the temperate and tropical zones of both hemispheres. The name *goatsucker* is based on an ancient belief that these birds fed on goats' milk by night, but their presence near such animals was no doubt due to the insects attracted by the goats. With their long, pointed wings, weak feet, and small, wide-gaping bills fringed with bristles, goatsuckers have been called flying insect traps. Like their relatives the owls, they are protected by brown, gray, and black coloring, and their lax and fluffy feathers render their flight almost noiseless. This and their monotonous, repetitious song are factors in their superstitious significance. Their weird cries are reflected in the common names for many of the species, e.g., whippoorwill, chuck-will's-widow, poorwill, poor-me-one, potoo, and pauraque. The whippoorwill is common in the E United States. Ornithologists have discovered that the whippoorwill, unlike other birds, hibernates during the winter instead of migrating. Its body temperature drops from 102°F (39°C) to 65°F (18.3°C), its breathing slows, and its digestion ceases until spring brings the return of the insects that constitute its diet. The whippoorwill's flight, like that of the swift, is graceful and erratic; it sometimes swoops downward and then stops abruptly, producing a booming sound as it spreads its wings to brake. The larger (12 in./30 cm) chuck-will's-widow (*Caprimulgus carolinensis*) is found in the South and the poorwill (7 in./17.5 cm) in the West. The nighthawk (*Chordediles popetue*), or bull bat, common in all parts of North America N to Labrador, is the most diurnal of the goatsuckers; it is active at twilight and daybreak, whereas the others fly only at night. The nighthawk's familiar cry is a nasal "peent." The oilbirds of South America have sonar devices that enable them to fly in total darkness. The pauraque, or cuiejo, is a Central American goatsucker, and the aptly named frogmouths are native to Australia and the Orient. Goatsuckers are classified in the phylum CHORDATA, subphylum Vertebrata, class Aves, order Caprimulgiformes.

Gob (gŏb), town, SW Palestine. 2 Sam. 21.18,19. In the parallel passage, 1 Chron. 20.4, GEZER is given instead.

Gobabis (gōbä'bĭs), town (1970 pop. 4,428), E central South West Africa. Manufactures include processed karakul sheepskins and dairy products. Gobabis was founded in 1840 as a German missionary station. There was heavy fighting in the area in 1904 during the war between the Herero and the Germans.

Gobat, Charles Albert (shärl älbĕr' gōbä'), 1843–1914, Swiss statesman. He took part in government affairs, wrote on international law, and helped found (1902) an international peace bureau. He received, with Élie Ducommun, the 1902 Nobel Peace Prize.

Gobelins, Manufacture nationale des (mänüfäktür' näsēōnäl' dā gôblăN'), state-controlled tapestry manufactory in Paris. It was founded as a dye works in the mid-15th cent. by Jean Gobelin. A tapestry works started by two Flemish weavers, Marc de Comans and François de la Planche, called to France by Henri IV in 1601, was later added. In 1662, Louis XIV purchased the Gobelins manufactory and there Colbert united all the royal craftsmen, creating a royal tapestry and furniture works. Charles Le Brun was director and chief designer from 1663 to 1690. The Gobelins was temporarily closed from 1694 to 1697, after which the works specialized in tapestry. Both low- and high-warp weaving were done until about 1825, when the low-warp power frames were moved to the manufactory of Beauvais; they were returned to Gobelins after World War II. The Gobelins factory has always been noted for excellence of materials, dyes, and workmanship; it originated the exquisite Gobelins blue. Famous tapestries from its looms include a set based on copies of Raphael's frescoes in the Vatican and 14 great pieces commemorating the achievements of Louis XIV.

Gobi (gō'bē), Mandarin *Sha-moh*, great desert of central Asia, c.500,000 sq mi (1,295,000 sq km), extending c.1,000 mi (1,610 km) from east to west across SE Mongolia and N China from the Great Khingan mts. to the Tien Shan; one of the world's largest deserts. The Gobi, located on a plateau from 3,000 to 5,000 ft (910–1,520 m) high, consists of a series of shallow alkaline basins; the western portion of the desert is entirely sandy. The Kerulen River is the Gobi's largest permanent stream; intermittent streams flow into small salt lakes or disappear into the sand. Nearly all the region's soil has been removed by the prevailing northwesterly winds and deposited in N central China as loess; fierce sand and wind storms are common. The Gobi has cold winters and short hot summers. Precipitation is in the form of widely-spaced cloudbursts. The Gobi's grassy fringe supports a small population of nomadic Mongolian tribes engaged in sheepherding and goatherding. The Gobi is crossed by a highway and by the Trans-Mongolian RR, which links Ulan Bator with Chi-ning, China. The railway shortens the Moscow-Peking run by c.700 mi (1,130 km). Coal is mined at Tawan-Tolgoi, Mongolia; oilfields are located at Saynshand, Mongolia, and Yümen, China. Many paleontological finds, including dinosaur eggs, have been made in the Gobi. Prehistoric stone implements, some c.100,000 years old, have also been excavated.

Gobineau, Joseph Arthur, comte de (zhôzĕf' ärtür' kôNt də gōbēnō'), 1816–82, French diplomat and man of letters. The chief early French proponent of the theory of Nordic supremacy, he was antidemocratic and anti-Semitic. His major work was *Essai sur l'inégalité des races humaines* (1853–55, tr. *The Inequality of Human Races*, 1915). He also wrote short stories, notably *Nouvelles asiatiques* (1876, tr. *Five Oriental Tales*, 1925).

goblin or **hobgoblin,** in French folklore, small household spirit, similar to the Celtic BROWNIE. Goblins perform household tasks but also can make mischief, such as pulling the covers off sleepers. They like wine and pretty children.

goby, common name for a member of the family Gobiidae, small marine fishes familiar in shallow waters, especially along southern shores. Gobies may be either scaled or scaleless; all species have the ventral fins modified into a sucking disk, as in the clingfish of the family Gobiesocidae. The naked goby (3 in./7.5 cm) is found S of Cape Cod and the sharptail goby (6 in./15 cm) in brackish bays along the Atlantic coast. The sleeper, or guavina, occasionally grows large enough to be used as food. On the Pacific coast the longjaw goby, or mudsucker, is a common bait fish. The most popular of many aquarium species is the bumblebee goby, native to S Asia. Gobies are classified in the phylum CHORDATA, class Osteichthyes, order Perciformes, family Gobiidae.

God, divinity of the three great monotheistic religions, Judaism, Christianity, and Islam. In the Old Testament various names for God are used. YHWH is the most celebrated of these; the Hebrews considered the name ineffable and, in reading, substituted the name *Adonai* [my Lord]. The ineffable name, or tetragrammaton [Gr.,=four-letter form], is of unknown origin; the reconstruction *Jehovah* was based on a mistake, and the form *Yahweh* is not now regarded as reliable. The name *Jah* occurring in names such as ELIJAH is a form of YHWH. The most common name for God in the Old Testament is *Elohim*, a plural form, but used as a singular when speaking of God. The name *El*, not connected with Elohim, is also used, especially in proper names, e.g., Elijah. The name *Shaddai*, used with other words and in names (e.g., ZURISHADDAI), appears rarely. Of these names only Adonai has a satisfactory etymology. It is generally not possible to tell from English translations of the Bible what was the exact form of the name of God in the original. The general conception of God may be said to be that of an infinite being (often a personality but not necessarily anthropomorphic) who is supremely good, who created the world, who knows all and can do all, who is transcendent over and immanent in the world, and who loves mankind. By the majority of Christians He is believed to have lived on earth in the flesh as Jesus Christ (see TRINITY). In the Old Testament, the concept of God is not a unified one. The attitude of believers to this apparent inconsistency has generally been that God, unchanging, revealed Himself more and more to Israel. Scholars belonging to the rational schools of the 19th cent. developed a view of the Bible as primarily a history of Judaism that evolved naturally without the benefit of divine intervention in the world. They see a series of stages in which God was first held by the Jews as simply the head of a tribal pantheon, then gradually assumed all the attributes of His fellow divinities, but was still worshiped more or less idolatrously. Gradually, according to these scholars, the Jews considered their God as more and more powerful until they made Him creator and ruler of all men but still preferring Israel as His special people. His higher attributes of goodness, love, and mercy these critics consider as very late in this development. More recent scholars have refuted this latter position, seeing these very qualities in the God of the Exodus. Although the idea of God, through its long acceptance by Jews, Christians, and Muslims, has come to be associated with the concept of a good, infinite personality, in recent times the name has been extended to many principles of an utterly different sort; thus, a philosopher may consider the unifying concept in his philosophy (e.g., cosmic energy, mind, world soul, number) as God. There are several famous arguments for the existence of God. The argument from the First Cause maintains that since in the world every effect has its cause behind it (and every actuality its potentiality), the first effect (and first actuality) in the world must have had its cause (and potentiality), which was in itself both cause and effect (and potentiality and actuality), i.e., God. The cosmological argument maintains that since the world, and all that is in it, seems to have no necessary or absolute (nonrelative) existence, an independent existence (God) must be implied for the world as the explanation of its relations. The teleological argument maintains that, since from a comprehensive view of nature and the world everything seems to exist according to a certain great plan, a planner (God) must be postulated. The ontological argument maintains that since the human conception of God is the highest conception humanly possible and since the highest conception humanly possible must have existence as one attribute, God must exist. Immanuel Kant believed that he refuted these arguments by showing that existence is no part of the content of an idea. This principle has become very important in contemporary philosophy, particularly in existentialism. The consensus among theologians now is that the existence of God must in some way be accepted on faith. See RELIGION; also articles on individual religions.

Godard, Jean-Luc (zhäN-lük gôdär'), 1930–, French film director and scriptwriter, b. Paris. Godard is probably the most influential of the French New Wave directors. His highly personal films are marked by a free-wheeling approach to style, content, and story structure, and by a growing interest in radical politics and the brutal illogic of modern society. His first full-length film, *Breathless* (1959), gained wide attention with its boldly elliptical editing techniques. His other films include *Vivre sa Vie* (1962), *Les Carabiniers* (1963), *Alphaville* (1965), *La Chinoise* (1967), and *Weekend* (1968). See *Jean-Luc Godard: A Critical Anthology* (ed. by Toby Mussman, 1968).

Godavari (gōdä'vərē), river, c.900 mi (1,450 km) long, rising in the Western Ghats in Maharashtra state, W central India, and flowing SE across the Deccan Plateau to the Bay of Bengal. The Manjra and Indravati rivers are its chief tributaries. Below RAJAHMUNDRY, c.50 mi (80 km) from the coast, the river divides into two streams that form a huge delta. The delta, site of some of the earliest European settlements in India, has an extensive navigable irrigation-canal system. A dam northwest of Rajahmundry provides water for irrigation and generates hydroelectricity. The Godavari River is sacred to Hindus and has several pilgrimage centers on its banks.

Goddard, John, 1724–85, American furniture maker, b. Dartmouth, Mass. He worked in Newport, R.I., and is recognized as having been one of the finest cabinetmakers in early America. Examples of his work are rare. He is noted for his stately pieces, especially secretaries, on which he developed the blockfront design, often surmounted by finely executed carvings in a shell motif.

Goddard, Robert Hutchings, 1882–1945, American physicist and rocket expert, b. Worcester, Mass., grad. Worcester Polytechnic Institute (B.S., 1908), Ph.D. Clark Univ., 1911. From 1914 he was associated with Clark Univ., becoming a professor of physics in 1919. Goddard designed and built early high altitude rockets. In 1926 he completed and successfully fired the world's first liquid fuel rocket. He developed the first smokeless powder rocket, the first practical automatic steering device for rockets, and innumerable other rocket devices. He was one of the first to develop a general theory of rocket action and to prove experimentally the efficiency of rocket propulsion in a vacuum. See his papers ed. by his wife, Esther C. Goddard (3 vol., 1970).

Godden, Rumer (gŏd'ən), 1907–, English novelist. Subtlety of characterization, especially of children, and the charm of her style contribute to the precise yet delicate artistry for which she is praised. The settings of many of her novels reflect her residence in India as a child and at various other times. Of her novels the most popular are *Black Narcissus* (1939), *Breakfast with the Nikolides* (1942), *The River* (1946), which in 1951 was made into a superb motion picture by Jean Renoir, *A Candle for St. Jude* (1948), *An Episode of Sparrows* (1955), *The Battle of the Villa Fiorita* (1963), *In This House of Brede* (1969), which is about life in a Roman Catholic convent in England, and *The Diddakoi* (1972). Among her other writings are translations, several books for children, two verse narratives, and a volume of short stories, *Swans and Turtles* (1968). Her sister **Jon Godden,** 1908–, is also a novelist; her works include *In The Sun* (1965) and *Mrs. Starr Lives Alone* (1971). The sisters have collaborated on *Two Under the Indian Sun* (1966), about their childhood in India, and *Shiva's Pigeons* (1971), a study of India.

Godefroy (gôdfrwä'), family of French scholars. **Denis Godefroy,** 1549–1622, was a Calvinist who fled (c.1580) to Geneva and later became a professor of law at Strasbourg and Heidelberg. He compiled an edition (1583) of the *Corpus Juris Civilis,* which may be called the first modern edition. His son, **Théodore Godefroy,** 1580–1649, became a Roman Catholic, was royal historiographer of France, and took part in the negotiation of the Peace of Westphalia. Another son, **Jacques Godefroy,** 1587–1622, remained a Calvinist and was professor of law at Geneva. His edition of the THEODOSIAN CODE (1665) is one of the masterpieces of legal scholarship.

Gödel, Kurt (gö'dəl), 1906–, American mathematician and logician, b. Brünn, Czechoslovakia, grad. Univ. of Vienna (Ph.D., 1930). He came to the United States in 1940 and was naturalized in 1948. He was a member of the Institute for Advanced Study, Princeton, until 1953, when he became professor of mathematics at Princeton Univ. He is best known for his work in mathematical logic, particularly for his theorem (1931) stating that the various branches of mathematics are based in part on propositions that are not provable within the system itself, although they may be proved by means of logical (metamathematical) systems external to mathematics. Gödel shared the 1951 Albert Einstein Award for achievement in the natural sciences with Julian Schwinger, Harvard mathematical physicist. His writings include *Foundations of Mathematics* (1969). See Ernest Nagel and J. R. Newman, *Gödel's Proof* (1958); Martin Davis, ed., *The Undecidable* (1965); C. S. Chihara, *Ontology and the Vicious-Circle Principle* (1973).

Goderich, Frederick John Robinson, Viscount: see RIPON, FREDERICK JOHN ROBINSON, 1ST EARL OF.

Godesberg, West Germany: see BAD GODESBERG.

godetia (gōdēsh'ə): see EVENING PRIMROSE.

Godey, Louis Antoine (gō'dē), 1804–78, American publisher, b. New York City. He was joint founder in 1830 of the *Lady's Book* (known after his partner's withdrawal as *Godey's Lady's Book*), the first successful woman's magazine. The magazine, which featured articles by famous authors and colored plates of the latest fashions, attained a circulation of 150,000 by 1858 and was considered an arbiter of morals and taste. Godey also owned a publishing house that produced such works as *The Young People's Book or Magazine of Useful or Entertaining Knowledge* (1841) and the *Lady's Musical Library* (1842).

Godfrey, Thomas, 1736–63, American poet and playwright, b. Philadelphia. The son of Thomas Godfrey, who invented the quadrant, he became apprenticed to a watchmaker after his father's early death. Godfrey is remembered as the author of *The Prince of Parthia* (1767), a blank verse tragedy reminiscent of Shakespeare and Marlowe. It was the first professionally produced drama written by an American. *The Court of Fancy* (1762) is his most notable volume of poetry.

Godfrey of Bouillon (bo͞oyôN'), c.1058–1100, Crusader, duke of Lower Lorraine. He fought for Holy Roman Emperor Henry IV against Pope Gregory VII and against Rudolf of Swabia and was rewarded (c.1082) with the duchy of Lower Lorraine, which he claimed through his mother. With his brothers Eustace and Baldwin, he was among those who set out (1096) for Jerusalem on the First Crusade. On the way to Constantinople, he allowed his army to pillage the countryside, but after his arrival he made peace (Jan., 1097) with the Byzantine emperor, ALEXIUS I. He played a minor role at Nicaea and Antioch, but achieved prominence in the siege of Jerusalem (1099) and was elected ruler of the city after its capture. Having refused the title of king on religious grounds, he was designated defender of the Holy Sepulcher. He won the battle of Ascalon (1099) and brought several Syrian towns under tribute. Godfrey was distinguished for his piety and simplicity. As the first Latin ruler of Jerusalem, he became the central figure of various legends, and his deeds were glorified in the CHANSONS DE GESTE. His brother, Baldwin I, succeeded him as ruler of Jerusalem and took the title king. See J. C. Andressohn, *The Ancestry and Life of Godfrey of Bouillon* (1972).

Godfrey of Strasbourg: see GOTTFRIED VON STRASSBURG.

Godfrey of Viterbo (vētĕr'bō), 12th cent., German or Italian priest. He was long attached to the courts of Holy Roman emperors Conrad III, Frederick I, and Henry VI in Italy. His *Gesta Friderici* is a contemporary account of Frederick, and his *Pantheon,* a universal history, freely mixes fact with legend.

Godhavn (gô*th*'houn), town (1969 pop. 863) in Godhavn dist. (1969 pop. 977), W Greenland, on Disko Island; founded in 1773. It is a fishing base, and has a geophysical observatory and an arctic research station (established 1906 by the Univ. of Copenhagen).

Godiva, Lady (gōdī'və), fl. c.1040–80, wife of Leofric, earl of Mercia; famous for her legendary ride through the city of Coventry. She was a benefactor of several monasteries, especially that at Coventry, which she and her husband founded (1043). The legend about her, which first appears in the chronicle of ROGER OF WENDOVER, states that her husband agreed to remit the heavy taxation on the people of Coventry if she would ride naked through the town on a white horse. The story of Peeping Tom, the only person who looked through the closed shutters, did not enter the legend until the 17th cent. Michael Drayton (1613), Tennyson (1842), and others made Lady Godiva the subject of poems. A bronze statue of her by Sir William Reid Dick was erected in Coventry in 1949. See J. C. Lancaster, *Godiva of Coventry* (1967).

Godkin, Edwin Lawrence (gŏd'kĭn), 1831–1902, American editor, b. Moyne, Ireland, of English parentage. His idealism found expression in his *History of Hungary and the Magyars* (1853) and won him the job of correspondent (1853–55) to the London *Daily News* during the Crimean War. In 1856 he came to the United States and studied law. During the Civil War he traveled in the South, sending letters to the *Daily News.* In 1865, Godkin established the *Nation* on stockholders' money but shortly after was compelled to buy the paper to maintain it. In 1881 he became an editor of the New York *Evening Post* and in 1883 editor in chief, carrying the *Nation,* by then an influential critical weekly, with him as a weekly in connection with the *Post.* He was absolutely independent politically and attacked the carpetbag regime, corruption under President Grant, free silver, organized labor, and high tariffs. His self-assurance and integrity gave his opinion weight among editors as well as readers. He wrote *Problems of Modern Democracy* (1896) and *Unforeseen Tendencies of Democracy* (1898). See Rollo Ogden, *Life and Letters of Edwin Lawrence Godkin* (1907); studies by W. M. Armstrong (1957) and L. H. Rifkin (1959).

Godolphin, Sidney Godolphin, 1st **earl of,** 1645–1712, English statesman. He early established a lasting friendship with John Churchill (later duke of MARLBOROUGH), and their political fortunes were closely linked. They had a small bloc of supporters in Parliament, but Godolphin's power was based on his considerable financial knowledge and expertise and resulting favor at court rather than on parliamentary strength. A member of Parliament from 1668, he was appointed a lord of the treasury in 1679 and first lord of the treasury in 1684. Charles II created him a baron in the same year. Although he had supported the attempt (1680) to exclude the future James II from the throne, he remained at the treasury on James's accession (1685) and was one of his closest advisers. He was reappointed (1689) by William III and served as treasury commissioner until he was implicated (1696) in a supposed plot to restore James II. He was again first lord of the treasury from 1700 to 1701. On the accession (1702) of Queen Anne, Godolphin was reappointed to the treasury and became in effect chief minister. The early stability of his ministry, based on a Tory majority and his own and the Marlboroughs's friendship with the queen, was gradually eroded. He became increasingly dependent on the support of the Whig Junto, especially in order to carry on the War of the Spanish Succession. The unpopularity of the war was a major factor in the fall of the ministry in 1710. See biography by Sir Tresham Lever (1952).

Godoy, Manuel de (mänwĕl' dā gō*th*oi'), 1767–1851, Spanish statesman. An army officer, he won the favor of Queen MARÍA LUISA, whose lover he became, and rose rapidly at the court of CHARLES IV. The king made him chief minister in 1792. Godoy favored the war (1793) against revolutionary France, but in 1795 he made peace (the second Treaty of Basel) and was awarded the title *príncipe de la Paz* [prince of the peace]. The following year he allied Spain with France (Treaty of San Ildefonso) in the war against England. After a brief eclipse, Godoy returned to power in 1801 and commanded the victorious Spanish army in the War of the Oranges against Portugal. His alliance with Napoleon I involved Spain in renewed war with England and led to the Franco-Spanish defeat at Trafalgar (1805). The unpopularity of Godoy's corrupt government became acute after Godoy concluded the Convention of Fontainebleau (1807) with Napoleon (see PENINSULAR WAR). Prince Ferdinand (later FERDINAND VII) led the opposition and in 1808 was proclaimed king after Charles IV's first abdication. Godoy who was captured and mauled by a mob in Aranjuez, was rescued by the French and sent to France. He died in Paris.

Godthåb (gôt'hôp), town (1969 pop. 7,166) in Godthåb dist. (1969 pop. 7,963), W Greenland, on the Godthåb Fjord. The largest town and capital of Greenland, it is the seat of the national council and of the supreme court, and it has foreign consulates. Godthåb also has radio stations and newspapers and is a fishing center. The town was founded in 1721 by Hans Egede, a Norwegian missionary. The Godthåb Fjord region has fine pastures and supports reindeer herds. At the head of the fjord are the remains of Vesterbygd, a 10th-century Norse settlement.

Godunov, Boris (bərēs' gədōōnôf'), c.1551–1605, czar of Russia (1598–1605). A favorite of IVAN IV (Ivan the Terrible), he helped organize Ivan's social and administrative system. After Ivan's death (1584), Boris became virtual ruler of Russia, ostensibly as regent for Ivan's young son Feodor I, who was married to Boris's sister. Boris was popularly believed to have ordered the murder (1591) of Feodor's younger brother and heir, DMITRI, in order to secure the succession for himself. Upon Feodor's death (1598), an assembly of the ruling class chose Boris as czar. Under his rule the Russian church was recognized (1589) as an independent patriarchate, equal to other Eastern churches; peace was obtained with Poland and Sweden; and colonization of the southern steppes and W Siberia was spurred. Most important, Boris continued Ivan's policy of strengthening the power of state officials and townspeople at the expense of the BOYARS. Yet famine (1602–4) and popular distrust undermined his support, and when a pretender to the throne appeared claiming to be Feodor's brother Dmitri, many rallied to his support and he easily invaded Russia in 1604. Boris died, and his son, FEODOR II, was unable to defend the throne against the false Dmitri. Boris's life is the subject of a drama by Pushkin that was the basis for Moussorgsky's famous opera. See biography by S. F. Platonov (tr. 1973).

Godwin or **Godwine** (both: gŏd'wĭn), d. 1053, earl of Wessex. He became chief adviser to King Canute, was created (c.1018) an earl, and was given great wealth and lands. After Canute's death (1035) Godwin and Queen Emma, Canute's widow, supported the claims to succession of her son HARTHACANUTE, against those of Canute's illegitimate son HAROLD HAREFOOT. Godwin apparently permitted the murder of another claimant to the throne, Alfred Ætheling, son of Queen Emma by her first husband, Æthelred the Unready, and brother of Edward (later EDWARD THE CONFESSOR). This brutality seems to have earned Godwin the enmity of Harthacanute and of Edward, who succeeded Harthacanute. Nevertheless, Godwin became even more powerful; he secured earldoms for his sons Sweyn and HAROLD and married (1045) his daughter, Edith, to Edward. In 1051, when Edward ordered Godwin to punish the people of Dover for a fracas with EUSTACE II of Boulogne and his retinue, Godwin took the opportunity to challenge the king's strength by refusing. Edward met the challenge and exiled Godwin and his family. However, in 1052, taking advantage of the popular dislike of the king's Norman friends, Godwin and his sons led an armed invasion of England, and the settlement they forced upon Edward restored Godwin to his former importance and outlawed many of the Norman newcomers. Godwin was succeeded as earl of Wessex by his son Harold. See F. M. Stenton, *Anglo-Saxon England* (3d ed. 1971).

Godwin, Mary Wollstonecraft: see WOLLSTONECRAFT, MARY.

Godwin, Parke, 1816–1904, American journalist, b. Paterson, N.J. He became associated while working on the New York *Evening Post* with William Cullen BRYANT, whose daughter he married. He later published a biography of Bryant (1883) and edited his works (4 vol., 1883–84). He retained his connection with the *Post* for nearly 45 years, following Bryant as editor in 1878, but, because of differences with the owners, he resigned in 1881 and became editor of the *Commercial Advertiser.* Godwin, sympathetic with Brook Farm and with Fourierism (see under FOURIER, CHARLES), wrote *A Popular View of the Doctrines of Fourier* (1844), and for a time edited the *Harbinger*, the Fourierist magazine. He translated part of Goethe's autobiography (1846–47) and other works from the German. See Allan Nevins, *The Evening Post* (1922).

Godwin, William, 1756–1836, English author and political philosopher. A minister in his youth, he was, however, plagued by religious doubts and gave up preaching in 1783 for a literary career. His *Enquiry Concerning Political Justice* (1793) recorded the view that men are ultimately guided by reason and therefore, being rational creatures, could live in harmony without laws and institutions. His views are also reflected in his novels—*Adventures of Caleb Williams* (1794), *St. Leon* (1799), and *Fleetwood* (1805). In 1797, Godwin married Mary Wollstonecraft, who died the same year after giving birth to a daughter, Mary. He remarried in 1801 and in 1805 established a small juvenile publishing business. His last years were an unceasing struggle against poverty and debt. Godwin's works strongly influenced his younger contemporaries, particularly SHELLEY, whose elopement with Mary (1814) drew from Godwin an exhibition of sternness at variance with his earlier views. However, he was later reconciled to their marriage. See biographies by F. K. Brown (1926) and E. K. Paul (2 vol., 1896; repr. 1970); studies by H. N. Brailsford (2d ed. 1951) and D. H. Munro (1953).

Godwin-Austen, Henry Haversham, 1834–1923, English topographer and geologist. An officer in the British army (1851–77), he was assigned to several government surveys in N India, especially in the Himalayas. He explored and surveyed the region around Mt. Godwin-Austen (in the Karakorum range), which was named for him.

Godwin-Austen, Mount, or **K2,** peak, 28,250 ft (8,611 m) high, in the Karakorum range, N Kashmir; 2d-highest peak in the world. It was discovered and measured by the Survey of India in 1856, and named for English topographer Henry Godwin-Austen, who explored and surveyed the region. "K2" is taken from the first letter of Karakorum, and the number indicates that it was the second peak in the range to be measured. An Italian team led by Ardito Desio reached the summit in 1954.

Godwine: see GODWIN (d. 1053).

godwit: see SHORE BIRD.

Goebbels, Paul Joseph (poul yō'zĕf gŏb'əls), 1897–1945, German National Socialist propagandist. He was kept out of the service in World War I by a clubfoot. After graduating from the Univ. of Heidelberg (Ph.D., 1921), be began a journalistic career and wrote some unsuccessful novels. He joined the National Socialist, or Nazi, party and worked with Gregor Strasser, who controlled the party in N Germany. As the split between Hitler and Strasser developed, he switched his loyalty to Hitler and was appointed (1926) district party leader in Berlin, where he founded a new organ for party propaganda, *Der Angriff* [*Attack*]. By exploiting mob emotions and by employing all modern methods of propaganda he helped Hitler into power. In 1928, Goebbels was elected to the Reichstag, and when Hitler seized power in 1933 he made Goebbels propaganda minister. This position gave him complete control over radio, press, cinema, and theater; later he also regimented all German culture. Goebbels placed his undeniable intelligence and his brilliant insight into mass psychology entirely at the service of his party. His most virulent propaganda was against the Jews. As a hypnotic orator he was second only to Hitler, and in his staging of mass meetings and parades he was unsurpassed. Utterly cynical, he seems to have believed only in the self-justification of power. He remained loyal to Hitler until the end; in April, 1945, he killed his family and himself while Berlin was falling to Soviet troops. See *The Early Goebbels Diaries 1925–1926*, ed. by H. Heiber (1963); *The Goebbels Diaries, 1942–43*, ed. and tr. by L. P. Lochner (1948, repr. 1970); *The Secret Conferences of Dr. Goebbels: The Nazi Propaganda War, 1939–43*, ed. by W. A. Boelcke (tr. 1970); biographies by R. Manvell and H. Fraenkel (1960) and H. Heiber (tr. 1972); study by E. K. Bramsted (1965).

Goerdeler, Carl Friedrich (kärl frē'drĭkh görd'ələr), 1884–1945, German civil servant, leader of resistance to Hitler. Lord mayor of Leipzig (1930–37) and price commissioner (1931–32, 1934–35), he resigned after continuously protesting measures taken by the Nazi regime. A conservative and a dedicated nationalist, he opposed Hitler's tactics and feared the consequences of war. After his resignation he organized the opposition to Hitler and conspired with Ludwig BECK in the unsuccessful attempt to assassinate Hitler on July 20, 1944. Goerdeler went into hiding but was arrested in Aug., 1944, and executed in Feb., 1945. See study by Gerhard Ritter (tr. 1958, repr. 1970).

Goering or **Göring, Hermann Wilhelm** (both: hĕr'män vĭl'hĕlm gö'rĭng), 1893–1946, German National Socialist leader. In World War I he was a hero of the German air force. An early member of the Nazi party, he participated (1923) with Hitler in the Munich "beer-hall putsch" and after its failure escaped eventually to Sweden, where he stayed until 1927. On his return he reestablished contact with Hitler and was elected (1928) to the Reichstag, of which he became president in 1932. When Hitler came to power (1933) he made Goering air minister of Germany and prime minister and interior minister of Prussia. Until 1936 Goering headed the Gestapo (secret police), which he had founded. He became director of Hitler's four-year economic plan in 1936, supplanted Hjalmar Schacht as minister of economy in 1937, and was virtual dictator over the German economy until 1943. Goering was responsible for the German rearmament program and especially for the creation of the German air force. In 1939 Hitler designated Goering as his successor and in 1940 made him marshal of the empire, a unique rank. Goering was notorious for his love of high-sounding titles, of extraordinary uniforms, of pageantry, and of voluntary or enforced gifts. In later years he spent more and more time at his palatial estate and was addicted to narcotics. Behind his facade of good humor he hid a vindictive temperament. In World War II he was responsible for the total air war waged by Germany; his immense popularity in Germany declined after the Allied air forces, contrary to Goering's emphatic predictions, began to lay Germany to waste. From 1943 on, Hitler deprived him of all formal authority and finally dismissed him shortly before the end of the war, when Goering attempted to claim his right of succession. He surrendered (May, 1945) to American troops and was the chief defendant at the Nuremberg trial for war crimes (1945–46). He defended himself with brilliant cynicism but was convicted and sentenced to death. Two hours before his scheduled hanging, he committed suicide by swallowing a poison capsule. See biographies by C. H. Bewley (1962), Roger Manvell, Heinrich Fraenkel (1962, repr. 1972), Asher Lee (1972), and Leonard Mosley (1974).

Goes, Hugo van der (hōō'gō vän dĕr gōōs), d.1482, Flemish painter. Probably born in Ghent, he was a member of the painters' guild there in 1467 and became dean of the guild in 1474, a year before his semiretirement to a monastery near Brussels. Early works, such as *The Fall of Man* (c.1468; Vienna), recall earlier Flemish art, such as that of the van Eycks and Justus of Ghent. The *Monforte Altarpiece* (c.1472; Berlin) reveals a classical sonority in color and serene figures. Later works, such as the great *Portinari Altarpiece* (c.1476; Uffizi), begin to show the tension and the dissonances in color and spatial arrangement that characterize his last works. His *Death of the Virgin* (c.1480; Bruges) is remarkable for the staring melancholy of the apostles' faces. Hugo suffered an attack of madness c.1481, which resulted in his death the following year. The ducal court and Italian and local merchants in Flanders admired his exquisite technique, powers of observation, and representation of human character, to be seen in his portraits at the Metropolitan Museum and Walters Art Gallery, Baltimore. See study by F. Winkler (1964).

Goethals, George Washington (gō'thəlz), 1858–1928, U.S. army engineer, b. Brooklyn, N.Y., grad. West Point, 1880. After serving on various inland water projects, he was appointed chief engineer of the Panama Canal when John F. Stevens resigned (1907). Goethals found the difficulty of the work increased by the climate, yellow fever, labor troubles, unexpected complications in building the locks, and crumbling substrata in the Culebra Cut. By taking intense personal interest in the men and expressing satisfaction in their individual achievements, he created an atmosphere of cooperation and completed the project ahead of schedule. He was governor of the Canal Zone (1914–16). In World War I he was briefly (1917) general manager of the Emergency Fleet Corporation, then (Jan.–April, 1918) head of the Bureau of Purchase and Supplies, and finally assistant chief of staff in charge of supplies.

Goethe, Johann Wolfgang von (yō'hän vôlf'gäng fən gö'tə), 1749–1832, German poet, dramatist, novelist, and scientist, b. Frankfurt. His genius embraced most fields of human endeavor; his art and thought are epitomized in his great dramatic poem *Faust.* Goethe describes his happy and sheltered childhood in his autobiography, *Dichtung und Wahrheit* (1811–33). In 1765 he went to Leipzig to study law. There, besides indulging in dissipations that ended with a hemorrhage and a long convalescence at Frankfurt, Goethe took lessons in art and music, in which he was talented. His earliest lyric poems, set to music, were published in 1769. In 1770–71 he completed his law studies at Strasbourg, where the acquaintance of Herder filled him with enthusiasm for Shakespeare, for Germany's medieval past, and for the German folk song. His lyric poems for Friederike Brion, daughter of the pastor of nearby Sesenheim, were written at this time as new texts for folk-song melodies. Among the lasting influences of Goethe's youth were J. J. Rousseau and Spinoza, who appealed to Goethe's mystic and poetic feeling for nature in its ever-changing aspects. It was in this period that Goethe began his lifelong study of animals and plants and his research in biological morphology. Goethe first attracted public notice with the drama *Götz von Berlichingen* (see BERLICHINGEN, GÖTZ VON), a pure product of STURM UND DRANG. Still more important was the epistolary novel *Die Leiden des jungen Werthers* [the sorrows of young Werther] (1774), which Goethe, on the verge of suicide, wrote after his unrequited love for Charlotte Buff. *Werther* gave him immediate fame and was widely translated. While the writing had helped Goethe regain stability, the novel's effect on the public was the opposite; it encouraged morbid sensibility. In 1775, Goethe was invited to visit Charles Augustus, duke of Saxe-Weimar, at whose court he was to spend the rest of his life. For 10 years Goethe was chief minister of state at Weimar. He later retained only the directorship of the state theater and the scientific institutions. A trip to Italy (1786–88) fired his enthusiasm for the classical ideal, as Goethe tells us in his travel account *Die italienische Reise* (1816) and in *Winckelmann und sein Jahrhundert* [WINCKELMANN and his century] (1805). Also written under the classical impact were the historical drama *Egmont* (1788), well known for Beethoven's incidental music; *Römische Elegien* (1788); the psychological drama *Torquato Tasso* (1789); the domestic epic *Hermann und Dorothea* (1797); and the final, poetic version (1787) of the drama *Iphigenie auf Tauris*. In 1792, Goethe accompanied Duke Charles Augustus as official historiographer in the allied campaign against revolutionary France. He appreciated the principles of the French Revolution but resented the methods employed; a reformer in his own small state, Goethe wished to see social change accomplished from above. Later he refused to share in the patriotic hysteria that swept Germany during the Napoleonic Wars. Napoleon met Goethe at Erfurt in 1808, and his remark was "Voilà un homme!" [there is a man!]. One of the two major works that occupied Goethe from adolescence until old age, the novel *Wilhelm Meisters Lehrjahre* [the apprenticeship of Wilhelm Meister] (1796), was destined to become the prototype of the German *Bildungsroman*, or novel of character development. In 1829 appeared the last installment of *Wilhelm Meisters Wanderjahre* [Wilhelm Meister's journeyman years], a series of episodes. More important, in fact, one of the great poetic and philosophical works of world literature, is the dramatic poem *Faust*. The first part was published in 1808, the second after Goethe's death. Goethe recast the traditional FAUST legend and made it one of the greatest poetic and philosophic creations the world possesses. His main departure from the original is no doubt the salvation of Faust, the erring seeker, in the mystic last scene of the second part. The friendship of Friedrich von Schiller and his death (1805) made a deep impression on Goethe. Many women passed through Goethe's life, and, of them, probably the most intellectual was Charlotte von Stein. He married (1806) Christiane Vulpius (1765–1816), who had borne him a son. Goethe's unsuccessful marriage offer (1822) to young Ulrike von Levetzow inspired his poems *Trilogie der Leidenschaft* [trilogy of passion]. *Westöstlicher Diwan* (1819), a collection of Goethe's finest lyric poetry, was inspired by his young friend Marianne von Willemer, who figures as Suleika in the cycle. The *Diwan* strikes a new note in German poetry, introducing Eastern elements derived from Goethe's reading of the Persian poet Hafiz. Increasingly aloof from national, political, or even literary partisanship, Goethe became more and more the Olympian divinity, to whose shrine at Weimar all Europe flocked. The variety and extent of his accomplishments and activities was monumental. Goethe knew French, English, Italian, Latin, Greek, and Hebrew and translated works by Diderot, Voltaire, Cellini, Byron and others. His approach to science was one of sensuous experience and poetic intuition. Well known is his stubborn attack on Newton's theory of light, in *Zur Farbenlehre* (1810). A corresponding treatise on acoustics remained unfinished. An accomplished amateur musician, Goethe conducted instrumental and vocal ensembles and directed opera performances in Weimar. His search for an operatic composer with whom he could collaborate failed; although many of his operetta librettos were composed, none achieved lasting fame. Goethe's exquisite lyrical poems, often inspired by existing songs, challenged contemporary composers to give their best in music, and such songs as "Nur wer die Sehnsucht kennt" [only the lonely heart], "Kennst du das Land" [know'st thou the land], and *Der Erlkönig* are among the song texts most often set to music. Goethe's aim was to make his life a concrete example of the full potentialities of man, and he succeeded as did few others. He is buried, alongside Schiller, in the ducal crypt at Weimar. The opinions of Goethe are recorded not only in his own writings but also in conversations recorded by his secretary J. P. Eckermann and in extensive correspondence with the composer Zelter and with Schiller, Byron, Carlyle, Manzoni, and others. The bulk of Goethe's work is immense; the most recent complete edition is the so-called Weimar edition (133 vol. in 140, 1887–1919). Most of his works have been translated into English, notably by Thomas Carlyle. Biographies and literary studies are numerous; for bibliographies see Eugene Oswald, *Goethe in England and America* (2d ed. 1909), and A. J. Dickson, *Goethe in England, 1909–1949* (1951). The following biographies may be mentioned: G. H. Lewes (1855), James Sime (1888), Friedrich Gundolf (1916, in German), and J. G. Robertson (1927); Ludwig Lewisohn, ed., *Goethe: The Story of a Man* (1949). Among well-known studies are essays by Carlyle, Emerson, Calvin Thomas, George Santayana, André Gide, Albert Schweitzer, and Thomas Mann. Recent studies include Karl Viëtor, *Goethe, the Thinker* (tr., 1950); Wolfgang Leppmann, *The German Image of Goethe* (1961); R. Peacock, *Goethe's Major Plays* (1959, repr. 1966); R. Gray, *Goethe: A Critical Introduction* (1967); E. C. Mason, *Goethe's Faust* (1967).

Goffe, William (gôf), d. c.1679, English soldier and regicide. A personal adherent of Oliver Cromwell, he fought in the English civil war, signed the death warrant of Charles I, and became an administrative major general during the Protectorate. He was excepted from the Act of Indemnity (at the Restoration) and fled with his father-in-law, Edward WHALLEY, to America. After short periods in Cambridge (Mass.), New Haven, and Milford (Conn.) he lived in seclusion at Hadley (Mass.). The tradition that he headed the citizens of Hadley in repelling an Indian attack was used by Sir Walter Scott in his *Peveril of the Peak* and by James Fenimore Cooper in his *Wept of Wish-ton-Wish*. See L. A. Welles, *History of the Regicides in New England* (1927, repr. 1971).

Gog, in the Bible. **1** Reubenite. 1 Chron. 5.4. **2** In the prophecy in Ezek. 38–39, a leader who will attack Israel and be defeated. Magog is his country. Gog is often identified with the Scythians. The same theme is used in Rev. 20.8, where the assailants are Gog and Magog.

Gogarten, Friedrich, 1887–1968, German theologian. He was professor of theology at the Univ. of Jena from 1927 until 1933, when he began to teach at the Univ. of Göttingen. He adopted the anti-idealism of Søren Kierkegaard, and his work is close to that of Karl Barth and Rudolf Bultmann. Using Barth's dialectical theology, he formulated a fresh interpretation of culture and history but from a Lutheran rather than Calvinist point of view. In his works *Politische Ethik* (1932) and *Der Mensch Zwischen Gott und Welt* (1952) he is concerned with the problem of man's relation to his religion and to the state. In his chief work, *Entmythologisierung und die Kirche* (1953; tr. *Demythologization and the Church*, 1955), he examines and expands on Bultmann's attempt to remove the elements of myth from the New Testament. See study by L. E. Shiner (1966).

Gogarty, Oliver St. John (gō'gərtē), 1878–1957, Irish author. A physician, he also served (1922–36) in the parliament of the Irish Free State. Gogarty is perhaps best known as the model for Buck Mulligan in James Joyce's *Ulysses*. *As I Was Going down Sackville Street* (1937) and *It Isn't This Time of Year at All!* (1954) contain reminiscences of Joyce, Yeats, and others in the Irish literary renaissance. See his collected poems (1954); his essays, *A Week End in the Middle of the Week* (1958); biography by Ulick O'Connor (1963).

Gogebic (gōgē'bĭk), east-west mountain range, 80 mi (129 km) long and .5 to 1 mi (.8–1.6 km) wide, extending from the W Upper Peninsula, N Mich., into N Wis. It is known for its iron deposits, discovered in 1848, which lie in some of the world's deepest mines. High-grade iron-oxide deposits have been depleted. New techniques make it possible to mine the vast reserves of taconite, a low-grade iron ore. Jasper is also mined. The name Penokee is sometimes given to parts of the range.

Gogh, Vincent Van: see VAN GOGH, VINCENT.

Gogol, Nikolai Vasilyevich (nyĭkəlī' vəsē'lyəvĭch gô'gəl), 1809–52, Russian short-story writer, novelist, and playwright, considered the father of Russian realism. Of Cossack origin, he first won literary success with fanciful and romantic tales of his native Ukraine in *Evenings on a Farm near Dikanka* (1831–32). His next stories, in *Mirgorod* (1835), contained elements of romance, humor, and the supernatural. "Taras Bulba," part of the collection, is a vigorous description of the adventures of a 17th-century Cossack. Gogol then wrote several tales set in St. Petersburg. The most famous of these is *The Overcoat* (1842), about a downtrodden clerk who sacrifices much to buy a new overcoat that is stolen the first time he wears it. As a dramatist Gogol's fame rests on *The Inspector-General* (1836), a satire on provincial officials. Petty vice and human folly are caricatured in this as in all his mature work. His picaresque novel *Dead Souls* (1842) concerns the rogue Chichikov who buys the names of dead serfs from landowners in order to mortgage them as property. This work is the culmination of Gogol's gift for caricature, imagery, and invention. Haunted throughout his life by moral and religious problems, and adverse criticism from his contemporaries, his powers declined as he attempted to write a second part to his novel, embodying positive spiritual values. In a frenzy he destroyed the manuscript; greatly depressed, his health ruined by fanatical fasting, he died shortly thereafter. Gogol's work is realistic in its concern for rich detail, but he is famed primarily for creating a fantastic world of the imagination. Most of his works have been translated into English. See his letters, ed. by C. R. Proffer (1968); his *Selected Passages from Correspondence with Friends* (tr. 1969); biographies by Janko Laurin (1926, repr. 1973) and Henri Troyat (tr. 1973); studies by Victor Erlich (1969) and T. S. Lindstrom (1974).

Gogra (gō'grä), river, major tributary of the Ganges, c.640 mi (1,030 km) long, rising in the Himalayas, SW Tibet (China), and flowing generally SE through Nepal (where it is called the Karnali) to join the Ganges in Bihar state, E India. The river is used extensively for trade. Its lower reaches are navigable by river steamers. It is also known as the Ghaghara.

Goiânia (go͞oyä'nyə), city (1970 pop. 388,926), capital of Goiás state, S central Brazil. A modern planned city, it was built to replace the old city of Goiás as state capital and was inaugurated as such in 1937. It is a shipping and processing center for a region producing cattle, minerals, and agricultural commodities. Goiânia is the seat of a federal university (est. 1964) and of several technical schools.

Goiás (goi-äs'), state (1970 pop. 2,941,107), 247,912 sq mi (642,092 sq km), central Brazil. GOIÂNIA is the capital.

Goidelic (goidĕl'ĭk), or Gaelic, group of languages belonging to the Celtic subfamily of the Indo-European family of languages. See CELTIC LANGUAGES; IRISH LANGUAGE.

goiter: see THYROID GLAND.

Gokcha: see SEVAN, USSR.

Gokhale, Gopal Krishna (gōpäl krĭsh'nə gōkä'lā), 1866–1915, Indian nationalist leader. A Brahman from Maharashtra, he was educated in India and became involved in the nationalist movement when he was quite young. A moderate, he stressed negotiation and conciliation rather than non-cooperation or violence. He was elected to the Bombay Legislative Council in 1899 and to the Imperial Legislative Council in 1902. The conflict of Gokhale's moderate views with the more militant ideas of Bal Gangadhar TILAK led to a breach in the Indian National Congress that nearly immobilized it from 1907 to 1916. Gokhale was instrumental in founding the Servants of India Society, a nationalist organization whose members, sworn to poverty and obedience, were enlisted to serve as volunteers for the social, political, and economic welfare of India. See biography and collected works by J. S. Hoyland (1948); M. K. Gandhi, *Gokhale, My Political Guru* (1955); Stanley Wolpert, *Tilak and Gokhale* (1962); D. B. Mathur, *Gokhale, a Political Biography* (1966).

Golan (gō'lən), refuge city, somewhere in Manasseh E of the Jordan. Deut. 4.43; Joshua 20.8; 21.27; 1 Chron. 6.71.

Golconda (gŏlkŏn'də), ruined city, Andhra Pradesh state, SE India. It was the capital (c.1364–1512) of the Bahmani kingdom, but after 1512 it became the capital of the Muslim sultanate of Golconda. The legions of Aurangzeb, the Mogul emperor, captured the city in 1687, after which Golconda gradually fell into ruin. The main feature of the city is its fort on a hill 400 ft (120 m) above the plain; it was large enough to house the administration, the army, and families of the rulers. There are also ruins of palaces and mosques. At its peak, the city was famed for the diamonds found to the southeast and cut in Golconda; its name has come to mean "Source of great wealth."

gold, metallic chemical element; symbol Au [Lat. *aurum*=shining dawn]; at. no. 79; at. wt. 196.9665; m.p. 1064.43°C; b.p. 2940°C; sp. gr. 19.32 at 20°C; valence +1 or +3. Gold is very ductile and is the most malleable metal; it can be beaten into extremely thin sheets of gold leaf. Only silver and copper, which are above it in group Ib of the PERIODIC TABLE, are better electrical conductors. Gold is chemically inactive. It is unaffected by moisture, oxygen, or ordinary acids but is attacked by the HALOGENS. Aqua regia (a mixture of nitric and hydrochloric acids that liberates chlorine) is so named for its ability to dissolve gold, the "king" of the metals. Gold forms both aurous (univalent) and auric (trivalent) compounds; auric chloride and chloroauric acid are its most common compounds. A relatively soft metal, gold is usually hardened by alloying with copper, silver, or other metals. White gold, a substitute for platinum, is an alloy of gold with platinum, palladium, nickel, or nickel and zinc. Green gold, also used by jewelers, is usually an alloy of gold with silver. Alloys of gold with copper are a reddish yellow and are used for coinage and jewelry. Gold is often found in nature alloyed with other metals; when more than 20% of silver is present the alloy is called electrum. The gold content of an alloy is commonly stated in carats, a carat being 1/24 part by weight of the total mass. Pure gold is therefore 24 carats fine; an alloy that is 75% gold is 18 carats fine. Fineness is sometimes expressed in terms of parts per thousand; thus gold containing 10% of other metals is said to have a fineness of 900. Gold is widely distributed on the earth; although large amounts are present also in sea-water, the cost of current methods for recovering it exceeds its value. Most gold is found in the metallic state in the form of dust, grains, flakes, or nuggets. It occurs, usually in association with silver or other metals, in quartz veins or lodes so finely disseminated that it is not visible. It is found also in alluvial placer deposits, which are worked by panning, dredging, and hydraulic mining. Gold is extracted from its ores by mechanical means and separated from other metals by chemical processes, notably the CYANIDE PROCESS, the AMALGAMATION PROCESS, and the chlorination process (in this the ore is oxidized and chlorinated and the gold precipitated with hydrogen sulfide). It also occurs in compounds, notably telluride minerals. Gold has been known from prehistoric times and was possibly the first metal used by man. It was valued for ornaments (see GOLDWORK), and magical efficacy was attributed to it. In the Middle Ages alchemists sought to transmute baser metals into gold. The quest for gold stimulated European explorations and conquests in the Western Hemisphere, and its discovery has led to many a GOLD RUSH. The chief producers are South Africa, the USSR, Canada, and the United States (especially in South Dakota and Nevada). For a discussion of the monetary function of gold, see BIMETALLISM; COIN; GOLD STANDARD; MONEY.

Goldberg, Arthur, 1908–, American labor lawyer and jurist, Associate Justice of the U.S. Supreme Court (1962–65), b. Chicago. He received his law degree from Northwestern Univ. in 1929. A corporation lawyer, he became a labor specialist after representing the Chicago newspaper guild in a strike (1938) against the Hearst papers. In World War II he served in the Office of Strategic Services as contact man with the European underground labor movement. He was (1945–48) professor of law at the John Marshall Law School in Chicago. In 1948 he was appointed by Philip Murray to be general counsel of the Congress of Industrial Organizations (CIO) and the United Steelworkers Union. Goldberg was a central figure in the merger (1955) of the American Federation of Labor (AF of L) and the CIO, and he led the fight to expel the International Brotherhood of Teamsters from the AFL-CIO. Appointed U.S. Secretary of Labor in 1961, he was credited with settling several serious labor disputes. In 1962 he was appointed by President Kennedy to the Supreme Court, where he joined the liberal faction. He resigned (1965) when President Lyndon B. Johnson appointed him U.S. representative to the United Nations; he held that post until 1968. In 1970, he was the unsuccessful Democratic candidate for governor of New York state. He wrote *AFL-CIO: Labor United* (1956).

Goldberg, Rube (Reuben Lucius Goldberg), 1883–1970, American cartoonist and sculptor, b. San Francisco. After drawing cartoons for San Francisco newspapers, he moved to New York City. There he worked for the New York *Evening Mail* until his cartoons became syndicated in 1921. Goldberg originated the successful comic strip "Boob McNutt" and the panel series "Foolish Questions." He is known for his drawings of ludicrously intricate machinery meant to perform simple operations. Goldberg worked as a political cartoonist for the New York *Sun* and later for the New York *Journal American*. After 1964 he concentrated on sculpture. He is the author of *How to Remove the Cotton from a Bottle of Aspirin* (1959) and *Rube Goldberg vs. the Machine Age* (1968). See biography by P. C. Marzio (1973).

Goldberger, Joseph, 1874–1929, American medical research worker, b. Austria-Hungary, grad. Bellevue Hospital Medical College, 1895. He came to the United States at the age of six. He joined the U.S. Public Health Service in 1899, specializing in preventive medicine, infectious diseases, and nutrition. Working on pellagra, he discovered the cause to be deficiency of a nutritive factor that he called "pellagra preventive" (P-P), now known to be niacin (nicotinic acid).

Gold Coast: see GHANA, republic.

Gold Coast, city (1971 pop. 66,558), Queensland, E Australia, on the Pacific Ocean. The city, a major resort, stretches for many miles along the coast.

Golden Age, in classical mythology: see AGE.

Golden Ass, The: see APULEIUS, LUCIUS.

Golden Bough, The: see FRAZER, SIR JAMES.

Golden Bull, term translated from the Latin *bulla aurea* and generally referring to a bull (edict) with a golden seal. Golden bulls were promulgated by medieval Byzantine rulers and by Western European monarchs, for example, by Holy Roman Emperor Frederick II (Golden Bull of 1213) and by King ANDREW II of Hungary (Golden Bull of 1222). However, the term is most frequently used in reference to the Golden Bull of 1356, issued by Holy Roman Emperor CHARLES IV. Mindful of the dissension caused by the disputed imperial election of his predecessor, Louis IV, Charles IV devised a series of detailed procedural regulations intended to prevent similar controversies. The measures were discussed and approved at the imperial diets of Nuremberg and Metz (1355–56). The "king of the Romans" was thereafter to be elected only by the majority vote of seven electoral princes (see ELECTORS). By omitting any mention of the papacy, the document virtually nullified papal claims to intervene in or to confirm an election. The electoral right was to descend by male primogeniture in the henceforth indivisible lay electorates (except in Bohemia, where the crown was elective). The Golden Bull sanctioned a long-developing trend against a centralized empire and gave the electors a constitutional basis on which to consolidate their holdings into sovereign states. It granted them regalian rights over coinage, mining, and the judiciary; conspiracy against them was to be considered lese-majesty. In codifying the princes' independence of imperial jurisdiction, the Golden Bull of 1356 set the constitutional form of the Holy Roman Empire, which with but a few modifications, survived until the empire's dissolution in 1806.

golden chain: see LABURNUM.

Golden Fleece, in Greek mythology, the magic fleece of the winged ram that saved Phrixus and Helle, the children of Nephele and Athamas, from the jealousy of Ino, Athamas' second wife. The ram flew to Colchis, but Helle fell into the sea, which was thereafter known as the Hellespont. Phrixus arrived safely, sacrificed the ram, and hung its fleece in a wood guarded by a dragon. The ram became the constellation Aries. Phrixus married a daughter of King Aeëtes of Colchis and begot Argus and three other sons. The quest of JASON and the Argonauts was for this fleece.

Golden Gate, strait, 4 mi (6.4 km) long and 1 to 2 mi (1.6–3.2 km) wide, linking San Francisco Bay with the Pacific Ocean. It was discovered in 1579 by the English explorer Sir Francis Drake. Known as the Golden Gate before the California gold rush, its name became popular during this period because of its new connotation. The strait is the drowned mouth of the united Sacramento and San Joaquin rivers and forms an excellent channel, c.400 ft (120 m) deep, into San Francisco Bay.

Golden Gate Bridge, across the Golden Gate from San Francisco to Marin Co., W Calif.; built 1933–37. Its overall length is 9,266 ft (2,824 m); its main span across the strait, 4,200 ft (1,280 m), is one of the longest bridges in the world. Joseph B. Strauss was the chief engineer.

Golden Gate National Recreation Area, Calif.: see NATIONAL PARKS AND MONUMENTS, table.

golden glow: see BLACK-EYED SUSAN.

Golden Horde, Empire of the, Mongol state comprising most of Russia, given as an appanage to Jenghiz Khan's oldest son, Juchi, and actually conquered and founded in the mid-13th cent. by Juchi's son, BATU KHAN, after the Mongol or Tatar (see TATARS) conquest of Russia. The name was derived from the Russian term *Zolotaya Orda*, used by the Russians to designate the Mongol host that had set up a magnificent gleaming tent camp along the Volga River. The empire, also called the Kipchak Khanate, had its capital first at Sarai Batu near Astrakhan on the lower Volga and later at Sarai Berke on the Volga near present-day Volgograd. Its ascendancy terminated the rise of Kievan Russia (Kiev was razed in 1240) and ultimately, although indirectly, contributed to the predominance of Muscovite Russia (see MOSCOW, GRAND DUCHY OF). Under the Empire of the Golden Horde, the Russian principalities retained their own rulers and internal administration. However, they were tributaries of the khan, who confirmed princely succession and exacted exorbitant taxes. Until the disintegration of the Mongol empire (14th cent.) the khans themselves were under the suzerainty of the great khan at Karakorum. In the early 14th cent. the empire of the Golden Horde adopted Islam as its official religion. Thus, Russia was exposed to both Muslim and Asian civilization. Internecine warfare among the Tatar leaders and attempts by the Russian princes, such as DMITRI DONSKOI, to end tributary payments contributed to the decline of the Empire of the Golden Horde in the late 14th cent. The state was conquered by TAMERLANE, who in 1395 dealt a final blow by sacking Sarai Berke. After his death the empire broke up into the independent khanates of Astrakhan, Kazan, Crimea, and Sibir. See Jeremiah Curtis, *The Mongols in Russia* (1908); A. E. Presniakov, *The Formation of the Great Russian State* (tr. 1970).

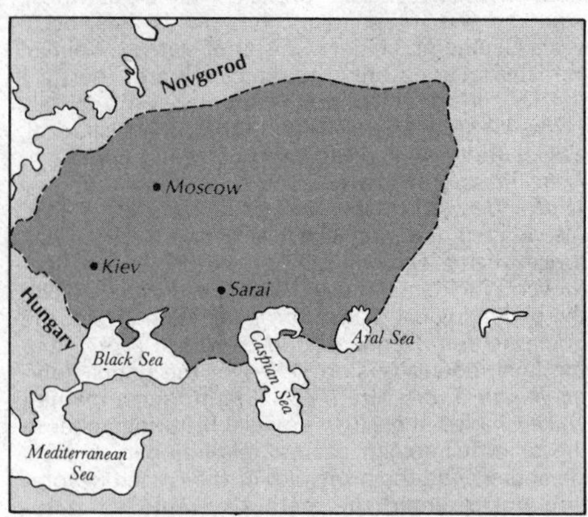

Khanate of the Golden Horde (c.1300)

Golden Horn: see ISTANBUL.

Golden Legend, The, collection of saints' lives written in the 13th cent. by JACOBUS DA VARAGINE. Originally entitled *Legenda sanctorum* [readings in the lives of the saints], it soon came to be called *Legenda aurea* [the golden legend] because of its popularity, which continued until the Reformation. It is a saints' calendar, with an introduction for each division of the year and a section on each great feast day. It is a compilation of wonder stories, presenting the ideals of saintly living; not critical or historical in purpose, it is a devotional book rather than a collection of biographies. It was early translated from Latin into the vernacular languages, and William Caxton published one of the English translations. The fantastic nature of some of the stories and the simple, graceless style of the Latin brought the scorn of Renaissance humanists. Yet the immense popularity the book enjoyed is evident from the wide influence it had on medieval literature. An excellent, somewhat abridged adaptation by Granger Ryan and Helmut Ripperger appeared in 1941.

Golden Rectangle: see GOLDEN SECTION.

golden retriever, breed of large SPORTING DOG developed primarily in Scotland in the mid-19th cent. It stands about 23 in. (58.4 cm) high at the shoulder and weighs from 60 to 75 lb (27.2–34.1 kg). Its golden-brown, water-repellent coat is made up of a dense undercoat and a longer, straight or wavy outercoat that lies flat against the body. There is a moderate to heavy fringe, or feathering, of hair on the chest, back of legs, and tail. A dog of great endurance, the golden retriever was originally developed as a retriever of waterfowl. However, it has been widely used to hunt upland birds as well, and has been successfully trained as a guide dog. See DOG.

goldenrod, any species of the large genus *Solidago* of the family Compositae (COMPOSITE family), chiefly North American weedy herbs. They have small yellow flowers clustered, often in panicles, along a wandlike stem. The few species that have white flowers are called silverrod. The goldenrods were, at one time, incorrectly considered a chief cause of hay fever, probably because they bloom in late summer and autumn, at the same time as the less conspicuous ragweeds. Goldenrods attracted short-lived commercial attention when Thomas Edison found that certain species contain latex. Some species (sometimes called dyer's-weed) have yielded a dye, and the leaves of many species have long been used for medicinal preparations and teas, whence the botanical name [Lat. *solidare*=to make whole]. The goldenrod adds beauty to fields, roadsides, and salt marshes in so many parts of the United States that it has been chosen as the state flower of Alabama, Kentucky, and Nebraska and has even been suggested for the national flower. Goldenrod is classified in the division MAGNOLIOPHYTA, class Magnoliopsida, order Asterales, family Compositae.

Golden Rule, saying of Jesus, "As ye would that men should do to you, do ye also to them likewise." Luke 6.31; Mat. 7.12. It is stated negatively in Tobit 4.15.

Golden Section, in mathematics, division of a line segment into two segments such that the ratio of the original segment to the larger division is equal to the ratio of the larger division to the smaller division. If c is the original segment, b is the larger division, and a is the smaller division, then $c = a + b$ and $c/b = b/a$. Thus, b is the geometric mean of a and c; the ratio is known as the Divine Proportion. The Golden Rectangle, whose length and width are

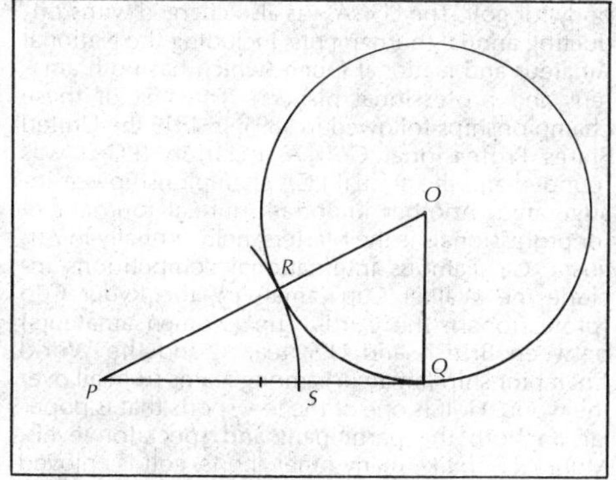

The Golden Section: To divide line PQ into extreme and mean ratio (the Golden Section, or Divine Proportion), first bisect PQ, then erect a perpendicular to PQ at Q and lay off OQ=½PQ. Draw the circle with center O and radius OQ and draw OP. On PQ lay off PS=PR. Point S divides PQ into extreme and mean ratio.

the segments of a line divided according to the Golden Section, occupies an important position in painting, sculpture, and architecture, because its proportions have long been considered the most attractive to the eye. The constructions of regular polygons of 5, 10, and 15 sides depend on the division of a line by the Golden Section. The numerical ratio of the greater segment of the line to the shorter segment as determined by the Golden Section is symbolized by ϕ (the Greek letter phi) and has the approximate value 1.618. It occurs in many widely varying areas of mathematics. For example, in the Fibonacci sequence (the sequence of numbers formed by adding successive members to find the next member—0,1,1,2,3,5,8,13, . . .), the values of the ratios 1, 2/1, 3/2, 5/3, 8/5, 13/8, . . . approach ϕ. See H. E. Huntley, *The Divine Proportion* (1970).

golden shower: see SENNA.

Golden Spike National Historic Site: see NATIONAL PARKS AND MONUMENTS (table).

golden stars: see TUNICATE.

golden tuft: see ALYSSUM.

Golden Valley, village (1970 pop. 24,246), Hennepin co., SE Minn., a suburb adjacent to Minneapolis; inc. 1886. It is chiefly residential, with some light industry and research activity.

Goldfaden, Abraham (gōldfäd'ən), 1840–1908, Ukrainian playwright who wrote in Yiddish and Hebrew. He was the first important Yiddish playwright and the founder of Yiddish theater. In 1876 he combined some of his songs and poems to form his first plays, which were initially performed in Jassy, Rumania. Russian authorities banned Yiddish theater in 1883, and Goldfaden and his followers founded Yiddish troupes in Paris, London, and New York City. Goldfaden settled in New York in 1903 and opened a drama school. Of his 400 plays the most famous is probably *Shulamit* (1880).

Goldfield, town, SW Nev., a former gold-mining center. Gold was discovered there in 1902, and after an early period of disappointment, large yields of high quality gold were extracted. A rush in 1903 built a lusty city, which was soon remarkable for its exuberant elegance, with a theater, a large hotel (still standing), and various fine residences. Tex Rickard, a saloonkeeper there, promoted the noted prizefight between Joe Gans and Battling Nelson in 1906. A strike by the miners caused Federal troops to be brought to Goldfield in 1907. Production reached its height in 1910, then fell off. The boom ended in 1918, and Goldfield declined almost as fast as it had risen.

goldfinch: see FINCH.

goldfish, freshwater fish, genus *Carassius*, of the family Cyprinidae, popular in aquariums and ponds. Native to China, it was first domesticated centuries ago from the wild form, an olive-colored carplike fish up to 16 in. (40 cm) long. It reverts to this type when it escapes from domestication and has been known to hybridize with the CARP. Breeders have developed bizarre varieties with fan, fringe, or veil tails and sometimes with double or triple fins. Some have bulging "telescope" eyes. The majority of those bred commercially are known as scaled goldfish and have a metallic sheen of red, gold, white, silver, or black. The rarer forms, which are called scaleless, actually have transparent scales and appear in bright red, blue, shades of purple, and calico patterns. Marketed goldfish range in length from 1 to 4 in. (2.5–10 cm). In pools, they are beneficial as well as ornamental, since they feed on mosquito larvae; however, their carplike feeding habits make them a nuisance in lakes and streams. Goldfish are classified in the phylum CHORDATA, subphylum Vertebrata, class Osteichthyes, order Cypriniformes, family Cyprinidae.

Goldie, Sir George (George Goldie Taubman), 1846–1925, British colonial administrator, b. Isle of Man. Goldie entered the Niger River trade in the 1870s, and his company soon dominated trade on the lower river. In 1886 the British government chartered his Royal Niger Company, giving it political and economic control over the hinterland of Nigeria. It was Goldie's objective, in which he was largely successful, to extend British control over the Niger and Benue rivers as far as they were navigable. He defeated French and German attempts to establish posts in Nigeria and conquered several of the Fulani emirates. See biographies by Dorothy Wellesley (1934) and J. E. Flint (1960).

Golding, Arthur, c.1536–c.1605, English translator. He translated many Latin classics, including Caesar's *Gallic War* and Ovid's *Metamorphoses*. A Calvinist, Golding tried to infuse the *Metamorphoses* with a stern moral tone. He also translated noted French works.

Golding, William, 1911–, English novelist. A highly imaginative and original writer, he is basically concerned with the eternal nature of man. In his best-known work, the allegorical *Lord of the Flies* (1954), he describes the nightmarish adventures of a group of English schoolboys stranded on an island and traces their degeneration from a state of innocence to that of blood lust and savagery. His later works include *The Inheritors* (1955), *Pincher Martin* (1956), *Free Fall* (1959), *The Spire* (1964), *The Pyramid* (1967), and *The Scorpion God* (1971).

Goldman, Edwin Franko, 1878–1956, American bandmaster and composer, b. Louisville, Ky.; pupil of Dvořák at the National Conservatory of Music, New York City. He played solo cornet in the Metropolitan Opera orchestra (1899–1909) and in 1911 organized his first band. In 1918 he inaugurated a series of public outdoor concerts. He composed over 100 marches and commissioned many works from leading composers. His son, Richard Franko Goldman (1911–), who succeeded him as leader of the Goldman band, is also a composer and writer on music.

Goldman, Emma, 1869–1940, American anarchist, b. Russia. She emigrated to Rochester, N.Y., in 1886 and worked there in clothing factories. After 1889 she was active in the anarchist movement, and her speeches attracted attention throughout the United States. In 1893, Goldman was imprisoned for inciting to riot. From 1906 she was associated with Alexander BERKMAN in publishing the anarchist paper *Mother Earth*. In 1916 she was imprisoned for publicly advocating birth control, and in 1917 for obstructing the draft. With Berkman, Goldman was deported in 1919 to Russia but left that country in 1921 because of her disagreement with the Bolshevik government. In 1926 she married James Colton, a Welshman. She was permitted to reenter the United States for a lecture tour in 1924 on condition that she refrain from public discussion of politics. She took an active part in the Spanish civil war in 1936. She died in Toronto. See her *Living My Life* (1931). Other writings include *Anarchism and Other Essays* (1911), *Social Significance of Modern Drama* (1914), and *My Disillusionment in Russia* (1923). See biographies by Richard Drinnon (1961) and Alix Shulman (1971).

Goldmark, Karl, 1830–1915, Hungarian composer. His concert overture *Sakuntala* (1865), his symphony *A Rustic Wedding* (1870), and an opera, *The Queen of Sheba* (1875), were very popular. His nephew, **Rubin Goldmark,** 1872–1936, a pupil of Dvořák in New York, was a composer and educator. From 1924 to 1936 he was chairman of the composition department at the Juilliard School of Music. His works include a *Negro Rhapsody* (1923).

Goldoni, Carlo (kär'lō gōldô'nē), 1707–93, Italian dramatist. He was enamored of comedy from childhood, having sketched his first comic drama at eight. He took a degree in law at Padua but thereafter devoted himself to the theater. He created a new Italian character comedy, considered artistically superior to the old commedia dell' arte. This he achieved by building on the old comedy of masks, amplifying written parts; by judicious imitation of Molière and adaptation of classical themes; and by applying his own excellent comedic sense. Goldoni wrote more than 260 dramatic works of all sorts, including opera. Among the most notable of his 150 comedies are *La locandiera* (1753, tr. *The Mistress of the Inn*, 1856), *Il ventaglio* (1763, tr. *The Fan*, 1911), *Il burbero benefico* (1771, tr. *The Beneficent Bear*, 1849), and *La buona figliuola* (1756, tr. *The Accomplished Maid*, 1767), which was set to music by Niccolò Piccinni. Toward the end of his life he was supported in France by a royal pension that was cut off by the Revolution. He died in poverty. See Goldoni's memoirs (1787, in French; tr. by John Black, 1926); biography by H. C. Chatfield-Taylor (1913); study by Heinz Riedt (tr. 1974).

gold rush, influx of prospectors, merchants, adventurers, and others to newly discovered gold fields. One of the most famous of these stampedes in pursuit of riches was the California gold rush. The discovery of gold at Sutter's Mill early in 1848 brought more than 40,000 prospectors to California within two years. Although few of them struck it rich, their presence was an important stimulus to economic growth. Agriculture, commerce, transportation, and industry grew rapidly to meet the needs of the settlers; mining, too, soon became big business as corporations replaced the individual prospector. Vigilante justice and ad hoc political structures quickly gave way to the complex organization of state government. Other large gold rushes took place in Australia (1851–53); WITWATERSRAND, South Africa (1884); and the KLONDIKE, Canada (1897–98). The excitement of the California gold-rush days has been captured in the works of Bret Harte and Jack London. See Oscar Lewis, *Sea Routes to the Gold Fields* (1949); Evelyn Wells and Harry Peterson, *The '49ers* (1949); Pierre Barton, *The Klondike Fever* (1958); R. W. Paul, ed., *The California Gold Discovery* (1966); D. B. Chidsey, *The California Gold Rush* (1968).

Goldsboro, city (1970 pop. 26,810), seat of Wayne co., E central N.C.; inc. 1847. Goldsboro is a marketplace for bright-leaf tobacco and a shipping center for timber, livestock, and farm products. Furniture, textiles, shoes, leather, metal, and electronic goods are manufactured. Wayne Community College and a branch of East Carolina Univ. are there. Seymour-Johnson Air Force Base is nearby.

Goldsborough, Louis Malesherbes, 1805–77, American naval officer, b. Washington, D.C. Appointed a midshipman in 1812, he fought in the Mediterranean and in the Mexican War and was superintendent (1853–57) of Annapolis. In the Civil War, Goldsborough, commanding the North Atlantic Blockading Squadron, directed the fleet that supported Gen. A. E. BURNSIDE in the successful expedition against the North Carolina coast (1862). His James River Squadron was defeated at Drewrys Bluff in the Peninsular campaign (May, 1862). Goldsborough maintained that he could not take Richmond without supporting successes on land by McClellan. The Dept. of the Navy thought otherwise, and the James River Squadron was given to Charles Wilkes as an independent command. Goldsborough was subsequently relieved at his own request but remained in the navy until 1873.

Goldschmidt, Meïr Aaron, (mī'ər ä'rôn gôl'shmĭt), 1819–97, Danish novelist, dramatist, and journalist. In his critical weekly *Corsaren,* he first spared, then ridiculed, Kierkegaard. Goldschmidt's novel *The Jew of Denmark* (1845, tr. 1852) was the first work to portray Jewish life for the Danish public; *The Heir* (1863, tr. 1865) was the first Danish novel to deal with divorce. One of his most popular novels was *The Homeless* (1853–57; tr., 3 vol., 1861).

Goldschmidt, Richard Benedikt, 1878–1958, American zoologist and geneticist, b. Germany, Ph.D. Univ. of Heidelberg, 1902. Goldschmidt taught at the Univ. of Munich (1903–14) and was at the Kaiser Wilhelm Institute, Berlin, from 1914 to 1936. He came to the United States and was professor of zoology at the Univ. of California (1936–48). He studied such phases of heredity and evolution as sex determination and the theory of genes as independent regulators of complex systems. He did much to unify genetic and evolutionary theory, and greatly influenced contemporary biologists. Among his many works are *The Mechanism and Physiology of Sex Determination* (tr. 1923), *The Material Basis of Evolution* (1940), *Theoretical Genetics* (1955), *Portraits from Memory* (1956), and his autobiography, *In and Out of the Ivory Tower* (1960). See biography by Curt Stern (1967).

Goldsmith, Oliver, 1730?–1774, Anglo-Irish author. The son of an Irish clergyman, he was graduated from Trinity College, Dublin, in 1749. He studied medicine at Edinburgh and Leiden, but his career as a physician was quite unsuccessful. In 1756 he settled in London, where he achieved some success as a miscellaneous contributor to periodicals and as the author of *Enquiry into the Present State of Polite Learning in Europe* (1759). But it was not until *The Citizen of the World* (1762), a series of whimsical and satirical essays, that he was recognized as an able man of letters. His fame grew with *The Traveler* (1764), a philosophic poem, and the nostalgic pastoral *The Deserted Village* (1770). However, his literary reputation rests on his two comedies, *The Good-natur'd Man* (1768) and *She Stoops to Conquer* (1773), and his only novel, *The Vicar of Wakefield* (1766). His comedies injected a much-needed sense of realism into the dull, sentimental plays of the period. They are lively, witty, and imbued with an endearing humanity. *The Vicar of Wakefield* is the warm, humorous, if somewhat melodramatic, story of a country parson and his family. Although he earned a great deal of money in his lifetime, Goldsmith's improvidence kept him poor. Boswell depicted him as a ridiculous, blundering, but tender-hearted and generous creature. He had the friendship of many of the literary and artistic great of his day, the most notable being that of Samuel Johnson. See biography by R. M. Wardle (1957); studies by C. M. Kirk (1967), R. Quintana (1967), and R. H. Hopkins (1969).

gold standard: see BIMETALLISM; MONEY.

Goldwater, Barry Morris, 1909–, U.S. Senator (1953–65, 1969–), b. Phoenix, Ariz. He studied at the Univ. of Arizona, but left in 1929 to enter his family's department-store business. After serving in World War II he won two elections to the Phoenix city council. In the U.S. Senate, Goldwater took a consistently conservative position, advocating state right-to-work laws, a reduction of public ownership of utilities, and decreases in appropriations for public welfare and foreign aid. He was vigorous in his attacks on subversive activities and opposed the senatorial censure of Joseph R. McCarthy. Goldwater became the acknowledged leader of the extreme conservative wing of the Republican party. He was reelected Senator in 1958. In 1964, he secured the Republican presidential nomination but was decisively defeated by President Lyndon B. Johnson in the election. He was again elected to the Senate from Arizona in 1968 and reelected in 1974. He wrote *The Conscience of a Conservative* (1960), *Why Not Victory?* (1962), and *The Conscience of a Majority* (1970). See biographies by Jack Bell (1962) and Stephen Shadegg (1962); studies by Karl Hess (1967) and J. H. Kessel (1968).

Goldwater, Robert, 1907–73, American art historian, b. New York City. Goldwater taught at Queens College, N.Y., from 1934 to 1957, when he was appointed professor of fine arts at New York Univ. The same year he also became the director of the Museum of Primitive Art, New York City. Known primarily for his work in African sculpture and modern art, he is the author of *Primitivism in Modern Art* (rev. ed. 1967), *Rufino Tamayo* (1947), *Jacques Lipchitz* (1954), *Gauguin* (1957), *Sculpture from Africa* (1963), and *What Is Modern Sculpture?* (1970).

goldwork. Ornaments, jewelry, and vessels of gold have figured in almost every stage of civilization as symbols of wealth and power. The earliest-known fine goldwork is from Ur in Mesopotamia. Dating from c.3000 B.C. to 2340 B.C., it was executed with great technical proficiency. Egyptian goldwork dating from the Middle Kingdom, including gold jewelry with inlaid gems, and the objects found in the tomb of Tutankhamen, are examples of the fine work done by Egypt's goldsmiths. Goldwork of the Aegean civilization shows the many metalworking techniques—openwork, REPOUSSÉ, EMBOSSING, and INLAYING—used by craftsmen of that time. The VAPHIO CUPS are the most outstanding treasures to survive this period, although many fine examples of goldwork (jewelry, death masks, drinking cups, vases, weapons, and dress ornaments) have been found at Troy, Mycenae, and Tiryns. The goldwork of the Achaemenid dynasty of Persia (6th–4th cent. B.C.) is noted for its extreme opulence and for the technical skill with which it was executed; examples of these treasures are in the British Museum and the Louvre. Archaic Greek and Etruscan goldwork dating from c.700 B.C. to 500 B.C. was strongly influenced by Middle Eastern craftsmen. With its rich and barbaric design, Etruscan goldwork was among the finest in the ancient world. Later Greek work developed exquisite FILIGREE and combined delicate geometric ornament with mythological figures. Roman goldwork followed Greek forms but placed greater emphasis on massive proportion and over-elaborate detail. Greek forms also influenced the goldsmiths of the Byzantine Empire. During the early Middle Ages the best European goldwork was produced by the Celts, particularly in Ireland—the Tara brooch (National Mus., Dublin) is characteristic of their intricate design and fine workmanship. The Anglo-Saxon and Merovingian schools employed spiral, animal, and interlacing ornament, with a splendid display of color and inlaid jewels. In the later Middle Ages a wealth of ecclesiastical crosses, reliquaries, sacred vessels, and altar fronts were produced throughout Europe in a diversity of styles and techniques but consistently with greater emphasis on gem setting and ornamentation. During the Italian Renaissance, the rediscovery of classical forms gave fresh spirit to representational figure work, and the art of the goldsmith was in great demand for both secular as well as sacred ornament. Renaissance goldsmiths, the most celebrated of whom was CELLINI, produced works of great refinement and detail. Later European goldwork tended to repeat Renaissance forms until the CLASSIC REVIVAL of the early 19th cent., when the excavations at Pompeii and Herculaneum revived interest in classical antiquity. Goldwork was equally important in many parts of Asia. India had many centers noted for ornate goldwork and other metalwork. Tibetan goldsmiths created figures having a religious significance. Chinese goldwork is rare because of the scarcity of the metal in China; the examples that survive are exquisite. Central and South America had excellent goldsmiths, and Aztec, Panamanian, and especially INCA goldwork is of extremely high quality. During the craft revival of the 1960s and 70s in the United States, the techniques of gold working that were developed in the past have been used to create complex, innovative designs, principally in jewelry making. To these have been added new techniques including electroforming. See C. H. V. Sutherland, *Gold* (1959).

Goldwyn, Samuel, 1882–1974, American film producer, b. Warsaw, Poland. Goldwyn arrived in the United States in 1896, and with Jesse L. Lasky and Cecil B. DE MILLE he organized the Jesse Lasky Feature Photoplay Company, coproducing *The Squaw Man* (1913). In 1916 he formed the Goldwyn Pictures Corp., which later merged with the company organized by Louis B. MAYER to become Metro-Goldwyn-Mayer. To promote superior screenwriting he founded Eminent Authors Pictures, Inc. (1919). Goldwyn later produced many major films independently, including *Wuthering Heights* (1939), *Guys and Dolls* (1955), and *Porgy and Bess* (1959). He won an Academy Award for *The Best Years of Our Lives* (1947). See his *Behind the Screen* (1923); study by R. E. Griffith (1956).

golem (gō'ləm) [Heb.,=embryo or anything incompletely developed], in medieval Jewish legend, an automatonlike servant made of clay and given life by means of a charm, or *shem* [Heb.,=name, or the name of God]. Golems were attributed in Jewish legend to several rabbis in different European countries. The most famous legend centered around Rabbi Löw, of 16th-century Prague. After molding the golem and endowing it with life, Rabbi Löw was forced to destroy the clay creature after it ran amok. See Joshua Trachtenberg, *Jewish Magic and Superstition* (1939, repr. 1961); Bedrich Thieberger, *The Great Rabbi Loew of Prague: His Life and Work and the Legend of the Golem* (1954).

golf, game of hitting a small hard ball with specially made clubs over an outdoor course sometimes called a links. The object is to deposit the ball in a specified number of cups, or holes, using as few strokes as possible. Although its origin is unknown, the game is identified with Scotland, where as early as 1457 it was banned as a threat to archery practice, which was considered vital to national defense. The Royal and Ancient Golf Club of St. Andrews, Scotland (founded 1754), became the international shrine of golf, and its basic rules are accepted throughout the world. The first British championship was held in 1857, when 11 clubs participated at St. Andrews, and three years later the annual British Open Tournaments were begun with a match at the Prestwick course in Scotland. Canada's Royal Montreal Golf Club (formed 1873) was the first golf club in the Western Hemisphere. There is evidence that golf was played in America in the 17th cent., but it was not until 1888 that the first permanent golf club, the St. Andrews Golf Club of Yonkers, N.Y., was organized by John G. Reid, a Scot. A dispute between the sponsors of two "national" championships led American golfers to found (1894) the United States Golf Association (USGA) as the nation's governing body for golf. The USGA was also charged with conducting annual tournaments, including the National Amateur and National Open (which has both amateur and professional players). The first of these championships followed in 1895. In 1916 the United States Professional Golf Association (PGA) was founded and the annual PGA championship was inaugurated. Another important annual tournament for professionals is the Masters, held annually in Augusta, Ga. Famous international competitions include the Walker Cup (amateur), the Ryder Cup (professional), the Curtis Cup (women amateurs) between British and U.S. teams, and the World Championship (amateur) among teams from all over the world. Golf is one of the few sports that is popular on both the participant and spectator levels. Moreover, unlike many other sports, golf is enjoyed by both men and women, and its self-regulating pace allows it to be played by persons of all ages. Because of such advantages, the growth in golf's popularity has been phenomenal, especially in the United States. Between 1891 and the outbreak of World War II the number of golf courses in the United States grew from fewer than 10 to more than 5,700. Professionals have also benefitted from golf's popularity. Today it is not unusual for a top-ranking professional golfer to earn $100,000 or more in a year. The standard golf course, usually more than 6,000 yd (about 5,500 m) around, is divided into 18 consecutively numbered "holes," each marked by a tall flag and measuring 4.5 in. (11.43 cm) in diameter and 4 in. (10.16 cm) in depth. Each hole is located in a green, a smooth surface of closely cropped grass. The ball is initially driven toward the hole from the tee, a rectangular area approximately 7 ft (2.4 m) long and 3 ft (.9 m) wide. Between the tee and the green is the fairway, often bounded by tall grass and trees (the rough) and containing natural or artificial obstacles (hazards), such as water, sand pits, and mounds (traps). Fairways vary in length from 100 to 650 yd (90–600 m). At present there are two types of ball in use. Americans play with a ball that measures 1.68 in. (4.27 cm) or more in diameter. The British and most others use a ball whose diameter is 1.62 in. (4.11 cm) or more. Both types of ball weigh 1.60 oz (45 grams) or less, and each has a pitted rubberlike surface with a steel or liquid core. A complete set of golf clubs consists of 4 woods, used for long drives; 10 irons, used for shorter shots; and a putter, used for the short distances on the green. Formerly, each of the woods and irons had a name. Now they are simply standardized with the numbers 1 through 4 and 1 through 10 respectively. Play may be for two (a twosome), three (a threesome), or four individuals (a foursome), each using a separate ball. In match play, as in the U.S. amateur tournaments, the winner is determined on the basis of the number of holes won from an opponent; in medal play, as in the U.S. Open tournament, victory is decided by the lowest stroke total for all holes. Competition in both match and medal play may be at 18, 36, 54, or 72 holes as the precontest rules determine. Golf is popular in Australia, Canada, and South Africa, in addition to the United States and Great Britain. The most famous golfer of modern times was Robert Tyre ("Bobby") Jones, Jr., who in 1930 won the U.S. Amateur and Open, and the British Amateur and Open championships, a feat accomplished by no other golfer. Other outstanding golfers, past and present, include Thomas D. Armour, Walter C. Hagen, William Benjamin ("Ben") Hogan, John Byron Nelson, Jr., Francis D. Ouimet, Gene Sarazen, Samuel Jackson Snead, Patricia ("Patty") Berg, Glenna Collett (Glenna Collett Vare), Thomas Henry Cotton, James Newton Demaret, Mildred ("Babe") Didrikson (Mildred Didrikson Zaharias), Arthur D'Arcy ("Bobby") Locke, Cary Middlecoff, Lloyd Mangrum, John Henry Taylor, Harry Vardon, Arnold Palmer, Jack Nicklaus, and Lee Trevino. See Charles Price, *The World of Golf* (1962); William Grimsley, *Golf: Its History, People and Events* (1966); Ben Bruce and Evelyn Davies, *Beginning Golf* (1968); Nevin H. Gibson, *Great Moments in Golf* (1972) and *A Pictorial History of Golf* (1974); Webster Evans, *Encyclopedia of Golf* (1974).

Golgi, Camillo (kämēl'lō gôl'jē), 1844–1926, Italian physician, noted as a neurologist and histologist. He shared with Ramón y Cajal the 1906 Nobel Prize in Physiology and Medicine for work on the structure of the nervous system. He introduced (c.1870) a method of staining nerve tissue with silver nitrate that he used (1883) to demonstrate certain nerve cells (Golgi cells) in the central nervous system. He observed (1909) the Golgi apparatus, a part of the cytoplasm distinguishable by special staining and known as the Golgi bodies when in the form of separate particles. He recognized that the three types of malaria are caused by different protozoan organisms. Golgi taught at the Univ. of Pavia from 1875.

Golgotha (gŏl'gəthə), the same as CALVARY.

Goliad (gō'lēăd), city (1970 pop. 1,709), seat of Goliad co., S Texas, on the San Antonio River, SE of San Antonio. It is a market for the surrounding farm region. A Spanish mission and presidio, originally established on Lavaca Bay, moved to Goliad, then called La Bahia, in 1749. An unthriving frontier town, it was captured and briefly held by filibustering expeditions from the United States in 1812 and 1821. After the start of the Texas Revolution (1836), Goliad was seized by Texan forces under Col. J. W. FANNIN. With the advance of Mexican troops into Texas, Fannin evacuated Goliad with more than 300 men and headed for Victoria. He was overtaken by the Mexicans and on March 20, 1836, after a hopeless battle, surrendered unconditionally. On March 27 most of the prisoners were shot in cold blood by the Mexicans. This Goliad massacre contributed to the battle cry of the victorious Texans at San Jacinto, "Remember the Alamo! Remember Goliad!" The American settlement grew up across the river, and the restored mission and the ruins of the old presidio are today in a state park. The ruins of another mission (1754) are a few miles to the southwest.

Goliardic songs (gōlēär'dĭk), Late Latin poetry of the "wandering scholars," or Goliards. The Goliards included university students who went from one European university to another, scholars who had completed their studies but were unable to buy benefices (ecclesiastical offices), unfrocked priests, runaway monks, and clerks. They begged and sang their way from place to place. Their existence is seen as a reaction against the medieval ascetic ideal and as evidence of the decline in popularity of the increasingly rigorous church. First appearing in large numbers in the 11th cent., the *vagi* or *vagantes* multiplied into a horde of unruly vagabonds. It was formerly believed that in the 13th cent. they joined to form a burlesque religious order, but it is now thought that the *ordo vagorum*, with its legendary archpoet Bishop Golias (Goliath) as grand master, was a literary fiction. The name *Goliards* may have derived from this same Golias. Although the church began (c.1230) to take measures against the Goliards, later church edicts against them testify to their continued, though dwindled, existence. The scandal associated with the Goliards should not obscure the merits of their verse. Their songs, in lilting bastard Latin verse with stressed rhymes, mimic the form of medieval hymns. They include lusty paeans to love and wine and the vagabond life as well as skillful attacks on the immorality of church life and churchmen. Although most of the songs are anonymous or bear pseudonyms, some of the best are attributed to Archipoeta, or the Archpoet (fl. 1161–65), and others to Primus, who was Hugo d'Orléans (fl. early 12th cent.). Many were formerly wrongly attributed to Walter MAP. The songs are often called *carmina burana*, after the title of the collection found in the abbey of Benediktbeuern and edited by J. A. Schmeller (4th ed., 1907). Widely collected and edited, the songs appear in English translation in *The Cambridge Songs* (ed. by Karl Breul, 1915), J. A. Symonds, *Wine, Women, and Song* (1884), H. J. Waddell, *Mediaeval Latin Lyrics* (rev. ed. 1933), and G. F. Whicher, *The Goliard Poets* (1949). Carl Orff set many of them to music simply and impressively in a secular cantata entitled *Carmina burana* (1937). See H. J. Waddell, *The Wandering Scholars* (7th ed. 1967).

Goliath (gōlī'əth), gigantic Philistine, who challenged the Israelites. The young David, fortified by faith, accepted the challenge and killed him with a stone from a sling. 1 Sam. 17; 21.9; 22.10; 2 Sam. 21.19.

Gollancz, Sir Hermann (gŏl'ənts), 1852–1930, English rabbi and authority on Hebrew language and literature. He was professor of Hebrew (1902–24) at University College, London. In 1902 he edited an English version of the Bible for Jewish use. His publications include translations from Hebrew and Aramaic. He was knighted in 1923.

Golovnin, Vasily Mikhailovich (vəsē'lyē mēkhī'ləvĭch gələvnyĕn'), 1776–1831, Russian explorer and writer. Sent in 1807 to make a geographical survey of Kamchatka and the Russian possessions in Alaska, he was captured and imprisoned (1811–13) by the Japanese. Later, in circumnavigating the world, he made a second trip (1817–19) to Kamchatka and the Aleutians. He wrote *Narrative of My Captivity in Japan, during the Years 1811, 1812, 1813* (1816, tr. 1818 and 1824).

Goltz, Colmar, Freiherr von der (kôl'mär frī'hĕr fən dər gôlts), 1843–1916, Prussian field marshal and military historian. A soldier, he served in the Austro-Prussian War (1866) and the Franco-Prussian War (1870–71). He later gained renown as a professor of military history. His writings include the much-celebrated *Nation in Arms* (1883, tr. 1913). In Turkish service from 1883 to 1896, he reorganized the Turkish army. He was (1914) governor general of Belgium in World War I, but was soon transferred to the Turkish front, where he commanded the Turkish 1st Army in Mesopotamia until April, 1916, when he died, possibly of poison.

Goltzius, Hendrik (hĕn'drĭk gôlt'sēŭs), 1558–1617, Dutch line engraver and painter; son of a glass painter. Early in life he established himself as a printer in Haarlem, to which he returned after extensive travel in Italy and Germany. As an engraver he was extremely versatile, imitating successfully the styles of Lucas van Leyden and Dürer. He is best known for his engravings after the work of these and of various Italian masters and for his engraved portraits. He produced 500 plates of great virtuosity and considerable beauty.

Golytsin: see GALLITZIN.

Gombert, Nicolas (nēkôlä' gôNbĕr'), c.1500–c.1560, Flemish composer. Gombert was the greatest follower of Josquin des Prés. He served at the court of Emperor Charles V. His sacred works make great use of imitative counterpoint; his secular songs express delight in nature.

Gombos, Julius (göm'bōsh), Hung. *Gömbös Gyula*, 1886–1936, Hungarian premier and officer. He was minister of war under the premiership of Stephen Bethlen (1921–31) and of Julius Károlyi (1931–32). In 1932, Gombos became premier. He ruled with authoritarian methods and introduced anti-Semitic bills in the legislature. Although favoring a national brand of fascism at home, Gombos opposed the spread of Nazi German influence and for this purpose drew close to Italy and Austria. After his sudden death, however, Hungary drifted toward the new Rome-Berlin Axis.

Gombrich, Ernst H., 1909–, British art historian and scholar, b. Vienna. Gombrich is best known for his superb art survey *The Story of Art* (1950), in which he distinguishes between representational art based on seeing and that based on understanding. This theory of visual perception is further developed in *Art and Illusion (1956),* in which he applies contemporary work in psychology to the framework of art history. Among his later works are two studies of Renaissance art, *Norm and Form* (1966) and *Symbolic Images* (1972).

Gombrowicz, Witold (vē'tōld gōmbrō'vĭch), 1904–69, Polish writer. After studying law at the Univ. of Warsaw, Gombrowicz published his first collection of short stories (1933). This was followed in 1937 by his satirical novel *Ferdydurke* (tr. 1961), which created a literary scandal. From 1938 to 1962 he lived in Buenos Aires; his work was not published in Poland until the 1950s. His reputation was established with the translation of his works into French, German, and English. From 1964 until his death Gombrowicz lived in France. His later major novels include *Trans-Atlantyk* (1953), *Pornografia* (1960, tr. 1966) and *Kosmos* (1965; tr. *Cosmos*, 1967). Gombrowicz is recognized as an original satirist, an existential innovator who mingled the real with the unreal to convey a highly personal vision of the world. His plays include *Princess Ivona* (1938, tr. 1969) and *The Marriage* (1947, tr. 1969). See his *A Kind of Testament* (tr. 1972).

Gomel (gō'mĕl, –məl, Rus. gô'mĭl), city (1970 pop. 272,000), capital of Gomel oblast, W European USSR, on the Sozh River, a tributary of the Dnepr. A river port and a large railroad junction in an agricultural area, it is the second largest city in Belorussia. The city's industries produce machinery, textiles, building materials, food products, electrical equipment, and fertilizers. First mentioned as Gomiy in 1142, when it was included in Kievan Russia, it became part of Lithuania in 1537. It was much fought over and passed to Poland by the Treaty of Andrusov (1667) and to Russia in 1772. Until World War II about 40% of the population was Jewish. In a park in Gomel are a palace and the Petropavlovsk Cathedral (founded 1819).

Gomer (gō'mər). **1** Wife of the prophet HOSEA. Hosea 1.3. **2** Son of Japheth and eponym of a people, probably the Cimmerians. Gen. 10.2; 1 Chron. 1.5; Ezek. 38.6.

Gómez, José Miguel (hōsā' mēgĕl' gō'mĕs), 1858–1921, president of Cuba (1909–13). He took part in the Ten Years War (1868–78) and the successful revolution begun in 1895. A liberal, he was defeated for the presidency in 1906 by ESTRADA PALMA but led an uprising that caused U.S. intervention and his own successful election. Affable and popular, he made some attempt to increase Cuba's material progress, but his administration was marred by corrupt practices. He was succeeded by Mario G. MENOCAL. In 1920, after unsuccessfully running against Alfredo ZAYAS, he charged his opponents with fraud, failed to gain support, and went into exile in New York City, where he died.

Gómez, Juan Vicente (hwän vēsän'tā), 1857–1935, caudillo of Venezuela (1908–35). Of Indian and white parentage, Gómez was born on a ranch in the Western Andes and grew up a nearly illiterate cattle herdsman. He catapulted into the national scene in 1899 when he led his guerrilla henchmen in support of Cipriano CASTRO, under whom he was vice president. When Castro was overthrown, Gómez became president, and although he relinquished the title for long intervals, he ruled continuously from his estate near Maracay. Congress conferred on him the title El Benemérito (the meritorious), but his enemies dubbed him El Bagre (the catfish) because of a supposed facial resemblance enhanced by a bushy mustache. Though cordial and simple in manner, Gómez was an absolute tyrant whose secret police ferreted out opposition and subjected victims to imprisonment and torture. He was also a patriot whose shrewdness and industry brought his country economic stability. Even before the oil development at Lake Maracaibo after 1918, he had put Venezuela on a sound financial basis; he was noted for fair dealing with foreign investors, and the capital he attracted made it possible for him to build Venezuela into a modern nation of railroads, highways, and other public works. Public education during his regime advanced little. In enriching the nation, he made himself enormously wealthy. He attempted to make the country a personal fief; nepotism was rife. Though unmarried, he sired between 80 and 100 offspring, and many of these, as well as his local henchmen, filled civil positions; he dominated them as he did other men by savage force of character. See biographies by D. J. Clinton (1936), Thomas Rourke (1936), and John Lavin (1954).

Gómez de Avellaneda, Gertrudis (hĕrtro͞o'thĕs gō'mĕth dā ävĕlyänä'thä), 1814–73, Spanish poet, b. Cuba. She went to Spain in 1836. Her passionate and poignant verses reflecting an unhappy love affair won her a high place among Spanish romantic poets. She also wrote problem novels, such as the antislavery *El Mulato Sab* (1841), and dramas on historical and religious subjects, including *Alfonso Munio* (1844), *Saúl* (1849), and *Baltasar* (1858).

Gómez de la Serna, Ramón (rämōn' gō'māth dā lä sĕr'nä), 1888–1963, Spanish novelist, biographer, and critic, b. Madrid. One of the most prolific and imaginative of modern Spanish writers, Gómez de la Serna was a precursor of surrealism. He sought to express the subconscious and portrayed modern man as a mannequin. He invented the *greguería*, a kind of surrealist metaphor in epigram form combining humor and poetic insight. Two collections of these are his *Flor de greguerías* (1933) and *Some Greguerías* (tr. 1944). Gómez de la Serna is known simply as Ramón, and his mode of literary expression as *ramonismo.* Among his many works are an autobiography (1948), lives of El Greco and Goya, and the novels *El doctor inverosímil* (1921) and *El torero Caracho* (1926). *Antología* (1955) and *Obras completas* (1956) are later collections of his works.

Gómez Palacio: see TORREÓN.

Gómez y Báez, Máximo (mäk'sēmō, ē bä'ās), 1836–1905, Cuban revolutionary, b. Dominican Republic. He served in the Spanish army but joined the Cuban revolutionists in 1868 and became commander in chief in 1873. At the end (1878) of the Ten Years War, he left Cuba but returned to serve in the successful revolution of 1895.

Gomorrah or **Gomorrha** (both: gəmŏr'ə), city, destroyed with SODOM.

Gompers, Samuel (gŏm'pərz), 1850–1924, American labor leader, b. London. He emigrated to the United States with his parents in 1863. He worked as a cigar maker and in 1864 joined the local union, serving as its president from 1874 to 1881, when he helped to found the Federation of Organized Trades and Labor Unions. It was reorganized in 1886 and became the American Federation of Labor, of which Gompers was first president and of which he remained president, except for the year 1895, until his death. He directed the successful battle with the KNIGHTS OF LABOR for supremacy, kept the union free from political entanglements in the early days, and refused to entertain various cooperative business plans, socialistic ideas, and radical programs, maintaining that more wages, shorter hours, and greater freedom were the just aims of labor. He came to be recognized as the leading spokesman for the labor movement, and his pronouncements carried much weight. During World War I, he organized and headed the War Committee on Labor; and as a member of the Advisory Commission to the Council of National Defense, he helped to hold organized labor loyal to the government program. A man of great personal integrity, he did much to make organized labor respected. See AMERICAN FEDERATION OF LABOR AND CONGRESS OF INDUSTRIAL ORGANIZATIONS. See his autobiography, *Seventy Years of Life and Labor* (1925, repr. 1967); biographies by Will Chasan (1971) and G. E. Stearn, ed. (1971); L. S. Reed, *The Labor Philosophy of Samuel Gompers* (1930, repr. 1966); F. C. Thorne, *Samuel Gompers, American Statesman* (1957, repr. 1969); S. B. Kaufman, *Samuel Gompers and the Origins of the American Federation of Labor, 1848–1896* (1973).

Gomułka, Władysław (vlädĭs'läf gəmōōl'kə), 1905–, Polish Communist leader. Long a Communist, he helped establish the Polish Workers' party and was (1943–49) secretary of its central committee. After World War II, he served (1945–49) as deputy premier of Poland. A Polish nationalist, he was purged in 1949 for alleged sympathy with the Yugoslav Communist leader, Josip Broz Tito, and was arrested in 1951. Freed in 1954, he was readmitted (1956) to the United Workers' (Communist) party. In Oct., 1956, on the wave of Polish resentment of USSR domination, Gomułka became first secretary of the party despite Soviet pressures. From this post he dominated the Polish government, continuing close ties with the USSR but establishing greater freedom of action for Poland and bringing some social and economic liberalization. He was forced to resign as first secretary in Dec., 1970, following widespread rioting by Polish workers in protest against food price increases announced by the government. In 1971 he was suspended from the party's central committee and removed from the council of state. See biography by Nicholas Bethell (rev. ed. 1972).

gonadotropic hormone (gō"nădətrŏp'ĭk) or **gonadotropin,** any one of three glycoprotein (see PROTEIN) HORMONES released by either the anterior PITUITARY GLAND or the placenta (the organ in which maternal and fetal blood exchange nutrients and waste products) that have various effects upon the OVARIES and testes (see TESTIS). The release of follicle-stimulating hormone (FSH), one of the pituitary hormones, is triggered by the action of follicle-stimulating hormone-releasing factor (FSH-RF); the release of lutenizing hormone (LH), the other pituitary hormone, is triggered by lutenizing hormone-releasing factor (LH-RF). This latter factor has been purified extensively and appears to be a peptide composed of ten amino acids. Both releasing factors are synthesized in the hypothalamus (that portion of the brain nearest the pituitary) and travel in the blood stream to the anterior pituitary, where—by means that are not clearly understood—they cause the release of their respective gonadotropic hormones. In the female, FSH causes an increase in the weight of the ovaries and encourages the growth of Graafian follicles (containing maturing eggs); in males FSH produces spermatogenesis in the testes. In females, secretion of LH is associated with the maturation of the follicles, the manifestation of heat (or estrus), and the release of the egg from the follicle, which is transformed into a corpus luteum. In males LH stimulates the testes to release testosterone. Sex hormones released from the ovaries and testes eventually reach the hypothalamus and help to regulate the hormonal cycle. Human chorionic gonadotropin (HCG), produced in the placenta, helps to maintain pregnancy once a fetus begins to develop. It appears in the urine in approximately the first week after the first missed menstrual period and is the basis for two kinds of pregnancy tests; in the Ascheim-Zondek test it causes the ovaries of an immature female rat or mouse to gain weight and produce ripened follicles and in the Friedman test it stimulates female rabbits to ovulate.

Gonaïves (gōnāēv'), city (1971 pop. 29,261), W Haiti, a port on the Gulf of Gonaïves. The region's agricultural products (including cotton, sugar, and bananas) are exported from the city's fine harbor. Gonaïves is also a major commercial center. Haiti's independence was proclaimed there in 1804. The Gulf of Gonaïves, situated in the pincers of two mountainous peninsulas, is considered one of the most beautiful in the world.

Gonbad-e Kavus (gōnbäd'ĕ kävōōs'), city (1966 pop. 40,667), Mazanderan prov., N Iran, on the Gorgan River. It is an agricultural trade center.

Gonçalves Dias, Antônio (əntō'nyōō gōōnsäl'vəs dē'əs), 1823–64, Brazilian poet and dramatist. A leading writer of the romantic school, he is noted for his strong nativist feeling and his glorification of the Brazilian Indian. His nostalgic poem "Canção in exílio" might be called the Brazilian national poem. His volumes of poetry include *Primeiros cantos* (1846), *Segundos cantos* (1846), *Últimos cantos* (1851), and *Os Timbiras* (1857). Gonçalves Dias wrote several plays and a dictionary of the Tupi language (1858). He was drowned in a shipwreck.

Goncharov, Ivan Aleksandrovich (ēvän' əlyĭksän'drəvĭch gənchərôf'), 1812–91, Russian novelist. Goncharov was a governmental official from 1834 to 1867. His realistic and satirical novel *Oblomov* (1858, tr. 1929) is a portrayal of the indolent nobleman common in Russia c.1860. The Russian word *Oblomovism* was coined to describe the lassitude the protagonist of the novel typified. Goncharov's other novels, *A Common Story* (1847, tr. 1894) and *The Precipice* (1869, tr. 1915), are variations on the same theme. He also wrote *The Frigate Pallas* (1858), based on his voyage to England, Africa, and Japan. See biography by Alexandra and Sverre Lyngstad (1971); study by Milton Ehre (1973).

Goncourt, Edmond Louis Antoine Huot de (ĕdmôN' lwē äNtwän' üō' də gôNkōōr'), 1822–96, and **Jules Alfred Huot de Goncourt** (zhül älfrĕd'), 1830–70, French authors. Brothers, they were known, for their close association in art and literature, as "les deux Goncourt." They began as artists, touring France in 1849 and keeping notes that were soon to turn them toward literature. They became art critics and historians of art, unsuccessful dramatists, promoters of Japanese art, and, in collaboration, the authors of a number of well-known novels of the naturalist school, including *Sœur Philomène* (1861), *Renée Mauperin* (1864, tr. 1887), *Germinie Lacerteux* (1864), *Mme Gervaisais* (1869), and a study, *The Woman of the Eighteenth Century* (1862, tr. 1927). In 1851 the brothers began the *Journal des Goncourt* (9 vol., 1887–96; tr. of selections by Lewis Galantière, 1937), an immensely successful publication devoted to an intimate account of Parisian society for 40 years. They affected an elaborate and contorted style, employed telegraphic brevity on occasion, and often selected subjects of sensational value. Their work paved the way for both naturalism and impressionism. After Jules's death Edmond wrote the novels *La Fille Élisa* (1877, tr. *Elisa*, 1959), *Les Frères Zemganno* (1879), and *Chérie* (1884). In his will Edmond provided for the founding of the Goncourt Academy (officially recognized 1903), which makes an annual award, the Goncourt Prize, for fiction. See André Billy, *The Goncourt Brothers* (1954, tr. 1960).

Gond (gŏnd), ethnic group in central India. The group is now divided among the states of Andhra Pradesh, Maharshtra, and Madhya Pradesh; in Madhya Pradesh there was a small but powerful Gond kingdom until the 18th cent. The Gonds, predominantly Hindu, speak a Dravidian language and are mainly organized into tribes in small villages. They number approximately 3,300,000. See Verrier Elwin, *Leaves from the Jungle; Life in a Gond Village* (2d ed. 1958); Stephen Fuchs, *The Gond and Bhumia of Eastern Mandla* (2d ed. 1968).

Gonda (gōn'də), town (1971 pop. 52,647), Uttar Pradesh state, N India, on the Sarayu River and the Lucknow-Gorakhpur railroad. Gonda is a district administrative center and a market for maize, sugarcane, pulses, and wheat. It was founded by the Rajput Man Singh in the early 16th cent. during the reign of Mogul emperor Akbar.

Gondar (gŏn'dər), town (1970 est. pop. 35,300), capital of Begemdir and Simen prov., NW Ethiopia, at an altitude of c.7,300 ft (2,225 m). It is a regional trade center and a tourist spot. Once Ethiopia's largest city and a center of religion and art, Gondar served as the capital of Ethiopia from c.1635 to 1867. In the 19th cent. the city declined, and in 1887 it was sacked by Sudanese Mahdists (see MAHDI). Gondar is noted for its architectural ruins and for its handicrafts.

Gondi, Paul de: see RETZ, JEAN FRANÇOIS PAUL DE GONDI, CARDINAL DE.

Gondola, Giovanni: see GUNDULIĆ, IVAN.

Gondomar, Diego Sarmiento de Acuña, conde de (gŏn'dəmär, Span. dyā'gō särmyān'tō thā äkōō'nyä kōn'dā thā gōndōmär'), 1567?–1626, Spanish ambassador to England (1613–18, 1620–22). He gained great influence over JAMES I and dissuaded him from giving real assistance to James's son-in-law, FREDERICK THE WINTER KING, at the outset of the Thirty Years War. He also demanded the execution (1618) of Sir Walter Raleigh. Gondomar was highly unpopular in England and was attacked in Thomas Middleton's play *A Game at Chess.*

Gondwanaland (gŏnd"wä'nəlănd"): see CONTINENTAL DRIFT.

gong, percussion instrument consisting of a disk with upturned edges, 3 ft (91 cm) or more in diameter in the modern orchestra, usually made of bronze, and struck with a mallet or drumstick. It is

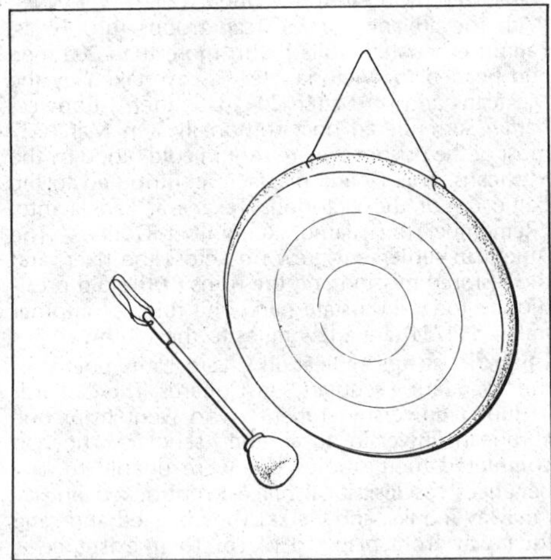

Gong

of ancient Oriental origin and is also called tamtam. First used in European music in the funeral march of Gossec's *Mirabeau* (1791), the gong has since been a regular member of the orchestra, but it is used sparingly.

Góngora y Argote, Luis de (lōōēs' dā gōn'gōrä ē ärgō'tā), 1561–1627, poet of the Spanish Golden Age; b. Cordova. Of a cultured family, he studied in Salamanca and became a prebendary (1585?) and later a priest (1617). In his youth he was gay and pleasure loving. His early religious duties were largely diplomatic and took him through much of Spain. Later he spent two years at court and became involved in a controversy with young Quevedo, who lampooned him. Góngora, who has been called Spain's greatest poet, successfully wove Renaissance and popular poetry into an original and elegant form. A poet of great sophistication, wit, and culture, he expressed an extraordinary visual imagination. The countervailing qualities of irony and melancholy enhanced his work as well. His earlier poetry includes sonnets, at which he excelled, and ballads. His fame, however, rests primarily upon the great, complex, stylized works of his maturity; these include *Panegyrico al duque de Lerma* (1609), *Fábula de Polifemo y Galatea* (1613?), and the unfinished pastoral idyll, *Las Soledades* (1613), now considered his masterpiece. Góngora's style gave rise to the term *Gongorism,* signifying a baroque tendency in Spanish literature that is the equivalent of euphuism in England. Characteristic elements of his style include an innovative use of the metaphor, latinization of vocabulary, and classical and mythological allusion. The critical controversy over *Las Soledades* continued for three centuries. Although his collected works were not published until 1921, Góngora greatly influenced modern Spanish poetry.

gonorrhea (gŏnərē'ə), infectious disease caused by a gonococcus (*Neisseria gonorrheae*), involving chiefly the mucous membranes of the genitourinary tract. It may occasionally spread to membranes in other parts of the body, especially those of the joints and the eyes. Since the principal mode of transmission is sexual contact, gonorrhea is classified as a VENEREAL DISEASE; contaminated clothing or bath water may also transmit the disease to extremely susceptible individuals such as female infants and children. Gonorrheal conjunctivitis was once a prominent cause of blindness in the newborn, the infection being transmitted from an infected birth canal in the mother. Routine use of silver nitrate solution in the eyes of every infant at birth has largely overcome this problem. Gonorrhea in the adult causes inflammation of the genital organs and urethra and, if not checked, there is extension to the deeper urinary and genital structures that can result in sterility. Examination of urethral discharge reveals the presence of the gonococcus organisms. The organisms are highly sensitive to most antibiotics, especially penicillin. There was an upsurge in the incidence of gonorrhea in the United States from 1960 to 1972.

Gonsalvo de Córdoba: see FERNÁNDEZ DE CÓRDOBA, GONZALO.

Gonzaga (gōntsä'gä), Italian princely house that ruled MANTUA (1328–1708), MONTFERRAT (1536–1708), and GUASTALLA (1539–1746). The family name is derived from the castle of Gonzaga, a village near Mantua. **Luigi Gonzaga,** 1267–1360, became captain general of Mantua in 1328. The power of his descendants grew in the 14th cent., and in 1433, Holy Roman Emperor Sigismund made **Gian Francesco Gonzaga,** 1395–1444, marquis of Mantua. His grandson, **Francesco Gonzaga,** 1466–1519, married Isabella d'ESTE. At the outset of the ITALIAN WARS, in which Spain and France vied for control of Italy, he led the allied troops that defeated (1495) King Charles VIII of France at Fornovo. In order to preserve the independence of Mantua, Francesco fought in turn for Venice, for the French, and for Pope Julius II. The court of Mantua, long a center of the arts and letters, was particularly brilliant under Francesco and Isabella. Their son and successor, **Federico** or **Federigo Gonzaga,** 1500–40, was made (1530) duke of Mantua by Holy Roman Emperor Charles V. In 1536 he acquired Montferrat, which continued to be claimed by Savoy. His brother **Ercole Gonzaga,** 1505–63, cardinal of the Roman Catholic Church, was long regent of the duchy. He furthered learning and the arts and presided (1562–63) over the Council of Trent. A younger brother, **Ferrante Gonzaga,** 1507–57, was generalissimo of Charles V in Italy, France, and Flanders. He acquired (1539) the county of Guastalla, which remained with his direct descendants until their extinction in 1746; in 1748 it was annexed to the duchy of Parma. In 1627 the senior male line of the older branch, ruling Mantua and Montferrat, became extinct. A cadet line, established in France, had succeeded, by marriage, to the duchies of Nevers or NIVERNAIS and RETHEL and in 1627 began to claim the succession to Mantua and Montferrat, which were strategically located on the Lombard plain near the Alpine passes. Its claim was strengthened by the marriage of Maria Gonzaga, sole heiress of the senior line, to Charles de Rethel, son of the duke of Nevers. France supported the Nevers branch, while Hapsburg Spain and Austria, anxious lest France gain a foothold in N Italy, supported the claims of the Guastalla branch. War between France and Spain broke out over the contested succession. The Nevers branch ultimately won with the signing of the Treaty of Cherasco (1631) and ruled Mantua and Montferrat until it in turn became extinct (1708) during the War of the Spanish Succession. Hapsburg Austria then annexed Mantua, and Savoy annexed Montferrat. See S. J. C. Brinton, *The Gonzaga* (1927).

Gonzales, Richard Alonzo (gŏnzăl'ĭs), 1928–, American tennis player, known as Pancho Gonzales, b. Los Angeles, of Mexican parentage. After two straight wins in both the U.S. lawn and clay court singles championships (1948, 1949), he gained an international reputation in 1949 as a member of the U.S. teams that won the Wimbledon, England, and Davis Cup competitions. Gonzales, noted for his powerful service and strong court play, turned professional in 1949. After an unsuccessful cross-country tour he went into semiretirement. Making a spectacular comeback in 1954, he remained the professional champion (except for 1960) until he retired in 1961. Returning again to competition, he reached the U.S. professional finals in 1964 and remained an active competitor throughout the 1960s. See his autobiography, *Man with a Racket* (1959).

González, Fernán: see FERNÁN GONZÁLEZ.

González, Julio (ho͞ol'yō gōnthä'lĕth), 1876–1942, Spanish sculptor. The son of a goldsmith and sculptor, González went to Paris in 1900. There he met Picasso and taught him techniques of iron welding and was in turn influenced by certain of Picasso's cubist ideas. Executed with ingenuity, González's semiabstract sculptures (e.g., *Hombre-Cactus,* 1939–40) are often free interpretations of the human figure. They distinguish him as one of the outstanding sculptors of the 20th cent. Some of his work is in the Museum of Modern Art, New York City. See study by Andrew Ritchie (1956).

González de Ávila, Gil (hĕl gōnthä'lĕth dā ä'vēlä), d. 1543, Spanish conquistador. Despite the opposition of Pedro ARIAS DE ÁVILA, he conquered Honduras, Costa Rica, and Nicaragua in 1522. He then fled to the island of Hispaniola to avoid trouble with Arias de Ávila. His claims were usurped (1523) by Francisco FERNÁNDEZ DE CÓRDOBA.

González Martínez, Enrique (ānrē'kā gōnsä'lĕs märtē'nĕs), 1871–1952, Mexican poet, physician, and diplomat. His early poetry, written during the 17 years of his medical practice, showed the influence of the modernist Rubén Darío and the French symbolists. In 1911 he rejected the artificial aestheticism of MODERNISMO in his poem *Los senderos ocultos* [hidden paths], beginning with the famous exhortation, "Wring the necks of the deceitful swans." He served in later years as ambassador to Argentina, Chile, and Spain. He collected and edited his poetry in three volumes of *Poesías* (1938–40).

González Prada, Manuel (mänwĕl' gōnsä'lĕs prä'thä), 1848–1918, Peruvian writer and political reformer, b. Lima. One of the most brilliant figures in Spanish American letters, he was a master of satire and invective. With apostolic zeal he took up the defense of the exploited Indian, and in his eloquent essays, speeches, and polemical writings he hurled demolishing broadsides at the landowning oligarchy that had ruled Peru since colonial days. He advocated radical social reform along nationalistic lines and became the mentor of a generation of young radicals. González Prada was also an innovator in poetry, introducing new devices and revitalizing Spanish verse by cultivating unusual forms, such as the triolet, the rondel, and the Malayan pantun. More than nine books of poetry and many editions of his essays were published, a number of them posthumously. Some of his prose collections are *Páginas libres* (1894), *Nuestros Indios* (1904), and *Horas de lucha* (1908).

goober: see PEANUT.

Gooch, George Peabody, 1873–1968, English historian. He was educated at the Univ. of London and at Cambridge. He had practical experience in politics as a Liberal member of Parliament from 1906 to 1910, and his interest in democratic political ideas was expressed especially in his *History of Democratic Ideas in the Seventeenth Century* (1898; new ed., with additions by Harold J. Laski, 1927; 2d ed. 1959) and *Political Thought in England from Bacon to Halifax* (1914). Gooch was associated with Harold W. V. Temperley in diplomatic studies; they edited *British Documents on the Origins of the War 1898–1938* (13 vol., 1926–38). With Sir Adolphus W. Ward, he edited *The Cambridge History of British Foreign Policy, 1783–1919* (3 vol., 1922–23). Gooch also became an authority on the history of Germany and wrote a useful survey of that country in the time of the Weimar Republic, *Germany* (1925); a biography of Frederick II (1947); and essays in *Studies in German History* (1948). His *History and Historians in the Nineteenth Century* (1913; 2d ed. 1946) is one of the most valuable books of modern historiography. Among his numerous other works is the textbook, *History of Modern Europe, 1878–1919* (1923). Gooch's historical writing is characterized by a scrupulous attention to detail.

Gooch, Sir William, 1681–1751, colonial governor of Virginia (1727–49), b. Yarmouth, England. He came to Virginia after distinguished service with the British army. Nominally, Gooch was only lieutenant governor, but he was in fact the real chief executive in the colony for 22 years. He defended the colonists before the Board of Trade, was an influence in their favor with Parliament, promoted tobacco growing, and was on generally good terms with the burgesses. His resignation because of failing health was profoundly regretted by the Virginians. Gooch was created baronet in 1746 and promoted major general in 1747. See biography by P. S. Flippin (1926).

Good, James Isaac, 1850–1924, American clergyman of the German Reformed Church, b. York, Pa. He held pastorates in York, Philadelphia, and Reading, Pa., and in 1890 he became professor in the School of Theology of Ursinus College. He was dean from 1893 to 1907, and in 1907 he became professor of church history and liturgics at the Central Theological Seminary, Dayton, Ohio. From 1911 to 1914 he was president of the General Synod of the Reformed Church in the United States. He wrote many books on the origins and history of the Reformed Church in Germany and the United States. See biography by C. H. Gramm (1944).

Goode, John Paul (go͝od), 1862–1932, American geographer and cartographer, b. Stewartville, Minn., grad. Univ. of Minnesota, 1889, Ph.D. Univ. of Pennsylvania, 1901. He taught geography at the Univ. of Pennsylvania (1901–17) and at the Univ. of Chicago (1917–28). Goode is noted for devising the interrupted homolosine projection, which combines the best qualities of the homolographic (or Mollweide) and sinusoidal projections; it is widely used for maps that portray global distribution. Goode edited many maps and books on geography, including the well-known *Goode's School Atlas* (1923; many later editions), now entitled *Goode's World Atlas.*

Goodell, William (go͝odĕl'), 1792–1867, American missionary in the Near East, b. Templeton, Mass. He went in 1823, for the American Board of Commissioners for Foreign Missions, to what is now Beirut, Lebanon, where he established the Congregationalist mission. In 1831 he went to Constantinople and there established a mission for the Armenians of the city. His translation of the Bible into Armeno-Turkish occupied 20 years. The success of Congregational missions in Turkey is largely founded upon his work. His memoirs were edited by E. D. G. Prime under the title *Forty Years in the Turkish Empire* (1876).

Goodenough's Island: see RAROTONGA.

Good Friday [probably from *God's Friday*], anniversary of Jesus' death on the Cross, the Friday before Easter, observed as a day of mourning and penitence. In the Orthodox, Roman Catholic, and Anglican churches, the celebration of Mass is suspended. In the Roman Catholic Church, a special Good Friday service is held, beginning at three o'clock in the afternoon, consisting of readings (Isa. 52.15–53.12; Heb. 4.14–16, 5.7–9; John 18.1–19.42), solemn prayers, the adoration of the cross, and the communion service (using a previously consecrated Host). The altar is completely bare. The present observance replaces the former Mass of the Presanctified, following the liturgical changes enacted by Pope Pius XII in 1956 and the general liturgical reform initiated at the Second Vatican Council.

Good Hope, Cape of: see CAPE PROVINCE.

Goodhue, Bertram Grosvenor, 1869–1924, American architect, b. Pomfret, Conn. He studied under James Renwick in New York City and in 1891 entered the office of Ralph Adams CRAM in Boston. Later he was made a partner in this firm but left it (1914) to begin independent practice. Goodhue was particularly successful in evolving a distinctive style for his ecclesiastical work, which was Gothic in form yet permeated with a modern spirit. Examples are the churches of St. Thomas and of St. Vincent Ferrer, New York City, and the buildings of the U.S. Military Academy at West Point. In his later years he turned from historical design and endeavored to create forms more harmonious with contemporary life and methods of construction, but he died before he could fully accomplish this aim. The most important works of this last period are the building at Washington, D.C., to house the National Academy of Sciences and National Research Council and the state capitol, Lincoln, Neb. Among his other works are St. Bartholomew's Church and the Chapel of the Intercession, New York City, and the First Baptist Church, Pittsburgh. See biography by C. H. Whitaker (1925).

Goodman, Benny (Benjamin David Goodman), 1909–, American musician and band leader, b. Chicago. Goodman studied clarinet at Hull House. In Chicago he had the opportunity to hear (and eventually to play beside) some of the outstanding jazz musicians of the era. He played the clarinet for many years in Chicago and later in California. In 1928 he went to New York City, where in 1934 he organized his own orchestra. In 1935 he formed the Benny Goodman trio with Gene Krupa and Teddy Wilson; it became a quartet in 1936 when Lionel Hampton joined it. Performing for radio, motion pictures, and records, Goodman's orchestra became nationally famous. After 1939 he became known as the King of Swing. In the 1950s Goodman's many tours abroad gained him international esteem. He also achieved success playing classical music for clarinet, particularly with the Budapest String Quartet. He commissioned Béla Bartók to compose *Contrasts,* for violin, clarinet, and piano, in 1938. Aaron Copland, Leonard Bernstein, and Morton Gould wrote music for him. Goodman wrote *The Kingdom of Swing* (1939) with Irving Kolodin. See bio-discographies by D. R. Connor (1958 and 1969).

Goodman, Nelson, 1906–, American philosopher, b. Somerville, Mass., grad. Harvard (Ph.D. 1941). He taught at Tufts (1945–46), the Univ. of Pennsylvania (1946–64), and Brandeis Univ. (1964–67) before becoming professor of philosophy at Harvard (1967). A proponent of nominalism, he worked with theories of inductive logic and helped to identify strategic problems in many areas of philosophy. He believes that philosophy should work to give precise structural descriptions of the world. His works include *The Structure of Appearance* (1951), *Languages of Art* (1968), *Problems and Projects* (1971), and *Fact, Fiction, and Forecast* (3d ed. 1973). See Alan Hausman, *Carnap and Goodman: Two Formalists* (1967).

Goodnight, Charles, 1836–1929, Texas cattleman, b. Macoupin co., Ill. He went to Texas in 1846, where he joined the Texas Rangers and became a noted scout and Indian fighter. He was later a pioneer in cattle ranching in New Mexico and Colorado and in 1866 laid out the Goodnight cattle trail from Texas to Wyoming, later extended (1875) to Colorado. In 1877, in partnership with John Adair, he established in the Texas Panhandle the J A Ranch of nearly 1 million acres (404,700 hectares), on which he maintained about 100,000 head of cattle. He improved his herds by crossing shorthorns and Herefords with the native longhorns. By crossing bison and Polled Angus cattle he produced the first herd of cattalo. He also bred bison and is thereby credited with preserving the remnant of the South Plains herd. In 1880 he organized the Panhandle Stockmen's Association, which suppressed lawlessness and introduced purebred cattle. See biography by J. E. Haley (1949).

Goodnow, Frank Johnson (go͝od'nō), 1859–1939, American expert on government; grad. Amherst (B.A., 1879; M.A., 1887) and Columbia (LL.B., 1882). After study abroad, he taught administrative law at Columbia for 30 years, was an adviser (1913–14) to the revolutionary Chinese government on drafting the new constitution, and was president (1914–29) of Johns Hopkins Univ. He is best remembered as a pioneer in the study of modern municipal government. Among his many books are *Politics and Administration* (1900, repr. 1967) and *Social Reform and the Constitution* (1911, repr. 1970).

Goodrich, Leland Matthew, 1899–, American political scientist, b. Lewiston, Maine, grad. Bowdoin College, 1920, and Harvard (M.A., 1921; Ph.D., 1925). He taught political science at Brown Univ. (1922–23, 1926–50) and was professor of international organization and administration at Columbia Univ. from 1950 until 1967, when he became emeritus professor of international relations. Goodrich was director of the World Peace Foundation from 1942 to 1946 and a member of the secretariat at the founding conference of the United Nations at San Francisco in 1945. His works, many of them collaborations, include *Charter of the United Nations: Commentary and Documents* (1946, with Edvard Hambro; 3d ed. 1969), *The United Nations and the Maintenance of International Peace and Security* (1955, with Anne Simons), *Korea: A Study of U.S. Policy in the United Nations* (1956), *The United Nations* (1959), and *The United Nations in a Changing World* (1974). He edited *Documents on American Foreign Relations,* Vol. IV (1942, with S. S. Jones and Denys Myers) and Vol. V–VII (1945, with M. J. Carroll).

Goodspeed, Edgar Johnson, 1871–1962, American Greek scholar, b. Quincy, Ill., grad. Denison Univ. (B.A., 1890; D.D., 1928) and Univ. of Chicago (B.D., 1897; Ph.D., 1898). He taught at the Univ. of Chicago from 1898 to 1937 and gained recognition as a biblical critic. He is principally known for his new translation of the Bible: *The New Testament—an American Translation* appeared in 1923; the wide esteem given it was extended also to *The Complete Bible—an American Translation* (with J. M. P. Smith, 1939), which is generally known as the Goodspeed Bible.

Good Thief or **Penitent Thief,** the malefactor crucified with Jesus who did not revile Him; Jesus promised him Paradise that day. Luke 23.39–43. In the Roman martyrology his feast is March 25. His name in tradition is Dismas or Desmas, that of the other thief Gesmas.

Goodwin Sands, stretch of shoals and sand bars, c.10 mi (20 km) long, lying off the east coast of Kent, SE England. It forms a breakwater E of The Downs, a roadstead. Shipwrecks were formerly frequent on the Sands. The shifting sands do not allow the construction of lighthouses, but there are several lightships and numerous buoys. Traditionally, the Sands were once a fertile isle called Lomea, the property of Godwin, earl of Wessex; Lomea was submerged by a great storm in the late 11th cent.

Goodwood, town (1970 pop. 21,000), Cape Prov., SW South Africa, a residential and commercial suburb of Cape Town. The town has some light industry and is on an important railroad line. Goodwood, founded in 1905, was named after the village of Goodwood in Sussex, England, which has a famous racecourse.

Goodyear, Charles, 1800–1860, American inventor, b. New Haven, Conn., originator of vulcanized rubber. He failed in his earlier business ventures and was in jail for debt when he began his experiments with rubber, searching for a way to prevent it from sticking and melting in hot weather. He experimented endlessly, kneading various chemicals into the raw rubber. He achieved some success in 1837 with a patented acid and metal coating, but it was not until 1839 that he discovered the process of vulcanization. He spent further years in perfecting the process, patenting it in 1844. Goodyear had carried on his research in the face of poverty and debt and was forced to market his patent rights for a fraction of their value. He went to Europe to try to establish the rubber business there but was unsuccessful. He died, poor and overworked, leaving his family in debt. See studies by R. F. Wolf (1939) and A. C. Regli (1941). His son **Charles Goodyear,** 1833–96, b. Germantown, Pa., assisted him in the manufacturing and marketing of rubber articles. He later turned to shoe manufacturing, being one of the first to see the application of Howe's sewing machine to the making of shoes. He organized in 1871 the Goodyear Boot & Shoe Machinery Company of New York to manufacture machines. He was only partially successful until the consolidation in 1880 with Gordon McKay, his chief competitor.

Googe, Barnabe (go͞oj, go͝oj), 1540–94, English poet and translator. In 1574 he was sent to Ireland as the representative of Sir William Cecil, Queen Elizabeth I's secretary of state. From 1582 to 1585 he was provost marshal of the presidency court at Connaught. Googe's *Ecologues, Epitaphs, and Sonnets* (1563) contains some of the earliest examples of English pastoral poetry. He also translated some contemporary Latin works into English.

Goole (go͞ol), municipal borough (1971 pop. 18,066), West Riding of Yorkshire, N England, at the confluence of the Ouse and Don rivers. A significant inland port, it has extensive dockyards. Coal and textiles are exported, and shipbuilding, iron casting, sugar refining, flour milling, and the manufacture of farm machinery, fertilizers, and clothing are leading industries. There is passenger service from Goole to Amsterdam, Copenhagen, and other continental ports. Goole is also a market town. In 1974 it became part of the new nonmetropolitan county of Humberside.

goose, common name for large wild and domesticated swimming birds related to the duck and the swan. Strictly speaking, the term *goose* is applied to the female and *gander* to the male. In North America the wild (or Canada) goose, *Branta canadensis,* is known by its honking call and by the migrating V-shaped flocks in spring and fall. Other wild geese are the BRANT (any species of the genus *Branta,* particularly *B. bernicla*) and the blue, snow, and white-fronted (or laughing) geese. Among the domestic geese are the popular Toulouse (or gray) goose (descended from the graylag, *Anser anser,* of Europe), the African goose, the Embden goose, and the Oriental breeds (developed from the wild Chinese goose). Geese were raised in ancient times by the Romans and other Europeans and were sacred in Egypt 4,000 years ago. Forcible feeding is used to fatten geese and to enlarge the liver for use in making pâté de foie gras. Geese are classifed in the phylum CHORDATA, subphylum Vertebrata, class Aves, order Anseriformes, family Anatidae.

gooseberry: see CURRANT.

goose bumps and **goose pimples:** see GOOSEFLESH.

goosefish: see ANGLER.

gooseflesh, temporary rumpling of the skin into tiny bumps, also called goose bumps and goose pimples. In response to cold or certain emotional states, such as fear or rage, the smooth muscles of the subsurface layer (dermis) of skin tend to contract, causing the skin to pucker and body hair to stand erect. In furred animals this can serve a dual purpose. Erection of the fur may make an animal seem larger than it actually is and act to frighten away a potential aggressor. Secondly, the erect fur traps a blanket of air close to the skin thus providing the organism with additional insulation against loss of body heat. In man, this response would seem to be vestigial.

goosefoot, common name for some members of the Chenopodiaceae, a family of widely distributed shrubs and herbs that includes the BEET, SPINACH, and mangelwurzel. Most species thrive in soils with a high mineral concentration and grow in such regions as the alkali plains of the SW United States and the pampas of Argentina. Aside from the vegetables of this family, most members are not commercially valuable. Of the genus *Chenopodium* (goosefoot) the lamb's-quarters (*C. album*) is a native of W Asia that has become a widespread weed. The Russian thistle (*Salsola tragus*) is a TUMBLEWEED of arid regions in the W United States and Eurasia. *Sarcobatus vermiculatus,* one of several shrubs called greasewood, is a grazing plant of the alkali plains also used locally as fuel. Goosefoot is classified in the divison MAGNOLIOPHYTA, class Magnoliopsida, order Caryophyllales, family Chenopodiaceae.

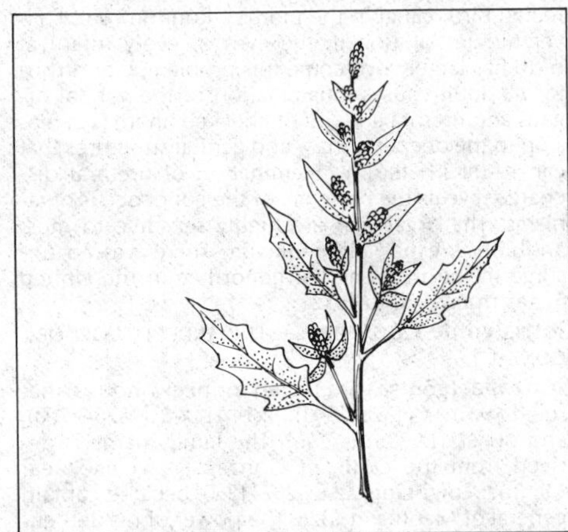

Lamb's-quarters, Chenopodium album, *a member of the goosefoot family*

Goossens, Sir Eugene (go͞o'sənz), 1893–1962, English conductor and composer, of Belgian parentage, studied in Bruges, in Liverpool, and in London at the Royal College of Music. First violinist (1911–15) in the Queen's Hall Orchestra, he was associated (1915–20) with Sir Thomas Beecham's opera company. He conducted at Covent Garden and was a conductor (1919–23) of the orchestra of Diaghilev's ballet company. In 1923 he came to the United States to be conductor of the Rochester Philharmonic. He then conducted the Cincinnati Symphony from 1931 to 1947, when he moved to Australia to become director of the New South Wales Conservatory of Music and conductor of the Sydney Symphony Orchestra. He was knighted in 1955. A prolific composer, he combined impressionistic harmonies with neoclassic polyphony. His works include two operas, two symphonies, and much vocal and chamber music. His brother Leon Goossens, a noted oboe virtuoso, made his American debut in 1928. Their father, Eugène Goossens, and their grandfather, Eugène Goossens, were both conductors.

gopher or **pocket gopher,** name for the burrowing RODENTS of the family Geomyidae, found in North America and Central America. The gopher is gray, buff, or dark brown. Its combined head and body length is 5 to 12 in. (13–30 cm) depending on the species; its tail is short. The name POCKET GOPHER refers to the fur-lined pouches that open on the outside of its cheeks and are used for carrying food and nesting material. The gopher has extremely long upper and lower teeth, which are always exposed, and broad forepaws armed with enormous claws; it uses its teeth as picks and its forepaws as shovels as it tunnels through the ground. Because gophers do not hibernate, they must accumulate stores of food for the winter. They live and do most of their foraging underground, feeding chiefly on roots and tubers. Except for brief pairing during the mating season, gophers are solitary—a single animal occupies each tunnel system. Although their extensive, ramifying tunnels sometimes damage earth dams and banks, gophers are of some value as agents of soil aeration and in forming humus by burying organic matter. Eastern pocket gophers, species of the genus *Geomys,* are found in the United States from the Rocky Mts. to the Mississippi valley and on the Gulf Coast. Western pocket gophers, species of *Thomomys,* are found from the Rocky Mts. to the Pacific and from S Canada to the Mexican border. The Mexican pocket gopher, *Cratogeomys castanops,* ranges from the SW United States to central Mexico. Other genera are found in Mexico and Central America. The name *gopher* is also applied to the GROUND SQUIRREL in some regions. Gophers are classified in the phylum CHORDATA, subphylum Vertebrata, class Mammalia, order Rodentia, family Geomyidae.

Göppingen (gŏp'ĭng-ən), city (1970 pop. 47,973), Baden-Württemberg, S West Germany. Its manufactures include machinery, precision instruments, chemicals, pharmaceuticals, wood and leather products, and textiles. Mineral water is bottled and shipped. Göppingen was chartered by the Hohenstaufen in the mid-12th cent. The city was twice (1425, 1782) devastated by fire. Noteworthy buildings include a church (15th cent.) and a castle (1559–69).

Gorakhpur (gō'rəkpo͝or''), city (1971 pop. 230,701), Uttar Pradesh state, N central India, on the Rapti River. Founded c.1400, it is a conglomeration of farm villages in a very densely populated area.

Gorboduc (gôr'bədək), legendary early British king mentioned by Geoffrey of Monmouth. In his lifetime he divided his kingdom between his sons Ferrex and Porrex, thereby creating great civil strife in which the two sons were killed. *Gorboduc,* or *Ferrex and Porrex,* the first English blank verse tragedy, was performed by the players of the Inner Temple in 1561. The first edition of the play, published in 1565, attributes the first three acts to Thomas Norton (1532–84) and the last two to Thomas SACKVILLE. The play is modeled on Senecan tragedy.

Gorchakov, Aleksandr Mikhailovich, Prince (əlyĭksän'dər mēkhī'ləvĭch, gərchəkôf'), 1798–1883, Russian diplomat. After serving (1854–56) as ambassador at Vienna, he became Alexander II's foreign minister and chancellor (1867). His wit and oratorical gifts made him known as a brilliant diplomat. Gorchakov's chief aim was to nullify the Treaty of Paris that closed the Crimean War (1854–56) and to find allies against Austria and England, who had been mainly responsible for the treaty, which thwarted Russian expansion in SE Europe. A rapprochement with France failed when Napoleon III gave diplomatic support to the Poles in their rebellion (1863) against the Russians. Gorchakov maintained neutrality in the Austro-Prussian War (1866) and the Franco-Prussian War (1870–71) in return for Bismarck's support of Russian intervention in Poland. He unilaterally ended (1870) the limitations imposed in the Treaty of Paris on Russia's Black Sea fleet. Despite the THREE EMPERORS' LEAGUE with Germany and Austria-Hungary, in 1875 Gorchakov sided with France when Franco-German relations grew tense. He was an opponent of Pan-Slavism but was unable to halt the agitation that led to the Russo-Turkish War of 1877–78. He attended the Congress of Berlin (1878), where most advantages gained in the war were lost. From 1879, N. K. GIERS guided Russian foreign policy, and in 1882, Gorchakov resigned.

Gorchakov, Mikhail Dmitreyevich, Prince (mēkhəyēl' dəmē'trēəvĭch), 1793–1861, Russian general. He served in the Russo-Turkish War of 1828–29, the suppression of the Polish insurrection (1830–31), and the campaign in Hungary (1849). In 1853 he became chief of staff of the Russian army. He succeeded A. S. Menshikov as Russian commander in chief in the Crimean War and heroically defended Sevastopol.

Gordian (gôr'dēən), name of three Roman emperors. **Gordian I** (Marcus Antonius Gordianus Africanus), d. 238, was a Roman of great wealth and was colleague in the consulship with Caracalla and with Alexander Severus, who appointed him proconsul in Africa. After the usurpation of MAXIMIN (d. 238), a rebellion broke out in Africa over the unscrupulousness of one of Maximin's men, and Gordian at the age of 81 was made coemperor (238) with his son. They were recognized by the Roman senate. Soon afterward, however, Vitallianus, a partisan of Maximin, attacked them in Carthage. Gordian I committed suicide, ending a reign of only 22 days, after learning that his son and colleague, **Gordian II**, 192–238, had been killed in battle. The senate named two new emperors, Balbinus and Pupienus. Gordian II's son, **Gordian III**, c.223–244, was made caesar. Balbinus and Pupienus defeated and killed Maximin but were soon murdered by the Praetorian Guard, whereupon Gordian III became emperor (238–44). In 242, Gordian attacked the Persians in Mesopotamia. He defeated them, but his best general, his father-in-law Timesitheus, died. The troops became disorderly, and PHILIP (Philip the Arabian) had Gordian murdered.

Gordian knot: see GORDIUS.

Gordimer, Nadine, 1923–, British writer, b. Springs, Transvaal, South Africa. She has taught in universities all over the world. Her novels are often bleak studies of South African life, and she tenders no moral hope for whites who live under apartheid. She has a talent for precise observation and beautifully conveys psychologically complex moments. Her novels include *The Voice of the Serpent* (1953), *The Late Bourgeois World* (1966), *A Guest of Honor* (1970), and *The Conservationist* (1975).

Gordin, Jacob Mikhailovich, 1853–1909, American writer of Yiddish plays, b. Russia. He was for some years a teacher and a newspaper writer in St. Petersburg, Odessa, and elsewhere. In 1880 he founded the Bible Brotherhood, a reform movement of Judaism. After the movement was suppressed, he left Russia in 1891 for the United States. In New York City he found the Yiddish stage in need of good plays, and for the rest of his life he wrote (more than 70), translated, and adapted plays in the vernacular. Among the best of these were *Siberia; God, Man, and the Devil; The Jewish King Lear; The Jewish Sappho;* and *The Kreutzer Sonata* (an English translation was produced in 1907). His collected plays were published (1910) in Yiddish in New York.

Gordium (gôr'dēəm), ancient city of Asia Minor, in Phrygia, now in Turkey, 50 mi (80 km) SW of Ankara. It was the capital of Phrygia from c.1000 to 800 B.C. Excavations conducted since 1950 have revealed Hittite, Phrygian, Persian, and Graeco-Roman remains. It was here that Alexander the Great is said to have cut the Gordian knot.

Gordius (gôr'dēəs), in Greek mythology, king of Phrygia. An oracle had told the Phrygians that the king who would put an end to their troubles was approaching in an oxcart, and, thus, when Gordius, a peasant, appeared in his wagon, he was hailed king. In gratitude, Gordius dedicated his wagon to Zeus. The pole of the wagon was fastened to the yoke with an intricate knot of bark that defied all efforts to untie it. This was the Gordian knot. An oracle declared that he who untied it would become leader of all Asia. A later legend states that when Alexander the Great came to Phrygia, he severed the knot with one blow of his sword. Hence the saying, "to cut the Gordian knot," meaning to solve a perplexing problem with a single bold action.

Gordon, Adam Lindsay, 1833–70, Australian poet, b. the Azores. In 1853 he went to South Australia, where he joined the mounted police and later became famous as a steeplechase rider and horse owner. His works include *Sea Spray and Smoke Drift* (1867), *Ashtaroth* (1867), and the vigorous *Bush Ballads and Galloping Rhymes* (1870). Depressed by debts, he committed suicide at 36. His collected poems were published in 1912.

Gordon, Charles George, 1833–85, British soldier and administrator. He served in the Crimean War, went to China in the expedition of 1860, taking part in the capture of Peking, and in 1863 took over the command of F. T. WARD, who had raised a Chinese army to suppress the TAIPING REBELLION. For the achievements of this Ever-Victorious Army he was popularly known as Chinese Gordon. In 1873 he entered the service of the khedive of Egypt, succeeding Sir Samuel BAKER as governor of Equatoria (S Sudan). Appointed governor of the Sudan in 1877, he waged a vigorous campaign against slave traders. He resigned in 1879, but after various appointments in India, China, Mauritius, and Cape Colony (Cape Province), he was sent back to the Sudan, where Muhammad Ahmad (see under MAHDI) had acquired control. Although under orders to evacuate the Egyptian garrison from Khartoum, Gordon took it upon himself to attempt to defeat the Mahdi. He was cut off and besieged at Khartoum for 10 months. A relief expedition belatedly dispatched from England reached the garrison two days after it had been stormed by the Mahdists, who killed Gordon. Gordon's death stirred public indignation and contributed to the collapse of the Gladstone government in 1885. See Gordon's journals at Khartoum (1885, repr. 1969); biographies by H. E. Wortham (1933) and G. R. Elton (1954); studies by Paul Charrier (1965), Anthony Nutting (1966), and John Marlowe (1969).

Gordon, Charles William, pseud. **Ralph Connor,** 1860–1937, Canadian clergyman and novelist. His popular stories were based on his experience as a Presbyterian missionary in the lumber and mining camps of the Canadian Northwest. Of the long list of his somewhat didactic and romantic novels, the most widely read are *The Sky Pilot* (1899) and *The Man from Glengarry* (1901). See his autobiography, *Postscript to Adventure* (1938).

Gordon, George, earl of Huntly: see HUNTLY.

Gordon, Lord George, 1751–93, English agitator, whose activities resulted in the tragic Gordon riots of 1780 in London. In 1779, Gordon assumed leadership of the Protestant Association, an organization formed to secure repeal of the Catholic Relief Act of 1778 (see CATHOLIC EMANCIPATION). On June 2, 1780, he led a huge crowd to present a petition to Parliament, and the demonstration rapidly turned into an orgy of destruction and plunder that lasted a week. The jails were broken open, and probably more than 800 people were killed and injured. Some 21 rioters were executed, but Gordon was acquitted through the efforts of his lawyer, Thomas Erskine. Dickens vividly described the riots in *Barnaby Rudge.* See Christopher Hibbert, *King Mob* (1958).

Gordon, John Brown, 1832–1904, U.S. public official and Confederate general, b. Upson co., Ga. Gordon began his Civil War service as an infantry captain and so distinguished himself through four years of campaigning in the Virginia area that at Lee's surrender he was a lieutenant general commanding a corps. His fighting in the Wilderness campaign and in the Shenandoah Valley under J. A. EARLY in 1864 was particularly brilliant. After the war he became an outstanding leader in Georgia politics. With Alfred H. Colquitt and Joseph E. Brown, he dominated the state government for many years. He was U.S. Senator (1873–80, 1891–97) and governor (1886–90). Despite charges that he mixed politics and railroad affairs, he remained the idol of his state. See his *Reminiscences of the Civil War* (1903); D. S. Freeman, *Lee's Lieutenants* (3 vol., 1942–44); biography by John B. Gordon (1955).

Gordon, Judah Leon, 1830–92, Russian-Hebrew novelist and poet, b. Vilna. His name in patronymic style was Jehudah Löb ben Asher. As teacher and writer he was one of the leaders in the renaissance of progressive culture among the Jews (*Haskalah*) and was an indefatigable foe of obscurantism. His historic poems were followed by satirical works attacking the severity of traditional Judaism. He wrote in incomparable classical Hebrew and in Russian; his influence on modern Hebrew letters has not diminished. A complete edition of his works was published (1928–35) in Tel-Aviv. See biography by A. B. Rhine (1910).

Gordon, Patrick, 1635–99, Scottish soldier of fortune and Russian general, b. Scotland. After serving alternately on both sides in the war between Sweden and Poland (1655–60), he entered the Russian army (1661) and later became the devoted friend of the youthful czar Peter I (Peter the Great). The greatest service he rendered Peter was his aid (1689) in thwarting the coup d'etat by Peter's half sister, the regent SOPHIA ALEKSEYEVNA, who wished to become ruler in her own right. Excerpts from Gordon's diary were published in 1859.

Gordon, Ruth, 1896–, American actress and playwright, b. Wollaston, Mass. Since her debut as Nibs in *Peter Pan* (1915), Gordon has had broad stage and film experience. Among the plays she has written are *Over Twenty-One, Years Ago,* and *The Leading*

Lady. She and her husband, the playwright and director Garson Kanin, have collaborated in writing many successful film scripts, including *A Double Life* (1948), *Adam's Rib* (1949), and *Born Yesterday* (1951). Gordon won an Academy Award for her performance in *Rosemary's Baby* (1968). In 1974 she appeared in the play *Dreyfus in Rehearsal.* See her autobiography, *Myself Among Others* (1971).

Gordon riots: see GORDON, LORD GEORGE.

Gordon setter, breed of large SPORTING DOG developed over centuries in Scotland and brought to prominence there by the fourth duke of Gordon in the early 1800s. It stands from 23 to 27 in. (58.4–68.6 cm) high at the shoulder and weighs from 45 to 75 lb (20.4–34.1 kg). The flat or slightly wavy coat is long and shiny and forms fringes, or feathers, of longer hair on the ears, chest, underside of body, back of legs, and tail. It is coal black in color with tan markings, usually chestnut or mahogany, on the head, throat, chest, and inside of hind legs. The Gordon was introduced into the United States by Daniel Webster and his friend George Blunt in 1842, and since then the breed's popularity has spread widely. Although slower than the other setters, it hunts with great accuracy and endurance. See DOG.

Gore, Charles, 1853–1932, English prelate and theologian. As the first principal (1884–93) of Pusey House, a theological center at Oxford, he influenced many undergraduates and was a leading figure in the High Church movement (see ENGLAND, CHURCH OF). In 1887 he founded the Society of the Resurrection, a community of celibate priests living under vows; this later became the Community of the Resurrection. He was also a founder-member of the Christian Social Union. In 1889 he edited *Lux Mundi*, a collection of essays that stated the views of modernists in the High Church. His Bampton Lectures (1891) upheld their position. He was made canon of Westminster in 1894. In 1902 he was consecrated bishop of Worcester, in 1905 bishop of Birmingham, and in 1911 bishop of Oxford. Among his many works are *The Church and the Ministry* (1889), *Christ and Society* (1928), and *The Philosophy of the Good Life* (1930). See biographies by Gordon Crosse (1932) and G. L. Prestige (1935).

Goremykin, Ivan Longinovich (ēvän' lən-gē'nəvĭch gəryĭmĭ'kĭn), 1839–1917, Russian statesman. A conservative, he was (1895–99) interior minister under Czar Nicholas II and succeeded (1906) COUNT WITTE as premier. The first Duma (1906) opposed his reactionary government, and his incompetence in handling the Duma led to his dismissal. Premier again from 1914 to 1916, Goremykin was regarded as the embodiment of reaction and a tool of Grigori Rasputin and was forced to resign. He was arrested briefly after the February Revolution (1917) in Russia, but was allowed to retire to his estate in the Caucasus, where he was murdered by a mob, probably Bolsheviks.

Goren, Charles Henry, 1901–, American expert on bridge, b. Philadelphia, grad. McGill Univ., 1922. Goren played bridge as a law student and by 1931 was competing in major tournaments. He wrote the first of his many books on bridge, *Winning Bridge Made Easy,* in 1936 and shortly thereafter gave up his law practice to teach bridge, write additional books, and play in tournaments. He won two world championships (1950, 1957) and 26 U.S. titles (including two ties) and became one of the nation's leading experts on the game. His books and syndicated articles have made his point-count bidding system the most popular in bridge. See his *Goren's Bridge Complete* (rev. ed. 1973).

Gorenko, Anna Andreyevna: see AKHMATOVA, ANNA.

Gorey, Edward, 1925–, American illustrator and writer, b. Chicago. Gorey is celebrated for more than 30 small volumes of gothic fables, most of them in verse and remarkably macabre. These he has illustrated lavishly in dark and abundant Edwardian detail. Many of his early works, published in small editions, have become collector's items; they include *The Unstrung Harp* (1953), *The Listing Attic* (1954), and *The Object-Lesson* (1958). His more recent single works include *The Awdrey-Gore Legacy* (1972), a spoof on English murder mysteries, and *The Lavender Leotard* (1973), concerning ballet.

Gorgan (gôrgän') or **Jurjan** (jo͝orjän'), town (1971 est. pop. 55,000), N Iran, E of the Caspian Sea. The surrounding region yields rice, wheat, barley, and nuts and has extensive forests and marshes. Gorgan is a trading center. The surrounding area, the ancient Hyrcania, was captured by the Arabs (716) and conquered by the Mongols (13th cent.). Aga Muhammad Khan, the founder of the Kajar dynasty, was born there, and the town flourished (c.1800) with the rise of the dynasty. It was formerly called Astrabad or Asterabad.

Gorgas, Josiah (gôr'gəs), 1818–83, chief of ordnance in the Confederate army during the American Civil War, b. Dauphin co., Pa.; father of William Crawford Gorgas. He was commissioned in the ordnance corps and served in the Mexican War. In April, 1861, he resigned his Union commission and was appointed major and chief of ordnance in the Confederate army, rising to the rank of brigadier general in 1864. The Confederacy's supply of arms was dangerously low and manufacturing facilities almost nonexistent. Although Gorgas sent purchasing agents to Europe, no shipments were received before 1862. Despite the enormous difficulties, however, Gorgas built up the South's war machine and supplied munitions to the Confederate armies until the war's end. In 1869 he joined the faculty of the Univ. of the South, becoming vice chancellor in 1872. He was named president of the Univ. of Alabama in 1878. See biography by F. E. Vandiver (1952).

Gorgas, William Crawford, 1854–1920, American disease and sanitation expert, surgeon general of the United States, b. Mobile, Ala., grad. Bellevue Hospital Medical College, 1879. He served with the U.S. army medical corps after 1880. Stricken with yellow fever while stationed at Fort Brown, Texas, Gorgas soon recovered and thereafter remained immune to the disease. In 1898 he was sent to Cuba as sanitation director. Applying the findings of Carlos J. Finlay and Walter Reed, Gorgas after a short time permanently rid Havana of yellow fever. He then went (1904) to the Isthmus of Panama, where amid administrative difficulties he succeeded in cleansing the Canal Zone of the dreaded yellow fever by eliminating the breeding places of mosquitoes and segregating stricken patients. He improved health conditions in the cities of Colón and Panama while insuring the completion of the Panama Canal. These events he discussed in his book, *Sanitation in Panama* (1915). He later made several trips to clear up disease-infested places throughout the world, and he made notable progress in Guayaquil, Ecuador, a city long scourged with yellow fever. He served (1914–19) as surgeon general of the United States and was attached, after 1916, to the International Health Board. See biographies by Marie Gorgas and B. J. Hendrick (1924), J. M. Gibson (1950), and E. F. Dolan and H. T. Silver (1968).

Gorges, Sir Ferdinando (gôr'jĭz), c.1566–1647, English colonizer, proprietor of MAINE. He was knighted (1591) for his services to Henry IV of France in the French Wars of Religion and was subsequently (1596–1601, 1603–29) military governor of Plymouth, England. Gorges was a leading figure in the Plymouth Company, chartered in 1606, and one of the two chief backers of the Sagadahoc colony, which was planted in 1607 at the mouth of the Kennebec River, Maine, and failed in 1608. In the following years he directed the many fishing and trading expeditions that the company carried on along the New England coast and defended its monopoly of the fisheries. He procured the services of Capt. John Smith to head a new settlement, but three successive expeditions foundered soon after leaving harbor, and the discouraged Smith withdrew. In 1620, Gorges obtained a revised charter for the Plymouth Company in which its territory, for the first time called New England, was established as lying between lat. 40°N and 48°N. The company reconstituted itself as the Council for New England, and grants were made to the individual members in the hope that they would become more interested in the project. Interest, however, centered in the more southern ventures, and Gorges found no financial support. The Pilgrim colony at Plymouth, patented under the London Company, had mistakenly settled within the bounds of the New England Council grant, but in 1621 it received a patent from the council and had Gorges's interest henceforth. Not so the Massachusetts Bay colony, against which Sir Ferdinando carried a long struggle in England on the ground that its patent was irregular. In order to make the whole of New England a royal colony, over which Gorges was to be governor general, the Council for New England surrendered its charter in 1635. The territory of New England was to be divided between the eight lords of the council, who were to hold it under new patents, but because of the growing intensity of the struggle between Charles I and Parliament in England the new arrangement was never consummated, and the Puritan commonwealth of Massachusetts was left free. In 1622, Gorges had received, with John MASON (1586–1635) a grant of the territory lying between the Merrimack and Kennebec rivers. They divided that area in 1629, Gorges taking the land east of the Piscataqua River, which became the province of Maine. His grant was confirmed by royal charter in 1639. Events in England prevented him from raising funds to colonize his domain. His grant passed to his heirs. His grandson, **Ferdinando Gorges,** 1630–1718, in 1677 finally sold to Massachusetts all rights to Maine for £1,250. See James P. Baxter, ed., *Sir Ferdinando Gorges and His Province of Maine* (3 vol., 1890, repr. 1967); Henry S. Burrage, *Gorges and the Grant of the Province of Maine* (1923); R. A. Preston, *Gorges of Plymouth Fort* (1953).

Görgey, Arthur (gör'gĕĭ), 1818–1916, Hungarian revolutionary general. He fought the Austrians in 1848–49 as a commander of the Hungarian republican army and distinguished himself as a strategist. He captured Buda (May, 1849), but when Russia sent aid to the Austrians, Görgey decided to surrender to the Russians rather than continue a lost cause. He forced Louis KOSSUTH, with whom he had often differed, to resign. Görgey was interned in Austria until 1867.

Gorgias (gôr'jēəs), c.485–c.380 B.C., Greek Sophist. From his native city, Leontini, Sicily, he was sent as an ambassador to Athens, where he settled to teach and practice rhetoric. Gorgias pursued the negative implications of the Eleatic school and asserted: (1) Nothing exists; (2) If anything does exist, it cannot be known; (3) If it can be known, the knowledge of it cannot be communicated. Objective truth being thus impossible, there remains only the art of the SOPHISTS, persuasion. Such arguments undermined the foundations of polytheism and led to open challenges of current moral standards. His challenge to speculative thought stimulated a more sophisticated approach to the problems of philosophy. A dialogue of Plato's bears his name.

Gorgon (gôr'gən), in Greek mythology, one of three monstrous sisters, Stheno, Euryale, and Medusa; daughters of Ceto and Phorcus. Their hair was a cluster of writhing snakes, and their faces were so hideous that all who saw them were turned to stone. Only MEDUSA was mortal. They were much represented in Greek art.

Gori (gô'rē), city (1970 pop. 48,000), SE European USSR, in Georgia. It has textile plants. Mentioned in the 7th cent. as Tontio, it was later named after a fortress. Gori passed to Russia in 1801. Stalin was born in the city.

gorilla, an APE, *Gorilla gorilla,* native to the forests of western equatorial Africa. It is the largest of the apes, the males reaching a height of 5 to 6 ft (150–190 cm) with a 9-ft (144-cm) arm spread. They weigh about 450 lb (200 kg) in the wild; in zoos they become fat and may reach 600 lb (270 kg) or more. Males have prominent saggital crests and brow ridges and enormous canine teeth; in females these features are much less developed. Females are smaller than males, weighing about half as much. Gorillas are enormously muscular and powerful animals capable of bending tempered steel bars of 2 in. (5.1 cm) thickness. They have shaggy coats of brown or black, sometimes with areas of silvery gray, especially on the back, or with red topknots. There are local and family differences in coloration, but females tend to be uniformly dark. Mostly terrestrial, gorillas are capable of standing erect, but normally walk on all fours, using the outside of the feet and the knuckles of the hands. They move about in groups of 5 to 20 animals, climbing trees in search of food and to build nests of leaves and twigs for sleeping. Often the oldest male of the group stays on the ground while the others remain in trees. They are chiefly vegetarians, living on a variety of leaves, fruit, roots, and bark. Quiet and retiring in temperament, they seldom, if ever, initiate an attack on humans; in their native regions they are less feared than chimpanzees, which are much more excitable animals. Gorillas roar and beat their chests to frighten intruders; if severely threatened they may rush at and bite a person. Their only enemies, aside from man, are leopards, which sometimes eat the young. Females bear one infant about every four years; the child is carried in the mother's arms and then on her back. Females mature in 6 or 7 years, males in 9 or 10; gorillas may live up to 35 years. Gorillas are classified in the phylum CHORDATA, subphylum Vertebrata, class Mammalia, order Primates, family Pongidae. See C. P. Groves, *Gorillas* (1970); G. B. Schaller, *The Year of the Gorilla* (1964, repr. 1971).

Gorinchem (gôr'ĭnkhəm) or **Gorkum** (gôr'kəm), town (1971 pop. 26,972), South Holland prov., W central Netherlands, on the Upper Merwede River.

It is a manufacturing center. Gorinchem became a major trade center in the 15th cent. It was captured by the Beggars of the Sea (see GUEUX) in 1572. Much of the old town and its walls have been preserved.

Goring, George Goring, Baron, 1608–57, English royalist commander in the civil war. He was a court gallant who had previously served in the Dutch army. In 1641 a group of army officers formed the "first army plot" with the intent of asserting the king's will against Parliament by force. Goring, then governor of Portsmouth, was one of the conspirators. Dissatisfied at having to play a secondary role, he betrayed the plot to the parliamentarians. In 1642 after playing a double game, Goring declared for the king. He held high commands until 1645, but his considerable ability as a general was offset by his ambition and intrigues that were disastrous for the royalist cause. He lived on the Continent from 1645 until his death.

Göring, Hermann Wilhelm: see GOERING, HERMANN WILHELM.

Gorizia (gôrē'tsēä), Ger. *Görz* (gûrts), city (1971 pop. 42,980), capital of Gorizia prov., Friuli-Venezia Giulia, NE Italy, on the Isonzo River and on the Yugoslav border. It is an industrial, commercial, transport, and tourist center. Manufactures include textiles, leather goods, paper, and machines. Located in the historic region of FRIULI, Gorizia was the seat of a duchy from c.1000 to 1500. It passed to the Hapsburgs in 1508 but preserved a remarkable autonomy until the 18th cent. From 1815 to 1918 the Austrian crown land of Görz-Gradisca (Slovenian *Gorica*) was included in Küstenland prov. In World War I, Gorizia and the surrounding area in the Karst were the scene of bloody battles (see ISONZO). The Italians took Gorizia in 1916, evacuated it in 1917, and recovered it in 1918. Gorizia was excepted from the cession in 1947 of E Friuli to Yugoslavia; on the eastern limit of the Italian city is the new Yugoslav community of Nova Gorica. Gorizia has a 16th-century fortress, a Gothic cathedral (14th cent., rebuilt 17th cent.), and the Church of St. Ignatius (1680–1725).

Gorki: see GORKY, USSR.

Gorkum, Netherlands: see GORINCHEM.

Gorky, Arshile (är'shīl gôr'kē), 1904–48, American painter, b. Armenia. He immigrated to the United States in 1920. Inspired by Ingres and Picasso, Gorky developed a figurative style of great refinement. A more radical turn in his art was prompted by the spontaneous automatism found in surrealism and in the works of Miró and Matta. Gorky began (c.1940) to create abstractions consisting of involved organic shapes enveloped in an aura of mystery. He pioneered in the development of ABSTRACT EXPRESSIONISM. His reputation had already been established when he committed suicide at the age of 44. Gorky is well represented in American collections. *Water of the Flowery Mill* is in the Metropolitan Museum, and there are works at the Museum of Modern Art and the Whitney Museum, New York City. See catalog by Julien Levy (1966); biography by Harold Rosenberg (1963).

Gorky, Maxim or **Maksim** (both: məksyēm gôr'kē) [Rus.,=Maxim the Bitter], pseud. of **Aleksey Maximovich Pyeshkov,** 1868–1936, Russian writer, b. Nizhny Novgorod (now Gorky). Gorky is considered the father of Soviet literature and the founder of the doctrine of SOCIALIST REALISM. Instilled by his grandmother with a love of romantic tales and great sympathy for mankind, Gorky began a nomadic life at 12, wandering the Volga area. Since the czar's schools were closed to peasants, he educated himself, an experience he describes in *My Universities* (1923). He held dozens of menial jobs, publishing his first story in 1892. Gorky then became a journalist and married a colleague on the *Samarskaya Gazeta.* His articles exposed local corruption and he soon lost his job. In 1898 his collection *Sketches and Stories* was published by a radical press and Gorky was an immediate sensation. These romantic tales concern the vigor and nobility of the Russian peasants and workers. About 1900 he turned to writing novels of social realism. Of these, *Mother* (1907) had the greatest impact on Soviet literature. Describing the awakening of revolutionary feeling in an ill-treated peasant woman, it became the prototype of the revolutionary novel. At this time Gorky became close friends with Leo Tolstoy and Chekhov, about both of whom he later wrote superb *Reminiscences* (tr. 1946). Gorky donated most of his income to the revolutionary movement. He was arrested frequently but treated warily because of his tremendous popularity. The czar rescinded his election to the Academy of Sciences in 1902, whereupon Chekhov and Korolenko resigned in protest. Gorky wrote 15 plays, two of which, heavily censored, were enormously successful at the Moscow Art Theatre. One of them, *The Lower Depths* (1902), a study of the wretched lives of derelicts, remains a classic. His plays, at first modeled on Chekhov's, emphasized characterization over plot. After the failure of the 1905 revolution, in which he took part, Gorky sought to raise funds for the movement abroad. Following an initial triumphant reception in the United States (1906), he was insulted and mistreated there because his traveling companion was not his wife. Settling in Capri (1906–13), he set up a Bolshevik propaganda school before he returned to Russia in 1914. Although philosophically at odds with Lenin, Gorky was able to extract from him aid for many intellectuals and artists in an era of intellectual restriction. Exhausted from his work as head of the State Publishing House and by bouts with tuberculosis, he sought rest abroad (1921) and returned in 1928. His final, unfinished work, often considered his masterpiece, is *The Life of Klim Samgin* (1927–36), a panoramic four-volume novel of Russian social conditions from 1880 to 1917. Gorky's death at 68 has been ascribed to assassination by poison, perpetrated by an anti-Soviet group. His work was remarkable for its vitality and optimism; it revealed, within its devotion to realism, a strong poetic strain and an eternal passion for justice. By the example of his work and life and by his literary criticism Gorky exerted a profound influence on Soviet thought. Most of his works have been translated. See his autobiography (tr. 1949); his letters to Andreev, ed. by Peter Yershov (1958); biographies by Filia Holtzman (1948) and Dan Levin (1965); studies by Alexander Kaun (1931, repr. 1960) and B. D. Wolfe (1967).

Gorky or **Gorki** (both: gôr'kē), formerly **Nizhny Novgorod** (nyēsh'nyī nôf'gərəd), city (1970 pop. 1,170,000), capital of Gorky oblast, E European USSR, on the Volga and Oka rivers. A major river port and a rail and air center, it is one of the chief industrial cities of the USSR. Heavy machinery, steel, chemicals, and textiles are produced. The city is the site of the largest automobile factory in the Soviet Union. In 1221 a prince of Vladimir founded the city as a frontier post against the Volga Bulgars and Mordvinians. Known as Nizhny Novgorod, it was a major trading point for Russia and the East. In 1350 it became the capital of the Suzdal-Nizhny Novgorod principality and was annexed in 1392 by Moscow. From 1608 to 1612 the city was the rallying point for the Russian army that defeated the Polish, Lithuanian, and Cossack armies. Nizhny Novgorod was famous for its annual trade fairs, held from 1817 to 1930, except during the Bolshevik Revolution and the civil war. Its turreted stone kremlin dates from the 13th cent. There are two 13th-century churches, a palace (1625–31), the Uspensky church (1672–74), and the Stroganov and Christmas churches (late 17th-early 18th cent.). The university was founded in 1918. Nizhny Novgorod was renamed in 1932 for Maxim Gorky, who was born there.

Gorky (gôr'kē) or **Gorky Leninskoye** (lyĕ'nyĭnskəyə), suburb of Moscow, central European USSR. The country home of Lenin, who died there, is now a memorial museum.

Görlitz (gör'lĭts), city (1970 pop. 87,308), Dresden district, SE East Germany, on the Görlitzer Neisse River, at the Polish border. Manufactures include textiles, metal goods, furniture, and beer. Lignite is mined nearby. Formerly a major city of LUSATIA, Görlitz was founded c.1200 and in 1377 became the capital of the duchy of Görlitz. It developed as an important cloth-weaving and trade center. The city passed to the Hapsburgs in 1526 and to Saxony in 1635. In 1815, Görlitz was annexed by Prussia. After World War II the section of the city on the right bank of the Neisse was placed in Poland and is called Zgorzelec (1970 pop. 28,400). Görlitz has numerous well-preserved 18th-century baroque houses. Jakob Boehme (1575–1624), the religious mystic, lived there.

Görlitzer Neisse, river: see NEISSE, river.

Gorlovka (gôr'ləfkə), city (1970 pop. 335,000), S European USSR, in the Ukraine, in the Donets Basin. It is a major coal-mining and industrial center, with a major chemical complex.

Gorman, Arthur Pue, 1839–1906, American legislator, b. Woodstock, Md. After serving from 1869 to 1879 in the Maryland legislature, he was elected to the U.S. Senate in 1880. Gorman had by this time virtually become Democratic boss of Maryland. As chairman of the Democratic National Committee in 1884, he directed Grover Cleveland's successful campaign for the presidency. His share in the Wilson-Gorman Tariff Act of 1894 consisted in leading a group of Senators, who, by adding over 600 amendments, turned the low-tariff Wilson Bill into a high-tariff act, as high as the act passed by the Republicans in 1883. Cleveland declared the bill a betrayal of the Democratic stand and denounced it, allowing it to become law without his signature. Gorman, who had become one of his party's leaders in the Senate, was defeated in 1898, but he was reelected again in 1903 and served as minority leader until his death.

Gorno-Altai Autonomous Oblast (gôr'nə-ältī', äl'tī, ältī'), oblast (1970 pop. 168,000), 35,800 sq mi (92,722 sq km), Altai Kray, SE Siberian USSR. Bordering on Mongolia in the south, it contains most of the Altai Mts. and is drained by the Biya, Katun, and Chuya rivers. The region is mountainous, and gold, manganese, and mercury are mined. Livestock raising and dairy farming are important, and grain is cultivated. The oblast capital is Gorno-Altaisk (1970 pop. 34,000), a processing center for the agricultural products of the region. The majority of Gorno-Altai's population are Russians; the rest are Altaians (Oirots, Temuts, Shors, Tilengets, and Kumands). The Altaians, numbering about 45,000, are a Turkic-speaking people with Mongolian strains. Some are nomadic or seminomadic herdsmen and hunters, but most are now settled on state and collective farms. A primitive communal society existed in the area from the 3d millennium B.C., and there is evidence of a Mongolian civilization in the 5th cent. B.C. The Turkish khanate ruled the region from the 6th to the 10th cent. A.D., and the Altaians were under the control of the Mongolian khans from the beginning of the 13th to the 18th cent. In 1756 the Altaians came under Russian hegemony. From 1918 to 1922 there was civil war as the mountain groups fought the Bolshevik forces. Between 1922 and 1948 the state was called the Oirot Autonomous Oblast. It was renamed in 1948. The oblast is sometimes known as Mountain-Altai.

Gorno-Badakhshan Autonomous Oblast (gôr'-nə-bədəkhshän'), oblast (1970 pop. 98,000), c.24,600 sq mi (63,710 sq km), Central Asian USSR, in Tadzhikistan, in the PAMIR. It is bordered by China on the east and by Afghanistan on the south and west and is separated from Pakistan and Kashmir by a narrow strip of Afghan territory. The eastern section (East Pamir) is a high plateau, and the western part (West Pamir) is cut by high ranges and deep, narrow valleys. Khorog is the capital. The population is mainly Tadzhik, with small Kirghiz and Russian minorities. Gold, salt, mica, limestone, and peat are mined. In the east livestock is raised (yaks, sheep, cattle, and goats), and in the western valleys grain, vegetables, and beans are grown. Formerly under the control of the Mongols and the Arabs, the region passed to Russian control in 1895. The autonomous oblast was formed in 1925. It is sometimes known as Mountain-Badakhshan.

Gorostiza, José (hōsā' gōrōstē'zä), 1901–, Mexican poet. Gorostiza is regarded as one of Mexico's foremost poets. Meticulous craftsmanship and intense subjectivity mark the poetry in *Canciones para cantar en las barcas* (1925) and *Muerte sin fin* (1939; tr.*Death without End,* 1969). The latter work is a long, complex, technically brilliant, and profoundly pessimistic meditation on the meaninglessness of life. Gorostiza's work is collected as *Poesía* (1964) and *Prosa* (1969).

Görres, Joseph von (yō'zĕf fən gör'əs), 1776–1848, German historian, journalist, and writer. As lecturer on philosophy at the Univ. of Heidelberg he befriended Joachim von Arnim and Clemens Brentano, whose folk song collection he followed with a collection of folk tales, *Deutsche Volksbücher* (1807). A typical romantic, Görres investigated Oriental myths and edited the epic *Lohengrin* (1813). At first he supported the French Revolution, but he later became a liberal nationalist with a violent hatred for Napoleon I; his principal work, *Germany and the Revolution* (1819, tr. 1820), greatly influenced contemporary politics. From 1814 to 1816, Görres edited the *Rheinische Merkur.* This newspaper, although suppressed in the period of reaction, set the style of modern political journalism. A Roman Catholic, Görres wrote books and essays on religious subjects and many works on literature, history, and folklore.

gorse: see FURZE.

Gorter, Herman (hĕr'män gôr'tər), 1864–1927, Dutch poet. He wrote two notable long poems, *Mei* (1889) and *Pan* (1912). A Marxian socialist, Gorter was a well-known political journalist.

Gorton, John Grey, 1911–, Australian political leader. A fruit grower, he entered politics after serving as a fighter pilot in World War II and was elected to the senate in 1949 as a Liberal party member. He held a number of cabinet posts in the Liberal-Country coalition government of Robert G. Menzies and under his successor, Harold E. Holt, became (Dec., 1966) minister for education and science. After Holt's death Gorton was chosen (Jan., 1967) to replace him as Liberal party leader and prime minister. In 1971, Gorton was ousted as party chief and prime minister in a dispute with Liberal party leaders; he served for a time as defense minister and deputy party leader, but he resigned these posts late in 1971. He served (1973-74) as minister for the environment.

Gorton, Samuel, c.1592-1677, Anglo-American religious leader, founder of Warwick, R.I., b. near Manchester, England. Seeking religious freedom, he immigrated to America (1637) but, because of his unorthodox religious teachings, was banished successively from Boston and Plymouth. At Portsmouth, R.I., he joined Anne Hutchinson in ousting William CODDINGTON (1639) but on Coddington's return to power was himself turned out. In 1642, Gorton bought Indian land south of Providence and founded Shawomet. Massachusetts authorities, with designs on that territory, jailed him (1643) for holding erroneous religious opinions. The earl of Warwick finally obtained for Gorton freedom from molestation on his land, which he renamed (1648) Warwick and on which he preached to colonists and Indians. His followers called themselves "Gortonites" for many decades after his death. His tenets included denial of the Trinity, denial of actual heaven and hell, and a belief that every man should be his own intercessor.

Gortyna (gôrtī'nə), ancient city, S central Crete. Under Rome it was one of the leading cities of the island. Many ancient Greek remains have been discovered on the site. An inscription dating from c.450 B.C. of a code of laws of inheritance, marriage, divorce, and other family matters was found on a wall in 1884.

Görtz, Georg Heinrich von (gā'ôrk hīn'rĭkh fən görts), 1668-1719, Swedish diplomat and financial expert, a German. While in the service of Frederick V, duke of Holstein-Gottorp, he helped create the duke's alliance with Sweden, which threatened Danish power in SCHLESWIG-HOLSTEIN. He won the favor of CHARLES XII of Sweden and became his chief minister in 1714. He tried to improve the position of Sweden by conducting (1718) peace negotiations with Russia to end the Northern War, but Charles would make no concessions. The unpopular measures of the reign were blamed upon Görtz, who had financed Charles's wars by depreciating Swedish currency. After Charles's death the new queen had Görtz executed as a traitor because of his past acts and because he supported the duke of Holstein-Gottorp, who was her rival for the throne.

Goryn (gô'rĭn), Pol. *Horyń*, river, W European USSR. It rises 65 mi (105 km) E of Lvov and flows 410 mi (660 km) N into the Pripyat River.

Görz: see GORIZIA, Italy.

Gorzów Wielkopolski (gôr'zo͞of vyĕlkôpôl'skē), Ger. *Landsberg an der Warthe*, city (1970 pop. 74,267), W Poland, on the Warthe River. A transportation and trade center, it also has shoe mills, chemical works, and lignite mines. Chartered in 1257, it was destroyed by the Swedes in the Thirty Years War. The town rose again in the 18th cent. as part of the Prussian province of Brandenburg. In World War II it again suffered great destruction.

Goschen, George Joachim Goschen, 1st **Viscount** (gō'shən), 1831-1907, British statesman. A leading financier, he was elected (1863) to Parliament as a Liberal and was president of the Poor Law Board (1868-71) and first lord of the admiralty (1871-74). In 1876 he was sent to Cairo to negotiate the establishment of Anglo-French control over Egypt's finances. He later served (1880-81) as ambassador to Turkey. Goschen was one of the leading Liberal Unionists, who in 1886 broke with William Gladstone over Irish Home Rule. As chancellor of the exchequer (1886-92) in the Conservative government he successfully converted the national debt and reduced currency stringencies, and as first lord of the admiralty (1895-1900) he supervised expansion of the navy. See his *Theory of Foreign Exchanges* (1861; 4th ed., with biographical preface by B. F. Hopper, 1932); study by T. J. Spinner, Jr. (1973).

Gosford, Archibald Acheson, 2d **earl of** (gŏz'fərd), 1776-1849, governor in chief of British North America (1835-37). He served in the British House of Commons and, after succeeding (1807) to his Irish peerage, was elected Irish representative peer in the House of Lords in 1811. While in Parliament, he urged a conciliatory policy toward Ireland. In 1835 he was appointed governor of British North America—excepting Newfoundland—and a royal commissioner to inquire into the state of affairs in Lower Canada. His policy of "conciliation without concession" toward Louis Joseph Papineau and other French Canadians alienated the English element without winning the French extremists. He resigned on Nov. 14, 1837, on the eve of the rebellion of 1837. On his return to England, he unsuccessfully opposed (1840) the Act of Union, which united Upper and Lower Canada.

Gosforth (gŏz'fərth), urban district (1971 pop. 26,826), Northumberland, NE England. Formerly a coal-mining center, Gosforth is now residential. In 1974 it became part of the new metropolitan county of Tyne and Wear.

goshawk: see HAWK.

Goshen (gō'shən). **1** Unidentified fertile region of Egypt occupied by the Israelites. Gen. 47.6; Ex. 8.22; 9.26. **2** Unidentified region, S Palestine, conquered by Joshua. Joshua 10.41; 11.16. **3** Town of Judah. Joshua 15.51.

Goshen, city (1970 pop. 18,004), seat of Elkhart co., N Ind., on the Elkhart River; inc. 1868. Goshen is in a farm and dairy region; poultry is also raised and processed. Its manufactures include rubber goods, electronic controls, wood products, metal products, mobile homes, and boats. There are Amish and Mennonite colonies in the area. Goshen College is there.

Goshogawara (gōshōgä'wärä), city (1970 pop. 47,567), Aomori prefecture, N Honshu, Japan, on the Iwaki River. It is an agricultural market and a communications center.

Goslar (gôs'lär), city (1970 pop. 40,045), Lower Saxony, E West Germany, at the northern foot of the Harz mts., near the border with East Germany. Since its founding in the 10th cent. Goslar has been a mining center. Today, copper, lead, zinc, iron, and sulfur are mined. Manufactures of the city include textiles, clothing, chemicals, and machinery. Goslar was a favorite residence of many early German emperors and was the scene of several imperial diets. It long was a member of the Hanseatic League and was a free imperial city until 1802, when it passed to Prussia. Goslar was awarded to Hanover in 1815 but was regained by Prussia in 1866. The city has preserved much of its medieval character. The Zwinger, a round tower built in 1517, is a remnant of its old fortifications. The Kaiserpfalz, a large Romanesque palace, was built (mid-11th cent.) for Emperor Henry III. There are several Romanesque and Gothic churches, a Gothic city hall (15th cent.), and many half-timbered houses, including the noted Brusttuch (1526).

Gosnold, Bartholomew (gŏz'nōld), fl. 1572-1607, English explorer and colonizer. In 1602 he commanded the *Concord* on a voyage of exploration, in which he navigated the coast from Maine to Narragansett Bay, naming Cape Cod and several islands and building a small fort on Cuttyhunk, westernmost of the Elizabeth Islands. In 1606 he commanded the *God Speed*, which carried a portion of the first settlers to Virginia. He protested against the site of Jamestown but was overruled. He died there of malaria several months later. See biography by W. F. Gookin (1963).

Gospel [M.E.,=good news; cf. *evangel* from Gr.,=good news], one of the four biographies of Jesus that begin the New Testament. The Gospels are named MATTHEW, MARK, LUKE, and JOHN. The first three are called SYNOPTIC GOSPELS because they present a comprehensive view, agreeing in subject matter and order. The solemn reading of the Gospel of the day is a special feature of the liturgy in many churches. Formerly the Gospel (i.e., a book of the Gospels) was used instead of the Bible for the oath in courts in Christian countries. This sort of honor paid to the book resulted in some of the glories of ILLUMINATION; e.g., the Lindisfarne Gospels (see HOLY ISLAND) and the Book of KELLS. For apocryphal Gospels, see PSEUDEPIGRAPHA.

gospel music, American religious musical form that owes much of its origin to the conversion to Christianity of the W African black man enslaved in the American South. Gospel music partly evolved from the songs slaves sang on plantations, notably work songs and the "field holler" with which they greeted one another or expressed emotion; and from the white Protestant hymns they sang in church. However, gospel music did not derive as much from Protestant hymns as did AMERICAN NEGRO SPIRITUALS. Gospel music, more emotional and jubilant, also stemmed from the call and response singing between preacher and congregation, which became common in slave churches. Gospel lyrics often call for obedience to God and avoidance of sin in order to obtain the reward of heaven's kingdom, and they also celebrate God's love. Gospel style makes use of choral singing in unison or harmony, often, but not always, led by a lead singer or singers. The songs are performed with fervent enthusiasm and vigor, and spiritual inspiration is conveyed sometimes by tight, intense control, and other times by abandon. In the black culture of the first half of the 20th cent., gospel music was considered antithetical to blues and JAZZ, despite their similarity of origins, and gospel performers rarely sang in nonreligious settings. Later, as all three forms became popular outside the black community, they were less mutually exclusive. There is a strong gospel element in "soul" jazz and in black ROCK MUSIC of the 1950s and 60s. Important modern performers of gospel music include Mahalia JACKSON, Sister Rosetta Tharpe, The Swan Silver Tones, The Clouds of Joy, and The Five Blind Boys of Mississippi. Black gospel music has its counterpart in white gospel music, which is, to a large and ironic degree, inspired by black gospel music. See Tony Heilbut, *The Gospel Sound* (1971); Linell Gentry, *A History and Encyclopedia of Country & Western & Gospel Music* (1954, repr. 1972).

Gosport (gŏs'pôrt), municipal borough (1971 pop. 75,947), Hampshire, S England. It is a major port and shares its harbor with Portsmouth. There are ship- and yacht-building facilities and various light industries. Formerly a victualing station for the Royal Navy, Gosport was an embarkation point for the invasion of France in 1944. Holy Trinity Church has an organ on which G. F. Handel played.

Gossaert or **Gossart, Jan:** see MABUSE, JAN DE.

Gosse, Sir Edmund William (gŏs), 1849-1928, English biographer and critic. He was lecturer in English literature at Trinity College, Cambridge (1884-90) and librarian of the House of Lords (1904-14). Although he wrote with enthusiasm and wit, his scholarship was often inaccurate and thus much of his critical work has been superseded. He did, however, introduce English readers to Ibsen and other Scandinavian writers as well as to some modern French writers and painters. Among the many biographies he wrote were those of Gray (1882), Donne (1899), Sir Thomas Browne (1905), Ibsen (1907), Swinburne (1917), and Congreve (rev. ed. 1924). *Father and Son* (1907), his best work, describes his relation with his father, Philip Henry Gosse (1810-88), English naturalist and author of zoological works, whose biography Edmund had written (1890). Included among Edmund's several volumes of verse are *On Viol and Flute* (1873) and *New Poems* (1879). He was knighted in 1925. See his essays on Scandinavian poetry and *Studies in the Literature of Northern Europe* (1879); his correspondence with André Gide, 1904-28 (ed. by L. F. Brugmans, 1959); his diary, ed. by R. L. Peters and D. G. Halliburton (1966); biography by J. D. Woolf (1972).

Gossec, François Joseph (fräNswä' zhôzĕf' gôsĕk'), 1734-1829, Belgian composer; pupil of Rameau. In 1784 he organized the École Royale de Chant and taught (1795-1816) composition at its successor school, the Paris Conservatory. Enthusiastic about the French Revolution, he wrote many works to celebrate patriotic events, such as a Te Deum for 1,200 singers and 300 wind instruments. Among his works are chamber music, more than 30 symphonies, and many operas. His clarity of form and innovations in orchestral color strongly influenced the development of French instrumental music.

Gossen, Hermann Heinrich (hĕr'män hīn'rĭkh gô'sən), 1810-58, German economist, little known in his lifetime. His work, *Entwicklung der Gesetze des menschlichen Verkehrs und der daraus fliessenden Regeln für menschliches Handeln* [development of the laws of human intercourse and their resulting rules for human behavior] (1854), anticipated the theory of marginal utility as formulated by William Stanley Jevons and others.

Gosson, Stephen (gŏs'ĭn), 1554-1624, English writer, b. Canterbury, grad. Oxford, 1576. He wrote three plays, all of which are lost and none of which seems to have been successful. He is best known for his attack on plays, poetry, and other arts in *The School of Abuse* (1579), which evoked in reply a defense from Thomas Lodge and Sir Philip Sidney's *Apology for Poetry*. See study by William Ringler (1942).

Göta älv (yö"tä ĕlv'), river, 56 mi (90 km) long, SW Sweden, draining Vänern lake into the Kattegat. It is part of the **Göta Canal,** a 240-mi (386-km) system of rivers, lakes, and canals, which crosses S Sweden from Göteborg to Arkosund on the Baltic Sea and to Stockholm by way of the sea. The canals, which account for one half of the waterway's length, were opened in 1832 and ascend and descend c.300 ft (90 m) by means of 58 locks. The section that passes around the rapids at Trollhättan was modernized in 1916 to accommodate small oceangoing vessels.

Gotaland or **Gotarike:** see SWEDEN.

Göteborg (yötəbôr'yə) or **Gothenburg** (gŏth'-ənbûrg", gŏt'ən-), city (1970 pop. 445,483), capital of Göteborg och Bohus co., SW Sweden, on the Kattegat at the mouth of the Göta älv River. It is Sweden's most important seaport and its second largest city; it is also a major commercial and industrial center and a rail junction. Manufactures include iron and steel, ball bearings, motor vehicles, textiles, processed food, and refined petroleum. There are large shipyards and fisheries in the city. Göteborg was founded in 1604 by Charles IX, but was soon after destroyed by the Danes in the Kalmar War. It was rebuilt by Gustavus II in 1619 and quickly became a major commercial center with large colonies of Dutch and English merchants. The Swedish East India Company was founded at Göteborg in 1731. The city's port was expanded in the mid-18th cent.; in the early 20th cent. it became the terminus of an important transatlantic shipping service. In 1865 the Göteborg licensing system for the control of liquor sales (see LIQUOR LAWS) was originated there. Göteborg has two universities, several academies, and one of the country's largest sports stadiums.

Gotha (gō'tä), city (1970 pop. 57,328), Erfurt district, SW East Germany. It is an industrial, administrative, and cultural center. Manufactures include wood and rubber products, processed food, and printed materials. Gotha was known in the late 12th cent. In 1485 it passed to the Ernestine line of the house of WETTIN and became (1640) the capital of the duchy of SAXE-GOTHA (from 1826 to 1918, Saxe-Coburg-Gotha). Gotha has long been a center of geographical research and publishing. The well-known publishing house of Justus Perthes (founded in 1785 and now called Hermann Haack) began (1863) the publication of the *Almanach de Gotha*, an authoritative reference work on the royal houses and the nobility of numerous countries. In 1875 an important congress of the German Social Democratic Party was held in Gotha. Among the chief historic buildings of the city are the early 15th-century Church of St. Margaret; Friedenstein, a 17th-century ducal palace; and Friedrichstal Palace (18th cent.).

Gotham, name for New York City first used by Washington Irving and others in the *Salmagundi Papers*, with satirical reference to Gotham, England.

Gothenburg: see GÖTEBORG, Sweden.

Gothic architecture and art. The character of the Gothic visual aesthetic was one of immense vitality; it was spikily linear and restlessly active. Informed by the scholasticism and mysticism of the Middle Ages, it reflected the exalted religious hysteria, the pathos, and the self-intoxication with logical formalism that were the essence of the medieval. Gothic style was the dominant structural and aesthetic mode in Europe for a period of 400 years. It is generally agreed that Gothic architecture made its initial appearance (c.1140) in the Île-de-France, the royal domain of the Capetian kings. However, the inception of the style owes much to several generations of prior experimentation, particularly in Normandy (see NORMAN ARCHITECTURE). Although individual components in Gothic architecture, such as ribbed vaulting and the pointed arch, had been employed in Romanesque construction, they had not previously received such a purposeful and consistent application. While the structural value of the Gothic rib has been contested, its formal significance cannot be overestimated. It served above all to delineate the vaults with a skeletal web that gave to the entire structure an articulation of impressive clarity. Unlike Romanesque architecture, with its stress on heavy masses and clearly delimited areas, Gothic construction is characterized by its lightness and soaring spaces. The overall effect of the Gothic cathedral combined this lightness with an innumerable subdivision and multiplicity of forms. The introduction (c.1180) of a system of flying buttresses (see BUTTRESS) made possible the reduction of wall surfaces by relieving them of part of their structural function. Great windows could be set into walls, admitting light through vast expanses of stained glass. Wall surfaces of High Gothic churches thus have the appearance of transparent and weightless curtains. The spiritual and mysterious quality of light is an important element of the religious symbolism of Gothic cathedrals. In plan the High Gothic cathedral remained faithful to the traditional basilican form. It consisted of a central nave flanked by aisles, with or without transept, and was terminated by a choir surrounded by an ambulatory with chapels. These elements, however, were no longer treated as single units but were formally integrated within a unified spatial scheme. The exterior view was dominated by twin towers crowning the facade. The facade was pierced by entrance portals often lavishly decorated with sculpture, and at a higher level appeared a rose window. Additional towers often rose above the crossing and the arms of the transept, which might have entrance portals and sculpture of their own. Around the upper part of the edifice was a profusion of flying buttresses and pinnacles. The first landmark of Gothic architecture was the ambulatory of the abbey of Saint-Denis, constructed between 1140 and 1144. Saint-Denis embodies the first daring use of large areas of glass, coupled with a brilliant organization of space. Its influence was immediate, and the possibilities of the new style were eagerly explored in structures such as the cathedrals of Sens, Noyon, Laon, and Paris, begun in the ensuing decades of the 12th cent. The High Gothic phase of architecture was ushered in by the Cathedral of Chartres, begun after 1194 and followed in rapid succession by the cathedrals of Bourges, Rheims, Amiens, and Beauvais. These structures surged to unprecedented heights. A further reduction of opaque wall surfaces in favor of graceful screens of stone tracery and glass led toward the formation of the Gothic RAYONNANT STYLE around the mid-13th cent. The most striking achievements of Rayonnant design, the Sainte-Chapelle in Paris and the Church of St. Urban in Troyes, have walls almost entirely of glass, held in place by only a thin skeletal frame of masonry. The adoption of Gothic architecture in various parts of Western Europe resulted in interesting variations and developments of the style. The cathedrals of Lincoln and Salisbury typify the early English style (late 12th–early 13th cent.); they retain much of the ponderous mural quality of earlier Norman architecture. In Italy height was usually subordinated to width, in a perpetuation of Romanesque proportions. French models served as inspiration for German churches of the 13th cent., notably at the cathedral in Cologne. Spanish Gothic architecture of this period was also based largely on French monuments; the forms, however, were modified, as in Toledo and Burgos, in the direction of greater ornamental display, partly derived from Moorish precedents. In the 13th cent. the newly founded orders of Franciscans and Dominicans erected large hall churches of unassuming sobriety. The simplicity and functional character of these buildings, shown in such structures as the interior of Santa Maria Novella in Florence or the Church of the Jacobins in Toulouse, contrasts with the trend toward richness in ornamental elaboration apparent in later Gothic art. In the 14th and 15th cent., these tendencies culminated in intricate webs of tracery, as in the towers of the cathedrals at Ulm and Strasbourg in Germany and in the FLAMBOYANT STYLE of the Church of Saint-Maclou in Rouen in France. In England the same exuberance of decoration is manifested in the DECORATED STYLE of Bristol and Ely cathedrals and the even more elaborate PERPENDICULAR STYLE, exemplified in the choir of the cathedral at Gloucester. Building activity, however, was seriously affected by the economic crises of the 14th cent. and by the Black Death, and later Gothic constructions were far less ambitious in scope than those of the preceding period. However, the Gothic tradition never completely died, and in the 19th cent. it enjoyed a revival inspired chiefly by the romantic movement (see GOTHIC REVIVAL). The essential character of the Gothic period, particularly at the outset, was the predominance of architecture; all the other arts were determined by it. Sculpture and stained glass were formally and spiritually integrated within the Gothic cathedral to express a theological program or scheme. The Royal Portal at Chartres (mid-12th cent.) exemplifies the early achievements in the development toward a coherent sculptural scheme; the tympanum, archivolts, and jamb figures are newly united structurally and iconographically to emphasize the importance of Christ on earth. Images of Christ begin to reveal a tendency toward greater humanization. By the first half of the 13th cent., the role of the Virgin Mary as the intermediary between God and man is stressed in the sculptural programs of Laon, Notre-Dame de Paris, and the north transept of Chartres. At the same time figures began to protrude more strongly from their architectural background. Whereas the jamb figures of the Royal Portal at Chartres were formally no more than splendid humanized columns, by the 13th cent. individual sculptural elements became more important and less united with the architecture. The portal figures of the cathedral at Rheims provide an eloquent example of the trend toward sculptural independence. From the mid-13th cent., mannerisms in gesture developed, such as the "hip-shot" pose, notable in the statue of the Virgin and Child at Amiens. This swaying posture further separated sculpture from architecture. In the 14th cent., after the completion of the great cathedrals, sculpture became an independent artistic form. Mannerisms were exaggerated into an elegant style that continued into the 16th cent. There was a parallel trend toward greater realism, which had its origin in sepulchral portrait sculpture. The tendency toward realism reached monumental form in the *Well of Moses* (Dijon; 1395–1403) by Claus Sluter. The influence of French Gothic sculpture spread throughout the Continent and England. The finest and most individual examples are found in Germany in the middle of the 13th cent. in the facades of Bamberg, Strasbourg, and Naumbourg cathedrals, the last showing evidence of a powerfully realistic, wholly German style. In Italy the late 13th-century works of Giovanni Pisano in Siena and Pistoia and of Lorenzo Maitani at Orvieto reflect the heightened expressiveness found in French Gothic art. Monumental fresco painting was rare in the Gothic period except in Italy, where the massive walls remained instead of yielding to the tall skeletal structure found elsewhere. In the rest of Europe STAINED GLASS and TAPESTRY assumed greater importance and showed a stylistic development analogous to that of sculpture. Another aspect of Gothic painting was manuscript illumination, in which text and pictures formed a united composition. From the beginning of the 13th cent., illuminations were done for the courts by lay schools. The Paris school achieved a perfection which made it the center of Gothic painting for nearly two centuries. English miniatures are often indistinguishable from the French in this period. The painters of the Avignon school flourished from 1309, when the papal court was moved there from Rome. This school produced one work, a *Pietà* from Villeneuve-lès-Avignon (Louvre; c. 1460), of such originality of expression that it stands outside the established categories of Gothic painting. Toward the end of the 14th cent., many Flemish artists went to France, and a Franco-Flemish style was created, showing an elegance and interest in minute detail; so wide was its diffusion that it came to be known as the International Style. At about this time panel painting, under the lead of Flanders and Italy, achieved preeminence over all other forms of painting. In the 15th cent. individual painters, such as Stephan Lochner, Martin Schongauer, and Grünewald in Germany, mark the culmination of Gothic art. Others, such as Jean Fouquet in France and the Van Eycks in Flanders, point the way to the Renaissance, while retaining much of the Gothic spirit. In 15th-century Italy, where the Gothic style had never really taken root, the early Renaissance was already in full swing. See Émile Mâle, *The Gothic Image* (1958); Paul Frankl, *The Gothic* (1960); Erwin Panofsky, *Gothic Architecture* (new ed. 1964); Wilhelm Worringer, *Form in Gothic* (rev. ed. 1964); Andrew Martindale, *Gothic Art* (1967); Wim Swaan, *The Gothic Cathedral* (1969); John Harvey, *The Master Builders* (1971).

Gothic language, dead language belonging to the now extinct East Germanic group of the Germanic subfamily of the Indo-European family of languages (see GERMANIC LANGUAGES). Gothic has special value for the linguist because it was recorded several hundred years before the oldest surviving texts of all the other Germanic languages (except for a handful of earlier runic inscriptions in Old Norse). Thus it sheds light on an older stage of a Germanic language and on the development of Germanic languages in general. The earliest extant document in Gothic preserves part of a translation of the Bible made in the 4th cent. A.D. by ULFILAS, a Gothic bishop. This translation is written in an adaptation of the Greek alphabet, supposedly devised by the bishop himself, which was later discarded. See Joseph Wright, *Grammar of the Gothic Language and the Gospel of St. Mark* (2d ed. 1954).

Gothic revival, term designating a return to the building styles of the Middle Ages. Although the Gothic revival was practiced throughout Europe, it attained its greatest importance in the United States and England. The early works were designed in a fanciful late rococo manner, exemplified by Horace Walpole's remodeled "gothick" house, Strawberry Hill (1770). By 1830, however, architects turned to more archaeological methods. Thus, just as the classical revivalists had done, they began to copy the original examples more literally. A. W. N. Pugin wrote two of the basic texts of the Gothic revival. In *Contrasts* (1836) he put forth the idea that the Middle Ages, in its way of life and art, was superior to his own time and ought to be imitated. He amplified his ideas in *The True Principles of Pointed or Christian Architecture* (1841), propounding that not only must Gothic detail be authentic but that the contemporary architect should achieve the structural clarity and high level of craftsmanship that were found in the Middle Ages by using the methods of medieval builders. John Ruskin elaborated on these ideas in *The Stones of Venice.* Followers of Ruskin and Pugin soon came into conflict with proponents of the CLASSIC REVIVAL, and the resulting conflict has often been called a battle of the two styles. The Church of England supported the Gothic movement, however, and provided for the restoration of a great number of medieval religious buildings. Sir George Gilbert Scott was the noted English restorer of the day, while in France, Viollet-le-Duc led the exponents of the Gothic revival there. Many architects found it advantageous to work in both styles, as did Sir Charles Barry, a leading classicist. Working with A. W. N. Pugin, he won a competition in 1840 with Gothic designs for the houses of parliament. In the United States the picturesque aspect of the style took precedence over the doctrinaire approach of Pugin. The first works of note in the Gothic style appeared in the 1830s in buildings designed by A. J. Davis and Richard Upjohn. The younger James Renwick became important in the 1840s and was especially renowned for his Grace Church and St. Patrick's Cathedral in New York City, both prime examples of the Gothic revival in the United States. The Gothic movement foundered because of the impossibility of reproducing medieval buildings when there was no longer a medieval economy or technology. Only superficial effects of the style lingered in some eclectic works of the 19th and 20th cent. However, the ideals of earlier theoreticians, the clear expression of structure and materials have influenced modern architecture. See Kenneth Clark, *Gothic Revival* (3d ed. 1963); P. B. Stanton, *The Gothic Revival and American Church Architecture* (1968); C. L. Eastlake, *History of the Gothic Revival* (rev. ed. 1972).

Gothic romance, type of novel that flourished in the late 18th and early 19th cent. in England. Gothic romances were mysteries, often involving the supernatural and heavily tinged with horror, and they were usually set against dark backgrounds of medieval ruins and haunted castles. *The Castle of Otranto* by Horace Walpole was the forerunner of the type, which included the works of Ann RADCLIFFE, Matthew Gregory LEWIS, and Charles R. MATURIN, and the novel *Frankenstein* by Mary SHELLEY. Jane Austen's novel *Northanger Abbey* satirizes Gothic romances. The influence of the genre can be found in some works of Coleridge, Le Fanu, Poe, and the Brontës. During the 1960s so-called Gothic novels became enormously popular in England and the United States. Seemingly modeled on Charlotte Brontë's *Jane Eyre* and Daphne du Maurier's *Rebecca,* these novels usually concern spirited young women, either governesses or new brides, who go to live in large gloomy mansions populated by peculiar servants and precocious children and presided over by darkly handsome men with mysterious pasts. Popular practitioners of this genre are Mary Stewart, Victoria Holt, Catherine Cookson, and Dorothy Eden.

Gothic type: see TYPE.

Goths: see OSTROGOTHS; VISIGOTHS.

Gotland (gŏt'lənd), Swed. *Gotlands län* (gôt' länts lĕn'), county (1970 pop. 54,093), 1,225 sq mi (3,173 sq km), SE Sweden, in the Baltic Sea. The county comprises the large island of Gotland and several smaller islands, including Fårön, Gotska Sandön, and Karlsö. VISBY is the capital. Gotland island is made up of a limestone plateau and has a steep coastline and a few hills. Its climate is temperate, and there is much fertile soil. Cereals, sugar beets, and vegetables are grown, and sheep are raised. Fishing, cement making, and tourism are the main industries. Archaeological remains indicate that Gotland, inhabited since the Stone Age, had wide commercial contacts from early times, especially under the Vikings (9th–11th cent.). In the 12th cent. German merchants settled at Visby, which became one of the chief towns of the HANSEATIC LEAGUE. From the 11th to the 14th cent. Gotland prospered as a major trade center of N Europe, but internal strife between the Hanse merchants and local tradesmen weakened the county. Gotland was conquered by the Swedish king, Magnus I (Magnus Ladulas) in 1280, and later was taken by Waldemar IV of Denmark in 1361 and by the Hanseatic League in 1370. Soon after Gotland became the base of wide-ranging pirates, and it gradually declined in importance. By the Treaty of Stettin in 1570, Gotland passed under Danish rule; by the Peace of Brömsebro in 1645 it was returned to Sweden. The county has many fine churches and ruined castles.

Goto-retto (gōtō'-rĕt'tō), group of more than 125 islands, 249 sq mi (645 sq km), Nagasaki prefecture, in the East China Sea, off W Kyushu, Japan. Fukue is the largest island. Whaling and fishing are the major occupations.

Gottfried von Strassburg (gôt'frēt fən shträs'-bo͝orkh), fl. 13th cent., German poet, also called Godfrey of Strasbourg. He is thought to have been official scribe of Strasbourg, but little is known of him. As author of the Middle High German *Tristan* (c.1210), he ranks as one of the great medieval German poets and is noted for his fluency and psychological depth. His style, although smooth and artful, is sometimes mannered. Gottfried's *Tristan* breaks off at the meeting of Tristan with Isolt of the White Hands. The poem was concluded by Ulrich von Türheim and Heinrich von Freiberg. See TRISTRAM AND ISOLDE. See translations of Gottfried's *Tristan* by J. L. Weston (1899) and E. H. Zeydel (1948) and studies by M. S. Balls (1971) and W. T. H. Jackson (1971).

Gottheil, Gustav (gŏt'hīl), 1827–1903, American Reform rabbi, b. Prussia. He served as assistant (1855–60) in the Berlin Reform Temple and as rabbi (1860–73) in Manchester, England. From 1873 until his retirement in 1899 he was assistant rabbi, and then rabbi, of Temple Emanu-El, New York City. His influence on Reform Judaism in the United States was great; he was the founder of several Jewish societies and a governor of the Cincinnati Hebrew Union College. In 1886 he prepared the first American Jewish hymnbook, much of which was incorporated in the Union Hymnal adopted by most of the American Reform congregations. Gottheil was the most prominent American rabbi at the first World Zionist Congress (1897), and he became one of the founders of the Federation of American Zionists, later the Zionist Organization of America. See biography by his son, R. J. H. Gottheil (1936).

Gottheil, Richard James Horatio, 1862–1936, American Orientalist and Semitic scholar, b. Manchester, England; son of Gustav Gottheil. He taught Semitic languages at Columbia from 1886 (as professor from 1887), and he was head of the Oriental department of the New York Public Library from 1896. An ardent Zionist, he was interested in the rebuilding of Palestine and was head (1909–10) of the American School of Archaeology at Jerusalem. His contributions to the study of Syriac are noteworthy. His works include *The Syriac Grammar of Mar Elia of Zobha* (1887); *The Syriac-Arabic Glosses of Isha bar Ali* (1908–28); many articles in *The Jewish Encyclopedia,* of which he was an editor; and a biography of his father (1936).

Gotthelf, Jeremias (yārāmē'äs gôt'hĕlf), 1797–1854, Swiss writer and clergyman. His real name was Albert Bitzius, but he adopted for his pen name that of the hero of his autobiographical *Bauernspiegel* (1837). Gotthelf, working as Protestant pastor in the Emmental valley in Bern canton, took an active interest in the education and economic improvement of the poverty-stricken rural population. His 38 volumes of prose—novels, stories, and essays—are characterized by Christian fervor, humor, sincerity, and vigor, and express his faith in the goodness and strength of rural people. Many were written in the Swiss-German idiom. Best known are *Ulric, the Farm Servant* (1840, tr. 1888), a novel; and *Die schwarze Spinne* [the black spider], a novella in which the peasant milieu and everyday realism are expanded into religious myth. See biography by H. M. Waidson (1953).

Göttingen (gŏt'ĭng-ən), city (1970 pop. 108,991), Lower Saxony, E West Germany, on the Leine River. It is noted for its university, founded in 1734 (opened 1737) by Elector George Augustus (George II of England). Manufactures of the city include optical and precision instruments, printed materials, textiles, and aluminum. Known in the 10th cent., Göttingen was granted (1210) a city charter and joined the Hanseatic League. When, in 1837, King Ernest Augustus of Hanover revoked the liberal constitution of Hanover, seven professors at the Univ. of Göttingen issued a strong protest and were summarily dismissed. They were the brothers Jakob and Karl Grimm, the founders of comparative philology; the historian and critic G. G. Gervinus; the historian F. C. Dahlmann; the physicist W. E. Weber; the Orientalist and theologian G. H. A. von Ewald; and the jurist Wilhelm Eduard Albrecht. This celebrated incident led to the decline of the university's reputation. It was revived at the end of the 19th cent. by the growth of world-famous departments of mathematics and physics. The university's reputation in mathematics dates back to 1807, when Karl Friedrich Gauss, who was born in the city, began to teach there. Göttingen was the seat of the *Göttinger Dichterbund* or *Göttinger Hainbund,* a group of early Romantic poets, formed there in 1772 by J. H. Voss and others. The city was virtually undamaged in World War II and has retained numerous historic buildings, including a 14th-century town hall, half-timbered houses, and student taverns. There are several museums.

Gottlieb, Adolph, 1903–74, American painter, b. New York City. Gottlieb studied under John Sloan and Robert Henri. In the 1940s he created pictographs, stylized, primitive symbols set in a gridlike pattern. His abstract dynamic canvases of the following decade (e.g., *Frozen Sounds, Number One,* 1951; Whitney Mus., New York City) placed him in the front ranks of ABSTRACT EXPRESSIONISM. Many of his later works, called bursts, display large fiery circles over a network of spiky lines.

Gottschalk or **Gottschalck** (both: gôt'shälk), d. c.868, German theologian; son of the count of Saxony. He was placed as a boy in the monastery of Fulda (c.822). He did not wish to be a monk but was forced by RABANUS MAURUS MAGNENTIUS, his superior, to remain. In 829 a synod freed him of his vows, but he went to the monastery of Orbais, where he was ordained a priest. He soon began to teach an extreme doctrine of predestination, holding that God had selected in advance whom He would save and whom condemn. His views, which he apparently derived from St. Augustine, created great interest. He preached in Italy and elsewhere. Rabanus and HINCMAR worked to suppress him, and Gottschalk was condemned in 848 and 849, deposed from the priesthood, and imprisoned in the monastery of Hautvilliers.

Gottschalk, Louis Moreau (gŏt'shôk), 1829–69, American pianist and composer, b. New Orleans, of English-French parentage, studied in Paris. Chopin and Berlioz praised his playing, and he appeared successfully in Europe, the United States, and South America. His orchestral compositions include two symphonic poems, *La Nuit des Tropiques* and *Montevideo.* His piano pieces, such as *The Last Hope* and *The Dying Poet,* were immensely popular in his lifetime. See his *Notes of a Pianist* (1881).

Gottsched, Johann Christoph (yō'hän krĭs'tôf gôt'shĕt), 1700–1766, German literary critic, disciple of the Enlightenment. As professor of poetry and philosophy at the Univ. of Leipzig, he virtually dictated intellectual life in that city, and he exerted great influence upon 18th-century German letters, largely through the controversies he aroused. His rationalistic *Versuch einer critischen Dichtkunst* [a critical approach to poetry] (1730) rejects poetic fancy and conceits, stressing purity of language and classic construction. Gottsched's theories were convincingly refuted by BODMER and Breitinger. Gottsched wrote much on dramatic theory and also engaged the troupe of Karoline Neuber to perform plays that he and his wife, Luise Adelgunde, wrote or adapted, notably *The Dying Cato* (1732).

Gottwald, Klement (klāmənt' gôt'vält), 1896–1953, Czechoslovak Communist leader, b. Moravia. After World War I he helped found the Czechoslovak Communist party and served on the party's central committee from 1925. From 1928 to 1943 he was on the executive committee of the COMINTERN, serving as Comintern secretary from 1935. After the German occupation of Czechoslovakia (1938), Gottwald went to Moscow, where he edited a newspaper that propagandized for Czechoslovakian liberation. In 1945 he became deputy premier in the coalition government of President Eduard Beneš. He was named premier in 1946 and also became chairman of the Czechoslovak Communist party. After the Communist coup in Feb., 1948, Gottwald succeeded Beneš as president of Czechoslovakia, a post he held until his death. He dominated government and party through a system of purges and trials, making Czechoslovakia into a satellite of the USSR. His large-scale purge of his opponents in the party culminated in the execution (Dec., 1952) of 11 prominent Communists. Gottwald's death inaugurated a cautious, but short-lived liberalization of the Czechoslovak Communist regime.

Gottwaldov (gôt'väldôf), city (1970 pop. 65,216), central Czechoslovakia, in Moravia, on the Dřevnice River. Formerly called Zlin, it was renamed (1949) in honor of Klement Gottwald, Czechoslovakia's first Communist president. One of the world's largest shoe-manufacturing cities, it is the center of the Czech shoe industry, which was founded in 1913 by Thomas Bata. Under the Bata family, the city grew into an almost self-sufficient factory community. Branches of the Bata shoe industry opened throughout the world. After World War II the Bata industries were nationalized and renamed Svit. Tires and other rubber goods, machinery, and timber are also important to Gottwaldov's economy.

Götz von Berlichingen: see BERLICHINGEN, GÖTZ VON.

gouache (gwäsh): see WATERCOLOR PAINTING.

Goucher College (gou'chər), at Towson, Md., formerly at Baltimore; primarily for women; inc. 1885, opened 1888 by Methodists. It is named after John Franklin Goucher (president of the college 1890–1908) and his wife, who were among the founders.

Gouda (gou'də, gō͞o'-, Du. gou'dä), city (1971 pop. 46,718), South Holland prov., W Netherlands, at the confluence of the Gouwe and Hollandsche IJssel rivers. It has an important cheese market. Its manufactures include smoking pipes, textiles, candles, and pottery. Chartered in 1272, Gouda was a center of the medieval cloth trade. Erasmus studied there prior to 1475, and in 1486 he entered a nearby Augustinian monastery. The city's notable buildings include the Gothic town hall (15th cent.) and the Sint Janskerk or Groote Kerk (16th cent.), one of the largest churches in the Netherlands.

Goudy, Frederic William, 1865–1947, American type designer, b. Bloomington, Ill. Goudy is celebrated as one of the finest and most prolific type designers in history. In 1905, Goudy established his first press, which he moved to New York City the next year. His wife, Bertha M. Sprinks Goudy, acted as typesetter. Kennerley, Deepdene, Garamont, and Forum are a few of his more than 100 typefaces. About 75 of his designs were destroyed when his plant burned down in 1939. Goudy is the author of *The Alphabet* (1918), *Elements of Lettering* (1922), and *Typologia* (1940). See his *Half Century of Type Design and Typography, 1895–1945* (1947).

Gough, Richard (gŏf), 1735–1809, English antiquary, authority on British topography. His valuable collection of books and manuscripts is in the Bodleian Library, Oxford. Chief among his many works are *Anecdotes of British Topography* (1768; enl. ed. *British Topography*, 2 vol., 1780) and *Sepulchral Monuments* (3 vol., 1786–99).

Goujon, Jean (zhäN gō͞ozhôN'), c.1510–c.1566, French Renaissance sculptor and architect. Although his work reflects the Italian mannerist style, particularly of Cellini, he developed his own extremely elegant, elongated, and often lyrical forms. Goujon is first recorded (1540) as having made columns for the organ loft of the Church of Saint-Maclou, Rouen. The classical quality of their design presupposes a firsthand knowledge of the monuments of Rome. He was associated with the architect Pierre Lescot, with whom he first worked on the rood screen of Saint-Germain-l'Auxerrois, Paris; some reliefs from the screen are now in the Louvre. Goujon also made the celebrated decorations for the *Fountain of the Innocents* (1547–49), several panels of which are also in the Louvre. Again in collaboration with Lescot, he worked on the Louvre itself, designing ornaments for the ground floor and attic, that have since been heavily restored; he also worked on the *Tribune of Caryatids.* Goujon, a Huguenot, died in exile in Italy.

Goulart, João (zhwouN gō͞olär'), 1918–, president of Brazil (1961–64). A rancher and attorney, he served as minister of labor, industry, and commerce (1953–54) and as vice president (1956–61). His succession to the presidency upon the resignation of President Janio Quadros (Aug., 1961) was opposed by the military because of his pro-Communist leanings. He was finally permitted to take office with severely limited powers although a plebiscite in Jan., 1963 gave him full presidential powers. Goulart's administration was beset with economic problems and political opinion polarized as the Communists' influence increased. Goulart was overthrown in a rightist revolution (April, 1964); he fled and was given asylum in Uruguay.

Goulburn, city (1971 pop. 21,568), New South Wales, SE Australia, at the confluence of the Wollondilly and Mulwaree rivers. It is a rail center and wool market.

Gould, George Jay, 1864–1923, U.S. railroad owner, b. New York City; son of Jay Gould. He was associated with his father, inherited all the holdings on Jay Gould's death, and adopted daring policies. To compete with E. H. Harriman he bought the Denver & Rio Grande RR. When Harriman bought the Southern Pacific and bottled up the Gould roads, Gould purchased the Western Pacific and completed it to San Francisco to get an outlet to the sea. In the east he also bought or built lines from Toledo to Baltimore via Pittsburgh to give the Wabash RR an outlet to the Atlantic and to challenge the monopoly of the Pennsylvania RR. He seemed to have a transcontinental system in his grasp, but his financing was unsound, and he crashed in the Panic of 1907. By 1918 all the roads had been lost. See E. P. Hoyt, Jr., *Goulds* (1969).

Gould, Glenn, 1932–, Canadian pianist and composer. A prodigy, he began study at the Royal Conservatory of Music in Toronto at the age of 12. He was piano soloist with the Toronto Symphony at 14, and by the time he was 19 he was making concert tours in Canada. Despite his idiosyncratic behavior while performing, Gould is regarded as a great pianist. He is particularly noted for his interpretations of the work of Bach and the romantic composers. As a composer, Gould has been influenced by the post-romantic music of the late 19th century. His first published composition, a string quartet, had its premiere on television in 1956. During the 1960s Gould reduced his concert appearances to a minimum, preferring to concentrate on recording.

Gould, Jay, 1836–92, American speculator, b. Delaware co., N.Y. A country-store clerk and surveyor's assistant, he rose to control half the railroad mileage in the Southwest, New York City's elevated railroads, and the Western Union Telegraph Company. With savings of $5,000 at 21 he became a speculator, particularly in small railroads. After some years he became a director of the Erie RR. Aided by James Fisk and Daniel Drew, he defeated Cornelius Vanderbilt for control of this road and manipulated its stocks in his own interest and that of his group, including "Boss" Tweed. The Gould-Fisk scheme to corner gold in 1869 caused the Black Friday panic. Public protest forced the Gould group out of the Erie, ending with Gould's expulsion in 1872. He then bought into the Union Pacific and other Western roads. By sharp practice he gained control of four lines which made up the Gould system. For years his name was a symbol of autocratic business practice, and he was widely disliked. After his death his estate and interests were managed by his son, George Jay Gould. See C. F. and Henry Adams, *Chapters of Erie* (1871); Julius Grodinsky, *Jay Gould: His Business Career, 1867–1892* (1957); Richard O'Connor, *Gould's Millions* (1962); E. P. Hoyt, Jr., *Goulds* (1969).

Gounod, Charles François (shärl fräNswä' gō͞onō'), 1818–93, French composer, studied at the Paris Conservatory and received the Grand Prix de Rome in 1839. His fame rests chiefly on his operas *Faust* (1859) and *Romeo and Juliet* (1867), marked by their richly lyrical romantic music. One other opera, *Mireille* (1864), had some success. His oratorios *La Rédemption* (1882) and *Mors et Vita* (1885), his funeral cantata, *Gallia* (1870), and his *Messe à Sainte Cécile* (1882) are worthy of note. He spent some years in the study of theology and greatly admired the church music of Palestrina. See his reminiscences (tr. 1896, repr. 1970); biography by James Harding (1973).

Goupil, René (Saint René Goupil) (rənā' gō͞opēl'), c.1607–1642, French missionary, one of the Jesuit Martyrs of North America. He went to Canada in 1640, spent two years assisting the Jesuits as a lay brother, and at the request of Father Isaac JOGUES accompanied him on his return to the Huron Indians from Quebec in 1642. Captured on the journey by Iroquois, they were enslaved and cruelly tortured. At that time Goupil took his vows. Not long afterward he was tomahawked near the site of the present Auriesville, N.Y. Feast: Sept. 26 or (among the Jesuits) March 16.

gourami (gō͞orä'mē), tropical freshwater fish of the labyrinth fish family. Like other members of their family, gouramis have a labyrinthine breathing apparatus connected to each gill chamber that enables them to utilize atmospheric oxygen. They can therefore live in oxygen-poor water. Gouramis are native to SE Asia and Africa. The true gourami, *Osphronemus goramy*, reaches a length of 2 ft (60 cm). It originated in Indonesia, but has been introduced in China and S Asia, where it is cultivated as an important food fish. Certain smaller members of the family, popular as aquarium fishes, are also called gouramis. Best known is the white, 10-in. long (25-cm) kissing gourami (*Helostoma temmincki*). Other popular gouramis are the moonlight gourami (*Trichogaster microlepis*) of Thailand, a 6-in. (15-cm) long, silvery-blue fish with long, threadlike ventral fins, and other *Trichogaster* species. The talking, or croaking, gourami (*Trichopsis vittatus*), a 2-in. (5-cm) long fish, is noted for the curious sounds produced by the males when they surface for air at night. The labyrinth fishes also include the BETTA, or fighting fish, and the so called CLIMBING PERCH, or walking fish, of SE Asia. They are classified in the phylum CHORDATA, subphylum Vertebrata, class Osteichthyes, order Perciformes, family Anabantidae.

gourd (gôrd, gŏŏrd), common name for some members of the Cucurbitaceae, a family of plants whose range includes all tropical and subtropical areas and extends into the temperate zones. Almost all members of the family are annual herbs that grow as climbing or prostrate vines with spirally coiled tendrils. The characteristic large and fleshy fruit of many genera is often called a pepo; several genera have dry fruits, some with a single seed. The family is known for its many edible and otherwise useful plants. The name *gourd* is applied to those whose fruits have hard, durable shells used for ornament and as utensils, e.g., drinking cups, dippers, and bowls. The Old World genus *Lagenaria* includes the calabash, dipper, and bottle gourds. *Luffa cylindrica* is the loofah, dishcloth gourd, or vegetable sponge;

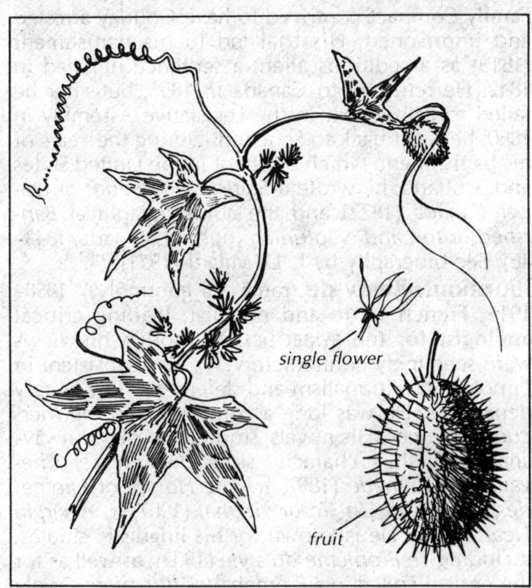

Wild balsam apple, Echinocystis lobata, *a member of the gourd family*

when the edible fruit—called California okra in the S United States—is bleached dry, the inner fibrous network is used as a filter or a scrubbing sponge. Among the many other gourds are the serpent, or snake, gourd (*Trichosanthes anguina*) of Indomalaysia, whose slender fruit reaches 6 ft (1.8 m) in length, and several members of the pumpkin and squash genus *Cucurbita;* in Europe the term *gourd* refers to this genus only. The gourd under which Jonah rested (Jonah 4.6) has been identified with both the gourds and the castor bean. Many of the edible members of the family have been cultivated for so long—often since prehistoric times—that a single species may include several quite different varieties. *Cucurbita* (see PUMPKIN) includes the pumpkin, the vegetable marrow, and the summer squashes (all varieties of *C. pepo*); the winter squashes (varieties of *C. maxima*); and the crooknecks and the cheese pumpkin (varieties of *C. moschata*). *Cucumis* (see MELON) includes the cucumbers (*C. sativus*) and the gherkins (*C. anguria*); *C. melo* includes all melons except the WATERMELON, which, together with the citron, or preserving, melon, is *Citrullis vulgaris.* Of the few members of the family indigenous to the United States, the colocynth, or bitter-apple (*Citrullis colocynthis*), yields a powerful laxative from the dried pulp, and the wild balsam apple, or prickly cucumber (*Echinocystis lobata*), characteristically explodes when ripe, shooting out its seeds—as does the Mediterranean squirting cucumber (*Ecballium elaterium*). Bryony (two species of *Bryonia*), cultivated in Central Europe as a cover vine, has long been valued locally for the medicinal properties of its roots. The African genus *Dendrosicyos* is a unique member of the family in that it grows as a small, bushy tree. Gourds are classified in the division MAGNOLIOPHYTA, class Magnoliopsida, order Violales, family Cucurbitaceae. See L. H. Bailey, *The Garden of Gourds* (1937); U.S. Dept. of Agriculture publications on melons and squash.

Gourgues, Dominique de (dômēnēk' də go͝org), c.1530–1593, French soldier and adventurer. He served in the French army in Italy, was captured by the Spanish, then by the Turks, served as galley slave under both, and after his release led expeditions to Africa and South America. Stirred by the massacre (1565), by Pedro MENENDEZ DE AVILÉS, of the French Huguenot colony at Fort Caroline on the Florida coast, he fitted out three ships and, joining forces with the Indians of the region, captured the Spanish fort of San Mateo (formerly Fort Caroline). He ruthlessly put all the surviving garrison to death and nailed to a tree a sign saying, "Hanged, not as Spaniards, but as traitors, robbers, and murderers"; this was in reply to the Spanish claim that the French colonists were "hanged, not as Frenchmen, but as Lutherans and heretics."

Gourlay, Robert Fleming (go͝or'lē), 1778–1863, Scottish writer and agitator, b. Fifeshire. He emigrated to Upper Canada (Ontario) in 1817 and at Kingston attempted to establish himself as a land agent, but he quickly discovered that land grants were largely controlled by the powerful clique known as the FAMILY COMPACT. At his instigation a convention of pioneer farmers from all over Upper Canada met (1818) at York to discuss their grievances. Alarmed at this threat to their power, the Family Compact contrived to have Gourlay arrested and imprisoned. His trial led to his banishment (1819) as a seditious alien, a sentence nullified in 1842. He returned to Canada in 1856, but after he failed to gain a seat in the Legislative Assembly in 1860, he went back to Scotland. During the years of his banishment, which he spent in the United States and Scotland, he wrote a *Statistical Account of Upper Canada* (1822) and the autobiographical *Banished Briton and Neptunian* (pub. in 38 parts, 1843–46). See biography by L. D. Milani (1971).

Gourmont, Remy de (rəmē' də go͝ormôN'), 1858–1915, French critic and novelist, leading critical apologist for the SYMBOLISTS. Although his views were seemingly contradictory, he was consistent in opposing traditionalism and defending new literary departures. He was long a contributor to the *Mercure de France.* His novels, stories, and plays, always analytic in their character study, include *Les Chevaux de Diomède* (1897, tr. *The Horses of Diomedes,* 1923) and *Un Cœur virginal* (1907, tr. *A Virgin Heart,* 1921). He is known for his linguistic studies, including *Le Problème du style* (1902), as well as for the critical collection *Promenades littéraires* (7 vol., 1904–28).

Gournay, Vincent de (văNsäN' də go͝ornā'), 1712–59, French economist, precursor of the PHYSIOCRATS and of Adam Smith. A wealthy merchant, he was in government service as intendant of commerce from 1751 to 1758. He translated and annotated the chief work of Josiah CHILD and gathered around him a group of men interested in reforming the economy of France and in abolishing trade restrictions. His favorite phrase was *"Laissez faire, laissez passer,"* and he is generally credited with being its originator. Unlike the physiocrats, he regarded industry and commerce as well as agriculture to be important sources of wealth.

gout, condition that manifests itself as recurrent attacks of acute arthritis, which may become chronic and deforming. About 95% of patients with this disorder are men, usually over 30. It is not caused by alcohol or dietary excesses as was once thought, but there seems to be a hereditary factor involved. The presence of increased uric acid in the body distinguishes gout from other forms of arthritis, although hyperuricemia alone, which often occurs in complete absence of gout, is not thought to be the sole causative factor. Gout usually begins with an acute attack of pain, inflammation, extreme tenderness, and redness in the affected joint—often the big toe and sometimes the ankle or knee. After repeated attacks the disease can cause the deposition of sodium urate crystals in the tissues about the joints, causing stiffness and deformity. The aim of treatment is to minimize the formation of uric acid crystals. A high liquid intake that increases daily urine output is usually recommended. Colchicine is used to relieve acute attacks, and uricosuric drugs facilitate the excretion of urates by the kidneys.

Gouthière, Pierre (pyĕr go͞otyĕr'), 1732?–c.1813, French metalworker. The greatest artist of ornamental bronzes of the period of Louis XVI, he produced a vast number of superb cast and chiseled gilt bronzes, executed chiefly for the adornment of fine clocks, Oriental and Sèvres porcelains, and furniture. The Wallace Collection in London includes a red jasper bowl adorned by Gouthière that once belonged to Mme Du Barry, a clock bearing his signature, and many other fine works.

Gouvion-Saint-Cyr, Laurent, marquis de (lōräN' märkē' də go͞ovyôN'-săN-sēr), 1764–1830, marshal of France. He served in the French Revolutionary and Napoleonic Wars and was made marshal following his victory at Polotsk (1812). After the Bourbon restoration he served twice (1815, 1817–19) as minister of war and was instrumental in passing a law to organize military recruitment by voluntary pledges and lottery and limit the arbitrariness of promotions. Because of these attempts to limit the influence of the émigré nobility in the officer corps, he was forced from office by the ultraroyalists. He wrote on the Napoleonic Wars and left personal memoirs.

Governador Valadares (go͞ovərnədo͞or' vəlathä'-rəs), city (1970 pop. 162,333), Minas Gerais state, SE Brazil, on the Doce River. Beans, rice, maize, sugarcane, coffee, avocados, and manioc are raised, and cattle are bred. Food processing, lumbering, and the mining of mica and beryl are also carried on.

government, system of social control under which the right to make laws, and the right to enforce them, is vested in a particular group in society. There are many classifications of government. According to the classical formula, governments are distinguished by whether power is held by one man, a few, or a majority. Today, it is common to distinguish between types of government on the basis of institutional organization and the degree of control exercised over the society. Organizationally, governments may be classified into parliamentary or presidential systems, depending on the relationship between executive and legislature. Government may also be classified according to the distribution of power at different levels. It may be unitary—i.e., with the central government controlling local affairs—or it may be federated or confederated, according to the degree of autonomy of local government. The basic law determining the form of government is called the CONSTITUTION and may be written, as in the United States, or largely unwritten, as in Great Britain. Modern governments perform many functions besides the traditional ones of providing internal and external security, order, and justice; most are involved in providing welfare services, regulating the economy, and establishing educational systems. The extreme case of governmental regulation of every aspect of people's lives is TOTALITARIANISM. See R. M. MacIver, *The Web of Government* (rev. ed. 1965); S. H. Beer, *Patterns of Government* (3d ed. 1973); G. A. Almond and G. B. Powell, *Comparative Politics: A Developmental Approach* (1966); S. E. Finer, *Comparative Government* (1970).

government ownership: see PUBLIC OWNERSHIP.

Government Printing Office, United States, Federal bureau that performs printing and binding for Congress and Federal departments and agencies, distributes government publications, and reprints documents for public purchase. The Government Printing Office was authorized (1860) by joint resolution of Congress and purchased (1861) for $135,000 by congressional appropriation. Its present activities are defined by a 1968 congressional act, and today its plant in Washington, D.C., is probably the largest in the world.

governor, chief executive of a dependent or component unit in a political system. In the United States, a governor is the chief executive of each state and is elected by the people of the state. In the British, French, and Dutch empires a governor was traditionally appointed to rule over each of the colonies. Governors in the United States originally lacked much power. They were often subordinate to the state legislatures and had little control over administrative agencies. However, political reforms in the early 20th cent. shifted power from the legislative to the executive branches of state governments, and today governors are among the most powerful political figures in the United States. At the National Governors Conference, developed from a meeting called (1908) by President Theodore Roosevelt, the nation's governors meet annually to discuss common political and governmental problems.

governor, automatic device used to regulate and control such variables as speed or pressure in the functioning of an engine or other machine. A governor may be an electric, hydraulic, or mechanical device, or it may employ some combination of electric, hydraulic, and mechanical components. The constant-speed governor serves to keep the speed of an engine constant under changes in load and other disturbances. It is very often a mechanical device, employing centrifugal force. Such a governor contains weights, called flyballs, each attached to the end of an arm. The arms are arranged, like the spokes of wheels, around a central spindle and are connected to the inlet valve (commonly called the governor valve). The flyballs are so attached that they move away from the spindle as the speed increases (decreasing the fuel or steam to the inlet) and come closer to the spindle as the speed decreases (increasing the fuel or steam), thereby keeping the speed constant. Varying degrees of closure and the speeds at which they are to occur can be set in advance. Where changes are required while an engine is in operation, a variable-speed governor is employed. A governor-synchronizing device is used to equalize the speed of two or more engines driving electric generators before they engage the generators. In order to control the speed of some engines, a governor's output must be strengthened by connecting the output to a hydraulic amplifier.

Governors Island, 173 acres (70 hectares), in Upper New York Bay, S of Manhattan island, SE N.Y. Bought from the Indians by the Dutch in 1637, it was the site of an early NEW NETHERLANDS settlement. The island received its present name in 1698 (officially 1784), when the British set it aside as the colonial governors' residence. Historic landmarks include Fort Jay (completed c.1800) and Castle William (1811), a military prison. Governors Island is now a U.S. military base and the East coast headquarters of the U.S. coast guard.

Gower, John (gou'ər, gôr), 1330?–1408, English poet. He was the best-known contemporary and friend of Chaucer, who addressed him as "Moral Gower," at the end of *Troilus and Criseyde.* Apparently he was a Kentish landowner who lived in London until his last years, when he became blind and retired as a layman to the priory of St. Mary Overey. In the 15th and 16th cent. Gower was frequently paired with Chaucer as a master of English poetry. Each of his three major works, characterized by metrical smoothness and serious moral criticism, was written in a different language. *Speculum Meditantis* (or *Miroir de l'omme,* 28,603 French octosyllabic lines, written before 1381) is an allegorical manual of the vices and virtues; *Vox Clamantis* (10,265 Latin elegiac verses, written c.1381) expresses horror at the Peasants' Revolt led by Wat Tyler and goes on to condemn the baseness of all classes of society; *Confessio Amantis,* Gower's masterpiece (c.34,000 English lines, written c.1390) is a collection of stories that illustrate the Seven Deadly Sins. Among his minor works are *Cinkante Ballades,* which are love poems in French, and *In Praise of Peace,* a poem in English. See his complete works (ed. by G. C. Macaulay, 4 vol., 1899–1902); selections, ed. by R. A. Peck (1968); study by J. H. Fisher (1964).

Gower (gou'ər), peninsula, c.15 mi (24 km) long and 5 mi (8 km) wide, West Glamorgan, S Wales, between Swansea Bay and Carmarthen Bay. Composed of limestone, the peninsula has scenic cliffs and numerous caves, many of which contain Paleolithic and Bronze Age relics. Farming is the chief economic activity. There are several coastal resorts. Most of the peninsula has been officially designated as a natural beauty area.

Gowon, Yakubu (yäko͞o'bo͞o gô'wŏn), 1934–, Nigerian head of state. A member of the small Angas tribe, he attended military schools in Nigeria and Great Britain, entered (1954) the Nigerian army, and advanced (1966) to battalion commander. After Nigeria had suffered two bloody coups in 1966, he was appointed commander in chief of the armed forces and head of the military government. He led (1967–70) the fight against the secessionist Biafran government of General OJUKWU, finally reuniting Nigeria after a vicious struggle. In 1971, Gowon became a full general.

Gowrie, earls of: see RUTHVEN, family.

Gowrie, Carse of (kärs, kĕrs, gou'rē), alluvial lowland, c.15 mi (24 km) long, Perthshire and Angus, central Scotland, along the northern shore of the Firth of Tay, between Perth and Dundee. A farm belt, it is famous for its fruit.

Goya y Lucientes, Francisco José de (fränthēs'kō hōsā' thā gō'yä ē lo͞othēän'tās), 1746–1828, Spanish painter and graphic artist. After studying in Saragossa and Madrid and then in Rome, Goya returned c.1775 to Madrid and married Josefa Bayeu, sister of Francisco Bayeu, a prominent painter. Soon after his return he was employed to paint a series of tapestry designs for the royal manufactory of Santa Barbara (Huelva) that focused royal attention on his talent. Depicting scenes of everyday life, they are painted with ROCOCO freedom, gaiety, and charm, enhanced by a certain earthy reality unusual in such CARTOONS. In these early works he revealed the candor of observation that was later to make him the most graphic and savage of satirists. Goya possessed a driving ambition throughout his life. His first important portrait commission, to paint Floridablanca, the prime minister, resulted in a painting intended to flatter and please an important sitter, heavy with technical display but less penetrating of vision than the portraits he made of the rich and powerful thereafter. He became court painter to Charles III in 1786, and during the reign of Charles IV and Maria Luisa he was a great favorite at court. His royal portraits are painted with an extraordinary realism revealing explicitly the contempt the artist felt for the crass stupidity, the mediocrity, and the corruption he was portraying. Nevertheless, his portraits were acceptable and he was commissioned to repeat them. In 1793, Goya suffered a terrible illness, now thought to have been either labyrinthitis or lead poisoning, that was nearly fatal and left him deaf. This created for him an even greater isolation than was his by nature and his works after 1793 were cheerless. His portraits of the duchess of Alba, who enjoyed the painter's close friendship and love, are elegant and direct and not flattering. Almost all the notables of Madrid posed for him during those years. Two of his most celebrated paintings, *Maja nude* and *Maja clothed* (both: Prado), were painted c.1797-1800. Goya did his chief religious work in 1798, creating a monumental set of dramatic frescoes in the Church of San Antonio de la Florida, Madrid. But it is in the etching and aquatint media that his profound disillusionment with mankind is most brutally revealed. In 1799 his *Caprichos* appeared, a series of etchings in the nature of grotesque social satire. They were followed (1810-13) by the terrible *Desastres de la guerra* [disasters of war], magnificent etchings suggested by the Napoleonic invasions of Spain. They constitute an indictment of human evil and an outrage at a world given over to war and corruption. Only his credit at court made their publication possible. Two frenzied paintings known as *May 2* and *May 3, 1808* (both: Prado) also record atrocities of war. Goya executed two other series of etchings, the *Tauromaquia* [the bullfight] and the *Proverbios*, the flowers of a tortured, nightmare vision. Throughout the Napoleonic period Goya retained favor under changing regimes. At the age of 70 he retired to his villa, where he decorated his walls with a series of "Black Paintings" of macabre subjects, such as *Saturn Devouring His Children, Witches' Sabbath*, and *The Three Fates* (all: Prado). His last years, harried by further illness, were spent in voluntary exile in Bordeaux, where he began work in lithography that foreshadowed the style of the great 19th-century painters. Goya is generally conceded to be the greatest painter of his century. The only masters he acknowledged were "Nature," Velázquez, and Rembrandt. All phases of his enormous and varied production can be appreciated only in Madrid. He is represented in many European and American galleries, notably in the Hispanic Society of America, the Metropolitan Museum, and the Frick Collection, all in New York City, and in the museums of Boston and Chicago. See André Malraux, *Saturn: An Essay on Goya* (tr. 1957); Pierre Gassier and Juliet Wilson, *Goya: His Life and Work* (with a catalogue raisonné, tr. 1971); Pierre Gassier, *Francisco Goya: Drawings* (tr. 1973).

Goyen, Jan Josephszoon van (yän yō'zəfsōn vän gō'yən), 1596-1656, Dutch landscape painter. He studied at Leiden and Haarlem. In 1631 he settled at The Hague. His typically Dutch landscapes of harbors, canals, riverbanks, and winter scenes with skaters and sleighs are naturalistically painted in a grayish-green tonality. He was one of the first landscape painters to sacrifice minute detail for atmospheric effect and space, and he had a considerable influence on later Dutch landscapists. His paintings are in many collections in Europe and the United States. Famous examples are *Panorama of The Hague* (The Hague); *Banks of a Canal* (Louvre); and *View of Dordrecht* (Rijks Mus.). The Metropolitan Museum has five of van Goyen's works, and the Pennsylvania Academy, two.

Goytisolo, Juan (hwän goitēsō'lō), 1931-, Spanish writer, b. Barcelona. His works usually denounce the absurdity and injustice of the world. Among his novels are *Fiestas* (1958, tr. 1960), *Duelo en el paraíso* [grief in paradise] (1955), *Fin de fiesta* (1962; tr. *The Party's Over*, 1966), *Señas de indentidad* (1966; tr. *Marks of Identity*, 1969), and *Count Julian* (tr. 1974).

Gozan (gō'zăn), fertile country bordering on the Habor, to which the Assyrians carried the Israelites. 2 Kings 17.6; 18.11; 19.12; Isa. 37.12.

Gozzi, Carlo, Conte (kär'lō kôn'tā gôt'tsē), 1720-1806, Italian dramatist. A defender of traditional Italian culture, he wrote comedies based on the old commedia dell' arte. To show the potential of the old forms and to ridicule Goldoni, their adversary, he conceived the idea of dramatizing the tales of Basile's *Pentamerone*. Thus he founded the fable play in Italy. His *Fiaba dell' amore delle tre melarance* (1761; set to music by Prokofiev as *The Love for Three Oranges*) was followed by more plays of the type, among them *Re Turandot* (1762), made into an opera by Puccini. Written in Venetian dialect, these were very popular in their day. See Gozzi's memoirs (1797; tr. with a critical essay by J. A. Symonds, 1890).

Gozzi, Gasparo (gäs'pärō), 1713-86, Italian critic and poet; brother of Carlo Gozzi. Struggling to support a large family, he wrote plays, stories, articles, and poems. He founded the literary journals *Gazzetta veneta* (1760) and *Osservatore veneto* (1761), which were urbane, satirical, and moralizing in the manner of the *Spectator*. His *Difesa di Dante* (1758) contributed to the 19th-century revival of interest in Dante.

Gozzoli, Benozzo (bānôt'tsō gôt'tsōlē), 1420-97, Florentine painter, whose real name was Benozzo di Lese. He was apprenticed to Fra Angelico, first in Florence and later in Rome. Becoming independent in 1449, he chose to stay in Montefalco for a few years. There he created an altarpiece of a *Madonna and Child with Saints* and also frescoes depicting the life of St. Francis. Upon his return to Florence in 1459, he began his famous *Journey of the Magi* for the chapel in the Medici Palace. There he painted a magnificent cavalcade of pilgrims to Bethlehem, including animated portraits of contemporary Florentines. To represent the Magi he painted Lorenzo de' Medici and two leaders of the East, Patriarch Joseph and Emperor John Paleologus. Gozzolzi depicted them in exotic Oriental dress against a background of fantastic landscape and strange animals. From 1468 until almost his last days he decorated the Camposanto, Pisa, with scenes from the Old Testament.

GPU: see SECRET POLICE.

Graaff Reinet (gräf rī'nət), town (1970 pop. 23,706), Cape Prov., S South Africa, on the Great Karroo. It is the center of an important farming and stock-raising area. Founded in 1786, it served as the capital of a short-lived Boer republic (1795-96). Andries Pretorius was born in Graaff Reinet. The city has a teachers college.

Grabbe, Christian Dietrich (krĭs'tēän dē'trĭkh gräb'ə), 1801-36, German dramatist and journalist. Critical of "Shakespearomania," Grabbe strove for a national German drama and wrote original, poetic historical tragedies. *Hannibal* (1835) and *Hermannsschlacht* [Hermann's battle] (1838) depict the genial individual shattered by others' lack of understanding. *Napoleon* (1831), *Scherz, Satire, Ironie und tiefere Bedeutung* (1822; tr. *Comedy, Satire, Irony and Deeper Meaning*, 1955), and *Don Juan und Faust* (1829) are among his other notable works. See studies by R A. Nicholl (1969) and C. D. Grabbe (1972).

Gracchi (grăk'ī), two Roman statesmen and social reformers, sons of the consul Tiberius Sempronius Gracchus and of CORNELIA. The brothers were brought up with great care by their mother. **Tiberius Sempronius Gracchus,** d.133 B.C., the elder of the Gracchi, fought at Carthage (146 B.C.) and in Spain (137). Alarmed at the state of Italy and the provinces, where the middle class was being totally eliminated by concentration of wealth and lands in the hands of a few, Tiberius stood for the tribunate of the people in 133 B.C. as an avowed reformer. On his election he immediately proposed and succeeded in passing the Sempronian Law (*Lex Sempronia Agraria*), a modification of the Licinian Rogations (see AGRARIAN LAWS), which sought to redistribute the public lands that the rich had taken over. Tiberius' colleague Octavius vetoed the law, and Tiberius, by immediately holding an unconstitutional referendum, deposed Octavius. Later in the year Attalus III, king of Pergamum, died and bequeathed his property to Rome; Tiberius proposed to use the bequest to provide capital for the paupers who were to settle the lands allotted under the Sempronian Law. It was now election time, and Tiberius renominated himself; the senate declared this action illegal and had the election postponed. In a great riot on the following day Tiberius was killed. His brother, **Caius Sempronius Gracchus,** d.121 B.C., became the organizer of the reform movement begun by Tiberius. After serving (126) as quaestor in Sardinia, he returned to Rome and was elected (123) tribune of the people. Setting out to complete his brother's work, he immediately initiated a series of remarkable social reforms. The chief aim of these reforms was to unite the plebs and the EQUITES, thus undermining the authority of the senate. The *Lex Frumentaria* benefited the small landholders by reappropriating the proceeds of the tax on allotted lands. The senate, which had formerly used this money for the aggrandizement of the aristocracy, was now required to use it for the good of the poor. In the *Lex Judiciaria*, Caius won over the equites by granting them control over the judgeships that had heretofore belonged to the senate. Caius was reelected (122) tribune, but the counterproposals of Marcus Livius Drusus began to gain popularity, and the following year Caius was defeated for reelection. Repeal of his measures was proposed, and in the ensuing riots Caius was killed. Within 10 years the reaction had annulled every Gracchan reform, and the social and political war began again, this time to culminate in the fatal and bloody struggle of MARIUS and SULLA. See study by Henry C. Boren (1969).

Grace, William Russell, 1832-1904, American financier, b. Queenstown, Ireland. He was in business in England and Peru before establishing (1865) W. R. Grace & Company in New York City. After Peru's defeat by Chile, Grace was among those who underwrote the Peruvian national debt, in return for extensive business concessions. The Grace firm established branches in many Latin American countries after 1895 and developed steamship operations. In 1880, Grace became the first Roman Catholic mayor of New York City and in two reform administrations opposed Tammany. See biography by his grandson, J. P. Grace (1953).

grace, in Christian theology, the free favor of God toward men, which is necessary for their salvation. A distinction is made between natural grace (e.g., the gift of life) and supernatural grace, by which God makes man (born sinful because of original sin) capable of enjoying eternal life. In general, the term *grace* is restricted to supernatural grace, usually considered as the keystone of the whole Christian theological system. Supernatural grace is usually defined as being actual or sanctifying. Actual grace turns the soul to God; sanctifying grace confirms and perpetuates the ends of this conversion and makes the soul habitually good. Most theologies (except in CALVINISM), wishing to maintain man's freedom in addition to God's complete freedom in granting grace, distinguish prevenient grace, which frees man and awakens him to God's call, from cooperating grace, by which God assists to salvation the free man who seeks it. When God seems to confer on a man such actual grace that his conversion appears inevitable, the grace is said to be efficacious. The apparent difficulty of claiming that grace may be efficacious while man is free was explained by St. THOMAS AQUINAS on the ground that it was a peculiar nature of this grace granted to some men that it should be ineluctable; it was this doctrine that Luis MOLINA and the Molinists disputed. Differing in effect from efficacious grace is merely sufficient grace, which, while sufficient to conversion, may be rejected by man at will. Calvinism rejects merely sufficient grace, holding instead that grace is irresistible. In every Christian theology God is considered to grant grace quite freely, since its gift is far greater than man can merit. As to which men are offered this grace, there is great difference. The generality hold that it is offered to men who place no obstacle in the way of salvation rather than to those who neglect what ways to grace they have been given; the Jansenists (see JANSEN, CORNELIS), however, believed that grace was not given outside the church, and the Calvinists hold that it is offered only to those predestined to election. Sanctifying grace may be said to succeed justification as actual grace precedes it. The operation of sanctifying grace brings holiness to the individual soul. The indwelling of God in the soul and the soul's actual participation in God's nature (in an indefinable manner) are the perfections of sanctifying grace. As to the means, there is a serious cleavage in Christianity, notably in regard to sacramental grace. According to Roman Catholics and Orthodox, the grace accompanying a sacrament is *ex opere operato*, i.e., by

God's ordinance the sacrament actually confers grace, the good disposition of the minister being unimportant and that of the recipient being not always a condition; Protestants hold that the sacraments are *ex opere operantis,* i.e., the faith of the recipient is all-important, and the sacrament is the sign, not the source of grace. Certain Christian systems have developed quite different ideas of grace, and PELAGIANISM has its advocates in liberal, 20th-century Protestantism. The great emphasis on grace is a distinction of Christianity. In recent years among orthodox theologians there has been a renewed interest in the theology of grace. Among traditional usages, they distinguish three forms of grace: God's communication of Himself to the Christian soul is grace; the favorable attitude of God toward the soul is grace; the ontological modification of Christian life by God's favor is grace.

Graces, in Greek mythology, personifications of beauty, charm, and grace; daughters of Zeus and the oceanid Eurynome. Also known as the Charites, they were usually three in number and were called Aglaia, Thalia, and Euphrosyne. The Graces were associated with Aphrodite and those gods associated with the arts, such as the Muses. Their worship at Athens suggests that they were ancient fertility or vegetation goddesses. In Rome they were called Gratiae.

Gracián, Baltasar (bältäsär' gräthyän'), 1601–58, Spanish Jesuit philospher and writer. A scholar, satirist, and epigrammatist, Gracián frequently ran afoul of Jesuit authority. *El héroe* (1637) and *El político* (1640) are treatises on the ideal qualities for political leaders. *Agudeza y arte de ingenio* [the wit and art of genius] (1643) is an analysis of poetry. *Oráculo manual y arte de prudencia* (1647) contains maxims and instructions for acquiring worldly wisdom. Gracián's masterpiece is the allegorical and pessimistic novel *El criticón* (3 parts, 1651–57), which contrasts an idyllic primitive life with the evils of civilization. It brought him exile and disgrace. See study by M. Z. Hafter (1966).

Graciosa (gräsēô'zə), island (1960 pop. 8,700), 24 sq mi (62 sq km), Angra do Heroísmo dist., in the N Atlantic, one of the central AZORES. The chief town is Santa Cruz.

grackle, common name applied to some members of the New World family Icteridae, which also includes blackbirds, orioles, meadowlarks, cowbirds, and others. The plumage of the purple, or common, grackle of the Atlantic coastal region is black with metallic hues, iridescent in the sunlight. It feeds on grain and harmful insects, but it is a cannibalistic nest robber. Grackles invade cities and roost in huge flocks. The bronzed grackle, which interbreeds with the purple, is found further inland and W to the Rocky Mts.; in the South are found the Florida and boat-tailed grackles, in Texas and Mexico the great-tailed grackles, or jackdaws. Grackles are classified in the phylum CHORDATA, subphylum Vertebrata, class Aves, order Passeriformes, family Icteridae.

gradation: see ABLAUT.

Gradisca d'Isonzo (grädē'skä dēsōn'tsō), town, Friuli-Venezia Giulia, NE Italy, on the Isonzo River, near the Yugoslav border. It is an agricultural center. The town was founded (late 15th cent.) by Venice as a fortress against the Turks. From 1754 to 1918 it formed with Gorizia (Görz) the crown land of Görz-Gradisca in the Austrian province of Küstenland.

Grado: see AQUILEIA, Italy.

Grady, Henry Woodfin, 1850–89, American journalist and orator, b. Athens, Ga. In 1879 a gift from Cyrus W. Field enabled him to buy into the Atlanta *Constitution.* He gained fame with his editorials and addresses, which attempted to reconcile North and South, and particularly with his stirring speech "The New South," delivered in New York in 1886. His speeches were posthumously published in *The New South and Other Addresses* (1904) and *Complete Orations and Speeches* (1910). See study by J. C. Harris (1972).

Graeae or **Graiae** (both: grē'ī), in Greek mythology, daughters of Ceto and Phorcus, called Deino, Enyo, and Pemphredo. The personifications of old age, they were born with gray hair and only one eye and one tooth among them. They were the protectors of their sisters, the Gorgons.

Graetz, Heinrich: see GRÄTZ, HEINRICH.

Graevius, Johann Georg (yō'hän gā'ôrk grā'vēōōs), 1632–1703, German antiquary. His German name was Gräve or Greffe. He was historiographer to William III of England and is remembered for his vast catalogs of Roman and Italian antiquities.

Graf or **Graff, Urs** (ōōrs), c.1485–1528, Swiss wood engraver, etcher, painter, and goldsmith, studied at Basel. He was influenced by the work of Dürer and Hans Baldung. One of the first to employ effectively the technique of white-line engraving, he was known for his lively humor and fantasy, as well as for his more serious religious aspect. A pen drawing of 1523 (Kupferstichkabinett, Basel), thought to be Lucretia, is representative of his vigorous, Dürer-esque style.

graffito (gräf-fē'tō). **1** Method of ornamenting architectural plaster surfaces. The designs are produced by scratching a topcoat of plaster to reveal an undercoat of contrasting and deeper color. The technique of graffito was used in ancient cultures including those of Egypt and Greece. It was refined in Italian decorative art of the 15th and 16th cent., being then used to treat the entire facades of buildings as great formal mural decorations. Around windows and doors were architectural borders depicting pilasters, colonnettes, and caryatids; remaining surfaces were covered with medallions, garlands, and arabesque bands. Fine examples remain, especially at Florence, and the medium has occasionally been revived in modern buildings. Graffito decoration is applied to pottery by coating an unfired piece with a contrasting color of clay and scratching a design through it to show the color underneath. The slip ware of the Pennsylvania Germans is a good example of graffito work. It is also spelled *sgraffito.* **2** An irreverent inscription on a wall in a public place is also called a graffito (pl. graffiti). The term *graffiti* was first used in this sense by archaeologists to designate informal writings on tombs and ancient monuments. Today, as then, graffiti deal with a wide variety of subjects and are often satirical in tone.

Graf Spee, German battleship: see SPEE, MAXIMILIAN, GRAF VON.

graft, in surgery: see TRANSPLANTATION, MEDICAL.

grafting, horticultural practice of uniting parts of two plants so that they grow as one. The scion, or cion, the part grafted onto the stock or rooted part, may be a single bud, as in BUDDING, or a CUTTING that has several buds. The stock may be a whole mature plant, such as an apple tree, or it may be a root (usually of a seedling). The most important reason for grafting is to propagate hybrid plants that do not bear seeds or plants that do not grow true from seed. It is also used in dwarfing and in tree surgery, to increase the productivity of fruit trees by adding to the number of buds, to adapt a plant to an unfamiliar soil or climate by using the roots of another plant which thrives in that environment, and to combat diseases and pests (e.g., the PHYLLOXERA) by using a resistant stock. Grafting, which was employed in Roman times, is used extensively by nurserymen and other horticulturists. Usually only closely related plants can be grafted successfully: grafting cannot produce new plant varieties. As a rule, the process is begun when the scion is dormant and the stock is just resuming growth. There are many methods of grafting, all of which depend on the closest possible uniting of the CAMBIUM layers of both scion and stock. See G. W. Adriance and F. R. Brison, *Propagation of Horticultural Plants* (2d ed. 1955); Norman Taylor, ed., *Encyclopedia of Gardening* (4th ed. 1961); R. J. Garner, *The Grafter's Handbook* (3d ed. 1968).

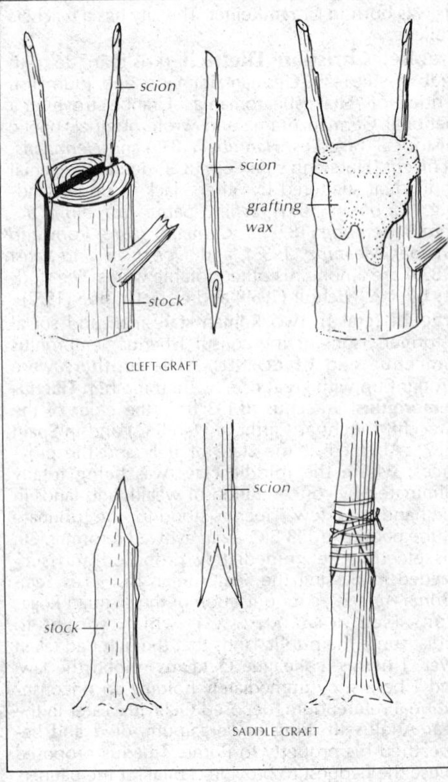

Two methods of grafting

Grafton, Augustus Henry Fitzroy, 3d **duke of,** 1735–1811, British statesman. After serving as a secretary of state (1765–66), he became first lord of the treasury in Lord Chatham's administration (1766–68) and, because of Chatham's illness, effective chief minister. He officially became chief minister in 1768. His handling of the John WILKES affair and the growing crisis in the American colonies led to the breakup of his ministry, and he resigned in 1770. He was lord privy seal under Lord North (1771–75) and under lords Rockingham (1782) and Shelburne (1782–83).

Grafton, Richard, d. c.1572, London publisher and printer. In 1539 with Edward Whitchurch he printed the Great Bible in black letter. He printed the first edition of the Book of Common Prayer, also in black letter. Grafton was printer to King Edward VI, and a protégé of Thomas Cromwell. He earned a minor place among English chroniclers.

Grafton, town (1970 pop. 11,659), Worcester co., S central Mass.; inc. 1731. Leather products and abrasives are produced there. An Indian reservation is nearby.

Graham, Billy (William Franklin Graham), 1918–, American evangelist, b. Charlotte, N.C. He was a lay preacher while a student (1936–40) at Bob Jones Univ. and the Florida Bible Seminary. In 1939 he was ordained a minister in the Southern Baptist Church. Graham, a fiery and persuasive preacher, began (1944) his career as evangelist for the American Youth for Christ movement. His first sustained evangelistic campaign (in Los Angeles in 1949) was a popular success and brought him national attention. He subsequently made preaching tours in most major U.S. cities and in Europe, Africa, South America, Asia, and Australia. The Minneapolis-based Billy Graham Evangelical Association, founded in the early 1950s, publishes *Decision* magazine and produces weekly radio shows, television specials, and movies. Among his many books are *Revival in Our Times* (1950), *The Seven Deadly Sins* (1955), *My Answer* (1960), *World Aflame* (1965), and *Challenge* (1969). See biographies by W. C. McLaughlin (1960), J. C. Pollock (1966), and J. E. Kilgore (1968); J. E. Barnhart, *The Billy Graham Religion* (1972).

Graham, George, 1674?–1751, English instrument maker. A clockmaker by trade, Graham designed clocks and watches that earned him membership in the Royal Society and were still manufactured into the present century. In 1725 he built a very accurate 8-ft (2.4-m) quadrant for the royal astronomer, Edmund Halley, at Greenwich; it was widely copied. His most important invention remains the micrometer screw, which enabled him to build zenith sectors and calipers of unprecedented precision. Graham is buried in Westminster Abbey.

Graham, James: see MONTROSE, JAMES GRAHAM, 5TH EARL AND 1ST MARQUESS OF.

Graham, Martha, 1895–, American dancer, teacher, and choreographer, b. Pittsburgh. After 1916, Graham attended the Denishawn School, Los Angeles; in 1920 she made her debut in Ted Shawn's *Xochitl,* which was created for her. She left the Denishawn company in 1923 to dance in musical revues and to make her independent debut (1926). Graham first appeared with her own group of dancers in 1929, began her tours after 1939, and became a leading figure in MODERN DANCE. Her highly individual, stark, and angular works often draw upon historical and mythological subjects. They include *Primitive Mysteries* (1931), *Letter to the World* (1940), *Deaths and Entrances* (1943), *Appalachian Spring* (1944), *Phaedre* (1962), *A Time of Snow* (1968), and *Archaic Hours* (1969). See her notebooks (1973); biography by Don McDonagh (1973).

Graham, Sylvester, 1794–1851, American reformer and Presbyterian minister, b. West Suffield, Conn. He advocated a vegetable diet as a cure for intemperance and the use of coarsely ground whole-wheat flour. Graham flour was named for him.

Graham, Thomas, 1805–69, Scottish chemist, best known for research in DIFFUSION in both gases and liquids that led to his formulation of Graham's law. His discovery that certain substances (e.g., glue, gelatin, starch) pass through a membrane more slowly than others (inorganic salts, e.g., common salt, or sodium chloride) led him to draw a distinction between the two groups, calling the former (the slower) colloids and the latter crystalloids. In this connection he discovered dialysis. His work was the earliest in colloidal chemistry. His investigation of phosphoric acid led to the present chemical concept of polybasic acids.

Grahame, Kenneth, 1859–1931, English author. He was a secretary in the Bank of England from 1908 until 1918. His works, noted for their humor and charm, include *The Golden Age* (1895) and *Dream Days* (1898), scenes of his childhood in England, and the children's classic *The Wind in the Willows* (1908). Grahame compiled the *Cambridge Book of Poetry for Young People* (1916). See his biography, with letters and unpublished work by P. R. Chalmers (1933, repr. 1971).

Graham Island, 2,485 sq mi (6,436 sq km), off the coast of British Columbia, Canada, northernmost and largest of the Queen Charlotte Islands.

Graham of Claverhouse: see DUNDEE, JOHN GRAHAM OF CLAVERHOUSE, 1ST VISCOUNT.

Graham's law: see DIFFUSION.

Grahamstown, city (1970 pop. 42,184), Cape Prov., SE South Africa. It manufactures pottery and is the commercial center for a rich agricultural region. Founded in 1819 as a military post, Grahamstown was repeatedly attacked in the early 19th cent. by the Xhosa and other black African peoples. Rhodes Univ. (1904) and the Albany Museum, with collections of prehistoric and natural history materials, are in the city.

Graiae: see GRAEAE.

Grail, Holy, a feature of medieval legend and literature. It appears variously as a chalice, a cup, or a dish and sometimes as a stone or a caldron into which a bleeding lance drips blood. It was identified by Christians as the chalice of the Last Supper brought to England by St. Joseph of Arimathea. Miraculous in its powers, it could provide food and healing. However, it would be revealed only to a pure knight, and the Grail Quest appears in different stories. In ARTHURIAN LEGEND the purest knight is variously PARSIFAL or GALAHAD. The Grail is one of the most difficult problems of Arthurian legend, introducing as it does features of Christian story, Celtic myth, and ancient fertility cults. See R. S. Loomis, *The Grail* (1963); Emma Jung and Marie-Louise von Franz, *The Grail Legend* (tr. 1971).

grain, in agriculture, term referring to the caryopsis, or dry FRUIT, of a cereal GRASS. The term is also applied to the seedlike fruits of BUCKWHEAT and of certain other plants and is used collectively for any plant that bears such fruits. The food content of the seeds (as they are commonly called) is mostly carbohydrate, but some protein, oil, and vitamins are also present. Grain, whole or ground into meal or flour, is the principal food of man and of domestic animals. The seeds of most grains grow in concentrated clusters that are gathered efficiently by modern mechanical harvesting machines (see COMBINE). Grain is easy to handle and, because of its low water content, can be stockpiled and stored for long periods, unlike other starch foods (e.g., the potato). Grains, both living and stored, are attacked by a variety of insect pests (e.g., the corn borer, locust, and grasshopper) and by smuts, rusts, blights, rots, and other DISEASES OF PLANTS. The principal grain crops, in order of total world output, are WHEAT, RICE, Indian CORN, OATS, BARLEY, and RYE; together, these grains occupy about half of all the land under crops. All the staple grains were domesticated in the Neolithic period, or New Stone Age, and their cultivation was a powerful factor in drawing men into settled communities. Many religious beliefs and rites have been associated with grains; the cereals derive their name from Ceres, the Roman goddess of grain. Grain has been an article of commerce in nearly all civilizations. See publications of the U.S. Dept. of Agriculture.

grain, in weights and measures: see ENGLISH UNITS OF MEASUREMENT.

grain alcohol: see ETHANOL.

Grain Coast, W Africa, former name of a part of the Atlantic coast that is roughly identical with the coast of modern Liberia. In the 15th cent. "grains of paradise," i.e., seeds of the melegueta pepper, became a major export item; hence the name Grain Coast.

grain drill: see DRILL.

Grainger, Percy Aldridge, 1882–1961, Australian-American pianist and composer. A friend of Grieg, whose music he often played, he settled (1914) in the United States after establishing an international reputation as a pianist and composer. His interest in folk music is exemplified in his many settings of English folk melodies.

graining, process of painting by which natural wood grain is imitated. It was common practice in the late 19th cent. to grain cheap, soft woods to give them the appearance of rare, expensive ones. A light general tone with the brush was followed by darker streaks applied with a comb and wiped with a rag. This art is rarely practiced today except in matching old work. The term is also applied to mechanical methods for producing an artificial texture of any kind, as in bookbinding, and refers to a process of artificially coarsening the smooth metal sheets to be used as plates in offset printing.

gram, abbr. g, unit of MASS equal to 0.001 KILOGRAM, the basic unit of mass in the METRIC SYSTEM. The gram is the unit of mass in the CGS SYSTEM. It is approximately equal to 0.035 avoirdupois ounce, or 0.0022 pound; a 1-pound mass equals about 453.6 grams.

gram-atomic weight, amount of an atomic substance whose weight, in grams, is numerically equal to the ATOMIC WEIGHT of that substance. For example, 1 gram-atomic weight of atomic oxygen, O (atomic weight approximately 16), is 16 grams. See GRAM-MOLECULAR WEIGHT.

gram-calorie: see CALORIE.

gramicidin (grăm″ĭsĭd′ən), ANTIBIOTIC obtained from the bacterial species *Bacillus brevis*, which is found in soil. Gramicidin is particularly effective against gram-positive bacteria (see GRAM'S STAIN). Because the drug is highly toxic, it cannot be administered internally and so is used only on the skin as a lotion or ointment. It is used primarily in the treatment of infected surface wounds, and in eye, nose, and throat infections. In 1939 the American microbiologist René Dubos isolated the substance tyrothricin and later showed that it was composed of two substances, gramicidin and tyrocidine. These were the first antibiotics to be manufactured commercially.

grammar, description of the structure of a language, consisting of the sounds (see PHONETICS); the meaningful combinations of these sounds into words or parts of words, called morphemes; and the arrangement of the morphemes into phrases and sentences, called syntax. Morphemes may contain lexical meaning, as the word *bird*, or syntactic meaning, as the plural *-s* (see INFLECTION; ETYMOLOGY). Words are minimal free forms, but a word may contain more than one morpheme, e.g., *treatment* contains two, *treat* and the derivational noun-forming suffix *-ment*. In traditional grammar, parts of speech are defined semantically, i.e., a noun is a person, place, or thing; but in linguistic morphology, parts of speech are defined according to their syntactic function: The difference between nouns and verbs is that they cannot appear in the same environment in a sentence. One method of language classification is based on structure; languages are classified according to the degree of synthesis, or the number of morphemes per word. Analytic languages, such as Chinese, have only one morpheme per word, while in synthetic languages one word represents more than one morpheme; in the case of some American Indian languages, a single word may have so many morphemes that it is the equivalent of an English sentence. The list of morphemes and their meanings (see SEMANTICS) in a language is usually not part of a grammar but is isolated in a DICTIONARY or vocabulary. In syntax, units larger than morphemes, such as phrases and sentences, are isolated, reflecting a hierarchical structure; thus the sentence "My sister Mary slowly took the cake from the shelf" would have as primary constitutents "My sister Mary" and "slowly took the cake from the shelf." Each primary constituent then may be broken down into a series of hierarchical secondary constituents. Syntax is also concerned with ordering grammatical sequences within the phrase, with agreement between concomitant entities (i.e., agreement of number and gender among subject and verb, nouns and pronouns), and with case, as mandated by the position and function of a word within a sentence. Also studied are such sentence transformations as negativization, interrogation, coordination, subordination, passivization and relativization. The first attempts to study grammar began in about the 4th cent. B.C., in India with Panini's grammar of Sanskrit and in Greece with Plato's dialogue *Cratylus*. The Greeks, and later the Romans, approached the study of grammar through philosophy. Concerned only with the study of their own language and not with foreign languages, early Greek and Latin grammars were devoted primarily to defining the parts of speech. It was not until the Middle Ages that grammarians became interested in foreign languages. The scientific grammatical analysis of language began in the 19th cent. with the realization that languages have a history and with subsequent attempts at the genealogical classification of languages through comparative linguistics. Grammatical analysis was further developed in the 20th cent. and was greatly advanced by the theories of structural linguistics and transformational-generative grammar (see LINGUISTICS). School grammars for the speakers of a standard language (e.g., English grammars for English-speaking students) are not descriptive but prescriptive, that is, they are rule books of what is considered correct. Such grammars have popularized many unsound notions because they often fail to take into account common usage and they do not differentiate language styles and levels, such as formal or colloquial; standard, nonstandard, or substandard; or dialect differences. See. C. F. Hockett, *A Course in Modern Linguistics* (1958); B. L. Liles, *An Introductory Transformational Grammar* (1971); Noam Chomsky, *Aspects of the Theory of Syntax* (1965) and *Language and Mind* (rev. ed. 1972); R. W. Langacker, *Language and Its Structure* (2d ed. 1973).

Gramme, Zénobe-Théophile (zānôb′ tāôfēl′ gräm), 1826–1901, Belgian electrical engineer. While working as a model maker for a Parisian manufacturer of electrical devices, Gramme became interested in improving them. He knew little of electrical theory, but he had seen the Italian physicist Antonio Pacinotti's direct-current dynamo, and in 1869 he built one of his own that proved practical in applications such as electric illumination. By reversing the principle of his dynamo, he invented the electric engine. In 1872, with the engineer Marcel Deprez and the physicist Arsène d'Arsonval, he successfully transmitted direct current electricity over a long distance.

gram-molecular volume, the volume occupied by one GRAM-MOLECULAR WEIGHT of any substance at STP (see separate article). See MOLAR VOLUME.

gram-molecular weight, amount of a molecular substance whose weight, in grams, is numerically equal to the MOLECULAR WEIGHT of that substance. For example, one gram-molecular weight of molecular oxygen, O_2 (molecular weight approximately 32), is 32 grams, and one gram-molecular weight of water, H_2O (molecular weight approximately 18) is 18 grams. The term MOLE is often used in place of gram-molecular weight. See GRAM-ATOMIC WEIGHT.

Grammont: see GERAARDSBERGEN, Belgium.

Gramont, Agénor, prince de Bidache, duc de Guiche et de (äzhānôr′ prăNs′ də bēdäsh′ dük də gēsh ā də grämôN′), 1819–80, French diplomat. He served as plenipotentiary at Stuttgart (1852) and Turin (1853) and was ambassador to Rome (1857) and Vienna (1861). As foreign minister in 1870, he instructed the French ambassador to Prussia, Vincent Benedetti, to hold the ill-fated interview with King (later Emperor) William I that led to the publication of the EMS DISPATCH, the flimsy pretext on which France declared war against Prussia (see FRANCO-PRUSSIAN WAR).

Gramont, Philibert, comte de (fēlēbâr′ kôNt də), 1621–1707, French courtier at the court of King Louis XIV. He fought with distinction in the early campaigns of the prince de CONDÉ and at first followed Condé in the FRONDE, but in 1654 he made his peace with the court, of which he was thereafter a chief member. Exiled (1662) for having attempted to rival Louis in a love affair, he went (1663) to the court of King Charles II of England. A prominent figure there, he married Elizabeth Hamilton, with whom he returned to France in 1664. It was to her brother, Anthony HAMILTON, that the aged courtier gave the anecdotal material Hamilton used in writing Gramont's memoirs. The memoirs, although they reveal Gramont as a witty and insolent cad, are an invaluable source for the social history of his period. The spelling Grammont, always used in the title of the memoirs, is an old error.

Grampians, the, or **Grampian Mountains,** highest mountain system of Great Britain, extending northeast to southwest along the southern fringe of the Highlands, central Scotland. Ben Nevis (4,406 ft/1,343 m) is the tallest peak. The scenic Grampians, extensively forested, have many lakes and contain the headwaters of many of Scotland's rivers. Numerous hydroelectric power plants are found there. The Grampians are a popular vacation area.

grampus, name applied to two members of the DOLPHIN family (Delphinidae): *Grampus griseus*, also known as Risso's dolphin, of worldwide distribution, and *Orcinus orca*, also known as the KILLER WHALE.

Gram's stain, laboratory staining technique that distinguishes between two groups of bacteria by the identification of differences in the structure of their cell walls. The Gram stain, named after its developer, Danish bacteriologist Christian Gram, has become an important tool in bacterial taxonomy, distinguishing between so-called gram-positive bacteria, which remain colored after the staining procedure, and gram-negative bacteria, which do not retain dye. In the staining technique, cells on a microscope slide are heat-fixed (killed) and stained with a basic dye, crystal violet, which stains all bacterial cells blue; then they are treated with an iodine-potassium iodide solution that allows the iodine to enter the cells and form a water-insoluble complex with the crystal violet dye. The cells are treated with alcohol or acetone solvent in which the iodine-crystal violet complex is soluble. Following solvent treatment, only gram-positive cells remain stained, possibly because of their thick cell wall, which is not permeable to solvent. After the staining procedure, cells are treated with a counterstain, i.e., a red acidic dye such as safranin or acid fuchsin, in order to make gram-negative (decolorized) cells visible. Counterstained gram-negative cells appear red, and gram-positive cells remain blue. Although the cell walls of gram-negative and gram-positive bacteria are similar in chemical composition, the cell wall of gram-negative bacteria is a thin layer sandwiched between an outer lipid-containing cell envelope and the inner cell membrane, whereas the gram-positive cell wall is much thicker, lacks the cell envelope, and contains additional substances, such as teichoic acids, polymers composed of glycerol or ribitol. The difference in reactivity between gram-positive and gram-negative bacteria is linked with differences in physiological properties of the two groups. Gram-positive bacteria are generally more sensitive to growth inhibition by dyes, halogens, many ANTIBIOTICS, and to attack by PHAGOCYTOSIS, and are more resistant to digestion by the enzymes PEPSIN and TRYPSIN and enzymes in animal sera.

Gran: see ESZTERGOM, Hungary.

Granada (gränä'thä), city (1970 est. pop. 51,363), W Nicaragua, on Lake Nicaragua. It is the center of commerce on Lake Nicaragua. Located in a rich agricultural region, it has been the stronghold of Nicaragua's landed aristocracy. Granada was founded in 1524 by Francisco FERNÁNDEZ DE CÓRDOBA. It was the object of repeated Indian raids by French and English pirates. After independence from Spain (1821) Granada became the conservative center, engaging in bloody rivalry with LEÓN, the city of the liberals. The struggle led to the founding of MANAGUA (1885). Granada was captured (1855) by the filibuster William WALKER.

Granada, city (1970 pop. 190,429), capital of Granada prov., S Spain, in Andalusia, at the confluence of the Darro and Genil rivers. Beautifully situated at the foot of the Sierra Nevada, it is a major tourist center, attractive because of its art treasures and rich history. Formerly (17th cent.) a silk center, Granada is now a trade and processing point for an agricultural area that is also rich in minerals. It was originally a Moorish fortress and rose to prominence during the Almoravid and Almohad dynasties. In 1238 it became the seat of the kingdom of Granada, last refuge of the Moors whom the Christian reconquest had driven south; the kingdom occupied the present provinces of Almería and Málaga and parts of Jaén and Cádiz. The concentration of Moorish civilization in Granada gave the city great splendor and made it a center of commerce, industry, art, and science. However, the kingdom was weakened by continuous feuds among noble families, notably the Zegris and the Abencerages, and was conquered by Ferdinand V and Isabella I during the reign of Boabdil. With the surrender (Jan., 1492) of the city of Granada, the Moors lost their last hold in Spain, and the kingdom was united with Castile. The city became an archiepiscopal see and, in 1531, the seat of a university. Located in Granada is the famous Alhambra, an old Moorish citadel and royal palace, which dominates the city from a hill; on the same hill is the palace of Emperor Charles V. The Palacio del Generalife, summer residence of the Moorish rulers, has celebrated gardens. Christian edifices include a 16th-century cathedral, in late Gothic and plateresque style; the adjoining royal chapel, containing the tombs of Ferdinand and Isabella; and a Carthusian monastery (16th cent.). Across the Darro River and facing the Alhambra is the Sacromonte hill, honeycombed with gypsy caves.

Granados, Enrique (änrē'kä gränä'thōs), 1867–1916, Spanish composer and pianist, b. Havana; studied at Barcelona with Felipe Pedrell. His most significant works are those for the piano in which he created the peculiarly Spanish manner later used by de Falla. *Goyescas* (1912–14), a set of piano pieces that later formed the basis for an opera of the same name, is his outstanding work. He appeared as a pianist in Paris and Spain, and Casals and Saint-Saëns were among artists who performed with him and admired his style.

Granby (grăn'bē, grăm'-), city (1971 pop. 34,385), S Que., Canada, on the North Yamaska River, E of Montreal. Located in a farming area, Granby has textile mills and plants that manufacture furniture, tobacco and rubber products, and precision instruments.

Gran Chaco (grän chä'kō) or **Chaco,** c.250,000 sq mi (647,500 sq km), extensive lowland plain, central South America. It is sparsely populated and is divided among Paraguay, Bolivia, and Argentina. Some of the highest temperatures in the southern continent are reached there. To the north of the Pilcomayo River and to the west of the Paraguay River is the section known as the Chaco Boreal, most of which belongs to Paraguay. This is arid land, dotted with swamps in the rainy season and with stretches of dense forest in which the QUEBRACHO tree abounds. Tannin extraction from the quebracho is an important economic activity there. The Chaco Central, in Argentina S of the Pilcomayo River, has much the same aspect. Cotton and quebracho are important there. The plains grow increasingly arid toward the west. The eastern part—the Chaco Austral and the region W of the Paraguay River—is the only habitable section of the Gran Chaco. The discovery of oil in a narrow strip of the barren section of the Chaco Boreal, at the foot of the Bolivian Andes, precipitated the **Chaco War,** 1932–35, between Bolivia and Paraguay. This territory of the Gran Chaco had been disputed since 1810. Technically the Gran Chaco was intended to be part of Bolivia since it had been part of the audiencia of Charcas, but Bolivia paid little attention to this wasteland and Paraguayan settlers opened up the region while Paraguayan soldiers pushed back the Indians. Thousands of Paraguayan colonists brought wealth to Paraguay by gathering quebracho and raising cattle. An armed conflict between Paraguay and Bolivia resulted as Bolivia sought access to the Paraguay River to ship oil to the sea and Paraguay refused to give up the lands. More than 100,000 lives were lost, and the war was concluded in 1935 only when both sides were exhausted. After three years of mediated negotiation following the end of hostilities, Paraguay and Bolivia signed (1938) a treaty. Three quarters of the disputed Chaco Boreal went to Paraguay; at the same time Bolivia was granted a corridor to the Paraguay River, the privilege of using Puerto Casado, and the right to construct a Bolivian port.

Grand Alliance, War of the, 1688–97, war between France and a coalition of European powers, known as the League of AUGSBURG (and, after 1689, as the Grand Alliance). Louis XIV of France took advantage of the absence of Emperor Leopold I on a campaign against the Turks and of the promised support of James II of England to invade the empire and devastate (1689) the Palatinate. The revolution in England overthrew James, and William, prince of Orange, became William III of England (1688–89). In an attempt to keep William from leading troops to the Continent, Louis supported a counterrevolution in Ireland but was frustrated at the battle of the Boyne (1690). The naval war, of which the first major battle was the French victory at Beachy Head (1690), was practically ended by the English victory of La Hogue (1692). On land, however, Louis and Vauban took Namur (1692); Marshal LUXEMBOURG was victorious at Fleurus (1690) over the Dutch and at Steenkerke (1692) and Neerwinden (1693) over William III; and the duke of Savoy was defeated at Marsaglia by CATINAT (1693), while another French army entered Catalonia. The exhaustion of the belligerents and the defection of Savoy from the Grand Alliance (1696) finally led to the Treaty of RYSWICK. This war was known on the American continent as King William's War (see FRENCH AND INDIAN WARS). See G. N. Clark, *The Dutch Alliance and the War against French Trade, 1688–97* (1923, repr. 1971).

Grand Army of the Republic (GAR), organization established by Civil War veterans of the Union army and navy. Principal figures in the founding of the GAR were John A. LOGAN and Richard J. Oglesby. The first post was formed (April 6, 1866) at Decatur, Ill., and at the first national encampment, held at Indianapolis, Ind., on Nov. 20, 1866, 10 states and the District of Columbia were represented. Gen. Stephen A. Hurlbut, the first commander in chief, was succeeded by Logan, who was followed in office by Gen. Ambrose E. Burnside. They were the most prominent military men to head the GAR. Membership increased rapidly in the 1880s, so that by 1890, when the GAR reached its peak, more than 400,000 members were reported. The members sought to strengthen the bonds of comradeship, to preserve the memory of their fallen comrades (they secured the general adoption of MEMORIAL DAY to achieve this purpose), to give aid to soldiers' widows and orphans and to handicapped veterans, and, most of all, to fight for pension increases and other benefits. Although the organization was nonpolitical, GAR members were overwhelmingly Republican and formed a reliable bloc of that party's strength in the years up to 1900. Soldier preference in Federal appointments became the rule, and pension legislation was usually enacted by the Republicans with their support in mind. The *National Tribune,* founded (1877) by George E. Lemon, a powerful pensions attorney of Washington, D.C., kept GAR members posted on pension matters. The organization scored a great victory in 1879 with the passage of the Arrears of Pension Act, which led many more veterans to apply for pensions. Theoretically, only those who suffered disabilities in service were entitled to pensions, but it became the practice for lenient Congressmen to introduce private pension bills. These were almost always granted until Grover Cleveland, the first President to examine the bills critically, found many of them to be fraudulent. The fact that Cleveland was a Democrat further confirmed GAR members in their staunch Republicanism. Auxiliary societies associated with the GAR were the Sons of Veterans (1881), the Women's Relief Corps (1883), and the Ladies of the Grand Army of the Republic (1886). A separate veterans organization, the United Confederate Veterans, was organized in 1889, but its membership (less than 50,000 at its peak) never approached that of the GAR. With the coming of the 20th cent. the GAR declined rapidly in numbers and influence. The 83d and last encampment was also held at Indianapolis, on Aug. 28–31, 1949, with 6 of the 16 surviving members in attendance. The last member of the GAR died in 1956. See M. R. Dearing, *Veterans in Politics: The Story of the G.A.R.* (1952).

Grand Bahama: see BAHAMA ISLANDS.

Grand Banks, submarine plateau rising from the continental shelf, c.36,000 sq mi (93,200 sq km), off SE N.F., Canada. It is c.300 mi (480 km) long and c.400 mi (640 km) wide; depths range from 20 to 100 fathoms. The cold Labrador Current flows over most of the banks; the warmer Gulf Stream sweeps along the eastern edge, sometimes crossing the southern part. The Grand Banks are noted for the persistent dense fog (formed as warm air passes over the cold water) that engulfs the area. The mingling of the two currents along with the shallowness of the water forms a favorable environment for plankton and other small sea life upon which cod, haddock, halibut, and other fish feed. Lobsters are also found there. The Grand Banks are probably the world's most important international fishing ground. However, fog, icebergs, and the nearby transatlantic shipping lanes make fishing hazardous.

Grand-Bassam (gräN-bäsäm'), town (1964 est. pop. 12,330), SE Ivory Coast, a port on the Atlantic Ocean. It is an administrative center in a region where coffee, cacao, pineapples, bananas, palm products, and timber are produced and fishing is important. In 1842–43, French merchants gained treaty rights at Grand-Bassam, which was a center of the gold and palm oil trade. From about 1900, when a wharf was built, until the mid-20th cent., when the seaport at Abidjan was constructed, Grand-Bassam handled most of the Ivory Coast's foreign trade.

Grand Canal, Chinese *Yün-ho* [transit river], longest in the world, extending c.1,000 mi (1,600 m) from Peking to Hangchow, E China, and forming an important north-south waterway on the N China plain. The canal was started in the 6th cent. B.C. and was constructed over a 2,000-year period. Its largest sections were completed in A.D. 610 under Emperor Yang Ti of the Sui dynasty and were built by dredging and linking existing canals. Tree-shaded roads, postal stations, and imperial pavilions were built along the canal. Between the 10th and the early 13th cent. the waterway fell into disrepair. Kublai Khan reconstructed the canal in the 13th cent. and extended it to Peking. Improvements were made during the Ming dynasty (1368–1644). Today the canal follows the Pai River south from Peking to Tientsin. The 250-mi (412-km) section S of Tientsin, which ties into the Wei River, is navigable in all seasons by junks and small steamers. Leaving the Wei, the canal runs through the elongated lakes of Shantung prov. past Su-chou, where it crosses the Yangtze at Chen-chiang. It runs generally south through the Yangtze delta, past Wu-hsi and on to Hangchow, the southern terminus. The canal is 100 to 200 ft (30-61 m) wide and from 2 to 15 ft (.6-4.6 m) deep. Railroads, roads, and widespread silting have reduced its economic importance.

Grand Canary: see CANARY ISLANDS, Spain.

Grand Canyon, great gorge of the Colorado River, one of the natural wonders of the world; c.1 mi (1.6 km) deep, from 4 to 18 mi (6.4-29 km) wide, and 217 mi (349 km) long, NW Ariz. The canyon shows in its rocks, exposed by more than 8 million years of erosion, the repeated geological sequence of uplift, erosion, submergence, and deposition of materials. The multicolored rocks, the steep and embayed rims, and the isolated towers, mesas, "temples," and other eroded rock forms catch the contrast of sun and shadow and glow with constantly changing hues of great beauty. Plant life on the canyon walls varies from subtropical at the base to sub-Arctic near the rims. Hundreds of ancient Indian pueblos dot the lower canyon walls and the rim. The first white man to see the canyon was the Spanish explorer García López de Cárdenas in 1540. In 1869, U.S. explorer John W. Powell was the first man to lead a party through the canyon in a boat. The Grand Canyon, set aside by the U.S. government in 1908 as a national monument, was expanded in 1919 and designated **Grand Canyon National Park** (673,575 acres/272,596 hectares). The park contains 105 mi (169 km) of the most spectacular part of the canyon. Along the forested northern rim and the more accessible southern rim are numerous lookouts; trails wind to the canyon floor. More than 2 million tourists visit the park each year. **Grand Canyon National Monument** (198,280 acres/80,244 hectares), est. 1932, is a primitive area adjoining the park on the west.

Grand Coulee Dam (ko͞o'lē), 550 ft (168 m) high and 4,173 ft (1,272 m) long, on the Columbia River, N central Wash., NW of Spokane; built 1933-42 as a key unit in the COLUMBIA BASIN PROJECT of the U.S. Bureau of Reclamation. Grand Coulee Dam, one of the world's largest concrete dams, is used for flood control, river navigation, irrigation, and power production. The dam has the largest power-producing capacity (2,025,000 kw) in the United States, and will be the world's largest hydroelectric generating plant (9,771,000-kw capacity) when completed c.1983. The dam impounds **Franklin D. Roosevelt Lake,** 130 sq mi (337 sq km), which extends to the Canadian border; it is one of the largest reservoirs in the United States. Power generated at the dam is used to pump water into Grand Coulee, a vertical-walled gorge, c.30 mi (48 km) long, carved by the Columbia River through the Columbia Plateau. The coulee, dammed at each end, is used as a reservoir (Banks Lake); it supplies water to more than 1,000,000 acres (404,700 hectares) on the plateau and acts as a back-up against pump and power failures. Franklin D. Roosevelt Lake is part of Coulee Dam National Recreation Area (see NATIONAL PARKS AND MONUMENTS, table). Located on the Pacific flyway, a chief north-south migratory route, the area has a great variety of waterfowl and land birds. Grand Coulee (1970 pop. 1,302) and Coulee Dam (1970 pop. 1,425) were founded by the U.S. government in 1935-36 as construction, operational, and housing bases for the dam.

Grande Prairie (Fr. gräNd prâ"rē'), city (1971 pop. 13,079), W Alta., Canada, NW of Edmonton. It is the chief business center for the Peace River valley farming area. The Northern Winter Carnival is held in the city annually.

Grand Falls. 1 City (1971 pop. 1,643), W N.B., Canada, on the St. John River. The nearby falls in the river and its 1-mi- (1.6-km) long gorge attract many visitors. The falls power a large hydroelectric development. **2** Town (1971 pop. 7,677), central N.F., Canada, on the Exploits River. In the town are large pulp and paper mills that produce large amounts of newsprint.

Grand Falls, Labrador: see CHURCHILL FALLS.

Grand Forks, city (1970 pop. 39,008), seat of Grand Forks co., E N.Dak., at the confluence of the Red and the Red Lake rivers; inc. 1881. In a spring wheat, livestock, and farm area, the city has grain elevators, state-operated flour mills, and plants that process and distribute meat, dairy products, sugar beets, and potatoes. The area was settled by French fur traders who traveled the two rivers by canoe and camped at the junction. They called their campsite La Grandes Fourches [Fr.,=the grand forks]. Grand Forks became an important stop on the Great Northern Railway. In 1928 the line built huge switching and storage yards in the city. The Univ. of North Dakota is there, as is a U.S. Bureau of Mines lignite research laboratory. Nearby is the Grand Forks Air Force Base.

Grand Haven, city (1970 pop. 11,844), seat of Ottawa co., SW Mich., at the mouth of the Grand River; inc. 1867. It is a port on Lake Michigan that ships sand and gravel. Grand Haven manufactures automobile parts, restaurant equipment, tools, and machinery. The city is also a popular resort. A state park is within the city limits.

Grand Island, city (1970 pop. 31,269), seat of Hall co., S Nebr., on the Wood River near its junction with the Platte; settled 1857 on the Platte by Germans, moved 1866 to its present location on the Union Pacific RR, inc. c.1872. The city, which is known as a horse, mule, and cattle market, is also a railroad, manufacturing, and shipping center for a rich, irrigated livestock, grain, and dairy region. A veterans hospital and a state soldiers and sailors home are in Grand Island. The Stuhr Museum of the Prairie Pioneer, on an island in a nearby man-made lake, was designed by Edward Durrell Stone. A state park is also in the area.

Grand Island, 13,000 acres (5,260 hectares), N Mich., in Lake Superior; one of Michigan's largest islands. Heavily wooded, it is a resort area and has a game refuge.

Grand Junction, city (1970 pop. 20,170), seat of Mesa co., W Colo., at the junction of the Gunnison and Colorado rivers; inc. 1882. The shipping and processing center of a large ranch and irrigated farm region, it also serves the area's uranium, oil shale, and coal-mining industries. Electronic equipment is manufactured there, and tourism is important to the city. Grand Junction's airport permits access to many Colorado skiing resorts; the city is also a center during the regional hunting season and serves as headquarters for Grand Mesa National Forest. Uranium production was curtailed in 1970 after a radiation hazard arose from the radioactive wastes (tailings) used as construction fill for building projects. The city has a junior college.

grand jury, body of persons selected according to law to inquire into crimes committed within a certain jurisdiction. It is called a grand jury because it usually has a greater number of jurors than the trial JURY, or petit jury. The grand jury, which has ancient origins in the COMMON LAW, has no function at a trial, but rather receives complaints and accusations in criminal cases, hears the evidence adduced by the state, and approves INDICTMENTS when satisfied that there is enough evidence against the accused to warrant a trial.

Grandma Moses: see MOSES, ANNA MARY ROBERTSON.

Grand Manan (mənăn'), island c.16 mi (26 km) long and c.7 mi (11.3 km) wide, S N.B. Canada, in the Bay of Fundy. On the north and west sides are bold cliffs, rising from 200 ft to 400 ft (61-122 m) high, visible from the Maine coast. The principal villages and harbors, North Head, Grand Harbor, and Seal Cove, are on the south and east sides. The chief occupation is fishing, and the island is a summer resort. It was settled after the American Revolution by Loyalists; British possession was disputed by the United States until 1817.

Grand Marnier: see CURAÇAO.

Grand'Mère (gräNmĕr'), city (1971 pop. 17,137), S Que., Canada, on the St. Maurice River, N of Trois Rivières. The Grand'Mère falls furnish power for paper and pulp mills. The city also has clothing and textile factories.

Grand Portage National Monument: see NATIONAL PARKS AND MONUMENTS (table).

Grand Prairie, city (1970 pop. 50,904), Dallas and Tarrant counties, N Texas, halfway between Dallas and Fort Worth; inc. 1909. Located in a highly urbanized area, it is a distribution center with a large aerospace industry. Other manufactures include mobile homes, metal goods, plastics, medical supplies, and concrete pipes. An African wildlife preserve and the spectacular "Six Flags over Texas" amusement park are there.

Grand Pré (grăn prā, Fr. gräN prā) [Fr.,=large field], village, W central N.S., Canada, on an arm of the Bay of Fundy. The area is famous for having been an early settlement of the Acadians, whose expulsion in 1755 is the subject of Longfellow's poem *Evangeline.* Grand Pré National Historic Park contains several remains from the Acadian period. The village was also the birthplace of Sir Robert Borden, prime minister of Canada from 1911 to 1920. See J. F. Herbin, *The History of Grand-Pré* (4th ed. 1911); W. R. Bird, *Done at Grand Pré* (1955).

Grand Rapids, city (1970 pop. 197,649), seat of Kent co., W central Mich., on the Grand River; inc. 1850. It is a distribution, wholesale, and industrial center for an area that yields fruit, farm produce, gypsum, and gravel. Furniture manufacturing (begun in 1859) remains an important industry. Among the city's other manufactures are appliances, electronic equipment, automotive parts, and paper products. It has an art gallery, a furniture museum, and a symphony orchestra. Also in Grand Rapids are Aquinas College, Calvin College, Grand Rapids Baptist Bible College and Seminary, a junior college, and a horticultural experiment station.

Grand River, c.165 mi (270 km) long, rising in the highlands of the Ontario Peninsula, S Ont., Canada, and flowing S past Kitchener and Brantford, then SE to Lake Erie at Port Maitland. It is navigable for c.70 mi (110 km) upstream. The river drains one of the most populated regions of Canada.

Grand River. 1 River, 260 mi (418 km) long, rising in S Mich. and flowing N to Lansing, then NW to Lake Michigan at Grand Haven. It is the longest river in the state and is navigable to the city of Grand Rapids, which grew there because of the availability of waterpower. **2** River, rising in SW N.Dak. and flowing 209 mi (336 km) SE through S.Dak. to the Missouri River near Mobridge. Shadehill Dam (1951), located on the river, was built for flood control and irrigation as part of the Missouri River basin project. **3** River in Okla.: see NEOSHO, river; PENSACOLA DAM.

Grand River Dam: see PENSACOLA DAM.

Grandson (gräNsôN'), Ger. *Grandsee,* town (1970 pop. 2,135), Vaud canton, W Switzerland, at the southwestern end of the Lake of Neuchâtel. An important town in the Middle Ages, Grandson is known chiefly as the scene of the defeat (1476) of Charles the Bold of Burgundy by the Swiss Confederates. Cigars are made there today. It has a noted Romanesque-Gothic church. The town is also known as Granson.

Grand Teton National Park (tētŏn', tē'tŏn), 310,443 acres (125,636 hectares), NW Wyo.; est. 1929. The park, which includes Jackson Hole and Jackson Lake, embraces the most scenic portion of the glaciated, snow-covered Teton Range; Grand Teton (13,766 ft/4,196 m) is the highest peak. The Snake River flows through the park, which is dotted with small lakes and has several glaciers, forests, and a great variety of wildlife. Hiking, floating down the Snake on rafts, camping, and mountain climbing are popular activities in the park, which is also headquarters for the famous Exum School of Mountaineering. American trapper John Colter in 1807-8 was probably the first white man to see the Tetons. Fur trapping thrived there until the 1840s.

Grand Traverse Bay, arm of Lake Michigan, 32 mi (52 km) long and 10 mi (16 km) wide, W central Mich. The bay is known for its fishing and boating. The surrounding area is an important cherry-growing and resort region. Traverse City is located at the head of the bay.

Grandview, city (1970 pop. 17,456), Jackson co., W Mo., S of Kansas City; inc. 1912. Grandview is in a farm region. Hardware and electrical equipment are manufactured in the city, and Richards-Gebaur Air Force Base is nearby.

Grandville: see GÉRARD, JEAN IGNACE ISIDORE.

Grandville, city (1970 pop. 10,764), Kent co., W Mich., on the Grand River, in a farm area; settled 1833, inc. as a city 1933. Aircraft parts, boxes, structural steel, die castings, and electrical products are made. Indian mounds, some of which were opened in 1964, are preserved in the northeastern section of the city.

Granet, François Marius (fräNswä' märyüs' grä-nā'), 1775-1849, French painter; student of J. L. David. Granet is known for his depictions of church interiors, among them his numerous versions of the *Choir of the Capuchin Monastery,* one of which is in the Metropolitan Museum. He bequeathed much of his own best work and also his fine collection of paintings to the museum of his native Aix-en-Provence.

Grange, Harold Edward (Red Grange), 1903-, American football player, b. Forksville, Pa. Grange was All-America halfback in 1923, 1924, and 1925 at the Univ. of Illinois. In his spectacular college career he scored 31 touchdowns and gained 3,367 yards by running and another 643 yards with 42 completed passes. Turning professional, he played with the

New York Yankees (1926–27) and the Chicago Bears (1928–35); in his professional career he scored 1,058 points. He appeared in several films, and after his retirement from football he became a radio and television sportscaster.

Grangemouth (grănj'məth, -mouth), burgh (1971 pop. 24,572), Stirlingshire, central Scotland, on the Forth River at the eastern terminus of the Forth and Clyde canal. Large quantities of scrap metal are imported for the production of steel. Oil refining is important, and there are large chemical works. The timber trade and sawmilling are also significant. Grangemouth was founded in 1777 to be the terminus of the canal, which opened in 1790. It was the scene of many experiments in steam navigation; the *Charlotte Dundas* was launched there in 1802. In 1975, Grangemouth became part of the new Central region.

Granger, Francis, 1792–1868, American political leader, b. Suffield, Conn. He practiced law in Canandaigua, N.Y., and served (1826–28, 1830–32) in the New York state legislature. A prominent leader of the ANTI-MASONIC PARTY, he was twice (1830, 1832) defeated for governor as its nominee. He was elected as a Whig to Congress in 1834. Appointed Postmaster General by President William Henry Harrison, Granger resigned (1841) with other cabinet members at Harrison's death. After another term (1841–43) in Congress, he became a leader of the conservative Whigs who opposed their party's drift toward radical antislavery views. He favored the Compromise of 1850, and with a small following withdrew (1850) from the Whig convention at Syracuse when resolutions were adopted endorsing William H. Seward's opposition to the compromise measures.

Granger, James, 1723–76, English clergyman and biographer. He published his *Biographical History of England from Egbert the Great to the Revolution* in 1760. By 1824 various editors had increased it to six volumes by adding illustrations and biographies taken from other books. Because many books were robbed of steel engravings to put into Granger's history, such mutilation came to be known as *grangerizing*.

Granger movement, American agrarian movement taking its name from the National Grange of the Patrons of Husbandry, an organization founded in 1867 by Oliver H. KELLEY and six associates. Its local units were called granges and its members grangers. The movement grew slowly until after the Panic of 1873, when it expanded rapidly, reaching its membership peak in 1875. Although established originally for social and educational purposes, the local granges became political forums and increased in number as channels of farmer protest against economic abuses of the day. The granges sought to correct these abuses through cooperative enterprise. They were in part successful with the establishment of stores, grain elevators, and mills, but they met disaster in their attempt to manufacture farm machinery. Through political activity the grangers captured several state legislatures in the Middle West and secured the passage in Illinois, Wisconsin, Minnesota, and Iowa of the so-called Granger laws, setting or authorizing maximum railroad rates and establishing state railroad commissions for administering the new legislation. There was also legislation covering warehouses and elevators. Railroads and other interested parties challenged the constitutionality of these laws in the Granger Cases. But the U.S. Supreme Court, in MUNN VS. ILLINOIS (1876), established as constitutional the principle of public regulation of private utilities devoted to public use. The Granger movement thus revealed the farmer as a political power and forced the older parties to give more attention to his demands. Inadequacy of state regulation, plus the weakening of the *Munn* vs. *Illinois* ruling by the WABASH CASE (1886), led to demands for national legislation. After 1876 the Greenback party, the Farmers' Alliance, and, finally, the Populist party expressed much of the agrarian protest, and the granges reverted to their original role, as purely social organizations. They continued to exist in the East, especially in New England, where they had been least active politically. See studies by J. D. McCabe (1873, repr. 1969) and S. J. Buck (1913, repr. 1963).

granite, coarse-grained igneous ROCK of even texture and light color, composed chiefly of quartz and feldspars. It usually contains small quantities of mica or hornblende, and minor accessory minerals may be present. Depending on the feldspar present, granite may be pink, dark gray, or light gray. It is commonly believed to have solidified from molten rock (called magma) under pressure. However, some granites show no contacts with surrounding wall rock, but instead gradually grade into metamorphic rock. Others show relic features found in sediments. This evidence suggests that some granites are not igneous in origin, but metamorphic. Some granites are the oldest known rocks on earth; others were formed during younger geologic periods. Crystallized at depth, granite masses are exposed at the earth's surface by crustal movement or by the erosion of overlying rocks. Very coarse-grained granite, called pegmatite, may contain minerals and gemstones of economic value. Such pegmatites are found in the Black Hills of South Dakota. Granite has been used by man since ancient times as a building material.

Granite City, city (1970 pop. 40,440), Madison co., SW Ill., an industrial suburb of East St. Louis, on the Mississippi; inc. 1896. It is a transportation center, with a port and rail connections.

Granja, La: see SAN ILDEFONSO, Spain.

Granjon, Robert (grăn'jən, Fr. rōbĕr' gräNzhôN'), fl. 1545–88, French designer of type and printer. He began his work in Paris and afterward worked in Lyons, Antwerp, and Rome. The types that he designed and made included roman, italic, Greek, Hebrew, and Syriac. He is known especially for his *caractères de civilité*, based on a beautiful French handwriting and intended to take the place in France that italic type then held in Italy. The greater legibility of italic caused the Granjon style to fall into disuse. Printers who used types designed and made by Granjon included Christophe Plantin, of Antwerp.

Gran Paradiso (grän pärädē'zō), mountain, 13,323 ft (4,061 m) high, in Valle d'Aosta, NW Italy. In the Graian Alps, it is the highest Alpine peak entirely in Italian territory.

Gran Quivira National Monument: see NATIONAL PARKS AND MONUMENTS (table).

Gran Sasso d'Italia (grän säs'sō dētä'lyä), mountain group of the central Apennines, in Abruzzi, central Italy. It rises to c.9,560 ft (2,914 m) in Monte Corno, the highest peak in the Apennines. Campo Imperatore, a mountaineering and skiing resort, may be reached by cable car. Mussolini was confined there after his fall from power but was rescued by German paratroopers.

Granson: see GRANDSON, Switzerland.

Grant, Cary, 1904–, British movie actor, b. Bristol as Archibald Leach. One of the most sought-after leading men in Hollywood from the mid-1930s until he retired from the screen in 1969, Grant expressed to perfection the essence of debonair British charm and elegance in hundreds of comic-romantic roles. In 1933 he was chosen by Mae West to play opposite her in *She Done Him Wrong*, his first major film. His most popular movies include *I'm No Angel* (1933), *The Awful Truth* (1937), *Bringing Up Baby* (1938), *Holiday* (1938), *His Girl Friday* (1940), *The Philadelphia Story* (1940), *Arsenic and Old Lace* (1944), *Notorious* (1946), *North by Northwest* (1959), and *Charade* (1963). See biography by Albert Govoni (1972).

Grant, Sir Francis, 1803–78, Scottish portrait painter. He was self-taught in painting, for which he abandoned a career in law. He began as a painter of hunting scenes (*The Melton Hunt* and *The Cottesmore Hunt*) but gained success as a fashionable portrait painter. Among his sitters were Scott, Macaulay, Disraeli, Palmerston, and Landseer. Sir Francis was president (1866–78) of the Royal Academy.

Grant, George Munro, 1835–1902, Canadian educator and author, b. Nova Scotia, educated at the Univ. of Glasgow. From 1877 to 1902 he was principal of Queen's Univ., Kingston, Ont.; under him the university made great gains in size and prestige. Grant was a cogent writer on education and public affairs. His best-known book, *Ocean to Ocean* (1873, rev. ed. 1925), is an account of his experiences with the western surveying expedition of Sir Sandford Fleming, chief engineer of the Canadian Pacific Railway. The book stirred much popular interest in the Canadian West and thus contributed to the settlement of the area.

Grant, Ulysses Simpson, 1822–85, commander in chief of the Union army in the Civil War, 18th President of the United States (1869–77), b. Point Pleasant, near New Richmond, Ohio. He was originally named Hiram Ulysses Grant. Grant spent his youth in Georgetown, Ohio, was graduated from West Point in 1843, and served creditably in the Mexican War. Grant was forced to resign from the army in 1854 because of his excessive drinking. He failed in his attempts at farming and business, and was working as a clerk in the family leather store in Galena, Ill., when the Civil War broke out. He was commissioned colonel of the 21st Illinois Volunteers, and in Aug., 1861, became a brigadier general of volunteers. Grant assumed command of the Dist. of Cairo, Ill., in September and fought his first battle, an indecisive affair, at Belmont, Mo., on Nov. 9, 1861. In Feb., 1862, aided by Union gunboats, he captured Fort Henry on the Tennessee River and FORT DONELSON on the Cumberland. It was the first major Union victory, and Lincoln at once made him a major general of volunteers. However, in April at Shiloh (see SHILOH, BATTLE OF), the arrival of the army of Gen. Don Carlos Buell probably saved him from defeat. The VICKSBURG CAMPAIGN (1862–63) was one of Grant's greatest successes. After repeated failures to get at the city, he made a brilliant advance in cooperation with a fleet and finally took Vicksburg by siege. The victory of Braxton Bragg, the Confederate general, at Chickamauga (see CHATTANOOGA CAMPAIGN), led to Grant's accession to the supreme command in the West, Oct., 1863. At Chattanooga in November his forces thoroughly defeated Bragg. The President, in March, 1864, made him commander in chief with the rank of lieutenant general, a grade especially revived by Congress for him. Grant himself directed George G. Meade's Army of the Potomac against Gen. Robert E. Lee in the WILDERNESS CAMPAIGN. His policy of wearing Lee out by sheer attrition was effective, though it resulted in the horrible slaughter of Spotsylvania and Cold Harbor. Failing to carry PETERSBURG by assault in June, 1864, Grant had that city under partial siege until April, 1865. Philip H. Sheridan's victory at FIVE FORKS made Petersburg and Richmond no longer tenable. Lee retreated, but was cut off at APPOMATTOX COURTHOUSE, where he surrendered, receiving generous terms from Grant, April 9, 1865. Grant went about the distasteful business of war realistically and grimly. He was a skilled tactician and at times a brilliant strategist (his Vicksburg campaign is regarded by many as one of the great battles of history). His courage as a commander of forces and his powers of organization and administration made him the outstanding general of the North. Grant also was notably wise in supporting good commanders, especially SHERIDAN, William T. SHERMAN, and George H. THOMAS. Made a full general in 1866, he was the first U.S. citizen after Washington to hold that rank. Grant at first seemed to favor the RECONSTRUCTION policy of President Andrew Johnson. In April, 1867, Johnson appointed him interim Secretary of War, replacing Edwin STANTON. Johnson expected him to hold the office against Stanton and thus bring about a court test of the constitutionality of the TENURE OF OFFICE ACT, but Grant turned the office back to Stanton when the Senate refused to sanction Stanton's removal. It was apparent then that the general had thrown in his lot with the radical Republicans. The inevitable choice of the Republicans for President, Grant was victorious over the Democratic candidate, Horatio Seymour, in 1868. Characterized chiefly by bitter partisan politics and shameless corruption, his administrations were a national disgrace. The punitive Reconstruction program of the radicals was pushed with new vigor, and monetary legislation favorable to the commercial and industrial interests was passed (see GREENBACK). The President associated with disreputable politicians and financiers; James Fisk and Jay Gould deceived him when they tried to corner the gold market in 1869 (see BLACK FRIDAY). In foreign affairs, however, much was accomplished by the able Secretary of State, Hamilton FISH. The party unanimously renominated Grant in 1872, and he was reelected easily over Horace Greeley, the candidate of the LIBERAL REPUBLICAN PARTY and the Democrats. Toward the end of his second term his Secretary of War, William W. Belknap, and his private secretary, Orville E. Babcock, were implicated in graft scandals. Through the loyalty of the deceived Grant, both escaped punishment. The two years following his retirement from the White House were spent in making a triumphal tour of the world. In 1880 the Republican "Old Guard," led by Roscoe Conkling, tried to secure another nomination for Grant but failed. He took up his residence in New York City, where he invested money in a fraudulent private banking business. It collapsed in 1884, leaving Grant bankrupt. Fatally ill from cancer of the throat, he set about writing his *Personal Memoirs* (2 vol., 1885–86; new ed., ed. by E. B. Long, 1952, repr. 1962) in order to provide for his family. He died a few days after manuscript was completed. As solid and unpolished as Grant himself, these memoirs rank among the great military narratives of history. The remains of the general and his wife lie in New York City in Grant's Tomb (completed in 1897; made a national memorial in 1959). See, in addition to his memoirs, his papers ed. by J. Y. Simon (5 vol., 1967–73); biography by U. S. Grant III (1969); J. F. C. Fuller, *The Generalship of U. S. Grant* (1929, repr. 1968); W. B. Hesseltine, *Ulysses S. Grant, Politician* (1935, repr. 1957); Lloyd Lewis, *Captain Sam Grant* (1950); Bruce Catton, *U. S. Grant and the American Military Tradition* (1954); *Grant Moves South* (1960), and *Grant Takes Command* (1969); Allan Nevins, *Hamilton Fish: The Inner History of the Grant Administration* (2 vol., rev. ed. 1957); J. H. Marshall-Cornwall, *Grant as Military Commander* (1970).

Grantham (grăn'təm, -thəm), municipal borough (1971 pop. 27,913), in the Parts of Kesteven, Lincolnshire, E central England, on the Witham River. Grantham is an agricultural center and railroad junction. There are mechanical engineering works. Landmarks include St. Wulfram's Church, mainly 13th cent., with its 280-ft (85-m) steeple; Angel Inn, where in 1483 Richard III condemned the duke of Buckingham to death; a bronze statue (on St. Peter's Hill) of Sir Isaac Newton, who attended King's School in Grantham; and George Hotel, described by Dickens in *Nicholas Nickleby*. At Grantham in 1643 Oliver Cromwell won his first victory over the royalists.

Grant-Kohrs Ranch National Historic Site, Mont.: see NATIONAL PARKS AND MONUMENTS (table).

Grants Pass, city (1970 pop. 12,455), seat of Josephine co., SW Oregon, on the Rogue River, in a heavily forested area; inc. 1887. It has important lumbering enterprises and is also the commercial center of a large region producing flower bulbs (especially gladioli), fruits, nuts, vegetables, and dairy products.

Grant's Tomb: see General Grant National Memorial under NATIONAL PARKS AND MONUMENTS (table).

granule, in astronomy: see PHOTOSPHERE.

granuloma inguinale: see VENEREAL DISEASE.

Granvelle, Antoine Perrenot de (äNtwän' pĕrənō' də gräNvĕl'), 1517–86, statesman in the service of Holy Roman Emperor Charles V and of King Philip II of Spain; cardinal of the Roman Catholic Church. He was born at Besançon (then an imperial city), the son of Nicolas Perrenot de Granvelle, whom he succeeded as imperial councillor. The younger Granvelle negotiated the marriage of the Infante Philip (later Philip II) to Queen Mary I of England. After Philip's accession (1556) he became president of the council of state under MARGARET OF PARMA, regent of the Netherlands. He was, in effect, governor and incurred the hostility of all Dutch and Flemish patriots (Protestants and Catholics alike) by retaining Spanish troops and increasing religious persecution. WILLIAM THE SILENT and the counts EGMONT and HOORN headed the opposition. In 1564, Granvelle was advised by Philip II to retire to Besançon. Granvelle subsequently served Philip as viceroy of Naples and adviser on Italian affairs. He was recalled as councillor to Philip in 1579 but lost influence after 1582.

Granville, Granville George Leveson-Gower, 2d **Earl,** 1815–91, British statesman. He entered Parliament as a Whig in 1836 and held various cabinet positions under Lord John Russell, the earl of Aberdeen, and Viscount Palmerston. As colonial secretary (1868–70, 1886) under William Gladstone, he had a large part in passing the bills that disestablished the Church of Ireland and began reforms in Irish land tenure. He was also foreign secretary (1870–74, 1880–85) under Gladstone.

Granville, John Carteret, 1st **Earl,** 1690–1763, English statesman, better known as Lord Carteret. While ambassador to Sweden (1719–20), he performed notable service as a mediator in negotiating the treaties that ended (1721) the Northern War. He served (1721–24) as a secretary of state, but his favor with George I posed a threat to Robert WALPOLE, who finally forced his resignation and sent (1724) him to Ireland as lord lieutenant. There he dealt skillfully with the agitation against the new English currency patent, which was attacked by Jonathan SWIFT in his *Drapier Letters* and withdrawn in 1725, and he became quite popular. Returning to England in 1730, Carteret led the opposition that in 1742 finally accomplished Walpole's downfall. He was the chief minister in the new cabinet but soon became unpopular because he supported George II's Hanoverian policies and aided Maria Theresa in the War of the Austrian Succession. He was dismissed in 1744 and, although he served (1751–63) as lord president of the council, he never regained much influence. He became Earl Granville in 1744. See biography by W. B. Pemberton (1936); Basil Williams, *Carteret and Newcastle* (1943).

Granville-Barker, Harley Granville, 1877–1946, English dramatist, actor, producer, and critic. As comanager of the Court Theatre from 1904 to 1907 he was one of the leading forces in the theater of his time. Granville-Barker was the chief producer of the plays of new dramatists as well as those of the great masters; he presented the works of Euripides, Shakespeare, Schnitzler, Shaw, and Galsworthy. His own realistic dramas, including *The Voysey Inheritance* (1905), *Waste* (1907), and *The Madras House* (1910), were not remarkable successes. His real literary distinction is in the field of criticism; his *Prefaces to Shakespeare* (6 vol. 1927–74) is a monumental work. See biography by C. B. Purdom (1956, repr. 1971).

grape, common name for the Vitaceae, a family of mostly climbing shrubs, widespread in tropical and subtropical regions and extending into the temperate zones. The woody vines, or lianas, climb by means of tendrils, which botanically are adaptations of terminal buds. The principal genera are *Cissus,* chiefly tropical, *Parthenocissus* (including the VIRGINIA CREEPER and Boston IVY), *Ampelopsis* (see AMPELOPSIS), and *Vitis;* the latter three include species native to the United States. Plants of the grape genus *Vitis* are extensively cultivated throughout the Northern Hemisphere. *V. vinifera,* which probably originated in the Mediterranean area and W Asia, is the grape (often called "the vine") of agriculture known since ancient times and frequently mentioned in the Bible. It is cultivated in the Old World and has been introduced successfully in South America and on the west coast of North America. Attempts to naturalize it E of the Rockies failed, chiefly because of the insect pest PHYLLOXERA; the grapes now grown in this area are either hybrids of *V. vinifera* with resistant American grapes or varieties derived from native American species. Chief among these are *V. rotundifolia,* the muscadine, or scuppernong, grape, and its varieties (James, Eden, and others) of the Gulf and southeastern states, and *V. labrusca,* the fox grape, from which are derived the Concord, Catawba, Delaware, and many other cultivated varieties of the eastern and northern states. California produces some two thirds of the grapes grown in the United States, and New York state ranks second in output. Grapes are sometimes classed according to their use, e.g., WINE, RAISIN, table, juice, or canning grapes. The cultivated grapevine is prey to numerous pests and diseases and requires a great deal of care (see VINEYARD). The art of grape growing was said in Greek legend to have been introduced by DIONYSUS; BACCHUS was the god of wine. Throughout history, the grape has been a symbol in art and literature of revelry and joy. Grapes are classified in the division MAGNOLIOPHYTA, class Magnoliopsida, order Rhamnales, family Vitaceae.

grapefruit or **pomelo** (pŏm'əlō), CITRUS FRUIT (*Citrus paradisi*) of the family Rutaceae (ORANGE family). The grapefruit is so named because it grows in grapelike bunches. The large globular fruit weighs from 1 to 5 lb (0.45–2.27 kg). It is believed that the progenitor of the grapefruit was the pomelo (*C. maxima*), native to and long a popular fruit in India and other parts of Asia. The pomelo (also called shaddock, for the man who first took it to England as a curiosity) was introduced into the West Indies, where it is thought that a seedling sport or mutation resulted in the grapefruit. Brought to Florida in 1809, the grapefruit had become an important commercial product of that state by the turn of the century. It is now grown in many varieties—chiefly in Florida, Texas, and California in the United States and also in some Mediterranean countries. The tree, an attractive evergreen, is usually propagated by budding. Like other citruses, it is prey to frost and hybridizes easily; the tangelo is a cross between the grapefruit and the tangerine. Grapefruits are classified in the division MAGNOLIOPHYTA, class Magnoliopsida, order Sapindales, family Rutaceae.

grape hyacinth, any plant of the genus *Muscari* of the family Liliaceae (LILY family), low plants with dense spikelike clusters of small, nodding flowers that are usually deep blue. Of more than 50 Old World species several have been successfully naturalized in the United States and are especially popular as rock-garden plants. Grape hyacinths are classified in the division MAGNOLIOPHYTA, class Liliatae, order Liliales, family Liliaceae.

grape sugar: see GLUCOSE.

graph, figure that shows relationships between quantities. In a line graph the relationship to be studied is treated as a FUNCTION and is plotted as in a coordinate system; such a system consists of two straight lines intersecting at right angles, each line having a unit length or scale indicated on it. The position of any point in this coordinate system can be described by giving its distances (with plus and minus signs to indicate respectively the distances to the right and left or up and down) from these lines. The graph of a function $y=f(x)$ is the set of points with coordinates $[x, f(x)]$ in the xy-plane, when x and y are numbers. A similar definition can be given for functions involving more general kinds of variables. In mathematics interest is almost exclusively in line graphs and what these reveal about the functions they represent. Statistics makes extensive use of both line graphs and bar graphs, in which the lengths of the various bars show the quantities to be compared.

graphic arts: see AQUATINT; DRAWING; DRYPOINT; ENGRAVING; ETCHING; ILLUSTRATION; LINOLEUM BLOCK PRINTING; LITHOGRAPHY; MEZZOTINT; NIELLO; PASTEL; POSTER; SILK-SCREEN PRINTING; SILHOUETTE; SILVERPOINT; SKETCH; STENCIL; WOODCUT AND WOOD ENGRAVING.

graphic terminal, special input or output station of a data-processing system. It is capable of handling data such as photographs, sketches, handwritten material, and printed matter and converting it to or from a form used by a COMPUTER. One common type uses a CATHODE-RAY TUBE. When it acts as an output device, the arrangement is essentially the same as a TELEVISION display in which the video signal is generated by the computer; the result is a varying beam of electrons that strikes the tube's phosphor-coated screen and causes it to glow. When it is used as an input device, the tube's screen develops electric charges where it has been struck by an external source of light and then is scanned, as in a television camera, to develop a signal proportional to the stored charges; this signal is converted to digital form and stored in the computer. For entering handwritten or drawn information in this way, a pencillike device called a light pen, which produces an intense spot of light at its tip, is traced over the surface of the cathode-ray tube. Other types of graphic terminals are also possible. For example, an output, or readout, screen can be made using an array of small light-emitting DIODES or neon glow tubes. Similarly, an input screen can use an array of small PHOTOELECTRIC CELLS.

graphite (grăf'īt), an allotropic form of CARBON, known also as plumbago and black lead. It is dark gray or black, crystalline (often in the form of slippery scales), greasy, and soft, with a metallic luster. It is a good conductor of electricity and does not fuse at very high temperatures or burn easily. It occurs in nature in grayish-black masses, massive or crystalline, and is obtained in various parts of the world—in the United States (massive) in Nevada, Michigan, and Rhode Island and (crystalline) in Alabama and North Carolina; in Brazil; in the British Isles and on the Continent; and in Sri Lanka, the Malagasy Republic, and Siberia. It is also prepared artificially by treating hard coal in the electric furnace, a process discovered by E. G. Acheson. The uses of graphite are wide and diverse. The so-called lead of pencils is in reality a mixture of graphite with clay. Crucibles required to withstand high temperatures and also electrodes are commonly made of graphite. It is used also in stove polish, in some paints, and as a lubricant.

Grasmere, village, Westmorland, NW England, in the Lake District, near Lake Grasmere. Dove Cottage was the home of William Wordsworth from 1799 to 1808; it now contains a Wordsworth museum. The Wordsworth family and the writer Hartley Coleridge are buried in the churchyard of St. Oswald's. Thomas De Quincey and Samuel Taylor Coleridge also lived in Grasmere.

Grass, Günter (gün'tər gräs), 1927–, German novelist, lyricist, artist, and playwright, b. Danzig (now Gdańsk). Writing from his experience in the Luftwaffe and as a prisoner of war, Grass deplores fascist militarism. The anguish of war and the present social and political problems of West Germany are his principal concerns in his novels. *Die Blechtrommel* (1959; tr. *The Tin Drum,* 1961), which brought him world renown, reveals his bizarre sense of humor. His second novel, *Hundejahre* (1963; tr. *Dog Years,* 1965), is a monumental work that aroused considerable controversy. Grass's early poems and plays are marked by a sensitivity for imagery and a tendency toward symbolism and ambiguity (see *Selected Poems,* tr. 1966; *New Poems,* tr. 1968; *Four Plays,* tr. 1967). His later works reflect a period of intense political activism. Student unrest in Berlin and the political "generation gap" are the themes of his novel *Örtlich betäubt* (1969; tr. *Local Anaesthetic,* 1970) and a play adaptation, *Davor* (1970; tr. *Max,* 1972).

Grass's reflections on his life in Berlin and his political activities are the basis for the novel *Aus dem Tagebuch einer Schnecke* (1972, tr. *From the Diary of a Snail*, 1973). His other works include a collection of speeches and open letters entitled *Speak Out!* (tr. 1969), and the novel *Inmary praise* (tr. 1974). See biographies by K. L. Tank (1965, tr. 1969) and W. G. Cunliffe (1969); study by Edward Diller (1974).

grass, any plant of the family Gramineae, the largest and most widely distributed group of vascular plants, having an extraordinary range of adaptation. Numbering approximately 500 genera and 4,500 species, the grasses form the climax vegetation (see ECOLOGY) in great areas of low rainfall throughout the world: the prairies and plains of North America, the savannas and pampas of South America, the steppes and plains of Eurasia, and the veldt of Africa. Most grasses are annual or perennial herbs with fibrous roots and, often, rhizomes. The stems are always noded and are typically hollow and swollen at the nodes, although many genera have solid stems. The leaves have two parts: a sheath surrounding the stem (called the culm in grasses); and a blade, usually flat and linear. The flowers are of a unique form, the inflorescence being subdivided into spikelets each containing one or more tiny florets. (In other flowering plants the inflorescences are clusters of separate flowers, never spikelets.) The dry seedlike fruit is called a caryopsis, or grain. Economically the grass family is of far greater importance than any other. The cereal grasses, e.g., WHEAT, RICE, CORN, OATS, BARLEY, and RYE, provide the GRAIN that is the staple food of most of mankind and the major type of feed. The grasses also include most of the hay and pasture plants, e.g., SORGHUM, TIMOTHY, BENT GRASS, BLUEGRASS, ORCHARD GRASS, and FESCUE. Popularly the word *grass* is used chiefly for these latter and for the LAWN grass types; it is also loosely applied to plants which are not true grasses (e.g., clover and alfalfa) but which resemble them and are similarly grown. Molasses and sugar are products of SUGARCANE and sorghum, both grasses. Many liquors are made from grains and molasses. Plants of the grass family are also a source of industrial ethyl alcohol, corn starch and by-products, newsprint and other types of paper, and numerous lesser items. Especially in the tropics, species of REED, BAMBOO (one of the few woody types), and other genera are used for thatching and construction. As food, grasses are as important for wildlife as for domesticated animals. Because of the tenacious nature of their large underground root system, grasses (e.g., BEACH GRASS) are often introduced to prevent erosion. Grasses are classified in the division MAGNOLIOPHYTA, class Liliatae, order Cyperales, family Gramineae. See U.S. Dept. of Agriculture, *Grass: The Yearbook of Agriculture* (1948); A. S. Hitchcock, *A Manual of Grasses of the United States* (2 vol., 2d ed. 1971); J. W. Bews, *The World's Grasses* (1929, repr. 1973).

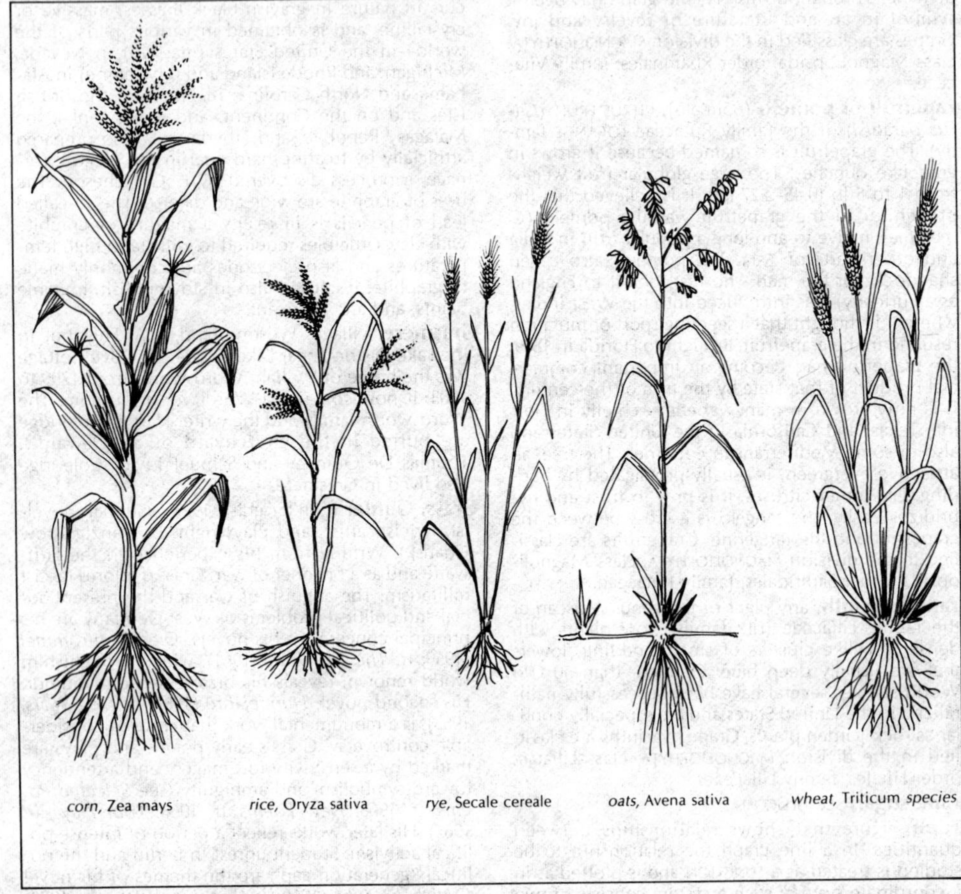

Edible grasses

Grasse, François Joseph Paul, comte de (fräNswä' zhôzĕf' pōl kôNt də gräs), 1722–88, French admiral. In 1781, in command of a French fleet sent to cooperate with the Continental forces in the American Revolution, he defeated a British naval force under Admiral Hood and captured Tobago. Then he came N to Virginia at the request of generals Washington and Rochambeau. There he used his fleet to blockade the York and James rivers, thus bottling up General Cornwallis at Yorktown. He outmaneuvered and defeated a British force under Admiral Graves, and men from his ships also took part in the land fight. His efforts led to the great victory of the YORKTOWN CAMPAIGN. After the Revolution was won, Admiral de Grasse was severely defeated (1782) by the British under Admiral Rodney in the West Indies.

Grasse, town (1968 pop. 32,096), Alpes-Maritime dept., SE France. Probably founded in Roman times, Grasse was a commercial center during the Middle Ages. Destroyed many times by the SARACENS, it was an independent republic from the 12th cent. until its union with the earldom of Provence in 1226. In 1536 the town was destroyed by Francis I to prevent the advance of Emperor Charles V. Surrounded by fields of flowers and rose gardens, Grasse is a center of the French perfume industry. Points of interest include a splendid early Gothic cathedral (12th cent.); a town hall built partially in the Middle Ages; and a museum containing paintings by Jean-Honoré Fragonard, who was born in Grasse.

grasshopper, name applied to almost 9,000 different species of singing, jumping INSECTS in two families of the order Orthoptera. Grasshoppers are long, slender, winged insects with powerful hind legs and strong mandibles, or mouthparts, adapted for chewing. They range from ½ to 4 in. (1–10 cm) in length. They have a front pair of rigid wings and a hind pair of larger, membranous wings, often brightly colored. When the wings are at rest, the hind pair folds and is covered by the front pair. Some species fly well, others poorly or not at all. There are three pairs of legs, all used for walking. The muscular hind legs are also used for jumping and for initiating flight. Grasshoppers can jump up to 20 times their body length. In most species the singing, or stridulating, is performed only by the males. Both sexes possess auditory organs. The long-horned grasshoppers (family Tettigoniidae) are characterized by antennae longer than the body and auditory organs on the forelegs. This family includes the KATYDIDS as well as the cave CRICKET and sand cricket. The short-horned grasshoppers (family Acrididae) are characterized by antennae shorter than the body and auditory organs on the abdomen. This group includes the LOCUST. There are many common species in each family. Most grasshoppers mate in the fall, after which the female lays the eggs in the ground or in plant tissues. The eggs of most species hatch in the spring. Newly hatched grasshoppers are similar to the adults except for their smaller size and lack of wings. After several molts, in which the young shed their old body coats and grow new ones, the winged adult stage is attained. Most grasshoppers are plant feeders, attacking crops such as wheat, barley, corn, rye, and oats. The migratory grasshoppers, including the locusts, are a serious threat to agriculture. A few long-horned grasshoppers are carnivorous. Grasshoppers are typically found in temperate regions. They are classified in the phylum ARTHROPODA, class Insecta, order Orthoptera, suborders Caelifera and Ensifera, families Tettigoniidae and Acrididae respectively.

Grassi, Giovanni Battista (jōvän'nē bät-tē'stä gräs'-sē), 1854–1925, Italian zoologist. He demonstrated (1898) that the *Anopheles* mosquito carries the plasmodium of malaria in its digestive tract. He is known also for his research on parasites, on migrations and metamorphosis in eels, on the vine parasite phylloxera, and on termites.

grassing: see BLEACHING.

Grassmann, Hermann Günther (hĕr'män gün'tər gräs'män), 1809–77, German mathematician and Sanskrit scholar, educated in Berlin. He invented a new algebra of vectors (somewhat similar to quaternions), presented in his book *Die Ausdehnungslehre* (1844, 4th ed. 1969). He composed a translation of the Rig-Veda (1876–77). The linguistic law reformulated by (and named for) him holds that in Indo-European bases, especially in Sanskrit and Greek, successive syllables may not begin with aspirates.

Grasso, Ella Tambussi, 1919–, U.S. politician, governor of Connecticut (1975–), b. Windsor Locks, Conn. A Democrat, she was elected to the Connecticut legislature in 1952 and served (1958–70) as secretary of the state. In 1970 she won election to the U.S. House of Representatives, and in 1974 she won the Connecticut gubernatorial election. She was the first woman to become governor of a state without achieving that office on the political coattails of her husband.

grass-of-Parnassus: see SAXIFRAGE.

grass pink: see ORCHID.

Gratiae: see GRACES.

Gratian (grā'shən), 359–83, Roman emperor of the West (375–83). At the death of his father, VALENTINIAN I, he accepted the army's election of his brother, VALENTINIAN II, as his colleague. Gratian took Britain, Gaul, and Spain as his own share of the empire and acted as guardian for Valentinian in Italy, Illyricum, and Africa. After the death of Valens (378), he made THEODOSIUS I emperor of the East. Gratian fought successfully against the barbarians. He appointed St. AMBROSE as an adviser and vigorously attacked paganism, ordering the removal of the altar of Victory from the senate house and the confiscation of the revenues of the vestal virgins and refusing the title *pontifex maximus.* Toward the end of his reign he neglected public affairs for hunting. In 383 he was assassinated by the followers of Maximus.

Gratian, fl. 1140, Italian legal scholar, founder of the science of CANON LAW. Almost nothing is known of his life beyond the fact that he was a monk, almost certainly Camaldolite, and that he taught at the convent of saints Felix and Nabor (San Felice) in Bologna. He was apparently very learned in scholasticism and Roman law. His great work, commonly known as the *Decretum,* appeared c.1140. It is a synthesis of church law, divided into three parts: the first deals with sources and principles of canon law and with ecclesiastical persons; the second, with ecclesiastical jurisdiction and property and to some extent with marriage and penance; the third, with sacraments and liturgy. Gratian, by his method, makes the compilation a systematic treatise; his commentaries, the *dicta Gratiani,* make up a large part of the work. The *Decretum* was used by the later popes and became the kernel of the *Corpus juris canonici.* See study by Stanley Chodorow (1972).

Grattan, Henry (grăt′ən), 1746–1820, Irish statesman. A lawyer, he entered (1775) the Irish Parliament and soon became known as a brilliant orator. Aided by Britain's preoccupation with the American Revolution and its fear of the revolutionary potential of the Irish volunteer army (see IRELAND), Grattan led the successful fight for abolition of the restrictions on Irish trade and the repeal of Poynings's Law (see under POYNINGS, SIR EDWARD). Having thus gained nominal legislative independence for the Irish Parliament, he worked to eliminate the system by which English patrons continued to control it, advocating CATHOLIC EMANCIPATION as the only means for making the Irish Parliament truly representative. The Catholic Relief Act (1793) gave Catholics the right to vote in Ireland, but hopes raised in 1795 that Catholics would be allowed to sit in Parliament were soon dashed, and Grattan retired (1797) in indignation at the government's policy. In 1800, on the last day of the debate on the parliamentary union with England, Grattan appeared in the Irish Parliament and made the greatest speech of his career in opposition to the Act of Union. He sat in the British Parliament from 1805, taking little part except to support Catholic Emancipation. See biographies by Roger McHugh (1936) and Stephen Gwynn (1939, repr. 1971).

Gratz, Barnard (grăts), 1738–1801, American merchant, b. Langensdorf, Upper Silesia. Having worked in his cousin's countinghouse in London, Gratz emigrated (1754) to Philadelphia, where he became a fur trader. Within a few years he and his brother **Michael Gratz,** 1740–1811, established a firm that acquired tracts of land in Ohio, Kentucky, Indiana, and Illinois for pioneer settlement and ran boats on the Ohio River. The brothers signed the nonimportation resolutions against the Stamp Act and gave invaluable aid to the patriot cause in the American Revolution when they ran supplies through the British blockade. Later, Barnard helped to amend Pennsylvania's and Maryland's constitutions so that Jews could hold office. Michael was the father of Rebecca Gratz. See W. V. Byars, ed., *B. and M. Gratz* (1916).

Grätz or **Graetz, Heinrich** (both: hīn′rĭkh grĕts), 1817–91, German Jewish historian. He was the first modern historian to write, from a Jewish perspective, a comprehensive history of the Jewish people. His *Geschichte der Juden* (11 vol., 1853–75), of which there have been numerous English translations as *History of the Jews,* had enormous influence on subsequent Jewish historiography. See S. W. Baron, *History and Jewish Historians* (1964).

Gratz, Michael: see GRATZ, BARNARD.

Gratz, Rebecca (grăts), 1781–1869, American philanthropist, b. Philadelphia; daughter of Michael Gratz. Well known for her philanthropies in Philadelphia, she is remembered chiefly as the probable prototype of Rebecca in Scott's *Ivanhoe,* her charm and beauty having been described to Scott by Washington Irving. Her letters were edited by David Philipson (1929). See biography R. G. Osterweis (1935).

Grau, Jacinto (hăthēn′tō grou), 1877–1958, Spanish dramatist, b. Barcelona. He participated in the Spanish literary Renaissance of the early 20th cent. Grau slowly gained recognition as the creator of strikingly original plays. *El conde Alarcos* (1917) and an impressive biblical drama, *El hijo pródigo* (1918), are well known, but his masterpiece is *El señor de Pigmalión* (1921), a blend of allegory, lyrical fantasy, and buffoonery. After the Spanish civil war Grau went to Argentina, where he spent the rest of his life.

Graubünden: see GRISONS, Switzerland.

Graudenz: see GRUDZIĄDZ, Poland.

Graun, Carl Heinrich (kärl hīn′rĭkh groun), 1704–59, German composer, best known for his oratorio *Der Tod Jesu* (1755), for many years performed annually in Germany. As musical director to Frederick the Great, who wrote the libretto of Graun's *Montezuma* (1755), he was also director of the opera at Berlin, where his own Italianate operas and those of Johann Hasse dominated the stage. His brother, **Johann Gottlieb Graun** (1703–71), also in the service of the court as a violinist, was the composer of 100 symphonies and many other works.

Graupner, Christoph (krĭs′tôf group′nər), 1693–1760, German composer, studied at Leipzig with Johann Heinichen and Johann Kuhnau. After playing harpsichord at the Hamburg opera (1706–9) under Keiser, he became (1712) conductor to the court at Darmstadt, where he remained until his death. He was elected successor to Kuhnau as cantor of St. Thomas's, Leipzig, but events at Darmstadt prevented him from taking the post, which was then given to J. S. Bach. At Hamburg he wrote a number of operas, but he turned to instrumental and sacred music at Darmstadt.

Graupner, Gottlieb (Johann Christian Gottlieb), 1767–1836, German-American musician, b. near Hanover. After playing the oboe in a regimental band in Hanover, he went (1788) to England, where he played (1791–92) in an orchestra conducted by Haydn. In 1795 he came to the United States, settling in Charleston, S.C., where he played in the City Theatre Orchestra. He moved to Boston in 1798. For nearly a quarter of a century a leading figure in that city's musical life, Graupner was a founder of the Handel and Haydn Society. He organized (c.1810) the Philharmonic Society, which was the first semiprofessional orchestra in Boston and played an important role in the development of Boston's cultural life.

Grau San Martín, Ramón (rämōn′ grou sän märtēn′), 1887–1969, president of Cuba (1933–34, 1944–48). Professor of medicine at the Univ. of Havana, Grau San Martín opposed Gerardo Machado. He then joined with student radicals and the military junta that ousted Carlos Manuel de CÉSPEDES and was named provisional president. Grau was in turn removed from office by a coup led by Fulgencio BATISTA Y ZALDÍVAR. He lost the presidential election to Batista in 1940, but he won in the free election of 1944 and as president launched a widely hailed program of social and economic readjustment. Corruption and nepotism were soon rife, and former supporters turned against him. A booming economy, however, favored the election (1948) of Grau's candidate, Carlos Prío Socarrás. Grau's political influence remained strong during Prío's regime, and when Batista ousted Prío (1952) in a second coup, he retained a measure of popularity. In 1954 he ran against Bastista but charged fraud before the election and retired. After Batista's ouster (1959) by Fidel Castro, Grau remained in Cuba.

grave, space excavated in the earth or rock for the burial of a corpse. When a grave is marked by a protective or memorial structure it is often referred to as a TOMB. See BURIAL; FUNERAL CUSTOMS.

gravel, particles of rock, i.e., stones and pebbles, usually round in form and intermediate in size between sand grains and boulders. Gravel is composed of various kinds of rock, the most common constituent being the mineral quartz. Deposits of gravel are formed as a result of the weathering of rocks and the erosive and concentrating action of rivers and waves. Sometimes gravel becomes consolidated into the sedimentary rock called conglomerate. Gravel is used extensively in building roads and in making concrete. For road building it is crushed into angular particles of uniform size. One or more layers of gravel underlie the road surface. A small percentage of clay must be present to act as a binder when gravel is used in macadam for road surfaces. When used as a coarse aggregate for CONCRETE, gravel must be clean and free from clay and organic matter. Commercially, it is classified according to the size of the particles. In areas where natural deposits are inadequate, gravel is produced by quarrying and crushing durable rocks, such as sandstone, limestone, or basalt.

Gravelot, Hubert (üběr′ grävlō′), 1699–1772, French engraver. Gravelot was instrumental in introducing the French ROCOCO pictorial tradition to England. The books he illustrated include the works of Shakespeare, Richardson's *Pamela,* and Fielding's *Tom Jones.* His *Treatise on Perspective* was widely read.

Gravenhage, 's: see HAGUE, THE.

Gravenhurst (grā′vənhûrst), town (1971 pop. 7,133), S Ont., Canada, N of Toronto. It is the gateway to the Muskoka Lakes area and has some light industry.

Graves, Alfred Percival, 1846–1931, Irish poet. An inspector of schools, he was also twice president of the Irish literary society. He complied several volumes of Irish music and folksongs. Included among his own writings are *Irish Songs and Ballads* (1880) and *Father O'Flynn* (1889). See his collected poems (1908); his autobiography, *To Return to All That* (1930). Robert Graves is his son.

Graves, Frank Pierrepont, 1869–1956, American educator, b. Brooklyn, N.Y., grad. Columbia (B.A., 1890; Ph.D., 1912). He taught Greek and classical philology at Tufts College (1891–96), was president of the Univ. of Wyoming (1896–98) and of the Univ. of Washington (1898–1903), and later served as professor of education and dean at the Univ. of Missouri, Ohio State Univ., and the Univ. of Pennsylvania. From 1921 until his retirement in 1940 he was commissioner of education and president of the Univ. of the State of New York. He wrote several works on both the Greek language and the history of education, as well as three volumes of addresses and papers.

Graves, Robert Ranke, 1895–, English poet, novelist, and critic; son of Alfred Percival Graves. He established his reputation with *Good-bye to All That* (1929), an outspoken book on his war experiences. A versatile and highly prolific writer, Graves, by his own admission, is primarily a poet. His early verse, dealing with themes of war and love, is generally considered his best, but all his poems are characterized by gracefulness and lucidity. In addition to his unorthodox novels of Roman history, *I, Claudius* (1934) and *Claudius the God* (1934), he wrote many fictionalized reappraisals of history and legend, including *King Jesus* (1946) and *Homer's Daughter* (1955). Graves is also known for studies of the mythological and psychological sources of poetry, such as *The White Goddess* (1947), and for his *Greek Myths* (2 vol., 1955). Other works of criticism include *The Common Asphodel (1949), Poetic Craft and Principle* (1967), and *On Poetry: Collected Talks and Essays* (1969). Among his translations are *The Golden Ass* of Apuleius and the *Iliad.* From 1961 until 1966 he was professor of poetry at Oxford. See his *Collected Poems* (1965), *Collected Short Stories* (1965), *Poems, 1968–1970* (1970), and *Poems 1970–72* (1973). See study by Michael Kirkham (1969), and a collection of essays, *Difficult Questions, Easy Answers* (1974).

Graves, Thomas Graves, Baron, 1725?–1802, British admiral. During the American Revolution his fleet was routed (1781) by the comte de GRASSE at the mouth of Chesapeake Bay, a defeat that led directly to the surrender of Lord Cornwallis at Yorktown (see YORKTOWN CAMPAIGN). In the French Revolutionary Wars Graves was second in command to Admiral Richard HOWE in the victory over the French in 1794 and was raised to the peerage.

Graves, William Sidney, 1865–1940, American army officer, b. Hill co., Texas, grad. West Point, 1889. He served (1899–1901) in the Philippines and commanded (1918–20) American forces in Siberia. Graves wrote *America's Siberian Adventures* (1931, repr. 1971).

Graves' disease: see THYROID GLAND.

Gravesend (grāv′zĕnd′), municipal borough (1971 pop. 54,044), Kent, SE England, on the Thames River. The town's industries include shipbuilding, metal casting, engineering, paper making, printing, and the production of tires and rubber products and cement. Known as the "gateway to the Port of London," Gravesend has been for centuries the place of the official reception of London's distinguished visitors and the starting point of expeditions. It is a station of pilots and customhouse officers. Pocahontas is buried in the parish churchyard.

graveyard school, 18th-century school of English poets who wrote primarily about human mortality. Often set in a graveyard, their poems mused on the vicissitudes of life, the solitude of death and the grave, and the anguish of bereavement. Their air of pensive gloom presaged the melancholy of the romantic movement. The most famous graveyard poems were Robert Blair's *The Grave* (1743), Edward Young's nine-volume *The Complaint, or Night Thoughts on Life, Death, and Immortality* (1742–45), and Thomas Gray's "Elegy Written in a Country Churchyard" (1750).

Gravier, Jacques (zhäk grävyā′), 1651–1708, French Jesuit missionary to the Illinois Indians. He went to Canada in 1685. He was sent W to the St. Ignace mission at Mackinac in 1687 and from there (1688) to Illinois to aid Claude Jean ALLOUEZ with the tribes of that region. He succeeded (1689) Father Allouez as vicar general of Illinois. Except for three years at St. Ignace and two trips to New Orleans (1700 and 1706), Gravier spent the remainder of his life with the Illinois Indians, putting their language into written form and preparing a grammar for it.

gravitation, the attractive FORCE existing between any two particles of MATTER. Since this force is experienced by all matter in the universe, from the largest galaxies down to the smallest particles, it is often called universal gravitation. Sir Isaac NEWTON was the first to fully recognize that the force holding any object to the earth is the same as the force holding the moon, the planets, and other heavenly bodies in their orbits. According to Newton's law of universal gravitation, the force between any two bodies is directly proportional to the product of their masses (see MASS) and inversely proportional to the square of the distance between them. The constant of proportionality in this law is known as the gravitational constant; it is usually represented by the symbol G and has the value 6.670×10^{-11} N-m²/kg² in the meter-kilogram-second (mks) system of units. Very accurate early measurements of the value of G were made by Henry Cavendish. **Gravity** is commonly used synonymously with gravitation, but in correct usage a definite distinction is made. Whereas gravitation is the attractive force acting to draw any bodies together, gravity indicates that force in operation between the earth and other bodies, i.e., the force acting to draw bodies toward the earth. The force tending to hold objects to the earth's surface depends not only on the earth's gravitational FIELD but also on other factors, such as the earth's rotation. The measure of the force of gravity on a given body is the WEIGHT of that body; although the mass of a body does not vary with location, its weight does vary. It is found that at any given location, all objects are accelerated equally by the force of gravity, observed differences being due to differences in air resistance, etc. Thus, the ACCELERATION due to gravity, symbolized as g, provides a convenient measure of the strength of the earth's gravitational field at different locations. The value of g varies from about 9.832 meters per second per second (m/sec²) at the poles to about 9.780 m/sec² at the equator. Its value generally decreases with increasing altitude; the maximum value occurs at sea level for any given latitude. Because variations in the value of g are not large, for ordinary calculations a value of 9.8 m/sec², or 32 ft/sec², is commonly used. Newton's theory of gravitation was long able to explain all observable gravitational phenomena, from the falling of objects on the earth to the motions of the planets. However, as centuries passed, very slight discrepancies were observed between the predictions of Newtonian theory and actual events, most notably in the motions of the planet Mercury. The general theory of RELATIVITY proposed in 1916 by Albert EINSTEIN explained these differences and provided a geometric explanation for gravitational phenomena, holding that matter causes a curvature of the space-time framework in its immediate neighborhood. A more recent alternate theory of gravitation is the scalar-tensor theory (Dicke-Brans theory), which has many assumptions in common with the Einstein theory and makes predictions differing only slightly from those of the other theory. Experiments have not yielded firm evidence in favor of either theory of gravitation over the other. Modern research has concentrated on those aspects of gravitation that parallel the electromagnetic force (see ELECTROMAGNETIC RADIATION). Gravity waves, first detected in 1969, are analogous to electromagnetic waves. A hypothetical particle, given the name *graviton*, has been suggested; it is analogous to the PHOTON, the particle embodying the quantum properties of electromagnetic waves (see QUANTUM THEORY). See A. S. Eddington, *Space, Time and Gravitation* (1920); P. G. Bergmann, *The Riddle of Gravitation* (1968), Steven Weinberg, *Gravitation and Cosmology* (1972).

gravitational collapse, in astronomy, theoretically predicted final stage in the life history of a star (see STELLAR EVOLUTION). A star in the last phases of gravitational collapse is often referred to as a "black hole." Gravitational collapse may begin when a star has depleted its steady sources of nuclear energy and can no longer produce the expansive force, which is a result of normal gas PRESSURE, that supports the star against the compressive force of its own GRAVITATION. As the star shrinks in size (and increases in density), it may assume one of several forms depending upon its mass. A less massive star may become a WHITE DWARF, a SUPERNOVA, or a NEUTRON STAR. However, if a star is too massive, its evolution will not stop at one of these stable configurations. According to present knowledge, nothing remains to prevent the star from collapsing without limit to an indefinitely small size. At this point, the effects of Einstein's general theory of RELATIVITY become paramount. According to this theory, space becomes curved in the vicinity of matter; the greater the concentration of matter, the greater the curvature. When the star (or supernova remnant) shrinks below a certain size determined by its mass, the extreme curvature of space seals off contact with the outside world. For a star with a mass equal to that of the sun, this limit is a radius of only 0.9 mi (1.5 km). The former star is now a black hole. Even light cannot escape the black hole but is turned back by the enormous pull of gravitation. Because light and other forms of energy and matter are permanently trapped inside the black hole, it can never be observed directly. However, a black hole could be detected by its effects on external objects or during the collapse while it was forming.

Gray, Asa, 1810–88, America's leading botanist and taxonomist, b. Oneida co., N.Y. As professor of natural history at Harvard from 1842, he was the teacher of many eminent botanists. Through his voluminous writings in periodicals and his well-known textbooks, he helped popularize the study of botany. With John Torrey he explored the W United States and helped to revise the taxonomic procedure of Linnaeus on the basis of a more natural classification, based primarily on fruit anatomy rather than on gross morphology (e.g., similarity of leaf shapes). This system is still used, although most modern botanists consider evolutionary and genetic evidence as the definitive indication of plant relationships. Gray's *Manual of Botany* was edited by M. L. Fernald (8th centennial ed. 1950); it is the standard reference work for the flora of the United States E of the Rockies. He initiated the quarterly *Gray Herbarium Card Index*, listing all the vascular plants of the Western Hemisphere described since 1873. Among his many other writings, still highly valued, are *Structural Botany* (6th ed. 1879) and *The Elements of Botany* (1887). See his letters (ed. by J. L. Gray, 1893, repr. 1968); biography by A. H. Dupree (1968).

Gray, Elisha, 1835–1901, American inventor, b. Barnesville, Ohio. He patented many electrical devices, most of them having to do with the telegraph. His telautograph (1888) for transmitting handwriting and line drawing has been widely used. While experimenting in 1875 with the idea of sending musical notes by wire, as a means of sending several messages simultaneously over the same wire, he hit upon the idea of transmitting the human voice and early in 1876 filed with the patent office a caveat for such an invention. Alexander Graham Bell's final patent had been registered just a few hours before. The Western Union Telegraph Company, which acquired both Gray's and Edison's patents, was defeated by the Bell Telephone Company in one of the most famous patent cases in American litigation.

Gray, George, 1840–1925, American jurist, b. New Castle, Del. A lawyer, he was (1879–85) attorney general of Delaware and was a Democratic U.S. Senator from 1885 to 1899. From 1898 to 1916, Gray often served on international commissions to arbitrate differences between the United States and other countries. He was instrumental in drawing up the treaty that ended the Spanish-American War, in negotiating a settlement of the dispute over fisheries of the N Atlantic, and in calming trouble with Mexico in 1916. He also served (1900–1920) on the panel of the Permanent Court of Arbitration at The Hague. In 1902, as chairman of a presidential arbitration commission, Gray settled the anthracite coal strike.

Gray, Horace, 1828–1902, American jurist, Associate Justice of the U.S. Supreme Court (1881–1902), b. Boston. At first a reporter (1854–61) to the Massachusetts supreme court, he later entered into law practice. Originally a member of the Free-Soil party, he became a Republican. After an unsuccessful attempt (1860) to secure the nomination for Massachusetts attorney general, he was appointed (1864) to the state supreme court and later (1873) became chief justice of the court. He was appointed by President Arthur to the U.S. Supreme Court, where he served the last 21 years of his life. As a lawyer and jurist, Gray was noted for using analytical case study as an approach to the historical development of legal principles and for his use of precedent in arguing and deciding cases.

Gray, John Chipman, 1839–1915, American lawyer and teacher, b. Brighton, Mass. A graduate of Harvard Law School, (1861), he served in the Civil War and then entered law practice in Boston; in 1869 he began teaching at Harvard Law School. He continued both practice and teaching until the last years of his life and was Royall professor at Harvard from 1883 until 1913. A leading advocate of the case system of teaching law, he was a recognized authority in both England and the United States on the law of real property. His best-known work is *The Nature and Sources of the Law* (1909). See Roland Gray, *John Chipman Gray* (1917).

Gray, Robert, 1775–1806, American sea captain, discoverer of the Columbia River, b. Tiverton, R.I. He probably served in the Continental navy in the American Revolution. In 1787 he and Capt. John Kendrick were sent by Boston merchants to the northwest coast of North America with two vessels, the *Columbia Rediviva* and the sloop *Lady Washington*. In 1789, Gray was transferred to command of the *Columbia*, took a rich cargo of sea otter skins to Canton, and in 1790 returned to Boston, the first American to circumnavigate the globe. In 1791 he went back to the Northwest coast and wintered there. On May 11, 1792, he took the *Columbia* past the dangerous bar and up the river later named after the ship. Though Spanish and English navigators had been familiar with the bar at the Columbia's mouth, Gray was the first to enter the river itself.

Gray, Stephen, 1666–1736, English physicist. Gray, a dyer by trade, cultivated science as a hobby. In 1696 he published an account of a magnifying glass that interested the Royal Society and from then on he frequently sent the Society and his patron, English Astronomer Royal John Flamsteed, ideas for simple but revealing experiments and reports of geological and astronomical observations. Gray's most important work, published in 1732, announced the discovery of electrical induction and the distinction between conductors and insulators.

Gray, Thomas, 1716–71, English poet. He was educated at Eton and Peterhouse, Cambridge. In 1739 he began a grand tour of the Continent with Horace Walpole. They quarreled in Italy, and Gray returned to England in 1741. He continued his studies at Cambridge, and he remained there for most of his life, living in seclusion, studying Greek, and writing. In 1768 he was made professor of history and modern languages, but he did no real teaching. Although he was reconciled with Walpole, and formed other close relationships in his lifetime, his shy and sensitive disposition was ill adapted to the robust century in which he lived. He was offered the laureateship in 1757 but refused it. His first important poems, written in 1742, include "To Spring," "On a Distant Prospect of Eton College," and a sonnet on the death of his close friend Richard West. After years of revision he finished his great "Elegy Written in a Country Churchyard" (1751), a meditative poem presenting thoughts conjured up by the sight of a rural graveyard; it is probably the most quoted poem in English. In 1757, Walpole published Gray's Pindaric odes, "The Progress of Poesy" and "The Bard." Gray's poetry illustrates the evolution of English poetry in the 18th cent.—from the classicism of the 1742 poems to the romantic tendencies of "The Fatal Sisters" and "The Descent of Odin" (1768). He did not write a large amount of poetry. Much of his verse is tinged with melancholy, and even more of it reflects his extensive learning. His letters, which contain much humor, are among the finest in the English language. See his collected works, ed. by E. Gosse (4 vol., rev. ed. 1902–6; repr. 1968); his correspondence, ed. by P. Toynbee and L. Whibley (1935, repr. 1971); selected letters, ed. by J. W. Krutch (1952); biographies by R. W. Ketton-Cremer (1955), M. Golden (1964), and W. P. Jones (1937, repr. 1965).

Gray Eminence: see JOSEPH, FATHER.

grayling, common name for a brilliantly colored fish belonging to the genus *Thymallus*, of the family Salmonidae (SALMON family), and closely allied to the smelt. Graylings are found chiefly in clear, cold, fresh waters of the Northern Hemisphere. They average 1 ft (30 cm) in length and 1 lb (.45 kg) in weight and exhibit hues of silver, gold, violet, blue, and olive brown. The American species include the arctic grayling, said to reach 4 lb (1.8 kg), the now scarce Michigan grayling, and the Montana grayling, found in the tributaries of the Missouri. The genus name, *Thymallus*, refers to the odor of wild thyme characteristic of the delicious flesh of fresh specimens. Graylings are classified in the phylum CHORDATA, subphylum Vertebrata, class Osteichthyes, order Clupeiformes, family Salmonidae.

gray matter: see NERVOUS SYSTEM.

Gray's Inn: see INNS OF COURT.

Grayson, Cary Travers, 1878–1938, American naval officer and surgeon, b. Culpeper co., Va. As a physician he entered (1903) the U.S. navy, was graduated (1904) from the navy medical school, and after further service and study became (1916) medical director with the rank of rear admiral. He was personal physician to Presidents Theodore Roosevelt, William Howard Taft, and Woodrow Wilson. Grayson was twice (1933, 1937) inaugural committee chairman for Franklin Delano Roosevelt and was chosen (1935) chairman of the American Red Cross.

Grayson, David: see BAKER, RAY STANNARD.

Graz (gräts), city (1971 pop. 248,500), capital of Styria prov., SE Austria, on the Mur River. The second largest city in Austria, it is an industrial, rail, and cultural center. Manufactures include iron and steel, paper, and machinery. Probably founded in the 12th cent., Graz is built around the Schlossberg, a mountain peak, on which are the ruins of a 15th-century fortress and the famous Uhrturm [clock tower]. The city has a 15th-century Gothic cathedral; several medieval churches (13th–15th cent.); and a twin-naved Gothic parish church that contains Tintoretto's *Assumption of the Virgin.* The Landhaus [provincial parliament] dates from the 16th cent. The Johanneum museum (founded 1811) is one of the finest provincial museums in Austria. The astronomer Johannes Kepler (1571–1630) taught at the state university in Graz (founded in the 16th cent.). The new university (built 1890–95) is noted for medical studies. Emperor Ferdinand II is buried in Graz.

Graziani, Rodolfo (rōdôl'fō grätsēä'nē), 1882–1955, Italian soldier and colonial administrator. After serving in World War I and in Libya (1921–33), he was made (1935) governor of Italian Somaliland. For his part in the Italo-Ethiopian War, he was widely acclaimed in Italy, was promoted to marshal, and served (1936–37) as viceroy of Ethiopia. Created marquis of Neghelli (1937), Graziani was made chief of staff of the Italian army (1939) and became governor of Libya (1940). In World War II, Graziani's army was completely routed (winter 1940–41) by the British in the Libyan campaign, and he resigned his command. Arrested in 1945, Graziani was indicted for high treason for his collaboration with the Germans in N Italy after the Italian armistice with the Allies in 1943. After two trials he was convicted (1950) by a military court. He was released from custody a few months later and became active in the neofascist party.

Grazzini, Antonio Francesco (äntō'nyō fränchä'skō grät-tsē'nē), 1503–84, Italian author, one of the founders of the ACCADEMIA DELLA CRUSCA (1550). He was an apothecary by trade. As a founder of the Accademia degli Umidi, each of whose members had to assume the name of a fish, he took the name Il Lasca [the roach]. He is best known for *Le Cene* [the suppers], tales of Florentine life. He also wrote comedies of intrigue and burlesque verses in the style of Berni in which he attacked Petrarchan humanism.

grease, mixture of lubricant and thickener. It is used to reduce friction between surfaces from which oils would leak away or cause damage by dripping, or where lubrication must be assured for extended periods. Many greases are mixtures of mineral oil and soap. The more common of them contain a calcium-base soap that withstands water but not high temperature, or a sodium-base soap that withstands higher temperatures and adheres well but dissolves in water. Other soaps used in greases have bases of lithium, aluminum, barium, or strontium. Nonsoap thickeners include carbon black, which is unaffected by temperature and is therefore used with extreme low-temperature lubricants; silica gel; and bentonite, a clay developed for universal greases. Solid lubricants are sometimes used for extreme bearing pressures and high temperatures. Synthetic oils are sometimes used for special conditions, generally temperature extremes.

greasewood: see GOOSEFOOT.

Great Alföld: see ALFÖLD, plain, Hungary.

Great Artesian Basin, c.670,000 sq mi (1,735,300 sq km), between the Eastern Highlands and the Western Plateau, E central Australia, extending S from the Gulf of Carpentaria, Queensland, to NE South Australia and N New South Wales. It is the world's largest artesian water-bearing area. Extremely arid, the basin receives water from the Eastern Highlands as rain is absorbed by porous rock and flows underground toward the center of the saucer-shaped basin. Thousands of wells, some more than 1 mi (1.6 km) deep, tap underground water-bearing rock formations. The rolling surface of the basin supports a pastoral economy based on irrigated grasslands. The highly mineralized artesian water cannot be used for agriculture.

great auk: see AUK.

Great Australian Bight, wide bay of the Indian Ocean, indenting the southern coast of Australia. An unbroken line of cliffs c.200 ft (60 m) high runs along the coast and extends inland as the arid and desolate Nullarbor Plain. The bight is very stormy during winter months.

Great Awakening, series of religious revivals that swept over the American colonies about the middle of the 18th cent. It resulted in doctrinal changes and influenced social and political thought. In New England it was started (1734) by the rousing preaching of Jonathan EDWARDS. Although there were early local stirrings in New Jersey in the 1720s under the evangelical preaching of Theodorus Frelinghuysen of the Dutch Reformed Church, the revival in the Middle Colonies actually began in New Jersey largely among the Presbyterians trained under William TENNENT. His son Gilbert TENNENT became the leading figure of the Great Awakening in the Middle Colonies. Other preachers followed, and with the tour (1739–41) of the famous Methodist preacher George WHITEFIELD, the isolated currents of revivalism united and flowed into all the colonies. The revival reached the South with the preaching (1748–59) of Samuel DAVIES among the Presbyterians of Virginia, with the great success of the Baptists in North Carolina in the 1760s, and with the rapid spread of Methodism shortly before the American Revolution. In New England the movement died out rapidly, leaving behind bitter doctrinal disputes between the "New Lights" and the "Old Lights," the latter led by Charles CHAUNCY, a Boston clergyman, who opposed the revivalist movement as extravagant and impermanent. The theology of the "New Lights," a slightly modified Calvinism, crystallized into the Edwardian, or New England, theology that became dominant in W New England, whereas the liberal doctrines of the "Old Lights," strong in Boston and the vicinity, were destined to develop into the Universalist or Unitarian positions. A similar division between "New Sides" and "Old Sides" took place in the Middle Colonies, causing a schism (1741–58) in the Presbyterian Church. The Great Awakening also resulted in an outburst of missionary activity among the Indians by such men as David BRAINERD, Eleazar WHEELOCK, and Samuel KIRKLAND; in the first movement of importance against slavery; and in various other humanitarian undertakings. It led to the founding of a number of academies and colleges, notably Princeton, Brown, Rutgers, and Dartmouth. It served to build up interests that were intercolonial in character, to increase opposition to the Anglican Church and the royal officals who supported it, and to encourage a democratic spirit in religion. See Joseph Tracy, *A History of the Revival of Religion in the Time of Edwards and Whitefield* (1845, repr. 1969); C. H. Maxson, *The Great Awakening in the Middle Colonies* (1920, repr. 1958); W. M. Gewehr, *The Great Awakening in Virginia* (1930, repr. 1965); E. S. Gaustad, *The Great Awakening in New England* (1957, repr. 1965); R. L. Bushman, ed., *The Great Awakening* (1969); D. B. Rutman, *The Great Awakening: Events and Exegesis* (1970).

Great Barrier Reef, largest coral reef in the world, c.1,250 mi (2,000 km) long, in the Coral Sea, forming a natural breakwater for the coast of Queensland, NE Australia. Composed of several individual reefs, the Great Barrier Reef is separated from the mainland by a shallow lagoon from 10 to 100 mi (16–161 km) wide. In some places it is more than 400 ft (122 m) thick. A major tourist attraction, the reef has many islets, coral gardens, and unusual marine life.

Great Basin, desert region of W United States, mostly in Nevada and extending into California, Oregon, Idaho, and Utah. It is bordered by the Sierra Nevada on the west, the Columbia Plateau on the north, the Rocky Mts. on the northeast, the Colorado Plateau on the east, and the Mojave Desert on the south. The region is a complex topographic basin, the surface of which is broken by numerous short fault-block mountains, trending mostly north-south and rising sharply in places to more than 10,000 ft (3,048 m) above arid, sediment-floored basins. DEATH VALLEY NATIONAL MONUMENT, 282 ft (86 m) below sea level, is the lowest basin; it is also the hottest (134°F/57°C in the shade is the highest temperature recorded) and one of the driest (less than 3 in./7.6 cm of rain annually) parts of the nation. Throughout the Great Basin rainfall is limited (2–20 in./5.1–51 cm annually) and sporadic. The region was recognized as an area of interior drainage by J. C. FRÉMONT, who explored (1843–45) and named it. The rivers of the region have no outlet to the sea; they either dry up as they cross the desert, like the Humboldt, or empty into large lakes or into playas that temporarily fill with water after heavy rain. Klamath and Utah lakes contain fresh water; most other lakes are brackish or salty. The lakes are remnants of a much larger system of ancient lakes that occupied the region during the Pleistocene epoch: Great Salt, Sevier, and Utah lakes are remnants of ancient Lake BONNEVILLE; North Carson, South Carson, Walker, Honey, Pyramid, and Winnemucca are remnants of ancient Lake LAHONTAN; and ancient Lake Manly is thought to have occupied Death Valley. The Great Basin is one of the least populated areas of the United States; its principal economic activities are mining and ranching. There are important copper mines at Bingham, Utah, and Ely, Nev.; silver is mined at Tonapah and Virginia City, Nev., site of the famous Comstock Lode discovery in 1859. Salt deposits, including the borax once mined in Death Valley, and a variety of commercial salts worked today near Great Salt Lake, are found in the region's ancient lake floors. Some cattle are grazed on the unfenced sagebrush-covered basins, and more intensive forms of cattle production, based on irrigated feed crops, are concentrated along the Humboldt and Reese rivers and along streams draining into the margins of the Great Basin from the Wasatch Mts. and the Sierra Nevada. See W. D. Thornbury, *Regional Geomorphology of the United States* (1965); Gloria G. Cline, *Exploring the Great Basin* (1963, repr. 1972).

Great Bear Lake, largest lake of Canada and fourth largest of North America, c.12,275 sq mi (31,800 sq km), c.190 mi (310 km) long and from 25 to 110 mi (40–177 km) wide, N central Mackenzie dist., Northwest Territories, on the edge of the Canadian Shield. It is drained to the W by the Great Bear River (c.100 mi/160 km long), which flows into the Mackenzie River. Even though it is one of North America's deepest (1,356 ft/413 m) lakes, its waters are open only about four months each year. The lake was discovered (c.1800) by traders of the North West Company, and a trading post was later established there. Fort Franklin, on the southwest shore, was built by Sir John Franklin, a British explorer, in 1825. Discoveries of rich radium ores (now exhausted) on the eastern side of the lake in 1930 caused much mining activity in the years immediately following; the Eldorado Mines, at Port Radium, were located there.

Great Belt: see STORE BAELT, strait, Denmark.

Great Bend, city (1970 pop. 16,133), seat of Barton co., central Kansas, on a bend in the Arkansas River; settled and inc. 1871. It is a trade and shipping center for a wheat and oil region.

Great Blasket: see BLASKET ISLANDS, Ireland.

Great Britain, officially the United Kingdom of Great Britain and Northern Ireland, constitutional monarchy (1971 pop. 55,346,551), 94,226 sq mi (244,044 sq km), on the British Isles, off the Western European continent. The country is often referred to simply as Britain. It comprises England (1971 pop. 45,870,062), 50,334 sq mi (130,365 sq km); Wales (1971 pop. 2,723,596), 8,016 sq mi (20,761 sq km); and Scotland (1971 pop. 5,227,706), 30,414 sq mi (78,772 sq km) on the island of Great Britain; and Northern Ireland (1971 pop. 1,525,187), 5,462 sq mi (14,146 sq km) on the island of Ireland. The Isle of Man (1971 pop. 49,743), 227 sq mi (588 sq km), in the Irish Sea, and the Channel Islands (1971 pop. 125,240), 75 sq mi (195 sq km), in the English Channel, both dependencies of the British crown, are not legally part of Great Britain. For physical geography and local administrative divisions, see ENGLAND, WALES, SCOTLAND, and IRELAND, NORTHERN. The capital of Great Britain is LONDON.

Economy. Great Britain is one of the world's leading industrialized nations. It has achieved this position despite the lack of most of the raw materials, except coal, needed for industry. Great Britain also must import about half of its food supplies. Thus the country's prosperity is heavily dependent upon the export of manufactured goods in exchange for raw materials and foodstuffs. The per capita national income was $1,513 in 1969. In 1970, manufacturing industries accounted for about 33% of the gross national product, service industries for 23%, distributive industries for 11%, transportation and communications for 8%, utilities for 3%, and mining for less than 2%. Manufacturing employs more people—more than one third of the total work force—than any other sector of the economy; the financial, professional, and scientific fields employ less than one fifth; the distributive trades slightly more than one tenth; and agriculture, forestry, fishing, and mining together less than one twentieth. Within the manufacturing sector itself, the largest employers were, in 1968, the textile, mechanical engineering, electrical engineering, and food processing industries. By value of production, the most important industries are food processing; the manufacture of textiles, vehicles, metals, and chemicals; and mechanical and electrical engineering. Except for foods, the products of these industries are also the leading exports. The chief imports are petroleum, foodstuffs, textile raw materials, metals, ores, and manufactured goods. The leading trade partners are the countries of the Commonwealth of Nations, the Common Market (which Britain joined in 1973), the European Free Trade Association, and the United States. Britain is the third most active trading nation in the world, accounting for about 7% of the world's trade. The main industrial and commercial areas of Great Britain are the great conurbations, where about one third of the country's population lives. The administrative and financial center and most important port is Greater London (1971 pop. 7,379,014), which also has various manufacturing industries. London remains an important international financial center, although it has lost the paramount position it once held. Metal goods, vehicles, and electronic equipment are made in the West Midlands conurbation (1971 pop. 2,369,205), which with the addition of COVENTRY roughly corresponds to the metropolitan county of West Midlands, created in the local government reorganization of the 1970s. The BLACK COUNTRY and the city of BIRMINGHAM are in the West Midlands. Cotton and synthetic textiles, coal, and chemicals come from South East Lancashire (1971 pop. 2,386,774), which includes MANCHESTER and with the addition of WIGAN roughly corresponds to the new county of Greater Manchester. LIVERPOOL, Britain's second port, is in the Merseyside conurbation (1971 pop. 1,262,467), which with SOUTHPORT and SAINT HELENS corresponds to the new Merseyside county. West Yorkshire (1971 pop. 1,726,097), including LEEDS and BRADFORD, is the center of woolen and worsted production and roughly corresponds to the new West Yorkshire county. Tyneside (1971 pop. 804,402), with NEWCASTLE UPON TYNE as its center, has coal mines and steel, chemical, and shipbuilding industries. With the addition of DURHAM it corresponds to the new county of Tyne and Wear. The South Wales conurbation (1971 pop. 1,833,653), with the ports of SWANSEA, CARDIFF, and NEWPORT (respectively in the new counties of West Glamorgan, South Glamorgan, and Gwent), has coal, steel, plastics, and synthetic-fibers industries. In Scotland, Central Clydeside (1971 pop. 1,727,625), including GLASGOW, is noted for shipbuilding, marine engineering, and steel production. The BELFAST area in Northern Ireland is a shipbuilding and textile center. Iron ore, tin, zinc, china clay, fluorspar, and oil shale are found in Britain in addition to coal. But, of the country's mineral requirements, only coal is present in sufficient quantity. The chief fishing ports of Great Britain are Grimsby and Hull, both on the Humber estuary in England. Whitefish, herrring, and shellfish make up the bulk of the catch. About half of Great Britain's land area is devoted to agriculture. The widespread dairy industry makes the country self-sufficient in milk, and nearly all the eggs needed are also home-produced. Beef cattle, raised in SE England, the Midlands, and NE Scotland, are the second largest agricultural commodity after dairy products. Large numbers of sheep are also raised for meat and wool. Barley, potatoes, and wheat are the main cereal crops. The coal, gas, electricity, railroad, and aviation industries and most of the steel industries are publicly owned.

Government and Religion. Great Britain is a constitutional monarchy. The constitution exists in no one document but is a centuries-old accumulation of statutes, judicial decisions, usage, and tradition. The hereditary monarch, who must belong to the Church of England according to the Act of Settlement of 1701, is almost entirely limited to exercising ceremonial functions. Sovereignty rests in Parliament, which consists of the House of Commons (with 635 members popularly elected from single-member constituencies), the House of Lords, and the crown. Effective power resides in the Commons; the executive—the cabinet of ministers headed by the prime minister—is usually drawn from the party holding the most seats in Commons. The monarch asks the leader usually of the majority party to be prime minister. Elections must be held at least once in five years, but within that period the prime minister may at any time request the crown to dissolve Parliament and call for new elections. Most legislation originates in the Commons. Theoretically, more than 1,000 persons—the hereditary and life peers of the realm, high officials of the Church of England, and the lords of appeal (who exercise judicial functions)—have the right to sit in the House of Lords; actually only about 265 attend regularly. The House of Lords may take a part in shaping legislation, but it cannot permanently block a bill passed by the Commons, and it has no authority over money bills. The lords of appeal constitute the highest court in Great Britain. The crown must not assent to all legislation, but assent has never been withheld since 1707. The two main parties are the CONSERVATIVE PARTY, descended from the old Tory party, and the LABOUR PARTY, which was organized in 1906 and is moderately socialist. The LIBERAL PARTY, formerly the Conservatives' main opponent, is now a weak third. The Church of England, also called the Anglican church (see ENGLAND, CHURCH OF), is the officially established church in England (it was disestablished in Wales in 1914); the monarch is its supreme governor. The Presbyterian Church of Scotland is legally established in Scotland. There is complete religious freedom throughout Britain. In England and Wales in the early 1970s there were about 28 million adherents of the Church of England, 4 million Roman Catholics, 760,000 Methodists, and 450,000 Jews. In Scotland the Church of Scotland has 1,200,000 members and there are 810,000 Roman Catholics and 90,000 Episcopalians (affiliated with the Church of England). In Northern Ireland there are 500,000 Roman Catholics, 410,000 Presbyterians, and 340,000 members of the Church of Ireland (Anglican). There are 44 universities in Great Britain and Northern Ireland (33 in England alone), the most famous being those at Oxford, Cambridge, Edinburgh, and London.

History. Until 1707, this section deals primarily with English history. England and Wales were formally united in 1536. In 1707, when Great Britain was created by the Act of Union between Scotland and England, English history became part of British history. For the early history of SCOTLAND and WALES, see separate articles. See also the articles on IRELAND; IRELAND, NORTHERN.

Early Period to the Norman Conquest. Little is known about the earliest inhabitants of Britain, but the remains of their dolmens and barrows and the great stone circles at STONEHENGE and Avebury are evidence of the developed culture of the prehistoric Britons. They had developed a Bronze Age culture by the time the first Celtic invaders (early 5th cent. B.C.) brought their energetic Iron Age culture to Britain. It is believed that Julius Caesar's successful military campaign in Britain in 54 B.C. was aimed at preventing incursions into Gaul from the island. In A.D. 43 the emperor Claudius began the Roman conquest of Britain, establishing bases at present-day London and Colchester. By A.D. 85, Rome controlled Britain south of the Clyde River. There were a number of revolts in the early years of the conquest, the most famous being that of BOADICEA. In the 2d century A.D., Hadrian's Wall was constructed as a northern defense line. Under the Roman occupation towns developed, and roads were built to ensure the success of the military occupation. These roads were the most lasting Roman achievement in Britain (see WATLING STREET), long serving as the basic arteries of overland transportation in England. Colchester, Lincoln, and Gloucester were founded by the Romans as *colonia*, settlements of ex-legionaries. Trade contributed to town prosperity; wine, olive oil, plate, and furnishings were imported, and lead, tin, iron, wheat, and wool were exported. This trade declined with the economic dislocation of the late Roman Empire and the withdrawal of Roman troops to meet barbarian threats elsewhere. The garrisons had been consumers of the products of local artisans as well as of imports; as they were disbanded, the towns decayed. Barbarian incursions became frequent. In 410 an appeal to Rome for military aid was refused, and Roman officials subsequently were withdrawn. As Rome withdrew its legions from Britain, Germanic peoples—the ANGLO-SAXONS and the Jutes—began raids that turned into great waves of invasion and settlement in the later 5th cent. The Celts fell back into Wales and Cornwall and across the English Channel to Brittany, and the loosely knit tribes of the newcomers gradually coalesced into a heptarchy of kingdoms (see KENT, SUSSEX, ESSEX, WESSEX, EAST ANGLIA, MERCIA, and NORTHUMBRIA). Late in the 8th cent., and with increasing severity until the middle of the 9th cent., raiding VIKINGS (known in English history as Danes) harassed coastal England and finally, in 865, launched a full-scale invasion. They were first effectively checked by King ALFRED of Wessex and were with great difficulty confined to the DANELAW, where their leaders divided land among the soldiers for settlement. Alfred's successors conquered the Danelaw to form a united England, but new Danish invasions late in the 10th cent. overcame ineffective resistance (see AETHELRED, 965?–1016). The Dane CANUTE ruled all England by 1016. At the expiration of the Scandinavian line in 1042, the Wessex dynasty (see EDWARD THE CONFESSOR) regained the throne. The conquest of England in 1066 by William, duke of Normandy (WILLIAM I of England), ended the Anglo-Saxon period. The freeman (ceorl) of the early Germanic invaders had been responsible to his king and superior to the serf. Subsequent centuries of war and subsistence farming, however, had forced the majority of freemen into serfdom, or dependence on the aristocracy of lords and thanes, who came to enjoy a large measure of autonomous control over manors granted them by the king (see MANORIAL SYSTEM). The central government evolved from tribal chieftainships to become a monarchy in which executive and judicial powers were usually vested in the king. The aristocracy made up his witan, or council of advisers (see WITENAGEMOT). The king set up shires as units of local government ruled by earldormen. In some instances these earldormen became powerful hereditary earls, ruling several shires. Subdivisions of shires were called hundreds. There were shire and hundred courts, the former headed by sheriffs, the latter by reeves. Agriculture was the principal industry, but the Danes were aggressive traders, and towns increased in importance starting in the 9th cent. The Anglo-Saxons had been Christianized by missionaries from Rome and from Ireland, and the influence of Christianity became strongly manifest in all phases of culture (see ANGLO-SAXON LITERATURE). Differences between Irish and continental religious customs were decided in favor of the Roman forms at the Synod of Whitby (663). Monastic communities, outstanding in the later 7th and in the 8th cent. and strongly revived in the 10th, developed great proficiency in manuscript illumination. Church scholars, such as Bede, Alcuin, and Aelfric—as well as King Alfred himself—preserved and advanced learning.

Medieval England. A new era in English history began with the NORMAN CONQUEST. William I introduced Norman-style political and military FEUDALISM. He used the feudal system to collect taxes, employed the bureaucracy of the church to strengthen the central government, and made the administration of royal justice more efficient. After the death of William's second son, HENRY I, the country was subjected to a period of civil war that ended one year before the accession of HENRY II in 1154. Henry II's reign was marked by the sharp conflict between king and church that led to the murder of THOMAS À BECKET. Henry carried out great judicial reforms that increased the power and scope of the royal courts. During his reign, in 1171, began the English conquest of Ireland. As part of his inheritance he brought to the throne Anjou, Normandy, and Aquitaine. The defense and enlargement of these French territories engaged the energies of successive English kings. In their need for money the kings stimulated the growth of English towns by selling them charters of liberties. Conflict between kings and nobles, which had begun under RICHARD I, came to a head under JOHN, who made unprecedented financial demands and whose foreign and church policies were unsuccessful. A temporary victory of the nobles bore fruit in the most noted of all English constitutional documents, the MAGNA CARTA (1215). The recurring baronial wars of the 13th cent. (see BARONS' WAR; MONTFORT, SIMON DE) were roughly contemporaneous with the first steps in the development of PARLIAMENT. EDWARD I began the conquest of Wales and Scotland. He also carried out an elaborate reform and expansion of the central courts and of other aspects of the legal system. The HUNDRED YEARS WAR with France began (1337) in the reign of Edward III. The Black Death (see PLAGUE) first arrived in 1348 and had a tremendous effect on economic life, hastening the breakdown (long since under way) of the manorial and feudal systems, including the institution of serfdom. At the same time the fast-growing towns and trades gave new prominence to the burgess and artisan classes. In the 14th cent. the English began exporting their wool, rather than depending on foreign traders of English wool. Later in the century, trade in woolen cloth began to gain on the raw wool trade. The confusion resulting from such rapid social and economic change fostered radical thought, typified in the teachings of John WYCLIF (or Wycliffe; see also LOLLARDRY), and the revolt led by Wat TYLER. Dynastic wars (see ROSES, WARS OF THE), which weakened both the nobility and the monarchy in the 15th cent., ended with the accession of the Tudor family in 1485.

Tudor England. The reign of the Tudors (1485–1603) is one of the most fascinating periods in English history. HENRY VII restored political order and the financial solvency of the crown, bequeathing his son, HENRY VIII, a full exchequer. In 1536, Henry VIII brought about the political union of England and Wales. Henry and his minister Thomas CROMWELL greatly expanded the central administration. During Henry's reign commerce flourished and the New Learning of the RENAISSANCE came to England. Several factors—the revival of Lollardry, anticlericalism, the influence of humanism, and burgeoning nationalism—climaxed by the pope's refusal to grant Hen-

SHETLAND ISLANDS
ORKNEY ISLANDS
THE HEBRIDES
LEWIS
NORTH UIST
SOUTH UIST
SKYE
Sea of the Hebrides
ATLANTIC OCEAN
SCOTTISH HIGHLANDS
Moray Firth
Loch Ness
Aberdeen
THE GRAMPIANS
SCOTLAND
NORTH SEA
Loch Lomond
Firth of Forth
Glasgow
Edinburgh
Firth of Clyde
NORTHERN IRELAND
Lough Neagh
Belfast
GREAT BRITAIN
Newcastle upon Tyne
PENNINES
ACHILL I.
ISLE OF MAN
LAKE DISTRICT
IRISH SEA
York
Leeds
Hull
ISLE OF ANGLESEY
Dublin
ARAN ISLANDS
IRELAND
Liverpool
Manchester
Sheffield
ENGLAND
The Wash
Cardigan Bay
CAMBRIAN MTS.
WALES
Birmingham
Coventry
Ouse R.
Norwich
St. George's Channel
Severn R.
Cardiff
Bristol
Thames R.
London
Bristol Channel
Strait of Dover
Southampton
Portsmouth
ISLE OF WIGHT
Plymouth
SCILLY IS.
ENGLISH CHANNEL
ATLANTIC OCEAN
CHANNEL ISLANDS
FRANCE

The key to pronunciation appears on page xi.

RULERS OF ENGLAND AND GREAT BRITAIN *(including dates of reign)*

Saxons and Danes

Egbert, 802–39
Æthelwulf, son of Egbert, 839–58
Æthelbald, son of Æthelwulf, 858–60
Æthelbert, 2d son of Æthelwulf, 860–65
Æthelred, 3d son of Æthelwulf, 865–71
Alfred, 4th son of Æthelwulf, 871–99
Edward (the Elder), son of Alfred, 899–924
Athelstan, son of Edward, 924–39
Edmund, 3d son of Edward, 939–46
Edred, 4th son of Edward, 946–55
Edwy, son of Edmund, 955–59
Edgar, younger son of Edmund, 959–75
Edward (the Martyr), son of Edgar, 975–78
Æthelred (the Unready), younger son of Edgar, 978–1016
Edmund (Ironside), son of Æthelred, 1016
Canute, by conquest, 1016–35
Harold I (Harefoot), illegitimate son of Canute, 1037–40
Harthacanute, son of Canute, 1040–42
Edward (the Confessor), younger son of Æthelred, 1042–66
Harold II, brother-in-law of Edward the Confessor, 1066

House of Normandy

William I (the Conqueror), by conquest, 1066–87
William II (Rufus), 3d son of William I, 1087–1100
Henry I, youngest son of William I, 1100–1135

House of Blois

Stephen, grandson of William I, 1135–54

House of Plantagenet

Henry II, grandson of Henry I, 1154–89
Richard I (Coeur de Lion), 3d son of Henry II, 1189–99
John, youngest son of Henry II, 1199–1216
Henry III, son of John, 1216–72
Edward I, son of Henry III, 1272–1307
Edward II, son of Edward I, 1307–27
Edward III, son of Edward II, 1327–77
Richard II, grandson of Edward III, 1377–99

House of Lancaster

Henry IV, grandson of Edward III, 1399–1413
Henry V, son of Henry IV, 1413–22
Henry VI, son of Henry V, 1422–61, 1470–71

House of York

Edward IV, great-grandson of Edward III, 1461–70, 1471–83
Edward V, son of Edward IV, 1483
Richard III, brother of Edward IV, 1483–85

House of Tudor

Henry VII, descendant of Edward III, 1485–1509
Henry VIII, son of Henry VII, 1509–47
Edward VI, son of Henry VIII, 1547–53
Mary I, daughter of Henry VIII, 1553–58
Elizabeth I, younger daughter of Henry VIII, 1558–1603

House of Stuart

James I (James VI of Scotland), descendant of Henry VII, 1603–25
Charles I, son of James I, 1625–49

Commonwealth and Protectorate

Council of State, 1649–53
Cromwell, Oliver, lord protector, 1653–58
Cromwell, Richard, lord protector, 1658–59

House of Stuart (restored)

Charles II, son of Charles I, 1660–85
James II, younger son of Charles I, 1685–88
William III, grandson of Charles I; ruled jointly with Mary II, 1689–94; ruled alone, 1694–1702
Mary II, daughter of James II; ruled jointly with William III, 1689–94
Anne, younger daughter of James II, 1702–14

House of Hanover

George I, great-grandson of James I, 1714–27
George II, son of George I, 1727–60
George III, grandson of George II, 1760–1820
George IV, son of George III, 1820–30
William IV, 3d son of George III, 1830–37
Victoria, granddaughter of George III, 1837–1901

House of Saxe-Coburg

Edward VII, son of Victoria, 1901–10

House of Windsor (family name changed during World War I)

George V, son of Edward VII, 1910–36
Edward VIII, son of George V, 1936
George VI, 2d son of George V, 1936–52
Elizabeth II, daughter of George VI, 1952–

ry a divorce from Catherine of Aragón so that he could remarry and have a male heir, led the king to break with Roman Catholicism and establish the Church of England. As part of the English Reformation (1529–39), Henry suppressed the orders of monks and friars and secularized their property. Although these actions aroused some popular opposition (see PILGRIMAGE OF GRACE), Henry's judicious use of Parliament helped secure support for his policies and set important precedents for the future of Parliament. England moved farther toward Protestantism under EDWARD VI; after a generally hated Roman Catholic revival under MARY I, the Roman tie was again cut under ELIZABETH I, who attempted without complete success to moderate the religious differences among her people. The Elizabethan age was one of great artistic and intellectual achievement, its most notable figure being William SHAKESPEARE. National pride basked in the exploits of Sir Francis DRAKE, Sir John HAWKINS, and the other "sea dogs." Overseas trading companies were formed and colonization attempts in the New World were made by Sir Humphrey Gilbert and Sir Walter Raleigh. A long conflict with Spain, growing partly out of commercial and maritime rivalry and partly out of religious differences, culminated in the defeat of the Spanish ARMADA (1588), although the war continued another 15 years. Inflated prices (caused, in part, by an influx of precious metals from the New World) and the reservation of land by the process of INCLOSURE for sheep pasture (stimulated by the expansion of the wool trade) caused great changes in the social and economic structure of England. The inclosures displaced many tenant farmers from their lands and produced a class of wandering, unemployed "sturdy beggars." The Elizabethan POOR LAWS were an attempt to deal with this problem. Rising prices affected the monarchy as well, by reducing the value of its fixed customary and hereditary revenues. The country gentry were enriched by the inclosures and by their purchase of former monastic lands, which were also used for grazing. The gentry became leaders in what, toward the end of Elizabeth's reign, was an increasingly assertive Parliament.

The Stuarts. The accession in 1603 of the Stuart JAMES I, who was also James VI of Scotland, united the thrones of England and Scotland. The chronic need for money of both James and his son, CHARLES I, which they attempted to meet by unusual and extralegal means; their espousal of the divine right of kings; their determination to enforce their high Anglican preferences in religion; and their use of royal courts such as STAR CHAMBER, which were not bound by the common law, to persecute opponents, together produced a bitter conflict with Parliament that culminated (1642) in the ENGLISH CIVIL WAR. In the war the parliamentarians, effectively led at the end by Oliver CROMWELL, defeated the royalists. The king was tried for treason and beheaded (1649). The monarchy was abolished, and the country was governed by the Rump Parliament, the remainder of the last Parliament (the Long Parliament) Charles had called (1640), until 1653, when Cromwell dissolved it and established the PROTECTORATE. Cromwell brutally subjugated Ireland, made a single commonwealth of Scotland and England, and strengthened England's naval power and position in international trade. When he died (1658), his son, Richard, succeeded as Lord Protector but governed ineffectively. The threat of anarchy led to an invitation by a newly elected Parliament (the Convention Parliament) to Charles, son of Charles I, to become king, ushering in the RESTORATION (1660). It was significant that Parliament had summoned the king, rather than the reverse; it was now clear that to be successful the king had to cooperate with Parliament. The WHIG and TORY parties developed in the Restoration period. Although CHARLES II was personally popular, the old issues of religion, money, and the royal prerogative came to the fore again. Parliament revived official Anglicanism (see CLARENDON CODES), but Charles's private sympathies lay with Catholicism. He attempted to bypass Parliament in the matter of revenue by receiving subsidies from Louis XIV of France. His brother and successor, JAMES II, was an avowed Catholic. James tried to strengthen his position in Parliament by tampering with the methods of selecting members; he put Catholics in high university positions, maintained a standing army (which later deserted him), and claimed the right to suspend laws. The birth (1688) of a male heir, who, it was assumed, would be raised as a Catholic, precipitated a crisis. In the GLORIOUS REVOLUTION, Whig and Tory leaders offered the throne to William of Orange (WILLIAM III), whose Protestant wife, Mary, was James's daughter. William and Mary were proclaimed king and queen by Parliament in 1689. The BILL OF RIGHTS confirmed that sovereignty resided in Parliament. The Act of Toleration (1689) extended religious liberty to all Protestant sects; in subsequent years, religious passions slowly subsided. By the ACT OF SETTLEMENT (1701) the succession to the English throne was determined. Since 1603, with the exception of the 1654–60 interregnum, Scotland and England had remained two kingdoms united only in the person of the monarch. When it appeared that William's successor, Queen ANNE, Mary's Protestant sister, would not have an heir, the Scottish succession became of concern, since the Scottish Parliament had not passed legislation corresponding to the Act of Settlement. England feared that under a separate monarch Scotland might ally itself with France, or worse still, permit a restoration of the Catholic heirs of James II—although a non-Protestant succession had been barred by the Scottish Parliament. On its part, Scotland wished to achieve economic equality with England. The result was the Act of Union (1707), by which the two kingdoms became one. Scotland obtained representation in (what then became) the British Parliament at Westminster, and the Scottish Parliament was abolished.

The Growth of Empire and 18th-Century Political Developments. The beginnings of Britain's national debt (1692) and the founding of the BANK OF ENGLAND (1694) were closely tied with the nation's more active role in world affairs. Britain's overseas possessions (see BRITISH EMPIRE) were augmented by the victorious outcome of the War of the Spanish Succession, ratified in the PEACE OF UTRECHT (1713). Britain emerged from the War of the Austrian Succession and from the Seven Years War as the possessor of the world's greatest empire. The peace of 1763 (see PARIS, TREATY OF) confirmed British predominance in India and North America. Settlements were made in Australia toward the end of the 18th cent; however, a serious loss was sustained when 13 North American colonies broke away in the American Revolution. Additional colonies were won in the wars against NAPOLEON I, notable for the victories of Horatio NELSON and Arthur Wellesley, duke of WELLINGTON. In Ireland, the Irish Parliament was granted independence in 1782, but in 1798 there was an Irish rebellion. A vain attempt to solve the centuries-old Irish problem was the abrogation of the Irish Parliament and the union (1801) of Great Britain and Ireland, with Ireland represented in the British Parliament. Domestically the long ministry of Sir Robert WALPOLE (1721–42), during the reigns of GEORGE I and GEORGE II, was a period of relative stability that saw the beginnings of the development of the cabinet as the chief executive organ of government. The 18th cent. was a time of transition in the growth of the British parliamentary system. The monarch still played a very active role in government, choosing and dismissing ministers as he wished. Occasionally, sentiment in Parliament might force an unwanted minister on him, as when GEORGE III was forced to choose Rockingham in 1782, but the king could dissolve Parliament and use his considerable patronage power to secure a new one more amenable to his views. Great political leaders of the late 18th cent., such as the earl of Chatham (see CHATHAM, WILLIAM PITT, 1st EARL OF) and his son William PITT, could not govern in disregard of the crown. Important movements for political and social reform arose in the second half of the 18th cent. George III's arrogant and somewhat anachronistic conception of the crown's role produced a movement among Whigs in Parliament that called for a reform and reduction of the king's power. Edmund BURKE was a leader of this group, as was the eccentric John WILKES. The Tory Pitt was also a reformer. These men also opposed Britain's colonial policy in North America. Outside Parliament, religious dissenters (who were excluded from political office), intellectuals, and others advocated sweeping reforms of established practices and institutions. Adam Smith's *Wealth of Nations,* advocating LAISSEZ FAIRE, appeared in 1776, the same year as the first publication by Jeremy BENTHAM, the founder of utilitarianism. The cause of reform, however, was greatly set back by the French Revolution and the ensuing wars with France, which greatly alarmed British society. Burke became the leading intellectual opponent of the Revolution in Britain, while many British reformers who supported (to varying degrees) the changes in France were branded by British public opinion as extreme Jacobins.

Economic, Social, and Political Change. George III was succeeded by GEORGE IV and WILLIAM IV. During the last 10 years of his reign, George III was insane, and sovereignty was exercised by the future George IV. This was the "Regency" period. In the mid-18th cent., wealth and power in Great Britain still resided in the aristocracy, the landed gentry, and the commercial oligarchy of the towns. The mass of the population consisted of agricultural laborers, semiliterate and landless, governed locally (in England) by justices of the peace. The countryside was fragmented into semiisolated agricultural villages and provincial capitals. However, the late 18th and early 19th cent. was a time of dynamic economic change. The factory system, the discovery and use of steam power, improved inland transportation (canals and turnpikes), the ready supply of coal and iron, a remarkable series of inventions, and men with capital who were eager to invest—all these elements came together to produce the epochal change known as the INDUSTRIAL REVOLUTION. The impact of these developments on social conditions was enormous, but the most significant socioeconomic fact of all from 1750 to 1850 was the growth of population. The population of Great Britain (excluding Northern Ireland) grew from an estimated 7,500,000 in 1750 to about 10,800,000 in 1801 (the year of the first national census) and to about 23,130,000 in 1861. The growing population provided needed labor for industrial expansion and was accompanied by rapid urbanization. Urban problems multiplied. At the same time a new period of inclosures (1750–1810; this time to increase the arable farmland) deprived small farmers of their common land. The Speenhamland System (begun in 1795), which supplemented wages according to the size of a man's family and the price of bread, and the Poor Law of 1834 were harsh revisions of the relief laws. The social unrest following these developments provided a fertile field for METHODISM, which had been begun by John Wesley in the mid-18th century. Methodism was especially popular in the new industrial areas, in some of which the Church of England provided no services. It has been theorized that by pacifying social unrest Methodism contributed to the prevention of political and social revolution in Britain. In the 1820s the reform impulse that had been largely stifled during the French Revolution revived. CATHOLIC EMANCIPATION (1829) restored to Catholics political and civil rights. In 1833 slavery in the British Empire was abolished. (The slave trade had been ended in 1807.) Parliamentary reform was made imperative by the new patterns of population distribution and by the great growth during the industrial expansion in the size and wealth of the middle class, which lacked commensurate political power. The general elections that followed the death of George IV brought to power a Whig ministry committed to parliamentary reform. The Reform Bill of 1832 (see REFORM BILLS) enfranchised the middle class and redistributed seats to give greater representation to London and the urban boroughs of N England. Other parliamentary legislation established the institutional basis for efficient city government and municipal services and for government inspection of factories, schools, and poorhouses. The competitive advantage British exports had gained from the Industrial Revolution lent new force to the arguments for free trade. The efforts of the Anti-Corn-Law League, organized by Richard COBDEN and John BRIGHT, succeeded in 1846 when Robert PEEL was converted to the cause of free trade, and the CORN LAWS were repealed. But CHARTISM, a mass movement for more thorough political reform, was unsuccessful (1848). Further important reforms were delayed nearly 20 years. The Reform Bill of 1867, sponsored by Disraeli and the Conservatives for political reasons, enfranchised the urban working classes and was followed shortly (under Gladstone and the Liberals) by enactment of the secret ballot and the first steps toward a national education system. In 1884 a third Reform Bill extended the vote to agricultural laborers. (Women could not vote until 1918.) In the 1880s trade unions, which had first appeared earlier in the century, grew larger and more militant as increasing numbers of unskilled workers were unionized. A coalition of labor and socialist groups, organized in 1900, became the Labour party in 1906. In the 19th cent. Britain's economy took on its characteristic patterns. Trade deficits, incurred as the value of food imports exceeded the value of exports such as textiles, iron, steel, and coal, were overcome by income from shipping, insurance services, and foreign investments.

PRIME MINISTERS OF GREAT BRITAIN (*including party* and dates in office*)

Sir Robert Walpole, 1721–42	Viscount Palmerston [Liberal] 1859–65
Earl of Wilmington, 1742–43	Earl Russell [Liberal] 1865–66
Henry Pelham, 1743–54	Earl of Derby [Conservative] 1866–68
Duke of Newcastle, 1754–56	Benjamin Disraeli [Conservative] 1868
Duke of Devonshire, 1756–57	William Gladstone [Liberal] 1868–74
Duke of Newcastle, 1757–62	Benjamin Disraeli [Conservative] 1874–80
Earl of Bute, 1762–63	William Gladstone [Liberal] 1880–85
George Grenville, 1763–65	Marquess of Salisbury [Conservative] 1885–86
Marquess of Rockingham, 1765–66	William Gladstone [Liberal] 1886
William Pitt the Elder (earl of Chatham), 1766–68	Marquess of Salisbury [Conservative] 1886–92
Duke of Grafton, 1768–70	William Gladstone [Liberal] 1892–94
Lord North, 1770–82	Earl of Rosebery [Liberal] 1894–95
Marquess of Rockingham, 1782	Marquess of Salisbury [Conservative] 1895–1902
Earl of Shelburne, 1782–83	Arthur Balfour [Conservative] 1902–5
Duke of Portland, 1783	Sir Henry Campbell-Bannerman [Liberal] 1905–8
William Pitt the Younger [Tory] 1783–1801	Herbert Asquith [Liberal] 1908–15
Henry Addington (later Viscount Sidmouth) [Tory] 1801–4	Herbert Asquith [Coalition] 1915–16
William Pitt the Younger [Tory] 1804–6	David Lloyd George [Coalition] 1916–22
Baron Grenville [Whig] 1806–7	Andrew Bonar Law [Conservative] 1922–23
Duke of Portland [Tory] 1807–9	Stanley Baldwin [Conservative] 1923–24
Spencer Perceval [Tory] 1809–12	Ramsay MacDonald [Labour] 1924
Earl of Liverpool [Tory] 1812–27	Stanley Baldwin [Conservative] 1924–29
George Canning [Tory] 1827	Ramsay MacDonald [Labour] 1929–31
Viscount Goderich (later earl of Ripon) [Tory] 1827–28	Ramsay MacDonald [National (Coalition)] 1931–35
Duke of Wellington [Tory] 1828–30	Stanley Baldwin [National] 1935–37
Earl Grey [Whig] 1830–34	Neville Chamberlain [National] 1937–40
Viscount Melbourne [Whig] 1834	Winston Churchill [Coalition] 1940–45
Sir Robert Peel [Tory] 1834–35	Clement Attlee [Labour] 1945–51
Viscount Melbourne [Whig] 1835–41	Sir Winston Churchill [Conservative] 1951–55
Sir Robert Peel [Conservative] 1841–46	Sir Anthony Eden [Conservative] 1955–57
Lord John Russell (later Earl Russell) [Whig] 1846–52	Harold Macmillan [Conservative] 1957–63
Earl of Derby [Conservative] 1852	Sir Alec Douglas-Home [Conservative] 1963–64
Earl of Aberdeen [Peelite Conservative] 1852–55	Harold Wilson [Labour] 1964–70
Viscount Palmerston [Liberal] 1855–58	Edward Heath [Conservative] 1970–74
Earl of Derby [Conservative] 1858–59	Harold Wilson [Labour] 1974–

* The modern party system did not evolve until the end of the 18th cent.

Victorian Foreign Policy. The reign of VICTORIA (1837–1901) covered the period of Britain's commercial and industrial leadership of the world and greatest political influence. Initial steps toward granting self-government for Canada were taken at the start of Victoria's reign, while in India conquest and expansion continued. Great Britain's commercial interests, advanced by the British navy, brought on in 1839 the first OPIUM WAR with China, which opened five Chinese ports to British trade and made Hong Kong a British colony. The aggressive diplomacy of Lord Palmerston in the 1850s and 60s, including involvement in the CRIMEAN WAR, was popular at home. From 1868 to 1880 political life in Great Britain was dominated by Benjamin DISRAELI and William E. GLADSTONE, who differed dramatically over domestic and foreign policy. Disraeli, who had attacked Gladstone for failing to defend Britain's imperial interests, pursued an active foreign policy, determined by considerations of British prestige and the desire to protect the route to India. Under Disraeli (1874–80) the British acquired the Transvaal, the Fiji Islands, and Cyprus, fought frontier wars in Africa and Afghanistan, and became the largest shareholder in the Suez Canal Company. Gladstone strongly condemned Disraeli's expansionist policies, but his later ministries involved Britain in Egypt, Afghanistan, and Uganda. Gladstone's first ministry (1868–74) had disestablished the Church of England in Ireland, and in 1886, Gladstone unsuccessfully advocated Home Rule for Ireland. The proposal split the Liberal party and overturned his ministry. In the last decades of the 19th cent. competition with other European powers and enchantment with the glories of empire led Britain to acquire vast territories in Asia and Africa. By the end of the century the country was entangled in the SOUTH AFRICAN WAR (1899–1902). Great Britain's period of hegemony was ending, as both Germany and the United States were surpassing it in industrial production.

World War I and Its Aftermath. Victoria was succeeded by her son EDWARD VII, then by his son, GEORGE V. The Liberals, in power 1905–15, enacted much social legislation, including old-age pensions, health and unemployment insurance, child health laws, and more progressive taxation. The budget sponsored by David LLOYD GEORGE to finance the Liberals' program brought on a parliamentary struggle that ended in a drastic reduction of the power of the House of Lords (1911). Growing military and economic rivalry with Germany led Great Britain to form ententes with its former colonial rivals, France and Russia (see TRIPLE ALLIANCE AND TRIPLE ENTENTE). In 1914, Germany's violation of Belgium's neutrality, which since 1839 Britain had been pledged to uphold, caused Britain to go to war against Germany (see WORLD WAR I). In the peace settlement (see VERSAILLES, TREATY OF) Britain acquired, as League of Nations mandates, additional territories in Africa, Asia, and the Middle East. But the four years of fighting had drained the nation of wealth and manpower. (About 750,000 men had died and 7 million tons of shipping had been lost.) The postwar years were a time of great moral disillusionment and material difficulties. To the international problems stemming directly from the war, such as disarmament, REPARATIONS, and WAR DEBTS, were added complex domestic economic problems, the task of reorganizing the BRITISH EMPIRE, and the tangled Irish problem. Northern Ireland was created in 1920, and the Irish Free State (see IRELAND, REPUBLIC OF) in 1921–22. The basic domestic economic problem of the post-World War I years was the decline of Britain's traditional export industries, which made it more difficult for the country to pay for its imports of foods and raw materials. A Labour government, under Ramsay MACDONALD, was in power for the first time briefly in 1924. In 1926 the country suffered a general strike. Severe economic stress increased during the worldwide economic depression of the late 1920s and early 30s. During the financial crisis of 1931, George V asked MacDonald to head a coalition government, which took the country off the gold standard, ceased the repayment of war debts, and supplanted free trade with protective tariffs modified by preferential treatment within the empire (see COMMONWEALTH OF NATIONS) and with treaty nations. Recovery from the depression began to be evident in 1933. Although old export industries such as coal mining and cotton manufacturing remained depressed, other industries, such as electrical engineering, automobile manufacture, and industrial chemistry, were developed or strengthened. George V was succeeded by EDWARD VIII, after whose abdication (1936) GEORGE VI came to the throne. In 1937, Neville CHAMBERLAIN became prime minister. The years prior to the outbreak of World War II were characterized by the ineffective attempts to stem the rising tide of German and Italian aggression. The League of Nations, in which Britain was a leader, declined rapidly by failing to take decisive action, and British prestige fell further because of a policy of nonintervention in the SPANISH CIVIL WAR. Appeasement of the Axis powers, which was the policy of the Chamberlain government, reached its climactic failure (as became evident later) in the MUNICH PACT of Sept., 1938. Great Britain had begun to rearm in 1936 and, after Munich, instituted conscription. With the signing of the Soviet-German pact of Aug., 1939, war was recognized as inevitable.

World War II and the Welfare State. On Sept. 1, 1939, Germany attacked Poland. Great Britain and France declared war on Germany on Sept. 3, and all the dominions of the Commonwealth except Ireland followed suit (see WORLD WAR II). Chamberlain broadened his cabinet to include Labour representatives, but after German victories in Scandinavia he resigned (May, 1940) and was replaced by Winston S. CHURCHILL. France fell in June, 1940, but the heroic rescue of a substantial part of the British army from Dunkirk (May-June) enabled Britain, now virtually alone, to remain in the war. The nation withstood intensive bombardment (see BATTLE OF BRITAIN), but ultimately the Royal Air Force was able to drive off the Luftwaffe. Extensive damage was sustained, and great urban areas, including large sections of London, were devastated. The British people rose to a supreme war effort; American aid (see LEND-LEASE) provided vital help. In 1941, Great Britain gained two allies when Germany invaded the USSR (June) and the United States entered the war following the Japanese attack on Pearl Harbor (Dec. 7). Britain declared war on Japan on Dec. 8. The wartime alliance of Great Britain, the USSR, and the United States led to the formation of the UNITED NATIONS and brought about the defeat of Germany (May, 1945) and Japan (Sept., 1945). The British economy suffered severely from the war. Manpower losses had been severe, including about 420,000 dead; large urban areas had to be rebuilt, and the industrial plant needed reconstruction and modernization. Leadership in world trade, shipping, and banking had passed to the United States, and overseas investments had been largely liquidated to pay the cost of the world wars. This was a serious blow to the British economy because the income from these activities had previously served to offset the import-export deficit. In 1945, the first general elections in 10 years were held (they had been postponed because of the war) and Clement ATTLEE and the Labour party were swept into power. Austere wartime economic controls were continued, and in 1946 the United States extended a large loan. The United States made further assistance available in 1948 through the MARSHALL PLAN. In 1949 the pound was devalued (in terms of U.S. dollars, from $4.03 to $2.80) to make British exports more competitive. The Labour government pursued from the start a vigorous program of nationalization of industry and extension of social services. The Bank of England, the coal industry, communications facilities, civil aviation, electricity, and internal transport were nationalized, and in 1948 a vast program of socialized medicine was instituted (many of these programs followed the recommendations of wartime commissions). Also in 1948, Labour began the nationalization of the steel industry, but the law did not become effective until 1951, after Churchill and the Conservatives had come into office. The Conservatives denationalized the trucking industry and all but one of the steel companies and ended direct economic controls, but they retained Labour's social reforms. ELIZABETH II succeeded George VI in 1952. In postwar foreign affairs Great Britain's loss of power was also evident. Britain had undertaken to help Greece and Turkey resist Communist subversion, but the financial burden proved too great, and the task was assumed (1947) by the United States. The British Empire underwent rapid transformation. British India was partitioned (1947) into two self-governing states, India and Pakistan. In Palestine, unable to maintain peace between Arabs and Jews, Britain turned its mandate over to the United Nations. Groundwork was laid for the independence of many other colonies; like India and Pakistan, most of them remained in the Commonwealth after independence. Great Britain joined the North Atlantic Treaty Organization (1949) and fought on the United Nations side in the Korean War (1950-53). The Conservative governments of Churchill and his successor, Anthony EDEN (1955), were beset by numerous difficulties in foreign affairs, including the nationalization (1951) of British petroleum fields and refineries in Iran, the Mau Mau uprising in Kenya (1952-56), turmoil in Cyprus (1954-59), and the problem of APARTHEID in South Africa. The nationalization (1956) of the Suez Canal by Egypt touched off a crisis in which Britain, France, and Israel invaded Egypt. Opposition by the United States brought about a halt of the invasion and withdrawal of the troops.

Recent Developments. Great Britain helped to form (1959) the European Free Trade Association (EFTA; see INTERNATIONAL GOVERNMENTAL ORGANIZATIONS). In 1961 the government of Harold MACMILLAN announced its decision to seek membership in the COMMON MARKET. Because of French opposition as well as Britain's request for special considerations for the countries of the Commonwealth and of EFTA, agreement with the Market on British entry was not reached until 1971. Britain finally entered the Market, after Parliament approved British membership, in Jan., 1973. Labour returned to power in 1964 under Harold WILSON with a tiny majority; this was sizably increased in the election of 1966. The steel industry was renationalized. The country faced the compound economic problems of a very unfavorable balance of trade, the instability of the pound sterling, a lagging rate of economic growth, and inflationary wages and prices. Crises arising from heavy speculation in the pound were halted in 1964 by strong U.S. and other financial support, and in 1965 by measures that included borrowing from the International Monetary Fund and government controls and cutbacks. Following another sterling crisis in 1966, Wilson announced stringent deflationary measures. Britain supported U.S. policy in Vietnam. The policy of granting independence to colonial possessions continued; but RHODESIA became a problem when its government, representing only the white minority, unilaterally declared its independence in 1965. Another problem was Spain's demand for the return of Gibraltar. Great Britain signed the nuclear test-ban treaty (1963) and the treaty banning the use of nuclear weapons in outer space (1967). A major crisis erupted in Northern Ireland in late 1968 when Catholic civil rights demonstrations turned into violent confrontations between Catholics and Protestants. British Army units were dispatched in an unsuccessful attempt to restore calm. In 1972 the British government suspended the Northern Ireland Parliament and government and assumed direct control of the province. The Conservatives under Edward HEATH returned to power in Britain in 1970 after winning an upset victory in the general elections. In 1971, Britain's currency was converted to the decimal system. At the end of 1973 the country underwent its worst economic crisis since World War II. Several factors contributed to the crisis. The balance of payments deficit, after improving in the late 1960s, had worsened. Serious inflation had led to widespread labor unrest, including slowdowns and refusals to work overtime in the critical coal-mining, railroad, and electrical industries. This in turn had caused a shortage of coal, Britain's main energy source. A further blow, following the war in the Middle East in Oct., 1973, was the reduction in oil shipments by several Arab states, accompanied by a steep increase in the price of oil. From Jan. 1, until early March, 1974, the nation was on a three-day work week, which resulted in high unemployment and reduced wages. When coal miners voted to strike in early 1974, Heath called an election in an attempt to bolster his position in resisting the miners' demands. Neither Labour nor the Conservatives emerged from that election with a plurality in the Commons; Labour had won 301 seats, the Conservatives 296, and the Liberals 14, with various nationalist parties holding the balance. After an unsuccessful attempt to form a minority government, Heath resigned (Mar., 1974) and was succeeded as prime minister by Harold Wilson, who moved immediately to settle the miners' dispute. In the elections of Oct., 1974, the Labour party won a slim majority (319 of the 635 seats in the House of Commons), and Wilson continued as prime minister. Useful analytical guides to the vast body of literature on Great Britain are G. R. Elton, *Modern Historians on British History, 1485-1945: A Critical Bibliography, 1945-1969* (1971) and E. C. Furber, ed., *Changing Views on British History: Essays on Historical Writing since 1939* (1966). For the different periods, see Charles Gross, *The Sources and Literature of English History from the Earliest Times to about 1485* (2d rev. ed. 1915, repr. 1951); Michael Altschul, *Anglo-Norman England, 1066-1154* (1969); Conyers Read, *Bibliography of British History: Tudor Period, 1485-1603* (2d ed. 1959); Mortimer Levine, *Tudor England, 1485-1603* (1968); Godfrey Davies, *Bibliography of British History: Stuart Period, 1603-1714* (1928; 2d ed., ed. by M. F. Keeler, 1970); S. M. Pargellis and D. J. Medley, ed., *Bibliography of British History: The Eighteenth Century, 1714-1789* (1951); C. L. Mowat, *Great Britain since 1914* (1971). For general histories, see Sir George Clark, ed., *The Oxford History of England* (2d ed.; 15 vol., 1937-1965); *Pelican History of England* (9 vol., 1950-64; several vol. in new ed., some repr.). Other useful sources of information include: *Britain: An Official Handbook*, prepared by the Central Office of Information (published annually since 1948); F. M. Powicke and E. B. Fryde, *Handbook of British Chronology* (2d ed. 1961); Sir David Keir, *The Constitutional History of Modern Britain since 1485* (9th ed. 1969); Peter Mathias, *The First Industrial Nation: An Economic History of Britain, 1700-1914* (1969); G. S. Graham, *A Concise History of the British Empire* (1971); S. H. Steinberg and I. H. Evans, ed., *Steinberg's Dictionary of British History* (2d ed. 1971); Sir Adolphus Ward and G. P. Gooch, ed., *The Cambridge History of British Foreign Policy, 1783-1919* (3 vol., 1922-23; repr. 1971); N. W. Wilding and Philip Laundy, *An Encyclopaedia of Parliament* (4th ed. 1971); L. W. Cobie, *A Dictionary of British Social History* (1973). See F. S. Stacey, *The Government of Modern Britain* (1968); Sir Lawrence Stamp and S. H. Beaver, *The British Isles: A Geographic and Economic Survey* (6th ed. 1971); Correlli Barnett, *The Collapse of British Power* (1972); C. B. Cox and A. E. Dyson, ed., *The Twentieth-Century Mind: History, Ideas and Literature in Britain* (3d vol., 1972); Peter Mauger and Leslie Smith, *The British People, 1902-1968* (1972); Anthony Sampson, *The New Anatomy of Britain* (1972); Jack Revell, *The British Financial System* (1973).

Great Dane, breed of very large, powerful WORKING DOG developed in Europe more than 400 years ago. It may stand as high as 36 in. (91.4 cm) at the shoulder and weigh up to 150 lb (68.1 kg). Its short, dense, glossy coat may be brindle, fawn, blue, black, or the combination of white with black patches that is called harlequin. Although its origins are obscure, dogs of similar appearance were depicted in the art of ancient China, Egypt, Greece, and Rome. Despite the name, the Great Dane in its present-day form is of German development, and records testify to its use as a boarhound in the 16th cent. in that country. Today it is raised for show competition and is also valued as a gentle, devoted pet. See DOG.

Great Depression, in U.S. history, the severe economic crisis supposedly precipitated by the U.S. stock-market crash of 1929. Although it shared the basic characteristics of other such crises (see DEPRESSION), the Great Depression was unprecedented in its length and in the wholesale poverty and tragedy it inflicted on society. Economists have disagreed over its causes, but certain causative factors are generally accepted. The prosperity of the 1920s was unevenly distributed among the various parts of the American economy—farmers and unskilled workers were notably excluded—with the result that the nation's productive capacity was greater than its capacity to consume. In addition, the tariff and war-debt policies of the Republican administrations of the 1920s had cut down the foreign market for American goods. Finally, easy-money policies led to an inordinate expansion of credit and installment buying and fantastic speculation in the stock market. The American depression produced severe effects abroad, especially in Europe, where many countries had not fully recovered from the aftermath of World War I; in Germany, the economic disaster and resulting social dislocation contributed to the rise of Adolf Hitler. In the United States, at the depth (1933) of the depression, there were 16 million unemployed—about one third of the available labor force. The gross national product declined from the 1929 figure of $103,828,000,000 to $55,760,000,000 in 1933. The economic, agricultural, and relief policies of the NEW DEAL administration under President Franklin Delano Roosevelt did a great deal to mitigate the effects of the depression and, most importantly, to restore a sense of confidence to the American people. Yet it is generally agreed that complete business recovery was not achieved and unemployment ended until the government began to spend heavily for defense in the early 1940s. See Dixon Wecter, *The Age of the Great Depression, 1929-1941* (1948, repr. 1956); Arthur M. Schlesinger, Jr., *The Crisis of the Old Order, 1919-1933* (1957); D. A. Shannon, ed., *The Great Depression* (1960); A. U. Romasco, *The Poverty of Abundance* (1965); Goronwy Rees, *The Great Slump* (1970); C. P. Kindleberger, *The World in Depression, 1929-1939* (1973).

Great Divide: see CONTINENTAL DIVIDE.

Great Dividing Range, crest line of the Eastern Highlands of Australia. For the most part it separates rivers draining into the Pacific Ocean from those flowing into the Indian Ocean and the Arafura Sea. Erosion and earth movements have pushed the watershed west of the range in several places.

Great Elector, the: see FREDERICK WILLIAM.

Greater Lebanon: see LEBANON.

Greater London: see LONDON.

Greater Manchester, metropolitan county (1972 est. pop. 2,727,000), W central England, created under the Local Government Act of 1972 (effective 1974). It is subdivided into 10 metropolitan districts. Greater Manchester comprises the county boroughs of BOLTON, BURY, MANCHESTER, OLDHAM, ROCHDALE, SALFORD, STOCKPORT, and WIGAN as well as parts of the former counties of Cheshire, Lancashire, and Yorkshire (West Riding).

greater wax moth: see BEE MOTH.

Great Falls, city (1970 pop. 60,091), seat of Cascade co., N central Mont., second-largest city in the state, at the confluence of the Missouri and Sun rivers and near the falls that give the city its name; inc. 1888. As the center of extensive hydroelectric power development, Great Falls is popularly called the "Electric City." There are oil and copper refineries, a zinc-reduction plant, and flour mills. The city is a market for an irrigated farm and livestock district and for the Sun River project. Great Falls is also a wholesale and retail trade and service center. The log cabin of the cowboy artist Charles M. Russell is preserved as a museum. Outside the city is Giant Springs, which discharges a large flow of water into the Missouri River. The College of Great Falls is there. Malmstrom Air Force Base is nearby.

Great Glen or **Glen More,** valley, 60 mi (97 km) long, across Inverness-shire, N central Scotland, extending from Moray Firth SW to Loch Linnhe. It was formed by a fault in the earth's surface. Loch Ness, Loch Oich, and Loch Lochy, glacial lakes located on the fault line, extend hundreds of feet below sea level. The CALEDONIAN CANAL traverses Great Glen.

Great Indian Desert, S Asia: see THAR DESERT.

Great Lakes, group of five freshwater lakes, central North America, between the United States and Canada; largest body of fresh water in the world, with a combined surface area of c.95,000 sq mi (246,050 sq km). From west to east they are Lake SUPERIOR, Lake MICHIGAN, Lake HURON, Lake ERIE, and Lake ONTARIO, out of which flows the Saint Lawrence River. The distance from Duluth, Minn., at the western end of Lake Superior, to the outlet of Lake Ontario is 1,160 mi (1,867 km). The international boundary passes approximately through the center of all the lakes except Lake Michigan, which lies entirely within the United States. The Great Lakes were formed at the end of the Ice Age when the glacier-carved lake basins were filled with meltwater. The lakes are connected to each other by straits, short rivers, and canals. The height above sea level of the lake surfaces varies from Lake Superior's 602 ft (183 m) to Lake Ontario's 246 ft (75 m); the greatest sudden drop occurs at Niagara Falls (167 ft/51 m) between lakes Erie and Ontario. All the lake bottoms, except that of Lake Erie, extend below sea level. French traders were the first Europeans to see any of the Great Lakes; Étienne Brulé visited Lake Huron c.1612. In 1614, Brulé and French explorer Samuel de Champlain explored Lake Huron and Lake Ontario. In 1679, French explorer Robert LaSalle sailed from Lake Erie to Lake Michigan. The Great Lakes region, rich in furs, was contested for many years by the French, English, and Americans. The close of the War of 1812 finally ended the struggle for possession of the Great Lakes, and settlement of the region rapidly followed. The opening of the Erie Canal in 1825 accelerated the development of commerce on the Great Lakes, which now carry great quantities of iron ore and grain, much coal, petroleum and steel, and manufactured articles from April until December, when ice closes most of the ports and winter storms hinder navigation. Large concentrations of population and industry along the lakes' shores have led to increasing pollution, especially of Lake Erie. The large industrial lakefront cities include Toronto, Hamilton, Buffalo, Cleveland, Detroit, Milwaukee, and Chicago. The opening of the St. Lawrence Seaway in 1959 has made the Great Lakes a truly international water body. The Illinois Waterway connects the lakes with the Mississippi River and the Gulf of Mexico; the New York State Barge Canal joins the Great Lakes with the Hudson River and the Atlantic Ocean. The Great Lakes region, with its national parks and lakeshores, state parks, and many natural and scenic features, has become an important year-round recreation area.

Great Meadows: see FORT NECESSITY.

Great Miami, river: see MIAMI, river.

Great Mother of the Gods, in ancient Middle Eastern religions, mother goddess, the great symbol of the earth's fertility. She was worshipped under many names and attributes. Similar figures have been known in every part of the world. Essentially she was represented as the creative force in all nature, the mother of all things, responsible particularly for the periodic renewal of life. The later forms of her cult involved the worship of a male deity, variously considered her son, lover, or both (e.g., Adonis, Attis, and Osiris), whose death and resurrection symbolized the regenerative powers of the earth (see FERTILITY RITES). Although the Great Mother was the dominant figure in ancient Middle Eastern religions, she was also worshiped in Greece, Rome, and W Asia. In Phrygia and Lydia she was known as Cybele; among the Babylonians and Assyrians she was identified as Ishtar; in Syria and Palestine she appeared as Astarte; among the Egyptians she was called Isis; in Greece she was variously worshiped as Gaea, Hera, Rhea, Aphrodite, and Demeter; and in Rome she was identified as Maia, Ops, Tellus, and Ceres. Even this listing, however, is by no means complete. Many attributes of the Virgin Mary make her the Christian equivalent of the Great Mother, particularly in her great beneficence, in her double image as mother and virgin, and in her son, who is God and who dies and is resurrected. See E. O. James, *The Cult of the Mother Goddess* (1959, repr. 1961).

Great Neck, village (1970 pop. 10,724), Nassau co., SE N.Y., on the north shore of Long Island, a primarily residential suburb of New York City; settled c.1634, inc. 1921. Its manufactures include aeronautical, electronic, and marine instruments and systems.

Great Northern Peninsula or **Petit Nord Peninsula,** comprising NW Newfoundland island, Canada, extending 170 mi (274 km) NE from Bonne Bay on the west to Cape Bauld at the tip; White Bay borders it on the east. The Long Range, along the west coast, rises to 2,651 ft (808 m) in Gros Morne. Fishing villages dot the indented coastline.

Great Ouse, river: see OUSE **1,** England.

Great Plains, high, extensive grassland region of North America. It extends from the Canadian provinces of Alberta, Saskatchewan, and Manitoba south through W central United States into Texas. In the United States the plains include parts of North Dakota, South Dakota, Nebraska, Kansas, Oklahoma, Montana, Wyoming, Colorado, New Mexico, and Texas. The Great Plains slope gently eastward from the foothills of the Rocky Mts. at an elevation of 6,000 ft (1,829 m) to merge into the prairies at an elevation of 1,500 ft (457 m). The 1,500 ft (457 m) contour line, the 100th meridian of longitude, and the 20-in. (51-cm) isohyet of precipitation are arbitrarily used to mark the region's eastern border. In places, however, it is clearly marked by an escarpment. Much of the Great Plains was once covered by a vast inland sea, and sediments deposited by the sea make up the nearly horizontal rock strata that underlie the area. Intrusive igneous rocks account for sections of higher elevation. The Great Plains region has generally level or rolling terrain; its subdivisions include Edwards Plateau, the Llano Estacado, the High Plains, the Sand Hills, the Badlands, and the Northern Plains. The Black Hills and several outliers of the Rocky Mts. interrupt the region's generally low profile. The Saskatchewan, Missouri, Platte, Republican, Arkansas, Cimarron, and Canadian rivers flow in wide beds, generally from west to east, and are important sources of water. The Great Plains has a semiarid climate; rainfall decreases from east to west, and, outside of the higher regions, the annual average precipitation is less than 20 in. (51 cm). The region has the highest occurrence of hail in North America. There are wide seasonal temperature ranges and winds of high velocity. In western sections the chinook, a warm winter wind, brings relief from bitterly cold and snowy winters. Grass is the dominant type of vegetation; trees are found in moister areas and along water courses. The Great Plains are sparsely populated, with huge ranches and farms occupying much of the grassland. Cattle and sheep grazing is an important economic activity in the western plains. The fertile soils of the eastern plains are very productive when water is available. Wheat is the principal farm crop; sorghum and flax are also grown. The westward expansion of the wheat belt during World War I resulted in the creation of the DUST BOWL. A variety of minerals are found on the Great Plains, including oil, natural gas, coal, and gold. First explored by the Spanish in the 1600s, the Great Plains were called the Great American Desert until well into the 19th cent. They were long inhabited by buffalo and Indians. American pioneers bypassed the region at first in the belief that an area that could not grow trees could not support agriculture. The railroads were largely responsible for populating the region. See Walter Prescott Webb, *The Great Plains* (1931, repr. 1957); Evans Jones, *The Plains States* (1968); Isaac Cooper, *The Plains* (1972).

Great Pyrenees, breed of large WORKING DOG whose fossil remains date its existence in Europe from the Bronze Age (1800–1000 B.C.). It stands from 25 to 32 in. (63.5–81.3 cm) high at the shoulder and weighs from 90 to 125 lb (40.8–56.7 kg). Its weather-resistant double coat is composed of dense, fine underhairs and a thick, coarse, straight or slightly wavy outercoat. Believed to be related to an ancient mastiff of central Asia or Siberia and to have been brought into Europe by the invading Aryan hordes, the Great Pyrenees was for centuries the guardian of shepherds and flocks in the mountains of Europe. Later, it became popular at the French court and as a guard dog on large estates. Today it is commonly raised for show competition and as a pet. See DOG.

Great Rift Valley, geological FAULT system of SW Asia and E Africa. It extends c.3,000 mi (4,830 km) from N Syria to central Mozambique. The northernmost extension runs S through Syria, the Jordan valley, the Dead Sea, and the Gulf of Aqaba. It continues into the trough of the Red Sea and at the southern end branches into the Gulf of Aden, where it continues as part of the Mid-Oceanic Ridge of the Indian Ocean. The main section of the valley in Africa continues from the Red Sea SW across Ethiopia and S across Kenya, Tanzania, and Malawi to the lower Zambezi River valley in Mozambique. Many small lakes in Ethiopia and several long narrow lakes, notably lakes Rudolf and Nyasa, lie on its course. Just N of Lake Nyasa there is a western branch, which runs north, chiefly along the eastern border of Zaïre; this branch is marked by a chain of lakes, including lakes Tanganyika, Kivu, Edward, and Albert. Victoria Nyanza does not lie in the Great Rift Valley but between its main and western branches. The Great Rift Valley ranges in elevation from c.1,300 ft (395 m) below sea level (the Dead Sea) to c.6,000 ft (1,830 m) above sea level in S Kenya. Erosion has concealed some sections, but in places, notably in Kenya, there are sheer cliffs several thousand feet high. The present configuration of the rift, which dates from the mid-Pleistocene epoch, is probably a result of a rifting process associated with thermal currents in the earth's mantle (see RIFT VALLEY);there is evidence of earlier rift structures.

Great Saint Bernard, pass: see SAINT BERNARD.

Great Salt Lake, shallow body of salt water, c.1,000 sq mi (2,590 sq km), NW Utah, between the Wasatch Range on the west and the Great Salt Lake Desert on the east; largest salt lake in North America. Fed by the Weber, Jordan, and Bear rivers, the lake varies in size and depth from year to year and with climatic changes; its average depth is 13 ft (4 m). Storage of spring run-off in reservoirs to meet domestic and industrial demands for water has caused a general decrease in the lake's area. Its salt content, now c.276,000 parts per million (saltier than sea water) increases as its area decreases. Magnesium chloride, potash, and common table salt have been commercially extracted from the lake. The heavy brine supports no life except brine shrimp and colonial algae. The Great Salt Lake is a remnant of prehistoric Lake Bonneville, which covered an extensive area of the Great Basin and was once c.1,000 ft (305 m) deep. Its various levels are marked by former beachlines on the mountains and by rich soil deposits on the terraces to the east, where the Mormons used to practice irrigated farming. Antelope and Fremont islands are the largest islands in the lake; the smaller islands are rookeries for sea gulls and other birds. Promontory Point, a mountainous peninsula 20 mi (32 km) long, extends into the lake from the north; a railroad cutoff passes through the neck as it crosses the lake and the Great Salt Lake Desert from Ogden to Lucin, Utah. The Bonneville Salt Flats, in the western part of the desert, is a world-famous automobile racing ground. In 1825 an American fur trader, James Bridger, was probably the first white man to see Great Salt Lake. In 1845 the U.S. explorer John Frémont became the first man to cross the salt desert.

Great Salt Plains Dam, on Salt Fork, a tributary of the Arkansas River, NW Okla., near Enid. The dam was authorized in 1936 as a Federal project and completed in 1941. In a salt-encrusted plains area, it provides flood control and impounds a large reservoir that is part of a national wildlife refuge.

Great Sand Dunes National Monument: see NATIONAL PARKS AND MONUMENTS (table).

Great Schism: see SCHISM, GREAT.

Great Seal of the United States: see UNITED STATES, GREAT SEAL OF THE.

Great Slave Lake, second largest lake of Canada, c.10,980 sq mi (28,400 sq km), S Mackenzie dist., Northwest Territories, named for the Slave (Dogrib) Indians. It is c.300 mi (480 km) long and from 12 to 68 mi (19–109 km) wide and is the deepest lake (2,015 ft/614 m) of North America. The Hay and Slave rivers are its chief tributaries; it is drained by the Mackenzie River. The western shores are wooded, but the long east and north arms reach into tundralike country. Samuel Hearne, a British fur trader, discovered the lake in 1771. Gold was discovered in the 1930s on the northern shore, and the town of YELLOWKNIFE was established as a mining center. The area is still important for gold mining; lead and zinc are found near Pine Point on the southern shore. The lake has commercial fisheries. Fort Providence, Hay River, and Fort Resolution are the chief towns on the lake.

Great Smoky Mountains, part of the Appalachian system, on the N.C.-Tenn. border; highest range E of the Black Hills, and one of the oldest uplands on earth. The mountains are named for the smokelike haze that envelops them. More than 25 peaks rise over 6,000 ft (1,829 m); Clingmans Dome, 6,642 ft (2,024 m), and Mt. Guyot, 6,621 ft (2,018 m), the highest points in Tennessee, were named after geologists T. L. Clingman and Arnold Guyot, who explored the mountains in the late 1800s. The Great Smokies are noted for their luxuriant vegetation; there are about 100 species of trees and more than 1,300 kinds of flowering plants. Nearly half of the forest is virgin growth. Black bears are the most frequently seen of the many animals and birds in the Great Smokies. Although the region's coves and valleys have been settled since pioneer times, they remained isolated and inaccessible until the 20th cent., when loggers began harvesting the virgin forest. **Great Smoky Mountains National Park,** 516,626 acres (209,079 hectares), est. 1930, straddles the crest of the Great Smokies for 71 mi (114 km). The park includes c.600 mi (965 km) of trails (the APPALACHIAN TRAIL follows the crest) and many streams and waterfalls. A number of former farmsteads with log cabins and barns, and a grist mill have been preserved; there are several museums.

Great South Bay, arm of the Atlantic Ocean, c.45 mi (72 km) long, between the southern shore of Long Island and offshore barrier islands, SE N.Y. With the rapid population growth along its shores, the shallow bay has suffered accelerated deposition, pollution, and rampant growth of eel grass. Major recreation areas on the bay include Jones Beach State Park and Fire Island National Seashore.

Great Trek: see TREK.

Great Wall of China: see CHINA, GREAT WALL OF.

Great War: see WORLD WAR I.

Greb, Harry, 1894–1926, American boxer, b. Pittsburgh. Although blind in one eye, Greb was one of the most feared fighters in American ring history. He was a natural middleweight, but fought light heavyweights and heavyweights with considerable success. In 1922 he won the light heavyweight title from Gene Tunney (the only loss of Tunney's career); the following year Greb took the middleweight title. In his professional career (1913–26), Greb fought 288 matches, winning 115, losing 9 (only one of which was by knockout), and having 164 no-decision bouts.

grebe (grēb), common name for swimming birds found on or near quiet waters in most parts of the world. Grebes resemble the related loon and the unrelated duck; they have short wings, vestigial tails, and long, individually webbed toes on feet that are set far back on a short, stubby body. They float lower in the water than do ducks, and at the approach of danger they sink progressively lower and then submerge, a practice which has given them the name helldiver. They are poor fliers and awkward on land; their loosely constructed nests are either hidden in the rushes and weeds at the water's edge or placed on floating vegetation fastened to growing plants. Many grebes cover their eggs with refuse when they leave the nest, and some carry the young on their backs. Grebes have complex courtship rituals, including dancing in pairs on the water. They eat crustaceans, fish, and aquatic insects and plants. Unique among birds is their unexplained habit of swallowing feathers. The best-known representative in the Western Hemisphere is the pied-billed grebe, *Podilymbus podiceps,* locally called dabchick, water witch, and didapper. Other grebes are the western and Holboell's grebes of North America and the eared and horned grebes of North America, Europe, Asia, and Africa. There is a flightless species in South America. Grebes were formerly hunted for their silky breast feathers. Grebes are classified in the phylum CHORDATA, subphylum Vertebrata, class Aves, order Podicipediformes, family Podicipedidae.

Grechko, Andrei Antonovich (əndrā' əntô'nəvĭch grĕch'kō), 1903–, Russian army officer and minister of defense. As a World War II commander he took part in the liberation of the Caucasus, the Ukraine, Czechoslovakia, and Poland. In 1953 he assumed command of Soviet troops in East Germany, suppressing the East German workers' rebellion of that same year. He became first deputy minister of defense in 1957, under the ailing Marshal Malinovsky. Assuming the top defense post in 1967, he deftly organized the 1968 invasion of Czechoslovakia by Soviet and other Warsaw Pact troops (see WARSAW TREATY ORGANIZATION) to suppress liberalization in that country. In 1973 he became a member of the Politburo, the ruling body of the Communist party.

Greco, El (ĕl grĕk'ō), c.1541–1614, Greek painter in Spain, b. Candia, Crete. His real name was Domenicos Theotocopoulos, of which several Italian and Spanish versions are current. Trained first in the school of icon painting, he is known to have studied in Venice under Titian and to have painted in Rome. In 1577 he was established in Toledo at work on the altar of the Church of Santo Domingo el Antiguo. The center painting of this group, the *Assumption,* now in the Art Institute of Chicago, shows marked Italian influence. His next great works, *El espolio de las vestiduras* (cathedral, Toledo) and *San Mauricio* (Escorial) indicate a rapid development. The second was commissioned by Philip II, but he rejected it. In any case, El Greco remained in Toledo, then an abandoned and rapidly dwindling capital whose proud and recalcitrant nobility were driven wholesale into the church as their only remaining vocation. He has left superb portraits of their ascetic faces, and in the foreground of his famous *Burial of the Count Orgaz* (Church of San Tomé, Toledo) it is they who are assembled at the funeral of the count, whose soul is seen ascending to Christ in the upper part of the painting. This masterpiece, painted in 1586, was followed by many others in which the artist, then mature, brought into play every resource of his dynamic art to express religious ecstasy. Flamelike lines, accentuated by vivid highlights, elongated and distorted figures, and full vibrant color contrasted with subtle grays all combine to produce a unique art. Among his many great works of this period are the *Baptism, Crucifixion,* and *Resurrection* (Prado); portrait of the inquisitor Cardinal Don Fernando Niño de Guevara (Metropolitan Mus.); two similar versions of St. Jerome (one in the National Gall., London; one in the Frick Coll., New York City); and a long series of paintings of St. Francis. To his last period belong such works as the *Assumption* (Mus. of San Vicente Anejo, Toledo); *Adoration* and *View of Toledo* (Metropolitan Mus.); the *Pentecost* (Prado); a portrait of Hortensio Felix Paravicino (Mus. of Fine Arts, Boston); and the *Laocoön* (National Gall. of Art, Washington, D.C.). The debt to El Greco of the later Spanish masters is incalculable. He unquestionably influenced Velázquez, who knew and esteemed his work. In his own day his admirers seem to have been intellectuals. Paravicino, the court preacher, was his friend and apologist. Overshadowed by the more popular masterpieces of Velázquez and Murillo, his work became less and less known, especially outside of Spain. It is only in the 20th cent. that he has become widely celebrated. Modern criticism ranks him among the greatest of inspired, visionary artists. Splendid examples of his vast production exist in many European and American galleries and collections. He is best seen in Toledo, Madrid, and the Escorial. A museum has been devoted to his work in what is said to have been his home in Toledo. See studies by L. Goldscheider (3d ed. 1954), P. Kelemen (1961), H. E. Wethey (1962), L. Bronstein (1967), and José Gudiol (tr. 1973).

Greco, José (hōsā' grĕk'ō), 1918–, Spanish-American dancer and choreographer, b. Italy. Greco emigrated to the United States as a child. He first appeared as a professional dancer in New York in *Carmen* in 1937, dancing thereafter in night clubs and resorts, in films, and in touring ballet companies. In 1948 he organized his own company, Ballets y Bailes de España, which has made numerous world tours. Greco is noted for his FLAMENCO.

Greece, Gr. *Hellas* or *Ellas,* republic (1971 pop. 8,745,084), 50,944 sq mi (131,945 sq km), SE Europe, occupying the southernmost part of the Balkan Peninsula and bordering on the Ionian Sea in the west, on the Mediterranean Sea in the south, on the Aegean Sea in the east, on Turkey and Bulgaria in the northeast, on Yugoslavia in the north, and on Albania in the northwest. ATHENS is the capital and largest city of the country, which is divided into 10 administrative regions. About 75% of Greece is mountainous and only about 25% of the land is arable. The country falls into four main geographical regions. Northern Greece includes portions of historic EPIRUS, MACEDONIA, and THRACE. It takes in part of the Pindus Mts. (which continue into central Greece); low-lying plains along the lower Nestos and Struma rivers; and the KHALKIDHIKÍ peninsula, on which THESSALONÍKI, Greece's second largest city, is located. Central Greece, situated N of the Gulf of Corinth, includes the low-lying plains of THESSALY, ATTICA, and BOEOTIA; Mt. Olympus (Ólimbos; 9,570 ft/2,917 m), the highest point in Greece; and Athens. Southern Greece is made up of the PELOPONNESUS. The fourth region of Greece comprises numerous islands (with a total area of c.9,600 sq mi/24,900 sq km), the most notable of which are CRETE, in the Mediterranean; KÉRKIRA, KEFALLENÍA, ZÁKINTHOS, LEVKÁS, and ITHÁKI, in the Ionian Sea; and the CYCLADES, the Northern SPORADES, the DODECANESE (including RHODES), ÉVVOIA, LESBOS, KHÍOS, SÁMOS, LÍMNOS, SAMOTHRACE, and THÁSOS, in the Aegean. Greece has few rivers, none of them navigable. The Greek people are only partly descended from the ancient Greeks, having mingled through the ages with the numerous invaders of the Balkans. There are two forms of the modern Greek language; one is the vernacular, used in popular literature, and the other is the official language of the state, the press, and the universities, employing classical terms and forms. There is a small Turkish-speaking minority. The Greek Orthodox Church is the established church of the country, and it includes the great majority of the population. The Greek primate is the archbishop of Athens, who recognizes the Ecumenical Patriarch of İstanbul. The Greek economy suffered severe dislocations in World War II and in the civil war that followed. Since 1950 there has been considerable investment in economic infrastructure and in industrial plant. However, in the early 1970s, Greece remained a relatively poor agricultural country. Farming contributed about 20% of the annual national product and manufacturing about 16%; tourism was an important source of income. The chief agricultural products are wheat, citrus fruits, olives and olive oil, grapes, currants, cotton, tobacco, sugar beets, tomatoes, and potatoes. Large numbers of sheep and goats are raised. The country's main industrial centers are Athens, Thessaloníki, PIRAIÉVS, PÁTRAI, and IRÁKLION. The principal manufactures are construction materials, textiles, food products, chemicals, refined petroleum, and ships. The chief minerals produced are lignite, bauxite, high-grade iron ore, magnesite, and iron pyrites. The output of hydroelectricity is low, but is being increased rapidly to help offset the country's dearth of other energy resources. Greece has a large merchant fleet, and its chief ports are Piraiévs and Thessaloníki. Although the country has easy access to the sea, fishing is relatively undeveloped; sponge fishing is important at KALÁMAI and on some of the islands. The value of imports into Greece is usually considerably higher than the value of exports from the country. The main exports are food, wine, tobacco, metals, and textiles; the leading imports are manufactured consumer goods, food, fuel, chemicals, and machinery. The principal trade partners are West Germany, the United States, Italy, and France. In 1962, Greece became an associate member of the European Economic Community (COMMON MARKET). Universities in Greece are located at Athens, Ioánnina, Pátrai, and Thessaloníki.

Ancient Greece. Important aspects of ancient Greek culture are covered in separate articles—GREEK ARCHITECTURE, GREEK ART, GREEK LANGUAGE, GREEK LITERATURE, GREEK MUSIC, and GREEK RELIGION. See also the articles on the cities, e.g., ATHENS, SPARTA, CORINTH, and THEBES. At various times in its history Greece included all of Epirus, Macedonia, and Thrace, part of Asia Minor, and MAGNA GRAECIA. Archaeological remains show that Greece had a long prehistory, dating from the Neolithic Age (c.4000 B.C.). By the Bronze Age (c.2800 B.C.) important cultures had developed. The AEGEAN CIVILIZATION had several phases, two of the most important being the MINOAN CIVILI-

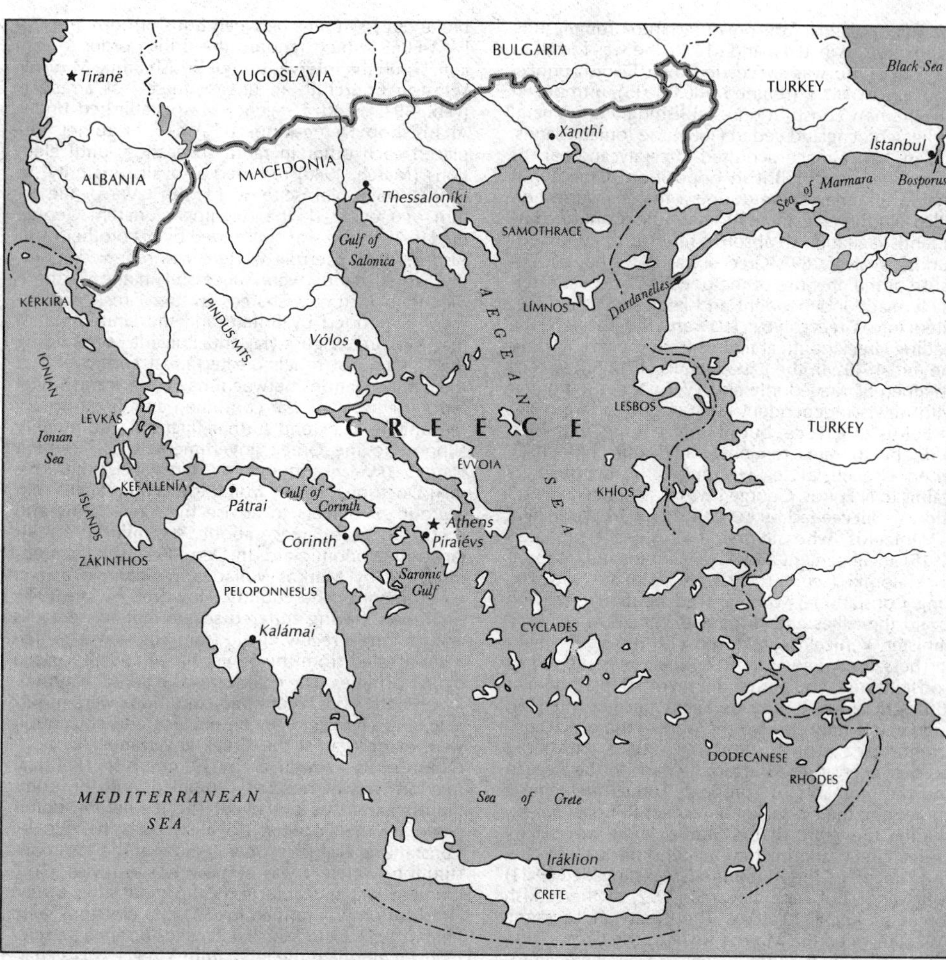

ZATION and the MYCENAEAN CIVILIZATION. These cultures had disappeared by 1100 B.C. The Greek-speaking ACHAEANS migrated into the Peloponnesus during the 14th and 13th cent. B.C. The Aeolians and the Ionians apparently preceded the Dorians, who migrated into Greece before 1000 B.C. The Ionians, moving forth, possibly as refugees, possibly as conquerors, settled in the Ionian Islands and on the shores of Asia Minor, which became a part of the Greek world. After the Dorian invasion, the peoples of Greece, under the influence of the divisive geography and the great variety of tribes, developed the CITY-STATE—small settlements that grew into minor kingdoms. Homeric Greece (named for the great epic poet HOMER) was dependent on the agriculture of relatively unproductive fields but was already open to the sea. Although the Greeks never rivaled the Phoenicians or the later Carthaginians and Romans as mariners, the sea offered them an opportunity for expansion and commerce. In the 8th, 7th, and 6th cent. B.C., the Greeks established colonies, many of which became separate city-states, from the Black Sea and the Bosporus (where Byzantium was founded) to Sicily, S Italy (Magna Graecia), Mediterranean France, the northern shores of Africa, and Spain. These colonies had a great influence on the history of the Greek mainland, where the city-states were developing in quarrelsome freedom. Because of their independence, the cities developed separately. However, there was a general pattern of development, which varied somewhat in each particular instance. Monarchies yielded to aristocracies, which were in turn replaced by tyrants, who usually gained power by espousing the cause of the underprivileged and by using force. Although the tyrants usually tried to establish dynasties, the hold established by their families was short-lived. Pisistratus, Hipparchus, and Hippias in Athens and the later Gelon, Dionysius the Elder, and Dionysius the Younger in Sicily were typical tyrants. On the Greek mainland the tyrannies soon yielded to oligarchies or to democracies tempered by limited citizenship and by slaveholding; it was in Greece that the idea of political democracy came into being. SOLON established a democracy in Athens. Militaristic Sparta had a unique constitutional and social development. The warring city-states had a sense of unity; all their citizens considered themselves Hellenes, and religious unity gave rise to leagues known as amphictyonies, notably the great amphictyony centered at Delphi. The celebration of contests such as the Olympian Games also fostered unity. However, the Ionian cities in Asia Minor received little help from Greece when they revolted (499 B.C.) against Persia, which also threatened the Greek mainland, and the mainland cities were poorly united in the PERSIAN WARS that continued until 449 B.C. Out of these successful wars, however, came the powerful surge of Greek civilization. Athens, in particular, with the support of the DELIAN LEAGUE as the basis of an empire, grew dramatically, and in the age of Pericles (c.495–429 B.C.) developed a culture that left its mark on the course of Western and Eastern civilization. Drama, poetry, sculpture, architecture, and philosophy flourished, and there was a vigorous intellectual life. The leading Greeks of the 5th and 4th cent. B.C. included Aeschylus, Sophocles, Euripides, Aristophanes, Phidias, Myron, Polykleitos, Heraclitus, Socrates, Plato, Aristotle, and Hippocrates. Although Athens succumbed in the PELOPONNESIAN WAR (431–404 B.C.) and Sparta triumphed briefly before continued fighting gave the hegemony of Greece to Corinth and Thebes, the civilization that had been created lived on. When PHILIP II of Macedon attacked the warring city-states and conquered Greece by defeating the Athenians and the Thebans in the battle of CHAERONEA (338 B.C.), he paved the way for his son, ALEXANDER THE GREAT, who spread Greek civilization over the known Western world and across Asia to India. After Alexander's death, his empire was torn apart by his warring generals (see DIADOCHI; PTOLEMY I; SELEUCUS I; ANTIGONUS I; DEMETRIUS I) in the period from 323 to 276 B.C. Some Greek cities formed the AETOLIAN LEAGUE to oppose Macedonian rule, but members of the ACHAEAN LEAGUE took the Macedonian side. The Greek city-states continued their rivalries, and Macedonia under the Antigonids became thoroughly Hellenized. Incessant warfare made Greece increasingly weak, while Rome grew stronger. In 146 B.C., after the Fourth Macedonian War (see MACEDON), the remnants of the Greek states fell definitively into the hands of Rome. Under Roman rule, the cities long retained a measure of independence and intellectual life, but had little political or economic importance. Hellenism, however, had triumphed, and Greek intellectual supremacy continued for many centuries. The Byzantine Empire was thoroughly Greek in origin, and HELLENISTIC CIVILIZATION, centered at Alexandria, Pergamum, Dura, and other cities, spread Greek influence and preserved the Greek heritage for later ages. The Greeks were the first to write narrative secular history, and the works of HERODOTUS, THUCYDIDES, XENOPHON, and POLYBIUS are basic sources of events and contemporary ideas as well as classics of world literature. The histories of Greece by Adolf Holm (tr., 4 vol., 1894–98) and George Grote (rev. ed., 12 vol., 1906–38) were long standard and are still useful. See Werner Jaeger, *Paideia* (tr., 3 vol., 1943–45); J. B. Bury, *The History of Greece to the Death of Alexander the Great* (3d ed., rev. by Russell Meiggs, 1951); A. E. Zimmern, *The Greek Commonwealth* (5th ed. 1961); W. W. Tarn, *Hellenistic Civilization* (3d rev. ed. 1966); A. R. Burn, *A Traveller's History of Greece* (1967); W. G. Forrest, *The Emergence of Greek Democracy, 800–400 B.C.* (1967); N. G. Hammond, *A History of Greece to 322 B.C.* (2d ed. 1967); Victor Ehrenberg, *From Solon to Socrates* (1968) and *The Greek State* (2d ed. 1969, repr. 1972); J. A. Larsen, *Greek Federal States* (1968); Pierre Lévêque, *The Greek Adventure* (tr. 1968); G. L. Huxley, *Early Sparta* (1971); M. I. Rostovtsev, *A History of the Ancient World* (tr., 2 vol., 2d ed. 1930–33; repr. 1971); V. R. Desborough, *The Greek Dark Ages* (1972); H. D. F. Kitto, *The Greeks* (1954, repr. 1972); Russell Meiggs, *The Athenian Empire* (1972); A. W. Adkins, *Moral Values and Political Behavior in Ancient Greece* (1973); John Ferguson, *The Heritage of Hellenism* (1973).

Medieval and Modern Greece. From the division (A.D. 395) of the Roman Empire into East and West until the conquest (15th cent.) of Greece by the Ottoman Turks, Greece shared the fortunes and vicissitudes of the BYZANTINE EMPIRE. The victory (378) of the VISIGOTHS over Emperor Valens at Adrianople marked the beginning of the frequent and devastating barbarian invasions of Greece; the Huns, Avars, Slavs, and Bulgars followed. Greek power and prestige were restored by the Macedonian dynasty of Byzantine emperors (867–1025); however, the center of the Greek world was CONSTANTINOPLE, not Greece proper. In the 11th cent. began the inroads of the Seljuk Turks into the empire, the Norman attacks on Epirus, and the age of the CRUSADES. The Fourth Crusade led in 1204 to the temporary disintegration of the Byzantine Empire and the creation of a feudal state (see CONSTANTINOPLE, LATIN EMPIRE OF) under the rule of French, Flemish, and Italian nobles and of Venice. The restored Byzantine Empire (1261–1453) recovered only parts of Greece, most of which continued under the rule of French and Italian princes until conquered by the Ottoman Turks (completed in 1456). Genoa held Khíos until 1566; Venice retained Crete until 1669 and the Ionian Islands until 1797. In its numerous wars with the Ottomans, Venice also held Athens, Évvoia, and several other ports and islands for brief intermittent periods prior to 1718. Under the OTTOMAN EMPIRE, Greece was merely one of many exploited territories. The Turks practiced religious tolerance, but otherwise their regime was grasping and oppressive. Many Greek families (notably the Phanariots; see under PHANAR) were important in the administration of the empire, and the Greek merchants living in Constantinople and in the ports of Asia Minor, notably İZMIR (Smyrna), were very prosperous; but Greece itself languished in obscurity and poverty. In the early 19th cent. the desire of the Greeks for independence was stimulated by growing nationalism, by the influence of the French Revolution, by the Turkish reverses in the Russo-Turkish Wars, by the rebellion (1820) of ALI PASHA against the Ottoman Empire, and by the sympathetic attitude of Alexander I of Russia, whose foreign minister, CAPO D'ISTRIA, was Greek. In 1821 the Greek War of Independence began under the leadership of Alexander and Demetrios YPSILANTI. European sentiment was overwhelmingly in favor of the Greek cause; financial aid poured in, and many foreign volunteers (of whom Lord Byron was the most celebrated) joined the Greek forces. Russia and England agreed (1826) to mediate between the Greeks and Turkey, and in 1827 the Greek political factions set aside their bitter rivalries to elect Capo d'Istria president of Greece. England, Russia, and France joined in demanding an armistice. Turkey having refused, the allied fleets attacked and defeated the fleet of MUHAMMAD ALI, viceroy of Egypt and the Ottoman sultan's chief supporter against the Greeks, in the battle of NAVARINO (1827). Only Russia, however, declared war (1828) on Turkey. Defeated, Turkey accepted the Treaty of Adrianople (1829; see ADRIANOPLE, TREATY OF) and recognized Greek autonomy. In 1832, Greece obtained from the European powers recognition of its independence. The powers chose, and Greece accepted (1832), a Bavarian prince as king of the Hellenes. OTTO I proved authoritarian and unpopular. He was pressured into promulgating a constitution in 1844, and in 1862 he was forced to abdicate. Otto was succeeded by a Danish prince, who as GEORGE I (reigned 1863–1913) introduced (1864) a new constitution establishing a unicameral parliament. England ceded (1864) the Ionian Islands, and in 1881 Greece acquired Thessaly and part of Epirus. Because of British opposition, Greece was unable to annex Crete during a major insurrection (1866–69) there against Ottoman rule. Continued irredentist agitation to absorb Crete led to the Greco-Turkish War of 1897; Greece was defeated, but because of the pressure of the powers Crete was eventually made independent and later (1913) incorporated into Greece. VENIZELOS and ZAÏMIS were the leading Greek political figures from the late 1890s to the mid-1930s. In the BALKAN WARS (1912–13) Greece obtained SE Macedonia and W Thrace; the frontier with newly independent ALBANIA gave a larger part of Epirus to Greece, but neither country was satisfied, and the area remained in dispute until 1971, when Greece, at least temporarily, dropped its claims to N Epirus. George I was assassinated in 1913 and was succeeded by CONSTANTINE I. In World War I, Venizelos, who favored the Allies, negotiated (1915) an agreement allowing them to land troops at Thessaloníki (see SALONICA CAMPAIGNS). However, King Constantine, who favored neutrality, refused to aid the Allies and dismissed Venizelos as prime minister. Venizelos organized (1916) a government at Thessaloníki, and in 1917 Allied pressure led to Constantine's abdication in favor of his younger son, ALEXANDER. Venizelos again became premier, and Greece fully entered the war. At the peace conference (see NEUILLY, TREATY OF; SÈVRES, TREATY OF) Greece received the Bulgarian coast on the Aegean and the remnants of European Turkey including E Thrace and the Dodecanese (except Rhodes) but excluding the Zone of the Straits. İzmir was placed under Greek administration pending a plebiscite. Encouraged by the Allies, the Greeks invaded (1921) Asia Minor, but were defeated (1922) by the Turkish forces of Kemal ATATÜRK. The Treaty of Lausanne (1923) restored the Maritsa River as the Greco-Turkish frontier in Europe. A separate agreement provided for the compulsory exchange of populations. Under the supervision of a League of Nations commission about 1.5 million Greeks of Asia Minor were resettled in Greece and about 800,000 Turks and 80,000 Bulgarians left Greece and were repatriated in their respective countries. Constantine, who had returned after the death (1920) of King Alexander, was again deposed in 1922. GEORGE II succeeded Alexander, but was soon also deposed (1923), and in 1924 a republic was proclaimed and then confirmed by a plebiscite. The years 1924–35 were marked by unsettled economic conditions and by violent political strife (including coups d'etat and countercoups), in which KONDOURIOTIS, PANGALOS, George KONDYLIS, Panayoti TSALDARIS, Zaïmis, and Venizelos were the chief protagonists. The defeat (1935) of the rebelling Venizelists in Crete marked the end of the republic. Kondylis ousted Tsaldaris and arranged for a plebiscite that resulted in the restoration of the monarchy and the return of George II. In 1936, Premier METAXAS, supported by the king, established a dictatorship, ostensibly to avert a Communist takeover of the country. In foreign relations, Greece abandoned its anti-Turkish policy by establishing (1934) the BALKAN ENTENTE with Yugoslavia, Rumania, and Turkey. When World War II broke out (1939) Greece remained neutral. In Oct., 1940, however, Italy, after a farcical ultimatum, invaded Greece. The Greeks resisted successfully, carrying the war into S Albania. Metaxas, who had strong pro-German leanings, died in Jan., 1941. When Germany began to gather troops on the Greek borders, Greece allowed the landing (March, 1941) of a small British expeditionary force, but by the end of April the Greek mainland was in German hands, and in May Crete fell. The Greek government fled to Cairo, then to England, and in 1943 settled in Cairo. The German occupation, in which Bulgarian and Italian troops also took part, plunged Greece into abject misery, including an acute shortage of food. Resistance grew despite ruthless reprisals, and successive puppet governments were failures. Guerrilla bands controlled large rural areas. In 1943 sporadic civil war began between the Communist guerrilla group (EAM-ELAS) and the royalist group (EDES). The guerrillas held most of Greece after the Germans began to withdraw in Sept., 1944. British troops landed, and by November all Germans were expelled. The appalling financial and economic conditions faced by the Greek government on its return (Oct., 1944) to Athens were complicated by an explosive political situation. In Dec., 1944, fighting broke out in Athens between British troops and the EAM-ELAS, which ignored the British order to disarm. Upon the intervention of British Prime Minister Winston Churchill, an uneasy truce was arranged (Feb., 1945), and a regency was established under Archbishop Damaskinos of Athens. Cabinets replaced each other in rapid succession, until elections (March, 1946) returned a royalist majority. In Sept., 1946, a plebiscite decided in favor of the return of George II, the reigning monarch; George died in 1947 and was succeeded by his brother PAUL. Also in 1946, guerrilla warfare was renewed; Communist-led bands were successful in the northern mountain districts. Charges by the Greek government, supported by Britain and the United States, that Albania, Yugoslavia, and Bulgaria were aiding the Communist rebels created great controversy at the United Nations between the Western and Soviet blocs. As the civil war continued and Great Britain felt unable to extend further financial and military support to the Greek government, U.S. President Harry S. TRUMAN announced (March, 1947) the "Truman Doctrine," under which the United States sent a group of officers to advise the Greek army and eventually gave Greece about $400 million in military and economic aid. In Dec., 1947, the Communists, led by Markos Vafiades, proclaimed a rival government of the country. However, by late 1949, the rebels, having suffered severe military setbacks and no longer receiving aid from Yugoslavia (which had defected from the Soviet bloc in 1948), ceased open hostilities. The civil war was marked by brutality on both sides. Economic conditions were miserable, and charges of incompetence and corruption were made against the Greek government by non-Communists as well as by Communists. Political freedom was of necessity curtailed, and the Communist party was outlawed. The legislature, dominated by the Populist (royalist) party headed by Constantine Tsaldaris, operated under the 1911 constitution, which it was empowered to revise. Government was unstable in 1950–51, but after a new constitution was ratified in 1951 and elections were held in 1952, Field Marshal Papagos became premier with a majority in the legislature. Greece was a charter member of the UN, and in 1951 it was admitted to the North Atlantic Treaty Organization (NATO). When Papagos died in 1955, he was succeeded by Constantine KARAMANLIS, whose National Radical Union party increased its majority in subsequent elections (1956, 1958, 1961). Under Papagos and Karamanlis, the Greek economy improved considerably, despite a series of damaging earthquakes in 1953–54; the United States continued to give Greece considerable economic and military aid. In 1954, Greece signed an alliance with Turkey and Yugoslavia, but friction with Turkey (and also with Great Britain) soon arose over the sovereignty of CYPRUS, the majority of whose population is ethnically Greek, and continued after Cyprus became independent in 1960. The moderately liberal Center Union gained a plurality of seats in the legislature in elections in 1963, but its leader George PAPANDREOU failed to win a vote of confidence for his government, and new elections were held in 1964. This time the Center Union gained a majority of seats and Papandreou became prime minister. Also in 1964, Paul died and was succeeded by his son, CONSTANTINE II. In mid-1965, Gen. George Grivas accused Papandreou's son Andreas (an economist who had taught in the United States) of helping to organize a secret leftist group among army officers; similar accusations against both Papandreous were made by the defense minister. In the resulting furor Constantine forced the resignation of George Papandreou, who long had been an opponent of the monarchy. After a period of uncertainty, a new government headed by Stefanos Stephanopoulos was formed in Sept., 1965. This government fell in Dec., 1965, and Constantine authorized Ioannis Paraskevopoulos to form an extraparliamentary government pending elections set for May, 1967. Paraskevopoulos gained the support of George Papandreou and of Panayotis Kanellopoulos, the leader of the National Radical Union, but was forced to resign in March, 1967, and was replaced as prime minister by Kanellopoulos. Before the elections (which the Center Union seemed likely to win) could be held, rightist army officers staged (April 21, 1967) a successful coup d'etat, claiming that a Communist takeover of Greece was imminent. Constantine KOLLIAS was made prime minister, but real power was held by three army officers, George PAPADOPOULOS, Gregory Spandidakis, and Stylianos Patakos. Many liberals and leftists were placed under arrest, and rigid controls were placed over Greek life. After failing in a countercoup (Dec., 1967), Constantine went into exile. Shortly thereafter, Gen. George Zoitakis was made regent, and Papadopoulos and Patakos, after resigning their army posts, became, respectively, prime minister and deputy prime minister. Some clandestine opposition groups were organized in Greece, and there was international protest against the dictatorial ways of the new regime. In 1968, a new constitution that drastically curtailed the power of the monarchy and expanded that of the prime minister was overwhelmingly approved in a referendum. Controls over Greek life were relaxed somewhat, and most political prisoners had been released by the early 1970s. In 1972, Papadopoulos, by then the most powerful person in the country, also assumed the post of regent. In May, 1973, members of the navy staged an unsuccessful coup d'etat. In June, 1973, the monarchy was abolished, and Greece became a presidential republic. After this move was approved by a plebiscite later in the year, Papadopoulos became provisional president, and Spyros Markezinis replaced him as prime minister. In an effort to eliminate the remaining traces of military rule and thus to gain greater international acceptance of the new order in Greece, elections were scheduled for 1974. However, on Nov. 25, 1973, Papadopoulos was ousted in a bloodless military coup led by Lt. Gen. Phaedon Gizikis, who became president. In the aftermath of its failure to gain control of Cyprus by political manipulation there, the Gizikis government, in July, 1974, voluntarily turned over power to a civilian government headed by Karamanlis, who returned from exile. Most exiled politicians (notably A. Papandreou) returned to Greece, all political parties (including the Communist party) were allowed to operate freely, and the 1951 constitution was reinstated. In a referendum in mid-Dec., 1974, Greek voters rejected by a large margin the reestablishment of the monarchy. See Edgar O'Ballance, *The Greek Civil War, 1944–49* (1966); J. K. Campbell and Phillip Sherrard, *Modern Greece* (1968); J. P. Carey and A. G. Carey, *The Web of Modern Greek Politics* (1968); C. M. Woodhouse, *A Short History of Modern Greece* (1968); Constantine Tsoucalas, *The Greek Tragedy* (1969); George Finlay, *A History of Greece* (7 vol., 1877; repr. 1970); A. G. Papandreou, *Democracy at Gunpoint* (1970); Joseph Braddock, *The Greek Phoenix* (1972); Richard Clogg, *Inside the Colonel's Greece* (tr. 1972) and with George Yannopoulos, ed., *Greece under Military Rule* (1972); Douglas Dakin, *The Unification of Greece: 1770–1923* (1972); Dominique Eudes, *The Kapetanios, Partisans and Civil War in Greece, 1943–1949* (tr., 1972); A. B. Herrick et al., *Area Handbook for Greece* (1972); David Holden, *Greece Without Columns: The Making of the Modern Greeks* (1972); D. G. Kousoulas, *Greece, Uncertain Democracy* (1973).

Greek Anthology, collection of short epigrammatic poems representing Greek literature from the 7th cent. B.C. to the 10th cent. A.D. It contains more than 6,000 poems on a variety of subjects by some 320 authors. Meleager compiled a collection of epigrams (which he called the *Garland*) probably between 90 B.C. and 80 B.C. Later others made additions or new collections. Early in the 10th cent. Constantius Cephalas made a compilation that is known as the *Palatine Anthology* because the sole manuscript was found in the library of the count Palatine in Heidelberg. In the first half of the 14th cent. a monk, Planudes Maximus, rearranged this collection, making additions and excluding many poems from the older compilation. The Planudes version was used until the *Palatine Anthology* was rediscovered in 1606. There are several good English translations of the Greek poems, particularly those by J. W. Mackail (3d ed. 1911), W. R. Paton (with Greek texts, 5 vol., 1916–26), and Dudley Fitts (rev. ed. 1956).

Greek architecture arose on the shores of the Aegean Sea. Palaces of the MINOAN CIVILIZATION remain at Cnossus and Phaestus on Crete. Of the later MYCENAEN CIVILIZATION, surviving examples are the Lion's Gate at Mycenae and palaces at Mycenae and Tiryns. When the Dorians migrated into Greece (before 1000 B.C.) true Hellenic culture began, and the architecture that eventually developed seems to have borrowed little or nothing from the preceding civilizations. In Greece the Dorians developed their building forms with such rapidity that between the 10th and the 6th cent. B.C. a definite system of construction was established. However, prior to the creation of the great marble temples of the 5th cent. B.C., there were undoubtedly evolutionary stages in which walls were made of sun-dried bricks and roofs, columns, and uprights of wood. The Heraeum at Olympia, considered one of the most ancient temples yet discovered, represents such a stage; in its later alterations (7th cent. B.C.), it is illustrative of the beginnings of the Doric temple of stone. Between 700 B.C. and the Roman occupation (146 B.C.), all the chief works were produced. The period in which all the major masterpieces were erected extended from 480 B.C. to 323 B.C.; it includes the reign of Pericles, in which the architects Callicrates, Mnesicles, and Ictinus flourished and in which the PARTHENON and other great works were produced. The products of the following Hellenistic period show a decline from the Athenian tradition and reveal Asian influences. Of the three great styles or ORDERS OF ARCHITECTURE (Doric, Ionic, and Corinthian), the Doric was the earliest and the one in which the noblest monuments were erected. Theories of the origin of the DORIC ORDER are numerous. The great remaining examples of the 6th cent. B.C. are found chiefly in Sicily and at Paestum in Italy. After 500 B.C. the archaic features of the Doric disappeared; harmonious proportions were achieved; and the final exquisitely adjusted type took form at Athens, in the Hephaesteum (465 B.C.), the Parthenon (c.447–432 B.C.), and the Propylaea (437–432 B.C.). The Greek colonies of the Asia Minor coast had evolved their own special order, the IONIC ORDER, stamped with Oriental influences. This style appeared in temples in Greece proper after 500 B.C., challenging with its slenderly proportioned columns and carved enrichments the supremacy of the simple, sturdy Doric. The most magnificent Ionic temples were those at Miletus. In Greece proper the Ionic appeared in only one temple of major importance, the ERECHTHEUM at Athens, and otherwise the form was restricted to minor buildings, as the temple of Nike Apteros, Athens (438 B.C.), and to interiors as in the Propylaea, Athens. The third Greek order, the still more ornate CORINTHIAN ORDER, appeared in this period, but was little used. The chief examples, both at Athens, are the CHORAGIC MONUMENT of Lysicrates (c.335 B.C.) and the Tower of the Winds (100 B.C.–35 B.C.). The Greeks laid their masonry without mortar but with joints cut to great exactness. Marble was not generally used until the 5th cent. B.C. Where coarse stonework or crude bricks were used, a coating, composed of marble dust and lime rubbed and highly polished, was applied to them. Even marble itself was sometimes so treated. Although it was long thought that buildings in ancient Greece retained the unbroken white of the marble, in fact colors and gilding were customarily applied to emphasize decorative sculpture and certain details, and remaining traces of these have been found. Having found in the simple column and lintel an adequate method of construction, they used it exclusively, drawing from it the maximum of dignity and beauty. Greek cities were often built in the vicinity of a steep hill called an acropolis that served as a citadel and upon which the principal temples were located for safety. The Acropolis at Athens is the most celebrated example. Throughout Greece numerous temples were built. Many illustrated the most rudimentary temple type—a simple rectangular chamber called the naos, the side walls extending to the front to form terminations for an open entrance porch containing two columns. This loggia was sometimes repeated at the other end. The next stage was the forming of freestanding porticoes, then a continuing of columns, flanking sides and ends, the naos thus being completely surrounded by a colonnade. This type was termed peripteral and was exemplified in most of the important monuments of the great period. In dipteral temples the surrounding colonnade was doubled. No public mass worship took place within the temples, the naos being designed primarily to house the statue of the deity. The structures of the culminating period are unique for the subtle proportionings and refinements of all the members, which are integrated into a superbly adjusted whole. To prevent an appearance of sagging, as in the temple platform (stylobate), or of concavity, as in the outlines of columns, subtly curved or slanting lines were substituted for straight or vertical ones and served as optical corrections. To insure the desired proportions and delicate relationships, a body of traditional formulas was accumulated, using mathematical and geometrical devices. The Greeks also built monumental tombs; agoras, or public meeting places; stoas, or colonnaded shelters; stadiums; palaestrae, or gymnasiums for athletic training; propylaea, or entrance gateways to cities; and amphitheaters. After the passing of power from Athens and Sparta to Asia Minor the pure traditions of the mainland were lost. Hellenistic architecture thus arose (4th–3d cent. B.C.), with florid and opulent elements and more complicated design. City planning, ignored by the mainland Greeks, was cultivated by the Hellenistic architects, among them Hippodamus; from them the Romans doubtless acquired their concepts of monumental civic design. See A. W. Lawrence, *Greek Architecture* (1967); V. Scully, *The Earth, the Temple, and the Gods* (rev. ed. 1970); J. J. Pollitt, *Art and Experience in Ancient Greece* (1972).

Greek art. The Aegean basin was a center of artistic activity from early times (see AEGEAN CIVILIZATION). Two great cultures—the MINOAN CIVILIZATION and the MYCENAEAN CIVILIZATION—had developed complex and delicate art forms. Before 1000 B.C., invasions of Dorians and other barbarian tribes from the north laid waste the earlier Aegean cultures. While there was not the definite cultural break once envisaged by archaeologists, the chaotic conditions caused by the invasions produced at first a decline in artistic production and then a slow transformation into a new art. A geometric scheme with linear patterns replaced the curvilinear designs and naturalistic representations of the Mycenaean age. When human and animal life was again represented, the forms assumed were schematized and formal. The pottery of the late geometric period (c.900–700 B.C.) is characterized by two-dimensional stylized patterns, effectively designed but bearing little relation to nature. Between 700 and 600 B.C. this geometric style gave way to new interest in representation, and Oriental influence encouraged the use of floral and arabesque designs and the adoption of Oriental monster and animal themes. During the archaic period (c.660–480 B.C.) sculpture emerged definitely as a principal form of artistic expression. Dating from the beginning of this period are magnificent statues of nude walking youths, *kouroi,* which suggest Egyptian prototypes but which are distinctive in stylization and tension of movement (e.g., *Kouros,* Metropolitan Mus.). Draped female sculptures from the archaic period suggest Near Eastern influence (e.g., *Hera of Samos,* Louvre). Vase painters depicted mythological scenes and, toward the end of the archaic period, many scenes from contemporary life. Outstanding was the Athenian school of black-figured vase painting led by the painter Execias. The appearance of the red-figured style of vase painting (c.525 B.C.) showed increased concern with the rendering of three-dimensional space and naturalistic detail. Euthymides and Euphronius were among the great early masters in this medium. About a generation later masterpieces were produced by the painters Brygos and Duris. In the early classical, or transitional, period (c.480–450 B.C.) a new humanism began to find its aesthetic expression in terms of a perfect balance between verisimilitude and abstraction of form. The largest surviving single group of sculpture is from the temple of Zeus at Olympia. Although certain conventions in rendering hair and draperies persist from the archaic period, the magnificent marble figures from the pediments reveal a new kind of insight into the structure of the human figure. Rare surviving works in bronze are the famous *Charioteer* (museum, Delphi) and the *Zeus* or *Poseidon* found in an ancient shipwreck off Cape Artemision (Athens, National Mus.). The height of the classical period or Golden Age (c.450–400 B.C.) was the time of Pericles and Thucydides, of the great dramatists Sophocles and Euripides, and of the young Socrates. The aesthetic ideal based on the representation of human character as an expression of a divine system embodying a rational ethic and ordered reality was integral to the culture. Polykleitos sought to arrive at a rational norm for the structure of the ideal human figure. The most magnificent original sculptures from this period are those from the temples of the Athenian ACROPOLIS. Earliest of these are the PARTHENON sculptures including the frieze representing the Panathenaic procession and the pedimental sculptures (see ELGIN MARBLES). The sculptors are anonymous, but Phidias is believed to have drawn up the designs. Somewhat later in date are the sculptures of the Hephaesteum, the Erechtheum, and the Nike Balustrade. In the late classical period (400–300 B.C.) there was increased emphasis on the expression of emotion in art. Works attributed to Praxiteles are characterized by elegance of proportion and graceful beauty. Powerful emotional effects are typical of the sculpture in the style of Scopas, and a new feeling for individualization and three-dimensional movement appeared in the art of Lysippos. Other sculptors of the period between 500 and 300 B.C. were Myron, Kresilas, Timotheus, and Bryaxis; painters included Polygnotus, Apollodorus, Zeuxis, Parrhasius, and Apelles. Aside from literary references, little is known about the actual work of these men. The style of the sculptors is adduced from fragments and Roman copies. Even less is known about the painters. From the vase paintings some reconstruction of the Greek school of mural painting is possible. With the conquests of Alexander the Great, Greek art entered its last great phase, the Hellenistic period. The importance of Athens gradually declined, and cultural centers rose at Pergamum, Rhodes, and Alexandria. Masterpieces of this period include the *Nike* (*Victory*) *of Samothrace* and *Aphrodite of Melos* (both: Louvre) and the *Pergamum Frieze* (Berlin Mus.). Especially charming among the minor arts are terra-cotta figurines from Tanagra. Marked tendencies toward heightening spatial illusionism are revealed in sculpture and, judging from Roman copies, prevailed also in painting (e.g., *Odyssey Landscapes,* Vatican). From the 2d cent. B.C. onward copies of former masterpieces of sculpture, which only approximate their prototypes, appear frequently along with vigorous group compositions closely related to the Pergamene school (e.g., *Laocoön and His Sons,* Vatican). Greek and Roman artists produced these copies of former masterpieces for private patrons or the Roman state and most of our knowledge of classical Greek art is derived from them. Although the inventive originality of Greek culture declined at this time, its influence remained of paramount importance during the Roman and Byzantine periods, and has continued to be an inspiring force throughout the history of Western culture. See also articles on individual artists, e.g., SCOPAS. See J. D. and A. B. Beazley, *Greek Sculpture and Painting* (1965); E. Homan-Wedeking, *Art of Archaic Greece* (1968); A. Liberman, *Greece, Gods, and Art* (1968); G. M. A. Richter, *Handbook of Greek Art* (5th ed. 1967); J. Charbonneaux, *Archaic Greek Art* (1971); John Boardman, *Greek Art* (rev. ed. 1973).

Greek Church: see ORTHODOX EASTERN CHURCH.

Greek fire, a flammable composition believed to have consisted of sulfur, naphtha, and quicklime. Although known in antiquity, it was first employed on a large scale by the Byzantines. Bronze tubes that emitted jets of liquid fire were mounted on the prows of their galleys and on the walls of Constantinople. The Byzantines in 673 and again in 717–18 destroyed two Saracen fleets with Greek fire.

Greek language, member of the Indo-European family of languages (see INDO-EUROPEAN). It is the language of one of the major civilizations of the world and of one of the greatest literatures of all time. By the 16th cent. B.C., Greek-speaking people were established in Greece, probably having come as invaders from the north. In antiquity there were a number of dialects of the Greek language, the most important of which were Aeolic, Arcadian, Attic, Cyprian, Doric, and Ionic. Ancient Greek was prevalent in the Balkan peninsula, the Greek islands, W Asia Minor, S Italy, and Sicily. Because of the political and cultural importance of Athens in the classical period of Greek history, the Athenian dialect, Attic, became dominant. From Attic there developed an idiom called the koinē, which means "common" or "common to all the people" and which became a standard form of Ancient Greek. After Alexander the Great the koinē developed into an international language that remained current in the central and E Mediterranean regions and in parts of Asia Minor and Africa for many centuries. Most of the New Testament was written in the koinē, which helped to gain a wide audience for Christianity. Byzantine Greek, based on the koinē, was the language of the Byzantine or East Roman Empire, which lasted from A.D. 395 until it was crushed by the Turks in 1453. The earliest surviving texts in Ancient Greek are of the 15th cent. B.C. and are written in a script known as Linear B, which was deciphered in 1953 by Michael VENTRIS. Later documents, including inscriptions and literary works, are written in the Greek alphabet, which was derived from the script of the Phoenicians c.9th cent. B.C. A variety of the Greek alphabet is still used today for the Greek language. Both the nouns and verbs of Ancient Greek were highly inflected. The verb had active, middle, and passive voices; indicative, subjunctive, optative, and imperative moods; singular, dual, and plural numbers; and many tenses. The noun had three genders (masculine, feminine, and neuter) and five cases (nominative, genitive, dative, accusative, and vocative). Unlike Latin, Greek had a word for the definite article. Three accents are used for Greek, the acute (´), the grave (`), and the circumflex (ˆ). In Ancient Greek they denoted a pitch accent related to the length of vowels, but in Modern Greek they serve as a stress accent. A symbol known as a rough breathing (ʻ) over an initial vowel represented the *h* sound in Ancient Greek, while the symbol for a smooth breathing (ʼ) over an initial vowel made clear the absence of aspiration. Though still retained today, the breathing marks no longer indicate pronunciation. In punctuation, the semicolon (;) stands for the question mark, and a raised dot (·) denotes the semicolon and colon. Modern Greek stems directly from the Attic koinē and dates from the fall of the Byzantine Empire in 1453 to the present. The official language of Greece and one of the official languages of Cyprus, Modern Greek is spoken today by about 10 million people, chiefly in Greece and the Greek islands (8 million speakers), Turkey (500,000), Cyprus (450,000), and the United States (400,000). The Greek language has not changed much in its long history. The differences are largely in pronunciation and vocabulary, but they also include divergences in grammar. Modern Greek, for example, has absorbed a number of loan words from Turkish and Italian, although its vocabulary is essentially that of Ancient Greek. However, the spoken form of Modern Greek differs markedly from the written form. The latter, referred to as *katharevousa,* is used by the government, the Greek Orthodox Church, the schools, and the mass media. It is much more like Ancient Greek than the former, which is called *dēmotikē. Dēmotikē* is the language of popular speech and is employed for conversation generally, although a literature in *dēmotikē* has recently developed. It has more foreign loan words and a simpler grammar than *katharevousa.* Many modern scientific and technical words in English and other Western languages are derived from Greek. It has been estimated that 12% of the English vocabulary is of Greek origin. See P. S. Costas, *An Outline of the History of the Greek Language* (1936); Edgar H. Sturtevant, *The Pronunciation of Greek and Latin* (2d ed. 1940); C. D. Buck, *Comparative Grammar of Greek and Latin* (3d ed. 1948) and *Greek Dialects* (rev. ed. 1955).

Greek-letter society: see FRATERNITY.

Greek literature, ancient. The Greek Isles are recognized as the birthplace of Western intellectual life. The earliest extant European literary works are the *Iliad* and the *Odyssey,* both written in ancient Greek probably before 700 B.C., and attributed to Homer. Among other early epic poems, most of which have perished, those of HESIOD, the first didactic poet, remain. The poems dealing with mythological subjects and known as the *Homeric Hymns* are dated 800–500 B.C. Only fragments survive of the works of many early Greek poets, including the elegiasts CALLINUS, TYRTAEUS, THEOGNIS, SOLON, PHOCYLIDES, SEMONIDES OF AMORGOS, ARCHILOCHUS, and HIPPONAX. The most personal Greek poems are the lyrics of ALCAEUS, SAPPHO, and ANACREON. The Dorian lyric for choral performance, developed with ALCMAN, IBYCUS, and STESICHORUS, achieved perfection in PINDAR, SIMONIDES OF CEOS and BACCHYLIDES. From the song and dance in the ceremonies honoring Dionysus at Athens, the drama evolved. Within a century tragedy was developed by three of the greatest playwrights in the history of the theater, AESCHYLUS, SOPHOCLES, and EURIPIDES. Equally exalted was the foremost exponent of Attic Old Comedy, ARISTOPHANES. Other writers who developed this genre included Cratinus and Eupolis, of whom little is known. The rowdy humor of these early works gave way to the more sedate Middle Comedy and finally to New Comedy, which set the form for this type of drama. The best-known writer of Greek New Comedy is MENANDER. The writing of history came of age in Greece with the rich and diffuse work of HERODOTUS, the precise and exhaustive accounts of THUCYDIDES, and the rushing narrative of XENOPHON. Philosophical writing of unprecedented breadth was produced during this brief period of Athenian literature; the works of PLATO and ARISTOTLE have had an incalculable effect in the shaping of Western thought. Greek oratory, of immense importance in the ancient world, was perfected at this time. Among the most celebrated orators were ANTIPHON, ANDOCIDES, LYSIAS, ISOCRATES, Isaeus, LYCURGUS, AESCHINES, and, considered the greatest of all, DEMOSTHENES. "Classical" Greek literature is said to have ended with the deaths of Aristotle and Demosthenes (c.322 B.C.). The greatest writers of the classical era have certain characteristics in common: economy of words, direct expression, subtlety of thought, and attention to form. The next period of Greek literature reached its zenith in Hellenistic Alexandria, where a number of major philosophers, dramatists, poets, historians, critics, and librarians wrote and taught. Hellenistic literature was imitative and specialized as to subject matter. It was appreciated less by Renaissance humanists than it is today. The poems of CALLIMACHUS, the bucolics of THEOCRITUS, and the epic of APOLLONIUS RHODIUS are now recognized as major works of world literature. The production of literary works just before and after the birth of Christ was enormous, but most were characterized by artificiality, pedantry, and self-consciousness. With the Roman political subjugation of Greece, Greek thought and culture, introduced largely by slave-tutors to the Roman aristocracy, came to exert enormous influence in the Roman world. Among the greatest writers of this period were the historians POLYBIUS, JOSEPHUS, and DION CASSIUS; the biographer, PLUTARCH; the philosophers PHILO and DION CHRYSOSTOM; and the novelist LUCIAN. Yet the conscious cultivation of Greek writing in general produced many works that seemed strained and precious. One great exception was the philosophical meditations of MARCUS AURELIUS. With the spread of Christianity, Greek writing took a new turn, and much of the writing of the Greek Fathers of the Church is eloquent. Religion dominated in the literature of the Byzantine Empire, and a vast treasury of writing was produced which is not generally well known to the West, with the exception of some historians (e.g., PROCOPIUS, ANNA COMNENA, George Acropolita, and Emperor JOHN VI) and some anthologists (e.g., Photius). The Loeb Classical Library offers text and translations of most of the extant ancient Greek literature. See W. W. Jaeger, *Paideia: The Ideals of Greek Culture* (3 vol., tr. 1943–45); Gilbert Highet, *The Classical Tradition* (1949); Moses Hadas, *A History of Greek Literature* (1950); Gilbert Murray et al., ed., *The Oxford Book of Greek Verse* (1954); Gilbert Murray, *The Literature of Ancient Greece* (3d ed. 1956); C. M. Bowra, *Ancient Greek Literature* (1960); H. D. F. Kitto, *Form and Meaning in Drama* (1956, repr. 1960); C. M. Bowra, *Greek Lyric Poetry from Alcman to Simonides* (rev. ed. 1961); H. J. Rose, *A Handbook of Greek Literature from Homer to the Age of Lucian* (4th ed. 1961); H. D. F. Kitto, *Poiesis: Structure and Thought* (1966); D. A. Campbell, ed., *Greek Lyric Poetry* (1967); John Ferguson, *A Companion to Greek Tragedy* (1972).

Greek literature, modern. Under Turkish rule, Greek literature virtually ceased, except in Crete. In the late 18th cent. two patriots, the poet Rhigas Pheraios (1751–98) and the intellectual Adamantios Koraës (1748–1833), sought to encourage a revival of Greek letters. The founding (1816) of the revolutionary society Philike Hetairea not only furnished the intellectual framework for the War of Independence (1821–27) but also spurred the postwar nationalist revival that awakened a modern Greek literature. Literature was hampered, however, by conflict between supporters of the demotic, or popular, literary style, and adherents of a reformed classical style. The Greeks had been completely cut off from the classical tradition by centuries of Turkish occupation and the successful revolution had created such pride in the new nation that there were many champions of a demotic style. Other hoped to restore the classical language which, until the 15th cent., had had an unbroken tradition. Throughout the rest of the 19th cent. and also in the 20th cent., the reformed classical and demotic styles were upheld by uncompromising adherents. Alexandros RANGABE was the outstanding literary figure of the classical trend. Demetrios Vernadakis (1834–1907) and Spyridon Vasiliadis (1845–74) were 19th-century dramatists who wrote romantic plays in classical speech forms. The demotic style, however, won increasing acceptance in all literary genres, particularly in poetry, which flourished above all other forms in modern Greek literature. The Ionian poets of the middle and late 19th cent. freely used the vernacular. Their leader was Dionysios Solomos (1798–1857), whose "Ode to Liberty" became the national anthem. Others were Andreas Kalvos (1796–1869), Andreas Lascaratos (1811–1901), the satirist Aristotle Valaoritis (1824–79), and the critic Jacob Polylas (1824–96). John Psiharis (1854–1929) aroused a storm with his satire of the purists, *The Voyage* (1888), and the publication in 1901 of a demotic translation of the New Testament caused a riot in Athens among university students. But the demotic has had the staunch support of such outstanding poets as Kostes PALAMAS; the classicist Constantine Cavafy (1863–1933); the popular George Drossinis (1859–1950); and the collector of folk poetry, Apostolos Melachrinos. The short stories of Alexandros Papadiantis (1851–1911) and Argyris Eftaliotis (1849–1933) expressed indigenous themes in the vernacular. Demotic dramatists include the naturalists Ioannis Kambisis (1872–1902) and Spyros Melos; the socialist Demetrios Tangopoulos (1867–1926); and the psychological dramatist Gregorios Xenopoulos (1867–1951), also an outstanding novelist. In 1927 the poet Angelos Sikelianos and his wife furthered the demotic cause with presentations at Delphi of classic Greek drama in the vernacular. In recent years Greek writers have been influenced by other European literary movements, notably the French. Symbolism appears in the work of George SEFERIS and George Kostiras and surrealism has an exponent in Odysseus Elytis. The effort of modern Greek writers to achieve a synthesis of the rich traditions of the Greek heritage is well represented in the work of Nikos KAZANTZAKIS. Seferis and Kazantzakis received the Nobel Prize in Literature. In 1967 the government of King Constantine II was overthrown in a bloodless coup by a group of army colonels; although the new regime policed the publishing industry and enforced strict newspaper censorship, antigovernment works still found their way into print. With the fall of the military government in 1974 civil liberties were restored and censorship ceased. See M. P. Gianes, ed., *Introduction to Modern Greek Literature* (1969); Willis Barnstone, ed., *Eighteen Texts: Writings by Contemporary Greek Authors* (1972); Kimon Friar, ed., *Modern Greek Poetry* (1973); and two histories of modern Greek literature by C. Th. Dimaras (1948, tr. 1973) and Linos Politis (1973).

Greek music. The music of ancient Greece was inseparable from poetry and dancing. It was entirely monodic, there being no harmony as the term is understood today. The earliest music is practically unknown to us, but in the Homeric era there existed a national musical culture looked upon by later generations as a "golden age." The chief instrument was the *phorminx,* a lyre used to accompany poet-singers who composed melodies from *nomoi,* short traditional phrases that were repeated. The earliest known musician was TERPANDER of Lesbos (7th cent. B.C.). The lyric art of Archilochus, Sappho, and Anacreon was also musical in nature. In the 6th cent. choral music was used in the drama, for which Pindar developed the classical ODE. The main instruments were at this time the *aulos,* a type of oboe associated with the cult of Dionysus, and the KITHARA, associated with Apollo and restricted to religious and hymnic use. This classical style of composition decayed in the last quarter of the 5th cent. After the fall of Athens in 404 B.C. there was an anti-intellectual reaction against the classical art, and it was almost forgotten by about 320 B.C. The new style, which resulted in the rise of professional musicians, was marked by subjective expression, free forms, more elaborate melody and rhythms, and chromaticism. The chief musical figures were Phrynis of Mitylene (c.450 B.C.), his pupil TIMOTHEUS of Miletus, and the dramatist Euripides. In the 4th cent. Plato described this muscial revolution in his *Laws* and *Republic.* The professionals developed solo instrumental music, and large massed choirs were popular in the huge theaters of the Hellenistic era. Finally, ancient Greek music lost its vitality and dwindled to insignificance under the Roman domination. There were two systems of MUSICAL NOTATION, a vocal and an instrumental, both of which are, though still problematic, decipherable, largely because of the *Introduction to Music* written by ALYPIUS (A.D. c.360). In spite of the prominent position of music in the cultural life of ancient Greece, only 15 musical fragments are extant, all of which are dated from the postclassical period. Early in its history Greek music benefitted from the discovery, usually attributed to Pythargoras of Samos, of the numerical relations of tones to divisions of a stretched string. The TEMPERAMENT, or Pythagorean tuning, derived from this series of ratios has been important throughout subsequent music history. Later theorists wrote about the science of harmonics, not as a part of musical art, but as a part of the mathematical view of the universe. ARISTOXENUS OF TARENTUM alone based his theories on musical practice. Practical music theory was based on the Greater Perfect System (a gamut of two octaves on the white keys of the piano from A above middle C down to the second A below middle C) and the Lesser Perfect System (the lowest octave of the Greater Perfect System plus B flat, middle C and D above it). A scale could be constructed by placing together two tetrachords—either diatonic, chromatic, or enharmonic (the latter using quarter-tones)—starting from any tone in the gamut. Thus, such scales, or *harmoniai,* were specific arrangements of tones and semitones within an octave compass, roughly corresponding to the modern concept of keys. An octave species was transposed to the kithara by tuning the strings so that they reproduced the intervallic relationships (but not the same pitches) of the octave species. This tuning of the kithara was called a *tonos.* The system of *harmoniai* and *tonoi* became so complicated by the time of Alypius that the whole concept lost significance for practical music. The Greeks invested much of their music with philosophical symbolism, as did the ancient Chinese. According to the Greek doctrines of *ethos* and *pathos* (character and feeling), the *harmoniai* were assigned certain ethical qualities. That is, because of melodic practices associated with a *harmonia,* it was considered to affect the character of a hearer in certain ways. This is discussed in Book III of Plato's *Republic,* but discussion and terminology vary with other writers. Greek music was subject to foreign domination for nearly two thousand years. In the 19th cent. a musical rebirth occurred with the works of the opera composers Nikolaos Mantzaros (1795–1872), Spyridion Xyndas (1812–96), and Spyros Samaras (1861–1917). Elements of nationalism are prevalent in the folklike songs of George Lambalet (1875–1945), Manos Hadjidakis, and Mikis Theodorakis. Introduced in Greece by Nikos Skalkottas (1904–49), SERIAL MUSIC has been composed by Yorgos Sisilianos and by Iannis XENAKIS, who also writes ELECTRONIC MUSIC. See Curt Sachs, *The Rise of Music in the Ancient World* (1943); Solon Michaelides, *The Neohellenic Folk-Music* (1948); E. A. Lippman, *Musical Thought in Ancient Greece* (1964).

Greek religion. Although its exact origins are lost in time, Greek religion is thought to date from about the period of the ARYAN invasions of the 2d millennium B.C. Those invaders encountered two other peoples who had existed in the region of Greece from Neolithic times: the Aegeans (Pelasgians) and the Minoans of Crete. The Aryans fused with the Aegean and Minoan cultures to create what is now considered Greek culture. The result, known as the Minoan-Mycenean civilization, flourished in the period from 1600 B.C. to 1400 B.C. Previous to the invasions, the Helladic communities had been widely separated geographically, but the attacking foreigners swept everything along in their path, including various beliefs that were prevalent in the outlying districts. At first the result was a confused conglomeration, but gradually a certain systematization of the gods began to take place. The marriage of Zeus, a sky god of the conquerors, and Hera, a fertility goddess of the conquered, symbolized the attempt at fusion, although the constant conflict between the divine pair, as seen in the *Iliad,* indicates the tensions of the match. The classical Greek pantheon was peopled with gods from all the cultures involved: Zeus the sky father, Demeter the earth mother, and Hestia, the virgin goddess of the hearth, were borrowed from the Indo-European invaders; Rhea was an indigenous Minoan goddess; Athena was Mycenean; Hera and Hermes were Aegean; Apollo was Ionian; Aphrodite came from Cyprus and Dionysus and Ares from Thrace. Just before the violent Doric invasions, the Achaeans fought the Trojans of Asia Minor. The chronicle of that war, the *Iliad,* furnishes the first clear picture of the early Greek religion as it evolved from a blending of Achaean, Dorian, Minoan, Egyptian, and Asian elements. This phase of Greek religion is called Homeric, after the author of the *Iliad,* or Olympian, after Mount Olympus, the Thessalian mountain where the gods dwelt. The early Egyptian influences represented by half-man, half-animal deities vanished, and the Olympians were purely anthropomorphic figures. Zeus was the supreme lord of the skies, retaining his original Aryan importance; he shared his dominion with his two chthonic and pre-Aryan brothers, Hades, lord of the underworld, and Poseidon, lord of the waters. Through a vast set of myths and legends (the clearest illustration is Hesiod's *Theogony*) the other gods and goddesses were carefully related to one another until a divine family was established with Zeus as its titular head. The Homeric pantheon was a tightly knit family group in charge of natural forces but not equal to the natural forces themselves. The gods had supernatural powers (particularly over human life), but their power was severely limited by a concept of fate (Moira) as the relentless force of destiny. The gods were not thought to be omnipresent, omniscient, or omnipotent. Shorn of the usual godly attributes, the Olympians often took on the property of being simply bigger than men, but not different or alien. The Olympians fought one another and often meddled in the affairs of men (this intervention was called the *deus ex machina,* or divine intervention). The superhuman features of the Olympians were their immortality and their ability to reveal the future to men. The Greeks did not consider immortality a particularly enviable property. Action was crucial and exciting by the very fact of life's brevity, and men were expected to perform by their own particular heroic arete, or virtue. Death was a necessary evil; the dead were impotent shades without consciousness, and there are only vague images of the Isles of the Blest in an Olympian world. The Greek, however, did expect information about his future life on earth from the gods. Thus divination was a central aspect of religious life (see ORACLE). The Olympians were, perhaps, most important in their role as civic deities, and each of the Greek city-states came to consider one or more of the gods as its particular guardian. There were public cults that were devoted to insuring the city against plague, conquest, or want. The religious festival became the occasion for a great assembly of citizens and foreigners. The civil strife that followed the classical period (from c.500 B.C.) placed the old gods on trial. Often the gods did not answer with the visible and immediate rewards that were expected. Although the Homeric gods had distinctive personalities, their reality still had to be accepted intellectually. This form of religion suited the sophisticated city dwellers, among whom there was even a strong monotheistic tendency; however, it did not meet the needs of the people of the provinces, the farmers and shepherds, who retained primitive notions steeped in superstition (see ANIMISM). Once the gods were placed on trial, the door was open for the popular religion of the Greek countryside. Since the gods could no longer be trusted to make life agreeable, an emphasis was placed on regeneration and on the afterlife. The MYSTERIES gained importance after Homeric religion was established, but the origins in the seasonal festivals that underlie many of them go back as far as 1400 B.C. The ELEUSINIAN MYSTERIES were perhaps the most widely practiced of the mysteries. Other popular rites were the mysteries of DIONYSUS and the ORPHIC MYSTERIES. In reaction to Dionysian excesses, Apollo eventually appropriated many of the virtues of the older gods, such as justice, harmony, legalism, and moderation. The tension between the Apollonian and Dionysian strains was particularly illustrated in the work of the tragic poets of Greece, the dramatists such as Aeschylus, Sophocles, and Euripides, who had begun to question the justice and integrity of the gods. It was in the area of philosophical thought that a clear-cut monism developed to augment and also shift Greek religious thought to a new type of speculation. The Greek philosophers sought a more rational and scientific approach in man's relation to nature, espousing a logical and important connection between man and nature, not a mysterious and secret one between man and god. It was Plato who made an absolute abstraction of the highest virtue, giving to that abstraction the quality of Absolute Good to which even the gods must be true. Philosophical inquiry led to the rationalization of myths and completed the destruction of the Homeric pantheon. The vacuum was eventually filled by Christianity. See M. P. Nilsson, *A History of Greek Religion* (tr. 1925, 2d ed. 1964); Gilbert Murray, *Five Stages of Greek Religion* (1925, repr. 1955); Werner W. Jaeger, *Paideia* (4 books in 3 vol., 1939–45, repr. 1960–62); H. J. Rose, *Ancient Greek Religion* (1946); W. K. C. Guthrie, *The Greeks and Their Gods* (1950, repr. 1956); Robert Graves, *The Greek Myths* (2 vol., 1955, repr. 1959); B. C. Dietrich, *The Origins of Greek Religion* (1974).

Greek revival: see CLASSIC REVIVAL.

Greeley, Horace, 1811–72, American newspaper editor, founder of the New York *Tribune,* b. Amherst, N.H. His irregular schooling, ending at 15, was followed by a four-year apprenticeship (1826–30) on a country weekly at East Poultney, Vt. When the paper failed, he went briefly to Erie co., Pa., where his impoverished farming family had moved. In Aug., 1831, he went to New York City, worked as a newspaper compositor, and in Jan., 1833, opened a job printing office in partnership with another printer. Greeley's great interest in public questions led him to found (1834), with a new partner, the *New Yorker,* a weekly journal "devoted to literature, the arts and sciences," which he edited ably but unprofitably for seven years. He supplemented his income by writing regularly for the *Daily Whig* and by editing Whig campaign sheets. His success in political journalism cemented Greeley's friendship with Whig leaders in New York state, and with their encouragement he issued the first number of the New York *Tribune* on April 10, 1841. He edited this paper for over 30 years; during much of that time it was the greatest single journalistic influence in the country. From the first, Greeley's object was to provide for the laboring classes a paper that was as cheap as those of his rivals but less sensational and more intelligent. Therefore, sensational police news and objectionable medical advertising were eliminated from the *Tribune.* Greeley's chief editorial assistant for 15 years after 1846 was Charles A. DANA. Beginning in 1849, George RIPLEY conducted for 30 years the first regular literary and book review department in a U.S. newspaper. Other talented men joined Greeley's staff (he was the first editor to allow by-lines), but his own clear, timely, vigorous editorials were the feature that made the *Tribune* known and quoted throughout the nation. Although Greeley styled both himself and his paper Whig, they were conservative only in so far as they thundered for a protective tariff. Other causes that Greeley promoted were hardly Whig-inspired. He advocated the organization of labor and led the way by organizing *Tribune* printers; New York printers elected (1850) him the first president of their chapel, the first in the nation. He also believed that a successful business should share its profits and ownership with its employees; this practice was observed at the *Tribune.* Among other social reforms advocated by Greeley were temperance, a homestead law, and woman's rights. He opposed all monopoly and disapproved of land grants to railroads, which he felt would lead to monopoly. He gave space in his paper to Fourierism when that movement was at its height and sponsored several experiments in cooperative living, including, later, the colony named for him at GREELEY, Colo. Even Karl Marx contributed to the *Tribune* from London. "Greeley's isms," as scoffers contemptuously called his plans for social reform, annoyed many *Tribune* readers, but he never apologized for them, and the paper continued to grow. After 1850 slavery overshadowed all other questions, and Greeley's antislavery views became more intense as the crisis approached. Some of his best editorials were directed against the Kansas-Nebraska Act. In this period the circulation (a total of 200,000 by 1860) of the weekly edition of the *Tribune* became so extensive in the rural districts of the West that Bayard Taylor could declare that it "comes next to the Bible." Everyone had heard and thousands had acted on his advice, "Go West, young man, go West." One of the first members of the new Republican party, he was a delegate to the national organizing convention in Feb., 1856. Barred as a New York delegate to the 1860 Republican convention, because of strained relations with the state leaders, he attended as a representative of Oregon. He was a leader in the successful fight to prevent Seward's nomination; and although at first favoring Edward Bates, he eventually threw his support to Abraham Lincoln. Seward had his revenge later by helping to block Greeley's election to the U.S. Senate (Greeley had served in the House of Representatives from Dec., 1848, to March, 1849). Greeley's course in the Civil War lost him many admirers. At first disposed to let the "erring sisters go in peace," he soon came around to vigorous support of the war. However, he persistently denounced Lincoln's policy of conciliating the border slave states. On Aug. 19, 1862, he published over his signature in the *Tribune* an open letter to the President, which he titled "The Prayer of Twenty Millions," demanding that Lincoln commit himself definitely to emancipation. Lincoln's reply (Aug. 22) "to an old friend, whose heart I have always supposed to be right" was masterly (see EMANCIPATION PROCLAMATION). Only reluctantly and belatedly did Greeley support Lincoln for reelection in 1864. The editor's humanitarian hatred of war led him to advocate peace negotiations of any sort, often to the embarrassment of the administration. In 1864, Lincoln sent him on what turned out to be a futile mission to Canada to treat with Confederate emissaries. After the war Greeley favored Negro suffrage and advocated amnesty for all Southerners. He was one of those who signed the bail bond to release Jefferson Davis from prison, and this magnanimous act cost him half the subscriptions to the *Weekly Tribune.* Greeley supported Ulysses S. Grant during the first years of his administration but came to resent what he considered Grant's subservience to that wing of the Republican party in New York state dominated by Roscoe Conkling. In 1871 he began to encourage the movement that grew into the LIBERAL REPUBLICAN PARTY and avidly sought the nomination for President in 1872. The new party's Cincinnati convention was cleverly stampeded toward Greeley, much to the disappointment of many of the reformers. Although the Democrats also endorsed him, many of them refused to support a man who had spent his life opposing the principles for which they had stood, especially that of a tariff for revenue only.

During the campaign all Greeley's shortcomings were caricatured, and he was denounced as a traitor and a crank. Despite his strenuous campaign he was overwhelmingly defeated by Grant. His disappointment at the result and his sorrow at the death of his wife a few days before the election unbalanced his mind, and he died insane on Nov. 29, 1872. Greeley wrote *The American Conflict* (1866), a history of the Civil War, and the autobiographic *Recollections of a Busy Life* (1868, repr. 1968). His other books, while interesting, were journalistic in character. See biographies by W. H. Hale (1950) and G. G. Van Deusen (1953, repr. 1964); Don C. Seitz, *Horace Greeley, Founder of the New York Tribune* (1926, repr. 1970); Ralph R. Fahrney, *Horace Greeley and the Tribune in the Civil War* (1936, repr. 1970); Jeter A. Isley, *Horace Greeley and the Republican Party, 1853–1861: A Study of the New York Tribune* (1947, repr. 1965).

Greeley, city (1970 pop. 38,902), seat of Weld co., N Colo., at the base of the Front Range of the Rocky Mts.; inc. 1885. It is a rail, trade, and processing center for a rich irrigated farm area. Greeley was founded (1870) by Horace Greeley through his agent, Nathan C. Meeker, as a cooperative farm and temperance colony. Meeker was killed in the Ute uprising of 1879; his home is now a museum. The city is the seat of the Univ. of Northern Colorado and a junior college. It has a symphony orchestra, a theater, and an art gallery. An annual rodeo is held there.

Greely, Adolphus Washington, 1844–1935, American army officer and arctic explorer, b. Newburyport, Mass. Entering the Union army at 17, he emerged a brevet major of volunteers at the end of the Civil War. In 1881, as a lieutenant in the regular army, Greely was given command of the Lady Franklin Bay Expedition to establish one of a chain of international circumpolar meteorological stations. Although he was without previous arctic experience, he and his party performed notable feats of exploration; many hitherto unknown miles along the coast of NW Greenland were added to the map, Ellesmere Island was crossed from east to west, and Lt. James B. Lockwood achieved a new northern record of 83°24′. Relief ships failed to reach Greely's party encamped at Cape Sabine; when the third relief vessel, under command of Capt. Winfield Scott Schley, arrived in 1884, all but Greely and six others had perished from starvation, drowning, or exposure. The survivors themselves were near death, and one died on the homeward journey. Greely's account of his tragic polar expedition is *Three Years of Arctic Service* (1886); another record is the diary of David L. Brainard, published as *Six Came Back* (ed. by B. R. James, 1940). Promoted chief signal officer and brigadier general in 1887 and later (1906) major general, Greely made a name for himself as builder of telegraphic communications for the army in Puerto Rico, Cuba, the Philippine Islands, and Alaska. He was director of relief operations after the San Francisco earthquake (1906). He retired in 1908. The Congressional Medal of Honor was awarded him in 1935. His writings include *Handbook of Alaska* (rev. ed. 1925) and *The Polar Regions in the Twentieth Century* (1928). See his autobiographical *Reminiscences of Adventure and Service* (1927); biography by William Mitchell (1936).

Green, Andrew Haswell, 1820–1903, American civic leader, b. Worcester, Mass. He read law under Samuel J. TILDEN and became his partner. Prominent in civic affairs of New York City, he held a number of offices, was largely responsible for much of the park system (notably Riverside Drive, Morningside, and Fort Washington parks), and accomplished financial reform. However, he is mainly remembered as the chief advocate of a plan to merge New York City and neighboring cities to make up Greater New York. He was chairman of the commission that in 1897 drew up the plan by which Greater New York was established in 1898. He also helped to bring about the union of the Astor and Lenox foundations into the New York Public Library with funds left by Tilden. See biography by John Foord (1913).

Green, Anna Katherine, 1846–1935, American detective-story writer, b. Brooklyn, N.Y., grad. Ripley Female College, Poultney, Vt., 1867. Of her many thrillers, characterized by logical construction and a knowledge of criminal law, *The Leavenworth Case* (1878) is the best known.

Green, Bartholomew, 1666–1732, early American printer, b. Cambridge, Mass.; the son of Samuel GREEN. He inherited his father's press in Cambridge in 1692 and moved it to Boston. He had the patronage of the government and of Harvard and became the foremost printer in New England. Except for four years Green printed the Boston *News-Letter,* the first American newspaper, from its inception in 1704 until his death. In 1722 he became its publisher also. His son-in-law, John Draper, succeeded to the *News-Letter.*

Green, Duff, 1791–1875, American journalist and politician, b. Woodford co., Ky. After service in the War of 1812, he settled in Missouri, where he became (1824) editor of the St. Louis *Enquirer.* He moved (1825) to Washington, D.C., purchased the *United States Telegraph,* and backed Andrew Jackson for President. After Jackson was elected (1828), Green's newspaper became the administration journal and Green was admitted to Jackson's Kitchen Cabinet. He backed John C. Calhoun against Jackson in the NULLIFICATION controversy, however, and thereafter he increasingly defended the South on the issues of slavery and the tariff. He left (1836) the *Telegraph,* and—having staunchly supported the Harrison-Tyler ticket in 1840—served Tyler on diplomatic missions to England (1843) and to Texas and Mexico (1844–45). He started (1844) in New York City the *Republic,* a newspaper devoted to tariff reduction and sympathetic toward the South. He became increasingly involved in Southern industrial development and railroad building. He had secured charters and funds for a Southern Pacific railroad and was about to start construction when the Civil War began. During the war he operated various ironworks for the Confederacy.

Green, George, 1793–1841, English mathematician and physicist. He was largely self-taught until, in 1833, he entered Caius College, Cambridge. In addition to making a number of contributions to the calculus, Green was especially interested in the equilibrium of fluids and was the first to introduce the potential in its application to the theories of the magnetic and electric fields. He also studied light and sound. His papers were edited, with a memoir, by N. M. Ferrers (1871).

Green, Henry, 1905–, English novelist, whose real name is Henry Vincent Yorke. For many years he worked as managing director of his family's industrial engineering business. His novels, with laconic titles such as *Party Going* (1939), *Nothing* (1950), and *Doting* (1952), are tantalizing and enigmatic. Viewing man's failures and inadequacies in an essentially comic light, Green achieves his unique effects through the techniques of a poet, relying on allusion, symbolism, and imagery. His most representative works are *Living* (1929), *Caught* (1943), *Loving* (1945), and *Concluding* (1948). See his autobiographical account *Pack My Bag* (1952); study by R. S. Ryf (1967).

Green, Hetty, 1835–1916, American financier, b. Henrietta Howland Robinson, New Bedford, Mass. She inherited a large fortune from her father and managed it so shrewdly that she was considered the greatest woman financier in the world. Extremely miserly during her lifetime, she left an estate valued at $100 million. See biography by Boyden Sparkes and S. T. Moore (1930); A. H. Lewis, *The Day They Shook the Plum Tree* (1963).

Green, John Richard, 1837–83, English historian, educated at Oxford. An Anglican clergyman, he became (1869) librarian of Lambeth Palace. His first historical work, *A Short History of the English People* (1874), was immediately popular and remains a work of high literary merit. As history it showed a marked emphasis on social rather than political change and stressed the significance of local events in the larger national picture. He expanded the *Short History* into a less popular four-volume *History of the English People* (1877–80). His later works were *The Making of England* (1882) and *The Conquest of England* (1883), which was edited by his widow, Alice Stopford Green. See biography by W. G. Addison (1946).

Green, Julian, 1900–, French writer, b. Paris, of American parentage. Except for the years from 1918 to 1922 and from 1940 to 1945, Green has lived in France. His novels, written in French, are somber psychological tales concerning vice and near madness. Among the best-known are *The Closed Garden* (1927, tr. 1928), *The Dark Journey* (1929, tr. 1929), *Midnight* (1936, tr. 1936), *Moira* (1950, tr. 1951), and *L'Autre* (1971, tr. 1973). His plays include *Sud* (1953), *L'Ennemi* (1954), and *L'Ombre* (1956). See his autobiography (1942); *Diary* (1964), a partial translation of the journal that he began keeping in the 1920s; studies by G. S. Burne (1971) and Samuel Stokes, Jr. (1955, repr. 1972).

Green, Matthew, 1696–1737, English poet. His one important poem, *The Spleen* (1737), marked by its wit, was in praise of the contemplative life.

Green, Paul, 1894–, American dramatist, b. Lillington, N.C., grad. Univ. of North Carolina, 1921. He is known for his realistic plays depicting the folk life of the South, especially that of the Negroes and the white tenant farmers. His first full-length play, *In Abraham's Bosom* (1926; Pulitzer Prize) was followed by such works as *The Field God* (1927), *The House of Connelly* (1931), *Johnny Johnson* (with music by Kurt Weill, 1936), and *Native Son* (with Richard Wright, 1941). Green also wrote symphonic outdoor dramas, short stories, and novels. His essays on the theater were collected in *The Hawthorn Tree* (1943), *Dramatic Heritage* (1953), and *Drama and the Weather* (1958). See his *Five Plays of the South* (1963); study by B. H. Clark (1974).

Green, Samuel, 1615–1702, early American printer. He established himself at Cambridge, Mass., in 1649, using a press owned by Henry Dunster, the first president of Harvard. Green succeeded Stephen DAYE and was the only printer in the colonies until 1665. The press that was sent to the colony in 1654 by the Society for the Propagation of the Gospel in New England was given to Green. He used it to produce his most famous imprints, John Eliot's Indian tracts and the Indian Bible. Green continued in business until 1692, when his son Bartholomew GREEN succeeded him; his imprints number nearly 300, among them editions of the *Bay Psalm Book* and *The Book of the General Lawes and Libertyes.*

Green, Samuel Swett, 1837–1918, American librarian, b. Worcester, Mass. Green was librarian of the Worcester, Mass., Free Public Library (1871–1909) and was a member of the Free Public Library Commission of Massachusetts from its beginning in 1890. One of the founders of the American Library Association, he was its president in 1891 and president of the World's Congress of Librarians at Chicago in 1893. Green promoted direct librarian assistance to users of library facilities. His writings include *The Public Library Movement in the United States, 1853–1893* (1913). See biography by R. K. Shaw (1926).

Green, Theodore Francis, 1867–1966, American politician, b. Providence, R.I. After studying law at Harvard and in Europe, he was admitted to the bar (1892) and practiced in Providence. Active in Democratic party politics, he held minor offices before being elected (1933) governor of Rhode Island. Green was first elected to the U.S. Senate in 1936 and served until his retirement in 1961 at the age of 93, the oldest Senator in history. From 1957 to 1959 he was chairman of the Senate Foreign Relations Committee. See biography by E. L. Levine (2 vol., 1963–71).

Green, Thomas Hill, 1836–82, English idealist philosopher. Educated at Oxford, he was associated with the university all his life. He was professor of moral philosophy there from 1878 until his death. In his *Introduction to Hume's Treatise on Human Nature* (1874), Green struck a heavy blow at traditional British empiricism. Rejecting sensationalism, he argued that all reality lies in relations, that relations exist only for a thinking consciousness, and that therefore the world is constituted by mind. In his *Prolegomena to Ethics* (1883) Green submitted an ethics of self-determination, which he epitomized in the phrase "Rules are made for man and not man for rules." Self-determination is present when man is conscious of his own desires, and freedom occurs when man identifies himself with what he considers morally good. Green's ethics are believed to have influenced, among others, John Dewey and Alfred North Whitehead. Politically, Green was a liberal; he asserted that government must represent general will and that when it fails to do so it should be changed. See his *Lectures on the Principles of Political Obligation* (1895). See also studies by Y. L. Chin (1920), J. C. McKirachan (1941), Melvin Richter (1964), and A. K. Mukhopadhyay (1967).

Green, William, 1872–1952, American labor leader, president of the American Federation of Labor (1924–1952), b. Coshocton, Ohio. He rose through the ranks of the United Mine Workers of America, of which organization he was (1912–24) secretary-treasurer. With backing from John L. Lewis, Green was elected president of the American Federation of Labor (AFL) to succeed Samuel Gompers. He led the organization of skilled labor into craft unions and gradually built up AFL membership. After eight of the largest unions split away (1935) under the leadership of John L. Lewis and formed the Committee for Industrial Organization (CIO) to organize workers in industrial unions, Green led the AFL in the subsequent struggle with the CIO. He set forth his philosophy in *Labor and Democracy* (1939). Green was succeeded as president of the AFL by George Meany. See AMERICAN FEDERATION OF LABOR AND CONGRESS OF INDUSTRIAL ORGANIZATIONS.

green algae: see ALGAE; CHLOROPHYTA.

Greenaway, Kate, 1846-1901, English illustrator and watercolorist. She is famous for her fanciful, humorous, delicately colored drawings of child life. She influenced children's clothing and the illustrating of children's books and was often imitated, though never successfully. Among the books for which she provided text as well as illustrations are *Under the Window* (1879), *A Day in a Child's Life* (1881), *Kate Greenaway's Birthday Album,* and *The Language of Flowers* (1885). See *The Kate Greenaway Treasury* ed. by Edward Ernest (1967).

greenback, in U.S. history, legal tender notes unsecured by specie (coin). In 1862, under the exigencies of the Civil War, the U.S. government first issued legal tender notes (popularly called greenbacks) that were placed on a par with notes backed by specie. By the end of the war such notes were outstanding to the amount of more than $450 million. They had been issued as temporary, and in accordance with the Funding Act of 1866 Secretary of State Hugh MCCULLOCH began retiring them. The hard times of 1867 caused many, especially among Western debtor farmers, to demand that the currency be inflated rather than contracted, and Congress suspended the retirement. George H. PENDLETON advanced the so-called Ohio Idea, recommending that all government bonds not specifying payment in specie should be paid in greenbacks. John SHERMAN, more conservative, was nevertheless willing to let the greenbacks stay in circulation on a redemption basis. The question was warmly debated in 1869 and was ended by a compromise, which left greenbacks to the amount of $356 million in circulation. The law creating them was declared constitutional in the later LEGAL TENDER CASES, and the matter rested until the Panic of 1873. The hard-hit agrarians then wanted to inflate the currency with more greenbacks. An inflation bill passed Congress in 1874, but so intense was conservative opposition that President Grant reversed his former position and vetoed the bill. Although the Greenback party worked hard to oppose them, the conservatives triumphed in Jan., 1875, with the Resumption Act, which fixed Jan. 1, 1879, as the date for redeeming the greenbacks in specie. The Secretary of the Treasury accumulated a gold reserve of $100 million, and confidence in the government was so great that few greenbacks were presented for surrender in 1879. Congress provided in 1878 that the greenbacks then outstanding ($346,681,000) remain a permanent part of the nation's currency. See Wesley Clair Mitchell, *A History of the Greenbacks* (1903, repr. 1960); D. C. Barrett, *The Greenbacks and the Resumption of Specie Payments, 1862-1879* (1931, repr. 1965); I. Unger, *Greenback Era* (1964).

Greenback party, in U.S. history, political organization formed in the years 1874-76 to promote currency expansion. The members were principally farmers of the West and the South; stricken by the Panic of 1873, they saw salvation in an inflated currency that would wipe out the farm debts contracted in times of high prices. They were opposed by the conservatives, who managed to get the Resumption Act of 1875 passed. The Greenbackers had in 1874 hoped to capture the Democratic party, but the nomination of Samuel J. Tilden killed that hope, and the Greenback party nominated Peter COOPER as its own candidate for President in 1876. The Greenbackers got only 81,737 votes. In 1878, however, certain labor organizations, embittered by the labor troubles in 1877, united with the advocates of cheap money in the Greenback-Labor party, and the combination party polled over 1 million votes and elected 14 Representatives to Congress that year. The Greenbackers' hopes for 1880 were high, and bidding for wider support they broadened their program by endorsement of woman suffrage, federal regulation of interstate commerce, and a graduated income tax. For the presidency in 1880 the party nominated its most notable figure, Gen. James B. WEAVER, but the return of prosperity, the passage of the BLAND-ALLISON ACT (1878), and the success of the Resumption Act had allayed the discontent on which the party had grown, and the Greenback-Labor vote declined in 1880 to just a little over 300,000. When the candidate in 1884, Gen. Benjamin Franklin BUTLER (1818-93), did very badly, the party dissolved. Some members joined the Union Labor party in 1888, but more of them went back to the old parties. Later many Greenbackers, among them Weaver and Ignatius Donnelly, became leading figures in the Populist party.

Green Bay, city (1970 pop. 87,809), seat of Brown co., NE Wis., at the mouth of the Fox River on Green Bay; inc. 1854. One of the best Great Lakes harbors and a railroad center, Green Bay is a port of entry, with heavy shipping and a large wholesale and jobbing trade. Its industries include papermaking, food and dairy processing, and machine building. Jean Nicolet established a trading post on the site of Green Bay in 1634; many notable French explorers and missionaries followed. The permanent settlement, the oldest in the state, dates from 1701. The key to the Fox-Wisconsin water route and thus the gateway to the Midwest, Green Bay became a fur-trading center and was occupied successively by the French (1717), the British (1761), and the Americans (1816). With the settlement of the Old Northwest after the War of 1812 and the decline of the fur trade, Green Bay became the trade center of a lumber and farm area. Of interest are the National Railroad Museum and many historical buildings, including the Tank Cottage (1776). A branch of the Univ. of Wisconsin is in the city, which is also the home of the Green Bay Packers professional football team.

Green Bay, western arm of Lake Michigan, c.100 mi (160 km) long and from 10 to 20 mi (16-32 km) wide, NE Wis. and NW Mich.; separated from the lake by the Door Peninsula. The Fox River flows into the head of the bay at Green Bay, Wis., a port city. The southern part of the bay is frozen from December to May.

Greenbelt, city (1970 pop. 18,199), Prince Georges co., W central Md., a residential suburb of Washington, D.C.; chartered 1937. Greenbelt was planned and built by the Federal government as an experimental model community. The huge National Agricultural Research Center surrounds the city on two sides, and the NASA Goddard Space Flight Center is nearby.

Greenberg, Clement, 1909-, American art critic, b. New York City. Greenberg's criticism is primarily concerned with art produced after ABSTRACT EXPRESSIONISM. This art he has termed POST-PAINTERLY ABSTRACTION, reflecting Heinrich Wölfflin's theory that painterly and linear styles alternate through the ages. In *Art and Culture* (1961), a collection of essays, Greenberg argues that the essence of modern art, especially painting, lies in its purely visual content.

Greenberg, Joseph Harold, 1915-, American anthropologist, b. New York City, grad. Columbia (A.B., 1936) and Northwestern Univ. (Ph.D., 1940). From 1948 to 1962 he was a professor of anthropology at Columbia. In 1962 he became a member of the faculty of Stanford Univ. His major areas of study are the classification of African languages and the ethnology of Africa. Among his writings are *The Languages of Africa* (1963), *Anthropological Linguistics* (1968), and *Language, Culture, and Communication* (1971).

greenbottle fly: see BLOWFLY.

greenbrier: see SMILAX.

Greendale, village (1970 pop. 15,089), Milwaukee co., SE Wis., a suburb of Milwaukee; inc. 1938. Automotive and machine parts are produced. Greendale is one of three original Greenbelt planned communities built by the Federal government in the 1930s.

Greene, Evarts Boutell, 1870-1947, American historian, b. Kobe, Japan, where his parents were missionaries, grad. Harvard (B.A., 1890; Ph.D., 1893). In 1894 he began teaching American history at the Univ. of Illinois, where from 1906 to 1913 he was also dean of the college of arts and literature. Called to Columbia in 1923, Green was appointed (1926) the first De Witt Clinton professor of history and held that chair until his retirement in 1939. From 1936 to 1939 he also served as chairman of the Institute of Japanese Studies at Columbia. Greene was a noted authority on the colonial and Revolutionary periods of American history. His principal works were *The Provincial Governor in the English Colonies of North America* (1898); *The Government of Illinois: Its History and Administration* (1904); *Provincial America, 1690-1740* ("American Nation" series, 1905, repr. 1964); *The Foundations of American Nationality* (1922; rev. ed. 1935, repr. 1968); *A New Englander in Japan: Daniel Crosby Greene* (1927), a biography of his father; *A Guide to the Principal Sources for Early American History (1600-1800) in the City of New York* (with Richard B. Morris, 1929); *American Population before the Federal Census of 1790* (with Virginia D. Harrington, 1932, repr. 1953); *Religion and the State: The Making and Testing of an American Tradition* (1941); and *The Revolutionary Generation, 1763-1790* ("History of American Life" series, Vol. IV, 1943, repr. 1971).

Greene, Graham, 1904-, English novelist and playwright. Although in most of his works he combines elements of the detective story, the spy thriller, and the psychological drama, his novels are essentially parables of the damned. Greene's heroes, like those of Dostoyevsky, realize their sins and achieve salvation only through great pain and soul-searching agony. A Roman Catholic convert, he is intensely concerned with the moral problems of man in relation to God. Some of his novels have been ranked as thrillers, and Greene himself calls such works as *Orient Express* (1942) and *The Ministry of Fear* (1943) "entertainments" to distinguish them from his more serious efforts. His four major works, *Brighton Rock* (1938), *The Power and the Glory* (1940), *The Heart of the Matter* (1948), and *The End of the Affair* (1951), mark him as a novelist of high distinction. Greene is a superb journalist, and many of his novels are set in sites of topical journalistic interest; e.g., *The Quiet American* (1955) is set in French Indochina; *Our Man in Havana* (1958), in pre-Castro Cuba; *A Burnt-Out Case* (1961), in the Congo just before its independence from Belgium; *The Comedians* (1966), in François Duvalier's Haiti; and *The Honorary Consul* (1973), in Argentina. His fine sense of comedy is displayed in the short-story collection *May We Borrow Your Husband?* (1967) and the novel *Travels with My Aunt* (1969). Greene is also the author of several plays, including *The Living Room* (1953) and *The Potting Shed* (1957), both thinly disguised religious dramas, and *The Complaisant Lover* (1959), a witty and intelligent play about marriage and infidelity. He is also noted for his short stories, essays, film criticism, and film scripts, including the mystery melodrama *The Third Man* (1950). Written when he was a young man, Greene's biography of John Wilmot, 2d earl of Rochester, *Lord Rochester's Monkey,* was published in 1974. See his autobiography, *A Sort of Life* (1971); studies by D. J. Lodge (1966), J. A. Atkins (rev. ed. 1966), and F. L. Kunkel (rev. ed. 1973).

Greene, Nathanael, 1742-86, American Revolutionary general, b. Potowomut (now Warwick), R.I. An iron founder, he became active in colonial politics and served (1770-72, 1775) in the Rhode Island assembly. At the beginning of the American Revolution he commanded a detachment of militia at the siege of Boston and was in charge of the city after the British evacuation (1776). Greene helped plan the defense of New York (1776), but illness kept him from the battle of Long Island. He was with Washington (1776-77) at Trenton, Brandywine, GERMANTOWN, and Valley Forge. In Feb. 1778, he became quartermaster general while still holding his field command; he reorganized the department, found supplies for the army, and rendered fine service in this capacity. His notable ability at organization also appeared in his field work. He fought (1778) at Monmouth and in the Rhode Island campaign and was president (1780) of the court-martial board that sentenced Major John André. After Gates was defeated at Camden (1780), Greene became the commander in the CAROLINA CAMPAIGN. He reorganized the Southern army, and he and his lieutenants (notably Daniel MORGAN and Henry LEE), with aid of partisan bands under Francis MARION, Thomas Sumter, and Andrew PICKENS, turned the tide in Carolina. Greene's forces were defeated at Guilford Courthouse, Hobkirks Hill, and Eutaw Springs, but each time the British victory was reversed, and he pushed south to surround Charleston until the British evacuated it (1782). The campaign is generally considered an example of excellent strategy, and Greene's generalship is much admired. To get supplies for the Continental Army, Greene often had been forced to endorse personal notes. After the war the dishonesty of a contractor forced him to sell his estates to honor those pledges. The people of Georgia, however, gave him a plantation. See biographies by his grandson, G. W. Greene (3 vol., 1867-71), and T. G. Thayer (1960); William Johnson, *Sketches of the Life and Correspondence of Nathanael Greene* (1822, repr. 1973).

Greene, Robert, 1558?-1592, English author. His short romances, written in the manner of Lyly's *Euphues,* include *Pandosto* (1588), from which Shakespeare drew the plot for *A Winter's Tale,* and *Menaphon* (1589). His best plays, *Friar Bacon and Friar Bungay* (1594) and *The Scottish History of James IV* (1598), are a potpourri of romance, fantasy, and history. He wrote numerous tracts and pamphlets reflecting his knowledge of the London underworld as well as his own bohemian life. An alleged attack on Shakespeare—one of the earliest references to the man—is in Greene's *Groatsworth of Wit Bought with a Million of Repentance* (1592). *A Quip for an Upstart Courtier* (1592), a social allegory, is considered his best pamphlet. Greene's short life ended in dire poverty. After his death he became the subject of a heated quarrel between Gabriel HARVEY and Thomas NASHE. See his *Life and Complete Works* (ed. by A. B. Grosart, 15 vol., 1881–86; repr. 1964).

Greeneville, town (1970 pop. 13,722), seat of Greene co., NE Tenn., in a tobacco, dairy, and cattle area; founded 1783, inc. 1903. It is a leading tobacco market and has plants that produce televisions and radios, gas pumps, lock sets, and condensed milk. In 1785, Greeneville succeeded Jonesboro as the capital of the State of Franklin (see FRANKLIN, STATE OF); a replica of the log cabin capitol is in the city. Andrew Johnson's home, tailor shop, and grave are in Andrew Johnson National Monument. In the courthouse square are monuments to Gen. John H. Morgan, who was killed there in the Civil War, and to Union soldiers. Tusculum College is in Greeneville, and a tobacco experiment station of the Univ. of Tennessee College of Agriculture and a state hospital and school for the handicapped are nearby. David Crockett was born at Limestone, to the northeast.

Greenfield. 1 Town (1970 pop. 18,116), seat of Franklin co., NW Mass., at the confluence of the Deerfield and Green rivers, near their junction with the Connecticut; settled 1686, set off from Deerfield and inc. 1753. It is an industrial center in a prosperous agricultural area. The first cutlery factory in the United States was established there in the early 1800s. Other products include silverware, electronic components, lumber, and paper and wooden boxes. The town, the eastern terminus of the Mohawk Trail, was ravaged by Indian attacks until 1735. It has a junior college and a historical museum. Asher Benjamin was born in Greenfield, and several buildings designed by him remain. Poet's Seat Tower provides a spectacular view of the town. **2** City (1970 pop. 24,424), Milwaukee co., SE Wis., a residential suburb of Milwaukee; inc. 1957.

Greenfield Village, reproduction of an early American village, est. 1933 by Henry Ford at Dearborn, Mich., as part of the Edison Institute. A white-spired church, a town hall, an inn, a school, a courthouse, a general store, and other buildings are grouped about a typical New England village green. Many of the structures were brought from their original location; others are reconstructions. Among them are Thomas Edison's Menlo Park workshop and his Fort Myers laboratory, a William McGuffey group including a school in which classes are regularly held, Noah Webster's birthplace, Stephen Foster's home, Luther Burbank's birthplace and office, and the Wright brothers' cycle shop and home. There are also mills and craft shops that illustrate early methods of production. The village has a blacksmith shop, a cobbler's shop, and a tintype studio. Nearby is the Henry Ford Museum, which has a large collection of Americana.

greenfly: see APHID.

greenhouse, enclosed glass house used for growing plants in regulated temperatures, humidity, and ventilation. A greenhouse can range from an unheated small room, carrying a few plants over the winter, to an immense heated glass building, or hothouse, covering acres of ground and used for forcing fruits or flowers out of season. Greenhouses have long been used for holding plants over cold seasons and to some extent for growing tropical plants and hothouse fruit, but only in this century has the greenhouse been used for forcing vegetables. Now millions of dollars' worth of plant products are raised yearly in greenhouses. See COLD FRAME. See Alex Laurie et al., *Commercial Flower Forcing* (6th ed. 1958); Harry Ibbotson, *Build Your Own Greenhouse* (rev. ed. 1965); H. T. and R. T. Northen, *Greenhouse Gardening* (2d ed. 1973).

greenhouse effect, process whereby heat is trapped at the surface of the earth by the atmosphere. Visible light from the sun passes through the atmosphere and is absorbed by the earth, warming the surface and providing energy for all life activities. Much of the incoming light energy is reradiated, directly or as a result of metabolism in living organisms, in the form of heat, i.e., infrared radiation. However, while the carbon dioxide, ozone, water vapor, and clouds of the atmosphere let incoming light energy through to the earth's surface, they keep the outbound infrared from leaving and actually reemit much of it back down to the ground. Thus, the atmosphere acts like a greenhouse. During the past century the combustion of enormous amounts of fossil fuels has raised the carbon dioxide content of the air 5% to 10%, leading some authorities to predict a long-term warming of the earth's climate. Others, predicting a cooling trend, contend that particulate matter entering the atmosphere from AIR POLLUTION will block out more incoming solar radiation and so counteract the heat-trapping action of carbon dioxide.

Greenland, Dan. *Grønland,* the largest island in the world (1969 est. pop. 46,000), c.840,000 sq mi (2,175,600 sq km), part of the kingdom of Denmark, lying largely within the Arctic Circle. It is surrounded by the Arctic Ocean in the north; the Greenland Sea in the east; the Denmark Strait in the southeast, which separates it from Iceland; the Atlantic Ocean in the south; and Davis Strait and Baffin Bay in the west, which separate it from Baffin Island, Canada. Greenland is 1,659 mi (2,670 km) long from Cape Farewell (lat. 59°46'N) to Cape Morris Jesup (lat. 82°39'N) and has a maximum width of about 800 mi (1,290 km). Geologically, the island is part of the Canadian Shield and, therefore, of North America; more than 50% of its ice-free area consists of rocks of the Precambrian era, mostly granites and gneisses. Mountain chains parallel Greenland's east and west coasts; Mt. Gunnbjørn (12,139 ft/3,700 m) and Mt. Forel (11,024 ft/3,360 m), both in SE Greenland, are the highest peaks. The entire coastline of Greenland is deeply indented by fjords. There are many offshore islands, of which Disko island, W Greenland, is the largest. Except for about 132,000 sq mi (341,880 sq km) of coastland and coastal islands, an ice sheet covers the island. The extreme northern peninsula (Peary Land) has no ice cap. Recent surveys indicate that the thickness of the ice sheet reaches c.14,000 ft (4,300 m) in some places; in a joint U.S.-Danish operation at Camp Century in the northwestern part of the ice sheet, a 4,560-ft (1,390-m) hole was drilled completely through the ice cap. Studies of the ice cores have permitted new insights into the climatic history of the last 100,000 years. The ice moves outward from the center, entering the sea in walls or debouching in glaciers, of which Humboldt Glacier is the largest. These rapidly moving glaciers calve tremendous icebergs, notably into the Davis Strait, through which they frequently reach the Atlantic ship lanes. Cold winds rush out from Greenland's interior, making the weather uncertain and foggy. A polar ocean current flows south along the entire east coast and around Cape Farewell, carrying immense ice flows that make the sea approach to E Greenland hazardous. The North Atlantic Drift gives the southwest coast of Greenland a warmer climate and heavy rainfall. More than 90% of the island's population live along the west coast. There are no forests in Greenland; dwarf trees are found in the southern coastal areas. Natural vegetation also includes mosses, lichens, grasses, and sledges.

Administration and Economy. A Danish colony until 1953, Greenland is now governed through several agencies. The Danish ministry for Greenland (est. 1955) is responsible for general administration and for control of trade. In Greenland itself, the ruling authorities are the governor and the provincial council. Greenland sends two representatives to the Danish Folketing. Godthåb is the capital. Other important settlements are Holsteinborg, Egedesminde, Julianehåb, Sukkertoppen, and Jakobshavn. About 10% of the people are European; the others are of mixed Eskimo and Danish ancestry. Fishing (cod, shrimp, halibut, and salmon) is the main industry, and dozens of processing plants have been constructed in the southern and southwestern areas. Some of the world's largest shrimp beds are in Disko Bay. Sealing is also important along the southeast and northwest coasts; about 40,000 seals are caught annually. There is extensive sheep breeding in the southern area. The only large-scale mining operation has been for cryolite at Ivigtut. This mine, the largest cryolite mine in the world, has now been exhausted, although an aboveground stockpile will continue to supply normal shipments for some time. Molybdenum, uranium, and coal are also found in Greenland. The polar bear, musk ox, polar wolf, lemming, Arctic hare, and reindeer are the chief land animals. Sea birds are hunted for their flesh, eggs, and down.

History and Change. Known in ancient times by the Greeks and later by the Irish, Greenland was discovered and colonized (c.982) by Eric the Red, a Norseman, who named it Greenland in order to make it seem attractive to potential settlers. It was in sailing to Greenland (c.1000) that Leif Ericsson, the son of Eric the Red, probably reached North America. Greenland became a bishopric c.1110, and ruins of churches of that period remain. By the 12th cent. the population numbered some 10,000. Greenland became self-governing, with its own Althing, but failed to achieve political stability. In 1261 the colony came under Norwegian rule, but in the 14th and 15th cent. it was neglected, and the colonists either died out or assimilated with the Eskimos. The British explorers Martin Frobisher and John Davis rediscovered Greenland in the 16th cent. but found no trace of Norsemen. Other explorers looking for the NORTHWEST PASSAGE subsequently charted much of the coast. Modern colonization was begun (1721) by the Norwegian missionary Hans Egede. Danish trading posts were established shortly afterward, and colonization was furthered by deporting undesirable subjects to Greenland. Soon, the native Greenlanders began to suffer from European diseases. Tuberculosis remains a problem. In 1815, at the Congress of Vienna, Denmark retained the colony through an oversight of the delegates, who detached Norway from Denmark, but forgot to mention the outlying Norwegian possessions. In the 19th and 20th cent. Greenland was explored and mapped by numerous arctic explorers. In World War II, after the German occupation (1940) of Denmark, the United States invoked the Monroe Doctrine for Greenland and reached an agreement (1941) with the Danish minister at Washington which permitted the establishment of U.S. military bases and meteorological stations. A Danish-American agreement for the common defense of Greeland was signed in 1951, and U.S. bases were retained, notably at Thule. In recent years Greenland has made great economic progress. A more specialized economy, based on trade, has been replacing the old subsistence economy, and the population has grown rapidly. Denmark has taken much interest in the country and, in addition to allowing a measure of self-government and implementing economic development, has provided free medical care and modern schools. See Vilhjalmur Stefansson, *Greenland* (1942); Gwyn Jones, *The Norse Atlantic Saga* (1964); Finn Gad, *The History of Greenland From Earliest Times to 1700* (Vol. I, tr. 1971); Erik Erngaard, *Greenland Then and Now* (1972).

Greenland Sea, arm of the Arctic Ocean, off the northeast coast of Greenland. It is the main outlet of the Arctic Ocean to the Atlantic. Because of drifting arctic ice, the northern part is rarely open to navigation. Jan Mayen island is there.

Greenland whale: see RIGHT WHALE.

Greenleaf, Simon, 1783–1853, American legal writer, b. Newburyport, Mass. A member of the Maine bar, he won a high reputation for legal scholarship early in his career. With the admission (1820) of Maine as a state, he was elected to a term in the legislature and was appointed reporter of the Maine supreme court. In 1833 he resigned this position and accepted the invitation of Joseph Story to become a professor of law at Harvard. Much of the excellence of Harvard Law School is attributed to these two men. Greenleaf's *Treatise on the Law of Evidence* (3 vol., 1842–53) for many years was the standard American work on the subject. Another text used for many years was his revision (5 vol., 1849–50) of William Cruise's *Digest of the Law of Real Property.*

greenling, common name for any of several species of the genus *Hexagrammos,* carnivorous, spiny-finned fishes of the family Hexagrammidae, common in the Pacific Ocean, especially in the waters N of Monterey, Calif. Greenlings have fleshy flaps on the top of the head. They are found in kelp beds and among rocks and are also called rock trout. Several species grow to a length of 20 in. (50 cm) and are valued as game fishes. Most important of the greenlings is the Atka mackerel, found near the Aleutian Islands, a handsome food fish with striking vertical stripes. The kelp greenling is unusual in that the male and female exhibit different coloration and markings, a rare phenomenon among fish. Greenlings are classified in the phylum CHORDATA, subphylum Vertebrata, class Osteichthyes, order Perciformes, family Hexagrammidae.

Green Mountain Boys, popular name of armed bands formed (c.1770) under the auspices of Ethan ALLEN in the Green Mountains of what is today Vermont. Their purpose was to prevent the NEW HAMPSHIRE GRANTS, as Vermont was then known, from becoming part of New York, to which it had been awarded by the British. Land speculators, such as Allen and his brothers, and settlers banded together in armed groups to defend their lands. Their methods were threat, intimidation, and actual violence against the New Yorkers, and they managed to keep the region free from New York control, establishing (1777) instead a separate government that ultimately achieved (1791) statehood for Vermont. In the American Revolution the Green Mountain Boys figured prominently in 1775, when, under Allen's leadership, they captured Ticonderoga. In 1777 Seth

Warner and John STARK led them to victory at Bennington—one of the notable achievements of the revolutionaries in the Saratoga campaign.

Green Mountains, range of the Appalachian Mts., extending 250 mi (402 km) from north to south, mainly in Vt. and extending into W Mass. and S Que., Canada. Mt. Mansfield, 4,393 ft (1,339 m) high, in Vermont, is the tallest peak. Composed of some of the oldest rocks in North America, the range has low, rounded peaks, fertile valleys, and streams that have furnished water power for many years. Timber and maple syrup are the main products of the heavily forested mountains, much of whose area is in national and state forests. The mountains also yield high-quality marble and granite, with world-famous quarries in Barre, Vt. The scenic Green Mts. are a year-round resort area. The Long Trail for hikers runs 261 mi (420 km) from Massachusetts to Canada; the Appalachian Trail runs through the southern part of the Green Mts.

Greenock (grĕn'ək, grĭn'-, grĕn'-), burgh (1971 pop. 69,004), Renfrewshire, W Scotland, on the Firth of Clyde. Greenock is a port, and shipping and shipbuilding are important industries. Others include engineering, textile manufacturing, sugar refining, and the production of office equipment. Greenock is the birthplace of James Watt, who is commemorated by Watt Institution and a statue by Sir Francis Chantrey. Robert Burns's "Highland Mary" (Mary Campbell) was buried in the cemetery of North Kirk. The church (founded 1591) with windows by William Morris, Edward Burne-Jones, D. G. Rossetti, and Ford Madox Brown, was removed to nearby Seafield to make room for expanding shipyards. In 1975, Greenock became part of the new Strathclyde region.

Greenough, Horatio (grē'nō), 1805–52, American sculptor and writer, b. Boston, grad. Harvard, 1824, and studied in Italy under Thorvaldsen. A protégé of Washington Allston, he was a man of ideas in advance of his time. His colossal statue of Washington, commissioned for the Capitol, was too heavy for the floor and was set up on the grounds; it was later placed in the Smithsonian Institution. *The Rescue* is on the east stairway of the Capitol. Greenough is admired now for his writings, in which he heralded the modern concept of functionalism in architecture. See his *Travels, Observations, and Experiences of a Yankee Stonecutter* (1852); his letters (ed. by Nathalia Wright, 1972); his collected writings, *Form and Function* (1958).

Green Revolution, popular term referring mainly to the tremendous increases in cereal-grain production in certain underdeveloped areas—especially India, Pakistan, and the Philippines in the late 1960s—through the cultivation of hybrid strains by new techniques; also used to refer to the social and economic changes wrought by the new agricultural practices in those countries. Beginning in Mexico in the mid-1940s, multidisciplined research in plant physiology and genetics, plant pathology, entomology, soil fertility, and cereal biochemistry led to the development of short-strawed, high-yielding, disease-resistant, nutritious varieties of wheat, rice, and maize that make efficient use of artifical fertilizer and irrigation. With the new cereals, agronomists also introduced new crop strategies and harvesting methods. Foremost among the scientists contributing to the Green Revolution has been American agronomist Norman E. BORLAUG, who was awarded the 1970 Nobel Peace Prize for his efforts in helping to solve the world's food problems.

Green River. 1 River, 370 mi (595 km) long, rising in central Ky. and flowing generally NW, through Mammoth Cave National Park, to the Ohio River near Evansville, Ind. Locks make the Green River navigable upstream to the park; coal barges dominate the traffic. **2** River, 730 mi (1,175 km) long, rising near the Continental Divide, W Wyo., and flowing generally S through W Wyo., NW Colo., and E Utah to the Colorado River in Canyonlands National Park, SE Utah; it is the largest tributary of the Colorado. Most of its course flows through deep canyons, including Canyon of the Lodore in Dinosaur National Monument (see NATIONAL PARKS AND MONUMENTS, table); the White, Yampa, and San Rafael rivers are its main tributaries. The Colorado River storage project of the U.S. Bureau of Reclamation has extensively developed the Green River basin for irrigation and hydroelectric power; Flaming Gorge Dam, NE Utah, is the major unit in this project.

Greens, political faction: see BLUES AND GREENS.

Greensboro, city (1970 pop. 144,076), seat of Guilford co., N central N.C.; inc. 1829. The second-largest city in North Carolina, it has an important textile industry and is a financial, insurance, and distribution center for the region. The manufacture of tobacco products and electrical machinery is also important. Greensboro was settled in 1749. The nearby site of the Revolutionary War battle of GUILFORD COURTHOUSE is now a national military park. Dolley Madison and O. Henry were born in Greensboro. Among its educational institutions are the Univ. of North Carolina at Greensboro, Greensboro College, Guilford College, North Carolina Agricultural and Technical State Univ., and Bennett College.

Greensburg, city (1970 pop. 15,870), seat of Westmoreland co., SW Pa.; settled c.1770, inc. as a city 1928. Paper products, building materials, electrical equipment, plate glass, and control systems are made in Greensburg. Col. Henry Bouquet defeated (1763) Indian warriors of Pontiac near there and opened up W Pennsylvania for settlement. Greensburg (originally New Town) was located midway between Fort Ligonier and Fort Pitt. It became county seat in 1785. Seton Hill College and a branch of the Univ. of Pittsburgh are there.

green turtle: see SEA TURTLE.

Greenville. 1 City (1970 pop. 39,648), seat of Washington co., W Miss., on Lake Ferguson, a deepwater harbor adjoining the Mississippi River; inc. 1886. It is the trade, processing, and shipping center of the Mississippi-Yazoo delta, a fertile region producing soybeans, oats, corn, timber, and especially cotton. It is also an industrial city, and its many manufactures include saws, metal products, concrete items, and automobile parts. **2** City (1970 pop. 29,063), seat of Pitt co., E N.C., on the Tar River; founded 1786. It grew as a tobacco center, and while still an important tobacco-processing and marketing city, it now has diversified manufacturing industries. East Carolina Univ. is there. **3** City (1970 pop. 12,380), seat of Darke co., W Ohio, in a farm area; settled 1808, inc. as a city 1900. Gen. Anthony Wayne built (1793) a fort on what is now Greenville as a base for his Indian campaign. After his victory at FALLEN TIMBERS, Wayne returned and in 1795 negotiated a treaty with the Indians, who ceded a large part of the Old Northwest to the United States. The fort was then abandoned. In 1805, Tecumseh and his brother, the Shawnee Prophet, lived there. When they were forced out (1808), white settlement began. A memorial marks the site of the signing of the treaty, and the famous mural by Howard Chandler Christy depicting the event now hangs in the rotunda of the state capitol. **4** City (1970 pop. 61,436), seat of Greenville co., NW S.C., on the Reedy River, in the Piedmont area near the Blue Ridge Mts.; laid out 1797, inc. as a city 1907. It is one of the principal industrial and commercial centers of the SE United States, and the heart of a large industrial region of mill towns. In Greenville are many huge textile mills, garment factories, farm produce processing and packing establishments, and plants making pharmaceuticals, fabricated metals, furniture, chemicals, plastics, electronic equipment, and turbine engines. Textile Hall is the scene of the biennial Southern Textile Exposition. Greenville is the seat of Furman Univ., Bob Jones Univ., a two-year branch of Clemson Univ., a technical center, and a Shriners' hospital for crippled children. It has an art museum, a zoo, and a historic park. Its Little Theater and symphony orchestra are especially popular. Two state parks are nearby. **5** City (1970 pop. 22,043), seat of Hunt co., E Texas, in a prosperous blackland cotton region; inc. 1874. Among its manufactures are electronic systems, clothing, and oil field equipment.

green vitriol, the heptahydrate of FERROUS SULFATE.

Greenwich (grĭn'ĭj, grĕn'-), borough (1971 pop. 216,441) of Greater London, SE England, on the Thames River. The borough was created in 1965 by the merger of the metropolitan boroughs of Greenwich and Woolwich. Manufactures include telephone equipment and underwater cable. The system of geographic longitude and time-keeping worked out at the famous Royal Observatory there have become standard in most countries of the world; the prime meridian, or long. 0°, passes through the observatory. The functions of the observatory were transferred to Herstmonceaux, Sussex, in 1950. The area has strong links with the sea. Greenwich has nearly 9 mi (14.5 km) of river frontage, and Woolwich's docks and shipbuilding facilities were important from the 16th to the mid-19th cent. The Royal Naval College is in the borough. The college building, partially designed by Christopher Wren, was originally a home for disabled sailors. On the site of the present structure (begun in the late 17th cent.) stood a palace that was the birthplace of Henry VIII, Mary I, and Elizabeth I; Edward VI died there. The National Maritime Museum is also in Greenwich, partly housed in a building designed by Inigo Jones for Anne of Denmark. The Royal Military Academy is in Woolwich. On the site of the once famous Royal Arsenal in Woolwich a new residential community is being developed. Both Greenwich and Woolwich are mentioned in documents dating from the 10th cent. and appear in the DOMESDAY BOOK.

Greenwich (grĕn'ĭch), residential and resort town (1970 pop. 59,755), Fairfield co., SW Conn., on the Mianus and Byram rivers and Long Island Sound; settled 1640, inc. 1955. This attractive suburban community with a prosperous New England atmosphere is noted as the home of many New York City executives. In recent years it has also become the seat of more than 100 national and international corporate headquarters. Settled on land bought from the Indians, Greenwich was long inhabited by farmers and oystermen. In the American Revolution it was plundered (1779) by the British under General Tryon; a house (built 1731) from which Gen. Israel Putnam supposedly made a dramatic escape is still preserved. In the late 19th cent. Greenwich began to attract artists and summer residents. Comprised of numerous villages (including Greenwich, Riverside, Quaker Ridge, Old Greenwich, and Cos Cob), it has over 32 mi (52 km) of shoreline on Long Island Sound, with many good harbors, beaches, and small islands.

Greenwich mean time (G.M.T.) or **universal time** (U.T.), local CIVIL TIME at the former site of the Royal Observatory in Greenwich, England, which is located on the PRIME MERIDIAN. It is used as the basis for standard time in most countries of the world.

Greenwich meridian: see PRIME MERIDIAN.

Greenwich Village (grĕn'ĭch, grĭn'-), residential district of lower Manhattan, New York City, extending S from 14th St. to Houston St. and W from Washington Square to the Hudson River. A separate village in colonial times, it later became an exclusive residential section. An influx of foreign immigrants settled there after 1880. Around 1910, the Village gained renown as the home and workshop of artists and of freethinkers. Barns, stables, and houses along the narrow, crooked streets were converted into studios, eating places, night clubs, theaters, and shops, and the Village acquired a reputation for bohemianism. Interesting old buildings, many dating from the early and mid-1800s, remain, although there is an increasing number of modern apartment houses. Washington Square Park, with its arch, is a meeting place. New York University's original campus surrounds the park. Outdoor art exhibits are held in the Village.

Greenwood, John, 1727–92, American artist, b. Boston, Mass. An engraver and painter, Greenwood executed some of the first GENRE paintings in America. He is also noted for his satirical works peopled with small, energetic figures reminiscent of Hogarth's.

Greenwood. 1 City (1970 pop. 11,408), Johnson co., central Ind.; settled 1822, inc. as a city 1960. Primarily residential, it has some industry. **2** City (1970 pop. 22,400), seat of Leflore co., W central Miss., on the Yazoo River in the Mississippi Delta; inc. 1844. It is a retail and trade center for a productive farm region and one of the largest cotton markets in the world. The area's original inhabitants were Choctaw Indians, and the city and county derive their names from a Choctaw chief and cotton planter, Greenwood Leflore. After the area was ceded to the United States in 1830 by the Treaty of Dancing Rabbit Creek, settlers poured in, carving vast cotton plantations out of the delta swamplands. A Civil War battle was fought at nearby Fort Pemberton from Feb. 24 to April 8, 1863. **3** City (1970 pop. 21,069), seat of Greenwood co., W S.C.; settled 1824, inc. as a city 1927. It is a rail center, with textile, wood product, and meat-packing industries. A trading post was established there in 1751, and a Revolutionary War battle was fought at nearby Old Star Fort in 1775. The first railroad came in 1852, and by 1911 five lines were operating through the city. Lander College is there.

Greer, town (1970 pop. 10,642), Greenville and Spartanburg counties, NW S.C., in a farm region. It has textile mills, food-processing plants, and some light manufacturing.

Gregg, David McMurtie, 1833–1916, Union general in the Civil War, b. Huntingdon, Pa., grad. West Point, 1855. Gregg served with the cavalry of the Army of the Potomac and was particularly distinguished in the fighting of July 3 at Gettysburg, when he checked Jeb Stuart's attempt to get to the Union rear.

Gregg, Josiah, 1806–50, American trader and historian of the SANTA FE TRAIL, b. Overton co., Tenn. He moved with his family to Illinois (1809) and then to Missouri (1812). He gained wide knowledge from his diverse readings. He journeyed to Santa Fe for the first time in 1831 and later, having become a trader, made many expeditions, sometimes going as far as Chihuahua, Mexico. He recorded his observations, which were published as *Commerce of the Prairies* (1844, new ed. 1954), later regarded as a classic of American frontier history and literature. He served under Gen. John W. Wool in the Mexican War and 1849 joined the California gold rush. He died when leading a prospecting party across the Coast Range in the winter. See his diary and letters, ed. by M. G. Fulton (1941–44).

Gregg, William, 1800–67, American industrialist, known as the "father of Southern cotton manufacture," b. Monongalia co., Va. (now W.Va.). He devoted his life to building up Southern industry. His views were expressed in *Essays on Domestic Industry* (1845), a collection of articles published first in the Charleston *Courier.* At a time when limited-liability corporations were very unpopular in the South, Gregg convinced the South Carolina legislature to grant him a charter for the formation (1846) of Graniteville, the first Southern mill town, built with local materials and labor and consisting of a large mill and houses for its 300 employees. Under his personal direction, the mill continued to bring Gregg steady profits through financial depression and the Civil War. He introduced an advanced factory-welfare program. As a state legislator (1856–57) his interest in economic issues was aimed at strengthening local industrial enterprises. See biography by Broadus Mitchell (1928).

Grégoire, Henri (äNrē' grāgwär'), 1750–1831, French priest, writer, and revolutionist. A Jansenist (see under JANSEN, CORNELIS), he was prominent in the States-General of 1789 and supported the union of the lower clergy with the third estate. He fought clerical and noble privilege and proposed abolition of the law of primogeniture. Grégoire took the oath of the Civil Constitution of the Clergy (even though it was condemned by the pope) and became constitutional bishop of Blois in 1791. He maintained his religious beliefs throughout the Terror and fought for religious freedom under the Directory. As a senator under the Consulate, he opposed the CONCORDAT OF 1801 and, resigning his see, became a simple priest. Although he opposed the empire, Napoleon I made him a count. In 1819 he was elected to the chamber of deputies but, as a radical and a dissident priest, was refused his seat. Grégoire died in poverty; his burial was the scene of a great liberal demonstration. His writings, some of which have been translated, deal chiefly with Jansenism, racial equality, and international cooperation.

Gregoras, Nicephorus (nīsĕf'ərəs grĕg'ərəs), c.1295–c.1359, Byzantine historian and theologian, one of the most learned men of his time. Among his scientific and philosophical works is a plan for a calendar reform similar to that effected by Pope Gregory XIII two centuries later. His chief book is the *Roman History,* covering the period from 1204 to 1359. This and the *Histories* of John Cantacuzene (see JOHN VI, Byzantine emperor) are the primary sources for 14th-century Byzantine history. The two works supplement each other. A staunch adherent of Byzantine Emperor Andronicus II, Gregoras temporarily fell out of favor with his successor and grandson, Andronicus III. Later, however, Gregoras was appointed (1333) to conduct the negotiations for the union of the Greek and Roman churches proposed by Pope John XXII. Gregoras was by then a famous man, but after he opposed doctrines that were approved (1351) by the Greek church, he was discredited and confined to a monastery until 1355.

Gregorian chant: see PLAINSONG.

Gregorovius, Ferdinand (grĕgərō'vēəs, Ger. fĕr'dēnänt grā"gōrō'vēo͝os), 1821–91, German historian. He spent many years in Rome, where he produced his authoritative *History of the City of Rome in the Middle Ages* (8 vol., 1859–72; tr. 1894–1900). Other works include his *Life of the Emperor Hadrian* (1851, tr. 1898).

Gregory I, Saint (Saint Gregory the Great), c.540–604, pope (590–604), a Roman; successor of Pelagius II. A Doctor of the Church, he was distinguished for his spiritual and temporal leadership. He was born to a wealthy patrician family and at the age of 30 he was made prefect of Rome, Rome's highest civil office. He felt the call to monasticism, however, and converted (c.575) his home and others of his houses into Benedictine convents. Later (c.586), he reluctantly became abbot. In 578 he was made a deacon of Rome. From 579 to c.586 he was ambassador at Constantinople, then he served as chief adviser of Pelagius II. When commencing a missionary voyage to England, he was recalled to Rome and accomplished his aim only by sending St. AUGUSTINE OF CANTERBURY (596) and a later mission (601). He was elected pope by acclamation, accepting against his will and despite chronic illness. The two chief features of Gregory's lasting work are the enforcement of the papal supremacy and the establishment of the temporal position of the pope. Gregory not only legislated minutely and carefully for his immediate charges, but he interfered when necessary outside Italy; e.g., he attacked Donatism in Africa and simony in Gaul. Most significantly, he refused to recognize *ecumenical* as a title of the patriarch of Constantinople, since that title was not consistent with the divine vicegerency of the pope. The exarch of Ravenna, representative of the Byzantine emperor in the West, claimed secular jurisdiction over Rome, and Gregory acknowledged it de jure. However, the exarch, Romanus, did nothing to help the city when it was threatened by a Lombard attack in 592. Gregory, as bishop of Rome, took command and negotiated a peace. It was ignored by the exarch, and the Lombards resumed their attack on Rome. Since Romanus deferred making peace, Gregory began independent negotiations, a new affront to the imperial dignity and an extralegal act. In his dealings with the Lombards and the exarch, Gregory showed that if the emperor would not defend the pope, the pope would defend himself and by doing so would make himself temporally independent. Thus he set a precedent that enabled the papacy to prevent the total destruction of Rome. Yet Gregory was the important exponent of the doctrine of divided powers: the emperor was God's vicar in things temporal, the pope in things spiritual. Gregory's encouragement of monasticism was significant historically, and his insistence on clerical celibacy and the exemption of the clergy from trial in civil courts bore great fruit later. He was succeeded by Sabinian. Gregory's works included *Moralia* (tr. *Morals on the Book of Job,* 1844–50); *Dialogues,* lives of saints, including St. Benedict, a widely read work all through the Middle Ages; *Liber pastoralis curae* (various Eng. tr., *Pastoral Care, Pastoral Charge,* and *Pastoral Rule*); homilies on the Gospel; and many invaluable letters. The Gregorial Sacramentary, a revision of the Gelasian Sacramentary (see GELASIUS I, SAINT), and the Gregorian antiphonary are spurious. St. Gregory contributed to the development of the Gregorian chant or PLAINSONG. Feast: March 12. See F. H. Dudden, *Gregory the Great* (2 vol., 1905; repr. 1967); Pierre Batiffol, *Saint Gregory the Great* (1929); E. C. Butler, *Western Mysticism* (3d ed. 1968).

Gregory II, Saint, d. 731, pope (715–31), a Roman; successor of Constantine. When Byzantine Emperor LEO III tried to impose iconoclasm in Italy by an imperial edict, Gregory answered that the emperor could not decide tenets of faith. He was supported by a popular uprising directed at the exarch of Ravenna, the emperor's viceroy in Italy. The Lombards, long the enemies of Rome, took up the Roman cause, with the result that its Byzantine suzerainty over Rome was virtually ended. It was Gregory who sent St. Boniface to evangelize Germany. He was succeeded by Gregory III. Feast: Feb. 11.

Gregory VII, Saint, d. 1085, pope (1073–85), an Italian (b. near Rome) named Hildebrand (Ital. Ildebrando); successor of Alexander II. He was one of the greatest popes. As a Benedictine, Hildebrand came to the attention of Gregory VI, who made him his chaplain. Thereafter his rise in power was rapid. Under Leo IX, Hildebrand became administrator of the Patrimony of Peter (see PAPAL STATES); he recovered much of the ecclesiastical property held by Italian nobles, and he restored the papal finances. About this time Hildebrand began his program of reform directed at the widespread corruption and laxity in the church. Opposition quickly sprang up from clergy and noblemen alike, but Hildebrand found continued support from popes Victor II and Stephen IX. Under Nicholas II two measures were accomplished that furthered the cause of reform—the papal election was taken out of the hands of the Romans and put into the college of cardinals, and a treaty was signed with the Normans of S Italy (1059) providing the pope with an ally against the German king. Hildebrand's course was not easy, however; a powerful party had arisen to oppose him. By 1073, when Hildebrand became Pope Gregory VII, the struggle was nearing a climax. Gregory's first action was to call reform synods and issue decrees that forbade, under pain of excommunication, clerical marriage (and concubinage) and simony. Gregory appointed legates, many from among the reforming Cluniac order, to travel throughout Europe and enforce the new laws. They met with opposition and violence almost everywhere. Gregory saw the root of all the evils afflicting the church in the practice of lay INVESTITURE, whereby abbacies and bishoprics became virtually the property of secular powers, who used them to their own advantage. In 1075 he condemned it and anyone who practiced it. Gregory's ensuing struggles with the royal houses of Europe, who opposed the decree, dominated the remaining years of his pontificate. In Germany, HENRY IV joined with the nobles against the reform, and in an investiture dispute with Gregory he was excommunicated (1076). The excommunication cost Henry much of his popularity, and in 1077 he humbled himself before the pope at CANOSSA. Gregory remained neutral in the civil war that followed in Germany but decreed (1079) Henry deposed when it became clear Henry would not cooperate with the forces working for peace in the empire. Henry answered by setting up an imperial antipope, GUIBERT OF RAVENNA (Clement III). When the civil war ended in Henry's favor, he marched (1081) into Italy. Gregory led the defense of Rome, but when Henry returned a second time (1083) the Romans, beguiled by Henry's generosity, betrayed Gregory. He fortified himself in the Castel Sant' Angelo until rescued by his Norman ally, ROBERT GUISCARD. The Normans plundered the city. With the antipope and Henry still in Italy, Gregory decided to join the Normans in their withdrawal south. He died a year later at Salerno, shorn of all support but that of the Normans. He was succeeded by Victor III. During all his struggles Gregory kept a watchful eye on the developments of the church in Norway, Denmark, and in the new Slavic nations. The troubles with the Saracens in the East led him to conceive the first plan for a holy war against the Turks. Gregory's contribution to the church is incalculable. His reform was a turning point in the history of the church. His struggle against the sovereignties of Europe is sometimes criticized as a bid for inordinate power, but generally his efforts are recognized as a stubborn and noble defense of the liberty of the church against domination by secular powers. The cause was not won by Gregory, but he had drawn the issue clearly. After the example of his pontificate the moral level of the church rose, and his successors were inspired to carry the investiture struggle to victory at the Concordat of Worms (1122). Feast: May 25. See his *Correspondence* (tr. 1932, repr. 1969); W. Schafer, ed., *The Gregorian Epoch* (1964); *Gregory VII–Church Reformer or World Monarch?* (1967); H. E. Cowdrey, *The Cluniacs and the Gregorian Reform* (1970).

Gregory IX, 1143?–1241, pope (1227–41), an Italian named Ugolino di Segni, b. Anagni; successor of Honorius III. As cardinal under his uncle, Innocent III, he became, at St. Francis' request, the first cardinal protector of the Franciscans. About 84 when he was elected, he was a vigorous pope despite his age. He immediately commanded Holy Roman Emperor FREDERICK II to keep his vow to go on crusade and excommunicated (1227) him when he delayed. The imperialists in Rome forced (1228) the pope into exile until 1230, when emperor and pope were reconciled. Five or six years later the struggle broke out again, this time over Italian liberties. Gregory again excommunicated (1239) Frederick and ordered his dethronement. Frederick prevented publication of the bulls in Germany and blocked a general council summoned by Gregory. Gregory died at 98 when Frederick was about to attack the city. He was succeeded by Celestine IV. Gregory ordered the collection of the decretals, a step toward codifying canon law, and he organized (1233) the Inquisition and gave special responsibility for it to the Dominicans.

Gregory X, d. 1276, pope (1271–76), an Italian named Tebaldo Visconti, b. Piacenza; successor of Clement IV. After Clement IV's death the cardinals took 34 months to elect a pope. Gregory was archdeacon of Liège when elected and neither a cardinal nor a priest. At the time he was in the Holy Land. He became a conciliator in European politics and helped to end civil war in Germany by supporting the election of Rudolf of Hapsburg as emperor. He convoked the Second Council of Lyons (1274; see LYONS, SECOND COUNCIL OF) and led in its work, particularly in the temporary reunion with the Orthodox of Constantinople. He was succeeded by Innocent V. Gregory was beatified in 1713.

Gregory XI, 1330–78, pope (1370–78), a Frenchman named Pierre Roger de Beaufort. He was the successor of Urban V, who had made an unsuccessful attempt to remove the papacy from Avignon to Rome (1367–70). From the time of his election Gregory heard prophetic admonitions to go to Rome, first from St. Bridget of Sweden and then from St. CATHERINE OF SIENA, who visited him (1376). But the Avignon court was opposed, and Italy had again become inhospitable. The pope's absence and the death of Cardinal de ALBORNOZ had plunged the entire Italian peninsula into anarchy and violence. Florence, Milan, and Perugia revolted against papal authority. With Gregory's sanction, ROBERT OF GENEVA led a marauding army into Italy, returning violence for violence. Gregory finally heeded St. Catherine's pleas and returned to Rome (Jan., 1377), thus ending the Babylonian Captivity of the popes on French soil. All his efforts to bring about peace failed. He was the last of the French popes and was succeeded by Urban VI. The elections after his death began the Great SCHISM. Gregory issued the first condemnation of the teachings of John Wyclif.

Gregory XII, c.1327–1417, pope (1406–15), a Venetian named Angelo Correr; successor of Innocent VII. As a condition of election, Gregory promised to do everything possible to end the Great SCHISM, including the relinquishing of his office. Negotiations were opened with the Avignon antipope, Benedict XIII (see LUNA, PEDRO DE), but soon broke down under pressure from Gregory's family. Seven of his cardinals thereupon defected and together with a group of Avignon cardinals convoked the Council of Pisa (see PISA, COUNCIL OF) which elected a second antipope, Alexander V. The Council of Constance (see CONSTANCE, COUNCIL OF) deposed the two antipopes, accepted Gregory's resignation (1415), and saw to the proper election of Martin V (1417). Gregory died as cardinal bishop of Porto.

Gregory XIII, 1502–85, pope (1572–85), an Italian named Ugo Buoncompagni, b. Bologna; successor of St. Pius V. He is best known for his work on the CALENDAR, and the reformed calendar, the Gregorian, is named for him. He was prominent at the Council of Trent (1545, 1559–63; see TRENT, COUNCIL OF) and in the work of reform thereafter. He was created (1564) cardinal and later was legate to Spain. As pope, Gregory's absorbing interests were the education of the clergy and the conversion of Protestants. He especially patronized the Jesuits, whom he encouraged on their many missions, particularly in N Europe and in Japan. He proposed the deposition of Queen Elizabeth of England, and he advocated no compromise with German Protestants. He has been much criticized for a public thanksgiving at Rome for the massacre of SAINT BARTHOLOMEW'S DAY, but he had been told that it was the suppression of a rebellion. He issued a new edition of the canon law. His government of the Papal States was execrable. He was succeeded by Sixtus V.

Gregory XVI, 1765–1846, pope (1831–46), an Italian named Bartolomeo Alberto Capellari, b. Belluno; successor of Pius VIII. In 1783 he became a Camaldolite and was (1825) created cardinal. Gregory was a conservative both in politics and theology, and he was continually opposed by liberals throughout Europe. His most famous act was the condemnation of Father LAMENNAIS with the encyclical *Mirari vos* (1832). In 1831 the CARBONARI outbreaks spread to Rome, and only Austrian help suppressed them. He nearly came to an open break over anticlerical legislation in Spain and Portugal, and he had a long controversy with Prussia. Gregory was actively interested in propagating the faith in England and the United States. He was succeeded by Pius IX.

Gregory, Lady Augusta (Persse), 1859–1932, Irish dramatist. She married Sir William Gregory, a retired governor of Ceylon, in 1880. After his death in 1892, she devoted herself entirely to literature. A vital force in the Irish drama, she was a founder and the omnipresent manager and director of the ABBEY THEATRE. Her most successful pieces, written for the Abbey players, include *Spreading the News* (1904), *The Gaol Gate* (1906), *The Rising of the Moon* (1907), and *The Workhouse Ward* (1908). Her short plays, mainly comedies, are rich in portrayals of Irish peasantry. Among her other works are *Our Irish Theater* (1913) and several long plays dealing with Irish history. See her journals (ed. by Lennox Robinson, 1946); studies by Elizabeth Coxhead (rev. ed. 1970) and Hazard Adams (1973).

Gregory, Horace, 1898–, American poet and critic, b. Milwaukee, Wis., grad. Univ. of Wisconsin, 1923. His poetry is noted for its dramatic structure and penetrating insights into the harshness of contemporary life. Among his volumes of poetry are *Chelsea Rooming House* (1930), *Poems, 1930–1940* (1941), and *Medusa in Gramercy Park* (1961). As a critic, Gregory is the author of *Pilgrim of the Apocalypse* (1933), a study of D. H. Lawrence; *The Shield of Achilles* (1944), essays on poetry; *A History of American Poetry, 1900–1940* (1946), written with his wife, the poet Marya Zaturenska; *The Dying Gladiators* (1961), essays; and *Dorothy Richardson: An Adventure in Self-Discovery* (1967). He has also made translations of the poems of Catullus and of Ovid's *Metamorphoses.* See his reminiscences (1971) and his collected essays (1973).

Gregory, James, 1638–75, Scottish mathematician. He invented a reflecting telescope (1661), which he described in his *Optica promota* (1663). In 1668 he became professor of mathematics at the Univ. of St. Andrews and, in 1674, professor of mathematics at the Univ. of Edinburgh. He originated a photometric mode of measuring the distance of stars and wrote *Geometriae pars universalis* (1668) and *Exercitationes geometricae* (1668).

Gregory Nazianzen, Saint (nāzēăn'zĭn), c.330–390, Cappadocian theologian, Doctor of the Church, one of the Four Fathers of the Greek Church. He is sometimes called Gregory Theologus. He studied widely in his youth and was from his student days a friend of St. Basil the Great. Basil appointed the unwilling Gregory to a bishopric, and Gregory succeeded him as principal leader of the conciliatory party in the church struggle against Arianism. In 379, Gregory was chosen Roman Catholic bishop of Constantinople. By his preaching he wrought a great revival of Catholicism there. He was deposed by the chicanery of an Alexandrian, but the first Council of Constantinople restored him. When St. Meletius died during the session, he took the chair, but on failing to settle the Antiochene schism, he gave up his patriarchate and returned home. Feast: May 9.

Gregory of Nyssa, Saint (nĭs'ə), d. 394?, Cappadocian theologian; brother of St. BASIL THE GREAT and his successor as champion of orthodoxy. He became bishop of Nyssa in Cappadocia in 371, was removed in 376, and was restored in 378. He was prominent in the First Council of Constantinople (see CONSTANTINOPLE, FIRST COUNCIL OF). His fame rests on his theological works, most of which were controversial, against Eunomius, Appollinarians, and against the teachings of Jews and pagans (*Oratio catechetica*). Feast: March 9.

Gregory of Tours, Saint, 538–94, French historian, bishop of Tours (from 573), b. Clermont-Ferrand, of a prominent family. He had a distinguished and successful career as bishop. Gregory wrote accounts of miracles of the saints, an astronomical work to determine movable feasts, and a commentary on the Psalms. His masterpiece, *Historia Francorum* [history of the Franks], in 10 books, is a universal history; its account of contemporary events is of great importance. Gregory's Late Latin is of linguistic interest. Feast: Nov. 17. See O. M. Dalton, *Gregory of Tours* (1927).

Gregory the Illuminator, Saint, d. c.330, churchman, called the Apostle of Armenia. He was the first metropolitan of Armenia and is revered as founder of the ARMENIAN CHURCH. Feast: Sept. 30.

Greifswald (grīfs'vält), city (1970 pop. 47,083), Rostock district, N East Germany, near the Baltic Sea. It is an industrial and commercial center. Manufactures include wood products and machinery. Greifswald was chartered in 1250, and in 1648 it became part of Swedish Pomerania. In 1815 it passed to Prussia. Noteworthy buildings include the 14th-century town hall and several churches of the 13th and 14th cent. The city has a noted university (founded 1456).

Greiz (grīts), city (1970 pop. 39,058), Gera district, S East Germany, on the White Elster River. Manufactures include textiles, paper and paper products, and machinery. From 1306 to 1918, Greiz was the capital of the principality of Reuss (Older Line).

Grellet, Stephen (grĕlĕt'), 1773–1855, Quaker missionary, b. France; son of well-to-do Roman Catholic parents. His name originally was Étienne de Grellet du Mabillier. He fled France at the time of the Revolution and eventually immigrated (1795) to the United States, where at Newtown (now part of Queens, New York City) he was converted to the beliefs of the Quakers. In 1796 he joined the Society of Friends; in 1798 he was recorded a minister of that body. He engaged in trade in New York City; his profits financed his extraordinary missionary tours. In the United States they extended through all the settled parts W to Illinois, N into Canada, and S to New Orleans. Four extended tours were made in Europe, where every major country was visited; interviews were granted to Grellet by many of the reigning sovereigns. He was deeply interested in education, in prison and hospital conditions, in provision for the poor, and in other social problems. He inquired into conditions and made recommendations in every country that he visited. His memoirs (1860) were edited by Benjamin Seebohm. See W. W. Comfort, *Stephen Grellet, 1773–1855* (1942).

gremlin, in American folklore, malicious, airborne supernatural being. Gremlins were first heard of during World War II as creatures responsible for unexplainable mechanical failures and disruptions in aircraft.

Grenada (grĭnā'də), island (1970 est. pop. 87,300), 120 sq mi (311 sq km), in the West Indies. It is part of the independent state of Grenada in the Windward Islands. The state includes the southern half of the archipelago known as the Grenadines. The capital, main port, and commercial center is SAINT GEORGE'S. Grenada is a volcanic, mountainous island with crater lakes. Its agricultural products include

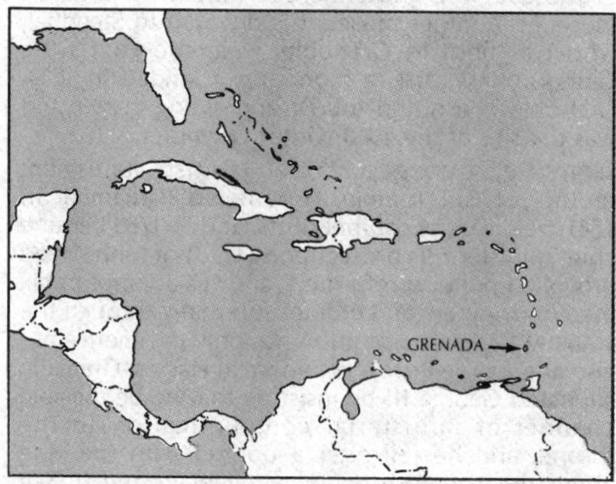

bananas, cacao, nutmeg, mace, sugar, and coconuts; cotton and limes are exported. Tourism is a leading industry. The population is overwhelmingly black or mulatto. Although English is the official language, a French patois is widely spoken. From its discovery by Christopher Columbus in 1498 until French settlement began in 1650, the hostility of the native Carib Indians prevented colonization on Grenada. A point of dispute between England and France, the island became permanently British in 1783. The British colonists imported African slaves and established sugar plantations. In 1967, Grenada became an associated state of Britain with full internal self-government. Complete independence was achieved in Feb. 1974, and Grenada became a full member of the Commonwealth of Nations.

grenade (grĭnād'), small bomb filled with explosives, gas, or chemicals and either thrown by hand or shot from a modified rifle or a grenade launcher. Grenades were in use as early as the 15th cent., and men trained to use them were called grenadiers. As the grenade fell into disfavor, however, the name *grenadier* was applied to members of various elite guards, such as those of Frederick II of Prussia and Napoleon I. Grenades were later reintroduced in warfare and have been widely used in the wars of the 20th cent.

grenadine: see POMEGRANATE.

Grenadines: see GRENADA; WINDWARD ISLANDS.

Grenchen (grĕn'khən), Fr. *Granges,* town (1970 pop. 20,051), Solothurn canton, NW Switzerland. It is a watchmaking center.

Grenfell, Bernard Pyne (grĕn'fĕl), 1869–1926, English classical scholar and Egyptologist. With Arthur Surridge Hunt he discovered at Oxyrhynchus the Logia of Jesus (see AGRAPHA OF JESUS). He became in 1908 professor of papyrology at Oxford and helped edit the *Oxyrhynchus Papyri* (9 vol., 1897–1912) and other similar works.

Grenfell, Sir Wilfred Thomason, 1865–1940, English physician and missionary, famous for his work among Labrador fishermen. After serving as a missionary to fishermen of the North Sea, Dr. Grenfell went to Labrador in 1892. During more than 40 years of service there and in Newfoundland, he built hospitals and nursing stations, established cooperative stores, agricultural centers, schools, libraries, and orphanages, and opened the King George V Seamen's Institute in St. John's, N.F., in 1912. Grenfell cruised annually in the hospital steamer *Strathcona II,* keeping in touch with his centers of missionary work. Among his many books are his autobiography, *Forty Years for Labrador* (1932), and *The Romance of Labrador* (1934). See biographies by Joyce Reason (1941), E. H. Hayes (1946), J. L. Kerr (1959), and S. Z. Starr (1971).

Grenoble (grənô'blə), city (1968 pop. 165,902), capital of Isère dept., SE France, on the Isère River at the foot of the Alps. It is the hydroelectric center of France and has an important nuclear-research center. Metals, electrical equipment, chemicals, and food products are the chief manufactures. An ancient city of the Allobroges and a Roman city, Grenoble came under the Burgundians (5th cent.), the Franks (6th cent.), and the kingdom of Provence (9th-11th cent.). When that kingdom broke up, Grenoble became a possession of the dauphins of Viennois; DAUPHINÉ along with its capital, Grenoble, passed to the French crown in 1349. The parlement of Grenoble was strongly anti-Royalist during the French Revolution. In Grenoble are a famous university (founded 1339); the Cathedral of Notre Dame (12-13th cent.); the Church of St. André (13th-14th cent.), which contains the tomb of the military hero Pierre Bayard; the Renaissance palace of the dauphins (now the courthouse); and an art museum. Another museum is devoted to Stendhal, who was born in Grenoble. Near the city is the Grande CHARTREUSE, a monastery founded in 1084. Grenoble is a noted tourist and skiing center and was the site of the 1968 winter Olympics.

Grenville, George, 1712-70, British statesman, brother of Earl Temple. He entered Parliament in 1741, held several cabinet posts, and in 1763 became chief minister. His prosecution (1763) of John WILKES provoked political reformers, and his attempt to tax the North American colonies internally through the STAMP ACT raised opposition not only in America but also among the British commercial classes. Grenville alienated George III by insisting that he be the sole channel of ministerial communication to the throne, and he fell after a quarrel with the king about the composition of a regency council. See L. M. Wiggin, *The Faction of Cousins* (1958).

Grenville, George Nugent Temple, 1st **marquess of Buckingham,** 1753-1813, British statesman; second son of George Grenville. He sat in the House of Commons from 1774 until 1779, when he succeeded his uncle as 2d Earl Temple. While lord lieutenant of Ireland (1782-83) he worked for enactment of the Irish Judicature Act (1783), which furthered Irish legislative independence. In 1783 he was George III's agent in defeating the East India bill of Charles James FOX in the House of Lords. Created (1784) marquess of Buckingham, he served again as lord lieutenant of Ireland (1787-89). He resigned after being censured by the Irish Parliament for not sending to England its invitation to the prince of Wales (later George IV) to assume the regency.

Grenville, Sir Richard, 1542?-1591, English naval hero. His cousin, Sir Walter RALEIGH, gave him command of the fleet of seven vessels carrying the first colonists to ROANOKE ISLAND in 1585. In 1591, Grenville was second in command, under Lord Thomas Howard, of the fleet sent to capture the Spanish treasure ships off the Azores. When Lord Thomas withdrew on finding the odds against him too heavy, Grenville's ship, the *Revenge,* became separated from the rest of the fleet, and Grenville tried to break through the Spanish line. He fought 15 Spanish ships all one evening and night, was mortally wounded, and died in Spanish captivity. His exploit is celebrated in Tennyson's poem "The Revenge." See biography (1937, repr. 1963) and study (1957) by A. L. Rowse.

Grenville, William Wyndham Grenville, Baron, 1759-1834, British statesman; youngest son of George Grenville. He was foreign secretary in the ministry of his cousin William Pitt from 1791 to 1801. During the French Revolutionary Wars, Grenville led the British war party and favored Pitt's repressive internal measures. He was also a champion of free trade and of CATHOLIC EMANCIPATION. In 1806 he formed the "ministry of all the talents," which abolished (1807) the slave trade. See study by E. D. Adams (1904).

Gresham, Sir Thomas (grĕsh'əm), 1519?-1579, English merchant and financier. As the royal financial agent in Antwerp after 1551 he proved himself very able, though his methods were frequently more effective than ethical. After the accession of Elizabeth I to the throne he spent most of his time in London but went on diplomatic and financial missions. He also accumulated a great private fortune as banker, mercer, and merchant. He was the principal figure in the founding of the Royal Exchange, and he endowed Gresham College in London. His name was given to **Gresham's law,** the economic principle that in the circulation of money "bad money drives out good," i.e., when depreciated, mutilated, or debased coinage (or currency) is in concurrent circulation with money of high value in terms of precious metals, the good money automatically disappears. It was thought that Gresham was the first to state the principle, but it has been shown that it was stated long before his time and that he did not even formulate it. See J. W. Burgon, *Life and Times of Sir Thomas Gresham* (2 vol., 1839, rep. 1968); biography by F. R. Salter (1925).

Gresham, Walter Quintin, 1832-95, American public official, b. Harrison co., Ind. A lawyer, he entered politics as a Whig and helped organize the Republican party. President Grant appointed (1869) him district judge in Indiana, and President Arthur chose him as Postmaster General (1883) and Secretary of the Treasury (1884), but he was soon made circuit judge (1884). Gresham supported Grover Cleveland on the tariff issue in 1892 and declined the Populist nomination for President. He served (1893-95) ably as Secretary of State under President Cleveland. See biography by his wife, Matilda Gresham (1919, repr. 1970).

Gresham's law: see under GRESHAM, SIR THOMAS.

Gresset, Jean Baptiste Louis (zhäN bätēst' lwē grĕsā'), 1709-77, French poet and dramatist. He was the author of a mock epic, *Vairvert* (1734), and of a successful comedy, *Le Méchant* (1747), satirizing the society of his period.

Gretchaninov, Aleksandr Tichonovich (əlyĭksän'dər tēkônô'vĭch grĕchänē'nôf), 1864-1956, Russian composer; pupil of Rimsky-Korsakov. Among his works are four symphonies, two operas, a setting of the Russian Orthodox service, and sacred choral works. His music has the rich sonorities and harmonic variety typical of late romanticism. In 1939 he came to the United States, where he remained until his death.

Gretna, city (1970 pop. 24,875), seat of Jefferson parish, SE La., on the Mississippi River. Its manufactures include cottonseed oil, alcohol, insecticides, and fertilizer. Founded in the early 19th cent. as Mechanicsham, Gretna merged with McDonoghville in 1913 and is now a suburb of New Orleans.

Gretna Green, village, Dumfriesshire, S Scotland, on the English border. It was famous as a place of runaway marriages from 1754, when English marriage law was tightened, until 1856, when a law was passed requiring that one of the parties to marriage in Scotland must reside in Scotland for at least 21 days before issuance of the license.

Grétry, André Ernest Modeste (äNdrā' ĕrnĕst' môdĕst' grātrē'), 1741-1813, French operatic composer. Enormously prolific and successful in his lifetime, he was a master of the 18th-century opéra comique. His works combined the melodic grace of Italian opera with the imagination, delicacy, and dramatic interest of the French. His masterpiece is *Richard Cœur de Lion* (1784).

Greuze, Jean-Baptiste (zhäN bätēst' gröz), 1725-1805, French genre and portrait painter. He studied at the Académie royale and won recognition in 1755 with his *Blind Man Deceived.* He traveled in Italy and on his return painted a series of popular pictures of a moralizing character—*The Village Bride, The Father's Curse, The Wicked Son Punished, The Broken Pitcher* (all: Louvre). His artificial, often slightly prurient compositions are less interesting to modern taste than his portraits, which include one of his wife called *The Milkmaid* (Louvre) and those of the dauphin, Robespierre, and Napoleon (all: Versailles). In the Revolution he lost both fortune and popularity and died in poverty. Examples of his work are in the Louvre, the Wallace Collection, London, the Edinburgh National Gallery, and the Metropolitan Museum. See study by Anita Brookner (1972).

Greville, Charles Cavendish Fulke (grĕv'ĭl), 1794-1865, English diarist. As clerk of the Council in Ordinary (1821-59), he was closely associated with Wellington, Palmerston, and other political leaders of the reigns of George IV, William IV, and Victoria. His memoirs (1874-87; ed. by Lytton Strachey and Roger Fulford, 1938) are an invaluable record of the period. See Louis Kronenberger, ed., *The Great World: Portraits and Scenes from Greville's Memoirs* (1962).

Grévy, Jules (zhül grāvē'), 1807-91, French statesman, president of France (1879-87). As a republican deputy after the February Revolution (1848), he sought to eliminate the danger of a single strong executive. He opposed the Second Empire of Napoleon III. Grévy, a provincial lawyer, abstained from politics from 1851 until he became a deputy in 1868. President of the national assembly (1871-73) and of the chamber of deputies (1876-77), he was chosen to succeed Marshal MacMahon as president of France. His moderate republicanism secured his reelection, but in 1887 he was forced to resign because of a scandal over his son-in-law's traffic in decorations of honor. Sadi Carnot succeeded him.

Grew, Joseph Clark, 1880-1965, American diplomat, b. Boston. Entering diplomatic service in 1904, he held posts of increasing importance in different capitals until 1924, when he became Under Secretary of State. In this position he supervised the establishment of the new Foreign Service. After serving (1927-32) as ambassador to Turkey, Grew was appointed (1932) ambassador to Japan and remained there until after the attack on Pearl Harbor. Afterward he was special assistant (1942-44) to Secretary of State Cordell Hull and again was Under Secretary of State (1944-45). See his autobiographical *Turbulent Era* (1952); biography by W. H. Heinrichs (1967).

Grew, Nehemiah, 1641-1712, English botanist and physician. Grew practiced medicine in London and made important microscopic studies of plants. He made what were probably the first observations of sex in plants. His most noted book is his *Anatomy of Plants* (1682), in which are included a number of papers on chemistry. He also wrote *Anatomy of Vegetables Begun* (1672) and *Comparative Anatomy of Trunks* (1675).

Grey, Albert Henry George Grey, 4th **Earl,** 1851-1917, English statesman, nephew of the 3d Earl Grey. In 1880 he entered the House of Commons as a Liberal, but he lost his seat as a result of his opposition to Gladstone's Home Rule Bill of 1886. Grey returned to Parliament as a member of the House of Lords when he succeeded his uncle to the earldom in 1894. Administrator (1896-97) of Rhodesia, he was appointed governor general of Canada in 1904. In this post he served with such success that his term of office was twice extended (to 1911) at the request of the Canadian government. See Harold Begbie, *Albert, Fourth Earl Grey: A Last Word* (3d ed. 1918).

Grey, Charles Grey, 2d **Earl,** 1764-1845, British statesman. Elected to Parliament in 1786, he was one of those appointed to manage the impeachment of Warren HASTINGS. From 1792 he was a leader of the movement for parliamentary reform and opposed the repressive policies of Sir William Pitt. He succeeded (1806) Charles James Fox as foreign secretary in the "ministry of all talents" and Whig leader of the House of Commons, putting through the measure to abolish the African slave trade (1807). As prime minister (1830-34) he secured the passage of the REFORM BILL of 1832 by threatening to force William IV to create enough Whig peers to carry it in the House of Lords. See biography by G. M. Trevelyan (1929, repr. 1971).

Grey, Sir Edward: see GREY OF FALLODON, EDWARD GREY, 1ST VISCOUNT.

Grey, Sir George, 1812-98, British colonial administrator. He explored the Swan River district in NW Australia (1838) and later was governor of South Australia (1841-45) and of New Zealand (1845-53). As governor of Cape Colony (1854-60), he was a firm advocate of federation for the South African territories. When war broke out between Maori natives and English settlers, Grey was called back to New Zealand to serve his second term as governor (1861-68). His efforts to end the fighting were fruitless, and he was recalled to Great Britain in 1868. After brief residence in London he returned to live in New Zealand and served (1877-79) as premier, advocating important social reforms, all later adopted. *Polynesian Mythology* (1855) is his most important book. See biography by James Rutherford (1961).

Grey, Lady Jane, 1537-54, queen of England for nine days. She was the daughter of Henry Grey, marquess of Dorset (later duke of SUFFOLK), and Frances Brandon, niece of Henry VIII. She became a ward of Baron Seymour of Sudeley, who tried unsuccessfully to bring about a marriage between her and Edward VI. After Seymour's execution (1549) for treason, she fell under the control of John Dudley, duke of NORTHUMBERLAND, who married (1553) her to his youngest son, Lord Guilford Dudley. Northumberland persuaded the boy king, Edward, to change the order of succession and name Lady Jane to follow him on the throne. After Edward's death Lady Jane, only 15 years old, was proclaimed queen on July 10, 1553. The English people, however, rallied to the cause of MARY I, and Northumberland's army deserted. After nine days as nominal queen, Lady Jane was imprisoned. Because of her youth and innocence her life would probably have been spared had not her father joined the rebellion of Sir

Thomas WYATT. Lady Jane, her husband, and her father were beheaded. See R. P. Davey, *The Nine Days' Queen* (1910); H. W. Chapman, *Lady Jane Grey* (1962).

Grey, Zane, 1875–1939, American writer of Western stories, b. Zanesville, Ohio, grad. Univ. of Pennsylvania, 1896. His melodramatic tales of the West and Southwest are vivid in topographical detail but improbable in character and situation. During his lifetime over 13 million copies of his books were sold. Grey was best known for *Riders of the Purple Sage* (1912). See study by Carleton Jackson (1973).

greyhound, breed of tall, swift, sight HOUND developed nearly 5,000 years ago in Egypt. It stands about 26 in. (66 cm) high at the shoulder and weighs about 65 lb (29.5 kg). Its short, smooth coat may be colored black, white, or various shades of fawn, brindle, blue, or red. Known in England before the 9th cent., the greyhound was bred and raised by the aristocracy. In fact, for approximately 700 years it was illegal under English law for a commoner to own a greyhound. It was used to hunt small game, especially hares, and by the early 19th cent. the coursing of hares had developed into an organized sport. In recent years, with the invention by Owen Patrick Smith of the mechanical rabbit for use on a round or oval track, the racing of greyhounds has grown widely in popularity. See DOG.

Greylock, Mount, Mass.: see BERKSHIRE HILLS.

Grey of Fallodon, Edward Grey, 1st Viscount (făl'ədən), 1862–1933, British statesman. He entered Parliament as a Liberal in 1885 and became (1905) foreign secretary in the difficult period preceding World War I. Coming to office in the middle of the Moroccan crisis (see MOROCCO), Grey continued the policy of support of France initiated by the 5th marquess of LANSDOWNE and authorized secret military conversations with France. In 1907 he concluded the Anglo-Russian entente, thus completing the so-called Triple Entente against Germany (see TRIPLE ALLIANCE AND TRIPLE ENTENTE). He again stood firmly in support of France during the AGADIR crisis (1911). Having successfully convened a conference of the Great Powers during the BALKAN WARS, Grey attempted the same course after the assassination (1914) of Archduke Francis Ferdinand of Austria. This time he failed, however, and World War I began. Remaining as foreign secretary until 1916, Grey maintained good relations with the United States and concluded the secret Treaty of London (1915), which brought Italy into the war. He was created a peer in 1916. Grey was president of the League of Nations Union from 1918 and served (1919–20) as a special ambassador to the United States. His chief publications are *Twenty-five Years, 1892–1916* (1926), *Fallodon Papers* (1926), and *Speeches on Foreign Affairs, 1904–1914* (1931). See biographies by G. M. Trevelyan (1937) and Keith Robbins (1971).

Greytown: see SAN JUAN DEL NORTE, Nicaragua.

Griboyedov, Aleksandr Sergeyevich (əlyĭksän'dər sĭrgā'əvĭch grēbəyĕ'dəf), 1795–1829, Russian playwright and diplomat. His fame rests upon his finest play, *Wit Works Woe* (1825; tr. in *Masterpieces of Russian Drama,* Vol. I, ed. by N. R. Noyes, 1933). A verse satire of Moscow society, the play is reminiscent of Molière's *Misanthrope,* but is typically Russian in scene and character. While serving as Russian minister to Persia, Griboyedov was killed defending the Tehran embassy against a Persian attack.

grid, electrode placed between the cathode and anode of an ELECTRON TUBE to control the stream of electrons passing from the cathode to the anode; it is usually made of a fine wire mesh or similar material. In a triode, or three-electrode vacuum electron tube, there is a single grid, the control grid, which is usually kept at a negative voltage, called a bias, with respect to the cathode. If a signal voltage, e.g., a radio signal, is added to the bias, the flow of electrons through the tube will vary in response to the signal, thus allowing the tube to be used as an amplifier. A tetrode, or four-electrode vacuum tube, has an additional grid, called a screen grid, between the control grid and the anode. In a pentode, or five-electrode vacuum tube, a third grid, called a suppressor grid, is placed between the screen grid and the anode. Certain special-purpose tubes contain multiple control grids.

Gridley, Charles Vernon, 1844–98, U.S. naval officer, b. Logansport, Ind. After serving in the Civil War, he continued in naval service. He was flagship commander under Commodore Dewey at Manila in 1898. Dewey's command to him, "You may fire when you are ready, Gridley," began the battle of Manila Bay in the Spanish-American War. Already in ill-health, Gridley died while returning to the United States.

Grieg, Edvard Hagerup (ĕd'vär hä'gərōōp grĕg), 1843–1907, Norwegian composer. Grieg developed a strongly nationalistic style which made him known as "the Voice of Norway." He received piano lessons from his mother and later studied at the Leipzig Conservatory. Influenced by N. V. GADE, Grieg at first wrote in the idiom of German romanticism, but after 1864, when the composer Richard Nordraak (1842–65) introduced him to Norwegian folk music, he turned to the heritage of his own country. In 1867 he founded the Norwegian Academy of Music. For his original and characteristically lyrical songs, he used texts by Norwegian poets, and he made settings of Norwegian folk songs that he had collected. His wife, the singer Nina Hagerup Grieg, was an outstanding interpreter of his songs. He continued, however, to write songs with German texts in the style of Mendelssohn and Schumann, a style that also permeates his piano pieces. In 1869, Grieg established his fame as a leading composer with his Concerto in A Minor for piano and orchestra, appearing himself as the solo pianist in its first performance. His subsequent compositions, generally confined to short lyric forms, include the cantata *Olav Trygvason* (1873) and the suite of incidental dramatic music, *Peer Gynt* (1876). Grieg's impressionistic harmonies, and his use of short melodic phrases, influenced later composers such as Debussy, Tchaikovsky, MacDowell, and Sibelius. See biography by David Monrad-Johansen (tr. 1938, repr. 1972); study ed. by G. E. H. Abraham (1948).

Grien, Hans Baldung: see BALDUNG.

Grierson, Sir George Abraham, 1851–1941, Irish philologist. Besides writing grammars of many modern Indian vernaculars, Grierson directed the compilation of the great *Linguistic Survey of India* (19 vol., 1894–1927).

Griffenfeld, Peder Schumacher, Count (pā'thər shōō'mäkhər, grĭf'ənfĕlt), 1635–99, Danish politician. The son of a merchant, he became (1665) secretary to FREDERICK III. In 1665 Griffenfeld drew up the *Kongelov* [king's law], which established an absolute monarchy in Denmark. He delivered (1670) the document, which had been kept secret until Frederick's death, to CHRISTIAN V. From 1671 to 1676, Griffenfeld dominated the government. In 1673 he was created count. He encouraged trade and industry and centralized the administration. His bourgeois origins and his support of absolutism antagonized the nobles, and his policy of peace, by which he hoped to restore Danish prestige, alienated the army. Denmark was drawn into war with Sweden (1675), and Griffenfeld's plans were overruled. On trivial evidence he was tried for treason and sentenced to death, but Christian commuted the sentence to life imprisonment.

Griffes, Charles Tomlinson (grĭf'ĭs), 1884–1920, American composer, b. Elmira, N.Y.; pupil of Humperdinck in Germany. Among his outstanding larger compositions are *The Pleasure-Dome of Kubla Khan* (Boston, 1920), for orchestra; his *Poem,* for flute and orchestra (1918); and *Roman Sketches* (1915–16), for piano, which includes *The White Peacock.* His piano sonata (pub. 1921) represents his mature style, in which he was free from earlier influences of German romanticism and of impressionism. See biography by E. M. Maisel (1943, repr. 1972).

Griffin, city (1970 pop. 22,734), seat of Spalding co., W central Ga., in a farm and cotton area; inc. 1843. The city has large textile and garment industries. Food processing is also important. Nearby is a state agricultural station.

griffin, in ancient and medieval legend, creature with the head and wings of an eagle and the body of a lion. Its name also appears as griffon and gryphon. The griffin originated in ancient Middle Eastern legend and is often found in Persian sculpture and the decorative arts. Although its significance is obscure, it is often thought to have been a protective symbol, representing strength and vigilance.

Griffith, Arthur, 1872–1922, Irish statesman, founder of SINN FEIN. He joined the nationalist movement as a young man. In 1899 he founded the *United Irishman,* in which he advocated that Irish members of Parliament withdraw from Westminster and organize their own assembly. His goal was the creation of a dual monarchy of England and Ireland, like that of Austria-Hungary. His ideas found adherents who, in 1905, formed the Sinn Fein. Griffith took no part in the Easter Rebellion of 1916, but he was imprisoned several times (1916–18) by the British. Elected to Parliament in 1918, he joined the other Sinn Feiners in forming DÁIL ÉIREANN and was elected its vice president. He led the Irish delegation that negotiated the treaty (1921) establishing the Irish Free State. When Eamon De Valera, president of the Dáil, rejected the treaty, Griffith succeeded to his office. He died suddenly at the beginning of the civil war. See biography by Padraic Colum (1959); Calton Younger, *A State of Disunion* (1972).

Griffith, D. W. (David Wark Griffith), 1880–1948, American movie director and producer, b. La Grange, Ky. Griffith was the first major American film director. He began his film career as an actor and a scenario writer in 1908 with the Biograph Company. He soon began to direct, evolving the principles of film technique. He introduced the fade-in, the fade-out, the long shot, the full shot, the close-up, the moving-camera shot, the flashback, crosscutting, and MONTAGE. He initiated scene rehearsals before shooting and took great pains with lighting effects. Carefully edited, his stories were not limited in time and space. In 1913 he made the first American film of four reels, *Judith of Bethulia,* and in 1915 his *Birth of a Nation,* which utilized his discoveries to their fullest, was a landmark in the history of the cinema. His *Intolerance* (1916) was the first "spectacle" film. In 1919 with Charlie Chaplin, Douglas Fairbanks, and Mary Pickford, he founded United Artists. Griffith was also the first to use dialogue in a feature film (1921). Among his other important films are *Hearts of the World* (1918), *Broken Blossoms* (1918), *Way Down East* (1920), and *Orphans of the Storm* (1922). The final years of Griffith's filmmaking were marked by diminished creativity, both technical and artistic. His last films, produced on much-tightened budgets, were rejected as outmoded. His career ended bitterly 17 years before his death. See Mrs. D. W. Griffith, *When the Movies Were Young* (1925); Lillian Gish's autobiography (1969); R. M. Henderson, *D. W. Griffith, His Life and Work* (1972); Karl Brown, *Adventures with D. W. Griffith* (1973).

Griffith, residential town (1970 pop. 18,168), Lake co., extreme NW Ind.; inc. 1904.

griffon: see BRUSSELS GRIFFON; WIREHAIRED POINTING GRIFFON.

Grignard, Victor (vĕktôr' grēnyär'), 1871–1935, French chemist. He shared the 1912 Nobel Prize in Chemistry for his work in organic synthesis based on his discovery (1900) of the Grignard reagent. He taught at the Univ. of Nancy (1909–19) and at the Univ. of Lyons (from 1919).

Grignard reagent (grēnyärd' rēā'jənt), any of an important class of extremely reactive chemical compounds used in the synthesis of hydrocarbons, alcohols, carboxylic acids, and other compounds. Chemically, a Grignard reagent is an organic magnesium halide dissolved in a nonreactive solvent (typically dry ethyl ether). The substance is made up of an organic group, e.g., an alkyl or aryl group, joined by a highly polar covalent bond (see CHEMICAL BOND) to magnesium, while the magnesium is joined by an ionic bond to a halogen ion, e.g., bromide or iodide. A Grignard reagent will react with water, oxygen, carbon dioxide, or almost any organic compound. The reaction of Grignard reagents with aldehydes to form alcohols is of particular importance in the laboratory. Because Grignard reagents are so unstable, they are generally prepared just before use by reacting an organic halide, e.g., methyl iodide, with magnesium metal in a completely dry solvent; air is usually excluded from the reaction vessel, e.g., by flushing it with nitrogen. Grignard reagents are named after Victor Grignard, a French chemist, who received a Nobel Prize (1912) for their discovery.

Grijalva, Juan de (hwän dā grĕhäl'vä), d.1527, Spanish explorer, commander of an expedition for the purpose of furthering the discoveries of Francisco FERNÁNDEZ DE CÓRDOBA (d.1518?). Leaving Santiago de Cuba in April, 1518, he sailed to Yucatán and explored the coast of Mexico at least as far as the neighborhood of Veracruz. Grijalva was the first Spaniard to hear of the empire of Montezuma. In 1523 he went to Mexico; later he took part in the conquest of Nicaragua. See H. R. Wagner, ed., *The Discovery of New Spain in 1518 by Juan de Grijalva* (1942).

Grijalva, river, c.400 mi (640 km) long, rising in SW Guatemala and flowing NW into S Mexico and N through Chiapas and Tabasco states to the Gulf of Campeche. It is navigable for c.60 mi (100 km) upstream. Several branches of the Usumacinta River flow into it. The Grijalva Project was begun in the 1960s along the lower Grijalva and Usumacinta rivers for flood control and sanitation. Named for the Spanish explorer Juan de Grijalva, who discovered it in 1518, the river is also called the Río Grande de Chiapas in the highland region.

grille, in architecture, a system of bars, usually of decorative metalwork, forming an openwork barrier or enclosure. In its usual materials of wrought iron or bronze, it has been favored for decorative treatment in all periods. Besides its almost universal function of protecting window and door openings, the grille since early medieval times has been used widely as an ornamental enclosure, especially in churches and for tombs, chapels, and shrines. An early example, of pierced bronze, is in the Church

Grille

of the Nativity at Bethlehem (5th or 6th cent.). Other major grilles are those around the tombs of the Scalas, Verona (13th cent.); that which formerly enclosed the tomb of Edward IV, St. George's Chapel, Windsor (15th cent.); and the railing of the tomb of Emperor Maximilian I, Innsbruck, Austria (16th cent.). The Renaissance was remarkable for its lavish employment of decorative metalwork; in England one of the great names in the art is that of Jean Tijou (17th cent.), who executed many notable grilles at St. Paul's Cathedral and Hampton Court Palace; in 18th-century France the works of Jean Lamour, especially at Nancy, are noteworthy. But it was in Spain that the Renaissance grille reached its apex in the *rejas*, or monumental altar and choir screens, in the great cathedrals (see REJERÍA). They were usually of gilded wrought iron. The stone grilles of the Muslim world are also famous, e.g., the marble ornamentation at the Taj Mahal. Edward Stone brilliantly revived and expanded the use of the grille, or screen, in architecture in the 20th cent. His design for the American Embassy at New Delhi is particularly successful.

Grillparzer, Franz (fränts grĭl'pärtsər), 1791-1872, Austrian dramatist. His work combines German classicism and exuberant lyricism. Considered Austria's greatest playwright, he wrote *Der Traum: ein Leben* (1817-34, tr. *A Dream is Life,* 1946), which influenced Hauptmann and Maeterlinck; a trilogy, *Das goldene Vliess* (1822, tr. *The Guest-Friend, The Argonauts, Medea,* 1942); the historical tragedy *König Ottokars Glück und Ende* (1825, tr. *King Ottocar, His Rise and Fall,* 1938); the lyric tragedy *Des Meeres und der Liebe Wellen* (1831, tr. *Hero and Leander,* 1938); *Libussa* (1844, tr. 1941); and *Die Jüdin von Toledo* (1855, tr. *The Jewess of Toledo,* 1953). Grillparzer was also a master of lyric poetry and prose. His finely wrought novella, *Der arme Spielmann* (1844, tr. *The Poor Minstrel,* 1915) contains autobiographical elements. See studies by F. E. Coenen (1951), G. A. Wells (1969), and W. E. Yates (1972).

Grimald, Grimalde, or **Grimoald, Nicholas** (all: grĭm'ôld), 1519?-1562?, English poet. He contributed 40 poems to the first edition (1557) of Tottel's miscellany, of which "A Funeral Song upon the Decease of Annes, His Mother" is the most noteworthy. His other works include two Latin dramas and translations of Vergil and Cicero.

Grimaldi, Francesco Maria (fränchās'kō märē'ä grĕmäl'dē), 1618?-1663, Italian physicist and mathematician. A Jesuit and professor at Bologna, he studied in detail and named the dark areas on the moon. Noted for his discoveries in the field of optics, he was the first to describe the diffraction of light (in a posthumous work published 1665) and the first to attempt a wave theory of light.

Grimaldi, Giovanni Francesco (jōvän'nē), 1606-80, Italian painter and architect, called Il Bolognese. He was a pupil of the Carracci and of Francesco Albani. With the exception of two years in France (1649-51), where he decorated the Mazarin Palace (now the Bibliothèque nationale) and other buildings for Cardinal Mazarin, most of his life was spent in Rome. He was employed as architect and painter by several popes. His paintings, chiefly landscapes in the manner of the Carracci, are found in the Borghese and Colonna galleries and the Quirinal, Rome; the Louvre; and in Vienna.

Grimaldi, Joseph (grĭmăl'dē), 1779-1837, English pantomime actor and clown. He made his debut at the age of three in *Robinson Crusoe* at Sadler's Wells, London. For many years he performed there and at Drury Lane. By the time he played the clown in his production of *Mother Goose* at Covent Garden in 1806, he was a legend. His last appearance was in *Harlequin Hoax* (1828). He was a master of pantomime; dynamic energy was the essence of his humor. The songs he made famous were sung long after his death at the insistence of the gallery. See his memoirs (ed. by Charles Dickens, 1838).

Grimaldi man: see MAN, PREHISTORIC.

Grimké, Angelina Emily (grĭm'kē), 1805-79, American abolitionist and advocate of woman's rights, b. Charleston, S.C. Converted to the Quaker faith by her elder sister Sarah Moore Grimké, she became an abolitionist in 1835, wrote *An Appeal to the Christian Women of the South* (1836) in testimony of her conversion, and with her sister began speaking around New York City. She developed into an orator of considerable power and was invited (1837) to lecture in Massachusetts. Her three appearances before the Massachusetts legislative committee on antislavery petitions early in 1838 constituted a triumph. The same year she married Theodore Dwight WELD, also an active abolitionist. Ill health after her marriage led her to abandon the lecture platform, but she continued to aid Weld in his abolitionist work and maintained a lasting, lively interest in the cause to which they had contributed so much. See C. H. Birney, *The Grimké Sisters* (1885, repr. 1969); G. H. Barnes and D. L. Dumond, ed., *Letters of Theodore Dwight Weld, Angelina Grimké Weld, and Sarah Grimké, 1822-1844* (2 vol., 1934); Gerda Lerner, *The Grimké Sisters from South Carolina* (1967, repr. 1971); K. D. Lumpkin, *The Emancipation of Angelina Grimké* (1974).

Grimké, Archibald Henry, 1849-1930, American Negro author and crusader for Negro advancement, b. near Charleston, S.C. The son of a white father and a slave mother, he was graduated from Lincoln Univ. (B.A., 1870; M.A., 1872) and, with the help of his aunt, Sarah Moore Grimké, from Harvard (LL.B., 1874). He then practiced law in Boston. His many articles and pamphlets on race problems focused attention on the double standard of justice applied to the Negro. He wrote biographies of William Lloyd Garrison (1891) and Charles Sumner (1892). From 1894 to 1898 he was American consul to Santo Domingo. He was president of the American Negro Academy from 1903 to 1916, and in 1919 was awarded the Spingarn medal by the National Association for the Advancement of Colored People for his services on behalf of the Negro. See biography by Janet Stevenson (1969).

Grimké, Sarah Moore, 1792-1873, American abolitionist and advocate of woman's rights, b. Charleston, S.C. She came from a distinguished Southern family. On a visit to Philadelphia, Sarah joined the Society of Friends. She converted her younger sister Angelina to the Quaker faith, and the two moved to the North permanently in Jan., 1832. Angelina became an abolitionist in 1835 and in turn converted Sarah. These two timid daughters of an aristocratic slaveholding family became the first women who dared to speak in public for the Negro slave and then for woman's rights. Sarah wrote *An Epistle to the Clergy of the Southern States* (1836), urging abolition, and *Letters on the Equality of the Sexes and the Condition of Woman* (1838). In 1838 the sisters persuaded their mother to give them, as their share of the family estate, slaves, whom they immediately freed. See bibliography under GRIMKÉ, ANGELINA EMILY.

Grimm, Jakob (yä'kôp), 1785-1863, German philologist and folklorist, a founder of comparative philology. His interest in the relationship among Germanic languages led to his formulation of GRIMM'S LAW. His German grammar (1819-37) and his *German Mythology* (1835, tr. 1880-88) were works of first importance. He is best known, however, for his work on German folk tales, known as *Grimm's Fairy Tales* (1812-15), which he collected with his brother, **Wilhelm Grimm,** 1786-1859, and which did much to encourage the romantic revival of folklore. The brothers Grimm also planned and inaugurated the great German dictionary (16 vol., 1854-1954). See biography of the brothers by M. B. Peppard (1971); Lore Segal and Maurice Sendak, eds. *The Juniper Tree and Other Tales from Grimm* (1973).

Grimmelshausen, Hans Jakob Christoffel von (häns yä'kôp krĭs'tôfəl fən grĭm'əlshou"zən), 1625-76, German novelist. Impressed into the THIRTY YEARS WAR at the age of 10, he educated himself in letters and the law. His *Simplicissimus* (*The Adventuresome Simplicius Simplicissimus;* 1669), a picaresque romance, is often called the first German biographical novel. Immediately successful, by virtue of its vigor, humor, and realistic characterizations, it gave rise to numerous "Simpliciades," many by Grimmelshausen writing under a pseudonym.

Grimm's law, principle of relationships in Indo-European languages, first formulated by Jakob Grimm in 1822 and a continuing subject of interest and investigation to 20th-century linguists. It shows that a process—the regular shifting of consonants in groups—took place once in the development of English and the other Low German languages and twice in German and the other High German languages. The first sound shift, affecting both English and German, was from the early phonetic positions documented in the ancient, or classical, Indo-European languages (Sanskrit, Greek, Latin) to those still evident in the Low German languages, including English; the second shift affected only the High German languages, e.g., standard German. Grimm's law shows that the classical voiceless stops (*k,t,p*) became voiceless aspirates (*h,th,f*) in English and mediae (*h,d,f*) in German, e.g., the initial sounds of Latin *pater,* English *father,* German *Vater,* and in the middle of Latin *frater,* English *brother,* German *Bruder.* It also shows that the classical unaspirated voiced stops (*g,d,b*) became voiceless stops (*k,t,p*) in English and voiceless aspirates (*kh,ts,f*) in German, e.g., the initial sounds of Latin *decem,* English *ten,* German *zehn,* and that the classical aspirated voiced stops (*gh,dh,bh*) became unaspirated voiced stops (*g,d,b*) in English and voiceless stops (*k,t,p*) in German, e.g., the initial sounds of Sanskrit *dhar,* English *draw,* German *tragen.*

Grimoald, Nicholas: see GRIMALD, NICHOLAS.

Grimsby, county borough (1971 pop. 95,685), in the Parts of Lindsey, Lincolnshire, E central England, at the mouth of the Humber River. It is one of the largest fishing ports in the world. Grimsby has an extensive trade in fish, coal, grain, and timber and an important frozen food industry. Other industries include the production of rayon, titanium oxide, and chemicals. There is a college of technology in Grimsby. In 1974, Grimsby became part of the new nonmetropolitan county of Humberside.

Grimsel (grĭm'zəl), pass, 7,159 ft (2,182 m) high, S Switzerland, between the Rhône and Aare valleys. The Grimsel Road (built 1891-94), over the pass, connects Bern and Valais cantons. The Grimsel Lake nearby is formed by two dams on the upper Aare River that supply water to the Oberhasli hydroelectric works.

Grindelwald (grĭn'dəlvält), town (1970 pop. 3,511), Bern canton, S central Switzerland, at the foot of the Eiger, Schreckhorn, and Wetterhorn peaks. It was one of the first Alpine resorts.

grinding, process by which surface material is removed from an object, usually metal, by the abrasive action of a rotating wheel or a moving belt. The wheel or belt contains abrasive grains that chop the surface of an object into tiny chips (see GRINDING WHEEL). Grinding is used in many manufacturing processes to produce a fine surface finish on an object and to bring the size of an object to within very fine tolerances. A grinding machine has devices that hold an unfinished object and move it past the machine's abrasive wheel or belt, which is driven by a motor. For less exacting work, such as sharpening cutting tools, objects can be hand held and ground by a machine consisting mainly of an abrasive wheel or belt. For many products grinding is only one step in a finishing process that involves additional similar operations such as HONING, lapping, polishing (see POLISHES), and buffing.

grinding wheel, wheel impregnated with abrasive grains and mounted so that it can be used for GRINDING. A grinding wheel can be made by mixing a bonding material, usually clay, with abrasive grains of such substances as silicon carbide or aluminum oxide. The mixture is then shaped into a wheel and hardened. A grindstone is a grinding wheel made by shaping naturally occurring sandstone, which contains abrasive quartz grains.

Gringore, Pierre (pyĕr grăNgôr'), c.1475-c.1539, French dramatist and poet. He produced ceremonial pageants and mystery plays and wrote the *Jeu du prince des sots* (1512), a dramatic tetralogy on contemporary politics, as well as a number of political and moral poems.

Grinnell, George Bird, 1849-1938, American naturalist and student of Indian life, b. Brooklyn, N.Y., grad. Yale (B.A., 1870; Ph.D., 1880). He accompanied Custer's Black Hills expedition as naturalist (1874), was with William Ludlow's expedition to Yellowstone Park (1875), and was a member of the Harriman Alaska expedition in 1899. He was editor (1876-1911) of *Forest and Stream* and was prominent in preservation of wildlife and in conservation movements. He organized the first Audubon Society and was an organizer of the New York Zoological Society. In 1885 he discovered the glacier in Montana that now bears his name and was influential in legislation that led to the establishment (1910) of Glacier National Park. He is best known, however, for his books on the Plains Indians, such as *Pawnee Hero Stories* (1889), *The Story of the Indian* (1895), *The Fighting Cheyennes* (1915), and *The Cheyenne Indians* (1923). See his selected papers ed. by J. F. Reiger (1972).

Grinnell, Josiah Bushnell, 1821-91, American pioneer, clergyman, and abolitionist, b. New Haven, Vt. As pastor (1851-52) of the First Congregational Church in Washington, D.C., he created a sensation by preaching an antislavery sermon, which cost him his pastorate. It was to him that Horace Greeley gave the famous advice, "Go West, young man, go West!" Go Grinnell did—to Iowa, where he founded (1854) the town of Grinnell and gave land and buildings (1859) to Iowa College, which was later named Grinnell College. An abolitionist political leader, he aided in the formation of the Republican party and served as a Congressman (1863-67). He also helped to extend education in Iowa, to promote railroads, and to aid agriculture and stock raising (especially by introducing new breeds). See his autobiographical *Men and Events of Forty Years* (1891); biography by C E. Payne (1938).

Grinnell College, at Grinnell, Iowa; coeducational; incorporated 1847 as Iowa College, opened 1848 by Congregationalists at Davenport. The college moved to Grinnell in 1859 and merged with Grinnell Univ. (chartered 1856; founded by Josiah B. Grinnell). It was named Grinnell College in 1909 and, although related to the Congregational Church, is a nonsectarian school.

grippe: see INFLUENZA.

Gripsholm (grĭps-hôlm'), castle, SE Sweden, near Stockholm, on Malaren Lake. Now an art museum, it was begun in the 1380s and was reconstructed by Gustavus I in the 16th cent.

Gris, Juan (hwän grēs), 1887-1927, Spanish cubist painter, whose original name was José Victoriano González. After studying in Madrid he settled in Paris in 1906, where he held his first exhibition at the Salon des Indépendents of 1912. Gris played an important role in the development of synthetic CUBISM. His paintings are composed of simple forms; at first they reflected an architectonic logic of design, but later they were given a more sumptuous, decorative treatment. The majority of his works are still-life oils and collages. Gris also painted several portraits. The Museum of Modern Art, New York City, has several still lifes. See his letters (ed. and tr. by Douglas Cooper, 1956); catalog by J. T. Soby (1958); D. H. Kahnweiler, *Juan Gris: His Life and Work* (rev. ed. 1969).

grisaille (grĭzī', -zāl', Fr. grēzä'yə), a monochrome painting and drawing technique executed in tones of gray. Such works were often produced in the Renaissance to simulate sculpture, as in Uccello's equestrian portrait of Sir John Hawkswood (Cathedral of Florence). Painters of stained glass frequently used grisaille. In the 17th cent. grisaille was prized for interior decoration.

Griselda (grĭzĕl'də), long-suffering heroine of medieval story, whose husband subjects her to numerous trials in order to test her devotion. The story originated in a widespread W European folktale patterned in part upon the story of Cupid and Psyche. The tale of Griselda was used by Boccaccio in the *Decameron*, by Petrarch, by Chaucer in the "Clerk's Tale," and by Thomas Dekker in the comedy *Patient Grissell.*

Grisi, Giulia (jo͝o'lyä grē'zē), 1811-69, Italian operatic soprano. She toured the United States in 1854 with Giuseppe Mario, whom she married in 1856. Roles were written for her by Bellini, in *I Puritani*, and by Donizetti, in *Don Pasquale.* Her first teacher was her sister, **Giuditta Grisi,** 1805-40, a mezzo-soprano, who married and retired in 1834.

Grisons (grēsŏnz', Fr. grēzôN'), Ger. *Graubünden,* canton (1970 pop. 162,086), 2,746 sq mi (7,112 sq km), E Switzerland, bordering on Italy and Austria. CHUR is the capital. The largest and most sparsely populated of the cantons, it is a region of Alpine peaks and glaciers, of forested highlands, and of fertile valleys. The Engadine Valley and the Swiss National Park, in the eastern part of the canton, attract large numbers of tourists. St. Moritz, Davos, and Arosa are the chief resorts. Industry is generally limited and is centered at Chur. About a fourth of the population speaks Romansh, a Rhaetic-Romantic language, which was made a national language in 1938; a smaller minority speaks Italian, and the rest, German. A part of Rhaetia under the Roman Empire, the territory preserved Roman laws and customs, although it nominally passed to the Ostrogoths (493) and to the Franks (537). In the 9th cent. the bishops of Chur began to attain prominence in the region. The bishops (after 1170 the prince-bishops) allied themselves with the rising power of the Hapsburgs. Their power, however, was checked and gradually broken by three local leagues founded between 1367 and 1436—the League of God's House, the *Graubünden,* or Gray League, and the League of Ten Jurisdictions. The three leagues, composed of communes and feudal lords, allied and joined with the Swiss Confederation. In 1512 they conquered the VALTELLINA from Milan. Only part of the population accepted the Reformation (1524-26). In the Thirty Years War the country was rent by bloody strife between the Catholic party, siding with Spain and the Holy Roman emperor, and the Protestants, supporting Venice and France. With the Valtellina the chief bone of contention, the struggle was one of European importance. In 1799 the Grisons was forced by the French to enter the HELVETIC REPUBLIC, and in 1803 it became a Swiss canton under Napoleon's Act of Mediation. The Valtellina was definitively lost at the Congress of Vienna (1815).

gristle: see CARTILAGE.

Griswold, Matthew (grĭz'wəld), 1714-99, American jurist and politician, b. Lyme, Conn. Admitted to the bar in 1743, he was very learned in the law and was active in Connecticut politics. As deputy governor (1769-84) before and during the American Revolution he was ex officio judge of the highest court in Connecticut, and by his wisdom contributed much to the new state in troubled times. He was later governor (1784-86) and presided over the state convention (1788) that ratified the Constitution. Roger Griswold was his son.

Griswold, Roger, 1762-1812, American political leader, b. Lyme, Conn.; son of Matthew Griswold. A Connecticut lawyer, he entered politics and, as U.S. Congressman (1795-1805), was a vigorous Federalist and a virulent critic of President Jefferson's administration, going so far as to advocate seriously the separation of New England from the Union. He was lieutenant governor of Connecticut (1809-11), and governor (1811-12). As governor he expressed Connecticut's attitude toward the war with England by withholding the state militia from the command of Federal officers, thereby causing a test case on the clause in the Constitution dealing with the authority of the President to requisition the state militia. Ruling on the case, the U.S. Supreme Court affirmed the President's authority.

Griswold, Rufus Wilmot, 1815-57, American editor, b. Benson, Vt. He was influential as editor of *Graham's Magazine* (1842-43) and the *International Monthly Magazine* (1850-52) and as anthologist of *The Poets and Poetry of America* (1842) and several similar books. He had known Edgar Allan Poe since 1842 and on Poe's death was named his literary executor. The obituary he wrote emphasized the scandals attached to Poe's name, and in his edition of Poe's writings he added passages in Poe's letters favorable to himself and had them published as Poe's own. See his selected letters and papers (ed. by his son, W. McC. Griswold, 1898).

Grivas, George (grē'väs), 1898-1974, Greek and Cypriot general, b. Cyprus. He joined the Greek army and early became an advocate of enosis (the union of Cyprus with Greece). After World War II, he returned to Cyprus to head a guerrilla army, Ethniki Organosis Kyprion Agoniston (National Organization for the Cyprus Struggle), or EOKA, which conducted the military struggle against the British in Cyprus from 1955 to 1959; he opposed the 1959 agreements establishing the independent republic of Cyprus. In Aug., 1964, after fighting broke out between Greek and Turkish Cypriots, he became commander of the Cypriot national guard. He also headed Greek forces on the island. Grivas was forced to leave Cyprus for Greece, however, in Nov., 1967, after an incident in which a number of Turkish Cypriots were killed in a battle with Grivas's national guard. In 1971, he returned secretly to the island to press for enosis, launching a terrorist campaign against the government of President Makarios. See his *Memoirs,* ed. by Charles Foley (1965); biography by Dudley Barker (1960).

grizzly bear or **grizzly,** large, powerful North American brown BEAR, characterized by silver-tipped, or grizzled, fur. Grizzlies are 6 to 7 ft (180 to 210 cm) long and stand 3½ to 4 ft (105 to 120 cm) at the humped shoulder; they weigh up to 750 lb (340 kg). They are more highly carnivorous than most bears and prey on large mammals such as deer. Formerly widespread in the western half of North America, from the Arctic Circle to central Mexico, they were nearly exterminated because of their predation on livestock. They are now found in wild and protected regions of Alaska, W Canada, and the U.S. Rocky Mts. Sometimes considered a distinct species (*Ursa horriblis*), the grizzly is now more commonly regarded as one of the many varieties of brown bear, which together constitute a single species, *Ursa ursa,* spread throughout North America and N Eurasia. It is classified in the phylum CHORDATA, subphylum Vertebrata, class Mammalia, order Carnivora, family Ursidae.

Grocyn, William (grō'sĭn), 1446?-1519, English humanist. An associate of John COLET and Thomas LINACRE, he reputedly introduced the teaching of Greek at Oxford.

Grodno (grôd'nô), Belorussian *Horodno*, city (1970 pop. 132,000), capital of Grodno oblast, W European USSR, in Belorussia, on the Neman River. A river port and an important railway center, it has industries producing machinery, electrical products, textiles, and processed food and tobacco. Dating back to the 10th cent., Grodno was the capital of an independent principality until 1398, when it was included in the grand duchy of Lithuania. It became the second capital of Lithuania and passed to Poland after the union of Lithuania with Poland in 1569 (see LUBLIN). In 1673 it became a seat of Polish diets, the last of which (1793) was forced to consent to the second partition of Poland. Grodno passed to Russia in 1795 and was the capital of Grodno province from 1801 to 1914. It was transferred to Poland in 1920 and was incorporated into the Belorussian Republic in 1939. Grodno has many historic buildings of great interest. Ruins of the ducal residence (12th cent.) are the oldest example of secular brick architecture in this part of Europe. Its medieval castle was restored in the 1930s. Other notable buildings include a 12th-century Orthodox Eastern church, the Stephen Báthory palace (16th cent.), and the Bernardine church (16th cent.). Stephen Báthory had his residence in Grodno, where he died in 1586, and STANISLAUS II abdicated there in 1795.

Groenendael (gro͞o'nəndäl''): see BELGIAN SHEEPDOG.

grog, originally a mixture of rum and water. It is named after Admiral Grogram Vernon, who first ordered the dilution of the British Royal Navy's daily rum ration. The term is now applied to almost any unsweetened mixture of spirits and water, hot or cold, and it is sometimes used for any intoxicating drink: hence, groggy.

groin, in oceanography: see COAST PROTECTION.

Grolier de Servières, Jean, vicomte d'Aguisy (grōl'yər, Fr. zhäN grôlyā' də sĕrvyĕr' vĕkôNt' dägēzē'), 1479-1565, French bibliophile. Grolier served Francis I as government treasurer and was later ambassador to Italy. There he met the printer Aldus Manutius and began collecting books. His library consisted of some 3,000 richly bound volumes, which remained in his family until 1675. About 350 volumes are now known to be in existence; many are in the Bibliothèque nationale. These books bear their owner's *ex libris,* "J. Grolerii et amicorum," which probably indicates that he also secured copies of the book for his friends. A New York club of bibliophiles, the Grolier Club (1884), and the American publishing company Grolier Incorporated are named after him. See Brander Matthews, *Bookbindings . . . with an Account of the Grolier Club* (1895).

Gromyko, Andrei Andreyevich (grōmē'kō, Rus. əndrā' əndrā'yəvĭch grəmĭ'kə), 1909-, Soviet diplomat. A member of the Communist party from 1931, he entered (1939) the diplomatic service, rising rapidly to become Soviet ambassador to the United States (1943-46) and chief permanent Soviet delegate to the United Nations (1946-48). He was (1952-53) ambassador to Great Britain. In 1956, Gromyko was elected to the central committee of the Communist party. He became foreign minister in 1957, maintaining his position despite changes in the leadership in the USSR and in foreign policy. In the early 1970s he was active in preparing the summit talks between Soviet leader Leonid Brezhnev and U.S. President Richard M. Nixon and in drawing up the nonaggression pact with West Germany.

Gronchi, Giovanni (jōvän'nē grôn'kē), 1887–, Italian political leader. He entered parliament in 1919 as a member of the new Popular party. When Benito Mussolini seized power in 1922 and formed a coalition ministry, Gronchi became undersecretary for industry and commerce. He joined the opposition a few months later and was soon forced to retire from political life. After Mussolini's downfall, he helped to found the Christian Democratic party and served (1944–46) as minister for commerce, industry, and labor. He was later (1948–55) speaker of the chamber of deputies and served as president of Italy from 1955 to 1962. See his autobiography (1962).

Groningen (grō'nĭng-ən), province (1971 pop. 522,400), c.900 sq mi (2,330 sq km), NE Netherlands, bordering on West Germany in the east and the North Sea in the north. Groningen is the capital of the province, which has a largely agricultural economy. There is a fertile coastal strip; the interior consists largely of reclaimed fenland and peat bogs and is drained by numerous canals. Vast reserves of natural gas were discovered there in 1961. In 1536, Charles V, the Hapsburg ruler, added Groningen to his Netherlands possessions. During the revolt of the Netherlands against Spain, the nobles living in the province's countryside signed the Union of Utrecht in 1579. The capital, however, remained loyal to the Hapsburgs until 1594.

Groningen, city (1971 pop. 171,334), capital of Groningen prov., NE Netherlands. It is an important trade and transportation center. Manufactures include clothing, food products, furniture, and machinery. In the 11th cent. Groningen came under the temporal power of the bishops of Utrecht. It soon rose to prominence and in the 12th cent. supplied ships for the Crusades. In 1284 it joined the Hanseatic League and later gained control over the central section of Friesland, which now constitutes Groningen prov. The city remained loyal to the Hapsburgs at the beginning of the revolt of the Netherlands against Spain, but was captured by the Dutch under Maurice of Nassau in 1594. A picturesque city, Groningen has several fine churches, notably the Martinikerk (15th cent.) and the Nieuwe Kerk (17th cent.), and many museums. It is the site of the Univ. of Groningen (1614).

Gronlund, Laurence (grŏn'lənd), 1846–99, American Socialist, b. Denmark, educated at the Univ. of Copenhagen. He emigrated to the United States in 1867 and became a lawyer in Chicago. His *Cooperative Commonwealth* (1884), the first adequate exposition in the English language of German socialism, went through many editions and was influential both in the United States and in England. He wrote *Our Destiny* (1891), *The New Economy* (1898), *Socializing a State* (1898), and a number of pamphlets against the single-tax doctrines of Henry GEORGE. He lectured in all parts of the country and, for a time, was an executive of the Socialist Labor party.

Grooms, Red, 1937–, American artist, b. Nashville, Tenn. Grooms was one of the earliest practitioners of the HAPPENING. He worked in other theatrical forms, but is best known for his POP ART constructions. Grooms's style is satirical and cartoonlike, as in his film *Fat Feet* (1965).

Groote, Gerard or **Geert** (gā'rärt, gārt', grō'tə), 1340–84, Dutch Roman Catholic reformer. He studied at Paris and elsewhere and because of his learning in theology, philosophy, jurisprudence, and medicine, he was appointed professor at Cologne. Converted from a worldly life c.1374, he retired to a Carthusian monastery near Arnhem, urged probably by John RUYSBROECK. He was ordained deacon, but never priest, and under episcopal auspices he preached all over the Netherlands, denouncing clergy and laity impartially and making many converts. In 1383 his clerical enemies procured an episcopal ban on his preaching. In his preaching period he formed the Brothers of the Common Life, or Modern Devotion, a voluntary monastic communal organization. Before his death he asked his followers to become Augustinian canons. His society and the Augustinians he inspired were pioneers in a general reform of German monastic life. Some scholars hold that Groote is the author of the devotional classic *The Imitation of Christ* (see IMITATION OF CHRIST, THE), ascribed by tradition to THOMAS À KEMPIS. *The Following of Christ* (tr. 1941) is purportedly based on the original Groote manuscripts in diary form.

Groote Eylandt (grōōt ī'lənd) [Dutch,=large island], 950 sq mi (2,461 sq km), Northern Territory, N Australia. It is the largest island in the Gulf of Carpentaria. Manganese ore is mined there.

Groote Schuur (khrōō'tə skür) [Afrik.,=large barn], estate, Cape Town, Cape Prov., SW South Africa. The main building of the estate, which is a good example of Dutch colonial architecture, was erected on the site of a large barn dating from 1657. It once was the home of Cecil Rhodes and is now the residence of South Africa's prime minister. The Univ. of Cape Town is on the grounds of the estate; in 1967, Dr. Christiaan Barnard performed the world's first human heart transplant operation there.

Gropius, Walter (väl'tər grō'pēōōs), 1883–1969, German-American architect, one of the leaders of modern functional architecture. In Germany his Fagus factory buildings (1910–11) at Alfeld, with their glass walls, metal spandrels, and discerning use of purely industrial features, were among the most advanced works in Europe. In his buildings for the Cologne Exposition (1914), using extensive areas of glass, modern engineering and materials received a frank architectural expression. After World War I, Gropius became (1918) director of the Weimar School of Art, reorganizing it as the BAUHAUS. It was moved in 1925 to Dessau. The complete set of new buildings for it, which Gropius designed (1926), remains one of his finest achievements. He built the Staattheater at Jena (1923), some experimental houses at Stuttgart (1927), and designed residences, workers' dwellings, and industrial buildings. He practiced (1934–37) in London with Maxwell Fry and in 1937 emigrated to America, where he headed the school of architecture at Harvard until 1952. Practicing his principles of cooperative design, Gropius worked with a group of young architects on the design of the Harvard graduate center. He continued his architectural activity with this group, the Architects Collaborative (TAC), in such works as the U.S. embassy at Athens, the Univ. of Baghdad (1961), and the Grand Central City building, New York City (1963). His writings include *The New Architecture and the Bauhaus* (tr. 1935) and *Scope of World Architecture* (1955). See studies by S. Giedion (1954), J. M. Fitch (1960), and M. Franciscono (1971).

Gropper, William, 1897–, American painter and cartoonist, b. New York City. Gropper studied painting at night under Henri and Bellows. Employed as cartoonist by the New York *Tribune*, he went to work for the *Rebel Worker* in 1919. He became a leading painter of the '20s and '30s, his works being primarily concerned with social responsibilities and class inequalities. Gropper is also known for his murals, such as those in the Dept. of the Interior Building, Washington, D.C. *The Senate* (Mus. of Modern Art, New York City) is characteristic of his bold, satiric style. See study by A. L. Freundlich (1968).

Groppi, James, 1931–, American Roman Catholic cleric and political activist, b. Milwaukee. Groppi, who grew up in the Milwaukee slums, attended St. Francis' Seminary and was ordained in 1960. In 1967 he helped lead Milwaukee's black population in more than 100 demonstrations against segregated housing; his actions resulted in an open housing ordinance. Groppi has directed his protest activities primarily to the state and city levels; he maintains a ministry in St. Michael's Parish, Milwaukee.

Gros, Antoine-Jean, Baron (äNtwän' zhäN bärôN' grō), 1771–1835, French painter. He studied with his father, a miniaturist, and with J. L. David, whose classical theory he adopted. Napoleon appointed him painter of war campaigns, and his realistic treatment of this subject was much admired. In 1797 he was commissioned to select Italian masterpieces, the spoils of war, to enrich the Louvre. Between 1802 and 1808 he painted his best-known works, *The Plague at Jaffa* and *The Battle of Eylau* (both: Louvre) and *The Battle of Aboukir* (Versailles). His romantic treatment of color and the emotional tone of his works were at odds with the painter's professed classicism. His fame endured until, after the Restoration, he tried to reinstate the classical manner in his work. He failed and, condemned to obscurity, drowned himself in the Seine. Delacroix and Géricault were influenced by his vivid color and his sense of movement.

grosbeak (grōs'bēk) [great beak], common name for various members of the family Fringillidae (FINCH family). Grosbeaks are characterized by their large conical bills. The male rose-breasted grosbeak (*Zamelodia ludoviciana*) is striking with its white bill and summer plumage of black and white accented by a rose-red breast. Sometimes called potato-bug bird, it destroys these and other insects. The pine grosbeak of the Old and New Worlds, the largest of the finches, feeds on conifer seeds and wild fruits; the western, or black-headed, grosbeak is an enemy of scale insects, codling moths, and flower beetles. The eastern, or evening, grosbeak is metallic yellow with black and white wings and tail. The common European grosbeak is the hawfinch. Grosbeaks are classified in the phylum CHORDATA, subphylum Vertebrata, class Aves, order Passeriformes, family Fringillidae.

Groseilliers, Médard Chouart, sieur des (mādär' shwär syör dā grôsāyā'), 1618?–c.1690, French trader and explorer in North America. He was the brother-in-law of Pierre Esprit RADISSON and his companion in his great journeys.

Gros Morne (grō môrn), mountain, 2,644 ft (806 m) high, W Newfoundland island, Canada, in the Long Range N of Bonne Bay; second highest point on Newfoundland. **Gros Morne National Park** (690 sq mi/1,787 sq km; est. 1970) contains a shifting sand dune region of the coast and the most spectacular section of the Long Range.

Gross, Samuel David, 1805–84, American surgeon, b. near Easton, Pa., M.D. Jefferson Medical College, Philadelphia, 1828. He taught at the medical colleges of several universities and at Jefferson from 1856. He made outstanding contributions to his profession as teacher of pathological anatomy and surgery; as inventor of surgical instruments and techniques; as author of *Elements of Pathological Anatomy* (1839), *A System of Surgery* (1859), and other works; and as a founder of the American Medical Association. See his autobiography (1887).

Grossbeeren (grōsbār'ən), village, Potsdam dist., central East Germany. There, in 1813, Friedrich Wilhelm von Bülow, using the Prussian militia for the first time, defeated the French under Oudinot, thus protecting Berlin.

Grosse Pointe Farms, city (1970 pop. 11,701), Wayne co., SE Mich., a residential suburb of Detroit, on Lake St. Clair; inc. 1893. The mansion of John Dodge and the Alger House, a branch of the Detroit Institute of Arts, are of interest.

Grosse Pointe Park, village (1970 pop. 15,585), Wayne co., SE Mich., a residential suburb of Detroit, on Lake St. Clair; inc. 1907.

Grosse Pointe Woods, village (1970 pop. 21,878), Wayne co., SE Mich., a residential suburb of Detroit; inc. 1926.

Grosseteste, Robert (grōs'tĕst), c.1175–1253, English prelate. Educated at Oxford and probably also at Paris, he became one of the most learned men of his time. He taught at Oxford and later, as rector, made the university an important center of learning. In 1224 he became lector of the Franciscans there and founded the Oxford Franciscan school, which profoundly influenced medieval thought. His most illustrious pupils, Adam MARSH and Roger BACON, continued Grosseteste's work at Oxford after he was made (1235) bishop of Lincoln, then the most populous see of England. As bishop, he was an indefatigable administrator and zealous reformer, visiting the monasteries, assigning suitable candidates to parish offices, and preaching to the people. Grosseteste fought for the maintenance of the Magna Carta. He thwarted efforts of HENRY III to control ecclesiastical appointments, and as a member of the baronial council he supported the reforms of Simon de MONTFORT (1208–65). Grosseteste did not hesitate to censure Pope Innocent IV for his excessive exactions and for appointing foreigners to rich English benefices; he also attacked the Curia for its corruption and indolence. Some historians see in Grosseteste's protests against Rome an influence upon Wyclif and a foreshadowing of the Reformation. Grosseteste was a prolific scholar. He knew Greek and probably Hebrew; his translations of, and commentaries on, Aristotle served as a foundation for the scholasticism of Albertus Magnus and Thomas Aquinas. His prolific writing included treatises on physics, optics, light, motion, color, mathematics, astronomy, psychology, pastoral works, and polemical poems in French for the layman. For 50 years after his death he was venerated in his diocese as a saint. In recent years he has been accounted one of the early practitioners of modern scientific method. Few of his writings are available in English. Three treatises are translated in Richard McKeon, *Selections from Medieval Philosophers* (1928–31). See S. H. Thomson, *The Writings of Robert Grosseteste* (1940); D. A. Callus, ed., *Robert Grosseteste, Scholar and Bishop* (1955); A. C. Crombie, *Robert*

Grosseteste and the Origins of Experimental Science (1953).

Grosseto (grōs-sä'tō), city (1971 pop. 62,634), central Italy, capital of Grosseto prov., Tuscany region, on the Ombrone River near the Tyrrhenian Sea. Situated in the reclaimed MAREMMA area, it is an agricultural market. Nearby are the ruins of RUSSELLAE, an Etruscan town deserted in the 12th cent.

Grossglockner (grōs'glôknər), peak, 12,460 ft (3,797 m) high, in Tyrol, S Austria, the highest point in the Hohe Tauern range and in Austria. It is traversed by the Grossglocknerstrasse (built 1930–35), a magnificent Alpine highway rising up to 7,770 ft (2,368 m). The great Pasterze glacier (12 sq mi/31 sq km; 5 mi/8 km long) descends the peak.

Grossgörschen or **Gross Görschen:** see LÜTZEN, East Germany.

Grossi, Tommaso (tôm-mä'zō grôs'sē), 1791–1853, Italian novelist and poet. Imitating his friend Manzoni, he wrote romantic historical novels, among them *Marco Visconti* (1834, tr. 1836). Other works include lyrics in the Milanese dialect.

Grosvenor, Gilbert Hovey (hŭv'ē grōv'nər), 1875–1966, American editor, b. Constantinople, Turkey. As director (1899–1919) and later as president (1920–54) of the National Geographic Society and as editor (1903–54) of the *National Geographic Magazine*, he encouraged worldwide exploration and greatly increased the circulation of his magazine, especially by using colored photographs. While he was director the society membership grew from 900 to 1,900,000. He was active in promoting conservation and the protection of wildlife.

Grosvenor Gallery, founded in London (1877) by Sir Coutts Lindsay (1839–1913), for the independent exhibition (opening May 1 annually) of paintings and sculpture by established artists, both Academicians and moderns being represented. There is no jury. The gallery has the atmosphere of the private dwelling for which the work shown is usually destined.

Gros Ventre Indians (grō văN'trə) [Fr.,=big belly], name used by the French for two quite distinct North American Indian tribes. One was the Atsina, a detached band of the ARAPAHO INDIANS, whose language belongs to the Algonquian branch of the Algonquian-Wakashan linguistic stock (see AMERICAN INDIAN LANGUAGES); the other was the HIDATSA INDIANS, whose language belongs to the Siouan branch of the Hokan-Siouan linguistic stock. The Indian sign language designated the two groups by somewhat similar gestures on the torso, one referring to the Hidatsa chest tattoos and the other, designating the Atsina, conveying the meaning of hunger. In the 18th cent. the Atsina roamed the plains between the Missouri and the Saskatchewan rivers under the protection of the powerful Blackfoot Indians to the west. Today the Atsina live with the Assiniboin Indians on the Fort Belknap Reservation in Montana, where together they number some 1,700. See Regina Flannery, *The Gros Ventres of Montana* (2 vol., 1953–57).

Grosz, George (grōs), 1893–1959, German-American caricaturist, draughtsman, and painter, b. Berlin. Before and during World War I he contributed drawings on proletarian themes to *Illustration* and other German periodicals. He was associated with the Dada group at that time. In postwar Germany, Grosz was famous for his vitriolic, satirical drawings attacking the corruption of German bourgeois society. On three occasions he was brought to trial by the state for allegedly defaming public morals and for blasphemy. In his caricatures he evoked a nightmare world, an inferno, made credible with a few jagged pen-and-ink lines. In 1924, Grosz began to paint, and in 1933 he accepted a position as art instructor at the Art Students League, New York City. He became a U.S. citizen in 1938. At first the fiery work of his German period was supplanted by a more traditional rendering of figures and landscapes. However, World War II impelled him to create a symbolic series of ravaged figures. His drawing *Street Scene* (Philadelphia Mus. of Art) is characteristic. Other works are at the Museum of Modern Art. Two collections of his drawings were published in 1944. See his autobiography, *A Little Yes and a Big No* (tr. 1946) and *Ecce Homo* (new ed. 1966); studies by John Baur (1954), H. Bittner (1960), and B. I. Lewis (1971).

Grote, George (grōt), 1794–1871, English historian of ancient Greece. He did not attend a university, but pursued his studies in classical literature and history by himself. One of Jeremy Bentham's circle of friends, he pushed his own utilitarian economic and political doctrines as a member of Parliament (1832–41). Thereafter he worked for public improvement of the Univ. of London. His great work, *History of Greece* (12 vol., 1846–56), was begun to refute an earlier conservative history by William Mitford and is colored by Grote's liberal and democratic sentiments. His careful workmanship, however, and his singularly wide and practical sympathy with Greek life make the book a classic of historical writing. Among his other works are *Plato and the Other Companions of Socrates* (3 vol., 1865) and the unfinished *Aristotle* (ed. by Alexander Bain and G. C. Robertson, 1872). See H. L. Grote, *The Personal Life of George Grote* (2d ed. 1873); biography by M. L. Clarke (1962).

Grotefend, Georg Friedrich (gä'ôrkh frē'drĭkh grō'təfĕnt), 1775–1853, German archaeologist and philologist. He specialized in Latin and Italian and wrote works on the Umbrian and Oscan languages and other subjects, but his greatest achievement was deciphering INSCRIPTIONS of Persian CUNEIFORM.

Grotius, Hugo (grō'shəs), 1583–1645, Dutch jurist and humanist, whose Dutch name appears as Huigh de Groot. He studied at the Univ. of Leiden and became a lawyer when 15 years old. In Dutch political affairs Grotius supported OLDENBARNEVELDT against MAURICE OF NASSAU. After Maurice gained power he had Grotius condemned (1619) to prison for life, but Grotius made a daring escape in 1621 and fled to Paris. There, expanding certain views he had earlier recorded but had never published, he wrote *De jure belli ac pacis* [concerning the law of war and peace] (1625, definitive ed. 1631), usually considered the first definitive text on international law. In it Grotius contended that natural law prescribes rules of conduct for nations as well as for private individuals. He derived much of the specific content of international law from the Bible and from classical history. Although he did not condemn war as an instrument of national policy, he maintained that it was criminal to wage war except for certain causes. Much of his book is an attempt to make the conditions of warfare more humane by inducing respect for private persons and their property. Grotius returned briefly to Holland in 1631, but was forced to flee in 1632. From 1635 to 1645 he represented Sweden at the French court. Although generally regarded as the founder of international law, Grotius was indebted for much of his work to earlier scholars, especially GENTILI. Grotius was also a leading student of theology and biblical criticism, and he wrote an authoritative account of contemporary Dutch political affairs. See study by E. Dumbauld (1969).

Groton (grŏt'ən), town (1970 pop. 38,244), New London co., SE Conn., on the Thames River opposite New London; settled c.1650, inc. 1705. Shipbuilding, the manufacture of chemicals and metal products, and the distribution of fuel oil are among the town's principal industries. The huge New London Naval Submarine Base, famous for the construction of submarines, is on the Thames; the *Nautilus*, the first nuclear submarine, was launched there in 1954. Groton is the site of Fort Griswold (1775), unsuccessfully defended against the British in 1781. Of interest are guided tours of the submarine base, an annual art festival, and a number of well-maintained colonial homes. A U.S. coast guard training school and a branch of the Univ. of Connecticut are in Groton. Silas Deane was born there. Groton includes the borough of Groton and the unincorporated villages of Conning Towers, Noank, and West Mystic.

Grotowski, Jerzy (yĕ'zhĭ grôtôf'skē), 1933–, Polish stage director. Grotowski was founder and director of the Polish Laboratory Theatre (1959). Using his small but influential avant-garde group, Grotowski propounds "poor theater," which eliminates all nonessentials, i.e., costumes, sound effects, makeup, sets, lighting, and a strictly defined playing area. See his *Towards a Poor Theatre* (tr. 1968).

Grouchy, Emmanuel, marquis de (ĕmänüĕl' märkē' də grōōshē'), 1766–1847, French general in the French Revolutionary and Napoleonic wars. Made a marshal after Napoleon's return from Elba during the Hundred Days, he is said to be responsible for Napoleon's defeat in the WATERLOO CAMPAIGN through his failure to prevent the Prussians from joining the English.

ground bass, melodic phrase used repeatedly as a bass line. In its earlier form, developed in the 13th and 14th cent., the ground or *basso ostinato* [Ital.= obstinate] never varied in harmonization or pitch. The tenor, or pes, of SUMER IS ICUMEN IN is such a ground. Another sort was developed during the 17th cent. by Purcell and his contemporaries. This ground was not rigid as to pitch, sometimes moving from bass to soprano. It was composed with varying melodies and harmonies in the upper parts. The result was often a series of variations as in the baroque passacaglia and CHACONNE. The device often has great dramatic effect. J. S. Bach and Handel made remarkable use of it.

ground-effect machine: see AIR-CUSHION VEHICLE.

groundhog: see WOODCHUCK.

ground ivy, trailing perennial herb of the genus *Glechoma* of the family Labiatae (MINT family), closely related to catnip and naturalized from Europe. It forms a dense ground cover and spreads rapidly, thriving in cool, damp places. Its leaves were once used to brew a cough remedy; in quantity it is reputed to be poisonous to horses. Gill-over-the-ground is another of its many names. Ground ivy is classified in the division MAGNOLIOPHYTA, class Magnoliopsida, order Lamiales, family Labiatae.

ground laurel: see TRAILING ARBUTUS.

groundmass: see PORPHYRY.

groundnut, common name for several different genera of twining leguminous plants with edible tuberous roots, chiefly the PEANUT. Groundnuts are classified in the division MAGNOLIOPHYTA, class Magnoliopsida, order Rosales, family Leguminosae.

ground pine, common name for several creeping plants, particularly species of CLUB MOSS.

groundsel, any plant of the very large genus *Senecio*, widely distributed herbs and (in the tropics) shrubs or trees of the family Compositae (COMPOSITE family). Many grow as vines. Most North American species have small, yellow, daisylike flowers; they are especially abundant in the plains region. Some species of the genus are better known as ragworts. The golden ragwort, or squawweed (*S. aureus*), has been used as an emmenagogue and a vulnerary by Indians and white men. Other species have also been used medicinally. A few have been found to be poisonous to livestock, although others are useful for grazing. The common groundsel (*S. vulgaris*), naturalized from Europe, is one of the species that is sometimes cultivated. The fruits of groundsels usually have a conspicuous white down (pappus), a characteristic shared by *Baccharis halmifolia*, the groundsel tree, which is a related shrub of the E United States. The florists' cineraria, a popular pot plant existing in many horticultural kinds, was derived from *S. cruentes*, native to the Canary Islands. This and particularly other related species are sometimes classified in a separate genus, *Cineraria*. Groundsel is classified in the division MAGNOLIOPHYTA, class Magnoliopsida, order Asterales, family Compositae.

ground speed indicator: see AIR NAVIGATION.

ground squirrel, name applied to certain terrestrial rodents of the SQUIRREL family. In North America the name refers to members of the genus *Citellus* and sometimes to the closely related genera *Tamias* (CHIPMUNK), *Cynomys* (PRAIRIE DOG), and *Marmota* (MARMOT and WOODCHUCK). *Citellus* species are found in Asia, E Europe, and North America. In the Old World they are called sousliks. Other ground squirrel genera are found in Africa and S Asia. The approximately 30 North American species of *Citellus* are found W of Hudson Bay, from the Arctic Ocean to central Mexico. These ground squirrels have rounded heads, short ears and legs, and shorter, less bushy tails than tree squirrels. Their combined head and body length is 4½ to 13½ in. (11.4–33 cm) depending on the species; the tail is usually a third to two thirds as long. Most are gregarious, living in extensive underground burrows; they hibernate in colder parts of their range. Members of different species are found in prairie grasslands, arctic tundra, mountain meadows, open forest, desert, and scrub country. In some regions the ground squirrel is called GOPHER, a name more commonly applied to burrowing rodents of a different family. Primarily vegetarian in their diet, ground squirrels may become agricultural pests, but they destroy insects and mice as well as crops. Their tunnels cause landslides and erosion, but also serve to mix and aerate the soil. Ground squirrels are classified in the phylum CHORDATA, subphylum Vertebrata, class Mammalia, order Rodentia, family Sciuridae.

group, in mathematics, system consisting of a set of elements, or mathematical objects, and an operation defined for combining the elements such that the following requirements are satisfied: (1) The set is closed under the operation; i.e., if *a* and *b* are elements of the set, then the element that results from combining *a* and *b* under the operation is also an element of the set; (2) the operation satisfies the

ASSOCIATIVE LAW; i.e., $a \circ (b \circ c) = (a \circ b) \circ c$, where $\circ$ represents the operation and *a, b,* and *c* are any three elements; (3) there exists an identity element *I* in the set such that $a \circ I = a$ for any element *a* in the set; (4) there exists an inverse a^{-1} in the set for every *a* such that $a \circ a^{-1} = I$. If, in addition to satisfying these four axioms, the group also satisfies the COMMUTATIVE LAW for the operation, i.e., $a \circ b = b \circ a$, then it is called a commutative, or Abelian, group. The real numbers (see NUMBER) form a commutative group both under addition, with 0 as identity element and $-a$ as inverse, and, excluding 0, under multiplication, with 1 as identity element and $1/a$ as inverse. The elements of a group need not be numbers; they may often be transformations, or mappings, of one set of objects into another. For example, the set of all permutations of a finite collection of objects constitutes a group. Group theory has wide applications in mathematics, including number theory, geometry, and statistics, and is also important in other branches of science, e.g., elementary particle theory and crystallography. See books on the theory of groups by A. G. Kurosh (tr. of 2d ed., 2 vol., 1960), I. D. MacDonald (1968), and J. J. Rotman (2d ed. 1973).

group dynamics: see GROUP PSYCHOTHERAPY.

grouper, common name for a large carnivorous member of the family Serranidae (sea BASS family), abundant in tropical and subtropical seas and highly valued as food fish. There are several genera, notably *Epinephelus* and *Mycteroperca,* including some 100 species, most of which are characterized by bright markings that change in color and pattern to match the background. In the West Indies and the Florida Keys are found the yellowfin grouper, noted for its many beautiful color phases; the coney, the smallest (9 in./22.5 cm) grouper, colored a livid reddish gray with blue spots; and the Nassau grouper, the rock hind, and the gag. The largest of the sea bass are the groupers called jewfishes—the black jewfish, or Warsaw grouper, *Hemichromis bimaculatus,* reaches a length of 6 ft (183 cm) and a weight of 500 lb (225 kg) and the spotted jewfish is even larger (up to 600 lb/270 kg). The red grouper and the black grouper, common N to the Carolinas, form the bulk of the commercial catch; both species weigh up to 50 lb (22.5 kg). Groupers are classified in the phylum CHORDATA, subphylum Vertebrata, class Osteichthyes, order Perciformes, family Serranidae.

group insurance: see INSURANCE.

group psychotherapy, a means of changing behavior and emotions that is based on the fact that much of human behavior and feeling involves the individual's adaptation and response to other persons. It is a process carried out in formally organized small groups of 5 to 12 persons who view themselves as in need of change. The group therapist is experienced in identifying, categorizing, and defining the behaviors and subjective responses that are revealed in the interaction of the members. Generally, he does not dispense advice or information. The tone and climate of such a group is set primarily by the predispositions and training of the therapist. The group becomes a "sample" of the outside world, reproducing most conditions of interpersonal relationships; its members jointly participate in observing personal motivation and styles of interaction. They also participate in attempting new behaviors and dealing with the consequences of such behaviors. The end of the process comes at that time when those desired interactions and communications about which the member was hesitant or in which he felt discomfort are able to take place with greater ease in the world outside the group. In observing the totality of the events that take place in group therapy, the process by which elements of personality are developed in each member is also studied. This process, called group dynamics, may be broken down into four primary areas of interest: the influence of the group on individual behavior; the group as an organized social system with a communications network that may be studied in terms of its interdependence qualities and its structure; the influence of the individual personality on the character of the group; and factors that lead to cohesion or disruption within the group. The composition of a group may be heterogeneous or homogeneous with reference to the age of the members or the type of problem, e.g., homosexuality, phobias. Group therapy may be the sole method employed to change behavior or it may be combined with individual treatment, either concurrently or separated in time. The principle of using interactions in a group for the purpose of change is inherent in society. The technique of a group formally organized for this purpose, however, is said to have been devised by J. H. Pratt in 1905 in general-care instruction classes for recently discharged tuberculosis patients, when he noticed the impact of this experience on their emotional states. In 1925, Trigant Burrow, a psychoanalyst, became dissatisfied with individual psychoanalysis and used group techniques in an attempt to decrease the authoritarian position of the therapist and to more thoroughly examine interpersonal interactions. The application of group therapy methods to prison inmates and discharged mental hospital patients was pioneered by Paul Schilder and Louis Wender in the 1930s. At that time group therapy was found to be particularly useful in the treatment of children and adolescents. The development of group therapy was given impetus during World War II as a result of the need for a prompt method of treatment for many patients simultaneously. (See PSYCHOANALYSIS and PSYCHOTHERAPY.)

Behavior Group Therapy. Behavior therapy attempts to apply the methods and conclusions of experimental psychology to the treatment of human behavior disorders. The disorders are seen as the result of maladaptive, undesirable habits that are changeable through learning. The main focus of treatment is on overt, observable behaviors and not on a patient's reports of subjectively felt experiences. Treatment consists of learning new behaviors by the reward and punishment of various responses. In many instances this process is facilitated in the group setting wherein additional aspects of a problem are revealed in group interaction and wherein the sharing of problems and solutions aids the learning process by the addition of social rewards and punishments.

Encounter Group. Derived from work done in sensitivity training (see below), this form of group therapy is designed to help a person become aware of all aspects of himself, both those aspects revealed in group interaction and those he can learn from contemplation of self. A series of specially designed, often nonverbal exercises and games are undertaken by participants in the group to facilitate this process and to enable each to derive a sense of belonging. The Esalen Institute of California is a well-known center for encounter group activities and studies.

Experiential-Existential Group Therapy. Existential anxiety is defined as the feeling of dread of nonbeing. In daily living private ideas must be shared. Life-styles that interfere with this sharing are discarded in order to reduce the feeling of being alone. Despair is a natural reaction to a situation in which meaningful contact cannot be made with another person. Unable to experience completely the present as a shared reality, a person is alone. He clings to his early childhood life, wherein he was cared for, and he worries about the future. An internal emptiness provokes him to frantic attempts to obtain a craved-for experience of others. The purpose of experiential-existential group therapy is to change the nature of his shared existence here and now, rather than to examine conflicts generated during his growth. Reality is assumed to be reflected completely in the experience of the group interaction. By revealing alternate modes of coping derived from studies of group dynamics, adherents of this system, e.g., Albert Ellis, Carl Rogers, Thomas Whitaker, and Thomas Malone, teach new methods by which a person can relate to others.

Gestalt Group Therapy. The background of this form of therapy may be found in psychoanalysis, Gestalt psychology, and existentialist philosophy. Its basic assumption is that the fulfillment of needs necessitates the forming and changing of patterned wholes that are central to attention and that must be differentiated from their backgrounds, which are merely peripheral to attention. These wholes, or gestalten (from the German *Gestalt,* whose basic meaning is shape or form), include not only aural and visual figures, but the perceptions of one's own body's motor behavior and one's feeling processes. When there is interference with the mechanisms of attention, as from the inadequate perception of the world itself, the blocking of the expression of needs, or the inhibition of the body from adequate expression, the person's organization of and dealings with the phenomenological world become disturbed. The aim of Gestalt therapy is to break up the patient's standard ways of perceiving and acting in relation to a need and to emphasize newly emerging patterns that might become central to attention as part of a new whole of experience. Much attention is paid to the nonverbal aspect of behavior and the focusing of awareness on the body itself. Emphasis is on present experience rather than on explanations and explorations of the past. A Gestalt group takes the form of the workshop model. Rather than strive for group interaction, participants observe the therapist in an experiencing of the present moment with a particular member. The therapist focuses on lingering emotions and memories that have survived unexpressed and are still part of the unconscious. As in psychodrama (see below), observation of the dramatic dialogue between therapist and patient is found to have great impact on the other members of the group as well, because they experience within themselves that patient's response.

Marathon Group Therapy. This is a form of group therapy conducted in one uninterrupted event varying from one to three days. Its origins lie in the sensitivity-training movement; among its earliest adherents are Frederick H. Stoller, Ronald C. Waller, and George R. Bach. The emphasis in such a group is on intimacy, face-to-face encounter, and the expression of personal reactions rather than the exploration or explanation of behavior. Its goal is to create an intimate group of participants, including the leader, who reveal much of themselves and their styles of coping. Its setting is usually informal apart from a defined starting and stopping time. All activities other than those of toilet and sleep are performed together, although there are groups that take no time out for sleeping and continue the session for twenty-four hours or more. The leader, in addition to participation as a member, sets the tone of the group and determines the times of the various pauses and the type of activity. Members are involved in a series of events in which role changes occur; thereby it may be perceived that rigidity leads to increased dissatisfaction and difficulty, while the adoption of a more fluid role is rewarding. New ways of expressing one's self are fostered. It is thought that such a setting, where a full range of interpersonal reaction and change can take place, is conducive to the resolution of personal crises, and that under such conditions of heightened feelings of anxiety and involvement learning is accelerated.

Psychodrama. This is a form of group therapy designed by Romanian-born Jacob L. Moreno in which hidden feelings are expressed and conflicting demands resolved through the interaction of patients acting out the various roles they assume in daily life. An individual may be defined in terms of his daily rules, i.e., his actual functioning in a given social situation. A role is shaped by a combination of personal past experience and the cultural patterns of society. An individual's roles must constantly change in order to meet the requirements of new situations; old roles form the patterns for new ones. The therapeutic theater used in psychodrama is intended to provide a setting where the individual can act out various roles freed of the psychologically restraining limits of his daily reality. The subject presents his private world spontaneously and through interaction with other people. He also assumes the roles of the significant other people in his life as he perceives them, and he involves other group members in his private drama. The participation of any one member stimulates others in the group to examine their own role functioning. Various techniques are utilized to facilitate the process, among which are soliloquy, role reversal, and projection. The therapist-director catalyzes the process, relating conflicts and problems from one member to another, identifying participation, and designing new situations wherein facets of the personality might be revealed. Also taking part are therapeutic aides, or auxiliary egos, persons who, at the direction of the therapist, assume various roles in interaction with any particular group member. Members of the audience assist the patient by functioning as a sounding board; they themselves benefit by simultaneously working out their own roles and by becoming participants in the various dramas either of their own volition or at the direction of the therapist-director. The analysis of role behaviors and the catharsis of emotions that develop in psychodrama are assumed to make the individual more flexible in role assumption and in the confrontation of reality.

Psychoanalytic Group Therapy. The aim of psychoanalytic group therapy is the resolution of the conflicts that develop as a person learns to control his biological drives, integrate the rules of his family and culture, and manage his day-to-day affairs. Undesirable behaviors and distressing feelings are interpreted as being the result of unconscious adaptations to conflicting demands. This type of treatment proceeds by the analysis of the transference, i.e., the repetition of particular, individual patterns of behavior and feelings in unconsciously equating the analyst with significant persons in the patient's past. Multiple transference may be defined as a simultaneous repetition of multiple social and familial behavior patterns wherein the group members as well as the therapist are equated with the significant others. Conflicts between the demands of biological drives, current life situations, and familial-cultural patterns are reflected in these relationships. Through psychoanalytic group therapy the past is recovered and made part of a conscious system, in order to remove or redefine the situations which gave rise to the conflict. The conflict is then resolved with the help of the therapist, who is dissociated from the patient's struggles.

Sensitivity-Training Group. Developed in 1946 by social scientists, the sensitivity training group is used as a vehicle to reinforce learning. Its operation is based primarily on the learners' experiencing of themselves in various social situations wherein attitudes are influenced and competencies are developed. The training group, or T group, uses and develops better skills for giving and receiving FEEDBACK, a term used to describe the way in which a particular personality has impact on the self and on others. The teacher is anyone in the group who supplies data for learning, recognizes available choices, and knows what he is feeling; he is not a traditional authority. The focus is on understanding what happens and not on inducing change in the participants—that is left to the decision of the members. While originally designed as a learning experience, principles derived from sensitivity training are used in treatment of mental disorders and in personality change, particularly the experiential approach wherein learning is related to the basic frustrations concerning intimacy and feelings of despair.

Transactional Analysis. Developed by the psychiatrist Eric Berne, transactional analysis is a systematized description of human behavior based on the simultaneous existence in every human being throughout his life of three ego states: the child, the adult, and the parent. In this system, living is seen as a problem of the organization of one's time. It is solved in one of six ways at any given time: withdrawal, rituals, pastimes, games, activity, and intimacy. The goal of transactional analysis is to give the adult ego state decision-making power over the parent and child ego states, with regard to time structuring. Group therapy is considered an optimal setting to observe time structuring and the confrontation of the parent-adult-child combination of one individual with that of other patients. See C. R. Rogers, *On Becoming a Person* (1961); Frederick Perls et al., *Gestalt Therapy* (1965); Eric Berne, *Transactional Analysis in Psychotherapy* (1961, repr. 1973) and *Principles of Group Treatment* (1966); Gerard Egan, ed., *Encounter Groups: Basic Readings* (1971); K. W. Back, *Beyond Words* (1972); Albert Ellis, *Humanistic Psychotherapy: The Rational-Emotive Approach* (1973); D. G. Appley and A. E. Windsor, *T-Groups and Therapy Groups in a Changing Society* (1973).

Group Theatre, organization formed in New York City in 1931 by Harold Clurman, Cheryl Crawford, and Lee STRASBERG. Its founders, who had worked earlier with the Provincetown Players, wished to establish a permanent company that would present contemporary plays of social significance and would work to develop the art of the theater. Although never financially secure, the group was recognized as a vital theatrical force. It was at its height between 1935 and 1937, during which time it produced *Awake and Sing, Waiting for Lefty,* and *Golden Boy,* all by Clifford Odets. In 1937, Clurman became sole director. Although the group disbanded in 1941, its influence is still greatly felt; many of its members have become prominent actors, teachers, and directors. See Harold Clurman, *The Fervent Years* (1945).

grouse, common name for a game bird of the colder parts of the Northern Hemisphere. There are about 18 species. Grouse are henlike terrestrial birds, protectively plumaged in shades of red, brown, and gray. The nostrils are entirely hidden by feathers, and the legs are partially or completely feathered. The most common eastern American grouse is the ruffed grouse (sometimes miscalled partridge or pheasant), *Bonasa umbellus,* a forest bird noted for the drumming sound made by the male during its elaborate courtship dance. The ptarmigan (*Lagopus lagopus*), or snow grouse, is an arctic species that migrates to the NW United States in winter, when its plumage changes from rusty brown to white, matching the snow. Western American grouse include the prairie chicken, *Tympanuchus cupido,* once common in the East, and the sage grouse, *Centrocercus urophasianus.* The latter, called also sage hen, sage cock, or cock of the plains, is the largest of the group (25–30 in./62.5–70 cm long) and so named because its flesh tastes strongly of sage—the result of feeding on sagebrush buds. The males of both these species are distinguished by yellow air sacs on the neck that inflate to an enormous size during courtship. European species include the capercaillie and the black grouse. The red grouse is found in Great Britain. Striking fluctuations in the abundance of all grouse species occur in intervals of 7 to 10 years. A combination of factors, rather than a single explanation, appears to be the cause for this not entirely understood phenomenon. Fortunately, grouse have high reproductive rates, which enable them to restore their populations after a low-level period. Grouse are classified in the phylum CHORDATA, subphylum Vertebrata, class Aves, order Galliformes, family Tetraonidae.

Grove, Sir George, 1820–1900, English musicographer, whose *Dictionary of Music and Musicians* (1879–89) has become a standard reference work. Originally an engineer, he assisted in the establishment of the Crystal Palace in London and for many years annotated the programs of the concerts there. From these notes he later drew material for *Beethoven and His Nine Symphonies* (1896). He served (1868–83) as editor of *Macmillan's Magazine,* and directed the Royal College of Music from 1883 to 1894. He was knighted in 1883.

Grove, Robert Moses (Lefty Grove), 1900–, American baseball player, b. Lonaconing, Md. A left-handed pitcher, he played (1925–33) for the Philadelphia Athletics. In 1931 he attained the season pitching record of 31 victories against four defeats for a percentage of .886 and equaled the American League mark of 16 consecutive victories. From 1934 until 1941, Grove played with the Boston Red Sox. In his 17 years of major-league pitching, he won 300 and lost 141 games for a lifetime pitching percentage of .680; he struck out over 2,200 batters, an outstanding record. Grove was elected to the Baseball Hall of Fame in 1947.

Grove City, village (1970 pop. 13,911), Franklin co., central Ohio, in a rich agricultural region. It has some manufacturing. Horse races are held there.

Groves, city (1970 pop. 18,067), Jefferson co., SE Texas, a residential suburb of Port Arthur.

Groveton, town (1970 pop. 11,750), Fairfax co., N Va.

growing season, period during which plant growth takes place. In temperate climates the growing season is limited by seasonal changes in temperature and is defined as the period between the last killing frost of spring and the first killing frost of autumn, at which time annual plants die and biennials and perennials cease active growth and become dormant for the cold winter months. In tropical climates, in which there is little seasonal temperature change, the amount of available moisture often determines the periods of plant growth; in the rainy season growth is luxuriant and in the dry season many plants become dormant. In desert areas, growth is almost wholly dependent on moisture. In arctic regions the growing season is short but concentrated; the number of daylight hours is so large that the total amount of sunlight equals that of a temperate growing season with shorter days. The length of the growing season often determines which crops can be grown in a region; some require long growing seasons and others mature rapidly. Plants that are perennials in a warm climate may sometimes be grown as annuals in cooler areas; by crossing hardy plant species with less hardy but more productive types, plant breeders have developed desirable new strains that mature in a shorter period. Other factors also affect the growing season; in the sheltered valleys and coastal slopes of the Pacific Northwest of the United States, the heavy winter rainfall and the dry summers have produced a unique area with a Mediterranean type of climate where plant growth occurs during the winter and dormancy during the summer. See CLIMATE; SEASONS.

growth hormone or **somatotropin** (sōmăt″ətrō′-pən), glycoprotein HORMONE released by the anterior PITUITARY GLAND that is necessary for normal skeletal growth in man (see PROTEIN). There is evidence that the secretion of growth hormone is regulated by the release of certain PEPTIDES by the hypothalamus of the brain. One such substance, called somatostatin, has been shown to inhibit the secretion of growth hormone. Somatotropin is known to act upon many aspects of cellular metabolism, but its most obvious effect is the stimulation of the growth of cartilage and bone in children. A deficiency of growth hormone secretion before puberty (by the end of which the synthesis of new bone tissue is complete) results in pituitary dwarfism. Pituitary dwarfs, who can be as little as 3 to 4 ft (91–122 cm) tall, are generally well-proportioned except for the head, which may be relatively large when compared to the body (this relationship of head to body is similar to that of normal children). Unlike cretins, whose dwarfism is caused by a deficiency of THYROXINE, pituitary dwarfs are not mentally retarded; they are often sexually immature. An excess of growth hormone in children results in gigantism; these children grow to be over 7 ft (213 cm) in height and have disproportionately long limbs. Excess growth hormone produced after puberty has little effect on the growth of the skeleton, but it results in a disease affecting terminal skeletal structures known as ACROMEGALY. In plants growth is regulated by a hormone called AUXIN.

Grozny (grôz′nē), city (1970 pop. 341,000), capital of the Chechen-Ingush Autonomous Soviet Socialist Republic, SE European USSR, in the northern foothills of the Greater Caucasus. It is the center of one of the USSR's richest oil fields, linked by pipelines to Makhachkala on the Caspian Sea, to Tuapse on the Black Sea, and to Gorlovka in the Ukraine. Grozny has oil refineries, chemical plants, and machinery factories. One of the Soviet Union's oldest oil-producing areas (production began in 1893), Grozny was a major strategic goal of invading German armies in World War II. Soviet troops halted the German advance just short of the city.

grub: see LARVA.

Gruber, Franz (frănts′ grōō′bər), 1787–1863, Austrian organist. On Christmas Eve in 1818 he composed his one published work, the music for the poem *Silent Night* by the local curate, Josef Mohr.

Grudziądz (grōō′jôNts), Ger. *Graudenz,* city (1970 pop. 75,511), N central Poland, a port on the Vistula River. Industries include flour milling, brewing, distilling, and light manufacturing. The city is also a railway junction. Founded and fortified by the TEUTONIC KNIGHTS, it was chartered in 1233. Grudziądz passed to Poland in 1466 and to Prussia in 1772; it was restored to Poland in 1919. Notable buildings include a Gothic church and an 18th-century Jesuit collegium.

Gruen, Victor, 1903–, American architect and city planner, b. Vienna. Gruen specialized in building suburban shopping centers. In the 1950s he designed such developments in and around Rochester, Detroit, Indianapolis, Minneapolis, Salt Lake City, Los Angeles, and the San Francisco Bay area. He sought solutions to city planning problems, particularly central congestion, in projects for Fort Worth, Texas, and the Palos Verdes Peninsula, Los Angeles. See his *Shopping Towns USA* (1960; with Larry Smith), *The Heart of Our Cities* (1964), and *Centers for Urban Environment* (1972; with Larry Smith).

Gruenberg, Louis (grōō′ənbûrg), 1884–1964, American composer, b. Russia; pupil of Busoni. After concert tours as a pianist in Europe and America, he settled in the United States as a composer in 1919. A champion of modern music, he helped found (1923) the League of Composers and was one of the first American composers to incorporate jazz rhythms into works of major dimensions, such as *Daniel Jazz* (1923) and *Jazz Suite* (1925). His opera *The Emperor Jones,* based on O'Neill's play, was presented at the Metropolitan Opera in 1933. From 1940 he composed music for motion pictures.

Gruening, Ernest Henry (grēn′ĭng), 1887–1974, American political leader, governor of Alaska (1939–53), and U.S. Senator (1959–69), b. New York City. He became interested in journalism and worked on Boston newspapers until 1917. From 1920 to 1923 he edited the *Nation.* He directed (1924) publicity for Robert La Follette's campaign for the presidency, and later founded (1927) the Portland, Maine, *Evening News.* He edited *These United States* (2 vol., 1923–24) and also wrote the highly regarded *Mexico and Its Heritage* (1928). Gruening directed (1934–39) the territories and island possessions division of the U.S. Dept. of the Interior and headed (1935–37) the Puerto Rico Reconstruction Administration. He was appointed governor of Alaska, lobbied for statehood, and became one of Alaska's first Senators. A Democrat, he was an early opponent of the Vietnam War, voting with Wayne Morse of Oregon against the Gulf of Tonkin Resolution in Aug., 1964. He was defeated in the 1968 primary. His works include *The State of Alaska* (1954) and *The Battle for Alaska Statehood* (1967). See his autobiography, *Many Battles* (1973); Sherwood Ross, *Gruening of Alaska* (1968).

Gruenther, Alfred Maximilian, 1899–, U.S. general, b. Platte Center, Nebr. A brilliant staff officer, during World War II he was deputy chief of staff to

Dwight D. Eisenhower in London (1942–43), chief of staff of the 5th Army (1943–44), and chief of staff of the 15th Army Group under Mark W. Clark (1944–45). In 1951, General Eisenhower chose him as chief of staff of the forces in the North Atlantic Treaty Organization. He continued in this post under Matthew B. Ridgway and then succeeded Ridgway as supreme allied commander in Europe (1953–56). Retiring from the army in 1956, Gruenther was (1957–64) president of the American Red Cross and served on various governmental advisory commissions.

Gruffydd ap Llewelyn (grōō'fĭth äp lōōĕl'ĭn, grĭf'ĭth, thōōĕl'ĭn), d. 1063, ruler of Wales (1039–63). A series of campaigns against other Welsh princes made him the ruler of virtually all Wales. Allied with the outlawed Ælfgar of Mercia, he launched a series of raids into W England, but his power was broken by HAROLD in two invasions (1062–63). His defeat plunged Wales into confusion and paved the way for the conquest of Wales by the Normans. The name also appears as Griffith ap Llewelyn.

Grumantbyen (grōō'mäntbü"ən), town, Spitsbergen island, Svalbard, N Norway, on the Isfjorden. It is a coal-mining settlement, established (1919) by an Anglo-Russian company. Its mines have been worked by the USSR since 1931. German battleships destroyed it in Sept., 1943, but it was quickly rebuilt. It is connected by rail with modern harbor facilities on Colesbukta Bay.

Grün, Hans Baldung: see BALDUNG, HANS.

Grünberg: see ZIELONA GÓRA, Poland.

Grundtvig, Nikolai Frederik Severin (nĭ'kōlī' frĭth'ərĭk sĕvərĕn' grōōnt'vĭg), 1783–1872, Danish educator, minister, and writer, founder of the Danish FOLK HIGH SCHOOL. He came into doctrinal conflict with church authorities and was forbidden to preach but was reinstated (1832) and became titular bishop (1861). In education Grundtvig stressed national history and literature. A champion of mass education, he was responsible for evolving a system of folk high schools that has aroused international interest. Grundtvig's many literary works include his epoch-making *Northern Mythology* (1808, rev. ed. 1832), which loosely retells the Old Norse myths. His poems and songs treat historical, mythological, and religious subjects. He was influential in reviving interest in Anglo-Saxon literature, and he translated *Beowulf* into Danish (1820). Svend Grundtvig, the folklorist, was his son. See studies by Hal Koch (tr. 1952), Johannes Knudsen (1955), and E. D. Nielsen (1955).

Grundy, Felix, 1777–1840, American political leader, b. Berkeley co., Va. After a successful career in Kentucky, he moved to Nashville, Tenn., where he became a noted criminal lawyer. A member (1811–14) of Congress, he joined the "war hawks" in strongly urging the War of 1812. His political power in Tennessee forced Andrew Jackson to keep his support, and Grundy succeeded to John H. Eaton's seat in the U.S. Senate when Eaton entered (1829) Jackson's cabinet. Grundy gave Jackson little support in the nullification crisis, but was reelected (1833) despite Jackson's opposition. He was appointed (1838) Attorney General by President Van Buren and resigned (1839) to return to the Senate. See biography by J. H. Parks (1940).

Grünewald, Mathias (mäte'äs grün'əvält), c.1475–1528, German painter of religious subjects. His original name was Mathis Gothart Neithart. Although he assimilated various compositional elements of three other great German masters (Schongauer, Dürer, and Cranach), he is unique in expressive power and in the visionary revelation of spiritual drama. From 1501 to 1521 he had his workshop in Seligenstadt, and from there he traveled to Alsace and Halle on commissions. He created several altarpieces for two powerful bishops of Mainz, and at his death in Halle he was listed as a painter and designer of waterworks. Grünewald's earliest work of certain date is the *Mocking of Christ* of 1503 (Munich), a linear, energetic and colorful painting in which the blindfolded figure of Christ is beaten by a group of grotesque men. This work incorporates a number of stylistic components that Grünewald employed in his later works: the dramatic use of silhouette and unusual color; the striking contrast of light with shadowed areas, called chiaroscuro; and the exaggeration and distortion of the human form. This array of expressionist devices conveys terror and anguish in terms of powerful images rather than beautiful ones. In this respect, Grünewald's approach differs strikingly from that of the Renaissance humanists such as Dürer. The most frequent subject in his few surviving works is the crucifixion of Christ, which he depicted again and again in harrowing detail. His masterpiece is the complex *Isenheim Altarpiece* of 1515, now at Colmar. It contains a central crucifixion panel, a figure of the wounded St. Sebastian, the annunciation, the resurrection, and a fearsome temptation of St. Anthony. There is a remarkable individualization of the characters of the drama, but more important are the spectacular effects of the light and color and the intense pain expressed in the tortured figures. Other of his crucifixion scenes are in Basel, Karlsruhe, and Washington, D.C. Although Grünewald's vision was almost unrelentingly terrible, the Karlsruhe crucifixion, apparently his last work, incorporates a new heroism and restraint. Completed in about 1525, it marked Grünewald's personal High Renaissance. See Eberhard Ruhmer, *Grunewald: The Paintings* (tr. 1958) and *Grunewald: The Drawings* (tr. 1970); Nicholas Pevsner and Michael Scheja, *The Isenheim* Altarpiece (tr. 1969); study by N. B. L. Pevsner and M. Meier (1958).

grunion: see SILVERSIDES.

grunt, common name for members of the family Pomadasyidae, carnivorous fish of warm seas, most species of which are small and brightly colored. They are sound-producers, creating their noises by grinding their pharyngeal teeth together. CROAKERS, which belong to another family, are also sound-producing fish. Grunts are bottom-feeders with large mouths vividly colored in red or orange on the inside. The common, or white, grunt is a favorite food fish found on shallow sandy bottoms from the West Indies to the Carolinas; it averages 1 ft (30 cm) in length and 1 lb (.5 kg) in weight. The many species abundant off the Florida coasts include the margate, blue-striped, and gray grunts and the bizarre porkfish, with a blue-striped yellow body and black head-bands. The California sargo is common along the Pacific coast and the commercially important pigfish is found from Long Island Sound to Texas. Grunts are classified in the phylum CHORDATA, subphylum Vertebrata, class Osteichthyes, order Perciformes, family Pomadasyidae.

Grünwald, battle of, 1410: see TANNENBERG.

Grütli: see RÜTLI.

Gruyère (grüyĕr'), district in Fribourg canton, W Switzerland. It is famous for its cattle and for Gruyère cheese.

Gruziya: see GEORGIAN SOVIET SOCIALIST REPUBLIC.

Gryphius, Andreas (ändrā'äs grü'fēōōs), 1616–64, German poet-dramatist, originally named Andreas Greif. He wrote in Latin, new High German, and Silesian dialect. Among his many sonnets, odes, epigrams, and religious lyrics is the famous "Vanitas! Vanitatum Vanitas!" His tragedies include *Leo Armenius* (1646) and *Carolus Stuardus* (1649); more noteworthy are his lively satiric comedies, such as *Horribilicribrifax* (1663) and *Peter Squenz* (1663).

grysbok: see ANTELOPE.

Gstaad (kshtät), village, Bern canton, W Switzerland. It is a fashionable winter sports resort. Cheese and wood products are made in the village.

GTP (guanosine triphosphate): see GUANINE.

guacharo: see OILBIRD.

Guadalajara (gwä"thälähä'rä), city (1970 pop. 1,196,218), capital of Jalisco state, SW Mexico, second largest city of Mexico. Guadalajara is a beautiful, spacious city on a plain more than 5,000 ft (1,524 m) high and surrounded by mountains. It is a modern commercial metropolis with many picturesque survivals of the Spanish colonial era. The mild, clear, dry climate has made it a popular health resort, and because of its charm it is often called "Perla del Occidente" (Pearl of the West). Guadalajara is also an important communications and industrial center. Industry is aided by direct rail service to the United States and by a hydroelectric plant utilizing the Juanacatlán falls on the Santiago River. Auto assembly plants and the manufacture of xerographic and photographic equipment are among the leading industries. The region around the city is important for agriculture and livestock raising; some coal is also mined. The most famous products of Guadalajara and its environs are intricately designed and finely worked glassware and pottery. Founded by Cristóbal de Oñate c.1530, Guadalajara was moved twice, before and during the Mixtón War, because of Indian raids; it was permanently established in 1542, the date chosen as its official founding. Guadalajara became the seat of the audiencia of Nueva Galicia. Easily captured in 1810 by Hidalgo y Costilla during the war against Spain, the city was the center of reform activities. Again in 1858, in the War of Reform, it was briefly occupied by the liberals under Benito Juárez. Its notable public buildings include the cathedral, finished in 1618 after more than 50 years of work, and the governor's palace, begun in 1643. The cathedral, which houses B. E. Murillo's *The Assumption of the Blessed Virgin*, has been partially destroyed several times by earthquakes and represents a conglomerate of architectural styles. The governor's palace, with murals by J. C. Orozco, is an excellent example of Spanish colonial architecture. The Univ. of Guadalajara and the orphanage chapel also contain Orozco murals. The city is the seat of an archbishop.

Guadalajara, town (1970 pop. 31,917), capital of Guadalajara prov., central Spain, in New Castile, on the Henares River. It flourished as a Roman colony and belonged to the Moors from the 8th to the 11th cent.

Guadalcanal (gwädəlkənăl'), volcanic island (1970 pop. 23,922), c.2,510 sq mi (6,500 sq km), South Pacific, largest of the SOLOMON ISLANDS. Honiara (1970 pop. 11,389), capital of the British Protectorate of the Solomon Islands, is on Guadalcanal. The island is largely jungle, with Mt. Popomanasiu rising to c.8,000 ft (2,440 m). There are coconut plantations, and some gold has been mined. The inhabitants, mostly Melanesians, live along the coasts. Discovered by English navigators in 1788, Guadalcanal became a British protectorate in 1893. During World War II the island was occupied by the Japanese. In Aug., 1942, U.S. forces landed, marking the first large-scale invasion of a Japanese-held island; after bitter jungle fighting, the island was conquered (Feb., 1943). Points of interest on Guadalcanal include a museum of Melanesian artifacts, and Henderson Field, the main objective of the American invasion and now an international airport.

Guadalquivir (gwä"thälkēvēr'), river, c.350 mi (560 km) long, rising in the Sierra de Cazorla, SE Spain, and flowing generally SW past Córdoba and Seville into the Atlantic Ocean near Sanlúcar de Barrameda. Known to the Arabs as *Wadi al-Kebir* [the large river], it is the longest stream in the Andalusia region of S Spain. There are several hydroelectric plants along its course. In its middle course it flows through a populous fertile region at the foot of the Sierra Morena, where it is used extensively for irrigation. The lower course of the Guadalquivir traverses extensive marshlands (Las Marismas) that are used for rice cultivation. The river is tidal to Seville (c.50 mi/80 km upstream), a major inland port and head of navigation for oceangoing vessels, and it is canalized between Seville and the sea.

Guadalupe (gwäthälōō'pā), town (1968 est. pop. 26,750), central Costa Rica. It is an agricultural center and a suburb of San José.

Guadalupe, city (1970 pop. 153,454), Nuevo León state, NE Mexico, on the Santa Catalina River. Its economy is based on agriculture, especially maize, and livestock raising.

Guadalupe (gwä"dəlōōp', Span. gwäthälōō'pā), town (1970 pop. 3,069), Cáceres prov., W central Spain, in Estremadura. It is noted for its monastery (formerly Hieronymite, now Franciscan) and the shrine of Our Lady of Guadalupe, whose cult was transferred in the 16th cent. to Guadalupe Hidalgo, Mexico.

Guadalupe, Sierra de (syĕr'rä thā gwäthälōō'pā), mountain range, W Spain, in Estremadura, between the Tagus and Guadiana rivers. The highest elevation is 4,734 ft (1,443 m).

Guadalupe Hidalgo (gwäthälōō'pā ēdäl'gō, wä–), shrine, central Mexico, in the Federal District. The basilica of Guadalupe containing the shrine of Our Lady of Guadalupe (feast: Dec. 12) is the focal point of the most famous pilgrimage in the Western Hemisphere. In 1531 an Indian, Juan Diego, reported to Archbishop Zumárraga a series of miraculous visions of the Virgin Mary on the hill of Tepeyacac. The Spanish prelate attempted to discredit the visions, but the spot was nevertheless renamed Guadalupe in honor of the shrine of Our Lady of Guadalupe, Spain. To this was added later the name of the revolutionary priest HIDALGO Y COSTILLA, who adopted her banner as his standard. She is the patroness of Mexico, especially beloved by the Indians. See Donald Demarest and C. B. Taylor, ed., *Dark Virgin: the Book of Our Lady of Guadalupe* (1956).

Guadalupe Hidalgo, Treaty of, 1848, peace treaty between the United States and Mexico that ended the Mexican War. Negotiations were carried on for the United States by Nicholas P. TRIST. The treaty was signed on Feb. 2, 1848, in the village of Guadalupe Hidalgo, just outside Mexico City. It confirmed U.S. claims to Texas and set its boundary at the Rio Grande. Mexico also agreed to cede to the United

States California and New Mexico (which included present-day California, Arizona, Nevada and Utah, and parts of New Mexico, Colorado, and Wyoming) in exchange for $15 million and assumption by the United States of claims against Mexico by U.S. citizens. The treaty was ratified by the U.S. Senate on March 10, 1848, and by the Mexican Congress on May 25.

Guadalupe Mountains National Park (gwä'dəlo͞op), 81,077 acres (32,812 hectares), W Texas; est. 1966. Located in the Guadalupe Mts., the park contains parts of the world's largest and most significant Permian limestone fossil reef. In the park are McKittrich Canyon; Guadalupe Peak, 8,751 ft (2,667 m), the highest point in Texas; and El Capitan, 8,078 ft (2,462 m), a noted landmark for westward-traveling pioneers.

Guadalupe Victoria (gwäthälo͞o'pä vēktōr'yä), 1786?–1843, Mexican general, first president of Mexico (1824–29), whose original name was Manuel Félix Fernández. He joined (1811) the revolution proclaimed by Hidalgo y Costilla, and even after the defeat and death of MORELOS Y PAVÓN he continued, as a fugitive, to support the revolutionary cause. His name, Guadalupe Victoria [Our Lady of Guadalupe Triumphant], was adopted in honor of the revolutionary standard. The achievement of independence under Agustín de ITURBIDE did not satisfy him, but he adhered to the Plan of Iguala (1821). Two years later he joined Santa Anna in his revolt against Iturbide's empire. Guadalupe Victoria was chosen as a member of the provisional government and then as president. Factional strife between the conservatives and liberals marred his administration, and the conservatives, under Vice President Bravo, started an unsuccessful revolt. He was succeeded by Vicente GUERRERO.

Guadarrama, Sierra de (syār'rä thä gwäthärä'mä), mountain range rising from the plateau of central Spain, N of Madrid, and extending c.120 mi (190 km) between the Tagus and Douro rivers. The rugged mountains rise to Peñalara (7,972ft/2,430 m), the highest peak. The range is crossed by several passes, such as the Guadarrama and Navacerrada, which link Madrid with Segovia. The passes are usually blocked by heavy winter snowfalls. Numerous streams have been dammed and supply water for irrigation, hydroelectric-power generation, and municipal needs. Largely forested, the mountains yield fine timber. There are skiing resorts on the slopes.

Guadeloupe (gwädəlo͞op'), overseas department of France (1970 est. pop. 327,000), 687 sq mi (1,779 sq km), in the Leeward Islands, West Indies. The department comprises the islands of Basse-Terre (Guadeloupe proper) and Grande-Terre, and the dependencies of Marie-Galante and Les Saintes to the south, Désiderade to the east, and St. Barthélemy and the northern half of SAINT MARTIN to the north.

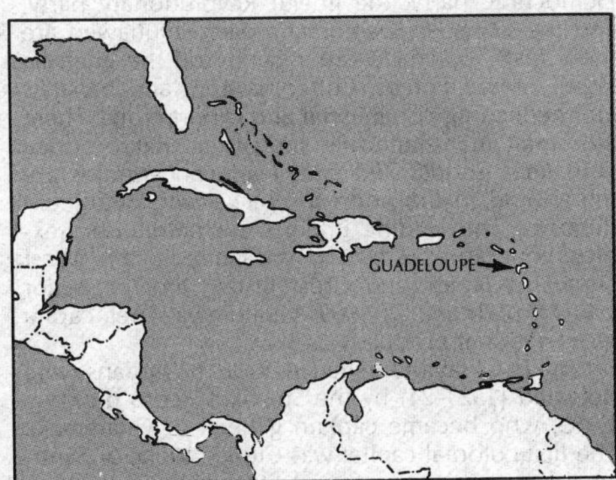

BASSE-TERRE, on the island of the same name, is Guadeloupe's capital; POINTE-À-PITRE, on Grande-Terre, is the chief port and commercial center. The islands have a mild, humid climate and are subject to hurricanes. Tourism is a major industry. Basse-Terre, volcanic in origin and extremely rugged, is settled along the coasts and produces bananas, coffee, cacao, and vanilla beans. Grande-Terre has low limestone cliffs and little rainfall; sugar and rum are its chief products. Subsistence farming, livestock raising, and fishing are carried on, and some salt and sulfur are mined. The population is overwhelmingly Negro or mulatto. Although French is the official language, a French patois is widely spoken. Discovered by Christopher Columbus in 1493, Guadeloupe was only feebly colonized by the Spanish and was finally abandoned in 1604. In 1635 settlement was begun by the French, who eliminated the native Caribs and imported slaves from Africa for plantation work. By the end of the 17th cent., Guadeloupe was a leading world sugar producer and one of France's most valuable colonies. The islands were hotly contested with the English until they were confirmed as French possessions in 1815. During World War II, Guadeloupe at first adhered to the Vichy regime in France, but an accord with the United States in 1942 led to its support of the Free French. In 1946 the colony of Guadeloupe became an overseas department of France. Its deputies sit in the French National Assembly in Paris.

Guadet, Marguerite Élie (märgərēt' älē' güädā'), 1758–94, French revolutionary. A leader of the GIRONDISTS, he was outlawed (1793) for his attacks on Maximilien Robespierre and Jean Paul Marat. He hid for 10 months before being captured and executed.

Guadiana (gwäthyä'nä), river, 510 mi (821 km) long, rising in the La Mancha Plateau, E Spain. It flows west through central Spain, then south, forming part of the Spanish-Portuguese border (except for a swing into Portugal), to the Gulf of Cádiz in the Atlantic Ocean. Although one of the longest rivers of the Iberian Peninsula, it is only navigable to Mértola, c.40 mi (60 km) upstream. Copper ore from Pomarão is moved down the river. The Guadiana is used to irrigate the fertile Mérida region of Spain and to generate hydroelectric power.

Guadix (gwäthēsh'), town (1970 pop. 19,840), Granada prov., S Spain, in Andalusia. It is the center of a farm area growing olives, flax, wheat, and hemp. Guadix was a Roman colony and, under the Visigoths, an episcopal see. It contains an 18th-century cathedral and the remains of a Moorish citadel. Just outside the city are many picturesque caves inhabited by gypsies.

Guam (gwäm), island (1970 pop. 84,996), 209 sq mi (541 sq km), W Pacific, an unincorporated territory of the United States; the largest, most populous, and southernmost of the MARIANAS ISLANDS. The southern part of the island is mountainous, rising on Mt. Lamlam to 1,332 ft (406 m). AGANA is the seat of government, and APRA HARBOR, a large U.S. naval base, is nearby. The interior of the island is dense jungle; most of the native villages are on the coast. Guam's inhabitants are chiefly of Chamorros stock (mixed Spanish, Filipino, and Micronesian descent); about one fourth of the island's population consists of U.S. military personnel and their dependents. Discovered in 1521 by Ferdinand MAGELLAN, Guam belonged to Spain until 1898, when it was taken by the United States in the Spanish-American War. From 1917 to 1950, Guam, under the Dept. of the Navy, was governed by a naval officer who was advised by a local congress. The Organic Act of 1950 transferred jurisdiction to the Dept. of the Interior and provided for a governor, appointed every four years by the President of the United States, and a 21-member unicameral legislature elected biennally by the residents. Guamanians are U.S. citizens but cannot vote in U.S. elections. Guam was attacked and captured by Japan in 1941, was retaken by U.S. forces in 1944, and became a major base for assaults on the Japanese mainland. During the Vietnam War in the 1960s Guam was an important base for air assaults on North and South Vietnam and Laos. Providing goods and services for the huge U.S. bases is the major industry. Most inhabitants practice subsistence farming, but large-scale agriculture is no longer possible because military installations occupy so much of the available land.

guan: see CURASSOW.

Guanabacoa (gwänäbäkō'ä), city (1970 pop. 69,706), La Habana prov., W Cuba, a commercial suburb of Havana. Numerous mineral springs are located near Guanabacoa, whose Indian name means "place of waters." The city was founded in 1555 on the site of an Indian settlement.

Guanabara (gwänäbä'rä), state (1970 pop. 4,252,009), 524 sq mi (1,357 sq km), SE Brazil, on the Atlantic Ocean. RIO DE JANEIRO is the capital. **Guanabara Bay,** a deep inlet of the Atlantic Ocean, is noted for its beauty. The site of the city of Rio, it is also called Rio de Janeiro Bay.

guanaco (gwänä'kō) or **huanaco** (hwän'äko), wild, hoofed mammal of the CAMEL family, *Lama guanicoe,* found on arid plains in the Andes mts. It is about 3½ ft (105 cm) high at the shoulder, with a long neck; it is brown on the back and sides, with light underparts and a dark face. Regarded by some authorities as the ancestor of the domestic LLAMA and ALPACA, the guanaco is not domesticated, but Indians use its flesh for food and make its hide into clothing and other coverings and its bones into various implements. Encroachments on its grazing land have reduced its numbers. The guanaco is classified in the phylum CHORDATA, subphylum Vertebrata, class Mammalia, order Artiodactyla, family Camelidae.

Guanahani: see SAN SALVADOR, island.

Guanajuato (gwänähwä'tō), state (1970 pop. 2,285,249), 11,805 sq mi (30,575 sq km), W central Mexico, on the central plateau. The city of Guanajuato is the capital. The state's high average elevation (6,000 ft/1,829 m) provides a moderately cool, healthful climate. Guanajuato is crossed in the north by transverse ranges of the Sierra Madre Occidental, some of which reach heights of 11,000 ft (3,353 m). In the south are fertile plains supporting stock raising and the cultivation of wheat (of which Guanajuato is a leading national producer), maize, other grain crops, and beans. The Lerma and its tributaries form the chief river system. Despite the steadily growing importance of agriculture, Guanajuato is noted primarily as Mexico's foremost mining state; much silver and gold is extracted, and mercury, lead, tin, copper, and opals are also produced. Industrial products from the cities—Guanajuato, Celaya, León, and Irapuato—include textiles, saddles and other leather goods, pottery, and foodstuffs. Joined with Querétaro, the state was a Spanish intendancy until 1824. A leading silver producer of Spanish America, Guanajuato declined in economic importance during the wars of the 19th cent.

Guanajuato, city (1970 pop. 33,762), capital of Guanajuato state, W central Mexico. The city, with an altitude of c.6,600 ft (2,000 m), is situated in the Cañada de Marfil [ivory ravine], a precipitous ravine encircled by barren hills. Guanajuato has narrow, winding, steep cobblestone streets, sometimes pieced out by stone steps, and the ground underneath is honeycombed with silver-mine shafts. Its geographic position and economic importance (as one of Spanish America's chief silver-producing centers) gave the city a key role in the wars and revolutions that racked Mexico in the 19th and early 20th cent. Guanajuato has recently become a resort city. There are several noteworthy colonial churches and buildings, including the Alhóndiga de Granaditas, originally a granary that was besieged and captured (1810) by Hidalgo y Costilla at the outset of the war against Spain.

guanine (gwä'nēn), organic base of the PURINE family. It was reported (1846) to be in the GUANO of birds; later (1879–84) it was established as one of the major constituents of NUCLEIC ACIDS. The accepted structure of the guanine molecule was proposed in 1875, and the compound was first synthesized in 1900. When combined with the sugar ribose in a glycosidic linkage, guanine forms a derivative called guanosine (a nucleoside), which in turn can be phosphorylated with from one to three phosphoric acid groups, yielding the three NUCLEOTIDES GMP (guanosine monophosphate), GDP (guanosine diphosphate), and GTP (guanosine triphosphate). Analogous nucleosides and nucleotides are formed from guanine and deoxyribose. The nucleotide derivatives of guanine perform important functions in cellular metabolism. GTP acts as a COENZYME in carbohydrate metabolism and in the biosynthesis of proteins; it can readily donate one of its phosphate groups to adenosine diphosphate (ADP) to form ADENOSINE TRIPHOSPHATE (ATP), an extremely important intermediate in the transfer of chemical energy in living systems. GTP is the source of the guanosine found in RNA and deoxyguanosine triphosphate (dGTP) is the source of the deoxyguanosine in DNA, and thus guanine is intimately involved in the preservation and transfer of genetic information. Guanine is said to account for the iridescence of fish scales and the white, shiny appearance of the skin of many amphibians and reptiles.

guano (gwä'nō), dried excrement of sea birds and bats found principally on the coastal islands of Peru, Africa, Chile, and the West Indies. It contains about 6% phosphorus, 9% nitrogen, 2% potassium, and moisture. Guano is found mixed with feathers and bones and is used as a fertilizer.

Guantánamo (gwäntä'nämō), city (1970 pop. 130,061), Oriente prov., SE Cuba, on the Guaso River. It is the processing center for a rich sugar- and coffee-producing region and has road and rail connections with Santiago de Cuba. Founded in the early 19th cent. by Frenchmen fleeing the slave rebellion in Haiti, Guantánamo retains many vestiges of French architecture. The city is c.20 mi (30 km) inland from its port, Caimanera, on landlocked **Guantánamo Bay,** where the United States maintains an important naval station. Often called the Pearl Harbor of the Atlantic, the base has naval installations covering c.28,000 acres (11,300 hectares). Its site was leased to the United States in 1903 by a treaty that was renewed in 1934; consent of both governments is needed to revoke the agreement. Since 1960 the Castro government has refused to accept the token annual rent ($5,000) from the United States and has pressured for the surrender of the base.

Guaporé (gwəpo͝orĕ'), river, c.750 mi (1,207 km) long, rising in the mountains of Mato Grosso state, W Brazil. It flows northwest through rain forest and forms part of the Brazil-Bolivia border before joining the Mamoré River. The federal territory formerly called Guaporé was renamed (1956) Rondônia. The river is also called Iténez.

Guaraní Indians (gwäränē'), people of the Tupí-Guarani linguistic stock, on the north and east coasts of South America from the Guianas to the Río de la Plata and W to the Paraná, Uruguay, and Paraguay rivers. The term *Tupí* or *Tupinambá* is used for the Brazilian Indians of the Amazon region and the term *Guaraní* for the groups in S Brazil and Paraguay. At the time of the Spanish conquest (16th cent.), the Guaraní, like the Tupí, lived in patrilineal communities of up to 60 families; each unit was ruled by a chief, but generally the SHAMAN had more power than the chief. The Guaraní cultivated maize, manioc, and other crops in small farms. Their religion was based on an impressive and elaborate mythology. The shaman was believed to possess supernatural powers and used these to ward off evil and cure sickness. Among the ancient Guaraní, ritual cannibalism was common. Although their material culture was not advanced, Guaraní songs, dances, and myths constituted a rich body of folklore. Guaraní influence on present-day Paraguayan musical folklore is strong. It was in Guaraní territory that early Jesuit missionaries established the historically controversial system of REDUCTIONS. The Indians today continue to practice communal agriculture in some rural areas. The Guaraní language is widely spoken in Paraguay. In Brazil, Tupian groups were generally assimilated into European culture. See Charles Wagley, *The Tenetehara Indians of Brazil* (1949); E. R. Service, *Spanish Guaraní Relations in Early Colonial Paraguay* (1954, repr. 1971); R. F. Murphy, *Headhunter's Heritage* (1960).

Guarda (gwär'də), city (1970 municipal pop. 40,529), capital of Guarda dist., N central Portugal, in Beira Alta. On the slopes of the Serra da Estrela, it is Portugal's highest city (c.3,400 ft/1,040 m) and is a winter sports resort. Guarda is also the commercial center of an agricultural region. It has an old fort, a castle, and a Gothic cathedral.

Guardi, Francesco (frănchās'kō gwär'dē), 1712–93, Venetian landscape and architectural painter. A follower of Canaletto, he developed a freer style of great brilliance. Guardi's work ranges from elaborate architectural scenes to spontaneous and delightful *capricci*, both in painting and drawings. His many charming landscapes are in the galleries of London, Paris, Venice, and Boston. The Metropolitan Museum and the National Gallery of Art, Washington, D.C., each have several. See monograph by Vittorio Moschini (tr. 1957); J. Byram Shaw, *The Drawings of Francesco Guardi* (1951).

Guardia, Tomás (tōmäs' gwär'dēä), 1832–82, president of Costa Rica. An army general, he led a revolt that eventually placed him in control and enabled him to rule the country from 1870 to 1882 with only brief interruptions. Under a repressive military dictatorship he exiled the leading families and halted the destructive Liberal-Conservative rivalry that had torn Costa Rica for nearly 50 years. Guardia undertook the building of a costly ocean-to-ocean railroad, financed and directed by the United Fruit magnate Minor Cooper KEITH. Although basically a military strong man, Guardia is generally credited with having laid the groundwork of Costa Rican political stability.

guardian and ward, in law. A guardian is someone who legally has the care of the person or property, or both, of a person, the ward, who is legally considered incapable of acting for himself; e.g., an infant (see INFANCY), an insane person, or a spendthrift. Guardianship is designed to safeguard the rights and interests of the ward. In Anglo-American law the three principal classes of guardianship over infants are testamentary, by nature, and by judicial appointment. In the first, statutes give parents the right to appoint a guardian by will. The right was originally restricted to a father, but many U.S. states now grant it to the surviving spouse or give a mother preference over a testamentary guardian named by the father. Guardianship by nature is the natural guardianship arising out of the relation of PARENT AND CHILD. At common law it belongs first to the father, and after his death to the mother, and in default of both to the grandfather, the grandmother, or next of kin. It extends to the person of the child only and not to the separate property of the child. The rights and duties of the guardian by nature are usually treated as those of a parent rather than of a guardian. The guardian by judicial appointment is one appointed by the court that by statute is given the jurisdiction over such relations. A court may, when no testamentary guardian has been appointed by the will of a deceased parent, appoint a guardian for the children. The selection of the guardian, if not made by the parent, is generally at the discretion of the ward if over a certain age. The welfare of the ward being primary, a guardian either of the person or of the property may be set aside by the court at its discretion. The same person is usually appointed guardian of the person and the property of the ward, but this is not necessary, the two being legally separate. The guardian is held to standards of prudence such as a businessman would exercise in his own affairs. He is bound by the FIDUCIARY relationship existing between his ward and himself and must render an accounting both annually and at the termination of the guardianship.

Guareschi, Giovanni (jōvä'nē gwärĕs'kē), 1908–68, Italian journalist and novelist. Guareschi edited a humorous weekly before World War II and in 1945 helped to found the popular weekly *Candido*. A master of warm but satirical humor, he is best known as author of *The Little World of Don Camillo* (tr. 1950) and its sequels, tales of a village priest's struggles with the local Communists. See his *Family Guareschi* (tr. 1970).

Guarini, Guarino (gwärē'nō gwärē'nē), 1624–83, Italian architect, mathematician, and writer. He was one of the first to analyze with perceptivity the structure of medieval architecture, in his *Architettura civile*, posthumously edited by Vittone in 1737. After studying in Rome, he returned to his birthplace, Modena, where he was ordained in the Theatine order. In 1660 he moved to Messina and designed several important church buildings there. Soon after, he traveled to Paris, where he built the Theatine church of Sainte-Anne-la-Royale (destroyed 1823) and wrote a mathematical-philosophical treatise, *Placita philosophica* (1665). Settling in Turin, he designed two palaces and three centralized churches; the Sindone Chapel and the Church of San Lorenzo are considered two of the finest examples of baroque architecture. Guarini reached the pinnacle of his achievement in his planning of domes that suggest the loftiness and openwork of the spires of Gothic churches.

Guarino da Verona (gwärē'nō dä vārô'nä), 1374?–1460, Italian humanist, considered the greatest teacher of his time. Associated with several universities, he translated various Greek and Latin classics and wrote a Latin grammar (1487).

Guarneri (gwärnĕ'rē) or **Guarnerius** (gwärnĕr'ēəs), family of violinmakers of Cremona, Italy. The first craftsman of the family was **Andrea Guarneri,** c.1626–1698, a pupil of Niccolò AMATI. He designed and built his instruments in the Amati fashion. Andrea's two sons, who were his pupils, surpassed him in his work. They were **Pietro Giovanni Guarneri,** 1655–c.1740, who worked in Mantua and made several innovations, and **Giuseppe Giovan Battista Guarneri,** 1666–c.1738, who made superb violins in an original style. The son of Giuseppe Guarneri, **Pietro Guarneri,** 1695–1765?, made his best violins in his later years, following his uncle's pattern for the most part. The greatest violinmaker of the family was **Giuseppe Guarneri,** 1687?–1745, grandnephew of Andrea, called "del Gesù" because he signed his labels with a cross and the letters IHS. He was second only to STRADIVARI in the history of violinmaking. He followed the school of Brescia instead of the Amati in his designs. Giuseppe built varied models to achieve a superb tone so that his instruments are not uniform. See W. H. Hill, *The Violin-Makers of the Guarneri Family* (1931).

Guasave (gwäsä'vā), city (1970 pop. 148,475), Sinaloa state, W Mexico, on the Sinaloa River. The growing of cotton and maize and the raising of livestock are the chief occupations. The city was established in 1595 as a Spanish mission among the Guasave Indians.

Guastalla (gwästäl'lä), town (1971 pop. 14,229), Emilia-Romagna, N Italy, on the Po River. It is an agricultural and industrial center. Probably founded in the 7th cent., Guastalla was held by various lords and in 1539 was bought by Ferrante Gonzaga of Mantua. It was made a duchy in 1621. After the Guastalla branch of the Gonzagas became extinct in 1746, the duchy passed (1748) to Parma. In 1806, Napoleon I conferred Guastalla on his sister, Pauline Borghese, but it later reverted to Parma.

Guatemala (gwätəmä'lə), republic (1970 est. pop. 5,110,000), 42,042 sq mi (108,889 sq km), Central America. The capital is GUATEMALA City. Other cities are PUERTO BARRIOS, SAN JOSÉ, QUEZALTENANGO, and ANTIGUA. The country is bounded on the N and W by Mexico, on the E by British Honduras (Belize) and the Caribbean Sea, on the SE by Honduras and El Salvador, and on the S by the Pacific Ocean. A highland region, where most of the population lives, cuts across the country from west to east. The rugged main range includes the inactive volcano Tajumulco, which is the highest point in Central America (13,816 ft/4,211 m). The range is flanked on the Pacific side by a string of volcanoes (some active), such as Tacaná, Acatenango, and Agua. Volcanic eruptions and floods have plagued Guatemala throughout history. In the center of the range is Lake Atitlán, and south of the highlands is the Pacific coastal lowland. North of them are the Caribbean lowland and the vast tropical forest known as the PETÉN. Lake Petén Itza is in N central Guatemala. The largest river is the Motagua, which flows into the Caribbean at the port of Puerto Barrios. North of the Motagua is the Lake Izabal-Río Dulce system,

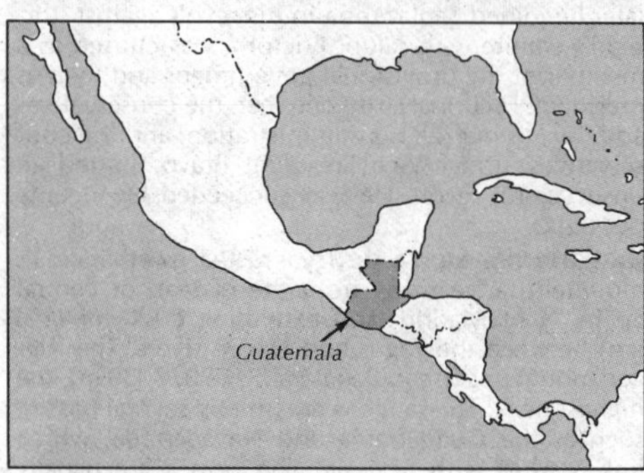

which was a major waterway in colonial times. The population, mainly Roman Catholic, is about half Indian and nearly half mestizo (who predominate in the cities), with a small number of whites and blacks. The Indians own small plots in the highlands and provide most of the agricultural labor. The Indian town of CHICHICASTENANGO is a tourist attraction. Guatemala's current constitution was adopted in 1965. It provides for a president, directly elected for a four-year term, who cannot succeed himself. A unicameral legislature is also elected for a four-year term. The legal political parties are the right-wing National Liberation Movement, the Institutional Democratic party, the liberal Revolutionary party, and the Christian Democratic party. Outlawed are the leftist Guatemala Labor party and the guerrilla Rebel Armed Forces. Coffee, cotton, and bananas are the leading commercial and export crops. There are small manufacturing industries that produce consumer goods. Zinc and lead concentrates are mined and in the north are nickel and petroleum deposits. The leading imports are petroleum, textiles, flour, and machinery. The United States, West Germany, Japan, and Great Britain are the major trading partners. In 1969, Guatemala's per capita gross national product was $325.

History. The Maya-Quiché (see QUICHÉ) Indians were defeated (1523–24) by the Spaniard Pedro de ALVARADO, who became captain general of Guatemala. The first colonial capital was Ciudad Vieja, or Santiago. The conquerors found little of the gold they sought, but cocoa and indigo were raised. Central America became independent from Spain in 1821. Guatemala was first a part of the Mexican Empire of Agustín de Iturbide and then became a nucleus of the CENTRAL AMERICAN FEDERATION. After the federation collapsed, Guatemala became a separate nation (1839). Guatemalan interference in the affairs of other Central American republics during the 19th and early 20th cent., under the conservative dictatorships of Rafael CARRERA and Manuel ESTRADA CABRERA and under the liberal, Justo Ruffino BARRIOS, caused intense hostility and finally led to the Washington Conference of 1907, which established the Central American Court of Justice. The boundary between Guatemala and British Honduras has remained in dispute since 1859; since 1945 Guatemala has actively sought to regain control of British Honduras, over which it claims sovereignty. Jorge UBICO became president in 1931, and his tenure was marked by repressive rule and an improvement in the nation's finances. After Guatemala declared war on the Axis powers in 1941, the large German-owned coffee holdings were expropriated. Popular discontent led to Ubico's overthrow in 1944 and his replacement by Juan José Arévalo. Arévalo launched a series of labor and agrarian reforms that were continued by Jacobo Arbenz Guzmán, who succeeded him in 1951. A law expropriating large estates angered foreign plantation owners, particularly the United Fruit Company. As Communist influence in the Arbenz government increased, relations with the United States deteriorated. In 1954 the United States aided the anti-Arbenz military force that placed Col. Carlos Castillo Armas in power. When Castillo Armas was assassinated three years later, Miguel Ydígoras Fuentes became president. Guatemalan bases were used to train anti-Castro guerrillas in the early 1960s. In 1963 the prospect of the return to power of Arévalo led to a military coup under the defense minister, Enrique Peralta Azurdia. However, leftist terrorism mounted and in turn provoked rightist terrorism. In 1966 the moderate leftist Julio César Méndez Montenegro was elected president. Political violence continued under his administration. In Aug., 1968, the U.S. ambassador was assassinated. In the election of 1970, Col. Carlos ARANA OSORIO, an extreme conservative, was chosen president. He imposed a one-year state of siege in an attempt to end the violence. In the early 1970s many labor and political leaders were killed and several foreign diplomats were kidnapped. When no candidate received an absolute majority in the presidential election of 1974, the legislature declared Gen. Kjell Laugerud Garcia the winner, even though Gen. Efrain Rios Montt, the anti-government candidate, had allegedly won a plurality. See Vera Kelsey and Lilly de Jongh Osborne, *Four Keys to Guatemala* (rev. ed. 1967); E. H. Galeano, *Guatemala: Occupied Country* (tr. 1969); R. N. Adams, *Crucifixion by Power: Essays on Guatemalan National Social Structure, 1944–1966* (1970); John Dombrowski et al., *Area Handbook for Guatemala* (1970); Thomas Melville and Marjorie Melville, *Guatemala: The Politics of Land Ownership* (1971); Pedro de Alvarado, *An Account of the Conquest of Guatemala in 1524* (tr. 1924, repr. 1972); R. E. Moore, *Historical Dictionary of Guatemala* (rev. ed. 1973).

Guatemala, city (1971 est. pop. 730,991), S central Guatemala, capital of the republic. Its full name is Santiago de los Caballeros de Guatemala la Nueva. In a broad, fertile, highland valley, c.5,000 ft (1,520 m) high, it enjoys an equable climate the year round. It is the largest city in Central America, with a cosmopolitan atmosphere and many fine public buildings. It is served by international and local airways, modern highways, and railroads and is the industrial and commercial center of the republic. To the city's markets come the fruits and vegetables of the tropical coasts and temperate highlands and also native handicrafts, especially textiles. Much of the produce is carried in from the countryside by Indians, who sell it in the market stalls. There is also a modern business section. The present city is the third permanent capital of Guatemala and was founded in 1776 after ANTIGUA was abandoned. An earthquake destroyed Guatemala City in 1917–18, but it was rebuilt on the same site. From the city excursions may be made to the ruined sites of Antigua and Ciudad Vieja, the first capital. Many interesting remains of Mayan civilization have been unearthed in the vicinity of Guatemala City, notably at Lake Amatitlán. The Univ. of San Carlos de Guatemala is in the city.

Guatémoc or **Guatemozín:** see CUAUHTÉMOC.

guava (gwä'və), small evergreen tree or shrub of the genus *Psidium* of the family Myrtaceae (MYRTLE family), native to tropical America and grown elsewhere for its ornamental flowers and edible fruit. The fruit (a fleshy berry with many hard seeds) of the common tropical guava *(P. guajava)* is shaped like an apple or a pear and has white, pink, or red flesh (depending on the variety) with a sweet, musky flavor and, usually, a yellow rind. The strawberry guava *(P. cattleyanum),* native to Brazil, bears a red fruit with a rough rind and reddish pulp, supposedly strawberrylike in flavor. At the time of the Spanish explorations the guava was found from Peru to Mexico; it is now grown commercially in Florida and California, where it has also escaped cultivation and become naturalized. Much of the perishable fruit is made into jellies, beverages, and similar products. It is a rich source of minerals and of vitamins A and C. Guava is classified in the division MAGNOLIOPHYTA, class Magnoliopsida, order Myrtales, family Myrtaceae.

Guayama (gwäyä'mä), town (1970 pop. 20,318), SE Puerto Rico. It is the processing and distribution center for a region producing sugarcane, tobacco, coffee, and livestock and is also the headquarters of a major irrigation and electrification project.

Guayaquil (gwīäkēl'), city (1970 est. pop. 794,300), capital of Guayas prov., W Ecuador, on the Guayas River near its mouth on the Gulf of Guayaquil, an inlet of the Pacific Ocean. The chief port and largest city of Ecuador and one of the best ports along Latin America's Pacific coast, Guayaquil has industries manufacturing textiles, leather goods, cement, alcohol, soap, and iron products. Through its modern harbor are shipped the principal exports of Ecuador, cacao and bananas, as well as tagua nuts, cattle, sugar, coffee, alligator skins, and Panama hats. Guayaquil was founded by the Spanish conquistador Sebastián de BENALCÁZAR in 1535. It was often subjected to attacks by buccaneers in the 17th cent. and in the 18th and 19th cent. was destroyed repeatedly by fires. The occupation of the city in 1821 by patriot forces under Antonio José de SUCRE was the first major step in Ecuador's final liberation from Spain. The fateful meeting between Simón BOLÍVAR and José de SAN MARTÍN that was to influence the course of independence in South America took place in Guayaquil in 1822. Because of its hot and humid climate the city was frequently scourged by yellow fever until the sanitation work of the U.S. surgeon-general William C. GORGAS. Guayaquil has several colonial landmarks and a university.

Guaymas (gwī'mäs), city (1970 pop. 84,730), Sonora state, NW Mexico, on the bay of Guaymas. A port on the Gulf of California, it is also the outlet for Hermosillo. Guaymas stands on a scenic inlet girt by desert mountains. Its fine beaches, excellent deep-sea fishing, and good transportation facilities have made it a popular tourist resort. Although the surrounding area was explored as early as 1539, the city was not established until the early 18th cent. by Jesuit missionaries. U.S. forces occupied Guaymas in 1846, during the Mexican War, and it was held by the French in 1865–66.

Gubbio (go͞ob'byō), town (1971 pop. 31,031), in Umbria, central Italy. It is an agricultural center and has long been known for its ceramics. Originally an Umbrian town (coins and the IGUVINE TABLES were found there), it later flourished under the Romans. Gubbio was a powerful free commune in the 11th–12th cent., came under the dukes of Urbino in 1384, and was held by the papacy from 1624 to 1860. A local school of painting (14th–15th cent.) included Guido Palmerucci and Ottaviano Nelli. The town retains a medieval character. Notable structures include the Gothic Palazzo dei Consoli (14th–15th cent.), the Palazzo Ducale (begun 1476), and a well-preserved Roman theater (1st cent. B.C.).

Guchkov, Aleksandr Ivanovich (əlyĭksän'dər ēvä'-nəvĭch go͞och'kôf), 1862–1936, Russian political leader. A prominent businessman, during the 1905 revolution he helped found the Octobrist party, which was based on acceptance of Czar Nicholas II's October Manifesto; the manifesto in effect made Russia a constitutional monarchy. Guchkov led the Octobrists in the third DUMA (1907–12) but resigned in 1911 in protest against the Czar's usurpation of the Duma's authority. During World War I he served as chairman of the central war industries committee. Prior to the overthrow of the autocracy in March, 1917, he urged Nicholas's abdication in favor of his son. In the provisional government set up after the Russian Revolution he served briefly as minister of defense. Following the Bolshevik seizure of power, Guchkov emigrated to France.

Gudbrandsdalen (go͝od'brändsdäl"ĕn), valley region of Oppland co., S central Norway. It extends c.100 mi (160 km) from the Dovrefjell southeastward to Lillehammer on Mjøsa lake. A rich agricultural and timber district, the valley is also a tourist area. The Lågan River, which traverses the valley, is a valuable source of hydroelectric power. The valley has long been an important trade route and a main invasion route through S Norway and has a rich history; many Gudbrandsdalen farmers trace their ancestry back to saga times. Much of the action in Ibsen's *Peer Gynt* is set there.

Gudenå (go͞o'thənô"), river, 98 mi (158 km) long, E Jutland, Denmark. The only Danish river of importance, it flows generally north, traversing several lakes, past Silkeborg, then NE past Randers (the chief port) to Randersfjørd and the Kattegat. It is partly navigable and has salmon fisheries.

Gudgodah (gŭd'gōdə, gŭdgō'-), desert camping place of the Israelites: see HOR-HAGIDGAD.

Guðmundsson, Kristmann (krĭst'män gvüth'-münsôn), 1902–, Icelandic novelist. Guðmundsson lived in Norway from 1924 to 1937 and has written in both Norwegian and Icelandic. His novels and stories of love, remarkable for profound psychological insight, include *The Bridal Gown* (1927, tr. 1931), and *Morning of Life* (1929, tr. 1936). Among Guðmundsson's later works are *Winged Citadel* (1937, tr. 1940), *Playthings* (1961), and *The Square* (1965).

Gudrun (go͞o'dro͞on) or **Kudrun** (ko͞o'-), in Germanic literature. **1** Heroine of the VOLSUNGASAGA. **2** Heroine and title person of an anonymous Middle High German epic written shortly after and strongly influenced by the Nibelungenlied (see under NIBELUNGEN). The epic tells the story of Hilde, Hagen's sister, and of the abduction of her daughter Gudrun. **3** Principal character of the Icelandic *Laxdaelasaga,* introduced to English readers by William Morris through his "Lovers of Gudrun" in *The Earthly Paradise.* Wagner's Gutrune (in the *Götterdämmerung)* is not Gudrun but corresponds to Kriemhild of the *Nibelungenlied.*

Guébriant, Jean Baptiste Budes, comte de (zhäN bätēst' büd kôNt də gābrēäN'), 1602–43, marshal of France and general in the Thirty Years War. He commanded the French auxiliaries of Bernhard of Saxe-Weimar and succeeded to his command. Guébriant, with Swedish aid, defeated (1641) the imperial troops at Wolfenbüttel. Made a marshal in 1642, he was killed at Rottweil.

Guebwiller, Ballon de: see VOSGES, mountains.

Guelderland or **Guelders:** see GELDERLAND.

guelder-rose: see HONEYSUCKLE.

Guelph (gwĕlf), city (1971 pop. 60,087), S Ont., Canada, on the Speed River. It is an industrial city located in a rich farm area. Manufactures include electrical, construction, and farm equipment, textiles, clothing, fiber glass, and tobacco products. The Univ. of Guelph, comprising the Ontario Agricultural College and other institutions, was founded in 1964. The city was founded in 1827 by the Scottish novelist John Galt.

Guelph, University of, at Guelph, Ont., Canada; provincially supported; nondenominational; coeducational; founded 1964. It has a faculty of graduate studies and schools of engineering, hotel and food administration, landscape architecture, and physical education as well as colleges of agriculture, arts, social science, family and consumer studies, physical science, biological science, and veterinary medicine.

Guelphs (gwĕlfs), European dynasty tracing its descent from the Swabian count Guelph or Welf (9th cent.), whose daughter Judith married the Frankish emperor Louis I. Guelph III (d. 1055) was made (1047) duke of Carinthia and margrave of Verona. Without male heirs, he was succeeded by his nephew, Guelph IV, whose father was a member of the Italian house of ESTE. He became (1070) the first Guelph duke of Bavaria. His grandson, HENRY THE PROUD, inherited the duchy of Saxony from Holy Roman Emperor Lothair II through his marriage to Lothair's daughter Gertrude. Henry's control of both Bavaria and Saxony made the Guelphs powerful rivals to the house of HOHENSTAUFEN for the imperial title; when Conrad III of Hohenstaufen became German king in 1138 he deprived Henry of his duchies, and war ensued. Amity between the two dynasties was restored with the accession of FREDERICK I of Hohenstaufen as Holy Roman emperor in 1155. His mother, Judith, was the sister of Henry the Proud, and Frederick I thus united in his person the two chief rival houses of Germany. Frederick reconfirmed HENRY THE LION, successor of Henry the Proud, as duke of Saxony and Bavaria. Later in Frederick's reign friction between the two developed, and in 1180, Frederick confiscated Henry's duchies; the Guelphs retained only Brunswick and Lüneburg. Henry's son OTTO IV briefly became Holy Roman emperor but was deposed (1215). In 1235, Brunswick and Lüneburg were raised to the duchy of BRUNSWICK under Henry's grandson Otto I of Brunswick. The line of Brunswick-Lüneburg or Hanover (see HANOVER, HOUSE OF) ascended (1714) the throne of Great Britain in the person of George I, but because of the Salic law of succession Hanover was separated (1837) from the British crown on the accession of Queen Victoria. After the annexation of Hanover by Prussia and the deposition (1866) of George V, last king of Hanover, the so-called Guelphic party was founded and unsuccessfully sought to restore the kingdom.

Guelphs and Ghibellines (gwĕlfs, gĭb'əlēnz, -lĭnz), opposing political factions in Germany and in Italy during the later Middle Ages. The names were used to designate the papal (Guelph) party and the imperial (Ghibelline) party during the long struggle between popes and emperors, and they were also used in connection with the rivalry of two princely houses of Germany, the Welfs or Guelphs, who were dukes of Saxony and Bavaria, and the HOHENSTAUFEN (the name *Ghibelline* is supposedly derived from Waiblingen, a Hohenstaufen castle). The rivalry between the German families, both of which had large holdings in Swabia, dates from their rise to power under Holy Roman Emperor Henry IV. The struggle began in earnest with HENRY THE PROUD and his son and successor, HENRY THE LION, and last flared up with the election of OTTO IV as Holy Roman emperor. In Italy the party names were perpetuated by two rival factions that for many years plunged the country into internal warfare. The names were first used in 13th-century Florence to designate the supporters of Otto IV (a Guelph) and the Hohenstaufen Frederick II (a Ghibelline). The terms, however, soon lost their original significance. Among the Ghibellines were EZZELINO DA ROMANO, Castruccio CASTRACANI, Della Scala of VERONA, the MONTEFELTRO family of Urbino, and the Visconti family of Milan (although Milan itself was Guelph). Unlike the noble families, towns seldom had fixed party loyalties, although Milan, Florence, and Genoa were usually Guelph; Cremona, Pisa, and Arezzo were usually Ghibelline. Venice remained neutral. In Rome the Ghibellines were represented by the pope's enemies, notably the Colonna family, and by the republicans. In S Italy the terms were rarely used, although the Angevin kings of Naples were strongly Guelph. In Florence, after the Ghibellines had finally been expelled in the late 13th cent., the Guelphs soon divided into Blacks and Whites. By the 15th cent. the names fell into disuse. At no time did either party clearly represent any particular political doctrine or social class. See Oscar Browning, *Guelphs and Ghibellines* (1894); T. F. Tout, *The Empire and the Papacy, 918-1273* (8th ed. 1924, repr. 1965); R. E. Herzstein, ed., *The Holy Roman Empire in the Middle Ages* (1966).

Guenevere: see GUINEVERE.

guenon: see MONKEY.

Guercino (gwĕrchē'nō), 1591-1666, Italian painter whose original name was Giovanni Francesco Barbieri, b. near Bologna. He studied with Ludovico Carracci. Between 1621 and 1623 he was in Rome, where he painted the ceiling frescos of the Casino Ludovisi and his superb *Burial of St. Petronilla* (Capitoline Mus., Rome). The classicist tendencies prevalent in Rome caused him to alter his style so that he never equaled the dramatic intensity of his early work. An extensive collection of his drawings is in the Royal Library at Windsor. See Denis Mahon, *Studies in Seicento Art and Theory* (1947).

Guéret (gārā'), town (1968 pop. 14,080), capital of Creuse dept., central France. It is a market center and an industrial town. Metals (especially aluminum), shirts, jewelry, and handicrafts are the principal manufactures. In the 13th cent. Guéret became the capital of the county of MARCHE. Points of interest include the Hotel de Moneyroux (15th-16th cent.), which is now an archive, and the Church of Saint Peter and Saint Paul (13th and 16th cent.), which was reconstructed in the 19th cent.

guereza: see MONKEY.

Guericke, Otto von (ô'tō fən gā'rĭkə), 1602-86, German physicist, noted for his study of pneumatics. He carried out his most important researches while burgomaster (1646-81) of Magdeburg. In the course of his attempts to create a vacuum he made the first air pump (c.1650). To demonstrate the pressure of air he devised the so-called Magdeburg hemispheres—two hollow copper hemispheres fitted together to form a globe c.14 in. (36 cm) in diameter from which the air could be pumped. A famous woodcut depicts the claim that it required two opposing eight-horse teams to pull the hemispheres apart. He invented (1660) a machine to generate electricity from the friction of the hand held against a rotating sulfur ball; he also predicted the periodicity of comets.

Guérin, Jules (gĕr'ĭn), 1866-1946, American mural painter and illustrator, b. St. Louis. His illustrations appeared in leading magazines. He executed decorations for the Lincoln Memorial, Washington, D.C.; the Pennsylvania RR station, New York City; the Federal Reserve Bank, San Francisco; the Civic Opera, the Merchandise Mart, and the Illinois Merchants' Bank, Chicago; the Cleveland Terminal, Cleveland; and the Louisiana state capitol, Baton Rouge.

Guérin, Maurice de (Georges Maurice de Guérin) (zhôrzh mōrēs' də gărăN'), 1810-39, French writer. At his early death he left two fragmentary prose poems, *Le Centaure* and *La Bacchante,* a handful of other poems, letters, journals, and scraps of prose. His works, infused with a mingling of pantheism and Christian mysticism, are classical in form. They were collected and edited by G. S. Trébutien as *Reliquiae* (1861). Guérin's sister, **Eugénie de Guérin,** 1805-48, was also a writer of distinction. An early collection of her journals and letters, also called *Reliquiae,* was made by Barbey d'Aurevilly and Trébutien (1885).

Guérin, Pierre Narcisse, Baron (pyĕr närsēs' bär-ôN), 1774-1833, French painter. He won enthusiastic recognition in 1800 for his *Marius Sextus* (Louvre). A defender of the classicism of J. L. David, he became director of the École de Rome in 1822. He counted among his pupils Delacroix, Géricault, and Ary Scheffer, who were to launch the romantic school. Among his best-known works are *Aeneas and Dido, Clytemnestra,* and *Andromache,* all in the Louvre.

Guernica (gärnē'kä), historic town (1970 pop. 14,678), Vizcaya prov., N Spain, in the Basque Province. It has metallurgical, furniture, and food manufactures. The oak of Guernica, under which the diet of Vizcaya used to meet, is a symbol of the lost liberties of the Basques. In April, 1937, German planes, aiding the insurgents in the Spanish civil war, bombed and destroyed Guernica. The indiscriminate killing of women and children aroused world opinion, and the bombing of Guernica became a symbol of fascist brutality. The event inspired one of Picasso's most celebrated paintings. Guernica is also called Guernica y Luno.

Guernsey (gûrn'zē), island (1971 pop. 51,458), 25 sq mi (65 sq km), in the English Channel, second largest of the Channel Islands. Guernsey bailiwick includes Alderney, Sark, Herm, Brechou, Jethou, and smaller islands. Guernsey has a low beach in the north and bold rocky cliffs along the south shore. The shipping and distributing center and chief town is Saint Peter Port. Exports include dairy products, fruits, flowers, vegetables, and Guernsey cattle. It is a tourist site.

Guernsey cattle, breed of dairy cattle developed on the islands of Alderney, Guernsey, and Sark near the north coast of France. First imported to the United States in about 1830, they are fawn-colored with white markings and are of medium size. Their milk is golden in color and rich in vitamin A. The average milk yield is a little higher than that of the Jersey, but the butterfat content is slightly lower.

Guerra Junqueiro, Abílio (äbē'lyō gĕr'ə zhōōnkā'-rō), 1850-1923, Portuguese poet. A revolutionary, he wrote violent satiric poems attacking conservatism, romanticism, and the Church. Typical are *A morte de Dom Jõas* (1874) and *A velhice do Padre Eterno* (1885). He later turned to writing simple, touching lyrics of rural life, as in *Os simples* (1892). For a time he served as minister to Switzerland.

Guerrazzi, Francesco Domenico (fränchās'kō dō-mān'nēkō gwär-rät'tsē), 1804-73, Italian patriot and writer, b. Leghorn. A radical republican and nationalist, he was repeatedly imprisoned for his activities in the RISORGIMENTO. He became minister and dictator (1848-49) of Tuscany in the government established there during the revolution of 1848, and after its fall he was exiled until 1859. After the unification of Italy (1861), Guerrazzi was a member in the Italian parliament until 1870. His romantic historical novels were written as calls to Italian patriotism; the best known of them is *L'assedio di Firenze* [the siege of Florence] (1836).

Guerrero, Vicente (vēsān'tā gär-rā'rō), 1782-1831, Mexican revolutionist and president (April-Dec., 1829). He fought under the command of MORELOS Y PAVÓN, spreading the revolution in the south. Guerrero won victory after victory. When Morelos was defeated and executed, Guerrero continued to wage guerrilla warfare, harassing the royalists. He fought on when most of the revolutionary leaders had been defeated or had given up the struggle for freedom. When Agustín de ITURBIDE was sent out in 1820 to defeat him, Guerrero won minor victories over Iturbide's troops but was later persuaded to adhere to the Plan of IGUALA (1821) and to accept Iturbide's leadership. Thus the revolution lost its popular cast and passed into the hands of the landowning creoles and the clergy. Guerrero accepted Iturbide's empire in 1822 but later joined the revolution begun by SANTA ANNA. The flimsy structure of Iturbide's government fell, and Guerrero was elected a member of the provisional government. He became a liberal party leader in opposition to the conservative Nicolás Bravo, and helped to put down Bravo's revolution against President GUADALUPE VICTORIA (1828). Defeated in the election of 1828, Guerrero charged fraud and, with the help of Santa Anna, led a successful revolution and was made president (1829). In his administration the Spanish invaders of Mexico were driven back by Santa Anna. In Dec., 1829, Anastasio Bustamante, the vice president, led a revolt against Guerrero, who retired to the south, where he conducted sporadic warfare throughout 1830. He was finally captured and shot. See biography by W. F. Sprague (1939).

Guerrero, state (1970 pop. 1,573,098), 24,887 sq mi (64,457 sq km), S Mexico, on the Pacific Ocean. The capital is CHILPANCINGO. Dominated by the Sierra Madre del Sur, which reaches 12,149 ft (3,703 m) in the Pico de Teotepec, Guerrero is extremely mountainous except for a narrow coastal strip, which has a good harbor at ACAPULCO. The state's major river is the Río de las Balsas. The climate of the coast and the deep valleys is hot and rainy, but the highlands are temperate and drier. Agriculture (the growing of coffee, tobacco, cotton, cacao, and cereals) and cattle breeding are the chief economic activities. Guerrero's extensive forests yield rubber, vanilla, and woods for cabinetmaking and for dyes. Mineral resources include gold, silver, lead, mercury, iron, coal, precious stones, and sulfur. The silverwork of TAXCO is famous. Little industrialization has occurred in Guerrero, despite its abundant hydroelectric power. Historically, Guerrero was divided among the states of Michoacán, Mexico, Puebla, and Oaxaca; it did not become a state in its own right until 1849. Some of the heaviest fighting of the Mexican war (1810-21) against Spain took place in the area, which was later named for Vicente Guerrero, one of the revolutionary leaders.

Guerrière: see CONSTITUTION, ship.

guerrilla warfare (gərĭl'ə) [Span.,=little war], fighting by groups of irregular troops (guerrillas) within areas occupied by the enemy. Guerrilla groups are sometimes merely robber bands using the war as a cover for their plundering; like pirates on the high seas, such guerrillas, when captured, do not have the rights of ordinary prisoners of war and are usually executed as robbers and murderers. More often, guerrilla forces are under the command of a leader commissioned by the power for whom he is fighting. When guerrillas obey the laws of conventional warfare they are entitled, when captured, to be treated as ordinary prisoners of war; nevertheless they are often executed by their captors. Guerrilla warfare has played a significant role in modern history, expecially as waged by Communist "liberation" movements after World War II in Southeast Asia and elsewhere. In the Vietnam War the United States was involved in a major conflict in support of South Vietnam against Viet Cong guerrillas aided by North Vietnamese troops. During the same period guerrilla warfare was waged in the other countries of Indochina, Laos, and Cambodia. The tactics of guerrilla warfare stress the sneak attack, as opposed to mass confrontation, and require an irregular, preferably forested, terrain and a sympathetic population, which guerrillas often seek to win over by propaganda as well as by terrorism. Large-scale guerrilla fighting accompanied the American Revolution, and the development of guerrilla tactics under such partisan leaders as Francis MARION, Andrew PICKENS, and Thomas SUMTER has been called the great contribution of the American Revolution to the development of warfare. The term *guerrilla* itself was coined during the Peninsular War (1808-14), when the Spanish partisans, under such leaders as Francisco Mina, proved unconquerable even by the armies of Napoleon I. From Spain the use of the term spread to Latin America and then to the United States. During the U.S. Civil War, William C. QUANTRILL, who operated in Missouri and Kansas, was the most notorious of the Confederate guerrilla leaders, but John S. MOSBY, in N. Virginia, was undoubtedly the most effective. During the Franco-Prussian War (1870-71) the Germans suffered so much from French partisans, or francs-tireurs, that Field Marshall von Moltke ordered the shooting of all prisoners not fully uniformed and led by regular officers. In the Philippines after the Spanish-American War, the U.S. army conducted a long campaign against Filipino guerrillas, such as Emilio AGUINALDO, and Moro bands. There has been frequent guerrilla warfare in Latin America. Notable among early 20th-century Latin American guerrillas are Francisco (Pancho) VILLA, Emiliano ZAPATA, and Augusto C. SANDINO. In World War I the most spectacular theater of guerrilla operations was the Arabian peninsula, where, under the leadership of T. E. LAWRENCE and Faisal al-Husayn (later Faisal I), various Arab guerrilla bands were used against superior Turkish forces. In the late 1920s and 30s the Chinese Communists under the leadership of MAO TSE-TUNG, perhaps the world's leading theorist of modern guerrilla warfare, conducted a large-scale guerrilla war against both the Kuomintang and the Japanese in N China. Guerrilla tactics, aided by the development of the long-range portable radio and the use of aircraft as a means of supply, reached new heights in World War II. The Germans failed to establish a complete hold on Yugoslavia because of the guerrilla resistance, which was led by the Communist partisan leader TITO and supplied by Allied airdrops. In the Soviet Union guerrilla warfare was included in instruction at the military academy; in the field it was so brilliantly organized that it constituted a continual threat to the German rear and contributed greatly to the German disaster on the Eastern Front. In Western Europe the Allies organized guerrilla forces in France, Norway, Denmark, Holland, Belgium, Italy, and Greece. These forces (known collectively as the underground and, in France, as the maquis) were supplied by Allied airdrops and coordinated from London by radio. The resistance forces in Western Europe, led mainly by British- and American-trained officers, conducted not only guerrilla operations but also industrial sabotage, espionage, propaganda, and the organization of escape routes for Allied prisoners of war. By the end of World War II resistance forces had played a major role in the defeat of Germany. Throughout the war the United States and Britain also carried on guerrilla warfare in the Philippines and Southeast Asia, while in China large-scale guerrilla operations were conducted against the Japanese by both Communists and Nationalists. In the years after World War II guerrilla warfare was employed by various nationalist groups in the colonies of the European powers and was a major strategy used by Communist powers in their conflict with the West. Pro-Communist Chinese elements in Malaya began guerrilla operations against the British in 1945 and continued to fight for about 10 years. Soon after the Philippines gained (1946) their independence, the Hukbalahap (Huk) guerrillas began operating there and were not subdued until some years later. Just after World War II large-scale guerrilla warfare broke out in Indochina between the French and the Communist Viet Minh, led by Ho Chi Minh and Vo Nguyen Giap. After the French defeat at DIENBIENPHU (1945), France withdrew from the conflict; but the 1954 GENEVA CONFERENCE brought no permanent peace, and Communist guerrilla activity continued in Laos, Cambodia, and South Vietnam. In the early 1960s the Vietnam conflict became a major war in which regular North Vietnamese and U.S. forces participated. In Algeria guerrilla warfare against the French was begun by the nationalists in 1954 and conducted with ever-increasing violence until Algeria won its independence in 1962. Greek nationalists in Cyprus carried on guerrilla warfare against the British from 1954 until that country gained independence in 1959. Fidel CASTRO and Ernesto (Che) GUEVARA in 1956 launched a guerrilla war in Cuba against the government of Fulgencio Batista; in 1959, Batista fled the country and Castro assumed control. This success gave encouragement to rebel guerrilla bands throughout Latin America, to whom the Cuban leaders gave various kinds of aid. In 1967, Guevara himself was killed by the Bolivian army while leading such a rebel band in the jungles of Bolivia. Beginning in the late 1960s, Palestinian Arab guerrillas intensified their activities against the state of Israel. In 1971, after a full-scale war with the Jordanian army, they were ousted from their bases in Jordan. However, they continued their raids on Israel from other Arab countries and engaged increasingly in acts of outright terrorism. See C. A. Dixon and Otto Heilbrunn, *Communist Guerrilla Warfare* (1954); Mao Tse-Tung, *On Guerrilla Warfare* (tr. 1961); Otto Heilbrunn, *Partisan Warfare* (1962); George Grivas, *General Grivas on Guerrilla Warfare* (1965); Baljit Singh, *The Theory and Practice of Modern Guerrilla Warfare* (1971); L. H. Gann, *Guerrillas in History* (1971).

Guesclin, Bertrand Du: see DU GUESCLIN, BERTRAND.

Guesde, Jules (zhül gĕd), 1845–1922, French socialist, whose original name was Basile. Exiled for his support of the Paris commune, he became a confirmed Marxist after 1876 and, with Paul Lafargue, led in advocating socialism in France and a policy of noncompromise with the existing government. Guesde was largely responsible for the formation (1905) of the unified Parti socialiste, which marked the triumph of Marxism over variant forms of French organized socialism. He was a deputy (1893–1921) and served in the cabinet during World War I, when his patriotism overcame his former uncompromising stand. He wrote many socialist pamphlets and articles.

Guess, George: see SEQUOYAH.

Guest, Edwin, 1800–1880, English archaeologist and philologist. A founder of the Philological Society (1842), Guest wrote articles on English philology and on archaeology, especially on the remains of Roman Britain. His writings are still valuable for the extensive material cited. His only book was *A History of English Rhythms* (1838; ed. by W. W. Skeat, 1882); his papers were republished as *Origines Celticae* (ed. by William Stubbs and C. Deedes, 1883).

Guettard, Jean-Étienne (zhän-ātyĕn' gĕtär'), 1715–1786, French geologist, botanist, and natural historian. He was curator of the natural history collection of the French scientist René de Réaumur (1741) and a member of the Faculty of Medicine of Paris (1742). From 1747 to 1752 he was *médecin botaniste* to the French prince Louis, duc d'Orléans, and later was also supported by Louis's son Louis-Philippe. He discovered the volcanic nature of the Auvergne region in France, mapped the mineralogical distributions of much of Europe, and collaborated with the French scientist Antoine Lavoisier on the preparation of a geological survey of France.

Gueux (gö) [Fr.,=beggars], 16th-century Dutch revolutionary party. In 1566 more than 2,000 Dutch and Flemish nobles and burghers (both Protestants and Roman Catholics) signed a document—the so-called Compromise of Breda—by which they bound themselves in solemn oath to resist the curtailment of liberties imposed by the Spanish government in the NETHERLANDS. The document was drafted chiefly by Philip van MARNIX. Its radical tone displeased the great nobles; on the advice of William the Silent the original wording was considerably toned down when, in the same year, a petition on behalf of the signers of the compromise was presented to the Spanish regent, Margaret of Parma. Margaret's adviser, Barlaymont, referred to the petitioners as "these beggars," whereupon the revolutionary party adopted both the sobriquet and the insignia of beggars. The "Beggars of the Sea" (Fr. *Gueux de la mer*) were crews of patriotic privateers first chartered in 1569 by WILLIAM THE SILENT to harass Spanish shipping. Their most notable action was the raising of the siege of LEIDEN (1574). Their activity marked the beginning of Dutch sea power.

Guevara, Antonio de (antō'nyō thā gävä'rä), 1480?–1545, Spanish moralist and chronicler. Guevara was chronicler for Charles V and holder of two bishoprics. His most famous work is a didactic novel, *Libro llamado Relox de príncipes y Libro áureo del emperador Marco Aurelio* (1529). The English translation by Sir Thomas North, *The Diall of Princes* (1557), was once thought to have influenced the rise of euphuism in English literature.

Guevara, Ernesto (ārnĕs'tō gävä'rä), 1928–67, Cuban revolutionary and political leader, b. Argentina. Originally trained as a physician at the Univ. of Buenos Aires, he took part (1952) in riots against the dictator Juan Perón in Argentina, joined agitators in Bolivia, and worked in a leper colony. In 1953 he went to Guatemala, joined the pro-Communist regime of Jacobo Arbenz Guzmán, and when Arbenz was overthrown (1954) fled to Mexico, where he met Fidel CASTRO and other Cuban rebels. "Che" Guevara became Castro's chief lieutenant soon after the rebel invasion of Cuba in 1956. He proved to be a resourceful guerrilla leader and was soon one of Castro's closest and most trusted friends. As president of the national bank after the fall (Jan., 1959) of Fulgencio Batista he was instrumental in cutting Cuba's traditional economic ties with the United States and in directing the flow of trade to the Communist bloc. He served (1961–65) as minister of industry. At heart a revolutionary rather than an administrator, he left Cuba in 1965 to foster revolutionary activity in other countries. In 1967, while directing a guerrilla movement in Bolivia, he was wounded in a clash with government troops, captured, and executed. He wrote *Guerrilla Warfare* (1961), *Man and Socialism in Cuba* (1967), and *Reminiscences of the Cuban Revolutionary War* (1968). See his diaries, ed. by Robert Scheer (1968) and by Daniel James (1968); his speeches and writings, ed. by John Gerassi (1968); Daniel James, *Che Guevara* (1969); Martin Ebon, *Che: The Making of a Legend* (1969); L. J. González and G. A. Sánchez Salazar, *The Great Rebel* (tr. 1969); Richard Harris, *Death of a Revolutionary* (1970); Leo Sauvage, *Che Guevara: the Failure of a Revolutionary* (1974).

Guevara, Luis Vélez de: see VÉLEZ DE GUEVARA.

Guggenheim (go͝og'ənhīm), family of American industrialists and philanthropists. **Meyer Guggenheim,** 1828–1905, b. Aargau canton, Switzerland, emigrated (1847) to the United States, prospered as a retail merchant in Philadelphia, and in time built up a flourishing business importing Swiss embroidery. When nearly 60 he purchased from friends some Colorado mining property. Sensing that sure profits were in processing rather than in mining, he built large smelters in Colorado and Mexico and a refinery at Perth Amboy, N.J. The expansion of the Guggenheim enterprises was accelerated by seven well-trained sons—Isaac, Daniel, Murry, Solomon, Benjamin, Simon, and William—who filled strategic places in the Guggenheim organization. **Daniel Guggenheim,** 1856–1930, b. Philadelphia, was largely responsible for combining (1901) the Guggenheim interests with the American Smelting and Refining Company, of which he became president. The Daniel and Florence Guggenheim Foundation, devoted to aeronautical research and development, represents his principal philanthropy. His son, **Harry Frank Guggenheim,** 1890–1971, b. West End, N.J., fought in the two world wars, served in international conferences, was (1929–33) ambassador to Cuba, and was cofounder with his wife of the Long Island newspaper *Newsday.* Daniel's brother, **Simon Guggenheim,** 1867–1941, b. Philadelphia, served (1907–13) as U.S. Senator from Colorado. With his wife he established (1925) in memory of their son the John Simon Guggenheim Memorial Foundation, which grants fellowships to scholars, writers, and artists. Another brother of Daniel, **Solomon Robert Guggenheim,** 1861–1949, b. Philadelphia, established a foundation to increase public appreciation of modern art. The foundation created (1937) in New York City the Solomon R. Guggenheim Museum for modern art, now located in a famous building designed by Frank Lloyd Wright. See Harvey O'Conner, *The Guggenheims* (1937).

Guggenheim Museum: see SOLOMON R. GUGGENHEIM MUSEUM.

Guiana (gēăn'ə, -än'-), region, NE South America. It faces the Atlantic Ocean on the north and east and is enclosed on the west and south within a vast semicircle formed by the linked river systems of the Orinoco, the Rio Negro, and the lower Amazon. It includes SE Venezuela, part of N Brazil, FRENCH GUIANA, SURINAM (Dutch Guiana), and GUYANA (formerly British Guiana). The region consists of a cultivated coastal plain, where most of the population lives, and a forested, hilly interior, the GUIANA HIGHLANDS. Descending from plateaus as high waterfalls, such as Kaieteur Falls (Guyana) and Angel Falls (Venezuela), the rivers, notably the Caroni, Essequibo, Courantyne, Maroni, and Oiapoque, flow through low mountains, savannas, and tropical rainforests into coastal swamps and lagoons. Most of the streams are navigable only for short distances, a feature that has hindered exploitation of the region. The coastal plain contains rich alluvial deposits carried by ocean currents from the Amazon. The Dutch and subsequently the English reclaimed much of the tidal lands for planting sugarcane and rice, but the acreage is tiny in comparison to Guiana as a whole. Most of coastal Guiana suffers from a monotonously hot and humid climate. Rainfall is heavy. The interior is peopled by native Indians and Bush Negroes, descendants of freed slaves or MAROONS. The Guiana coast was discovered (1498) by Columbus, who did not, however, land there. The legend of El Dorado drew Sir Walter Raleigh to the region in 1595. The Spanish had also come in search of easy wealth, but, finding none, they left the coast open to exploitation by the Dutch, English, and French. The Dutch were the first to settle, but ownership of territory changed hands many times. After the emancipation of the slaves in the 19th cent., labor shortage proved a major problem on the European-owned plantations. It was partially offset by importing Asian Indians and Indonesians. In recent years, however, mechanization has caused chronic unemployment in some areas.

Guiana Highlands, mountainous tableland, c.1,200 mi (1,930 km) long and from 200 to 600 mi (322–966 km) wide, N South America, bounded by the Orinoco and Amazon river basins, and by the coastal lowlands of the Guianas. It is located in SE Venezuela, Guyana, Surinam, French Guiana, and N Brazil. The Pakaraima Mts., which culminate in Mt. Roraima (9,219 ft/2,810 m high) on the Venezuela-Guyana-Brazil border, form the highest section of the highlands. Geologically, the Guiana Highlands is a shield—a stable mass of Precambrian rock—and is related to the Brazilian Highlands. It consists of vast plateaus of ancient crystalline rocks overlaid by geologically recent sandstone and lava caps. The tablelands rise one after another, like gargantuan steps, in sheer escarpments hundreds to thousands of feet high. Numerous rivers, fed by heavy rainfall, rise in the highlands and pour over the edges to create deep gorges and magnificent waterfalls. Angel Fall (3,212 ft/979 m high) in Venezuela is the world's highest waterfall. The sparsely populated region, romantically depicted in W.H. Hudson's *Green Mansions,* is famous for the exuberance of its semideciduous tropical rain forests and for its rich fauna, including many varieties of brilliantly colored tropical birds. Its inaccessibility is attested by the discovery in the mid-1900s of the headwaters of the Orinoco River in the southwestern section and of a hitherto unknown tribe of tall Indians, the Panares. The crystalline rocks of the Guiana Highlands yield gold and diamonds. Large deposits of iron ore, manganese, and bauxite have been made accessible by new roads and railroads, but the enormous potential wealth of the highlands is still largely untapped because of the dense cover of vegetation. The region has great hydroelectric-power potential that could form the base for industrial development. The highlands remains one of the world's few frontiers although it is yielding to the development process that has transformed Santo Tomé de Guayana, Venezuela, into the region's chief industrial center and the gateway to the interior.

Guibert of Ravenna (gwĭb'ərt, gēbĕr'), d. 1100, Italian churchman, antipope (1080–1100) with the name Clement III; b. Parma. As imperial chancellor of Italy (1057–63), he consistently supported the Holy Roman emperor's opposition to papal reform efforts, and he led the party that repudiated Pope Alexander II. Emperor HENRY IV made him archbishop of Ravenna (1072), and Guibert continued to intrigue against GREGORY VII. In 1080, after Gregory excommunicated the emperor, Guibert summoned a council that declared the pope deposed and chose Guibert to replace him. The antipope entered Rome in 1083 in Henry's train, was enthroned in 1084, and crowned the emperor. His name is sometimes spelled Wibert.

Guicciardini, Francesco (frănchās'kō gwĕtchärdē'nē), 1483–1540, Italian historian and statesman. He represented (1512–14) his native Florence at the court of Spain, held offices in the Florentine government, and in 1516 entered the service of Pope Leo X. An able administrator, he was appointed governor of Modena (1516), commissary of the papal army (1521), and president of the Romagna (1524). After 1527, when he lost his high office as a result of the invasion of the papal states by the army of Emperor Charles V, Guicciardini devoted himself chiefly to writing. Breaking with medieval tradition, he removed history from the realm of literature and related it to the development of states. His history of Italy, written in his maturity and covering the period 1492–1534 (the period of the Italian Wars), is the masterwork of Italian historical literature of the Renaissance. It is distinguished by its clear-eyed analysis of motives, events, and persons. A follower of Machiavelli, Guicciardini has been accused of cynical realism. His history of Florence from 1378 to 1509, written in his youth, was published in 1859. It is marked by extreme simplicity and directness of style. Guicciardini also wrote a collection of maxims, translated as *Counsels and Reflections* (1890). See studies by F. Gilbert (1965) and R. Ridolfi (1968).

guidance, concept that institutions, especially schools, should promote the efficient and happy life of the individual by helping him adjust to social realities. The disruption of community and family life by industrial civilization convinced many people that experts in guidance should be trained to handle problems of individual adjustment. Though the need for attention to the whole individual had been recognized by educators since the time of Socrates, it was only during the 20th cent. that researchers actually began to study and accumulate information about guidance. This development, occurring largely in the United States, was the result of two influences: John Dewey and others insisted that the object of education should be to stimulate the fullest possible growth of the individual and that the unique qualities of personality require individual handling for adequate development; in this same period (i.e., the early 20th cent.), social and economic conditions stimulated a great increase in school enrollment. These two forces encouraged a reexamination of the curricula and methods of secondary schools with special reference to the needs of students who did not plan to enter college. The academic curriculum was revised to fit their cultural and vocational requirements (see VOCATIONAL EDUCATION). Early guidance programs dealt with the immediate problem of vocational placement. The complexities of the industrial economy and the unrealistic ambitions of many young people made it essential that machinery for bringing together jobs and workers be set up; vocational guidance became that machinery. Counseling organizations were established to help people understand their potentialities and liabilities, as well as to help them make intelligent vocational decisions. The first vocational counseling service was the Boston Vocational Bureau, established (1908) by Frank Parsons, a pioneer in the field of guidance. His model was soon copied by many schools, municipalities, states, and private organizations. With the development of aptitude and interest tests, such as the Stanford-Binet Intelligence Test and the Strong Vocational Interest Blank, commercial organizations were formed to analyze people's abilities and furnish career advice. Schools, especially those in industrial areas, organized testing and placement services, many of them in cooperation with interested Federal and state agencies. Under the provisions of the National Defense Education Act (1958), the Federal government provided assistance for guidance and counseling programs in the public secondary schools and established a testing procedure to identify students with outstanding abilities. The U.S. Dept. of Labor has been an active force in establishing standards and methods of vocational guidance. It has helped all of the states to form their own vocational guidance and counseling services. The personnel departments of many large corporations have also instituted systems of guidance to promote the better utilization of their manpower. The field of guidance includes educational counsel that goes beyond vocational considerations into questions of avocation, creative interest, financial resources, and family background. Modern high school guidance programs also include academic counseling for those students planning to attend college. Since guidance deals with the fields of personal social adjustment, counselors must be conversant with the psychology of personality. Virtually all teachers colleges offer major courses in guidance, and graduate schools of education grant advanced degrees in the field. See Arthur E. Traxler, *Techniques of Guidance* (3d ed. 1966); Percival W. Hutson, *The Guidance Function in Education* (2d ed. 1968); C. H. Miller, *Foundations of Guidance* (2d ed. 1971).

guided missile, self-propelled, unmanned space or air vehicle carrying an explosive warhead. Its path can be adjusted during flight, either by automatic self-contained controls or by distant human control. Guided missiles are powered either by ROCKET engines or by JET PROPULSION. Although an American, R. H. GODDARD, did much of the early work on missile research, guided missiles were first developed in their modern, practical form by the Germans, who in World War II employed V-1 and V-2 guided missiles against Great Britain and the Low Countries. The V-1 was an aerodynamic missile, i.e., it was controlled by aerodynamic surfaces and followed a straight-line trajectory to its target. The V-2 was the world's first operational ballistic missile, powered during flight and following a parabolic trajectory. Advances in electronics, radar, jet propulsion, and other areas of technology, together with the development of nuclear warheads, have made guided missiles the key strategic weapon of modern warfare. Guided missiles are of various types and ranges; long-range missiles generally have nuclear warheads, while short-range missiles usually have high-explosive warheads. Aerodynamic missiles are of four types. Air-to-air missiles supplement antiaircraft guns and are often guided by self-contained controls that detect and target the missile toward heat sources. Air-to-surface missiles, launched by aircraft against ground positions, are generally radio-controlled. There are also surface-to-air missiles, which operate against aircraft or other missiles, and surface-to-surface missiles, which include antitank and naval missiles. Most long-range missiles are ballistic; the intermediate-range ballistic missile (IRBM) can reach targets up to 1,500 nautical miles away, while the intercontinental ballistic missile (ICBM) has a range of many thousands of miles. Early ICBMs were set on course by radio command, but modern ICBMs are controlled by inertial guidance, which is more accurate and is immune to electronic interference. The key offensive ballistic missiles employed by the United States are the Minuteman ICBM, which is launched from silos, and the submarine-launched Polaris, a replacement of the earlier Poseidon. Both missiles can be equipped with Multiple Independent Reentry Vehicles (MIRV), which permit one booster to carry several warheads, each guided to a separate target. The Soviet Union completed the first operative ICBMs in 1958, and the United States, reacting to a supposed "missile gap," gained overwhelming missile superiority by 1962. After that time, the Soviet Union engaged in an intensive buildup and regained superiority in both the number and size of its warheads. Meanwhile, the major powers organized antiballistic missile (ABM) systems, such as the U.S. Safeguard program, for the detection and interception of enemy missiles. In 1972 an agreement was reached in the strategic arms limitation talks (SALT) between the United States and the Soviet Union. By the terms of the SALT agreement each side was restricted to 200 launchers in two ABM sites and required to limit the number of land-based and sea-based missiles to their total at that time. The agreement left the Soviet Union with an overall total of 2,358 missiles and the United States with a total of 1,710.

guide dog, a dog trained to lead a blind person. The first school for training such dogs was established by the German government after World War I for the benefit of blinded veterans. Schools now exist in several European countries and the United States, where the pioneer Seeing Eye, Inc., founded by Dorothy Harrison Eustis in 1929 and established near Morristown, N.J., in 1932, is the best known. The master spends about a month at the school training with the already trained dog and is usually charged a nominal fee. Although the German shepherd is by far the most widely used breed for guide-dog work, several other breeds, e.g., the golden retriever, the Labrador retriever, and the Doberman pinscher, have been trained successfully for this work. Approximately 10% of the blind population can use seeing-eye dogs successfully, that fraction including scores of persons who have achieved new independence through their assistance. Applicants may be rejected on the basis of sufficient useful vision, advanced age, poor health, or unsuitable temperament. See Dickson Hartwell, *Dogs against Darkness* (3d ed. 1968); V. B. Scheffer, *Seeing Eye* (1971).

Guidi, Tommaso: see MASACCIO.

Guido d'Arezzo (gwē'dō därĕt'tsō) or **Guido Aretinus** (ârətī'nəs), c.990–1050, Italian Benedictine monk, known for his contributions to musical notation and theory. His theoretical work *Micrologus* (c.1025) is one of the principal sources of our knowledge of ORGANUM, an early form of polyphony. His work in MUSICAL NOTATION included the addition of two lines (one red, one yellow) to the two already serving as a staff and the use of both the lines and the spaces. Also important was his system of SOLMIZATION (sometimes called, after him, Aretinian syllables), whereby the syllables *ut, re, mi, fa, sol, la* are used as names for the six tones, C to A, known as the hexachord. As the octave replaced the hexachord, an additional syllable, *si* or *ti*, was added, and eventually *ut* was replaced by the more singable *do.* Other revisions of Guido's system that have been suggested from time to time have not survived.

Guido of Siena (sēĕn'ə), fl. 13th cent., Italian painter. All that is known of him is an inscription on a large and almost completely repainted *Virgin and Child Enthroned,* formerly in San Domenico at Siena, now in the Palazzo Pubblico, that reads "Guido de Senis" and bears the date 1221. If this dating is accurate, then he is one of the innovators in Italian art after the dominance of the Byzantine style. However, some authorities are inclined to believe that the picture was painted as late as 1280. See study by J. H. Stubblebime (1964).

Guido Reni: see RENI, GUIDO.

Guienne, Fr. *Guyenne* (both: gēĕn', gwē–), region of SW France. The name referred to different territories at different times. Guienne as it existed from the time of Henry IV (late 16th–early 17th cent.) to the French Revolution covered the present departments of Gironde, Dordogne, Lot, Lot-et-Garonne, and Aveyron and most of Tarn-et-Garonne. It thus had no geographic unity and included part of the Aquitaine basin and part of the MASSIF CENTRAL. BORDEAUX is the historical capital, the chief port, and the center of the wine industry. Guienne was synonymous with AQUITAINE until the Hundred Years War (1337–1453). It passed to England through the marriage (1152) of Eleanor of Aquitaine to Henry II. In 1453, Guienne was reconquered by France. To its main components—Bordelais, PÉRIGORD, and Agenois (see AGEN)—two former dependencies of Toulouse were added, QUERCY and ROUERGUE. From the 17th cent. to 1792 it formed part of the vast province of Guienne and Gascony under the jurisdiction of the PARLEMENT of Bordeaux. The birth of the lyric poetry of the TROUBADOURS occurred in Guienne (11th–12th cent.).

Guildford (gĭl'fərd), municipal borough (1971 pop. 56,887), county town of Surrey, SE England, on the Wey River. It is a market town and produces knitwear, plastics, and engineered goods. Sheep and cattle fairs are held in Guildford. There are several old buildings, and the Univ. of Surrey is in Guildford. Lewis Carroll is buried in the town.

guilds or **gilds,** economic and social associations of persons engaging in the same business or craft, typical of Western Europe in the Middle Ages. Membership was by profession or craft, and the primary function was to establish local control over that profession or craft by setting standards of workmanship and price, by protecting the business from competition, and by establishing status in society for members of the guild. Similar associations of merchants and craftsmen have been known at various times in many parts of the world. Greek merchants' associations were of considerable significance in both the Hellenistic and Roman periods. Under the Roman Empire each provincial city had, as did Rome, its various *collegia* (some of which were clubs as well as economic guilds); Constantinople later had its efficiently organized *corpora.* Those guilds were continued in the East and in some of the cities of Italy, where they persisted at least until the 10th cent. Their effect on the creation of medieval guilds is, however, debatable.

Medieval Europe. Some scholars have found the origin of guilds in the old tribal or religious guilds of the Germans. At any rate, by the 11th cent. associations of merchants had begun to form for the protection of commerce against the feudal governments. Those merchant guilds became extremely powerful as trade in the Mediterranean and across Europe increased. Some of the Italian merchant guilds, such as those in Genoa and Florence, became dominant in local government. In England and in Germany the merchant guilds also exercised enormous power in the growing towns. Commerce was becoming less and less a local affair, and the guilds in some cases developed into intercity leagues for the promotion and protection of trade. The most striking example was the HANSEATIC LEAGUE of N Europe, which established and controlled some of its own trading cities. The merchant guilds had vast influence in the development of commerce during that period. No less important were the craft guilds, the associations of artisans of a particular industry, e.g., the weavers guild. These grew with great rapidity as towns developed in the 12th cent. and tended to share power with the merchants or even, in some cases, to supplant them in power. Generally the members were divided into masters, apprentices, and journeymen. The masters were the owners of the shops and instructors of the apprentices. The apprentices were bound to the masters; they were accepted for a stipulated sum paid to the masters for training and were given a subsistence wage for a number of years; the amount paid and the length of time varied from one craft to another and one place to another. The apprentices were strictly under the control of the masters, but the conditions of control were set by guild regulation. The journeymen were men who had finished their training as apprentices but could not attain the status of masters, the number of masters being limited. The guild reflected a predilection for ordering society. Each guild set the terms of its craft: the forms of labor, standard of product, and methods of sale. With the rise of nationalism in the West, those things were increasingly subject to royal and national law. The relationship of the feudal ruler to the guilds was ideally one of cooperation. Actually the wealthy guilds were able to gain some immunity from interference by noble or king either by paying them large sums of money or by intimidating them. Sometimes, as in the weaving towns of Flanders, the guilds led revolts against feudal authority (e.g., in BRUGES and GHENT). The tendency in the industrial towns was for the guilds to assume dominance in municipal government, and traces of that control have persisted in the local governments of Western Europe. The guilds of London (see LIVERY COMPANIES) had wide social obligations and prominence in the city government. The strengthening of the power of nations in the 15th and 16th cent. tended to increase royal power, and the king in some instances was able to reduce the guilds to subservience. The improvement of communications, the expansion of trade, with the introduction of foreign-made goods, and finally the appearance of the capitalist and the entrepreneur hastened the end of the guild system. The guilds, with their rigorous controls and emphasis on stability and quality, were not equipped to cope with the expanding production of a more capitalistic age. They tended to guard their monopolies jealously and to oppose change. As time went on, the guild system became increasingly rigid, and the trend toward hereditary membership grew very marked. Thus the development of new trade and industry fell to the capitalists, who adapted themselves to new demands in an age of exploration and expansion. By the 17th cent. the power of the guilds had withered in England, and they were officially abolished in 1835. In France the guilds were abolished (1791) in the French Revolution. The German and Austrian guilds were abolished in the 19th cent. as were those in the Italian cities. In Eastern Europe guilds grew numerous in the great market cities, and the power of some long persisted, notably in Novgorod and Kraków. In the Western world today the term *guild* is used for certain associations that appear to have little connection with the medieval institution. Some of the great professional associations (e.g., in medicine and law) fulfill some of the functions of the old guilds but are rarely given that name.

Asia. Elsewhere in the world associations of merchants and of artisans developed and followed a similar pattern, flourishing as protective devices or as regulatory instruments of the state. The guilds of the Muslim Middle East developed in the 9th cent. and persisted into the 20th cent., although they never attained political influence equivalent to that of the guilds of medieval Europe. In India, guilds were highly developed before the time of the Maurya empire, and they continued in existence long after British control was established. The history of the Indian guilds was closely tied in with the caste system. The guilds in Japan were opposed and weakened by the stronger medieval rulers, but they were later used as powerful regulatory devices; they were swept away in the Meiji restoration in 1868. In China, guilds of unknown antiquity persisted as powerful bodies into the 20th cent. See Charles Gross, *The Gild Merchant* (1890, repr. 1964); L. F. Salzman, *English Industries of the Middle Ages* (new ed. 1964); Henri Sée, *Economic and Social Conditions in France during the Eighteenth Century* (tr. 1927, repr. 1968); Stella Kramer, *The English Craft Gilds* (1927); H. B. Morse, *The Gilds of China* (2d ed. 1932, repr. 1967); George Unwin, *Gilds and Companies of London* (4th ed. 1963); R. S. Smith, *The Spanish Guild Merchant* (1940); George Clune, *The Medieval Gild System* (1943); G. A. Williams, *Medieval London* (1963).

guild socialism, form of socialism developed in Great Britain that advocated a system of industrial self-government through national worker-controlled guilds. The theory, as originated by Arthur J. Penty in his *Restoration of the Gild System* (1906), stressed the spirit of the medieval craft guilds. In later elaborations by A. R. Orage, S. G. Hobson, and G. D. H. Cole, aspects of Marxism and SYNDICALISM were adopted. Guild socialists held that workers should work for control of industry rather than for political reform. The function of the state in a guild-organized society was to be that of an administrative unit and owner of the means of production; to it the guilds would pay rent, while remaining independent. In 1915 the National Guilds League was created; it had a number of notable writers and speakers, including Bertrand Russell. After World War I several working guilds were formed. However, the most powerful of these, the National Building Guild, collapsed in 1922, and thereafter the movement waned. The National Guilds League was dissolved in 1925. During its existence it had considerable influence on British trade unions. See G. D. H. Cole, *Guild Socialism Restated* (1920); Niles Carpenter, *Guild Socialism* (1922); S. T. Glass, *The Responsible Society* (1966).

Guilford (gĭl'fərd), town (1970 pop. 12,033), New Haven co., S Conn., on Long Island Sound; founded 1639. It has fishing and poultry-raising industries. Metal castings and boats are made. The town includes several summer shore communities. Some of the oldest houses in the state are there; the stone Whitfield House (1639–40) was restored in 1936 and is now a state historical museum. Also of interest are the Hyland House (1660) and the Thomas Griswold House Museum (1735).

Guilford Courthouse, battle of, in the CAROLINA CAMPAIGN of the American Revolution, fought March 15, 1781. The site is included in a national military park near Greensboro, N.C. (see NATIONAL PARKS AND MONUMENTS, table).

Guillaume de Lorris (də lôrēs'), c.1215–c.1278, French poet, author of the first part of the ROMAN DE LA ROSE. He handled the chivalric conventions with subtlety and charm, and his work shows taste, psychological perception, and wide familiarity with French letters.

Guillaume de Machaut: see MACHAUT, GUILLAUME DE.

guillemot (gĭl'əmŏt"), northern sea bird, genus *Cephas,* of the AUK family. The black guillemot, or tystie, *Cephus grylle,* is about 13 in. (33 cm) long and is very striking in its breeding plumage, being entirely black from bill to tail except for large white wing patches and bright red legs. In winter its plumage is a mixture of black, white, and gray. It inhabits coasts all around the North Atlantic Ocean, but is more abundant on the American side, where it is found as far south as Cape Cod. The pigeon guillemot, *C. columba,* is very similar to the black guillemot, and may be a geographic variety rather than a distinct species. It is found on Pacific coasts from the Bering Sea to S California and N Japan. Guillemots are distinctive among auks in a number of ways: they are better fliers than most, they are not very gregarious, and the female lays two or three eggs at a time instead of the usual one. Pairs of guillemots tend to occupy particular territories in the water, where they swim and dive for food. Like other auks, they build no nest, but lay their eggs on the rocks. In Great Britain a related bird, called MURRE in North America, is also called guillemot. Guillemots are classified in the phylum CHORDATA, subphylum Vertebrata, class Aves, order Charadriiformes, family Alcidae.

Guillén, Jorge (hôr'hā gĕlyān'), 1893–, Spanish poet. Guillén left Spain after the civil war (1939) and taught Spanish in the United States. His verse is difficult, terse, and lyrical. *Cántico,* his volume of poems, has appeared in four successively augmented editions (1928, 1936, 1945, 1950; tr. 1965). Among the most intellectual of modern Spanish poets, he has been compared to Paul Valéry, whose work he translated. *Affirmation: 1919–1966* (1968) is a bilingual anthology of Guillén's work. See study by Ivar Ivask (1969).

Guillén, Nicolás (nēkōläs' gēyān'), 1904–, Cuban poet. A leading exponent of *poesia negra*—an Afro-Antillean genre developed in the Caribbean—Guillén writes poetry charged with intense racial and political feelings. In *Motivos de son* (1930) and *Sóngoro cosongo* (1931) he employed native incantations, dances, and street cries. Guillén's later poetry, more traditional in form, is devoted to social and economic problems. It includes *Balada* (1962), *Antología mayor* (1964), and *El gran zoo* (1967, tr. 1972). See his *Man-Making Words* (tr. 1972); Wilfred Cartey *Three Antillian Poets* (1965).

Guilmant, Félix Alexandre (fālĕks' älĕksäN'drə gēlmäN'), 1837–1911, French organist, one of the foremost performers of his day. He taught at the Schola Cantorum, of which he was a founder, and at the Paris Conservatory, where Marcel Dupré, Joseph Bonnet, René Vierné, and Nadia Boulanger were among his pupils. He composed much organ music.

Guimarãis (gēmərīNsh') or **Guimarães** (-räNsh'), city (1960 pop. 23,598), Braga dist., NW Portugal, in Minho. It has textile and cutlery manufactures, but its main importance is historical. The town was the seat of Duke Henry of Burgundy and of his son, Alfonso I, first king of Portugal. Alfonso VII of León besieged (1127) Guimarãis and forced Alfonso of Portugal to swear fealty, but the Portuguese later established his independence. Guimarãis was a favorite royal residence. It has several splendid churches, particularly the Nossa Senhora da Oliveira, and a notable old castle.

Guimard, Hector (ĕktôr' gēmär'), 1867–1942, French architect and furniture designer. Influenced by Victor Horta, he became the first and foremost French architect of art nouveau. The most familiar landmarks created by Guimard (c.1900) are the entrance gates to the *métro* (subway) stations in Paris, of metal cast into elegant, flowerlike forms. However, nearly all of them have been destroyed. On the Rue La Fontaine, Paris, he built the Castel Béranger (1894–98) and an apartment house (1911). He went to New York City in 1938, where he remained until his death. Several examples of his decorative work can be found at the Museum of Modern Art, New York.

Guimerà, Ángel (än'zhĕl gēmärä'), 1845?–1924, Catalan poet and dramatist. His first successful play, *Mar y cel* [sea and sky] (1888), was followed by many others, among them *Maria Rosa* (1894) and his masterpiece, *Terra baixa* (1896; tr. *Marta of the Lowlands*, 1914). These were translated into Spanish by Echegaray. Guimerà's work is characterized by vigor and imagination and tends toward the sensual and macabre.

Guinea (gĭn'ē), an archaic term for the west coast of Africa. In its widest sense it has been applied to the region from Angola to Senegal. Parts of the region bore names originating in early colonial trade, notably Grain Coast, Ivory Coast, Gold Coast, and Slave Coast. Characteristic of the coast are dense tropical forests, heavy rainfall, and a hot, humid climate. Today the term refers to the Republic of Guinea, Guinea-Bissau, and Equatorial Guinea.

Guinea, Fr. *Guinée*, republic (1973 est. pop. 4,150,000), 94,925 sq mi (245,856 sq km), W Africa. CONAKRY is the capital and chief city. The country is bounded on the north by Guinea-Bissau, Senegal, and Mali; on the east by the Ivory Coast; on the south by Sierra Leone and Liberia; and on the west by the Atlantic Ocean. A humid and tropical country, Guinea comprises an alluvial coastal plain, the mountainous Fouta Jallon region, a savanna interior, and the forested Guinea Highlands, which rise to c.5,800 ft (1,770 m) in the Nimba Mts. The main ethnic groups are the pastoral Fulani and the agrarian Malinké, Susu, and other tribes. French is the country's principal language and Islam the chief religion. Predominantly agricultural, Guinea produces rice, millet, manioc, cassava, coffee, bananas, palm kernels, and citrus fruits. Stock raising is important in the highlands. Some of the world's largest bauxite

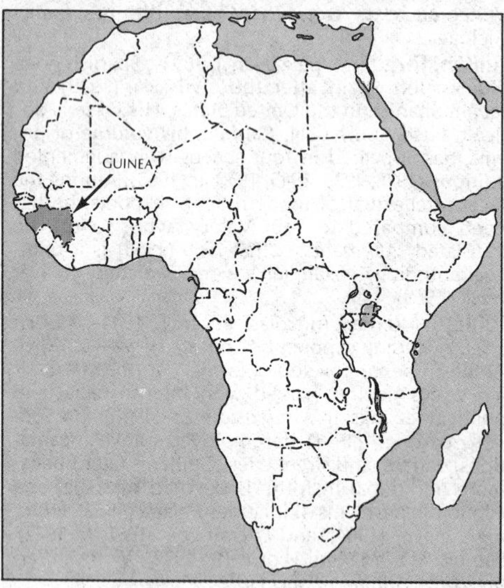

deposits lie in Guinea, and iron ore, gold, and diamonds are also mined. Alumina, made from bauxite, is a leading export; other exports include iron ore and a variety of agricultural products. Mineral exports go mostly to the United States and Western Europe, while the Soviet Union and Eastern Europe take much of Guinea's farm products. Guinea has some light industry, but inadequate transportation facilities have hampered industrialization. Rail lines connect some large cities, and there are airports at Conakry and KANKAN; the road network is underdeveloped. The northeastern plains of present-day Guinea belonged to medieval Ghana and later to the Mali empire. In the early 18th cent., a Fulani feudal state was established in the Fouta Jallon region. European exploration of the Guinean coast began with the Portuguese in the mid-15th cent.; by the 17th cent. French, British, and Portuguese traders were competing for slaves and by the 19th cent. for palm oil, peanuts, and other products. Anger over excessive levies exacted from French traders by local chieftains led France to proclaim a protectorate over the Boké area of Guinea in 1849. After a series of wars and agreements with other tribal chiefs, France took control of much of the rest of Guinea and annexed it under the name Rivières du Sud [rivers of the south]. In 1891 it was constituted as a French colony separate from Senegal, of which it had hitherto been a part. Its name was changed to French Guinea in 1893, and two years later it became part of French West Africa. Guinean resistance to French rule was not quelled until 1898, however, and sporadic revolts continued into the 20th cent. Little economic development occurred under the colonial regime until just before World War II, when exploitation of Guinea's rich bauxite deposits began. The parallel growth of a radical labor movement led to the rise of Sékou TOURÉ, a union leader who also headed the Parti Démocratique de Guinée (PDG), a branch of the intercolonial Rassemblement Démocratique Africain. Under his leadership, Guinea became the only colony to vote against the constitution of the French Community in 1958 and to opt for complete independence. France retaliated by severing relations and withdrawing all financial and technical aid and personnel; ties were reestablished in 1963. Guinea cultivated close relations with the Soviet Union but expelled the Soviet ambassador in 1961 for alleged interference in the country's internal affairs. Touré also advocated African unity and steered the country into a union (largely symbolic) with Ghana in 1958; Mali joined in 1961. In the late 1960s, Guinea sought improved relations with the West, although its basic international posture has remained one of nonalignment. Touré has continued to foster Pan-Africanism; the limitation or renunciation of sovereignty in favor of African unity is written into Guinea's constitution. In 1966, when Ghana's President Kwame Nkrumah was deposed, Touré welcomed him to Guinea as joint president. Guinea is a one-party socialist republic; Touré, who has held the presidency since independence, heads both the government and the PDG, which exercises ultimate authority. In 1972 he relinguished the post of premier to Louis Lansana Beavogui. The national assembly is elected every five years on a single slate by universal adult suffrage. In 1970 the country was invaded from Guinea-Bissau (then Portuguese Guinea) by a small force that included Guinean exiles opposed to Touré. The invasion was unsuccessful, and several political trials and executions followed. Guinea actively supported the independence movement in Guinea-Bissau, and Conakry was the movement's headquarters. In 1973, Guinea took greater control of the foreign-owned bauxite industry and in 1974 became one of the seven charter members of the International Association of Producers of Bauxite. See Ruth Schachter Morgenthau, *Political Parties in French-speaking West Africa* (1964); Samir Amin, *Trois expériences africaines de développement: Le Mali, la Guinée et le Ghana* (1965); A. Mabileau, and I. Meyriat, ed., *Décolonisation et régimes politiques en Afrique noire* (1967).

Guinea, Gulf of, large open arm of the Atlantic Ocean formed by the great bend of the coast of W Africa. It extends from the western coast of the Ivory Coast to the Gabon estuary and is bounded on the south by the equator. The bights of Benin and Biafra belong to the gulf. Islands in the gulf include Fernando Po, São Tomé, and Principe.

Guinea-Bissau (bĭs''sou'), formerly **Portuguese Guinea,** independent country (1970 pop. 487,448), 13,948 sq mi (36,125 sq km), W Africa, bordering on the Atlantic Ocean in the west, on Senegal in the north, and on the Republic of Guinea in the east

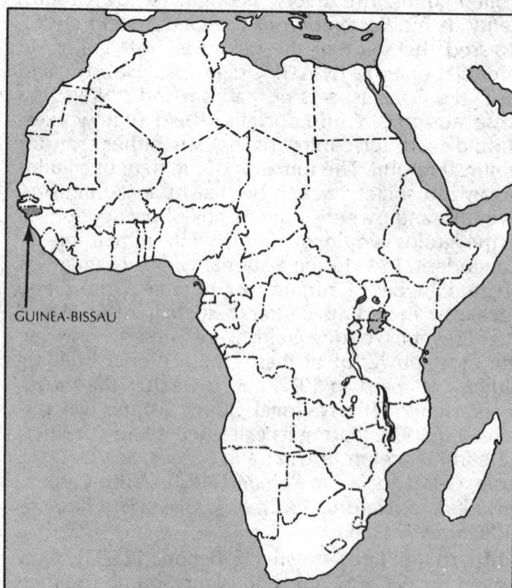

and south. The country includes the nearby Bijagós (Bissagos) Archipelago and other islands in the Atlantic. The capital and chief city is Bissau; other important towns are Cacheu and Bolama. The country is largely a low-lying coastal plain and has many rivers, some with wide swampy estuaries. Farming is by far the leading occupation; rice, palm oil, groundnuts, and coconuts are the main products. Bauxite is mined. Most of the inhabitants adhere to traditional animist beliefs; about one third are Muslim. There are virtually no European settlers. The area that became Portuguese Guinea was first visited by the Portuguese in 1446–47, and in the 16th cent. it was an important source of slaves sent to South America. The territory was administered as part of the Portuguese Cape Verde Islands possession until 1879, when it became a separate colony. In 1951 it was constituted an overseas province. In 1956 the African Party for the Independence of Guinea and Cape Verde (PAIGC) was founded; it was led by Amilcar Cabral until his assassination in 1973. After some years of sporadic violence, the PAIGC launched a war of independence in Portuguese Guinea in the early 1960s. By 1972, Portugal had about 35,000 troops in the province; the rebels held S and SE Portuguese Guinea, while the Portuguese retained control of the major towns. In Sept., 1973, the PAIGC declared the province, renamed Guinea-Bissau, independent of Portugal. A government was established and elections for a national assembly were held in PAIGC-controlled areas. Following the coup in Portugal (April, 1974), the new Portuguese government initiated (May) negotiations with the PAIGC. Although the PAIGC wanted to include the Cape Verde Islands (which they contended were part of Guinea-Bissau) in the discussions, Portugal refused but agreed to hold a referendum to decide the future status of the islands. In August an agreement was reached under which Portugal granted (Sept. 10) independence to Guinea-Bissau. Luis de Almeida Cabral, the leader of the PAIGC, became the first president. Guinea-Bissau was admitted to the United Nations in 1974.

guinea fowl, common name for any of the seven species of gallinaceous birds of the family Numididae, native to Africa and Madagascar. The helmeted guinea fowl, *Numida meleagris,* from which the domesticated strains are descended, is typical of the family, with its bare head and neck, sleek body, smooth dark feathers dotted with white, and short tail. It is named for its bony casque. Guinea fowls are raised, mainly for their gamey flesh, in many parts of the world. Of the three domestic varieties (the pearl, the white, and the lavender), the purplish-gray colored pearl is the most common. The largest member of the family is the 24-in. (60-cm) vulturine guinea fowl, *Acryllium vulturinum,* found in tropical E Africa. Guinea fowls are extremely good runners and use this method, rather than flying, to escape predators. Guinea fowls are known to have been domesticated by the ancient Greeks and Romans. They are classified in the phylum CHORDATA, subphylum Vertebrata, class Aves, order Galliformes, family Numididae.

guinea pig, domesticated form of the CAVY, *Cavia porcellus,* a South American RODENT. It is unrelated to the pig; the name may refer to its shrill squeal. Guinea pigs were raised by the Incas and have long been used as food in South America. They were first imported into Europe from Guiana in the 16th cent. There are a number of varieties, some with short, smooth hair and others with longer hair, and a great range of color combinations, including mixtures of black and white and many shades of brown. They have rounded bodies, large heads, and blunt noses and reach a length of 6 to 10 in. (15–25 cm) and a weight of 1 to 2 lb (450–900 grams). Females produce three to five litters, usually of three or four young, per year. The guinea pig's rapid reproductive rate and high resistance to disease make it a valuable laboratory animal; it is used for testing serums and antitoxins and for experiments in genetics and nutrition. It is also sometimes kept as a pet. It is classified in the phylum CHORDATA, subphylum Vertebrata, class Mammalia, order Rodentia, family Caviidae.

Güines (gwē'nās), city (1970 pop. 41,407), La Habana prov., W Cuba. It is located in one of the island's most heavily farmed areas. Güines was founded in 1737 as the commercial and financial center of the rich surrounding farm region.

Guinevere, in ARTHURIAN LEGEND, wife of King Arthur. Her illicit and tragic love for Sir LAUNCELOT, which foreshadowed the downfall of Arthur's kingdom, ends with her retirement to a convent. She also figures in several early romances and Celtic legends, her name appearing in various forms (e.g., Guanhamara, Gvenour, and Gwenhwyfars). In different versions of the Arthurian story her name appears as Guenevere and Guinever.

Guinicelli or **Guinizelli, Guido** (gwē'dō gwēnēchĕl'lē; gwēnētsĕl'lē), c.1230–1276?, Italian poet. In his best verse he wrote of love as an inner spirituality or nobility, disassociated from courtly connotations. For this, and for his style—delicate, intelligent, and brilliant in imagery—he is often seen as precursor and even as formulator of the style of poetry adopted by Cavalcanti, Dante, and others. His influence was marked; Dante called him his literary father. Little of Guinicelli's verse remains.

Guinness, Sir Alec, 1914-, English actor. After his stage debut in 1934, Guinness performed with John Gielgud's company and the Old Vic. He is known especially for his enormous versatility in numerous films, including *Oliver Twist* (1948), *Kind Hearts and Coronets* (1949, performing eight roles), The *Lavender Hill Mob* (1951), *The Prisoner* (1955), *The Horse's Mouth* (1959), *Tunes of Glory* (1960), and *Cromwell* (1969). Guinness won an Academy Award for his performance in *The Bridge on the River Kwai* (1957). He was knighted in 1959. See study by Kenneth Tynan (3d ed. 1961).

Guipúzcoa: see BASQUE PROVINCES.

Güiraldes, Ricardo (rēkär'dō gwĕräl'dās), 1886-1927, Argentine writer. He spent his boyhood on a ranch where he learned the ways of the gauchos, later traveling to Europe. In his novels and short stories he applied postmodernist techniques to Argentine regional themes. His masterpiece, *Don Segundo Sombra* (1926, tr. *Shadows in the Pampas,* 1935), in part autobiographical, captured the heroic spirit of the gaucho amid exquisite descriptions of the pampas.

Guiscard, Norman rulers in Sicily: see ROBERT GUISCARD; ROGER I.

Guise (gēz, gwēz), influential ducal family of France. It was founded as a cadet branch of the ruling house of LORRAINE by **Claude de Lorraine**, 1st **duc de Guise**, 1496-1550, who received the French fiefs of his father, René II, duke of Lorraine and Bar. In 1513, Claude connected himself by marriage with the French royal family. He fought in the ITALIAN WARS under King Francis I and was wounded (1515) at Marignano; as governor of Champagne he fought successfully against the English and the imperial troops. He was created a duke and peer by Francis I, who, however, ultimately came to regard him with distrust. Claude's daughter, MARY OF GUISE, married King James V of Scotland and was the mother of Mary Queen of Scots (Mary Stuart). His son **François de Lorraine**, 2d **duc de Guise,** 1519-63, became conspicuous, at the accession (1547) of Henry II, as the rival for power of Anne, duc de MONTMORENCY. In the final stages of the Italian Wars, François distinguished himself in the defense of Metz (1552), led the expedition to Italy against King Philip II of Spain, and after the failure of the expedition returned to defend France from English and Spanish attacks; in 1558 he took Calais from the English. With the accession (1559) of the youthful Francis II, who was married to the duke's niece, Mary Stuart, François de Guise and his brother the Cardinal de Lorraine were given control of the government. Their arrogance, their persecution of the Protestants, and their enmity toward the princes of Bourbon and Condé led to the conspiracy of Amboise (see AMBOISE, CONSPIRACY OF), which they suppressed (1560). Shortly afterward, however, the death of Francis II deprived the Guises of power; CATHERINE DE' MEDICI, as regent, dominated the government. As a result, in 1561, the duke joined with Montmorency and Marshal Saint-André in the so-called triumvirate, which, at the head of the Catholic party, opposed both the HUGUENOTS and the tolerant policy of the regent. The murder of Protestants at Vassy by Guise's troops brought about the outbreak of the WARS OF RELIGION (1562-98), and Guise took the field against the Huguenots. Victorious at Dreux (1562), he was assassinated while preparing to attack Orléans. His brother **Charles de Guise, Cardinal de Lorraine,** c.1525-1574, was largely responsible for the persecution of the Protestants during the reign of Francis II. At the Colloquy of POISSY (1561) he defended Catholicism against Theodore BEZA; at the Council of Trent (1562-63) he at first upheld the independence of the Gallican church but later reversed his position and attempted to have the decrees of the council proclaimed in France. He subsequently negotiated with Philip II of Spain for Spanish support of the Catholic cause in France. After the downfall of Michel de L'HÔPITAL, Charles temporarily returned to power until 1570. He was the most consummate politician in his family and a master of intrigue. His nephew **Henri de Lorraine**, 3d **duc de Guise**, 1550-88, son of François, fought in the Wars of Religion and cooperated with Catherine de' Medici in planning the massacre of the Huguenots on Aug. 24, 1572 (see SAINT BARTHOLOMEW'S DAY, MASSACRE OF). After the peace of 1576 he formed the Catholic League (see LEAGUE), and King Henry III, although secretly afraid of the League, became its nominal head. After the death of FRANCIS, duke of Alençon and Anjou (1584), Henri de Lorraine revived (1585) the League in opposition to the Protestant Henry of Navarre (later King HENRY IV), who had become heir presumptive to the throne. War broke out between the League and Henry of Navarre. Although the king was the nominal head of the League, he was overshadowed by the immensely popular Guise, who had designs on the throne. In May, 1588, when Guise returned to Paris, the Parisians revolted against the king on the Day of the Barricades (May 12). Instead of taking the throne Guise helped Henry III to escape, and the king named him lieutenant general of France. Later in the same year, however, the king brought about his assassination. Henri's brother **Louis de Lorraine, Cardinal de Guise**, 1555-88, was killed at the same time. After their deaths the leadership of the League devolved upon their brother, Charles, duc de MAYENNE. Henri was succeeded by his son **Charles de Lorraine,** 4th **duc de Guise**, 1571-1640. **Henri de Lorraine,** 5th **duc de Guise**, 1614-64, son of the 4th duke, was archbishop of Rheims but became duke after the death of his older brother (1639) and of his father. He conspired (1641) against Cardinal Richelieu and was forced to live in exile for a time in Flanders. In 1647 he took part, as representative of the house of Anjou, in the insurrection at Naples against Spanish rule. Captured by the Spanish (1648), he was a prisoner until 1652. He made a new attack on Naples in 1654, then returned to Paris, where, as grand chamberlain, he played a prominent role in the social life of the court. He was succeeded by his nephew, **Louis Joseph de Lorraine,** 6th **duc de Guise,** 1650-71. With **François Joseph de Lorraine**, 7th **duc de Guise,** 1670-75, son of the 6th duke, the line came to an end. See H. N. Williams, *The Brood of False Lorraine* (1918); H. D. Sedgwick, *The House of Guise* (1938).

Guise, Jean d'Orléans, duc de: see ORLÉANS, family.

guitar, musical instrument related to the lute, modern guitars normally having six strings that are plucked with the fingers. Earlier versions had pairs of strings like the lute. The guitar has a flat back, sides that curve inward to form a waist, and a fretted neck (see FRETTED INSTRUMENT). It appeared as early

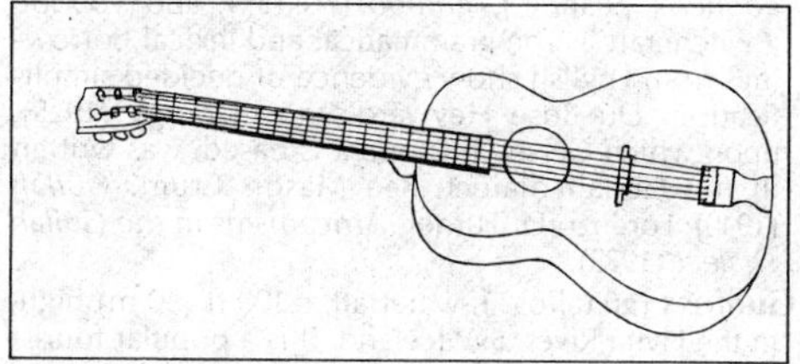

Guitar

as the 12th cent. in Spain, the country with which it is particularly associated. It was very popular there in the 16th cent., when much music was written for it. The composer Fernando Sor (1778-1839) was a brilliant guitarist who wrote many important works for that instrument. In the late 19th cent. there was revived interest in the guitar, aroused largely by the playing of Francisco Tárrega (1852-1909), one of the greatest guitar players of all time. Andrés SEGOVIA is one of the foremost contemporary guitarists; he has done much to stimulate interest in the instrument and its repertory, especially in 16th-century music. See Alexander Bellow, *The Illustrated History of the Guitar* (1970).

guitarfish: see RAY.

Guitry, Lucien Germain (lüsyăN' zhĕrmăN' gētrē'), 1860-1925, French actor and producer. Guitry succeeded Coquelin as France's most versatile actor. He made his debut in 1878 in *La Dame aux camélias* and then played nine years at the Michel Theater, St. Petersburg, before returning to Paris. There Guitry worked in the Théâtre de la Renaissance (1902-9). He created 73 of his 144 roles. After 1919 these included several roles in the plays of his son, **Sacha Guitry** (sâshä'), 1885-1957, actor and dramatist. Guitry was a prolific and enormously popular playwright from the age of 21. His skillful and witty dramas include *Nono* (1905), *Deburau* (1918), *Jean de la Fontaine* (1922), and *Mozart* (1925). He also acted in and directed motion pictures, of which two of the best were *The Story of a Cheat* (1937) and *Pearls of the Crown* (1938). See his memoirs (tr. 1935); biography by James Harding (1968). His second wife, **Yvonne Printemps** (1895-), French actress and singer, won great success in Guitry's *Nono* and had an outstanding career, directing and performing at her own Paris theater (1937-58).

Guizot, François (fräNswä' gēzō'), 1787-1874, French statesman and historian. The son of a Protestant family of Nîmes, he was educated at Geneva. He began a legal career in Paris in 1805, but soon took up literary work and later became a professor of modern history at the Univ. of Paris. His lectures there formed a center of political opposition to the Restoration. His friendship with ROYER-COLLARD and his sympathy with the moderate royalists soon drew him into minor political office. As an opposition deputy he was involved in the JULY REVOLUTION of 1830 and became one of the leading intellectual exponents of the bourgeois July Monarchy of LOUIS PHILIPPE. As minister of public instruction (1832-37), Guizot introduced (1833) a new system of primary education. Turning more and more to conservatism, he became (1840) the chief power in the ministry nominally headed by Soult, who had displaced the more liberal THIERS as premier. In 1847, Guizot became premier. His leadership provided a stable government, but his complacent acceptance of the established order led to his overthrow in the FEBRUARY REVOLUTION of 1848, which forced the abdication of Louis Philippe. Guizot devoted the rest of his life to writing. The best known of his many works, *Histoire de la révolution d'Angleterre* [history of the revolution in England] (6 vol., 1826-56), illustrates his critical approach and his devotion to original sources as well as his admiration for middle-of-the-road British revolutionism. He also wrote *Mémoires pour servir à l'histoire de mon temps* [memoirs to serve as a history of my time] (8 vol., 1858-67) and the brilliant *General History of Civilization in Modern Europe* (6 vol., 1829-32; tr. by William Hazlitt, 3 vol., 1846). The last work, never completed, covers principally the civilization of France up to the 14th cent. See study by D. W. Johnson (1963). See his memoirs (8 vol., tr. 1974).

Gujarat (gōōjərät'), state (1971 pop. 26,687,186), c.72,000 sq mi (186,480 sq km), W India, on the Arabian Sea and almost all of the Kathiawar peninsula. Gujarat was constituted in 1960 from the Gujarati-speaking areas in the northern and western portions of the former state of Bombay. The population is concentrated in the cities of AHMEDABAD (the capital), SURAT, BARODA, BHAVNAGAR, RAJKOT, and JAMNAGAR. The state is the center of the Indian cotton-textile industry. It is a fertile, well-watered region, except for the arid Kutch area in the north; rice, wheat, and cotton are grown. Salt, limestone, manganese, calcite, and bauxite are mined. Hydroelectric power is utilized. Archaeological discoveries have linked Gujarat with the Indus valley civilization (c.3,000-1,500 B.C.) and have suggested that it was a part of the Mauryan empire (c.320-185 B.C.). The Gujarat region was the center of Jainism under the Hindu Anhilvada kingdom (founded c.755), which fell (1233) to the DELHI SULTANATE. In 1401, Gujarat became an independent sultanate. Its immense wealth invited attack, and in 1509 the Portuguese wrested from it the colony of Diu (see GOA, DAMAN, AND DIU). In 1572 the sultanate was annexed to the Mogul empire. The MAHRATTAS were powerful in the area in the first half of the 18th cent. Under the British the region retained its local princely rulers. In 1947 the region was organized into the state of Bombay. Gujarat is governed by a chief minister and cabinet responsible to a unicameral elected legislature and by a governor appointed by the president of India.

Gujarati (gōō"jərä'tē), language belonging to the Indic group of the Indo-Iranian subfamily of the Indo-European family of languages. See INDO-IRANIAN LANGUAGES.

Gujranwalla (gōōj"rän'välə), city (1972 metropolitan area est. pop. 335,000), NE Pakistan. It is a commercial center trading in wheat, rice, sugar, oilseed, and oranges. There are varied manufactures. Gujranwalla rose to prominence under Ranjit Singh, the great Sikh ruler, who was born in the city. A mausoleum houses the ashes of Ranjit Singh and his father, Mahan Singh.

Gujrat (gōōjərät'), town (1969 est. pop. 73,000), E Pakistan. It is noted for its furniture, brassware, pottery, and cotton goods. Boots, shawls, and electric fans are also produced. Standing on the site of a fort built by the Mogul emperor Akbar in 1580, Gujrat was the location of the final battle between the British and the Sikhs in 1849. The town has two colleges affiliated with Punjab Univ.

Gulbarga (gŭl'bərgä), town (1971 pop. 145,630), Karnataka state, S central India. Peanuts and locally spun cotton and silk fabrics are marketed. Gulbarga, a district administrative center, was the capital (1347–1432) of the Muslim Bahmani kingdom and is the site of the tomb of Firuz Shah Bahmani. The large 13th-century mosque is modeled after that in Córdoba, Spain.

Gülek Boğazı: see CILICIAN GATES.

Gulf. For names beginning thus, see second part; e.g., for Gulf of Mexico, see MEXICO, GULF OF.

Gulf Islands National Seashore: see NATIONAL PARKS AND MONUMENTS (table).

Gulfport, city (1970 pop. 40,791), seat of Harrison co., SE Miss., on Mississippi Sound, in a farm and resort area; inc. 1898. It is a port of entry, receiving large shipments of bananas. The city's industries include seafood packaging and the manufacture of chemicals, pharmaceuticals, metal products, and clothing. Gulfport was settled (1891) as the site for a railroad terminus. In 1902 its harbor was opened, and the city developed as an important lumber-shipping center. With the depletion of timber resources, Gulfport extended its shipping facilities and turned to manufacturing and to a growing tourist trade. There are several military installations in Gulfport. A number of antebellum houses remain. De Soto National Forest is to the north, and historic Ship Island, with its Civil War Fort Massachusetts, is 12 mi (19 km) out in the sound.

Gulf Stream, warm ocean current of the N Atlantic Ocean, off E North America. It was first described (1513) by Ponce de León, the Spanish explorer. The Gulf Stream originates in the Gulf of Mexico and, as the Florida Current, passes through the Straits of Florida and along the coast of SE United States with a breadth of c.50 mi (80 km). Off Cape Hatteras it is separated from the coast by a narrow southern extension of the cold Labrador Current and flows NE into the Atlantic Ocean, where it spreads out and merges with the North Atlantic Drift. At lat. 40°N and long. 60°W, the Gulf Stream is no longer distinguishable from the rest of the ocean drift. The Gulf Stream has an average speed of 4 mi (6.4 km) per hr but slows down as it widens to the north. At the beginning of the Gulf Stream the water temperature is 80°F (27°C), but the temperature decreases as the stream moves north. A dense fog is formed, especially off Newfoundland, SE Canada, as warm air above the Gulf Stream moves over the cold water of the Labrador Current. It is a common error to confuse the Gulf Stream with the North Atlantic Drift, which is responsible for the warm climate of Western Europe. See T. F. Gaskell, *The Gulf Stream* (1973).

gulfweed: see SEAWEED.

Gulick, Luther Halsey (gyo͞o'lĭk), 1865–1918, American pioneer in physical education, b. Honolulu, of American missionary parents. He studied at Oberlin College, Sargent School of Physical Training (now part of Boston Univ.), and the New York Univ. medical college (M.D., 1889). From 1887 to 1903 he was secretary of the physical training department of the YMCA. He devised the emblem of the organization and, with James Naismith, originated the game of basketball. He was director of physical training in the New York City public schools from 1903 to 1908; in 1907 he founded the child hygiene department of the Russell Sage Foundation, directing it until his retirement in 1913. With others he founded (1910) the Camp Fire Girls movement. He devoted much of his time to associations interested in hygiene and physical education, wrote several books in these fields, and lectured extensively. In 1917 he surveyed the work of the YMCA in France, returning to write his last and best-known book, *The Dynamic of Manhood* (1917). See biography by E. J. Dorgan (1934, repr. 1973).

Gulick, Luther Halsey, 1892–, American public administrator and educator, b. Osaka, Japan, grad. Oberlin College, 1914. He studied at the Training School for Public Service, New York and at Columbia (Ph.D., 1920). A widely recognized specialist in municipal finance and administration, he became (1920) a staff member of the New York Bureau of Municipal Research (renamed 1921 as the Institute of Public Administration). From 1931 to 1942, Gulick was Eaton professor of municipal science and administration at Columbia. He later became director of the Institute of Public Administration, a post he held until his retirement in 1961. Gulick's many works include *Evolution of the Budget in Massachusetts* (1920), *Administrative Reflections from World War II* (1948), *American Forest Policy* (1951), and *The Metropolitan Problem and American Ideas* (1962).

Gulistan, Treaty of (go͞olĭstän'), 1813, signed by Russia and Iran (Persia) at Gulistan, a village in what is now NW Azerbaijan SSR. It ended the Russo-Persian war that had begun in 1804. Persia ceded the khanates forming the present-day Azerbaijan SSR and renounced its claim on Georgia and Dagestan.

gull, common name for an aquatic bird of the family Laridae, which also includes the TERN and the JAEGER. It is found near all oceans and many inland waters. Gulls are larger and bulkier than terns, and their tails are squared rather than forked. Their plumage is usually white with gray or black markings on the back, wings, and head. Their long, narrow wings are adapted to soaring and their webbed feet to swimming. They have strong bills, hooked at the end; they eat clams and fish and sometimes insects, but are most useful as scavengers in harbors and bays. They are often seen hovering over the wakes of ships, seeking refuse, and frequenting garbage dumps. The common gull—called sea gull in North America—is the herring gull *Larus argentatus smithsonianus,* a subspecies of the common European gull *L. argentatus.* It is found on the Atlantic and Pacific coasts and on the Great Lakes. The larger great black-backed gull, *L. marinus,* is more northern; the ring-billed, Bonaparte's, and laughing gull are smaller. The Franklin's gull of the Great Plains is called the "prairie dove." The California and western gulls are common on the Pacific coast. The kittiwake is a small oceanic gull of the genus *Rissa,* seldom seen on land. The lesser black-backed and little gulls are European. Gulls are classified in the phylum CHORDATA, subphylum Vertebrata, class Aves, order Charadriiformes, family Laridae.

Gullah (gŭl'ə), a CREOLE LANGUAGE spoken by the Gullah Negroes of the Carolina Sea Islands and the Middle Atlantic coast of the United States. The word is probably a corruption of the African *Gola* or *Gora,* names of African tribes living in Liberia, but it may also be derived from Angola, whence many of the modern Gullahs' ancestors came. The Gullah dialect is a mixture of 17th- and 18th-century English and of a number of West African languages (among them Hausa, Ibo, and Yoruba). The African influence on Gullah can be seen in the phonology, vocabulary, and grammar. Some African words in Gullah have entered American English, including *goober* ("peanut"), *gumbo* ("okra"), and *voodoo* ("witchcraft"). The grammatical and lexical borrowings from English show evidence of decided simplification. Du Bose Heyward's novel *Porgy* (1925), upon which Gershwin's opera is based, was written in the Gullah dialect. See Mason Crum, *Gullah* (1940); Lorenzo D. Turner, *Africanisms in the Gullah Dialect* (1973).

Gullfoss (gü'təlfôs"), waterfall, c.100 ft (30 m) high, in the Hvítá River, SW Iceland. It is a popular tourist attraction.

Gullstrand, Allvar (äl'vär gŭl'stränd), 1862–1930, Swedish ophthalmologist. He was professor (1894–1927) successively of eye therapy and of optics at the Univ. of Uppsala. He applied the methods of physical mathematics to the study of optical images and of the refraction of light in the eye. For this work he received the 1911 Nobel Prize in Physiology and Medicine. He is noted also for his research on astigmatism and for improving the ophthalmoscope and corrective lenses for use after removal of a cataract from the eye.

gum, in anatomy: see TEETH.

gum, term commonly applied to any of a wide variety of colloidal substances somewhat similar in appearance and general characteristics, exuded by or extracted from plants. In this classification, however, many substances that are not true gums are included, among them many RESINS, so-called gum resins, and such substances as frankincense, myrrh, labdanum, copal, amber, chicle, and rubber (gum elastic, India rubber). True gums are complex organic substances mostly obtained from plants, some of which are soluble in water and others of which, although insoluble in water, swell up by absorbing large quantities of it. With water they form thick, gluey fluids. Their chemical nature is complex. In general, they contain in various proportions carbon, hydrogen, oxygen, and such metals as calcium, magnesium, and potassium in the form of salts of various organic acids. Gum arabic, or gum acacia, is a typical, water-soluble gum obtained from various plants of the genus *Acacia,* chiefly those found in Africa. A complex polysaccharide containing metal salts, gum arabic varies in color from white to red and is used extensively in making inks, adhesives, and confections; in the textile industry for filling fabrics; and in medicine as an emollient. Gum senegal is very similar. Among the gum resins (mixtures of gums and resins) are AMMONIAC, asafetida, BDELLIUM, GAMBOGE, and myrrh. See also TRAGACANTH. See C. L. Mantell et al., *The Technology of Natural Resins* (1942); C. L. Mantell, *The Water-Soluble Gums* (1947, repr. 1965).

gum ammoniac: see AMMONIAC.

gumbo, another name for okra (see MALLOW); also applied in the W United States to a rich, black, alkaline alluvial soil, which is soapy or sticky when wet.

Gumilev, Nikolai Stepanovich (nyĭkəlī' styĭpä'nəvĭch go͞omĕlyôf'), 1886–1921, Russian poet. With his wife, the poet Anna AKHMATOVA, and Gorodetsky Gumilev founded the ACMEIST school of poetry in 1912. He traveled widely in Europe and, especially, in Africa, and his poetic imagery is enhanced by the frequent use of foreign and exotic elements. *The Pillar of Fire* (1921) contains much of his best work. *Abinger Garland* (1945) is an English translation of some of his work. Gumilev was executed by the Bolsheviks for alleged conspiratorial activities.

Gumma (go͞om'mä), prefecture (1970 pop. 1,658,897), 2,446 sq mi (6,335 sq km), central Honshu, Japan. MAEBASHI is the capital; other important cities are Isezaki, Kiryu, and Takasaki. The prefecture is mountainous and has many hot springs. Rice and wheat are raised, and raw silk is produced.

Gumplowicz, Ludwig (lo͞ot'vĭkh go͞om'plōvĭch), 1838–1909, Austrian sociologist, political scientist, and jurist. From 1897 to 1909 he was a professor at Graz. He held that social development rose out of conflict, first among races, then among states, then among other social groups. His theories, influential although extreme, are expressed chiefly in *Der Rassenkampf* [race conflict] (1883) and *Grundriss der Soziologie* (1885, tr. *The Outlines of Sociology,* 1899).

Gumri: see LENINAKAN, USSR.

gum tragacanth: see TRAGACANTH.

gum tree, name for the eucalyptus (see MYRTLE) and for several other trees, e.g., the sweet gum, of the family Hamamelidaceae (WITCH-HAZEL family), and the BLACK GUM.

gun, in general, any weapon that discharges shot, shell, or bullets by the explosion of gunpowder or some other explosive from a straight tube. See FIREARM; ARTILLERY; SMALL ARMS.

gunboat, small warship for use on rivers and along coasts in places inaccessible to vessels of larger displacement. In the U.S. Civil War both sides used as gunboats, on the Mississippi and other rivers, any boat that had an engine and had room to mount a gun. Gunboats were widely employed by the European powers in the Far and Middle East and Africa during the late 19th and early 20th cent. for police duty. More recently, gunboats equipped with gas-turbine propulsion plants were used by the U.S. navy for coastal patrol operations during the Vietnam War. See *Jane's Fighting Ships* (pub. annually since 1897).

guncotton: see NITROCELLULOSE.

Gundulić, Ivan (ē'vän go͞ondo͞o'lĭch), or **Giovanni Gondola** (jōvän'nē gŏnda'lä), 1588–1638, Croatian poet. Born in Ragusa (Dubrovnik) of an aristocratic Dalmatian family, he became chief magistrate of Ragusa. In his early work he imitated Italian models. His greatest work, the epic poem *Osman* (1626), concerning the Polish wars against the Turks, reveals early Slavic nationalism and shows the influence of ancient native song. Possessing great lyric ability, Gundulić was considered the foremost figure of the South Slav literary renaissance.

Guni (gyo͞o'nī). **1** Son of Naphtali. Gen. 46.24; Num. 26.48. **2** Descendant of Gad. 1 Chron. 5.15.

Gunib (go͞onyĕp'), village, SE European USSR, in Dagestan. Now a mountain resort in the North Caucasus, it was historically important as a natural fortress during the Caucasian wars of the 19th cent. SHAMYL, leader of the Circassian tribes, made his last stand against the Russians at Gunib, where he was captured in 1859.

gunmetal, a BRONZE, an alloy of copper, tin, and a small amount of zinc. Although originally used extensively for making guns (from which it received its name), it has been superseded by steel, and it is now chiefly employed in casting machine parts. The so-called 88-10-2 (copper-tin-zinc) alloy is the "government bronze," composed of 88% copper, 10% tin, and 2% zinc. The percentages of the three elements are varied slightly in gunmetals produced for different purposes. The metal commonly called gunmetal today is very often steel treated to simulate the bronze alloy. In other cases, copper and tin are used alone; in still others, copper, tin, and lead are used.

Gunnarsson, Gunnar (gü'när gü'närsôn), 1889–, Icelandic novelist. Gunnarsson lived abroad until 1938, when he returned to Iceland. Through his early works, written in Danish, he helped interest Europeans in Icelandic culture. *Guest the One-eyed* (4 vol., 1912–14; tr. 1920) is an Icelandic family saga; *Seven Days' Darkness* (1920, tr. 1930) concerns the problem of war. *The Heath Laments* (1940) and *Sonata on the Sea* (1954) are written in Icelandic. His masterpiece, the semiautobiographical *Church on the Mountain* (5 vol., 1923–28), illustrates his rich imagination and poetic skill. It was partly translated as *Ships in the Sky* (1938) and *The Night and the Dream* (1938). Among his later works that have been translated into English is *Black Cliffs* (1969).

Gunnison, river, 180 mi (290 km) long, rising in W central Colo. and flowing SW, W, and NW to the Colorado River at Grand Junction. It flows through magnificent canyons, notably the **Black Canyon of the Gunnison,** a national monument (see NATIONAL PARKS AND MONUMENTS, table). Gunnison Tunnel, c.5 mi (8 km) long, was built between 1905 and 1909 to divert the river's water to the Uncompahgre Valley for irrigation.

gunpowder, explosive mixture of saltpeter (75%), sulphur (10%), and carbon (15%) in the form of charcoal. An increase in the percentage of saltpeter (potassium nitrate) increases the speed of combustion. In the past gunpowder was widely used for blasting and for propelling bullets from guns but it has been largely replaced by more powerful EXPLOSIVES. Another form of powder containing potassium chlorate instead of the nitrate is commonly used in fireworks and in matches.The origin of gunpowder was probably Chinese, for it seems to have been known in China at least as early as the 9th cent. and was there used for making firecrackers. There is some evidence that it came to Europe through the Arabs. Roger Bacon was long credited with inventing it because a formula for making it is given in a work attributed to him, and some German scholars have credited its invention to the alchemist-monk Berthold Schwarz. However, it is now generally agreed that gunpowder was introduced and not invented in Europe in the 14th cent. Its use revolutionized warfare completely and ultimately played a large part in the alteration of European patterns of living up until modern times Gunpowder was the only explosive in wide use until the middle of the 19th cent., when it was superseded by nitroglycerine-based explosives.

Gunpowder Plot, conspiracy to blow up the English Parliament and King James I on Nov. 5, 1605, the day set for the king to open Parliament. It was intended to be the beginning of a great uprising of English Catholics, who were distressed by the increased severity of penal laws against the practice of their religion. The conspirators, who began plotting early in 1604, expanded their number to a point where secrecy was impossible. They included Robert Catesby, John Wright, and Thomas Winter, the originators, Christopher Wright, Robert Winter, Robert Keyes, Guy Fawkes, a soldier who had been serving in Flanders, Thomas Percy, John Grant, Sir Everard Digby, Francis Tresham, Ambrose Rookwood, and Thomas Bates. Percy hired a cellar under the House of Lords, in which 36 barrels of gunpowder, overlaid with iron bars and firewood, were secretly stored. The conspiracy was brought to light through a mysterious letter received by Lord Monteagle, a brother-in-law of Tresham, on Oct. 26, urging him not to attend Parliament on the opening day. The 1st earl of Salisbury and others, to whom the plot was made known, took steps leading to the discovery of the materials and the arrest of Fawkes as he entered the cellar. Other conspirators, overtaken in flight or seized afterward, were killed outright, imprisoned, or executed. Among those executed was Henry GARNETT, the superior of the English Jesuits, who had known of the conspiracy. While the plot was the work of a small number of men, it damaged the cause of all English Catholics and led to an increase in the harshness of laws against them. Guy Fawkes Day, Nov. 5, is still celebrated in England with fireworks and bonfires, on which effigies of the conspirator are burned. See John Langdon-Davies, ed., *Gunpowder Plot* (1964); John Gerard, *What Was the Gunpowder Plot?* (2d ed. 1897); S. R. Gardiner, *What the Gunpowder Plot Was* (1897, repr. 1971).

Gunsaulus, Frank Wakeley (gənsôl'əs), 1856–1921, American Congregational clergyman and educator, b. Chesterville, Ohio. Ordained a minister of the Methodist Church in 1875, he entered the Congregational ministry in 1879. He then filled pastorates in Ohio, Massachusetts, Maryland, and Chicago. From 1899 he preached to large congregations in the independent Central Church, Chicago. He resigned in 1919 to devote his energies fully to the Armour Institute of Technology (now Illinois Institute of Technology), of which he was president from its establishment in 1893. He took a leading part in the affairs of the city of Chicago and was noted throughout the country as a lecturer. His writings include *The Man of Galilee* (1899), *Paths to Power* (1905), and *Martin Luther and the Morning Hour in Europe* (1917).

Gunter, Edmund, 1581–1626, English mathematician and astronomer, educated at Westminster School, London, and Christ Church, Oxford. He invented (1618) a small portable quadrant and discovered (1622) the variation of the magnetic compass. His Gunter's chain is a surveyor's chain graduated on the decimal scale. He devised Gunter's scale, a logarithmic scale of equal parts as well as trigonometric functions, which with the aid of compasses served as a SLIDE RULE.

Günther, Ignaz (ĭg'näts gün'tər), 1725–75, German sculptor. Günther produced numerous wood carvings that reveal mannerist and ROCOCO influences. His elegant figures are elongated to the point of distortion, and the wood is brightly painted, as in his works for the church at Rott-am-Inn in Bavaria.

Günther, Johann Christian (yō'hän krĭs'tyän), 1695–1723, German lyric poet. The young Goethe was inspired by the naturalness and vigor of Günther's verse. Among his remembered poems is the drinking song "Brothers, Let's Be Merry."

Gunton, George, 1845–1919, American economist, b. England. In 1874 he went to Fall River, Mass. His activities as a labor leader prevented his obtaining employment there in his trade as a weaver, and in 1878 he became manager of *Labor Standard.* Appointed (1889) director of economics and sociology for the Young Men's Christian Association of North America, he founded in 1890, in association with the Rev. Heber Newton, the Institute of Social Economics, in New York City, and the *Social Economist* (known after 1896 as *Gunton's Magazine*), which he edited until 1904. He wrote *Wealth and Progress* (1887), *Principles of Social Economy* (1891), *Trusts and the Public* (1899), and, with Hayes Robbins, *Outlines of Social Economics* (1900) and *Outlines of Political Science* (1901).

Guntram (gŭn'trəm), c.525–592, Frankish king of Burgundy and Orléans (561–92), son of Clotaire I. He intervened in the wars of his relatives in order to maintain the balance of power in the Frankish lands. After the death (575) of his brother King Sigebert I of Austrasia he aided Sigebert's son Childebert II, to whom he eventually left his domains. Supposedly good to his people, he was made a saint of the Roman Catholic Church. Feast: March 28.

Guntur (go͝ontoor'), city (1971 pop. 269,941), Andhra Pradesh state, SE India. It is a railroad junction and a cotton and tobacco market. Founded by the French in the 18th cent., Guntur was ceded to Great Britain in 1823.

guppy: see KILLIFISH.

Gupta (go͝op'tə), Indian dynasty, c.320–c.550, whose empire at its height encompassed much of India. Ancient Indian culture reached a high point during this period. Gupta paintings adorned the caves of Ajanta, its sculpture embellished the temples of Ellora, and its metaphysical speculations flowered in Vedantic philosophy and in the study of mathematics. The dynasty was founded by Chandragupta I (reigned c.320–c.330), who married a princess of the Licchavi tribe, acquired the kingdom of Magadha, and expanded his domains to include all of Bihar and some of Bengal. His brilliant son, Samudragupta (reigned c.330–c.380), conquered almost all of N India and much of the Deccan. The third and greatest of the Guptas, Chandragupta II (reigned c.380–c.414), further expanded the kingdom to include Ujjain. His reign, vividly described in the writings of Fa Hsien, a Chinese Buddhist pilgrim, was marked by prosperity throughout the land. Embassies were sent to many foreign courts, among them Rome, and a single code of law was promulgated for India. In this period also, the splendid Iron Pillar was erected (c.400) near what is now New Delhi, and KALIDASA wrote his dramas. Chandragupta II's successors were Kumaragupta (reigned c.414–455) and Skandagupta (reigned 455–c.467). The latter repelled the invasions of the White Huns, but after his death they overran much of N India. The dynasty lingered on in Bengal until c.550. See O. P. Bhatia, *The Imperial Guptas* (1962); J. F. Fleet, *Inscriptions of the Early Gupta Kings and Their Successors* (2d ed. 1963).

Gur (gûr), ascent near Ibleam. 2 Kings 9.27.

Gur-baal (gûr-bā'ăl), unidentified town, Palestine, in the Negev, inhabited by Arabs. 2 Chron. 26.7.

Gurkha (go͝or'kə), ethnic group of NEPAL. They claim descent from the Rajputs of N India and entered Nepal from the west after being driven from India. They conquered (early 16th cent.) the small Nepalese state of Gurkha and henceforth called themselves Gurkhas. They expanded eastward, and by the mid-18th cent. had established their authority over all of Nepal. Their invasion of Tibet in 1791 brought Chinese retaliation, and a war (1814–16) with the British in India resulted in bringing strong British influence to Nepal. The Gurkhas, predominantly Tibeto-Mongolians, speak Khas, a Rajasthani dialect of Sanskritic origin. Under the Gurkha dynasty, Hinduism became the state religion of Nepal. Gurkhas have served in the armies of India and of Great Britain; over 200,000 fought alongside the British in World War I, and 40 battalions served in World War II. Gurkha regiments were still in the Indian and British armies in the 1960s. Gurkha soldiers bear the famed kukri, a short curved sword. See studies by Harold James and Denis Sheil-Small (1965) and D. L. Bolt (1967, repr. 1969).

Gürsel, Cemal (jĕmäl' gürsĕl'), 1895–1966, Turkish army officer and political leader. He fought in World War I and in most of the military campaigns during the war of independence (1920–23). Gürsel remained in the army and in 1958 became commander of Turkish ground forces. A popular army figure, he led the coup of May, 1960, which overthrew the government of Adnan Menderes (see TURKEY). Gürsel resisted attempts to continue military rule and was elected president of the republic in 1961. Because of illness, he was succeeded as president by Cevdet Sunay in March, 1966, and died in September.

guru (go͞o'ro͞o), in Hinduism and Buddhism, spiritual teacher. The guru gives initiation into spiritual practice and instructs his disciples, often maintaining a close relationship with them. Among the SIKHS the title guru was given to the 10 leaders of the community from Nanak (c.1469–c.1539), founder of Sikhism, to Govind Singh (1666–1708). Govind appointed no successor, declaring that the Granth (the Sikh scriptures) was the true guru.

Guryev (go͝or'yĭf), city (1970 pop. 114,000), capital of Guryev oblast, Central Asian USSR, in Kazakhstan, on the Ural River and near the Caspian Sea. A seaport and an industrial center of the Emba oil fields, it has refineries, shipyards, and varied manufactures. Fishing is also important. The city is linked by oil pipeline (550 mi/885 km long) with Orsk. Founded in 1645 as a military outpost, Guryev was a fishing center until the development of the region's petroleum industry in the 1930s.

Gusau (go͞ozou'), town (1969 est. pop. 80,000), NW Nigeria, on the Sokoto River. It is a regional trade center for peanuts, cotton, and tobacco and a collection point for hides and skins. In 1929 a railroad reached Gusau, which then developed as an entrepôt for NW Nigeria.

Gustaf Adolf: see GUSTAVUS VI.

Gustavo A. Madero (go͞ostä'vō ä mädā'rō), city (1970 pop. 1,182,895), Federal District, S central Mexico. Formerly called Guadalupe Hidalgo, it was renamed in 1931. It is the site of the Guadalupe Hidalgo shrine and is a major pilgrimage center. The treaty of Guadalupe Hidalgo (1848), which ended the Mexican War, was signed there.

Gustavus I (gəstā'vəs), 1496–1560, king of Sweden (1523–60), founder of the modern Swedish state and the VASA dynasty. Known as Gustavus Eriksson before his coronation, he was the son of Erik Johansson, a Swedish senator and follower of the STURE family. Gustavus was treacherously imprisoned by CHRISTIAN II, the Danish king who was attempting to assert his control over Sweden under the KALMAR UNION. In 1520 his father was one of the nationalist leaders killed in the massacre Christian ordered at Stockholm after he had defeated Sweden. Having escaped from prison, Gustavus led the peasants of Dalarna to victory over the Danes and was elected (1521) protector of Sweden. In 1523 the Riksdag at Strangnas elected him king, ending the Kalmar Union. In 1527, Gustavus convinced the Riksdag at Vasteras to establish a national Protestant Church. To help create a strong monarchy, he wanted the revenue controlled by the Roman Catholic Church and a state Church subservient to his needs. Gustavus organized a national army of Swedish volunteers and built an efficient navy. Because the German city of LÜBECK had supported Gustavus against Christian, it had gained extensive trading privileges in Sweden. A temporary Danish-Swedish alliance led to victory over Lübeck in 1537 and freedom for the Swedish economy to grow; native industries were developed and foreign trade expanded. Gustavus firmly established royal authority, crushed several peasant and clerical revolts, limited the power of the nobility, and in 1544, by the Pact of Succession, made the throne hereditary in the Vasa family, thereby ending the practice of electing Swedish kings. At his death his eldest son succeeded him as Eric XIV, while his other three sons were named royal dukes with wide powers.

Gustavus II (Gustavus Adolphus), 1594–1632, king of Sweden (1611–32), son and successor of Charles IX. His excellent education, personal endowments, and early experience in affairs of state prepared him for his crucial role in Sweden and Europe. With the help of his great chancellor, Axel OXENSTIERNA, he insured internal stability by granting concessions to the turbulent nobility, and he terminated (1613) the Kalmar War with Denmark by buying off the Danes. This enabled him to undertake a successful campaign against Russia, which was forced to cede (1617) Ingermanland. Gustavus at first stayed out of the THIRTY YEARS WAR, which had begun in 1618. However, his resumption (1621) of the intermittent warfare between the Swedish and Polish branches of the house of VASA led to his entry into that vast conflict. His primary objects in invading Poland were to consolidate Swedish hegemony over the Baltic by acquiring Polish LIVONIA and to reduce the threat posed by the Catholic SIGISMUND III of Poland to Swedish Protestantism. The victories of the armies of Holy Roman Emperor Ferdinand II in the Thirty Years War soon caused the king to draw closer to the German Protestant princes. In 1628 he promised his aid to CHRISTIAN IV of Denmark in the defense of Stralsund. In 1629, through the mediation of Cardinal RICHELIEU of France, he obtained the truce of Altmark with Poland, gaining a large part of Livonia and several good Baltic ports; a secret treaty with France promised a French subsidy if Gustavus entered Germany. For the Protestant cause and also to gain control of the S Baltic coast, the king landed in Pomerania with 13,000 troops in 1630; these were soon augmented until 40,000 were at his disposal. Gustavus's invasion of Mecklenburg failed when the Mecklenburgers refused to heed his appeal to rise against the chief imperial general, WALLENSTEIN, who was their new ruler. Early in 1631 the Franco-Swedish treaty was openly ratified at Bärwalde, and after the fall of MAGDEBURG, Saxony and Brandenburg accepted the king's conditions for an alliance with Sweden. The spectacular sweep of the Swedish army through Germany then began. In Sept., 1631, Gustavus defeated the new imperial commander, TILLY, at Breitenfeld near Leipzig in the first Protestant victory of the war. He then marched west, reaching Mainz by Christmas, while the Saxon army moved into Bohemia. Resuming his campaign early in 1632, Gustavus returned east, defeated (April) the imperial troops at the crossing of the Lech (where Tilly was mortally wounded), and entered Bavaria. Wallenstein, reinstated as commander by the emperor, speedily put a large army into the field and forced the king to fall back to Nuremberg. Wallenstein set up his camp at a short distance, and the two armies remained facing each other for more than two months (July–Sept.) without giving battle. Finally Gustavus attacked Wallenstein's camp, but he failed and retired toward Würzburg, leaving a strong garrison at Nuremberg. Wallenstein then invaded unprotected Saxony, causing Gustavus to hasten north. At Lützen the two armies met on Nov. 16. The Swedes won the battle, but Gustavus was killed. Oxenstierna continued to direct Swedish policy under Gustavus's daughter, Queen Christina, while eventually Baner, and later Torstensson, took the king's place in the field. In military organization and strategy, Gustavus was ahead of his time. While most powers relied on mercenary troops, he organized a national standing army that distinguished itself by its discipline and relatively high moral standard. Deeply religious, the king desired his soldiers to behave like a truly Christian army; his stern measures against the common practices of looting, raping, and torture were effective until his death. His successes were due to this discipline, his use of small and mobile units, the superiority of his firearms, and also his personal magnetism. Although he was deeply interested in the internal progress of his kingdom, much of the credit for the development of Swedish industry and the fiscal and administrative reforms of his reign belongs to Oxenstierna. See biographies by G. F. MacMunn (1931) and N. G. Ahnlund (tr. 1940); Michael Roberts, *Gustavus Adolphus: A History of Sweden, 1611–1632* (2 vol., 1953, 1958), and *Gustavus Adolphus and the Rise of Sweden* (1973).

Gustavus III, 1746–92, king of Sweden (1771–92), son and successor of Adolphus Frederick. When Gustavus ascended the throne, he found his kingdom torn by civil strife. To the conflicting interests of peasants, nobles, priests, and officials was added the struggle between the aggressive, pro-French, and aristocratic Hat party and the more conservative, pro-Russian Cap party. His efforts at conciliation having failed, the king placed himself in complete control by a coup d'etat. He imposed (1772) upon the estates a new constitution that restored to the sovereign the prerogatives lost by his predecessors. He immediately inaugurated a policy of rigid financial reform, made his fleet one of the most powerful in Europe, and proclaimed complete religious toleration. His extravagance and his emulation of the court of Versailles, however, offset many of his improvements. Because of the aggressive policy of Russian Empress Catherine II, Gustavus embarked (1788) upon a war with Russia, having first forced the rebellious Swedish gentry into promising their support. An officers' mutiny threatened the campaign with disaster, but when the Danes invaded Sweden at Catherine's instigation, the king rallied the lower classes and, with the moral support of Prussia and England, repulsed the attackers. In a second coup d'etat, Gustavus strengthened (1789) the regal authority. The following year he defeated the Russians, who then entered a defensive alliance with him. He was attempting to form a coalition to intervene in the French Revolution in favor of the royalists when he was assassinated at a masked ball by a representative of the nobles. He was succeeded by his son, Gustavus IV. A gifted and learned monarch, Gustavus was the author of dramas and poems. He patronized science and literature and founded (1786) the Swedish Academy. See R. N. Bain, *Gustavus III and His Contemporaries, 1746–92* (1894).

Gustavus IV, 1778–1837, king of Sweden (1792–1809). On the assassination of his father, Gustavus III, he succeeded under the regency of his uncle, later King CHARLES XIII, a liberal. Attaining his majority in 1796, Gustavus dismissed his uncle's ministers and embarked on a reactionary policy at home. His adoption of INCLOSURE advanced the agricultural economy. The king directed his foreign policy against the French Revolution, and in 1805 he joined the Third Coalition against Napoleon I. Swedish Pomerania was occupied by the French, and Finland was taken (1808) by Russia, which in 1807 had made peace with France at Tilsit. Gustavus's despotism, his mental unbalance, and his disastrous policies led to his forced abdication when the Russians threatened Stockholm (March, 1809). The crown was tendered to Charles XIII, who made peace with Russia, and Gustavus's descendants were barred from succession. Gustavus spent most of his exile as "Colonel Gustafsson" at St. Gall, Switzerland, where he died.

Gustavus V, 1858–1950, king of Sweden (1907–50), son and successor of Oscar II. During his reign Sweden evolved toward political equality and economic prosperity and avoided military involvement in two world wars. He married (1881) Victoria of Baden. He was succeeded by his son, Gustavus VI.

Gustavus VI (Gustaf Adolf), 1882–1973, king of Sweden (1950–73), son and successor of Gustavus V. After the death (1920) of his first wife, Princess Margaret of Connaught, he married (1923) Lady Louise Mountbatten (d. 1965). He participated in archaeological expeditions in Sweden, Greece, and China, and founded the Swedish Institute in Rome. A botanist, his work in that field gained his admission (1958) to the British Royal Academy. He was succeeded by his grandson, Carl Gustaf (King Charles XVI Gustavus).

Gustavus Adolphus: see GUSTAVUS II.

Guston, Philip, 1913–, American painter, b. Montreal. Guston emigrated to the United States in 1916. He gained renown in the 1930s as a painter of social themes. Later he developed an abstract style of concentrated forms, as in *The Painter's City* (1956; Janis Gall., New York City). His works are often suggestive of impressionism. See study by Dore Ashton (1960).

Gutenberg, Johann (gōō'tənbərg, Ger. yō'hän gōō'tənbĕrk), c.1397–1468, German printer, believed to have been the first European to print with movable types cast in molds. His type was hand set, the characters equal in height, and printed on handmade paper. Similar PRINTING had been done earlier in China and Korea, but there is no evidence that Oriental printing was known in Europe in Gutenberg's time. Europeans who have been thought by some to have preceded Gutenberg in the practice of his art include Laurens Janszoon KOSTER, of Holland, and Pamfilo CASTALDI, of Italy. Gutenberg's name does not appear on any printing attributed to him, and details of his life and work remain doubtful. The evidence indicates that he was born in Mainz, trained as a goldsmith, and became a partner in a printing office in the 1430s. He is believed to have lived in Strasbourg for some years, and he may have made his great invention there in 1436 or 1437; but he returned to Mainz, where the printing attributed to him was produced. The masterpiece of Gutenberg's press was the MAZARIN BIBLE (c.1455). He borrowed money from the lawyer and goldsmith Johann FUST to finance his great venture, was unable to repay it, and lost both his press and types. Fust continued the work of the press with his son-in-law Peter Schöffer. Gutenberg was exiled from Mainz during the sack of 1462 but returned in 1465 and was awarded a pension and tax exemption. Although the separate elements (type, ink, press, and paper) of his printing were not entirely Gutenberg's own invention, he printed in quantity work of excellent quality and thereby contributed significantly to the technology of human communication. There is a Gutenberg Museum in Mainz. See O. W. Fuhrmann, *The Five Hundredth Anniversary of the Invention of Printing* (1937); J. M. Fontana, *Mankind's Greatest Invention* (rev. ed. 1964); D. C. McMurtrie and Don Farran, *Wings for Words* (1940, repr. 1971).

Gütersloh (güt'ərslō), city (1970 pop. 75,297), North Rhine-Westphalia, W West Germany. Its manufactures include textiles, household appliances, furniture, and printed materials. Gütersloh passed from the bishopric of Osnabrück to Prussia in 1815 and was chartered in 1825.

Guthrie, Samuel, 1782–1848, American physician, b. Brimfield, Mass. In Sackets Harbor, N.Y., where he settled after serving as surgeon in the War of 1812, he invented a percussion powder and a punch lock for exploding it, thus making obsolete the flintlock musket. In 1831 he discovered chloroform, anticipating by a few months its discovery by Eugène Soubeiran in France and Justus von Liebig in Germany.

Guthrie, Thomas Anstey: see ANSTEY, F.

Guthrie, Sir Tyrone, 1900–1971, English stage director, playwright, and writer. After his first stage appearance at Oxford in 1924, Guthrie was director of the Scottish National Players (1926–28), the Festival Theatre, Cambridge (1929–30), and the Old Vic-Sadler's Wells Company. He later mounted plays in many other parts of the world and he directed the theater named for him in Minneapolis, Minn. Creative and experimental and noted for his Shakespearean productions, Guthrie was among the first to write plays for radio. See his *A Life in the Theatre* (1959), *In Various Directions* (1965), and *Tyrone Guthrie on Acting* (1971).

Guthrie, Woody, 1912–67, American folk singer, guitarist, and composer, b. Okemah, Okla. Having learned harmonica as a boy and guitar as an adolescent, Guthrie was an itinerant musician and laborer from the age of 13. He was always deeply involved in union and left-wing politics, and he wrote many of his over 1,000 published songs on themes of social injustice, poverty, and politics. A friend of Huddie LEDBETTER, Pete SEEGER, and Ramblin Jack Elliott, Guthrie exerted a strong influence on younger performers, notably Bob DYLAN. His most famous song is probably "This Land Is Your Land." Guthrie died of Huntington's Chorea. See his autobiography, *Bound for Glory* (1943, rev. ed. 1968). See also Robert Shelton, ed., *Born to Win* (1965); and Henrietta Yurchenco and Marjorie Guthrie, *A Mighty Hard Road* (1970). Guthrie's son, **Arlo Guthrie,** 1947–, b. New York City, is also a folk singer and composer. He is best known for "Alice's Restaurant," a rambling, witty song that was the basis of a successful motion picture in which Arlo starred (1969).

Gutiérrez Nájera, Manuel (mänwĕl' gōōtyār'rās nä'hārä), 1859–95, Mexican poet and journalist. One of the precursors of MODERNISMO, he founded the literary periodical *Revista azul.* His elegant poetry, edited after his death, is delicately musical and wistful; it reflects the influence of Bécquer and of the French symbolists and shows the transition from romanticism to modernism. He also wrote exquisite, often humorous prose, notably in *Cuentos frágiles* [gossamer stories] (1883) and *Cuentos de color de humo* [smoke-colored stories] (1898). See Nell Walker, *The Life and Works of Manuel Gutiérrez Nájera* (1927).

gutta-percha (gŭt'ə-pûr'chə), natural LATEX obtained from *Palaquium gutta* and several other evergreen trees of the Far East. The latex, collected by felling or girdling the tree, is allowed to coagulate and is then washed, purified, and molded into bricks for shipping. Like CAOUTCHOUC, gutta-percha is a polyterpene, i.e., a polymer of isoprene (see RUBBER), but, unlike caoutchouc, it is not very elastic; the reason for the difference is that the polymer molecules in gutta-percha have a *trans* structure, whereas those of caoutchouc have a *cis* structure (see ISOMER). Gutta-percha is an excellent nonconductor and is often employed in insulating marine and underground cables. It is also used for golf-ball coverings, surgical appliances, and adhesives.

Gutzkow, Karl Ferdinand (kärl fĕr'dēnänt go͞ots'kō), 1811–78, German writer. He entered journalism in 1831 and became a leader of the antiromantic and nationally conscious literary movement known as Young Germany. For his *Wally die Zweiflerin* [Wally the doubter] (1835), an attack on marriage and religious orthodoxy, he was briefly jailed. Gutzkow's controversial writings furthered German social and political liberalism, and his novel *Die Ritter vom Geiste* [knights of the spirit] (9 vol., 1850–52) is important in the development of the modern German social novel. Among his plays is *Uriel Acosta* (1847, tr. 1860), which, although derivative, is perhaps his best work.

Guy, Thomas, 1645?–1724, English philanthropist, founder of Guy's Hospital, London (1721). As a printer and bookseller, Guy amassed a fortune, which he devoted to private and institutional charity. He contributed largely to St. Thomas's Hospital and Christ's Hospital in London and founded an almshouse in Tamworth, Staffordshire.

Guyana (gīăn'ə, -än'-), formerly **British Guiana,** republic (1970 pop. 714,233), 83,000 sq mi (214,969 sq km), NE South America, on the Atlantic Ocean. The capital is GEORGETOWN. On the east Guyana is separated from Surinam by the Courantyne River. The Akarai Mts. form the southern border with Brazil. Several rivers make up much of the western border with Brazil and Venezuela, and the Essequibo River flows through the center of the country (for a more detailed description of the physical characteristics of the area, see GUIANA). Most of the population lives along the coast. More than 50% of the people are East Indian (both Hindu and Muslim), about 33% are Negro, about 4% native Indian, and the rest mixed, European, and Chinese. English is the official language. Christianity, Hinduism, and Islam are the main religions. The Univ. of Guyana in Georgetown was founded in 1963. Guyana, which became independent of Great Britain in 1966, is a member of the Commonwealth of Nations. It has a parliamentary form of government. The popularly-elected national assembly, chosen by proportional representation, elects the president, who is the head of state. Guyana's politics largely reflect ethnic differences. The main parties are the Communist-oriented People's Progressive party (PPP), supported mainly by East Indians; the socialist People's National Congress (PNC), supported largely by Negroes; and the conservative United Force party (UF), which draws its support from the smaller ethnic groups. Agriculture and mining are the principal economic activities. Sugarcane, rice, and coconuts are the leading crops, and cattle and other livestock are raised. Bauxite, manganese, gold, and diamonds are mined. There are large forest resources (notably greenheart and balata) that are just beginning to be exploited. The processing of bauxite and sugarcane are the largest industries; the bauxite industry was nationalized in the early 1970s. The chief exports are bauxite, alumina, sugar and rum, and rice. The United States, Great Britain, and Canada are the most important trading partners. In 1974, Guyana became one of the seven charter members of the International Association of Producers of Bauxite. In the early 17th cent. the Dutch established settlements about the Essequibo River, and England and France also founded colonies in the Guiana region. By the Treaty of Breda (1667) the Dutch gained all the English colonies in Guiana. Possessions continued to change hands in the late 18th and early 19th cent. until the Congress of Vienna (1815) awarded the settlements of Berbice, Demerara, and Essequibo to Great Britain; they were united as British Guiana in 1831. Slavery was abolished in 1834. In 1879 gold was discovered, thus speeding British expansion toward the Orinoco delta and resulting in the VENEZUELA BOUNDARY DISPUTE. After World War II significant progress toward self-government was begun. Under the 1952 constitution, elections were won (1953) by the PPP headed by Cheddi JAGAN, who formed a government. However, the British deemed the government pro-Communist and suspended the constitution. Subsequently the PPP split, and Forbes BURNHAM formed the PNC. The PPP again won elections in 1957 and (after self-government was granted) in 1961. Proportional representation was introduced in 1964 in response to charges by the PNC that the electoral system was unfair. After the 1964 elections the PNC and the UF formed a coalition, and Burnham became prime minister. Full independence was negotiated in 1966. In the elections of 1968 and 1973 the PNC won a majority, and Burnham continued as prime minister. Antagonism between the East Indians, who control a substantial portion of the nation's commerce, and the Negroes led to frequent clashes and bloodshed in the 1960s, but violence subsided by the 1970s. Guyana became a republic in 1970. The boundaries with Venezuela and Surinam became a matter of dispute in the 1960s, with Venezuela laying claim to some 60% of Guyana's territory. Tensions on both fronts eased in 1970 when a 12-year truce was declared with Venezuela and a mutual troop withdrawal agreement was made with Surinam. See R. T. Smith, *British Guiana* (1962); V. T. Daly, *A Short History of the Guyanese People* (1966), Johnson Research Associates, *Area Handbook for Guyana* (1969), R. A. Glasgow, *Guyana: Race and Politics among Africans and East Indians* (1970), Henry Kirke, *Twenty-Five Years in British Guiana* (1898, repr. 1970), A. H. Adamson, *Sugar Without Slaves: The Political Economy of British Guiana, 1838–1904* (1972).

Guy of Chauliac: see CHAULIAC, GUY DE.

Guy of Lusignan (lüsēnyäN'), d. 1194, Latin king of Jerusalem (1186–92) and Cyprus (1192–94), second husband of Sibylla, sister of King BALDWIN IV of Jerusalem. In 1183 he was briefly regent for his brother-in-law, who was incapacitated by leprosy, but Baldwin made Guy's stepson king as Baldwin V, and the Latin nobles forced Guy to yield command to Raymond of Tripoli. On Baldwin V's death (1186) Guy became king with the support of both his wife and Reginald of Châtillon. He was defeated and captured (1187) by SALADIN at the decisive battle of Hattin, which led to the fall of Jerusalem. Released in 1188, he laid siege (1189) to Acre (see AKKO), which was captured (1191) in the Third Crusade with the help of Richard I of England and Philip II of France. After the death (1190) of Sibylla, Guy's right to the throne was contested by CONRAD, marquis of Montferrat, who was supported by Philip II. In spite of Richard I's support, Guy was compelled (1192) to resign his title, but was given the island of Cyprus. His descendants (see LUSIGNAN) ruled Cyprus and Lesser Armenia. His brother, AMALRIC II, succeeded him in Cyprus.

Guy of Warwick (wŏr'ĭk), English legendary hero, popularized by a 14th-century rhymed romance. Guy won the earl of Warwick's daughter and saved England from the Danes by killing the giant Colbrand; he later renounced worldly vanities and ended his days as a hermit. The story probably has a historical basis. Its popularity lasted through the 17th and 18th cent.

Guyon, Jeanne Marie Bouvier de la Motte (zhän märē' bo͞ovyā' də lä môt güēyôN'), 1648–1717, French mystic and author of writings dealing largely with QUIETISM. Confined by the government (1688) in a convent because of her heretical opinions and her correspondence with Miguel de MOLINOS, she was released through the efforts of Mme de Maintenon. François FÉNELON, who became her disciple, defended her in a famous controversy with BOSSUET. She was later condemned and imprisoned (1695–1702) in the Bastille. Her collected works appeared (1767–91) in 40 volumes. See her autobiography (tr. 1897); biographies by T. C. Upham (1847) and Michael de La Bedoyère (1956).

Guys, Constantin (gois), 1805?–1892, French watercolorist and draftsman, b. Holland. He accompanied Byron in the Greek struggle for liberty in 1824. His friend Baudelaire recognized his talent, but he was not generally known, as his work was published anonymously, most frequently in the *Illustrated London News*. Most of his witty drawings deal with the elegant society of his period, but he also drew, from life, scenes of the Crimean War. See P. G. Konody, *The Painter of Victorian Life* (1930), which includes an essay by Baudelaire.

Guyton de Morveau, Louis Bernard, Baron (lwē bĕrnär' bärôN' gētôN' də môrvō'), 1737–1816, French chemist and lawyer. He wrote the chemical section of the *Encyclopédie méthodique* (Vol. I, 1786) and collaborated with Lavoisier and others in establishing a system of chemical nomenclature. He taught chemistry (1794–1811) at the École Polytechnique, Paris, served in the Legislative Assembly and in the National Convention during the French Revolution, and was master of the mint (1799–1814). He was created baron in 1811.

Guzmán, Martín Luis (märtēn' lo͞oēs' go͞osmän'), 1887–, Mexican novelist and journalist. Guzmán worked as a journalist during the Mexican revolution, in which he joined the forces of Francisco Villa. He recorded his impressions of the war years in *The Eagle and the Serpent* (1928, tr. 1930) and depicted the political intrigue of the 1920s in *La sombra del caudillo* (1929). From 1914 to 1934 he lived in exile. Returning to Mexico, he edited his monumental *Memorias de Pancho Villa* (5 vol., 1938–51; tr. 1965) and founded *Tiempo,* an influential weekly. His *Muertes históricas* (1958) contains studies of Porfirio Díaz and Venustiano Carranza. Guzmán's works are collected in *Obras completas* (1961–63).

Guzmán, Nuño de (no͞o'nyō thā go͞othmän'), or **Núñez Beltrán de Guzmán** (no͞o'nyĕth bĕlträn'), d. 1544, Spanish conquistador. After serving as governor of Panuco in NE Mexico, he became president of the first audiencia of New Spain (1528). His notorious rule brought an outcry from the colonists; in 1530 the audiencia was excommunicated by Bishop ZUMÁRRAGA; later it was replaced by a second audiencia. Meanwhile, Guzmán left Mexico City (Dec., 1529), conquered NUEVA GALICIA, and was responsible for the founding of Culiacán and Guadalajara. He blocked several expeditions sent out by CORTÉS, his bitter rival. Guzmán's conquest was, however, not very productive. He stirred up trouble with the Indians and with his own men. Superseded in the governorship, he was imprisoned (1536–38); he then returned to Spain, where he died in obscurity. See study by D. E. Chipman (1966).

Guzmán (go͞osmän') or **Ciudad Guzmán** (syo͞othäth'), city (1970 pop. 40,031), Jalisco state, SW Mexico. It is a marketing and processing center, especially for hogs, with some minor industries. The city is the starting point for ascents of the Nevado de Colima (14,235 ft/4,339 m) and the smoking volcano, Colima (12,631 ft/3,850 m). Formerly called Zapotlán el Grande, Guzmán was the site of the pre-Columbian kingdom of Zapotlán, which was conquered by the Spanish in 1526.

Guzmán Blanco, Antonio (äntō'nyō go͞osmän' blän'kō), 1829–99, president of Venezuela, a caudillo who dominated the nation from 1870 to 1888. Son of the founder of the Liberal party, Guzmán Blanco was a magnetic and energetic figure with considerable diplomatic and administrative ability. He became a general in the revolution that deposed José Antonio Páez and was vice president (1863–68) in the Liberal administration that followed. In 1870 he led a successful counterrevolution against MONAGAS and was elected president. A benevolent despot, he alternately suppressed and supported the Church; he was a foe of civil liberties but made free education compulsory; he reformed governmental administration and instituted many public works that brought material advancement to Venezuela. The egocentric Guzmán Blanco filled Venezuela with portraits and statues of himself. Several times he relinquished his office to make diplomatic and pleasure trips to Europe but kept control of the country through presidential puppets, notably Joaquín CRESPO. In 1888, when he was abroad, his power was destroyed by revolution. He spent the rest of his life in Paris. See biography by G. S. Wise (1951, repr. 1970).

Gvozdena Vrata: see IRON GATE, gorge, Rumania and Yugoslavia.

Gwalior (gwä'lēôr), city and former princely state, 26,008 sq mi (67,361 sq km), central India. Part of Madhya Pradesh state since 1956, the region of Gwalior formerly consisted of one large territory and numerous enclaves. Wheat, millet, oilseed, and cotton are the regional crops. The state was formed in the mid-18th cent. by Ranoji Sindhia, a Mahratta chief who became independent of the peshwa (hereditary Mahratta prime minister). Forces of Gwalior overran much of central India until they were checked by the British in the early 19th cent., and the state was temporarily annexed to the British domain. It was restored to the Sindhias in 1886. When India became independent in 1947, Gwalior and several other princely states were combined into the state of Madhya Bharat. In 1956, Madhya Bharat merged with Madhya Pradesh. The city of **Gwalior** (1971 pop. 406,755) was the capital of Gwalior state. It lies at the foot of Gwalior fort, a stronghold on the Rock of Gwalior, a plateau 2 mi (3.2 km) long and 300 ft (91 m) high. Within the battlemented walls of the fort are elaborately carved palaces and temples. Huge Jain reliefs are carved in the cliffs of the Rock of Gwalior. Among the city's manufactures are textiles, porcelain ware, leather and plastic goods, and processed food. There are several colleges and an experimental farm.

Gwathmey, Robert, 1903–, American painter, b. Richmond, Va. Gwathmey taught at Cooper Union from 1942 to 1968. His paintings combine a human sympathy for the impoverished Negro with intense atmospheric effects of harsh sun and parched earth. Representative of his works, which are found in many museums, is *Sowing* (Whitney Mus., New York City).

Gwelo (gwĕl'ō), city (1973 est. pop., with suburbs, 55,000), central Rhodesia. It is an industrial and commercial center. Manufactures include footwear, ferroalloys, metal goods, and cement. Gwelo was founded in 1894 and in 1896 was a major point of defense for Europeans during the rebellion by the Ndebele.

Gwent (gwĕnt), nonmetropolitan county (1972 est. pop. 442,000), SE Wales, created under the Local Government Act of 1972 (effective 1974). It comprises the county borough of NEWPORT and portions of the former counties of MONMOUTHSHIRE and BRECONSHIRE.

Gwin, William McKendree, 1805–85, American politician, b. Sumner co., Tenn. He received (1828) a degree in medicine from Transylvania Univ. and practiced in Clinton, Miss., until 1833. He represented Mississippi in the U.S. House of Representatives (1841–43) and went to California in 1849. There he threw himself into the movement for statehood and was an outstanding leader in the state constitutional convention. One of the first U.S. Senators from California (1850–55, 1857–61) and chief spokesman for the slavery interests there, he became involved in several battles with his ambitious antislavery rival, David C. BRODERICK. During the Civil War, Gwin was imprisoned several times as a Southern sympathizer. In 1863 he went to France where he won the support of Napoleon III for a scheme to colonize N Mexico with settlers from the Confederacy, but his plans were thwarted by the opposition of Emperor Maximilian. See biography by Lately Thomas (1969).

Gwinnett, Button, c.1735–1777, American political figure, signer of the Declaration of Independence, b. Gloucestershire, England. Emigrating to America, he became a Georgia planter and merchant. In 1776–77, he was a Georgia delegate to the Continental Congress. He was briefly president (governor) of Georgia in 1777, but was killed in a duel. See biography by C. F. Jenkins (1926).

Gwyn or **Gwynn, Nell** (Eleanor Gwyn), 1650–87, English actress. Once an orange-seller at the Theatre Royal, she became a member of Killigrew's company, making her debut there in 1665. Her charm and vivacity in comic roles endeared her to the public, as did her witty renditions of prologues and epilogues. She became the mistress of Charles II (1669) and bore him two sons, one of whom was created the duke of St. Albans. Her portrait was painted by Sir John Lely; she is the subject of several plays including *Sweet Nell of Old Drury*, by Paul Kester. See Clifford Bax, *Pretty Witty Nell* (1932).

Gwynedd (gwĭn'ĕth), nonmetropolitan county (1972 est. pop. 221,000), NW Wales, created under the Local Government Act of 1972 (effective 1974). It comprises the former counties of ANGLESEY and CAERNARVONSHIRE and portions of the former counties of MERIONETHSHIRE and DENBIGHSHIRE.

gymnastics, exercises for the balanced development of the body, practiced usually in a room or building called a gymnasium. In Greece the gymnasium was originally a place of training for the OLYMPIC GAMES and other athletic contests; the Lyceum and Academy of Athens were large enough for cavalry parades, besides containing a running track, pits for jumping, and ranges for throwing the discus and javelin. By the end of the 4th cent. B.C. the gymnasium became an educational and cultural center for Greek youths. Modern gymnastics date from the early 19th cent., when Ludwig Jahn established several *Turnplätze* in Berlin. Gymnastics spread on the Continent, to England, then to the United States, and became part of the modern Olympic meets. Gymnastics (see PHYSICAL EDUCATION AND TRAINING) became part of the American school curriculum, were adopted by the army, and became a featured college sport in the United States. Besides free calisthenics, the principal gymnastic events in the United States are the side and long horse, the parallel and horizontal bars, trampoline, rope climbing, the flying rings, and tumbling. Except for rope climbing, which is scored on speed, events are scored on the basis of form, execution, and difficulty of optional exercises. There are competitions for women as well as for men. All around champions are selected on the basis of excellence in a number of events. Team competitions are scored on the basis of total points for all events. The Amateur Athletic Union holds annual national championship meets for men and women. See H. D. Price, and others, *Gymnastics and Tumbling* (3d ed., 1959); N. C. Loken, *Complete Book of Gymnastics* (1967); F. J. Fogel, *Gymnastics Handbook* (1971).

gymnosperm: see ANGIOSPERM.

gymnure: see HEDGEHOG.

Gympie (gĭm'pē), city (1971 pop. 11,131), Queensland, E Australia. It is an agricultural center. A silver mine is nearby. Gympie was formerly a gold-mining center.

gynecology (gīn"əkŏl'əjē), branch of medicine specializing in the disorders of the female reproductive system. Modern gynecology deals with menstrual disorders, the menopause, infectious disease and maldevelopment of the reproductive organs, disturbances of the sex hormones, benign and malignant tumor formation, and the prescription of contraceptive devices. Some gynecologists also practice OBSTETRICS. The "diseases of women" were recognized and written about even in ancient times. An encyclopedia of gynecology was published in 1566 under the direction of Caspar Wolf of Zürich. William Hunter and other famous physicians of the subsequent era made intensive studies of various pelvic abnormalities and devised procedures for their correction. Surgical gynecology, however, made no real progress until the 19th cent., when, as in other fields of surgery, the introduction of ANESTHESIA and antisepsis (see ANTISEPTIC) paved the way for many advances. The American physician J. M. SIMS was largely responsible for gaining acceptance of gynecology as a medical and surgical specialty. Until then there had been opposition to it on moral grounds from midwives and the clergy and from the medical profession.

Gyöngyös (dyön'dyösh), city (1970 pop. 33,149), N Hungary, at the foot of the Matra Mts. It is the commercial center of a wine-producing and tobacco-growing region. Lead and zinc are mined nearby. Gyöngyös has a large Franciscan college (founded 1634), a 14th-century church, and a castle.

Győr (dyör), Ger. *Raab* (räb), city (1970 pop. 100,065), NW Hungary, near the Czechoslovak border and at the confluence of the Rába and Danube rivers. Győr is a road and rail hub, a river port, a county administrative center, and a leading industrial city, known especially for its engineering works and textile plants. Its location about midway between Budapest and Vienna makes the city an important communications point. The site of Győr was a Roman military outpost called Arabona that was evacuated in the 4th cent. A.D. and later destroyed. The Magyars built fortifications there in the 9th cent., and Győr grew around the fortress, which was later (17th cent.) used as a defensive position against the Turks. Győr became an episcopal see in 1001 and was made a royal free town in 1743. In 1849, Hungarian revolutionary forces were decisively defeated by the Austrians near Győr. The city's industrialization dates from the second half of the 19th cent. Present-day landmarks include a 12th-century cathedral (rebuilt 17th cent.), an episcopal palace, and several impressive monuments and baroque houses from the 17th and 18th cent.

Gypsophila (jĭpsŏf'ələ): see PINK.

gypsum (jĭp'səm), mineral composed of calcium sulfate (calcium, sulfur, and oxygen) with two molecules of water, $CaSO_4 \cdot 2H_2O$. It is the most common sulfate mineral, occurring in many places in a variety of forms. A transparent crystalline variety is selenite. A massive gypsum of delicate color and texture, readily worked into ornamental vases, boxes, and the like, is called alabaster. A lustrous gypsum with fibrous structure, called satin spar, is used in jewelry and for other ornaments, but it is soft and easily marred. Plaster of Paris, a fine white powder, is produced by heating gypsum to expel the water. If this powder is moistened and then allowed to dry, it becomes hard, or sets. Its major use is in the manufacture of gypsum lath and wall board, and for casts and molds. It is widely used for staff, the material of which temporary exposition buildings are made. Uncalcined gypsum is added to Portland cement as a retarder.

gypsy or **gipsy** [from *Egypt,* because of an inaccurate idea that gypsies came from a so-called Little Egypt], an essentially nomadic people with particular FOLKWAYS and a unique language, found on every continent. Gypsies usually travel in small caravans and make their living as metalworkers, singers, dancers, musicians, horse dealers, and auto mechanics. Gypsy women are famous as fortunetellers. Most gypsies are dark-complexioned, short, and lightly built. It is believed that they came originally from NW India, which they left for Persia in the 1st millennium A.D. Probably during their sojourn in Persia, they became divided into three main tribal divisions: the Gitanos, the Kalderash, and the Manush. Later they moved northward and westward, and are recorded as first appearing in Western Europe in the 15th cent. Alternately welcomed and persecuted by civil and religious authorities, they moved from country to country until they had spread to every part of Europe by the beginning of the 16th cent. They arrived in North America in the late 1800s. Their language, called ROMANY, belongs to the Indo-Iranian family and is closely related to the languages of NW India, while their blood groupings have also been found to coincide with those of S Himalayan tribes. In the course of their wanderings, gypsies have sometimes mixed with nongypsy neighbors and have occasionally settled down, but they have clung tenaciously to their identity and customs. Their physical type has remained largely unaltered; their bands are still ruled by elders. Traditionally sorcerers and necromancers, gypsies usually adopt the religion of their country of residence; probably the greater number are Roman Catholic or Orthodox Eastern Christian. Each year in May they gather in S France from all over the world for a pilgrimage to Saintes-Maries-de-la-Mer. Gypsies are estimated to number about 5,000,000, although some 500,000 of them perished in gas chambers and concentration camps during World War II. In modern times, and especially since the beginning of the 20th cent., various nations have attempted to curb their nomadic habits by requiring them to register, to go to school and learn trades, and to observe certain rules of sanitation. In 1956 the Soviet Union decreed that the last wandering gypsy bands in that country be gradually settled in places of their choice. Other socialist countries in E Europe have adopted similar measures. Other countries are attacking the problem with mobile school units and special educational facilities. See George Borrow, *The Romany Rye* (1857, new ed. 1949, repr. 1959); I. H. Brown, *Gypsy Fires in America* (1924); Gipsy Petulengro's autobiography, *A Romany Life* (1935); Jan Yoors, *The Gypsies* (1967); Donald Kenrick and Gratton Puxon, *The Destiny of Europe's Gypsies* (1972).

Gypsy language: see ROMANY.

gypsy moth, common name for a moth, *Porthetria dispar,* of the tussock moth family. Its caterpillars, or larvae, defoliate deciduous and evergreen trees and shrubs. Introduced from Europe into Massachusetts c.1869, the gypsy moth became a serious pest within 20 years. The adult moths have hairy bodies. Females, with a wingspread of about 2 in. (5 cm), are white with dark lines on the wings; the smaller males are gray. The female covers the egg mass with body hair and scales. The larvae emerge in the spring; their blackish bodies have yellow stripes and rows of blue or red tubercles bearing tufts of hair. When full grown they are about 2 in. long. Pupation (see INSECT) lasts about two weeks, and the adults emerge from the cocoon in midsummer. Because the females rarely fly, dispersal of the gypsy moth occurs chiefly in the egg and larval stages. In North America the gypsy moth has been confined to the NE United States and adjacent parts of Canada. Its spread has been checked by stringent quarantine and its numbers controlled by such measures as importing insect parasites, destroying the egg masses, and spraying trees with insecticide. In recent years, however, the gypsy moth population has increased, causing considerable damage to trees. The gypsy moth is classified in the phylum ARTHROPODA, class Insecta, order Lepidoptera, family Liparidae.

gyre: see OCEAN.

gyrefalcon: see FALCON.

gyrocompass: see GYROSCOPE.

gyroplane: see AUTOGIRO.

gyroscope (jī'rəskōp"), symmetrical mass, usually a wheel, mounted so that it can spin about an axis in any direction. When spinning, the gyroscope has special properties. Many spinning objects exhibit some of these properties; the rotation of the earth about its axis gives it the properties of a huge gyroscope. Once a gyroscope starts to spin, it will resist changes in the orientation of its spin axis. For example, a spinning top resists toppling over, thus keeping its spin axis vertical. If a TORQUE, or twisting force, is applied to the spin axis, the axis will not turn in the direction of the torque, but will instead move in a direction perpendicular to it. This motion is called precession. The wobbling motion of a spinning top is a simple example of precession. The torque that causes the wobbling is the weight of the top acting about its tapering point. The modern gyroscope was developed in the first half of the 19th cent. by the French physicist Jean B. L. Foucault, and its first notable use was in a visual demonstration of the earth's rotation. In the second half of the 19th cent., with the invention of the electrically driven rotor, its uses multiplied. It became possible to rotate the gyroscope's wheel at desired speeds without interfering with the precession. Large gyroscopes are used in ship stabilizers to counteract rolling. The gyroscope is the nucleus of most automatic steering systems, such as those used in airplanes, missiles, and torpedoes. It is also used in the gyrocompass, a directional instrument used on ships. Unaffected by magnetic variations, its spinning axis, when brought in line with the north-south axis of the earth, provides an accurate line of reference for navigation. See J. B. Scarborough, *The Gyroscope: Theory and Applications* (1958); Walker Wrigley et al., *Gyroscopic Theory, Designs and Instrumentation* (1969).

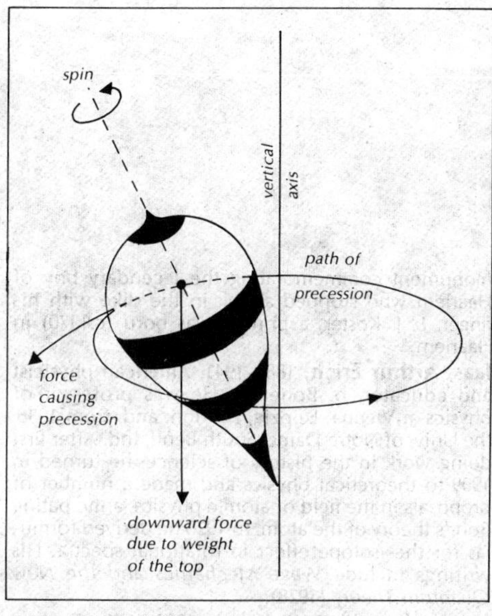

A spinning top illustrates the gyroscopic principle. If the top is not vertical, the downward force of its weight produces a torque, causing the top to precess, or wobble, in a circle about the vertical axis. The force causing precession is perpendicular to both the downward force causing the torque and the axis of spin.

Gyula (dyo͝o'lŏ), town (1970 pop. 26,266), SE Hungary, on the White Koros River near the Rumanian border. It is an agricultural center and has a fine château and a 14th-century castle. Ferenc Erkel, composer of the Hungarian national anthem, was born in Gyula.

Gyulafehérvár: see ALBA IULIA.

H, 8th letter of the ALPHABET. It is a usual symbol for a glottal spirant, murmured (as in the English *house*) or voiceless (as in the English *herb*). In some Greek alphabets eta, the long *e*, had this form. In chemistry H is the symbol for the element HYDROGEN.

Haag, Den: see HAGUE, THE.

Haahashtari (hā″əhăsh'tărī, -hăshtā'-), descendant of Judah. 1 Chron. 4.6.

Haakon I (hä'kən, Nor. hô'ko͝on) (Haakon the Good), c.915–961, king of Norway (c.935–961), son of Harold I. He was brought up as a Christian at the court of King Athelstan in England. His brother, Eric Bloodyaxe, had succeeded Harold as chief king, but the other sons of Harold refused to obey Eric and helped Haakon seize power. Haakon strengthened the national army and fleet. His effort to introduce Christianity was unsuccessful. He died from a battle wound, and Eric's sons succeeded him with Danish support.

Haakon IV (Haakon Haakonsson), 1204–63, king of Norway (1217–63), illegitimate son of Haakon III and grandson of Sverre. Secretly reared by the Birkebeiner faction (see SVERRE), he was chosen king (1217) on the death of Haakon III's successor, King Inge. Haakon Haakonsson overcame the rival claims of Earle Skule (Inge's brother), and in 1223 a great council at Bergen reaffirmed his kingship. Skule, after a renewed attempt at rebellion, was slain by the Birkebeiners in 1240. Haakon, then recognized by Pope Innocent IV, was solemnly crowned in 1247 at Bergen by a papal legate. Under Haakon IV medieval Norway reached its zenith. Iceland and Greenland were acquired, and important legal reforms were carried out. Haakon's court was splendid, and Old Norse literature flowered during his reign. SNORRI STURLUSON lived for some time at the court. Haakon died at Kirkwall in the Orkney Islands when campaigning against Scotland. He was succeeded by his son, Magnus VI.

Haakon VII, 1872–1957, king of Norway (1905–57). Formerly Prince Charles, second son of King Frederick VIII of Denmark, he was elected by the Storting to the throne on the separation of Norway from Sweden in 1905 and took the name Haakon. He married Princess Maud, the daughter of Edward VII of England. During the German occupation of Norway (1940–45) in World War II, Haakon headed a government in exile at London. He was succeeded by his son, Olaf V. See M. A. Michael, *Haakon, King of Norway* (1958).

Ha'am, Ahad: see GINZBERG, ASHER.

Haardt, Georges Marie (zhôrzh märē' ärt, härt), 1886–1932, French explorer. Traveling by automobile, he crossed the Sahara and then traversed Africa from Cape Town to Cairo. In April, 1931, he led a trans-Asian motor expedition of which one section started from Beyrouth (Beirut), Lebanon, and the other from Peiping (Peking), China; they met in Sinkiang. The expedition ended in Peiping in Feb., 1932 after an 8,000-mi (12,875-km) journey. With Louis Audouin-Dubreuil, Haardt wrote *Across the Sahara by Motor Car* (tr. 1924) and *The Black Journey* (tr. 1927). See Georges Le Fèvre, *An Eastern Odyssey* (tr. 1935).

Haarlem (här'ləm), city (1971 pop. 172,235), capital of North Holland prov., W Netherlands, on the Spaarne River, near the North Sea. Although an industrial center with shipyards, machinery plants, and textile mills, Haarlem is chiefly noted as the center of a famous flower-growing district and the export point for bulbs (especially tulips). Haarlem was chartered in 1245. In 1573 it was sacked by the Spanish during the revolt of the Netherlands. During the 16th and 17th cent. Haarlem was a center of Dutch painting; Frans Hals, Jacob van Ruisdael, and Adriaen van Ostade worked there. Since that period the city has been the center of tulip raising. Among Haarlem's numerous historic buildings are the Church of St. Bavo, or Groote Kerk (15th cent.), which has a world-famous organ; the Stadhuis [city hall], formerly a palace of the counts of Holland, begun in 1250; and many fine medieval gabled houses. The city has many museums. Nearby is a monument commemorating the legendary boy of Haarlem who stopped a leak in the dike with his finger. L. J. Koster, a printer, was born (c.1370) in Haarlem.

Haas, Arthur Erich, 1884–1941, American physicist and educator, b. Bohemia. He was professor of physics at Vienna, Leipzig, London, and, from 1936, the Univ. of Notre Dame, South Bend, Ind. After first doing work in the history of science, he turned in 1909 to theoretical physics and made a number of proposals in the field of atomic physics, anticipating Bohr's theory of the atom. In 1920 he derived formulas for the isotope effect in rotational spectra. His writings include *Wave Mechanics and the New Quantum Theory* (1928).

Haase, Hugo (ho͞o'gō hä'zə), 1863–1919, German Socialist leader. A Social Democratic member of the Reichstag, he opposed World War I, but initially followed his party's position in supporting the war. In Dec., 1915, he split with the Social Democrats under Friedrich EBERT, who replaced him as leader in the Reichstag. In 1917, Haase and his followers formed the Independent Social Democratic party. After the proclamation of a German republic in Nov., 1918, Haase joined with Ebert and Philipp SCHEIDEMANN in forming the new government, but his party was unwilling to accept the "bourgeois revolution" of the Social Democrats and withdrew late in December. Haase was murdered by a personal enemy.

Habacuc (həbăk'ək), variant of HABAKKUK.

Habaiah (hăbī'ə, hăbā'yə), priestly family. Ezra 2.61; Neh. 7.63.

Habakkuk, Habacuc, or **Habbacuc** (all: həbak'ək), book of the Old Testament, 35th in the order of the Authorized Version, eighth of the books of the Minor Prophets. It is a set of poems, perhaps three (1.1–2.4; 2.5–20; 3.1–19), on the punishment of the wicked by God, using the Chaldaeans (i.e., Babylonians) as His instrument, and the triumph of divine justice and mercy. The third (3.1–19), in which Habakkuk praises God, resembles a psalm and has a musical direction like one. Some believe that Habakkuk lived at the time of the fall of Nineveh (612 B.C.). A prophet of this name is mentioned in the story of BEL AND THE DRAGON. A commentary on the book of Habakkuk was found among the DEAD SEA SCROLLS. See F. E. Gaebelein, *Four Minor Prophets: Obadiah, Jonah, Habakkuk, and Haggai* (1970); H. E. Freeman, *Nahum, Zephaniah, Habakkuk* (1973).

Habana: see HAVANA, Cuba.

Habash al-Hasib (häbäsh' äl-häsēb'), d. c.870, Arab mathematician and astronomer. Habash al-Hasib was born in what is now Mary, Turkmen SSR, and worked in Baghdad. He calculated tables of sines, tangents, and standard astronomical functions. He found formulas for calculating the positions and orbits of celestial bodies that go beyond the Ptolemaic theory on which they are based.

Habaziniah (hăb″əzĭnī'ə), ancestor of Jaazaniah the Rechabite. Jer. 35.3.

Habbacuc (həbăk'ək), variant of HABAKKUK.

habeas corpus (hā'bēəs kôr'pəs) [Lat.,=you have the body], WRIT directed by a judge to some person who is detaining another, commanding him to bring the body of the person in his custody at a specified time to a specified place for a specified purpose. The writ's sole function is to release from unlawful imprisonment; through this use it has come to be regarded as the great writ of liberty. The writ tests only whether a prisoner has been accorded due process, not whether he is guilty. The most common present-day usage of the writ is to APPEAL state criminal convictions to the Federal courts when the petitioner believes his constitutional rights were violated by state procedure. It is mentioned as early as the 14th cent. in England and was formalized in the Habeas Corpus Act of 1679. The privilege of the use of this writ as a safeguard against illegal imprisonment was highly regarded by the British colonists in America, and wrongful refusals to issue the writ were one of the grievances before the American Revolution. As a result, the Constitution of the United States provides that "The Privilege of the Writ of Habeas Corpus shall not be suspended, unless when in Cases of Rebellion or Invasion the public Safety may require it" (Article 1, Section 9).

Haber, Fritz (hä'bər), 1868–1934, German chemist. He was a professor of physical chemistry at Karlsruhe and became director of the Kaiser Wilhelm Institute at Dahlem in 1911. During World War I he directed Germany's chemical warfare activities, which included the introduction of poison gas; following the Nazi rise to power in 1933, however, he resigned his posts and went into exile in England. Haber won the 1918 Nobel Prize in Chemistry for his discovery of the HABER PROCESS for synthesizing ammonia from its elements. He also did studies of autoxidation and pyrolysis. See biography by M. H. Goran (1967).

Haberle, John (hăb'ərlē″), 1856–1933, American painter, b. New Haven, Conn. Noted for his photographically precise still-life paintings, Haberle is often compared in style with William HARNETT. He is remembered chiefly for his rigorously detailed paintings of paper scraps and money. Haberle's art is a celebration of the ordinary.

Haber process (hä'bər), commercial process for the synthesis of AMMONIA, NH_3. Pure hydrogen and nitrogen gases are mixed in the appropriate proportion, heated to between 450°C and 600°C, compressed to about 1,000 atmospheres pressure, and passed over a catalyst. The reaction is $3H_2+N_2 \rightleftharpoons 2NH_3+\text{heat}$. The ammonia gas is liquefied by rapid cooling; unreacted nitrogen and hydrogen are returned to the reaction chamber. This process, developed by Fritz HABER in 1909, was the first commercially important high-pressure chemical process.

Habersham, James (hă'bərshəm), 1713–75, colonial statesman, acting governor of Georgia (1771–73), b. Beverley, Yorkshire, England. He came to Georgia (1738) and was associated with George WHITEFIELD and the Bethesda Orphanage until he became (1744) a merchant. He favored the introduction of slavery into the colony and played an important role in the colonial politics after Georgia became a royal province. Unlike his son Joseph, he was a strong Loyalist, and he dissolved (1773) the assembly for its radical actions in the unrest preceding the American Revolution.

Habersham, Joseph, 1751–1815, political leader in the American Revolution and U.S. Postmaster General (1795–1801), b. Savannah, Ga.; the son of James Habersham. From the beginning, he was active in the Revolutionary cause and rose to be a colonel in the Continental Army. He also served in the Continental Congress and was a member of the Georgia convention that ratified the Constitution of the United States. After service in the cabinet, he was (1802–15) president of the Georgia branch of the Bank of the United States.

Habima Theater (häbē'mä), the national theater of Israel. Founded in 1917 in Moscow by Nahum Zemach and at first affiliated with the Moscow Art Theatre, it was the first established Hebrew-language theater. Based in Tel-Aviv, the company tours abroad; it has visited the United States twice, in 1926 and in 1948. The troupe is characterized by a passionate acting style. Among its best-known productions are *The Dybbuk, The Golem,* and *Oedipus Rex.* See Raikin Ben-Ari, *Habima* (tr. 1957); Mendel Kohansky, *The Hebrew Theatre* (1969).

Habington, William (hăb'ĭngtən), 1605–54, English poet. His one volume of verse, *Castara* (1634), originally included only love poems to his wife, Lucy (daughter of Sir William Herbert), on the theme of chastity. A later edition (1635) contained some elegies to a friend, and the final edition (1640) included a number of sacred poems. He was also the author of a play, *The Queen of Aragon* (1640). See his poems ed. by Kenneth Allott (1948, repr. 1973).

haboob: see SANDSTORM.

Habor, river: see KHABUR, river.

Habsburg, family: see HAPSBURG.

Habsburg (häps'bo͝orkh), castle, Aargau canton, N Switzerland, near the Aare River. Built c.1030, it served during the 12th and 13th cent. as the seat of the counts of Habsburg or HAPSBURG, whose name derives from the castle [Ger. *Habichtsburg*=hawk's castle].

Habte-Wold, Aklilou (äklē'lo͞o hābtā'wôld), 1912–, Ethiopian government official. He held numerous posts, including those of minister of foreign affairs (1949–57) and prime minister (1961–74). In 1974 he was forced to resign during the civil and military disturbances that accompanied demands for reform.

Hachaliah (hăkəlī'ə), Nehemiah's father. Neh. 1.1; 10.1.

Hachijo-shima (hä"chējō'-shĭmä), island, c.40 sq mi (100 sq km), S Japan, in the Philippine Sea. Ogago is the chief town of this mountainous island, which has two active volcanoes. Dairying, fishing, and weaving are the main occupations.

Hachilah (hăk'īlə), unidentified hill, S Palestine. 1 Sam. 23.19; 26.1,3.

Hachinohe (hächē'nōhä), city (1970 pop. 208,801), Aomori prefecture, N Honshu, Japan, on the Oirase River and the Pacific Ocean. It is a major fishing and commercial port, agricultural market, and industrial and commercial center. The city has important steam power plants and is the center of an iron and sand-mining district.

Hachmoni (hăk'mōnī) or **Hachmonite** (hăk'-mōnīt), name of a family. 1 Chron. 11.11; 27.32. Tachmonite: 2 Sam. 23.8. The passages are obscure.

hackberry: see ELM.

Hackensack, city (1970 pop. 36,008), seat of Bergen co., NE N.J., on the Hackensack River, a residential and industrial suburb of New York City; settled 1647, inc. as a city 1921. Dutch settlers from Manhattan established a trading post there in 1647. During the Revolution the city served as camping grounds for armies of both sides. It grew as a commercial and shipping center in the early 1800s. Although informally called Hackensack (after the Ackenack Indians), it was officially New Barbados until 1921. Of interest are the Church on the Green (First Dutch Reformed; built 1696, rebuilt 1728) and the von Steuben House (1739), a state historic site and the headquarters of the county historical society.

Hackensack, river, c.45 mi (70 km) long, rising in SE N.Y. and flowing S through the Jersey Meadows, NE N.J., to Newark Bay. The lower Hackensack is heavily industrialized (and polluted) and economically tied to the ports on Newark Bay and to the industrial development on the Passaic River. It is navigable by oceangoing vessels to Kearny, N.J., and by tugs and barges to Hackensack, N.J. The river's upper course is unpolluted and dammed to form three reservoirs that supply water to Rockland (N.Y.) and Bergen (N.J.) counties.

Hackett, James Henry, 1800–1871, American actor, b. New York City. After his debut in 1826, he gained fame through his impersonations of peculiarly American character types. However, one of his most successful roles was that of Falstaff, which he performed in London in 1833 and which made him the first prominent American actor to appear on the English stage. Besides acting, he managed theaters and wrote a volume of commentary on Shakespeare (1863). His son, **James Keteltas Hackett,** 1869–1926, b. Wolfe Island, Ont., was also an actor. One of the first matinee idols, he was outstanding in such romantic plays as *The Prisoner of Zenda.*

hackmatack: see LARCH.

Hackney, borough (1971 pop. 216,659) of Greater London, SE England, on the Lea River. The borough was created in 1965 by the merger of the metropolitan boroughs of Hackney, Shoreditch, and Stoke Newington. Clothing manufacture (in Hackney) and printing and furniture making (in Shoreditch) are the borough's chief industries. London's first theater was built in Shoreditch (c.1575). The parish church of St. Mary in Stoke Newington is one of the few remaining Elizabethan churches. The writer Daniel Defoe lived in Stoke Newington. The London College of Furniture, the Shoreditch College for the Clothing Industry, and Cordwainer's Technical College are in the borough. Hackney Marshes, a large sports and recreation area intersected by the Lea, lies just outside the borough.

Haco. For rulers of Norway thus named, see HAAKON.

Hadad (hā'dăd). **1** Son of Ishmael. 1 Chron. 1.30. Hadar: Gen. 25.15. **2** King of Edom. Gen. 36.35; 1 Chron. 1.46. **3** Last king of Edom. 1 Chron. 1.50. Hadar: Gen. 36.39. **4** Scion of the kings of Edom, who escaped Joab's massacre. He fled to Egypt and married the pharaoh's sister-in-law. Later he seems to have relieved Edom from Solomon's oppression. 1 Kings 11.14–25.

Hadad (hā'dăd) or **Adad** (ā'dăd), ancient weather god of Semitic origin, worshiped in Babylonia and Assyria. Important throughout the Middle East, he was worshiped under many names. As god of the storm, he was, according to one legend, responsible for the great flood that overwhelmed the world.

Hadadezer (hădədē'zər), king of Zobah, who led a Syrian coalition against David. The allies were eventually defeated and became tributaries. 2 Sam. 8.3–12; 1 Kings 11.23. Hadarezer: 2 Sam. 10.16,19; 1 Chron. 18.3–10; 19.16,19.

Hadadrimmon (hā"dădrĭm'ən), proper name, occurring in Zech. 12.11. It is usually regarded as a compound of the names of Aramaean and Akkadian gods.

Hadano (hădä'nō), city (1970 pop. 75,226), Kanagawa prefecture, E central Honshu, Japan. An important communications center and agricultural market, the city has textile mills and sake and soy-sauce production plants.

Hadar (hā'där), variant of HADAD **1, 3.**

Hadar or **Beta Centauri,** bright star in the constellation CENTAURUS; 1970 position R.A. 14ʰ01.7ᵐ, Dec. −60°13′. A bluish-white giant of SPECTRAL CLASS B1 II, it has an apparent MAGNITUDE of 0.63, making it one of the 10 brightest stars in the sky. Its distance from the earth is more than 400 light-years. Hadar is a visual BINARY STAR.

Hadarezer (hădərē'zər), variant of HADADEZER.

Hadashah (hăd'əshə, hədā'-), unidentified town, SW Palestine. Joshua 15.37.

Hadassah (hədăs'ə), Hebrew name of ESTHER. Esther 2.7.

Hadassah, women's Zionist organization of the United States founded (1912) by Henrietta Szold. It has done important work in Israel in medical service, child welfare, and aid to refugees. Most of the budget of Youth Aliyah, the organization that transports children and youths to Israel and supports them there, is met by Hadassah. Its principal activities in the United States are educational and charitable work. See study by Marlin Levin (1973).

Hadattah (hədăt'ə), in the Bible: see HAZOR **6.**

Haddington, burgh (1971 pop. 6,505), county town of East Lothian, SE Scotland. It has a large corn exchange. Farm machinery and textiles are manufactured, flour is milled, and grain is malted in the town. There is a trade in hides. Haddington was burned by raiding English armies in 1216, 1244, and 1355. Giffordgate, a suburb, was the birthplace of the Protestant reformer John Knox. Lennoxlove, built for Frances Stuart, mistress of Charles II, is now a seat of the dukes of Hamilton. In 1975, Haddington became part of the new Lothian region.

haddock: see COD.

Haddonfield, borough (1970 pop. 13,118), Camden co., SE N.J., a residential suburb of Camden; settled c.1713, inc. 1875. Of interest is Indian King Tavern (1750), where the first state legislature met in 1777.

Haden, Sir Francis Seymour (hā'dən), 1818–1910, English etcher, writer, and surgeon. He was a successful practicing surgeon in London (1847–87) and founded there a hospital for the treatment of incurable diseases, but is better known as an etcher and an authority on etching. He did much to familiarize the public with Rembrandt's etchings. Haden's own works, for the most part hard-ground etchings and drypoints, are of a very high quality. The best examples of his art are in the New York Public Library; the Albright Art Gallery, Buffalo; the Metropolitan Museum; and the British Museum. He was Whistler's brother-in-law.

Hadera (hədā'rä), town (1972 pop. 31,900), W Israel, on the plain of Sharon, near the Mediterranean Sea. Manufactures include tires, paper, and processed foods. Hadera was founded in 1891 by Jewish settlers, who drained vast malarial swamps and planted groves of citrus fruit and fields of grain. The ruins of CAESAREA PALASTINAE are nearby.

Haderslev (hä'thərslĕv), Ger. *Hadersleben,* city (1970 com. pop. 29,680), Sønderjylland co., S Denmark, a seaport on the Haderslev Fjord, an inlet of the Lille Baelt. It is a commercial and industrial center. Haderslev was held by Prussia from 1864 to 1920. Of note is the Church of St. Mary (13th cent.).

Hades (hā'dēz), in Greek mythology. **1** The ruler of the underworld: see PLUTO. **2** The world of the dead, ruled by Pluto and Persephone, located either underground or in the far west beyond the regions inhabited by man. It was separated from the land of the living by the rivers Styx [hateful], Lethe [forgetfulness], Acheron [woeful], Phlegethon [fiery], and Cocytus [wailing]. The newly arrived dead were ferried across the Styx by the avaricious old ferryman Charon, whom they paid with the coin left in their mouths when they were buried. Unauthorized spirits who tried to enter or leave Hades were challenged by the fearful dog Cerberus. The honey cake that the Greeks buried with the dead was intended to quiet him. All the dead drank of the river of forgetfulness. The judges of the dead—Minos, Aeacus, and Rhadamanthus—assigned to each soul its appropriate abode. The virtuous and the heroic were rewarded in the ELYSIAN FIELDS, while the wrongdoers were sent to TARTARUS.

Hadewijch (hä'dəvĭkh), fl. early 13th cent., Dutch mystical poet, a nun. Her works, beautiful lyrics on the love of God and a number of letters in rhyme and visions in prose, are a monument alike of early Dutch literature and of Roman Catholic mysticism.

Hadhramaut or **Hadramaut** (both: hädrəmout', -môt'), region, S Arabia, on the Gulf of Aden and the Arabian Sea, occupying the eastern part of Southern Yemen. Historically, the name refers to the former Hadhramaut states, a collective term for the Quaiti and Kathiri sultanates. The chief port and city of the region is MUKALLA. The Hadhramaut extends c.400 mi (640 km) from east to west. It consists of a narrow, arid coastal plain, a broad plateau averaging 4,500 ft (1,370 m) high, a region of deeply sunk wadis (watercourses), and an escarpment fronting the desert. The sedentary population, the Hadranis, live in towns built along the wadis and harvest crops of wheat, maize, millet, dates, coconuts, and coffee. On the plateau the Bedouins raise sheep and goats. The Hadhramaut is called HAZARMAVETH in the Bible.

Hadid (hā'dĭd), town, NE of Lydda (Lod), settled by Benjamites after the Exile. Ezra 2.33; Neh. 7.37; 11.34.

Hadlai (hădlā'ī, hăd'lāī, hăd'lā), Ephraimite. 2 Chron. 28.12.

Hadley, Arthur Twining, 1856–1930, American economist and educator, b. New Haven, Conn.; son of James Hadley. A graduate (1876) of Yale, he was on the faculty (1879–99) and later was president (1899–1921) of the university. As president of Yale, Hadley guided the wide expansion and improvement of the university. His *Railroad Transportation* (1885), the first comprehensive treatment of the subject, was long a standard work, and he served on several government commissions dealing with railroad problems. His other works include *Economics: An Account of the Relations between Private Property and Public Welfare* (1896), a strong defense of capitalism; *Undercurrents in American Politics* (1915); and *The Conflict between Liberty and Equality* (1925). See biography by his son Morris Hadley (1948).

Hadley, Henry Kimball, 1871–1937, American composer and conductor, b. Somerville, Mass., studied at the New England Conservatory and in Vienna. He composed and conducted in Europe from 1904 until 1909. Upon his return he became conductor of the Seattle Symphony Orchestra. From 1911 to 1915 he was conductor of the San Francisco Symphony Orchestra. Hadley's compositions, which displayed his facility and craftsmanship, won a number of awards.

Hadley, Herbert Spencer, 1872–1927, American lawyer, b. Olathe, Kansas. As attorney general of Missouri (1905–9), he successfully prosecuted the Standard Oil Company for violating the state antitrust law. He was governor of Missouri from 1909 to 1913 and was a prominent supporter of Theodore Roosevelt. In 1923 he became chancellor of Washington Univ. in St. Louis. He was on the committee of the American Law Institute which prepared the *Code of Criminal Procedure,* a model code published in 1930.

Hadley, John, 1682–1744, English instrument maker. An optician by trade, Hadley built reflecting telescopes, based on Newton's model, that had greater resolution than the cumbersome refractors then in use. In 1731 he built a reflecting octant, based on Newton's sketch, that prefigured the modern nautical sextant. Hadley was a leading member of the Royal Society.

Hadoram (hədō'rəm). **1** The same as JORAM **3. 2** Descendant of Eber. Gen. 10.27; 1 Chron. 1.21. **3** The same as ADONIRAM.

Hadrach (hā'drăk), region, N Syria. Zech. 9.1.

Hadramaut: see HADHRAMAUT.

Hadrian. For popes of that name, see ADRIAN.

Hadrian (hā'drēən) or **Adrian,** A.D. 76–138, Roman emperor (117–138), b. Spain. His name in full was Publius Aelius Hadrianus. An orphan, he became the ward of Trajan. Hadrian distinguished himself as a commander (especially in Dacia) and as an administrator. Nevertheless, Trajan's choice, announced after his death, of Hadrian as his successor, caused some discontent in Rome. Hadrian's reign was vigorous and judicious. He proved his military skill in pacifying (118) Moesia. Abandoning the aggressive policy of Trajan in Asia, he withdrew to the boundary of the Euphrates. In Palestine, however, he proved himself ruthless. His Romanizing policy aroused opposition, especially when he excluded the Jews from Jerusalem. He put down (A.D. 132) the insurrection of Bar Kokba with great severity; the ensuing war (132–135) was the most difficult of his reign. In Rome he was generous in offering circuses and in giving alms to the poor, and he enlarged and reformed the civil service. He traveled extensively in the empire, interesting himself in all the local affairs of state and adorning the provincial cities. In Germany he built great protective walls, and in Britain (where he had visited c.121) he had Hadrian's Wall built. He carried out his plan of building a temple of Jupiter Capitolinus on the site of the ruined Temple at Jerusalem and renamed Jerusalem Colonia Aelia Capitolina. He built the Arch of Hadrian in Athens, and in Rome he rebuilt the Pantheon, added to the Roman Forum, and erected a mausoleum (now Castel Sant'Angelo). His last years were spent more or less quietly in Rome and in his villa at Tibur (which has been excavated), cultivating the arts. He was learned in Greek and was accomplished in poetry and music. He patronized artists, and his regard for the young ANTINOÜS was imperishably recorded by sculptors and architects. As his successor he chose ANTONINUS PIUS. See biographies by Sulamith Ish-Kishor (1935) and S. H. Perowne (1960); B. W. Henderson, *Life and Principate of the Emperor Hadrian* (1923).

Hadrian's Mausoleum or **Hadrian's Mole:** see CASTEL SANT' ANGELO.

Hadrian's Wall, ancient Roman wall, 73.5 mi (118.3 km) long, across the narrow part of the island of Great Britain from Wallsend on the Tyne River to Bowness at the head of Solway Firth. It was mainly built from A.D. c.122 to 126 by Emperor Hadrian and was extended by Emperor Severus a century later. The wall demarcated the northern boundary and defense line of Roman Britain. Fragments of the wall, 6 ft (1.8 m) high and 8 ft (2.4 m) thick, and many of the "mile stations" (stone blockhouses along the wall constructed every Roman mile) remain. The British government has undertaken the preservation of the wall, which is one of the largest and most significant remains of the Roman occupation.

Hadrumetum: see SUSAH, Tunisia.

Haeckel, Ernst Heinrich (ĕrnst hīn'rĭkh hĕ'kəl), 1834–1919, German biologist and philosopher. He taught (1862–1909) at the Univ. of Jena. An early exponent of Darwinism in Germany, he evolved a mechanistic form of MONISM based on his interpretation of Darwin's theories and set forth in his speculative popular works on science, *Generelle Morphologie* (1866), *The History of Creation* (1868, tr. 1906), and *The Evolution of Man* (1874, tr. 1910). Although many of his conclusions have been proved erroneous, they attracted a large following and stimulated research. He developed a theory of RECAPITULATION, illustrated by his gastraea theory, wherein he postulated a hypothetical ancestral form (gastraea) represented by the gastrula stage of individual development. He is known also for his study of invertebrate marine organisms, especially the Radiolaria and sponges.

Haedui: see AEDUI.

haemo-. For words beginning thus, see HEMO-.

Ha-erh-pin: see HARBIN, China.

Hafez, Amin al- (āmēn' äl-hä'fāz), 1911–, Syrian army officer and politician. He served (1963–65) as chief of state in Syria's Ba'athist government but had to flee to Lebanon (1965) after radical Ba'athist military officers, led by Nurreddin Attassi and Hafez al-Assad, toppled his government in a coup d'etat. He moved his exile to Iraq in 1968 and was sentenced to death *in absentia* in 1971.

Hafiz (häfēz') [Arabic,=one who has memorized the Koran], d. 1389?, Persian lyric poet, b. Shiraz. His original name was Shams ad-Din Muhammad. He was a teacher of the Koran and was in close association with dervishes, whom he continually satirized. According to Muslim critics he was a Sufi (see SUFISM), and in this light they interpret his passionate lines as allegorical. Critics of the West incline to construe them literally. His lyrics are always vehement, especially his amatory verses, his drinking songs, and his invective. Hafiz's favorite form is the gazel, in rhyming couplets, comparable to the sonnet. His poetry has appeared as the *Divan*, an anthology published in many hundreds of variations. Hafiz is buried in a splendid tomb near Shiraz.

Hafnarfjörður (häp'närfyör"thür), town (1970 pop. 9,696), SW Iceland, S of Reykjavík. It is a distribution, industrial, and fishing center with an excellent harbor. During the 15th and 16th cent. German and English traders fought over the port. The town was chartered in 1908.

hafnium (hăf'nēəm), metallic chemical element; symbol Hf; at. no. 72; at. wt. 178.49; m.p. about 2150°C; b.p. above 5400°C; sp. gr. 13.31 at 20°C; valence +4. Hafnium is a lustrous, ductile, silvery metal with a hexagonal, close-packed crystalline structure. Its chemical properties are almost identical to those of ZIRCONIUM, the element directly above it in group IVb of the PERIODIC TABLE. The two elements are among the most difficult to separate—zirconium is almost always an impurity in hafnium and affects its physical properties. Finely powdered hafnium can spontaneously ignite in air; because of this reactivity the metal has found use in the manufacture of light bulbs and vacuum tubes as a scavenger for small amounts of oxygen and nitrogen. Hafnium reacts directly with the halogens to form tetrahalides, and when heated it reacts with carbon, boron, sulfur, and silicon. Hafnium carbide is a refractory material with an extremely high melting point. Hafnium metal is produced by the Kroll process, in which a hafnium tetrahalide is reacted with magnesium or sodium metal. Because it is a good neutron absorber, hafnium metal is often used for nuclear reactor control rods. It has been alloyed with several other metals, among them iron and titanium. Hafnium is found widely distributed in nature, usually in association with zirconium minerals such as zircon. The existence of hafnium was suspected for many years before it was demonstrated (1923) through X-ray spectroscopic analysis by Dirk Coster and Georg von Hevesy. They named the element for Hafn, Latin for Copenhagen, the city where they had made the discovery.

Hafrsfjord or **Hafsfjord** (both: häfs'fyôrd), inlet of the North Sea, Rogaland co., SW Norway, near Stavanger. Harold I won (872) a decisive victory there that made him king of all Norway.

Hagab (hā'găb), family that returned from the Exile. Ezra 2.46.

Hagaba or **Hagabah** (both: hăg'əbə), family of Nethinim. Neh. 7.48; Ezra 2.45.

Hagar (hā'gər) or **Agar** (ā'gər), handmaid of Abraham's wife Sarah and mother of his eldest son, Ishmael. She and her son were sent out into the wilderness because of Sarah's jealousy. An angel comforted her there. Gen. 16; 21.9–21. St. Paul uses Hagar as a symbol for the bondage of the Old Law. Gal. 4.24. The Hagarites, Hagrites, or Agarenes were a tribe hostile to Israel and probably had no connection with Hagar. 1 Chron. 5.10; Ps. 83.6; Baruch 3.23.

Hagen, Johannes Georg (yōhä'nəs gā'ôrk hä'gən), 1847–1930, American astronomer and mathematician, b. Austria. A Jesuit, he came in 1880 to the United States to teach. In 1888 he was made director of the astronomical observatory at Georgetown Univ., Washington, D.C., where he remained until 1905. In 1906 he was called to Rome to be at the head of the Vatican Observatory. Much of his research and writing was devoted to the variable stars and to nebulas and cosmic clouds.

Hagen, Walter (hā'gən), 1892–1969, American golfer, b. Rochester, N.Y. Hagen won the U.S. Open championship in 1914 and again in 1919; he took the British Open title in 1922, 1924, 1928, and 1929. "The Haig," as he was known to his admirers, also won the U.S. Professional Golfers Association championship five times (1921, 1924–27), the Australian, Canadian, French, and Belgian open tournaments, and many other titles of lesser importance. He played on five British Ryder Cup teams. See his autobiography (1956).

Hagen (hä'gən), city (1970 pop. 200,909), North Rhine-Westphalia, W West Germany, on the Ennepe River. It is an industrial center in the Ruhr district. Its manufactures include iron and steel, chemicals, machinery, paper, and motor vehicles. Hagen was chartered in 1746 and became famous for its textiles in the late 18th cent. Its main industrial growth dates from 1870.

Hagerstown, city (1970 pop. 35,862), seat of Washington co., NW Md., on Antietam Creek near its junction with the Potomac River, in the fertile Cumberland valley; inc. 1791. A junior college is located there. The Hager house (1743), home of the town's founder, is open to the public. The numerous historic sites in the area include the Antietam National Battlefield Site and Cemetery (see NATIONAL PARKS AND MONUMENTS, table) and Fort Frederick (1756), a fort of the French and Indian Wars era.

Hägerstrom, Axel (äk'səl häg'ərstrôm), 1868–1939, Swedish philosopher. He was a student (1886–93) at Uppsala Univ. and taught there from 1893 until his retirement in 1933. The son of a Lutheran minister, his interests shifted from theology to philosophy soon after he began his studies at Uppsala. Influenced by Kant, he explored the concept of reality in *The Principle of Science* (1908). He was critical of subjectivism and the Austrian school of value theory, holding that all value statements are essentially emotive and lack any truth value. Hägerstrom, with Adolf Phalén, founded the Uppsala school of philosophy, which flourished in the 1920s and 30s, although most members of the school disagreed with much of his work. Near the end of his career Hägerstrom's interest was in practical philosophy, particularly the philosophy of morals, religion, and law.

hagfish, primitive marine fish of the order Cyclostomata, or jawless fishes (see CYCLOSTOME), of worldwide distribution in cold and temperate waters. Its rudimentary skeleton, of cartilage rather than bone, has a braincase, but no jaw. The circular sucking mouth has rows of horny teeth. There is a single median nostril and the eyes are poorly developed. Like the other jawless fishes, the LAMPREYS, hagfish retain the NOTOCHORD, a supporting structure found in higher vertebrates only in the embryo, throughout life. They lack a sympathetic nervous system, a spleen, and scales. Hagfish, or hags, spend much time embedded in muddy bottoms. They are chiefly scavengers, but also parasitize slow-moving fishes, eating their way into the victim's body and leaving only the skin and skeleton. Also known as slime eels, hagfish have glands on either side of their bodies that produce enormous quantities of mucoid material, probably as a defense mechanism. The sexes are separate, although an individual may have rudimentary organs of the opposite sex. Spawning occurs throughout the year; no larval stage is known. There are 3 genera and about 20 species of hagfishes. The Atlantic hagfish, *Myxine glutinosa*, may reach a length of 30 in. (76 cm). The Pacific hagfish, *Eptatretus stouti*, has been extensively used in physiological studies. The hagfish is classified in the phylum CHORDATA, subphylum Vertebrata, class Agnatha, order Cyclostomata, family Myxinidae.

Haggai (hăg'āī) or **Aggeus** (ăgē'əs), book of the Old Testament, 37th in the order of the Authorized Version, 10th of the books of the Minor Prophets. Dated 520–519 B.C., it is a call to the Jews, newly returned from the Babylonian exile, to renew work on the restoration of the Temple. It is addressed to the leader Zerubbabel and the high priest Joshua, saying that the new Temple will be less in material splendor than Solomon's, but its glory will be greater. The book includes a Messianic prophecy (2.7). Haggai is mentioned in the book of Ezra (5.1; 6.14), which gives a narrative account of the rebuilding of the Temple. See study by J. G. Baldwin (1972); see also bibliography under OLD TESTAMENT.

Haggard, Sir Henry Rider, 1856–1925, English novelist. From 1875 to 1881 he served in the government of South Africa, which was the scene of many of his highly popular romances. *King Solomon's Mines* (1885), *Allan Quatermain* (1887), and *She* (1887), all in rough but colorful prose, are among his best-known works. He also wrote a study of colonization in South Africa and works on agricultural problems. He was knighted in 1912 for his welfare work in England. See his autobiography, *The Days of My Life* (1926); biography by his daughter L. R. Haggard (1951).

Haggeri (hăg'ərī, hăgē'rī), father of MIBHAR.

Haggi (hăg'ī), founder of a Gadite family. Gen. 46.16; Num. 26.15.

Haggiah (həgī'ə), Merarite Levite. 1 Chron. 6.30.

Haggith (hăg'ĭth), mother of ADONIJAH **1**.

Hagi (hä'gē), city (1970 pop. 52,541), Yamaguchi prefecture, W Honshu, Japan, on the delta of the Abu River. It is a fishing and commercial port and was a castle town of the Mori clan during the Tokugawa era.

Hagia Sophia (hä'jə sōfē'ə, hä'jēə,) [Gr.,=Holy Wisdom] or **Santa Sophia**, Turkish *Aya Sofia,* originally a Christian church at Constantinople (now İstanbul), later a mosque, but now converted into a museum of Byzantine art. The supreme masterpiece of Byzantine architecture, it stands on the site of an earlier basilican church erected by Constantius II in 360, some 30 years after Byzantium had become the capital of the Roman Empire. This church was burned in 404 and rebuilt by Theodosius II in 415, only to be again destroyed by fire in 532. The present structure, which is entirely fireproof, was built in 532-37 by Emperor Justinian from designs of his imperial architects Anthemius of Tralles and Isidorus of Miletus. As a result of severe earthquakes, the dome collapsed in 558, but it was rebuilt by 563 on a somewhat higher curve. With the Turkish conquest of Constantinople in 1453, Hagia Sophia became a mosque, and in subsequent years all the interior figure mosaics were obscured under coatings of plaster and painted ornament; most of the Christian symbols elsewhere were obliterated. The four slender minarets, which rise so strikingly at the outer corners of the structure, were added singly and at different times; the crescent supplanted the cross on the summit of the dome, and the altar and the pulpit were replaced by the customary Muslim furnishings. The spacious nave is covered by a lofty central dome carried on pendentives, a device not previously employed in monumental construction. Pendentives make possible support of the dome on a square framework of four huge equal arches resting on huge piers. The arches at the east and west are extended and buttressed by great half domes, while the half domes in turn are carried on smaller semidomed exedrae. A vast oblong interior, 102 ft (31 m) by 265 ft (81 m), is thus created from a succession of domical elements that build up to the main dome, 102 ft (31 m) in diameter and 184 ft (56 m) high, in which a corona of 40 arched windows sheds a flood of light on the interior. At the east end of the nave is the vaulted sanctuary apse and at the west end a great narthex or vestibule, beyond which an exonarthex opens to the forecourt, or atrium. Flanking the nave to the north and south are side aisles with galleries over them. Their massive vaults, carried at both levels by monolithic columns of green and white marble and purple porphyry, serve as buttresses to receive the thrust of the great dome and its supporting arches. The vast interior is thus wholly free of suggestion of ponderous load, and its effect is that of a weightless golden shell that seems to possess a miraculous inherent stability. In one structural organism are epitomized the Roman methods of construction, modified and enriched by new aesthetic theories and realized in strikingly colorful materials and ornamental techniques, which although often considered Eastern, are in fact the logical outgrowth of trends already apparent in Roman imperial buildings of the first three centuries A.D. All interior surfaces are sheathed with polychrome marbles and gold mosaic, encrusted upon the brick core of the structure; most of the magnificent figure mosaics have been cleaned and restored to view. Externally, the broad, smooth surfaces of stuccoed walls and the great unconcealed masses of vaults and domes pile up impressively. Hagia Sophia served as model for several of the great Turkish mosques of Constantinople. See H. Kahler, *Hagia Sophia* (tr. 1967).

Hague, Frank, 1876-1956, American politician, mayor of Jersey City, N.J., b. Jersey City. He worked his way up through the ranks of the local Democratic machine and was elected (1913) to the city board of commissioners. As mayor of Jersey City (1917-47), Hague built one of the strongest urban political machines in the nation. After his election to the Democratic National Committee in 1922, he was the most powerful Democrat in the state and a force to be reckoned with at national conventions. Accused of corruption and large-scale intimidation of municipal employees, Hague was a controversial figure. He lost much of his power in the 1949 elections, when his nephew, Frank Hague Eggers, was defeated in the mayoralty race; and in 1952 the state Democratic organization ousted him from his post as national committeeman. See biography by R. J. Connors (1971); study by D. D. McKean (1940, repr. 1967).

Hague, The (hāg), Du. *'s Gravenhage* or *Den Haag,* Fr. *La Haye,* city (1971 pop. 537,643), capital of South Holland prov. and seat of the government of the Kingdom of the Netherlands, W Netherlands, on the North Sea. Although it has some industries (the manufacture of clothing, metal goods, printed materials, and food products), The Hague's economy revolves around government administration, which is centered there rather than in Amsterdam, the capital of the Netherlands. The Hague is the seat of the Dutch legislature, the Dutch supreme court, the International Court of Justice, and foreign embassies. The city is the headquarters of numerous companies, including the Royal Dutch Shell petroleum company. The Hague was (13th cent.) the site of a hunting lodge of the counts of Holland (*'s Gravenhage* means "the count's wood"). In about 1250, William, count of Holland, began the construction of a palace, around which a town grew in the 14th and 15th cent. In 1586 the States-General of the United Provs. of the Netherlands convened in The Hague, which later (17th cent.) became the residence of the stadtholders and the capital of the Dutch republic. In the 17th cent. The Hague rose to be one of the chief diplomatic and intellectual centers of Europe. In the early 19th cent., after Amsterdam had become the constitutional capital of the Netherlands, The Hague received its own charter from Louis Bonaparte. It was (1815-30) the alternative meeting place, with Brussels, of the legislature of the United Netherlands. The Dutch royal residence from 1815 to 1948, the city was greatly expanded and beautified in the mid-19th cent. by King William II. In 1899 the First Hague Conference met there on the initiative of Nicholas II of Russia; ever since, The Hague has been a center for the promotion of international justice and arbitration. Among the numerous landmarks of The Hague is the Binnenhof, which grew out of the 13th-century palace and which now houses both chambers of the legislature; it contains the 13th-century Hall of Knights (Dutch *Ridderzaal*), where many historic meetings have been held. Nearby is the Gevangenenpoort, the 14th-century prison where Jan de Witt and Cornelius de Witt were murdered in 1672. The Mauritshuis, a 17th-century structure built as a private residence for John Maurice of Nassau, is now an art museum and contains several of the greatest works of Rembrandt and Vermeer. The Peace Palace (Dutch *Vredespaleis*), which was financed by Andrew Carnegie and opened in 1913, houses the Permanent Court of Arbitration and, since 1945, the International Court of Justice. Among the other notable buildings are the former royal palace; the Groote Kerk, a Gothic church (15th-16th cent.); the Nieuwe Kerk, containing Spinoza's tomb; and the 16th-century town hall. Educational institutions in The Hague include schools of music and international law. Northwest of the city is SCHEVENINGEN, a popular North Sea resort and a fishing port. William III, king of England (1689-1702), was born in The Hague.

Hague Conferences, term for the International Peace Conference of 1899 (First Hague Conference) and the Second International Peace Conference of 1907 (Second Hague Conference). Both were called by Russia and met at The Hague, the Netherlands. Neither succeeded in the main announced purpose of effecting a reduction in armaments, but a number of declarations and conventions respecting the laws of war were adopted and were later ratified by many states. Ratified prohibitions of aerial bombardment and of the use of submarine mines and poison gas proved ineffective, but more heed was given to conventions respecting the rights of neutral shipping (particularly respecting contraband) and the protection of noncombatants. A substantial achievement was the founding by the First Hague Conference of the Permanent Court of Arbitration, popularly called the Hague Tribunal (see separate article). However, at the second conference the United States failed in its effort to secure the establishment of a world court. A third conference, scheduled for 1916, was canceled because of World War I. In the attempt to formulate certain rules of international law, the Hague Conferences furnished an example for both the League of Nations and the United Nations.

Hague Tribunal, popular name for the Permanent Court of Arbitration established in 1899 by a convention of the First Hague Conference. Its headquarters are at The Hague, the Netherlands. In 1973 there were 71 countries adhering to the convention. Each member nation may appoint to the court up to four jurists versed in international law. A case is initiated when two or more nations sign a compromis, an agreement to submit a dispute to arbitration. The disputants may either select arbitrators from the panel to hear their case or they may have two arbitrators choose an umpire before whom the hearing will be held. Tribunals sit at The Hague unless another place is specified in the compromis. The Hague Tribunal is administered by the International Bureau, which has custody of archives, and by the Administrative Council, which is composed of the diplomatic envoys of member nations accredited to the Netherlands. The tribunal has arbitrated more than 20 international disputes. Important cases were final settlement (1904) of the VENEZUELA CLAIMS and the North Atlantic Coast Fisheries Arbitration (1910) between the United States and Great Britain. After World War I the Hague Tribunal lost most of its importance to the WORLD COURT, which was in 1945 superseded by the INTERNATIONAL COURT OF JUSTICE.

Hahn, Otto (ô'tō hän), 1879-1968, German chemist and physicist. His important contributions in the field of radioactivity include the discovery of several radioactive substances, the development of methods of separating radioactive particles and of studying chemical problems by the use of radioactive indicators, and the formation of artificial radioactive elements by bombarding uranium and thorium with neutrons. He received the 1944 Nobel Prize in Chemistry for splitting the uranium atom (1939) and discovering the possibility of chain reactions. The development of the atomic bomb was based on this work. Hahn was a member of the Kaiser Wilhelm Institute of Chemistry, Berlin, from 1912 and director from 1928 to 1944. He was in Allied custody (1944-46) and on his return to Germany became head of the Kaiser Wilhelm Gesellschaft, Göttingen (later reorganized as the Max Planck Gesellschaft).

Hahn, Reynaldo, 1875-1947, French musician. Hahn was born in Venezuela and was taken to Paris at three. Among his teachers was Massenet. He wrote much incidental music, songs, operettas, and other works. As a conductor he specialized in Mozart operas. In 1945 he became a director of the Paris Opéra.

Hahnemann, Samuel (zä'mo͞oēl hä'nəmän), 1755-1843, German physician, founder of HOMEOPATHY. He expounded his system in *Organon of the Rational Art of Healing* (1810, tr. 1913). He practiced in Leipzig, Köthen, and Paris and despite opposition, gained a large following.

Hai (hä'ī), variant of AI **1.**

Haida Indians (hī'də), North American Indians living on the Queen Charlotte Islands, off British Columbia, and on the southern end of the Prince of Wales Island, off Alaska. They speak the Haida language, which forms a branch of the family of Nadene languages (see AMERICAN INDIAN LANGUAGES). In physical and cultural characteristics they are closely related to the Tlingit and the Tsimshian Indians; the three tribes belong to the Northwest Coast cultural area. Before the advent (early 19th cent.) of white fur traders, the Haida lived in large cedar-plank houses, fished for salmon, and hunted sea mammals; they were noted for their large and well-made dugout canoes. Their society was divided into the Raven and Eagle clans, and their customs featured the conspicuous display of wealth (see POTLATCH). They then numbered some 8,000, but by 1880 disease, particularly smallpox and venereal infections, had reduced them to some 2,000. Today most of the 900 remaining Haida are employed in fishing and in canning. The artwork of the Haida is widely acclaimed. See Charles Harrison, *Ancient Warriors of the North Pacific* (1925); Polly Miller, *Lost Heritage of Alaska* (1967).

Haidar Ali or **Hyder Ali** (both: hī'dər älē'), 1722-82, Indian ruler. A Muslim of peasant stock, he rose by military brilliance to command the army of the Hindu state of Mysore. By 1761 he was virtual ruler of Mysore and began expanding the dominions of that kingdom at the expense of the Mahratta states and Hyderabad. In 1767 the British, in alliance with Hyderabad and the Mahrattas, took the field against Haidar. They were soon deserted by their allies, however, and Haidar, after some initial reverses, took his army to the outskirts of Madras and dictated the peace (1769). Angered by the British refusal to honor a defensive alliance (formed in accordance with the 1769 peace terms) in 1772 and by their seizure of Mahé from the French in 1779, Haidar invaded the Carnatic in 1780 and routed a British force. In 1781 he was defeated near Madras by Sir Eyre Coote. Haidar died a year later, but the war was continued by his son TIPPOO SAHIB. See biography by N. K. Sinha (3d ed. 1959); study by L. B. Bowring (1969).

Haifa (hī'fä), city (1972 pop. 217,400), NW Israel, a port on the Mediterranean Sea, at the foot of Mt. Carmel. Haifa, the chief city of N Israel, is a major industrial center. Along with Ashdod, Haifa is one of Israel's main ports and handles oceangoing vessels, including oil tankers. It is a railroad hub and has an international airport. Haifa is known to have existed by the 3d cent. A.D. but was of little importance during early Muslim times. The Crusaders, who called it Caiffa or Caiphas, developed it commercially. Destroyed by SALADIN in 1191, it began to revive in the late 18th cent. It was captured by Napoleon in 1799. The city's main growth occurred in the 20th cent. with the development of its port. Haifa Univ. and the Technion (Israel Institute of Technology; est. 1924) are there. Haifa is the world center of BAHAISM and the site of the shrine of Bab and a Bahai temple.

Haig, Douglas Haig, 1st **Earl,** 1861–1928, British field marshal. He saw active service in the Sudan (1898) and in the South African War (1899–1902) and upon the outbreak of World War I (1914) was given command of the 1st Army Corps in France. In Dec., 1915, he became commander in chief of the British expeditionary force. Under pressure from the French commander, Joseph Joffre, he undertook the battle of the Somme (July–Nov., 1916), which resulted in very heavy casualties and little territorial gain. The British prime minister, David Lloyd George, constantly antagonistic to Haig and unreceptive to his requests from the field, exacerbated the situation by putting the British troops under the orders of the French commander in 1917. Haig thus conducted the Passchendaele campaign (July–Nov., 1917; see YPRES, BATTLES OF) under orders from Gen. Robert Nivelle, while the French army was being reorganized after a mutiny. Haig was under continual French pressure to take over more of the front, and until the joint command of himself and Gen. Ferdinand Foch was instituted (1918), the strategy and conduct of the war were tragically mismanaged. Haig has been much criticized for the staggering casualties sustained. He was made an earl (1919) and devoted the remainder of his life to organizing the British Legion and raising funds for disabled ex-servicemen. See his private papers, ed. by Robert Blake (1952); biography by Duff Cooper (2 vol., 1935–36); study by Sir James Marshall-Cornwall (1973); G. S. Duncan, *Douglas Haig as I Knew Him* (1967).

Hai-k'ou (hī-kō) or **Hoihow** (hoi'hou'), city (1970 est. pop. 500,000), Hainan island, Kwangtung prov., China. A seaport on Hainan Strait, it is the largest city on the island and an industrial center, with food-processing establishments, cement plants, machine shops, and a large integrated steel complex. Hai-k'ou has an airport.

haiku (hī'ko͞o), an unrhymed Japanese poem recording the essence of a moment keenly perceived, in which nature is linked to human nature. It usually consists of 17 *jion* (Japanese symbol-sounds). The term is also used for foreign adaptations of the haiku, notably the poems of the IMAGISTS. These poems are usually written in three lines of five, seven, and five syllables. See SENRYU. See the anthology ed. by H. G. Henderson, *Introduction to Haiku* (1958).

Hail (hä'ēl, hīl), city (1960 est. pop. 20,000), N central Saudi Arabia, in an oasis. It was the capital of the independent emirate of Jabal Shammar, which Ibn Saud conquered in 1921.

hail, precipitation in the form of pellets composed of ice or of ice and snow, occurring at any time of the year, usually during the passage of a cold front or during a thunderstorm. Small hailstones have a soft center and a single outer coat of ice. They are formed when the surfaces of snow clumps melt and refreeze or become coated with water droplets that subsequently freeze. Large hailstones usually have alternate hard and soft layers. There are various explanations of how these large stones form and grow. Some believe that they form in clouds when supercooled raindrops, i.e., ones chilled below the freezing temperature without solidifying, freeze on dust particles or snowflakes. These tiny hailstones are then blown repeatedly up and down by the winds in a cloud. Each time they are blown downward to a region whose temperature is above freezing, the stones collect more moisture, and each time they are blown upward to a region below freezing, the moisture solidifies into ice, and some snow may collect. The stones continue to grow, adding layer after layer, until they are too heavy to be supported by the winds and fall to the ground. In another explanation, it is suggested that hailstones continuously descend, gaining layers by passing through regions of the air that contain different amounts of water. Hailstones are spherical or irregularly spherical and usually vary in diameter up to ½ in. (1.3 cm); in rare cases hailstones having diameters up to 5 in. (12.7 cm) have been observed. Hail causes much damage and injury to crops, livestock, property, and airplanes. See SLEET.

Hai-la-ehr: see HAILAR, China.

Hailar (hī'lär'), Mandarin *Hai-la-erh*, city, NW Heilungkiang prov., China, on the Hailar (Argun) River. It is an agricultural production center on the Chinese Eastern RR. Formerly known as Hulun, Hailar consists of an old and a new city—the old section, founded in 1734 as a fort, is typically Chinese; the new section is a modern, industrial quarter. Before boundary changes (1969–70), Hailar was in Inner Mongolian Autonomous Region.

Haile Selassie (hī'lē səläs'ē, -lä'sē), [Amharic,= power of the Trinity], 1891–, emperor of Ethiopia. He was born Tafari Makonnen, the son of a noted general and the grandnephew of Emperor Menelik II. A brilliant student, he became a favorite of Menelik, who made him a provincial governor at 14. As a Coptic Christian, Tafari opposed Menelik's grandson and successor, who became a Muslim convert, and in 1916 compelled his deposition and established Menelik's daughter Zauditu as empress with himself as regent. In 1928, Tafari was crowned king of Ethiopia, and in 1930, after the empress's mysterious death, he became emperor as Haile Selassie, supposedly the 111th descendant of King Solomon and the Queen of Sheba to rule. He attempted internal reforms and took great pride in the suppression of slavery. When Italy invaded Ethiopia in 1935, he personally led defending troops in the field, but in 1936 he was forced to flee to British protection. Twice (1936, 1938) he vainly appealed to the League of Nations for effective action against Italy. In 1940, after Italy entered World War II, he returned to Africa with British aid, and in 1941 he reentered Ethiopia and regained his throne. In the postwar period he instituted social and political reforms, such as establishing (1955) a national assembly. In the 1960s and 70s he worked for pan-African aims, particularly through the Organization of African Unity. In 1960 a revolt by a group of young intellectuals and army officers, who demanded an end to oppression and poverty, was crushed. In 1974, however, the army was successful in seizing control. Haile Selassie was progressively stripped of his powers and finally, on Sept. 12, 1974, deposed. See H. M. Hanson and D. Hanson, *For God and Emperor* (1958); Leonard Mosley, *Haile Selassie: The Conquering Lion* (1965); Peter Schwab, ed., *Ethiopia and Haile Selassie* (1972).

Hailsham, Quintin McGarel Hogg, Baron, 1907–, British politician. He was (1938–50) a Conservative member of Parliament for Oxford. In 1950 he succeeded his father as Viscount Hailsham and sat in the House of Lords, but in 1963 he renounced the title for his lifetime and returned to the House of Commons, where he served until 1970. He was first lord of the admiralty (1956–57), deputy party leader and then leader in the House of Lords (1957–60 and 1960–63), lord president of the council (1957–59 and 1960–64), and minister for science and technology (1959–64). Given a life peerage in 1970, he held (1970–74) the post of lord chancellor. Lord Hailsham has written widely, including *The Purpose of Parliament* (1946) and *Science and Politics* (1963).

Hainan or **Hai-nan** (hī'nän'), island (1953 pop. 2,800,000), in the South China Sea; administratively part of Kwangtung prov., China. The second largest island off the China coast (Taiwan is the largest), Hainan is separated from the mainland (Liu-chou Peninsula) by Hainan Strait (c.30 mi/50 km wide). HAI-K'OU is its largest city and major port. The year-round growing season and monsoon climate favor the cultivation of coffee, rubber, tea, coconuts, sugarcane, and tropical fruit; the island is fast becoming the country's largest rubber plantation. The mountainous interior is thickly forested, yielding tropical hardwoods. Hainan is rich in minerals, notably high-grade iron and tungsten, but also tin, copper, manganese, lead, silver, coal, graphite, antimony, and crystal. The many aboriginal Li, who inhabit the forested interior, have been constituted with the Miao into a large Li-Miao autonomous district. Under Chinese control since the 1st cent. A.D., Hainan was not fully incorporated into China until the 13th cent. It became part of Kwangtung in the late 14th cent. In World War II it was occupied (1939) by the Japanese, who developed the industries and exploited the great iron-ore deposits. The island was liberated (1945) by the Nationalists. The Chinese Communists landed in April, 1949, and, with the aid of Communist guerrillas from the mountains, gained control in 1950. The Yülin naval base, a natural harbor developed by the Japanese, has been expanded under the Communist government.

Hainaut (ĕnō'), Flemish *Henegouwen*, province (1970 pop. 1,317,453), 1,437 sq mi (3,722 sq km), S Belgium, bordering on France in the south. The chief cities of the predominately French-speaking province are MONS, the capital; CHARLEROI; and TOURNAI. It is low-lying, except in the southeast, and has considerable productive farmland where primarily wheat, sugar beets, and dairy cattle are raised. Coal is mined in the BORINAGE region. Manufactures of Hainaut include glass, ceramics, chemicals, electrical equipment, processed food, and cement. The province is drained by the Scheldt, Dender, and Sambre rivers and is served by a dense rail network and the Charleroi-Brussels Canal. The county of Hainaut was created in the late 9th cent., and in the divisions of the Carolingian empire became a fief of Lotharingia. Count Reginar Long-Neck made himself master (late 9th–early 10th cent.) of the duchy of Lower Lorraine, which continued under his elder son (see LOTHARINGIA) while his younger son inherited Hainaut. The widow of Reginar V, the last count of Hainaut, married (1036) Count Baldwin V of FLANDERS, but at his death (1070) Hainaut and Flanders were again separated. In 1191, Flanders once more passed, through marriage, to the counts of Hainaut. Baldwin VI of Hainaut (as Baldwin IX, count of Flanders) took part in the Fourth Crusade and became (1204) emperor of Constantinople as BALDWIN I. After Baldwin's death the two counties were united, but in 1278 they were again separated. In 1433, Philip the Good of Burgundy added Hainaut and Holland to his dominions after overcoming the resistance of his cousin, Countess Jacqueline. Hainaut remained under the house of Burgundy until the death (1482) of MARY OF BURGUNDY, when its history became that of the Austrian Netherlands (see NETHERLANDS, AUSTRIAN AND SPANISH). By the treaties of the Pyrenees (1659) and of Nijmegen (1678) parts of Hainaut, including the city of Valenciennes, were permanently annexed by France; they form part of the present NORD dept. Hainaut is sometimes spelled Hainault.

Hainisch, Michael (mĭ'khäĕl hī'nĭsh), 1858–1940, president of Austria (1920–28). He was a leading agriculturist and a noted writer. Politically acceptable to all major parties, he was elected first president of the new republic in 1920 and was reelected in 1924. He was (1929–30) minister of commerce and transportation in the Schober cabinet. Throughout his political career Hainisch strongly favored a union of Austria and Germany.

Haiphong (hī'fŏng'), city (1960 pop. 182,496), NE North Vietnam, on a large branch of the Red River delta c.10 mi (20 km) from the Gulf of Tonkin. It is connected with the sea by a narrow access channel that requires continual dredging. The major port of North Vietnam and one of the largest ports in SE Asia, Haiphong was developed (1874) by the French and became the chief naval base of French Indochina. A shipbuilding industry and cement, glass, porcelain, and textile works were established by the French. At the beginning of the French-Indochina War (Nov., 1946), French naval vessels shelled the city, killing c.6,000 Vietnamese. After the French departed and the new state of North Vietnam was created (1954), the silted-up harbor was reconstructed with Chinese and Soviet aid and the docks and shipbuilding yards were repaired and modernized. The old French cement plant was enlarged, and fish-canning, chemical-fertilizer, machine-tool, and additional textile industries were established. During the VIETNAM WAR, Haiphong was severely bombed from 1965 to 1968 and again from April to Dec., 1972; the shipyards and the industrial section of the city were devastated, rail connections with Hanoi were disrupted, and thousands of homes were destroyed. The harbor was mined by U.S. naval planes in May, 1972, and effectively sealed until the mines were swept by U.S. forces after the cease-fire agreement in early 1973. Reconstruction, while slow, has been aided by the fact that many of the factories were dismantled during the bombings and relocated in rural areas; when returned to Haiphong, much of the machinery was able to function in ruined structures. Haiphong is a special municipality administered directly by the central government. About 10% of its inhabitants are Chinese.

hair, slender threadlike outgrowth from the skin of mammals. In some animals hair grows in dense profusion and is called FUR or WOOL. Although all mammals show some indication of hair formation, dense hair is more common among species located in colder climates and has the obvious function of insulation against the cold. Other functions include camouflage and protection against dust and sand. The long, sensitive hairs, called tactile hairs, that are located around the mouth area of most mammals are extremely sensitive to touch. Each hair filament originates in a deep pouchlike depression of the epidermis, called a hair follicle, which penetrates into the dermis. The root of the hair extends down into the hair follicle and widens into an indented bulb at its base. Extending into the indentation is the papilla, the center of hair growth, which contains the capillaries and nerves that supply the hair. Newly dividing cells at the base of the hair multiply, forcing the cells above them upward. As the cells move upward, they gradually die and harden into the hair shaft. The hair shaft has two layers, the cuticle and the cortex. The cuticle (outer layer) consists of flat, colorless overlapping cells; below the cuticle is the cortex, containing pigment and a tough protein called keratin; it forms the bulk of the hair shaft. Coarse hair, such as that of the scalp, contains

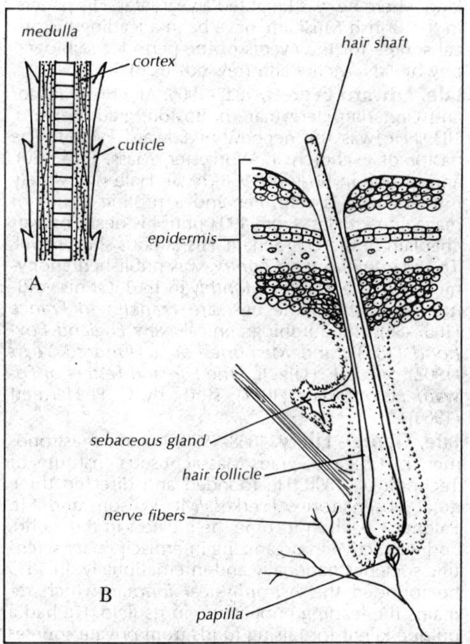

A. *Cross section of a hair shaft*
B. *General structure of a hair*

an additional inner core called the medulla. Hair is lubricated by SEBACEOUS GLANDS that are located in the hair follicle. Illness or stress may lessen the secretion of pigment, which normally gives color to hair, and cause the hair shaft to whiten. However, the normal process of whitening that comes with age is determined by heredity. In humans, scalp hairs are generally shed every two to four years, while body hairs are shed more frequently. Straight-textured hair, round in cross section, is common among American Indians, Eskimos, and Mongoloid peoples. Kinky or woolly hair, flat in cross section, prevails among the dark peoples of Africa, Australia, and elsewhere. Wavy or curly hair, common among Caucasians, is oval in cross section. The color of hair is determined by the amount of pigment and air spaces in the cortex and medulla. Hair color and texture are inherited characteristics.

hairdressing, arranging of the hair for decorative, ceremonial, or symbolic reasons. Primitive men plastered their hair with clay and tied trophies and badges into it to represent their feats and qualities. Among women, a band to keep the hair from the eyes was the forerunner of the fillet. Much early hairdressing is traditional, as in the feather tufts or stiffened coronet of some primitive peoples, the queue of the Chinese, the tonsure of ecclesiastics, the flowing locks of the maid, and the bound or cut tresses of the wife. From ancient times hair has been dyed, bleached, curled, braided, waxed and oiled, hennaed, powdered, perfumed, cut, shaved, enhanced with false hair, covered with a WIG, concealed by nets and veils, or adorned with beads, jewels, pins, combs, feathers, ribbons, and flowers, natural and artificial. In the world of fashion, hairdressing developed as an art during the Middle Ages, when an appropriate coiffure became as important as the proper costume. Since that time, styles, especially for women, have been created and re-created, from long to short, from the high pompadour or use of chignons to the close bob, in a repetitive cycle. In the 1960s hair styles for men in the United States and Western Europe changed dramatically from short fashions, popular since the late 18th cent., to varying degrees and styles of long hair, often accompanied by beards, moustaches, and long sideburns. Hairdressers, especially those employed by motion picture companies, have become personally renowned for the styles they create.

hairfly: see GNAT.

hairworm, worm of the class Nematomorpha in the phylum ASCHELMINTHES.

Haiti (hā'tē), Fr. *Haïti* (äētē'), independent republic (1971 pop. 4,314,628), 10,700 sq mi (27,713 sq km), West Indies, on the western third of the island of Hispaniola. It is bounded on the N by the Atlantic Ocean, on the S by the Caribbean Sea, and on the E by the Dominican Republic. Jamaica lies to the west and Cuba to the northwest. The capital is PORT-AU-PRINCE; other important cities are CAP-HAÏTIEN and GONAÏVES. The offshore islands of Tortuga and Gonâve also belong to Haiti. Agriculture is the principal economic activity in Haiti. The country is mostly mountainous, but about one third of the land is arable. Subsistence crops include cassava, rice, sugarcane, sorghum, yams, corn, and plantains. Most Haitians own and farm tiny plots of land, and great population density has caused rural poverty. Haiti's major export is coffee; other exports include cotton, sugar, sisal, bauxite, and essences. Spiny lobsters constitute an important share of Haitian exports to the United States, the country's leading trading partner. Industry in Haiti consists largely of light manufacturing; products include foodstuffs, liquors, essential oils, leather goods, soap, and footwear. Some bauxite and copper are mined but other mineral deposits have barely been tapped. Haiti is the most densely populated country in Latin America and has the lowest per capita income. About 95% of the inhabitants are blacks (the descendants of African slaves) who still follow West African cultural patterns. Since the mid-19th cent., however, Haiti has been dominated by the mulatto minority, which clings to the French cultural tradition; Haiti is the only French-speaking republic in the hemisphere, although most of the people speak a dialect called Creole. Only about 2,000 whites, mainly foreigners, live in Haiti. Roman Catholicism is the predominant religion, but African nature gods are still worshipped and *vodun* (voodoo) rites are practiced. Economic hardship and dictatorial government have caused numerous Haitians to emigrate, especially to the United States. The island of Hispaniola was discovered and named by Columbus in 1492. Disease and ill treatment by the Spaniards decimated the native Arawak Indians, who gave Haiti ("land of mountains") its name. While establishing plantations in E Hispaniola (now the Dominican Republic), however, the Spanish largely ignored the western part of the island, which by the 17th cent. became a base for French and English buccaneers. Gradually French colonists, importing African slaves, developed sugar plantations on the northern coast. Unable to support its claim to the region, Spain ceded Haiti (then called Saint-Domingue) to France in 1697. It became France's most prosperous colony in the Americas and one of the world's chief coffee and sugar producers. The pattern of settlement took the French south in the 18th cent. and society became stratified into Frenchmen, Creoles, freed blacks, and black slaves. Between the blacks and whites were the mulattoes, who aspired to the privileges of the whites and who feared the blacks. Politically and socially, Haiti was a tinderbox; the spark was the French Revolution. When French-descended Creole planters sought to prevent mulatto representation in the French National Assembly and in local assemblies in Saint-Domingue, the mulattoes revolted under the leadership of Vincent OGÉ. This rebellion destroyed the entire structure of Haitian society. The blacks formed guerrilla bands led by TOUSSAINT L'OUVERTURE, a former slave who had been made an officer of the French forces on Hispaniola. When the English invaded Haiti in 1793 during the Napoleonic Wars, Toussaint maintained an uneasy alliance with the mulatto André RIGAUD and cooperated with the remnant of French governmental authority. In 1795, Spain ceded its part of the island to France, and in 1801 Toussaint conquered it, abolished slavery, and proclaimed himself governor general of an autonomous government over all Hispaniola. Napoleon sent his brother-in-law, Gen. Charles LECLERC, with a huge punitive force to restore order in 1802, but he was unable to conquer the interior. A peace was patched up, and Toussaint, taken by trickery, died in a French prison; but the revolt continued and forced the French troops, already ravaged by yellow fever, to withdraw. The rebels received unexpected aid from U.S. President Thomas Jefferson, who feared that Napoleon would use Saint-Domingue as a base to invade Louisiana. In 1804, Haiti became the second nation in the Western Hemisphere, after the United States, to win complete independence. The remaining whites were expelled, and Jean-Jacques DESSALINES, an ex-slave, proclaimed himself emperor. His assassination (1806) led to the division of Haiti into a black-controlled north under Emperor Henri CHRISTOPHE and a mulatto-ruled south under President Alexandre PÉTION. After their deaths Haiti was unified by Jean Pierrre BOYER, who also brought (1822–44) Santo Domingo under Haitian control. Seeking to indemnify French planters, Boyer brought financial ruin to Haiti; he was exiled in 1843. Haiti's last emperor (1847–59) was Faustin SOULOUQUE. Since the end of his reign, the country has been a republic. Anarchy persisted, intensified by the mulatto-Negro

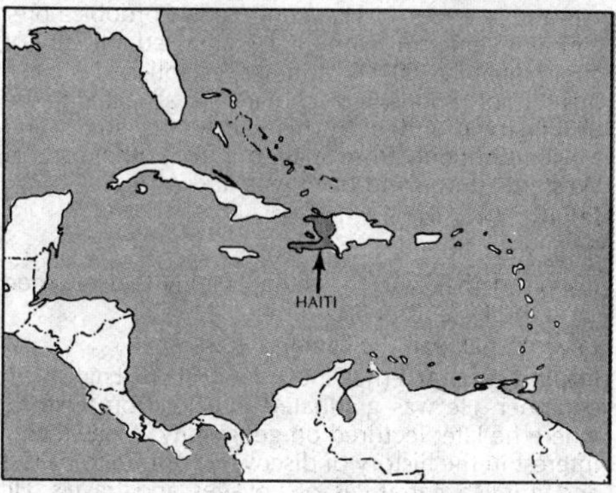

hostility, and Haiti's economy, which had never recovered from the violent independent struggle, declined further. Heavy international indebtedness invited foreign intervention. After the dictator Guillaume Sam was killed by a mob in 1915, the United States, troubled over its property and investments in the country and fearing Germany might seize Haiti, took the opportunity to land marines in Port-au-Prince. The Haitian congress was forced to accept an agreement permitting U.S control over customs receipts; two years later the resident American naval commander dissolved the congress and dictated a new constitution. Although financial and general material progress advanced under American control, Haiti protested against U.S. violation of its sovereignty, and a U.S. Senate investigation in 1921 found that the avowed purpose of preparing Haiti for responsible self-government had been ignored. In 1930 a U.S. presidential commission recommended that Haiti be allowed to elect a legislature that would, in turn, name a president. Sténio Vincent, a vocal opponent of U.S. military occupation, was chosen by the legislators. The marines were finally withdrawn in 1934, although U.S fiscal control was maintained until 1947. Political instability persisted in Haiti after World War II, and the country's future was clouded by rising turbulence in the Dominican Republic and by the emergence of a Communist Cuba. François ("Papa Doc") DUVALIER, who was elected president in 1957, used voodoo as an instrument of control over the masses and instilled fear through his paramilitary secret police, the *tonton macoutes.* In 1964 he proclaimed himself president for life. Upon his death in 1971 he was succeeded by his 19-year-old son, Jean-Claude, who also became president for life. The new regime disbanded the *tonton macoutes* and embarked upon economic reforms. Tourism and foreign investment were encouraged and Haitian exiles were urged to return. Besides the president, Haiti's government consists of a unicameral legislature, which is elected by direct popular vote for a six-year term. The country has one official political party and several unofficial opposition groups, some operating abroad. See Harold Courlander and Rémy Bastien, *Religion and Politics in Haiti* (1966); R. W. Logan, *Haiti and the Dominican Republic* (1968); Bernard Diederich and Al Burt, *Papa Doc: The Truth about Haiti Today* (1969); Katherine Dunham, *Island Possessed* (1969); R. I. Rotberg and C. K. Clague, *Haiti, The Politics of Squalor* (1971); Hans Schmidt, *The United States Occupation of Haiti, 1915–1934* (1971); O. E. Moore, *Haiti: Its Stagnant Society and Shackled Economy* (1972); T. O. Ott, *The Haitian Revolution, 1789–1804* (1973).

Hajduki Wielkie: see CHORZÓW, Poland.

Hajj Omar (häj ō'mär), 1797–1864, Muslim religious and military leader in W Africa. A chieftain of the large Tukulor tribe of Senegal, he desired to convert the pagan tribesmen of the W Sudan. Declaring a holy war in 1852, he used modern weapons against the pagan Africans. In several engagements (1857–59) against the French in Senegal, he was repulsed. Thereafter he turned eastward, conquering the kingdoms of Segu and Massina and sacking Timbuktu. He was killed in 1864 while attempting to put down a revolt by the Fulanis, a Muslim group living in Massina. Bitter quarrels over his domain by his sons weakened it, and in 1890 it was annexed by the French.

Hakam II, al- (äl-häkäm'), 914–76, Umayyad caliph of Córdoba (961–76), son and successor of Abd ar-Rahman III. In the early part of his reign he successfully waged war against the Christian kings, Sancho I of León and Castile and García of Navarre. His naval forces defeated Norman sea raiders and seized (976) Tangier from the Idrisids, thereby annexing Morocco to Moorish Spain. A scholar and patron of the arts and sciences, al-Hakam II made Córdoba a preeminent center of learning. He amassed a library of approximately 400,000 volumes, established numerous schools, sponsored scholars and attracted to the university founded by his father Christians and Muslims not only from Spain but from other parts of Western Europe and from Asia and Africa.

Hakata: see FUKUOKA, Japan.

hake: see COD.

Hakkatan (hăk'ətăn, hăkā'tăn), family that returned from the Exile. Ezra 8.12.

Hakkoz (hăk'ŏz), the same as KOZ.

Hakluyt, Richard (hăk'lo͞ot), 1552?–1616, English geographer. He was graduated in 1574 from Oxford, where he later lectured on geography. A passionate interest in the history of discovery led him to collect and publish narratives of voyages and travels. He was active in promoting English discovery and colonization, especially in North America, and was a member of the London Virginia Company. His chief work, called by J. A. Froude "the prose epic of the English nation," is *The Principal Navigations, Voyages, Traffics, and Discoveries of the English Nation* (3 vol., 1598–1600), an enlargement of a one-volume version (1589). Other publications include *Divers Voyages touching the Discovery of America and the Islands Adjacent* (1582) and an account of the discoveries of Hernando De Soto under the title *Virginia Richly Valued* (1609). Manuscripts left at his death were included by Samuel Purchas in his *Pilgrims* (4 folios, 1625); others are preserved at the Bodleian Library, Oxford. The publication of narratives of early explorations has been continued by the Hakluyt Society, founded in 1846. See *The Original Writings and Correspondence of the Two Richard Hakluyts* (1935, repr. 1967); G. B. Parks, *Richard Hakluyt and the English Voyages* (2d ed. 1961); Hakluyt Society, *Richard Hakluyt and His Successors* (1946, repr. 1967).

Hakodate (häkō'dä'tā), city (1970 pop. 241,663), extreme SW Hokkaido, Japan, on the Tsugaru Strait. Opened (1854) to U.S. ships and a little later (1857) to general foreign trade, it is today the chief port of the island. A commercial and industrial center, the city has ironworks, shipyards, and an extensive fishing industry. Of interest is the Goryokaku, the fort where the Tokugawa shogun made his last stand.

Hakon. For rulers of Norway thus named, see HAAKON.

Hakone (hä"kō'nā), resort region, Kanagawa prefecture, central Honshu, Japan. Famous for its mountains, lakes, and hot springs, it is included in Fuji-Hakone-Izu National Park, of which the central feature is Fujiyama. The Hakone Shrine (built 757), a major shrine of central Japan, is one of the many religious monuments that dot the area.

Hakupha (hăkyo͞o'fə), family that returned from the Exile. Ezra 2.51; Neh. 7.53.

Hal: see HALLE, Belgium.

halacha: see HALAKAH.

Halah (hā'lə), unidentified region or city of Assyria, N Mesopotamia, to which Israelites were deported. 2 Kings 17.6; 18.11; 1 Chron. 5.26.

halakah or **halacha** (both: hälä'khä, häläkhä') [Heb.,=law], the legal portion of the Talmud and of post-Talmudic literature concerned with personal, communal, and international activities, as well as with religious observance. Halakah is the term used to designate both a particular ordinance and the law in the abstract. The adjective halakic means "of a legal nature," e.g., halakic Midrash. The plural, halakoth, designates a collection of laws. Halakah usually refers to the Oral Law as codified in the MISHNA, and in particular to those statements of law that appear in categorical form without immediate regard for scriptural derivation. Halakah is contrasted with aggada (plural aggadoth), the literary, aesthetic element in the Oral Law and in the Talmud and MIDRASH generally, which elaborates scriptural meaning through legends, tales, parables and allegories. Both the halakic and aggadic elements have been extracted and made the subject of commentary.

Halberstadt (häl'bərshtät), city (1970 pop. 46,774), Magdeburg district, W East Germany. It is an industrial center and rail junction. Manufactures include textiles, paper, processed food, and machinery. Halberstadt was made an episcopal see in 814. It was burned (1179) by Henry the Lion; after Henry's fall (1180) the bishopric of Halberstadt was given in temporal fief to the bishops by Emperor Frederick I. The city became (13th–14th cent.) a flourishing trade center. In 1648 it was annexed by Brandenburg. Halberstadt was severely damaged in World War II. Noteworthy buildings include the Cathedral of St. Stephen (13th–17th cent.) and the Liebfrauenkirche, a 12th-century church.

Halcyone (hălsī'ənē) or **Alcyone** (ăl-), in Greek mythology, daughter of Aeolus and wife of Ceyx. When her husband drowned, Halcyone in despair threw herself into the sea. Out of pity the gods changed the pair into kingfishers or halcyons, and Zeus forbade the winds to blow seven days before and after the winter solstice, the breeding season of the halcyon. The expression "halcyon days" comes from this myth and figuratively means a time of peace and tranquility. Another legend says that they were changed to birds as punishment for calling themselves Zeus and Hera.

Haldane, John Scott, 1860–1936, British scientist, b. Edinburgh. He made many important contributions to mine safety, investigating principally the action of gases, the use of rescue equipment, and the incidence of pulmonary disease. He devised a decompression apparatus for the safe ascent of deep-sea divers, and in 1905 he discovered that regulation of breathing is determined by the effect of the amount of carbon dioxide in the blood on the respiratory center of the brain. He studied barometric pressure on an expedition to Pikes Peak, Colo., in 1911. He founded the *Journal of Hygiene*, and his published works include *Organism and Environment* (1917), *New Physiology* (1919), *Respiration* (1922), *The Sciences and Philosophy* (1929), and *The Philosophy of a Biologist* (1936). His son, **John Burdon Sanderson Haldane,** 1892–1964, is known for his work as a geneticist, for the application of mathematics to biology, and for his graphic expositions of science for the layman. His publications are numerous, including (with John S. Huxley) *Animal Biology* (1927). See biography by R. W. Clark (1969); study ed. by K. R. Dronamraju (1968).

Haldane of Cloan, Richard Burdon Haldane, Viscount, 1856–1928, British statesman. He entered (1885) the House of Commons as a Liberal. As war secretary (1905–12) he effected drastic army reforms, creating a British expeditionary force, an imperial general staff, an officers training corps, and the territorial army. On a diplomatic mission to Germany (1912), he rejected a proposal of British neutrality in any war into which Germany might be drawn. His tenure of office as lord chancellor (1912–15) ended after the outbreak of World War I, when popular clamor mistakenly attacked him as pro-German. In Ramsay MacDonald's first short Labour ministry (1924) he was again lord chancellor. He was first chancellor of the Univ. of Bristol and was elected lord rector of Edinburgh. He wrote a number of philosophical works, including *Pathway to Reality* (1903), *Reign of Relativity* (1921), *The Philosophy of Humanism* (1922), and *Selected Addresses and Essays* (1928, repr. 1970). He also wrote an autobiography (1929). See biographies by Dudley Sommer (1960) and Sir F. B. Maurice (2 vol., 1937–39, repr. 1970); study by S. E. Koss (1969).

Halden (häl'dən), town (1970 pop. 26,687), Østfold co., SE Norway, a port on the Iddefjord (an arm of the Skagerrak), near the Swedish border. Manufactures include forest products, footwear, and textiles. The first atomic reactor plant in Scandinavia was built there to furnish power for industry. The town was chartered in 1665 and developed around Fredrikssten Fortress, which three times (1716, 1718, 1814) withstood Swedish attacks. Charles XII fell before its walls in 1718. From 1665 to 1928 Halden was known as Frederikshald or Fredrikshald.

Haldimand, Sir Frederick (hôl'dĭmənd), 1718–91, British general and colonial governor of Quebec, b. Neuchâtel canton, Switzerland. A soldier of fortune in several European armies before joining (1756) the British forces, he commanded a battalion in America in the last of the French and Indian Wars. Later he was military governor (1762–66) of Trois Rivières dist. in Quebec; commander in chief (1767–73) in Florida, which then extended to the Mississippi River; and commander in chief of North America (1773–74) during Thomas Gage's absence in England. His patience with the colonists during the time of the Boston Tea Party helped to prevent hostilities. Recalled to England at the opening of the American Revolution because it was considered best to have a person of English birth in chief command, he was sent (1778) to Quebec to replace Guy CARLETON as governor. There, aided by his native knowledge of French, he succeeded in keeping the loyalty of the French Canadians when France was aiding the Americans. He efficiently organized the defenses of the province, inaugurated a system of canals, and provided admirably for the Loyalist refugees from the revolting colonies. In 1784 he returned to England where he was knighted a year later. His papers, in the British Museum, have been a leading historical source for the events of the period. See biography by J. N. McIlwraith (rev. ed. 1926).

Hale, Edward Everett, 1822–1909, American author and Unitarian clergyman, b. Boston, grad. Harvard, 1839. He was the nephew of Edward Everett. The pastor of a church in Worcester, Mass. (1842–56), and of one in Boston (1856–1903), Hale was widely influential as a reformer and a prolific writer of magazine articles. From 1903 until his death he was chaplain of the U.S. Senate. His famous short novel, *The Man without a Country*, was published anonymously in the *Atlantic Monthly* in 1863. Of his voluminous writings the best are *Franklin in France* (1887–88), the autobiographical *New England Boyhood* (1893), and *Memories of a Hundred Years* (1902). See E. E. Hale, Jr., *The Life and Letters of Edward Everett Hale* (1917); study by C. P. Hartnett (1966).

Hale, George Ellery, 1868–1938, American astronomer, b. Chicago, grad. Massachusetts Institute of Technology, 1890. He founded and directed three great observatories (Yerkes, Mt. Wilson, and Mt. Palomar), each in its time the greatest in the world, and was active in organizing interdisciplinary scientific societies nationally and internationally. In 1895 he founded the *Astrophysical Journal*, which remains the leading publication in its field. He had a unique talent for raising funds from private sources in the days before massive governmental support of scientific research. The 200-in. (50.8-cm) reflector at Mt. Palomar is named the Hale telescope in his honor, and the Mt. Wilson and Palomar observatories were renamed the Hale Observatories in 1969. In his own work he pioneered the experimental study of the physical nature of the sun and stars. His observatories were also laboratories employing the latest in photographic and spectrographic techniques. In 1890 he invented the SPECTROHELIOGRAPH, which led to the discovery of magnetic fields and vortices in sunspots. Although he studied in Germany with Helmholtz and Planck, served as the first professor of astrophysics at the University of Chicago, and received many prizes and medals from scientific academies around the world, he never completed the requirements for his Ph.D. Besides technical monographs, he wrote *Depths of the Universe* (1924), *Beyond the Milky Way* (1926), and *Signals from the Stars* (1931).

Hale, John Parker, 1806–73, American politician, b. Rochester, N.H. He practiced law at Dover, N.H., and had remarkable success with juries. He was U.S. district attorney (1834–41) and a member of the House of Representatives (1843–45). His refusal to vote for the annexation of Texas caused his expulsion from the Democratic party. He then (1847–53) served in the Senate as an independent and was nominated (1852) for President by the Free-Soil party. Again (1855–64) in the Senate, he was accused of questionable practices as naval committee chairman, and he was defeated (1864) for reelection. He was minister to Spain (1865–69). See R. H. Sewell, *John P. Hale and the Politics of Abolition* (1965).

Hale, Sir Matthew, 1609–76, English jurist. He was successively a judge in the Court of Common Pleas (1654), chief baron of the Exchequer (1660), and chief justice of the Court of King's Bench (1671). Because of his lack of partisanship, he served under Charles I, Oliver Cromwell, and Charles II. Hale is best known for his scholarly works on criminal law, including *Pleas of the Crown* (1678) and *History of the Pleas of the Crown* (2 vol., 1736–39). His *History of the Common Law of England* (1713) was a pioneer work. See biography by Gilbert Burnet (1682, repr. 1972).

Hale, Nathan, 1755–76, American soldier, hero of the American Revolution, b. Coventry, Conn. A young schoolteacher when the Revolution broke out, he was commissioned an officer in the Connecticut militia, served in the siege of Boston, then went to take part in operations in New York. He volunteered for the dangerous mission of getting information about the British forces on Long Island, where he went in the natural disguise of a schoolmaster. He was discovered, captured, and hanged without trial. He is remembered especially for the statement he is said to have uttered on the gallows, "I only regret that I have but one life to lose for my country." See biography by H. P. Johnston (1914); Morton Pennypacker, *General Washington's Spies on Long Island and in New York* (1939).

Hale, Philip, 1854–1934, American music critic, b. Norwich, Vt., grad. Yale, 1876, studied music in Germany and France. He was music critic of the Boston *Post* (1890–91), Boston *Journal* (1891–1903), and Boston *Herald* (1903–34) and annotated the program notes of the Boston Symphony Orchestra from 1901 until his death. A collection of his writings was published in 1935.

Hale, Sarah Josepha (Buell), 1788–1879, American author, editor, and feminist, b. near Newport, N.H. In 1828 she became editor of the *Ladies' Magazine*, Boston, and in 1837 of *Godey's Lady's Book*, Philadelphia, where she remained over 40 years. The illustrated *Lady's Book* strongly influenced fashions and manners of her day. Mrs. Hale cultivated female authors and constantly urged the higher education of women. She also advocated a national Thanksgiving holiday. Her poem "Mary Had a Little Lamb" was published in her *Poems for Our Children* (1830). See O. W. Burt, *First Woman Editor* (1960).

Hale, William Bayard, 1869–1924, American journalist, b. Richmond, Ind. An Episcopal minister, he served in several parishes before attaining a national reputation as a journalist. In 1900, Hale became managing editor of *Cosmopolitan*. He wrote (1912) the campaign biography of Woodrow Wilson and helped in the publicity campaign to elect him president. His report (1913) as confidential agent in Mexico implicated ambassador Henry Lane Wilson in the murder of Francisco MADERO by Victoriano HUERTA. The report influenced the president to recall Wilson and initiate a campaign to drive Huerta from Mexico. In 1915, Hale turned propaganda adviser for Germany until the United States entered World War I. His book, *American Rights and British Pretensions on the Seas* (1915), stirred American resentment of the British blockade. Denounced and ostracized in the United States, he lived in Europe after the war.

Haleakala National Park (hä"lää"kälä'), 27,283 acres (11,041 hectares), on Maui island, Hawaii; est. 1961. Haleakala volcano, 10,023 ft (3055 m) high, has been dormant since the mid-1700s. Its crater, 2,720 ft (829 m) deep with an area of 19 sq mi (49 sq km), is one of the largest in the world. Rare silversword plants and many native and migratory birds are found in the park.

Hale Observatories, two astronomical OBSERVATORIES located in California on Mt. Wilson, near Pasadena, and on Palomar Mt., NE of San Diego. The observatories have a single staff and are jointly administered by the California Institute of Technology and the Carnegie Institution of Washington, D.C. Mt. Wilson Observatory was founded in 1904 by George E. Hale. Its equipment includes 100-in. (250-cm) and 60-in. (150-cm) reflecting TELESCOPES and two solar tower telescopes of length 150 ft (46 m) and 60 ft (18 m). Beginning in 1928, with funds provided by the Rockefeller Foundation, Hale began construction of a 200-in. (500 cm) reflector to be located on Palomar Mt. As a result of the long process of casting and grinding the giant mirror and interruptions caused by World War II, completion of the Hale telescope was delayed until 1948, 10 years after the death of Hale himself. The immense light-gathering power of the 200-in. telescope is used primarily in studies of very faint objects and very distant galaxies. Also at Palomar Mt. are a 60-in. (150-cm) reflector and 48-in. (120-cm) and 18-in. (46-cm) Schmidt camera telescopes. The larger Schmidt camera was used to prepare a monumental photographic atlas covering about three fourths of the entire sky. A third observatory in Chile, housing 40-in. (100-cm) and 100-in. (250-cm) reflectors, was completed in 1974. Principal research programs conducted by Hale Observatories are on the structure and dimensions of the universe and on the physical nature, chemical composition, and evolution of celestial bodies.

Hales, Alexander of: see ALEXANDER OF HALES.

Hales, John, 1584–1656, English clergyman and scholar, often alluded to as the Ever-Memorable. He won distinction by his lectures on Greek at Oxford, his preaching, and his writings. From 1613 to 1649 he held a fellowship at Eton College. As chaplain to Sir Dudley Carleton, he was an observer at the Synod of Dort (1618–19), an important meeting of Calvinists. Hales's tolerance in religion found expression in *Schism and Schismatics*, published anonymously (and without consent) in 1642. Archbishop Laud in 1639 made Hales a canon of Windsor, but he was ejected from that post in 1642 and from his Eton fellowship in 1649. His remaining years, under the Commonwealth, were spent in obscurity and poverty. In the *Golden Remains of the Ever Memorable Mr. John Hales* (1659), with a preface by John Pearson, are included a number of his writings. See biography by J. H. Elson (1948).

Hales, Stephen, 1677–1761, English physiologist and clergyman. From 1709 he was perpetual curate of Teddington. His experimental studies in animal and plant physiology contributed greatly to the progress of science. In his investigations of circulation he made the first measurements of blood pressure by inserting a tube in a horse's artery. Plant physiology was given impetus by his work on transpiration, root pressure, circulation of sap, and the relationship between green plants and air. His inventions included apparatus for ventilating buildings. Some of his studies are described in his *Vegetable Staticks* (1727), *Haemostaticks* (1733), and *A Description of Ventilation* (1743).

Halesowen (hālz'ōwən), municipal borough (1971 pop. 53,933), Worcestershire, central England. Listed in the Domesday Book as Hala, Halesowen is a manufacturing town with coal mines and steel plants. It was the birthplace of the printer William Caslon and the poet William Shenstone. In 1974, Halesowen became part of the new metropolitan county of West Midlands.

Halévy, Élie (ālē' älāvē'), 1870–1937, French historian, an authority on 19th-century England; son of Ludovic Halévy. In *The Growth of Philosophic Radicalism* (3 vol., 1901–4; tr., new ed. 1949) Halévy made a major contribution to the intellectual history of utilitarianism. His masterpiece, a historical classic, is *A History of the English People in the Nineteenth Century* (6 vol., 1912–30; tr., 2d ed. 1949–52). Based on massive research, it describes and analyzes the development of ideas and institutions. Particularly notable is the first volume, *England in 1815*, a brilliant re-creation of social, political, economic, and religious conditions.

Halévy, Jacques François Fromental Élie (zhäk fräNswä' frômäNtäl'), 1799–1862, French operatic composer. He studied with Cherubini at the Paris Conservatory, where he became a professor in 1827. Bizet, who later became his son-in-law, was one of his pupils. Halévy's one big success was *La Juive* (1835), although others, such as *L'Éclair* (1835) and *La Reine de Chypre* (1841), enjoyed popularity in their time.

Halevy, Judah: see JUDAH HA-LEVI.

half-life, measure of the average lifetime of a radioactive substance (see RADIOACTIVITY). One half-life is the time required for one half of any given quantity of the substance to decay. For example, if the half-life of a particular RADIOACTIVE ISOTOPE is 6 days and 100 grams of the isotope are originally present, then only 50 grams will remain after 6 days, 25 grams after 12 days (2 half-lives), 12.5 grams after 18 days (3 half-lives), and so on. Of course the 87.5 grams that are no longer present as the original substance after 18 days have not disappeared but remain in the form of one or more other substances in the isotope's radioactive decay series. The half-life of a radioactive isotope is a characteristic of that isotope and is not affected by any change in physical or chemical conditions.

half-timber house, type of construction of the Middle Ages in N Europe, used chiefly for dwellings. Some French examples date from the 12th cent., and by the 13th cent. the medium had reached high development. In this form of construction the skeleton frame of the building, with all supporting and bracing members, was of timber, usually oak. The outside enclosing walls were of wattle and daub, plaster, or brick, the material being used as a filling between the exposed structural timbers. The work of the 14th, 15th, and 16th cent. gave increasing decorative emphasis to the timbers, which had richly carved Gothic or Renaissance ornamentation. Many cottages, farmhouses, and manors in England used half-timber, but in France and Germany it was chiefly employed for town dwellings. In these three countries many fine examples remain, particularly in the Rhine towns of Germany and at Rouen, Lisieux, and Caen in France. Half-timber, used in some of the 17th-century dwellings of the American colonists, proved unsuited to the climate and was soon abandoned for more weathertight methods. See A. W. Jackson, *The Half-Timber House* (1912).

half tone: see PHOTOENGRAVING; PRINTING.

Half-Way Covenant, a doctrinal decision of the Congregational churches in New England. The first generation of Congregationalists had decided that only adults with personal experience of conversion were eligible to full membership but that children shared in the covenant of their parents and therefore should be admitted to all the privileges of the church except the Lord's Supper. The question arose (c.1650) whether this privilege should be extended to the children of these children, even though the parents of the second generation may have confessed no experience that brought them into full communion. It was proposed (1657) and adopted (1662) by a church synod that the privileges should be extended. The measure, to which the nickname Half-Way Covenant became attached, provoked much controversy and was never adopted by all the churches. Portions of many congregations seceded to form new settlements, among them Newark, N.J.

Halhul (hăl'həl), town, S Palestine, N of Hebron. Joshua 15.58.

Hali (hā'lī), unidentified town, N Palestine. Joshua 19.25.

Haliburton, Thomas Chandler (hăl'ĭbûrtən), pseud. **Sam Slick,** 1796–1865, Canadian jurist and author. Haliburton was a judge of the court of common pleas in 1829 and a judge of the provincial supreme court in 1841; he retired in 1856. He then moved to England, where he was a member of the House of Commons from 1859 until his death. His *Historical and Statistical Account of Nova Scotia* (1829) was the first history of that province. Haliburton's most popular work was a series about the sayings and doings of Sam Slick, which he began in the *Nova Scotian;* they were collected in *The Clockmaker* (1836). He continued writing about this humorous Yankee clock peddler, a medium for satirizing both Canadians and Americans, in *The Attaché; or, Sam Slick in England* (1843–44) and *Sam Slick's Wise Saws and Modern Instances* (1853). Haliburton also wrote other humorous and historical works. See biographies by V. L. O. Chittick (1924) and J. D. Logan, ed. (1925).

halibut: see FLATFISH.

Halicarnassus (hăl"ĭkärnă'səs), ancient city of Caria, SW Asia Minor, on the Ceramic Gulf (now the Gulf of Kos) and on the site of the modern city of Bodrum, Turkey. Halicarnassus was Greek in origin, but there were Carian inhabitants. Except for a brief period in the 5th cent. B.C., the city was not intimately concerned with Greek affairs. As a Persian vassal it was ruled by tyrants and participated in Xerxes' invasion of Greece (480 B.C.), but after the expulsion of the tyrants (460–455) it joined the Delian League. A dynasty of Carian kings in the 4th cent. B.C. was made famous by MAUSOLUS, whose wife, Artemisia, built him a magnificent tomb (see MAUSOLEUM), considered one of the Seven Wonders of the World. Alexander the Great conquered the city (c.334 B.C.). It was the birthplace of Herodotus and of Dionysius of Halicarnassus. See G. E. Bean and J. M. Cook, *The Halicarnassus Peninsula* (1955).

halide: see HALOGEN.

Halifax, Charles Montagu, earl of (hăl'əfăks), 1661–1715, English statesman. He and Matthew PRIOR were coauthors of a parody of John Dryden's *The Hind and the Panther,* entitled *The Town and The Country Mouse* (1687). As a lord of the treasury, Halifax proposed (1692) the system of government borrowing that established the British national debt. In 1694 he adopted the proposal of William PATERSON to found the Bank of England and was appointed chancellor of the exchequer. The following year he designated Isaac Newton as warden of the mint to effect a recoinage and issued the first exchequer bills. Halifax succeeded Sidney Godolphin as first lord of the treasury (1697–99) and was twice impeached (1701, 1703) for breach of trust as auditor of the exchequer, but he was not convicted. He was reappointed first lord of the treasury on the accession (1714) of George I.

Halifax, Edward Frederick Lindley Wood, 1st earl of, 1881–1959, British statesman. He entered the House of Commons (1910) as a Conservative and was president of the Board of Education (1922–24) and of the Board of Agriculture (1924–25). Created Baron Irwin in 1925, he served (1926–31) as viceroy of India. Confronted with the civil disobedience campaign of Mohandas GANDHI and his followers, he promised (1929) dominion status for India and induced Gandhi to participate in the further round-table conferences on India's future. Succeeding his father as Viscount Halifax in 1934, he became Conservative leader of the House of Lords in 1935, serving also as secretary for war (1935) and lord privy seal (1935–38). As foreign secretary (1938–40) Halifax firmly supported Neville Chamberlain's policy of appeasement toward Nazi Germany. From 1941 to 1946 he was ambassador to the United States. He was created an earl in 1944. He wrote *John Keble* (1932); his speeches are collected as *Indian Problems* (1932), *Speeches on Foreign Policy* (1940), and *American Speeches* (1947). See his autobiography, *Fullness of Days* (1957); biographies by Alan Johnson (1941) and the earl of Birkenhead (1965).

Halifax, George Savile, 1st marquess of, 1633–95, English statesman. A protégé of the 2nd duke of Buckingham, he was made Viscount Halifax (1668) and sat (1672–76) in the privy council. An opponent both of the pro-Catholic faction that arranged the alliance (1670) with France and of the ministry of Lord Danby, which reversed that policy, Halifax became known as the Trimmer because of his practice of "trimming," or balancing between factions. He was expelled from the council for opposing Danby, but he regained favor with Charles II and was readmitted (1679) to the council, created an earl (1679) and a marquess (1682), and made lord privy seal (1682). He led the successful opposition to the bill (1680) to exclude the future James II from the throne. On the accession (1685) of James II, Halifax was made lord president of the council, but he resigned almost immediately in opposition to James's pro-Catholic policies. When William of Orange landed in England in 1688, Halifax at first sought to mediate between William and James, but then joined William. As leader of the Whig peers, he formally requested (1689) William to accept the crown of England. He was appointed (1689) lord privy seal and chief minister, but lack of a supporting group in Parliament made it impossible for him to form a viable ministry, and he resigned (1690). His most famous political pamphlet, *The Character of a Trimmer* (written 1684, published 1688), describes the virtues of his middle course in politics. See his complete works, ed. by Walter Raleigh (1912, repr. 1970); his life and letters by H. C. Foxcroft (2 vol., 1898; repr. 1969); biography by H. C. Foxcroft (1946).

Halifax, city (1971 pop. 122,035; metropolitan area pop. 222,637), provincial capital, S central N.S., Canada, on the Atlantic Ocean. It is the largest city in the Maritime Provinces and is Canada's principal ice-free Atlantic port. Halifax is the eastern terminus of Canada's two great railroad systems and of its transcontinental highway. Its many industries include commercial fishing, fish processing, shipbuilding, oil refining, and the manufacture of electronics. It is the home port of the Canadian Atlantic fleet and the headquarters of its eastern army. Halifax was founded in 1749 and named for the earl of Halifax, then president of the Board of Trade and Plantations. It was intended originally to be a British naval stronghold comparable to that of France at LOUISBURG. It served as a naval base for the expedition against Louisburg in 1758, against the American colonies in the American Revolution, and against the United States in the War of 1812. The first transatlantic steamship service, from Halifax to Great Britain, began in 1840. During both world wars the port was an important naval and air base, convoy terminal, and embarkation center. In 1917 a vessel carrying explosives was rammed in the harbor, causing an explosion that killed about 1,800 people, injured thousands more, and destroyed the northern part of the city. Places of interest include the Citadel fortress; Province House (1818); St. Paul's Church, the oldest (1750) Anglican church in Canada; and Point Pleasant Park. The Halifax *Gazette,* founded in 1752 and the first newspaper in Canada, still exists as the *Nova Scotia Royal Gazette.* Educational institutions include Dalhousie Univ. (1818), the Univ. of Kings College, Mount St. Vincent Univ., St. Mary's Univ., and technical and art schools. See M. J. Bird, *The Town that Died* (1963); S. H. Prince, *Catastrophe and Social Change* (1920, repr. 1968); T. H. Raddall, *Halifax: Warden of the North* (rev. ed. 1971).

Halifax, county borough (1971 pop. 91,171), West Riding of Yorkshire, central England, on a small tributary of the Calder River. The borough's industries include the manufacture of carpets; cotton, wool, and worsted goods; and engineered products, machine tools, and boilers. Noteworthy are the Bankfield Museum, the 18th-century Piece Hall, the 15th-century parish church of St. John the Baptist, the Renaissance town hall designed by Sir Charles Barry, and Heath Grammar School (1585). Halifax carried on an important wool trade in the Middle Ages. In 1974, Halifax became part of the new metropolitan county of West Yorkshire.

halitosis (hăl″ĭtō′sĭs), unpleasant odor carried on the breath. It is usually the result of gum disorder, tooth decay, smoking, indulgence in aromatic foods, or a mild digestive upset. Known commonly as bad breath, halitosis may also be indicative of lung or sinus infection, uremia, or cirrhosis of the liver. The minty odor of acetone on the breath is a symptom of diabetes mellitus. Successful treatment of halitosis consists of eliminating or controlling the underlying cause. Proper diet and dental hygiene is often helpful. Mouthwashes and scented toothpastes mask the condition but do not alleviate it. A physician should be consulted for persistent cases of halitosis.

Hall, Basil, 1788–1844, British naval officer and traveler. In the service from 1802 to 1823, he commanded vessels on scientific assignments and voyages of exploration. He wrote of them in his *Account of a Voyage of Discovery to the West Coast of Corea and the Great Loo-Choo* (1818); in *Extracts from a Journal Written on the Coasts of Chile, Peru, and Mexico* (2 vol., 1823, repr. 1968); and in *Fragments of Voyages and Travels* (1831–33), in three series, each series in three volumes. After leaving the navy he traveled in the United States, his *Travels in North America* (3 vol., 1829) forming a valuable description of America.

Hall, Charles Francis, 1821–71, American arctic explorer, b. Rochester, N.H. He became interested in the many search expeditions for Sir John Franklin's party, and with Eskimo companions he explored (1860–62) the southeast corner of Baffin Island, finding traces of Sir Martin Frobisher's party but none of Franklin's. Hall was the first explorer in three centuries to visit Frobisher Strait, which he found to be a huge bay almost bisecting Baffin Island. His *Arctic Researches and Life among the Esquimaux* (1864, repr. 1970) is a narrative of this journey. On his second arctic expedition (1864–69) he found traces of the fate of Franklin's party on Boothia Peninsula and King William Island and in his searching added much to the geographical knowledge of the whole area. In 1871 he was placed in command of a government expedition to the North Pole. In the *Polaris* his party went northward in the passages between Greenland and Ellesmere Island to the Arctic Ocean and achieved a new northern record of 82°11′. Hall died suddenly at the party's wintering quarters. On the homeward journey most of the crew died aboard the *Polaris* when it was struck by an enormous ice floe. See biography by Chauncey Loomis (1971).

Hall, Edward, 1499?–1547, English chronicler. He wrote *The Union of the Noble and Ilustre Famelies of Lancastre and York* (1548), usually called *Hall's Chronicle.* A glorification of the Tudors, it is important for the light it sheds on social life early in the reign of Henry VIII and for the use Shakespeare made of it in his historical plays.

Hall, Granville Stanley, 1844–1924, American psychologist and educator, b. Ashfield, Mass., grad. Williams, 1867. G. Stanley Hall taught at Antioch and Harvard, studied experimental psychology in Germany, and in 1882 organized at Johns Hopkins a psychological laboratory that rapidly took a leading position in the field. He founded (1887) the *American Journal of Psychology* and was one of the organizers (1891) of the American Psychological Association. As first president (1889–1920) of Clark Univ., he raised it to prominence for its courses in education. Among his works are *The Contents of Children's Minds* (1883), which inaugurated the child-study movement in the United States; *Adolescence* (1904); *Educational Problems* (1911); *Jesus, the Christ, in the Light of Psychology* (1917); and his autobiography (1923). See biographies by Lorine Pruette (1926, repr. 1970) and Dorothy Ross (1972); R. Jackson Wilson, *In Quest of Community* (1970).

Hall, James, 1811–98, American geologist and paleontologist, b. Hingham, Mass., grad. Rensselaer School (later Rensselaer Polytechnic Institute), 1832. An authority on stratigraphy and invertebrate paleontology, he joined the New York state geological survey in 1836 and in 1839 became state geologist for New York. He wrote *Paleontology of New York* (8 vol. in 13, 1847–94), a monumental report on the paleontology of the state; his work formed the basis for the later geological histories of North America. He also served briefly as state geologist for Iowa and Wisconsin and was director (1866–94) of the New York State Museum at Albany. See studies by R. C. Randall (1964) and J. M. Clarke (1921, repr. 1973).

Hall, Joseph, 1574–1656, English prelate and author. He was educated at Emmanuel College, Cambridge, and became bishop of Exeter, 1627–41, and of Norwich, 1641–47. The rise of Puritanism involved him in serious church difficulties, and his vigorous defense of the episcopacy against its attackers resulted in his imprisonment in 1641 on charges of high treason. He was eventually released, but his living was confiscated and he lived the remainder of his life in poverty. Hall's most notable work, his verse satires, modeled after the Roman satirist Juvenal, appeared in two parts: *Virgidemiarum* or *Toothless Satires* (1597) and *Biting Satires* (1598). He also wrote prose satires, poems, meditations, and autobiographical tracts. See his poems, ed. by Arnold Davenport (1949, repr. 1969); biography by T. F. Kinloch (1951).

Hall, Lyman, 1724–90, political leader in the American Revolution, signer of the Declaration of Independence, b. Wallingford, Conn. He was a Congregational minister for some time before practicing medicine. Hall moved to Georgia, became involved in politics, and was sent (1775) to the Continental Congress as a delegate from St. John's Parish before the colony sent any official delegation. Hall served until 1780, when he returned to Georgia. He became governor in 1783. It was at his suggestion that Georgia chartered a state university in 1785.

Hall, Marshall, 1790–1857, English physician and physiologist, M.D. Univ. of Edinburgh, 1812. He practiced medicine in Nottingham and in London. He opposed bloodletting and devised a method of artificial respiration named for him. As a result of his experiments with animals he advanced (1833) the theory of reflex action in a paper before the Royal Society; despite some opposition the theory was later universally accepted. His works also include *The Diagnosis of Diseases* (1817) and *Memoirs on the Nervous System* (1837).

Hall, Samuel Read, 1795–1877, American educator and clergyman, b. Croydon, N.H. After teaching in Rumford, Maine, and Fitchburg, Mass., he founded (1823) at Concord, Vt., a training school for teachers, one of the first in the United States. He also helped to organize (1830) the American Institute of Instruction, the oldest educational association in the United States. Hall became principal of the teachers seminary at Phillips Academy (1830–37), of Holmes Plymouth Academy (1837–40), and of Craftsbury Academy, to which he added a teachers training department (1840–46). From 1846 to 1875 he served as pastor in Brownington and in Granby, Vt. He wrote numerous textbooks, and his famous *Lectures on School-Keeping* (1829) were republished in 1929, with a biography of Hall and a bibliography of his works by A. D. Wright and G. E. Gardner.

hall, a communicating passageway or, in medieval buildings, the large main room. In the feudal castle of N Europe it was the single apartment, and in it lord and retainers lounged, ate, and slept. From the hearth in its center the smoke rose to an outlet in the roof. At one end was the raised dais reserved for the master and those of his own rank. With developing amenities extra spaces were added for cooking and sleeping, and the hall advanced beyond its early rude and unfinished appearance. In English manor houses of the 14th and 15th cent. the characteristic great hall was covered by a fine open-timber roof, heated by one or more huge fireplaces, and lighted with lofty windows often arranged in deep, projecting bays. Westminster Hall, part of the ancient royal palace commenced in the 11th cent. and rebuilt in the 14th cent., was the most splendid. By the 17th cent., with the addition of drawing room, library, and bedrooms, the hall of the English house was no longer of great size and dominance. The English colleges of the Middle Ages and Renaissance also had halls or commons, chiefly for dining, that were architecturally similar to the baronial examples. Some were covered with fine fan vaults, others with timber roofs as at Christ Church, Oxford, perhaps the most splendid hall next to Westminster. The various guilds of N Europe had their halls, especially impressive in Flanders, e.g., the cloth halls at Bruges, Brussels, and Ypres. In Italy communal independence produced the remarkable series of local civic halls, often with imposing towers, as at Siena and Florence. The word *hall* came to be used in the title of many great English houses (Haddon Hall) and similarly in that of some Southern estates in the American colonies. See J. A. Gotch, *Growth of the English House* (1909).

Hall, Fort: see FORT HALL.

Hallam, Henry, 1777–1859, English historian, educated at Oxford. His most famous work, *A View of the State of Europe during the Middle Ages* (1818), stressed institutional and legal history but revealed little understanding of European history prior to the 12th cent. In a subsequent work, *The Constitutional History of England from the Accession of Henry VII to the Death of George II* (1827), he showed his Whig hatred of political and ecclesiastical tyranny by condemning James I and Charles I and glorifying the Revolution of 1688. He was the earliest authoritative exponent of the Whig historical philosophy, and his *Constitutional History* remained a model for the writing of English constitutional history until William Stubbs.

Hallam, Lewis, c.1714–1756, Anglo-American actor and manager of the first professional theatrical company in the United States. He arrived from England with his company in 1752 and opened at Williamsburg, Va., with Shakespeare's *Merchant of Venice.* In 1753 he built the first theater in New York City, on Nassau St., where he presented Elizabethan and Restoration dramas, farces, and operettas. The company played in Philadelphia, toured the South, and then went to Jamaica, where Hallam died. His widow married David Douglass, and in 1758 they formed the American Company, in which Hallam's son, **Lewis Hallam, Jr.,** c.1740–1808, performed. The younger Hallam excelled in comedy. In 1767 he played in Thomas Godfrey's *Prince of Parthia,* the first American drama to be produced professionally. On the death of Douglass, Hallam took over the management and subsequently produced (1787) the first American comedy, *The Contrast,* by Royall Tyler.

Hallandale, city (1970 pop. 23,849), Broward co., SE Fla., on the Atlantic coast and the Intracoastal Waterway; settled 1897, inc. 1927. Horse and greyhound racetracks there are major sources of employment. The beautiful residential community of Golden Isles is located on finger islands within the city.

Hallé, Sir Charles (hăl'ē), 1819–95, German-English conductor and pianist, originally named Karl Halle. As a young pianist in Paris he knew Chopin, Liszt, and Berlioz. During the Revolution of 1848 he moved to England. There, in 1857, he founded the Hallé Orchestra in Manchester. He conducted many music festivals and was a noted educator. Hallé was knighted in 1888. See the partly autobiographical *Life and Letters of Sir Charles Hallé* (ed. by C. E. Hallé and Marie Hallé, 1896, repr. 1973); biography by Charles Rigby (1952).

Halle (hä'lə), Fr. *Hal,* town (1970 pop. 20,017), Brabant prov., central Belgium, on the Charleroi-Brussels Canal. It is a commercial and industrial center. Manufactures include textiles, paper, machines, processed food, and chemicals. Halle's Gothic Church of Our Lady (14th–15th cent.) contains a celebrated miraculous image of the Virgin and is a place of pilgrimage.

Halle (häl'ə), city (1970 pop. 257,300), capital of Halle district, S central East Germany, on the Saale River. It is an industrial center and a major transportation hub. Manufactures include chemicals, refined sugar and other food products, paper, and machinery. Salt and potash are mined in the region. Located on the site of Bronze Age and Iron Age settlements, Halle was first mentioned in the 9th cent. In 968 it was given to the archbishops of Magdeburg, who frequently resided there. The city was a member (1281–1478) of the Hanseatic League and accepted (1544) the Reformation. Halle was annexed by Brandenburg in 1648. The famous Univ. of Halle was founded in 1694, and in 1817 it absorbed the Univ. of Wittenberg. In Halle in 1695 the philanthropist A. H. Francke founded a school for paupers, the first of the Francke Institutes. The first Bible Society was founded at Halle in 1710. Noteworthy buildings include the Gothic Red Tower (1418–1506) and the Marienkirche, a 16th-century church. The composer Handel was born (1685) in Halle.

Halleck, Fitz-Greene (hăl'ĭk), 1790–1867, American poet, b. Guilford, Conn. He was joint author, with Joseph Rodman Drake, of the humorous lampoons "Croaker Papers," most of which were printed in the New York *Evening Post* in 1819. In the same year he published his long satire, *Fanny* (1819), in the style of Byron's *Beppo.* His poem "Marco Bozzaris," popular as a recitation, and his "Green Be the Turf above Thee," an elegy on the death of Drake, were the best known of Halleck's graceful verses. For many years he was personal secretary to John Jacob Astor. See biographies by J. G. Wilson (1869) and N. F. Adkins (1930).

Halleck, Henry Wager, 1815–72, Union general in the American Civil War, b. Oneida co., N.Y., grad. West Point, 1839. He entered the Corps of Engineers and became an expert on fortifications; his *Elements of Military Art and Science* (1846) was influential in the Civil War. In the Mexican War he served in California, holding various positions in the military government there. Halleck resigned from the army in 1853 and entered the leading law firm of the state. In the Civil War he was made a major general in the regular army (Aug., 1861) and was sent to succeed John C. Frémont in command of the Dept. of the Missouri. In March, 1862, the departments of the Ohio and Kansas were added to his jurisdiction. Although he was an able organizer, the prestige that he gained was due to the successes of Ulysses S. GRANT, Don Carlos BUELL, Samuel R. CURTIS, and John POPE—all under his command. After Shiloh (April, 1862) Halleck took the field himself and advanced on Corinth, which General Beauregard abandoned to him in May. In July, 1862, he was appointed general in chief with the understanding that he was to remain in Washington as military adviser to the President and the Secretary of War. His failure to act decisively made him ineffective as general in chief, however, and he was grateful when, upon Grant's being given supreme command in March, 1864, he was demoted to chief of staff. He remained in the army after the war and held command of the Division of the South at the time of his death. See study by S. E. Ambrose (1962).

Hallein (häl'īn), town (1971 pop. 14,400), in Salzburg prov., W Austria, on the Salzach River, near the West German border. It is a spa and has a noted marble industry. An ancient Celtic settlement, Hallein was first mentioned in the 13th cent. There is a noted pilgrimage church (1594–1612) there.

hallel (həlāl', hăl'ĕl) [Heb.,=praise], group of Psalms (113–118) sung, as in the days of the Temple, every morning of Hanukkah, at the Passover service, and on most other Jewish holidays as an expression of joy and thanksgiving.

Hallelujah (hăl"əlōō'yə) or **Alleluia** (ăl-) [Heb.,=praise the Lord], joyful expression used in Hebrew worship; cf. Pss. 104–6, 111–13, 115–17, 135, 146–50. Christian liturgies make wide use of it, particularly at Easter time. The *Hallelujah Chorus* is the brilliant concluding piece of Part II of Handel's *Messiah.*

Haller, Albrecht von (äl'brĕcht fən hä'lər), 1708–77, Swiss scientist and writer. He had already won distinction as botanist and poet when he was appointed (1736) professor of anatomy, medicine, and botany at the Univ. of Göttingen. There he carried on the research in experimental physiology for which he is especially famed and on which he based his theory of the irritability (known today as contractility) of muscle tissue, set forth in *A Dissertation on the Sensible and Irritable Parts of Animals* (1732, tr. 1936). He returned (1753) to his native Bern, where he continued his research and took part in public affairs. Among his voluminous writings are *Elementa physiologiae corporis humani* (8 vol., 1757–66); noted bibliographies in anatomy, surgery, botany, and medicine; and a volume of poems, *Versuch schweizerischer Gedichte* (1732).

Hallet, Étienne Sulpice (ātyĕn' sülpēs' älā'), 1755–1825, French architect. He emigrated c.1789 to the United States, where he became known as Stephen Hallet. Before the opening of the public competition for the design of the Capitol, at Washington, D.C., Hallet had submitted designs to Thomas Jefferson, then Secretary of State. His plan consisted of a monumental central dome with flanking wings, and he was encouraged to go on with the project. In 1793, however, the design submitted by William THORNTON was approved and adopted by the President, who, in justice to Hallet, retained him as supervisor of the execution of Thornton's plans. When, however, Hallet attempted to introduce some alterations in Thornton's design, he was dismissed from the post.

Hallet, Stephen: see HALLET, ÉTIENNE SULPICE.

Halley, Edmund (hăl'ē), 1656–1742, English astronomer and mathematician. He is particularly noted as the first astronomer to predict the return of a comet and the first to point out the use of a transit of Venus in determining the parallax of the sun. In 1676 he went to St. Helena to observe the southern skies and as a result made a catalog of 341 stars of the Southern Hemisphere. In 1677 he made the first complete observation of a transit of Mercury. He financed the publication of Isaac Newton's *Principia* and helped to prepare it for the press. On the basis of Newton's theory, Halley calculated the orbit of the great comet of 1682—since known as HALLEY'S COMET. In 1698–1700 he made one of the first studies of compass variations in the North Atlantic. He was made astronomer royal in 1720. He observed the moon through the complete revolution of its nodes; this took 18 years. Other discoveries of Halley's are the proper motions of the stars, the long-inequality of Jupiter and Saturn, and the acceleration of the moon's mean motion. His noted synopsis of known comets appeared in 1705; his *Tabulae astronomicae* (1749, tr. 1752) was published posthumously. See his *Correspondence and Papers* (ed. by E. F. MacPike, 1932); biography by C. A. Ronan (1970).

Halley's comet, periodic COMET named for Edmund Halley, who observed it in 1682 and identified it as the one observed in 1531 and 1607. Halley did not live to see its return early in 1759, close to the time he predicted. It reappeared in 1910 and is expected to return in 1985.

hallmark, mark impressed on silverwork or goldwork to signify official approval of the standard of purity of the metal, also called plate mark. The hallmark was introduced by statute in England in 1300 and enforced by the Goldsmiths' Hall, London. Similar marks, many of them unofficial, were used on the Continent and in America. Other marks used on plate include one for the place of assay; a date mark, usually a letter; the maker's touch, at first a symbol, later his initials or name; a duty mark, to signify payment of a tax; the artisan's mark. Marks have also been used on plated ware, baser metals, and pottery. See CHINA MARKS.

Hall of Fame, national shrine for great Americans, in the Bronx, New York City; est. 1900. The Hall of Fame, a 630-ft (192-m) colonnade resting on a corridor above a terrace, was instituted by Chancellor Henry M. MacCracken from a $250,000 donation by philanthropist Helen Gould Shepard. The names of 50 outstanding Americans, selected by the 100-member College of Electors (with at least one member from each state), were inscribed on bronze tablets under the busts of those elected in 1900; five people were to be added each fifth year. However, this plan has not been followed with any great regularity. There are now more than 100 persons enshrined there.

Hallohesh (hălō'hĕsh), signer of the Covenant. Neh. 10.24.

Halloween: see ALL SAINTS' DAY.

Hallowell, Alfred Irving, 1892–1974, American anthropologist, b. Philadelphia, Pa., grad. Univ. of Pennsylvania (B.S., 1914; A.M., 1920; Ph.D., 1924). He was a professor of anthropology at the Univ. of Pennsylvania from 1927 to 1944 and from 1947 to 1963. From 1944 to 1947 he was professor of anthropology at Northwestern Univ. He concerned himself especially with personality and culture, American Indians, and social organization. Among his writings are *Bear Ceremonialism in the Northern Hemisphere* (1926), *The Role of Conjuring in Saulteaux Society* (1942), and *Culture and Experience* (1955).

Hallstatt (häl'shtät), village (1964 est. pop. 1,340), Upper Austria prov., W central Austria, in the SALZKAMMERGUT, on the Lake of Hallstatt. It is a tourist center, with salt mines and a wood-carving industry. Hallstatt is one of the oldest settlements in Austria. Archaeologists excavated (19th cent.) in a nearby cemetery the remains of a culture known as the Hallstatt epoch of the IRON AGE.

Hallström, Per (pâr häl'ström), 1866–1960, Swedish short-story writer, dramatist, and poet. Before devoting himself to writing, Hallström worked in London and Chicago as a chemist. He is appreciated primarily for his collections of short stories, such as *Purpur* [purple] (1895) and *Thanatos* [death] (1900). His major works, written before 1910, combine profound compassion with a sensitive awareness of beauty.

hallucination, false sensory perception characterized by a lack of external stimulus. The two most common types of hallucination are auditory, i.e., hearing voices or noises and visual, i.e., seeing people or things that are not actually present. Hallucinations play a prominent part in SCHIZOPHRENIA and their interpretation is important to the psychiatrist in his attempt to understand the underlying emotional conflicts of the psychotic patient. However, hallucinations occur to normal people under conditions of sensory deprivation, emotional stress, or great fatigue. Hallucinations can also be induced by various drugs (see PSYCHOTOMIMETIC DRUG).

hallucinogenic drug (həlōō"sənōjĕn'ĭk): see PSYCHOTOMIMETIC DRUG.

Halmahera (hälmähä'rä) or **Jailolo** (jīlô'lô), island (c. 7,000 sq mi/18,100 sq km), E Indonesia, between New Guinea and Celebes, on the equator. The largest of the Moluccas and irregular in shape, it consists of two intersecting mountain ranges (rising to c.5,000 ft/1,520 m), which form four rocky peninsulas separated by three deep bays. There are several active volcanos, lush jungles, streams, and a few lakes. The natives, mostly Malayans, engage in subsistence farming, hunting, and fishing. The chief products are spices, resin, sago, rice, tobacco, and coconuts. There are anchorages at Galela and Weda. Known to the Portuguese and the Spaniards as early as 1525, Halmahera came under Dutch influence in 1660. Taken by the Japanese (1942) in World War II, it was frequently bombed by the Allies. The island is sometimes called Jilolo or Gilolo.

Halmstad (hälm'städ''), city (1970 pop. 44,448), capital of Halland co., SW Sweden, a seaport on the Kattegat at the mouth of the Nissan River. It is an industrial center and summer resort. Manufactures include steel, textiles, and paper, and shipbuilding is carried on. Chartered in 1307, Halmstad was an important fortified city of Denmark before being conquered by Sweden in 1645. Of note are a Gothic church (14th cent.) and a 17th-century castle.

halo, in art: see NIMBUS.

halo, in meteorology, circle of light surrounding the moon or sun. It may be white or it may show the colors of the spectrum—more or less blurred, with the red on the inside. A halo occurs when the light from the sun or the moon is refracted and reflected by ice crystals in the atmosphere, usually in a thin layer of high cirrostratus clouds. Under certain circumstances a second, or outer, halo appears, fainter than the inner one. At times another ring, white and luminous, is also seen lying parallel with the horizon and passing through the source of light. On this parhelic circle mock suns, or parhelia, sometimes appear; a single mock sun, the anthelion, directly opposite the sun, may be added. In general a white halo results from the reflection of light by ice crystals, while one which appears as colored rings results from the refraction of light by ice crystals. Halos are more brilliant and complex near the poles than in other parts of the world. The theory attributing their formation to the presence of ice crystals was first given by the French philosopher Descartes. The study of the scientist Auguste Bravais on the subject is considered most authoritative. Similar to a halo and sometimes confused with it is the CORONA. In X-ray electron diffraction, the term *halos* refers to the broad rings that appear on a photographic film as a result of the diffraction of a monoenergetic beam of X rays or electrons from a crystalline powder located at the center of the camera.

halogen (hăl'əjĕn) [Gr.,=salt-bearing], any of the chemically active elements found in group VIIa of the PERIODIC TABLE; the name applies especially to FLUORINE (symbol F), CHLORINE (Cl), BROMINE (Br), and IODINE (I). ASTATINE (At), formerly known as alabamine, is a radioactive element also classed as a halogen; its most stable isotope (which does not occur in nature) has a half-life of less than 8½ hr. The chemical and physical properties of astatine are not well known; it is believed to resemble iodine. The halogens are the best-defined family of chemical elements. Chemically they closely resemble one another; they are nonmetallic and form monovalent negative ions. They also exhibit an almost perfect gradation of physical properties. Fluorine, a pale yellow gas, is the least dense and chemically the most active, displacing the other halogens from their compounds and even displacing oxygen from water. Chlorine, a yellow-green gas, is more dense and less reactive than fluorine. Bromine is a dark red liquid. Iodine is a grayish black solid and is the least chemically active of the four; however, among the nonmetals only oxygen is more reactive than iodine. Pure halogens exist as diatomic molecules, e.g., Cl_2; they form interhalogen compounds, i.e., compounds between two halogens. The halogens form numerous compounds with other elements. With hydrogen they form hydrogen halides, whose water solutions are called hydrohalic acids, e.g., the water solution of HYDROGEN CHLORIDE is called hydrochloric acid. They form numerous metal halides, or SALTS, e.g., sodium chloride, common table salt. They also form halocarbons, compounds with carbon and often other elements such as hydrogen and oxygen. CHLOROFORM, IODOFORM, and CARBON TETRACHLORIDE are halocarbons. Some other halogen compounds are calomel (mercurous chloride), FLUORITE, sal ammoniac (AMMONIUM CHLORIDE), corrosive sublimate (MERCURIC CHLORIDE), and chlorine bleaches.

Halohesh (hălō'hĕsh) [Heb.,=HALLOHESH], father of Shallum, ruler in Jerusalem. Neh. 3.12.

halophyte (hăl'əfīt''), any plant, especially a seed plant, that is able to grow in habitats excessively rich in salts, such as salt marshes, sea coasts, and saline or alkaline semideserts and steppes. These plants have special physiological adaptations that enable them to absorb water from soils and from sea water, which have solute concentrations that nonhalophytes could not tolerate. Some halophytes are actually succulent, with a high water-storage capacity.

Halprin, Lawrence, 1917–, American landscape architect, b. New York City. Halprin values mobility above static structure in urban life, and his designs emphasize human participation and interaction. His fountain blocks in Portland, Ore., in which water cascades down concrete tiers, invite wading. Halprin's designs for Nicollet Mall (1962) in Minneapolis, Minn., and the Student Union Plaza of the Univ. of California at Berkeley also reflect an awareness of human movement. He is the author of several books, including *Cities* (1963) and *Freeways* (1966).

Hals, Frans (fräns häls), c.1580–1666, Dutch painter of portraits and genre scenes, b. Antwerp. Hals spent most of his life in Haarlem, where he studied with Karel van Mander. Although his reputation was established early, much of his long life was passed in poverty. Hals's pictures of scenes from everyday life were painted during the first half of his career, in a freer style than his formal portraits. During the 1620s and 1630s, Hals was commissioned to paint large group portraits of various companies of the civic guards in full regalia. Some of these "corporation pictures" are among his finest works. Each individual, and the group as a whole, is portrayed with remarkable vivacity and informality. *Banquet of the Officers of the St. George Militia* (1616; Haarlem) is an imposing early work of this type. In his later work Hals developed a cool palette, alternating blacks and grays with brilliant and sparkling color. The master reached the height of his renown in the 1630s. He painted, in these years, several groups and a number of important single portraits (e.g., *Lucas de Clercq;* Rijks Mus.). His possessions were seized for debt in 1652, and difficult years followed. Four years before his death he was granted a pension by the town. At the age of 84 he painted two masterpieces, *The Governors of the Almshouse* and *Lady Regents of the Almshouse* (both: Haarlem). These portrait groups have the same brilliant lighting and cool clarity as his gayer canvases. Hals employed Caravaggesque lighting to capture momentary effects and give them authentic life. He worked rapidly, detailing his subjects with the utmost frankness and economy of means. His work is best seen in the Frans Hals Museum, Haarlem. His notable paintings include *Archers of St. George* (three paintings), *Archers of St. Adrian* (two paintings), and *Governors of St. Elizabeth Hospital* (all: Haarlem); *The Rael and Blaeuw Company, Married Couple,* and *The Merry Drinker* (all: Rijks Mus.); *Laughing Cavalier* (1624; Wallace Coll., London); *Malle Bobbe* and *The Smoker* (both: Metropolitan Mus.). Hals's work was not highly valued until the 19th cent. About one third of his 250 extant works are in American collections; the Metropolitan Museum has 12. See catalog by N. S. Trivas (2d ed. 1949); studies by P. Descargues (tr. 1968) and S. Slive (3 vol. 1970–74). Five of Hals's sons became painters. The foremost was **Frans Hals,** c.1618–c.1669, a skillful painter of still life and rustic scenes. **Dirk Hals,** c.1591–1656, brother of the elder Frans Hals, imitated his style but lacked his genius. He specialized in festivals and drinking scenes, his *Merry Party* (National Gall., London) being characteristic.

Halsey, William Frederick (hôl'sē), 1882–1959, American admiral, b. Elizabeth, N.J., grad. Annapolis, 1904. He commanded destroyers in World War I, and after 1935 he served with naval air units. In World War II he led (Jan., 1942) a spectacular carrier raid against the Marshall Islands and Gilbert Islands, and during the campaign in the Solomon Islands he assumed command of the South Pacific area. As commander (1944–45) of the U.S. 3d Fleet, he commanded the naval action in the Philippines and led (July, 1945) the seaborne bombardment of Japan. He was promoted (Nov.) to admiral of the fleet (five-star admiral). He retired from the navy in 1947 because of ill health. His experiences in World War II were published as *Admiral Halsey's Story* (1947). See biographies by R. B. Jordan (1946), Jack Pearl (1962), and Wyatt Blassingame (1970).

Hälsingborg (hĕlsĭngbôr'yə), city (1970 pop. 93,609), Malmöhus co., S Sweden, a seaport on the Øresund, connected by ferry with Helsingør, Denmark. It is a commercial and industrial center. Manufactures include processed copper, rubber, electrical goods, textiles, and refined sugar. A trade center and stronghold since the 9th cent., Hälsingborg was destroyed during the Danish-Swedish conflicts in the 17th cent. and passed to Denmark. The city was rebuilt after its return to Sweden in 1710. Its modern industrial development dates from the mid-19th cent. Of note are a well-preserved castle (12th–15th cent.), the Church of St. Mary (13th–15th cent.), and numerous half-timber houses.

Halsted, William Stewart (hôl'stĭd), 1852–1922, American surgeon, b. New York City, M.D. College of Physicians and Surgeons, 1877. He practiced in New York and in 1886 became the first professor of surgery at Johns Hopkins, where he was associated with Sir William Osler, W. H. Welch, and H. A. Kelly in developing the great medical school and hospital. His surgical contributions include an operative technique based on minimum injury of tissues, anesthesia by the injection of cocaine into the nerves, a method of operating for cancer of the breast and for hernia, experimental work on the thyroid, and the introduction of the use of rubber gloves. See his *Surgical Papers* (2 vol., 1924); biography by A. J. Beckhard and W. D. Crane (1960).

Haltemprice (hô'təmprīz), urban district (1971 pop. 52,239), East Riding of Yorkshire, E central England, on the Humber River. Haltemprice was originally the name of an Augustinian canonry founded in 1322 at Cottingham, a village in the district. There is a shipyard at Hessle village. Other industries in the district include horticulture, mink farming, and carpet manufacturing. Haltemprice is also a residential suburb of Hull. In 1974 it became part of the new nonmetropolitan county of Humberside.

Halychyna: see GALICIA, Poland and Ukraine.

Halys, river of Asia Minor: see KIZIL IRMAK.

Ham. 1 Son of Noah and father of Cush, Mizraim, Phut, and Canaan. Gen. 9; 10. **2** City, E of the Jordan, the modern Ham (Jordan). Gen. 14.5. **3** Name used in connection with the cities of Simeon. 1 Chron. 4.40. The "Land of Ham" is a designation for Egypt. Ps. 78.51; 105.23,27; 106.22. The Hamitic languages were named after the son of Noah (see HAMITO-SEMITIC LANGUAGES).

ham, hind leg of a hog above the hock joint, prepared for food by curing or smoking. Ham is one of the earliest of preserved meats; it is now a leading product of the meat-packing industry. The flavor and quality of ham depend on the age, condition, and feeding of the swine and on the smoke used in curing. The Westphalian hams of Germany are smoked with juniper brush; birchwood also is used in N Europe; hickory is favored in the United States. The delicate flavor of the relatively lean Smithfield hams of Virginia is attributed in part to the roots, acorns, and nuts upon which the hogs feed. The major consumers of ham are Denmark, Germany, and the United States.

Hamada (hämä'dä), city (1970 pop. 49,407), Shimane prefecture, SW Honshu, Japan, on the Japan Sea. It is a fishing and commercial port, with a huge fish market and an important fish-canning industry.

Hamadan (hämädän'), city (1966 pop. 124,167), capital of Hamadan governorate, Kermanshah prov., W Iran, at the foot of Mt. Alvand. Located at an altitude of 6,000 ft (1,829 m), it is the trade center for a fertile farm region where fruit and grain are grown. The city is noted for its rugs, leatherwork, and wood and metal products. In ancient times, as Hangmatana or Agbatana, it was a capital of Media. It was known to the Greeks as Ecbatana. In the 7th cent. Hamadan passed to the Arabs, and it was later held by the Seljuk Turks (12th–13th cent.) and the Mongols (13th–14th cent.). The city has had a Jewish colony for many years; the reputed tombs of Mordecai and Esther are there. Avicenna (980–1037), the physician and philosopher, is buried in Hamadan.

hamadryad, in zoology: see COBRA.

hamadryads: see NYMPH.

Hamaguchi, Osachi or **Yuko** (ō'sächē hämägōō'chē, yōō'kō), 1870–1931, Japanese statesman. He was finance minister (1924–26) and home minister (1926–27) before becoming (1927) president of the Minseito party. As prime minister (1929–30, 1931), he failed in combating economic depression. He pursued a conciliatory policy toward China and compromised with the United States in the London Naval Treaty of 1930 (see NAVAL CONFERENCES). These measures were unpopular with the militarists. He was shot by an ultranationalist in 1930 and died in 1931.

Hamah or **Hama** (both: hä'mä), city (1970 est. pop. 137,000), capital of Hamah governorate, W central Syria, on the Orontes River. It is the market center for an irrigated farm region where cotton, wheat, barley, millet, and maize are grown. Manufactures include cotton and woolen textiles, silk, underclothes, cloaks, towels, carpets, and dairy products. Famous old waterwheels, some as much as 90 ft (27 m) in diameter, bring water up from the Orontes for irrigation. Hamah is a road and rail center, and an airport is nearby. The city has a long history, having been settled as far back as the Bronze Age and Iron Age. In the 2d millennium B.C., it was a center of the Hittites. As Hamath it is often mentioned in the Bible, where it is said to be the northern boundary of the Israelite tribes. The Assyrians under Shalmaneser III captured the city in the mid-9th cent. B.C. Later included in the Persian Empire, it was conquered by Alexander the Great and, after his death (323 B.C.), was claimed by the Seleucid kings, who renamed it Epiphania, after Antiochus IV (Antiochus Epiphanes). The city later came under the control of Rome and of the Byzantine Empire. In A.D. 638 it was captured by the Arabs. Christian Crusaders held Hamah briefly (1108), but in 1188 it was taken by Saladin, in whose family it remained until it passed to Egyptian Mameluke control in 1299. An early Mameluke governor of Hamah was Abd al-Fida (reigned 1310–30), the historian and geographer. In the early 16th cent. the city came under the Ottoman Empire. After World War I it was made part of the French Levant States League of Nations mandate, and in 1941 it became part of independent Syria. Points of interest in Hamah include the remains of the Roman aqueduct (still in use) and the Great Mosque of Djami al-Nuri (until 638 a Christian basilica). Hemath is the AV form, Hamath the RV, in Amos 6.14. The Hamath-zobah taken by Solomon (2 Chron. 8.3) may have been Hamah, or it may have been a city of Zobah E of the Jordan River.

Hamamatsu (hämä'mätso͞o), city (1970 pop. 432,221), Shizuoka prefecture, S central Honshu, Japan. Its chief products are textiles, musical instruments, motorcycles, and compact cars; the weaving and dyeing industry is also important. Hamamatsu was a castle town in the 16th cent.

Haman (hā'mən) or **Aman** (ā'-), favored minister of Ahasuerus. He commanded that all Jews be put to death. ESTHER interceded for her people, and Haman was hanged on the gallows he had set up for Mordecai. Esther 3–7.

Hamann, Johann Georg (yō'hän gā'ôrk hä'mən), 1730–88, German Protestant theologian, b. Königsberg (now Kaliningrad, USSR). Although opposed to the rationalism of Kant and the German Enlightenment of Herder and Lessing, he was highly esteemed by the leading thinkers of his day. He was an advocate of religious immediacy, stressing the rights of the individual personality and the importance of inner religious experience. For Hamann, faith was the faculty of perceiving God's acts in history and His works in nature. Because of the aphoristic and occasional nature of his writings, he was called "The Magus of the North." His works, chief of which are *Sokratische Denkwürdigkeiten* (1759), *Aesthetica in nuce* (1761), and *Golgatha und Scheblimini* (1784), greatly influenced Søren Kierkegaard. See studies by R. G. Smith (1960), J. C. O'Flaherty (1952, repr. 1966), and W. M. Alexander (1966).

Hamar (hä'mär), city (1970 pop. 15,777), capital of Hedmark co., SE Norway, on Lake Mjøsa. It is a commercial, industrial, and winter-sports center. Hamar was founded in 1152 as an episcopal see by Nicholas Breakspear (later Pope Adrian IV) and is now a Lutheran episcopal see.

Hamasa (hämä'sä, həmä'sə) [Arabic,=valor], one of the great anthologies of Arabic literature. It was gathered together in the 9th cent. by ABU TAMMAM when he was snowbound in Hamadan, where he had access to an excellent library. There are 10 books of poems, classified by subject. Some of them are selections from long poems. This is one of the treasuries of early Arabic poetry, and the poems are of exceptional beauty. A later anthology by the same name was compiled by the poet al-Buhturi (c.820–897). The term has been used in modern times to mean "heroic epic."

Hamath or **Hamath-zobah:** see HAMAH, Syria.

Hambletonian (hămbəltō'nēən), 1849–76, American trotting horse, foaled at Chester, N.Y. Originally owned by Jonas Seely, Hambletonian was bought for little money by Bill Rysdyk and won few honors as a trotting horse. But Hambletonian, a very muscular bay with well-formed hind legs, became the foundation sire of the strain of trotting horses bearing his name. The Hambletonian Association, formed in 1923 to promote trotting races, offered a stake for three-year-old trotters, and the famous Hambletonian trotting event—also named for Rysdyk's horse—first took place in Syracuse in 1926. From 1930 to 1942 and from 1944 to 1956 the Hambletonian was held annually at Goshen, N.Y.; in 1957 it was moved to Du Quoin, Ill.

Hamburg (häm'bo͝orkh), officially *Freie und Hansestadt Hamburg* (Free and Hanseatic City of Hamburg), city (1970 pop. 1,793,823), coextensive with, and capital of, Hamburg state (288 sq mi/746 sq km), N West Germany, on the Elbe River near its mouth in the North Sea, and on the Alster River. It is West Germany's largest city and its busiest port. Hamburg has large shipyards and various industries whose manufactures include machinery, food products, chemicals, metal goods, and printed materials. It is a rail and road junction and serves as the base of an important fishing fleet. Most of the dock area is part of a free port. Hamburg originated (early 9th cent.) in the Carolingian castle of Hammaburg, probably built by Charlemagne as a defense against the Slavs. It became (834) an archiepiscopal see (united in 847 with the archdiocese of Bremen) and a missionary center for northern Europe. The city quickly grew to commercial importance and in 1241 formed an alliance with Lübeck, which later became the basis of the HANSEATIC LEAGUE. Hamburg accepted the Reformation in 1529. In 1558 the first German stock exchange was founded there; with the arrival of Dutch Protestants, Portuguese Jews, and English cloth merchants (expelled from Antwerp), and with the expansion of commercial ties with the United States after 1783, Hamburg continued to prosper. It was occupied by the French in 1806 and in 1815 joined the German Confederation. In 1842 a fire destroyed much of the city. After World War I Hamburg was briefly (1918–19) a socialist republic. In 1937 the city ceded CUXHAVEN, its outlying port, to Prussia, but incorporated the neighboring towns of ALTONA, HARBURG, and Wandsbek. During World War II (especially in 1943) Hamburg was severely damaged by aerial bombardment, and some 55,000 persons were killed. Rebuilt after 1945, Hamburg today is an elegant, modern city and a cultural center, widely known for its opera, theaters, magazine and book-publishing houses, radio and television broadcasting centers, and film studios. At its center are two lakes, the *Binnenalster* (Inner Alster) and the *Aussenalster* (Outer Alster). The St. Pauli district, with its well-known street, the Reeperbahn, includes numerous places of entertainment. Hamburg is the seat of a university (founded 1919), several museums, and medical and technical institutes. There are extensive zoological and botanical gardens. Noteworthy buildings include the baroque St. Michael's Church (1750–62), rebuilt (1907–12) after a fire; the Church of St. Jacobi (begun in the 14th cent.); and the Renaissance-style city hall (1886–97). Felix Mendelssohn and Johannes Brahms were born in the city.

Hamburg, village (1970 pop. 10,215), Erie co., W N.Y., S of Buffalo; settled c.1808, inc. 1874. Part of a township of 48,000 people, Hamburg is near Buffalo, where many of its inhabitants work. The village is primarily residential.

Hamden, town (1970 pop. 49,357), New Haven co., S Conn.; inc. 1786. The town, settled c.1638, was named for John Hampden, the English Puritan patriot. A residential and manufacturing suburb of New Haven, of which it was once a part, Hamden makes firearms, machinery, electrical products, metal goods, rolled steel, and handbags. The town's industrial development dates back to 1798, when Eli Whitney set up an arms factory using techniques of mass production; a plaque now marks the site. Hamden also has many early mill sites and pre-Revolutionary and Civil War houses. Quinnipiac College is in the town.

Hämeenlinna (hä'mānlĭn"nä), Swed. *Tavastehus,* city (1970 pop. 37,629), capital of Häme prov., S Finland. It is a lake port and a manufacturing town with plywood mills and spool mills. Built around a 13th-century castle on Lake Vanajavesi, the city was chartered in 1638. The beautiful Aulanko-Karlberg natural park nearby is a tourist center. Jean Sibelius was born in Hämeenlinna.

Hameln (häm'əln), Eng. *Hamelin,* city (1970 pop. 47,414), Lower Saxony, N central West Germany, a port on the Weser River. It is an industrial center and rail junction. Its manufactures include carpets, chemicals, and metal products. The city is also a tourist center, known as the scene of the legend of the PIED PIPER OF HAMELIN. Frescoes illustrating the tale adorn the so-called Ratcatcher's House (built 1602–3). An ancient Saxon settlement, Hameln became a missionary outpost c.750, received city rights c.1200, and, while frequently changing hands, acquired considerable independence. It was a member of the Hanseatic League from 1426 to 1572. The city passed to Hanover in 1814 and to Prussia in 1866. It has retained many historic buildings, including an early Gothic church (14th cent.), the Rattenkrug (built 1568), and the Wedding House (1610–17; now the city hall).

Hamhung (häm'ho͝ong'), Jap. *Kanko,* city (1962 est. pop. 125,000), capital of South Hamgyong prov., E central North Korea. It is a leading port for Korean foreign trade as well as a major industrial center. Metalware, cotton textiles, and fertilizers are manufactured. Coal mines are nearby. The founder of the Yi dynasty, the last imperial line of Korea, was born in Hamhung.

Hamilcar (hămĭl'kär, həmĭl'-), fl. 480 B.C., Carthaginian general. Little is known of him, although he was a member of the powerful Barca family. He commanded an army against GELON and the Greeks in Sicily, who severely defeated him (480 B.C.) at Himera. Hamilcar was killed in the battle.

Hamilcar Barca, d. 229 or 228 B.C., Carthaginian general. He was assigned the command in Sicily in 247 in the First Punic War (see PUNIC WARS). From mountain bases near Palermo he made repeated raids on the Romans and relieved the Punic garrison in Lilybaeum. However, the Carthaginians were defeated, and Hamilcar Barca negotiated the terms of the peace that led to Carthage's withdrawal from Sicily. The Carthaginian mercenaries shortly afterward revolted and besieged Carthage, but Hamilcar defeated them in 238. After that his popularity made him virtual dictator. He then set out (237) to conquer Spain as a new base against Rome and had won considerable territory when he died. Hamilcar was probably the ablest general and statesman that Carthage had before his son HANNIBAL.

Hamilton, Alexander, 1755–1804, American statesman, b. on Nevis in the West Indies, illegitimate son of James Hamilton (of good Scottish family) and Rachel Faucett Lavien (daughter of a doctor-planter on Nevis, estranged wife of a merchant). The brilliant, ambitious youth went to the North American colonies late in 1772 and studied (1773–74) at King's College (now Columbia). In the troubled times leading to the American Revolution, he wrote articles and pamphlets espousing the colonial cause so well that the works were then popularly attributed to John JAY. In the war he became a captain of artillery, attracted George Washington's notice, and, as Washington's secretary and aide-de-camp, performed invaluable services. Desiring more active duty, he left Washington's staff in 1781 and performed brilliantly in the field at Yorktown. His marriage to Elizabeth Schuyler, daughter of Gen. Philip J. SCHUYLER, connected him with an old and powerful New York family. He was a lawyer in New York City and a member of the Continental Congress. By 1780 he had already outlined a plan of government with a strong central authority to replace the weak system of the Articles of Confederation, and as delegate (1782–83) to the Continental Congress he pressed continually for the strengthening of the national government. It was Hamilton who proposed at the unsuccessful Annapolis Convention (1786) that a constitutional convention be called at Philadelphia in May, 1787, and he was one of New York state's three delegates to the convention when it was convened. Although he believed the Constitution to be deficient in the limited powers that it gave the national government, he did much to get it ratified, particularly by impressive contributions to The FEDERALIST. In New York, Hamilton fought vigorously against the opposition of George CLINTON to the Constitution, and of all the advocates of the new instrument of government Hamilton had perhaps the strongest voice of any except James MADISON. In the first decade of the republic, he played a decisive role in shaping domestic and foreign policy. As Secretary of the Treasury under George Washington, Hamilton presented (1790) a far-reaching financial program to the first Congress. He proposed that the debt accumulated by the Continental Congress be paid in full, that the Federal government assume all state debts, and that a Bank of the United States be chartered. For revenue, Hamilton advocated a tariff on imported manufactures and a series of excise taxes. He hoped by these measures to strengthen the national government at the expense of the states and to tie the government to men of wealth and prosperity. Hamilton was a well-to-do lawyer and banker (he helped to found the Bank of New York), and his own high connections aroused suspicion among the less conservative members of the government; his policies alienated the agrarian interests and drew opposition from those who feared concentration of power in the Federal government. A widespread antipathy to party divisions muted the opposition, however, and Congress adopted the Hamiltonian program. Foreign affairs soon brought this unity to an end. Hamilton's program depended on continued trade with Great Britain for success. He favored friendship with Great Britain and supported JAY'S TREATY (1794); he was opposed to the French Revolution and encouraged strong measures against France in the near-war of 1798—measures bitterly opposed by the pro-French Thomas Jefferson. Two opposing parties formed around these issues: the Federalists, led by Hamilton and John Adams, and the Democratic Republicans, led by Jefferson and James Madison. By that time, John Adams was President. Hamilton was perhaps the most powerful of the Federalists, but he was not in complete command of the party (he had even resigned his cabinet post in 1795, largely for financial reasons). There was little personal liking between Hamilton and Adams, and friction between them grew in the course of the Adams administration. Both were swept under in the election of 1800. Because the Constitution did not provide for the election of the President and Vice President on separate ballots, a tie between Jefferson and his running mate, Aaron BURR, left the choice of the chief executive to the House of Representatives. Hamilton's influence made Jefferson President and Aaron Burr Vice President—an outcome in accord with the popular will. Burr was, however, disgruntled, and when in 1804 Hamilton again thwarted Burr, keeping him from the governorship of New York, trouble followed. Burr accused Hamilton of having called him a "dangerous" man and, when Hamilton replied forthrightly to the charge, challenged him to a duel. The two men met at Weehawken Heights, N.J., and Hamilton was mortally wounded. Publication of the definitive edition of the Hamilton papers was begun in 1961 (ed. by Harold C. Syrett), and 22 volumes have been published. Publication of Hamilton's law papers, (ed. by Julius Goebel, Jr.) was begun in 1964. See biographies by Nathan Schachner (1946, repr. 1961), Broadus Mitchell (2 vol., 1957-62), John C. Miller (1959, repr. 1964), and one in his own words, ed. by M. J. Kline (2 vol., 1973); Richard Morris, ed., *Alexander Hamilton and the Founding of the Nation* (1957); Jacob E. Cooke, ed., *Alexander Hamilton: A Profile* (1967); Gerald Stourgh, *Alexander Hamilton and the Idea of Republican Government* (1969); Broadus Mitchell, *Alexander Hamilton: The Revolutionary Years* (1970).

Hamilton, Alice, 1869-1970, American toxicologist, physician, and educator, b. New York City, M.D. Univ. of Michigan, 1893; she continued her studies in Germany. A pioneer in industrial diseases and hygiene, she joined the faculty of Harvard Medical School in 1919 and became emeritus professor of industrial medicine in 1935. Her services as an outstanding authority on industrial conditions, ailments, and poisons were eagerly sought by political and government agencies. She worked with the state of Illinois, the U.S. Dept. of Commerce, and the health committee of the League of Nations. Her publications include *Industrial Poisoning in the United States* (1925), *Industrial Toxicology* (1934), and *Exploring the Dangerous Trades,* an autobiography (1943).

Hamilton, Andrew, d. 1703, colonial governor of New Jersey, b. Scotland. Becoming deputy governor of East Jersey in 1687, Hamilton defended the proprietors against popular opposition and shortly had to leave the colony. In 1692 he was commissioned governor of East and West Jersey, but after five years of effective administration he was removed by the proprietors to please the crown. When he was recalled he could not restore authority. Appointed deputy postmaster general for the colonies in 1692, Hamilton induced several colonies to set up uniform postal rates. In 1701, William Penn appointed him deputy governor of Pennsylvania, a post he held until his death.

Hamilton, Andrew, 1676?-1741, colonial American lawyer, defender of John Peter ZENGER, b. Scotland. He practiced law in Maryland and then Pennsylvania, where he became (1717) attorney general and held other offices. When the governing party in New York had disbarred all local lawyers who ventured to defend Zenger, Hamilton was brought in and by his brilliant defense secured Zenger's acquittal (1735), establishing truth as a defense against libel charges. See biography by A. B. Konkle (1941).

Hamilton, Andrew Jackson, 1815-75, American politician, b. Huntsville, Ala. Moving to Texas in 1846, he served (1849) as attorney general, was a member of the legislature (1851-53), and in 1859 was elected as a Unionist to the U.S. House of Representatives. He returned (1861) to the state legislature, but after the outbreak of the Civil War he fled (1862) to Washington. Abraham Lincoln appointed him a brigadier general of volunteers and military governor of Texas, and in June, 1865, he was made provisional governor by Andrew Johnson. Hamilton pressed for equal civil rights for whites and blacks, but the state constitutional convention (1866) rejected his program. As leader of the conservative Republicans, he ran (1869) unsuccessfully for governor. See biography by J. L. Waller (1968).

Hamilton, Anthony, 1646?-1720, French author of Scottish descent, b. Ireland. He spent much time in France, where he became a master of the French language. He fought in the Dutch Wars for Louis XIV and commanded an Irish regiment for James II in 1687. His most celebrated work is the *Mémoires du comte de Grammont* (1713), based on the life of his brother-in-law, Philibert, comte de GRAMONT. They are especially valuable for their pictures of life at the court of Charles II. See translation by Peter Quennell (1930).

Hamilton, Emma, Lady, 1765?-1815, mistress of the British naval hero Horatio NELSON. Born Emma Lyon, she became the mistress of Charles Greville, then of Sir William HAMILTON, ambassador to Naples, whom she married (1791). She gained enormous influence with Neapolitan Queen Marie Caroline. Her intimacy with Nelson began in 1798, and after returning to England with him, she bore him a daughter, Horatia, in 1801. Although she received legacies from both her husband and Nelson, she died in debt and obscurity. Portraits of her were painted by many of the famous artists of her day; many are by George Romney. See biographies by Walter Sichel (1905), Marjorie Bowen (1935), and Mollie Hardwick (1970).

Hamilton, Sir Ian Standish Monteith (ē'ən, mŏntēth'), 1853-1947, British general. He served in many campaigns in Asia and Africa, distinguishing himself in the South African War (1899-1902). He was military attaché with the Japanese in the Russo-Japanese War (1904-5). During World War I he commanded (1915) the Mediterranean expeditionary force in the abortive GALLIPOLI CAMPAIGN. Relieved of his command, he spent his later years in pacifistic activities. His books include *The Millennium?* (1918), *Gallipoli Diary* (1920), and *Listening for the Drums* (1944). See biography by his nephew, I. B. M. Hamilton (1966).

Hamilton, James, 1st **earl of Arran** (ăr'ən), 1477?-1529, Scottish nobleman; son of the 1st Baron Hamilton and Mary, daughter of James II of Scotland. He was privy councilor to James IV, by whom he was created (1503) earl of Arran. After the death (1513) of James and the marriage of his widow, MARGARET TUDOR, to Archibald DOUGLAS, 6th earl of Angus, Arran opposed their custody of the young JAMES V. He rebelled against the new regent, John STUART, duke of Albany, in 1515 but thereafter supported him, serving on the council of regency during Albany's absences (1517-20 and 1522-24). When Angus returned (1524) to Scotland, Arran had to come to terms with him and assisted him in keeping the king prisoner. After James's escape (1528), however, Arran joined the royal party.

Hamilton, James, 2d **earl of Arran,** d. 1575, Scottish nobleman; son of James Hamilton, 1st earl of Arran. After the death (1542) of James V, he stood next in line to the throne after the infant MARY QUEEN OF SCOTS. A Protestant and member of the pro-English party, he was chosen regent in preference to Cardinal David BEATON. However, in 1543 he became a Catholic and joined the French party. Although he had previously negotiated a marriage treaty with England, he consented to the marriage of the young queen to the French dauphin (later Francis II) and was created (1548) duc de Châtelherault in France. Forced (1554) to give up the regency to the queen mother, MARY OF GUISE, he joined (1559) the Protestant uprising of the lords of the congregation. He was exiled from Scotland after Queen Mary married Lord Darnley (1565). In 1569 he returned and was imprisoned until he agreed (1573) to recognize James VI (later James I of England) as king.

Hamilton, James, 3d **earl of Arran,** 1530-1609, Scottish nobleman; son of James Hamilton, 2d earl of Arran. He spent some years (1550-58) as a soldier in France, but his espousal of Protestantism brought his recall to Scotland, where his father, with the concurrence of John Knox, unsuccessfully proposed him as a suitor for Elizabeth I of England and then for Mary Queen of Scots. In 1562 he accused the earl of BOTHWELL of conspiring to abduct Queen Mary. He was clearly insane, however, and as a result was imprisoned until 1566. Arran succeeded to his father's estates in 1575, but because of his insanity he was placed under the care of his brother, John Hamilton, 1st marquess of Hamilton. The Arran estates and title were forfeited to James Stuart (see STUART, JAMES, EARL OF ARRAN) in 1580 but restored in 1585. Arran, however, remained in confinement for the rest of his life.

Hamilton, James Douglas, 4th **duke of,** 1658-1712, Scottish nobleman. He served at the courts of Charles II and James II and remained, after his grudging acceptance of William III, a sympathizer with the Jacobites. He became duke of Hamilton in 1698 and, although he had opposed the union of Scotland with England, entered the united Parliament as a representative Scottish peer in 1708. Coming into favor with the Tory regime after 1710, he was made privy councilor (1710), duke of Brandon (1711), and ambassador to Paris (1712). He was killed in a duel by Lord Mohun before he could go to France. Suspicion of foul play caused the Tories to accuse the Whigs of murdering him, alleging that the Whigs feared he was about to engineer a Jacobite restoration from France. The duel is described in Thackeray's *Henry Esmond.*

Hamilton, James Hamilton, 3d **marquess** and 1st **duke of,** 1606-49, Scottish nobleman; grandson of John Hamilton, 1st marquess of Hamilton. He succeeded (1625) his father as marquess of Hamilton and earl of Cambridge and was appointed (1628) privy councilor in Scotland. He raised (1630) an army to fight under Gustavus Adolphus of Sweden in the Thirty Years War, but his expedition ended in disaster (1633). As Charles I's commissioner in Scotland, he tried to conciliate the COVENANTERS in 1638 and, failing, led a force against them in the first Bishops' War. Later his attempt to come to terms with Archibald Campbell, 8th earl of ARGYLL, apparently gave rise (1641) to the obscure plot known as the Incident, devised by James Graham, 5th earl of MONTROSE, to seize and probably murder Hamilton, his brother William (later 2d duke of Hamilton), and Argyll. Hamilton escaped and managed to retain the confidence of the king, being created duke in 1643. In 1644, however, he was imprisoned by Charles on suspicion of treachery, and he was freed only by parliamentary troops in 1646. In 1648, Hamilton secured ratification in the Scottish Parliament of the agreement known as the Engagement between Charles and the Scots and led the Scottish army that invaded England. Defeated at Preston, he was captured, tried by the same court that condemned Charles, and executed.

Hamilton, John Hamilton, 1st **marquess of,** 1532-1604, Scottish nobleman; second son of James Hamilton, 2d earl of Arran. He was in his earlier years hostile to Mary Queen of Scots, but he later became her supporter and as a result forfeited his lands. In revenge he was party to the murder (1570) of the regent, James Stuart, 1st earl of Murray. In 1573 Hamilton represented his family at the Pacification of Perth, when the Hamiltons acknowledged Mary's son, James VI (later James I of England), as king. The death of his father in 1575 made him the nearest heir to the throne of Scotland and placed him at the head of the Hamilton family because of the insanity of his elder brother James, 3d earl of Arran. In 1579 proceedings were started against him in connection with Murray's murder, and he fled to England, where he tried unsuccessfully to secure support. With other banished lords he returned to Scotland in 1585, was reconciled with James, and thereafter enjoyed possession of his family's estates and the favor and confidence of the king. He was created marquess in 1599.

Hamilton, Patrick, 1504?-1528, Scottish Protestant martyr. While at St. Andrews, he was suspected of Lutheran sympathies. He fled (1527) to Germany, where, during his short stay, he met Luther and Melanchthon. In Germany he wrote *Loci communes,* known as *Patrick's Places,* embodying the doctrines of the Reformation. When Hamilton returned in 1527 to Scotland, he was charged with heresy, sentenced by Archbishop Beaton, and burned at the stake in 1528. See biographies by Peter Lorimer (in *Precursors of John Knox,* 1857), T. P. Johnston (1882), and A. Cameron (1929).

Hamilton, William, 1704-54, English poet, b. Scotland. He is best known for the poem "The Braes of Yarrow" (1724).

Hamilton, Sir William, 1730-1803, British diplomat and archaeologist, ambassador to Naples (1764-1800). He is chiefly remembered as the husband of Lady Emma Hamilton, mistress of Horatio Nelson. His fine collection of antiquities from Pompeii was sold to the British Museum in 1772. His publications include *Antiquités étrusques, greques et romaines* (1766-67) and *Mount Vesuvius* (1772). See biography by Brian Fothergill (1969); Jack Russell, *Nelson and the Hamiltons* (1969).

Hamilton, Sir William, 1788-1856, Scottish philosopher. He was widely interested in law, physiology, and literature and was professor of history and philosophy at the Univ. of Edinburgh. Hamilton helped to reestablish the waning fame of the Scottish school of metaphysics. His "Philosophy of the Unconditioned" (1829), a critique of Cousin's *Cours de philosophie* published in the *Edinburgh Review,* publicized his views on the infinite, which he considered unknowable. Under the influence of Kant, he conceived of the world that man knows as finite and conditioned in terms of space, time, and degree. In logic his attempt to "quantify the predicate" was a crude anticipation of later developments in mathematical logic. The British academic outlook was broadened by his emphasis on the German philosophers and on Aristotle. His son, Francis, published his *Lectures on Metaphysics and Logic* (ed. by H. L. Mansel and John Veitch, 4 vol., 1859–60, repr. 1969).

Hamilton, William Hamilton, 2d duke of, 1616–51, Scottish nobleman. With his brother James Hamilton, 3d marquess and 1st duke of Hamilton, he gained favor with Charles I of England. He was created (1639) earl of Lanark and made (1640) secretary of state for Scotland. In 1643, on Charles's orders, he was arrested with his brother for supposed implication in the latter's intrigues, but he escaped (1644). He regained favor when he went in 1646 as one of the Scottish commissioners to treat with Charles at Newcastle. In 1647 he was one of the signers for the Scots of the treaty with Charles known as the Engagement, and he helped to organize the second civil war. After the Scottish defeat at Preston (1648), he fled to Holland. He returned in 1650 with Charles II and joined the Scottish invasion of England. He died of wounds received at the battle of Worcester.

Hamilton, Sir William Rowan, 1805–65, British mathematician, b. Dublin. A child prodigy, he had mastered 13 languages by the age of 13 and was still an undergraduate when he became professor of astronomy at the Univ. of Dublin (1827). Hamilton was one of the most original and creative mathematicians of his time. In his *Theory of Systems of Rays* (1828) he predicted the existence of conical refraction (later confirmed experimentally by H. Lloyd) and unified the field of optics under the principle of varying action, which he later extended to dynamics and which has become of fundamental importance in modern physics, particularly quantum theory. His later years, which were marred by personal problems, were largely devoted to the invention and development of his theory of quaternions. Although he believed this work to be his most important, quaternions have been superseded in most applications by the methods of vector and tensor analysis. Of some import, however, was his discovery that the algebra of quaternions does not follow the commutative law; it opened the way for the discovery and development of numerous types of abstract algebras by later mathematicians. See E. T. Bell, *Men of Mathematics* (1937).

Hamilton, city (1970 est. pop. 2,127), capital of Bermuda, on Bermuda Island. It is a free port at the head of Great Sound, a huge lagoon protected by coral reefs. The city is the focus of Bermuda's commercial and social life and is a major tourist resort.

Hamilton, city (1971 pop. 309,173), S Ont., Canada, at the western end of Lake Ontario. It is situated on a narrow plain between its harbor (connected by canal with the lake) and the Niagara escarpment. Hamilton, one of Canada's largest cities, is an important port, transportation center, and manufacturing city. It is Canada's leading producer of iron and steel; other manufactures include automobiles, heavy machinery, and paper and textile products. The site was settled by UNITED EMPIRE LOYALISTS in 1778. Places of interest include the Royal Botanical Gardens, the open-air market, and the historical museum in Dundern Park. McMaster Univ. (1887) is in the city.

Hamilton, city (1971 pop. 74,784), N central North Island, New Zealand, on the Waikato River. Hamilton is the urban center of a densely populated dairy area. It was founded as a military settlement on the site of a deserted Maori village in 1864. The Univ. of Waikato, founded in 1964, is in the city.

Hamilton, burgh (1971 pop. 46,347), Lanarkshire, S central Scotland, at the confluence of the Avon and the Clyde rivers. The administrative center of Lanarkshire, it is a market town with metal products and other industries. Rudolf Hess landed near Hamilton after his flight from Germany in May, 1941. In 1975, Hamilton became part of the new Strathclyde region.

Hamilton, city (1970 pop. 67,865), seat of Butler co., SW Ohio, on the Great Miami River; inc. 1857. A manufacturing center in a highly industrialized valley, Hamilton has paper and pulp mills, huge blast furnaces, and many factories that make a great variety of products, including safes, machinery, chemicals, and pumps and motors. Hamilton was settled on the site of Fort Hamilton, built in 1791 by Arthur St. Clair. William Dean Howells lived there as a boy. Miami Univ. has a branch in Hamilton.

Hamilton, river, Labrador: see CHURCHILL 1, river.

Hamilton, Mount, peak 4,372 ft (1,333 m) high, W Calif., in the Coast Ranges, E of San Jose. It is the site of Lick Observatory (built 1876–88), directed by the Univ. of California. In 1959 a 120-in. (305-cm) telescope was installed by the California Institute of Technology.

Hamilton College, at Clinton, N.Y.; for men; founded 1793 by Samuel Kirkland as Hamilton-Oneida Academy, chartered 1812 as Hamilton College. It was named for Alexander Hamilton. Hamilton is noted for its liberal arts curriculum. The school has a cooperative program with nearby Kirkland College (founded 1968; for women).

Hamilton Grange National Memorial: see NATIONAL PARKS AND MONUMENTS (table).

Hamilton Inlet: see MELVILLE, LAKE, Canada.

Hamina (hä'mĭnä), Swed. *Fredrikshamn*, city (1970 pop. 11,028), Kymi prov., SE Finland, on the Gulf of Finland. Hamina is an important port. Timber and wood products are exported. Originally named Veckelaks, it was a noted trade center in the Middle Ages. The Treaty of Fredrikshamn (1809), by which Sweden ceded all of Finland to Russia, was signed in Hamina.

Hamites, African people of caucasoid descent who occupy the Horn of Africa (chiefly Somalia and Ethiopia), the western Sahara, and parts of Algeria and Tunisia. They are believed to be the original settlers of N Africa. The Hamitic cradleland is generally agreed to be in Asia—perhaps S Arabia or possibly an area farther east. The Hamites entered Africa in a long succession of migrations, of which the earliest may have been as far back as the end of the pluvial period. They are commonly divided into two great branches, Eastern and Northern. The Eastern Hamites comprise the ancient and modern Egyptians, the Beja, the Berberines, the GALLA, the Somali, the Danakil, and most Ethiopians. The Northern Hamites include the BERBERS of Cyrenaica, Tripolitania, Tunisia, and Algeria, the Berbers of Morocco, the TUAREG and Tibu of the Sahara, the Fulbe of the Western Sudan, and the extinct Guanche of the Canary Islands.

Hamitic languages, subfamily of the Hamito-Semitic family of languages. See HAMITO-SEMITIC LANGUAGES.

Hamito-Semitic languages (hăm'ĭtō-səmĭt'ĭk), family of languages spoken by approximately 130 million people in N Africa; much of the Sahara; parts of E, central, and W Africa; and W Asia (especially the Arabian peninsula, Iraq, Syria, Jordan, Lebanon, and Israel). Since four of the Semitic tongues, Arabic, Hebrew, Coptic, and Syriac, are also respectively the languages of Islam, Judaism, and two sects of the Christian faith, the Hamito-Semitic family reaches many millions in addition to its native speakers. Recently it has been recommended that the term *Afroasiatic* be used instead of *Hamito-Semitic* to designate this language family, partly because it is the only one whose member tongues are found in both Africa and Asia and partly because the new name is regarded by some authorities as more accurate from the standpoint of modern linguistics. However, many scholars still consider the older term, Hamito-Semitic, satisfactory if used in a linguistic rather than an anthropological sense. Traditionally, the Hamito-Semitic language family is said to have two subfamilies: Semitic (with languages spoken by about 100 million persons) and Hamitic (with languages native to about 30 million people). Although some scholars regard Hamitic and Semitic as two distinct language families, they possess a number of grammatical similarities and have a larger common vocabulary than borrowing would account for. The most satisfactory explanation is that the Hamitic and Semitic groups, despite their divergences, are subfamilies of a single Hamito-Semitic linguistic family, as evidenced by their marked grammatical, lexical, and phonological resemblances. The Hamitic subfamily is generally considered to include ancient Egyptian (see EGYPTIAN LANGUAGE) and its descendant, COPTIC; the Berber languages; and the Cushitic languages. Ancient Egyptian and Coptic are extinct. Some linguists also place the Chad languages within the Hamitic subfamily. Those Hamitic tongues are or were spoken in N Africa, much of the Sahara, the Horn of E Africa, and parts of central and W Africa. They were named after Ham, the second son of the biblical Noah, whose descendants supposedly were the original speakers of the Hamitic languages. Whereas ancient Egyptian, Coptic, and the Berber tongues were or are the languages of white people, the Cushitic and Chad tongues are spoken largely by blacks. Why native speakers of the Hamitic subfamily are both white and black is not known. The Berber languages are the mother tongues of more than 10 million persons in N Africa. The oldest known Berber inscriptions are from the 4th cent. B.C., but Berber-speaking peoples have lived in N Africa since c.3000 B.C., and Berber names appear in ancient Egyptian inscriptions of the Old Kingdom. The Berber tongues have survived Phoenician, Roman, and Arab conquests. Today they are spoken in Morocco, Tunisia, Algeria, Libya, Egypt, Mauritania, Chad, and Niger. Many Berbers are bilingual, speaking also Arabic. The modern Berber variants include Tamachek, Zenaga, Kabyle, Rif, Siwi, and others. Grammatically, gender and number are indicated by prefixes and suffixes. The vocabulary has been enriched by borrowings from Latin, Arabic, French, and Spanish. The Arabic alphabet is employed, except in the case of the Tamachek dialect, which continues to use an ancient Berber alphabet known as Tifinagh. The name *Cushitic* is derived from *Cush*, a son of Ham. The principal Cushitic languages are Galla, the tongue of 6 million people in Ethiopia and Kenya, and Somali, spoken by 3 million people in the Somali Republic, Ethiopia, and Afars and Issas. Among the many other Cushitic languages are Saho-Afar, Agau, Beja, Burji, Geleba, Gimira, Janjero, Konso, Kaffa, Maji, and Sidamo. Galla is written in the Ethiopic script (see discussion of writing below) and Somali in the Roman alphabet. The Chad group of languages is found near Lake Chad in central Africa. Its most important tongue is Hausa, native to 9 million people, of whom more than 7 million live in N Nigeria, 1 million in Niger, and 1 million in the Cameroons, Togo, and Dahomey. In addition, Hausa is widely used in W Africa as a lingua franca by large numbers of nonnative speakers. Hausa has long employed an alphabet based on that of Arabic, but today it is turning increasingly to a writing system based on Roman characters. The written literature in Hausa includes both poetry and prose. Among the many other Chad languages are Angas, Bolewa, Gwandara, Hiji, Kuseri, Kotoko, Mandara, Ron, Shirawa, and Sokoro. The Semitic languages are named after Shem or Sem, the oldest son of Noah, from whom most of their speakers were said to be descended. These languages are believed to have evolved from a hypothetical parent tongue, proto-Semitic. The place of origin of proto-Semitic is still disputed; Africa, Arabia, and Mesopotamia are the most probable locations. The Semitic subfamily may be divided into North Semitic and South Semitic. The former has the subdivisions Northeast Semitic and Northwest Semitic, while the latter is made up of Southeast Semitic and Southwest Semitic. An example of a Northeast Semitic language is AKKADIAN, also called Assyro-Babylonian. The principal subdivisions of the Northwest Semitic group are Canaanite, Ugaritic, and ARAMAIC (which embraced many dialects in the course of its long history, including SYRIAC). The name *Canaanite* is derived from *Canaan*, the ancient region that comprised Palestine, Phoenicia, and part of Syria. Included among the Canaanite languages are Phoenician, Moabite, and HEBREW. Phoenician, a dead language, was the tongue of the Phoenician people. The earliest inscriptions in Phoenician that can be deciphered are dated c.10th cent. B.C. The language is also preserved in inscriptions from ancient Phoenician colonies, especially Carthage, whose language was a variant of Phoenician known as Punic. The existence of Moabite is known from a single inscription in that language dating back to about the 9th cent. B.C., from proper names that occur in the Old Testament, and from the inscriptions of other peoples. The Ugaritic language was first encountered in 1929 at Ras Shamra, Syria, a village where ancient clay tablets with writing in this tongue were found. Since Ras Shamra, which flourished before the 12th cent. B.C., was called Ugarit in antiquity, the language discovered there was named after that ancient city. The Ugaritic language has variously been regarded as an early form of Hebrew, an early form of Phoenician, an early dialect of Canaanite, and an independent dialect of Northwest Semitic. Its classification is still unresolved. The writings in Ugaritic are important in the study of the Hebrew language and biblical literature of the early period. To the Southwest Semitic group belong both classical ARABIC and the modern Arabic dialects. Southeast Semitic is represented by the South Arabic language of ancient South Arabia, which is preserved in inscriptions, and by the Semitic languages of Ethiopia, such as classical ETHIOPIC or Geez, AM-

HARIC, Tigre, and Tigrinya. About 5,000 stone inscriptions in South Arabic (or Himyaritic) were found in what are now Yemen and Southern Yemen. Ancient South Arabic had two principal dialects, Sabaean and Minaean. Sabaean inscriptions were also discovered in parts of Ethiopia. The earliest Minaean inscriptions belong to the 8th cent. B.C. or even earlier; the Sabaean inscriptions are of a later date. Some dialects spoken today in parts of S Arabia are called Modern South Arabic. Their relationship to the ancient South Arabic dialects of the inscriptions has not yet been determined. A Semitic language (or languages) was brought from S Arabia to Ethiopia during the first millennium B.C. by Semites. At that time the native languages of Ethiopia were Cushitic, and these languages strongly influenced the imported Semitic tongues. The Semitic languages of Ethiopia are classified as North Ethiopic (to which Geez or classical Ethiopic, Tigre, and Tigrinya belong) and South Ethiopic (consisting of Amharic, Harari, Gurage, and others). A distinctive feature of the Semitic languages is the triliteral or triconsonantal root, composed of three consonants separated by vowels. The basic meaning of a word is expressed by the consonants, and different shades of this basic meaning are indicated by vowel changes. An example from Arabic is the root *KTB*, "write." This can become *KaTaBa*, "he wrote," *KuTiBa*, "it was written," *yaKTuBu*, "he will write," *yuKTaBu*, "it will be written," *aKTaBa*, "he caused someone to write," *KiTaB*, "book," *KuTuB*, "books," *KaTiB*, "writer," and *KaTBun*, "act of writing." The plural can be formed either by adding a suffix to the singular or by an internal vowel change, as in Arabic *kitab*, "book," but *kutub*, "books." The use of internal change for the plural has all but died out except in Arabic, South Arabic, and North Ethiopic, but there are traces of it in other Semitic languages. Two genders, masculine and feminine, are found in Semitic languages. The feminine is often indicated by the suffixes *-t* or *-at*. The Semitic verb is distinguished by its ability to form from the same root a number of derived stems that express new meanings based on the fundamental sense, such as passive, reflexive, causative, and intensive. These stems can be formed in several ways, as by a change in the internal vowels or by the addition of a prefix. Proto-Semitic apparently lacked a definite article, but later a number of the Semitic languages developed one. There were three cases in proto-Semitic: nominative, genitive, and accusative. Akkadian and classical Arabic retain the cases, of which there are merely traces in the other Semitic languages. There were three numbers in proto-Semitic: singular, dual, and plural. The dual is found in Akkadian, Hebrew, South Arabic, and Arabic; and traces of it are preserved in the other Semitic languages. The proto-Semitic verb originally had aspects rather than tenses. These aspects were the perfect, expressing a completed action, and the imperfect, expressing an uncompleted action. Later on the perfect was used to indicate the past and the imperfect to denote the present or future. Reviewing the entire Hamito-Semitic family grammatically, one finds two genders, masculine and feminine. The feminine is usually indicated in nouns and adjectives by the suffixes *-t* or *-at*. Gender is found in the noun, the adjective, the pronoun, and the verb. The plural of nouns may be formed by internal change, the addition of suffixes, or partial reduplication. The verb tends to be more highly developed in connection with aspect or mood than with regard to tense. Verbal conjugation is marked by a combination of internal change and the use of prefixes and suffixes. The formation of derivative verbs (as of a causative, reflexive, or passive nature), often by prefixes, is characteristic. In Egyptian and Berber, as well as in the Semitic languages, one finds the triliteral or triconsonantal root mentioned earlier. The languages of the Hamito-Semitic family are thought to have first been spoken along the shores of the Red Sea. One theory holds that the Hamito-Semitic, or Afroasiatic, language family came into being in Africa, for only in Africa are all its members found, aside from some Semitic languages encountered in W Asia. The existence of the Semitic languages in W Asia is explained by assuming that the Semites of Africa migrated from E Africa to W Asia in very ancient times. At a later date, some Semites returned from Arabia to Africa. The writing used for Semitic languages is either CUNEIFORM or alphabetic writing. The latter has two principal divisions, the North Semitic script and the South Semitic script. The oldest known writing system employed by Semitic-speaking peoples is cuneiform. It was adopted by the Akkadians (see AKKAD) c.2500 B.C. from the Sumerians (see SUMER), whose language was not a Semitic tongue. The Sumerian cuneiform goes back to about 4000 B.C., and it was used by various peoples until about the 2d cent. B.C. Babylonian and Assyrian, which were later dialects of Akkadian, also employed cuneiform. At first cuneiform was written from right to left vertically, but at a later date the direction of writing was reversed, that is, from left to right horizontally. The North Semitic and South Semitic scripts are thought by some scholars to go back to a common source, a hypothetical proto-Semitic writing system. Although proto-Semitic writing has not survived, the assumption of its existence is considered by certain authorities to be the most satisfactory explanation of the close resemblances between very early examples of North Semitic and South Semitic writings. Others dispute this and regard the origin of the South Semitic ALPHABET as a still unsolved problem. The source of the proto-Semitic alphabetic script has been variously conjectured to be Egyptian HIEROGLYPHICS, Babylonian cuneiform, or other writing systems. It has been claimed that the proto-Semitic writing system, which probably took form in the territory of Syria and Palestine some time between 2000 and 1500 B.C., is the ancestor of all the alphabets of the world, both ancient and modern. The North Semitic writing is alphabetic in that each sign or symbol represents a consonantal sound of the language. Vowels for some time were omitted. Symbols of various kinds to indicate the vowels for Hebrew, Arabic, and Syriac probably date from the 8th cent. A.D. The North Semitic script consists of a Canaanite branch and an Aramaic branch. The Canaanite branch gave rise to Early Hebrew writing and Phoenician writing. Another descendant of the Canaanite branch is the Greek alphabet, which is the parent of all modern European alphabets, including the Roman and the Cyrillic. According to a Greek tradition the Phoenicians passed on their alphabet to the Greeks. The oldest extant Early Hebrew text is dated at about the 11th or 10th cent. B.C. Early Hebrew writing was the alphabet of the Jews until they adopted Aramaic instead of Hebrew as their spoken language some time before the Christian era, when they also began to use the Square Hebrew letters derived from the Aramaic writing. The only descendant of the Early Hebrew alphabet still in use is the Samaritan writing. Records of the Aramaic script go back to the 9th cent. B.C. After about 500 B.C. the Aramaic alphabet was used throughout the Middle East. In addition to being the parent of Square Hebrew letters, from which evolved modern Hebrew writing, the Aramaic alphabet is the ancestor of Arabic writing, the Syriac scripts, and other Semitic alphabets. Aramaic writing probably also gave rise to the significant alphabetic writing systems of Asia, such as the Devanagari alphabet so widely used in India. As Islam spread to various nations in Africa and Asia, it was accompanied by the Arabic alphabet. For example, Arabic writing was adapted for Persian, Pushtu, Urdu, Malay, the Berber languages, Swahili, Hausa, and Turkish. (Since 1928 the Roman alphabet has been used for Turkish.) The South Arabic inscriptions mentioned earlier employed the South Semitic alphabet, which is no longer used on the Arabian peninsula. This alphabet was taken to Ethiopia during the first millennium B.C. and is still used there, in modified form, for the Ethiopic languages. In fact, the sole noteworthy South Semitic script to survive until modern times is the one employed for the Ethiopic languages. All other known alphabets are believed to be derived from North Semitic writing. Although the South Arabic letters form a consonantal alphabet, the Ethiopic writing is syllabic in nature. Ethiopic consonants have six or more forms, each depending on the vowel following the consonant. This may be a later development. In any case, the origin of the syllabic nature of the Ethiopic script is an unsolved problem. All Semitic languages are writtten from right to left except Ethiopic, Assyrian, and Babylonian, which are written from left to right. See L. H. Gray, *Introduction to Semitic Comparative Linguistics* (1934); M. A. Bryan, *Notes on the Distribution of the Semitic and Cushitic Languages of Africa* (1947); Sabatine Moscati, ed., *An Introduction to the Comparative Grammar of the Semitic Languages* (1964); J. H. Greenberg, *The Languages of Africa* (2d ed. 1966); De Lacy E. O'Leary, *Comparative Grammar of the Semitic Languages* (1923, repr. 1969).

Hamlin, Hannibal, 1809-91, Vice President of the United States (1861-65), b. Paris, Maine. Admitted to the bar in 1833, he practiced at Hampden, Maine. He was a Maine legislator (1836-40, 1847), a U.S. Representative (1843-47), and a U.S. Senator (1848-57). As a Democrat he supported Franklin Pierce's administration, but left (1856) his party when it adopted a strong proslavery platform, and joined the Republican party; in the same year he was elected governor of Maine. After a few weeks he resigned to reenter (1857) the U.S. Senate, where he became increasingly prominent. Geographical and political considerations made him a natural choice as Abraham Lincoln's running mate in 1860. As Vice President during the Civil War he presided over the Senate with ability and took part in a variety of governmental wartime activities. He returned to the Senate (1869-81), supporting the Reconstruction and the economic policies of his party. He was minister to Spain in 1881-82. See biographies by his grandson Charles E. Hamlin (1899, repr. 1971) and H. D. Hunt (1969).

Hamlin, Talbot Faulkner, 1889-1956, American historian of architecture, writer, and theoretician, b. New York City. He was librarian of Avery Library, Columbia Univ., and later professor of architecture there. Hamlin wrote *Some European Architectural Libraries* (1939), *Architecture through the Ages* (1940), *Greek Revival Architecture in America* (1944), *Architecture: An Art for all Men* (1947), and *Benjamin Henry Latrobe* (1955). He also edited the basic reference text *Forms and Functions of Twentieth Century Architecture* (1952).

Hamm (hăm), city (1970 pop. 84,942), North Rhine-Westphalia, W West Germany, on the Lippe River, in the RUHR district. The city contains iron and steel foundries and manufactures textiles and machinery. Founded in 1226, Hamm was the capital of the county of Mark until 1809. An active member of the Hanseatic League, it passed to Cleves in the 14th cent. and later (1614) to Brandenburg. The city was badly damaged in World War II.

Hamm, village, S Grand Duchy of Luxembourg, near Luxembourg city. Gen. George S. Patton is buried in the large U.S. military cemetery there.

Hammarskjöld, Dag (däg häm'ərshōld", Swed. häm'ärshöld'), 1905-61, Swedish statesman, secretary general of the United Nations (1953-61). He attended the universities of Uppsala and Stockholm (Ph.D., 1934). The son of a former prime minister of Sweden, Hjalmar Hammarskjöld, he entered government service in 1930. He was chairman of the board of the Bank of Sweden (1941-48), performed many diplomatic missions, and entered (1951) the Swedish cabinet as deputy foreign minister. Hammarskjöld served (1951-53) in the Swedish delegation to the United Nations and in 1953 was elected to succeed Trygve Lie as secretary general. He was reelected in 1957. During his tenure Hammarskjöld greatly extended the influence of the United Nations as well as the prestige of the secretary general. A quiet, tactful, and highly active diplomat, he personally led missions to Peking (1955), the Middle East (1956, 1958), and elsewhere to lessen tensions or to arrange peace settlements. Under his guidance a UN emergency force was established to help maintain order in the Middle East after the 1956 Suez crisis, and UN observation forces were sent to Laos and Lebanon. He initiated and directed (1960-61) the United Nation's vigorous role in the Republic of the Congo (now ZAÏRE) against the strong opposition of the Soviet Union. He was on a mission to the Congo when his plane crashed in Northern Rhodesia (now Zambia) on Sept. 18, 1961. He was succeeded as secretary general by U Thant. Hammarskjöld was posthumously awarded the 1961 Nobel Peace Prize. See his book of personal reflections, *Markings* (1964) and his *Public Papers, 1953-1956*, ed. by A. W. Cordier and Wilder Foote (1972); study by Brian Urquhart (1972).

Hammath (hăm'ăth). **1** Fortified Naphtalite city. Joshua 19.35. It is probably the Hammon of 1 Chron. 6.76 and the Hammothdor of Joshua 21.32. **2** Father of the founder of the house of Rechab. 1 Chron. 2.55.

Hammedatha (hămĕd'əthə,-ədā'thə), father of Haman. Esther 3.1.

Hammelech (hăm'ēlĕk) [Heb.,=the king], in the Bible, form occurring in Jer. 36.26 and 38.6. The translators of KJV took it for a name, but it is better translated "the king."

Hammerfest (hä'mərfĕst), town (1970 est. pop. 7,060), Finnmark co., N Norway, on Kvaløy island. It is the northernmost town of Europe, but its harbor is always ice-free. The town has sealing and fishing industries and fish-processing plants. Tourists are attracted by its uninterrupted daylight from May 17 to July 29. Chartered c.1795, Hammerfest was heavily damaged by British naval bombardment in 1809, by fire in 1890, and by retreating German forces in 1944.

hammerhead, common name for a heavy-looking, heronlike bird, *Scopus umbretta*. Its plumage is brown with light and dark glossy, purplish streaks on the wings and body. It has short legs, partially webbed feet, and a heavy, wide, moderately long, black bill. Its stiff, backward-pointing crest, along with its peculiar bill, give its head a hammer-shaped appearance. Both sexes are similarly arrayed. Long-winged and long-tailed, the hammerhead, or hammerkop (as it is called in Africa), may reach a body length of 20 in. (51 cm). It is an inhabitant of the marshes and mangrove swamps of southern Arabia, Africa, and Madagascar, where it feeds primarily on aquatic animals, such as water insects, small fish, and amphibians. It often perches on the back of hippopotamuses, searching for frogs. Hammerheads reside singly, in pairs, or in small flocks, near water and seldom far from trees, in the forks of which they build intricate domed nests, some 3 to 6 ft (91.5–183 cm) or more in diameter. The nests, to which the birds return each year, are complex, three-compartment structures, lined with mud and dung, and ornamented outside with bright-colored objects. The female lays a clutch of three to six white eggs. Both sexes care for the highly dependent young. According to native superstitions, hammerheads are evil omens, and it is considered bad luck to harm them. Such superstitions have kept the birds somewhat protected. Hammerheads are classified in the phylum CHORDATA, subphylum Vertebrata, class Aves, order Ciconiiformes, family Scopidae.

hammerhead shark, active, surface-living shark, genus *Sphyrina.* Its curious head has lateral projections resembling the crossbar of a T, and its eyes and ears are located in the outer tips of the projections. It has been suggested that the extension of the head in the plane of the pectoral fins may give the fish increased lift, but there is no evidence that hammerheads are better swimmers than other sharks. Found in inshore, brackish water, hammerheads are both predators and scavengers. They feed on a variety of fishes including skates, rays, and other hammerheads, and large hammerheads have been known to attack and eat humans without provocation. The largest species is the widely distributed great hammerhead, *Sphyrina mokarran,* which typically reaches 15 ft (4.6 m) in length; the distance between its eyes may be as much as 3 ft (90 cm). The common hammerhead, *S. zygaena,* is found in all tropical waters, summering as far N as Newfoundland. It may reach a length of 12 ft (3.7 m). The bonnet, or shovelhead, shark is a small, harmless hammerhead found in the W Atlantic from Brazil to Massachusetts. It reaches a length of 5 ft (150 cm) and its lateral lobes are much shorter than in other species, giving the head a rounded appearance. There are several other species distributed throughout tropical and temperate oceans. Hammerhead sharks are classified in the phylum CHORDATA, subphylum Vertebrata, class Chondrichthyes, order Selachii, family Sphyrnidae.

hammerkop: see HAMMERHEAD (bird).

Hammersmith, borough (1971 pop. 184,935), of Greater London, SE England, on the Thames River. The borough was created in 1965 by the merger of the metropolitan boroughs of Hammersmith and Fulham. Hammersmith has pottery works and varied other industries and is the site of the British Broadcasting Corp. Television Centre. Fulham Palace, with 37 acres (15 hectares) of grounds, is the residence of the bishop of London. William Morris's Kelmscott Press was in Hammersmith, and St. Paul's School for boys was moved there in 1884.

Hammerstein, Oscar (hăm'ərstīn), 1846–1919, German-American operatic impresario. In 1888 he built the Harlem Opera House, and in 1906 the Manhattan Opera House, where he gave noteworthy productions. He brought many fine singers to the United States, and introduced *Louise, Pelléas et Mélisande,* and *Elektra* to the American public. In 1910 the Metropolitan Opera Company bought his interests. Upon the failure (1913) of an operatic venture in London, he returned to New York and built the Lexington Theater, where he produced varied entertainments. See biography by Vincent Sheean (1956).

Hammerstein, Oscar, 2d, 1895–1960, American lyricist and librettist, b. New York City, grad. Columbia Univ., 1916; grandson of Oscar Hammerstein. His first success was *Wildflower* (1923), with music by Vincent Youmans. Thereafter, he collaborated with Rudolf Friml on *Rose Marie* (1924); with Jerome Kern on *Sunny* (1925) and *Show Boat* (1927); and with Sigmund Romberg on *Desert Song* (1926) and *The New Moon* (1928). With the composer Richard RODGERS he brought to the stage musicals such as *Oklahoma!* (1943; Pulitzer Prize), *Carousel* (1945), *South Pacific* (1949; Pulitzer Prize), and *The King and I* (1951)—all of which gave new distinction to the American musical through their integration of musical, dramatic, and dance elements. Hammerstein wrote the lyrics to many famous songs, including "The Last Time I Saw Paris" and "It Might As Well Be Spring," which won Academy Awards. See biographies by D. Taylor (1953), S. Green (1963), J. F. Cone (1966), and J. Hammond (1970).

Hammett, Dashiell (dəshēl'), 1894–1961, American writer. Hammett originated the "hard-boiled" school of detective fiction. His stories are realistic, fast-paced, and marked by a certain sophistication. He was the creator of Nick Charles and Sam Spade, the latter the original tough "private eye." Hammett's novels *The Maltese Falcon* (1930), *The Glass Key* (1931), and *The Thin Man* (1932), are considered classics of the genre; they were all made into successful motion pictures. See posthumous collections of his stories, *The Big Knockover,* ed. by Lillian Hellman (1966) and *The Continental Op,* ed. by Steven Marcus (1974); study by W. F. Nolan (1969).

hammock, suspended bed, usually of netting, canvas, or leather. The hammock and its name were introduced to Europeans by Christopher Columbus, who learned of them from American Indians. While the plaited hammock seems to be native to the Western Hemisphere, blankets have served the same purpose among primitive tribes in other parts of the world. The hammock was formerly used to conserve space on naval vessels. It has served as a means of conveyance in tropical areas.

Hammoleketh (hămŏl'ĕkĕth), mother of Ishod. 1 Chron. 7.18.

Hammon (hăm'ən). **1** Unidentified Asherite town. Joshua 19.28. **2** See HAMMATH.

Hammond, James Henry, 1807–64, American statesman, b. Newberry co., S.C. A lawyer and the owner of large plantations on the Savannah River, Hammond was an early believer in secession. He voiced this belief in the U.S. House of Representatives (1835–36) and as governor of South Carolina (1842–44) during the turmoil of the tariff of 1842. In 1857, Hammond was elected to the U.S. Senate and there, in reply to William Seward, made his famous "Cotton is King" speech. As the crisis approached, however, he began to doubt the wisdom of secession, thinking the South could attain its desired ends within the Union. He later supported the Confederacy, however, although he criticized the government of Jefferson Davis. See biography by Elizabeth Merritt (1923); study by R. C. Cinnamond (1949).

Hammond. 1 City (1970 pop. 107,790), Lake co., extreme NW Ind., bounded by Lake Michigan, the Ill. state line, and the Little Calumet River, and traversed by the Grand Calumet River; inc. 1884. Originally important as a slaughterhouse site, Hammond was a meat-packing town until its great packing house was destroyed by fire in 1901. It is now a highly industrialized center in the great Calumet region. It has steel foundries, a publishing industry, and a great variety of manufactures, including petroleum products, soaps and toilet articles, railroad equipment, forgings, valves, and hospital and surgical supplies. A campus of Purdue Univ. is there. **2** City (1970 pop. 12,487), Tangipahoa parish, SE La.; inc. 1888. It has feed mills and a lumber and wood-products industry. The city is the seat of Southeastern Louisiana Univ., a state school for retarded children, and a state agricultural experiment station.

Hammonton, town (1970 pop. 11,464), Atlantic co., S N.J.; inc. 1866. It is the trade and shipping center of a fertile fruit region.

Hammoth-dor (hăm'əth-dôr): see HAMMATH.

Hammurabi (hămŏŏrä'bē), fl. 1792–1750 B.C., king of BABYLONIA. He founded an empire that was eventually destroyed by raids from Asia Minor. Hammurabi may have begun building the tower of Babel (Gen. 11.4), which can now be identified with the temple-tower in Babylon called Etemenanki. His code of laws is one of the greatest of ancient codes. It is carved on a diorite column, in 3,600 lines of cuneiform; it was found at Susa and is now at Paris. The laws are generally humanitarian, but one severe feature is the retributive nature of the punishment, which follows "an eye for an eye" literally. See study by F. M. T. Böhl (1946).

Hamonah (hāmō'nə), name to be given a city in the prophecy in Ezek. 39.16.

Hamon-gog (hā'mən-gŏg), name to be given a valley in the prophecy in Ezek. 39.11–16.

Hamor (hā'môr), head of the family from whom Abraham bought his tomb. Gen. 34.2–31. Emmor: Acts 7.16.

Hampden, John (hămp'dən, hăm'-), 1594–1643, English parliamentary leader; cousin of Oliver Cromwell. He entered Parliament in 1621, became closely associated with Sir John ELIOT, and was imprisoned (1627) for refusing to pay the forced loan demanded by CHARLES I. With Viscount SAYE AND SELE, John PYM, and other parliamentary leaders, he involved himself in various colonization schemes. In 1637, Hampden challenged the king's right to raise revenue by the device of ship money, a tax originally levied on ports for defense purposes but extended by Charles to inland counties. He was convicted (1638) by a very narrow margin for his refusal to pay the tax, and the case inflamed popular resentment against the king. Conspicuous as a leader of both the Short and Long Parliaments, Hampden was one of the five members whose attempted arrest by Charles (1642) helped to precipitate the ENGLISH CIVIL WAR. He raised a regiment for the parliamentarians and was mortally wounded at Chalgrove Field, fighting Prince Rupert. See biography by Hugh Ross Williamson (1933).

Hampden, Walter (hăm'dən), 1879–1955, American actor, b. Brooklyn, N.Y., whose original name was Walter Hampden Dougherty. He made his first appearance in London in 1901. Returning to the United States in 1907, he supported Nazimova in an Ibsen series and later appeared in Kennedy's *Servant in the House* and in Shakespearean drama. In 1923 he was first seen as Cyrano de Bergerac, a role that he often repeated. After assuming management of the Colonial Theatre, he renamed it Hampden's and appeared there (1925–30) with his own company. A revered figure of the American theater, Hampden was president of the Players' Club for 27 years.

Hampshire, Stuart Newton, 1914–, British philosopher, grad. Oxford. He taught at Oxford, University College (London), and London Univ. before joining (1963) the faculty of Princeton Univ. His work includes contributions in epistemology, metaphysics, philosophy of mind, ethics, and aesthetics. His philosophic approach reflects his interest in psychoanalysis and in the history and criticism of painting and literature. Hampshire has been especially concerned with the relationship between meaning and confirmation, and he has emphasized the importance of introspection in the determination of human action. Beginning with the psychological observation that men assume certain dispositions as a result of experiences in early childhood, he argues that some measure of control over these dispositions can be obtained through an understanding of their origins. The importance he places on introspection has led him to reject the strict behaviorist position, favoring instead Spinoza's connection of freedom and knowledge, a connection also made in psychoanalytic theory. Consequently, his position in the area of ethics is that any system must take account of human nature as being historically and genetically conditioned but essentially revisable—because of the possibility of self-conscious intentional action. Hampshire's works include *Spinoza* (1951); the important article on "On Referring and Intending," in the *Philosophical Review* (1956); *Thought and Action* (1959); *Freedom of the Individual* (1965); and *Freedom of Mind and Other Essays* (1971).

Hampshire, county (1971 pop. 1,561,605), 1,503 sq mi (3,893 sq km), S central England. WINCHESTER is the county town. The terrain is undulating and is crossed by two chalk downs, rising in places to more than 800 ft (244 m). The principal rivers are the Test, the Itchen, and the Avon. Hampshire is an agricultural county, devoted to sheep raising and dairy farming. There is oil refining at Fawley and aircraft engineering at Farnborough. SOUTHAMPTON and PORTSMOUTH are two of Britain's leading ports. BOURNEMOUTH is a large resort. There is much evidence of prehistoric and Roman settlement in the county. Hampshire was part of the Anglo-Saxon kingdom of WESSEX and has numerous historical and literary associations. In 1974, Hampshire was reorganized as a nonmetropolitan county; a small area in the southwest, including Bournemouth, was transferred to the new nonmetropolitan county of Dorset.

Hampshire College, at Amherst, Mass.; coeducational; opened 1970. The emphasis of the academic program is on the individual needs of the students. The college participates in a cooperative arrangement with Amherst, Smith, Mount Holyoke College, and the Univ. of Massachusetts.

Hampshire sheep, large sheep bred originally in Hampshire, England, by crossing Southdowns, Cotswolds, and other breeds. Hampshires are large in size and hornless, have black faces and legs, and are characterized by rapid growth. Recognized as one of the popular meat breeds, they are raised all over the world on farms and ranges and are one of the leading breeds in the United States, particularly in Kentucky and California.

Hampshire swine, breed of swine that originated in S England and was introduced to the United States in the early 1800s. Major improvement of the breed took place in the state of Kentucky. Hampshire swine are black with a white belt encircling the front of the body including the front legs and feet. They are meaty, medium-sized hogs with a smooth appearance and are active and alert animals.

Hampstead, England: see CAMDEN.

Hampton, Wade, c.1752–1835, American planter and soldier, b. Halifax co., Va. He served in the American Revolution and took part in South Carolina politics, opposing the ratification of the Federal Constitution and serving as a U.S. Representative (1795–97, 1803–5). He developed large cotton plantations in South Carolina before 1800, held sugar plantations in Mississippi after 1811, and was reputed to be the wealthiest planter of his day in America. A major general in the War of 1812, Hampton commanded a force that was to march from N New York to the St. Lawrence River and then, after effecting a union with Gen. James Wilkinson's army, move against Montreal. He was defeated by a smaller British force in the battle of CHATEAUGAY; and, blamed by Wilkinson for the failure of the campaign, he resigned his command. Wade Hampton (1818–1902) was his grandson.

Hampton, Wade, 1818–1902, Confederate general in the American Civil War, b. Charleston, S.C.; grandson of Wade Hampton (c.1752–1835). Hampton, a wealthy planter, served (1852–61) in the South Carolina legislature. In the Civil War he raised Hampton's Legion, which he led at the first battle of Bull Run. He commanded an infantry brigade in the Peninsular campaign, being made a brigadier general in May, 1862, but in July was given a brigade in the cavalry. He was active in most of Jeb Stuart's operations (1862–64) and upon Stuart's death in 1864 succeeded to the command of the cavalry corps. He took part in the fighting around Richmond and Petersburg and later with part of his force was engaged in covering Joseph E. Johnston's army until the surrender to General Sherman in April, 1865. He had been promoted lieutenant general in Feb., 1865. In the election of 1876, the Democrats of South Carolina were led to victory by Hampton, their candidate for governor. Daniel H. Chamberlain, the carpetbagger incumbent, disputed the result, but when Federal troops were withdrawn (April, 1877), he had no support. More for this political triumph, which restored home rule, than for his military prowess Hampton is considered a state hero. He was reelected as governor in 1878 and in 1879 became a U.S. Senator. Hampton remained the dominant figure in South Carolina politics until 1890, when Benjamin TILLMAN led a successful revolt against Hampton's rule, and Hampton lost his Senate seat. He was (1893–99) commissioner of Pacific railroads. See E. L. Wells, *Hampton and His Cavalry* (1899) and *Hampton and Reconstruction* (1907); A. B. Williams, *Hampton and His Red Shirts* (1935, repr. 1970); M. W. Wellman, *Giant in Gray* (1949); H. M. Jarrell, *Wade Hampton and the Negro* (1949, repr. 1969).

Hampton, since 1965 part of the Greater London borough of RICHMOND UPON THAMES, SE England, on the Thames River. It is the site of **Hampton Court Palace,** begun by Cardinal Wolsey in 1514 as his private residence. After his downfall it was taken by Henry VIII and remained a royal residence until the time of George II. William III had part of it torn down and rebuilt by Christopher Wren. Much of it is open to the public. Many of its rooms are occupied by royal pensioners. The **Hampton Court Conference** was held in 1604, early in the reign of James I, to consider reforms of the Established Church for which its Puritan clergy had petitioned. Few concessions were made to the Puritans. The conference authorized a new version of the Bible (the King James Version).

Hampton, city (1970 pop. 120,779), independent and in no county, SE Va., a port of Hampton Roads at the mouth of the James River, connected to Norfolk by bridge and by tunnel; settled 1610 by colonists from Jamestown, inc. 1849. It has a large seafood packing and shipping industry (fish, crabs, and oysters) and some light manufacturing. Nearby military installations contribute greatly to the economy: Langley Air Force Base (est. 1917), a tactical air command installation; a large shipyard; the National Aeronautics and Space Administration's Langley Research Center; and historic Fort Monroe (built 1819–34 to command the entrance to Chesapeake Bay), now the headquarters of the U.S. Continental Command. One of the oldest continuous English settlements in the country, Hampton was founded on the site of the Indian village Kecoughtan. It was attacked by pirates in the late 17th cent. (Blackbeard was captured off the coast), shelled in the Revolutionary War, sacked by the British in 1813, and burned almost to the ground by evacuating Confederates in 1861 to prevent its possession by Union troops. It is the seat of Hampton Institute. Points of interest include St. John's Episcopal Church (1728; original church est. 1610), with a Bible dating from 1599 and communion silver that belonged to the Jamestown settlers; and a nearby reproduction of an Indian village.

Hampton Court Conference and **Hampton Court Palace:** see under HAMPTON, England; JAMES I.

Hampton Institute, at Hampton, Va.; coeducational; opened 1868, chartered 1870 as a normal and agricultural school. Founded by Samuel Chapman Armstrong, it was among the first Negro colleges and also pioneered in Indian education. Hampton's library is noted for its collection relating to Negro history.

Hampton National Historic Site: see NATIONAL PARKS AND MONUMENTS (table).

Hampton Roads, roadstead, 4 mi (6.4 km) long and 40 ft (12.2 m) deep, SE Va., through which the waters of the James, Nansemond, and Elizabeth rivers pass into Chesapeake Bay. One of the finest natural harbors in the world, it has been a major anchorage point since colonial times and has extensive harbor facilities and shipyards; Newport News and Hampton are on the north shore and Norfolk and Portsmouth on the south. The Port of Hampton Roads, established in 1926 under the State Port Authority of Virginia, is one of the busiest U.S. seaports. Hampton Roads has long been important to the U.S. navy; Norfolk is headquarters for the Atlantic Fleet. The tunnel under the roads, opened in 1957, is one of the longest vehicular tunnels (7,479 ft/2,280 m) in the United States. Hampton Roads was the site of the Civil War battle (March, 1862) between the ironclads MONITOR AND MERRIMACK.

Hampton Roads Peace Conference, meeting held on Feb. 3, 1865, on board the Union transport *River Queen* in Hampton Roads, Va., with the object of ending the Civil War. President Lincoln and Secretary of State William H. Seward represented the Union, and A. H. Stephens, R. M. T. Hunter, and J. A. Campbell, the Confederacy. The meeting was brought about through the efforts of Francis P. BLAIR (1791–1876). Unofficially, but with Lincoln's knowledge, Blair had discussed the possibility with Jefferson Davis of restoring peace through a united opposition to European intervention in Mexico. Lincoln's terms—reunion, acceptance of emancipation, immediate cessation of hostilities, and the disbanding of all Confederate forces—proved unacceptable to the South, and the conference failed.

hamster, Old World RODENT, related to the voles, lemmings, and New World mice. There are many hamster species, classified in several genera. All are solitary, burrowing, nocturnal animals, with chunky bodies, short tails, soft, thick fur, and large external cheek pouches used for holding food. Some of the larger species have scent glands on the flanks; the scent is used for territorial marking. Hamsters feed on grain and other plant matter and are serious agricultural pests in many parts of their range. The common, or European, hamster, *Cricetus cricetus,* of the temperate parts of Europe and W Asia, is reddish brown with black underparts and white patches on the nose, cheeks, throat and flanks. It is about 12 in. (30 cm) long, with a very short tail. It stores grain in its chambered burrow for use in winter during interruptions of hibernation. The Syrian, or golden, hamster, *Mesocricetus auratus,* of E Europe and W Asia, is familiar as a laboratory animal and pet, but is little known in the wild state; all of the domestic stock is descended from a single group captured in 1930. About 6 in. (15 cm) long, it is lighter colored than the common hamster, with white underparts. Rat-tailed, or Eurasian, hamsters *(C. cricetulus)* are widely distributed through Europe and Asia; these somewhat longer-tailed forms are quite fierce, preying on other rodents as well as on lizards and small birds, although their diet is mostly vegetarian. Other hamsters are found in Europe and Asia, and species of the hamster genus *Mystromys,* called white-tailed rats, are found in Africa. Hamsters are classified in the phylum CHORDATA, subphylum Vertebrata, class Mammalia, order Rodentia, family Cricetidae. See MOUSE.

Hamsun, Knut (kəno͞ot' häm' so͞on), 1859–1952, Norwegian novelist. In his youth, virtually without formal education, he led a wandering life, and on his second visit to the United States (1886–88) he worked as a streetcar conductor, lecturer, peddler, clerk, and harvest hand. The theme of the wanderer is prominent in many of his novels, including the naturalistic *Hunger* (1890, tr. 1899), which aroused a furor of criticism and gained him a large audience. He also wrote the lyrically beautiful *Pan* (1894), a trilogy of plays, and a volume of poems (1903). His masterpiece, *The Growth of the Soil* (1917, tr. 1920), sets simple agrarian values against those of the new industrial society. It was awarded the 1920 Nobel Prize in Literature. Hamsun's largely autobiographical work reflects an intense love of nature. His concern is often for the material condition of the individual and its effect on his spirit. His later works include *Vagabonds* (1927, tr. 1930), *The Road Leads On* (1933, tr. 1934), and *The Ring Is Closed* (1936, tr. 1937). During World War II Hamsun lost popularity because he acclaimed the Nazi invasion of Norway. See his memoir, *On Overgrown Paths* (1949, tr. 1967); A. Gustafson, *Six Scandinavian Novelists* (1940, repr. 1967).

Hamtramck (hămtrăm'ĭk), city (1970 pop. 27,245), Wayne co., SE Mich., within the confines of Detroit; inc. as a city 1922. Automobiles and automotive parts, paint, plastic products, and sausages are manufactured there. The site was settled by Frenchmen in the late 18th cent. The city grew quickly after the coming of the automobile industry c.1910. Points of interest include St. Florian's Church (a fine example of Gothic architecture); and the memorial and grave of Col. John F. Hamtramck, first U.S. commander of the Detroit garrison.

Hamuel (hămyo͞o'əl), Simeon's grandson. 1 Chron. 4.26.

Hamul (hā'məl), grandson of Judah. Gen. 46.12.

Hamun-e Helmand or **Hamun-i-Helmand** (both: hämo͞on'-ē hĕl'mänd), marshy lake in the Seistan, c.5,000 sq mi (12,950 sq km), on the Iran-Afghanistan border. It is the largest single expanse of fresh water within the central plateau of Iran. The lake, fed by the Helmand, Farah, and other rivers, varies in size during the year, achieving its maximum extent in the late spring, when it overflows via the Shalaq River (in Iran) into the Gowd-e Zereh, an area of salt flats and swamps in SW Afghanistan. The Hamun-e Helmand has the potential to support irrigated agriculture in the area.

Hamutal (hămyo͞o'təl), mother of Jehoahaz and Zedekiah. 2 Kings 23.31; 24.18; Jer. 52.1.

Han (hän), dynasty of China that ruled from 202 B.C. to A.D. c.220. Liu Pang, the first Han emperor, had been a farmer, minor village official, and guerrilla fighter under the Ch'in dynasty. During the period of civil strife that followed the fall of the CH'IN, he advanced from the Hwai River valley, defeated his rivals for the throne, and then established himself in Ch'angan near the old Ch'in capital. Under Liu Pang and the succeeding Han emperors the task of unification begun by the Ch'in was carried further. However, the harsh laws of the Ch'in were repealed, taxes were lightened, the absolute autocracy of the emperor was lessened, and, most importantly, Confucianism was made the basis of the state. The pyramidal bureaucracy of Ch'in administration was retained, and the Han period saw the beginnings of one of the distinguishing features of the Chinese educational and state system, the recruiting of members of the bureaucracy through civil service examinations. The dynasty attained its greatest territorial expanse under the emperor Wu Ti (reigned 140 B.C.–87 B.C.), who extended Han power W to Sinkiang and Central Asia, N to Manchuria and Korea, and S to Yünnan, Hainan island, and Annam (in modern South Vietnam). One of China's greatest historians, SSU-MA CH'IEN, flourished during the reign of Wu Ti. The Han emperors ruled for 400 years with one interruption; in A.D. 8 an agrarian reformer usurped the throne and established the Hsin dynasty. This short-lived dynasty has come to mark the division between the Early, or Western, Han period and the Later, or Eastern, Han period, which began A.D. 25, when the Han capital was moved east to Loyang. The entire Han era was one of political and cultural centralization and expansion. The writing brush and paper and ink came into wide use and the manufacture of porcelain had its beginnings in this period. Many classic texts were edited, and the first dictionary was compiled. The coming of Buddhism increased cultural ties with India and parts of the Middle East. Trade with border states was increased to pacify these regions and to gain their allegiance. The dynasty collapsed A.D. c.220 and was followed by some 350 years of smaller political units, including the THREE KINGDOMS and the TSIN dynasty. China was eventually reunited under the SUI dynasty. See Pan Ku, *The History of the Former Han Dynasty* (tr., 3 vol., 1938–55); Ssu-ma Ch'ien, *Records of the Grand Historian of China* (tr., 2 vol., 1961); Michael Loewe, *Everyday Life in Early Imperial China* (1968); Jacques Gernet, *Ancient China from the Beginnings to the Empire* (tr. 1968); Tung-hsi Ch'u, *Han Social Structure* (1972).

Han. **1** River of S China, 210 mi (338 km) long, rising in W Fukien prov. and flowing S through Kwangtung prov. to the South China Sea at Shan-t'ou; navigable for about 100 mi (160 km) upstream. The densely populated delta is a rich agricultural area; two crops of rice are grown annually. Manganese and tungsten are mined in the upper valley. **2** River of central China, c.700 mi (1,130 km) long, rising in SW Shensi prov. and flowing E between the Tsinling and the Ta-pa mts., then SE through Hupeh prov. to join the Yangtze at Wu-han; navigable for about 300 mi (480 km) upstream. The river floods its fertile lower valley in summer. There is a hydroelectric power station near Hsiang-fan, Hupeh prov.

Hanaford, Phoebe Ann (Coffin) (hăn'əfərd), 1829–1921, American Universalist minister. She was the first woman ordained (1868) in New England. Hanaford was the author of fiction, history, and a chronicle of American women, *Daughters of America* (1882).

Hanameel (hānăm'ēēl, hăn'əmēl), son of Jeremiah's uncle Shallum. Jer. 32.7–9,12.

Hanan (hā'nən). **1** Reader with Ezra in explaining the law. Neh. 8.7. **2** Sealer of the covenant, probably the same as the preceding. Neh. 10.10. **3** Descendant of Saul. 1 Chron. 8.38; 9.44. **4** One of David's guard. 1 Chron. 11.43. **5** One of Nehemiah's treasures. Neh. 13.13. **6** Father whose sons had a room in the Temple. Jer. 35.4. **7, 8** Sealers of the covenant. Neh. 10.22,26. **9** Family of Nethinim. Ezra 2.46; Neh. 7.49. **10** Benjamite chief. 1 Chron. 8.23.

Hananeel (hānăn'ēēl, hăn'ənēl), tower, on the Jerusalem wall. Neh. 3.1; 12.39; Jer. 31.38; Zech. 14.10.

Hanani (hăn'ənī, hānā'-). **1** Chief singer of David. 1 Chron. 25.4,25. **2** Seer who reproved Asa. 2 Chron. 16.7. Apparently this is the father of Jehu. 1 Kings 16.1,7. **3** Governor of Jerusalem. Neh. 1.2; 7.2. **4** Priest. Ezra 10.20. **5** Singer. Neh. 12.36.

Hananiah (hănənī'ə). **1** One of the THREE HOLY CHILDREN. **2** False prophet. Jer. 28. **3** Son of Zerubbabel. 1 Chron. 3.19. **4** Musician. 1 Chron. 25.23. **5** Father of ZEDEKIAH **4**. **6** Grandfather of IRIJAH. **7** Benjamite. 1 Chron. 8.24. **8** Captain under King Uzziah. 2 Chron. 26.11. **9** Man who had a foreign wife. Ezra 10.28. **10** Sealer of the Covenant. Neh. 10.23. **11, 12** Repairers of the wall. Neh. 3.8,30. **13** Chief priest. Neh. 12.12. **14** Priest at the dedication of the walls. Neh. 12.41. **15** Governor in Jerusalem. Neh. 7.2,3. Ananias and Annas are Greek forms of this name.

Hanau (hä'nou), city (1970 pop. 55,379), Hesse, central West Germany, on the Main and Kinzig rivers. It is an important rail and road junction and is a center of the West German jewelry industry. Other manufactures include rubber goods, lamps, and machinery. Hanau was chartered in 1303 and in the 16th cent. accepted refugees from the Low Countries who contributed significantly to the city's economic growth. Hanau passed to Hesse-Kassel in 1736, and with it to Prussia in 1866. The philologists Jakob and Wilhelm Grimm and the composer Paul Hindemith were born in Hanau.

Han-chung (hän-jŏŏng) or **Hanchung** (hän'-chŏŏng'), city (1970 est. pop. 120,000), SW Shensi prov., China, on the Han River, near the Szechwan border. It is a major agricultural and trade center. The city was formerly called Nancheng.

Hancock, John, 1737–93, political leader in the American Revolution, signer of the Declaration of Independence, b. Braintree, Mass. From an uncle he inherited Boston's leading mercantile firm, and naturally he opposed the STAMP ACT (1765) and other British trade restrictions. In 1768 his ship *Liberty* was seized as a smuggler and confiscated by the crown. A riot ensued, and later the ship was burned. Hancock was hailed as a martyr and elected (1766) to the legislature, where he joined Samuel ADAMS in advocating resistance to England. In 1775, Gen. Thomas Gage issued a warrant for their arrest, but they escaped. Hancock was a member (1775–80) and president (1775–77) of the Continental Congress. His name appears first (and largest) on the Declaration of Independence, and the term "John Hancock" is often used to mean a signature. He was governor of Massachusetts (1780–85, 1787–93). See biographies by Lorenzo Sears (1912, repr. 1972) and H. S. Allan (1953).

Hancock, Winfield Scott, 1824–86, Union general in the American Civil War, b. Montgomery Square, near Norristown, Pa. He served with distinction in the Mexican War and was chief quartermaster on the Pacific coast when the Civil War broke out. Made a brigadier general of volunteers in Sept., 1861, Hancock fought in the Peninsular campaign (1862); in the Antietam campaign he succeeded to the command of a division. His command was heavily engaged in the battles of Fredericksburg (1862) and Chancellorsville (1863). Hancock, commanding the 2d Corps, played a conspicuous role in the GETTYSBURG CAMPAIGN. Gen. George G. Meade chose to fight at Gettysburg on Hancock's recommendation, and in the last two days of the battle Hancock was foremost in repulsing the Confederate attacks, particularly General Pickett's charge on July 3, 1863. He was severely wounded. Hancock led the 2d Corps in the Wilderness campaign and in the operations around Petersburg until Nov., 1864, when he left to recruit a new corps. His course as chief of the military department of Louisiana and Texas after the war was characterized by a wise moderation, which was not approved by the radicals in Congress. He was transferred to another command at his own request. The Democratic party nominated him for President in 1880, on his military record. James Garfield defeated him, but with only a slight popular plurality. See Almira Hancock, *Reminiscences of Winfield Scott Hancock* (1887); biography by Glenn Tucker (1960).

Hand, Learned, 1872–1961, American jurist, b. Albany, N.Y. He received his law degree from Harvard in 1896. He was judge of a Federal district court (1909–24) and of a Federal circuit court of appeals (1924–51). Often called the "tenth justice of the Supreme Court," Hand delivered more than 2,000 opinions and gained a reputation as a defender of free speech. His appellate decisions are frequently cited by the Supreme Court. *The Spirit of Liberty,* a collection of his papers and addresses, was published in 1952; his *Bill of Rights,* a series of lectures, was published in 1958. See studies by Hershel Shanks, ed. (1968), Marvin Schick (1970), and K. P. Griffith (1973).

Hand, Wayland Debs, 1907–, folklorist, b. Auckland, New Zealand. Hand is the author of *Popular Beliefs and Superstitions from North Carolina* (1964), which is ranked among the finest published studies of superstition. It is remarkable for its logical arrangement of material, accurate comparative information, and completeness of informant attributions. Hand also wrote two volumes of essays on folklore and literature, *Humaniora* (1960) and *Folklore International* (1967), as well as *Eyes on Texas: Fifty Years of Folklore in the Southwest* (1967).

hand, terminal part of the forelimb in primates. The human hand consists of the wrist, palm, four fingers, and thumb. In man and other primates the thumb is opposable, i.e., it can be moved into a position opposite to the other four digits. Opposable thumbs make possible precise movements such as grasping small objects. The opposable thumb, in combination with a well-developed brain, is considered to be responsible for man's achievement of dominance over other animals. There are 27 bones in the human hand. The wrist, which joins the hand to the forearm, contains eight cubelike bones arranged in two rows of four bones each. The metacarpus, or palm, is composed of five long metacarpal bones. Fourteen phalangeal bones constitute the four fingers and thumb (three in each finger, two in the thumb). The bones of the hand are firmly interconnected by ligaments; the bones of the digits are anchored to muscles in the hand and, through tendons, to muscles in the arms and shoulders, permitting a wide range of movements.

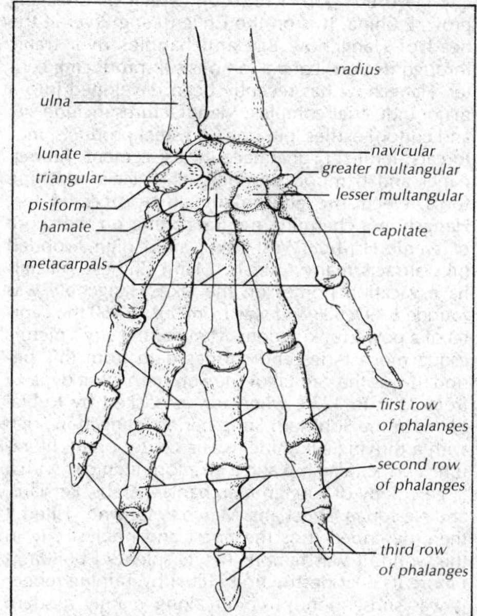

Bones of right wrist and hand, dorsal view

Handa (hän'dä), city (1970 pop. 80,653), Aichi prefecture, S central Honshu, Japan, on the Chita Peninsula and Chita Bay. Handa, a fishing port, is a production center for cotton textiles, sake, and soy sauce.

handbag: see PURSE.

handball, indoor or outdoor game played by striking a ball against a wall or walls with the palm of the hand. Play may be for singles or doubles on a court with one, three, or four walls. In the one-wall game, the court is 20 ft (6.1 m) by 34 ft (10.4 m). The short line, from behind which the ball is served, is marked off 16 ft (4.9 m) from, and parallel to, the wall, which is 16 ft high. With either hand the player hits the ball against the wall before or after it has struck the floor once. His object is to keep the ball out of reach of the opponent (who tries to strike it back against the wall) but within the bounds of the court. In the three-wall and four-wall games, the court is 20 ft (6.1 m) by 40 ft (12.2 m), and it has three walls 20 ft high and a back wall 12 ft (3.7 m) high. The ball is played off all four walls in the four-wall game. There is no back-wall play in three-wall competition. In all games, a point is scored when the nonserver (individual or team) cannot return the ball—made of hard black rubber, 1⅞ in. (4.76 cm) in diameter, and 2.3 oz in weight—against the front wall. The serve changes hands when the server (two in doubles) cannot return the ball, and the first player or team to score 21 points wins. Special gloves are used to protect the hands. Four-wall handball has been played in Ireland since the Middle Ages and was introduced at the end of the 19th cent. into the United States; one-wall handball, an American variation of the game, originated in Brooklyn, N.Y. National, regional, and intercollegiate championships are played annually. The major U.S. organizing body for the sport is the U.S. Handball Association, located in Skokie, Ill.

handedness, habitual or more skillful use of one hand as opposed to the other. Although the majority of persons (between 90% and 95%) are right-handed, and fossil evidence indicates that this has been the case for as much as a million years, there is as yet no satisfactory explanation of why this should be. It was traditionally argued that there is a slight tendency toward asymmetrical physiological development favoring the right side of the body and that the center of gravity is to the right of the body's midline. This, however, would seem to be the consequence of greater dependence upon the right hand rather than the cause of right-handedness. The neurological argument, formerly predominant, has also come under criticism. This hypothesis holds that since the right and left sides of the body are controlled by the opposite hemispheres of the brain the greater development of the left hemisphere will result in right-handedness. However, recent anatomical studies have demonstrated that Broca's center, the area of the cerebral cortex that controls speech and muscular coordination, is almost always better developed in the left hemisphere, even in left-handed individuals. Psychologists have revived the possibility of a cultural explanation. They have shown that up to the age of one year infants will use either hand indiscriminately. It is only between the ages of one and three that a preference appears and becomes established. Whether this indicates that the preference is learned during that period is not clear. The period is also the time of anatomical sophistication of the nervous system, and it may be that the organism must develop neurologically to a certain extent before a preference for handedness can be demonstrated and sustained. Strongly encouraging left-handed children to switch to right-handedness in many cases causes no serious psychological harm and may even make an individual facile in the use of both hands (ambidexterity). In other cases, however, stuttering and certain difficulties with reading, sports participation, and social behavior have been at least partially attributed to this cause. If it is not clear that culture is the causative agent in handedness, it is certain that the high incidence of right-handedness has shaped human society in almost every conceivable aspect. Tools, machinery, and even clothing are largely designed for the right-handed.

Handel, George Frideric (hăn'dəl), 1685–1759, English composer, b. Halle (now in East Germany). Handel was one of the greatest masters of baroque music, most widely celebrated for his majestic oratorio *The Messiah.* Of German descent, he was originally named Georg Friedrich Handel. Son of a barber-surgeon, he early displayed musical talent and was sent to Friedrich Zachow, an organist and composer at Halle, for three years of training. After studying law at the Univ. of Halle (1703), he joined the opera orchestra at Hamburg. There his first two operas, *Almira* and *Nero,* were produced in 1705. The following four years were spent in Italy, where his operas *Rodrigo* (1707?) and *Agrippina* (1709) were staged, the latter very successfully. In Italy he met Alessandro Scarlatti and other masters and absorbed the Italian style and forms. In 1710 he became musical director to the elector of Hanover but obtained leave to visit England in 1711, when his *Rinaldo* was produced in London. He returned to England in 1712 and took up permanent residence there. His employer, the elector, became George I of England in 1714. It was for the king that Handel composed his celebrated orchestral *Water Music* (1717). In 1719 an opera company, the Royal Academy of Music, was formed under the musical direction of Handel, Attilio Ariosti, and Giovanni Battista Bononcini, all of whom composed operas for it. The company was dissolved in 1728, but Handel continued trying to present Italian opera in London until 1741, when his last opera, *Deidamia,* failed. Handel's 46 operas include much of his finest music; among them are *Julius Caesar* (1724), *Atalanta* (1736), *Berenice* (1737), and *Serse* (1738), which contains the tenor aria now known as *Largo.* His *Messiah* was presented in Dublin in 1742. An essentially contemplative work, it stands apart from the rest of his 32 oratorios, which are dramatically conceived, and its immense popularity has resulted in the erroneous conception of Handel as primarily a church composer. Other outstanding oratorios are *Acis and Galatea* (1720), *Esther* (1732), *Israel in Egypt* (1736–37), *Saul* (1739), and *Judas Maccabeus* (1747). He also composed about 100 Italian solo cantatas; numerous orchestral works, including the Twelve Grand Concertos, Op. 6 (1739); two books of harpsichord suites (1720, 1733); three sets of six organ concertos (1738, 1743, 1760, the last published posthumously); and the anthem "Zadok, the Priest" (1727) for the coronation of George II, which has been used for all subsequent coronations. While composer to the duke of Chandos (1715–19), he wrote the 11 Chandos Anthems. Handel's sight became impaired in 1751, and by 1753 he was totally blind, but he continued to conduct performances of his works on occasion. He is buried in Westminster Abbey. Handel's musical style exemplifies the vigor and grandeur of the late German baroque and at the same time has English and Italian qualities of directness, clarity, and charm. He strongly influenced English composers for a century after his death, and, following a period of relative neglect, he has again come to be recognized as one of the giants in music. See his letters and writings, ed. by E. H. Müller (1937); biographies by Herbert Weinstock (2d ed. 1959), P. H. Young (rev. ed. 1963), and P. H. Lang (1966); Winton Dean, *Handel and the Opera Seria* (1970).

handicraft: see ARTS AND CRAFTS.

handkerchief. In classical Greece pieces of fine perfumed cotton, known as mouth or perspiration cloths, were often used by the wealthy. From the 1st cent. B.C., Roman men of rank used an oblong cloth of linen (the *sudarium*) chiefly to wipe perspiration from the face and hands. During the empire a square handkerchief of cotton or silk was carried, especially by women. The handkerchief was dropped by the praetors as a starting signal in the Roman games and was waved by spectators as a sign of approval. In the Middle Ages it was a prized possession and was conspicuously displayed by the wealthy. It was worn by knights in tournament as the symbol of a lady's favor. It came into general use in the Renaissance and was called a napkyn. Silk, cambric, and lawn, lavishly embroidered or laced, became fashionable for both men and women. Shapes were also varied. Today the handkerchief is more practical than decorative. Disposable paper handkerchiefs are used for all but very formal occasions. The handkerchief carried in the left hand of the officiating priest in the early Christian church evolved into a folded band that by the 12th cent. had become the maniple, worn on the left arm.

Handlin, Oscar, 1915–, American historian, b. Brooklyn, N.Y. He received his Ph.D. from Harvard in 1940 and has taught there since 1939. Most of his work is in U.S. social and economic history, particularly in the influence of immigration on American culture. With his wife, Mary F. Handlin, he wrote *Commonwealth* (1947), a study of the economy and of the role of government in Massachusetts during the period 1774–1861. He won the 1952 Pulitzer Prize in history for *The Uprooted* (1951, 2d enl. ed. 1973), a history of the immigration movements to America after 1820. Among his other works are *Boston's Immigrants, 1790–1865* (1941, rev. and enl. ed. 1959); *Adventure in Freedom; 300 Years of Jewish Life in America* (1954); *Race and Nationality in American Life* (1957); *The Newcomers—Negroes and Puerto Ricans in a Changing Metropolis* (1959); and *The Dimensions of Liberty* (1961). He also edited, with others, the *Harvard Guide to American History* (1954).

Handsome Lake, 1735?–1815, Seneca Indian religious prophet; half brother of CORNPLANTER. After a long illness he had a vision (c.1800) and began to preach new religious beliefs. His moral teachings showed a similarity to Christian ethics and had a profound effect among the Iroquois Indians. He advocated giving up the Indian mode of life and taking up agriculture, much to the disgust of RED JACKET. Though Christian missionaries opposed Handsome Lake's religion, it nevertheless persisted alongside Christianity. See *The Code of Handsome Lake* (tr. by A. C. Parker, 1913, repr. 1968); Anthony Wallace, *The Death and Rebirth of the Seneca* (1969, repr. 1972).

Handy, W. C. (William Christopher), 1873–1958, American songwriter and band leader, b. Florence, Ala. Largely self-taught, Handy began his career as a cornet player in a minstrel show in 1896, and later organized various small bands. He was among the first to set down the blues, and with his *Memphis Blues* (1912), originally entitled *Mr. Crump* (1909), he rose to prominence. His songs, such as *St. Louis Blues* (1914) and *Beale Street Blues* (1917), are the classic examples of their type. In 1918 he moved from Memphis to New York City and remained active as a writer and publisher of music, in spite of growing blindness, until shortly before his death. His other songs include *Yellow Dog Blues* (1914), *Joe Turner Blues* (1915), and *Loveless Love* (1921). He was publisher of many of his own compositions and was author of several books, including *Blues: An Anthology* (1926) and his *Collection of Negro Spirituals* (1938). See his autobiography, *Father of the Blues* (1941).

Hanes (hā'nēz), unidentified place, Egypt. Isa. 30.4.

Hanford, city (1970 pop. 15,179), seat of Kings co., central Calif.; inc. 1891. It is a trade and processing center of the San Joaquin Valley. Rubber and oil companies are located in Hanford.

Hang-chou: see HANGCHOW, China.

Hangchow or **Hang-chou** (hăng'chou, häng'-jō'), city (1970 est. pop. 1,100,000), capital of Chekiang prov., E China. It is on the Ch'ien-t'ang River at the head of Hangchow Bay and handles river traffic through its port. Long a famous silk-producing center, Hangchow has recently been developed into a major industrial complex. Manufactures include silk and cotton textiles, pig iron and steel products, motorcars, fertilizer, pharmaceuticals, cement, rubber, paper and bamboo products, chemicals, machine tools, electronic equipment, and processed tea. Hangchow's charming natural setting on the shore of scenic Hsi-hu (West Lake) amid high, wooded hills attracts many tourists. Many Chinese officials have vacation homes on the lake. Hangchow was founded A.D. 606 and was from 907 to 960 the capital of a powerful kingdom. Many of the city's picturesque monasteries and shrines date from this period. It was the capital of the Southern Sung dynasty from 1132 to 1276, when it was sacked by Kublai Khan. In the Southern Sung period Hangchow, rich with a thriving silk trade, was a center of art, literature, and scholarship and a cosmopolitan city with a large colony of foreign merchants—Arabs, Persians, and Nestorian Christians. Marco Polo, who visited it then, described it as the finest and noblest city in the world. It was famous for its splendid buildings before its near destruction (1861) by Taiping rebels; it was subsequently rebuilt along mainly modern lines. Its modern prosperity dates from the opening of the Shanghai-Hangchow-Ning-po RR in 1909. It was occupied by the Japanese from 1937 to 1945, and it fell to the Communists in 1949. Hangchow is the seat of Chekiang Univ., Hangchow Univ., an agricultural institute, a medical college, and an institute of fine arts. Also in the city are botanical gardens and an astronomical observatory. **Hangchow Bay** is an arm of the East China Sea and begins at the mouth of the Ch'ien-t'ang River. When the tide is coming in, the funnel shape of the bay creates a spectacular bore, 5 to 15 ft (1.5–4.6 m) high, which sweeps past Hangchow, menacing shipping. Choushan Archipelago lies across the southern entrance of the bay.

Hanging Gardens of Babylon: see BABYLON.

Hangö (häng'ö) or **Hanko** (häng'kō), city (1970 pop. 9,686), Uusimaa prov., SW Finland, at the tip of the Hanko peninsula on the Baltic Sea. A popular bathing resort and a manufacturing town, it is the most important winter port in Finland. It was leased to the Soviet Union for 30 years as a naval base after the Finnish-Russian War (1939–40). The USSR exchanged it for a 50-year lease on the Porkkala district in 1944; however, in 1956 the Soviet Union evacuated Porkkala.

Haniel (hăn'ĭēl, hənī'–), Asherite chief. 1 Chron. 7.39.

Hankey, Maurice Pascal Alers Hankey, 1st Baron, 1877–1963, British soldier and civil servant. Educated at the Royal Naval College, Greenwich, he served in the Royal Marines artillery (1895–1901) and in naval intelligence (1902–6). As secretary to the Committee of Imperial Defence (1912–38) and secretary to the cabinet (1916–38), he represented Great Britain at imperial and international conferences and was extremely influential in a back-room capacity. In 1939 he was made a baron and a privy councillor, and he held minor cabinet posts until 1942. He became an active member of the House of Lords, a director of the Suez Canal Company, and an author. His writings include *Government Control in War* (1945), *Diplomacy by Conference* (1946), and *The Supreme Command, 1914–1918* (1961). See biography by S. W. Roskill (2 vol., 1970–72).

Hanko, Finland: see HANGÖ.

Han-k'ou (hän-kō) or **Hankow** (hăng'kou'), former city, since 1950 part of the WU-HAN conurbation, E Hupeh prov., China. Built on an alluvial plain on the left banks of both the Han and Yangtze rivers, it is the largest city in the conurbation and contains its port, a major facility handling oceangoing vessels. The city has many industries. Han-k'ou owes much of its development to the Peking-Canton RR, which crosses the Yangtze at Han-k'ou. The city was opened as a treaty port in 1862, held (1938–45) by the Japanese, and in 1949 passed to the Chinese Communists. It is linked by bridges with Han-yang and Wu-ch'ang.

Hanna, Marcus Alonzo (Mark Hanna), 1837–1904, American capitalist and politician, b. New Lisbon (now Lisbon), Ohio. He attended Western Reserve College for a short time, then entered his father's wholesale grocery and commission business at Cleveland in 1858. He became a partner in 1862 and rapidly developed as a characteristic American capitalist of the Gilded Age. Hanna became a dealer in coal and iron mines, furnaces, lake shipping and shipbuilding; his financial enterprises included ownership of a bank, a newspaper, an opera house, and a street-railway system. He was active in politics and by 1890 was the ruling power in the Ohio Republican party. He was instrumental in having William MCKINLEY elected governor of Ohio in 1891 and again in 1893. Hanna saved McKinley's reputation when financial ruin threatened, groomed him for the presidency in 1895, and was responsible for his nomination by the Republicans in 1896. As chairman of the Republican National Committee, Hanna boldly made that campaign a defense of business and property against the doctrines of the Democrats enunciated by William Jennings Bryan; on that basis he received heavy financial contributions from big business. He was appointed Senator from Ohio in 1897 after John Sherman resigned and was subsequently elected to the seat. Hanna continued to dominate Republican party councils until he died. He supported ship subsidies and advocated construction of the Panama Canal, opposing the Nicaraguan route. At the time of his death Hanna was being considered as a possible presidential candidate by old guard Republicans disenchanted with Theodore Roosevelt's progressive policies. Although sympathetic at times to organized labor, Hanna looked upon the great industrialists as the natural leaders of the country. His leadership of the party exemplified the union between business and politics for the purposes of economic policy rather than for personal graft. See biographies by Herbert Croly (1912, repr. 1965) and Thomas Beer (1929, repr. 1973); Margaret Leech, *In the Days of McKinley* (1959); C. A. Stern, *Resurgent Republicanism: The Handiwork of Hanna* (1968).

Hannah, Samuel's mother. Her song is recalled in the MAGNIFICAT. 1 Sam. 1; 2.1-21. The names Anna and Ann are variants of Hannah.

Hannathon (hăn'əthən), unidentified place, N Palestine. Joshua 19.14.

Hannibal, b. 247 B.C., d. 183 or 182 B.C. Carthaginian general, an implacable and formidable enemy of Rome. From his father, HAMILCAR BARCA, the defender of Sicily in the First Punic War (see PUNIC WARS), he learned to hate Rome. He succeeded as general in Spain on the death of his brother-in-law, HASDRUBAL, in 221 B.C. After consolidating his position for two years, he besieged Rome's ally Saguntum (now Sagunto), which fell eight months later. Carthage supported him, and Rome declared war (the Second Punic War, 218-201 B.C.). With a relatively small army of select troops, Hannibal set out to invade Italy by the little-known overland route. He fought his way over the Pyrenees and reached the Rhône River before the Romans could block his crossing, moved up the valley to avoid their army, and crossed the Alps. This crossing of the Alps, with elephants and a full baggage train, is one of the remarkable feats of military history. Which pass he used is unknown; some scholars believe it was the Mont Genèvre or the Little St. Bernard. He descended into Italy and with his superior cavalry overran the Po valley, winning recruits from the Gallic tribes. A Roman force tried to stop him on the Trebbia only to be wiped out. In the spring of 217 he crossed the Apennines and marched toward Rome. At Lake Trasimeno he destroyed the main Roman army, but he avoided the strong walls of Rome and moved southward, hoping to stir up a general revolt. In 216 the Romans, having replaced Quintus Fabius Maximus Verrucosus (see under FABIUS), attacked the Carthaginians at Cannae, but by brilliant cavalry tactics Hannibal managed to surround the entire force and cut it to pieces. Most of S Italy then allied itself with him, including the important city of Capua. Insufficiently supported from home, Hannibal could not assail Rome and had to content himself with ravaging and reducing smaller places. From 212 the tide gradually turned against him. In 211 the Romans retook Capua, despite his rapid march toward Rome to entice them away. In 207 he fought his way for the last time into a position near Rome, but the defeat and death (207) of his brother Hasdrubal on the Metaurus (Metauro) River made his position hopeless, and he withdrew into the mountains of Bruttium. Recalled to Carthage in 203 to check the advance of SCIPIO AFRICANUS MAJOR in Africa, he was decisively beaten at ZAMA (202). After the conclusion of peace (201), Hannibal became (probably in 196) a suffete, or chief magistrate, of Carthage. He reformed the government and reorganized the revenues in order to pay the heavy tribute imposed by Rome. Denounced to the Romans for allegedly intriguing against Rome, he fled (195) to Antiochus III of Syria. He took a small part in Antiochus' war with Rome, and after the Syrian defeat he fled again, this time to Bithynia. About to be delivered to the Romans, he poisoned himself. Although knowledge of him is based primarily on the reports of his enemies, Hannibal appears to have been both just and merciful. He is renowned for his tactical genius. See G. P. Baker, *Hannibal* (1930, repr. 1967); Leonard Cottrell, *Hannibal: Enemy of Rome* (1961); Gavin De Beer, *Hannibal: Challenging Rome's Supremacy* (1969); W. J. Jacobs, *Hannibal: An African Hero* (1973).

Hannibal, city (1970 pop. 18,698), Marion and Ralls counties, NE Mo., on the Mississippi River; inc. 1845. It is a river port and railroad center. Its industries include meat canning, printing, and the manufacture of boats, candy, cement, and lumber and metal products. The city is famous as the boyhood home of Mark Twain; his house has been preserved, and a museum, a statue, a lighthouse, and a bridge across the Mississippi commemorate him. The famous Tom Sawyer cave is another landmark. Hannibal has a junior college.

Hanniel (hăn'ĭel) [Heb.,=HANIEL], Manassite prince. Num. 34.23.

Hanno, fl. c.480? B.C., Carthaginian navigator. He founded seven towns on the Atlantic shore of Morocco and probably explored the Atlantic coast of Africa to Sierra Leone.

Hanno, fl. 250-200 B.C., Carthaginian statesman, leader of the conservative land-owning party and consistent opponent of the Barca family. His refusal to pay the mercenaries of HAMILCAR BARCA brought on their great revolt (240-238 B.C.). He favored expansion in Africa (where he extended the Carthaginian conquests to Theveste) and opposed war with Rome. Hanno's unwillingness to send help overseas was a factor in Hannibal's final failure in Italy.

Hanno (hän-nō), city (1970 pop. 52,066), Saitama prefecture, central Honshu, Japan, on the Naguri River. It is a commercial town with a large logging industry.

Hannover, West Germany: see HANOVER.

Hanoch (hā'nək) [Heb.,=ENOCH]. **1** Son of Midian. Gen. 25.4. Henoch: 1 Chron. 1.33. **2** Reuben's eldest son. Gen. 46.9; 1 Chron. 5.3; Ex. 6.14; Num. 26.5.

Hanoi (hăn'oi, hənoi'), city (1965 est. pop. 850,000), capital of North Vietnam, on the right bank of the Red River. It is the transportation hub of the country, with an international airport and rail connections to Kun-ming, China, as well as to the main Chinese system centering on Peking; it is also linked by rail with Haiphong and, before the VIETNAM WAR, was linked with Saigon. The center of a network of roads and waterways as well, Hanoi is an important shipping point for agricultural and industrial products. It is the manufacturing center of the country; before the heavy 1972 U.S. bombings its products included locomotives, machine tools, plywood, textiles, chemicals, matches, tires, building materials, distillery items, and handicrafts. The city, while containing an old Vietnamese section, is known for its modern European-style buildings and broad, tree-lined avenues. Hanoi became (7th cent.) the seat of the Chinese rulers of Vietnam. Its Chinese name, Dong Kinh or Tong King, became Tonkin and was applied by Europeans to the entire region. Hanoi was occupied briefly by the French in 1873 and passed to them 10 years later. It became the capital of French Indochina after 1887. The French developed Hanoi industrially, centering railway repair shops and small processing industries there. Occupied by the Japanese in 1940, Hanoi was liberated in 1945, when it became the seat of the Vietnam government. From 1946 to 1954, it was the scene of heavy fighting between the French and Viet Minh forces. After the French evacuated Hanoi in accordance with the Geneva Conference (July, 1954), the city became the capital of North Vietnam. Under the North Vietnamese it was greatly expanded industrially. During the Vietnam War its transportation facilities were continually disrupted by the bombing of bridges and railways, which were, however, immediately repaired. The city remained remarkably intact despite heavy U.S. bombings (1965-68, 1972), although widespread destruction occurred after the massive attacks of Dec. 18-30, 1972, when many nonmilitary targets, including the French embassy and large residential areas, were hit. Much of the civilian population had been evacuated and factories had been dismantled and reassembled in forested and rural areas. After the cease-fire, much of the machinery was returned and functioned again in ruined structures. Hanoi is also a cultural center; in the city are the Univ. of Hanoi, the Hanoi Polytechnical College, the Institute of Oriental Medicine (a major teaching and research center), and several ancient monuments, notably the Pagoda of the Great Buddha.

Hanotaux, Gabriel (gäbrēĕl' änōtō'), 1853-1944, French historian and statesman. Twice minister of foreign affairs (1894-95, 1895-98), he greatly furthered the Franco-Russian rapprochement. His chief fame is as a historian, notably as the author of *Contemporary France* (4 vol., 1903-8; tr., 4 vol., 1903-9) and *Histoire de la fondation de la troisième république* (4 vol., 1925-26). He also edited the *Histoire de la nation française* (15 vol., 1925-27). See studies by T. M. Iams (1962), and A. A. Heggoy (1972).

Hanover (hăn'ōvər), Ger. *Hannover,* former independent kingdom and former province of Germany; Lower Saxony, N West Germany. Hanover, Osnabrück, Stade, Wilhelmshaven, Hildesheim, Emden, Lüneburg, Celle, and Göttingen were its chief cities. Very irregular in outline, Hanover stretched from the Dutch border and the North Sea in the northwest to the Harz mts. in the southeast. The name Hanover originally applied only to the city, becoming the name of a state in 1815. Most of the territory was included in the duchy of Brunswick, which the house of the GUELPHS retained after 1180. In the repeated subdivisions of Brunswick among the various branches of the family, the branch of Brunswick-Lüneburg (and its offshoots, the duchies of Lüneburg, Celle, and Lüneburg-Calenberg) emerged as the most powerful. The dukes of Brunswick-Lüneburg played an important part in the Thirty Years War (1618-48) on the Protestant side, and in 1692 Duke Ernest Augustus of Calenberg was raised to the rank of elector. His lands became known as the electorate of Hanover. The marriage of Ernest Augustus to SOPHIA, granddaughter of James I of England, brought (1714) the English throne to his son, Elector George Louis (GEORGE I of England). Personal union of Great Britain and Hanover continued under the house of Hanover (see separate article). Napoleon I gave the electorate to Prussia in 1805, but in 1807 he assigned part of Hanover to the kingdom of Westphalia under his brother Jérôme Bonaparte, the remainder being divided in 1810 between France and Westphalia. In 1813, Great Britain regained possession, and in 1815 the Congress of Vienna raised Hanover to a kingdom, with membership in the GERMAN CONFEDERATION. At the accession (1837) of Queen Victoria in England, Hanover was separated from the British crown because of the Salic law of succession. ERNEST AUGUSTUS, son of George III, became king of Hanover and began his reign by rescinding the liberal Hanoverian constitution of 1833, thus evoking the well-known protest of the seven professors at GÖTTINGEN; the Revolution of 1848 forced him to grant a liberal constitution. His son, GEORGE V, succeeded him in 1851. George V refused to support Prussia in the AUSTRO-PRUSSIAN WAR (1866) and, as a consequence, lost his kingdom, which was made a Prussian (from 1871 a German) province. After World War II the province was incorporated into LOWER SAXONY.

Hanover, Ger. *Hannover,* city (1970 pop. 523,941), capital of Lower Saxony, N West Germany, on the Leine River and the Midland Canal. It is a major industrial, commercial, and transshipment center, also serving as a rail and road junction. Manufactures include iron and steel, tires, food products, printed materials, machinery, textiles, and motor vehicles. The city is the site of a noted annual industrial fair. Hanover was chartered in 1241 and in 1369 passed to Brunswick. In 1386 it joined the Hanseatic League. In 1692 it became the capital of the electorate (from 1815 kingdom; from 1866 province) of Hanover (see separate article). Hanover was badly damaged in World War II, but after 1945 numerous old buildings were reconstructed and many modern structures were erected. Points of interest include the Gothic former city hall (15th cent.); the Marktkirche (14th cent.), a red-brick church with a high (318 ft/97 m) tower; the Leineschloss (17th cent.), a château that now houses the parliament of Lower Saxony; and the remains of Herrenhausen castle (17th cent.). Hanover is the seat of technical, medical, and veterinary universities and several museums. The city has numerous parks and gardens. Elector Ernest Augustus, his wife Sophia, and their son, George I of England, are buried in Hanover.

Hanover. 1 Town (1970 pop. 10,107), Plymouth co., SE Mass., on the North River, in a farm area; settled 1649, set off from Scituate and Abington 1727. It has some light manufacturing. The anchor of the U.S.S. *Constitution* is said to have been made there. **2** Borough (1970 pop. 15,623), York co., SE Pa.; inc. 1815. Industries include food processing and the manufacture of shoes, textiles, twine, and metal products. Standardbred horses are raised there (many famous trotters have "Hanover" in their names). A cavalry action preceding the battle of Gettysburg was fought in Hanover in June, 1863.

Hanover, house of, ruling dynasty of Hanover (see HANOVER, province), which was descended from the GUELPHS and which in 1714 acceded to the British throne in the person of GEORGE I. George was the grandson of James I's daughter Elizabeth, queen of Bohemia, and the son of SOPHIA, electress of Hanover, and his succession to the throne was based on the Act of SETTLEMENT (1701). His successors were George II, George III, George IV, and William IV. The Salic law barred women from the succession in Hanover, and when William IV's niece, VICTORIA, succeeded (1837) to the British throne, the crowns of Hanover and Great Britain were separated. Victoria married Prince Albert of Saxe-Coburg-Gotha, so her descendants belonged to the house of WETTIN. ERNEST AUGUSTUS, son of George III, became (1837) king of Hanover and was succeeded by GEORGE V, who lost the crown in 1866. See Alvin Redman, *The House of Hanover* (1960, repr. 1968).

Hansa: see HANSEATIC LEAGUE.

Hansard (hăn'sərd), name given to the official record of the proceedings of the British Parliament, named after the Hansard family of printers. Luke

Hansard (1752–1828) was printer to the House of Commons and published *Journals of the House of Commons* (1774–1828) based on information from other printed sources. William COBBETT began (1804) a series of unofficial reports of the debates that was printed by Luke's son, Thomas Curson Hansard (1776–1833), who took over the enterprise in 1812. The reports were published by the family firm until 1890 and by different contractors until 1909, when the House of Commons instituted a series of official reports. The House of Lords followed suit in 1917, and substantially verbatim daily reports became available. Published by Her Majesty's Stationery Office, the reports are still generally referred to as Hansard, and the name appears on the title page. See J. C. Trewin and E. M. King, *Printer to the House* (1952).

Hansberry, Lorraine, 1930–65, American playwright, b. Chicago. She grew up on Chicago's South Side. In 1959 she became the first black woman to have a play produced on Broadway when *A Raisin in the Sun* opened to wide critical acclaim. The play dealt in human terms with the serious and comic problems of a black family in modern America. Her next play, *The Sign in Sidney Brustein's Window* (1964) was less successful. Hansberry died of cancer at 35. A collection of her writings, *To Be Young, Gifted, and Black,* was published in 1969.

Hanseatic League (hăn″sēăt′ĭk, hăn″zē–), mercantile league of medieval German towns. It was amorphous in character; its origin cannot be dated exactly. Originally a Hansa was a company of merchants trading with foreign lands. After the German push eastward and the settlement of German towns in the Slavic lands of the Baltic, the merchant guilds and town associations led (13th cent.) to leagues. Most notable was the company of German merchants with headquarters at VISBY; pushing east, they founded a branch at NOVGOROD. In London, where German merchants had traded since the 11th cent., the privileges granted to Cologne merchants were extended to other Germans, and a Hansa of German merchants was formed (see STEELYARD, MERCHANTS OF THE). A major impetus to the league's development was the lack of a powerful German national government to provide security for trade. In order to obtain mutual security, exclusive trading rights, and, wherever possible, trade monopoly, the towns drew closer together. In 1241 LÜBECK and HAMBURG concluded a treaty of mutual protection. Other cities joined this association, and a strong league grew up led by Lübeck. Ports and inland towns from Holland to Poland entered the league, but the north German cities remained the principal members. The league vigorously extended its operations, founding principal foreign branches at BRUGES and BERGEN. The Hansa towns reached their summit in their victories over WALDEMAR IV of Denmark, gaining in the Treaty of Stralsund (1370) a virtual trade monopoly in Scandinavia. Their Baltic hegemony continued through numerous wars until their defeat by the Dutch in 1441. Despite its success, the league suffered from lack of organization. Although assemblies of the league met irregularly at Lübeck, many towns did not send representatives, and decisions were subject to review by the individual towns. The number of members fluctuated, probably from less than 100 to over 160. By the 16th cent. internal dissension, curtailment of freedom by the German princes, growth of centralized foreign states and consequent loss of Hanseatic privileges, advances of Dutch and English shipping, and various changes in trade all operated against the league. The last diet was held in 1669, but the league was never formally dissolved. Lübeck, Hamburg, and BREMEN are still known as Hanseatic cities. See Philippe Dollinger, *The German Hansa* (tr. 1970).

Hansen, Duane, 1925–, American sculptor, b. Alexandria, Minn. A member of the superrealist movement of the late 1960s and early 70s, Hansen produced life-sized tableaux of realistic figures and props. These frequently depict violent events such as *Vietnam Scene* (1969). Many of his single figures, including *Hard Hat* (1970), portray familiar types of modern Americans.

Hansen, Marcus Lee, 1892–1938, American historian, b. Neenah, Wis. He spent almost four years in Europe gathering material for his studies on immigration. For *The Atlantic Migration, 1607–1860* (1940), first volume of a projected trilogy, he was awarded (posthumously) the 1941 Pulitzer Prize for history. In 1928 he began teaching history at the Univ. of Illinois, where he was made full professor in 1930. Among his other books are *Old Fort Snelling, 1819–1858* (1918), *Welfare Campaigns in Iowa* (1920), *German Schemes of Colonization before 1860* (1924), and *The Immigrant in American History* (posthumous, 1940).

Hansen, William Webster, 1909–49, U.S. physicist, b. Fresno, Calif. Hansen received his doctorate in physics from Stanford in 1933 and joined the faculty there in 1934. He invented the high-quality cavity resonator on which the linear electron accelerator depends. During World War II he worked in New York on defense applications of physics and electronics, including radar. He is considered a founder of the field of microwave electronics.

Hansen's disease: see LEPROSY.

Hanse towns: see HANSEATIC LEAGUE.

Hanson, Howard, 1896–, American composer, teacher, and conductor, b. Wahoo, Nebr. In 1921, Hanson won the Prix de Rome, becoming the first composer to enter the American Academy there. From 1924–64 he was director of the Eastman School of Music, Rochester, N.Y.; in 1964 he became director of the Institute of American Music at the Univ. of Rochester. Among his works are the Romantic Symphony (Symphony No. 2., 1930) and his Pulitzer Prize-winning Fourth Symphony (1944). Hanson's opera *Merry Mount,* based on a tale by Nathaniel Hawthorne, appeared in 1934. His works for chorus and orchestra include *The Lament for Beowulf* (1925), the *Hymn for the Pioneers* (1948), the *Cherubic Hymn* (1950), and *The Song of Democracy* (1957). Hanson's music is strongly romantic. His influence as a teacher was profound.

Hanson, John, 1715–83, first "President of the United States in Congress Assembled," b. Charles co., Maryland. He served in the Maryland provincial legislature, was active in the patriot cause in the Revolution, and was (1780–82) a member of the Continental Congress. Since he was the first President to serve the one-year term (1781–82), under the Articles of Confederation, Hanson is sometimes referred to as the first President of the United States. His duties were, however, merely those of a presiding officer and bore no relation to the duties of the President under the Constitution. See biography by S. W. Smith (1932).

Han-tan or **Hantan** (both: hän-dän), city (1970 est. pop. 500,000), SW Hopeh prov., China. It is a newly flourishing industrial center, with an iron mine, cotton mills, and chemical and cement plants. There are coal mines at nearby Feng-feng.

Hanukkah (hä′nəkə, –no͝okä), Jewish holiday, the Festival of Lights, the Feast of Consecration, or the Feast of the Maccabees; also transliterated Chanukah. According to tradition, it was instituted by Judas Maccabeus and his brothers in 165 B.C. to celebrate the dedication of the new altar in the Temple at Jerusalem. Three years earlier Antiochus Epiphanes (Antiochus IV) had profaned the Temple when he tried to force the Jews to offer sacrifices to heathen deities. The festival occurs in December near the time of the winter solstice, as does Christmas, and lasts eight days. Hanukkah later came to be linked also with a miraculous cruse of oil that burned for eight days, leading to the practice of lighting special Hanukkah candles, one the first evening, two the second, and so on. The eight-branched candlestand (menorah) used in that ceremony is a frequent symbol for the holiday.

Hanun (hā′nən). **1** King of Ammon. His insolent reception of David's messengers brought on a disastrous war. 2 Sam. 10; 1 Chron. 19. He may be the same as SHOBI. **2, 3** Two workers on the wall of Jerusalem. Neh. 3.13,30.

Han-yang or **Hanyang** (both: hän-yäng), former city, now part (since 1950) of the WU-HAN conurbation, E Hupeh prov., China, on the right bank of the Han River at its junction with the Yangtze. It is a heavy industrial center. Han-yang was founded during the Sui dynasty (A.D. 581–618). It is linked by bridge with Han-k'ou.

Haphraim (hăfrā′ĭm), border town of Issachar. Joshua 19.19.

haploid cell: see MEIOSIS.

happening, an artistic event of a theatrical nature, but presented without the framework of a plot. Happenings, developed in the early 1960s, were influenced by DADA notions of the nature of art. The term originated with the creation and performance in 1959 of Allan Kaprow's "18 Happenings in 6 Parts." This work emphasized various sorts of performances and experiences, including slide projection, dance, and taste and odor sensations. Many examples of the genre required audience participation and the aesthetic effect produced was a result of the combination of events experienced. Celebrated happenings include Claes Oldenburg's "Store" (1961), "Autobodies" (1963), and "Washes" (1965); Robert Rauschenberg's "Map Room II" (1965); Robert Whitman's "The American Moon" (1960); and Kaprow's "Calling" (1965).

Hapsburg or **Habsburg** (both: hăps′bûrg, Ger. häps′bo͝ork), ruling house of AUSTRIA (1282–1918). The family, which can be traced to the 10th cent., originally held lands in Alsace and in NW Switzerland. Otto (d. 1111) took the name Hapsburg from a castle near Aargau, Switzerland, when he was designated count. Vast estates in Upper Alsace, Baden, and Switzerland were inherited (1173) by his grandson Count Albert III (d. 1199) and passed to Rudolf II (d. 1232) and Albert IV (d. c.1240). The extinction of the houses of Lenzburg, ZÄHRINGEN, and Kyburg facilitated family acquisitions. The election (1273) of Count Rudolf IV as RUDOLF I, king of the Germans, provoked war with King Ottocar II of Bohemia. Ottocar's defeat and death at the Marchfeld (1278) confirmed Hapsburg possession of Austria, Carniola, and Styria; these lands and the Austrian ducal title were declared hereditary by Rudolf in 1282. In 1335, Carinthia too was claimed. Possession of these dominions marked the rise of the Hapsburgs to European significance. Held in common by the sons of Albert I and of Albert II, these lands were divided, after the death (1365) of Duke Rudolf IV, between the Albertine and Leopoldine lines (named for his brothers) and were reunited under Maximilian I only at the end of the 15th cent. Tyrol (1363), NE Istria (1374), and Trieste (1382) were added to the Hapsburg domain. Albert V of Austria, married to a daughter of Holy Roman Emperor SIGISMUND, succeeded him as king of Bohemia and Hungary and was chosen (1438) German king as ALBERT II. Henceforth, with one exception, the head of the house of Hapsburg was elected German king and Holy Roman emperor (see HOLY ROMAN EMPIRE for a complete list of emperors). Though Holy Roman Emperor FREDERICK III raised (1453) Austria to an archduchy and acquired (1471) Fiume, he had to struggle to maintain the Hapsburg realms during his constant warfare against Matthias Corvinus, king of Hungary and Bohemia. Under Frederick and his son, MAXIMILIAN I, a series of marriages greatly increased the hereditary holdings of the dynasty and gave rise to the motto, "Let others wage war; thou, happy Austria, marry." Most of the Low Countries (see NETHERLANDS, AUSTRIAN AND SPANISH) were acquired by the marriage of Maximilian to MARY OF BURGUNDY. The marriage of their son, Philip I, to Joanna of Castile, brought Philip's elder son, Holy Roman Emperor CHARLES V, to the throne of SPAIN. The marriage of Charles's younger brother, Ferdinand, to Anna, daughter of Louis II of BOHEMIA and HUNGARY, strengthened the Hapsburg claim to these possessions after the death (1526) of Louis at MOHACS. Hapsburg power reached its zenith under Charles V. The reigns of Maximilian I and Charles V also witnessed the emergence of the enduring struggles that eventually sapped Hapsburg strength: the defense of Central Europe against the Turks; the support of the Catholic Church against the Protestant Reformation; and the defense of the dynastic position against the rise of France. Charles V divided his dominions between his son, PHILIP II of Spain, and his brother, Ferdinand of Austria, Bohemia, and Hungary, who succeeded Charles as Holy Roman Emperor FERDINAND I. The Spanish and Austrian branches of the dynasty cooperated in the Thirty Years War (1618–48) and opposed the French in the Third Dutch War (1672–78) and in the War of the Grand Alliance (1688–97). The division of the family holdings, the acquisition of the royal crowns of Bohemia and Hungary, and the wars against the Turks in the 17th cent.—these factors transformed the dynasty into a polyglot monarchy, interested more in extending the family power in the Balkans than in purely German affairs. The Hapsburgs lost Alsace, Franche-Comté, Artois, and part of Flanders and Hainaut during the wars against Louis XIV. In the War of the SPANISH SUCCESSION, caused by the extinction of the Spanish Hapsburgs at the death (1700) of King CHARLES II, the family lost their claim to Spain. However, they retained the Austrian Netherlands and Lombardy and reconquered Hungary from the Turks. By the PRAGMATIC SANCTION (1713), Holy Roman Emperor CHARLES VI guaranteed the indivisibility of the Hapsburg domains and the succession of his daughter, MARIA THERESA. In the War of the AUSTRIAN SUCCESSION (1740–48) and in the Seven Years War (1756–63), Maria Theresa lost Silesia to Prussia but successfully defended the rest of her inheritance. On the death of Charles Albert of Bavaria, Holy Roman emperor as Charles VII (1742–45), the imperial title was bestowed on Archduchess Maria Theresa's husband, Francis, grand duke of Tuscany and former duke of Lorraine, who became FRANCIS I. Maria Theresa inaugurated the bureaucratic centralization that was carried forward by her son Holy Roman Emperor JOSEPH II. With him began the line of **Hapsburg-Lorraine.** An enlightened despot, Joseph II instituted reforms that included abolition of serfdom, revision of the penal code, religious toleration, and reduction of the power of the church. Leadership in the Hapsburg empire was given to the Germans. TUSCANY, separated (1790) from the main family holding, was held until 1860 by a junior branch of the dynasty (except during the French Revolutionary and Napoleonic eras). The duchy of MODENA, acquired (1806) by marriage, was also possessed until 1859 by a junior branch. The senior line was continued by the brother of Joseph II, Holy Roman Emperor LEOPOLD II, who repealed many of the reforms of Joseph II. Leopold's son, Francis II, abdicating as Holy Roman emperor, assumed (1806) the title Francis I, emperor of Austria. Though repeatedly humbled by Napoleon I, Francis emerged at the Congress of Vienna (1815) as one of the most powerful European monarchs. Giving up the Austrian Netherlands, the Hapsburgs regained Dalmatia, Istria, and Tyrol. They were compensated with Salzburg and in N Italy with Lombardy and Venetia, which, with Tuscany, Modena, and Parma, made the Italian peninsula virtually a Hapsburg appendage. In the 19th cent. the Hapsburg position was challenged in Germany by Prussia, in Italy by Sardinia, and in the Balkans by Russia. During the REVOLUTIONS OF 1848, Francis's son Ferdinand abdicated in favor of his nephew FRANCIS JOSEPH, whose long rule (1848–1916) saw Austria lose (1859) its dominance in Italy and surrender (1866) leadership in Germany to Prussia. In 1867 the Hapsburg lands were reorganized as the AUSTRO-HUNGARIAN MONARCHY. Buffeted by the twin forces of liberalism and nationalism and torn by the fratricidal hostilities of the polyglot national groups, the Hapsburg monarchy failed to create any ideological basis for its existence, failed to curb the domineering national groups (Magyars, Germans, and Poles), and failed to satisfy the demands of the rising middle and industrial classes. The assassination of heir apparent FRANCIS FERDINAND precipitated World War I; the death (1916) of Francis Joseph left his grandnephew, Emperor CHARLES I, to witness the defeat of Austria-Hungary, which was dissolved immediately after Charles's abdication in 1918. Charles's son, Archduke Otto, succeeded him as head of the Hapsburgs. The unresolved problems of the Hapsburg monarchy remained to torment the Balkan successor states. See R. A. Kann, *The Habsburg Empire* (1957) and *Multinational Empire* (1950, repr. 1964); O. Jászi, *Dissolution of The Habsburg Monarchy* (1929, repr. 1961); H. Kohn, *The Hapsburg Empire: 1804–1918* (1961); A. J. May, *The Passing of The Hapsburg Monarchy, 1914–1918* (2 vol., 1966) and *The Hapsburg Monarchy, 1867–1914* (1951, repr. 1968); Edward Crankshaw, *The Hapsburgs* (1971); V. L. Tapié *The Rise and Fall of the Hapsburg Monarchy* (1971).

Hara, Takashi (Kei) (täkä'shē hä'rä), 1856–1921, Japanese statesman, prime minister (1918–21). As secretary general and later president (1914), Hara established the SEIYUKAI as the first powerful majority party by compromise with the oligarchs (see GENRO), distribution of patronage posts to cooperative bureaucrats, exploitation of public works legislation, and lavish use of election money. He was the first prime minister to form a party cabinet in accordance with principles of parliamentary government. He encouraged the extension of suffrage but suppressed labor organization. His administration was notable for the expedition to Siberia, the independence movement in Korea, Japanese participation in the Paris Peace Conference, labor unrest, and naval armament. He was assassinated by a fanatic. See Tetsuo Najita, *Hara Kei in the Politics of Compromise, 1905–1915* (1967).

Hara (hā'rə), unidentified district to which the Assyrians deported the tribes of Reuben, Gad, and Manasseh. 1 Chron. 5.26.

Haradah (hăr'ədə), unidentified desert encampment during the Exodus, S of Kadesh. Num. 33.24,25.

Harahan, city (1970 pop. 13,037), Jefferson parish, SE La., a suburb of New Orleans, on the Mississippi River. The Huey P. Long Bridge over the Mississippi is nearby.

hara-kiri (hăr'ə-kēr'ē, hăr'ə-) [Jap.,=belly-cutting], the traditional Japanese form of honorable suicide, also known by its Chinese equivalent, *seppuku.* It was practiced by the Japanese feudal warrior class in order to avoid falling into enemy hands. Around 1500, it became a privileged alternative to execution, granted to DAIMYO and SAMURAI guilty of disloyalty to the emperor. The condemned man received a jeweled dagger from the emperor. He then selected as his second a faithful friend, received a delegation of official witnesses, and with much ceremony and formality plunged the dagger into the left side of his abdomen, drew it across to the right, and made a slight cut upward; at this point, his second beheaded him with one stroke of a sword, and the bloody dagger was returned to the emperor. Around 1700, it became permissible to go through a mere semblance of disembowelment prior to beheading. However, many nobles continued to fulfill the entire rite. Voluntary hara-kiri, performed in the same manner, was resorted to after a private misfortune, out of loyalty to a dead master, or in protest against the erroneous conduct of a living superior. Obligatory hara-kiri was abolished in 1868, but its voluntary form has persisted. It was performed by 40 military men in 1895 as a protest against the return of conquered territory, the Liaotung peninsula, to China; by General NOGI on the death of Emperor Meiji in 1912; and by numerous soldiers as an alternative to surrender in World War II. See BUSHIDO, KAMIKAZE, SUICIDE. For detailed accounts of hara-kiri, see A. B. F. Redesdale, *Tales of Old Japan* (1919).

Harald: see HAROLD.

Haran (hā'răn). **1** Abraham's brother. Gen. 11.26, 27–29. **2** Caleb's son. 1 Chron. 2.46. **3** Levite. 1 Chron. 23.9.

Haran or **Harran** (both: härän'), ancient city of Mesopotamia, now in SE Asiatic Turkey, 24 mi (39 km) SE of Urfa. It was an important center on the trade route from Nineveh to Carchemish and the seat of the Assyrian moon god. The Babylonians defeated the Assyrian army at Haran in 609 B.C. Frequently mentioned in the Bible, it was the home of Abraham's family after the migration from Ur. The Greek form of the name is Charan or Charran. In Roman times it was CARRHAE.

Harappa: see INDUS VALLEY CIVILIZATION.

Harar or **Harrar** (both: hä'rər), city (1968 est. pop. 42,771), capital of Harar prov., E central Ethiopia, at an altitude of c.6,000 ft (1,830 m). It is the trade center for a region where coffee, cereals, and cotton are produced. Harar was probably founded in the 7th cent. After 1520 the Somali conqueror Ahmad Gran made it the capital of a considerable Muslim state, but an invasion by the Galla people brought an end (1577) to its political power. The city maintained a precarious independence until its occupation (1875–85) by Egypt. In 1887 it was incorporated into Ethiopia by Menelik II. A walled city, Harar was long a center of Islamic learning. Today it is the site of a military academy and of teacher-training and agricultural schools.

Hararite (hā'rərīt), obscure epithet used of five names in the lists of mighty men. 2 Sam. 23.11,33; 1 Chron. 11.34,35.

Harbin (här'bĭn), or **Ha-erh-pin** (hä-ĕr-bĭn), Rus. *Kharbin,* city (1970 est. pop. 2,750,000), capital of Heilungkiang prov., China, on the Sungari River. It is the major trade and communications center of central Manchuria, the junction of the two most important railroads in Manchuria, and the main port on the Sungari. Part of the great Manchurian industrial complex of metallurgical, machinery, chemical, petroleum, and coal industries, Harbin also has railroad shops, food-processing establishments (soybeans are a major commodity), and plants making aircraft, tractors, ball bearings, precision instruments, cutting tools, electrical and electronic equipment, cement, fertilizer, and lead pencils. Harbin was unimportant until Russia was granted a concession (1896) and built a modern section alongside the old Chinese town. (Russia surrendered its concession in 1924.) Flooded by White Russian refugees after 1917, Harbin had one of the largest European populations in the Far East. Most of the Europeans left the city following the rise to power of the Chinese Communists. Harbin's institutions of higher learning include Harbin Polytechnical Univ., a medical college, and several technical institutes.

Harbona or **Harbonah** (both: härbō'nə), chamberlain of King Ahasuerus. Esther 1.10; 7.9.

harbor: see PORT.

harbor seal, most commonly seen SEAL of the Northern Hemisphere, *Phoca vitulina.* Harbor seals are found along coasts and in sheltered bays and harbors of North America, Europe, and NE Asia. They range farther south than any other northern seal, being found in North America as far S as New Jersey and S California. They range north to the southernmost limits of the ice cap. Also known as common seals, hair seals, and leopard seals, they enter rivers, and are even found in the Great Lakes. Small seals, they reach a length of up to 6 ft (180 cm) and a weight of up to 250 lb (110 kg). Their coats are gray with white spots or yellowish with gray or black blotches. Harbor seals are solitary hunters; they feed on fish, mollusks, and crustaceans, coming ashore to rest and sleep. They may gather in large numbers on rocks or beaches, especially at the mating season. They are polygamous and the female produces a single pup in early spring. Small colonies of several families each occupy particular locations in the water, usually near rocky shores or islands, and may remain there for many generations. Their greatest enemies are sharks and killer whales. Harbor seals are classified in the phylum CHORDATA, subphylum Vertebrata, class Mammalia, order Carnivora, suborder Pinnipedia, family Phocidae.

Harbour Grace, town (1971 pop. 2,771), E N.F., Canada, on Conception Bay. It is a leading fishing port and has fish-processing plants. It was settled c.1550 and is one of the oldest towns in the province. An airport is nearby.

Harburg (här'bo͝orkh), district of Hamburg, N West Germany; a port on the Elbe River. Refined petroleum and rubber goods are produced in the district. Formerly an independent town, Harburg was incorporated into Hamburg in 1937.

Harcourt, Sir William George Granville Venables Vernon, 1827–1904, English statesman. A brilliant parliamentarian and a supporter of Gladstone, he entered Parliament in 1868 and had a notable career as solicitor general (1873–74), home secretary (1880–85), and chancellor of the exchequer (1886, 1892–95). In his 1894–95 budgets he devised a new system of death duties and extended graduated taxation. On Gladstone's retirement (1894) he was passed over for the office of prime minister (see VICTORIA), but he effectively led (1894–99) the Liberal party in the Commons. He was also a noted writer on international law. See biography by A. G. Gardiner (1923).

Hardangerfjord (hārdäng'ərfyôr'), second largest fjord of Norway, penetrating 114 mi (183 km) from the Atlantic Ocean into Hordaland co., SW Norway. A southern branch, the Sørfjord, cleaves the Hardangervidda, a barren and rocky plateau, for 25 mi (40 km); at its head are the village of Odda and the famous Skjeggedalsfoss, a waterfall 525 ft (160 m) high. An eastern branch, the Eidfjord, extends 15 mi (24 km) to the quaint village of Vik near the Vøringfoss, a waterfall 535 ft (163 m) high. The valleys of the Hardangerfjord are fertile and dotted with picturesque villages. Embroidery and violinmaking are traditional home industries. The region is a favorite tourist area. Extending inland from the fjord is the Hardangerfjell, a mountain mass rising to 6,153 ft (1,875 m) in the Hardangerjøkel.

hardboard: see COMPOSITION BOARD.

Hardecanute: see HARTHACANUTE.

Hardee, William Joseph, 1815–73, American army officer, Confederate general, b. Camden co., Ga. A graduate of West Point, he served with distinction in the Mexican War and compiled *Rifle and Light Infantry Tactics,* a standard army textbook of the time (1853–55). In 1856, he was appointed commandant of cadets at West Point. When Georgia seceded, he resigned his commission as lieutenant colonel and became a Confederate brigadier general. After organizing an Arkansas brigade, Hardee joined A. S. Johnston's army and fought at Shiloh (April, 1862). He was promoted to lieutenant general in October and was an able corps commander in the Army of Tennessee, fighting at Perryville, Murfreesboro, and Missionary Ridge and in the ATLANTA CAMPAIGN. He commanded against General SHERMAN in Georgia and South Carolina (1864–65), abandoning Savannah and Charleston to union troops and surrendering to Sherman in North Carolina in April, 1865. See study by N. C. Hughes (1965).

Harden, Maximilian (mäk"sēmē'lyän här'dən), 1861–1927, German journalist, whose real name was Witkowski. One of the leading publicists of his time, he was an admirer of Bismarck. After Bismarck's fall he used his own paper, the *Zukunft,* to attack the men surrounding William II, and in World War I he censured the military leaders. Later he sharply criticized the statesmen of the German republic. Essentially Harden was a popular journalist appealing to mass prejudices and beliefs. Among his many books are *Germany, France, and England* (tr. 1924) and *I Meet My Contemporaries* (tr. 1925). See biography by H. F. Young (1959).

Hardenberg, Friedrich von: see NOVALIS.

Hardenberg, Karl August, Fürst von (kärl ou'-gŏost fürst fən här'dənbĕrk), 1750-1822, Prussian administrator and diplomat, b. Hanover. After service for Hanover and Brunswick, he entered the Prussian service. As Prussian delegate he signed the Treaty of Basel (1795) with France (see FRENCH REVOLUTIONARY WARS). He became chief minister in charge of foreign affairs (1804-6), but was dismissed upon pressure from Napoleon I. After war had broken out against France a few months later, Hardenberg was recalled (1807) to the ministry, only to be ousted again after Prussia's defeat and the disastrous Treaty of Tilsit. In 1810 he was made prime minister with the title of state chancellor. His immediate task was to restore state finances so that Prussia would be able to pay the huge indemnity imposed by Napoleon at Tilsit. He introduced a general tax system, and, continuing the reform program begun by Karl vom und zum STEIN, abolished trade monopolies, secularized remaining church property, turned feudal lands into freeholds, and extended legal equality to the Jews. His reforms helped modernize the Prussian state, preparing it for the final struggle against Napoleon I. In 1813 he persuaded the vacillating FREDERICK WILLIAM III to join the coalition against Napoleon. Following Napoleon's defeat he was delegate to the Congress of Vienna. He remained in office until his death, but from 1815 he was forced to cooperate with the Prussian reactionaries.

hardening, in metallurgy, treatment of metals to increase their resistance to penetration. A metal is harder when it has small grains, which result when the metal is cooled rapidly. Sometimes small areas on the surface of a casting are given a fine-grain structure by chill hardening; metal pieces (chills) are inserted in the wall of a sand mold. The area next to the chill cools faster and becomes harder than the surface next to the sand. Metals worked cold, as by being rolled into thinner pieces, become hardened, partly by reducing grain size and partly by distorting the shape of the grains so that they increasingly resist further distortion. Alloying may harden a metal by changing its chemical composition. In hardening by precipitation, one constituent of a supersaturated solid solution separates from the solution. Usually the process is carried out at above room temperature. At room temperature the process takes longer; it is then known as age-hardening. Aluminum-copper alloys are hardened by precipitation. Iron-carbon alloys, steel and cast iron, for example, respond well to heat treatments. By varying the percentage of carbon and the rate of cooling from a high temperature, many gradations of hardness, softness, toughness, and other properties are achieved. To impart hardness the metal is rapidly cooled from a high temperature by quenching in water, oil, or molten salt. Later heat treatment by tempering or annealing modifies the metal slightly to give other desirable qualities. Steels with a low percentage of carbon can be given a hard surface by increasing the amount of carbon at the surface so that they will respond to heat treatment, a process known as carburizing, or casehardening. One way to do this is to pack steel in charcoal and then heat it. Another way is to heat the metal in a furnace with a hydrocarbon gas atmosphere; still another is to heat the metal in a molten-salt bath containing potassium and sodium cyanides. If the salt bath cited is of a lower temperature, the steel surface will also pick up nitrogen, which helps harden it; the process is then called cyaniding. At even lower temperatures the steel picks up only nitrogen, and is nitrided.

hardening of the arteries: see ARTERIOSCLEROSIS.

hardhack: see SPIRAEA.

Hardicanute: see HARTHACANUTE.

Hardie, James Keir (kēr' här'dē), 1856-1915, British labor leader and socialist, b. Scotland. A coal miner, he became a union organizer and in 1888 founded the Scottish Labour party. In 1892, Hardie entered Parliament, becoming the first independent workers' representative to secure election. He was a founder (1893) and first president (1893-1900) of the Independent Labour party and was instrumental in forming (1900) the Labour Representation Committee, which became the LABOUR PARTY. See biographies by William Steward (1921), Emrys Hughes (1956), and K. O. Morgan (1967); H. M. Pelling, *Origins of the Labour Party* (2d ed. 1965).

Hardin, John, 1753-92, American Indian fighter, b. Fauquier co., Va. He served in Lord Dunmore's War (1774) and was a noted member of Daniel Morgan's riflemen during the Revolution. His services at Saratoga were particularly noteworthy. He moved to Washington co., Ky., in 1786 and afterwards took part in many expeditions against the Indians N of the Ohio, winning general recognition for his courage and his ability as a woodsman and a leader of men. He was sent in 1792 to negotiate a treaty with the Miami Indians and was murdered by Indians at what is now Hardin, Ohio.

Hardin, John Wesley, 1853-95, American desperado, b. Bonham, Texas. In the lawless violence of the frontier the boy early became a gambler and a gunman, but was able by his shooting skill and the help of friends to escape capture until 1877, when he was sentenced to 25 years for killing a sheriff. He studied law in prison and, pardoned in 1894, began practice in El Paso but was shot down a year later by a local constable. See his autobiography, introd. by R. G. McCubbin (1961); biography by Lewis Nordyke (1957).

Harding, Chester, 1792-1866, American portrait painter, b. Conway, Mass. He worked as an itinerant portrait painter long enough to enable him to study at the Pennsylvania Academy of Design. Later he practiced in St. Louis, Washington, D.C., and Boston and had three years of artistic and social success in London. On returning to the United States he became the fashionable painter of Boston. His principal portraits are those of Daniel Webster (one in the Bar Association, New York City, and one in the Cincinnati Art Mus.); John Randolph (Corcoran Gall.); as well as effective characterizations of Chief Justice Marshall, Henry Clay, and Washington Allston.

Harding, Stephen: see STEPHEN HARDING, SAINT.

Harding, Warren Gamaliel (gəmā'lēəl), 1865-1923, 29th President of the United States (1921-23), b. Blooming Grove (now Corsica), Ohio. After study (1879-82) at Ohio Central College, he moved with his family to Marion, Ohio, where he devoted himself to journalism. He bought the Marion *Star*, built up the newspaper, and became a member of the small group that dominated local affairs. He entered Ohio Republican politics and was (1899-1903) a member of the state legislature. Harding served as lieutenant governor (1904-5), but he was defeated (1910) as Republican candidate for governor. His talent for public speaking and his affable personality won Harding the support of the political leaders as well as of the people and enabled him to rise into national politics; he was picked to nominate William Howard Taft at the convention of 1912, and he was elected (1914) to the U.S. Senate. His six-year stay in the Senate was undistinguished, for he followed the party whips on domestic legislation and Henry Cabot Lodge on issues concerning the peace. In 1920, Harding was nominated for the presidency, largely through the efforts of a group of Senators, after successive balloting for Gen. Leonard WOOD and Frank O. LOWDEN had deadlocked the Republican convention. His vague pronouncements on the League of Nations and his noncommittal utterances in the campaign helped him to win the election, defeating the Democratic candidate, James M. COX, by an impressive majority. The administration that followed was marked by one achievement, the calling of the Washington Conference (see NAVAL CONFERENCES). Harding, conscious of his own limitations, had promised to rely on a cabinet of "best minds," but unfortunately he chose—along with more capable advisers—men who lacked any sense of public responsibility. At the time of the legislative deadlock of 1923 came rumors of scandals in the Veterans' Bureau, in the Office of the Alien Property Custodian, and in the departments of the Interior and Justice. In the midst of these rumors Harding died suddenly (Aug., 1923) in San Francisco on his return from a journey to Alaska. Thus he was not troubled by the exposure of the TEAPOT DOME scandal and was spared the humiliation of seeing his appointees Secretary of the Interior Albert B. FALL and Attorney General Harry M. DAUGHERTY brought to the bar of justice. Lesser scandals were also exposed, and Harding's administration has been stigmatized as one of the most corrupt in American history. See Samuel Hopkins Adams, *Incredible Era* (1939, repr. 1964); Francis Russell, *Shadow of Blooming Grove* (1968); R. K. Murray, *Harding Era* (1969); Andrew Sinclair, *Available Man* (1969); R. C. Downes, *The Rise of Warren Gamaliel Harding* (1970).

hardness, property of matter commonly described as the resistance of a substance to being scratched by another substance. The degree of hardness is relative, different substances being compared with one another. Mohs's scale of hardness (named for Friedrich Mohs), used commonly in mineralogy, lists certain minerals in order of hardness: talc, 1; gypsum, 2; calcite, 3; fluorite, 4; apatite, 5; orthoclase, 6; quartz, 7; topaz, 8; corundum, 9; diamond, 10. The listing indicates merely that gypsum (hardness=2) is harder than—i.e., capable of scratching—talc (hardness=1). The listing does not indicate that gypsum (2) is twice as hard as talc (1). The hardness of many minerals falls between those included in the list. For example, the hardness of barite is 3.3. Hardness may differ with the direction of the scratch made on the substance. Thus the mineral kyanite has a hardness of 5 parallel to the length of its crystals, and of 7 at right angles to this direction. There are several other methods based on the resistance to indentation for testing engineering materials. The solid elements have been thus classified: diamond (an allotropic form of carbon) is hardest and listed as 10, with cesium the softest, rated as 0.2, the same degree of hardness as wax (hardness=0.2 at 0°C). The hardness numeral of the Brinell scale is based upon the indentation produced when pressure is exerted by a sphere on the substance. The value thus obtained has a direct relation to the tensile strength of the substance. The hardness of a material may be modified by the presence of small quantities of another substance, as in metallic alloys, or by impurities in minerals.

Hardouin, Jules: see MANSART, JULES HARDOUIN.

hardpan, condition of the soil or subsoil in which the soil grains become cemented together by such bonding agents as iron oxide and calcium carbonate, forming a hard, impervious mass. It is disadvantageous to farming, interfering with the circulation of moisture in the soil and with the growth of roots through the soil. When the condition is caused by the filling of the air spaces in the soil with fine particles of clay, the subsoil is called a clay pan. This usually occurs in acid soil.

Hardwar (hərdwär'), town (1971 pop. 77,940), Uttar Pradesh state, N India, on the Ganges River. Annual and duodecennial pilgrimages are associated with the town's Hindu temple and with the Ganges. The Gurukul school, founded in 1902, is a center of Vedic studies.

Hardwicke, Philip Yorke, 1st earl of, 1690-1764, English jurist. As lord chancellor (1737-56) he did much to systematize the laws of EQUITY and established the principle that equity must follow its precedents. An influential member of the government, he was active in suppressing the Jacobite uprising of 1745.

hardwood: see WOOD.

Hardy, Alexandre (älĕksäN'drə ärdē'), b. between 1569 and 1575, d. 1631 or 1632, French dramatist. His more than 600 plays are unexceptional, but he played a transitional role as innovator of the less lyrical, more dramatic theater later developed by CORNEILLE.

Hardy, Thomas, 1840-1928, English novelist and poet, b. near Dorchester, one of the great English writers of the 19th cent. The son of a stonemason, he derived a love of music from his father and a devotion to literature from his mother. Hardy could not afford to pursue a scholarly career and was apprenticed to John Hicks, a local church architect. He continued, however, to study the Greek and Latin classics. From 1862 to 1867 he served as assistant to Arthur Blomfield, a London architect; ill health forced him to return to Dorset, where he worked for Hicks and his successor until 1874. He was, however, continually writing. Such early novels as *Desperate Remedies* (1871) and *A Pair of Blue Eyes* (1873) met with small success and may be considered formative works. After the appearance of *Far From the Madding Crowd* (1874), popular as well as critical acclaim enabled him to devote himself exclusively to writing. His success also made marriage feasible, and in 1874 he married Emma Lavinia Gifford. Over the next 22 years he wrote many novels—including those he referred to as "romances and fantasies"—most of which were first serialized in popular magazines. His major works are *The Return of the Native* (1878), *The Mayor of Casterbridge* (1886), *Tess of the D'Urbervilles* (1891), and *Jude the Obscure* (1896), the latter two considered masterpieces. They are all set against the bleak and forbidding Dorset landscape (known as Wessex in the novels), whose physical harshness echoes that of an indifferent, if not malevolent, universe. Hardy's characters, who are for the most part of the poorer rural classes, are sympathetically and often humorously portrayed. Their lives are ruled not only by nature but also by rigid Victorian social conventions. Hardy's style is accordingly roughhewn, sometimes awkward, but always commanding and intense. He had always written poetry and regarded the novel as an inferior genre. After *Jude the Obscure* was attacked on grounds of supposed immorality (it dealt sympathetically with open sexual relations between men and women), Hardy abandoned fiction. However, the compelling reason was probably that his thought had become too abstract to be adequately expressed in novels. Beginning at the age of 58, Hardy published many volumes of poetry, including *Wessex Poems* (1898), *Satires of Circumstance* (1914), *Moments of Vision* (1917), and *Winter Words* (1928). His poetry is spare, unadorned, and unromantic, and its pervasive theme is man's futile struggle against ineluctable cosmic forces. Hardy's verse drama *The Dynasts* (written 1903–8), one of his finest works, is a historical epic of the Napoleonic era, expressing the view that history, too, is guided by forces far more powerful than individual will. Hardy's vision reflects a world in which Victorian complacencies were dying but its moralism was not, and in which science had eliminated, for the thinking person, all the comforting certainties of religion. Hardy's wife died in 1912, and in 1914 he married Florence Emily Dugdale, a writer of children's books, some 40 years his junior. He lived the latter half of his life at Max Gate, a house built after his own designs in his native Dorset, and died there. His ashes are interred in Westminster Abbey; but his heart is buried separately, with a certain dark propriety, near the Egdon Heath made famous by his novels. See Evelyn Hardy and F. B. Pinion, eds., *One Rare Fair Woman,* his letters to Florence Henniker (1972); biographies by his wife F. E. Hardy (1928 repr. 1971), and by Evelyn Hardy (1953, repr. 1973); studies by C. J. Weber (2d ed., 1965; and 1942, repr. 1965), R. C. Carpenter (1964), Irving Howe (1967), J. I. M. Stewart (1971), F. R. Southerington (1971), Micheal Millgate (1971), and Merryn Williams (1972); studies on his poetry by J. O. Bailey (1971), Ernest Brennecke (1924, repr. 1973), and Paul Zietlow (1974); bibliographical study by R. L. Purdy (1954).

Hare, Sir John, 1844–1921, English actor-manager, whose original name was John Fairs. From 1856 to 1874 he was a prominent actor with the Bancrofts' company in the plays of Tom Robertson. He managed (1875–79) the Court Theatre and later with the Kendals co-managed (1879–88) the St. James Theatre. In 1889 he became manager of the Garrick Theatre, built for him by W. S. Gilbert. He was knighted in 1907.

Hare, Robert, 1781–1858, American chemist, b. Philadelphia. He was professor of chemistry (1819–47) at the medical college of the Univ. of Pennsylvania. Hare made important contributions to early American chemistry. Among his inventions were the oxyhydrogen blowpipe, an electric furnace, and a deflagrator, and his research included work on salts. See biography by E. F. Smith (1917).

hare, name for certain herbivorous mammals of the family Leporidae, which also includes the RABBIT and PIKA. The name is applied especially to species of the genus *Lepus,* sometimes called the true hares. Hares generally have longer ears and hind legs than rabbits and move by jumping rather than by running. Unlike rabbits, hares are born covered with fur and with their eyes open. Hares are native to Eurasia, Africa, and North and Central America; they have been introduced into Australia in recent times. They range in weight from 3 to 13 lb (1.4–5.9 kg) and from 13 to 25 in. (33–63 cm) in length. They are usually brown or grayish in color, but northern species acquire a white coat in winter. Hares live in meadows, brushy country, and woodland clearings; they are largely nocturnal although they may forage in the day if undisturbed. Members of most species rest in shallow hollows, called forms, that they make in vegetation; they have regular trails from these forms to their feeding spots. Females make nests of their own fur for receiving the young. Hares feed on grasses, leaves, and bark. Like rabbits, they reingest their own droppings so that food passes twice through the digestive system. Most North American hares are very large, with extremely long ears, and are called JACKRABBITS. Other North American species are the VARYING HARE (or snowshoe rabbit), *Lepus americanus,* which ranges over the northern half of the continent; the Arctic hare, *L. arcticus,* found on the coasts and islands of the Arctic Ocean; and the Alaska, or tundra, hare, *L. othus,* found in N and W Alaska. The brown hare, *L. europaeus,* is a large hare native to Europe, where it is valued as game. Introduced as a game animal in the NE United States, it has become an agricultural pest. The so-called Belgian hare is actually a domestic rabbit. Hares are classified in the phylum CHORDATA, subphylum Vertebrata, class Mammalia, order Lagomorpha, family Leporidae.

harebell: see BELLFLOWER.

harelip, congenital abnormality in which there is a cleft or split in the upper lip. There may be a single opening in the middle portion of the lip or an opening on each side. The condition frequently occurs along with a CLEFT PALATE, an opening in the roof of the mouth. Harelip is usually corrected by plastic surgery soon after birth.

harem (hâr'əm) [Arabic], term applied to women's apartments in a Muslim household. In the ancient Arab world women enjoyed a certain amount of freedom. However, with the advent of Islam, the veiling and seclusion of women into harems became more common. The most famous harem, that of the sultans of Turkey, dates from the 15th cent. and included the old and new palaces on Seraglio Point, Constantinople. It was abolished with the downfall (1909) of Abd al-Hamid II. The sultan's harem often contained several hundred women, all subject to the control of the sultan's mother and guarded by eunuchs. In India the harem is called a *purdah* or *zenana;* in Iran, *andarun.* Although the harem is rapidly disappearing in the 20th cent., there nevertheless are still some in existence in the more remote areas of the Muslim world. See N. M. Penzer, *The Harem* (1937); Dorothy Van Ess, *Fatima and Her Sisters* (1961).

Haren, Willem van (vĭl'əm văn hä'rən), 1710–68, Dutch poet, b. Friesland, of a noble family. His chief work is an epic poem, *Friso* (1741). His brother, **Onno Zwier van Haren,** 1713–79, also a poet, wrote patriotic verse, notably a series about the GUEUX, entitled first *Aan de Vaderland* (1769), in final form *De Geusen* (1772).

Hareph (hā'rĕf), Judah's descendant. 1 Chron. 2.51.

Hareth (hā'rĕth), forest, apparently near ADULLAM. 1 Sam. 22.5.

Harfleur (ärflör'), town (1968 pop. 15,598), Seine-Maritime dept., N France, at the mouth of the Seine River on the English Channel. It was a flourishing port during the later Middle Ages but declined because of silting in the 16th cent. The seige and capture (1415) of Harfleur by the English in the Hundred Years War is described by Shakespeare in *Henry V.*

Hargeisa: see HARGHESSA, Somalia.

Harghessa or **Hargeisa** (both: härgā'sä), town (1963 est. pop. 40,000), N Somalia. It is a commercial center and watering place for nomadic stock herders. The town was taken in 1870 by Egyptian forces, who withdrew in 1884 to fight the Mahdi in Sudan. The British later took control and, in 1941, made Harghessa the capital of British Somaliland.

Hargreaves, James (här'grēvz), 1720?–1778, English engineer. In 1762 he made an unsuccessful attempt to develop a machine for carding, a process preparatory to SPINNING, and in 1764 he invented the spinning jenny, which resulted in doubling production in the carding process.

Harhaiah (härhā'ə, -hā'yə), father of UZZIEL **6.**

Harhas (här'hăs), ancestor of Huldah's husband. 2 Kings 22.14. Hassah: 2 Chron. 34.22.

Har-heres: see HERES.

Harhur (här'hər), post-Exilic family. Ezra 2.51; Neh. 7.53.

Hari, Mata: see MATA HARI.

Harim (hā'rĭm). **1** Family of priests in the return from the Exile. Neh. 12.15. Rehum: Neh. 12.3. **2** Another family of priests in the return from the Exile. Ezra 2.39; 10.21; Neh. 7.42; 10.5. **3** Priest, probably the ancestor of **2.** 1 Chron. 24.8. **4** Family of laymen in the return from the Exile. Ezra 2.32; 10.31; Neh. 7.35; 10.27. **5** Father, or family, of a repairer of the wall of Jerusalem, probably the same as **1, 2,** or **4.** Neh. 3.11.

Haringey (hâr'ĭng-gā"), borough of Greater London (1971 pop. 236,956), SE England. Haringey was created in 1965 by the merger of the municipal boroughs of Hornsey, Tottenham, and Wood Green. It is mainly residential. Tottenham has furniture, light engineering, children's clothing, and printing industries. The studios of BBC television news are in Wood Green. Bruce Castle in Tottenham, built in the 16th cent., houses a postal museum in honor of Sir Rowland Hill, founder of the penny postage system.

Harington, Sir John, 1560?–1612, English author. He spent most of his career at the court of Queen Elizabeth I, where he became known for his indelicate humor. His Rabelaisian *Metamorphosis of Ajax* (1596, ed. by E. S. Donno, 1961) uses ornate style and classical allusions to discuss at length the construction of an Elizabethan privy. He also did a translation (1591) of Ariosto's *Orlando Furioso.* His *Letters and Epigrams* (ed. by N. E. McClure, 1930) are vivid sketches of Elizabethan social life and writings.

Hariph (hā'rĭf), a signer of the covenant. Neh. 7.24; 10.19. Jorah: Ezra 2.18.

Hariri (Abu Muhammad al-Kasim al-Hariri) (härē'rē), 1054–1122, Arabian writer of Basra. His principal work is one of the most popular of Arabian books. It is called *Makamat* [literary assemblies], the name of a literary genre that was much affected at this time. It consists of 50 episodes, in which an old rogue, Abu Zaid, goes from place to place earning his living by his clever talk and his wits. It is written in an almost euphuistic style. Numerous Western translations have been made since the 17th cent.

Hari Rud (hä'rē rōōd), river, c.700 mi (1,130 km) long, rising in the Kuh-e Baba range, central Afghanistan, and flowing west and then north into the steppes S of the Kara Kum desert in the Turkmen SSR; its lower course forms part of the Afghanistan-USSR border. The river irrigates the fertile valley of Herat, NW Afghanistan, and flows through the Tedzhen oasis in the Turkman SSR, a wheat, cotton, and cattle raising area. In the USSR the river is called Tedzhen or Tejend; in ancient times it was known as the Arius.

Harkness, Edward Stephen, 1874–1940, American philanthropist, b. Cleveland. He inherited a fortune from his father, a partner of John D. Rockefeller, Sr. His extensive philanthropies, many of them anonymous, were extended especially to colleges, hospitals, and museums. He served as president of the COMMONWEALTH FUND. See biography by J. W. Wooster (1949).

Harlan, John Marshall, 1833–1911, American jurist, Associate Justice of the U.S. Supreme Court (1877–1911), b. Boyle co., Ky., grad. Centre College, 1850. Admitted to the bar in 1853, he served in the Civil War as a colonel in the Union army until 1863, when he became attorney general of Kentucky. He took a leading part in the violent political struggles of the day, becoming after the war a leader of the conservative Republicans; he was defeated for the governorship, however, in 1872 and 1875. As head of the Kentucky delegation to the Republican national convention in 1876, he played a leading role in the nomination of Rutherford B. Hayes. In Oct., 1877, Hayes appointed him to the U.S. Supreme Court. A man of strong and independent convictions and, on the whole, a strict constructionist, he became known as a dissenter. In the "insular cases" (1901) he protested against the decision that did not give the residents of the new U.S. possessions the national benefits of the Constitution. He upheld the police power of the states, dissented in the civil-rights cases (1883) and the income-tax case (1894), and argued that the court had no right to read the word *unreasonable* into the Sherman Act in the decisions against the Standard Oil and American Tobacco trusts. A firm defender of civil liberties and civil rights, Justice Harlan dissented vigorously in *Plessy* vs. *Ferguson* (1896), in which the Supreme Court enunciated the "separate but equal" doctrine justifying segregation. In 1893, President Benjamin Harrison appointed him to the tribunal to settle the Bering Sea Fur-Seal Controversy at Paris. See F. B. Clark, *The Constitutional Doctrines of Justice Harlan* (1915); Frank Latham, *The Great Dissenter* (1970).

Harlan, John Marshall, 1899–1971, Associate Justice of the U.S. Supreme Court (1955–1971), b. Chicago; grandson of John Marshall Harlan. He received his law degree from New York Law School and was admitted to the bar in 1925; he practiced in New York City. He was an assistant U.S. attorney (1925–27), special assistant attorney general of New York state (1928–30), and chief counsel to the New York State Crime Commission (1951–53). Harlan was a judge of the U.S. Court of Appeals, 2d Circuit, from 1954 to 1955, when he was appointed by President Eisenhower to replace Justice Robert H. Jackson on the Supreme Court. A conservative on the court, he held a narrow view of the court's power, believing that the Federal judiciary should not interfere in state and local matters, and that political and social evils should be corrected through the political process and not through court action; he nevertheless sided with the majority on many civil rights cases. Harlan resigned from the court in late 1971, shortly before his death.

Harland, Henry, 1861–1905, American novelist, b. St. Petersburg, Russia, studied at Harvard. He traveled extensively in Europe during his childhood. His first novels were written under the pseudonym Sidney Luska and dealt with immigrant Jewish life in the United States. He later abandoned this type of writing and in 1889 left the United States to live in London. There he became one of the leading exponents of fin de siècle aestheticism and with Aubrey BEARDSLEY founded (1894) the YELLOW BOOK. During the three years of the *Yellow Book's* publication, Harland was its literary editor and contributed many stories to it. His later novels, including *The Cardinal's Snuff Box* (1900) and *The Lady Paramount* (1902), were noted for their wit and highly polished prose style.

Harlech (här'lĕkh, -lĕk, här'lē), village, Merionethshire, W Wales. The ancient village with its 13th-century castle rests on a cliff 200 ft (61 m) above the modern seaside village. The heroic defense of the castle against the Yorkists (1468; see ROSES, WARS OF THE) is the theme of the Welsh battle song, "The March of the Men of Harlech."

Harleian Library (här'lēən, härlē'-), manuscript collection of more than 7,000 volumes and more than 14,000 original legal documents, formed by Robert Harley, 1st earl of Oxford, and his son Edward, 2d earl of Oxford. In 1753 it was purchased for £10,000 by the British government and with the collections of Sir Robert Bruce COTTON and Sir Hans Sloane formed the basis of the British Museum library.

Harlem, residential and business section of upper Manhattan, New York City, bounded roughly by 110th St., the East River and Harlem River, 168th St., Amsterdam Ave., and Morningside Park. The Dutch settlement of Nieuw Haarlem was established by Peter Stuyvesant in 1658. To the W of Harlem, near the present site of Columbia Univ., British and Continental forces fought (Sept. 16, 1776) the Battle of Harlem Heights. Harlem remained rural until the 19th cent., when improved transportation facilities linked it with lower Manhattan. It then became a fashionable residential section of New York City. With the rapid influx of blacks that began c.1910, Harlem became one of the largest black communities in the United States. After World War II many Puerto Ricans and other Hispanic-Americans settled in East Harlem (also called Spanish Harlem), located E of Fifth Ave. Seventh Ave. at 125th Street is generally considered the heart of Harlem; Lenox Ave., once internationally known for its entertainment spots, is now mainly lined with housing developments. Harlem is the site of the Abyssinian Baptist Church (est. 1808), headed for many years by Adam Clayton Powell, Jr., and the Apollo theater, noted for performances by black musicians and entertainers. An extensive scholarly collection is housed at the Schomburg Center for Research in Black Culture (part of the New York Public Library), which is adjacent to the Countee Cullen branch of the Library, since the 1920s a meeting place of leading black writers and artists. Richard Wright, Countee Cullen, James Baldwin, and Langston Hughes lived in Harlem and wrote of its culture. Harlem today is a depressed economic area with considerable unemployment; much of its housing is substandard. In 1974 a large New York state office building was opened on 125th Street as part of an attempt to improve the economy of Harlem.

Harlem Ballet: see DANCE THEATRE OF HARLEM.

Harlem River, navigable tidal channel, 8 mi (12.9 km) long with Spuyten Duyvil Creek, in New York City, SE N.Y., separating Manhattan from the Bronx. Connecting the Hudson and East rivers, it is a shipping shortcut between Long Island Sound and river ports north of New York City. Several railroad and highway bridges span the river.

Harlequin (här'ləkwĭn, -kĭn): see COMMEDIA DELL' ARTE.

harlequin snake: see CORAL SNAKE.

Harley, Robert, 1st **earl of Oxford,** 1661-1724, English statesman and bibliophile. His career illustrates the power of personal connections and intrigue in the politics of his day. When he entered (1689) Parliament, he was generally associated with the Whigs and introduced (1694) the Triennial Bill (which required new parliamentary elections every three years) in the House of Commons. His sympathies soon shifted, however, and before the accession (1702) of Queen ANNE he was a leader of the Tories. He was secretary of state for the north (1704-8) but was forced out of office by John Churchill, 1st duke of MARLBOROUGH, because of his intrigues against the predominantly Whig government. His influence on the queen continued, however, through his kinswoman Abigail MASHAM. The unpopularity of the War of the Spanish Succession and the uproar caused by the trial of Henry SACHEVERELL brought the fall of the Whigs, and Harley came to power with Henry ST. JOHN (later Viscount Bolingbroke) in 1710. He survived an attempt on his life in 1711 and was made earl and lord treasurer. Consolidating his power, he undertook secret peace negotiations that led to the Peace of Utrecht (1713) and founded the South Sea Company (see SOUTH SEA BUBBLE). His position, however, was undermined by the intrigues of St. John, and he lost office just before Queen Anne's death (1714). After the accession of George I, he was imprisoned (1715) and impeached (1716) for his conduct of the peace negotiations and for dealings with the Jacobites, but he was acquitted. The manuscript collection gathered by Harley and his son Edward constitutes the HARLEIAN LIBRARY in the British Museum. See biographies by E. S. Roscoe (1902), Elizabeth Hamilton (1969), and Angus McInnes (1970).

Harlingen (här'lĭnjən), city (1970 pop. 33,503), Cameron co., extreme S Texas; inc. 1910. It is a shipping and processing center in the lower Rio Grande valley, an irrigated farming area yielding citrus and other fruits, truck crops, and cotton. The city, which is linked to the Intracoastal Waterway by a barge channel, has canneries, cotton-processing plants, and factories making wearing apparel, aircraft, and metal and concrete products. Harlingen was founded (c.1904) with the coming of the railroad and grew with the agricultural development of the surrounding area. It is the seat of a boys' preparatory marine academy and a state technical institute. An airfield there maintains flying models of all U.S. World War II aircraft.

Harlow, Jean, 1911-37, American movie star, b. Kansas City, Mo.; her original name was Harlean Carpenter. Harlow was Hollywood's first real sex goddess. A wisecracking platinum blonde, she had genuine talent as a comedienne. Her films include *Hell's Angels* (1930), *Red Dust* (1932), *Blonde Bombshell* (1933), *Dinner at Eight* (1933), *Libelled Lady* (1936), and *Saratoga* (1937). She died of uremic poisoning at 26.

Harlow, new town and urban district (1971 pop. 77,684), Essex, E England. Harlow was designated one of the NEW TOWNS in 1946 to alleviate overpopulation in London. Among its industries are furniture making, metallurgy, and printing. There is a technical college in Harlow.

Harmás Körös, river: see KÖRÖS, river, Hungary.

Harmensen, Jacob: see ARMINIUS, JACOBUS.

Harmhab: see HOREMHEB.

Harmodius and Aristogiton (härmō'dēəs, ăr"-ĭstōjī'tən), d. c.514 B.C., Athenian tyrannicides. Provoked by a personal quarrel, the two friends planned to assassinate HIPPARCHUS and his brother, the tyrant HIPPIAS. The plans miscarried; Hipparchus was killed, but Hippias was not hurt. Harmodius was killed on the spot, and Aristogiton was executed. In spite of their mixed motives, they were soon made heroes of Athens and were given public recognition after the expulsion (510 B.C.) of Hippias. Two public statues, executed by ANTENOR, were erected, and coins were struck with their image.

Harmon, Judson, 1846-1927, U.S. Attorney General and governor of Ohio, b. Newton, Ohio. He was a lawyer and a judge in Cincinnati for many years and served (1895-97) ably as U.S. Attorney General under President Cleveland. Harmon was elected (1908) governor of Ohio on the Democratic ticket, thus breaking a long Republican rule. He was reelected in 1910, defeating Warren G. Harding. As governor he put through many reforms, including a corrupt-practices act, a workmen's compensation act, and Ohio's ratification of the Sixteenth and Seventeenth amendments to the U.S. Constitution.

Harmonia: see CADMUS.

harmonic. 1 Physical term describing the VIBRATION in segments of a sound-producing body (see SOUND). A string vibrates simultaneously in its whole length and in segments of halves, thirds, fourths, etc. These segments form what is known in algebra as a harmonic series, or progression, since the rate of vibration of each segment is an integral multiple of the frequency of the whole string, i.e., each segment vibrates respectively twice, three times, four times, etc., as fast as the whole string. The vibration of the whole string produces the fundamental tone, and the segments produce weaker subsidiary tones. A similar phenomenon occurs in an air column in a pipe. At most the first 16 tones in such a series can be heard by the human ear; the character or timbre of a fundamental tone is determined by the number of its subsidiary tones heard and their relative intensity. The subsidiary tones have been loosely called harmonics (as a noun), but they are properly called partials, the fundamental tone being the first partial. They are also called overtones (a synonym for "upper partials"), although this term includes a number of sounds that do not fit in with the harmonic series, and are therefore not considered musical. **2** Term describing the silvery sound produced separately when the fundamental and possibly more partial tones are damped by touching a string at a nodal point. Similarly harmonics are produced separately in an air column by overblowing or in brass wind instruments by the use of valves.

harmonica. 1 The simplest of the musical instruments employing free reeds, known also as the mouth organ or French harp. It was probably invented in 1829 by Sir Charles Wheatstone, who called his instrument the aeolina. The major production of the instrument has been in Germany since the early 19th cent. The reeds are set in a small, narrow case of wood or metal. For each reed there is a hole, through which the player draws or blows air with the mouth. Commonly the instrument is diatonic, having a compass of about two octaves, but the comparatively few virtuoso harmonica players

Harmonica

use larger instruments having the full chromatic scale. The low cost and very small size of the harmonica adapt it well to class instruction among school children, but it remains a novelty in concert music. Milhaud, Vaughan Williams and Arthur Benjamin wrote music for the harmonica virtuoso Larry Adler. **2** Musical glasses, introduced in Dublin in 1743 by Richard Pockrich, played upon in London by Gluck in 1746, and improved by Benjamin Franklin c.1761. Franklin's instrument consisted of a series of glass bowls, graduated in size and fitting one inside another. They were supported by a horizontal spindle passing through all of the bowls. As the spindle was made to revolve by means of a lever the edges of the bowls passed through a trough filled with water. Contact of the player's fingertip with the moistened revolving edges of the bowls produced a penetrating, ethereal sound. A later form of the instrument had a keyboard. Both Mozart and Beethoven, as well as a few lesser composers, wrote works for it. **3** Strips of metal or glass, played upon with hammers or, later, having a keyboard, as described by Berlioz in his treatise on instrumentation. Related to this obsolete form are the CELESTA and GLOCKENSPIEL.

harmonic motion, regular VIBRATION in which the ACCELERATION of the vibrating object is directly proportional to the displacement of the object from its EQUILIBRIUM position but oppositely directed. A single object vibrating in this manner is said to exhibit simple harmonic motion (SHM). More complex harmonic motion can be analyzed as combinations of two or more simple harmonic motions. Examples of objects whose motion approximates SHM are a PENDULUM swinging in a small arc, a mass bouncing at the end of a stretched spring, and air molecules vibrating back and forth as a SOUND wave passes. Simple harmonic motion is a periodic motion; that is, it repeats itself at regular intervals. The time required for one complete vibration of the object is the period of the motion. The inverse of the period is the frequency, which is the number of vibrations per unit of time. The maximum displacement of the object from its central position of equilibrium is the amplitude of the motion. At maximum displacement the velocity of the object is zero; the velocity is greatest when the object passes through its equilibrium position. These terms are commonly used to describe any periodic phenomenon, e.g., WAVE motion and the rotation or revolution of an astronomical body. For any real harmonic motion, various forces act to reduce the amplitude with each vibration, i.e., to damp the motion. If these forces are small compared to the restoring force arising from the original displacement, then the object will vibrate a number of times with successively smaller amplitudes until the motion gradually dies out; this is known as damped harmonic motion. For a certain value of the damping forces, the object returns to its original position in a minimum amount of time and comes to rest at that position; such motion is termed critically damped. If the damping forces are large compared to the restoring force, the object returns slowly to its original position without vibrating at all; the system is said to be overdamped.

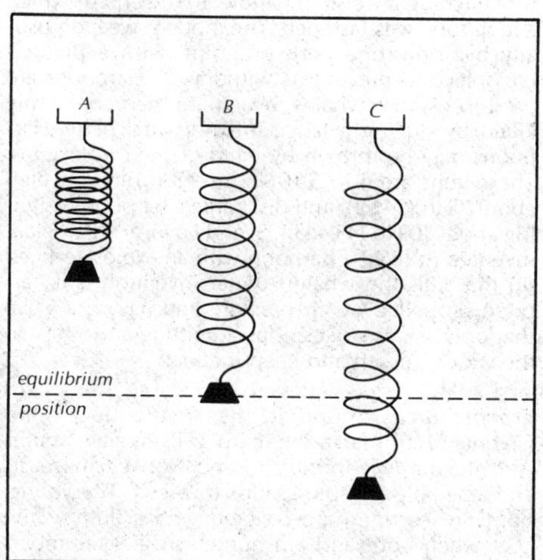

Harmonic motion is exhibited by a weight vibrating on the end of a spring. In A, the displacement of the object from its equilibrium position and the acceleration of the object are at a maximum; the velocity of the object is zero. In B, the displacement and acceleration are zero, while the velocity is at a maximum. In C, the displacement and acceleration are again at a maximum, and the velocity is again zero.

harmonic progression: see PROGRESSION.

harmonium: see REED ORGAN.

harmony, in music, simultaneous sounding of two or more tones and, especially, the study of chords and their relations. Harmony was the last in the development of what may be considered the basic elements of modern music—harmony, melody, rhythm, and tone quality or timbre. The polyphonic superposition (see POLYPHONY; COUNTERPOINT) of horizontal melodic lines prevailed until the 16th cent., when the perpendicular or harmonic construction of chords was established. Rameau, in 1722, presented the idea that different groupings of the same notes were but inversions of the same chord. During the 18th cent. the concept of TONALITY, with the major and minor modes as its basis and with a certain chord serving as the key center of a composition, became general. The polyphonic music of Bach has a harmonic structure. As the system of triads and their relations was explored, the principle of MODULATION appeared and composers developed freer concepts of tonality; finally, in the 20th cent., some have discarded tonality in favor of music that is composed in terms of horizontal contrapuntal lines. (See ATONALITY; SERIAL MUSIC) See Vincent Persichetti, *Twentieth-Century Harmony* (1961); Walter Piston, *Harmony* (3d ed. 1962); W. J. Mitchell, *Elementary Harmony* (3d ed. 1965); Arnold Schoenberg, *Structural Functions of Harmony* (rev. ed. 1969).

Harmony Society, religious society founded by German Separatists under the leadership of George Rapp. The Harmonists (or Rappites) held property in common and subscribed to the austere doctrines of their leader, including that of celibacy. In 1805 the society founded the village of Harmony, Pa., and developed it into a prosperous agricultural and industrial community. Led by Rapp, the Harmonists moved in 1814–15 to Indiana and founded another Harmony. They prospered there too, but in 1825 they sold their holdings to Robert Owen (see NEW HARMONY) and returned to Pennsylvania to create their third village at Economy (now Ambridge), NW of Pittsburgh. In 1832 a part of the colony, under "Count Leon," a German adventurer, withdrew to form a separate community. The society was weakened by the death of Rapp (1847), dwindled as the members grew older, and went out of existence after 1906. See studies by Aaron Williams (1866, repr. 1971); John S. Duss (1943), and K. J. R. Arndt (2 vol., 1972).

Harmsworth, Alfred Charles William: see NORTHCLIFFE, ALFRED CHARLES WILLIAM HARMSWORTH, VISCOUNT.

Harmsworth, Harold Sidney: see ROTHERMERE, HAROLD SIDNEY HARMSWORTH, 1ST VISCOUNT.

Harnack, Adolf von (ä'dôlf fən här'näk), 1851–1930, German theologian and church historian. He was professor of church history successively in the universities of Leipzig, Giessen, Marburg, and Berlin. He was director (1905–21) of the Royal Library, Berlin, and president of the scientific research foundation, Kaiser Wilhelm-Gesellschaft. His great work, *Lehrbuch der Dogmengeschichte* (4 vol., 1886–90; tr. *The History of Dogma,* 7 vol., 1895–1900), has exerted an important influence upon modern theological study. Other translated works include *Monasticism* (1895), *What Is Christianity?* (1901), *The Apostles' Creed* (1901), *The Expansion of Christianity in the First Three Centuries* (2 vol., 1904–5), and *Luke the Physician* (1907). See studies by G. W. Glick (1967) and Wilhelm Pauck (1968).

Harnepher (här'nēfər, härnē'fər), son of Zophah the Asherite. 1 Chron. 7.36.

harness, comprehensive term for the gear of a draft animal, excluding the yoke, by which it is attached to the load that it pulls. Although harnesses are used on dogs (for drawing travois and dogsleds), on goats, and sometimes on oxen, the typical harness is for horses. There are two main kinds—the collar harness and the breast harness. In the collar harness a padded leather collar fits over the horse's shoulders; to it are fastened the hames, linked metal parts with two curved projections to which are attached the traces, leather straps that pass down the sides of the horse and by which the load is drawn. In the breast harness the traces are attached to a breastband that crosses the shoulders below the neck. The horse is controlled by reins or lines attached to the bit, a metal mouthpiece held in place by the bridle, i.e., the various straps and buckles that make up the headgear of the horse, including the blinders. A long, narrow saddle pad is held in place on the horse's back by a bellyband (or girth), a backband, and a crupper, a loop under the tail. The reins pass through rings on the hames and on the saddle pad; looped straps on the pad hold the shafts of a vehicle. The breeching, a strap that passes around the hindquarters below the tail and is held in place by hip straps, bears the stress when the horse is backed up or is going downhill. There are many individual parts of the various harnesses, each of them having a specific name; the different kinds of bits alone are innumerable. Harness making is an ancient craft, dating from the domestication of the horse; the SADDLE was a later invention.

harness racing: see HORSE RACING.

Harnett, William Michael, 1848–1892, American painter, b. Ireland. He immigrated to Philadelphia as a child; he first learned engraving and then studied painting at the Pennsylvania Academy of the Fine Arts and at the National Academy of Design and Cooper Union. He executed mainly still lifes and excelled in the rendering of textures and *trompe-l'œil* (eye-deceiving) realistic effects. Examples of his work are *After the Hunt* (Calif. Palace of the Legion of Honor, San Francisco), *Emblems of Peace* (Springfield Mus. of Fine Arts, Mass.), and *The Faithful Colt* (Wadsworth Atheneum, Hartford, Conn.). See Alfred Frankenstein, *After the Hunt* (rev. ed. 1969).

Harney, William Selby, 1800–1889, American general, b. Haysboro, near Nashville, Tenn. He entered the army in 1818 and gained a colonel's rank in the Florida Indian campaigns. Ranking cavalry officer under Winfield Scott in the Mexican War, Harney was disliked by that general, who arbitrarily relieved him of his command and had him court-martialed for resuming it in defiance of orders. Harney apologized, but at the same time appealed to superiors in Washington, who supported him. Restored to his position, he performed brilliantly at CERRO GORDO (1847). In the Platte country after the war, Harney defeated the Sioux. As commander of the Dept. of Oregon, he ordered (1859) the occupation of San Juan Island, which the British claimed; the SAN JUAN BOUNDARY DISPUTE was thus brought to a crisis. For this action he was recalled. At the opening of the Civil War, Harney commanded the Dept. of the West, with headquarters in St. Louis. He agreed with Gen. Sterling PRICE of the pro-secessionist Missouri militia to make no hostile move if the militia kept the peace. The radical Unionists, irked at his conciliatory policy, had him deprived of his command in May, 1861. He was retired in 1863. See biography by L. U. Reavis (1878).

Harney Peak, S. Dak.: see BLACK HILLS.

Härnösand (hĕrnösänd'), city (1970 pop. 16,624), capital of Västernorrland co., E Sweden, on the Gulf of Bothnia at the mouth of the Ångermanälven River. Its harbor, icebound in winter, is a center of the coastal trade of N and E Sweden. Forest products are the chief exports of Härnösand. Manufactures include machinery, processed tobacco, and ships. The city was chartered in 1585 and has long been a cultural center of Norrland. It was burned in 1721 by Russians.

Harod (hā'rŏd). **1** Spring, near Mt. Gilboa, where Gideon mustered his men. Judges 7.1–8. **2** Home of David's warrior Shammah. 2 Sam. 23.25.

Haroeh (hă'rōē, hārō'ē), descendant of Judah. 1 Chron. 2.52.

Harold, 1022?–1066, king of England (1066). The son of GODWIN, earl of Wessex, he belonged to the most powerful noble family of England in the reign of EDWARD THE CONFESSOR. Through Godwin's influence Harold was made earl of East Anglia. He went into exile with his father in 1051, returning to help him regain power the next year. His succession (1053) to the earldom of Wessex and to Godwin's great estates made Harold the most powerful figure in England except for the king, and he aspired to become heir to the throne. He gained glory by a successful campaign against the Welsh leader GRUFFYDD AP LLEWELYN in 1062–63. Shortly after this (probably in 1064), Harold was apparently shipwrecked on the coast of Ponthieu and was surrendered by the count of Ponthieu to William, duke of Normandy (later WILLIAM I of England). Harold then, possibly under coercion, took an oath to support William's candidacy to the English throne. When the Northumbrians revolted (1065) against Harold's brother TOSTIG and chose Morcar in his place as earl of Northumbria, Harold took Morcar's part. The family was thus divided when Edward the Confessor died (1066), naming Harold his heir instead of William. Harold was also the choice of the council to be king. William of Normandy immediately undertook an invasion. At the same time, Tostig, with Harold III of Norway, invaded England in the north. Harold went north and soundly defeated them (Sept. 25, 1066) at the battle of Stamford Bridge, in which both Tostig and Harold III were slain. Then the harassed king hurried south to oppose William, who had landed at Pevensey. Harold established his forces in hastily built earthworks near Hastings. They fought valiantly but were finally put to rout, and Harold was killed. See biography by Piers Compton (1961); F. M. Stenton, *Anglo-Saxon England* (3d ed. 1971).

Harold I or **Harold Fairhair,** Norse *Harald Haarfager,* c.850–c.933, first king of Norway, son of Halfdan the Black, king of Vestfold (SE Norway). After succeeding his father, Harold initiated a series of battles against the other petty kings, climaxed by a great victory at Hafrs Fjord (872) that made him ruler of Norway. Although he is considered Norway's first king, Harold controlled only the west coast. Migration to Iceland reached its peak during Harold's reign, as did the raids by Norsemen on the coasts of Europe. The king maintained friendly relations with Athelstan, king of the English. The Viking civilization of 9th-century Norway flourished at his court. On his death his lands were divided among his sons; Eric Bloodyaxe was made overlord, but another son, Haakon I, seized power.

Harold III or **Harold Hardrada** (härdrä'də), Norse *Harald Harđráđi* [Harold stern council], d. 1066, king of Norway (1046–66), half brother of Olaf II. After Olaf's defeat (1030), Harold went to serve Zoë, the Byzantine empress, in campaigns against the Seljuk Turks, but he returned (1042) to Scandinavia to join the revolt against Magnus I. Made joint king in 1046, he became sole king at Magnus's death in 1047 and engaged in the turbulent warfare of the time. In 1066 he accompanied TOSTIG, the exiled earl of Northumbria, on an invasion of N England. At the same time, William of Normandy was preparing an invasion of S England. The hard-pressed king of the English, HAROLD, defeated the Norse invasion at Stamford Bridge; both Harold III and Tostig fell in the battle. However, the way had been prepared for the Norman victory at Hastings.

Harold Bluetooth, d. c.985, king of Denmark. Succeeding (935) his father, Gorm the Old, who had united Denmark, Harold consolidated the kingdom. He tried to assert suzerainty over Norway but was defeated by the Germans. He was forced to accept Christianity, which he introduced into Denmark. While fighting the forces of his son SWEYN, he was defeated and killed.

Harold Fairhair: see HAROLD I.

Harold Hardrada: see HAROLD III.

Harold Harefoot, d. 1040, king of the English (1037–40), illegitimate son of Canute and Ælfgifu of Northampton. On his father's death (1035) he disputed the succession of his half brother HARTHACANUTE to the English throne. A compromise was reached (1036) by which Harold would be regent while Harthacanute would remain in Denmark, but in 1037 Ælfgifu succeeded in having her son recognized as king. His brief reign was one of bloodshed and confusion, and he died as Harthacanute was preparing to invade England and claim his throne.

Harorite (hā'rōrīt), in the Bible, apparently a copyist's error for Harodite. 1 Chron. 11.27.

Harosheth (hā'rōshĕth), home or camp of Sisera. Judges 4.2,13,16.

harp, stringed musical instrument of ancient origin, the strings of which are plucked with the fingers. The existence of the harp is recorded in paintings from the 13th cent. B.C. at Thebes. In different forms it was played by peoples of nearly all lands throughout the ages. The harp was particularly popular with the Irish from the 9th cent. They adopted the small instrument still in use, called the Irish harp, as a national symbol. The larger instrument was well known on the Continent by the 12th cent. During

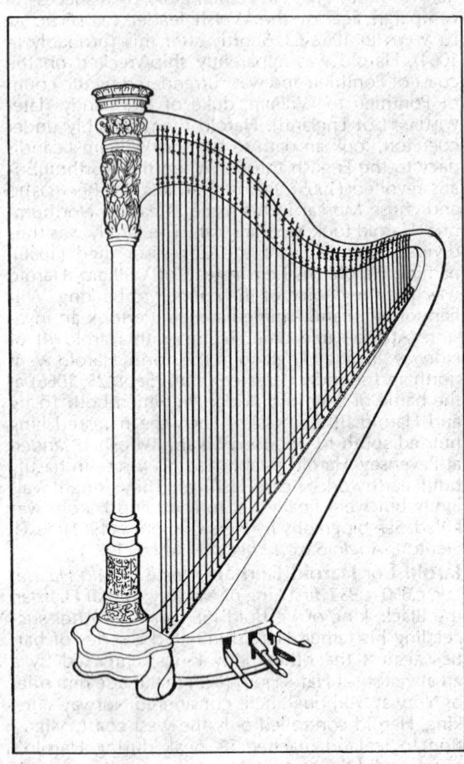

Harp

the 15th cent. the harp came to be made in three parts, as it is today: sound box, neck, and pillar. The strings are stretched between the sound box and the neck; into the neck are fastened the tuning pegs. Chromatic harps, having a string for each tone of the chromatic scale, have appeared since the late 16th cent., but none has been as practical as the diatonic harp, made in the late 17th cent. in the Tyrol and equipped with hooks capable of altering the pitch of any string by a semitone. A pedal mechanism that shortened the strings was devised (c.1720) for this purpose in Germany. The harp was perfected with Sébastien Érard's invention (c.1810) of the double-action pedals, which can shorten each string twice, raising the pitch by a semitone or a tone. The harp appeared occasionally in the orchestra in the 18th cent., but its regular inclusion there, as well as most of its solo literature, dates from the late 19th cent. See Roslyn Rensch, *The Harp* (1970).

Harpenden (här'pəndən), urban district (1971 pop. 24,161), Hertfordshire, E central England. Mainly residential, it is the site of Rothamsted Experimental Station (for agricultural research).

Harper, Ida Husted, 1851–1931, American woman suffragist. Allied with the woman-suffrage movement from 1898, she became the official reporter and historian of the National American Woman Suffrage Association. She wrote *The Life and Works of Susan B. Anthony* (3 vol., 1898–1908, repr. 1969) and later volumes (IV–VI, 1900–1922) of the *History of Woman Suffrage* started by Susan B. Anthony, who also contributed to Vol. IV.

Harper, William Rainey, 1856–1906, American educator and Hebrew scholar, b. New Concord, Ohio, grad. Muskingum College, 1870, Ph.D. Yale, 1875. The author of many texts on Hebrew language and literature, Harper taught Hebrew at Baptist Union Theological Seminary in Chicago after 1879 and also gave (after 1883) courses at Chautauqua Institution. In 1886 he went to Yale as professor of Semitic languages, resigning in 1891 to become first president of the Univ. of Chicago. With vast funds at his disposal, Harper was able to recruit an outstanding faculty. He was committed to fostering advanced instruction and research in his university and maintained a policy whereby promotion for members of the faculty was directly related to their scholarly research. See biography by T. W. Goodspeed (1928); R. J. Storr, *Harper's University* (1966).

Harpers Ferry, town (1970 pop. 423), Jefferson co., easternmost W Va., at the confluence of the Shenandoah and Potomac rivers; inc. 1763. The town is a tourist attraction, known for its history and its scenic beauty. John Brown's seizure of the U.S. arsenal there on Oct. 16, 1859, and the town's subsequent strategic importance during the Civil War, when it was considered the key to the Shenandoah valley, brought it into national prominence. In 1747, Robert Harper, a millwright, established a ferry at the junction of the two rivers—hence the town's name. The U.S. arsenal was located there in 1796, and by the mid-19th cent. Harpers Ferry was an important arms-producing center, with mills, numerous gun factories, and huge stores of weapons and ammunition. The development of the Chesapeake and Ohio Canal and of the Baltimore & Ohio RR also increased its importance, making it a vital transportation link between the Ohio valley and the East. During the Civil War it was held mostly by Union soldiers, but changed hands a number of times. Its industrial plant was repeatedly destroyed by retreating troops of both sides and during the occasional attacks on the town. Harpers Ferry never recovered economically, and a series of devastating floods in the late 19th cent. ended all hopes for revival. Despite continued flooding during the 20th cent., many old buildings remain. Of particular interest are the fire engine house in which John Brown was captured; the John Brown Museum; and the old steps, hand-carved (early 1800s) into the natural stone, which lead to Robert Harper's house (1775–82) and to the Jefferson Rock (a bluff above the rivers where Thomas Jefferson once stood). The Harpers Ferry National Historical Park (est. 1963; 1,530 acres/619 hectares) receives many visitors annually.

Harper Woods, city (1970 pop. 20,186), Wayne co., SE Mich., a residential suburb of Detroit; inc. 1951.

Harpocrates (härpŏk'rətēz), the Greek name for the Egyptian sky god HORUS. He was represented as a small boy with his finger held to his lips and came to be considered the god of silence. His cult, combined with that of Isis and Serapis, was very popular in the Roman Empire.

harpoon (härpo͞on'), weapon used for spearing whales and large fish. The early type was a flat triangular piece of metal with barbed edges and a socket for attaching a wooden handle, to the end of which a long rope was fastened. The modern weapon usually has only one barb or point, with a pivoted crosspiece to prevent its withdrawal. Harpoons are used to capture whales, which are then commonly killed by driving a lance into the vital parts. Harpoons may be thrown by hand or fired from guns. These guns are 4 to 5 ft (1.2 m–1.5 m) long, weigh about 75 lb (34 kg), and discharge a harpoon weighing about 100 lb (45.4 kg). Svend Foyn, a Norwegian, invented (c.1856) a harpoon with an explosive-filled tip that kills the whale. A later invention is a harpoon propelled by air pressure and having a valve that opens as it strikes, thus admitting air to hasten the whale's death and keep it afloat.

harp seal, crested earless, or true, SEAL, *Pagophilus groenlandicus,* found in the N Atlantic around Greenland. In the spring, harp seals migrate southward to the Newfoundland and Norwegian coasts and assemble in large groups to breed. The young, born on ice floes, are covered with a fluffy white coat when born and are hunted in great numbers for their fur. The fur gradually darkens to gray as the young seals mature; the old males are marked with a brown crest on each side, suggesting the outline of a harp. Harp seals, sometimes seen as far S as Maine, are classified in the phylum CHORDATA, subphylum Vertebrata, class Mammalia, order Carnivora.

harpsichord, stringed musical instrument played from a keyboard. Its strings, two or more to a note, are plucked by quills or jacks. The harpsichord originated in the 14th cent. and by the 16th cent. Venice was the center of its manufacture. At that time its prevailing shape was winglike, similar to that of a grand piano. The square harpsichord, often called SPINET, became more common in the late 16th cent., when harpsichord making in the northern countries surpassed that of Italy. Perhaps the greatest craftsmen were the Ruckers family of Antwerp, who worked from the late 16th cent. through most of the 17th cent. Varying the touch in harpsichord playing does not alter the quality or volume of tone; to provide dynamic variety, octave couplers and various stops that change the tone were introduced. Contrast in volume and in tone color is made easier by the addition of a second keyboard, or manual, found on German harpsichords from the late 16th cent. and on Italian ones from c.1665. The instrument provided the basic support of virtually all the various combinations of instruments as chamber music and orchestral forms developed. In the 19th cent. the harpsichord, which required frequent tuning and replacement of quills, was superseded in general use by the piano. In the mid-20th cent. the older instrument has had a revival in popularity. See F. T. Hubbard, *Three Centuries of Harpsichord Making* (1965); W. I. Zuckermann, *The Modern Harpsichord* (1969).

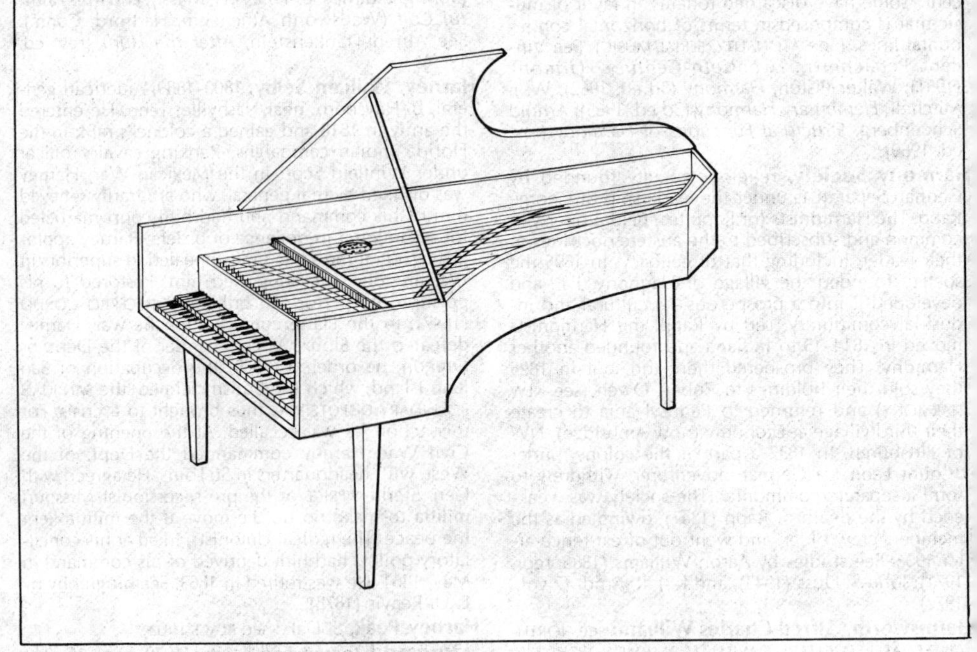

Harpsichord

Harpy, in Greek mythology, a predatory monster with the head of a woman and the body, wings, and claws of a bird. The Harpies snatched food from tables or else befouled tables, leaving filth and stench and causing famine. They were the daughters of Electra, the sea nymph, and Thaumas, son of Pontus and Gaea.

harpy or **harpy eagle:** see EAGLE.

Harran: see HARAN, Mesopotamia.

Harrar, Ethiopia: see HARAR.

harrier, breed of medium-sized HOUND whose origin is obscure but whose existence in England dates from the 13th cent. It stands from 19 to 21 in. (48.3–53.3 cm) high at the shoulder and weighs from 40 to 50 lb (18.1–22.7 kg). Its short, dense coat is glossy and usually a combination of black, tan, and white in color. Many authorities believe the harrier to be a descendant of hounds brought to England by the Normans. However, the dog we know today is most probably a bred-down version of the foxhound (see ENGLISH FOXHOUND), of which it is an exact replica except for its smaller size. The harrier was originally and still is used in packs to hunt hares. In England, this sport had a much broader-based popularity than foxhunting since harriers can be followed on foot. Today it is also kept as a house pet. See DOG.

harrier, bird: see HAWK.

Harriman, Edward Henry, 1848–1909, American railroad executive, b. Hempstead, N.Y.; father of William Averell Harriman. He became a stockbroker in New York City and soon entered the railroad field, where he attracted attention by able management of the Illinois Central RR, of which he became a director (1883) and vice president (1887). He became executive committee chairman of the Union Pacific in 1898 and repossessed for it the Oregon Short Line. By purchase of the holdings of Collis P. HUNTINGTON, he secured control not only of the Southern Pacific RR, but also of the Central Pacific RR. His attempt to secure an entrance into Chicago by seizing control of the Burlington & Quincy RR was blocked by James J. HILL in a struggle famous in American financial history. In a later compromise, he joined with Hill and J. P. Morgan in organizing the Northern Securities Company, a holding company formed to prevent railroad competition. But in 1904 the trust was ordered dissolved by the U.S. Supreme Court. Harriman used the financial strength of his roads to buy widely and speculatively in railroad stocks elsewhere. His practices were investigated and condemned by the Interstate Commerce Commission (1907). He conducted the Harriman Alaskan expedition of 1899, a scientific undertaking; sponsored boys' clubs; and pledged $1 million and 10,000 acres (4,047 hectares) of forest land to New York state for park purposes. The reservation, now the 42,500-acre (17,200-hectare) Harriman State Park, is part of the Palisades Interstate Park. See biographies by George Kennan (2 vol., 1922, repr. 1969) and H. J. Eckenrode and P. W. Edmunds (1933).

Harriman, William Averell, 1891–, American public official; son of E. H. Harriman. Expanding his railroad inheritance, W. Averell Harriman became a banker and shipbuilder and later (1932) board chairman of the Union Pacific. He was administrative officer (1934–35) of the NRA and an official (1937–40) in the Dept. of Commerce, then became (1941) chief overseas administrator of lend-lease. He was ambassador to the USSR (1943–46) and to Great Britain (1946). After serving (1946–48) as Secretary of Commerce, he was appointed (April, 1948) U.S. representative abroad for the European Recovery Program and later (1951–53), director of the Mutual Security Agency. He was elected governor of New York (1955–59) and was an unsuccessful candidate for the Democratic presidential nomination in 1956. Defeated for reelection in 1958 by Nelson A. Rockefeller, he became in 1961 President John F. Kennedy's special roving ambassador. He was Undersecretary of State for Political Affairs (1963–65) and ambassador-at-large (1965–68) for President Lyndon B. Johnson. In 1968, when the Paris peace talks on Vietnam opened, he was chief U.S. negotiator. He is the author of *Peace with Russia* (1959) and *America and Russia in a Changing World* (1971).

Harrington, James, 1611–77, English political writer. His *Commonwealth of Oceana* (1656) pictured a utopian society in which political authority rested entirely with the landed gentry. Harrington advocated definite agrarian reforms, however, in order to achieve a greater equality of power. He sought to abolish primogeniture and to limit the amount of land an individual could hold. He also advocated division of the powers of government, a written constitution, and the principle of rotation in office. Penn's government in Pennsylvania is said to owe much to the *Oceana*. Harrington's ideas can be seen in the doctrines of the American Revolution and the French Revolution. See studies by Charles Blitzer (1960, repr. 1970) and H. F. Russell-Smith (1971).

Harriot, Thomas (hâr'ēət), 1560–1621, English mathematician and astronomer. He was tutor to Sir Walter Raleigh, who sent him in 1585 to Virginia as surveyor with Sir Richard Grenville. Returning to England, Harriot wrote *A Brief and True Report of the New Found Land of Virginia* (1588), one of the earliest known large-scale statistical surveys. He made valuable contributions to algebra, introducing new symbols and notation. His *Artis analyticae praxis* appeared in 1631. See biography by Muriel Rukeyser (1971).

Harris, Sir Arthur Travers, 1892–, British air chief marshal. In World War I he served for a time in German West Africa before transferring to the Royal Flying Corps in France. Prominent in the Royal Air Force from its beginning, he was chief of the bomber command (1942–45) and proponent of the saturation bombing tactics used against German targets. He was created baronet in 1953.

Harris, Chapin Aaron, 1806–60, American dentist, b. Pompey, N.Y. One of the founders of dentistry as a profession, he was the author of *The Dental Art* (1839; later called *Principles and Practice of Dental Surgery*) and *Dictionary of Dental Science* (1849) and founder (1840) of the first dental school—the Baltimore College of Dental Surgery (now part of the Univ. of Maryland). He also founded the *American Journal of Dental Science* (1839) and helped to organize the American Society of Dental Surgeons (1840).

Harris, Frank, 1856–1931, British-American author, b. Galway, Ireland. He studied at the Univ. of Kansas, became a U.S. citizen, and returning to England, edited successively a number of periodicals. A controversial figure in both his private life and his writings, he is primarily known for his scandalously frank and highly unreliable autobiography, *My Life and Loves* (3 vol., 1923–27), which was banned in the United States and England for many years. Much of his other work, such as his first novel, *The Bomb* (1908), shows a similar leaning toward eroticism. His biographical series *Contemporary Portraits* (1915–27), portraying such men as Shaw, Wells, Galsworthy, and Kipling, many of whom he knew, and his biography of Oscar Wilde (1916) reveal his facility for maliciousness and imaginative speculation. Among his other works are the volume of short stories, *Montes the Matador* (1900) and the novel *Great Days* (1913).

Harris, Isham Green (ī'shəm), 1818–97, American political leader, b. Franklin co., Tenn. Admitted to the bar in 1841, he was elected in 1847 to the Tennessee senate. Harris, a states' rights Democrat, served (1849–53) in Congress and was (1857–61) governor of Tennessee. It was largely through his efforts that Tennessee joined the Confederacy in May, 1861. Forced by Union victories to leave the state, he served on the staffs of various Confederate generals from 1862 to 1865, when he fled to Mexico and then to England. In 1867 he returned to Memphis. From 1877 to his death he was a U.S. Senator from Tennessee.

Harris, Joel Chandler, 1848–1908, American short-story writer and humorist, b. Eatonton, Ga., considered one of the greatest American regionalist writers. As an apprentice to the editor of the *Countryman,* a newspaper published on a Southern plantation, Harris gained firsthand knowledge of Negro slaves and their folklore. His stories and sketches of the South were originally published in the Atlanta *Constitution,* with which he was associated from 1876 to 1900. Harris's first collection, *Uncle Remus: His Songs and His Sayings* (1881), brought him immediate fame. Featuring as their narrator a lovable, shrewd former slave, the Uncle Remus stories drew upon Negro folklore and humor and captured the authentic life, character, and dialect of Southern Negroes. The demand for his stories and sketches was so great that Harris followed with nine more books in a similar vein, including *The Tar Baby* (1904) and *Uncle Remus and Br'er Rabbit* (1906). In other notable works, such as *Mingo and Other Sketches in Black and White* (1884) and *Free Joe and Other Georgian Sketches* (1887), Harris portrayed with accuracy and insight the aristocrats and poor whites of Georgia. See his life and letters by J. C. Harris (1918); biography by P. M. Cousins (1968).

Harris, Julie, 1925–, American actress, b. Grosse Point, Mich. Harris made her New York debut in *It's a Gift* (1945). Her versatility and power have won her enormous critical acclaim. Outstanding among her many stage performances were leading roles in *Macbeth* (1948), *Member of the Wedding* (1950; film, 1952), *I Am a Camera* (1951; film, 1956), *The Lark* (1955), *Forty Carats* (1968), *The Last of Mrs. Lincoln* (1972), and *In Praise of Love* (1974). Harris's notable films include *East of Eden* (1955), *The Haunting* (1963), and, for television, *Johnnie Belinda, Little Moon of Alban, A Doll's House,* and *Ethan Frome.*

Harris, Marvin, 1927–, American anthropologist, b. New York City, grad. Columbia (A.B., 1949; Ph.D., 1953). A member of the faculty of Columbia (1952–), he was chairman of the department of anthropology (1963–66). His major areas of research have been community studies in Latin America and ethnologies in Africa. He wrote *Minorities in the New World* (1958), *The Nature of Cultural Things* (1964), *The Rise of Anthropological Theory* (1968), *Culture, Man and Nature* (1971), and *Cows, Pigs, Wars, and Witches* (1974).

Harris, Roy, 1898–, American composer, b. Lincoln co., Okla. Harris was the pupil of Arthur Farwell and Nadia Boulanger. He began to compose c.1925; his early compositions displayed the vital, melodic, and personal expression that is characteristic of all his works. His most significant works include his First Symphony (1934); *When Johnny Comes Marching Home* (1934), a choral work; Symphony for Voices (1936) to poems by Walt Whitman; the Folksong Symphony (1940); Cumberland Concerto (1951); and the Seventh Symphony (1956). Outstanding among his numerous works of chamber music is his Piano Quintet (1936). Since 1960 he has been composer in residence at the Univ. of California.

Harris, Thomas Lake, 1823–1906, American Christian mystic. Born in England, he was brought to the United States as a child. In 1845 he was called to the pulpit of the Fourth Universalist Society, in New York City, but three years later, deeply impressed by spiritualism, Harris organized the First Independent Christian Society. During that period he dictated long poems for which he said he had received inspiration while in trances. He wove the ideas of Swedenborgianism into his religious teachings. Under his leadership, the Brotherhood of the New Life, to which adherents had been drawn in Great Britain as well as the United States, established (1861) a community in Wassaic, N.Y., later moving it (1863), to nearby Amenia and (1867) to Brocton, near Buffalo, where it was known as Salem-on-Erie. In that year Laurence OLIPHANT joined this communal religious settlement. Harris and part of the community moved to Santa Rosa, Calif., in 1875; Oliphant remained behind and in 1881 broke completely with Harris. Ten years later Harris left the Santa Rosa community. See H. W. Schneider and George Lawton, *A Prophet and a Pilgrim* (1942).

Harris, Townsend, 1804–78, American merchant and diplomat, b. Sandy Hill, N.Y. A merchant in New York City for many years, he became (1846) a member of the board of education, served as its president (1846–48), and helped obtain the legislation chartering the present College of the City of New York. Appointed (1855) consul general to Japan, he arrived at Shimoda in 1856, the first U.S. diplomat in Japan after that country had been opened up by Commodore Matthew C. Perry. In 1859, Harris was raised to be minister. Having previously negotiated a commercial treaty with Siam, he won the confidence of the Japanese and obtained a commercial treaty (1858) that, in contrast to the demands of other Western powers, was notably moderate. He returned to the United States in 1861. See M. E. Cosenza, ed., *The Complete Journal of Townsend Harris* (1930, 2d ed. 1959); Carl Crow, *He Opened the Door of Japan* (1939).

Harris, William Torrey, 1835–1909, American educator and philosopher, b. Windham co., Conn., educated at Yale. He was superintendent (1868–80) of the St. Louis public school system and was U.S. commissioner of education (1889–1906). In 1873, with Susan Blow, he established in St. Louis the first permanent kindergarten in the United States. He interpreted German philosophical thought, particularly Hegelianism, in his books and in the pages of the *Journal of Speculative Philosophy,* which he founded and edited (1867–93). His books include *Hegel's Logic* (1890, repr. 1970) and *The Psychologic Foundations of Education* (1898, repr. 1969). See biography by J. S. Roberts (1924); K. F. Leidecker, *Yankee Teacher* (1946, repr. 1971).

Harris, Scotland: see LEWIS WITH HARRIS.

Harrisburg, city (1970 pop. 68,061), state capital and seat of Dauphin co., SE Pa., on the Susquehanna River; settled c.1710 by John Harris, who established a trading post and operated a ferry there; inc. 1791. It is a commercial, wholesale, and administrative center and railroad hub. Rich iron and coal mines are nearby, and the city has a large steel industry. Food processing is also important. Other manufactures include metal products, rails, airplane parts, clothing, textiles, and shoes. Harrisburg became the state capital in 1812 and grew as an inland transportation center with the opening of the Pennsylvania Canal in 1827 and the arrival of the railroad in 1836. The city has numerous parks. Its sprawling Italian Renaissance state capitol (completed 1906) has a 272-ft (83-m) dome modeled after St. Peter's in Rome. Other notable structures are the education building, which contains the state library; the Pennsylvania State Museum; the William Penn Memorial Museum; the John Harris Mansion (1766), headquarters of the county historical society; and the Soldiers' and Sailors' Memorial Bridge. A junior college and a state mental hospital are in Harrisburg.

Harrison, Benjamin, 1726?–1791, political leader in the American Revolution, signer of the Declaration of Independence, b. Charles City co., Va. As a member (1749–75) of the house of burgesses, he protested against the Stamp Act (1765). He was a delegate (1774–78) to the Continental Congress and later governor of Virginia (1781–84). His son William Henry Harrison and his great-grandson Benjamin Harrison were U.S. Presidents.

Harrison, Benjamin, 1833–1901, 23d President of the United States (1889–93), b. North Bend, Ohio, grad. Miami Univ. (Ohio), 1852; grandson of William Henry Harrison. After reading law in Cincinnati, he moved (1854) to Indianapolis, where he was a lawyer and politician. He served in the Civil War as commander of an Indiana volunteer regiment and in 1865 was brevetted brigadier general of volunteers. A well-established corporation lawyer, he was (1881–87) a member of the U.S. Senate as a Republican but was defeated for reelection. The Republicans chose him (1888) as presidential candidate against Grover Cleveland. After what has been called the most corrupt campaign in American history, he was elected in the electoral college, though Cleveland had the larger popular vote. Harrison as President approved all regular Republican measures, including the highly protective McKinley Tariff Act. His equivocal stand on civil service reform displeased both reformers and spoilsmen. The first Pan-American Conference was held (1889) in his administration. Defeated for reelection in 1892 by Cleveland, Harrison returned to his Indianapolis law practice. He later represented Venezuela in the Venezuela Boundary Dispute. Harrison wrote *This Country of Ours* (1897) and *Views of an Ex-President* (1901). See his public papers and addresses (1893, repr. 1969); biography by H. J. Sievers (3 vol., 1952–68).

Harrison, Frederic, 1831–1923, English jurist and sociologist. He served on various law commissions and was (1877–89) professor of jurisprudence and international law under the Council of Legal Education. Most prominent as the leader of English POSITIVISM, he was cofounder of, and contributor to, the *Positivist Review* and was president of the English Positivist Committee. Regarding positivism as an approach to social reform, he worked to obtain a broader electoral franchise, wider primary education, and beneficial labor legislation. Harrison's voluminous works include studies of the law and of literature, biographies, a novel, and a long poem. See his *Autobiographic Memoirs* (1911); study by his son Austin Harrison (1926).

Harrison, Jane Ellen, 1850–1928, English classical scholar. She applied archaeological discoveries in the interpretation of Greek religion. Her works include *Prolegomena to the Study of Greek Religion* (1903), *Themis* (1912), *Ancient Art and Ritual* (1913), and *Epilegomena to the Study of Greek Religion* (1921). See biography by J. G. Stewart (1959).

Harrison, Pat (Byron Patton Harrison), 1881–1941, U.S. Congressman, b. Crystal Springs, Miss. A lawyer, he served as a Democrat in the U.S. House of Representatives (1911–19) and in the U.S. Senate from 1919 until his death. He became (1933) chairman of the Senate finance committee and was active in putting early New Deal legislation through Congress. Harrison was opposed to President Franklin Delano Roosevelt's tax measures but supported his foreign policy.

Harrison, Rex, 1908–, English actor. Born Reginald Carey, he entered repertory theater at 16 as an apprentice. Harrison, noted for his suave, insouciant style, has appeared in many plays, including *Anne of the Thousand Days* (1949), *Bell, Book, and Candle* (1950), and *In Praise of Love* (1974). His performances in both the stage (1956) and film (1964) versions of *My Fair Lady* won enormous popular and critical acclaim. Harrison's other films include *The Ghost and Mrs. Muir* (1947), *The Fourposter* (1952), and *Cleopatra* (1962).

Harrison, Ross Granville, 1870–1959, American biologist and anatomist, b. Germantown, Pa., Ph.D. Johns Hopkins, 1894. He went to Yale as professor of comparative anatomy in 1907 and held various honorary positions there until his death. He is known for his work on nerve development in the embryo and on nerve regeneration as well as for his discovery of a method of tissue culture that permits study of isolated living cells in a controlled environment.

Harrison, Wallace Kirkman, 1895–, American architect and city planner, b. Worcester, Mass. Harrison designed the trylon and perisphere, the symbolizing structures for the New York World's Fair, 1939. In 1945 he entered into partnership with Max Abramowitz, who was later famed for his designs for Philharmonic Hall at LINCOLN CENTER FOR THE PERFORMING ARTS and the Columbia Univ. law school (both: 1962). Harrison has been responsible for numerous large buildings, such as those for Alcoa in Pittsburgh (1952) and the Time & Life Building (1960) and the Exxon Corp. headquarters (1973), both in New York City. He has also acted as the coordinator of many architects on important projects in New York City, including the UN Headquarters, Lincoln Center, and the New York World's Fair, 1964. Harrison is especially noted for having found solutions to many complex problems in construction.

Harrison, William Henry, 1773–1841, 9th President of the United States (March 4–April 4, 1841), b. "Berkeley," Charles City co., Va.; son of Benjamin Harrison (1726?–1791) and grandfather of Benjamin Harrison (1833–1901). He attended Hampden-Sydney College and studied medicine briefly under Benjamin Rush in Philadelphia before joining (1791) the army and taking part in campaigns against the Indians in the Northwest Territory. In 1798 he resigned to become secretary of the territory, and the next year he became territorial delegate to Congress. He helped secure the division of the territory into Ohio and Indiana and served (1800–1812) as governor of Indiana Territory at Vincennes. He was perhaps more important than any other man in opening Ohio and Indiana to settlement, negotiating a number of treaties with the Indians, notably the Treaty of Fort Wayne (1809). Indian opposition to the white advance then concentrated in hostile demonstrations directed by TECUMSEH. Harrison engaged the forces of Tecumseh at the famous battle of TIPPECANOE. In the War of 1812, after the failure of Gen. William Hull, Harrison was made commander in the Northwest. Taking Detroit (Sept. 29, 1813), he advanced to defeat Gen. Henry Procter and establish American hegemony in the West at the battle of the Thames River on Oct. 5, 1813 (see THAMES, BATTLE OF THE), in which Tecumseh was killed. Later Harrison concluded treaties with the Indians—Greenville (1814) and Spring Wells (1815)—that ushered in an era of peace and white expansion in the Old Northwest. He served in the House of Representatives (1816–19) and the Senate (1825–28). He was appointed (1828) minister to Colombia but was recalled (1829) by Andrew Jackson. His political fortunes rose as he became regarded as a compromise Whig candidate between Henry Clay and Daniel Webster. A group of Whig Anti-Masons nominated him for President in 1836, and in 1840, Webster went over to Harrison's candidacy for the presidency as a Whig. Clay, although bitterly disappointed, had to support Harrison. The campaign that followed was the first of the "rip-roaring" campaigns in U.S. history. Harrison and his running mate, John TYLER, were transformed by publicity. Harrison, an aristocratic Virginian, was made into a simple backwoods frontiersman, Tyler into his faithful lieutenant. The "Log Cabin and Hard Cider" campaign was launched in answer to ill-judged jeers from the supporters of the Democratic candidate, Martin VAN BUREN. Van Buren was pictured as an effete, "silver-spoon" man, Harrison as a rugged Westerner, despite his Virginia upbringing. "Tippecanoe and Tyler too" won—partly because the Panic of 1837 had turned many against Van Buren. Harrison then selected a brilliant Whig cabinet headed by Webster and adopted a program outlined by Clay, but the strain of the campaign was too much. He died a month later, Tyler became President, and the WHIG PARTY fell prey to factionalism. See biographies by D. B. Goebel (1926, repr. 1973), Freeman Cleaves (1939, repr. 1969), and J. A. Green (1941); R. G. Gunderson, *The Log Cabin Campaign* (1957).

Harrison, town (1970 pop. 11,811), Hudson co., NE N.J., an industrial suburb on the Passaic River opposite Newark; inc. 1869.

Harrisonburg, city (1970 pop. 14,605), seat of Rockingham co., NW Va., in the Shenandoah Valley; settled 1739, inc. 1916. It is a processing center in a poultry, dairy, and livestock area. Its manufactures include air conditioners, automobile parts, aluminum doors and windows, cardboard boxes, plastic bottles, clothing, furniture, and animal feeds and fertilizers. Gen. T. J. (Stonewall) Jackson ended his renowned Valley Campaign just E of Harrisonburg in 1862, and his leading cavalry chief, Gen. Turner Ashby, was killed there. Madison College, Eastern Mennonite College, and the headquarters of George Washington National Forest are in the city. Limestone caverns and the Shenandoah National Park are nearby.

Harrod, James, 1742–93, American frontiersman, b. Bedford co., Pa. He fought in the French and Indian Wars and in 1773 made a journey down the Ohio River to Kentucky. In 1774 he returned to Kentucky and began a settlement, the first in the state; it was named Harrodsburg in his honor. Later he opposed the colonization schemes of Richard HENDERSON and his Transylvania Company. In 1777, 1779, and 1782 he took part in campaigns against the Indians and was a member of the Virginia assembly (1779). Harrod disappeared mysteriously while trapping with two companions and never returned. He probably was murdered. See biography by K. H. Mason (1951).

Harrodsburg, city (1970 pop. 6,741), seat of Mercer co., central Ky., S of Frankfort. It is a trade center in a bluegrass area producing livestock, grain, and tobacco. Clothing, glass, and dairy products are made there. It is also a tourist and resort city, with mineral springs. Harrodsburg, the oldest settlement in the state, was founded in 1774 by James HARROD. One of the settlement's early leaders was George Rogers Clark. The city has a number of early-19th-century buildings. Pioneer Memorial State Park contains a replica of old Fort Harrod (where the state's first school was conducted) and the cabin in which Nancy Hanks and Thomas Lincoln were married.

Harrogate (hăr'ōgĭt, –gāt), municipal borough (1971 pop. 62,290), West Riding of Yorkshire, N central England. The borough is a health resort, with more than 80 mineral springs. It is a popular trade exhibition center and has varied light industry. In 1974, Harrogate became part of the new nonmetropolitan county of North Yorkshire.

Harrow, borough (1971 pop. 202,718), of Greater London, SE England. Until 1965, Harrow was a municipal borough in the former county of Middlesex. For centuries Harrow grew foodstuffs for London. Now it is mainly residential and contains parts of the Green Belt, areas set aside as parkland. Optical and photographic goods and glass are manufactured. The famous Harrow public school, founded in 1571, is in the borough. Among its illustrious graduates were the writers Byron and Galsworthy and the statesmen Peel and Palmerston.

harrow, farm implement, consisting of a wooden or metal framework bearing metal disks, teeth, or sharp projecting points, called tines, which is dragged over plowed land to pulverize the clods of earth and level the soil. Harrows are also used to uproot weeds, aerate the soil, and cover seeds. Primitive harrows were twiggy branches drawn over the soil to smooth it; in India a ladderlike device of bamboo is still used. In modern large-scale farming, harrows are of varied types. Some are simply dragged behind a tractor or draft animal; some are suspended on wheels; many have levers to adjust the depth of the cut. There may be one or more gangs (sets) of cutting parts per harrow, and one or more harrows may be drawn at a time. In disk harrows, which next to the plow are the most widely used tillage implements, the saucer-shaped disks are set at angles to the line of pull for maximum pulverization. Spike-tooth harrows have rigid teeth, and spring-tooth harrows have curved tines that adjust to obstacles. The rotary crossharrow has power-driven rotating toothed disks; another type of harrow slices through topsoil and vegetation with curved knives. In general, the harrow is similar to the CULTIVATOR, except that it penetrates the soil to a lesser depth. See Claude Culpin, *Farm Machinery* (8th ed. 1969); Michael Partridge, *Farm Tools through the Ages* (1973).

Harrowing of Hell, the victorious descent of Jesus Christ into hell after his death, to release the souls held captive there and confound the realms of hell. It is not a Christian dogma but is an idea ancient in Christianity; some analogous idea is behind the phrase of the Apostles' Creed (see CREED 3), "He descended into hell" (omitted by the Nicene Creed). The apocryphal Gospel of Nicodemus, one of the PSEUDEPIGRAPHA, gives an elaborate account of the Harrowing of Hell. The story became very popular in the Middle Ages; it is included in the Medieval collection *Cursor Mundi. The Harrowing of Hell* is the name of a 13th-century poem in dialogue, sometimes called the first English religious drama. See Early English Text Society, *The Middle English Harrowing of Hell and Gospel of Nicodemus* (1907).

Harsha (hûr'shə), b. c.590, Indian emperor (606–47). He briefly restored the GUPTA empire. Harsha became (606) king of a small state in the upper Ganges valley, and by 612 he had built up a vast army with which he forged nearly all India N of the Narbada River into an empire. An extremely able military leader, his only defeat was at the hands of the Chalukyas, when he attempted (c.620) to invade the Deccan. His capital at Kanauj was an artistic and literary center, and Harsha himself was a distinguished poet and dramatist. A Hindu early in life, Harsha later became a devout Buddhist and forbade the killing of animals in his realm. He built innumerable stupas, established many monasteries, and founded several state hospitals. His great Buddhist convocation at Kanauj (643) was reputedly attended by 20 kings and thousands of pilgrims. The life and times of Harsha are described in the *Harsha-charita,* a flowery work by Bana, the court poet, and in the *Si-yu-ki* [records of the Western world] written by the Chinese pilgrim Hsüan-tsang. After Harsha's death, N India relapsed into anarchy. See R. K. Mookerji, *Harsha* (1926); studies by D. Devahuti (1970) and Baijnath Sharma (1970).

Harsha (här'shə), family that returned from the Exile. Ezra 2.52; Neh. 7.54.

Harspranget, village: see LULEÄLV, river, Sweden.

Harstad (här'stä), town (1970 pop. 19,986), Troms co., NW Norway, on Hinnøya, the largest island of Norway. It is a fishing center and a bunkering place for coastal steamers and trawlers. Nearby is the fortified church of Trondenes (13th cent.).

Hart, Albert Bushnell, 1854–1943, American historian, b. Clarksville, Greene co., Pa. He began teaching history at Harvard in 1883, became a full professor in 1897, and from 1910 until his retirement in 1926 was professor of government. Hart was a prodigious worker who was responsible for the publication of about 100 volumes, notably the "American Nation" series (28 vol., 1904–18), of which he was editor and for which he wrote Vol. XVI, *Slavery and Abolition, 1831–1841* (1906) and Vol. XXVI, *National Ideals Historically Traced* (1907, repr. 1968). He also edited *Epochs of American History* (4 vol., 1891–1926), contributing *Formation of the Union, 1750–1829* (Vol. II, 1892; new ed. 1925) to the series; *American History Told by Contemporaries* (5 vol., 1897–1929); *Source Readers in American History* (5 vol., 1901–27); and *Commonwealth History of Massachusetts* (5 vol., 1927–30, repr. 1967). He was joint editor, with Edward Channing, of *American History Leaflets* (1892–1910) and, with Andrew C. McLaughlin, of the *Cyclopedia of American Government* (3 vol., 1914). With Channing again he also compiled the *Guide to the Study and Reading of American History* (1896; rev. and enl. ed. by Channing, Hart, and Frederick J. Turner, 1912), still one of the most valuable single-volume bibliographies of American history. Hart also edited, with Herbert E. Bolton, the *American History Atlas* (1918; 4th ed., with Bolton and David M. Matteson, 1940) and was editor of *The American Yearbook* (1911–20, 1923–32). Long an admirer and supporter of his Harvard classmate Theodore Roosevelt, he edited, with Herbert R. Ferleger, the *Theodore Roosevelt Cyclopedia* (1941). Of the individual books he wrote, *Salmon Portland Chase* (1899, repr. 1970), *The Foundations of American Foreign Policy* (1901, repr. 1970), and *Actual Government as Applied under American Conditions* (1903, 4th ed. 1919) were probably most important.

Hart, Basil Henry Liddell: see LIDDELL HART, BASIL HENRY.

Hart, John, 1711?–1779, political leader in the American Revolution, signer of the Declaration of Independence, b. Stonington, Conn. Moving to Hopewell, N.J., as a youth, he became prosperous as a farmer and a miller. He was a member of the provincial assembly from 1761 to 1771, of several provincial congresses, and of the Continental Congress of 1776.

Hart, Lorenz Milton, 1895–1943, American lyricist, b. New York City, studied at Columbia. Hart began collaborating with Richard RODGERS in 1919; their initial success was *The Garrick Gaieties* (1925). Thereafter, the team of Rodgers and Hart produced such popular musicals as *Connecticut Yankee* (1927), *The Boys from Syracuse* (1938), *Pal Joey* (1940), and *By Jupiter* (1942). Their many famous songs include "Manhattan," "Blue Moon," and "The Lady Is a Tramp." Hart was noted for his witty, literate, but always expressive lyrics; his rhymes were distinctly original. He was the first lyricist to receive equal billing with the composer.

Hart, Moss, 1904–1961, American dramatist, b. New York City, studied at Columbia. His first important play, *Once in a Lifetime* (1930), was the beginning of a long collaboration with George S. KAUFMAN. Among their other successful comedies are *You Can't Take It with You* (1936; Pulitzer Prize), *I'd Rather Be Right* (1937)—written with George M. Cohan, *The Man Who Came to Dinner* (1939) and *George Washington Slept Here* (1940). Hart collaborated on musicals with Irving Berlin and Cole Porter; his most successful musical was *Lady in the Dark* (1941), written with Kurt Weill and Ira Gershwin. Among his plays, produced between 1941 and 1952, are *Winged Victory, Christopher Blake, Light Up the Sky,* and *The Climate of Eden.* In 1956 he directed the long-running musical hit *My Fair Lady.* See his autobiographical *Act One* (1959).

Hart, William S., 1870–1946, American film actor, b. Newburgh, N.Y. He made his stage debut in 1889, appearing on Broadway and in road companies until he began his film career in 1914. An excellent horseman, he became the prototype of "the strong, silent man of the West" in such films as *Wild Bill Hickok* (1923) and *Tumbleweeds* (1926; his last film). His horse, Paint, was equally famous. He appeared in 27 films over a period of 8 years. See his autobiography, *My Life East and West* (1929).

Harte, Bret (Francis Brett Harte) (härt), 1836–1902, American writer of short stories and humorous verse, b. Albany, N.Y. At 19 he went to California. After trying his hand at teaching, clerking, and mining, he turned to journalism and in 1868 helped establish the *Overland Monthly,* where his short stories and verse first appeared. He gained enormous success with the publication of "The Luck of Roaring Camp," the first of his picturesque stories of Western local color. Another triumph was scored with the humorous dialect poem "Plain Language from Truthful James," also known by the title "The Heathen Chinee." Although Harte did not greatly develop character and motivation, he had an observant eye and a brisk reportorial style that ranged from rough humor to romance. Other well-known stories, such as "The Outcasts of Poker Flat," "Tennessee's Partner," "Miggles," and "Brown of Calaveras," still retain their freshness and pathos. After achieving wide recognition, Harte returned East in 1871. He was U.S. consul in Germany and Scotland from 1878 to 1885. The remainder of his life was spent near London. Although he continued to write, his final years added little to his literary development. See his letters, ed. by G. B. Harte (1926); biography by Richard O'Connor (1966); Margaret Duckett, *Mark Twain and Bret Harte* (1964).

hartebeest (här'tĭbēst"), large African ANTELOPE of the genus *Alcelaphus.* The hartebeest resembles a horse with horns. It has a very long face and a small hump between the shoulders; its coat is fawn or reddish and its ringed horns curve up and inward in a U shape. Most kinds of hartebeest stand about 4 ft (120 cm) at the shoulder and weigh about 400 lb (180 kg). Swift animals of the plains, hartebeests usually live in herds of around a dozen animals and are often found associated with other herd animals, such as zebras, gnus, and gazelles. The common hartebeest *(A. buselaphus)* has many races, distributed through most of Africa. Although the races are given different common names (e.g., the kongoni, or Coke's hartebeest, of E Africa), they are quite similar in appearance and behavior and interbreed readily. The N African bulbul and the S African red hartebeest are extinct races of the common hartebeest. The former was known to the Romans and was very numerous until the 19th cent. Swayne's hartebeest, a small Ethiopian race, is in danger of extinction. A second species, Lichtenstein's hartebeest *(A. lichtensteini),* is found in SE Africa. An antelope related to the hartebeests, *Damaliscus hunteri,* is known as Hunter's hartebeest, but is more properly called a DAMALISK. The hartebeest is classified in the phylum CHORDATA, subphylum Vertebrata, class Mammalia, order Artiodactyla, family Bovidae.

Hartford, city (1970 pop. 158,017), state capital, Hartford co., central Conn., on the west bank of the Connecticut River; settled as Newtown 1635–36 under Thomas Hooker and Samuel Stone on the site of a Dutch trading post (1633; abandoned 1654), inc. 1784. It is the largest city in the state, a port of entry, a world-famous insurance center, and a commercial, industrial, and cultural hub. Its insurance business began in 1794; today more than 35 insurance companies have their headquarters there. Manufactures include firearms, typewriters, precision instruments, computers, auto parts, electric equipment, and brushes. One of the earliest and strongest colonial centers, Hartford formed (1639) with two other towns the Connecticut Colony, adopting the FUNDAMENTAL ORDERS. From 1701 to 1875 it was joint capital with New Haven. It was an important military supply depot during the Revolution, and in 1814–15 it hosted the HARTFORD CONVENTION. Landmarks include the old statehouse (1796; designed by Charles Bulfinch), where the Hartford Convention met; the site of the CHARTER OAK; the capitol (completed 1878; designed by Richard M. Upjohn); and the famous Travelers Insurance tower. The Connecticut state library includes the Colt collection of firearms. The city has a noted art museum (the Wadsworth Atheneum) and a symphony orchestra. Other attractions are the Harriet Beecher Stowe House (1871), where Stowe lived from 1873 to 1896; and the Mark Twain Memorial (1873–74), which was occupied for about 30 years by the author. Noah Webster, John Fiske, and the elder J. P. Morgan were born in Hartford, and the theologian Horace Bushnell, the author Charles Dudley Warner, and the poet Wallace Stevens also lived there. The Hartford *Courant,* founded in 1764, is one of the oldest newspapers in the United States. The city's many parks include Colt Park (formerly the estate of Samuel Colt) and Elizabeth Park, scene of an annual rose festival. Hartford is the seat of Trinity College, Diocesan Sisters College, Hartford Seminary Foundation, a branch of the Univ. of Connecticut and its schools of law and social work, three junior colleges, the American School for the Deaf, and the Connecticut Institute for the Blind. Constitution Plaza, a 15-acre (6-hectare) development project, was completed in 1964.

Hartford Convention, Dec. 15, 1814–Jan. 4, 1815, meeting to consider the problems of New England in the WAR OF 1812; held at Hartford, Conn. Prior to the war, New England Federalists (see FEDERALIST PARTY) had opposed the Embargo Act of 1807 and other government measures; many of them continued to oppose the government after fighting had begun. Although manufacturing (fostered by isolation) and contraband trade brought wealth to the section, "Mr. Madison's War" (as the Federalists called the War of 1812) and its expenses became steadily more repugnant to the New Englanders. The Federalist leaders encouraged disaffection. The New England states refused to surrender their militia to national service (see GRISWOLD, ROGER), especially when New England was threatened with invasion in 1814. The Federal loan of 1814 got almost no support in New England, despite prosperity there. Federalist extremists, such as John LOWELL and Timothy PICKERING, contemplated a separate peace between New England and Great Britain. Finally, in Oct., 1814, the Massachusetts legislature issued a call to the other New England states for a conference. Representatives were sent by the state legislatures of Connecticut, Massachusetts, and Rhode Island; other delegates from New Hampshire and Vermont were popularly chosen by the Federalists. The meetings were held in secret. George Cabot, the head of the Massachusetts delegation and a moderate Federalist, presided. Other important delegates were Harrison Gray OTIS (1765–1848), also a moderate, and Theodore DWIGHT, who served as secretary of the convention. The moderates prevailed in the convention. The proposal to secede from the Union was discussed and rejected, the grievances of New England were reviewed, and such matters as the use of the militia were thrashed out. The final report (Jan. 5, 1815) arraigned Madison's administration and the war and proposed several constitutional amendments that would redress what the New Englanders considered the unfair advantage given the South under the Constitution. The news of the Treaty of Ghent ending the war and of Andrew Jackson's victory at New Orleans made any recommendation of the convention a dead letter. Its importance, however, was twofold: It continued the view of states' rights as the refuge of sectional groups, and it sealed the destruction of the Federalist party, which never regained its lost prestige. See J. T. Adams, *New England in the Republic* (1926, repr. 1960); J. M. Banner, *To the Hartford Convention* (1970).

Hartford Foundation, fund established (1929) by retail food merchants John A. Hartford (1872–1951) and George L. Hartford (1864–1957) as a philanthropic institution with the general purpose of doing "the greatest good for the greatest number." Incorporated in 1942, the foundation has concentrated on financing biomedical research carried on by teaching hospitals and medical schools. Its aim has been to work for the prevention, diagnosis, and treatment of those diseases about which medical knowledge is limited. The foundation helped bring about the clinical application of several lifesaving devices, particularly in connection with heart and kidney disease treatment. In 1972 its assets exceeded $190 million.

Hartford Wits: see CONNECTICUT WITS.

Harthacanute (här'thăkənōōt), **Hardicanute,** or **Hardecanute** (both: här'dĭkənōōt), d. 1042, king of Denmark (1035–42) and of the English (1040–42); son of Canute and Emma. On his father's death (1035) he succeeded to the throne of Denmark, where he was already the effective ruler. In England his illegitimate half brother, HAROLD HAREFOOT, first acted as regent, then as king (1037–40), while Harthacanute in Denmark was reaching a settlement with MAGNUS I of Norway. Harold's death in 1040 allowed Harthacanute to take over the English throne peaceably, although he arrived in England with 62 warships. His reign was quarrelsome and oppressive, but by indicating as his heir EDWARD THE CONFESSOR he averted a possible dynastic struggle when his own death ended the male line of the royal Danish house in England.

Hartigan, Grace, 1922–, American painter, b. Newark, N.J. Hartigan began painting semiabstract canvases after her introduction to the works of the abstract expressionists in 1949. She integrates recognizably representational images into abstract compositions. Her works are characterized by broad shapes executed with loose brushwork and a strong, heavy line.

Hartington, Spencer Compton Cavendish, marquess of: see DEVONSHIRE, SPENCER COMPTON CAVENDISH, 8TH DUKE OF.

Hartlepool (härt'lēpōōl, härt'əl-), county borough (1971 pop. 96,898), Durham, NE England. The county borough was created in 1966 by the merger of the municipal borough of Hartlepool, the rural district of Stockton, and the county borough of West Hartlepool. A seaport, Hartlepool exports coal and imports timber, wood pulp, petroleum, and iron ore. There are shipbuilding, iron and steel manufacturing, engineering, and brewing industries. Hartlepool is also the home of a herring fleet. A convent founded on the site in 640 was famous under St. Hilda (649–657) and was destroyed by the Danes in 800. In the 12th and 13th cent. Hartlepool was the chief port of the palatinate of Durham. West Hartlepool developed in the 19th cent. as a port for coal export. Seaton Carew, a suburb, is a seaside resort. In 1974, Hartlepool became part of the new nonmetropolitan county of Cleveland.

Hartley, David, 1705–57, English physician and philosopher, founder of associational psychology. In his *Observations on Man* (2 vol., 1749) he stated that all mental phenomena are due to sensations arising from vibrations of the white medullary substance of the brain and spinal cord. He conceived the whole mind as resulting from the association of simple sensations. See ASSOCIATIONISM.

Hartley, Marsden, 1877–1943, American landscape and still-life painter, b. Lewiston, Maine. He was educated in Cleveland, but early in his career he went to New York City, where he studied under William Chase and at the National Academy of Design. In 1909 his landscapes were shown at the Stieglitz gallery. During the next 12 years he made three trips to Europe and one to the Southwest. His work showed the influence successively of the French and German moderns. He exhibited in Munich with Klee and Kandinsky. His reputation was established about 1921, and in 1931 he was awarded a Guggenheim fellowship. Although his early works were often almost entirely abstract, Hartley later returned to depicting nature with a forceful simplicity. He is best known for his paintings of people and scenery of Maine. Hartley is represented in leading American museums. See catalog by William Mitchell (1970).

Hartmann, Eduard von (ā'dōōärt fən härt'män), 1842–1906, German philosopher. His *Philosophy of the Unconscious* appeared in 1869 (tr., 3 vol., 1884; new ed. 1931). By the unconscious, Hartmann meant the inexplicable forces of nature which activate the world process, whether in atoms or in organisms. Influenced by Schopenhauer and Hegel, he saw the world process as a struggle between blind impulse and reason. In ethics, he overcame an early pessimism founded on the irrational characteristics of life and later formulated a qualified optimism based on the evolutionary forces of reason.

Hartmann, Nicolai (nē'kōlī), 1882–1950, German philosopher, b. Latvia. He taught at Marburg (1922–25), Cologne (1925–31), Berlin (1931–45), and Göttingen (1945–50). Abandoning his early adherence to idealism, he propounded instead a philosophical realism based on the intelligibility of being. For Hartmann, ontology was the source of philosophy. He saw philosophy's mission as the statement of the problems of being and the unraveling of the irrational and the puzzling. Although a nontheistic humanist, he posited three levels of the spirit, which he considered to be a process rather than a substance. He held the world to be a unity, but said that one would not be justified in calling that unity God. His ontological disagreement with Heidegger provides two of the mainstreams of modern European philosophy. In his *Ethik* (1926, tr., 3 vol., 1932), he sought to develop a system of values from the ethics of Max SCHELER; Hartmann's ethics, like Scheler's, are distinctive in their treatment of the freedom of the will. Among his other works are *Gründzuge einer Metaphysik der Erkenntnis* (1921); *Das Problem des geistigen Seins* (1933); *Möglichkeit und Wirklichkeit* (1938); *Der Aufbau der realen Welt* (1940); *Neue Wege der Ontologie* (1949, tr. *New Ways of Ontology,* 1952); and *Ästhetik* (1953). See study by Otto Samuel (tr. 1954).

Hartmann von Aue (härt'män fən ou'ə), c.1170–c.1220, German poet whose name is also spelled von Ouwe. His chivalric romances *Erec* and *Iwain* are tales of Arthurian legend. Other works include the religious legend *Gregorius;* the idyl *Der arme Heinrich* [poor Henry], upon which Longfellow based his *Golden Legend;* and lyrics.

hartshorn, spirits of: see AMMONIA.

Hartung, Hans (häns här'tōōng), 1904–, French painter, b. Germany. Hartung rejected the early influence of German EXPRESSIONISM and developed an entirely abstract style in which a strong linear element creates a rhythmic unity. In his works black lines are grouped together in bunches on a luminescent background. Characteristic is his *Composition* (1951; Cavellini Coll., Brescia). See study by Umbro Apollonio (tr. 1973).

Harum (hā'rəm), descendant of Judah. 1 Chron. 4.8.

Harumaph (häryōō'măf, hā'-), father of JEDAIAH **2.**

Harun ar-Rashid (härōōn är-răshēd') [Arabic,=Aaron the Upright], c.764–809, 5th and most famous ABBASID caliph (786–809). He succeeded his brother Musa al-Hadi, fourth caliph, a year after the death of his father, Mahdi, the third caliph. In his youth he had been very successful as a general in invasions of Asia Minor; on one of these he reached the Bosporus. Harun's empire included all SW Asia and the northern part of Africa, but by the end of his caliphate much of Africa had withdrawn from all but nominal obedience. He had diplomatic relations with China and with Charlemagne. The most famous incident of his career was the fall of the Barmecides, a Persian family that had become very powerful under Mahdi. Yahya the Barmecide had aided Harun in obtaining the caliphate, and he and his sons were in high favor until 798, when the caliph threw them in prison and confiscated their land; the reasons for this are not known, but it was probably a result of an extended intrigue by the Arabian group at court. Harun was repeatedly faced with insurrections in his empire. These grew more frequent after the fall of the Barmecides, who were adroit statesmen. After this Harun's prime minister was Fazl ibn-Rabi. Harun was a munificent patron of letters and of arts, and under him Baghdad was at its apogee. He became a great figure to the Arabs, who tell about him in many of the stories of the *Thousand and One Nights.* See F. W. Buckler, *Harunu'l-Rashid and Charles the Great* (1931); H. St. John B. Philby, *Harun al Rashid* (1933).

Harunobu, Suzuki (sōōzōō'kē härōō'nō'bōō), 1725–70, Japanese color-print artist of the ukiyo-e school. He was the first to use a wide range of colors effectively in printing. In 1765 he created multicolored calendar prints from wood blocks. He continued to produce works notable for their pure color harmony, delicacy of line, and subtlety of feeling. From popular portrayals of actors and courtesans, he progressed to interpretations of domestic life, idyllic love, and graceful figures of young girls. His works are called *nishiki-e* [Jap.,=brocade pictures]. See catalog of his works by Jack Hillier (1970); biography by Ichitaro Kondo (1956); study by Seiichiro Takahashi (1968).

Haruphite (häryōō'fīt, hâr'yōōfīt), obscure designation of Shephatiah. 1 Chron. 12.5.

Haruz (hā'rəz), father of Meshullemeth. 2 Kings 21.19.

Harvard, John, 1607–38, chief founder of Harvard College, b. Southwark, England, M.A. Emmanuel College, Cambridge, 1635. He immigrated in 1637 to Charlestown, Mass., where he was assistant to the pastor and teaching elder of the First Church. He bequeathed £780 (half his estate) and his library of 320 volumes toward the founding of a new college at Cambridge, Mass., which was named in his honor.

Harvard, town (1970 pop. 12,536), Worcester co., E central Mass.; inc. 1732. A Shaker house and cemetery, an Indian museum, and a Harvard Univ. observatory are there. Nearby is a museum on the site of Fruitlands, a cooperative vegetarian community founded by Bronson Alcott. Fort Devens is also in the vicinity.

Harvard College Observatory, astronomical OBSERVATORY located in Cambridge, Mass., operated by Harvard Univ. (Harvard College at the time of the observatory's founding in 1839). Its equipment includes a 61-in. (155-cm) reflecting telescope and 15-in. (38-cm) and 12-in. (30-cm) refracting telescopes. The observatory maintains a radio-astronomy station at Fort Davis, Texas (site of McDonald Observatory), with an 84-ft (26-m) steerable dish for galactic studies, including the study of quasars and pulsars, and dynamic spectrum analyzers covering a wide range of frequencies for studies of solar activity. Other programs of the Harvard Observatory include various aspects of solar physics, stellar and nebular spectroscopy and photometry, and theoretical cosmology. Among the noted directors of the observatory have been W. C. Bond, G. P. Bond, E. C. Pickering, and Harlow Shapley. In 1973 the research programs of the Harvard College Observatory were merged with those of the Smithsonian Astrophysical Observatory to form the Center for Astrophysics, under a single directorship; the observatory itself, however, maintains its separate status under the control of Harvard.

Harvard University, mainly at Cambridge, Mass. The oldest American college, Harvard College, for men, was founded in 1636 with a grant from the General Court of the Massachusetts Bay Colony. In 1638 it was named for John HARVARD, its first benefactor. During the 1640s the college expanded despite inadequate finances, and in 1650 it was incorporated and chartered by the General Court. Intended to be an institution for the education of Puritan ministers, it grew to be an institution of general education, and new and more liberal subjects and policies were introduced. In the 18th cent., particularly under John Leverett (1708–24), enrollment and campus facilities increased and the religious attachment to Congregationalism declined. Systematic theological instruction was inaugurated in 1721 with the establishment of a professorship of divinity, and by 1827, with the opening of Divinity Hall, Harvard became a nucleus of theological teaching in New England. In its early years the college was largely supported by the colony and the New England community as a whole, but support soon came in the form of gifts, and in 1823 the last state grant was received. Under Charles W. ELIOT, the college became a great modern university. Its physical plant and curriculum were expanded, the graduate school was established, and the law and medical schools were reorganized. Eliot is also noted for his introduction of the elective system at Harvard. Besides Harvard College, the university includes graduate schools of divinity (1816), law (1817), arts and sciences (1872), education (1920), engineering (1935; reorganization of Lawrence Scientific School of 1847), and public administration (1935). Harvard also has schools of business administration (1908), medicine (1782), public health (1922), and dental health (1941). Radcliffe College for women (est. 1879, chartered 1894) is affiliated with Harvard; Radcliffe students are instructed by Harvard professors and receive diplomas granted by Harvard. The university library, among the nation's finest, houses over 8 million volumes, and the Fogg Museum of Art is one of the finest university museums in the world. Harvard is closely associated with numerous research facilities, including the Astrophysical Observatory of the Smithsonian Institution and the Peabody Museum of Archaeology and Ethnology. The university also operates a center for Byzantine studies at Dumbarton Oaks in Washington, D.C. See histories by S. E. Morison (1936) and E. J. Kahn (1969).

harvest customs, practices associated with the celebration of the gathering of agricultural crops. The gathering of the harvest—the climax of the year's labors wherever the soil is cultivated—has been celebrated from ancient times, by both primitive and civilized people, with merrymaking or with the performance of symbolic rites of a religious or magical significance. The corn mother, symbolizing the spirit of the grain, was a common figure of harvest time. Usually made of the last or the best sheaf cut, her image was carried in triumph from the field, drenched with water to invoke rain for the next season. Other harvest customs, such as the baking of a loaf in the figure of a child, suggest ancient sacrificial rites of harvest time. An important feature of ancient Greek religion was the worship of Demeter, the corn goddess, her daughter Kore (Persephone), and the god Dionysus. The Romans adopted this worship, identifying the Greek deities with their own indigenous crop deities, Ceres (from whom the word *cereal* derives), Libera, and Liber. Pagan rites associated with the harvest continued into Christian times, and such religious festivals as Corpus Christi, All Saints, and the Festival of Lughnasa in Ireland retain traces of the ancient customs. The Jewish feasts of Shavuot and Sukkoth are harvest festivals. In the United States the harvest season is annually celebrated on Thanksgiving Day.

harvester, farm machine that mechanically harvests a crop. Small-grain harvesting has been mechanized to a certain extent since early times. In the modern period the first harvester to gain general acceptance was made by Cyrus McCormick in 1831 (see REAPER). More recently the COMBINE has been developed for small-grain harvesting. The first mechanical cotton picker was patented in 1850, but, due to the supply of cheap labor, cotton harvesters did not gain acceptance until after World War II. Labor shortages have led to the development of a variety of harvesters adapted for almost every kind of agricultural crop, including tomatoes, grapes, nuts, cucumbers, and root crops, e.g., beets and potatoes. The most common exceptions are certain tree fruits. Nuts and some fruits, such as figs, are allowed to mature and fall to the ground where they are mechanically picked up. Hydraulic shakers have also been developed so that nuts and fruits, such as apricots, grapes, and plums, can be shaken from the tree or vine onto the ground, or onto nets or belts. With some plants, such as tomatoes, special varieties have had to be developed that can withstand mechanical contact. The culinary quality of crops developed for mechanical harvesting is presently the cause of concern by consumer groups. See Claude Culpin, *Farm Machinery* (8th ed. 1969).

harvest fish, common name for a fish of the family Stromateidae (butterfish family), a family of fishes with almost circular bodies and small mouths. The butterfish, or dollarfish (genus *Peprilus*), is found from Maine to South Carolina during the summer. The harvest fish (*Poronotus triacanthus*), a more southerly species, is called whiting in the Chesapeake Bay area, where it is most abundant. Members of the butterfish family range from 6 to 9 in. (15–23 cm) in length and average ½ lb (0.23 kg) in weight. They are found in schools on sandy bottoms close to shore. They are known for their habit of swimming under certain species of jellyfishes, where they find shelter and perhaps a food supply of small invertebrates that have become entangled in the tentacles, but they are also subject to fatal stings inflicted by these tentacles. The so-called California pompano is a common Pacific harvest fish. Harvest fishes are classified in the phylum CHORDATA, subphylum Vertebrata, class Osteichthyes, order Perciformes, family Stromateidae.

harvest fly: see CICADA.

harvestman, arachnid, often called daddy longlegs because of its eight long, slender legs. The harvestman has a rounded or oval body possessing glands that give off an acrid scent. Its food consists of a variety of organic materials, including fluids from fruits and vegetation, animal tissue, and even other harvestmen. The unrelated CRANE FLY is also called daddy longlegs because of its long legs. Harvestmen are classified in the phylum ARTHROPODA, class Arachnida, order Opiliones.

harvest moon, full moon occurring nearest to the autumnal EQUINOX, about Sept. 23. During harvest moon the retardation (later rising each night) of the moon is at a minimum because of the relation of the moon's path to the horizon. On several nights in succession the moonrise is at nearly the same time, and there is full moonlight almost from sunset to sunrise if the sky is unclouded.

Harvey, Gabriel, 1545?–1630?, English author. An ardent scholar, he studied at Cambridge and became a fellow of Pembroke Hall. There he became close friends with Edmund Spenser, who later celebrated Harvey as Hobbinol in *The Shepherd's Calendar.* In 1578, Harvey became a fellow of Trinity Hall and began the study of law, but the publication of some satirical verses in 1579 involved him in considerable trouble with the authorities, and his appointment as master was recalled. The publication of the *Four Letters* (1592), a scurrilous post-mortem attack on Robert GREENE, involved Harvey in the heated Martin MARPRELATE CONTROVERSY, which was terminated in 1599 by the intervention of the government. Much of Harvey's Martinist writings contained personal rebuffs, particularly to Thomas NASHE, who had described Harvey as an arrogant, tactless misfit. See his complete works edited by A. B. Grosart (3 vol., 1884–85).

Harvey, George Brinton McClellan, 1864–1928, American journalist and diplomat, b. Peacham, Caledonia co., Vt. After a career in journalism and insurance, he became involved in the construction and administration of electric railroads, a venture that brought him a fortune. In 1899 he bought the *North American Review,* and, with the backing of J. P. Morgan, he assumed control (1901) of *Harper's Weekly.* Harvey retired (1913) from the editorship of *Harper's Weekly,* but later (1918) founded *Harvey's Weekly* as a medium for virulent attacks on Woodrow Wilson (his former friend and protégé), the Wilson administration, and the peace negotiations. Harvey supported (1920) the candidacy of Warren G. Harding and aided in the preparation of Harding's campaign speeches. After Harding's election, Harvey was appointed ambassador to Great Britain. His works include *Women* (1908) and *Henry Clay Frick, the Man* (1928).

Harvey, William, 1578–1657, English physician considered by many to have laid the foundation of modern medicine, b. Folkestone, studied at Cambridge, M.D. Univ. of Padua, 1602. Returning to London, he became a physician of St. Bartholomew's Hospital and a lecturer at the College of Physicians, and he was later appointed court physician. Harvey was first to demonstrate the function of the heart and the complete circulation of the blood, a feat especially remarkable because it was accomplished without the aid of a microscope. Acceptance of his theories was slow in coming, and it was not until 1827 that they were fully substantiated. He also contributed greatly to the advance of comparative anatomy and embryology. His famous *Exercitatio anatomica de motu cordis et sanguinis in animalibus (On the Movement of the Heart and Blood in Animals)* was published in 1628. See the translation of his writings by K. J. Franklin (1963); biography by G. L. Keynes (1966); study by Gweneth Whitteridge (1971).

Harvey, William Henry, 1811–66, Irish botanist. An authority on algae, he wrote *A Manual of the British Algae* (1841), *Phycologia Britannica* (4 vol., 1846–51), and *Phycologia Australica* (5 vol., 1858–63), which are classics in their field. He spent several years in South Africa, and as a result of his studies there, he wrote, with O. W. Sonder, *Flora Capensis* (7 vol. in 11, 1859–1933).

Harvey, William Hope, 1851–1936, American writer on economics, called Coin Harvey, b. Buffalo, Putnam co., W.Va. He studied at Marshall College, practiced law, and interested himself in monetary problems. He was a vigorous advocate of BIMETALLISM at the time the argument over coinage of silver was at its height. His *Coin's Financial School* (1894) attempted to explain the money question in simple terms. Harvey's sturdy pamphleteering had great influence on the Populist party, and his demand for free coinage of silver was given full expression when William Jennings Bryan ran for President in 1896. Bryan's famous "cross of gold" speech in 1896 embodied Harvey's ideas. Among Harvey's other works are *Coin on Money, Trusts, and Imperialism* (1899) and *The Remedy* (1915).

Harvey, city (1970 pop. 34,636), Cook co., NE Ill., a suburb S of Chicago; inc. 1895. Its manufactures include steel, cranes, automobile parts, and other metal products. Harvey has an oil research center and a junior college. The city was founded by Turlington W. Harvey, a wealthy lumberman, in 1890.

Harvey Mudd College: see CLAREMONT COLLEGES.

Harwich (hăr'ĭj), municipal borough (1971 pop. 14,892), Essex, E central England, on the estuary of the Stour and the Orwell rivers. An important port, Harwich imports foodstuffs, iron and steel, and machinery and exports chemicals and automobiles. In wartime it has been an important naval base; it also serves as a port for passenger ships to the Continent, especially Antwerp. There is also container-ship service from Harwich to Zeebrugge, Belgium. The borough's other industries are boatbuilding, fishing, light engineering, and cement manufacture. The borough includes Dovercourt Bay, a popular seaside resort. Harwich, an ancient town, was known in the Middle Ages for its port and had an important shipbuilding industry in the 17th cent.

Haryana (hărēän'ə), state (1971 pop. 9,971,165), 17,120 sq mi (44,341 sq km), N central India. CHANDIGARH is the capital, and Ambala, Karnal, Panipat, Rohtak, and Bhiwani are other important cities. The terrain is generally dry, flat, and barren. Cotton is the main product. There are iron-ore deposits in the southwestern part of the state. Haryana was created in 1966 out of the Hindi-speaking portions of Punjab state. It is governed by a chief minister and cabinet responsible to an elected unicameral legislature and by a governor appointed by the president of India.

Harz (härts), mountain range, on the East German–West German border, extending c.60 mi (100 km) between the Elbe and Leine rivers. The rugged mountains were once densely forested. They culminate in Brocken peak (3,747 ft/1,142 m high). The region has good waterpower potential. Intensive uranium-ore prospecting began there after World War II. The Upper Harz has extensive wastelands and a severe, rainy climate. It is noted for its mineral deposits (especially silver). Gosler, West Germany, is the chief town of the region, which also has some summer resorts. The Lower Harz has a mild climate. It is an agricultural region where grains and cattle are raised. Wernigerode, East Germany, is the main town.

Hasa, Al (äl hä'sä, hă'sə), region, E Saudi Arabia, on the Persian Gulf. HOFUF is the chief town. Oil, dates, wheat, and rice are produced. It was taken from the Turks in 1914 by Ibn Saud.

Hasadiah (hăsədī'ə), one of Zerubbabel's sons. 1 Chron. 3.20.

Hasan (häsän'), c.625–c.669, 5th caliph; son of ALI and FATIMA (daughter of Muhammad the Prophet). When Ali was killed in 661, Hasan became caliph, but he was not strong enough to withstand the threat of arms of the Umayyads and under pressure abdicated in favor of MUAWIYA. He retired to Medina and died, reputedly of poison. His more active brother, HUSEIN, took up the family cause. The Shiites believe that Hasan was murdered by the Umayyads and venerate him as a martyr.

Hasbeya (häsbä'ə), small town, S Lebanon, at the foot of Mt. Hermon. It was a center of the Druses from the 13th cent. to the 19th cent. The Khulwat el-Bujad, a sacred shrine of the Druses, is on the hillside.

Hasbrouck Heights (hăz'brŏŏk), borough (1970 pop. 13,651), Bergen co., NE N.J., a residential suburb adjoining Hackensack; settled c.1685, inc. 1894.

Hasdrubal (hăz'drŏŏbəl), d. 221 B.C., Carthaginian general. He fought under his father-in-law, HAMILCAR BARCA, in Africa and in Spain, where he succeeded (229 or 228 B.C.) Hamilcar as general. He increased the empire in Spain, where he founded Carthago Nova (modern Cartagena). By treaty with Rome (226), he fixed the northern boundary of Carthaginian Spain at the Ebro River.

Hasdrubal, d. 207 B.C., Carthaginian general; son of HAMILCAR BARCA. During the Second Punic War (see PUNIC WARS), his brother HANNIBAL, on leaving for Italy, made Hasdrubal commander in Spain. Hasdrubal conducted a long campaign against the Romans, led by Publius and Cneius SCIPIO, who prevented him from joining Hannibal at a critical moment in 216. Both Scipios fell in battle in 211, but in 209 SCIPIO AFRICANUS MAJOR took Cartagena. Hasdrubal eluded him by crossing the Pyrenees at their western extremity and, after crossing the Alps, arrived in central Italy. On the Metaurus (Metauro) River he met (207) the army of Caius Claudius Nero. Hasdrubal died in the battle. His defeat is considered decisive in the war, for it prevented Hannibal from receiving Carthaginian aid.

Hašek, Jaroslav (yä'rōsläf hä'shĕk), 1883–1923, Czech writer, b. Prague. His experiences as a soldier in World War I inspired his famous novel *The Good Soldier Schweik* (4 vol., 1920–23; tr. 1930), a satire on the Austrian military bureaucracy and on war in general. The ludicrous adventures of the good-hearted Schweik make the business of war an absurdity. The novel won Hašek international fame and was adapted for stage and film. Brecht wrote a sequel to the book in 1944. Hašek also wrote many volumes of short stories.

Hasenuah (hăsĭnyo͞o'ə), Benjamite. 1 Chron. 9.7.

Hashabiah (hăshəbī'ə). **1** Chief priest. Ezra 8.24. **2** Priest. Neh. 12.21. **3,4,5** Chief Levites. 1 Chron. 27.17; 2 Chron. 35.9; Neh. 12.24. **6** Kohathite. 1 Chron. 26.30. **7** Harpist. 1 Chron. 25.3,19. **8,9,10** Merarites. 1 Chron. 6.45; 9.14; Ezra 8.19. **11** Sealer of the Covenant. Neh. 10.11. **12,13** Levites in the Temple. Neh. 11.15,22. **14** Worker on the wall. Neh. 3.17.

Hashabnah (hăshăb'nə), signer of the covenant. Neh. 10.25.

Hashabniah (hăsh"ăbnī'ə). **1** Father of a repairer of the wall of Jerusalem. Neh. 3.10. **2** Signer of the covenant. Neh. 9.5.

Hashbadana (hăshbăd'ənə), companion of Ezra. Neh. 8.4.

Hashem (hā'shĕm), the same as JASHEN.

Hashima (hăshē'mä), city (1970 pop. 49,156), Gifu prefecture, central Honshu, Japan, on the Kijo River. It is a major center for the production of kimonos.

hashish (hăsh'ēsh, -ĭsh), resin extracted from the flower clusters and top leaves of the hemp plant, *Cannabis sativa*. Hashish, called charas in India, is the most potent grade of cannabis and is obtained from cultivated plants grown in hot, moist climates. MARIJUANA, a cheaper and poorer quality substance, is usually obtained from the cut tops of uncultivated plants and plants growing in colder climates. Like marijuana, hashish is usually smoked, but in a pipe or water pipe; in N Africa it is also eaten. It is an intoxicant, producing exaggerations of sensations, much like mescaline (see PSYCHOTOMIMETIC DRUGS).

Hashmonah (hăshmō'nə), unidentified desert place of encampment on the Exodus. Num. 33.29,30.

Hashub (hā'shəb). **1,2** Repairers of the wall of Jerusalem. Neh. 3.11,23. **3** Signer of the covenant. Neh. 10.23. **4** Merarite. Neh. 11.15. Hasshub: 1 Chron. 9.14.

Hashubah (həsho͞o'bə), one of Zerubbabel's sons. 1 Chron. 3.20.

Hashum (hā'shəm). **1** Family that returned with Zerubbabel, several of whom had foreign wives. Ezra 2.19; 10.33; Neh. 7.22; 10.18. **2** Companion of Ezra at his reading of the Law. Neh. 8.4.

Hashupha (hashyo͞o'fə), the same as HASUPHA.

Hasidim or **Chassidim** (both: hăsē'dĭm) [Heb.,=the pious], term used by the rabbis to describe those Jews who maintained the highest standard of religious observance and moral action. The term has been applied to movements at three distinct times. The first Hasidim, also called the Assideans or Hasideans, were an ancient Jewish sect that developed between 300 B.C. and 175 B.C. They were the most rigid adherents of Judaism in contradistinction to those Jews who were beginning to be affected by Hellenistic influences. The Hasidim led the resistance to the hellenizing campaign of Antiochus IV of Syria, and they figured largely in the early phases of the revolt of the MACCABEES. Their ritual strictness has caused some to see them as forerunners of the Pharisees. Throughout the Talmudic period numerous figures were referred to as Hasidim. During the 12th and 13th cent., however, there arose in Germany a specific group known as the Hasidei Ashkenaz. Influenced by Saadia ben Joseph and with messianic and mystical elements, it held as its central ideology the unity of God, the application of justice in all situations, social and economic equality, and martyrdom at the hands of the crusaders rather than compromise of any kind. The chief ethical work that derived from the group was the *Sefer Hasidim* (tr. *Book of the Pious*, 1973). The third movement to which the term Hasidim is applied is that founded in the 18th cent. by Baal-Shem-Tov and known as HASIDISM. See Saul Lieberman, *Hellenism in Jewish Palestine* (1962); S. G. Kramer, *God and Man in the Sefer Hasidim* (1966); A. L. Lowenkopf, *The Hasidim* (1973). See also bibliography under HASIDISM.

Hasidism (hăs'ĭdĭz"əm), Jewish movement founded in Poland in the 18th cent. by BAAL-SHEM-TOV. Its name derives from HASIDIM. Hasidism arose in reaction to persecutions, which produced several false messiahs (most notably SABBATAI ZEVI), and to the academic formalism of rabbinical Judaism, which had stiffened in the face of these messianic developments. The movement, which stressed the mercy of God and encouraged joyous religious expression through music and dance, spread rapidly, especially among the uneducated masses. Baal-Shem taught that purity of heart is more pleasing to God than learning. He drew his teaching chiefly from Jewish legends and aroused much opposition among the Talmudists, who in 1781 pronounced the movement heretical. Hasidism shows the influence of the Lurianic cabala (see CABALA; LURIA, ISAAC BEN SOLOMON). Although the sect lost its original enthusiasm and the appointed holy men (*Zaddikim*) at times used their power to exploit, Hasidism continued to be a notable force in Jewish life. There are Hasidic communities in the United States living in the manner of the early Hasidim. Hasidic doctrine has influenced modern Christian theology through the interpretative works of Martin Buber. See Gershom Scholem, *Major Trends in Jewish Mysticism* (1946, repr. 1961); Martin Buber, *The Legend of the Baal-Shem* (1955, repr. 1969), *Hasidism and Modern Man* (1958, repr. 1966), and *The Origin and Meaning of Hasidism* (1960); S. H. Dresner, *The Zaddick* (1960); Elie Wiesel, *Souls on Fire* (1972).

Haskins, Charles Homer, 1870–1937, American historian, an authority on medieval history, b. Meadville, Pa. At Harvard (1902–31) he was professor and dean of graduate studies (1908–24); in the latter capacity he greatly influenced contemporary graduate training. He served (1918–19) on the American commission at the Paris Peace Conference. Chairman (1920–26) of the American Council of Learned Societies and president (1922) of the American Historical Association, he was also founder and president (1926–27) of the Medieval Academy of America. His work in medieval history stimulated an entire school of American medievalists. Among his works are *The Normans in European History* (1915, repr. 1959 and 1966), and *Norman Institutions* (1918, repr. 1960); cultural and intellectual works include *The Rise of Universities* (1923), *Studies in the History of Medieval Science* (2d ed., 1927, repr. 1960), and *The Renaissance of the Twelfth Century* (1927, repr. 1957).

Hasköy: see İSTANBUL.

Hasmoneans: see MACCABEES, Jewish family.

Hasrah (hăs'rə), the same as HARHAS.

Hassam, Childe (chīld hăs'əm), 1859–1935, American painter and etcher, b. Boston, studied in Paris. Hassam's sprightly landscapes and interiors show the strong influence of impressionism. Examples of his work are: *Isles of Shoals, Church at Gloucester,* and *July 14th Rue Daunou* (Metropolitan Mus.); *The New York Window; Broad and Wall Streets; Fifth Avenue; Aphrodite;* and *Evening Bells.* He is represented in the Pennsylvania Academy of the Fine Arts, Art Institute of Chicago, Museum of Fine Arts, Boston, Corcoran Gallery, and numerous other museums. See his lithographs with text by Fuller Griffith (1962).

Hassan (häsän'), d. 1894, sultan of Morocco (1873–94). He brought the weak and disorganized country firmly under his control and held in check attempts by European powers at domination. He placed (1877) the instruction of his army under a French military mission.

Hassan II (hä'sän), 1929–, king of Morocco (1961–), Formerly crown prince Moulay Hassan, he ascended the throne on the death (1961) of his father, Muhammad V. A graduate of the Univ. of Bordeaux, Hassan became chief of staff of the Moroccan army in 1957. In 1965 political unrest in Morocco caused him to assume full executive and legislative control, but an abortive coup (July, 1971) led him to yield some of his powers to the Moroccan parliament. As king, Hassan has pursued a neutralist foreign policy, receiving aid from both the West and from Communist nations.

Hasse, Johann Adolph (yō'hän ä'dôlf häs'ə), 1699–1783, German composer; pupil of Alessandro Scarlatti. Hasse was court composer at Dresden (1731–60). He wrote masses, oratorios, sonatas, and symphonies but was known chiefly for his operas, written in a thoroughly Italianized style. They include *Artaserse* (first version, 1730), which was written for his wife, Faustina Bordoni Hasse (1700–1781), one of the most celebrated singers of the period.

Hasselt (hä'səlt), city (1970 pop. 39,663), capital of Limburg prov., NE Belgium, in the Campine region, a port on the Albert Canal. It is a commercial and industrial center and a rail junction. Hasselt was chartered in 1232. The Dutch defeated the Belgians there in 1831.

Hassenaah (hăsēnā'ə), family name of workers on the wall of Jerusalem. Neh. 3.3. Senaah: Ezra 2.35; Neh. 7.38.

Hasshub (hăsh'əb), variant of HASHUB.

Hassi Messaoud (häs'sē mĕs"säo͞od') [Arab.,= blessed well], town, E Algeria. Formerly a water hole in the Sahara desert, Hassi Messaoud rose to prominence with the discovery of oil in 1954. A pipeline c.400 mi (640 km) long carries oil to the port of Bejaïa on the Mediterranean; a second pipeline was built in 1966.

Hasting (hā'stĭng), fl. last half of 9th cent., leader of the VIKINGS, called Hasting the Pirate. He ravaged the coasts of France, Spain, and Italy, went into Morocco, plundered in the south of France, and took a fleet to England late in Alfred's reign.

Hastings, Francis Rawdon-Hastings, 1st marquess of (hā'stĭngz), 1754–1826, British soldier and administrator. He fought with distinction against the colonists in the American Revolution. Created (1783) Baron Rawdon and then succeeding (1793) his father as earl of Moira, he played an active role in the House of Lords and was a partisan of the prince of Wales (later George IV). As governor general of Bengal (1813–22), he successfully waged war on the Gurkhas of Nepal (1814–16), the marauding Pindaris, and the Mahrattas, meanwhile maintaining a vigorous and progressive government. He was rewarded (1817) for his services with the title marquess of Hastings. He was governor of Malta when he died.

Hastings, Serranus Clinton, 1814–93, American judge, b. Jefferson co., N.Y. He was admitted to the Indiana bar in 1836 and moved to Iowa soon afterward. He served in the first Iowa territorial legislature and in 1846 became the first representative of Iowa in Congress. In 1849 he moved to California and became chief justice of the state supreme court while the fusion of common law and Spanish custom was being effected. He established and endowed Hastings College of Law in San Francisco, now part of the Univ. of California.

Hastings, Thomas, 1784–1872, American composer, b. Washington, Conn. Of his hymns, *Rock of Ages* is most famous. He compiled several books of hymns, including *Musica Sacra* (1816) and *Spiritual Songs* (with Lowell Mason, 1831).

Hastings, Thomas, 1860–1929, American architect, b. New York City, grad. École des Beaux-Arts, Paris. He worked in the office of McKim, Mead, and White, New York City, and in 1886 commenced practice in partnership with John M. Carrère. The New York Public Library is their best-known work. Hastings's designs after the death of Carrère (1911) include the Chapel of St. Ambrose in the Cathedral of St. John the Divine and the architectural ensemble of the 59th St. Plaza, all in New York City, and the memorial amphitheater in the National Cemetery at Arlington, Va.

Hastings, Warren, 1732–1818, first governor general of British India. Employed (1750) as a clerk by the East India Company, he soon became manager of a trading post in Bengal. When Calcutta was captured (1756) by Siraj ud-Daula, Hastings was taken prisoner but soon released. After the British recapture (1757) of the city, he was made British resident at Murshidabad. Good service there brought appointment to the Calcutta council (1761), but Hastings returned to England (1764) disgusted with the corruption of the administration in Bengal. In 1769 he went back to India as a member of the Madras council, and in 1772 became governor of Bengal. He immediately embarked on a course of judicial and financial reform, law codification, and the suppression of banditry, taking measures that laid the foundation of direct British rule in India. In 1774, Hastings was appointed governor general of India. This position was created by Lord North's Regulating Act (1773), which also set up a four-member governing council. In the succeeding years Hastings was greatly hampered by opposition in the council, especially from Sir Philip FRANCIS. Another problem he encountered in his new position was the ill-defined relationship with and resulting lack of control over the subordinate provincial governors. The interference of the Bombay government in Mahratta affairs led to a war with the Mahrattas, while the blunders of the Madras government provoked conflict with HAIDAR ALI of Mysore. In both cases Hastings, conscious of the danger of French intervention, dispatched armies from Bengal that saved the British position. Nonetheless he was criticized for interference with the provincial governments. Hastings resigned in 1784 and returned to England, where he was charged with high crimes and misdemeanors by Edmund BURKE and Sir Philip Francis, whom he had wounded in a duel in India. The chief charges against him concerned his extortion of money from the rajah of Benares and the begum of Oudh, his hiring out of British troops to the nawab of Oudh to subdue the Rohillas (a warlike Afghan tribe), and his alleged responsibility for the judicial murder of an Indian merchant, Nandkumar. He was impeached in 1787; but the trial, begun in 1788, ended with acquittal in 1795, despite the bitter prosecution of Burke, Francis, Richard B. Sheridan, and Charles James Fox. Hastings's fortune was spent in the defense, but the East India Company contributed to his later support. He became popular and was made a privy councilor (1814). See biographies by A. M. Davies (1935) and K. G. Feiling (1955, repr. 1967); studies by Penderel Moon (1947, repr. 1962) and P. J. Marshall (1965).

Hastings, county borough (1971 pop. 72,169), East Sussex, SE England. A resort and residential city, it is backed by cliffs and has a 3-mi (4.8-km) marine esplanade, parks, and bathing beaches. The site was occupied in Roman times and probably earlier. It was made famous by the battle of Hastings, which took place at nearby BATTLE on Oct. 14, 1066, between the Normans under William, duke of Normandy (later William I) and the Anglo-Saxons under Harold. This battle, one of the most celebrated in history, was won by William's force—probably smaller but better trained and better rested—after a whole day's fighting. This was the first and most decisive victory of the Norman Conquest of England. Hastings became one of the CINQUE PORTS.

Hastings, city (1971 pop. 29,753), SE North Island, New Zealand. It has extensive food-processing industries.

Hastings. 1 City (1970 pop. 12,195), seat of Dakota co., SE Minn., on the Vermillion River and on bluffs above the Mississippi opposite its confluence with the St. Croix; inc. 1857. It is a farm trade and manufacturing center. **2** City (1970 pop. 23,580), seat of Adams co., S central Nebr.; inc. 1874. Farm equipment is the leading industrial product. Hastings College is located there.

Hasupha (həshyo͞o'fə), family of Nethinim. Ezra 2.43. Hashupha: Neh. 7.46.

hat, headdress developed from the simple close-fitting cap and hood of antiquity. The first known type of hat, which was distinguished as such by having a brim, was the felt *petasus* of the Greeks, which tied under the chin and was worn by travelers. The decorative peaked cap was most popular in the Middle Ages. Later the medieval hood evolved into the 14th cent. turbanlike chaperon with hanging ends, called liripipes; the liripipes originated with the tassels on strings that had been added to the hoods of cloaks. The simple close-fitting coifs, gorgets, wimples, and veils of early medieval women gave way (in the 14th cent.) to netlike headdresses of jeweled gold wire known as cauls and crespins, and later to conical hennins and large decorative butterfly and horn-shaped headdresses with starched veils. In the 16th cent. the beret, of colorful velvet or silk and richly jeweled, feathered, and slashed, was made fashionable by Henry VIII. Women's head coverings progressed from the nunlike gable headdress to the French hood set back on the head to the small heart-shaped Mary Stuart cap. The 17th cent. saw the high-crowned beaver of the Puritan and the wide plumed hat of the cavalier; by 1660 the brim had become so wide that the corners were turned up forming the tricorne. Women during that century generally wore hoods, although the high-standing, wired lace fontanges and commodes were popular; after 1700 the lace cap became fashionable. By the 19th cent. straw was used in making the recently introduced bonnets for women and Panamas for men. At the same time the beaver, or English round hat, of the 17th and 18th cent. gave way to the silk top hat, or stovepipe; caps and soft felt hats came back into favor; and the derby was introduced by William Bowler in England. Women's hats increased in size with their coiffures, culminating in the plumed and flowered "Merry Widows" of the late 19th cent.; with the advent of the closed automobile, hats became smaller. The 1960s saw a considerable decrease in the wearing and manufacture of hats. See HEADDRESS.

Hatach (hā'tăk), Esther's eunuch. Esther 4.5,6,9,10.

Hatay: see ALEXANDRETTA, SANJAK OF.

Hatch, William Henry, 1833-96, U.S. Congressman (1879-95), b. Scott co., Ky. He was admitted (1854) to the bar and moved to Hannibal, Mo. He became prominent in Democratic politics in Missouri and was elected to the U.S. House of Representatives. Hatch devoted himself to agricultural legislation and became chairman of the Committee on Agriculture. He successfully pushed through Congress the act (1884) that created the Bureau of Animal Industry, the Hatch Act (1887), which provided for direct Federal aid for the study of scientific agriculture, and the act (1889) that elevated the Dept. of Agriculture to the status of an executive department in the cabinet.

hatchet: see TOMAHAWK.

Hatfield, new town and civil parish (1971 pop. 25,211), Hatfield Rural District, Hertfordshire, SE England. Hatfield was designated one of the NEW TOWNS in 1948 to alleviate overpopulation in London. The plans for this new town were coordinated with those of nearby WELWYN GARDEN CITY. Aircraft works are the town's most notable industry.

Hathath (hā'tăth), son of Othniel. 1 Chron. 4.13.

Hathaway, Anne: see SHAKESPEARE, WILLIAM.

Hathor (hăth'ôr), in Egyptian religion, celestial goddess of love and festivity. The personification of the sky, she was represented as a star-studded cow or as a woman with the head of a cow. She was identified with many other goddesses of fertility and love, such as Aphrodite. Her name also appears as Athor.

Hatipha (hātī'fə, hăt'ĭ-), family that returned from the Exile. Ezra 2.54; Neh. 7.56.

Hatita (hăt'ĭtə, hātī'-), family that returned from the Exile. Ezra 2.42; Neh. 7.45.

Hatogaya (hätō'gäyä), city (1970 pop. 51,377), Saitama prefecture, E central Honshu, Japan. It is a residential suburb of Tokyo.

Hatoyama, Ichiro (ēchē'rō hätō'yämä), 1883-1959, Japanese statesman. A graduate of the law school of Tokyo Univ., he was first elected to the lower house of the Japanese legislature in 1915. Hatoyama was education minister in the Inukai and Saito cabinets (1931). A leader of the prewar Seiyukai party, he organized the conservative postwar Liberal party, and became its first president. In 1954, Hatoyama led his faction out of the party, absorbed the Progressive party, and formed the Democratic party. By this move, he deposed Shigeru YOSHIDA, and was himself prime minister (1954-56) until he lost support of the new conservative Liberal-Democratic party.

Hatshepsut (hätshĕp'so͞ot), d. 1468 B.C., queen of ancient Egypt, of the XVIII dynasty; daughter of THUTMOSE I. She managed to rule Egypt by relegating her husband, Thutmose II (see under THUTMOSE), to the background. After his death, she continued in power as regent to his son, Thutmose III (see under THUTMOSE). Her reign (1486-1468) was peaceful, and she developed the resources of Egypt, reviving the mining at Sinai. She built the famous temple at Deir el Bahari in W Thebes.

Hatta, Mohammad (hăt'ə), 1902-, Indonesian political leader. He was born on Sumatra into an aristocratic family. Interested in economics, he went to the Netherlands to study. There he joined the Indonesian independence movement and edited the journal *Indonesia Merdeka*. He was arrested in 1927 by the Dutch, tried, but released. Hatta returned to Sumatra in 1932. He became chairman of the Pendikan Nasional Indonesia, a nationalist propaganda organization. For his activities, Hatta was again arrested by the Dutch and exiled in 1935. He was freed by the Japanese early in 1942 when they occupied Indonesia. Hatta and Sukarno, another nationalist leader, decided to cooperate with the Japanese to further the purpose of Indonesian independence. In Aug., 1945, Hatta and Sukarno joined in proclaiming the birth of the independent Republic of Indonesia. Sukarno became president and Hatta was vice president. The Dutch resisted the nationalists, and Hatta became premier and defense minister in 1948 to direct the fight against the Dutch troops. Again imprisoned by the Dutch in 1949, Hatta was released to head a delegation to the Hague and there successfully negotiated a settlement. He was (1949-50) again prime minister before serving (1950-56) as vice president of the republic; he resigned 1956 after a dispute with Sukarno. Hatta withdrew from political life and devoted himself primarily to the cooperative movement in Indonesia. See his *Portrait of a Patriot: Selected Writings* (1973).

Hatteras, Cape (hăt'ərəs), promontory on Hatteras Island, a low, sandy, barrier bar between the Atlantic Ocean and Pamlico Sound, E N.C. Called the Graveyard of the Atlantic, the cape experiences frequent storms that drive ships landward. **Cape Hatteras National Seashore** (28,500 acres/11,534 hectares; est. 1937), a vast expanse of sand and water, is made up of Hatteras, Bodie, and Ocracoke islands and comprises one of the largest stretches of undeveloped seashore on the U.S. Atlantic coast. Cape Hatteras Lighthouse (built 1870) is the only lighthouse owned by the National Park Service.

Hattiesburg, city (1970 pop. 38,277), seat of Forrest co., SE Miss., on the Leaf River; inc. 1884. It is the rail, trade, and industrial center of a farm and timber area. Once a great lumbering city, it now has many diverse industries. Hattiesburg is the seat of the Univ. of Southern Mississippi and of William Carey College. Camp Shelby, a U.S. army and national guard training station, is in nearby De Soto National Forest. A state park is also in the area.

Hattil (hăt'ĭl), family that returned from the Exile. Ezra 2.57; Neh. 7.59.

Hatton, Sir Christopher, 1540-91, English courtier. He became a favorite of Queen Elizabeth I, from whom he received offices, honors, and lands. Knighted in 1578, he acted as Elizabeth's spokesman in the House of Commons and, although not a lawyer, was lord chancellor from 1587 until his death. He was a friend and patron of Edmund Spenser. Hatton himself wrote the fourth act of *Tancred and Gismund* (first pub. 1591), a tragedy by Robert Wilmot, Henry Noel, Hatton, and others. Ely Place in Holborn, formerly in the possession of the bishops of Ely, was granted to him, and the name of the garden there was changed to Hatton Garden. See biography by E. S. Brooks (1946).

Hattusas: see BOĞAZKÖY; HITTITES.

Hattush (hăt'əsh). **1,2** Descendants of David. 1 Chron. 3.22; Ezra 8.2. **3** Signer of the covenant. Neh. 10.4; 12.2. **4** Worker on the wall of Jerusalem. Neh. 3.10.

Hauer, Josef Matthias (yō'zĕf mätēäs hou'ər), 1883-1959, Austrian music theorist and composer. Primarily self-taught, Hauer devised a method of atonal composition that used the 12 tones of the scale divided into 44 melodic patterns, or "tropes." He also developed a new system of musical notation for 12-tone music. Hauer, a prolific composer, wrote music in all the major forms.

Haugesund (hou'gəso͞on), city (1970 pop. 27,219), Rogaland co., S Norway, a port on the North Sea. It has large fisheries and industries producing processed fish and aluminum. Nearby are numerous Viking monuments, including the grave of Harold I (9th cent.).

Haugwitz, Christian August Heinrich, Graf von (hĭn'rĭkh gräf fən houk'vĭts), 1752-1832, Prussian foreign minister (1802-4, 1805-6). In 1805, after the French victory at Austerlitz, Haugwitz tried to appease Napoleon I by concluding treaties with France that involved humiliating Prussian subservience to French policy and open Franco-Prussian alliance. Dissatisfaction with the terms and continued French mobilization on Prussia's frontiers finally led in Oct., 1806, to Prussia's declaration of war against France and subsequent defeat at Jena. Haugwitz, dismissed from office, retired to Italy, where he died.

Hauptmann, Bruno Richard, 1899-1936, convicted kidnapper and murderer, b. Germany. The infant son of Charles and Anne Morrow LINDBERGH was abducted (March 1, 1932) at Hopewell, N.J., and a ransom of $50,000 for his release was paid through the intercession of Dr. John F. Condon. The child's battered body was found (May 12, 1932) near Hopewell, and on Sept. 19, 1934, Hauptmann, a carpenter, was found with part of the ransom. In a sensational trial at Flemington, N.J., he was convicted of murder. Hauptmann maintained his innocence to the last, and although temporarily reprieved, he was electrocuted on April 3, 1936. The case precipitated (1934) congressional action against KIDNAPPING. See S. B. Whipple, *The Trial of Bruno Richard Hauptmann* (1937); George Waller, *Kidnap* (1961).

Hauptmann, Gerhart (gĕr'härt houpt'män), 1862-1946, German dramatist, novelist, and poet. His play *Before Dawn* (1889, tr. 1909) inaugurated the naturalistic movement in the German theater and won overnight fame. His other realistic plays include the famous tragedy of the working class, *The Weavers* (1892, tr. 1899), the comedy *The Beaver Coat* (1893, tr. 1905), and the tragedies *Drayman Henschel* (1899, tr. 1913) and *Rose Bernd* (1903, tr. 1913). Responsive to changing moods in literature, Hauptmann reflected the trend away from naturalism with the dream play *Hannele* (1893, tr. 1894) and the popular romantic play *The Sunken Bell* (1897, tr. 1898). His prose works include the novel of a modern mystic, *The Fool in Christ, Emanuel Quint* (1910, tr. 1911) and *The Heretic of Soana* (1918, tr. 1923). *Till Eulenspiegel* (1928) is an epic of postwar Germany. A leading figure in German literature for three generations, Hauptmann received many honors, notably the 1912 Nobel Prize in Literature. See study by H. F. Garten (1954).

Hauraki Gulf (hourä'kē, -rä'kē), arm of the Pacific Ocean, N North Island, New Zealand, forming the entrance to Auckland harbor. Numerous islands are found in the gulf; Great Barrier Island acts as a breakwater.

Hauran: see HAWRAN, Syria.

Hausa or **Haussa** (both: hou'sə, -sä), black African ethnic group, numbering about 6,800,000, chiefly in N Nigeria and S Niger. The Hausa are almost exclusively Muslim and practice agriculture. Their widespread trading activities have contributed to making their language a lingua franca in much of W Africa. In earlier times the Hausa were organized in the **Hausa States.** Long the vassals of BORNU, the states were conquered by the Songhay in 1513 and by the Fulani in the early 19th cent. In colonial Nigeria the traditional Hausa-Fulani social and political structure was largely maintained under the British policy of indirect rule. The Hausa are a major force in the politics of independent Nigeria. See Ibrahim Madauci, *Hausa Customs* (1968); Polly Hill, *Rural Hausa* (1972).

Hausa language, member of the Chad group of languages frequently assigned to the Hamitic subfamily of the Hamito-Semitic family of languages. See HAMITO-SEMITIC LANGUAGES.

Hauser, Kaspar (käs'pär hou'zər), 1812?–1833, mysterious German foundling. He appeared in Nuremberg in 1828 in a state of semi-idiocy, producing dubious documents and giving an incoherent account of his past, which, he said, he had spent in a dark prison hole. He awakened immediate interest and sympathy. Subsequently the earl of Stanhope, the British historian, became interested in him and assumed responsibility for his education. The boy's death from a knife wound was regarded as a political assassination by those who believed him—without any serious grounds—to be the son of the grand duke of Baden by his first wife. Others believe that the wound was self-inflicted and that Hauser was a psychopath. Much has been written on him; he is the subject of Jakob Wassermann's novel *Caspar Hauser* (tr. 1928) and is used as the main character in *Kaspar*, a play by Peter Handke (tr. 1970). See Andrew Lang, *Historical Mysteries* (1904); J. A. L. Singh, *Wolf Children and Feral Man* (1942, repr. 1966).

Haushofer, Karl (kärl hous'hōfər), 1869–1946, German geographer, theorist of Nazi GEOPOLITICS. After a successful military career he became (1921) professor of geography at Munich. Among his students was Rudolf Hess, who introduced Haushofer to Hitler. Haushofer's influence on Hitler is evident in *Mein Kampf*, and he remained one of Hitler's closest advisers on foreign affairs. In 1946, Haushofer and his wife committed suicide by taking poison. Haushofer's writings were much influenced by those of Sir Halford John Mackinder. They include *Geopolitik des Pazifischen Ozeans* (1925), *Bausteine zur Geopolitik* (1928), and *Weltpolitik von heute* (1934). Haushofer also edited the periodical *Zeitschrift für Geopolitik.* See Andreas Dorpalen, *The World of General Haushofer* (1942, repr. 1966); E. A. Walsh, *Total Power* (1948).

Haussmann, Georges Eugène, Baron (zhôrzh özhěn' bärôN' ōsmän'), 1809–91, French civic official and city planner. Distinguished for his bold alterations in the layout of Paris under Napoleon III, he is largely responsible for the city's present appearance. To create adequate traffic circulation, old streets were widened and new ones cut, while the great railway stations were placed in a circle outside the old city and provided with broad approaches. For the enhancement of monuments, open spaces and vistas were contrived, including the Place de l'Opéra, the Étoile, and the Place de la Nation, which became focusing points for radiating avenues. The Bois de Boulogne was laid out, as well as a number of smaller parks. The Boulevard Haussmann in Paris commemorates his name. See Howard Saalman, *Haussman: Paris Transformed* (1971).

hautboy: see OBOE.

Haute-Garonne (ōt-gärôn'), department (1968 pop. 690,712), S France, in Languedoc, bordering Spain. TOULOUSE is the capital.

Haute-Loire (ōt-lwär), department (1968 pop. 208,337), S central France, largely in the Massif Central. LE PUY is the capital.

Haute-Marne (ōt-märn), department (1968 pop. 214,336), NE France, largely in Champagne. CHAUMONT is the capital.

Hautes-Alpes (ōt-zälp), department (1968 pop. 91,790), SE France, mainly in Dauphiné, bordering on Italy. GAP is the capital.

Haute-Saône (ōt-sōn), department (1968 pop. 214,176), E France, in Franche-Comté. It is mainly agricultural. VESOUL is the capital.

Haute-Savoie (ōt-sävwä') department (1968 pop. 378,550), E France, in the northern part of the old duchy of SAVOY. ANNECY is the capital.

Hautes-Pyrénées (ōt-pērānā'), department (1968 pop. 225,730), SW France, in parts of Bigorre, Gascony, and the Basque Provinces. TARBES is the capital.

Haute-Vienne (ōt-vyěn), department (1968 pop. 341,589), central France, in the Massif Central. LIMOGES is the capital.

Haute-Volta: see UPPER VOLTA.

Haut-Rhin (ō-răN), department (1968 pop. 585,018), E France, in lower ALSACE. Its capital is COLMAR.

Hauts-de-Seine (ōt-də-sěn), department (1968 pop. 1,461,619), N central France, W of Paris. NANTERRE is the capital.

Haut-Zaïre (ōt-zäēr'), formerly **Orientale** (ôrēäNtäl'), region (1970 pop. 3,356,419), c.204,000 sq mi (528,360 sq km), N Zaïre. Kisangani is the capital. The region borders the Central African Republic and the Sudan on the north and Uganda on the east. Gold is mined, and cotton, coffee, and palm oil are produced. The province was the political stronghold of Patrice Lumumba. In 1960, Lumumba's followers, led by Antoine Gizenga and centered at Kisangani (then Stanleyville), attempted to establish a government to rival the central government at Kinshasa (then Leopoldville). The Stanleyville regime controlled most of the region until the central government reestablished control in 1962. There were further rebellions in 1964, 1966, and 1967.

Haüy, René Just, Abbé (rənā' zhüst äbā' äüē'), 1743–1822, French mineralogist, an authority on crystals. He discovered the geometric law of crystallization and wrote many books and papers on crystallography. He was professor at the Museum of Natural History, Paris, from 1802.

Havana (həvăn'ə), Span. *La Habana* (lä ävä'nä), city (1970 pop. 1,130,634), capital of Cuba and of La Habana prov., W Cuba; largest city and chief port of the West Indies and one of the oldest cities in the Americas. An important hub of air and maritime transportation, it is the focal point of Cuba's commerce, exporting sugar, tobacco, and fruits and importing mainly foodstuffs, cotton, and machinery and technical equipment. Industries include oil refineries, assembly plants, rum distilleries, sugar refineries, a steel mill, and factories making the famous Havana cigars. Good hotels and entertainment made the city a popular winter resort, but tourism from the United States ended after Fidel Castro took power in Cuba in 1959. Havana's hot, humid climate is moderated by sea winds. Severe hurricanes are frequent. Founded c.1515, probably by the Spanish explorer Diego de Velázquez, Havana possesses one of the best natural harbors in the Caribbean and has long been strategically and commercially important. The original settlement, called San Cristóbal de la Habana, was moved from Cuba's southern coast to the site of present-day Havana in 1519. Spanish treasure galleons assembled in Havana's harbor for their return voyage to Spain, and the city tempted many English, French, and Dutch buccaneers. It became the capital of Cuba in the late 16th cent. In 1762, during the French and Indian Wars, Havana fell to Anglo-American forces, but the following year it was returned to Spain in exchange for the Floridas. By the early 19th cent. the city ranked as one of the wealthiest and busiest commercial centers in the Western Hemisphere. The blowing up of the U.S. battleship *Maine* in Havana harbor in Feb., 1898, was the immediate cause of the Spanish-American War. U.S. troops occupying Havana in the wake of their victory there improved sanitary conditions and eliminated yellow fever from the city. Havana is still noted for its cleanliness. In the old city, dominated by MORRO CASTLE and other fortresses, are narrow streets, numerous churches, and fine examples of colonial architecture. The modern section of the city has wide boulevards, impressive public buildings (notably the lavishly decorated capitol), and magnificent residences. Havana Univ. was founded in 1721. The city has many cultural facilities.

Havant and Waterloo (hă'vănt), urban district (1971 pop. 108,999), Hampshire, S England. Manufactures include pharmaceuticals, toys, kitchen equipment, electronic components, and automobiles. The old town of Havant was known for its parchment.

Havel (hä'fəl), river, c.215 mi (350 km) long, rising in the lake region of Mecklenburg, N East Germany. It flows generally S through West Berlin to Potsdam where it turns west. At Brandenburg it turns northwest and enters the Elbe River near Havelberg. It is navigable for most of its length. The Spree River, its chief tributary, joins it at Spandau. The Havel is linked with the Oder River by the Oder-Spree Canal. During the Soviet blockade of Berlin (1948) the Havel was used as a runway for amphibian aircraft.

Havelock, Sir Henry (hăv'lŏk), 1795–1857, British general. Entering the army in 1815, he was sent (1823) to India, where he served in the first Burma War (1824–26), the first Afghan War (1839), and the Sikh Wars (1843–49). During the Indian Mutiny, Havelock recaptured (July, 1857) Cawnpore (KANPUR) from the rebels, but he was too late to save the British population from massacre. In Sept., 1857, he relieved Lucknow from siege, but he and his forces were then caught in the renewed siege. He died a few days after the relief of the city in November. See J. C. Pollock, *Way to Glory* (1957).

Havelok the Dane, English 13th-century metrical romance. It concerns a prince brought up as a scullion, who, after discovering his true identity, wins the kingdoms of Denmark and England. The poem's emphasis on the simple virtues suggests that it was written for a bourgeois rather than an aristocratic audience. The hero has been identified with the 10th-century king, Olaf Cuaran, who ruled at different times in Northumberland and in Dublin.

Havemeyer, Henry Osborne (hăv'əmī"yər), 1847–1907, American industrialist, b. New York City. He inherited large family interests in sugar refining and, with his brother Theodore, expanded them. At his death his American Sugar Refining Company controlled about half the sugar refining of the country. A large part of his notable art collection was bequeathed in 1929 by his widow to the Metropolitan Museum of Art.

Haverfield, Francis John (hăv'ərfēld), 1860–1919, English historian and archaeologist. Educated at Oxford, he also worked under Theodor Mommsen. In 1907 he became Camden professor of ancient history at Oxford. He was the first scientific historian of Roman Britain. His works include *The Romanization of Roman Britain* (1905), *Ancient Town Planning* (1913), and *The Roman Occupation of Britain* (1924), many monographs, and the authoritative chapters he contributed to the *Victoria History of the Counties of England.*

Haverford College, at Haverford, Pa.; Quaker; for men; opened 1833, called a school until 1856. Its collection of Quaker literature and history is notable.

Haverfordwest, municipal borough (1971 pop. 9,101), county town of Pembrokeshire, SW Wales, on the Western Cleddau River. It is a market town. There is a notable 13th-century church there. In 1974, Haverfordwest became part of the new nonmetropolitan county of Dyfed.

Haverhill (hā'vərĭl), city (1970 pop. 46,120), Essex co., NE Mass., on the Merrimack River; inc. as a town 1641, as a city 1870. Formerly one of the nation's leading shoe producers, Haverhill now processes leather and makes leather products and electronic components. Points of interest there are John Greenleaf Whittier's birthplace (the house dates from c.1688) and the home of Hannah Dustin. The Haverhill branch of Northeastern Univ. and two junior colleges are also in the city.

Havering, borough (1971 pop. 246,778), of Greater London, SE England. Havering was created in 1965 by the merger of the municipal borough of Romford and the urban district of Hornchurch. The borough is largely residential but plastics, chemicals, clothing, beer, and other items are manufactured there. A market has been held in Romford since 1247. Until 1892, Romford was the capital of Havering-atte-Bower, a group of parishes united since the time of Edward the Confessor.

Havilah (hăv'ĭlə, həvĭl'ə). **1,2** Descendants of Noah. Gen. 10.7, 29; 1 Chron. 1.9,23. **3** Region, probably to be identified with some part of N or NE Arabia. Gen. 2.11; 25.18; 1 Sam. 15.7.

Haviland, John, 1792–1852, American architect, b. Philadelphia. Haviland was noted as a pioneer in prison architecture. His design for the Pennsylvania Eastern State Penitentiary was imitated internationally and heralded prison reform in the 19th cent. Haviland's prisons were characterized by light, airy cells occupied by a single inmate; his designs were soon outmoded by the rise of prison populations.

Havířov (hä'vĕrzhôf), town (1970 pop. 81,317), E Czechoslovakia, in Moravia. An important manufacturing and mining town, Havířov was founded in the 1950s and belongs to the Ostrava-Karviná industrial complex. It contains large blocks of workers' housing.

Havoth-jair (hā'vŏth-jā'ər), group of villages in Bashan and Gilead, E of the Jordan. They were named for Jair son of Manasseh or for Jair the judge. Num. 32.41; Judges 10.4. Bashan-havoth-jair: Deut. 3.14. The "towns of Jair" also are mentioned in Joshua 13.30, 1 Kings 4.13, and 1 Chron. 2.23.

Havre (hăv′ər), city (1970 pop. 10,558), seat of Hill co., N Mont., on the Milk River; inc. 1892. Founded in 1887 with the coming of the railroad, it is today an important railroad point with large diesel shops. It is also the center of a cattle, sheep, and wheat area served by the Milk River project. Northern Montana College is there.

Havre, Le (lə ä′vrə), city (1968 pop. 200,940), Seine-Maritime dept., N France, in Normandy, at the mouth of the Seine River on the English Channel. It was founded in 1517 as Le Havre-de-Grâce by Francis I. Le Havre became a major seaport in the 19th cent. Crude oil is the largest import; refined oil and agricultural products lead the exports. Among the city's industries are oil refining and the manufacture of automobiles, cement, synthetic rubber, and fertilizers. During World War II the British bombed the city to prevent its use by the Germans for an invasion of England.

haw, common name for several plants, e.g., the HAWTHORN and the black haw (see HONEYSUCKLE).

Hawaii (həwī′ē, hävä′ē), state (1970 pop. 769,913), 6,450 sq mi (16,706 sq km), central Pacific, admitted to the Union in 1959 as the 50th state. Hawaii consists of a group of eight major islands and numerous islets in the Pacific Ocean, c.2,100 mi (3,380 km) SW of San Francisco. The capital is HONOLULU on OAHU. Hawaii island is the largest and geologically the youngest of the group, and Oahu is the most populous and economically important. The other principal islands are KAHOOLAWE, KAUAI, LANAI, MAUI, MOLOKAI, and NIIHAU. The PALMYRA atoll and Kingman Reef, which were within the boundaries of Hawaii when it was a U.S. territory, were excluded when statehood was achieved. The Hawaiian islands are of volcanic origin and are edged with coral reefs. Generally fertile with a mild climate, they are sometimes called "the paradise of the Pacific" because of their spectacular beauty: abundant sunshine; acres of green plants and gaily colored flowers; coral beaches with rolling white surf and fringed with palms; and, rising with sober majesty to solitary heights, cloud-covered volcanic peaks. Some of the world's largest active and inactive volcanoes are found on Hawaii and Maui; eruptions of the active volcanoes have provided spectacular displays but their lava flows have occasionally caused great property damage. Mauna Kea and Mauna Loa are volcanic mountains on Hawaii island; Haleakala volcano is on Maui in Haleakala National Park. Vegetation is generally luxuriant throughout the islands, with giant fern forests in Hawaii Volcanoes National Park. Kahoolawe, however, is arid, and Niihau and Molokai have very dry seasons. Although many species of birds and domestic animals have been introduced on the islands, there are few wild animals other than boars and goats, and there are no snakes. The coastal waters abound with fish. Sugarcane and pineapples, grown chiefly on large company-owned plantations, are the major agricultural products and the basis of the islands' principal industry, food processing. Hawaii is one of the world's leading producers of canned pineapple. Other products include coffee, cattle, calves, and dairy products. Commercial fishing is also carried on; tuna is the principal species caught. U.S. military defense installations at PEARL HARBOR and elsewhere in the state are extremely important to Hawaii's economy. Tourism is another leading source of income. The first known settlers of the Hawaiian islands were Polynesian voyagers (the date of final migration is believed to be c.750). The islands were discovered in 1778 by the English explorer Capt. James Cook, who named them the Sandwich Islands for the English Earl of Sandwich. At the time of Cook's discovery, the islands were under the rule of warring native kings. In 1810, Kamehameha I became the sole sovereign of all the islands, and, in the peace that followed, agriculture and commerce were promoted. As a result of Kamehameha's hospitality, American traders were able to exploit the islands' sandalwood, which was much valued in China at the time. Trade with China reached its height during this period. However, the period of Kamehameha's rule was also one of decline. Europeans and Americans brought with them devastating infectious diseases, and over the years the native population was greatly reduced. The adoption of Western ways—trading for profit, using firearms, and drinking liquor—contributed to the decline of native cultural tradition. This period also marked the breakdown of the traditional Hawaiian religion, with its belief in idols and human sacrifice. The period was followed by years of religious unrest. When missionaries arrived in 1820 they found a less idyllic Hawaii than the one Captain Cook had discovered. Kamehameha III, who ruled from 1825 until his death in 1854, relied on the missionaries for advice and allowed them to preach Christianity. The missionaries established schools, developed the Hawaiian alphabet, and used it for translating the Bible into Hawaiian. In 1839, Kamehameha III issued a guarantee of religious freedom, and the following year a constitutional monarchy was established. From 1842 to 1854 an American, G. P. Judd, held the post of prime minister, and under his influence many reforms were carried out. Although Hawaiian independence was recognized by the United States in 1842, French and British interests in the islands continued to be of concern to the Americans. In the following decades, however, commercial ties between Hawaii and the United States were in ascendancy. An American trade treaty had been made in 1842, and the supplying of American whaling ships began to replace the waning sandalwood trade. In 1848 the islands' feudal land system was abolished, making private ownership possible and thereby encouraging capital investment in the land. By the time the whaling industry collapsed in the 1860s, the sugar industry, which had been introduced in the 1830s, was well-established. Hawaiian sugar gained a favored position in U.S. markets under a reciprocity treaty made with the United States in 1875. The treaty was renewed in 1884, but not ratified. Ratification came in 1887 when an amendment was added giving the United States exclusive right to establish a naval base at Pearl Harbor. The amount of sugar exported to the United States increased sharply, and thousands of Oriental immigrants were brought into Hawaii to work on large sugar plantations. After the sugar boom, American businessmen invested in the Hawaiian sugar industry. Along with the Hawaiians in the industry, they came to exert powerful influence over the islands' economy and government, a dominance that was to last until World War II. Toward the end of the 19th cent. agitation for constitutional reform in Hawaii led to the overthrow of the monarchy (1893). The reformers, many of them Americans in Hawaii, deposed Queen Liliuokalani, who had ruled since 1891. A provisional government was established and John L. Stevens, the U.S. Minister to Hawaii, proclaimed the country a U.S. protectorate. The provisional government sought U.S. annexation of the islands, but President Grover Cleveland refused after a special investigation revealed that most Hawaiians had not supported the revolution and that Hawaiians and Americans in the sugar industry had played a leading role in overthrowing the monarchy. The United States tried to bring about the restoration of Queen Liliuokalani, but the provisional government on the islands refused to give up power and instead established (1894) a republic with Sanford B. Dole as president. Cleveland's successor, President William McKinley, favored annexation, which was finally accomplished in 1898. In 1900 the islands were made a territory, with Dole as governor. In this period Hawaii's pineapple industry expanded as pineapples (cultivated since the early 19th cent.) were first grown for canning purposes. In 1937 statehood for Hawaii was proposed and refused by the U.S. Congress—the territory's mixed population and distance from the U.S. mainland being among the obstacles. On Dec. 7, 1941, Japanese aircraft made a surprise attack on Pearl Harbor, plunging the United States into World War II. During the war the Hawaiian islands were the chief Pacific base for U.S. forces and were under martial law (Dec. 7, 1941–March, 1943). The post-war years ushered in important economic and social developments. There was a dramatic expansion of labor unionism, marked by major strikes in 1946, 1949, and 1958. The International Longshoremen's and Warehousemen's Union organized the waterfront, sugar, and pineapple workers. The tourist trade, which had grown to major proportions in the 1930s as a result of skillful advertising and the construction of luxury hotels, expanded further with post-war advances in air travel and with further investment and development. The building boom that accompanied the rise in tourism brought construction of new hotels and housing developments, and the establishment of new industries stimulated further economic growth. After having sought statehood for many decades, Hawaii was finally admitted to the Union on Aug. 21, 1959. More ethnic and cultural groups are represented in Hawaii than in any other state, although whites continue to control the state: some 40 individuals own about 97% of the land. Chinese laborers, who came to work in the sugar industry, were the first of the large groups of immigrants to arrive (starting in 1852), and Filipinos and Koreans were the last (after 1900). Other immigrant groups—including Portuguese, Germans, Japanese, and Puerto Ricans—came in the latter part of the 19th cent. Japanese now represent roughly a third of the population. Intermarriage with other races has brought a further decrease in the number of pureblooded Hawaiians who make up only a very small percentage of the population. In the 1960s tourism continued to grow, creating problems of overcrowding and damage to the islands' natural beauty. The state legislature attempted to deal with these problems through environmental legislation. In 1969 construction of a new state capitol was completed. Hawaii's constitution was drafted in 1950 and became effective in 1959 upon attainment of statehood. A governor elected every four years heads the executive. The legislature has a senate with 25 members elected for four-year terms and a house of representatives with 51 members elected for two-year terms. The state elects two Representatives and two Senators to the U.S. Congress and has four electoral votes. John A. Burns, a Democrat, was elected governor in 1962 and reelected in 1966 and 1970. In 1974, George R. Ariyoshi, a Democrat, was elected governor. The Univ. of Hawaii is located at Honolulu. In 1961 the Center for Cultural and Technical Interchange between East and West was dedicated at the university and drew graduate students and technical trainees from Asia and the Pacific area. See James Michener, *Hawaii* (1959); L. H. Fuchs, *Hawaii Pono: A Social History* (1961); R. S. Kuykendall, *The Hawaiian Kingdom* (3 vol., 1938, 1953, 1957); A. G. Day, *Hawaii and Its People* (rev. ed., 1968); Gavan Daws, *Shoal of Time* (1968); E. G.

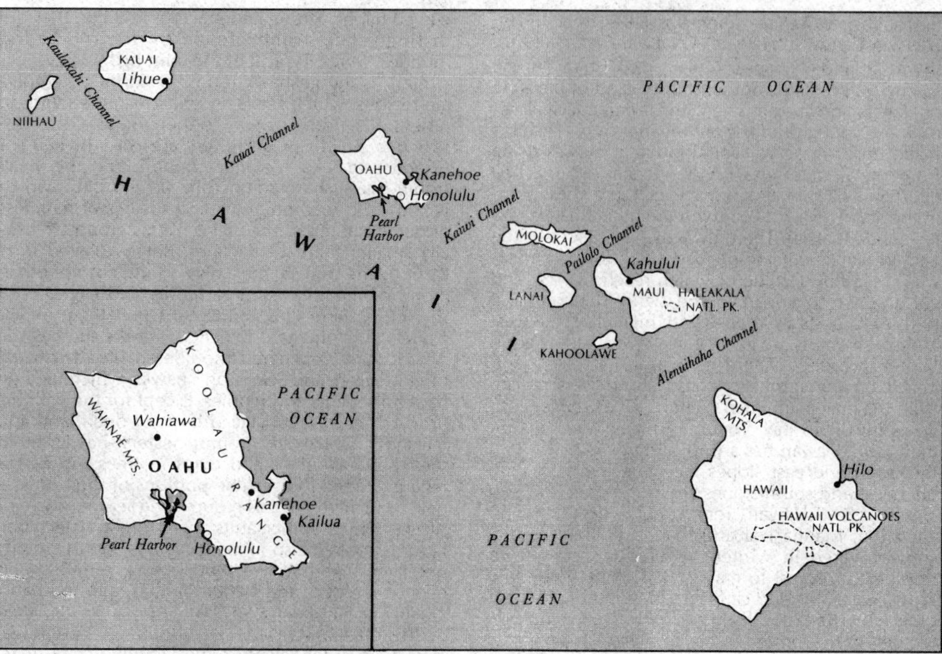

Burroughs, *Hawaiian Americans* (1947, repr. 1970); Sherwin Carlquist, *Hawaii: A Natural History* (1970).

Hawaii, island (1970 pop. 63,468), 4,037 sq mi (10,456 sq km), largest and southernmost island of the state of Hawaii and coextensive with Hawaii co. Geologically the youngest of the Hawaiian group, Hawaii is made up of three volcanic mountain masses rising from the floor of the Pacific Ocean—Mauna Kea (13,796 ft/4,205 m above sea level, the highest point in the state); Mauna Loa (with the huge Kilauea crater); and Hualalai. The only active volcanoes in the United States, outside of Alaska, are found on Hawaii. Lava flows, some of which reach the sea, and volcanic ash cover parts of the island. The north and northeast coasts are rugged with high cliffs; the west and south coasts are generally low, with a few good bathing beaches. There is an unusual black-sand beach on the southeast coast. Short rivers radiate from the major summits; Wailuku River, the longest, flows into Hilo Bay. There are many waterfalls on the island. Hawaii has a tropical-rainy climate, with the north and east slopes receiving the most rain. The west and south slopes are much drier; the Kau Desert is in S Hawaii. Temperatures decrease with elevation; Mauna Loa and Mauna Kea are usually snow-covered in winter. Vegetation varies from tropical rain forest to grasslands to barren volcanic areas. Sugarcane and cattle are the island's principal products. The KONA district of W Hawaii is the coffee belt of the United States. It is also known for its health resorts and for its offshore deep-sea fishing. Hilo, on the east coast, is the island's largest city and chief port and is the county seat. A highway, linking the coastal towns, encircles the island. At Kealakekua Bay there is a monument to Capt. James Cook, the English explorer. Hawaii Volcanoes National Park and City of Refuge National Historical Park are on Hawaii. All over the island *heiaus* (ancient temples) may be found.

Hawaii, University of, mainly at Honolulu; land-grant and state supported; coeducational; chartered 1907, opened 1908 as the College of Agricultural and Mechanic Arts. It became the College of Hawaii in 1911 and assumed its present name in 1920. In 1960 the Federal government created the Center for Cultural and Technical Interchange between East and West on the Manoa campus.

Hawaii Volcanoes National Park, 229,616 acres (92,926 hectares), on Hawaii island, Hawaii; est. 1916. The park contains two of the most active volcanoes in the world—KILAUEA with its fire pit, called Halemaumau, and MAUNA LOA with the active Mokuaweoweo crater on its summit. The vegetation around Kilauea is varied—a few miles west of the arid Kau Desert is a lush fern jungle. The Haleakala section was made a separate park in 1961 (see HALEAKALA NATIONAL PARK).

Hawarden (hôr'dən, här'-), rural district (1971 pop. 42,467), Flintshire, NE Wales. There are ruins of a 13th-century castle on the grounds of Hawarden Castle (built 1752), which was the home of W. E. Gladstone until his death there in 1898. Gladstone established St. Deiniol's Hostel and library for theological students. The Early English church has a window memorial to Gladstone by Burne-Jones. In 1974, Hawarden became part of the new nonmetropolitan county of Clwyd.

Hawes, Stephen, c.1475–1530, English poet. His best-known works, the two allegories *Example of Virtue* (1504?) and *Pastime of Pleasure* (1505?), use typically medieval conventions, but they differ from medieval allegory in their humanist emphasis on learning, fame, and the perfection of life in this world.

Haw-Haw, Lord: see JOYCE, WILLIAM.

Hawick (hô'ĭk), burgh (1971 pop. 16,286), Roxburghshire, S Scotland, on the Teviot River. Hawick is famous for its fine woolens and tweeds. Besides the manufacture of knitwear, Hawick's industries include dye works and light engineering plants. There is also an important stock market. The house of the barons of Drumlanrig was the only building not burned by the English during a border raid in 1570. St. Mary's Church (1763) stands on the site of a 7th-century Celtic church. Nearby Branxholm Tower figures in Scott's *Lay of the Last Minstrel* as Branksome Hall. In 1975, Hawick became part of the Borders region.

hawk, name generally applied to the smaller members of the Accipitridae, a heterogeneous family of diurnal birds of prey such as the EAGLE, the KITE, the Old World VULTURE, and the SECRETARY BIRD. Hawks belong to the same order as the FALCON, the New World vulture, and the OSPREY. Hawks have keen sight, sharply hooked bills, and powerful feet with curved talons. Strong and graceful in flight, they are distinguished from falcons by their broader, rounded wings. Typical of the hunting hawks, or accipiters, is the goshawk found in northern temperate regions, which feeds on small mammals and on other birds, riding its prey to the ground. Other destructive American accipiters are the chicken, or Cooper's, hawk, *Accipiter cooperi,* and the small (robin-sized) sharp-shinned hawk, *A. fuscus,* which is known to feed on at least 50 species of harmless or beneficial birds. The males of this group are usually smaller than the females. Buteos (called buzzards by the English) are a diverse and cosmopolitan group of medium to large hawks and eagles with shorter legs and tails and larger wings than the accipiters. They include beneficial hawks such as the American red-tailed, red-shouldered, broad-winged, rough-legged, and Swainson's hawks, which feed on harmful rodents and reptiles. Except for the harriers, or marsh hawks (owl-faced birds of open land and marshes), which are ground nesters, hawks build their nests of sticks and twigs in trees. All hawks regurgitate the indigestible portions of their prey as pellets. Included in this group is the serpent eagle of Africa, which somersaults in its flight. The name hawk is applied also to many falcons and the totally unrelated nighthawk (a GOATSUCKER), certain members of the GULL and JAEGER families, and the hawk swallow, a European SWIFT. True hawks are classified in the phylum CHORDATA, subphylum Vertebrata, class Aves, order Falconiformes, family Accipitridae.

Hawke of Towton, Edward Hawke, 1st Baron (tou'tən), 1705–81, British admiral. He entered the navy in 1720 and first saw fighting as commander of a ship in the battle of Toulon (1744). He was promoted (1747) to rear admiral and in the same year inflicted a major defeat on a French squadron off La Rochelle. In the Seven Years War, Hawke relieved (1756) Admiral John Byng as commander in the Mediterranean and was appointed an admiral. In Nov., 1759, after blockading the French ports in the Bay of Biscay for six months, he won a decisive victory over the French fleet in Quiberon Bay. His victory averted the danger of a French invasion of Great Britain. He served (1766–71) as first lord of the admiralty and was raised (1776) to the peerage. During his long career Hawke did much to improve conditions in the fleet. See biography by R. F. Mackay (1965).

Hawkes, John, pseud. of Clendennin Burne, Jr., 1925–, American writer, b. Stamford, Conn., grad. Harvard, 1949. He has taught English at Brown Univ. since 1958. Hawkes is considered one of the most original American writers of the 20th cent. His highly experimental works blend everyday reality with menacing hallucinations. Complex, ambiguous, and grimly humorous, they often focus on the emptiness, brutality, and terror of modern life. His works include *The Goose on the Grave* (1954), a collection of short fiction, as well as the novels *The Cannibal* (1949), *The Beetle Leg* (1951), *The Lime Twig* (1951), *Second Skin* (1964), *Blood Oranges* (1971), and *Death, Sleep & The Traveler* (1974).

Hawkesbury, town (1971 pop. 9,276), SE Ont., Canada, on the Ottawa River. It has lumber and paper mills and manufactures clothing and prefabricated homes.

Hawkesworth, John, 1715?–1773, English author. He succeeded his friend Samuel Johnson in 1744 as reporter of parliamentary debates in the *Gentleman's Magazine.* With Johnson and Joseph Warton he wrote the periodical *Adventurer* (1752–54).

hawking: see FALCONRY.

Hawkins, Sir Anthony Hope: see HOPE, ANTHONY.

Hawkins, Coleman, 1907–69, American jazz musician, b. St. Joseph, Mo. He began playing saxophone at the age of 9. He was part of Fletcher HENDERSON'S band from 1924 until 1934. Hawkins established the tenor saxophone as a major jazz instrument. His enormous tone, vigorous attack, and improvisatory genius both in ballads and up-tempo pieces made his influence pervasive. Because his style constantly evolved, Hawkins was distinguished even in the company of avant-garde jazz musicians from 1945 until 1969.

Hawkins or **Hawkyns, Sir John,** 1532–95, English admiral. In 1562–63 and in 1564–65 he led extremely profitable expeditions that captured slaves on the W African coast, shipped them across the Atlantic, and sold them, despite Spanish prohibition, in Spanish ports in the West Indies. Hawkins set out on a similar expedition in 1567, but he fell afoul of a Spanish squadron in San Juan de Ulúa, the port of Veracruz, and barely escaped with three of his boats, one of which was commanded by his kinsman Francis DRAKE. Probably acting as an agent for Lord Burghley, Hawkins pretended to betray Queen Elizabeth I in offering (1571) his services to the Spanish, in order to obtain the release of prisoners and to discover plans for the proposed Spanish invasion of England. In 1571 he entered Parliament and subsequently became treasurer and comptroller of the navy. In this capacity he made a number of important improvements in ship construction and rigging. His enemies charged him with using his office to his personal financial advantage, but he was exonerated after an inquiry by a royal commission. In the great defeat of the Spanish ARMADA (1588), Hawkins commanded the *Victory* and was knighted for his services. In 1595 he set out on a new expedition to the West Indies under Drake, but died and was buried at sea off Puerto Rico. See biography by J. A. Williamson (2d. ed. 1969); K. R. Andrews, ed., *The Last Voyage of Drake and Hawkins* (1972).

Hawkins, Sir Richard, 1562?–1622, English admiral, son of Sir John Hawkins. He served under Sir Francis DRAKE in the 1585–86 expedition to the West Indies, commanded the *Swallow* in the defeat of the Spanish Armada in 1588, and served under his father in 1590 in an unsuccessful expedition against Portugal. In 1593 he set out on an expedition in the ship *Dainty,* sailed down the Brazilian coast and through the Strait of Magellan, plundered Valparaiso, and took a number of prizes. However, he was captured (1594) by two Spanish ships, taken to Peru, and sent to Spain (1597), where he remained in prison until 1602. He was knighted (1603), served in Parliament (1604), and as vice admiral of Devon was active in defending the Devonshire coast from pirates. He also served in a disastrous expedition (1620–21) against the Barbary pirates.

hawksbill: see SEA TURTLE.

Hawksmoor or **Hawksmore, Nicholas,** 1661–1736, English architect involved in the development of most of the great buildings of the English baroque. From the age of 21 he assisted Sir Christopher Wren in the design of Chelsea Hospital, city churches, royal residences, and St. Paul's Cathedral. He became deputy surveyor (1705–29) in the construction of Greenwich Hospital. In the building of the great residences, Castle Howard and Blenheim Palace, he was associated with Sir John Vanbrugh. Under the act of 1711, Hawksmoor was appointed one of the architects to design 50 churches in London. He planned (1714–30) six highly original churches, which included St. George's, Bloomsbury; Christ Church, Spitalfields; and the rebuilding of St. Mary Woolnoth. At Oxford he designed the north quadrangle of All Souls' College. Influenced by architectural elements of many periods, Hawksmoor arrived at an individuality of design that makes him a significant figure in the history of the international baroque. See study by Kerry Downes (1959).

hawkweed, any species of the genus *Hieracium* of the family Compositae (COMPOSITE family), widely distributed perennials, chiefly of open fields. The small, dandelion-like flower heads are borne in clusters at the top of a long, hairy stem; the basal leaves are also hairy. Some species of the W United States are used for forage; in the East, hawkweeds are generally considered pests. In the fall the orange hawkweed, or devil's-paintbrush, the rattlesnake weed, and the king devil often turn whole fields a ruddy orange or yellow. Other species are red or white; a few are cultivated in rocky soil where other plants cannot grow. In folklore, hawks sharpened their eyesight by eating hawkweed sap. Hawkweed is classified in the division MAGNOLIOPHYTA, class Magnoliopsida, order Asterales, family Compositae.

Hawkwood, Sir John de, d. 1394, English soldier. He fought in the French wars of Edward III and was knighted, although it is not known when or where. With his "white company" of mercenaries, he entered (1362) Italy and became a CONDOTTIERE. He served sometimes one republic, sometimes another, but he was employed most regularly by Florence, where he died. The cathedral in Florence contains an equestrian portrait of Hawkwood by Paolo Uccello.

Hawley, Joseph, 1723–88, political leader in the American Revolution, b. Northampton, Mass. He was a leader of the opposition to the revivalist preaching of Jonathan EDWARDS and helped bring about Edwards's dismissal from his Northampton church. A lawyer, he served in the General Court of Massachusetts, where he became prominent in the struggle for political freedom before the Revolution. A leader of pre-Revolutionary activities in W Massachusetts, he was a strong supporter and frequent correspondent of John Adams. See biography by E. F. Brown (1931, repr. 1966).

Hawley-Smoot Tariff Act, 1930, passed by the U.S. Congress; it brought the U.S. tariff to the highest protective level yet in the history of the United States. President Hoover desired a limited upward revision of tariff rates with general increases on farm products and adjustment of a few industrial rates. A congressional joint committee, however, in compromising the differences between a high Senate tariff bill and a higher House tariff bill, arrived at new high rates by generally adopting the increased rates of the Senate on farm products and those of the House on manufactures. Despite wide protest, the tariff act, called the Hawley-Smoot Tariff Act because of its joint sponsorship by Representative Willis C. Hawley and Senator Reed Smoot, both Republicans, was signed (June, 1930) by President Hoover. The act brought retaliatory tariff acts from foreign countries, and U.S. foreign trade suffered a sharp decline.

Hawran or **Hauran** (hourän') [Heb.,=hollow or cavernous land], district, SW Syria. It is a largely treeless region marked by conical volcanic peaks, barren lava fields, and rich lava soil. In the northeast are the Druse mts., many of whose numerous caverns were once inhabited. Grains and fruits (including grapes) are grown in Hawran. Most of the inhabitants are DRUSES, who migrated from Lebanon in the 18th and 19th cent. The Hawran district belonged, at least in part, to the biblical kingdom of Bashan, which the Israelites conquered. Designated the northeast boundary of the Promised Land (Ezek. 47.16, 18), Hawran later became the Roman province of Auranitis. The region was converted to Christianity by the late 2d cent. and was considerably disturbed by the Arab invasion of the 7th cent. During the Crusades, Muslims who were driven out of Palestine moved to Hawran to make a stand against the Christians. The district has many ancient towns whose buildings and furniture are made entirely of lava; about 300 of these "giant cities of Bashan" have been located. Inscriptions in Greek, Latin, Arabic, and Sabean (southern Arabic) abound.

hawthorn, any species of the genus *Crataegus* of the family Rosaceae (ROSE family), shrubs and trees widely distributed in north temperate climates and especially common in E North America. They usually have thorns, clusters of white flowers in the spring, and colorful orange, red, or yellow fruits in the fall. The fruits, called haws, resemble tiny apples; some are used in jellies. In some species the flowers are rose-colored and the fruits blue or black. Hawthorns are cultivated for ornament and, especially in England, for hedges (*haw* also means *hedge*). In England the flowers are associated with May Day, and the hawthorn (called also may, thorn, haw, whitethorn, and thorn apple) has long been used as a symbol of spring in English poetry. There are many legends surrounding the hawthorn, e.g., that of the Glastonbury thorn (see GLASTONBURY, England). English hawthorns are of two species, *C. oxyacantha* and *C. monogyna;* the common American hawthorn, with bright red haws, is *C. coccinea,* called scarlet, or red, haw (as are other similar species). A hawthorn is the state flower of Missouri. Hawthorn wood is very hard and is used for such small items as tool handles. The black haw is a viburnum (see HONEYSUCKLE). Hawthorn is classified in the division MAGNOLIOPHYTA, class Magnoliopsida, order Rosales, family Rosaceae.

Hawthorne, Nathaniel, 1804–64, American novelist and short-story writer, b. Salem, Mass., one of the great masters of American fiction. His novels and tales are penetrating explorations of moral and spiritual conflicts. Descended from a prominent Puritan family, he was the son of a sea captain who spelled his name as Hathorne. From his widowed mother Hawthorne acquired his gloomy outlook and solitary ways. After attending Bowdoin College (1821–25), he spent 12 years in the seclusion of his home, devoting himself to writing. His first novel, *Fanshawe* (1829), was unsuccessful, but his short stories won notice and were collected in *Twice-Told Tales* (1837; second series, 1842). Unable to support himself by writing and editing, he took a job at the Boston customhouse but found the work distasteful. For about six months he tried living at the experimental community BROOK FARM, but he did not share the optimism and idealism of the transcendentalist participants, and his solitary personality was not suited to communal life. In 1842 he married Sophia Peabody, a friend and follower of Emerson, Thoreau, and Margaret Fuller, and they settled in Concord. There he wrote the tales and sketches in the collection *Mosses from an Old Manse* (1846). For a livelihood he served as surveyor of the port at Salem (1846–49), where he began writing his masterpiece, *The Scarlet Letter* (1850). Set in 17th-century Puritan New England, the novel delves deeply into the human heart, presenting the problems of moral evil and guilt through allegory and symbolism. It is often considered the first American psychological novel. Hawthorne's next novel, *The House of the Seven Gables* (1851), takes place in the New England of his own period but nevertheless deals with the effects of Puritanism. For a time the Hawthornes lived at "Tanglewood," near Lenox, Mass., where he wrote *A Wonder Book* (1852), based on Greek mythology, which became a juvenile classic, and *Tanglewood Tales* (1853), also for children. At this time he befriended his neighbor Herman Melville, who was one of the first to appreciate Hawthorne's genius. Returning to Concord, Hawthorne completed *The Blithedale Romance* (1852), a novel based on his Brook Farm experience. A campaign biography of his college friend Franklin Pierce earned Hawthorne the post of consul at Liverpool (1853–57) after Pierce became President. Hawthorne's stay in England is reflected in the travel sketches of *Our Old Home* (1863), and a visit to Italy resulted in the novel *The Marble Faun* (1860). After returning to the United States, he worked on several novels that were never finished. He died during a trip to the White Mts. with Franklin Pierce. Aside from his importance as a novelist, Hawthorne is justly celebrated as a short-story writer. He helped to establish the American short story as a significant art form with his haunting tales of human loneliness, frustration, hypocrisy, eccentricity, and frailty. Among his most brilliant stories are "The Minister's Black Veil," "Roger Malvin's Burial," "Young Goodman Brown," "Rappaccini's Daughter," "The Great Stone Face," and "Ethan Brand." See the centenary edition of his complete works, ed. by William Charvat, R. H. Pearce, and C. M. Simpson (8 vol., 1965—); biographies by his son, Julian Hawthorne (2 vol., 1884, repr. 1968), Newton Arvin (1928, repr. 1961), H. H. Hoeltje (1962), and Randall Stewart (1948, repr. 1970); studies by his son-in-law, G. P. Lathrop (1876, repr. 1968), Henry James (1879, repr. 1956), F. C. Crews (1966), J. C. Stubbs (1970), and M. D. Bell (1971).

Hawthorne. 1 City (1970 pop. 53,304), Los Angeles co., S Calif., a suburb of Los Angeles; inc. 1922. Toys, cash registers, and defense-related products are made there. **2** Borough (1970 pop. 19,173), Passaic co., NE N.J.; settled 1850, inc. 1898. Primarily residential, it produces chemicals and plastics.

Hay, John: see TWEEDDALE, JOHN HAY, 2D EARL AND 1ST MARQUESS OF.

Hay, John (Milton), 1838–1905, American author and statesman, b. Salem, Ind. He practiced law at Springfield, Ill., where he met Abraham LINCOLN. Hay accompanied Lincoln to Washington and was the President's assistant private secretary until Lincoln's death. The next five years were spent in minor posts in the U.S. legations at Paris, Vienna, and Madrid. Then followed four years of journalism in New York City, in which period he published *Castilian Days* (1871) and his famous *Pike County Ballads* (1871). Marriage to the daughter of a wealthy Cleveland banker enabled him to pursue the profession of man of letters, to travel, and to fill political posts of distinction. He was appointed Assistant Secretary of State in 1878 and moved to Washington, D.C., where he became the intimate of Henry ADAMS and Clarence King. In this period he published anonymously *The Bread-Winners* (1884), a social novel, and, with John G. Nicolay, the monumental *Abraham Lincoln: A History* (10 vol., 1890), a work for which the young secretaries, while serving under Lincoln, had gathered material with his knowledge and permission. In March, 1897, McKinley appointed Hay ambassador to Great Britain, and there he served his country well during the trying time of the Spanish-American War. From Sept. 20, 1898, until his death, July 1, 1905, he was Secretary of State under Presidents McKinley and Theodore Roosevelt. In the McKinley administration he was a maker of policies; in the Roosevelt administration he was, in his chief's own words, a "fine figurehead." Hay was responsible for the OPEN DOOR policy (1899) with regard to China, which stressed freedom of commercial enterprise for American merchants; for U.S. involvement in the BOXER UPRISING; and for the HAY-PAUNCEFOTE TREATIES. See W. R. Thayer, *Life and Letters of John Hay* (1915, repr. 1972); Tyler Dennett, *John Hay* (1933, repr. 1961).

Hay, river, c.530 mi (850 km) long, rising in several headstreams in NE British Columbia and NW Alta., Canada, and flowing generally NE through NW Alta., over Alexander Falls, and into Great Slave Lake. Its valley, a principal north-south route, is followed by a highway and a railroad.

hay, wild or cultivated plants, chiefly grasses and legumes, mown and dried for use as livestock fodder. Hay is an important factor in cattle raising and is one of the leading crops of the United States. Alfalfa, timothy, and red clover are the principal hay crops. After mowing, the hay is left spread in the field or is stacked in windrows or in cocks for drying. It must dry quickly and uniformly; its nutritive value and palatability are reduced by overexposure to sunlight or rain, and unequal drying often results in loss of the leaves, which form two thirds of its feed value. Hay stored while still moist may build up heat and ignite by spontaneous combustion.

Haya, people of Africa living on Lake Victoria in the extreme northwest of Tanzania. They originally came from W Uganda, a region they left because of endless wars. There are now about 300,000 Haya; they grow bananas and coffee in a country that is rich and populous. They belong to a group of peoples known collectively as the Interlacustrine Bantu. The Haya include the Basiba, Heia, Kiziba, Wahaya, Wassiba, and Ziba.

Haya de la Torre, Víctor Raúl (vēk'tôr räo͞ol' ä'yä dā lä tô'rē), 1895–, Peruvian political leader, founder of the APRA (see APRA) party. Although he never held power and spent much of his political life in exile or in prison, he had great influence on contemporary hemispheric politics. A leading advocate of nationalist revolutions in Latin America, he championed the cause of the Indians and fought for radical, although expressly non-Communist, social and economic reforms. He was exiled in 1923 and after eight years returned to Peru, where he ran unsuccessfully for the presidency in 1931 and was imprisoned for 15 months. Because APRA advocated the overthrow of the oligarchy that had ruled Peru since colonial days, the party was outlawed from 1931 to 1934 and from 1935 to 1945, when José Luis Bustamante became president with its support. Dissident *Apristas* revolted in Callao in Oct., 1948; the party was again outlawed. In November, Manuel ODRÍA seized power and forced Haya to seek asylum in the Colombian embassy in Lima. The Peruvian government granted him safe conduct in 1954 only after years of bitter denunciations from liberals throughout the hemisphere. APRA was legalized in 1956, but Haya continued to live mostly abroad until 1962 when he returned to campaign for the presidency. He obtained a slim plurality but not enough to be constitutionally elected; a military junta nullified the elections. Running again in 1963, Haya was defeated, but his party continued to be popular in the 1970s.

hay baler, farm implement that packs and ties field-dried hay into bundles, called bales, for convenient handling, storage, and shipping. It ordinarily picks up hay that has been raked into rows (see RAKE), packs it, ties it into a bale, and then delivers the bale back to the ground for later pickup. More modern balers have automatic stacking or loading devices. Nearly all hay in the United States is baled. See Claude Culpin, *Farm Machinery* (8th ed. 1969).

Hayden, Robert, 1913–, American poet, b. Detroit, Mich. After earning his M.A. at the Univ. of Michigan, he taught there and later at Fisk Univ., where he has been professor of English since 1946. Although the tone of his poems is quiet and often loving, he has a considerable gift for irony and his insights can be shattering. In 1966 he was awarded a prize for *Ballad of Remembrance* (1962) at the World Festival of Negro Arts in Dakar, Senegal. See his *Collected Poems* (1967).

Haydn, Franz Joseph (fränts yō'zĕf hī'dən), 1732–1809, Austrian composer, one of the greatest masters of classical music. As a boy he sang in the choir at St. Stephen's, Vienna, where he received his principal musical training. He struggled in poverty for years, earning a meager living as a teacher and accompanist. Eventually, his compositions came to the attention of some of Vienna's music-loving aristocrats, and under their patronage his career progressed rapidly. Most of his prodigious musical output was produced during the 29 years of his service as musical director to the princes Esterházy, beginning in 1761. During the 1780s, when he received commissions from London and Paris and honors from all over Europe, he formed a close friendship with Mozart, an association that influenced the music of each. In 1791 and 1794 he made visits to London. During this period he wrote the 12 so-called Salomon Symphonies (after the impressario who had arranged his tours), much chamber music, and a large number of songs with English texts. Haydn's works are notable for their originality, liveliness, optimism, and instrumental brilliance. He established the basic forms of symphonic music, which were to be a model and inspiration for the works of Mozart, and of Beethoven, who studied under Haydn. Important in the development of the classic sonata form, his string quartets and symphonies expanded the three-movement sonata form of C. P. E. Bach, adding one or two minuets before the last movement. Two great oratorios, *The Creation* (1798) and *The Seasons* (1801), were written in his old age. His works include over 100 symphonies, many known by such names as the Farewell Symphony (1772), the Surprise Symphony (1791), the Military Symphony (1794), and the Clock Symphony (1794); over 80 string quartets; much other chamber music; more than 50 piano sonatas; and numerous operas, masses, and songs. See biographies by Karl Geiringer (2d ed. 1968), Rosemary Hughes (rev. ed. 1970), and Ludwig Nohl (1902, repr. 1971); H. C. R. Landon, *The Symphonies of Joseph Haydn* (1955).

Haydn, Michael (mĭkh'äĕl), 1737–1806, Austrian composer, younger brother of Franz Joseph Haydn. Haydn, largely self-taught, was noted especially for his sacred music. He was a friend of Mozart, whose Symphony No. 37 is actually Haydn's work with an introduction by Mozart. Toward the end of his life Haydn taught the Czech composer Antonín Reicha and Carl Maria von Weber.

Haydon, Benjamin Robert, 1786–1846, English historical painter and writer. A painter in the Grand Manner expounded by Reynolds, Haydon was also a popular teacher, writer, and lecturer. His lectures on design were published in 1847. Among his admirers were most of the great literary figures of the day, including Wordsworth and Keats, who sat for him for their portraits (both: National Portrait Gall., London). See his *Correspondence and Table-Talk* (1876) and his autobiography and journals (1926 ed., with introduction by Aldous Huxley).

Hayes, Carlton Joseph Huntley, 1882–1964, American historian and diplomat, b. Afton, N.Y. He began teaching history at Columbia in 1907, and from 1935 to his retirement in 1950 he held the Seth Low chair of history. He was noted for his studies in nationalism, *Essays on Nationalism* (1926) and *Historical Evolution of Modern Nationalism* (1931). His many other works include *A Generation of Materialism (1871–1900)* (1941) and the textbooks *A Political and Cultural History of Modern Europe* (2 vol., 1932–36; rev. ed. 1939) and *History of Europe* (with Marshall W. Baldwin and Charles W. Cole, 1949). Hayes was U.S. ambassador to Spain from May, 1942, to March, 1945, a period recorded in his *Wartime Mission in Spain, 1942–1945* (1945). Though some criticized him as being too friendly with Franco, it was generally held that he played an important role in preventing an outright Spanish alliance with the Axis in World War II. A convert to Roman Catholicism, Hayes became a leading Catholic layman and was long cochairman (1925–45) of the National Conference of Christians and Jews.

Hayes, Helen, 1900–, American actress, b. Washington, D.C., as Helen Hayes Brown. Hayes made her New York stage debut in 1908. Her performances in *Dear Brutus, Mary of Scotland, Caesar and Cleopatra,* and *What Every Woman Knows* brought her fame; her portrayal (1935–39) of the title role in Laurence Housman's *Victoria Regina* established her as an actress of the first rank. She won an Academy Award (1932) for *The Sin of Madelon Claudet.* In 1928 she married the playwright Charles MacArthur. Hayes returned to Broadway in *Harvey* in 1970. Her later films include *Anastasia* (1956) and *Airport* (1969). See her *Gift of Joy* (1965; with Lewis Funke), *On Reflection* (1968; with Sandford Dody), and *Twice Over Lightly* (1972; with Anita Loos); biography by her mother, Catherine Hayes Brown (1940).

Hayes, Isaac Israel, 1832–81, American physician and arctic explorer, b. Chester co., Pa. While serving as ship's surgeon on the second expedition (1853–55) of E. K. KANE, Hayes led an exploring party across Kane Basin and northward along the east shore of Ellesmere Island; he named Grinnell Land after Henry Grinnell, the financier of arctic explorations. On his own expedition (1860–61) he sought an open seaway to the North Pole, which he incorrectly believed he had found at a point that seems to have been the south end of Kennedy Channel. His astronomer had died during the early part of the expedition, and Hayes's astronomical calculations were inaccurate. Nevertheless, he brought back fossils and relics and made some valuable meteorological observations. In 1869 he made another journey to Greenland, on which he was accompanied by the marine artist, William Bradford. Hayes wrote several books on his arctic experiences, including *Cast Away in the Cold* (1868) and *The Land of Desolation* (1872).

Hayes, Roland, 1887–, American tenor, b. Curryville, Ga. The son of a former slave, Hayes studied at Fisk Univ. and with private teachers in Boston and in Europe. As one of the foremost interpreters of modern French songs, German lieder, and Negro spirituals, Hayes was the first Negro singer to achieve enormous international recognition. See MacKinley Helm, *Angel Mo' and Her Son, Roland Hayes* (1942).

Hayes, Rutherford Birchard, 1822–93, 19th President of the United States (1877–81), b. Delaware, Ohio, grad. Kenyon College, 1843, and Harvard law school, 1845. He became a moderately successful lawyer in Cincinnati and was made (1858) city solicitor. In the Civil War he began as a major of volunteers, took part in some 50 engagements, was several times wounded, and rose in rank to be (1865) major general of volunteers. Elected to Congress while still in the field, he served (1865–67) as a regular Republican, quietly supporting the radical Reconstruction program. He was three times (1867, 1869, 1875) elected governor of Ohio and was chosen as the Republican candidate for President in 1876, opposing Samuel J. TILDEN, the Democratic candidate. The election marked the resurgence of the Democrats and the political reentry of the South into the Union. The chaotic political conditions brought on by Reconstruction resulted in disputed elections in South Carolina, Florida, Louisiana, and Oregon. Congress created an electoral commission to decide the elections. The commission awarded all disputed returns to Hayes and thereby gave him a majority of one in the electoral college. Indignation over the obviously partisan decision affected Hayes's administration, which was generally conservative and efficient and no more. He withdrew Federal troops from Louisiana and South Carolina, and the Reconstruction era was ended. His conciliatory policy toward the South and his genuine interest in civil service reform alienated important Republican groups, notably the "Old Guard" led by Roscoe Conkling. An advocate of hard money, he vetoed the BLAND-ALLISON ACT, which was passed over his veto and provided for resumption of specie payments in gold. After his presidential term Hayes was active in philanthropic foundations. See his diary ed. by T. H. Williams (1964); biographies by Harry Barnard (1954, repr. 1967), H. J. Eckenrode (1957, repr. 1963), and T. H. Williams (1965); study by K. E. Davison (1972).

Hayes, river, c.300 mi (480 km) long, rising in a lake NE of Lake Winnipeg, central Manitoba, Canada, and flowing NE to Hudson Bay. It was the chief route used by Hudson's Bay Company traders from Hudson Bay to Lake Winnipeg and the interior; York Factory, an important establishment of the company, is at its mouth.

hay fever, seasonal ALLERGY causing inflammation of the mucous membranes of the nose and eyes. It is characterized by itching about the eyes and nose, sneezing, a profuse watery nasal discharge, and tearing of the eyes. The cause is a sensitivity to one or more species of pollens or fungi. In addition, many patients with hay fever develop other allergic conditions, e.g., ASTHMA and sinusitis. In the spring, hay fever may be caused by tree pollens (oak, elm, maple); in summer, by grass pollens, wheat or corn rusts, or fungus spores; in late summer and fall, by ragweed pollen, which is the most common cause. Temporary relief of symptoms may be obtained from antihistamines and decongestants, such as ephedrine. Physicians may resort to corticosteroids in severe cases. Sometimes desensitization measures are taken, consisting of repeated injections of small amounts of the allergen (pollen) until its presence produces no symptoms; however, the treatment must be continued from year to year, since immunity is not permanent. Some relief can be obtained by removing pollen from the air by air conditioners and filters.

Hay-Herrán Treaty (hä-ĕrän'), 1903, aborted agreement between the United States and Colombia providing for U.S. control of the prospective PANAMA CANAL and for U.S. acquisition of a canal zone. It was signed by U.S. Secretary of State John Hay and Colombian foreign minister Tomás Herrán on Jan. 22, 1903. The treaty stipulated that the New Panama Canal Company, which held an option on the canal route, might sell its properties to the United States; that Colombia lease a strip of land across the Isthmus of Panama to the United States for construction of a canal; and that the United States pay Colombia $10 million and, after nine years, an annuity of $250,000. Although it did not give the United States complete governmental control over the proposed canal zone, the treaty was ratified by the U.S. Senate. The Colombian congress delayed ratification, hoping to increase the price offered by the United States; finally, it rejected the treaty because of dissatisfaction with the financial terms and fear of "Yankee imperialism" and loss of national sovereignty. See D. C. Miner, *The Fight for the Panama Route* (1940).

Hayman, Francis, 1708–76, English painter. Influenced by the French ROCOCO style, Hayman painted conversation pieces—landscape scenes peopled by fashionable contemporaries (see PORTRAITURE). He also worked as a designer at the Drury Lane Theatre.

Haymarket Square riot, outbreak of violence in Chicago on May 4, 1886. Demands for an eight-hour working day became increasingly widespread among American laborers in the 1880s. A demonstration, largely staged by a small group of anarchists, caused a crowd of some 1,500 people to gather at Haymarket Square. When policemen attempted to disperse the meeting, a bomb exploded and rioting ensued. Seven policemen and four other persons were killed, and more than 100 persons were wounded. Public indignation rose rapidly, and punishment was demanded. Eight anarchist leaders were tried, but no evidence was produced that they had made or thrown the bomb. They were, however, convicted of inciting violence. Four were hanged, one committed suicide, and the remaining three—after having served in prison for seven years—were pardoned (1893) by John P. Altgeld, governor of Illinois, on the ground that the trial had been unjust. The incident was frequently used by the adversaries of organized labor to discredit the waning KNIGHTS OF LABOR movement. See Henry David, *History of the Haymarket Affair* (1936, repr. 1964).

Hayne, Paul Hamilton, 1830–86, American poet, b. Charleston, S.C., grad. Charleston College. Considered the last of the Southern literary cavaliers, he wrote a book of nature poetry (1855) and edited *Russel's Magazine* (1857–60). He was left impoverished by the Civil War and took refuge on a small estate in Georgia. There he wrote *Legends and Lyrics* (1872), a collection of delicate, charming poems that is considered his most mature work. See study by R. S. Moore (1972).

Hayne, Robert Young, 1791–1839, American statesman, b. Colleton District, S.C. Having served in the South Carolina legislature (1814–18) and as attorney general of South Carolina (1818–22), Hayne was a U.S. Senator (1823–32) and gained attention as a leading Southern spokesman against the tariff. His famous debate with Daniel Webster in Jan., 1830, precipitated by the FOOT RESOLUTION, covered all the issues of political and economic difference between the South and the North. Hayne upheld the doctrines of states' rights and NULLIFICATION, thus provoking Webster's impassioned defense of a nationalistic interpretation of the Constitution. Hayne resigned from the Senate (1832) and was governor of South Carolina (1832–34) at the time the nullification convention met. Henry Clay's compromise tariff satisfied Hayne, and the latter's influence palliated the ensuing high feeling. After serving (1835–37) as mayor of Charleston, Hayne devoted the rest of his life to unsuccessful railroad projects designed to ally the West with the South. See biography by T. D. Jervey (1909, repr. 1970).

Haynes, John, c.1594–1654, colonial governor of Massachusetts and then of Connecticut. He emigrated (1633) from England to Massachusetts and as governor (1635) banished Roger Williams, an act he later regretted. Haynes moved (1637) to Hartford, Conn., and became (1639) the first governor of Connecticut under the FUNDAMENTAL ORDERS. He held the office on alternate years until his death. He urged the union of the New England colonies and later served as Connecticut commissioner to the New England Confederation.

Hay-Pauncefote Treaties (hā-pôns'fo͝ot), negotiated in 1899 and 1901 by Secretary of State John Hay, for the United States, and Lord PAUNCEFOTE OF PRESTON, British ambassador to the United States, for Great Britain, with the object of modifying the CLAYTON-BULWER TREATY, concerning the construction of an Isthmian canal in Central America. The draft of the first treaty was submitted to London in January, 1889. The proposed agreement granted to the United States the exclusive right to build and maintain a canal. It further provided for a neutralization scheme (to be governed by rules similar to the Suez Canal regulations adopted at Constantinople in 1888) calling for the nonfortification of the canal and equal transit rights to ships of all nations, even in time of war. After a delay of almost a year the treaty was signed and submitted to the U.S. Senate in Feb., 1900. Resistance to ratification grew steadily, particularly among those concerned over the neutralization rules. On Dec. 20, 1900, the Senate finally ratified the agreement, but with three amendments: abrogation of the Clayton-Bulwer Treaty, provision for the fortification of the canal, and deletion of the article providing that other powers join the treaty. Since Great Britain refused to ratify the treaty as amended, negotiations were immediately reinstated. A new treaty was signed by Hay and Pauncefote on Nov. 18, 1901, and was ratified by the U.S. Senate on Dec. 16, 1901. The new compromise treaty, superseding the Clayton-Bulwer Treaty, provided that the United States might construct a canal and have full control in its management and regulation. It nominally retained the principle of neutrality under the sole guarantee of the United States, stipulated that the canal be open to ships of all nations on equal terms, but omitted the clause contained in the first draft forbidding fortifications. The Panama Canal Act, passed in 1912, which exempted from tolls American ships engaged in coastwise trade, was protested by Great Britain as a violation of the treaty and was repealed in 1914 through the efforts of President Wilson. See Tyler Dennett, *John Hay* (1933, repr. 1961); J. W. Pratt, *A History of United States Foreign Policy* (1955).

Hays, Arthur Garfield, 1881–1954, American lawyer, b. Rochester, N.Y. He was admitted (1905) to the bar and practiced in New York City. He was active in many cases concerned with civil liberties; he distinguished himself as a defense attorney in the Scopes Case (1925) in Tennessee and in the Sacco-Vanzetti Case (1927). He was counsel for the American Civil Liberties Union and conducted (1937) the investigation of civil liberties in Puerto Rico. He wrote *Let Freedom Ring* (1928, rev. ed. 1937), *Democracy Works* (1939), and an autobiography (1942).

Hays, Will H., 1879–1954, American politician and motion-picture executive, b. Sullivan, Ind.; his original name was William Harrison Hays. Hays became active in Indiana political affairs, was chairman of the Republican state committee, and served (1918–21) as chairman of the Republican National Committee. He was (1921–22) Postmaster General under President Harding. As president (1922–45) of the Motion Picture Producers and Distributors of America, he administered the motion-picture moral code (popularly called the "Hays Code"), which was promulgated (1934) by agreement of the leading men of the industry. See his memoirs (1955).

Hays, city (1970 pop. 15,396), seat of Ellis co., W central Kansas; inc. 1885. It is a rail, trade, and medical center in a grain, cattle, and oil area. Medical and hospital supplies and hydraulic cylinders are manufactured. For protection against the Indians, Fort Hays was established (1865) 14 mi (23 km) southeast of the present city, on a stagecoach road to Denver. Floods in 1867 forced the fort's relocation to its present site, and the city of Hays grew just east of it. The fort was abandoned in 1889 and the land turned over to the state with the understanding that it be used for a school, an agricultural experiment station, and a state park. Today the school has grown into Fort Hays Kansas State College; the agricultural experiment station (laid out 1901) is one of the world's largest; and the park, a state historic site, contains the fort's surviving buildings.

Hayward, city (1970 pop. 93,058), Alameda co., W Calif.; settled 1851, inc. 1876. It is an important commercial and distributing center for an agricultural area. Food processing is its major industry. It is the seat of California State Univ. at Hayward and a junior college, and is the eastern terminus of the San Mateo toll bridge across San Francisco Bay.

Haywood, Eliza (Fowler), 1693?–1756, English author. Separated from her husband, she supported herself and her two children by writing plays and novels. Two of her books, *Utopia* (1725) and *The Court of Carmania* (1727), scandalized well-known society figures, and earned her the disapproval of Pope who satirized her in *The Dunciad.* She also conducted the periodical the *Female Spectator* (1744–46).

Haywood, William Dudley, 1869–1928, American labor leader, known as Big Bill Haywood, b. Salt Lake City, Utah. He began work as a miner at 15 years of age. In 1896 he joined the newly organized Western Federation of Miners, and in 1900 became a member of the executive board and national secretary-treasurer of the organization, with headquarters in Denver. His leadership was militant, and he was often accused of inciting to violence, especially in the Colorado troubles culminating in the Cripple Creek strike (1904), which he led. He was also accused of instigating the assassination of former governor Steunenberg of Idaho in 1905, but was acquitted in a trial in which he was defended by Clarence S. Darrow; the trial attracted nationwide attention. In 1905 he was one of the organizers of the INDUSTRIAL WORKERS OF THE WORLD (IWW). He joined the Socialist party and became a member of its national executive board, but because of his advocacy of violence was forced out of the party. He led the famous Lawrence and Paterson textile workers' strikes in 1912 and 1913. Repudiating the crafts union ideal and the cooperation policy of the American Federation of Labor, he preached the IWW doctrines of class struggle, no compromise, and mass action. When the United States entered World War I he was arrested on a charge of sedition, was tried, convicted, and sentenced to 20 years' imprisonment. While awaiting a new trial in 1921, he forfeited bail and escaped to the Soviet Union, where he lived for the rest of his life. Haywood wrote many articles and prepared his own autobiography, published as *Bill Haywood's Book* (1929, repr. 1958). See P. F. Brissenden, *The I.W.W.* (2d ed. 1920, repr. 1957); S. H. Holbrook, *The Rocky Mountain Revolution* (1956).

Hazael (hăz'āĕl, həzā'əl), fl. 840 B.C., king of Damascus; successor and murderer of BENHADAD **2.** From the Bible he appears as the ally of the party of Elisha in Israel and later as the conqueror, taking all the Hebrew possessions E of the Jordan, ravaging Judah, and rendering Israel impotent. From inscriptions of Shalmaneser III of Assyria it appears that Hazael withstood an attack by the Assyrian army and kept Damascus, Syria, and Palestine independent. He was succeeded by his son Benhadad (fl. 800 B.C.). 1 Kings 19.15; 2 Kings 8–10.

Hazaiah (həzā'yə, hā"zī'ə), descendant of Judah. Neh. 11.5.

Hazar-addar (hā'zär-ăd'är), boundary town, S Palestine. Num. 34.4. In the parallel verse, Joshua 15.3, textual error seems to have made two names, Hezron and Adar, out of one.

Hazard, Ebenezer, 1744–1817, American public official and historian, b. Philadelphia. He became a publisher in New York City. He was appointed (1775) first postmaster of the city under the Continental Congress, made (1776) surveyor general of the Continental Post Office, and in 1782 succeeded Richard Bache as Postmaster General. This office he held until Sept., 1789, when, under the new Federal Constitution, the Post Office establishment was reorganized. Under him the mail was first carried in stagecoaches on main routes, displacing the old horse-and-rider system. He edited two volumes of *Historical Collections* (1792–94, repr. 1969).

Hazard, Paul (pôl äzär'), 1878–1944, French scholar. He began his teaching at the Univ. of Lyons in 1910. After World War I he taught at the Sorbonne and in 1925 was appointed to the chair of comparative literature in the Collège de France. In alternate years between 1932 and 1940 he was a visiting lecturer at Columbia Univ. Recognized as an authority on comparative literature, Hazard was elected to the French Academy in 1939. Among his important writings are *Histoire illustrée de la littérature française* (comp. with Joseph Bédier, 2 vol., 1923–24); *Books, Children and Men* (1932, tr. 1944); *The European Mind, the Critical Years, 1680–1715* (3 vol., 1935, tr. 1953); and *European Thought in the Eighteenth Century* (3 vol., 1946, tr. 1954).

Hazar-enan (hā'zär-ē'nən), unidentified northern boundary limit of Israel. Num. 34.9; Ezek. 47.17; 48.1.

Hazar-gaddah (hā'zär-găd'ə), town, S Palestine. Joshua 15.27.

Hazar-hatticon (hā'zär-hăt'ĭkŏn), town of Israel. Ezek. 47.16.

Hazaribagh (həzä'rĭbäg), town (1971 pop. 54,703), Bihar state, E central India. Located on the Chota-Nagpur plateau, 2,000 ft (610 m) above sea level, the town is a district administrative center and a market for rice, maize, and mustard. There is a sanatorium in the town.

Hazarmaveth (hā'zärmā'vĕth), son of Joktan and eponym of the present-day region of HADHRAMAUT. Gen. 10.26; 1 Chron. 1.20.

Hazar-shual (hā'zär-shōō'əl), unidentified town, S Palestine. Joshua 15.28; 19.3; 1 Chron. 4.28; Neh. 11.27.

Hazar-susah (hā'zär-syōō'sə) or **Hazar-susim** (-syōō'səm), unidentified town, S Palestine. Joshua 19.5; 1 Chron. 4.31.

Hazazon-tamar: see HAZEZON-TAMAR.

haze, suspension in the atmosphere of minute dust or salt particles that are not individually seen but that nevertheless reduce visibility. So-called damp haze and dry haze produce different optical effects because the particles of which each consists are of different sizes, the dry haze particles being smaller. Damp haze may develop from dry haze when water condenses on moisture-absorbing dry haze particles. Continuation of condensation in such cases leads to the formation of FOG. A hazy condition prevalent on hot days, known as optical haze, or "shimmer," is caused by unequal heating of the air, which results in unequal refraction of light as it passes through air of varying density.

hazel, any plant of the genus *Corylus* of the family Betulaceae (BIRCH family), shrubs or small trees with foliage similar to the related alders. They are often cultivated for ornament and for the edible nuts. Hazels are also called filberts, although the latter is more strictly a name for European kinds (*C. maxima, C. avellena,* and their varieties, e.g., the cobnut) that are cultivated, chiefly in Europe, for the filbert of commerce. Nuts of the American hazel (*C. americana*) are often gathered but seldom sold. Winter hazel and WITCH HAZEL are not related to hazel. Hazel is classified in the division MAGNOLIOPHYTA, class Magnoliopsida, order Fagales, family Betulaceae.

Hazel Crest, village (1970 pop. 10,329), Cook co., NE Ill., a residential suburb of Chicago; inc. 1911.

Hazelelponi (hā'zĕlĕlpō'nī), Judahite woman. 1 Chron. 4.3.

hazelmouse: see DORMOUSE.

Hazel Park, city (1970 pop. 23,784), Oakland co., SE Mich., a suburb of Detroit; inc. 1942. Hazel Park has varied light manufacturing industries and a racetrack. Most of the early settlers were Germans. Ottawa Indian chief Pontiac made his headquarters in Hazel Park.

Hazelwood, city (1970 pop. 14,082), St. Louis co., E. Mo., a suburb of St. Louis; inc. as a village 1949, city charter approved 1969. Its manufactures include automobile and aircraft parts, food products, and furniture.

Hazen, William Babcock, 1830–87, American general, b. West Hartford, near Hartford, Vt. In the Civil War he fought at Shiloh, Perryville, and Murfreesboro, and in the Chattanooga campaign. Promoted to major general of volunteers (1864), he led a division in General Sherman's campaign through Georgia and the Carolinas. After the war he served many years in the West. His criticism of army contracts and the post-trader system helped to expose the misdealings of William Worth BELKNAP in the War Dept. Hazen was appointed chief signal officer in 1880. As ex officio head of the Weather Bureau, he organized the polar expedition of Adolphus W. Greely. See his *Narrative of Military Service* (1885); E. I. Stewart, ed., *Penny-an-Acre Empire in the West* (1968).

Hazerim (həzē'rĭm, hăz'ə-), Hebrew word meaning villages. It is erroneously given in ancient translations as the name of a place. Deut. 2.23.

Hazeroth (həzē'rŏth, hăz'ə-) [Heb.,=camping grounds], camp of the Hebrews, N of Mt. Sinai. Num. 11.35; 12.16; 33.17; Deut. 1.1.

Hazezon-tamar (hăz'əzŏn-tā'mär), unidentified town, Palestine. Gen. 14.7. The identification of Hazezon-tamar with En-gedi in 2 Chron. 20.2 is probably an error.

Haziel (hā'zēĕl, hāzī'-), Gershonite Levite. 1 Chron. 23.9.

Hazleton (hā'zəltən), city (1970 pop. 30,426), Luzerne co., E Pa., on a mountain top in an anthracite-coal region; inc. as a borough 1856, as a city 1892. The once dominant coal industry has declined; the economy is now based on diversified industries, and the city's manufactures include textiles, metal products, foam rubber, electronic equipment, shoes, furniture and fixtures, and paper products. Hazleton was settled c.1809. Its name derives from the hazel bushes that grew in the swamp called Haselschwamm by the early German settlers. The settlement began to grow after coal was discovered nearby in 1826. Coal production reached its peak in the two World Wars. A junior college affiliated with Pennsylvania State Univ. and a state hospital, with a school of nursing, are in Hazleton.

Hazlitt, William, 1778–1830, English essayist. Abandoning the idea of entering the clergy, he took up painting and later journalism. He acted as parliamentary reporter and theatrical critic for the *Morning Chronicle* and later contributed to Leigh Hunt's *Examiner*, the *Edinburgh Review*, the *London Magazine*, and the *New Monthly*. Hazlitt's penetrating literary criticism is collected in *Characters of Shakespeare's Plays* (1817), *Lectures on the English Poets* (1818), *Lectures on the English Comic Writers* (1819), *Table Talk* (1821–22), and *The Spirit of the Age* (1825), portraits of his contemporaries. His essays on Shakespeare and his *Dramatic Literature of the Age of Elizabeth* (1820) renewed enthusiasm for Elizabethan drama. Hazlitt was one of the great masters of the miscellaneous essay, displaying a keen intellect, sensibility, and wide scope of interest and knowledge. His most notable single essays include "On Going a Journey," "My First Acquaintance with Poets," "On the Feeling of Immortality in Youth," and "Going to a Fight." His interest in the French Revolution and his strong beliefs in the principles of liberty and the rights of man inspired him to write a life of Napoleon (4 vol., 1828–30). See biographies by H. C. Baker (1962) and P. P. Howe (1947, repr. 1972); studies by J. B. Priestley (1960), R. Park (1971), and R. M. Wardle (1971). *The Memoirs of William Hazlitt* (1867) is by his grandson, **William Carew Hazlitt,** 1834–1913, bibliographer. Among W. C. Hazlitt's works are a valuable *Handbook to the Popular, Poetical, and Dramatic Literature of Great Britain* (1867) and its supplements and *Four Generations of a Literary Family: The Hazlitts* (1897).

Hazo (hā'zō), nephew of Abraham. Gen. 22.22.

Hazor (hā'zôr) **1** Fortified city of N Galilee, 5 mi (8 km) SW of Lake Hula, in present-day Israel. Strategically located in ancient Palestine on the road leading from Egypt to Syria and Asia Minor, it was occupied from the early Bronze Age to Hellenistic times. Joshua destroyed it because it was the center of the league of Canaanite kingdoms. Joshua 11.1; 19.36. Solomon rebuilt it as one of his strongholds in the north. 1 Kings 9.15; 2 Kings 15.29. Tiglathpileser III later destroyed it. Excavations have revealed both the Canaanite and Israelite cities and have confirmed the biblical data. **2** Unidentified town, Palestine. Joshua 15.23 **3** See KERIOTH **2. 4** town, the modern Khirbat Hazzar, Jordan, 4 mi (6 km) NW of Jerusalem, occupied after the Exile. Neh. 11.33. **5** collective name used for the seminomadic Arabs. Jer. 49.28–33. **6** Unidentified town, S Palestine. Joshua 15.25. AV gives at this point "Hazor, Hadattah," but RV is more likely correct with Hazor-hadattah.

H. D.: see DOOLITTLE, HILDA.

He, chemical symbol of the element HELIUM.

Head, Edith: see under FASHION.

Head, Sir Edmund Walker, 1805–68, British governor general of Canada (1854–61), cousin of Sir Francis Bond Head. An Oxford scholar and tutor, he published several books. His success as lieutenant governor of New Brunswick (1848–54) led to his appointment as governor general of Canada in 1854. He faced difficult problems during his administration, primarily caused by the antagonism between French and British inhabitants, but he retired from office before the political issues that led to confederation (1867) reached a peak. See biography by D. G. Kerr (1954).

Head, Sir Francis Bond, 1793–1875, British administrator in Canada. A soldier (1811–25) and unsuccessful mining adventurer in South America, he had had little experience to prepare him for the post of lieutenant governor of Upper Canada (Ontario), to which he was appointed in 1835. Sir Francis's reactionary policy in Canada and his alliance with the FAMILY COMPACT estranged Robert Baldwin and the moderate reformers and drove William Lyon Mackenzie and other radical reformers into open rebellion in 1837. Head, who had resigned but had not yet been replaced in his post, quelled this uprising. He left Canada in 1838, never again to hold public office, and devoted his later years to writing.

Head, Richard, c.1637–c.1686, English writer. His best-known work is *The English Rogue* (1665), written with Francis Kirkman, a collection of crude picaresque stories. Among his other fictional biographies of rogues are *The Life and Death of Mother Shipton* (1667) and *Floating Island* (1673).

headdress, head covering or decoration, protective or ceremonial, which has been an important part of COSTUME since ancient times. Its style is governed in general by climate, available materials, religion or superstition, and the dictates of fashion. The most primitive form consisted of varied styles of HAIRDRESSING. Protective head coverings include the HAT, cap, hood, helmet, WIG, and VEIL. Ceremonial headdress, which is often highly symbolic and steeped in tradition, includes all head coverings and headdressings that indicate rank, profession, or religion, as well as those worn in ritualistic ceremonies, games, and contests. Examples are the feathered war bonnet of the American Indian, the peacock feathers of the Manchu, the Eastern turban, the Turkish fez, the cardinal's hat, the nun's coif and veil, the marriage crowns, the judge's wig, the academic cap (mortarboard), and many others.

Heade, Martin Johnson, 1819–1904, American painter, b. Lumberville, Pa. He studied under Thomas Hicks and in Europe and later traveled in Central and South America. He painted portraits, dramatic seascapes, and landscapes but is best known for exotic paintings in which scientifically exact birds and plants are set against poetic backgrounds in eerie colors. Among his paintings in museums are *Orchids and Hummingbirds* (Detroit Inst. of Arts) and *Approaching Storm: Beach near Newport* (Mus. of Fine Arts, Boston). See study by R. G. McIntyre (1948).

head-hunting, practice of taking and preserving the head of a slain enemy. It has occurred throughout the world from ancient times into the 20th cent. In Europe it flourished in the Balkans until the early 20th cent. The practice often has magico-religious motives. Head-hunting tribes usually believe that there is soul matter concentrated in the head; therefore, taking the head of an enemy not only adds to the totality of soul matter in one's community but also weakens the power of the enemy tribe. Heads are also secured as tokens of courage and manhood. As a rule in these tribes young men are allowed to marry only after they have taken their first head, and for each trophy they may wear a distinctive feather or special tattoo. In some parts of the world, notably among the Indians of North America, the scalp alone was taken (see SCALPING), and the hair was often used in the making of amulets. Heads may be mummified in various ways, as in New Guinea, where both skull and skin are preserved, or among the Jívaro of South America, where the skin alone is preserved to produce a so-called shrunken head. See also CANNIBALISM. See L. M. Cotlow, *Amazon Head Hunters* (1953).

Head Start, U.S. educational program for disadvantaged preschool children, established under the Economic Opportunity Act of 1964. Aimed initially only at poor children, its purpose was to organize programs that would prepare preschool children for elementary school. Money was appropriated through the Office of Economic Opportunity, which made individual grants to cities and other localities to set up Head Start centers. In 1969 the program was transferred to the Dept. of Health, Education, and Welfare. It was later extended to children above the poverty level, whose parents, however, had to pay according to their income.

heal-all: see SELF-HEAL.

Health, Education and Welfare, United States Department of, Federal executive department established to improve the administration of programs in the fields of health, education, and social security. The department was formed in 1953 as the successor to the Federal Security Agency and its chief executive officer, the Secretary, was given cabinet rank. Among its principal constituent organizations are the Public Health Service (which includes the Food and Drug Administration), the Office of Education, the Social Security Administration, and the Social and Rehabilitation Service. Oveta Culp HOBBY was the first Secretary. The department's history has been a stormy one as it has served as the vehicle for many controversial programs, such as Federal aid to education and medical care for the aged.

health insurance, prepayment plan providing services or cash indemnities for medical care needed in times of illness or disability. It is effected by voluntary plans, either commercial or nonprofit, or by compulsory national insurance plans, usually connected with a social security program. Compulsory accident and sickness insurance was initiated (1883–84) in Germany by Otto von Bismarck; it was adopted by Great Britain, France, Chile, the Soviet Union, and other nations after World War I. In Britain the National Health Insurance Act of 1946, which went into effect in 1948, provided the most comprehensive compulsory medical care plan introduced anywhere up to that time. Under the plan the individual is free to obtain medical attention from any doctor participating in the national health service, the cost of which is met by the national government and local taxation. In 1958 the Canadian Hospital and Diagnoses Act provided full hospital service almost free of charge in public wards. The program is financed by the federal government but administered by the provinces. Before 1965, when MEDICARE and MEDICAID were introduced, the United States was the only Western industrial nation without some form of compulsory national health insurance. Advocacy of government health insurance in the United States began in the early 1900s. Theodore Roosevelt made national health insurance one of the major planks of the Progressive party in the 1912 presidential campaign, and in 1915 a model bill for health insurance was presented in numerous state legislatures but was defeated. Opposition to such plans was led, after 1920, by the American Medical Association and was motivated by the fear that government participation in medical care might lead to SOCIALIZED MEDICINE. In the past, health insurance in the United States took the form of voluntary programs. Such programs date from about 1850, when health insurance was provided chiefly by cooperative mutual benefit and fraternal beneficiary associations. Limited coverage by commercial companies was also introduced during that period, and subsequently many plans were established by industries and labor unions. After 1920 the emphasis was on hospitalization and medical care policies. Many plans have been set up by societies of practicing physicians, but the largest enrollment has been in Blue Cross and Blue Shield plans. These are community-sponsored, nonprofit service plans based on contracts with hospitals and with subscribers. By the 1970s, Blue Cross, which covers expenses for hospital care, had more than 75 million subscribers in the United States, and Blue Shield, which covers doctors' fees, had almost 67 million members. Most general voluntary plans accept subscribers, in groups or as individuals, without medical examination and regardless of income; they extend coverage to dependents and exclude accidents and diseases covered by workmen's compensation laws. Although valuable in cushioning the financial distress caused by illness or injury, voluntary health insurance not only limits benefits in order to avoid prohibitive rates, but excludes many people, particularly the needy aged. It became apparent that it was necessary to obtain legislation that would provide medical care for the elderly. A voluntary Federal-state grant-in-aid program providing medical care to the aged began to be implemented in 1961. Legislation proposed by President Kennedy to provide medical care for the aged through the social security mechanism was defeated in 1961, but in 1965, during President Lyndon B. Johnson's administration, Federal legislation in the form of MEDICARE for the aged and MEDICAID for the indigent was enacted. See Harry Eckstein, *The English Health Service: Its Origins, Structure, and Achievements* (1958); H. M. Somers and A. R. Somers, *Doctors, Patients, and Health Insurance* (1961); O. W. Anderson, *The Uneasy Equilibrium* (1968); D. S. Hirshfield, *The Lost Reform* (1970); R. J. Myers, *Medicare* (1970); M. V. Pauly, *Medical Care at Public Expense* (1971).

Healy, George Peter Alexander, 1813–94, American painter, b. Boston. He began painting portraits at the age of 18 and, disregarding background, concentrated on producing a good likeness. Examples of his art are the portraits of Louis Philippe, François Guizot, and a self-portrait (Uffizi); Daniel Webster and Longfellow (Mus. of Fine Arts, Boston); Mrs. John C. Cruger and a self-portrait (Metropolitan Mus.); Chief Justice Taney (Capitol, Washington, D.C.); a series of the Presidents (Corcoran Gall.); and Lincoln (Newberry Library, Chicago). See his *Reminiscences of a Portrait Painter* (1894).

Healy, Timothy Michael, 1855–1931, Irish statesman, first governor general of the Irish Free State (1922–27). Elected to Parliament in 1880, he worked closely with Charles Stewart PARNELL until the O'Shea divorce scandal (1890). Thereafter he led the anti-Parnell nationalists in Parliament. He was expelled from the party in 1902 but retained his seat in Parliament until 1918, when he resigned it to a Sinn Feiner. In the meantime he practiced at the bar, especially in the interests of Irish tenants and woman suffragists. On the foundation (1922) of the Irish Free State he was appointed governor general and showed a remarkable spirit of conciliation in the performance of his duties. He resigned in 1927.

hearing: see EAR.

hearing aid, device used in some forms of deafness to amplify sound before it reaches the auditory organs. Modern hearing aids are electronic. They contain a tiny receiver and a transistor amplifier, and are battery powered. Some are small enough to fit into an arm of a pair of eyeglasses, or into the outer ear. The bone-conduction hearing aid, placed behind the ear, channels sound waves to the adjacent bony part of the skull, which then transmits the vibrations to the auditory nerve of the cochlea. The air-conduction hearing aid amplifies sounds and directs them into the ear towards the tympanic membrane. The oldest form of hearing aid is the ear trumpet, a large horn-shaped device that collects sound at its large mouth and channels it into its small earpiece, which is inserted into the ear.

Hearn, Lafcadio (lăfkä'dēō hûrn), 1850–1904, American author, b. Leucadio, Ionian Islands, of Irish-Greek parentage. He was educated in Ireland, England, and France before immigrating to the United States in 1869. There he eked out a living by doing odd jobs and newspaper work. Handicapped throughout most of his life by partial blindness, Hearn was a colorful, imaginative, but morbidly discontented man. Most admired for his sensitive use of language, he was at his best in writing about the macabre and in creating strange exotic moods. Hearn first attracted attention with the originality and highly polished style of his "Fantastics," a series of weird sketches that appeared in a New Orleans paper. His first published book was *One of Cleopatra's Nights* (1882), a translation of six Gautier stories. This was followed by *Stray Leaves from Strange Literature* (1884); *Gombo Zhèbes* (1885), a collection of Creole proverbs; *Some Chinese Ghosts* (1887), Oriental folk tales; *Chita: A Memory of Last Island* (1889); and *Two Years in the French West Indies* (1890). In 1890 he went to Japan, commissioned to write a series of articles for an American publisher. There he spent the rest of his life, writing what is considered his best work. He married a Japanese woman, taught in Japanese universities, and became a Japanese citizen in 1895, taking the name Yakumo Koizumi. Of his 12 books written during this period, *Glimpses of Unfamiliar Japan* (1894), *Kokoro* (1896), *Japanese Fairy Tales* (1902), and *Japan: An Attempt at Interpretation* (1904) are most memorable. See biography by Elizabeth Stevenson (1961).

Hearne, Samuel (hûrn), 1745–92, British fur trader, explorer in N Canada. He entered the British navy at the age of 11 and saw service in the naval battles of the Seven Years War. In 1766 he was hired by the Hudson's Bay Company, and he was mate of the sloop *Churchill*, serving at and about Fort Prince of Wales (now Fort Churchill) until 1768, when he became mate of the brigantine *Charlotte*. In 1769 he was chosen to head a land expedition to the north to investigate Indian reports of a great river and large copper mines. His first two attempts met with failure, but finally in Dec., 1770, guided by a Chipewyan Indian, he set off on the third and successful expedition, which took him across the barren grounds to the Coppermine River and down to its mouth. He came back by Great Slave Lake and arrived at Fort Prince of Wales on June 30, 1772. Although the copper mines proved disappointing, the trip was of great importance. In spite of his inaccurate geographical data, Hearne opened up an unknown territory. He gave an accurate and valuable account of the Chipewyan Indians, and he proved that there was no short Northwest Passage. In June, 1774, Hearne set out from York Factory and established Cumberland House for the Saskatchewan trade, the first inland post of the Hudson's Bay Company. He returned in 1775 and set off immediately again for the west but was recalled to Fort Prince of Wales, where he was put in charge until the French captured the fort in 1782. Hearne made his way to England, but returned to Canada in 1783, where he remained until 1787. His *Journey from Prince of Wales Fort on Hudson's Bay to the Northern Ocean* appeared in 1795. See the Champlain Society editions of that work (ed. by J. B. Tyrrell, 1911) and of his later journals (ed. by J. B. Tyrrell, 1934, repr. 1968). See also selections from his *Journey* (ed. by Farley Mowat, 1958, repr. 1968); Agnes Laut, *Pathfinders of the West* (1904, repr. 1969); Gordon Speck, *Samuel Hearne and the Northwest Passage* (1963).

Hearst, George (hûrst), 1820–91, American mining magnate, U.S. Senator (1886–91), b. Franklin co., Mo. He went to California in 1850 and became a mining prospector and geologist. He successfully selected and invested in numerous mining properties, notably the Ophir in Nevada, the Homestake in South Dakota, and the Anaconda in Montana. He bought (1880) the San Francisco *Examiner*, which his son William Randolph Hearst managed after 1887. An unsuccessful Democratic candidate (1885) for U.S. Senator, George Hearst was later appointed (1886) and then elected (1888) to the Senate. His wife, Phoebe Apperson Hearst (1842–1919), became a prominent philanthropist and donated freely to the Univ. of California for buildings, expeditions, and facilities. See biography by C. M. B. and Fremont Older (1933, new ed. 1966).

Hearst, William Randolph, 1863–1951, American journalist and publisher, b. San Francisco. During his lifetime Hearst established a vast publishing empire that included 18 newspapers in 12 cities and 9 successful magazines. He persuaded his father, George Hearst, to place him in charge of the San Francisco *Examiner*, where he experimented profitably with flamboyant pictures, shrieking typography, and earthy, mass-appeal news coverage. In 1895 he invaded New York City with his purchase of the *Morning Journal* and began a bitter war with the other yellow, or sensational, journals. Hearst provided aggressive news coverage, bought distinctive talent, enticed employees of other papers from their jobs with higher salaries and greater prestige, and increased the size of his paper while cutting its price to a penny—a move his competitors were forced to follow. Into the circulation battle between the rival newspapers Hearst brought wild reports of Cuba's struggle for independence from Spain. Other papers replied with further lurid accounts. Leaving the truth behind, the papers' anti-Spanish outcry fanned public sentiment and helped to drive the United States to war with Spain (1898). By the time Hearst had established his supremacy in "penny journalism," his funds were almost exhausted, but he had gained a foothold for the great newspaper empire he was to erect. He served in the House of Representatives (1903–7) but was defeated as candidate for mayor of New York City in 1905 and 1909 and for governor of New York in 1906. While a congressman he sought the Democratic party's presidential nomination without success. Hearst's papers originally supported public ownership, antitrust laws, and legislation favorable to labor unions. Support for Franklin D. Roosevelt's New Deal gave way, however, to vigorous opposition to the President's policies on taxes, trusts, and labor. The publisher became stridently conservative. His castle at San Simeon, Calif., erected from 1919 on, won fame for its huge art collections, which often overflowed into warehouses. At his estate Hearst entertained friends in the motion-picture industry, which he had entered as a financier on a large scale. The property was presented to the state as a museum after Hearst's death. The publisher's holdings embraced not only his newspapers and magazines (which included *Good Housekeeping, Cosmopolitan,* and *Harper's Bazaar*) but also the *American Weekly* syndicated supplement and services supplying news, features, and photographs. A flamboyant, highly controversial figure, Hearst was nonetheless an intelligent, extremely competent newspaperman. Although he occasionally manipulated the news, he was not afraid to espouse unpopular causes even at great cost in money and popularity. See biography by W. Swanberg (1961).

Heart, river, 180 mi (290 km) long, rising in the low prairie country near the Little Missouri River, SW N.Dak., and flowing E to the Missouri at Mandan, N.Dak. The Heart Butte and Dickinson dams, irrigation and flood control units built by the U.S. Bureau of Reclamation as part of the MISSOURI RIVER BASIN PROJECT, have created the region's largest lakes, which are major recreation areas.

heart, muscular organ that pumps blood to all parts of the body. The rhythmic beating of the heart is a ceaseless activity, lasting from before birth to the end of life. The human heart is a pear-shaped structure about the size of a fist. It lies obliquely within the chest cavity just left of center, with the apex pointing downward. The heart is constructed of a special kind of MUSCLE called myocardium, whose contractions are entirely self-stimulated The organ is enclosed in a double-layered, membranous sac, the pericardium. The heart is divided into two cavities by a wall of muscle. The left cavity pumps blood throughout the body, while the right cavity pumps blood only through the lungs. Each cavity is in turn divided into two chambers, the upper ones called atria, the lower ones ventricles. Venous blood from the body, containing large amounts of carbon dioxide, returns to the right atrium. It enters the right ventricle, which contracts, pumping blood through the pulmonary artery to the lungs. Oxygenated blood returns from the lungs to the left atrium and enters the left ventricle, which contracts, forcing the blood into the AORTA, from which it is distributed throughout the body. Blood flows one way only. It is prevented from backing up by a series of valves at various openings: the tricuspid valve between the right atrium and right ventricle, the bicuspid, or mitral, valve between the left atrium and left ventricle, and the semilunar valves in the aorta and the pulmonary artery. Each heartbeat, or cardiac cycle, is

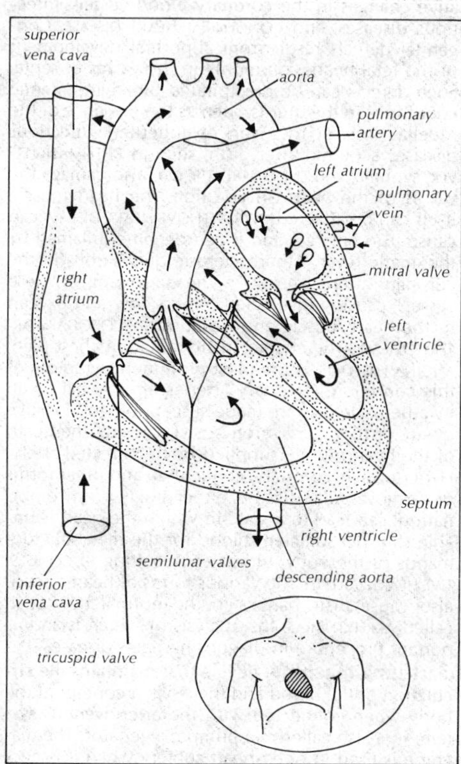

Cross section of heart, with arrows indicating direction of blood flow

divided into two phases. In the first phase, a short period of ventricular contraction, or systole, the tricuspid and mitral valves snap shut, producing the familiar "lub" sound heard in the physician's stethoscope. In the second phase, a slightly longer period of ventricular relaxation, or diastole, the pulmonary and aortic valves close up, producing the characteristic "dub" sound. Both sides of the heart contract, empty, relax, and fill simultaneously; therefore, only one systole and one diastole are felt. The normal heart has a rate of 72 beats per min, but in infants the rate may be as high as 120 beats, and in children about 90 beats, per min. Each heartbeat is stimulated by an electrical impulse that originates in a small strip of heart tissue known as the sino-atrial (S-A) node, or pacemaker. One of the important advances in cardiology is the artificial pacemaker used to electrically initiate a normal heartbeat when the patient's own pacemaker is defective; it may be surgically implanted in the patient's body. Another familiar tool of the cardiologist is the electrocardiograph (EKG), which is used to detect abnormalities that are not evident from a physical examination (see ELECTROCARDIOGRAPHY). One of the most important advances in heart surgery during the 1960s was the transplantation of the healthy heart immediately after the death of an individual (the donor) to a recipient suffering from incurable heart disease (see TRANSPLANTATION, MEDICAL). However, new advances in the design and construction of an artificial heart—both the entire organ and such parts as the valves and large blood vessels—show even more promise in treating cardiovascular disease. See CIRCULATORY SYSTEM.

heartburn, burning sensation beneath the breastbone, also called pyrosis. Heartburn does not indicate heart malfunction but results from nervous tension or overindulgence in food or drink. The sensation is produced by spasmodic constrictions of the esophagus, accompanied or occasioned by regurgitation of stomach acids, which spread upward into the throat and jaw, and may result in belching or vomiting. Physical activity immediately following ingestion of food may exaggerate the symptoms. The discomfort can usually be relieved by taking alkaline preparations to counteract the excessive acidity. Proper dietary habits, e.g., eating slowly, avoiding spicy foods, and a period of physical inactivity after eating, may prevent heartburn. Sometimes the condition is symptomatic of a disease of the digestive system, such as a stomach ulcer or gall-bladder disorder, and persistent recurrence should be called to the attention of a physician.

heart disease, any of several abnormalities of the heart and its function in maintaining blood circulation. Among the most common causes are degenerative changes in the coronary blood vessels, infectious diseases, and CONGENITAL HEART DISEASE. Congenital defects result from abnormal development of the fetal heart, commonly in the valves or septa. Such defects can be precipitated by environmental conditions in the uterus, such as the presence of the rubella virus, or they can be inherited. Infectious diseases acquired after birth, such as RHEUMATIC FEVER, syphilis, and ENDOCARDITIS, can also damage the valves of the heart. In addition, the heart muscle itself can be affected: HYPERTENSIVE HEART DISEASE can cause it to enlarge, and it can become inflamed by rheumatic fever. Atherosclerotic depositions in the coronary arteries result in the narrowing of these vessels, causing insufficient blood flow and oxygen to the heart muscle and resulting in CORONARY ARTERY DISEASE. The characteristic radiating chest pain, ANGINA PECTORIS, is the most prominent symptom of this condition. Coronary arteries already narrowed by atherosclerosis are made susceptible to blockage by a clot (coronary thrombosis), causing the death of the heart muscle supplied by the affected artery. Hypertensive, coronary, congenital, and other forms of cardiovascular disease, either singly or in combination, can lead to a state in which the heart is unable to expel sufficient blood for the metabolic demands of the body, ultimately resulting in CONGESTIVE HEART FAILURE. The various forms of heart disease also cause disturbances in the normal heartbeat, called ARRHYTHMIAS, the analysis of which is an important procedure in diagnosing heart disease.

heart-lung machine, device that maintains the circulation of the blood and the oxygen content of the body when connected with the arteriovenous system; it is also called the pump oxygenator. The machine is used in open-heart surgery when it is necessary to effect a bypass of the circulatory system of the heart and lungs. The oxygenator repeatedly draws off the blood from the veins, reoxygenates it, and pumps it into the arterial system. The contractions of the heart are halted by running a potassium citrate solution through the coronary vessels. The surgeon is thus enabled to open the heart and make the necessary repairs while the heart is still and his view is not obstructed by blood.

heart murmur: see ARRHYTHMIA.

hearts, card game played by three to six players with an ordinary deck. All the cards are dealt to the players. When a card is led, each hand must follow suit if possible. The object is to avoid taking tricks that contain cards of the heart suit, but a larger premium is given if every heart is taken. In black lady, a popular variation of hearts, the queen of spades is to be equally avoided. Other variations include omnibus hearts, domino hearts, and auction hearts.

heartsease, name for several plants, particularly a species of VIOLET also known as pansy.

heartwood, the central, woody core of a tree, no longer serving for the conduction of water and dissolved minerals; heartwood is usually denser in texture and darker in color than the outer SAPWOOD. Before the synthesis of aniline dyes, the heartwood of several tropical trees (sold collectively under the commercial name *brazilwood*) was used to produce blue, purple, and red dyes. As a tree becomes older, the heartwood increases in diameter, whereas the sapwood remains about the same thickness. See WOOD.

heat, internal ENERGY of a substance associated with the positions and motions of the individual molecules (or atoms or ions) composing the substance rather than with the position or motion of the substance as a whole. The average kinetic energy of the molecules, which is due to their motions, is measured by the TEMPERATURE of the substance, while the potential energy is associated with the state, or phase, of the substance (see STATES OF MATTER). Heat energy is commonly expressed in either of two units: the CALORIE, a metric unit, is used by scientists everywhere, and the BRITISH THERMAL UNIT (Btu), an English unit, is used by engineers in the United States. It has also become common for scientists to express heat energy in the unit JOULE, a unit used to express all forms of energy. As heat is added to a substance in the solid state, the molecules of the substance gain kinetic energy and the temperature of the substance rises. The amount of heat needed to raise a unit of mass of the substance one degree of temperature is called the SPECIFIC HEAT of the substance. Because of the way in which the calorie and the Btu are defined, the specific heat of any substance is the same in either system of measurement. For example, the specific heat of water is 1 calorie per gram per degree Celsius; i.e., 1 calorie of heat is needed to raise the temperature of 1 gram of water by 1 degree Celsius; it is also 1 Btu per pound per degree Fahrenheit. When the solid reaches a certain temperature, it changes to a liquid. This temperature is a particular property of the substance and is called its MELTING POINT. While the solid-liquid transition is taking place, there is no change in temperature. All of the heat being added is being converted to the internal potential energy associated with the liquid state. The amount of heat needed to convert one unit of mass of a substance from a solid to liquid is called the heat of fusion, or latent heat of fusion, of the substance. Like specific heat, LATENT HEAT is also a property of the particular substance. The latent heat of fusion for the ice-to-water transition is 80 calories per gram. After the substance is completely changed from a solid to a liquid, further addition of heat again causes the temperature to rise until it reaches the BOILING POINT, the particular temperature at which the given substance changes from a liquid to a gas. During the liquid-gas transition, the temperature remains constant until the change is completed. The heat of vaporization, or latent heat of vaporization, is the heat that must be added to convert one unit of mass of the substance from a liquid to a gas. Heat may be transferred from one substance to another by three means—CONDUCTION, CONVECTION, and RADIATION. Conduction involves the transfer of energy from one molecule to adjacent molecules without the substance as a whole moving. Convection involves the movement of warmer parts of a substance away from the source of heat and takes place only in fluids, i.e., liquids and gases. Radiation is the transfer of heat energy in the form of ELECTROMAGNETIC RADIATION, principally in the INFRARED RADIATION portion of the spectrum. The analysis of heat on the basis of the structure of matter is considered in the KINETIC-MOLECULAR THEORY OF GASES and provides an explanation for various of the GAS LAWS. The gas laws in turn serve to define an absolute temperature scale based on theoretical considerations (see KELVIN TEMPERATURE SCALE). The study of heat and its relationship to useful work is called THERMODYNAMICS and involves macroscopic quantities such as pressure, temperature, and volume without regard for the molecular basis of these quantities. LOW-TEMPERATURE PHYSICS is concerned with phenomena that occur at extremely low temperatures. See M. C. Mott-Smith, *Heat and Its Workings* (1933, repr. 1962); Richard Becker, *Theory of Heat* (tr. 1967).

heat capacity, or **thermal capacity,** ratio of the change in HEAT energy of a unit mass of a substance to the change in TEMPERATURE of the substance; like its melting point or boiling point, the heat capacity is a characteristic of a substance. The measurement of heat and heat capacity is called CALORIMETRY. In the metric system, heat capacity is often expressed in units of CALORIES per gram per degree Celsius (cal/g-°C); in the English system, BRITISH THERMAL UNITS per pound per degree Fahrenheit (Btu/lb-°F) are often used. Because of the definitions of the calorie and Btu, these two heat capacity units are equivalent; the heat capacity of pure water is 1 cal/g-°C and 1 Btu/lb-°F. Other units are used also; for example, the heat capacity of pure water is 4.184 joules/g-°C and 1.16×10^{-6} kilowatt-hours/g-°C. The heat capacity of a system such as a calorimeter refers to the ratio of the change in heat energy of the system as a whole to the change in its temperature and is expressed in such units as calories per degree Celsius. It has been found by experiment that the value of the heat capacity depends on the conditions under which the heat energy of a substance or system changes. See also SPECIFIC HEAT.

heat engine, device that turns thermal energy into mechanical energy. See ENTROPY.

heat exhaustion, condition caused by overexposure to sunlight or another heat source and resulting in dehydration and salt depletion, also known as heat prostration. The symptoms are severe headaches, weakness, dizziness, blurred vision, and sometimes unconsciousness. However, the body temperature is not elevated as in HEATSTROKE. The condition is usually temporary and rarely fatal. Salt depletion may be so severe that painful spasms of the muscles, commonly called heat cramps, occur. Treatment includes administering a salt solution to replace the sodium chloride and water that have been depleted from the body. See FIRST AID.

Heath, Edward Richard George, 1916–, British statesman. He was educated at Oxford. After serving in the army during World War II, he worked for a merchant bank. Elected to Parliament as a Conservative in 1950, he held several posts in the party whip's office (1951–55) before becoming government chief whip and parliamentary secretary to the treasury (1955–59), minister of labor (1959–60), and lord privy seal with foreign office responsibilities (1960–63). In the last capacity he negotiated unsuccessfully for Great Britain's entry into the European Common Market, a policy to which he remained firmly committed. He was secretary of state for industry and trade and president of the Board of Trade (1963–64) and was elected leader of the Conservative party, then in opposition, in 1965. The Conservatives lost the 1966 general election, but they won an unexpected victory in 1970, largely on the issue of the country's economy, and Heath became prime minister. Heath's administration was marked by the entry of Britain into the Common Market (Jan., 1973), by legislation to restrict immigration from Commonwealth countries, and also by legislation, which proved ineffective, to regulate industrial relations. The intensification of strife in Northern Ireland led to the suspension of the Northern Irish Parliament and government in 1972. A new provincial assembly and a coalition executive were created (1973) but both proved short-lived. Soaring inflation forced Heath to abandon his earlier opposition to wage and price controls in 1972. However, the attempt to enforce wage controls worsened the government's already bad relations with the trade unions. A series of major industrial disputes culminated in a confrontation (Nov., 1973–Feb., 1974) with the miners' union. The miners' ban on overtime, followed by a full strike, so reduced energy supplies that the country was forced onto a three-day work week schedule. Heath finally called an election (Feb., 1974), asking for a mandate for his tough policy toward the unions. He did not receive sufficient support to form a Conservative government and resigned as prime minister. Continuing under Heath's leadership, the Conservatives were again defeated in Oct., 1974. He has written *Old World, New Horizons* (1970). See biographies by M. I. Laing (1972) and Andrew Roth (1972).

heath, in botany, common name for some members of the Ericaceae, a family of chiefly evergreen shrubs with berry or capsule fruits. Plants of the heath family form the characteristic vegetation of many regions with acid soils, particularly the moors, swamps, and mountain slopes of temperate regions throughout the world and, to a lesser extent, of tropical and subarctic regions (see HEATH, in ecology). Many species have attractive blossoms and are consequently popular as wild flowers or, when possible, as cultivated ornamentals, e.g., the RHODODENDRON, AZALEA, MOUNTAIN LAUREL (not a true laurel), TRAILING ARBUTUS, and heather. The BEARBERRY and MADROÑO are sometimes grown for the shiny, leathery leaves typical of the family. Other species valued commercially for their edible fruits include the BLUEBERRY, CRANBERRY, and HUCKLEBERRY. WINTERGREEN is the source of a flavoring. Sometimes considered a part of the heath family are the pipsissewa and related perennial herbs and the INDIAN PIPE and related saprophytic (nongreen) plants. The common heather—the heather of Scotland—is *Calluna vulgaris,* sometimes called ling. Native to Europe and Asia Minor, it is now common also in Greenland and in North America. Its multiple branches have been used for brooms. The names heath and

Rhododendron, Rhododendron maximum, *a member of the heath family*

heather are often used interchangeably. Although both are somewhat similar low evergreen shrubs of the Old World, heather has short, scalelike, overlapping leaves and a profusion of long-lasting rosy flowers; the true heaths (genus *Erica*) have needlelike leaves and white, rose, or yellow flowers. Species of this large genus are characteristic of vast moor areas in W Europe and, especially, South Africa and the Mediterranean area. The root of the tree heath (*E. arborea*), called also *bruyère*, brier, brierroot, French brier, and other names, is the major source of brier pipes (see SAINT-CLAUDE). Heather and a few species of heath are grown as ornamentals; cultivated forms of heather usually have red to purple flowers of a deeper shade than those of the wild types. Other plants of similar habit, particularly those of the same family, are sometimes also called heath or heather. Heath is classified in the division MAGNOLIOPHYTA, class Magnoliopsida, order Ericales, family Ericaceae.

heath, tract of open land characterized by a few scattered trees, abundant moss cover, and numerous low shrubs, principally of the heath family (see HEATH, in botany). In high-latitude regions with minimal variation in climate, the undershrub vegetation may persist indefinitely on shallow, peaty soils rather than undergoing succession to the climax vegetation (see ECOLOGY), e.g., temperate forests. Alpine azalea, bearberry, dwarf birch, and some insectivorous plants are among the additional flora found on heaths.

Heathcote, Caleb, 1666–1721, merchant and public official in colonial New York, b. England. He arrived in New York in 1692. He became a member of the governor's council and, in Westchester co., a colonel of militia, county judge, and after 1696 mayor of Westchester borough town. Later he held the offices of mayor of New York City (1711–13) and surveyor general of customs for all northern colonies. He engaged in contracting, milling, and land speculation in large tracts in Westchester, Dutchess, and Ulster counties. In 1701 he received the manor of Scarsdale (Westchester co.), the last manor to be granted in the British colonies. His enthusiasm for the Anglican church led him to take five missionary journeys into Connecticut, and both there and in Westchester he established new congregations. See D. R. Fox, *Caleb Heathcote, Gentleman Colonist* (1926).

heather: see HEATH, in botany.

Heathfield, 1st Baron: see ELIOTT, GEORGE AUGUSTUS, 1ST BARON HEATHFIELD OF GIBRALTAR.

heating, means of making a building comfortably warm relative to a colder outside temperature. Old, primitive methods of heating a building or a room within it include the open fire, the fireplace, and the STOVE. In ancient Rome a heating system, called a hypocaust, warmed a building by passing hot gases from a furnace through enclosed passages under the floors and behind the walls before releasing them outside. The principal modern systems that are used to heat a building are classified as warm air, hot water, steam, or electricity. In the warm-air system air, heated in a furnace, rises through warm-air ducts and enters the rooms through outlets, while cooler air in the rooms passes into return ducts that lead back to the furnace. The air circulates through the system by convection, i.e., the tendency of a fluid such as air to rise when warm and sink when cool. In newer buildings the circulation is assisted by a fan. The hot-water system has a boiler for heating the water that is sent through connecting pipes to RADIATORS and convectors, the latter devices being metal enclosures containing hot-water pipes surrounded by metal fins. The circulation is maintained by pumps or, in older buildings, by convection. In the steam-heating system, steam generated in a boiler is circulated by its own pressure (sometimes aided by a vacuum pump) through radiators. There are many kinds of electric heating systems. In one type current is sent through wires into electric resistors that are contained in convectors in rooms. The resistors convert the current into heat. In a radiant panel heating system a room is warmed by heat emitted from wall, floor, or ceiling panels. They are warmed by the circulation of warm air, hot water, or steam or by an electric current in resistors within or behind the panels. Experiments are being made to utilize solar energy for heating buildings. In many large buildings, such as theaters, public libraries, and municipal buildings, the heating, ventilating, and air-conditioning units are combined in one system. In district heating, heat is distributed from a heating plant to buildings in a section (usually commercial) of a city. See J. R. Allen et al., *Heating and Air Conditioning* (6th ed. 1946); R. W. Shoemaker, *Radiant Heating* (1948); W. K. Carrier et al., *Modern Air Conditioning, Heating, and Ventilation* (3d ed. 1959).

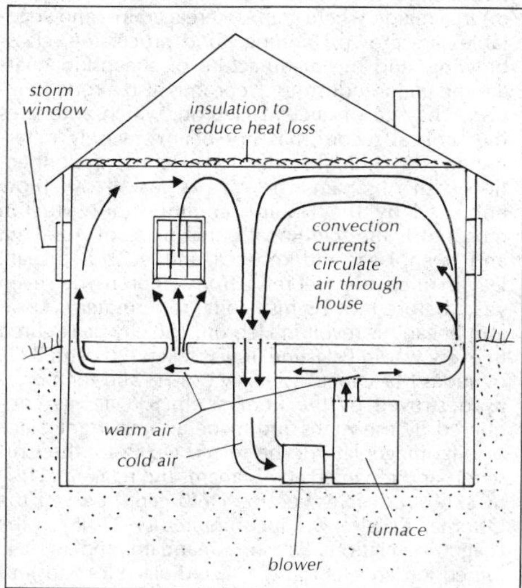

Typical warm-air heating system

heat of combustion, HEAT released during COMBUSTION. In particular, it is the amount of heat released when a given amount (usually 1 MOLE) of a combustible pure substance is burned to form incombustible products (e.g., water and carbon dioxide); this amount of heat is a characteristic of the substance. Heats of combustion are used as a basis for comparing the heating value of fuels, since the fuel that produces the greater amount of heat for a given cost is the more economic. Heats of combustion are also used in comparing the stabilities of chemical compounds. For example, if equal quantities of two isomeric hydrocarbons burn to produce equal amounts of carbon dioxide and water, the one releasing more energy (i.e., with the higher heat of combustion) is the less stable, since it was the more energetic in its compounded form.

heat prostration: see HEAT EXHAUSTION.

heatstroke, profound disturbance of the heat-regulating mechanism of the body, also known as sunstroke. It is characterized by extremely high body temperatures and sometimes by convulsions and coma. The skin is usually hot and dry because the body-cooling process of sweating has ceased. However, in some cases the skin may feel relatively cool because blood vessels just below the skin have constricted and the overheated blood is not being carried to the surface. Heatstroke is a rare disorder and is more common among elderly and obese people and those with debilitating diseases. Heatstroke, unlike HEAT EXHAUSTION, is considered a serious threat to life; treatment must be swift to prevent death or serious brain damage from high body temperature. The body should be cooled as quickly as possible by removing the patient to a cool shady place and applying cold water or ice water to the skin. See FIRST AID.

heaven, in Judaeo-Christian belief, state of bliss in which the just see God face to face. This privilege is called the beatific vision; it constitutes the principal joy of the redeemed. Many Christians believe that after the general RESURRECTION the human body will be glorified and reunited forever with the soul in heaven. The Roman Catholic Church teaches that before entering heaven many souls must pass through PURGATORY to be made ready. The Orthodox Eastern churches hold a doctrine somewhat similar, but not so definite. In the popular mind and in literature heaven is often represented as full of material delights. Much of the conventional imagery—e.g., golden streets—is based on the Book of REVELATION. Poetical names for heaven are Paradise, Holy City, and New Jerusalem. Islam is commonly accused of teaching that heaven is full of delights of the flesh, but there is good ground for supposing that the passages of the Koran telling of the delights of heaven are allegorical. For comparable ideas see ELYSIAN FIELDS; FORTUNATE ISLES; VALHALLA.

heaves, chronic pulmonary emphysema in horses. Heaves is characterized by the disruption of normal lung tissue with resultant loss of the lung's elastic recoil. A forced expiratory effort is needed to empty the lungs of air. The cause is not known, but the disease is associated with prolonged feeding of poor-quality roughage and dusty feeds. These conditions may incite an allergic reaction in association with chronic bronchitis, thus leading to emphysema. Treatment consists of substituting dampened hay and grain or pelleted rations for the dusty feeds and administering anti-inflammatory drugs. Complete recovery is rare.

Heaviside, Oliver (hĕv'ēsīd), 1850–1925, English physicist. He did valuable work in telephony and in the theory of electrical conduction in cables and other areas of electric theory. He suggested (1902) the existence of a layer in the upper atmosphere responsible for altering the path of certain radio waves and thus making possible long-distance transmission of signals. The same conclusion was reached independently by Arthur E. Kennelly; its existence was proven, and it is known both as the Kennelly-Heaviside layer and as the Heaviside layer. See IONOSPHERE.

heavy spar: see BARITE.

heavy water: see DEUTERIUM.

Hebbel, Christian Friedrich (krĭs'tyän frē'drĭkh hĕb'əl), 1813–63, German tragic dramatist. Born poor, he was largely self-educated. Hegel's historical theories influenced his work, which is a link between romantic and realist drama. Hebbel's first play, *Judith* (1840, tr. 1914), introduced a new type of tragic character, heroic through degradation and retribution rather than through virtue. Other works include *Maria Magdalena* (1844, tr. 1913–15); the historical tragedies *Herod and Mariamne* (1850, tr. 1912) and *Agnes Bernauer* (1852, tr. 1909); *Gyges and His Ring* (1856, tr. 1914); and the great trilogy *The Nibelungs* (1862, tr. 1903). His tragedies contain much violent emotion, and they usually portray a struggle between old and new sets of values. See studies by S. G. Flygt (1968) and Mary Garland (1973).

Hebburn, urban district (1971 pop. 23,597), Durham, NE England, on the Tyne River. It has shipbuilding, electrical industries, and engineering works. In 1974, Hebburn became part of the new metropolitan county of Tyne and Wear.

Hebe (hē'bē), in Greek religion, goddess of youth; daughter of Zeus and Hera and wife of Hercules. She appears only occasionally in legend as a cupbearer and attendant of the gods. The Romans identified her as Juventas.

Hebel, Johann Peter (yō'hän pā'tər hā'bəl), 1760–1826, German short-story writer and dialect poet. Editor of *Der rheinländische Hausfreund* [Rhineland home companion] from 1801 to 1811, Hebel gained popularity as author of realistic, often humorous folk anecdotes with overtones of Christian ethic. A collection of these, *Schatzkästlein* [treasure box], appeared in 1811. In his *Alemannische Gedichte* [Alemannic poems] (1803), dialect is employed for fine poetic expression in verses that extol youth, mother love, and the beauties of nature.

Heber (hē'bər). **1** Eponym of the Hebrews. Luke 3.35. Eber: Gen. 10.21. **2** Kenite, husband of Jael. Judges 4.11, 17; 5.24. **3,4** Benjamites. 1 Chron. 8.17,22. **5** Gadite. 1 Chron. 5.13. **6** Judahite. 1 Chron. 4.18. **7** Asherite. Gen. 46.17; Num. 26.45; 1 Chron. 7.31,32. **8** Eber, priest. Neh. 12.20.

Heber, Reginald, 1783–1826, English clergyman and hymn writer. He became bishop of Calcutta in 1823. Several volumes of his poems and of his sermons were published, but he is best known as the author of the familiar hymns *The Son of God Goes Forth to War; Holy, Holy, Holy;* and *From Greenland's Icy Mountains.* He also edited the works of Jeremy Taylor.

Hébert, Jacques René (zhäk rənā' ābĕr'), 1757–94, French journalist and revolutionary. An ardent supporter of the French Revolution, he gained the support of the working classes through his virulent paper *Le Père Duchesne* and was prominent in the CORDELIERS. He became one of the leaders of the COMMUNE OF PARIS, and, as such, his power was a counterforce to that of Maximilien ROBESPIERRE. He was largely responsible for the tightening of the maximum price laws during the REIGN OF TERROR and for the Law of Suspects. An atheist, he and Pierre CHAUMETTE were the founders of the cult of the worship of Reason. Hébert's policies and his power over the commune threatened the government and aroused Robespierre's opposition. When Hébert and his followers made preparations for a popular insurrection, they were arrested (March, 1794), tried by the Revolutionary Tribunal, and guillotined.

Hébert, Louis, 1575–1627, French pioneer, known as the first Canadian farmer. A Paris apothecary, he spent 10 years (1604–14) in Acadia, and at Port Royal (now Annapolis Royal, N.S.) he made some attempts to farm. Soon after his return to France, Hébert, at the urging of his friend Samuel de Champlain, again set forth for Canada. With his family he settled at Quebec in 1617, the first permanent settler and farmer in Canada. In 1623 he received a grant of land on the site of what is now Upper Town, Quebec.

Hébert, Philippe, 1850–1917, Canadian sculptor, b. Halifax. He studied in Italy (1869–71) and in Paris, and after 1902 he became the most noted sculptor and monument designer of his time in Canada. His works include patriotic statues of Queen Victoria, and Sir John Macdonald (Ottawa); Laval (Quebec); and King Edward and Maisonneuve (Montreal). His son, Henri Hébert, was also a sculptor.

Hebrew language, member of the Canaanite group of the Northwest Semitic subdivision of the Semitic subfamily of the Hamito-Semitic family of languages (see HAMITO-SEMITIC LANGUAGES). Hebrew was the language of the Jewish people in Biblical times, and most of the Old Testament was written in Hebrew. The oldest extant example of Hebrew writing dates from the 11th or 10th cent. B.C. Hebrew began to die out as a spoken tongue among the Jews after they were defeated by the Babylonians in 586 B.C. Well before the time of Christ it had been replaced by Aramaic as the Jewish vernacular, although it was preserved as the language of the Jewish religion. From A.D. 70, when the dispersion of the Jews from Palestine began, until modern times, Hebrew has remained the Jewish language of religion, learning, and literature. During this 2,000-year period, Hebrew has always been spoken to some extent. At the end of the 19th cent. the Zionist movement brought about the revival of Hebrew as a spoken language, which culminated in its designation as an official tongue of the state of Israel in 1948. There it is spoken by most of the 2.5 million Jews of that country. Grammatically, Hebrew is typical of the Semitic tongues in that so many words have a triconsonantal root consisting of three consonants separated by vowels. Changes in, or omissions of, the vowels alter the meaning of a root. Prefixes and suffixes are also added to roots to modify the meaning. There are two genders, masculine and feminine, which are found in the inflection of the verb as well as in noun forms. Modern Hebrew has experienced some grammatical changes and has updated its vocabulary by adding many new words, especially words of a scientific nature. The earliest alphabet used for Hebrew belongs to the Canaanite branch of the North Semitic writing and is known as Early Hebrew. Later the Jews adapted the Aramaic writing (see ARAMAIC) and evolved from it a script called Square Hebrew, which is the source of modern Hebrew writing. Today the Hebrew alphabet has 22 letters, all consonants. Symbols for the vowels were apparently introduced about the 8th cent. A.D. and are usually placed below the consonants if employed. Their use is generally limited to the Bible, verse, and children's books. Hebrew is written from right to left. See William Chomsky, *Hebrew: The Eternal Language* (1957); Moshe Greenberg, *Introduction to Hebrew* (1965); Edward Horowitz, *How the Hebrew Language Grew* (1967).

Hebrew literature. The great monuments of the earliest period of Hebrew literature are the OLD TESTAMENT and the APOCRYPHA; parts of the PSEUDEPIGRAPHA and of the DEAD SEA SCROLLS were also produced before the conquest of Judaea by Titus. The literature of the Jews developed mainly in the Hebrew language, although there were also works in Greek, Aramaic, and Arabic. In the 2d cent. began the Talmudic period, which lasted well into the 6th cent.; in these centuries the great anonymous encyclopedic work of religious and civil law, the TALMUD, was compiled, edited, and interpreted. The MIDRASH—a collection of HALAKAH (found also in the Talmud) and haggadic material—likewise forms part of the Hebrew literature of that period. In the 4th cent. the TARGUM to the Pentateuch and to the Prophets was finished. The 6th and 7th cent. saw the development of the MASORA in Palestine. In Babylonia meanwhile many valuable additions to Hebrew literature were made by the Geonim (see SCRIBE) after the 6th cent. Commentaries on the Talmud and haggadic material continued to be written until the 11th cent., when the Babylonian academies were suppressed and the center of Jewish literary activity shifted to Spain. There, and to some extent in Italy, Hebrew literature flourished for centuries. The finest work was accomplished in the realms of poetry—which was influenced by Arabian and Indian literature—and philosophy. Philology, exegesis, and codification also flourished. Literature on philosophy and ethics was subsequently eclipsed by writings on mysticism (see CABALA), and by the 14th cent. the great cabalistic work, the *Zohar,* appeared. Famous scholars and authors of Hebrew literature in the Middle Ages included AHA OF SHABCHA, SAADIA BEN JOSEPH AL-FAYUMI, DUNASH BEN TAMIM, DUNASH BEN LABRAT, GERSHOM BEN JUDAH, AL-FASI, Solomon ben Judah IBN GABIROL, RASHI, JUDAH HA-LEVI, Abraham ben Meir IBN EZRA, MAIMONIDES, IMMANUEL BEN SOLOMON, Isaac ABRAVANEL, and Joseph ben Ephraim CARO. In the persecutions following the Crusades, when the Jews were driven from country to country, they clung to their literature—which leaned increasingly to mysticism and asceticism—and especially to the Old Testament. On the threshold of the transition from the old isolated life was the poet Moses Hayyim LUZZATTO—a contemporary of the Gaon of Vilna, ELIJAH BEN SOLOMON—but the modern period of Hebrew literature really began with Moses MENDELSSOHN. While Nachman Kohen KROCHMAL and Shloime ANSKY (Solomon Seinwel Rapoport) were contributing to biblical criticism and historical scholarship, writers such as Peretz (Peter) SMOLENSKIN were devoting themselves to Haskalah, or literature of enlightenment, intended to shake the Jews of Central Europe from their medieval attitudes. Other important figures of the period are the scholar Joseph Halévy, the poet Leon GORDON, and the novelist Solomon Yakob Abramovich, whose pseudonym was MENDELE MOCHER SFORIM. The rise of ZIONISM, particularly reflected in the writings of Asher GINZBERG (Ahad Ha'am), gave Hebrew literature fresh impetus, and Palestine became again the center of publication in Hebrew. Hebrew was proclaimed the national language of the Jews, and after the establishment (1948) of the state of Israel, greater opportunities were given to Hebrew writers and scholars. The two great poets of modern Hebrew literature are Hayyim Nahman BIALIK and Saul TCHERNIHOVSKY, who was strongly influenced by ancient Greek literature. The poetry of Abraham Shlonsky, Lea Goldberg, and Nathan Alterman deals with social and political themes. Among the many writers of prose are Joseph H. Brenner, who described Jewish life in Eastern Europe and pioneer life in Palestine, and Salman Shneur, who wrote of the simple and uneducated Jews. The Nobel laureate S. Y. AGNON portrayed the Eastern European milieu and pioneer life in Palestine; his works have become classics in modern Hebrew epic literature. Hebrew writers who are native to Israel seek inspiration in the classical Hebrew past or in the new life of Israel. The most outstanding writer of this group is Moshe Shamir, who in his two novels—one depicting a Hasmonean king and the other dealing with the Arab-Israeli War of 1948—gave new dimensions to Hebrew fiction. Aron David Gordon (1856–1922) was one of the greatest social and political essayists of Hebrew literature. The leading literary critics are David Frishman (1861–1922) and Yosef Klausner (1874–1958). Outside of Israel, the writing of the Jews is ordinarily in the language of the countries in which they live or in YIDDISH, whose literary use developed rapidly after the middle of the 19th cent. See Nahum Slouschz ben David, *The Renascence of Hebrew Literature, 1743–1885* (1909, repr. 1973); H. T. Fowler, *The History of the Literature of Ancient Israel from the Earliest Times to 135 B.C.* (1912); R. H. Charles, ed., *Apocrypha and Pseudepigrapha of the Old Testament in English* (1913); Lewis Browne, ed., *The Wisdom of Israel* (1945); Menachem Ribalow, *The Flowering of Modern Hebrew Literature* (tr. 1959); Meyer Waxman, *A History of Jewish Literature* (6 vol., 1960); Joel Blocker, ed., *Israeli Stories* (1963); Samuel Halkin, *Modern Hebrew Literature* (rev. ed. 1970); Nathan Kravitz, *Three Thousand Years of Hebrew Literature* (1972); Eisig Silberschlag, *From Renaissance to Renaissance: Hebrew Literature from 1492–1970* (vol. I, 1973).

Hebrew music: see JEWISH LITURGICAL MUSIC.

Hebrews. For history, see JEWS; for religion, see JUDAISM.

Hebrews, epistle of the New Testament, the 19th book in the usual order. It was traditionally ascribed to St. Paul, but few scholars accept his authorship. It was written before A.D. 96. Because of its title, it was long assumed that the book was addressed to Jewish Christians who, through the pressure of persecution, were tending to return to Judaism. However, most modern scholars reject that view and believe that the epistle was directed toward Christians who were lapsing, not into their old religion, but into indifference. The first part (1.1–4.13) is an argument that Christ is superior to the angels (1–2) and to Moses (3.1–6); it closes with an exhortation to faith in the form of a commentary on Ps. 95.7–11 (3.7–4.13). The second part (4.14–10.18) treats the priesthood of Jesus Christ (the order of Melchizedek), which replaces the priesthood of Aaron; it ends with Christ's sacrifice of himself, which supersedes all other sacrifices and serves to expiate sin (9.1–10.18). The doctrine is followed by an exhortation (10.19–12.13) to perseverance in the faith, including a famous chapter (11) on faith in Old Testament lives. The teachings of Hebrews are very significant in the history of theology. See Ronald Williamson, *Philo and the Epistle to the Hebrews* (1970); William MacDonald, *The Epistle to the Hebrews* (1971).

Hebrews, Gospel according to the: see PSEUDEPIGRAPHA.

Hebrew University, at Jerusalem, coeducational. First proposed in 1882, formally opened 1925. The university is famous for its work on the Dead Sea Scrolls and its experiments in atomic and solar energy. It has numerous foreign students. It has faculties of humanities, science, medicine, law, agriculture, social sciences, and dental medicine. The Harry S. Truman International Center for the Advancement of Peace, the Institute of Contemporary Jewry, and the National and University Institute of Agriculture are affiliated.

Hebrides, the (hĕb'rĭdēz), or **Western Islands,** group of more than 500 islands, W and NW Scotland, in Ross and Cromarty co., Inverness-shire, and Argyllshire. Less than a fifth of the islands are inhabited. The Outer Hebrides (sometimes also referred to as the Long Island) are separated from the mainland and from the Inner Hebrides by the straits of Minch and Little Minch and by the Sea of the Hebrides; they extend for 130 mi (209 km) from the Butt of Lewis on LEWIS WITH HARRIS to Barra Head island. Other islands are North UIST, Benbecula, South Uist, Barra, the Flannan Islands (Seven Hunters), and Saint Kilda. The Inner Hebrides include the islands of SKYE, Raasay, Rum, Eigg, Coll, Tiree, STAFFA, IONA, MULL, Scarba, COLONSAY, ORONSAY, Jura, and ISLAY. Fishing, crop raising, sheep grazing, manufacturing of tweeds and other woolens, quarrying (slate), and catering to tourists are the chief means of livelihood. The original Celtic inhabitants, converted to Christianity by St. Columba (6th cent.), were conquered by the Norwegians (starting in the 8th cent.). They held the Southern Islands, as they called them, until 1266. From that time the islands were ruled by various native Scottish chiefs, until the Macdonalds established themselves (1346) as lords of the isles. Since the 16th cent. the Hebrides have belonged to the crown of Scotland. The tales of Sir Walter Scott did much to make the islands famous. The climate is mild, the scenery is beautiful, and there are interesting prehistoric and ancient historical remains and geological structures. There has been much emigration from the overpopulated islands, especially to Canada in the 20th cent. Under the Local Government Act of 1973, the Outer Hebrides were included in a new administrative region, the Western Isles Island Area; the Inner Hebrides were included in the new Strathclyde and Highland regions.

Hebron (hē'brən). **1** Kohathite Levite. Ex. 6.18; Num. 3.19; 1 Chron. 6.2,18; 23.12. **2** Judahite. 1 Chron. 2.42,43.

Hebron, city (1968 est. pop. 38,000), W Jordan, near Jerusalem. It is situated at an altitude of 3,000 ft (910 m) in a region where grapes, cereal grains, and vegetables are grown. Tanning, food processing, glassblowing, and the manufacture of sheepskin coats are the major industries. Hebron is also a road junction. The site of ancient Hebron, which antedates the biblical record, has not been precisely determined. The Bible first mentions Hebron in connection with Abraham. The cave of MACHPELAH (now enclosed by the Haram, an important Muslim mosque) is the traditional burial place of Abraham and Sarah, Isaac and Rebecca, and Jacob and Leah. David ruled the Hebrews from Hebron for seven years before moving his capital to Jerusalem. Absalom began his revolt in Hebron. The city has figured in every war in Palestine. It was taken (2d cent. B.C.) by Judas Maccabeus (see MACCABEES) and temporarily destroyed by the Romans. In 636 it was conquered by the Arabs and made an important place of pilgrimage, later to be seized (1099) by the Crusaders and renamed St. Abraham, and retaken (1187) by SALADIN. It later became (16th cent.) part of the Ottoman Empire, was incorporated (1922–48) in the League of Nations Palestine mandate, and in 1948 joined Jordan. Hebron is a sacred place for Muslims and Jews. It has usually had a significant Jewish population, although following Arab riots in 1929 most Jews left and did not return until after the Israeli occupation following the 1967 Arab-Israeli War. Hebron's modern Arabic name is Al-Khalil.

Hecate (hĕk'ətē, hĕk'ĭt), in Greek mythology, goddess of ghosts and witchcraft. Originally she seems to have been an extremely powerful and benevolent goddess, identified with three other goddesses—Selene (in heaven), Artemis (on earth), and Persephone (in the underworld). From the three supposedly came her image in Greek art as a figure with three bodies or three heads. Generally she is identified as a spirit of black magic, Persephone's attendant, with the power to conjure up dreams, phantoms, and the spirits of the dead. In the upper world she haunted graveyards and crossroads and was invisible to all eyes except those of the hounds who attended her.

Hecatoncheires: see GAEA; TITAN.

Hecht, Ben (hĕkt), 1894–1964, American writer, b. New York City. He grew up in Wisconsin and, while still in his teens, worked on newspapers in Chicago. Early in his career he became involved in the Chicago literary movement of the time, founding in 1923 the Chicago *Literary Times,* an iconoclastic review that he edited for two years. A stormy and controversial figure, Hecht was known for a variety of literary and theatrical activities. He wrote novels, short-story collections, and plays, and he wrote, directed, and produced for the motion-picture industry. With Charles MacArthur, he collaborated on several film scripts and plays, of which *The Front Page* (1928), an irreverent drama of newspaper life, is the most famous. See his autobiography, *A Child of the Century* (1954).

Hecht, Selig, 1892–1947, American biophysicist, b. Glogow, Austria (now Poland). He moved to the United States in 1898 and was graduated from the College of the City of New York (B.S., 1913) and from Harvard (Ph.D., 1917). After organizing the laboratory of biophysics at Columbia Univ., he was professor of biophysics there from 1926. He pioneered in applying physiochemical principles to sensory physiology and is known for his determination of minimal quantal requirements at the threshold of vision and for his successful laboratory regeneration of visual purple. An advocate of popular scientific education, he wrote *Explaining the Atom* (1947).

Heckel, Erich (ā'rĭkh hĕk'əl), 1883–1970, German painter. In 1905, Heckel, together with KIRCHNER and SCHMIDT-ROTTLUFF, founded the BRÜCKE in Dresden. His paintings of this period (e.g., *Scene in a Forest,* 1913; Wallraf-Richartz Mus., Cologne) are characterized by violent color and slashing brushwork. His later works, primarily landscapes, are more tranquil in feeling.

Hecker, Friedrich Franz Karl (frē'drĭkh fränts kärl hĕk'ər), 1811–81, German revolutionary. A lawyer, he was a leader of the radical republicans in the grand duchy of Baden and during the revolutionary agitation of 1847–49 in Germany, he helped organize the demands for democratic parliamentary government. Prior to the meeting of the FRANKFURT PARLIAMENT in 1848 he led an unsuccessful uprising in Baden, proclaiming a constitutional republic. Forced into exile, he settled permanently in the United States. A Republican, he supported Lincoln and fought in the Civil War.

Hecker, Isaac Thomas, 1819–88, American Roman Catholic priest, founder of the Paulist Fathers; son of Prussian immigrants. Feeling the general discontent of his day in the dying Puritanism of New England, he associated with the transcendentalists, stayed for a short time at Brook Farm, and was a friend of Thoreau, Emerson, Bronson Alcott, and Orestes Brownson. Still dissatisfied, he entered (1844) the Roman Catholic Church, joined the Redemptorist order, and was ordained a priest (1849). Returning (1851) from abroad, he worked with immigrant Catholics in the United States. He was a successful missionary, but his intense zeal, doubts of his own worthiness, ill health, and his fixed purpose caused a somewhat stormy career. Difficulties with his order caused him to be expelled, but the pope dispensed him and his colleagues of their vows and allowed them in 1858 to found the Missionary Priests of St. Paul the Apostle (the Paulist Fathers)—an order that achieved prominence in the United States. Father Hecker, who was the superior until his death, founded the Paulist magazine the *Catholic World.* Although ideas allegedly based on those of Hecker were later condemned as the heresy of "Americanism," the whole controversy was settled by an encyclical (1899) of Pope Leo XIII, without Father Hecker or any other American priest ever being specifically charged with holding the heretical views. See biographies by Walter Elliott (1891, repr. 1972) and V. F. Holden (1939, repr. 1974).

Heckewelder, John Gottlieb Ernestus (hĕk'əvĕldər), 1743–1823, Moravian missionary in the United States, b. Bedford, England. Settling (1754) in Bethlehem, Pa., with his parents, he later was indentured to a cedar cooper, while acting occasionally as a messenger to the Indians on the Susquehanna. By 1771 he was an accredited missionary and assistant to David ZEISBERGER. After years with the Pennsylvania Indians who had been removed to Ohio, he retired to Bethlehem, Pa. (1786), but he aided the U.S. government on several occasions with Indian treaties. In 1801 he managed the Indian lands at Gnadenhutten, and he supervised the removal of the Indians to Canada. He spent his last years writing numerous accounts of Indian life, notably his *Account of the History, Manners and Customs of the Indian Nations, Who Once Inhabited Pennsylvania* (1819). See his journals, *Thirty Thousand Miles with John Heckewelder* (ed. by Paul Wallace, 1958).

Heckscher, Eli Filip (ē'lē fĭl'ĭp hĕk'shər), 1879–1952, Swedish economic historian. Influenced by the neoclassical economics of Alfred Marshall, Heckscher advocated the use of monetary policy to combat inflation. His views were adopted by the Bank of Sweden in 1920. His best-known work, *Mercantilism* (tr. 1935), was the first modern synthesis of mercantile thought and practice. Heckscher saw the mercantile system as embodying the political and economic values of competitive young nation states, and he questioned the validity of mercantile theory. Other works include an outstanding economic history of Sweden (4 vol., 1935–49; tr. of abridged ed. 1954).

hectare, abbr. ha, unit of area in the METRIC SYSTEM, equal to 10,000 sq m, or about 2.47 acres. It is commonly used instead of the are, a metric unit equal to 100 sq m, which is too small for practical use in the measurement of land area.

Hector, in Greek mythology, leader and greatest hero of the Trojan troops during the Trojan War. He was the eldest son of Priam and Hecuba, the husband of Andromache, and the father by her of Astyanax. In the *Iliad* he is portrayed as the courageous mainstay of Trojan resistance. He was killed by Achilles in revenge for the death of Patroclus. Hector had several hero cults, most notably at Troy and Thebes.

Hecuba (hĕk'yo͝obə), in Greek mythology, chief wife of Priam, king of Troy. Hecuba bore to Priam 19 children, including Paris, Hector, Troilus, Cassandra, and others who were prominent in the Trojan War. To save Polydorus, her youngest son, from the Greeks, Hecuba sent him to Polymnestor, king of Thrace. After the sack of Troy she was allotted to Odysseus, who on his way home stopped at Thrace. Learning there that Polymnestor had murdered Polydorus, Hecuba, in revenge, blinded the king and killed his children. She is an important character in Euripides' plays *Hecuba* and *The Trojan Women.*

Heda, Willem Claasz (vĭl'əm kläs hä'dä), 1594–c.1678, Dutch still-life painter. His excellent studies of tables laden with food, called *ontbijt* [breakfast piece] still life, are seen in many important European galleries. They are characterized by delicate lighting effects and somber colors.

Hedge, Frederic Henry, 1805–90, American Unitarian clergyman and author, b. Cambridge, Mass., educated in Germany and at Harvard. He held several New England pastorates. In 1836 he joined Emerson and others in forming the Transcendental Club. His edition of *Prose Writers of Germany* (1848) established him as a German scholar. Hedge also wrote for periodicals, edited (1857–61) the *Christian Examiner,* and wrote *Reason in Religion* (1865) and many other books. He was professor of ecclesiastical history in the Harvard Divinity School (1857–76) and professor of German at Harvard (1872–81).

hedge, ornamental or protective barrier composed of shrubs or small trees growing in close rows. The plants may be allowed to grow naturally or may be trimmed to various heights and shapes (see TOPIARY WORK). Thorny hedge plants include barberry, Osage orange, buckthorn, and hawthorn. Popular evergreen hedge plants are box, privet, azalea, yew, arborvitae, rhododendron, mountain laurel, and holly. Decorative deciduous shrubs often used are lilac, forsythia, mock orange, spiraea, euonymus, and viburnum. Hedges may also serve in erosion control, e.g., *Rosa rugosa* planted along highway embankments and the rows of poplars, hemlocks, and other trees planted as shelter belts.

hedgehog, Old World insectivorous mammal of the family Erinaceidae, related to moles and shrews. The spiny hedgehogs are found in Africa and Eurasia, except SE Asia. They have rounded bodies up to 13 in. (33 cm) long, very short tails, and pointed snouts; their backs and sides are covered with stiff spines and their undersides with coarse hair. They are usually brown and yellow in color. When frightened, a hedgehog rolls itself into a tight ball with its spines pointing outward; when rolled up it is invulnerable to almost any predator. The European hedgehog, *Erinaceus europaeus,* is about 9 in. (23 cm) long, with small ears. It is strictly nocturnal, spending the day in a burrow in the undergrowth; it hibernates in midwinter. The name hedgehog describes the tendency of these animals to make their burrows in the hedgerows that surround English fields. Hedgehogs are not related to hogs, but they root in the ground for food in the manner of hogs. Their diet consists of small animals, including worms, insects, frogs, mice, and even poisonous snakes; they have a high level of immunity to viper venom. A hedgehog will bite a snake and then roll itself up as the snake strikes, repeating this procedure until the snake is dead. *E. europaeus* is found throughout Europe and N Asia, as far north as the limits of the deciduous forest. Other spiny hedgehog species are found in Africa and Asia; many are desert dwellers. Some are wholly nocturnal and others only partially so; all either hibernate or aestivate and tend to hole up during dry weather. Some species have large pointed ears like those of dogs. The hairy hedgehogs, or gymnures, are found instead of spiny hedgehogs in SE Asia. They resemble long-snouted rats and have coarse bristles but no spines. They give off a distinctive musky odor, produced by anal glands. The largest of the gymnures is the moon rat, *Echinosorex gymnurus,* with a 15-in. long (38-cm) body and an 8-in. (20-cm) tail. There are no New World hedgehogs, although the North American PORCUPINE, which is not an insectivore but a rodent, is sometimes erroneously called a hedgehog. The spines of hedgehogs differ from those of porcupines; they are not barbed and do not pull out of the animal's skin easily. Both spiny and hairy hedgehogs are classified in the phylum CHORDATA, subphylum Vertebrata, class Mammalia, order Insectivora, family Erinaceidae.

hedging, in commerce, method by which traders contract both to buy and to sell a particular good so as to minimize any losses caused by price fluctuations. It is generally used by traders on the commodities market. For example, a miller may buy wheat that is to be converted into flour. At the same time, he will contract to sell an equal amount of wheat, which he does not presently own, to another trader. The miller agrees to deliver the second lot of wheat at the time his flour is ready for market and at the price current at the time of the agreement. If the price of wheat declines during the period between the miller's purchase of the grain and the flour's entrance onto the market, there will also be a resulting drop in the price of flour. That loss must be sustained by the miller. However, since he has a contract to sell wheat at the older, higher price, the miller makes up for his loss on the flour sale by his gain on the wheat sale. Hedging is also employed by export-import traders and certain manufacturers.

Hedin, Sven Anders (svĕn än'dərs hĕdēn'), 1865–1952, Swedish explorer in central Asia. Following soon after PRZHEVALSKY, Hedin explored Tibet, Sinkiang, and the Kunlun and Trans-Himalaya ranges and discovered the sources of the Brahmaputra and the Indus rivers; his account was published in *Scientific Results of a Journey in Central Asia, 1899–1902* (8 vol., 1904–8) and in *Transhimalaya* (3 vol., 1909–12). His explorations in Tibet were reported in *Southern Tibet* (12 vol., 1917–22). Hedin also wrote popular accounts of his travels, including *Across the Gobi Desert* (1931, repr. 1968); *Jehol, City of Emperors* (1931); *The Conquest of Tibet* (1934); and a trilogy, *The Flight of the Big Horse* (1936), *The Silk Road* (1938), and *The Wandering Lake* (1940), dealing with the Lob Nor of Sinkiang. He also wrote *My Life as an Explorer* (7th ed. 1942) and *Great Men I Met* (2 vol., 1952).

Hedjaz: see HEJAZ, Saudi Arabia.

Hedmark (hĕd'märk), county (1972 est. pop. 180,000), c.10,600 sq mi (27,500 sq km), SE Norway, bordering on Sweden in the east. The capital is Hamar. It is the chief forest area of Norway; production is especially important in the upper Glåma River valley. The county also has productive farms.

hedonism (hē'dənĭzəm, hĕd'-) [from Gr.,=pleasure], the doctrine that pleasure is the highest good. Ancient hedonism expressed itself in two ways: the cruder form was that proposed by ARISTIPPUS and the early CYRENAICS, who believed that pleasure was achieved by the complete gratification of all one's sensual desires; on the other hand, EPICURUS and his school, though accepting the primacy of pleasure, tended to equate it with the absence of pain and taught that it could best be attained through the rational control of one's desires. Ancient hedonism was egoistic; modern British hedonism, expressed first in 19th cent. UTILITARIANISM, is universalistic in that it is conceived in a social sense—"the greatest happiness for the greatest number." See J. C. Gosling, *Pleasure and Desire* (1969).

Hedwig, Johann (yō'hän hāt'vĭkh), 1730–99, German botanist, b. Transylvania. He was an authority on the lower plants, especially mosses, and was professor at the Univ. of Leipzig from 1786. The moss *Hedwigia* is named for him.

Heem, Jan Davidszoon de (yän dä'vĕtsōn də hām), 1606–84, Dutch painter of fruit and flower pieces. He studied with his father, David de Heem, and became one of Holland's foremost still-life painters. His paintings are found in many leading European museums; the Metropolitan Museum possesses three examples. His son and pupil, **Cornelis de Heem** (kōr'nā"lĭs), c.1631–1695 painted works that were often confused with his father's.

Heemskerck, Maarten van (mär'tən vän hāms'-kĕrk), 1498–1574, Dutch painter. His family name was van Veen. He studied in Haarlem under Scorel and in Rome from 1532 to 1534. His Italianate paintings won him a high reputation in Haarlem, but his most valuable work is contained in his sketchbooks (Berlin), which include drawings of ancient monuments in Rome and sketches of the construction of St. Peter's. The Metropolitan Museum has his portrait of his father.

Heerlen (hār'lən), city (1970 pop. 75,140), Limburg prov., SE Netherlands. It is an industrial and transportation center; its manufactures include textiles and food products. The city was a major coal-mining center from the late 19th cent. to the early 1970s, when mining operations were substantially reduced.

Heflin, James Thomas, 1869–1951, U.S. politician, b. Randolph co., Ala. He was admitted (1893) to the bar and in 1920 entered the U.S. Senate where he was known at first as "Cotton Tom" because of his championing of the Southern farmer. He later became a vigorous anti-Roman Catholic crusader and supporter of white supremacy, famous for his theatrical oratory and distinctive dress. His opposition to the presidential campaign of Alfred E. Smith in 1928 promoted Heflin's defeat for reelection in 1930, and he was subsequently unsuccessful in regaining office. See A. A. Michie and Frank Ryhlick, *Dixie Demagogues* (1939).

Hefner, Hugh M., 1926–, American publisher and entrepreneur, b. Chicago. Raised according to strict Methodist principles, Hefner reacted by becoming the originator and publisher of *Playboy*, an extremely popular magazine for men. First issued in 1953, *Playboy* features photographs of nude women, advice on hedonistic living, and stories and articles by well-known writers. Hefner has multiplied his success by worldwide ventures into related businesses, such as nightclubs, hotels, movies, games, and real estate.

Hegai (hĕg'āī) or **Hege** (hē'gē), chamberlain of Ahasuerus. Esther 2.3,8,15.

Hege, the same as HEGAI.

Hegel, Georg Wilhelm Friedrich (gā'ôrkh vĭl'-hĕlm frē'drĭkh hā'gəl), 1770–1831, German philosopher, b. Stuttgart; son of a government clerk. Educated in theology at Tübingen, he acted as a private tutor at Bern and Frankfurt. In 1801 he became *privatdocent* [tutor] and in 1805 professor at the Univ. of Jena. While considered a follower of Schelling, he was developing his own system, which he first presented in *Phenomenology of Mind* (1807). During the Napoleonic occupation Hegel edited (1807–8) a newspaper, which he left to become rector (1808–16) of a *Gymnasium* at Nuremberg. He then returned to professorships at Heidelberg (1816–18) and Berlin (1818–31), where he became famous. In his lectures at Berlin he set forth the system elaborated in his books. Chief among these were *Science of Logic* (1812–16); *Encyclopedia of the Philosophical Sciences* (1817), an outline of his whole philosophy; and *Philosophy of Right* (1821). He also wrote books on ethics, aesthetics, history, and religion. His interests were wide, and all were incorporated into his unified philosophy. His absolute idealism envisaged a world-soul that develops out of, and is known through, the dialectical logic. In this development, known universally as the Hegelian dialectic, one concept (thesis) inevitably generates its opposite (antithesis), and the interaction of these leads to a new concept (synthesis). This in turn becomes the thesis of a new triad. Hegel regarded Kant's study of categories as incomplete. The idea of being is fundamental, but it evokes its antithesis, not being. However, these two are not mutually exclusive for they necessarily produce the synthesis, becoming. Hence activity is basic, progress is rational, and logic is the basis of the world process. The study of nature and mind reveal reason as it realizes itself in cosmology and history. The world process is the absolute, the active principle which does not transcend reality but exists through and in it. The universe develops by a self-creating plan, proceeding from astral bodies to the world, from the mineral kingdom to the vegetable, from the vegetable kingdom to the animal. In society the same progress can be discovered; man's activities lead to property, which leads to law. Out of the relationship between the individual and law develops the synthesis of ethics, where both the interdependence and the freedom of individuals interact to produce the state. The state thus is a totality above all individuals, and since it is a unit, its highest development is rule by monarchy. Such a state is an embodiment of the absolute idea. In his study of history, Hegel reviews the story of states which hold sway over lesser peoples until a higher representative of the absolute evolves. Though much of his development was questionable, the concept of the conflict of cultures stimulated historical analysis. Hegel considered art as a closer approach to the absolute than government. In the history of art he distinguishes three periods—the Oriental, the Greek, and the romantic. He believed that the modern romantic form of art cannot encompass the magnitude of the Christian ideal. Hegel taught that religion moved from worship of nature through a series of stages to Christianity, where Christ represents the union of God and man, of spirit and matter. Philosophy goes beyond religion as it enables man to comprehend the entire historical unfolding of the absolute. Hegel has influenced many subsequent philosophies—post-Hegelian idealism, the existentialism of Kierkegaard and Sartre, the socialism of Marx and Lasalle, and the instrumentalism of Dewey. His theory of the state was the guiding force of the group known as the Young Hegelians, who sought the unification of Germany. His lectures on philosophy, religion, aesthetics, and history were collected in eight volumes after his death. See biography by Franz Wiedmann (1968); W. T. Stace, *The Philosphy of Hegel* (1923, repr. 1955); Sidney Hook, *From Hegel to Marx* (1936, repr. 1962); Israel Knox, *The Aesthetic Theories of Kant, Hegel, and Schopenhauer* (1936); Herbert Marcuse, *Reason and Revolution* (1955, repr. 1963); J. N. Findlay, *Hegel: A Re-examination* (1958, repr. 1964); W. A. Kaufman, *Hegel: Reinterpretation, Texts and Commentary* (1965); Z. A. Pelczynski, ed., *Hegel's Political Philosphy: Problems and Perspectives* (1971); Stanley Rosen, *Hegel* (1974).

hegemony (hĭjĕm'ənē, hē–, hĕj'əmō"nē, hĕg'ə-), [Gr.,=leadership], dominance, especially of one Greek city-state over others. The free Greek city-states produced excellent soldiers, but the governments so weakened themselves by wars over hegemony that they fell prey to Macedon and later to Rome. When the city-states lost their independence, they declined politically and culturally. The greatest of the wars over hegemony was the Peloponnesian War between Athens and Sparta, each strengthened by allies. The subjugation of all GREECE by Macedon resulted.

hegira or **hejira** (hĭjī'rə, hĕj'ərə) [Arabic *hijra*= breaking off of relations], flight of the prophet MUHAMMAD from Mecca in Sept., 622. Muhammad was a monotheist and preached against the polytheism of the Meccan religion. This aroused the hostility of the merchant leaders of his native city, who derived much of their wealth from pilgrimages to Mecca and its surrounding cities. Forced to flee from his enemies, Muhammad went to Yathrib (laber renamed MEDINA), where he became ruler. The Muslim era is dated from the first day (July 16, 622) of the lunar year in which the hegira took place. The abbreviation A.H. is used before years of the hegira, like A.D. in Christendom.

Heiberg, Gunnar Edvard Rode (gōōn'är ĕd'värd rō'də hā'bârg), 1857–1929, Norwegian dramatist. His plays include *Aunt Ulrikke* (1883), *The Balcony* (1894, tr. 1922), and *King Midas* (1890), a satire on Bjørnson. *The Tragedy of Love* (1904), probably his best work, deals with love as an uncivilized passion.

Heiberg, Johan Ludvig (yōhăn' lōōth'vē hī'bâr), 1791–1860, Danish writer, director of the National Theater. In the play *Christmas Fun and New Year's Jesting* (1817), he satirized leading contemporary writers. As a defender of classical drama, Heiberg became an influential figure in Danish literature and criticism. He composed many vaudevilles, or musical comedies, based on French models but Danish in subject and humor. Among his plays is *The Hill of the Elves* (1828), probably the most frequently performed of Danish plays.

Heide (hī'də), town (1970 pop. 22,992), Schleswig-Holstein, N West Germany, in the center of the Dithmarschen oil fields. It is a trade center, with one of the largest market squares in West Germany. Heide was the capital of the peasant republic of DITHMARSCHEN from 1447 until 1559, when it was destroyed by fire.

Heidegger, Martin (mär'tĕn hī'dĕger), 1889–, German philosopher. As a student at Freiburg, Heidegger was influenced by the neo-Kantianism of Heinrich Rickert and the phenomenology of Edmund Husserl. In 1923 he became professor at Marburg, where he wrote and published the only completed part of his major work, *Sein und Zeit* (1927; tr. *Being and Time*, 1962). On the basis of this work Heidegger was called (1928) to Freiburg to succeed Husserl in the chair of philosophy, which he occupied until his retirement in 1951. He supported Adolf Hitler during the dictator's first years in power, but he soon became disillusioned with Nazism. Although generally considered an existentialist, Heidegger vehemently rejected this title, just as he came to reject Husserl's phenomenology. Heidegger's fundamental concern, as announced in *Sein und Zeit* and developed in his subsequent works, is the problem of being. In *Sein und Zeit*, being is shown to be intimately linked with temporality; the relationship between them is investigated by means of an analysis of human existence. Strongly influenced by Sören Kierkegaard, Heidegger delineated various aspects of human existence such as "care," "moods," and man's relationship to death. It was those studies and their influence upon Jean Paul Sartre that have led many critics to consider Heidegger an existentialist. The ontological aspect of Heidegger's thought assumed greater prominence in his later writings. He considers himself the first thinker in the history of Western philosophy to have raised explicitly the question concerning the "sense of being," and he locates the crisis of Western civilization in mass "forgetfulness of being." In addition to its influence on Sartre, Heidegger's thought has influenced modern Protestant theology through Paul Tillich and Rudolph Bultmann. Among his works are *Kant and the Problem of Metaphysics* (1929, tr. 1962), *What Is Metaphysics?* (1929, tr. 1949), *An Introduction to Metaphysics* (1953, tr. 1959), *What Is Philosophy?* (1956, tr. 1958), and *The End of Philosophy* (1956, tr. 1973). See studies by Thomas Langan (1959), Magda King (1964), James M. Demske (1963, tr. 1970), and L. M. Vail (1972).

Heidelberg (hī'dəlbĕrkh), city (1970 pop. 121,023), Baden-Württemberg, SW West Germany, picturesquely situated on the Neckar River. Manufactures include printing presses and other machinery, precision instruments, textiles, and leather goods. Heidelberg was first mentioned in the 12th cent. In 1225 it was acquired by the count palatine of the Rhine and until 1720 was the residence of the electors palatine (see PALATINATE). The Univ. of Heidelberg (Ruprecht-Karl-Universität) was founded in 1386 by Elector Rupert I and is the oldest German-speaking university after those in Prague and Vienna. It became a bulwark of the Reformation in the 16th cent., declined after the Thirty Years War (1618–48), and, recovering after the French Revolutionary Wars, became the leading university of 19th-century Germany. Student life in 19th-century Heidelberg, with its duels, songs, and romance, has been much publicized. The university's professors have included noted theologians, the chemist R. W. Bunsen, and the sociologist Max Weber. Since 1952 the city has been the headquarters of the U.S. army in Europe. Heidelberg is famous for its ruined castle (built mainly in the 16th and early 17th cent.), which was largely destroyed by French troops in the late 17th cent. In the castle's cellar is the Heidelberg Tun, a gigantic wine cask with a capacity of c.58,080 gal (2,200 hectoliters). Other points of interest in Heidelberg include the city hall (1701–03) and the *Philosophenweg* (Philosopher's Way), a path overlooking the city. The **Heidelberg Catechism** was a profession of faith of the German Reformed (Calvinistic) Church, drawn up at the request of Elector Frederick III and published in

1563. It gained wide repute and was adopted by several REFORMED CHURCHES.

Heidelberg man: see HOMO ERECTUS.

Heidenstam, Verner von (vĕr'nər fən hā'dənstäm), 1859–1940, Swedish lyric poet, novelist, and essayist. His first volume of poetry, *Pilgrimage and Wanderyears* (1888), challenged the contemporary realistic and utilitarian Swedish literature. His subjective and personal style was also evident in *Poems* (1895) and *New Poems* (1915), which established him as one of Sweden's great lyric poets. In the historical novels *The Charles Men* (1897–98, tr. 1920), *Saint Birgitta's Pilgrimage* (1901), and *The Tree of the Folkungs* (2 vol., 1905–7; tr. 1925) he evoked a sense of national continuity. Essays, notably "Renascence" (1889), supported a truly Swedish literary approach, linking realism with imagination and a sense of the beautiful. Heidenstam received the 1916 Nobel Prize in Literature. Some of his poems appeared in translation in 1919. See Alrik Gustafson, *Six Scandinavian Novelists* (1940).

Heifetz, Jascha (yä'shə hī'fĭts), 1901–, Russian-American violinist, b. Vilna. He studied first with his father and in 1910 became a pupil of Leopold Auer at the St. Petersburg Conservatory, giving his first public concert the next year. After great success as a child prodigy in Europe, he immigrated to the United States in 1917. Heifetz became an even greater artist in his mature years, combining brilliantly reasoned, tranquil interpretation with unsurpassed virtuoso technique. He has arranged a number of works for the violin and commissioned several concertos from contemporary composers.

Heijermans, Herman (hĕr'män hī'ərmäns), 1864–1924, Dutch dramatist. Much of his work treated life among the Dutch Jews. His dramas include *Op Hoop van Zegen* (1900, tr. *The Good Hope*, 1928).

Heijo: see PYONGYANG, North Korea.

Heilbronn (hīlbrôn'), city (1970 pop. 101,660), Baden-Württemberg, S West Germany, a port on the Neckar River. A commercial and industrial center, its manufactures include metal products, textiles, chemicals, and wine. Heilbronn was the site (early 9th cent.) of a Carolingian palace and in the 14th cent. became a free imperial city. Although it suffered in the wars of the 16th cent., particularly in the Peasants' War, the city rose to great commercial prosperity in the late 16th and early 17th cent. In 1802, Heilbronn passed to Württemberg, and later in the 19th cent. it acquired industrial importance. In World War II (especially 1944) much of the city was destroyed. Points of interest include the church of St. Kilian (13th–15th cent.) and the Götzenturm, a tower built in 1392, which is mentioned in Goethe's drama *Götz von Berlichingen* (1772).

Heiligenblut (hī'lĭgənblōōt') [Ger.,=holy blood], village, Carinthia prov., SW Austria, at the foot of the Grossglockner. It is a winter sports and mountain-climbing center. Heiligenblut is a famous place of pilgrimage; in its Gothic church (late 15th cent.) is a vial that, according to tradition, contains some of Christ's blood.

Heilprin, Angelo (hīl'prĭn), 1853–1907, American naturalist, b. Hungary. He was taken to the United States in 1856, but furthered his scientific education in Europe (1876–79). He was long associated with the Academy of Natural Sciences and the Wagner Free Institute of Science, both in Philadelphia. He accompanied Robert Peary on his first arctic expedition (1891) and headed the relief expedition of 1892, as described in his *Arctic Problem* (1893). He wrote travel books and two works on the eruption in Martinique of Mont Pelée.

Heilungkiang (hā'lōōng'kyäng', –jēäng'), Mandarin *Hei-lung-chiang* [black dragon river (the Amur)], province (1967 est. pop. 21,000,000), c.272,000 sq mi (704,480 sq km), NE China. The capital is HARBIN. Heilungkiang constitutes the northern part of the region known as Manchuria and is separated from the USSR by the Argun River in the west, the Amur in the north, and the Ussuri in the east. Both the Greater Khingan and Lesser Khingan mountain ranges traverse the province; their heavily forested slopes contain some of the finest timber in China. Lumbering is a major industry. The northwest (that area W of the Greater Khingan) was formerly (before 1969) a part of Inner Mongolia; it has a large Mongol population and is predominantly pastureland, with related industries (dairy products, leather). HAILAR is the principal town of this region. The south, which contains the agricultural, industrial, and economic base of the province, is watered by the Sungari, the Nen, the Hulan, and the Mutan rivers, and is known as the Manchurian plain. It is a great wheat area; millet, kaoliang, soybeans, sugar beets, and flax are also grown. Heilungkiang has more tractor farming than any other Chinese province, and vast reclamation projects have been instituted under the Communist government. The Chinese Eastern RR crosses S Heilungkiang and has many branches to the north; Harbin is the junction point with the South Manchurian railway system. Heilungkiang contains the great Ta-ch'ing oilfield, first worked in 1959, and has oil-refining operations. Major coal mines are in Chi-hsi and Hao-kang. Iron and magnesite are also mined, and aluminum is produced. Gold is extracted in the Greater and Lesser Khingan. Harbin is one of the country's leading industrial centers, known especially for its heavy machinery. CH'I-CH'I-HA-ERH, CHIA-MU-SSU, and MU-TAN-CHIANG are also industrial cities, with manufactures ranging from processed foods to locomotives. The boundaries of Heilungkiang have been changed several times. The former provinces of Hingan and Nunkiang were added to it in 1950 and Sungkiang was incorporated in 1954. The northwest section became part of Inner Mongolian Autonomous Region in 1949 and was returned to Heilungkiang in the 1969–70 redistricting.

Heimdall: see ASGARD.

Heine, Heinrich (hīn'rĭkh hī'nə), 1797–1856, German poet, b. Düsseldorf, of a Jewish family. One of the greatest of German lyric poets, he had a varied career. After failing in business he tried law but found it uncongenial and finally turned to history and literature. His first published poems and plays established him as a young romantic. In the literary salon of Rahel Varnhagen von Ense he met, among others, Fouqué, Chamisso, Hoffmann, Grabbe, and Immermann; some of these became life-long friends, others bitter enemies. Disillusioned with Germany and in political disgrace because of his liberal sympathies, he left for Paris (1831), where he supported the social ideals of the French Revolution, becoming for a time a Saint-Simonist. As the towering figure of the revolutionary literary movement Young Germany, he continued from Paris to disseminate French revolutionary ideas in Germany. He received a French government pension, worked as correspondent for German newspapers, and died after years of severe illness, during which he was nursed by his faithful "Mouche" (who used the pen name Camille Selden). Heine's writing reflects the dualism of his nature; it shows strong influences of both classic and romantic German literature. Nationalistic as well as international in orientation, Heine also revealed French, English, and Jewish strains in his work. His *Buch der Lieder* (1827, tr. *Book of Songs*, 1846), which contains the lyric cycles "Nordsee" and "Lyrisches Intermezzo," shows his indebtedness to the romantic folk-song poets. Other collections of poems are *Neue Gedichte* (1847), *Romanzero* (1851), and *Letzte Gedichte* (1853). Schumann composed music for Heine's poems, as did Schubert, Mendelssohn, Liszt, and many others. His lyrics have been used in more than 3,000 compositions, the most popular perhaps being "Die Lorelei," with melody by Franz Silcher (1789–1860). Heine's later poems and especially his prose works established him as a satirist of barbed wit and as an embittered critic of romanticism, of jingoistic patriotism, and of current social and political affairs. Most poignant are *Die Harzreise* [Harz journey] (1826) and *Reisebilder* [travel pictures] (1827–31), which combine poetry and prose. *Atta Troll* (1843) and *Deutschland* (1844) reflect his reaction to German anti-Semitism, as do his earliest dramatic work, *Almansor*, and an unfinished novel, *Der Rabbi von Bacharach*. Possibly because of their cosmopolitan character, Heine's works have never been as popular in Germany as they have in other lands. Virtually all of Heine's works have been translated into English, notably by E. A. Bowring, Havelock Ellis, C. G. Leland, Louis Untermeyer, and Humbert Wolfe. See biography by E. M. Butler (1956); studies by M. Brod (1957), S. S. Prower (1961), L. Hofrichter (1963), M. Spann (1966).

Heinemann, Gustav (gōōs'täf hīn'əmän), 1899–, West German political leader. A corporation lawyer and wartime leader of the CONFESSING CHURCH, he helped found the Christian Democratic Party, although he quit its first cabinet to establish a splinter party advocating a unified, disarmed, and neutral Germany. In 1957 he joined the Social Democrats. As minister of justice (1966–69) in Kurt Georg Kiesinger's coalition cabinet, Heinemann instituted many legal reforms. He served from 1969 to 1974 as president of the German Federal Republic.

Heinse, Wilhelm (vĭl'hĕlm hīn'sə), 1746–1803, German novelist. His principal novels, *Ardinghello; or, An Artist's Rambles in Sicily* (1787, tr. 1839) and *Hildegard von Hohenthal* (1795–96), typify elements of STURM UND DRANG (Storm and Stress).

Heinsius, Daniel (dä'nēĕl hīn'sēəs), 1580–1655, Dutch classicist. One of the most famous Renaissance scholars, he edited many Latin works, composed fine Latin poetry, and wrote in Dutch as well. His son **Nikolaas Heinsius,** 1620–81, rivaled his father as an author and editor of Latin poetry.

Heinze, Frederick Augustus (hīn'zē), 1869–1914, American copper magnate, b. Brooklyn, N.Y. He went in 1889 to Butte, Mont., as engineer for a mining company. In 1893 he organized the Montana Ore Purchasing Company and challenged the claims of the Amalgamated Copper Company, which was controlled by Standard Oil. Brilliant and aggressive, Heinze won sympathy as a knight pitted against the "interests," but he was unsuccessful. In 1906 he sold most of his holdings, and the United Copper Company, which he founded, went down in the Panic of 1907. See John Fahey, *Inland Empire* (1965); Sarah McNelis, *Copper King at War* (2d ed. 1968).

heir, person designated by law to succeed to the ownership of PROPERTY of another if that owner does not make a contrary disposition of it by WILL. A person who takes property left to him by will is not an heir but a legatee. The property that the heir receives is his inheritance. Originally the common law confined the term *heir* to an inheritor of real estate; the persons to whom the personal property of the deceased went were called the next of kin. The group of heirs of a person may differ from the group that the law recognizes as his next of kin, but the law that dictates the constitution of both is now largely statutory, and in many states of the United States the statutes have abolished all distinction. When TITLE to property is in a living person and his heirs, the meaning is merely that the person has absolute ownership of the property and can do with it what he wishes. No person may be the heir of a living person; the relationship arises only at the death of another. If the other person is still living, the person who may become an heir is called an heir apparent or heir presumptive. An heir presumptive is in the same position as an heir apparent except that his claim may be superseded, as by the birth of one more closely related to the owner. These terms are much used with regard to dynastic succession; an heir apparent is in such connection the undisputed heir to the throne if he survives the incumbent; an heir presumptive is one who will inherit the throne if nothing intervenes—especially the birth of a child to the incumbent.

Heisenberg, Werner (vĕr'nər hī'zənbĕrk), 1901–, German physicist. One of the founders of the quantum theory, he is best known for his UNCERTAINTY PRINCIPLE, or indeterminacy principle, which states that it is impossible to determine with arbitrarily high accuracy both the position and momentum (essentially velocity) of a subatomic particle like the electron. The effect of this principle is to convert the laws of physics into statements about relative probabilities instead of absolute certainties. In 1926, Heisenberg developed a form of the quantum theory known as matrix mechanics, which was quickly shown to be fully equivalent to Erwin Schrödinger's wave mechanics. His 1932 Nobel Prize in Physics cited not only his work on quantum theory but also work in nuclear physics in which he predicted the subsequently verified existence of two allotropic forms of molecular hydrogen, differing in their values of nuclear spin. He was a student of Arnold Sommerfeld, an assistant to Max Born, and later a close associate of Niels Bohr. He taught at the universities of Leipzig (1927–41) and Berlin (1942–45). Since 1958 he has been director of the Max Planck Institute for Physics and Astrophysics, now located in Munich. His most recent work concerns the so-called S-matrix approach to nuclear forces and the possibility that space and time are quantized, or granular, in structure. His *Physics and Philosophy* (1962) and *Physics and Beyond* (1971) are popular accounts of the revolutions in modern physics.

Heisman, John William, 1869–1936, American football coach, b. Cleveland, Ohio. He studied and played football at Brown (1887–89) and the Univ. of Pennsylvania (1890–91). He coached football for 36 years—at Oberlin (1892, 1894), Akron (1893), Auburn (1895–99), Clemson (1900–1903), Georgia Tech (1904–19), Pennsylvania (1920–22), Washington and Jefferson (1923), and Rice (1924–27). Heisman was most successful at Georgia Tech, where from 1914 to 1918 his teams played 33 games without defeat. He was noted for a high-scoring attack, and Georgia Tech's 222–0 victory over Cumberland in 1916 stands as a record in collegiate competition. One of football's most successful coaches, Heisman was also one of its most inventive. He is credited with legalizing the forward pass (1906) and with originating the hidden-ball trick. From 1927 until his death, Heisman was athletic director of the Downtown Athletic Club in New York City. The trophy presented annually since 1935 by that club to the most outstanding college football player in the nation is named in his memory.

Heister, Lorenz (lō'rĕnts hī'shtər), 1683–1758, German surgeon. Having studied anatomy under the famous Dutch master Frederik Ruysch (1638–1731), Heister served as an army surgeon in several campaigns before becoming professor of anatomy and surgery at Altdorf. Distressed at the inferior state of surgery in Germany he published his *Chirurgie* (Nuremberg, 1718), based on extensive readings of the foremost French authorities. This influential and profusely illustrated work became the standard text on the subject and was widely reprinted and translated. The English version (1748) was the first systematic treatise on surgery to appear in that language. Heister was the first to study the pathology of appendicitis (1711), as well as the first to use the term *tracheotomy* (1718).

Hejaz or **Hedjaz** (both: hĕjăz', hĕjäz'), region (1963 est. pop. 2,000,000), c.150,000 sq mi (388,500 sq km), NW Saudi Arabia, on the Gulf of Aqaba and the Red Sea. MECCA is the chief city. Extending S to Asir, Hejaz is mainly a dissected highland region lying between the narrow, long coastal strip and the interior desert. There are several oases and some wadis (watercourses) where crops, such as dates, wheat, and millet, and livestock are raised. Hejaz is, however, more important as a place of pilgrimage. Each year many thousands of Muslim pilgrims come into Hejaz, mainly through JIDDA, the chief port, to visit the holy cities of Mecca and MEDINA; non-Muslims are excluded from much of the region. Following the fall (1258) of the caliphate of Baghdad, Hejaz came under Egyptian control. In 1517 it came under Turkish suzerainty, although nominal rule remained in the hands of the sherifs of Mecca of the Hashemite family. In the early 19th cent. Hejaz was raided by the Wahabis, and peace was restored only in 1817 by the governor of Egypt. After 1845, Hejaz came again under direct Turkish control. To improve communications, the Turks built the Hejaz railway (completed 1908; in disuse since World War I) from Damascus to Medina. The Hejaz was in 1916 proclaimed independent by Husayn ibn Ali, the sherif of Mecca, who with the aid of T. E. Lawrence destroyed Turkish authority. Husayn was himself defeated in 1924 by Ibn Saud, ruler of Nejd and founder of SAUDI ARABIA, who annexed his domain. The formal union of Hejaz and Nejd into Saudi Arabia was proclaimed in 1932.

hejira: see HEGIRA.

Hekinan (hākē'nän), city (1970 pop. 56,933), Aichi prefecture, central Honshu, Japan, near Chita Bay. It is an agricultural, commercial, and communications center.

Hekla (hĕk'lä), volcano, c.4,900 ft (1,490 m) high, SW Iceland; one of the highest in Europe. Since the early 11th cent. more than 20 eruptions have been recorded; the worst occurred in 1766 and the most recent in 1947. Hekla emits steam and has several crater lakes. In medieval Icelandic folklore Hekla was believed to be one of the gates to purgatory; it is also a legendary gathering place for witches.

Hel (hĕl), in Norse mythology, the underworld (sometimes called Niflheim) and the goddess who ruled there. In early Germanic mythology, Hel was the goddess who ruled the majestic abode for the dead. Later, particularly after the advent of Christianity, Hel became a place of punishment, similar to the Christian hell.

Helah (hē'lə), wife of Ashur. 1 Chron. 4.5.

Helam (hē'ləm), unidentified city, Jordan; there David defeated Hadarezer. 2 Sam. 10.16–19.

Helbah (hĕl'bə), town, NE Palestine, the same as Ahlab. Judges 1.31.

Helbon (hĕl'bŏn), ancient place, Syria, NW of Damascus. It was noted for its wine. Ezek. 27.18.

Held, Anna, 1873?–1918, American musical comedy actress, b. Paris. She is remembered for her beauty and charm and for her tempestuous off-stage life. After she had small singing and dancing parts in Paris, success came to her when Florenz Ziegfeld (whom she subsequently married) persuaded her to come to the United States to star in the first of his lavish productions, *A Parlor Match* (1896). She was long a favorite on the New York stage; some of her outstanding performances were seen in *The Little Duchess, The Parisian Model,* and *Miss Innocence.*

Held, Julius Samuel, 1905–, American art historian, b. Germany. Held emigrated to the United States in 1934. In 1937 he began to teach at Columbia Univ., where he was professor of art history from 1944 to 1970. Distinguished as a connoisseur of Dutch and Flemish art, he is the author of *Rubens in America* (with Jan-Albert Goris, 1947), *Flemish Painting* (1953), *Peter Paul Rubens* (1953), *Rubens: Selected Drawings* (1959), *Rembrandt's Aristotle and Other Rembrandt Studies* (1969), and *17th and 18th Century Art* (1971; with Donald Posner).

Heldai (hĕl'dāī). **1** See HELEB. **2** Man who was to have a memorial in the temple. Zech. 6.10. Helem: Zech. 6.14.

Heleb (hē'lĕb), mighty man. 2 Sam. 23.29. Heled: 1 Chron. 11.30. He may be the captain Heldai of 1 Chron. 27.15.

Heled (hē'lĕd), the same as HELEB.

Helek (hē'lĕk), descendant of Manasseh. Num. 26.30.

Helem (hē'lĕm). **1** Asherite. 1 Chron. 7.35. **2** The same as HELDAI **2.**

Helen, in Greek mythology, the most beautiful of women; daughter of Leda and Zeus, and sister of Castor, Pollux, and Clytemnestra. While still a young girl Helen was abducted to Attica by Theseus and Polydeuces, but Castor and Pollux rescued her. Later, when she was courted by the greatest heroes and chieftains of Greece, her foster father, Tyndareus, fearful of their jealousies, demanded that each suitor swear to defend the rights of the man Helen chose. She then married MENELAUS, who, when PARIS carried her off to Troy, reminded her former suitors of their oath. They then recruited an army and defeated the Trojans in the Trojan War. Some legends say that Paris forcibly abducted Helen; others that she fell in love with him and went willingly. In one peculiar account, originating in Stesichorus and used by Euripides, Helen was rescued by Proteus in Egypt, who substituted in her stead a phantom that sailed to Troy with Paris. Proteus then cared for Helen until Menelaus finally claimed her. In the *Iliad* and *Odyssey,* Helen becomes Paris' wife but is in sympathy with the Greeks. She is easily reconciled with Menelaus after the war, and they return to a peaceful life at Sparta. There are several other accounts of the story of Helen. Some say that after she and Menelaus returned to Greece, Orestes vengefully tried to kill her but that Zeus deified her. She bore Menelaus one daughter, Hermione, and, by some accounts, a son, Pleisthenes. Helen had cults in Sparta and elsewhere and is considered by some scholars to be a "faded" goddess—perhaps an ancient fertility goddess—who became a mortal woman.

Helena, Saint (hĕl'ənə), c.248–328?, mother of Constantine I. She became a Christian in 313. According to tradition she found (327) the relic of the True Cross in Jerusalem and identified the location of the Holy Sepulcher. Feast: Aug. 18.

Helena, 1 City (1970 pop. 10,415), seat of Phillips co., E central Ark., on the Mississippi, in the delta cotton country, and at the southern end of Crowley's Ridge; inc. 1833. It is a rail terminus and river port. The city was occupied by Union troops in the Civil War; they were attacked unsuccessfully by Confederates in a battle there July 4, 1863. A junior college is in Helena, and antebellum homes and Indian mounds are in the area. The county museum contains mound artifacts. St. Francis National Forest is to the north. **2** City (1970 pop. 22,730), state capital and seat of Lewis and Clark co., W central Mont., on the eastern slope of the Continental Divide; inc. 1870. It is a commercial and shipping center in a ranching and mining area. Helena's manufactures include machine parts, concrete, and paints. The city was founded after the discovery of gold (1864) in Last Chance Gulch (now Helena's main street), and grew rapidly. In 1874 a general election ratified the choice of Helena to replace Virginia City as territorial capital. In the 1890s it maintained its position as state capital against the rivalry of Anaconda. Rich silver and lead strikes in the neighborhood kept its mining wealth high. Helena is the seat of Carroll College. A veterans hospital is at nearby Fort Harrison, and Canyon Ferry Dam (completed 1954) is on the Missouri. The city is undergoing extensive urban renewal, with emphasis on allaying ecological damage from the mining and smelting operations.

Helenus, in Greek mythology, Trojan who was gifted with prophetic powers; son of Priam and Hecuba. When Helen was given to Deiphobus after the death of Paris, Helenus in anger betrayed Troy by revealing to the Greeks that Hercules' poisoned arrows were needed to defeat the Trojans. After the fall of Troy he went to Greece. He later married Andromache and founded Bathrotus, where, in the *Aeneid,* he is visited by Aeneas, who seeks his advice.

Heleph (hē'lĕf), unidentified town, NE Palestine. Joshua 19.33.

Helez (hē'lĕz). **1** One of David's guard. 2 Sam. 23.26; 1 Chron. 11.27. **2** Descendant of Jerahmeel. 1 Chron. 2.39.

Helgoland (hĕl'gōlänt") or **Heligoland** (hĕl'ĭgōlănd"), island (1967 est. pop. 3,200), c.150 acres (60 hectares), Schleswig-Holstein, N West Germany, in the North Sea. Formed of red sandstone, it rises to c.200 ft (60 m) above the sea and is largely covered with grazing land. The island is a popular tourist resort. Strategically located near the mouths of the Weser and the Elbe rivers, Helgoland was captured by the Danes in 1714, was occupied by the English in 1807, and was formally ceded to England by Denmark in 1814. In exchange for rights in Africa, England gave the island to Germany in 1890. The Germans installed fortifications, which were razed after World War I according to the terms of the Treaty of Versailles. However, Germany refortified Helgoland in 1936 and used it as a naval base in World War II. In 1947, British occupation authorities, after evacuating the islanders (mostly fishermen), blew up the fortifications and part of the island in one of the largest known nonatomic blasts.

Heli (hē'lī), father of St. Joseph. Luke 3.23.

Heliand (hĕl'ēənd, hā'lēänd) [Old Saxon,=Savior], Old Saxon poem of 5,983 lines, a narrative of the life of Christ in alliterative verse, written c.825.

Helianthus (hē"lēăn'thəs): see SUNFLOWER.

Helicon (hĕl'ĭkŏn), Gr. *Elikón,* mountain group, c.20 mi (30 km) long, central Greece, in Boeotia; it rises to 5,736 ft (1,748 m). Helicon formed part of the border between ancient Boeotia and Phocis. In Greek legend it was the abode of the Muses and sacred to Apollo. The fountains of Hippocrene and Aganippe are on the slopes of Mt. Helicon. The temple of the Muses was situated in the eastern part of the mountain, at the foot of which were Thespiae and Ascra, home of Hesiod.

helicopter, type of aircraft in which the lift is obtained by means of one or more power-driven horizontal propellers called rotors. In a single-rotor helicopter the reaction torque from the spinning rotor tends to make the craft spin also. A small rotor near the tail compensates for this torque. On twin-rotor craft the rotors spin in opposite directions so that their reactions cancel each other. The helicopter is propelled in any given direction by inclining the axis of the main rotor in that direction. This method of flight was one of the earliest considered; Leonardo da Vinci, in the 16th cent., described its possibilities. Best known among its developers are the French inventor Louis Breguet and the engineers Igor Sikorsky of the United States and Juan de la Cierva of Spain. The helicopter has not been used for long-distance transportation, but because of its maneuverability and ability to land and take off in small areas it has been adopted for a wide range of services, e.g., air-sea rescue, fire fighting, crop sowing, traffic control, and many others. However, it is more difficult to fly than fixed-wing aircraft. Helicopters were widely used during the Korean War for carrying supplies and as ambulances. In the fighting in the 1960s and 70s in Southeast Asia, guns and rockets were mounted on helicopters so that they could be used in attacks as well as in reconnaissance and troop transportation. See J. W. Taylor, *Helicopters and VTOL Aircraft* (1968); Charles Gablehouse, *Helicopters and Autogiros* (rev. ed. 1969).

heliocentric system: see COPERNICAN SYSTEM.

Heliodorus (hē"lēōdôr'əs), fl. 175 B.C., Syrian statesman. The treasurer of Seleucus IV (Seleucus Philopator), he murdered the king and attempted unsuccessfully to usurp the throne. According to 2 Mac. 3 he entered the Temple at Jerusalem but was prevented from taking the treasure by three angels.

Heliodorus of Emesa (ĕm'əsə), fl. 3d cent., Syrian Greek writer. He wrote the romance *Aethiopica,* one of the oldest and best of surviving Greek romances. Little is known of his life except that he was a Phoenician from Emesa, Syria.

Heliogabalus (hē"lēōgăb'ələs) or **Elagabalus** (ĕləgăb'ələs), c.205–222, Roman emperor (218–22). He was a priest of the local sun god, Elagabalus, at Emesa and was named Varius Avitus Bassianus. He was a cousin of CARACALLA; according to the claims (almost certainly false) of his ambitious mother and grandmother, he was the son of Caracalla. He was chosen by the troops in Syria as emperor in opposition to the legitimate heir, Macrinus. When Macrinus was defeated and killed at Antioch, Heliogabalus became emperor as Marcus Aurelius Antoninus. His reign was a tragic farce. He imported the cult of which he was priest, and Rome was shocked and disgusted by the indecency of the rites as well as by the private life of the emperor, who gave high offices to an actor, a charioteer, and a barber. His grandmother, Julia Maesa, induced him to adopt his young cousin, ALEXANDER SEVERUS, but Heliogabalus later tried to have the boy killed. Heliogabalus and his mother were murdered in an uprising of the Praetorian Guard. Alexander Severus succeeded.

heliograph (hē'lēəgrăf) [Gr.,=sun-writer], signaling device using flashes of sunlight. It has two mirrors that are used to reflect sunlight on a distant point and a shutter through which the sunlight passes so that messages may be transmitted in telegraphic code by means of long and short flashes. It was used in ancient times and as recently as the 19th cent. by the U.S. army in the SW United States and by the British army in India.

Heliopolis (hēlēŏp'əlĭs) [Gr.,=city of the sun], ancient city, N Egypt, in the Nile delta, 6 mi (10 km) below modern Cairo. It was noted as the center of sun worship, and its god Ra or Re was the state deity until Thebes became capital (c.2100 B.C.). The god Amon was then joined with Ra as Amon-Ra or Amon-Re (see EGYPTIAN RELIGION). Under the New Empire (c.1570 B.C.–c.1085 B.C.), Heliopolis was the seat of the viceroy for N Egypt. The obelisks called Cleopatra's Needles were erected there. Its schools of philosophy and astronomy declined after the founding of Alexandria in 332 B.C., but the city never wholly lost importance until the Christian era. The Egyptian name was On, and by this name it appears in the Bible (Gen. 41.45,50; 46.20). Elsewhere in the Bible, Heliopolis is referred to as Beth-shemesh (Jer. 43.13) and Aven (Ezek. 30.17).

Heliopolis, Syria: see BAALBEK.

Helios (hē'lēŏs) [Gr.,=sun], in Greek mythology, the sun god, son of the Titans Hyperion and Theia. Each morning he left a palace in the east and crossed the sky in a golden chariot. In the evening he rested in another palace in the west and then sailed to the east along the river Oceanus. Although he was often invoked for serious oaths, his worship in Greece was negligible, except on Rhodes. There the famous Colossus represented him, and an important festival was celebrated in his honor. In later times he was identified with Apollo. Helios was the father of Aeëtes and Circe by Perse, and of Phaëthon by the nymph Rhode (or Clymene). He was often referred to simply as Titan, especially in Rome, where he was also known as Sol, and where he was an important god. His sister was Eos.

heliotrope [Gr.,=sun-turning] or **turnsole,** name for any plant that turns to face the sun, especially members of the genus *Heliotropium* of the family Boraginaceae. The garden heliotrope is a valerian, and the winter heliotrope, or sweet coltsfoot, is a composite.

heliotrope (hē'lēətrōp"), in mineralogy: see BLOODSTONE.

heliport, AIRPORT designed exclusively for HELICOPTER traffic.

helium (hē'lēəm), gaseous chemical element; symbol He; at. no. 2; at. wt. 4.0026; m.p. below −272°C at 26 atmospheres pressure; b.p. −268.6°C at 1 atmosphere pressure; density 0.1785 grams per liter at STP (see separate article); valence usually 0. Helium is less dense than any other known gas except hydrogen and is about one seventh as dense as air. Extremely unreactive, it is an INERT GAS in group 0 of the PERIODIC TABLE. Its noncombustibility and buoyancy (second only to hydrogen) make helium the most suitable gas for balloons and other lighter-than-air craft. A mixture of helium and oxygen is often supplied as a breathing mixture for deep-sea divers and caisson workers and is used in decompression chambers; because helium is less soluble in human blood than nitrogen, its use reduces the risk of caisson disease, or the bends. Helium can also be used wherever an unreactive atmosphere is needed, e.g., in electric arc welding, in growing crystals of silicon and germanium for semiconductors, and in refining titanium and zirconium metals. It is also used to pressurize the fuel tanks of liquid-fueled rockets. Liquid helium is essential for many low temperature applications (see LOW-TEMPERATURE PHYSICS). Helium is a rare and costly gas. The United States is the major producer. Natural gas from wells in Texas, Oklahoma, and Kansas is the principal source. Crude helium is separated by liquefying the other gases present in the natural gas; it is then either further purified or stored for later purification and use. Some helium is extracted directly from the atmosphere; the gas is also found in certain uranium minerals and in some mineral waters, but not in economic quantities. It has been estimated that helium makes up only about 0.000001% of the combined weight of the earth's atmosphere and crust; it is most concentrated in the exosphere, which is the outermost region of the atmosphere, 600 to 1500 mi (960–2400 km) above the earth's surface. Helium is abundant in outer space; it makes up about 23% of the mass of the visible universe. It is the end product of energy-releasing fusion processes in STARS. (See INTERSTELLAR MATTER.) Spectroscopic evidence for the presence of helium in the sun was first obtained during a solar eclipse in 1868. A bright yellow emission line was observed and was later shown to correspond to no known element; the new element was named by J. N. Lockyer and E. Frankland from *helios* [Gr.,=sun]. Helium was isolated (1895) from a sample of the uranium mineral cleveite by Sir William Ramsay. Natural helium is a mixture of two stable isotopes, helium-3 and helium-4. In helium obtained from natural gas about one atom in 10 million is helium-3. The unstable isotopes helium-5, helium-6, and helium-8 have been synthesized. The alpha particles that are emitted from certain radioactive substances are identical to helium-4 nuclei (two protons and two neutrons). Helium-4 is unusual in that it forms two different kinds of liquids. When it is cooled below 4.22°K (its boiling point at atmospheric pressure) it condenses to liquid helium-I, which behaves as an ordinary liquid. When liquid helium-I is cooled below about 2.18°K (at atmospheric pressure), liquid helium-II is formed. Liquid helium II has a number of unusual properties. It is sometimes called a superfluid because it has extremely low viscosity. It also has extremely high heat conductivity and expands on cooling. It cannot be contained in an open beaker since a thin film of it creeps up the side, over the lip, and flows down the outside. The study of these phenomena is a part of low-temperature physics. When helium-3 is liquefied and cooled it does not exhibit the properties of liquid helium-II; this difference in properties between helium-3 and helium-4 can be explained in terms of quantum mechanics.

Helkai (hĕl'kāī, hĕlkā'ī), priest with Zerubbabel. Neh. 12.15.

Helkath (hĕl'kăth), unidentified town, N Palestine. Joshua 19.25; 21.31. Hukok: 1 Chron. 6.75.

Helkath-hazzurim (hĕl'kăth-hăzh'o͝orĭm), field, where 12 champions of David fought 12 champions of Ish-bosheth. 2 Sam. 2.12–17.

hell, in Christian theology, eternal abode of souls damned by the judgment of God. Its characteristic is that the souls in hell are deprived forever of the sight of God. The punishment of hell is generally analogized to earthly fire. Hell has been treated in legend and literature, especially in the *Divine Comedy* of Dante. A constant feature is SATAN or Lucifer, considered as the ruler of hell. Other religions have similar conceptions. Islam has a hell that is virtually the same. The Sheol or Tophet of the ancient Jews is a gloomy place of departed souls, where they are not tormented but wander about unhappily. The ethical aspect was apparently developed gradually, and Sheol became much like the hell of Christianity. Gehenna, in the New Testament, which drew its name from the Vale of HINNOM, was certainly a place of punishment. In Greek religion the great underworld was HADES, ruled by the god of that name, who was also known as Pluto. The Romans called this underworld also Orcus, Dis, and, poetically, Avernus. The idea of HEL that appears in the elaborate cosmology of the *Edda* was probably heavily influenced by Christian writings. See HEAVEN; SIN.

Helladic culture: see MYCENAEAN CIVILIZATION.

Hellas: see GREECE.

hellbender: see SALAMANDER.

Helle: see GOLDEN FLEECE.

hellebore (hĕl'əbôr), name for plants of the genus *Helleborus* of the family Ranunculaceae (BUTTERCUP family), Eurasian perennials with attractive palmately divided leaves and flowers of various colors. Hellebores are noted for their early blooming, particularly the black hellebore or Christmas rose (*H. niger*), with evergreen leaves and white or greenish blossoms that resemble wild roses. Hellebores and other species are used medicinally but are highly toxic. Species of the genus *Veratrum*—which are also poisonous and medicinal and which yield an insecticide—are variously known as false, or American, hellebore and white hellebore; they are unrelated plants of the family Liliatae (LILY family). Hellebore is classified in the division MAGNOLIOPHYTA, class Magnoliopsida, order Ranunculales, family Ranunculaceae.

Hellen, in Greek mythology, ancestor of the Hellenes, or Greeks; son of DEUCALION and Pyrrha. He was the father of Dorus, Xuthus, and Aeolus, who were the progenitors of the principal nations of the Greeks—the Dorians, the Ionians, the Achaeans, and the Aeolians.

Hellenism, the culture, ideals, and pattern of life of ancient Greece in classical times. It usually means primarily the culture of ATHENS and the related cities during the Age of Pericles. The term is also applied to the ideals of later writers and thinkers who draw their inspiration from ancient Greece. Frequently it is contrasted with Hebraism—Hellenism then meaning pagan joy, freedom, and love of life as contrasted with the austere morality and monotheism of the Old Testament. The Hellenic period came to an end with the conquest of Alexander the Great in the 4th cent. B.C. It was succeeded by the HELLENISTIC CIVILIZATION. See GREECE; GREEK ARCHITECTURE; GREEK ART; GREEK LITERATURE, ANCIENT; GREEK RELIGION. See Rex Warner, *Eternal Greece* (rev. ed. 1962); D. Garman, tr., *A Literary History of Greece* (1964); John Ferguson, *The Heritage of Hellenism* (1973).

Hellenistic civilization. The conquests of Alexander the Great spread HELLENISM immediately over the Near East and far into Asia. After his death in 323 B.C., the influence of Greek civilization continued to expand over the Mediterranean world and W Asia. The wars of the DIADOCHI marked, it is true, the breakup of Alexander's brief empire, but the establishment of Macedonian dynasties in Egypt, Syria, and Persia (the Ptolemies and the Seleucidae) helped to mold the world of that day into a wider unity of trade and learning. While the city-states of Greece itself tended to stagnate, elsewhere cities and states grew and flourished. Of these the chief was ALEXANDRIA. So great a force did Alexandria exert in commerce, letters, and art that this period is occassionally called the Alexandrian Age, and the end of Hellenistic civilization is generally set at the final triumph of Roman power in Alexandria in the 1st cent. B.C. PERGAMUM was also prominent, and there were other cities of influence (e.g., Dura). The bounds of the known world were extended by navigators, who learned, for example, about the North Sea. The upsurge of commerce brought a great increase of wealth to merchants and in general to the upper classes; this wealth was also reflected in a tendency toward the ornate and superimpressive in architecture, although town plans and buildings of the period have proportions and grace rarely excelled. It should be noted, however, that the increase of wealth did not reach the poor, who in general were more impoverished than they had previously been. Education, however, was much more widespread than ever before, and Greek was the fashionable language of the educated world. The result was a great increase of volume in literature (see GREEK LITERATURE, ANCIENT) and a tendency for writing to divide into popular literature for the wide audience and specialized writing for narrow, highly intellectual circles. The libraries of Alexandria and Pergamum were centers of literary criticism and the compiling of anthologies and catalogs. The literature of the Hellenistic period has been stigmatized since the Renaissance as imitative and ponderous, but actually there was a great richness in some of the writing. Not only were there outstanding poets such as Callimachus and Theocritus but there were also new forms that emerged, such as the complicated but frequently charming romances and the works of Lucian. Similarly some of the finest—and some of the most familiar—ancient sculptures to survive to our day are Alexandrian (e.g., the Venus of Milo and the Dying Gaul). Philosophical disputation was popular among the educated, and the contributions of the Stoics and the Epicureans to the world were great. The greatest contribution of the age was the preservation and enrichment of the Greek heritage for the use of Rome and succeeding civilizations. As Rome gradually overshadowed the Mediterranean world, the Romans learned much from the peoples they conquered, and Hellenistic civilization was absorbed rather than extinguished. See studies by M. I. Rostovtzeff (3 vol., 1941), M. Hadas (1959), J. C. Stobart (3d ed. 1960), G. T. Griffith and W. W. Tarn (rev. ed. 1961), P. Grimal, ed. (1969), and F. E. Peters (1971).

Heller, Joseph, 1923–, American writer, b. Brooklyn, N.Y. Heller is best known for his novel *Catch-22* (1961). The work has received high praise for its comic treatment of the absurdities of war and for its narrative technique, which reflects the illogic of computerized military strategies. Heller has also published a play, *We Bombed in New Haven* (1968), dealing with the changes in the American attitude toward war, and another novel, *Something Happened* (1974).

Heller, Stephen (shtĕf'ən hĕl'ər), 1814-88, French pianist and composer, b. Budapest. Heller toured as a piano virtuoso, ruining his health before settling in Paris in 1838. There he developed close friendships with many of the leading artists of the day. He wrote a large number of subtle and entertaining piano pieces.

Heller, Walter, 1915-, American economist, b. Buffalo, N.Y., grad. Oberlin College (A.B., 1935), Univ. of Wisconsin (M.A. 1938, Ph.D. 1941). He worked (1942-46) for the U.S. Treasury before joining the Univ. of Minnesota faculty to serve (1946-) as a professor of economics. After service as a consultant to the United Nations (1952-60) and to the state of Minnesota (1955-60), he was appointed (1961) chairman of the Council of Economic Advisers by President John F. Kennedy. He left the council in 1964, but continued to serve as a consultant to President Lyndon B. Johnson until 1969.

Helles, Cape (hĕl'əs), southernmost point of the Gallipoli peninsula, NW Turkey. It commands the entrance to the Dardanelles.

Hellespont: see DARDANELLES.

Helleu, Paul César (pôl sāzär' ĕlö'), 1859-1927, French drypoint etcher and painter. He is best known for his drypoint studies and portraits of fashionable women, which have the spontaneity of rapid sketches. His nearly 1,500 drypoints were often printed in two or more colors. An example of his painting, *The Windows of Saint Denis,* is in the Museum of Fine Arts in Boston.

Hell Gate, narrow channel of the East River, SE N.Y., between Wards Island and Astoria, Queens, New York City. Named Hellegat by the Dutch navigator Adriaen Block, who passed through it into Long Island Sound in 1614, it was dangerous to ships because of its strong tidal currents and rocks. Cleared of all obstacles, it allows oceangoing vessels to sail between New York harbor and Long Island Sound. It is crossed by the Triborough highway bridge and by the Hell Gate railroad bridge.

hellgrammite: see DOBSONFLY.

Hellín (ĕlyēn'), town (1970 pop. 22,152), Albacete prov., SE Spain, in Murcia. An important marketing and distributing center, it is noted for its sulfur mines, worked since Roman times. Clay and gypsum are also quarried, and footwear and chemicals are manufactured.

Hellman, Lillian, 1905-, American dramatist, b. New Orleans. Her plays, although often melodramatic, are marked by intelligence and craftsmanship. *The Children's Hour* (1934), her first drama, concerns the devastating effects of a child's malicious charge of lesbianism against two of her teachers. *The Little Foxes* (1939) and *Another Part of the Forest* (1946) constitute a chilling study of a wealthy and rapacious Southern family. Several of Hellman's dramas—notably *Watch on the Rhine* (1941) and *The Searching Wind* (1944)—treat international political themes such as isolationism and the rise of fascism. She has made several English adaptations of French plays and, with Richard Wilbur, wrote the libretto for a musical version of Voltaire's *Candide* (1955). Her other plays include *Days to Come* (1936), *The Autumn Garden* (1951), and *Toys in the Attic* (1960). See her autobiographical works, *An Unfinished Woman* (1969) and *Pentimento* (1973).

Helmand or **Helmund** (hĕl'mənd), river, c.700 mi (1,130 km) long, rising in the Hindu Kush Mts., NE Afghanistan and flowing generally SW to the Seistan basin, SW Afghanistan, where it helps form the Hamun-e Helmand, a marshy lake that extends into Iran; longest river in Afghanistan. The Arghandab is its chief tributary. The Helmand's ancient irrigation and river-control system was destroyed by Jenghiz Khan (13th cent.) and Tamerlane (14th cent.); the modern irrigation works, though not so extensive, are vital to both Iranians and Afghans, and in times of drought there are disputes over water rights.

Helmholtz, Hermann Ludwig Ferdinand von (hĕr'män lo͞ot'vĭkh fĕr'dēnänt fən hĕlm'hōlts), 1821-94, German scientist. Although known especially as a physicist and biologist, he was also a physician, mathematician, philosopher, and lecturer on popular science. He extended the application of the law of conservation of energy and in 1847 formulated it mathematically. He contributed to the knowledge of thermodynamics and electrodynamics and studied vortex motion in fluids. A pioneer in physiological optics and author of a *Treatise on Physiological Optics* (1867; tr., 3 vol., 1924-25), he extended Thomas Young's theory of color vision, explained the mechanism of lens accommodation in the eye, and invented (1851) the ophthalmoscope. He was an authority on acoustics, especially on the perception of tone quality, and wrote *On the Sensations of Tone* (4th ed. 1877, tr. 1954). Helmholtz was professor of physics at the Univ. of Berlin from 1871 and also director of the physicotechnical institute at Charlottenburg from 1887. See his *Selected Writings,* ed. by Kahl Russell (1971); study by R. M. Warren and R. P. Warren (1968).

Helmond (hĕl'mônt), city (1971 pop. 58,003), North Brabant prov., SE Netherlands, on the Aa River. Manufactures include textiles and food products. Its 15th-century castle is now the town hall.

Helmont, Jan Baptista van (yän bäptĭs'tä vän hĕl'-mônt), 1577-1644, Flemish physician, chemist, and physicist. He attributed physiological changes to chemical causes, but his conclusions were colored by his speculative mysticism. He discovered carbon dioxide, distinguished gases as a class of substances (as contrasted with solids and liquids), and is credited with introducing the term *gas* in its present scientific sense. His chief work is *Ortus medicinae* (1648).

Helms, Richard McGarrah, 1913-, U.S. government official, b. St. Davids, Pa. After working (1935-42) as a journalist, he joined (1942) the U.S. navy where he engaged in intelligence work for the Office of Strategic Services. After the war Helms continued in intelligence work and was one of the architects of the legislation creating (1947) the Central Intelligence Agency (CIA). He worked for the CIA for many years, becoming its chief expert on espionage operations. Helms was appointed (1965) CIA deputy director and later served (1966-73) as director. He left the CIA in 1973 to become U.S. ambassador to Iran.

Helmstedt (hĕlm'shtĕt), city (1970 pop. 27,363), Lower Saxony, E West Germany, a major frontier station at the East German border. Manufactures include machines and textiles. Helmstedt was founded in the 9th cent. and later (15th-16th cent.) was a member of the Hanseatic League. From 1576 to 1810 it was the seat of a noted university, whose Renaissance-style buildings still stand.

Helmund, river, Afghanistan: see HELMAND.

Heloise: see ABELARD, PETER.

Helon (hē'lŏn), father of ELIAB **1.**

helots: see SPARTA, Greece.

Helou, Charles (hĕl'ō), 1911-, Lebanese political leader. After working as a newspaper publisher, he was appointed (1947) Lebanon's representative to the Vatican. He served (1954-55) as minister of justice and health in the government of Camille Chamoun. Helou served as Lebanon's president from 1964 to 1970.

Helper, Hinton Rowan, 1829-1909, American writer, b. Davie co., N.C. He was in California during the gold rush and later returned east to write *The Land of Gold* (1855). His next book, *The Impending Crisis of the South* (1857), an attack on slavery, enraged the South. In 1860 the Republican party distributed 100,000 copies of the book. Helper condemned slavery not on humanitarian or moral grounds, but because it was an economic threat to the poor whites of the South. Three subsequent books, including *Nojoque* (1867), were vicious attacks on the Negro for his alleged basic inferiority. See biography by H. C. Bailey (1965); study by Harvey Wish (1960).

Helpmann, Robert, 1909-, Australian dancer and choreographer. In 1933, Helpmann joined what later became the Sadler's Wells Ballet and was soon a leading soloist. He starred in many productions, often as partner to Margot Fonteyn, and won acclaim in a wide variety of roles ranging from romantic to comic. Helpmann was best known for his appearances in *Apparitions, The Rake's Progress,* and *A Wedding Bouquet.* As a choreographer he is noted for such strongly dramatic works as *Miracle in the Gorbals* (1944). Since 1950 he has also worked as an actor and stage director and has performed in several films, including *The Red Shoes* (1948) and *Tales of Hoffmann* (1950).

Helps, Sir Arthur, 1813-75, English historian and author. His works include *Friends in Council* (3 series, 1847-59), dialogues on social and intellectual subjects; *The Spanish Conquest in America* (4 vol., 1855-61); *Realmah* (1868), a political novel; and *The Life of Columbus* (1869). He edited the published speeches of Prince Albert and the works of Queen Victoria.

Helsingfors, Finland: see HELSINKI.

Helsingør (hĕl"sĭng-ör') or **Elsinore** (ĕl'sĭnôr"), city (1970 est. pop. 30,200), Frederiksborg co., E Denmark, on the Øresund opposite Hälsingborg, Sweden. It is an industrial center, fishing port, and summer resort. Manufactures include ships, machinery, beer, and textiles. Known since the 13th cent., Helsingør experienced its greatest prosperity from the 15th cent. to 1857, when it served as the port where the Danish kings collected tolls from ships passing through the Øresund. It is the site of Kronborg castle (1754-85; completely restored 1925-37), which, although the strongest fortress in Denmark at the time, was taken by the Swedes in 1660. The castle is now a maritime museum and is also used for performances of Shakespeare's *Hamlet,* which is set there. Also of note in Helsingør is the Church of St. Mary (15th cent.).

Helsinki (hĕl'sĭngkē), Swed. *Helsingfors,* city (1970 pop. 523,677), capital of Finland and of Uusimaa prov., S Finland, on the Gulf of Finland. Situated on a peninsula, sheltered by islands, and fortified by SUOMENLINNA, the city is a natural seaport (blocked by ice from January to May) and the commercial, administrative, and intellectual center of Finland. It has machine shops, shipyards, food-processing plants, textile mills, clothing and china factories, and chemical plants. The city, founded (1550) by Gustavus I of Sweden, was devastated by a great fire in 1808; it was rebuilt as a well-planned, spacious metropolis. Helsinki grew rapidly after Alexander I of Russia moved (1812) the capital there from Turku. When the Univ. of Helsinki (founded 1640) was moved from Turku in 1828, Helsinki became the center of Finnish nationalism. The construction of the first Finnish railway (1860), connecting Helsinki and Hämeenlinna, led to renewed prosperity for the capital. In the older part of the city are the state council building, the residence of the president, the Univ. of Helsinki, the Church of St. Nicholas, the national art gallery, and the impressive railway station (designed by Eliel Saarinen). Other cultural landmarks include an opera house, the house of representatives building, the technical university (1879), and the sports stadium (scene of the 1952 Olympic games).

Helst, Bartholomeus van der (bär"tōlōmā'əs vän dər hĕlst), 1613-70, Dutch portrait painter. In Amsterdam the wealthy citizens preferred his flattering, tasteful portraits to those of Rembrandt. He painted several group portraits for the city fathers; among the best are *Banquet of the Civic Guard* (1648) and *Syndics of the Arquebusiers* (both: Rijks Mus.). He was one of the founders of the painters' Guild of St. Luke (1654). *The Musician* and two portraits are in the Metropolitan Museum.

Helvellyn (hĕlvĕl'ĭn), mountain, 3,118 ft (950 m) high, in the Lake District, NW England, SE of Keswick. Near the summit is a memorial to Charles Gough, who died (1805) there of exposure. He was commemorated in poems by Sir Walter Scott and William Wordsworth.

Helvetia (hĕlvē'shə), region of central Europe, occupying the plateau between the Alps and the Jura mts. The name is derived from the Roman term for its inhabitants, the predominantly Celtic Helvetii, who were defeated (58 B.C.) at Bibracte by Julius Caesar in the GALLIC WARS. The Helvetii later prospered under Roman rule; their achievements are evidenced by the remains at AVENCHES. Helvetia corresponds roughly to the western part of modern Switzerland, and the name is still used in poetic reference to that country and on its postage stamps.

Helvetic Republic (hĕlvē'tĭk), 1798-1803, Swiss state established under French auspices. In Sept., 1797, several exiled Swiss leaders in France (notably Frédéric César de LA HARPE) formally urged the French Revolutionary government (the Directory) to help in liberating the subject districts of SWITZERLAND and in overthrowing the aristocratic cantonal governments. The Directory, eager to secure the Alpine passes as well as the treasury of BERN, ordered the invasion of Switzerland (Jan., 1798); resistance was brief. A unified state, the Helvetic Republic, was set up. Lack of funds and constant French political and military intervention proved troublesome; finally, the French Revolutionary Wars shifted (1799) into Switzerland. An Austrian army defeated the French at Zurich (June), but Austro-Russian discord led to the victory (Sept.), again at Zurich, of André Masséna over a Russian army under General Korsakov. General Suvorov, who arrived from Italy to aid Korsakov, was obliged to retreat to Lindau in Germany. The survival of the Helvetic Republic until 1803 was largely due to the presence of French troops, since the Swiss were hostile to centralization. In Feb., 1803, Napoleon, imposing the Act of

Mediation, established a confederation of 19 cantons, with a federal diet subservient to France.

Helvétius, Claude Adrien (hĕlvē'shəs, Fr. klōd ädrēăN' ĕlvāsyüs'), 1715–71, French philosopher, one of the Encyclopedists. He held the post of farmer-general (i.e., tax collector), an exceedingly remunerative position. In 1751 he retired to the country, devoting himself to writing and philanthropic enterprises. His book *De l'esprit* (1758, tr. *Essays on the Mind,* 1807) was regarded as a godless book and was condemned by the pope and by the Parlement of Paris. Agreeing with Locke's doctrine that the minds of men are originally blank tablets, Helvétius maintained that all men are born with equal ability and that distinctions develop from the totality of educational influences. Like Condillac he maintained that all forms of intellectual activity have their beginning in sensation. In ethics a utilitarian, he judged the good in terms of self-satisfaction and regarded self-interest as the sole motive for action. Both Jeremy Bentham and James Mill acknowledge his influence. Another book, *De l'homme,* posthumously published (1772) and translated, is called in English *A Treatise on Man: His Intellectual Faculties and His Education* (1777, tr. 1810, repr. 1969). The complete works of Helvétius were published in 1796 and 1818. See G. V. Plekhanov, *Essays in the History of Materialism* (tr. 1934, repr. 1967); study by David W. Smith (1965).

Helwan: see HULWAN, Egypt.

Hemam (hē'məm), descendant of Esau. Gen. 36.22. Homam: 1 Chron. 1.39.

Heman (hē'mən, hĕm'-). **1** Wise man. 1 Kings 4.31; 1 Chron. 2.6; title of Ps. 88. **2** Chief singer. 1 Chron. 6.33; 15.16–19; 25.1–7.

Hemans, Felicia Dorothea (Browne) (hĕm'ənz), 1793–1835, English poet. She married Capt. Alfred Hemans in 1812, had five children, and separated from him in 1818. Although she wrote much mild and sentimental poetry, today she is known only for "Casabianca," which has the famous first line, "The boy stood on the burning deck. . . , "The Landing of the Pilgrim Fathers," and "England's Dead."

Hemath (hē'măth). **1** Ancestor of the Rechabites. 1 Chron. 2.55. **2** The same as HAMAH.

hematite (hĕm'ətīt), mineral, an oxide of iron, Fe_2O_3, containing about 70% metal, occurring in nature in red to reddish-brown earthy masses and in steel-gray to black crystalline forms. Hematite that has a metallic luster is called specular hematite, or specular iron. The red powdered hematite is used as a pigment (OCHER) and as rouge in polishing. Hematite is the most important ore of iron. Extensive and richly productive deposits occur in the Lake Superior region (Michigan, Minnesota, and Wisconsin) and the Birmingham district (Alabama). The mineral is widely distributed throughout the world and is responsible for the red coloration of many sedimentary rocks. See LIMONITE.

Hemdan (hĕm'dăn), Edomite. Gen. 36.26. Amram: 1 Chron. 1.41.

heme: see COENZYME.

Hemel Hempstead (hĕm'əl), municipal borough (1971 pop. 69,371), Hertfordshire, SE England. It is a market town and suburb of London. Manufactures include paper, electrical and light engineering products, office machinery, and photographic apparatus.

Hemet (hĕm'ĭt), city (1970 pop. 12,252), Riverside co., S Calif., in the fertile San Jacinto valley; inc. 1910. Leading manufactures include mobile homes, metal castings, electronic components, and nursery stock; potatoes are shipped. Mt. San Jacinto College is there. A special tourist attraction is the Ramona Outdoor Play, staged annually by residents of the twin cities of Hemet and San Jacinto.

Hemichordata (hĕmĭkôr"dā'tə), small phylum of marine invertebrates closely related to both the echinoderms (phylum ECHINODERMATA) and chordates (phylum CHORDATA). Acorn worms, or enteropneusts, are the most common hemichordates. The body is composed of an anterior, conical proboscis, a short collar, and a long, wormlike trunk. Gill clefts in the pharynx and a hollow nerve cord in the collar suggest relationship to chordates, while the ciliated larvae are similar to those of echinoderms. Hemichordates live in burrows or under objects in shallow water and feed on detritus. *Balanoglossus gigas* may reach a length of nearly 5 ft (1.5 m), but most species are considerably smaller. A small number of deep-sea tube-dwelling creatures known as pterobranchs are also members of the phylum.

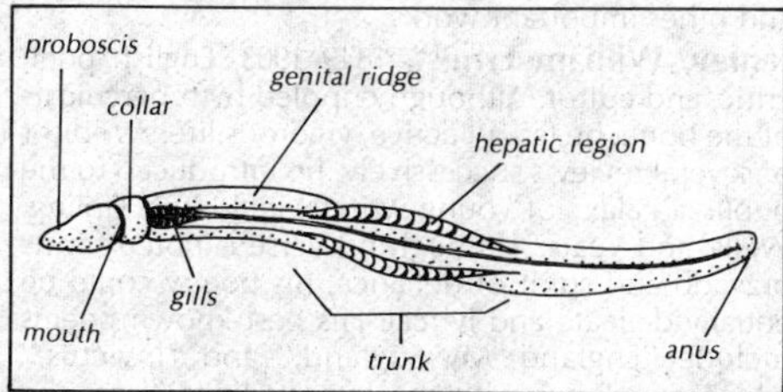

Dorsal view of an acorn worm, Saccoglossus, *representative of the phylum Hemichordata*

Hemingway, Ernest, 1899–1961, American novelist and short-story writer, one of the great American writers of the 20th cent., b. Oak Park, Ill. Hemingway's fiction usually focuses on people living essential, dangerous lives—soldiers, fishermen, athletes, bullfighters—who meet the pain and difficulty of their existence with stoic courage. His celebrated literary style, influenced by Ezra Pound and Gertrude STEIN, is direct, terse, and often monotonous, yet particularly suited to his elemental subject matter. The son of a country doctor, Hemingway worked as a reporter for the Kansas City *Star* after graduating from high school in 1917. During World War I he served as an ambulance driver in France and in the Italian infantry and was wounded just before his 19th birthday. Later, while working in Paris as a correspondent for the Toronto *Star,* he became involved with the expatriate circle surrounding Gertrude Stein. His first books, *Three Stories and Ten Poems* (1923), *In Our Time* (short stories, 1924), and *The Torrents of Spring* (a novel, 1926), attracted attention primarily because of his stunning literary style. With the publication of *The Sun Also Rises* (1926), he was recognized as the spokesman of the "lost generation" (so called by Gertrude Stein). The novel concerns a group of psychologically bruised, disillusioned expatriates living in postwar Paris, who take psychic refuge in such immediate physical activities as eating, drinking, traveling, brawling, and lovemaking. His next important novel, *A Farewell to Arms* (1929), is about a tragic wartime love affair between an ambulance driver and an English nurse. Hemingway also published such volumes of short stories as *Men Without Women* (1927), *Winner Take Nothing* (1933), and *The Fifth Column* [a play] and the *First Forty-nine Stories* (1938), which include such famous stories as "The Killers," "The Undefeated," and "The Snows of Kilimanjaro." His nonfictional works, *Death in the Afternoon* (1932), about bullfighting, and *Green Hills of Africa* (1935), about big-game hunting, glorify virility, bravery, and the virtue of a primal challenge to life. During the Spanish Civil War, Hemingway served as a correspondent on the loyalist side; from this experience came his great novel, *For Whom the Bell Tolls* (1940), which, in detailing an incident in the war, argues for human brotherhood. Hemingway fought in World War II and then settled in Cuba in 1945. His novella *The Old Man and the Sea* (1952) celebrates the indomitable courage of an aged Cuban fisherman. In 1954, Hemingway was awarded the Nobel Prize in Literature. After his expulsion from Cuba by the Castro regime, he moved to Idaho. He was increasingly plagued by ill health and diminishing mental faculties, and in July, 1961, he committed suicide by shooting himself. Among Hemingway's works are the novels *To Have and Have Not* (1937) and *Across the River and into the Trees* (1950); he also edited an anthology of stories, *Men at War* (1942). Posthumous publications include *A Moveable Feast* (1964), a memoir of Paris in the 1920s; a novel, *Islands in the Stream* (1970); and *The Nick Adams Stories* (1972), a collection that includes previously unpublished pieces. See the memoir of his brother, Leicester (1962); biographies by Marcelline (Hemingway) Sanford (1962) and C. H. Baker (1969); studies by J. M. DeFalco (1963), Philip Young (2d. ed. 1966), and C. H. Baker (4th ed. 1972).

hemipode (hĕm'ĭpōd): see BUSTARD QUAIL.

Hemling, Hans: see MEMLING, HANS.

hemlock, any tree of the genus *Tsuga,* coniferous evergreens of the family Pinaceae (PINE family) native to North America and Asia. The common hemlock of E North America is *T. canadensis,* an ornamental tree (sometimes cultivated as a hedge) with small cones and short, dark green leaves so arranged as to give the branchlets a flattened appearance. The tree has been highly valued as a source of tanbark but is now seriously reduced in number. Its wood is soft and light. One of the two Western hemlocks (*T. heterophylla,* the tallest tree of the genus) has more valuable wood, which is used in construction work. The ground hemlock is a species of YEW. The POISON HEMLOCK and water hemlock are herbs of the family Umbelliferae (CARROT family) of the division MAGNOLIOPHYTA. True hemlock is classified in the division PINOPHYTA, class Pinopsida, order Coniferales, family Pinaceae.

Hemmer, Jarl Robert (yärl rō'bərt hĕm'ər), 1893–1944, Finnish author who wrote in Swedish. Inwardly troubled, he experienced several religious crises and finally committed suicide. His poems, e.g., *Realm of the Rye* (1922, tr. 1938), show a fresh, lyrical love of nature. He is best known for *A Fool of Faith* (1931, tr. 1935), a powerful novel of suffering and tragedy.

hemoglobin (hē'məglō"bĭn), respiratory pigment found in the red BLOOD cells of all vertebrates and some invertebrates. A hemoglobin molecule is composed of a protein group, known as globin, and four heme groups, each associated with an iron atom. Each iron atom combines reversibly with a molecule of oxygen in the lungs and carries it through the body to a tissue capillary, where it is exchanged for carbon dioxide. Hemoglobin is produced in bone marrow by erythrocytes and is circulated with them until their destruction. It is then broken down in the spleen, and some of its components, such as iron, are recycled to the bone marrow; other components, such as the heme groups, are broken down into bilirubin, transported to the liver, and secreted with the BILE into the intestine for eventual elimination from the body. Hemoglobin deficiency may be a result of structural abnormality in the hemoglobin molecules themselves or of malfunction or destruction of the red blood cells, a condition known as ANEMIA.

hemolysis (hĭmŏl'ĭsĭs), destruction of red blood cells in the bloodstream. Although new red blood cells, or erythrocytes, are continuously created and old ones destroyed, an excessive rate of destruction sometimes occurs. The dead cells, in sufficiently large numbers, overwhelm the organ that destroys them, the spleen, so that serum pigments resulting from hemoglobin breakdown appear in the blood serum, a condition known as JAUNDICE. Large-scale destruction of red blood cells, from any of a variety of causes, results in ANEMIA. Rh disease, or ERYTHROBLASTOSIS FETALIS, is a hemolytic disease of newborns caused by an immune reaction between fetal red blood cells and maternal antibodies to them. Some hemolytic conditions, e.g., those in which red blood cells are fragile and rupture easily, are treated by removal of the spleen to slow cell breakdown or by administration of STEROIDS.

Hémon, Louis (lwē āmôN'), 1880–1913, French Canadian novelist, b. France. After working as a journalist for French publications in England (1903–11), he moved to Quebec, where he worked as a farm hand. He was killed by a train in 1913. Of his four posthumously published novels, one, *Maria Chapdelaine* (1914), has become a classic of French Canadian literature. A harsh, realistic story of pioneer life in Quebec, it profoundly influenced subsequent Canadian authors.

hemophilia (hē"məfĭl'ēə,–fēl'yə), hereditary disorder in which the clotting ability of the blood is impaired and excessive bleeding results. The disease is transmitted through females but almost invariably affects male offspring only. Hemophilia is classified according to the clotting factor that is lacking in the blood. In hemophilia A, the so-called classical hemophilia, the antihemophiliac globulin is missing. In hemophilia B the plasma thromboplastin component is lacking. Small wounds and punctures that in an ordinary individual are sealed over by coagulated blood become vital crises in a hemophiliac. The hemophiliac bleeds uncontrollably after a small cut or bruise, after rigorous exertion, and even spontaneously. A minor surgical procedure such as a tooth extraction is extremely hazardous. Hemorrhages into the spaces about the joints often lead to disability. Local hemorrhage in a hemophiliac may be treated with a pressure pad soaked with one of the substances that aid in coagulating blood, such as globulin or fibrin foam. For hemophilia A, transfusions with either whole blood or plasma that contains the missing clotting factor or administration of the clotting factor in concentrated form may be necessary from time to time. Examples of the transmission of hemophilia have been found in several royal families, including those of Queen Victoria of England and Alfonso XIII of Spain.

hemorrhage (hĕm'ərĭj), escape of blood from the circulation (arteries, veins, capillaries) to the internal or external tissues. The term is usually applied to a loss of blood that is copious enough to threaten health or life. Slow bleeding may lead to anemia, while the sudden loss of a large amount of blood may cause shock. Hemorrhage from a cerebral artery can be fatal because of interference with brain function. Many diseases and disorders (e.g., peptic ulcer, hemorrhoids, tuberculosis, hemophilia, typhoid fever, and scurvy) as well as childbirth and many injuries can give rise to hemorrhage. Internal hemorrhage may require surgical intervention. See FIRST AID.

hemorrhoids (hĕm'əroidz) or **piles,** dilatations of the veins about the anus (external hemorrhoids) or those higher up inside it (internal hemorrhoids). They appear as small, rounded, purplish tumors, often complicated by inflammation, clotting, and bleeding. Hemorrhoids are very common phenomena and are brought about by factors that produce venous congestion, such as constipation, diarrhea, or pregnancy. In some instances, the pain from inflamed hemorrhoids can be intense, and the bleeding so profuse as to pose the threat of anemia. Hemorrhoids that are uncomplicated or bleed only slightly at infrequent intervals do not require specific treatment except to improve the condition that may be causing them, such as constipation. Hemorrhoids that are very painful or bleed excessively are treated by warm baths and suppositories and, if necessary, by injection or surgery.

hemp, common name for a tall annual herb (*Cannabis sativa*) of the family Cannabinaceae, native to Asia but now widespread because of its cultivation for the bast fiber (also called hemp) and for the drug it yields. Known and cultivated in ancient China, the plant was introduced into Europe, now the center of its production, before the Christian era. In the United States it is cultivated chiefly in the Midwest. The fiber, retted from the stem, is one of the most important for various kinds of cordage; it is also used in making paper, cloth (canvas and other kinds), oakum for calking ships, and other products. The male and female flowers are borne on separate plants. The chemical derived from the female flowering tops (cannabis indica) is used medicinally and is the source of the powerful narcotics MARIJUANA and HASHISH. Hemp seed is used as bird food, and the oil from the seeds is used in the manufacture of paints, varnishes, and soap. The dried leaves are used in Asia for a beverage. The word *hemp* is used in combination for several other kinds of fiber plants, notably MANILA HEMP and SISAL HEMP. The true hemp plant is related to the hop, which is used in making beer. Hemp is classified in the division MAGNOLIOPHYTA, class Magnoliopsida, order Urticales, family Cannabinaceae.

Hempstead, village (1970 pop. 39,411), Nassau co., SE N.Y., on W Long Island; inc. 1853. It is a retail center for the area. Electronic equipment, tools, chemicals, metal products, and furniture are made in the village. Hempstead was settled in 1644 by English colonists who named it for their old home in England, Hemel-Hempstead. Hofstra Univ. is there.

Hems: see HIMS, Syria.

Hen, man who was to have a memorial in the temple. Zech. 6.14.

Hena (hē'nə), unidentified town, on the Euphrates. 2 Kings 18.34; 19.13; Isa. 37.13.

Henadad (hĕn'ədăd), chief of a family active in rebuilding the Temple. Ezra 3.9.

henbane or **black henbane,** herb (*Hyoscyamus niger*) native to the Mediterranean region and naturalized in parts of North America. It belongs to the family Solanaceae (NIGHTSHADE family) and contains a narcotic poison (similar to that of the related belladonna) that is extracted from the leaves for medicinal use. The drug, also called henbane, is composed of alkaloids, chiefly hyoscyamine and SCOPOLAMINE. Henbane is produced chiefly in Egypt, the USSR, and Hungary; the United States is a major importer. The name henbane refers to the fact that the seeds of this herb are very poisonous to poultry. It is sometimes also called nightshade. Henbane is classified in the division MAGNOLIOPHYTA, class Magnoliopsida, order Polemoniales, family Solanaceae.

Hench, Philip Showalter, 1896–1965, American physician, b. Pittsburgh, M.D. Univ. of Pittsburgh, 1920. Associated with the Mayo Foundation of the Univ. of Minnesota school of medicine after 1921, he was made head of the department of rheumatic diseases in 1926, began teaching in 1928, and was made professor in 1947. In 1946 he became consultant to the surgeon general of the U.S. army. He shared with Edward C. Kendall and Tadeus Reichstein the 1950 Nobel Prize in Physiology and Medicine for his pioneering work in the treatment of rheumatoid arthritis with cortisone and ACTH.

Henderson, Alexander, 1583–1646, Scottish churchman. He is often regarded as the greatest figure in the Church of Scotland after John Knox. Although he was presented to the parish of Leuchars by a prelate, he soon became a leading opponent of prelacy and of English domination in the church. In 1638, after the signing of the National Covenant (see COVENANTERS), he was elected moderator of the general assembly at Glasgow, which deposed the bishops and set up Presbyterianism in spite of royal threats. Henderson met King Charles I to settle the problem and was favorably received. In 1640 he was elected rector of the Univ. of Edinburgh. In 1641 and 1643 he was moderator of the general assembly and in 1643 presented a draft of the Solemn League and Covenant. He sat thereafter (1643–46) in the Westminster Assembly. In the year of his death he again met Charles for a conference on church government during the course of the king's alliance with the Scottish army. Henderson wrote many speeches and sermons. See biographies by J. P. Thomson (1912) and R. L. Orr (1919).

Henderson, Arthur, 1863–1935, British statesman, organizer and leader of the British LABOUR PARTY. In early life he was an ironworker and a labor union leader. Elected (1903) to Parliament, he was chairman of the parliamentary Labour party (1908–10, 1914–17), president of the Board of Education (1915–16), paymaster general (1916), and a member of the war cabinet (1916–17). In Ramsay MacDonald's first ministry (1924) he was home secretary. As foreign secretary (1929–31) Henderson worked to moderate Franco-German problems and supported the League of Nations. He led Labour opposition to the formation of the National government in 1931 and lost his seat in Parliament. From 1932 until his death he was president of the World Disarmament Conference, and he was awarded the 1934 Nobel Peace Prize. His writings include *The Aims of Labour* (1919). See biography by M. A. Hamilton (1938); study by David Carlton (1970).

Henderson, Fletcher (James Fletcher "Smack" Henderson), 1898–1952, American jazz composer, arranger, and pianist, b. Cuthbert, Ga. Henderson played piano from childhood. Short of funds after coming to New York City in 1920 to study graduate chemistry, he took a job with W. C. Handy's music company. During the 1920s and 30s, Henderson led superbly dynamic jazz orchestras. The hallmarks of his arrangements include two- and four-bar repetitions, bursting section choruses, and solo showcasing. He is considered the creator of "swing" and influenced many musicians, notably Benny GOODMAN.

Henderson, Leon, 1895–, American economist, administrator of the Office of Price Administration (1941–42), b. Millville, N.J. An official of the Russell Sage Foundation (1925–34), Henderson held several posts as economic adviser in the administration of President Franklin Delano Roosevelt before his appointment to the Securities and Exchange Commission in 1939. After leaving the OPA, he entered upon a career in business.

Henderson, Richard, 1735–85, American colonizer in Kentucky, b. Hanover co., Va. An associate justice of the North Carolina superior court (1769–73), Henderson was long interested in Western lands and was the chief promoter of the TRANSYLVANIA COMPANY. He followed (1775) Daniel BOONE, an agent for the company, to the company's first settlement at Boonesboro on the Kentucky River and in 1779 employed James ROBERTSON to settle the Cumberland River area. Virginia and North Carolina voided the company's land grants, and Henderson and his associates were left with a very small portion of the vast territory they had claimed. Although primarily a land speculator, Henderson was one of the most important figures in the early expansion of the frontier. See Archibald Henderson, *The Conquest of the Old Southwest* (1920); W. S. Lester, *The Transylvania Colony* (1935).

Henderson. 1 City (1970 pop. 22,976), seat of Henderson co., NW Ky., on the Ohio River, in an oil, coal, tobacco, corn, and livestock area; founded 1797 and named for Richard Henderson, inc. as a city 1867. Furniture, clothing, truck axles, and plastics are made. John J. Audubon lived in Henderson from 1810 to 1819; nearby is Audubon Memorial State Park, with a museum and a bird sanctuary. A junior college is in the city. **2** City (1970 pop. 16,395), Clark co., SE Nev., in a desert area overlooking Las Vegas and surrounded by mountains; inc. 1953. Limestone, titanium, ammonium perchlorate, chlorine, hydrogen, and manganese are produced, and water heaters are manufactured. Hydroelectric power is supplied by Hoover Dam. The city was founded (1942) to provide houses for employees of a magnesium plant. Southern Nevada Museum is there. Nearby Mt. Charleston and Lake Mead offer recreational activities. **3** City (1970 pop. 13,896), seat of Vance co., N N.C.; settled c.1811, inc. 1841. It is an important bright leaf tobacco market, with food-processing industries. Nearby Kerr Reservoir on the Roanoke River offers water sports. **4** City (1970 pop. 10,187), seat of Rusk co., NE Texas; inc. 1877. It is a prosperous oil city, with wells and refineries. There are also foundries and lumber and cotton mills. Originally a pinewoods lumbering town, then a cotton center, the city was transformed in 1830 when C. M. Joiner struck the first gusher of the fabulously rich East Texas Oil Field nearby. The site of an Old Shawnee Indian village is in the area.

Hendrick, c.1680–1755, chief of the Mohawk Indians, known also as Tiyanoga. He became a Christian and was an ally of the British. He represented his people at the Albany Congress (1754). The next year he was killed fighting for the British at Lake George in the French and Indian War.

Hendricks, Thomas Andrews, 1819–85, American political leader, b. near Zanesville, Ohio. As U.S. Senator from Indiana (1863–69) he opposed radical Reconstruction. He was (1873–77) governor of Indiana. Defeated for Vice President on the Tilden ticket in 1876, he won on the Cleveland ticket in 1884. Hendricks died after eight months in office. See biography by John W. Holcombe (1886).

henequen (hĕn'əkĭn): see SISAL HEMP.

Hengchow: see HENG-YANG, China.

Hengelo (hĕng'əlō), city (1971 pop. 69,685), Overijssel prov., E Netherlands. Manufactures include heavy machinery and metal products.

Hengist and Horsa (hĕng'gĭst, hôr'sə), names of two brothers who, according to tradition, led the Jutish invasion of Britain and founded the kingdom of KENT. Hengist would more properly be written Hengest. They are said to have been invited by VORTIGERN in 449 to help the Britons defend themselves against the Picts and Scots to the north, to have settled in Kent, and to have fought a battle with Vortigern, in which Horsa was killed (c.455). The names may all be mythical, but historians generally agree that in the 5th cent. a Jutish chief and his retinue did arrive in Kent, did serve a British king, and did revolt and that various battles prepared the way for the later settlement of Kent by the Jutes.

Heng-yang or **Hengyang** (both: hŭng-yăng), city (1970 est. pop. 240,000), central Hunan prov., China, on the Hsiang River, at the mouth of the Lei River. It is the leading transportation center of Hunan, linking water, rail, and highway routes. Manufactures include chemicals, machine tools, textiles, paper, processed foods, and fertilizer. Lead and zinc mines are nearby. Its former name was Hengchow.

Henie, Sonja (sō'nyə hĕn'ē), 1913–1969, Norwegian-American figure skater and movie actress, b. Oslo, Norway. She began ice skating at the age of eight and two years later won the first of six straight Norwegian figure-skating championships. She won the world's figure-skating crown ten consecutive years, the European title eight times in a row, and the Olympic figure-skating championship in 1928, 1932, and 1936. After her last Olympic win she moved permanently to the United States and turned professional. Her ice carnivals attracted millions. She starred in a number of motion pictures and wrote the autobiographical *Wings on My Feet* (1940).

Henle, Jacob (Friedrich Gustav Jakob Henle) (frē'drĭkh go͞os'täf yä'kôp hĕn'lə), 1809–85, German anatomist and histologist. A pupil of J. P. Müller, he taught at Zürich, Heidelberg, and Göttingen. He contributed pioneer work on the microscopic structure of tissues, including the renal tubules that bear his name, epithelium, hair, and blood vessels. He anticipated Pasteur in his theory that microorganisms cause infectious diseases. He wrote *Handbuch der systematischen Anatomie* (3 vol., 1866–71) and other important works.

Henley, William Ernest, 1849–1903, English poet, critic, and editor. Although crippled by tuberculosis of the bone, he led an active, vigorous life. As editor of several reviews successively, he introduced to the public a galaxy of young writers, including Kipling, Wells, and Yeats. Although his verse is noted for its bravado and spirit of defiance, his poetry could be equally delicate and lyrical. His best-known poems include "England, My England," and "Invictus," which concludes with the famous lines "I am the master of my fate, I am the captain of my soul." Henley's volumes of verse include *A Book of Verses* (1888), *The Song of the Sword* (1892), and *For Eng-*

land's Sake (1900). He collaborated on four plays with Robert Louis Stevenson, with whom he enjoyed a long friendship. See biography by John Connell (1949, repr. 1971); study by J. H. Buckley (1945, repr. 1971).

henna, name for a reddish or black hair dye obtained from the powdered leaves and young shoots of the mignonette tree, or henna shrub (*Lawsonia inermis*), an Old World shrub of the LOOSESTRIFE family. Henna dye has long been in use, as evidenced by Egyptian mummies.

Hennepin, Louis (hĕn'əpĭn), 1640–1701?, French cleric and explorer in North America. A Franciscan Recollect friar, Hennepin came to Canada in 1675, meeting on the journey LA SALLE, who made him chaplain of his proposed Western expedition in 1678. After some time spent at Fort Frontenac the party sailed (1679) in the *Griffon,* the first ship on the Great Lakes, for Green Bay. La Salle crossed to the Mississippi by the Illinois route and from there sent Hennepin with the expedition, led by Michel ACO, which was the first to explore the upper Mississippi valley. They ascended the river to Minnesota, where they were captured by the Sioux. In the course of his captivity Hennepin first saw and named the Falls of St. Anthony, where Minneapolis was located afterward. He was rescued by DULUTH. After returning to France, Hennepin claimed in his *Description de la Louisiane* (1682) the leadership and all the credit for the upper Mississippi expedition. Later, in his *Nouveau Voyage* (1696) and *Nouvelle Découverte* (1697), he falsely claimed to have descended the Mississippi to its mouth. His narratives, however, have undeniable charm and importance. He was the first to describe such parts of America as the upper Mississippi and Niagara Falls. R. G. Thwaite's translation, *Hennepin's New Discovery* (1903, repr. 1972) contains a biography and bibliography.

Henoch (hē'nək): see ENOCH **2** and HANOCH **1.**

Henri, Robert (hĕn'rī), 1865–1929, American painter and teacher, b. Cincinnati. He studied at the Pennsylvania Academy of the Fine Arts. In 1888 he went to Paris, where he worked at Julian's and the Beaux-Arts until, dissatisfied with the schools, he set up his own studio. In 1891 he returned to Philadelphia. As a member of the group of artists known as the EIGHT, he participated in the rebellion against academic art. Henri became one of the foremost American art teachers. First in Philadelphia, then at the Chase School in New York City, at his own school (1909–12), and at the Art Students League he inspired his students with his dynamic concept of art. Opposed to the formalization of style, he viewed art as a medium to express life and especially humanity. Among his pupils were George Bellows, Rockwell Kent, and Edward Hopper. In his own work, Henri excelled in dramatic portraits. Characteristic are his *Spanish Gypsy* (Metropolitan Mus.); *Young Woman in Black, Himself,* and *Herself* (Art Inst., Chicago); and *Girl with a Fan* (Pennsylvania Acad. of the Fine Arts). See his *Art Spirit* (1960); study by W. I. Homer (1969).

Henrietta Maria (mərī'ə), 1609–69, queen consort of CHARLES I of England, daughter of Henry IV of France. She married Charles in 1625. Although she was devoted and loyal to her husband, she lacked judgment, and her Roman Catholic faith made her suspect in England. By her negotiations with the pope, with foreign powers, and with English army officers, she added greatly to the suspicions against Charles that helped to precipitate (1642) the English civil war. After 1644 she lived in France, making continual efforts to secure foreign aid for her husband until his execution in 1649. She returned (1660) to England after the Restoration, but resumed living in France in 1665. Her influence may have affected the religious beliefs of her sons Charles II and James II, although she herself was unsuccessful in her attempts to convert them to Catholicism. See biography by Carola Oman (1936); study by Quentin Bone (1972).

Henrietta of England (Henrietta Anne), 1644–70, duchesse d'Orléans, called Madame; sister-in-law of King Louis XIV of France. The daughter of King Charles I and Queen Henrietta Maria of England, she was taken (1646) to France when civil war raged in England; in 1661 she married Philippe I, duc d'ORLÉANS, brother of Louis XIV. In Louis's behalf she negotiated the Treaty of Dover with her brother, King CHARLES II (1670). She died shortly after her return from England; it was rumored that she had been poisoned by her husband. Jacques Bossuet's funeral oration for Madame is one of his best-known sermons. See her correspondence with Charles, ed. by Cyril Hartmann (rev. ed. 1954); Mme de La Fayette, *Secret History of Henrietta Princess of England* (tr. 1929).

Henry I or **Henry the Fowler,** 876?–936, German king (919–36), first of the Saxon line; precursor of the Holy Roman emperors. He succeeded his father as duke of Saxony in 912. A foe of King CONRAD I, who futilely tried to subdue the rebellious Henry, he was nevertheless named (918) by Conrad as his successor. Designated king by Saxon and Franconian nobles in 919, Henry refused to be crowned by the bishops, thus maintaining his independence of the church. During his reign he changed his attitude toward the church, probably because of a growing awareness of its political importance. As king he immediately turned to restoring monarchical authority, which had been whittled away by the dukes. By 921 he had secured recognition of his royal authority from the dukes of Swabia and Bavaria. In 925 he won LOTHARINGIA from its allegiance to France. Henry also dealt with the Magyar raids, which Conrad had failed to halt. In 924 after a Magyar invasion of Saxony, Henry arranged a nine-year truce and agreed to pay yearly tribute to the Magyars. He used this respite to introduce military reforms in Saxony and Thuringia. Saxon soldiers were trained for mounted combat, and the new efficiency of his army enabled him to take Brandenburg from the Wends. In the marches, or frontier regions, Henry built large fortresses, primarily for military purposes; however, he attracted some permanent settlers in these regions. In 933 the truce with the Magyars ended when Henry refused to pay tribute; he defeated the Magyars in a great battle at Riade, near the Unstrut River. He expanded his frontier at Danish expense in 934. Before his death Henry secured from the nobles the succession of his son as OTTO I. The restorer of the imperial tradition, Henry was recognized even in his lifetime as founder of a new realm, Germany. His wife, Matilda, founded many monasteries, including Quedlinburg where she lies buried with her husband. She is a saint of the Roman Catholic Church; her feast is March 14.

Henry II, 973–1024, Holy Roman emperor (1014–24) and German king (1002–24), last of the Saxon line. He succeeded his father as duke of Bavaria. When Otto III died without an heir, Henry, who was Otto's third cousin and the grandson of HENRY I, was elected German king. After some opposition he was recognized by the German duchies. In 1004 he entered Italy and at Pavia was crowned king of the rebellious Lombards by the bishops. Italian resistance appeared to be broken when Pavia was destroyed in a conflict between the citizens and Henry's German followers, but his supremacy was still uncertain when he went north to meet BOLESLAUS I of Poland. Henry expelled (1004) Boleslaus from Bohemia, but the war dragged on until 1018, when Boleslaus was able to obtain territories in E Germany in fief from Henry. Returning (1013) to Italy, Henry was crowned (1014) Holy Roman emperor at Rome. On his third Italian campaign (1021–22), undertaken at the pope's behest, he restored order in Lombardy, reasserted his sovereignty in all Italy, and attended a synod at Pavia where he advocated far-reaching church reform. Always relying heavily on ecclesiastic support, Henry opposed the regular clergy in its jurisdictional struggle with the bishops, and he forcefully exercised his right of nominating bishops. However, both Henry and his empress, Kunigunde of Luxembourg, were distinguished for piety and have been canonized. By his attention to German affairs Henry counteracted the ill effects of his predecessor's exclusive concern with Italy. Henry died childless; he was succeeded by CONRAD II. Feast: July 15.

Henry III, 1017–56, Holy Roman emperor (1046–56) and German king (1039–56), son and successor of Conrad II. He was crowned joint king with his father in 1028, and acceded on Conrad's death in 1039. Under Henry III the medieval Holy Roman Empire probably attained its greatest power and solidity. In 1041, Henry defeated the Bohemians, who had been overrunning the lands of his vassals the Poles and compelled Duke Bratislaus I of Bohemia to renew his vassalage. Although several expeditions to Hungary against the raiding Magyars failed to establish his authority in that country, Henry was able in 1043 to fix the frontier of Austria and Hungary at the Leitha and Morava rivers, where it remained until the end of World War I. In the West, Henry attempted with some initial success to control particularist tendencies among the duchies. The dukes of Saxony and Lorraine (Lotharingia) offered the most resistance. In Saxony, Henry managed to avert rebellion, which, however, erupted after his death. On the death of Duke Gozilo of Lorraine (1044), Henry divided the duchy between the duke's two sons. Duke Godfrey, the elder, who received Upper Lorraine, organized numerous revolts against Henry; in 1047–50 the counts of Holland and Flanders (Lower Lorraine) joined in the revolt. Godfrey was successively defeated, imprisoned, restored, and expelled again. He went to Italy (1051), where he married (1054) Marchioness Beatrice of Tuscany, mother of MATILDA; Godfrey used his Tuscan position to bolster his strength in Germany, and Henry was unable to subdue him. Despite his political involvement Henry made religious matters his prime concern and supported monastic reform movements, including the CLUNIAC ORDER. He branded as simony the customary payments made to the king by new bishops and in 1046 undertook to reform the church. Descending into Italy, he had three rival claimants to the papacy set aside at the synods of Sutri and Rome and was accorded the decisive vote in papal elections. The four German popes named by Henry (including LEO IX) renewed the strength of the papacy, which was to prove the nemesis of his successors. On his death his wife Agnes of Poitou assumed the regency for his infant son, HENRY IV.

Henry IV, 1050–1106, Holy Roman emperor (1084–1105) and German king (1056–1105), son and successor of HENRY III. He was the central figure in the opening stages of the long struggle between the Holy Roman Empire and the papacy. During his minority the papacy, the German nobles, and the high ecclesiastics greatly increased their power at the expense of the imperial authority. In 1062, Archbishop Anno of Cologne abducted Henry and assumed the regency, which had been held by Henry's mother Agnes; Anno enriched his see from the royal lands and revenues. He allowed Archbishop ADALBERT of Hamburg-Bremen to share the authority and plunder, and Adalbert soon became sole regent. Henry attained his majority in 1065, but Adalbert retained the regency until jealous nobles persuaded Henry to dismiss (1066) him. The first task of Henry after assuming control was to restore his authority in the duchies, especially in Saxony, where a revolt (1073) was subdued in 1075. He then turned his attention to Italy, where he sought to restore imperial authority; this provoked a conflict with the papacy. Henry disregarded the opposition of Pope GREGORY VII to lay INVESTITURE and invested a new bishop of Milan. Gregory supported the previous bishop, who had been put in office by a revolutionary movement in the city, and threatened Henry with deposition. Henry summoned a council at Worms, which declared Gregory deposed (Jan., 1076). Gregory, at a synod in Feb., 1076, declared Henry excommunicate and deposed and absolved his subjects of their oaths of fealty. A powerful coalition of German nobles, including the rebellious Saxons, agreed (Oct., 1076) not to recognize the king unless he obtained absolution by February; his fitness to rule was to be decided at a diet to be held at Augsburg under the chairmanship of the pope. To forestall the action of this diet, Henry crossed the Alps in the dead of winter to seek absolution. By his humiliation and penitence he moved the pope to grant him absolution at CANOSSA in Jan., 1077. The rebel dukes, however, were determined to depose him, and they elected Duke Rudolf of Swabia antiking, thus plunging Germany into civil war. Gregory remained neutral until March, 1080, when he renewed Henry's excommunication and deposition and recognized Rudolf's title. But Henry was now supported by a large party; German and Italian bishops joined him in declaring Gregory deposed and in electing an antipope, Clement III (see GUIBERT OF RAVENNA). Rudolf died in 1080 and his supporters elected a Lotharingian count, Herman of Salm, to succeed him. By this time, however, the German revolt was practically broken, and in 1081 Henry carried the war into Italy. After several unsuccessful attempts he occupied Rome in 1084, installed Clement III as pope, and was crowned emperor. He retired before the advance of Gregory's Norman allies under ROBERT GUISCARD, who rescued Gregory but plundered Rome. The Normans then withdrew from Rome, taking Gregory, who had gained the hatred of the Romans, with them. In Germany, Henry broke (1088) the power of Herman, but his stubborn support of Clement III against Gregory's successors made his own family turn against him because they felt he was endangering the monarchy. When his son Henry (later HENRY V) rebelled in 1104, only the Rhenish cities were loyal to the emperor. Trapped by a promise of conciliation, Henry IV was imprisoned and forced to abdicate (1105). In 1106, just before his death, he escaped and received considerable support. During his reign Henry was caught between the rising particularism of the princes and the reformist demands of a revivified papacy, but he managed to salvage enough of his father's legacy to make possible a restoration of imperial power under the Hohenstaufens.

Henry V, 1081–1125, Holy Roman emperor (1111–25) and German king (1105–25), son of Henry IV. Crowned joint king with his father in 1099, he put himself at the head of the party desiring reconciliation with the pope and, with the approval of Pope PASCHAL II, rebelled (1104) against his father and compelled him to abdicate (1105). Formally reconciled with the church, Henry V practiced lay INVESTITURE from the beginning of his reign. The pope protested against the practice. In 1110, Henry entered Italy with his army to settle the conflict and receive the imperial crown. At this time the pope proposed a compact that provided that if the king abandoned lay investiture and confirmed the pope's right to the Patrimony of St. Peter (see PAPAL STATES), the bishops of the empire would give up the temporal powers and estates they had received from former emperors. Henry accepted the compromise, but when it was announced at St. Peter's as a preliminary to his imperial coronation (1111), a violent tumult arose from the clergy, who saw their wealth and power being given away. Henry thereupon left the city with the pope and cardinals as his prisoners; in order to procure his release, Paschal conceded to Henry the right to appoint and invest at will and crowned him emperor. Henry returned to Germany, but in 1112 Paschal repudiated his concessions. Henry was faced (1114–21) by rebellions in Saxony that he was unable to put down; he nevertheless went to Italy in 1116 to take possession, as suzerain, of the fiefs of MATILDA of Tuscany and, as heir, of her alodial lands. In 1118, Paschal died. Henry set up an antipope to the new pope, Gelasius II, whereupon Gelasius excommunicated the emperor. In 1119, Henry entered upon negotiations with Pope CALIXTUS II, Gelasius's successor, and a compromise on the investiture question was reached at last in the Concordat of Worms (1122; see WORMS, CONCORDAT OF). Henry made peace with his domestic enemies at the Diet of Würzburg (1121). His empress, MATILDA, daughter of Henry I of England, bore him no heir; the nobles elected the duke of Saxony to succeed him as Holy Roman Emperor Lothair II. Henry was the last emperor of the Salian line.

Henry VI, 1165–97, Holy Roman emperor (1191–97) and German king (1190–97), son and successor of Holy Roman Emperor Frederick I (Frederick Barbarossa). He was crowned German king at Aachen in 1169 and king of Italy at Milan in 1186 after his marriage to CONSTANCE, heiress presumptive to the throne of Sicily. Henry remained in Italy as his father's representative, ravaging central Italy and forcing it to submit to imperial domination. He became regent at his father's departure (1189) for the Third Crusade and succeeded Frederick, who died in 1190. In 1191, Henry entered Italy on an expedition to secure Constance's Sicilian inheritance from TANCRED of Lecce, who had illegally assumed the crown. Stopping at Rome he was crowned Holy Roman emperor by Pope Celestine III. He continued southward, but failed in the initial attempt to take Sicily. He returned to Germany, where he faced a rebellion fomented by the GUELPHS and the nobles of the Lower Rhine, who opposed his attempt to absorb Thuringia into the royal demesne. Henry secured a powerful bargaining weapon when he obtained custody (1193) of King RICHARD I of England, brother-in-law and ally of the Guelph leader, HENRY THE LION. Soon after Richard had paid a ransom, sworn fealty to Henry, and been released (Feb., 1194), peace was made. In Sicily, the death of Tancred favored the success of Henry's second expedition (May, 1194). Palermo fell in November, and on Christmas Day Henry was crowned king of Sicily. Insatiable, Henry dreamed of further expansion in the Mediterranean. He began to promote (1195) a new crusade and intimidated the Byzantine emperor, ALEXIUS III, into paying him tribute. At the Diet of Würzburg (1196) Henry proposed that the empire be made hereditary in his family, the Hohenstaufen, and in return offered unrestricted rights of inheritance to those who held fiefs from him. The proposal was defeated, though it found many supporters, and Henry contented himself with securing the election of his infant son (later Emperor FREDERICK II) as king. Henry died of a fever at Messina just as he was preparing to invade the Holy Land. He was succeeded in Sicily by Frederick II and in the rest of the empire by PHILIP OF SWABIA.

Henry VII, c.1275–1313, Holy Roman emperor (1312–13) and German king (1308–13). A minor count of the house of Luxembourg, Henry was elected German king on the death of King ALBERT I after the electors had set aside the two main contenders, Albert's eldest son, Frederick of Austria, and the French prince CHARLES OF VALOIS. By accepting Elizabeth of Bohemia's offer (1310) to marry his son, John of Luxembourg, he gained Bohemia for his house and made it the main rival to the house of Hapsburg. He secured the German princes' approval for the acquisition by lavishly distributing the imperial domain. Henry's chief concern, however, was to renew the Hohenstaufen policy of making Italy the main source of imperial power. Pope Clement V and, among others, Dante welcomed his rule as a means of ending the by now almost meaningless strife of the GUELPHS AND GHIBELLINES. Entering the peninsula in 1310, Henry proclaimed himself above all parties and received the homage of leaders of both of the chief factions; in Jan., 1311, he was crowned king of the Lombards at Milan, a Guelph city. A revolt occurred in Milan, however, when Henry levied taxes on the city to support his army; although the revolt was suppressed, it drove Henry into the Ghibelline camp and precipitated war with the Guelph cities. Henry did not reach Rome until the following year, where on June 29, 1312, he was crowned Holy Roman emperor. Leaving Rome, he besieged Florence, but without success; in 1313, having allied himself with King FREDERICK II of Sicily, he pronounced the ban of the empire against King Robert of Naples, who opposed Henry's policy in Italy. While preparing to attack Robert, Henry died of fever. Henry VII's abortive Italian campaign only served to prove the futility of any attempt to revive the ancient imperial policy at a time when the papacy and S Italy were controlled by France and the N Italian towns were autonomous. Henry was succeeded by Holy Roman Emperor LOUIS IV. See W. M. Bowsky, *Henry VII in Italy* (1960).

Henry I, 1068–1135, king of England (1100–1135), youngest son of William I. He was called Henry Beauclerc because he could write. He quarreled with his elder brothers, WILLIAM II of England and ROBERT II, duke of Normandy, and attempted with little success to establish a territorial base for himself on the Continent. When William II was killed, Henry seized the treasury and had himself elected and crowned king while Robert was away on crusade. Henry issued a charter promising to right injustices inflicted by William and to refrain from unjust demands on the church and the barons. He also recalled ANSELM from exile. His marriage (1100) to Edith (thereafter known as Matilda), daughter of Malcolm III of Scotland and niece of EDGAR ATHELING, gained him some popularity with his English (as opposed to Norman) subjects. Robert invaded England in 1101, but the brothers reached an agreement by which Robert renounced his claim to the English throne in return for the promise of a pension and the surrender of Henry's possessions in Normandy. In the succeeding years Henry defeated and banished Robert's leading supporters in England. He then invaded (1105) Normandy, defeated (1106) Robert at Tinchebrai, and became duke of Normandy. In the meantime Henry had become involved in a quarrel with Anselm over the lay INVESTITURE of bishops and abbots. In a compromise settlement (1107) the king gave up investiture but retained the right to receive homage from the prelates. Henry's reign continued to be troubled by uprisings in Normandy centering about Robert's son and encouraged by Louis VI of France, who was almost constantly at war with Henry. Henry's only legitimate son, William Atheling, was drowned (1120), and Henry I's second marriage was childless. The latter years of his reign were marked therefore by his attempts to secure the succession for his daughter MATILDA. Henry's reign in England was one of order and progress. Royal justice was strengthened and expanded; the Norman legal system gradually fused with the old Anglo-Saxon. The first of the extant PIPE ROLLS and the first appearance of the court of EXCHEQUER date from this reign. See A. L. Poole, *From Domesday Book to Magna Carta* (2d ed. 1955); Frank Barlow, *The Feudal Kingdom of England, 1042–1216* (2d rev. ed. 1962).

Henry II, 1133–89, king of England (1154–89), son of MATILDA, queen of England, and GEOFFREY IV, count of Anjou. He was the founder of the ANGEVIN, or Plantagenet, line in England and one of the ablest and most remarkable of the English kings. His early attempts to recover the English throne, which he claimed through his mother, were unsuccessful. He was made duke of Normandy in 1150, and at Geoffrey's death (1151) inherited Anjou, Maine, and Touraine. His marriage (1152) to ELEANOR OF AQUITAINE brought him Aquitaine, Poitou, and Auvergne. By an invasion of England in 1153, he finally forced King STEPHEN to acknowledge him as heir, and in 1154 Henry ascended the English throne. Henry's vast Continental domains (he ruled about half the area of present-day France) were to occupy him for much of his reign, but his first objective was to restore order and royal authority to an England ravaged by civil war. He did this (by razing unlicensed castles, reclaiming royal castles and alienated crown lands, and appointing capable crown officials) so effectively that the country was free of major disorder until 1173. Henry's desire to restore royal authority to the level of that in Henry I's reign brought him into conflict with THOMAS À BECKET, whom he had made (1162) archbishop of Canterbury. The quarrel, which focused largely on the jurisdiction of the church courts, came to a head when Henry issued (1164) the Constitutions of CLARENDON, defining the relationship between church and state, and it ended (1170) in Becket's murder, for which Henry was indirectly responsible. The crime aroused such indignation that Henry had to make his peace with the papacy in the Compromise of Avranches (1172). But, though he made some concessions, most clauses of the Constitutions remained in force. Henry's most significant achievement lay in his development of the structure of royal justice. With the aid of such competent jurists as Ranulf de GLANVILL, he clearly established the superiority of the royal courts over private, feudal jurisdictions. His justices toured the country, administering a strengthened criminal law and a revised land law, based on the doctrine of seisin (possession). Procedural advances included the greatly extended use of writs and juries. While these developments were taking place, Henry was also engaged in consolidating his possessions. He recovered (1157) the northern counties of England from Scotland and undertook (1171–72) an expedition to Ireland, where he temporarily consolidated the conquests already made by Richard de Clare, 2d earl of PEMBROKE. He was less successful in his attempts (1157 and 1165) to extend his authority in Wales. Henry also expanded his holdings in France, acquiring Vexin, Brittany, and Toulouse. In 1169 the king distributed among his three oldest sons the titles to his possessions: Henry was to receive Normandy, Maine, and Anjou (he was also crowned king of England in 1170); Richard (later RICHARD I), Aquitaine; and GEOFFREY, Brittany. They did not receive actual authority, however, and, encouraged in their discontent by their mother and supported by Louis VII of France, they rebelled against Henry in 1173–74. The rebellion collapsed, but the king's sons continued to conspire against him. Richard and the youngest son, JOHN, in alliance with PHILIP II of France, were actually in the course of another rebellion in 1189 when their father died. Since the young Henry had died (1183), Henry II was succeeded by Richard. See biographies by L. F. Salzman (1914, repr. 1967), J. T. Appleby (1962), R. W. Barber (1964, repr. 1967), and W. L. Warren (1973); A. L. Poole, *From Domesday Book to Magna Carta* (2d ed. 1955); Frank Barlow, *The Feudal Kingdom of England, 1042–1216* (2d rev. ed. 1962); J. E. A. Joliffe, *Angevin Kingship* (2d ed. 1963).

Henry III, 1207–72, king of England (1216–72), son and successor of King John. He became king under a regency; William Marshal, 1st earl of PEMBROKE, and later PANDULF acted as chief of government, while Peter des ROCHES was the king's guardian. At the time of Henry's accession, England was torn by civil war and partially occupied by the French prince Louis (later King LOUIS VIII). In 1217, however, the French were defeated and withdrew. Some of the English barons, Louis's former allies, continued to cause trouble; but Hubert de BURGH, chief justiciar and the greatest power in the government after 1221, gradually restored order. In 1227, Henry was granted full powers of kingship, and in 1230, with typical willfulness and against the advice of the justiciar, he led an unsuccessful expedition to Gascony and Brittany. In 1232 the king dismissed Hubert, and for the next two years the government was controlled by Peter des Roches and his nephew (or son), Peter des Rivaux. This administration, which consisted of trained civil servants (many of them Poitevin), was hated by the barons, and a baronial revolt (1233–34) forced Henry to dismiss it. Henry then assumed direct control of the government, but despite frequent protests from the barons and from his brother, RICHARD, EARL OF CORNWALL, the king continued to surround himself with French favorites, including relatives of ELEANOR OF PROVENCE (whom he married in 1236) and his own Poitevin half brothers. The latter involved him in a disastrous campaign (1242) to expel Louis IX of France from Poitou. In 1238, Henry had weathered a storm of baronial protest caused by the secret marriage of his sister, Eleanor, to Simon de MONTFORT, earl of Leicester. The king subsequently (1248) sent Montfort to restore English authority in Gascony, but he totally alienated his former friend when he recalled him (1252) to answer charges of unjust administration. In 1254, Henry accepted the papal offer of the kingdom of Sicily for his younger son, Edmund, earl of Lancaster (see LANCASTER, HOUSE OF), agreeing in return to finance the conquest of the kingdom from the Hohenstaufen dynasty. However, the English barons, disturbed by the king's subservience to the papacy (which had already resulted in large papal exactions and an influx of foreign clergy into England) and angry that they had not been consulted, refused the necessary funds. Threatened by the pope with excommunication, Henry was forced to come to terms with the baronial opposition, now led by Simon de Montfort. The king accepted its plan for conciliar government set forth in the PROVISIONS OF OXFORD (1258), supplemented by the Provisions of Westminster (1259). Divisions in the baronial party enabled Henry to repudiate (1261) the provisions, with papal sanction, and in 1263 war broke out (see BARONS' WAR). An attempt to have Louis IX of France arbitrate the dispute led to the Mise of Amiens (1264), a declaration completely in the king's favor, and the war was renewed. Montfort won (1264) the battle of Lewes and summoned (1265) his famous representative PARLIAMENT. However, the heir to the throne, Prince Edward (later EDWARD I), led the royal troops to decisive victory at Evesham (1265), where Simon de Montfort was killed. By 1267 the barons had capitulated. From 1267 on, Prince Edward actually ruled the realm and Henry was king in name only. Henry III has suffered at the hands of many historians not only because of his manifest incapacity for rule but also because of the hostility of contemporary chroniclers. His long reign, however, showed progress in several respects. Learning flourished, particularly at Oxford, where Robert GROSSETESTE and Roger BACON inspired others by their intense pursuit of knowledge and their championing of the natural sciences. Many magnificent buildings were erected, including Salisbury Cathedral and Westminster Abbey. Commerce and industry thrived, even though interrupted by warfare. See Kate Norgate, *The Minority of Henry III* (1912); F. M. Powicke, *King Henry III and the Lord Edward* (1947, repr. 1966) and *The Thirteenth Century* (2d ed. 1962).

Henry IV, 1367–1413, king of England (1399–1413), eldest son of JOHN OF GAUNT and grandson of Edward III; called Henry of Bolingbroke. By 1377 he had become the earl of Derby, and in 1380 he married Mary de Bohun, coheiress of the earl of Hereford. In 1387 he joined the opposition to King RICHARD II led by his uncle, Thomas of Woodstock, duke of GLOUCESTER, and became one of the five "lords appellant" who ruled England in 1388–89. In the early 1390s he served in Lithuania with the Teutonic Knights and went on pilgrimage to Jerusalem. He supported the king when Richard took his revenge on three of the "lords appellant," including Gloucester, and was made duke of Hereford in 1397. However, in 1398 after a quarrel with Thomas Mowbray, 1st duke of NORFOLK, whose confidence he betrayed to Richard, Hereford was banished for 10 years by the king. When John of Gaunt died in 1399, Richard confiscated the vast Lancastrian estates, which were Hereford's inheritance. The irate duke, taking advantage of Richard's absence in Ireland and the widespread dissatisfaction with Richard's rule, landed in England in July, 1399. He gained ample support, and Richard, who surrendered to him in August, was forced to abdicate. Henry's claim to the throne was confirmed by Parliament in September. He thus, by revolution and election, founded the Lancastrian dynasty. The new king was immediately faced with insurrections. Early in 1400, supporters of Richard rebelled, but the revolt was easily suppressed and most of its leaders were subsequently executed. Richard himself died at Pontefract Castle, either by self-starvation or murdered on Henry's orders. The Welsh, aided by France, also revolted in 1400, and Henry led an ineffective invasion of Scotland. The Scots were decisively defeated in 1402 at Homildon Hill, but the Welsh continued their rebellion under OWEN GLENDOWER. The Percys (Sir Henry PERCY, his father, the 1st earl of NORTHUMBERLAND, and his uncle, the earl of WORCESTER), once the king's partisans, unexpectedly rebelled and were defeated at Shrewsbury in 1403. A rebellion of 1405 in the north was crushed, and the leaders, among them Richard Le SCROPE, archbishop of York, were executed; Henry was severely criticized for their deaths. Despite the capture (1406) of James (later JAMES I), heir to the Scottish throne, trouble with Scotland continued under Robert STUART, 1st duke of Albany. Northumberland's new rebellion was put down at Bramham Moor in 1408, the Welsh were crushed shortly afterward (though Owen Glendower was not captured), and the French armies ceased to harry English possessions in France. No sooner had these troubles ended than others began for Henry—an illness that left him an invalid for much of his few remaining years and a somewhat obscure struggle between two parties, one of them led by his son, the future Henry V, for control of the council. Henry V came to a throne made temporarily secure by the military efforts of his father. But Henry IV had lacked the skill and patience to restore the financial stability of the crown, now enormously in debt, and to provide a satisfactory administration of civil justice. See biography by J. L. Kirby (1971); V. H. H. Green, *The Later Plantagenets* (1955, repr. 1966); E. F. Jacob, *The Fifteenth Century* (1961).

Henry V, 1387–1422, king of England (1413–22), son and successor of HENRY IV. He was probably brought up under the care of his uncle, Henry BEAUFORT. He was knighted by Richard II in 1399 and created prince of Wales when his father usurped the throne in the same year. With his father, with Sir Henry PERCY, and later by himself, he led armies against OWEN GLENDOWER in Wales and there gained valuable military and administrative experience. Although wounded, he figured largely in the royal victory over the Percys at Shrewsbury (1403). Henry began (c.1409) to work actively in the privy council, which he and his friends dominated in 1410–11. In favoring the Burgundians rather than the Armagnacs in France (see ARMAGNACS AND BURGUNDIANS), he disagreed with the king, and a suggestion by his followers that he should succeed immediately to his father's throne led to his dismissal from the council (1411). He became king, however, upon his father's death in 1413, dismissed the incumbent ministers, and made Henry Beaufort lord chancellor. A rebellion by the Lollards, led by Sir John OLDCASTLE, resulted in a strong parliamentary statute (1414) against the sect, but trouble continued intermittently until the execution of Oldcastle in 1417. Determined to regain the lands in France held by his ancestors, Henry arranged a secret pact with Burgundy and prepared to attack France, thus reopening the HUNDRED YEARS WAR. Launching his first invasion in 1415, he laid successful siege to Harfleur and marched toward Calais, having announced his claim to the throne of France. He met and defeated a superior French force in one of the most famous battles of English history at AGINCOURT (1415). The enthusiastic acclaim that Henry received for this victory for the time overshadowed English political and economic unrest. Henry formed (1416) an alliance with Holy Roman Emperor Sigismund and extended his agreement with the Burgundians. In 1417 he led another expedition to France. In 1419, Rouen capitulated, and Normandy was in English hands. In 1420, Henry concluded the Treaty of TROYES, by which he agreed to marry CATHERINE OF VALOIS and to rule France in the name of her father, Charles VI, who accepted Henry as his successor. The English king continued his conquests to consolidate his holdings and late in 1420 entered Paris. The following year he returned with his wife to England, there made further military preparations despite considerable popular opposition to the continuation of war, and embarked on his third invasion of France. After a year of minor victories, he fell ill and died in Sept., 1422. Henry had abandoned his early recklessness (celebrated and probably exaggerated by Shakespeare) and had ruled with justice and industry. He lifted England from the near anarchy of his father's reign to civil order and a high spirit of nationalism. His main interest, however, was in gaining control of lands in France—lands that he sincerely believed to be his right. His strong personality, his military successes, and his care for his less fortunate subjects made him a great popular hero. He exhibited military genius, characterized by brilliant daring, patient strategy and diplomacy, and attentiveness to detail. The wars, however, placed the crown further in debt and left the nation with economic and military problems that could not be met in the reign of his son, Henry VI. See biography by H. F. Hutchison (1967); E. F. Jacob, *Henry V and the Invasion of France* (1947, repr. 1963); K. H. Vickers, *England in the Later Middle Ages* (7th ed. 1950); V. H. Green, *The Later Plantagenets* (1955).

Henry VI, 1421–71, king of England (1422–61, 1470–71). The only son of Henry V and Catherine of Valois, he became king of England when he was not yet nine months old. When his grandfather, Charles VI of France, died, Henry was proclaimed king of France by the English, in accordance with the terms of the Treaty of TROYES (1420). The French, however, recognized the son of Charles VI as CHARLES VII. During Henry's early years, England was under the protectorate of his uncles, John of Lancaster, duke of BEDFORD, who was regent in France, and Humphrey, duke of GLOUCESTER. Gloucester did not wield full authority, however, for much of the actual power resided in a council dominated by Henry BEAUFORT. After the English defeat by Joan of Arc at Orléans in 1429 and Charles VII's coronation at Rheims shortly thereafter, the council attempted to protect English interests in France by crowning Henry king of France at Paris in 1431. After the death of Bedford in 1435 and the defection of Burgundy from the Anglo-Burgundian alliance, however, the English cause in France became hopeless. From c.1435, Henry fell under the dominance of a faction headed first by Henry Beaufort and later by William de la POLE, 4th earl of Suffolk, both of whom opposed continuing the war in France. Suffolk negotiated a marriage for Henry with MARGARET OF ANJOU in 1445. This marriage was at first favorably received in England, but when Henry, now under the influence of his wife, surrendered Maine to Charles VII, Suffolk and the queen lost their popularity. Suffolk was impeached in 1450 and mysteriously murdered at sea while on his way to France. The rebellion of Jack CADE, which broke out after Suffolk's death, was but one of many riots and uprisings indicating popular dissatisfaction with the government. The faction headed by Queen Margaret and Edmund Beaufort, 2d duke of SOMERSET, which dominated the king after Suffolk's death, was opposed by Richard, duke of YORK, the most powerful noble in the kingdom and heir presumptive to the throne. The struggle between these two factions developed into the dynastic battle between the Lancasters and the Yorks known as the Wars of the ROSES. In 1453, shortly before the birth of his son, Edward, the king became insane. The duke of York was made protector (1454) in spite of the protests of Margaret, but when the king recovered, York was excluded from the council. In 1455, York met the Lancastrians at St. Albans in a conflict generally regarded as the first battle of the Wars of the Roses; Somerset was killed, and the Yorkists gained control of the council. York was again protector (1455–56), but thereafter Margaret was in control until 1460 when the Yorkist party won another victory at Northampton. Henry was made a prisoner, and York was named protector and heir apparent to the throne to the exclusion of Henry's own son. York was killed at Wakefield in 1460, but his son Edward defeated the Lancastrian forces at Mortimer's Cross, entered London, and was proclaimed king as EDWARD IV in Feb., 1461. Henry, who had been rescued from Yorkist captivity at the second battle of St. Albans a few days earlier, now fled to Scotland. He remained there during most of the subsequent fighting until 1465, when he was captured and put in the Tower of London. When Richard Neville, earl of WARWICK, allied himself with Queen Margaret and invaded England in 1470, Henry was restored to the throne, but his second reign was short-lived. The unfortunate king was captured at the battle of Barnet and returned to the Tower. He was murdered there only days after Edward IV's final victory at Tewkesbury in May, 1471. Henry was a mild, honest, and pious man, a patron of literature and the arts and the founder of Eton College (1440). He was, however, unstable, weak-willed, and politically naïve. It was his complete inability to cope with the pressures and responsibilities of kingship that probably drove him to insanity. See biography by Mabel Christie (1922); K. H. Vickers, *England in the Later Middle Ages* (7th ed. 1950); E. F. Jacob, *The Fifteenth Century* (1961).

Henry VII, 1457–1509, king of England (1485–1509). He was the son of Edmund Tudor, earl of Richmond, who died before Henry was born, and Margaret BEAUFORT, a descendant of Edward III through John of Gaunt, duke of Lancaster. Although the Beaufort line, which was originally illegitimate, had been specifically excluded (1407) from all claim to the throne, the death of the imprisoned Henry VI (1471) made Henry Tudor head of the house of Lancaster. At this point, however, the Yorkist Edward IV had established himself securely on the throne, and Henry, who had been brought up in Wales, fled to Brittany for safety. The death of Edward (1483) and accession of RICHARD III left Henry the natural leader of the party opposing Richard, whose rule was very unpopular. Henry made an unsuccessful attempt to land in England during the abortive revolt (1483) of Henry STAFFORD, 2d duke of Buckingham. Thereafter he bided his time in France until 1485 when, aided by other English refugees, he landed in Wales. At the battle of Bosworth Field he defeated the royal forces of Richard, who was slain. Henry advanced to London, was crowned, and in 1486 fulfilled a promise made earlier to Yorkist dissidents to marry Edward IV's daughter, Elizabeth. He thus united the houses of York and Lancaster, founding the Tudor royal dynasty. Although Henry's accession marked the end of the Wars of the Roses, the early years of his reign were disturbed by Yorkist attempts to regain the throne. The first serious attempt, an uprising in favor of the imposter Lambert SIMNEL, was easily crushed (1487). The French invasion of Brittany aroused great antagonism in England, and ultimately, in concert with Spain and Archduke Maximilian (later Holy Roman Emperor Maximilian I), Henry led (1492) an army against Boulogne. He soon made peace with France, however. In 1494, Henry sent Sir Edward POYNINGS to Ireland to consolidate English rule there. Poynings drove out of Ireland the Yorkist pretender Perkin WARBECK, who then sought support from the Scottish king, JAMES IV. James attempted (1496) to invade England, but the next year, under pressure from Spain, he expelled Warbeck. The latter was defeated shortly thereafter in an attempted invasion of Cornwall. A truce (1497) between England and Scotland was followed by the marriage (1503) of Henry's sister MARGARET TUDOR to James—a marriage that led ultimately to the union of England and Scotland. Another threat to Henry's throne was posed by the Yorkist claimant Edmund de la Pole, earl of Suffolk (see under POLE, family), who received some support on the Continent but in 1506 was surrendered to Henry by Philip of Burgundy (soon recognized as Philip I of Castile). In 1501, Henry had married his son Arthur to KATHARINE OF ARAGÓN, daughter of Ferdinand and Isabella of Spain. After Arthur died in 1502, an agreement was reached by which Katharine married Arthur's brother Henry (later HENRY VIII). On the death of Philip I (1506) Henry VII, then a widower, proposed that he should marry Philip's widow and Katharine's sister, Joanna, but Joanna's madness made the match impossible. The English king then opened unsuccessful negotiations for the marriage of his daughter Mary to Philip's son (later Holy Roman Emperor Charles V). Relations between Henry and Ferdinand became strained; the latter allied himself with the French while Henry arranged treaties with Maximilian. Shortly thereafter Henry contracted an illness from which he never recovered. Henry was an astute political leader. He established the Tudor tradition of strong rule tempered by a sense of justice that endeared him, as it did his great successors, Henry VIII and Elizabeth I, to the English people. In Henry's later years, however, his extortionist practices alienated many. His marriage and his relentless suppression of Yorkist plots to regain the throne brought order out of the chaos of civil war. In his suppression of the recalcitrant nobles he was greatly assisted by the use of the court of STAR CHAMBER as a supremely powerful judiciary body. His diplomatic abilities kept England at peace, and he arranged a favorable commercial treaty with the Netherlands. England's navy was developed, and explorations in the New World begun. See biographies by Roger Lockyer (1968), R. L. Storey (1968), and S. B. Chrimes (1973); A. F. Pollard, *The Reign of Henry VII* (1913–14); S. T. Bindoff, *Tudor England* (1950); J. D. Mackie, *The Earlier Tudors, 1485–1558* (1952); G. R. Elton, *England Under the Tudors* (1955).

Henry VIII, 1491–1547, king of England (1509–47), second son and successor of Henry VII. In his youth he was educated in the new learning of the Renaissance and developed great skill in music and sports. He was created prince of Wales in 1503, following the death of his elder brother, Arthur. At that time he also received a papal dispensation to marry Arthur's widow, KATHARINE OF ARAGÓN. The marriage took place shortly after his accession in 1509. Henry inherited from his father a full exchequer and a precedent for autocratic rule.

Wolsey and Foreign Policy. In 1511, Henry joined Pope Julius II, King Ferdinand II of Aragón, Holy Roman Emperor Maximilian I, and the Venetians in their HOLY LEAGUE against France. Accompanied by the increasingly influential Thomas (later Cardinal) WOLSEY, he led (1513) his army to France, captured Thérouanne and Tournai, and won the BATTLE OF THE SPURS. During his absence invading Scottish forces under JAMES IV were defeated at FLODDEN by the earl of Surrey. When Ferdinand deserted the anti-French alliance, Henry, now deep in the intricacies of continental politics, married (1514) his sister MARY OF ENGLAND to Louis XII of France. The alliance ended the next year, however, at the death of Louis and the accession of FRANCIS I, who aroused Henry's personal jealousy and tried to stir up the Scots against England. Rapid changes in the diplomatic situation following the death of Ferdinand (1516) enabled Wolsey, now chancellor, to conclude a new alliance with France, soon expanded to include all the major European powers in a pledge of universal peace (1518). As part of the alliance Henry's daughter Mary (later MARY I) was betrothed to the French dauphin. With the election of Ferdinand's grandson, already king of Spain, as Holy Roman Emperor CHARLES V in 1519, England held the balance of power between the empire and France. Despite a show of amity between Henry and Francis on the FIELD OF THE CLOTH OF GOLD (1520), Henry joined Charles in war against France in 1522. When Charles won a decisive victory over Francis at Pavia in 1525 and refused England any part of the spoils, Henry and Wolsey tried to curb the alarming rise of imperial power by an unpopular alliance (1527) with France. By this time Henry had determined to divorce Katharine, and English diplomacy became a series of maneuvers to win the approval of Pope CLEMENT VII, who was in the power of the emperor, Katharine's nephew.

The Reformation. Katharine seemed unlikely to have more children and was persistently loyal to her nephew, and Henry was not only anxious for a male heir but had become infatuated with Anne BOLEYN. The king wished to invalidate the marriage on the grounds that the papal dispensation under which he and Katharine had been permitted to marry was illegal. The pope reluctantly authorized a commission consisting of cardinals Wolsey and CAMPEGGIO to decide the issue in England. Katharine denied the jurisdiction of the court, and before a decision could be reached Clement had the hearing adjourned (1529) to Rome. The failure of the commission, followed by a reconciliation between Charles and Francis I, led to the fall of Wolsey and to the initiation by Henry of an antiecclesiastical policy intended to force the pope's assent to the divorce. Under the guidance of the king's new minister, Thomas CROMWELL, the anticlerical Parliament drew up (1532) the *Supplication Against the Ordinaries,* a long list of grievances against the church, and in a document known as the *Submission of the Clergy,* the convocation of the English church accepted Henry's claim that all ecclesiastical legislation was subject to royal approval. Acts stopping the payment of annates to Rome and forbidding appeals to the pope followed. The pope still refused to give way on the divorce issue, but he did agree to the appointment (1533) of the king's nominee, Thomas CRANMER, as archbishop of Canterbury. Cranmer immediately pronounced Henry's marriage with Katharine invalid and crowned Anne (already secretly married to Henry) queen, and the pope excommunicated Henry. In 1534 the breach with Rome was completed by the Act of Supremacy, which made the king head of the Church of England (see ENGLAND, CHURCH OF). Any effective opposition was suppressed by the Act of Succession entailing the crown on Henry's heirs by Anne, by an extensive and severe Act of Treason, and by the strict administration of the oath of supremacy. A number of prominent churchmen and laymen, including Sir Thomas MORE, were executed. Under Cromwell's supervision, a visitation of the monasteries in 1535 led to an act of Parliament in 1536 by which smaller monasteries reverted to the crown, and the others were confiscated within the next few years. By distributing some of this property among the landed gentry, Henry acquired the loyalty of a large and influential group.

The Aftermath. In 1536, Anne Boleyn, who had given birth to Elizabeth (later Elizabeth I) but failed to have a male heir, was convicted of adultery and incest and beheaded. Soon afterward, Henry married Jane SEYMOUR, who in 1537 bore a son (later EDWARD VI) and died. Meanwhile in 1536–37 Henry had dealt brutally but effectively with rebellions in the north by subjects protesting economic hardships and the dissolution of the monasteries (see PILGRIMAGE OF GRACE). In 1536, Henry authorized the Ten Articles, which included some Protestant doctrinal points, and he approved (1537) publication of the Bible in English. However, the Six Articles passed by Parliament in 1539 reverted to the fundamental principles of Roman Catholic doctrine. Another temporary peace (1538) between France and the empire seemed to pose the threat of Catholic intervention in England and helped Cromwell persuade the king to ally himself with the German Protestant princes by marrying (1540) ANNE OF CLEVES. However, Henry disliked Anne and divorced her almost immediately, while Cromwell was beheaded. The king then married Catherine HOWARD, but in 1542 she met the fate of Anne Boleyn. He married his sixth wife, Catherine PARR, in 1543. In 1542 war had begun again with Scotland, still controlled through JAMES V by French and Catholic interests. The fighting culminated in the rout of the Scots at Solway Moss and the death of James. Henry forced the Scots to agree to a treaty (1543) of marriage between MARY QUEEN OF SCOTS and his own son, Edward, but this was to come to nothing. In 1543, Henry once more joined Charles in war against France and was able to take Boulogne (1544). The expensive war dragged on until 1546, when Henry secured a payment of indemnity for the city. During Henry's reign the navy was organized for the first time as a permanent force. Wales was officially incorporated into England in 1536 with a great improvement in government administration there. Although he derived considerable funds from the dissolution of Irish monasteries and assumed (1542) the titles of king of Ireland and head of the Church of Ireland, Henry was forced to adopt a conciliatory policy toward Irish leaders. In 1521, Henry had been given the title "Defender of the Faith" by the pope for a treatise against Martin Luther, and he remained orthodox in his doctrinal views throughout his reign. However, the Six Articles were only fitfully enforced, the use of the English Bible was cautiously increased, seizure of church property continued, and the destruction of relics and shrines was begun. The way had been opened for Protestantism. At Henry's death, the council that he had appointed for the minority of Edward VI leaned toward the new doctrines.

Henrician Despotism. Henry was a supreme egotist. He advanced personal desires under the guise of public policy or moral right, forced his ministers to pay extreme penalties for his own mistakes, and summarily executed many with little excuse. Nonetheless he possessed considerable political insight, and he could have imposed his sometimes arbitrary rule only upon a nation willing to accept it. Although Henry dominated his Parliaments, the importance of that institution increased significantly during his reign. Under his strong hand England enjoyed a comparatively peaceful and prosperous transition at a time when severe wars and religious strife were ravaging the rest of Europe. See biographies by A. F. Pollard (1902, repr. 1966), Theodore Maynard (1949; a Roman Catholic view), John Bowle (1965), J. J. Scarisbrick (1968), and L. B. Smith (1971); Kenneth Pickthorn, *Early Tudor Government* (1934, repr. 1951); H. M. Smith, *Henry VIII and the Reformation* (1948).

Henry I, c.1008–1060, king of France (1031–60), son and successor of King Robert II. To defend his throne against his mother, his brothers Robert and Eudes, and subsequently against the count of Blois, he secured, at the cost of territorial concessions, the aid of Robert I, duke of Normandy, and of Geoffrey Martel, count of Anjou. After the submission of his brother Robert, Henry unwisely invested him with the duchy of Burgundy, setting up a powerful rival to the French kingdom. He found the chief enemy of his later reign in Robert of Normandy's son William, later William I of England, who successfully resisted two invasions by Henry. Henry was succeeded by his son Philip I.

Henry II, 1519–59, king of France (1547–59), son of King Francis I. His robust physique contrasted with his weak and pliant disposition. Throughout his reign he was governed by Anne de MONTMORENCY, by his mistress DIANE DE POITIERS, and by François and Charles de GUISE. He renewed the struggle against Holy Roman Emperor CHARLES V (Charles I of Spain), allying himself with the German Protestants despite his own strong Catholicism. War continued under Charles's son King PHILIP II of Spain, who was allied with Mary Tudor of England, until the Treaty of CATEAU-CAMBRÉSIS (1559) ended French pretensions in Italy. In 1558, Calais was conquered from the English. Henry issued a series of increasingly severe edicts against the Protestants and established more firmly the absolute royal power. His queen, CATHERINE DE' MEDICI, played a minor role during her husband's reign. Henry, accidentally killed by Gabriel de Montgomery in a tournament, was succeeded by Francis II. See H. N. Williams, *Henry II: His Court and Times* (1910).

Henry III, 1551–89, king of France (1574–89); son of King Henry II and Catherine de' Medici. He succeeded his brother, Charles IX. As a leader of the royal army in the Wars of Religion (see RELIGION, WARS OF) against the French Protestants, or Huguenots, Henry, then duke of Anjou, defeated (1569) the Huguenots at Jarnac and Moncontour. He refused (1571), on religious grounds, to proceed with negotiations for his marriage to the Protestant queen of England, Elizabeth I. With his mother, the duke helped instigate the massacre of the Huguenots (see SAINT BARTHOLOMEW'S DAY, MASSACRE OF). Elected king of Poland (1573), he returned to France at his brother's death to assume the French crown. By the Edict of Beaulieu (1576) at the end of the fifth war of religion, he made concessions to the moderates and the Protestants, which led to the formation of the Catholic League (see LEAGUE) at the behest of Henri, 3d duc de GUISE. The king, fearing the League's power, proclaimed himself its head. It was dissolved after he revoked some of his earlier concessions to the Protestants. The League was revived by Henri de Guise, however, when the death (1584) of the king's brother, Francis, duke of Alençon, made the Protestant Henry of Navarre the legal heir to the French throne. De Guise forced Henry III to issue an edict suppressing Protestantism and excluding Henry of Navarre from the throne. In the war that ensued, known as the War of the Three Henrys, Navarre defeated the king's troops at Coutras (1587). Taking advantage of the king's weakness, Henri de Guise revolted against him, and, with the help of the Parisian populace, expelled him from Paris on May 12, 1588 (the Day of the Barricades). Henry III procured the assassination of de Guise and his brother Louis in the hope of quelling the rebellion, but his action only further provoked the Catholics. Joining forces with Henry of Navarre, the king attempted to regain Paris. In the siege he was stabbed by Jacques CLÉMENT. The last male member of the house of Valois, Henry III left France torn by civil war. Henry of Navarre succeeded him as Henry IV.

Henry IV, 1553–1610, king of France (1589–1610) and, as Henry III, of Navarre (1572–1610), son of Antoine de BOURBON and JEANNE D'ALBRET; first of the Bourbon kings of France. Raised as a Protestant, he was recognized (1569) by the Huguenot leader Gaspard de COLIGNY as the nominal head of the Huguenots. As a result of the temporary reconciliation (1570) between the Huguenots and the crown, Henry was betrothed to MARGARET OF VALOIS, sister of King CHARLES IX. A few days after his marriage (Aug. 18, 1572) the massacre of the Huguenots (see SAINT BARTHOLOMEW'S DAY, MASSACRE OF) took place. Henry saved his life by abjuring Protestantism; however, he remained a virtual prisoner of the court until 1576, when he escaped, returned to the Protestant faith, and joined the combined Protestant and moderate Roman Catholic forces in the fifth of the Wars of Religion (see RELIGION, WARS OF). He became the legal heir to the French throne upon the death (1584) of Francis, duke of Alençon, brother and heir to King HENRY III, who had succeeded Charles IX in 1574. The Catholic LEAGUE, led by Henri, 3d duc de GUISE, refused to recognize a Protestant as heir and persuaded the king to revoke concessions to the Protestants and to exclude Henry of Navarre from the succession. In the resulting war, known as the War of the Three Henrys, Henry of Navarre defeated (1587) the king's forces at Coutras but was reconciled with Henry III when the League revolted against him (1588). After Henry III's death (1589), Henry IV defeated the League forces under the duc de MAYENNE at Arques (1589) and Ivry (1590) but was forced to abandon the siege of Paris when the League received Spanish aid. In 1593 he again abjured Protestantism, allegedly with the remark, "Paris is well worth a Mass." He was received in Paris in 1594. His conciliatory policy soon won him general support. To rid France of Spanish influence, Henry declared war on Spain (1595) and brought it to a successful conclusion with the Treaty of Vervins (1598). He then turned to the internal reconstruction of his war-ravaged kingdom. With the Edict of Nantes (1598; see NANTES, EDICT OF), he established political rights and a measure of religious freedom for the Huguenots. Aided by baron de Rosny (later duc de SULLY), Henry restored some measure of financial order, encouraged agriculture, founded new industries, built roads and canals, expanded foreign trade through commercial treaties with Spain, England, and Turkey, and encouraged colonization of Canada. Anxious to see prosperity reach all classes, he is reputed to have said, "There should be a chicken in every peasant's pot every Sunday." In his foreign policy Henry sought to weaken the Spanish and Austrian Hapsburgs. He was preparing to oppose them on the question of the succession to the duchies of Cleves and Jülich when he was stabbed to death by a fanatic, François Ravaillac. Henry's marriage with Margaret of Valois was annulled in 1599. His mistresses included Gabrielle d'ESTRÉES and Henriette d'Entragues. In 1600 he married Marie de' Medici, who was regent during the minority of their son Louis XIII. Numerous anecdotes and legends about Henry bear witness to his gallantry, his Gallic wit, and his concern for the common people, which have made him probably the most popular king among the French. See biographies by P. G. Willert (1893), Quentin Hurst (1938), Heinrich Mann (2 vol., tr. 1937–39), and Desmond Seward (1971); Roland Mousnier, *The Assassination of Henry IV* (tr. 1973).

Henry I, 1204–17, Spanish king of Castile (1214–17), son and successor of Alfonso VIII. At his death after a short, uneventful reign, his sister Berenguela renounced her rights to the crown in favor of her son, Ferdinand III.

Henry II or **Henry of Trastámara** (trăstəmär'ə), 1333?–1379, Spanish king of Castile and León (1369–79), illegitimate son of Alfonso XI. After taking part in several unsuccessful revolts against his half brother, PETER THE CRUEL, he secured the aid of DU GUESCLIN and Peter IV of Aragón and drove Peter from the throne in 1366. Peter allied himself with England and, with the help of EDWARD THE BLACK PRINCE defeated Henry at Nájera (1367), but after Edward's departure, Henry defeated and killed Peter at Montiel (1369). John of Gaunt, son-in-law of Peter the Cruel, and FERDINAND I of Portugal unsuccessfully contested his title as king and the succession of his son, John I.

Henry III, 1379–1406, Spanish king of Castile and León (1390–1406), son and successor of John I. His marriage (1388) to Catherine, daughter of John of Gaunt, ended a long dynastic conflict. Henry consolidated royal authority against the nobles. He also sent a fleet that destroyed (1400) Tetuán in N Africa, dispatched envoys to Tamerlane, and sponsored the colonization of the Canary Islands. He was succeeded by his son John II.

Henry IV, 1425–74, Spanish king of Castile and León (1454–74), son and successor of John II. His weakness opened the way to civil strife and anarchy. The Castilian nobles refused to recognize Henry's alleged daughter JUANA LA BELTRANEJA as his heiress and forced the king to designate first his half brother Alfonso (d. 1468) and then his half sister Isabella (later ISABELLA I) as his successor. After Isabella's marriage (1469) to Ferdinand of Aragón, however, Henry again recognized Juana. On Henry's death civil war broke out among the contenders for the succession. See study by Townsend Miller (1972).

Henry, Alexander, two fur traders, uncle and nephew, of the Old Northwest, each of whom left a valuable journal of his travels and experiences. **Alexander Henry,** the elder, 1739–1824, b. New Brunswick, N.J., served under Jeffrey Amherst in the last of the French and Indian Wars. As a fur trader he barely escaped massacre (1763) by the Indians at Michilimackinac in Pontiac's Rebellion. Captured by the Ojibwa, he was later adopted and protected by a family and made his way back to Fort Niagara in time to join Bradstreet's army in lifting the siege of Detroit. He returned to fur trading and in 1775 penetrated the Old Northwest to the region of the Saskatchewan. Competition with the Hudson's Bay Company caused a body of the free traders, among them Henry, Peter Pond, and the Frobishers, to unite as the group that eventually became the powerful North West Company. See his *Travels and Adventures in Canada and the Indian Territories* (new ed. with biographical notes by James Bain, 1972). The date and place of birth of his nephew, **Alexander Henry,** the younger, d. 1814, are not known. His journal of 1799–1814, edited by Elliott Coues (together with the journal of David Thompson) as *New Light on the Early History of the Greater Northwest* (1897), describes his adventures as a trader of the North West Company on the Red, Pembina, Saskatchewan, and Columbia rivers and is particularly valuable for its account of the Indian tribes of those regions. Henry was drowned near Astoria, Oregon. See Walter O'Meara, *The Savage Country* (1960).

Henry, John: see JOHN HENRY.

Henry, Joseph, 1797–1878, American physicist, b. Albany, N.Y., educated at Albany Academy. He taught (1826–32) mathematics and natural philosophy at Albany Academy and was professor of natural philosophy (1832–46) at Princeton (then the College of New Jersey). From 1846 he served as the first secretary and director of the newly founded Smithsonian Institution; he introduced and developed many of its activities and established its general policies. Before assuming his responsibilities at the Smithsonian Institution, he had made notable contributions to the physical sciences, especially in electromagnetism. Henry improved the electromagnet, increasing its strength and fitting it for practical use. He invented and operated the first electromagnetic telegraph, which formed the basis for the commercial telegraphic system. He discovered self-inductance, and the unit of inductance is often called the henry in his honor. Independently of Michael Faraday he discovered the principle of the induced current, basic to the dynamo, transformer, and many other devices. Henry invented a small electromagnetic motor, and extended the work on induced currents to show that an induced current can be used to induce another current in a nearby circuit and that resulting currents in turn can induce others. His numerous other contributions include the institution of the weather report system. See his *Papers,* ed. by Nathan Reingold et al. (15 vol., 1972–); biography by S. R. Riedman (1961).

Henry, O.: see O. HENRY.

Henry, Patrick, 1736–99, political leader in the American Revolution, b. Hanover co., Va. Largely self-educated, he became a prominent trial lawyer. Henry bitterly denounced (1765) the Stamp Act and in the years that followed helped fan the fires of revolt in the South. As an orator he knew no equal. Several phrases attributed to him—e.g., "If this be treason, make the most of it" and "Give me liberty or give me death"—are familiar to all Americans. Henry became a leader among the so-called radicals and spoke clearly for individual liberties. He was a delegate to the house of burgesses (1765–74), the Continental Congress (1774–76), and the Virginia provincial convention (1775). His hopes for a military career in the American Revolution were frustrated, but as governor of Virginia (1776–79) he sent George Rogers CLARK to the Illinois country. He was (1784–86) again governor and led the fight for the Virginia Religious Freedom Act of 1785. Although he later became a Federalist, Henry opposed ratification of the Federal Constitution, believing that it endangered state sovereignty, and he worked successfully to have the first 10 amendments (Bill of Rights) added to the Constitution. See W. W. Henry, *Patrick Henry: Life, Correspondence, and Speeches* (3 vol., 1891; repr. 1970); biographies by M. C. Tyler (1898; repr. 1972), R. D. Meade (2 vol., 1957–69), and R. R. Beeman (1974).

Henry, Cape, SE Va., at the entrance to Chesapeake Bay, E of Norfolk. Cape Henry Memorial marks the approximate spot where the Jamestown settlers landed April 26, 1607. In 1939 the site was included in Colonial National Historical Park.

Henry, Fort, Tenn.: see FORT HENRY.

Henry E. Huntington Library and Art Gallery: see HUNTINGTON, HENRY EDWARDS.

Henry of Burgundy, d. 1112, count of Portugal. One of a group of French nobles called by Alfonso VI of León to assist in the fight against the Moors, he arrived in Spain c.1095. He was assigned a portion of land previously held by his cousin Raymond, who was the husband of Alfonso's daughter Urraca. To Henry, Alfonso gave his illegitimate daughter Teresa and the title count of Coimbra—later exchanged for the title count of Portugal. After the death of Alfonso VI, Henry tried to enhance his position by war and intrigues with and against Urraca, her son Alfonso (later Alfonso VII of Castile), and her second husband, Alfonso I of Aragón. In this he failed, but he died leaving a territory that was to become the independent kingdom of Portugal under his son Alfonso I.

Henry of Flanders, c.1174–1216, Latin emperor of Constantinople (1206–16), brother and successor of Emperor BALDWIN I. The ablest and most respected of the Latin emperors, he fought successfully against the Bulgarians and with varying success against Emperor THEODORE I of Nicaea. He was succeeded by his brother-in-law, Peter of Courtenay.

Henry of Huntingdon, d. 1155, English chronicler, archdeacon of Huntingdon. His *Historia Anglorum* is important not because it gives many new facts but because it was much used by later writers. It is based on Bede and the *Anglo-Saxon Chronicle* for the earlier period but is original work for the years 1126–54. The *Historia Anglorum* was translated by Thomas Forester (1853, repr. 1968).

Henry of Navarre: see HENRY IV, king of France.

Henry's law, chemical law stating that the amount of a gas that dissolves in a liquid is proportional to the partial pressure of the gas over the liquid, provided no chemical reaction takes place between the liquid and the gas. It is named after William Henry (1774–1836), the English chemist who first reported the relationship.

Henryson, Robert, c.1425–c.1506, Scottish poet. It is thought that he was a schoolmaster at Dunfermline Abbey. His principal poem is *The Testament of Cresseid,* which was written as a harshly moral epilogue to Chaucer's *Troilus and Criseyde.* In Henryson's version the heroine dies a destitute leper. Partly because of this poem, Henryson has been called a Scottish Chaucerian. That his temper is more Scottish than Chaucerian is shown by the dry, macabre humor of such pieces as the *Moral Fables of Æsop.* Other notable works include *Orpheus and Eurydice* and *Robene and Makyne.* See edition of his work by H. H. Wood (rev. ed. 1958, repr. 1968); study by John MacQueen (1967).

Henry Street Settlement: see WALD, LILLIAN D.

Henry the Fowler: see HENRY I, German king.

Henry the Lion, 1129–95, duke of Saxony (1142–80) and of Bavaria (1156–80); son of HENRY THE PROUD. His father died (1139) while engaged in a war to regain his duchies, and it was not until 1142 that Henry the Lion became duke of Saxony. Bavaria was restored to him after the accession of his cousin, Holy Roman Emperor FREDERICK I, who wished to end the strife in Germany between the rival families of Welfs, or GUELPHS, and HOHENSTAUFEN. Henry took part in Frederick's earlier Italian expeditions but devoted his attention chiefly to Saxony and to expansion beyond the Elbe, where he extended his authority with Frederick's support. With ALBERT THE BEAR and other Saxon nobles he took part in the crusade against the WENDS in 1147. In subsequent years he gradually extended his power over the pagan lands bounded by the Elbe, the Oder, and the Baltic. He encouraged settlement in the conquered regions, which became Christianized; he also fostered commercial activity, especially that of Lübeck. In 1168 he married Matilda, daughter of Henry II of England. Henry pursued an independent foreign policy, intervening in the Danish civil wars (1147–57) in support of Waldemar I, whose protector he became. His greed and ambition brought him into conflict with other German nobles, particularly Albert the Bear. Throughout this period Henry retained the support of the emperor. In 1176, however, a breach occurred when Frederick, engaged in war in Italy, requested Henry's aid. Henry demanded the imperial city of Goslar in exchange for military support, but Frederick refused, was defeated, and was forced to make peace with the pope. As a result of Frederick's reconciliation with the pope, Henry was ordered to restore Saxon church lands that he had seized. He failed to comply immediately, and the bishop of Halberstadt and the Saxon nobles allied against him. The emperor, called in to judge the case, confiscated (1180) Henry's fiefs. The partitioning of the duchies of Bavaria and Saxony marked the change to smaller territorial units in Germany, which from then on was a patchwork of principalities. Henry's armies were defeated. He retained only Brunswick and Lüneburg and was banished (1182) for three years, which he spent in England. While Frederick was on the Third Crusade, Henry sought to occupy Saxony (1189). Temporary peace was made, but Henry continued to intrigue against the Hohenstaufen. Shortly before his death he reached an accord with Frederick's successor HENRY VI. Conflict between Guelphs and Hohenstaufen continued after his death. Henry's younger son became emperor in 1209 as Otto IV. See A. L. Poole, *Henry the Lion* (1912).

Henry the Minstrel: see BLIND HARRY.

Henry the Navigator, 1394–1460, prince of Portugal, patron of exploration. Because he fought with extraordinary valor in the Portuguese conquest of Ceuta (1415), he was created duke of Viseu by his father, John I, king of Portugal. The Moroccan campaign inspired Henry with a desire to extend his knowledge of Africa. In 1416 he established at Sagres in SW Portugal a base for explorations, later adding a naval arsenal and an observatory and a school for the study of geography and navigation. The nearby port of Lagos provided a convenient harbor. One of his navigators rediscovered the Madeira Islands (1418–20), and by degrees the west coast of Africa was explored. Cape Bojador was reached in 1434, Cape Blanco was passed in 1441, and the Bay of Arguim was discovered in 1443. When Henry's captains returned with slaves and gold, African exploration, long derided, became very popular; from 1444 to 1446 between 30 and 40 vessels sailed for the W African coast under the prince's authority. His navigators discovered the Senegal River and rounded Cape Verde (1444) and finally (1460) reached a point near the present Sierra Leone. The abuses of the slave trade caused Henry to forbid the kidnapping of Negroes in 1455. Henry played an important political role in the minority of Alfonso V, establishing his brother Pedro as regent. His position as grand master of the wealthy and powerful Order of Christ (Portuguese successor to the Knights Templars) increased his influence, and much of the revenue for his ventures was derived from his ecclesiastical tithes. His military reputation, dimmed by a disastrous expedition (1437) against Tangier, was recovered by a subsequent Moroccan campaign (1458), and he was offered the command of several foreign armies. Henry's chief importance, however, lay in his notable contributions to the art of navigation and to the progress of exploration, which provided the groundwork for the development of Portugal's colonial empire and for the country's rise to international prominence in the 16th cent. See biographies by E. D. S. Bradford (1960), R. H. Major (1967), C. R. Beazley (1895, repr. 1968), and Elaine Sanceau (1969).

Henry the Proud, c.1108–1139, duke of Bavaria (1126–38) and of Saxony (1137–38). A member of the GUELPH family, he inherited the duchy of Bavaria and enormous private wealth. By his marriage (1127) with Gertrude, only child of German King LOTHAIR II (later Holy Roman emperor), he became the most powerful German noble. He fought with Lothair against the HOHENSTAUFEN dukes, Frederick of Swabia and his brother Conrad, who refused to recognize Lothair's election. In 1136 he accompanied Lothair to Italy, where the pope invested Henry with lands in Tuscany. Although he was Lothair's intended successor to the German kingship, Henry was defeated in the election of 1138 by Conrad of Hohenstaufen (CONRAD III), who shortly afterward deprived Henry of his duchies. Henry, however, retained the loyalty of his subjects. He succeeded in expelling ALBERT THE BEAR from Saxony and was preparing to attack Bavaria when he suddenly died, leaving as his heir his young son HENRY THE LION.

Henschel, Sir George (hĕn'shəl), 1850–1934, German-English conductor, composer, and baritone. His first appearance (1877) in England was as a singer, and there he and his wife inaugurated (c.1880) the song recital. In 1881 he became the Boston Symphony Orchestra's first conductor. He returned to England in 1884 and was professor of singing (1886–88) at the Royal College of Music, London. He founded (1886) the London Symphony Concerts, which he conducted until they ceased in 1897. In his musical compositions, which include operas, songs, choral works, and instrumental music, he was strongly influenced by Brahms and Wagner. He was knighted in 1914. His first wife, **Lillian June (Bailey) Henschel,** 1860–1901, was an American soprano. She made her debut in Boston in 1876, then studied (1878) with Viardot-Garcia in Paris and later with Henschel, whom she married in 1881.

Henschke, Alfred: see KLABUND.

Henselt, Adolf von (ä'dôlf fən hĕn'zəlt), 1814–89, German pianist and composer. One of the most brilliant performers of his time, he gave up his concert career in 1838 to become court pianist and teacher in St. Petersburg. He composed a concerto, salon pieces, and studies for the piano.

Henslow, John Stevens (hĕnz'lō), 1796–1861, English botanist. He was professor of mineralogy (1822–27) and of botany (1827–61) at Cambridge Univ. Henslow was a teacher and friend of Charles Darwin, whom he recommended as naturalist to the *Beagle* expedition. He wrote on scientific farming and also *A Catalogue of British Plants* (1829) and *Dictionary of Botanical Terms* (1857).

Henslowe, Philip, d. 1616, English theatrical manager. Although he managed the Rose Theatre, Bankside, London, and the Fortune Theatre, Cripplegate, London, he is best remembered for his association with Edward ALLEYN and the ADMIRAL'S MEN. He employed a number of dramatists, including Dekker, Chapman, Drayton, and Thomas Heywood. His diary (ed. with supplementary material by R. A. Foakes and R. T. Rickert, 1961) contains valuable information on the Elizabethan stage.

Henson, Josiah, 1789–1883, Negro slave, reputedly the basis of the character of Uncle Tom in *Uncle Tom's Cabin,* b. Charles co., Md. In 1825 he faithfully led a party of his master's slaves from Maryland, across free territory in Ohio, to Kentucky. Tricked out of the freedom he had purchased and threatened with being sold down South, he escaped with his wife and children in 1830. He became a leader of the community of escaped Negroes at Dresden, Upper Canada (now Ontario). Henson, who had become a Methodist Episcopal preacher while in Kentucky, traveled widely, visiting England three times. His autobiography, *The Life of Josiah Henson* (1849), was enlarged in 1858 as *Truth Stranger than Fiction* and in 1879 as *"Truth is Stranger than Fiction";* the later editions contained introductions by Harriet Beecher Stowe. See Brion Gysin, *To Master—a Long Goodnight* (1946); Henry Blesby, *Josiah, the Maimed Fugitive* (1873, repr. 1969).

Henty, George Alfred, 1832–1902, English author. Initially a war correspondent, he later wrote boys' adventure tales that were very popular. Henty's books all focused on an ideal of manly virtue. They include *The Young Bugler* (1880) and *With Clive in India* (1884).

Henze, Hans Werner (häns vĕr'nər hĕn'tsə), 1926–, German composer, b. Gütersloh. Henze was a pupil of Wolfgang Fortner and René Leibowitz. His early works were influenced by Stravinsky, Hindemith, and Bartók. In his first violin concerto (1947) he took up 12-tone writing but has not confined himself to that method (see also SERIAL MUSIC). Henze's leftist politics are manifested in works such as the *Essay on Pigs* for baritone and chamber orchestra (1969) and the oratorio *The Raft of the Frigate "Medusa"* (1968). He has also written six symphonies (1947–69), concertos for various instruments, and several operas. Among the latter are *Elegy for Young Lovers* (1961) and *The Bassarids* (1965), both to texts by W. H. Auden; and *The Young Lord* (1965).

heparin (hĕp'ərĭn), ANTICOAGULANT produced by cells in many animals. A polysaccharide, heparin is found in the human body and occurs in greatest concentration in the tissues surrounding the capillaries of the lungs and the liver. The substance, extracted from animal tissues, is used clinically to delay BLOOD CLOTTING.

hepatica (hĭpăt'ĭkə) or **liverleaf,** any plant of the genus *Hepatica* of the family Ranunculaceae (BUTTERCUP family), low, woodland, spring wild flowers of the north temperate zone, popular for wild gardens. The delicate blossoms, of shades of lavender, pink, and blue, may appear while there is still snow; the three-lobed leaves persist through winter. Hepaticas were formerly used as a domestic remedy. Although often called liverworts, they are unrelated to the primitive plants commonly called LIVERWORTS that are classified with the mosses in the division Bryophyta. Hepatica is classified in the division MAGNOLIOPHYTA, class Magnoliopsida, order Ranunculales, family Ranunculaceae.

hepatitis (hĕp"ətī'tĭs), inflammation of the liver. Two forms of the disease, both transmitted by a virus, are most common: infectious hepatitis and serum hepatitis. The infectious type occurs sporadically or in epidemics, the virus being present in the feces and transmittable via contaminated food or water. Serum hepatitis is usually transmitted by transfusions of infected blood or plasma or the use of poorly sterilized hypodermic needles or other medical instruments. The incubation period for serum hepatitis is 6 weeks to 6 months, and it is estimated that 30,000 cases of the disease result from blood transfusions each year in the United States. The incubation period for infectious hepatitis is only 2 to 6 weeks. In this form, the disease can be attenuated in exposed persons by injections of gamma globulin. Symptoms of the disease in either form are nausea, fever, weakness, loss of appetite, sudden distaste for tobacco smoking, and (except in the mildest form) jaundice. Treatment usually consists of bed rest until the acute phase is over, gradual return to activities, and adequate diet. Recovery ordinarily takes place in 6 to 8 weeks, but in some cases residual illness persists for a year or more. Hepatitis can be incurred as a complication of several other disorders in addition to viral infection, among them amebic dysentery, cirrhosis of the liver, and mononucleosis. Also, alcohol, carbon tetrachloride, some tranquilizers and antibiotics, and many other substances can produce a toxic reaction in the liver, resulting in hepatitis.

Hepburn, Alonzo Barton, 1846–1922, American legislator and banker, b. Colton, St. Lawrence co., N.Y. He served (1875–80) in the New York state legislature and became chairman of the legislative committee to investigate railroad rate discrimination. The published proceedings of this committee—popularly called the Hepburn Report—strongly influenced subsequent corrective legislation and helped bring about the adoption (1887) of the Federal Interstate Commerce Act. Later Hepburn devoted himself to banking and to government fiscal administration. See biography by J. B. Bishop (1923).

Hepburn, Katharine, 1909–, American actress, b. Hartford, Conn. Periodically on the stage from 1928, she has enhanced the screen with her individual and commanding presence since 1932. She won three Academy Awards, for *Morning Glory* (1933), *Guess Who's Coming to Dinner?* (1967), and *The Lion in Winter* (1968). Together in nine films, Hepburn and Spencer TRACY formed a team remarkable for humor and intelligence. Her best film work includes *Alice Adams* (1935), *Bringing Up Baby* (1938), *The Philadelphia Story* (1940, written for her), *State of the Union* (1948), *The African Queen* (1951), *The Rainmaker* (1956), *Long Day's Journey into Night* (1962), and *A Delicate Balance* (1973). The play *Coco* (1969) was her first musical. See H. Dickens, *The Films of Katharine Hepburn* (1971).

Hepburn, Mitchell Frederick, 1896–1953, Canadian political leader. A member of the House of Commons (1926–34), he was chosen (1930) leader of the Liberal party in Ontario and became (1934) premier of the province. Several years later, he became involved in struggles with labor organizations and with Mackenzie King and his Liberal administration, which caused a split in the Liberal party. He resigned the premiership in 1942 and retired (1945) after an election defeat.

Hepburn, William Peters, 1833–1916, American legislator, b. Wellsville, Ohio. He was raised in Iowa and entered law there. He was a Civil War cavalry officer. From 1881 to 1887 he served as a Republican Congressman from Iowa. After four years as solicitor of the Treasury, he reentered Congress in 1893, serving 16 years. He was vitally interested in railroad regulation and was for many years chairman of the Committee on Interstate and Foreign Commerce. He drafted the Hepburn Act of 1906, which strengthened the INTERSTATE COMMERCE COMMISSION (see also REBATE), and was joint author of the Pure Food and Drugs Act (1906). See biography by J. E. Briggs (1919).

Hephaestus (hĕfĕs'təs), in Greek mythology, Olympian god. According to Homer he was the son of Hera and Zeus, but Hesiod states that he was conceived and borne by Hera alone. Originally an oriental fire god, in Greece he became the divine smith and god of craftsmen. He was worshiped primarily in cities such as Athens, where he had a temple. It was said that he was either born lame or was lamed by Zeus, who threw him down from Olympus when Hephaestus took Hera's side in a dispute. He was represented as bearded, with mighty shoulders, but crippled legs. At huge furnaces, worked by Cyclopes, he fashioned ornaments, weapons, and magical contrivances for the gods and heroes (e.g., Achilles' shield). But in mythology he was usually a comic figure. Most scholars agree that he was the husband of Aphrodite, who was unfaithful to him. The Romans identified Hephaestus with Vulcan.

Hepher (hē'fər). **1** Head of a Manassite family. Num. 26.32; 27.1; Joshua 17.2,3. **2** A Judahite. 1 Chron. 4.6. **3** One of David's warriors. 1 Chron. 11.36. **4** Unidentified Canaanite royal city. Joshua 12.17; 1 Kings 4.10.

Hephthalites: see WHITE HUNS.

Hephzi-bah (hĕf'zĭ-bə). **1** Mother of Manasseh. 2 Kings 21.1. **2** Name for Jerusalem restored. Isa. 62.4.

Hepplewhite, George (hĕp'əlhwīt), d. 1786, English cabinetmaker and furniture designer. His style is characterized by light, curvilinear forms, painted or inlaid decoration, and distinctive details such as slender tapering legs (plain, fluted, or reeded) and the spade foot. Decorative motifs include designs introduced by Robert ADAM and his brother James, ribbons, rosettes, prince of Wales feathers, ears of wheat, and the lyre. He is noted for distinctive chair backs in shield, oval, interlaced hearts, ladder, and wheel forms and for the use of much satinwood and painted beechwood as well as mahogany. His small pieces, e.g., inlaid work tables, fire screens, knife boxes, and tea caddies, are especially prized by collectors. Hepplewhite's firm was continued by his widow, who published in 1788 his *Cabinet-Maker and Upholsterer's Guide* (repr. 1969).

heptachlor (hĕp'təklōr''): see INSECTICIDE.

Heptameron: see MARGARET OF NAVARRE.

heptarchy (hĕp'tärkē) [Gr.,=seven-kingdom], name traditionally applied to the kingdoms of Anglo-Saxon England in the period prior to the Danish conquests of the 9th cent. The term was probably first used by 16th-century writers who believed that England was then divided into seven kingdoms—NORTHUMBRIA, EAST ANGLIA, MERCIA, ESSEX, SUSSEX, WESSEX, and KENT. Actually the political and geographical divisions were neither so orderly nor permanent. At one time (c.600) there appear to have been as many as 12 independent states, but the number of kingdoms, their boundaries, and their political status shifted constantly throughout this period.

Hepworth, Dame Barbara, 1903–, English sculptor. Hepworth's smooth, usually nonfigurative sculptures recall those of Jean Arp. Working in Cornwall, she has consistently sought perfection of form and surface texture. She has worked primarily in stone, more recently in bronze. Her sculpture is represented in the Tate Gallery, London. Until 1951, Hepworth was married to the painter Ben NICHOLSON. See studies by A. M. Hammacher (tr. 1968) and Alan Bowness, ed. (1971).

Hera (hĕr'ə), in Greek religion, queen of the Olympian gods, daughter of Cronus and Rhea. She was the wife and sister of Zeus and the mother of Ares and Hephaestus. A passionately jealous wife, she fought constantly with Zeus and plagued his mistresses and children. She was the protectress of women, presiding over marriage and childbirth, and frequently punished offending husbands. A powerful divinity, Hera was worshiped in all parts of Greece, especially at Argos and Salmos, where she had splendid temples. She is usually represented as a majestic figure, fully draped, crowned with a wreath or diadem, and carrying a scepter. Frequently she is associated with the pomegranate, symbol of marital love and fruitfulness. The peacock was sacred to her. The Romans identified Hera with Juno.

Heraclea (hĕrəklē'ə), ancient Greek city, in Lucania, S Italy, not far from the Gulf of Tarentum (Taranto). There Pyrrhus defeated the Romans in 280 B.C. Bronze tablets giving Roman municipal laws were found nearby.

Heraclea Pontica (pŏn'tĭkə), ancient Greek city, a port on the southern shore of the Black Sea. Founded in the 6th cent. B.C. by colonists from Megara and Boeotia, it rose to a position of great prominence, controlling much of the coast and sending out colonies. It was at its height in the 4th cent. B.C. but was hindered by the rise of Bithynia also in Asia Minor. It was destroyed by the Romans in the wars against Mithridates VI of Pontus. Modern Ereğli, Turkey, is on the site.

Heracleopolis (hərăk''lēŏp'əlĭs), ancient city, N Egypt, just S of Al Fayyum. One of the oldest Egyptian cities, it was in existence before 3000 B.C. and was the capital (c.2155–c.2050) of the IX and X dynasties. The temple of the local god was enlarged in the XII dynasty and again by Ramses II.

Heracles: see HERCULES.

Heraclitus (hĕrəklī'təs), c.535–c.475 B.C., Greek philosopher of Ephesus, of noble birth. According to Heraclitus, there was no permanent reality except the reality of change; permanence was an illusion of the senses. He taught that all things carried with them their opposites, that death was potential in life, that being and not-being were part of every whole—therefore, the only possible real state was the transitional one of becoming. He believed fire to be the underlying substance of the universe and all other elements transformations of it. He identified life and reason with fire and believed that no man had a soul of his own, that each shared in a universal soul-fire. See his *Cosmic Fragments*, ed. by G. S. Kirk (1954, repr. 1962); study by P. E. Wheelwright (1959).

Heraclius (hĕrəklī'əs, hĭrăk'lēəs), c.575–641, Byzantine emperor (610–41). The son of a governor of Africa, he succeeded the tyrant Phocas, whom he deposed and had executed. In the early years of his reign Avars and Bulgars threatened, attacking even Constantinople, and the Persians conquered Syria, Palestine, and Egypt. In three costly campaigns (622–28) Heraclius recovered the provinces from the Persians, but they fell (629–42) to the Muslim Arabs. He sought to reconcile the Monophysites with the Orthodox Church; this attempt led to the compromise of MONOTHELETISM, which was rejected by both sides. Heraclius began the reorganization of the empire into military provinces (*themes*). He was succeeded briefly by his son Constantine III and then by his grandson Constans II.

Herakles: see HERCULES.

heraldry, system in which inherited symbols, or devices, called charges are displayed on a shield, or escutcheon, for the purpose of identifying individuals or families. In the Middle Ages the herald, often a tournament official, had to recognize men by their shields; thus he became an authority on personal and family insignia. As earlier functions of the herald grew obsolete, his chief duties became the devising, inscribing, and granting of armorial bearings. Personal and family insignia are common to primitive tribes (e.g., TOTEM) and are mentioned by Homer, but heraldry proper is a feudal institution developed by noblemen using personal insignia on seals and shields that came to be transmitted to their families. It is thought to have originated in Germany in the late 12th cent., and to have been adopted and improved in France, Spain, and Italy, and imported into England by the Normans. The crusades and tournaments which drew together knights from many countries caused heraldry to flourish in Western Europe. The practice of embroidering family emblems on the surcoat, or tabard, worn over chain mail in the 13th cent. accounts for the term "coat of arms." The use of armorial bearings spread rapidly thereafter through all grades of feudal rank above squire. Private assumption of arms became so common that Henry V forbade it, and on the chartering of the Heralds' College in 1483 the regulations pertaining to heraldry were placed in the hands of the Garter King-of-Arms. Arms were borne by families, corporations, guilds, religious houses, inns of court, colleges, boroughs and cities, and kingdoms. In the United States the seals and insignia of colleges, cities, and the like are examples of the persistence of the heraldic tradition. For methods of displaying armorial bearings, see BLAZONRY. See A. R. Wagner, *Heralds and Heraldry in the Middle Ages* (2d ed. 1956); Hubert Allcock, *Heraldic Design* (1962); A. C. Fox-Davies, *A Complete Guide to Heraldry* (rev. ed. 1969); Charles Boutell, *Manual of Heraldry* (1863; rev. ed. by J. P. Brooke-Little, 1970).

Heralds' College, body first chartered in 1483 by Richard III of England. It has been reorganized several times. Its purpose is to assign new coats of arms and to trace lineages to determine heraldic rights and privileges (see HERALDRY). It has collected and combined the rule of BLAZONRY into a system. The college consists of the Garter king of arms (principal king of arms of both England and the Order of the Garter), the kings of arms of Norroy and of Clarenceux, and several heralds and pursuivants (attendants). In Scotland, heraldic matters are regulated by the Lyon king of arms; in Northern Ireland, the jurisdiction of the Ulster king of arms passed in 1943 to the king of arms of Norroy. The kings of arms and heralds also proclaim a new king's accession and attend at state occasions such as the opening of Parliament and the introduction of new peers into the House of Lords. See Roger Milton, *The English Ceremonial Book* (1972).

Herat (hĕrät'), city (1971 pop. 103,915), capital of Herat prov., NW Afghanistan, on the Hari Rud. The fertile river valley is renowned for its fruits, especially grapes. Herat has textile weaving and carpet industries and is a market for wool, carpets, dried fruits, and nuts. The city walls are gone, but the great earthwork of the citadel remains. Herat, whose inhabitants are mainly Tadzhiks, is also noted for its bazaars and its highly decorated gharries (horse-drawn cabs). Landmarks include the Great Mosque (first built 12th cent.) and several exquisite minarets. Paved roads lead to the USSR border. Herat, an ancient city, is identified with the Haroyu of the *Vendidad* (Zoroastrian priestly code), the Haraiva of Achaemenian inscriptions, and the Aria of the Greeks. Its strategic location on the old trade route from Persia to India and on the caravan road from China and central Asia to Europe has long made Herat an object of contention among the powers of the day. Although taken by various conquerors, it remained under the Persian empire for several centuries. From the 11th cent. nomads from the East pressed in. The Mongols under Jenghiz Khan devastated Herat in 1221. Tamerlane took the city in 1383; under his later successors, Shah Rukh and Husayn, it enjoyed prosperity, and its court was a center of art and learning. The Uzbeks took Herat in the early 16th cent.; later it was disputed between the Persians and the rulers of an emerging Afghanistan. In the mid-19th cent., British pressure checked Persian claims to Herat, which in 1881 was taken by Abd ar-Rahman and finally confirmed as part of a united Afghanistan.

Hérault (ārō'), department (1968 pop. 591,397), S France, in LANGUEDOC. MONTPELLIER is the capital, and SÈTE is the chief port.

Hérault de Séchelles, Marie Jean (märē' zhäN ārō' də sāshĕl'), 1759–94, French revolutionary. A lawyer, he became a favorite of Queen Marie Antoinette, but nevertheless joined the revolutionary cause in 1789. A member of the Legislative Assembly and of the Convention and the Committee of Public Safety, he was prominent in shaping the war measures of 1792 and in establishing the revolutionary tribunal that was to be the main instrument of the Reign of Terror. Ironically, he was also chief author of the republican constitution of 1793, which was superseded by the dictatorship of the Terror. He was guillotined with Georges Danton and his supporters.

herb (ûrb, hûrb), name for any plant that is used medicinally or as a spice and for the useful product of such a plant. Herbs as condiments and seasonings are still important in culinary art; the use of medicinal herbs, however, has waned since the advent of prescription and synthetic medicines, although plants remain a major source of drugs. The term *herb* is also applied to all herbaceous plants as distinguished from woody plants. See R. E. Clarkson, *Herbs, their Culture and Uses* (1966); G. B. Foster, *Herbs for Every Garden* (rev. ed. 1973); Arnold and Connie Krochmal, *A Guide to the Medicinal Plants of the United States* (1974).

herbaceous plant (hûrbā'shəs), plant whose STEM is soft and green and shows little growth of wood. The term "herbaceous plant" is used to distinguish such plants from woody plants. Herbaceous plants, or herbs, as they are commonly called, may be ANNUAL—that is, their stems and leaves die after a year's growth, and the plants are propagated by seed—or they may be produced each year by new shoots from dormant roots. The stems of woody plants, e.g., most shrubs and trees, are tough, are covered with nongreen bark, and enlarge in diameter by the accumulation of annual layers of WOOD produced by the CAMBIUM. They are PERENNIAL.

herbal, early botanical book containing descriptions and illustrations of herbs and plants with their properties, chiefly those qualities that made them useful to man as medicines or condiments. Most of the herbals were written between c.1470 and c.1670; they were especially popular in England and Germany. Among the famous herbalists were Gaspard Bauhin, Otto Brunfels, Hieronymus Bock, and Leonhard Fuchs, all active during the 16th cent. Mingled with illustrations of often painstaking accuracy were fantastic figures and many superstitious descriptions of the magical powers of plants, e.g., the doctrine of signatures. This theory of herb medicine was based on the superficial resemblance of certain plants or plant parts to specific human organs or parts. The appropriate herb was used for any disorder of its human counterpart. Thus certain heart-shaped leaves were thought to relieve heart disease; the convoluted walnut, brain disease; and the figworts, whose flowers have deep throats, were given for scrofula (hence the figwort family name Scrophulariaceae). The herbal began to disappear as medicine acquired a scientific basis and the herb garden ceased to supply family medicines. See A. R. Arber, *Herbals, Their Origin and Evolution* (2d ed. 1938); B. C. Harris, *The Compleat Herbal* (new ed. 1972).

herbarium, collection of dried and mounted plant specimens used in systematic botany. To preserve their form and color, plants collected in the field are spread flat in sheets of newsprint and dried, usually in a plant press, between blotters or absorbent paper. The specimens, mounted on sheets of stiff white paper, are labeled with all essential data, e.g., date, where found, natural coloration, altitude, special habitat conditions, and placed in a protective case. As a precaution against insect attack the pressed plant is poisoned and the cases disinfected. Herbariums are essential for the preservation of type specimens, the verification of plant classification, and the standardizing of nomenclature. Thus inclusion of as much of the plant (e.g., flowers, leaves, seed, and fruit) as possible is desirable. Linnaeus' herbarium now belongs to the Linnaean Society in England. Most universities maintain herbariums. Notable herbariums in the United States include the Gray Herbarium at Harvard Univ. and those at the U.S. National Museum (of the Smithsonian Institution) and at the New York and Missouri botanical gardens. See Joseph Lanjouw, ed., *Index Herbariorum: The Herbaria of the World* (1954–72); P. W. Leenhouts, *A Guide to the Practice of Herbarium Taxonomy* (1968).

Herbart, Johann Friedrich (yō'hän frē'drĭkh hĕr'bärt), 1776–1841, German philosopher and educator. Influenced by Leibniz, Kant, and Fichte, Herbart made many important contributions to psychology. In 1805 he lectured at Göttingen and from 1809 to 1833 held the chair of philosophy at Königsberg. He then returned to Göttingen as professor of philosophy. *Psychologie als Wissenschaft* (1824–25) was his major psychological work and *Allgemeine Metaphysik* (1828–29) his most important philosophical study. Herbart held that the concepts of change and becoming harbored a contradiction that destroyed the reality of continuous identity. He maintained that true being consists of a plurality of simple reals, which were modeled after the Leibnizian monads. Change is nothing but alteration in the various relationships among reals. The reactions of reals to these changing relationships are their efforts at self-preservation, as in the case of the soul, whose efforts are ideas. Ideas themselves strive for self-preservation, each one having resistance to change. This makes possible mathematical treatment of ideas and opens the way to scientific psychology. Though he denied the possibility of psychological experiment, Herbart sought to develop the mathematical and empirical, as well as the metaphysical, aspects of psychology. In education he emphasized the importance of relating new concepts to the experience of the learner so that there would be less resistance to apperception of new ideas. He stressed the need for moral education through experience and brought the work of teaching into the area of conscious method. Many of Herbart's educational works have been translated into English. See his *Application of Psychology to the Science of Education* (tr. 1892); biography by A. M. Williams (1911); R. D. Chalke, *A Synthesis of Froebel and Herbart* (1912); H. B. Dunkel, *Herbart and Herbartianism* (1970).

herb Christopher: see BANEBERRY.

Herbert, A. P. (Sir Alan Patrick Herbert), 1890–1971, English author and member of Parliament. He was a regular contributor to the comic magazine *Punch* from 1910 until his death. Herbert served in Parliament from 1935 until 1950 as a representative for Oxford Univ. and was largely responsible for the bill (1937) liberalizing English divorce law. His numerous books include *The House by the River* (1921), *The Water Gipsies* (1930), and *The Singing Swan* (1968). He was knighted in 1945. See his autobiography *A. P. H.: His Life and Times* (1970).

Herbert, George, 1593–1633, one of the English METAPHYSICAL POETS. Of noble family, he was the brother of Baron Herbert of Cherbury. He was graduated from Cambridge. His early determination to enter the church was temporarily deflected by an appointment as public orator in 1619, a post he held until 1627. In 1630 he was ordained an Anglican priest and made rector at Bemerton. Herbert's devotional poems combine a homely familiarity with religious experience and a reverent sense of its magnificence. His verse is marked by quietness of tone, precision of language, metrical versatility, and the use of conceits. All unpublished at his death, the poems were left by Herbert to his friend Nicholas Ferrar, who had them published as *The Temple* (1633). Herbert also wrote Latin poems and a prose manual of clerical life, *A Priest of the Temple* (first printed in *Herbert's Remains,* 1652). The 20th-century revival of interest in the metaphysical poets has stressed Herbert. See his complete works edited by F. E. Hutchinson (2d ed. 1953); biographies by Izaak Walton (1670) and G. H. Palmer (1905); studies by M. K. Rickey (1966) and Arnold Stein (1968).

Herbert, Mary: see PEMBROKE, MARY HERBERT, COUNTESS OF.

Herbert, Victor, 1859–1924, Irish-American cellist, composer, and conductor, studied at the Stuttgart Conservatory. In 1886 the Metropolitan Opera Company engaged his wife, Therese Herbert-Föster, as a singer and Herbert as first cellist, and together they immigrated to the United States. From 1898 to 1904 he was conductor of the Pittsburgh Symphony Orchestra, but after 1904 he was chiefly engaged in composition. Two of Herbert's serious operas, *Natoma* (1911) and *Madeleine* (1914), were produced, but he achieved his major success with his melodious operettas, some of which are *Babes in Toyland* (1903), *The Red Mill* (1906), *Naughty Marietta* (1910), *Sweethearts* (1913), and *Eileen* (1917). He also wrote music for some of the Ziegfeld Follies, and composed some orchestral music and a cello concerto. See biography by E. N. Waters (1955).

Herbert, William: see PEMBROKE, WILLIAM HERBERT, 3D EARL OF.

Herbert Hoover National Historic Site: see NATIONAL PARKS AND MONUMENTS (table).

Herbert of Cherbury, Edward Herbert, 1st **Baron,** 1583–1648, English philosopher, poet, and diplomat; elder brother of George Herbert, the metaphysical poet. He was ambassador to France (1619–24) and was created Baron Herbert of Cherbury in 1629. A precursor of deism, Lord Herbert laid down his principles of natural religion in *De veritate* (1624), *De religione laici* (1645), and *De religione gentilium* (1663). His secular metaphysical poetry also shows the influence of his philosophy, for even his love poems in *Poems* (1665) reflect the serious, analytic approach of the rationalist. He also wrote a biography of Henry VIII (1649) and an autobiography, first published by Horace Walpole in 1764.

herbicide (hûr'bəsīd"), chemical compound that kills plants or inhibits their normal growth. Herbicides may be described as selective or nonselective. Selective herbicides kill or stunt weeds in a germinating or growing crop without permanent injury to the crop plants; nonselective herbicides are toxic to all plants and are used to stop plant growth, for instance on roadsides, ditch banks, irrigation channels, railroad rights-of-way, and industrial sites. Contact herbicides kill only the plant parts to which they are applied; systemic herbicides are absorbed either by the foliage or by the roots and are translocated to other portions of the plant. Some herbicides, when incorporated with the soil, will kill germinating seeds and small seedlings. Herbicides may be used in lieu of tillage, but are most often used in combination with tillage and other agronomic practices; they may be most advantageously used where cultivation is impossible or not desirable. The early use of chemical herbicides was limited to inorganic compounds. Herbicides such as ashes, common salts, and bittern have been used in agriculture since ancient times. Observation in 1896 that BORDEAUX MIXTURE, a fungicide, also provided control of certain weeds, led to the use of copper sulfate as a selective weed killer to control charlock in cereals. By 1900, solutions of sulfuric acid, iron sulfate, copper nitrate, and ammonium and potassium salts were known to act as selective herbicides; soon thereafter sodium arsenite solutions became the standard herbicides, and they were used in large quantities until about 1960. Other popular inorganic herbicides include ammonium sulfamate, carbon bisulfide, sodium chlorate, sulfuric acid solutions, and formulations containing borate. Although certain oils have been used as herbicides for many years, the development of organic chemicals as herbicides essentially began with the use of dinitrophenol compounds in 1932. A monumental breakthrough occurred in the 1940s with the development of 2,4-D (2,4-dichlorophenoxyacetic acid), a compound similar to plant hormones that acts as a highly selective systemic herbicide when used in very small quantities; 2,4-D rapidly gained widespread usage in the control of broadleaved weeds in corn, sorghum, small grains, and grass pastures. The phenoxyaliphatic acids and their derivatives constitute a major group of organic herbicides because of their selectivity and their ease of translocation. Other groups of organic herbicides include organic arsenicals, substituted amides and ureas, nitrogen heterocyclic acids, and phenol derivatives. See PESTICIDE.

herbivore: see CARNIVORE.

Hercegovina: see BOSNIA AND HERCEGOVINA, Yugoslavia.

Herculaneum (hərkyo͞olā'nēəm), ancient city of S Italy, on the gulf of Naples at the foot of Mt. Vesuvius. Damaged by an earthquake in A.D. 63, it was completely buried, along with POMPEII, by the volcanic eruption of Mt. Vesuvius in A.D. 79. Before the earthquake, it was a popular Roman resort and residential town with fine villas. The first discovery of ruins was made in 1709, and excavations have continued since. Important early finds were the sumptuous so-called Villa of the Papyri (with a large library, and bronze and marble statues), a basilica with fine murals, and a theater. The modern towns of Resina and Portici are on the site. See J. J. Deiss, *Herculaneum* (1966, repr. 1968).

Herculano de Carvalho e Araújo, Alexandre (əlēshäN'drə ərko͞olä'no͞o thĭ kərvä'lyo͞o ĕ ərou'zho͞o), 1810–77, Portuguese historian. One of the outstanding thinkers of his time, he is considered the first modern Portuguese historian. His great four-volume history of Portugal (1846–53) is notable for its treatment of feudal institutions and of social conditions. He is also known for his history of the Inquisition in Portugal (tr. 1926, repr. 1972).

Hercules (hûr'kyo͞olēz), **Heracles,** or **Herakles** (both: hĕr'əklēz), most popular of all Greek heroes, famous for extraordinary strength and courage. Alcmene, wife of Amphitryon, made love to both Zeus and her husband on the same night and bore two sons, Hercules (son of Zeus) and Iphicles (son of Amphitryon). Hercules incurred the everlasting wrath of Hera because he was the child of her unfaithful husband. A few months after his birth Hera set two serpents in his cradle, but the prodigious infant promptly strangled them. When he was a young man, Hercules defended Thebes from the armies of a neighboring city, Orchomenus, and was rewarded with Megara, daughter of King Creon. But Hera later drove Hercules insane, and in his madness he killed his wife and children. After he had recovered his sanity, he sought purification at the court of King Eurystheus of Tiryns for 12 years. During those years Hercules performed 12 arduous labors: he killed the Nemean lion and the Hydra; caught the Erymanthian boar and the Cerynean hind; drove off the Stymphalian birds; cleaned the stables of Augeas; captured the Cretan bull and the horses of Diomed; made off with the girdle of the Amazon queen Hippolyte; killed Geryon; captured Cerberus; and finally took the golden apples of Hesperides. After his labors were completed, Hercules was involved in many other adventures and combats, including the Calydonian hunt and the Argonaut expedition. He killed Iphitus, son of the king of Oichalia, because the king would not give him his daughter Iole. When Neleus, king of Pylos, refused him absolution for that crime, Hercules sacked his kingdom and killed all his sons except Nestor. For that outrage the Delphic oracle bade him serve Omphale, queen of Lydia, who, in some legends, dressed him in women's clothes and had him work with her maids spinning wool. He later was her lover, but after he finished his servitude he returned to Oichalia and carried off Iole. When his second wife, Deianira, daughter of King Oeneus, was seized by the centaur Nessus, Hercules killed Nessus with arrows dipped in the poisonous blood of Hydra. As he died, Nessus told Deianira that blood from his wound would restore Hercules' love for her if ever it were to wane. Later, when Deianira sought to win back her husband's love, she contrived to have him don a robe smeared with the blood. The robe stuck fast to Hercules' skin, burning him unbearably. In agony, he built a huge pyre atop Mt. Oite and had it set afire. His mortal parts burned away, but the rest rose to heaven, where he was finally reconciled with Hera and married Hebe. Although worshiped as a god, Hercules was properly a hero, frequently appealed to for protection from various evils. In art Hercules was portrayed as a powerful, muscular man wearing a lion's skin and armed with a huge club. Perhaps the most famous statue of him is the Farnese Hercules in the National Museum in Naples. He is the hero of plays by Sophocles, Euripides, and Seneca.

Hercules, in astronomy, northern CONSTELLATION located between Lyra and Corona Borealis. It is traditionally depicted as the hero Hercules in a kneeling position. There are no very bright stars in Hercules and only three of third magnitude, the brightest of which, Ras Algethi (Alpha Herculis), is a red giant and possibly the largest visible star in the sky. The constellation contains the globular STAR CLUSTER M13, barely visible to the naked eye but spectacular even in a small telescope. Hercules reaches its highest point in the evening sky in late July.

Hercules'-club, common name for several small, thorny trees, chiefly the devil's-walking-stick of the family Aralaceae (GINSENG family) and the prickly ash of the family Rutaceae (ORANGE family). The families are classified in the division MAGNOLIOPHYTA, class Magnoliopsida, orders Umbellales and Sapindales, respectively.

Hercules cluster, giant globular STAR CLUSTER in the northern constellation HERCULES; cataloged as M13 or NGC 6205. The cluster is just visible to the naked eye and is the best example of a globular cluster visible in the Northern Hemisphere. Its angular diameter is about ⅔ that of the full moon, and its linear diameter is 100 LIGHT-YEARS. The entire cluster contains perhaps 100,000 or more stars. In its central portion, the stars are so close together that they cannot be resolved, despite the cluster's relatively near distance of 35,000 light-years; the separation between stars is estimated to be only a few ASTRONOMICAL UNITS as compared to the normal interstellar separation of a few light-years.

Herczeg, Ferenc (fĕ'rĕnts hĕr'tsĕg), 1863–1954, Hungarian writer. Herczeg wrote popular romantic farces as well as historical and social novels, plays, and stories, which were generally ironic and detached in tone. He spoke for the Hungarian gentry, although the mild satire of such social novels as *The Golden Violin* (1916) partly transcended this orientation. Some of his plays have been translated.

Herder, Johann Gottfried von (yō'hän gôt'frēt fən hĕr'dər), 1744–1803, German philosopher, critic, and clergyman, b. East Prussia. Herder was an enormously influential literary critic and a leader in the STURM UND DRANG movement. After an impoverished childhood, he studied theology at Königsberg and came under the influence of Kant. During an appointment at Riga, Herder gained attention with his *Fragmente über die neuere deutsche Literatur* [fragments concerning current German literature] (1767). In 1776 he became court preacher at Weimar through the influence of Goethe, whose work was greatly affected by Herder's ideas, particularly by his *Über den Ursprung der Sprache* [on the origin of language] (1772). In this treatise Herder held that language and poetry are spontaneous necessities of human nature, rather than supernatural endowments. At Weimar, Herder became the leading theorist of German romanticism and a significant contributor to the most brilliant court of the era. There he produced his anthology of foreign folk songs, *Stimmen der Völker* (1778–79) and also made some of the earliest studies of comparative philology, comparative religion, and mythology. His vast work *Ideen zur Philosophie der Geschichte der Menschheit* (1784–91; tr. *Outlines of the Philosophy of Man,* 1800) developed a major evolutionary approach to history in which he propounded the uniqueness of every historical age. See biography by R. T. Clark (1955); studies by F. M. Barnard (1965) and H. B. Nisbet (1970).

herd's-grass: see TIMOTHY; BENT GRASS.

Heredia, José María (hōsā' märē'ä ārā'thēä), 1803–39, Cuban journalist and poet. He is considered the most lyrical of the poets writing during the period of the wars of independence. Although Heredia's poetry is classic in form, it is imbued with romantic melancholy and joy in nature. His subjectiveness and passionate nature appear in his two best-known poems, "On the Teocalli of Cholula" (written 1820) and "Niagara" (written 1824). Exiled from Cuba as a revolutionary (1823), he spent two years in New York City, where he published his poems, and spent the rest of his life in Mexico. He was a cousin of the French poet Heredia.

Heredia, José María de, 1842–1905, French poet, a leading exponent of the poetic ideals of the PARNASSIANS, b. Cuba. His reputation rests on *Les Trophées* (1893), containing 118 masterful sonnets in the Petrarchan manner. This work displays an almost unparalleled effort to reproduce the sensory effects of painting, music, and sculpture in poetic terms.

Heredia, city (1970 pop. 24,021), capital of Heredia prov., central Costa Rica. On the central plateau, it is a center of the coffee and cattle industries and, with its colonial architecture, a tourist attraction. Heredia was founded in 1571.

heredity, transmission from generation to generation through the process of REPRODUCTION in plants and animals of factors which cause the offspring to resemble their parents. That like begets like has been a maxim since ancient times. Although the fact of heredity has been generally known for centuries, the actual mechanism by which inherited characteristics may be transmitted to successive generations could not be satisfactorily explained until powerful enough microscopes and sufficiently refined research techniques disclosed the true nature of the universal reproductive process in which the sperm and the ovum, containing the hereditary material (see CHROMOSOME) in their cell nuclei, unite to give rise to the new individual. Thus the science of heredity developed long after practical observations of breeding and of parent-child resemblance had been noted and also after the theory of evolution had been established. In the 18th cent. the popular concept of heredity was the theory of preformation: that the prototypical members of each kind of organism (e.g., Adam and Eve among humans) contained within them all future generations, perfectly formed but in miniature, arranged one inside the next like a series of Chinese boxes. In the early 19th cent. Lamarck developed a theory of evolution to which the then current belief in the inheritance of ACQUIRED CHARACTERISTICS became linked as an explanation of its mechanism. The theory of pangenesis, as it was termed in a modified version in DARWINISM, was strongly reminiscent of the ideas of Hippocrates and Aristotle. It hypothesized tiny particles called pangens, or gemmules—each bearing the hereditary potential for a specific body part—which circulated in the body and eventually collected in the reproductive cells. Finally, in 1875, Oscar Hertwig's principle of the universality of fertilization in sexual reproduction confirmed that whatever hereditary material existed must be transmitted through the two sex cells. August Weismann's theory of germ plasm continuity (1892) established that the germ (sex) cells are set apart from other body cells early in embryonic development and thus that only changes in the germ plasm, and not influences on the adult body, can affect the characteristics of future generations. In 1900 the neglected work of Gregor MENDEL was rediscovered and the first scientific laws for the mechanisms of heredity were presented. These, correlating beautifully with the microscopic and experimental observations of the mechanics of fertilization, have provided the basis for all modern genetic studies (see GENETICS). It has been demonstrated that MUTATION is the mechanism for evolution, initiating new variations and alterations in the individual. The mutant's ability to survive and to produce offspring bearing the same variation results from the action of natural SELECTION in a manner similar to that proposed in the original evolutionary theories. See T. G. Dobzhansky, *Heredity and the Nature of Man* (1964); L. C. Dunn, *Heredity and Evolution in Human Populations* (1965).

Hereford (hĕr'əfərd), municipal borough (1971 pop. 46,503), county town of Herefordshire, W central England. It is a cattle-market town. There is also food processing, brewing, and light manufacturing. At the great cathedral, which probably dates from the 11th cent., the Festival of the Three Choirs is held every third year. (In the other years it is held at Gloucester or Worcester.) The White Cross, near the town, commemorates the termination of the great plague in the mid-14th cent. There is a grammar school founded in the 14th cent. Hereford was the birthplace of Nell Gwyn, mistress of Charles II, and the actor David Garrick. In 1974, Hereford became part of the new nonmetropolitan county of Hereford and Worcester.

Hereford (hûr'fərd), city (1970 pop. 13,414), seat of Deaf Smith co., N Texas, in the Panhandle; inc. 1906. Fine livestock is raised in Hereford, and cattle feeding is an important industry, along with meat packing and sugar refining. Vegetables and grains are grown on irrigated farms in the semiarid plains.

Hereford and Worcester, nonmetropolitan county, W central England, created under the Local Government Act of 1972 (effective 1974). It is composed of the county borough of Worcester and most of the former counties of Herefordshire and Worcestershire.

Hereford cattle (hûr'fərd), breed of beef cattle originated in Herefordshire, England, and thought to be descended from the primitive cattle of the country. They are medium-to-large, deep-bodied, thick-fleshed animals with white faces and white markings. Probably first brought to the United States in 1817 by Henry Clay, they are now the predominating breed on the Western ranges. A polled (hornless) Hereford strain developed in the United States by selective breeding is now very popular. Herefords are also widely raised in Australia and South America.

Herefordshire, county (1970 pop. 138,425), 842 sq mi (2,181 sq km), W central England, on the Welsh border. The county town is HEREFORD. A land of many streams and woods, the county has undulating terrain, reaching its greatest height in the Black Mts. in the southwest and the Malvern Hills in the east. The chief rivers are the Wye, the Teme, and the Frome. The region is primarily agricultural and is famous for its orchards and livestock (Hereford cattle and Ryeland sheep). Food processing and brewing are important, and there is some tile manufacture and metal-working. In the Middle Ages, Herefordshire was the scene of much border warfare with the Welsh, and there are many ruins of castles and fortifications, the most remarkable of which is Offa's Dyke (8th cent.). Herefordshire had a flourishing woolen and cloth trade in the Middle Ages. In 1974 the county was combined with almost all of Worcestershire to form the new nonmetropolitan county of Hereford and Worcester.

Herero (hərār'ō), Bantu people, mainly in South West Africa and Botswana. They number about 55,000. A pastoral tribe, noted for their large cattle herds, the Herero probably migrated from the region of Lake Tanganyika in the 18th cent. They warred against their neighbors, the Khoikhoi, and enslaved many smaller tribes. Their territory was annexed (1885) as a part of German South West Africa, and from 1903 to 1907 they rebelled against German rule and were almost exterminated. In more recent times the Herero have often pressed for independence. See J. M. White, *The Land God Made in Anger* (1969).

Heres (hē'rēs) or **Har-heres** (hä-), town, S Palestine, probably the same as BETH-SHEMESH **2.** Judges 1.35.

Heresh (hûr'ĕsh), servant of the Tabernacle. 1 Chron. 9.15.

Hereward the Wake (hĕr'ĭwərd), fl. 1070, Anglo-Saxon rebel against WILLIAM I. He apparently held land in Lincolnshire. In 1070 he sacked Peterborough with the aid of a Danish fleet and then consolidated his forces on the Isle of Ely. After William captured (1071) the island, Hereward seems to have continued resistance as an outlaw. It is said that he was later pardoned by William. He became a folk hero to the conquered Anglo-Saxons.

Herford (hĕr'fôrt), city (1970 pop. 65,531), North Rhine-Westphalia, N central West Germany, on the Werre River. Its manufactures include textiles, carpets, furniture, and processed food. Herford developed around a 13th-century church (still standing) that formerly had been a Benedictine convent (founded in the 9th cent.). It was a member of the Hanseatic League and passed to Brandenburg in 1647.

Hergenröther, Joseph Adam Gustav (yō'zĕf ä'däm gŏŏs'täf hĕr'gənrötər), 1824-90, German theologian and scholar, cardinal of the Roman Catholic Church. He was a professor at Munich and Würzburg. In 1879, Leo XIII made him cardinal and first prefect of the newly opened Vatican archives. Hergenröther wrote polemical works and church history. A zealous advocate of ULTRAMONTANISM, he refuted DÖLLINGER with *Anti-Janus* (1870, tr. 1870). His historical works include *The Catholic Church and the Christian State* (1876, tr. 1876) and *Manual of Universal Church History* (3 vol., 1876-80). His monumental work on PHOTIUS, written to dispel charges of papal responsibility for the Eastern schism, is fundamental, but considered by later scholars to be unfair to Photius. See American Catholic Historical Association, *Church Historians* (1926).

Hergesheimer, Joseph (hûr'gəshī'mər), 1880-1954, American novelist, b. Philadelphia. He first achieved literary distinction with the publication of *The Three Black Pennys* (1917). This novel, set against the background of the Pennsylvania iron industry, portrays the changing fortunes of a family of ironmasters. His other important works include *Java Head* (1919), dealing with miscegenation in a New England sea-trading family, and *Linda Condon* (1919), a character study of an emotionally repressed girl. Among his later colorful novels, generally considered less artistic, are *Balisand* (1924) and *Tampico* (1926). Hergesheimer, who has been called a naturalist writing of the romantic past, is also the author of short stories, essays, biographies, and the autobiography, *From an Old House* (1925).

Herisau (hä'rĭzou), town (1970 pop. 14,597), capital of Appenzell Ausser-Rhoden half canton, NE Switzerland. Embroideries, cotton textiles, machinery, precision instruments, and other goods are made. Among its historic monuments is a partly 10th-century church.

Héristal: see HERSTAL, Belgium.

Herkimer, Nicholas, 1728-77, American Revolutionary general. He was born in a German colony near the present town of Herkimer, N.Y. He served in the French and Indian War and was appointed (1776) brigadier general in the New York militia. In 1777 in the SARATOGA CAMPAIGN, Herkimer was leading a relief party to the Americans besieged by General St. Leger at Fort Stanwix when at Oriskany Creek they were ambushed by a force of Loyalists and Indians. Herkimer was mortally wounded, and his force had to retreat, but St. Leger later abandoned his plan to join Burgoyne.

Herm: see CHANNEL ISLANDS, Great Britain.

herm (hûrm), in 6th-century Greek art, vertical pillar surmounted by a bearded human head and often having a phallus below. These structures were considered sacred to Hermes. They were placed on street corners in Athens and used outside the city as milestones. By the end of the Hellenistic era the form was employed for portraiture.

hermandad (ārmändäth') [Span.,=brotherhood], league or federation of towns, a characteristic feature of municipal life in late medieval Spain, especially in Castile. Since the medieval Spanish kings were for the most part unable to offer adequate protection, protective municipal leagues against bandits and other rural criminals, as well as against the lawless nobility, began to emerge in the 12th cent. These bodies, at first temporary but eventually permanent, took into custody and summarily tried suspects. Among the most powerful was the league of N Castilian and Basque ports, the *Hermandad de las Marismas,* formed in 1296 to safeguard domestic and foreign trade. The crown, which was only partly successful in regulating the activities of the *hermandades,* finally suppressed them in the late 15th cent. As one of their first acts after the war of succession, Ferdinand and Isabella established the centrally organized and efficient Holy Hermandad (Span. *Santa Hermandad*). Especially effective in rural Castile, this combined rural constabulary and judicial tribunal ensured personal security and public order, serving the additional purpose of reasserting royal jurisdiction and curbing aristocratic power. Each town provided archers and militia, and the tribunals consisted of unpaid local judges (*alcaldes*). A supreme council under the bishop of Cartagena as royal representative oversaw the entire organization. Although the *Santa Hermandad* soon achieved its purpose, the Spanish rulers, who had found it indispensable in fighting the Moors as well, kept the supreme council until 1498. *Hermandades* continued locally as modest local police units until their suppression in 1835.

Hermann, d. A.D. 21: see ARMINIUS.

hermaphrodite (hərmăf'rədīt''), animal or plant that normally possesses both male and female reproductive systems, producing both eggs and sperm. Many plants, including most flowering plants (angiosperms), are hermaphroditic, or monoecious; in these, male and female reproductive structures are present in the same plant, often in the same flower, and many monoecious plants are self-pollenators. Many lower animals, especially immobile species, are hemaphroditic; in some, such as earthworms, two animals copulate and fertilize each other. Some parasitic species, e.g., the tapeworm, are self-fertile as well as hermaphroditic, insuring reproduction where the parasite may be the only member of its species in the host. Many hermaphrodites are protandric, i.e., gametes of the two sexes are produced in the same organism, sometimes in the same gonad, but at different times; in such organisms (e.g., the oyster and the sage plant) self-fertilization is impossible.

Hermaphroditus (hərmăfrədī'təs), in Greek mythology, beautiful son of Hermes and Aphrodite. He scorned the nymph Salmacis, who prayed that they might never be separated. When Hermaphroditus swam in her stream, she combined with him, uniting male and female characteristics in one body—hence the origin of the word *hermaphrodite.*

Hermas (hûr'məs), Roman Christian. Rom. 16.14.

Hermas, Shepherd of, Christian apocalyptic work, composed in Rome A.D. c.139-155. It is a collection of revelations given to Hermas, a devout Christian, by an angel (Shepherd) and is divided into three sections: Visions, Mandates, and Similitudes. The teachings are concerned mostly with matters of penance, morals, and the condition of the church; they were highly regarded by early Christians. The book is extant in fragments of the original Greek and in complete Latin and Ethiopic texts. It has been published in English translation in collections of patristic literature.

Hermes (hûr'mēz), Roman Christian. Rom. 16.14.

Hermes, in astronomy: see ASTEROID.

Hermes, in Greek religion, son of Zeus and Maia. His functions were many, but he was primarily the messenger of the gods, particularly of Zeus, and conductor of souls to Hades. He was god of travelers and roads, of luck, of music and eloquence, of merchants and commerce, of young men, and of cheats and thieves. He was credited with having invented the lyre and the shepherd's flute. His most typical monument, the herma or herm, was a stone pillar which usually had a carved head on top and a phallus in the center, probably representing the god in his original role as the giver of fertility. The Hermaea, a riotous festival, was celebrated in his honor. In art, as exemplified by the statue *The Flying Mercury* by Giovanni Bologna (Bargello, Florence) Hermes is represented as a graceful youth, wearing a wide-brimmed winged hat and winged sandals and carrying the CADUCEUS. A famous statue by Praxiteles, which is located in the Heraeum at Olympia, Greece, shows Hermes with the child Dionysus. The Romans identified Hermes with Mercury.

Hermes Trismegistus: see HERMETIC BOOKS.

Hermetic books, ancient metaphysical works dealing essentially with the idea of the complete community of all beings and objects. Authorship of the books was attributed to the Egyptian god of wisdom, Thoth, whose name was sometimes translated into Greek as Hermes Trismegistus [Thoth the thrice great] and was therefore equated with the Greek god Hermes. The books treat of a variety of subjects, including magic, astrology, and alchemy, and were particularly influential in the 3d cent. with the Neoplatonists and in France and England in the 17th cent.

Hermione (hərmī'ənē), in Greek mythology, the only daughter of Helen and Menelaus. When Helen eloped with Paris, Hermione was abandoned to the care of Clytemnestra. She later married Neoptolemus, the son of Achilles. In Euripides' *Andromache,* she is carried off by Orestes who marries her after he has contrived the murder of Neoptolemus at Delphi.

hermit [from Gr.,=desert], one who lives in solitude, especially from ascetic motives. Hermits are known in many cultures. Permanent solitude was common in ancient Christian ASCETICISM; St. ANTHONY of Egypt and St. SIMEON STYLITES were noted hermits. Many extreme Franciscans (Spirituals) of the 13th and the 14th cent. were hermits, among them Pope St. Celestine. In the East the hermit, or eremetical, life was widely held to be the more perfect form of MONASTICISM and was open only to those who had first passed years in a monastic community. Monasticism in the West developed along the less rigorous communal lines; the CARTHUSIANS are well-known exceptions. The hermit or anchorite of the ancient church lived in the desert, commonly walled up in a cell with only a window. In medieval Europe the cell usually connected with a church. The ANCREN RIWLE was written for English anchoresses. JULIANA OF NORWICH was a famous English anchoress.

Hermitage, in France: see MONTMORENCY, France.

Hermitage, museum in Leningrad, one of the world's foremost houses of art. It was reconstructed in the neoclassical style in the 19th cent. from the original pavilion palace erected by Catherine II. Although opened to the public in 1852, it contained only the imperial collections until 1917. There are now more than 40,000 drawings, 500,000 engravings, and 8,000 paintings of the Flemish, French, Dutch, Spanish, and Italian schools, including many by Rembrandt, Rubens, Picasso, and Matisse, which represent only a fraction of the riches of the museum. The most popular section, "The Heroic Past of the Russian People," includes the War Museum and a tribute to Peter the Great. Another part is devoted to the life and works of Pushkin. The collections include the art of India, China, Egypt, pre-Columbian America, Greece, and Rome, as well as Scythian art from the Eurasian steppe. There are also tapestries, ivories, and furniture. Russian art is exhibited separately in Mikhailovsky Palace, which was opened in 1898.

Hermitage, home of Andrew Jackson, built 1819-31, central Tenn., E of Nashville. The house, a handsome example of a Tennessee planter's home, with a fine formal garden, was constructed of bricks made on the estate. It was rebuilt in 1835 after fire had seriously damaged the first structure. Jackson and his wife are buried in the plantation graveyard. A church that he built (1823) is on the grounds. See Stanley Horn, *The Hermitage* (1938).

hermit crab, a CRUSTACEAN distinguished from true crabs by its long, soft, spirally coiled abdomen terminating in an asymmetrically hooked tail. Most hermit crabs protect this vulnerable portion of their bodies by occupying the empty shells of periwinkles, whelks, and other gastropod mollusks. A few find other homes; for example, a species that inhabits the Indian Ocean lives in sections of old bamboo cane. When the hermit crab grows out of one shell it seeks a larger one, fighting for it if challenged. Sea anemones often attach themselves to these shells, obtaining free transportation and scraps of food in return for protecting their hosts. Hermit crabs are common beach scavengers in most parts of the world. Most species are marine, but some tropical forms, such as the robber crab, *Birgus latro,* are largely terrestrial. This species, the largest hermit crab, generally reaches over 1 ft (30 cm) in length. It becomes increasingly terrestrial and develops heavy armor as it matures into an adult, at which stage it is able to completely discard its adopted shell. With its great pincers the robber crab has been known to crack coconuts, which it obtains by climbing palm trees. Hermit crabs are classified in the phylum ARTHROPODA, class Crustacea, order Decapoda.

Hermite, Charles (shärl ĕrmēt'), 1822-1901, French mathematician. A professor at the École polytechnique, Paris (1869-76), and at the Faculty of Sciences (1869-97), he exerted a strong influence on the French school of mathematics. He made valuable contributions to the theory of numbers, the theory of elliptic functions, and the theory of equations (especially of the fifth degree). In 1873, Hermite proved the transcendence of the irrational number *e* (see separate article).

Hermit Kingdom: see KOREA.

Hermogenes (hərmŏj'ənēz), man at odds with Paul. 2 Tim. 1.15.

Hermon, Mount, Arabic *Jabal Ash Shaykh* [mountain of the chief] and *Jebel-eth-Thelj* [snowy mountain], on the Syria-Lebanon border. The highest of its three peaks (all of which are snow-covered in winter and spring) rises to 9,232 ft (2,814 m). Mt. Hermon, a sacred landmark in ancient Palestine, is mentioned often in the Bible as Hermon, Sion, Senir, and Shenir; its beauty is extolled in the Psalms. The name Baal-Hermon (Judges 3.3; 1 Chron. 5.23) records the reverence in which it was held by the worshipers of Baal. The Romans also revered it, as did the Druses (there is a Druse shrine near Hasbaya). The ancient city of CAESAREA PHILIPPI was at its foot. Mt. Hermon is traditionally designated as the scene of the Transfiguration.

Hermonthis (hərmŏn'thĭs), ancient city, N Egypt, 8 mi (13 km) S of Thebes. It was founded in prehistoric times and was prominent during the period of Roman supremacy. Originally the shrine of Month, a hawk-headed deity, Hermonthis has a fine temple built c.1500 B.C. and reconstructed by the Ptolemies. Modern Armant or Erment is on the site.

Hermopolis Magna, ancient city, S Egypt, on the Nile and near the modern Ashmunein. It was the chief seat for the worship of Thoth. At the modern Tunneh el Gebel, 7 mi (11 km) southwest of the site, is a Greco-Egyptian cemetery.

Hermosa Beach (hûrmō'sə), resort city (1970 pop. 17,412), Los Angeles co., S Calif., on Santa Monica Bay; inc. 1907. Surfboards are made there.

Hermosillo (ārmōsē'yō), city (1970 pop. 206,663), capital of Sonora state, NW Mexico, at the entrance to the gorge of the Sonora River. Hermosillo is a transportation and agricultural center in an irrigated area where cereals and cotton are grown and cattle are raised. Established in 1700 as an Indian town with a Jesuit missionary, the city was later renamed in honor of the Spanish general José María Gonzalez de Hermosillo.

Hermoupolis (ĕrmōō'pôlĭs) or **Síros** (sē'rôs), city (1971 pop. 13,502), capital of Cyclades prefecture, SE Greece, on the east coast of SÍROS island. It is the chief city of the CYCLADES and a major Aegean port and commercial center. It grew rapidly after being founded (c.1820) by refugees from Khíos and Psará islands.

Hernandarias: see ARIAS DE SAAVEDRA, HERNANDO.

Hernández. For some Spaniards thus named, see FERNÁNDEZ.

Hernández, José (hōsā' ārnän'dĕs), 1834–86, Argentine poet, journalist, and soldier. Hernández lived in the pampas as a child. He was the author of the national classic of gaucho literature, *Martín Fierro* (1872), and its sequel, *La vuelta de Martín Fierro* [the return of Martin Fierro] (1879, tr. 1936, 1948). The poem, written in colorful dialect, recounts the adventures of a wandering soldier-minstrel and glorifies the vanishing free life of the GAUCHO in the solitude of the Pampa.

Hernández, Miguel (mēgĕl'), 1910–42, Spanish poet, b. Orihuela. A completely self-taught writer, he absorbed the influence of the poets of the Golden Age and of the generation of GARCÍA LORCA. His poetry, both tender and vigorous, reflects his own experience with war, death, and social injustice. His works include *El hombre acecha* [man lies in wait] (1939) and *Cancionero y romancero de ausencias (1939; tr. Songbook of Absences,* 1972).

Hernández Colón, Rafael (räfäĕl' ĕrnän'dĕs kōlōn'), 1936–, governor of Puerto Rico (1973–). An honors graduate of Johns Hopkins Univ. (1956) and the Univ. of Puerto Rico law school (1959), he practiced law in Ponce, and was elected to the senate in 1968. He served as president of the senate and as president of the Popular Democratic party. In 1972 he decisively defeated Gov. Luis Ferré to become, at 36, the island's youngest governor; the election was a virtual referendum on statehood, which Hernández, who wanted a continuation of the commonwealth status, opposed.

Hernández Martínez, Maximiliano (mäk"-sēmēlyä'nō ĕrnän'dĕs märtē'nĕs), 1882–1966, president of El Salvador (1931–44). An admirer of fascist theories, he seized power during a palace revolt, then was elected president in 1935. He ruled dictatorially until he was ousted by a general strike led by students, which erupted after his bloody suppression of an army uprising. The revolt spread to Guatemala, where Jorge UBICO was similarly deposed. Hernández Martínez lived in exile in Honduras.

Herndon, William Henry, 1818–91, friend, law partner, and biographer of Abraham LINCOLN, b. Greensburg, Ky. In 1844 he became the junior member of the Springfield, Ill., law firm of Lincoln and Herndon, a partnership that was never dissolved. The two became close friends, and Herndon played a major role in Lincoln's early political career, managing the 1858 campaign against Senator Stephen Douglas. After Lincoln's assassination Herndon collected reminiscences of Lincoln's boyhood and youth from those who had known him and in his old age wrote, with Jesse Weik, *Herndon's Lincoln: The True Story of a Great Life* (3 vol., 1889). In it, Herndon presented a picture of Lincoln intended to counteract the heroic, almost mythical, view of him held by the public. The focus on Lincoln's personal life led to many distortions, however, and in the case of the Ann RUTLEDGE romance, serious inaccuracies. Although his work has been largely discredited, Lincoln scholars owe Herndon a large debt for his assiduous collection of materials relating to Lincoln's life. See D. H. Donald, *Lincoln's Herndon* (1948).

Herne, James A. (hûrn), 1839–1901, American actor and dramatist, b. Cohoes, N.Y., whose original name was James Aherne. He first appeared on the stage in 1859 and later gained prominence in San Francisco as stage manager and character actor. In association with David BELASCO he wrote and adapted several plays, the most notable being *Hearts of Oak.* In 1878, Herne married the actress Katherine Corcoran, for whom he wrote most of his plays. His dramas, distinguished by a homely as well as melodramatic realism, include *Margaret Fleming* (1891), *Shore Acres* (1893), and *The Reverend Griffith Davenport* (1899). Herne used American material, and his influence on the development of realistic character was enormous.

Herne (hĕr'nə), city (1970 pop. 104,077), North Rhine-Westphalia, W West Germany, a port on the Rhine-Herne Canal. It is an industrial center of the RUHR district; manufactures include textiles, radio and television sets, and machinery.

Herne Bay (hûrn), urban district (1971 pop. 25,117), Kent, SE England. It is a resort with 7 mi (11 km) of coast and 5 mi (8 km) of promenades. The town developed after a railroad was built in 1833.

hernia, protrusion of an internal organ or part of an organ through the wall of a body cavity. The hernia is enclosed by a sac formed by the lining of the cavity. It results from a weakness or rupture in the wall, usually where there is already a natural weakness. A hernia may be present at birth or acquired later in life after heavy strain on the musculature. Structurally weak points, e.g., where various blood vessels, nerves, and ducts enter or leave a body cavity, occur in areas such as the lower abdomen, the diaphragm, and the region around the navel. If the protruding structure is caught in the muscular aperture of the wall, the result is a strangulation of the part, or an incarcerated hernia. Prompt medical attention must be received or loss of blood and eventual gangrene may result. A small hernia usually bulges spontaneously under exercise and strain and recedes into the cavity when the subject relaxes. A truss or external pad held against the weak spot may be used to control a hernia. However, surgery is usually recommended, even for a mild hernia, since it may eventually enlarge.

Herning (hĕr'nĭng), city (1970 com. pop. 52,759), Ringkøbing co., central Denmark. It is an important manufacturing center with textile mills and machine shops. An annual textiles fair is held there.

Hero, Greek mathematician: see HERON OF ALEXANDRIA.

Hero, in Greek mythology, priestess of Aphrodite in Sestos. Her lover, Leander, swam the Hellespont nightly from Abydos to see her. During a storm the light by which she guided him blew out, and he drowned. Hero, in despair, then threw herself into the sea. Christopher Marlowe's poem *Hero and Leander* is based on the story.

hero, in Greek religion, famous person, who after his death, was worshiped as quasi-divine. The heroes might be actual great men and women, real or imaginary ancestors, or "faded" gods and goddesses (i.e., ancient gods who for some reason were demoted to human status). Homer treats his heroes as nobles and fighting men, but many Homeric heroes, such as Hector and Achilles, later became objects of worship. Hero cults were distinctly different from the attendance to the dead, which was to afford comfort in the afterlife. In hero w in the worship of all infernal powers, ritua performed at night, black animals were sacri and blood and other liquid offerings were pour beside the hero's tomb. The worship centered in general on the supposed place of the hero's tomb; the cult of some heroes, notably Hercules, was, however, widespread.

Herod, dynasty reigning in Palestine at the time of Christ. Antipater, fl. c.65 B.C., was founder of the family fortune. He was an Idumaean and gave refuge to Hyrcanus II (see MACCABEES), thus gaining a stronghold in Palestine. His son Antipater (d. 43 B.C.) was favored by Julius Caesar who made him (c.55 B.C.) virtual ruler of all of Palestine. The son of the second Antipater was Herod the Great (d. 4 B.C.) who gave the family its name. He was friendly with Marc Antony who secured him (37 B.C.–4 B.C.) the title of king of Judaea; after the battle of Actium he made peace with Octavian (later AUGUSTUS), who thereafter showed him great favor. He made great efforts to mollify the Jews by publicly observing the Law, by building a temple, and by reestablishing the Sanhedrin. He promoted Hellenization and adorned most of his cities, especially Jerusalem. Herod married 10 times, and the various families in the palace intrigued against each other continually. In his last years Herod was subject to some sort of insanity, and he became bloodthirsty. He executed (6 B.C.) Aristobulus and Alexander, his sons by Mariamne, granddaughter of Hyrcanus II. He executed (4 B.C.) Antipater, son of his first wife, when he found out that Antipater had instigated the intrigues that led to the execution of Aristobulus and Alexander. This was the Herod who was ruling at the time of Jesus' birth and who ordered the massacre of the Innocents (see Mat. 2). Herod divided his kingdom among his sons Archelaus, Herod Antipas, and Philip. Archelaus (d. after A.D. 6) ruled Palestine S of the Vale of Jezreel from 4 B.C. to A.D. 6 (Mat. 2.22); he was removed by Augustus after complaints by the Jews. Herod Antipas (d. after A.D. 39), tetrarch of Galilee and Peraea, was the Herod who executed John the Baptist and who was ruling at Jesus' death. He repudiated his wife, daughter of ARETAS, to marry his niece Herodias, wife of his half brother Herod Philip, whom she divorced to marry Herod Antipas. This affair gained Herod Antipas many enemies, and the vaulting ambitions of Herodias eventually ruined him. She drove him to seek a royal title, and he was banished by Caligula in A.D. 39 (Mat. 14; Mark 6; Luke 3; 23; Acts 13). Herod the Great's son Philip (d. A.D. 34) was tetrarch of the region E of Galilee; his kingdom was non-Jewish, and he pursued a successful romanizing and hellenizing policy. He was probably the best of his family; his wife was SALOME **1.** He built Caesarea Philippi. The eldest son of Aristobulus, Herod Agrippa I (d. A.D. 44), was a man of some ability. Out of friendship Caligula made him king (A.D. 39) of Philip's tetrarchy; later he was made (A.D. 41) ruler of S Syria and of Palestine E and W of the Jordan. He was strongly pro-Jewish, and he built extensively at Berytus (modern Beirut). He is mentioned in Acts 12. His son, Herod Agrippa II (b. c.100), received only the northern part of his father's kingdom, and that not until c.52. He was a poor ruler and alienated his subjects. His sister was BERENICE (d. A.D. c.28). After the fall of Jerusalem he went to Rome. See also Acts 25; 26. He was the last important member of his family. As a dynasty the Herods depended largely on the power of Rome. They are usually blamed for the state of virtual anarchy in Palestine at the beginning of the Christian era. The prime source is the history of JOSEPHUS. See studies by A. H. Jones (1938, repr. 1967), Samuel Sandmel (1967), Michael Grant (1971), and H. W. Hoehner (1972).

Herodas: see HERODES.

Herodes (hĭrō'dēz), fl. 3d cent. B.C., Greek poet. He wrote realistic mimes in choliambic verse often depicting vulgar situations. A papyrus containing some 700 readable lines by Herodes is extant. His name is also spelled Herodas or Herondas.

Herodes Atticus (Tiberius Claudius Atticus Herodes) (ăt'ĭkəs), c.101–c.177, Greek Sophist, rhetorician, and patron of learning, b. Marathon. A great public benefactor, he used his fortune to adorn Athens and other Greek cities. One speech, doubtfully attributed to him, is extant. The name also appears as Atticus Herodes.

Herodians (hĕrō'dēənz), Jewish political party of the early 1st cent. A.D., related to the dynasty of HEROD. Some have supposed that they were largely SADDUCEES. In the New Testament the Herodians are referred to, with the Pharisees, as being in opposition to Jesus (Mat. 22.16; Mark 3.6; 12.13).

Herodias (hērō'dēəs): see HEROD.

Herodion (hĭrō'dēən), Christian at Rome. Rom. 16.11.

Herodotus (hērŏd'ətəs), 484?–425? B.C., Greek historian, called the Father of History, b. Halicarnassus, Asia Minor. Only scant knowledge of his life can be gleaned from his writings and from references to him by later writers, notably Suidas. He may have been exiled from Halicarnassus for taking part in a revolution, and certainly he spent some time abroad (possibly in Samos); then he seems to have returned to his native city, where he may have had a part in overthrowing the tyrant Lygdamis before he left Halicarnassus permanently. He traveled along the coast of Asia Minor to the northern islands and to the shore of the Black Sea; he also at some time visited Mesopotamia, Babylon, and Egypt. By 447 B.C. he was in Athens, and in 443 he seems to have helped to found the Athenian colony of Thurii in S Italy, where he probably spent the rest of his life completing his history. That classic work, the first comprehensive attempt at secular narrative HISTORY, is the starting point of Western historical writing. It is primarily concerned with the story of the PERSIAN WARS, but the earlier books embody great quantities of material about the ancient world as Herodotus knew it, with long digressions and stories of all sorts, illustrating the diverse cultures of his time and earlier. It is divided into nine books named for the Muses (a division made by a later editor). The value of the work lies not in its accuracy but in its scope and the rich diversity of information as well as the charm of its anecdotal style. See the translation of his history by A. D. Godley (1922); studies by T. R. Glover (1924, repr. 1970), J. E. Powell (1938, repr. 1960), J. L. Myres (1953, repr. 1971), and C. W. Fornara (1971); W. W. How and Joseph Wells, *A Commentary on Herodotus* (2 vol., rev. ed. 1928); H. R. Immerwahr, *Form and Thought in Herodotus* (1966).

Heroic Age, in classical mythology: see AGE.

heroic couplet: see PENTAMETER.

heroin, narcotic drug synthesized from MORPHINE (see NARCOTIC). Originally produced in 1898, it was thought to be not only nonaddictive but useful as a cure for addiction, as well as capable of relieving morphine withdrawal symptoms. Later it was discovered to have the same pharmacologic effects as morphine and to be just as addictive. Although the manufacture and importation of the drug is restricted in the United States, and it is not used medically, heroin predominates in illicit narcotics traffic because it provides more potency for less bulk than morphine and is thus easier to smuggle. Drug pushers dilute it with milk sugar, or lactose, before selling it to addicts; QUININE is also added to imitate the bitter taste of heroin so the addict cannot tell how much heroin he is actually getting. See DRUG ADDICTION AND DRUG ABUSE.

Hérold, Louis Joseph Ferdinand (lwē zhôzĕf' fĕrdēnäN' ārôld'), 1791–1833, French composer. He composed a number of operas, two of which—*Zampa* (1831) and *Le Pré aux clercs* (1832)—were for a time very popular.

heron (hĕr'ən), common name for members of the family Ardeidae, large wading birds including the bittern and the egret, found in most temperate regions but most numerous in tropical and subtropical areas. Unlike the remotely related cranes and ibises, which fly with their heads extended straight forward, herons fly with their necks folded back on their shoulders. Their plumage is soft and drooping and, especially at breeding time, there may be long, showy plumes on the head, breast, and back. Herons are usually solitary feeders, patiently stalking their prey (small fish and other aquatic animals) in streams and marshes and then stabbing them with their sharp, serrated bills. Most herons roost and nest in large colonies called heronries; others are gregarious only at breeding time; and some are entirely solitary. The nests vary from a sketchy platform of twigs high in a tree to a bulky mass of weeds and rushes built on the ground among the marsh reeds. American herons include the great and little blue herons, the green heron, the yellow-crowned and the black-crowned night herons (the latter known also as night quawk, because of its cry), and the Louisiana heron, called by Audubon "the lady of the waters." The great white heron of Florida, a little larger (50 in./125 cm long) than the great blue, is a striking bird sometimes confused with the American egret. Other large white herons are common in Africa. The European night heron ranges to India and N Africa. The odd looking shoe-billed heron (or stork, a misnomer) is found along the White Nile and the boat-billed heron in tropical America. Herons are classified in the phylum CHORDATA, subphylum Vertebrata, class Aves, order Ciconiiformes, family Ardeidae.

Herondas: see HERODES.

Heron of Alexandria (hēr'ŏn) or **Hero,** mathematician and inventor. The dates of his birth and death are unknown; conjecture places them between the 2d cent. B.C. and the 3d cent. A.D. He is believed to have lived in Alexandria; although he wrote in Greek, his origin is uncertain. Several of his works survive either in Greek or in Latin translation. He wrote on the measurement of geometric figures, and a formula for finding the area of a triangle has been ascribed to him. Known for his study of mechanics and pneumatics, he invented many contrivances operated by water, steam, or compressed air; these include a fountain, a fire engine, siphons, and an engine in which the recoil of steam revolves a ball or a wheel.

Herophilus (hĭrŏf'ələs), fl. 300 B.C., Greek anatomist, called by some the father of scientific anatomy. A contemporary of Erasistratus at Alexandria, he made public dissections, comparing human and animal morphology. He studied the structure of the brain (which he regarded as the site of intelligence) and the spinal cord and distinguished between motor and sensory nerves. He also investigated the eye, the alimentary canal (he is credited with naming the duodenum), the reproductive organs, and the arteries and veins.

herpes simplex (hûr'pēz), an acute virus infection of the skin characterized by one or more blisters filled with clear fluid. These vesicles usually appear around the lips (where they are commonly known as cold sores), in the mouth (where they take the form of canker sores), and about the genitals. It is believed that invasion of the causative agent occurs in most persons during infancy and childhood, either as a systemic or severe local infection, which subsequently becomes dormant. The reappearance of blisters may be triggered by such factors as fever, infectious diseases, exposure to sunlight, menstruation, or pregnancy. The blisters usually last from 10 to 14 days. Treatment for recurrent herpes includes elimination of the precipitating conditions and local antibiotic treatment to prevent bacterial infection. See also HERPES ZOSTER (shingles).

herpes zoster, infection of a ganglion (nerve center) with severe pain and a blisterlike eruption in the area of the nerve distribution, also called shingles. The causative organism is a filtrable virus believed to be the same virus that causes chicken pox. Herpes zoster usually affects persons past middle life. It most often involves the area of the upper abdomen and lower chest, but may appear along other nerve pathways including that leading to the eye; serious ocular complications can lead to blindness. Although there is no specific treatment for the disease, it is generally nonrecurrent. Aspirin and other analgesics are used to relieve pain, although there is often residual neuralgic pain that is difficult to control.

Herrera, Abraham Cohen de (ār-rā'rä), c.1570–1635, Jewish philosopher and cabalist, also called Alonso Nuñez de Herrera and Abraham Irira. Born possibly in Portugal of a noble Marrano family, he may have been related to Gonzalo Fernández de Córdoba, conqueror and viceroy of Naples. Herrera went with his family to Italy, later becoming assistant to his uncle, the trading agent of the Moroccan sultan. As such, he was captured by the British while in Cadíz and held for ransom. Freed in 1600, he made his way to the Lowlands, finally settling in Amsterdam. His studies of Neoplatonism, as taught in the Florentine Academy according to the interpretation of Marsilio Ficino and as found in the Neoplatonic *Dialoghi d'Amore* of Judah ABRAVANEL, and his studies of Lurianic cabala (see LURIA, ISAAC BEN SOLOMON), prompted him to attempt a synthesis of these two traditions in his *Puerta del cielo* (n.d.). This work, circulating in the original Spanish only in manuscript and in its Hebrew translation and Latin abridgment, had a profound effect on religious developments in the Jewish and Christian communities and upon philosophers into the 19th cent., including Baruch Spinoza and Gottfried Wilhelm Leibniz. Herrera also wrote *Casa de Dios,* dealing with pneumatology and angels, and *Epítome y compendio de la lógica o dialéctica,* a treatise on logic (his only published work, n.d.).

Herrera, Fernando de (fārnän'dō thā ārā'rä), 1534–97, Spanish poet. One of the outstanding poets of the 16th cent. and the leader of the Seville school, he earned the name Herrera el Divino. He is remembered for his Neoplatonic love lyrics and sonnets inspired by Doña Leonor de Gelves and for his heroic odes on Don Juan of Austria and the victory of Lepanto. His annotated edition of the poetry of Garcilaso was a masterpiece of Renaissance criticism and analysis. Herrera's *Tomás Moro* (1592) was a defense of Sir Thomas More.

Herrera, Francisco de (fränthēs'kō), c.1576–1656, Spanish painter, engraver, miniaturist, and draftsman. He worked in Seville most of his life, executing religious and genre subjects. His style is broad and dynamic, with powerful accents of light and dark and expressive distortions. Herrera's most famous works are the *Triumph of St. Hermengild* (Seville) and *St. Basil Dictating His Rule* (c.1639; Louvre). From 1640 until his death he worked in Madrid. His son, **Francisco de Herrera,** the younger, 1622–85, studied still-life painting in Naples. Returning to Seville in 1656, he executed religious works. His masterpieces, the *Triumph of St. Hermengild* (Prado) and the *Triumph of St. Francis* (Seville Cathedral), both of the 1660s, show his loose and sketchy technique and bright, warm colors. In 1677 he became Charles II's court painter and master of royal works, designing architectural plans, including one, never executed, for the cathedral at Saragossa.

Herrera, José Joaquín (hōsā' hwäkēn'), 1792–1854, president of Mexico (1844–45, 1848–51). Rising to power after the collapse of Santa Anna's second presidential administration, he incurred the disfavor of ultraconservatives by attempting to avoid war with the United States; a revolution led by PAREDES Y ARRILLAGA resulted in his resignation. After the war he again held the presidency and attempted to reform the government, but his administration was hampered by Indian insurrections, political unrest, and a staggering national debt. He was succeeded by Mariano ARISTA. See biography by T. E. Cotner (1949, repr. 1969).

Herrera y Reissig, Julio (hōō'lyō ārā'rä ē rāsēk'), 1875–1910, Uruguayan poet. He belonged to a family prominent in public affairs but withdrew along with his bohemian followers to an attic known as the Tower of the Panoramas. He became the Uruguayan leader of MODERNISMO. The obscurity and preciosity of his verses and their fantastic, extravagant imagery show the influence of Luis de Góngora and of the French SYMBOLISTS. His *Obras completas* (1911–13) was published posthumously.

Herrera y Tordesillas, Antonio de (äntō'nyō thā ārā'rä ē tôrthāsē'lyäs), 1559?–1625, Spanish historian. Appointed official historiographer of Castile and the Indies under Philip II, he wrote a general history of the New World (1601), a history of Philip's reign (1601–12), and various other works dealing with his own times. He had access to official documents, and his facts are generally reliable.

Herreshoff, John Brown (hĕr'əs-hŏf), 1841–1915, American yacht and ship builder. Though totally blind from the time he was 15, he managed his own sail-boat building company until his brother, **Nathaniel Green Herreshoff,** 1848–1938, became his partner in 1878. Together they produced steam yachts and torpedo boats, but in 1891 they resumed the construction of sailing yachts, introducing new and radical features of design. The *Gloriana* won them a reputation, and they subsequently produced five successful defenders of the America's Cup—the *Vigilant* (1893), the *Defender* (1895), the *Columbia* (1899), the *Reliance* (1903), and the *Resolute* (built 1914; raced 1920). See C. B. Burnett, *Let the Best Boat Win: The Story of America's Greatest Yacht Designer* (1957).

Herrick, Robert, 1591–1674, English poet, generally considered the greatest of the CAVALIER POETS. Although he was born in London, he spent most of his childhood in Hampton. In 1607 he became apprenticed to his uncle, jeweler to the king, and remained in London until 1613. He was graduated from Cambridge, and sometime before 1627 he took orders. In 1627 he was chaplain in the duke of Buckingham's disastrous expedition to the Isle of Ré. Two years later Herrick was given the country living of Dean Prior in Devonshire, remaining there until 1647, when he was ejected because of royalist sympathies. He was restored to his living in 1662 and remained there until his death. Herrick never married, and the many women mentioned in his poems are probably imaginary. The bulk of his work is contained in the *Hesperides* (1648), which when it first appeared included his sacred songs called *Noble Numbers.* He was a disciple of Ben Jonson and his lyrics show considerable classical influence, but his greatness rests on his simplicity, his sensuousness, his care for design and detail, and his management of words and rhythms. Among the best known of his lyrics are "The Night Piece, to Julia"; the song commencing "Gather ye rosebuds while ye may"; "Corinna's Going a-Maying"; "To Anthea"; "Cherry-ripe"; and "Upon Julia's Clothes." Among his sacred poems is the fine piece "His Litany to the Holy Spirit." Herrick also excelled in the writing of epigrams and epitaphs. His reputation declined after his death, but in the 19th cent. he was recognized as a great lyricist. See edition of his poetical works by L. C. Martin (new ed. 1965); his memoirs ed. by D. Aaron (1963); studies by Frederick Moorman (1910, repr. 1962), and R. B. Rollin (1966).

Herrick, Robert, 1868–1938, American novelist, b. Cambridge, Mass., grad. Harvard, 1890. He was professor of English at the Univ. of Chicago from 1893 to 1923. Herrick wrote realistic social novels about the conflict between professional and personal values in American capitalistic society. His works include *The Common Lot* (1904), *The Memoirs of an American Citizen* (1905), *The Master of the Inn* (1908), *Together* (1908), *Clark's Field* (1914), *Waste* (1924), *Chimes* (1926), and *The End of Desire* (1932). See study by B. R. Nevius (1962).

Herrin, city (1970 pop. 9,623), Williamson co., S Ill.; settled 1818, inc. 1900. It is a trade center of an extensive coal-mining area. The Herrin Massacre occurred in 1922 during a countywide coal strike; clashes between unionized strikers and nonunion miners, who had been imported by the coal company, resulted in the deaths of about 25 people.

herring, common name for members of the large, widely distributed family Clupeidae, comprising many species of marine and fresh-water food fishes, including the sardine *(Sardinia)*, the menhaden *(Brevoortia)*, and the SHAD *(Alosa)*. Herrings are relatively small but very abundant; they swim in huge schools, feeding on plankton and small animals and plants. The adult common herring, *Clupea harengus*, found in temperate and cold waters of the North Atlantic, is about 1 ft (30 cm) long with silvery sides and blue back. It lays up to 30,000 eggs, which sink to the sea bottom and develop there; the young mature in three years. Other species lay their eggs in seaweed in shallow waters, and still others, the anadromous types, spawn in large rivers. Best known of these is the American shad, *Alosa sapidissima*. Another common anadromous herring is the alewife, *A. pseudoharengus* (15 in./37.5 cm), found along the Atlantic coast from Nova Scotia to South Carolina and landlocked in Lake Ontario and the Finger Lakes of New York. The menhaden is an extremely abundant species of the Atlantic coast of North America. It was used by the Indians to fertilize their cornfields (its name is the Narraganset word for "fertilizing"); a billion pounds of menhaden per year is converted into oil and fish meal. The skipjack, a streamlined, steel-blue herring 15 in. long, is found in the Mississippi River and the Gulf of Mexico. Its name, which is also applied to the much smaller and unrelated SILVERSIDES and to a much larger and unrelated bonito (see TUNA), describes any fish with a habit of leaping clear of the water. Of the smaller food herrings and related species, the anchovies and sardines are the most important. The American anchovies, *Engraulis encrasicholus*, belong to the closely related family Engraulidae, are about 4 in. (10 cm) long, inhabit warm seas, and are chiefly valuable as food for other fishes. Spanish and Italian anchovies, abundant in the Mediterranean area, are cured by a process involving fermentation; the small European herrings (called sprats, or brislings) are cured without fermentation and are sold as Norwegian, or Swedish, anchovies and sardines. The name sardine is also applied to various small fish packed with oil or sauce in flat cans. The true sardine from France, Spain, and Portugal is usually the young pilchard *(Sardinia pilchardus)* of Mediterranean and Atlantic coastal waters. Sardine fishing and canning are an important industry in Maine, where small herrings are used, and in California, where the sardine is a species closely related to the European pilchard. The larger herrings are dried, smoked, salted, or pickled and sold in nearly all parts of the world under such names as bloaters, kippers, and red herrings. The name sprat is sometimes applied to certain American species of commercial herring. Herrings are classified in the phylum CHORDATA, subphylum Vertebrata, class Osteichthyes, order Clupeiformes, family Clupeidae.

Herrings, Battle of the, 1429, episode in the siege of Orléans by the English in the Hundred Years War. The French, under Jean, comte de Dunois, attacked a supply train commanded by Sir John FASTOLF. The English, barricaded behind the wagons with herring barrels, repelled the attack. The action took place at Rouvray, a hamlet NW of Orléans.

Herriot, Édouard (ādwär' ĕryō'), 1872–1957, French statesman and man of letters. After beginning an academic career he turned to politics. A moderate leftist, anticlerical, and antimilitarist, he rose to leadership of the Radical Socialist (Radical) party, a dominant party in France from 1899 to 1940. In 1904 he was elected mayor of Lyons, an office he held until 1941 and again after 1945. He subsequently became a deputy, president of the chamber of deputies, member of several ministries, and three times premier (notably 1924–25 and 1932). His first premiership saw the evacuation of the Ruhr, occupied under his predecessor, Raymond POINCARÉ; the continued fall of the franc led to Herriot's resignation in 1925. During his term in 1932, Herriot sought a conciliatory policy among France, Great Britain, the United States, the Soviet Union, and Germany. At the DISARMAMENT CONFERENCE of 1932 he upheld in principle the demand for French security but submitted a modified plan to keep the conference from foundering. He was one of the few French statesmen to advocate payment by France of the WAR DEBTS to the United States; on this question his cabinet fell. An opponent of the Vichy government in World War II, Herriot was arrested in 1942 and taken to Germany in 1944. Freed in 1945, he resumed leadership of the Radicals, who had dwindled in size and had long ceased to be a leftist group. In 1956 he resigned the party presidency in protest against a party split. Long held in high personal esteem, Herriot served (1947–54) as president of the national assembly, which had replaced the chamber of deputies. He was also an ardent advocate of a European confederation, for which he set forth a plan in *The United States of Europe* (tr. 1930). Among his nonpolitical writings are *Madame Récamier* (tr. 1925) and a biography of Beethoven (tr. 1935).

Herrnhut (hĕrn'hōōt), town (1965 est. pop. 1,800), Dresden dist., SE East Germany. It was founded (1722) by Graf von ZINZENDORF as a colony of Moravian Brethren (see MORAVIAN CHURCH), and is today a Moravian center with archives, a publishing house, and a museum.

Herschel, family of distinguished English astronomers. **Sir William Herschel**, 1738–1822, originally named Friedrich Wilhelm Herschel, was a great pioneer in the study of the stars. Born in Hanover, Germany, the son of a musician, he early became a skilled performer on several instruments. He went to England in 1757 and worked as a musical conductor, organist, and teacher of music and studied mathematics and astronomy in his leisure time. He constructed telescopes and systematically explored the sky. On March 13, 1781, he discovered a new planet later named Uranus. Because of this discovery he was appointed private astronomer to the king (1782), and was then able to devote his time to astronomy. In 1789 at his home in Slough, Herschel erected his great telescope, with a 48-in. (122 cm) mirror and a focal length of 40 ft (12.2 m). With his powerful reflecting telescopes, Sir William penetrated farther into the distances beyond our solar system, covering the whole of the heavens several times during his lifetime. He discovered the sixth and seventh satellites of Saturn, determined the rotation period of Saturn, and studied the rotation of other planets. He concluded from the motions of double stars that they are held together by gravitation and that they revolve around a common center, thus confirming the universal nature of Newton's theory of gravitation. He cataloged over 800 double stars. His researches in the field of nebulas suggested a possible beginning of new worlds from gaseous matter. Before this time only about 100 nebulas had been known; Sir William's catalog contained about 2,500. He concluded that the whole solar system is moving forward through space, and he was able to indicate the point toward which he believed it to be moving. From 1781 to the time of his death, he presented many papers before the Royal Society. See biographies by J. B. Sidgwick (1955), Angus Armitage (1962), and Deborah Crawford (1968); study by M. A. Hoskin (1963). His sister, **Caroline Lucretia Herschel**, 1750–1848, discovered eight comets and three nebulas and from 1772 collaborated with her brother. She revised (1798) John Flamsteed's catalog of stars and arranged her brother's catalog of star clusters and nebulas, for which she received the gold medal of the Royal Astronomical Society in 1828. See M. C. Herschel, *Memoirs and Correspondence of Caroline Herschel* (1876). Sir William's son, **Sir John Frederick William Herschel**, 1792–1871, first distinguished himself as a mathematician at Cambridge but later turned to astronomy. He confirmed his father's observations of double stars, was able to add numbers of previously unrecognized pairs to those in the catalog, and extended his examination to include nebulas. He presented his results to the Royal Society in the form of a catalog of stars in 1833. In order to complete the survey of the heavens, he went to the Cape of Good Hope in 1834 and discovered and measured many previously unseen nebulas and clusters of stars in the southern sky. Among his books are *Outlines of Astronomy* (1849) and *A General Catalogue of Nebulae* (1864). The latter was revised by Johan Dreyer as *A New General Catalogue of Nebulae and Clusters of Stars* (1888), and, generally known as the NGC, it still serves as a standard reference source. Sir John also made contributions to the field of photography. He was the first to use sodium thiosulfate (hypo) as a fixing agent, and he introduced the terms "positive image" and "negative image." See his diaries and correspondence, *Herschel at the Cape*, ed. by D. S. Evans et al. (1969); biography by Gunther Buttman (tr. 1970).

Hersey, John (hûr'sē), 1914–, American novelist, b. China, of American parents, grad. Yale, 1936. His writings, many of which reflect his experiences as a war correspondent in World War II, are concerned with the problem of man's inhumanity to man. His first novel, *A Bell for Adano* (1944; Pulitzer Prize), depicts the American occupation of a rural town in war-torn Italy. Later novels include *The Wall* (1950), depicting the uprising of the Jews in the Warsaw Ghetto against the Nazis; *The War Lover* (1959); *The Child Buyer* (1960); *Letter to the Alumni* (1970); *The Conspiracy* (1972); and *My Petition for More Space* (1974). His nonfiction works include *Hiroshima* (1946), a powerful, penetrating, and objective report of the effects of atomic bombing, and *The Algiers Motel Incident* (1968), concerning an occurrence in the 1967 Detroit race riot.

Herskovits, Melville Jean, 1895–1963, American anthropologist, b. Bellefontaine, Ohio; educated at the Univ. of Chicago (Ph.B., 1920) and Columbia (Ph.D., 1923). After teaching at Columbia and at Howard Univ. he went to Northwestern Univ., where he taught anthropology from 1927. He did ethnographic research in Surinam, Haiti, Trinidad, and Brazil, but his most important work was done in Africa. Herskovits pioneered in the application of the principles of modern cultural anthropology to Negro ethnology. Among his works are *The American Negro: A Study in Racial Crossing* (1928), *Dahomey* (1938), *The Myth of the Negro Past* (1941), *Man and His Works* (1949; reissued 1955 as *Cultural Anthropology*), *Franz Boas* (1953), *Dahomean Narrative: A Cross-Cultural Analysis* (1958, with his wife, Frances S. Herskovits), and *The Human Factor in Changing Africa* (1962). See study by G. E. Simpson (1973).

Herstal (hĕr'stäl), Fr. *Héristal*, city (1970 pop. 29,600), Liège prov., E Belgium, on the Meuse River, an industrial suburb of Liège. It is the center of Belgium's armaments industry; other manufactures include iron and steel, motor vehicles, aircraft engines, and electrical equipment. Herstal was the residence of the early Carolingian mayors of the palace, including Pepin II, who was born there (8th cent.).

Herter, Christian Archibald, 1895–1966, U.S. Secretary of State (1959–61), b. Paris. After holding minor positions in the Dept. of State (1916–19) and the Dept. of Commerce (1921–24), he became editor of a Boston newspaper and later served (1931–43) in the Massachusetts state assembly, acting (1939–43) as its speaker. As a Republican member of the U.S. House of Representatives (1943–52), Herter gained a reputation as an internationalist and helped win passage of the Marshall Plan. He served as governor of Massachusetts (1953–57) and Undersecretary of State (1957–59) and in 1959 succeeded John Foster Dulles as Secretary of State. He wrote *Toward an Atlantic Community* (1963). See biography by G. B. Noble (1970).

Hertford, William Seymour, 1st **marquess and** 2d **earl of** (här'fərd, härt'-), 1588–1660, English nobleman; great grandson of Edward Seymour, duke of SOMERSET, and grandson of Lady Catherine Grey, through whom he had a claim to the throne. His secret marriage (1610) to Arabella STUART, cousin of James I, enraged the king, and he was imprisoned. He escaped and fled the country, but returned in 1616 after Arabella's death. Made a privy councilor (1640) and marquess of Hertford (1640), he fought well for Charles I in the civil war. He received his ancestor's dukedom of Somerset at the Restoration (1660).

Hertford, municipal borough (1971 pop. 20,379), county town of Hertfordshire, E central England, on the Lea River. Hertford is an agricultural market. There are several light industries, including brewing, flour milling, and the manufacture of leather goods and stationery. It was important even in Saxon times; there, in 672, the archbishop of Canterbury convened the first national church council. Near Hertford is one of England's leading schools, Haileybury College, founded in 1862. The school merged with the Imperial Service College in 1942.

Hertfordshire (här'fərdshĭr, härt'-), county (1971 pop. 922,128), 631 sq mi (1,634 sq km), E central England. The county town is Hertford, but Watford, Hemel Hempstead, Stevenage, and St. Albans are more important urban centers. The terrain is level except for an extension of the Chiltern Hills in the northwest. The chief streams are the Colne, the Lea, and the Stort, which drain into the Thames. Although one of London's "Home Counties," Hertfordshire is primarily an agricultural region, producing large quantities of wheat and hay as well as dairy products, vegetables, and flowers for the nearby London market. There are brickmaking, printing, brewing (especially in Watford), papermaking, and engineering industries. The county figured prominently in the military history of England, particularly during the Wars of the Roses (see ROSES, WARS OF THE).

Hertling, Georg, Graf von (gā'ôrkh gräf fən hĕrt'-lĭng), 1843–1919, German statesman and philosopher, imperial chancellor (Nov., 1917–Sept., 1918). He was professor of philosophy and a right-wing leader of the Catholic Center party in the Reichstag before he became (1912) prime minister and minister of foreign affairs of Bavaria. As chancellor he was unable to meet the conflicting demands of the military commanders, the Reichstag, and public opinion. His age and conservatism rendered him incapable of meeting the crisis that followed the collapse of the German war effort in the fall of 1918. He resigned and was succeeded by MAXIMILIAN, PRINCE OF BADEN. His philosophic works are strongly Roman Catholic; he was an authority on medieval scholasticism. He left memoirs.

Hertogenbosch, 's, Netherlands: see 'S HERTOGENBOSCH.

Hertwig, Oscar (ôs'kär hĕrt'vĭkh), 1849–1922, German embryologist. He studied medicine with Haeckel and Gegenbaur. In 1875 he established the fact that fertilization consists of the union of the nuclei of a male and a female sex cell. He studied the germ-layer theory (introducing the term *coelom*) and malformations of vertebrate embryos.

Hertz, Gustav (go͞os'täf hĕrts), 1887–, German physicist. He is noted for his work on the atom, and he shared with James Franck the 1925 Nobel Prize in Physics for research on the effects of the impact of electrons on atoms. He became professor at the Technical Institute, Berlin, in 1928 and also director of research at the Siemens works in 1935; in 1947 he undertook atomic research for the USSR.

Hertz, Heinrich Rudolf (Ger. hīn'rĭkh ro͞o'dôlf), 1857–94, German physicist. He confirmed J. C. Maxwell's electromagnetic theory and in the course of experiments (1886–89) produced and studied electromagnetic waves (known also as hertzian waves, or radio waves). He demonstrated that these are long, transverse waves that travel at the velocity of light and can be reflected, refracted, and polarized like light. Hertz also investigated electric discharge in rarefied gases. The unit of frequency called hertz was named in his honor. His writings include *Electric Waves* (1890, tr. 1893) and *Principles of Mechanics* (1894, tr. 1899).

hertz (hûrts), [for Heinrich R. Hertz], abbr. Hz, unit of frequency, equal to 1 cycle per second. The term is combined with metric prefixes to denote multiple units such as the kilohertz (1,000 Hz), megahertz (1,000,000 Hz), and gigahertz (1,000,000,000 Hz).

Hertzog, James Barry Munnik (hûrt'sŏg, hĕrt'-sôkh), 1866–1942, South African military and political leader. Before the South African War, in which he commanded a division of the Boer forces (1899–1902), he had been a judge in the Orange Free State. As minister of education in the Orange River Colony (1907–10), he insisted upon the teaching of Dutch as well as English in the schools. In the first cabinet of the Union of South Africa he was minister of justice (1910–12), but his active resistance to Louis Botha, then premier, and to the supremacy of Great Britain brought about a crisis, and he was dropped from the government. Hertzog then took the lead in organizing the National party, opposed to imperialism and aiming at a state independent of the British Empire. After 1924, when by an alliance between that party and the Labour party a coalition government was formed, he was prime minister for 15 years until Sept., 1939. His administrations protected domestic industries, passed measures of racial segregation, and disenfranchised the Bantu of the Cape Prov. Hertzog was at first inclined to appease Hitler, favoring a return of German colonial territories, but he advocated neutrality in World War II. Parliament then repudiated his anti-British stand. See biographies by C. M. van den Heever (1946) and Oswald Pirow (1958).

Hertzsprung, Ejnar (ī'när hĕrts'spro͝ong), 1873–1967, Danish astronomer. Although trained as a chemical engineer, Hertzsprung made his career in astronomy, specializing in exact photographic observations of stars. In 1905 he discovered high-luminosity, or giant, stars. In 1913 he calculated the distance to the Small Magellanic Cloud by a method still used for measuring galactic and intergalactic distances. His 1922 catalog of star colors and luminosities disclosed the absence of bright stars of intermediate color, called the Hertzsprung gap. Working independently, both Hertzsprung and the American astronomer H. N. Russell developed a graph in which the luminosity of a star is plotted against its surface temperature. Such a graph is now called a HERTZSPRUNG-RUSSELL DIAGRAM.

Hertzsprung-Russell diagram [for Ejnar Hertzsprung and H. N. Russell], graph showing the luminosity of a star as a function of its surface temperature. Each single point on the Hertzsprung-Russell (H-R) diagram represents a star in some collection of stars, such as a STAR CLUSTER or GALAXY. The position of the point representing a given star is determined by the star's luminosity and surface temperature. The luminosity, or absolute MAGNITUDE, increases upwards on the vertical axis; the temperature (or some temperature-dependent characteristic such as SPECTRAL CLASS or color) decreases to the right on the horizontal axis. It is found that the majority of stars lie on a diagonal band that extends from hot stars of high luminosity in the upper left corner to cool stars of low luminosity in the lower right corner. This band is called the main sequence. Stars called WHITE DWARFS lie sparsely scattered in the lower left corner. The giant stars—stars of great luminosity and size (see RED GIANT)—form a thick, approximately horizontal band that joins the main sequence near the middle of the diagonal band. Above the giant stars, there is another sparse horizontal band consisting of the supergiant stars. The stars in the lower right corner of the main sequence are frequently called red dwarfs, and the stars between the main sequence and the giant branch are called subgiants. The significance of the H-R diagram is that stars are concentrated in certain distinct regions instead of being distributed at random. This regularity is an indication that definite laws govern STELLAR STRUCTURE and STELLAR EVOLUTION. In population I regions (see STELLAR POPULATIONS) like the spiral arms of galaxies or open star clusters, the stars fall almost exclusively on the main sequence. In population II regions like the nuclei of galaxies and globular clusters, the stars are older and have evolved significantly. The most luminous stars have evolved furthest, and an H-R diagram of such a region will show the upper end of the main sequence depopulated and will show a well-developed giant branch. In such a diagram it appears that the main sequence has "burned down" from the top like a candle. Thus, the point at which the main sequence terminates and the giant branch begins is an indication of the age of a star cluster. A modified H-R diagram of the stars in a cluster of unknown distance can be used to determine the absolute magnitude, or luminosity, of the stars. Since the apparent magnitude of a star of given absolute magnitude depends on the star's distance, the observed apparent magnitude of the stars can be used to calculate the distance to the cluster. This method of determining distances is called spectroscopic parallax.

Heruli: see GERMANS.

Hervey of Ickworth, John Hervey, Baron (här'vē, hûr'vē), 1696–1743, English memoirist. A temperamental figure who served in various minor offices under Robert Walpole, he is chiefly remembered for his *Memoirs of the Reign of George II,* which provide an excellent source for the politics and intrigue of the court of George II. See edition by Romney

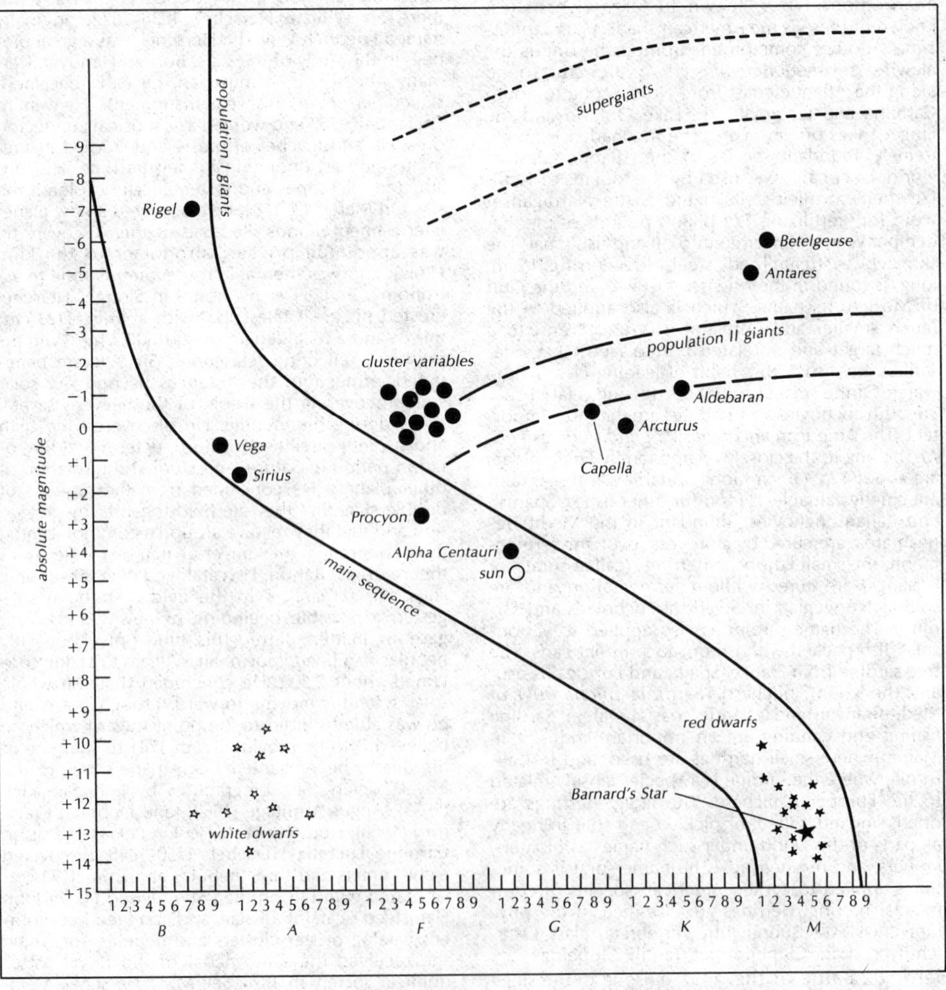

The Hertzsprung-Russell (H-R) diagram shows the absolute magnitudes of stars as a function of their spectral class, which is related to their temperature. Most stars fall along a diagonal, the main sequence, that extends from cool, dim red dwarf stars to hot, bright blue giant stars.

Sedgwick (3 vol., 1931, repr. 1970); biography by Robert Halsband (1973).

Herwegh, Georg (gā'ôrkh hĕr'vāk), 1817-75, German revolutionary poet. His best-known work, *Gedichte eines Lebendigen* [poems of a living man] (1841) stirred much liberal enthusiasm. Herwegh remained in exile after taking a leading part in the unsuccessful revolution (1848) in Baden.

Herzen, Aleksandr Ivanovich (ŭlyĭksän'dər ēvä'nəvĭch hâr'tsĭn), 1812-70, Russian revolutionary leader and writer. In 1834 he was sent to the provinces as a civil servant because he had belonged to a socialist political circle. In 1840 he returned to Moscow, where he met and influenced Belinsky. In 1847, Herzen left Russia, never to return. He settled first in Paris, where he supported the Revolution of 1848, and later in England, where he set up the first free Russian press abroad. *From the Other Shore,* a series of articles written mainly in 1848-49 (1855, tr. 1956), is a critique of the European revolutions of the period. In 1855 he published a survey of Russia under serfdom, together with a history of the revolutionary movements he had witnessed, in *My Past and Thoughts* (tr., 4 vol., 1968). He also published the influential weekly journal *Kolokol* (1857-62), which was officially banned but nevertheless widely read in Russia. Herzen wrote a popular novel, *Who Is to Blame?* (1847), about a liberal hero who becomes disillusioned with Russian society. He was a leading Westernizer until 1848, but then he modified his views toward the Slavophile faith in Russia's communal institutions, although he viewed the peasant communes as forerunners of a socialist society rather than as strongholds of tradition. See his *Selected Philosophical Works* (published in English in Moscow, 1956), and *My Past and Thoughts* (abr. by Dwight Macdonald, 1973); Richard Hare, *Pioneers of Russian Social Thought* (1951); Martin Malia, *Alexander Herzen and the Birth of Russian Socialism, 1812-1855* (1961, repr. 1965); E. H. Carr, *The Romantic Exiles* (1968).

Herzl, Theodor (tā'ōdôr hĕr'tsəl), 1860-1904, Hungarian Jew, founder of modern ZIONISM. Sent to Paris as a correspondent for the Vienna *Neue Frei Presse,* he reported on the Dreyfus affair. Appalled by the vicious anti-Semitism he observed, he decided that Jewish assimilation in Europe was impossible and that the only solution to the Jewish problem was the establishment of a Jewish national state. He stated his ideas in his famous pamphlet, *Der Judenstaat,* first published in 1896. Herzl organized the first Zionist World Congress (1897) and served as its president from its inception until his death. In 1949 his body was moved from Vienna to Jerusalem, for burial with the highest honors by the Israeli nation. See his diaries (ed. by Raphael Patai, tr. 1960); biographies by Jacob De Haas (2 vol., 1927), Alex Bein (tr. 1962), and Desmond Stewart (1974); study by Joseph Adler (1962).

Herzlia: see HERZLIYYA, Israel.

Herzliyya (hĕrtslē'ə), town (1970 est. pop. 38,500), central Israel, near the Mediterranean Sea. It is a resort with fine beaches. It was founded in 1924 and named for Theodor Herzl, the founder of modern Zionism. There are flour mills in the town, and citrus fruits are grown in the vicinity. The name is also spelled Herzlia.

Herzog, Johann Jakob (yō'hän yä'kôp hĕr'tsōkh), 1805-82, German Protestant theologian. His most important contribution was the founding and editing of the *Realencyklopädie für protestantische Theologie und Kirche* (22 vol., 1853-68).

Heschel, Abraham Joshua, 1907-1972, American Jewish philosopher and theologian, b. Warsaw. He succeeded Martin Buber as director of the Central Organization for Jewish Adult Education in Frankfurt and then taught in Warsaw and London before going to the United States in 1940. He taught philosophy and rabbinics at the Hebrew Union College, Cincinnati, and in 1945 became professor of Jewish ethics and mysticism at the Jewish Theological Seminary in New York City, where he remained until his death. He developed an influential philosophy and theology that sought to renew in man the ability to grasp the reality of the God-man relationship and of the holiness of life. He played a significant role in the civil rights movement and in the Christian-Jewish dialogue. Heschel's major works are *Man Is Not Alone: A Philosophy of Religion* (1951), *God in Search of Man: A Philosophy of Judaism* (1955), *The Prophets* (1962), *Who Is Man?* (1965), *Israel: An Echo of Eternity* (1969), and *A Passion for Truth* (1973). See F. A. Rothschild, ed., *Between God and Man* (1959); A. A. Cohen, *Natural and Supernatural Jew* (1962).

Hesdin, Jacquemart de (zhäkmär' də ādăN'), fl. c.1384-1411, Franco-Flemish manuscript illuminator. Jacquemart illustrated numerous BOOKS OF HOURS, including a number of manuscripts for Jean, duc de Berry. Influenced by Sienese painting, his ILLUMINATIONS included elaborate architectural interiors used to place figures in a believable space. Jacquemart is notable also for his marginalia—fanciful foliage and animal shapes forming a sort of frame to encompass the manuscript page.

Hesed (hē'sĕd), father of a steward of Solomon. 1 Kings 4.10.

Heshbon, ancient city, E of the Jordan. It was an Amorite capital, located at the crossroads of the east-west road to Jericho and the north-south road paralleling the Jordan. It was first allotted to Reuben, later to Gad. Num. 21.26; 32.37; Joshua 13.17; 21.39; Isa. 15.4; Jer. 48.2,34,35.

Heshmon (hĕsh'mŏn), town, in the Negev, near Beersheba. Joshua 15.27.

Hesiod (hē'sēəd, hĕs'-), fl. 8th cent.? B.C., Greek poet. He is regarded as having lived later than Homer, but there is no absolute certainty about the dates of his life. Hesiod portrays himself as a Boeotian farmer. Little is known of his life, however, except for the few scant references he makes to his family's origin and to a quarrel over property with his brother. He seems to have lost the dispute, and his most famous poem, the didactic *Works and Days,* is filled with caustic advice for his brother and maxims for farmers to pursue; its aim is to inculcate righteousness and efficiency. The "days" are days lucky or unlucky for particular tasks. Also ascribed to him are the *Theogony,* a genealogy of the gods, and *The Shield of Heracles.* He gave his name to the Hesiodic school of poets, rivals of the Homeric school. Homer and Hesiod codified and preserved the myths of many of the Greek gods of the classical pantheon. See F. Solmsen, *Hesiod and Aeschylus* (1949).

Hesperides (hĕspĕr'ĭdēz), in Greek mythology, daughters of Atlas. They lived in a fabulous garden located at the western extremity of the world. There they guarded (with the aid of the dragon Ladon) a tree that bore golden apples. Hercules killed the dragon and obtained the apples as one of his 12 labors.

Hess, Moses, 1812-75, German socialist. He was responsible for converting Engels to communism, and he early introduced Marx to social and economic problems. Hess played a prominent role in transforming Hegelian theory by conceiving of man as the initiator of history rather than as a mere observer. He was reluctant to base all human destiny on economic causes and class struggle, and he came to see the struggle of races, or nationalities, as the prime factor of past history. In *Rom und Jerusalem* (1862, tr. 1958) he declared that the freeing and uniting of humanity was the mission of the Jewish people and urged the establishment of a Jewish state in Palestine. See biographies by John Weiss (1960) and Mary Schulman (1963).

Hess, Dame Myra, 1890-1965, English pianist, studied at the Royal Academy of Music. She made a brilliant debut in London in 1907 and first appeared in the United States in 1922. Her playing was acclaimed for both virtuosity and poetic sensitivity. In 1939, and during World War II, Hess organized a series of lunch-time concerts in the National Gallery, London. These concerts, many of which she herself played, were immensely popular. In 1941 she was made Dame of the British Empire.

Hess, Rudolf, 1894-, German National Socialist leader, b. Alexandria, Egypt; son of a German merchant. In 1920 he became an ardent follower of Adolf Hitler and after the Munich "beer-hall putsch" (1923) shared Hitler's imprisonment. Hitler dictated *Mein Kampf* to him. In 1933 he became deputy Führer and minister without portfolio. In 1939, Hitler named him second in line of succession after Hermann GOERING. Hess created a worldwide sensation when he stole an airplane and flew (May, 1941) from Augsburg to Scotland (where he was arrested), apparently in an attempt to negotiate a peace agreement with Great Britain. At the Nuremberg war-crimes trial he was sentenced (1946) to life imprisonment at Spandau prison. Hess's behavior both before and during his trial raised questions as to his sanity. See James Douglas-Hamilton, *Motive for a Mission* (1971).

Hess, Victor Francis, 1883-1964, American physicist, b. Austria, Ph.D. Univ. of Graz, 1906. After teaching at the universities of Graz and Innsbruck, he came to the United States in 1938 and was later naturalized. He became professor of physics at Fordham Univ. in 1938. By means of instruments carried aloft in balloons, Hess and others proved that radiation that ionizes the atmosphere is of cosmic origin. For this discovery of cosmic rays he shared with C. D. Anderson the 1936 Nobel Prize in Physics. He attributed (1939) a 27-day cycle of cosmic-ray intensity to the magnetic field of the sun and correlated it with the 27-day period of rotation of the sun. He also worked on devising methods for detecting minute quantities of radioactive substances. His works include *Cosmic Radiation and Its Biological Effects* (with Jakob Eugster, 1940, 2d ed. 1949).

Hess, Walter Rudolf, 1881-1973, Swiss physiologist. For his work on the control of organs by certain areas of the brain he shared with Egas Moniz the 1949 Nobel Prize in Physiology and Medicine. He was (1917-51) professor and director of the physiology institute at the Univ. of Zurich.

Hesse, Eva (hĕs'ə), 1936-70, American sculptor, b. Hamburg, Germany. Hesse's sculpture displays an antiformalism that developed in the late 1960s in reaction against conventional geometric constructivism. Using such materials as latex, fiberglass, wire, and rope, she built numerous repeating series of large and eccentric forms. These were grouped irregularly over the floor or hung from the ceiling. Hesse's innovative work was cut short by her death from a brain tumor at 34.

Hesse, Hermann (hĕr'män), 1877-1962, German novelist and poet. A pacifist, he went to Switzerland at the outbreak of World War I and became (1923) a Swiss citizen. The spiritual loneliness of the artist and his estrangement from the modern world are recurring themes in Hesse's works. His novels, increasingly psychoanalytic and symbolic, include *Peter Camenzind* (1904, tr. 1961), *Unterm Rad* (1905, tr. *The Prodigy,* 1957), *Rosshalde* (1914), and *Demian* (1919, tr. 1923). One of his most famous and most complex novels, *Steppenwolf* (1927, tr. 1929), treats the dual nature of man; this theme is pursued in *Narziss und Goldmund* (1930, tr. *Death and the Lover,* 1932), perhaps his masterpiece. Among other works are *Das Glasperlenspiel* (1943, tr. *Magister Ludi,* 1949) and *Siddhartha* (1922, tr. 1951), a novella reflecting Hesse's interest in Oriental mysticism. The gentle, lyric quality of Hesse's prose is shared by the wistful, lamenting verse of his *Gedichte* (1922) and *Trost der Nacht* (1929). He was awarded the 1946 Nobel Prize in Literature. See his *Wandering* (autobiographical notes) (tr. 1972); studies by R. Rose (1965), T. Ziolowski (1965 and 1966), M. Boulby (1967), and G. W. Field (1972).

Hesse, Philip of: see PHILIP OF HESSE.

Hesse (hĕs, hĕs'ē, hĕs'ə), Ger. *Hessen,* state (1970 pop. 5,382,000), 8,150 sq mi (24,604 sq km), central West Germany. WIESBADEN is the capital. It is bounded by Baden-Württemberg and Bavaria in the south, Rhineland-Palatinate in the west, North Rhine-Westphalia and Lower Saxony in the north, and East Germany in the east. It includes the former Prussian province of Hesse-Nassau, which extended from the East German border in the east to the Rhine in the west and contained the cities of Kassel, Fulda, Marburg, Frankfurt, and Wiesbaden; it also includes, except for Rhenish Hesse, the former grand duchy (after 1918, state) of Hesse or Hesse-Darmstadt. Hesse-Darmstadt consisted of three territories—the northern portion, including the city of Giessen, was called Upper Hesse (Ger. *Oberhessen*); the southern portion, with Darmstadt, the former capital of the grand duchy, was called Starkenburg; the portion W of the Rhine, containing the historic cities of Mainz and Worms, was called Rhenish Hesse (Ger. *Rhein-Hessen*). In 1946, Rhenish Hesse was incorporated into the new state of Rhineland-Palatinate. Nearly all of Hesse is a hilly, agricultural land, heavily forested in parts. It has the Odenwald hills and the Taunus range and is drained by the Rhine, Main, Lahn, Eder, and Fulda rivers. Grain, potatoes, and fruit are grown, and cattle are raised there. Along the beautiful Rhine valley some of the finest German wines are produced. Industry is centered in the Frankfurt area and at Kassel, Wiesbaden, and Darmstadt. The chief manufactures include chemicals, machinery, and metal goods. Lignite, potash, and iron ore (notably along the Lahn River) are mined, and there are deposits of petroleum and natural gas in the state. Wiesbaden, Bad Homburg, and Bad Nauheim are among the numerous health resorts of Hesse. Frankfurt, Marburg, Giessen, and Darmstadt have noted universities. Hesse has no unified history. The cities of W Hesse—Frankfurt, Mainz, and Worms—are among the oldest in Germany and have played important roles in its history.

Frankfurt and Worms, however, were free imperial cities under the Holy Roman Empire, and Mainz was the capital of an archbishopric-electorate that included much of the present-day state. The prince-abbots of Fulda also were independent territorial princes. The history of the western part of Hesse-Nassau until 1866 is that of NASSAU. Other parts of present-day Hesse long belonged to the Rhenish Palatinate. Enfeoffed first to the dukes of Franconia, later to the counts of Thuringia, Hesse emerged in 1247 as a landgraviate immediately subject to the emperor under a branch of the house of Brabant. Landgrave Philip the Magnanimous (see PHILIP OF HESSE) was a leading figure in the German Reformation. At his death (1567) Philip's lands were divided among his four sons, with Kassel, Marburg, Rheinfels, and Darmstadt their respective capitals. Upon the demise, shortly afterward, of the Marburg and Rheinfels lines, the whole territory was held by the two remaining lines—Hesse-Kassel and Hesse-Darmstadt. Out of Hesse-Darmstadt the small landgraviate of Hesse-Homburg was taken in 1622. In the 18th cent. the rulers of Hesse improved their finances by letting mercenaries for hire; many of the Hessians who fought for the British in the American Revolution settled in the United States after the war. In 1803 the landgrave of Hesse-Kassel was raised to the rank of elector, and thereafter Hesse-Kassel became known as Electoral Hesse (Ger. *Kurhessen*). When Napoleon I created (1806) the Confederation of the Rhine, the landgraviate of Hesse-Darmstadt was raised to a grand duchy but Electoral Hesse was absorbed (1807) into the kingdom of Westphalia, created by Napoleon for his brother, Jérôme Bonaparte. The Congress of Vienna (1814–15) restored Electoral Hesse and awarded it and Hesse-Darmstadt substantial territorial gains. Electoral Hesse, the free city of Frankfurt, and Nassau, having all three sided with Austria in the Austro-Prussian War (1866), were annexed by Prussia and were merged (1868) in the province of Hesse-Nassau, of which Kassel became the capital. The former state of WALDECK was incorporated into Hesse-Nassau in 1929. The grand duchy of Hesse-Darmstadt also had sided against Prussia. It ceded Hesse-Homburg (which it had just acquired through the extinction of that line), but it continued under its own dynasty until the German revolution of 1918. In 1871, Hesse-Darmstadt joined the newly founded German Empire. Louis IV (reigned 1877–92) married Alice of Great Britain, daughter of Queen Victoria; through their daughter, who became the last empress of Russia, the disease of hemophilia was transmitted to the imperial house of Russia. The BATTENBERG (Mountbatten) family is a morganatic branch of the house of Hesse. In World War II nearly all the major cities of Hesse suffered severe damage.

Hesse-Darmstadt, Hesse-Homburg, Hesse-Kassel: see HESSE, West Germany.

Hesselius, Gustavus (hĕsē'lēəs), 1682–1755, American portrait painter, b. Sweden, settled c.1712 in Philadelphia. He was the earliest portrait painter and organ builder in the United States. His *Last Supper* (1721–22) for St. Barnabas Church in Prince Georges co., Md., was the first recorded public commission awarded an artist in the United States. Hesselius's portraits of himself and his wife (c.1740) are owned by the Pennsylvania Historical Society. In later life he was assisted by his son, **John Hesselius,** 1728–78, who later settled in Maryland and painted more than a hundred portraits of Southern and Philadelphia families. He was an early instructor of Charles Willson Peale.

Hesse-Nassau, former Prussian province: see HESSE; NASSAU.

Hessian fly, European gall GNAT, *Phytophaga destructor*, so named because it was first observed in America shortly after the Hessian troops landed on Long Island in the American Revolution. It is one of the most destructive pests of wheat, barley, and rye. There are usually two generations a year but may be up to five. The adults, 1/10 in. (0.25 cm) long, live only a few days. They lay their eggs on plants, usually where the stems are covered by leaves; the larvae feed on the sap and weaken the plants so that they cannot bear grain. In its winter pupa stage the INSECT looks like and is called a flaxseed. Some control is achieved by planting winter wheat late, after the adult females have laid their eggs. The Hessian fly is classified in the phylum ARTHROPODA, class Insecta, order Diptera, family Cecidomyiidae. See bulletins of the U.S. Dept. of Agriculture.

Hestia (hĕs'tēə), in Greek religion, goddess of the hearth; daughter of Cronus and Rhea. Both public and private worship of Hestia were widespread; she represented personal and communal security and happiness. An Olympian goddess (although some said she resigned her seat on Olympus to Dionysus), she was thought of as the kindest and mildest of the gods. She was of little mythological importance, appearing in only a few stories. The Romans identified her with VESTA.

Hesychius of Alexandria (hēsĭk'ēəs), fl. 5th cent.?, Alexandrian grammarian. Hesychius is known as the compiler of an invaluable lexicon, a glossary of unusual words and expressions occurring in Greek writings. The material is drawn from special languages (e.g., medical), from older poets, and from various dialects and languages. It is the source of virtually all the material now available on certain vanished languages, such as Macedonian.

Hetch Hetchy Valley, in Yosemite National Park, central Calif., on the Tuolumne River. It once rivaled Yosemite Valley in beauty and grandeur. O'Shaughnessy Dam (completed 1923; enlarged 1938) turned the valley into a lake c.9 mi (14 km) long, which is used for generating power and for supplying water to San Francisco by an aqueduct 156 mi (251 km) long.

heterosis (hĕt"ərō'sĭs): see HYBRID.

heterotroph, living organism that obtains its energy from carbohydrates and other organic material. All animals and most bacteria and fungi are heterotrophic. In contrast, AUTOTROPHS are organisms that use inorganic substances as energy sources and carbon dioxide as a carbon source.

heterozygote (hĕt"ərōzī'gōt): see GENETICS.

Heth, eponym of the Hittites. Gen. 10.15; 23.3; 25.10; 49.32; 1 Chron. 1.13.

Hethlon, unidentified town, on the northwest boundary of the Promised Land. Ezek. 47.15; 48.1.

Hettner, Alfred (äl'frĕt hĕt'nər), 1859–1942, German geographer and teacher; a founder of modern German geography. His methodology and his materialistic philosophy have had a great influence on Russian and Soviet geographers. He founded (1895) the journal *Geographisches Zeitschrift* and published *Die Geographie: ihre Geschichte, ihre Wesen und ihre Methoden* (1927).

Hevelius, Johannes (yōhän'əs hävā'lēo͝os), 1611–87, Polish astronomer, b. Danzig. From a finely equipped observatory in his house at Danzig, assisted by his wife Elizabeth, he made valuable observations of the moon's surface, discovered four comets, and collected data for his catalog of 1,564 stars. He recorded his pioneer study of lunar topography in *Selenographia* (1647), noted for excellent lunar maps. Many of the names given by him to the lunar mountains, craters, and other features are still used. He was one of the first to observe (1661) a transit of Mercury. He improved astronomical instruments but resisted the introduction of telescopic sights. His surname appears in various spellings, among them Hevel, Hewel, Hewelcke, and Höwelcke. See E. F. McPike, *Hevelius, Flamsteed, and Halley* (1937).

Hevesy, Georg von (gā'ôrkh fən hĕ'vĕshĕ), 1885–1966, Hungarian physicist and chemist. He received the 1943 Nobel Prize in Chemistry for his work on the use of isotopes as tracers in studying chemical processes. Hevesy was the first to apply the radioactive tracer technique to biology, and he later used it in medical research. He also discovered X-ray fluorescence analysis. He was codiscoverer of hafnium, element 72 in the periodic table. Hevesy became an associate of the Institute of Theoretical Physics, Copenhagen, in 1920 and also of the Institute for Research in Organic Chemistry, Stockholm, in 1943.

Hewes, Joseph, 1730–79, political leader in the American Revolution, signer of the Declaration of Independence, b. Kingston, N.J. He moved (1760) to Edenton, N.C., and became a wealthy merchant and shipper. As a member of the Continental Congress (1774–77), Hewes helped establish the American navy and obtained a commission for John Paul Jones in 1775. Reelected to Congress in 1779 he died during the session.

Hewitt, Abram Stevens (hyo͞o'ĭt), 1822–1903, American industrialist and political leader, b. Haverstraw, N.Y. He became a lawyer, and friendship with a son and marriage to a daughter of Peter COOPER shaped his career. Together he and Edward Cooper became (1847) iron manufacturers with Peter Cooper's backing. Hewitt promoted advanced methods of iron making and steel making and was interested in railroad development and mining. He built up one of the great fortunes of his day. Elected as a Democratic Representative to Congress in 1874, he served continuously, except for one term, until 1886. As chairman of the Democratic National Committee he directed Samuel J. Tilden's presidential campaign in 1876. During Rutherford Hayes's administration he led a Democratic House majority in securing the repeal of a number of radical Reconstruction measures. In 1886 he was elected mayor of New York City on a Tammany ticket, defeating Henry GEORGE and Theodore Roosevelt. As a reform mayor, he did not suit Tammany and was not renominated. He became a trustee of Columbia Univ. and was for many years connected with Cooper Union. Selections of his writings, edited by Allan Nevins, appeared in 1937. See study by Allan Nevins (1935, repr. 1967).

hex, witchcraft or one who works it. The word is of German origin, and beliefs connected with it spread from Europe to the United States, especially to the Pennsylvania Dutch country. The hex can be worked by either sex, but more commonly by a man, usually an amateur or professional hex "doctor." Such a person is thought to be able to control the forces of nature, cure sickness, and thwart the intentions of evildoers by means of stock magic formulas handed down from the Middle Ages and from gypsy practitioners. The colorful, geometric hex signs found on Pennsylvania Dutch barns are meant to protect the animals within from malicious curses, spells, and the EVIL EYE. Belief in hexerei, or witchcraft, remains widespread.

hexahedron (hĕk"səhē'drən): see CUBE; POLYHEDRON.

hexameter (hĕksăm'ətər) [Gr.,=measure of six], in prosody, a line to be scanned in six feet (see VERSIFICATION). The most celebrated hexameter measure is dactylic, which was the meter for most Greek and Latin poetry. In dactylic hexameter each foot may have a long syllable followed by two shorts, except the last, which has only two syllables, the first being long; any of the first four feet may have two long syllables. The origin of the dactylic hexameter is not known, but it appears first, and in its purest form, in Homer. Classical epic poets thereafter, including Vergil, used this meter, and it was extended to didactic and satirical literature, as in the works of Lucretius and Martial. In modern languages the only possible substitute for the quantitative differences that were essential to classical meters is in the stress accent; hence we have a noticeably singsong effect when English dactylic hexameter is read aloud. One of the few examples of its use in modern languages is in Longfellow's *Evangeline:* "Thís is the fórest priméval. The múrmuring pínes and the hémlocks." A famous dactylic hexameter in English prose is in Isa. 14.12: "Hów art thou fállen from héaven, O Lúcifer, són of the mórning!" The ALEXANDRINE is the only important modern hexameter.

Hexapla (hĕk'səplə) [Gr.,=sixfold], polyglot version of the Old Testament made by ORIGEN. It was mainly in six columns—a Hebrew text (probably the Masoretic), a Greek transliteration of it, and four Greek versions (Aquila's, Symmachus', Origen's Septuagint, Theodotion's). Some fragments survive.

Heyden, Jan van der (yän vän dər hī'dən), 1637–1712, Dutch architectural and landscape painter. He worked chiefly in Amsterdam. His charming pictures of towns, buildings, and public squares are painted with accuracy and precision. He is represented in many leading European collections. The Metropolitan Museum has two of his paintings. Van der Heyden improved the construction of fire engines and was made head of the Amsterdam fire department.

Heydrich, Reinhard (rīn'härt hī'drĭkh), 1904–42, German police official under the Nazi regime. Forced to resign (1931) from the navy for misconduct, Heydrich joined the SS (see NATIONAL SOCIALISM). He soon won Heinrich Himmler's confidence and in 1934 was appointed deputy chief of the Gestapo (see SECRET POLICE). He was deeply involved in planning the extermination of the Jews. In 1941, Heydrich was appointed protector of Bohemia and Moravia. His ruthless methods there and elsewhere and his numerous executions earned him the name "the Hangman of Europe." In May, 1942, he was shot by Czech patriots. Several days later the entire male population of the village of LIDICE was murdered in retaliation.

Heyerdahl, Thor, 1914–, Norwegian explorer and anthropologist, b. Larvik, Norway. He carried out research in the Marquesas Islands in 1937–38 and studied the Indians of British Columbia in 1939–40. To support his thesis that the first settlers of Polynesia were of South American origin, he made the crossing from Peru to the Tuamotu Islands on a primitive raft with five companions in 1947. This voyage is described in *Kon Tiki* (tr. 1950). In 1970,

Heyerdahl sailed, in a papyrus boat, from Morocco to Barbados, in an attempt to prove that ancient Mediterranean civilizations could have sailed in reed boats to America. This adventure is described in *The Ra Expeditions* (tr. 1971). His other writings include *American Indians in the Pacific* (1952); *Aku-Aku* (tr. 1958); *Sea Routes to Polynesia* (1968). See biography by Arnold Jacoby (1967).

Heym, Georg (gā'ôrkh hīm), 1887–1912, German poet and novelist of early EXPRESSIONISM. Rebelling against the new romanticism, Heym created the "demon" metropolis. This became his symbol for the tyrannization of man and nature, which he embodied in grotesques of fear and chaos. His works include the poetry collections *Der ewige Tag* [the eternal day] (1911) and *Umbra vitae* (1912), a novel, *Der Dieb* [the thief] (1913), and the tragedies *Die Athener Ausfahrt* [the Athenians' sally] (1907) and *Atalanta* (1911).

Heymans, Corneille (kôrnā'yə hī'mäns), 1892–1968, Belgian physiologist. His contributions to the physiology of circulation include a study of the sensory mechanism through which arterial blood pressure is maintained under a reflex mechanism. He discovered the importance of the carotid sinus in regulating the respiratory center; for this finding he received the 1938 Nobel Prize in Physiology and Medicine. He became professor at the Univ. of Ghent in 1930.

Heyse, Paul (poul hī'zə), 1830–1914, German realistic writer. Besides the 120 novellas on which his reputation rests, he wrote some 50 plays, 6 novels, and many fine translations, especially of Italian poets. He was the first German to receive the Nobel Prize in Literature (1910). His most famous story is *L'Arrabbiata* (1855, tr. *The Fury,* 1855); other well-known works include the novels *Children of the World* (1873, tr. 1882) and *The Romance of the Canoness* (1886, tr. 1887), as well as *The Maiden of Treppi* (1858, tr. 1874) and *Andrea Delfin* (1859, tr. 1864), which are novellas. Heyse's writings are elegant, polished, and psychologically probing.

Heyward, DuBose (dəbōz' hā'wərd), 1885–1940, American author, b. Charleston, S.C. His first published work was a volume of poetry, *Carolina Chansons* (1922), written with Hervey Allen. Heyward's story of Negro life on the Charleston waterfront, *Porgy* (1925), was dramatized by Heyward and his wife Dorothy in 1927. In 1935 it was made into a folk opera, *Porgy and Bess,* with the score by George Gershwin. Heyward's later works include *Mamba's Daughters,* a story of Negro life, which the Heywards also successfully dramatized (1939).

Heyward, Thomas, 1746–1809, political leader and soldier in the American Revolution, signer of the Declaration of Independence, b. near Charleston, S.C. He was a delegate to the Continental Congress (1775–78), but he resigned to become a judge in South Carolina. Heyward fought at Charleston and was captured (1780) when the British took the city.

Heywood, John (hā'wo͝od), 1497?–1580?, English dramatist. He was employed at the courts of Henry VIII and Mary I as a singer, musician, and playwright. At the accession of Elizabeth I in 1564 Heywood, who was a Roman Catholic, fled to Belgium, where he stayed for the rest of his life. Important in the development of English comedy, Heywood was the most famous writer of the interlude, a short comic dialogue. Chief among his interludes are *The Play of the Weather* (1533) and *The Four P's* (c.1543). His other works include epigrams, proverbs, and ballads. See his works (ed. by B. A. Milligan, 1956).

Heywood, Thomas, 1574?–1641, English dramatist. A prolific writer, he claimed to have written and collaborated on more than 200 plays, most of which are now lost. Although he wrote dramas based on English history, classical mythology, and romantic adventure, he is most famous for those dealing with contemporary English life. Heywood's best play, *A Woman Killed with Kindness* (1603), is one of the finest examples of domestic tragedy in the English drama. His other notable plays include *The Fair Maid of the West* (1631) and *The London Traveler* (1633). A professional actor as well as a playwright, he wrote an *Apology for Actors* (1612) in reply to attacks against the theater by the Puritans. See studies by Otelia Cromwell (1928, repr. 1969), A. M. Clark (1931, repr. 1967), and F. S. Boas (1950).

Heywood, municipal borough (1971 pop. 30,418), Lancashire, NW England. Products include cotton goods, metal goods, boilers, industrial inks, carpets, paper, rope, and machinery. In 1974, Heywood became part of the new metropolitan county of Greater Manchester.

Hezeki (hĕz'ēkī), descendant of Benjamin. 1 Chron. 8.17.

Hezekiah (hĕzəkī'ə), king of Judah, son and successor of Ahaz. During his reign Sennacherib of Assyria routed (701 B.C.) the rebellious Jews and exacted a high indemnity from them. However, a plague in the Assyrian army saved (690 B.C.) Judah from a second invasion by Sennacherib. Hezekiah's reign was marked by the prophecies of ISAIAH and MICAH and by reforms to purify the religion of Israel by eliminating certain Canaanite practices. The country also experienced great material prosperity. His son and successor was Manasseh. 2 Kings 18–20; 2 Chron. 29–32; Isa. 36–39; Prov. 25.1. Ezekias: Mat. 1.10. The Hezekiah of 1 Chron. 3.23 is a different person, otherwise unknown. See HIZKIJAH.

Hezion (hē'zēŏn), Syrian king, the grandfather of BENHADAD **1.** 1 Kings 15.18.

Hezir (hē'zĭr). **1** Chief priest in the time of David. 1 Chron. 24.15. **2** Signer of the covenant. Neh. 10.20.

Hezrai (hĕz'rāī) or **Hezro** (-rō), one of David's guard. 2 Sam. 23.35; 1 Chron. 11.37.

Hezron (hĕz'rən). **1** Ancestor of David. Gen. 46.12; Num. 26.21; Ruth 4.18. Esrom: Mat. 1.3; Luke 3.33. **2** Son of Reuben. Gen. 46.9; Num. 26.6. For towns called Hezron, see HAZAR-ADDAR and KERIOTH **2.**

Hf, chemical symbol of the element HAFNIUM.

Hg, chemical symbol of the element MERCURY.

Hialeah (hīəlē'ə), city (1970 pop. 102,452), Dade co., SE Fla., NW of Miami; inc. 1925. Its industries include printing and the manufacture of apparel, furniture and fixtures, metal and plastic goods, transportation equipment, and building supplies. Nearby Miami International Airport is a major employer. Hialeah Park Race Track, featuring the famed flamingos, is in the city.

Hiawatha (hī'əwä'thə), fl. c.1550, legendary chief of the Onondaga Indians of North America. He is credited with founding the IROQUOIS CONFEDERACY. He is the hero of the well-known poem by Henry Wadsworth Longfellow. See T. R. Henry, *Wilderness Messiah* (1955).

Hibben, John Grier, 1861–1933, American educator, b. Peoria, Ill., grad. Princeton (B.A. 1882; Ph.D., 1893) and studied at the Univ. of Berlin and Princeton Theological Seminary. He was minister of the Presbyterian Church at Chambersburg, Pa., from 1887 to 1891. He taught logic at Princeton from 1891 to 1912, when he succeeded Woodrow Wilson as president of the university. While president, Hibben inaugurated the schools of architecture, engineering, and public affairs. His textbooks *Inductive Logic* (1896) and *Deductive Logic* (1905) were widely used; his educational ideas are revealed in *A Defense of Prejudice* (1911, repr. 1970).

Hibbing, village (1970 pop. 16,104), St. Louis co., NE Minn., on the Mesabi iron range 90 mi (145 km) from the Canadian border; inc. 1893. Iron mining, formerly the major industry, has declined, but the manufacture of mining equipment is important. In 1917, Hibbing was moved 2 mi (3.2 km) south to make room for a large open-pit iron mine. A junior college is there.

hibernation (hī"bərnā'shən) [Lat.,= wintering], practice, among certain animals, of spending part of the cold season in a more or less dormant state, apparently as protection from cold when a normal body temperature cannot be maintained and food is scarce. Hibernating animals are able to store enough food in their bodies to carry them over until food is again obtainable. They do not grow during hibernation, and all body activities are reduced to a minimum: there may be as few as one or two heartbeats a minute. Cold-blooded animals (e.g., insects, reptiles, amphibians, and fish) must hibernate if they live in environments where the temperature—and hence their own body temperature—drops below freezing. Some insects pass their larval stage in a state of hibernation; in such cases hibernation is closely associated with the reproductive cycle (see LARVA; PUPA). However, most warm-blooded animals, i.e., birds and mammals, can survive freezing environments because their metabolism controls their body temperatures. Many hibernating animals seek insulation from excessive cold; bears and bats retire to caves, and frogs and fish bury themselves in pond bottoms below the frost line. Analogous to hibernation is aestivation, a dormant period of escape from heat and drought. Other methods of avoiding excessively high or low temperatures and destructive increases or decreases in the water supply are encystment and ensuing dormancy, e.g., in plant seeds and bacteria, and migration. Some animals, such as rabbits, raccoons, and squirrels, store food against scarcity and spend cold periods asleep in their burrows, though they may emerge on warm days.

Hibernia: see IRELAND.

hibiscus: see MALLOW.

hiccup or **hiccough,** involuntary spasmodic contraction of the diaphragm followed by a sharp intake of air, which is abruptly stopped by a sudden, involuntary closing of the glottis (opening between the vocal cords); the consequent blocking of air produces a repeated characteristic sharp sound, or *hic.* It is believed that hiccup is caused by stimulation of the nerve pathways or centers that control the muscles of respiration, particularly the diaphragm. In most instances hiccups are transient, although their course may sometimes be shortened by such measures as holding the breath, deep regular breathing, or rebreathing into a paper bag to increase the carbon dioxide content of the body. However, persistent hiccups may last for weeks, months, or even years. When hiccups are prolonged, therapy may include the administering of certain drugs, inhalation of carbon dioxide, and even interruption of the phrenic nerve either by injection of an anesthetic or by surgery.

Hickel, Walter Joseph, 1919–, U.S. Secretary of the Interior (1969–70), b. Ellinwood, Kan. After moving to Alaska in 1940, he founded (1947) a construction company and built it into a multimillion-dollar firm. He led the fight for Alaskan statehood and served (1966–69) as governor. Appointed Secretary of the Interior by President Nixon, Hickel proved to be a strong environmentalist; he supported a bill that placed liability on oil companies for offshore oil spills and demanded environmental safeguards in the construction of the Alaskan pipeline. After he sharply criticized (May, 1970) President Nixon's hostility to student antiwar demonstrators, relations between the two men deteriorated until Hickel was forced (Nov., 1970) to resign. He is the author of *Who Owns America?* (1971).

Hickok, Laurens Perseus, 1798–1888, American philosopher, b. Bethel, Conn. Trained for the ministry, he served as a clergyman (1823–36) and professor of theology (1836–55) before going to Union College as professor of philosophy (1855–66) and president (1866–68). He was one of the first American philosophers to utilize the work of Immanuel Kant. Among Hickok's many works were *The Logic of Reason, Universal and Eternal* (1875), *A System of Moral Science* (1853, rev. ed. 1880), and *Empirical Psychology* (1854, rev. ed. 1882).

Hickok, Wild Bill, 1837–76, American frontier marshal, b. Troy Grove, near Ottawa, Ill. His real name was James Butler Hickok. He took part in the Kansas struggle preceeding the Civil War, was a driver of the Butterfield stage line, and gained fame as a gunfighter. He served as a Union scout in the Civil War. After the war he became deputy U.S. marshal at Fort Riley (1866), marshal of Hays, Kansas (1869), and marshal of Abilene (1871). His reputation as a marksman in desperate encounters with outlaws made him a figure of frontier legend. After a tour of the East with BUFFALO BILL (1872–73), Hickok went to Deadwood (now in S. Dak.) where he was murdered by Jack McCall. See biographies by F. J. Wilstach (1926), W. E. Connelley (1933), Richard O'Connor (1959), and J. G. Rosa (1964).

Hickory, city (1970 pop. 20,569), Burke and Catawba counties, W N.C., at the foot of the Blue Ridge Mts.; inc. 1870. The city's manufactures include hosiery, furniture, porcelain, electrical and electronic products, and textiles. Lenoir Rhyne College is there. The city also has a museum of art and an Indian museum.

hickory, any plant of the genus *Carya* of the family Junglandaceae (WALNUT family); deciduous nut-bearing trees native to E North America except for a single species found in SE Asia. The pecan (*C. pecan*) is one of the most important nut trees of the United States. The tree, the tallest of the hickories, is native from S Illinois through the Mississippi valley to central Texas and Mexico. A rich food (containing 70% or more fat), the pecan is the most popular American nut after the peanut and is used as a table delicacy, in ice cream, and for confectionery, especially the traditionally Southern pecan pies and pralines. Cultivated varieties with unusually thin shells, called paper-shelled pecans, have been developed, but wild pecans are also gathered and sold in quantity. Other hickories having edible nuts that are marketed to a lesser extent include the shagbark hickory (*C. ovata*) of the E United States, the shellbark hickory (*C. laciniosa*), chiefly of the Midwest and South, and the mockernut, or white, hickory (*C. alba* or *C.*

tomentosa) of the E United States. The hickory nut of commerce is usually that of the shagbark (the names shagbark and shellbark are often used interchangeably), which has a relatively thin shell. The Indians made a food of ground hickory nuts. The abundant oil or fat of the nuts was a staple article in the diets of both Indians and early colonists. The pignut (*C. glabra*) has small nuts of variable quality, usually bitter, that have been used as mast for fattening hogs. Hickories have been so exploited for their valuable wood that they are in danger of extinction. The wood of several species is extremely hard, heavy, strong, and elastic. It is a preferred wood for golf clubs, wheel spokes, and tool handles and wherever strength and resilience are required. Prairie schooners often carried hickory sticks on their westward treks to replace broken wagon parts and ox yokes. The wood, used also for furniture, is prone to decay in moisture. Shagbark hickory is the most valuable for timber. Hickory is classified in the division MAGNOLIOPHYTA, class Magnoliopsida, order Junglandales, family Junglandaceae.

Hickory Hills, village (1970 pop. 13,176), Cook co., NE Ill., a suburb of Chicago; inc. 1951.

Hicks, Edward, 1780–1849, American painter and preacher, b. Bucks co., Pa. A member of the Society of Friends, he became a noted back-country preacher. At the same time he supported himself by painting carriages, signs, furniture, and the like. Hicks's fame rests on *The Peaceable Kingdom,* of which nearly 100 versions exist (among them two at the N.Y. State Historical Association and the Brooklyn Mus., respectively). A completely untrained primitive artist, he borrowed many of his animal groups from European engravings. His paintings have great charm and appeal. In his day Hicks was famed only as a preacher. See study by Alice Ford (1952, repr. 1973).

Hicks, Elias, 1748–1830, American Quaker preacher, b. Hempstead, N.Y. He worked on his Long Island farm between his preaching tours, which established his reputation as one of the most able Quaker preachers of the times. Hicks worked against slavery, publishing his *Observations on Slavery* in 1811. When a division in the Society of Friends occurred in 1827, he was the leader of the liberal separation party, to which the name Hicksite was unofficially given. See biographies by H. W. Wilbur (1910) and Bliss Forbush (1956).

Hicks, Granville, 1901–, American writer, b. Exeter, N.H. A member of the Communist party, he edited *The New Masses* and wrote a Marxist interpretation of American literature, *The Great Tradition* (1933). In 1939 he resigned from the party and in the 1950s was a "cooperative" witness before the House Committee on Un-American Activities. In addition to several novels he has written *John Reed: The Making of a Revolutionary* (1968) and *Literary Horizons: A Quarter Century of American Fiction* (1970). See his autobiography, *Part of the Truth* (1965).

Hicks, Sir John Richard, 1904–, British economist, grad. Balliol College, Oxford, 1931. He was a professor at the Univ. of Manchester (1938–46) before joining the faculty of Oxford (1946). At the time of his retirement in 1971, Hicks was a research fellow at Oxford's All Souls College. A specialist in equilibrium theory, his writings stress the interrelationships among economic markets. He was knighted in 1964 and, with Kenneth ARROW, received the 1972 Nobel Memorial Prize in economics. His most important book is *Value and Capital* (1939).

Hicks, Thomas, 1823–90, American portrait painter, b. Newtown, Pa. He studied at the Pennsylvania Academy of the Fine Arts and abroad, where he lived for several years. He settled in New York City in 1849 and there became one of the outstanding portraitists of his day. The New-York Historical Society has some interesting portraits; others of President Lincoln, Henry Ward Beecher, Harriet Beecher Stowe, Edwin Booth as Iago, Hamilton Fish, and Daniel W. Middleton are in the Capitol, Washington, D.C. The Metropolitan Museum has a portrait of the artist's wife.

Hicks, Thomas Holliday, 1798–1865, American statesman, b. Dorchester co., Md. In 1857 he was elected governor of Maryland as a Know-Nothing. After the states of the lower South seceded in 1860–61, he refused to yield to the popular demand to call a special session of the Maryland legislature because he feared that the legislators would rush blindly into secession. Subsequently, with Federal troops occupying the state and secessionists, including legislators, under arrest, Maryland elected a thoroughly Unionist legislature, which sent Hicks to the U.S. Senate, where he served from Dec., 1862, until his death. See G. L. P. Radcliffe, *Governor Thomas H. Hicks of Maryland and the Civil War* (1901); W. B. Hesseltine, *Lincoln and the War Governors (1948).*

Hicksville, uninc. city (1970 pop. 48,075), Nassau co., SE N.Y., on Long Island; founded 1648. It is chiefly residential, with some manufacturing.

Hidalgo (ēthäl'gō), state (1970 pop. 1,156,177), 8,058 sq mi (20, 870 sq km), central Mexico. PACHUCA DE SOTO is the capital. Crossed by the Sierra Madre Oriental, the state is extremely mountainous; in the southern and western areas, however, are plains and fertile valleys lying within Mexico's central plateau. The climate is warm in the lower valleys, temperate on the plateau, and cold in the mountains. Hidalgo's chief crop is maguey (see AMARYLLIS), grown on the central plateau. Tobacco, cotton, and coffee are also cultivated, and textiles are manufactured in Hidalgo. The state's main industry, however, is mining (particularly around Pachuca). Hidalgo is a leading national producer of silver, gold, copper, lead, iron, and sulfur. The territory was occupied successively by the Toltec (whose capital was Tollán—now TULA), the Chichimec, and the Aztec Indians. Conquered by the Spanish in 1530, it was part of the province and state of Mexico until it became the separate state of Hidalgo in 1869. There are several hot springs in Hidalgo.

Hidalgo (hĭdăl'gō), in astronomy: see ASTEROID.

hidalgo (hēdäl'gō) [contraction of Span. *hijo de algo*=son of something], term designating the lowest degree of Spanish nobility, a rank above the ordinary gentry but below the great lords. The status was granted either directly from the crown (*hidalgo de carta*) or was inherited through birth (*hidalgo de sangre*). The term was known as early as the 12th cent.; the prolonged warfare to reconquer Spain from the Moors especially necessitated the continuous expansion of this knightly class. Although it did not have any political importance, the rank gave its members privileges such as use of the title *Don* and considerable exemption from taxation. The hidalgo is a familiar character in Spanish literature, often being portrayed as a vagabond knight.

Hidalgo del Parral (ēthäl'gō dĕl päräl') or **Parral,** city (1970 pop. 61,729), Chihuahua state, N Mexico, on the Parral River. The city, a rail and highway junction, is one of Mexico's large mining centers, especially for silver, which has been mined in the region since the 16th cent. From 1640 to 1731, the city was the capital of the colonial province of Nueva Vizcaya. One of the first cities to take up arms during Francisco Madero's revolution of 1917, it was later (1923) the site of the assassination of Francisco (Pancho) Villa.

Hidalgo y Costilla, Miguel (mēgĕl' ēthäl'gō ē kōstē'yä), 1753–1811, Mexican priest and revolutionary, a national hero. A creole intellectual, he was influenced by the French Revolution. As parish priest of the village of Dolores, Hidalgo attempted to improve the lot of the natives. Under his direction the Indians set out olive groves and vineyards, built a porcelain factory, engaged in the silk industry, and began other forbidden projects. As a result he antagonized the government and was also brought before the Inquisition to be tried for heresy, but the case was suspended. When Napoleon invaded Spain and captured Ferdinand VII, the aftermath in Mexico, as in other South American countries, was the birth of separatist movements. Hidalgo was one of a group of creoles who met at Querétaro and planned a revolution. The plot was soon discovered, but he took a bold step and openly adopted the cause of independence. On Sept. 16, 1810, he issued the *Grito de Dolores* [cry of Dolores], launching the revolt against Spain. Hidalgo gathered an immense army of Indians. With the banner of Our Lady of Guadalupe (see GUADALUPE HIDALGO) as his standard, he injected religious zeal into the insurrection, but the Indians' cry for freedom and land was just as fervent. Ignacio ALLENDE and other creole officers who had taken part in the conspiracy now brought colonial militia into Hidalgo's ranks, and certain radical creoles also joined. The church and the landowning creoles remained hostile. Success attended Hidalgo's ill-organized army: Guanajuato, Guadalajara, and Valladolid fell to the revolutionaries, and they set out for Mexico City. They defeated a royalist force at Monte de los Cruces (Oct. 30, 1810) but did not pursue their victory. Rather, on Hidalgo's orders, the insurgents turned away from the capital and, retiring northwestward, were routed at Aculco. At Guadalajara, Hidalgo reorganized the army that was sent forth only to be crushed by CALLEJA DEL REY, the royalist general, at CALDERÓN BRIDGE (Jan. 17, 1811). Hidalgo, Allende, and the other leaders made their way north, hoping to reach the United States, but were betrayed and captured. Hidalgo, after being degraded (defrocked) by the Inquisition, was shot. His schemes for social reform, exemplified in the emancipation of slaves, the cessation of the tribute tax, and the return of the land to the Indians, had come to nothing, but the war for Mexican independence continued; leadership of the movement was passed on to MORELOS Y PAVÓN. See studies by Hugh Hamill (1966) and J. A. Canuso (1967).

Hidatsa Indians (hēdät'sä), North American Indians, also known as the Minitari and the Gros Ventre. Their language belongs to the Siouan branch of the Hokan-Siouan linguistic stock (see AMERICAN INDIAN LANGUAGES). After their separation from the CROW INDIANS, with whom they were united before the historic period, they occupied several agricultural villages on the upper Missouri River in North Dakota and were in close alliance with the occupants of other villages, the ARIKARA INDIANS and the MANDAN INDIANS. The Hidatsa villages, with circular earth lodges, were enclosed by an earthen wall. Among other Hidatsa traits were the cultivation of corn and an annual organized buffalo hunt. They had a complex social organization and elaborate ceremonies, including the sun dance. After the smallpox epidemic of 1837, they moved up the Missouri and established themselves close to the trading post of Fort Berthold. Together with the Arikara and Mandan they reside on the Fort Berthold Reservation in North Dakota and number some 2,700. See A. W. Bowers, *Hidatsa Social and Ceremonial Organization* (1965).

Hiddai (hĭd'āī, hĭdā'ī), one of David's guard. 2 Sam. 23.30. Hurai: 1 Chron. 11.32.

Hiddekel, Hebrew name for the TIGRIS.

Hideyoshi (Hideyoshi Toyotomi) (hēdāō'shē), 1536–98, Japanese warrior and dictator. He entered the service of NOBUNAGA as a common soldier and rose to become his leading general. After Nobunaga's death Hideyoshi ruled as civilian dictator. He set out to unify Japan, violently disrupted by a century of civil strife. Hideyoshi subdued the military Buddhist sects, conquered Kyushu, and in 1584 came to terms with IEYASU. He froze the class structure, then forbade (1587) peasants to bear arms; by 1590, with the defeat of the Hojo clan, Hideyoshi was ruler of a united Japan. Although best remembered for his military exploits, Hideyoshi as a civil administrator decreed a land survey, revised the land tax, developed a code of maritime law, and encouraged foreign trade. He at first received Christian missionaries cordially. Then, believing them a political danger because of their proselytizing zeal, he proscribed (1587) their activities and persecuted some of them. In 1592 he attempted to conquer China but succeeded only in subduing Korea; after his death the Japanese withdrew from Korea. He erected monuments, beautified Osaka, his capital, and encouraged the arts.

Hiel (hī'ĕl), rebuilder of Jericho. 1 Kings 16.34.

Hierapolis (hīərăp'əlĭs), ancient city of Phrygia, W Asia Minor, 7 mi (11.3 km) N of Laodicea and on a plateau 500 ft (152 m) above the Lycus valley (in present-day Turkey). Devoted to the worship of Leto in ancient times, it became an early seat of Christianity (Colossians 4.13). The Romans greatly enlarged and improved the city, building a large theater and numerous baths about the hot springs for which the site is famous. Today these springs still feed falls that cover the rocks with gleaming white deposits of lime, creating vast falls of crystal incrustations. Near the city was a deep chasm called the Plutonium, which the ancients thought led to the nether regions; the fissure no longer exists. Extensive ruins survive from the Roman and Christian periods.

hierarchy: see MINISTRY and ORDERS, HOLY.

hieratic: see HIEROGLYPHIC.

Hiero I (hī'ərō), 5th cent. B.C., Greek Sicilian ruler, tyrant of Syracuse (478–467 B.C.). He succeeded his brother Gelon. A noted patron of literature, Hiero had Simonides, Pindar, and Aeschylus at his court. Some of them honored him in verse for his victorious contests in the Greek games. The greatest glory of his career was his part in the defeat of the Etruscans at sea at Cumae in 474 B.C. As a ruler Hiero was a despot. The name also appears as Hieron I.

Hiero II, d. c.215 B.C., Greek Sicilian ruler, tyrant of Syracuse (c.270–c.215 B.C.). He showed such ability and distinction after PYRRHUS left Sicily (275 B.C.) that he was made commander in chief of the Syracusans and was later chosen (c.265 B.C.) tyrant or king. Against the Mamertines, who had taken possession of Messana, Hiero's forces and those of the

Carthaginians laid siege (265 B.C.), but when the Romans under Appius Claudius intervened successfully, the Syracusans withdrew, defeated. Hiero then entered into a treaty with the Romans, which recognized his dominion over SE Sicily and the east coast to Tauromenium (Taormina). As an ally of Rome, Syracuse furnished money and fighting forces against Carthage in the Punic Wars. Hiero faithfully abided by the terms of the peace. As a ruler he was just, prudent, and generous, and he was a patron of the arts. ARCHIMEDES, his relative, had his encouragement in the construction of great engines of warfare. The name also appears as Hieron II.

hieroglyphic (hī″rəglĭf′ĭk, hī″ərə-) [Gr.,=priestly carving], type of WRITING used in ancient EGYPT. Similar pictographic styles of Crete, Asia Minor, and Central America and Mexico are also called hieroglyphics (see MINOAN CIVILIZATION; ANATOLIAN LANGUAGES; MAYA; AZTEC). Interpretation of Egyptian hieroglyphics, begun by Jean-François CHAMPOLLION, is virtually complete; the other hieroglyphics are only very imperfectly understood. The distinguishing feature of hieroglyphics is that they are conventionalized pictures used chiefly to represent meanings that seem arbitrary and are seldom obvious. Egyptian hieroglyphics appear in several stages: the first dynasty (3110–2884 B.C.), when they were already perfected; the Old Kingdom; the Middle Kingdom, when they were beginning to go out of

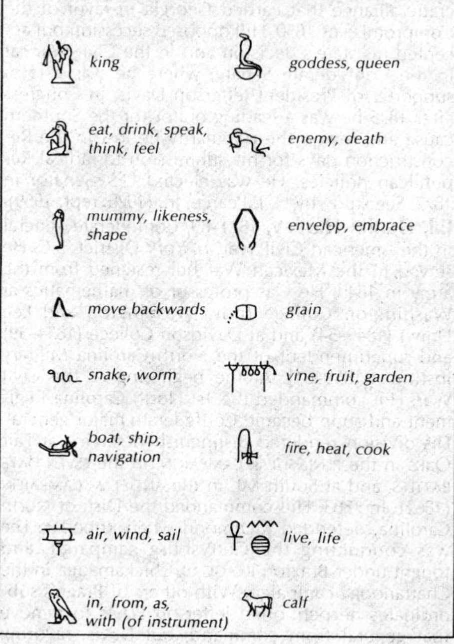

Examples of hieroglyphics

use; the New Empire, when they were no longer well understood by the scribes; and the late hieroglyphics (from 500 B.C.), when the use of them was a tour de force. With a basic number of 604 symbols, hieroglyphics were written in several directions, including top to bottom, but usually from right to left with the pictographs facing the beginning of the line. There were in general three uses to which a given hieroglyphic might be put (though very few were used for all three purposes): as an ideogram, as when a sign resembling a man meant "man" or a closely connected idea (thus a man carrying something meant "carrying"); as a phonogram, as when an owl represented the sound *m*, because the word for owl had *m* for its principal consonant; or as a determinative, an unpronounced symbol placed after an ambiguous sign to indicate its classification (e.g., an eye to indicate that the preceding word has to do with looking or seeing). As hieroglyphic developed, most words came to require determinatives. The phonograms were, of course, the controlling factor in the progress of hieroglyphic writing, because of the fundamental convenience of an ALPHABET. In the Middle Kingdom a developed cursive, the hieratic, was extensively used for private documents where writing speed was essential. In the last centuries B.C. a more developed style, the demotic, supplanted the hieratic. Where the origin of most hieratic characters could be plainly seen in the hieroglyphics, the demotics were too conventionalized to bear any resemblance to the hieroglyphics from which they had sprung. See A. H. Gardiner, *Egyptian Grammar* (3d ed. 1957); Nina Davies, *Picture Writing in Ancient Egypt* (1958); E. A. Budge, *Egyptian Language* (8th ed. 1966).

Hieron: see HIERO.

Hieronymus: see JEROME, SAINT.

Higashikurume (hēgä″shēko͞oro͞o′mä), city (1970 pop. 78,075), Tokyo Metropolis, E central Honshu, Japan. It is a residential suburb of Tokyo.

Higashi-Matsuyama (hēgä′shē-mätso͞oyä′mä), city (1970 pop. 50,383), Saitama prefecture, E central Honshu, Japan. It is a suburb of Tokyo and an agricultural and communications center.

Higashi-Osaka (hēgä′shē-ōsä′kä), city (1970 pop. 500,173), Osaka prefecture, W central Honshu, Japan, on the Onii River. It is a residential and industrial suburb of Osaka.

Higden, Ranulf, d. c.1364, English chronicler. He wrote the *Polychronicon*, a universal history, interesting chiefly for its display of the geographical, scientific, and historical knowledge of its time. It was translated from Latin into English by John of Trevisa in 1387 and again by an anonymous translator in the early 15th cent. William Caxton printed (1482) Trevisa's translation plus several continuations to bring it to 1460. See study by John Taylor (1966).

Higgaion (hĭgā′yən), in Ps. 9.16, musical direction of unknown significance.

Higgins, William, b. 1762 or 1763, d. 1825, Irish chemist. After study at Oxford he became supervisor of the Royal Dublin Society's mineralogical collection and in 1800 the Society's professor of chemistry. He worked on the chemistry of bleaching and the detection of adulterants in commercial alkalies. Although the discovery of the chemical atomic theory is usually credited to English scientist John Dalton, Higgins claimed that the discovery was his own.

Higginson, Francis, 1586–1630, American colonial clergyman, b. Leicestershire, England, M.A. Cambridge, 1613. Admitted (1614) to the ministry of the Church of England, he later became a nonconformist and in 1629 sailed with a group of settlers for Salem, Mass. His journal of the first months at Salem was sent back to England and printed with the title *New-England's Plantation* (1630). Elected minister of the settlement, he drew up a confession of faith and a covenant that were adopted. He soon died as a result of hardships suffered the first winter. See biography by T. W. Higginson (1891), which contains his complete journal.

Higginson, Henry Lee, 1834–1919, American philanthropist. He founded (1881), and for many years supported, the Boston Symphony Orchestra. He also donated to schools and colleges. See Bliss Perry, ed., *Life and Letters of Henry Lee Higginson* (1921).

Higginson, Thomas Wentworth, 1823–1911, American author, b. Cambridge, Mass. A Unitarian minister, he was one of the early leaders in the abolitionist movement. His *Army Life in a Black Regiment* (1870) recounts his experiences as colonel of the first regiment of Negroes in the Civil War. He retired from the army in 1864 and devoted his time primarily to writing and to furthering liberal reforms. A versatile author and an able scholar, he wrote essays; several popular histories; a novel, *Malbone* (1869); biographies of Margaret Fuller (1884), H. W. Longfellow (1902), and J. G. Whittier (1902); and such reminiscences of political and literary friends as *Cheerful Yesterdays* (1898). In 1890–91, with M. L. Todd, he edited in two volumes the *Poems* of Emily Dickinson. Although he failed to realize the true measure of her genius, he encouraged Dickinson's writing. See his *Letters and Journals, 1846–1906* (1921); biography by his wife Mary Thatcher Higginson (1914, repr. 1972).

high-bush cranberry: see HONEYSUCKLE.

High Church: see ENGLAND, CHURCH OF.

higher criticism, name given to a type of biblical criticism distinguished from textual or lower criticism. The aim of higher criticism was to apply to the Bible the same principles of science and historical method applied to secular works for which no claim of divine inspiration could be made. It depended largely on the study of internal evidence, although available data from linguistics and archaeology were incorporated. The primary questions were determination of authenticity, chronological order of the different parts, and identity of the writers. Higher criticism may be said to have begun with the French scholar Jean Astruc in the middle of the 18th cent.; it was continued principally by German scholars such as Johann Gottfried Eichhorn, Ferdinand Christian Baur, and Julius Wellhausen in the 19th cent. Their findings were disputed among themselves and bitterly attacked by others, who felt that the sole purpose of the criticism was to discredit the Christian religion. The term fell into disuse as biblical archaeology and related sciences expanded; it is not used by biblical scholars today.

Highet, Gilbert Arthur, 1906–, American classicist, b. Glasgow, Scotland. He was educated at the Univ. of Glasgow (M.A., 1929) and at Oxford, where he was a fellow (1932–38) of St. John's College. In 1951 Highet became a citizen of the United States. He was a professor of Greek and Latin at Columbia Univ. from 1938 to 1950 and has been Anthon professor of Latin language and literature since 1950. His writings include *The Classical Tradition* (1949); *The Art of Teaching* (1950); *Juvenal the Satirist* (1954); *Poets in a Landscape* (1957); *The Anatomy of Satire* (1962); *Vergil's Aeneid* (1972). His wife, the novelist **Helen MacInnes,** 1907–, b. Glasgow, is noted for her fast-paced, intricately plotted novels of espionage, including *Above Suspicion* (1941), *While Still We Live* (1944), *Decision at Delphi* (1960), and *The Snare of the Hunter* (1974).

Highgate, residential area within Camden, Islington, and Haringey boroughs, London, England. The house where Francis Bacon died is in Highgate, and Herbert Spencer, George Eliot, and Karl Marx are buried in Highgate cemetery in Camden. Highgate School, a public school founded in 1565, is there.

Highland. 1 Uninc. community (1970 pop. 12,669), San Bernardino co., SE Calif., in a citrus-grove area at the foot of the San Bernardino Mts. It has citrus-packing plants and some light industry. A state hospital is there, and Norton Air Force Base is adjacent to the community. **2** Residential town (1970 pop. 24,947), Lake co., extreme NW Ind., in the Chicago metropolitan area; settled 1850 as Clough Postal Station, inc. 1910.

Highland fling, national dance of Highland Scotland. Composed in the duple rhythm of the strathspey, a variety of reel, it is characterized by the Scotch snap (a succession of sixteenth notes alternating with dotted eighths). The "fling" emphasizes a kicking gesture.

Highland Park. 1 City (1970 pop. 32,263), Lake co., NE Ill., a suburb of Chicago on Lake Michigan; inc. 1869. It is a retail business and medical center for the North Shore area, and the summer home of the Chicago Symphony Orchestra. Fort Sheridan is adjacent to the city. **2** City (1970 pop. 35,444), Wayne co., SE Mich., within the confines of Detroit; laid out 1818, inc. as a city 1917. Tractors, auto parts, packaging equipment, and food products are made, and there are trucking and warehousing industries. The world headquarters (designed by Minoru Yamasaki) of the Chrysler Corp. are there. Highland Park grew mainly after Henry Ford established a factory in the city in 1909. A junior college is there. **3** Residential borough (1970 pop. 14,385), Middlesex co., N central N.J., on the Raritan River opposite New Brunswick; inc. 1905. **4** Town (1970 pop. 10,133), Dallas co., N Texas, a residential suburb within the confines of Dallas; inc. 1913.

Highlands, mountain region in the northern extremity of Scotland. It consists roughly of that part of Scotland north of the imaginary line from Dumbarton to Stonehaven excluding the Orkneys, the Shetlands, Caithness co., and the lower coastal area of the northern mainland; the Hebrides are usually included. Famous for its rugged beauty, the land is unsuitable for farming and since the 18th cent. has suffered from a steady decline of population—partly caused, initially, by the failure of the JACOBITE rebellions. Crofting, fishing, and distilling are the main occupations; in recent years the tourist trade has been an important source of income. Since World War II the British government has sponsored the forestry industry and several schemes of hydroelectric development in the Highlands as part of a comprehensive effort to stem the flow of emigration and to relieve poverty and chronic depression. The early history of the region is not well known. By the 11th cent. the Scottish monarchy was definitely centered in the Lowlands, and except when raids of Highland marauders in the Lowlands spurred punitive expeditions by the king, the Highland lairds were left to run their own affairs. Until its decline in the 19th cent. the Scottish Gaelic language was the core of Highland culture, which resisted innovations from England and the Lowlands with singular tenacity. The distinctive marks of the Highlands, the dress and the clan system, now in disuse except as sentimental archaisms, were products of the late Middle Ages. The dress, including the kilt, tartan, sporran, tam, and dirk, was outlawed by the British government in the 18th cent., when it became alarmed at the continued interest in the Jacobites that animated the Highlands—the Highlands had furnished the backbone of the Jacobite uprisings of 1715 and 1745. Not all the Highlanders rose to support the Stuarts, but enough did to make the lost cause the inspiration for a great revival in Gaelic literature and regional self-consciousness. The British government set out systematically—and successfully—to crush the clans that had led the revolts. In the 19th cent., as the language and sectional feeling declined, the government allowed the revival of clan dress and the use of bagpipes, long the national musical instrument of Scotland. In the remote areas, old customs survive more than anywhere else in the British Isles, and many of the Highlanders have remained Roman Catholic to the present despite the vigor of the Scottish Reformation. This persistence of old ways and the beautiful scenery have made the Highlands popular in literature. See D. S. Thomson and Ian Grimble, *The Future of the Highlands* (1968); L. G. Pine, *The Highland Clans* (1972); A. J. Youngson, *After the Forty-Five: The Economic Impact of the Scottish Highlands* (1973).

High Point, city (1970 pop. 63,259), Davidson, Guilford, and Randolph counties, N N.C., in a heavily forested Piedmont region; settled before 1750, inc. 1859. It is an industrial center noted for the production of furniture and hosiery. Four annual furniture expositions are held there. Of interest is the restored home of a blacksmith (1786). High Point College is in the city.

highway: see ROAD.

High Wycombe (wĭk'əm), municipal borough (1971 pop. 59,298), Buckinghamshire, S England. The town is well known for its furniture industry and also has paper mills, saw mills, and engineering works. Other industries include printing and the manufacture of precision instruments and clothing. Ancient British and Roman remains are found nearby. The parish church dates from the 13th cent. Wycombe Abbey, a mansion built in 1795, is now a girls' public school.

Hilary of Arles, Saint (hĭl'ərē, ärl), d. 449, Gallo-Roman churchman. Forsaking riches, he entered the monastery at Lérins. He was made archbishop of Arles (c.429) against his wishes. As head of the church in Gaul, Hilary hastily deposed two bishops. They appealed to Pope LEO I, who thereupon deprived the see of Arles of its metropolitan powers, declaring the sovereignty of Rome. Later, Leo referred to him as "Hilary of sacred memory." Feast: May 5.

Hilary of Poitiers, Saint (poitĕrz', poi'tyā), c.315-367?, bishop of POITIERS from c.350, Doctor of the Church. A convert from paganism, he distinguished himself as a supporter of Athanasius against ARIANISM. For his zeal he was exiled (c.356). After his return (360) he aided Pope Liberius in the attempted purge of Arianism in the West. He wrote many theological works, mostly against the Arians, including the historically invaluable *De synodis* and the *De trinitate* (tr. by Stephen McKenna, 1954). He composed allegorical interpretations of the Bible and sacred poetry. His hymns were important in the early development of that form. Feast: Jan. 14; in England, Jan. 13 (Hilarymas). Hilary term, in English courts and schools, begins Jan. 11. See W. N. Myers, ed. and tr., *The Hymns of Saint Hilary of Poitiers* (1928); C. F. A. Borchardt, *Hilary of Poitiers' Role in the Arian Struggle* (1966).

Hilda, Saint, 614-80, English abbess of Whitby, princess of Northumbria. She became a Christian at the age of 13 and a nun at 33. About 647 she set out for a convent in France, but was recalled by St. Aidan to found a convent on the banks of the Wear River. In 657, St. Hilda founded the abbey later called Whitby. It was a double monastery, housing both men and women. The poet Cædmon became a lay brother there during her abbacy. Her strong personality made her a great figure in the Church in N England, and the Synod of Whitby (663) met in her abbey to settle differences between the Roman and the Celtic ecclesiastical uses. St. Hilda herself favored the Celtic rite, but the Roman rite was adopted. Feast: Nov. 17.

Hildebert of Lavardin (hĭl'dəbərt, lăv'ərdĭn; lävärdăN'), c.1056-1133, French churchman, bishop of Le Mans (1096-1125), and archbishop of Tours (1125-33). He was taken prisoner when Le Mans was captured (1099) by William II of England and was carried away to England, where he spent a year. When he was at Tours he came into conflict with Louis VI of France over the king's supposed right to present the deanery of Tours. Hildebert attended the First Lateran Council. He completed the cathedral at Le Mans. He was one of the most prolific writers of his period; especially noteworthy are his Latin hymns and poems. He wrote several elegies, a mythological poem on the destruction of Troy, lives of St. Hugh of Cluny and St. Mary of Egypt, and miscellaneous works, such as an interpretation of the Mass.

Hildebrand: see GREGORY VII, SAINT.

Hildebrand, Adolf von (ä'dôlf fən hĭl'dəbränt), 1847-1921, German sculptor and author. He studied in Munich and in Italy, where he spent 18 years. He is best known for his dignified public monuments, such as the equestrian statue of Bismarck in Bremen, and for his realistic portrait busts. Hildebrand defined his art theory in *The Problem of Form* (tr. 1907), urging that sculpture should emphasize clarity of form rather than meticulous detail.

Hildebrand, Lay of, fragment of an epic in mixed Low and Old High German composed c.800 in the monastery of Fulda. Hildebrand, armorer of Dietrich of Bern (THEODORIC THE GREAT), returns home after many years on the battlefield and is insulted by his son Hadubrand, who does not recognize him. The inevitable tragic ending, in which Hildebrand must kill his warrior son, is confirmed by a later "Hildebrandslied" manuscript of the 13th century.

Hildesheim (hĭl'dəs-hīm), city (1970 pop. 93,800), Lower Saxony, N central West Germany. The city is an industrial and transportation center. Its manufactures include stoves, chemicals, radio and television sets, rubber goods, and motor vehicles. In 815, Emperor Louis I made Hildesheim the seat of a bishopric; Hildesheim's bishops later became territorial princes of the Holy Roman Empire. The city received a charter in 1249 and soon afterwards joined the Hanseatic League. The bishopric was secularized at the beginning of the 19th cent.; in 1813 it passed to Hanover, and in 1866 it passed, with Hanover, to Prussia. Hildesheim owes much of its architectural beauty to one of its early bishops, St. Bernward (d. 1022). Among the splendid buildings, all Romanesque in style, are the cathedral (11th cent.), the Church of St. Michael (11th-12th cent.), and the Church of St. Godehard (12th cent.). Many old buildings were badly damaged in World War II. The city also contains a noted museum of ancient Egyptian materials.

Hildreth, Richard, 1807-65, American historian, b. Deerfield, Mass. From 1832 to 1838 he was the leading editorial writer for the Boston *Daily Atlas*. In addition to writing controversial pamphlets and contributing to magazines, Hildreth wrote *Banks, Banking, and Paper Currencies* (1840); a discussion of slavery, *Despotism in America* (1840); a novel, *The Slave; or, Memoirs of Archy Moore* (1836), which went through many editions in England, France, and America; and two books written in an inductive, scientific manner, *Theory of Morals* (1844) and *Theory of Politics* (1853). His chief work, however, was *The History of the United States* (6 vol., 1849-52), an accurate though uninspired treatment of American history to the year 1821 from a Federalist point of view. See biography by D. E. Emerson (1946); M. M. Pingel, *An American Utilitarian* (1948).

Hilen (hī'lən), the same as HOLON **1.**

Hilgard, Eugene Woldemar (hĭl'gärd), 1833-1916, American agricultural chemist and geologist, Ph.D. Univ. of Heidelberg, 1853. Born in Germany, he was brought to the United States in 1836. An authority on soil chemistry and reclamation of alkali soils, he was professor (1875-1904) of agriculture at the Univ. of California and director of the agricultural experiment station in Berkeley, Calif. His works include *Soils* (1906).

Hilkiah (hĭlkī'ə). **1** High priest under King Josiah and a leader in his revival of religion. 2 Kings 22; 23; 2 Chron. 34; 35. **2** Father of Jeremiah. Jer. 1.1. **3** Father of ELIAKIM **2. 4** Merarite Levites. 1 Chron. 6.45; 26.11. **5** Father of GEMARIAH **2. 6** Companion of Ezra. Neh. 8.4. **7** Levite who returned with Zerubbabel. Neh. 12.7, 21.

Hill, Ambrose Powell, 1825-65, Confederate general in the American Civil War, b. Culpeper, Va. He served briefly in the Mexican War and had a varied army career until he resigned in March, 1861, to support the Confederacy. After fighting at Williamsburg in the Peninsular campaign, Hill became (May, 1862) the youngest major general in the Army of Northern Virginia. His division was heavily engaged in the SEVEN DAYS BATTLES. He fought under Stonewall Jackson from July, 1862, until Jackson's death. Hill's division, noted for its fast marching, saved the day for Stonewall at Cedar Mt., just before the second battle of BULL RUN (Aug., 1862), and its opportune return from Harpers Ferry enabled it to repulse Gen. Ambrose Burnside's attack in the ANTIETAM CAMPAIGN. When Jackson was mortally wounded in the battle of CHANCELLORSVILLE, he turned his command over to Hill, but Hill himself was soon wounded, and Jeb Stuart took over. In the reorganization of the Army of Northern Virginia after Jackson's death, Hill was given command of the new 3d Corps. He was thereupon promoted to lieutenant general (May, 1863). His corps brought on the fighting in the GETTYSBURG CAMPAIGN, and Hill directed the battle on July 1, 1863. He was at the head of his corps through most of the Wilderness campaign (1864) and in the defense of PETERSBURG (1864-65). In the assault that finally broke the Confederate lines at Petersburg (April 2, 1865), Hill, with characteristic impulsiveness, went out to rally his troops and was killed. See D. S. Freeman, *Lee's Lieutenants* (3 vol., 1942-44); biography by W. W. Hassler (1957, repr. 1962).

Hill, Archibald Vivian, 1886-, British physiologist, b. Bristol. He received (with Otto Meyerhof) the 1922 Nobel Prize in Physiology and Medicine for discoveries relating to the production of heat in muscles. He also studied production of heat in stimulated nerves. He was (1940-46) a member of the war cabinet scientific advisory committee. His publications include *Muscular Activity* (1926), *Muscular Movement in Man* (1927), and *First and Last Experiments in Muscle Mechanics* (1970).

Hill, Benjamin Harvey, 1823-82, American statesman, b. Jasper co., Ga. A highly successful lawyer and Whig politician, he supported the Whig-Democratic alliance that carried Georgia in favor of the Compromise of 1850. Hill opposed secession but accepted his state's decision and in the Civil War sat in the Confederate Senate, where he was a loyal supporter of President Jefferson Davis. In Congress after 1875 he was a leading orator for the Southern cause and rewon the popularity he lost in the Reconstruction days for his submission to radical Republican policies. He was elected U.S. Senator in 1877. See study by H. J. Pearce, Jr., (1928, repr. 1969).

Hill, Daniel Harvey, 1821-89, Confederate general in the American Civil War, b. York District, S.C. He served in the Mexican War but resigned from the army in 1849. He was professor of mathematics at Washington College (now Washington and Lee Univ.) (1849-54) and at Davidson College (1854-59) and superintendent of the North Carolina Military Institute (1859-61). At the beginning of the Civil War, Hill commanded the 1st North Carolina Regiment and soon became Confederate major general. His division rendered distinguished service at Fair Oaks in the PENINSULAR CAMPAIGN, in the SEVEN DAYS BATTLES, and at South Mt. in the ANTIETAM CAMPAIGN (1862). In 1863, Hill commanded the Dist. of North Carolina, defended Richmond when Robert E. Lee was conducting the Gettysburg campaign, and fought under Braxton BRAGG at Chickamauga in the Chattanooga campaign. With others of Bragg's subordinates he petitioned Jefferson Davis to remove that general from command, but Davis, favoring Bragg, removed Hill himself. He then had no active command until the last days of the war, when he fought at Bentonville, N.C. After the war he settled in Charlotte, N.C., where he established a monthly magazine and a weekly newspaper. He was president of the Univ. of Arkansas (1877-84) and of the Middle Georgia Military and Agricultural College (1886-89). See D. S. Freeman, *Lee's Lieutenants* (3 vol., 1942-44); biography by L. H. Bridges (1961).

Hill, David Bennett, 1843-1910, American politician, b. Montour Falls, N.Y. He entered law and politics, becoming the upstate boss of the Democratic party in New York. He served as state legislator and, as lieutenant governor, succeeded to the governorship in 1885 upon Grover Cleveland's resignation. He was elected governor in 1885, and reelected (1888). As U.S. Senator (1892-97), he fought the free-silver wing in his own party. See biography by H. J. Bass (1961).

Hill, David Octavius, 1802-70, and **Robert Adamson,**1821-48, Scottish pioneer photographers. Hill was a painter of romantic Scottish landscapes. In 1843 he was commissioned to make a group portrait of the 470 clergymen who founded the Free Church of Scotland. He required an assistant to make the calotypes from which he would work, and he hired Adamson as a partner. Distinguished persons from many fields came to be photographed by the partners. Together they made (1843-48) more than 1,000 portraits and numerous views of Edinburgh before Adamson died at 27. Hill returned to painting and the partners' great work was not rediscovered until 1872. See study by Heinrich Schwarz (tr. 1931).

Hill, James Jerome, 1838-1916, American railroad builder, b. Ontario, Canada. He went to St. Paul,

Minn., in 1856. He became a partner of Norman Kittson in a steamboat line and, with Kittson, Donald Alexander Smith (later Baron Strathcona and Mount Royal), and Sir George Stephen, he bought (1878) the St. Paul and Pacific RR. It was completed to the Canadian border, but Hill, having early envisioned the expansion of farming, trade, and industry from Minnesota to the Rockies and beyond, set about to carry the line westward in what was probably the greatest feat of railroad building in the United States. In 1887, Great Falls, Mont. (which Hill had helped to found), was reached; by 1893 the road was completed across the mountains to the Pacific at Seattle. The line's expansion was accomplished despite the appalling difficulties of the terrain and the lack of the Federal assistance showered so generously on the earlier transcontinental roads. Furthermore, the construction involved no financial scandals. Hill pioneered in having "farm demonstration" trains and by his eloquent publicity persuaded thousands of farmers to settle in Montana, where unfortunately many of them were later ruined by drought. Hill in 1890 consolidated his rail properties into the Great Northern Railway Company. His great rival, the Northern Pacific, got into difficulties in the Panic of 1893, and he was the leader in its reorganization. When the courts prevented a union of the two roads, Hill's financial ally, J. Pierpont Morgan, took over the Northern Pacific, and a community of interests was maintained. In 1901 the two acted jointly to gain entrance to Chicago by purchasing the Chicago, Burlington & Quincy (commonly called the Burlington). Morgan and Hill thus forestalled Hill's rival, E. H. Harriman, who also wanted the Burlington. A violent financial struggle ensued, precipitating the stock market panic of May 9, 1901. In a compromise measure, Harriman, Hill, and Morgan set up the Northern Securities Company as a holding company for the Great Northern and Northern Pacific systems, but the organization was dissolved by order of the U.S. Supreme Court as a violation of the Sherman Anti-Trust Act. Hill retired from the presidency of the Great Northern in 1907, but remained on the board until 1912. He also assisted in the construction of the Canadian Pacific. He built and endowed the Hill Reference Library in St. Paul. Hill wrote *Highways of Progress* (1910). See biographies by J. G. Pyle (2 vol., 1944; repr. 1968) and S. H. Holbrook (1955).

Hill, Joe (Joseph Hillstrom), 1879–1915, Swedish-American union organizer, b. Jevla, Sweden. In 1902, Hill emigrated to the United States. He worked for a while in a Bowery saloon in New York City, then he went to Chicago and finally to California, where he became a maritime worker in San Pedro. In 1910 he became a member of the San Pedro local of the INDUSTRIAL WORKERS OF THE WORLD (IWW). His activities during the four years that he was an active Wobbly (as members of the IWW were known) are obscure. It is known that in 1911, with an international brigade, he took part in the Mexican Revolution and that he unceasingly wrote labor songs. Among them are "The Preacher and the Slave," "Casey Jones," "The Union Scab," "Scissor Bill," "Mr. Block," and "The Tramp." In 1915 he was tried for the murder of a prominent Salt Lake City man. He was found guilty and executed by firing squad. About 30,000 people attended his funeral in Chicago, and on the following May Day his ashes were scattered in every state (except Utah) and many countries. Since then he has become a legendary hero of radical labor. See biography by G. M. Smith (1969).

Hill, Sir Rowland, 1795–1879, English educator, inventor, and postal reformer. He introduced the system of self-government in his school at Hazelwood in Birmingham. In his *Plans for the Government and Education of Boys in Large Numbers* (1822) he argued that moral influence of the highest kind should be the predominant power in school discipline. After his retirement from teaching (1833), Hill invented a rotary printing press and evolved a system of prepaid penny postage that was finally adopted in 1839. From 1854 to his retirement from public office in 1864 he was secretary to the Post Office. He was knighted in 1860. See biographies by G. Birkbeck Hill (1880) and E. C. Smythe (1907).

Hillah: see AL HILLAH, Iraq.

Hillary, Sir Edmund Percival, 1919–, New Zealand mountain climber and explorer. He went on many mountain-climbing expeditions before taking part in the Mt. EVEREST expedition in 1953; he and Tenzing Norkay of Nepal were the first men to reach the summit of the highest mountain in the world. He was later knighted by Queen Elizabeth II. In 1958, leading a five-man group by dog sled and snow tractor across 1,200 mi (1,931 km) of Antarctica to the South Pole, he became part of the first group since 1912 to reach the Pole by overland route. His *No Latitude for Error* (1961) recounts this experience. In 1960 he embarked on a fruitless search for the ABOMINABLE SNOWMAN, and a year later he suffered a mild cerebral stroke while climbing Mt. Makalu (27,790 ft; 8,470 km) in Nepal. He wrote *High Adventure* (1955), which concerns the Mt. Everest expedition, *The Crossing of Antarctica* (with Sir Vivian Fuchs, 1959), and *High in the Thin Cold Air* (with Desmond Doig, 1962).

Hillcrest Heights, uninc. town (1970 pop. 24,037), Prince Georges co., W central Md., a suburb of Washington, D.C.

Hillel (hĭl'ĕl), father of ABDON **1.**

Hillel, fl. 30 B.C.–A.D. 10, Jewish scholar, ancestor of the patriarchs who led the Jews until A.D. c.400, b. Babylon. He was president of the Sanhedrin and laid the foundation of a systematic legal interpretation of Hebrew Scriptures. He was the great spiritual and ethical leader of his generation. His most famous maxim is "Do not unto others that which is hateful unto thee." Many others of his sayings resemble the teachings of Jesus Christ. His teachings were opposed by SHAMMAI. See biography by A. H. Blumenthal (1973).

Hillerød (hĭl'ərōth), city (1970 est. pop. 23,500), capital of Frederiksborg co., E Denmark. It is an industrial and tourist center. The city developed around the famous Renaissance-style Frederiksborg castle (1602–20), which was once a royal residence and today houses the national museum. From 1640 to 1840, Danish kings were crowned in the castle church.

Hilliard, Henry Washington (hĭl'yərd), 1808–92, American statesman and diplomat, b. Fayetteville, N.C. After teaching English literature (1831–34) at the Univ. of Alabama, he began to practice law in Montgomery, Ala. He was a state representative (1836–38) and U.S. chargé d'affaires (1842–44) in Belgium before serving (1845–51) in Congress. Hilliard led a losing fight against adoption of Alabama's ordinance of secession. However, he considered Abraham Lincoln's call for volunteers to be unconstitutional, and he thereupon briefly joined the Confederate forces. He was U.S. minister to Brazil from 1877 to 1881. He wrote *Politics and Pen Pictures at Home and Abroad* (1892).

Hilliard, Nicholas, 1537–1619, English miniature painter, son of a goldsmith. Trained first as a jeweler, he was court painter to Elizabeth and to James I. The first true miniaturist in England, Hilliard was self-taught. He painted meticulous linear portraits on card or vellum, even on the backs of playing cards. His works were highly individual, elegant and subtle, particularly well suited to their form. He and his pupil Isaac OLIVER led their field. Hilliard's reputation gained him many distinguished Elizabethans as subjects. Much of his work is at Windsor Castle and in the private collections of England; *Queen Elizabeth* (1572) is in the National Portrait Gallery and his *Portrait of a Youth* (c.1588) is in the Victoria and Albert Museum, both in London. An essay on miniature painting, *The Art of Limning,* is attributed to Hilliard. See monograph by Emma Auerbach (1961).

Hillingdon, borough (1971 pop. 234,718) of Greater London, SE England. Hillingdon was created in 1965 by the merger of the municipal borough of Uxbridge and the urban districts of Hayes, Harlington, Ruislip-Northwood, Yiewsley, and West Drayton. Among the borough's industries are printing, motion-picture production, and the manufacture of aircraft, food products, and electrical and musical instruments. The area includes a portion of London (Heathrow) Airport and part of the Grand Union Canal, which links the coalfields and other sources of raw materials in the Midlands with London. Uxbridge was an ancient market town on the Colne River. Charles I and representatives of Parliament negotiated unsuccessfully in the "Treaty House" in Uxbridge in 1645. The parish church in Hayes was used by St. Anselm, archbishop of Canterbury.

Hillis, Newell Dwight, 1858–1929, American Congregational minister. He was pastor (1899–1924) of the famous Plymouth Church (Congregational), Brooklyn, N.Y. He was an eloquent preacher and a widely known lecturer. His books include *Great Books as Life-Teachers* (1899) and *Great Men as Prophets of a New Era* (1922, repr. 1968).

Hillman, Sidney, 1887–1946, American labor leader, b. Lithuania. He emigrated to the United States in 1907. Beginning as a garment worker, he became a union leader after his key participation in a successful clothing workers' strike (1910) in Chicago. In 1914 he began his long tenure as president of the Amalgamated Clothing Workers. He promoted union-management cooperation and started many novel union practices, such as cooperative housing and banking. One of the founders of the Congress of Industrial Organizations (CIO), he was its vice president from 1935 to 1940. A moderate, opposed to labor schism, he directed the labor sections of the Office of Production Management from 1940 to 1942. Through the CIO Political Action Committee, which he headed from its start (1943) until his death, he sought labor support for political programs favored by unions. His strong support of President Franklin Delano Roosevelt's policies made him influential in the Democratic party. He was also a founder of the American Labor party and its chairman (1944–45). As CIO delegate at world labor parleys, he helped create (1945) the World Federation of Trade Unions. See biography by Matthew Josephson (1952).

Hillquit, Morris, 1869–1933, American lawyer and Socialist leader, b. Riga, Latvia (then in Russia, now Latvian SSR). He came to the United States in 1886. He was the leader of the right-wing, or constitutional, Socialists in their revolt against the radical leadership of Daniel DE LEON in 1899. This revolt split the Socialist Labor party and led (1900) to the founding of the Social Democratic party, which evolved into the Socialist party. Hillquit from the beginning was the dominant theorist and tactician of the party, representing it on the executive committee of the Socialist and Labor International. He vigorously opposed U.S. entry into World War I and served as the defense lawyer in many espionage cases against socialists. He also served for many years as counsel to a number of labor unions. He was his party's candidate for mayor of New York City twice and for Congressman five times. In 1924 he led the Socialists into Robert M. La Follette's Progressive party. He wrote *History of Socialism in the United States* (1903), *Socialism in Theory and Practice* (1909), *From Marx to Lenin* (1921), and the autobiography *Loose Leaves from a Busy Life* (1934, repr. 1971). See F. G. Ham and C. S. Warmbrodt, *The Morris Hillquit Papers* (1969).

Hillsboro, city (1970 pop. 14,675), seat of Washington co., NW Oregon, in the Tualatin valley; inc. 1876. Fruits and vegetables are frozen and packed, and kitchen cabinets and electric organs are manufactured. Settled c.1845, Hillsboro has a pioneer museum and cemetery and a notable old Scottish church.

Hillsdale, borough (1970 pop. 11,768), Bergen co., NE N.J.; inc. 1923. It is primarily residential.

Hilo (hē'lō), city (1970 pop. 26,353), seat of Hawaii co., on Hilo Bay of Hawaii island; settled by missionaries c.1822, inc. as a city 1911. The second largest city of Hawaii, a port of entry, and the only metropolitan area on the island, Hilo is the trade and shipping center for a sugarcane, orchid, papaya, and macadamia-nut region. The economy is based heavily on sugar and on tourism, which was spurred by the inauguration in 1967 of direct air service to the U.S. mainland. Among Hilo's points of interest are the peaks of Mauna Kea and Mauna Loa, which rise behind the city; the Lyman House (c.1839), now a museum with a collection of Hawaiiana; a state park in the bayfront area; and an island-park in Hilo Bay. Hilo College, part of the Univ. of Hawaii, and a junior college are also in the city. Hilo was badly damaged by tidal waves in 1946 and 1960.

Hilprecht, Hermann Volrath (hĕr'män fôl'rät hĭl'prĕkht), 1859–1925, American Assyriologist, b. Germany; Ph.D. Univ. of Leipzig, 1883. He is noted as an authority on cuneiform writing. Hilprecht went to the United States in 1886 and was professor of Assyriology (1886–1911) at the Univ. of Pennsylvania and curator (1887–1911) of the Semitic department of its museum. He was scientific director of four expeditions (1895–1914) to Nippur and reorganized (1893–1909) the Babylonian collection of the Imperial Ottoman Museum, Constantinople. Retiring to Germany in 1914, Hilprecht later returned to the United States and was naturalized.

Hilton, Walter, d. 1396, English religious writer, an Austin canon of Thurgarton, Nottinghamshire. His spiritual treatise *The Scale of Perfection* (ed. by Evelyn Underhill, 1923) is a general manual for holy living. Although it was addressed to a Carthusian recluse, it became popular among English laymen before the Reformation. Hilton also composed a shorter *Treatise Written to a Devout Man.* His mysticism, typically English, resembles that of Richard ROLLE OF HAMPOLE. See studies by J. E. Milosh (1966) and Phyllis Hodgson (rev. ed. 1967).

Hilversum (hĭl'vərsəm), city (1971 pop. 114, 862), North Holland prov., central Netherlands. It is the center of Dutch radio and television broadcasting. Its manufactures include chemicals, machinery, and carpets. There are several sanatoriums in the city.

Himachal Pradesh (hĭmä'chəl prədāsh'), state (1971 pop. 3,424,332), 21,629 sq mi (56,019 sq km), NW India, in the W Himalayas, bordered by the Tibet region of China on the east. SIMLA is the capital. The state is covered with forested mountains, and the valleys are extensively cultivated. The forests supply large quantities of timber, the main source of income. Potatoes and fruits are the chief crops. Salt mining and the making of handicrafts are also practiced there. Pahari-speaking Hindus inhabit the lower hill area; peoples of Tibetan origin live in the high mountain regions. Himachal Pradesh was formed as a union territory in 1948 by the merger of 30 former Punjabi princely states. The small state of Bilaspur was merged with it in 1954. In 1966 five more districts and parts of two others from Punjab were added to the territory. Himachal Pradesh became a state in 1971. It is governed by a chief minister and cabinet responsible to an elected unicameral legislature and by a governor appointed by the president of India.

Himalayan cat: see CAT.

Himalayas (hĭmäl'əyəz, hĭməlā'əz) [Sanskrit,= abode of snow], great Asian mountain system, extending c.1,500 mi (2,410 km) E from the Karakorum range through Pakistan, India, China, Nepal, Sikkim, and Bhutan to the southern bend of the Brahmaputra River in SE Tibet (China). For most of its length, the Himalayas comprise two nearly parallel ranges separated by a wide valley in which the Indus River flows westward and the Brahmaputra flows eastward. The northern range is called the Trans-Himalayas. The southern range has three parallel zones: the Great Himalayas, the perpetually snow-covered main range in which the highest peaks (average elevation 20,000 ft/6,100 m) are found; the Lesser Himalayas with 7,000 to 15,000 ft (2,130–4,570 m) elevations; and the southernmost Outer Himalayas, 2,000 to 5,000 ft (610–1,520 m) high. A relatively young and still growing system subject to severe earthquakes, the Himalayas' main axis was formed c.25 to 70 million years ago as the earth's crust folded against the northward-moving Indian subcontinent. Some 30 Himalayan peaks rise to more than 25,000 ft (7,620 m), including Mt. Everest (29,028 ft/8,848 m) and Kanchenjunga (28,208 ft/8,598 m), the highest and third highest peaks in the world. Himalayan peaks have long been the goal of mountaineers. The towering ranges present an almost insuperable barrier to travel, even by air. Railroads reach only the southern foothills from where the main route follows footpaths across primitive bridges, ropeways, and high mountain passes. Improved roads run between Kashmir and China and from India through Nepal and Sikkim to China. The aridity of S and W China results from the interception of the moisture-laden northwest monsoon by the Himalayas' southern face. Consequently, the northern slopes receive relatively light snowfall and have little drainage, while the snow-covered and extensively glaciated southern slopes give rise to the Indian subcontinent's major rivers, including the Indus, Sutlej, Ganges, and Brahmaputra. Little of the Himalayan region is inhabitable or of great current economic value. The southern approaches are malarial jungle and swamps with many wild animals. Grazing is possible on some of the gentler slopes, and farming is carried on in the valleys; there is some lumbering in the extensive forests found below 12,000 ft (3,660 m). Limited amounts of iron ore, gold, and sapphires are worked in the west. The Himalayan rivers, with their perennial flow, offer much scope for hydroelectric power and irrigation development. Hill resorts such as Simla, Naini Tal, Mussoorie, and Darjeeling are popular summer retreats from the heat of the Indian plains. The Himalayas are associated with many legends in Asian mythology (see ABOMINABLE SNOWMAN); on isolated slopes are found the retreats of rishis (holy sages), gurus (teachers), and Tibetan monks.

Himeji (hēmä'jē), city (1970 pop. 407,954), Hyogo prefecture, SW Honshu, Japan. A railroad and market center, it manufactures cotton textiles and supplies iron and steel for the Osaka-Kobe industrial area. The ruins of a 14th-century castle have been completely restored.

Himera (hĭm'ərə), ancient city on the north coast of Sicily, founded by Greeks in the 7th cent. B.C. Here in 480 B.C. (a traditional date) forces led by Gelon routed the Carthaginians led by Hamilcar. Years later the Carthaginians destroyed (409 B.C.) the city. The citizens moved to nearby Thermae (modern Termini). The poet Stesichorus was born in Himera.

Himi (hē'mē), city (1970 pop. 60,883), Toyama prefecture, W central Honshu, Japan, on Toyama Bay. It is a fishing port and agricultural distribution center.

Himmler, Heinrich (hīn'rĭkh hĭm'lər), 1900–1945, German Nazi leader. An early member of the National Socialist German Workers' (Nazi) party, Himmler took part in Adolf Hitler's "beer-hall putsch" of 1923, and in 1929 HITLER appointed him head of the SS, or *Schutzstaffel*, the party's black-shirted elite corps. When Hitler came to power he made Himmler head of police in Munich and then chief of the political police throughout Bavaria. After the party purge of June, 1934, which eliminated Ernst ROEHM, head of the SA, or Nazi militia, Himmler's SS became the major police organ of the state. In 1936, Himmler was named chief of the German police; this brought him formal control over the Gestapo, the SECRET POLICE that had been set up in 1933 by Hermann GOERING. From his preeminent position Himmler terrorized his own party hierarchy as well as all German-held Europe, establishing and overseeing CONCENTRATION CAMPS and ordering incarceration and death for millions, particularly after the beginning of World War II. A superb bureaucrat and one of the most cold-blooded of the Nazi leaders, he was a fanatic racist. In Aug., 1943, he became minister of the interior, and after putting down the conspiracy against Hitler in July, 1944, he was the virtual dictator of German domestic policy. In April, 1945, just before Germany's defeat in World War II, Himmler secretly attempted to negotiate German surrender, hoping to save himself. Upon hearing of this, Hitler expelled him from the party. Himmler attempted to escape, but was arrested by British troops in May, 1945, and committed suicide by swallowing poison. See biographies by Willi Frischauer (1953), Roger Marvell and Heinrich Fraenkel (1965, repr. 1972), and B. F. Smith (1971).

Hims (hĭmsh) or **Homs** (hômz), city (1970 est. pop. 216,000), capital of Hims governorate, W central Syria, on the Orontes River. It is a commercial center located in a fertile plain where wheat, grapes, barley, and onions are grown. Manufactures include refined petroleum, flour, fertilizer, processed foods, and silk, cotton, and woolen textiles. The city is a road and rail junction. In ancient times Hims, then called Emesa, was the site of a great temple to Baal (or Helios-Baal), the sungod. Emesa came into startling prominence in the early 3d cent. A.D. when a priest of the temple became Roman emperor as Heliogabalus, or Elagabalus. Aurelian defeated the forces of Zenobia of Palmyra there in 272. The Arabs took the town in 636, renaming it Hims. The Arab soldier Khalid died there in 642; a shrine and mosque in his honor were erected in 1908. Hims was part of the Ottoman Empire from the 16th cent. until after World War I, when it became part of the French League of Nations mandate.

Himyaritic (hĭm"yərĭt'ĭk), another name for South Arabic. See ARABIC LANGUAGES; HAMITO-SEMITIC LANGUAGES.

Hinayana Buddhism: see BUDDHISM.

Hinckley, urban district (1971 pop. 47,982), Leicestershire, central England, near WATLING STREET. Hosiery and shoes are the chief manufactures. There are also dyeing and engineering industries.

Hincks, Sir Francis, 1807–85, Canadian journalist and statesman, b. Ireland. Settling (1832) in York (now Toronto), he was soon drawn into the Reform party. In 1839 he became editor of the Toronto *Examiner,* a newspaper founded by the reformers, which under his direction ably argued the cause of responsible government. Entering the Canadian legislative assembly in 1841, Hincks was twice (1842–43, 1848–51) inspector general (or finance minister). He worked to effect an alliance between the reformers of Upper Canada and Lower Canada, vigorously opposed the movement for annexation by the United States, and in the interval between his terms of office as inspector general founded a new Reform party journal, the Montreal *Pilot.* As prime minister in the joint Hincks-Morin administration (1851–54), he directed his efforts toward achieving a reciprocal trade treaty with the United States and promoting railroad construction, but his failure to resolve differences between Roman Catholic and Protestant factions led to his resignation (1854). Hincks served as British governor of Barbados and the Windward Islands (1855–62) and of British Guiana (1862–69); he then returned to Canada to serve (1869–73) as minister of finance in Sir John A. Macdonald's coalition government. In 1869 he was knighted. See his reminiscences (1884); biography by R. S. Longley (1943).

Hincmar (hĭngk'mär), 806–82, Frankish churchman, archbishop of Rheims (from 845). He was a supporter of Carolingian Emperor LOUIS I and a counselor of his son CHARLES II (Charles the Bald). As a metropolitan he tried to depose a bishop in 862 and brought on himself the censure of Pope St. NICHOLAS I. Later (876), in a different contention, he upheld the rights of metropolitans. Hincmar vigorously opposed GOTTSCHALK and urged (850) ERIGENA to write on predestination. Dissatisfied with Erigena's tract, Hincmar wrote three treatises on the subject himself. He strongly opposed the divorce of LOTHAIR, king of Lotharingia, and he spent much of his time in defending the claims of Charles in various dynastic struggles, particularly against LOUIS THE GERMAN. As a strong upholder of tradition, Hincmar defended the practice of public penance and initiated a reform in the French clerical life of the period.

hindbrain: see BRAIN.

Hindemith, Paul (hĭn'dəmĭth), 1895–1963, German-American composer and violist, b. Hanau, Germany. Hindemith is one of the foremost composers of the early 20th cent., combining experimental and traditional techniques into a distinctively modern style. After studying at the Frankfurt Conservatory, he began his career as a viola player. He taught (1927–37) composition at the Berlin Hochschule, but during the Nazi regime his compositions were banned because of their dissonance and modernity. In 1935 he was commissioned by the Turkish government to reorganize that country's musical education. Later he taught at Yale Univ. (1940–53), becoming a U.S. citizen in 1946; but in 1952 he returned to Europe to teach at the Univ. of Zürich. Hindemith's early compositions are highly contrapuntal and often atonal. Later works display a return to tonality that has often been termed neoclassical. His best-known work is the symphony (1934) drawn from his opera *Mathis der Maler* [Mathis the painter] (1938), which is based on the life of the painter Mathias Grunewald. Other operas include *Cardillac* (1926) and *Neues vom Tage* [news of the day] (1929). Many of Hindemith's works might be classed as *Gebrauchsmusik* [utility music], written for specific performance by amateur school groups or chamber music organizations. His aim was to establish closer contact between composer and public. Included in this group are the children's opera *Wir bauen eine Stadt* [we are building a city] (1931) and numerous sonatas and chamber works. Other important works are the *Ludus Tonalis* (1943) for piano; the song cycle *Das Marienleben* (1923, 1948) set to poems by Rilke; the viola concerto *Der Schwanendreher* (1935), based on medieval German folk songs; the ballet *Nobilissima Visione* (1938); and the setting for chorus and orchestra of Walt Whitman's *When Lilacs Last in the Dooryard Bloom'd* (1946). His writings include *Traditional Harmony* (2 vol., 1943, 1948) and *A Composer's World* (1952). See study by Ian Kemp (1970).

Hindenburg, Paul von (hĭn'dənbûrg, Ger. poul fən hĭn'dənbo͝ork), 1847–1934, German field marshal and president (1925–34), b. Poznan (then in Prussia). His full name was Paul Ludwig Hans Anton von Hindenburg und Beneckendorff. He fought in the Austro-Prussian War (1866) and in the Franco-Prussian War (1870–71) and was appointed (1878) to the general staff. Though retired after 1911, he was made commander in East Prussia early in World War I. General LUDENDORFF, who was his chief of staff throughout the war, was the real author of Hindenburg's victories. Victory in the battle of TANNENBERG (Aug., 1914) over a much larger Russian force was followed (1914–15) by German occupation of Poland and part of the Baltic provinces. As commander in chief of the German armies in the East from Sept., 1914, Hindenburg's prestige was greatly enhanced by these victories. In 1916, Hindenburg, by then a field marshal, succeeded General FALKENHAYN as commander of all German armies; Ludendorff was made quartermaster general. Subsequently, the two men became virtual dictators of Germany, intervening in civilian affairs, regulating labor, and mobilizing the rest of the economy for total warfare. In the military sphere they stemmed the Allied advance in the West and consolidated the Hindenburg Line, running roughly from Lens through Saint-Quentin to Rheims. Rumania was crushed, and Russia withdrew from the war (1917). From March to July, 1918, Hindenburg launched a costly offensive into France, but the Allied counteroffensive, spearheaded by fresh American troops, led to the German defeat and surrender. Although Ludendorff was forced to resign in Oct., 1918, Hindenburg remained in office. After the overthrow of the emperor (November),

Hindenburg and the army swore an oath of allegiance to the republican government. Although Hindenburg was to be tried as a war criminal under the terms of the Treaty of Versailles, the special German court at Leipzig never even indicted him. After the death of the German president Freidrich Ebert in 1925, Hindenburg was persuaded to run for the office by a coalition of nationalists, Prussian Junkers, and other conservative groups. As president, his powers were very limited. In 1932 he was reelected with the help of his chancellor, Heinrich BRÜNING. Shortly after the election, at the instigation of his advisors, Hindenburg dismissed Brüning. Finally, in Jan., 1933, the nearly senile president, fearing civil war, gave in to his advisers and appointed Adolf HITLER chancellor. Hindenburg continued as a figurehead until his death. See J. W. Wheeler-Bennett, *The Wooden Titan* (1936, repr. 1967), Andreas Dorpalen, *Hindenburg and the Weimar Republic* (1964).

Hindenburg: see ZABRZE, Poland.

Hindenburg: see AIRSHIP.

Hindi (hĭn'dē), language belonging to the Indic group of the Indo-Iranian subfamily of the Indo-European family of languages (see INDO-IRANIAN LANGUAGES). The official language of India, Hindi is the written or literary variant of HINDUSTANI that is used by Hindus. It is written in the Devanagari alphabet employed for SANSKRIT and has a vocabulary of Indic origin. There are two main dialectal groups of the Hindi language: Western Hindi and Eastern Hindi. The former has four principal dialects. The latter is the medium of an extensive and outstanding literature. Some 133,500,000 people in India understand Hindi. See H. C. Scholberg, *Concise Grammar of the Hindi Language* (3d ed. 1955); Suniti K. Chatterji, *Indo-Aryan and Hindi* (2d ed. 1960); Ernest Bender, *Hindi Grammar and Reader* (1967); Franklin Southworth, *Student's Hindi-Urdu Reference Manual* (1971).

Hinduism (hin'do͞oĭzəm), Western term for the religious beliefs and practices of the vast majority of the people of India. One of the oldest living religions in the world, Hinduism is unique among the world religions in that it had no single founder but grew over a period of 4,000 years in syncretism with the religious and cultural movements of the Indian subcontinent. Hinduism is composed of innumerable sects and has no well-defined ecclesiastical organization. Its two most general features are the CASTE system and acceptance of the VEDA as the most sacred scriptures. Hinduism is a synthesis of the religion brought into India by the ARYANS (c.1500 B.C.) and indigenous religion. The first phase of Hinduism was early Brahmanism, the religion of the priests or BRAHMANS who performed the Vedic sacrifice, through the power of which proper relation with the gods and the cosmos is established. The Veda comprises the liturgy and interpretation of the sacrifice and culminates in the UPANISHADS, mystical and speculative works that state the doctrine of *Brahman,* the absolute reality that is the self of all things, and its identity with the individual soul, or *atman* (see INDIAN PHILOSOPHY; VEDANTA). Later Upanishads refer to the practices of YOGA and contain theistic elements that are fully developed in the BHAGAVAD-GITA. Post-Vedic Hinduism in all its forms accepts the doctrine of KARMA, according to which the individual reaps the results of his good and bad actions through a series of lifetimes (see TRANSMIGRATION OF SOULS). Also universally accepted is the goal of *moksha* or *mukti,* liberation from suffering and from the compulsion to rebirth, which is attainable through elimination of passions and through knowledge of reality and finally union with God. In the middle of the first millennium B.C., an ossified Brahmanism was challenged by heterodox, i.e., non-Vedic, systems, notably BUDDHISM and JAINISM. The priestly elite responded by creating a synthesis that accepted yogic practices and their goals, recognized the gods and image worship of popular devotional movements, and adopted greater concern for the daily life of the people. There was an increase in writings, such as the Laws of Manu (see MANU), dealing with DHARMA, or duty, not only as applied to the sacrifice but to every aspect of life. Their basic principle is *varna-ashrama-dharma,* or *dharma* in accordance with *varna* (class or caste) and *ashrama* (stage of life). The four classes are the Brahmans, Kshatriyas (warriors), Vaishyas (farmers and merchants), and Shudras (laborers). The four stages of life are *brahmacharya* or celibate student life (originally for study of the Veda), *grihastha* or householdership, *vanaprastha* or forest hermitage, and *sannyasa,* complete renunciation of all ties with society and pursuit of spiritual liberation. (In practical terms these stages were not strictly adhered to. The two main alternatives have continued to be householdership and the ascetic life.) The entire system was conceived as ideally ensuring both the proper function of society as an integrated whole and the fulfillment of the individual's needs through his lifetime. The post-Vedic *Puranas* deal with these themes and also elaborate the myths of the popular gods. They describe the universe as undergoing an eternally repeated cycle of creation, preservation, and dissolution, represented by the trinity of BRAHMA the creator, VISHNU the preserver, and SHIVA the destroyer as aspects of the Supreme. In medieval times the esoteric ritual and yoga of TANTRA and sects of fervent devotion (see BHAKTI) arose and flourished. The groundswell of devotion produced poet-saints all over India who wrote religious songs and composed versions of the epics in their vernaculars. This literature plays an essential part in present-day Hinduism, as do puja, or worship of enshrined deities, and pilgrimage to sacred places. The most popular deities include Vishnu and his incarnations Rama and KRISHNA, Shiva, the elephant-headed god Ganesha, and the Mother-Goddess or *Devi,* who appears as the terrible KALI or Durga but also as Sarasvati, the goddess of music and learning, and as Lakshmi, the goddess of wealth. All the gods and goddesses, each of which has numerous aspects, are regarded as different forms of the one Supreme Being. Modern Hindu leaders such as Swami VIVEKANANDA, Mohandas GANDHI, and Aurobindo GHOSE, have given voice to a movement away from the traditional ideal of world-renunciation and asceticism and have asserted the necessity of uniting spiritual life with social concerns. See J. N. Farquhar, *A Primer of Hinduism* (1912); C. N. E. Eliot, *Hinduism and Buddhism* (3 vol., 1921; repr. 1968); A. B. Keith, *The Religion and Philosophy of the Veda and Upanishads* (1925, repr. 1971); Sarvepalli Radhakrishnan, *The Hindu View of Life* (1927, repr. 1962); Louis Renou, *Religions of Ancient India* (1953, repr. 1968) and *Hinduism* (1961); R. G. Zaehner, *Hinduism* (1962); A. T. Embree, ed., *The Hindu Tradition* (1966, repr. 1972); T. J. Hopkins, *The Hindu Religious Tradition* (1971); P. H. Ashby, *Modern Trends in Hinduism* (1974).

Hindu Kush (hĭn'do͞o ko͝osh), 2d highest mountain system in the world, extending c.500 mi (800 km) W from the Pamir Knot, N Pakistan, into NE Afghanistan; rises to 25,236 ft (7,692 m) in Tirich Mir, N Pakistan. Glaciated and receiving heavy snowfall, the mountains have permanently snow-covered peaks and little vegetation. Meltwater feeds the headstreams of the Amu Darya and the Indus rivers. Virtually uninhabited, the system is crossed by several high-altitude passes; once followed by Alexander the Great and Tamerlane in their invasions of India, they are now trade routes. The Hindu Kush were formerly called the Caucasus Indicus.

Hindu music. The music of India is entirely monodic. To Westerners it is the most accessible of all Oriental musical cultures. Its tonal system divides the octave into 22 segments called srutis, not all equal but each roughly equal to one quarter of a whole tone of Western music. The basic scales are *sa-grama* and *ma-grama.* The more important of these, the *sa-grama,* closely approximates the C Major scale. *Ma-grama,* which differs from the *sa-grama* in only one interval, is said to have disappeared from use about the 16th cent. Other scales are derived from these by the sharping or flatting of some of the intervals or by leaving out some of the tones. Melody is based on the system of ragas, which are melody types used as the basis for improvisation. There are innumerable ragas, and with each there is an accompanying set of rules for improvisation in that raga. To each is ascribed certain ethical and emotional properties, and each is associated with a certain season and a certain time of day. For a single raga, however, these connotations vary in different parts of India. The ragas were the inspiration for much Rajput miniature painting the iconography of which varied according to its period, place of production, and creator. Legend celebrates the powers of the ragas; e.g., a raga associated with darkness could, if sung in the middle of the day by a singer whose skill was great enough, bring darkness upon the earth. In the performance of the ragas, great importance is attached to the *gamakas,* the ornaments, or graces, that are characteristic of this music. Accompanied song is considered the highest type of music. In the accompaniment, rhythm is very complex and is based on certain rhythmic patterns, called *talas,* which are often combined in the most intricate ways. The oldest instrument is the drum, of which there are several types; it can be tuned by means of special kinds of coating given the skin. The most important instrument is the vina. In antiquity the name was given to a harp, but the modern vina is a zither with gourd resonators. A similar instrument is the SITAR, the most popular instrument in N India. It has movable frets, is played with a plectrum, and has greater volume than the vina. In addition, various types of bagpipe, lute, fiddle, oboe, trumpet, flute, cymbal, and gong have been known in India. Many of the instruments are of Islamic origin. Hindu music has, since the mid-1960s, enjoyed considerable popularity in the West. See A. H. Fox-Strangways, *The Music of Hindostan* (1914); Walter Kaufman, *The Ragas of North India* (1968); Alain Daniélou, *Northern Indian Music* (new ed. 1969); H. A. Popleg, *The Music of India* (3d ed. 1970).

Hindustan (hĭn"do͞ostăn') [Persian,=Hindu land], vague term, usually applied to the Ganges Plain of N India, between the Himalayas in the north and the Deccan plateau in the south. Used variably throughout Indian history—generally in contradistinction to the Deccan of peninsular India—it gradually came to mean the whole of N India from the Punjab to Assam. The term *Hindustan* has also been applied to the whole Indian subcontinent.

Hindustani (hĭndo͞ostän'ē), subdivision of the Indic group of the Indo-Iranian languages, which themselves form a subfamily of the Indo-European family of languages. Some authorities define Hindustani as the spoken form of HINDI and URDU. Others prefer to call Hindi and Urdu written varieties of Hindustani. The term *Hindustani* can also be used to include some vernacular dialects of northern India. Hindi is the variety of Hindustani used by Hindus; it is also the official language of India. Written in the Devanagari alphabet employed for SANSKRIT, Hindi is read from left to right and has a vocabulary that is strictly Indic. Urdu, on the other hand, is the form of Hindustani used by Muslims and is official in Pakistan; it is written in a modified form of the Arabic alphabet, is read from right to left, and has added a number of words borrowed from Arabic and Persian to its originally Indic vocabulary. Despite these differences, both Hindi and Urdu are written variants of the same Indic subdivision, Hindustani. The latter goes back to the Prakrits or vernacular dialects of classical Sanskrit (see INDO-IRANIAN LANGUAGES) and has been greatly influenced by Sanskrit itself. The grammar of Hindustani is much simpler than that of the older Indic tongues, such as Sanskrit. For instance, the neuter gender, the dual number, and the old case endings for the noun have been discarded. The conjugation of the verb has also been greatly simplified. Instead of prepositions, Hindustani uses postpositions, or particles placed after words to make clear their grammatical function or relationship. Hindustani plays an important role in modern India as a LINGUA FRANCA; the number of people who speak or understand Hindustani in India and Pakistan has been variously estimated, but it probably exceeds 150 million persons. Thus Hindustani ranks third, after Chinese and English, among the world's language communities. See INDO-IRANIAN. See Gordon H. Fairbanks and Bal G. Misra, *Spoken and Written Hindi* (1966); R. S. MacGregor, *An Outline of Hindi Grammar* (1972).

Hine, Lewis, 1874–1940, American photographer, b. Oshkosh, Wis. Hine dedicated much of his photographic career, which began in 1908, to exposing in sharp, painful images the social evils of the industrial revolution in the United States. He photographed the poverty of the newly arrived immigrants and the street life and factory life of working children. He also detailed the effects of war on the land and people of Europe, the complex relationship of man and machine, the construction of the Empire State Building, and the influence of a Tennessee Valley Authority dam program on the life of a rural community. Hine's work reflects concern, compassion, and a crusading idealism. The power of his images placed him at the forefront of 20th-century documentary photographers. See study by Judith M. Gutman (1967).

Hingan (hĭng'än'), Mandarin *Hsing-an,* former province (c.100,000 sq mi/259,000 sq km), NE China. The capital was Hailar. The region, a part of Manchuria, is bordered on the north by the Amur River and on the west by the Argun River; both separate it from Siberia. There are immense coal and timber reserves. In 1950, Hingan became part of Heilungkiang prov.

Hingham (hĭng'əm), resort town (1970 pop. 18,845), Plymouth co., E Mass., on the south shore of Hingham Bay; inc. 1635. The Old Ship Church (1681), a fine example of American Gothic architecture, has been in continuous use since it was built.

Hinkle, Beatrice Mores (Van Geisen), 1874–1953, American psychiatrist, b. San Francisco, M.D. Cooper Medical College (now part of Stanford Univ.), 1889. In 1908 she opened at Cornell Medical College, New York City, the first psychotherapeutic clinic in the United States. She wrote *The Re-Creating of the Individual* (1923) and translated Jung's work as *Psychology of the Unconscious* (1916).

Hinnom, valley, W of Jerusalem. It was of ill repute because of the connection of TOPHET, a high place in the valley, with MOLECH worship. In later Jewish literature it was called Ge-Hinnom and in the Greek of the New Testament, Gehenna (a corruption of Ge-Hinnom); it came to mean Hell. Joshua 15.8; 18.16; 2 Kings 23.10; 2 Chron. 28.3; 33.6; Jer. 7.31; 32.35.

hinny: see MULE.

Hino (hē'nō), city (1970 pop. 98,557), Tokyo Metropolis, E central Honshu, Japan, on the Asa River. It is a residential suburb of Tokyo and an agricultural center.

Hinsdale, residential village (1970 pop. 15,918), Cook and Du Page counties, NE Ill., part of the greater Chicago metropolitan area; inc. 1873.

Hinsley, Arthur, 1865–1943, English prelate, cardinal of the Roman Catholic Church. Born in Yorkshire, he attended Catholic schools in England and Rome. He was ordained in 1893 and spent several decades as a schoolmaster and rector. He served as a missionary in Africa, first as visitor apostolic (1926–30) and then as archbishop of Sardis and apostolic delegate (1930–34). In 1934 he retired but was called from retirement in 1935 to be enthroned as archbishop of Westminster, primate of the Roman Catholic Church in England. He was created cardinal in 1937. Cardinal Hinsley was noted as a foe of German and Italian fascism.

Hiogo: see KOBE, Japan.

Hiouentang: see HSÜAN-TSANG.

hip, side of the human body, between the waist and thigh, formed by the edge of the hipbone, the top of the thighbone, and the surrounding flesh. The adult hipbone consolidates three bones separate in youth: the ilium, ischium, and pubis. The two prominences commonly called the hipbones are the crests of the ilia. The bones of the buttocks that support the seated body are projections of the ischia. At the body midline fibrous tissue bands the two pubis bones, thus stabilizing the hips and preventing them from spreading or buckling. With maturity, the ilium, ischium, and pubis meet and grow together at a Y-shaped junction, the site of the acetabulum, a deep cavity that receives the rounded head of the thighbone. The resulting ball-and-socket joint allows great latitude of thigh movement. See PELVIS; LEG.

hip dysplasia (dĭsplā'zhə), congenital malformation of the hip, or coxofemoral, joint. It occurs mostly in largebreed dogs but is reported in almost all species of large animals. The malformation of the hip prevents the head of the femur from fitting properly into the socket joint of the pelvis. This condition causes joint instability and leads to partial or complete dislocation, pain in the joint, and secondary osteoarthritis. Visible symptoms may include difficulty in rising and lameness of varying severity. A hereditary disease, hip dysplasia may be definitely diagnosed only after X-ray examination. Treatment consists of the use of pain relievers, moderate exercise, weight control, and, finally, surgical removal of the head of the femur. Cutting a small muscle (pectineus) will often help in restoring joint stability. Because this is a genetically related disease, animals suffering from hip dysplasia should not be used for breeding.

Hipparchus (hĭpär'kəs), c.555–514 B.C., Athenian political figure, son of PISISTRATUS. After the death of his father, he was closely associated with his brother Hippias, tyrant of Athens, in ruling the Athenian city-state. Under Hippias he was a patron of the arts and sponsored the poets Anacreon and Simonides. He was slain by HARMODIUS AND ARISTOGITON because of his personal vices.

Hipparchus, fl. 2d cent. B.C., Greek astronomer, b. Nicaea, Bithynia. He is the first systematic astronomer of whom there are records. He made his observations chiefly on the island of Rhodes. Ptolemy's geocentric theory of the universe was based largely on the conclusions of Hipparchus, a record of whose researches is preserved in the *Almagest* of Ptolemy. In it Hipparchus is credited with the discovery of the precession of the equinoxes, the eccentricity of the sun's apparent orbit, and certain inequalities of the motions of the moon. He also made the first known comprehensive chart of the heavens giving the positions of at least 850 stars; this was expanded by Ptolemy. Hipparchus suggested a method of determining longitude by observing the parallax of the moon in eclipse. He is believed to have been the first to make systematic use of trigonometry, and he computed a table of chords roughly equivalent to trigonometrical sines. Only one of his works, a commentary on the work of Aratus and Eudoxus, survives.

Hippias (hĭp'ēəs), tyrant (527 B.C.–510 B.C.) of Athens, eldest son of PISISTRATUS. Hippias governed Athens after the death of his father. His younger brother Hipparchus was closely associated in office with him until Hipparchus was assassinated in 514 B.C. At first Hippias attempted to work with his opponents, the Alcmaeonidae, but his rule became harsher as the Persians advanced. In 510 B.C. he was overthrown by the Alcmaeonidae and the Spartans and went into exile. He lived at the court of Darius and was with the Persian forces at Marathon.

Hippius, Zinaida Nikolayevna: see GIPPIUS, ZINAIDA NIKOLAYEVNA.

Hippocrates (hĭpŏk'rətēz), c.460–c.370 B.C., Greek physician, recognized as the father of medicine. He is believed to have been born on the island of Cos; to have studied under his father, a physician; to have traveled for some time, perhaps studying in Athens; and to have then returned to practice, teach, and write at Cos. The Hippocratic or Coan school that formed around him was of enormous importance in separating medicine from superstition and philosophic speculation, placing it on a strictly scientific plane based on objective observation and critical deductive reasoning. Although Hippocrates followed the current belief that disease resulted from an imbalance of the four bodily HUMORS, he maintained that the disturbance was influenced by outside forces and that the humors were glandular secretions. He believed that the goal of medicine should be to build the patient's strength through appropriate diet and hygienic measures, resorting to more drastic treatment only when the symptoms showed this to be necessary. This was in contrast to the contemporary Cnidian school, which stressed detailed diagnosis and classification of diseases to the point of ignoring the patient. Hippocrates noted not only many of the signs of disease but also that these symptoms could appear throughout a family or a community or even over successive generations. Of the large collection of writings that derived from the Coan school, only a few are generally ascribed to Hippocrates himself, although his influence is felt throughout; of these, *The Aphorisms,* summing up his observations and deductions, and *Airs, Waters, and Places,* which recognized a link between environment and disease, are considered the most important. The collection has appeared in several translations, notably that by Littré, and many volumes are in the Loeb Classical Library. While the **Hippocratic oath** cannot be directly credited to him either, it undoubtedly represents his ideals and principles. One of the abridged versions in which it is administered to medical graduates in many modern universities is as follows: "You do solemnly swear, each man by whatever he holds most sacred, that you will be loyal to the profession of medicine and just and generous to its members; that you will lead your lives and practice your art in uprightness and honor; that into whatsoever house you shall enter, it shall be for the good of the sick to the utmost of your power, you holding yourselves far aloof from wrong, from corruption, from the tempting of others to vice; that you will exercise your art solely for the cure of your patients and will give no drug, perform no operation, for a criminal purpose, even if solicited, far less suggest it; that whatsoever you shall see or hear of the lives of men which is not fitting to be spoken, you will keep inviolably secret. These things do you swear. Let each man bow the head in sign of acquiescence. And now, if you will be true to this, your oath, may prosperity and good repute be ever yours; the opposite, if you shall prove yourselves forsworn." See study by E. B. Levine (1971).

Hippocrene (hĭp'əkrēn"): see MUSES and PEGASUS, in mythology.

Hippodamus (hĭpŏd'əməs), fl. 5th cent. B.C., Greek architect, b. Miletus. He was the first to plan cities according to geometric layouts. For Pericles he remodelled Piraeus (the port of Athens). He also planned (408) the city of Rhodes and went with the Athenian colonists to replan (c.440) the new city of Thurii in Italy. Other cities of the ancient world followed his methods.

Hippolyte (hĭpŏl'ĭtē), in Greek mythology, an Amazon queen. One of the 12 labors of Hercules was to take the golden girdle of Ares from her. To accomplish his task Hercules captured Hippolyte and then ransomed her for the girdle, although some said that he killed her for it. According to one legend, after Theseus abducted her sister Antiope, Hippolyte led a vengeful army to Athens but was defeated and died of grief. She is sometimes confused with Antiope and said to be the mother of Hippolytus.

Hippolytus, Saint (hĭpŏl'ĭtəs) [Gr.,=loosed horse], d. c.236, first antipope (c.217–235), theologian, and martyr. Probably a disciple of St. Irenaeus, he became the most astute theologian in the Roman Church of his time —he was the West's equivalent of ORIGEN in the East. He taught a Logos doctrine similar to that of Tertullian. Perhaps out of Montanistic leanings, he fell into dispute with Popes Zephyrinus and CALIXTUS I, accusing them of laxness on the question of heresy and of leniency with lapsed Christians; they in turn rejected his doctrine of the Trinity. Hippolytus withdrew from the Roman Church and with a small band of followers set himself up as antipope. During the reign of Pope Pontian (by which time Hippolytus was reconciled with the Roman Church) he composed his *Philosophumena*—a refutation of prevalent heresies, important today as a source for the period. Under Maximin's persecution he and Pontian were banished to the mines of Sardinia where before his death he was reconciled with the church. The ancient tradition of a St. Hippolytus who was torn apart by wild horses seems to refer to an earlier martyr. Feast: Aug. 13.

Hippolytus, in Greek mythology, son of Theseus and Antiope (or Hippolyte). After the death of Antiope, Theseus married Phaedra, daughter of Minos. Because Hippolytus worshiped only Artemis, the jealous Aphrodite punished him by causing his stepmother to fall in love with him. When he rejected her advances, Phaedra accused him of violating her and hanged herself. Theseus then drove him from Athens and prayed to his father, Poseidon, to have him killed. Poseidon frightened Hippolytus' horses, and he was dragged to his death. The legend is the subject of plays by Euripides, Seneca, and Racine.

Hippomedon (hĭpŏm'ədŏn): see SEVEN AGAINST THEBES.

Hippomenes (hĭpŏm'ĭnēz): see ATALANTA.

Hipponax (hĭpō'năks), fl. 540 B.C., Greek iambic poet. Banished from Ephesus after insulting the tyrants there, he went to live in Clazomenae. He is believed to have been the inventor of the choliambic, or "limping" iambic verse. He wrote spirited satire, fragments of which are extant.

hippopotamus, herbivorous, river-living mammal of tropical Africa, related to the pig. The large hippopotamus, *Hippopotamus amphibius,* has a short-legged, broad body with a tough gray or brown hide. The male stands about 5 ft (160 cm) high at the shoulder and weighs about 5 tons (4500 kg); the female is slightly smaller. The mouth is wide and the incisors and lower canines are large ivory tusks that grow throughout life. The eyes are located near the top of the head, so the animal can see when it is nearly submerged. Hippopotamuses usually live in herds of about 15 animals. Much of their time is spent in the water, where they feed on aquatic plants. When standing or swimming underwater they must rise to breathe every 5 min. At night groups of animals feed on the shore. The hippopotamus is hunted for meat and Africans use the hide for shields and whips. Once widespread in Africa, the animal is now rare except in unsettled areas and on reserves. The pygmy hippopotamus, *Choeropsis liberiensis,* is found in W Africa. It is about 30 in. (75 cm) tall at the shoulder and weighs about 400 lb (180 kg). More piglike in appearance and behavior than the large hippopotamus, it tends to be solitary and spends much of its time on the shore, sleeping by day in thickets. Hippopotamuses are classified in the phylum CHORDATA, subphylum Vertebrata, class Mammalia, order Artiodactyla, family Hippopotamidae.

Hippo Regius: see ANNABA, Algeria.

Hirado (hērä'dō), town (1970 pop. 32,863), on Hirado island, off NW Kyushu, Japan. It is known for its fine porcelains. The Portuguese traded at its port c.1550, and Dutch and English factories were established in the early 17th cent. There was also trade with China and Korea.

Hirah (hī'rə), Judah's father-in-law. Gen. 38.12.

Hiram (hī'rəm). **1** King of Tyre, a friend of David and Solomon. Solomon and Hiram shared in the trade with India and the Mediterranean, and they constantly exchanged gifts. Hiram sent much fine material for the Temple. 2 Sam. 5.11; 1 Kings 5; 9; 10.

Huram: 2 Chron. 2; 8; 9. **2** King of Tyre, mentioned in the inscriptions of Tiglath-pileser. **3** Artisan in metals from Tyre, sent for by Solomon to work on the ornamentation of the Temple. 1 Kings 7.13-45. Huram: 2 Chron. 4.11-22.

Hiranuma, Kiichiro, Baron (kē"ē'chērō hērä'nōōmä), 1865-1952, Japanese statesman, founder of the Kokuhonsha, a powerful militaristic and reactionary society. He became minister of justice in 1923. The following year he founded the Kokuhonsha, which drew support from high military, business, and political circles. By 1926, Hiranuma was vice-president of the privy council. He influenced Japan's withdrawal from the League of Nations, the abrogation of the Washington Naval Treaty, and the signing of the Anti-Comintern Pact. After the abortive military coup of Feb., 1936, Hiranuma became president of the privy council. He was prime minister for eight months in 1939, resigning after the Russo-German pact was signed. He continued to serve as president of the privy council, was home minister in 1940, and supported Tojo's call for a fight to the finish in 1945. Arrested as a war criminal in 1946, he was condemned to life imprisonment. Released from prison in 1951, he died in 1952.

Hiratsuka (hērä'tsōōkä), city (1970 pop. 163,671), Kanagawa prefecture, central Honshu, Japan, on Sagami Bay and the Sagami River. It is a commercial and industrial center with industries producing rubber goods, electronic equipment, and fountain pens.

Hirohito, (hĭr"ōhē'tō, hērō'hētō), 1901–, emperor of Japan. He was made regent in 1921 and succeeded his father, TAISHO, as emperor in 1926. He married (1924) Princess Nagako Kuni; a son and heir, Prince AKIHITO, was born in 1933. For 20 years he exerted little influence on Japanese politics, but in the summer of 1945 he, along with several moderate statesmen, persuaded the Japanese government to accept unconditional surrender rather than fight to the death. Under Allied pressure, the emperor publicly renounced (Jan., 1946) the idea of imperial divinity. The constitution of 1946 made him "symbol of the state and of the unity of the people," and stripped him of all but ceremonial powers. The emperor is well known for his studies in marine biology.

Hirosaki (hērō'säkē), city (1970 pop. 157,603), Aomori prefecture, N Honshu, Japan. A commercial center, it has industries that produce sake and lacquer ware. It is a former castle town and has 17th-century ruins.

Hiroshige, Ando (än'dō hērō'shēgä"), 1797-1858, Japanese painter and color-print artist of the ukiyo-e school. Among his prolific work is a series of landscapes (1833) entitled *Fifty-three Stages of the Tokaido Highway.* He painted flowers, fish, and birds, but his important prints are landscapes, frequently snow, rain, mist, or moonlight scenes. From him Whistler drew inspiration for his nocturnal scenes. Hiroshige is represented in the major museums of Tokyo, London, New York City, and Boston, and in many private collections. Hiroshige II, his son-in-law, and Hiroshige III, his adopted son, were pupils who took the name of their master. See his *Fifty-three Stages of the Tokaido,* ed. by Ichitaro Kondo (1960, repr. 1965); study by E. F. Strange (1925).

Hiroshima (hĭr"ōshē'mə, hērō'shmä), city (1970 pop. 541, 834), capital of Hiroshima prefecture, SW Honshu, Japan, on Hiroshima Bay. It is an important commercial and industrial center manufacturing textiles, sake, ship components, automobiles, machinery, tools, furniture, and canned foods. The city is also a market for agricultural and marine products. Founded c.1594 as a castle city on the Ota River delta, Hiroshima is divided by the river's seven mouths into six islands connected by 81 bridges. After 1868, Hiroshima's port, Ujina, was enlarged, and rail lines were built to link it with Kobe and Shimonoseki. Hiroshima was the target (Aug. 6, 1945) of the first atomic bomb ever dropped on a populated area; almost 130,000 people were killed, injured, or missing, and 90% of the city was leveled. Much of the city has been reconstructed, but a gutted section has been set aside as a "Peace City" to illustrate the effect of an atomic bomb. Since 1955 an annual world conference against nuclear weapons has met in Hiroshima. Hiroshima prefecture (1970 pop. 2,435,910), 3,258 sq mi (8,438 sq km), is generally mountainous, with fertile valleys. Silkworms, rice, and wheat are grown extensively. Hiroshima, Kure, and Onomichi are among the important cities.

Hirota, Koki (kō'kē hē'rōtä), 1878-1948, Japanese statesman. He trained at the Genyosha, a nationalist political society, and graduated from the law school of Tokyo Univ. A career diplomat, he served as ambassador to Russia (1930-32) and as foreign minister (1933-36). He became prime minister in March, 1936, and followed army dictates. His regime saw increased military spending, government interference in the economy, growth of aggression in China, and the signing of the Anti-Comintern Pact. He resigned under army pressure in Feb., 1937. Later he was (1937-38) foreign minister and president of the cabinet planning board under Fumimaro Konoye. In 1945 he negotiated to keep the USSR from declaring war on Japan. After the war he was arrested as a war criminal, and in 1948 he was convicted and hanged.

Hirsch, Emil Gustav (hûrsh), 1851-1923, American rabbi, b. Luxembourg. He was rabbi in Baltimore, Md., and Louisville, Ky., but is best known for his work as rabbi of the Sinai congregation of Chicago. In 1892 he became professor of rabbinical literature and philosophy at the Univ. of Chicago, and he was president (1885-97) of the Chicago Public Library board. He was an influential exponent of advanced thought and Reform Judaism. He edited the Milwaukee *Der Zeitgeist* (1880-82) and the *Reform Advocate* (1891-1923). See *My Religion*, a compilation of Hirsch's addresses and sermons, by G. B. Levi (1925); biography by D. C. Hirsch (1968).

Hirsch, Maurice, baron de (mōrēs' bärôN' də hĭrsh), 1831-96, German Jewish financier and philanthropist. The benefactor of numerous organizations and causes, his most ambitious project was the Jewish Colonization Association (1891), an organization designed to facilitate the emigration of Jews from Russia to colonies in North and South America. He formulated this colonization plan after the Russian government had refused his offer of $10 million for the establishment of proper educational conditions for Jews in that country. His other philanthropic contributions included immense sums donated to the Alliance Israélite Universelle (the first international Jewish organization), to Galician schools, and to various London hospitals.

Hirsch, Samson Raphael, 1808-88, German rabbi and chief exponent of Neo-Orthodoxy. As rabbi in Frankfurt-am-Main, he advocated the organization of autonomous Orthodox congregations outside of the state-recognized Jewish communal structure because of the latter's failure to support traditional ideals and practices. He was not an isolationist, however; he sought to combine traditional Jewish studies with secular learning. He first promoted that notion in his *Nineteen Letters* (1836, tr. 1899). He maintained in *Horeb* (1837, tr. 1962) that the reason for the Jews' existence was—in keeping with Biblical teachings—to exemplify the righteous life for all the world as revealed by God. He further saw Judaism as an organic institution and condemned the breaks in tradition advocated by the Reform movement. See Isidor Grunfeld, *Three Generations: The Influence of Samson Raphael Hirsch on Jewish Life and Thought* (1958); J. L. Blau, *Modern Varieties of Judaism* (1966).

Hirschberg: see JELENIA GÓRA, Poland.

Hirshhorn Museum and Sculpture Garden, Washington, D.C. Part of the Smithsonian Institution, the museum was designed by Gordon Bunshaft to house 6,000 pieces of the enormous art collection amassed by the industrialist Joseph H. Hirshhorn and presented by him to the nation in 1966. Opened in 1974, it is the capital city's first museum devoted exclusively to modern art. The building is a circular, windowless slab of concrete faced with pink granite. The sculpture garden extends from the glass-walled interior courtyard of the building; it contains a shallow pool and a fountain surrounded by masterworks of 19th- and 20th-century sculpture that are considered the chief strength of the collection. The painting collection is especially strong in works by Eakins and examples of pop art, op art, color-field painting, and the new realism. In addition to works from the collection and new acquisitions, temporary exhibitions organized in collaboration with other museums are presented. The museum's full name is the Joseph H. Hirshhorn Museum and Sculpture Garden.

Hirtius, Aulus (ô'ləs hûr'shēəs), d. 43 B.C., Roman soldier. He was a friend of Julius Caesar, with whom he served in Gaul. After Caesar's assassination (44 B.C.) Hirtius and Caius Vibius Pansa were consuls and took sides with the senate against Marc Antony, who was at Mutina (Modena) besieging Decimus Junius Brutus. Hirtius was killed in the successful lifting of the siege. He was probably the author of the eighth book of Caesar's *Gallic Wars.* He may also have been the author of *Bellum Alexandrinum*, a work that continues Caesar's commentary on the civil war.

His, Wilhelm (vĭl'hĕlm hĭs), 1831-1904, German biologist, b. Basel. He stressed the importance of mechanical principles in embryological development and introduced the use of the microtome for preparing tissue sections for microscopic study. He taught at the universities of Basel (1857-72) and Leipzig (from 1872).

Hishikawa Moronobu: see MORONOBU, HISHIKAWA.

Hispaniola (hĭs"pănyō'lə), Span. *Española* (āspänyō'lä), second largest island of the West Indies, 29,530 sq mi (76,483 sq km), between Cuba and Puerto Rico. HAITI occupies the western third of the island and the DOMINICAN REPUBLIC the remainder. Discovered by Columbus in 1492, the island was called Española. The later French colony was called Saint-Domingue, after Santo Domingo, the Spanish colony in the eastern part of the island. The terrain, dominated by the Cordillera Central, is rugged; Pico Duarte (10,417 ft/3,175 m high) is the tallest peak. Extending far westward, like the claws of a crab, two mountain ranges form the scenic Golfe de la Gonâve. The island's climate is subtropical, and agriculture (coffee, cocoa, sugarcane) flourishes in the abundant rainfall. Bauxite is mined there. Port-au-Prince, Haiti, and Santo Domingo, the Dominican Republic, are the largest cities.

Hiss, Alger, 1904–, American public official, b. Baltimore. After serving (1929-30) as secretary to Justice Oliver Wendell Holmes, Hiss practiced law (1930-33) in Boston and New York City. He then was attached to the Agricultural Adjustment Administration (1933-35) and to the Dept. of Justice (1935-36). He entered the Dept. of State in 1936 and rose rapidly to become an adviser at various international conferences and a coordinator of American foreign policy. In 1947, Hiss resigned his government post to become president of the Carnegie Endowment for International Peace. In Aug., 1948, Whittaker CHAMBERS, a magazine editor who confessed to having been a Communist party courier, accused Hiss of having helped in transmitting confidential government documents to the Russians. Hiss denied these charges and since, under the statute of limitations, he could not be tried for espionage, he was indicted (Dec., 1948) on two counts of perjury by a grand jury. When he was first brought to trial in New York City in 1949, the jury was unable to reach a decision (July, 1949). At a second trial Hiss was found guilty (Jan., 1950) and sentenced to a five-year prison term. His trial created great public controversy; many people believed that the Federal Bureau of Investigation had tampered with evidence in order to secure Hiss's conviction. Hiss was released from prison in Nov., 1954, his term having been shortened for good conduct. In 1957 he wrote *In the Court of Public Opinion,* in which he denied all the charges that had been made against him. See Whittaker Chambers, *Witness* (1952); Ronald Seth, *The Sleeping Truth: The Hiss-Chambers Affair Reappraised* (1968).

Hissar (hĭs-sär'), town (1971 pop. 89,463), Haryana state, NW India, on the West Jumna Canal. It is a district administrative center in a well-irrigated area and is a market for cotton, grain, and oilseed. An agricultural experimental farm is on Hissar's outskirts. Cotton and silk fabrics are made by handloom in the town. Hissar, founded in 1356, became important under the MOGUL empire. Depopulated by famine in 1783, Hissar was occupied by the British in 1803.

Hissarlik: see TROY, ancient city.

histamine (hĭs'təmēn"), organic compound derived in the body from the amino acid HISTIDINE by the removal of a carboxyl group (COOH). Although found in many plant and animal tissues, histamine is specifically important in human physiology because it is one of the chemicals released from certain cells (particularly mast cells) upon tissue injury or during the neutralization of foreign material (antigens) by certain types of antibodies. Released histamine tends to dilate blood capillaries, often causing the skin to appear red and feel warm, and makes the capillaries more permeable, allowing fluid to escape into the tissues. This causes edema (swelling), usually manifested as acute urticaria (rapidly-appearing hives, accompanied by severe itching). This sort of reaction is common to many allergies, such as food allergies, and the symptoms can often be controlled well with ANTIHISTAMINES. Unfortunately, histamine is not the only substance released under these conditions, and some allergies, particularly chronic ones such as asthma, are relatively resistant to antihistamine therapy.

histidine (hĭs'tĭdēn), organic compound, one of the 22 α-AMINO ACIDS commonly found in animal proteins. Only the L-stereoisomer appears in mammalian protein. Histidine is the direct precursor of HIS-

TAMINE; it is also an important source of carbon atoms in the synthesis of PURINES. The imidazole group on the side chain of histidine can act as both an acid and a base, i.e., it can both donate and accept protons under some conditions. This turns out to be an important property when histidine is incorporated into PROTEINS, particularly when it becomes a part of the primary structure of some ENZYMES. It is thought that the side chain of this amino acid acts as a general acid and base as it participates in the catalytic functions of CHYMOTRYPSIN, as well as those of a number of enzymes dealing with the metabolism of carbohydrates, proteins, and nucleic acids. It has even been implicated in the workings of cocoonase, the enzyme that allows adult silk moths to escape from their cocoons. Histidine is considered to be an essential amino acid for infants (it must be supplied in the diet); experiments with adults indicate that they can go for at least short periods without dietary intake of this amino acid. It was isolated from protein in 1896; its structure was confirmed by chemical synthesis in 1911.

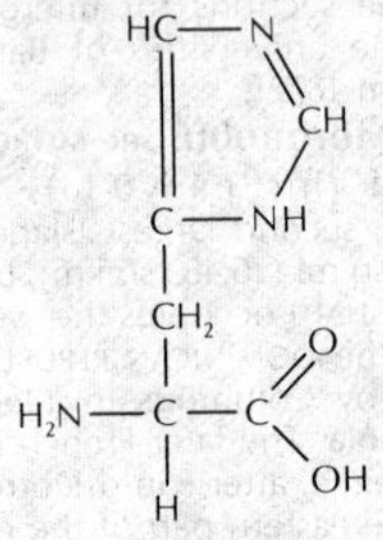

histidine

histocompatibility: see TRANSPLANTATION, MEDICAL.

histology (hĭstŏl'əjē), study of the groups of specialized cells called tissues that are found in most multicellular plants and animals. Histologists study the organization of tissues at all levels, from the whole organ down to the molecular components of cells. Animal tissues are classified as epithelium, with closely spaced cells and very little intercellular space; connective tissue, with large amounts of intercellular material; muscle, specialized for contraction; and nerve, specialized for conduction of electrical impulses. Blood is also sometimes considered a separate tissue type. These types are combined in different ways in the organism to form characteristic organs. Plants are composed of relatively undifferentiated tissue known as meristematic tissue; storage tissue, or parenchyma; vascular tissue; photosynthetic tissue, or chlorenchyma; and support tissue, or sclerenchyma and collenchyma. A variety of techniques are used for histological studies, including tissue culture, use of various fixatives and stains, the use of a microtome for preparing thin sections, light microscopy, electron microscopy, and X-ray diffraction. The field is divided into developmental histology, the study of tissue formation and specialization in growing embryos; histophysiology, the study of relations between morphological changes and physiological activity; and histochemistry, the study of the chemical composition of tissue structures. Histological investigation includes study of tissue death and regeneration and the reaction of tissue to injury or invading organisms. Because normal tissue has a characteristic appearance, histologic examination is often utilized to identify diseased tissue.

histone (hĭs'tōn), any one of a family of heterogenous PROTEIN molecules that are strongly basic and of relatively small size (molecular weight less than 25,000 grams per mole). The histones are rich in the amino acids ARGININE and LYSINE; members of the class differ from one another chiefly in the relative amounts of these two amino acid residues. The histones appear to be strongly, but not covalently, complexed to the deoxyribonucleic acid (DNA) of somatic cell nuclei; the combination of the protein and DNA is called a nucleoprotein. The precise function of the histone molecule is unknown, but it seems likely to play a role in regulation of the expression of the genetic material.

histoplasmosis: see FUNGUS INFECTION.

historical materialism: see DIALECTICAL MATERIALISM.

history, in its broadest sense, is the story of mankind's past. More specifically it means the records of that past, not only in chronicles and treatises on the past but in many material forms (e.g., monuments, buildings, artifacts, business papers, and newspapers). The early time, for which those records do not exist in any organized form, is prehistory, although that term is more generally used for the period in any civilization before inscriptions and other written records were preserved. In the older civilizations, as in Egypt, Mesopotamia, and China, historical records appear immediately after the appearance of writing, for conquering kings wished to record their triumphs for all posterity. There was also some interest in the remote past, particularly genealogical interest in the glorification of royal ancestors and their achievements. There appears early, too, a strain of religious interest in showing the lessons of history, religious and ethical. Thus the early historical sections of the Bible are concerned with the manifestation of God's will in the events of man's existence, while they show the same genealogical interests as the king lists of other peoples. It was not until the time of the Greeks, however, that historiography, the writing of organic history, emerged. The compilations of the *logographoi* in the 6th cent. B.C. were organized records. It is with some justice, however, that HERODOTUS is considered the first historian, because in his work appears the conscious desire to record all the significant and noteworthy circumstances surrounding a set of events and motivating the actions of people in those events. The element of causation was strong. Herodotus was remarkable, too, for the scope of his interests; he recorded myths, described customs, and made speculations. He used much unverified information, however, and failed to differentiate clearly between fact and fable. The second great Greek historian, THUCYDIDES, was of a different stamp. In writing the history of the Peloponnesian War he limited himself to matters of state and war; he tried to establish chronology and facts with some exactitude, avoiding the digressions of Herodotus; and he wrote a neat, grave work, conveying the lessons he drew from his story. The third of the great Greek historians, XENOPHON, was more devoted to the purely narrative aspects of history. These types of history writing, set thus early, persisted and are to be seen in various writers today. The influence of Thucydides was early in the ascendant, and the two important Greek historians of the Roman period, POLYBIUS and DION CASSIUS, more or less modeled themselves on that master. The Roman historian LIVY tended more to the narrative form, and he invoked the intervention of the gods to explain cause and effect. The great commentaries of Julius CAESAR were more like inspired reporting than pure history writing, and the personal element in them was strong. TACITUS followed more or less the pattern of Thucydides but with a brooding moral interest in the decay of Roman society. He showed a tremendous regard for accuracy and for testing the value of his sources that was not evident in many of the ancient historians. It did appear to some extent in the scrupulous work of the Jewish historian JOSEPHUS, but it was to disappear almost totally in medieval historiography. Medieval works tended to divide into two types of historiography. One was the universal history, which found some inspiration in St. Augustine's *City of God;* it was outstandingly illustrated by Paulus OROSIUS and continued by such lesser men as ISIDORE OF SEVILLE. The other was the chronicle, ranging from the crude and simple annals of local monasteries to more orderly and organized accounts such as those of SAXO GRAMMATICUS, OTTO OF FREISING, ROGER OF WENDOVER, and MATTHEW OF PARIS. The two forms were not infrequently mixed. Attempts at broader histories of peoples such as the history of the Goths by CASSIODORUS (preserved only in the compendium of JORDANES) and the history of the Franks by GREGORY OF TOURS were early and had few successors. The chronicles tended to be parochial. Since learning was restricted to the church, the chroniclers were generally biased in favor of the church, and they often were little concerned with politics and secular rule. They were criticized most by the humanists of the Renaissance and later generations for their readiness to supply without evidence facts that accorded with their opinions and for their credulous acceptance of many stories of miracles. They retained, however, some idea of the universal history of the world as it was then known as well as some idea of pattern in history. Furthermore, there were works of decided merit. Bede's *Ecclesiastical History* was an early model in a branch of historiography that has been of great importance. The biographical or semibiographical accounts of knightly deeds in the Crusades gave rise to the critical history of WILLIAM OF TYRE. Contact with Byzantines and Muslims broadened history writing by showing the Westerners other points of view. Byzantine historians had also early fallen into the writing of chronicles, although the greater unity of the Byzantine Empire and the persistence of a unified culture gave somewhat more literary quality to the Byzantine works, from PROCOPIUS through ANNA COMNENA to the 13th-century writings of George Acropolita and the Acominatus brothers. The effect on the West of the works of the celebrated Muslim historians is debatable, although IBN KHALDUN must be placed among the world's great historians. Other important Arab historians were TABARI and MASUDI. The new learning of the 12th cent. did, however, affect all writing and attitudes. The emergence of the secular historian, shown in the work of Geoffroi de VILLEHARDOUIN, became more pronounced in the chronicles of Jean, sire de JOINVILLE, Jean FROISSART, and Philippe de COMINES in successive centuries. The humanism of the Renaissance revolutionized historiography, for it placed emphasis on textual criticism and on a critical attitude toward documents and sources. Men such as PETRARCH, Lorenzo VALLA, MARSILIUS OF PADUA, and Juan Luis VIVES did much to sweep away old myths and produce a more critical attitude. Revival of classical learning immediately affected historians, and in one sense Niccolò MACHIAVELLI and Francesco GUICCIARDINI followed in the steps of Greek and Roman historians, although their work was original and immediate. Both the Reformation and the Catholic Reformation furthered historical scholarship, as both sides used the past to support their religious views. Critical methods in history were forwarded in the 16th and 17th cent. by the writings of Jean BODIN and Jean MABILLON, and great critical collections of sources were begun (e.g., the *Acta sanctorum*), while antiquaries everywhere discovered, questioned, and emended old texts. The way was prepared for the beginning of modern history. The men of the ENLIGHTENMENT lifted history writing to a new level. VOLTAIRE not only stressed accuracy and refused to accept the judgments of conventional historiographers but cultivated the wider, universal view of history, stressing its social and moral aspects. The attempt to get back to the fundamental natural bases of human development was implicit in the *Esprit des lois* of MONTESQUIEU. The 18th cent. saw, too, the great attempt made by Giovanni Battista VICO to synchronize history into meaningful general patterns. From England came the masterful work of Edward GIBBON. The end of the century also brought the budding of archaeology out of antiquarianism and of philology out of classical scholarship. These two sciences were essential to the development, in the 19th cent., of critical objective history as an academic discipline. The father of the new objective school was the great Leopold von RANKE. His efforts and those of his successors, notably Theodor MOMMSEN, Johann Gustav DROYSEN, and Heinrich von TREITSCHKE, established canons of criticism and historical methods. This German school made history writing into a profession and founded the formal academic study of history. In France, serious modern history began with Numa Denis FUSTEL DE COULANGES. It was continued by such men as Ernest LAVISSE, Charles SEIGNOBOS, and Achille LUCHAIRE, who were among those who turned history into a wide study. In the United States, earlier historians, such as George BANCROFT, William H. PRESCOTT, and John L. MOTLEY, were followed by the thorough Edward CHANNING and such brilliant and questioning men as Henry ADAMS, Francis PARKMAN, and Frederick J. TURNER; they in quite different ways developed the study of history. In England such men as Samuel R. GARDINER and Charles H. FIRTH challenged the older Whig historians such as Thomas B. MACAULAY. Meanwhile, however, the broader interest in the philosophy of history had not died, and the philosophy of Georg Wilhelm Friedrich HEGEL had created a school of idealistic historians; his influence continues. Other philosophical views were reflected in general theories, some of the later figures being Oswald SPENGLER, Benedetto CROCE, and Arnold TOYNBEE. The theories of Karl MARX not only set in motion a continuing series of interpretations of history from the Marxist economic point of view but also affected historians of all other schools. There were, too, other schools of economic history, such as the "new history" of James Harvey ROBINSON and Charles A. BEARD in the United States. The trend was toward broader social and economic history and that trend continued in the 20th cent. Anthropology and sociology contributed new ideas to history and opened the way to the history of cultures in the round (related to, but different from, such theories of spiritual cultural history as that of Karl LAMPRECHT). Modern psychology also began to be applied to the interpretation of history, and the growth of technological society stimulated some historians' concern with the development of science. The constant growth of the body of critical professional historiography led in the 20th cent. to historical research in extraordinary detail, stimulated by the techniques of Sir Lewis NAMIER. Perhaps in reaction to this increasing emphasis, there arose also a tendency to reassert the principle of history as an art as well as a scientific study and to extend the boundaries of history to study mass movements and society as a whole. However, at the same time the detailed scientific approach was reinforced by the development of computer analysis of historical materials. The quantitative analysis made possible by computers seemed to allow detailed study of far broader areas than had been possible for the historian using traditional methods. Quantitative history was, however, still in an early and controversial stage of development in the mid-1970s. The New Columbia Encyclopedia includes articles on most leading historians.

History in Asia. As in Europe, from early times the writing of history in Asia was concerned with the recording of events, chiefly as chronicles, annals, or archives. It was only with the impact of Western civilization that the writing of interpretative history began in Asia. In China by the middle of the Chou dynasty, histories of the royal house and of the various states (notably the *Shu Ching*, or *Document of History*, and the *Annals of Lu* by CONFUCIUS) were being compiled. Ssu-ma Chien (d. c.87 B.C.) wrote the first general history of China; his work was the model for later dynastic histories. He was followed in the 1st cent. A.D. by Pan Ku, compiler of the *History of the Former Han.* Under the T'ang dynasty, imperial commissions completed or compiled eight standard histories to fill in the period from the Three Kingdoms. A pioneer collection of early inscriptions was made, and Ssu-ma Kuang wrote (1066–84) an integrated history of China from 403 B.C. to A.D. 959. The Manchu rulers were noted for fraudulent histories glorifying their past. Critical treatment of Chinese history was forwarded in the late 19th and early 20th cent. with the work of K'ang Yu-wei, Wang Hsien-ch'ien, and Wang Kuo-wei. Japan's early tradition of historiography was derived from China. About the 3d cent. A.D. the Japanese began to keep imperial archives, and an accurate chronology was developed by the early 6th cent. The *Kojiki* (early 8th cent.) purported to be a history of the royal line since mythological times. It was supplemented by the more detailed *Nihonshiki*, which was continued to the end of the 9th cent. by five official histories. In the 17th cent. Tokugawa Mitsukuni (1628–1701) started to compile a history of Japan modeled on the Chinese dynastic histories; supplements appeared until 1906. Motoori Norinaga (1730–1801) was the leading figure in a movement to revive Shinto and imperial prestige; his commentary on the *Kojiki* was completed in 1798. Surviving Indian records date from the 6th cent. B.C., when anthologies were being made from older collections. Genealogies of native rulers appeared in the *Puranas*. However, the writing of history was not highly developed in India; the principal products were the *artha* or handbooks on politics and practical life. In the 7th cent. the work of HSÜAN-TSANG gave much valuable information about India. Arab works on India, notably that of Alberuni of Khiva, began to appear in the 10th cent.; notable later Muslim historians were FIRISHTA and Khafi Khan. After the coming of Europeans in the 15th cent. many accounts of India appeared, and, under British rule, histories of the British raj predominated. After 1947, Indian scholars resurrected older sources and began to rewrite Indian history in the light of this research. See London University School of Oriental and African Studies, *Historical Writing on the Peoples of Asia* (4 vol., 1961–62); C. V. Langlois and Charles Seignobos, *An Introduction to the Study of History* (tr. 1898, repr. 1966); E. R. A. Seligman, *The Economic Interpretation of History* (2d ed. rev. 1924, repr. 1961); Allen Johnson, *The Historian and Historical Evidence* (1926, repr. 1965); M. A. Fitzsimons et al., ed., *The Development of Historiography* (1954, repr. 1967); John Hale, *The Evolution of British Historiography: From Bacon to Namier* (1964); R. F. Berkhofer, *A Behavioral Approach to Historical Analysis* (1969); S. W. Halperin, ed., *Essays in Modern European Historiography* (1970); J. H. Hexter, *The History Primer* (1971); B. B. Wolman, ed., *The Psychoanalytic Interpretation of History* (1971); Peter Gay et al., ed., *Historians at Work* (2 vol., 1972).

history painting, the painting of scenes from classical and Christian history and mythology. It was taught in the ACADEMIES OF ART, from the Renaissance to the 19th cent., as the highest form of art in an hierarchical grouping that ranked still-life painting lowest on the list. Included in the category were scenes from contemporary history, such as Velázquez's *Surrender at Breda,* and commemorative works and apotheoses, such as Rubens's *Life of Marie de' Medici.* Scenes from antiquity dominated 18th-century painting, and modern subjects were exalted by treating them in classical terms. A modern work cited as falling within the history-painting tradition is Picasso's *Guernica.*

Hita (hē'tä), city (1970 pop. 64,866), Oita prefecture, N central Kyushu, Japan, on the Chikugo River and the Hita plain. It is an agricultural and industrial center with lumbering and wool industries.

Hitachi (hētä'chē), city (1970 pop. 193,210), Ibaraki prefecture, E central Honshu, Japan, on the Kashima Sea. It is an important industrial city where cement, electrical equipment, and chemicals are produced. It is the site of one of Japan's largest copper mines.

Hitchcock, Alfred, 1899–, English-American film director, writer, and producer, b. London. Hitchcock began his career as a director in 1925 and became prominent with his *39 Steps* in 1935. In 1938 he began working in the United States. Hitchcock's brilliant technique in creating suspense is seen in such films as *The Lady Vanishes* (1938), *Rebecca* (1940), *Suspicion* (1941), *Spellbound* (1945), *Notorious* (1946), *Strangers on a Train* (1951), *Rear Window* (1954), *Vertigo* (1958), *North by Northwest* (1959), the classic horror film *Psycho* (1960), *The Birds* (1963), and *Frenzy* (1972). Hitchcock had two successful television series (1955–62 and 1963–65). His work had considerable influence on French filmmakers of the 1960s. See François Truffaut, *Hitchcock* (tr. 1967); study by Robin Wood (2d ed. 1969).

Hitchcock, Ethan Allen, 1835–1909, U.S. Secretary of the Interior (1898–1907), b. Mobile, Ala. He was appointed minister to Russia in 1897 but was called into McKinley's cabinet the next year. Under Presidents McKinley and Theodore Roosevelt, Hitchcock prosecuted a vigorous program for the conservation of natural resources and reorganized the administration of Indian affairs.

Hitchcock, Frank Harris, 1867–1935, U. S. Postmaster General (1909–13), b. Amherst, Ohio. After service in the Dept. of Agriculture (1897–1903), the Dept. of Commerce and Labor (1903–5), and as Assistant Postmaster General (1905–8), he became Postmaster General. He organized the parcel post and the postal savings bank system and urged the initiation of an airmail system.

Hitchcock, Gilbert Monell, 1859–1934, American newspaper publisher and political leader, b. Omaha, Nebr. A lawyer, he founded (1885) the Omaha *Evening World,* combined it (1889) with the *Morning Herald,* and was proprietor of the *World-Herald* until his death. He was a supporter of William Jennings Bryan until in 1910 the two split in a quarrel that shook Democratic politics. He was a U.S. Representative (1903–5, 1907–11), and, as Nebraska's first Democratic Senator (1911–23), he was notable for his strong support of President Wilson's policies in World War I. As chairman of the Committee on Foreign Affairs and then as Democratic minority leader, he led the fight in the Senate for the Treaty of Versailles and the League of Nations.

Hitchcock, Henry-Russell, 1903–, American architectural historian, b. Boston. Hitchcock taught at various universities and in 1947 became professor of art at Smith. His writings on architecture are among the foremost in the field. They include *Frank Lloyd Wright* (1928), *Modern Architecture* (1929), *The Architecture of H. H. Richardson and His Times* (1936), *Early Victorian Architecture in Britain* (1954), *Latin American Architecture since 1945* (1955), *Architecture: Nineteenth and Twentieth Centuries* (1958), and *Rococo Architecture in Southern Germany* (1968).

Hitchcock, Lambert, 1795–1852, American chairmaker, b. Cheshire, Conn. In 1818 in Barkhamsted, Conn., Hitchcock established a factory whose employees came to number about 100. The village that the factory created was named Hitchcockville (changed in 1866 to Riverton). Hitchcock at first made parts of chairs and sold the parts to chairmakers. Later, he discontinued this business and manufactured complete chairs that were sold throughout the United States. The **Hitchcock chair** is characteristic of its time and has come to be sought by collectors. It is a factory product, typically not carved or upholstered, and is painted black over red, often with designs stenciled in colors or bronze. It is of good wood and is sturdily built. The legs and rungs are simple and well turned. The seat is of wood, cane, or rush. The name of L. Hitchcock or of a firm that he formed (Hitchcock, Alford & Company) is stenciled on the back edge of the seat. See J. T. Kenney, *The Hitchcock Chair* (1971).

Hitchcock, Thomas, Jr., 1900–1944, American polo player and aviator, b. Aiken, S.C., grad. Harvard, 1922. Trained at polo at an early age by his parents, both of whom were outstanding polo players, Tommy Hitchcock played in his first tournament at the age of 13. In World War I he joined the Lafayette Escadrille, distinguished himself in aerial combat, and became a hero after he was shot down behind the German lines and escaped to Switzerland. Hitchcock's polo playing in 1921 won for the United States the International Polo Challenge Cup, and later he excelled in several international tournaments. Probably the outstanding polo player of all time, Hitchcock received from the U.S. Polo Association its highest polo rating, the 10-goal handicap, from 1922 until 1940 (except in 1935, when he received a 9-goal rating). In 1937 he became a partner in a prominent banking firm. In World War II, Hitchcock was killed in an airplane crash in England while commanding a U.S. fighter-plane group.

Hitchcock chair: see HITCHCOCK, LAMBERT.

Hitchin, urban district (1971 pop. 28,680), Hertfordshire, SE England. Hitchin was the site of a monastery in OFFA's time and appears in the Domesday Book as a royal manor named Hiz. Corn and cattle are traded at a biweekly market. Industries include building contracting, engineering, tanning, parchment making, medicinal distilling, and rose growing. Henry Bessemer, the inventor, and George Chapman, the translator, were born in Hitchin.

Hitler, Adolf (ä'dôlf hĭt'lər), 1889–1945, German dictator, founder and leader of NATIONAL SOCIALISM. He was born in Braunau in Upper Austria, the son of Alois Hitler (1837–1903), an Austrian customs official. Alois Hitler was the illegitimate son of Maria Anna Schicklgruber, a servant, who later married Johann Georg Heidler or Hitler. A poor student, Adolf Hitler dropped out of high school, and after his mother's death in 1907 he moved to Vienna, where he twice failed the admission examination for the academy of arts. He lived on an inheritance and, when that ran out, on charity and the sale of picture postcards, which he copied. His vicious anti-Semitism (perhaps influenced by that of Karl LUEGER), political harangues, and moodiness drove acquaintances away. In 1913 he settled in Munich, and upon the outbreak of World War I he joined the Bavarian army. During the war he was gassed and wounded; he rose no higher than corporal but received the Iron Cross (first class) for bravery. The war hardened his extreme nationalism, and he wildly blamed the German defeat on betrayal by Jews and Marxists. Upon his return to Munich he joined with a handful of nationalistic veterans in the German Workers' party.

Hitler and the Nazi Party. In 1920 the German Workers' party was renamed the National Socialist German Workers', or Nazi, party; in 1921 it was reorganized with Hitler as near-dictatorial party chairman. He welded it into a paramilitary organization and won the support of such prominent nationalists as Field Marshal LUDENDORFF. On Nov. 8, 1923, Hitler attempted the "beer-hall putsch," intended as a coup to overthrow the republican government. Leading Bavarian officials (themselves discontented nationalists) were surrounded at a meeting in a Munich beer hall by the Nazi militia, or storm troopers, and made to swear loyalty to this "revolution." On regaining freedom the officials used the *Reichswehr* [army] to defeat the coup. Hitler fled, but he was soon arrested and sentenced to five years in the Landsberg fortress. He served only nine months; the authorities did not look unkindly on extreme nationalists. The putsch made Hitler known throughout Germany. In prison he dictated to Rudolf HESS the turgid *Mein Kampf* [my struggle], filled with anti-Semitic outpourings, worship of power, disdain for morality, and strategy for world domination. It became the bible of National Socialism. Under the tutelage of Hitler and Gregor STRASSER, aided by Paul GOEBBELS and from 1928 by Hermann GOERING, the party grew slowly until the economic depression, beginning in 1929, brought it mass support. Hitler then made prime use of his frenzied but magnetic oratory of hate and power, his insight into mass psychology, and his mastery of deceitful strategy. To the economically depressed he promised to despoil "Jew financiers," and to the workers he promised security. He gained the financial support of bankers and industrialists with his virulent anti-Communism and his promises to control trade unionism. After acquiring German citizenship through the state of

Brunswick, he ran in the presidential elections of 1932 in a whirlwind campaign. He lost the election to the popular war hero Paul von HINDENBURG but strengthened his position by falsely promising to support Chancellor Franz von PAPEN, who lifted the ban on the storm troops (June, 1932). When the Nazis were elected the largest party in the Reichstag (July, 1932), Hindenburg offered Hitler a subordinate place in the cabinet. Hitler unsuccessfully held out for the chief post and for sweeping powers. The chancellorship fell to Kurt von SCHLEICHER, who resigned on Jan. 28, 1933. Amid collapsing parliamentary government and rising civil violence between Nazis and Communists, Hindenburg, on the urging of von Papen, called Hitler to be chancellor of a coalition cabinet, refusing him extraordinary powers. Supported by Alfred HUGENBERG, Hitler took office on Jan. 30.

Hitler in Power. Germany's new ruler had a superb mastery of Machiavellian politics (in matters of culture he was unoriginal and sometimes mawkish, and his education was erratic, although he pretended to artistic and intellectual accomplishments). Although never insane Hitler had a paranoid fear of plots and persecutions; his belief in his mission to achieve the supremacy of the so-called Aryan race, which he termed the master race, was clear evidence of a warped mind. Having legally come to power, Hitler used brutality and subversion to pervert the state in favor of his dictatorship. He blamed the Communists for the fire in the REICHSTAG of Feb. 27, and by fanning anti-Communist hysteria the Nazis and Nationalists won a bare majority of Reichstag seats in the elections of March 5. After the Communists had been barred, and amid a display of storm trooper strength, the Reichstag voted to give Hitler dictatorial powers. From the first days of Hitler's "Third Reich" (for its history, see GERMANY; NATIONAL SOCIALISM; WORLD WAR II) political opponents such as von Schleicher and Gregor Strasser were murdered or incarcerated, and Nazis, among them Ernst ROEHM, were themselves purged. Jews, Socialists, and others were hounded, arrested, and deprived of rights or were assassinated. Government, law, and education became appendages of National Socialism. From Hindenburg's death in 1934 the chancellorship and presidency were united in the person of the Führer [leader]. *Heil Hitler!* became the obligatory form of greeting, and a cult of Führer worship was propagated. In 1938, in the midst of a carefully nurtured scandal, Hitler dismissed the top army commanders and divided their power between himself and faithful subordinates like Wilhelm KEITEL. As Hitler prepared for war he replaced professional diplomats with Nazis such as Joachim von RIBBENTROP. Many former doubters in Germany were converted by Hitler's bold diplomatic coups, beginning with German rearmament and culminating in the triumph of the MUNICH PACT. Hitler bullied smaller nations into making territorial concessions and played on the desire for peace and fear of Communism among the larger European states to achieve his expansionist goals. To forestall retaliation he claimed to be merely rectifying the onerous Treaty of Versailles. Benito MUSSOLINI became his ally and later made Italy his satellite, and Hitler helped Franco to dictatorship in Spain. On Hitler's order the Austrian chancellor Engelbert DOLLFUSS was assassinated, and Austria was amalgamated with the Reich. Hitler used the issue of "persecuted" Germans in Czechoslovakia as pretext for taking (1939) parts of that nation. He concluded a nonaggression pact (Aug., 1939) with Stalin in order to invade Poland but honored it only until he found it convenient to attack the USSR (June, 1941). Meanwhile, his invasion of Poland had begun World War II. In Dec., 1941, he assumed personal command of war strategy. A poor defense strategist, he refused to admit defeat after the battle of Stalingrad (now VOLGOGRAD) and in pursuing the war brought death to vast numbers of German troops. As the tide of war turned against Hitler, his mass assassination of the Jews, overseen by Adolf EICHMANN, was speeded, and he increasingly gave power to Heinrich HIMMLER and the dread SECRET POLICE, the Gestapo and SS (*Schutzstaffel*).

The End of the Third Reich. By July, 1944, the German military situation was desperate, and a group of high military and civil officials (including Field Marshal Erwin von Witzleben and Karl GOERDELER) executed a long-fomented plot against Hitler. Hitler escaped a bomb explosion with some injury; a vicious purge followed. Although the war was hopelessly lost by early 1945, Hitler insisted that the Germans fight on to the death. During the final German collapse in April, 1945, Hitler denounced Nazi leaders who wished to negotiate and remained in Berlin when it was stormed by the Russians. On April 29 he married his long-time mistress, Eva Braun, and on April 30 they committed suicide in an underground shelter of the chancellery building, having ordered that their bodies be burned. He left Germany a devastated nation. Hitler's legacy is the memory of the most dreadful tyranny of modern centuries. See his *Mein Kampf* (complete tr. 1940), *Hitler's Secret Conversations, 1941–1944* (tr. 1953), and *Hitler's Secret Book* (tr. 1962). See biographies by Konrad Heiden (1944), Alan Bullock (rev. ed., 1964), B. F. Smith (1968), and J. C. Fest (tr. 1974); H. R. Trevor-Roper, *The Last Days of Hitler* (1947); W. A. Jenks, *Vienna and the Young Hitler* (1960); Werner Maser, *Hitler* (tr. 1973); R. E. Hertzstein, *Adolf Hitler and the German Trauma, 1913–1945* (1974); Richard and Clara Winston, *Hitler* (1974).

Hitopadesa: see SANSKRIT LITERATURE.

Hitoyoshi (hētō'yōshē), city (1970 pop. 42,196), Kumamoto prefecture, W central Kyushu, Japan, on the Kuma River. It is an agricultural center, railway junction, and popular resort area noted for its hot springs. It is a former Edo era castle town noted for its Aoi Asho (Shinto) shrine built in 1611 A.D.

Hitti, Philip Khuri, 1886–, American orientalist, b. Syria. Educated at the American Univ. at Beirut and at Columbia, he settled in 1913 in the United States. There he taught Oriental languages and Semitic literature at Columbia (1915–1919) and at Princeton from 1926 until his retirement in 1954. Among his writings are *History of the Arabs* (1937, 7th ed. 1960), *History of Syria* (1951), *The Near East in History* (1961), and *Islam: A Way of Life* (1970).

Hittite: see ANATOLIAN LANGUAGES.

Hittite art. The Hittite invaders of central Anatolia (the area that is present-day W Turkey) came from the east c.2000 B.C. and by 1400 B.C. were masters of all of Asia Minor. Their most important period of artistic activity lasted from 1450 to 1200 B.C. Hittite art drew upon far earlier sources developed in Sumer and Babylon (see SUMERIAN AND BABYLONIAN ART) and upon local Anatolian culture of the 3d millennium B.C., characterized by elaborate gold and bronze ornamental work found at Alaça Hüyük and earlier neolithic remains found at Chatal Hüyük dating from the 7th millennium B.C. The Hittites quickly assimilated many aspects of the cultures they overran. They adopted a pantheon of Mesopotamian and N Syrian gods and represented them in their art—the males with high pointed hats, short-skirted robes, and boots with long, curling toes, and the females with long, pleated robes and square hats. The Hittites were accomplished carvers and metalworkers. Among the most impressive late representatives of Hittite deities is a series of ornaments from CARCHEMISH made to adorn a royal golden robe; they are carved in steatite and lapis lazuli and mounted in gold cloisons, each ⅝ in. (14.5 cm) high (7th cent. B.C.; British Mus.). The Hittites adapted the Babylonian CUNEIFORM to their language and also employed an elaborate HIEROGLYPHIC script for the engraving of monuments. Although animal figures are to be found in abundance in the artistic remains of the Hittites, their chief concern was human activity, particularly religious ritual. At the Great Sanctuary of Yazılıkaya near BOĞAZKÖY is a magnificent series of mythological scenes in carved rock depicting lions and sphinxes attending gods and goddesses. At İvriz another rock relief represents King Warbalawa praying before the god Tarhan, a capped and booted figure hung about with grapes and holding grain to symbolize fertility (8th cent. B.C.). There remain fewer representations of royal domestic life, including a hunting scene from Alaça Hüyük (200 B.C., Archaelogical Mus., Ankara), a family procession with King Araras with his children and their nurse and pets from Carchemish (750 B.C.), and a few polychrome vase paintings from Bitik, near Ankara, one of which is thought to depict a marriage. Other vases were made in animal shapes (e.g., duck vase, c.1700 B.C., from Beycesultan, Archaeological Mus., Ankara) and in the form of domestic items (e.g., boot vase, 19th cent. B.C., from Kültepe, Archaeological Mus., Ankara). A minor art of considerable development was the signet seal, generally containing figures and a cuneiform inscription, which the Hittites used instead of the cylinder seal popular with neighboring cultures. The principal architectural remnant of the Hittite civilization is at Boğazköy, where temple structures and the city walls may be seen. The Hittites developed the *bit-hilani*, a porticoed entrance hall built with a stairway approach flanked by pillars. Another characteristic form was the double gateway with corbeled arch, decorated with friezes and protected on either side by a threatening beast figure. Among the best-known of these is the lion gate at Hattuşaş, the ancient Hittite capital (c.1600 B.C.). These gate figures were later to be copied and used in the churches of Western Europe. In building interiors wall painting was evidently practiced with considerable sophistication, but only a few fragments of this work remain, principally at Boğazköy and Atchana in N Syria. The art of the Hittite Empire merged stylistically with Syrian art gradually, beginning in the 11th cent. B.C. The modern interest in Hittite culture was aroused in the mid-19th cent. by the Rev. Archibald Henry Sayre of Oxford, England. See ASSYRIAN ART; PHOENICIAN ART. See Maurice Vieyra, *Hittite Art* (1955); Seton Lloyd, *Early Anatolia* (1956); Ekrem Akurgal, *The Art of the Hittites* (tr. 1962); Carel J. Du Ry, *Art of the Ancient Near and Middle East* (1969).

Hittites (hĭt'īts), ancient people of Asia Minor and Syria, who flourished from 1600 to 1200 B.C. The Hittites, a people of Indo-European connection, were supposed to have entered Cappadocia c.1800 B.C. To the southwest, in the Taurus and Cilicia, were the Luites, relatives of the Hittites; to the southeast, in the Upper Euphrates, the Hurrians (Khurrites). In the country the Hittites then occupied, the aboriginal inhabitants were apparently the Khatti, or Hatti. Hittite names appear c.1800 B.C. on the tablets written by Assyrian colonists (see ASSYRIA) at Kultepe (Kanesh) in Cappadocia. However, real evidence of Hittite existence does not occur until the Old Hittite Kingdom (1600–1400 B.C.). This kingdom, which was centered in Cappadocia, was opposed by the Syrians. The Hittites tried to invade Babylonia but were halted by Egypt and Mitanni. The Hittite Empire that followed the Old Kingdom, with its capital at BOĞAZKÖY (also called Hattusas), was the chief power and cultural force in W Asia from 1400 to 1200 B.C. The famous Hittite rulers date from this period. Among these are Supiluliumash (fl. 1380 B.C.) who is mentioned in the TEL EL AMARNA letters, Mursilish II (fl. 1335 B.C.), and Hattusilish III (fl. 1300 B.C.). The Hittite Empire was a loose confederation that broke up under the invasions of the Thracians, Phrygians, and Assyrians c.1200 B.C. Several small states arose, with CARCHEMISH becoming an outstanding city. The neo-Hittite kingdom (c.1050–c.700 B.C.) was conquered by the Assyrians, who installed Hittite princes as vassals to their throne. The artistic work of the Hittites, as in reliefs, round sculptures, and seals, shows a high state of culture and considerable Babylonian and Assyrian influence. A great number of inscriptions have been uncovered in the Hittite area; these are for the most part in cuneiform. Besides the Babylonian inscriptions, there are many in Hittite hieroglyphs, or Kanesian. The Hittite language is Indo-European in relationship. There are several other languages meagerly represented in the Hittite archives: the so-called Luwian (similar to Hittite) and Khattian and Hurrian (both non-Indo-European and apparently unrelated to one another). There is also a hieroglyphic alphabet (or syllabary) liberally represented; the decipherment of this script was aided by the bilingual texts found at Karatepe and was published by H. T. Bossert. The Hittite civilization clearly had many foreign elements, notably from Mesopotamia; its pantheism borrowed most of its concepts from Babylonian, Assyrian, and Hurrian sources. The Hittite law codes are interesting partly because they are to some extent independent of the Babylonian. The Hittites were one of the first peoples to smelt iron successfully. See D. G. Hogarth, *Hittite Seals* (1920) and *Kings of the Hittites* (1926); E. H. Sturtevant, *Comparative Grammar of Hittite* (2d ed. 1951); Maurice Vieyra, *Hittite Art, 2300–750 B.C.* (1955); C. W. Cerám, *The Secret of the Hittites* (1956); John Garstang, *The Hittite Empire* (1929) and *The Geography of the Hittite Empire* (1959); O. R. Gurney, *The Hittites* (rev. ed. 1961); Ekrem Akurgal, *The Art of the Hittites* (tr. 1962).

Hittorff, Jacques Ignace (zhäk ēnyäs' ētôrf'), 1792–1867, French architect. He became a leading exponent of the classical revival in France, and his chief work is the Neo-Greek Church of St. Vincent de Paul, in Paris, which he built (1824–44) with his father-in-law, J. B. Lepère. Hittorff was appointed (1833) architect for the embellishments of the Place de l'Étoile, the Champs Élysées, and the Place de la Concorde. He designed the column in the Place Vendôme and other civic adornments. He also built (1861–63) the Gare du Nord. A pioneer in the study of the color ornament used in ancient Greek buildings, he published *Restitution du temple d'Empédocle à Sélinonte; ou, L'Architecture polychrome chez les Grecs* (1851).

Hiva Oa (hē'vä ō'ä), volcanic island (1967 est. pop. 1,000), 154 sq mi (399 sq km), South Pacific, second largest and the most important of the MARQUESAS ISLANDS, FRENCH POLYNESIA. Hiva Oa is the seat of Atuona, capital of the Marquesas. The Bay of Traitors, protected by ridges c.3,000 ft (910 m) high, provides a good harbor. Copra is the chief export.

hives (urticaria), rash consisting of blotches or localized swellings (wheals) of the skin, caused by an allergic reaction (see ALLERGY). The swelling is caused by distention of the skin capillaries and escape of serum and white cells into the skin and tissues. Hives are usually extremely itchy, and they may occur in a small area or cover virtually the entire body. The allergic reaction is commonly to a food or a drug, although injections of serum, insect bites, inhalants (pollen), and physical factors (cold, light, heat) may also be causative. Usually crops of hives come and go, remaining at one site for several hours and then reappearing at another; commonly an acute attack subsides spontaneously in a week or two. However, chronic cases of hives may last for long periods of time. Antihistamines and cortisone are considered helpful in relieving the itching and reducing the swelling.

Hivites (hī'vīts), peaceful tribe probably living in the vicinity of Jerusalem. They were crushed in the Hebrew occupation. Gen. 10.17; Ex. 3.8,17; Joshua 9.1,7; 11.3,19; 2 Sam. 24.7.

Hizkiah (hĭzkī'ə) [Heb., variant of HEZEKIAH], ancestor of Zephaniah. Zeph. 1.1.

Hizkijah (hĭzkī'jə) [Heb., variant of HEZEKIAH], one who returned from captivity to Palestine. Neh. 10.17. Hezekiah: Ezra 2.16; Neh. 7.21.

Hjälmaren (yĕl'märən), lake, c.190 sq mi (490 sq km), S central Sweden. It is drained into Mälaren lake by the Eskälven. Canals connect the lake with Arboga and Öreboro.

Hjørring (yör'ĭng), city (1970 com. pop. 31,100), Nordjylland co., N Denmark. The center of an agricultural region, it has food-processing plants, textile mills, and machine shops. Hjørring dates from the 12th cent. and has retained several medieval churches.

Hkakabo Razi (kä'käbō rä'zē), peak, 19,296 ft (5,881 m) high, N Burma, on an outlier of the Himalayan system. It is the highest point in Burma.

Ho, chemical symbol of the element HOLMIUM.

Hoadly, Benjamin (hōd'lē), 1676–1761, English prelate, center of the BANGORIAN CONTROVERSY within the Church of England. He was a leader in the Low Church group. In 1715 he was appointed bishop of Bangor, Wales, and chaplain to George I. His pamphlet, *A Preservative against the Principles and Practices of the Non-Jurors* (1716), and especially his sermon (1717) before the king on the text "My kingdom is not of this world," in which he maintained that Christ had not delegated authority to ecclesiastics, started the Bangorian Controversy. The ablest replies to Hoadly were those of William LAW. Hoadly was transferred to Hereford (1721), to Salisbury (1723), and to Winchester (1734).

Hoar, Ebenezer Rockwood, 1816–95, American lawyer, U.S. Attorney General (1869–70), b. Concord, Mass. While serving (1846) in the Massachusetts senate, he declared that he would rather be a "Conscience Whig" than a "Cotton Whig," thus originating an antislavery slogan. He was appointed U.S. Attorney General by President Grant, one of Grant's few good appointments. When Grant named him (1870) Associate Justice of the U.S. Supreme Court, the Senate, hostile to Hoar because he had insisted on filling new judgeships in the Federal circuit courts with able rather than political appointees, refused to confirm the appointment. Grant, seeking Senate support for his project of annexing Santo Domingo, in June, 1870, abruptly requested Hoar's resignation as Attorney General. Later Hoar helped negotiate the Treaty of Washington that settled the ALABAMA CLAIMS, and in 1873–75 he served in Congress.

Hoar, George Frisbie, 1826–1904, American legislator, b. Concord, Mass. He practiced law, became a Republican in politics, and was U.S. Representative (1869–77) and U.S. Senator (1877–1904). Hoar served on the congressional electoral commission that decided the contested election of 1876 in favor of the Republican Rutherford B. Hayes. He fought political corruption and avoided much of the partisan bitterness of the day. Hoar was a leader among the group of New Englanders who opposed President McKinley's expansionist policy. His *Autobiography of Seventy Years* (1903) is an excellent commentary on American political history. See biography by F. H. Gillett (1934); study by R. E. Welch (1971).

Hoare, Samuel: see TEMPLEWOOD, SAMUEL JOHN GURNEY HOARE, 1ST VISCOUNT.

hoarfrost: see FROST.

hoatzin (wätsēn') [from Aztec], common name for a peculiar marsh bird, *Opisthocomus hoatzin.* The hoatzin is a slender bird with a brownish plumage spotted with white above and reddish-yellow to rust below. It may reach up to 25 in. (64 cm) in length, but weighs no more than 1¾ lb (810 grams). It has a long tail of 10 loosely bound feathers, and a large, bristly crest mounted on a tiny skull. Its young are good swimmers and are peculiar in having claws on their first and second wing digits, which they use along with their short curved bills and weak toes for climbing trees. In this respect the hoatzin is reminiscent of the extinct lizard-bird Archaeopteryx. As the young mature and begin to fly (though never especially well), the claws dwindle. Hoatzins are sometimes called reptile-birds because of their crocodilian odor and harsh, monotonous call. In yet another respect, they are the most advanced of avians. In other birds, food is broken up in the gizzard, but the hoatzin accomplishes this in its well-developed, muscular, horny-walled crop, and its gizzard is much reduced. The hoatzin's specialized diet consists of certain marsh plants, including the mangrove, and the bird is thus restricted to the riverine forests centering around the Amazon Basin where it lives in small colonies of 10 to 50 birds. Both sexes participate in the building of loosely entwined stick nests, 5 to 20 ft (1.5–6.1 m) over the water, in the forks of riverbank trees. The female lays two to four small eggs per clutch, which are yellowish in color with pink or brown spots. Little is known of the incubation period or of parental responsibilities. Hoatzins are classified in the phylum CHORDATA, subphylum Vertebrata, class Aves, order Galliformes, family Opisthocomidae.

Hobab (hō'băb): see JETHRO.

Hobah (hō'bə), unidentified city or region, to which Chedorlaomer fled. Gen. 14.15.

Hoban, James (hō'bən), c.1762–1831, American architect, b. Ireland. By 1789, Hoban had immigrated to the United States. He designed the South Carolina statehouse, which was burned in 1865. In 1792 he moved to Washington, D.C., and won the competition for the design of a mansion for the President (later called the White House), which he built from 1792 to 1799 and rebuilt after it was burned by the British in 1814. He was one of the supervising architects who served at the Capitol in the execution of Dr. William Thornton's design, and he worked on public buildings for more than 25 years.

Hobart, Garret Augustus, 1844–99, Vice President of the United States (1897–99), b. Long Branch, N.J. A lawyer and businessman, he was prominent in New Jersey Republican politics for many years. Elected Vice President on the ticket with McKinley, he died in office.

Hobart (hō'bärt, -bərt), city (1971 pop. 52,425; urban agglomeration pop. 129,808), capital and principal port of Tasmania, SE Australia, at the foot of Mt. Wellington (4,166 ft/1,270 m high). Hobart's harbor is one of the finest in the world. The city has diverse industries, including meat-packing, food processing, and the making of textiles, chemicals, and glass. It was founded in 1804 and named for Robert Hobart, the British colonial secretary. Hobart is the seat of the Univ. of Tasmania (1890) and of Roman Catholic and Anglican cathedrals. The Hobart Theatre Royal (1836) is the oldest major theater in Australia.

Hobart (hō'bərt), city (1970 pop. 21,485), Lake co., extreme NW Ind.; settled c.1849, inc. 1921. Welding machinery and supplies, tools and castings, and aluminum doors and windows are made in Hobart.

Hobart College, at Geneva, N.Y.; for men; Episcopalian; founded 1822 as Geneva College. It adopted its present name in 1860. Hobart's medical school was noted for having graduated (1849) the first woman physician (Dr. Elizabeth Blackwell) in the United States. In 1872 the medical college was transferred to Syracuse Univ. In 1943, Hobart College joined William Smith (nonsectarian; for women; founded 1908) to form The Colleges of the Seneca. Classes are attended in common by students from both colleges, and teaching is done by a common faculty; each college, however, awards its own degrees.

Hobbema, Meindert (mīn'dərt hôb'əmä), 1638–1709, Dutch landscape painter. In landscape art Hobbema was second only to his contemporary Jacob van Ruisdael, with whom he may have studied. Most of his life was spent in a poor district of Amsterdam, where he died a pauper. Hobbema was little appreciated in his day but he is now recognized as the last of the great 17th-century Dutch masters of landscape. He painted most of his surviving work before 1668, when he took a clerical position with the city; thereafter he produced very few paintings. While lacking Ruisdael's scope and imagination, Hobbema equals him in draftsmanship, bold execution, and color. His works are full of life and luminosity and loving observation of nature. He painted chiefly woodland scenes, country villages, water mills, and other rustic subjects, his great mastery of detail never detracting from the general effect of his large and vigorous compositions. Much of his work is in England where it greatly influenced the later English landscapists. Among his well-known works are *Avenue at Middelharnis* (1689; National Gall., London); *The Mill* (Louvre); *Water Mill* (Rijks Mus.); and *Entrance to a Village* (Metropolitan Mus.). The National Gallery, London, has the best collection of his work.

Hobbes, Thomas (hŏbz), 1588–1679, English philosopher, grad. Magdalen College, Oxford, 1608. For many years a tutor in the Cavendish family, Hobbes took great interest in mathematics, physics, and the contemporary rationalism. On journeys to the Continent he established friendly relations with many learned men, including Galileo and Gassendi. In 1640, after his political writings had brought him into disfavor with the parliamentarians, he went to France (where he was tutor to the exiled Prince Charles). His work, however, aroused the antagonism of the English group in France, and his thorough materialism offended the churchmen, so that in 1651 he felt impelled to return to England, where he was able to live peacefully. Among his important works, which appeared in several revisions under different titles (see Sir W. Molesworth's edition of the complete works, 11 vol., 1839–45), are *De Cive* (1642), *Leviathan* (1651), *De Corpore Politico* (1650), *De Homine* (1658), and *Behemoth* (1680). In the *Leviathan,* Hobbes developed his political philosophy. He argued from a mechanistic view that life is simply the motions of the organism and that man is by nature a selfishly individualistic animal at constant war with all other men. In a state of nature, men are equal in their self-seeking and live out lives which are "nasty, brutish, and short." Fear of violent death is the principal motive which causes men to create a state by contracting to surrender their natural rights and to submit to the absolute authority of a sovereign. Although the power of the sovereign derived originally from the people—a challenge to the doctrine of the divine right of kings—the sovereign's power is absolute and not subject to the law. Temporal power is also always superior to ecclesiastical power. Though Hobbes favored a monarchy as the most efficient form of sovereignty, his theory could apply equally well to king or parliament. His political philosophy led to investigations by other political theorists, e.g., Locke, Spinoza, and Rousseau, who formulated their own radically different theories of the social contract. See biographies by Leslie Stephen (1904, repr. 1961), A. E. Taylor (1908, repr. 1970), John Laird Stephen (1934, repr. 1968); studies by Leo Strauss (1952), Clarence de Witt Thorpe (1940, repr. 1964), T. A. Sprague, Jr. (1973), and J. W. N. Watkins (rev. ed. 1973).

hobblebush: see HONEYSUCKLE.

Hobbs, city (1970 pop. 26,025), Lea co., SE N.Mex.; inc. 1929. With the discovery (1927) of oil and natural gas in the area, Hobbs became one of the last great oil-boom towns in the United States. Chemical production is of increasing importance, as are feedlots for livestock and the raising of thoroughbred horses. Cotton and other crops are grown on irrigated farms in the area; there are also truck farms for vegetables. Beef cattle have long been important in Hobbs; dairy farming is more recent. New Mexico Junior College is in the city.

Hobby, Oveta Culp, 1905–, American public official and newspaper publisher, Secretary of Health, Education and Welfare (1953–55), b. Killeen, Texas. She served as parliamentarian of the Texas house of representatives from 1925 to 1931 and from 1939 to 1941. In 1931 she married William Pettus Hobby, former governor of Texas (1917–21) and publisher of the Houston *Post.* She held various responsible positions on the newspaper. In World War II she became (1942) director of the Women's Army Auxiliary Corps (WAAC), which, in 1943, became the Women's Army Corps (WAC). She was commissioned colonel in 1943 and remained director until 1945. Appointed Federal Security Administrator under President Eisenhower, she became (April, 1953) the first Secretary of the newly created Dept. of Health, Education and Welfare, the only woman in the cabinet. In July, 1955, she resigned to succeed her ailing husband as president of the Houston *Post* and in 1965 she became chairman of the board.

hobgoblin: see GOBLIN.

Hobhouse, Leonard Trelawney, 1864–1929, English philosopher, sociologist, and journalist. He taught at Oxford and at the Univ. of London. Hobhouse sought to show with evidence from anthropology and comparative psychology that the evolution of the human mind was correlated with the development of societies. A liberal, Hobhouse ardently opposed imperialism. His books include *The Theory of Knowledge* (1896), *Morals in Evolution* (1906), and *Social Development* (1924). See studies by Hugh Carter (1927, repr. 1968) and J. A. Hobson and Morris Ginsberg (1931).

Hobkirks Hill, battle of: see CAROLINA CAMPAIGN.

Hoboken (hō'bōkən), city (1970 pop. 33,693), Antwerp prov., N Belgium, on the Scheldt River, an industrial suburb of Antwerp. It has large shipyards, metal refineries, and wool-processing plants.

Hoboken (hō'bōkən, -bəkən), city (1970 pop. 45,380), Hudson co., NE N.J., on the Hudson River adjoining Jersey City and opposite Manhattan; settled by the Dutch c.1640, inc. as a city 1855. It is a port of entry, a railroad terminal, and a busy seaport. Its long waterfront, shipyards, dry docks, marine shops, and warehouses accommodate oceangoing vessels. The city has a large food-processing industry. There are also factories making electronic equipment, precision instruments, chemicals, machinery, paper products, and furniture. The site changed title many times before John Stevens gained possession in 1784. He built his home at Castle Point (an unusual rock formation overlooking the river) and laid out the town in 1804. Its name was taken from the Indian *hobocan,* meaning "tobacco pipe." Stevens built (c.1825) and ran on his estate the first locomotive to pull a train on tracks in the United States. Before the mid-19th cent. Hoboken was a resort and amusement center for New Yorkers. In the latter 19th cent. it became an important industrial and commercial center. It was a major embarkation port for the American Expeditionary Force in World War I. John Jacob Astor lived in Hoboken, and his home was a gathering place for authors, including Fitz-Greene Halleck, Washington Irving, and William Cullen Bryant. Hoboken is the seat of Stevens Institute of Technology.

Hobson, John Atkinson, 1858–1940, English economist and journalist. He achieved wide popularity as a lecturer and writer. Criticizing classical economics, which centered on man's mechanical response to inflexible economic laws, he held that economic theory was bound up with the ethical problems of social welfare and should be a guide to reform. The economic measures he supported prefigured the more fully developed ideas of John Maynard Keynes. Hobson advocated partial socialization, and in *Imperialism* (1902) he interpreted imperialism as a product of the economic excesses of capitalism. His other works include *The Evolution of Modern Capitalism* (1894), *The Economics of Distribution* (1900), *The Economics of Unemployment* (1922), and the autobiographical *Confessions of an Economic Heretic* (1938). See H. N. Brailsford, *The Life-Work of J. A. Hobson* (1948).

Hoccleve or **Occleve, Thomas** (hŏk'lēv, ŏk'-), c.1368–c.1450, English poet, an imitator of Chaucer. He was a clerk in the office of the Privy Seal. His longest work, *The Regiment of Princes,* a didactic poem on the virtues and vices of a ruler, was addressed to the future King Henry V. Hoccleve's main importance is historical. His typically medieval lyrics to the Virgin, his ballades to patrons, and his versified moral tales are characteristic of his times.

Hoche, Lazare (läzär' ôsh), 1768–97, French general in the French Revolutionary Wars. Having distinguished himself at Dunkirk he was given command of the army of the Moselle in 1793. He recaptured the Wissembourg lines and occupied Speyer. Accused of treason by his rival, General Pichegru, Hoche was imprisoned in 1794. After his release, he was given the command in the VENDÉE. He pacified (1795) that province, but his attempted invasion of Ireland (1796) was thwarted by bad weather. In 1797 he defeated the Austrians at Neuwied and served briefly as minister of war.

Hochelaga (hō"shəlăg'ə, -lä'gə), former Indian village, Canada, discovered by Jacques Cartier on his second voyage (1535). It was situated at the foot of Mt. Royal in what is now the central part of the city of Montreal. The town was the capital of the Hochelagan people (probably of Iroquoian stock), the chief inhabitants of the St. Lawrence valley. Excavations in Montreal have unearthed hearths, kitchen middens, and burial places of the ancient village.

Hochhuth, Rolf (rôlf hōkh'ho͞ot), 1931–, German dramatist. His controversial first drama, *Der Stellvertreter* (1963; tr. *The Deputy,* 1963), brought him worldwide fame because of its provocative theme. An inquiry into Christian duty, it accuses Pope Pius XII, Christ's deputy, and the Roman Catholic clergy of tolerating Nazi crimes against the Jews. His second play, *Die Soldaten* (1967; tr. *Soldiers,* 1968), is a skillful documentary treatment of the fire-bombing of cities during World War II. *Liebe in unserer Zeit* [love in our time] (1961) and *Die Hebamme* (1971; tr. *The Midwife,* 1972) are among his other works.

Ho-chiang or **Hokiang** (both: hô-jēäng), former province (c.52,300 sq mi/135,500 sq km), NE China. The capital was Chia-mu-ssu (Kiamusze). Created in 1945, largely out of the former province of Kirin, it was one of nine provinces established in Manchuria by the Chinese Nationalist government after World War II. However, the Nationalists never gained effective control of Manchuria, and the provinces existed only on paper. In 1949 Ho-chiang was included in the Communist province of Sungkiang, which in 1954 became part of Heilungkiang prov.

Ho Chi Minh (hô chē mĭn), 1890–1969, Vietnamese nationalist leader, president of North Vietnam (1954–69). His given name was Nguyen That Thanh. In 1911 he left Vietnam, working aboard a French liner. He later lived in London and in the United States during World War I before going to France near the end of the war. There he became involved in the French socialist movement and was (1920) a founding member of the French Communist party. He studied revolutionary tactics in Moscow, and, as a Comintern member, was sent (1925–27) to Canton, China. While in the Far East, he organized Vietnamese revolutionaries and founded the Communist party of Indochina (later the Vietnamese Communist party). In the 1930s, Ho lived mainly in Moscow and China. He finally returned to Vietnam after the outbreak of World War II, organized a Vietnamese independence movement (the VIET MINH), and raised a guerrilla army to fight the Japanese. He proclaimed the republic of Vietnam in Sept., 1945, and later agreed that it would remain an autonomous state within the French Union. Differences with the French, however, soon led (1946) to an open break. Warfare lasted until 1954, culminating in the French defeat at DIENBIENPHU. After the Geneva Conference (1954), which divided Vietnam at the 17th parallel, Ho became the first president of the independent republic of North Vietnam. The accord also provided for elections to be held in 1956, aimed at reuniting North and South Vietnam; however, South Vietnam, backed by the United States, refused to hold the elections. The reason was generally held to be that Ho's popularity would have led to reunification under Communist rule. In succeeding years, Ho consolidated his government in the North. He organized a guerrilla movement in the South, the National Liberation Front, or VIET CONG, which was technically independent of North Vietnam, to win South Vietnam from the successive U.S.-supported governments there (see VIETNAM WAR). See biographies by Jean Lacouture (1968), David Halberstam (1971), Jean Sainteny (1972), and Charles Fenn (1974).

Hochkirch (hōkh'kĭrkh), village (1965 est. pop. 900), Dresden dist., SE East Germany. At Hochkirch in 1758 the Austrians under Daun defeated Frederick II of Prussia. In 1813, Napoleon I defeated a Prussian-Russian army near the village.

Höchst (hökhst), industrial district of Frankfurt, in Hesse, central West Germany. It is a leading center of the West German chemical industry and was formerly the site of the I. G. Farben chemical and dye works. Höchst was chartered in 1355 and in 1928 was incorporated into Frankfurt. In the Thirty Years War (1618–48), Tilly defeated (1622) Christian of Brunswick there.

hock: see WINE.

hockey, field, outdoor stick and ball game similar to soccer. Field hockey, of ancient origin, was played in England for several centuries, and after it was standardized by the Wimbledon Hockey Club (organized 1883), it spread to other countries. Field hockey for men has been played in the United States since 1890, but the Field Hockey Association of America, which regulates men's play, was not formed until 1930. Field hockey for men enjoys limited popularity in the United States and is played on the amateur level only. The sport became an Olympic event in 1908, and competition has since been dominated by India, Great Britain, and Pakistan. Field hockey for women has been a popular amateur sport in the United States, especially among college girls, since 1901; the U.S. Field Hockey Association (formed 1921) governs the women's game. Rules for men and women are essentially the same. The game is played on a level field, measuring 50 to 60 yd by 90 to 100 yd (46 to 55 m by 82 to 91 m), by two teams of 11 players each (five forwards, three halfbacks, two fullbacks, and a goalkeeper). A face-off in the center of the field starts the game. Teams direct their play toward advancing the ball—made of cork and twine, covered with white leather, and about 9 in. (23 cm) in circumference—down the field with their sticks (wooden, with a flat head on only one side of the striking surface). A point is scored by delivering the ball past the goalkeeper through the goal posts, which are 7 ft (2.13 m) high, 12 ft (3.66 m) apart, and joined by a net. Illegal use of the stick and roughness are penalized by temporarily relegating a player to the penalty corner. See M. J. Barnes, *Field Hockey* (1969); Caroline Haussermann, *Field Hockey* (1970); Melvyn Hickey, *Hockey for Women* (2d ed. 1970).

hockey, ice, winter skating sport in which players use sticks to propel a rubber disk into a net-enclosed goal area. Ice hockey, played exclusively by men, originated in Canada in the 1870s and later spread to the United States. There are at present two major professional ice hockey conferences, each with teams in both the United States and Canada. The National Hockey League (founded 1917) is the older group and is made up of 18 teams in two conferences, the Clarence Campbell conference and the Prince of Wales conference. Each conference, in turn, is divided into two divisions. The Lester Patrick division of the Campbell conference consists of the Atlanta Flames, New York Islanders, New York Rangers, and Philadelphia Flyers. The Conn Smythe division of the Campbell conference includes the Chicago Black Hawks, Kansas City Scouts, Minnesota North Stars, St. Louis Blues, and Vancouver Canucks. The James Morris division of the Prince of Wales conference includes the Detroit Red Wings, Los Angeles Kings, Montreal Canadiens, Pittsburgh Penguins, and Washington Capitals. The Charles F. Adams division of the Prince of Wales conference contains the Boston Bruins, Buffalo Sabres, California Golden Seals, and Toronto Maple Leafs. The World Hockey Association was formed (1971) as a rival league. By 1975 it consisted of the following 14 teams: Chicago Cougars, Cleveland Crusaders, Edmonton Oilers, Houston Aeros, Indianapolis Racers, Michigan Stags, Minnesota Fighting Saints, New England Whalers, Phoenix Road Runners, Quebec Nordiques, San Diego Mariners, Toronto Toros, Vancouver Blazers, and Winnipeg Jets. Because amateur and school-age hockey is poorly developed in the United States, most players in both professional leagues are Canadian. The Stanley Cup, now signifying world professional hockey supremacy, was first awarded (1893) for the Canadian amateur championship. From 1912 to 1925 it was awarded to the winner of competition between champions of the Pacific Coast League and Eastern League, but since 1926 it has been decided by a play-off among the best teams of the National Hockey League. Stanley Cup champions since 1926 have been: 1926, Montreal; 1927, Ottawa; 1928, New York; 1929, Boston; 1930, 1931, Montreal; 1932, Toronto; 1933, New York; 1934, Chicago; 1935, Montreal; 1936, 1937, Detroit; 1938, Chicago; 1939, Boston; 1940, New York; 1941, Boston; 1942, Toronto; 1943, Detroit; 1944, Montreal; 1945, Toronto; 1946, Montreal; 1947, 1948, 1949, Toronto; 1950, Detroit; 1951, Toronto; 1952, Detroit; 1953, Montreal; 1954, 1955, Detroit; 1956, 1957, 1958, 1959, 1960, Montreal; 1961, Chicago; 1962, 1963, 1964, Toronto; 1965, 1966, Montreal; 1967, Toronto; 1968, 1969, Montreal; 1970, Boston; 1971, Montreal; 1972, Boston; 1973, Montreal; 1974, Philadelphia. Amateur hockey is a popular international sport and has been played in the Winter Olympic Games since 1920. The International Ice Hockey Federation (founded 1908), the world governing body for amateur ice hockey, also sponsors an annual world championship. Since the 1950s both the Olympic competitions and the world championships have been dominated by the Soviet Union and, to a lesser extent, Czechoslovakia. Although Canada has an elaborate system of amateur hockey leagues, as well as many college teams, the country has not excelled in international amateur hockey since the early 1950s, mainly because the best Canadian amateurs quickly become professional and thus ineligible for amateur competition. In the United States, amateur ice hockey is generally confined to northern areas, such as New England and the Great Lakes region. Ice hockey is played on a rink that may vary from 184 to 200 ft (56–61 m) in length, and from 85 to 98 ft (26–30 m) in width. Six players—a goalie, a center, two defensemen, and two forwards—all of whom are on ice skates, make up a team. The rink is surrounded on all sides by walls 3½ to 4 ft (1.06–1.22 m) high. The goal nets are 4 ft (1.22 m) high and 6 ft (1.83 m) wide and are set 10 ft (3.05 m) out from each end of the rink, which is divided by colored lines under the ice into three zones (attacking, neutral, and defending), each 60 ft (18.29 m) long. A vulcanized rubber puck, 1 in. (2.54 cm) thick and 3 in. (7.62 cm) in circumference, is used, and the weight, size, and shape of ice-hockey sticks are standardized. After the face-off, teams concentrate on defending their own goals or, when in possession of the puck, on hitting it into the attacking zone and from there maneuvering it past the opposing defense into the net. Each goal counts one point. The game is divided into three 20-min periods; overtime periods in case of ties are only used in Stanley Cup play-off games. In this fast and body-bruising game, players use heavy protective equipment, and unlimited substitution is allowed. A player detected by the referee in roughing, tripping, high-sticking, or other violations is removed from the game to the penalty box for two minutes (a minor penalty) or more (major penalties), and his team must continue play shorthanded. Linesmen, goal judges, a timekeeper, and a scorer also officiate in ice hockey. The Hockey Hall of Fame was officially opened at the Canadian National Exhibition in Toronto in 1961. See G. A. Walford, *Ice Hockey* (1971); Harry Brown, *Ice Hockey Skating* (1972); S. K. Farrington, Jr., *Skates, Sticks, and Men* (1972).

Hocking, William Ernest, 1873–1966, American idealist philosopher, b. Cleveland, grad. Harvard (B.A., 1901; Ph.D., 1904). He was professor of philosophy at Harvard from 1914 until his retirement in 1943. His writings, which emphasize in particular the religious aspects of philosophy, include *The Meaning of God in Human Experience* (1912), *Human Nature and Its Remaking* (1923), *The Lasting Elements of Individualism* (1937), *Science and the Idea of God* (1944), *The Coming World Civilization* (1956), and *The Meaning of Immortality in Human Experience* (1957). See studies by D. S. Robinson (1968), A. R. Luther (1969), and R. B. Thigpen (1972).

Hockney, David, 1937–, English painter. Moving from a distorted, semiexpressionist form of POP ART, Hockney developed a highly personal realistic style. His clearly illuminated compositions often deal with homosexual life.

Hod, Asherite. 1 Chron. 7.37.

Hodaiah (hōdā'yə) [Heb., = Hodaviah], descendant of David. 1 Chron. 3.24.

Hodaviah (hŏdəvī'ə). **1** Chief Manassite. 1 Chron. 5.24. **2** Benjamite. 1 Chron. 9.7. **3** Levitical family. Ezra 2.40. Hodevah: Neh. 7.43. Judah: Ezra 3.9.

Hoddesdon (hŏdz'dən), urban district (1971 pop. 26,071), Hertfordshire, E central England. A residential suburb of London, Hoddesdon has light industries and horticultural enterprises. Broxbourne Woods attracts many London visitors, and there are several old inns and houses. Izaak Walton, author of *The Compleat Angler,* fished in the Lea River, which flows through Hoddesdon.

Hodeida (hōdā'də) or **Al Hudaydah** (äl ho͝odā'dä), city (1970 est. pop. 90,000), W Yemen, on the Red Sea. The chief port of the country, it exports coffee, dates, and hides. It was developed as a seaport in the mid-19th cent. by the Turks. After a disastrous fire in Jan., 1961, destroyed much of the city, it was rebuilt, particularly the port facilities, with Soviet aid. A highway from Hodeida to Sana, the capital, was completed in 1961.

Hodesh (hō'dĕsh), wife of Shaharaim. 1 Chron. 8,9.

Hodevah (hōdē'və), the same as HODAVIAH **3** .

Hodge, Charles, 1797–1878, American Calvinist theologian, b. Philadelphia. He was associated with Princeton Theological Seminary, where, after graduation, he taught first Oriental and biblical literature and later theology for 58 years. His chief work is his *Systematic Theology* (3 vol., 1872–73). He also wrote *The Constitutional History of the Presbyterian Church in the United States of America* (2 vol., 1839–40), *Discussions of Church Polity* (1878), and several widely used volumes of commentaries. He contributed the equivalent of many volumes to the *Princeton Review,* which he founded and edited for over 40 years. His biography was written (1880, repr. 1969) by his son **Archibald Alexander Hodge,** 1823–86, who succeeded to his place at the seminary.

Hodge, Frederick Webb, 1864–1956, American anthropologist, b. England. He was taken to the United States at the age of seven. He entered the field of archaeology through service (1884–86) in the Southwest with the U.S. Geological Survey and as secretary (1886–89) to the Hemenway Archaeological Expedition. Hodge became associated with the Bureau of Ethnology in 1889, led many of its expeditions in the Southwest, edited its *Handbook of the American Indians North of Mexico* (2 vol., 1907–10), and served (1910–18) as ethnologist in charge. A founder of the American Anthropological Association (1902), he edited its journal, the *American Anthropologist,* from 1902 to 1914. He was also associated (1918–31) with the Museum of the American Indian (Heye Foundation), New York City, conducting several of its archaeological expeditions to the Southwest. In 1932 he became director of the Southwest Museum, Los Angeles.

Hodges, George, 1856–1919, American Protestant Episcopal clergyman, b. Rome, N.Y. While at Calvary Church, Pittsburgh (1881–94), he attracted attention by the quality of his preaching. He was an early exponent of the SOCIAL GOSPEL and founder of Kingsley House and other philanthropic agencies in Pittsburgh. From 1894 until his death he was dean of the Episcopal Theological School, Cambridge, Mass. He was the author of many books and articles. See biography by his wife, Julia Shelley Hodges (1926).

Hodges, Luther Hartwell, 1898–1974, American politician, U.S. Secretary of Commerce (1961–65), b. Pittsylvania co., Va. From 1919 to 1950 he pursued a successful career in the textile industry. After his retirement from business he was elected (1952) lieutenant governor of North Carolina and succeeded to the governorship on the death of the incumbent in 1954. A Democrat, he was elected to a full term in 1956, and his administration achieved considerable success in attracting new industries to North Carolina. Appointed to the Dept. of Commerce by President John F. Kennedy, he worked to improve relations between business and government. He resigned in 1965.

Hodgkin, Alan Lloyd, 1914–, British biophysicist, educated at Trinity College, Cambridge. As a government research scientist during World War II, he worked on radar development. At Cambridge he became a Royal Society research professor in 1952 and in 1959 became a member of the Medical Research Council. He shared the 1963 Nobel Prize in Physiology and Medicine with A. F. Huxley and Sir John Carew Eccles for work in analyzing the electrical and chemical events in nerve cell discharge.

Hodgkin's disease, chronic systemic disorder manifested chiefly by enlargement of the lymph nodes, resulting from the proliferation of neoplastic cells. The spleen is also frequently enlarged, and, in later stages of the disorder, invasion of the bone marrow, liver, lungs, and other organs by atypical cells is common. Although Hodgkin's disease is generally considered to be a malignant neoplasm, there is also some evidence that it is caused by an infection. Itching of the skin is a prominent symptom, and in the advanced stages there are fever, anemia, and loss of weight. Radiation therapy is the treatment of choice in early stages of the disease, i.e., if it is limited to one or two abnormal lymph nodes. Patients in early stages who undergo such therapy and who experience no reappearance of symptoms for 5 years or more have at least a 95% chance of complete cure. At present the overall recovery rate is about 30%. Nitrogen mustard and certain other drugs are used to alleviate constitutional symptoms in the advanced stages of the disease.

Hodgson, Ralph, 1871–1962, English poet. He wrote five volumes of poetry before his collected poems appeared in 1917. After a silence of nearly 40 years—during which time he taught in Japan and emigrated to the United States—he published two more volumes. Hodgson treated his subject matter, nature, lyrically and simply. Some of his poems, e.g., "Eve" and "Time, You Old Gypsy Man," have been highly acclaimed.

Hodiah (hōdī'ə), name in an obscure passage. 1 Chron. 4.19.

Hodijah (hōdī'jə). **1** Levite in the return from the Exile. Neh. 8.7; 9.5; 10.10. **2, 3** Sealers of the covenant. Neh. 10.13, 18.

Hodler, Ferdinand (hōd'lər), 1853–1918, Swiss painter and lithographer. At first he worked in an ornamental style akin to art nouveau. Inclined toward mysticism, he visited Paris in 1891 and was attracted to the symbolist group around Gauguin. Hodler then evolved his own powerful means of expression with strong rhythmic patterns and a tight linear structure, which he called parallelism. He influenced the expressionists of the next generation. Characteristic paintings are *Eurythmy* (1894–95) and *The Woodcutter* (both: Bern).

Hódmezővásárhely (hôd'mĕzövä''shärhā), city (1970 pop. 52,797), SE Hungary, near the Tisza River. An agricultural center, it also produces machinery, textiles, and pottery. The city has many churches.

hoe, usually a flat blade, variously shaped, set in a long wooden handle and used primarily for weeding and for loosening the soil. It was the first distinctly agricultural implement. The earliest hoes were forked sticks. Heavy flaked-stone implements mounted with bitumen were used in Mesopotamia in the 5th millennium B.C. They occur together with flint-bladed sickles and grinding stones—all of which are indications of farming settlements. Hoe blades were made of animal antlers and scapulae, or shoulder blades, and of shells. Variations on the hoe, such as the pick, the adz, and the PLOW, appeared as the blade progressed from stone to copper, bronze, iron, and steel. Modern garden hoes are of two types, the drag hoe and the thrust hoe. Truck farms use light scraping hoes, chopping hoes, and multibladed hoes, and in large-scale agriculture a cultivating implement called a rotary hoe is used for weeding. The hoe symbolizes the garden horticulture that sustained high civilizations, such as those of pre-Columbian America. See Michael Partridge, *Farm Tools through the Ages* (1973).

Hoek van Holland (ho͝ok vän hôl'änt) or **Hook of Holland,** district of Rotterdam, W Netherlands, on the North Sea. It is an outer port of Rotterdam, with which it is connected by the New Waterway. It is a terminus of ships that cross the English Channel from Harwich, England.

Hoel, Sigurd (sē'go͞or hō'əl), 1890–1960, Norwegian novelist. Hoel's sophisticated novels of urban life include the witty satire *Sinners in Summertime* (1927, tr. 1930) and the more serious *One Day in October* (1931, tr. 1932). *Meeting at the Milestone* (1947, tr. 1951) probes the psychology of the Nazi conquerors. Hoel also wrote warm and evocative stories of childhood, notably *Road to the World's End* (1933).

Hof (hōf), city (1970 pop. 54,424), Bavaria, E central West Germany, on the Saale River, near the borders with East Germany and Czechoslovakia. The city's industries produce textiles, chemicals and dyes, metal goods, beer, and paper. Hof was first mentioned in the early 13th cent. and in 1373 passed to the Hohenzollern burgraviate of Nuremburg. It went to Bavaria in 1810 and was included in Upper FRANCONIA. Among its points of interest are two churches, the Lorenzkirche (11th cent.) and the Michaelskirche (c.1230).

Ho-fei or **Hofei** (both: hô-fā), city (1970 est. pop. 400,000), capital of Anhwei prov., China. A rapidly growing industrial city, it has textile mills, iron works and steelworks, food and cotton processing plants, and a variety of other manufactures. It is a transportation hub, with rail links to major cities and industrial centers. In Ho-fei are Anhwei Univ., a polytechnical university, a medical college, and agricultural and mining institutes. The city was formerly called Luchow.

Hofer, Andreas (ändrā'äs hō'fər), 1767–1810, Austrian patriot; son of a Tyrolean innkeeper. After its defeat by Napoleon I in 1805 Austria was forced to cede the TYROL to France's ally Bavaria. In 1809, when Austria renewed war on France, Hofer led the Tyrolean peasants in rebellion against Bavaria and the French. After several military successes he was made governor of the Tyrol by the Austrians. In Oct., 1809, Austria was obliged by the Treaty of Schönbrunn to abandon the Tyrol, but Hofer continued to resist. He was betrayed to the French, court-martialed, and shot at Mantua.

Hofer, Karl, 1878–1955, German painter. After a stay in Paris, where he was influenced by Cézanne's works, Hofer settled in Berlin (1913). He developed a restrained expressionist style revealing melancholic psychical isolation in works such as *Three Maskers* (1922; Wallraf-Richartz Mus., Cologne). In 1943, Hofer's studio was destroyed by the Nazis.

Hoffa, James Riddle (hôf'ə), 1913–, U.S. labor leader, b. Brazil, Indiana. As a young warehouseman he organized (1932) a union that was admitted two years later into the TEAMSTERS UNION. A successful organizer, he rose swiftly in the union so that in 1952 he became international vice president and in 1957 succeeded Dave Beck as president of the union. Evidences of corruption in the union revealed by a Senate investigating committee led to the expulsion of the Teamsters from the American Federation of Labor-Congress of Industrial Organizations in 1957, and Hoffa was forced to accept a three-man board of monitors to supervise his activities as Teamsters president. Despite efforts from outside the union to remove Hoffa, he was reelected president by acclamation in 1961. In 1962 he was indicted by a Federal grand jury and charged with accepting illegal payments from a Detroit trucking company; the case ended in a mistrial when the jury was deadlocked. Hoffa's power in the union continued to grow, and by 1964 he was able to effect the trucking industry's first national contract. However, in the same year Hoffa was convicted in two separate trials for jury tampering and fraud in handling the union benefits fund, and he was sentenced to a 13-year prison term. After all appeals had been exhausted, Hoffa began (1967) serving his sentence, but he retained the Teamster presidency until 1971, when he resigned. In the same year, President Nixon commuted Hoffa's sentence, with the parole provision that he not engage in union activity until 1980. After his release, Hoffa was active in promoting prison reform. See his autobiography, *The Trials of Jimmy Hoffa* (1970); Walter Sheridan, *The Fall and Rise of Jimmy Hoffa* (1972).

Høffding, Harald (hä'räl hôf'dĭng), 1843–1931, Danish philosopher. He was professor at Copenhagen (1883–1915). His histories of philosophy have been enjoyed by a large audience, especially his *History of Modern Philosophy* (1894–95; tr., 2 vol., 1900, repr. 1955).

Hoffman, Malvina, 1887–1966, American sculptor, b. New York City. She was a pupil of Rodin. Of her spirited figures representative examples are *Pavlowa gavotte* (Stockholm, Sweden) and *Russian Dancers*. Her portraits include those of John Muir (American Mus. of Natural History, New York City), Ivan Mestrovic (Brooklyn Mus., N.Y.), and busts of Paderewski as artist and as statesman. Her most impressive achievement is a series of 100 bronze portraits of racial types (Hall of Man, Field Mus., Chicago). To procure material for this anthropological gallery, Miss Hoffman traveled about the world for five years. She wrote an account in *Heads and Tales* (1936); her *Sculpture Inside and Out* was published in 1939.

Hoffmann, Ernst Theodor Amadeus (ĕrnst tā'ōdōr ämädā'o͞os hôf'män), 1776–1822, German romantic novelist and composer, a lawyer. At one time an opera director at Bamberg and a gifted music critic, he is most famous as a master of the gothic tale. His stories of madness, grotesquerie, horror, and the supernatural include *Fantasiestücke in Callots Manier* (1814–15), *Die Serapionsbrüder* (1819–21, tr. *The Serapion Brethren,* 1886–92), *Die Elixiere des Teufels* (1815–16, tr. *The Devil's Elixir,* 1824–26), and *Lebensansichten des Katers Murr* (1820–22, tr. *Kater Murr, the Educated Cat,* 1892). Offenbach's opera *Tales of Hoffmann* is based on three of his stories. He greatly influenced the composer Schumann. See studies by K. Negus (1965), H. W. Hewett-Thayer (1948, repr. 1971), and H. S. Daemmrich (1973).

Hoffmann, Friedrich (frē'drĭkh), 1660–1742, German physician. He taught and practiced at Halle from 1693. He studied and wrote on such varied topics as pediatrics, mineral waters, and meteorology; introduced many drugs into practice (e.g., Hoffmann's anodyne, or compound spirit of ether); and was among the first to describe several diseases, including appendicitis and German measles, and to recognize the regulatory role of the nervous system. His approach to physiology was mechanistic, viewing disease as a disruption of the body's tonus (hence the term *tonic* for his remedies).

Hoffmann, Josef, 1870–1956, Austrian decorator and architect. A student of Otto Wagner, he was a leader of Austrian decoration in the first three decades of the 20th cent. His sophisticated compositions, based on rectangles and squares, with delicate ornamental trimming, can best be seen in the architecture and decor of his masterpiece, the Palais Stoclet in Brussels (1905–11).

Hoffmann, Max, 1869–1927, German general in World War I. A brilliant strategist, he contributed to the German victory over the Russians at Tannenberg and in 1916 became chief of staff of the eastern armies. As military representative he helped negotiate the Treaty of Brest-Litovsk with Russia. In his war diary and later books he bitterly criticized the German high command.

Hofmann, August Wilhelm von (ou'go͝ost vĭl'hĕlm fən hôf'män), 1818–92, German organic chemist. He was professor at the Univ. of Berlin from 1865 and was a founder (1868) of the German Chemical Society. He studied the constitution of aniline and was the first to prepare rosaniline and its derivatives, thereby laying the basis for the aniline dye industry. He also discovered a reaction for deriving amines from amides and developed the Hofmann method of finding the vapor densities, and from these the molecular weights, of liquids. He also helped to popularize the concept of valence (the word comes from his term *quantivalence*).

Hofmann, Hans, 1880–1966, American painter, b. Germany. After earning a considerable reputation as a teacher in Munich, Hofmann moved permanently to the United States in 1930. He opened his own schools of art in New York City and in Provincetown, which were central to the development of ABSTRACT EXPRESSIONISM. Hofmann's work, influenced by Kandinsky, expresses his tremendous exuberance in his handling of violent, clashing colors. Representative examples of his art are *Germania* (Baltimore Mus. of Art) and *Elegy* (Walker Art Center, Minneapolis). See his writings, ed. by Sam Hunter (2d ed. 1964) and by W. C. Seitz (1963, repr. 1972).

Hofmann, Joseph, 1876–1957, Polish-American pianist, b. near Cracow; pupil of Anton Rubinstein. He toured Europe as a child prodigy, making his American debut in 1887 at the Metropolitan Opera House, New York City. That same year he ceased giving concerts but resumed his career in 1894. He returned (1924) to the United States, where he was director (1926–38) of the Curtis Institute of Music, Philadelphia. He composed under the pseudonym Michel Dvorsky but is best known for his great virtuosity as a performer.

Hofmannsthal, Hugo von (ho͞o'gō fən hōf'mänstäl), 1874–1929, Austrian dramatist and poet. His first verses were published when he was 16 years old, and his play *The Death of Titian* (1892, tr. 1913) when he was 18. His varied gifts as poet and as dramatist are shown in his librettos for Richard Strauss: *Electra* (1903, tr. 1908), *Der Rosenkavalier* (1911, tr. *The Rose Bearer,* 1912), *Ariadne auf Naxos* (1912, tr. 1913), *Arabella* (1929), and others. Also notable are his *Poems* (1903, tr. 1918), the tragedy *Der Turm* (1925), his adaptation of *Everyman* (1911, tr. 1917), and his correspondence with Strauss (1955, tr. 1961). *Everyman* is performed annually at the Salzburg festival, of which Hofmannsthal was a founder.

Hofmeister, Wilhelm (vĭl'hĕlm hōf'mī"stər), 1824–77, German botanist. Although self-taught, he made such valuable studies of the reproduction and development of plants that he was appointed professor, successively, at the universities of Heidelberg (1863) and Tübingen (1872). He demonstrated alternation of generations, especially in nonflowering plants, and described the behavior of the nucleus in cell formation.

Hofstadter, Richard, 1916–70, American historian, b. Buffalo, N.Y. He received his Ph.D. from Columbia in 1942 and began teaching there in 1946, becoming full professor in 1952 and De Witt Clinton professor of American history in 1959. One of the most brilliant of 20th-century American historians, Hofstadter wrote widely, delving into intellectual, social, and political history and covering the entire span of U.S. history. He won Pulitzer Prizes for *The Age of Reform* (1956) and *Anti-Intellectualism in American Life* (1963). His other major works include *Social Darwinism in American Thought* (1944, rev. ed. 1955), *The American Political Tradition and the Men Who Made It* (1948), *The Paranoid Style in American Politics* (1965), *The Progressive Historians* (1968), *The Idea of a Party System* (1969), and *America at 1750* (1971). See biographical memoir by L. A. Cremin (1972); S. M. Elkins and E. L. McKitrick, ed., *The Hofstadter Aegis* (1974).

Hofstra University, at Hempstead, N.Y.; coeducational. Founded as a division of New York Univ. in 1935, it became independent in 1940, and its name was changed to Hofstra College. In 1963 the school gained university status. A school of law was opened in 1970.

Hofu (hō'fo͞o), city (1970 pop. 97,009), Yamaguchi prefecture, SW Honshu, Japan, on the Suo Sea. It is a center of chemical industries producing artificial fibers, liquors, medicines, and salt.

Hofuf (hōfo͞of') or **Al Hufuf** (äl–), town (1960 est. pop. 100,000), E Saudi Arabia. Textiles, brass, and copper wire are made in Hofuf. It is also a trade center for dates, wheat, and fruit and has a large mosque. Originally called Hasa, it was the center of the Karmathian movement in the 10th cent. The oil fields of Shimanya are nearby.

hog: see SWINE.

Hogan, Ben (hō'gən), 1912–, American golfer, b. Stephenville, Texas. A former caddy, Hogan taught golf until he began his professional playing career in 1937. One of the game's great money winners, he won every major golf championship. After service in World War II, Hogan gained the Professional Golfers Association (PGA) championship in 1946 and again took the PGA title in 1948, when he also won the U.S. Open golf crown. After sustaining serious injuries in an automobile accident (Feb., 1949), Hogan made a dramatic comeback with his second U.S. Open victory in 1950. He repeated this in 1951 and added his first Master's crown. In 1953, Hogan won the three major golf titles—the U.S. Open, the Master's, and the British Open. His final (1953) U.S. Open triumph made him the first since Bobby Jones to win four U.S. Open titles. He wrote *Power Golf* (1948) and, with H. W. Wind, *Modern Fundamentals of Golf* (1957).

Hogarth, David George (hō'gärth), 1862–1927, English archaeologist, keeper (1909–27) of the Ashmolean Museum, Oxford. He explored and excavated (1887–1907) in Cyprus, Crete, Egypt, Syria, and Melos. Among his published works are *A Wandering Scholar* (1896), *The Archaic Artemisia of Ephesus* (1908), *Ionia and the East* (1909), *The Ancient East* (1914, 2d ed. 1950), *Hittite Seals* (1920), *Arabia* (1922), and *Kings of the Hittites* (1926). See biography by A. H. Sayce (1928).

Hogarth, William, 1697–1764, English painter, satirist, engraver, and art theorist, b. London. At the age of 15 he was apprenticed to a silver-plate engraver. He soon made engravings on copper for bookplates and illustrations—notably those for Butler's *Hudibras* (1726). He studied drawing with Thornhill, whose daughter he married in 1729. Hogarth tried to earn a living with small portraits and portrait groups, but his first real success came in 1732 with a series of six morality pictures, *The Harlot's Progress.* He first painted, then engraved them, selling subscriptions for the prints, which had great popularity. *The Rake's Progress,* a similar series, appeared in 1735. The series *Marriage à la Mode* (1745) is often considered his masterpiece. With a wealth of detail and brilliant characterization he depicts the profligate and inane existence of a fashionable young couple. Hogarth invented a sort of visual shorthand that enabled him to recall with perfect clarity whatever sight he wished to retain. He became, by this means, an enormously learned artist possessing a profound visual understanding. His *Analysis of Beauty* (1753) is a brilliant formal exposition of the ROCOCO aesthetic. In such prints as *Gin Lane* and *Four Stages of Cruelty* Hogarth is very sincerely didactic, employing the weapons of satire against the cruelty, stupidity, and bombast that he observed in all levels of the society of his day. His portraits *The Shrimp Girl* (National Gall., London) and *Captain Coram* (1740) are two of the masterpieces of British painting. Hogarth's major works are in England. In New York City the Metropolitan Museum and the Frick Collection possess examples of his work. See his *Analysis of Beauty,* ed. by Joseph Burke (1955); his graphic works, ed. by R. Paulson (rev. ed. 1970); biographies by P. Quennell (1955) and R. Paulson (1971); studies by F. Antal (1962) and G. C. Lichtenberg (tr. 1966).

hogback, sharp-crested ridge with steep slopes on both sides, formed by the erosion of steeply tilted rock layers. Hogbacks are commonly formed along the eroded flanks of large, tightly folded anticlines and synclines (see FOLD). Impressive hogbacks are seen in the foothills east of the Front Range of the Rocky Mts. in Colorado, where they are formed by the vertical or steeply dipping layers of Dakota sandstone. This region forms the intake area for the Dakota artesian system. Hogbacks are also common in the Black Hills of South Dakota where sedimentary rocks were uplifted by the intrusion of Black Hills granite. See CUESTA.

hog cholera, acute, highly infectious viral disease of swine, also called swine fever. It is perhaps the most serious disease of swine in North America. It is characterized by dullness and listlessness, loss of appetite, rise in temperature to between 105°F (41°C) and 107°F (42°C), diarrhea, and often death. Purple hemorrhagic areas will appear on the abdomen and many pigs display nervous signs, such as circling, incoordination, muscle tremors, and convulsions. Mortality is very high and recovered animals are permanently stunted. The disease is transmitted readily by direct or indirect contact. The virus may enter a herd through contaminated feed, water, equipment, or by contact with an infected animal or person. At one time, feeding pigs raw garbage containing pork scraps from infected pigs was a common cause of infection. For this reason the United

States and many other countries now prohibit the feeding of uncooked garbage to pigs. A national hog cholera eradication program has been established in the United States to eliminate all possible sources of virus introduction. A vaccine is available in areas where the disease is still present.

Hogg, James, 1770–1835, Scottish poet, called the Ettrick Shepherd. Sir Walter Scott established Hogg's literary reputation by including some of his poems in *Border Minstrelsy.* Hogg's verse, notable for its earthy vigor, includes *The Mountain Bard* (1807) and *The Queen's Wake* (1813). He also wrote several prose works, including recollections of Scott (1834). See his memoirs, *Confessions of a Fanatic* (1824); study by Louis Simpson (1962).

Hogg, James Stephen, 1851–1906, governor of Texas (1891–95), b. Cherokee co., Texas. He was admitted (1875) to the Texas bar, and was county attorney (1879–81), district attorney (1881–85), and state attorney general (1887–91). As soon as he became (1891) governor of Texas, Hogg established (1891) a state railroad commission with broad powers of regulation and then successfully pushed through other sweeping economic reforms. He was reelected governor of Texas in 1893. He retired from political life in 1895 to practice law. See his addresses and state papers, ed. by R. C. Cotner (1951); biography by R. C. Cotner (1959).

Hogg, Quintin: see HAILSHAM, QUINTIN MCGAREL HOGG, BARON.

Hogg, Thomas Jefferson, 1792–1862, friend and biographer of Percy Bysshe SHELLEY. He was dismissed in 1811 from Oxford for defending Shelley's atheism. Authorized by Mary Shelley to write a life of her husband, Hogg issued (1858) the first two volumes, which were biased, inaccurate, and overly devoted to incidents in Hogg's own life; the family eventually withdrew the materials from his use. His account of Shelley at Oxford, written earlier, was published separately in 1904 as *Shelley at Oxford.* Throughout his life Hogg was a successful lawyer.

Hoggar, mountains, Africa: see SAHARA.

Hoglah (hŏg'lə), daughter and coheiress of Zelophehad. Num. 26.33; 27.1–11.

Hogue, La (lä ôg), or **La Hougue** (lä o͞og), cape on the northeast coast of the Cotentin peninsula, France, on the English Channel. Off the cape, during the War of the Grand Alliance, a French fleet under Tourville was defeated (1692) by the English and Dutch. The battle ended French naval supremacy in the war.

Hoham (hō'hăm), king of Hebron, whom Joshua defeated. Joshua 10.3.

Hohenfriedeberg (hō"ənfrē'dəbərk), Pol. *Dobromierz,* town, SW Poland. In 1745 it was the site of the victory of Frederick II of Prussia over the Austrian and Saxon forces in the War of the Austrian Succession. Hohenfriedeberg was ceded to Poland after World War II.

Hohenlohe-Schillingsfürst, Chlodwig Karl Viktor, Fürst zu (klōt'vĭkh kärl vĭk'tôr fürst tso͞o hō"ə-nlō"ə-shĭl'ĭngsfürst), 1819–1901, German chancellor (1894–1900). As premier of Bavaria (1866–70), he favored German unification, and in 1871 he entered the service of the German Empire and became one of Bismarck's staunchest supporters. He was ambassador to Paris (1874–80) and governor of Alsace-Lorraine (1885–94). Succeeding Leo von Caprivi as chancellor in 1894, he delegated most of his duties to his cabinet, especially the foreign secretaries Marschall von Bieberstein and Bernhard von BÜLOW. The latter succeeded Hohenlohe when he retired in 1900. See his memoirs (tr. 1906).

Hohensalza: see INOWROCŁAW, Poland.

Hohenstaufen (hō"ənshtou'fən), German princely family, whose name is derived from the castle of Staufen built in 1077 by a Swabian count, Frederick. In 1079, Frederick married Agnes, daughter of Holy Roman Emperor Henry IV, and was created duke of Swabia. The line of German kings and Holy Roman emperors began (1138) with Frederick's son CONRAD III, who was succeeded by FREDERICK I, HENRY VI, and PHILIP OF SWABIA. Their chief rivals were the GUELPHS (see also GUELPHS AND GHIBELLINES), whose scion, Otto IV, was Holy Roman emperor from 1209 to 1215; but the Hohenstaufen heir, FREDERICK II, was elected king by a rival party in 1212. The most spectacular representative of the house, Frederick shifted the center of the family interests to Sicily and S Italy. His involvement in Italy brought him into conflict with the popes, who worked at bringing about the downfall of the house. Shortly after Frederick's death (1250) his son CONRAD IV died and CONRADIN, the last legitimate Hohenstaufen, became titular king of Sicily; his uncle MANFRED, an illegitimate son of Frederick II, seized the regency for him. Manfred's death (1258) and Conradin's execution (1268) ended the family power, and with the death of Frederick's illegitimate son ENZIO (1272) the family became extinct. Memories of the German empire's greatness under the Hohenstaufen played a part in later German history and inspired legends such as that of the KYFFHÄUSER. See T. F. Tout, *The Empire and the Papacy, 918–1273* (8th ed. 1941); James W. Thompson, *Feudal Germany* (1928, repr. 1962); G. Barraclough, *The Origins of Modern Germany* (2d rev. ed. 1966).

Hohentwiel (hōəntvēl'), mountain, 2,260 ft (689 m) high, in Baden-Württemberg, SW West Germany. On the summit of Hohentwiel are the ruins of an ancient castle that was the seat of the dukes of Swabia in the 10th cent.

Hohenzollern (hō"ən-tsôl'ərn), German princely family that ruled Brandenburg (1415–1918), Prussia (1525–1918), and Germany (1871–1918). Originating in S Germany and traceable to the 11th cent., the family probably took its name from the German word *zôller,* meaning "watchtower" or "castle," and in particular from the Swabian castle of Hohenzollern, the ancestral seat in the Black Forest. Conrad of Hohenzollern, appointed (c.1170) burgrave (imperial representative) of Nuremberg by Holy Roman Emperor Frederick I, was succeeded (1192) by Frederick of Hohenzollern (d. c.1200), whose sons founded the Swabian and Franconian lines of the family. (For the Swabian line see Hohenzollern-Hechingen and Hohenzollern-Sigmaringen under HOHENZOLLERN, province). The Franconian line acquired the margraviates of Ansbach (1331) and Kulmbach (1340). In 1415, Holy Roman Emperor Sigismund made Frederick VI of Hohenzollern elector of Brandenburg, and in 1417 Frederick formally received the electoral dignity as Frederick I. Brandenburg then became the center of Hohenzollern power. Frederick II (reigned 1440–70) bought New Mark from the Teutonic Knights and Lower Lusatia from the Holy Roman emperor; he made Berlin the political capital. Elector ALBERT ACHILLES (reigned 1470–86) issued a family law that made Brandenburg indivisible. Roman law was introduced by Joachim I (1499–1535), who tried to suppress the Protestant movement. In 1525, ALBERT OF BRANDENBURG, grand master of the Teutonic Knights, secularized the domains of his order as the duchy of Prussia. Joachim II (reigned 1535–71) converted to Lutheranism. When John Sigismund (reigned 1608–19) converted to Calvinism, his subjects remained Lutheran; thus religious toleration became a mark of the dynasty. John Sigismund's acquisition (1614) of Cleves, Mark, and Ravensburg and his inheritance (1618) of the duchy of Prussia (East Prussia) marked the Hohenzollern rise as a leading German power. FREDERICK WILLIAM, the Great Elector (reigned 1640–88), obtained E Pomerania, the secularized bishoprics of Cammin, Minden, and Halberstadt, and the expectancy to Magdeburg upon the death of its administrator. His reign brought centralization and absolutism to the Hohenzollern lands. In 1701 his son was crowned "king in Prussia" as FREDERICK I and at the Peace of Utrecht was recognized (1713) as king of Prussia. The royal title was a new symbol of the unity of the family holdings. FREDERICK WILLIAM I (reigned 1713–40), through his administrative, fiscal, and military reforms, was the real architect of Hohenzollern greatness. As a result of the Northern Wars, he obtained (1721) part of W Pomerania, including Stettin. FREDERICK II (reigned 1740–86) seized Silesia from Holy Roman Empress Maria Theresa and acquired (1772) West Prussia and Ermeland from the first partition of Poland. An enlightened despot, he achieved the reform and codification (1794) of Prussian law. FREDERICK WILLIAM II (reigned 1786–97), FREDERICK WILLIAM III (reigned 1797–1840), and FREDERICK WILLIAM IV (reigned 1840–61) were mediocre rulers; their ministers were more important in the history of Prussia. WILLIAM I (reigned 1861–88) entrusted his affairs to Otto von Bismarck, under whose direction Prussia triumphed over its rival Austria and over France. In 1871, William was proclaimed emperor (kaiser) of a united Germany. He was succeeded by FREDERICK III (1888) and by WILLIAM II (reigned 1888–1918), whose instability and ambition contributed to the involvement of Germany in World War I; his abdication ended the family's rule in Germany.

Hohenzollern, former province of Germany. After 1945 it became part of the temporary state of Württemberg-Hohenzollern, which was included in the state of BADEN-WÜRTTEMBERG in 1952. Its chief city was Sigmaringen, located in a mountainous region of the Swabian Jura. The impressive castle of Zollern or Hohenzollern (first mentioned 1267) in the north gave its name to the ruling house of Prussia. In 1575, Count Charles I divided the territory among his three sons, founding three lines—**Hohenzollern-Hechingen, Hohenzollern-Sigmaringen,** and **Hohenzollern-Haigerloch.** In 1634 the Hohenzollern-Haigerloch line died out and the territory was absorbed by Hohenzollern-Sigmaringen. Hohenzollern-Hechingen and Hohenzollern-Sigmaringen, both principalities, in 1850 renounced their rights in favor of Prussia. Charles of Hohenzollern-Sigmaringen was chosen (1866) prince of Rumania and later (1881) assumed the royal title as Carol I; his successors in Rumania were Ferdinand, Carol II, and Michael. The candidature (1870) of Leopold of Hohenzollern-Sigmaringen to the Spanish throne helped to precipitate the Franco-Prussian War.

Hohe Tauern (hō'ə tou'ərn), range of the Eastern Alps, S Austria, extending c.70 mi (110 km) E from the Italian border. It rises to 12,460 ft (3,798 m) in the Grossglockner. The Tauern railroad (built 1901–8) traverses the range through a tunnel (5 mi/8 km long).

Hohokam Pima National Monument, Ariz.: see NATIONAL PARKS AND MONUMENTS, table.

Hoie: see HUY, Belgium.

Hoihow: see HAI-K'OU, China.

hoist: see WINCH.

Hojeda, Diego de (dyā'gō thā hōhā'thä), 1571–1615, Peruvian poet, b. Seville. He settled in Peru in 1590 and became a Dominican priest. As a poet he represents the transition between the Renaissance and baroque periods. His long religious narrative poem *La Cristiada* (1611) treats the life and Passion of Jesus; it is replete with religious and profane stories and digressions.

Hokan-Siouan (hō'kən-so͞o'ən), linguistic stock, or family, whose member languages are spoken by Indians in North and Central America. See AMERICAN INDIAN LANGUAGES.

Hokiang: see HO-CHIANG, China.

Hokkaido (hōkī'dō), island (1970 pop. 5,184,287), c.30,130 sq mi (78,040 sq km), N Japan, separated from Honshu island by the Tsugaru Strait and from Sakhalin, USSR, by the Soya Strait. It is the second largest, northernmost, and most sparsely populated of the major islands of Japan. Once called Yezo, it received the name Hokkaido [region of the northern sea] in 1869. Its rugged interior with many volcanic peaks rises to 7,511 ft (2,289 m) in Asahi-dake. The Ishikari, second longest river of Japan, traverses W Hokkaido; its valley is an important urban and industrial region. Hokkaido has a humid continental climate and receives much snow. Forests, covering most of the island, are a source of lumber, pulp, and paper (milled in Hokkaido). Coal, iron, and manganese are mined; the Ishikari coal field produces a major part of Japan's supply. Although large areas of the island are unsuited to farming, agriculture is an important occupation. Hokkaido is one of the major fishing centers of the world. The island is the chief winter resort and sports area in Japan; the 1972 Winter Olympics were held there, at Sapporo. Hokkaido's scenic beauty is preserved in several national parks. The population is concentrated largely in the west and southwest. Sapporo, Hakodate, and Otaru are the chief cities. Kushiro is the main port for E Hokkaido. The island was originally inhabited by AINU, aborigines of uncertain ancestry. Until 1800 the Ainu outnumbered the Japanese, who had begun (16th cent.) to settle the southwest peninsula; there are now c.17,000 Ainu in Hokkaido. With the Meiji restoration (1868) Japan began the first serious effort to people the island as a means of strengthening the northern frontier. Under a government-sponsored plan to develop the island, Horace Capron, an American agriculturalist, introduced (1872–76) scientific methods of farming. In 1885, Hokkaido was made an administrative unit and was granted a central government. The growth of the railroads helped speed settlement, but despite subsidies, the severe winters discouraged emigration from S Japan. Parts of the island, particularly in the north, are still largely uninhabited.

Hokusai, Katsushika (kätso͞oshē'kä hōksī'), 1760–1849, Japanese painter, draftsman, and wood engraver, one of the foremost ukiyo-e print designers. After producing wood engravings for several years, he became a pupil of the celebrated designer Shunsho Katsukawa, adopting the name Shunro. In the 1790s he illustrated books and printed cards for greetings and announcements. About 1798 he took the name Hokusai. In all he used over 50 different names. His output was prodigious and his fame widespread, but to the end of his life Hokusai lived in poverty and retained his simplicity. He was distinguished for the variety of his styles, his extraordinary technical excellence, and his observant delineation of contemporary life. His landscapes reveal a startling imagination and a dramatic sense of composition. Of his astounding output some of the best-known works are the famous *Mangwa*, or *Ten Thousand Sketches*, in 15 volumes (1814–78); the color-print series *Views of Famous Bridges and Views of Lu-chu Islands*; and *Views of Mount Fuji*. Hokusai's work has had a marked influence on the art of the West. See his *Thirty-Six Views of Mount Fuji* (1966); studies by J. R. Hillier (1955) and James Michener (1958).

Hokushu: see HOKKAIDO, Japan.

Holbach, Paul Henri Thiry, baron d' (pôl äNrē' tērē' bärôN' hôlbäk'), Ger. *Paul Heinrich Dietrich, Baron von Holbach* (poul' hīn'rĭkh dētrĭkh bärōn' fŭn hôl'bäkh), 1723–89, French philosopher, one of the Encyclopedists. Although a native of the Palatinate, he lived in Paris from childhood. He became a member of a group of notable thinkers and literary men including Diderot, Helvétius, Condorcet, and Rousseau. A supporter of naturalistic and materialistic views, he was a vigorous opponent of Christianity and all positive forms of religion. His best-known work is *Système de la nature* (1770), first published under the name of Mirabaud. See biography by W. H. Wickwar (1935, repr. 1968); study by Max Cushing (1914, repr. 1971).

Holbaek (hôl'bĕk), city (1970 com. pop. 26,215), Vestsjaelland co., E Denmark, a seaport on Holbaek Fjord, an arm of the Isefjord; chartered 1288. It is a commercial and industrial center.

Holbein, Hans (häns hôl'bīn), the elder, c.1465–1524, German painter and draftsman. He worked principally in Augsburg and Ulm, painting altarpieces for churches and probably portraits. Such early works as the altarpiece depicting the *Life of the Virgin* (Augsburg Cathedral) and the large *Basilica of Santa Maria Maggiore* altarpiece (Augsburg) show little divergence from the common practice of the Swabian school, which was influenced by the Flemish style. In later altarpieces done after c.1500, such as those of the *Basilica of St. Paul* (Augsburg) and of *St. Catherine* (Augsburg) and especially in his masterly *St. Sebastian* altarpiece (Munich), Holbein's art shows the influence of Italy. In addition to his painting, Holbein designed stained-glass windows for the cathedral at Eichstatt and for the Church of Saints Ulrich and Afra at Augsburg. He also produced a number of remarkable silverpoint portrait drawings that show something of the same talent for which his son Hans became renowned. His older son, **Ambrosius Holbein,** c.1495–c.1519, is best known for his book illustrations and portraits. The Basel Museum has several works attributed to him. The younger son, **Hans Holbein,** the younger, c.1497–1543, outstanding portrait and religious painter of the northern Renaissance, was influenced by his father and by Hans Burgkmair. The first half of his life was spent in Basel except for short intervals in Lucerne, Lombardy, and France. He early showed his diverse talents by designing woodcuts and glass paintings, illustrating books, and painting portraits and altarpieces. From youth he enjoyed the friendship of the great humanist Erasmus, and he made pen drawings illustrating Erasmus' *Praise of Folly*. Of this period are the portraits of Jacob Meyer and his wife and the beautiful preliminary drawing of Meyer in red chalk and silverpoint (all: Basel). In 1519 he was admitted to the painters' guild of Basel. Between 1519 and 1526 he decorated many buildings there, including the Town Hall, and painted the *Passion Scenes* and the celebrated *Dead Christ* (both in Basel), the altarpiece in Solothurn of the *Madonna with St. Ursus and a Bishop Saint*, and the famous *Madonna of Burgomaster Meyer* altarpiece (Darmstadt). Also of this period are several of his numerous portraits of Erasmus and a portrait of Boniface Amerbach (Basel). In these works the artist, now mature, shows his full genius without relinquishing the polished surface and enameled color of the earlier paintings. He reveals Italian influence in his larger conception and monumental composition and in the design and idealism of the characterization. A bold and subtle line, both precise and flowing, distinguishes these works. From 1526 to 1528, Holbein was in England, where he painted a fine group of portraits, including those of Sir Thomas More (Frick Coll., New York City) and Sir Henry Guildford (Windsor Castle) and his wife (City Art Mus., St. Louis). After another residence (1528–32) in Basel, where he executed a second group of frescoes for the Town Hall (both series later destroyed), he settled in England and worked on portraits and wall paintings. Among the many famous portraits of these last years are those of Christine of Denmark and *The French Ambassadors* (both: National Gall., London). In 1536 he became court painter to Henry VIII and made numerous portraits and drawings of the king and his wives. His own wife and children, of whom there is a beautiful group portrait (Basel Mus.), remained in Basel. At 46 Holbein died of the plague in London. In addition to his paintings, he left to the world magnificent preliminary portrait drawings in which he combined chalk, silverpoint, pen and ink, and other media. Today they are prized as highly as his paintings and may constitute a freer expression of his gift for exquisite characterization. In the beautiful simplicity of their design and in the subtle suggestion of both form and character, they are unsurpassed. Also famous are his woodcuts, which include the *Dance of Death* series and illustrations for Luther's Bible. Many European museums possess examples of his paintings. At Windsor Castle are 80 Holbein portrait drawings. In the United States, the Metropolitan Museum has several portraits; the Frick Collection, New York City, has two; and the National Gallery of Art, Washington, D.C., has two. See studies by P. Ganz (2d ed. 1956) and M. Kay (1966).

Holberg, Ludvig, Baron (lo͞oth'vē bärōn' hōl'bĕr), 1684–1754, Danish dramatist, essayist, poet, and historian, apostle of the Enlightenment in Scandinavia. Born in Norway, he studied theology in Bergen and in Copenhagen. After 1708 he made Denmark his home, residing there between European travels. Professor of metaphysics and later of history at the Univ. of Copenhagen, Holberg was the foremost Danish author of his time. His comedies, which brought him world stature, include the early mock-heroic epic poem *Pedar Paars* (1719–20), the satirical drama *The Political Tinker* (1722), and numerous other plays (he wrote 26 in the period 1722–24 alone). The ideas of the Enlightenment were publicized in *Niels Klim's Subterranean Journey* (1740, tr. 1960), a utopian novel, and in *Moral Thoughts* (1744) and *Epistles* (5 vol., 1748–54), collections of essays. He also wrote many popular scientific works; histories of Denmark, of Christianity, and of the Jews; and an autobiography (3 parts, in Latin, 1728–43, tr. 1827). Translations of his works include selected plays (1914, 1946, 1950) and essays (1955).

Holborn: see CAMDEN, England.

Holbrook, Josiah (hōl'bro͝ok), 1788–1854, American educator, founder of the LYCEUM movement, b. Derby, Conn., grad. Yale (1810). He experimented with various schools where manual training, farming, and formal instruction were combined. After the failure (1825) of his Agricultural Seminary, he began lecturing on popular scientific subjects. In 1826, at Millbury, Mass., he organized the first lyceum that became a part of a national system. He manufactured scientific apparatus for schools and lyceums and edited *Scientific Tracts* (1830–32) and *The Family Lyceum* (1832–33). In 1837, at Berea, Ohio, he established the Lyceum Village, which failed after a few years. He continued to promote the lyceum movement until his death.

Holbrook, town (1970 pop. 11,775), Norfolk co., E Mass.; settled 1710, set off from Randolph and inc. 1872. It has some light manufacturing.

Holcroft, Thomas (hōl'krôft), 1745–1809, English dramatist and novelist. Sometimes credited with having introduced melodrama to the London stage, he is the author of the sentimental play *The Road to Ruin* (1792). His novels include *Alwyn* (1780) and two inspired by the revolutionary ideas of his friend William Godwin, *Anna St. Ives* (1792) and *Hugh Trevor* (1794–97). See his memoirs (1816); study by Elbridge Colby (2 vol., 1968).

Holden, Oliver (hōl'dən), 1765–1844, American composer and compiler of hymns, b. Shirley, Mass. His popular tune *Coronation*, to Edward Perronet's hymn *All Hail the Power of Jesus' Name*, first appeared in his *Union Harmony* (1793). With Samuel Holyoke and Hans Gram he edited *The Massachusetts Compiler* (1795), an important collection and study of sacred vocal music.

Holden, town (1970 pop. 12,564), Worcester co., central Mass., a residential suburb of Worcester; settled 1723, set off and inc. 1741. It has some light manufacturing.

Hölderlin, Friedrich (frē'drĭkh höl'dərlĭn), 1770–1843, German lyric poet. Befriended and influenced by Schiller, Hölderlin produced, before the failure of his mind at 36, lofty yet subjective poetry, modeled on classic Greek verse. Little known outside Germany, he is highly regarded by critics and is generally considered to be a link between the classic and romantic schools. Besides lyrics (1820), he wrote an elegiac novel in prose, *Hyperion* (1797–99; tr. in Pierce and Schreiber, *Fact and Fancy of German Romance*, 1927), and a dramatic fragment, *Der Tod des Empedokles* (1799). A selection of his verse was translated (1943) by Frederic Prokosch. See study ed. by E. E. George (1972).

holding company: see CORPORATION.

Holdsworth, Sir William Searle, 1871–1944, British legal historian. He was (1903–8) professor of constitutional law at University College, London. After 1922 he was Vinerian professor of English law at Oxford. Holdsworth's greatest achievement is his *History of English Law* (12 vol., 1903–38). The work begins with Anglo-Saxon times, and it is an account of legal procedure and court organization down to the Judicature Acts of 1875 and of the important phases of substantive law through the 18th cent. Many authorities consider Holdsworth's history among the most thorough scholarly accounts of English law ever written. He was knighted in 1929. His other books include *The Historians of Anglo-American Law* (1928, repr. 1966) and *Charles Dickens as a Legal Historian* (1928, repr. 1972). See biography by R. W. Lee (1945).

Holguín (ōlgēn'), city (1970 pop. 131,508), Oriente prov., E Cuba. It is a prosperous commercial center and transportation hub in a fertile region of diversified agriculture. Often called "Cuba's granary," Holguín is located in a region where sugarcane, coffee, tobacco, and cattle are raised. Most exports are handled by its port, Gibara. The city, founded in 1523, was named for Garcia Holguín, a 16th-century conquistador in Mexico. It was moved to its present site in the 18th cent.

Holiday, Billie, 1915–59, American singer, b. Baltimore. Her original name was Eleanora Fagan. She began singing professionally in 1930, and after performing with numerous bands—especially those of Benny Goodman, Teddy Wilson, Count Basie, and Artie Shaw—she embarked in 1940 on a career of solo appearances in nightclubs and theaters. Her highly personal approach to a song, her individual phrasing and intonation, and the often rough but highly emotional quality of her voice soon earned her a supreme position among modern jazz singers. Although she was financially successful, she suffered many personal disasters, complicated by the drug addiction that she could not overcome and that eventually destroyed her career and hastened her death. She was also known as Lady Day. See her autobiography (1956).

holiday [altered from holy day], day set aside for the commemoration of an important event. Holidays are often accompanied by public ceremonies, such as parades and carnivals, and by religious observances; they may also be simply a time of rest and recreation. Days of commemoration are observed throughout the world, e.g., Bastille Day in France, May Day in the Soviet Union, and the New Year in China. National holidays are observed throughout a country and are considered legal if proclaimed by the central government. In the United States the state governments have jurisdiction over the celebration of holidays, except with regard to Federal employees and agencies. On legal holidays banks and schools are closed and there are restrictions on business transactions. New Year's Day, George Washington's birthday, the Fourth of July (Independence Day), Labor Day, Veterans Day, Thanksgiving Day, and Christmas Day are legal holidays observed by all the states. Abraham Lincoln's birthday, Memorial Day, Election Day, and Columbus Day are legal in some states. There are many special occasions that are observed by a single state or by a group of states, such as Patriots' Day (in Boston and Maine) and the Confederate Memorial Day. In 1971 the U.S. Congress created several three-day weekends for federal employees by proclaiming Washington's birthday, Memorial Day, Columbus Day and Veterans Day be held on Mondays regardless of their actual dates. Later these Monday holidays were adopted by a number of individual states. For religious holidays, see FEAST. See also BANK HOLIDAYS. See E. M. Deems, ed., *Holy-days and holidays* (1902, repr. 1968); R. J. Myers, *Celebrations; The Complete Book of American Holidays* (1972).

Holinshed, Raphael (hŏl'ĭnz-hĕd", hŏl'ĭn-shĕd"), d. c.1580, English chronicler. He was a translator who also assisted one Reginald Wolfe in the preparation of a universal history, which was never finished. In 1577, four years after Wolfe's death, appeared Holinshed's *Chronicles of England, Scotland,*

and Ireland, which he wrote with the assistance of William Harrison and Richard Stanihurst. Many Elizabethan dramatists drew plots for plays from the book in this and later editions. Shakespeare used it for several plays, especially *Macbeth, King Lear,* and *Cymbeline.* See study by Stephen Booth (1968).

Holland, Henry Richard Vassall Fox, 3d **Baron,** 1773–1840, British politician, nephew of Charles James Fox. He was a member of the Whig opposition party from 1797 and served as lord privy seal in the coalition ministry of 1806–7. An opponent of the Act of Union with Ireland (1801), he continually advocated its repeal, at the same time working for Catholic Emancipation. Although a loyal and active member he was never personally powerful in the Whig party. When the Whigs returned to power, he served as the chancellor of the duchy of Lancaster (1830–34, 1835–40). Lord Holland is, perhaps, best known for his influence on literature, politics, and letters through the hospitality that HOLLAND HOUSE in London provided for the brilliant and distinguished people of his day. His son, the 4th baron, edited Holland's *Foreign Reminiscences* (1850) and *Memoirs of the Whig Party* (1852). See L. C. Sanders, *The Holland House Circle* (1908, repr. 1960).

Holland, former county of the Holy Roman Empire and, from 1579 to 1795, chief member of the United Provinces of the Netherlands. Its name is popularly applied to the entire Netherlands. Holland has been divided since 1840 into two provinces, NORTH HOLLAND and SOUTH HOLLAND. The county was created in the early 10th cent. and originally controlled not only present North and South Holland, but also Zeeland and part of medieval FRIESLAND. William II was elected (1247) German king, but was unable to exert his authority. He was killed (1255) in a campaign against the West Frisians, who had always been difficult to control. In 1299, John of Avesnes, count of Hainaut, seized Holland, which in 1345, through marriage, came into the hands of the Bavarian house of Wittelsbach. The house of Wittelsbach retained possession of Holland until 1433, when Philip the Good, duke of Burgundy, wrested it from Jacqueline (or Jacoba), countess of Hainaut, Holland, Zeeland, and Friesland. In the civil strife that accompanied this event the party of the Kabeljaauws [codfish], representing the cities, fought the Hoeks [fish hooks], the nobles who supported Jacqueline. The Hoeks again rebelled when Archduke Maximilian (later Emperor Maximilian I) assumed the guardianship over the Netherlands after the death (1482) of Mary of Burgundy; their fleet was annihilated and their leaders were executed in 1490. The cloth industry and commerce of Holland, though they developed later than those of Flanders and Brabant, began to rival those of Bruges and Antwerp in the 15th cent. The ports of Holland were closely linked with the Hanseatic League and later became, after the Netherlands had gained independence, major entrepôts and shipbuilding centers. Holland led in the struggle (16th–17th cent.) for Dutch independence, and, because it dominated the States-General, its history became virtually identical with that of the NETHERLANDS.

Holland, city (1970 pop. 26,337), Allegan and Ottawa counties, SW Mich., near Lake Michigan, on Lake Macatawa, in a dairy and poultry area; founded 1847 by Dutch settlers, inc. 1867. Furnaces have been made there since 1906. Other products include furniture and boats. Tulip growing is an important industry, and the flowers have been planted along the streets and in the public parks. The city's many Dutch descendants hold a week-long tulip festival each spring. In Windmill Island Park is a Dutch windmill imported from the Netherlands and a miniature Dutch village; Dutch dancers perform there during the summer months. The Dutch Reformed Church operates Hope College and Western Theological Seminary in Holland. A coast guard station is on Lake Macatawa, and a state park is nearby.

Holland, Parts of: see LINCOLNSHIRE.

Holland House, residence of the Holland family in Kensington, London, made famous in the first 40 years of the 19th cent. by the hospitality of Henry Fox, 3d Baron HOLLAND, and his wife. Built in 1606 by John Thorp, the mansion was bought in 1767 by Henry Fox, grandfather of the 3d baron. Holland House was an intellectual headquarters for English liberals and other distinguished men. Reformers such as Jeremy Bentham, Sir Samuel Romilly, and Lord Brougham, scientists such as Michael Faraday and Sir Humphry Davy, writers such as Thomas Moore, Lord Byron, and Sir Walter Scott, and statesmen such as Viscount Melbourne, George Canning, and Viscount Palmerston were frequent guests at the famous dinners at Holland House.

Hollandia: see DJAJAPURA, Indonesia.

Holland Land Company, Dutch enterprise active in the settlement of much of W New York and some of NW Pennsylvania. Organized by Dutch bankers in 1796, it secured lands in New York (known as the Holland Purchase) from Robert MORRIS, who had assembled them as part of a gigantic land speculation. The company developed its holdings, planned town sites, and sold the lands on liberal terms directly to settlers. Its main land office was opened (1801) in Batavia, N.Y. About 1846 the affairs of the company in the United States were liquidated. See studies by P. D. Evans (1924) and William Chazanof (1970).

Hollar, Václav or **Wenzel** (väts'läf, vĕn'tsəl hôl'ər), 1607–77, Bohemian etcher. He studied with Merian and after a period in Strasbourg and Cologne, he settled in England, working for Charles I. Despite distinguished patrons, ability, and industry, he lived and died in poverty. Much of his best work was done during his stay in Antwerp (1645–52). Hollar produced more than 2,500 plates of great variety, including portraits; animal studies; landscapes; and religious, still-life, and architectural subjects. His *Theatrum Mulierum* illustrates the costumes of his day. Other works include *Views of London* (before the Great Fire) and *Edinburgh.* See study by A. M. Hind (1922, repr. 1973).

Hollins, George Nichols, 1799–1878, American naval officer, b. Baltimore. His active career spanned the years from the War of 1812, in which he served under Decatur, to the end of the Civil War, in which he fought for the Confederacy. In 1854, while commanding the *Cyane,* he shelled SAN JUAN DEL NORTE, Nicaragua, in retaliation for attacks on American life and property. With a few hastily assembled vessels, he defeated part of the Union blockading squadron of the Mississippi in Oct., 1861. Hollins commanded Confederate naval forces in the heavy fighting on the upper Mississippi in 1862.

Hollins College, at Hollins College, Va., N of Roanoke; primarily for women; opened 1842 as a seminary, renamed Hollins Institute 1855, became a college 1911.

Holliston, town (1970 pop. 12,069), Middlesex co., E Mass.; settled c.1659, inc. 1724. Its manufactures include plastics, quartz glass, wood panels, and paper products.

holly, common name for members of the Aquifoliaceae, a family of widely distributed trees and shrubs, most numerous in Central and South America. The evergreen English holly (*Ilex aquifolium*), the common holly of Europe, cultivated also in North America, is closely associated with Christmas tradition. The American holly (*I. opaca*), native to the E United States, is very similar; both are so popular for their decorative spiny leaves and red berries that they are becoming scarce. The hard white wood of both species is used for cabinetmaking and related purposes; it is close grained and polishes easily. Yerba maté, MATÉ, or Paraguay tea (*I. paraguariensis*) is very important commercially in South America as the source of a popular tealike beverage. Teas and medicinal preparations are also made from some other members of the family, e.g., yaupon and winterberry, or feverbush, both of E North America. Wild or mountain holly (*Nemopanthus mucronata*) is a deciduous shrub of E North America. Many species of this family are cultivated as ornamentals. Holly is classified in the division MAGNOLIOPHYTA, class Magnoliopsida, order Celastrales, family Aquifoliaceae.

hollyhock: see MALLOW.

Hollywood. 1 Community (1970 pop. c.194,000), part of the city of Los Angeles, S Calif., on the slopes of the Santa Monica Mts.; inc. 1903, consolidated with Los Angeles 1910. Although several major film studios are now in nearby sections and many films are shot on location throughout the world, Hollywood is still the center of the country's motion-picture industry and draws many tourists. It is also the home of numerous television, radio, and recording companies. Hollywood, whose first film was made c.1911, has come to signify the U.S. motion-picture industry in general—its morals, manners, and characteristics. Points of interest include Hollywood Blvd., Sunset Strip, and Grauman's Chinese Theatre. In surrounding hills are the Hollywood Bowl, Griffith Park (with an observatory and planetarium), and the homes of film celebrities. The Univ. of Judaism and a junior college are in Hollywood. **2** City (1970 pop. 106,873), Broward co., SE Fla., on the Atlantic Ocean; inc. 1925. A resort and retirement center, it also produces electronic equipment and building materials. Most of Port Everglades, the area's largest port, is within the city limits. Gulf Stream Park race track and a U.S. navy ordnance laboratory are nearby. Hollywood is the winter home of Riverside Military Academy.

Holmes, John Haynes, 1879–1964, American clergyman, b. Philadelphia, grad. Harvard, 1902, and Harvard Divinity School, 1904. For 42 years (1907–49) he was minister of the Community Church, New York City; in 1949 he became pastor emeritus. The church belonged to the Unitarian denomination until 1919, when it became nondenominational. The causes supported by Holmes's effective public addresses included the abolition of intolerance and of war. A founder of the National Association for the Advancement of Colored People and of the American Civil Liberties Union, he was long actively associated with both organizations. Among his many books are *A Sensible Man's View of Religion* (1932) and *The Affirmation of Immortality* (1947). See his autobiography (1959); study by C. H. Voss (1964).

Holmes, Oliver Wendell, 1809–94, American author and physician, b. Cambridge, Mass., grad. Harvard (B.A., 1829; M.D., 1836); father of Oliver Wendell Holmes, Jr. He began his medical career as a general practitioner but shifted into the academic field, becoming professor of anatomy and physiology at Dartmouth (1838–40), dean of the Harvard medical school (1847–53), and Parkman professor of anatomy and physiology at Harvard (1847–82). A stimulating and popular speaker, he published two important medical lectures, one in opposition to the practice of homeopathy and the other on the nature of fevers. His first important poem, "Old Ironsides" (1830), was a protest against the scrapping of the fighting ship *Constitution.* A collection of his witty occasional poems was published in 1836. In 1857 he began to contribute to the *Atlantic Monthly* (which he named) the famous series of "Breakfast-table" sketches, which were collected in *The Autocrat of the Breakfast-Table* (1858) and several subsequent volumes. These urbane pieces present imaginary conversations at a Boston boardinghouse, reflecting Holmes's opinions, charm, and wit. The first volume includes several poems, of which the most famous are the ironic "Deacon's Masterpiece" and "The Chambered Nautilus." Among his other notable works are three novels presenting a scientific approach to psychological traits, most notably *Elsie Venner* (1861); and biographies of his friends John Lothrop Motley (1879) and Ralph Waldo Emerson (1855). See biographies by E. M. Tilton (1947) and M. R. Small (1962); study by M. A. De Wolfe Howe (1939, repr. 1972); bibliography by T. F. Currier, ed. by E. M. Tilton (1953, repr. 1971).

Holmes, Oliver Wendell, 1841–1935, American jurist, Associate Justice of the U.S. Supreme Court (1902–32), b. Boston; son of the writer Oliver Wendell Holmes. He served (1861–64) with distinction in the Civil War, took a law degree at Harvard (1866), and began practice in Boston in 1867. Holmes taught (1870–73) constitutional law and jurisprudence at Harvard while editing the *American Law Review* and the 12th edition (1873) of Kent's *Commentaries.* In 1880, Holmes delivered a series of lectures on common law at the Lowell Institute. In them he attacked prevailing views of jurisprudence and proposed new conceptions of the origin and nature of law. He maintained that the law could be understood only as a response to the needs of the society it regulated, and that it was useless to consider it merely a body of rules developed logically by legal theorists. With the publication of the Lowell lectures in 1881, Holmes achieved international recognition. He became (1882) professor of law at Harvard and several months later was appointed to the Massachusetts supreme judicial court. There he served for 20 years, becoming chief justice in 1899. He was appointed to the U.S. Supreme Court by President Theodore Roosevelt in 1902. The canons of Holmes's judicial faith were strict and demanding. He preached "judicial restraint" and firmly believed that popular majorities through their elected representatives should not have their will thwarted capriciously; when his colleagues on the court nullified social legislation—e.g., minimum wage and hour laws—as unconstitutional, Holmes vigorously objected. From his eloquent opinions in these cases he came to be regarded as the Great Dissenter. In cases dealing with free speech, however, Holmes felt it necessary for the judge to loose the bonds of restraint and prevent legislatures from assuming censorious powers. In defense of the First Amendment, he developed the "clear and present danger" rule, which allows for restrictions only when the public interest is faced with immediate threat. Set forth in the Abrams and Gitlow cases in dissenting opinions, the rule was generally accepted by the Supreme Court. Holmes's published works include *The Common Law* (1881), *Speeches* (1891, 1913), and *Collected Legal Papers* (1920). See S. J. Konefsky, *The Legacy of Holmes and Brandeis* (1956, repr. 1974); Felix Frankfurter, *Mr. Justice Holmes and the Supreme Court* (2d ed. 1961); biographies by M. D. Howe (Vol. I 1957, Vol. II 1963) and Silas Bent (1932, repr. 1969).

Holmes, Sherlock: see DOYLE, SIR ARTHUR CONAN.

Holmes, William Henry, 1846–1933, American geologist, anthropologist, and museum director, b. Harrison co., Ohio. He was internationally recognized for his work in museum science. In 1872 he became an artist with the F. V. Hayden survey, and after it was absorbed (1879) into the U.S. Geological Survey, he was appointed geologist. He contributed pioneer reports on the phenomena of Yellowstone Park, the classic illustrative material in the famous Grand Canyon atlas, and reports of much geological reconnaissance work in Colorado. Holmes was a noted mountain climber, and peaks in Yellowstone Park and the Henry Mts. of Utah were later named in his honor. While directing the reconnaissance survey of the San Juan River district of SE Utah in 1875, he was fascinated by the cliff-dwelling remains in the region and increasingly turned to that field, becoming one of the great pioneers of Southwestern archaeology. His *Art in Shell of the American Indians* (1883), *Pottery of the Ancient Pueblos* (1886), and many essays on Indian textiles, were among the first serious contributions to the study of Indian art. His work in ceramics was especially important in the study of ethnographical relationships. Holmes left the Geological Survey in 1889 to become archaeologist of the Bureau of American Ethnology, and from 1902 to 1909 he served as its chief. From 1910 to 1920 he was chief curator of anthropology at the U.S. National Museum. In 1910 he also became curator of the National Gallery of Art and from 1920 served as its director. His later books included the important *Handbook of Aboriginal American Antiquities* (1919).

holmium (hōl'mēəm) [Lat.,=Stockholm], metallic chemical element; symbol Ho; at. no. 67; at. wt. 164.93; m.p. about 1465°C; b.p. about 2700°C; sp. gr. 8.78 at 25°C; valence +3. Holmium is a soft, malleable, lustrous, silvery metal of the LANTHANIDE SERIES in group IIIb of the PERIODIC TABLE. It is prepared by reduction of a holmium halide with calcium metal. Holmium is stable in dry air at room temperature but is rapidly oxidized in moist air or when heated. Holmia, the oxide, is found in nature, with other RARE EARTHS, in the minerals gadolinite and monazite. Holmium, its oxide, and its salts have no commercial uses. The metal was discovered spectroscopically in 1878 by the Swiss chemists Soret and Delafontaine and independently in 1879 by the Swedish chemist Per T. Cleve; it is named for Cleve's native city.

Holocaust, name given to the period of persecution and extermination of European Jews by National Socialist, or Nazi, Germany. Persecution of German Jews began with Adolf Hitler's rise to power in 1933; in the succeeding years most of those Jews who did not flee the country were sent to CONCENTRATION CAMPS. After the outbreak of World War II, Hitler began implementation of what he called "the final solution of the Jewish question," the extermination of the Jewish people in all of the countries conquered by his armies. By the end of the war 6 million Jews had been systematically murdered. This destruction of European Jews brought to an end a creative religious and secular life that had fed the Jewish communities throughout the world. The void has forced the Jewish community in the United States, the world's largest, to reevaluate its goals and to devote its resources to the building of a new center of Jewish life in the Diaspora. The renascent Jewish community in the state of Israel, itself largely a by-product of the Holocaust, now serves as a focal point for much of this activity. A vast literature consisting of histories, diaries, memoirs, poetry, novels, and prayers has been composed in an effort to understand the Holocaust in terms of its religious and secular implications. The secular materials attempt to explain the motivations of those who proposed and implemented the extermination policies and the reactions, both communal and personal, of their victims. The religious materials focus on the problem of whether, in view of what happened, one can still speak in traditional Jewish terms of a God, active in history, who rewards the righteous and who maintains a unique relationship with the Jewish people. See Martin Buber, *Eclipse of God* (1952); R. L. Rubenstein, *After Auschwitz* (1966); A. H. Friedlander, ed., *Out of the Whirlwind: A Reader of Holocaust Literature* (1968); Nora Levin, *The Holocaust* (1968); Elie Wiesel, *Night* (1960) and *Legends of Our Time* (1968); A. A. Cohen, ed., *Arguments and Doctrines: A Reader of Jewish Thinking in the Aftermath of the Holocaust* (1970); Raul Hilberg, *Destruction of European Jews* (1967) and *Documents of Destruction* (1971); Gerd Korman, ed., *Hunter and Hunted* (1973).

Holocene epoch (hŏl'əsēn) or **Recent epoch,** most recent of all subdivisions of geologic time, ranging from the present back to the time (c.11,000 years ago) of almost complete withdrawal of the glaciers of the preceding PLEISTOCENE EPOCH. During the Holocene epoch, the sculpturing of the earth's surface to its present form was completed. Withdrawal of the glacial ice resulted in the development of the present-day drainage basins of the Missouri and Ohio rivers, the development of the Great Lakes, and a general worldwide rise in sea level of up to 450 ft (140 m) as the glacial meltwater was returned to the seas. In the W United States and Canada, the Coast Ranges continued to be uplifted. Warming climates resulted in the poleward migration of plants and animals. The most significant development during the Holocene was the rise of modern man, who is thought to have first appeared in the late Pleistocene. All of the races of modern man were fully developed, with eventual worldwide distribution. Man's culture developed during this epoch from a primitive one to the complex industrial society of today, in which man himself has become a significant factor in altering the earth's surface environment. See GEOLOGIC ERAS (table).

Holofernes (hŏləfûr'nēz, hōlŏf'ərnēz), invading general killed by Judith to save her city, Bethulia. Judith 2–13.

holography (hōlŏg'rəfē, hō-), method of reproducing a three-dimensional image of an object by means of light wave patterns recorded on a photographic plate or film. Holography is sometimes called lensless photography because no lenses are used to form the image. The plate or film with the recorded wave patterns is called a *hologram*. The light used to make a hologram must be coherent, i.e. of a single wavelength or frequency and with all the waves in phase. (A coherent beam of light can be produced by a LASER.) Before reaching the object, the beam is split into two parts; one (the reference beam) is recorded directly on the photographic plate and the other is reflected from the object to be photographed and is then recorded. Since the two parts of the beam arriving at the photographic plate have travelled by different paths and are no longer necessarily coherent, they create an INTERFERENCE pattern, exposing the plate at points where they arrive in phase and leaving the plate unexposed where they arrive out of phase (nullifying each other). The pattern on the plate is a record of the waves as they are reflected from the object, recorded with the aid of the reference beam. When this hologram is later illuminated with coherent light of the same frequency as that used to form it, a three-dimensional image of the object is produced; it can even be photographed from various angles. This technique of image formation is known as wave front reconstruction. Since waves from all parts of the object are recorded on all parts of the hologram, any part of the hologram, however small, can be used to reproduce the entire image. The theoretical principles of holography were developed by Dennis Gabor in 1947. However, no adequate source of coherent light was available until the invention of the laser in 1960. Holography using laser light was developed during the early 1960s and has had several applications. In research, holography has been combined with microscopy to extend studies of very small objects; it has also been used to study the instantaneous properties of large collections of atmospheric particles. In industry, holography has been applied to stress analysis and vibrational analysis. Color holograms have been developed, formed using three separate exposures with laser beams of each of the primary colors (see COLOR). Another new technique is acoustical holography, in which the object is irradiated with a coherent beam of ultrasonic waves (see SOUND; ULTRASONICS); the resulting interference pattern is recorded by means of microphones to form a hologram, and the photographic plate thus produced is viewed by means of laser light to give a visible three-dimensional image. See J. B. De Velis and G. O. Reynolds, *Theory and Applications of Holography* (1967); G. W. Stroke, *An Introduction to Coherent Optics and Holography* (2d ed. 1969).

Holon (hō'lŏn). **1** Unidentified city, apparently near Hebron. Joshua 15.51; 21.15. Hilen: 1 Chron. 6.58. **2** Unidentified town of Moab. Jer. 48.21.

Holon (hōlôn'), city (1972 pop. 98,000), W central Israel. Manufactures include textiles, metal and leather goods, processed foods, furniture, glassware, plastics, and construction materials. Holon was founded in 1940 with the merger of several residential neighborhoods. About half the Samaritan population of Israel lives in the city.

Holst, Gustav (hōlst), 1874–1934, English composer, studied at the Royal College of Music. Grieg, Richard Strauss, and Ralph Vaughan Williams influenced his early work, but most of his music is highly original. Outstanding compositions are *The Planets* (1914–16), a suite for orchestra; *The Hymn of Jesus* (1917), for chorus and orchestra; *The Perfect Fool* (1920–22), an opera; and *Egdon Heath* (1927), an orchestral piece. See biography (1938) and study (2d ed., 1968) by his daughter, Imogen Holst.

Holst, Hermann Eduard von (fən hôlst), 1841–1904, American historian, b. Livonia (then part of Russia), of German parents. He was barred from Russia because of a pamphlet attacking the czarist government. He immigrated (1867) to the United States, where hardship and labor undermined his health. While in the United States he studied American institutions. In 1872 he returned to Europe to teach in the universities of Strasbourg (1872–74) and Freiburg (1874–92). His *Constitutional and Political History of the United States* (7 vol., 1876–92), written in German and translated, is chiefly the constitutional and political history of slavery and the struggle to preserve the Union. He fervently supported and vividly portrayed the Union cause. His other works include a biography of John C. Calhoun (1882) and *The French Revolution Tested by Mirabeau's Career* (1894). From 1892 to 1900 he was head of the history department at the newly founded Univ. of Chicago.

Holstebro (hôl'stəbrō''), city (1970 com. pop. 33,092), Ringkøbing co., W central Denmark, on the Storå River. It is a commercial and industrial center and a rail junction.

Holstein, Friedrich von (frē'drĭkh fən hôl'shtīn), 1837–1909, German diplomat. After the Congress of Berlin (1878) he became a powerful figure in shaping German foreign policy. His official position was (1878–1906) political counselor in the foreign office, and during his life he was almost totally unknown outside government circles. During the 1880s he attempted to thwart Chancellor Bismarck's Russian policy, favoring instead closer ties with Austria-Hungary; after Bismarck's fall (1890) he allowed the 1887 Reinsurance Treaty with Russia to lapse. He favored rapprochement with Great Britain but set the terms too high, mistakenly believing that Britain would never come to terms with France or Russia. When Britain and France reached agreement in 1904, Holstein tried to break their entente by provoking (1905) a crisis over Morocco. His advice was ignored by Chancellor Bülow, who feared war with Britain, and Holstein resigned. Germany subsequently found itself isolated at the international conference at Algeciras on Morocco. See his papers, ed. by Norman Rich and M. H. Fisher (4 vol., tr. 1955–63); study by Norman Rich (2 vol., 1965).

Holstein, former duchy, N West Germany, the part of Schleswig-Holstein S of the Eider River. Kiel and Rendsburg were the chief cities. For a description of Holstein and for its history after 1814, see SCHLESWIG-HOLSTEIN. For a time part of the duchy of Saxony, Holstein was created (1111) a county of the Holy Roman Empire and was bestowed on Adolf of Schauenburg. In 1386 the count of Holstein received the duchy of SCHLESWIG as a hereditary fief. On the death (1459) of Adolf VIII, last of the Schauenburg line, Schleswig and Holstein passed to Christian I of Denmark, son of Adolf's sister and the count of OLDENBURG. Christian in two charters (1460) established the relationship of Denmark, Schleswig, and Holstein as a personal union; the opposition of the German nobles in the two territories to direct Danish rule was a powerful factor in this arrangement, which lasted for four centuries. In 1474, Emperor Frederick III awarded DITHMARSCHEN to Christian and raised Holstein to a duchy under the immediate suzerainty of the Holy Roman Empire (as distinct from Schleswig, which was outside the imperial jurisdiction). Both duchies were divided in the 16th cent. into a royal portion, ruled by the Danish kings; a ducal portion, ruled by the dukes of Holstein-Gottorp, a younger branch of the Danish royal line; and a common portion, ruled jointly by the kings and dukes. In 1658 the Treaty of Roskilde abolished Danish suzerainty over the ducal portion, but in 1721, at the end of the Northern War, the ducal portion of Schleswig was united with the royal portion. In 1773, Grand Duke Paul (later Paul I) of Russia, heir of the Gottorp line, ceded the ducal portion of Holstein to the Danish dynasty in exchange for the county of Oldenburg. Thus all Schleswig-Holstein was once more united under the Danish kings.

Holstein-Friesian cattle (hōl'stēn-frē'zhən, -stīn-), breed of dairy cattle originated in N Holland and Friesland. Commonly called Holsteins, these large cattle with sharply defined black and white spotted markings are believed to have been bred for their dairy qualities for 2,000 years. The region from which they come was famous even in Caesar's time for its cattle. In milk production the cows average a higher yield than that of any other breed, although the milk has a relative low butterfat content; as a dairy breed, they rank high for beef and veal production. Large numbers of Holsteins were imported in the late 19th cent. to the United States, where they are now the most numerous of dairy cattle. They are also widely raised in Canada, Australia, South America, and South Africa.

Holsteinsborg (hôl'stănsbôr"), town (1969 pop. 3,232), Holsteinsborg dist. (1969 pop. 4,166), W Greenland. The second-largest town in Greenland, it is a fishing center and has a modern canning factory.

Holston, river, c.120 mi (190 km) long, formed by the uniting of its northern and southern forks, NE Tenn., and flowing SW through the Great Appalachian Valley, joining the French Broad River at Knoxville to form the Tennessee River. Settlement along the Holston began before the American Revolution, and it was a major route of westward migration. On the river is Cherokee Dam, a flood control unit of the Tennessee Valley Authority that impounds Cherokee Lake; several smaller dams on the Holston's southern fork.

Holt, Harold Edward, 1908-67, Australian political leader. After studying law, he entered politics and became associated with Robert Gordon Menzies. He held a number of cabinet offices in Menzies's governments and was minister of labor and national service (1949-58), minister of immigration (1949-56), and treasurer (1958-66) in Menzies's Liberal-Country party coalition. When Menzies retired in 1966, Holt succeeded as Liberal party leader and prime minister. During his short tenure he increased the number of Australian troops in South Vietnam, a policy that caused controversy in Australia. He died by drowning Dec., 1967.

Holt, Helen Maud: see TREE, SIR HERBERT BEERBOHM.

Holt, Henry, 1840-1926, American author and publisher, b. Baltimore. In 1866 he became a partner in the publishing firm that became (1873) Henry Holt & Company. He was the author of several novels and the autobiographical *Garrulities of an Octogenarian Editor* (1923). In 1960, Henry Holt & Company became Holt, Rinehart, & Winston.

Holt, Joseph, 1807-94, American public official, judge advocate general of the U.S. army (1862-75), b. Breckinridge co., Ky. He began to practice law in Elizabethtown, Ky., and became a widely known lawyer and political speaker in the old Southwest. For his services to the Democratic party, President Buchanan appointed him commissioner of patents in 1857, and in 1859 he became Postmaster General. He was Secretary of War from January to March, 1861. After the secession movement began, Holt, who had previously been sympathetic to the South, gave unhesitating allegiance to the Union and influenced Kentucky's ultimate loyal stand. Appointed (Sept., 1862) to the new office of judge advocate general, Holt supported and carried out President Lincoln's desires for an extension of military jurisdiction over many civil matters, including the trials of political prisoners. The trial and punishment of John Wilkes Booth's accomplices, however, especially the hanging of Mary E. SURRATT, on questionable evidence and with evidence favorable to the defendants suppressed, brought a reaction against Holt and the power he had assumed. However, the radical Republicans in Congress kept him in office until 1875.

Holy Alliance, 1815, agreement among the emperors of Russia and Austria and the king of Prussia, signed on Sept. 26. It was quite distinct from the Quadruple Alliance (Quintuple, after the admission of France) of Great Britain, Russia, Austria, and Prussia, arrived at first in 1814 and revived in 1815. Nevertheless, both were a part of the resettlement of European political boundaries after the fall of the Napoleonic empire. The alliance was essentially an attempt by the conservative rulers to preserve the social order. It was particularly the product of the religious zeal of Czar ALEXANDER I. Specifically, it accomplished nothing, since it was merely a vague agreement that the sovereigns would conduct themselves in consonance with Christian principles. Ultimately all the princes of Europe signed the alliance except three—George IV of England, who could not, for constitutional reasons; the pope, who could not, for religious reasons; and the sultan, who was not a Christian prince. The agreement was not important, but the name was applied to the cooperation of Russia, Austria, and Prussia, particularly in the period of the European conferences of Aachen, Troppau, Laibach, and Verona. The Holy Alliance became a symbol of the reaction dominated by METTERNICH. Austria repressed revolution in Italy, and France interfered in Spain in the name of the Holy Alliance. It was against that reactionary solidarity that the British foreign policy under George CANNING was directed. The MONROE DOCTRINE was, in part, an outgrowth of that same fear of the European reactionary powers.

Holy City: see ALLAHABAD; VARANASI; JERUSALEM; MECCA; ROME.

Holy Cross, College of the, at Worcester, Mass.; Jesuit; for men; founded and opened 1843, chartered 1865. Noteworthy among its facilities is the O'Callahan Science Library. It is a member college of the Harvard Univ. Graduate School of Education.

Holy Family, term referring to the Child Jesus, Mary, and Joseph. In the Roman Catholic Church the feast in its honor falls usually on the first Sunday after the Epiphany. In art the theme of the Holy Family became popular during the Renaissance, probably deriving from the larger theme of the Nativity in medieval representations. There are fine examples by Signorelli, Michelangelo, and Rubens.

Holy Ghost or **Holy Spirit** [*ghost,* i.e., spirit, a translation of Gr. *pneuma*=breath, air], in Christian doctrine, the third person of the TRINITY. The Holy Ghost is sometimes defined as the aspect of God immanent in this world, in men, and in the church. Jesus' promise to his disciples of a Comforter (or Paraclete, i.e., advocate), in John 14, is considered his principal reference to the Holy Ghost, and the descent of the Holy Ghost on the apostles and the communication of the gift of tongues, as recounted in Acts 2, are thought to be the chief manifestations of the Holy Ghost in time. This incident is commemorated on Pentecost (Whitsunday). Certain Christian groups, such as the Montanists and the Society of Friends, have attributed utterances of their members to the inspiration of the Holy Ghost. The dove is the symbol of the Holy Ghost. For the controversy over the procession of the Holy Ghost, see CREED.

Holy Grail: see GRAIL, HOLY.

Holy Innocents, children of Bethlehem "from two years old and under" (Mat. 2.16-18) who were killed by the order of Herod the Great, who hoped to destroy the Infant Jesus. They are believed to have numbered between 12 and 25 and have been venerated in the Christian Church as martyrs since ancient times. In the Eastern Church they are known as the Holy Children. Their feast, formerly known in England as Childermas, is Dec. 28.

Holy Island or **Lindisfarne** (lĭn'dĭsfärn), off the coast of Northumberland, NE England. At low tide the island is connected with the mainland by a stretch of sand. The island is partly cultivated. Tourism and fishing are important. A church and monastery, built in 635 by St. Aidan, represented the first establishment of Celtic Christianity in England. Saint Cuthbert was the most famous of the bishops of Holy Island. The settlement was burned by the Danes in 793 but rebuilt. When the Danes invaded in 875, the monks fled, wandering for eight years until they settled at Chester-le-Street in 883. The bishopric was maintained for 112 years there and moved to Durham in 995. A Benedictine priory was set up on the island in 1083 by monks from Durham. There are remains of a church and of an early 16th-century castle. The Lindisfarne Gospels or Book of Durham is an illuminated Latin manuscript of the Gospels, now in the British Museum, written at Holy Island before 700; an Anglo-Saxon gloss was added at Durham in the 10th cent.

Holy Land: see PALESTINE.

Holy League, in French history: see LEAGUE.

Holy League, in Italian history, alliance formed (1510-11) by Pope JULIUS II during the ITALIAN WARS for the purpose of expelling LOUIS XII of France from Italy, thereby consolidating papal power. Venice, the Swiss cantons, Ferdinand II of Aragón, Henry VIII of England, and Holy Roman Emperor Maximilian I were the chief members of the league. The Swiss, who did most of the fighting, routed the French at Novara (1513), but in the same year Julius II died and the league fell apart. The French victory (1515) at MARIGNANO reestablished the French in Lombardy.

Holyoake, Keith Jacka, 1904–, New Zealand political leader. A farmer, he was active in agricultural organizations in the 1930s and 1940s. He entered Parliament in 1932. As a member of the National party, he became deputy leader of the party in Parliament in 1947. In 1949 he was named deputy prime minister and minister of agriculture in the National party government. He served briefly as prime minister in 1957, when Sidney G. Holland resigned the post, and was subsequently leader of the Nationalist opposition. When his party won the 1960 elections, he became prime minister, serving until 1972 when he resigned the post to deputy prime minister John Marshall in order to revitalize the party for the coming elections (which the Nationalists lost). He was knighted in 1970.

Holyoke, city (1970 pop. 50,112), Hampden co., SW Mass., on the Connecticut River; settled 1745, inc. 1873. The city is an industrial center. Paper and paper products are the leading manufactures; others include printed material, metals, detergents, plastics, machinery, and textiles. Holyoke Community College is there.

holy orders: see ORDERS, HOLY.

Holy Roman Empire, designation for the political entity that originated at the coronation as emperor (962) of the German king OTTO I and endured until the renunciation (1806) of the imperial title by FRANCIS II. The term itself did not come into usage until several centuries after Otto's accession. The Holy Roman Empire was a successor state to the empire founded in 800 by CHARLEMAGNE (see also CAROLINGIANS), who revived the title of Roman emperor in the West. According to Carolingian theory, the Roman Empire had merely been suspended, not ended, by the abdication of the last Roman emperor in 476; Charlemagne thus claimed legitimate succession from the Romans. From the death of Arnulf (899), the last Carolingian to hold the imperial title, until Otto's coronation in Rome by Pope John XII, various rulers bore the imperial title but exercised no authority; among them were Louis III, king of Provence, and Berengar I, king of Italy. When Otto I became emperor, he renewed the traditions of the Carolingian empire that had been eroding since Arnulf's death. Otto's empire comprised the German duchies, Lorraine (or Lotharingia), Italy, and Burgundy, which had its own nominal king. Burgundy (see ARLES, KINGDOM OF) was formally annexed in 1033. From the time of Otto's reign the imperial office was based on the German kingship. The German king, elected by the German princes, automatically sought imperial coronation by the pope. After 1045 a king who was not yet crowned emperor was known as king of the Romans, a title that asserted his right to the imperial throne and implied that he was emperor-designate. Not every German king became emperor, however, because the popes, especially when elections to the kingships were disputed, often claimed that the selection of the emperor was their prerogative. Despite the fact that the German kingship and the imperial office were technically elective, they tended to become hereditary. At times the ELECTORS, the German princes who approved the succession to the German kingship, exercised real authority in choosing the king, although papal confirmation was still necessary for accession to the imperial throne. In 1338 at the diets of Rhense and Frankfurt the German princes proclaimed the electors' right to choose the emperor without papal intervention. The Golden Bull of 1356 issued by CHARLES IV reaffirmed this and regulated the election procedure. Emperors continued to be crowned by the pope until after the coronation (1530) of Charles V. Thereafter, following the precedent (1508) of Maximilian I, they were crowned at Frankfurt. Several early emperors were also crowned king of Italy with the iron crown of the Lombards. After 1438 the imperial office was held, with one exception, by the house of HAPSBURG.

Foundations of Imperial Authority. In theory, just as the pope was the vicar of God on earth in spiritual matters, so the emperor was God's temporal vicar; hence he claimed to be the supreme temporal ruler of Christendom. Actually, the power of the emperor never equaled his pretensions. Although the emperors were accorded diplomatic precedence over other rulers, their suzerainty early ceased over France, S

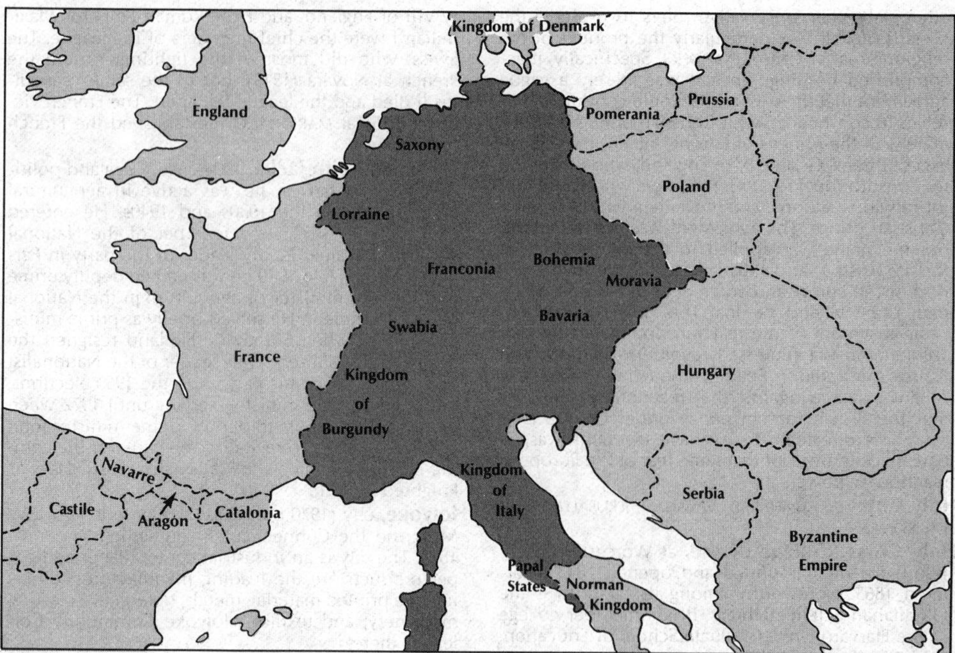

Holy Roman Empire (c.1100)

Italy, Denmark, Poland, and Hungary; and their control over England, Sweden, and Spain was never more than nominal. The authority of the emperors in Italy and Germany was sometimes nonexistent, sometimes real. The territorial limits of the empire varied, but it generally included GERMANY, AUSTRIA, BOHEMIA and MORAVIA, parts of N ITALY, present-day BELGIUM, and, until 1648, the NETHERLANDS and SWITZERLAND. Some countries (e.g., HUNGARY) were ruled by the emperor or imperial prince but were outside the empire, while others (e.g., FLANDERS, POMERANIA, SCHLESWIG, and HOLSTEIN) were part of the empire but were ruled by foreign princes who held their lands in fief from the emperor and took part in the imperial DIET.

Weaknesses of the Empire. The imperial position was precarious from the start. A conflict over the relationship of the spiritual papal power to the temporal imperial power resulted in the INVESTITURE controversy during the reign of HENRY IV (1084–1105) and in the subsequent struggles between the popes ALEXANDER III, GREGORY IX, and INNOCENT IV and the emperors FREDERICK I and FREDERICK II concerning papal sovereignty in Italy. The papacy was victorious, and the emperors ceased to interfere seriously with papal affairs except during the Great Schism (see SCHISM, GREAT) of the 15th cent. and in the ITALIAN WARS of the 16th cent. Also untenable was the dual position of the emperors as rulers of Germany and of Italy; geography as well as cultural and political conditions separated the two countries. The defense of the empire against foreign attack was made more difficult by the repeated attempts of the emperors to maintain their authority in Italy against the opposition of the city-states (see COMMUNE), the papacy, and the petty princes. Frederick I failed to suppress the LOMBARD LEAGUE, which had papal support. Frederick II, after inheriting Naples and Sicily, was primarily interested in Italian affairs; his conflict with the papacy produced the feud between GUELPHS AND GHIBELLINES throughout Italy and ruined the imperial authority there. The death (1254) of his heir, CONRAD IV, the last ruling HOHENSTAUFEN, was followed by an interregnum of 19 years. Opposing claimants to the imperial crown were unable to exercise authority during this period, and the power of the emperor declined considerably. The election (1273) of RUDOLF I as the first Hapsburg German king restored some order, but after his death rival claimants renewed the strife. The effect of continued warfare and weak monarchs increased the power of the German princes, particularly the dukes of the great duchies of Bavaria, Saxony, Swabia, Franconia, Thuringia, and Upper and Lower Lorraine. The Golden Bull of 1356 conceded the princes' dominance over the monarchy.

Preservation of Imperial Dignity. The emperors maintained some authority against the nobles with the support of the towns and of the great ecclesiastical princes (e.g., the archbishop-electors of COLOGNE, MAINZ, and TRIER), who were imperial appointees. As the German towns grew in wealth and power, they entered leagues for defense against the nobles. Since they acted as a counterbalance to the nobility, they were generally favored by the emperors, who made them free imperial cities with a voice in the diet. The power of the emperors, however, had come to depend largely on the size and wealth of the emperors' hereditary domains. Thus, the Luxemburg emperors (HENRY VII, CHARLES IV, WENCESLAUS, and SIGISMUND) and the Hapsburg emperors concerned themselves with their own lands, to the detriment of the unity of the empire. During the reign of MAXIMILIAN I (1493–1519) the conflict between the dynastic policy of the Hapsburg emperors and the interests of the German empire (then known as the Holy Roman Empire of the German Nation) became pronounced. The princes attempted to remove the administration of the empire from the emperor and put it in the hands of an imperial council; the council would control all external and internal affairs of the empire. Under pressure Maximilian I created (1500) a council (see REICHSREGIMENT) and an imperial court of justice. However, these were only temporary measures, since the Hapsburgs had no intention of pursuing German policy, which would conflict with their dynastic interests, particularly in Austria.

Dissolution of the Empire. In the 16th cent., under CHARLES V and FERDINAND I, imperial and Austrian affairs were practically identical. This identity was furthered by the REFORMATION, which generally aligned the German Protestant princes against the emperors, who championed Roman Catholicism. In the THIRTY YEARS WAR (1618–48; see FERDINAND II; FERDINAND III; WALLENSTEIN; PROTESTANT UNION) the emperor, allied with Spain, opposed the Protestant princes, who were allied chiefly with Sweden and France. The struggle ended with the virtual dissolution of the empire in the Peace of Westphalia (1648; see WESTPHALIA, PEACE OF), which recognized the sovereignty of all the states of the empire; the only limitation was that the princes could not make alliances directed against the empire or the emperor. Although the imperial title became largely honorific, the outward forms of the empire were retained; the emperors, with their hereditary lands, remained powerful monarchs. While the peace generally legalized the situation that had existed in the empire since the Reformation, it also advanced the growth of particularism and absolutism in the German states. The emperors suffered further loss of prestige in their wars against Louis XIV (see DUTCH WARS **3**; GRAND ALLIANCE, WAR OF THE; SPANISH SUCCESSION, WAR OF THE). The death (1740) of CHARLES VI ended the male Hapsburg line, precipitating further conflict (see AUSTRIAN SUCCESSION, WAR OF THE; SEVEN YEARS WAR). While the elector of Bavaria was chosen (1742) emperor as Charles VII, MARIA THERESA, daughter of Charles VI, defended her Hapsburg inheritance against the claims of Bavaria, Prussia, and Saxony. By the peace of Hubertusburg (1763), FRANCIS I, husband of Maria Theresa, was recognized as emperor; however, PRUSSIA, under King FREDERICK II, had emerged as the leading German power. Joseph II, successor of Francis I, adhered to the principles of the Enlightenment; he attempted to rationalize the administration of the imperial government but failed in the face of resistance by the particularist princes, especially Frederick II of Prussia. During the FRENCH REVOLUTIONARY WARS the empire was completely reorganized by the treaty of Lunéville (1801) and by action of the diet in 1803. The number of states was greatly reduced, and the remaining states were aggrandized at the expense of the petty princedoms and ecclesiastical estates. In 1804, Holy Roman Emperor FRANCIS II took the title Francis I, emperor of Austria, and after the establishment (1806) of the CONFEDERATION OF THE RHINE under Napoleon I, Francis renounced his title as Holy Roman Emperor. After the fall of Napoleon no attempt was made to restore the empire, but a GERMAN CONFEDERATION was established that lasted until 1866. See H. A. L. Fisher, *The Medieval Empire* (1898, repr. 1969); J. W. Thompson, *Feudal Germany* (1928, repr. 1962); G. Barraclough, *The Origins of Modern Germany* (1946, rev. ed. 1947, repr. 1966); T. F. Tout, *The Empire and the Papacy, 918–1273* (8th ed. 1965);

HOLY ROMAN EMPERORS *(including dates of reign)*
Saxon dynasty
Otto I, 936–73 Otto II, 973–83 Otto III, 983–1002 Henry II, 1002–24
Salian or Franconian dynasty
Conrad II, 1024–39 Henry III, 1039–56 Henry IV, 1056–1105 Henry V, 1105–25
Lothair II, duke of Saxony, 1125–37
Hohenstaufen dynasty and rivals
Conrad III, 1138–52 Frederick I, 1152–90 Henry VI, 1190–97 Philip of Swabia, 1198–1208 *antiking:* Otto IV (Guelph), 1198–1208 Otto IV (king, 1208–12; emperor, 1209–15), 1208–15 Frederick II (king, 1212–20; emperor, 1220–50), 1212–50 Conrad IV, 1237–54 *antiking:* Henry Raspe, 1246–47 *antiking:* William, count of Holland, 1247–56
Interregnum, 1254–73
Richard, earl of Cornwall and Alfonso X of Castile, rivals
Hapsburg, Luxemburg, and other dynasties
Rudolf I (Hapsburg), 1273–91 Adolf of Nassau, 1292–98 Albert I (Hapsburg), 1298–1308 Henry VII (Luxemburg), 1308–13 Louis IV (Wittelsbach), 1314–46 Charles IV (Luxemburg), 1346–78 Wenceslaus (Luxemburg), 1378–1400 Rupert (Wittelsbach), 1400–10 Sigismund (Luxemburg), 1410–37
Hapsburg dynasty
Albert II, 1438–39 Frederick III, 1440–93 Maximilian I, 1493–1519 Charles V, 1519–58 Ferdinand I, 1558–64 Maximilian II, 1564–76 Rudolf II, 1576–1612 Matthias, 1612–19 Ferdinand II, 1619–37 Ferdinand III, 1637–57 Leopold I, 1658–1705 Joseph I, 1705–11 Charles VI, 1711–40
Interregnum, 1740–42
Charles VII (Wittelsbach-Hapsburg), 1742–45 Francis I (Lorraine), 1745–65
Hapsburg-Lorraine dynasty
Joseph II, 1765–90 Leopold II, 1790–92 Francis II, 1792–1806

James Bryce, *The Holy Roman Empire* (new ed. 1968); see also bibliographies under MIDDLE AGES; GERMANY.

Holyrood Palace (hŏl'ērōōd) [i.e., holy cross], royal residence, Edinburgh, Midlothian, SE Scotland. In 1128, David I founded Holyrood Abbey on this site, where according to legend he was saved from an infuriated stag by the miraculous interception of a cross. The abbey's Chapel Royal, still standing, contains the remains of David II, James II, James V, Lord Darnley, and others. James IV began the present building c.1500. The palace, partially destroyed by the English in 1544, was the scene of the murder of David Rizzio in 1566. It was almost completely destroyed by fire in 1650. Charles II rebuilt it between 1671 and 1679 according to plans by Sir William Bruce of Kinross.

Holy Sepulcher (sĕp'əlkər), church in Jerusalem, officially the Church of the Resurrection. It is in the east central part of the Christian quarter, on the supposed site of Jesus' tomb. Steps connect it with chapels of St. Helena and of the Finding of the True Cross (see HELENA, ST.; CROSS). The center of the church is Romanesque, the shrine itself being at the west end of the nave in a great rotunda; the entrance of the church is from the south. The fabric built by the Crusaders is preserved, somewhat disguised, in the present building. The church has been much quarreled over by various Christian groups. The Orthodox Eastern secured control of most of it from the Turks, but there are partitioned areas for the use of Roman Catholics (in the custody of the Franciscans), the Copts, the Syrian Jacobites, and the Gregorian Armenians. See study by Charles Coüasnon (1974).

Holy Spirit: see HOLY GHOST.

Holy Thursday: see ASCENSION.

holy water, in Christian churches, water blessed to symbolize spiritual cleansing. In Roman Catholic churches there is a bowl (stoup or font) of holy water near the doors, so that the faithful may bless themselves with it on entering. Holy water is a SACRAMENTAL and is used in formal blessings, including the ASPERGES.

Holy Week, week before EASTER. Its chief days are named PALM SUNDAY, MAUNDY THURSDAY, GOOD FRIDAY, and Holy Saturday. In Christian life it is a week of devout observance, commemorating the Passion and Jesus' death on the cross. The liturgies have special features and services, e.g., TENEBRAE. In the Roman Catholic Church these rise to a climax with the vigil of the Resurrection on the evening of Holy Saturday. At this time the paschal CANDLE is blessed with the hymn *Exsultet,* and Lent with its fast ends at midnight.

holy year: see JUBILEE.

Holz, Arno (är'nō hôlts), 1863–1929, German critic and poet. His influence as a founder of the German naturalist school and as a critic is more important than his work itself. He was particularly influential in the development of Hauptmann. Among his works are the realistic sketches *Papa Hamlet* (with Johannes Schlaf, 1889); the drama *Die Familie Selicke* (also with Schlaf, 1890); *Die Kunst* [art] (1891); and the poems *Phantasus* (1898–99).

homage: see FEUDALISM.

Homam (hō'măm), the same as HEMAM.

Homayun: see HUMAYUN.

Homburg: see BAD HOMBURG VOR DER HÖHE, West Germany.

Home, 14th **earl of:** see DOUGLAS-HOME, SIR ALEC.

Home, Daniel Dunglas (hyōōm), 1833–86, Scottish spiritualist medium, b. Edinburgh, Scotland. He was taken to the United States when a small child. At age 13 he claimed to have discovered his gifts for dealing with spirits, and from 1850 to his death he had a triumphant career as a medium, always retaining his amateur status by refusing money, although he did accept expensive gifts. In his drawing room séances furniture moved with no apparent cause, ghostly hands appeared, and furniture and Home himself would levitate in the air. There was much dispute about the validity of these highly physical manifestations of spirits. Though numerous efforts were made to expose him, none was successful. See his *Incidents in My Life* (2 vol., 1863–72); Jean Burton, *Heyday of a Wizard* (1944).

Home, Henry: see KAMES, HENRY HOME, LORD.

home economics, study of homemaking and the relation of the home to the community. Formerly limited to problems of food (nutrition and cookery), clothing, sewing, textiles, household equipment, housecleaning, housing, hygiene, and household economics, it later came to include many aspects of family relations, parental education, consumer education, and institutional management. The application of scientific techniques to home economics was developed under the leadership of Ellen Henrietta Swallow RICHARDS; later an emphasis was placed on the social, economic, and aesthetic aspects. Although called in some countries home science, household arts, domestic science, or domestic economy, the subject is known today in the United States as home economics, and specialized terms are used for its subdivisions. The field of home economics has, at different times, emphasized training in needlework, cookery, the management of servants, the preparation of medicines, and food preservation; such instruction was once given mainly in the home and from a practical rather than a scientific standpoint. In the United States the teaching of cooking and sewing in the public schools was coincident with manual training for boys, beginning in the 1880s. State institutions, notably in Iowa, Kansas, and Illinois, pioneered in introducing home economics courses on the college level in the 1870s. In 1914, the Smith-Lever Act made Federal funds available for extension work in home economics and agriculture, in cooperation with the states; through this provision, supplemented by later acts, home demonstration work is carried on in many rural localities. The Smith-Hughes Act of 1917 instituted secondary school vocational education in home economics and other fields. Home economics, once taught only to women, is now taught to both men and women; in the United States home economics courses are taught mainly at the secondary school level, more commonly in rural than in urban areas. The International Federation of Home Economics, an organization devoted to the teaching of home economics on a worldwide basis, has members in over 60 countries. See Stanley Schuler and E. M. Schuler, *The Householders' Encyclopedia* (1973); M. B. Tate, *Home Economics As a Profession* (2d ed. 1973).

home missions: see MISSIONS.

Home of Franklin D. Roosevelt National Historic Site: see NATIONAL PARKS AND MONUMENTS (table).

Home of Polwarth, Sir Patrick, or **Sir Patrick Hume of Polwarth** (both: hyōōm, pōl'wərth), 1641–1724, Scottish statesman. Devoted to Presbyterianism, he opposed the policies of the duke of LAUDERDALE, took part in the unsuccessful rebellion of the 8th earl of ARGYLL in support of the duke of MONMOUTH, and fled to France. He returned (1688) with William III, who made him Baron Polwarth (1689), sheriff of Berwick (1692–1710), lord chancellor of Scotland (1696–1702), and earl of Marchmont (1697). See G. H. Rose, ed., *The Marchmont Papers* (1831).

homeopathy (hōmēŏp'əthē), system of medicine whose fundamental principle is the law of similars—that like is cured by like. It was first given practical application by Samuel Hahnemann of Leipzig, Germany, at the beginning of the 19th cent. and was designated homeopathy to distinguish it from the established school of medicine which he called allopathy. It had been observed that quinine given to a healthy person causes the same symptoms that malaria does in a person suffering from that disease; therefore quinine became the preferred treatment in malaria. When a drug was found to produce the same symptoms as did a certain disease, it was then used in small doses in treatment of that disease. U.S. medical schools do not presently emphasize the homeopathic approach.

Home Owners' Loan Corporation, (HOLC), former U.S. government agency established in 1933 to help stabilize real estate that had depreciated during the depression and to refinance the urban mortgage debt. It granted long-term mortgage loans amounting to over $3 billion at low interest rates (5% and later 4.5%) to some 1 million homeowners facing loss of their property. The HOLC ceased its lending activities in June, 1936, by the terms of the Home Owners' Loan Act. Later it made additional advances to borrowers, and by 1951 its assets were liquidated. See C. L. Harriss, *History and Policies of the Home Owners' Loan Corporation* (1951).

Homer, principal figure of ancient Greek literature, the first European poet. Two epic poems are attributed to him, the *Iliad* and the *Odyssey,* written in a literary type of Greek, Ionic in basis with Aeolic admixtures. Ranked among the great works of Western literature, these two poems together constitute the prototype for all subsequent epic poetry. The "Homeric question" was the great dispute of scholarship in the 19th cent. Scholars tried to analyze the two works by various tests, usually to show that they were strung together from older narrative poems. A recent project using a computer has presented strong evidence that the *Iliad* is the work of a single poet. Modern scholars are generally agreed that there was a poet named Homer who lived before 700 B.C., probably in Asia Minor, that he wrote for an aristocratic society, and that the *Iliad* and the *Odyssey* are each the product of one poet's work, developed out of older legendary matter. Some assign the *Odyssey* to a poet who lived slightly after the author of the *Iliad.* Legends about Homer were numerous in ancient times. He was said to be blind. His birthplace has always been disputed, but Chios or Smyrna seems most likely. The study of Homer was required of all Greek students in antiquity, and his heroes were worshiped in many parts of Greece. The *Iliad* and the *Odyssey* are written in dactylic hexameter and are of nearly the same length. Divided into 24 books, the *Iliad* tells of the wrath of ACHILLES and its tragic consequences, an episode in the TROJAN WAR. The action is in several sections. Achilles quarrels with Agamemnon over possession of the girl Briseis, and Achilles retires from the war to sulk in his tent. The Greek position gradually weakens until Agamemnon offers amendment to Achilles (Books I–IX). Book X tells of an expedition by Odysseus and Diomed leading to Greek reverses in the war. Thereupon Patroclus, Achilles' friend, is inspired to go into battle wearing Achilles' armor. He is killed by Hector (Books XI–XVII). Book XVIII tells of the visit of Thetis, mother of Achilles, to comfort her grieving son and of the forging of new armor by Hephaestus for Achilles. Achilles then determines to avenge his friend, kills Hector, buries Patroclus, and finally, at the entreaty of Priam, gives Hector's body to the aged father (Books XIX–XXIV). The *Iliad* is a highly unified work, splendid in its dramatic action. Written in a simple yet lofty style, it contains many perceptive characterizations that make exalted personages like Hector and Achilles believable as human beings. The *Odyssey* is written in 24 books and begins nearly 10 years after the fall of Troy. In the first part, Telemachus, Odysseus' son, visits Nestor at Pylos and Menelaus at Sparta, seeking news of his absent father. He tells them of the troubles of his mother, Penelope, who is beset by mercenary suitors. Menelaus informs him that his father is with the nymph Calypso (Books I–IV). The scene then shifts to Mt. Olympus with an account of Zeus' order to Calypso to release Odysseus, who then builds a raft and sails to Phaeacia. There he is entertained by King Alcinoüs and his daughter Nausicaä; he relates to them the story of his wanderings in which he has encountered Polyphemus, Aeolus, Circe, Scylla, and Charybdis, the Sirens, the Laestrygones, and the lotus-eaters (Books V–XII). Dramatic tension mounts with the return of Odysseus and Telemachus to Ithaca; together they plan and execute the death of the suitors. Afterwards Odysseus makes himself known to his wife and his father, with whose aid he repulses the suitors' angry kinsmen. Athena intervenes, peace is restored, and Odysseus once again rules his country (Books XIII–XXIV). The atmosphere of adventure and fate in the *Odyssey* contrasts with the heavier tone and tragic grandeur of the *Iliad. The* HOMERIC HYMNS were falsely attributed to Homer. Among the many notable translations of the *Iliad* and the *Odyssey* are the prose translations by Andrew Lang et al and the modern poetic translations by Richmond Lattimore. See J. A. Scott, *The Unity of Homer* (1921); D. L. Page, *The Homeric Odyssey* (1955); R. Bespaloff, *On The Iliad* (1947, repr. 1962); A. J. B. Wace and F. H. Stubbings, ed., *A Companion to Homer* (1962); C. H. Whitman, *Homer and the Heroic Tradition* (1958, repr. 1965); C. R. Beye, *The Iliad, The Odyssey and The Epic Tradition* (1966); W. F. J. Knight, *The Many Minded Homer* (1971); M. Parry, *The Making of Homeric Verse,* ed. by A. Parry (1971); and C. M. Bowra, *Homer* (1972).

Homer, Louise, 1871–1947, American contralto, whose maiden name was Louise Dilworth Beatty, b. Pittsburgh. She studied in Philadelphia, Boston, and Paris and made her debut (1898) in Vichy, France. After her American debut (1900) with the Metropolitan Opera Company in San Francisco, she sang major roles with that company until 1919. Later she sang with the Chicago Opera (1920–25) and the San Francisco and Los Angeles opera companies (1926). In 1894 she married her harmony teacher, **Sidney Homer,** 1864–1953, an American composer known for his many songs. See Homer's *My Wife and I* (1939); biography by their daughter Anne Homer (1974).

Homer, Winslow, 1836–1910, American landscape, marine, and genre painter. Homer was born in Boston, where he later worked as a lithographer and illustrator. In 1861 he was sent to the battlefront as correspondent for *Harper's Weekly*, his work winning international acclaim. Many of his postwar studies of everyday life, such as *Crack the Whip* (Metropolitan Mus.), date from this period, during which he was a popular magazine illustrator. In 1876, Homer abandoned illustration to devote himself to painting. He found his inspiration in the American scene and, eventually, in the sea, which he painted at Prouts Neck, Maine, in the summer and in Florida or the Bahamas in the winter. His oils and watercolors alike are characterized by their directness, realism, objectivity, and splendid color. But it is above all as a watercolorist that Homer excelled. After 1884 he lived the life of a recluse. His powerful and dramatic interpretations of the sea in watercolor have never been surpassed and hold a unique place in American art. They are in leading museums throughout the United States. Characteristic watercolors are *Breaking Storm* and *Maine Coast* (both: Art Inst. of Chicago) and *The Hurricane* (Metropolitan Mus.). Characteristic oils include *The Gulf Stream* (1899) and *Moonlight—Wood's Island Light* (both: Metropolitan Mus.), and *Eight Bells* (1886; Addison Gall., Andover, Mass.). See biographies by Lloyd Goodrich (1959), P. C. Beam (1966), and John Wilmerding (1972); studies by Lloyd Goodrich (1968 and 1972); Barbara Gelman, ed., *The Wood Engravings of Winslow Homer* (1969); Donelson Hoopes, *Winslow Homer's Watercolors* (1969).

Homeric Hymns (hōmĕr'ĭk), name applied to a body of hexameter poems falsely attributed to HOMER by the ancients. Composed probably between 800 and 400 B.C., they are complimentary verses to the various gods, such as Aphrodite, Apollo, Demeter, and Hermes. Although sometimes of great beauty, they are important mainly as prime sources for information about Greek religion and cults. The *Margites* (7th or 6th cent. B.C.), a comic poem, and *The Battle of the Frogs and Mice* (5th–2d cent. B.C.), a mock epic, were also incorrectly attributed to Homer.

Home Rule, in Irish and English history, political slogan adopted by Irish nationalists in the 19th cent. to describe their objective of self-government for Ireland. A basic theme in the history of Ireland through the centuries of English dominance was the desire for control over its domestic affairs. The modern Home Rule movement began in 1870 under the leadership of Isaac BUTT, whose program appealed most strongly to the Irish middle classes. The long agricultural depression beginning in 1873 increased economic stimulus for Home Rule, and under the leadership of Charles Stewart PARNELL the movement gained support from the agricultural laborers and erstwhile members of the FENIAN MOVEMENT. In this period only a minority had recourse to violence, and Parnell disavowed the murder of two British officials in Dublin in 1882 (see PHOENIX PARK MURDERS). In 1886, William GLADSTONE committed the LIBERAL PARTY to Home Rule. His bill of 1886 would have established a separate Irish legislature, while reserving many powers, including taxation, to the British Parliament at Westminster. The bill failed to pass, and the incoming Conservative government developed a policy of land reform (see IRISH LAND QUESTION) to mollify the Irish. The unity of the Irish party in Parliament collapsed after Parnell was ruined by a divorce scandal in 1890. In 1893 the Liberals passed in the House of Commons the Second Home Rule Bill providing a bicameral legislature for purely local matters and Irish representation at Westminster to vote on Irish taxation. This was generally considered by Home Rule advocates to be unsatisfactory, but the bill was, in any event, defeated in the House of Lords. Advocates of constitutional means to Home Rule began to lose ground to republicans and revolutionaries. The Gaelic League and Irish Ireland ideals of an increasingly self-conscious Irish people culminated in the founding (c.1900) of SINN FEIN. The Irish Council Bill of 1907, which was to establish a purely Irish body to direct the spending of Irish tax proceeds, failed to pass because of Irish dissatisfaction with the plan. In 1912 the Third Home Rule Bill passed the House of Commons. The most notable difference from the bill of 1893 was that it would have eventually given control of the police to Ireland. A tremendous outcry arose in Protestant Ulster, which feared Roman Catholic domination. Private armies—the Ulster Volunteers (in the North) and the Irish Volunteers (in the South)—were raised, and civil war threatened if the bill became law. In 1914, Commons again passed the bill, but the House of Lords excluded Ulster from its provisions. The Commons voted to allow Ulster to vote itself out of Home Rule for six years. At the outbreak of World War I the bill was passed once again with the proviso that it should not go into effect until after the war. The law never took effect. By this time Irish labor leaders like James CONNOLLY had been drawn into the struggle, and Irish radicalism—along with impatience and doubts as to Britain's good faith—brought about the Easter Rebellion of 1916. In 1918, S Ireland elected to Parliament only Sinn Fein members pledged to republicanism instead of Home Rule. These members did not go to Westminster, however; instead they set up their own Irish assembly, the DÁIL ÉIREANN, which declared Ireland independent. There followed a period of guerrilla war between the nationalist IRISH REPUBLICAN ARMY (IRA) and a force of British irregulars known as the Black and Tans. In 1921 the British government entered into negotiations with the *de facto* Irish government headed by Eamon DE VALERA. The Irish Free State, with dominion status, was created by an Anglo-Irish treaty in 1921. Remaining ties with Great Britain were gradually discarded (see IRELAND, REPUBLIC OF). The six counties of Northern Ireland (see IRELAND, NORTHERN) remained part of the United Kingdom, their government being established under the provisions of the Fourth Home Rule Bill of 1920, which was meant to set up two parliaments, but which was rendered void in the South by the establishment of the Irish Free State. The continued British presence in Northern Ireland was abhorrent to Irish nationalists, but apart from short periods of terrorist activity by the IRA, the issue was allowed to lie fairly dormant until the late 1960s. Then the repressive Protestant reaction to a movement to end discrimination against Catholics within Northern Ireland revived militant nationalist sentiment. Escalating violence between Protestants and Catholics and a new, intensive campaign of terror by the IRA caused the British cabinet to suspend the Northern Ireland government in 1972. New machinery of government was established in 1973, in which the Roman Catholics shared power for the first time and provision was made for increased cooperation between the Northern and Southern governments. However, Protestant pressure brought the collapse of the new system and the resumption of direct British rule of Northern Ireland in 1974. The nationalist goal of unifying Ireland still appeared far from reach. For an economic interpretation see Erich Strauss, *Irish Nationalism and British Democracy* (1951); for an opposing political interpretation see Nicholas Mansergh, *The Irish Question, 1840–1921* (rev. ed. 1965). See W. K. Hancock, *Survey of British Commonwealth Affairs* (2 vol., 1937–1942; repr. 1964); A. T. Q. Stewart, *The Ulster Crisis* (1967).

home rule, municipal, system adopted in many states of the United States by which a city is given the right to draft and amend its own CHARTER and to regulate purely local matters without interference from the state legislature. The rapid growth of urban centers in the latter part of the 19th cent. brought new and complex problems; the state legislatures, which had controlled most CITY GOVERNMENT, found themselves incapable of handling the fast-growing cities. In 1875, Missouri adopted the first municipal home rule clause in its constitution; other states have followed its lead. The form of the rule varies greatly from state to state. There are two principal types of municipal home rule: constitutional home rule, by which cities are given the right by the state constitution to form their own charters; and legislative home rule, by which local autonomy is granted through an act of the state legislature. Local and general concerns cannot, of course, be strictly delimited, and there are frequent legal and political contests concerning jurisdiction. The growing importance of the suburbs and the relative decline of cities have led to the concept of metropolitan government as an intermediary between city and state government. See J. D. McGoldrick, *Law and Practice of Municipal Home Rule, 1916–1930* (1933, repr. 1972); R. P. Bolan, *Fundamentals of Home Rule* (1960); bibliography by N. C. Burg (1973).

Homestead. 1 City (1970 pop. 13,674), Dade co., SE Fla.; inc. 1913. It is a trade and shipping center for the redland district, known for its many varieties of citrus and other fruits and vegetables. Nearby Homestead Air Force Base is important to its economy. The city is also a vacation center—the gateway to Everglades National Park (see NATIONAL PARKS AND MONUMENTS, table) and the Florida Keys. Local attractions include several tropical gardens, a pioneer museum, and a castlelike building furnished with coral items. A state subtropical experiment station is there, and an atomic power plant is nearby. **2** Borough (1970 pop. 6,309), Allegheny co., SW Pa., on the Monongahela River just S of Pittsburgh; inc. 1880. It is famous for large iron and steel works (most of which are now in the neighboring borough of Munhall). The works, formerly owned by the Carnegie company, in 1892 saw the outbreak of the HOMESTEAD STRIKE, one of the most bitterly fought industrial disputes in U.S. labor history.

Homestead Act, 1862, passed by the U.S. Congress. It provided for the transfer of 160 acres (65 hectares) of unoccupied public land to each homesteader on payment of a nominal fee after five years of residence; land could also be acquired after six months of residence at $1.25 an acre. The government had previously sold land to settlers in the West for revenue purposes. As the West became politically stronger, however, pressure was increased upon Congress to guarantee free land to settlers (see FOOT RESOLUTION; PREEMPTION ACT). Several bills providing for free distribution of land were defeated in Congress; in 1860 a bill was passed in Congress but was vetoed by President Buchanan. With the ascendancy of the Republican party (which had committed itself to homestead legislation) and with the secession of the South (which had opposed free distribution of land), the Homestead Act, sponsored by Galusha A. Grow, became law.

Homestead National Monument of America: see NATIONAL PARKS AND MONUMENTS (table).

Homestead strike, in U.S. history, a bitterly fought labor dispute. On June 29, 1892, workers belonging to the Amalgamated Association of Iron and Steel Workers struck the Carnegie Steel Company at Homestead, Pa. to protest a proposed wage cut. Henry C. Frick, the company's general manager, determined to break the union. He hired 300 Pinkerton detectives to protect the plant and strike-breakers. After an armed battle between the workers and the detectives on July 6, in which several men were killed or wounded, the governor called out the state militia. The plant opened, nonunion workers stayed on the job, and the strike, which was officially called off on Nov. 20, was broken. The Homestead strike led to a serious weakening of unionism in the steel industry until the 1930s.

Homewood. 1 City (1970 pop. 21,137), Jefferson co., N central Ala., a residential suburb of Birmingham; inc. 1921. **2** Village (1970 pop. 18,871), Cook co., NE Ill., a residential suburb of Chicago; platted 1852, inc. 1892.

homicide (hŏm'əsīd), taking of human life. Homicides that are neither justifiable nor excusable are crimes. A criminal homicide committed with MALICE aforethought is MURDER, otherwise it is MANSLAUGHTER. A homicide is excusable if it is the result of an accident that occurred during a lawful act and that did not amount to culpable NEGLIGENCE. Justifiable homicides are intentional killings done in accordance with legal obligation or in circumstances where the law recognizes no wrong. They include the execution of criminals, killings necessary to prevent a FELONY or to arrest a suspected felon, and killings in self-defense. The plea of self-defense is allowable only when the slayer reasonably feared death or serious bodily injury to himself at the hands of the person slain. In some states of the United States one may lawfully use killing force, if needed, in resisting the unlawful invasion of a home or real PROPERTY. Other states require that the home or property be abandoned if homicide would be required for its protection.

homily (hŏm'əlē), type of oral religious instruction delivered to a church congregation; a sermon. A distinction, not always observed, between homily and sermon is that the homily renders practical moral advice, rather than discussing doctrine, whereas the sermon is usually based on a scriptural theme. Works of literature giving moral advice are also called homilies. ÆLFRIC wrote many homilies.

hominy [Algonquian], hulled corn with the germ removed and served either ground or whole. The pioneers in North America prepared it by soaking the kernels in weak wood lye until the hulls floated to the top. Hominy is boiled until tender and served as a vegetable. Hominy grits (hominy ground into small grains) are boiled and served as a vegetable or as a cereal, or they may be shaped into patties and fried; they are especially popular in the S United States. Samp is a type of coarse hominy.

Homoeans, homoion, homoiousion, and **homoousion:** see ARIANISM.

Homo erectus (hō'mō ērĕk'təs), extinct species of man dating from 1,000,000 to 300,000 years ago. Fossils of this species were first discovered in 1891 by Eugene Dubois in Java, and classified as *Pithecanthropus. Homo erectus* remains were also found in

China, at Choukoutien, near Peking, in 1927, and were initially termed Peking man or *Sinanthropus pekinensis.* Other examples were discovered in E Africa (Chellean Man), Germany (Heidelberg Man), and Algeria (*Atlanthropus*). Some fossils that are transitional between AUSTRALOPITHECUS and *Homo erectus* are sometimes classified in the latter group; they include *Homo habilis* (E Africa), *Telanthropus* (South Africa), and *Meganthropus,* or Java man (Java). In body size and brain development, *Homo erectus* is intermediate between the earlier *Australopithecus* and the later *Homo sapiens,* the species to which modern man belongs. The limb bones of *Homo erectus* do not differ from those of *Homo sapiens.* The species achieved an erect posture in motion, and developed such cultural items as the use of fire and stone tools, such as the hand axe.

homogenization, process in which a mixture is made uniform throughout. Generally this procedure involves reducing the size of the particles of one component of the mixture and dispersing them evenly throughout the other component. Probably the most familiar example of a homogenized product is commercially sold milk. In milk that has not been homogenized the globules of fat range in diameter from approximately 1 to 20 micrometers (millionths of a meter), or 40 to 800 millionths of an inch. This allows them to separate out from the rest of the milk if it is allowed to stand. After homogenization the globules are reduced to a range of sizes clustering closely about 1 micrometer and remain stably dispersed through the milk. Homogenization is usually accomplished by pumping the milk through a small opening at high pressure. Milk that has been homogenized is better suited for shipment in paper containers but deteriorates more rapidly than unhomogenized milk.

homograft: see TRANSPLANTATION, MEDICAL.

homology, in biology, correspondence between structures of different species that is attributable to the inheritance of the structures from a common ancestor. The forelimbs of vertebrates, such as the wing of a bird, the wing of a bat, and the foreleg of an amphibian, are homologous; there is an almost identical number of bones in the limbs, and the pattern of construction is identical. Homologous structures do not necessarily have the same function in the different organisms; the bird wing and whale flipper are also homologous structures. ANALOGY is the functional similarity between structures that do not have a common origin; for example, the wings of birds and those of insects are analogous.

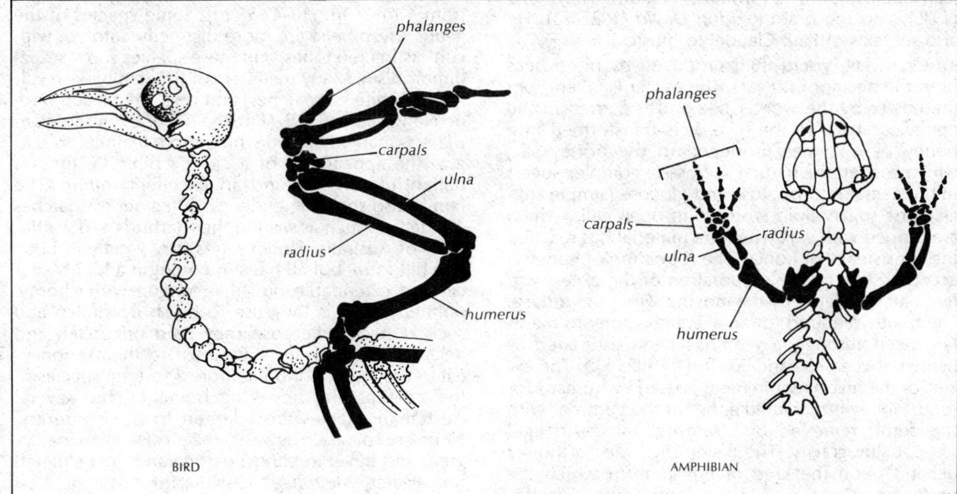

Homology in bones of a bird wing and an amphibian foreleg

homolosine (həmŏl'əsīn, -sīn"), map projection: see GOODE, JOHN PAUL.

homophony (hōmŏf'ənē), species of musical ensemble texture in which all voice parts move more or less to the same rhythm. A listener tends to hear the highest voice as the melody and the lower voices as its accompaniment. Homophony can be contrasted with imitative texture, in which each voice part is heard as equally important melodically.

homosexuality, sexual and emotional interest in members of one's own sex. Homosexuality is sometimes accompanied by fear of, or aversion to, sexual activity with the opposite sex. Medical and psychological research has yielded little evidence that homosexuality is caused by biological predisposition or primary gender identity disorder (i.e., the feeling that one is really a member of the opposite sex). Psychoanalytic theory attributes homosexuality to an inability to resolve issues in the Oedipal stage of development (see OEDIPUS COMPLEX). Oedipal theory suggests that identification with the parent of the same sex is the normal developmental defense toward anxiety caused by amorous feelings for the parent of the opposite sex (e.g., a male child identifies with his father in order to freely express his feelings for his mother). Resolution of the Oedipal complex through identification is considered a major step in the socialization of the child. Both female homosexuals (lesbians) and male homosexuals often retain an attachment for the mother and fear of the father. Other psychiatric theories that have gained some acceptance include the following: that homosexuality is a regression to the earliest (oral) stage of development; that most families of homosexuals are characterized by an overprotective mother and an absent or brutal father; or that homosexuals feared engulfment by a dominant mother in the pre-Oedipal phase. Other authorities suggest that male homosexuality may be an expression of nonsexual problems, such as fear of adult responsibility, or may be triggered by various experiences, such as association with homosexuals. Female homosexuality has been little studied and is poorly understood. Many of the theoretical causes of male homosexuality may also hold true for female homosexuality if the father-mother relationship patterns are considered in reverse. Although female homosexuality has become more common, it is believed that males are more likely to seek refuge in homosexuality because of the greater status and cultural demands attached to the heterosexual male role. Evidence also indicates that females have less trouble adjusting to the homosexual role than do their male counterparts. Bisexuals are sexually active with members of both sexes, but their core gender identity is that of their own biological sex. Biological bisexuals (hermaphrodites and intersexes), who possess some organs of both sexes, are psychologically the gender of their assignment and rearing. Transvestism, or dressing in the clothing worn by members of the opposite sex, is engaged in by some homosexuals but also by heterosexual fetishists and by transsexuals, whose gender role is that of the biologically opposite sex (see FETISHISM). Transsexuals are distinguished from homosexuals by the feeling that they are really members of the opposite sex. The use of hormones, psychotherapy, and sex-change operations have become increasingly common in dealing with transsexuals. Many Western men have pseudohomosexual longings toward other men at times of crisis in their cultural roles, such as an occupational failure. Also, otherwise heterosexual men often engage in homosexual acts when deprived of female companionship, e.g., in prison. Many individuals experiment homosexually during preadolescence and adolescence but grow up to assume the heterosexual role. In the United States the penalties for homosexual acts vary from state to state; in many states unharmful private sexual acts of any kind between consenting adults are considered outside the province of legal authority. Some authorities, as well as homosexual groups, believe that instances of mental disorder in homosexuals result more from societal pressures and bias against homosexuality than from any psychopathology. The prejudices against homosexuals in culture and law are related to society's emphasis on the family as the means of acculturation of the child.

homozygote (hō"mōzī'gōt): see GENETICS.

Homs: see HIMS, Syria.

Honan or **Ho-nan** (both: hō-năn, Chin. hô-năn), province (1968 est. pop. 50,000,000), c.65,000 sq mi (168,350 sq km), NE China. The capital is CHENG-CHOU. It is sparsely settled in the mountainous western region but densely populated and cultivated in the east. Though the climate is dry, the loess provides fertile soil. Honan is a major wheat and cotton producing province; other agricultural products include kaoliang, rice, millet, sweet potatoes, tobacco, fruit, oakleaf silk, and oilseed crops (sesame, peanuts). The province is well-watered, with the Huang Ho (Yellow River) flowing through the northern section and the Huai River in the east; both are generally navigable. Floods and droughts, long suffered in Honan, have been alleviated by the building (1960s) of the San Men dam on the Huang Ho in the southwest, the construction of the People's Victory Canal (which diverts water from the Huang Ho to the Chin River), forestation efforts, and other irrigation and drainage programs. In addition to its excellent waterways, Honan has many good highways and a fine railway system; the principal north-south and east-west railroad lines of China cross the province, intersecting at Cheng-chou. Coal, abundantly found in Honan, and hydroelectric power from the San Men project supply burgeoning industries in Chenchou, Lo-yang, and K'ai-feng. An aluminum plant is at the San Men gorge. In addition to coal, iron is mined, and lead and pottery clay are found. Stone Age remains have been discovered in Honan, and from c.2000 B.C. the region was a center of Chinese civilization; An-yang, Lo-yang, and K'ai-feng are historic cities. In the early 1930s, N Honan was part of the Anhwei-Honan-Hupeh soviet area (also called the Oyuwan Republic). The area N of the Huang Ho was a part of P'ing-yüan prov. from 1949 to 1952.

Honanfu: see LO-YANG, China.

Hondecoeter, Melchior d' (mĕl'khēôr də hŏn'də-kōōtər), 1636–95, Dutch animal painter. His grandfather, Gillis d'Hondecoeter (d. 1638) and his father, Gysbert d'Hondecoeter (1604–1653), were landscape and animal painters. After four years at The Hague, where he painted *The Menagerie of William III at Loo,* Melchior settled in Amsterdam. He painted all forms of animal life, but is best known for his depiction of birds and fowl, in which he has few equals. Representative works, executed in a smooth, precise style, include the *Dead Cock* (Brussels) and *The Floating Feather* (Amsterdam).

Hondo: see HONSHU, Japan.

Honduras (hŏndŏŏr'əs, -dyŏŏr'-; Span., ōndōō'räs), republic (1973 est. pop. 2,800,000), 43,277 sq mi (112,088 sq km), Central America. TEGUCIGALPA is the capital and chief commercial center. Second largest of the Central American countries, Honduras is bounded on the N by the Caribbean Sea, on the E and S by Nicaragua, on the SW by El Salvador, and on the W by Guatemala. The short stretch of southern coast on the Gulf of Fonseca, with a small port, AMAPALA, is the sole Pacific outlet. Honduras has a tropical, rainy climate. Over 80% of the land is mountainous; ranges extend from east to west at altitudes of 5,000 to 9,000 ft (1,520–2,740 m) and limit heavy rainfall to the north. In the east are the swamps and forests of the MOSQUITO COAST. Two river systems, the Patuca and the Ulua, drain most of the north. The economy is based on agriculture; bananas are by far the most important product, comprising 50% of all exports. The vast banana plantations, established by U.S. companies, are mainly along the northern coast; the UNITED FRUIT COMPANY, fiercely resented by many Latin Americans as an exploitative monopoly, has had much social and political influence in Honduras. Coffee (grown chiefly by small farmers), timber, minerals (silver, lead, zinc), and beef are also exported. Other important food crops include corn, beans, rice, and sugarcane. Honduras has rich forest resources and deposits of silver, lead, zinc, gold, cadmium, antimony, and copper, but exploitation is hampered by inadequate road and rail systems, and the country remains underdeveloped. Its only railroads link the banana plantations in the north to SAN PEDRO SULA and the principal ports, La Ceiba (see CEIBA, LA), PUERTO CORTÉS, TELA, and Trujillo; they do not penetrate more than 75 mi (121 km) inland. Air transportation, however, has opened up remote areas. Industry, concentrated chiefly in San Pedro Sula, is small and consumer-oriented. Food processing, especially sugar refining, is the most important, followed by lumber, chemicals, clothing, and cement. About half

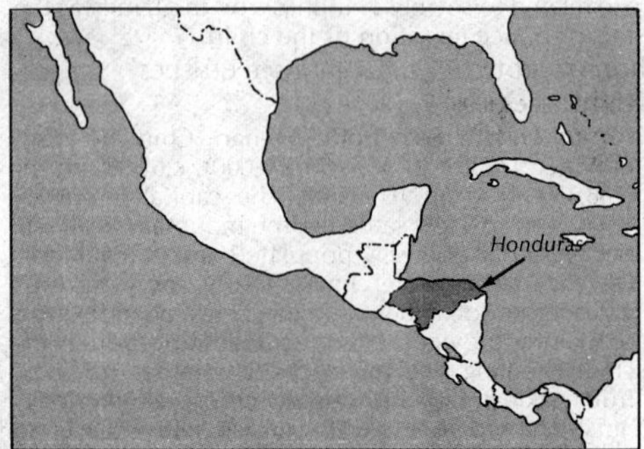

of the population (about 90% mestizo) is illiterate. The restored Mayan ruins of COPÁN in the west, first discovered by the Spaniards in 1576 and rediscovered in dense jungle in 1839, reflect the great Mayan culture that arose in the 4th cent. It had declined when Columbus sighted the region in 1502, naming it Honduras (meaning "depths") for the deep water off the coast. Hernán CORTÉS arrived in 1524 and ordered Pedro de ALVARADO to found settlements along the coast. Comayagua and Tegucigalpa developed as early mining centers. In 1821, Honduras gained independence from Spain and became part of Iturbide's Mexican Empire; from 1825 to 1838 it was a member of the CENTRAL AMERICAN FEDERATION. Thereafter, conservative and liberal factions fought bloody wars to control the republic, and Honduras was subjected to frequent interference from its Central American neighbors. Great Britain long controlled the Mosquito Coast and the BAY ISLANDS; William WALKER attempted a "liberation" in 1860. Although Honduras often sought to reestablish Central American unity, the attempts were frustrated by political and personal animosities. Foreign capital, plantation life, and conservative politics constituted a trio of dominant forces that held sway in Honduras from the late 19th cent. to the end of the regime (1933–48) of Tiburcio CARÍAS ANDINO, when the liberal movement was reawakened. The rights of workers were not effectively defined and protected until a labor code was adopted in 1955 and a new constitution was promulgated in 1957. That year Ramón Villeda Morales became the first liberal president in 25 years. Shortly before the scheduled presidential election in 1963, Villeda was overthrown and replaced by a military junta under Osvaldo López Arellano. It ruled until the adoption of a new constitution in 1965 (the country's 12th), at which time López was elected president for a six-year term. The illegal immigration of several hundred thousand Salvadorans across the ill-defined El Salvador-Honduras border and the expulsion of many of the immigrants by Honduras led to a war with El Salvador in July, 1969. Although the war lasted only five days, its effects were serious. The Organization of American States mediated the dispute and established a demilitarized zone along the border, but border incidents continued for several years. Honduras withdrew from the Central American Common Market as a result of the war, with subsequent economic hardship. When Ramón Ernesto Cruz, who was elected president in 1971 to succeed López, moved too slowly on reentering the Common Market, he was overthrown (Dec., 1972) by López in the country's 137th coup d'etat (in 151 years). López announced that he would govern for not less than five years and promised social and economic reforms. In late 1974 the Caribbean coast of Honduras was devastated by a hurricane. See D. Z. Stone, *The Archaeology of Central and Southern Honduras* (1957); R. S. Chamberlain, *The Conquest and Colonization of Honduras, 1502–1550* (1966); T. B. Villanueva, *The Role of Institutional Innovation in the Economic Development of Honduras* (1968); T. E. Wright, *Into the Maya World* (1969); E. G. Squier, *Honduras* (1870, repr. 1970); H. I. Blutstein et al., *Area Handbook for Honduras* (1971).

Honduras, British: see BRITISH HONDURAS.

Hone, Nathaniel, 1718–84, Irish miniaturist and portrait painter. Hone is noted for his smoothly painted, informal portraits of middle-class subjects. His painting *The Conjurer* (1775) formed part of the first recorded one-man show in Great Britain.

Hone, Philip, 1780–1851, American diarist and politician, b. New York City. With his brother he built up a successful auctioneering business, which he later abandoned for politics. He was mayor of New York City in 1825. His diary (1828–51), opinionated and shrewd, contains valuable records of life in New York and of the development of the Whig party during that period. See selections from his diary, ed. by Bayard Tuckerman (2 vol., 1889) and by Allan Nevins (2 vol., 1927; repr. 1971).

Hone, William, 1780–1842, English writer and bookseller. He was tried and acquitted three times in 1817 for publishing parodies on the church and the government. Besides writing political satires (illustrated by Cruikshank), he published highly popular compilations of miscellaneous information on such subjects as manners, e.g., the *Every-Day Book* (2 vol., 1826–27).

hone, stone of fine texture or an artificial substitute for it used as an abrasive for sharpening edged tools such as the chisel, knife, and razor. It may be used dry, with water, or with oil. The whetstone is similarly used, but is coarser. The oilstone is a hone or a whetstone used with oil.

Honecker, Erich (ä'rĭkh hôn'ĕkər), 1912–, East German political leader. The son of an ardent Communist, Honecker was imprisoned for 10 years under the Nazis for his party activities. After the war he joined Walter Ulbricht's Socialist Unity (Communist) party and began a steady rise in the East German party bureaucracy. He became a member of the secretariat of the Communist party central committee in 1958, with particular responsibility for security matters. When Ulbricht resigned as party leader in 1971, Honecker succeeded him and later that year replaced him as head of the national defense council.

Honegger, Arthur (hŭn'ĕgər, Fr. ärtür ônägĕr'), 1892–1955, Swiss-French composer, studied at the conservatories of Zürich and Paris. One of the group of Parisian composers called Les Six, he wrote music ranging from satire to intensely religious works that are marked by incisive rhythms and sharp dissonances, often the result of his use of polytonality. Besides *Pacific 231* (1923)—the first of three *mouvements symphoniques*—his outstanding works are of a theatrical nature, such as ballets, the operas *Judith* (1926) and *Antigone* (1927, libretto by Jean Cocteau), music for films, including *Mayerling* (1935), and the oratorio *King David* (1921–23). He also set texts of Paul Claudel to music.

honey, sweet, viscid fluid produced by honeybees from the nectar of flowers. The nectar is taken from the flower by the worker bee and is carried in the honey sac back to the hive. It is transformed into honey by enzymes produced in the honey sac, which convert the natural sucrose (a complex sugar) in the nectar into fructose and glucose (simple sugars). The sugary fluid is stored in open cells, which are capped with wax when the material has reached the consistency of honey. The formation of honey is accomplished by the evaporation of the excess water in air circulated by the moving wings of workers. The honey required for an average colony to maintain itself through a year has been estimated as being between 400 and 500 lb (180–225 kg). The excess of the hive's requirement is used by humans for food. Honey is marketed either in the comb or with the comb removed by straining, by centrifugal force, or by gravity. The flavor and color of honey depend upon the kind of flower from which the nectar was taken, e.g., linden honey from Czechoslovakia, lavender honey from France, and wild rose honey from Greece. Much of that produced in the United States is the pale, delicately flavored alfalfa and clover honey. Among the numerous other blossoms yielding nectar are those of the basswood, buckwheat, orange, palmetto, sage, and tupelo. The leading producers of honey are Argentina, Australia, Canada, and the United States. From earliest times until cane sugar became commercially important, honey was a major sweetening agent. Honey is easily absorbed and utilized by the body. It contains about 70 to 80% sugar; the rest is water, minerals and traces of protein, acids, and other substances. See U.S. Agricultural Research Service, *Beekeeping in the United States* (rev. ed. 1971).

honey badger or **ratel** (rāt'əl), carnivore, *Mellivora capensis*, of the forest and brush country of Africa, the Middle East, and India; it is a member of the badger and skunk family. The honey badger has short legs and stout claws and is a strong burrower and a good climber. About 2 ft (61 cm) long excluding the tail, it has a coat that is black on the lower half of the body and pale gray above. The honey badger resembles its distant relative the skunk in coloration and in the possession of an anal scent gland. It is nocturnal, feeds on rodents, reptiles, and insects, and has a thick loose coat that protects it against snake bites and insect stings. The honey badger collaborates with the HONEYGUIDE, or indicator bird, in obtaining honey, a favorite food. The bird searches for a bee colony, and when one is found, the honey badger rips it open. The bird and the honey badger then share the honey. Honey badgers travel singly or in pairs. The young, usually two, are born in burrows. Honey badgers are classified in the phylum CHORDATA, subphylum Vertebrata, class Mammalia, order Carnivora, family Mustelidae.

honey bear: see BEAR; KINKAJOU.

honey-buzzard, common name for a medium-sized, buzzardlike hawk, *Pernis apivorus*. The color of its plumage varies, but is predominantly reddish brown, and its tail is marked by three lateral brown bands. As with many birds of prey, the female tends to be larger than the male, with a wingspan of up to 60 in. (152 cm). The honey-buzzard has a pointed, decurved bill, and a unique (among birds of prey) patch between eyes and bill, which is covered with scalelike, rather than large, bristly feathers. It has powerful toes and strong claws. Honey-buzzards are found throughout the Old World, where they feed on a diet of bees, wasps, and honey, which the birds steal from the hives of the insects. In winter, the European and northern Asian members of this species migrate to breeding grounds in Africa and India. The entire breeding season, from nest building to independence of the young, takes as long as five months. For this reason, many breed only every second year. The female lays two white, brown-spotted eggs per clutch, which are incubated for a period of 30 days. Honey-buzzards are classified in the phylum CHORDATA, subphylum Vertebrata, class Aves, order Falconiformes, family Accipitridae.

honeycomb moth: see BEE MOTH.

honeycreeper: see WARBLER.

honeydew melon: see MELON.

honeyeater or **honeysucker,** common name for arboreal birds comprising some 160 species of the family Meliphagidae, and found in Australia, New Zealand, and the SW Pacific. There is a single South American genus. The plumage tends to be dull, ranging from greenish to grayish brown, with little difference between the sexes. They range in length from 4 to 17 in. (10–42.5 cm). Some species of the genus *Myzomelia* are more distinctly colored, with contrasting red tones, and these species show sexual dimorphism. Many members of the family have yellow or white ear patches, and one, the parson bird, or New Zealand tui (*Prosthemadera novaeseelandiae*), is marked by two white throat feathers, said to give the appearance of a cleric's bib. The tui is a delightful songster and an excellent mimic. The family also shows a tendency to featherless patches on the face such as seen in the friarbirds and wattlebirds of Australia. Honeyeaters vary greatly in body and bill form, but all have in common a highly specialized, extendable, brushlike tongue, with a horny, pointed tip. This they use to brush up pollen and suck at nectar. Because they feed on pollen and nectar (and the insects attracted to them), honeyeaters are important pollinators. Most are species of the treetops and flowering branches, but several Australian species are adapted to open country. None are solitary. They are gregarious to varying degrees and travel in bands, particularly the helmeted honeyeater, *Meliphaga cassidix*, of Australia. Nest and nesting habits also vary, but none of the honeyeaters are ground nesters. The number of eggs per clutch ranges from two in the tropical species to four in those of temperate areas. Male participation in rearing also varies, but most help in feeding the young. Honeyeaters are classified in the phylum CHORDATA, subphylum Vertebrata, class Aves, order Passeriformes, family Meliphagidae.

honeyguide, small plainly colored Old World bird of the family Indicatoridae, known for its habit of leading man and some lower animals (notably the HONEY BADGER) to the nests of wild bees. Honeyguides are native to Africa, the Himalayas, and the East Indies. The largest and best-known species is the 8-in. long (20-cm) black-throated African honeyguide, *Indicator indicator*. It leads tribesmen to bees' nests, waits for them to open the hive, and then feeds on bits of honeycomb, bees, and larvae; it has special bacteria in its stomach to aid in the digestion of beeswax. Honeyguides lay their eggs in the nests of hole-nesting birds and the young, on hatching, kill their nest mates with special needle-sharp bill hooks; they are then able to consume all the food brought by their foster parents. Honeyguides are classified in the phylum CHORDATA, subphylum Vertebrata, class Aves, family Indicatoridae, order Piciformes.

honey locust, leguminous deciduous tree (*Gleditsia triacanthos*) of the family Leguminosae (PULSE family), native to the eastern half of the United States but planted as a shade tree in many regions of the United States and in other countries, where it is sometimes naturalized. It has heavily fragrant flowers attractive to bees, compound leaves made up of small leaflets, and large branching thorns. The pods, which usually twist with age, are brown, flat, about 12 to 18 in. (30.5–45.7 cm) long, and have a sweet, edible pulp that has been used to make beer. Pulp of Oriental species has substituted for soap. Wood of the honey locust is durable and is used chiefly for fence posts and crossties. Other trees called locust belong to the same family. The honey locust is classified in the division MAGNOLIOPHYTA, class Magnoliopsida, order Rosales, family Leguminosae.

honeysucker: see HONEYEATER.

honeysuckle, common name for some members of the Caprifoliaceae, a family comprising mostly vines and shrubs of the Northern Hemisphere, especially abundant in E Asia and E North America. The family includes the elders, viburnums, weigelas, and snowberries as well as the honeysuckles; all are hardy plants that are sometimes cultivated as ornamentals. One of the best-known North American species of the true honeysuckles (genus *Lonicera*) is the trumpet honeysuckle (*L. sempervirens*), an evergreen plant with fragrant, trumpet-shaped scarlet blossoms. The Japanese honeysuckle (*L. japonica*), with small white to yellow flowers, is naturalized in the United States and has become a ubiquitous and noxious weed, strangling the living plants on which it climbs. Woodbine, a name for several vines, is

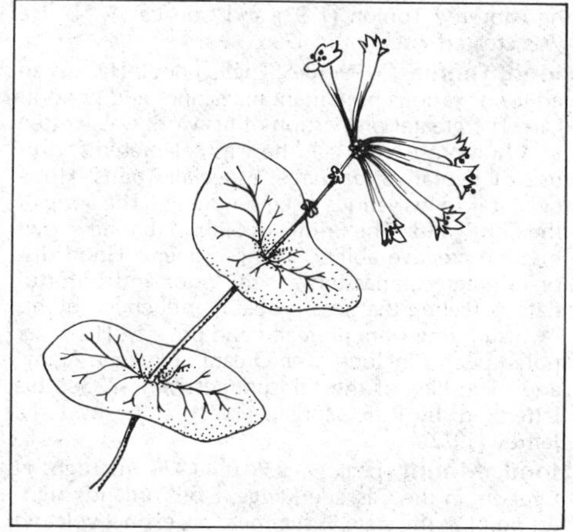

Trumpet honeysuckle, Lonicera sempervirens

most often *L. periclymenum,* also called eglantine. Bush honeysuckles are of the genus *Diervilla.* Some plants of other families are also called honeysuckle, e.g., the swamp and purple honeysuckles of the heath family. *Sambucus* (elder or elderberry) and *Viburnum* are shrubs and trees usually having showy flat-topped clusters of white flowers. The berries of some species are edible, e.g., those of the common North American elder (*S. canadensis*), used in preserves, pies, and wine. The European elder (*S. nigra*) and the "Spirit of the Elder" have figured prominently in folklore of N Europe. Among the better known viburnums (also having edible berries) are the black haw, or stagbush (*V. prunifolium*), of E North America; the straggling-branched hobblebush, or wayfaring tree (*V. alnifolium* in America, *V. lantana* in the Old World); and the high-bush cranberry, or cranberry tree (*V. opulus;* the American plants are sometimes designated as *V. trilobum*). The snowball, or guelder-rose, is a cultivated variety of the cranberry tree in which the rounded blossom-clusters are composed of large sterile flowers. Arrowwood (*V. dentatum* and similar species) was formerly used for making arrows. The waxy-fruited snowberries are species of the genus *Symphoricarpos.* Weigela (or weigelia), shrubs of the E Asian genus *Weigela,* are sometimes cultivated elsewhere for their funnel-shaped blossoms. Twinflower (*Linnaea borealis*), unusual for this family in that it is herbaceous, was the favorite flower of Linnaeus. Honeysuckle is classified in the division MAGNOLIOPHYTA, class Magnoliopsida, order Dipsacales, family Caprifoliaceae.

Hong Kong (hŏng kŏng), Mandarin *Hsing-kang,* British crown colony (1971 pop. 3,948,179), land area 399 sq mi (1,034 sq km), adjacent to Kwangtung prov., SE China, on the estuary of the Canton (Pearl) River, 40 mi (64 km) E of Macao and 90 mi (145 km) SE of Canton. The colony comprises Hong Kong island (29 sq mi/75 sq km), ceded by China in 1842 under the Treaty of Nanking; Kowloon or Cowloon (Mandarin, *Chiu-lung*) peninsula (3.5 sq mi/9 sq km), ceded (with Stonecutters Island) in 1860 under the Peking Convention; and the New Territories (366 sq mi/948 sq km), a mountainous mainland area adjoining Kowloon, which, with Deep Bay on the west and Mirs Bay on the east and some 235 offshore islands, was leased in 1898 for 99 years. The capital, officially named Victoria but commonly called Hong Kong, is on the northwest shore of Hong Kong island, at the foot of Victoria Peak (1,805 ft/550 m), the center of an extensively quarried granite range covering much of the island. Hong Kong has many natural harbors, that of Victoria (c.17 sq mi/44 sq km) being one of the finest in the world. The colony grew around this beautiful, sheltered, deepwater port, and today an estimated 80% of the population is concentrated there. Hong Kong is a free port, a bustling trade center, and a shipping and banking emporium—one of the greatest trading and transshipment centers in the Far East. After 1950, when much of its entrepôt trade with Communist China was halted because of UN and U.S. embargoes, Hong Kong began to industrialize. Overcoming such handicaps as a scarcity of minerals, power sources, usable land, and fresh water, and utilizing its abundant supply of cheap labor, Hong Kong has become a leading light-manufacturing center. The textile and garment industry is the colony's largest; there are vast complexes of spinning, carding, and weaving mills that run nonstop 24 hours a day. Other industries include shipbuilding, food processing, and the manufacture of plastics, electrical and electronic equipment, rubber products, machinery, chemicals, ceramics, furniture, jewelry, and toys. Tourism is a major source of revenue, and motion-picture production, insurance, and printing and publishing are also important. Because of the mountainous and rocky terrain, only about one seventh of the land is arable; farming is carried on principally in the New Territories; the Yuen Long valley has the best farmland. Rice and a variety of vegetables, including cabbage, eggplant, maize, red pepper, leek, and watercress, are grown. The yield cannot begin to meet the needs of the overcrowded colony, however, and food must be imported, much of it from the People's Republic of China. Fishing is a common occupation, and Deep Bay is known for its oyster beds. Although over 98% of the population is Chinese, Hong Kong has substantial British and American communities. The Univ. of Hong Kong is a coeducational institution under government control, organized on the model of British universities. Chinese Univ. was established in 1963 with the merger of three existing colleges. The region of Hong Kong, which had long been barren, rocky, and sparsely settled—its many islands and inlets a haven for coastal pirates—was occupied by the British during the Opium War (1839–42). The colony prospered as an east-west trading center, the commercial gateway to, and distribution center for, S China. It was efficiently governed, and its banking, insurance, and shipping services quickly became known as the most reliable in SE Asia. In 1921 the British agreed to limit the fortifications of the colony, and this contributed to its easy conquest (Dec. 25, 1941) by the Japanese. It was reoccupied by the British on Sept. 16, 1945. Since 1949, when the Communists took control of mainland China, hundreds of thousands of refugees have crossed the border, making Hong Kong's urban areas the most densely populated in the world. Refugees are crammed into hillside squatter huts or on junks in the harbors; many are homeless, sleeping on sidewalks and rooftops and in alleys, stairwells, and basements. The government has built a large number of low-rent, skyscraper housing developments, but many of the new units have become as crowded as the squatter areas, and thousands of people remain homeless. The colony's long-standing water problem has been eased by the construction of an elaborate system of giant reservoirs as well as by the piping in of a considerable amount of water from China. Serious problems of housing, health, drug addiction, and crime continue, however, aggravated by a soaring birth rate and the illegal influx of refugees from China (immigration controls were first instituted in May, 1950). The wretched poverty that exists side by side with great wealth in a boomingly prosperous colony provides fertile ground for Communist activity. In May, 1967, Hong Kong was struck by a wave of riots and strikes inspired by China's Cultural Revolution. The government reacted firmly, and, although the Chinese retaliated by briefly stopping the piping of water and by attacking British representatives in Peking, relations between Hong Kong and Communist China soon resumed the surface harmony that has existed since about 1959, following a decade of Communist harassment. For Communist China, Hong Kong remains a major source of foreign exchange and an important commercial link with the outside world. Hong Kong's rail link with the mainland is by the Kowloon-Canton Railway; it is run by the Hong Kong government for its 22 mi (35 km) to the Chinese border; there, passengers cross the Luhu Bridge spanning the Sham Chun River to transfer to the Chinese section of the railway. Kowloon is connected with Hong Kong island, 1 mi (1.6 km) away, by ferry and by a vehicular tunnel (opened 1972). Hong Kong has shipping connections with all major world ports and is an international air hub; the modern airport at Kai Tak (opened 1958) was built on land reclaimed from Kowloon Bay. See Richard Hughes, *Hong Kong: Borrowed Place, Borrowed Time* (1968); I. C. Jarvie and Joseph Agassi, ed., *Hong Kong: A Society in Transition* (1969); James Pope-Hennesy, *Half-Crown Colony* (1970); W. H. Ingrams, *Hong Kong* (1952, repr. 1972); G. B. Endicott, *A History of Hong Kong* (1964, repr. 1973).

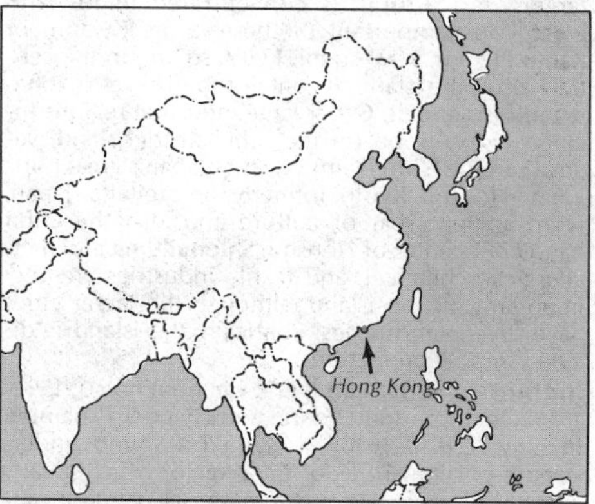

Honiara: see GUADALCANAL.

honing, process using abrasive stones in which a tiny amount of material is removed from a surface to produce an extremely smooth finish. A hone holds a number of stones in a circular pattern. In internal honing the hone moves against a workpiece, such as an engine cylinder; in external honing, a workpiece, such as a piston, is moved against the hone.

Honjo (hōn'jō), city (1970 pop. 47,116), Saitama prefecture, central Honshu, Japan, on the Tone River. It is an agricultural center and a market for raw silk.

Honolulu (hŏn"əlōō'lōō, hōnō-), city (1970 pop. 324,871), capital of the state of Hawaii and seat of Honolulu co., on the southeast coast of the island of OAHU. The city and county are legally coextensive, and both are governed by the same mayor and council. With steamship and air connections to the U.S. mainland, the Orient, Australia, and New Zealand, Honolulu is the crossroads of the Pacific, as well as the economic center and principal port of the Hawaiian Islands. The city is famous for its beauty and the variety of its ethnic groups. It lies on a narrow plain between the sea and the Koolau Range and climbs the slopes of Punchbowl. Bypassed by Capt. James Cook when he explored the islands in 1778, Honolulu's harbor was entered in 1794 by William Brown, an English captain. Honolulu's history from 1820, when missionaries arrived on the islands, is much the same as that of Hawaii. Growing from a settlement of mud huts into the main residence of Hawaiian royalty and later of foreign consuls, Honolulu became the permanent capital of the kingdom of Hawaii in 1845. In the 19th cent. American and European whalers and sandalwood traders visited its port, and Honolulu was occupied successively by Russian, British, and French forces. It remained Hawaii's capital when the islands were annexed by the United States in 1898 and achieved statehood in 1959. The Japanese bombed Pearl Harbor, the naval base at Honolulu, on Dec. 7, 1941, and during World War II the port became a strategic naval base and a staging area for U.S. forces in the Pacific. Since the war, a rise in tourism, diversification of industry, and construction of luxury hotels and housing developments have made Honolulu the business and population center of Hawaii. Sugar processing and pineapple canning have long been Honolulu's major industries. Increased peacetime defense activity at the many military installations in the area (Pearl Harbor Naval Shipyard, Schofield Barracks, and Camp H. M. Smith, headquarters of the U.S. Pacific Command), expansion of harbor facilities, and the completion of an international airport further aided the city's growth. The largest of Honolulu's parks is Kapiolani, containing a zoo, an aquarium, and Waikiki Shell, where the Honolulu Symphony gives concerts. Notable institutions are the Univ. of Hawaii; the Bishop Museum, noted for its studies of Polynesia; the Honolulu Academy of Arts; and Kawaiahao Church (1841), where funerals for Hawaiian monarchs and nobility were held. Iolani Palace, the former home of Hawaii's kings, is the only royal palace in the United States. The beach at Waikiki is noted for fine bathing and surf riding. The famous Diamond Head crater is nearby.

Honorius I (hōnôr'ēəs), pope (625–38), an Italian; successor of Boniface V. He showed great interest in the church in Spain and the British Isles, and he did a great deal to improve the churches in Rome. In the course of the dispute over MONOTHELETISM, he was asked as pope for an opinion on its orthodoxy. In reply he wrote a letter using the words "one will" to express the reality of the hypostatic union, apparently confirming the heresy. Pope and letter were both declared heretical at the Third Council of Constantinople. The letter is not considered an argument against papal infallibility, as he was not speaking ex cathedra. Honorius was succeeded by Severinus.

Honorius II, d. 1130, pope (1124–30), an Italian named Lamberto, b. Bologna; successor of Calixtus II. Before becoming pope he spent several years in Germany adjusting the quarrel over investiture between Holy Roman Emperor Henry V and the papacy. The matter was settled by the Concordat of Worms (1122). Honorius supported Lothair II in the disputed imperial election, and Lothair, after becoming emperor, conceded the Church's demands in the matter of episcopal elections. Honorius had an extended dispute with Henry I of England over the pope's right to send special legates to England. He was succeeded by Innocent II.

Honorius III, d. 1227, pope (1216–27), a Roman named Cencio Savelli; successor of Innocent III. He was created cardinal in 1197 and was an able administrator of the papal treasury. He was also very learned, and Innocent made him the tutor of Frederick (later Holy Roman Emperor FREDERICK II). On his accession to the papacy Honorius tried to persuade Frederick to go on crusade. He crowned (1220) Frederick, from whom he received another promise to go, but throughout Honorius's pontificate Frederick postponed departure. Honorius intervened in English politics to force the barons to support the young Henry III, a papal ward. Elsewhere he worked for peace in Christendom—in Italy, Spain, Hungary, and Denmark. He was succeeded by Gregory IX.

Honorius, 384–423, Roman emperor of the West (395–423). On the death (395) of Theodosius I, the Roman Empire was divided; ARCADIUS, the elder son, received the East, and Honorius, the younger son, received the West. This division proved to be a permanent one. The general STILICHO, as guardian of Honorius, at first controlled the government of the West and defended the empire against the Visigoths. Honorius married (398) Stilicho's daughter, but in 408, influenced by a malicious favorite, Honorius ordered the execution of his general. ALARIC I, king of the Visigoths, invaded Italy again in 409 and installed a puppet ruler at Rome, while Honorius remained at Ravenna. Negotiations with Alaric were mishandled by Honorius; infuriated, Alaric stormed and sacked Rome in 410. Alaric's death left ATAULF in command of the Visigoths, who then left Italy to invade Gaul. In 412, Honorius made peace with Ataulf, whom he reluctantly accepted (414) as husband for his sister GALLA PLACIDIA. A rival emperor, CONSTANTINE, was defeated (411) by Honorius' general Constantius, who soon exercised the actual power and who married (417) the widowed Galla Placidia. In 421, Honorius was obliged to accept Constantius as joint emperor (see CONSTANTIUS III), but Constantius died in the same year. Honorius died two years later; after a usurper was put down by forces from the East, the son of Galla Placidia and Constantius became (425) emperor as Valentinian III. The weak reign of Honorius marked an important stage in the decline of the Western Empire.

Honshu (hŏn'shōō), island (1970 pop. 81,560,590), c.89,000 sq mi (230,510 sq km), central Japan. It is c.800 mi (1,290 km) long and from c.30 to 150 mi (50–240 km) wide and is the largest and most important island of Japan. It is separated from Hokkaido by the Tsugaru Strait, from Kyushu by Shimonoseki Strait, and from Shikoku by the Inland Sea. Honshu is predominantly mountainous, rising to 12,389 ft (3,776 m) at Fujiyama (the highest peak of Japan), and has many volcanoes. It has valuable forest, but a limited amount of arable land. Oil, zinc, and copper are found on the island. The Shinano, the longest river of Japan, traverses central Honshu. Most of the rivers of the island are short and swift, feeding many small hydroelectric plants. Earthquakes are common, especially around Fujiyama. The climate of Honshu has a wide range from the north with its snowy winters to the subtropical south. Agriculture is varied; rice, other grains, cotton, fruits, and vegetables are grown. The bulk of Japan's tea and silk comes from Honshu. The population, which is still largely agricultural, is concentrated in lowland areas. Most important of these is the Kwanto or Kanto Plain (c.5,000 sq mi/12,950 sq km) in the central part of the island; it contains the Tokyo-Yokohama industrial belt. Other large industrial regions include Osaka-Kobe (in the Kinki district), and Nagoya (on the Nobi Plain). Most of Japan's great ports are on Honshu. Kyoto, formerly the capital of Japan, is an ancient seat of culture and also the chief handicraft center of Honshu. Shipbuilding and metallurgical, chemical, and textile industries are very important on the island, although the larger cities have diverse industries. Politically the island is divided into 34 prefectures.

Honthorst, Gerrit van (gĕr'ĭt vän hŏnt'hôrst), 1590–1656, Dutch portrait, genre, and allegorical painter. In Italy (c.1610–1620) he gained a sound understanding of the works of Caravaggio, which greatly affected his style. He was a master at painting candlelit genre pieces and biblical scenes. Upon his return to Holland, he introduced the Italian manner of illusionistic decoration into Dutch interiors, as in his decorative scheme for the palace of Honselaarsdijk. In 1628, Charles I invited him to England, where he decorated Whitehall and painted portraits of the king and nobility. Several of these are now in the National Gallery, London. He also worked for the court of Denmark, and from 1637 to 1652 at The Hague. Together with TERBRUGGHEN and Baburen he led the influential Utrecht school of painting that introduced Caravaggesque dramatic realism into Dutch art. Honthorst's *Winter King of Bohemia* is in the Metropolitan Museum. See study by J. R. Judson (1959).

Hooch or **Hoogh, Pieter de** (both: pē'tər də hōkh), b. c.1629, d. after 1677, Dutch genre painter. He worked in Delft, Leiden, and Amsterdam, painting intimate interiors that may have been influenced by those of Vermeer. Usually he preferred to paint rooms opening into other rooms or to the outdoors, intriguing the imagination with half-seen vistas, and displaying his ability to handle complicated lighting effects. His warm tone and subtle colors show Rembrandt's influence. De Hooch repeated his basic compositions many times, so that his later works are static and less interesting. One of his finest paintings is *Courtyard of a Dutch House* (National Gall., London). His works are housed in many European museums, and the Metropolitan Museum has seven.

Hood, John Bell, 1831–79, Confederate general in the American Civil War, b. Owingsville, Ky. After serving in California and Texas, he resigned from the army (April, 1861) and entered the Confederate service, being made a brigadier general in March, 1862. He fought in the Peninsular campaign and at the second battle of Bull Run (Aug., 1862) and was promoted to the rank of major general in October. As a division commander under James LONGSTREET, he distinguished himself at Antietam, Fredericksburg, and Gettysburg and at Chickamauga, where he lost a leg and won his lieutenant generalcy (Sept., 1863). In the ATLANTA CAMPAIGN of 1864 he fought under Joseph E. JOHNSTON until Jefferson Davis, displeased with that general's retreat, made Hood commander. Hood, faring no better against General SHERMAN, was obliged to abandon Atlanta on Sept. 1. To prevent a further Union advance Hood moved against Sherman's long line of communications in October. Sherman followed, but later, satisfied that George H. THOMAS at Nashville could cope with Hood, returned to Atlanta and marched to the sea. Hood then began to advance through Tennessee. John M. SCHOFIELD slowly withdrew before him, repulsing his attack in a bloody battle at Franklin (Nov. 30) before joining Thomas. Hood went on to Nashville, where he entrenched his greatly depleted forces. Thomas attacked and in the battle of Nashville (Dec. 15–16) won the most complete victory of the war, virtually annihilating the Confederates. Hood resigned his command (Jan., 1865) and surrendered at Natchez, Miss., in May. See his *Advance and Retreat* (1879, new ed. 1959, repr. 1969); S. F. Horn, *The Army of Tennessee* (1941, repr. 1959); biographies by Richard O'Connor (1949, repr. 1959) and J. P. Dyer (1950).

Hood, Raymond Mathewson, 1881–1934, American architect, b. Pawtucket, R.I. He studied at Brown Univ., Massachusetts Institute of Technology, and the École des Beaux-Arts, Paris. In 1922 he was the winner, with John Mead Howells, of the international competition for the design of the Tribune Tower, Chicago (completed 1925). He practiced from 1927 to 1931 in the firm of Hood, Godley, and Fouilhoux. In New York City, Hood was architect for the American Radiator Building and for the Daily News Building (with J. M. Howells). He was a consultant in the rebuilding of the Univ. of Brussels, and his firm was one of the three associated in the Radio City development in New York. He designed buildings for the Century of Progress Exposition in Chicago.

Hood, Samuel Hood, 1st **Viscount,** 1724–1816, British admiral. Entering the navy in 1741, he served with distinction in the Seven Years War. In 1781 he was sent to the West Indies as second in command to Lord RODNEY. He fought in many engagements in the American Revolution, including the victory (1782) over the French fleet under the comte de GRASSE (who had earlier defeated Hood) off Dominica. As commander in chief in the Mediterranean he captured Toulon (1793) and Corsica (1794). He was created viscount in 1796.

Hood, Thomas, 1799–1845, English poet. He was an editor of various prominent magazines and periodicals. The greater proportion of his work was written in a humorous vein, and he was celebrated for his use of figurative language, especially puns. However, it is in his serious poems, notably "The Song of the Shirt" and "The Bridge of Sighs," that he shows his true creative ability. In these poems Hood displays great compassion for the poor and unfortunate, a feeling that was probably influenced by his own suffering from ill-health and poverty. His other noted poems include "The Dream of Eugene Aram" and "The Plea of the Midsummer Fairies." See his letters ed. by P. F. Morgan (1973); study by L. N. Jeffrey (1972).

Hood, Mount, peak, 11,235 ft (3,424 m) high, N Oregon, in the Cascade Range, E of Portland; highest point in the state. A symmetrical, extinct volcano with glaciers and forested lower slopes, it is a favorite mountain-climbing and skiing center.

hoof, horny epidermal casing at the end of the digits of an ungulate (hoofed) MAMMAL. In the even-toed ungulates, such as swine, deer, and cattle, the hoof is cloven; in the odd-toed ungulates, such as the horse and the rhinoceros, it is solid. Hoofs are adapted to the habits of the animal—e.g., flat, thick cloven hoofs enable the camel to walk on soft sand without sinking into it.

hoof-and-mouth disease: see FOOT-AND-MOUTH DISEASE.

Hooft, Pieter Corneliszoon (pē'tər kôrnā'lĭsōn hōft), 1581–1647, Dutch historian, poet, and dramatist. His great work was a history of the revolt of the Netherlands against Spain, *Nederlandsche Historien* (1628–47). Hooft was also a lyric poet of the first order and introduced French and Italian Renaissance lyricisms into Dutch poetry.

Hoogh, Pieter de: see HOOCH, PIETER DE.

Hooghly, river, an arm of the Ganges, c.160 mi (260 km) long, formed by the confluence of the Bhagirathi, Jalangi, and Matabhanga rivers, West Bengal state, E India, and flowing S to the Bay of Bengal; navigable to oceangoing vessels to Calcutta, c.120 mi (190 km) upstream. It is the major shipping artery through the important Hooghlyside industrial area, despite its sandbars and strong tidal currents. The Hooghly's headwaters are important for inland traffic. Portuguese trading posts were established along the river in 1537.

Hooghly-Chinsura (hōō'glē-chĭn'sŏŏrə), town (1971 pop. 105,341), West Bengal state, E India, on the Hooghly River. A center of the Hooghlyside industrial district, the town has many large rice mills. It was founded by the Portuguese in 1537 and was of commercial importance in the 16th and 17th cent.

Hoogstraten, Samuel van (sä'müĕl vän hōkh'-strätən), 1627–78, Dutch portrait painter and etcher, studied with his father, Dirk van Hoogstraten (1596–1640), and with Rembrandt. His best works, such as *The Old Jew* (Vienna), reflect the influence of Rembrandt. He was director of the Academy in Dordrecht and author of a treatise (1678) in which he analyzed the theory and practice of the art of Rembrandt and other artists of the period. He was also known for his experiments in perspective.

Hook, Sidney, 1902–, American philosopher, b. New York City, grad. City College (B.S., 1923), Ph.D. Columbia Univ., 1927. He taught at New York Univ. (1927–72) and was long head of its philosophy department (1948–69). Originally a Marxist, he wrote *The Meaning of Marx* (1934) and *From Hegel to Marx* (1936). Hook later became disenchanted with Marxism and became active in anti-Communist causes. His opinions on American life were expressed in such works as *Heresy Yes, Conspiracy No* (1953), *Common Sense and the Fifth Amendment* (1957), *The Place of Religion in a Free Society* (1968), and *Academic Freedom and Academic Anarchy* (1970). See Paul Kurtz, ed., *Sidney Hook and the Contemporary World* (1968).

Hooke, Robert (hŏŏk), 1635–1703, English physicist, mathematician, and inventor. He became curator of experiments for the Royal Society (1662), professor of geometry at Gresham College (1665), and city surveyor of London (1667). Considered the greatest mechanic of his age, he made many improvements in astronomical instruments and in watches and clocks, was the first to formulate the theory of planetary movements as a mechanical problem, and anticipated universal gravitation. In 1684 he devised a practicable system of telegraphy. He invented the spiral spring in watches and the first screw-divided quadrant and constructed the first arithmetical machine and Gregorian telescope. He stated Hooke's law (see ELASTICITY). In his *Micrographia* (1665) he described his microscopic observations of plant tissues. Hooke coined the term *cell.* See studies by Margaret 'Espinasse (1956) and F. F. Centore (1970); bibliography by Sir Geoffrey Keynes (1960).

Hooker, Joseph, 1814–79, Union general in the American Civil War, b. Hadley, Mass. He fought against the Seminole and, as a staff officer in the Mexican War, was thrice brevetted for gallantry. Hooker resigned from the army in 1853 and was for several years a farmer in California. At the outbreak of the Civil War he became a brigadier general of volunteers. He distinguished himself in subordinate commands in the Peninsular campaign, at the second battle of Bull Run, and in the Antietam campaign, and was made a brigadier general in the regular army in Sept., 1862. After the battle of FREDERICKSBURG, Hooker severely criticized Ambrose BURNSIDE, whom he succeeded (Jan., 1862) in command of the Army of the Potomac. In April, 1863, he advanced against Robert E. Lee, but in the resulting battle of CHANCELLORSVILLE, he failed to justify his nickname of "Fighting Joe." Hooker followed Lee closely in the subsequent Confederate invasion of Pennsylvania, but, angered at General Halleck's refusal to send him reinforcements from Harpers Ferry, he asked on June 28, 1863, to be relieved. A few days later his successor, George G. MEADE, fought the battle of Gettysburg. Hooker ably commanded reinforcements from the East in the CHATTANOOGA CAMPAIGN, and in 1864 he fought in the Atlanta campaign until General Sherman passed him over as successor to John B. McPherson. He then commanded various departments until his retirement in 1868. See biography by W. H. Hebert (1944).

Hooker, Richard, 1554?–1600, English theologian and clergyman of the Church of England. He studied and lectured at Oxford and preached at Drayton-Beauchamp, Buckinghamshire; at the Temple Church, London; at Boscombe, Wiltshire; and at Bishopsbourne, Kent. His famous *Of the Laws of Ecclesiastical Polity* (in 8 books, of which only 5 were published in his lifetime) was an epoch-making discussion of church government, written in an excellent prose style. It helped to formulate the intellectual concepts of Anglicanism, and its influence on the theory of government (civil as well as ecclesiastical) as based on rules of reason was widely felt in England. An edition of Hooker's works (1666) contained a celebrated biography by Izaak Walton (1665). A new critical edition of his complete works is in preparation, sponsored by the Folger Shakespeare Library under the general editorship of W. Speed Hill. Two volumes have appeared: *Richard Hooker: A Descriptive Bibliography of the Early Editions, 1593–1724* (1970) and *Studies in Richard Hooker: Essays Preliminary to an Edition of His Works* (1972). Six more volumes are projected.

Hooker, Thomas, 1586–1647, Puritan clergyman in the American colonies, chief founder of Hartford, Conn., b. Leicestershire, England. A clergyman, he was ordered to appear before the court of high commission for nonconformist preaching in England and fled (1630) to Holland. In 1633, Hooker immigrated to Massachusetts, where he was pastor at Newtown (now Cambridge). He had a dispute with John Cotton and apparently was discontented with the strict theological rule in Massachusetts. After a group of settlers had been sent ahead in 1635, he and many of his flock moved in 1636 to found Hartford, where he was pastor until his death. Hooker was one of the drafters of the Fundamental Orders (1639), under which Connecticut was long governed and which represent his political views. He also promoted a plan for the New England Confederation. See biography by G. L. Walker (1891, repr. 1969).

Hooker, Sir William Jackson, 1785–1865, English botanist. A leading authority of his time on ferns, he formed a famous herbarium and built up the Glasgow and Kew botanical gardens. In Kew Gardens he founded the first museum of economic botany. Among his many works are *British Jungermanniae* (1816), *Flora Scotica* (1821), *British Flora* (1830), and a number of works on ferns, including *Genera Filicum* (1838), *Species Filicum* (5 vol., 1846–64), and *Synopsis Filicum* (1868). He edited many botanical journals. His son **Sir Joseph Dalton Hooker,** 1817–1911, was also a botanist. After his first scientific expedition he wrote on the flora of New Zealand and Tasmania. Sir Joseph's great works include *Antarctic Flora* (1844–47), *Genera Plantarum* (with George Bentham, 3 vol., 1862–83), and *The Flora of British India* (7 vol., 1875–97). He edited the *Index Kewensis* (2 vol., 1895), by B. D. Jackson. He was a friend of Darwin and a supporter of his theories. See Mea Allan, *The Hookers of Kew, 1785–1911* (1967).

Hooke's law: see ELASTICITY.

Hook of Holland: see HOEK VAN HOLLAND.

hookworm, any of a number of bloodsucking nematodes in the order Strongiloidae that live as parasites in man and other mammals and attach themselves to the host's intestines by means of hooks. Hookworm infection in man is caused by infestation with *Ancylostoma duodenale* (the European species) or with *Necator americanus* (the American species). It is found in tropical and subtropical climates, especially where the inhabitants do not wear shoes or stockings and where the soil is contaminated by human excrement. The larva of the hookworm, living in moist soil or mud, easily penetrates the exposed skin, usually the sole of the foot, and is then carried by the blood to the lungs. An early sign of hookworm infestation is a dermatitis at the site of entry, known as ground itch. As the larva passes through the lungs, it causes episodes of coughing with bloody sputum. Raised with the mucus into the mouth, the larva is then swallowed. It may also be swallowed with polluted drinking water or with unclean vegetables eaten raw. By means of its hooks the larva attaches itself to the upper portion of the small intestine, where it nourishes itself on the blood of its host. The larva matures and the female produces eggs, as many as 30,000 per day, that are passed from the intestine with the feces, usually to contaminate the soil still further. The drain on the blood of the host results in anemia. This, together with the resulting abdominal pain and diarrhea, causes general debility. Hookworm is treated with drugs, notably tetrachloroethylene, that loosen and destroy the parasite, as well as with specifics for the anemia and abdominal symptoms. Incidence of this disease, which was once seriously prevalent, has been much reduced by improved sanitation and the wearing of shoes.

Hoopa Indians (hōō'pə), North American Indians whose language belongs to the ATHABASCAN branch of the Nadene linguistic stock (see AMERICAN INDIAN LANGUAGES). In the 19th cent. they occupied the valley of the Trinity River from Hoopa valley to the Klamath River in NW California. Their cedar-planked houses, dugout canoes, basket hats, and many elements in their mythology identify them with the Northwest Coast culture, of which they are the southernmost representatives; however, some of their customs—e.g., the use of a sweat house for ceremonies and the manufacture of acorn bread—are not characteristic of that culture area. In 1864 the U.S. government made their lands a reservation (Hoopa Valley), where they now reside with their neighbors, the Yurok Indians. The Hoopa today number about 950. The name is sometimes spelled Hupa. See P. E. Goddard, *Life and Culture of the Hupa* (1903).

Hooper, William, 1742–90, political leader in the American Revolution, signer of the Declaration of Independence, b. Boston. He became a lawyer and moved (1764) to Wilmington, N.C. Hooper served on the local committee of correspondence and was a North Carolina delegate (1774–77) to the Continental Congress.

hoopoe (hōō'pōō, -pō), common name for a shy, solitary, Old World woodland bird, *Upupa epops.* Its body color ranges from cinnamon to chestnut, with white-barred, black wings and tail, and a head topped by a prominent, erectile crest. Hoopoes measure from 10½ to 12 in. (27–30 cm) bill to tail. They are primarily ground feeders and use their long, slender, decurved bills to probe for large insects, worms, and lizards. Less frequently, the hoopoe feeds while airborne, exhibiting its characteristic undulating erratic flight. Hoopoes are excellent runners. Found throughout the Old World, hoopoes frequent warm, dry areas, which are at least partially open. They are common in Israel and surrounding countries. The northernmost species, which reach the English Channel and the Baltic Sea, are migratory in winter. The nest is built in a tree cavity or a rock crevice, sometimes lined with debris, or sometimes bare. The female lays and incubates from four to six pale blue to olive colored eggs per clutch and is fed during incubation by her mate. Both sexes care for the naked, helpless young. In addition to its beautiful plumage, the hoopoe is also noted for its filthy, malodorous nest. The bad odor comes from a combination of putrefying excrement, which the bird does not trouble to remove, and from defensive musty-smelling secretions released from the preen gland of the female when she is disturbed. Woodhoopoes belong to the same family as the hoopoe. They are uncrested and are more gregarious than the hoopoe. Found only in the forests of Africa, woodhoopoes are metallic greens, blues, and purples in color, and travel in small, noisy groups. They share the same foul nesting habits as the hoopoes. Hoopoes and woodhoopoes are classified in the phylum CHORDATA, subphylum Vertebrata, class Aves, order Coraciiformes, family Upupidae.

Hoorn or **Horn, Philip de Montmorency, count of** (both: hôrn), 1518?–1568, Netherlands nobleman, member of the council of state during the regency of Margaret of Parma. In 1562 he joined with the count of EGMONT and William the Silent in opposition to Cardinal GRANVELLE, who had introduced Spanish troops and the Spanish Inquisition into the Netherlands. When the duke of Alba replaced (1567) Margaret of Parma, he had Egmont and Hoorn arrested and, after an irregular trial, beheaded. That event caused great public outrage and marked the beginning of the open revolt against the Spanish.

Hoorn, town (1970 pop. 18,574), North Holland prov., N central Netherlands, on an inlet of the IJsselmeer. It is a commercial and processing center for a vegetable-growing and dairy-farming region. Hoorn was founded in 1311. In the 17th cent., the golden age of Dutch exploration, the city sent forth many native sons, including Willem Schouten, who was the first to round (and who also named) Cape Hoorn (later Horn); A. J. Tasman, who discovered New Zealand and Tasmania; and J. P. Coen, founder of Batavia (now Djakarta), Indonesia.

Hoosac Range (hōō'sək), southern continuation of the Green Mts., NW Mass. and SW Vt., running from north to south. Its maximum height is c.3,000 ft (910 m). A railroad tunnel, c.5 mi (8 km) long, built from 1852 to 1873, at the cost of nearly 200 lives, crosses the range from east to west.

Hooton, Earnest Albert (hōō'tən), 1887–1954, American anthropologist, b. Clemansville, Wis.; grad. Lawrence College, 1907, Ph.D. Univ. of Wisconsin, 1911, Rhodes scholar, 1910–13. He began teaching at Harvard in 1913 and became professor of anthropology in 1930, a post he held until his death. Hooton is known particularly for his researches on early man and primates. He also sought by meticulous study to establish scientifically a correlation between body build and social, cultural, and racial factors. He is the author of *Ancient Inhabitants of the Canary Islands* (1925), *Up from the Ape* (1931, rev. ed. 1946), *Apes, Men, and Morons* (1937), *Crime and the Man* (1939), *Man's Poor Relations* (1942), *Young Man, You are Normal* (1945), and with collaborators, *The Physical Anthropology of Ireland* (1955).

Hoover, Herbert Clark, 1874–1964, 31st President of the United States (1929–33), b. West Branch, Iowa. After graduating (1895) from Stanford, he worked as a mining engineer in many parts of the world. He became an independent mining consultant and established offices in New York City, San Francisco, and London. When World War I broke out in 1914, Hoover, then in London, was made chairman of the American Relief Commission. In this post he arranged the return to the United States of some 150,000 Americans stranded in Europe. As chairman (1915–19) of the Commission for Relief in Belgium, he secured food and clothing for civilians of war-devastated Belgium and N France. After the United States entered the war, he became U.S. Food Administrator, a member of the War Trade Council, and chairman of the Interallied Food Council. Appointed a chairman of the Supreme Economic Council and director of the European Relief and Reconstruction Commission at the Paris Peace Conference, he coordinated the work of the various relief agencies; he was given direct authority over the transportation systems of Eastern Europe in order to ensure efficient distribution of supplies. After the signing of the Treaty of Versailles, Hoover returned (1919) to the United States, although he continued to direct the American Relief Administration, which was to feed millions in the 1921–23 famine in the USSR. As Secretary of Commerce (1921–29) under Presidents Harding and Coolidge, Hoover reorganized and expanded the department, sponsored conferences on unemployment, fostered trade associations, and gave his support to such engineering projects as the St. Lawrence Waterway and the Hoover Dam. He gained much popular approval and easily won the Republican nomination for President in 1928. He defeated Democratic candidate Alfred E. Smith. In the first year of his administration Hoover established the Federal Farm Board, pressed for tariff revision (which resulted in the HAWLEY-SMOOT TARIFF ACT), and appointed the National Commission on Law Observance and Law Enforcement, with George W. WICKERSHAM as chairman, to study the problem of enforcing prohibition. The rest of his administration was dominated by the major economic depression ushered in by the stock market crash of Oct., 1929. Hoover, believing in the basic soundness of the economy, felt that it would regenerate spontaneously and was reluctant to extend Federal activities. Nonetheless he did recommend, and Congress gave the funds for, a large public works program, and the RECONSTRUCTION FINANCE CORPORATION was created (1932) to stimulate industry by giving loans unobtainable elsewhere. Congress, which had a Democratic majority after the 1930 elections, passed the Emergency Relief Act and created the Federal home loan banks. As the depression deepened, veterans demanded immediate payment of bonus certificates (issued to them in 1924 for redemption in 1945). In 1932 some 15,000 ex-servicemen, known as the BONUS MARCHERS, marched on Washington; Hoover ordered Federal troops to oust them from Federal property. In foreign affairs Hoover was confronted with the problems of disarmament, reparations and war debts, and Japanese aggression in the Far East. The United States participated in the London Conference of 1930 (see NAVAL CONFERENCES) and signed the resulting treaty; it also took part in the abortive DISARMAMENT CONFERENCE. In 1931, Hoover proposed a one-year moratorium on reparations and war debts to ease the financial situation in Europe. The administration's reaction to the Japanese invasion (1931) of Manchuria was expressed by Secretary of State Henry L. STIMSON, who declared that the United States would not recognize territorial changes achieved by force or by infringement of American treaty rights. Hoover ran for reelection in 1932 but was overwhelmingly defeated by Franklin Delano Roosevelt. Except for major speeches before the Republican conventions and a 1938 European tour, Hoover retired from public life until the close of World War II, when he undertook (1946) the coordination of food supplies to countries badly affected by the war. He then headed (1947–49) the Hoover Commission, a committee empowered by Congress to study the executive branch of government. Many of its recommendations were adopted, including establishment of the Department of Health, Education, and Welfare. Under President Eisenhower he headed the second Hoover Commission (1953–55), which made recommendations on policy as well as organization. The Herbert Hoover Library was dedicated at West Branch, Iowa, in 1962. Hoover died on Oct. 20, 1964, in New York City. Among Hoover's writings are *Principles of Mining* (1909), *The Challenge to Liberty* (1934), *The Ordeal of Woodrow Wilson* (1958), and *An American Epic* (3 vol., 1959–61). With his wife, Lou Henry Hoover (1875–1944), he translated Agricola's *De re metallica* (1912). See his memoirs (3 vol., 1951–52); biographies by Eugene Lyons (1948, repr. 1964), Harold Wolfe (1956), and Carol Wilson (1968); H. G. Warren, *Herbert Hoover and the Great Depression* (1959); A. U. Romasco, *Poverty of Abundance* (1965, repr. 1968).

Hoover, John Edgar, 1895–1972, American administrator, director of the FEDERAL BUREAU OF INVESTIGATION (FBI), b. Washington, D.C. Shortly after he was admitted to the bar, he entered (1917) the Dept. of Justice and served (1919–21) as special assistant to Attorney General A. Mitchell PALMER. In this capacity he directed the so-called Palmer Raids against allegedly radical aliens. Director of the Bureau of Investigation (renamed the Federal Bureau of Investigation in 1935) after 1924, J. Edgar Hoover built an efficient crime-detection agency, establishing a centralized fingerprint file, a crime laboratory, and a training school for police. During the 1930s he sought to publicize the work of the agency in fighting organized crime, and he himself participated in the arrest of several major gangsters. After World War II, Hoover concentrated his attention on the threat of Communist subversion in the United States. Remaining in office until his death, he became a very controversial figure. His many critics considered his anti-Communism obsessive and charged him with harassment of left-wing dissenters and violation of their civil liberties. Hoover accumulated enormous power, but, serving under eight Presidents, he kept the FBI free of outside political pressure. His writings include *Persons In Hiding* (1938), *Masters of Deceit* (1958), and *A Study of Communism* (1962). See biographies by Hank Messick (1972) and J. R. Nash (1972); W. W. Turner, *Hoover's F. B. I.* (1970).

Hoover Dam, 726 ft (221 m) high and 1,244 ft (379 m) long, on the Colorado River between Nev. and Ariz.; one of the world's largest dams. Built between 1931 and 1936 by the U.S. Bureau of Reclamation, the dam is named for President Herbert Hoover; from 1933 to 1947 it was known as Boulder Dam. A key unit on the Colorado River, the dam is one of the world's largest suppliers of hydroelectric power (1,344,800-kw capacity), and provides for flood control, river regulation, and improved navigation. Hoover Dam impounds Lake Mead, the world's largest reservoir; water is used to irrigate c.650,000 acres (263,000 hectares) in S California and Arizona, and c.400,000 acres (162,000 hectares) in Mexico. Hoover Dam is part of Lake Mead National Recreation Area (see NATIONAL PARKS AND MONUMENTS, table). Boulder City, Nev., was built to house workers on the project.

Hoover Institution on War, Revolution, and Peace, at Stanford, Palo Alto, Calif. It was established in 1919 as the Hoover War Library by Herbert Hoover to extend his collection of documents of World War I, but its scope has been expanded to include source material on social and political developments arising from both world wars. Research, publication, and advanced study are conducted by the institution.

hop, herbaceous perennial vine of the family Moraceae (MULBERRY family), widely cultivated since early times for brewing purposes. The commercial hop (*Humulus lupulus*) is native to Eurasia but is now grown in many temperate regions, notably England, Germany, the United States, South America, and Australia. The conelike ripened female flowers, called hops, are borne on different plants from the male; their loose scales contain lupulin, a yellow powder that is added to beer to impart a bitter flavor and is used medicinally as a tonic and soporific. Oil of hops is used for some perfumes, and the hop stem is used for fiber. The fruit of the unrelated hop tree (*Ptelea trifoliata*) of North America is occasionally used as a substitute for hops. Hops are classified in the division MAGNOLIOPHYTA, class Magnoliopsida, order Urticales, family Moraceae.

Hope, Anthony, pseud. of **Sir Anthony Hope Hawkins,** 1863–1933, English novelist. A lawyer, he wrote novels in his spare time. *The Prisoner of Zenda* (1894), a romantic novel of impersonation set in an imaginary kingdom, was an international success. None of his later novels—including a sequel, *Rupert of Hentzau* (1898)—or plays approached its enormous popularity. See his *Memories and Notes* (1927).

Hope, Bob, 1903–, American comedian, b. London; his original name was Leslie Townes Hope. Famous for his "ski-jump" nose, topical humor, and rapid-fire delivery, Hope is a perennially popular radio and television entertainer and has made more than 50 films. They include *Road to Morocco* (1942), *Monsieur Beaucaire* (1946), *The Paleface* (1947), and *How to Commit Marriage* (1969). From 1940 to 1972 he made annual trips overseas to entertain American troops. See his autobiographical *Have Tux, Will Travel* (1959).

Hopeh (hō'pā') or **Ho-pei** (hô-bā), province (1968 est. pop. 47,000,000), 75,000 sq mi (194,250 sq km), NE China, on the Po Hai, an arm of the Yellow Sea. The capital is Shih-chia-chuang. The province contains two autonomous municipalities administered directly by the central government: PEKING, the capital of China, and TIENTSIN, a major port. Another large port on the relatively unindented coast line is CH'IN-HUANG-TAO. Other important cities are T'ANG-SHAN and PAO-TING. Hopeh is mountainous in the north and the west, where rich iron and coal deposits are extensively mined. S Hopeh is part of the North China plain. The land is fertile and rainfall is adequate, but until water conservation programs were instituted, the province was subject to severe drought and flooding. These recent improvements, along with the enlargement of farms and the expansion of mechanization, have greatly increased agricultural output. Hopeh is a major cotton-producing province and an important producer of wheat. Other crops include rice, millet, kaoliang, potatoes, sweet potatoes, barley, corn, soybeans, and fruit. Stock raising is important, and fishing and salt production are significant along the coast. Heavy industry (mainly metallurgical, iron and steel, machinery, and textile) is concentrated in and around Peking, Tientsin, and T'ang-shan. With many good roads and railroad systems centering on Peking and Tientsin, and with the Grand Canal and other excellent waterways, Hopeh has one of the best communications systems in China. One of the earliest regions of Chinese settlement, Hopeh has many prehistoric sites. Parts of the former provinces of Jehol and Chahar were incorporated into Hopeh in 1956. The province was formerly called Chi and Chihli. Hopeh Univ. is in Tientsin.

Hopetown or **Hope Town,** town (1970 pop. 4,210), Cape Prov., central South Africa, on the Orange River; founded 1854. Nearby, diamonds were first discovered (1867) in South Africa. Today the town is mainly an agricultural trade center.

Hopewell, city (1970 pop. 23,471), within Prince George co. but independent, at the confluence of the James and Appomattox rivers, SE Va.; founded 1913, inc. 1916. Hopewell is a port and an industrial center in which chemicals, synthetic textiles, and paper products are manufactured. The city was founded as a munitions center and during World War I had a population of 40,000. In 1926, Hopewell absorbed contiguous City Point, General U.S. Grant's base of operations in 1864–65. Fort Lee is nearby.

Hopewell Village National Historic Site: see NATIONAL PARKS AND MONUMENTS (table).

Hophni (hŏf'nī), son of Eli. With his brother he met death because of sacrileges. 1 Sam. 1–4.

Hophra (hŏf'rə): see APRIES.

Hopi Indians (hō'pē), group of the PUEBLO INDIANS, formerly called Moki, or Moqui, Indians. They speak the Hopi language, which belongs to the Uto-Aztecan branch of the Aztec-Tanoan linguistic stock, at all their pueblos except Hano, where the language belongs to the Tanoan branch of the Aztec-Tanoan linguistic stock (see AMERICAN INDIAN LANGUAGES). They occupy several mesa villages in NE Arizona and number some 6,000. In 1540 they were visited by some of Coronado's men under Pedro de Tovar, but because of their geographical isolation they remained more independent of European influence than the other Pueblo tribes. In 1629 the Spanish began to establish missions at the pueblos of Awatobi, ORAIBI, and Shongopovi. These missions were destroyed in the revolt of 1680 (see POPÉ), and when the Indians of Awatobi invited the missionaries to return, the other Hopi destroyed their village. After the revolt, pueblos in the foothills were abandoned and new villages were built on the mesas for defense against possible attack by the Spanish. The pueblo of Hano was built by Tewa Indians, who had fled from the area of the Rio Grande valley that the Spanish reconquered. In the 1820s, about the time that Mexican rule replaced Spanish rule in the Southwest, the Navaho Indians began to raid Hopi villages and encroach on Hopi land. This encroachment did not cease with the establishment of a Hopi reservation in 1882; since 1943 the Navaho have legally occupied three fourths of the original reservation. The Hopi are now faced with the problem of insufficient and seriously eroded land. They are sedentary farmers, mainly dependent on corn, beans, and squash; they also raise wheat, cotton, and tobacco and herd sheep. Each village is divided into clans and is governed by a chief, who is also the spiritual leader. Political and religious duties devolved upon the clans, e.g., the Badger clan, which still conducts the KACHINA (fertility) ceremony, and the Antelope and Snake clans, which perform the famous snake dance at Walpi and other pueblos. A Hopi tribal council and constitution was established in 1936, but internal dissension has limited tribal unity. See L. M. Thompson, *The Hopi Way* (1944, repr. 1965) and *Culture in Crisis* (1950); W. C. O'Kane, *The Hopis* (1953); H. C. James, *The Hopi Indians* (1956); Frank Waters, *Book of the Hopi* (1963, repr. 1972); Mischa Titiev, *Hopi Indians of Old Oraibi* (1972).

Hopkins, Edward, 1600-1657, colonial governor of Connecticut, b. England. He migrated (1637) to Hartford, where he soon became a leader because of his wealth and ability. He became governor of the Connecticut colony in 1640 and was governor, assistant governor, or deputy governor every year until 1656, the law not allowing the office of governor to be held two years in succession. As a delegate from Connecticut he helped to form the New England Confederation, and he was elected one of the confederation commissioners. He returned to England shortly before his death to become warden of the fleet, keeper of the palace at Westminster, and member of Parliament.

Hopkins, Esek, 1718-1802, American Revolutionary naval hero, b. Scituate, R.I.; brother of Stephen Hopkins. He commanded a privateer in the French and Indian War, and in Dec., 1775, he was appointed commander in chief of the newly established Continental navy. In 1776 he made a successful raid on New Providence in the Bahamas. After a dispute with the Continental Congress, he was suspended from command in 1777 and then dismissed from the service in 1778. See biography by Edward Field (1898, repr. 1972).

Hopkins, Sir Frederick Gowland, 1861-1947, English biochemist, educated at Cambridge and the Univ. of London. He was professor of biochemistry at Cambridge (1914-43). Among his contributions were important studies in carbohydrate metabolism and muscular activity, including the discovery of the relationship of lactic-acid formation to muscular contraction. Through his feeding experiments with laboratory animals he concluded that "accessory food factors" (later named vitamins) are essential to health. For this work he shared with Christian Eijkman the 1929 Nobel Prize in Physiology and Medicine. He was knighted in 1925. His works include *Newer Aspects of the Nutrition Problem* (1922), *The Problems of Specificity in Biochemical Catalysis* (1931), and *Chemistry and Life* (1933). See J. G. Crowther, *British Scientists of the Twentieth Century* (1952).

Hopkins, Gerard Manley, 1844-89, English poet, educated at Oxford. Entering the Roman Catholic Church in 1866 and the Jesuit novitiate in 1868, he was ordained in 1877. Upon becoming a Jesuit he burned much of his early verse and abandoned the writing of poetry. However, the sinking in 1875 of a German ship carrying five Franciscan nuns, exiles from Germany, inspired him to write one of his most impressive poems "The Wreck of the *Deutschland.*" Thereafter he produced his best poetry, including "God's Grandeur," "The Windhover," "The Leaden Echo," and "The Golden Echo." Since Hopkins never gave permission for the publication of his verse, his *Poems,* edited by his friend Robert Bridges, did not appear in print until 1918. His life was continually troubled by inner conflict, which arose, not from religious skepticism, but from an inability to give himself completely to his God. Both his poems and his letters often reflect an intense dissatisfaction with himself as a poet and as a servant of God. Though he produced a small body of work, he ranks high among English poets, and his work profoundly influenced 20th-century poetry. His verse is noted for its piercing intensity of language and its experiments in prosody. Of these experiments the most famous is "sprung rhythm," a meter in which Hopkins tried to approximate the rhythm of everyday speech. See his journals and papers (ed. by Humphrey House and completed by Graham Storey, 1959); his letters (ed. by C. C. Abbott, 1955-56); biographies by John Pick (2d ed 1966) and Eleanor Ruggles (1944, repr. 1969); studies by W. H. Gardner (2 vol., 2d ed. 1948), Alan Heuser (1958, repr. 1969), Bernard Kelly (1935, repr. 1972), and A. G. Sulloway (1973).

Hopkins, Harry Lloyd, 1890-1946, American public official, b. Sioux City, Iowa. A social worker, he was appointed (1931) head of New York's Temporary Emergency Relief Administration by Franklin Delano Roosevelt, then governor of New York. Two years later, after Roosevelt became President, Hopkins was made chief of the Federal Emergency Relief Administration (FERA) and of the Civil Works Administration, which grew out of the FERA. In 1935 he became head of the Works Progress Administration. Hopkins was made Secretary of Commerce in Dec., 1938, but resigned in Aug., 1940, because of ill health. An intimate friend of President Roosevelt, Hopkins was a special assistant to the President during World War II. He administered the lend-lease program in 1941 and went on several missions to London and Moscow. After Roosevelt's death, he went as President Truman's representative to Moscow to settle problems that had arisen over Poland and the organization of the United Nations. In July, 1945, he retired from public life. See studies by R. E. Sherwood (rev. ed. 1950, repr. 1972) and S. F. Charles (1963).

Hopkins, Johns, 1795-1873, American financier and philanthropist, founder of Johns Hopkins Univ., b. Anne Arundel co., Md. In 1819 he founded his own commission firm, later known as Hopkins Brothers, and also went into banking. He later had a large part in the growth of the Baltimore & Ohio RR, of which he became a director in 1847. His cognizance of Baltimore's lack of medical facilities in times of epidemic and his own scant education led him to bequeath, a few years before his death, $7 million for the founding of a free hospital and Johns Hopkins Univ. See biography by H. H. Thom (1929).

Hopkins, Lemuel, 1750-1801, American poet and physician, b. Waterbury, Conn. One of the CONNECTICUT WITS, he collaborated with several others in writing popular political satires. He was one of the most advanced and distinguished physicians of his time and founder of the Medical Society of Connecticut.

Hopkins, Mark, 1802-87, American educator, b. Stockbridge, Mass., grad. Williams, 1824, and Berkshire Medical School, 1829. After a few months of medical practice he returned (1830) to Williams as professor of moral philosophy and rhetoric. President of the college from 1836 to 1872 and professor of intellectual and moral philosophy until his death, he was renowned as a teacher and administrator. He was ordained in the Congregational Church in 1836, preached frequently, and was president of the American Board of Commissioners for Foreign Missions (1857-87). His works include the Lowell Institute lectures for 1844, which later appeared as *Evidences of Christianity* (1863; rev. for text use), *Lectures on Moral Science* (1862), *The Law of Love and Love as a Law* (1869), and *The Scriptural Idea of Man* (1883). See biographical studies by Franklin Carter (1892) and Frederick Rudolph (1956).

Hopkins, Mark, 1813-78, American railroad builder and merchant, b. Henderson, N.Y. A clerk in a village store and later a commission merchant in New York City, he was more than 35 years old when he went to California. There he became (1853) a partner of Collis P. HUNTINGTON and was later one of the incorporators of the Central Pacific RR, of which he became treasurer. See Oscar Lewis, *The Big Four* (1938, repr. 1963); E. C. Latta and M. L. Allison, *Controversial Mark Hopkins* (2d rev. ed. 1963).

Hopkins, Samuel, 1721-1803, American clergyman and theologian, b. Waterbury, Conn., grad. Yale, 1741. He was a leading disciple of Jonathan EDWARDS, whose theology was the foundation for his own system, later known as Hopkinsianism. For 60 years Hopkins held pastorates at Great Barrington, Mass., and at Newport, R.I. His preaching, noninspirational and severely logical, was less influential than his writings, notably his *System of Doctrines* (1793). His views remained potent in American religious life until after the Civil War. Hopkins was one of the first New England ministers to denounce slavery and the slave trade.

Hopkins, Stephen, 1707-85, colonial governor of Rhode Island and political leader in the American Revolution, b. Providence, R.I. A member of the colonial assembly for many years, he also served as assistant justice (1747-49) and chief justice (1751-55) of the superior court. Between 1755 and 1768 he held the office of governor for nine years. The period was one of bitter strife in the colony between Newport and Providence, with Hopkins leading the Providence faction. In 1754, Hopkins was a delegate to the Albany Congress, where he energetically supported Benjamin Franklin's plan of union, writing *A True Representation of the Plan Formed at Albany* (1755) in hope of converting the opposition in Rhode Island. He was an early and strenuous defender of colonial rights, and his *Rights of Colonies Examined* (1765), attacking the sugar and stamp acts, was widely read. Again chief justice of the superior court, Hopkins refused to allow the burners of the GASPEE to be prosecuted. He was a member (1774-76) of the Continental Congress, a member of the committee that prepared the Articles of Confederation, and a signer of the Declaration of Independence. He was the first chancellor of Rhode Island College (now Brown Univ.). See biography by W. E. Foster (2 vol., 1884).

Hopkins, William, 1793-1866, English geologist. Hopkins studied mathematics at Cambridge, and then supported himself as a private mathematics tutor. Many of England's best mathematicians and mathematical physicists of the time were his students. In his early forties he became interested in geology. He proposed mathematical models of shifts of the earth's crust, of the nature of the earth's interior, of the transport of erratic boulders, and of the causes of climatic change. Modern geologists have discarded Hopkins's original conclusions, but his application of mathematics remains a valuable contribution to geological methods.

Hopkins, city (1970 pop. 13,428), Hennepin co., SE Minn., a suburb of Minneapolis; inc. as West Minneapolis 1893, name changed 1928. Foods, especially raspberries, are processed and distributed, and farm machinery, heavy equipment, ordnance, and automotive parts are made in Hopkins. An annual raspberry festival is held there.

Hopkinson, Francis, 1737-91, American writer and musician, signer of the Declaration of Independence, b. Philadelphia. A practicing lawyer, Hopkinson was also an accomplished poet, essayist, and musician and is considered the first native American composer of a secular song, *My Days Have Been So Wondrous Free* (1759). During the American Revolution he wrote propaganda supporting the colonial cause, best displayed in *The Battle of the Kegs* (1778). Hopkinson represented (1776) New Jersey in the Continental Congress and later (1776-78) served as chairman of the navy board (as such he may have designed the American flag) and as treasurer of the Continental loan office (1778-81). He returned to public office in Pennsylvania and served as judge of admiralty (1779-89) and as judge of the U.S. district court (1789-91). He later wrote in support of the adoption of the U.S. Constitution. See his essays and writings (3 vol., 1792; repr. 1968); biography by G. E. Hastings (1926, repr. 1968).

Hopkinson, Joseph, 1770-1842, American jurist, b. Philadelphia; son of Francis Hopkinson. A successful lawyer, he helped to defend (1804) Justice Samuel Chase in impeachment proceedings and was associated with Daniel Webster in the Dartmouth College Case; he was also a Federalist Congressman (1815-19) and a Federal judge. He is mainly remembered as the author (1798) of the words of *Hail, Columbia.* See biography by B. A. Konkle (1931).

Hopkinsville, city (1970 pop. 21,250), seat of Christian co., SW Ky.; inc. 1804. Rich agricultural lands surround the city, which is a leading tobacco market. Light fixtures, wire, and other hardware as well as clothing and bowling balls are manufactured in the city. Hopkinsville Community College, part of the Univ. of Kentucky, is there.

Hoppe, Willie (William Frederick Hoppe) (hŏp'ē), 1887-1959, American billiards champion, b. Cornwall, N.Y. He practiced billiards from a very early age and gave exhibitions before he won (1906) his first world championship in Paris. Hoppe subsequently won many balkline and three-cushion billiard championships, and when he retired in 1952 after winning his 12th world three-cushion championship (the last 6 in a row), he had won 51 world billiards titles in 46 years of tournament competition. He wrote *Thirty Years of Billiards* (1925) and *Billiards as It Should Be Played* (1941).

Hopper, DeWolf, 1858-1935, American singer and comedian, b. New York City. He made his debut in 1879 and thereafter became popular in musical comedy and light opera. He is best remembered for his recitation of "Casey at the Bat," first presented in 1888. His fifth wife was Hedda Hopper (1890-1966), the actress and Hollywood gossip columnist. In collaboration with W. W. Stout, Hopper wrote *Once a Clown Always a Clown* (1927).

Hopper, Edward, 1882-1967, American painter and engraver, b. Nyack, N.Y., studied in New York City with Robert Henri. Hopper lived in France for a year but was little influenced by the artistic currents there. His early paintings had slight success; he gained a reputation, however, through his etchings, which remain popular. In 1920 the first one-man show of his paintings was held; in 1933 a retrospective exhibition of his works took place at the Museum of Modern Art, New York City. He excelled in creating realistic pictures of clear-cut, sunlit streets and houses, often without figures. In his paintings there is a frequent atmosphere of loneliness, an almost menacing starkness, and a clear sense of time of day or night. His work in oil and watercolor is slowly and carefully painted, with light and shade used for pattern rather than for modeling. Hopper is represented in many leading American museums. *Early Sunday Morning* (1930; Whitney Museum, New York City) is a characteristic oil. See catalog (1971) and study (1971) by Lloyd Goodrich.

hopping mouse: see MOUSE.

Hoppner, John, 1758–1810, English portrait painter. He was a protégé of George III, whose illegitimate son he was rumored to be. He imitated, without total success, the style of Sir Joshua Reynolds. Hoppner achieved a lifelong popularity rivaled only by that of Sir Thomas Lawrence. He painted with facility and lively color, though many paintings have now faded badly. Under the patronage of the Prince of Wales, many of Hoppner's best works were hung in St. James's Palace, where they remain. Among his famous portraits are those of the countess of Oxford (National Gall., London) and the duke of Kent (Windsor Castle). The Metropolitan Museum has many of his portraits. See study by William McKay and William Roberts (1914 ed.).

hops: see HOP.

Hoquiam (hō'kwēəm), city (1970 pop. 10,466), Grays Harbor co., W Wash., on Grays Harbor; inc. 1890. With its twin city, Aberdeen, it has fishing (including shellfishing), lumbering, cranberry, and tourist industries. Olympic National Park is to the north.

Hor, unlocated mountain, on the boundary of Edom, the place of Aaron's death. Num. 20. It was traditionally identified with Jabel Harun, a mountain in SW Jordan, but it does not correspond with the biblical description. The Hor of Num. 34.7,8 is probably Mt. Hermon.

Horace (Quintus Horatius Flaccus) (hôr'əs), 65 B.C.–8 B.C., Latin poet, one of the greatest of lyric poets, b. Venusia, S Italy. He studied at Rome and Athens and, joining Brutus and the republicans, fought (42 B.C.) at Philippi. Returning to Rome, he was introduced by Vergil to MAECENAS, who became (c.38 B.C.) his intimate friend and constant benefactor. Maecenas gave him the famous Sabine Farm, where he lived thereafter except for lengthy visits to Rome. His first book of *Satires* appeared in 35 B.C., the *Epodes* c.30 B.C., the second book of *Satires* in 29 B.C., three books of *Odes* c.24 B.C., and the first book of *Epistles* c.20 B.C. The fourth book of *Odes,* the second book of *Epistles,* a hymn (the *Carmen Saeculare*), and the *Ars Poetica,* or *Epistle to the Pisos,* appeared c.13 B.C. Horace was a master of poetic form. His early poems show the influence of the Greek Archilochus, but his later verse displays complete and individualized adaption of Greek meters to Latin. As his genius matured, Horace's themes turned from personal vilification to more generalized satire and to literary criticism. He gives a vivid picture of contemporary Roman society and represents especially the spirit of the Augustan age of Rome—a time of peace, when the arts were cultivated earnestly without pretense. He had much influence on English poetry. See Loeb translations by H. R. Fairclough (rev. ed. 1929) and C. E. Bennett (rev. ed. 1964); poetic translations by H. R. Henze (1961) and J. Michie (1965); studies by E. Fraenkel (1957), S. Commager (1962), L. P. Wilkinson (1951, repr. 1965), H. D. Sedgwick (1947, repr. 1967), D. A. West (1967), M. O. Lee (1970), and C. D. N. Costa, ed. (1973).

Horae (hō'rē), in Greek religion, goddesses of the seasons; daughters of Zeus and Themis. Although they controlled the recurrence of the seasons, they also attended other gods and had no cults of their own. The number and names of the Horae differed from region to region. According to Hesiod, there were three Horae—Eirene or Irene (peace), Dice or Dike (justice), and Eunomia (order).

Horam (hôr'ăm), king of Gezer. He was defeated and killed by Joshua. Joshua 10.33.

Horatii (hōrā'shēī), in Roman legend, male triplets who represented Rome in a battle against Alba, which was represented by the Curiatii, also triplets. After two of the Horatii had been killed, the remaining brother defeated the Curiatii. When the sister of the Horatii bemoaned the death of one of the Curiatii, who had been her lover, her brother killed her. Condemned to death, he was spared when he appealed to the people. To do penance he was led, veiled, under a yoke.

Horatius (Horatius Cocles) (hōrā'shəs, hə–), legendary Roman hero. With two companions he held Lars Porsena's Etruscan army at bay while the Romans cut down the Sublician Bridge (connecting Rome with the road westward) behind them. Horatius swam the Tiber River to safety and received as much land as he could plow around in a day. Horatius is the subject of the most popular poem in Macaulay's *Lays of Ancient Rome* (1842).

Hordaland (hôr'dälän), county (1972 est. pop. 377,000), c.6,030 sq mi (15,600 sq km), SW Norway, bordering on the North Sea in the west. Bergen is the capital. Hordaland includes the Hardangerfjord region and numerous islands and is a favorite tourist area. Fishing, farming, and manufacturing (including chemicals and metal goods) are the chief occupations.

Horeb (hō'rĕb), mountain, another name for Mt. Sinai. Ex. 3.1; 17.6; 33.6; Deut. 1.6,19; 4.10,15. It is mentioned in Ps. 106.19 as the place of the making of the golden calf. Elijah fled to Horeb. 1 Kings 19.8.

horehound, aromatic Old World perennial herb (*Marrubium vulgare*) of the family Labiatae (MINT family), naturalized in North America. It has woolly white foliage and tiny white clustered flowers and is called the common, or white, horehound. The dried leaves and flower tops are used in making horehound candy and remedies for coughs and colds. The black horehound and the water horehound belong to other genera of the mint family. Horehound is classified in the division MAGNOLIOPHYTA, class Magnoliopsida, order Lamiales, family Labiatae.

Horem (hō'rĕm), unidentified fortified city, N Palestine. Joshua 19.38.

Horemheb (hō'rĕmhĕb") or **Harmhab** (härm'hăb), d. c.1303 B.C., king of ancient Egypt (c.1342 B.C.–c.1303 B.C.), founder of the XIX dynasty. A powerful noble under Ikhnaton, he seems to have been an army commander under the successors of that ruler, most notably under Tutankhamen. As king, Horemheb repaired the temples of Amon, abandoned or demolished buildings erected under Ikhnaton, and by untiring effort suppressed corruption in the government and restored prosperity to Egypt. He was succeeded by Ramses I.

Horgan, Paul, 1903–, American writer, b. Buffalo, N.Y. His diverse works reflect his fascination with the effects of history and landscape on people. Among his works are the novels *Main Line West* (1936), *Things As They Are* (1964), and *Whitewater* (1970); also *Great River: The Rio Grande in North American History* (1954), *Peter Hurd: A Portrait Sketch From Life* (1965), *Encounters With Stravinsky* (1972), an account of his friendship with the Russian composer, and *Approaches to Writing* (1975).

Horgen (hôr'gən), town (1970 pop. 15,691), Zürich canton, N Switzerland, on the Lake of Zürich. A textile center in the 17th cent., Horgen today has manufactures of machinery, appliances, and electrical goods. There is a noteworthy 18th-century church in the town.

Hor-hagidgad (hôr-həgĭd'găd), wilderness camp of the Israelites. Num. 33.32. The camping place called Gudgodah may have been the same. Deut. 10.7.

Hori (hō'rī). **1** Edomite. Gen. 36.22; 1 Chron. 1.39. **2** Simeonite. Num. 13.5.

Horims (hō'rĭmz) or **Horites** (–rīts), inhabitants of Seir, who were conquered by the Edomite invaders. Gen. 14.6; 36.20–30; Deut. 2.12,22.

horizon, in astronomy, roughly circular line bounding an observer's view of the surface of the earth where the sky and earth seem to meet. This is the visible horizon. At sea the visible horizon is a perfect circle with the observer at its center, but on land it is irregular due to topographic features. The distance to the horizon varies as the square root of the observer's elevation; at four times the height the distance to the horizon is twice as great. The CELESTIAL HORIZON, the principal axis in the HORIZON COORDINATE SYSTEM, lies halfway between the observer's ZENITH and NADIR. In geology *horizon* refers to sedimentary deposits of a certain period, usually marked by characteristic fossils.

horizon coordinate system or **altazimuth coordinate system** (ăltăz'əməth), astronomical coordinate system in which the position of a body on the CELESTIAL SPHERE is described relative to an observer's CELESTIAL HORIZON and ZENITH. The coordinates of a body in this system are its ALTITUDE and AZIMUTH. Altitude is measured from the celestial horizon along the vertical circle through the body and the zenith of the observer. Azimuth is measured along the celestial horizon from the observer's south point (the point on the horizon directly south of him) to the point where the body's vertical circle intersects the horizon. Because the earth rotates on its axis, the altitude and azimuth of a celestial body are constantly changing.

horizontal sounding balloon: see WEATHER BALLOON.

Hormah (hôr'mə), unidentified city, extreme S Palestine, earlier called Zephath. Here the invading Israelites were defeated by the Canaanites. Later the Israelites destroyed the city. Num. 14.45; 21.3; Deut. 1.44; Joshua 12.14; 15.30; 19.4; Judges 1.17; 1 Sam. 30.30.

hormone, secretory substance carried from one gland or organ of the body via the blood stream to more or less specific tissues, where it exerts some influence upon the metabolism of the target tissue. Normally, various hormones are produced and secreted by the endocrine, or ductless, glands, including (in the mammal) the pituitary, thyroid, parathyroids, adrenals, ovaries, testes, pancreatic islets, certain portions of the gastrointestinal tract, and the placenta. As lack of any one of them may cause serious disorders, many hormones are now produced synthetically and used in treatment where a deficiency exists. The hormones of the anterior pituitary include THYROTROPIC HORMONE, ADRENOCORTICOTROPIC HORMONE, the GONADOTROPIC HORMONES, and GROWTH HORMONE; the posterior pituitary secretes ANTIDIURETIC HORMONE and OXYTOCIN. The thyroids secrete THYROXINE, and the parathyroids secrete PARATHYROID HORMONE. The adrenal medulla secretes EPINEPHRINE and NOREPINEPHRINE while the cortex of the same gland releases ALDOSTERONE, CORTICOSTERONE, CORTISOL, and CORTISONE. The ovaries primarily secrete ESTROGEN and PROGESTERONE and the testes TESTOSTERONE. The adrenal cortex, ovaries, and testes in fact produce at least small amounts of all of the STEROID hormones. The islets of Langerhans in the pancreas secrete INSULIN and GLUCAGON. The passage of chyme (see DIGESTIVE SYSTEM) from the stomach to the duodenum causes the latter to release secretin, which stimulates the flow of pancreatic juice. The duodenum can also be stimulated by the presence of fats in the chyme to secrete cholecystokinin, a hormone that stimulates the gall bladder to contract and release BILE. There is evidence that the upper intestine secretes pancreatozymin, which enhances the amount of digestive enzymes in the pancreatic juice. In addition, the pyloric region of the stomach secretes gastrin, a hormone that increases the secretion of hydrochloric acid into the stomach. The placenta has been shown to secrete progesterone and chorionic gonadotropin. There is evidence that it even contains a substance similar to growth hormone. Insects have a unique hormonal system that includes ecdysone, a steroid that influences molting and metamorphosis, and juvenile hormone, needed for early development. Plants, too, have a hormonal system, which includes the AUXINS, the gibberellins, the cytokinins, and substances associated with the formation of flowers, tubers, bulbs, and buds. Ethylene is said to function as a hormone in plants, acting to hasten the ripening of fruits.

Hormoz (hôr'mōz") or **Ormuz** (ôr'mŭz", ôrmōōz'), island (1966 est. pop. 600), 5 mi (8.1 km) long and 3.5 mi (5.6 km) wide, S Iran, in the Strait of Hormoz, between the Persian Gulf and the Gulf of Oman. Salt and red ochre are produced. The town of Hormoz, originally built on the mainland, was moved (c.1300) to the island after repeated attacks by marauding raiders. The new port prospered and served as a center of trade with India and China. It was attacked by the Portuguese under Alfonso de Albuquerque in 1507 and was captured by them in 1514. Its recapture in 1622 by Shah Abbas I with the aid of an English fleet marked the end of the island's prosperity; the shah abandoned Hormoz for the new mainland port of Bandar Abbas. The name is also spelled Hormuz.

Horn, Philip de Montmorency, count of: see HOORN, PHILIP DE MONTMORENCY, COUNT OF.

Horn, Cape, headland, 1,391 ft (424 m) high, S Chile, southernmost point of South America, in the archipelago of Tierra del Fuego. It was discovered and first rounded by Willem Schouten, the Dutch navigator, on Jan. 29, 1616, and named for Hoorn in the Netherlands. Lashing storms and strong currents made "rounding the Horn" one of the great hazards of sailing-ship days. It is still a formidable challenge to navigation.

Horn: see KING HORN.

horn, in symphonic and chamber music: see FRENCH HORN.

horn, in zoology, one of a pair of structures projecting from the head of a hoofed animal, used chiefly as a weapon. In cattle, sheep, Old World antelopes, and related animals the horns are permanent and unbranched and are usually present in both sexes. They are composed of a sheath of keratin—a tough fibrous material derived from epithelial tissue—overlying a bony core projecting from the skull. In the deer family the branched structures, called antlers, are composed entirely of bone with no actual horn substance; they are usually present only in the male and are shed annually. The horns of the pronghorn have characteristics of both true horns and antlers. Rhinoceros horns are not true horn but greatly modified hair, derived entirely from the epidermis. Horns have long been used for many purposes, e.g., drinking cups, spoons, trumpets, containers for gunpowder, and combs. Carved pieces of horn have been found dating from prehistoric times. In art and religion horns symbolize power. The "horns of the altar" (Amos 3.14) symbolized divine protection. Hornlike protuberances appear on other animals, e.g., on the horned toad and the horned pout.

Hornaday, William Temple (hôr'nədā), 1854–1937, American naturalist, b. Plainfield, Ind. He was educated at Iowa State College, continued his study of zoology and museology in Europe, and was chief taxidermist (1882–90) of the U.S. National Museum. As the first director (1896–1926) of the New York Zoological Park and as an author, Hornaday was a leader in wildlife conservation. His book *Extermination of the American Bison* (1887) helped to save the bison from extinction. His works also include the classic *American Natural History* (1904), books on wild animals, and *Thirty Years' War for Wild Life* (1931).

hornbeam or **ironwood,** name in North America for two trees of the family Betulaceae (BIRCH family), native to the eastern half of the continent. *Carpinus caroliniana,* also called blue beech and water beech, has smooth gray bark. The hop hornbeam, *Ostrya virginiana,* has thin, narrowly ridged, light-brown bark. The strong, heavy wood of both species is used for tool handles, mallets, and vehicle parts. The names hornbeam and ironwood are also applied to other species of *Carpinus.* Many valuable hardwood timber trees of other families are called ironwood, especially in Australia and in the Old World tropics. Hornbeams are classified in the division MAGNOLIOPHYTA, class Magnoliopsida, order Fagales, family Betulaceae.

hornbill, common name for members of the family Bucerotidae, Old World birds of tropical and subtropical forests, named for their enormous downcurved bills surmounted by grotesque horny casques. From 2 to 5 ft (61–152.5 cm) in length, they are the largest of an order that also includes the kingfishers. Hornbills are black and dark brown with patches of white or cream on the body, wings, and tail. The bill is usually brownish, though in some species it is black, red, or yellow. Omnivorous, hornbills eat fruits, berries, insects, and small animals. They have loud, far-carrying voices and a variety of calls, including brays, toots, bellows, and cackles. They are noted for their unusual nesting habits; presumably as a defense against monkeys and snakes, the female is sealed into the nesting cavity by the male, who feeds her through a bill-sized aperture for a period of from 6 weeks to 3 months while she incubates the eggs. This practice, and the fact that hornbills mate for life, has made them the subject of superstition among native tribes, who use them (or representations of them) in religious rituals as symbols of purity and fidelity. The great hornbill, *Buceros bicornis,* ranges from India to Indochina and Sumatra. Hornbills are classified in the phylum CHORDATA, subphylum Vertebrata, class Aves, order Coraciiformes, family Bucerotidae.

hornblende: see AMPHIBOLE.

hornbook, primer of a kind in use from the 15th to the 18th cent. On one side of a sheet of parchment or paper the matter to be learned was written or printed; over the sheet, for its protection, a transparent sheet of horn was placed; and the two were fastened to a thin board, which usually projected to form a handle, perforated so that the hornbook might be attached to a girdle. The matter printed or written included the alphabet in capitals and small letters and other material, varying in different hornbooks, such as numerals and the Lord's Prayer. Sometimes the base and handle were made of metal, stone, or ivory and had letters carved or cast on them. See A. W. Tuer, *History of the Hornbook* (2 vol., 1896, repr. 1968).

Hornchurch, England: see HAVERING.

Horne, Marilyn, 1934–, American mezzo-soprano, b. Bradford, Pa. She had established her reputation in concerts and opera in Italy and West Germany before her highly successful American debut as Marie in Alban Berg's *Wozzeck* at the San Francisco Opera in 1960. In 1970 she made her debut at the Metropolitan Opera singing Adalgisa in Bellini's *Norma.* Horne is noted for the power and smoothness ("seamlessness") of her voice, evident in the ease with which she glides from one register to another. Among her notable roles have been Eboli in Verdi's *Don Carlos,* Arsace in Rossini's *Semiramide,* and the title role in Bizet's *Carmen.*

Horne, Richard Henry, or **Richard Hengist Horne,** 1802–84, English author. His chief work was the allegorical poem *Orion* (1843). *A New Spirit of the Age* (1844), written with Elizabeth Barrett (later Elizabeth Barrett Browning) and others, contains social and literary studies. His correspondence with Miss Barrett was published in 1877. Of his plays, he was best known for the tragedies *Cosmo de' Medici* and *The Death of Marlowe* (both: 1837).

horned lizard or **horned toad,** broad, flat-bodied lizards of the genus *Phrynosoma,* found in arid regions from extreme SW Canada to Guatemala. There are several species in the United States W of the Mississippi. The body is 3 to 5 in. (7.6 to 12.7 cm) long; it has a short, thin tail, a short neck, and short legs. There are spines on the head, sides, and back. Horned lizards are protectively colored, usually in dull grays and browns. They feed on insects, especially ants, and are often found buried in the sand, with only their heads exposed. In some species the female lays eggs; in others the eggs are incubated internally and the young are born alive. When alarmed, members of some species eject a thin stream of blood from the nictitating membrane of the eye for a distance of several feet. Horned lizards are classified in the phylum CHORDATA, subphylum Vertebrata, class Reptilia, order Squamata, family Iguanidae.

horned pout: see CATFISH.

horned toad: see HORNED LIZARD.

Hornell (hôrněl'), city (1970 pop. 12,144), Steuben co., SW N.Y., on the Canisteo River; settled 1790, inc. 1906. Textiles and steel bearings are manufactured there.

hornet: see WASP.

Horne Tooke, John: see TOOKE, JOHN HORNE.

Horney, Karen, 1885–1952, American psychiatrist, b. Germany, M.D. Univ. of Berlin, 1913. She married Oscar Horney in 1909. Previous to her arrival (1932) in the United States, she was secretary of the Berlin Psychoanalytic Institute, where she taught for 12 years. Associate director (1932–34) of the Chicago Institute for Psychoanalysis, Horney then came to New York City, where she lectured at the New School for Social Research. She deviated from orthodox Freudian analysis by emphasizing environmental and cultural, rather than biological, factors in the genesis of neurosis. Anxiety, she held, is created by anything that jeopardizes a person's means of gaining security. The neurotic's rigid adherence to his safety devices protects him in some ways but renders him helpless toward other possible dangers. To further her work based on these beliefs, she founded (1941) and became dean of the American Institute of Psychoanalysis. Her works include *The Neurotic Personality of Our Time* (1937), *Self-Analysis* (1942), *Our Inner Conflicts* (1945), and *Neurosis and Human Growth* (1950).

hornpipe, English folk dance known since the 16th cent., when it obtained its name from the wind instrument that accompanied it. The hornpipes of the 17th and 18th cent. have moderate 3–2 time and 4–4 time. As a solo dance it was popular with sailors, who performed it with folded arms and numerous gestures and steps. The hornpipe appears in the works of Purcell and Handel.

Hornsby, Rogers, 1896–1963, American baseball player and manager, b. Winters, Texas. He started in major-league baseball in 1915 as a shortshop for the St. Louis Cardinals and later (1920) became a second baseman. He was the National League batting champion seven times (1920–25, 1928) and in 1924 had a batting average of .424, which is still the major-league record for the 20th cent. As manager (1925–26) of the Cardinals, "Rajah" Hornsby led the team to the pennant and world-series victories in 1926. He was traded to the New York Giants in 1927 and then was player-manager with the Boston Braves (1928) and Chicago Cubs (1930–32). After another short stay with the Cardinals in 1933, Hornsby went over to the American League as manager (1933–37) of the St. Louis Browns. A right-handed hitter, he maintained a lifetime batting average of .358, second only to Ty Cobb's .367 record average. He was voted the most valuable player in 1925 and 1928 and was elected in 1942 to the National Baseball Hall of Fame.

horology (hōrŏl'əjē), science of measuring TIME and technology of constructing instruments for its measurement or recording. Early measurements of the passage of time were based on observations of seasonal cycles and of the apparent motion of celestial bodies. Shorter intervals were measured by observing the shadow cast by an upright object; the shadow clock and the SUNDIAL were probably the first devices constructed. Later came the HOURGLASS and the CLEPSYDRA and finally the CLOCK and the WATCH. The most accurate type of timekeeping device in existence today is the ATOMIC CLOCK. Highly accurate time, which is necessary for such purposes as navigation and the tracking of artificial satellites, is provided throughout the world by time signals that are transmitted by certain radio stations. The age of ancient objects can be estimated by various techniques, e.g., radiocarbon dating (see DATING).

Horonaim (hŏrōnā'ĭm), unlocated Moabite town. Isa. 15.5; Jer. 48.3,5,34.

Horonite (hôr'ōnīt): see SANBALLAT.

horoscope: see ASTROLOGY.

Horowitz, Vladimir (hôr'ōwĭts), 1904–, Russian-American virtuoso pianist, b. Kiev. Horowitz studied at the Kiev Conservatory. After a Russian debut at the age of 17, he appeared with overwhelming success in Berlin and Paris in 1924 and made his American debut with the New York Philharmonic in 1928. Possessing remarkable technical virtuosity, he soon became one of the most popular pianists in the United States. In 1933 he married the daughter of Arturo Toscanini and settled (1940) in New York City. Horowitz gave few recitals after 1953.

Horrocks or **Horrox, Jeremiah** (both: hŏr'əks), 1618?–1641, English astronomer. He made the first observation of the transit of Venus. His *Venus in sole visa,* which narrates this experience, was printed by Hevelius in 1662. The transit occurred on Nov. 24, 1639; Horrocks watched the small shadow of the planet move part way across the disk of light on a white screen, where the sun's image was focused through a telescope adjusted to an aperture in the shutter. Other fragments of his works besides the *Venus* were edited by John Wallis (1672). Horrocks estimated more correctly than anyone else had yet done the distance of the sun from the earth.

Horsa: see HENGIST AND HORSA.

horse, hoofed, herbivorous mammal of the family Equidae, now represented by a single living genus, *Equus.* The name horse is commonly applied only to the domestic horse, *Equus caballus,* and to the wild PRZEWALSKI'S HORSE, *E. przewalski.* All other wild horse species are now extinct; horses called wild are actually feral, i.e., descendants of domesticated animals. In addition to these two species, the genus *Equus* includes the ASS (two species) and the ZEBRA (three species). All of these equids are plains-dwelling animals, adapted for swift running. They have greatly lengthened footbones (metapodials) in both front and hind limbs, which act as an extension of the leg and end in a single, highly developed toe, covered by a hoof. Their teeth are adapted for grinding coarse, gritty grass; digestion of cellulose occurs in the intestine with the aid of protozoa. All species have tufts of hair on the tail, used for switching away insects, and crests of hair on the neck and shoulders. The wild and domestic horses are large, sturdy animals with big hooves. Their tail tufts are long, flowing plumes, and in the domestic horse the crest is a long mane. Asses are smaller, lighter animals with slender legs and hooves, long ears, and short crests and tail tufts. Zebras are intermediate in build and are distinguished by their striped hide markings. Horses, zebras, and asses can interbreed, but the offspring are usually sterile. The offspring of a horse and a donkey (domestic ass) is called a mule. In addition to the genus *Equus* the family Equidae includes about 20 known fossil genera, and the evolutionary history of the family is well known. The earliest known direct ancestor of *Equus,* the eohippus [Gr., =dawn horse] or *Hyracotherium,* lived approximately 50 million years ago during the Eocene epoch. Eohippus species varied in height from 10 to 20 in. (25–50 cm) and had four toes on each front foot and three on each hind foot.

They were found in both the Old and New Worlds; in the Old World, however, they eventually became extinct. Modern horses evolved in the region that is now the Great Plains of North America and spread from there to the rest of the world. The major changes in the New World descendants of the eohippus were a gradual increase in size, adaptation of the teeth for grazing on grass rather than browsing on foliage, and the development of the one-toed foot. Horses ascribable to the genus *Equus* had appeared in North America by the late Pliocene epoch, about three million years ago, and quickly spread to all continents except Australia. Horses still existed in North America when people first settled the continent after the last ice age; but they suddenly disappeared from that region about 10,000 years ago, along with many other large New World mammals (e.g., camels, mastodons, and mammoths). The cause of extinction is not known, but it is possible that the balance of nature was upset by human settlement and hunting. Horses were thereafter confined to the Old World until they were reintroduced to the Americas by European settlers, c.1500 A.D. Many species of *Equus* arose in the Old World; several were hunted by Old Stone Age (Paleolithic) peoples of Europe, as evidenced by cave paintings and by fossil remains. Horses were probably first domesticated by central Asian nomads in the 3d millennium B.C. There are records of horses from Mesopotamia and China (c.2000 B.C.), Greece (c.1700 B.C.), Egypt (c.1600 B.C.), and India (c.1500 B.C.). Horses were domesticated in W Europe no later than 1000 B.C. It is not known whether these early breeds were all products of a single original domestication, or of independent domestications of local races of the wild horse (*E. przewalski* or similar species). It is widely held that the two major groups of modern horses—the light, swift southern breeds, called LIGHT HORSES, and the heavy, powerful northern breeds, called DRAFT HORSES—are of independent origin, although later modified by interbreeding. The small breeds called PONIES are variously held to be descended from the southern type of horse or independently domesticated from a small European wild race. The horse was swifter and more manageable than the ass, which had been domesticated much earlier. Its first known use was for drawing the two-wheeled Mesopotamian war chariots, and it continued to be used primarily for warfare and for transportation of aristocracy until quite recent times, while cheaper animals (e.g., oxen, mules, and donkeys) were used for work purposes. Possession of horses was an important element in the conquest of central Asia and the Middle East by successive peoples for over 3,000 years. Early mounted warriors rode bareback or with saddle cloths. The SADDLE and the STIRRUP were probably developed in China in the early Christian era; their use was spread by Asian horsemen (such as the Huns) and was adopted by Arabs and Europeans in the early Middle Ages. The Arabs established the first breed of known lineage that survives in modern times; the Arabian horse is also ancestral to many other light breeds. The Arab cavalry conquered the Middle East and N Africa in the 7th cent. A.D.; during the same period the use of armored knights developed in Europe. The horse played a major role in the culture of the Mongols, who developed cavalry warfare to its highest peak and in the 13th cent. established an empire extending from China to E Europe. The horse was brought to the Americas by the Spanish conquistadors, and Indians soon acquired them from ranches and missions. The Plains Indians of North America quickly developed a horse culture that led to the ascendancy of these tribes in numbers and power. Horses were used for hunting buffalo and other game, for warfare, and for pulling loads on a TRAVOIS. Escaped Indian horses were ancestral to the MUSTANG, the so-called wild horse of the W United States. Draft horses, used primarily for work rather than for riding, were developed in Europe. During Roman times the Gauls and other Europeans used horses of the heavy, northern type for pulling loads. In the Middle Ages such horses were used to breed the Great Horse of the Low Countries. This horse, developed for use in warfare, was in turn the ancestor of the modern draft breeds; it stood over 16 hands (64 in./160 cm) high and was strong enough to carry an armored knight as well as its own coat of armor. The Middle Ages also saw technological advances such as the nailed horseshoe and the rigid horse-collar (see HARNESS), which made the use of draft horses more practical. As armored cavalry warfare declined, heavy horses were used increasingly for farm labor. By the 19th cent. the draft horse had replaced the ox in N Europe and was also the chief draft animal of North America. Draft breeds common in the United States are the BELGIAN, CLYDESDALE, PERCHERON, and SHIRE; the last is the best-known draft horse in England. Light horses, used for saddle, harness, or racing, are all descended in part from the ARABIAN HORSE, the oldest living breed. They include the THOROUGHBRED, distinguished as a racehorse; the AMERICAN SADDLE HORSE, a riding horse known for its easy gaits; the MORGAN and the QUARTER HORSE, all-purpose breeds used for riding and cow herding; and the STANDARDBRED, or trotter, developed for light harness racing. The light breeds APPALOOSA and PINTO, both much used in cow herding, are distinguished by their color patterns. The PALOMINO, another popular light horse, is not considered a breed but a color type. Ponies are small horses used as children's mounts and for light work; among them are the SHETLAND PONY and WELSH PONY. The terms cow pony and polo pony refer to the use to which the horse is put, rather than its size or breed. Polo ponies are usually a cross between a Thoroughbred and some other light breed. The use of work horses has declined rapidly with the advance of mechanization, but the demand for horses for show and sport has increased. In horse terminology, a male is a stallion, or if castrated, a gelding; a female is a mare; her offspring are foals—the males colts, the females fillies. A male parent is a sire and a female parent a dam. Mating usually occurs in the spring, and a single foal is born after a gestation of about 11 months. Horses reach sexual maturity in about two years, but are not fully grown for about five years. The average life span is 18 years, but 30-year-old horses are not uncommon. The standard unit of height is a hand, equal to 4 in. (10 cm). Horses are classified in the phylum CHORDATA, subphylum Vertebrata, class Mammalia, order Perissodactyla, family Equidae. See HORSE RACING; HORSEMANSHIP. See R. W. Howard, *The Horse in America* (1965); Luigi Gianoli, *Horses and Horsemanship through the Ages* (tr. 1969); Roger Longrigg, *The History of Horse Racing* (1972); P. D. Rossdale, *The Horse from Conception to Maturity* (1972); Donald Braider, *The Life, History and Magic of the Horse* (1973); C. E. Hope and G. N. Jackson, ed., *The Encyclopedia of the Horse* (1973).

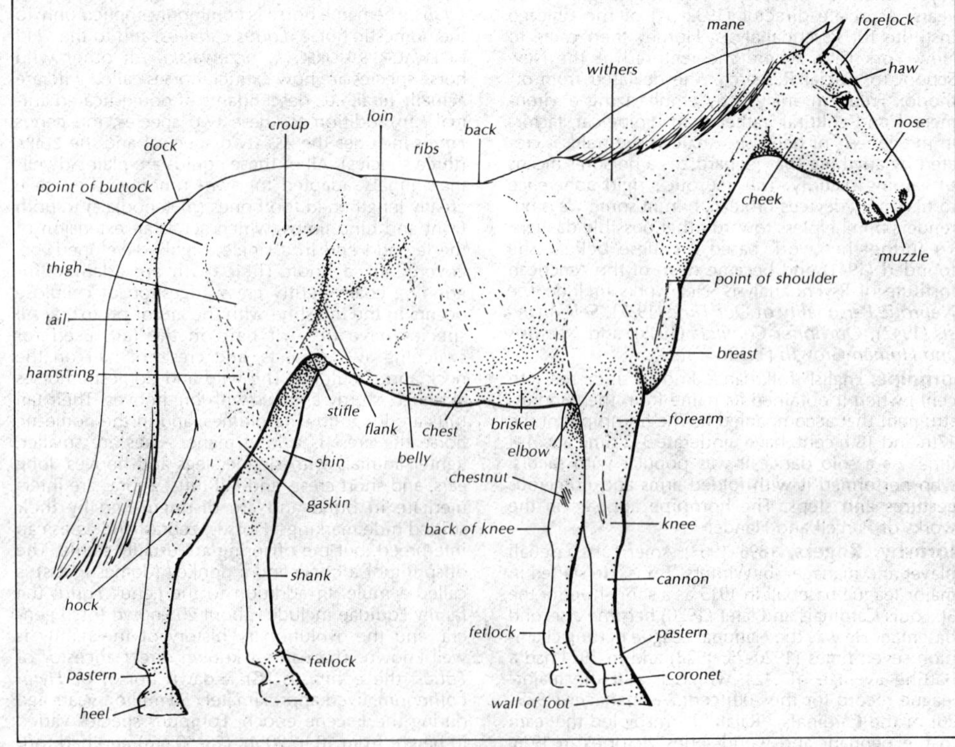

General anatomy of a horse

horseback riding: see HORSEMANSHIP.

horse chestnut, common name for some members of the Hippocastanaceae, a family of trees and shrubs of the north temperate zones and of South America. The horse chestnut tree, *Aesculus hippocastanum*, a native of the Balkan peninsula, is now cultivated in many countries for shade and ornament. Buckeyes are several similar but often smaller North American species of the same genus. Horse chestnuts and buckeyes (as the nuts too are called) somewhat resemble true chestnuts in appearance but are edible only after careful preparation. Some American Indian tribes ate buckeyes in large quantity after thorough roasting or leaching. Buckeyes, with their eyelike markings, are still carried as charms by some rural people. Ohio is called the Buckeye State from the prevalence of the Ohio buckeye, *A. glabra*. The wood of the horse chestnut and of the buckeye is soft; it is used for paper pulp and for carpentry, woodenware, and other similar purposes. The only other genus of the family is *Billia*, evergreens ranging from Colombia to Mexico. Horse chestnuts are classified in the division MAGNOLIOPHYTA, class Magnoliopsida.

horse collar: see HARNESS.

horsefly, common name for the large hairy FLIES of the family Tabanidae. Male horseflies feed on pollen and nectar, but the females suck blood as well and are common pests of animals and sometimes of humans. The bites of many species are very painful. The larger horseflies, e.g., the mourning horsefly and the 1-in. (2.5-cm) black horsefly, belong to the genus *Tabanus*; the smaller and more common banded horseflies, with black, brown, or yellow bodies and brilliantly colored eyes, are members of the genus *Chrysops*. The deerflies, which carry the diseases ANTHRAX and TULAREMIA, and in Africa, a filarial worm infestation, belong to this group. Horseflies are most abundant in hot weather. The eggs are laid on plants or stones close to water. The somewhat flattened ½-in. (1.3-cm) larvae have fleshy protuberances on each body segment, aiding in locomotion; they live in water or in moist earth and feed on snails and on other insect larvae. Horseflies are classified in the phylum ARTHROPODA, class Insecta, order Diptera, family Tabanidae. See INSECT.

horsehair worm, worm of the class Nematomorpha in the phylum ASCHELMINTHES.

Horsehead Nebula, dark NEBULA located in the constellation Orion; designated IC 434 or B 33. It consists of a cloud of nonluminous INTERSTELLAR MATTER resembling the outline of a horse's head and appears against the background of a bright emission nebula. The Horsehead Nebula measures about 4 min of arc at its greatest width. It is located near the belt of Orion at a distance of about 300 light-years from the earth.

horse latitudes, two belts of latitude where winds are light and the weather is hot and dry. They are located mostly over the oceans, at about 30° lat. in each hemisphere, and have a north-south range of about 5° as they follow the seasonal migration of the sun. The horse latitudes are associated with the subtropical ANTICYCLONE and the large-scale descent of air from high-altitude currents moving toward the poles. After reaching the earth's surface, this air spreads toward the equator as part of the prevailing trade winds or toward the poles as part of the westerlies. The belt in the Northern Hemisphere is sometimes called the "calms of Cancer" and that in the Southern Hemisphere the "calms of Capricorn." The term *horse latitudes* supposedly originates from the days when Spanish sailing vessels transported horses to the West Indies. Ships would often become becalmed in mid-ocean in this latitude, thus severely prolonging the voyage; the resulting water shortages would make it necessary for crews to throw their horses overboard.

horse mackerel: see TUNA.

horsemanship, art of riding and handling a horse. Horseback riding was practiced as far back as the Bronze Age and was thereafter adapted to commerce, industry, war, sport, and recreation. Diverse styles of riding developed, and the SADDLE, as well as the STIRRUP and other riding aids, were manufactured along with the other appurtenances to horseback riding. At the two extremes of riding are the jockey's riding style, sacrificing comfort and security in the interest of speed, and the cowboy's style, more relaxed for long hours of work. Riding as a skilled sport developed from the style of mounted knights in the medieval period. The so-called academy style is popular in the E United States as well as in Europe. Riding as recreation has become increasingly popular in the United States, particularly in metropolitan and suburban areas. Horse shows, originated by Ireland's Royal Dublin Society (1864), offer riders a chance to test their skills in competition. Contests are held among hunters, jumpers, ponies, and three- and five-gaited horses; a test of overall training and obedience, known as the dressage event, is also held. The major horse show in the United States is the National Horse Show at New York City (originated 1883). Equestrian events have been held in the Olympic games since 1912. Olympic competitions include dressage, jumping (Prix de Nations), and a three-day all-around competition that involves dressage, jumping, and endurance. See also HORSE RACING. See Margaret C. Self, *Riding Step by Step* (1965); C. P. Chenevix Trench, *A History of Horsemanship* (1970); R. S. Summerhays, *Summerhays' Encyclopaedia for Horsemen* (5th. ed. 1970); Henry Wynmalen, *Equitation* (1972).

horse nettle: see NIGHTSHADE.

Horsens (hôr'səns), city (1970 com. pop. 52,203), Vejle co., central Denmark, a port at the head of the Horsens Fjord, an inlet of the Kattegat. It is a commercial and industrial center. Horsens was a fortified town in the Middle Ages. It retains a noteworthy 13th-century monastery and church.

horsepower, unit of POWER in the English system of units. It is equal to 33,000 FOOT-POUNDS per minute or 550 foot-pounds per second or approximately 746 watts. The term *horsepower* originated with James Watt, who determined by experiment that a horse could do 33,000 foot-pounds of work a minute in drawing coal from a coal pit.

horse racing, trials of speed between two or more horses. It involves races among harnessed horses with a particular gait, saddled thoroughbreds along a flat track (the "flats"), or saddled horses over an obstacle course (the steeplechase). Horse races, today popular throughout most of the Western world as well as in many other areas, are recorded as early as 1500 B.C., in Egypt. In the earliest days there were no race courses or established race distances. Horse owners became involved in friendly arguments and wagers as to which horse was faster and which owner was the better rider. The saddle-horse races of the ancient Olympic games are believed to be the first public exhibitions of horse racing. Harness-horse racing began some years later when horses hauled chariots. In the Roman era the chariot race was a favorite pastime. The desire for faster and stronger horses led to the development of highly bred strains of horses. Organized horse racing dates from the 12th cent. in England, where royalty fostered the sport. It is still known popularly as the "sport of kings." The Arabs were the first to breed fine horses, but the ancestry of most of the thoroughbreds of the world is traceable to English horses. As early as the 16th cent., prizes were awarded for horse racing, but the 12th earl of Derby originated (1780) the first horse-racing event on a sweepstakes basis at his estate in Epsom, England. The event is still known as the Epsom Derby, or the English Derby. Steeplechase racing (the riding of horses over an obstacle course with hurdles and water holes to approximate rough natural conditions) was officially organized in the 19th cent. and became popular in England and Ireland. The Grand National Steeplechase, held annually since 1839 at Aintree course, Liverpool, England, is the most difficult and the most famous. Horse racing was introduced into France in the reign of Louis XIV. There, in the 19th cent., Pierre Oller invented and introduced the PARIMUTUEL BETTING system as a means of reforming race track gambling. In the early American colonies, horse racing was common among couriers and also among members of the leisured classes, and later moved westward with the pony-express riders and cowboys. Racing and trotting horses were carefully bred in the United States in the 18th and 19th cent. (see JUSTIN MORGAN; HAMBLETONIAN). Harness-horse racing became very popular in the 1870s, and in 1891 the modern low-wheel sulky replaced the high-wheeler. Harness racing features two differently gaited horses—pacers (laterally gaited), who move with a swaying motion, bringing the right front and right hind legs forward at the same time, and trotters (diagonally gaited), who move with a high-stepping, straight ahead gait with left front and right hind legs moving forward in unison. Harness racing, formerly a favorite event at country fairs, became increasingly popular after World War II at racing centers near urban areas. The United States Trotting Association (formed 1938) governs the sport. Notable harness races include the Hambletonian, Kentucky Futurity, Cane Futurity, and Yonkers International. The first thoroughbred racing in the United States was held at the Saratoga Springs, N.Y., track (1863). Churchill Downs, at Louisville, Ky., opened its flat-racing track in 1875; other flat tracks soon began to appear all over the country. Gambling on horse races, though the subject of constant attack by reform groups and religious leaders, flourished, often falling into the hands of unscrupulous elements. Steps were taken to reform flat racing, and in England much of the responsibility for organization and supervision was placed in the hands of the Jockey Club (founded 1750). In the United States individual states set up racing commissions, which now govern the sport. The Thoroughbred Racing Association (founded 1942) is one of the leading regulatory organizations in the sport. In the United States the three most important flat-racing events (all for 3-year-olds) are the Kentucky Derby at Churchill Downs, the Preakness at the Pimlico track near Baltimore, Md., and the Belmont Stakes at Belmont Park, Elmont, N.Y. Together these events are known as the Triple Crown. Other important thoroughbred races include the St. Leger Stakes (Great Britain), Queen's Plate (Canada), Melbourne Cup (Australia), Gran Premio Carlos Pellegrini (Argentina), Japan Derby, Prix de l'Arc de Triomphe (France), and Preis von Europa (West Germany). The last two, as international events, attract horses from all over the world. With the institution of legalized parimutuel betting at most tracks, and government regulation of horse racing, the U.S. sport has grown greatly. Since the early 1950s horse racing has been the most popular spectator sport in the country, with a paid attendance of almost 75 million people in 1972 alone. Taxation of parimutuel betting has made horse-race wagering an important source of tax funds. In order to further increase this revenue, New York City instituted the nation's first legalized off-track betting system in 1971. It was modeled somewhat on the system in effect in Great Britain. Famous horses in the history of thoroughbred racing include Assault, Citation, Count Fleet, Gallant Fox, Omaha, Secretariat, Sir Barton, War Admiral, and Whirlaway—all winners of the Triple Crown—Carry Back, Kelso, Man o' War, Nashua, Native Dancer, Round Table, Seabiscuit, and Tom Fool. Outstanding jockeys include Eddie Arcaro, Ted Atkinson, Ed (Snapper) Garrison, Bill Hartack, Isaac Murphy, Sir Gordon Richards, Earl Sande, Willie Shoemaker, and Tod Sloan. Some famous harness-racing horses were Adios Butler, Bye Bye Byrd, Bret Hanover, Cardigan Bay, Su Mac Lad, Speedy Scot, and Duke Rodney. Notable drivers include William Haughton, Robert Farrington, Stanley Dancer, and Herve Fillion. See W. H. P. Robertson, *The History of Thoroughbred Racing in America* (1964); Roger Longrigg, *The History of Horse Racing* (1972).

horse-radish, perennial herb (*Armoracia lapathifolia*, but sometimes classified in other genera) of the family Cruciferae (MUSTARD family), native to central and S Europe (where it has long been cultivated in gardens) and naturalized in many parts of North America. It is grown mainly for its roots, which formerly were used medicinally, particularly as an antiscorbutic. Today the roots make a popular condiment and are usually grated and mixed with vinegar to make a sauce or relish for meats and sea food. The lively pungency of the root is caused by its volatile oil, which resembles mustard oil. It has a stimulating effect, exciting the action of the stomach and promoting secretions. The wilted foliage may be used as a poultice to relieve toothache and facial neuralgia. An old name for it is German mustard. Horse-radishes are classified in the division MAGNOLIOPHYTA, class Magnoliopsida, order Capparales, family Cruciferae.

horseshoe, narrow plate, commonly of iron or steel, shaped to fit a horse's hoof and attached to the hoof by nailing it to the inner edge of the horny wall of the hoof. Horseshoes vary from the light plate worn by race-horses to the heavy shoe with sharp pointed wedges, or calks, worn by horses of logging camps in drawing heavy loads over roads of ice. The earliest extant shoe dates from the 6th cent. B.C. A horseshoe used by the Romans was a leather boot with a metal plate at the bottom. Before the advent of motor vehicles, shoeing horses was an important trade, often combined with general blacksmithing. Often the horseshoer's skill cured lameness, and before veterinary medicine became a profession the horseshoer, or farrier, treated horses for all their diseases. The horseshoe is an emblem and talisman of good luck.

Horseshoe Bend, a turn on the Tallapoosa River, near Dadeville, E central Ala., site of a battle on March 27, 1814, in which the CREEK INDIANS, led by William Weatherford, an Indian chief, were defeated by militia under the command of Andrew Jackson. This defeat broke the Indians' power, and they surrendered soon afterward. Horseshoe Bend National Military Park is there (see NATIONAL PARKS AND MONUMENTS, table).

horseshoe crab, large, primitive marine arthropod related to the SPIDER. The heavy dark brown exoskeleton, or carapace, is domed and shaped like a horseshoe. The body is divided into a broad, flattened, semicircular front part (the prosoma), a tapering middle part (the opisthosoma), and a pointed, spiky taillike part (the telson). Horseshoe crabs, also called king crabs, have no jaws, and the mouth is flanked by a pair of pincerlike chelicera that are used to crush worms and other invertebrates taken as food. Five pairs of walking legs attached to the prosoma enable the animals to swim awkwardly or burrow through the sand or mud. The respiratory organs are called book gills and are unique to horseshoe crabs. Each book gill is made of about 100 thin leaves, or plates; these are fitted like pages of a book onto one pair of flaplike appendages on the opisthosoma. Rhythmic movement of the appendages circulates water over the gill surfaces and drives blood into and out of the gill leaves. Horseshoe crabs first appeared in the Upper Silurian period, and a number of fossil species have been described. Five species still survive; four of these are found along the Pacific coast of Asia. The American species, *Limulus polyphemus*, is common along the Atlantic coast from Nova Scotia to Florida. It lives in shallow water, preferring soft or sandy bottoms, and reaches a maximum length of nearly 2 ft (61 cm). Horseshoe crabs are considered living fossils; they resemble fossil TRILOBITES and eurypterids of the Paleozoic era. They are classified in the phylum ARTHROPODA, subphylum Chelicerata (with the spiders), class Merostomata.

horseshoe pitching, game played by two or more persons using horseshoes, the object being to throw the shoes so as to encircle a vertical iron peg that is 14 in. (35.6 cm) high. Regulation courts are at least 50 ft (15 m) long and 10 ft (3 m) wide; pitching distance is 40 ft (12.2 m) for men and 30 ft (9.1 m) for women. Shoes cannot exceed 7⅝ in. (19.4 cm) in length, 7¼ in. (18.4 cm) in width, or weigh more than 42 oz (1.18 kg). Quoit pitching is played on the same principle as horseshoe pitching except that pegs are 1 in. (2.54 cm) high, and pitching distance is 30 ft (9.1 m) for men and 20 ft (6.1 m) for women. The metal, circular rings, or quoits, with one rounded and one flat surface, differ in size and weight from area to area. In the United States they must exceed 3 lb (1.4 kg) in weight, and are generally 9 in. (22.9 cm) in diameter with a concentric bore 4 in. (10.2 cm) in diameter. Points in horseshoe pitching and in quoits are scored on a similar basis. Each ringer (horseshoe or quoit circling the peg) counts 3 points; each hobber, or leaner (horseshoe or quoit leaning against the peg), 2 points; and each horseshoe or quoit nearer the peg than that of the opponent, 1 point. A tally of 50 points wins at horseshoe pitching, while 21 points usually wins at quoits. At sea, the game of deck quoits is played, the quoits being made of rings of rope. Horseshoe and quoit pitching developed concurrently, and although their origins are obscure, they were both played in ancient Greece and Rome. The games were brought to England, where quoits attained great popularity. It is also popular in Ireland, Scotland, and Canada. Quoits was played in colonial America, but horseshoe pitching rapidly became more popular. Today it is a common form of recreation among the elderly. The National Horseshoe Pitchers Association of America (organized 1914) conducts annual world's championships for men and women. Jukskei, a variant of horseshoe and quoit pitching, is played in South Africa.

horsetail, any plant of the genus *Equisetum* [Lat.,= horse bristle], the single surviving genus of a large group (Equisetophyta) of primitive vascular plants. Like the ferns and club mosses, relatives of the living horsetails thrived in the Carboniferous period (when they contributed to coal deposits); the group as a whole is now nearly extinct. Horsetails have whorls of small scalelike leaves around a hollow, jointed stem that is green and carries on photosynthesis. They reproduce by an alternation of generations (see REPRODUCTION) similar to that of the ferns; in some horsetails, special nongreen shoots have at their tops strobili (see CONE) that bear the spores. Fossil evidence indicates that many extinct horsetails were treelike and attained a far greater size than do living types, although one tropical American species (*E. giganteum*) grows to more than 30 ft (9.1 m). Other species, mostly under 3 ft (91 cm), are found in all temperate and tropical regions except New Zealand and Australia; the common types of North America and Eurasia are *E. arvense* in drier habitats and *E. hyemale*, the scouring rush, in moist and wooded areas. The latter was formerly utilized for scouring purposes and it is still included in some scouring and abrasive powders; its typical coarse texture is due to the presence of silica. Other horsetails have been used for home remedies. Horsetails are classified in the division EQUISETOPHYTA, class Equisetopsida, order Equisetales.

Horsham (hôr'shəm), urban district (1971 pop. 26,378), West Sussex, SE England. It is a residential area and a market town with tanneries and mills. The Causeway, an old cobbled street, has Tudor and Stuart houses and a 13th-century parish church. "Field Place," birthplace of Shelley, is nearby. Christ's Hospital, a public school whose pupils included Charles Lamb and Samuel Taylor Coleridge, was moved from London to Horsham in 1902.

Horsley, Samuel, 1733-1806, English prelate, noted as a scientist. He became bishop of St. David's in 1788, of Rochester in 1793, and of St. Asaph in 1802. Science was the field in which he first became widely known. In 1767 he was elected a fellow of the Royal Society, of which he was for many years a secretary. Horsley completed an edition of Sir Isaac Newton's works in 1785, but he is particularly remembered for the controversy (1783-90) with Joseph Priestly concerning the doctrine of Christ's incarnation, in which Horsley defended the orthodox view. His books include mathematical and theological works. See biography by H. H. Jebb (1909).

Horsley, Sir Victor Alexander Haden, 1857-1916, English surgeon and neurologist. A specialist in surgery of the endocrine glands and the nervous system, he devised a noted operation for spinal-cord tumor. He wrote *Functions of the Marginal Convolutions* (1884) and, with others, *Experiments upon the Functions of the Cerebral Cortex* (1888) and *Alcohol and the Human Body* (1907). See studies by Stephen Paget (1919) and C. J. Bond (1939).

Horta, Victor, Baron, 1861-1947, Belgian architect. The Tassel House in Brussels (1892-93), his first mature work, was the earliest monument of art nouveau. It was excelled only by his later works, such as the Baron von Eetvelde house (1895) and the Maison du Peuple (1896-99), both in Brussels. The houses are especially significant for their interior architecture. The irregularly shaped rooms open freely onto one another at different levels. The plantlike design of the iron balustrade is echoed in the curving decorative lines of the mosaic floors, plaster walls, and other surfaces. The decorative beauty and undulating quality of his ironwork is found again in the Maison du Peuple, a great market and communal complex built for the city of Brussels. Even before World War I, Horta was officially acclaimed and given a peerage. He later reverted to a more traditional mode of architectural expression.

Horta (hôr'tə, Port. ôr'tə), town (1970 pop. 17,475), capital of Horta dist., in the AZORES, Portugal, on Fayal island. It has an excellent harbor with shipyards and is a military air base.

Horten (hôr'tən), town (1970 pop. 14,252), Vestfold co., SE Norway, a port on the Oslofjord (an arm of the Skagerrak); chartered 1907. It is a commercial and industrial center. Horten was the main Norwegian naval base until after World War II, when its facilities were moved to Bergen.

Hortensius, Quintus (kwĭn'təs hôrtĕn'shəs), 114 B.C.-50 B.C., Roman orator. He was the favorite lawyer of the patrician party and made his name as defense counsel in the bribery and embezzlement trials so frequent in Rome. At one of these trials he defended Caius VERRES, who was successfully prosecuted by Cicero, Hortensius' friendly rival. Hortensius was a master of the flowery Asian style of oratory. None of his speeches have survived.

Horthy de Nagybanya, Nicholas (hôr'tĭ də nŏ'dyəbä''nyŏ), Hung. *Nagybányai Horthy Miklós*, 1868-1957, Hungarian admiral and regent. He commanded the Austro-Hungarian fleet in World War I. After Béla KUN seized (1919) power in Hungary, the counterrevolutionary government put Horthy in command of its forces. When the Rumanian forces that had defeated Kun evacuated Budapest (Nov., 1919), Horthy entered it and in 1920 was made regent and head of the state. He checked two attempts (March and Oct., 1921) of former Emperor CHARLES I to regain his throne in Hungary—once by persuasion and once by armed force. Charles was then formally barred from the throne and exiled, and Horthy found himself regent of a kingless kingdom. A nationalist who was distinctly inclined toward the right, he guided Hungary through the years between the two world wars. After the suicide (1941) of the premier, Paul TELEKI, Hungary entered World War II as an ally of Germany. Despite Horthy's opposition, German troops occupied Hungary in March, 1944. When Russian troops entered Hungary, Horthy sent an armistice commission to Moscow and announced (Oct., 1944) the surrender of Hungary. The Germans immediately forced Horthy to countermand his order and resign. He was taken to Bavaria and later was freed by U.S. troops. After appearing as a witness at the Nuremberg war-crimes trial (1946), he settled (1949) in Portugal, where he died. His memoirs appeared in English in 1956. See his papers, ed. by Miklós Szinai and László Szücs (1965); J. Szemak, *Living History of Hungary* (1969).

horticulture [Lat. *hortus*=garden], science and art of gardening and of cultivating fruits, vegetables, flowers, and ornamental plants. Horticulture generally refers to small-scale gardening and agriculture to the growing of field crops, usually on a large scale, although the distinction is not always precise (for example, MARKET GARDENING could be classed either way). A horticultural variety of a plant is one produced under cultivation, as distinguished from the botanical species, the wild form which occurs in nature. Although many horticultural practices are very ancient (see BOTANY), comparatively recent knowledge of genetics, plant physiology, biochemistry, ecology, plant pathology, entomology, and soils, and the systematic application of such knowledge to practical use (e.g., in plant BREEDING), has expanded horticulture into an extremely complex science. Agencies such as the various bureaus of the Dept. of Agriculture, the state experimental stations, and the many agricultural colleges; organizations such as the American Horticultural Society and the various state horticultural societies and local granges and garden clubs; and the commercial flower-growing and experimental nurseries (see NURSERY)—all are engaged in developing, analyzing, systematizing, and disseminating improved horticultural practices for the benefit of both amateur and professional gardeners. See also GARDEN. See E. P. Christopher, *Introductory Horticulture* (1958); J B. Edmond et al., *Fundamentals of Horticulture* (3d ed. 1964).

Horton, Lester, 1906-53, American modern dancer, choreographer, and teacher, b. Indianapolis. Moving to California in 1928, Horton formed his own company in Los Angeles and also performed in theater, films, and nightclubs. He became one of the country's most influential choreographers, incorporating such diverse elements as American Indian dances and modern jazz into works of striking originality and drama. His influence is reflected in the work of his pupil Alvin AILEY. Other well-known dancers who worked in his company include Carmen deLavallade, Arthur MITCHELL, and James Truitte. Horton's company continued to perform after his death until 1960.

Horton, river, c.275 mi (440 km) long, rising in a lake N of Great Bear Lake, Mackenzie dist., Northwest Territories, Canada, and flowing NW to Franklin Bay, a part of the Beaufort Sea.

Horus (hôr'əs), in Egyptian religion, sky god, god of light and goodness. One of the most important of the Egyptian deities, Horus was the son of Osiris and Isis. In a famous myth he avenged the murder of his father by defeating Set, the god of evil and darkness. As Horus the Elder he was represented as a falcon-headed solar deity, who was perhaps originally a king or high priest of predynastic Egypt. As Horus the Child, called HARPOCRATES by the Greeks and Romans, he was represented as a small boy with a finger held to his lips.

Horyu-ji: see NARA, Japan.

Hosah (hō'sə). **1** Temple doorkeeper. 1 Chron. 16.38; 26.10,11,16. **2** Unidentified city of Asher. Joshua 19.29.

Hosanna (hōzăn'ə) [perhaps Heb.,=save now; cf. Ps. 118.25,26], reverent ejaculation, shouted by the crowd on Jesus' entrance to Jerusalem on Palm Sunday. Mat. 21.9,15; Mark 11.9,10; John 12.13. It is used in Christian worship, e.g., in the SANCTUS.

hose, covering for the legs and feet. In the Middle Ages the leg was bound from the ankle to the knee with hides or cloth and then cross-gartered with thongs or strips of cloth; later a loose trouser, bound at the ankle, was worn. As the lower legs of the trousers became more fitted, they were called breeches, and as the breeches were shortened to the knee, fitted cloths called hose (also known by the French *chausses*) were worn. By the 12th cent. feet were added to the hose. As breeches grew shorter, hose became longer; by c.1450 the hose reached the hips and were attached by points (laces) to the doublet. By c.1490 the breeches and hose formed one garment; thus tights were first known. Silk and velvet were used, as was wool, and color became extravagant. The tights were multicolored and often each leg was in a contrasting color. As the upper part of the hose became more decorated and puffed out, a separation occured (c.1500); the upper part was called trunk hose, and the leg coverings were for the first time called stockings and recognized as a separate accessory of dress. Knitted hose were first known in Scotland (1499); in France, Henry II is said to have worn (c.1559) the first knitted silk hose. Knitting thereafter became general, and machines came into use after 1589. Colored and embroidered hose were worn in the 17th cent., though white silk was the fashion. In the 17th cent. the decorative boot hose of the cavalier were of white linen and lace. Cotton came into use after 1680. Nylon, because of its strength and elasticity, became the leading hosiery fiber after World War II. In the 1960s women began to wear pantyhose, a one-piece garment that extends from waist to feet. As men's trousers grew longer their stockings grew shorter, and the word sock came into use. Women's hose, although hidden until modern times by their long skirts, have always been an important part of their costume. See M. N. Grass, *History of Hosiery* (1956).

Hosea (hōzē'ə, -zā'ə) or **Osee** (ōsē'), book of the Old Testament, 28th in the order of the Authorized Version, first of the books of the Minor Prophets. It consists of the career and sermons of the prophet Hosea, who preached against the sins of the northern kingdom of Israel in the 8th cent. B.C. The book opens with an account of Hosea's marriage to the prostitute Gomer and his apparent remarriage to her after she has deserted him, to show God's love for Israel, a wayward nation (1-3); then come sermons against the apostasy and moral decadence of the people, followed by the promise that after punishment will come redemption (4-14). It is not clear whether the marriage story represents Hosea's actual experience or is purely allegorical.

Hoseyn: see HUSAYN; HUSEIN; HUSSEIN.

Hoshaiah (hŏsh''ā'ə). **1** A leader at the dedication of the wall. Neh. 12.32. **2** Father of JAAZANIAH **2.**

Hoshama (hŏsh'əmə, hōshā'-), one of the house of David. 1 Chron. 3.18.

Hoshea (hōshē'ə). **1** See JOSHUA. **2** Died after 722 B.C., last king of Israel (c.730-722 B.C.). He succeeded Pekah, whom he murdered. He was a tributary of Assyria but made the fatal mistake of aligning himself with Egypt against his Assyrian overlord, who overran (c.728 B.C.) Israel and, after a long siege, took (722 B.C.) Samaria. This was the end of the northern kingdom. 2 Kings 15.30; 17. **3** Ruler of Ephraim. 1 Chron. 27.20. **4** One who sealed the Covenant. Neh. 10.23. **5** Hebrew name for the prophet HOSEA.

Ho-shen (hô-shŭn), 1750-99, Manchu official noted for symbolizing the widespread corruption of the Ch'ing dynasty of China during its decline. As a favorite of emperor CH'IEN LUNG, he rose, within two years, from bodyguard to grand councilor and minister of the imperial household. Later, while president of the boards of revenue and civil office, he amassed a great fortune through extortion. After Ch'ien Lung's death, the new emperor Chia Ch'ing seized his wealth and ordered him to commit suicide.

Hosius (hō'zhēəs), c.255–c.358, Spanish prelate, bishop of Córdoba, leader against ARIANISM. He presided at the Council of Nicaea (325) and is credited by Athanasius with having authored the Nicene formulary. He was exiled to Sirmium in the Arian reaction and was forced to sign a semi-Arian formula. He renounced it before his death.

hospital, institution for the care of the sick, maintained by private endowment or public funds or both. General hospitals minister to all types of illness, while special hospitals are concerned with only one disease or group of diseases. Many hospitals are maintained solely for the treatment of military personnel and veterans. Once a pesthouse for the care of the indigent and the friendless, with a quality of treatment and nursing from which few emerged alive, the hospital has flourished with the progress of medicine and surgery. Toward the end of the 19th cent. hospital care was revolutionized by the discovery of anesthesia, improvement in sanitation, establishment of hospital nursing schools, and other advances. Hospitals in large cities have become huge medical centers equipped not only to treat the ill but also to further the education of the medical staff, train a nursing staff, perform vital research into the cause and cure of disease, and help the patient with convalescent and social problems.

Hospitalers: see KNIGHTS HOSPITALERS.

Host [Lat.,=sacrificial victim], in Roman Catholic practice, consecrated wafer of the EUCHARIST. The bread used is pure white and unleavened, baked in small disks. The Hosts not consumed at MASS are set aside especially for the viaticum, for the sick, and for adoration, as at BENEDICTION.

hostage, person held by another as a guarantee that certain actions or promises will be carried out. During periods of internal turmoil insurgents often seize hostages. Thus, in the early 1970s, dissident political groups in South America kidnapped prominent nationals and foreign diplomats and held them as hostages until the government met certain demands, such as release of political prisoners. Hostages are often taken among civilians in an occupied country in order to ensure the delivery of requisitions, to discourage hostile acts, or to take reprisals for hostile acts committed by unknown persons. This has been done in almost every war and was countenanced by international custom as long as hostages were not cruelly treated or made to pay for crimes committed by others. In World War II thousands of hostages were executed throughout Europe by the German authorities in an attempt to crush resistance movements. Because these massacres went beyond the then-accepted limits, some of those responsible were later sentenced as war criminals. A Geneva Convention of 1949 forbade entirely the taking of civilian hostages. In civil wars the taking of hostages is quite frequent. One victim of the practice was Georges Darboy, archbishop of Paris, executed during the uprising of the Commune of Paris in 1871. Early military custom also regulated the behavior and treatment of hostages; at that time a hostage was a person who had been delivered to an authority as a token of good faith. Such a person was usually a high-ranking member of his society and was to be treated according to his rank and as an honored guest. However, he might be imprisoned or even executed if the agreement guaranteed by his person was broken, although execution was considered an extreme measure. The code of honor was often very strictly observed in feudal times. Thus, during the Hundred Years War when the hostages that had been sent to England in exchange for the release of JOHN II of France escaped, King John felt bound to return to captivity in England. Until the 18th cent., hostages were often exchanged when treaties were concluded to guarantee that the terms of the treaties would be observed.

Hostos, Eugenio María de (āo͞ohä'nyō mārē'ä dā ō'stōs), 1839–1903, Latin American philosopher, sociologist, writer, and political and educational reformer, b. Puerto Rico, educated in Spain. He advocated a federation of the Antilles, including Puerto Rico, Cuba, and the Dominican Republic, and devoted his life to seeking the political independence of Cuba and Puerto Rico. In Santo Domingo (1879–88) he founded the first normal school and introduced advanced teaching methods. As professor in the Univ. of Chile, he was instrumental in having women admitted. He is widely known throughout Latin America as a publicist of civic reforms, as a rationalist in ethics who believed that "to be civilized and to be moral is the same thing," and as a writer of sober, graceful, and didactic prose. He wrote approximately 50 volumes, among which are *La peregrinación de Bayoán* (1863), a political novel; *Moral social* (1888); *Lecciones de derecho constitucional* (1887); and a superb essay, *Hamlet* (1873). See study by E. C. de Hostos (tr. 1954).

hotbed, low, glass-covered frame structure for starting tender plants. It differs from a COLD FRAME only in that the soil is heated—either artificially as by underground electric wiring or steampipes, or naturally with stable manure. The manure is first turned over daily until the initial period of strong fermentation is over; it is then mixed with dead leaves or straw, placed in the bottom of the hotbed frame, and covered with an appropriate amount of soil. Heat is produced by the decaying organic matter. Proper ventilation is important, as is thermostatic control of artificially heated hotbeds. Tomatoes, cucumbers, celery, and other crops can be grown in hotbeds in the spring. A heated frame (i.e., an artificially heated cold frame) can be used with a hotbed; this reduces the necessity of covering the frame with burlap or other insulation at night and during cold spells.

hotel [Fr., from O.Fr. (original of Eng. *hostel*), from Latin (original of Eng. *hospital*),=guest place], name applied since the late 17th cent. to an establishment supplying both food and lodging to the public (see INN). In common law of England and America, the hotelkeeper is a public servant and must receive all proper persons. The first American hotels, successors to the early inns, differed from their European prototypes by charging a fixed fee for food and lodging (American plan). For many years $1.00 per day was the accepted price. Fraunces Tavern (1762; see under FRAUNCES, SAMUEL) and the City Hotel (1793) were fashionable resorts of early New York City. The Tremont House, in Boston (1829), for years considered the most imposing hotel in the United States, was rivaled by the Astor, built in New York in 1836. The modern hotel in America dates from the early days of railroad travel, when the modest hostelry, prepared to entertain small groups of occasional guests, was forced to become a more commodious and efficient institution to accommodate the great number of traveling salesmen. Technical progress in the late 19th cent. permitted the construction of large, fireproof hotels. Hotels may be classed as transient, residential, or resort hotels; and, according to their clientele, as commercial, workers', women's, or family hotels. Semicommercial hotels with club features are maintained by organizations such as the YMCA. With the growth of suburban centers and the increase of travel by automobile, a form of transient hotel, called a MOTEL, became popular. See Herbert Weisskamp, *Hotels* (1968).

Hôtel de Bourgogne (ōtĕl' də bo͞orgô'nyə), first theater in Paris. It was built in 1548 by the Confraternity of the Passion, the Paris actors' monopoly. Its first days were marred by a ban on the presentation of religious dramas. The actors carried on in spite of their restricted repertory, which consisted of farces and secular plays. The audiences dwindled, and the players were forced to lease the theater to traveling companies until 1610, when the theater's first permanent company, called the King's Players, was established by Valleran-Lecomte (fl. 1590–1613). In 1634 another company, whose members included the tragedian Montdory and the comedian Jodelet, was established at the Théâtre du Marias, and competition between the two companies arose. However, after the retirement of Montdory, the Bourgogne reigned supreme, with actors such as Bellerose (c.1600–1670), Floridor (1608–72), and Montfleury (1600–67) setting the style of the day. The arrival in 1658 of MOLIÈRE interrupted this reign. The Théâtre du Marais combined with the Molière faction to challenge the Bourgogne hegemony. In 1680, however, the companies merged to form the COMÉDIE FRANÇAISE.

Hotham (hō'thăm), descendant of Asher. 1 Chron. 7.32.

Hothan (hō'thăn), father of two of David's guard. 1 Chron. 11.44.

Hothir (hō'thĭr), leader of musicians. 1 Chron. 25.4.

hothouse: see GREENHOUSE.

Ho-t'ien (hô-tyĕn) or **Khotan** (kō'tän'), town and oasis (1958 est. pop. 50,000), SW Sinkiang Uigur Autonomous Region, China, near the headstream of the Ho-t'ien River. It is the center of an area growing silk and cotton. Textiles, carpets, and felt goods are manufactured. On the southern part of the Silk Road, Ho-t'ien was an early center for the spread of Buddhism from India into China. It fell to the Arabs in the 8th cent., and soon after the town grew wealthy on the proceeds of the caravan trade that traveled the route between China and the West. Its prosperity ended with the conquest of Ho-t'ien by Jenghiz Khan. After many political changes the region became (1878) permanently part of China. Ho-t'ien is connected by road with Kashgar and Wu-lu-mu-ch'i (Urumchi).

Hotin: see KHOTIN, USSR.

Hotman, François (fräNswä' ôtmäN), 1524–90, French jurist. Converted (1547) to Protestantism and implicated (1560) in the conspiracy of Amboise (see AMBOISE, CONSPIRACY OF), he spent large parts of his life in Switzerland. In his most influential work, *Franco-Gallia* (1573), he was among the first to point out the Germanic origin of the early Frankish institutions, and on that basis he advocated an elective monarchy for France. See studies by Beatrice Reynolds (1931, repr. 1968) and D. R. Kelley (1973).

hot spring, natural discharge of groundwater having an elevated temperature. Most hot springs result from the emergence of groundwater that has passed through or near recently formed, hot, igneous rocks. Iceland, Yellowstone Park in the United States, and North Island of New Zealand are noted for their hot springs. In recent years the depletion of fossil fuels has resulted in a renewed interest in utilizing the energy contained in hot springs. This type of geothermal energy is already being utilized in California, Italy, and Iceland. See ENERGY, SOURCES OF.

Hot Springs, city (1970 pop. 35,631), seat of Garland co., W central Ark.; settled 1807, inc. 1876. The city nearly surrounds Hot Springs National Park. Hot mineral springs in the park have made the city a famous health resort. Lumber and metal and electrical products are produced in Hot Springs. Situated in the Ouachita Mts., the city is at the center of the lake system of the Ouachita River. The area was discovered by the Spanish explorer Hernando De Soto in 1541. The properties of the waters were investigated in 1804 under the authorization of President Thomas Jefferson. The city has a zoo that trains performing animals.

Hot Springs National Park, 3,535 acres (1,431 hectares), W central Ark.; est. 1921; nearly surrounded by the city of Hot Springs. Long used by the Indians for medicinal purposes, and visited by Spanish explorer Hernando De Soto in 1541, the springs became a Federal Reservation in 1832. More than a million gallons of water a day, with an average temperature of 143°F (62°C), flow from 47 springs. The National Park Service collects, cools, and supplies water to bathhouses in and out of the park.

Hotspur: see PERCY, SIR HENRY.

Hottentot bread: see YAM.

Hottentots: see KHOIKHOI.

Hötzendorf, Franz Conrad von: see CONRAD VON HÖTZENDORF, FRANZ.

Houbraken, Arnold (är'nōlt hou'brä"kən), 1660–1719, Dutch painter, etcher, and author of *The Great Theatre of Dutch Painters* (3 vol., 1718–21), containing important biographies. His son **Jacobus Houbraken,** 1698–1780, a well-known engraver, worked chiefly in Amsterdam, executing over 500 portraits and book illustrations including those for his father's volumes.

Houdin, Jean Eugène Robert (zhäN özhĕn' rōbĕr' o͞odăN'), 1805–71, French conjurer and magician. He was celebrated for his optical illusions and mechanical devices and for his attributing his "magic" to natural instead of supernatural means. Houdin was the first to use electromagnetism for his effects. He wrote an autobiography (1857) and *Secrets of Prestidigitation and Magic* (1868). Harry HOUDINI, who named himself for Houdin, wrote *The Unmasking of Robert-Houdin* (1908). See H. R. Evans, *The Master of Modern Magic* (1932).

Houdini, Harry (ho͞odē'nē), 1874–1926, American magician and writer, b. Appleton, Wis. His real name was Erich Weiss, and he took his stage name after the French magician HOUDIN. He was world-famed for his escapes from bonds of every sort—locks, handcuffs, straitjackets, and sealed chests under water. Houdini performed in silent films and was also noted for his exposure of fraudulent spiritualistic mediums and their phenomena. He left to the Library of Congress his library of magic, one of the most complete and valuable in the world. Among his writings are *The Unmasking of Robert-Houdin* (1908), *Miracle Mongers and Their Methods* (1920), and *A Magician among the Spirits* (1924). See *Houdini's Magic* (ed. from his notebooks, 1932); biographies by Harold Kellock (1928) and W. L. Gresham (1959); W. B. Gibson, *Houdini's Escapes* (1930).

Houdon, Jean-Antoine (zhäN-äNtwän' o͞odôN'), 1741–1828, French neoclassical sculptor. He studied with Michel Ange Slodtz, Lemoyne, and Pigalle, took the Prix de Rome at the age of 20, and spent four years in Italy. Many of his later works reveal his study of antique form, e.g., the marble *Diana* (Leningrad) and *The Bather* (Metropolitan Mus.). He quickly became famous in Paris for portrait sculpture and received commissions from all over the world. In 1785 he visited the United States briefly and stayed at Mt. Vernon while making studies for his statue of Washington (capitol, Richmond, Va.). He made portrait busts of Jefferson, Franklin, Diderot, Rousseau, John Paul Jones, Lafayette, Mirabeau, Buffon, and Prince Henry of Prussia, and a full-length statue of Voltaire (Comédie Française). He succeeded not only in creating sculptural documents of his time, but in developing a type of portraiture remarkable for its elegance, measured realism, and depiction of individuality. Houdon exerted a strong influence over European and American sculptors for several generations.

Hough, George Washington, 1836–1909, American astronomer, b. Montgomery co., N.Y., grad. Union College, 1856. He discovered 627 double stars and made systematic studies of the surface of Jupiter. Many instruments for use in astronomy, meteorology, and physics were designed and constructed by him. From 1862 to 1874, Hough was director of Dudley Observatory, Albany, N.Y. In 1879 he was appointed professor of astronomy at the Univ. of Chicago and director of Dearborn Observatory; when the observatory was removed to Evanston, Ill., he introduced original plans for the dome and electric control for the telescope.

Houghton, Richard Monckton Milnes, 1st Baron, 1809–85, English author. Throughout much of his life he was an active member of Parliament. He was among the first to recognize the genius of Keats and in 1848 published his *Life, Letters, and Literary Remains of John Keats.* In addition he secured a pension for Tennyson and widely proclaimed Swinburne's genius. His poetical works include *Poems of Many Years* (1838) and *Palm Leaves* (1844).

Houghton, William Stanley, 1881–1913, English dramatist. He was (1907–12) a critic for the Manchester *Guardian.* His plays, greatly influenced by Ibsen, include *The Dear Departed* (1908), *The Younger Generation* (1910), and his best work, *Hindle Wakes* (1912). He was one of the best of a group of realistic playwrights often called the Manchester school.

Houghton-le-Spring (hō'tən-lə-sprĭng, hou'-), urban district (1971 pop. 32,666), Durham, NE England. It is a market town, with coal mining as the chief industry. In 1974, Houghton-le-Spring became part of the new metropolitan county of Tyne and Wear.

Hougue, La: see HOGUE, LA.

Houma (hō'mə), city (pop. 30,922), seat of Terrebonne parish, SE La.; inc. 1848. Houma is a port on the Intracoastal Waterway. The processing of seafood, sugarcane, and oil are the leading industries. The city was founded in 1834 and has many fine antebellum buildings. South Louisiana Trade School is there; nearby is a U.S. sugarcane experiment station.

hound, classification used by breeders and kennel clubs to designate dogs bred to hunt animals. Most of the dogs in this group hunt by scent, their quarry ranging from such large game as bear or elk to small game and vermin; ground scenters trail slowly with the head low, and air scenters hunt with head breast-high. Also classified as hounds are several long-legged breeds that hunt mainly by sight. A third variety, called treeing hounds, also track by scent; these dogs pursue tree-climbing animals, such as raccoons and opossums. Many scent hounds have a coat characteristically patterned in "hound colors": black, white, and tan. The following 19 hound breeds are registered with the American Kennel Club: AFGHAN HOUND, AMERICAN FOXHOUND, BASENJI, BASSET HOUND, BEAGLE, BLOODHOUND, BORZOI, BLACK-AND-TAN COONHOUND, DACHSHUND, ENGLISH FOXHOUND, GREYHOUND, HARRIER, IRISH WOLFHOUND, NORWEGIAN ELKHOUND, OTTER HOUND, RHODESIAN RIDGEBACK, SCOTTISH DEERHOUND, SALUKI, and WHIPPET.

Hounslow, borough (1971 pop. 206,182) of Greater London, SE England, on the Thames River. Hounslow was created in 1965 by the merger of the municipal boroughs of Heston and Isleworth and of Brentford and Chiswick with the urban district of Feltham. Hounslow's manufactures include razor blades, soap, tires, biscuits, precision instruments, pharmaceuticals, and heating equipment. There were prehistoric and Roman settlements in the area. In 1016, Edmund Ironside defeated the Danes at Brentford. The Hounslow district of Heston and Isleworth was the site of the first stop on an important coach route to Southampton and Bath. The former Hounslow Heath, the location of a Roman camp, was a refuge for highwaymen; the area is now a military installation. The artist William Hogarth is buried in Chiswick. His house is open to the public.

Houphouët-Boigny, Félix (fālĕks' o͞ofwä'-bwä'-nyə), 1905–, African political leader, president (1960–) of the republic of the Ivory Coast. A descendant of wealthy Baoule chieftains, he practiced medicine (1925–40) in the Ivory Coast and then entered government service. At the Bamako Conference (1946), which was attended by most French African leaders, he was elected chairman of the newly formed African Democratic Rally, subsequently a powerful force in African politics. As minister delegate (1956–57), he was associated with the formulation of French colonial policy. In 1958 the Ivory Coast became a self-governing republic, with Houphouët-Boigny as president of the constituent assembly. He became prime minister in 1959 and president of the republic in 1960. He was reelected to five-year terms in 1965 and 1970.

hour angle, in astronomy, a coordinate in the EQUATORIAL COORDINATE SYSTEM. The hour angle of a celestial body is the angular distance, expressed in hours, minutes, and seconds (one hour equals 15 degrees), measured westward along the celestial equator from the observer's celestial meridian to the HOUR CIRCLE of the object being located. The hour angle is used in measuring astronomical time; local SIDEREAL TIME is equal to the hour angle of the vernal equinox.

hour circle, in astronomy, a secondary axis in the EQUATORIAL COORDINATE SYSTEM. The hour circle of a celestial body is the great circle on the CELESTIAL SPHERE that passes through both the body and the north celestial pole. A star's hour circle is used in determining its RIGHT ASCENSION and DECLINATION.

hourglass, glass instrument for measuring time, usually consisting of two bulbs united by a narrow neck. One bulb is filled with fine sand that runs through the neck into the other bulb in an hour's time. The date of its invention is unknown, but it was in use in ancient times. Similar devices for marking shorter periods of time, e.g., three-minute sandglasses for timing the cooking of eggs, are still used occasionally.

houri (ho͞o'rē, hou'-) [from Arabic, = black-eyed], one of the beautiful maidens said by some Muslims to dwell in paradise for the enjoyment of the faithful. The passages in the Koran detailing the physical delights of heaven are considered by many Muslim critics as allegorical.

hours of labor: see LABOR, HOURS OF.

Housatonic (ho͞osətŏn'ĭk), river rising in the Berkshires, W Mass., and flowing generally south c.130 mi (210 km) through W Connecticut to Long Island Sound at Stratford. The river has long been used as a source of power.

House, Edward Mandell, 1858–1938, American political figure, adviser to President Wilson, b. Houston, Texas. Active in Texas politics, he was (1882–92) campaign manager and adviser to Gov. James Hogg and his successors. He was known as "Colonel" House because of a Texas state office he held. He met Woodrow Wilson in 1911 and helped him secure (1912) the Democratic presidential nomination. After Wilson's election House became the President's closest adviser. He often served as the President's liaison with members of the administration and important men in the country. Greatly interested in foreign affairs, he was sent to Europe in 1914 in an attempt to prevent the outbreak of war and again in 1915 to propose a peace conference. After U.S. entry into World War I, he was U.S. representative at the conference for coordinating Allied activities. House also gathered data for the peace conference, was American delegate to negotiate the armistice, and was a member of the U.S. peace commission. He helped to draft the Treaty of Versailles and the Covenant of the League of Nations. More conciliatory and realistic than Wilson at the peace conference, his friendship with Wilson ended in 1919 because of conflict on the conduct of the negotiations. House and Charles Seymour edited the documentary *What Really Happened at Paris* (1921). Some of his papers, selected and edited by Seymour as *The Intimate Papers of Colonel House* (2 vol., 1926–28), are a valuable historical source. See Arthur D. Howden Smith, *The Real Colonel House* (1918) and *Mr. House of Texas* (1940); Sir Andrew MacPhail, *Three Persons* (1929); Alexander L. George and Juliette George, *Woodrow Wilson and Colonel House* (1956, repr. 1964).

housefly, common name of the FLY *Musca domestica,* found in most parts of the world. The housefly, a scavenger, does not bite living animals but is dangerous because it carries bacteria and protozoans that cause many serious diseases, e.g., TYPHOID FEVER, CHOLERA, and DYSENTERY. The housefly feeds by depositing a drop of digestive liquid on its food, which may be garbage, excrement, or other filth. Although most of the liquid drop is sucked back again through the insect's tubelike lower lip, or labium, a residue remains that may contain disease-causing organisms from previous meals. Disease is also transmitted on the fly's sticky foot pads and hairy body. Each female lays from 100 to 200 eggs in the garbage or manure on which the white larvae feed. With favorable temperatures, one generation or more per month may be produced. METAMORPHOSIS is complete, i.e., development is in four stages. The housefly is classified in the phylum ARTHROPODA, class Insecta, order Diptera, family Muscidae. For methods of control see bulletins of the U.S. Dept. of Agriculture.

House of Commons: see PARLIAMENT.

House of David, a religious colony founded in 1903 at Benton Harbor, Mich., by Benjamin Purnell. The colony was established in anticipation of the imminent establishment of the kingdom of God on earth and was run on a communistic basis. In the 1920s and 30s it was nationally known for its bearded baseball team. In the late 1960s there were about 70 members.

House of Lords: see PARLIAMENT.

House of Parliament: see WESTMINSTER PALACE.

House of Representatives: see CONGRESS OF THE UNITED STATES.

house plants, varied group of plants grown indoors and requiring no special treatment other than ordinary care. They are usually grown singly in pots, but can also be grouped and planted together in dish gardens and terrariums. Some are cultivated for their flowers, such as geraniums and African violets, while others, such as philodendron and sansevieria (snake plant), are grown for their decorative foliage. Growing house plants successfully can be greatly facilitated by maintaining a cool temperature and raising the atmospheric moisture either by the use of humidifiers or simply by placing evaporating pans on radiators. See Montague Free, *All about House Plants* (1947); E. D. Ballard, *Garden in Your House* (rev. ed. 1971); C. M. Fitch, *The Complete Book of Houseplants* (1972); George Taloumis, *House Plants for Five Exposures* (1973).

house sparrow: see ENGLISH SPARROW.

housing, in general, living accommodations available for the inhabitants of a community. Throughout the 19th cent., with the advent of the Industrial Revolution, housing as a problem worsened as urban populations expanded. The crowding of cities and factory towns by workers led not only to severe housing shortages but also to the deterioration of existing housing and the growth of slums. The problem was aggravated by the erection of substandard housing for workers and by speculators seeking high profits. Inadequate housing for the increasing urban population led, in the mid-19th cent. in Great Britain, to the development of a reform movement. Humanitarian and philanthropic groups first took up the cause of workers' housing. The Society for Improving the Dwellings of the Labouring Classes was established in 1845 and was followed by similar organizations dedicated to the building of low-rent dwellings. Ultimately, growing public opinion encouraged Parliament to pass (1851) the Shaftesbury Acts (the Labouring Classes Lodging Houses Acts). They provided for the construction of lodging houses according to certain minimum standards. Slum clearance began with the Torrens Act of 1868, which provided for the demolition or improvement of unsanitary dwellings. After the turn of the century much was done in Great Britain toward eliminating slums and constructing model tenements; the GARDEN CITY was one solution offered to the housing problem. A major step forward was taken with the passage of the first Housing and Town Planning Act in 1909; it granted local governments the power to oversee housing development. Other actions included legislation providing for low-rent dwellings and a continuing program of slum clearance. The large-scale destruction of housing during World War II resulted in severe shortages after 1945, and all efforts in the housing area were directed toward redressing that problem. Between 1945 and 1970 about 7 million new dwellings were built in

Great Britain. In the United States, housing problems—in particular the growth of slums—became extremely acute during the 19th cent. in the cities of the eastern seaboard and in the larger Midwestern cities. A leading cause was the heavy immigration from Europe that began in the middle of the 19th cent. and reached a peak at the turn of the century. However, until the 1930s, with the exception of the World War I period, governmental action to regulate housing construction was confined almost exclusively to local regulatory legislation. The first housing law was the New York City tenement house law of 1867. Its requirements were meager, but in 1879 a revised law was passed prohibiting windowless rooms. The findings of a tenement house commission resulted in a new law in 1901, requiring better provision for light and ventilation, fire protection, and sanitation. Most U.S. city and state housing laws in the following years were based on those of New York City. There had been some tenements in U.S. cities put up by philanthropists, but until World War I there was no government housing in the United States. Then temporary dwellings were put up for defense workers. In 1918 the U.S. Housing Corporation was established to guide the liquidation of the government's housing; it operated until 1942. The U.S. government lapsed into almost complete inaction with regard to building housing until the advent of the New Deal. The National Housing Act (1934) created the Federal Housing Administration (FHA) to undertake a nationwide system of home loan insurance. It also established, by means of mortgage insurance regulation, minimum standards for construction, for design, and for location. Low-cost housing projects, including farm-family homes sponsored by the Resettlement Administration, were, by the Wagner-Steagall Act (1937), coordinated under the U.S. Housing Authority, which financed urban low-rent and slum clearance developments by making loans at low interest rates. Such loans were later extended to rural housing. When the defense program in World War II brought about acute housing shortages, the Lanham Act (1940) authorized Federal operation of a large-scale housing program for defense workers, who also benefited by amended FHA rules (1941–42). To unify the many Federal housing agencies, President Franklin Delano Roosevelt created (1942) the National Housing Agency, which included the Federal Public Housing Authority, the Federal Home Loan Bank Administration, and the FHA. But the total wartime construction of permanent homes was far below peacetime levels, while the demand for housing rose sharply with a high marriage rate, migration from farms to cities, greater buying power, and later the return of veterans. Complicated by building codes, union practices, and labor and material shortages, the housing deficiency remained serious after the war, and Federal rent controls continued for some time. A national housing policy began to emerge when Congress passed the Housing Act of 1949; it directed action toward easing the housing shortage and eliminating slums, and it set forth the goal of a decent home for every family. The concept of urban renewal was developed in the Housing Act of 1954, which required local authorities to enforce a set of minimum standards with regard to slums. Federal aid for housing was further expanded with the Housing and Urban Development Act of 1965, which created a separate cabinet-level Dept. of Housing and Urban Development. A new focus was established by the government in 1966 with the passage of the Demonstration Cities and Metropolitan Development Act (the Model Cities Act); the act coordinated Federal, state, and local assistance to selected low-income areas of cities with reference to economic, social, and housing problems. The countries of continental Europe, as a result of the damages caused by World War II, faced housing shortages even more acute than those in Great Britain and the United States. Most postwar efforts were directed at rebuilding major industries, and house construction suffered as a result. However, once the economies were stable, attention turned to housing; the Soviet Union led in rate of construction, followed by Sweden and West Germany. Western Europe has led Eastern Europe in construction. In most countries of Africa, Asia, and Latin America, urban housing shortages are today particularly severe as a result of population increases and the migration from rural areas to cities. Since population growth in Latin America is the highest in the world, the housing problem there is the greatest. The problem is aggravated by the fact that the limited resources of governments engaged in the process of economic development have prevented their undertaking large-scale housing programs. See Peter Self, *Cities in Flood, Problems of Urban Growth* (1957); Paul Wendt, *Housing Policy: Search for Solutions, a Comparison of the United Kingdom, Sweden, West Germany, and the United States since World War II* (1962); Charles Abrams, *Housing in the Modern World* (1964); Horacio Caminos, *Urban Dwelling Environments* (1969); J. B. Cullingworth, *Housing and Labour Mobility* (1969); R. W. Bolling, *Housing Development and Urban Planning* (1970); Moshe Safdie, *Beyond Habitat* (1970); Robert Goodman, *After the Planners* (1971); R. J. Johnston, *Urban Residential Patterns* (1971); P. W. Martin, *The Ill-Housed* (1971); Martin Pawley, *Architecture versus Housing* (1971); United Nations Report, *Social Programming of Housing in Urban Areas* (1971); D. R. Mandelstam and Roger Montgomery, *Housing in America* (1973).

Housing and Urban Development, U.S. Department of, established 1965 to administer programs that provide assistance for housing and community development. It assists the President in achieving maximum coordination of the various Federal activities that have a major effect upon urban community, suburban, or metropolitan development. The department assists in finding solutions to the problems of housing and urban development through state, county, town, village, or other local or private action, including the promotion of interstate, regional, and metropolitan cooperation. It encourages the maximum participation of the private home-building and mortgage-lending industries in housing, urban development, and the national economy. The secretary of the department is a member of the President's cabinet. Robert Weaver, the department's first head, was also the first black cabinet member in U.S. history.

Housman, A. E. (Alfred Edward Housman), 1859–1936, English poet and scholar, whose verse exerted a strong influence on later poets. He left Oxford without a degree because he had failed his final examinations. Ever afterward he was a coldly reserved and aloof man, a recluse seemingly without emotional life. After serving for 10 years in the civil service, he became in 1892 a professor of Latin at University College, London, and in 1911 professor of Latin at Cambridge and fellow of Trinity College. Housman proved to be one of the finest classical scholars of his time. He produced a monumental edition of Manilius (5 vol., 1903–30), edited Juvenal (1905) and Lucan (1926), and wrote valuable classical studies. But it is as a poet that he is best known, although only two small volumes appeared during his lifetime, *A Shropshire Lad* (1896) and *Last Poems* (1922). His verse is noted for its economy of words and directness of statement, pictures of the English countryside, and the fusion of humor and pathos. The passing of youth and the inevitability of death is his most characteristic theme. His best-known poems include "When I Was One-and-twenty," "With Rue My Heart·Is Laden," "To an Athlete Dying Young," and "Far in a Western Brookland." His essay *The Name and Nature of Poetry* (1933) was originally given as a lecture at Cambridge. See his complete poems (ed. by T. B. Haber, with an introduction by Basil Davenport, 1959); biography by Grant Richards (1942, repr. 1973); studies by Norman Marlow (1958), Tom B. Haber (1967), and A. S. Sydenham (1936, repr. 1973).

Housman, Laurence, 1865–1959, English author; brother of A. E. Housman. He achieved success as the anonymous author of *An Englishwoman's Love Letters* (1900). Best known as a dramatist, he wrote *Little Plays of St. Francis* (1922–35) and *Palace Plays* (1930–33). His most famous play, *Victoria Regina* (1934), adapted from his *Palace Plays,* was banned from the English stage for representing living members of the royal family, but an American production with Helen Hayes in 1935 was highly successful.

Houssay, Bernardo Alberto (bärnär'dō älbār'tō ou'sī), 1887–1971, Argentine physiologist, b. Buenos Aires. He was a child prodigy, entering college at the age of 9 and becoming a hospital intern at 13. With C. F. and G. T. Cori he was awarded the 1947 Nobel Prize in Physiology and Medicine for his work on the functions of the pituitary gland. He demonstrated that a hormone secreted by the pituitary prevented metabolism of sugar and that injections of pituitary extract induced symptoms of diabetes. He was a founder and director of the Institute of Biology and Experimental Medicine in Buenos Aires. In 1949 he came to the United States as a special research fellow at the National Institute of Health.

Houston, David Franklin (hyōō'stən), 1866–1940, American cabinet officer and educator, b. Monroe, N.C., grad. South Carolina College, 1887, M.A. Harvard, 1892. He taught political science at the Univ. of Texas (1894–1902) and was later president of the Agricultural and Mechanical College of Texas (1902–5), president of the Univ. of Texas (1905–8), and chancellor of Washington Univ. in St. Louis (1908–16). He served in Woodrow Wilson's cabinent first as Secretary of Agriculture (1913–20), then as Secretary of the Treasury (1920–21). He later entered business in New York City. See his *Eight Years with Wilson's Cabinet* (1926).

Houston, Samuel, 1793–1863, American frontier hero and statesman of Texas, b. near Lexington, Va. He moved (c.1806) with his family to Tennessee and lived much of his youth with the Cherokee Indians, by whom he was adopted. Serving (1814) in the Creek campaign under Andrew Jackson, he was seriously wounded (1814) while fighting bravely at the battle of Horseshoe Bend. He returned to Tennessee, was admitted (1818) to the bar, practiced law in Lebanon, Tenn., and held many state offices. Tall, vigorous, and dramatic in speech and in action, Houston, like Jackson, captured the popular imagination. He was sent (1823, 1825) to the U.S. Congress as a Democrat. Elected (1827) governor of Tennessee, Houston seemed in 1829 to have a bright political future, with his reelection almost assured and the Democrats strengthening themselves in national politics. Suddenly, however, his wife, Eliza Allen Houston, left him, and he immediately resigned (1829) his governorship. He rejoined the Cherokee in what is now Oklahoma. There he lived with them as government post trader and as adviser, drinking heavily during much of this period. Then (1833) he moved on through Arkansas to Texas. He had little to do with the preliminaries of the Texas Revolution, although he watched the struggle closely. He was a member of the convention that set up a provisional government in Texas and of the convention (1836) that declared Texas independent. He was made commander in chief of the revolutionary troops. After the surrender of the Alamo (March, 1836), Houston's army persistently retreated before the numerically superior forces of SANTA ANNA, and there was panic among Texas settlers and much criticism of Houston. He brilliantly redeemed himself at the battle of SAN JACINTO (April 21, 1836), when by a surprise attack he decisively defeated the Mexicans and captured Santa Anna himself. Later that year Houston was elected the first president of the new republic of Texas. The independence of Texas was recognized by the United States and other countries. Replaced (1838) by Mirabeau LAMAR, Houston served as president again from 1841 to 1844, but during these years he was harassed by financial problems and by border troubles. Texas was admitted to the Union in 1845, and Houston was one of the first to represent his state in the U.S. Senate. After serving 14 years in the Senate, he was defeated because of his uncompromising Unionism. Challenging his opponents and drawing upon his popularity, Houston was elected (1859) governor of Texas. The aged statesman preached preservation of the U.S. Constitution in the face of secession, but the tide was against him. After the people of Texas voted (Feb., 1861) to secede from the Union, Houston refused to join the Confederacy and was removed (March, 1861) from the governorship. He accepted the verdict, refused help from the North to defend his prerogative, and retired. See his writings (ed. by A. W. Williams and E. C. Barker, 8 vol., 1938–43); biographies by Marquis James (1929, repr. 1971), Llerena Friend (1954, repr. 1969), and M. K. Wisehart (1962).

Houston, city (1970 pop. 1,232,802), seat of Harris co., SE Texas, a deepwater port on the Houston Ship Channel; inc. 1837. The sixth largest city in the nation and the largest in the entire South and Southwest, Houston is a port of entry; a great industrial, commercial, and financial hub; one of the world's major oil centers; and the third busiest tonnage-handling port in the United States (after New York and New Orleans). Houston has numerous space and science research firms; electronics plants; giant oil refineries; one of the world's greatest concentrations of petrochemical works; steel mills; shipyards; grain elevators; breweries; meat-packing houses; paper, rice, and cotton mills; and factories manufacturing and assembling a great variety of products. Harrisburg (now part of Houston) was settled in 1823, and Houston itself, founded in 1836 by J. K. and A. C. Allen and named for Sam Houston, was promoted as a rival to Harrisburg and soon served (1837–39) as capital of the Texas republic. In the course of the 19th cent. Houston grew from a muddy town on Buffalo Bayou to a prosperous railroad center. However, its phenomenal expansion came after the digging (1912-14) of a ship channel on Buffalo Bayou and Galveston Bay, linking it to the Gulf and making it a deepwater port. The development of the coastal oil fields poured quick wealth into the city; the natural gas, sulfur, salt, and limestone deposits also in the area laid the basis for its great chemical production; shipbuilding during World War II spurred further growth; and the establishment (1961) nearby of the National Aeronautics and Space Administration's Manned Spacecraft Center (renamed the Lyndon B. Johnson Space Center in 1973) brought the aerospace industry. In 1948 several suburbs were incorporated into the city, and today it spreads wide across the prairie. It is the seat of Rice Univ., Texas Southern Univ., the Univ. of Houston, the Univ. of St. Thomas, Dominican College, Gulf Coast Bible College, Houston Baptist College, Baylor College of Medicine, and South Texas Junior College. Its many parks include the large Hermann Park, which has a zoo, a museum of natural science, and a planetarium. Houston has several notable art museums, an arboretum, and a botanical garden. The civic center includes the Sam Houston Coliseum and Music Hall; the Jesse H. Jones Hall for the Performing Arts, home of the symphony orchestra; and a convention and exhibit center, featuring the National Space Hall of Fame. Other tourist attractions include Old Market Square; Sam Houston Historical Park, which contains restored homes (built 1824-68) and reconstructed buildings; the huge air-conditioned Astrodome (opened 1965) and its adjacent "Astroworld," an amusement center. Ellington Air Force Base is just southeast of the city, and the San Jacinto battlefield is in nearby Pasadena. Houston has an international airport. See G. M. Fuermann, *Houston: The Once and Future City* (1971).

Houston, University of, at Houston, Texas; coeducational; est. 1927 as a junior college, became a four-year institution in 1934, became a state-supported university in 1963. The school's various facilities include the Center for Research in Business and Economics; the Center for Human Resources; the Public Affairs Research Center; and the Clear Lake City Center, which is affiliated with the National Aeronautics and Space Administration Manned Spacecraft Center.

Houston Symphony Orchestra. Founded in 1913 with 35 players, the orchestra reorganized in 1930 and presented its first full season of concerts in 1931. Among its important conductors have been Leopold Stokowski (1955-60), Sir John Barbirolli (1960-67), André Previn (1967-69), and Lalwrence Foster (1970-). The permanent home of the symphony is the Jesse H. Jones Hall for the Performing Arts, which opened in 1966 as part of Houston's Civic Center.

Hove (hōv), municipal borough (1971 pop. 72,659), East Sussex, SE England. It is a modern residential seaside resort.

Hoveida, Amir Abbas (āmēr' äb-bäs' hōvā'dä), 1919-, Iranian political leader, prime minister of Iran (1965-). After serving (1958-64) with the National Iranian Oil Company, he became (1964) minister of finance in the liberal government of Hassan Ali Mansur. When Mansur was killed by right-wing Muslim extremists, Hoveida was named (1965) prime minister. He continued his predecessor's policy of land redistribution and sought to maintain friendly ties with both the United States and the Soviet Union. Hoveida was reelected in 1967 and 1971.

Hovenweep National Monument: see NATIONAL PARKS AND MONUMENTS (table).

hovercraft: see AIR-CUSHION VEHICLE.

Hovhaness, Alan (hōvhä'nəs), 1911-, American composer, b. Somerville, Mass. Hovhaness is of Armenian descent, and many of his works are based on Armenian culture or show Middle Eastern or Oriental influence. He is interested in unusual sonorities. Hovhaness is enormously prolific; although he destroyed many compositions in 1940, his extant works number in the hundreds. Among them are *Lousadzak* [coming of light] (1945), for piano and strings; the symphonic poem *Ukiyo-Floating World* (1965); and *And God Created Great Whales* (1970), for orchestra and recorded humpback whale.

Howard, English noble family. Landowners in Norfolk from the 13th cent., the Howards obtained the duchy of Norfolk through the marriage of Sir Robert Howard to Margaret Mowbray, daughter of Thomas Mowbray, 1st duke of Norfolk. Their son John Howard, 1st duke of NORFOLK (in the Howard line), received the title in 1483 when the direct Mowbray line died out. He was killed fighting for Richard III at Bosworth Field. His son, Thomas Howard, 2d duke of NORFOLK, was deprived of his title and estate by Henry VII, but he regained favor and was a prominent military commander under both Henry VII and Henry VIII. Two of Henry VIII's wives—Anne BOLEYN (mother of Elizabeth I) and Catherine HOWARD—were members of the Howard family; they were both nieces of Thomas Howard, 3d duke of NORFOLK. He came into conflict with Henry after the execution of Catherine, and in 1546 he and his son, Henry Howard, earl of SURREY, were both accused of treason. The latter was executed, but his father was restored to the title in 1553 on the accession of Mary I. His grandson, Thomas Howard, 4th duke of NORFOLK, was beheaded in 1572 for conspiring on behalf of Mary Queen of Scots. His forfeited titles were gradually restored to the family in the 17th cent.—earl of Surrey (1603), earl of Norfolk (1644), duke of Norfolk (1660). In 1672 the office of earl marshal was made hereditary to the dukes of Norfolk, but because of the family's Roman Catholicism, they were not able to exercise the office until empowered to by special statute in 1824. The present head of the Howard family is Miles Francis Fitzalan-Howard, 17th duke of Norfolk, b. 1915. Norfolk is the oldest and premier dukedom in England. The title of earl of Surrey passes to the heir presumptive of the dukedom. The cadet branches of the Howard house are numerous. Charles Howard, 1st earl of NOTTINGHAM, hero in the defeat of the Spanish Armada, was the grandson of the 2d duke of Norfolk. Henry Howard, earl of NORTHAMPTON, an important courtier in the reigns of Elizabeth I and James I, was the son of Henry Howard, earl of Surrey. Thomas Howard, 1st earl of SUFFOLK, another naval hero and courtier and son of the 4th duke of Norfolk, was the father of Frances Howard, who, with her husband Robert Carr, earl of Somerset, was implicated in the murder of Sir Thomas Overbury. The great-great-grandson of the 4th duke was Charles Howard, 1st earl of CARLISLE, who held important posts under Oliver Cromwell and Charles II. His descendant, Frederick Howard, 5th earl of CARLISLE, achieved some prominence in the latter part of the 18th cent.

Howard, Bronson, 1842-1908, American dramatist, b. Detroit. His plays are important in the development of American drama. He was a newspaper reporter in New York until the success of his first play, *Saratoga*, a farcical comedy produced in 1870. He wrote 12 subsequent plays, including *Young Mrs. Winthrop* (1882), one of the first American dramas of social criticism; *The Henrietta* (1887), a satire on business practice; and by far his most popular play, *Shenandoah* (1888), a Civil War drama, first unsuccessfully produced but revived the following year with great success. See his collected plays (ed. by A. G. Halline, 1941).

Howard, Catherine, 1521?-1542, fifth queen consort of HENRY VIII of England. She was the daughter of Lord Edmund Howard and the niece of the powerful Thomas Howard, 3d duke of NORFOLK. Henry married her soon after his divorce from Anne of Cleves in 1540. Late in 1541 she was accused of immoral conduct prior to her marriage. Although she confessed, Henry was at first inclined to clemency. When evidence was produced for similar misconduct after her marriage, she was attainted for treason and beheaded. See L. B. Smith, *A Tudor Tragedy* (1961).

Howard, Charles, 1st **earl of Carlisle:** see CARLISLE, CHARLES HOWARD, 1ST EARL OF.

Howard, Sir Ebenezer, 1850-1928, English town planner, principal founder of the English garden-city movement. His *To-morrow: a Peaceful Path to Real Reform* (1898), reissued as *Garden Cities of To-morrow* (1902), outlined a model self-sustaining town that would combine town conveniences and industries with the advantages of an agricultural location. As a result of the first publication he was able to form (1899) the Garden City Association, and, in 1903 Letchworth, the first English garden city, was founded. In 1920 he organized Welwyn Garden City. See Dugald Macfadyen, *Sir Ebenezer Howard and the Town Planning Movement* (1933).

Howard, Elizabeth Jane: see under AMIS, KINGSLEY.

Howard, Frederick, 5th **earl of Carlisle:** see CARLISLE, FREDERICK HOWARD, 5TH EARL OF.

Howard, Henry: see SURREY, HENRY HOWARD, EARL OF.

Howard, John, 1726-90, English prison reformer. He had great influence in improving sanitary conditions and securing humane treatment in prisons throughout Europe. He was responsible (1774) for persuading the House of Commons to enact a set of penal reform acts. See biographies by Martin Southwood (1958) and D. L. Howard (1963).

Howard, Leland Ossian, 1857-1950, American entomologist, b. Rockford, Ill., grad. Cornell (B.S., 1877), Ph.D. Georgetown Univ., 1896. Associated with the U.S. Bureau of Entomology from 1878 (as its chief, 1894-1927, and as its principal entomologist until 1931), he profoundly influenced the development of economic and medical entomology in the United States. He waged war against insect parasites of man (especially the mosquito and housefly) and against crop pests such as the boll weevil, corn borer, gypsy moth, and Japanese beetle. Among his best-known works are *The Insect Book* (1901), *The House Fly* (1911), *Mosquitoes of North and Central America and the West Indies* (et al., 4 vol., 1912-17), *The Insect Menace* (1931), and his autobiography, *Fighting the Insects* (1933).

Howard, Oliver Otis, 1830-1909, Union general in the Civil War, founder of Howard Univ., b. Leeds, Maine, grad. Bowdoin College, 1850, and West Point, 1854. Made a brigadier general of volunteers (Sept., 1861), he fought in the East from the first battle of Bull Run through the GETTYSBURG CAMPAIGN. Howard lost his right arm at Fair Oaks in the Peninsular campaign (1862). His 11th Corps was completely routed by Stonewall Jackson's flank attack in the battle of CHANCELLORSVILLE. On the first day at Gettysburg, Howard, assuming command after J. F. REYNOLDS was killed, was driven back with heavy losses to Cemetery Hill. His corps constituted part of the Union reinforcements under Hooker in the CHATTANOOGA CAMPAIGN. In the Atlanta campaign he commanded the Army of the Tennessee after the death of J. B. MCPHERSON, and he led it in Sherman's march through Georgia and the Carolinas. President Andrew Johnson made Howard, who was devoted to the cause of Negro betterment, chief commissioner of the FREEDMEN'S BUREAU in May, 1865. While the bureau rendered some good service, many of its officials were corrupt. Howard himself was honest but he was not an able administrator. A founder (1867) of Howard Univ. (named for him), he was its president (1869-73). He later helped to found Lincoln Memorial Univ. in Tennessee. As commander of the Dept. of the Columbia (1874-81), Howard directed several campaigns against the Indians and negotiated with Chief JOSEPH in 1877. In 1886 he was promoted to major general and assigned to command the Division of the East; he held this post until his retirement in 1894. He wrote biographies of Chief Joseph (1881) and Zachary Taylor (1892), as well as *Famous Indian Chiefs I Have Known* (1908) and an autobiography (1907). See biography by J. A. Carpenter (1964); study by W. S. McFeely (1968).

Howard, Sir Robert, 1626-98, English dramatist. He held several important government posts under Charles II. His introduction to his *Foure New Plays* (1665) initiated a dispute with his brother-in-law, John DRYDEN, about the use of blank verse or rhyme in drama. His best-known play is *The Committee* (1665).

Howard, Roy Wilson, 1883-1964, American newspaper publisher, b. Gano, Ohio. He became New York manager of the United Press (UP) in 1907. During World War I, as president and general manager of UP, Howard prematurely reported from Europe that an armistice had been signed; this caused widespread turmoil. In 1921 he was elected board chairman of the UP, of the Newspaper Enterprise Association, and of their parent concern, the Scripps-McRae newspaper chain. Howard became the partner of Robert P. Scripps, and the chain was renamed Scripps-Howard. Scripps died in 1938, and Howard was trustee for his heirs until they took control of the chain in the late 1940s. However, he retained control of the *New York World-Telegram and the Sun*, which he had built for the chain by purchasing the *Telegram* (1927), the *World* (1931), and the *Sun* (1950).

Howard, Sidney Coe, 1891-1939, American dramatist, b. Oakland, Calif., grad. Univ. of California, 1915, and studied under George Pierce BAKER at Harvard. His first successful play was *They Knew What They Wanted* (1924; Pulitzer Prize), a compassionate drama set in the wine-producing region of California. It was followed by such plays as *Ned McCobb's Daughter* (1926), about a courageous New England resort owner; *The Silver Cord* (1926), concerning possessive maternalism; and *Yellow Jack* (1934), a dramatization of man's struggle against yellow fever. Howard's other works include the adaptation *The Late Christopher Bean* (1932) and the Academy Award winning screenplay for the movie *Gone With the Wind* (1939).

Howard, William: see STAFFORD, WILLIAM HOWARD, 1ST VISCOUNT.

Howard of Effingham, Charles Howard, 2d Baron: see NOTTINGHAM, CHARLES HOWARD, 1ST EARL OF.

Howard University, at Washington D.C.; coeducational; with Federal support. It was founded in 1867 by Gen. Oliver O. HOWARD of the Freedmen's Bureau, to provide education for newly emancipated slaves. A normal and preparatory department was opened the same year. In 1868 the collegiate department and the departments of law, pharmacy, and medicine were opened, followed by the theological (1871), dentistry (1882), music (1883), and engineering and architecture (1910) departments. The Founders Library houses the Moorland-Spingarn and Channing Pollock collections on Negro literature and history dating back to the 16th cent. Although predominantly a Negro university, the school has been open since its founding to all qualified students.

Howe, Clarence Decatur (hou), 1886-1960, Canadian civil engineer and cabinet minister, b. Waltham, Mass. He went to Canada in 1908 as professor of civil engineering at Dalhousie Univ. He founded (1916) an engineering firm that became internationally famous for its design and construction of grain elevators. He entered the Canadian House of Commons as a Liberal in 1935 and was at once invited by Mackenzie King to join the cabinet as minister of railways and canals and minister of marine. He merged the two agencies into the ministry of transport in 1936 and thereafter devoted himself to the development of air transportation, founding and organizing the Trans-Canada Air Lines. Soon after the outbreak of World War II, he was appointed (1940) minister of munitions and supply and in 1944 accepted concurrent appointment as minister of reconstruction. He became minister of trade and commerce in 1948. In 1957 he resigned the post when the Liberal party was defeated. From 1957 until his death he was chancellor of Dalhousie Univ.

Howe, Edgar Watson, 1853-1937, American editor and author, b. Treaty, near Wabash, Ind. From 1877 to 1911 he was editor and proprietor of the Atchison, Kansas, *Daily Globe,* and in 1911 he established *E. W. Howe's Monthly.* Published until 1937, this periodical was noted for Howe's pithy editorials. His first and generally considered best book is *The Story of a Country Town* (1883), among the first realistic novels of small-town life in the Midwest and a precursor of the naturalistic novel in American fiction. Always a champion of the common people, Howe was nicknamed the "Sage of Potato Hill." See his autobiography, *Plain People* (1929).

Howe, Elias, 1819-67, American inventor, b. Spencer, Mass. He was apprenticed in 1838 to an instrument maker and watchmaker in Boston at whose suggestion he turned his attention to devising a sewing machine. He exhibited his first machine in 1845 and patented another in 1846. No financial backing was secured in the United States, and in 1846 a third machine was sold in England, together with all rights in Great Britain, to William Thomas. Howe worked with Thomas in London to produce a machine to stitch leather. After a breach between the two, Howe returned to the United States to find his machine being manufactured by others. He brought several suits (including one against Isaac M. Singer) for infringement of patent and finally obtained a judgment for royalty in 1854. With the royalties earned through an extension of his patent (1861-67), he supported during the Civil War an infantry regiment in which he served as a private and in 1865 established in Bridgeport, Conn., the Howe Machine Company.

Howe, Gordie (Gordon Howe), 1928-, Canadian hockey player. He began playing hockey at the age of five and in 1945 became a professional hockey player. From the 1946-47 season through 1970-71, Howe, possibly the greatest forward in the game's history, played with the Detroit Red Wings of the National Hockey League and gained nearly every league record in both regular-season and playoff competition. He scored 786 goals, 1,023 assists, and 1,809 total points. In 1973, after a two-year retirement, Howe signed a four-year contract, along with his two sons, to play for the Houston Aeros of the World Hockey Association.

Howe, Irving, 1920-, American literary and social critic, b. New York City. He is associated with the "Old Left," and, as editor of *Dissent* and frequent contributor to *The Partisan Review, The New Republic,* and *The New York Review of Books,* he is connected with the New York literary establishment. His works include *William Faulkner: A Critical Study* (1952), *Politics and the Novel* (1957), and *The Critical Point* (1974). He has edited such books as *The Idea of the Modern in Literature and the Arts* (1967).

Howe, John, 1630-1705, English Puritan clergyman. As domestic chaplain to Oliver Cromwell, he advocated religious toleration. After the Restoration, he preached in secret (1662-71) until, becoming chaplain to Lord Massereene of Antrim Castle, Ireland, he turned his attention to writing. He eventually settled at Utrecht until the Declaration of Indulgence (1687) permitted his return to England. Howe's principal work is *The Living Temple of God,* an expression of his Puritanism. It is included in his collected works (1724).

Howe, Joseph, 1804-73, Canadian journalist and political leader, b. Halifax, N.S. In 1828, Howe became proprietor and editor of the *Nova Scotian,* which under his direction became the leading journal of the province. In 1836 he entered the provincial assembly; there and in his newspaper he continued his campaign for responsible government and his struggle against successive governors, whom he forced from Nova Scotia, until the demands of his reform party were granted in 1848. From 1848 to 1854 he was provincial secretary; from 1860 to 1863 he was premier. Howe worked ardently for education and for an intercolonial railroad to link the Maritime Provinces with Canada proper, but although early an advocate of union, he opposed confederation. Even after confederation had been achieved (1867) he continued his opposition, but realizing the hopelessness of his position, he entered (1869) John Macdonald's dominion cabinet as president of the council, losing by this act many of his supporters in Nova Scotia. When he retired in 1873 to accept appointment as lieutenant governor of Nova Scotia, his homecoming was marked by little enthusiasm. He died soon after assuming office. See *Joseph Howe: Voice of Nova Scotia* (ed. by J. M. Beck, 1964); biographies by J. W. Longley (rev. ed. 1926) and J. A. Roy (1935).

Howe, Julia Ward, 1819-1910, American author and social reformer, b. New York City. She assisted her husband, Dr. Samuel Gridley HOWE, in his philanthropic projects and in editing the Boston *Commonwealth,* an abolitionist paper. Mrs. Howe wrote and lectured in behalf of woman suffrage, Negro emancipation, and other causes, and helped found a world peace organization. In Nov., 1861, after watching Union troops march into battle, she wrote "The Battle Hymn of the Republic," her most famous work. It was published in the *Atlantic Monthly* in Feb., 1862. The American Academy of Arts and Letters elected her as its first woman member. Besides writing several volumes of poetry, she was the author of *Sex and Education* (1874), *Modern Society* (1881), and a biography of Margaret Fuller (1883). See her *Reminiscences, 1819-1899* (1899); biography by her daughters Laura E. Richards and Maud Howe Elliott (1915, repr. 1970); L. H. Tharp, *Three Saints and a Sinner* (1956).

Howe, Richard Howe, Earl, 1726-99, British admiral; elder brother of Viscount HOWE. He won early recognition in the Seven Years War for his operations in the English Channel. After the outbreak of the American Revolution, he was given (1776) command of the North American fleet. He and his brother were commissioned to seek a peaceful settlement of the dispute with the colonies, but negotiations at Staten Island in 1776 came to nothing, and he supported (1777) his brother's successful campaign against Philadelphia. In 1778 he outmaneuvered the French fleet under the comte d'ESTAING in its attempt to cooperate with land troops to take British-held Newport, R.I. He resigned later that year, but in 1782 he assumed command of the Channel fleet and relieved the siege of Gibraltar. Howe is best remembered for his decisive victory over the French fleet in the battle called the First of June in 1794. Created Earl Howe in 1788, he was popularly known as Black Dick. See study by I. D. Gruber (1972).

Howe, Samuel Gridley, 1801-76, American reformer and philanthropist, b. Boston, Mass., grad. Brown, 1821, M.D. Harvard, 1824. He began his lifelong service to others by going to Greece to aid in the War of Independence and spending six years there. He is best remembered for his work with the blind; he was the organizer of the New England Asylum for the Blind (which later became the Perkins Institution) and was head of it for 44 years. The remarkable success of the education of Laura BRIDGMAN, who was both blind and deaf, did much to improve education of the handicapped in the United States. He was chairman of the Massachusetts state board of charities from 1865 to 1874. He also supported Dorothea Dix in her work for the insane, sought to help the mentally retarded, approved the educational reforms of Horace Mann, and with his wife, Julia Ward Howe, opposed slavery. The troubles in Crete (1866-67) took him again to Greece. His letters and journals have been published (1906-9). See biographies by Harold Schwartz (1956) and Milton Meltzer (1964).

Howe, William Howe, 5th Viscount, 1729-1814, English general in the American Revolution; younger brother of Admiral Richard Howe. He took up a military career, and in the last of the French and Indian Wars served with distinction at the capture of Louisburg and in the fight for Quebec (1759). He took part in the Havana expedition of 1762. In 1775 he arrived at Boston with British reinforcements for Gen. Thomas Gage, and he was a commander in the battle of Bunker Hill. He was knighted and succeeded (Oct., 1775) Gage as commander in chief in the colonies (the command in Canada being given to Gen. Guy Carleton). In 1776 he withdrew his men from besieged Boston to Halifax, then (May, 1776) went with his brother Richard to Staten Island. After negotiations for a peaceful settlement failed, Howe led his troops in the successful battle of Long Island, captured New York City, and defeated the Continental Army at White Plains. Although he gained control over SE New York and much of New Jersey, Howe missed several opportunities to capture George Washington's army. In 1777 he did not take the part planned for him in the British strategy in the SARATOGA CAMPAIGN. Instead he launched a successful drive for Philadelphia, defeating Washington in the battle of BRANDYWINE. He later repelled an attack on GERMANTOWN and held his position in Philadelphia, but again, as at New York, he did not wipe out the Continental forces. Charging that he was not properly supported by the home government, he resigned and in 1778 returned to England. His command in America was taken over by Sir Henry CLINTON. On his brother's death in 1799, Howe succeeded to the Irish title, becoming 5th Viscount Howe. See biography by Bellamy Partridge (1932); T. S. Anderson, *The Command of the Howe Brothers during the American Revolution* (1936, repr. 1971); I. D. Gruber, *The Howe Brothers and the American Revolution* (1972).

Howell, John Adams, 1840-1918, American naval officer and inventor, b. Bath, N.Y., grad. Annapolis, 1858. He served as a lieutenant throughout the Civil War, fighting under Admiral Farragut at Mobile Bay (1864). In the Spanish-American War he commanded a squadron of the North Atlantic Fleet and was promoted (1898) to rear admiral. Howell originated the gyroscopic steering torpedo, invented a flywheel torpedo, and developed torpedo-launching apparatus.

Howells, William Dean, 1837-1920, American novelist, critic, and editor, b. Martins Ferry, Ohio. Both in his own novels and in his critical writing, Howells was a champion of realism in American literature. His education was gained by voracious reading as he worked for his father, a town printer in various small towns in Ohio. Howells early turned to writing and to editorial work on the *Ohio State Journal* (1856-61). He wrote a campaign biography of Lincoln in 1860 and was given an appointment as consul in Venice in 1861. The first of his many travel books, *Venetian Life* (1866) and *Italian Journey* (1867), brought recognition. After his return to the United States in 1865, he worked for various periodicals; he was associated with the *Atlantic Monthly* for 15 years and later wrote the "Editor's Study" (1886-91) and the "Easy Chair" (1900-1920) of *Harper's Magazine.* His first novels, *Their Wedding Journey* (1872), *The Lady of the Aroostook* (1879), and others, were moralistic comedies of manners that aroused only mild interest. However, when he turned to realism with *A Modern Instance* (1882) and *The Rise of Silas Lapham* (1885), he became a leading novelist. In these two books, which are regarded as his major achievements, Howells portrayed with minute detail characters attempting to solve lifelike problems, often arising from social distinctions. His unromantic love story, *Indian Summer* (1886), was also highly popular. Howells' critical essays on the works of such realistic European writers as Tolstoy, Zola, and Ibsen helped to mold American taste, and he was a literary mentor of Mark Twain, Hamlin Garland, Thorstein Veblen, and Stephen Crane. He himself became more and more concerned with social conflict and the problem of industrialization. Socialist thought is apparent in his novels *A Hazard of New Fortunes* (1890), *The Quality of Mercy* (1892), and *An Imperative Duty* (1893), and even more forthright in his utopian works, *A*

Traveler from Altruria (1894) and *Through the Eye of the Needle* (1907). He was amazingly prolific; besides his many novels he wrote plays ranging from blank verse tragedy to farce; critical works; several volumes of reminiscence; and short stories. The most notable of his critical volumes is *Criticism and Fiction* (1891). His books of reminiscences include *A Boy's Town* (1890), *My Year in a Log Cabin* (1893), *Impressions and Experiences* (1896), *Literary Friends and Acquaintances* (1900), *My Mark Twain* (1910), and *Years of My Youth* (1916). See his life in letters, ed. by his daughter, Mildred Howells (1928); biographies by E. H. Cady (2 vol., 1956–58) and K. S. Lynn (1972); study by G. N. Bennett (1973); bibliography by V. J. Brenni (1973).

Howel the Good: see HYWEL DDA.

howitzer: see ARTILLERY.

Howland Island, uninhabited island (.73 sq mi/1.89 sq km), central Pacific near the equator, c.1,620 mi (2610 km) SW of Honolulu. The island was discovered by American traders and was claimed by the United States in 1856, along with JARVIS ISLAND and BAKER ISLAND. The three islands were worked for guano deposits by British and American companies during the 19th cent. The guano industry declined, and the islands were forgotten until they became a stop on the air route to Australia. American colonists were brought from Hawaii in 1935 in order to establish U.S. control against British claims, but the colony was disbanded at the outbreak of World War II. While en route to Howland Island in 1937 the aviator Amelia EARHART was lost in the Pacific. Howland Island is under the U.S. Dept. of the Interior.

Howrah (hou'rä), city (1971 pop. 740,622), West Bengal state, E central India, on the Hooghly River opposite Calcutta. A center of the Hooghlyside industrial complex, Howrah produces textiles, jute products, glass, steel, and other items.

Hoxha, Enver (ĕn'vĕr hô'jä), 1908–, Albanian Communist leader and general. A founder (1941) of the Albanian Communist party (Albanian Labor party from 1948), Hoxha headed the radical resistance group in Italian-occupied Albania during World War II. First secretary of the party from 1943, he was premier (1946–54) of Albania after its proclamation as a republic. Hoxha was also minister of foreign affairs (1946–53) and commander in chief of the army (1944–54). He maintained close ties with the Soviet Union until its rift with Communist China in 1961; he then joined Peking in its ideological struggle against Moscow and was branded as a Stalinist by Soviet and other Communist leaders. In the 1960s and early 1970s, Hoxha further strengthened Albania's relations with China.

Hoxie, Robert Franklin (hŏk'sē), 1868–1916, American economist, b. Edmeston, W of Cooperstown, N.Y., Ph.D. Univ. of Chicago, 1905. He taught at the Univ. of Chicago from 1906 to 1916. A realistic interpreter of the changing economic system in the United States, he was noted for his work in labor history. As special investigator (1914–15) for the U.S. Commission on Industrial Relations he produced *Scientific Management and Labor* (1915). His *Trade Unionism in the United States* (ed. by L. B. Hoxie and Nathan Fine, 1917; 2d ed. 1923, repr. 1966), though incomplete, is his most important work.

Hoy, island, 13 mi (21 km) long and 6 mi (9.7 km) wide, off N Scotland, second largest of the ORKNEY Islands. It is located at the southwestern side of the Scapa Flow anchorage. Ward Hill (1,565 ft/477 m) is one of many hills on the island; magnificent cliffs line the shore. There are some farms in the northeastern section, but the midland is a barren moor. Lyness, on the east coast, was headquarters of the Scapa Flow naval base. The Old Man of Hoy, a sandstone pinnacle 450 ft (137 m) high, is a famous sailors' landmark. The Dwarfie Stone, a huge sandstone block with hollowed rooms inside, is a Viking relic.

Hoya (hō'yä), city (1970 pop. 86,914), Tokyo Metropolis, E central Honshu, Japan, on the Shakoji River. It is a residential suburb of Tokyo and an agricultural center where raw silk is produced.

hoya: see MILKWEED.

Hoyerswerda (hoi''ərsvĕr'dä), city (1970 pop. 58,663), Cottbus dist., SE East Germany, on the Black Elster River; chartered 1371. Located in a lignite-mining area, it is an industrial city, manufacturing glass and other products.

Hoylake, urban district (1971 pop. 32,196), Cheshire, NW England, on the Wirral Peninsula at the mouth of the Dee River. It is a seaside resort with yachting facilities and a golf course. In 1974, Hoylake became part of the new metropolitan county of Merseyside.

Hoyle, Edmond (hoil), 1672–1769, English writer on games, b. London. He codified the rules of whist in his book *A Short Treatise on the Game of Whist* (1742) and in successive editions of the book he added new material on whist together with treatises on quadrille, piquet, and backgammon. He wrote several other books, and "according to Hoyle" has come to mean "by highest authority." Several modern encyclopedias of card games use the name *Hoyle* in their titles.

Hoysala, dynasty of S India, c.1110–1326. It had its origins in the last half of the 11th cent., when Vinayaditya ruled and established a base centered on Dorasamudra (modern Halebid), which became the dynasty's capital. His grandson Bittiga (later called Vishnuvardhana; reigned c.1110–42) made extensive conquests, including the Mysore plateau, and built magnificent temples at Dorasamudra that were noted for their intricate and elaborate sculpture. Under Bittiga the Hoysalas became worshippers of Vishnu. Bittiga's grandson, Vira Ballala II (reigned 1173–1220) extended Hoysala control N of Mysore and made the dynasty the most powerful in S India. The Hoysalas later came into conflict with the Muslim sultans of Delhi and were defeated by Malik Kafur, the sultan's general, in 1310. The last Hoysala rule was overthrown in 1326. At its height the dynasty ruled over parts of the modern states of Mysore, Andhra Pradesh, Kerala, and Tamil Nadu. See J. M. Derrett, *The Hoysalas* (1957).

Hoyt, John Wesley, 1831–1912, American educator, b. Worthington, Ohio, grad. Ohio Wesleyan Univ., 1849. In Madison, Wis., he published the *Wisconsin Farmer and Northwestern Cultivator.* A founder of the Republican party and first president of the Wisconsin Academy of Sciences, Arts, and Letters, he sponsored the establishment of the state agricultural college in a reorganization of the state university. From 1878 to 1882 he was governor of Wyoming Territory and from 1887 to 1890 served as first president of the Univ. of Wyoming. He devoted his later years to the promotion of a national university.

Hrabanus Maurus: see RABANUS MAURUS MAGNENTIUS.

Hradec Králové (hrä'dĕts krä'lôvā), Ger. *Königgrätz*, city (1970 pop. 69,587), N Czechoslovakia, in Bohemia, on the Elbe (Labe) River. It is an industrial center, manufacturing machinery, chemicals, photographic equipment, and musical instruments. Founded in the 10th cent., it was a leading town of medieval Bohemia. It suffered heavily in the Hussite and Thirty Years wars. The town became a Roman Catholic bishopric in 1653. The city has a 14th-century Gothic cathedral, a 14th-century town hall, a 17th-century baroque palace, and two huge marketplaces from medieval times. There is also a medical institute (founded 1946). The battle of SADOVÁ (1866, also called the battle of Königgrätz, was fought in the vicinity.

Hrdlicka, Ales (ä'lĕsh hûrd'lĭchkä), 1869–1943, American anthropologist, b. Bohemia. He received his medical education in the United States. In 1903 he began to organize the division of physical anthropology at the U.S. National Museum, Smithsonian Institution, in Washington and was its curator from 1910 to 1942. Hrdlicka founded the *American Journal of Physical Anthropology* (1918), which he edited until his death, and the American Association of Physical Anthropologists (1929). From 1898 to 1925 he carried out anthropological investigations throughout Europe and the Americas as well as in East Asia, Australia, Egypt, and South Africa. In 1926–37 he led expeditions to Alaska. His work on anthropometry, early man, and human evolution and his research on the supposed migration tracks of the American Indian in Siberia and Alaska won him an international reputation. His books include *Physical Anthropology* (1919), *Anthropometry* (1920), *Old Americans* (1925), and *Alaska Diary, 1926–1931* (1943).

Hrolf: see ROLLO.

Hrotswith (hrôtsvēt') or **Roswitha von Gandersheim** (rôsvē'tä fən gän'dərs-hīm), 10th-century German dramatist, a nun. Of a noble Saxon family, Hrotswith was well educated. Her long epic poems—one including a fragment on Emperor Otto I, one on the founding of the abbey of Gandersheim—and shorter poems on religious subjects were written in Latin hexameters. She is best known for six plays written in the style of Terence, with intent to supplant Roman immorality by Christian piety. They are *Passio Gallicanus, Dulcitius, Callimachus, Sapientia, Abraham,* and *Paphnutius.* Hrotswith's plays show considerable power of characterization, a happy sense of humor, and deep piety. The dialogues are lively and the scenes move quickly. The plays appear to have been written for actual presentation by students in the abbey. See study by M. M. Butler (1960).

Hrushevsky, Mikhailo (mĕkhəyĕl'ō hrōōshĕf'skē), 1866–1934, Ukrainian historian and statesman. Hrushevsky's monumental *History of Ukraine* (10 vol., 1899–1937) covers the period to 1658. Other works include *A History of Ukraine* (tr. 1941) and *History of Ukrainian Literature* (5 vol., 1922–27). Hrushevsky argued that the period of the Kievan state (10th–13th cent.) belonged to Ukraine only, thus repudiating the Russian nationalist tradition that traced the history of Russia from ancient Kiev. He became president of the republic of Ukraine on its proclamation in Jan., 1918. After the German occupation of Ukraine, he fled (1918) to Austria, returning in 1924. In 1930 he was exiled from Kiev by the Soviet authorities.

Hs-. For some Chinese names beginning thus, see S-; e.g., for Hsi, see SI.

Hsia (shēä), semilegendary first dynasty of China, which ruled, according to traditional dates, from c.2205 B.C. to c.1766 B.C. or, according to some modern scholars, from c.1994 B.C. to c.1523 B.C. This dynasty is said to have been founded by Yu, the culture hero of China who built canals to control floods and then divided the reclaimed land. Scanty archaeological remains suggest that the people had domestic animals, wheat and millet, the potter's wheel, bronze weapons, and war chariots. The Hsia dynasty was succeeded by the SHANG, the first historic dynasty of China. See Li Chi, *Beginnings of Chinese Civilization* (1957); Chang Kwang-chi, *Archaeology of Ancient China* (rev. and enl. ed. 1968).

Hsia Kuei (shyä gwā), c.1180–1230, Chinese painter of the Sung dynasty. Little is known of his life. He and his contemporary Ma Yüan were regarded as the greatest landscape painters of the day and were the founders of the so-called Ma-Hsia school of landscape painting. Hsia was especially known for his skillful use of empty spaces, which he outlined with firm, decisive strokes. Many later artists tried to recapture his style. *Twelve River Views* in the Nelson-Atkins Museum, Kansas City, Mo., is one of the better examples of many paintings attributed to him.

Hsia-men: see AMOY, China.

Hsi-an (shē-än) or **Sian** (sē'än', shē–), city (1970 est. pop. 1,900,000), capital of Shensi prov., China, in the Wei River valley. Situated on the Lung-hai RR, the principal east-west line of China, it is an important commercial center in a wheat- and cotton-growing area. It has textile mills, food-processing establishments, and plants making chemicals, cement, motor vehicles, and fertilizer. Hsien-yang, one of several cities which previously occupied this site, was (255–206 B.C.) the capital of the Ch'in dynasty. The present city, then called Chang-an, was the western capital of the T'ang dynasty (618–906), and it was then a center of Buddhist, Muslim, and Nestorian Christian missionary activity. In the "Sian Incident" (1936) Chiang Kai-shek was kidnapped by Chang Hsueh-liang and kept prisoner there until he agreed to form a united front against the Japanese. The site of the incident is now a lush hot-spring resort with memorial pavilions. The city has numerous T'ang dynasty pagodas and is noted for its museum of history, housed in an 11th-century Confucian temple containing large stone tablets from the T'ang dynasty; one (781) commemorates the establishment of a Nestorian church. The city wall, dating from the Ming dynasty (1368–1644), is still visible in places. In Hsi-an are botanical gardens, Northwestern Univ., a science and technology university, a medical college, and several technical institutes. The city has a major airport.

Hsiang or **Siang** (both: sēäng, shēäng), river, 715 mi (1,151 km) long, rising in NE Kwangsi prov. and flowing N through Hunan prov. to Tung-t'ing lake, SE China. The river is navigable to large vessels for most of its course; Ch'ang-sha is the largest city and major port. The upper Hsiang is connected by canal with the Kuei River, thus joining the Yangtze and Si river systems. The densely populated Hsiang valley is one of China's major industrial regions and yields manganese, lead, and zinc. The delta is an important rice-growing area.

Hsiang-t'an (shēäng-tän) or **Siangtan** (sēäng'tän', shē–), city (1970 est. pop. 300,000), E central Hunan prov., China, on the Hsiang River. Formerly an agricultural distribution center, it is now industrialized. Products include manganese ore, cement, machine tools, and trucks.

Hsi-k'ang or **Sikang** (both: shē-käng), former province, SW China. K'ang-ting was the capital before 1950 and Ya-an from 1950 to 1955. It is largely a region of high mountains (over 10,000 ft/3,050 m) cut by the gorges of several rivers. The area became a province c.1939. In 1955 the portion of Hsi-k'ang E of the Yangtze River was joined to Szechwan prov.; the autonomous region of Tibet received the remainder.

Hsin-chu (shĭn-jōō), city (1969 pop. 201,678), NW Taiwan. The city and surrounding area are noted for the production of tea, rice, oranges, and petroleum. Hsin-chu's major industries include petroleum refining and the manufacture of cement, fertilizers, and textiles. Immigrants from the China mainland formed a colony at Hsin-chu in the early 1700s. Since the 19th cent. the city has been a thriving commercial center.

Hsin-hui (shĭn-hwē) or **Sunwui** (sōōn'wē'), town, S Kwangtung prov., SE China, in the Si River delta, near Canton. It has fruit orchards, fruit-processing industries, and machine shops. Tungsten mines are in the area. A treaty port in 1904, it was an important outlet for Chinese emigrants to the United States.

Hsi-ning or **Sining** (both: shē-nĭng), city (1970 est. pop. 250,000), capital of Tsinghai prov., W China, on the Hsi-ning River. For centuries it has been the major commercial hub on the caravan route to Tibet, trading in wool, hides, salt, and timber. More recently it has developed as a processing (flour-milling, wool-spinning, meat-packing) and distribution center for the NE Tsinghai agricultural basin. Construction of a highway to the mineral-rich Tsaidam basin and completion in 1959 of a link to the Chinese rail network via Lan-chou in Kansu prov. has spurred industrial development. Manufactures include chemicals, machinery, motor vehicles, metal products, and textiles. Coal is mined in the area. Hsi-ning was the extraterritorial capital of the Koko Nor territory and remained in Kansu until 1928, when it became the capital of the newly-formed Tsinghai prov.

Hsin-kao Shan, Sinkao Shan (both: shĭn-gou-shän), or **Mt. Morrison,** 13,113 ft (3,997 m) high, S Taiwan; highest peak on the island. It was first ascended in 1896 by a Japanese expedition.

Hsinking: see CH'ANG-CH'UN, China.

Hsin-yang or **Sinyang** (both: shĭn-yäng), city (1970 est. pop. 125,000), S Honan prov., China. It is a transportation hub lying on the Peking-Canton RR and the major regional center for southernmost Honan and N Hupeh provs. Textiles are produced in the city.

Hsüan-tsang (shüän-dzäng) or **Hiouentang,** 605?–664, Chinese Buddhist scholar and translator. He early entered monastic life and later traveled in China, where he taught and studied. Between 629 and 645 he made a pilgrimage to India in search of authentic scriptures. He studied at TAXILA and Nalanda (see BARAGAON), the most celebrated center of Buddhist learning in India, and also visited Kashmir and the important holy places of Buddhism. Pious, learned, and fluent in Sanskrit, he was honored by the rulers of India whom he met, including the Emperor Harsha. On his return to China he translated the texts he had brought back with him and wrote his memoirs. His disciple K'uei-chi is known as the founder of the Fa-hsiang school of Buddhism, the Chinese branch of YOGACARA. See his *Si-yu-ki; Buddhist Records of the Western World* (2 vol., tr. 1884, repr. 1969); Arthur Waley, *The Real Tripitaka* (1952); Thomas Loatters, *On Yuan Chwang's Travels in India* (1961).

Hsüan Tsung (shüän dzōōng), 685–762, Chinese emperor (712–56), 9th of the T'ang dynasty. Under his brilliant early rule the T'ang reached the height of its power. Improved administration and new grain-transport facilities increased the flow of revenue to the central government, and T'ang armies restored Chinese suzerainty over Central Asia. In 751, however, the T'ang armies were defeated by the Arabs at Talas (near modern Fergana, Uzbek SSR) and by the Thai state of Nan-chao in the southwest. The revolt of the northeastern regional commander AN LU-SHAN in 755 forced Hsüan Tsung to abdicate. Peace was restored in 763 with the aid of foreign troops, but Central Asia was lost and control over the provinces of China proper was considerably weaker than that which had been achieved earlier by Hsüan Tsung. In Chinese legend Hsüan Tsung's infatuation with his concubine YANG KUEI-FEI is blamed for demoralizing the T'ang court and paving the way for the rebellion of An Lu-shan.

Hsüan T'ung: see PU YI, HENRY.

Hsü-chou or **Süchow** (both: shü-jō), city (1970 est. pop. 1,500,000), N Kiangsu prov., E central China. It is a rail center at the junction of railroads serving Kiangsu, Shantung, Anhwei, and Hunan provs. Iron and coal mines are nearby, and the city has a small integrated steel complex. Food is processed, and machine tools are also made. Hsü-chou was known as Tungshan from 1912 to 1945. It was in Shantung prov. from 1949 to 1952, when it was returned to Kiangsu.

Huai or **Hwai** (both: hwī), river, c.680 mi (1,090 km) long, rising in the Tung-pai mts., Honan prov., E China, and flowing E across Anhwei prov., through Hung-tse Lake, to the East China Sea. The Huai marks the boundary between the N China Plain and the Yangtze delta. More than two thirds of the fertile Huai basin is under cultivation; wheat, millet, and kaolin are the main crops. An irrigation canal branches from the river to the sea. Receiving many tributaries, the Huai floods more frequently and over a larger area than any river in N China; since 1950 extensive flood control facilities, including eight dams, have been built.

Huai-nan or **Hwainan** (both: hwī-nän), city (1970 est. pop. 350,000), N central Anhwei prov., China. Established after 1949 as the center of China's chief coal-mining region, it is the site of a major colliery. Chemicals are also manufactured.

Hua-lien (hwä-lĕn), city, E central Taiwan. It is an important port for the local area and is a market for sugarcane, rice, jute, and camphor wood grown in the surrounding region. The city also produces fertilizers, metal, small machinery, and canned foods.

Huambo: see NOVA LISBOA, Angola.

huanaco: see GUANACO.

Huancayo (wänkī'ō), city (1969 est. pop. 91,200), alt. 10,731 ft (3,721 m), capital of Junín dept., S central Peru. One of Peru's major agricultural centers, it markets and ships the wheat, maize, potatoes, and barley grown in the surrounding area. With a predominantly Indian population, Huancayo is an important market for Indian textiles. Silver, copper, and coal are mined in the region. The city is noted for its picturesque colonial architecture and has a church dating from 1617.

Huang Ho, Hwang Ho (both: hwäng' hō'), or **Yellow River,** great river of N China, c.3,000 mi (4,830 km) long, rising in the Kunlun mts., NW Tsinghai prov., and flowing generally east into the "great northern bend" (around the Ordos Desert), then east again to the Po Hai, an arm of the Yellow Sea. The turbulent upper Huang Ho meanders east through a series of gorges to the fertile Lan-chou valley. Hydroelectric power dams in the Liu-chia gorge and at Lan-chou, the largest city on the river, generate electricity and impound irrigation water. Past Lan-chou, the Huang Ho becomes a wide, slow-moving stream as it begins its bend around the Ordos and separates the northern uplands from the desert and loess lands of the south and west. It is navigable in places for small vessels. The west end of the "great northern bend" passes through the heavily populated Ninghsia agricultural region, an oasis c.60 mi (100 km) long, where cereals and fruits are raised. At the northwest corner of the "great northern bend," the Huang Ho divides into numerous branches that water a fertile area where ancient irrigation canals have been repaired and are now in use. At the northeast corner lies the most fertile land outside the Great Wall; it was farmed without irrigation until 1929. Turning south, the Huang Ho passes through the Great Wall and enters the extremely fertile loess region (where rich coal deposits are also found on both sides of the river). Cutting deep into the loess, the river receives most of the yellow silt from which its name is derived. After receiving the Wei and Fen rivers, its chief tributaries, the Huang Ho turns east and flows through San-men gorge, site of the huge San-men dam (completed 1962), which is used for power production, flood control, and navigation. The dam impounds a 907-sq-mi (2,350-sq-km) reservoir; however, because of excessive silt, the power plant has not yet been used. Silt dropped at the Huang Ho's mouth over the millennia has created a great delta called the North China Plain, which extends over much of Honan, Hopeh, and Shan-tung provs., and which merges with the Yangtze delta in N Kiangsu and N Anhwei provs.; the delta is constantly expanding eastward into the sea. The Huang Ho meanders over the fertile, densely populated plain to reach the Po Hai. The plain is China's agricultural heartland, producing corn, kaoliang, winter wheat, vegetables, and cotton. However, floods, insufficient rainfall, and overcrowding cause frequent famine. During the winter dry season the Huang Ho is slow-moving and silt-laden, and occupies only part of its huge bed; with the summer rains, it becomes a raging torrent. Since the 2nd cent. B.C., the lower Huang Ho has inundated the surrounding region some 1,500 times and has made nine major changes in its course. In an attempt to halt the Japanese invasion of China in 1938, the Chinese diverted the Huang Ho south, flooding more than 20,000 sq mi (51,800 sq km) and killing some 900,000 people; it was returned to its present course in 1947. The Chinese have long sought to control the Huang Ho by building dikes and overflow channels. Silt deposition, the principal cause of flooding, continually elevates the river bed; in places the river flows 60 to 70 ft (18–21 m) above the surrounding plains. During the summer high water period, water pressure against the dikes frequently breaks through the retaining walls to cause devastating floods, which have led the Huang Ho to be called "China's Sorrow." In 1955 the Chinese initiated a 50-year construction plan for control of the river. Dikes are being repaired and reinforced, and a series of 45 silt-retaining dams, when completed, will control the upper river, produce 23 million kw of electricity, and provide water for 20 million acres (8 million hectares). The People's Victory Canal, a 40-mi-long (64-km) diversion and irrigation channel, connects the Huang Ho with the Wei River.

Huang-pu (hwäng-bōō) or **Whampoa** (hwäm'pō'-ä'), city, S Kwangtung prov., SE China, on an island in the Canton River. It is c.9 mi (14.5 km) SE of Canton, of which it is an outer port; it has been enlarged and modernized since 1952 and now accommodates large oceangoing vessels. An important industrial city, Huang-pu is economically a part of Canton. The Whampoa Military Academy, founded there in 1924 as a Kuomintang training center, was organized by Chiang Kai-shek. Several of its officers, notably Chou En-lai, later became leaders of the Chinese Communist army.

Huang-p'u, river, China: see WHANGPOO.

Huang-shih or **Hwangshih** (both: hwäng-shŭr), city (1970 est. pop. 200,000), E Hupeh prov., China, on the Yangtze River. It is a new industrial center, built after 1950, with a giant iron and steel complex supplied with iron from the mines at Tayeh and with coking coal from P'ing-hsiang. Other manufactures include cement, building materials, textiles, and processed foods.

Huang Ti: see YELLOW EMPEROR.

Huarás or **Huaraz** (both: wäräs'), city (1961 est. pop. 20,300), capital of Ancash dept., W central Peru. It is in a high valley at an altitude of 9,931 ft (3,027 m), and has a predominantly Indian population. Huarás is the center of an agricultural district raising grains and potatoes. Some minerals (silver, cinnabar, and coal) are mined. HUASCARÁN peak forms a superb backdrop to the city. In 1941 an avalanche of mud and water wiped out a large section of the city and killed some 6,000 people.

Huáscar (wäs'kär), d. 1533, Inca of Peru; son of HUAYNA CAPAC. At his father's death (1525) he became emperor, but had to share the empire with his younger half brother, ATAHUALPA. Shortly before the beginning of the Spanish conquest under Francisco Pizarro, Atahualpa rebelled successfully and later secretly ordered Huáscar murdered.

Huascarán (wäskärän'), extinct volcano, 22,205 ft (6,768 m) high, W central Peru, near Huarás. The highest mountain in Peru and one of the highest in the Andes, Huascarán and other nearby peaks form an impressive snow-capped rampart. In 1962 an immense avalanche swept down its slopes and buried the village of Ranrahirca.

Huastec (wäs'tĕk), Indians of the PANUCO River basin, E Mexico. They speak a Mayan language but are isolated from the rest of the Mayan stock, from whom they may have been separated prior to the arrival of the Spanish. Their culture did not develop along with that of the Maya. They remained on the outer fringes of later civilizations of the central plateau, notably the Aztec. Huastecan music and dancing have influenced some of the musical folklore of Mexico. The contemporary Huastec population, maintaining aspects of their traditional culture and language, numbers several thousand in the areas of Veracruz and San Luis Potosí. See Robert Wauchope, *Handbook of Middle American Indians,* Vol. III: *Ethnology* (ed. by E. Z. Vogt, 1964).

Hua-yen Buddhism (hwä-yŭn) [Chin.,=garland], school of Chinese Buddhism, centering on the *Avatamsaka Sutra* [garland sutra]. There is no Indian counterpart of this school. Hua-yen makes a fivefold classification of Buddhist teachings and scriptures, from lower to higher, with its own teaching at the top. According to the school, all phenomena arise simultaneously from the universal principle of the *Dharma*-realm. The ultimate principle and manifested things mutually interpenetrate without any obstruction, and at the same time that they embody the Absolute, all phenomena reflect and are identified with one another. The first master of the school was Tu-shun (557-640). He was succeeded by Chih-yen (602-668), Fa-ts'ang (643-712), Ch'eng-kuan (737-838), and Ts'ung-mi (780-841), who was also a master of the Ch'an or Zen school. The name also appears as Hwa-yen. See C. C. Chang, *The Buddhist Teaching of Totality* (1971).

Huayna Capac (wī'nä kä'päk), d. 1525, Inca of Peru, last of the great emperors. The Inca empire reached its greatest extent and power under his rule, but disruptive forces were already at work. Their action was hastened by Huayna Capac's decision to divide the empire by leaving the recently conquered kingdom of Quito to his favorite son, ATAHUALPA, and the rest to the legitimate heir, HUÁSCAR. War between the brothers had just ended when Francisco Pizarro began his conquest. Huayna Capac's third son, MANCO CAPAC was the last Inca to succumb to the Spanish.

Hubbard, Elbert, 1856-1915, American author and publisher, b. Bloomington, Ill. He founded (1895) an artist colony in East Aurora, N.Y., and established there the Roycroft Press, emulating William Morris's idealistic experiment in fine books and hand craftsmanship. An ardent believer in rugged individualism, Hubbard edited the inspirational *Philistine* magazine and was the author of the essay "A Message to Garcia" (1899), a lesson in duty and efficiency based on an incident in the Spanish-American War. Hubbard died on the *Lusitania,* which was sunk in the Irish Sea by a German submarine on May 7, 1915.

Hubbard, Frank McKinney, 1868-1930, American humorist, b. Bellefontaine, Ohio. He worked (1891-1930), on the Indianapolis *News,* where, as Kin Hubbard, he wrote and illustrated stories about the rustic philosopher Abe Martin. These pieces were syndicated and won him nationwide fame. See *Abe Martin's Wisecracks* (ed. by E. V. Lucas, 1930).

Hubbell, Carl Owen, 1903-, American baseball player, b. Carthage, Mo. A left-handed pitcher, Hubbell played his entire major league career (1928-43) with the New York Giants. Hubbell, famous for his adept use of his "screwball" pitch, hurled brilliantly in the 1934 All-Star game, pitched 24 consecutive victories in the 1936-37 seasons, and won 253 games before he retired. Known as "the Meal Ticket," he was elected to the Baseball Hall of Fame in 1947.

Hubbell Trading Post National Historic Site: see NATIONAL PARKS AND MONUMENTS (table).

Hubble, Edwin Powell, 1889-1953, American astronomer, b. Marshfield, Mo., grad. Univ. of Chicago, 1910, Rhodes scholar, 1910-13. He discovered that there are large-scale galaxies, or independent star systems, lying far beyond the Milky Way and that these galaxies are distributed almost uniformly in all directions. He was the first to offer observational evidence to support the expanding theory of the universe, presenting his findings in what is now known as HUBBLE'S LAW. He did research (1914-17) at Yerkes Observatory, Williams Bay, Wis., and joined (1919) the staff of Mt. Wilson Observatory, Pasadena, Calif., of which he became director. Included in his writings are *A General Study of Diffuse Galactic Nebulae* (1926), *Extra-Galactic Nebulae* (1927), *Spiral Nebula as a Stellar System* (1929), *The Realm of Nebulae* (1936), and *The Observational Approach to Cosmology* (1937).

Hubble's law, in astronomy, statement that the distances between galaxies (see GALAXY) or clusters of galaxies are continuously increasing and that therefore the universe is expanding. The law applies to all galaxies or clusters sufficiently distant from one another that gravitational forces are negligible. According to the law, these galaxies are flying away from each other at tremendous speeds such that the greater the distance between any two galaxies, the greater their relative speed of separation. In other words, the expansion of the universe is roughly uniform. This empirical finding is more consonant with the theory that the universe began with an explosive "big bang" than the theory that the universe has always existed in an unchanging "steady state" (see COSMOLOGY). Edwin Hubble first proposed this law in 1929 based on a study of the light received from the distant galaxies. He observed that the characteristic colors, or spectral lines (see SPECTRUM), emitted by the stars in the galaxies do not have exactly the same wavelengths observed in the laboratory; rather they are systematically shifted to longer wavelengths, toward the red end of the spectrum. Such "red shifts" could occur because other galaxies are moving away from our own galaxy, the Milky Way. The change in the wavelength of light that results from the relative motion of the source and the receiver of the light is an example of the DOPPLER EFFECT. The precise definition of the red shift is the increase in the wavelength divided by the original wavelength; for a given relative velocity, this quantity is the same for all wavelengths or colors. For example, a red shift of 0.05 means that all wavelengths are increased by 5% because of the recessional velocity. Thus the velocity of any given galaxy is measured by its red shift. Hubble's law was deduced from observations that indicate that the more distant a galaxy, the greater its red shift and hence the greater its velocity relative to the Milky Way. The fact that all other galaxies seem to be receding from the Milky Way does not imply that there is anything special about our position in space. Because the expansion of the universe is approximately uniform, it would appear to an observer in any galaxy that all other galaxies, including the Milky Way, were receding from his galaxy. Subsequent work has confirmed the general features of Hubble's law, but the original value for the expansion rate—Hubble's constant—has been drastically corrected. The present value implies that for every billion light-years between any two galaxies, their relative speed of separation is roughly 10% of the speed of light. Hubble's original value for the expansion rate was between five and ten times too large because he underestimated the distances to the galaxies.

Hubertusburg, Peace of (hoo͝bĕr'to͞osbo͝orkh), 1763, treaty signed on Feb. 15 between Austria and Prussia at the end of the Seven Years War. It was signed at Hubertusburg, Saxony (in present-day E Germany), a castle (built 1721-33) then used as a hunting lodge by the electors of Saxony. Prussia retained possession of Silesia and emerged as the leading power in Germany. In return, it promised to support the Archduke Joseph (later Holy Roman Emperor Joseph II) at the election of the king of the Romans. Saxony, included in the peace, was restored to its prewar limits.

Hubli-Dharwar (ho͞o'blē-där'vär), city (1971 pop. 379,555), Karnataka (formerly Mysore) state, SW India. The cities of Hubli and Dharwar, 13 mi (21 km) apart, were incorporated as one city in 1961. Dharwar is the district administrative center for a rice- and cotton-growing area. Hubli is a trade and transportation center with cotton and silk factories. It is built around an 11th-century Hindu stone temple. Dharwar grew up around a fort thought to have been built in 1405 by an officer of the Hindu king of Vijayanagar. It was captured by the Muslims in 1685 and by the MAHRATTAS in 1753. Hyder Ali, ruler of Mysore, occupied Dharwar in 1778. It was ceded to the British in 1818.

Huc, Évariste Régis (āvärēst' räzhēs' ük), 1813-60, French Roman Catholic missionary and explorer, a Lazarist priest. In 1844 while in China on a mission, he and two companions began an overland trip from Peking to Tibet. After enduring great hardships in the mountains, they reached Lhasa in 1846 but were promptly expelled for fear they would proselytize. Huc's account of his travels, first published in 1850, was abridged and translated by Julie Bedier as *High Road in Tartary* (1948).

Hucbald (hŭk'bôld), c.840-930, Flemish monk, composer and writer, formerly thought to be the author of the *Musica enchiriadis* (see POLYPHONY). He wrote a musical treatise, *De institutione harmonica,* but he is more important as a biographer of saints.

Huch, Ricarda (rēkär'dä ho͞okh), 1864-1947, German novelist, historian, and poet. She is best known for her historical romances of Garibaldi, *Defeat* and *Victory* (1906-7, tr. 1928, 1929), and of the Thirty Years War, *Der grosse Krieg in Deutschland* (1912-14). Other works include the novels *Recollections of Ludolf Ursleu* (1893, tr. 1913-15) and *The Deruga Trial* (1918, tr. 1929), two historical studies on romanticism (1899, 1902), and poems (1891, 1904, 1929, 1944).

huckleberry, any plant of the genus *Gaylussacia,* shrubs of the family Ericaceae (HEATH family), native to North and South America. The box huckleberry (*G. brachycera*) of E North America is evergreen and is often cultivated. The common huckleberry (*G. baccata*), called black or high-bush huckleberry, is native E of the Mississippi; it is the best known and is valued for its edible blue or black fruit. The huckleberry and similar species are often confused with the blueberry (the names sometimes are used interchangeably), but the fruits are botanically distinct. Huckleberries for the market are nearly always gathered from the wild. Whortleberry, a name sometimes used for huckleberries, is more often used for blueberries. For the florists' huckleberry, see BLUEBERRY. Huckleberry is classified in the division MAGNOLIOPHYTA, class Magnoliopsida, order Ericales, family Ericaceae.

Hucknall (hŭk'nəl) or **Hucknall Torkard,** urban district (1971 pop. 26,349), Nottinghamshire, central England. It has coal mines and manufactures hosiery. Lord Byron is buried in the parish church.

Huddersfield, county borough (1971 pop. 130,964), West Riding of Yorkshire, N central England, on the Colne River. Its textile industry, including cotton, woolen, and rayon goods, is important. Other products are machinery, iron goods, chemicals, and dyed fabrics. The proximity of coal and good transportation facilities by river, canal, and rail have contributed greatly to the development of Huddersfield. Its history dates back to Roman times. In 1974, Huddersfield became part of the new metropolitan county of West Yorkshire.

Hudson, Henry, fl. 1607-11, English navigator and explorer. He was hired (1607) by the English Muscovy Company to find the Northeast Passage to the Orient. He failed, and another attempt (1608) to find a new route was also fruitless. Engaged (1609) for the same purpose by the Dutch East India Company, he sailed in the *Half Moon* to Spitsbergen, where extreme ice and cold brought his crew near mutiny. Hudson, determined not to lose his reputation as an explorer, disregarded his instructions and sailed westward hoping to find the NORTHWEST PASSAGE. He entered Chesapeake Bay, Delaware Bay, and later New York Bay. He was the first white man to ascend (1609) the Hudson River (named for him), nearly to present-day Albany. His voyage gave the Dutch their claim to the region. His fourth expedition (1610), financed by English adventurers, started from England. Again he sailed westward, hoping to find the Northwest Passage. Between Greenland and Labrador he entered Hudson Strait and by it reached Hudson Bay. After weeks of exploration, he was forced by ice to winter there. By the next summer (1611) his starved and diseased crew mutinied and set Hudson, with his son and seven men, adrift in a small boat, without food or water. He was never seen again. His discoveries, however, gave England its claim to the Hudson Bay region. See biography by Llewelyn Powys (1927).

Hudson, Henry Norman, 1814-86, American essayist, b. Cornwall, Vt., grad. Middlebury College, 1840. During the Civil War he served as chaplain with Gen. B. F. Butler. He later arraigned Butler in *A Chaplain's Campaigns with General Butler* (1865). Hudson was also a noted Shakespearean scholar and literary critic.

Hudson, William Henry, 1841-1922, English author and naturalist, b. Buenos Aires of American parents. He spent his childhood on the pampas but developed a heart condition and finally emigrated to England in 1870. Hudson was a sensitive observer of nature, particularly of birds. In his books he describes plants and animals in a highly personal manner with great force and beauty. His best-known work, *Green Mansions* (1904), is a romance set in a South American jungle. Included among his other works are *The Purple Land* (1885), *The Naturalist in La Plata* (1892), *A Shepherd's Life* (1910), *Far Away and Long Ago* (1918), and *A Hind in Richmond Park* (1922). See biographies by Morley Roberts (1924) and J. T. Frederick (1972); studies by Robert Hamilton (1946) and R. E. Haymaker (1954); bibliography by G. F. Wilson (1922, repr. 1968).

Hudson. 1 Industrial town (1970 pop. 16,084), Middlesex co., E central Mass., on the Assabet River, in an apple-growing region; settled c.1699, inc. 1866. It has various manufacturing industries. **2** Town (1970 pop. 10,638), Hillsborough co., S N.H., on the Merrimack River opposite Nashua; est. 1673 as part of Dunstable, Mass., included in New Hampshire as Nottingham West in 1746; name changed to Hudson in 1830. Synthetic furs, optical equipment, and shoes are among its manufactures. For many years a small farming community, it began industrializing in the 1960s, and its population almost doubled.

Hudson, river, c.315 mi (510 km) long, rising in Lake Tear of the Clouds, on Mt. Marcy in the Adirondack Mts., NE N.Y., and flowing generally S to Upper New York Bay at New York City; the Mohawk River is its chief tributary. One of the most important waterways of the world, the Hudson is navigable by ocean vessels to Albany and by smaller vessels to

Troy; pleasure boats and self-propelled barges use the canalized section between Troy and Fort Edward, the head of navigation. Divisions of the New York State Barge Canal connect the Hudson with the Great Lakes and with Lake Champlain and the St. Lawrence River. The Hudson is tidal to Troy (c.150 mi/240 km upstream), and this section is considered to be an estuary. The upper course of the river has many waterfalls and rapids. The middle course, between Albany and Newburgh, is dominated by the Catskill and Shawangunk mts. on the west and by the large estates (the Roosevelt home at Hyde Park is the most famous) on the east bank. From Newburgh to Peekskill the river crosses the mountainous and forested Hudson Highlands in a deep, scenic gorge. West Point Military Academy overlooks the river there, and Bear Mt. Bridge spans this section. Near Tarrytown the river widens to form the Tappan Zee (which is crossed by a causeway), and from there to its mouth the Hudson is flanked on the west by the sheer cliffs of the Palisades. At the mouth are the ports of New York and New Jersey, forming one of the world's largest and busiest harbors. The Hudson forms part of the New York–New Jersey border, and the two states are linked by the George Washington Bridge, the Holland and Lincoln vehicular tunnels, and railway tubes. First sighted by Verrazano in 1524, the river was explored by Henry Hudson in 1609. It was a major route for the Indians and later for the Dutch and English traders and settlers. During the American Revolution both sides fought for control of the Hudson, and there were many battles along its banks. In 1825 the Erie Canal linked the river with the Great Lakes, thus providing the first all-water trans-Appalachian route. Many industries are located on the Hudson's banks, and pollution by raw sewage and industrial wastes became a serious problem in the 1900s; antipollution legislation passed in 1965 has sought to protect the river from further contamination. A well-known school of painting is associated with the Hudson, and the river is featured in the legend of Rip Van Winkle and other stories of Washington Irving. See Carl Carmer, *The Hudson* (1939, repr. 1968); Robert H. Boyle, *The Hudson River* (1969); Roland Van Zandt, comp., *Chronicles of the Hudson* (1971); A. R. Talbot, *Power along the Hudson* (1972).

Hudson Bay, inland sea of North America, c.475,000 sq mi (1,230,000 sq km), c.850 mi (1,370 km) long and c.650 mi (1,050 km) wide, E central Canada. Hudson Bay and James Bay (its southern extension), and all their islands are part of the Northwest Territories. Hudson Strait (c.450 mi/720 km long) connects Hudson Bay with the Atlantic Ocean, and Foxe Channel leads to the Arctic Ocean. Mansel, Coats, and Southampton islands are at the northern end of the bay. Hudson Bay occupies the southernmost portion of the Hudson Bay Lowlands, a depression in the Canadian Shield formed during the Pleistocene epoch by the weight of the continental ice sheet. As the ice retreated, the region was flooded by the sea, and sediments were deposited in it. With the burden of ice removed, the floor of the lowlands has been slowly rising and the bay is gradually becoming shallower. The western shores are generally low and marshy and covered by tundra, while the east coast is barren and rocky, with the Ottawa and Belcher island groups offshore. Many rivers, including the Churchill and Nelson, drain into the bay. Hudson Bay moderates the local climate; it is ice-free and open to navigation from mid-July to October. The bay was explored and named (1610) by Henry Hudson in his search for the Northwest Passage. The surrounding region was a rich source of furs, and France and England struggled for its possession until 1713, when France ceded its claim by the Peace of Utrecht. Hudson's Bay Company set up many trading posts there, especially at river mouths; some of the posts have operated continuously since 1670. The Hudson Bay Railway (opened 1929) links the prairie provinces with Churchill, Man., a port for oceangoing freighters.

Hudson River school, group of American landscape painters, working from 1825 to 1875. The 19th-century romantic movements of England, Germany, and France were introduced to the United States by such writers as Washington Irving and James Fenimore Cooper. At the same time, American painters were studying in Rome, absorbing much of the romantic aesthetic of the European painters. Adapting the European ideas about nature to a growing pride in the beauty of their homeland, for the first time a number of American artists began to devote themselves to landscape painting instead of portraiture. They were particularly attracted by the grandeur of Niagara Falls and the scenic beauty of the Hudson River valley, the Catskills, and the White Mts. The works of these artists reflected a new concept of wilderness—one in which man was an insignificant intrusion in a landscape more beautiful than fearsome. First of the group of artists properly classified with the Hudson River school was Thomas Doughty; his tranquil works greatly influenced later artists of the school. Albert Bierstadt glorified the Rocky Mts. in the West, working in the same manner as the painters in the East. Thomas Cole, whose dramatic and colorful landscapes are among the most impressive of the school, may be said to have been its leader during the group's most active years. Among the other important painters of the school are Asher B. Durand, J. F. Kensett, S. F. B. Morse, Henry Inman, Jasper Cropsey, Frederick E. Church, and, in his earlier work, George Inness. See articles on individual painters. See Barbara Novak, *American Painting in the Nineteenth Century* (1969); J. K. Howat, *The Hudson River and Its Painters* (1972).

Hudson's Bay Company, corporation chartered (1670) by Charles II of England for the purpose of trade and settlement in the Hudson Bay region of North America and for exploration toward the discovery of the Northwest Passage to the Orient. The company was founded as a result of the exploration of the region by Pierre RADISSON and the sieur des Groseilliers in 1668–69 under the auspices of London merchants. The expedition's success in opening up the fur trade with the Indians prompted Prince Rupert, Charles's cousin, and others to appeal to the king for a charter. A preliminary charter seems to have been granted that year, but it was not until 1670 that the much-discussed permanent charter was granted to these "Gentlemen Adventurers trading into Hudson's Bay." It conferred on them not only a trading monopoly but practically sovereign rights in the region specified as that drained by rivers flowing into Hudson Bay. The extent of this vast region was not then known, nor was it fully known for about a century. The monopoly was not respected by other English traders. The Great Company, as the Hudson's Bay Company was known, did a highly profitable business, but Hudson Bay was claimed also by the French, who sent expeditions against the posts that were soon established near the mouths of the Moose, Albany, Severn, and Nelson rivers. Warfare went on, almost regardless of whether there was peace or war between the two nations in Europe, until after the Peace of Utrecht (1713–14). The French on the whole were more successful than the British in the conflict over control of the posts, but ultimately all of Hudson Bay was recognized as British territory. Rivalry, however, continued between the French traders from Montreal and Quebec and the Hudson's Bay men. The Great Company was content to remain at its seaboard posts and made little effort either to send traders inland or to search out the Northwest Passage. The only notable early voyages made westward that are known today were those of Henry KELSEY, the disastrous attempt of James Knight in 1719 to find by sea the Northwest Passage and fabulous gold mines, the expeditions of Anthony Hendry (1754), and the journey of Samuel Hearne across the barren grounds to the mouth of the Coppermine River in 1771, which definitely proved that there was no short Northwest Passage out of Hudson Bay. The company was harshly criticized in the middle of the 18th cent., chiefly on the ground of its failure to discover the Northwest Passage. With the transference of Canada from France to England by the Treaty of Paris in 1763, a new opposition to the company in the lands nominally held in monopoly developed. Scotsmen had assumed a large role in the Montreal fur trade, and their trade cut into the declining returns of the Hudson's Bay Company. Out of the combinations of these Montreal merchants grew the NORTH WEST COMPANY, which was to be the chief rival of the older company. The Hudson's Bay men were stirred out of their lethargy. Samuel Hearne founded Cumberland House on the Saskatchewan River in 1774, and thereafter the Hudson's Bay Company took a greater interest in the West. Other difficulties stood in the way of the company. In 1782 a French naval expedition took Fort Prince of Wales, on the Churchill River, one of the most important company posts. It was returned and became Fort Churchill, but trade there and at York Factory, the other great eastern post, declined. Brisk rivalry with the Northwesters (as the traders of the North West Company were known) in the West did not turn to the advantage of the Hudson's Bay Company. The company policy apparently did not encourage exploration; thus the great geographer, David THOMPSON, left it to join the Northwesters. The whole policy and nature of the Hudson's Bay Company was altered when the earl of SELKIRK gained control after 1808. His scheme to colonize Scottish and Irish farmers on company lands led to the RED RIVER SETTLEMENT trouble, which brought disaster to the company. The ruinous and bloody rivalry was brought to an end by the amalgamation of the companies in 1821. The name of the older company was retained. The amalgamation marked the beginning of a period of true monopoly. The new united company virtually had absolute rule over a vast territory that extended from the Atlantic to the Pacific, since all of Canada except the eastern settled provinces was leased to the company. Parts of the United States, especially the Columbia River country, were subject to joint Canadian and American occupancy, but virtually were under the company rule, especially during the long tenure of John MCLOUGHLIN, who acted as administrator there. The governorship (1821–56) of Sir George SIMPSON marked the peak of the company's fortunes. In 1857 the company was subjected to a parliamentary investigation. Although the company trade privileges were renewed, its position was not secure. In 1863 the stock of the company was bought up and reissued by the International Financial Society. The stock passed from a few to many holders. This internal reorganization had a vast effect on the company. It also was changed from without, particularly after confederation (1867). Opponents were able to challenge successfully its monopolistic operations. In 1869 the company territory was by governmental order transferred to Canada in return for £300,000. The nature of the company was thereafter entirely different. It began to change from being solely a fur-trading organization and eventually became a gigantic corporation of almost innumerable interests. The sales of company lands brought in much money. For many years (1889–1914) Lord STRATHCONA was governor. It was after his death that the real expansion of the company into retail trade and manufacturing of all sorts took place, in the administrations of Sir Robert Molesworth Kindersley (1915–25) and Charles Vincent Sale (1926–30). In World War I company ships were used as transports and the company rendered great services to the war effort. In 1930 the company was split up: the Canadian stores were segregated into a separate organization, and the London portion was once more turned to the fur trade. Partly because of the secrecy of the company concerning its records and partly because of the strong feeling for and against the company, there has been no adequate, impartial, and scholarly history of the Hudson's Bay Company in general; E. E. Rich's official history (3 vols., 1961) is based on the company's records, but is not annotated. See introductions to scholarly editions of traders's journals, such as those of the Champlain Society. See also George Bryce, *The Remarkable History of the Hudson's Bay Company* (1900, repr. 1968); H. A. Innis, *The Fur Trade in Canada* (1930, repr. 1962); Douglas MacKay, *The Honourable Company* (1936, repr. 1970); J. S. Galbraith, *The Hudson's Bay Company as an Imperial Factor, 1821–1869* (1957).

Hudson seal: see MUSKRAT.

Hue (hwā), city (1968 est. pop. 157,000), former capital of the historic region of ANNAM, South Vietnam, in a rich farming area on the Hue River near the South China Sea. The third largest city in South Vietnam, it is a market center and the northernmost base in the military coastal supply system. The nearby port of Lai An serves as the naval station. A cement plant 3 mi (4.8 km) southwest utilizes the fine limestone deposits in the area. Probably founded in the 3d cent. A.D., Hue was occupied in turn by the Chams and the Annamese. After the 16th cent. it was the seat of a dynasty that extended its power over S Annam, modern Cochin China, and parts of Cambodia and Laos. The first king of Vietnam, Nguyen Anh, was crowned there in 1802, and shortly thereafter Hue became the capital of the new kingdom, emerging as an artistic and literary center. The French occupied the city in 1883. During World War II the Japanese mined iron ore in the area. In the VIETNAM WAR, Hue was the scene of the longest and heaviest fighting of the Tet offensive (Jan.–Feb., 1968); some 4,000 civilians were killed and most of the city, including the palaces and tombs of the former Annamese kings, was destroyed. Much has since been rebuilt. Hue has an important airport and is the seat of the Univ. of Hue.

hue and cry, formerly, in English law, pursuit of a criminal immediately after he had committed a FELONY. Whoever witnessed or discovered the crime was required to raise the hue and cry against the perpetrator (e.g., call out "Stop, thief!") and to begin pursuit; all persons within hearing were under the same obligation, and it was a punishable offense not to join in the chase and capture. The perpetrator was promptly brought into court, and if there was evidence of his having been caught red-handed, he was summarily convicted without being allowed to testify in his own behalf. The hue and cry was abolished in the early 19th cent. Possible modern survivals are the obligation to serve on a sheriff's posse and to assist a police officer in pursuing a suspected culprit.

Huelva (wĕl'vä), city (1970 pop. 96,689), capital of Huelva prov., SW Spain, in Andalusia, on the Odiel River above its junction with the Río Tinto. A busy port with copper, sulfur, and cork exports, it also has large fisheries and summer resort facilities. A Roman aqueduct supplies the city with water. Nearby La Rábida monastery, where Columbus made his plans, is a summer university.

Huerta, Adolfo de la (ädôl'fō thā lä wăr'tä), c.1882–1955, Mexican revolutionist and president (May–Dec., 1920). As governor of Sonora, he broke with President CARRANZA and declared the secession of the state (1920). This was a signal for the successful revolt against Carranza led by OBREGÓN and supported by CALLES. After Carranza's murder, de la Huerta was provisional president until Obregón took office by election; during his tenure a settlement was reached with Villa. He was minister of finance under Obregón. Upon the designation of Calles as official presidential candidate, de la Huerta revolted (Dec., 1923); the uprising was crushed by Obregón in the spring of 1924, and de la Huerta was sent into exile in the United States. He was recalled (1935) by Lázaro Cárdenas to serve in diplomatic posts. See study by M. C. Meyer (1972).

Huerta, Victoriano (vēktōryä'nō), 1854–1916, Mexican general and president (1913–14). He served under Porfirio Díaz. After the revolution of Francisco I. MADERO (1911) he aided the new president, who, reluctantly, made him (1912) commander of the federal forces. In 1913 he plotted secretly with Madero's enemies, including U.S. ambassador Henry Lane Wilson, and overthrew the president. Huerta established a military dictatorship, notable for political corruption and rule by imprisonment and assassination. Numerous counterrevolutions broke out; the most important insurgent leaders were Venustiano CARRANZA, Francisco VILLA, and Emiliano ZAPATA. U.S. President Woodrow Wilson was openly hostile to Huerta, and unpleasant international incidents occurred at Tampico and Veracruz. Steady insurgent military pressure forced Huerta to resign in July, 1914. He fled to Europe and returned to the United States, where he was subsequently arrested for revolutionary activities; an alcoholic, he died in El Paso shortly after being released from an army jail.

Huesca (wā'skä), town (1970 pop. 33,185), capital of Huesca prov., NE Spain, in Aragón, at the foot of the Pyrenees. It is a farm center. In this ancient town Sertorius founded a school in 77 B.C. After Peter I of Aragón liberated it (1096) from the Moors, Huesca was the residence of the kings of Aragón until 1118. A university, later discontinued, was founded there in 1354. The 13th-century Gothic cathedral, the early Romanesque Church of San Pedro, and the royal palace of the Aragonese monarchs are notable landmarks.

Hügel, Friedrich, Baron von (frē'drĭkh bärōn' fən hü'gəl), 1852–1925, British Roman Catholic religious writer, b. Florence; son of an Austrian diplomat. After his marriage (1873), Hügel lived in England. He wrote *The Mystical Element of Religion as Studied in St. Catherine of Genoa and Her Friends* (1908), a classic in the study of mysticism. Other works include *Eternal Life* (1912) and *Essays and Addresses on the Philosophy of Religion* (1921 and 1926). Through letters and essays he exerted a profound influence on the MODERNISM movement within the Roman Catholic Church. Hügel defended the methods of modern biblical scholarship in the face of growing papal disapproval. Although a Catholic, Hügel saw divine truth in all religions, and he refused to proselytize. He regarded the adoration of God by the creature to be the essence of religion, and he stressed the values common to both the natural and the supernatural life. See biography by Michael de la Bedoyère (1951); studies by J. P. Whelan (1971) and L. F. Barmann (1972).

Hugenberg, Alfred (äl'frĕt hōō'gənbĕrkh), 1865–1951, German financier and politician. He was president of the directorate of the Krupp firm (1909–18), entered the Reichstag in 1919, and was chairman (1928–33) of the conservative German Nationalist party and a member of Hitler's first cabinet (Jan.–June, 1933). The Hugenberg combine, organized in 1916 and comprising newspapers, motion-picture companies, information services, and finance corporations, enabled him to influence public opinion. The combine was gradually absorbed by the state under the Nazis.

Huggins, Sir William, 1824–1910, English astronomer. Using a spectroscope, he began to study the chemical constitution of stars from the observatory attached to his home in Tulse Hill, London. He proved that while some nebulas are clusters of stars, others are uniformly gaseous. Huggins pioneered in spectroscopic photography and played a part in developing the combined use of the telescope, spectroscope, and photographic negative. He adapted the gelatin dry-plate negative for making astronomical photographs; this made possible exposures of any desired length. In 1866, Huggins made the first spectroscopic observations of a nova. He applied the Doppler effect to the measurement of stellar motions in the line of sight. Huggins was president (1900–1906) of the Royal Society. With his wife, Margaret Lindsay Murray, Lady Huggins, he prepared an *Atlas of Representative Stellar Spectra* (1899).

Hugh Capet (kā'pĭt, kăp'ĭt), c.938–996, king of France (987–96), first of the CAPETIANS. He was the son of HUGH THE GREAT, to whose vast territories he succeeded in 956. After the death of Louis V, last Carolingian king of France, the nobles and prelates elected him king, setting aside the last Carolingian claimant, CHARLES I of Lower Lorraine. In order to fix the succession, Hugh took as his associate his son Robert (later King Robert II). He spent much of his reign fighting Charles and later became involved in a controversy with the papacy—unsettled at his death—over deposition of the Carolingian archbishop of Rheims.

Hughes, Charles Evans, 1862–1948, American statesman and jurist, Associate Justice of the U.S. Supreme Court (1910–16), U.S. Secretary of State (1921–25), and eleventh Chief Justice of the United States (1930–41), b. Glens Falls, N.Y. A graduate of Columbia law school, he was admitted to the bar in 1884 and practiced law in New York City, where he rose rapidly in his profession. He served (1905) as counsel for a committee of the New York state legislature investigating gas companies and, as counsel (1905–6) for another state investigating committee, achieved national prominence for his exposure of corrupt practices of insurance companies in New York. This led to his election (1906) as Republican governor of New York. In this post (1907–10) Hughes brought about the establishment of the public service commission, the passage of various insurance-law reforms, and the enactment of much labor legislation. He resigned the governorship after President Taft appointed him (1910) Associate Justice of the U.S. Supreme Court but left the Court in 1916 to run for President on the Republican ticket. The election was one of the closest presidential contests in American history, Woodrow Wilson defeating Hughes by an electoral vote of 277 to 254 and a popular vote of 9,129,606 to 8,538,221. The vote of California, which went to Wilson by less than 4,000 votes largely because of the disaffection of Hiram JOHNSON, decided the election. Hughes again devoted himself to his law practice. In 1921, President Warren Harding appointed him Secretary of State. He continued in this office under President Coolidge. Hughes prepared plans for the limitation of naval armaments at the Washington Conference (see NAVAL CONFERENCES), directed negotiations for several important foreign treaties, and vastly increased the prestige of the U.S. Dept. of State. He afterward was a member of the Permanent Court of Arbitration (1926–30) and a judge of the Permanent Court of International Justice (1928–30). He was appointed (1930) Chief Justice of the United States by President Hoover; he retired in 1941. As Chief Justice, Hughes generally held a moderately conservative position, although he was thought by some to have become more liberal as he grew older. More often than not he voted to uphold controversial legislation of President Franklin Delano Roosevelt's New Deal, but he vigorously opposed Roosevelt's unsuccessful effort to reorganize the Supreme Court. Many of his addresses were published in *The Pathway to Peace* (1925), *The Supreme Court of the United States* (1928), *Our Relations to the Nations of the Western Hemisphere* (1928), *Pan-American Peace Plans* (1929), and *Nations United for Peace* (1945). See his autobiographical notes, ed. by D. J. Danelski and J. S. Tulchin (1973); biographies by Merlo Pusey (2 vol., 1951, repr. 1963) and Dexter Perkins (1956); studies by Samuel Hendel (1951), Betty Glad (1966), and R. F. Wesser (1967).

Hughes, Howard Robard, 1905–, U.S. business executive, b. Houston. As a young man he inherited (1925) the patent rights to an oil tool drill, which, manufactured by the Hughes Tool Company, formed the basis of his financial empire. His interest in aviation led to the formation of the Hughes Aircraft Corp. in the 1930s, which later became a major U.S. defense contractor. A pilot himself, he set a number of airplane records, including a world record (1935) of 352 mi (566 km) per hr in a plane of his own design. Hughes's interests in the 1920s and 30s also extended to the motion picture industry, and among the films that he produced were such classics as *Hell's Angels* and *The Front Page*. Through his parent concern, the Hughes Tool Company, he gained a controlling interest in Trans World Airways (TWA); when he divested himself of his TWA stock in 1966, he received $546.5 million. In the 1960s he purchased a number of gambling casinos in Las Vegas. A billionaire, he became a recluse in later years. His vast business interests have involved him in extensive litigation. He was married (1957–71) to the actress Jean Peters.

Hughes, John Ceiriog, 1832–87, Welsh lyric poet. By restoring simplicity of diction and emotional sincerity, he did for Welsh poetry what Wordsworth and Coleridge did for English poetry. Many of his songs were written to folk airs.

Hughes, John Joseph, 1797–1864, American Roman Catholic churchman, b. Co. Tyrone, Ireland. He joined his family in the United States in 1817 and on graduating from Mt. St. Mary's College, Emmitsburg, Md., was ordained (1826). He served mostly in Philadelphia until 1838, when he was consecrated bishop and became coadjutor to Bishop John Dubois in New York. In 1842, Hughes was made bishop, and in 1850 the first archbishop of New York. He obtained for the church complete control of its property by the clergy. A resolute and ardent defender of Catholicism, he engaged in debates, worked actively in behalf of Irish immigrants, and strongly urged the obliteration of European national affiliations in American Catholicism. His vigorous but unsuccessful attempt to secure state support for religious schools carried him into politics and led to the establishment of the independent Catholic school system. In the Civil War, Abraham Lincoln sent him to France to promote a friendly attitude toward the Union cause. He founded (1841) St. John's College (now Fordham Univ.) and laid (1858) the cornerstone of St. Patrick's Cathedral, New York City. See his works (ed. by Lawrence Kehoe, 1864); biography by J. R. G. Hassard (1866, repr. 1969); study by V. P. Lannie (1968).

Hughes, Langston (James Langston Hughes), 1902–67, American poet, b. Joplin, Mo., a major figure of the Harlem Renaissance. He worked at a variety of jobs and lived in several countries, including Mexico and France, before Vachel Lindsay discovered his poetry in 1925. The publication of *The Weary Blues* (1926), his first volume of poetry, enabled Hughes to attend Lincoln Univ. in Pennsylvania, from which he graduated in 1929. His writing, which often uses dialect and jazz rhythms, is largely concerned with depicting American Negro life, particularly the experience of the urban Negro. Among his later collections of poetry are *Shakespeare in Harlem* (1942), *One-Way Ticket* (1949), and *Selected Poems* (1959). Hughes's numerous other works include several plays, notably *Mulatto* (1935); books for children, such as *The First Book of Negroes* (1952); and novels, including *Not Without Laughter* (1930). His newspaper sketches about Jesse B. Simple were collected in *The Best of Simple* (1961). See his autobiographies, *The Big Sea* (1940) and *I Wonder As I Wander* (1956).

Hughes, Richard, 1900–, English novelist. After graduating from Oxford in 1922, he helped found the Portmadoc Players and was for a time vice president of the Welsh National Theatre. In addition, he wrote several plays, notably *The Sisters' Tragedy* (1922). Hughes is probably best known for his first novel, *A High Wind in Jamaica* (American ed., *The Innocent Voyage*, 1929), a bizarre tale about a group of children captured by pirates; the chilling unease of the story derives from the evil apparent, not in the pirates, but in the children. *In Hazard* (1938), Hughes's next novel, is a sea story reminiscent of Conrad. The novels *The Fox in the Attic* (1961) and *The Wooden Shepherdess* (1972) are part of a proposed long historical novel of contemporary times entitled *The Human Predicament*.

Hughes, Sir Samuel, 1853–1921, Canadian political leader, b. Ontario. A schoolteacher and newspaper editor, he entered the House of Commons in 1892 and held a seat until his death. As minister of militia and defense (1911–16) in Sir Robert Borden's government, he was responsible for organizing and dispatching the Canadian Expeditionary Force in World War I. To this task he brought great energy, but his outspoken criticism of those with whom he did not agree forced Borden to request his resignation in 1916. Hughes was knighted in 1915.

Hughes, Ted, 1930–, English poet, b. Mytholmroyd, W Yorkshire. In his poems, which are marked by controlled diction and style, Hughes attempts to bring order and meaning out of images of violence and passion. His works include *The Hawk in the Rain* (1957), *Lupercal* (1960), *Meet My Folks* (1961), *Wodwo* (1967), *Crow: From the Life and Songs of the Crow* (1971), *Selected Poems* (1973), and various children's books. Hughes was married to the American poet Sylvia PLATH.

Hughes, Thomas, 1822–96, English author. A lawyer, Hughes eventually became a judge; he was also a Liberal member of Parliament and worked assiduously for social reforms. His novel of school life, *Tom Brown's School Days* (1857), is a classic. Its sequel, *Tom Brown at Oxford* (1861), was less successful.

Hughes, William Morris, 1864–1952, Australian statesman, b. England. He emigrated in 1884 and after a varied career entered the New South Wales legislature (1894) and, with confederation, the first federal Parliament (1901). In 1904 he became minister for external affairs in the first Labour government and later was attorney general (1908–9, 1910–13, 1914–21). As prime minister of the commonwealth (1915–23), he gave great support to the British throughout World War I and upheld the position of Australia at the Paris Peace Conference. He held many cabinet posts during the 1930s and was (1940–41) minister of the navy. His writings include *Splendid Adventure: A Review of Empire Relations* (1929) and *Policies and Potentates* (1950). See Douglas Sladen, *From Boundary-Rider to Prime Minister* (1916).

Hugh of Lincoln, Saint, 1140–1200, bishop of Lincoln, b. Avalon, Burgundy, of a noble family. He became religious while still a child and joined (c.1160) the Carthusians, rising to become procurator general. About 1176 he was, at the request of King Henry II, sent to England to become prior of the charterhouse founded by Henry at Witham, Somerset. In 1186 he was consecrated bishop of Lincoln. He opposed Henry's forest laws and his demands for the preferment of unworthy courtiers. In 1198 he was spokesman for the barons in their refusal of money to Richard I and was also in conflict with Richard's successor, John. But the bishop's high courage, devotion to religion and justice, and ready tact helped him to convert the angry royal brothers to his own views. He was noted for his charity, love of the poor and oppressed, and the holiness of his life. He partially rebuilt Lincoln Cathedral, where his shrine was a place of pilgrimage until the Reformation. He is also known as St. Hugh of Avalon. Feast: Nov. 17. See Margaret Thompson, *The Carthusian Order in England* (1930); biographies by Herbert Thurston (tr. 1898) and Joseph Clayton (1931).

Hugh of Saint Victor, 1096–1141, French or German philosopher and theologian, a canon regular of the monastery of St. Victor, Paris, from c.1115. In 1133 he was made head of the monastery school, which became under him one of the principal centers of learning in medieval France. Hugh made St. Victor the chief competitor of Abelard's school (see ABELARD). It was out of the struggle between these schools that SCHOLASTICISM was born. Hugh used the same dialectic method that Abelard did, but his findings were never heterodox; the unquestionable orthodoxy of the school of St. Victor may have been an important cause of the eventual triumph in Roman Catholic theology of the dialectic method, which Abelard had brought under serious suspicion. Hugh's *Eruditionis didascaliae libri VII* expounds his new contribution to the division of knowledge. *De sacramentis Christianae fidei* (*On the Sacraments of the Christian Faith;* tr. by R. J. Defarrari, 1957), Hugh's chief work, is a general thesis on dogmatic theology, giving him his high place in medieval philosophy. Hugh also wrote many mystical works (e.g., *Arca Noë moralis, Arca Noë mystica, De amore sponsi ad sponsam*) and he was long best known for them. His mystical teaching was very influential in the history of his school, but he was not so extreme as his successors, notably RICHARD OF SAINT VICTOR. He was responsible for the celebrated division of the mystical ascent into three stages: thought (with which we see God in nature), meditation (with which we see God within ourselves), and contemplation (with which we see God as if face to face). See *The Didascalicon of Hugh of St. Victor* (with notes and tr. by Jerome Taylor, 1961); biography by Jerome Taylor (1957).

Hugh the Great, d. 956, French duke; son of King ROBERT I and father of HUGH CAPET. Excluded from the succession on his father's death by his brother-in-law RAOUL, he supported the candidacy of LOUIS IV, the Carolingian heir, after Raoul's death (936). Hugh hoped to rule through this weak king who had been raised in England. Louis IV attempted to increase his strength, however, and his reign was marked by warfare between king and vassal, in which Hugh, excommunicated (948) at the insistence of Louis, was forced to submit (950). Although Hugh never held the title of king, his vast possessions made him the virtual ruler of France.

Hugo, Victor Marie, Vicomte (hyo͞o'gō, Fr. vēktôr' märē' vēkôNt' ügō'), 1802–85, French poet, dramatist, and novelist, b. Besançon. His father was a general under Napoleon. As a child he was taken to Italy and Spain and at a very early age had published his first book of poems, resolving "to be Chateaubriand or nothing." The preface to his drama *Cromwell* (1827) placed him at the head of the romanticists; he remained the greatest exponent of the school and was considered by many the greatest poet of his day. His principal poetic works are *Les Orientales* (1829), *Les Feuilles d'automne* (1831), *Les Chants du crépuscule* (1835), *Les Voix intérieures* (1837), *Les Rayons et les ombres* (1840), *Les Châtiments* (1853), *Les Contemplations* (1856), and *La Légende des siècles* (1859). The production of his poetic drama *Hernani* (tr. 1830), which broke with conventions of the French theater, caused a riot between the classicists and the romanticists. The drama was the basis of Verdi's opera *Ernani;* Verdi also made use of Hugo's play *Le Roi s'amuse* (1832) for *Rigoletto.* Other plays include *Marion Delorme* (1831, tr. 1872), *Ruy Blas* (1838, tr. 1850), and *Les Burgraves* (1843), the failure of which spelled the end of the romantic drama. The tragic deaths in that year of Hugo's daughter and her husband were reflected in a moving series of poems of childhood, including *The Art of Being a Grandfather* (1877). Hugo's two greatest novels are *Notre Dame de Paris* (1831, tr. 1833) and *Les Misérables* (1862, tr. 1862), which are epic in scope and portray the sufferings of humanity with great compassion and power. His other important novels include *Les Travailleurs de la mer* (1866, tr. *Toilers of the Sea,* 1866), and *Quatre-vingt-treize* (1874, tr. *Ninety-three,* 1874). He began his political career as a supporter of the duke of Reichstadt, Napoleon's son; later Hugo espoused the cause of Louis Philippe's son, and then for a short time of Louis Bonaparte. Because he afterward opposed NAPOLEON III, Hugo was banished and went first to Brussels, then to the isle of Jersey, and later (1855) to Guernsey, where he lived until 1870, refusing an amnesty. In 1870 he returned to Paris in triumph. He was elected to the national assembly and the senate. His last years were marked by public veneration and acclaim, and he was buried in the Panthéon. Critics are divided as to his relative greatness, but he was a towering figure in 19th-century French literature. See biography by André Maurois (tr. 1956); studies by Richard B. Grant (1968), E. M. Grant, (1945, repr. 1966 and 1968), and J. P. Houston (1974).

Huguenots (hyo͞o'gənŏts), French Protestants, followers of John CALVIN. The term is derived from the German *Eidgenossen,* meaning sworn companions or confederates. Prior to Calvin's publication in 1536 of his *Institutes of the Christian Religion,* a reform movement already existed in France. Despite persecution, the movement grew. Under King Henry II reprisals became more severe. Nevertheless, in 1559, the first French national synod was held, and a Presbyterian church modeled on Calvin's reform in Geneva was founded. The adherence of a large number of the nobility to the movement gave it political meaning and added fuel to persecution. The conspiracy of Amboise (1560; see AMBOISE, CONSPIRACY OF) during the reign of King FRANCIS II, inflamed both Roman Catholic and Protestant sentiment. This, along with political rivalry, particularly among the BOURBONS and the GUISES, precipitated the Wars of Religion (1562–98; see RELIGION, WARS OF). Despite such heavy blows to the Huguenots as the massacre of SAINT BARTHOLOMEW'S DAY (1572), the formation of the Catholic League (see LEAGUE), and the intervention of Spain (1589–98) against the Protestant heir to the throne, the Bourbon HENRY IV, the Protestants were ultimately victorious. Their success was due largely to their unity under such admirable leaders as Louis I de CONDÉ, Gaspard de COLIGNY, JEANNE D'ALBRET, and her son, Henry IV. In 1598, Henry IV, by issuing the Edict of Nantes (see NANTES, EDICT OF), established Protestantism in 200 towns, proclaimed freedom of worship, and allowed substantial political independence. During the next 50 years, more and more skilled artisans and members of the bourgeoisie became Huguenots, who thus constituted one of the most industrious and economically advanced elements in French society. In the reign of King Louis XIII, Cardinal RICHELIEU decided to suppress Protestant political privileges. An uprising (1621–22) against the introduction of Catholicism in Béarn was put down by Richelieu, and the Protestants lost all the strongholds given to them under the Edict of Nantes, except Montauban and La Rochelle. Led by Henri de ROHAN and Benjamin de SOUBISE, the Huguenots revolted again in 1625 and in 1627. La Rochelle was captured (1628) by Richelieu after a 14-month siege, during which King Charles I of England attempted to send some aid to the Protestant defenders. The Peace of Alais (1629) stripped the Huguenots of all political power but assured them of continued religious tolerance. Cardinal Mazarin continued Richelieu's policy, but King Louis XIV, urged by the French Catholic clergy, moved to suppress the dissident religion. Conversion was encouraged; the Edict of Nantes was interpreted in the strictest way possible; and dragoons were quartered in the homes of Huguenots (see DRAGONNADES). Finally, in 1685, the Edict of Nantes was revoked. This act had disastrous results. Entire provinces were depopulated as countless Huguenots fled to England, the Netherlands, Germany, Switzerland, and America. The only important fragment of Huguenots left in France was in the Cévennes, where the war of the CAMISARDS (1702–10) broke out. In 1787, Louis XVI allowed the Huguenots tolerance, and in Dec., 1789, the revolutionary National Assembly restored their civil rights. Full religious freedom was not attained until church and state were separated in 1905. See history by H. M. Baird (6 vol., 1879–95); A. J. Grant, *The Huguenots* (1934, repr. 1969); Otto Zoff, *The Huguenots* (1942).

Huguenot Wars: see RELIGION, WARS OF.

Hu Han-min (ho͞o hän-mĭn), 1879–1936, Chinese statesman. While studying law in Japan (1905) he was associated with Sun Yat-sen in revolutionary activities. After the revolution of 1911, Hu opposed Yüan Shih-k'ai and served Sun Yat-sen. His position in the Kuomintang and the Canton government was such that he was considered a likely successor to Sun. However, he was forced to withdraw from political life in 1925 when his cousin was implicated in the murder of one of his rivals. He served the Nationalist government as president of the Legislative Yüan (1928–31). He led a Kuomintang faction opposed to Chiang Kai-shek, and his arrest by Chiang in 1931 led to a secessionist movement. Civil war was averted only by the need to unite following the Japanese takeover of Manchuria. After his release, Hu devoted himself to interpreting the political thought of Sun Yat-sen.

Huhehot: see HU-HO-HAO-T'E, China.

Hu-ho-hao-t'e (ho͞o-hô-hou-tä) or **Huhehot** (ho͞o-hähōt'), city (1970 est. pop. 700,000), capital of the Inner Mongolian Autonomous Region, N China. The terminus of caravan routes to Sinkiang and to the Mongolian People's Republic, Hu-ho-hao-t'e is also connected by rail with Peking and is a trade center for NW China. Manufactures include chemicals, textiles, fertilizers, motor vehicles, and beet sugar and other processed foods. Hu-ho-hao-t'e consists of two sections. The old town is a Mongolian political and religious center dating from the 9th cent. It was the seat of the Living Buddha until his removal (1664) to Urga (see ULAN BATOR). The newer Chinese section, which grew around the railway station after 1921, is the administrative center. Hu-ho-hao-t'e is the seat of Inner Mongolian Univ., a medical college, and several technical institutes. The city was called Kweisui until 1954.

Huidobro, Vicente (vēsän'tä wētho͞'brō), 1893–1948, Chilean poet, founder of a short-lived aesthetic movement known as *creacionismo,* which emphasized the value of the poet as creator. He lived for many years in Paris and was a founder of the review *Nord-Sud.* Striving for original imagery, he sought to deny the poetic past. Like other avant-garde movements of the post-World War I period, Huidobro's creationism had only a limited influence. Poems illustrative of his philosophy are included in *Tour Eiffel* (1917) and *Últimos poemas* (1948).

Hui-neng: see ZEN BUDDHISM.

Hui Shih (hwē shûr), c.380-c.300 B.C., Chinese logician, remembered for his paradoxes. Little is known about his life, except that he was a provincial prime minister, or about the thinking that led to his paradoxes, which range over physical, mathematical, and logical concepts. Of his voluminous writings, only ten paradoxes and some other fragments have survived.

Hui Tsung (hwē dzōōng), 1082-1135, Chinese emperor of the Northern Sung dynasty, painter, and a great patron of art. Politically he was a rather ineffectual ruler, but he was said to have devoted all his spare time to painting and to the reorganization of the Imperial Academy of Painting. Through his encouragement, art collecting came into vogue during his reign. The emperor himself was an accomplished artist, specializing in delicately colored bird-and-flower paintings. There are also many such paintings by others that have his seals and signatures—affixed by the emperor to signify his approval of the work of artists who laboriously copied his own paintings. Most of these works show intimate, detailed studies of nature, executed in a refined, sensitive, and meticulous manner. He abdicated in 1125 when his attempts to buy off the advancing Jurchens failed. In 1126 the Northern Sung capital at Kaifeng was overrun by the Jurchen hordes, and he was captured together with the new emperor and taken to Mongolia, where he died in captivity. A scroll painting in silk at the Museum of Fine Arts, Boston, known as *Ladies Preparing Silk,* is believed to be the copy made by the emperor after the work by the 8th-century painter Chang Hsüan. The same museum has a small painting called *The Five-Colored Parakeet,* which is one of the best bird-and-flower paintings attributed to him.

Huitzilopochtli (wē"tsēlōpōcht'lē), chief deity of the Aztec, god of war. He is said to have guided the Aztecs during their migration from Aztlán. Usually represented in sculptured images as hideous, he was the object of human sacrifice, particularly of war prisoners. He was also god of the sun, and it was believed that he was born each morning from the womb of Coatlicue, goddess of earth. His temple at Tenochtitlán was a great architectural achievement of pre-Columbian America.

Huizinga, Johan (yōhän' hoi'zĭngə), 1872-1945, Dutch historian. He began his academic career in philology, but his reputation rests on his work in the cultural history of the late Middle Ages, the Renaissance, and the Reformation. Huizinga's classic *Waning of the Middle Ages* (tr. 1924) deals with the Low Countries and N France in the 14th and 15th cent. and weakens Jacob Burckhardt's concept of the Renaissance. Huizinga considered the Renaissance the death of the Middle Ages rather than the birth of the modern world. Other notable works include *Erasmus of Rotterdam* (tr. 1954) and essays on the philosophy of history. In World War II he was imprisoned for his opposition to the Nazis.

Hukbalahap (Huk) (hōōk"bälähäp'), Communist-led guerrilla movement in the Philippines. It developed during World War II as a guerrilla army to fight the Japanese; the name is a contraction of a Tagalog phrase meaning "People's Anti-Japanese Army." After the war the army openly declared its Communist orientation, and launched an armed revolt against the Philippine government. The Huk's emphasis on land reform attracted many peasants, especially in central Luzon. The movement was also strong on Panay. By 1950 some five provinces were under virtual Huk control and the Philippine government launched a vigorous military campaign against them. After the Huk leader Luis Taruc voluntarily surrendered in 1954, the movement died out. The need for land reform continued, however, and in the late 1960s the Hukbalahaps became active again. In Aug., 1969, President Marcos launched a military campaign against them, and Huk activities ceased in late 1970. Other Communist groups, however, continued Huk terrorist activity.

Hukok (hyōō'kōk): see HELKATH.

Hul, descendant of Shem. Gen. 10.23.

Hula, Lake or **Lake Huleh** (both: hōō'lā), Arabic *Bahr al Hulah,* near sea-level lake formed by a natural dam of basalt, NE Israel; the united Jordan River exits from its southern end. Between 1950 and 1958, c.12,350 acres (5,000 hectares) of the lake's swampy shore were drained; this land, now irrigated by the Jordan, produces rice, cotton, and sugar beets. Lake Hula can undoubtedly be identified with the Waters of Merom, where Joshua won a great victory (Joshua 11).

Hulagu Khan (hōōlä'gōō khän), 1217-65, Mongol conqueror, grandson of Jenghiz Khan. His brother Mangu, grand khan of the Mongols, directed him to quell a revolt in Persia. In 1256, in the course of his successful campaign, his forces virtually exterminated the powerful ASSASSIN sect. Moving west to enlarge his conquests, he sacked and burned Baghdad in 1258 (executing the last Abbasid caliph) and captured Aleppo and Damascus in 1260. Further advances were checked by the Mamelukes, who defeated him (Sept., 1260) at the decisive battle of Ayn Jalut (Goliath's Well) in Syria. Hulagu withdrew to Azerbaijan, adopted Islam, and founded the Il-khan dynasty. His khanate, which included all of Persia, endured until 1335, when it was divided into five parts.

Huldah (hŭl'də), prophetess, consulted by Josiah on the finding of the Law. 2 Kings 22.14-20; 2 Chron. 34.22-28.

Huleh, Lake: see HULA, LAKE.

Hull, Bobby (Robert Marvin Hull, Jr.), 1939-, Canadian hockey player. Considered to be the best left wing in the sport's history, Hull was skating from age three and began playing with the Chicago Black Hawks of the National Hockey League (NHL) in the 1957-58 season. He played 15 seasons with them before joining the Winnipeg Jets of the World Hockey Association (WHA) for the 1972-73 season. Hull led the NHL in scoring three times (1959-60, 1961-62, 1965-66) and was most valuable player twice (1964-65, 1965-66). He was also named most valuable player in the WHA for 1972-73. He scored 604 goals in the NHL. His play is marked by a combination of speed, endurance, strength, and grace.

Hull, Cordell, 1871-1955, American statesman, b. Overton co. (now Pickett co.), Tenn. Admitted to the bar in 1891, he sat (1893-97) in the Tennessee legislature and, after service in the Spanish-American War, was appointed (1903) circuit court judge. He served (1907-21, 1923-31) in the U.S. House of Representatives, where he was the author of important tax legislation. He was elected (1930) to the U.S. Senate, but resigned (1933) when Franklin Delano Roosevelt named him Secretary of State. Hull placed great emphasis on international economic relations. Through his efforts, pacts were signed with several nations under the Reciprocal Agreements Act (1934), and he fostered the "good neighbor" policy toward Latin American countries. After World War II broke out in Europe he pushed for aid to the Allies and recommended revision of the Neutrality Act. After U.S. entry into the war, he worked to improve cooperation among the Allies, visiting Moscow in 1943, and backed the establishment of a world organization to maintain peace. Ill health caused his resignation as Secretary of State in 1944. He was awarded the 1945 Nobel Peace Prize. See his autobiography (1948); biography by J. W. Pratt (2 vol., 1964).

Hull, Isaac, 1773-1843, American naval officer, b. Derby, Conn. He served in the undeclared naval war with France (1798-1800) and in the Tripolitan War before being promoted to captain in 1806. In 1810 he was given command of the *Constitution.* Early in the War of 1812 he slipped his ship out of Chesapeake Bay and, evading seven enemy ships, succeeded in making his way through the British blockade to Boston Harbor. On Aug. 19, 1812, the *Constitution* met the *Guerrière* in one of America's great sea battles. Hull's superior seamanship forced the British vessel to surrender. See his papers, ed. by G. W. Allen (1929); biographies by Bruce Grant (1947) and L. T. Molloy (1964).

Hull, William, 1753-1825, American general, b. Derby, Conn. He served brilliantly in the American Revolution and became in 1805 governor of the newly created Michigan Territory. As the War of 1812 began he asked Congress for a larger U.S. fleet on Lake Erie and reinforcements for Detroit. Hull, in command of Detroit, failed to make a planned attack on Canada and instead remained in Detroit until British forces under Sir Isaac Brock seized the fort on Aug. 16, 1812, capturing many supplies. Hull was court-martialed for cowardice and neglect of duty, and only his Revolutionary War record prevented his execution. Subsequent evidence has shown that Hull was not solely to blame for the disastrous campaign.

Hull, city (1971 pop. 63,580), SW Que., Canada, at the confluence of the Ottawa and Gatineau rivers, opposite the city of Ottawa; inc. 1895. Hull has a hydroelectric power station. There are paper, pulp, and lumber mills, iron foundries, and cement and meat-packing plants. Nearby is Gatineau Park, a large recreation area.

Hull, officially **Kingston upon Hull,** county borough (1971 pop. 285,472), East Riding of Yorkshire, NE England, on the north shore of the Humber estuary at the influx of the small Hull River. Its port is one of the chief outlets for the industrial Yorkshire and Lincolnshire districts, with which there are excellent rail and water connections. Imports include oilseed, wood, foodstuffs, wool, metal ores, and petroleum; exports include coal, coke, machinery, automobiles, tractors, iron and steel products, and textiles. Hull is also one of the world's largest fishing ports. Among its many manufactures are processed foods, chemicals, iron and steel products, and machinery. Flour mills and sawmills are nearby. Hull was founded late in the 13th cent. by Edward I, and the construction of docks, which now extend for miles along the Humber, was begun c.1775. The Wilberforce House, Municipal Museum, and Ferens Art Galleries are noteworthy. The grammar school, founded in 1486, was attended by Andrew Marvell and William Wilberforce, who were born in Hull. Schools include the Univ. of Hull, Endsleigh College, and Kingston upon Hull College. Trinity House, established in 1369 to aid sailors, has been since 1787 Trinity House Navigation School. Hull's annual fair is one of the largest in England. In 1974, Hull became part of the new nonmetropolitan county of Humberside.

Hull House: see ADDAMS, JANE.

Hulun: see HAILAR; China.

Hulwan (hōōlwän') or **Helwan** (hĕl-), town (1966 pop. 203,500), N Egypt, on the Nile River, opposite the ruins of MEMPHIS; a suburb of Cairo. Manufactures include iron and steel, cement, and textiles. The town is a health resort, long known for its hot sulfur springs. It is the site of a metallurgical research center and an astronomical observatory. An ancient burial chamber, one of the largest in the world, was discovered at Hulwan in 1946.

Humacao (ōōmäkä'ō), town (1970 pop. 12,411), E Puerto Rico, on the Humacao River. It is a port of entry in an area growing sugarcane and fruit. The town was founded in 1790.

human chorionic gonadotropin (HCG): see GONADOTROPIC HORMONE.

humanism, philosophical and literary movement in which man and his capabilities are the central concern. The term was originally restricted to a point of view prevalent among thinkers in the Renaissance. The distinctive characteristics of Renaissance humanism were its emphasis on classical studies, or the humanities, and a conscious return to classical ideals and forms. The movement led to a restudy of the Scriptures and gave impetus to the Reformation. The term *humanist* is applied to such diverse men as Giovanni Boccaccio, Petrarch, Lorenzo Valla, Lorenzo de' Medici, Erasmus, and Thomas More. In the 20th cent., F. C. S. Schiller and Irving Babbitt applied the term to their own thought. Modern usage of the term has had diverse meanings, but some contemporary emphases are on lasting human values, cultivation of the classics, and respect for scientific knowledge. See Moses Hadas, *Humanism: The Greek Ideal and Its Survival* (1960, repr. 1972) and *The Living Tradition* (1966); Jacques Maritain, *Integral Humanism* (tr. 1968, repr. 1973); R. W. Southern, *Medieval Humanism* (1971).

Humayun or **Homayun** (both: hōōmä'yōōn), 1507-56, second Mogul emperor of India (1530-56), son and successor of Babur. Although he was a capable general, as emperor his indolence and erratic behavior proved disastrous for his rule. In 1535, pressed by enemy incursions into Rajasthan, Humayun defeated the formidable Bahadur Shah of Gujarat. However, he then spent a year enjoying the pleasures of his court at Agra, while military opposition, particularly that of SHER KHAN in Bihar, grew in strength. Sher Khan overran Bengal in 1537, and Humayun was finally forced into battle; he was surprised and routed at Chausa in 1539 and crushingly defeated at Kanauj in 1540. Humayun fled to Sind and finally obtained shelter from Shah Tahmasp of Persia in 1544. After the death of Sher Khan's son, Humayun, with Persian support, invaded (1555) India and reestablished Mogul authority. He died soon after, and his son Akbar became emperor. See his memoirs, *The Tezkereh al Vakiāt* (tr. 1970); Ishwari Prasad, *Life and Times of Humayun* (1955); study by R. S. Avasthy (1967).

Humber, river, c.75 mi (120 km) long, rising in the Long Mts., W N.F., Canada, and flowing SE then SW, through Deer Lake, to the Bay of Islands at Corner Brook.

Humber, navigable estuary of the Trent and Ouse rivers, c.40 mi (60 km) long and from 1 to 8 mi (1.6-

12.9 km) wide, NE England, in Humberside. Spurn Head, with a lighthouse, is at the mouth of the Humber. The shores are generally low, and shoals obstruct shipping in parts. Encroachment of the sea has destroyed former ports, notably Ravenspur. In early English history the Humber was significant as a means of ingress. Hull and Grimsby are the chief cities and major fishing ports. In 1973 construction was begun on a bridge across the Humber linking Hull with the estuary's southern shore. When completed it will be one of the longest (4,580 ft/1,396 m) suspension bridges in the world.

Humberside, nonmetropolitan county (1972 est. pop. 838,000), NE England, created under the Local Government Act of 1972 (effective 1974). It is composed of the county boroughs of GRIMSBY and KINGSTON UPON HULL, and parts of the former counties of YORKSHIRE (East Riding and West Riding), and LINCOLNSHIRE (Parts of Lindsey).

Humbert I, 1844–1900, king of Italy (1878–1900), son and successor of Victor Emmanuel II. A soldier by training, Humbert showed interest primarily in military affairs and foreign policy, and early expectations of his tolerance and liberalism were largely unfulfilled. Under the influence of his conservative wife, Margherita, Humbert became increasingly authoritarian, favoring the imperialistic and pro-German policies of premier Francesco Crispi and disregarding the recommendations of parliamentary leaders. His orientation helped lead to the conclusion of the Triple Alliance. Escaping two attempts on his life, he fell victim to an assassin at Monza. His son, Victor Emmanuel III, succeeded him.

Humbert II, 1904–, last king of Italy (1946), son and successor of Victor Emmanuel III. He married (1930) Marie José, daughter of Albert I of Belgium; a son, Victor Emmanuel, was born in 1937. In World War II, Humbert commanded Italian forces in various theaters of the war and in 1944 Victor Emmanuel III delegated his powers to him. On the abdication (May, 1946) of his father, Humbert succeeded to the throne, pending a referendum on the monarchy. The referendum (June, 1946) resulted in the establishment of a republic, and Humbert went into exile in Portugal.

Humboldt, Alexander, Freiherr von (hŭm'bōlt, Ger. älĕksän'dər frī'hĕr fən hōōm'bôlt), 1769–1859, German naturalist and traveler. His full name is Friedrich Heinrich Alexander von Humboldt. Educated at Göttingen, he studied for his vocation as scientific explorer at Hamburg, Freiberg, and Jena and made several scientific excursions in Europe. In 1792 he was appointed assessor of mines in Berlin. From 1799 to 1804 he made his renowned expedition with A. J. A. Bonpland to Central and South America and Cuba, a journey that did much to lay the broad foundations for the sciences of physical geography and meteorology. Humboldt explored the course of the Orinoco River and the sources of the Amazon River, establishing the connecting systems of the two. He ascended peaks in the Peruvian Andes to study the relation of temperature and altitude, made observations leading to the discovery of the periodicity of meteor showers, and investigated the fertilizing properties of guano. In 1808 he settled in Paris and published the findings of his New World expedition in *Voyage de Humboldt et Bonpland* (23 vol., 1805–1834), often cited by the title of Part I, *Voyage aux régions équinoxiales du nouveau continent.* Humboldt established the use of isotherms in map making; studied the origin and course of tropical storms, the increase in magnetic intensity from the equator toward the poles, and volcanology; and made pioneer investigations on the relationship between geographical environment and plant distribution. In 1827 he settled in his native Berlin at the request of the Prussian king. His interest in terrestrial magnetism led him to effect one of the first instances of international scientific cooperation, in the form of a system of meteorological stations throughout Russia and the British colonies. In 1829, Humboldt made an expedition to Russia and Siberia. In his *Kosmos* (5 vol., 1845–1862; tr. 1849–1858) he sought to combine the vague ideals of the 18th cent. with the exact scientific requirements of the 19th cent. and to formulate a concept of unity amid the complexity of nature. See biography by Charlotte Kellner (1963); Douglas Botting, *Humboldt and the Cosmos* (1973).

Humboldt, Wilhelm, Freiherr von (vĭl'hĕlm), 1767–1835, German statesman and philologist; brother of Alexander von Humboldt. As Prussian minister of education (1809–10) he thoroughly reformed the school system, largely on the basis of the ideas of PESTALOZZI, and he sent Prussian teachers to study the methods of Pestalozzi's school in Switzerland. He was one of the founders of the Univ. of Berlin. Humboldt was one of the great liberal reformers of Prussia along with Stein and Hardenberg. He remained prominent in the government until 1819, when he retired because of his opposition to the prevailing spirit of reaction. Humboldt was a friend of Goethe and Schiller. His lengthy treatise on Kavi, the ancient language of Java, published posthumously (1836–40), is a work of precision, clarity, and scientific caution.

Humboldt (hŭm'bōlt), city (1970 pop. 10,066), Gibson co., W central Tenn.; inc. 1865. It is a trade and processing center in a region yielding fruits (especially strawberries) and vegetables.

Humboldt, river, c.300 mi (480 km) long, rising in several branches in the mountains of NE Nev. It meanders generally west through the arid Great Basin to disappear in Humboldt Sink, W Nevada. Along with its tributaries, the Humboldt drains most of N Nevada. Its length varies with the season, and its volume decreases downstream. Most of the towns of N Nevada are located on the river. Near Lovelock the Humboldt project of the U.S. Bureau of Reclamation is served by the Rye Patch Dam (completed 1936), which impounds water for irrigation. Forage crops are raised along the river. Known to early explorers and named by J. C. Frémont, the river was an important route followed by many of the emigrants from Salt Lake City to central California. Its course supplied wagon trains with water and grass.

Humboldt Bay: see DJAJAPURA, Indonesia.

Humboldt Glacier, NW Greenland. The largest known glacier of the Northern Hemisphere, it debouches into Kane Basin along a front c.60 mi (100 km) wide and 300 ft (91 m) high. U.S. explorer E. K. Kane discovered it on his expedition of 1853–55.

Hume, David (hyōōm), 1711–76, Scottish philosopher and historian. Educated at Edinburgh, he lived (1734–37) in France, where he finished his first philosophical work, *A Treatise of Human Nature* (1739–40). His other philosophical works include *An Enquiry Concerning Human Understanding* (1748; a simplified version of the first book of the *Treatise*), *An Enquiry Concerning the Principles of Morals* (1751), *Political Discourses* (1752), *The Natural History of Religion* (1755), and *Dialogues Concerning Natural Religion* (1779). Hume also wrote an exhaustive *History of England* (1754–62), whose purity of style overcame the frequent faultiness of fact and made the work the standard history of England for many years. In 1763, Hume returned to Paris as secretary to the British embassy. It was at that time that he became a friend of Jean Jacques Rousseau, to whom he later gave refuge in England. In philosophy Hume pressed the analysis of John Locke and George Berkeley to the logical extreme of skepticism for which he is famous. He could see no more reason for hypothesizing a substantial soul or mind than for accepting a substantial material world. A complete nominalist in his handling of ideas of material objects, he carried the method into the discussion of mind and found nothing there but a bundle of perceptions. Causal relation derives solely from the customary conjunction of two impressions; the apparent sequence of events in the external world is in fact the sequence of perceptions in the mind. From this statement Hume argued that our expectation that the future will be like the past (e.g., that the sun will rise tomorrow morning) has no basis in reason; it is purely a matter of belief. However, he also asserted that such theoretical skepticism is irrelevant to the practical concerns of daily life. Hume's attack on rationalism is also evident in his two works on religion; in these he rejects any rational or natural theology. See his autobiography (1777); studies by Norman Kemp Smith (1941), J. B. Stewart (1963, repr. 1973), John Passmore (1968), and James Noxon (1973).

Hume, Joseph, 1777–1855, English politician and reformer. Although a Tory in early life, he sat in Parliament from 1818 to 1855 (with only one interruption) as an indefatigable member of the Radical party. Hume was a leader in almost all the reform issues of the day. He fought for repeal of the Combination Acts (laws against the nascent labor unions) and for CATHOLIC EMANCIPATION, financial retrenchment, parliamentary reform, freedom of the press, free trade, colonial self-government, and disestablishment of the Church of Ireland.

Hume of Polwarth, Sir Patrick: see HOME OF POLWARTH, SIR PATRICK.

Hume Reservoir, c.70 sq mi (180 sq km), on the Murray River, near Albury, on the Victoria–New South Wales border, Australia. It is the largest water-storage area in Australia. Impounded by Hume Dam (completed 1937), the reservoir irrigates most of the Murray basin. It receives additional water from the Snowy Mts. Hydroelectric Scheme.

Hume-Rothery, William, 1899–1968, English metallurgist. Prevented from pursuing a military career by an attack of meningitis that left him deaf, Hume-Rothery proceeded to study chemistry at Oxford and metallurgy at the Royal School of Mines. In 1925 he settled in Oxford, supporting himself and his work on external research grants; he had no offical position until 1938, and received his professorship, Oxford's first in metallurgy, in 1957. His work centered on the structure of alloys, which he approached as a chemist, physicist, and practicing metallurgist. His three rules of alloy formation (1934), which inspired much subsequent work, are perhaps his most notable achievement. He was a fine experimentalist, particularly in pyrometry, and an accomplished popularizer, whose books, especially *The Structure of Metals and Alloys* (with R. E. Smallman and C. W. Haworth, 1936; 5th ed., rev., 1969), have made the results of scientific metallurgy accessible to engineers and nonspecialists.

humerus: see ARM.

humidity, moisture content of the atmosphere, a primary element of CLIMATE. Humidity measurements include absolute humidity, the mass of water vapor per unit volume of natural air; relative humidity (usually meant when the term *humidity* alone is used), the ratio of the actual water-vapor content of the air to its total capacity at the given temperature; specific humidity, the mass of water vapor per unit mass of natural air; and the mixing ratio, the mass of water vapor per unit mass of dry air. Absolute humidity finds greatest application in ventilation and air-conditioning problems. Humidity is measured by means of a HYGROMETER. The rate of evaporation decreases as the moisture content of the air increases and approaches saturation. In addition, the saturation point (moisture-holding capacity of the air) increases rapidly as the temperture of the air rises (see DEW). Thus cold air, while its moisture content is necessarily quite low (low absolute humidity), may be almost saturated with respect to the maximum amount of water vapor it is capable of holding (high relative humidity). Cold air with high relative humidity "feels" colder than dry air of the same temperature because high humidity in cold weather increases the conduction of heat from the body. Conversely, hot air attended by relative humidity "feels" warmer than it actually is because of an increased conduction of heat to the body combined with a lessening of the cooling effect afforded by evaporation. On the other hand, a low relative humidity "modifies" the effect of temperature extremes on the human body. Humidity decreases with altitude. Proximity to large bodies of water and the prevalence of moisture-bearing winds favor high humidity. A temperature-humidity index has been developed by the U.S. National Weather Service that gives a single numerical value in the general range of 70 to 80 reflecting the outdoor atmospheric conditions of temperature and humidity as a measure of comfort (or discomfort) during warm weather. The temperature-humidity index, I_{TH}, is defined as follows: $I_{TH}=0.4$ (dry-bulb thermometer temperature F + wet-bulb thermometer temperature F) + 15. When the index is 70 most people feel comfortable; at 75 about one half of the population is satisfied; at 80 most are uncomfortable.

Humiliati (hōōmĭl"ēä'tē) [Lat.,=the humbled ones], Roman Catholic association of laymen formed in the 11th cent. in Lombardy. They wore plain clothes and lived under special vows, but mingled freely with the world. They were protected by the papacy in most of the 12th cent., and some of them were organized into an order or joined other orders. There were occasional defections from the Humiliati to the Waldensians, and some conversions in the other direction. The Humiliati were finally suppressed in the 16th cent. after their orthodoxy had long been questioned.

Hummel, Johann Nepomuk (yō'hän nā'pōmōōk hōōm'əl), 1778–1837, Hungarian-born pianist and composer. In 1785, Hummel was taken to Vienna, where he impressed Mozart and was his pupil for two years. Later he studied with Johann Albrechtsberger and Antonio Salieri. In piano technique and improvisatory ability Hummel was thought to rival Beethoven. His compositions—124 opus numbers, many written for piano and chamber groups—represent a link between the classical and romantic styles.

hummingbird, common name for members of the family Trochilidae, small, strictly New World birds, related to the swifts, and found chiefly in the mountains of South America. Hummingbirds vary in size from a 2¼-in. (6-cm) fairy hummingbird of Cuba (the smallest of all birds) to an 8½-in. (21.6-cm) giant hummer of the Andes, *Patagona gigas.* Their colors are brilliant and jewellike; the feathers have a prismatic construction that iridesces in changing light. Hummingbirds feed on insects and the nectar of flowers, for which their long, slender (sometimes curved) bills are especially adapted. They are usually seen hovering or darting (at speeds of up to 60 mi/97 km per hr) in the air as they feed in flight; their weak feet cannot support them on flat surfaces. Their wingbeats are so rapid (50–75 beats per sec) that the wings appear blurred. The enormous amount of energy expended on this continuous movement is supported by constant feeding; at night they lapse into a state of torpor like that of animals in hibernation. The nests vary but are usually tiny cups of soft vegetation fastened to the top of a branch. Several species are found in the W and SW United States, e.g., the black-chinned hummingbird and the calliope hummingbird, the smallest (3 in./7.6 cm) of the U.S. species. The only species found in the NE United States is the ruby-throated hummingbird, *Archilochus colubris.* The male is metallic green above and whitish below, with an iridescent ruby-red throat; the female is dull-colored. The sunbirds, small and brilliant passerine birds of India, Africa, and Australia, are sometimes called hummingbirds in those areas but belong to a different taxonomic order (Passeriformes). Hummingbirds are classified in the phylum CHORDATA, subphylum Vertebrata, class Aves, order Apodiformes, family Trochilidae.

humor, according to ancient theory, any of four bodily fluids that determined man's health and temperament. Hippocrates postulated that an imbalance among the humors (blood, phlegm, black bile, and yellow bile) resulted in pain and disease, and that good health was achieved through a balance of the four humors; he suggested that the glands had a controlling effect on this balance. For many centuries this idea was held as the basis of medicine and was much elaborated. Galen introduced a new aspect, that of four basic temperaments reflecting the humors: the sanguine, buoyant type; the phlegmatic, sluggish type; the choleric, quick-tempered type; and the melancholic, dejected type. In time any personality aberration or eccentricity was referred to as a humor. In literature, a humor character was one in whom a single passion predominated; this interpretation was especially popular in Elizabethan and other Renaissance literature. One of the most comprehensive treatments of the subject was the *Anatomy of Melancholy,* by Robert Burton. The theory found its strongest advocates among the comedy writers, notably Ben Jonson and his followers, who used humor characters to illustrate various modes of irrational and immoral behavior. In medicine, the theory lost favor in the 19th cent. after the German Rudolf Virchow presented his cellular pathology.

humpback: see HUNCHBACK.

Humperdinck, Engelbert (hŭm'pərdĭngk, Ger. ĕng'əlbĕrt ho͝om'pərdĭngk), 1854–1921, German composer and teacher, studied at the conservatories of Cologne and Munich. He was a friend of Wagner, whom he assisted in preparing *Parsifal* for production and whose son, Siegfried, was later his pupil. He is known chiefly for his first opera, *Hänsel und Gretel* (1893), successful because of its fairy-tale subject and its folk-inspired music. He wrote other operas and dramatic music which are mostly forgotten.

Humphrey, Doris, 1895–1958, American modern dancer and choreographer, b. Oak Park, Ill. Humphrey was a featured soloist with the Denishawn Company until 1927. One of the foremost figures of MODERN DANCE, she developed many experimental concepts in form and content in such works as *Water Study* (1928) and *Theater Piece No. 2* (1956). In 1955 she was instrumental in founding the Juilliard Dance Theater in New York City. See her autobiography, ed. by S. V. Cohen (1972).

Humphrey, Hubert Horatio, 1911–, U.S. Vice President (1965–69), b. Wallace, S.Dak. After practicing pharmacy for several years, Humphrey taught political science and became involved in state politics. An ardent New Dealer, he was appointed to several Federal offices in Minnesota. He was instrumental in getting the Democratic party and the Farmer-Labor party to merge, and with the combined backing of both parties he was elected mayor of Minneapolis in 1945 and reelected in 1947. In 1948, Humphrey (with the backing of the Farmer-Labor party) became the first Democrat from Minnesota ever elected to the U.S. Senate. He gained a national reputation by his strong stand for civil rights. Reelected in 1954, Humphrey campaigned in the 1960 presidential primaries against John F. Kennedy but withdrew after his defeat in the West Virginia primary. He was (1960) reelected to the U.S. Senate and became (1961) the assistant majority leader. In 1964, Lyndon B. Johnson chose Humphrey as his running mate on the Democratic national ticket, which won. In 1968, after Johnson decided not to run for reelection, Humphrey was a leading contender for the Democratic nomination. He was opposed by many critics of the Vietnam War, however, because he had supported the escalation of the war during Johnson's administration. Humphrey nevertheless secured the nomination but he was narrowly defeated by the Republican candidate, Richard M. Nixon, in the election. Humphrey successfully ran for the U.S. Senate in 1970. In 1972 he made another bid for the Democratic presidential nomination but failed to secure it. See his *War on Poverty* (1964), *The Cause is Mankind* (1964), *School Desegregation: Documents and Commentaries* (also publ. as *Integration vs. Segregation*; 1964), *Beyond Civil Rights* (1968), and *The Political Philosophy of the New Deal* (1970); biographies by Michael Amrine (1960), A. H. Ryskind (1968), and Robert Sherrill and H. W. Ernst (1968).

Humphrey Island: see MANIHIKI.

Humphreys, David, 1752–1818, American diplomat and poet, b. present Ansonia (then in Derby), Conn. His military talents and patriotism won the friendship of General Washington and a place on his staff during the American Revolution. From 1784 to 1786 Humphreys was secretary to a U.S. mission negotiating commercial treaties in Europe. While a member (1786–88) of the Connecticut assembly, he was one of the satirical CONNECTICUT WITS. His own copious poetry was largely patriotic and didactic. Sent abroad (1790) as a secret agent, he later served (1793) as commissioner for Algerian affairs and then (1796) as minister plenipotentiary to Spain. On his return in 1802 he brought 100 merino sheep to improve New England flocks; in 1806 he set up a large woolen mill at Humphreysville (now Seymour), Conn., and developed a paternalistic community there for his orphan boy laborers. See biography by F. L. Humphreys (1917, repr. 1971).

Humtah (hŭm'tə), unidentified city, apparently near Hebron, in S Palestine. Joshua 15.54.

humus (hyo͞o'məs), organic matter that has decayed to a relatively stable, amorphous state. It is an important biological constituent of fertile SOIL. Humus is formed by the decomposing action of soil microorganisms (e.g., bacteria and fungi), which break down animal and vegetable material into elements that can be used by growing plants. Technically, humus, as the end result of this process, is less valuable for plant growth than are the products formed during active decomposition (see FERTILIZER). Because of its low specific weight and high surface area, humus has a profound effect upon the physical properties of mineral soils with regard to improved soil structure, water intake and reservoir capacity, ability to resist erosion, and the ability to hold chemical elements in a form readily accessible to plants.

Huna Bay: see HÚNAFLÓI, Iceland.

Húnaflói (ho͞o'näflō"ē), inlet of the Greenland Sea, c.60 mi (100 km) long and 30 mi (50 km) wide, NW Iceland, between the Vestfjarđa and Skagafjarđa peninsulas. It has several fishing ports.

Hunan or **Hu-nan** (both: ho͞o'nän') [south of the lake], province (1968 est. pop. 38,000,000), c.80,000 sq mi (207,200 sq km), S central China, S of Tung-t'ing lake. CH'ANG-SHA is the capital. Largely hilly in the south and west, Hunan becomes an alluvial lowland in the Tung-t'ing basin in the northeast; the Hsiang River, which traverses the province from north to south, and the lesser Yüan and Tzu rivers drain into Tung-t'ing lake. The mountainous uplands include the Nan Ling range and Heng Shan mt. Rice is the outstanding crop, particularly in the "rice bowl" of Tung-t'ing lake; wheat, corn, sweet potatoes, ramie, tobacco, rapeseed, and tea are also produced. Almost one fourth of the province is forested, mostly in the southwestern hills. Hunan is famous for its cedar; pine, fir, oak, camphor, bamboo, and tung wood are also important. Pulp and paper mills are found along the upper Yüan and Tzu rivers. Hunan abounds in mineral resources; it has the country's largest lead-zinc mine and its leading antimony production center. Tungsten, manganese, coal, mercury, gold, tin, and sulfur are also found. The population of Hunan, concentrated mainly in the Hsiang and lower Yüan valleys and along the Han-k'ou-Canton RR, is overwhelmingly Chinese and speaks a variety of Mandarin. There are aboriginal Miao and Yao peoples in the hills of the south and west; since 1952 several autonomous reserves have been established for these minorities. Under Chinese rule since the 3d cent. B.C., the region was traditionally called Hsiang for its main river. It belonged to the kingdom of Wu at the time of the Three Kingdoms (A.D. 220–80) and later became part of the Chu kingdom of the Five Dynasties (907–60). Its present name, first used (12th cent.) under the Sung dynasty, was revived in the 17th cent. by the Manchus when the historic province of Hukwang was divided into the present provinces of Hupeh and Hunan. Hunan, traditionally the home of fighting men, supplied the troops that saved the Manchu dynasty from the Taiping rebels. Largely unoccupied by the Japanese in World War II, it passed to Communist rule in 1949. Mao Tse-tung was born in Hunan.

hunchback, abnormal outward curvature of the spine in the thoracic region. It is also known as kyphosis and humpback, and in its severe form a noticeable hump is evident on the back. Hunchback may be congenital, but it can also result from poor posture, uneven growth of the spine, fracture of vertebrae, or deficiency disorders that lead to a weakening or collapse of the vertebrae. Treatment may consist of exercises to strengthen the vertebral column, the application of orthopedic devices to hold the bones in proper position, or corrective surgery to fuse the bones together.

hundred, in English history, a subdivision of a shire, first mentioned in the 10th cent. and surviving as a unit of local government into the 19th cent. It is thought that in origin the hundred comprised 100 geld hides, the geld hide being the basic Anglo-Saxon land unit for taxation purposes; but the hundreds varied considerably in size. The number of hundreds in a shire also varied, and their boundaries were continually changed. The hundred had its own court. The Saxon tithing groups, which had corporate responsibility for the crimes committed by their members, came before it, and personal pleas of debt and trespass were also brought there. Originally presided over by the king's reeves, the hundred courts continued to meet regularly every four weeks until the 13th cent., by which time many of them had been taken over by local lords. They gradually lost importance and from the 16th cent. had little more than a formal existence. In Yorkshire, Lincolnshire, Nottinghamshire, Rutland, and Leicestershire the unit equivalent to the hundred was called a wapentake; in Northumberland, Cumberland, Westmorland, and Durham, a ward. See H. M. Cam, *The Hundred and the Hundred Rolls* (1930, repr. 1963); F. M. Stenton, *Anglo-Saxon England* (3d ed. 1971).

Hundred Days, name given to the period after the return of the deposed French emperor, NAPOLEON I, from Elba. The Hundred Days are counted from March 20, 1815, when Napoleon arrived in Paris, to June 28, 1815, when Louis XVIII was restored for the second time as king, following Napoleon's disastrous WATERLOO CAMPAIGN.

Hundred Years War, 1337–1453, conflict between England and France. Its basic cause was a dynastic quarrel that originated when the conquest of England by William of Normandy created a state lying on both sides of the English Channel. In the 14th cent. the English kings held the duchy of GUIENNE in France; they resented paying homage to the French kings, and they feared the increasing control exerted by the French crown over its great feudal vassals. The immediate causes of the Hundred Years War were the dissatisfaction of EDWARD III of England with the nonfulfillment by PHILIP VI of France of his pledges to restore a part of Guienne taken by Charles IV; the English attempts to control Flanders, an important market for English wool and a source of cloth; and Philip's support of Scotland against England. The war may be dated from 1337, when Edward assumed the title of king of France, a title held by Philip. Edward first invaded France from the Low Countries (1339–40), winning small success on land but defeating (1340) a French fleet at the battle of SLUIS. In 1346 he won the battle of CRÉCY and besieged Calais, which surrendered in 1347. In 1356 the English won the battle of Poitiers, capturing King JOHN II of France. After prolonged negotiations, the Treaty of BRÉTIGNY was signed (1360); England received Calais and practically all of Aquitaine, as well as a large ransom for the captive king. The Gascon nobles, oppressively taxed by EDWARD THE BLACK PRINCE, appealed (1369) to King CHARLES V. The war was renewed, and by 1373, DU GUESCLIN had won back most of the lost French territory. In 1415, HENRY V of England renewed the English claims, took Harfleur, and defeated France's best knights at AGINCOURT. By 1419 he had subdued Normandy, with the connivance of JOHN THE FEARLESS, duke of Burgundy. PHILIP THE GOOD, successor of John the Fearless, mediated between Henry V and CHARLES VI of France (see TROYES, TREATY OF), and Charles recognized Henry as heir to the crown of France. By 1429 the English and their Burgundian allies were masters of practically all France N of the Loire, but in that year JOAN OF ARC raised the siege of Orléans and saw CHARLES VII crowned king of France at Rheims. Her capture by the Burgundians and her judicial murder after extradition to the British did not stop the renewal of French successes. In 1435, Charles obtained the alliance of Burgundy (see ARRAS, TREATY OF). By 1450 the French reconquered Normandy, and by 1451 all Guienne but Bordeaux was taken. After the fall (1453) of Bordeaux, England retained only Calais, which was not conquered by France until 1558. England, torn by the Wars of the Roses, made no further attempt to conquer France. The Hundred Years War inflicted untold misery on France. Farmlands were laid waste, the population was decimated by war, famine, and the Black Death (see PLAGUE), and marauders terrorized the countryside. Civil wars (see JACQUERIE; CABOCHIENS; ARMAGNACS AND BURGUNDIANS) and local wars (see BRETON SUCCESSION, WAR OF THE) increased the destruction and the social disintegration. Yet the successor of Charles VII, LOUIS XI, benefited from these evils. The virtual destruction of the feudal nobility enabled him to unite France more solidly under the royal authority and to promote and ally with the middle class. From the ruins of the war an entirely new France emerged. For England, the results of the war were equally decisive; it ceased to be a continental power and increasingly sought expansion as a sea power. The great chronicler of the war was FROISSART. Shakespeare, taking liberties with history, dramatized the war in *Henry V* and *Henry VI*. See Édouard Perroy, *The Hundred Years War* (tr. 1951; repr. 1967); K. A. Fowler, *The Age of Plantagenet and Valois: The Struggle for Supremacy, 1328–1498* (1967).

Hunedoara (ho͞onädwä'rä), Hung. *Vajdahunyad*, city (1970 est. pop. 77,000), W central Rumania, in Transylvania. A major industrial center, it has ironworks and steelworks. Iron ore and coal are mined nearby. The city is noted for its historic Hunyadi Castle, built in the 15th cent. on the site of an old citadel.

Huneker, James Gibbons (hŭn'ĭkər), 1860–1921, American essayist and music critic, b. Philadelphia. The originality and pungency of his style and the soundness of his criticism made him one of the most important critics of his time. He was music, art, and drama critic for the New York *Sun* (1902–17), then music critic for the *Times* (1917–19), and later for the *World* (from 1919 until his death). His books include *Mezzotints in Modern Music* (1899), *Chopin* (1900), *Iconoclasts—a Book of Dramatists* (1905), *Franz Liszt* (1911), and *Unicorns* (1917). A collection of his essays, edited by H. L. Mencken, was published in 1929. See his *Letters* (1922) and *Intimate Letters* (1924).

Hungarian language, also called Magyar, member of the Ugric group of the FINNO-UGRIC LANGUAGES. These languages form a subdivision of the Uralic subfamily of the Ural-Altaic family of languages (see URALIC AND ALTAIC LANGUAGES). Hungarian is spoken in Hungary by approximately 9 million people and by an additional 3 million distributed in Rumania, Czechoslovakia, Yugoslavia, the USSR, the United States, and elsewhere. There are a number of dialects. Like the other Uralic and Altaic languages, Hungarian has vowel harmony and agglutination. Suffixes or postpositions are used extensively. The noun has about 25 cases, and the verb is inflected to a considerable degree. Hungarian has a definite article and an indefinite article, both of which are lacking in the related languages of Finnish and Turkish. There is no grammatical gender in Hungarian. The first syllable of a word is stressed. During the first millennium A.D., Hungarian was written in a script akin to that of the oldest Turkic writing, but in the 11th cent. A.D. the Roman alphabet was introduced and subsequently was adopted in a modified form. The earliest extant Hungarian documents in the Roman alphabet go back to the 13th cent. and are the oldest texts of a Uralic language. The vocabulary of Hungarian has borrowed words from other languages, especially the Turkic languages, the Slavic languages, and German. For grammars see R. A. Hall (1938) and Charles Wojatsek (1962).

Hungarian literature. Until the 19th cent. Latin was the official and literary language of Hungary. The *Funeral Oration* (c.1230) is the oldest surviving work in Magyar; some chronicles of the 14th and 15th cent. exist. The Reformation prompted various translations of the Bible. The poets Bálint Balassa (late 16th cent.) and Miklós Zrinyi and Stephen Gyongyossi (17th cent.) were succeeded in the 18th cent. by Vitez Michael Csokonai and Ferenc Faludi. In the last quarter of the same century, Hungarian literature was given fresh life with the work of György BESSENYEI, while Ferenc Kazinczy led a reform of the Hungarian language. The establishment of a national theater and the founding in 1825 of the Hungarian Academy of Science assured the development of a national literature. The leading literary figures in the 19th cent. were the poets Sandor KISFALUDY and his brother Károly (also a noted dramatist), János ARÁNY, Mihály VÖRÖSMARTY, and Sándor PETŐFI, and the novelist Mór JÓKAI. Endre ADY and Attila JÓZSEF were the outstanding poets of the early 20th cent.; the dramatists Ferenc HERCZEG and Ferenc MOLNÁR, of the same period, achieved international fame. Between the two World Wars, the novelists were divided in three groups—the Horthy regime defenders; the Populists, who sought amelioration of the peasants' lot; and the Communists. The most eminent Populist was László NÉMETH. After World War II, Hungarian literature fell under Soviet influence, and the Communist party exercised rigid control over writing and publishing. Writers who adhered to the Soviet doctrine of SOCIALIST REALISM include the poet György Somlyó and the prose writers Géza Hegedűasa and József Darvas. Diverging from this doctrine were the poet László Mecs, published only outside Hungary, and the novelist Tibor Déry, who was imprisoned for his nonconformity. The revolt of Oct., 1956, whose participants included a number of prominent writers, resulted in a diminishing of official supervision. See histories by Tibor Kloniczay et al. (1964) and Frigyes Riedl (tr. 1906, repr. 1968); Joseph Reményi, *Hungarian Writers and Literature* (1965); Linda Degh, ed., *Folktales of Hungary* (tr. 1965).

Hungarian pointer: see VIZLA.

Hungary, Hung. *Magyarország,* republic (1971 pop. 10,315,597), 35,919 sq mi (93,030 sq km), Central Europe. BUDAPEST is the capital. Hungary borders on Czechoslovakia in the north, on the USSR in the northeast, on Rumania in the east, on Yugoslavia in the south, and on Austria in the west. The Danube River forms the Czechoslovak-Hungarian border from near Bratislava to near ESZTERGOM, then turns sharply south and bisects the country. To the east of

the Danube the Great Hungarian Plain (Hung. *Alföld*) extends beyond the Hungarian boundaries to the Carpathians and the Transylvanian Alps. The Dráva and Tisza rivers are also important waterways. To the west of the Danube is the Little Alföld and the Transdanubian region, which are separated by the Bakony and Vértes mts. The Mátra Mts. in the north reach a height of 3,330 ft (1,015 m) at Kékes, the highest peak in Hungary. Lake Balaton, the largest lake in Hungary and in Europe, is a leading resort area. Hungary has cold winters and hot summers; springs and falls are short. It has long been an agricultural country but since World War II has become heavily industrialized. Agriculture employs less than one third of the population, although many industrial workers live in rural areas. Nearly all of the arable land is included in collective and state farms. Grains (especially corn and wheat), potatoes, turnips, and grapes and other fruit are grown, and livestock and poultry are raised. Sugar beets, flax, hemp, tobacco, and paprika are the chief industrial crops. Mineral resources are limited; bauxite is the most important. Other deposits include brown coal (lignite), and small amounts of manganese, petroleum, and natural gas. The greater part of Hungarian industry is located in or near Budapest. Other industrial centers are GYŐR, MISKOLC, PÉCS, DEBRECEN, SZEGED, and Dunapentele. Industry is nationally owned. Products include machinery, textiles, metal products, motor vehicles, and chemicals. Hungary exports transportation equipment, machinery, wine, bauxite, and textiles, and it imports petroleum, iron ore, coal, coke, nonferrous metals, timber, and cotton. The USSR, East Germany, and Czechoslovakia are the main trading partners. Situated on a plain near the geographic center of Europe, Hungary has been the meeting place and battleground of many peoples, and its heterogeneous population was a major problem before 1919. However, as a result of the separation of non-Hungarian territories after World War I, the great slaughter of the Jews in World War II, and the exchange after the war of Slavic and Rumanian minorities for their Magyar counterparts, Hungary is today essentially homogeneous. The Magyars constitute about 96% of the population. Hungarian is the official language. About two thirds of the people are Roman Catholic, but there is a large Calvinist minority.

Growth of a State. The Roman provinces of Pannonia and Dacia, conquered under Tiberius and Trajan (1st cent. A.D.), embraced part of what was to become Hungary. The HUNS and later the OSTROGOTHS and the AVARS settled there for brief periods. In the late 9th cent. the MAGYARS, a Finno-Ugric people from beyond the Urals, conquered all or most of Hungary and Transylvania. The semilegendary leader, ARPAD, founded their first dynasty. The Magyars apparently merged with the earlier settlers, but they also continued to press westward until defeated by King (later Holy Roman Emperor) Otto I, at the LECHFELD (955). Halted in its expansion, the Hungarian state began to solidify. Its first king, St. STEPHEN (reigned 1001–38), completed the Christianization of the Magyars and built the authority of his crown—which for 945 years remained the symbol of national existence—on the strength of the Roman Catholic Church. Under Bela III (reigned 1172–1196), Hungary came into close contact with Western European, particularly French, culture. Through the favor of succeeding kings, a few very powerful nobles—the magnates—won ever-widening privileges at the expense of the lesser nobles, the peasants, and the towns. In 1222 the lesser nobles forced the extravagant ANDREW II to grant the Golden Bull (the "Magna Carta of Hungary"), which limited the king's power to alienate his authority to the magnates and established the beginnings of a parliament. Under Andrew's son, BELA IV, the kingdom barely escaped annihilation: Mongol invaders, defeating Bela at Muhi (1241), occupied the country for a year, and OTTOCAR II of Bohemia also defeated Bela, who was further threatened by his own rebellious son STEPHEN V. Under Stephen's son, LADISLAUS IV, Hungary fell into anarchy, and when the royal line of Arpad died out (1301) with Andrew III, the magnates seized the opportunity to increase their authority. In 1308, Charles Robert of Anjou was elected king of Hungary as CHARLES I, the first of the ANGEVIN line. His autocratic rule checked the magnates somewhat and furthered the growth of the towns. Under his son, LOUIS I (Louis the Great), Hungary reached its greatest territorial extension, with power extending into Dalmatia, the Balkans, and Poland.

Foreign Domination. After the death of Louis I, a series of foreign rulers succeeded: SIGISMUND (later Holy Roman Emperor), son-in-law of Louis; ALBERT II of Austria, son-in-law of Sigismund; and LADISLAUS III of Poland (Uladislaus I of Hungary). During their reigns the Turks began to advance through the Balkans, defeating the Hungarians and their allies at Kossovo (1389), NIKOPOL (1396), and VARNA (1444). John HUNYADI, acting after 1444 as regent for Albert II's son, LADISLAUS V, gave Hungary a brief respite through his victory at Belgrade (1456). The reign of Hunyadi's son, MATTHIAS CORVINUS, elected king in 1458, was a glorious period in Hungarian history. Matthias maintained a splendid court at Buda, kept the magnates subject to royal authority, and improved the central administration. But under his successors ULADISLAUS II and LOUIS II, the nobles regained their power. Transylvania became virtually independent under the Zapolya family. The peasants, rising in revolt, were crushed (1514) by John Zapolya. Louis II was defeated and killed by the

Turks under Sulayman the Magnificent in the battle of MOHÁCS in 1526. The date is commonly taken to mark the beginning of Ottoman domination over Hungary. Ferdinand of Austria (later Emperor FERDINAND I), as brother-in-law of Louis II, claimed the Hungarian throne and was elected king by a faction of nobles, while another faction chose Zapolya as JOHN I. In the long wars that followed, Hungary was split into three parts: the western section, where Ferdinand and his successor, RUDOLF II, maintained a precarious rule, challenged by such Hungarian leaders as Stephen BOCSKAY and Gabriel BETHLEN; the central plains, which were completely under Turkish domination; and Transylvania, ruled by noble families (see BÁTHORY and RÁKÓCZY). The Protestant Reformation, supported by the nobles and well-established in Transylvania, nearly succeeded throughout Hungary. Cardinal PÁZMÁNY was a leader of the Catholic Reformation in Hungary. In 1557 religious freedom was proclaimed by the diet of Transylvania, and the principle of toleration was generally maintained throughout the following centuries. Hungarian opposition to Austrian domination included such extreme efforts as the assistance THÖKÖLY gave to the Turks during the siege of Vienna (1683). Emperor LEOPOLD I, however, through his able generals Prince EUGENE OF SAVOY and Duke CHARLES V of Lorraine, soon regained his lost ground. Budapest was liberated from the Turks in 1686. In 1687, Hungarian nobles recognized the Hapsburg claim to the Hungarian throne. By the Peace of Kalowitz (1699), Turkey ceded to Austria most of Hungary proper and Transylvania. Transylvania continued to fight the Hapsburgs, but in 1711, with the defeat of Francis II Rákóczy (see under RÁKÓCZY, family), Austrian control was definitely established. In 1718 the Austrians took the BANAT from Turkey.

Hungary and Austria. The Austrians brought in Germans and Slavs to settle the newly freed territory, destroying Hungary's ethnic homogeneity. Hapsburg rule was uneasy. The Hungarians were loyal to MARIA THERESA in her wars, but many of the unpopular centralizing reforms of JOSEPH II, who had wanted to make German the sole language of administration and to abolish the Hungarian counties, had to be withdrawn. In the second quarter of the 19th cent. a movement that combined Hungarian nationalism with constitutional liberalism gained strength. Among its leaders were Count SZECHENYI, Louis KOSSUTH, Baron EÖTVÖS, Sándor PETŐFI, and Francis DEAK. Inspired by the French Revolution of 1848, the Hungarian diet passed the March Laws (1848), which established a liberal constitutional monarchy for Hungary under the Hapsburgs. But the reforms did not deal with the national minorities problem. Several minority groups revolted, and, after FRANCIS JOSEPH replaced Ferdinand VII as emperor, the Austrians waged war against Hungary (Dec., 1848). In April, 1849, Kossuth declared Hungary an independent republic. Russian troops came to the aid of the emperor, and the republic collapsed. The Hungarian surrender at Vilagos (Aug., 1849) was followed by ruthless reprisals. But after its defeat in the Austro-Prussian War (1866), Austria was obliged to compromise with Magyar national aspirations. The *Ausgleich* of 1867 (largely the work of Francis Deak) set up the AUSTRO-HUNGARIAN MONARCHY, in which Austria and Hungary were nearly equal partners. Emperor Francis Joseph was crowned (1867) king of Hungary, which at that time also included Transylvania, Slovakia, Ruthenia, Croatia and Slovenia, and the Banat. The minorities problem persisted, the Serbs, Croats, and Rumanians being particularly restive under Hungarian rule. During this period industrialization began in Hungary, while the condition of the peasantry deteriorated to the profit of landowners. By a law of 1874 only about 6% of the population could vote. Until World War I, when republican and socialist agitation began to threaten the established order, Hungary was one of the most aristocratic countries in Europe. As the military position of Austria-Hungary in World War I deteriorated, the situation in Hungary grew more unstable. Hungarian nationalists wanted independence and withdrawal from the war; the political left was inspired by the 1917 revolutions in Russia; and the minorities were receptive to the Allies' promises of self-determination. In Oct., 1918, Emperor CHARLES I (King of Hungary as Charles IV) appointed Count Michael KÁROLYI premier. Károlyi advocated independence and peace and was prepared to negotiate with the minorities. His cabinet included socialists and radicals. In November the emperor abdicated, and the Dual Monarchy collapsed.

Independence. Károlyi proclaimed Hungary an independent republic. However, the minorities would not deal with him, and the Allies forced upon him very unfavorable armistice terms. The government resigned, and the Communists under Béla KUN seized power (March, 1919). The subsequent Red terror was followed by a Rumanian invasion and the defeat (July, 1919) of Kun's forces. After the Rumanians withdrew, Admiral HORTHY DE NAGYBANYA established a government and in 1920 was made regent, since there was no king. Reactionaries conducted a brutal White terror. The Treaty of Trianon (see TRIANON, TREATY OF), signed in 1920, reduced the size and population of Hungary by about two thirds, removing virtually all non-Magyar areas and depriving Hungary of valuable natural resources. The next twenty-five years saw continual attempts by the Magyar government to recover the lost territories. Early endeavors were frustrated by the LITTLE ENTENTE and France, and Hungary turned to a friendship with Fascist Italy and, ultimately, to an alliance (1941) with Nazi Germany. The authoritarian domestic policies of the premiers Stephen BETHLEN and Julius GOMBOS and their successors safeguarded the power of the upper classes, ignored the demand for meaningful land reform, and encouraged anti-Semitism. Between 1938 and 1944, Hungary regained, with the aid of Germany and Italy, territories from Czechoslovakia, Yugoslavia, and Rumania. It declared war on the USSR (June, 1941) and on the United States (Dec., 1941). When the Hungarian government took steps to withdraw from the war and protect its Jewish population, German troops occupied the country (March, 1944). The Germans were driven out by Soviet forces (Oct., 1944–April, 1945). The Soviet campaign caused much devastation. National elections were held in 1945 (in which the Communist party received less than one fifth of the vote), and a republican constitution was adopted in 1946. The peace treaty signed at Paris in 1947 restored the Trianon boundaries and required Hungary to pay $300 million in reparations to the USSR, Czechoslovakia, and Yugoslavia. A new coalition regime instituted long-needed land reforms. Early in 1948 the Communist party, through its control of the ministry of the interior, arrested leading politicians, forced the resignation of Premier Ferenc Nagy, and gained full control of the state. Hungary was proclaimed a People's Republic in 1949, after parliamentary elections in which there was only a single slate of candidates. Radical purges in the national Communist party made it thoroughly subservient to that of the USSR. Industry was nationalized, and collectivization of land was ruthlessly pressed. The trial of Cardinal MINDSZENTY aroused protest throughout the Western world. By 1953 continuous purges of Communist leaders, constant economic difficulties, and peasant resentment of collectivization had led to profound crisis in Hungary. Premier Mátyás Rákosi, the Stalinist in control since 1949, was removed in July, 1953, and Imre Nagy became premier. He slowed down collectivization and emphasized production of consumer goods, but he was removed in 1955, and the emphasis on farm collectivization was restored. In 1955, Hungary joined the Warsaw Treaty Organization and was admitted to the United Nations. On Oct. 23, 1956, a popular anti-Communist revolution, centered in Budapest, broke out in Hungary. A new coalition government under Imre Nagy declared Hungary neutral, withdrew it from the Warsaw Treaty, and appealed to the UN for aid. However, János KÁDÁR, one of Nagy's ministers, formed a counter-government and asked the USSR for military support. In severe and brutal fighting Soviet forces suppressed the revolution. Nagy and some of his ministers were abducted and were later executed. Some 190,000 refugees fled the country. Kádár became premier and sought to win popular support for Communist rule and to improve Hungary's relations with Yugoslavia and other countries. He carried out a drastic purge (1962) of former Stalinists (including Mátyás Rákosi), accusing them of the harsh policies responsible for the 1956 revolt. Collectivization, which had been stopped after 1956, was again resumed in 1958–59. Kádár's regime gained a degree of popularity as it brought increasing liberalization to Hungarian political, cultural, and economic life. Relations with the Catholic Church were improved by an agreement (1964) with the Vatican. The departure (1971) of Cardinal Mindszenty from Budapest after 15 years of asylum in the U.S. legation and his removal (1974) from the position of primate of Hungary further improved church-state relations. In 1968 economic reforms were introduced to bring a measure of decentralization to the economy and to allow for supply and demand factors. Consumer goods production rose sharply, and Hungary achieved great improvements in its standard of living. Hungary aided the USSR in the invasion of Czechoslovakia in 1968. The country is governed under the 1949 constitution, which was amended in 1972. There is a unicameral parliament, elected every four years, which elects a presidential council. The council chooses the ministers. Actual power resides in the Communist party, officially known as the Hungarian Socialist Workers Party, which heads the People's Patriotic Front. Since 1967 more than one candidate has been allowed to run in parliamentary constituencies, but all must support the Front's programs. See Paul Teleki, *The Evolution of Hungary* (1923); Denis Sinor, *History of Hungary* (1959); F. A. Vali, *Rift and Revolt in Hungary* (1961); C. A. McCartney, *A History of Hungary, 1929–1945* (1957, repr. 1962); Oszkar Jaszi, *Revolution and Counter-Revolution in Hungary* (tr. 1924, rep. 1969); N. M. Nagy-Talavera, *The Green Shirts and Others* (1970); D. G. Kosary, *A History of Hungary* (1941, repr. 1971); Paul Ignotus, *Hungary* (1972). See also bibliography under AUSTRO-HUNGARIAN MONARCHY.

Hung-chiang or **Hungkiang** (both: ho͝ong-jēäng), town, SW Hunan prov., China, a port on the upper Yüan River. It is a regional trade center, noted for its tung oil and lumber.

hunger strike, refusal to eat as a protest against existing conditions. Although most often used by prisoners, others have also employed it. For example, Mohandas GANDHI in India and Cesar CHAVEZ in California fasted as religious penance during otherwise political or economic disputes. An ancient device, the hunger strike was revived in England in the early 20th cent. by militant woman suffragists and became the accepted technique of those sentenced for suffragist activities. The passage of the so-called Cat-and-Mouse Act in 1913, by which the prisoners in ill health due to fasting could be temporarily discharged, ended the forced feeding to which the authorities had resorted. The Franchise Act of 1918 ended the suffragist hunger strikes. The hunger strike was used by Irish nationalists in 1912 and again later on. Hunger strikes were used by Sinn Feiners in 1920, and Terence MacSwiney, lord mayor of Cork, died in a London prison after a fast of 74 days. Thereafter, hunger striking was forbidden by the Sinn Fein. It was used again in the 1970s by imprisoned members of the Irish Republican Army. Hunger striking was used between 1917 and 1919 by American woman suffragists and also by conscientious objectors imprisoned in the United States. During the Vietnam War, the Roman Catholic priests Daniel and Philip Berrigan used the hunger strike in 1969 at Danbury Prison, Conn., where they had been imprisoned for destroying draft records. In 1970 inmates in California's Soledad Prison used it on a massive scale to protest prison conditions.

Hungkiang: see HUNG-CHIANG, China.

Hungry Horse Dam, 564 ft (172 m) high and 2,115 ft (645 m) long, NW Mont. on the southern fork of the Flathead River; one of the highest dams in the United States. A major unit in the development program for the Columbia River basin, it was built (1948–53) to provide hydroelectric power (285,000-kw capacity), flood control, and irrigation. Hungry Horse Reservoir, formed by the dam, extends c.35 mi (55 km) upstream.

Hung-tse or **Hungtse** (both: ho͝ong'-dzŭ), lake, 65 mi (105 km) long, E China, on the border of Anhwei and Kiangsu provs. It receives the Huai River and is connected with the Grand Canal. The San Ho dam, with the largest hydraulic works along the Huai River, is at the outlet of the lake.

Hunkers, conservative faction of the Democratic party in New York state in the 1840s, so named because they were supposed to "hanker" or "hunker" after office. In opposition to them stood the radical Democrats, or BARNBURNERS. The Hunkers favored internal improvements and liberal chartering of state banks; they opposed antislavery agitation. They generally controlled the party machinery and the patronage. In the 1846 gubernatorial nomination they turned against the Democratic candidate, Gov. Silas Wright, a Barnburner. The Barnburners retorted in kind by voting for and supporting the Free-Soil ticket in the 1848 presidential election, which thereby went to the Whig candidate, Zachary Taylor. Those Barnburners who did not persist in their antislavery views were welcomed back to the party fold in 1850. The Hunkers themselves, however, subsequently divided into the "Softs" led by William L. Marcy and Horatio Seymour, who supported President Pierce, and the "Hards" led by Daniel S. Dickinson, who did not give up their antislavery principles and who opposed Pierce. See J. D. Hammond,

History of Political Parties in New York State, Vol. III (1852).

Huns, nomadic and pastoral people of unknown ethnological affinities who originated in N central Asia, appeared in Europe in the 4th cent. A.D., and built up an empire there. They were organized in a predominantly military manner. Divided into hordes, they undertook extensive independent campaigns, living off the countries they ravaged. The Huns have been described as short and of somewhat Mongolian appearance. Their military superiority was due to their small, rapid horses, on which they practically lived, even eating and negotiating treaties on horseback. Despite the similarity of their tactics and habits with those of the White Huns, the Magyars, the MONGOLS, and the Turks, their connection with those peoples is either tenuous or—in the case of the Magyars and the Turks—unfounded. The Huns appear in history in the 3d cent. B.C., when part of the Great Wall of China was erected to exclude them from China. Called Hsiung-nu by the Chinese, the Huns occupied N China from the 3d cent. A.D. until 581. Having swept across Asia, they invaded the lower Volga valley c.372 and advanced westward, pushing the Germanic OSTROGOTHS and VISIGOTHS before them and thus precipitating the great waves of migrations that destroyed the Roman Empire and changed the face of Europe. They crossed the Danube, penetrated deep into the Eastern Empire, and forced (432) Emperor Theodosius to pay them tribute. ATTILA, their greatest king, had his palace in Hungary. Most of the territories that now constitute European Russia, Poland, and Germany were tributary to him, and he was long in Roman pay as Roman general in chief. When Rome refused (450) further tribute, the Huns invaded Italy and Gaul and were defeated (451) by AETIUS, but they ravaged Italy before withdrawing after Attila's death (453). Their later movements are little known; some believe that the WHITE HUNS were remnants of the Hunnic people. The word *Huns* has been used as an epithet, for German soldiers, for example, connoting destructive militarism. See Thomas Hodgkin, *Italy and Her Invaders,* Vol. I (rev. ed. 1892, repr. 1967); W. M. McGovern, *Early Empires of Central Asia* (1939); E. A. Thompson, *A History of Attila and the Huns* (1948); J. D. Maenchen-Helfen, *The World of the Huns* (1973).

Hunt, Gaillard (gĭlyärd'), 1862–1924, American historian and editor, b. New Orleans. He served (1887–1909, 1917–24) the Dept. of State in various capacities, his most important work being done as chief of the division of publications and as editor. From 1909 to 1917 he was chief of the division of manuscripts in the Library of Congress. Among his books are *The Life of James Madison* (1902), *John C. Calhoun* (1907), *Life in America One Hundred Years Ago* (1914), *The Department of State of the United States: Its History and Functions* (1914), and *Israel, Elihu, and Cadwallader Washburn* (1925). He edited *The Writings of James Madison* (9 vol., 1900–1910) and Vol. XVI to XXVII of the *Journals of the Continental Congress* (1909–1928).

Hunt, Henry, 1773–1835, English radical politician. A powerful orator, popular with the laboring classes, Hunt was quarrelsome and stubborn but a sincere proponent of electoral and other reforms. He took part with Arthur THISTLEWOOD in the Spa Fields meeting (1816) and gained his chief notice by presiding at the meeting in Manchester that ended in the PETERLOO MASSACRE (1819). He was imprisoned for two years, after a trial of doubtful legality. Hunt sat in Parliament (1830–32) but exerted little influence.

Hunt, Holman: see HUNT, WILLIAM HOLMAN.

Hunt, Leigh (James Henry Leigh Hunt) (lē), 1784–1859, English poet, critic, and journalist. He was a friend of the eminent literary men of his time, and his home was the gathering place for such notable writers as Hazlitt, Lamb, Keats, and Shelley. With his brother John, Hunt established in 1808 the *Examiner,* a liberal weekly to which he contributed political articles. Because of an outspoken article casting aspersions on the prince regent, the brothers were imprisoned from 1813 to 1815, but they continued to edit the journal from jail. In 1822, Hunt joined Shelley and Byron in Italy and launched the *Liberal* (1822–23), which proved a failure. During other periods Hunt contributed to the *Indicator* (1819–21), the *Tatler* (1830–32), and *Leigh Hunt's London Journal* (1834–35). His literary fame rests chiefly on his miscellaneous light essays, his lyrics "Abou Ben Adhem" and "Jenny Kissed Me," and his witty and informative autobiography (1850). *The Story of Rimini* (1816), based on the love of Paolo and Francesca, is his only long poem of consequence. A noted dramatic and literary critic, he was one of the first to praise the genius of Shelley and Keats. See L. H. Houtchens and C. W. Houtchens, ed., *Leigh Hunt's Dramatic Criticism* (1949), *Leigh Hunt's Literary Criticism* (1956), and *Leigh Hunt's Political and Occasional Essays* (1962); biography by Edmund Blunden (1930, repr. 1970).

Hunt, Richard Morris, 1828–95, American architect, b. Brattleboro, Vt., studied in Geneva, Switzerland, and at the École des Beaux-Arts; brother of William Morris Hunt. He was a conspicuous exponent of 19th-century eclecticism. Hunt worked under T. U. Walter on the extensions of the Capitol at Washington, D.C. In New York City he founded the first American studio for training young architects, and he was one of the organizers of the American Institute of Architects, of which he became president in 1888. Most of his work was closely imitative of historic styles. It included the Lenox Library, New York City (later torn down); the first building for the Fogg Museum of Art, Cambridge, Mass.; the U.S. naval observatory at Washington, D.C.; the pedestal for the Statue of Liberty in New York harbor; and numerous magnificent residences, such as those of the Vanderbilts in New York City and Newport, R.I. His Tribune Building in New York was one of the first elevator buildings. The Administration Building at the Columbian Exposition in Chicago was the most noted of his later works. See biography by Barr Ferree (1895).

Hunt, William Holman, 1827–1910, English painter. Hunt was a founder of the PRE-RAPHAELITE brotherhood and one of its most conscientious exponents. His paintings are often crude in color and laborious in technique, but are completely sincere in their devotion to Pre-Raphaelite principles. In 1854 he visited Palestine in order to have authentic material for his religious paintings. Among his best-known works are *The Light of the World* (Oxford Univ.) and *The Triumph of the Innocents* (Liverpool Gall.). See his *Pre-Raphaelitism and the Pre-Raphaelite Brotherhood* (1905–6); studies by F. G. Stephens (1860) and A. C. Gissing (1936).

Hunt, William Morris, 1824–79, American painter, b. Brattleboro, Vt., studied in Düsseldorf and Paris. He was greatly influenced by the Barbizon school and by J. F. Millet. During the Civil War he established himself in Boston, where he introduced the ideals and methods of the Barbizon school. As teacher and painter, Hunt exerted a widespread influence upon American art. He is thought to be the first American master to admit female students into his classes. His earliest works were usually figure pieces; he then turned to portraits and in his later years devoted himself chiefly to landscapes. Among his best-known paintings are *Girl at a Fountain, The Bathers,* and a landscape (Metropolitan Mus.); a portrait of Chief Justice Shaw (courthouse, Salem, Mass.); and *The Flight of Night* (Pennsylvania Acad. of the Fine Arts). See biography by his granddaughter, Diana Holman-Hunt (1969).

Hunter, Dard, 1883–1966, American printer-publisher, b. Steubenville, Ohio. Hunter is known for his researches and writings on the history and technique of papermaking. From 1938 he was curator of the Dard Hunter Paper Museum, which he founded (see MUSEUMS OF SCIENCE). His writings include *Papermaking* (rev. ed. 1948) and *Papermaking by Hand in America* (1950). See his autobiography, *My Life with Paper* (1958).

Hunter, John, 1728–93, Scottish anatomist and surgeon, studied under his brother, William Hunter. A pioneer in comparative anatomy and morphology, he made many valuable investigations and introduced several surgical techniques, including a method of ligating aneurisms that is still in use. His writings include *Natural History of the Human Teeth* (1771), a work on venereal disease (1786), and *Treatise on the Blood, Inflammation, and Gunshot Wounds* (1794). Hunter's anatomical collection, acquired in 1800 by the Royal College of Surgeons, London, formed the nucleus of the Hunterian Museum. See biographies by E. A. Gray (1952), John Kobler (1960), and Iris Noble (1971).

Hunter, Robert, d. 1734, royal governor of New York and New Jersey (1709–19), b. Ayrshire, Scotland. His administration was notably successful. He maintained a vigorous campaign against the French and Indians and cooperated with other colonies in military matters. He allayed the bitter political factionalism that had kept New York and New Jersey in turmoil for several decades, and he also straightened out financial and revenue matters. Hunter was less successful with several thousand Rhenish Palatinate refugees, whom he brought over and settled on the upper Hudson to produce naval stores for England. Unable to secure funds for the project from England or from his assembly, Hunter went in debt to the amount of £21,000 to save the colony. From 1727 until his death he was governor of Jamaica.

Hunter, Robert Mercer Taliaferro (tŏl'əvər), 1809–87, American statesman, b. Essex co., Va. He was a U.S. Representative for Virginia (1837–43, 1845–47), serving as speaker from 1839 to 1841. Hunter became a leading states' rights Democrat and supported John C. Calhoun for the presidency in 1844. He entered the U.S. Senate in 1847, where he became a prominent spokesman for the Southern cause. He resigned in 1861 to become the Confederate secretary of state (1861–62) and then a Confederate senator (1862–65). He participated in 1865 in the futile HAMPTON ROADS PEACE CONFERENCE. Imprisoned for several months after the war, Hunter helped organize (1867) a conservative party that won control of the Virginia state government from the radicals in 1869. See C. H. Ambler, ed., *Correspondence of Robert M. T. Hunter, 1826–1876* (1918); biography by H. H. Simms (1935).

Hunter, William, 1718–83, Scottish physician. He was famous as a lecturer, as London's leading obstetrician, as professor of anatomy and later president of the Royal Academy of Arts, and as head of a school and museum of anatomy where many noted men were trained. He bequeathed his valuable anatomical collection to the Univ. of Glasgow. His works include the important *Anatomy of the Human Gravid Uterus* (1774). See biography by Charles Illingworth (1967); study by R. H. Fox (1901); memoir by G. C. Peachey (1924).

Hunter, Port, or **Newcastle Harbour,** estuary of the Hunter River, New South Wales, Australia. The second-largest harbor of the state, it is 3 mi (4.8 km) long and 2 mi (3.2 km) wide. The coal-loading port of Newcastle is on the southern shore near the entrance.

Hunter College of the City University of New York; coeducational; opened 1870 as Normal College, chartered 1888, renamed in 1914. It is located in Manhattan. Its former Bronx campus became Lehman College in 1968. Residents of New York City are admitted to the baccalaureate program tuition free. See NEW YORK, CITY UNIVERSITY OF.

Hunter's hartebeest: see DAMALISK.

hunter's moon, the next full moon after the HARVEST MOON, which it resembles.

hunting, act of seeking, following, and taking wild animals for consumption or display. It differs from fishing in that it involves only land animals. Hunting was a necessary activity of early man. Through the Paleolithic period it was man's chief means of obtaining food and clothing. In the Neolithic period, when man first practiced agriculture, killing game was still an important part of his work. Hunting was popular among the ancients and became a sport in medieval Europe, where it was reserved, as far as possible, for the privileged classes by GAME LAWS. FALCONRY and fox hunting became increasingly popular in England in the Middle Ages, and the use of hunting dogs—hounds, setters, pointers, spaniels, and the like—became widespread in this period. Hunting can be divided into three branches, each of which is defined by the type of instrument used by the hunter. Hunting with weapons (now primarily firearms, formerly BOW AND ARROW, BOOMERANG, or sling) is probably the most popular, especially in the United States. TRAPPING and snaring with deceptive implements is popular in northern areas. In coursing (with dogs) and falconry (with hawks) hunters enlist the aid of trained animals. Coursing is especially popular in Great Britain and Western Europe. Types of hunting are also distinguished by the size of the animal being sought. Big-game hunting is the most glamorous and often the most dangerous. It became a popular sport among the wealthy Western colonists in Africa and India during the 19th cent., and even today the big-game safari remains an exciting pastime to many people. Notable big-game animals include the fox, moose, caribou, bear, and elk of North America; the reindeer, elk, and wolf of Europe; the tiger, leopard, elephant, and wild goat of Asia; and the antelope, gazelle, zebra, leopard, lion, giraffe, rhinoceros, and elephant of Africa. Small-game hunting, known as "shooting" in Great Britain, is practiced against birds such as the quail, partridge, grouse, pheasant, and goose, as well as against such small land animals as the hare, rabbit, woodchuck, and squirrel. Extensive hunting, both commercial and recreational, has made many species of game animals (for example, the American

BISON) nearly extinct. Game laws and WILDLIFE REFUGES in the United States have been designed to save game animals and birds from extinction. Many African nations have also instituted such measures, but illegal poaching for furs and skins remains a problem both there and in other areas of the world. See Gunnar Brusewitz, *Hunting* (1969); A. L. Cone, *The Complete Guide to Hunting* (1970); Michael Braider, *Hunting and Shooting from the Earliest Times to the Present Day* (1971).

Huntingdon, Henry Hastings, 3d **earl of,** 1535–95, English nobleman. Through his mother, Catherine Pole, a great granddaughter of the duke of Clarence (brother of Edward IV and Richard III), Hastings claimed the right to succeed Elizabeth I to the English throne. He received some support from the Protestant party. Hastings was custodian of the rival claimant, MARY QUEEN OF SCOTS, for a brief period in 1569. In 1572 he was president of the council of the north. See biography by Claire Cross (1966).

Huntingdon, Selina Hastings, countess of, 1707–91, English religious leader, patron of the Calvinistic Methodists. She was closely associated with the Wesleys and George WHITEFIELD. When they split, she took the side of Whitefield, whom she made one of her chaplains. Largely responsible for introducing Methodism to the upper classes, she established chapels in Bath and other centers of fashion and appointed chaplains to take charge of them. In 1768 she founded a seminary for the training of ministers at Trevecca House in Wales. Later it was removed to Cheshunt, Hertfordshire. Those associated with her establishments and under her moral control were known as "Lady Huntingdon's Connexion." Huntingdon College, Montgomery, Ala., is named for her. See Sarah Tytler, *The Countess of Huntingdon and Her Circle* (1907).

Huntingdon and Godmanchester, municipal borough (1971 pop. 16,540), county town of Huntingdon and Peterborough, E central England, traversed by the Ouse River. The boroughs of Huntingdon and Peterborough were merged in 1961. There are light industries and an agricultural market. Oliver Cromwell was born in Huntingdon; both he and Samuel Pepys went to school there. Huntingdon has many fine Georgian buildings. In 1974, Huntingdon and Godmanchester became part of the new nonmetropolitan county of Cambridgeshire.

Huntingdon and Peterborough, county (1971 pop. 202,337), 486 sq mi (1,259 sq km), E central England. The county was formed by the amalgamation of the counties of Huntingdonshire and the Soke of Peterborough in 1965. The county town is HUNTINGDON AND GODMANCHESTER. The terrain is level, and the eastern portion lies in the formerly marshy district known as the Fens, now drained and cultivated. The chief rivers are the Ouse and the Nene. The region is chiefly agricultural; its main crops are wheat, barley, oats, fruit, potatoes, sugarbeets, and vegetables. Peterborough has important industries. There are remains of two important Roman roads. In Anglo-Saxon times the area came under the control of EAST ANGLIA. In 1974, Huntingdon and Peterborough became part of the new nonmetropolitan county of Cambridgeshire.

hunting leopard: see CHEETAH.

Huntington, Collis Potter, 1821–1900, American railroad builder, b. near Torrington, Conn. A storekeeper of Oneonta, N.Y., before he went West in the gold rush of 1849, he became a storekeeper in California, and by 1853 he and his partner, Mark HOPKINS, were leading Sacramento hardware merchants. Seeing the desirability of a direct route to the silver mines newly opened in what is now Nevada, Huntington, Hopkins, Charles CROCKER, and Leland STANFORD organized a railroad company (the Central Pacific). Huntington's financial acumen and success in winning subsidies and favorable legislation from Congress gave him and his partners practical control of transportation in the West. They consolidated their power in forming (1884) the Southern Pacific, of which Huntington was president after 1890. His vast fortune was left mostly to his nephew, Henry Edward Huntington, except for bequests to the Hampton Normal and Agricultural Institute and the Tuskegee Normal and Industrial Institute. See Oscar Lewis, *The Big Four* (1938, repr. 1963); David Lavender, *Great Persuader* (1970).

Huntington, Ellsworth, 1876–1947, American geographer, b. Galesburg, Ill., grad. Beloit College, 1897, M.A. Harvard, 1902, Ph.D. Yale, 1909. He taught at Euphrates College, Turkey (1897–1901); accompanied the Pumpelly (1903) and Barrett (1905–6) expeditions to central Asia; and wrote of his Asian experiences in *Explorations in Turkestan* (1905) and *The Pulse of Asia* (1907). He taught geography at Yale (1907–15) and from 1917 was a research associate there, devoting his time chiefly to climatic and anthropogeographic studies. *The Climatic Factor* (1914), *Civilization and Climate* (1915, rev. ed. 1924), and, with S. S. Visher, *Climatic Changes* (1922) were notable contributions. He also wrote, in collaboration with others, a series of geography texts, which includes *Principles of Human Geography* (with S. W. Cushing, 5th ed. 1940). Other books are *The Character of Races* (1924), *The Human Habitat* (1927), and *Mainsprings of Civilization* (1945). See study by G. J. Martin (1973).

Huntington, Henry Edwards, 1850–1927, American financier, b. Oneonta, N.Y. He was prominent in railroad and other enterprises. Until the death of his uncle, Collis P. HUNTINGTON, the two were business associates. His estate at San Marino, near Pasadena, Calif., with botanical and other gardens, art collections, and library, together with a large endowment, was placed (1919–22) in the hands of trustees who were to maintain it for the public after his death. The **Henry E. Huntington Library and Art Gallery** has the largest collection of incunabula in America; it excels also in rare legal documents showing the growth of English and American constitutional law, Americana (especially West Coast material), and manuscript collections of English literature. Its special treasures include a Gutenberg Bible, Gainsborough's *Blue Boy*, and Thomas Lawrence's *Pinkie*. The library gives a certain number of research fellowships and scholarships. It publishes many descriptive catalogs of its collections.

Huntington, Lucius Seth, 1827–86, Canadian politician, b. Quebec prov. A lawyer, he served in the Legislative Assembly and in its successor, the House of Commons, from 1861 to 1882. In 1873, he launched in Parliament the charges of corruption against Sir John A. Macdonald's government, which led to the Pacific scandal and the fall of Macdonald's government. He was later postmaster general.

Huntington, Samuel, 1731–96, political leader in the American Revolution, signer of the Declaration of Independence, b. Windham, Conn. He was a delegate (1775–84) to and president (1779–81) of the Continental Congress before serving as governor of Connecticut (1786–96).

Huntington. 1 City (1970 pop. 16,217), seat of Huntington co., NE Ind.; inc. 1848. It is a farm trade center and an industrial city. Its manufactures include automotive parts and machinery. The city is the seat of Huntington College. The nearby Forks of the Wabash were an Indian gathering place and an early trade center. **2** Uninc. town (1970 pop. 12,130), Suffolk co., SE N.Y., on the northern shore of Long Island; settled 1653. It is the heart of a township containing 17 contiguous communities, noted for their precision manufactures. The town, which is chiefly residential, has numerous harbors and boatyards. **3** City (1970 pop. 74,315), seat of Cabell co., W W.Va., on the Ohio River; founded 1871 as the western terminus of the Chesapeake & Ohio RR and named for the president of the railway. The largest city in the state, it is a ranking commercial center and a river port with large shipments of bituminous coal. It has railroad yards and important glass and chemical industries. Other manufactures include electrical goods, wood and metal products, and mattresses. Marshall Univ. is there.

Huntington Beach, city (1970 pop. 115,960), Orange co., S Calif., on the Pacific coast, across from Santa Catalina Island, in a truck-farm, citrus-fruit, and oil area; inc. 1909. It has oil refineries and aerospace, communications, metallurgical, and food-packing industries. The city's population increased more than tenfold between 1960 and 1970 and is still rapidly climbing. It has long been known for its fine beaches.

Huntington Library and Art Gallery: see HUNTINGTON, HENRY EDWARDS.

Huntington Park, city (1970 pop. 33,744), Los Angeles co., S Calif., a residential and industrial suburb of Los Angeles; founded 1856, inc. 1906.

Huntington's chorea: see CHOREA.

Huntington Station, uninc. town (1970 pop. 28,817), Suffolk co., SE N.Y., on the north shore of Long Island. Walt Whitman was born there, and his birthplace is preserved.

Huntingtower or **Ruthven Castle,** Tayside region, E central Scotland, near Perth. James VI (later James I of England) was held in the castle by the earl of Gowrie in the "raid of Ruthven" in 1582.

Huntley, Chet (Chester Robert Huntley), 1911–74, American news broadcaster, b. Cardwell, Mont. He joined the National Broadcasting Company in 1955. Huntley and David BRINKLEY developed documentary techniques for televised analyses of public affairs. Their *Huntley-Brinkley Report* series (1956–71) won several awards, including the Academy of Television Arts and Sciences Award for news program achievement. In 1971, Huntley retired from television to Montana, where he planned to develop land. See his *Generous Years: Remembrances of a Frontier Boyhood* (1968).

Huntly, George Gordon, 4th **earl of,** 1514–62, Scottish nobleman. He was made lord high chancellor in 1546. Although a Roman Catholic, he led a revolt against MARY QUEEN OF SCOTS and was killed at the battle of Corrichie. His son, **George Gordon,** 5th **earl of Huntly,** d. 1576, was, however, a favorite of Mary and may have been an associate of the earl of Bothwell in the murder (1567) of Lord Darnley. He supported Mary's cause until 1572, when he resigned it as hopeless. His son, **George Gordon,** 6th **earl** and 1st **marquess of Huntly,** 1562–1636, plotted with Spain for the restoration of Catholicism in Scotland and raised a rebellion in 1589. He regained the favor of the young James VI (later James I of England), who commissioned him to murder (1592) the 2d earl of Murray. After another rebellion (1594), however, James blew up his castle at Strathbogie, and Huntly left the country. He was soon pardoned again and made (1599) marquess and lieutenant of the north, but he was in continual trouble with the Presbyterian Church, which doubted the sincerity of his abjuration of Catholicism, and he lost favor after the accession (1625) of Charles I.

Huntsville, town (1971 pop. 9,784), SE Ont., Canada, on the Muskoka River. It is a resort center and has lumber mills and a woodworking plant.

Huntsville. 1 City (1970 pop. 137,802), seat of Madison co., N Ala.; inc. 1811. A major center for U.S. space research, Huntsville is the site of the Redstone Arsenal, the U.S. army's control and procurement center for guided missiles and rockets. NASA's George C. Marshall Space Flight Center (est. 1960) and the Alabama Space and Rocket Center are also in the city. Although Huntsville's economy centers around the aerospace industries, tires, glass, and electrical equipment are also produced. The constitutional convention of the Alabama Territory was held in 1819 in Huntsville, where the first state legislature also met. Numerous antebellum buildings remain. Huntsville is the seat of Oakwood College, Alabama A&M Univ., and a branch of the Univ. of Alabama. Monte Sano State Park is nearby. **2** City (1970 pop. 17,610), seat of Walker co., E central Texas; inc. 1845. Located in a pine area, it has many sawmills and wood-processing plants. Huntsville, the home of Sam Houston, contains his grave (with an impressive monument), his restored home, and other memorials. Also in the city are Sam Houston State Univ. and the Texas Department of Corrections. An annual rodeo held by the prisoners draws many spectators.

Hunyadi, John (ho͝onʹyŏdĭ), Hung. *Hunyadi János,* c. 1385–1456, Hungarian national hero, leader of the resistance against the Turks. He was chosen (1441) voivode [governor] of Transylvania under King Uladislaus I (Ladislaus III of Poland) and won numerous victories over the Turks. In 1444, however, the Christians were routed at Varna and the king was slain. Hunyadi, after a period of confusion, was chosen (1446) regent by the Hungarian diet. Young LADISLAUS V, chosen king in 1444, was kept from his kingdom by his guardian, Holy Roman Emperor FREDERICK III, until 1453. When Ladislaus assumed his rule, Hunyadi laid down the regency and devoted his full energy to fighting the Turks. His fight was a Christian crusade and was aided by Pope Calixtus III. With St. John Capistran, Hunyadi defeated (1456) the Turks at Belgrade and thus staved off the Turkish conquest of Hungary for 70 years. Hunyadi was bitterly opposed by many of the Magyar nobles. His elder son Ladislaus was executed in 1457 by order of King Ladislaus V for assassinating the king's uncle. John Hunyadi's younger son became king as MATTHIAS CORVINUS.

Hunza (ho͝onʹsä), princely state, 3,900 sq mi (10,101 sq km), NW Kashmir, administered by Pakistan. Declared a British protectorate in 1893, Hunza acceded to Pakistan after the partition of British India (1947). The region is noted for the longevity of its inhabitants.

Hupa Indians: see HOOPA INDIANS.

Hupeh (ho͞oʹpāʹ), Mandarin *Hu-pei,* province (1968 est. pop. 32,000,000), c.72,000 sq mi (186,480 sq km), central China. The capital is WU-HAN (formerly it was Wu-ch'ang, which is now part of Wu-han). In this province the Yangtze River, flowing through the south, is joined by the Han River, coming from the northwest. At their junction lies Wu-han, a city comprising three former cities, Han-k'ou, Han-yang, and Wu-ch'ang; it is a transportation hub and the major industrial and commercial center of central China. The central part of Hupeh was once a huge lake and is now a basin, at or below sea level, formed from silt deposited by the Yangtze. Hupeh's lakes and many rivers provide excellent irrigation facilities, and the warm climate, adequate rainfall, and rich soil make the province one of the most productive in China. Wheat, barley, rapeseed, and beans are raised in the winter, and rice, cotton, tea, soybeans, and corn in the summer. Rice production has increased significantly as a result of water conservation, modern fertilizer, better seed, and double-cropping; the province produces a surplus, which is sent to N China. Wheat is raised in the drier areas. Cotton accounts for 53% of all commercial crops; sesame, peanuts, and ramie are also significant. The minerals in the province are mostly nonferrous, though there are two huge steel complexes, one at Wu-han and one at Huang-shih. Fish culture is important.

Hupham (hyo͞o'făm), the same as HUPPIM.

Huppah (hŭp'ə), chief priest. 1 Chron. 24.13.

Huppim (hyo͞o'pĭm), founder of a Benjamite family. Gen. 46.21; 1 Chron. 7.12,15. Hupham: Num. 26.39.

Hur. **1** One who upheld a hand of Moses at Rephidim. Ex. 17.12; 24.14. **2** Grandfather of BEZALEL **1**, perhaps the same as **1.** 1 Chron. 4.1,4. **3** Midianite king killed by the Hebrews. Num. 31.8; Joshua 13.21. **4** Father of an officer of Solomon. 1 Kings 4.8. **5** Father of REPHAIAH **4.**

Hurai (hyo͞o'rī, -rāī), the same as HIDDAI.

Huram (hyo͞or'əm). **1** Descendant of Benjamin. 1 Chron. 8.5. **2, 3** See HIRAM **1** and **2.**

Hurd, Peter, 1904–, American painter, b. Roswell, N.Mex. Hurd left West Point to study art at the Pennsylvania Academy of the Fine Arts. He worked as apprentice to the painter N. C. Wyeth and married his daughter, the painter Henrietta Wyeth. Hurd is known for his realistic paintings of Western scenes and for his illustrations. He decorated the Big Springs, Texas, post office and the post office annex at Dallas, Texas, with mural paintings. His portrait of President Lyndon Johnson is in the National Portrait Gallery, Washington, D.C. Hurd is represented in the major American museums. See his selected lithographs (1969).

Hurd, Richard, 1720-1808, English theologian, editor, and critic. From 1781 until his death he was bishop of Worcester. His best-known works are *Moral and Political Dialogues* (1757) and *Letters on Chivalry and Romance* (1762), an examination of knight-errantry and Gothic literature.

hurdy-gurdy, musical instrument, first described by St. Odo of Cluny in the 10th cent. and very popular in the early Middle Ages. It generally had three strings, caused to vibrate by a wooden wheel turned by a crank. Stopping was accomplished by keys that usually affected only one string that played the melody, the others acting as drones. Usually two players were required. In the late Middle Ages and the Renaissance the instrument was smaller and was relegated to beggars and peddlers. Haydn composed a few pieces for an 18th-century form of hurdy-gurdy with sympathetic strings and a set of organ pipes added. It was still used in provincial France and Spain and more rarely in London in the early 20th cent. The barrel organ has been called a hurdy-gurdy because of its crank and its use for street playing. See also VIELLE.

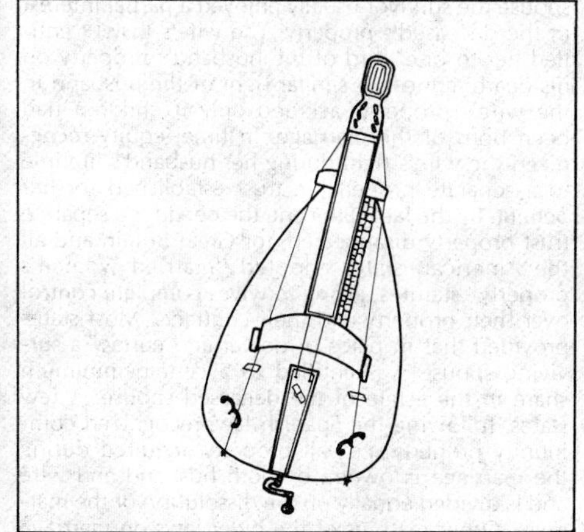

Hurdy-gurdy

Huri (hyo͞o'rī), father of ABIHAIL **2** .

Hurley, Patrick Jay, 1883-1963, U.S. cabinet officer, b. Choctaw Indian Territory (now in Oklahoma). Hurley practiced law in Tulsa, Okla., was (1912-17) national attorney for the Choctaw Nation, and fought in France in World War I as a colonel in the U.S. army. He was Under Secretary of War (1929) and Secretary of War (1929-33), served on diplomatic missions, and participated in Republican party politics. After the outbreak of World War II he saw active fighting in the Far East as the personal representative of Gen. George C. Marshall. Hurley served (1942) as the first U.S. minister to New Zealand and afterward was (1942-43) President Franklin Delano Roosevelt's personal representative in the Middle East. He was promoted (1944) major general, and was envoy (1944-45) and ambassador to China. A champion of Chiang Kai-shek's Nationalist Chinese government, he later charged that officials in the U.S. Department of State had subverted the U.S. policy of support to Chiang's government. See biography by Don Lohbeck (1956); study by R. D. Buhite (1973).

hurling, outdoor ball and stick game similar to field hockey (see HOCKEY, FIELD). The national pastime of Ireland, it was played for many centuries before the Gaelic Athletic Association standardized the rules in 1884. In the United States, hurling was played by early Irish immigrants, and it is still played by some Irish-Americans, especially in areas of recent immigration. An extremely rugged game, hurling is played on a field 80 by 140 yd (73.15 by 128.02 m) by two opposing teams of 15 players each. The ball, made of rubber, is 9 to 10 in. (22.86 to 25.4 cm) in circumference, cork-centered, and covered with horsehide. After it is picked off the ground or caught in the hurley—a tapering, curved, broad-bladed wooden stick 3 ft long—the player runs with the ball as far as he can and then hurls it toward a teammate or toward the goal his team is attacking. Only the hurley may be used in advancing the ball. The goalposts are 16 ft (4.88 m) high and 21 ft (6.4 m) wide, with a crossbar 8 ft (2.44 m) above the ground. Three points are scored by driving the ball into the net under the crossbar, one point by hitting it over the crossbar.

Hurok, Sol, 1888-1974, American impresario, b. Russia. Emigrating to the United States in 1906, Hurok was a peddler, streetcar conductor, bottle washer, and hardware salesman before becoming the foremost impresario of his age. By his own estimation, he presented more than 4,000 artists and companies, among them Pavlova, Marian Anderson, the Comédie Française, the Old Vic Company, the Royal Ballet, Andrés Segovia, Jean-Louis Barrault, and Victoria de los Angeles. The film *Tonight We Sing* (1953) was based on his autobiography, *Impresario* (1946).

Huron, city (1970 pop. 14,299), seat of Beadle co., E central S.Dak., on the James River; inc. 1883. A shipping and trade center for a large livestock and grain area, it has meat-packing and lumbering industries. It is also the administrative center for a number of state and Federal agencies. Huron College is there.

Huron, Lake, 23,010 sq mi (59,596 sq km), 206 mi (332 km) long and 183 mi (295 km) at its greatest width, between Ont., Canada, and Mich.; second largest of the GREAT LAKES. It has a surface elevation of 580 ft (177 m) above sea level and a maximum depth of 750 ft (229 m). Centrally located between the upper and lower Great Lakes, Lake Huron receives the waters of Lake Superior through the St. Marys River and those of Lake Michigan through the Straits of Mackinac; it drains into Lake Erie through the St. Clair River-Lake St. Clair-Detroit River system. Large tributaries flowing into the lake include the Mississagi, Wanapitei, Spanish, and French rivers from Ontario and the Au Sable and Saginaw rivers from Michigan. The northern shoreline is irregular, with many bays and inlets; the largest are Georgian Bay and North Channel, which indent the Ontario shore and are nearly landlocked by Manitoulin Island and Bruce Peninsula. Saginaw Bay is the principal indentation on the southern shores. Lake Huron is part of the Great Lakes-St. Lawrence Seaway system and is navigated by oceangoing and lake vessels. The chief cargoes are iron ore, grain, coal, and limestone. Navigation is impeded by ice in the shallower sections from mid-December to early April. The lake is subject to occasional violent storms. The principal lakeshore cities are Port Huron, Mich., and Sarnia, Ont., at the lake's outlet; Owen Sound, Midland, and Parry Sound, Ont.; and Bay City, Alpena, and Cheboygan, Mich. The waters of the lake are largely unpolluted, and commercial and sport fishing is important. Major salt deposits are worked at the south end of the lake. Georgian Bay, an arm of the lake, is a popular resort area, and recreational facilities are provided at Georgian Bay Islands National Park (Canada), on the islands in Mackinac Strait, and at numerous state and provincial parks along the lake's scenic shores. Étienne Brulé, the French explorer, was probably the discoverer (c.1612) of Georgian Bay, and Samuel de Champlain was the first white man to visit (1615) Lake Huron.

Huron Indians, confederation of four North American Indian groups who spoke the Wyandot language, which belongs to the Iroquoian branch of the Hokan-Siouan linguistic stock (see AMERICAN INDIAN LANGUAGES). Their name for themselves was *Wendat, Huron* being the name applied to them by the French. In the early 17th cent. they occupied the region between Lake Simcoe and Georgian Bay in Ontario and numbered some 20,000. Their culture was substantially that of the area of the Eastern woodlands. They lived in palisaded villages and cultivated tobacco. In 1615, when Samuel CHAMPLAIN visited the Huron, they were at war with the Iroquois. The long-standing enmity between the Huron and the Iroquois was climaxed in 1648, when the Iroquois, armed with Dutch firearms, invaded Huronia and subsequently disrupted (1649) the Huron confederacy as such. It was at this time that Father Jean de BRÉBEUF, who established (1626) a Roman Catholic mission among the Huron, and other Jesuit missionaries were killed by the Iroquois. The survivors of the Huron fled in all directions—southwest to the Tobacco Nation, south to the Neutral Nation, southeast to the Erie Indians, and northeast to a French fort near Quebec. The inexorable Iroquois hunted the Huron everywhere; in 1649 the Iroquois attacked the Tobacco Nation, causing the migration of these people in company with the Huron. In 1650 the Neutral Nation was invaded by the Iroquois and practically wiped out, and in 1656 the Erie Indians were almost exterminated. The Huron who had fled to Quebec ultimately received a small reservation at Lorette, where some 500 still live, but the remnants of the Huron and Tobacco Nation went, under pressure from the Iroquois, first to Michigan, then to Wisconsin and Illinois, where the Sioux attacked them. The Tobacco Nation and Huron eventually settled (1750) in villages near Detroit and at Sandusky, Ohio. In Ohio they became known to the British as the Wyandot Indians and as such fought with the British against the Americans in both the American Revolution and the War of 1812. After the War of 1812 possession of their lands was confirmed by the United States, but by 1842 they had sold their tracts and moved to what is now Wyandotte co., Kansas. In 1867 they were settled in NE Oklahoma, where some 900 now reside as citizens. See B. G. Trigger, *The Huron Farmers of the North* (1969).

hurricane, tropical CYCLONE in which winds attain speeds greater than 75 mi (121 km) per hr. The term is often restricted to those storms occurring over the N Atlantic Ocean; the identical phenomenon occurring over the W Pacific Ocean is called a typhoon; and over the Indian Ocean, a tropical cyclone. A cyclone that eventually reaches hurricane intensity first passes through two intermediate stages known as tropical depression and tropical storm. Incipient hurricanes usually form over the tropical N Atlantic Ocean and mature as they drift westward; hurricanes also occasionally form off the west coast of Mexico and move northeastward from that area. An average of 3.5 tropical storms per year eventually mature into hurricanes along the east coast of North America, usually over the Caribbean Sea or the Gulf of Mexico; one to three of these annually approach the U.S. coast, some changing their direction from west to northeast as they develop. Whereas hurricanes and N Pacific typhoons usually develop sometime between July and October, typhoons and tropical cyclones of the Southern Hemisphere favor the period from December through March; Bay of Bengal and Arabian Sea tropical cyclones occur either between April and June or between September and December, the times of the onset and retreat of the MONSOON winds. The precise mechanism and conditions that suffice for complete storm maturation are as yet not completely understood. The mature hurricane is nearly circularly symmetrical, and its influence often extends over an area 500 mi (805 km) in diameter. As a result of the extremely low central pressure (often around 28.35 in./72 cm but sometimes considerably lower, with a record 25.91

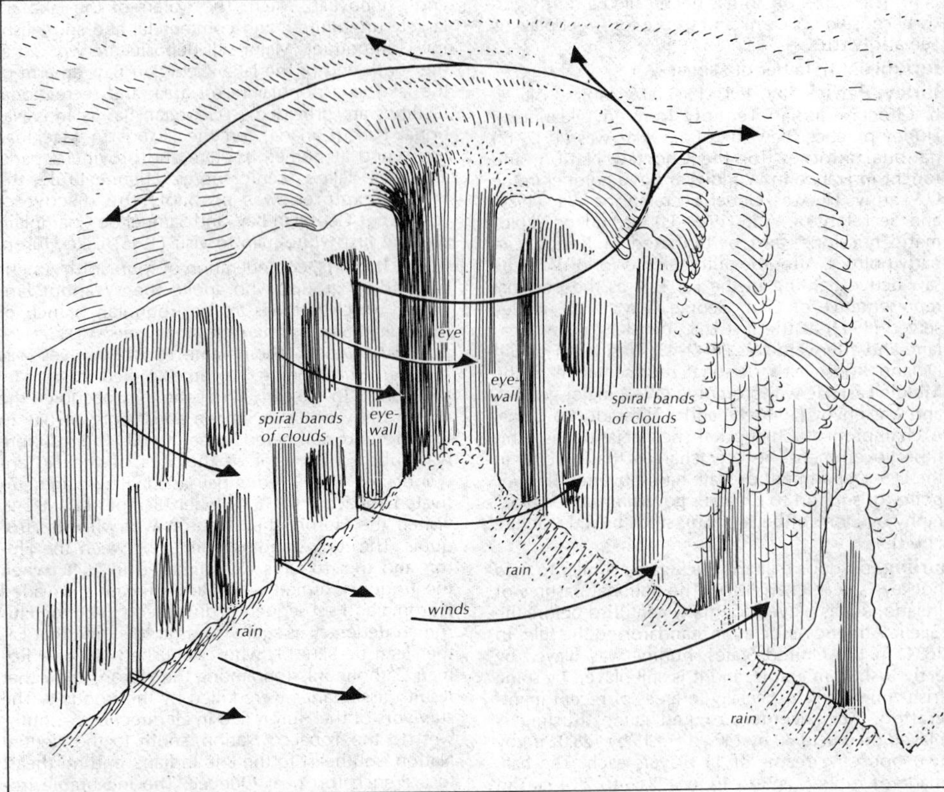

View into the eye of a hurricane showing the structure of the surrounding cloud wall

in./65.8 cm registered in a 1958 typhoon) surface air spirals inward cyclonically (counterclockwise in the Northern Hemisphere), converging on a circle of about 20 mi (30 km) diameter that surrounds the hurricane's "eye." The circumference of this circle defines the so-called eye-wall, where the inward-spiralling, moisture-laden air is forced aloft, causing condensation and the concomitant release of LATENT HEAT; after reaching altitudes of tens of thousands of feet above the surface, this air is finally expelled toward the storm's periphery. The upward velocity of the air and subsequent condensation make the eye-wall the region of heaviest precipitation and highest clouds. Because the outward increase in pressure is greatest there, the eye-wall is also the region of maximum wind speed. By contrast, the hurricane eye is almost calm, experiences little or no precipitation, and is often exposed to blue sky. Temperatures in the eye are 10°F to 15° F (5°C–8°C) warmer than those of the surrounding air as a result of sinking currents at the hurricane's core. Clouds are spread outward from the eye-wall in spiral bands parallel to the wind direction, giving the hurricane an appearance easily identifiable by satellite photography or airborne radar. Persistent rain gives way to more showery weather toward the outer regions of the storm. Hurricanes and typhoons usually move westward at about 10 mi (16 km) per hr during their early stages and then curve poleward as they approach the western boundaries of the oceans at 20° to 30° lat., although more complex tracks are common. Hurricanes have a lifespan of 1 to 30 days. They weaken and are transformed into extratropical cyclones after prolonged contact with the colder ocean waters of the middle latitudes, and they rapidly decay after moving over land areas. The source of a hurricane's energy is the tropical ocean, which supplies great quantities of moisture as well as thermal energy to the developing hurricane. In the average hurricane, the release of latent heat from the condensation of water vapor provides as much energy as the detonation of 400 20-megaton hydrogen bombs; fortunately, only 2% to 4% of this heat energy is converted naturally into the kinetic energy of the winds' motion. Nevertheless, high winds are a primary cause of hurricane-inflicted loss of life and property damage. Another cause is the flooding resulting from the coastal storm surge of the ocean and the torrential rains, both of which accompany the storm. The potential danger of a hurricane is enormous. The 1970 Bay of Bengal tropical cyclone killed about 300,000 persons, mainly by drowning, while in the United States, Hurricane Agnes (1972) caused about $3 billion damage. Project Stormfury is an experimental program sponsored by the U.S. government and aimed at finding ways to "defuse" hurricanes in their developing stages, before they are able to strike inhabited land areas. See I. R. Tannehill, *Hurricanes, Their Nature and History* (9th ed. 1956); G. E. Dunn and B. I. Miller, *Atlantic Hurricanes* (rev. ed. 1964); Thomas Helm, *Hurricanes* (1967).

Hurst, Fannie, 1889–1968, American author, b. Hamilton, Ohio, grad. Washington Univ., 1909. She is noted for her sympathetic, sentimental novels including *Lummox* (1923), *Back Street* (1930), *Imitation of Life* (1933), and *God Must Be Sad* (1961).

Hurst, John Fletcher, 1834–1903, American Methodist bishop and educator, b. Maryland. He was president of Drew Theological Seminary from 1873 until 1880, when he was elected bishop. Bishop Hurst was founder and chancellor (1891–1902) of American Univ., Washington, D.C., although the university did not open until after his death. His numerous writings include *A History of the Christian Church* (1897–1900).

Hurst, city (1970 pop. 27,215), Tarrant co., N Texas, an industrial and residential suburb of Fort Worth; inc. 1952. A large helicopter factory just south of the city is the major employer for Hurst, which also has a variety of retail and service industries. A campus of Tarrant County Junior College is in the city.

Hurtado de Mendoza, Diego (dyā'gō o͞ortä'thō dā mändō'thä), 1503–75, Spanish poet, historian, and statesman, b. Granada. An ambassador of Charles I (Holy Roman Emperor Charles V) to England and Venice and at the Council of Trent, he was banished by Philip II to Granada from 1568 to 1574. There he wrote his famous history of the Moorish rebellion, *Guerra de Granada,* which was not printed until 1627. He wrote poetry, especially elegies and epistles, in the traditional manner. The picaresque novel *Lazarillo de Tormes* was formerly attributed to him, but his authorship is now considered improbable. See biography by Erika Spivakovsky (1970).

Husák, Gustav (go͝os'täf ho͞o'säk), 1913–, Czechoslovakian political leader. A member of the Communist party from 1933, he helped to lead the Slovak national uprising against the German occupation in World War II. After the war he held government and party posts. During the 1951 party purges, he was arrested and imprisoned. He was released in 1960, and was allowed to rejoin the party in 1963. A critic of party secretary Antonín NOVOTNÝ, he called for political liberalization and Slovakian national autonomy. Following Novotný's resignation, Husák became (1968) deputy premier and was an architect of the 1968 reforms. After the invasion of Czechoslovakia by the USSR (Aug., 1968), he became increasingly pro-Soviet. In April, 1969, he replaced Alexander Dubček as Communist party secretary. He renewed Czechoslovakia's ties with the USSR and reinstituted strong party control over the Czech economy and state.

Húsavík (ho͞o'sävēk"), town (1970 pop. 1,993), N Iceland, on Skjálfandi bay. It is a fishing port and commercial center.

Husayn: see also HUSEIN; HUSSEIN.

Husayn ibn Ali (ĭ'bən ä'lē), 1856–1931, Arabian political and religious leader. In 1908 he succeeded as grand sherif of Mecca and thus became ruler of the Hejaz under Turkey. In World War I, after receiving British assurances that all Arab lands not under French control would be liberated, he began (1916) a successful revolt against the Turks in Arabia and proclaimed himself king of the Hejaz and even of all Arabia. Believing that the British had not kept their promises, he refused to sign the Treaty of Versailles. Great Britain lent him no support in his struggle with Ibn Saud, who defeated him in 1924, forcing him to abdicate and renounce his claim to the caliphate. That claim, advanced after the Turkish parliament abolished the Ottoman caliphate in 1924, was based on Husayn's membership in the Hashimite family, a branch of the Koreish tribe, to which Muhammad the Prophet had belonged. In 1925, Ibn Saud took Husayn's domain. Husayn lived (1924–30) in exile on Cyprus. He died in Amman, the capital of his son Abdullah, ruler of Trans-Jordan (now Jordan). Another son, Feisal I, founded the royal line of Iraq.

husband and wife. This article discusses only the legal aspects of the married state; for the sociological aspects, see MARRIAGE. In law, marriage is a contractual relationship between man and woman that vests the parties with a new legal status. Most of the requisites for other binding contracts must also be present in the case of marriage. Thus, the parties must have acted free from duress and must not have made fraudulent representations; otherwise the purported marriage may be dissolved by a judicial decree of NULLITY OF MARRIAGE. However, marriage is unlike other contractual relationships in that it creates a personal status that may not be terminated by the will of both parties but only by a court, e.g., by a DIVORCE. With few exceptions, a marriage validly contracted in one place is universally recognized. Thus a common-law marriage—i.e., a marriage solely by consent of the parties, without ceremony or registration—contracted in a state where such unions are valid will be deemed binding in states where a license to marry and a civil or religious ceremony of marriage are required. At an early period common-law marriages were frequent in Europe. The difficulties arising from common-law marriages—e.g., the doubtful legitimacy of children—led to their complete prohibition in Roman Catholic countries by the Council of Trent. Although common-law marriage was abolished in England in 1753, it continued lawful in Scotland and in the American colonies. Today most American states do not allow such marriages. The former Anglo-American law of marriage was chiefly characterized by the view that husband and wife are one legal personality for whom the husband acts. Accordingly, the husband determined the marital domicile, he was the dominant figure in the relation of PARENT AND CHILD, and nearly all the property of the wife passed to his absolute control for the duration of the marriage. The wife ordinarily could not make separate contracts, but if her husband refused support to her or to the children, she might pledge his credit to supply the needs of her station in life. After the death of a spouse the survivor usually enjoyed a partial interest in the deceased's property. The wife's DOWER entitled her to one third of the husband's property on his death; curtesy, a similar right of the husband in the wife's property, accrued only if children had been born of the marriage. In time, equity recognized the wife's right during her husband's lifetime to a separate property in trust established for her benefit. By the late 19th cent. the need for a separate trust property disappeared, for Great Britain and all the American states adopted "married women's property" statutes, giving to wives complete control over their property and their contracts. Most states provided that in place of dower and curtesy a surviving spouse was entitled to a certain minimum share in the estate of the deceased spouse. A few states, following the Spanish law, recognized community property, i.e., all property acquired during the marriage is owned by both husband and wife and is divided equally on the dissolution of the marriage. Other features of the older laws on marriage persisted, but by the early 1970s many were modified or eliminated. Thus, the husband in most cases still determines the marital residence, and he owes the wife a duty of support that she is not usually required to return. Certain old legal actions for injury to the marital relation that were once available only to the husband, such as actions for criminal conversation (i.e., a civil action against the paramour for adultery), actions for loss of consortium (marital services) because of physical injury to the wife; and actions for alienation of the wife's affections are now either extended to the wife or denied to the husband. See H. H. Clark, Jr., *The Law of Domestic Relations in the United States* (1968).

Husein: see also HUSAYN; HUSSEIN.

Husein (ho͞osīn') or **Husayn** (-sān'), c.626–680, Muslim saint of the Shiites; second son of ALI and FATIMA (daughter of Muhammad the Prophet). His elder brother, HASAN, was forced to abdicate as 5th caliph in favor of Muawiya. The CALIPHATE thus passed away from the Alid family, although many believers upheld the sons of Ali. On the death of Hasan, Husein tried to make good his own claim, but he proved irresolute in crises. Finally he did lead an insurrection, but he and his band were massacred by the Umayyads at KARBALA. The day of this defeat—the 10th of Muharram in the hegira year 61 (Oct. 10, 680)—became the great holy day of the Shiites, who uphold the legitimacy of the Alid claims. They commemorate the day with an extensive mourning ritual that culminates in a passion play, the Ashura. The tomb of Husein at Karbala is for them a holy place of pilgrimage. His name also appears as Hussein and Husain.

Hushah (hyo͞o'shə), descendant of Judah. 1 Chron. 4.4.

Hushai (hyo͞o'shāī), friend of David, who set him to spy on Absalom. 2 Sam. 15–17.

Husham (hyo͞o'shăm), king of Edom. Gen. 36.34,35; 1 Chron. 1.45,46.

Hushathite (hyo͞o'shəthīt"), designation of SIBBECAI, possibly derived from HUSHAH.

Hu Shih (ho͞o shŭr), 1891–1962, Chinese philosopher and essayist, leading liberal intellectual in the MAY FOURTH MOVEMENT (1917–23). He studied under John Dewey at Columbia Univ., becoming a lifelong advocate of pragmatic evolutionary change. While professor of philosophy at Peking Univ., he wrote for the iconoclastic journal *New Youth* (see CH'EN TU-HSIU). His most important contribution was promotion of vernacular literature to replace writing in the classical style. Hu Shih was also a leading critic and analyst of traditional Chinese culture and thought. He was ambassador to the United States (1938–42), chancellor of Peking Univ. (1946–48), and after 1958 president of the Academia Sinica in Taiwan. See J. B. Grieder, *Hu Shih and the Chinese Renaissance* (1970).

Hushim (hyo͞o'shĭm). **1** See SHUHAM. **2** Name in the genealogy of Benjamin. 1 Chron. 7.12. **3** Wife of a Benjamite. 1 Chron. 8.8,11.

Huskisson, William (hŭs'kĭsən), 1770–1830, British statesman. First elected to Parliament in 1796, he was secretary of the treasury (1804–5, 1807–9) but resigned with his close associate George Canning. He joined (1814) Lord Liverpool's administration, holding minor office until appointed president of the Board of Trade and treasurer of the navy in 1823. Although a Tory, Huskisson was an advocate of free trade and did much to liberalize Great Britain's trading regulations. He reformed the Navigation Acts, reduced import duties, and attempted to introduce a sliding scale to relax the effect of the CORN LAWS. He served (1827–28) as colonial secretary and leader of the House of Commons under Viscount Goderich and the duke of Wellington, resigning after a dispute with Wellington over parliamentary reform. He was killed by a locomotive at the opening of the Manchester and Liverpool Railway.

Huskvarna (hŭs'kvär"nä), city (1970 pop. 14,369), Jönköping co., S Sweden, at the southern end of Lake Vättern. In the late 17th-cent. it replaced nearby Jönköping as a weapons-manufacturing center. Other products include sewing machines, bicycles, textiles, and electrical goods. A hydroelectric power station is nearby.

husky: see SIBERIAN HUSKY.

Huss, John (hŭs), Czech *Jan Hus* (yän ho͞os), 1369?–1415, Czech religious reformer. Of peasant origin, he was born in Husinec, Bohemia (from which his name is derived). He studied theology at the Univ. of Prague, was ordained a priest c.1400, and in 1402 was appointed preacher of the Bethlehem Chapel, a foundation dedicated to preaching in the Czech language. He early came under the influence of the writings of John WYCLIF, and though he did not fully espouse Wyclif's doctrine, he opposed its condemnation (1403) by the Univ. of Prague and translated Wyclif's *Triologus* into Czech. In his sermons Huss attacked the abuses of the clergy, thus earning the hostility of many priests, who turned the archbishop of Prague against him. Huss, however, had the support of Wenceslaus IV (see WENCESLAUS, Holy Roman emperor). He furthermore represented the Czech national aspirations in conflict with the German elements in Bohemia. In 1408 the archbishop and the university opposed the king's scheme to have Bohemia observe neutrality between the rival popes Gregory XII and Benedict XIII (Pedro de Luna). Only the Czech members of the university supported Wenceslaus, who as a result changed (1409) the university charter, giving the Czechs a predominant position; he made Huss rector of the university. The Bohemian clergy thus were split into two groups. This situation was not helped when, in the same year, the Council of Pisa deposed both popes and chose Pietro Cardinal Philarghi as Alexander V, who was shortly succeeded by Baldassarre Cardinal Cossa as John XXIII. With papal support, the archbishop forbade preaching in the Bethlehem Chapel, ordered the burning of Wyclif's books, and excommunicated (1410) Huss and his followers. Wenceslaus stood by Huss and in 1411 brought about a truce, but the fight flared up again in 1412, when Huss openly denounced the bulls of the antipope John XXIII against King Lancelot of Naples and preached against indulgences. The pope excommunicated Huss, who—to save Prague from the papal interdict—retired to a castle near Tabor. During his two years of exile he wrote his chief works, including the *De ecclesia*, which increasingly reflected Wyclif's influence. He denied the infallibility of an immoral pope, asserted the ultimate authority of Scripture over the church, and accorded the state the right and duty to supervise the church. Because of these ideas he is generally considered a forerunner of the Protestant Reformation. At the invitation of Holy Roman Emperor SIGISMUND, who granted him a safe-conduct, Huss presented himself in 1414 at the Council of Constance to justify his views. The council refused to recognize his safe-conduct, and Huss was imprisoned and tried as a heretic. His friend JEROME OF PRAGUE was also seized and put on trial. Huss denied some of the beliefs attributed to him; others he refused to modify unless convinced of their error. The council condemned his writings and sentenced him to be burned at the stake, where he died heroically. By his death he became a national hero. He was declared a martyr by the university of Prague, and the modern Czechoslovak church claims to continue his tradition. See his *De ecclesia* (tr. by D. S. Schaff, 1915); letters (ed. by Matthew Spinka, 1973); biographies by D. S. Schaff (1915), Franz Lützow (2d ed., 1921), and Matthew Spinka (1968); H. B. Workman, *The Age of Huss* (Vol. II of *The Dawn of the Reformation*, 1902).

Hussein: see also HUSAYN; HUSEIN.

Hussein I (ho͞osān', -īn'), 1935–, king of Jordan; educated in England at Harrow and Sandhurst. He ascended the throne (1953) after his grandfather had been killed (1951) by a Palestinian extremist and after his father was declared mentally unfit to serve as king. The target of more than a dozen assassination attempts, Hussein espouses a moderate pro-Western policy that has repeatedly brought him into conflict with leftist leaders in other Arab countries, as well as with Palestinian elements in his country. He has maintained his throne largely through the support of the British-trained Arab Legion and the fierce loyalty of the Bedouin tribesmen of E Jordan. Although Hussein was generally moderate in his stance toward Israel, he led Jordan into the 1967 Arab-Israeli War, as a result of which Israel occupied all Jordan W of the Jordan River. This loss intensified the conflict between Hussein and the Palestinian guerrilla movement, and finally civil war erupted (1970) between royal forces and the Palestinians. Hussein was victorious and was thus able to strengthen his rule over his kingdom. However, at the 1974 Arab summit meeting, he agreed to relinquish any claim to responsibility over the future of West Bank Jordan to the Palestine Liberation Organization.

Husseini (Amin el Husseini) (ho͞osä'nē; ämēn' ĕl), 1896?–1974, Arab political and religious leader. He was inveterately opposed to the creation of a Jewish state in Palestine, and, suspected of complicity in anti-Jewish riots in Jerusalem (1920), he fled to avoid punishment. He returned under an amnesty and was appointed Grand MUFTI of Jerusalem by the British in 1921. He fled (1937) to Lebanon after being arrested for provoking violence between Arabs and Jews. Just before World War II he moved on to Iraq. After the abortive pro-Axis Iraqi revolt of 1941 he was flown to Rome, and in Berlin he broadcast Nazi propaganda and helped recruit Arab supporters for the Germans. In 1946 the mufti, escaping from house arrest near Paris, arrived in Egypt, where he lived until the early 1960s, when he moved again to Lebanon. Also called Haj Amin el Husseini, he retired from public life after serving as president of the 1962 World Islamic Congress, which he had founded in 1931.

Husserl, Edmund (ĕt'mo͞ont ho͞os'ərl), 1859–1938, German philosopher, founder of the phenomenological movement (see PHENOMENOLOGY). He was professor at Göttingen and Freiburg and was greatly influenced by Franz Brentano. His philosophy is a descriptive study of consciousness for the purpose of discovering the structure of experience, i.e., the laws by which experiences are had. His method was to "bracket" the data of consciousness by suspending all preconceptions, especially those drawn from the "naturalistic standpoint." Thus, objects of pure imagination are examined with the same seriousness as data taken from the objective world. Husserl concluded that consciousness has no life apart from the objects it considers. This characteristic he calls "intentionality" (object-directedness), following Brentano. In his later work, Husserl moved toward idealism and denied that objects exist outside of consciousness. His chief works are *Logische Untersuchungen* (1900–1901) and *Ideas for a Pure Phenomenology* (tr. 1952). See studies by Paul Ricoeur (1967), Joseph Kockelmans, ed. (1967), R. A. Mall (1973), and Maurice Natanson (1973).

Hussites (hŭs'īts), followers of John Huss. After the burning of Huss (1415) and Jerome of Prague (1416), the Hussites continued as a powerful group in Bohemia and Moravia. They drew up (1420) the Four Articles of Prague, demanding freedom of preaching, communion in both kinds (i.e., both wine and bread) for laymen as well as priests, the limitation of property holding by the church, and civil punishment of mortal sin, including simony. Meanwhile the HUSSITE WARS had begun, and in their course the Hussite movement splintered into several groups. The moderate group, called Utraquists [from Lat. *sub utraque specie*=in both kinds] or Calixtines [from Lat.,=chalice], consisted chiefly of the lesser nobility and the bourgeoisie. The Univ. of Prague was their center and Master Jan Rokycana their principal leader. Except for the demands made in the Four Articles, they agreed substantially with the Roman Catholic Church. The more radical Hussites, the Taborites, named after their religious center and stronghold at Tabor, went further than the Utraquists in accepting the doctrines of John Wyclif. Consisting largely of peasants, this group expressed the messianic hopes of the oppressed. They regarded the Four Articles as minimal concessions. Their real goal was the total abolition of the feudal system and the establishment of a classless society without private property. From among their number came such leaders as John ZIZKA and PROCOPIUS THE GREAT. Puritanical and iconoclastic, the Taborites reduced the sacraments to communion and baptism, denied the Real Presence, and abolished the veneration of saints and holy images. The Hussite Wars necessitated a temporary alliance between the two groups. However, when the Utraquists were reconciled (1436) with the church through the agreement known as the Compactata, the Taborites refused to acquiesce. Of the demands of the original Four Articles the Catholic Church conceded only on communion in both kinds. The obstinacy of the Taborites led to the alliance between the Utraquists and the Catholics and to the military defeat of the Taborites at Lipany (1534). After this, Taborite influence vanished from Bohemia. The Bohemian and Moravian Brethren are, however, probably descended from this group (see MORAVIAN CHURCH). The Utraquists obtained (1436) royal recognition of the Compactata, which remained the fundamental religious law of Bohemia until 1567. By that time Protestantism had made great progress in Bohemia, and the Utraquists themselves were divided. The Old Utraquists remained Catholic; the New Utraquists joined with the Lutherans and drew up (1575) the *Confessio Bohemia*, which achieved official status (1609) in the Letter of Majesty of Emperor Rudolph II (see BOHEMIA). The violation of this letter was the prelude to the Thirty Years War. Bohemia, which was overwhelmingly Protestant in the mid-16th cent., was returned to Catholicism by both force and persuasion. Nevertheless, the Evangelicals, as the Lutheran Utraquists were called, did not entirely disappear, and neither did the other major communion, the Moravian Church. In spite of its ultimate failure, the Hussite movement is of permanent historical significance. It was the first substantial attack upon the two bulwarks of medieval society, feudalism and the Roman Catholic Church. As such it helped pave the way for both the Protestant Reformation and the rise of modern nationalism. See Josef Macek, *The Hussite Movement in Bohemia* (tr. 1958); Howard Kaminsky, *A History of the Hussite Revolution* (1967).

Hussite Wars, series of conflicts in the 15th cent., caused by the rise of the HUSSITES in Bohemia and Moravia. It was a religious struggle between Hussites and the Roman Catholic Church, a national struggle between Czechs and Germans, and a social struggle between the landed and peasant classes. On the death (1419) of Wenceslaus IV of Bohemia (see WENCESLAUS, emperor), the Hussites in Bohemia and Moravia took up arms to prevent his brother—their archenemy, Emperor SIGISMUND—from entering into his succession. John ZIZKA, the Hussite military leader, expelled Sigismund in 1420 and routed him again at Kutna Hora in 1422. From 1419 to 1436, Bohemia had no effective king, although Witowt of Lithuania was elected (1421) antiking and sent his nephew, Sigismund Korybut, to Bohemia as his vicar. Korybut took the crown in 1424 and held it until 1427. After the death (1424) of Zizka the division between the radical and the moderate parties of the Hussites—the Taborites and the Utraquists—widened. A Taborite, PROCOPIUS THE GREAT, succeeded Zizka as military commander of the Hussites. In 1425-26 a Hussite army invaded Silesia and Saxony, and in 1429-30 the united Hussite forces penetrated as far as Franconia. Several crusades against the Hussites were utterly routed by the Czechs, whose military organization and tactics were much superior to those of their opponents. Negotiations with the Council of Basel began, especially through the Univ. of Prague, and in 1433 the Czech delegates arrived at Basel (see BASEL, COUNCIL OF). The result was the conclusion of the Compactata, by which the moderate Hussites were taken back into the Catholic Church. The Compactata were rejected by the Taborites. Civil war now broke out between the Utraquists and the Taborites (predominantly the party of the lower classes). At the decisive battle of Lipany (1434) the Taborites were routed and Procopius was killed. At a council meeting (1436) at Jihlava the Compactata were ratified and Sigismund was recognized as king of Bohemia. On the death (1439) of Sigismund's successor, Albert II, the Utraquist leader GEORGE OF PODEBRAD governed Bohemia—first in the name of LADISLAUS V and from 1458 as king. He refused to accept the papal revocation (1462) of the Compactata and was declared deposed in 1466. A new war began between George and the nobles, and in 1468, MATTHIAS CORVINUS of Hungary attacked Bohemia. By the time peace was made (1478), long after George's death, the religious element of the wars had largely disappeared. See Franz, Graf von Lützow, *The Hussite Wars* (1914); Howard Kaminsky, *History of the Hussite Revolution* (1967).

Husson or **Fleury, Jules** (zhül üsôN', flörē')1821-89, French novelist who wrote under the name Champfleury. Considered a pioneer of French realism, Champfleury was an avid collector of French art and artifacts and conducted extensive research into French history. His literary views are set forth in *Réalisme* (1857). Among his novels are *Les Bourgeois de Molinchart* (1854), a portrait of provincial life; and *Les Souffrances du Professeur Delteil* (1856), a comedy about student pranks. His other works include *Histoire de la cariacature* (1865-69). In later life he was director of the porcelain factory at Sèvres.

Huston, John (hyo͞os'tən), 1906-, American motion picture director, writer, and actor, b. Nevada, Mo. He wrote the screenplays for many of his films, notably *The Maltese Falcon* (1941), a classic detective movie. Among the many and diverse films he has directed are *The Treasure of the Sierra Madre* (1947), *The Asphalt Jungle* (1950), *The African Queen* (1951), *Beat the Devil* (1954), *Moby Dick* (1956), *The Misfits* (1960), and *Fat City* (1972). His father was **Walter Huston,** 1884-1950, American actor, b. Toronto, Canada. A character actor, he starred in Kurt Weill's *Knickerbocker Holiday* (1938). His films include *Dodsworth* (1936), *All That Money Can Buy* (1941), and *The Treasure of the Sierra Madre.*

Husum (ho͞o'zo͞om), city (1970 pop. 24,963), Schleswig-Holstein, N West Germany, a port on the North Sea. It is a fishing center and major cattle market. First mentioned in the 13th cent., Husum was chartered at the beginning of the 17th cent. and soon became a prosperous commercial city, but it later declined. Many fine patrician houses remain. The 19th-century poet and novelist Theodor Storm was born in Husum and is buried there.

Hutcheson, Francis, 1694-1746, British philosopher, b. County Down, Ireland. He was a professor at the Univ. of Glasgow from 1729 until his death. His reputation rests on four essays published anonymously while he was living in Dublin, prior to his college teaching. Two of them were included in *An Inquiry into the Original of Our Ideas of Beauty and Virtue* (1725) and two in *An Essay on the Nature and Conduct of the Passions and Affections, with Illustrations on the Moral Sense* (1728). Although one of the first to write on the subject of aesthetics, he was primarily known in the field of ethics. According to Hutcheson, man has many senses, the most important of which is the moral sense. This "benevolent theory of morals," in which man has a desire to do good, was a development of Shaftesbury's natural affection to benevolent action and was in opposition to Hobbes's theories. The criterion of moral action was the "greatest happiness for the greatest numbers," an anticipation of the utilitarian philosophers in word as well as spirit. See his *System of Moral Philosophy* (with memoir by Rev. William Leechman, 1755). See biography by W. R. Scott (1900, repr. 1966); study by W. L. Taylor (1965).

Hutchins, Robert Maynard, 1899-, American educator, b. Brooklyn, N.Y., studied at Oberlin College, grad. Yale, 1921, taught in the Yale law school (1925-27), and served as dean (1927-29). He became president of the Univ. of Chicago in 1929 at the age of 30 and held that position until 1945; he served as chancellor there from 1945 until 1951. After 1943 he was chairman of the board of editors for the *Encyclopaedia Britannica.* An enthusiast for adult education, he received in 1946 a year's leave of absence to promote the "great books" program. He was associate director of the Ford Foundation from 1951 to 1954, when he became president of the Fund for the Republic, and later president of the Center for the Study of Democratic Institutions in Santa Barbara, Calif. In 1969 he became chairman of the board. His books include *The Higher Learning in America* (1936), *Education for Freedom* (1943), *The Conflict in Education in a Democratic Society* (1953), and *The Learning Society* (1968).

Hutchins, Thomas, 1730-89, American frontiersman, surveyor, and geographer, b. Monmouth co., N.J. He took part in the French and Indian War and gained a reputation for his engineering ability through planning Fort Pitt and other works. His journals of military expeditions in the Western country are valuable historical sources. A captain in the British army and in London at the opening of the American Revolution, Hutchins refused to bear arms against the Revolutionaries and was imprisoned and charged with high treason. Released in 1780, he escaped to France and ultimately to Charleston, S.C., where he joined the Revolutionary forces. In July, 1781, he became geographer to the United States. In 1785 he took charge of the survey of the Northwest Territory.

Hutchinson, Anne, c.1591-1643, religious leader in New England, b. Anne Marbury in Lincolnshire, England. She emigrated (1634) with her husband and family to Massachusetts Bay, where her brilliant mind and her kindness won admiration and a following. The informal discussions at her home gave scope to Puritan intellects, but her espousal of the covenant of grace as opposed to the covenant of works (i.e., she tended to believe that faith alone was necessary to salvation) caused John COTTON, John WINTHROP, and other former friends to view her as an antinomian heretic. She defied them, was tried by the General Court, and was sentenced (1637) to banishment for "traducing the ministers." Several of her followers—including William CODDINGTON, John WHEELWRIGHT, John UNDERHILL, and John CLARKE—also left Massachusetts Bay. After helping Coddington to found the present Portsmouth, R.I., she quarreled with him and, with Samuel GORTON, ousted him in 1639. After Coddington's return to power, she moved (1642) to Long Island and then to what is now Pelham Bay Park in New York City. There she and all the other members of her family but one were killed by Indians. See Winifred K. Rugg, *Unafraid* (1930, repr. 1970); E. J. Battis, *Saints and Sectaries* (1962); D. D. Hall, comp., *The Antinomian Controversy, 1636-1638* (1968).

Hutchinson, Thomas, 1711-80, colonial governor of Massachusetts (1771-74) and historian, b. Boston. A descendant of Anne Hutchinson, he was a man of wealth and prominence, of learning, and of notable integrity. He entered public life when he became (1737) a member of the General Court, the Massachusetts legislature. When the cost of the Louisburg campaign was repaid to Massachusetts, he proposed (1748) that the money be used to redeem the colony's depreciated currency. The plan, which was ultimately successful in stimulating trade, caused Hutchinson to lose the election in 1749 and aligned him with the conservatives. He was a member of the governor's council (1749-66), a delegate to the Albany Congress (1754), chief justice (1760-61), and lieutenant governor (1758-71). When he was appointed royal governor in 1771, Hutchinson was perhaps the most powerful man in the colony, but he had bitter political enemies among the radicals, notably Samuel Adams. Though he considered the Stamp Act and other government measures unwise, he had favored strict enforcement, and his unpopularity caused a mob to sack and burn his mansion in 1765. His unpopularity increased after he became governor, and he favored strenuous measures against the growing discontent. These views were exposed when letters he had written to English friends were made public. In 1773 he refused to let the tea-laden ships clear Boston Harbor and thus brought on the BOSTON TEA PARTY. As tension grew worse he was replaced as governor by Gen. Thomas Gage and moved to England. He was the author of an accurate, scholarly, and useful book, *The History of the Colony and Province of Massachusetts Bay* (3 vol., 1764-1828; modern ed. by L. S. Mayo, 1936). See his diary and letters (ed. by P. O. Hutchinson, 1883-86, repr. 1971); study by Bernard Bailyn (1974).

Hutchinson, city (1970 pop. 36,885), seat of Reno co., S central Kansas, on the Arkansas River; inc. 1872. It is a commercial and industrial center in a grain (especially wheat), livestock, and oil region. Its many facilities include a giant grain elevator, over half a mile long. Farm equipment and aircraft parts are made, and salt is extracted from great beds beneath the city. Hutchinson has a junior college, a planetarium, and the Kansas state fairgrounds.

Hutten, Ulrich von (o͞ol'rĭkh fən ho͞ot'ən), 1488-1523, German humanist and poet, partisan of the Reformation, an outstanding figure in German political history. Hutten's career as poet was launched by his participation in the famous *Episculae obscurorum virorum* (1515), which supported the cause of REUCHLIN. In 1517 he was crowned poet laureate by Holy Roman Emperor Maximilian I. He wrote innumerable epigrams, speeches, and songs, although his main literary vehicle was dialogues; *Arminius,* the best known, is in the collection *Gesprachsbüchlein* (1521). A vehement patriot, he became an associate of Luther and joined SICKINGEN in his war on ecclesiastical princes. He died in exile, seeking asylum with Zwingli. See biography by D. F. Strauss (tr. 1874, repr. 1970); study by T. W. Best (1969).

Hutterian Brethren (hətēr'ēən), a body of Christians practicing strict communism based on religious principles. The brethren are descendants of those Moravian Anabaptists who were followers of Jacob Hutter, a minister from the Tyrol, who was burned at the stake in 1536. In the 17th cent. there were a number of Hutterian brotherhoods in Moravia. Persecution drove them eastward to eventual settlement in Russia. In 1874, in company with Russian Mennonites, a group emigrated to the United States, settling near Tabor, S.Dak. Other groups followed. Their doctrines and principles, aside from their practice of common ownership, are in accord with those of MENNONITES in general. There are 28 groups in South Dakota and 1 in Minnesota. They are also known as Hutterische Brethren. See studies by Victor Peters (1965) and J. W. Bennett (1967).

Hutton, James, 1726-97, Scottish geologist. Turning early from the study of chemistry and medicine to geology, he formulated controversial theories of the origin of the earth and of atmospheric changes (see UNIFORMITARIANISM) that paved the way to modern geological science. Hutton concluded that the earth's history can be explained by observing the geological forces now at work, because these forces are identical to the ones that operated in the past. His great work was *The Theory of the Earth* (2 vol., 1795; MS fragment for Vol. III ed. by Archibald Geikie, 1899); it was simplified by John Playfair as *Illustrations of the Huttonian Theory of the Earth* (1802). See study by E. B. Bailey (1967).

Huxley, Aldous Leonard, 1894-1963, English author; grandson of Thomas Henry Huxley. Educated at Eton and Oxford, he traveled widely and during the 1920s lived in Italy. He came to the United States in the late 1930s and settled in California. On the verge of blindness from the time he was 18, Huxley devoted much time and energy in an effort to improve his vision. He began his literary career writing critical essays and symbolist poetry, but he soon turned to the novel. *Crome Yellow* (1921), *Antic Hay* (1923), *Those Barren Leaves* (1925), and *Point Counter Point* (1928) are brittle, skeptical pictures of a decadent society. *Brave New World* (1932) presents a nightmarish, utopian civilization in the 25th cent. It was followed by *Eyeless in Gaza* (1936), *After Many a Summer Dies the Swan* (1939), *Ape and Essence* (1948), *The Devils of Loudon* (1952), and *The Genius and the Goddess* (1955). Marked by an exuberance of ideas and comic invention, his novels reflect, with increasing cynicism, his disgust and disillusionment with the modern world. His later writings, however, reveal a strong interest in mysticism and Eastern philosophy. Huxley's other works include collections of short stories, of which *Mortal Coils* (1922) is representative, and essays, such as *End and Means* (1937) and *Brave New World Revisited* (1958). See memoirs by his wife, Laura Archera Huxley (1968); biographies by George Woodcock (1972) and Sybille Bedford (2 vol., 1973–74); studies by J. A. Atkins (rev. ed. 1968), Peter Bowering (1969), Philip Thody (1973), and K. M. May (1973); R. W. Clark, *The Huxleys* (1968).

Huxley, Andrew Fielding, 1917–, British research scientist, educated at University College, London. He finished his studies at Cambridge after doing operational research for the admiralty during World War II. He was director of studies at Trinity College, Cambridge, from 1952 to 1960, when he became professor of physiology at University College, London. He is the half brother of Sir Julian Huxley and the late Aldous Huxley. He shared the 1963 Nobel Prize in Physiology and Medicine with A. L. Hodgkin and Sir John Carew Eccles for analysis of the electrical and chemical events in nerve cell discharge.

Huxley, Julian Sorell, 1887–, English biologist and writer, educated at Oxford; grandson of Thomas Henry Huxley. He taught at the Rice Institute, Houston, Texas (1912–16), at Oxford (1919–25), and at King's College, London (1925–35). During those years and subsequently, as secretary (1935–42) of the Zoological Society of London, he was also president of the National Union of Scientific Workers (1926–29). From 1946 to 1948 he served as director general of the United Nations Educational, Scientific, and Cultural Organization. A gifted exponent of science, his writings include *Animal Biology* (with J. B. S. Haldane, 1927), *Scientific Research and Social Needs* (1934), *We Europeans* (with A. C. Haddon, 1936), *The Living Thoughts of Darwin* (1939), *Man in the Modern World* (1947), *Heredity, East and West* (1949), and *Memories* (2 vol., 1971 and 1974). Also, he edited T. H. Huxley's *Diary of the Voyage of H.M.S. Rattlesnake* (1935), *The New Systematics* (1940), and *The Humanist Frame* (1962).

Huxley, Thomas Henry, 1825–95, English biologist and educator, grad. Charing Cross Hospital, 1845. Huxley gave up his own biological research to become an influential scientific publicist and was the principal exponent of Darwinism in England. An agnostic (see AGNOSTICISM), he doubted all things not immediately open to logical analysis and scientific verification. He held up truth as an ideal and spoke and wrote frequently on its tool, the scientific method, and its yield, the evolutionary theory. He placed human ethics outside the scope of the materialistic processes of evolution; he believed that civilization is man's protest against nature and that progress is achieved by the human control of evolution. Huxley held numerous public offices, serving on 10 royal commissions (1862–84). His many works include *Evolution and Ethics* (1893), *Collected Essays* (9 vol., 1893–94), *Scientific Memoirs* (4 vol., 1898–1902), and an autobiography (1903). See selected writings, ed. by Cyril Bibby (1967); biographies by Huxley's son Leonard (1920, repr. 1969) and Cyril Bibby (1972).

Huy (üē'), Flemish *Hoie,* town (1970 pop. 12,736), Liège prov., E Belgium, on the Meuse River; founded in the 9th cent. Below the citadel (19th cent.; now a military depot and a prison), which dominates the town, is a fine Gothic abbatial church (14th–15th cent.).

Huygens, Christiaan (krĭs'tyän hoi'gəns), 1629–95, Dutch mathematician and physicist; son of Constantijn Huygens. He improved telescopic lenses and discovered (1655) a satellite of Saturn and the rings of Saturn. These discoveries were described in his *Systema Saturnium* (1659). He was the first to use the pendulum in clocks. He developed a wave theory of light opposed to the corpuscular theory of Newton and formulated Huygens's principle, which holds that, concerning light waves, every point on a wave front is itself a source of new waves. In 1678 he discovered the polarization of light by double refraction in calcite. His chief work is *Horologium oscillatorium* (1673). See his *Oeuvres complètes* (22 vol. in 23, 1888–1950); study by A. E. Bell (1947); Aant Elzinga, *On a Research Program in Early Modern Physics* (1972).

Huygens, Constantijn (kônstäntīn'), 1596–1687, Dutch humanist and poet, b. The Hague. He was broadly educated in languages, law, and social protocol to follow a public career. From 1625 he was secretary to the stadtholder, or lieutenant governor, of The Hague. Huygens wrote verse in seven languages as well as in Dutch. His poems, descriptive and satirical, were highly esteemed; both the English and the French monarchs knighted him in recognition of his genius. His verse is graceful, highly ornamented, and sometimes moralistic. In his collection *Daghwerck* (1627–38) he wrote of his love for his wife. One of his last works, *Cluyswerck* (1683) is semiautobiographical. Huygens was also an accomplished musician and composer of many works for strings. The thousands of his letters that survive attest to his wide acquaintance among contemporary scholars, including Descartes, Corneille, and Jean Louis Guez de Balzac. Huygens was the father of the physicist-mathematician Christiaan Huygens.

Huysmans, Cornelis (kōr'nālĭs hois'mäns), 1648–1727, Flemish painter of landscapes and religious subjects. Most of his life was spent in Malines. His landscapes, painted with a broad brush, are rich in warm, dark tones; he emulated the coloring of the Venetians. His works may be seen in many important European museums. The Metropolitan Museum has two landscapes. His brother and pupil, **Jan Baptist Huysmans,** 1654–1716, landscape painter, was less skillful in his imitation of the Venetians. Examples of his few surviving works are in the museums of Brussels and Antwerp.

Huysmans, Jacob (yä'kōp), c.1633–1696, Flemish portrait painter. In the reign of Charles II he settled in England, where he became one of the fashionable painters of the court. His chief portraits are those of Izaak Walton and Catherine of Braganza, wife of Charles II (both: National Gall., London), done in the style of Lely.

Huysmans, Jan Baptist: see under HUYSMANS, CORNELIS.

Huysmans, Joris Karl (zhōrēs' kärl üēsmäNs'), 1848–1907, French novelist of Dutch family. He was at first a disciple of Zola; typical of his early, naturalistic novels is *Marthe* (1876). Huysmans sought to satisfy his mystical leanings through occultism, before eventually becoming absorbed in Roman Catholicism. His novel *À rebours* (1884, tr. *Against the Grain,* 1922) records his spiritual quest and expresses the mood of the DECADENTS. His luminous style influenced his contemporaries and later writers. See biographies by Robert Baldick (1955), H. R. Brandreth (1963), and G. R. Ridge (1968).

Huysum, Jan van (yän vän hoi'sōōm), 1682–1749, Dutch painter of still life and landscapes. His father was Justus van Huysum (1659–1716), a successful landscape and genre painter of Amsterdam. Although he painted landscapes in a classical style, Jan is best known for his flower and fruit still lifes in oil and in watercolor. These are distinguished for their brilliant light and shade effects, delicacy of coloring, and exquisite finish. They are to be found in most of the leading European museums, notably in the Louvre and the museums of Amsterdam and Vienna. See study by M. H. Grant (1954).

Huz, nephew of Abraham. Gen. 22.21.

Hvannadalshnúkur, peak: see ÖRAEFAJÖKULL, Iceland.

Hvar (khvär), Gr. *Pharos,* Ital. *Lesina,* island (1971 pop. 11,326), 112 sq mi (290 sq km), in the Adriatic Sea off the Dalmatian coast, W Yugoslavia. Fruit growing, cattle raising, and fishing are the chief occupations. The island is also a leading tourist center. The chief town, Hvar, was long a Croatian cultural center. Its architecture exemplifies its long history: It has a 12th-century Byzantine cathedral, a 15th-century Franciscan church, and a 16th-century Venetian fort.

Hwainan: see HUAI-NAN, China.

Hwaining: see AN-CH'ING, China.

Hwang-hai: see YELLOW SEA.

Hwang Ho, river, China: see HUANG HO.

Hwangpoo, river, China: see WHANGPOO.

Hwangshih: see HUANG-SHIH, China.

Hwa-yen Buddhism: see HUA-YEN BUDDHISM.

Hyacinth (hī'əsĭnth) or **Hyacinthus** (hīəsĭn'thəs), in Greek mythology, beautiful youth loved by Apollo. He was killed accidentally by a discus thrown by the god. According to another legend, the wind god Zephyr, out of jealousy, blew the discus to kill Hyacinth. From his blood sprang a flower which was named for him.

hyacinth, any plant of the genus *Hyacinthus,* bulbous herbs of the family Liliaceae (LILY family) native to the Mediterranean region and South Africa. The common, or Dutch, hyacinth of house and garden culture became so popular in the 18th cent. that 2,000 kinds were said to be in cultivation in Holland, the chief commercial producer. This hyacinth has a single dense spike of fragrant flowers in shades of red, blue, white, or yellow. A variety of the common hyacinth is the less hardy and smaller blue- or white-flowered Roman hyacinth (var. *albulus*) of florists. The flower of the Greek youth HYACINTH has been identified with a number of plants (e.g., iris) other than the true hyacinth. The related grape hyacinths (*Muscari*), sometimes called baby's-breath, are very low, mostly blue-flowered herbs similar in appearance to hyacinths and also commonly cultivated. Types of BRODIEA, CAMASS, SQUILL, and other lily-family plants with flower clusters borne along the stalk are also called hyacinth. Hyacinths are classified in the division MAGNOLIOPHYTA, class Liliatae, order Liliales, family Liliaceae.

hyacinth or **jacinth** (jā'sĭnth), terms commonly applied to a variety of cinnamon-brown GARNET (hessonite), but more correctly restricted to red, yellow, and brown zircon.

Hyacinthe, Père: see LOYSON, CHARLES.

Hyades (hī'ədēz), in astronomy, open STAR CLUSTER in the constellation Taurus, located immediately to the right of the bright star Aldebaran. The cluster is about 130 light-years from the earth. It consists of about 100 stars all moving in the same direction. Its shape is that of an oblate spheroid, with most of the stars lying within 20 light-years of the center. Most of the stars in this cluster are of SPECTRAL CLASS G and K and are average in size, with temperatures that are comparable to that of the sun.

Hyades, in Greek mythology, nymphs; daughters of Atlas and Aethra. They cared for both Zeus and Dionysius as infants. In recognition of these services, they were placed among the stars of the constellation Taurus, where their rising and setting corresponded to the rainy seasons.

hyaline membrane disease, respiratory distress syndrome of newborns, most common in infants born prematurely or by CESAREAN SECTION or having a diabetic mother. The immature lungs of such infants cannot retain air; the air spaces empty completely and collapse after the first (and each succeeding) exhalation. Plasma leaks out of the lung tissue and coats the air spaces with a pink coating that is glassy, or hyaline, in appearance, hence the name of the disease. Exhaustion, resulting from the extreme effort required to breathe, is responsible for the death of many afflicted infants. Hyaline membrane disease is thought to be caused by a lack, in the immature lung, of a surfactant agent; the substance, a mixture of lipids and proteins, contributes to the elasticity of lung tissue and stabilizes air passages so that the lung remains partly aerated after each exhalation. Intensive care, including help in breathing, can often bring infants with the disease through the first five or six days, after which most recover completely. There is some evidence that tests on amniotic fluid during pregnancy can identify fetuses that are likely candidates for hyaline membrane disease, and that STEROIDS administered to such fetuses will accelerate production of lung surfactant.

hyaluronic acid: see MUCOPOLYSACCHARIDE.

Hyannis (hīăn'ĭs), resort village (1970 pop. 6,847), Barnstable co., SE Mass., on Cape Cod; inc. 1639. It is the business center of the area; major industries are tourism and home construction. A junior college and a conservatory of music and arts are located there. Nearby Hyannisport is famous as the site of a compound of houses owned by the Kennedy family.

Hyatt, Alpheus, 1838–1902, American zoologist, b. Washington, D.C., grad. Harvard, 1862. He was a devoted follower of Louis Agassiz. From 1870, Hyatt was custodian and later curator of the Boston Society of Natural History. He also taught zoology and paleontology at the Massachusetts Institute of Technology (1870–88) and at Boston Univ. (1877–1902). At the Harvard Museum of Comparative Zoology he built up a remarkable collection of fossil cephalopods; his discoveries contributed to the knowledge of their evolution. He wrote extensively on the cephalopods, sponges, and other subjects. Hyatt helped to establish the Marine Biological Laboratory at Woods Hole, Mass.

Hyatt, John Wesley, 1837–1920, American inventor, b. Starkey, N.Y. He is known especially for his development of CELLULOID; with his brothers, he began its manufacture in 1872. He also invented the Hyatt filter, a means of chemically purifying water while it is in motion; a widely used type of roller bearing; a sugarcane mill superior to any previously used; a sewing machine for making machine belting; and a substitute for ivory in the manufacture of billiard balls and other articles.

Hyattsville, city (1970 pop. 14,998), Prince Georges co., W central Md., a suburb of Washington, D.C.; inc. 1886. Hyattsville is a residential community with some light industry and commercial activity.

Hybla (hī'blə), ancient town of Sicily, on the southern slope of Mt. Etna. It is possibly the modern Paternò. Another Hybla, or Hybla Heraea, was in S Sicily.

hybrid (hī'brĭd), term applied by plant and animal breeders to the offspring of a cross between two different subspecies or species, and by geneticists to the offspring of parents differing in any genetic characteristic (see GENETICS). Hybridization is often used in agriculture to obtain greater vigor or growth (heterosis); the MULE, the hybrid steer, and hybrid corn are examples. Hybrid vigor is achieved by crossing two inbred strains (see BREEDING). The first generation shows greatly increased vigor and a better yield primarily because many genes for recessive, often deleterious, traits from one parent are masked by corresponding dominant genes in the other parent.

hydatid disease: see TAPEWORM.

Hyde, Douglas, 1860–1949, Irish scholar and political leader. He was largely responsible for the revival of the Irish language and literature through his founding of the Gaelic League in 1893. After teaching modern Irish for many years (1909–32), Hyde became, in 1938, the president of Eire. He held the office until 1945. Known by his Gaelic name, An Craoibhin Aoibhinn, he was the author of many works, including a *Literary History of Ireland* (1899) and *Love Songs of Connacht* (1894). See biography by Diarmid Coffey (1938).

Hyde, Edward: see CLARENDON, EDWARD HYDE, 1ST EARL OF.

Hyde, municipal borough (1971 pop. 37,075), Cheshire, NW England. It has iron foundries and factories producing cotton, machinery, rubber, paper, and hats. In 1974, Hyde became part of the new metropolitan county of Greater Manchester.

Hyde Park, town (1970 pop. 2,805), Dutchess co., SE N.Y., on the Hudson River; settled c.1740. It is famous as the site of the Roosevelt estate, where Franklin D. Roosevelt was born and is buried. The Roosevelt Library (1941) contains historical material dating from 1910 until Roosevelt's death in 1945. Hyde Park is also the site of the Frederick W. Vanderbilt mansion and two state parks. Both the Roosevelt and Vanderbilt homes are national historic sites (see NATIONAL PARKS AND MONUMENTS, table).

Hyde Park, 361 acres (146 hectares) in Westminster borough, London, England. Once the manor of Hyde, a part of the old Westminster Abbey property, it became a deer park under Henry VIII. Races were held there in the 17th cent. In 1730, Queen Caroline had the artificial lake, the Serpentine, constructed. It curves diagonally through Hyde Park and Kensington Gardens. Today's distinctive features of the park are Hyde Park Corner (near the Marble Arch), the meeting place of soapbox orators, and Rotten Row, a famous bridle path.

Hyderabad (hī'dərəbăd"), former state, S central India. The region of Hyderabad is now divided among the states of Karnataka, Maharashtra, and Andhra Pradesh. Situated almost entirely within the Deccan plateau, it has abundant crops of cotton and rice in the north, while grains are grown in the heavily irrigated southern area. Cotton spinning, weaving, and food processing are the principal industries. There are large deposits of coal and iron in the area. The monuments of AJANTA and ELLORA are the chief relics of the region's ancient Hindu civilization. The Mogul empire conquered Hyderabad in the late 17th cent. In 1724 the viceroy Asaf Jah, founder of the last royal line, achieved independence for Hyderabad. The loyalty of the later nizams (rulers) to Great Britain was several times rewarded by gifts of territory. In 1903, Berar, then the northernmost section of the state, was transferred to British administration. When India was partitioned (1947), the nizam, a Muslim prince and one of the most important in India, wished to remain independent. In 1948 the Indian army invaded Hyderabad. The population, in a plebiscite, endorsed accession to India. Hyderabad became a state in 1950 but was partitioned among neighboring states in 1956. The nizam was made to renounce nearly all of his fortune and was removed from power. **Hyderabad,** city (1971 pop. 1,612,276), former capital of Hyderabad and now capital of Andhra Pradesh, was founded in 1589 as the capital of the GOLCONDA kingdom. An administrative and commercial center and a transportation hub, the city has fine ancient structures, notably the Char Minar (1591) and the Old Bridge (1593). It is also the seat of Osmania Univ. (founded 1918).

Hyderabad, city (1972 metropolitan area est. pop. 834,000), capital of Sind prov., S Pakistan. Pakistan's third largest city, it was long noted for its embroideries and cutlery and now has chemical, engineering, food-processing, cotton, cement, cigarette, glass, and match industries. Founded in 1768 by Ghulam Shah Kalhora, Hyderabad was laid out by his son, Sarfaraz Khan, in 1782 and was the capital of the emirs of Sind. The British East India Company occupied Hyderabad when the Sind became a British protectorate in 1839. In the city are the Univ. of Sind and several colleges. Umarkot, birthplace of the great Mogul emperor Akbar, is nearby.

Hyder Ali: see HAIDAR ALI.

Hydra, Greece: see ÍDHRA.

hydra (hī'drə), common name for freshwater organisms in the phylum Cnidaria, which includes jellyfish, sea anemones, and corals. Hydras are widely distributed in lakes, ponds, and sluggish streams. They are small, cylindrical, solitary organisms, the largest reaching about 1 in. (2.5 cm) in length. They attach themselves temporarily to water plants or submerged objects, using an adhesive pedal disk at the anal end. The simple body consists of an outer layer of epidermis, a middle noncellular layer of mesoglea, and an inner layer of gastrodermis lining the simple gastrovascular cavity, where the final stages of food digestion occur. A whorl of tentacles surrounds the mouth. Hydras feed on small plankton organisms, especially microcrustaceans, stunning them with stinging cells (nematocysts) in the tentacles. Hydras reproduce asexually by budding and sexually by means of gonadal cells formed on the sides of the body. The green hydra, *Chlorhydra viridissima,* contains green algae living symbiotically in its gastrodermal cells. The gray and brown hydras belong to the genus *Pelmatohydra.* Several species of hydra also occur in American waters. Hydras are classified in the phylum CNIDARIA, class Hydrazoa.

Hydra, in astronomy, southern CONSTELLATION lying S of Corvus, Crater, Virgo, Leo, and Cancer. It is a long, slender, winding constellation traditionally depicted as a snake and known also as the Water Monster or Sea Serpent. The only bright star in the constellation is Alphard (Alpha Hydrae); it is a double star, but the two components can be detected only with a telescope. Hydra reaches its highest point in the evening sky in the spring.

Hydra, in Greek mythology, many-headed water serpent; offspring of Typhon and Echidna. When one of its heads was cut off, two new heads appeared. The second labor of Hercules was to kill the monster. He did so by burning the neck after cutting off each head.

hydrangea (hīdrān'jə): see SAXIFRAGE.

hydrate (hī'drāt), chemical compound that contains water. A common hydrate is the familiar blue vitriol, a crystalline form of CUPRIC SULFATE. Chemically, it is cupric sulfate pentahydrate, $CuSO_4 \cdot 5H_2O$. When a crystal of the substance is formed, five molecules of water (H_2O) are combined in the crystal with each molecule of cupric sulfate ($CuSO_4$). This water is called water of crystallization. When cupric sulfate pentahydrate is heated above 150°C the water of crystallization is driven off and anhydrous cupric sulfate is formed. It has several properties different from the pentahydrate, e.g., color, density, and crystal structure. GLAUBER'S SALT is sodium sulfate decahydrate, $Na_2SO_4 \cdot 10H_2O$. Crystals of it readily give up their water of crystallization at ordinary temperatures, forming a powdery coating of the anhydrous salt; this phenomenon (efflorescence) is exhibited by many hydrates. The number of molecules of water present in a given hydrate is fixed. However, some substances form several different hydrates. There are four different hydrates of ferrous sulfate, each with its own unique physical properties. In organic chemistry a compound formed by addition of water to a carbon-carbon double bond is sometimes called a hydrate; it contains a hydroxyl functional group and usually cannot be dehydrated. In commerce a metal hydroxide is sometimes called a hydrate; e.g., calcium hydrate is calcium hydroxide.

hydraulic machine, machine that derives its power from the motion or pressure of water or some other liquid. Water falling from one level to a lower one is used to drive machines like the WATER WHEEL and the TURBINE. The difference in height between the highest and the lowest level is called the head. The amount of WORK produced per pound of falling water is proportional to the head. Water power can be produced in this way from many natural sources, such as waterfalls and dammed rivers. Where no natural sources are available, an artificial reservoir can be made. When energy is plentiful, it is used to pump water into the reservoir; the water is then available as a power source to drive turbines when energy becomes scarce. In driving certain industrial hydraulic machines an apparatus called an accumulator is employed to supply high power for short periods of time. One type consists essentially of a cylinder enclosing a piston loaded with weights. When water is slowly pumped into the cylinder, the piston and weights are forced up to a position where they are held. When they are released, they force the water out of the cylinder rapidly, providing the machine with hydraulic power. Water or oil under pressure is commonly used as a source of power for many types of presses, riveting machines, capstans, winches, and other machines. The **hydraulic press,** or **hydrostatic press,** was invented by Joseph Bramah and is therefore sometimes called the Bramah press. It consists essentially of two cylinders each filled with liquid and each fitted with a piston; the cylinders are connected by a pipe also filled with the liquid. One cylinder is of small diameter, the other of large diameter. According to PASCAL'S LAW, pressure exerted upon the smaller piston is transmitted undiminished through the liquid to the surface of the larger piston, which is forced upward. Although the pressure (force per unit of area) is the same for both pistons, the total upward force on the larger piston is as many times greater than the force on the smaller piston as the area of the larger piston is greater than the area of the smaller piston. If, for example, the smaller piston has an area of 2 sq in. and a force of 100 lb is exerted upon it, then the force on the larger piston having an area of 50 sq in. would be 2,500 lb $(100 \times 50/2 = 2{,}500)$. However, when the pistons move, the distance the smaller piston travels is proportionately greater than the distance the larger piston travels, satisfying the law of conservation of energy. If the smaller piston moves 25 in., the larger one will only move 1 in. The hydraulic press is used, for example, to form three-dimensional objects from sheet metal and plastics and to compress large objects. The **hydraulic jack,** also an application of Pascal's law, is used to exert large forces or to lift heavy loads. Like the hydraulic press it consists essentially of two different-sized pistons contained in cylinders that are connected by a pipe. When the smaller piston is moved back and forth by a handle connected to it, it pumps a liquid into the cylinder of the larger piston, forcing the larger piston to move. In this way a weak force applied to the smaller piston can raise a heavy load on the larger one. The hydraulic ELEVATOR is also an application of Pascal's law.

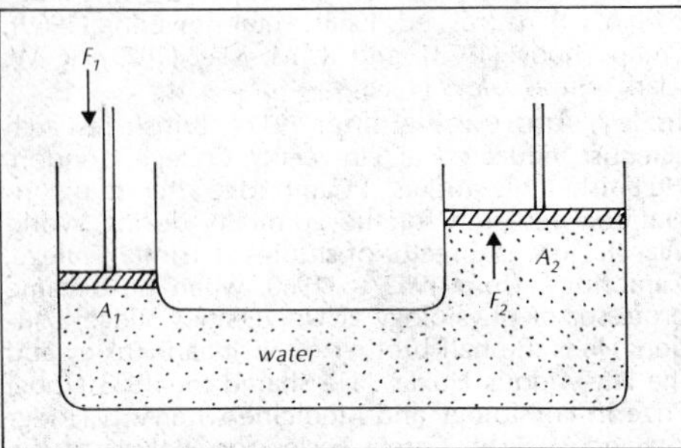

Hydraulic pressure: In any hydraulic device the pressure exerted by one piston is transmitted throughout the fluid. Since pressure equals force divided by area, a small force (F_1) exerted on a piston of small surface area (A_1) results in a large force (F_2) being exerted on a second piston of large surface area (A_2).

hydraulics, branch of engineering concerned mainly with moving liquids. The term is applied commonly to the study of the mechanical properties of water, other liquids, and even gases when the effects of compressibility are small. Hydraulics can be divided into two areas, hydrostatics and hydrokinetics. Hydrostatics, the consideration of liquids at rest, involves problems of buoyancy and flotation, pressure on dams and submerged devices, and hydraulic presses. The relative incompressibility of liquids is one of its basic principles. Hydrokinetics, the study of liquids in motion, is concerned with such matters as friction and turbulence generated in pipes by flowing liquids, the flow of water over weirs and through nozzles, and the use of hydraulic pressure in machinery.

hydrazine (hī'drəzēn"), chemical compound, formula NH_2NH_2, m.p. 1.4°C, b.p. 113.5°C, specific gravity 1.011 at 15°C. It is very soluble in water and soluble in alcohol. At ordinary temperatures it is a colorless, fuming liquid that has an ammonialike odor, but when frozen it forms white crystals. Hydrazine is corrosive and a strong reducing agent, but it is a weaker base than AMMONIA. It reacts with water to form hydrazine hydrate, $N_2H_4 \cdot H_2O$, a colorless liquid that boils at 120°C. Hydrazine can be prepared (usually as the hydrate) by reacting ammonia with chloramine, NH_2Cl, in the presence of glue or gelatin. The glue or gelatin inhibits decomposition of the hydrazine. Ammonium chloride is a by-product. The chloramine may be prepared by reacting ammonia with a hypochlorite or chlorine gas. Hydrazine is also prepared by reaction of sodium hypochlorite with urea in the presence of glue or gelatin. Hydrazine is dibasic and forms many salts, e.g., mono- and di-hydrochlorides, mono- and di-nitrates, and two sulfates. The major use of hydrazine is as a rocket fuel because it burns rapidly, producing a large amount of heat. Hydrazine and its derivatives are also used in the manufacture of algaecides, fungicides, insecticides, and agricultural chemicals; in rubber curing and the manufacture of foam rubber and plastics; in soldering fluxes; and as a corrosion inhibitor in boiler feedwater. ISONIAZID, a drug widely used in treatment of tuberculosis, is isonicotinic hydrazide.

hydria (hī'drēə), ancient Greek water jar with three handles—two lateral for lifting, a third vertical for pouring. In shape it was similar to the amphora, the early form having a narrower shoulder, while a later one, called the kalpis, was curved at the shoulder and had a smaller vertical handle.

hydrobromic acid (hī"drəbrō'mĭk): see BROMIDE.

hydrocarbon (hī"drōkär'bən), any organic compound composed solely of the elements hydrogen and carbon. The hydrocarbons differ both in the total number of carbon and hydrogen atoms in their molecules and in the proportion of hydrogen to carbon. The hydrocarbons can be divided into various homologous series. Each member of such a series shows a definite relationship in its structural formula to the members preceding and following it, and there is generally some regularity in changes in physical properties of successive members of a series. The ALKANES are a homologous series of saturated aliphatic hydrocarbons. The first and simplest member of this series is methane, CH_4; the series is sometimes called the methane series. Each successive member of a homologous series of hydrocarbons has one more carbon and two more hydrogen atoms in its molecule than the preceding member. The second alkane is ethane, C_2H_6, and the third is propane, C_3H_8. Alkanes have the general formula C_nH_{2n+2} (where n is an integer greater than or equal to 1). Generally, hydrocarbons of low molecular weight, e.g., methane, ethane, and propane, are gases; those of intermediate molecular weight, e.g., hexane, heptane, and octane, are liquids; and those of high molecular weight, e.g., eicosane ($C_{20}H_{42}$) and polyethylene, are solids. Paraffin is a mixture of high-molecular-weight alkanes; the alkanes are sometimes called the paraffin series. Other homologous series of hydrocarbons include the ALKENES and the ALKYNES. The various alkyl derivatives of BENZENE are sometimes referred to as the benzene series. Many common natural substances, e.g., natural gas, petroleum, and asphalt, are complex mixtures of hydrocarbons. The coal tar obtained from coal by coking is also a mixture of hydrocarbons. Natural gas, petroleum, and coal tar are important sources of many hydrocarbons. These complex mixtures can be refined into simpler mixtures or pure substances by fractional distillation. During the refining of petroleum, one kind of hydrocarbon is often converted to another, more useful kind by cracking. Useful hydrocarbon mixtures include cooking gas, gasoline, naphtha, benzine, kerosene, vaseline, paraffin, and lubricating oils. Many hydrocarbons are useful as fuels; they burn in air to form carbon dioxide and water. The hydrocarbons differ in chemical activity. The alkanes are unaffected by many common reagents, while the alkenes and alkynes are much more reactive, as a result of the presence of unsaturation (i.e., a carbon-carbon double or triple bond) in their molecules. Many important compounds are derived from hydrocarbons, either by substitution or replacement by some other chemical group or element of one or more of the hydrogen atoms of the hydrocarbon molecule, or by the addition of some element or group to a double or triple bond (in an unsaturated hydrocarbon). Such derivatives include alcohols, aldehydes, ethers, carboxylic acids, and halocarbons.

hydrocephalia: see MENTAL RETARDATION.

hydrocephalus, also known as water on the brain, developmental (congenital) or acquired condition in which there is an abnormal accumulation of body fluids within the skull. The congenital form may be associated with other abnormalities. The acquired form may follow meningitis or other cerebral inflammation or tumor. The accumulation of fluid causes compression of the brain and enlargement of the skull, sometimes with separation of bone structures. Paralysis and death may result or, at the least, mental retardation. Many forms of therapy, including surgery, have been attempted, but usually without much success in extreme cases.

hydrochloric acid: see HYDROGEN CHLORIDE.

hydrocyanic acid (hī"drōsīăn'ĭk): see HYDROGEN CYANIDE.

hydrodynamics: see MECHANICS.

hydroelectric power: see POWER, ELECTRIC; WATER POWER.

hydrofoil, flat or curved finlike device, attached by struts to the hull of a watercraft, that lifts the moving watercraft above the water's surface. The term is often extended to include the vessel itself. Like an aircraft wing in its appearance and function, the foil develops lift as it passes through the water; the hull is raised above the surface, and the drag caused by the vessel's contact with the water is thereby reduced. Hydrofoil vessels are capable of traveling faster than 70 mi (113 km) per hr. They are used for ferries in many countries in Europe and Asia; in the United States they are used mostly for military purposes. In addition to offering greater speeds, such vessels do not pitch and roll as do conventional watercraft. Foils may be of the submerged or the surface-piercing type. On ocean-going passenger ships a type of hydrofoil called a stabilizer is used to minimize wave action on the vessel. The first hydrofoil vessel was built in 1905 by the Italian engineer Enrico Forlanini. In 1918, Alexander Graham Bell built the HD-4, a vessel 60 ft (18.3 m) long that attained a speed of 70.86 mi (114.03 km) per hr. See Christopher Hook, *Hydrofoils* (1967); Roy McLeary, *Jane's Surface Skimmers* (annually, 1968–); W. T. Gunston, *Hydrofoils and Hovercraft* (1969).

hydrogen (hī'drəjən) [Gr.,=water forming], gaseous chemical element; symbol H; at. no. 1; at. wt. 1.007967; m.p. −259.14°C; b.p. −252.87°C; density 0.08988 grams per liter at STP; valence usually +1. Under ordinary conditions hydrogen is a colorless, odorless, tasteless gas that is only slightly soluble in water; it is the least dense gas known. It is the first element in group Ia of the PERIODIC TABLE. Ordinary hydrogen gas is made up of diatomic molecules (H_2) that react with oxygen to form water (H_2O) and hydrogen peroxide (H_2O_2), usually as a result of combustion. A jet of hydrogen burns in air with a very hot blue flame. The flame produced by a mixture of oxygen and hydrogen gases (as in the oxyhydrogen BLOWPIPE) is extremely hot and is used in welding and to melt quartz and certain glasses. Hydrogen gas must be used with caution because it is highly flammable; it forms easily ignited explosive mixtures with oxygen or with air (because of the oxygen in the air). At high temperatures hydrogen is a chemically active mixture of monohydrogen (atomic hydrogen) and the normal diatomic hydrogen (see ALLOTROPY). It has a great affinity for oxygen and is a powerful reducing agent (see OXIDATION AND REDUCTION). It reacts with nitrogen to form ammonia. With the halogens it forms compounds (hydrogen halides) that are strongly acidic in water solution. With sulfur it forms hydrogen sulfide (H_2S), a colorless gas with an odor like rotten eggs; with sulfur and oxygen it forms SULFURIC ACID. It combines with several metals to form metal hydrides such as calcium hydride. Combined with carbon (and usually other elements) it is a constituent of a great many organic compounds, such as HYDROCARBONS, CARBOHYDRATES, fats, oils, proteins, and organic acids and bases. Hydrogen is prepared commercially by catalytic reaction of steam with hydrocarbons, by the reaction of steam with hot coke (carbon), by the electrolysis of water, and by the reaction of mineral acids on metals. Millions of cubic feet of hydrogen gas are produced daily in the United States alone. Hydrogen was formerly used for filling balloons, airships, and other lighter-than-air craft, a dangerous practice because of hydrogen's explosive flammability; there were disastrous fires, e.g., the immolation of the German airship *Hindenburg* at its mooring at Lakehurst, N.J., in 1937. Helium is preferable for use in lighter-than-air craft since it is not flammable. Hydrogen is used in the Haber process for the fixation of atmospheric nitrogen, in the production of methanol, and in hydrogenation of fats and oils. It is also important in low-temperature research. It can be liquefied under pressure and cooled; when the pressure is released, rapid evaporation takes place and some of the hydrogen solidifies. The melting point of solid hydrogen is only about 13°C above absolute zero. Although under normal conditions hydrogen does not physically resemble the ALKALI METALS below it in the periodic table, it is believed that at very high pressures solid hydrogen would assume metallic properties. While hydrogen is only about one part per million in the atmosphere, it is the most abundant element in the universe. It is believed that hydrogen makes up about three quarters of the mass of the universe, or over 90% of the molecules. It is found in the sun and in other stars, where it is the major fuel in the fusion reactions (see NUCLEOSYNTHESIS) from which stars derive their energy. Atmospheric hydrogen is a mixture of three ISOTOPES. The most common is called protium (mass no. 1, atomic mass 1.007822); the protium nucleus (protium ion) is a proton. A second isotope of hydrogen is deuterium (mass no. 2, atomic mass 2.0140), the so-called heavy hydrogen, often represented in chemical formulas by the symbol D. The deuterium nucleus, or ion, is called the deuteron; it consists of a proton plus a neutron. The two isotopes are found in atmospheric hydrogen in the proportion of about 1 atom of deuterium to every 6,700 atoms of protium. Protium and deuterium differ slightly in their chemical and physical properties; for example, the boiling point of deuterium is about 3°C lower than protium. The properties of compounds they form differ depending on the ratio of the two isotopes present. Deuterium oxide (D_2O), the so-called heavy water, is present in ordinary water; the concentration of deuterium oxide is increased by electrolysis of the water. The melting point (3.79°C), boiling point (101.4°C), and specific gravity (1.107 at 25°C) of deuterium oxide are higher than those of ordinary water. Deuterium oxide is used as a moderator in nuclear reactors. Deuterium is also of importance because of the wide use it has found in scientific research; for example, chemical reaction mechanisms have been studied by the use of deuterium atoms as tracers (i.e., deuterium is substituted for atoms of ordinary hydrogen in compounds), making it possible to follow the course of individual molecules in a reaction. Tritium (mass no. 3, atomic mass 3.016), a third hydrogen isotope, is a radioactive gas with a half-life of about 12¼ years; it is often represented in chemical formulas by the symbol T. It is produced in nuclear reactors and occurs to a very limited extent in atmospheric hydrogen. It is used in the hydrogen bomb, in luminous paints, and as a tracer. The tritium nucleus, or ion, is called the triton; it consists of a proton plus two neutrons. Tritium oxide (T_2O) has a melting point (4.49°C) higher than that of deuterium oxide. Besides being a mixture of three isotopes, hydrogen is a mixture of two forms, an *ortho* form and a *para* form, which differ in their electronic and nuclear spins. At room temperature atmospheric hydrogen is about ¾ *ortho*-hydrogen and ¼ *para*-hydrogen. The two forms differ slightly in their physical properties. Although hydrogen was prepared many years earlier, it was first recognized as a substance distinct from other flammable gases in 1766 by Henry CAVENDISH, who is credited with its discovery; it was named by A. L. Lavoisier in 1783. Deuterium was discovered by H. C. UREY, F. G. Brickwedde, and G. M. Murphy in 1932, although its existence had been suspected for some years. Deuterium oxide was also discovered by Urey and was first obtained in nearly pure form by G. N. Lewis.

hydrogenation (hīdrôj'ənā"shən, hī"drəjənā'shən), chemical reaction of a substance with molecular hydrogen, usually in the presence of a catalyst. A common hydrogenation is the hardening of animal fats or vegetable oils to make them solid at room temperature and improve their stability. Hydrogen is added (in the presence of a nickel catalyst) to carbon-carbon double bonds in the unsaturated fatty acid portion of the fat or oil molecule:

$$\begin{array}{ccccccc} & \text{H} & \text{H} & & & \text{H} & \text{H} \\ & | & | & & & | & | \\ — & \text{C} = & \text{C} — & + \ \text{H}_2 \longrightarrow & — & \text{C} — & \text{C} — \\ & & & & & | & | \\ & & & & & \text{H} & \text{H} \end{array}$$

Another hydrogenation is the synthesis of METHANOL from carbon monoxide. Hydrogenation reactions are important in petroleum refining; production of gasoline by cracking involves destructive hydrogenation (hydrogenolysis), in which large molecules are broken down to smaller ones and reacted with hydrogen. Most hydrogenation reactions are reversible and proceed to favorable equilibria at high pressure and moderate temperature.

hydrogen bomb, weapon deriving a large portion of its energy from the nuclear fusion of HYDROGEN isotopes. In an ATOMIC BOMB, uranium or plutonium is split into lighter elements that together weigh less than the original atoms, the remainder of the mass appearing as energy. Unlike this fission bomb, the hydrogen bomb functions by the fusion, or joining together, of lighter elements into heavier elements. The end product again weighs less than its components, the difference once more appearing as energy. Because extremely high temperatures are required in order to initiate fusion reactions, the hydrogen bomb is also known as a thermonuclear bomb. The presumable structure of a thermonuclear bomb is as follows: at its center is an atomic bomb; surrounding it is a layer of lithium deuteride (a compound of lithium and deuterium, the isotope of hydrogen with mass number 2); around it is a tamper, a thick outer layer, frequently of fissionable material, that holds the contents together in order to obtain a larger explosion. Neutrons from the atomic explosion cause the lithium to fission into helium, tritium (the isotope of hydrogen with mass number 3), and energy. The atomic explosion also supplies the temperatures needed for the subsequent fusion of deuterium with tritium, and of tritium with tritium (50,000,000°C and 400,000,000°C, respectively). Enough neutrons are produced in the fusion reactions to produce further fission in the core and to initiate fission in the tamper. Since the fusion produces mostly neutrons and very little that is radioactive, the concept of a "clean" bomb has resulted: one having a small atomic trigger, a less fissionable tamper, and therefore less radioactive FALLOUT. Carrying this progression further would result in the suggested neutron bomb, which would have a minimum trigger and a nonfissionable tamper; there would be blast effects and a hail of lethal neutrons but almost no radioactive fallout. The proposed cobalt bomb is, on the contrary, a radioactively "dirty" bomb having a cobalt tamper. Like other types of nuclear explosion, the explosion of a hydrogen bomb creates an extremely hot zone near its center. In this zone, because of the high temperature, nearly all of the matter present is vaporized to form a gas at extremely high pressure. A sudden overpressure, i.e., a pressure far in excess of atmospheric pressure, propagates away from the center of the explosion as a shock wave, decreasing in strength as it travels. It is this wave, containing most of the energy released, that is responsible for the major part of the destructive mechanical effects of a nuclear explosion. The details of shock wave propagation and its effects vary depending on whether the burst is in the air, under water, or under ground. The first thermonuclear bomb was exploded in 1952 at Eniwetok by the United States, the second in 1953 by the USSR. Great Britain, France, China, and India have also exploded thermonuclear bombs. See NUCLEAR ENERGY.

hydrogen chloride, chemical compound, HCl, a colorless, poisonous gas with an unpleasant, acrid odor. It is very soluble in water and readily soluble in alcohol and ether. It fumes in moist air. It is not flammable, and the liquid is a poor conductor of electricity. Hydrogen chloride is prepared commercially by the reaction of sulfuric acid with sodium chloride (common salt); niter cake, a mixture of sodium bisulfite and sulfuric acid that is a by-product of nitric acid manufacture, is sometimes used in place of sulfuric acid. Hydrogen chloride is also produced as a by-product of the manufacture of chlorinated organic chemicals. It can be prepared directly by reaction of hydrogen and chlorine gases; the reaction is very exothermic and takes place readily in sunlight or at elevated temperatures. Although anhydrous (water-free) hydrogen chloride is commercially available as a high-pressure compressed gas in steel cylinders, most of the gas produced is dissolved in water to form hydrochloric acid (see ACIDS AND BASES), a commercially important chemical. Pure grades of hydrochloric acid are colorless, but technical grades, commonly called muriatic acid, are often yellow-colored because of impurities such as dissolved metals. Most hydrochloric acid produced has a concentration of 30% to 35% hydrogen chloride by weight. The major use of hydrochloric acid is in the manufacture of other chemicals. It is also used in large amounts in pickling (cleaning) metal surfaces, e.g., iron before galvanizing. It reacts with most common metals, releasing hydrogen and forming the metal chloride; with most metal oxides and hydroxides it reacts to form water and the metal chloride. Hydrochloric acid is also used in small amounts in processing glucose and other foods and for various other uses. Concentrated solutions are strong acids and highly corrosive. Hydrochloric acid is not an oxidizing agent but can be oxidized by very strong oxidizing agents, liberating chlorine gas. In dilute solutions of the acid the hydrogen chloride is almost completely dissociated into hydrogen and chloride IONS. A solution containing 20.24% hydrogen chloride by weight is azeotropic, boiling at a constant temperature of 110°C at atmospheric pressure. Hydrogen chloride also forms monohydrates, dihydrates, and trihydrates that are liquids at room temperature.

hydrogen cyanide, HCN, colorless, volatile, and extremely poisonous chemical compound whose vapors have a bitter almond odor. It melts at −14°C and boils at 26°C. It is miscible in all proportions with water or ethanol and is soluble in ether. Its water solution is a weak acid (see ACIDS AND BASES) commonly known as hydrocyanic acid or prussic acid. Its salts are called CYANIDES. Hydrogen cyanide may be synthesized directly from ammonia and carbon monoxide or from ammonia, oxygen (or air), and natural gas. It is a by-product of the production of coke from coal and is recovered (along with hydrogen sulfide) from coke-oven exhaust gases. It may also be prepared by reacting a cyanide salt, e.g., calcium cyanide, with a strong acid, e.g., sulfuric acid, or by thermal decomposition of formamide. Because impure hydrogen cyanide can undergo spontaneous explosive polymerization and decomposition, a small amount of stabilizer (usually phosphoric acid) is added to it. The principal use of hydrogen cyanide is in the manufacture of organic chemicals, e.g., acrylonitrile, methyl methacrylate, and adiponitrile, that are used in producing synthetic fibers and plastics. It is also used in the chemical laboratory, and is sometimes used in agriculture as a fumigant. Hydrogen cyanide is found in nature in some vegetable substances, e.g., bitter almond, peach stones, cherry and cherry laurel leaves, and sorghum; it is usually combined in glycoside molecules (see SUGAR) and is released when they are broken down by enzymes during metabolism.

hydrogen fluoride, chemical compound, HF, a colorless, fuming liquid or colorless gas that boils at 19.54°C. It is miscible with water and is soluble in benzene, toluene, and concentrated sulfuric acid. Hydrofluoric acid is a water solution of hydrogen fluoride; hydrofluoric acid containing 35.35% hydrogen fluoride by weight is an azeotrope with a constant boiling point of 120°C. Whether gaseous, liquid, or in solution, hydrogen fluoride is a dangerous chemical and must be handled with caution, since it attacks the skin and other tissue. Hydrogen fluoride has a number of properties that distinguish it from the other hydrogen halides. It polymerizes, forming molecules such as H_2F_2 and H_6F_6; this explains in part its relatively high boiling point. It is a relatively weak acid. It attacks glass, reacting with the silica, SiO_2, to form the gas silicon tetrafluoride, SiF_4, and water; this leaves the surface of the glass etched. Major industrial uses of hydrogen fluoride include the synthesis of fluorocarbons (e.g., FREON and TEFLON) and the production of aluminum fluoride and synthetic cryolite for use in aluminum refining. It is also employed in refining uranium for use as a nuclear fuel, in manufacturing various organic chemicals, in producing stainless steel, and for various other applications. Hydrogen fluoride is produced commercially by heating purified fluorspar (calcium fluoride) with concentrated sulfuric acid to produce the gas, which may be condensed by cooling or dissolved in water. Hydrogen fluoride is available commercially either in an anhydrous (water-free) state or in water solutions of various concentrations. Because it attacks glass, it is usually stored in steel tanks, cylinders, or drums, or, in small amounts, in plastic bottles.

hydrogen-ion concentration: see *p*H.

hydrogen peroxide, chemical compound, H_2O_2, a colorless, syrupy liquid that is a strong oxidizing agent and, in water solution, a weak acid. It is miscible with cold water and is soluble in alcohol and ether. Although pure hydrogen peroxide is fairly stable, it decomposes into water and oxygen when heated above about 80°C; it also decomposes in the presence of numerous catalysts, e.g., most metals, acids, or oxidizable organic materials. A small amount of stabilizer, usually acetanilide, is often added to it. Hydrogen peroxide has many uses. It is available for household use as a 3% (by weight) water solution; it is used as a mild bleaching agent and medicinally as an antiseptic. The 3% solution is sometimes called ten volume strength, since one volume of it releases ten volumes of oxygen when it decomposes. Hydrogen peroxide is available for commercial use in several concentrations. Highly concentrated solutions were first used in World War II by the military, e.g., in fuels for rockets and torpedoes. It is used as a bleaching agent for textiles, e.g., wool and silk, and in paper manufacture. It is also used in chemical manufacture. Hydrogen peroxide is prepared commercially by oxidation of alkylhydroanthraquinones and by electrolysis of ammonium bisulfate. It can also be prepared by reaction of barium peroxide with sulfuric acid and is prepared (with acetone) by oxidation of isopropanol. Hydrogen peroxide was discovered (1818) by L. J. Thenard.

hydrogen sulfide, chemical compound, H_2S, a colorless, extremely poisonous gas that has a very disagreeable odor, much like that of rotten eggs. It is slightly soluble in water and is soluble in carbon disulfide. Dissolved in water, it forms a very weak dibasic acid that is sometimes called hydrosulfuric acid. Hydrogen sulfide is flammable; in an excess of air it burns to form sulfur dioxide and water, but if not enough oxygen is present, it forms elemental sulfur and water. Hydrogen sulfide is found naturally in volcanic gases and in some mineral waters. It is often formed during decay of animal matter. It is a part of many unrefined carbonaceous fuels, e.g., natural gas, crude oil, and coal; it is obtained as a by-product of refining such fuels. It may be made by reacting hydrogen gas with molten sulfur or with sulfur vapors, or by treating a metal sulfide (e.g., ferrous sulfide, FeS) with an acid. Hydrogen sulfide reacts with most metal ions to form sulfides; the sulfides of some metals are insoluble in water and have characteristic colors that help to identify the metal during chemical analysis. Hydrogen sulfide also reacts directly with silver metal, forming a dull, grey-black tarnish of silver sulfide (Ag_2S).

hydrology, study of water and its properties, including its distribution and movement in and through the land areas of the earth. The hydrologic cycle consists of the passage of water from the oceans into the atmosphere, onto the lands, through and under the lands, and back to the ocean. Hydrology is principally concerned with the part of the cycle after the precipitation of water onto the land and before its return to the oceans. Hydrologists study the cycle by measuring such variables as the amount and intensity of precipitation, the amount of water stored as snow or in glaciers, the advance and retreat of glaciers, the rate of flow in streams, and the amount and flow of ground water. METEOROLOGY and OCEANOGRAPHY are closely related to hydrology. See WATER SUPPLY.

hydrolysis (hīdrŏl'ĭsĭs), chemical reaction of a compound with water, usually resulting in the formation of one or more new compounds. The most common hydrolysis occurs when a salt of a weak acid or weak base (or both) is dissolved in water. Water ionizes into negative hydroxyl ions (OH^-) and positive hydrogen ions (H^+), which become hydrated to form positive hydronium ions (H_3O^+). The salt also breaks up into positive and negative ions. For example, when sodium acetate is dissolved in water it readily dissociates into sodium and acetate ions. Because sodium hydroxide is a strong base, the sodium ions react only slightly with the hydroxyl ions already present in the water to form sodium hydroxide molecules. Acetic acid is a weak acid, so the acetate ions react readily with the hydrogen ions present in the water to form neutral acetic acid molecules. The net result of these reactions is a relative excess of hydroxyl ions, causing an alkaline solution. A chemical reaction has actually taken place between the water and the dissolved salt. There are relatively few instances in which water reacts directly with organic compounds under ordinary conditions. It does react with acid halides, acid anhydrides, and organometallic compounds, e.g., GRIGNARD REAGENTS. The addition of strong acids or bases or the use of steam will often bring about hydrolysis where ordinary water has no effect. Some industrially important hydrolysis reactions are the synthesis of alcohols from olefins (e.g., ethanol, CH_3COOH, from ethene, CH_2CH_2) in the presence of a strong acid catalyst, the conversion of starches to sugars in the presence of a strong acid catalyst, and the conversion of animal fats or vegetable oils to glycerol and fatty acids by reaction with steam. Hydrolysis is an important reaction in plants and animals (see METABOLISM). The catalytic action of certain ENZYMES allows the hydrolysis of proteins, fats, oils, and carbohydrates.

hydrometer (hīdrŏm'ətər), device used to determine directly the SPECIFIC GRAVITY of a liquid. It usually consists of a thin glass tube closed at both ends, with one end enlarged into a bulb that contains fine lead shot or mercury to cause the instrument to float upright in a liquid. In the glass tube is a scale so calibrated that the reading on it level with the surface of the liquid in which the hydrometer is floating indicates the number of times heavier or lighter the liquid is than water, i.e., the specific gravity of the liquid. The hydrometer is based upon ARCHIMEDES' PRINCIPLE. The level at which the hydrometer floats depends only on the DENSITY of the liquid. Hence this level can be used to measure both the density and the specific gravity, which is proportional to it. Commercial hydrometers are usually calibrated for ordinary room temperature, which is taken to be 20°C (68°F), or for 4°C (39.2°F). Because of the variation in the depth to which the instrument sinks in heavy and in light liquids, one type is made for use in liquids more dense than water and another for use in those less dense than water. The so-called bulb hydrometer consists of a small commercial hydrometer contained in a larger glass tube into which the solution to be tested is drawn by the action of a rubber bulb. It is used to measure the specific gravity of the sulfuric acid solution in automobile batteries. The two Baumé hydrometers (invented by Antoine Baumé), one for specific-gravity determinations in liquids denser than water and the other for liquids less dense than water, are calibrated with the special Baumé scale (also constructed by him).

hydrophobia: see RABIES.

hydrophone (hī'drəfōn"), device that receives underwater sound waves and converts them to electrical energy; the voltage generated can then be read on a meter or played through a loudspeaker. The hydrophone is the marine equivalent of the microphone, which receives and converts sound waves in air. It is used in sonar apparatus and in certain underwater weapons. The same device may also be used to generate sounds, converting electrical energy to motional mechanical energy; in this capacity it is called a projector.

hydroplane, small, high-powered racing boat designed to skim along the surface of the water. Its hull is so shaped that at high speeds the bow is tilted up out of the water, reducing the effect of frictional drag. Hydroplanes are commonly powered by outboard motors. A SEAPLANE is also frequently called a hydroplane.

hydroponics, growing of plants without soil in water to which nutrients have been added. Hydroponics has been known to scientists for over a century as an aid in the study of plant life processes, but not until 1929 were experiments conducted solely to determine its feasibility for the growing of commercial crops. There are now chemical garden installations scattered throughout the United States and on some Pacific islands. Under hydroponics, plants can be grown closer together than in the field, thereby increasing yields, and multiple cropping (the growing of several crops in the same tank) can be practiced. In addition to conserving space, hydroponics almost eliminates the problem of weeds and pests. The cost of equipment is high and the personnel must be specially trained. Although hydroponics is possible for most plants, a limiting factor is the amount of support required by a given plant. Usually the plants are held upright by wire supports or are rooted in a sterile medium, e.g., pure sand or gravel. The nutrient solutions must supply, in optimum concentrations and in correct balance, the elements, such as nitrogen, phosphorus, potassium, and other essentials to plant growth normally found in soil. Other names for hydroponics are soilless gardening, soilless culture, chemiculture, and water gardening. See R. Bridwell, *Hydroponic Gardening* (1972); J. S. Douglas, *Beginner's Guide to Hydroponics* (1972).

hydrostatics: see MECHANICS.

hydrosulfuric acid: see HYDROGEN SULFIDE.

hydrotherapy, use of water in the treatment of illness or injury. Although the medicinal and hygienic value of water was recognized by the early Greeks, hydrotherapy attained its widest use in the 18th and 19th cent. through the practice of the British physician Sir John Floyer and an Austrian peasant, Vincenz Priessnitz. Priessnitz is credited with a number of inventions still in use including the sponge bath, the douche, and the wet sheet pack, and he is acknowledged as an important contributor to the rise of the health spa movement in Europe. Scientific hydrotherapy is based on the conduction of heat to or from the body by means of a water medium. Heated water is used for its sedative effect, and hot water vapor is used in controlled situations to relieve pain. Patients who have suffered extensive burns are often immersed in water for long periods. Maintained at skin temperature, i.e., approximately 93°F (34°C), the water prevents loss of body heat. Fevers are reduced by cold sponge baths taken on rubber sheets. Whirlpool baths are used to relieve painful muscle and joint conditions, and underwater exercise has proved a useful physical therapy in cases of paralysis and stiffness of the extremities.

hydroxide (hīdrŏk'sīd), chemical compound that contains the hydroxyl (−OH) RADICAL. The term refers especially to inorganic compounds. Organic compounds that have the hydroxyl radical as a FUNCTIONAL GROUP are called ALCOHOLS; the hydroxyl radical is also present in the carboxyl group of organic acids. Most metal hydroxides are bases and form solutions that have a bitter taste and are slippery to the touch; the solutions have an excess of OH^- ions and a *p*H greater than 7, neutralize acids, and change the color of litmus from red to blue. Alkali metal hydroxides such as SODIUM HYDROXIDE are strong bases and are very soluble in water; alkaline-earth metal hydroxides such as CALCIUM HYDROXIDE (slaked lime) are much less soluble in water and are not as strongly basic. Magnesium hydroxide (MILK OF MAGNESIA) is only slightly basic. Some hydroxides (e.g., aluminum hydroxide) exhibit AMPHOTERISM, having either acidic or basic properties depending on the reaction in which they are involved. The hydroxides of some nonmetallic elements are acidic; the hydroxide of sulfur, $S(OH)_6$, spontaneously loses two molecules of water to form sulfuric acid, H_2SO_4. Ammonium hydroxide, NH_4OH, is a weak base known only in the solution that is formed when the gas AMMONIA, NH_3, dissolves in water.

hydroxyl group (hīdrŏk'sĭl), in chemistry, FUNCTIONAL GROUP that consists of an oxygen atom joined by a single bond to a hydrogen atom. An ALCOHOL is formed when a hydroxyl group is joined by a single bond to an ALKYL GROUP or ARYL GROUP. A metal hydroxide is formed when a hydroxyl group is joined to a metal (e.g., sodium hydroxide).

hydroxyl radical: see HYDROXIDE.

hydroxylysine (hīdrŏk"sĕlī'sēn), organic compound, one of the 22 α-AMINO ACIDS commonly found in animal proteins. Only the L-stereoisomer appears in mammalian protein. Hydroxylysine is present in COLLAGEN and collagen products, including gelatin and isinglass, but it is less frequently found in other proteins. The residues of hydroxylysine in collagen are evidently formed by the addition of a hydroxyl group to LYSINE residues already present in either the finished protein or a polypeptide precursor. As in the conversion of proline to hydroxyproline in the collagen molecule, ascorbic acid (vitamin C) might be required as a COENZYME for lysine hydroxylation (see VITAMIN). Hydroxylysine was purified from protein during the 1920s.

hydroxyproline (hīdrŏk"sēprō'lēn), organic compound, one of the 22 α-AMINO ACIDS commonly found in animal proteins. Only the L-stereoisomer appears in mammalian protein. Like HYDROXYLYSINE, hydroxyproline is often present in COLLAGEN, but is less frequently seen in other proteins. Mammals evidently cannot incorporate dietary hydroxyproline into collagen; instead a hydroxyl group is substituted for a hydrogen atom on PROLINE residues already forming a part of either the collagen molecule itself or a polypeptide precursor of the finished protein. Hydroxyproline was isolated from gelatin in 1902, and its synthesis was accomplished during the years 1905 to 1919.

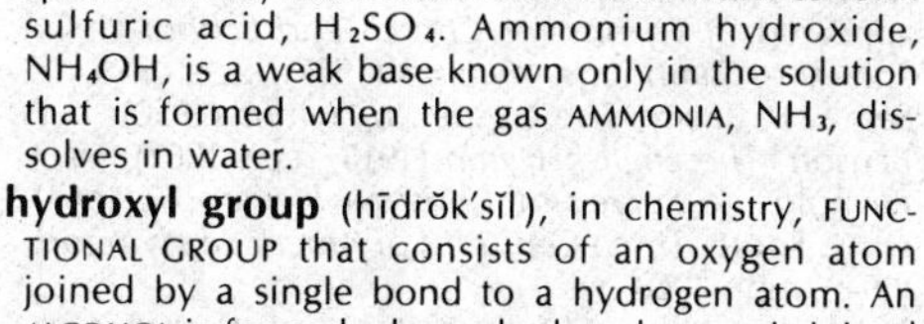

hydroxyproline

hydroxytoluene: see CRESOL.

hyena, carnivorous, chiefly nocturnal mammal of the Old World family Hyaenidae. Although doglike in appearance, hyenas are more closely related to cats (family Felidae) than to dogs. The front legs of a hyena are longer than the hind ones, giving the back a sloping appearance. Hyenas feed mostly on carrion and can crush bones with their strong teeth and jaws. They hunt small animals but usually flee if threatened. They sleep by day, in caves or burrows. Hyenas range over most of Africa and SW Asia. Three species are generally recognized. The spotted hyena, *Crocuta crocuta,* of Africa S of the Sahara, is the largest and boldest species; it stands 2½ ft (76 cm) high at the shoulder and has a gray coat with irregular patches. Often abroad in the day as well as at night, it pursues game in packs and even invades camps and villages in search of refuse and livestock. Occasionally it attacks children or sleeping adults, and it is famous as a grave robber. The smaller striped hyena, *Hyaena hyaena,* of Asia and N Africa and the brown hyena, or strand wolf, *H. brunnea,* of S Africa are shyer and more nocturnal and solitary in their habits. The former is grayish brown with darker stripes; the latter is dark brown over most of the body. The hyena is a valuable scavenger but is considered repulsive because of its stench and its cry, which resembles maniacal laughter. The AARDWOLF is a member of the hyena family. Hyenas are classified in the phylum CHORDATA, subphylum Vertebrata, class Mammalia, order Carnivora, family Hyaenidae. See Hans Kruuk, *The Spotted Hyena* (1972).

Hyères (yĕr), city (1968 pop. 34,875), Var dept., SE France, in Provence, on the Mediterranean Sea. A port in medieval times, Hyères is now a resort. Off the coast is a group of islands of the same name.

hygiene, science of preserving and promoting the health of both the individual and the community. It has many aspects, which may be categorized as follows: personal hygiene (proper living habits, cleanliness of body and clothing, healthful diet, a balanced regimen of rest and exercise); domestic hygiene (sanitary preparation of food, cleanliness, and ventilation of the home); public hygiene (supervision of water and food supply, containment of communicable disease, disposal of garbage and sewage, control of air and water pollution); industrial hygiene (measures that minimize occupational disease and accident); and mental hygiene (recognition of mental and emotional factors in healthful living).

hygrometer (hīgrŏm'ətər), instrument used to measure the moisture content of a gas, as in determining the relative humidity of air. The most common type of hygrometer is the dry- and wet-bulb PSYCHROMETER. It consists of two identical mercury THERMOMETERS, one of which has a wet cotton or linen wick around its bulb. The sling type is swung around in the air. Water evaporating from the wick absorbs heat from the thermometer bulb, causing the thermometer reading to drop. The observer, after reading the dry-bulb temperature and the drop in wet-bulb temperature, looks up the relative humidity in appropriate tables. An aspirated type depends on a fan to assure proper ventilation for the wet-bulb thermometer. The chief type of mechanical hygrometer uses human hair, which stretches as it absorbs moisture. A linkage connects the center of a bundle of hairs under tension to a pointer. Another commercial type uses goldbeater's skin, a membrane from the intestines of oxen. The temperature at which dew or frost forms is a measure of the absolute humidity—the weight of water vapor per unit volume of air or other gas at the temperature before cooling. Knowing absolute humidity and air temperature, the observer can calculate relative humidity. The temperature at which dew forms, called the dew point, is determined by a dew-point hygrometer, which is basically a mirror, usually of polished metal, cooled until dew or frost forms on it. Various cooling methods employ compressed carbon dioxide, dry ice, liquid air, or mechanical refrigeration. The mirror may be part of a mercury thermometer, but for more accuracy thermocouples are often fastened to the surface of the mirror or buried underneath it. After dew or frost forms, the mirror is allowed to warm in the air or is electrically heated until the dew or frost disappears. The mean between the temperatures read when dew appears and when it disappears is the dew point. Because human observation varies, photoelectric cells are sometimes used to register the time at which the mirror fogs. One kind of electric hygrometer works on the principle that electrical resistance varies in a material that absorbs moisture. An automatic version uses a pair of parallel wires wrapped around a piece of plastic; a coating of moisture-absorbing material fills the space between the wires. The resistance of the coating to a current passing between the wires may be measured by a Wheatstone bridge. Instruments based on this principle are now in use at most U.S. National Weather Service observatories for the routine monitoring of the local dew point. The most accurate way to measure humidity is to pass a known volume of gas over a hygroscopic, or moisture-absorbing, material such as phosphorus pentoxide. It is weighed before and after to determine how much water it took out of the gas. Some materials change color as they absorb moisture; the color can be compared with a color scale or measured photoelectrically to determine humidity.

Hyksos (hĭk'sōs) [Egyptian,=rulers of foreign lands], invaders of ancient EGYPT, now substantiated as the XV–XVIII dynasties. They were a northwestern Semitic (Canaanite or Amorite) people who entered Egypt sometime between 1720 and 1710 B.C. and subdued the pharaohs of the Middle Kingdom. They used Avaris-Tanis in the Nile delta as their capital rather than the Egyptian capital of Thebes. Under their hegemony, which lasted over a century, they established a powerful kingdom that included Syria and Palestine, and maintained peace and prosperity in their territories. They introduced the horse-drawn chariot and the composite bow, and their successful conquests were furthered by a type of rectangular fortification of beaten earth used as a fortress; archaeologists have uncovered examples of these mounds at Jericho, Shechem, and Lachish. Their most important contribution was perhaps the introduction into Egypt of Canaanite deities and Asian artifacts, which were instrumental in abrogating the despotism and isolationism of the Old and Middle kingdoms. The Hyksos were crushed by Amasis I at the battle of Tanis in 1550 B.C.

Hylan, John Francis (hī'lən), 1868–1936, American political leader, Democratic mayor of New York City (1918–25), b. Greene co., N.Y. He practiced law in Brooklyn and was city magistrate (1906–14) and judge of the county court (1914–18). In 1917, after a bitter campaign marked by charges that he was the candidate of the anti-American element of New York City's German and Irish population, Hylan defeated J. P. Mitchel for mayor. As mayor, "Red Mike" Hylan was at odds with Tammany. James J. Walker, his successor, appointed (1925) Hylan justice of the children's court.

Hylas (hī'ləs), in Greek mythology, beautiful youth. He was a favorite companion of Hercules. While on the expedition of the Argonauts, Hylas was dragged into a spring by water nymphs enchanted by his beauty and was never found.

Hymen (hī'mən) or **Hymenaeus** (hīmənē'əs), in Greek mythology, personification of marriage, represented as a beautiful youth carrying a bridal torch and wearing a veil.

Hymenaeus (hīmənē'əs), Christian denounced by Paul for heresy or apostasy. 1 Tim. 1.20; 2 Tim. 2.17.

Hymettus (hīmĕ'təs), Gr. *Imittós,* mountain range, E central Greece, in Attica, extending c.10 mi (16 km) between Athens and the Saronic Gulf. Mt. Hymettus (c.3,370 ft/1,030 m) is the highest point. It is noted for its honey. Marble has been quarried there since antiquity.

hymn, song of praise, devotion, or thanksgiving, especially of a religious character. Early Christian hymnody consisted mainly of the Psalms and the great canticles, *Nunc dimittis, Magnificat,* and *Benedictus,* from the Bible and of the Sanctus, Gloria in excelsis, and Te Deum. These were chanted in unison (see PLAINSONG). Metrical Latin Hymnody began with the hymns of St. Ambrose, bishop of Milan, and St. Hilary, bishop of Poitiers, in the 4th cent. This type of hymn, usually four-line stanzas in iambic tetrameter, was the basis of nearly all Christian hymnody until the 16th cent. Notable Latin hymns are *Corde natus ex parentis,* from Prudentius in the 4th cent., and Fortunatus' 6th-century processionals, *Vexilla Regis* and *Pange lingua* (whose meter was imitated in the PANGE LINGUA of St. Thomas Aquinas). From the 11th cent. came Wipo's Easter sequence, *Victimae paschali laudes.* The *Dies irae,* probably by Thomas of Celano, and the *Stabat Mater Dolorosa* by Jacopone da Todi are great hymns of the 13th cent. With the Reformation came the development of Protestant hymnody. The first hymnbooks in the vernacular are probably those published by the followers of John Huss in Bohemia in 1501 and 1505. In 1524 the first Lutheran hymnal was published at Wittenberg. The early Lutheran hymns were translations of Latin hymns, folksongs with new texts, or sometimes original melodies. Calvinism contributed the Genevan Psalter (final version, 1562). It consisted of the Psalms, translated into French verse by Clément Marot and Theodore Beza and set to music, most of which was supplied by Louis Bourgeois, who used some original tunes and adapted others. The familiar doxology tune *Old Hundredth* is the tune of Psalm 134 in this Psalter. The first collection of English church tunes was Sternhold's Psalter (1556), published at Geneva, consisting of metrical versions of the Psalms by Thomas Sternhold (d. 1549) and others, set to unharmonized tunes. John Wesley's hymnal (1737) contained metrical psalms, translations from Greek and German, and original lyrics and melodies, and was thus the first hymnal in the modern sense. Other notable English hymnists of the 18th cent. were Isaac Watts, Charles Wesley, and William Cowper, poets whose hymns are sung in nearly all Protestant churches. In the 19th cent. there was a revived interest in plainsong which resulted in many translations of ancient Latin hymns, such as those by John Mason NEALE. In America the Puritans used psalters brought with them from Europe until the *Bay Psalm Book* (1640), the earliest American hymnal, was published at Cambridge, Mass. William BILLINGS wrote the first original American hymns as distinguished from paraphrases of psalms and psalm tunes; another important composer was Lowell MASON, whose song collections, such as *Spiritual Songs* (1831), compiled jointly with Thomas Hastings, attained wide distribution. In the latter half of the 19th cent. the gospel hymn was developed (see GOSPEL MUSIC). It is marked by lively rhythm, constant alternation of the simplest harmonies, and sentimental text. Arthur Sullivan's "Onward Christian Soldiers" (1871) is a well-known example of the martial hymn of the period. In the 20th cent. radical variations in church music have emerged: folk-song and jazz elements have been integrated with older music and frequently replaced it. Troubadour-style "protest" songs with theological content were common in the 1960s alongside a newly vital, more conservative hymnody. Excellent examples of the latter appeared in *Hymns for Church and School* (1964) and *The Cambridge Hymnal* (1967). See CANTATA. See A. E. Bailey, *The Gospel in Hymns* (1950); L. F. Benson, *The English Hymn* (1915, repr. 1962); W. J. Reynolds, *A Survey of Christian Hymnody* (1963); H. W. Foote, *Three Centuries of American Hymnody* (1940, repr. 1968).

Hyndman, Henry Mayers (hīnd'mən), 1842–1921, English Socialist, an early advocate of Marxism in England. He was a journalist by profession. In 1881 he founded the parent organization of the Social Democratic Federation, which in 1911 became the British Socialist party, with Hyndman as chairman. In World War I the party was disrupted, many members becoming Communists. Hyndman reorganized the Social Democratic Federation in 1920. Among his works are *The Historical Basis of Socialism* (1883), *The Economics of Socialism* (2d ed. 1896), *A Record of an Adventurous Life* (1911), and *Further Reminiscences* (1912). See biography by Rosalind Hyndman (1923); study by Chushichi Tsuzuki (1961).

Hyogo (hyō'gō), prefecture (1970 pop. 4,667,928) 3,213 sq mi (8,322 sq km), SW Honshu, Japan. KOBE is the capital. Although largely agricultural, the prefecture has industrial centers at Kobe, Akashi, Amagasaki, Himeji, and Nishinomiya.

hyoscine (hī'ōsēn, -sĭn): see SCOPOLAMINE.

Hypatia (hīpā'shə), d.415, Alexandrian Neoplatonic philosopher and mathematician, a woman renowned for her learning, eloquence, and beauty. Little is known of her writings. Her fame is largely owing to her barbarous murder by a band of monks, said to have been encouraged by the archbishop, St. CYRIL of Alexandria (a personal and political enemy of the prefect of Egypt, who was believed to have been Hypatia's lover).

hyperbola (hīpûr'bələ), plane curve consisting of all points such that the difference between the distances from any point on the curve to two fixed points (foci) is the same for all points. It is the CONIC SECTION formed by a plane cutting both nappes of the CONE; it thus has two parts, or branches. The center of a hyperbola is the point halfway between its foci. The principal axis is the straight line through the foci. The vertices are the intersection of this axis

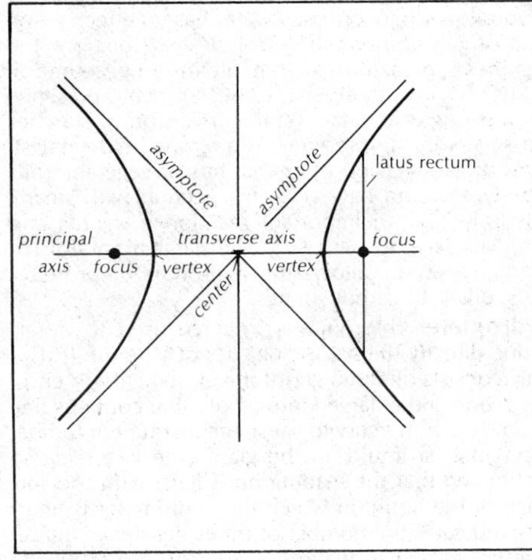

Hyperbola

with the curve. The transverse axis is the line segment joining the two vertices. The *latus rectum* is the chord through either focus perpendicular to the principal axis. The asymptotes are lines, in the same plane, which the curve approaches as it approaches infinity. An equilateral, or rectangular, hyperbola is one whose asymptotes are perpendicular. A second hyperbola may be drawn whose asymptotes are identical with those of the given hyperbola and whose principal axis is a perpendicular line through the center; the two hyperbolas thus related are called conjugate.

hyperbole (hīpûr'bəlē), a figure of speech in which exceptional exaggeration is deliberately used for emphasis rather than deception. Andrew Marvell employed hyperbole throughout "To His Coy Mistress":

An hundred years should go to praise
Thine eyes and on thy forhead gaze;
Two hundred to adore each breast;
But thirty thousand to the rest . . .

Hyperboreans (hī''pərbôr'ēənz, -bôrē'ənz), in Greek mythology, people dwelling in a state of perfect bliss in the Far North. They were especially associated with the worship of Apollo.

hyperglycemia: see DIABETES.

hyperinsulinism, presence in the system of an above-normal amount of INSULIN, the substance secreted by the PANCREAS and needed by the body to utilize sugar. An increased amount of insulin in the body results in below-normal amounts of sugar in the system, giving rise to such symptoms as headache, dizziness, weakness, and emotional instability. In severe cases there may be convulsions, coma, and death. The cause of oversecretion of insulin may be organic, i.e., a tumor of the pancreas, impaired liver function, or endocrine disorders, or it may be functional, e.g., unusual muscular exertion, pregnancy, or lactation. In diabetics, hyperinsulinism is known as insulin shock and may occur from overdosage with insulin in the course of treatment. Where there is some organic cause for hyperinsulinism, surgery may be required to eliminate it. Functional hyperinsulinism and insulin shock are treated by dietary measures designed to bring the insulin-sugar ratio into better balance.

Hyperion (hīpēr'ēən), in astronomy, one of the 10 known moons, or natural satellites, of SATURN.

Hyperion, in Greek religion, a Titan. He was the husband of his sister Theia and the father by her of Helios, Selene, and Eos. It is sometimes said that he was the original sun god.

hyperon (hī'pərŏn''), class of ELEMENTARY PARTICLES heavier than nucleons (PROTON and NEUTRON). The nucleons and the hyperons together make up the BARYON family of particles.

hyperopia (hī''pərō'pēə): see FARSIGHTEDNESS.

hyperplasia (hī''pərplā'zhə): see HYPERTROPHY.

hypersensitivity, heightened response in a body tissue to an antigen, or foreign substance. The body normally responds to the introduction of an antigen by producing specific ANTIBODIES against it. The antibodies impart IMMUNITY for any subsequent exposure to that antigen. When exposure takes place under certain physiological conditions or in allergic individuals with abnormal immune systems, a heightened immune response results that causes cell damage. Histamines, substances released from damaged cells, cause dilation of small blood vessels, tissue inflammation, and constriction of the bronchi of the lungs. ANAPHYLAXIS is the immediate, sometimes fatal, shocklike hypersensitivity reaction to drugs or serum to which an individual has been previously sensitized. SERUM SICKNESS is a similar but milder, more prolonged hypersensitivity to serum proteins or drugs that occurs several weeks after injection of foreign material. Delayed reaction allergies occur when cells of the immune system, the lymphocytes, that have previously been sensitized react to antigenic substances such as chemicals, drugs, or tubercle bacilli or other infecting organisms. The lymphocytes slowly infiltrate an area, such as skin exposed to poison ivy toxin, and cause tissue damage. Anaphylaxis, serum sickness, and delayed sensitivity may occur in otherwise normal, nonallergic individuals as well as allergics, as a response to substances that are highly sensitizing. Individuals with allergic, or atopic, hypersensitivity form special weak types of antibodies, called reagins, that give little immunological protection even to mildly antigenic substances but cause local tissue damage and such symptoms as HIVES, HAY FEVER, and ASTHMA. ANTIHISTAMINES are drugs that prevent histamine from acting on blood vessels, bronchioles, and other organs. Acute reactions, such as anaphylaxis, are treated by giving EPINEPHRINE and other sympathomimetic drugs. Steroids such as CORTISONE are also given to suppress inflammation and depress the immune system. In some cases, hypersensitized individuals are given injections of gradually increasing quantities of the antigenic material to which they are sensitive; the circulating antibodies that are produced in response to this material prevent the antigen from reaching tissue and causing the inflammatory response.

hypersonic speed: see AERODYNAMICS.

hypertension: see HYPERTENSIVE HEART DISEASE.

hypertensive heart disease, disorder of the heart, primarily enlargement of the left ventricle, caused by high blood pressure. Because blood pressure rises with age and state of excitation, the level at which hypertension is considered to be present varies greatly (see BLOOD PRESSURE). Hypertension becomes severe enough to damage the heart when the constriction of the arteries that causes high blood pressure is sufficiently advanced to force the left ventricle to compensate for the increased workload. If left untreated, hypertensive heart disease eventually causes death from CONGESTIVE HEART FAILURE or CORONARY ARTERY DISEASE, or complications such as cerebral hemorrhage and uremia. However, the development of antihypertensive drugs has greatly reduced the number of fatalities, especially when hypertension is not precipitated by other pathological conditions in the body such as kidney disease, adrenal tumors, or thyroid disease.

hyperthyroidism: see THYROID GLAND.

hypertrophy (hīpûr'trəfē), enlargement of a tissue or organ of the body resulting from an increase in the size of its cells. Such growth accompanies an increase in the functioning of the tissue. In normal physiology the growth in size of muscles (e.g., in an athlete as a result of increased exercise) and also the enlargement of a uterus in pregnancy are caused by hypertrophy of muscle cells. In pathology the thickening of the heart muscle from overstrain, as in high blood pressure, is the result of hypertrophy. An organ subjected to extra work (e.g., the one kidney left to function after surgical removal of the other) usually compensates by enlarging; in such cases hyperplasia, an increase in the number of cells, generally accompanies hypertrophy.

hyphen: see PUNCTUATION.

hypnotic drugs, general central nervous system DEPRESSANTS. In large doses such drugs, e.g., the BARBITURATES, act as soporifics, and in smaller doses they are used as SEDATIVES.

hypnotism (hĭp'nətĭzəm) [Gr.,=putting to sleep], term given by James Braid in 1842 to phenomena previously described as animal magnetism and mesmerism (see MESMER). Superficially resembling sleep, it is generally induced by the monotonous repetition of words and gestures while the subject is completely relaxed. In slight hypnosis the subject remains conscious and remembers what has happened after waking. In deep hypnosis the sensory system and the muscles are greatly affected. Although almost everyone can be hypnotized, individuals vary greatly in susceptibility. The hypnotic state is characterized by heightened suggestibility, e.g., the hypnotized individual can be induced to follow many, but not all, bizarre instructions or endure painful conditions. In the late 19th cent., it was used by a number of medical practitioners, including the Frenchmen J. M. Charcot, Pierre Janet, and others, who found that individuals susceptible to HYSTERIA are also highly suggestible and can be put into deep hypnosis and sometimes cured of symptoms. The method proved highly successful in demonstrating the emotional basis of hysteria and was used for a time by Freud in psychoanalysis. Hypnosis is still used by qualified doctors as an aid in medical practice and psychotherapy, e.g., to help AMNESIA sufferers recall traumatic events. See G. H. Estabrooks, *Hypnotism* (rev. ed. 1959); William Moodie, *Hypnosis in Treatment* (1960); M. M. Tinterow, ed., *Foundations of Hypnosis* (1970); Margaret Brenman and M. M. Gill, *Hypnotherapy* (1947, repr. 1972); Erika Fromm and R. E. Shor, *Hypnosis: Research Developments and Perspectives* (1972).

hypo: see SODIUM THIOSULFATE.

hypocaust (hī'pəkôst): see HEATING.

hypochondria (hī"pəkŏn'drēə), neurotic reaction characterized by habitual preoccupation with physical health and unwarranted concern with an imagined or negligible physical defect. Rarely appearing as an isolated symptom, it more frequently is a complicating factor in a psychopathological condition. It differs from HYSTERIA in that hysterics are usually indifferent to physical infirmities.

hypoglycemia: see DIABETES.

hypophysis: see PITUITARY GLAND.

hypostyle (hĭp'əstīl, hī'pə-), the chamber in Egyptian temples in which a number of columns supported a flat stone roof. Forming the chief and largest inner space of the temple, it was entered from the outer courtyard and, in turn, gave access to the holy of holies and the small inner sanctuaries occupying the rear of the structure. Its columns were arranged to form a wide center aisle flanked by two or more side aisles, the center one rising higher than the others to permit clerestory lighting. The ruined temple of Amon at Al Karnak shows the most celebrated hypostyle hall, constructed in the XIX dynasty.

hypothalamus, an important supervisory center in the BRAIN, rich in ganglia, nerve fibers, and synaptic connections. The hypothalamus regulates body temperature, blood pressure, heartbeat, metabolism of fats and carbohydrates, and sugar levels in the blood. Through direct attachment to the PITUITARY GLAND, the hypothalamus also meters secretions controlling water balance and milk production in the female. The role of the hypothalamus in awareness of pleasure and pain has been well established in the laboratory. There is evidence, moreover, that it organizes motor responses involved in expressing emotions, for example, the contortions of the face signifying anger. Despite its numerous vital functions, the hypothalamus in humans accounts for only 1/300 of total brain weight and is about the size of an almond. Structurally, the hypothalamus is joined to the THALAMUS, with which it works in tandem to monitor the sleep-wake cycle.

hypothyroidism: see THYROID GLAND.

Hypsicles of Alexandria (hĭp'sĭklēz), astronomer of ancient Greece. Some authorities place Hypsicles in the 2d cent. B.C. and some in the 2d cent. A.D. The 14th and 15th books of Euclid's *Elements,* which discuss regular many-sided solids, are attributed to him. His other works include a short treatise on astronomy that introduces the division of the circle into multiples of sixty.

Hypsilanti: see YPSILANTI.

hyrax (hī'răks), name for rabbit-sized mammals of Africa and SW Asia comprising the family Procavidae. Although rodentlike in appearance, hyraxes are hoofed mammals, or ungulates (see CHORDATA), most closely related to elephants and sea cows. The hyrax, also called coney, has a squat, furry body, with short slender legs, short ears, and a short tail. It has small hooves on its toes, and moist padded soles that cling to steep surfaces by suction, making it an excellent climber. There are about 14 hyrax species, classified in two genera. The genus *Procavia* includes the ground-living species, sometimes called dassies. Dassies are rock dwellers and live in colonies of up to 50 animals; they are found especially in deserts and hills. Most species of the genus *Dendrohyrax* are arboreal and are known as tree hyraxes; they are the only tree-dwelling hoofed mammals. Tree hyraxes are solitary and nocturnal; they are confined to forested regions of Africa. Hyraxes feed on seeds, fruit, and leaves, and in large numbers can be serious agricultural pests. They are classified in the phylum CHORDATA, subphylum Vertebrata, class Mammalia, order Hyracoidea, family Procavidae.

Hyrcania: see GORGAN, town, Iran.

Hyrcanus: see MACCABEES, Jewish family.

hyssop (hĭs'əp), aromatic, perennial, somewhat woody herb (*Hyssopus officinalis*) of the family Labiatae (MINT family), native to the Old World but growing as an escape from gardens in North America. The plant has small violet-blue, sometimes pink or white, flowers. Although now grown chiefly for ornament, it has been used to flavor soups and salads, as a tea for chest ailments, and as a poultice for bruises; oil of hyssop has been added to liqueurs and cologne. The hyssop of the Scriptures (1 Kings 4.33; Ps. 51.7; John 19.29) may have been a similar plant or the name may have referred to different plants. Hyssop is used as a symbol of humility in religious painting. North American plants of the related genus *Agastache* are called giant hyssop and were used medicinally and as flavoring by the Indians. Hyssop is classified in the division MAGNOLIOPHYTA, class Magnoliopsida, order Lamiales, family Labiatae.

Hystaspes (hĭstăs'pēz) or **Hystaspis** (hĭstăs'pĭs), Old Persian *Vishtaspa,* fl. 6th cent. B.C., ruler of ancient Persia, father of DARIUS I. Under him Darius was governor of Parthia. The legendary patron of Zoroaster is also called Hystaspes or Vishtaspa; he may or may not be the same as Darius' father.

hysterectomy (hĭstərĕk'təmē), surgical removal of the UTERUS. A hysterectomy may involve removal of the uterus only, or additional removal of the cervix (base of the uterus), FALLOPIAN TUBES, and OVARIES. It is performed in cases of malignant tumors or in cases of benign formations, e.g., fibroid tumors, that cause bleeding and pain. An emergency hysterectomy is sometimes necessary to end uterine hemorrhage or uncontrollable bleeding. Removal does not physically interfere with sexual activity, but since it eliminates the possibility of childbearing, it is avoided in younger women if more conservative treatment is feasible. Removal of the ovaries may precipitate the premature occurrence of MENOPAUSE.

hysteresis, phenomenon in which the response of a physical system to an external influence depends not only on the present magnitude of that influence but also on the previous history of the system. Expressed mathematically, the response to the external influence is a doubled-valued function; one value applies when the influence is increasing, the other applies when the influence is decreasing. Magnetic hysteresis occurs when a permeable material like soft iron is magnetized by being subjected to an external magnetic field. The induced magnetization tends to lag behind the magnetizing force. If a field is applied to an initially unmagnetized sample and is then removed, the sample retains a residual magnetization (it has become a permanent magnet). The graph of the magnetic induction B versus the magnetic field H is called a hysteresis loop. The area of the loop is proportional to the energy dissipated as heat when the system goes through a cycle; this represents a considerable energy loss in alternating-current machinery. Thermal hysteresis occurs when the value of a given property of a body depends not only on the body's temperature but also on whether the temperature is rising or falling. An example is the dielectric constant versus temperature for certain crystals. Another kind of hysteresis is a common feature of control or cybernetic systems. A familiar example is a thermostat controlling a source of heat and set at some temperature T_0. When the room temperature falls through T_0 to some lower temperature T_1, the heating power is switched on. When the room temperature rises through T_0 to some higher temperature T_2, the power is switched off. Thus, for temperatures lower than T_1, the heat is always on; for temperatures higher than T_2, the heat is always off; but for temperatures between T_1 and T_2, the heat may be on or off (double-valued response), depending on which of the two temperatures T_1 and T_2 occurred most recently in the system's history. Unlike the previous examples, this hysteresis effect is not naturally occurring; it is designed into the control system to prevent the damage to the system that would arise from switching on and off too frequently.

hysteria (hĭstĕr'ēə), one of the PSYCHONEUROSES, commonly referred to as the conversion neurosis, in which a psychological conflict is converted into a bodily disturbance. Hysteria is usually found in patients with immature, histrionic personalities who are under great stress, as in wartime. Hysterical symptoms, which are largely symbolic and which relieve the patient's anxiety, include paralysis of a limb, psychic blindness, or convulsive seizures. The specific hysterical illness usually does not correspond to the anatomy; e.g., an entire limb may be paralyzed rather than a specific group of muscles. The patient may also be unconcerned about the illness. Hysteria expressed through behavior rather than in physical infirmity may be manifested as AMNESIA or dual personality. At the end of the 19th cent. great advances were made in the understanding and cure of hysteria by the recognition of its psychogenic nature and by the use of hypnotism to influence the high degree of suggestibility that is one of the outstanding traits of the hysteric. The Austrian physician Josef Breuer, the French psychologists J. M. Charcot and Pierre Janet, and Freud were pioneers in the investigation of hysteria by the use of hypnosis. Freud concluded that hysterical symptoms were symbolic representations of a repressed unconscious event that had been accompanied by strong emotions that for one reason or another could not be adequately expressed or discharged at the time. Instead the strong effect associated with the event was diverted into the wrong somatic channels (conversion), and the symptom resulted. Freud and Breuer found that "catharsis" reactivation of the memory could remove the hysterical symptom. Hysteria is distinguished from psychosomatic disorders, e.g., ulcers, in that the latter involve organs under control of the involuntary (autonomic) nervous system. See PSYCHOSOMATIC MEDICINE.

Hythe (hīth), municipal borough (1971 pop. 11,949), Kent, SE England. A summer resort and market town, it was one of the CINQUE PORTS. Saltwood Castle, near Hythe, once the property of the archbishops of Canterbury, is supposed to have been the scene of the plotting of the murder (1170) of Thomas à Becket. At Hythe is the School of Small Arms.

Hyuga (hyo͞o'gä), city (1970 pop. 47,420), Miyazaki prefecture, E Kyushu, Japan, on the Pacific Ocean. It is a fishing port and agricultural center.

Hywel Dda (ho͞o'ĕl thä), or **Howel the Good,** d. 950?, king of Wales. He is credited with the uniform codification of medieval Welsh laws. The *Laws of Hywel Dda* are now extant only in manuscript fragments, but they suggest an enlightened code and are a valuable source for social history.

I

I, 9th letter of the ALPHABET. It is a usual symbol for a high front vowel, like *ī* as in the English *rip.* The Greek correspondent is iota. *J* is a formal development from *I.* English *ī* is pronounced as a diphthong of *ä* and *y.* In chemistry I is the symbol of the element IODINE.

iambic pentameter: see PENTAMETER.

Iamblichus (īăm′blĭkəs), d. c.330, Syrian philosopher, a leading exponent of NEOPLATONISM. A pupil of Porphyry, he was deeply impressed by the doctrines of Plotinus. In his own teachings he combined with Plato's ideas many of those of Pythagoras and much that was mystical and even magical, derived from the Orient. His following was large and enthusiastic in his own time, and in the 15th and 16th cent. he was studied with admiring interest. Of his writings on mathematical and philosophical subjects there remain several parts of an extensive work on the philosophy of Pythagoras. His work *On the Egyptian Mysteries* survives, but his commentaries on Plato and Aristotle have disappeared. See Thomas Whittaker, *The Neo-Platonists* (2d ed. 1928, repr. 1961).

Iapetus (īăp′ĭtəs), in astronomy, one of the 10 known moons, or natural satellites, of SATURN.

Iapetus, in Greek mythology, a Titan. By the nymph Clymene he fathered Atlas, Prometheus, Epimetheus, and Menoetius.

Iaşi (yäsh) or **Jassy** (yä′sē), city (1970 est. pop. 184,000), E Rumania, in Moldavia, near the USSR border. Iaşi is the administrative and commercial center of a fertile agricultural region. Textiles, pharmaceuticals, machinery, food products, furniture, plastics, and metal are produced. In 1565, Iaşi succeeded Suceava as the capital of the Rumanian principality of Moldavia, a position it held until Moldavia and Walachia were united in 1859. The city was repeatedly burned and sacked by Tatars, Turks, and Russians. A treaty signed there in 1792 ended the second of the Russo-Turkish Wars of Catherine II. In Iaşi, long an important cultural center, the first book in the Rumanian language was printed (1643) and the national theater was founded (1849). During World War I the city served as Rumania's temporary capital while German forces occupied Walachia. Iaşi's large Jewish population was massacred by the Nazis in one of the worst pogroms in history. Soviet troops took the city in 1944. Iaşi is the see of an Orthodox archbishop and has a university (founded 1860) and other institutions of higher education. Landmarks include the 17th-century cathedral, the Church of the Three Hierarchs (17th cent.), and the Church of St. Nicholas (15th cent.), all outstanding examples of the Moldavian adaptation of Byzantine architecture.

Ibadan (ēbä′dän, ēbädäN′), city (1971 est. pop. 758,000), SW Nigeria. The second largest city in Nigeria, it is a major commercial and industrial center. Manufactures include canned foods, metal products, furniture, soap, and chemicals. It is also an important market for cacao, which, along with cotton, is produced in the region. Ibadan was founded in the 1830s as a military camp during the YORUBA civil wars and developed into the most powerful Yoruba city-state. In 1840, Ibadan forces defeated FULANI invaders from the north at the battle of OSHOGBO, thus protecting S Yorubaland from attack. The city came under British protection in 1893. It contains some mosques and is the site of the Univ. of Ibadan (1962), formerly University College, Ibadan.

Ibagué (ēbägā′), city (1968 est. pop. 172,100), alt. 4,300 ft (1,311 m), capital of Tolima dept., W central Colombia. It is a major commercial center for the Magdalena and Cauca valleys. Coffee, flour, and sugar are produced in the city, and silver and sulfur are shipped. In 1854, Ibagué served briefly as the national capital. It grew rapidly as a result of the coffee boom in the 1890s.

Ibáñez, Vicente Blasco: see BLASCO IBÁÑEZ.

Ibáñez del Campo, Carlos (kär′lōs ēbä′nyās thĕl käm′pō), 1877–1960, president of Chile (1927–31, 1952–58). An army general who served as minister of war (1925–27) and vice president (1927), he became president upon the forced resignation of Pres. Emiliano Figueroa. He ruled dictatorially, suppressing all opposition. He launched many public works projects and instituted educational and labor reform, remaining popular until the worldwide depression hit Chile. Widespread demonstrations in 1931 forced him into exile in Argentina. After several attempts to regain power, he was elected (1949) to the senate. He won the presidency (1952) by a plurality after promising to curb inflation and to reform the bureaucracy. His administration was hampered, however, by opposition in congress and by his own old age.

Ibaraki (ēbä′räkē), prefecture (1970 pop. 2,143,551), 2,352 sq mi (6,092 sq km), central Honshu, Japan. MITO is the capital. The prefecture yields coal, tobacco, and raw silk.

Ibarbourou, Juana de (hwä′nä dā ēbärbo͞o′ro͞o), 1895–, Uruguayan poet also called Juana de América. One of the most popular poets of Spanish America, she caused a sensation with the exuberant and lilting sensuality of her lyrics in *Aguas de diamante* (1919) and *Raíz salvaje* (1920). Her early works also include the introspective *La rosa de los vientos* (1930). *Oro y tormenta* (1956), in which she uses biblical themes, reflects her increasing preoccupation with suffering and death. *Chico Carlo* (1944) contains her memoirs. Her work is collected in *Obras completas* (3d ed. 1968).

Ibarra, Francisco de (fränthēs′kō thā ēbä′rä), 1539?–1575, Spanish conquistador in Mexico. In 1554, after founding FRESNILLO, he headed an expedition to the N of Zacatecas. For the next 20 years he explored, founded settlements, and exploited mines in the vast region comprising present-day Durango, Chihuahua, and part of Sinaloa, which he called the Kingdom of Nueva Vizcaya. In 1562, after his most successful campaign, Ibarra was named governor, a post he retained until his death. See study by J. L. Mecham (1927, repr. 1968).

Iberia (ībēr′ēə), ancient country of Transcaucasia, roughly the eastern part of present-day Georgian SSR. It was inhabited in earliest times by various tribes, collectively called Iberians by ancient historians, although Herodotus called them Saspirams. Between the 6th and 4th cent. B.C. the kingdoms of COLCHIS (western Georgia) and Iberia were founded. Iberia was allied to the Romans, ruled by the Sassanids of Persia, and became (6th cent. A.D.) a Byzantine province. Its later history is that of Georgia.

Iberian Gates, pass, USSR: see DARYAL.

Iberian Mountains (ībēr′ēən), mountain system, extending c.250 mi (400 km) along the northeastern edge of the Meseta (central plateau), NE Spain. Moncayo (7,590 ft/2,313 m high) is the highest peak in the system. The Douro River and several tributaries of the Ebro River rise there.

Iberian Peninsula, c.230,400 sq mi (596,740 sq km), SW Europe, separated from the rest of Europe by the Pyrenees. Comprising SPAIN and PORTUGAL, it is washed on the N and W by the Atlantic Ocean and on the S and E by the Mediterranean Sea; the Strait of Gibraltar separates it from Africa. The Iberian Peninsula is dominated by the Meseta (central plateau), a great uplifted fault block (average elevation 2,000 ft/610 m) ringed and crossed by mountain ranges. It covers about two thirds of the peninsula. Coastal lowlands, the site of the major industrial cities, surround the primarily agrarian-oriented Meseta. Climatically, the Iberian Peninsula has hot summers, cold winters, and limited precipitation. Five major rivers drain the peninsula.

Iberians, ancient people of Spain. They are believed to have migrated from Africa in the Neolithic period and again at the end of the Bronze Age. They were first mentioned in the 6th cent. B.C., after they had settled in E Spain and the Ebro valley. The Iberian Peninsula, i.e., Spain and Portugal, is named for them. The high point of Iberian civilization was reached about the 4th cent. B.C., and thereafter their culture came under the influence of Carthaginian colonization. About the 4th cent. B.C. began the Celtic migration into Spain, and the two peoples later (probably 3d cent.) merged into the so-called Celtiberian nation. After the Roman conquest of Spain the Celtiberians gradually accepted Roman culture. The theory that the Iberians and the Basques were identical has been discredited by modern research. See Pierson Dixon, *The Iberians of Spain* (1940); Antonio Arribas Palau, *The Iberians* (1963).

Ibert, Jacques (zhäk ēbĕr′), 1890–1962, French composer. Ibert, a pupil of Fauré, won the Prix de Rome in 1919. His music is generally bright, colorful, and tuneful. Among the most popular of Ibert's works are *Escales* (*Ports of Call,* 1924) and *Divertissement* (1930), for orchestra; concertos for flute (1934) and for saxophone (1935); *Trois pièces brèves* (1930) for woodwind quintet; and the piano suite *Histoires.* He also wrote many ballets, operas, and sets of incidental music.

Iberville, Pierre le Moyne, sieur d' (pyĕr lə mwän syör dĕbĕrvēl′), 1661–1706, French Canadian naval officer, founder of the French territory of LOUISIANA, b. Ville Marie (in present Montreal), Canada; son of Charles le Moyne, sieur de LONGUEUIL, and brother of Jean Baptiste le Moyne, sieur de BIENVILLE. In 1675 he entered the French navy but after 10 years at sea returned to Canada. He led five expeditions (1686, 1689, 1691, 1694, 1697) against the British fur-trading posts on Hudson Bay. Despite these efforts, the British foothold was not broken, largely because Iberville received no support from France. In 1690 he took part in the raid on Schenectady led by his elder brother Jacques, sieur de Ste-Hélène. In 1692 he unsuccessfully attacked Fort Pemaquid, Maine, but in 1696 he destroyed that post and also captured St. John's, Newfoundland, temporarily ousting the British from that area. In 1698, Iberville, who was in France, was charged with planting a settlement in the lower Mississippi valley. With colonists and supplies in four ships, Iberville, accompanied by his younger brother Bienville, reached the Gulf of Mexico in 1699 and founded Old Biloxi (now Ocean Springs, Miss.). He was the first definitely to ascertain the mouth of the Mississippi from the Gulf approach and to explore its delta. He returned to the colony with supplies and reinforcements in 1700 and 1701–2. Illness prevented Iberville from returning again to the colony, which, under Bienville's direction, was moved to the Mobile area in 1702. Iberville recovered sufficiently to lead an expedition that captured (1706) the British islands of Nevis and St. Kitts in the West Indies and was ready to carry out an old plan to attack Boston and New York when, having put in at Havana, he was stricken with yellow fever and died. See biography by N. M. Crouse (1954).

ibex (ī′bĕks), wild GOAT, genus *Capra,* found in rugged country on mountain ranges from central Asia to the Himalayas, S Europe, and NE Africa. Ibexes are surefooted and agile; they usually travel in small herds of about a dozen animals, feeding on a wide variety of vegetation. Most of the isolated populations of the various ranges are races of the single species *Capra ibex* and differ chiefly in the size of their horns. Ibexes are brown to gray, from 2½ to 3½ ft (76–106 cm) tall at the shoulder, and very sturdily built. The chin is bearded, and the tail is short. The long, heavily ridged horns of the male curve up, back, and downward; in the Alpine race they form a semicircle and measure 30 in. (76 cm) along the edge. In some other races the male has still longer horns. The horns of the female are short and point straight back. The Alpine race is now found only on reserves in Switzerland. Closly related species are the tur, or Caucasian ibex (*C. caucasia*), of SE Russia; the Spanish ibex, or Spanish tur (*C. pyrenaica*), now extinct in the Pyrenees but still found in other parts of the Iberian Peninsula; and the MARKHOR (*C. falconeri*), of central Asia. Ibexes and other goats are classified in the phylum CHORDATA, subphylum Vertebrata, class Mammalia, order Artiodactyla, family Bovidae.

Ibhar (ĭb′här), son of David. 2 Sam. 5.15.

ibis (ī′bĭs), common name for wading birds with long, slender, decurved bills, found in the warmer regions of both hemispheres. The body is usually about 2 ft (61 cm) long. Most ibises nest in colonies. They feed in ponds, lakes, and brackish marshes on fish and other aquatic animals. The sacred ibis of ancient Egypt, *Threskiornis aethiopica,* a white and black bird, no longer frequents the Nile basin, although it inhabits other parts of Africa. In the southern part of North America are found the white ibis, *Eudocimus albus;* the white-faced and eastern glossy ibises, *Plegadis falcinellus;* and a bird that was formerly called the wood ibis, which is really a STORK. The scarlet ibis of South America, *E. ruber,* is occasionally seen in the S United States. Ibises are classified in the phylum CHORDATA, subphylum Vertebrata, class Aves, order Ciconiiformes, family Threskiornithidae.

Ibiza (ēvē'thä), island (1970 pop. 45,075), 221 sq mi (572 sq km), Baleares prov., Spain, one of the Balearic Islands, in the W Mediterranean. The town of Ibiza is the capital. There are fisheries and saltworks on the island. Subsistence farming, aided by irrigation, is mostly terraced. A picturesque island with Roman, Phoenician, and Carthaginian remains, Ibiza attracts tourists and artists.

Ibizan hound (ēbē'zŏn, ĭb'ə-), also called Ibizan Podenco, breed of tall, swift dog of ancient origin now found chiefly in the Balearic Islands and other areas of Spain. It stands from 22 to 28 in. (55.8–71.1 cm) high at the shoulder and weighs from 42 to 50 lb (19.1–22.7 kg). Its short coat is usually red with white markings, but it may also be solid red or white. It is generally believed that the Ibizan is a modern survivor of the ring-tailed, prick-eared greyhound of ancient Egypt, although similarities to both the afghan and the basenji suggest the possibility that the breed was originated by other people prior to its development in Egypt. Introduced into the United States in 1956, it is exhibited in the miscellaneous class at dog shows sanctioned by the American Kennel Club. See DOG.

Ibleam (ĭb'lēəm), town, Palestine, the present-day Tell Belameh (Jordan). Joshua 17.11; Judges 1.27; 2 Kings 9.27. Bileam: 1 Chron. 6.70. Gath-rimmon: Joshua 21.25.

Ibn al-Haytham (ĭb'ən äl-hīth-äm') or **Alhazen** (älhəzĕn'), 965–c.1040, Arab mathematician. Ibn al-Haytham was born in Basra, Persia, but made his career in Cairo, where he supported himself copying scientific manuscripts. Among his many original works, only those on optics, astronomy, and mathematics survive. His *Optics,* which relied on experiment rather than on past authority, introduced the important idea that light rays emanate in straight lines in all directions from every point on a luminous surface. Latin editions of the *Optics,* available from the 13th cent. on, influenced the work of Kepler and Descartes. As a cosmologist, al-Haytham tried to find mechanisms by which the heavenly bodies might be shown to follow the paths determined by Ptolemaic mathematics. In mathematics, al-Haytham elucidated and extended Euclid's *Elements* and suggested a proof of the parallel postulate.

Ibn Bajja: see AVEMPACE.

Ibn Batuta (ĭ'bən bätōō'tä), 1304?–1378?, Muslim traveler, b. Tangier. No other medieval traveler is known to have journeyed so extensively. In 30 years (from c.1325) he made a series of journeys recorded in a dictated account that was rediscovered during the French occupation of Algeria. He traveled overland in North Africa and Syria to make the pilgrimage to Mecca. Afterward he explored Arabia, Mesopotamia, Persia, and Asia Minor. He made a journey by way of Samarkand to India, where he resided for almost eight years at the court of the sultan of Delhi, who sent him to China as one of his ambassadors. Ibn Batuta visited the Maldive Islands, the Malabar coast, Ceylon, and Sumatra. He returned c.1350 to Tangier. Later he went to Spain, then to Morocco, and from there he crossed the Sahara to visit Timbuktu and the Niger River. Batuta is still considered a most reliable source for the geography of his period and an authority on the cultural and social history of Islam. For annotated selections from his writings, see *Travels of Ibn Battūta* (tr. by H. A. R. Gibb, 3 vol., rev. ed. 1958–71).

Ibneiah (ĭbnē'yə), son of a Benjamite chief. 1 Chron. 9.8.

Ibn Ezra, Abraham ben Meir (mâr), 1098–1164, Jewish grammarian, commentator, poet, philosopher, and astronomer, b. Tudela, Spain. He traveled widely and wrote a large number of books. His scholarly works of all kinds and his poems are of high quality, but he is best known as a biblical critic. He was the inspiration of Robert Browning's "Rabbi Ben Ezra." Aben Ezra is another form of his name. See Raphael Levy, *The Astrological Works of Abraham Ibn Ezra* (1927); Michael Friedländer, *Essays on the Writings of Abraham Ibn Ezra* (1877, repr. 1963–64).

Ibn Gabirol, Solomon ben Judah (ĭ'bən gäbē'rôl), c.1021–1058, Jewish poet and philosopher, known also as Avicebron, b. Malaga. His secular poetry deals partly with nature and love, but most of it reveals a gloom and bitterness engendered by his tragic life. Orphaned early, he spent much of his life contending with mediocre rivals and critics jealous of his scholarship. It is thought that he was murdered by a rival. Ibn Gabriol's religious poetry is filled with a mystic awe of God, and much of it has been incorporated into the Judaic liturgy. His great philosophical work, *The Well of Life,* showing the influence of Neoplatonism, was written in Arabic. In its Latin translation (*Fons vitae*), it exercised a great influence on Christian thought. The book is an attempt to explain the universality of matter, man's purpose in life, and the communion of man's soul with the spiritual sources that created it. His hundreds of poems and his book of ethics, *The Improvement of the Moral Qualities,* were also important. See study by Abraham Cohen (1925).

Ibnijah (ĭbnī'jə), member of the house of Benjamin. 1 Chron. 9.8.

Ibn Khaldun (ĭ'bən khäldōōn'), 1332–1406, Arab historian, b. Tunis. He held various offices under the rulers of Tunis and Morocco and served (1363) as ambassador of the Moorish king of Granada to Peter the Cruel of Castile. In 1382 he sailed to Cairo, where he spent most of the rest of his life as a teacher and lecturer. Many times grand Melikite cadi (judge) of Cairo, he made the pilgrimage to Mecca in 1387. In 1400 he accompanied the Egyptians in their campaign against Tamerlane, and he was sent to arrange for the capitulation of Damascus to Tamerlane. Ibn Khaldun is generally considered the greatest of the Arab historians. In his great work, the *Kitab al-Ibar* [universal history], he attempts to treat history as a science and outlines a philosophy of history, setting forth principles of sociology and political economy. The first part of the book, the Muqaddimah (translated into English by Franz Rosenthal, 3 vol. 1958), treats of Muslim life in general and of principles; the second deals with the history and culture of the Arabs; the third is a comprehensive survey of the history of the Berbers. To those he added an autobiography, completed in 1394 but expanded a few months before he died. See studies by Nathaniel Schmidt (1930), Muhsin Mahdi (1957), and W. J. Fischel (1967).

Ibn Rushd: see AVERROËS.

Ibn Saud (Abd al-Aziz ibn Saud) (ĭ'bən säōōd'), c.1888–1953, founder of SAUDI ARABIA and its first king. His family, with its regular seat at Ar Riyad in the Najd, were the traditional leaders of the ultra-orthodox WAHABI movement in Islam. During Ibn Saud's youth the Saud family was in exile in Kuwait. In 1900 he and a small party of relatives and servants recaptured Ar Riyad. By 1912 he had completed the conquest of the Najd and organized a well-trained army. During World War I the British made slight efforts to cultivate Ibn Saud's friendship but favored his rival, HUSAYN IBN ALI of the Hijaz. In 1924–25, Ibn Saud defeated Husayn and proclaimed himself king of Hijaz and Najd. After consolidating his power over most of the Arabian peninsula, he changed (1932) the name of his kingdom to Saudi Arabia. He forced many of the nomad tribes to adopt a settled way of life and to abandon their private wars and vendettas. He is credited with suppressing the robbery and extortion that formerly harassed pilgrims to Mecca and Medina. In 1936 and 1939 he granted oil concessions to American companies. The oil deposits of Arabia proved to be among the richest in the world, and Ibn Saud used some of the income derived from them on national improvements. The greater part of his oil revenues, however, was spent on the royal family. During World War II, Ibn Saud remained neutral but favored the Allies. Although anti-Zionist, he took only a minor part in the Arab-Israeli war of 1948. He was succeeded by Prince Saud, his eldest son. See H. S. J. Philby, *Arabian Jubilee* (1953) and D. A. Howarth, *The Desert King* (1967).

Ibn Sina: see AVICENNA.

Ibn Tufayl (ĭ'bən tōōfäl'), 12th-century Spanish-Arabian philosopher and physician, b. near Granada. His chief work was a philosophical romance, *Hayy ibn Yaqzan,* describing the development of a hermit, who, after long seclusion on an island, attains knowledge of the divine. He later comes into contact with a man trained in religion, the point of the work being the conflict between philosophy and religion. The book was translated into several European languages in the 17th cent. and was widely read. Ibn Tufayl, called Abubacer by Europeans, was famous as a physician and gained something of a reputation for magic in the West.

Ibn Tumart (ĭ'bən tōōmärt'), c.1080–1130, Berber Muslim religious leader, founder of the ALMOHADS. He went to the East in his youth and returned convinced that he was the MAHDI and that he was destined to reform Islam. He was a rigorist and purist in doctrine and morality. Believing in a mystical concept of the oneness of God, Ibn Tumart fought violently the anthropomorphism then current. He became increasingly fanatical, until he finally preached a holy war against Muslims who disagreed with him. He was esteemed as a man of compelling personality and of great sagacity.

Ibo (ē'bō), one of the largest ethnic groups in Nigeria, deriving mainly from SE Nigeria, numbering over 7 million. Originally settled in many autonomous villages, the Ibo nevertheless had a sense of cultural unity and the ability to unite for political action. They were receptive to Christianity and education under British colonialism and missionary influence. The Ibo became heavily represented in professional, managerial, technical, and commercial occupations, and many migrated to other regions of Nigeria. They played a major role in securing Nigerian independence from Britain in 1963. During the political conflict in 1966, thousands of Ibo immigrants were killed in the northern region, home of the Muslim Hausa and Fulani. Many Ibo fled to their eastern homeland, which seceded from Nigeria in 1967, calling itself the Republic of Biafra. Civil war followed, and, by 1970, Biafra was defeated. See George Basden, *Among the Ibos of Nigeria* (1921, repr. 1966); A. C. Smock, *Ibo Politics* (1971).

Ibrahim Pasha (ēbrähēm' pä'shä), 1789–1848, Egyptian general. He was the eldest son of MUHAMMAD ALI, governor of Egypt under the Ottoman Empire. Ibrahim conducted (1816–19) largely successful campaigns against the Wahabis in Arabia. He fought (1825–28) against the insurgent Greeks and sent large numbers into slavery in Egypt, but the landing of French troops forced him to withdraw from the country. After Muhammad Ali turned against the Ottoman sultan, Ibrahim conquered (1832–33) Syria. His attempts to apply to Syria the reforms that his father had introduced in Egypt caused a series of disorders. Warfare with the Turks was resumed in 1838, but British and Austrian military intervention on Turkey's behalf compelled Ibrahim to evacuate to Egypt. In 1848 he was regent of Egypt during his father's insanity.

Ibri (ĭb'rī), Merarite of the family of Jaaziah. 1 Chron. 24.27.

Ibsen, Henrik (hĕn'rĭk ĭb'sən), 1828–1906, Norwegian dramatist and poet. His early years were lonely and miserable and distressed by the consequences of his family's financial ruin. On his own at sixteen, he first was apprenticed to an apothecary. Not long after this he began writing poetry, and in 1850 he published his first play, *Catilina,* a tragedy in verse. In 1851 he began an extended apprenticeship in the theater, first as stage manager and playwright with the National Stage in Bergen and in 1857 as theater director for the Norwegian Theater in Oslo. His early plays for the most part went unrecognized or were greeted with opposition and critical hostility. As a man far in advance of his times, Ibsen was condemned for unveiling truths which society preferred to keep hidden. In 1864, dissatisfied with the backwardness of Norway, he went to Italy. He wrote the bulk of his drama there and in Germany. His career can be divided into three periods. The first phase, that of poetic dramas, dealt primarily with historical themes, folklore, and romantic pageantry. His name was established with the publication of *Love's Comedy* (1862). However, it was in 1866 that he reached prominent stature as a dramatist, when he published the first of his masterpieces, *Brand,* the tragedy of an idealist. *Peer Gynt,* another poetic drama and Ibsen's least understood work, appeared the following year. In this play Ibsen recounted the adventures of an egocentric but imaginative opportunist. With *The League of Youth* (1869) and *Pillars of Society* (1877), he began his second dramatic phase, that of the realistic social plays which are his best known. Ibsen rebelled against society's conventions through which the perpetuation of empty traditions restricts all intellectual, artistic, and spiritual growth. He was perhaps most successful in depicting the 19th-century woman, whose inner nature was in strong conflict with the role she was called on to perform. These feminist dramas include *A Doll's House* (1879), *Ghosts* (1881), *Rosmersholm* (1886), and *Hedda Gabler* (1890). Other notable plays, *An Enemy of the People* (1882) and *The Wild Duck* (1884), examine the effects of true and false idealism. Although nearly all Ibsen's plays contain symbolic elements, it was in his final works that the emphasis on symbolism became very strong. The chief plays of this group are *The Master Builder* (1892), *Little Eyolf* (1894), *John Gabriel Borkman* (1896), and *When We Dead Awaken* (1900). All have a firmly knit structure beneath the symbols; all blend an introspective realism with folk poetry. No playwright has exerted greater influence on 20th-century drama. His plays—there are many good English translations—are continually revived in the United States and Europe. See biographies by H. Koht (1928, new tr. 1971), H. Heiberg (tr. 1969), and M. Meyer (1971); studies by G. M. C. Brandes (1899, repr. 1964), G. B. Shaw (1913, repr. 1957), M. C. Bradbook (rev. ed. 1966), and J. R. Northam (1953 and 1973).

Ibycus (ĭb'ĭkəs), fl. before 500 B.C., Greek lyric poet, b. Rhegium, S Italy. The extant fragments of his work contain the earliest-known example of the triadic choral lyric. He spent some time at the court of Polycrates of Samos. The "cranes of Ibycus" as an expression of triumphant justice refers to the tale that Ibycus, murdered at sea, was revenged by cranes who saw the crime and eventually revealed the murderers. See C. M. Bowra, *Greek Lyric Poetry* (1936, repr. 1961).

Ibzan (ĭb'zăm), judge of Israel. Judges 12.8–10.

Ica (ē'kä), city (1969 est. pop. 69,400), capital of Ica dept., SW Peru, on the Pan-American Highway. It is a commercial center for the cotton, wool, and wine produced in the region. There are several summer resorts nearby. Ica is also the archaeological name of the Chincha empire of ancient Peru, which had one of its major centers in the adjacent valley. The empire fell to the Inca in the 15th cent. The Spanish settled the city in 1563. In Ica is the shrine of Our Lord of Luren, the site of colorful pilgrimages. The city has twice been leveled by earthquakes.

Içá, river, Brazil: see PUTUMAYO.

Icaria, Greece: see IKARÍA.

Icarus: see DAEDALUS.

Icarus, in astronomy: see ASTEROID.

Icaza, Jorge (hôr'hā ēkä'sä), 1906–, Ecuadorian novelist. Icaza writes in harsh, realistic terms against the exploitation of the Indian. His novel *En las calles* [in the streets] won him acclaim in 1935. Among his other works are the novels *Huasipungo* (1934), *Cholos* (1938), and *El chulla Romero y Flores* (1958) and the short stories collected in *Relatos* (1969).

Icazbalceta, Joaquín García: see GARCÍA ICAZBALCETA, JOAQUÍN.

ICBM: see GUIDED MISSILE.

ice: see WATER.

Ice Age: see PLEISTOCENE EPOCH.

Ice Age National Scientific Reserve: see NATIONAL PARKS AND MONUMENTS (table).

iceberg, mass of ice that has become detached, or calved, from the edge of an ice sheet or glacier and is floating on the ocean. Only about one ninth of the total mass of a berg projects above the water. Gravel and boulders carried by icebergs are gradually dropped to the ocean floor as the iceberg melts. By studying these materials, scientists have been able to determine the maximum range of icebergs during glacial periods. Greenland is the source of most of the icebergs in the N Atlantic, where the iceberg season lasts roughly from February to October. As a consequence of the loss of the *Titanic* through collision with an iceberg in 1912, a patrol of N Atlantic shipping channels was initiated in 1914 by the international agreement of 16 nations primarily concerned. In maintaining its share of this patrol the U.S. coast guard uses planes and surface vessels equipped with radar, loran, and underwater sound equipment. A constant census of bergs is maintained, and the location of an iceberg is reported to any ship in its vicinity.

iceboating, sport of sailing a specially prepared boat equipped with runners over ice. The first iceboats were probably sailed by the Dutch during the 18th cent., although the Finns and Lapps may have built similar vehicles at a much earlier date. During the 19th cent. in the United States iceboating was a popular winter sport among wealthy residents of the Hudson River area. They usually built huge and elaborately equipped vehicles, some of which had sails larger than 600 sq ft (183 sq m). In the 20th cent., however, the center of American iceboating shifted to the Midwest, where persons of more modest means built and maintained their own relatively small boats. In Europe iceboating was a very popular sport before World War II, with races held annually by the European Ice Yachting Union. Since the war, however, only Sweden continued regular competition. Iceboats are rated according to size of sail. The largest racing boats today have sails measuring 350 sq ft (107 sq m); the smallest sails are about 75 sq ft (23 sq m). Well-constructed boats can attain speeds up to 100 mi (161 km) per hr. One of the more interesting properties of an iceboat is that, under proper conditions, it can actually travel faster than the prevailing breeze; in a 10-mi (16.1-km) per hr wind, for example, an ice boat may travel up to 40 mi (64 km) per hr. The Ice Yacht Challenge Pennant of America (est. 1881) is open to boats of any size and is generally considered the most prestigious award in American iceboating.

icebreaker, ship of special hull design and wide beam, with relatively flat bottom, designed to force its way through ice. When the icebreaker charges into the ice at full speed, its sharply inclined bow, meeting the edge of the ice, rises upon it, and the weight of the vessel causes the ice to collapse. A well-designed icebreaker is able to force its way through ice up to 35 ft (10.7 m) thick. In many northern seaports, especially in the Soviet Union, Canada, and the Great Lakes area of the United States, all water-borne traffic in winter is made possible by the use of icebreakers. The first notable icebreaker was the *Pilot* (1870), used to maintain communication between Kronstadt and St. Petersburg. In 1959 the Soviet Union launched its first nuclear-powered icebreaker, the *Lenin*. Icebreakers have been widely used in the exploration of the Arctic and the Antarctic. In 1969 the *Manhattan*, a huge oil tanker fitted with an ice-breaking bow, successfully navigated a Northwest Passage from Newfoundland to Alaska's Prudhoe Bay, opening a new route to Arctic oil fields.

ice cream, sweet frozen food, made from milk fat and solids, sugar, flavoring, a stabilizer (usually gelatin), and sometimes eggs, fruits, or nuts. The mix is churned at freezing temperature to attain a light, smooth texture. Water ices existed in the Roman Empire, and Marco Polo brought back from the Far East reports of ice-flavored foods. From Italy the confection spread to France and England, reaching America early in the 18th cent. The manufacture of ice cream in the United States on a commercial scale began in 1851 in Baltimore and has become an important industry. Commercial ice cream is pasteurized and homogenized. Federal, state, local, and industry regulations as to percentage of milk fats and solids, purity of ingredients, and cleanliness of preparation and dispensing are designed to maintain the dietary value of ice cream and to inhibit bacterial multiplication, for which ice cream is a favorable medium. Similar frozen confections include the fat-rich bisque (with added bakery products), parfait (containing eggs), and mousse; frozen custard, generally low in fat; and ices and plain or milk sherbets, based on fruit juices and sugar.

Ice Fjord, Spitsbergen: see ISFJORDEN.

ice hockey: see HOCKEY, ICE.

İçel, Turkey: see MERSİN.

Iceland, Icel. *Ísland,* republic (1972 pop. 207,174), 39,698 sq mi (102,819 sq km), the westernmost state of Europe, occupying an island in the Atlantic Ocean just S of the Arctic Circle, c.600 mi (970 km) W of Norway and c.180 mi (290 km) SE of Greenland. REYKJAVÍK is the capital. The republic includes several small islands, notably the VESTMANNAEYJAR off the southern coast of Iceland. Deep fjords indent the coasts, particularly in the north and west. The island itself is a geologically young basalt plateau, averaging 2,000 ft (610 m) in height (Öraefajökull, c.6,950 ft/2,120 m high, is the highest point) and culminating in vast icefields, of which the Vatnajökull, in the southeast, is the largest. There are about 200 volcanoes, many of them still active; the highest is Mt. Hekla (c.4,900 ft/1,490 m). Hot springs abound and are used for inexpensive heating; the great Geysir is particularly famous. The watershed of Iceland runs roughly east-west; the chief river, the Jökulsá, flows N into the Axarfjörður (there are several other rivers of the same name). Only about one fourth of the island is habitable, and practically all the larger inhabited places are located on the coast; they are Reykjavík, Akureyri, HAFNARFJÖRÐUR, SIGLUFJÖRÐUR, AKRANES, and ISAFJÖRÐUR. The climate is relatively mild and humid (especially in the west and south), owing to the proximity of the North Atlantic Drift; however, N and E Iceland have a polar, tundralike climate. Grasses predominate; timber is virtually absent, and much of the land is barren. About 15% of the land is potentially productive, but agriculture,

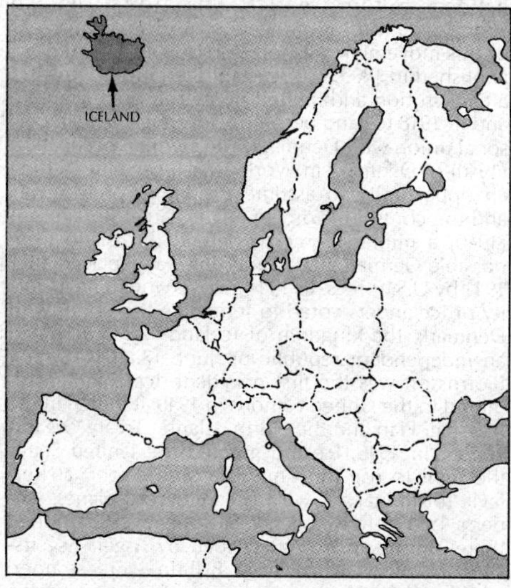

cultivating mainly hay, potatoes, and turnips, is restricted to .5% of the total area. Fruits and vegetables are raised in greenhouses. There are extensive grazing lands, used mainly for sheep raising, but also for horses and cattle. Fishing is the most important industry, with codfish and herring the chief exports. Aside from aluminum smelting, Iceland has little heavy industry and relies on imports for many of the necessities and luxuries of life. Most trade is with the United States and Europe. In 1968 the per capita national income was $1,487. Iceland is governed by parliamentary democracy, with a cabinet responsible to the ALTHING and a president elected by popular vote for a four-year term. The four major parties are the Independence, the Social Democratic, the Progressive, and the Labor Alliance. The republic possesses neither an army nor a navy. The government plays a major part in the economic life of the country and has established monopolies on the import and sale of several important articles. Social welfare legislation is extensive. The Lutheran Church is the sole established church, but there is complete religious freedom. The official language is Icelandic (Old Norse). Virtually all Icelanders are literate; they read more books per capita than any other people in the world. There is a university (est. 1911) at Reykjavík.

Settlement and Subjection. Iceland may be the Ultima THULE of the ancients. Irish monks visited it before the 9th cent. but abandoned it on the arrival (c.850–875) of Norse settlers, many of whom had fled from the domination of HAROLD I. The Norse settlements also contained Scottish and Irish slaves. In 930 a general assembly, the Althing, was established near Reykjavík at Thingvellir, and Christianity was introduced c.1000 by the Norwegian Olaf I, although paganism seems to have survived for a time. These events are preserved in the literature of 13th-century Iceland, where OLD NORSE LITERATURE reached its greatest flowering. (Modern Icelandic is virtually the same language as that of the sagas.) Politically, Iceland became a feudal state, and the bloody civil wars of rival chieftains facilitated Norwegian intervention. The attempt of SNORRI STURLUSON (1179–1241) to establish the full control of King Haakon IV of Norway over Iceland was a failure; however, Haakon incorporated Iceland into the archdiocese of Trondheim and between 1261 and 1264 obtained acknowledgment of his suzerainty by the Icelanders. Norwegian rule brought order, but high taxes and an imposed judicial system caused much discontent. When, with Norway, Iceland passed (1380) under the Danish crown, the Danes showed even less concern for Icelandic welfare; a national decline (1400–1550) set in. Lutheranism was imposed by force (1539–51) over the opposition of Bishop Jon ARESSON; the Reformation brought new intellectual activity. The 17th and 18th cent. were, in many ways, disastrous for Iceland. English, Spanish, and Algerian pirates raided the coasts and ruined trade; epidemics and volcanic eruptions killed a large part of the population; and the creation (1602) of a private trading company at Copenhagen, with exclusive rights to the Iceland trade, caused economic ruin. The private trade monopoly was at last revoked in 1771 and transferred to the Danish crown, and in 1786 trade with Iceland was opened to all Danish and Norwegian merchants. The exclusion of foreign traders was lifted in 1854.

National Revival. The 19th cent. brought a rebirth of national culture (see ICELANDIC LITERATURE) and strong agitation for independence. The great leader of this movement was Jón SIGURÐSSON. The Althing, abolished in 1800, was reestablished in 1843; in 1874 a constitution and limited home rule were granted; and in 1918 Iceland became a sovereign state in personal union with Denmark. The German occupation (1940) of Denmark in World War II gave the Althing an opportunity to assume the king's prerogatives and the control of foreign affairs. Great Britain sent (1940) a military force to defend the island from possible German attack, and this was replaced after 1941 by U.S. forces. In 1944 an overwhelming majority of Icelanders voted to terminate the union with Denmark; the kingdom of Iceland was proclaimed an independent republic on June 17, 1944. Sveinn Björrnsson was the first president. Iceland was admitted to the United Nations in 1946; it joined in the Marshall Plan and the North Atlantic Treaty Organization. In 1946, Iceland granted the United States the right to use the American-built airport at Keflavík for military as well as commercial planes. Under a 1951 defense pact, U.S. troops were stationed there. Björnsson was succeeded by Ásgeir Ásgeirsson. Relations with Great Britain were strained when Iceland, in order to protect its vital fishing industry, extended (1958) the limits of its territorial waters from 4 to 12 mi (6.4–19.3 km). The conflict, which at times led to exchanges of fire between Icelandic coast guard vessels and British destroyers, was resolved in 1961 when Great Britain accepted the new limits. Kristjárn Eldjárn was elected president in 1968 and 1972. Iceland joined the European Free Trade Association in 1970. In 1971 elections the Independence party–Social Democratic party coalition government, which had governed for 12 years, lost its majority. A leftist coalition, composed of the Progressive party, the Communist-led Labor Alliance party, and the Liberal Left party, came to power. The dispute with Britain over fishing rights was renewed in 1972 when Iceland unilaterally extended its territorial waters to 50 mi (80 km) offshore and forbade foreign fishing vessels in the new zone. Following confrontations between British warships and Icelandic coast guard vessels, an interim agreement was reached in Oct., 1973, whereby, reportedly, the British would limit their annual catch and restrict themselves to certain fishing areas and specified numbers and types of vessels. In Jan., 1973, the Helgafell volcano on Heimaey island erupted, damaging the town of Vestmannaeyjar. Later in the year Iceland and the United States began revising the 1951 defense pact, with a view toward ending the U.S. military presence. In May, 1974, the Althing was dissolved following a split in the ruling coalition over economic policies. In the June elections the Independence party won a large plurality and formed a new government. See V. H. Malmström, *A Regional Geography of Iceland* (1958); Amalia Líndal, *Ripples from Iceland* (1962); Barthi Guthmundsson, *The Origin of the Icelanders* (tr. 1967); W. H. Auden and Louis MacNeice, *Letters from Iceland* (1969); J. C. Griffiths, *Modern Iceland* (1969); Benedikt Gröndal, *Iceland: From Neutrality to NATO Membership* (1971); Vilhjalmur Stefansson, *Iceland: The First American Republic* (1939, repr. 1971).

Icelandic language, member of the North Germanic, or Scandinavian, group of the Germanic subfamily of the Indo-European family of languages. Spoken chiefly by about 200,000 people in Iceland, it stems from Old Norse, the language of the Vikings who settled in Iceland in the 9th cent. (see GERMANIC LANGUAGES; NORSE). The beginning of the modern period of the Icelandic language may be said to date from the translation of the New Testament in 1540 by Oddur Gottskálksson. Before that date the language is considered Old Icelandic, which is classified as belonging to the western branch of Old Norse. Unlike the other Scandinavian languages, Icelandic is noted for its conservatism in grammar, vocabulary, and spelling. For instance, it still has three genders (masculine, feminine, and neuter) and four cases for nouns (nominative, genitive, dative, and accusative), which survive from Viking times. Verbs have a highly developed inflectional system. In matters of vocabulary, there has been a strong purist movement for several centuries. For example, instead of directly adopting modern scientific terms, Icelandic renders them by translations or by newly created compounds and expressions formed from native words. Actually, Modern Icelandic has changed so little from its parent language, Old Norse, in the course of the centuries that Icelanders today read the Eddas and sagas of Old Norse literature more easily than the English and the Americans read Shakespeare. One reason for the relative stability and purity of Icelandic is that its speakers lived for centuries in comparative isolation on an island and thus were not much influenced by other languages. The Roman alphabet came to Iceland c.1000, along with Christianity. To it have been added several symbols: ð (pronounced *th*, as in *then*), þ (pronounced *th*, as in *think*), æ, and ö. In addition, six letters may take the acute accent: *á, é, í, ó, ú*, and *ý*. See Stefán Einarsson, *Icelandic: Grammar, Texts, Glossary* (1949); K. G. Chapman, *Icelandic-Norwegian Linguistic Relationships* (1962).

Icelandic literature. For the earliest literature of Iceland, see OLD NORSE LITERATURE. With the loss of Iceland's political independence (1261–64) came a decline in literature, though the linguistic tradition continued and the old writings were still venerated. In the 13th and 14th cent. the sagas of antiquity flourished; many were based on Eddic poems (see EDDA). Chivalric romances appeared c.1300, emphasizing classical and ecclesiastical themes and showing French influence. After 1550, German and Danish influences were strong. From the 14th cent. to the middle of the 16th, much literary activity was spent in translating foreign works, in copying and compiling Old Norse works, and in writing religious poems in the old meters. In the 14th cent. the rímur was developed; this metrically ingenious narrative poetry based on the sagas was popular until the 19th cent. and was revived in the 20th cent. The Protestant Reformation, thrust upon Iceland in the 16th cent., turned literary emphasis to hymns and illuminations of the Protestant faith. Einar Sigurdsson (1538–1626) was the great spiritual poet of the age. The first printing press was brought to Iceland in 1528 by Bishop Jón ARESSON, but from the Reformation until the late 18th cent. it was under church control. Secular works, however, were circulated in manuscript. The great secular poets of the 17th cent. were Hallgrímur Petursson (1614–74), author of the superb *Passion Hymns*, and the satirical Stefan Olafsson (1620–88). Árni MAGNUSSON, a noted literary antiquarian, compiled a library of ancient Icelandic masterpieces at this time. In 1773 a printing press was established for publishing secular works, and there followed the formation of a number of literary societies. Neoclassicism dominated literary style in the late 18th cent. A romantic revival, begun in the 1830s, brought to Icelandic literature a productivity and excellence unknown since the Eddas and sagas. Influenced both by the newly aroused nationalism and by continental romanticism, the revival was begun by the poets Bjarni Thorarensen (1786–1841) and Jónas Hallgrímsson (1807–45). The first writer of the modern Icelandic short story, Hallgrímsson also influenced Jón THÓRODDSEN, who wrote the first published Icelandic novel. This movement, whose practitioners created the classical Icelandic style of the 19th and 20th cent., was continued by Grimur Thomsen (1820–96), writer of heroic narrative poems; Benedikt Grondal (1826–1907), romantic and humorous poet; Steingrímur Thorsteinsson (1831–1913), lyric poet, satirist, and translator; and Matthías Jochumsson (1835–1920), whose plays were the real beginning of modern Icelandic drama. The towering figure of the period was the historian and statesman Jón SIGURÐSSON. The founding of the periodical *Verdandi* [the present], in 1882, marked the advent of a new realism, strongly socialistic, individualistic, and anticlerical. The movement was much influenced by the Danish critic Georg BRANDES. Among the notable realists were the short-story writer, reformer, and social critic Gestur Palsson (1852–91); the brilliant Icelandic-Canadian poet Stephan G. Stephansson (1853–1927); and the anticlerical satirist and lyric poet Thorsteinn Erlingsson (1858–1914). One of the most significant Icelandic writers of this period was Einar H. Kvaran (1859–1938). At first a realist, he later wrote of religious affirmation through spiritualism in short stories about the poor in Reykjavík. Jón Trausti (pseud. of Guðmundur Magnusson, 1873–1918) wrote of modern rural and town life and also of medieval Iceland in a series of superb novels and short stories. The 20th cent. saw the rise of a more introspective writing, influenced by the ideas of Nietzsche and by the French symbolists. One group of writers, part of the Icelandic colony in Copenhagen, wrote in Danish to reach a wider public. They were led by Johann Sigurjonsson (1880–1919), a romantic dramatist. Others were Gunnar GUNNARSSON, the romantic novelist of the Icelandic family saga, and the cosmopolitan dramatist Guðmundur KAMBAN. A neoromantic movement arose in the 1920s, which had as a leading spirit the poet, scholar, and critic Sigurdur Nordal, author of the prose poem *Hel* (1919), a work of great originality and lyric beauty. Among the neoromantics were the novelists Guðmundur Hagalin and Kristmann GUÐMUNDSSON and the lyric poets Davið Stefánsson and Stefan Sigurdsson. With the urbanization of Iceland's population came the rise of a working class and new patterns of life and thought. Kamban and Trausti early became socialists; Hagalin turned from conservative journalism to become thoroughly identified with the new socialist middle class. The most gifted writer to reach prominence in this period was the Nobel laureate Halldor K. LAXNESS. The establishment of British and American bases in Iceland during World War II introduced foreign literary influence, and Icelandic independence (1944) increased nationalist and patriotic emphasis. In the 1950s the introspective "atom poets," including Stefan H. Grimsson and Hannes Sigfursson, were acclaimed. Major contemporary writers include Agnar Thórðarson, Elias Mar, Oddur Björnsson, and Jökull Jakobsson. See Stefan Einarsson, *History of Icelandic Prose Writers, 1800–1940* (1948) and *A History of Icelandic Literature* (1957); Richard Beck, *History of Icelandic Poets, 1800–1940* (1950); Gabriel Turville-Petre, *Origins of Icelandic Literature* (1953); Gwyn Jones, ed., *Eirik the Red, and Other Icelandic Sagas* (1961).

Iceland moss: see LICHEN.

Iceland spar, colorless variety of crystallized CALCITE, characterized by its properties of transparency and double refraction. It is used chiefly in the manufacture of NICOL PRISMS, which are essential parts of polarizing microscopes and other optical instruments. The principal deposit is in Iceland, but small quantities are found in other countries, including the United States and Mexico.

ice plant, low, fleshy plant (*Cryophytum crystalinum*) of warm, dry, barren regions. It is cultivated chiefly as a curiosity because of its leaves, densely coated with small, glistening, bladder-shaped hairs. The ice plant and many other related herbs (e.g., New Zealand spinach), often with fantastic shapes, were formerly combined in the genus *Mesembryantheum.* They grow in abundance in South Africa, whence many had been introduced to European botanical gardens by 1600. Ice plants are classified in the division MAGNOLIOPHYTA, class Magnoliopsida, order Caryophyllales, family Aizoaceae.

Ichabod (ĭk'əbŏd) [Heb.,=inglorious], son of Phinehas and grandson of Eli. He was born at the hour of the capture of the Ark by the Philistines and was named to commemorate the unfortunate event. 1 Sam. 4.21; 14.3.

I-ch'ang or **Ichang** (both: ē-chäng), city (1970 est. pop. 160,000), SW Hupeh prov., China, a river port on the Yangtze. It is the western terminus for large oceangoing vessels traveling up the Yangtze from Shanghai; there goods are transshipped to smaller boats that can negotiate the gorges and rapids of the Yangtze. The gorges above the city are noted for their scenic beauty. I-ch'ang has food-processing and cement industries.

Ichihara (ēchē'härä), city (1970 pop. 156,016), Chiba prefecture, central Honshu, Japan, on Tokyo Bay. It is an industrial city with important petrochemical, shipbuilding, and steel industries.

Ichikawa (ēchē'käwä), city (1970 pop. 261,055), Chiba prefecture, central Honshu, Japan, on the Edo River. It is an industrial city with metallurgical, chemical, textile, and foodstuff industries.

Ichinomiya (ēchĭnō'mēyä), city (1970 pop. 219,274), Aichi prefecture, central Honshu, Japan. It is an industrial satellite of Nagoya and has spinning, weaving, and metallurgical industries.

ichneumon: see MONGOOSE.

ichneumon fly (ĭknōō'mən), common name for a family of INSECTS, related to the WASPS, whose larvae are parasitic on many other insects. Over 3,000 species of ichneumon flies, also known as ichneumon wasps, are found throughout the United States except in the Southwest. The female has an extremely long ovipositor capable of piercing through several inches of insect-infested tree trunk to the caterpillars and other larvae within. When the eggs hatch, the ichneumon larvae feed on the body of the host. One species parasitizes the aquatic larva of the caddisfly, and the female must dive to the underwater burrow of the host to deposit her eggs. Ichneumon flies are harmless to humans and trees, and in fact help to keep many insect pests under control. Other wasps, such as the braconid wasps, are also larval parasites of insect hosts. Ichneumon flies are classified in the phylum ARTHROPODA, class Insecta, order Hymenoptera, family Ichneumonidae.

Ickes, Harold LeClaire (ĭk'ēz), 1874–1952, American statesman, b. Blair co., Pa. As a Chicago newspaper reporter and later as a lawyer, he became interested in local reform politics. Originally a Republican, he joined (1912) the Progressive party and became that party's state leader, but he returned to the Republican party in 1916. President Franklin Delano Roosevelt appointed (1933) Ickes Secretary of the Interior and also made him head of the Public Works Administration (PWA). During World War II he was also administrator in control of the country's fuel resources. Ickes came into frequent conflict with business interests both as a conservationist and because of the public programs he set up. On the other hand he was criticized for spending PWA money too slowly to make an immediate impact on the depression. President Truman accepted Ickes's resignation (1946) from the cabinet in an argument over Truman's nomination of Edwin W. Pauley, an oil executive, as Undersecretary of the Navy. Ickes's reputation for outspoken bluntness is upheld by his *New Democracy* (1934) and *The Autobiography of a Curmudgeon* (1943). His *Secret Diary* (3 vol. 1953–54) provides a valuable view of the New Deal.

Icknield Street (ĭk'nēld), name for a prehistoric road in England, extending SW from the Wash, along the line of the Chiltern Hills and Berkshire Downs, to Salisbury Plain.

Icolmkill, Scotland: see IONA.

icon [Gr. *eikon*=image], single image created as a focal point of religious veneration, especially a painted or carved portable object of the Orthodox Eastern faith. Icons commonly represent Christ Pantocrator, the Virgin as Queen of the Heavens, or, less frequently, the saints; since the 6th cent. they have been considered an aid to the devotee in making his prayers heard by the holy figure represented in the icon. The icon grew out of the mosaic and fresco tradition of early Byzantine art (see BYZANTINE ART AND ARCHITECTURE). It was used to decorate the wall and floor surfaces of churches, baptisteries, and sepulchers, and later was carried on standards in time of war and in religious processions. Although the art form was in common use by the end of the 5th cent., early monuments have been lost, largely because of their destruction during the iconoclastic controversy (726–843; see ICONOCLASM). Little has survived that was created before the 10th cent. Byzantine icons were produced in great numbers until 1453, when Constantinople fell to the Ottoman Empire. The practice was transplanted to Russia, where icons were made until the Revolution (see RUSSIAN ART AND ARCHITECTURE). The anonymous artists of the Orthodox Eastern faith were concerned not with the conquest of space and movement as seen in the development of Western painting but instead with the portrayal of the symbolic or mystical aspects of the divine being. The stiff and conventionalized appearance of icons may bear some relationship to the two-dimensional, ornamental quality of the Oriental tradition. It is this effect more than any other that causes the icons in Byzantine and later in Russian and Greek Orthodox art to appear unchanging through the centuries; there is, however, a stylistic evolution in Byzanto-Russian art that can be seen through variations of a standard theme by local schools rather than through the development of an art style by periods. The term *icon* came to mean "subject matter" in the 19th-century German school of art historical study, and from this meaning were derived the terms ICONOGRAPHY and *iconology*. See V. K. Lazarev, *Russian Icons* (1962); Anneliese Schröder, *Introduction to Icons* (tr. 1967); Kurt Weitzmann et al., ed., *A Treasure of Icons* (tr. 1968); Heinz Skrobucha, *The World of Icons* (tr. 1971).

Icon Basilike: see EIKON BASILIKE.

Iconium (īkō'nēəm), ancient city of Asia Minor, the modern KONYA, Turkey. In ancient days it was at various times in Phrygia, Lycaonia, and Cappadocia, as the bounds of those regions changed. It was also for a time included in the Roman province of Galatia. It was visited by Paul, who converted part of the Greek and Jewish population and established an important church there (Acts 13.51,52; 14.19,21). In the 3d cent. A.D., Iconium became an active Christian colony.

iconoclasm (īkŏn'ōklăzəm) [Gr.,=image breaking], opposition to the religious use of images. Veneration of pictures and statues symbolizing sacred figures, Christian doctrine, and biblical events was an early feature of Christian worship (see ICONOGRAPHY; CATACOMBS). To combat the sort of heresy that denied the true humanity of Christ, the reality of Christ's humanity was increasingly emphasized, and images and crucifixes became common. Opponents of their use claimed they led to idolatry. Canon 36 of the Synod of Elvira (c.305) was one of the earliest to prohibit images in churches, "lest that which is worshiped and venerated be depicted on the walls." After the 5th cent. the increasingly superstitious practices of the masses reinforced this opinion. Iconoclasm flourished in Asia Minor, especially around Constantinople, in the 8th and 9th cent. The movement may have been influenced by the iconoclasm of Islam, Judaism, and Manichaeism and was certainly strengthened by the numerous PAULICIANS in the empire. LEO III, CONSTANTINE V, LEO IV, and LEO V were important iconoclastic emperors. Opponents of iconoclasm were Popes GREGORY II and ADRIAN I and Empress IRENE, who restored the images; St. THEODORE OF STUDIUM and St. JOHN OF DAMASCUS; and St. NICEPHORUS and St. Theophanes, who wrote histories of the controversy. Iconoclasm was rejected at Nicaea (see NICAEA, SECOND COUNCIL OF) but ended only during the minority of MICHAEL III. The iconoclastic controversy stimulated Byzantine artists to strive for spiritual revelation in religious art rather than for naturalistic representation. The churches of the Orthodox Eastern Church are generally decorated only with flat pictures, bas-reliefs, and mosaics (see BYZANTINE ART). Iconoclasm was also a feature of the Protestant Reformation. The Puritans were especially hostile to the use of religious images, and some Protestants still consider their use idolatrous. See E. J. Martin, *A History of the Iconoclastic Controversy* (1930).

iconography (ī"kŏnŏg'rəfē) [Gr.,=image-drawing] or **iconology** [Gr.,=image-study], in art history, study and interpretation of figural representations, either individual or symbolic, religious or secular; more broadly, the art of representation by pictures or images, which may or may not have a symbolic as well as an apparent or superficial meaning. When first used in the 18th cent. the term was confined to the study of engravings, which were then the standard mode of illustrating books on art and on antiquities in general. But it came shortly to be applied more specifically to the history and classification of Christian images and symbols of all sorts, in whatever medium they happened to be rendered originally or in whatever way they were reproduced for study. With the rise of the systematic investigation of art from prehistoric ages to modern times, it became apparent that each major phase or epoch in which figural representations occur had created and developed in varying degrees of richness and elaboration an iconography of its own. As used today, therefore, the term is necessarily qualified to indicate the field of iconographic study under discussion—e.g., the iconography of the various Egyptian deities, the iconography of Roman imperial portraits, early Christian iconography, Buddhist or Hindu iconography, Byzantine iconography, Gothic iconography. As a method of scholarly research the science of iconography strives also to recover and express the thought from which a given convention of representation has arisen, particularly when the convention has assumed the value of a symbol. The importance of identifying motifs is central to iconographical interpretation. For example, St. Catherine of Alexandria is traditionally portrayed in the presence of a wheel. This wheel is a familiar attribute that serves to identify her and that at the same time signifies a miracle connected with her martyrdom. Some attributes are more difficult to understand, and their obscurity has led scholars to consult other images or literary sources in order to interpret the motif more satisfactorily. Certain themes characteristic of a specific philosophy have been commonly represented during an era, and an iconography has been developed to express them. An example is the still life *vanitas vanitatum* of the Middle Ages, a reminder of the transitory quality of earthly pleasure symbolized by a skull, candle, and hourglass (or, in later versions, a watch). In every living art the conventions and symbols, as well as their meanings, change with the passage of time and the growth of ideas; many disappear, while others become almost unintelligible to a later generation and can be recovered only by intensive study. Among the foremost scholars in iconographic studies are Didron, Émile Mâle, Aby Warburg, and Erwin Panofsky. **Christian iconography,** by reason of its long history and the dynamic concepts that controlled its growth, is richer and more varied than that of any other art. Beginning with the catacomb frescoes in the early centuries of the Christian era, it deals with the perils faced by the human soul on earth in its journey toward eternal salvation. Figures from the Old Testament (e.g., Abraham, Judith and Holofernes), episodes from the life and passion of Christ (e.g., the Nativity, the Descent from the Cross, the Pietà), scenes from the life of the Virgin Mary (e.g., the Sacred Conversation, the Visitation), scenes from the lives of the saints (e.g., St. Francis Receiving the Stigmata, St. Jerome in the Wilderness, the Martyrdom of St. Agatha), and symbolic scenes of ultimate beatitude (e.g., the Majesty, the Savior of the World, the Coronation of the Virgin), all reveal the same purpose—to repeat in many forms and inculcate in every mind the moral aims and fundamental dogmas of the Christian religion. A long series of evolutionary stages unfolds in the representation of a given person or scene from the art of the catacombs to that of the Gothic cathedrals. Thus the art of the Middle Ages is above all a kind of sacred writing whose system of characters, i.e., the iconography, had to be learned by every artist. It was governed also by a kind of sacred mathematics, in which position, grouping, symmetry, and number were of extraordinary importance and were themselves an integral part of the iconography. From earliest times Christian iconography has likewise been a symbolic code, showing men one thing and inviting them to see in it the figure of another. Some examples are: the dove, which figures the Holy Spirit; the fish, symbol of Christ, from the Greek *icthus*, an anagram for Jesus Christ, Son of God, Savior; the monkey or reptile as symbol of evil; and the bowl or pitcher of water and the vase of lilies that signify the Virgin's purity in the Annunciation scene. In Christian art, form is thus merely the vehicle of spiritual meaning; in the expression and reading of this meaning lies the essence of Christian iconography. See Erwin Panofsky, *Studies in Iconology* (1939, repr. 1962); George Ferguson, *Signs and Symbols in Christian Art* (2d ed. 1955); A. N. Didron, *Christian Iconography* (2 vol., tr. 1851–86, repr. 1965); Gertrude Schiller, *Iconography of Christian Art* (tr. 1971).

icosahedron (īkō"səhē'drən): see POLYHEDRON.

Ictinus (ĭktī'nəs), fl. 2d half of 5th cent. B.C., one of the greatest architects of Greece. His celebrated work is the Parthenon (447–432 B.C.) upon the Acropolis at Athens, which he built with the architect Callicrates as associate. Ictinus also built the temple of Apollo Epicurius at Bassae, near Phigalia, c.430 B.C. and is said to have rebuilt the Telesterion at Eleusis.

id: see PSYCHOANALYSIS.

Ida, Mount (ī'də), Gr. *Ídhi*, 8,058 ft (2,456 m) high, central Crete, Greece; the highest mountain on Crete.

Idaho (ī'dəhō), state (1970 pop. 713,008), 83,557 sq mi (216,413 sq km), NW United States, one of the Rocky Mt. states, admitted as the 43d state of the Union in 1890. The capital and largest city is BOISE; other cities of importance are POCATELLO and IDAHO FALLS. Idaho is bounded on the N by the Canadian province of British Columbia, on the NE by Montana, on the E by Wyoming, on the S by Utah and Nevada, and on the W by Oregon and Washington. From the northern Panhandle, where Idaho is about 45 mi (72 km) wide, the state broadens S of the Bitterroot Range to 310 mi (499 km) in width. Much of Idaho has a primitive and unspoiled natural beauty,

with rugged slopes and towering peaks, a vast expanse of timberland, scenic lakes, wild rivers, cascades, and spectacular gorges. Hells Canyon, which at one point is 7,900 ft (2408 m) below the mountaintops, is the deepest gorge in North America. The climate of the state ranges from hot summers in the arid southern basins to cold, snowy winters in the high wilderness areas of central and northern Idaho. Across S Idaho the Snake River flows in a great arc; with its tributaries the river has been harnessed to produce hydroelectric power and to reclaim vast areas of dry but fertile land. To the N of the Snake River valley, in central and north central Idaho, are the massive Sawtooth Mts. and the Salmon River Mts., which shelter some of the most magnificent wilderness areas remaining in the United States, including the Selway Bitterroot Wilderness Area and the Idaho Primitive Area. In the central and north central regions and in the Panhandle there are tremendous expanses of national forests covering approximately two fifths of the state and constituting the largest gross area of national forests in any state except California. The state's jagged granite peaks include Mt. Borah, which reaches an altitude of 12,662 ft (3,859 m). Rushing rivers such as the Salmon and the Clearwater, and many lakes, notably Lake Pend Oreille, Lake Coeur d'Alene (often described as one of the world's loveliest), and Priest Lake, as well as the state's mountain areas, make Idaho a superb fish and game preserve and vacation land. The state is especially inviting to campers, anglers, and hunters (Idaho has one of the largest elk herds in the nation). Agriculture is still the most important sector of the state's economy. Cattle and calves are the leading agricultural products; dairy products are also important. Idaho's chief crops are potatoes (for which the state is nationally famous), hay, wheat, and sugar beets. Food processing is the chief industry; lumber and wood products and chemicals are other major manufactured items. Since the 1950s and 1960s tourism has become a major industry in Idaho; about 6 million people visit the state annually. Mining, once a major source of income, and still economically important, has been surpassed by agriculture, manufacturing, and tourism in annual income earned. Silver, antimony, phosphate rock, lead, and zinc are the principal minerals produced. Probably the first white men to enter the area that is now Idaho were members of the Lewis and Clark expedition in 1805. They were not far ahead of the fur traders who came to the region shortly thereafter. A Canadian, David Thompson of the North West Company, established the first trading post in Idaho in 1809. The next year traders from St. Louis penetrated the mountains, and Andrew Henry of the Missouri Fur Company established a post near present-day Rexburg, the first American trading post established in the area. In this period the fortunes of the Idaho region were wrapped up with those of the Columbia River region, and the area encompassed by what is now the state of Idaho was part of Oregon country, held jointly by the United States and Great Britain from 1818 to 1846. Fur traders in an expedition sent out by John Jacob Astor came to the Snake River region to trap for furs after having established (1811) a trading post at Astoria on the Columbia River. In 1821 two British trading companies operating in the Idaho region, the North West Company and the Hudson's Bay Company, were joined together as the Hudson's Bay Company which, after 1824, came into competition with American MOUNTAIN MEN also trapping in the area. By the 1840s the two groups had severely depleted the region's fur supply. Early American visitors to the area included the American army officer and trader, Benjamin L. E. Bonneville (1832); Nathaniel Wyeth, the explorer and trader, who in 1834 founded Fort Hall not far from Fort Boise; Henry Spaulding, chief assistant of missionary Marcus Whitman and founder (1836) of a mission at Lapwai, near present-day Lewiston; and John C. Frémont and Kit Carson, who passed through Idaho in 1843. Father P. J. De Smet, a Jesuit who did extensive missionary work in the West, also came to Idaho where he founded a mission. In 1846 the United States gained sole claim to Oregon country south of the 49th parallel by the Oregon Treaty with Great Britain. The area was established as a territory in 1848. Idaho still had no permanent settlement when Oregon Territory became a state in 1859 and the eastern part of Idaho was added to Washington Territory. A Mormon outpost founded at Franklin in 1860 is considered the first permanent settlement, but it was not until the discovery of gold that settlers poured into Idaho. Gold was discovered on the Clearwater River in 1860, on the Salmon in 1861, in the Boise River basin in 1862, and gold and silver were found in the Owyhee River country in 1863. The usual rush of settlers followed, along with the spectacular but ephemeral growth of towns. Most of these settlements are only ghost towns now, but the many settlers who poured in during the gold rush—mainly from Washington, Oregon, and California, with smaller numbers from the east—formed a population large enough to demand new government administration, and Idaho Territory was set up in 1863. The Indians, mostly Kootenai, Nez Percé, Western Shoshone, Bannock, Coeur d'Alene, and Pend d'Oreille, became upset by the incursion of whites and some attacked white settlements. The Federal government had subdued the northern tribes in 1858 and put most of the Indians on reservations. The Bannock were defeated in 1863 and again in 1878. In 1876–77 the Nez Percé Indians, led by Chief Joseph, made their heroic but unsuccessful attempt to flee to Canada while being pursued by U.S. troops. The late 19th cent. also witnessed the growth of cattle and sheep ranching, along with the strife that developed between the two groups of ranchers over grazing areas. A new mining boom started in 1882 with the discovery of gold in the Coeur d'Alene, and although the gold strike ended in disappointment, it prefaced the discovery there of some of the richest silver mines in the world. Coeur d'Alene and Kellogg became notable mining centers, and the Bunker Hill and Sullivan (a lead mine) became one of the most famous of mines. Severe labor troubles there at the end of the century led to political uprisings. Frank Steunenberg, who as governor had used Federal troops to put down the uprisings, was assassinated in 1905. The trial of William Haywood and others accused of involvement in the murder drew national attention and marked the beginning of the long career of William E. Borah (who had prosecuted the mine leaders) as an outstanding Republican party leader in the state and nation. The coming of the railroads (notably the Northern Pacific) through Idaho in the 1880s and the 1890s brought new settlers and aided in the founding of such cities as Idaho Falls, Pocatello, and American Falls. Farming expanded in the state and private interests developed irrigation projects. Some of these aroused public opposition, which led to establishment of state irrigation districts under the Carey Land Act of 1894. The Reclamation Act of 1902 brought direct Federal aid, and furthered reclamation work in Idaho. Notable among public reclamation projects are the Boise project and the Minidoka project. The projects, both public and private, have also helped to increase the development of Idaho's enormous potential of hydroelectric power. Three new private hydroelectric projects along the Snake River were put into operation between 1959 and 1968. The unspoiled quality of much of Idaho's land has nourished one of the youngest of Idaho's businesses—the tourist trade. SUN VALLEY, one of the nation's notable year-round vacation spots, is an example of the development of resorts in Idaho. The state also contains the Craters of the Moon National Monument. In 1949 a large Atomic Energy Commission project was begun in Idaho. The National Reactor Testing Station is situated near Arco, the first American town to be lighted by electricity obtained from atomic-power plants. Idaho's constitution was adopted in 1889 and became effective in 1890 upon statehood. The state's chief executive is a governor elected for a term of four years; the governor may succeed himself. The legislature consists of a 70-member house of representatives and a 35-member senate. State representatives and senators are elected every two years. The state also elects two Representatives and two Senators to the U.S. Congress and has four electoral votes. In 1970, Cecil Andrus, a Democrat, was elected governor, the first Democrat elected to Idaho's governorship in 24 years; he was reelected in 1974. Outstanding among Idaho's institutions of higher learning is the Univ. of Idaho, at Moscow. See Federal Writers' Project, *Idaho* (1938, rev. ed. 1950); M. D. Beal, *A History of Southeastern Idaho* (1942). and, with M. W. Wells, *History of Idaho* (1959) and *Idaho: A Student's Guide* (1965); F. T. Dubois, . . . *The Making of a State* (1971).

Idaho, University of, mainly at Moscow; land-grant and state supported; coeducational; chartered and opened 1889. Among its facilities are the Water Resources Research Institute (est. 1963) and the Forest, Wildlife and Range Experiment Station.

Idaho Falls, city (1970 pop. 35,776), seat of Bonneville co., SE Idaho, traversed by the Snake River; inc. 1900. The chief city of the extensively irrigated upper Snake valley (see MINIDOKA PROJECT), Idaho Falls is the prosperous commercial and processing center of a livestock, dairy, and farm region producing potatoes, wheat, sugar beets, and seed peas. Concrete, steel, and lumber are manufactured there. Tourism is important since the city lies near several national parks and major recreational areas. A nearby U.S. Atomic Energy Commission national reactor testing station is also a source of employment. The site of Idaho Falls was originally a miner's fording point over the Snake River, and the first settlers were Mormons. A beautiful Latter-Day Saints Temple was opened in 1945. The city also has a vocational-technical college. Special attractions in Idaho Falls include several annual rodeos and the performance each August of the sun dance by the Bannock Indian tribe.

Idalah (ĭd'ələ, īdā'lə), unidentified town, N Palestine. Joshua 19.15.

Idalium (īdā'lēəm), ancient town in Cyprus. It had a well-known temple of Aphrodite. An inscription in Phoenician and Cypriote, found on a temple site at Idalium, gave the key to the Cypriote language. Idalium is near the modern village of Dhali.

Ida Mountains: see KAZ DAĞI.

Idbash (ĭd'băsh), descendant of Judah. 1 Chron. 4.3.

Iddo (ĭd'ō). **1** Ruler of Manasseh. 1 Chron. 27.21 **2** Father of one of Solomon's stewards. 1 Kings 4.14. **3** Prophet, whose book is mentioned as a source. 2 Chron. 9.29; 12.15; 13.22. **4** Father or grandfather of the prophet Zechariah. Zech. 1.1; Ezra 5.1; Neh. 12.4,16. **5** A leader in the return from the Exile. Ezra 8.17. **6** See ADAIAH **2.**

ideal gas: see GAS LAWS; KINETIC-MOLECULAR THEORY OF GASES.

idealism, the attitude that places special value on ideas and ideals as products of the mind, in comparison with the world as perceived through the senses. In art idealism is the tendency to represent things as aesthetic sensibility would have them rather than as they are. In ethics it implies a view of life in which the predominant forces are spiritual and the aim is perfection. In philosophy the term refers to efforts to account for all objects in nature and experience as representations of the mind and sometimes to assign to such representations a higher order of existence. It is opposed to materialism. Plato conceived a world in which eternal ideas constituted reality, of which the ordinary world of experience is a shadow. In modern times idealism has largely come to refer the source of ideas to man's consciousness, whereas in the earlier period ideas were assigned a reality outside and independent of man's existence. Nevertheless, modern idealism generally proposes suprahuman mental activity of some sort and ascribes independent reality to certain principles, such as creativity, a force for good, or an absolute truth. The subjective idealism of George Berkeley in the 18th cent. held that the apparently objective world has its existence in the consciousness of individuals. Immanuel Kant developed a critical or transcendental idealism in which the phenomenal world, constituted by the human understanding, stands opposed to a world of things-in-themselves. The post-Kantian German idealism of J. G. Fichte and Friedrich von Schelling, which culminated in the absolute or objective idealism of G. W. F. Hegel, began with a denial of the unknowable thing-in-itself, thereby enabling these philosophers to treat all reality as the creation of mind or spirit. Forms of post-Kantian idealism were developed in Germany by Arthur Schopenhauer and Hermann Lotze and in England by Samuel Coleridge; forms of post-Hegelian idealism were developed in England and France by T. H. Green, Victor Cousin, and C. B. Renouvier. More recent idealists include F. H. Bradley, Bernard Bosanquet, Josiah Royce, Benedetto Croce, and the neo-Kantians such as Ernst Cassirer and Hermann Cohen. See J. H. Muirhead, *The Platonic Tradition in Anglo-Saxon Philosophy* (1931, repr. 1965); A. C. Ewing, ed., *The Idealist Tradition* (1957); G. A. Kelly, *Idealism, Politics, and History* (1969).

identification, in psychology: see DEFENSE MECHANISM.

identity, in philosophy, problem of distinguishing sameness from change, or unity from diversity; primarily examined in connection with personal identity, universals, and the law of identity in logic. In personal identity the concern has been to determine whether anything in the body or mind remains constant; philosophers have reached no general agreement on this point. The term *identity* has also become increasingly important in modern psychology, largely through the work of Erik Erikson. He has used the term to designate a sense of self that develops in the course of a man's life and that both relates him to and sets him apart from his social milieu. The terms "identity crisis" and "identity confusion," introduced by Erikson, have gained a wide usage, which often varies from their intended technical sense.

Ides: see CALENDAR.

Idfu (ĭd'fōō) or **Edfu** (ĕd'-), town (1966 pop. 27,300), S central Egypt, on the Nile River. It is an agricultural trade center and has paper mills. Idfu was the capital of a predynastic upper Egyptian kingdom that flourished c.3400 B.C. and worshipped HORUS. Later, a large sandstone temple of Horus was built there by Ptolemy III and Ptolemy IV. It is one of the finest extant examples of Egyptian temple architecture. Excavations have yielded a field of mastabas dating from the Old Kingdom, a Roman necropolis, and Coptic and Byzantine remains. The town was known to the Greeks, who identified Horus with Apollo, as Apollinopolis Magna.

Ídhra (ē'thrä) or **Hydra** (hī'drə), island (1971 pop. 2,531), 21 sq mi (54 sq km), SE Greece, in the Aegean Sea, off the Argolís peninsula of the Peloponnesus. It is mostly barren and rocky. Ídhra town (1971 pop. 2,381) is the center of population. Sponge fishing, shipbuilding, and textile manufacturing are the main occupations. Settled from the 15th cent. by Albanian-speaking Greeks from the Peloponnesus, the island became by the 17th cent. a shipbuilding and commercial center. It declined after the Greek War of Independence (1821–29), in which its seafaring people played an important role.

idiocy: see MENTAL RETARDATION.

Idlib (ĭd'lĭb), town (1961 est. pop. 36,000), capital of Idlib governorate, NW Syria. It is the market center for a fertile agricultural region where grains, grapes, olives, sesame, and cotton are grown. Idlib's chief industries are textile manufacture, olive pressing, and fig drying.

Ido (ē'dō), short name of Esperandido, an artificial language that is a simplified version of ESPERANTO. See INTERNATIONAL LANGUAGE.

idol, an object, frequently an image, which is worshiped as a deity. Idols are usually found in human or animal form and may be treated as though alive; they are fed, bathed, anointed, crowned, and sometimes even provided with a consort. Christians and Jews extend the term to include any deity other than their own; theologically, however, idol worship is generally applied to the adoration of what is seen and tangible as opposed to the worship of an unseen spiritual being.

Idomeneus (īdŏm'ənōōs"), legendary Cretan king. Although an old man, he led the Cretan contingent to the Trojan War and fought valiantly. On his way home he vowed in a storm that if the ship was saved he would sacrifice to Poseidon the first living thing he met after landing, which turned out to be his son. He fulfilled his vow, but killing his son caused a pestilence to be visited on Crete, and Idomeneus had to flee to Italy. The legend of the homecomer's vow is widespread, the best-known example being that of JEPHTHAH.

Idris I, 1890–, king of Libya (1950–69). A grandson of the founder of the Senussi Muslim sect, he became leader of the group in 1917. He was acknowledged (1920) by the Italians as emir of Cyrenaica but had to flee to Egypt in 1922 after quarreling with the Italian Fascists. He was restored to power by the British (1943) and became Libya's first king when independence was granted (1950). Deposed in a military coup d'etat (1969), he went into exile in Egypt.

Idrisi (ĭdrē'sē) or **Edrisi** (ĕ–), b. 1099?, d. after 1154, Arabian geographer, b. Ceuta. He traveled in Europe, Asia Minor, and Mediterranean lands and settled at the court of Roger II of Sicily, for whom he made a silver celestial globe and a map of the earth engraved on a plate of silver. He completed (1154) a description of the earth, compiled from his studies and observations and from the reports of travelers sent out by Roger II. This monumental compendium—called the *Kitab Rujjar* (the Book of Roger)—is the most important geographic work of the period. Idrisi divided the earth into seven horizontal climatic zones, each divided vertically into 11 arbitrary sections.

Idrisids (ĭd'rĭsĭdz"), two historic Muslim families. **1** An Arab Shiite dynasty of Morocco (788–974), founded by Idris I, a descendant of caliph Ali. It was the first Shiite dynasty in the history of Islam. Having failed in an anti-Abbasid rebellion in Arabia, Idris fled to central Morocco, where he later established a state. His son, Idris II, became known as the founder of Fez. Berber insurrections and invasions by the Umayyads of Spain and the Fatimids of Tunisia brought an end to the Idrisid dynasty. **2** A family of rulers in Arabia at the beginning of the 20th cent. The first ruler of the family was Sayyid Ahmad al-Idrisi, a descendant of the Idrisid family of Morocco, who established the Khardiriyah Idrisiyah, a strictly puritan religious brotherhood. Another member of the family, Sayyid Muhammad al-Sanusi, founded the SANUSI brotherhood in N Africa. Idrisid rule in Arabia came to an end when Saudi Arabia came into being in 1934.

Idumaea or **Idumea:** see EDOM.

idyl (ī'dəl), short poem. The ancient idyls, especially those of Bion and Moschus, were intended as little selections in the style of such longer poems as elegies or epics. There are 10 famous idyls by the Greek THEOCRITUS, and, since some of them dealt with pastoral or rural scenes, the term *idyl* came to be restricted to gently flowing, artistic pieces on rural subjects. In the 19th cent., Alfred Tennyson in his *Idylls of the King* used the term rather in its looser original sense than in the later restricted pastoral meaning. For idyls in their bucolic sense, see PASTORAL.

Ie-shima: see OKINAWA.

Ieyasu (Ieyasu Tokugawa) (ēā'yäsōō tōkōōgä'wə), 1542–1616, Japanese warrior and dictator. A gifted leader and brilliant general, he founded the TOKUGAWA shogunate. Early in his career he helped NOBUNAGA and HIDEYOSHI unify Japan. In 1590 he received the area surrounding Edo (Tokyo) in fief, and he later made Edo his capital. After Hideyoshi's death (1598), he became the most powerful daimyo by defeating rival barons in the battle of Sekigahara (1600). He became shogun in 1603, made his son Hidetada nominal ruler in 1605, subdued Hideyoshi's heirs in 1615, and at his death in 1616 was the undisputed dictator of Japan. He sought to perpetuate the supremacy of his family by freezing the status quo. Under his regime attendance at the shogunal court was compulsory, castle building was strictly controlled, and Confucianism was revived to strengthen the state. Like Hideyoshi, he encouraged foreign trade; Japanese vessels carried goods to China, the Philippines, and Mexico. Christians were at first tolerated because he wished to trade with Europe. Ieyasu was advised about European ways by the Englishman, Will ADAMS. After Ieyasu's death a great mausoleum was erected in his honor at Nikko, which became one of the most important shrines in Japan. His name also appears as Iyeyasu.

Ife (ē'fā), city (1969 est. pop. 151,000), SW Nigeria. Located in a farm region, the city is an important center for marketing and shipping cacao. According to tradition, Ife is the oldest YORUBA town (founded c.1300). All Yoruba chiefs trace their descent from the first mythological ruler of Ife, Oduduwa, and they regard the reigning *oni* (king) of Ife as their ritual superior. Ife was the most powerful Yoruba kingdom until the late 17th cent., when OYO surpassed it. Terracotta and naturalistic bronze sculptures made in the area as early as the 12th cent. are considered among the finest works of West African art; some are displayed in the Ife Museum. The Univ. of Ife is in the city, which is sometimes called Ile-Ife [old Ife].

Ifni (ēf'nē), former Spanish possession (580 sq mi/1,502 sq km), SW Morocco, on the Atlantic Ocean. The main industry is fishing. Ifni was ceded by Morocco to Spain in 1860, but Spanish administration was nominal until 1934; from then until 1958 its capital, Sidi Ifni, was the residence of the governor-general of SPANISH SAHARA. Border clashes between Spanish and Moroccan troops occurred in 1957. Spain returned Ifni to Morocco in 1969.

Igal (ī'găl). **1** Spy sent by Moses into Canaan. Num. 13.7. **2** One of David's guard. 2 Sam. 23.36. Joel: 1 Chron. 11.38.

Igarka (ēgär'kə), city (1970 pop. 16,000), NW Siberian USSR, on the lower Yenisei River. It has sawmills and is a major lumber port. Igarka was founded in 1928. During the Stalin period forced labor was used in the area, especially for logging.

Igdaliah (ĭg"dälī'ə), a holy man. Jer. 35.4.

Igeal (ī'gēəl), descendant of the house of David. 1 Chron. 3.22.

Iglau: see JIHLAVA, Czechoslovakia.

Iglesias, Miguel (mēgĕl' ēglā'syäs), 1822–1901, president of Peru (1881–85). A general, he fought in the war with Chile (see PACIFIC, WAR OF THE), distinguishing himself in the defense (1881) of Lima. Because the government failed to meet Chilean demands, Iglesias, supported by Chile, assumed the presidency and accepted the harsh terms of the Treaty of Ancón (1883). Many Peruvians refused to acknowledge him as president, and a revolution led by CÁCERES was successful. Defeated in the ensuing election, Iglesias left the country.

Iglesias (ēglā'zyäs), town (1971 pop. 28,047), SW Sardinia, Italy. Manufactures include furniture and metal goods. The zinc and lead mines of the region have been famous since the 13th cent. The influence of Pisa, which controlled Iglesias in the Middle Ages, is apparent in the Romanesque cathedral (14th–15th cent.) and the medieval castle.

igloo (ĭg'lōō) [Eskimo], dome-shaped dwelling of the Eastern ESKIMO constructed of blocks of snow placed in an ascending spiral with a low tunnel entrance. Although it can provide adequate protection for weeks in severe cold, it is used almost exclusively as a temporary shelter while traveling.

Ignatiev, Nikolai Pavlovich, Count (nyĭkəlī' päv'ləvĭch ĭgnä'tyəf), 1832–1908, Russian diplomat. He was sent to China as an envoy in 1859, where he cleverly played the Chinese against the British and French and secured the Ussuri region for Russia through the Treaty of Peking (1860). As ambassador to Constantinople (1864–1877), he promoted nationalist and Pan-Slav (see PAN-SLAVISM) aspirations in the Balkans and helped instigate the anti-Turkish rebellion in Bulgaria. His diplomacy led to the Russo-Turkish War of 1877–78, at the close of which he negotiated the Treaty of San Stefano, which greatly expanded Russian influence in the Balkans. Shortly afterwards, his influence waned and he retired. He served briefly as minister of the interior (1881–82).

Ignatius of Antioch, Saint (ĭgnā'shəs, ăn'tēŏk), d. c.107, bishop of Antioch and Christian martyr, called Theophorus [God-bearer]. He was probably a convert and a disciple of St. John the Evangelist. On his way to Rome to be martyred by the wild beasts of the amphitheater, he wrote the important letters to the churches in Rome and in Asia Minor, and to St. POLYCARP. The seven epistles are an invaluable testimony to the beliefs and internal organization of the early Christians. St. Ignatius is the first writer to stress the virgin birth. He firmly denounced DOCETISM and the Judaizing tendencies then prevalent. He taught a sound Christological theology, which viewed the mystery of the Trinity as an assumed doctrine of faith. The only guarantee against heresy, he taught, is the church united under a bishop. St. Ignatius is the first in Christian literature to use the word *Catholic.* Feast: Feb. 1. See J. A. Kleist, tr., *The Epistles of St. Clement of Rome and St. Ignatius of Antioch* (1946), Virginia Corwin, *Saint Ignatius and Christianity in Antioch* (1960).

Ignatius of Constantinople, Saint, c.800–877, Greek churchman, patriarch of Constantinople. A son of Byzantine Emperor Michael I, he was castrated and shut up in a monastery (813) by the man who deposed his father, Emperor Leo V, to prevent his succession to the throne. In 846 or 847, he was made patriarch of Constantinople by the Empress Theodora, who approved his uncompromising zeal against ICONOCLASM. After her banishment by her brother Bardas, who became regent for Michael III, St. Ignatius was asked to resign. PHOTIUS, whose politics were more acceptable, became patriarch. The Ignatian party refused to accept Photius and sought aid from the pope, St. NICHOLAS I. On the accession of BASIL I, St. Ignatius again became patriarch. In 869, St. Ignatius was declared to be the legal patriarch (see CONSTANTINOPLE, FOURTH COUNCIL OF). Ignatius is regarded as a father of the Church in the West and as a saint by both East and West. Feast: Oct. 23.

Ignatius of Loyola, Saint (loiyō'lə), 1491–1556, Spanish churchman, founder of the Jesuits (see JESUS, SOCIETY OF), b. Loyola Castle near Azpeitia, Guipúzcoa, Spain. He was of noble birth and was reared in the household of a prominent courtier. In 1517 he left his life at court to enter the army. During a convalescence (1521) from a serious wound, he was converted through reading a life of Christ. He went to Montserrat, where he was confessed and absolved, and from there he went to MANRESA. In 1523 he set out for the Holy Land. Prevented from entering Palestine, he returned with the decision to secure an education. He studied at Barcelona (1524–26); at Alcalá (1526–27), where for a short time he was imprisoned by the Inquisition; at Salamanca (1527–28), where he again suffered brief imprisonment; and at Paris. St. Ignatius's strength lay not in scholarship but in spiritual direction. The Inquisition again became suspicious, but he was cleared of any irregularities. He and six followers—among them St. Francis Xavier and Diego Lainez—took together vows of poverty and chastity. This group was the nucleus of the future Jesuits. They planned to go to the Holy Land and live in imitation of Christ, working to convert the Muslims, but the Turkish wars intervened, and they went to Rome instead. They were ordained (1537) and received by the pope (1538), who set them to work in Italy. In 1539, Ignatius drew up a *Formula* for a new order and secured (1540) papal approval. It served as the basis for the later *Constitutions,* published at his death, by which Jesuits have been governed ever since. Ignatius was elected (1541) general of the order and remained its leader, with headquarters in Rome, until his death. Although the Jesuits became a major force in the Catholic Reformation, the society was not founded particularly for that purpose. Ignatius's great interests seem to have been the foreign missions and the education of youth. Many schools were opened in Europe during his lifetime, and missions were begun in Japan, India, and Brazil. He was dominated all his life by a desire to imitate Christ. His *Spiritual Exercises,* written over a number of years, are a series of reflections, examinations of conscience, and prayers, grouped according to a traditional set of four steps leading to mystical union with God. The spirituality identified with St. Ignatius is characterized by emphasis on human initiative. His little book is a classic of Christian mysticism and is much used by devout Catholics. His concept of the "soldier of Christ" has often been understood too militaristically: Ignatius used the image in obvious imitation of St. Paul (Eph. 6.10-17). He is buried in the Gesù at Rome. He was canonized in 1622. Feast: July 31. See *Letters of St. Ignatius Loyola* (tr. 1959), and his quasi-autobiography, *The Testament of Ignatius Loyola* (tr. 1900). See also biographies by H. D. Sedgwick (1923), Paul Dudon (tr. 1949), and J. P. Brodrick (1956); J. P. Brodrick, *The Origin of the Jesuits* (1940, repr. 1971); Theodore Maynard, *Saint Ignatius and the Jesuits* (1956); Hugo Rahner, *Ignatius the Theologian* (tr. 1968).

igneous rock: see ROCK.

ignis fatuus (ĭg'nĭs făch'o͞oəs): see WILL-O'-THE-WISP.

ignition, apparatus for igniting a combustible mixture. The German engineer Nikolaus A. Otto, in his first gas engine, used flame ignition; another method was heating a metal tube to incandescence. Ignition systems in modern automobiles use an electric spark which ignites the compressed mixture of air and gasoline in the cylinders. A battery ignition system has a 6- or 12-volt battery charged by an engine-driven generator to supply electricity, an ignition coil to increase the voltage, breaker points, a distributor to direct current to the correct cylinder, and a spark plug projecting into each cylinder. Current goes from the battery through the primary winding of the coil, through the breaker points, and back to the battery. The breaker points comprise a switch with tungsten contacts to retard erosion. Driven at half engine speed, a breaker cam, which is a rotating object with a lobed surface, opens and closes the points. There is one lobe on the cam for each cylinder. When the breaker points are closed, current flows through the primary winding of the ignition coil. The primary winding consists of wire coiled around an iron core. Over this is a secondary winding of many more turns of finer wire attached to the distributor. Current flowing through the primary winding creates a magnetic field. When the breaker cam opens the breaker points, the circuit is broken and current stops. The magnetic field collapses, inducing in the secondary winding a much higher voltage that is led to the distributor. Inside the distributor a moving finger rotates at half engine speed. As it rotates it touches contacts, each of which runs to a different cylinder. Rotation is timed so that when the finger is touching the contact for a particular cylinder, a high voltage has just been induced in the secondary winding of the ignition coil and the piston has almost reached the top of the compression stroke. Thus a high voltage is impressed across the spark plug gap. The spark plug consists of a center electrode imbedded in insulating ceramic. Around the outside is a threaded metal shell that screws into a hole in the top of the cylinder. A ground electrode extends from the shell over the end of the center electrode. Between the two electrodes there is a small gap of .015–.040 in. (.038–.102 cm). At about 8,000 volts a spark jumps the gap and ignites the air-gasoline mixture. A centrifugal advance makes the spark fire earlier at high engine speeds; a vacuum advance makes it fire earlier at small throttle openings above idle. A magneto ignition system is essentially the same except that a permanent magnet generator supplies current directly. Where compactness is an advantage or where there are no other accessories that require a battery, a magneto system may be preferred. Aircraft, motorcycles, and farm equipment often have magnetos. In some modern ignition systems the current to the primary winding of the coil is electronically switched, producing a higher voltage at the spark plugs. Such systems generally reduce ignition maintenance and increase engine efficiency. In a Diesel engine the fuel ignites as soon as it is injected into the hot, highly compressed air in the cylinder.

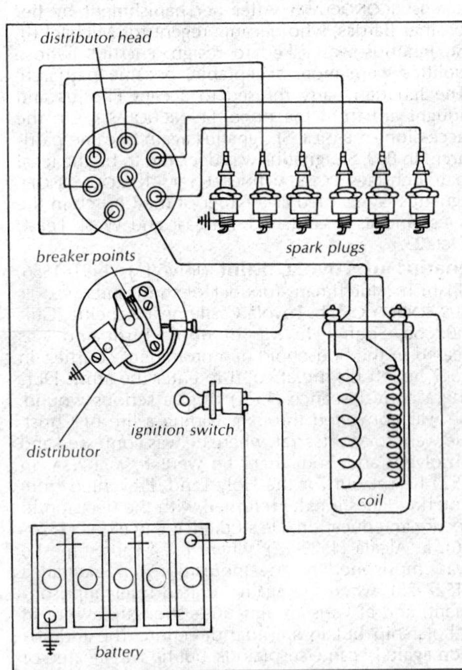

Ignition system

Igor (ē'gər), d. 945, duke of Kiev (912–45), successor of Oleg. According to the Russian *Primary Chronicle,* a medieval history, Igor was the son of Rurik, founder of the Russian princely line. Igor's expedition (941) against Constantinople was routed by the Greeks, and in 945 he concluded a new commercial treaty with the Byzantines. He was killed by rebellious Slavic tribesmen while attempting to collect tribute. His wife, St. OLGA, served as regent for their son Sviatoslav after Igor's death.

Igor (Igor Sviatoslavich) (ē'gər svyä"təslä'vĭch), 1151–1202, Russian prince. In 1185 he was defeated by the CUMANS in an expedition that was immortalized in the epic *Slovo o polku Igoreve* (tr. by Vladimir Nabokov, *The Song of Igor's Campaign,* 1960). The author is unknown, but the date of composition has been established as c.1187. The manuscript was discovered in 1795 in a 16th-century transcript containing many errors in copying. Although its authenticity has been questioned, it is considered the first notable work of Russian literature. It is remarkable for thematic unity and for imagery, particularly descriptions of nature and invocations of pagan magic. The work was used by BORODIN for his opera *Prince Igor.* It was earlier translated as *The Lay of the Host of Igor.*

Igorot (ĭgərōt', ēgə-), general name for the people of N central Luzon island, the Philippines. The Igorot form two subgroups: the largest group lives in the south, central, and western areas, and is very adept at rice-terrace farming; the other group lives in the east and north. They formerly practiced headhunting. The name Igorot is also used as a collective term for many of the warlike tribes of Luzon.

Iguaçu Falls or **Iguassú Falls** (both: ēgwəso͞o'), in the Iguaçu River, on the Argentina-Brazil border near the Paraguay line. Iguaçu Falls has two main sections that are composed of hundreds of waterfalls separated from each other by rocky islands along a 3-mi (4.8-km) escarpment. The highest fall is 210 ft (64 m) high; most of the falls are from 100 to 130 ft (30–40 m) high. Argentina and Brazil maintain national parks on each side of the falls. The surroundings, in the midst of beautiful scenery, abound in begonias, orchids, brilliant-hued birds, and myriads of butterflies. The Asunción-Paranaguá highway passes near the falls.

Iguala (ēgwä'lə), city (1970 pop. 60,980), Guerrero state, S Mexico, on the Cocula River. It is the communications, distribution, and processing center of the surrounding mining and agricultural region. There are frequent earthquakes. The city is famous historically as the place where Agustín de Iturbide, with the acquiescence of the guerrilla leader Vicente Guerrero, proclaimed the **Plan of Iguala** on Feb. 24, 1821. The plan's Three Guarantees provided for Roman Catholicism as Mexico's sole religion (thus confirming clerical privileges), absolute independence from Spain (preferably under a constitutional monarchy headed by Ferdinand VII or another member of the reigning Spanish family), and racial equality (the right of any person to hold office). The plan was discarded when Iturbide made himself emperor.

iguana (ĭgwä'nə), name for several large lizards of the family Iguanidae, found in tropical America and the Galapagos. The common iguana (*Iguana iguana*) is a tree-living, strictly vegetarian species found along streams from Mexico to N South America. Members of this species are 3 to 6 ft (90–180 cm) long, with the tail accounting for two-thirds of the length. They are bright green with dark stripes on the tail. A crest of spines runs from the neck to the tail. The flesh and eggs of the common iguana are valued as food. Spiny, or black, iguanas (species of *Ctenosaura*) are ground-living vegetarian lizards found from Baja California to Central America. The chuckwalla (*Sauromalus obesus*) and the desert iguana (*Dipsosaurus dorsalis*) are desert species of the SW United States and NW Mexico. The 16-in. long (40-cm), greenish chuckwalla is the largest U.S. lizard except for the gila monster and is known for its ability to inflate itself, making it difficult to extract from crevices. The gray-brown desert iguana is marked with dark spots and stripes; it lives in burrows made by other animals. Both feed on cactus flowers and fruits and tender desert plants. Basilisks (*Basiliscus* species), found along streams in tropical America, are large iguanas that can walk in an upright position; males are crested. A marine iguana (*Amblyrhynchus cristatus*), the only marine lizard, is found in the Galapagos Islands, where there is also a land species (*Conolophus subcristatus*). The large, diverse iguana family includes many smaller species not called iguanas. They are found throughout the temperate and tropical Americas, as well as in the Fiji Islands and on Madagascar. Most North American lizards belong to this family, including the collared lizards, the utas, the swifts, the so-called horned toads, or HORNED LIZARDS, and the American CHAMELEON, or anole (not a true chameleon). Most members of the family feed on insects and other small animals as well as some plant matter. In nearly all species the females lay eggs in the ground. Iguanas are classified in the phylum CHORDATA, subphylum Vertebrata, class Reptilia, order Squamata, family Iguanidae.

Iguanodon (ĭgwăn'ədŏn), biped vegetarian duck-billed DINOSAUR, characterized by teeth similar to those of the iguana, a powerful tail, and a horny beak. Complete skeletons of the 30-ft-long (9-m) reptile have been found in Belgium in rocks of the Cretaceous period. The *Iguanodon* is classified in the phylum CHORDATA, subphylum Vertebrata, class Reptilia, order Ornithischia.

Iguassú Falls, South America: see IGUAÇU FALLS.

Iguvine Tables (ĭ'gyo͞ovĭn), several inscribed bronze tablets dating from the 1st and 2d cent. A.D., discovered in 1444 at Gubbio, Italy (the ancient Iguvium and later Eugubium). Most of them are still preserved there. They set forth the acts of the Attidian Brethren, a corporation of 12 priests. The tablets proved an important aid in understanding the ancient Umbrian language and supplied information on ancient Italian religious rites.

Iida (ē'dä), city (1970 pop. 77,261), Nagano prefecture, central Honshu, Japan, on the Tenryu River. It is an agricultural market and railway junction.

Iim (ī'ĭm). **1** See IJE-ABARIM. **2** Town, S Palestine. Joshua 15.29.

Iizuka (ē'zo͞okä), city (1970 pop. 75,643), Fukuoka prefecture, N Kyushu, Japan, on the Onga River. It is a mining center in a coal mining area.

IJ or **Y** (both: ī), inlet of the IJsselmeer, North Holland prov., NW Netherlands, on which Amsterdam is located. It receives the Amstel River and is connected by canals with the North Sea and with the Lek and Waal rivers.

Ije-abarim (ī'jē-ăb'ərĭm), wilderness camping ground on the Exodus. Num. 21.11; 33.44. Iim.: Num. 33.45.

Ijebu-Ode (ējābo͞o'-ōdā'), town (1969 est. pop. 79,000), SW Nigeria. It is a commercial town and a collection point for cacao and palm products.

Manufactures include textiles, metal and clay products, processed timber and plywood, canned fruit and juice, and milled rice. Ijebu-Ode was the capital of the YORUBA Ijebu kingdom that was founded by the 15th cent. Long opposed to foreign contacts, the Ijebu kingdom remained closed to Europeans until 1892, when the British seized it in retaliation for the Ijebu's closing of the trade routes to the north during the Yoruba civil wars.

IJmuiden (īmoi'dən), city, North Holland prov., W Netherlands, on the North Sea, part of the municipality of VELSEN. It is a seaport and fishing center at the end of the North Sea Canal.

Ijon (ī'jŏn), unidentified town, N Palestine. It was looted by both Benhadad and Tiglath-pileser. 1 Kings 15.20; 2 Kings 15.29.

IJssel (ī'səl), river, 72 mi (116 km) long, branching from the Neder Rijn (Lower Rhine) River near Arnhem, E Netherlands, and flowing N into the IJsselmeer, near Kampen. The IJssel is connected to the Rhine and carries about one tenth of the Rhine's water. The river, which is canalized in places, passes through an industrial and truck-farming region; Deventer and Zutphen are the chief cities.

IJsselmeer (ī'səlmār"), shallow freshwater lake, NW Netherlands, bordering on the provinces of North Holland, Utrecht, Gelderland, Overijssel, and Friesland. It was formed from the old ZUIDER ZEE by the construction of a dam (completed 1932). The dam, 19 mi (31 km) long, has navigation locks and drainage sluices (which control the lake's level) and carries a roadway connecting North Holland with Friesland. The IJssel River, from which the lake takes its name, is the chief feeder of the IJsselmeer. Considerable areas have been reclaimed from the former Zuider Zee since 1932. The largest of the reclaimed areas is the Northeast Polder (185 sq mi/479 sq km). Parts of the polders were flooded in World War II but have been salvaged since, and further land reclamation is proceeding. Amsterdam, located on the IJ, an inlet of the IJsselmeer, is the chief city on the lake. The IJsselmeer is an important freshwater fishing ground. Since 1937 pike, perch, and eels have replaced saltwater fish.

Ikaría or **Icaria** (both: īkâr'ēə), mountainous island (1971 pop. 7,702), c.100 sq mi (260 sq km), SE Greece, one of the SPORADES, near Turkey. It has iron-ore deposits and sulfur springs. According to Greek mythology Icarus fell into the sea near the island.

Ikeda, Hayato (häyä'tō ēkä'dä), 1899–1965, Japanese political leader, prime minister (1960–64). After serving as an official in the finance ministry (1925–48) he entered politics, gaining election to Japan's house of representatives (1949). During the next decade he held a variety of ministerial posts, including finance minister (1949–52, 1956–57) and international trade and industry minister (1959–60). A moderate, he became prime minister in 1960 when adverse public reaction to the United States-Japan Security Treaty caused Nobusuke Kishi to resign. A member of Japan's dominant Liberal-Democratic party, Ikeda emphasized economic progress during his term in office. He left the prime ministry in late 1964, shortly before he died from cancer.

Ikeda, city (1970 pop. 94,333), Osaka prefecture, S Honshu, Japan, on the Ina River. It is an industrial and residential suburb of Osaka with a major industrial vehicles industry.

Ikhnaton (īknä'tən) or **Akhenaton** (ä"kənä'tən) [Egyptian,=Aton is satisfied], d. c.1354 B.C., king of ancient Egypt (c.1372–1354 B.C.), of the XVIII dynasty; son and successor of AMENHOTEP III. His name at his accession was Amenhotep IV, but he changed it to honor the god Aton. He is important for religious innovations. He abandoned polytheism to embrace monotheism. He held that the sun, named Aton, was god, and god alone, and that he was Aton's physical son. The solar monotheism was absolute; the new system allowed no accommodations and no exceptions. Through the rays of the sun everything that lived had its being. In honor of Aton the new capital was called Akhetaton (the modern TEL EL AMARNA), and new provincial capitals were founded in Nubia and Syria. The royal artists founded a new artistic school, characterized by the abandonment of convention and a turning to nature (because it showed the power of the sun). Ikhnaton's fanaticism was its own undoing. He defaced every monument on which appeared the name of Amon, previously the greatest god of Egypt. The Aton cult died with Ikhnaton because the sentiments of the priesthood and the people were outraged by his destruction of their traditions. Ikhnaton's religious zeal also lost Egypt the empire, because he had seriously neglected the provinces. As a result, his successors, Sakere and TUTANKHAMEN, received—instead of an empire including Nubia and Syria—only Egypt and some of the upper valley. There is a theory that Ikhnaton was coregent with his father, Amenhotep III, during the crucial years of change, but the question remains as yet unsolved. Of the many artistic achievements of the era of Ikhnaton, perhaps the most familiar today is the bust of his wife, Nefretete. See Joy Collier, *The Heretic Pharaoh* (1972); F. J. Giles, *Ikhnaton: Legend and History* (1970).

Ikkesh (ĭk'ĭsh), father of one of David's guard. 2 Sam. 23.26; 1 Chron. 11.28; 27.9.

Ikon Basilike: see EIKON BASILIKE.

Ilai (ī'lī, ī'lāī), one of David's mighty men. 1 Chron. 11.29. Zalmon: 2 Sam. 23.28.

Ilan (yē'län'), city, NE Taiwan. Located in an agricultural area, it is the largest rice market in Taiwan. Fertilizers and wood and paper products are among the city's manufactures.

ILAS, instrument low-approach system: see INSTRUMENT LANDING SYSTEM.

Île-aux-Noix (ēl-ō-nwä), island, 210 acres (85 hectares), in the Richelieu River near St. Jean, S Que., Canada; site of Fort Lennox National Historic Park (est. 1921). During the French and Indian War (1759) the French built a fort there to delay the British advance on Montreal but were forced to surrender it in 1760. Named Fort Lennox and occupied by a British garrison, the island fell (1775) to American forces and was used as a base by the American generals Schuyler and Montgomery for attacks on Montreal and Quebec until abandoned in 1776. The British then used the island to supply their operations against the American fleet on Lake Champlain. The present Fort Lennox dates from the 1820s, when the old fortifications were repaired and additions were built. It was a military post until 1870.

Île-de-France (ēl-də-fräNs), region and former province, N central France, in the center of the Paris basin, a fertile depression where the Marne and Ouse rivers join the Seine. Containing parts of the Beauce and Brie districts and of the Vexin, Île-de-France is now included in the departments of Paris, Seine-Saint-Denis, Val-de-Marne, Hauts-de-Seine, Val d'Oise, Yvelines, Essonne, Oise, Seine-et-Marne, and Aisne. The region has numerous large industrial towns and residential suburbs and supplies the Paris metropolis with fruits, vegetables, and dairy products. Places of economic or historic importance besides Paris include Beauvais, Compiégne, Fontainebleau, Laon, Meaux, Melun, Nemours, Saint-Cloud, Saint-Germain-en-Laye, Senlis, Soissons, and Versailles. Île-de-France was the cradle of the French monarchy. The name came into use only in the 14th cent. and was then applied to the land bounded by the Seine, the Ouse, and the Marne and their affluents. But the region, including the countship of Paris, had become part of the duchy of France or Francia by the 10th cent. When Hugh Capet, duke of France and count of Paris, was chosen as the French king in 987, his domains became the nucleus of the ever-growing crown land, which by the time of the death of Louis XI (1483) comprised the major part of present-day France. Île-de-France itself, which had been enlarged through the acquisition by the crown of various fiefs, was at that time constituted into a province subject to the parlement of Paris. After the French Revolution the province was divided.

Île de France: see MAURITIUS.

Île de la Cité, France: see PARIS.

Île Jésus, Que., Canada: see LAVAL.

Îles du Salut (ēl dü sälü') or **Safety Islands,** small archipelago, off French Guiana in the Caribbean. The best-known of the islands is DEVILS ISLAND.

Ilesha (ēlā'shä), city (1969 est. pop. 192,000), SW Nigeria. Formerly a caravan trade center, Ilesha is today an agricultural and commercial city. Cacao, kola nuts, and yams are shipped from there. There is a sawmill, and alluvial gold is found. Ilesha was the capital of the YORUBA Ilesha kingdom of the OYO empire. After Oyo's collapse in the early 19th cent., Ilesha became subject to IBADAN. The city was taken by the British in 1893.

ileum: see INTESTINE.

Ilf, Ilya Arnoldovich (ēlyä' ərnôl'dəvĭch ēlf), 1897–1937, Russian humorist whose original name was Ilya Arnoldovich Fainzilberg. In all his writing he collaborated with Yevgeny Petrovich Katayev (1903–42), who used the pseudonym Yevgeny Petrov and was a younger brother of the dramatist Valentin Katayev. The two wrote satiric stories and novels, including *Twelve Chairs* (1928, tr. *Diamonds to Sit On,* 1930), a chronicle of a rogue's search for hidden treasure. The rogue, Ostap Bender, is also the hero of their second novel, *The Little Golden Calf* (1931, tr. 1932). After a tour of the United States they wrote the witty and mildly critical *One-Storied America* (1936, tr. *Little Golden America,* 1937). Ilf died the next year of tuberculosis.

Ilford: see REDBRIDGE.

Ilhéus (ēlyĕ'o͞os), city (1970 pop. 107,738), Bahia state, E Brazil, a port on Ilhéus Bay, an inlet of the Atlantic Ocean. Founded in the mid-16th cent., it became the world's chief cacao port during the early 20th cent. Ilhéus is still the cacao center of Brazil and ships the agricultural produce of the surrounding hinterland.

Ili (ē'lē'), river of China and the USSR, 590 mi (950 km) long, rising in the Tien Shan, NW Sinkiang prov., and flowing W across the China-USSR border, through the sandy Sary-Ishik-Otrau Desert, in Kazakhstan, and into Lake Balkhash. I-ning (Kuldja), in Sinkiang, is the largest city on the river. The Ili is used for irrigation and is navigable in its middle course. West of the town of Ili is Karpachagay Gorge. The entire Ili valley was occupied by the Russians from 1871 to 1881, when the present border was established; China has regained only part of its original territory.

Iliad: see HOMER.

Iliamna (īlēăm'nə), lake, c.1,000 sq mi (2,590 sq km), 75 mi (120 km) long and up to 22 mi (35 km) wide, SW Alaska, at the base of the Alaska Peninsula; largest lake in Alaska and the third largest lake wholly within the United States. It is fed by many lakes and streams; the Kvichak River drains it SW into Bristol Bay. The lake is noted for sport fishing. Iliamna, Newhalen, and Kakhonak are the chief lakeside villages.

Iligan (ēlē'gän), city (1970 est. pop. 82,900), capital of Lanao del Norte prov., W central Mindanao, the Philippines, a port on Iligan Bay. It is the center of a rapidly growing heavy industry complex, powered by hydroelectricity from the new Maria Christina Falls plant on the Agus River. The nation's first steel mill was established there in 1964. The city also has chemical and fertilizer plants.

Ilion: see TROY.

Ilipa (ĭl'ĭpə), ancient town of Spain, near the modern Seville. Here SCIPIO AFRICANUS MAJOR defeated (206 B.C.) the Carthaginian forces after Hasdrubal had fled to Gaul. The overthrow of Carthaginian power in Spain paved the way for the defeat of HANNIBAL at Zama (202 B.C.).

Ilium: see TROY.

Ilkeston (ĭl'kĕstən), municipal borough (1971 pop. 34,123), Derbyshire, central England. There are iron and coal mines to the south. Rayon, lace, hosiery, and iron goods are manufactured. Ilkeston is mentioned in the DOMESDAY BOOK. Eastwood, a nearby mining village, is the birthplace of D. H. Lawrence, and many of his novels are set in the district.

Illampú (ēyämpo͞o'), peak, 21,276 ft (6,485 m) high, in the Cordillera Real of the Bolivian Andes, E Bolivia. Although lower than the adjacent peak, Ancohuma (21,489 ft/6,550 m high), Illampú is the name usually given to the whole mountain. It is sometimes called Sorata, from the village high on its slopes. Permanently capped with snow, Illampú dominates the mountain scenery visible from La Paz.

Illecillewaet (ĭləsĭl'əwĕt, -wăt), mountain stream, c.50 mi (80 km) long, rising in Illecillewaet glacier on the west slope of the Selkirk Mts., SE British Columbia, Canada. It flows southwest in a mountain valley to join the Columbia River near Revelstoke. For almost its entire distance it is followed by the Canadian Pacific Railway and is well known to travelers for its exceptional beauty.

Ille-et-Vilaine (ēl-ā-vēlĕn'), department (1968 pop. 652,722), NW France, in BRITTANY, on the English Channel. RENNES is the capital.

illegitimacy: see BASTARD.

Illia, Arturo (ärto͞o'rō ēl'yä), 1900–, president of Argentina (1963–66). A country physician, he entered politics after 1930, and from 1948 to 1952 he was one of the few non-Perónist representatives in the national legislature. He was elected president in 1963, but with only 25% of the vote; he was unable to deal effectively with the country's deteriorating economy and the political problems created by the followers of deposed Juan PERÓN. Illia canceled Argentina's petroleum contracts with foreign companies, a move that, while popular, soon destroyed the country's virtual self-sufficiency in oil. After the Perónists made gains in the 1966 elections, alarmed military leaders deposed Illia and replaced him with Gen. Juan Onganía.

Illimani (ēyēmä'nē), mountain, 21,184 ft (6,457 m) high, E Bolivia. One of the highest peaks of the Cordillera Real of the Bolivian Andes, it is permanently snow-capped. Illimani was first climbed by Baron Conway of Allington in 1898.

illinium (ĭlĭn'ēəm): see PROMETHIUM.

Illinois (ĭlənoi'), state (1970 pop. 11,113,976), 56,400 sq mi (146,076 sq km), N central United States, in the Midwest, admitted as the 21st state of the Union in 1818. SPRINGFIELD is the capital; CHICAGO, ROCKFORD, and PEORIA are the largest cities. Illinois is bounded on the N by Wisconsin, on the E by Lake Michigan and Indiana, on the SE and S by Kentucky (where the Ohio River forms the boundary), and on the W by Missouri and Iowa (where the Mississippi River forms the boundary). The broad level lands that

gave Illinois the nickname Prairie State were fashioned by Pleistocene glaciers, which leveled rugged ridges and filled valleys over the northern and central parts of the state. The fertile prairies are drained by more than 275 rivers, most of which flow to the Mississippi-Ohio systems; the Illinois is the largest river in the state. These rivers provided early explorers a way S from Lake Michigan into the interior of the continent and later, in the days of canal building, played a big part in hastening settlement of the prairies. The completion of the Erie Canal linked Illinois, through Lake Michigan, to the eastern seaboard of the United States. Today the Illinois Waterway links Chicago to the Mississippi basin as the old Chicago and Illinois and Michigan canals once did, and the St. Lawrence Seaway provides access for oceangoing vessels. The waterways are but a part of a transportation complex that includes railroads, airlines, and a very extensive modern highway system. Although the area's climate varies, with extreme temperatures in parts of the state, the rich land, adequate rainfall (32-36 in./81-91 cm annually), and a long growing season make Illinois an agricultural rival of its neighbor Iowa. Corn, hogs, cattle, and soybeans are the principal sources of farm income. Other major crops include hay and wheat. Beneath the fertile topsoil lies mineral wealth, and the state is a leading producer of fluorspar. Bituminous-coal fields and large oil deposits make S Illinois a major source of fuel; in 1972 Illinois ranked fourth among the states in the production of coal, and its reserves are greater than any other state E of the Rocky Mts. These agricultural and mineral resources encouraged the establishment of great industries along the state's excellent lines of communication and transportation, and by 1880 income from industry was almost double that from agriculture. Major industries include the manufacture of electrical and nonelectrical machinery, food products, fabricated and primary metal products, and chemicals; and printing and publishing. Metropolitan Chicago, one of the country's major rail centers, is also one of the great industrial centers of the world, famous for its meat-packing plants and huge grain mills and elevators. Outside Chicago is the Argonne National Laboratory, a major research and development installation of the Atomic Energy Commission. Scattered across the northern half of the state are cities with specialized industries—Elgin, Peoria, Rock Island, Moline, and Rockford. Industrially important cities in central Illinois include Joliet, Decatur, and East Saint Louis. At the end of the 18th cent. the Illinois, Sac, Fox, and other Indian tribes were living in the river forests, where many centuries before them the prehistoric Indian MOUND BUILDERS had dwelt. French explorers and missionaries came to the region early. Father Marquette and Louis Jolliet, on their return from a trip down the Mississippi, paddled up the Illinois River in 1673, and two years later Marquette returned to establish a mission in the Illinois country. In 1679 the French explorer Robert Cavelier, sieur de La Salle, went from Lake Michigan to the Illinois, where he founded (1680) Fort Creve Coeur and with his lieutenant, Henri de Tonti, completed (1682-83) Fort St. Louis on Starved Rock cliff. French occupation of the area was sparse, but the settlements of Cahokia and Kaskaskia achieved a minor importance in the 18th cent., and the area was valued for fur trading. By the Treaty of Paris of 1763, ending the French and Indian Wars, France ceded all of the Illinois country to Great Britain. However, the British did not take possession until Indian resistance, led by the Ottawa Indian chief, Pontiac, was quelled (1766). In the American Revolution, George Rogers Clark and his expedition captured (1778) the British posts of Cahokia and Kaskaskia before going on to take Vincennes. The Illinois region was an integral part of the Old Northwest that came within U.S. boundaries by the 1783 Treaty of Paris ending the Revolution. Under the ORDINANCE OF 1787 the area became the Northwest Territory. Made part of Indiana Territory in 1800, Illinois became a separate territory in 1809. Settlement was very slow until after the War of 1812, during which an Indian massacre occurred at Fort Dearborn. The fur trade was still flourishing throughout most of Illinois when it became a state in 1818, but already settlers were pouring down the Ohio River by flatboat and barge and across the Genesee wagon road. In 1820 the capital was moved from Kaskaskia to Vandalia. The BLACK HAWK WAR (1832) practically ended the tenure of the Indians in Illinois and drove them W of the Mississippi. Frontier conditions began to disappear in Illinois, and development eventually came after swamps had been drained and fields had been cleared. In the 1830s there was heavy and uncontrolled land speculation. Mob fury broke out in the murder (1837) of the abolitionist Elijah P. Lovejoy at Alton and in the lynching (1844) of the Mormon leader Joseph Smith and his brother Hyrum at Nauvoo. Industrial development came with the opening of an agricultural implements factory by Cyrus H. McCormick at Chicago in 1847 and the building of the railroads in the 1850s. During this period the career of Abraham Lincoln began. In the state legislature Lincoln and his colleagues from Sangamon co. had worked hard and successfully to bring the capital to Springfield in 1839. As Illinois moved toward a wider role in the country's affairs, Lincoln and another Illinois lawyer, Stephen A. Douglas, won national attention with their debates on the slavery issue in the senatorial race of 1858. In 1861, Lincoln became President and fought to preserve the Union in the face of the South's secession. During the Civil War, Illinois supported the Union, but there was much proslavery sentiment in the southern part of the state. By the 1860s industry was well established, and many immigrants from Europe had already settled in the state, foreshadowing the influx still to come. Immediately after the war, industry expanded to tremendous proportions, and the Illinois legislature, by setting aside acreage for stockyards, prepared the way for the development of the meat-packing industry. Economic development had outrun the construction of facilities, and Chicago was a mass of flimsy wooden structures when the fire of 1871 destroyed most of the city. In the latter part of the 19th cent. farmers in the state revolted against exorbitant freight rates, tariff discrimination, and the high price of manufactured goods. The Order of Patrons of Husbandry was founded in 1867 for cooperative buying, and later the Illinois farmers enthusiastically joined the GRANGER MOVEMENT. One of the major Granger cases (see MUNN VS. ILLINOIS) was contested in Illinois. Laborers in factories, railroads, and mines also became restive, and from 1870 to 1900 Illinois was the scene of such violent labor incidents as the HAYMARKET SQUARE RIOT of 1886 and the Pullman strike of 1894. In the 20th cent. labor conditions improved, but violent labor disputes persisted, notably the massacre at Herrin in 1922 during a coal-miners' strike and the bloody riot during a steel strike at Chicago in 1937. State politics became divided by the conflicting forces of farmers, laborers, and corporations, and opposing political machines came into being downstate and upstate. In 1937 new oil fields were discovered in southern Illinois, further enhancing the state's industrial development. During World War II the nation's first controlled nuclear reaction was executed at the Univ. of Chicago, paving the way for development of nuclear weapons during the war. World War II spurred the growth of the Chicago metropolitan area, and the opening (1959) of the Saint Lawrence Seaway made the city a major port for overseas shipping. Adlai E. Stevenson, governor of Illinois from 1949 to 1953, achieved national prominence in winning the Democratic presidential nomination in 1952 and 1956. Also during the 1950s the "gateway amendment" to the Illinois constitution simplified the state's constitutional amendment process. Southern Illinois experienced population declines in the 1950s and 1960s as farms in the south became more mechanized, providing fewer jobs in the area. In 1970, Illinois adopted a new state constitution that, among other reforms, banned discrimination in employment and housing. The governor of Illinois is elected for a term of four years. The state legislature, called the general assembly, consists of a house of representatives with 177 members elected to serve for two years and a senate with 59 members elected for two or four years. Illinois elects 24 Representatives and 2 Senators to the U.S. Congress and has 26 electoral votes. Daniel Walker, a Democrat, was elected governor in 1972. Institutions of higher learning in Illinois include the Univ. of Illinois, at Urbana-Champaign; Northwestern Univ., at Evanston; the Univ. of Chicago and the Illinois Institute of Technology, in Chicago; Illinois State Univ., at Normal; and Southern Illinois Univ., at Carbondale. Among Illinois's many tourist attractions are Shawnee National Forest, with recreational facilities; the Cahokia Mounds; and many state parks and historical sites, including New Salem and Lincoln's home and burial place in Springfield. An additional summer attraction is the Illinois State Fair. See N. F. Garvey, *The Government and Administration of Illinois* (1958); Walter Havighurst, *The Heartland: Ohio, Indiana, Illinois* (1962); T. C. Pease, *The Story of Illinois* (3d ed. 1965); W. L. Burton, *The Trembling Land: Illinois in the Age of Exploration* (1966); V. Hicken, *The Settlement of Illinois, 1700-1850* (1966) and *Illinois in the Civil War* (1966); Federal Writers' Project, *Illinois* (1939, repr. 1971).

Illinois, river, 273 mi (439 km) long, formed by the confluence of the Des Plaines and Kankakee rivers, NE Ill., and flowing SW to the Mississippi at Grafton, Ill. It is an important commercial and recreational waterway. The Illinois forms the greater part of the Illinois Waterway, which links the Great Lakes with the Mississippi. The chief city on the river is Peoria.

Illinois, University of, at Urbana, Champaign, and Chicago; land-grant with state and federal support; coeducational; chartered 1867, opened 1868 as Illinois Industrial Univ., renamed 1885. It pioneered in vocational education. In 1946 the university began a two-year undergraduate program in Chicago. Enrollment steadily increased at this branch until in 1965 it was made the four-year Chicago Circle campus. The university also operates the Medical Center in Chicago, which includes schools of medicine, dentistry, pharmacy, and nursing, and is closely affiliated with the other medical institutions in the city.

Illinois Indians, confederation of North American Indians, comprising the Cahokia, the Kaskaskia, the Michigamea, the Moingwena, the Peoria, and the Tamaroa tribes. They belong to the Algonquian branch of the Algonquian-Wakashan linguistic stock (see AMERICAN INDIAN LANGUAGES). In the mid-17th cent. they lived in S Wisconsin, N Illinois, and sections of Iowa and Missouri. They then numbered some 6,500. Jacques Marquette and Louis Jolliet are believed to have been the first Europeans to travel (1673) through Illinois territory. Father Claude Jean ALLOUEZ, a Jesuit missionary, visited them in 1676 and stayed with them for years. By 1750 wars with the Sioux, the Fox, and the Iroquois had reduced the population to some 2,000. In 1769 the assassination of the celebrated Ottawa chief PONTIAC by a Kaskaskia Indian provoked the Lake tribes (the Ojibwa, the Ottawa, the Potawatami, the Kickapoo, and the Sac and Fox) to vengeance. They began a war of extermination, which in a few years diminished the Illinois to a small number, who sought asylum at the French settlement at Kaskaskia. By 1800 there remained some 150 Illinois Indians. In 1833 the survivors, represented by the Kaskaskia and the Peoria, sold their lands in Illinois and moved W of the Mississippi. Their descendants now occupy a reservation in NE Oklahoma, which they share with the Wea and Piankashaw Indians.

Illinois Institute of Technology, in Chicago; coeducational; founded 1940 by a merger of Armour Institute of Technology (founded 1892) and Lewis Institute (1896). The school divisions include the IIT Research Institute (formerly the Armour Research Foundation), John Crerar Library, the Institute of Gas Technology, the Research Center of the Association of American Railroads, and the Institute for Psychological Services.

Illinois Waterway, 336 mi (541 km) long, linking Lake Michigan with the Mississippi River, N Ill.; an important part of the waterway connecting the Great Lakes with the Gulf of Mexico. The Illinois Waterway extends from the mouth of the Chicago River, on Lake Michigan, following the Chicago Sanitary and Ship Canal, the lower Des Plaines River, and the Illinois River to the Mississippi at Grafton, Ill. The Calumet channels branch southeast from the waterway and link it with the Calumet industrial region along the Ill.-Ind. border. Principal cargoes, carried chiefly by barges, are coal, petroleum, grain, and steel products. Recreational areas have been developed along the waterway.

Illinois Wesleyan University, at Bloomington, Ill.; United Methodist; chartered 1853. Founded for men, it became coeducational in 1870. The university includes schools of art, music, drama, and nursing.

illiteracy, inability to meet a certain minimum criterion of reading and writing skill. The exact nature of the criterion varies, so that illiteracy must be defined in each case before the term can be used in a meaningful way. In 1930 the U.S. Bureau of the Census defined as illiterate any person over ten years of age who was unable to read and write in any language. By the next census (1940), however, the concept of "functional" illiteracy was adopted, and any person with less than five years of schooling was considered functionally illiterate, or unable to engage in social activities in which literacy is assumed. Since that time, the concept of functional illiteracy has grown in popularity among American educators, but the standards of definition have changed with the increasing complexity of most social activities. Thus, by 1970, the U.S. Office of Education considered at least six years of schooling (and sometimes as many as eight) to be the minimum criterion for functional literacy. The United Nations, which defines illiteracy as the inability to read and write a simple message in any language, has conducted a number of surveys on world illiteracy. In the first survey (1950, pub. 1957) at least 44% of the world's population were found to be illiterate. A later study (1962, pub. 1965) showed little or no improvement. The highest illiteracy rates were found in the less developed nations of Africa and Asia; the lowest, in the more advanced nations of Europe and North America. Using the United Nations definition of illiteracy, the United States and Canada have an overall illiteracy rate of only 2% or 3%. In certain disadvantaged areas, however, such as the rural South in the United States, the illiteracy rate is much higher. Throughout most of history most people have been illiterate. In feudal society, for example, the ability to read and write was of value only to the clergy and aristocracy. The first known reference to "literate laymen" did not appear until the end of the 14th cent. Illiteracy was not seen as a problem until after the invention of printing in the 15th cent. The first significant decline in illiteracy came with the Reformation, when translation of the Bible into the vernacular became widespread and Protestant converts were taught to read it. Revolutionary political movements from the 18th to the 20th cent. generally included an attack on illiteracy as one of their goals. Direct attacks on illiteracy take two main forms: ADULT EDUCATION and the establishment of public schools with compulsory attendance for children. "Opportunity schools" have attempted to combat adult illiteracy in American urban areas. Soldiers have been used effectively in Turkey and Mexico as instructors for the general populace. In the United States, universal public education has almost eliminated illiteracy among the young. Literacy tests for voting still exist in some states of the union but have fallen into disfavor after charges that they were used unfairly. See UNESCO, *World Illiteracy at Mid-century* (1957); UNESCO, *Statistics of Illiteracy (1965);* Charles Jeffries, *Illiteracy: A World Problem* (1967); Frank Laubach, *Forty Years with the Silent Billion* (1970).

illuminance: see PHOTOMETRY.

Illuminati (ĭlo͞o″mĭnā'tī, -nä'tē) [Lat.,=enlightened], rationalistic society founded in Germany soon after 1776 by Adam Weishaupt, a professor at Ingolstadt. It had close affinities with the Freemasons and seemingly was organized on a Masonic plan. For 10 years it was very popular among German rationalists, but as a society it had limited influence. The Roman Catholic Church, which Weishaupt left in his youth and rejoined before his death, condemned the Illuminati; in 1785 the Bavarian government dissolved the organization. It did not long survive. In Spain and Italy in the 15th cent. the term *Illuminati* referred to persons believed to hold supranatural intellectual powers. Other groups using the name have included a mystical sect that flourished in the 16th cent. in Spain and France, the ROSICRUCIANS, and certain followers of Boehme and Swedenborg.

illumination, in art, decoration of manuscripts and books with colored, gilded pictures, often referred to as miniatures (see MINIATURE PAINTING); historiated and decorated initials; and ornamental border designs. Before the 14th cent. illuminated manuscripts in the West were nearly always made of vellum. Both ink outline and full color drawings were common. The color medium was usually TEMPERA, and the gilt was burnished to a high luster. Lavish illumination was most commonly applied to religious books, including early gospels, fashioned for rich patrons, then psalters and BOOKS OF HOURS. A few other sorts of manuscripts, such as the BESTIARY, were, by tradition, profusely illustrated. The earliest known illustrated rolls come from Egypt; they include the oldest example, the *Ramesseum Papyrus* (c.1980 B.C.) and fragments from the *Book of the Dead,* found in tombs. Little or nothing survives of ancient Greek illumination, although scientific treatises and epic poetry are said to have contained pictures. It is thought that by the 2d cent. A.D. the long papyrus roll began to be replaced by the parchment codex (or leaved book). Thus a new, compact format was introduced as the framework for the picture. From the late classical period (probably 5th cent. A.D.) come the illustrations of Vergil (Vatican) and the *Iliad* (Ambrosian Library, Milan). Most illuminations of the early Christian period, whose style was based on Hellenistic prototypes, are preserved only in medieval copies made in monasteries. Sumptuous Byzantine codices of the 6th and 7th cent., such as the Vienna *Genesis,* also show the adaptation of antique models to biblical subject matter. In the 7th and 8th cent. the work of the Irish, Anglo-Saxons, Franks, and Lombards displayed rich decorative geometric designs with intricate human and animal interlacing, largely concentrated in initials and title pages. Among the masterpieces of Hiberno-Saxon illumination are the *Book of Durrow,* the *Book of Kells* (both: Trinity Coll. Library, Dublin), and the *Lindisfarne Gospels* (British Mus.). The chief works of the Carolingian period date from the beginning of the 9th cent. and were created for the court of Charlemagne, whose aim was to revive the art of antiquity. The existence of several local monastic schools led to a variety of styles; prominent were the Ada group, characterized by splendid coloring and figures full of movement and expression, e.g., *The Gospel Book of Ada* (Municipal Library, Trier), and the Rheims school, known for vibrant pen drawings with little color, e.g., the *Utrecht Psalter* (9th cent.; University Library, Utrecht), which greatly influenced the English school of Winchester in the 10th and 11th cent. The *Benedictional of St. Aethelwold* (c.980) typifies this style, with sketchy drawings of elongated figures in fluttering drapery, enriched by foliated borders. Contemporary with the flowering of the Winchester school was the Ottonian renascence in Germany. Germanic illuminators used thick, luxurious colors with vigorous outlines and dynamic movement. Reichenau, Hildesheim, and Fulda were prominent centers of Ottonian art. In Byzantine miniatures a more classical mode continued into the 13th cent. in such works as the *Joshua Roll* (10th cent.; Vatican), along with images of a hieratic austerity. Italy was important for the diffusion of the Byzantine style; her most original works are the *Exultet* rolls (Pisa), containing joyous hymns. Byzantine work declined after the capture of Constantinople in 1204. In Spain, where there was a mixture of Christian and Arabic elements, a highly inventive work was the *Commentary of Beatus on the Apocalypse* (a 10th-century copy is in the Pierpont Morgan Library, New York City). The illumination of large books, Bibles and psalters, was fashionable in the Romanesque era. Richly decorated initials graced these books and, in the early 12th cent., stylized figures enhanced by complex garments and gestures were plentiful. Characteristic of mid-12th-century work is the Winchester Bible. Paris was the birthplace of new ideas in book ornamentation at the beginning of the 13th cent. Picture and text were more closely integrated. The most striking quality of the Gothic miniatures was their parallel to STAINED-GLASS windows in the use of similar colors, drawing, and medallion frameworks. Book size decreased, initials were expanded, and grotesque little monsters and drolleries appeared in the margins. Lay schools emerged in the 14th cent., directed by individual artists, such as MAÎTRE HONORÉ and Jean PUCELLE. Gold fields were replaced by colored and landscape backgrounds, although colors were sometimes abandoned for GRISAILLE, as in the *Hours of Jeanne d'Evreux* (c.1325; Metropolitan Mus.) by Jean Pucelle. Greater realism and a wealth of ornament in the margins can be seen in the works done in the early 15th cent. for the duc de Berry by the Burgundian court artists André Beauneveu, Jacquemart de Hesdin, and the Limbourg brothers. The epitome of elegance was reached in the *Très riches heures du duc de Berry* (Chantilly) by the Limbourg brothers, showing a fusion of the refined Parisian style with the more realistic art of Flanders and also the influence of Italian panel painting. Other notable works of the 15th cent. include the *Hours of Catherine of Cleves* (c.1428–45; Morgan Library) and illuminations of the Master of Mary of Burgundy (Bodleian, Oxford). The Boucicaut Master also made notable contributions. From the region of Tours came the highly accomplished *Hours of Étienne Chevalier* (Chantilly) by Jean FOUQUET and the work of his pupil Jean Bourdichon. In England the early 14th-century art of illumination was nearly indistinguishable from that of France, e.g. *Queen Mary's Psalter* (British Mus.). Italy was an important center of illumination in the 15th and 16th cent. Among those who worked as illuminators were Fra Angelico, Mantegna (briefly), Liberale da Verona, and Giulio Clovio. In general, illuminations were no longer closely related to the text but became little paintings in Renaissance frames. The decline of the art of the miniature was made inevitable by the invention of the printing press, and toward the end of the 15th cent. woodblock prints began to replace painted illumination. The art of illumination was also highly developed in the Middle East and in the Orient. See PERSIAN ART AND ARCHITECTURE; ISLAMIC ART AND ARCHITECTURE; MOGUL ART AND ARCHITECTURE; INDIAN ART AND ARCHITECTURE. Since the mid-1960s many illuminated books have been published in relatively inexpensive facsimile editions. See Sabrina Mitchell, *Medieval Manuscript Painting* (1965); David Diringer, *The Illuminated Book* (rev. ed. 1967); David Bland, *A History of Book Illustration* (2d ed. 1969); D. M. Robb, *The Art of the Illuminated Manuscript* (1972).

illumination, in physics: see LIGHTING; PHOTOMETRY.

illusionism, in art, a kind of visual trickery in which painted forms seem to be real. It is sometimes called trompe l'oeil [Fr.,=fool the eye]. The development of one-point PERSPECTIVE in the Renaissance advanced illusionist technique immeasurably. It was highly developed in the baroque period; Caravaggio's bowls of fruit included insects to enhance verisimilitude. American masters of trompe l'oeil include William M. HARNETT and John F. PETO.

illustration, any type of picture or decoration used in conjunction with a text to embellish its appearance or to clarify its meaning. It is as old as writing, both originating in the pictograph. With the advent of printing, the art of hand-painted ILLUMINATION declined as a means of book illustration. Modern book illustration originated in the 15th-century BLOCK BOOKS, in which the text and the illustration were cut on the same block. Book illustration has followed closely the development of the printing processes. Copperplate engraving and etching tended to replace the woodcut during the 16th and 17th cent., but it was not until the close of the 18th cent. that the art was revolutionized by Thomas Bewick's ingenious use of wood engraving and Senefelder's invention of lithography. These two processes greatly stimulated the production of illustrated books and magazines and were exploited by such masters as Daumier, Doré, and Gavarni. In the late 19th cent., wood engraving and lithography were superseded by the photomechanical processes that made possible the reproduction of a wide variety of painting and drawing techniques. The exploitation of these processes for cheap and rapid but sloppy mass production obscured their artistic potential so that the early hand processes were revived in book illustration by such artists as William Morris, Matisse, Rouault, Picasso, Chagall, Rockwell Kent, and many others. However, such major illustrators as Aubrey Beardsley, Howard Pyle, and Elihu Vedder have understood and exploited the photomechanical processes to great effect in the reproduction of their art works. Other great artists famous for illustration are Dürer, Holbein, William Hogarth, William Blake, Manet, and Winslow Homer. Illustration of fiction was more popular in the 19th cent. than in the 20th. Dickens's works were illustrated by John Leech, H. K. Browne ("Phiz"), and George Cruikshank. Sir John Tenniel's illustrations for *Alice in Wonderland* are almost as well known as the text itself. Today much of the finest illustration is done in the field of CHILDREN'S LITERATURE. From Beatrix POTTER to Ludwig Bemelmans and Maurice SENDAK a number of gifted writers of children's stories have illustrated their own books. Among the great illustrators of children's books are Kate Greenaway, Walter Crane, Randolph Caldecott, Edward Lear, Ernest Shepherd, Palmer Cox, A. B. Frost, and Wanda Gág (see CHILDREN'S BOOK ILLUSTRATION). In the Middle East fine printing of illustrated books is a very recent development. The lavish *King Fuad Koran* (1923, Egypt) is exceptional among Middle Eastern printed works. In the Orient the art of book illustration is very old. Printing was highly developed in China by the 9th cent., and exquisite block-printed illustrations enhanced many volumes. Japan borrowed Chinese techniques as early as the 9th cent. and used the ancient processes for wood-block printing of ukiyo-e (see JAPANESE ART) in books into the 18th cent. Twentieth-century printing of illustrated books in Japan involves the best and most recently developed processes. See J. N. Lewis, *The Twentieth Century Book* (1967); David Bland, *A History of Book Illustration* (2d ed. 1969); Diana Klemin, *The Illustrated Book* (1970); R. M. Slythe, *The Art of Illustration* (1972).

Illyés, Gyula (dyo͞o'lŏ ĭl'yās), 1902–, Hungarian poet and novelist. Illyés came from a poor peasant family. He was educated in Budapest and Paris and supported himself with menial jobs, writing only in his spare time. During World War II he was associated with the journal *Nyugat.* After the liberation of Hungary he became a member of parliament, withdrawing from public life when the Stalinists rose to power. In his poetry Illyés was a spokesman for the oppressed peasant class. Greater universality and an appeal for national and individual liberty mark his later work. See his autobiographical novel, *People of the Puszta* (tr. 1967); selected poetry in *A Tribute to Gyula Illyés,* ed. by Thomas Kabdebo and Paul Tabori (1968).

Illyria (ĭlĭr'ēə) and **Illyricum** (ĭlĭr'ĭkəm), ancient region of the Balkan Peninsula. In prehistoric times a group of tribes speaking dialects of an Indo-European language swept down to the northern and eastern shores of the Adriatic and established themselves there. The region that they occupied came to be know as Illyria, and therefore the name has vague limits. Among the Illyrian peoples were the tribes later called the Dalmatians and the Pannonians; therefore Illyria is sometimes taken in the widest sense to include the whole area occupied by the Pannonians, and thus to reach from Epirus N to the Danube. More usually Illyria is used to mean only the Adriatic coast N of central Albania and W of the Dinaric Alps. The Illyrians were much affected by the Celts and mingled freely with them; the inhabitants of the later Rhaetia were a compound of Illyrians and Celts. The Illyrians were warlike and frequently engaged in piracy. The mines of the region, located inland, attracted the Greeks, but the terrain was too difficult. Greek cities were established on the coast in the 6th cent. B.C., but they did not flourish, and generally the Greeks left the Illyrians alone. Philip II of Macedon and later Philip V warred against them, but without permanent results. An Illyrian kingdom was set up in the 3d cent. B.C. with the capital at Scodra (present-day Shkodër, Albania), but trouble over Illyrian piracy led the Romans to conduct two victorious wars against Scodra (229–228, 219 B.C.). After the Dalmatians had split from the kingdom, the Romans conquered Genthius, king of Scodra, and established (168–167 B.C.) one of the earliest Roman colonies as Illyricum. The colony was enlarged by the total conquest of Dalmatia in several wars (notably 156, 119, 78–77 B.C.). The southern Illyrians were finally conquered (35–34 B.C.) by Augustus—a conquest confirmed by the campaigns of 29–27 B.C. Illyricum was expanded by conquests (12–11 B.C.) of the Pannonians. At the time of the stubborn revolt of the Illyrians (A.D. 6–9) the territory was split into the provinces of Dalmatia and Pannonia, but the term *Illyricum* was still used. It was later given to one of the great prefectures of the late Roman Empire. Illyricum then included much of the region N of the Adriatic as well as a large part of the Balkan Peninsula. When Napoleon revived (1809) the name for the Illyrian Provs. of his empire he included much of the region N of the Adriatic and what is today E Yugoslavia. Roughly the same region was included in the administrative district of Austria called (1816–49) the Illyrian kingdom. See Stanley Casson, *Macedonia, Thrace, and Illyria* (1926).

Ilmen (ĭl'mən), shallow lake, varying in size from c.300 to c.800 sq mi (780–2,070 sq km), NW European USSR. It empties through the Volkhov River into Lake Ladoga. Novgorod and Staraya Russa are nearby.

ilmenite (ĭl'mĕnīt), black mineral, iron titanium oxide, $FeTiO_3$, crystallizing in the hexagonal system. It is sometimes found as tabular hexagonal crystals but occurs more commonly as small grains in igneous and metamorphic rocks and in sands derived from them. Ilmenite has been noted as an important constituent of lunar rocks. It is the commonest titanium mineral and is the most important source of this element and its compounds. Over 3 million tons of ilmenite are mined annually; important producers are the United States, Canada, Australia, and Norway.

Iloilo (ē"lōē'lō), city (1970 pop. 209,738), capital of Iloilo prov. (1970 pop. 1,168,454), SE Panay, the Philippines, on Iloilo Strait of Panay Gulf. With a fine harbor sheltered by Guimaras island, it is the principal port on Panay, with both interisland and overseas shipping. Sugar, rice, and corn are exported. Iloilo is also a busy commercial center, with some manufacturing. It is known for its delicate, handwoven fabrics, made from silk and pineapple leaves. Central Philippine Univ., the Univ. of San Augustín, and a branch of the Univ. of the Philippines are there.

Ilorin (ēlô'rēn), city (1969 est. pop. 242,000), SW Nigeria. It is an industrial city and the market (especially for cattle, poultry, palm products, and yams) and transport center for a wide region. Manufactures include cigarettes, matches, and sugar. Traditional artisans make woven goods, tin products, wood carvings, and pottery. Ilorin was the capital of a YORUBA kingdom that, with the assistance of the FULANI, successfully rebelled against the OYO empire in 1817 but soon thereafter was incorporated into the Fulani state of SOKOTO. Through warfare against Oyo and IBADAN in the later 19th cent., Ilorin considerably increased its territory. In 1897 it was conquered by troops of the British-chartered Royal Niger Company led by Sir George GOLDIE.

Il Ruzzante: see BEOLCO, ANGELO.

Imabari (ēmä'bärē), city (1970 pop. 111,125), Ehime prefecture, N Shikoku, Japan, on the Hiuchi Sea. It is a commercial and fishing port and a manufacturing center with industries producing cotton textiles and food products.

image, in optics, likeness or counterpart of an object produced when rays of light coming from that object are reflected from a MIRROR or are refracted by a LENS. An image of an object is also formed when this light passes through a very small opening like that of a pinhole camera (which has no lens). Images are classed as real or virtual. A real image occurs when the rays of light from the object actually converge to form an image and can be seen on a screen placed at the point of convergence. For example, the image produced by the refraction of light rays by a convex lens (when the distance between the object and the lens is greater than the focal length of the lens) is real, and it appears on the side of the lens opposite the one on which the object is present. On the other hand, a virtual image occurs when the prolongations of the light rays converge to form an image, but the light rays themselves do not reach the point of convergence. Thus a virtual image cannot be seen on a screen. The image in a plane mirror is virtual. It appears to be behind the mirror, at a distance equal to that of the object in front, although the rays of light from the object do not penetrate the mirror but are reflected from it. Images of the same size as the object are sometimes produced, as in the case of the plane mirror, but in other cases they are larger, and in still others, smaller. They are sometimes erect and in other cases are inverted. The size of the image and whether it is erect or inverted, real or virtual, depend on the distance of the object from the lens or mirror relative to the focal length and on the type of lens or mirror (plane, convex, or concave) employed.

imaginary number: see NUMBER.

imagists, group of English and American poets writing from 1909 to about 1917, who were united by their revolt against the exuberant imagery and diffuse sentimentality of 19th-century poetry. Influenced by classicism, by Chinese and Japanese poetry, and by the French SYMBOLISTS, the imagists stated that poetic ideas are best expressed by the actual rendering of concrete objects, not merely by commenting upon them. The poet must embody his feelings in specific physical analogies that exactly convey his meaning. He must produce a hard, clear, concentrated poetry, free of stilted and artificial vocabulary, meter, and imagery. Ezra Pound, as head of the group, edited the anthology *Des Imagistes* (1913) and organized the principal imagist organ, the *Egoist* (1914–19). When he deserted imagism, Amy Lowell and others, including Richard ALDINGTON, Hilda DOOLITTLE, D. H. Lawrence, John Gould FLETCHER, and James Joyce published three imagist anthologies (1915, 1916, 1917). In its revival of the clarity and conciseness of classical poetry and in its general liberating effect on literature, imagism has been an important influence. See *Imagist Anthology* (1930, repr. 1970); Peter Jones, ed., *Imagist Poetry* (1973); study by Glen Hughes (1960).

Imaichi (ēmī'chē), city (1970 pop. 43,201), Tochigi prefecture, central Honshu, Japan. It is an agricultural market and tourist center near Nikko National Park.

imam (ĭmäm') [Arab.,=leader], in Islam, a recognized leader. Among the SUNNI the term refers to the leader in the Friday prayer at the mosque; any pious Muslim may function as imam. An imam may also be a religious teacher. The term is also a synonym for caliph, the vicegerent of God. In this use it is applied by the SHIITES to Ali, to HASAN and HUSEIN, and to the rest of the caliphs in the family of Ali, whom the Shiites consider, alone of the orthodox caliphs, to have been the successors of the Prophet. Since the Umayyad family was so long in the caliphate the followers of the family of Ali came to believe that there was a hidden imamate, or succession of legitimate, unrecognized Alid imams, or true caliphs. The idea grew up in the Middle Ages that one in this succession (the twelfth, or the seventh, imam) would return at the end of this world to restore the true caliphate. The returning imam is called the MAHDI. The belief in the hidden imam and the variations in it have caused political trouble, notably in Persia and Africa. The FATIMIDS were particularly given to belief in the hidden imam. The DRUSES, the ISMAILIS, and the ASSASSINS hold doctrines related to the belief in the hidden imam.

Imandra (ē'məndrə), lake, 340 sq mi (881 sq km), NW European USSR, on the Kola Peninsula S of Murmansk. Deeply indented, it contains some 140 islands and receives about 20 large rivers. It empties into the Kandalaksha Bay of the White Sea through the Niva River.

Imari (ēmä'rē), city (1970 pop. 61,561), Saga prefecture, NW Kyushu, Japan, on Imari Bay. It is a fishing and commercial port.

Imari ware: see KYUSHU.

Imatra (ĭm'äträ), falls in the Vuoksijoki River, SE Finland, between Lake Saimaa (Finland) and Lake Ladoga (USSR). The river descends 60 ft (18 m) in a series of rapids c.½ mi (.8 km) long. The hydroelectric station there supplies power to all of S Finland. Imatra is a tourist attraction.

imbecility: see MENTAL RETARDATION.

Imeritia (ĭmərĭsh'ə), geographic and historic region, SE European USSR, in Georgia, in the upper Rion River basin. KUTAISI (the historic capital) and Chiatura are the main cities. Imeritia is an agricultural region, noted for its mulberry trees and vineyards. There are also manganese and coal deposits. The Imeritians, now numbering about 500,000, speak a Georgian dialect and probably represent a very early branch of the Caucasians. Imeritia has been known since 1442, when the Georgian ruler Alexander I divided his kingdom into three parts among his sons; one part was Imeritia. From 1510 it was often invaded by the Turks, to whom it was forced to pay tribute. It was an independent kingdom from the 16th to 18th cent. In 1804, Russia forcibly obtained an oath of allegiance from Imeritia, which, however, continued to fight until its annexation to the Russian Empire in 1810.

Imhoff tank: see SEPTIC TANK.

imitation, in music, a device of COUNTERPOINT wherein a phrase or motive is employed in more than one voice. The imitation may be exact, the same intervals being repeated at the same or different pitches, or it may be free, in which case numerous types of variation are possible. When the same motive is repeated at different pitches but in the same voice, the device is called sequence. Imitation was much used in both vocal and instrumental compositions of the 15th and 16th cent. The *ricercare, canzone,* capriccio, and fantasia—instrumental forms of this period—employed imitation to a great extent and without formal plan. They were forerunners of the fugue. The strictest form of imitation is the CANON. While imitation is found to some extent in the music of nearly all periods, it is of special significance in Renaissance and baroque music.

Imitation of Christ, The, Christian devotional book, of great popularity. It originated among the Brothers of the Common Life in the Netherlands and was written probably c.1425. Tradition (since c.1445) has ascribed it to THOMAS À KEMPIS, whose name appears on an early Latin manuscript. A popular contemporary theory holds that Thomas copied out and edited *The Imitation* from manuscripts originating with Gerard GROOTE. The work encourages a life of mystical devotion to Christ and a distrust of the human intellect. The four books treat liberation from worldly inclinations, recollection as a preparation for prayer, the consolations of prayer, and the place of eucharistic communion in a devout life. The work is a summary of the spirit of Groote's movement, the *devotio moderna.* The English translation by Richard Whitford (c.1530) has long been standard. It has been revised into modern English (Harold Gardiner, ed., 1955). The *Imitation* has also been rendered as *The Following of Christ* (tr. 1941). See J. E. G. De Montmorency, *Thomas à Kempis: His Age and Book* (1906, repr. 1970).

Imla or **Imlah** (both: ĭm'lə), father of Micaiah the prophet. 1 Kings 22.8,9; 2 Chron. 18.7,8.

Immaculate Conception of Our Lady: see MARY.

immanence (ĭm'ənəns) [Lat.,=dwelling in], in metaphysics, the presence within the natural world of a spiritual or cosmic principle, especially of the Deity. It is contrasted with transcendence. The immanence of God in the world is the basic feature of PANTHEISM. Among the most important philosophies using the concept of immanence are STOICISM and the systems of Giordano BRUNO and SPINOZA. In general, the great monotheistic religions have held that God is both immanent and transcendent, although individual thinkers have tended to emphasize one or the other aspect.

Immanuel or **Emmanuel** (both: ĭmăn'yo͞oəl) [Heb.,=God with us], name given by Isaiah to the child who would be a sign to Judah of her deliverance. It is a name of Jesus. Isa. 7.14; 8.8; Mat. 1.23.

Immanuel ben Solomon, c.1265–c.1330, Hebrew-Italian poet and scholar, b. Rome. He wrote biblical criticism and, in both Hebrew and Italian, satiric verse and lively stories. His work represents a synthesis of Jewish thought and reflects the spirit of Italian Renaissance. His collected poems were printed (1491) under the title *Mahberoth Immanuel* [the compositions of Immanuel]. His verse was notorious in his day and later for its satiric and erotic content. He introduced the Italian sonnet form into Hebrew poetry.

Immer (ĭm'ər). **1** Priestly family. 1 Chron. 9.12; 24.14; Ezra 2.37; 10.20; Neh. 3.29; 7.40; 11.13. This is probably the same as AMARIAH **8. 2** Priest. Jer. 20.1 **3** Unidentified place in Babylonia. Ezra 2.59; Neh. 7.61.

Immermann, Karl Leberecht (kärl lā'bərekht ĭm'ərmän), 1796–1840, German novelist and dramatist. As a Prussian official in Düsseldorf he was active in the local theater, and his stage direction (1835–37) introduced a new epoch in the German theater. His many plays, mostly historical tragedies, are forgotten, but his novels remain famous. The semiautobiographical novel *Die Epigonen* [men born too late] (3 vol., 1836), reminiscent of Goethe's *Wilhelm Meister,* describes the decay of the old social structure and the rise of industrial society, which Immermann deplored. *Der Oberhof* (separately pub. 1863), an episode of the satire *Münchhausen* (4 vol., 1838–39), is considered the best description of peasant life written before the period of realism. See study by A. W. Porterfield (1911).

immigration, entrance of a person into a new country for the purpose of establishing permanent residence. Motives for immigration, like those for migration generally, are chiefly economic, although religious and political factors may be important. Most immigration in the 19th and 20th cent. has been from Europe to the continents of Australia, North America, and South America. From 1820 to 1930 the United States received about 60% of the world's immigrants. This was a result partly of the great POPULATION expansion in the developed areas of the world and partly because of improved methods of transportation. Until the middle of the 19th cent. the bulk of immigrants were from the British Isles and NW Europe. By 1880 emigration from these countries had tapered off, and there was an influx of southern and eastern Europeans. At that time the United States was in the midst of a great industrial expansion. The desire for quantities of cheap, unskilled labor and the efforts of transportation companies to promote the profitable importation of immigrants were factors in the continuance of the movement. Immigration from Asia began in the middle of the 19th cent. Immigrants were largely responsible for the rapid expansion of the country, and their high birthrate did much to swell the general U.S. population. The majority of the later European arrivals settled in the northeastern cities. They usually formed distinct ethnic neighborhoods where they tended to remain somewhat isolated from the wider culture; thus assimilation was slow, and there was much social conflict. Often exploited, immigrants were accused by organized labor of lowering wages and living standards. Opposition was early manifested by such organizations as the KNOW-NOTHING MOVEMENT and, on the West Coast, in violent anti-Chinese riots. The first restrictions against any particular group were made in 1882 by the Chinese Exclusion Act, which denied entrance to Chinese laborers. In the same year, restrictions against the entrance of diseased persons, paupers, and other undesirables were strengthened, and laws were passed for the DEPORTATION of aliens. Despite strong opposition, a literacy test was imposed on all immigrants in 1917. The first permanent quota law was passed in 1924; it also provided for a national origins plan to be put into effect in 1929. This limited the entire number of European immigrants to 150,000 and fixed quotas for individual countries at ⅙ of 1% of the number of people of that origin living in the United States in 1920—thus favoring those from N and W Europe, especially the British, at the expense of those from S and E Europe. The act of 1924 also, in effect, excluded all Asians, and was bitterly resented by the Japanese. The Chinese Exclusion Act was repealed by Congress in 1943, and a small quota was set up. In 1952 the Immigration and Nationality Act (the McCarran-Walter Act) was passed; while abolishing race as an overall barrier to immigration, it kept particular forms of national bias. The act was amended in 1965, abolishing the national origins quota; however, an overall limitation was placed on non-Western Hemisphere nations, and Western Hemisphere countries for the first time came under quota restrictions. Canada, in the first third of the 20th cent., began to receive an increasing number of immigrants, mainly from Great Britain, the Commonwealth, and the United States; these immigrants were attracted to Canada by the expansion of agriculture in the west and the development of industry in the east. Australia and New Zealand received many European immigrants in the 19th cent.; the former country has been characterized by a preference for immigrants of British stock and by a policy of excluding Africans and Asians that dates from the late 19th cent. After 1965, however, Australia began to admit non-Europeans in particular categories, such as those with specialized skills. The Latin American countries with the highest rate of European immigration (from the late 19th cent. on) were Argentina (notably Germans), Brazil (mainly Portuguese), and Uruguay. Two major trends in immigration emerged after World War II: Australia and New Zealand became the countries with the highest rates of increase, and large numbers of Europeans moved into the countries of Africa. Exclusion policies are not limited to Australia and the United States. Great Britain, in acts passed in 1962 and 1968, began to limit immigration from Commonwealth countries. Besides the United States, the Republic of South Africa, Brazil, and the Philippine Republic all have numerical quotas, often as a method of restricting the immigration of Africans and Asians. Virtually all countries have educational and financial requirements for immigrants; those with criminal records may also be prohibited from becoming immigrants. See NATURALIZATION. See D. R. Taft, *International Migrations* (1955); John Higham, *Strangers in the Land* (rev. ed. 1963); Oscar Handlin, ed., *Immigration as a Factor in American History* (1959, repr. 1961); M. A. Jones, *American Immigration* (1960); John Thomas, *Planned International Migration and Multilateral Cooperation* (1971); Paul Tabori, *The Anatomy of Exile* (1972).

immortality, attribute of deathlessness ascribed to the soul in many religions and philosophies. Forthright belief in immortality of the body is rare. Immortality of the soul is a cardinal tenet of Islam and is held generally in Judaism, although it is not an essentially Jewish idea. The ancient Greeks and Romans believed in an afterlife, in which the souls of men lived on, but generally only the gods were considered truly immortal. The ancient Celts believed firmly in immortality. In the East, ZOROASTRIANISM posited immortality. The religions arising in India (Hinduism, Buddhism, and Jainism) generally consider individual immortality undesirable and believe in REINCARNATION of men as a chain eventually leading to reunion with the infinite (Nirvana). Christianity teaches the RESURRECTION of the body (in the sense of survival of personality) as well as immortality of the soul. See SPIRITISM; HEAVEN; HELL. See J. G. Frazer, *Man, God, and Immortality* (rev. ed. 1927, repr. 1968); C. H. Moore, *Ancient Beliefs in the Immortality of the Soul* (1931, repr. 1963); W. E. Hocking, *Thoughts on Life and Death* (1937, repr. 1957).

immortelle: see EVERLASTING.

immunity, ability of an organism to resist disease. A group of tissues in the body combats disease-causing agents by PHAGOCYTOSIS, the process by which body cells destroy invading microorganisms, and by inactivation of foreign agents (antigens) by ANTIBODIES and other defending substances. Antibodies are one group of globulin proteins, called gamma globulins, produced in vertebrates. Antibody molecules are able to chemically recognize surface portions, or epitopes, of large molecules that act as antigens, such as nucleic acids, proteins, and polysaccharides. About 10 amino acid subunits of a protein may compose a single epitope recognizable to a specific antibody. The fit of an epitope to a specific antibody is analogous to the way a key fits a specific lock. The amino acid sequence and configuration of an antibody molecule were determined in the 1960s by the biochemists Gerald Edelman, an American, and R. R. Porter, an Englishman; for this achievement they shared the 1972 Nobel Prize in Medicine. The antibody molecule is now known to consist of four polypeptide chains, two identical heavy (i.e., long) chains and two identical light (i.e., short) chains. All antibody molecules are alike except for certain small segments that, varying in amino acid sequence, account for the specificity of the molecules for particular antigens. In order to recognize and neutralize a specific antigen such as a virus, the body produces millions of antibodies, each differing slightly in the amino acid sequence of the variable regions; some of these molecules will chemically fit the invading antigen. Antibodies are produced and secreted by lymphocytes, cells originating from stem cells in bone marrow. According to the modified clonal selection theory originally postulated by the Australian immunologist Sir Macfarlane Burnet (for which Burnet and British zoologist P. B. Medawar won the 1960 Nobel Prize in Medicine), a lymphocyte is potentially able to secrete one particular, specific humoral, or free-circulating, antibody molecule. It is believed that early in life specific lymphocytes are formed to recognize thousands of different antigens, including a group of autoimmune lymphocytes, i.e., cells recognizing antigens of the organism's own body. The immune system is self-tolerant; i.e., it does not normally attack molecules and cells of the organism's own body, because those lymphocytes that are autoimmune are inactivated or destroyed early in life, and the cells that remain, the majority, recognize only foreign antigens. The presence of antigens in contact with receptor sites on the lymphocyte surface stimulates the lymphocyte to divide and become a CLONE (a line of descendant cells), with each cell of the clone specific for the same antigen. Some cells of the clone, called plasma cells, secrete large quantities of antibody; others, entering a resting state, remain prepared to respond to any later invasions by the same antigen. Antibody secretion by lymphocytes can be stimulated or suppressed by such variables as the concentration of antigens, the way the antigen fits the lymphocyte's receptor regions, the age of the lymphocyte, and the effect of other lymphocytes.Immunologic tolerance against foreign antigens can be induced experimentally by creating conditions of high-zone tolerance, i.e., by injecting large amounts of a foreign antigen into the host organism, or low-zone tolerance, i.e., injecting small amounts of foreign antigen over long periods of time. Antibodies act in diverse ways; for example, they combine with some antigens, such as bacterial TOXINS, and neutralize their effect; they remove other substances from circulation in body fluids; and they bind certain bacteria or foreign cells together, a process known as agglutination. Antibodies attached to antigens on the surfaces of invading cells activate a group of 11 blood serum proteins called complement, which cause the breakdown of the invading cells in a complex series of enzymatic reactions. Complement proteins are believed to cause swelling and eventual rupture of cells by making holes in the lipid portion of the cell's membrane. They also play a part in tissue inflammation by causing release of HISTAMINE and substances that attract phagocytes to the site of infection. Together with antibody, complement proteins make a bacterium more easily phagocytized, a process known as opsonization; they also accelerate blood clotting. Immunity has taken on increased medical importance; for instance, the ability of the body to reject foreign matter is the main obstacle to the successful TRANSPLANTATION of certain tissues and organs. In blood transfusions the immune response is the cause of severe cell agglutination or rupture (lysis) when the blood donor and recipient are not matched for immunological compatibility (see BLOOD GROUPS). An immune reaction can also occur between a mother and baby (see RH FACTOR). ALLERGY, ANAPHYLAXIS, and SERUM SICKNESS are all manifestations of undesirable immune responses. Many degenerative disorders of aging, e.g., ARTHRITIS, are thought to be disorders of the immune system. In AUTOIMMUNE DISEASES, such as rheumatoid arthritis and LUPUS, an individual produces antibodies against his own proteins and cell components. Combinations of foreign proteins and their antibodies, called immune complexes, circulating through the body may cause glomerulonephritis and Bright's disease (a kidney disease); circulating immune complexes following infection by the hepatitis virus may cause arthritis. Organisms are protected against infectious disease by a variety of preventive mechanisms. Nonsusceptibility is the inability of certain disease-carrying organisms to grow in a particular host species. Nonsusceptibility may be caused by such conditions as lack of availability of particular growth substances needed by the infecting microorganism, or body temperature unsuitable for the invading microorganism (for example, chickens are nonsusceptible to anthrax because the bacteria cannot grow at the body temperature normal for that animal). Natural resistance is a condition in which organisms are protected against infectious disease by a complex of factors, e.g., the physical and chemical barriers of skin, respiratory tract, and gastrointestinal system. Various chemical substances in tissue and fluid are antibacterial, such as lysozyme, a basic protein that impairs the integrity of the invading bacterial cell membrane. Interferon is a large protein produced by virus-infected cells that inactivates viruses. Many responses of tissue also contribute to natural resistance. One response to injury is release of histamine, resulting in increased local blood flow and an increase in the permeability of the capillaries. Leakage of the clotting protein fibrinogen and other substances into the injured area results in blockage of tissue by clots, which wall off the injured area to retard the spread of bacteria or their toxins. In natural immunity, antibodies are present or appear without any obvious external factor that stimulates their production. Thus, antibodies against typhoid antigens are normally found in human blood serums; these antibodies may be produced in response to the presence of substances chemically similar to the infectious agent. In active immunity, specific antibodies are generally produced in response to an initial invasion of disease-causing organisms. An individual who recovers from certain diseases, such as measles or diphtheria, will usually be immune to a second attack of the same diseases. Active immunity can also be acquired by exposing the individual to disease-causing organisms that are altered in form and unable to cause disease; when given to humans, preparations of attenuated, or weakened and nonvirulent, viruses or various TOXOIDS (i.e., heat-treated bacterial toxins) do not cause disease but are potent enough to elicit formation of antibodies. The toxins produced by bacteria are powerful antigens, too harmful to be used successfully in human immunization. Antibodies to these toxins, or antitoxins, can be obtained from horses that have been exposed to the toxins. The horse antitoxin, combined with toxin, can then be given to humans, because in combination the toxin is nearly neutralized and is released slowly in the body, where it stimulates the formation of human antibodies. In passive immunity, specific antibodies are injected into individuals who have been exposed to a disease to temporarily protect them from the disease or to lessen its severity. Young mammals are passively immune to many diseases because of specific maternal antibodies that pass through the placenta during pregnancy. The administration of the gamma globulin fraction of blood serum also provides some passive immunity to such diseases as measles, polio, and infectious hepatitis. Adoptive immunity, an immune state produced by transferring immunologically active lymphocytes from an immunized donor animal to a nonimmunized recipient, is used as an experimental tool. Lack of immunity, as in the congenital inability to produce antibodies or as a result of disorders of the immune system, leave an individual unprotected from disease; such individuals usually die before adulthood. See H. J. A. Parish, *A History of Immunization* (1965); G. J. V. Nossal, *Antibodies and Immunity* (1969); David Wilson, *Body and Antibody* (1972).

immunization: see IMMUNITY.

immunology, study of the resistance of organisms to INFECTION. Immunologists study pathogenic, or disease-causing, organisms to determine how they injure the host (see TOXINS); the genetic, physiological, and nutritional factors that enable the host to resist infection; and the defensive measures used by organisms to fight invading pathogens (see IMMUNITY). A large number of procedures have been developed to detect and measure quantities of immunologically active substances such as circulating ANTIBODIES.

immunosuppressive drug, any of a variety of substances used to prevent production of ANTIBODIES. They are commonly used to prevent rejection by a recipient's body of an organ transplanted from a donor. A transplant is rejected when the recipient's immune system acts against it; current methods aim at suppressing the activity of the lymphocytes, the cells that form antibodies (see IMMUNITY; TRANSPLANTATION). The STEROIDS, such as CORTISONE, which suppress the antibody-forming lymphocyte cells, have been used to prolong human organ transplants. Steroids may also prevent antigens from entering cells and thereby prevent local allergic inflammation reactions. In another immunosuppressive method, human lymphocytes are injected into horses, stimulating the animals to produce antilymphocyte serum. The serum, administered to humans with transplanted organs, in some way inactivates lymphocyte cells. The procedure will not work effectively for more than a few injections of serum. Another group of immunosuppressive drugs act by interfering with the synthesis of NUCLEIC ACIDS and are especially effective against proliferating cells such as stimulated lymphocytes. Some of these are analogs of purines and pyrimidines, substances that are nucleic acid subunits; the purine analog azothioprine has been used to suppress rejection of transplanted human kidneys. Most substances that inhibit nucleic acid synthesis, such as NITROGEN MUSTARD, cyclophosphamide (CYTOXAN), CHLORAMPHENICOL, ACTINOMYCIN, METHOTREXATE, and COLCHICINE, are not widely used clinically because they are too toxic. Many of the drugs that suppress the function of the immunological system are also used clinically to check growth of cancerous tissue, which is composed of rapidly dividing cells. The drugs currently used to suppress antibody formation also leave an individual susceptible to infection.

Imna (ĭm'nə), chief of the Asherites. 1 Chron. 7.35.

Imnah (ĭm'nə). **1** The same as JIMNA. **2** Father of KORE **2.**

Imola (ē'mōlä), city (1971 pop. 57,141), Emilia-Romagna, N central Italy, on the Aemilian Way. It is an agricultural and industrial center, known for its ceramics. A Roman town (*Forum Cornelii*), it later (11th cent.) became a free commune. The city was subsequently ruled by tyrants (including the Visconti and the Sforza) until it passed to the papacy in the early 16th cent. Landmarks include a Gothic cathedral, several Renaissance palaces, and the "Rocca," a large fortress (14th cent.).

impala, species of ANTELOPE, *Aepyceros melampus,* closely related to the gazelle and found in the savannah and bush country of E and S Africa. It is the antelope most commonly depicted in illustrations and in motion pictures. It is about 3 ft (90 cm) high at the shoulder, with a coat of rich reddish brown, shading to whitish on the underparts. The horns, borne only by the male, are long and curved in the shape of a lyre. Impalas are the most powerful jumpers of all antelopes; they can leap 10 ft (3 m) into the air and travel 30 ft (9 m) in a single bound. Impalas live in herds, sometimes numbering several hundred individuals; they feed on grasses and shrubs and always stay fairly near water. They are often found in association with herds of other animals, such as zebras and gnus. Impalas are still fairly numerous over most of their range. They are classified in the phylum CHORDATA, subphylum Vertebrata, class Mammalia, order Artiodactyla, family Bovidae.

impasto (ĭmpäs'tō, –pä'stō), thickly applied paint that projects from the picture surface. Such works as Childe Hassam's *Allies Day* (1917; National Gall. of Art, Washington, D.C.) and Hans Hoffman's abstraction *In Upper Regions* (1963; David N. Marks Coll.) exploit to advantage the vigorous effect inherent in impasto technique.

impatiens (ĭmpā'shēēnz"): see JEWELWEED.

impeachment, formal accusation issued by a legislature against a public official charging him with crime or other serious misconduct. In a looser sense the term is sometimes applied also to the trial by the legislature that may follow. Impeachment developed in England, beginning in the 14th cent., as a means of trying officials suspected of dereliction of duty. The English procedure was for the House of Commons to prosecute by presenting articles of impeachment to the House of Lords, which rendered judgment. Any penalty, including death, might be inflicted. The impeachment (1787) and trial (1788-95) of Warren HASTINGS was among the last of the English cases. In the United States impeachment of public officials is provided for in the Federal government and in most states. In Federal matters the U.S. Constitution gives the House of Representatives the power to impeach civil officers of the United States, including the President and Vice President, but not including members of Congress. Impeachments are tried by the Senate, with the concurrence of two thirds of the members present needed for conviction. The sole penalties on conviction are removal from office and disqualification from holding other Federal office; however, the convicted party is liable to subsequent criminal trial and punishment for the same offense. There have been 11 impeachments tried by the Senate and four convictions. Two of the best-known cases, which did not result in conviction, were those of Supreme Court Justice Samuel CHASE and of President Andrew JOHNSON. In 1974 the Judiciary Committee of the House of Representatives voted to bring impeachment charges against President Nixon (see WATERGATE AFFAIR), but Nixon resigned before the House took action. See studies by Irving Brant (1972), Raoul Berger (1973), and Charles L. Black, Jr. (1974).

impedance, in electricity, measure in ohms of the degree to which an electric circuit resists the flow of electric current when a voltage is impressed across its terminals. Impedance is expressed as the ratio of the voltage impressed across a pair of terminals to the current flow between those terminals. When a circuit is supplied with steady direct current, the impedance equals the total RESISTANCE of the circuit. The resistance depends upon the number of electrons that are free to become part of the current and upon the difficulty that the electrons have in moving through the circuit. When a circuit is supplied with alternating current, the impedance is affected by the INDUCTANCE and CAPACITANCE in the circuit. When supplied with alternating current, elements of the circuit that contain inductance or capacitance build up voltages that act in opposition to the flow of current. This opposition is called reactance, and it must be combined with the resistance to find the impedance. The reactance produced by inductance is proportional to the frequency of the alternating current. The reactance produced by capacitance is inversely proportional to the frequency of the alternating current. In order for a source of electricity that has an internal impedance to transfer maximum power to a device that also has an impedance, the two impedances must be matched. For example, in the simple case of pure resistances, the resistance of the source must also equal the resistance of the device. Impedance matching is important in any electrical or electronic system in which power transfer must be maximized.

imperative: see MOOD.

imperfect: see TENSE.

Imperia (ēmpĕ'rēä), city (1971 pop. 40,758), capital of Imperia prov., Liguria, NW Italy, on the Ligurian Sea. Located on the Italian Riviera, it is a port, industrial center, and winter resort. Manufactures include iron and steel, refined olive oil, and chemicals. The cathedral (1780–1832) dominates the modern city. Andrea Doria, the admiral and statesman, was born there (1468).

Imperial Beach, residential and resort city (1970 pop. 20,244), San Diego co., S Calif., on the Mexican border; inc. 1956. The southwesternmost city in the continental United States, Imperial Beach has several naval bases and air stations.

Imperial conference, assembly of representatives of the self-governing members of the British Empire, held about every four years until World War II. The meetings prior to 1907—in 1887, 1897, and 1902—were known as Colonial Conferences, and were chiefly concerned with defense problems and the possibility of imperial tariff preference. Relatively informal, they were held when colonial representatives came to Great Britain for royal celebrations. More formalized meetings were held 1907, 1911, 1917–18, 1921, 1923, 1926, 1930, 1936, and 1937. The conferences were designed to strengthen imperial ties by exchange of ideas, but their decisions had no legal effect. The two main focal points of discussion remained defense and economic policy. In 1917–18 the Imperial War Conference acknowledged the importance of the whole empire in defense policy by admitting India, not yet self-governing, to the conference. There was an acknowledged need on the part of Britain for practical support from the dominions in military and naval resources, and a parallel desire for participation in the decision-making initiative on the part of the dominions. The dominions also wanted to be able to pursue independent foreign policies, within the bounds of imperial cooperation. The constitution of the conferences themselves and the status of the dominions were the chief problems discussed at meetings during the 1920s. The resolutions of the conferences were given legal effect by the Statute of Westminster (1931; see WESTMINSTER, STATUTE OF), which declared the legislatures of the several dominions on an equal footing with that of the United Kingdom. A standing Imperial Economic Committee concerned itself with coordination of economic matters. Since World War II, Commonwealth policy has been coordinated through regular meetings of the prime ministers of the Commonwealth of Nations. See Maurice Ollivier, ed., *The Colonial and Imperial Conferences from 1887 to 1939* (1954).

imperialism, broadly, the extension of rule or influence by one government, nation, or society over another. Evidence of the existence of empires dates back to the dawn of written history in Egypt and in Mesopotamia, where local rulers extended their realms by conquering other states and holding them, when possible, in a state of subjection or semisubjection. An early, highly organized empire was that of Assyria, which was succeeded by the even more integrated Persian Empire. Ancient imperialism reached its climax under the long-enduring Roman Empire, the eastern part of which lasted until late into the Middle Ages as the Byzantine Empire. In Western Europe no true empire arose to replace Rome; the Holy Roman Empire, despite the aspirations of its rulers, was little more than a confederation of princely states. However, imperialism remained an important historical force elsewhere. In the Middle East and North Africa the Arabs and later the Turks built large empires. Farther east, besides the huge, if unstable, empires of the nomadic Mongols and others arising out of Central Asia, there were long-lasting and complex imperial organizations exemplified by various Chinese dynasties. Imperialism was reborn in the West with the emergence of the modern nation state and the age of exploration and discovery. It is to this modern type of empire building that the term *imperialism* is quite often restricted. Colonies were established not only in more or less sparsely inhabited places where there were few or no highly integrated native states (e.g., North America and Africa) but also in lands where ancient civilizations and states existed (e.g., India, Malaya, Indonesia, and the Inca lands of South America). The emigration of European settlers to people the Western Hemisphere and Africa, known as COLONIZATION, was marked by the same attitude of assumed superiority on the part of the newcomers toward the native populations that prevailed where the Europeans merely took over control without large-scale settlements. The Portuguese and the Dutch from the 15th to the 17th cent. built "trading empires" in Africa and the East for the exploitation of the resources and commerce of lands already developed. The Spanish and Portuguese established important colonies in the New World in the 17th cent., hoping to exploit the mineral wealth of the lands they conquered. The British and French imperialists became the foremost exemplars of colonial settlement in Africa and the East. Acting on mercantilist principles (see MERCANTILISM), the European nations in the 18th cent. attempted to regulate the trade of their colonies in the interests of the mother country. Later, the increase of manufactures in the INDUSTRIAL REVOLUTION introduced a new form of imperialism, as industrial nations scrambled both for markets and for raw materials. The eastward spread of Russia after the 16th cent. and the westward spread of the United States may also be termed imperialistic, although the United States did not actually acquire colonial possessions until the Spanish-American War. In the late 19th cent. Italy, Germany, and Japan also developed imperial ambitions; these nations, like the older colonial powers, were moved by a variety of aims, including commercial penetration, military glory, and diplomatic advantage. At its best, European imperialism brought economic expansion and new standards of official administration and public health to subject countries; at its worst, it meant brutal exploitation and dehumanization. In every instance, however, the pressure of an alien culture, with its different values and religious beliefs, and the imposition of new forms of social organization meant the breakdown of traditional forms of life and the disruption of native civilization. At the end of the 19th cent. there was a strong reaction against the most inhumane forms of imperialist exploitation. Efforts were made to improve the standards of colonial administration; and a new justification of the rule of non-Europeans by the European powers was found in the idea of "the white man's burden," which advanced the notion that the developed nations of Europe had a duty to rule Asians and Africans in order to lead them to a higher level of civilization and culture. Among the leading critics of imperialism at that time were the Marxists, who saw imperialism as the ultimate stage of capitalism and made much of the connection between imperialist rivalries and war. After World War I, antiimperialist feeling grew rapidly throughout the world, sparked by the development of movements for national liberation within subject countries. Nevertheless the major colonialist powers, Great Britain, France, and others, held on to their colonies, while Fascist governments in Italy and Germany, as well as militarist opinion in Japan, fostered even more extreme imperialist aims. In the years since World War II, most of the countries once subject to Western control have achieved independence. Much of the contemporary debate centers on the issue of neo-imperialism. Many of the less developed countries contend that their economic development is largely controlled and seriously retarded by the developed countries, both through unfair trading practices and by a lack of controls over international business corporations. See J. A. Schumpeter, *Imperialism and Social Classes* (tr. 1919, repr. 1960); J. A. Hobson, *Imperialism: A Study* (3d ed. 1948, repr. 1965); Ronald Robinson and Jack Gallagher, *Africa and the Victorians* (1961, repr. 1965); George Lichtheim, *Imperialism* (1970); K. E. Boulding and Tapan Mukerjee, ed., *Economic Imperialism* (1972).

Imperial Valley, fertile region in the Colorado Desert, SE Calif., extending S into NW Mexico. Once part of the Gulf of California, most of the region is below sea level; its lowest point is −232 ft (−71 m) at the southern shore of the Salton Sea. Receiving only c.3 in. (7.6 cm) of rain annually, the valley experiences extremely high temperatures (115°F/46°C) and has a great daily temperature range. Having one of the longest growing seasons in the United States (more than 300 days), the valley can, with irrigation, support two crops a year; it was first irrigated in 1901. Several disastrous floods on the Colorado River in 1905–6 inundated the area; not until 1935, with the completion of Hoover Dam, was the valley safe from floods. Approximately 1 million acres (404,700 hectares) have been irrigated, chiefly by the All-American Canal. The valley is an important source of winter fruits and vegetables for the northern areas of the United States; cotton, dates, grains, and dairy products are also important. Brawley, Calexico, and El Centro, Calif., are the main U.S. cities in the valley; Mexicali, Mexico, also in the valley, is the center of Mexico's important cotton-growing district.

impetigo (ĭmpətī'gō), contagious skin infection affecting mainly infants and children. The causative organism is either hemolytic streptococcus or staphylococcus. The eruption consists of red spots or blisters that rupture, discharge, and become encrusted. The infection is easily spread over the skin by dirty fingernails because of its symptomatic itching. Effective treatment with antibiotic ointments usually relieves the infection within 10 days. Systemic treatment with antibiotics is sometimes necessary to prevent the nephritis that occasionally develops.

Imphal (ĭm'pəl), city (1971 pop. 100,605), capital of Manipur state, NE India, in the Manipur River valley, 2,500 ft (762 m) above sea level. Industries include weaving and the manufacture of metalware. Until 1813, when Manipur was conquered by the Burmese, Imphal was the seat of the Manipuri kings. The inhabitants, of Tibeto-Burman origin, are famous for their music and dance. Imphal has three colleges affiliated with Gauhati Univ., as well as a technical college.

impotence (im'pətəns), inability of the male to perform sexual intercourse. Its equivalent in the woman is frigidity. Impotence should be distinguished from STERILITY, which is the inability to produce sperm or egg cells necessary for reproduction. Infrequently, impotence results from physical causes such as structural abnormalities of the genital organs; decreased activity of the thyroid, pituitary, or sex glands (resulting in a decreased secretion of male sex hormones); anemia or other debilitating diseases; or chronic poisoning such as in drug addiction or alcoholism. However, the most frequent cause of impotence is thought to be psychological in origin. For example, neuroses arising from negative attitudes toward interpersonal relationships established during childhood are sometimes proved to relate to habitual impotence.

impressionism, in music, a French movement in the late 19th and early 20th cent. It was begun by Debussy in reaction to the dramatic and dynamic emotionalism of romantic music, especially that of Wagner. Reflecting the impressionist schools of French painting and letters, Debussy developed a style in which atmosphere and mood take the place of strong emotion or of the story in program music. He used new chord combinations, whole-tone chords, chromaticism, and exotic rhythms and scales. In place of the usual harmonic progression, he developed a style in which chords are valued for their individual sonorities rather than for their relations to one another, and dissonances are unprepared and unresolved. Although conceived in reaction to romanticism, musical impressionism seems today the culmination of romanticism. Its influence was widespread and is evident in the music of Ravel, Dukas, Respighi, Albéniz, de Falla, Delius, C. T. Griffes, and J. A. Carpenter. See Christopher Palmer, *Impressionism in Music* (1973).

impressionism, in painting, late-19th-century French school. It was loosely structured in that many painters were associated with the movement for only brief periods in their careers. Their association came about more for the purpose of exhibiting their works than from an approach to painting held in common. Impressionism was generally characterized by the attempt to depict transitory visual impressions, often painted directly from nature, and by the use of pure, broken color to achieve brilliance and luminosity. The movement began with the friendship of four students of the academic painter Marc Gleyre: Monet, Renoir, Sisley, and Bazille. These four met regularly at the Café Guerbois with Cézanne, Pissarro, and Morisot, and later with Degas, Manet, the critics Duret and Rivière, and the art dealer Durand-Ruel. The painters repudiated academic standards and reacted against the romantics' emphasis on emotion as subject matter. They forsook literary and anecdotal subjects and, indeed, rejected the role of imagination in the creation of works of art. Instead they observed nature closely, with a scientific interest in visual phenomena. Although they painted everyday subjects, they avoided the vulgar and ugly, seeking visual realism by extraordinary stylistic means. When works by five of these painters were rejected by the Salon of 1873, the disgruntled artists organized an independent exhibit in 1874. They called themselves the *Société anonyme des artistes, peintres, sculpteurs, etc.*, but a hostile journalist dubbed them "impressionists" after Monet's *Impression: Sunrise, 1872* and they grudgingly accepted the name. The impressionists were a disparate group and their eight exhibits (in 1874, 1876, 1877, 1879, 1880, 1881, 1882, and 1886) were fraught with squabbles and hurt feelings. Manet, their prime influence, refused to exhibit with them although he was often in their company informally. The subject matter of their painting was as diverse as their personalities: Manet chose Old Master themes which he treated in a novel and stunningly direct way so that his canvases were the focus of acid controversy and scandal. Monet, Sisley, and Pissarro were the most consistently impressionist in style. Their subject was landscape and the changing effects of light. Degas painted horse races, the ballet, and portraits of ordinary people, all with a photographic sense of "accidental" composition. Renoir, painting his idealized women and children and his lush landscapes, developed DIVISIONISM; omitting black for shadows and outlines from his palette in the 1860's, he used pure, bright color to separate forms. Monet painted many series of the same subject at different times of day so that the character of light became his subject and the forms of objects seemed to dissolve, as in the series of Rouen Cathedral. The interests and attitudes of these painters influenced the postimpressionists Cézanne, Seurat, Gauguin, and Van Gogh. Toulouse-Lautrec gained from a study of Degas's paintings; Matisse, Vuillard, and Bonnard all owed a debt to the landscape painters. However, impressionist objectivity was limiting; the severe and total rejection of both the function of imagination and of the enduring aspects of reality began to pall. Gauguin and Van Gogh used color imaginatively and violently for its expressive emotional value. Immediate impressions and flickering light gave way to heavier subjects, solid with "meaning," in the works of the impressionists' successors. Impressionism ran its course and produced aesthetic revolution from within and without, putting hosts of painters to come greatly in its debt. The works of the impressionist school were received with hostility from critics and public alike, with a few exceptions, until the 1920s. By the 1930s impressionism had a large cult following, so that in the 1950s even the least works by painters associated with the movement commanded enormous prices. See POSTIMPRESSIONISM and articles on individual artists, e.g., RENOIR. See François Mathey, *The Impressionists* (tr. 1961); Alan Bowness, ed., *Impressionists and Post-Impressionists* (1965); Pierre Courthion, *Impressionism* (tr. 1972); John Rewald, *The History of Impressionism* (rev. ed. 1973).

impressment, forcible enrollment of recruits for military duty. Before the establishment of CONSCRIPTION, many countries supplemented their militia and mercenary troops by impressment. In England, impressment began as early as the Anglo-Saxon period and was used extensively under Elizabeth I, Charles I, and Oliver Cromwell. "Press gangs" forcibly seized and carried individuals into service; frequently subjects of foreign countries were taken. After 1800, England restricted impressment mostly to naval service. The Napoleonic Wars increased English need for sea power and led to the impressment of a large number of deserters, criminals, and British subjects who had become naturalized Americans. (Until 1850, England did not recognize the right of a man to renounce his nationality.) Frequent interception of American ships (see CHESAPEAKE) to impress American citizens was a major cause of the War of 1812. England generally abandoned such forcible measures after 1835. In Prussia, impressment was introduced by Frederick William I after 1713, laying the groundwork for Prussian military power in the 18th cent. It reached its height under Frederick II (Frederick the Great) who made forced recruitment on foreign soil an integral part of the Prussian military system. Impressment was used in many countries as a method of ridding society of undesirables. Persons of property, apprenticed youths, and other respectable citizens were often exempted by law. The system fostered gross abuses and was often a means of private vengeance. It filled the army and navy with a group ready for mutiny, desertion, or other disloyalty, and it adversely affected voluntary recruitment. After 1800 impressment tended to become a means of enforcing conscription, and it fell into disuse after 1850. See J. R. Hutchinson, *The Press-Gang Afloat and Ashore* (1914); J. F. Zimmerman, *Impressment of American Seamen* (1926, repr. 1966).

imprinting, form of early learning in many animal species, in which, at a critical period early in life, the animals form strong and lasting attachments. Imprinting is important for normal social development. The term was first used by the zoologist Konrad Lorenz to describe the way in which the social characteristics of greylag geese and other fowl become instilled in their young offspring (see ETHOLOGY). In natural circumstances imprinting, to the mother, food, or surroundings, occurs instinctively during a biologically fixed time span; it is very difficult to extinguish. Under experimental conditions chicks and ducklings readily become imprinted to an appropriate model such as a moving decoy or a human being. Subsequent learning may be tied to and reinforced by the imprinted object, and later social behaviors, such as the greeting ceremony and courtship, may be directed exclusively to the mother-substitute. In fowl, attachment increases with the amount of effort the offspring must exert to follow the imprinted object. The onset of fear in an organism is believed to end the period of imprintability. There is evidence that in fowl the imprinting period begins before hatching and is characterized by vocal communication between mother and unhatched ducklings.

impulse, in mechanics: see MOMENTUM.

Imrah (ĭm'rə), Asherite. 1 Chron. 7.36.

Imri (ĭm'rī). **1** Judahite. 1 Chron. 9.4. Probably the same as AMARIAH **8.** **2** Father of a builder of the walls. Neh. 3.2.

İmroz (ēmrōz') or **Imbros** (ĭm'brŏs), island (1970 pop. 6,786), 108 sq mi (280 sq km), NW Turkey, in the Aegean Sea, near the entrance to the Dardanelles. Grain and beans are grown there. The majority of the population is Greek.

Imru al-Kais: see AMRU AL-KAIS.

In, chemical symbol of the element INDIUM.

Ina (ē'nä), city (1970 pop. 51,922), Nagano prefecture, central Honshu, Japan, on the Tenryu River. It is an agricultural and industrial center with a famous agricultural school.

Inagua (ēnä'gwä), island group of the Bahama Islands. A virtually isolated cluster at the southern end of the archipelago, it includes Great Inagua, Little Inagua, and some islets. Matthew Town is the chief settlement of Inagua.

Inari (ē'närē), Swed. *Enare,* lake, c.500 sq mi (1,290 sq km), N Finland. It is fed by the Ivalojoki and empties into the Arctic Ocean through the Paatsjoki. Lake Inari contains more than 3,000 islands and is a tourist attraction.

Inazawa (ēnä'zäwä), city (1970 pop. 78,180), Aichi prefecture, central Honshu, Japan. It is a residential and industrial suburb of Nagoya and a textile production center.

inbreeding, mating of closely related organisms. Inbreeding is chiefly used as a means of insuring the preservation of specific desired traits among the offspring of purebred animals (see BREEDING). Continued inbreeding through many generations reduces the chances for diversity of characteristics in the offspring and tends to reduce vigor and fertility. Only in laboratory conditions can the unwanted characteristics that frequently result from inbreeding be selected out of the strain and selection for purely advantageous traits be carried out. The necessarily uncontrolled cases of inbreeding among humans (as in closed societies or within royal families) have generally proved deleterious, and inbreeding is therefore discouraged in most societies (see CONSANGUINITY; INCEST).

Inca (ĭng'kə), pre-Columbian Indian empire, W South America. Centered at CUZCO, Peru, the empire dominated at the time of the Spanish conquest (1532) the entire Andean area from Quito, Ecuador, S to the Río Maule, Chile. The name Inca may specifically refer to the emperor, but is generally used to mean the empire or the people. Since the people combined much AYMARA mythology with their own, their origin myth is obscure. The most common belief is that the legendary founder, MANCO CAPAC (who seems to have been a historical figure), brought his people from mountain caves to the Cuzco Valley. During the early Inca period (c.1200–c.1440) the tribe gradually established its hegemony over other peoples of the valley and under the emperor named Viracocha (the name also of the supreme creator in Inca cosmology) allied themselves with the QUECHUA. However, it was not until the reigns of Pachacuti (c.1440–1471) and his son Topa Inca, or Tupac Yupanqui (1471–93), that the Inca made their great conquests. The present Ecuador (the kingdom of Quito) was subjugated by HUAYNA CAPAC, giving the empire its greatest extent and power. At his death it was divided between his sons, HUÁSCAR and ATAHUALPA, and a long civil war ensued from which Atahualpa emerged triumphant just as Francisco PIZARRO landed on the shores of Peru and the Spanish conquest began. The Inca empire extended some 2,000 mi (3,200 km). Although the Inca showed a genius for organization, their conquests were facilitated by the highly developed social systems of some of the kingdoms that they absorbed, such as the CHIMU, and the established agrarian communities that covered the area of their conquest. The Inca empire was a closely knit state. At the top was the emperor, an absolute monarch ruling by divine right. Merciless toward its enemies, requiring an obedience close to slavery, the imperial government was responsible for the welfare of its subjects. Everything was owned by the state except houses, movable household goods, and some individually held lands. In addition to cultivating the land, the common people were drafted to work on state projects such as mining, public works, and army service. This obligation was known as *mita.* From well-stocked storehouses were drawn goods to support priests, government servants, special craftsmen, the aged and the sick, and widows. The royal family formed an educated, governing upper nobility, which at the time of the Spanish conquest numbered around 500. To further increase government control over an empire grown unwieldy, all who spoke Quechua became an "Inca class" by privilege and became colonists. Lesser administrative officials, formerly independent rulers, and their descendants were the minor nobility, or curaca class, also supported by the government. For purposes of administration the empire was divided into four parts, the lines of which met at Cuzco; the quarters were divided into provinces, usually on the basis of former independent divisions. These in turn were customarily split into an upper and a lower moiety; the moieties were subdivided into ayllus, or local communities. Much as it exists today as the basic unit of communal Indian society, so the ancient ayllu was the political and social foundation of Inca government. When a territory was conquered, surveys, consisting of relief models of topographical and population features, and a census of the population were made. With these reports, recorded on QUIPU, of the material and human resources in each province, populations were reshuffled as needed. Thus transplanted, and dominated by Quechua colonists, the subject peoples had less chance to revolt, and the separate languages and cultures were molded to the Inca pattern. Religion, controlled by a hierarchy similar to the government hierarchy, emphasized ritual and organization. Heading the Inca gods was Viracocha. His servants were the sun, the god of the weather or thunder, the moon, the stars, the earth, and the sea. The sun god was foremost among these. Divination, sacrifices (human only at times of crisis), celebrations and ceremonies, ritual, feasts, and fasts were all part of Inca religion. Although the Andean area offers a diversity of plant domestication, the handicaps of terrain and climate presented severe obstacles. To overcome them, Inca engineers demonstrated extraordinary skill in terracing, drainage, irrigation, and the use of fertilizers. They lacked draft animals, but domesticated animals (the llama, the alpaca, the dog, the guinea pig, and the duck) were important to daily living; from the wild vicuña, fine wool was sheared. Without paper or a system of writing, the architects and master masons who designed and supervised the construction of public buildings and engineering works in such cities as MACHU PICCHU and the fortress of SACSAHUAMÁN built clay models, employing in actual construction sliding scales, plumb bobs, and bronze and stone tools. Without wheeled vehicles for transport, the huge polygonal blocks for fortress, palace, temple, and storehouse were emplaced by ramp and rollers and were fitted with extraordinary precision. Wall corners were always carefully bonded. Adobe bricks and plaster were common, especially along the coastal desert. Buildings were usually of one story. One of the most remarkable evidences of Inca engineering skill was an elaborate network of roads, which in many places still survives. Streams were crossed by a log or stone bridge, placid rivers by balsa ferry or pontoon bridge, and chasms by a breeches-buoy contrivance or by a suspension bridge that might be as much as 200 ft (60 m) long. Road sections were maintained by the nearest village, as were the shelters and military storehouses, a day's travel apart; a village also supplied messengers for its sector. These men, serving 15-day shifts, relayed messages about every mile. Thus, 150 mi (240 km) could be traveled daily, a distance that later took the Spanish colonial post 12 to 13 days to cover. In the manufacture of textiles the Inca utilized almost every available kind of fiber and produced elaborate multicolored tapestries. In ceramics they achieved a fine-grained, highly polished, metallic hardness that stressed functional and utilitarian design. Mining was fairly extensive. Of the metals, copper and bronze were for public use; gold, silver, and tin were reserved for the emperor, the temples, and the upper nobility. Metallurgical processes included the techniques of smelting, alloying, casting, hammering, repoussé, incrustation, inlay, soldering, riveting, and cloisonné. When Francisco Pizarro landed in South America in 1532, he was welcomed by Atahualpa. By strategem the conquistador lured the emperor into his camp, captured, and then executed him. Shortly thereafter

(1533) Pizarro entered Cuzco. Although the Spaniards did not immediately subdue the Inca, the highly personal and centralized political structure of the Inca facilitated the Spanish conquest. Despite the heroic resistance carried on in many sections and the rebellion (1536–37) of Manco Capac, the conquest was assured. Under Spanish rule Inca culture was greatly modified and eventually Hispanicized. The Indians were reduced to a subordinate status, and only in recent years have efforts been made to make the Peruvian Indians (about 50% of the population) an integral part of the national life. See chapters on the Inca in the *Handbook of South American Indians*, Vol. II (1963). For accounts by early historians, see Pedro de Cieza de Léon, *The Incas* (tr. 1959) and Garcilaso de la Vega, *The Royal Commentaries of Peru* (tr. 1966). See also W. H. Prescott, *The History of the Conquest of Peru* (1855, repr. 1963); C. R. Markham, *The Incas of Peru* (1910, repr. 1969); P. A. Means, *Ancient Civilizations of the Andes* (1931, repr. 1964) and *The Fall of the Inca Empire* (1932, repr. 1964); Hiram Bingham, *Machu Picchu: Lost City of the Incas* (1948, repr. 1969); V. W. von Hagen, *Highway of the Sun* (1956); Bertrand Flornoy, *The World of the Inca* (tr. 1956); Louis Baudin, *A Socialist Empire: The Incas of Peru* (tr. 1961) and *Daily Life in Peru under the Last Incas* (tr. 1962); J. A. Mason, *The Ancient Civilizations of Peru* (rev. ed. 1968) and Alfred Métraux, *The History of the Incas* (tr. 1970).

incantation, set formula, spoken or sung, for the purpose of working MAGIC. An incantation is normally an invocation to beneficent supernatural spirits for aid, protection, or inspiration. It may also serve as a charm or spell to ward off the effects of evil spirits. In black magic an incantation may be the means of summoning or materializing the powers of darkness.

incarnation, the assumption of human form by a god, an idea common in religion. In early times the idea was expressed in the belief that certain living men, often kings or priests, were divine incarnations. India and Egypt were especially rich in forms of incarnation in men as well as in beasts. Incarnation is found in various phases in Greek religion, in which the human body of a god was a disguise or a temporary means of communication. The most widely accepted belief in incarnation is in that of JESUS Christ, held by Christians to be God in the flesh, partaking wholly both of divinity and of humanity, except in so far as human beings have a propensity to sin. This is the accepted understanding of the biblical "The Word was made flesh" (John 1.14). See AVATARA.

incense, perfume diffused by the burning of aromatic gums or spices. Incense was used in ancient Egypt, Greece, and Rome and is mentioned in the Old and the New Testaments. It is also found in the major religions of the Orient. It was introduced into public worship in the Roman Catholic Church in the 6th cent.

incense-tree, common name for members of the Burseraceae, a family of deciduous shrubs and large trees found chiefly in tropical America and NE Africa. The name derives from the characteristic aromatic oils or resins that are secreted from their stems. The incenses frankincense and myrrh are prepared from large irregular lumps of light reddish to yellowish brown gum exuded by some species. Frankincense (from several species of the genus *Boswellia,* chiefly *B. carterii*) is also used medicinally and for fumigation; another name for it is olibanum. Myrrh is obtained from several species of the genus *Commiphora,* whose native range extends from Somaliland to E India. The two principal species are *C. erythraea,* yielding bitter, or bisabol, myrrh, an important BDELLIUM, and the common myrrh (*C. myrrha*), yielding sweet, or harobol, myrrh. The rarer *C. opobalsam* of Arabia yields Mecca, or Duhnual, balsam (also called BALM OF GILEAD). All three are used in perfumes and sometimes medicinally; they were employed by the ancients for embalming. Frankincense and myrrh, together with gold, were the gifts of the Magi of the Gospels (Mat. 2.11). Both were used for incense in religious ceremonies, as frankincense still is. The Biblical myrrh, probably a mixture of several substances, may also have been derived in part from the unrelated rockrose (genus *Cistus*), a small evergreen plant of the Mediterranean area. The name myrrh is also used for sweet cicely, of the parsley family. Another genus (*Bursera*) of the incense-tree family, the tropical elephant tree, is the source of several gums and resins; the Mexican *B. jorullensis* yields COPAL de Penca. Incense-trees are classified in the division MAGNOLIOPHYTA, class Magnoliopsida, order Sapindales.

incest, sexual relations between persons to whom MARRIAGE is prohibited by custom or law because of their close KINSHIP. Ideas of kinship, however, vary widely from group to group, hence the definition of incest also varies. Customs prescribing whom one may and may not marry are found in primitive as well as advanced human groups, and these apparently anteceded knowledge of the genetic effects of the intermarriage of close relatives. Even modern prohibitions of incest are based only in part on the observed fact that inherited defects, like inherited excellences, tend to be transmitted, and in intensified form, when both parents possess the same genes. Among primitive as among advanced human groups the marriage of parents and offspring, or brothers and sisters, is prohibited and abhorred. Only in some royal families, as in ancient Egypt and among the Inca, have incestuous marriages (including marriages of brothers and sisters) been customary—perhaps to conserve royal prerogatives and property. Theories concerning the universality of incest taboos include sociological and psychological interpretations. In anthropology, the incest taboo is often considered in relation to rules of exogamy, by which marriage serves as a means of social alliance between kinship groups. Incest is a recurrent theme in mythology and literature across the world, and it has played an important role in psychoanalytical speculation and theory. See OEDIPUS. For the contemporary legal aspects of incest, see CONSANGUINITY. See R. E. L. Master, *Patterns of Incest* (1963); S. K. Weinberg, *Incest Behavior* (4th ed. 1966); Herbert Meisch, *Incest* (tr. 1972).

inch: see ENGLISH UNITS OF MEASUREMENT.

Inchbald, Elizabeth (ĭnch'bôld), 1753–1821, English author. The daughter of a farmer, Joseph Simpson, she went to London in 1772 to seek her fortune on the stage. The same year she married a fellow actor, Joseph Inchbald. In 1784 she turned from acting to writing. Her plays, moral and sentimental, include *I'll Tell You What* (1785) and *Wives as They Were, and Maids as They Are* (1797). However, she is better remembered for two romantic novels, *A Simple Story* (1791) and *Nature and Art* (1796). See biography by William McKee (1935); B. R. Park, *Thomas Holcroft and Elizabeth Inchbald* (1952).

Inchon (ĭn'chŏn), city (1970 pop. 646,013), NW South Korea, on the Yellow Sea. The country's second largest port, Inchon has an ice-free harbor (protected by a tidal basin) and is the port and commercial center for Seoul. Inchon's economy is heavily dependent on shipping and the transshipment of goods. The city is one of South Korea's major industrial centers: iron, steel, coke, light metals, textiles, chemicals, and fertilizers are among its manufactures. Fishing is also an important industry. Large salt fields have been developed in the tidal flats off Inchon. The city was opened to foreign trade in 1883. It was called Jinsen by the Japanese, who ruled Korea from 1904 to 1945. During the Korean War, U.S. troops landed at Inchon (Sept. 15, 1950) to relieve pressure on the Pusan perimeter and to launch the subsequent UN drive northward. Inchon has a technical college. The city was formerly called Chemulpo.

inchworm, name for the larvae of moths of the family Geometridae, a large, cosmopolitan group with over 1,200 species indigenous to North America. Also called measuring worms, spanworms, and loopers, inchworms lack appendages in the middle portion of their body, causing them to have a characteristic looping gait. They have three pairs of true legs at the front end, like other CATERPILLARS, but only two or three pairs of prolegs (larval abdominal appendages), located at the rear end. An inchworm moves by drawing its hind end forward while holding on with the front legs, then advancing its front section while holding on with the prolegs. Inchworms have smooth, hairless bodies, usually about 1 in. (2.5 cm) long. They are green, brown, or black and in many species have irregular projections that cause them to resemble the twigs of the trees they feed on. Many inchworms, when disturbed, stand erect and motionless on the prolegs, increasing the resemblance. Certain destructive inchworms are called CANKERWORMS. Adult geometrid moths range in wingspread from 3/8 in. to 2 in. (9.5–51 mm). Most are gray or brown with fine patterns and are well camouflaged on trees. The CABBAGE LOOPER is not an inchworm, but a caterpillar of a different family. Inchworms are classified in the phylum ARTHROPODA, class Insecta, order Lepidoptera, family Geometridae.

incinerator, furnace for burning refuse. The older and simpler kind is a brick-lined cell with a metal grate over a lower ash pit. There is an opening in the top or side for loading and another opening in the side for removing masses called clinkers, which are composed of incombustible materials. A home or apartment house may have a small incinerator in its basement connected by a chute to doors on each floor. A newer rotary-kiln type used by municipalities and by large factories has a long, slightly inclined passageway through which refuse is moved continuously. In the first section the refuse is dried on moving steps, then moved onto a rocking grate where it is ignited and partially burned. The third and last section is a refractory-lined cylinder where combustion is completed. Clinkers spill out at the end. The heat from the incinerator generates steam in a boiler, sometimes for producing electricity. A high stack, fan, or steam jet supplied from the boiler supplies a draft. Ash drops through the grate, but many particles are carried along with the hot gases. These particles and volatile gases are burned in a combustion chamber fed by several furnaces. However, because of the necessity to control air pollution, the ejection of the gases into the environment, even after this treatment, is considered undesirable. Therefore, incinerators are being equipped for more complete cleaning of flue gases or abandoned entirely.

inclination, in astronomy, the angle of intersection between two planes, one of which is an orbital plane. The inclination of the plane of the moon's orbit is 5°9′ with respect to the plane of the ecliptic (the plane of the earth's orbit around the sun). The inclination of the plane of the ecliptic relative to the plane of the earth's equator is 23°27′8″.26; this angle is called the obliquity of the ecliptic.

inclined plane, simple MACHINE, consisting of a sloping surface, whose purpose is to reduce the force that must be applied to raise a load. To raise a body vertically a force must be applied that is equal to the weight of the body, i.e., the product of its

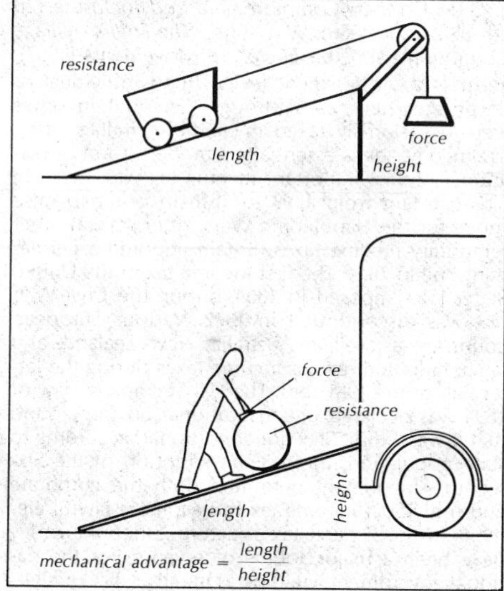

Inclined plane

mass and the acceleration of gravity. The amount of work done (i.e., energy expended) in raising the body is equal to its weight times the distance through which it is raised. By means of an inclined plane a force smaller than the weight of the body can be exerted over a distance greater than the direct vertical distance, doing work equal to the product of the force and the distance through which it acts. If friction is ignored, the work done using the inclined plane will be exactly equal to the work done in lifting the body directly. In any real system some work is done to overcome friction between the plane and the load. The actual mechanical advantage of an inclined plane is the ratio of the load lifted to the force applied; ideally it is equal to the ratio of the length of the sloping plane to its vertical rise. An inclined plane whose sloping length is 5 m and whose vertical rise is 1 m has a mechanical advantage of 5; a 300-newton load can be moved up such a plane by a 60-newton force. The inclined plane has been modified in many ways. The screw and wedge are applications of the principle of the inclined plane but do not require that the load be moved vertically for their successful operation. The chisel, carpenter's plane, auger bit, and ax are some of the many tools based on this principle. Switchbacks on mountain roads are inclined planes that reduce the effort of an automobile engine but increase the distance a car must travel to ascend the mountain.

inclosure or **enclosure,** in British history, the process of inclosing (with fences, ditches, hedges, or other barriers) land formerly subject to common rights. Such land included fields cultivated by the open-field or strip system, wasteland, and the common pasture land. Inclosure accompanied and accelerated the breakdown of the MANORIAL SYSTEM. In England the practice, dating from the 12th cent., received legal sanction through statutes (1235, 1285) permitting landlords to inclose wastelands on condition they left sufficient land for their free tenants. Its great development, however, came with the rapid expansion of the Flemish wool trade after the 14th cent. The monetary advantages resulting from intensive cultivation of large, fenced fields and particularly from the conversion of land into fenced sheep pastures moved landlords to make agreements with tenants or to expel them, illegally or for the slightest default, in order to inclose large areas. Under the Tudors, the hardship of dispossessed tenants, increasing vagrancy, and social unrest resulted in statutes designed to limit the practice. However, the process continued virtually unchecked, reaching its peak in the late 17th cent. In the early 18th cent. there was very little inclosure, but from 1750 to 1800 inclosure by private act of Parliament increased dramatically. The General Enclosure Act (1801) standardized much of the process, and an act of 1845 provided for the incorporation of all inclosures in a single act each year. By this time, however, the movement toward general inclosure was largely completed. Although the process remained harsh for the small farmer, the period of parliamentary inclosures paralleled a period of increasing industrial use of labor. Inclosed land did promote more efficient farming and was able to produce an ever-increasing agricultural output during the early 19th cent., when the population was growing rapidly. See E. C. K. Gonner, *Common Land and Inclosure* (2d ed. 1912, repr. 1966); W. E. Tate, *The English Village Community and the Enclosure Movements* (1967).

income tax, assessment levied upon individual or corporate incomes. Although personal incomes were occasionally taxed in medieval Italian cities, the income tax is essentially a modern form of taxation. The first important income tax was levied in Great Britain from 1799 to 1816 in order to raise funds for the Napoleonic Wars. After several other temporary income taxes, Britain adopted a permanent one in 1874. The first income tax in the United States was imposed in 1864, during the Civil War, but was discontinued in 1872. Various European countries, as well as Australia, New Zealand, and Japan, adopted regular income taxes during the latter half of the 19th cent. The U.S. income tax law of 1894 was declared unconstitutional on the ground that it was a direct tax not apportioned according to state population. In 1913 the adoption of the Sixteenth Amendment permitted both the corporate and individual income tax to become a lawful element in the Federal tax structure. Since then they have been a major source of revenue for the national government, yielding as much as 85% of all its receipts in some years. Income taxes had been levied sporadically by various states since 1789; since 1919 most states have adopted the tax. The first major American city to impose a tax on incomes was Philadelphia (1939). By 1972 cities with income tax laws included Baltimore, Cleveland, Detroit, New York, and St. Louis, in addition to Philadelphia. In general, personal incomes below a certain amount are exempted from the individual income tax, the amount varying for single and for married persons with or without dependents. The tax is applied to the net income above such exemptions, and the rate becomes progressively higher for larger incomes. Since the mid 1960s the tax rate has ranged from about 15% for the lowest brackets to about 70% for the highest. A similar graduated structure applies to corporate income taxes. See B. I. Bittker, *Federal Income, Estate, and Gift Taxation* (3d ed. 1964); B. E. V. Sabine, *A History of Income Tax* (1966); C. J. Gaa, *Contemporary Thought on Federal Income Taxation* (1969).

incorporation: see CORPORATION.

incubator, apparatus for the maintenance of controlled conditions in which eggs can be hatched artificially. Incubator houses with double walls of mud, a fireroom, and several compartments each holding about 6,000 hens' eggs were developed in ancient times; the Chinese have long used baskets with a capacity of about 5,000 eggs that are alternated with layers of heated wheat. In the United States small incubators were developed in the 1840s and large ones have been used since 1910; some commercial models have trays for as many as one million eggs. The modern apparatus, with automatic controls for temperature and humidity and devices for turning the eggs, is widely used by hatcheries in the baby-chick business. Eggs are selected for size, weight, and shell texture and often are candled after a week in the incubator in order to remove infertile eggs. The development of small-scale apparatus for hatching eggs led to the invention of incubators for the early care of prematurely born infants, whose lives are often saved in an environment of controlled heat, humidity, and ventilation. Another type of incubator has been developed for the culture of microorganisms. See E. M. Funk and M. R. Irwin, *Hatchery Operation and Management* (1955); M. O. North, *Commercial Chicken Production Manual* (1972).

incubus (ĭng'kyo͝obəs), lascivious male demon said to possess mortal women as they sleep and to be responsible for the birth of demons, witches, and deformed children. According to one legend the incubus and his female counterpart, the succubus, were fallen angels. The belief in these demons was especially prevalent in the Middle Ages, and stories of assaults by incubi were not uncommon.

incunabula (ĭn"kyo͝onăb'yo͝olə), plural of **incunabulum** [Late Lat.,=cradle (books); i.e., books of the cradle days of printing], books printed in the 15th cent. The known incunabula represent about 40,000 editions. The books include products of more than 1,000 presses, including such famous printers as Gutenberg, Jenson, Caxton, and Aldus Manutius and give evidence as to the development of typography in its formative period. These books were generally large quarto size, bound in calf over boards of wood, decorated with red initials (rubricated) and ornamental borders, and carrying a COLOPHON but no title page. Notable European collections of incunabula are in Paris, London (British Museum), Oxford (Bodleian Library), Vienna, Rome, Milan, Brussels, and The Hague. Notable American collections are in Washington, D.C. (Library of Congress), New York City (Morgan Library and others), Providence (John Carter Brown Library and Annmary Brown Memorial), San Marino, Calif. (Henry E. Huntington Library), and in the libraries of Harvard and Yale Univ. For an introduction to incunabula and a guide to further study, see Margaret B. Stillwell, *Incunabula and Americana 1450-1800* (2d ed. 1961).

Independence. 1 City (1970 pop. 10,347), seat of Montgomery co., SE Kansas, on the Verdigris River, near the Okla. line, in an important oil-producing area where corn and wheat are also grown. It is an oil refining center. The town was founded (1869) on a former Osage Indian reservation. It boomed with the discovery of natural gas in 1881 and oil in 1903. It has a junior college. Nearby is the site of the Rebel Creek battle, where a detachment of Confederate soldiers (except for one survivor) was wiped out by Osage Indians in 1863. **2** City (1970 pop. 111,630), seat of Jackson co., W Mo., a suburb of Kansas City; inc. 1849. Its manufactures include electrical equipment, dehydrated foods, and oil products. Especially in the 1830s and 1840s it was the starting point for expeditions over the Santa Fe Trail, the Oregon Trail, and the California Trail. A group of Mormons settled there in 1831, and the city is the headquarters of the Reorganized Church of Jesus Christ of Latter Day Saints. It was the home of President Harry S. Truman and is the seat of the Harry S. Truman Library and Museum, on whose grounds the former president is buried. Other points of interest include the old county jail and museum (1859; restored); the old county courthouse (1825; restored); and nearby Fort Osage (1808; reconstructed). Central Missouri State College has a residence center in Independence.

Independence, American War of: see AMERICAN REVOLUTION.

Independence, Declaration of: see DECLARATION OF INDEPENDENCE.

Independence Day: see FOURTH OF JULY.

Independence Hall, historic building on Independence Square, downtown Philadelphia, in Independence National Historical Park. Originally constructed as the Pennsylvania colony's statehouse in 1732, the hall was the scene of the proclamation of the U.S. Declaration of Independence (1776) and was the meeting place of the Continental Congress and the Constitutional Convention. The building has a small museum of historical and colonial objects, including the Liberty Bell.

Independence National Historical Park: see NATIONAL PARKS AND MONUMENTS (table).

Independents, in religion, those bodies of Christians who claim freedom from ecclesiastical and civil authority for their individual churches. They hold that each congregation should have control of its own affairs. In a historic sense, it is ordinarily applied to churches in Great Britain now known as Congregational. The name Independents came into use in the 17th cent. and was in use in Great Britain until the end of the 18th cent. See CONGREGATIONALISM; PURITANISM; SEPARATISTS.

Independent Treasury System. After President Andrew JACKSON vetoed the bill to recharter the Bank of the United States, he transferred (1833) government funds from the bank to state banks (the "pet banks"). Those banks, however, used the funds as a basis for speculation, which was already rampant and was soon to be further increased by the distribution of the Federal surplus among the states. The situation was brought to a head by Jackson's issue of the Specie Circular (1836), which led to a drain on the "pet banks" and their collapse in the Panic of 1837. President Martin VAN BUREN then proposed that an independent treasury be set up that would be isolated from all banks. The proposal met considerable opposition and failed to pass the House of Representatives in 1837 and again in the sessions of 1837-38 and 1838-39. In 1840 it was finally passed and approved by the President. However, the following year the Whigs repealed the law. The intention of the Whigs was to establish a new central bank, but the objections of President John TYLER on constitutional grounds prevented the creation of another Bank of the United States. The Democrats won the presidential election of 1844, and measures were inaugurated to restore the Independent Treasury System. The act of Aug., 1846, ordered that the public revenues be retained in the Treasury building and in subtreasuries (see SUBTREASURY) in various cities. The Treasury was to pay out its own funds and be completely independent of the banking and financial system of the nation; all payments by and to the government, moreover, were to be made in specie. The separation of the Treasury from the banking system was never completed, however; the Treasury's operations continued to influence the money market, as specie payments to and from the government affected the amount of hard money in circulation. Although the Independent Treasury did restrict the reckless speculative expansion of credit, it also tended to create a new set of economic problems. In periods of prosperity, revenue surpluses accumulated in the Treasury, reducing hard money circulation, tightening credit, and restraining even legitimate expansion of trade and production. In periods of depression and panic, on the other hand, when banks suspended specie payments and hard money was hoarded, the government's insistence on being paid in specie tended to aggravate economic difficulties by limiting the amount of specie available for private credit. The most serious weaknesses in the system were revealed during the Civil War; under the pressures created by wartime expenditures, Congress passed the acts of 1863 and 1864 creating national banks. Exceptions were made to the prohibition against depositing government funds in private banks, and in certain cases payments to the government could be made in national bank notes. After the Civil War, the Independent Treasury continued in modified form as each administration tried to cope with its weaknesses in various ways. Secretary of the Treasury Leslie M. Shaw (1902-7) made many innovations; he attempted to use Treasury funds to expand and contract the money supply according to the nation's credit needs. The Panic of 1907, however, finally revealed the inability of the system to stabilize the money market; agitation for a more effective banking system led to the passage of the Federal Reserve Act in 1913. Government funds were gradually transferred from subtreasuries to district banks, and an act of Congress in 1920 mandated the closing of the last subtreasuries in the following year, thus bringing the Independent Treasury System to an end. See David Kinley, *The History, Organization, and Influence of the Independent Treasury of the United States* (1893, repr. 1968) and *The Independent Treasury of the United States* (1910, repr. 1970); D. W. Dodwell, *Treasuries and Central Banks* (1934); Paul Studenski and Herman Krooss, *Financial History of the United States* (1963).

indeterminate sentence: see PAROLE; SENTENCE.

index, of a book or periodical, a list, nearly always alphabetical, of the topics treated. This list is usually at the back of a book, and the table of contents is in the front. The index seeks to direct the reader to all names and subjects on which the book has information. The subject, with the number of the page on which related information is to be found, is called the entry. In an index to a periodical the entries are less specific, referring usually to an article as a whole rather than to every subject touched upon in each article. Indexing requires experience and skill, since it is necessary not only to grasp the meaning of the author but to phrase that meaning clearly and in such a way as to place it alphabetically where the reader is likely to look first. Books written to give information are of little value unless properly indexed. Indexes to books were made long before the invention of printing. In the 16th cent. the term *index* began to be commonly applied to such a list; until the 17th cent. the index was rarely alphabetical. Diderot's famous ENCYCLOPÉDIE (1751–1772) had an alphabetical index. Indexes to periodicals are nearly as old as this form of literature. In 1848 in the United States a general index to the most widely circulated periodicals of the time was issued by William Frederick Poole. *Poole's Index,* later compiled cooperatively, continued until 1907, when it was superseded by the *Readers' Guide to Periodical Literature.* There are special indexes in various fields of knowledge, e.g., of law, medicine, art, education, engineering, industrial arts, agriculture. Newspaper indexes include those to the London *Times* (from 1906) and the New York *Times* (from 1913). An *International Index to Periodical Literature* has been issued since 1913. The H. W. Wilson Company of New York City is noted for its special annual indexes, particularly the *Readers' Guide to Periodical Literature* and the *Cumulative Book Index.* Indexes to illustrations, to artifacts, to formulas, and to various collections of materials are common. Some are alphabetical like book or periodical indexes; others may be by number, color, or some other scheme. Although indexes are usually compiled by skilled individuals, since the 1950s there have been some compiled by computers, notably the *New York Times Index.* The CATALOG of the books in a library is sometimes known as an index. See M. D. Anderson, *Book Indexing* (1971); R. L. Collison, *Indexes and Indexing* (4th ed. 1972).

Index, in the Roman Catholic Church, list of publications forbidden to be read, called *Index librorum prohibitorum* [list of forbidden books]. This censorship was exercised by the Holy See. Catholics are forbidden, as a natural part of ethics, to read anything they know may endanger their faith or moral life; the Index was a partial guide to such literature. Since it was made up only from decisions referred for judgment on specific works, there was no consistency of inclusion; the failure of a book to appear in it implied nothing. The last edition of the Index was published in 1948. In 1966 the Congregation for the Doctrine of the Faith (formerly, the Holy Office) announced that the Index and its related penalties of excommunication would no longer have the force of law in the church.

Index, cephalic: see CEPHALIC INDEX.

Index number, in econometrics, a figure reflecting a change in value or quantity as compared with a standard or base. The base usually equals 100 and the index number is usually expressed as a percentage. For example, if a commodity cost twice as much in 1970 as it did in 1960, its index number would be 200 relative to 1960. Index numbers are used especially to compare business activity, the cost of living, and employment. They enable economists to reduce unwieldly business data into easily understood terms. See Robin Marris, *Economic Arithmetic* (1958).

India, republic (1971 pop. 547,959,809), 1,261,810 sq mi (3,268,090 sq km), S Asia. The second most populous country in the world, it has also been known as the Union of India and as Bharat, its ancient name. NEW DELHI is the capital of the republic, which is divided into 21 states: ANDHRA PRADESH; ASSAM; BIHAR; GUJARAT; HARYANA; HIMACHAL PRADESH; Jammu and Kashmir (see KASHMIR); KARNATAKA; KERALA; MADHYA PRADESH; MAHARASHTRA; MANIPUR; MEGHALAYA; NAGALAND; ORISSA; PUNJAB; RAJASTHAN; TAMIL NADU; TRIPURA; UTTAR PRADESH; and West Bengal (see BENGAL). There are also nine union territories, administered by the federal government: the ANDAMAN AND NICOBAR ISLANDS; ARUNACHAL PRADESH; CHANDIGARH; DADRA AND NAGAR-HAVELI; DELHI; GOA, DAMAN, AND DIU; Lakshadweep (see LACCADIVE, MINICOY, AND AMINDIVI ISLANDS); MIZORAM; and PONDICHERRY. Kashmir is disputed with Pakistan. India's land frontier (c.9,500 mi/15,290 km long) stretches from the Arabian Sea on the west to Burma on the east and touches, from west to east, Pakistan; a small portion of Afghanistan atop the state of Jammu and Kashmir; China; Nepal; Sikkim; Bhutan; and Bangladesh. Sikkim is an Indian protectorate; Bhutan is advised in foreign affairs by India. The southern half of India is a triangular-shaped peninsula (c.1,300 mi/2,090 km wide at its base) that thrusts into the Indian Ocean between the Bay of Bengal on the east and the Arabian Sea on the west and has a coastline c.3,500 mi (5,630 km) long; at its southern tip is Cape Comorin. In the north, towering above peninsular India, is the Himalayan mountain wall, where rise the three great rivers of the Indian subcontinent—the Indus, the Ganges, and the Brahmaputra. The Indo-Gangetic alluvial plain, which has much of India's arable land, lies between the Himalayas and the dissected uplands of the Deccan, a plateau occupying most of peninsular India. The plain is limited in the west by the Thar (Great Indian) Desert of Rajasthan, which merges with the swampy Rann of Kutch to the south. The Narbada River, south of the plain, marks the beginning of the Deccan. The plateau, scarped by the mountains of the Eastern Ghats and Western Ghats, is drained by the Godavari, Kistna, and Cauvery rivers; they break through the Eastern Ghats and, flowing E into the Bay of Bengal, form broad deltas on the wide Coromandel Coast. Further north, the Mahanadi River drains central India into the Bay of Bengal. The much narrower western coast of peninsular India, comprising chiefly the Malabar Coast and the fertile Gujarat plain, curves around the Gulf of Cambay in the north to the Kathiawar peninsula. The coastal plains of peninsular India have a tropical climate. The Deccan and a part of the Indo-Gangetic plain are subtropical, with most of the latter area experiencing frost in winter and very hot summers. India's rainfall, which depends upon the monsoon, is variable; it is heavy in Assam and West Bengal and along the southern coasts, moderate in the inland peninsular regions, and scanty in the arid northwest, especially in Rajasthan and Punjab.

Economy. Agriculture supports about 70% of the Indian people. Vast quantities of rice are grown wherever the land is level and water plentiful; other crops are wheat, pulses, jowar and bajra (cereals), and corn. Cotton, tobacco, and jute are the principal nonfood crops. There are large tea plantations in Assam, Karnataka, and Tamil Nadu. India's food output and distribution is not sufficient for the needs of its enormous population. Fragmentation of holdings, peasant indebtedness (to parasitic moneylenders), outmoded methods of crop production, and social prejudice against certain improvements have been characteristic of Indian agriculture. The poverty-stricken lot of village India, ever threatened by drought, flood, famine, and disease, has been somewhat alleviated in recent years by government agricultural modernization efforts and reclamation and irrigation projects. India has perhaps more cattle per capita than any country in the world, but backward stock-raising techniques and the Hindu stricture against the killing of cows detract greatly from their economic value. Sheep are raised by pastoral peoples in grazing areas. Coastal fisheries and, to a lesser extent, inland fisheries as well as pearling grounds are locally important. India has forested mountain slopes, with stands of oak, pine, sal, teak, ebony, palms, and bamboo, and the cutting of timber is a major rural occupation. Aside from mica, manganese, and ilmenite, in which the country ranks high, India's mineral resources, although large, are not as yet fully exploited. There are very large iron ore deposits. The Chota Nagpur Plateau region of S Bihar, SW West Bengal, and N Orissa are the most important mining areas; they are the source of coal, iron, mica, and copper. There are workings of magnesite, gold (in the Kolar gold fields in Karnataka), bauxite, chromite, salt, and gypsum. Oil fields exist in Assam and Gujarat, but India is deficient in petroleum. Industry in India, traditionally limited to agricultural processing and light manufacture, especially of cotton, woolen, and silk textiles, jute, and leather products, has been greatly expanded in recent years but still employs less than 10% of the work force. There are large textile works at BOMBAY and AHMEDABAD and a huge iron and steel complex (mainly controlled by the Tata family) at JAMSHEDPUR. The government runs steel plants at ROURKELA, BHILAINAGAR, DURGAPUR, and Bokaro. BANGALORE has electronics and armaments industries. India's large motion picture industry is concentrated in Bombay. Handicrafts, especially handweaving and brasswork, are important in the rural areas. The major cities are connected by state-owned railroad systems, one of the most extensive nets in the world; however, a variety of gauges makes frequent transshipment necessary. Transportation by road is limited, and in rural India the bullock cart is still the chief means of transportation. There are international airports at New Delhi, CALCUTTA, and Bombay. The leading ports are Bombay, MADRAS, Calcutta, COCHIN, and VISAKHAPATNAM. The leading exports are jute, tea, iron ore, iron and steel, cotton goods, and leather. The chief imports are machinery, wheat, petroleum, raw cotton, iron and steel, and rice. India's major trade partners are the United States, the USSR, Great Britain, and Japan. In 1971, India had 18 cities with populations of more than 500,000: AGRA, Ahmedabad, Bangalore, Bombay, Calcutta, Delhi, HOWRAH, HYDERABAD, INDORE, JABALPUR, JAIPUR, KANPUR, LUCKNOW, Madras, MADURAI, NAGPUR, POONA, and VARANASI.

Government. India is a federal state with a parliamentary form of government. It is governed under the 1949 constitution (effective since Jan., 1950). The president of India is elected for a five-year term by the elected members of the federal and state parliaments. Theoretically he possesses full executive power, but actually that power is exercised by the prime minister (head of the majority party in the federal Parliament) and council of ministers (which includes the cabinet), who are appointed by the president. The ministers are responsible to the lower house of Parliament (Lok Sabha) and must be members of Parliament. The federal Parliament is bicameral. The upper house, the council of states (Rajya Sabha), consists of a maximum of 250 members; the great majority are apportioned by state—each state's delegates are elected by its elected assembly—and 12 members are appointed by the president. In addition, in 1973, 3 members represented the union territory of Delhi, and 1 member represented the union territory of Pondicherry. One third of the members retire every other year. The lower house is elected at least every five years, but it may be dissolved earlier by the president. It is composed of no more than 500 members apportioned among the states—directly elected in constituencies by universal adult suffrage—and a maximum of 25 representatives of the union territories. In addition, in 1973, 2 members appointed by the president represented Anglo-Indians. There is a supreme court appointed by the president. State governors are appointed by the president for five-year terms. States have either unicameral or bicameral parliaments and have jurisdiction over police and public order, agriculture, education, public health, and local government. The federal government has jurisdiction over any matter not specifically reserved to the states. In addition the president may intervene in state affairs during emergencies and may even suspend a state's government. The Congress party has dominated Indian politics since independence. It is moderately socialist and opposes communalism and the caste system. The Praja Socialist party and the Samyukta Socialist party both favor democratic socialism and sometimes join in a coalition. The Communist party has been strong in some parts of India, notably in Kerala and in West Bengal. In 1964 it split into pro-Soviet and pro-Chinese factions. The Jan Sangh is the leading Hindu communal party. The Dravida Munnetra Kazhagam supports the interests of the Dravidian peoples of S India. The Swatantra party stresses free enterprise. India is a member of the United Nations and of the Commonwealth of Nations.

Outline of Culture. The racial composition of modern India is exceedingly complex, but a mixture of Dravidian and Aryan elements forms a racial core; scattered in remote areas throughout India are still about 20 million aboriginal peoples, such as the Gonds, Bondos, Kani, Todas, and Nagas, of uncertain racial ancestry. India is a land of great cultural diversity, further intensified by the CASTE system and by the split between village India, with its traditional, centuries-old customs, and urban India, restless, educated, and international in outlook. There are more than 1,500 languages and dialects spoken in India. Hindi and English are used officially. The Indian constitution recognizes 15 languages. They are (listed in descending order by number of speakers in 1961) Hindi, Telugu, Bengali, Marathi, Tamil, Urdu, Gujarati, Kannada, Malayalam, Oriya, Punjabi, Assamese, Kashmiri, Sindhi, and Sanskrit (a classical language, not in current use). In fact, the administrative states of India are generally organized along linguistic lines. The constitution abolished the condition of "untouchability," and legislation has been used to reserve quotas for former untouchables (and also for tribal peoples) in the legislatures, in education, and in the public services. In addition to about 61 million Muslims, there are Christian, Sikh, Buddhist, Jain, and Parsi communities in India, but

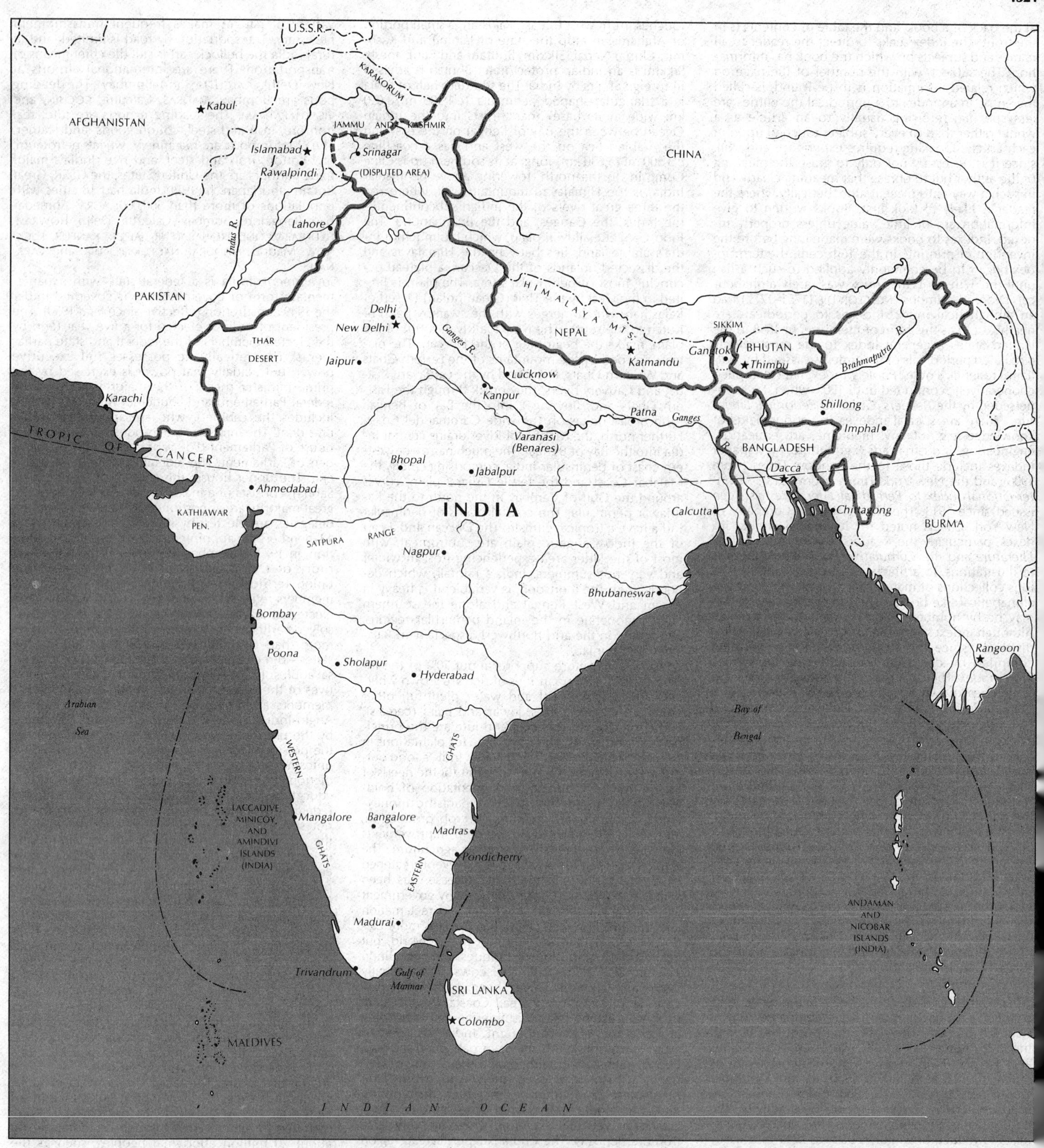

Hinduism is overwhelmingly the majority religion, with approximately 450 million followers. There is no state religion. The holy cities of India attract pilgrims from throughout the East: Varanasi (formerly Benares), Allahabad, Puri, and Nasik are religious centers for the Hindus; Amritsar is the holy city of the Sikhs; and Satrunjaya Hill near Palitana is sacred to the Jains. With its long and rich history, India retains many outstanding archaeological landmarks; preeminent of these are the Buddhist remains at Sarnath, Sanchi, and Bodh Gaya; the cave temples at Ajanta, Ellora, and Elephanta; and the temple sites at Madurai, Tanjore, Abu, Bhubaneswar, Konarak, and Mahabalipuram. For other aspects of Indian culture, see HINDU MUSIC; INDIAN ART AND ARCHITECTURE; INDIAN LITERATURE; MOGUL ART AND ARCHITECTURE; PALI LITERATURE; PRAKRIT LITERATURE; SANSKRIT LITERATURE. The historical discussion that follows deals, until Indian independence, with the Indian subcontinent, which includes the regions that are now BANGLADESH and PAKISTAN, and thereafter concentrates on the history of India.

From the Indus Valley to the Fall of the Mogul Empire. One of the earliest civilizations of the world, and the most ancient on the Indian subcontinent, was the INDUS VALLEY CIVILIZATION, which flourished c.2500 B.C. to c.1500 B.C. It was an extensive and highly sophisticated culture, its chief urban centers being Mohenjo-Daro and Harappa. The Aryans invaded through the mountain passes of the northwest, possibly destroyed (c.1500 B.C.) the Indus civilization, and established their homeland, Aryavarta, in the plains of the Punjab and along the upper Ganges. Over the next 2,000 years the Aryans developed a Brahmanic civilization (see VEDA) with a caste system, which evolved into Hinduism. From their homeland they spread E over the Gangetic plain and by c.800 B.C. were established in Bihar and Bengal. The first important Aryan kingdom was Magadha, with its capital near present-day Patna; it was there, during the reign of Bimbisara (540–490 B.C.), that the founders of JAINISM and BUDDHISM preached. KOSALA was another kingdom of the period. In 327–325 B.C., Alexander the Great invaded the province of Gandhara in NW India that had been a part of the Persian empire. The Greek invaders were eventually driven out by CHANDRAGUPTA of Magadha, founder of the Mauryan empire (see MAURYA). Hinduism was the religion of the early Mauryan empire. The Mauryan emperor ASOKA (d. 232 B.C.), Chandragupta's grandson, perhaps the greatest ruler of the ancient period, unified all of India except the southern tip. Under Asoka, Buddhism was established as the state religion and was also spread to Sri Lanka and SE Asia. During the 200 years of disorder and invasions that followed the collapse of the Mauryan state (c.185 B.C.), Buddhism in India declined. S India enjoyed greater prosperity than the north, despite almost incessant warfare; among the Tamil-speaking kingdoms of the south were the Pandya and CHOLA states, which maintained an overseas trade with the Roman Empire. Hindu culture was spread through the Malay Archipelago and Indonesia by Tamil-speaking colonists from the S Indian kingdoms. Meanwhile, Greeks following Alexander had settled in BACTRIA (in the area of present-day Afghanistan) and established an Indo-Greek kingdom. After the collapse (1st cent. B.C.) of Bactrian power, fierce tribes from central Asia, the Scythians, Parthians, Afghans, and Kushans, swept into NW India. There, small states arose and disappeared in quick succession; among the most famous of these kingdoms was that of the Kushans, which, under its sovereign KANISHKA, enjoyed (2d cent. A.D.) great prosperity. In the 4th and 5th cent. A.D., N India experienced a golden age under the GUPTA dynasty, when Hindu art and literature reached a high level. Gupta splendor rose again under the emperor HARSHA of Kanauj (c.606–647), and N India enjoyed a renaissance of Hindu art, letters, and theology. It was at this time that the noted Chinese pilgrim HSÜAN-TSANG visited India. While the Guptas ruled the north, in this, the classical period of Indian history, the Pallava kings of Kanchi held sway in the south, and the Chalukyas controlled the Deccan. During the medieval period (8th–13th cent.) several independent kingdoms, notably the Palas of Bihar and Bengal, the Sen, the Ahoms of Assam, a later Chola empire at Tanjore, and a second Chalukya dynasty in the Deccan, waxed powerful. In NW India, beyond the reach of the medieval dynasties, the RAJPUTS had grown strong and were able to resist the rising forces of Islam. Islam was first brought to Sind, W India, in the 8th cent. by seafaring Arab traders; by the 10th cent. Muslim armies from the north were raiding India. From 999 to 1026, MAHMUD OF GHAZNI several times breached Rajput defenses and plundered India. In the 11th and 12th cent. Ghaznavid power waned, to be replaced c.1150 by that of the Muslim principality of GHOR. In 1192 the legions of Ghor defeated the Hindus under Prithivi Raj, and the DELHI SULTANATE, the first Muslim kingdom in India, was established. The sultanate eventually reduced to vassalage almost every independent kingdom on the subcontinent, except that of Kashmir and the remote kingdoms of the south. The task of ruling such a vast territory proved impossible; difficulties in the south with the state of VIJAYANAGAR, the last Hindu kingdom in India, and the capture (1398) of the city of Delhi by Tamerlane finally brought the sultanate to an end. The small Muslim kingdoms that succeeded it were swept away by a great Muslim invader from Afghanistan, BABUR, a remote descendant of Tamerlane, who, after the battle of Panipat in 1526, founded the MOGUL empire. The empire was consolidated by AKBAR and reached its greatest territorial extent, the control of almost all of India, under AURANGZEB (ruled 1659–1707). Under the Delhi Sultanate and the Mogul empire a large Muslim following grew and a new culture evolved in India (see MOGUL ART AND ARCHITECTURE); Islam, however, never supplanted Hinduism as the faith of the majority.

The Arrival of the Europeans. Only a few years before Babur's triumph, Vasco da Gama had landed at Calicut (1498) and the Portuguese had conquered Goa (1510). The splendor and wealth of the Mogul empire (from it comes much of India's greatest architecture including the TAJ MAHAL) attracted British, Dutch, and French competition for the trade that Portugal had at first monopolized. The British East India Company (see EAST INDIA COMPANY, BRITISH), which established trading stations at Surat (1613), Bombay (1661), and Calcutta (1691), soon became dominant and with its command of the sea drove off the traders of Portugal and Holland. While the Mogul empire remained strong, only peaceful trade relations with it were sought; but in the 18th cent., when an Afghan invasion, dynastic struggles, and incessant revolts of Hindu elements, especially the MAHRATTAS, were rending the empire, Great Britain and France seized the opportunity to increase trade and capture Indian wealth, and each attempted to oust the other. From 1746 to 1763 India was a battleground for the forces of the two powers, each attaching to itself as many native rulers as possible in the struggle. The brilliant victories of Robert CLIVE, the British commander, over DUPLEIX and Lally ended all French threats to the power of the British company.

India under British Rule. Clive's defeat of the Nawab of Bengal at Plassey in 1757 traditionally marks the beginning of the British Empire in India (recognized in the Treaty of Paris of 1763). Warren HASTINGS, Clive's successor and the first governor-general of the company's domains to be appointed by Parliament, did much to consolidate Clive's conquests. By 1818 the British controlled nearly all of India S of the Sutlej River and had reduced to vassalage their most powerful Indian enemies, the state of Mysore (see HAIDAR ALI and TIPPOO SAHIB) and the Mahrattas. Only Sind and Punjab (the Sikh territory) remained completely independent. The East India Company, overseen by the government's India Office, administered the rich areas with the populous cities; the rest of British India remained under native princes, with British Residents in effective control. Great Britain regarded India as an agricultural reservoir and a market for British goods, which were admitted duty free. However, the export of cotton goods from India suffered because of the Napoleonic Wars and subsequently were barred from Britain by high tariffs at the same time that there was strong competition for the markets of continental Europe; national handicrafts, particularly textile weaving, were hard hit, throwing artisans upon the support of the already overcrowded land. On the other hand, the British initiated projects to improve transportation and irrigation. British control was extended over Sind in 1843 and Punjab in 1849. Social unrest, added to the apprehensions of several important native rulers about the aggrandizing policies of Governor General DALHOUSIE, led to the bloody INDIAN MUTINY of 1857. It was suppressed, and Great Britain, determined to prevent a recurrence, initiated long-needed reforms. The East India Company lost most of its functions, and its governor general became the crown's viceroy. The common soldiers in the British army in India were drawn more and more from among the Indians, and these troops were later also used overseas. Sikhs and Gurkhas became famous as British soldiers. Native rulers were guaranteed the integrity of their domains as long as they recognized the British as paramount. In 1861 the first step was taken toward self-government in British India with the appointment of Indian councilors to advise the viceroy and the establishment of provincial councils with Indian members. But the power of Britain was symbolized and reinforced when Queen Victoria was crowned empress of India in 1877. With the setting up of government universities, an Indian middle class had begun to emerge and to advocate further reform. Among the leaders who organized the INDIAN NATIONAL CONGRESS in 1885 were Allan Octavian Hume, retired from the Indian Civil Service, Dadabhai NAOROJI, Pherozeshah Mehta, and W. C. Bonnerjee. Later in the century, Bal Gangadhar TILAK, Surendranath BANERJEA, Gopal Krishna GOKHALE, Rabindranath TAGORE, and Aurobindo GHOSE also rose to prominence. The nationalist movement had been foreshadowed earlier in the century in the writings of Rammohun ROY. Popular nationalist sentiment was perhaps most strongly aroused when, for administrative reasons, Viceroy CURZON partitioned (1905) Bengal into two presidencies; newly created Eastern Bengal had a Muslim majority. (The partition was ended in 1911.) In the early 1900s the British had widened Indian participation in legislative councils (the Morley-Minto reforms). Separate Muslim and Hindu constituencies, introduced for the first time, were to be a major factor in the growing split between the two communities. Muslim nationalist sentiment was expressed by Sayyid Ahmad Khan, IQBAL, and Muhammad Ali. At the outbreak of World War I all elements in India were firmly united behind Britain, but discontent arose as the war dragged on. The British, in the Montagu declaration (1917) and later in the Montagu-Chelmsford report (1918), held out the promise of eventual self-government. However, Britain's prestige in India was shattered by the long, costly war. Crop failures and an influenza epidemic that killed millions plagued India in 1918–19. Britain passed the Rowlatt Acts (1919), which enabled authorities to dispense with juries, and even trials, in dealing with agitators. In response Mohandas K. GANDHI organized the first of his many passive resistance campaigns. The massacre of Indians by British troops at AMRITSAR further inflamed the situation. The Government of India Act (late 1919) set up provincial legislatures with "dyarchy," which meant that elected Indian ministers, responsible to the legislatures, had to share power with appointed British governors and ministers. Although the act also provided for periodic revisions, Gandhi felt too little progress had been made, and he organized new protests. Imperial conferences concerning the status of India were held in 1930, 1931, and 1932, and led to the Government of India Act of 1935. The act provided for the election of entirely Indian provincial governments and a federal legislature in Delhi that was to be largely elected. In the first elections (1937) held under the act, the Congress, led by Gandhi and Jawaharlal NEHRU, won well over half the seats, mostly in Hindu or general constituencies, and formed governments in 7 of the 11 provinces. The MUSLIM LEAGUE, led by Muhammad Ali JINNAH, won 109 of the 485 Muslim seats and formed governments in 3 of the remaining provinces. Fearing Hindu domination in a future independent India, Muslim nationalism in India henceforth became a totally separate movement. World War II found India by no means unified behind Great Britain. There was even an "Indian national army" of anti-British extremists, led by Subhas BOSE, which fought in Burma on the Japanese side. To procure India's more wholehearted support, Sir Stafford Cripps, on behalf of the British cabinet, in 1942 proposed establishing an Indian interim government, in which Great Britain would maintain control only over defense and foreign policy, to be followed by full self-government after the war. The Congress adamantly demanded that the British leave India and, when the demand was refused, initiated civil disobedience and the Quit India movement. Great Britain's response was to outlaw the Congress and jail Gandhi and other leaders. Jinnah, who offered to support the war, demanded the partition of India into Muslim- and Hindu-majority sections.

Independence. The British Labour government of Prime Minister Attlee in 1946 offered self-government to India, but it warned that if no agreement was reached between the Congress and the Muslim League, Great Britain, on withdrawing in June, 1948, would have to determine the apportionment of power between the two groups. Reluctantly the Congress agreed to the creation of Pakistan, and in Aug., 1947, British India was divided into the dominions of India and Pakistan. The princely states were nominally free to determine their own status, but realistically they were unable to stand alone. Partly by persuasion and partly by coercion, they joined one or the other of the new dominions. Hyderabad, in S central India, with a Muslim ruler and Hindu population, held out to the last and was finally incorporated (1948) into the Indian union by force. The future of Kashmir was never resolved. Nehru became prime minister of India, and Jinnah governor general of Pakistan. Partition left large minorities of Hindus and Sikhs in Pakistan, and Muslims in India. Widespread hostilities erupted between the communities and continued while large numbers of people—about 16 million in all—fled across the borders seeking safety. More than 500,000 people died in the disorders (late 1947). Gandhi was killed by a Hindu fanatic in Jan., 1948. The hostility between India and Pakistan was aggravated when warfare broke out (1948) over their conflicting claims to jurisdiction over the rich princely state of Jammu and Kashmir. India became a sovereign republic under a constitution adopted in 1949. In addition to staggering problems of overpopulation, economic backwardness, and inadequate social services, India had to achieve the integration of the former princely states into the union and the creation of national unity from diverse cultural and linguistic groups. The states of the republic were reorganized several times along linguistic lines. India consolidated its territory by acquiring the former French settlements (see PONDICHERRY) in 1956 and by forcibly annexing the Portuguese enclaves of Goa, Daman, and Diu in Dec., 1961. In world politics, India has been a leading exponent of nonalignment. The republic's major foreign problems have been a border dispute with China that first surfaced in 1957, and continual difficulties with Pakistan. The Chinese controversy climaxed on Oct. 20, 1962, when the Chinese launched a massive offensive against Ladakh in Kashmir and in areas on the NE Indian border. The Chinese announced a cease-fire on Nov. 21 after gaining much territory claimed by India. In the late 1960s there was friction with Nepal, which accused India of harboring Nepalese politicians hostile to the Nepalese monarchy. In Aug., 1965, fighting between India and Pakistan broke out in the Rann of Kutch frontier area and in Kashmir. The United Nations proclaimed a cease-fire in September, but clashes continued. India's Prime Minister SHASTRI, who succeeded Nehru after the latter's death in 1964, and Pakistan's President Ayub Khan met (1966) under Soviet auspices in Tashkent, USSR, to negotiate the Kashmir problem. They agreed on mutual troop withdrawals to the lines held before Aug., 1965. Shastri died in Tashkent and was succeeded, after bitter debate within the Congress party, by Indira GANDHI, Nehru's daughter. The Congress party suffered a setback in the elections of 1967; its parliamentary majority was sharply reduced and it lost control of several state governments. In 1969 the party split in two: Mrs. Gandhi and her followers formed the New Congress party, and her opponents on the right formed the Old Congress party. In the elections of March, 1971, the New Congress won an overwhelming victory. Rioting and terrorism by Maoists, known as Naxalites, flared in 1970 and 1971. The situation was particularly serious in West Bengal. In Pakistan, attempts by the government (dominated by West Pakistanis) to suppress a Bengali uprising in East Pakistan led in 1971 to the exodus of millions of Bengali refugees (mostly Hindus) from East Pakistan into India. Caring for the refugees imposed a severe drain on India's slender resources. India supported the demands of the Awami League, an organization of Pakistani Bengalis, for the autonomy of East Pakistan, and in Dec., 1971, war broke out between India and Pakistan on two fronts: in East Pakistan and in Kashmir. Indian forces rapidly advanced into East Pakistan; the war ended in two weeks with the creation of independent Bangladesh to replace East Pakistan, and the refugees returned from India. India's relations with the United States were strained because of U.S. support of Pakistan. In mid-1973, India and Pakistan signed an agreement (to which Bangladesh was a party but not a signatory) providing for the release of prisoners of war captured in 1971 and calling for peace and friendship on the Indian subcontinent. Also in 1973, India's ties with the USSR were strengthened by a new aid agreement that considerably increased Soviet economic assistance; at the same time, relations with the United States improved somewhat. In May, 1974, India became the world's sixth nuclear power by exploding an underground nuclear device in the Thar Desert in Rajasthan state. See Jawaharlal Nehru, *The Discovery of India* (1946, repr. 1960); S. S. Harrison, *India: The Most Dangerous Decades* (1960); R. C. Majumdar, ed., *The Bharatiya Vidya Bhavan's History and Culture of the Indian People* (6 vol., 1951–61); S. Abid Husain, *The National Culture of India* (1961); N. K. Bose, *Culture and Society in India* (1962); Bradford Smith, *Portrait of India* (1962); W. T. de Bary, ed., *Sources of Indian Tradition* (1958, repr. 1964); P. T. Bauer, *Indian Economic Policy and Development* (1961, repr. 1965); Percival Griffiths, *Modern India* (4th ed. 1965); Michael Brecher, *Nehru's Mantle: The Politics of Succession in India* (1966); Hugh Tinker, *India and Pakistan: A Political Analysis* (1966); O. H. K. Spate, *India and Pakistan: A General and Regional Geography* (3d ed. 1967); R. C. Majumdar et al., *An Advanced History of India* (rev. ed. 1961, repr. 1967); A. L. Basham, *The Wonder That Was India* (3d ed. 1968); R. L. Park, *India's Political System* (1968); V. M. Dean, *New Patterns of Democracy in India* (2d ed. 1969); P. B. Mukerji, *Critical Problems of the Indian Constitution* (1969); R. C. Dutt, *The Economic History of India* (2 vol., 2d ed. 1906, repr. 1970); D. N. Majumdar, *Races and Cultures of India* (4th ed. 1961, repr. 1973); T. G. P. Spear, *India: A Modern History* (1961, repr. 1973); *The Cambridge History of India* (6 vol., 1922–37, repr. 1973).

Indiana, state (1970 pop. 5,193,669), 36,291 sq mi (93,994 sq km), N central United States, in the Midwest, admitted as the 19th state of the Union in 1816. The capital and largest city is INDIANAPOLIS, in the central part of the state. Other major cities are FORT WAYNE and GARY. Indiana is bounded on the N by Michigan and Lake Michigan, on the E by Ohio, on the S by Kentucky, from which it is separated by the Ohio River, and on the W by Illinois. Northern Indiana is a glaciated lake area, separated by the Wabash River from the central agricultural plain,

which is rich with deep glacial drift. The southern portion of the state is a succession of bottomlands interspersed with knolls and ridges, gorges and valleys. Limestone caves, such as the big Wyandotte Cave, and mineral springs, as at French Lick and West Baden Springs, are found there. The unglaciated soil is shallow in S Indiana, and the cutting of timber has caused erosion, but there is some farming. Although Indiana as a whole is a great manufacturing state, about three quarters of the land is utilized for agriculture. With a growing season of about 170 days and an average rainfall of 40 in. (102 cm) per year, Indiana farms have rich yields. Grain crops, mainly corn and wheat, are important and also support the livestock and dairying industries. Soybeans and hay are also principal crops, and vegetables and fruits are produced in great quantity and variety. Livestock, especially hogs and cattle, are also major agricultural products. Meat-packing is chief among the many industries related to agriculture. Although the urban population exceeds the rural, many towns are primarily service centers for agricultural communities. There are, however, large cities with varied, heavy industries; prominent, besides Indianapolis, are EVANSVILLE, Fort Wayne, Gary, SOUTH BEND, and TERRE HAUTE. In the Calumet region along Indiana's Lake Michigan shoreline, marshy wastelands were drained and transformed into an area supporting a complex of factories and refineries. Indiana's leading manufactures are iron and steel, electrical equipment, transportation equipment, nonelectrical machinery, chemicals, food products, and fabricated metals. Rich mineral deposits of coal and stone (the S central Indiana area is the nation's leading producer of building limestone) have encouraged construction and industry; petroleum production is also substantial. Throughout the state the products of farms and factories are transported by truck and by train. Indiana calls itself the crossroads of America, and its extreme northwest corner—where transportation lines head east after converging on nearby Chicago from all directions—is one of the most heavily traveled areas in the world in terms of rail, road, and air traffic. Waterborne traffic, too, is important to Indiana. Tremendous improvements on the Ohio River and the opening (1959) of the St. Lawrence Seaway, linking the Great Lakes with the Atlantic Ocean, have benefited the state. With the opening in 1970 of the Burns Waterway Harbor on Lake Michigan, Indiana gained its first public port and greatly enhanced its shipping facilities. The MOUND BUILDERS were Indiana's earliest known inhabitants, and the remains of their culture have been found along Indiana's rivers and bottomlands. The region was first explored by white men, notably the French, in the late 17th cent. The leading French explorer was Robert Cavalier, sieur de La Salle, who came to the area in 1679. At the time of exploration, the area was occupied mainly by tribes of Miami, Delaware, and Potawatamie Indians. Vincennes, the first permanent settlement in what is now Indiana, was fortified in 1732, but for the first half of the 1700s most of the white men in the area were Jesuit missionaries or fur traders. By the Treaty of Paris of 1763 ending the French and Indian Wars (1689–1763), Indiana, which was then part of the area known as the Old Northwest, passed from French to British control, and, along with the rest of the Old Northwest, was united with Canada under the Quebec Act of 1774 (see INTOLERABLE ACTS). During the American Revolution an expedition led by George Rogers Clark captured, lost, and then recaptured Vincennes from the British. By the Treaty of Paris of 1783 ending the Revolutionary War, Great Britain ceded the Old Northwest to the United States. Indiana was still largely unsettled when the Northwest Territory, of which it formed a part, was established in 1787. Indians in the territory resisted white settlement, but with Gen. Anthony Wayne's victory at Fallen Timbers in 1794, the process of subduing the Indians of the Old Northwest began. U.S. forces led by Gen. William Henry Harrison also defeated the Indians in the battle of TIPPECANOE (1811) in the Wabash country, and they were finally forced out of the region in the War of 1812 when Harrison defeated both the British and the Indians in the battle of the Thames in Ontario (see THAMES, BATTLE OF THE). In 1800, Indiana Territory was formed and included the present-day states of Indiana, Illinois, and Wisconsin, and parts of Michigan and Minnesota. Vincennes was made the capital, which in 1813 was moved to Corydon. A constitutional convention met in 1816, and Indiana achieved statehood. Jonathan Jennings, an opponent of slavery, was elected governor. Indianapolis was laid out as the state capital, and the executive moved there in 1824–25. Indiana was the site of several experimental communities in the early 19th cent., notably the Rappite (1815) and Owenite (1825) settlements at New Harmony. An internal improvement scheme to construct canals and railroads for the young state was undertaken in 1836, but it was abandoned the following year with the advent of the Panic of 1837 when the state became deeply indebted. In the 1840s the Wabash and Erie Canal opened between Lafayette and Toledo, Ohio, giving Indiana a water route via Lake Erie to eastern markets. Also in the 1840s the state's first railroad line was completed between Indianapolis and Madison. The Hoosier spirit of simplicity and forthrightness that developed during Indiana's early years of statehood figured in the writings of Edward Eggleston in *The Hoosier Schoolmaster* and was represented in much later days by James Whitcomb Riley, George Ade, Gene Stratton Porter, and also in the nostalgic lyric by Paul Dresser (Theodore Dreiser's brother) for the song "On the Banks of the Wabash, Far Away." The Civil War brought great changes in the state. In the elections of 1860, Indiana voted for Lincoln, who had spent his boyhood in the Hoosier state. Although there was some proslavery sentiment in the state, represented by the KNIGHTS OF THE GOLDEN CIRCLE, Oliver P. Morton, governor during the war, held the state unswervingly to the Union cause even after constitutional government broke down in 1862. Confederate general John Hunt Morgan led a spectacular raid into Indiana in 1863, but otherwise little action occurred in the state. Manufacturing, which had been stimulated in Indiana by the needs of the war, developed rapidly after the war. Factories sprang up, and the old rustic pattern was broken. However, Indiana's farmers continued to be an important force in the state, and in the hard times following the Panic of 1873 indebted farmers expressed their discontent by supporting the GRANGER MOVEMENT and later the GREENBACK PARTY in 1876 and the POPULIST PARTY in the 1890s. Industrial development came to the Calumet region in the late 19th cent. with the establishment of an oil refinery at Whiting. As the 19th cent. drew to a close, industry continued to expand and the growing numbers of industrial workers in the state sought to organize through labor unions. Eugene V. Debs, one of the great early labor leaders, was from Indiana, and the labor movement at Gary in the Calumet area figured prominently in the nationwide steel strike just after World War I. In World War II, Indiana industries contributed heavily to the war effort. Indiana society in the first half of the 20th cent. has been described in a number of studies and books. The classic sociological study by Robert S. Lynd and Helen M. Lynd of an American manufacturing town, *Middletown* (1929), was based on data from Muncie, Ind. Midwestern life and American boyhood were portrayed realistically, and often with humor and optimism, in the novels of Booth Tarkington. Another Indiana author, Theodore Dreiser, wrote more generally of American society in a changing age. In the 1920s religious and racial intolerance was exploited in Indiana as in the South by the Ku Klux Klan. In the 1930s and 1940s, Wendell Willkie and Ernie Pyle, both natives of Indiana, became nationally prominent figures in politics and journalism, respectively. Concern for education has long been manifest in the state. Robert Dale Owen, son of the English reformer Robert Owen (who founded an idealistic community at New Harmony), promoted tax support of public schools, and this policy was incorporated into the state constitution of 1851. Among the institutions of higher learning in Indiana are Indiana Univ., at Bloomington; Purdue Univ., at Lafayette; the Univ. of Notre Dame, near South Bend; DePauw Univ., at Greencastle; Butler Univ., at Indianapolis; Valparaiso Univ., at Valparaiso; Earlham College, at Richmond; and Goshen College, at Goshen. Indiana Dunes National Lakeshore, with a 3-mi (4.8-km) frontage on Lake Michigan, is noted for its beautiful shifting sand dunes. Formerly a state park, the area was made a National Lakeshore in 1966. Four years earlier, in 1962, the U.S. Congress authorized the establishment of the Lincoln Boyhood National Memorial in S Indiana. The Indianapolis Motor Speedway is the site of the famous 500-mi (800-km) auto race, held annually. Indiana's constitution dates from 1851 and provides for an elected executive and legislature. A governor serves as the chief executive for a term of four years and may not succeed himself. The legislature, called the general assembly, has a senate with 50 members elected for four years and a house of representatives with 100 members elected for two years. Indiana elects 11 Representatives and 2 Senators to the U.S.

Congress and has 13 electoral votes. Although Indiana in the latter half of the 19th cent. was regarded as a "swing state" electorally, in the 1900s its voting pattern has been generally conservative and Republican. However, Democrats have had some successes in gubernatorial and congressional elections. Otis R. Bowen, a Republican, became governor in 1973. See Federal Writers' Project, *Indiana, A Guide to the Hoosier State* (1941); John D. Barnhart and Donald F. Carmony, *Indiana, from Frontier to Industrial Commonwealth* (1954); Walter Havighurst, *The Heartland: Ohio, Indiana, Illinois* (1962); Indiana Historical Society, *The History of Indiana* (1965); W. E. Wilson, *Indiana: A History* (1966); E. A. Leary, *The Nineteenth State* (rev. ed. 1967).

Indiana, industrial borough (1970 pop. 16,100), seat of Indiana co., W Pa.; inc. 1816. It is the principal supply and trading center for a bituminous coal mining area in the Alleghenies and has factories producing rubber goods, scientific instruments, and aluminum doors and windows. Indiana Univ. of Pennsylvania is there.

Indiana Dunes National Lakeshore: see NATIONAL PARKS AND MONUMENTS (table).

Indian Affairs, Bureau of, created (1824) in the U.S. War Dept. and transferred (1849) to the U.S. Dept. of the Interior. The War Dept. managed Indian affairs after 1789, but the separate bureau was not set up for many years. It had jurisdiction over trade with the Indians, their removal to the West, their protection from exploitation, and their concentration on reservations. Because of wide dissatisfaction in the West over army administration of Indian affairs, the Indian service was given to the Dept. of the Interior and reorganized. The new bureau was no more successful than its predecessor in preventing Indian wars or in protecting Indian rights. The Bureau of Indian Affairs instead developed primarily into a land-administering agency, a process speeded up by the Dawes Act of 1887, the Burke Act of 1906, and the Wheeler-Howard Act of 1934. The bureau also provides agricultural and economic guidance, a general health program, social services, educational facilities, and reclamation projects for Indians in the United States. The Bureau of Indian Affairs has also been officially called the Office of Indian Affairs and the Indian Service. In the early 1970s, Indian civil rights groups, such as the AMERICAN INDIAN MOVEMENT, began actively protesting their dissatisfaction with the Bureau of Indian Affairs.

Indiana Harbor, Ind.: see EAST CHICAGO.

Indianapolis (ĭn"dēənă'pəlĭs), city (1970 pop. 744,743), state capital and seat of Marion co., central Ind., on the White River; selected 1820 as the site of the state capital (which was moved there in 1825), inc. 1847. The largest city in Indiana and the eleventh largest in the United States, it is the chief processing point in a rich agricultural region and is a major grain and livestock market. It is also the commercial, transportation, and industrial center for a large area; its many manufactures include chemicals, pharmaceuticals, aircraft and automotive parts, telephone and electronic equipment, and road-building machinery. The city is the seat of Butler Univ., Marian College, Indiana Central College, Christian Theological Seminary, and Indiana Univ.-Purdue Univ. at Indianapolis, with many units, including the Medical Center and the Herron School of Art. The American Legion has its national headquarters there in a building erected as a war memorial. Landmarks are the state capitol (1878-88); the state library and historical building; the home and burial place of James Whitcomb Riley; the home of Benjamin Harrison; a Carmelite monastery; the Soldiers and Sailors Monument (1902); the Indiana National Bank Tower, highest structure in the state; and the Indianapolis Motor Speedway, site of the world famous annual 500-mi automobile race. Fort Benjamin Harrison, the U.S. army finance center, is nearby.

Indian art and architecture is essentially traditional and religious. Each work of art is not only a symbol but also a manifestation of a god or his powers. In both Buddhist and Hindu art, symbolism in every gesture, posture, and attribute contains many levels of meaning. In images of the Buddha, his different hand positions (mudras) signify religious states, such as the Enlightenment (Nirvana), the Way, Salvation. In Hindu sculpture, deities (see VISHNU, KRISHNA, and SHIVA) are frequently represented with many hands, each embodying a characteristic attribute. This article deals with that art and architecture belonging to the Indian subcontinent, now divided between India, Pakistan, and Bangladesh. With the exception of MOGUL ART AND ARCHITECTURE, which demands separate treatment, the major trends in Indian art, Hindu, Buddhist, and Jain, are discussed herein.

Indus valley civilization (c.3000 B.C.-c.1500 B.C.). The earliest Indian art emerged from the valley of the Indus River during the second half of the 3d millennium B.C. The best-known sites are Harappa, destroyed in the 19th cent., and Mohenjo-Daro; these are among the earliest examples of city planning. Houses, markets, storage facilities, offices, and public baths were arranged in a gridlike scheme. There was also a highly developed drainage system. At Mohenjo-Daro the appearance of the houses, without color or sculptural ornament, continued unchanged for 1,500 years. The Indus civilization produced many statuettes made of steatite and limestone. Some statuettes are related to the hieratic style of contemporary Mesopotamia, while others are done in the smooth, sinuous style that is the prototype of later Indian sculpture, in which the plastic modeling reveals the animating breath of life (prana). Also found in this region are square steatite seals, frequently adorned with naturalistically rendered bulls; ceramic storage jars with simple, stylized designs; toys with wheels; and crude figurines, which have been identified as mother goddesses. Bronze weapons, tools, and sculptures were significant in the Indus civilization; they indicate a sophistication in craftsmanship rather than a major aesthetic development. Of the period from the end of the Indus civilization (c.1500 B.C.) until Alexander the Great crossed (325 B.C.) the Indus, few traces remain. However, the principles of architecture were developed in wooden buildings, long since disintegrated. From the MAURYA dynasty the most famous remains are the edict pillars, erected throughout N India by the Emperor ASOKA to proclaim his devotion to Buddhism. The great, smooth columns are over 50 ft (15 m) high and are surmounted by lotus flowers and animal figures. These pillars, together with the vestiges of the capital city of Pataliputra, reveal strong Iranian and some Hellenistic influences. Also dating from the reign of Asoka is the earliest stone ogival chaitya window, found on the portal of a rock-cut sanctuary near Bodh Gaya. The chaitya halls were large monastic sanctuaries hewn out of rock. As they evolved, from the 3d cent. B.C. through the 1st millennium A.D., they became elaborate colonnaded halls, or walls embellished with painting or sculpture.

The Early Classic Period. The Sunga dynasty (2d-1st cent. B.C.) and early Andhra dynasty (1st cent. B.C.), have left the earliest extant STUPAS. These relic mounds are surrounded by railings and gateways covered with carved ornament. One of the main stupas is at Bharhut, where the sculpture is archaic in character. Relief medallions of the jatakas (tales of the incarnations of Buddha) are shallow cut, with all the incidents of each story arranged unchronologically into a single composition. The bodies of yakshis (female tree spirits) and other figures consist of rather awkwardly joined parts; prana is still emphasized. The remains of a stupa at Sanchi show the same archaisms. Important carving on the gateways of another stupa at Sanchi date from the early Andhra period. The yakshis have become full, graceful forms, and high-relief compositions are conceived in a continuous method of narration. The carved railing from Bodh Gaya, the place of the Buddha's enlightenment, and the earliest surviving wall paintings are also early Andhra; a painting in one of the caves at Ajanta shows the Buddha in his elephant incarnation. Under the Kushans, conquerors from the north, two of India's most important styles were developed between the 2d and 5th cent. A.D.: Gandhara art and art of Mathura. Gandhara art, named after the region of GANDHARA now in Pakistan, presents the first human images of the Buddha. Earlier his supernatural character had been represented by symbols, such as the pipal tree, the wheel of life, footprints, and an empty throne. Gandhara style was profoundly influenced by 2d-century Hellenistic art and was, itself, highly influential in central Asia and the Far East. Ornate stupas and monasteries, ivories, colossal gilt figures, and imported fine glass and lacquerware attest to the cosmopolitan tastes and extensive trade that characterized the period. Relief friezes, often carved in dark schist, show figures whose casual poses and draperies are reminiscent of Western style. However, farther east and south, contemporary Mathura created a wholly Indian sculptural art. Reddish limestone was the usual medium. Completely symmetrical, heavier Buddhas, whose limbs are formed according to religious canons, smile benignly at their worshipers. Reliefs of the ever-present yakshis are more frankly sensual and erotic than those at Sanchi. Buddhist iconography was developed in Gandhara; Mathura, however, preserved and developed Indian forms for three centuries. Still farther south, in the Deccan, the Andhra dynasty continued to flourish; its greatest monument is the carving from the Great Stupa at Amaravati, A.D. c.200. The complex but coherent composition, the chiaroscuro, and the liveliness of the crowded surfaces distinguish these bas-reliefs.

The Gupta Period (A.D. 320-600). This was the golden age of Buddhist art. Both rock-cut and free-standing chaitya halls remain; their facades and interiors are covered with smooth, elegant reliefs. The cella-and-porch temple, originating in this period as a Buddhist building, was soon adopted by Hinduism, as was the chaitya hall. In this period there is little difference in the images of the major Indian religions, Buddhist, Hindu, or Jain. Large stone figures, stone and terra-cotta reliefs, and large and small bronzes are made in the refined Gupta style; the level of production is remarkably and uniformly high. Most of the murals at AJANTA were executed in this period; they depict the joys of secular life and epitomize the beauty of the spiritual. Gupta style influenced the art of the lands neighboring India, but very little original art of the period survives. After the 7th cent., only the Pala and Sena dynasties (730-1197), in the Ganges valley, remained Buddhist. Images in bronze and in hard black stone from Nalanda and elsewhere are done in a degenerate Gupta manner; so much attention is paid to the ornamental details that Gupta calm is lost.

Architecture and Sculpture of the Hindu Dynasties. From the 6th cent. on, with the resurgence of Hindu dynasties throughout India, a characteristic temple plan was developed. An entrance portico led to a pillared hall (mandapa) into the cella. The shrine was often crowned by a large tower known as the shikhara. Frequently in S India the Dravidian tower rose in a series of terraces, each symbolizing a different divinity; in the north, Indo-Aryan or *nagara* spires ascended in a massive conical shape. Innumerable temples were built that were so exuberantly embellished with sculpture that their style is called "sculptural architecture." The Khajuraho temples in central India (c.1000) are the high point of the *nagara* buildings, and the unfinished Temple of the Sun at Konarak (c.1250) shows, in its famous erotic sculptures, the last carvings that combine balanced mass with delicate execution. The Jain temples at Mt. Abu, all made of imported white marble and dating from the 10th and 13th cent., are so ornately carved inside that the majesty of stone and form is lost in the airiness of effect. The 7th-century Pallava dynasty in S India introduced the Dravidian-style temple in five pyramidal *raths* (temples) at MAHABALIPURAM; also there is the contemporary giant boulder carved with a magnificent representation of the *Descent of the Ganges,* with all the gods, men, and beasts, including the elephant family, portrayed life size. The Dravidian plan was used also in the 8th cent. in the quarried temple at ELLORA and in the rock structures on ELEPHANTA island. The CHOLA dynasty of S India perfected this form in the 11th cent., when they probably also cast most of the fine S India bronzes, of which the *Nataraja* (dancing Siva) images are perhaps the best known and most beautiful. The Dravidian style ended in the comparatively crude stucco sculptured architecture of 17th-century Mandura. Medieval bronze sculpture was highly developed in S India. The chief subjects were the deities, figures of whom were used for processional and home ritual. Skilled CIRE-PERDUE sculptures were produced until the late 19th cent. in many regions of India.

Indian Painting. Adverse climate and other conditions have injured what wall painting existed. The most famous surviving Buddhist paintings are from the caves at Ajanta. Little is known of Hindu wall painting except for fragments at Ellora and Tanjore (see THANJAVUR). The earliest Indian manuscript paintings are Buddhist, of the Pala dynasty; they have a delicate line with no indication of depth. The 13th- to 15th-century Jain manuscript illuminations are square, brightly colored, and easily recognized by the characteristic protruding farther eye. Rajput miniature painting, which was practiced in N India from the 16th through the 19th cent., derives much of its technique and coloring from Mogul models, but it illustrates Hindu subjects: the *raga* and *ragini* series (modes and seasons), the legendary epics and romances, and the tantric texts, particularly Krishna's deeds. Rajput painting is characterized by an interest in nature and sinuous grace in the depiction of the human form.

The Modern Era. Little of the glorious tradition of Indian artistic achievement survived British rule. Indian artists adapted Western techniques and produced GOUACHE paintings for European buyers. The Patua scrolls, containing swiftly executed watercolor illustrations of many subjects, became a major basis for the revival of Indian themes in art during the 20th cent. A growing nationalist sentiment pervaded Indian art in the early decades of the 20th cent. simultaneously with the conscious assimilation of Western styles. Major modern painters include Abanindranath Tagore, Nandalal Bose, Jamini Roy, Amrita Sher Gil, N. S. Bendre, M. B. Samant, Francis Souza, Bhagwan Kapoor, and M. F. Husain. Among chief contemporary sculptors are Ram Kinker, Dhanraj Bhagat, Amar Nath Seghal, Chintamoni Kar, and Amina Ahmad. Fine collections of Indian art can be seen in the British Museum, in the Victoria and Albert Museum, and in the Museum of Fine Arts, Boston. See H. R. Zimmer, *The Art of Indian Asia* (2 vol., 2d ed. 1960); Benjamin Rowland, *The Art and Architecture of India* (3d ed. 1967); Curt Maury, *Folk Origins of Indian Art* (1970); W. G. Archer, *Indian Painting from the Punjab Hills* (1974).

Indiana State University, mainly at Terre Haute; coeducational; est. 1865 as a normal school, became Indiana State Teachers College in 1929, gained university status in 1965. There is a branch at Evansville (opened 1965). Although its curriculum has greatly expanded, the university still focuses on the preparation of teachers and school administrators.

Indiana University, mainly at Bloomington; state supported; coeducational; chartered 1820 as a seminary, opened 1824. It became a college in 1828 and a university in 1838. It has extension centers at Fort Wayne, Indianapolis, Kokomo, Gary, South Bend, Richmond, and Jeffersonville. It operates a medical center at Indianapolis. There is a noted nuclear energy laboratory. In cooperation with the universities of Chicago and Texas, Indiana operates McDonald Observatory on Mt. Locke, Texas. David Starr JORDAN was a noted president.

Indian bread: see TUCKAHOE.

Indian Head, town (1971 pop. 1,810), SE Sask., Canada, E of Regina. In a wheat-growing region, it has flour mills and grain elevators. A dominion experimental and forestry farm is in the town.

Indian literature. Oral literature in the vernacular languages of India is of great antiquity, but it was not until about the 16th cent. that an extensive written literature appeared. Chief factors in this development were the intellectual and literary predominance of Sanskrit until then (except in S India, where a vast literature in Tamil was produced from ancient times) and the emergence of Hindu pietistic movements that sought to reach the people in their spoken languages. Among the Muslims classical Persian poetry was the fountainhead of a later growth in the Urdu literature produced for the Mogul court, and elaborate Urdu verse on set themes was produced in abundance. In the early 19th cent., with the establishment of vernacular schools and the importation of printing presses, a great impetus was given to popular prose, with Bengali writers perhaps taking the lead. Foreign, particularly English, literature was eagerly studied and to some extent assimilated to classical Indian modes and themes. Today there is a written literature in all the important languages of India, Pakistan and Bangladesh, as well as a large literature in English intended to reach all the university-educated public regardless of native language. Among the best-known writers of the 19th and early 20th cent. are Rammohun ROY, Bankim Chandra CHATTERJEE, Vivekenanda, Rabindranath TAGORE, winner of the 1913 Nobel Prize in Literature, and Prem Chand, as well as Asadullah Khan Ghalib and Muhammad IQBAL, the Muslim poets who wrote in Urdu and in Persian. Later writers include R. K. NARAYAN, Raja RAO, Bhabhani BHATTACHARYA, Ahmed Ali, Khushwant Singh, and Thakazhi Sivasankara Pillai in the field of fiction; Sarojini NAIDU, Faiz Ahmed Faiz, and Nazrul Islam, in the field of poetry; and Mohandas GANDHI, M. N. Roy, Jawaharlal NEHRU, and Jayaprakash Narayan in the field of politics. See SANSKRIT LITERATURE; PALI LITERATURE; PRAKRIT LITERATURE. See Krishna Kripalani, *Modern Indian Literature* (1970); T. W. Clark, *The Novel in India* (1970); Maurice Winternitz, *A History of Indian Literature* (2 vol., tr. 1927; repr. 1973).

Indian music, of India: see HINDU MUSIC.

Indian Mutiny, 1857–58, revolt of the Indian soldiers in the Bengal army of the British East India Company that developed into a widespread uprising against British rule in India. It is also known as the Sepoy Rebellion, sepoys being the native soldiers. In the years just prior to the mutiny many factors combined to create a climate of social and political unrest in India. The political expansion of the East India Company at the expense of native princes and of the Mogul court aroused Hindu and Muslim alike, and the harsh land policies, carried out by Governor General Dalhousie and his successor Lord Canning, as well as the rapid introduction of European civilization threatened traditional India. In 1853, NANA SAHIB, leader of the Mahrattas, was denied his titles and pension by the British, and the aged BAHADUR SHAH II, last of the Mogul emperors, was informed that the dynasty would end with his death. These affronts to their native rulers deeply offended the Bengali soldiers, and their resentment grew with the British annexation (1856) of the kingdom of Oudh, from which many of them came. They interpreted a regulation of 1856 subjecting them to service overseas (which would have entailed the loss of caste in crossing the open sea) as part of a plot to force them to adopt Christianity. This belief was strengthened when the British furnished the soldiers with cartridges coated with grease made from the fat of cows (sacred to Hindus) and of pigs (anathema to Muslims). The handling of these cartridges would have constituted a serious breach of both Hindu and Muslim law. The British replaced the cartridges when the mistake was realized; but suspicion persisted, and in Feb., 1857, began a series of incidents in which sepoys refused to use the cartridges. On May 10 the sepoys revolted at Meerut; they captured Delhi and proclaimed Bahadur Shah II the emperor of all India. The mutiny spread rapidly through N central India, and, by the end of June, Cawnpore (KANPUR) had fallen to the sepoys of Nana Sahib, and Lucknow was besieged. In repressing the rebellion the British were aided by the loyalty of the Punjab (the Sikhs did not wish to see the restoration of Mogul rule) and the passivity of the south. Troops (largely British) under generals Colin Campbell and Henry Havelock accomplished the reconquest. Delhi was recaptured in Sept., 1857, and Lucknow (which had been abandoned in Nov., 1857) was retaken in March, 1858. The rebellion was marked by atrocities on both sides, the British (despite an official position of moderation) taking savage reprisals for the massacres perpetrated by the rebels. The British government did, however, recognize the urgent need for reform, and in 1858 the East India Company was abolished and rule assumed directly by the British crown. Expropriation of land was discontinued, religious toleration was decreed, and Indians were admitted to subordinate positions in the civil service. However, the rebellion was long remembered with bitterness by the British. Military precautions against further uprisings included increasing the proportion of British to native troops and restricting artillery service to Britons. Although it is too much to say that the mutiny constituted a nationalist uprising, it was at that time that the first stirrings of active Indian nationalism began to be felt. See Sir John Kaye and George Malleson, *History of the Indian Mutiny* (6 vol., 1896); T. P. Holmes, *History of the Indian Mutiny* (3 vol., 1904–12); R. C. Majumdar, *The Sepoy Mutiny and Revolt of 1857* (2d ed. 1963); Richard Collier, *The Great Indian Mutiny* (1963); A. T. Embree, ed., *1857 in India* (1963); S. B. Chaudhuri, *Theories of the Indian Mutiny* (1965).

Indian National Congress, Indian political party, founded in 1885. Its original members wanted economic reform and a larger say in the making of British policy for India. By 1907, however, the Congress, strained by slow progress, had split into a moderate group led by Gopal Krishna GOKHALE, who sought dominion status for India, and a militant faction under Bal Gangadhar TILAK, who demanded swaraj [complete independence]. The split was temporarily healed in 1916 when the Congress voted to support Great Britain in World War I; but in 1917 the more militant group forced the moderates out of power. In 1919 the Congress instituted a satyagraha [passive resistance] campaign, led by Mohandas Karamchand GANDHI, against legislation that restricted the press and political activities. On this and later occasions the Congress leaders were imprisoned. Claiming to represent all Indians and not, as charged, only upper-caste Hindus, the Congress urged unity in the struggle for swaraj; however, many Muslims, fearful of the vast Hindu majority, began to withdraw from the Congress at this time. Wide popular support of the party was achieved, even though Congress was divided by differing views on CASTE, especially untouchability, and by contrasting approaches to economic reform; the conservative right wing favored cautious reform while the left wing, of which Jawaharlal NEHRU was a leader, urged socialism. The great strength of the organization was shown by victories in 7 of the 11 provincial elections of 1937. At the outbreak of World War II, the Congress, after a long and heated debate, voted for neutrality, and when India was under Japanese attack it threatened (1942) refusal of cooperation with Great Britain unless immediate concessions were made toward a democratic central government. The British responded by outlawing the organization and arresting its leaders. The Congress reorganized in 1945 and promptly expelled the Communist faction, which had supported the war. In the 1946 elections to the Indian constituent assembly, the Congress won the Hindu vote, but it lost the Muslim vote to the MUSLIM LEAGUE. The Congress reluctantly agreed to the partition of the Indian subcontinent and the formation of the state of Pakistan. After partition Congress, as the largest party, began (1947) to govern the Union of India under Jawaharlal Nehru's leadership. For the next four years the Congress was in a period of transition and crisis. The organization was in essence a nationalist movement that had represented many people of diverse political opinions. It now, however, was required to operate as a political party; while endeavoring to satisfy some widely different demands, the programs that it adopted were largely socialist in character. Despite disorder in the party, its adaptability was shown in the 1951 elections, when it received overwhelming popular support. It retained this support into the 1960s, when, although still dominating the political system, it began to lose strength after the death (1964) of Nehru. The leadership of Nehru's daughter, Indira GANDHI, who became prime minister in 1966, was challenged by a powerful right-wing group within the Congress, and in 1969 the party formally split into two factions; the right-wing group, led by Morarji DESAI, called itself the Old Congress party, while Indira Gandhi's group became known as the New Congress. Although the position of the New Congress at first seemed very weak, in the 1971 national elections and the 1972 state elections it scored strong victories. See Bhogaraju Pattabhi Sitaramajya, *The History of the Indian National Congress* (2 vol., 1946–47; repr. 1969); C. F. Andrews and Girija Mukirji, *Rise and Growth of the Congress in India* (2d ed. 1967); Myron Weiner, *Party Building in a New Nation* (1967); Stanley Kochanek, *The Congress Party of India* (1968); B. K. Chatterjee, *Congress Splits* (1970).

Indian nut: see PINE NUT.

Indian Ocean, third largest ocean, c.28,350,000 sq mi (73,427,000 sq km), extending from S Asia to Antarctica and from E Africa to SE Australia; it is c.4,000 mi (6,400 km) wide at the equator. The Indian Ocean is connected with the Pacific Ocean by passages through the Malay Archipelago and between Australia and Antarctica; and with the Atlantic Ocean by the expanse between Africa and Antarctica and by the Suez Canal. Its chief arms are the Arabian Sea (with the Red Sea, the Gulf of Aden, and the Persian Gulf), the Bay of Bengal, and the Andaman Sea. The continental shelf of the Indian Ocean is narrow. Madagascar and Sri Lanka, the largest islands in the ocean, are structurally parts of the continents as are Socotra, the Andaman Islands, and the Nicobar Islands; the Seychelles and the Kerguelen Islands are exposed tops of submerged ridges. The Laccadives, the Maldives, and the Chagos are low coral islands, and Mauritius and Réunion are high volcanic cones. The floor of the Indian Ocean has an average depth of c.11,000 ft (3,400 m). The Mid-Oceanic Ridge, a broad submarine mountain range extending from Asia to Antarctica, divides the Indian Ocean into eastern and western sections. The ridge rises to an average height of c.10,000 ft (3,000 m), and a few peaks emerge as islands. A large rift, an extension of the eastern branch of the Great Rift Valley that runs through the Gulf of Aden, extends along most of its length (see SEA-FLOOR SPREADING). The Mid-Oceanic Ridge, along with other submarine ridges, encloses a series of deep-sea basins (abyssal plains). The greatest depth (25,344 ft/7,725 m) is in the Java Trench, S of Java, Indonesia. The Indian Ocean receives the waters of the Zambezi, Tigris-Euphrates, Indus, Ganges-Brahmaputra, and Irrawady rivers. The surface waters of the ocean are generally warm, although close to Antarctica pack ice and icebergs are found. The Indian Ocean has two water circulation systems—a regular counterclockwise southern system (South Equatorial Current, Mozambique Current, South Pacific Drift, West Australian Current) and a northern system whose currents are directly related to the seasonal shift of the monsoon winds. The southwest monsoon draws moisture from the Indian Ocean and drops heavy rainfall on W India and Southeast Asia.

Indian paintbrush: see FIGWORT.

Indian philosophy. Systematized Indian philosophy begins in the period of the UPANISHADS (900–500 B.C.), during which many philosophical views were formulated not only in the Upanishads themselves, but in all circles of Indian intellectual life. The rise of Buddhism (from the 5th cent. B.C.), with its strict reliance on logic and insight, necessitated a more systematic approach for rival systems; philosophical tenets were presented in the form of aphorisms or *sutras*, intended to serve as an aid to memory and as a basis for oral elaboration. Because of their extreme conciseness, however, the *sutras* are difficult to understand, and many commentaries were added by later thinkers. Indian philosophy developed through a process of controversy between existing schools, rather than through the construction of new systems by independent speculation, as in the West. The Indian systems grew in relation to one another, always attempting to adhere to traditional opinion, while at the same time restating the theories so as to be less open to refutation by opponents. Indian philosophical schools are divided into two categories: those that accept the authority of the VEDA (*astika*) and those that do not (*nastika*). Of the former there are six classical schools. Nyaya, traditionally founded by Akshapada Gautama (6th cent. B.C.) is a school of logic and epistemology that defined the rules of debate and canons of proof. Its views were accepted with modification by most of the other schools. The atomist school, Vaisheshika, founded by Kanada (3d cent. B.C.), posited a sixfold classification of reality into substance, quality, activity, generality, particularity, and inherence. The universe is made up of nine kinds of substance: earth, water, light, air, ether, time, space, soul (or self), and mind. The Samkhya system, founded by Kapila (6th cent. B.C.), admits two basic metaphysical principles, *purusha* (soul) and *prakriti* (nature or matter). *Prakriti* consists of three *gunas* or qualities: *sattva* (light or virtue), *rajas* (activity or passion), and *tamas* (darkness or inertia). When these constituents are in equilibrium, *prakriti* is static. However, disturbance of the equilibrium results in the evolution of *buddhi* (intelligence) and *ahamkara* (ego). From the latter are produced, on the cosmic level, the five subtle elements (earth, water, light, air, ether) and the five gross elements (the objects of the senses); and, on the individual level, the faculties of action, thought, and sense. The *purusha* (soul) appears to be bound to *prakriti* with all its modifications and may become free only through realization that it is distinct from *prakriti*. This freedom constitutes salvation. Early versions of Samkhya that are now lost may have been theistic, but the classical system does not include God. The YOGA system expounded by Patanjali (2d cent. B.C.) accepts the Samkhya metaphysics to explain the validity of yogic processes described in the *Yoga Sutras* and also accepts the concept of an *Ishvara*, God or supreme soul. *Yoga* is defined as "cessation of the modifications of consciousness" and is achieved by an eight-stage discipline of self-control and meditation. The Purva Mimamsa school, founded by Jaimini (2d cent. B.C.), set forth principles of interpretation of the Vedic texts, which were regarded as entirely analyzable into injunctions to ritual action. Its epistemology and theory of meaning was constructed to show that the words of the Veda had an eternal and intrinsic validity. The different schools of Uttara Mimamsa or VEDANTA all base themselves on the *Brahma-Sutras* of Badarayana (early centuries A.D.) and agree that these epitomize the teachings of the Upanishads but differ in their concepts of God, world, soul, and the relation between the three. The three main heterodox schools, which did not attempt to justify their theories by reference to the Veda and Upanishads, are BUDDHISM, JAINISM, and the materialist school called Charvaka or Lokayata. The Charvaka was the only Indian school to reject the ideas of KARMA and *moksha* (spiritual liberation). Its adherents held that only this world exists; there is no God or future life. Perception is the only valid form of knowledge, and matter, made up of the four gross elements—earth, air, fire, and water—is the only reality. Religious ideas are delusion and moral values convention only; therefore the aim of life is not salvation but the avoidance of pain and pursuit of pleasure. See F. M. Müller, *The Six Systems of Indian Philosophy* (1899, repr. 1963); S. N. Das Gupta, *History of Indian Philosophy* (4 vol., 1922–55); Sarvepalli Radhakrishnan and C. A. Moore, *Source Book in Indian Philosophy* (1957); D. M. Riepe, *The Philosophy of India and Its Impact on American Thought* (1970); R. A. Simari, *The Structure of Indian Thought* (1970); P. T. Raju, *The Philosophical Traditions of India* (1971); R. N. Sharma, *Indian Philosophy* (1972).

Indian pipe, common name for the genus *Monotropa* and for the family Monotropaceae, low flowering plants of north temperate zones. They are chlorophylless saprophytes with a funguslike appearance. Each stem has scalelike leaves and, with its nodding flower, resembles a pipe. The plant's waxy white or yellowish-white color has given rise to such names as corpse plant and ghost flower. The related snow plant (*Sarcodes sanguinea*) of the Sierra Nevadas is a bright red species that shoots up and blooms as soon as the snow melts. Indian pipes, snow plants, and related saprophytes are classed by some botanists as a separate family, the Monotropaceae; by others they are included in the family Ericaceae (HEATH family). Both families are classified in the MAGNOLIOPHYTA, class Magnoliopsida, order Ericales.

Indian Removal Act, in U.S. history, law signed by President Andrew Jackson in 1830 providing for the general resettlement of Indians to lands W of the Mississippi River. From 1830 to 1840 approximately 60,000 Indians were forced to migrate. Of some 11,500 Cherokees moved in 1838, about 4,000 died along the way.

Indian Reorganization Act, legislation passed in 1934 in the United States in an attempt to secure new rights for Indians on reservations. Its main provisions were to restore to the Indians management of their assets (mostly land); to prevent further depletion of reservation resources; to build a sound economic foundation for the people of the reservations; and to return to the Indians local self-government on a tribal basis. The objectives of the bill were vigorously pursued until the outbreak of World War II. Although the act is still in effect, its underlying purpose of gradual assimilation of Indians into American society is opposed by many Indians.

Indian rice: see WILD RICE.

Indian River, lagoon, c.100 mi (160 km) long, E Fla., parallel to the east coast from N of Titusville to Stuart. Resorts are on its shores.

Indians, antiquity and prehistory of, study of the origins of the aboriginal peoples of the Americas. It is generally accepted that the first humans to inhabit the Americas moved across the Bering Strait from NE Asia in waves of migration that began some time before 30,000 B.C. The fact that there are no fossil remains of higher apes or prehistoric humans (see MAN, PREHISTORIC) in the Americas and the close ethnic affinities between the American Indians and people of Mongoloid stock support this contention. Archaeological evidence has been collected that clearly demonstrates that humans occupied W North America more than 25,000 years ago. By 8000 B.C. successive waves of nomadic Indians had spread throughout the Americas.

Stone Age Cultures of the Americas. The major Paleolithic cultural horizons in North America were Sandia (c.20,000–15,000 B.C.), Clovis (c.12,000–10,000 B.C.), and Folsom (c.10,000–8000 B.C.). The people who created them were apparently seminomadic, big-game hunters of the Great Plains of North America. Characteristic of the remains of these cultures are lanceolated or fluted projectile points made out of stone by the pressure-flaking method. Later groups in the West, such as the Cochise (8000–5000 B.C.), seemed to have depended mostly on food collecting. The Cochise culture gave rise to the Mogollon, a basic culture in the southwest. In Middle and South America the earliest evidence of human occupation, a carved elephant bone from the vicinity of Puebla, Mexico, dates back to 30,000 B.C., but it is through such cultural horizons as Iztapan (c.8500 B.C.) in Mexico, Aympitín (c.6000 B.C.) in the Andes, and Magellan I (c.7000) in the area of Tierra del Fuego that one can visualize the tremendous range of Stone Age cultures in the Americas. With the decline of hunting and food-gathering groups (c.7000–5000 B.C.) came the rise of agriculture. Between 5000 and 1000 B.C., both in North and South America, the domestication and cultivation of manioc, maize, beans, and squash; the appearance of pottery; and the increasing abundance of sites revealing a complex social system marked the end of the fundamental life patterns of Stone Age hunters and heralded the rise of the high Indian civilizations. See H. M. Wormington, *Ancient Man in North America* (4th ed. 1957); J. D. Jennings, *Prehistory of North America* (1968); Franklin Folson, *America's Ancient Treasures* (1971); Kurt Marek, *The First American* (1971); Friedrich Katz, *The Ancient American Civilizations* (tr. 1972); R. S. MacNeish, comp., *Early Man in America* (1973).

Indians, Middle American, aboriginal peoples living in the area between present-day United States and South America. Although most of Mexico is geographically considered part of North America and although there have been cultural contacts between Mexican groups and the Pueblo Indians of the SW United States, the cultural development of most of Mexico belongs, in fact, to that of Middle America. In the southern portion of the valley of Mexico and in the jungle region of Yucatán, ancient Mexico reached its highest cultural achievements. The MAYA had links with the CHOROTEGA of Nicaragua and Honduras and these in turn had contacts with the CHIBCHA of Colombia, thus establishing a Central American cultural chain between the civilizations of Mexico and those of the Andean region. Highly developed civilizations flourished in Mexico after the domestication of maize and the rise of agricultural communities; the OLMEC, the Maya, and the cultures of the central plateau, Teotihuacán, TOLTEC, MIXTEC, ZAPOTEC and AZTEC, developed architecture, agriculture, the use of stone—and sometimes of metal—to a high, often remarkable, degree. The QUICHÉ and the Cakchiquel flourished in Guatemala; besides these and the Chorotega, the southern tip of Central America did not produce as highly developed civilizations as the rest of Middle America. In the Caribbean coastal region there was a constant influx of ARAWAK and CARIB INDIANS, and today many of the Indians of Panama, Nicaragua, and Honduras, such as the San Blas Indians, the Mosquitia Indians (see MOSQUITO COAST), and the Lenca of Honduras, bear the imprint of Carib ancestry or influence. The Mexican Indians after the Spanish conquest in the 16th cent. retained their ancestral mode of life in some regions, but they were mostly a subjugated group until the 20th cent. Indian artisans did make notable contributions to the early development of the arts, notably in painting and architecture, but the Indians were mostly used as laborers under the ENCOMIENDA and the repartimiento, and thousands eventually became the victims of PEONAGE. It was not until after the revolution of 1910 and the *indianismo* movement of Emiliano ZAPATA that efforts were made, notably by the Mexican president Lázaro Cárdenas, with regard to the economic and social development of the Indian. Today the descendants of the above-mentioned Indian groups, as well as such peoples as the HUASTEC, the TARASCAN, the YAQUI INDIANS, and the TARAHUMARA INDIANS, constitute a powerful cultural and economic element of Mexican life. See J. A. Graham, comp., *Ancient Mesoamerica* (1966); D. Z. Stone, *Pre-Columbian Man Finds Central America* (1972); M. P. Weaver, *The Aztecs, Maya, and their Predecessors* (1972).

Indians, North American, peoples who occupied North America before the arrival of the Europeans in the 15th cent. They are so called because of the belief prevalent at the time of Columbus that the Americas were the outer reaches of the Indies (i.e., the East Indies). Most scholars agree that the Indians came into the Western Hemisphere from Asia via the Bering Strait in a series of migrations. From Alaska they spread east and south. The several waves of migration are said to account for the many native linguistic families (see AMERICAN INDIAN LANGUAGES), while the common origin is used to explain the physical characteristics that the Indians have in common (though with considerable variation)—Mongoloid features, coarse, straight black hair, dark eyes, sparse body hair, and a skin color ranging from yellow brown to reddish brown. Evidence of Indian existence in the Americas extends back more than 25,000 years. In pre-Columbian times (prior to 1492) the Indian population of the area N of Mexico is estimated to have been between one and two million. From prehistoric times until recent historic times there were roughly six major cultural areas, excluding that of the Arctic (see ESKIMO), i.e., Northwest Coast, Plains, Plateau, Eastern Woodlands, Northern, and Southwest.

The Northwest Coast Area. The Northwest Coast area extended along the Pacific coast from S Alaska to N California. The main language families in this area were the Nadene in the north and the Wakashan (a subdivision of the Algonquian-Wakashan linguistic stock) and the Tsimshian (a subdivision of the Penutian linguistic stock) in the central area. Typical tribes were the Kwakiutl, the Haida, the Tsimshian, and the Nootka. Thickly wooded, with a temperate climate and heavy rainfall, the area had long supported a large Indian population. Salmon was the staple food, supplemented by sea mammals (seals and sea lions) and land mammals (deer, elk, and bears) as well as berries and other wild fruit. The

Indians of this area used wood to build their houses and had cedar-planked canoes and carved dugouts. In their permanent winter villages some of the groups had totem poles (see TOTEM), which were elaborately carved and covered with symbolic animal decoration. Their art work, for which they are famed, also included the making of ceremonial items, such as rattles and masks, weaving, and basketry. They had a highly classified society with chiefs, nobles, commoners, and slaves. Public display and disposal of wealth was a basic feature of the society (see POTLATCH). They had woven robes, furs, and basket hats as well as wooden armor and helmets for battle. This distinctive culture, which included cannibalistic rituals, was not greatly affected by European influences until after the late 18th cent., when the white fur traders and hunters came to the area.

The Plains Area. The Plains area extended from just N of the Canadian border S to Texas and included the grasslands area between the Mississippi River and the foothills of the Rocky Mts. The main language families in this area were the Algonquian-Wakashan, the Aztec-Tanoan, and the Hokan-Siouan. In pre-Columbian times there were two distinct types of Indians there, sedentary and nomadic. The sedentary tribes, who had migrated from neighboring regions and had initally settled along the great river valleys, were farmers and lived in permanent villages of dome-shaped earth lodges surrounded by earthen walls. They raised corn, squash, and beans. The foot nomads, on the other hand, moved about with their goods on dog-drawn TRAVOIS and eked out a precarious existence by hunting the vast herds of buffalo (bison)—usually by driving them into enclosures or rounding them up by setting grass fires. They supplemented their diet by exchanging meat and hides for the corn of the agricultural Indians. The horse, first introduced by the Spanish of the Southwest, appeared in the Plains about the beginning of the 18th cent. and revolutionized the life of the Plains Indians. Many Indians left their villages and joined the nomads. Mounted and armed with bow and arrow, they ranged the grasslands hunting buffalo. The other Indians remained farmers (e.g., the Arikara, the Hidatsa, and the Mandan). Indians from surrounding areas came into the Plains (e.g., the Sioux from the Great Lakes, the Comanche and the Kiowa from the west and northwest, and the Navaho and the Apache from the southwest). A universal sign language developed among the perpetually wandering and often warring Indians. Living on horseback and in the portable TEPEE, they preserved food by pounding and drying lean meat and made their clothes from buffalo hides and deerskins. The system of COUP was a characteristic feature of their society. Other features were rites of fasting in quest of a vision, warrior clans, bead and feather art work, and decorated hides. These Plains Indians were among the last to engage in a serious struggle with the white settlers in the United States.

The Plateau Area. The Plateau area extended from above the Canadian border through the plateau and mountain area of the Rocky Mts. to the Southwest and included much of California. Typical tribes were the Spokan, the Paiute, the Nez Percé, and the Shoshone. This was an area of great linguistic diversity. Because of the inhospitable environment the cultural development was generally low. The Indians in the Central Valley of California and on the California coast, notably the Pomo, were a sedentary people, who gathered edible plants, roots, and fruit and also hunted small game. Their acorn bread, made by pounding acorns into meal and then leaching it with hot water, was distinctive, and they cooked in baskets filled with water and heated by hot stones. Living in brush shelters or more substantial lean-tos, they had partly buried earth lodges for ceremonies and ritual sweat baths. Basketry, coiled and twined, was highly developed. To the north, between the Cascade Range and the Rocky Mts., the social, political, and religious systems were simple, and art was nonexistent. The Indians there underwent (c.1730) a great cultural change when they obtained from the Plains Indians the horse, the tepee, a form of the sun dance, and deerskin clothes. They continued, however, to fish for salmon with nets and spears and to gather camas bulbs. They also gathered ants and other insects and hunted small game and, in later time, buffalo. Their permanent winter villages on waterways had semisubterranean lodges with conical roofs; a few Indians lived in bark-covered long houses.

The Eastern Woodlands Area. The Eastern Woodlands area covered the eastern part of the United States, roughly from the Atlantic Ocean to the Mississippi River, and included the Great Lakes. The Natchez, the Choctaw, the Cherokee, and the Creek were typical inhabitants. The northeastern part of this area extended from Canada to Kentucky and Virginia. The people of the area (speaking languages of the Algonquian-Wakashan stock) were to a large extent deer hunters; the women tended small plots of corn, squash, and beans. The birchbark canoe gained wide usage in this area. The general pattern of existence of these Algonquian peoples and their neighbors, who spoke languages belonging to the Iroquoian branch of the Hokan-Siouan stock (enemies who had probably invaded from the south), was quite complex. Their diet of deer meat was supplemented by other game (e.g., bear), fish (caught with hook, spear, and net), and shellfish. Cooking was done in vessels of wood and bark or simple black pottery. The dome-shaped wigwam and the longhouse of the Iroquois characterized their housing. The deerskin clothing, the painting of the face and (in the case of the men) body, and the scalp lock of the men (left when hair was shaved on both sides of the head), were typical. The myths of Manitou (often called Manibozho or Manabaus), the hero who remade the world from mud after a deluge, are also widely known. The region from the Ohio River S to the Gulf of Mexico, with its forests and fertile soil, was the heart of the southeastern part of the Eastern Woodland cultural area. There before c.500 the Indians were seminomads, who hunted, fished, and gathered roots and seeds. Between 500 and 900 they adopted agriculture, tobacco smoking, pottery making, and burial mounds (see MOUND BUILDERS). By c.1300 the agricultural economy was well established, and artifacts found in the mounds show that trade was widespread. Long before the Europeans arrived, the peoples of the Natchez and Muskogean branches of the Hokan-Siouan linguistic family were farmers who used hoes with stone, bone, or shell blades. They hunted with bow and arrow and blowgun, caught fish by poisoning streams, and gathered berries, fruit, and shellfish. They had excellent pottery, sometimes decorated with abstract figures of animals or humans. The villages were enclosed by wooden palisades reinforced with earth. Some of the large villages, usually ceremonial centers, dominated the smaller settlements of the surrounding countryside. There were temples for sun worship; rites were elaborate and featured an altar with perpetual fire, extinguished and rekindled each year in a "new fire" ceremony. The society was commonly divided into classes, with a chief, his children, nobles, and commoners making up the hierarchy.

The Northern Area. The Northern area covered most of Canada in the belt of semiarctic land from the Rocky Mts. to Hudson Bay. The main languages in this area were those of the Algonquian-Wakashan and the Nadene stocks. Typical of the people there were the Chipewyan. Limiting environmental conditions prevented farming, but hunting, gathering, and activities such as trapping and fishing were carried on. Nomadic hunters moved with the season from forest to tundra, killing the caribou in semiannual drives. Other food was provided by small game, berries, and edible roots. Not only food but clothing and even some shelter (caribou-skin tents) came from the caribou, and with caribou leather thongs the Indians laced their snowshoes and made nets and bags. The snowshoe was one of the most important items of material culture. The SHAMAN featured in the religion of many of these people.

The Southwest Area. The Southwest area generally extended over Arizona, New Mexico, and parts of Colorado and Utah. The Uto-Aztecan branch of the Aztec-Tanoan linguistic stock was the main language group of the area. The higher material culture of the Aztecs to the south was early reflected in this region. Here a seminomadic people called the BASKET MAKERS, who hunted with a spear thrower, or ATLATL, acquired (c.1000 B.C.) the art of cultivating beans and squash, probably from their southern neighbors. They also learned to make unfired pottery. They wove baskets, sandals, and bags. By c.700 B.C. they had initiated intensive agriculture, made true pottery, and hunted with bow and arrow. They lived in pit dwellings, which were partly underground and were lined with slabs of stone—the so-called slab houses. A new people came into the area some two centuries later; these were the ancestors of the Pueblo Indians. They lived in large, terraced community houses set on ledges of cliffs or canyons for protection (see CLIFF DWELLERS) and developed a ceremonial chamber (the KIVA) out of what had been the living room of the pit dwellings. This period of development ended c.1300, after a severe drought and the beginnings of the invasions from the north by the ATHABASCAN-speaking Navaho and Apache. The known historic Pueblo cultures of such sedentary farming peoples as the Hopi and the Zuni then came into being. They cultivated corn, beans, squash, cotton, and tobacco, killed rabbits with a wooden throwing stick, and traded cotton textiles and corn for buffalo meat from nomadic tribes. The men wove cotton textiles and cultivated the fields, while women made fine polychrome pottery. The mythology and religious ceremonies were complex.

Contemporary Indian Life. In the 1890s the long struggle between the expanding European population and the Indian that had begun soon after the coming of the Spanish in the 16th cent. and the British and the French in the 17th cent. was brought to an end. Indian life in the United States in the 20th cent. has been marked by poverty, poor education, and unemployment (in the early 1970s the unemployment rate among Indians was about 40%, roughly 10 times the national average). The Indian population in the United States is some 792,000; another 244,000 reside in Canada. Information about particular Indian groups can be found in separate articles and in separate biographies and subject articles (e.g., PONTIAC'S REBELLION; DAWES ACT; NORTH AMERICAN INDIAN ACT). The Bureau of American Ethnology, The American Indian Historical Society, The American Museum of Natural History, and the Heye Foundation have published many useful works on the Indians. For some general works see A. L. Kroeber, *Cultural and Natural Areas of Native North America* (1939, repr. 1963); H. E. Driver, *Indians of North America* (1961, rev. ed. 1969); R. F. Spencer et al., *The Native Americans* (1965); Clark Wissler, *Indians of the United States* (rev. ed. 1966); R. C. Owens, ed., *The North American Indians: A Sourcebook* (1967); Wolfgang Haberland, *The Art of North America* (1968); Alvin Josephy, *The Indian Heritage of America* (1968); A. L. Marriott and C. K. Rachlin, *American Indian Mythology* (1968); A. L. Marriott, *American Epic* (1969); Angie Debo, *A History of the Indians of the United States* (1970); J. U. Terrell, *American Indian Almanac* (1971); Wayne Moguin and Charles Van Doren, eds., *Great Documents in American Indian History* (1973); W. H. Oswatt, *This Land Was Theirs* (2d ed. 1973).

Indians, South American, aboriginal peoples of South America. In the land mass extending from the Isthmus of Panama to Tierra del Fuego, Indian civilizations developed long before the coming of the European. It is estimated that about 30 million Indians lived in South America at the time Europeans arrived. Today the Indians of South America remain a major determinant in the social, political, economic, and cultural life of the various nations. Archaeological studies have shed light on the early cultures of the rugged Andean region. Extensive remains have established the existence of developed cultures at CHAVÍN DE HUÁNTAR and the PARACAS peninsula in Peru. The MOCHICA, the CHIMU, and the NAZCA were three other major early Peruvian cultures. In Bolivia the impressive ruins at TIAHUANACO bear witness to yet another early civilization. The CHIBCHA of the N Andes, the AYMARA of the central Andes, and the ARAUCANIAN INDIANS of Chile are considered to have produced some of the socially complex pre-Columbian cultures (see PRE-COLUMBIAN ART AND ARCHITECTURE) of the Andes, but the most impressive civilization, both from the point of view of technical achievement and of political structure, was unquestionably the empire of the INCA. The modern descendants of these Indians form an integral part of the populations of Ecuador, Peru, and Bolivia and to a lesser extent of NW Argentina and Chile. QUECHUA, the Inca language, is the most widespread linguistic stock, but Aymara is also important (see AMERICAN INDIAN LANGUAGES). Since colonial days Indians have been used extensively as agricultural and industrial laborers, mostly without adequate remuneration or political representation; often they have been brutally exploited. These conditions of semiservitude are still prevalent in some areas, although political upheavals, especially in Bolivia and Peru, have done much to create an awareness of the need for social and economic reform. The few remaining Indians of Venezuela, the Guianas, and Brazil N of the Amazon are mostly descendants of the ARAWAK and the CARIB INDIANS. A considerable number of seminomadic farmers and hunters survive in the hinterlands of the Guianas and in the basins of the upper Rio Branco and Rio Negro. In most of the Amazon basin, including the tropical regions of E Colombia, Ecuador, Peru, Bolivia, and NE Argentina, as well as in the basin of the Río de la Plata, the surviving Indians are mostly of

Tupí-Guaraní stock (see GUARANÍ INDIANS). Belonging to a separate linguistic stock are the Gê-speaking Indians of the eastern highlands of Brazil. Although not materially advanced, the Gê are characterized by a highly complex social organization. The Brazilian Tupí-Guaraní Indians practice a rudimentary form of subsistence agriculture and have not developed a high material civilization. Today the Indian population of Brazil is relatively small and scattered in isolated clusters. The Guaraní of Paraguay, on the other hand, are fairly numerous, skilled in minor arts, and play a significant role in the national life. Another tropical-forest Indian group is the JÍVARO, once practitioners of head shrinking. The Colorado Indians of W Ecuador are almost extinct but have often been the object of public attention because of their practice of painting their bodies with bright red paint. They are actually of Chibcha stock. The Motilones, who live along the border of Colombia and Venezuela in the marshes and hills W of Lake Maracaibo, have tenaciously resisted assimilation. The other major Indian groups of South America consisted of the nomadic hunters of PATAGONIA and the fishing people of the islands and fjords of S Chile and Argentina. The Puelches and Tehuelches, tall hunters of the Patagonian tableland, were encountered by early Spanish explorers; these people have virtually disappeared. In the rugged and wet region of the southernmost archipelagoes a dwindling number of Indians survives. Frequently called the Fuegians, because of their campsites at TIERRA DEL FUEGO, the Ona, Yahgan, and Alacaluf survive by hunting and fishing. The canoe is the chief mode of transportation of the Yahgan and the Alacaluf, and the social organization is not as advanced as other Indian groups. See J. H. Seward, ed., *Handbook of South American Indians* (7 vol., 1946–59, repr. 1969); J. H. Steward and L. C. Faron, *Native Peoples of South America* (1959); Carleton Beals, *Nomads and Empire Builders* (1965); Johannes Wilbert, *Survivors of Eldorado* (1972).

Indian shot: see CANNA.

Indian subcontinent, region, S central Asia, comprising the countries of PAKISTAN, INDIA, and BANGLADESH and the Himalayan states of NEPAL, SIKKIM, and BHUTAN. SRI LANKA, an island off the southeastern tip of the Indian peninsula, is often considered a part of the subcontinent.

Indian Territory, in U.S. history, name applied to the country set aside for the Indians by the Indian Intercourse Act (1834). In the 1820s, the Federal government began moving the Five Civilized Tribes (Cherokee, Creek, Seminole, Choctaw, and Chickasaw) of the Southeast to lands W of the Mississippi River. The Indian Removal Act of 1830 gave the President authority to designate specific lands for them, and in 1834 Congress formally approved the choice. The Indian Territory included present-day Oklahoma N and E of the Red River, as well as Kansas and Nebraska; the lands were delimited in 1854, however, by the creation of the Kansas and Nebraska territories. Tribes other than the original five also moved there, but each tribe maintained its own government. As white settlers continued to move westward, pressure to abolish the Indian Territory mounted. With the opening of W Oklahoma to whites in 1889 the way was prepared for the extinction of the territory, achieved in 1907 with the entrance of Oklahoma into the Union. See OKLAHOMA.

Indian tobacco, name for several plants, among them LOBELIA.

Indian turnip: see ARUM.

Indian wars, in American history, general term referring to the series of conflicts between Europeans and their descendants and the North American Indians. Each of the colonial powers in North America met and overcame Indian resistance. In the Southwest the most notable incident precipitated by the Spaniards was the ferocious Pueblo uprising led by POPÉ in 1680. New France was constantly menaced because of the hostility of the IROQUOIS CONFEDERACY, although the French missionaries and traders maintained better relations with other Northeastern tribes. The history of the English settlements is studded with Indian conflicts. The more memorable include the war of the PEQUOT INDIANS against the Connecticut settlers in 1637; the uprising of the WAMPANOAG INDIANS and NARRAGANSETT INDIANS against the New England colonies in 1675–76, known as KING PHILIP'S WAR; the wars with the YAMASEE INDIANS on the South Carolina frontier; and PONTIAC'S REBELLION in the Northwest Territory in 1763. After the American Revolution, the most pressing Indian problem facing the new government was the unwillingness of the tribes of the Northwest to acquiesce in the settlement of the Ohio valley. After unsuccessful expeditions under generals Josiah Harmar (1790) and Arthur ST. CLAIR (1791), Gen. Anthony WAYNE defeated the Indians at the battle of FALLEN TIMBERS in 1794. By the Treaty of Greenville (1795) the Indians agreed to give up their lands in Ohio and move to Indiana. However, the settlers then began to encroach on their lands in Indiana, provoking the Shawnee chief, TECUMSEH, and his brother, the SHAWNEE PROPHET, to organize a powerful Indian confederacy. In 1811, William H. HARRISON defeated the Shawnee Prophet at TIPPECANOE. Tecumseh allied himself with the British in the War of 1812 and was killed in the battle of the Thames (1813; see THAMES, BATTLE OF), which ended the Indian threat in the Northwest Territory. During the War of 1812 the CREEK INDIANS also rose and were defeated (1814) by Andrew JACKSON. After 1815 the policy of Indian removal to reservations across the Mississippi River was pursued by the U.S. government with such success that by 1860 the great majority of the tribes had been moved. Often, however, this was accomplished only with a struggle. The attempt to remove the SEMINOLE INDIANS from their lands in Florida resulted in a number of wars; the most notable SEMINOLE WAR involved the celebrated OSCEOLA. Similarly the refusal of the SAC AND FOX INDIANS to be removed led to the BLACK HAWK WAR of 1832. After 1860 the Indian wars continued but they now took place W of the Mississippi; the heaviest fighting occurred on the Great Plains, but there was also intermittent warfare in the Southwest and Northwest. In these conflicts most of the fighting was done by the regular army led by two of the more renowned fighters against the American Indians, generals George CROOK and Nelson MILES. Much of the opposition was furnished by four tribes: the SIOUX, the APACHE, the COMANCHE, and the CHEYENNE. Other tribes that presented courageous but generally futile opposition to the white man's rapacity were the ARAPAHO, the KIOWA, the UTE, the BLACKFOOT, the SHOSHONE, the NEZ PERCÉ, and the BANNOCK. The warfare was characterized by numerous atrocities on both sides. Until 1861 the Plains Indians had been relatively peaceful, but the advance of white settlers, with their wanton slaughter of the buffalo herds on which the Indians depended for their livelihood led to the first of the numerous outbreaks in the West. Dissatisfaction among the Indians continued; the contributing causes were corrupt Indian agents, transgressions by prospectors seeking valuable minerals in tribal lands, and the interference of the railroads with the Indians' traditional hunting practices. Notable incidents in this bloody warfare include the virtual siege of Tucson by a band of Apaches led by COCHISE, the massacre at SAND CREEK, the Fetterman Massacre (see under FETTERMAN, William Judd), Custer's last stand (see CUSTER, GEORGE ARMSTRONG), and the battle of WOUNDED KNEE. Among the fighting leaders of the Indians were GERONIMO, CRAZY HORSE, Chief JOSEPH, CAPTAIN JACK, RED CLOUD, and MANGAS COLORADAS. The fighting between the army and the Indians reached its height between 1869 and 1878, when over 200 pitched battles were fought. Although the Indians fought fiercely and courageously, the continuing flow of settlers to the West and the spread of a Western railroad network made their resistance ineffectual. Wounded Knee in 1890 is often considered the last battle of the Indian Wars although there was an expedition against the Ojibwa Indians in Minnesota in 1898. By 1887, with the passage of the DAWES ACT, a new era in Indian policy had begun. Indian resistance was at an end, and the government had successfully confined them to reservations. See the bibliographies under the various chiefs, tribes, and wars cited. See Albert Britt, *Great Indian Chiefs* (1938, repr. 1969); M. F. Schmitt and D. A. Brown, *Fighting Indians of the West* (1948, repr. 1966); R. H. Lowie, *Indians of the Plains* (1954, repr. 1963); A. M. Josephy, *The Patriot Chiefs* (1961); John Tebbel and K. W. Jennison, *The American Indian Wars* (1961); John Tebbel, *The Compact History of the Indian Wars* (1966); A. W. Eckert, *Wilderness Empire* (1969); D. A. Brown, *Bury My Heart at Wounded Knee* (1970); Stephen Longstreet, *War Cries on Horseback* (1970); Harrison Bird, *War for the West, 1790–1813* (1971); S. L. A. Marshall, *Crimsoned Prairie* (1972).

India-Pakistan Wars, name given to the series of conflicts between INDIA and PAKISTAN since 1947, when the Indian subcontinent was partitioned and the two countries became independent of Great Britain. The creation of Pakistan as a divided state, with West Pakistan separated from East Pakistan by about 1,000 mi (1,600 km) of Indian territory, was an important factor in the wars. The most violent outbreaks came in 1947–48, 1965, and 1971. The roots of the conflict lie in the hostility between Hindus and Muslims. Early in the 20th cent. the two groups worked together in the INDIAN NATIONAL CONGRESS (founded 1885) to oppose Britain's colonial policies, but Muslims gradually shifted their allegiance to the MUSLIM LEAGUE (founded 1906) because they feared Hindu domination in the Congress. Britain became more inclined to accede to Muslim demands for a separate state during World War II, when the league, under the dynamic leadership of Muhammad Ali JINNAH, supported Britain's aims, while the Congress, its demands for immediate concessions toward self-rule having been turned down, took a neutral position. As independence approached, tensions mounted, and bloody clashes between Hindus and Muslims increased. Religious rioting following independence (Aug., 1947) quickly assumed horrendous proportions, with the mass slaughtering by the majority groups in each country of minority group members. There are no reliable statistics on the casualties, but it is estimated that more than 1 million people died. Approximately 7.5 million Muslim refugees entered Pakistan, while about 10 million Hindus fled Pakistan for India. The delicate position of India's princely states played a key role in the violence, because the rulers were permitted by the terms of independence to determine the status of their states; through political necessity, however, their only realistic choice was to become part of either India or Pakistan and not to continue as independent states. Disagreements occurred in areas where rulers espoused a different religion from the majority of their subjects. The situation in KASHMIR, in NW India, was particularly controversial; the ruler was Hindu and elected to become part of India, while his Muslim subjects wanted to enter Pakistan. Conflicts also arose in the Punjab and in Bengal. India moved quickly to consolidate its position in the disputed areas. In Kashmir, in support of its coreligionists, Pakistan opposed India's actions. The undeclared war in Kashmir continued until Jan. 1, 1949, when a truce was arranged through UN mediation; negotiations between India and Pakistan began and lasted until 1954 without resolving the Kashmir problem. Pakistan controlled part of the area, Azad (Free) Kashmir, while India held most of the territory, which it completely annexed in 1957. An uneasy peace existed until April, 1965, when fighting broke out in the Rann of Kutch, a sparsely inhabited region along the West Pakistan–India border. In August fighting spread to Kashmir and to the Punjab, and in September Pakistani and Indian troops crossed the partition line between the two countries and launched air assaults on each other's cities. After threats of intervention by China had been successfully opposed by the United States and Britain, Pakistan and India agreed to a UN-sponsored cease-fire and withdrew to the pre-August lines. Prime Minister Shri Lal Bahadur SHASTRI of India and President AYUB KHAN of Pakistan met in Tashkent, USSR, in Jan., 1966, and signed an agreement pledging continued negotiations and respect for the cease-fire conditions. After the Tashkent Declaration another period of relative peace ensued. It began to deteriorate in early 1971 after civil war had erupted in Pakistan, with the more powerful West Pakistan pitted against East Pakistan, which was demanding greater autonomy. India sympathized with East Pakistan, which it bordered on three sides and which was populated by Muslim Bengalis culturally akin to India's Hindu Bengalis. Moreover, some 10 million East Pakistanis fled to India in the course of the civil war creating immense difficulties for India in providing for them. This was a major factor in India's decision to intervene in the war. The ferocity of the fighting in East Pakistan thus climaxed with India's invasion of that territory, which then declared its independence as BANGLADESH, in Dec., 1971. Concurrently, fighting broke out along the India–West Pakistan border. Through great-power diplomatic pressures and through the efforts of the United Nations, a cease-fire was arranged in mid-December, but by that time Pakistan had been defeated. It lost East Pakistan, about 100,000 of its troops were captured, and the country was severely damaged economically. The political dislocation of the war resulted in the emergence of Zulfikar Ali BHUTTO as the leader of Pakistan and of MUJIBUR RAHMAN as prime minister of Bangladesh. Tensions long remained high but were somewhat alleviated by the Simla accord of 1972, which reduced the chance of military clashes, and by Pakistan's recognition of Bangladesh in 1974. More than 25 years of intermittent conflict had left political-geographical and religious problems unresolved; in addition the commitment of the parties to the pursuit of peaceful solutions remained tenuous. See Sisir Gupta, *Kashmir: A Study of India-Pakistan Relations* (1966); Alastair Lamb, *Crisis in Kashmir, 1947–1966* (1966); W. J. Barnds, *India, Pakistan, and the Great Powers* (1972); W. N. Brown, *The United States and India, Pakistan, Bangladesh* (1972); Kalim Siddiqui, *Conflict, Crisis, and War in Pakistan* (1972).

India-rubber tree: see FIG.

indicative: see MOOD.

indicators, acid-base, organic compounds that, in aqueous solution, exhibit color changes indicative of the acidity or basicity of the solution. Common indicators include *p*-nitrophenol, which is colorless from *p*H 1 to 5 and yellow from *p*H 5 to 9; methyl orange, yellow in basic and neutral solutions and reddish below *p*H 3.7; phenolphthalein, colorless in acid and neutral solutions, pink at about *p*H 8.5, and purplish at *p*H 10; and LITMUS. Most indicators are also used in large amounts for dyeing; small quantities are nonetheless invaluable for use as indicators in chemical laboratories.

Indic languages, group of languages belonging to the Indo-Iranian subfamily of the Indo-European family of languages. See INDO-IRANIAN LANGUAGES.

indictment (ĭndīt'mənt), in CRIMINAL LAW, formal written accusation naming specific persons and crimes. It is made by a GRAND JURY when the jury's action is initiated by the public prosecutor's presentment of a bill of indictment. Persons suspected of crime may be rendered liable to trial by indictment, by presentment, or by information. A presentment is an accusation issued by the grand jury on its own knowledge, without any bill of indictment having been previously drawn up by the prosecutor. An information is an accusation presented directly by the prosecutor without consideration by a grand jury. The Fifth Amendment to the U.S. Constitution safeguards the right to a preliminary hearing by a grand jury in major Federal cases. It provides in effect that no person outside military service may be tried in a Federal court for a capital or otherwise infamous crime except on indictment or presentment. When an indictment or presentment is approved, the foreman of the grand jury marks it "true bill." Indictments, presentments, and informations are similar to the plaintiff's complaint in a civil action (see PROCEDURE).

Indies: see EAST INDIES; WEST INDIES.

indigestion or **dyspepsia,** discomfort during or after eating caused by some interference with the normal digestive process. Symptoms include nausea, heartburn, abdominal pain, gas distress, and a feeling of abdominal distention. Common indigestion may be a result of poor eating habits, including eating too much or too rapidly, eating during emotional upsets, and swallowing large amounts of air. Excessive smoking may also be a factor. Certain foods and drinks may contribute to indigestion, including such gas forming vegetables as beans, cabbage, and onions, as well as foods with a high fat content and carbonated or alcoholic beverages. Constipation may also be a cause. Indigestion may be a symptom of such conditions as ulcers and gall bladder inflammation. Persistent indigestion should be diagnosed by a physician.

Indigirka (ēndyĭgēr'kə), river, NE Siberian USSR, in the Yakut Autonomous Republic. It rises in the Oymyakon plateau and flows c.1,100 mi (1,770 km) N into the Arctic Ocean. It is navigable (June–September) from its confluence with the Moma River to the Arctic Ocean.

indigo [Span.; from Lat.,=Indian], important blue dyestuff used in printing inks and for vat dyeing of cotton (see DYE). It was anciently produced in India and was known in Egypt, probably c.1600 B.C.; mummies of the XVIII dynasty have been discovered wrapped in indigo-dyed cloth. Indigo is obtained from leguminous plants of the genus *Indigofera,* chiefly from the Asiatic species *Indigofera tinctoria,* but also from several other species. The plants contain a colorless, soluble glucoside called indican. When the macerated plants are allowed to ferment in vats of water the colorless form of indigo is liberated; stirring of the liquid causes oxidation of the colorless material to form a blue sediment. The natural indigo gives a strong blue color of great permanence. Use of the natural dye greatly decreased after the synthesis of indigo was accomplished. Adolf von Baeyer was the first to synthesize it, but others developed the methods used for its commercial production from ANILINE and chloroacetic acid.

indigo bunting or **indigo bird:** see BUNTING.

indigo snake: see RACER.

Indio, city (1970 pop. 14,459), Riverside co., SE Calif., in the Coachella Valley of the Colorado Desert, 22 ft (6.7 m) below sea level; founded 1876, inc. 1930. It is the trade and administrative center for a citrus, grape, and date area. The National Date Festival is held on the Indio county fairgrounds. Joshua Tree National Monument and a junior college are nearby.

indium (ĭn'dēəm), a metallic chemical element; symbol In; at. no. 49; at. wt. 114.82; m.p. 156.6°C; b.p. about 2080°C; sp. gr. 7.31 at 20°C; valence +1, +2, or +3. Indium is a soft, malleable, ductile, lustrous, silver-white metallic element; it crystallizes in a face-centered tetragonal structure. Its properties are similar to those of gallium, the element directly above it in group IIIa of the PERIODIC TABLE. Like gallium, it remains in the liquid state over a wide range of temperatures. It wets glass and can be used to form a mirror surface that is more corrosion-resistant than, and reflects as well as, one of silver. It is also used in low-melting fusible alloys and as a protective plating for bearings and other metal surfaces. Although indium resists oxidation at room temperature, when heated above its melting point it ignites and burns with a violet flame; the oxide that is formed is used in glassmaking to give a yellow color. Indium reacts readily with the halogens and (when warm) with other nonmetals, e.g., phosphorus, selenium, and sulfur. It has trivalent compounds that are similar to those of gallium and aluminum. Indium salts color the Bunsen flame a deep blue-violet. Indium phosphide, arsenide, and antimonide are semiconductor materials used in photocells, thermistors, and rectifiers. Indium is found in very low concentrations in many ores and minerals; it was first found in zinc blende and is produced commercially as a by-product of the smelting of zinc. Indium was discovered in 1863 by Ferdinand Reich and H. T. Richter, using spectroscopic analysis; it was named for a brilliant indigo line in its spectrum.

Indo-Aryan, variant name for Indic languages. Broader uses referring to racial stocks are now obsolete. See INDO-IRANIAN LANGUAGES.

Indochina, Fr. *Indochine,* former federation of states, SE Asia. It comprised the French colony of COCHIN CHINA and the French protectorates of TONKIN, ANNAM, LAOS, and CAMBODIA (Cochin China, Tonkin, and Annam were later united to form VIETNAM). The capital was HANOI. The federation formed the easternmost region of the Indochinese peninsula (which it shared with Burma, Thailand, and Malaya) and faced E on the South China Sea. The cultures of Indochina were influenced by China and India. The centuries before European intervention saw the growth and decline of the KHMER EMPIRE in Cambodia, the rise and fall of CHAMPA, and the steady expansion of Annam. European penetration began in the 16th cent.; in the 19th-century race for a colonial empire, the French took (1862, 1867) Cochin China as a colony and gained protectorates over Cambodia (1863), Annam (1884), and Tonkin (1884). In 1887 they formed those four states into a union of Indochina, with a governor general at its head; Laos was added to the union in 1893. In World War II, France was forced to accept Japanese intervention in N Indochina in 1940; the subsequent Japanese move into S Indochina (July, 1941) was viewed by the United States as a threat to the Philippines; it prompted the freezing of all Japanese assets in the United States and precipitated the diplomatic exchanges cut short by the Japanese attack on Pearl Harbor. Even before the end of the war, the French announced plans for a federation of Indochina within the French Union, with greater self-government for the various states. The federation was accepted in Cambodia and Laos. Vietnamese nationalists, however, demanded (1945) the complete independence of Annam, Tonkin, and Cochin China as Vietnam, and after Dec., 1946, these regions were plunged into bitter fighting between the French and the extreme nationalists, oftentimes led by Communists. The war in Vietnam dragged on for years, culminating in the French defeat at DIENBIENPHU. The GENEVA CONFERENCE in 1954 effectively ended French control of Indochina.

Indochina War: see VIETNAM WAR.

Indo-European, family of languages having more speakers than any other language family. It is estimated that about 1.6 billion people, or roughly half of the world's population, speak an Indo-European tongue as a first language. The Indo-European family is so named because at one time its individual members were prevalent mainly in an area between and including India and Europe, although not all languages spoken in this region were Indo-European. Today, however, the Indo-European languages have spread to every continent and a number of islands. It should be stressed that the term *Indo-European* describes language only and is not used scientifically in an ethnic or cultural sense. The languages classified as Indo-European are sufficiently similar to form one major linguistic division. The characteristics they share with respect to vocabulary and grammar have led many scholars to postulate that they are all descended from an original parent language, called Proto-Indo-European, which is believed to have been spoken some time before 2000 B.C. Since there are no written records of Proto-Indo-European, it apparently was in use before writing was known to its speakers. Even its existence is an assumption, although a plausible one and the only really satisfactory explanation of the common features of the modern Indo-European languages. There has been much speculation as to the region where the speakers of Proto-Indo-European first lived and the nature of their culture, but nothing definite is known. One theory of the origin of the individual Indo-European languages suggests that as the ancient speakers of Proto-Indo-European migrated or moved away from each other, losing contact, their language broke up into a number of tongues. These tongues later also split up still further, eventually giving rise to the many modern Indo-European languages. For a classification of Indo-European subfamilies, groups, subgroups, and individual languages, see table on page 1333. By studying the vocabulary and grammar of the various daughter languages of which there are records, scholars have tried to reconstruct Proto-Indo-European and infer some of its characteristics. It appears to have been highly inflected in a distinctive way. Apparently, it also had three genders (masculine, feminine, and neuter) for nouns, pronouns, and adjectives; no less than six cases for the noun; agreement between adjectives and nouns; and a free accent (i.e., one that could be placed on any syllable). The descendant languages have all tended to discard to a greater or lesser extent these features of the mother tongue and to become simplified. For example, they substitute increasingly the use of word order and prepositions for inflections to indicate the relationships of words in a sentence. There also exists among the Indo-European languages a similarity of basic words (such as words denoting kinship, numerals, and parts of the body) that points to a common origin. Different forms of writing for the various Indo-European languages used both in ancient and modern times include cuneiform, hieroglyphics, and a number of alphabets, among them the Devanagari, Greek, Roman, and Arabic scripts. See articles on many of the Indo-European subfamilies, groups, and languages. See also Antoine Meillet, *The Indo-European Dialects* (tr. 1967); W. D. Lockwood, *A Panorama of Indo-European Languages* (1972); Émile Benveniste, *Indo-European Language and Society* (tr. 1973).

Indo-Iranian, subfamily of the Indo-European family of languages, spoken by about 470 million people, chiefly in Afghanistan, Bangladesh, India, Iran, Nepal, Pakistan, and Sri Lanka (see INDO-EUROPEAN, table). The Indo-Iranian subfamily consists of three groups of languages: the Dardic (or Pisacha), the Indic (or Indo-Aryan), and the Iranian. Some scholars, however, include the Dardic tongues under the Indic classification.

Dardic Group. Among the Dardic, or Pisacha, languages are Kafiri, spoken in Afghanistan; Khowar, current in Pakistan; Shina, Kohistani, and Kashmiri, prevalent in Pakistan and Kashmir; and ROMANY, the language of the gypsies, spoken mainly outside of India. These languages share certain distinctive phonetic characteristics, feature the use of pronominal suffixes with various verb forms, and include in their vocabularies a number of words that among the languages of India are usually encountered only in Vedic Sanskrit. Kashmiri is the sole Dardic language that both has a literature and is recognized in the Indian constitution of 1950. The native tongue of 2 million people, it has been heavily influenced by Sanskrit, so that it is now partly Indic in character. Kashmiri is written in Persian letters by Muslims, whereas Hindus use a script similar to the Devanagari alphabet.

Indic Group. The Indic, or Indo-Aryan, languages form the largest group of the Indo-Iranian subfamily. The oldest written form of the Indic group is Vedic (or Vedic Sanskrit), in which the VEDA were composed. Although the Veda appear to have first been written down in the 3d cent. B.C., they were transmitted orally long before this time—possibly

THE INDO-EUROPEAN FAMILY OF LANGUAGES

Subfamily	*Group*	*Subgroup*	*Languages and Principal Dialects*
ANATOLIAN			Hieroglyphic Hittite*, Hittite (Kanesian)*, Luwian*, Lycian*, Lydian*, Palaic*
Baltic			LETTISH (Latvian), LITHUANIAN, Old Prussian*
CELTIC	Brythonic		Breton, Cornish*, Welsh
	Continental		Gaulish*
	Goidelic or Gaelic		IRISH (Irish Gaelic), Manx, Scottish Gaelic
GERMANIC	East Germanic		Burgundian*, GOTHIC*, Vandalic*
	North Germanic		Old Norse* (see NORSE): DANISH, Faeroese, ICELANDIC, NORWEGIAN, SWEDISH
	West Germanic (see GRIMM'S LAW)	High German	GERMAN, YIDDISH
		Low German	AFRIKAANS, DUTCH, ENGLISH, FLEMISH, FRISIAN, Plattdeutsch (see GERMAN LANGUAGE)
GREEK			Aeolic*, Arcadian*, Attic*, Byzantine Greek*, Cyprian*, Doric*, Ionic*, Koinē*, Modern Greek
INDO-IRANIAN	Dardic or Pisacha		Kafiri, Kashmiri, Khowar, Kohistani, ROMANY (Gypsy), Shina
	Indic or Indo-Aryan		PALI*, PRAKRIT*, SANSKRIT*, Vedic*
		Central Indic	HINDI, HINDUSTANI, URDU
		East Indic	Assamese, Bengali, Bihari, Oriya
		NW Indic	Punjabi, Sindhi
		Pahari	Central Pahari, Eastern Pahari (Nepali), Western Pahari
		South Indic	Marathi (including major dialect Konkani), Singhalese (Sinhalese)
		West Indic	Bhili, Gujarati, Rajasthani (many dialects)
	Iranian		Avestan*, Old Persian*
		East Iranian	Baluchi, Khwarazmian*, Ossetic, Pamir dialects, Pushtu (Afghan), Saka (Khotanese)*, Sogdian*, Yaghnobi
		West Iranian	Kurdish, Pahlavi (Middle Persian)*, Parthian*, PERSIAN (Farsi), Tadzhiki
ITALIC	(Non-Romance)		Faliscan*, LATIN*, Oscan*, Umbrian*
	ROMANCE or Romanic	Eastern Romance	ITALIAN, RHAETO-ROMANIC, RUMANIAN, Sardinian
		Western Romance	CATALAN, FRENCH, Ladino, PORTUGUESE, PROVENÇAL, SPANISH
SLAVIC or Slavonic	East Slavic		Belorussian (White Russian), RUSSIAN, UKRAINIAN
	South Slavic		BULGARIAN, CHURCH SLAVONIC*, Macedonian, SERBO-CROATIAN, Slovenian
	West Slavic		CZECH, Kashubian, Lusatian (Sorbian or Wendish), Polabian*, POLISH, Slovak
Thraco-Illyrian			Albanian, Illyrian*, Thracian*
Thraco-Phrygian			ARMENIAN, Grabar (Classical Armenian)*, Phrygian*
Tokharian (W China)			Tokharian A (Agnean)*, Tokharian B (Kuchean)*

* Asterisk indicates a dead language.

before the 15th cent. B.C. Vedic has been described as the parent language of SANSKRIT, which by the 4th cent. B.C. had become the sacred and literary language of the Hindus of India, and its classical form was in use (at least for literature) until A.D. c.1100. This tongue was called *Sanskrit* (that is, "polished") to distinguish it from the many vernacular dialects to which the label PRAKRIT (or "natural") was attached. Sanskrit, the most important source for all modern Indic languages, has survived to this day as a liturgical language in India. It is written in Devanagari, a development of the Brahmi script, believed to be derived from a form of ancient Semitic writing that may go back to Egyptian hieroglyphics. Most Indic languages are written in some modified form of the Devanagari alphabet. Extensive changes have taken place in the evolution of the Indic languages, and many languages show marked differences between the current speech form and the written form, which reflects older literary patterns. While the vocabulary of many Indic languages derives primarily from Sanskrit, Muslim influence over the centuries has added loan words from Arabic and Persian to such Indic tongues as Urdu and Sindhi. Aside from phonemic and vocabulary changes, the inflection of nouns and verbs has been considerably simplified. Prepositions are now often used in place of the earlier cases of the nouns, which have been reduced from eight to two. The principal modern Indic tongues include the Northwest Indic languages Punjabi and Sindhi; the central Indic languages HINDI and URDU; the East Indic tongues Assamese, Bengali, and Oriya; the West Indic language Gujarati; the South Indic tongues Marathi and Singhalese; and the northern or Pahari dialects or languages. Hindi, now the primary language of India, is understood by about 133.5 million persons, the majority of them in central India. Very similar to Hindi (but recorded in a form of the Arabic alphabet) is Urdu, the language of more than 20 million persons in Pakistan and India. Punjabi, or Panjabi, is spoken by about 37 million people in NW India and Pakistan. It is close to the Western Hindi dialect and to Urdu and is written in an alphabet based on the Devanagari script. Its vocabulary for the most part evolved from Sanskrit. Sindhi, the native tongue of about 7 million persons in Pakistan, is recorded in a modification of a Persian script by Muslims, although a variety of the Devanagari alphabet is employed by Hindus using Sindhi. Of the East Indic languages, Assamese is the tongue of 6 million people in Assam, and has a literature dating back to the 15th cent. Assamese has been influenced by Tibeto-Burman idioms and recalls Sanskrit in vocabulary, but is allied grammatically to Bengali, the language of 47 million inhabitants of Bangladesh and 37 million Indians living in and around the Calcutta region. Bengali is rich in literature; the greatest modern author who wrote in the language was Rabindranath TAGORE. Oriya, the language of about 20 million persons, chiefly in the Indian state of Orissa, is closer to Sanskrit phonetically and lexically than any other modern Indic tongue. The leading West Indic language is Gujarati, with 22 million speakers, chiefly in the states of Gujarat and Maharashtra in India. Gujarati was the language of Mohandas Gandhi and has an important literature dating from the 15th cent. Of the South Indic languages, Marathi, with between 35 million and 40 million speakers, is prevalent in the Indian state of Maharashtra. Its literature dates from the 13th cent. The other leading South Indic tongue is Singhalese, or Sinhalese, the language of about 8 million people on the island of Sri Lanka. Although it belongs to the Indic group, Singhalese is separated geographically from the other Indic languages of N and central India by an intervening region in S India, in which the Dravidian languages are spoken. Thus, the fundamentally Indic vocabulary of Singhalese is influenced by the nearby Dravidian languages. Although its oldest existing literary texts are from the 10th cent. A.D., written records have survived from as early as the 2d cent. B.C. The Pahari dialects or languages are spoken by about 2 million people in the kingdom of Nepal and in parts of N India. These idioms are classified as Eastern Pahari (or Nepali), which is the language of Nepal and has been influenced by Tibeto-Burman languages; Central Pahari, which has two main dialects, Garhwali and Kumaoni; and Western Pahari, noted for its numerous dialects. Both Central and Western Pahari are purely Indic and have not been affected by Tibeto-Burman forms of speech.

Iranian Group. The third and last group of the Indo-Iranian subfamily consists of the Iranian languages, spoken by about 40 million people, mainly in Iran, Afghanistan, Pakistan, and parts of the USSR. Historically, the oldest Iranian forms of which there are any records are Avestan and Old Persian, both highly inflected languages. Old Persian has survived in cuneiform inscriptions from the time of the Achaemenid kings, who ruled ancient Persia during the 6th to 4th cent. B.C. Avestan is the language in which was composed the Avesta, or sacred text of the Zoroastrian religion. The Avesta probably dates from about the 7th to the 5th cent. B.C., but apparently was handed down orally and was not recorded in writing until much later. Avestan is still in use today as the liturgical language of the Zoroastrian faith. The Middle Iranian period, dating from the 3d cent. B.C. to the 9th or 10th cent. A.D., is characterized by considerable grammatical simplification, as in the reduced inflection of the noun and verb. Among the languages surviving in written records that fall within this period are Parthian, Middle Persian, Khwarazmian, Sogdian, and Saka. Parthian was used by the Arsacid rulers of ancient Persia (3d cent. B.C.–3d cent. A.D.). Middle Persian, or Pahlavi, was the tongue of the Sassanid or Sassanian kings of Persia (3d–7th cent. A.D.). Khwarazmian, which was once spoken in Central Asia, survives in some glosses discovered in Arabic books and in texts of the 2d cent. A.D. found in the USSR. Sogdian, which had a base in Samarkand, flourished as a lingua franca in Central Asia from the 4th to 10th cent. A.D. Saka, or Khotanese, was at one time the tongue of Khotan, a region in Chinese Turkistan. The modern Iranian languages, dating from about the 9th or 10th cent. to the present, show phonetic and grammatical simplification. For example, case endings tend to be dropped and the use of prepositions substituted. The most important of the modern Iranian languages is Modern PERSIAN, the official tongue of Iran, which stems directly from Middle Persian, but has been influenced by Arabic and Turkish. It has a great literature of considerable age and is the native tongue of 12 million persons in Iran and 3 million in Afghanistan. There are a number of dialects of Modern Persian. Other modern Iranian languages include Pushtu (also called Pashto and Afghan), with 14 million speakers in Afghanistan, where it is the national language, and in Pakistan; Baluchi, which has more than 1 million speakers, chiefly in Pakistan and Iran; Kurdish, the language of close to 5 million Kurds living mainly in Turkey, Iran, and Iraq; the Pamir dialects or languages, spoken in parts of Afghanistan, Pakistan, and the USSR; Yaghnobi, which is derived from Sogdian and spoken in Tadzhikistan; and Tajiki, a tongue of more than 1 million people in Tadzhikistan. Today's Iranian languages are written in adaptations of the Arabic alphabet, except for Tajiki, which uses Cyrillic characters. See L. H. Gray, *Indo-Iranian Phonology* (1902); G. A. Grierson, ed., *Linguistic Survey of India* (1903–28); R. G. Kent, *Old Persian* (1950); S. K. Chatterji, *Indo-Aryan and Hindi* (2d ed. 1960); A. M. Ghatage, *Historical Linguistics and Indo-Aryan Languages* (1962); Jules Bloch, *Indo-Aryan, from the Vedas to Modern Times* (rev. ed. tr., 1965); Thomas Burrow, *The Sanskrit Language* (2d ed. 1965); J. A. Boyle, *Grammar of Modern Persian* (1966).

Indonesia, republic (1973 est. pop. 128,650,000), c.735,000 sq mi (1,903,650 sq km), SE Asia, in the Malay Archipelago. The capital and largest city is DJAKARTA, on Java. The fifth most populous country in the world, Indonesia comprises more than 3,000 islands extending c.3,000 mi (4,830 km) along the equator from the Malaysia mainland toward Australia; the archipelago forms a natural barrier between the Indian and Pacific oceans. Consisting of the territory of the former Netherlands East Indies, Indonesia's main island groups are the Greater SUNDA ISLANDS, which include JAVA, SUMATRA, central and S BORNEO (Kalimantan), and CELEBES (Sulawesi); the Lesser Sunda Islands, consisting of BALI, FLORES, SUMBA, LOMBOK, and the western part of TIMOR; the MOLUCCAS (Maluku), with AMBON, CERAM, and HALMAHERA; and the RIAU ARCHIPELAGO. IRIAN BARAT (West New Guinea), after years of dispute with the Dutch, was formally annexed by Indonesia in Aug., 1969. The most important islands, culturally and economically, are Java, Bali, and Sumatra. All the larger islands have a central volcanic mountainous area flanked by coastal plains; there are more than 100 active volcanoes. Earthquakes are frequent, although seldom severe. The animal life of Indonesia roughly forms a connecting link between the fauna of Asia and that of Australia. Elephants are found in Sumatra and Borneo, tigers as far south as Java and Bali, and marsupials in Timor and Irian Barat. Crocodiles, snakes, and richly colored birds are everywhere. The tropical climate, abundant rainfall, and remarkably fertile volcanic soils permit a rich agricultural yield. Rubber is the most valuable crop (in 1970, Indonesia ranked second in world production); other plantation crops include sugarcane, coffee, tea, tobacco, palm oil, cinchona, cacao, sisal, coconuts, and spices. Despite plantation cultivation, Indonesia has a wide landholding base; the majority of the people are largely self-sufficient in food. Rice is the major crop; cassava, maize, yams, soybeans, peanuts, and fruit are also grown. Fish are abundant, both in the ocean and in inland ponds. In natural resource potential, Indonesia is one of the wealthiest countries in the world. It has great timberlands; vast rain forests of giant trees (among the world's tallest) cover the mountain slopes, and teak, sandalwood, ironwood, camphor, and ebony are cut. Palms and bamboos abound, and a great variety of forest products are manufactured. In 1972 timber was the country's second most valuable export, outdistanced only by petroleum, which is by far the most important mineral. In 1972, Indonesia ranked eleventh in world production. It was fifth in the production of tin (1972), of which it is thought to have about one sixth of all world deposits. Bauxite, nickel (sixth in world production in 1972), coal, manganese, salt, gold, and silver are also mined. Iron and copper are believed to exist in great quantity, and uranium has been reported. Primarily a supplier of raw materials, the country has had little industrial development; 70% of its working force is still engaged in agriculture. Industry is limited to food, mineral, and wood processing and a variety of light manufactures. The population falls roughly into two groups, the Malayan and the Papuan, with many of the inhabitants of central Indonesia representing a transition between the two types. Within each group are numerous subdivisions, and cultural development ranges from the modern Javanese and Balinese to primitive, almost Stone Age, tribes in Borneo and Irian Barat. The complex ethnic structure is the result of several great migrations many centuries ago from Asia and the Pacific. More than 250 mutually unintelligible languages are spoken in Indonesia, but an official language, Bahasa Indonesia (regarded as the purest Malay) has been adopted; it has spread rapidly and is now understood in all but the most remote villages. English is the official foreign language. About 85% of the population are Muslim, some 5% are Christian, and about 5% are Hindu. Hindus are concentrated principally on Bali, which is known for its unique culture. Animism, sometimes combined with Islam, is common among some groups. The Chinese constitute by far the greatest majority of the nonindigenous population; they number about 2 to 3 million and play an important role in the country's economic life. There are smaller minorities of Arabs, Indians, and Pakistanis.

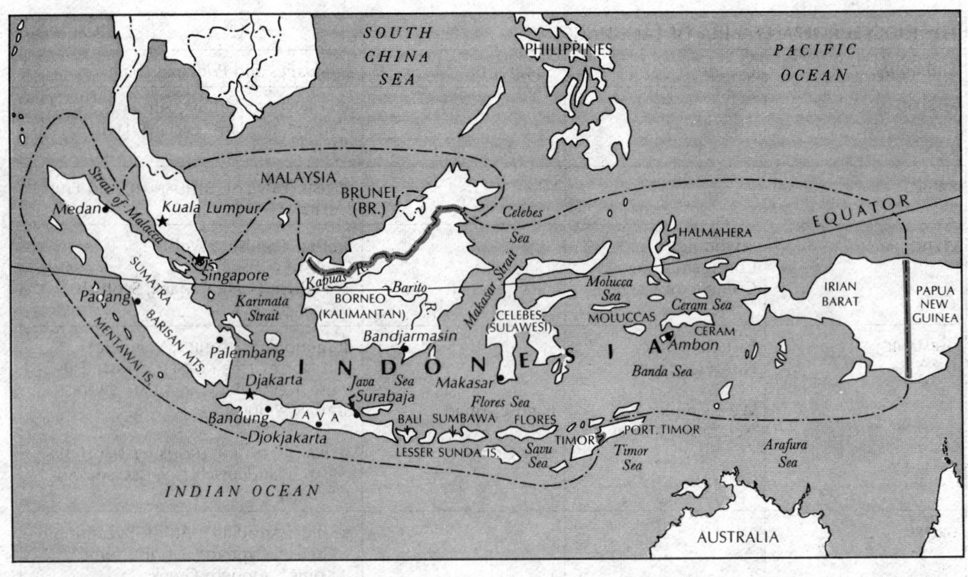

History. Early in the Christian era, Indonesia came under the influence of Indian civilization through the gradual influx of Indian traders and Buddhist and Hindu monks. By the 7th and 8th cent., kingdoms closely connected with India had developed in Sumatra and Java; the spectacular Buddhist temples of BOROBUDUR date from this period. Sumatra was the seat (7th–13th cent.) of the important Buddhist kingdom of Sri Vijaya. In the late 13th cent. the center of power shifted to Java, where the fabulous Hindu kingdom of Majapahit had arisen; for two centuries it held sway over Indonesia and large areas of the Malay Peninsula. A gradual infiltration of Islam began in the 14th and 15th cent. with the arrival of Arab traders, and by the end of the 16th cent. Islam had replaced Buddhism and Hinduism as the dominant religion. The once powerful kingdoms broke into smaller Islamic states that quarreled among themselves and fell easy prey to European imperialism. Early in the 16th cent. the Portuguese, in pursuit of the rich spice trade, began establishing trading posts in Indonesia, after taking (1511) the strategic commercial center of Malacca (see MELAKA) on the Malay Peninsula. The Dutch followed in 1596 and the English in 1600. By 1610 the Dutch had ousted the Portuguese, who were allowed to retain only the eastern part of Timor, but the English competition remained strong, and it was only after a series of Anglo-Dutch conflicts (1610–23) that the Dutch emerged as the dominant power in Indonesia. Throughout the 17th, 18th, and 19th cent. the Dutch East India Company steadily expanded its control over the entire area. When the company was liquidated in 1799, the Dutch government assumed its holdings, which were thereafter known in English as the Netherlands (or Dutch) East Indies. Dutch rule was briefly broken (1811–14) during the Napoleonic Wars when the islands were occupied by the British under Sir T. Stamford Raffles. The Dutch exploited the riches of the islands throughout the 19th cent., but their rule did not go unchallenged by the Indonesians. In 1825, Prince Diponegoro of Java launched a long and bloody guerrilla war against the colonists, and in 1906 and again in 1908 the native rulers of Bali led their subjects in suicidal charges against Dutch fortifications. The Indonesian movement for independence began early in the 20th cent., and in 1927 the Indonesian Nationalist party arose under the leadership of SUKARNO. It received its impetus during World War II, when the Japanese drove out (1942) the Dutch and occupied the islands. In Aug., 1945, immediately after the Japanese surrender, Sukarno and Muhammad Hatta, another nationalist leader, proclaimed Indonesia an independent republic. The Dutch bitterly resisted the nationalists, and four years of intermittent and sometimes heavy fighting followed. Under UN pressure, an agreement was finally reached (Nov., 1949) for the creation of an independent republic of Indonesia. A new constitution provided for a parliamentary form of government. Sukarno was elected president, and Hatta became premier. Although Sukarno had achieved a major accomplishment in uniting so many diverse peoples and regions under one government and one language, his administration was marked by inefficiency, injustice, corruption, and chaos. The rapid expropriation of Dutch property and the ousting of Dutch citizens (late 1950s) severely dislocated the economy; the country's great wealth was not exploited, and soaring inflation and great economic hardship ensued. A widespread native revolt, stemming from a desire for greater autonomy, began on Sumatra early in 1958 and spread to Celebes and other islands; the disorders led to increasingly authoritarian rule by Sukarno, who dissolved (1960) the parliament and reinstated the constitution of 1945, which had provided for a strong, independent executive (Hatta had resigned in 1956 following a conflict with Sukarno). The army, whose influence was strengthened by its role in quickly quelling the revolts, and the Communist party, whose ranks were growing very rapidly, constituted two important power blocs in Indonesian politics, with Sukarno holding the balance of power between the two. In early 1962, Sukarno dispatched paratroopers to Netherlands New Guinea—territory claimed by Indonesia but firmly held by the Dutch—forcing the Dutch to agree to transfer that area to the United Nations with the understanding that it would pass under Indonesian administration in May, 1963, pending a referendum that was to be held by 1970. After the referendum, in Aug., 1969, Netherlands New Guinea was formally annexed by Indonesia, and its name was changed to Irian Barat, or West Irian. Meanwhile, Sukarno made (1963) a major propaganda issue of Indonesian opposition to the newly created Federation of Malaysia and staged guerrilla raids into Malaysian territory on Borneo, beginning a conflict that was waged intermittently for three years. Sukarno began to lean increasingly toward the left, openly summoning Communist leaders for advice, exhibiting hostility toward the United States, and cultivating the friendship of Communist China. In 1965 he withdrew Indonesia from the United Nations. There is reason to believe that he may have known in advance of the abortive Communist coup against the army that began in Sept., 1965, with the assassination of six high army officials. The coup was swiftly thwarted by army forces under General SUHARTO, who gradually assumed power (although retaining Sukarno as symbolic leader). Thousands of alleged Communists were executed; people everywhere took the law into their own hands and a widespread massacre ensued (Oct.–Dec., 1965). As many as 750,000 people may have been killed; in E and central Java and in Bali entire villages were wiped out. The new government steadily increased its power, aided by massive student demonstrations against Sukarno. General Suharto brought an end (1966) to hostilities against Malaysia, reestablished close ties with the United States, and reentered (1966) the United Nations. On March 12, 1967, the national assembly voted Sukarno out of power altogether and named General Suharto acting president. Suharto was elected president in 1968 and was unanimously reelected by the assembly in 1973. Suharto has given top priority to the economic rehabilitation of Indonesia; he has stabilized the currency and restored domestic calm. Indonesian educational facilities have expanded enormously since independence. The literacy rate has risen from 7% to about 50%. Notable among the many state universities scattered throughout the islands are the Univ. of Indonesia, at Djakarta; Airlangga Univ., at Surabaja; Gadjah Mada Univ., at Jogjakarta; and the Univ. of North Sumatra, at Medan. Private schools include the Islamic Univ. of Indonesia, at Jogjakarta, and National Univ., at Djakarta. See R. T. McVey, ed., *Indonesia* (1963); S. T. Alisjahbana, *Indonesia: Social and Cultural Revolution* (tr., 2d ed. 1966); Bruce Grant, *Indonesia* (2d ed. 1966); J. W. Henderson et al., *Area Handbook for Indonesia* (1970); G. M. Kahin, *Nationalism and Revolution in Indonesia* (1952, repr. 1970); Bernhard Dahm, *History of Indonesia in the Twentieth Century* (tr. 1971); Bruce Glassburner, ed., *The Economy of Indonesia* (1971); H. R. Heekeren, *The Stone Age of Indonesia* (2d ed. 1972); Claire Holt et al., *Culture and Politics in Indonesia* (1972); W. T. Neill, *Twentieth-Century Indonesia* (1973).

Indore (ĭndôr'), city and former native state, W central India. The state is now part of Madhya Pradesh state. The region contains extensive forests and much building stone. Indore was established c.1728 by Malhar Rao Holkar, a soldier in the service of the MAHRATTAS and the founder of the ruling dynasty. In 1818, Indore became tributary to the British. **Indore,** city (1971 pop. 572,622), on the Saraswati and Khan rivers, became important in the late 18th cent. It was the capital of the maharajas of Indore and is the site of their imposing palace. Indore is now a major commercial and industrial center, with chemical, textile, and iron and steel industries. It has three colleges and a medical school.

Indra (ĭn'drə): see VEDA.

Indre (ăN'drə), department (1968 pop. 247,148), central France, in parts of Berry, Orléanais, Marche, Touraine, and Poitou. CHÂTEAUROUX is the capital.

Indre-et-Loire (ăNdrālwär'), department (1968 pop. 437,870), N central France. It occupies most of TOURAINE, and Tours is its capital.

indri: see LEMUR.

inductance, quantity that measures the electromagnetic INDUCTION of an electric circuit component; it is a property of the component itself rather than of the circuit as a whole. The self-inductance, *L*, of a circuit component determines the magnitude of the electromagnetic force (emf) induced in it as a result of a given rate of change of the current through the component. Similarly, the mutual inductance, *M*, of two components, one in each of two separate but closely located circuits, determines the emf that each may induce in the other for a given current change. Inductance is expressed in henrys (for Joseph Henry). An INDUCTOR is a device designed to produce an inductance, e.g., a coil; an ideal inductor, i.e., one having no resistance or capacitance (see IMPEDANCE), is often called an inductance.

induction, in electricity and magnetism, common name for three distinct phenomena. **Electromagnetic induction** is the production of an ELECTROMOTIVE FORCE (emf) in a conductor as a result of a changing magnetic FIELD about the conductor and is the most important of the three phenomena. It was discovered in 1831 by Michael Faraday and independently by Joseph Henry. Variation in the field around a conductor may be produced by relative motion between the conductor and the source of the magnetic field, as in an electric GENERATOR, or by varying the strength of the entire field, so that the field around the conductor is also changing. Since a magnetic field is produced around a current-carrying conductor, such a field can be changed by changing the current. Thus, if the conductor in which an emf is to be induced is part of an electric circuit, the induction can be caused by changing the current in that circuit; this is called self-induction. The induced emf is always such that it opposes the change that gives rise to it, according to LENZ'S LAW. Changing the current in a given circuit can also induce an emf in another, nearby circuit unconnected with the original circuit; this type of electromagnetic induction, called mutual induction, is the basis of the TRANSFORMER. **Electrostatic induction** is the production of an unbalanced electric charge on an uncharged metallic body as a result of a charged body being brought near it without touching it. If the charged body is positively charged, electrons in the uncharged body will be attracted toward it; if the opposite end of the body is then grounded, electrons will flow onto it to replace those drawn to the other end, the body thus acquiring a negative charge after the ground connection is broken. A similar procedure can be used to produce a positive charge on the uncharged body when a negatively charged body is brought near it. See ELECTRICITY. **Magnetic induction** is the production of a magnetic field in a piece of unmagnetized iron or other ferromagnetic substance when a magnet is brought near it. The magnet causes the individual particles of the iron, which act like tiny magnets, to line up so that the sample as a whole becomes magnetized. Most of this induced magnetism is lost when the magnet causing it is taken away. See MAGNETISM.

induction, in LOGIC, the process of reasoning from the particular to the general. It is the opposite of deduction, which is reasoning from the general to the particular. Francis Bacon in his *Novum Organum* (1620) elucidated the first formal theory of inductive logic, which he proposed as a logic of scientific discovery, as opposed to deductive logic, which is the logic of argumentation. Both processes, however, are used constantly in research. By observation of particular events (induction) and from already known principles (deduction), new hypothetical principles are formulated; the principles are tested by particular crucial applications; as the results of the tests satisfy the conditions of the hypotheses, laws are arrived at—by induction; from these laws future results may be determined by deduction. The process of deduction is infallible if the original proposition is true. Induction attains at most only a high degree of probability; its accuracy depends ultimately on the uniformity of the subject matter. For the classic formulation of the inductive procedure see J. S. Mill, *System of Logic* (1843). See also C. D. Broad, *Induction, Probability, and Causation* (1969); J. L. Cohen, *The Implications of Induction* (1970).

inductor, electric device consisting of one or more turns of wire and typically having two terminals. An inductor is usually connected into a circuit in order to raise the INDUCTANCE to a desired value. Since inductance is a property that varies with frequency, inductors range from a single loop in a length of wire (used at ultrahigh frequencies), through spirals in the copper coating of an etched circuit board (used at very high frequencies), to large coils of insulated wire wound onto iron or ferrite cores. For radio use, inductors often have air cores to avoid the losses caused by magnetic hysteresis and by eddy currents that occur when solid cores are used. Solid cores, however, offer the advantage of raising the inductance that can be obtained from a coil of a given number of turns of wire. Ferrites are often used, since they are nonconductors and are immune to eddy currents.

indulgence, in the Roman Catholic Church, the pardon of temporal punishment due for sin. It is to be distinguished from absolution and the forgiveness of guilt. The church grants indulgences out of the Treasury of Merit won for the church by Christ and the saints. Indulgences may be plenary, i.e., a full remission of all temporal punishment; or they may be partial, i.e., a remission of part of the temporal punishment. Contrary to popular understanding the number of days specified in a partial indulgence does not denote a reduction of time in purgatory. The practice of quantifying indulgences stems from ancient usage, when actual public penance was imposed and remitted for specified periods as the church saw fit. Hence, the penitent who is granted an indulgence receives merit as if he had performed actual penance for the length of time specified. The degree of merit varies with the disposition of the penitent. The notion that this practice encourages moral laxity is denied by the church, since the penitent must be in a state of grace and the attachment to even a single venial sin will reduce the effectiveness of the indulgence. Indulgences won for souls in purgatory are applied only as God wills. Martin LUTHER protested against the sale and abuse of indulgences and came to reject the teaching altogether. Since the Council of Trent (1562) the buying and selling of indulgences has been unlawful.

Indus (ĭn'dəs), chief river of Pakistan, c.1,900 mi (3,060 km) long, rising in the Kailas range in the Tibet region of China, and flowing W across Jammu and Kashmir, India, then SW through Pakistan to the Arabian Sea SE of Karachi. The upper Indus, fed by snow and glacial meltwater from the Karakorum, Hindu Kush, and Himalayan mts., flows through deep gorges and scenic valleys; its turbulence makes it unsuitable for navigation. Flowing onto the dry Punjab plains, the Indus becomes a broad, meandering, silt-laden stream and receives the combined waters of the five rivers of the Punjab (Chenab, Jhelum, Ravi, Beas, and Sutlej), its chief affluent. The Indus delta, unlike the deltas of many other rivers, is composed of clay and is infertile. The Indus valley is Pakistan's most densely populated region and its main agricultural area; wheat, corn, rice, millet, dates, and fruits are the chief crops. In Pakistan the Indus is extensively used for irrigation and hydroelectric-power generation. The Sukker and Kotri dams create the main reservoirs. The use of the Indus and its tributaries has long been a source of conflict between Pakistan and India, although a treaty by which the waters were to be shared was signed in 1960. The lower Indus is navigable for small boats but is little used for transportation. The river valley was the site of the prehistoric Indus Valley civilization. The river was once considered to be the western boundary of India.

industrial alcohol: see ETHANOL.

industrial engineering: see ENGINEERING.

industrial management, term applied to highly organized modern methods of carrying on industrial, especially manufacturing, operations. Before the Industrial Revolution men worked with hand tools, manufacturing articles in their own homes or in small shops. In the third quarter of the 18th cent. steam power was applied to machinery, and men and machines were brought together under one roof in factories, where the manufacturing process could be supervised. This was the beginning of shop management. In the next hundred years factories grew rapidly in size, in degree of mechanization, and in complexity of operation. The growth, however, was accompanied by much waste and inefficiency. In the United States many engineers, spurred by the increased competition of the post-Civil War era, began to seek ways of improving plant efficiency. The first sustained effort in this direction was made by Frederick Winslow TAYLOR, an assistant foreman in the Midvale Steel Company, who in the 1880s undertook a series of studies to determine whether workers used unnecessary motions and hence too much time in performing operations at a machine. Each operation required to turn out an article or part was analyzed and studied minutely, and superfluous motions were eliminated. Records were kept of the performance of workers and standards were adopted for each operation. Such time and motion studies, improved by experience, have become a permanent feature of shop management. The early studies resulted in a faster pace of work and the introduction of rest periods. Industrial management also involves studying the performance of machines. Specialists are employed to keep machines in good working condition and to ensure that replacement parts are always ready. Automatic machines are frequently checked and adjusted to prevent variation in the quality of their output; this is sometimes referred to as quality engineering. The flow of materials through the plant is supervised to ensure that neither men nor machines are idle. Constant inspection is made to keep output up to standard. Charts are used for recording the accomplishment of both men and machines and for comparing them with established standards. Careful accounts are kept of the cost of each operation. When a new article is to be manufactured it is given a design that will make it suitable for machine production, and each step in its manufacture is planned, including the machines and materials to be used. The tendency is to train workers on the job, and foremen are taught how to give this training and how to assist workers in overcoming job difficulties. Supervisors are trained in new techniques by means of periodic conferences with experts. The principles of scientific management have been gradually extended to every department of industry—office work, financing, marketing, and so on. With the development of industrial psychology, industrial management has come to include the whole field of industrial relations, not only those of workers to materials and machines, but those of workers to each other and to management. Soon after 1910, American firms established the first personnel departments, and eventually some of the larger ones took the lead in efforts to create in the plant an environment conducive to worker efficiency. Time and motion studies had taught management to take account of the limits of human physical and mental capacity and of the importance of a good physical environment, good lighting, heating, and ventilation. Safety devices, better sanitation, plant cafeterias, and facilities for rest and recreation have been provided, thus adding to the welfare of employees and enhancing morale. Many such improvements were made at the insistence of employee groups, especially labor unions. Workers and their unions have also sought higher wages and increased benefits, including group health and life insurance, and liberal retirement pensions. Some corporations permit employees to buy stock; others make provision for employee representation on the board of directors or on the shop grievance committee. Many corporations provide special opportunities for training and promotion for workers who desire advancement, and some have made efforts to solve such difficult problems as job security and a guaranteed annual wage. Modern technological devices, particularly in the areas of electronics, thermodynamics, and mechanics, have made automatic and semiautomatic machines a reality in recent years. The development of such automation is bringing about a second industrial revolution and is causing vast changes in commerce as well as industry. The basic difference between mass production and automation lies in the complete integration of fully automatic machines without the need for man as an intermediary. The fear of job displacement in many industries that are introducing techniques of automation has produced friction between labor and management. The protection of jobs against automation is presently a central issue in many industries, including printing, railroads, and freight handling. See Leon Alford, *Principles of Industrial Management* (rev. ed. 1951); Georges Friedmann, *Industrial Society: The Emergence of the Human Problems of Automation* (1955); J. R. Bright, *Automation and Management* (1958, repr. 1970); H. J. Leavitt, *Managerial Psychology* (3d ed. 1972); L. L. Bethel, *Industrial Organization and Management* (5th ed. 1973).

Industrial Revolution, term usually applied to the social and economic changes that mark the transition from a stable agricultural and commercial society to a modern industrial society relying on complex machinery rather than tools. It is used historically to refer primarily to the period in British history from the middle of the 18th cent. to the middle of the 19th cent. Dramatic changes in the social and economic structure took place as inventions and technological innovations created the factory system of large-scale machine production and greater economic specialization, and as the laboring population, formerly employed predominantly in agriculture (in which production had also increased as a result of technological improvements), increasingly gathered in great urban factory centers. The same process occurred at later times and in changed tempo in other countries. There has been much objection to the term because the word *revolution* suggests sudden, violent, unparalleled change, whereas the transformation was, to a great extent, gradual. Some historians argue that the 13th and 16th cent. were also periods of revolutionary economic change. However, in view of the magnitude of change between 1750 and 1850, the term seems useful. The ground was prepared by the voyages of discovery from Western Europe in the 15th and 16th cent., which led to a vast influx of precious metals from the New World, raising prices, stimulating industry, and fostering a money economy. Expansion of trade and the money economy stimulated the development of new institutions of finance and credit (see COMMERCIAL REVOLUTION).

The Industrial Revolution in Great Britain. In the 17th cent. the Dutch were in the forefront financially, but with the establishment (1694) of the Bank of England, their supremacy was effectively challenged. Capitalism appeared on a large scale, and a new type of commercial entrepreneur developed from the old class of merchant adventurers. Many machines were already known, and there were sizable factories using them, but these were the exceptions rather than the rule. Wood was the only fuel, water and wind the power of these early factories. In the 18th cent. this was changed. An expanding and wealthier population demanded more and better goods. In the productive process, coal came to replace wood. Early model steam engines were introduced to drain water and raise coal from the mines. The crucial development of the Industrial Revolution was the use of steam for power, and the greatly improved engine (1769) of James WATT marked the high point in this development. Cotton textiles was the key industry early in the Industrial Revolution. John Kay's fly shuttle (1733), James Hargreaves's spinning jenny (patented 1770), Richard Arkwright's water frame (1769), Samuel Crompton's mule (1779), which combined the features of the jenny and the frame, and Edmund Cartwright's power loom (patented 1783) facilitated a tremendous increase in output. The presence of large quantities of coal and iron in close proximity in Britain was a decisive factor in its rapid industrial growth. The use of coke in iron production had far-reaching effects. The coal mines from the early 1700s had become paramount i[illegible]nce, and the Black Country appeared in [illegible]me time that Lancashire and York[illegible] transformed into the greatest tex[illegible]he world. Factories and industrial [illegible]p. Canals and roads were built, and the advent of the railroad and the steamship widened the market for manufactured goods. The BESSEMER PROCESS made a gigantic contribution, for it was largely responsible for the extension of the use of steam and steel that were the two chief features of industry in the middle of the 19th cent. Chemical innovations and, most important of all, perhaps, machines for making machines played an important part in the vast changes. Actually, the revolution did not end at all in Britain. New periods came in with electricity and the gasoline engine. However, by 1850 the revolution was accomplished, in that industry had become a dominant factor in the nation's life.

The Worldwide Revolution. France had in the 17th and most of the 18th cent. kept pace with Britain, but it later lagged behind in industrial development, and the British victory in their long-standing commercial rivalry kept markets away from France. The revolution did not make the rapid progress that it did in Britain, but after 1830 it developed steadily. The railroad and improved transportation preceded the introduction of the revolution into Germany, which is conventionally said to have accompanied the formation of the ZOLLVEREIN; industrial Germany was created after 1850. The United States made some contributions to the early revolution, notably the cotton gin (1793) of Eli WHITNEY. But the transformation of the United States into an industrial nation took place largely after the Civil War and on the British model. The textile mills of New England had long been in existence, but the boom period of industrial organization was from 1860 to 1890. The Industrial Revolution was introduced by Europeans into Asia, and the last years of the 19th and the early years of the 20th cent. saw the development of industries in India, China, and Japan. However, Japan is the only country of E Asia that may be said to have had a real Industrial Revolution. The Russian Revolution had as a basic aim the introduction of industrialism. The Industrial Revolution has changed the face of nations, giving rise to urban centers requiring vast municipal services. It created a specialized and interdependent economic life and made the urban worker more completely dependent on the will of his employer than the rural worker had been. Relations between capital and labor were aggravated, and MARXISM was one product of this unrest. Doctrines of LAISSEZ FAIRE, developed in the writings of Adam SMITH and David RICARDO, sought to maximize the use of new productive facilities. But the revolution also brought a need for a new type of state intervention to protect the laborer and to provide necessary services. Laissez faire gradually gave way in the United States, Britain, and elsewhere to welfare capitalism. The economic theories of John Maynard KEYNES reflected this change. The Industrial Revolution provided the economic base for the rise of the professions, population expansion, and improvement in living standards, and remains a primary goal of less developed nations. See F. C. Dietz, *The Industrial Revolution* (1927, repr. 1973); T. S. Ashton, *The Industrial Revolution* (1948); W. O. Henderson, *The Industrialization of Europe, 1780–1914* (1969); R. M. Hartwell, *The Industrial Revolution and Economic Growth* (1971); J. W. Osborne, *The Silent Revolution: The Industrial Revolution in England as a Source of Cultural Change* (1970); P. N. Stearns, *The Impact of the Industrial Revolution* (1972); Brian Bracegirdle et al., *The Archaeology of the Industrial Revolution* (1973).

industrial union, labor union composed of all the workers in a given industry, regardless of skill, craft, or occupation (as opposed to the craft union, in which all members are of one skill, such as carpenters or electricians). The industrial union is sometimes referred to as a vertical union, since it accepts workers from the least to the most skilled as members. Prior to the 1870s, unions in the United States had been organized on a craft basis; a modified form of industrial union appeared with the KNIGHTS OF LABOR. After the downfall of that labor body in 1890, some 15 years elapsed before a new organization cutting across craft lines emerged in labor affairs. This was the INDUSTRIAL WORKERS OF THE WORLD, whose policy it was to accept everyone, skilled or unskilled and regardless of race, sex, or creed. The American Federation of Labor (AFL), the successor to the Knights of Labor, put great emphasis on craft unions, and industrial unions tended to disappear. However, within the AFL in the 1930s one segment of unions under the leadership of John L. LEWIS began to organize in the mass production industries, i.e., to form industrial unions. These unions, initially named the Committee for Industrial Organization, were expelled (1936) and were renamed (1938) the Congress of Industrial Organizations (CIO). The newly formed CIO was basically an industrial union. Three kinds of industrial unions were recognized—those consisting of all employees working on the same commodity (e.g., electrical workers or brewery workers), those using the same tools to work on different materials (e.g., textile and aluminum workers), and all employees of a given factory regardless of their particular skill. Following the merger of the AFL with the CIO in 1955, an Industrial Union Department (IUD) was organized within the merged organization. The IUD stated that it was open to any union organized in whole or in part on an industrial basis. See bibliography under AMERICAN FEDERATION OF LABOR AND CONGRESS OF INDUSTRIAL ORGANIZATIONS.

Industrial Workers of the World (IWW), revolutionary industrial union organized in Chicago in 1905 by delegates from the Western Federation of Mines, which formed the nucleus of the IWW, and 42 other labor organizations. It became the chief organization in the United States representing the doctrines of SYNDICALISM. Leaders included Eugene V. DEBS, William D. HAYWOOD, and Daniel DE LEON. Its members were called, among other nicknames, the Wobblies. The aim of the IWW was to unite in one body all skilled and unskilled workers for the purpose of overthrowing capitalism and rebuilding society on a socialistic basis. Its methods were DIRECT ACTION, propaganda, the boycott, and the strike; it was opposed to sabotage, to arbitration or collective bargaining, and to political affiliation and intervention. The organization spread to Canada and Australia and in a very small way to Europe, but its main activities were confined to the United States. It was especially strong in the lumber camps of the Northwest, among dock workers in port cities, in the wheat fields of the central states, and in textile and mining areas. The stand against political action led to controversy among the members, with De Leon emphasizing the Marxist point of view as against those opposing political action. De Leon and his followers were expelled in 1908 and set up an independent organization, which was never more than a splinter group and was dissolved in 1925. In 1924 a split took place in the parent organization between the Westerners and the Easterners over the question of centralization. It resulted in a victory for the Easterners, with the Westerners setting up a new organization with headquarters in Oregon, based on the so-called Emergency Program, which called for a loose federation of highly autonomous locals. Of the 150 strikes conducted by the IWW, the most notable occurred at Goldfield, Nev. (miners, 1906–7); at Lawrence, Mass. (textile workers, 1912); at Paterson, N.J. (silk workers, 1913); in the Mesabi range, Minn. (iron miners, 1916); in the lumber camps of the Northwest (1917); at Seattle (general strike, 1919); and in Colorado (miners, 1927–28). At the time of World War I the IWW was antimilitaristic; its members were accused of draft evasion, of fomenting German-paid strikes in order to cripple essential war industries; of sabotage; and of criminal syndicalism. Many of its leaders and members were thrown into jail, and to this loss was added the large number who joined the Communist party after 1917. A further cause of decline was the fact that a great portion of the membership was made up of migratory and casual laborers, and it was difficult to organize them into a cohesive group. From a probable strength of 30,000 in 1912, the membership fell to probably less than 10,000 in 1930. Among the colorful personalities in the IWW were Joe Hill and Ralph Chaplin. The IWW made several contributions to the American labor movement. It unionized skilled and unskilled labor; it organized migrant and Negro workers at least temporarily; it brought about improved working conditions and shorter hours, especially in the lumber camps; and it influenced the structure of later unions. See P. F. Brissenden, *The I.W.W.: A Study of American Syndicalism* (1920, repr. 1958); J. S. Gambs, *The Decline of the I.W.W.* (1932, repr. 1966); J. L. Kornbluh, ed., *Rebel Voices* (1964, repr. 1968); Patrick Renshaw, *Wobblies* (1967); Melvyn Dubofsky, *We Shall Be All* (1969).

Indus valley civilization, ancient civilization that flourished from about 2500 B.C. to about 1500 B.C. in the valley of the Indus River and its tributaries, in the northwestern portion of the Indian subcontinent, i.e., present-day Pakistan. Since 1921 this civilization has been revealed by spectacular finds at Mohenjo-Daro, an archaeological site in NW Sind, and at Harappa, in central Punjab near the Ravi River. These sites, each of which measures more than 3 mi (5 km) in circumference, were once great urban centers, the chief cities of the Indus civilization. They had large and complex hill citadels, housing palaces, granaries, and baths that were probably used for sacred ablutions; the great bath at Mohenjo-Daro was c.40 ft (12 m) long and 23 ft (7 m) wide. Beyond the citadels were well-planned towns, laid out in rectangular patterns. Houses, often two-storied and spacious, lined the town streets; they had drainage systems that led into brick-lined sewers. The economy of the Indus civilization was based on a highly organized agriculture, supplemented by an active commerce, probably connected to that of the ancient civilizations of Mesopotamia. The arts flourished there, and many objects of copper, bronze, and pottery, including a large collection of terracotta toys, have been uncovered. Most notable, however, are the steatite seals, exquisitely engraved with animal figures and often bearing a line of pictographic script. On some seals are depicted a bo tree or, as some authorities hold, a Babylonian tree of life, and others have as their central figure the god Shiva, who later became preeminent in the Hindu pantheon. The writing, long a riddle to archaeologists, was deciphered in 1969; the language appears to be structurally related to the Dravidian languages. The origin, rise, and decline of the Indus valley civilization remain a mystery, but it seems most probable that the civilization fell (c.1500 B.C.) to invading ARYANS. See Sir John Marshall, *Mohenjo-Daro and the Indus Civilization* (3 vol., 1931); Stuart Piggott, *Prehistoric India* (1950); K. N. Dikshit, *Prehistoric Civilization of the Indus Valley* (2d ed. 1967), Sir Mortimer Wheeler, *The Indus Civilization* (3d ed. 1968); J. H. Hawkes, *The First Great Civilizations* (1973).

Indy, Vincent d': see D'INDY, VINCENT.

Ine (ĭ'nə), king of Wessex (688–726). In 694 he forced the people of Kent to pay compensation for the murder of a kinsman, and he extended his sway over Sussex and Surrey and probably over Devon. He also forwarded the diocesan reorganization of the church, founding (705) a bishopric at Sherborne. His code of laws, the earliest West Saxon code, was appended to the later codification of Alfred. Ine abdicated and went to Rome, where he died.

inequality, in mathematics, statement that a mathematical expression is less than or greater than some other expression; an inequality is not as specific as an EQUATION, but it does contain information about the expressions involved. The symbols $<$ (less than), $>$ (greater than), $\leq$ (less than or equal to), and $\geq$ (greater than or equal to) are used in place of the equals sign in expressions of inequalities. As in the case of equations, inequalities can be transformed in various ways. The direction of the inequality remains unchanged if some number is added to both sides or subtracted from both sides or if both sides are multiplied or divided by some positive number; e.g., subtracting 10 from both sides of the inequality $x < 8$ gives $x - 10 < -2$, and multiplying the inequality by 2 gives $2x < 16$. Multiplication or division by a negative number reverses the sign of the inequality; e.g., if $-2x < 8$, then dividing both sides by -2 results in the inequality $x > -3$.

inert gas or **noble gas,** any of the elements in group 0 of the PERIODIC TABLE. In order of increasing atomic number they are: HELIUM, NEON, ARGON, KRYPTON, XENON, and RADON. They are colorless, odorless, tasteless gases and were once believed to be entirely inert, i.e., forming no chemical compounds; however, some compounds of these elements have been produced, i.e., fluorides of krypton, xenon, and radon. The low chemical activity of the inert gases is due to the fact that their outermost, or valence, electron shell is complete, containing two electrons in the case of helium and eight in the remaining cases. The inert gases are sometimes called the rare gases, although argon is not rare (it makes up about 1% of the atmosphere) and helium is commercially produced. See G. A. Cook, *Argon, Helium and the Rare Gases* (2 vol., 1961); Isaac Asimov, *The Noble Gases* (1966).

inertia (ĭnûr'shə), in physics, the resistance of a body to any alteration in its state of MOTION, i.e., the resistance of a body at rest to being set in motion or of a body in motion to any change of speed or change in direction of motion. Inertia is a property common to all matter. Newton's second law of motion states that the external force required to affect the motion of a body is proportional to that acceleration. The constant of proportionality is known as the MASS, which is the numerical value of the inertia; the greater the inertia of a body, the less is its acceleration for a given applied force.

Inez de Castro: see CASTRO, INÉS DE.

infallibility (ĭnfăl"əbĭl'ətē), in Christian thought, exemption from the possibility of error, bestowed on the church as a teaching authority, as a gift of the Holy Spirit. It has been believed since the earliest times to be guaranteed in such scriptural passages as John 14.16,17. The analogous attribute of the Bible is usually called inerrancy. Protestants widely reject infallibility of the church. The Orthodox hold that the ecumenical councils are infallible. Roman Catholics hold that the infallibility of the church is vested in the pope, when he speaks *ex cathedra* (i.e., from the chair of Peter, as the visible head of the church) on matters of faith and morals. However, definitive pronouncements resulting from an ecumenical council, when ratified by the pope, are also held to be infallible. The pope speaks *ex cathedra* only rarely and after long deliberation. The dogma of papal infallibility was enunciated by the First Vatican Council (1870).

infancy, stage of human development lasting from birth to approximately two years of age. The first year is characterized by rapid physical growth. A normal baby doubles its birth weight in six months and triples it in a year; during that time there is great expansion of the head and chest, thus permitting development of the brain, heart, and lungs, the organs most vital to survival. The bones, which are relatively soft at birth, begin to harden, and the fontanelles, the soft parts of the newborn skull, begin to calcify, the small one at the back of the head at about 3 months, the larger one in front at varying ages up to 18 months. Brain weight also increases rapidly during infancy: By the end of the second year, the brain has already reached 75% of its adult weight. Growth and size depend on environmental conditions as well as genetic endowment; for example, severe nutritional deficiency during the mother's pregnancy as well as in infancy are likely to result in irreversible impairment of growth and intellectual development, while overfed, fat infants are predisposed to become obese later in life. The newborn infant sleeps almost constantly, awakening only for feedings, but the number and length of waking periods gradually increase until at the age of three months most infants have acquired a fairly regular schedule for sleeping, feeding, and bowel movements. By the end of the first year, sleeping and waking hours are divided about equally. Human milk provides the basic nutritional elements necessary for growth; however, doctors generally prescribe supplemental foods to be added to the diet at intervals. Development of motor activity follows a fairly standard sequence. The infant learns to lift its head, to turn over on its back, and to develop the muscular coordination for refined, visually directed hand movements and for sitting, crawling, standing, and walking, generally in that order. Motor development proceeds more rapidly than actual physical growth by the beginning of the second year. Bowel and bladder control is sometimes possible after 18 months. However, many normal healthy infants show delay in one or several developmental activities or may apparently skip a stage altogether. An infant's early crying sounds are largely limited to the frontal vowels and a few consonants; the remaining vowel and consonant sounds gradually appear, first produced in a babbling manner, and the first meaningful words may appear at ten months. By the end of the second year the infant's active vocabulary may reach 250 words. Studies indicate that certain cognitive processes, the order of which is largely biologically controlled, begin as early as two months after birth. Up to six months of age, differences in motor and conceptual development are generally independent of the infant's rearing conditions and culture, but by one year of age, cultural differences affect intellectual development. From the early months on, the infant forms attachments to those who care for him, and on the basis of their behavior he begins to develop expectations of gratification, e.g., adult responses to his cries of distress. Social smiling appears early, and by the latter part of the first year the baby may depend on the presence of familiar faces and become apprehensive in the presence of strangers. See many studies by Jean Piaget; Arnold Gesell and Frances Ilg, *Infant and Child in the Culture of Today* (rev. ed. 1973).

infanticide (ĭnfăn'təsīd) [from Lat.,=child murder], the putting to death of the newborn with the consent of the parent, family, or community. It is believed that infanticide is most common among peoples whose food supply is often inadequate; among the Chinese and the Eskimo, it was once common for female babies to be killed for this reason. In certain societies children who are deformed or are believed tainted by evil (e.g., twins) may be slain at birth. In most of the Greek city-states and in ancient Rome a child was virtually its father's chattel—e.g., in Roman law, the *Patria Potestas* granted the father the right to sell, offer in sacrifice, kill, or otherwise dispose of his offspring. In Sparta the decision was made by a public official. An allusion to the custom of infanticide is made in the biblical account of Abraham's near-sacrifice of Isaac (Gen. 22). Christianity, like Islam and Judaism, condemns infanticide as murder, and in all countries the act is a crime. If infanticide served as a primitive form of birth control, as many anthropologists believe, then the introduction of contraceptives, abortion, and other methods of population control have helped to replace that function.

infantile paralysis: see POLIOMYELITIS.

infantile sexuality: see PSYCHOANALYSIS.

infantry, body of soldiers who fight on foot and are equipped with hand-carried weapons, in contradistinction to cavalry and other branches of an army. Infantry hordes armed with swords, spears, slings, and bows were used in all ancient wars. The Greek PHALANX was the first infantry to be organized in formations; phalanxes were the dominant tactical infantry formation until Roman times. The Roman LEGION attained its tactical supremacy over the phalanx because of its greater maneuverability. Infantry declined as a major fighting force in Europe after the 4th cent. when the more effective light cavalry was introduced by the nomadic tribes of central Asia. In the Middle Ages mounted knights formed the backbone of all European armies, but with the return of mass warfare at the end of the medieval period, infantry units of pikemen and archers reappeared. After the middle of the 14th cent., when firearms were first used, the infantry, armed with muskets and rifles, became the dominant element in modern European wars. Before the advent of automatic weapons at the end of the 19th cent., infantry fought in mass formations; in the Boer War and in World War I the mass formation gave way to trench warfare. Large numbers of infantrymen, supported by aircraft, tanks, and artillery, were also employed in World War II and in the Korean and Vietnam wars. Infantry forces are considered by most military authorities as the only arm of modern warfare that can secure a total military decision. See ARMY; STRATEGY AND TACTICS; WARFARE.

infarction, blockage of blood circulation to a localized area or organ of the body resulting in tissue death. In the acute emergency known as myocardial infarction, a common type of heart attack, a blood-clot (thrombus) or hemorrhage occurs in an artery that supplies blood to the heart muscle, i.e., a coronary artery. Usually the artery has previously been narrowed by ARTERIOSCLEROSIS. Death of heart muscle tissue and heart failure may result (see CORONARY ARTERY DISEASE; CONGESTIVE HEART FAILURE). Infarcts also commonly occur in the spleen, kidney, lungs, and brain. The healing of an infarction occurs through replacement of the dead tissue by scar tissue.

infection, invasion of body tissues by microorganisms, e.g., BACTERIA, VIRUSES, FUNGI, and PROTOZOA. Invading organisms such as bacteria produce TOXINS that damage host tissues and interfere with normal metabolism; some toxins are actually enzymes that, by breaking down host tissues, prevent the localization of infections. Other bacterial substances destroy the host's phagocytes (see PHAGOCYTOSIS). Viruses, which are parasitic on host cells, cause cellular degeneration, as in RABIES or POLIOMYELITIS, or cellular proliferation, as in WARTS and cold sores. Substances produced by many invading organisms cause allergic sensitivity in the host; the immune response to virus infection has been implicated in some diseases (see ALLERGY). IMMUNITY is the term used to describe the capacity of the host to respond to infection. The invasion of body tissues by parasitic worms and other higher organisms is commonly referred to as infestation.

infectious canine hepatitis, acute viral disease of canines, especially dogs and foxes. The causative agent, an adenovirus, is not infectious to humans. In foxes the disease is manifested primarily as encephalitis. Transmission occurs mainly by direct contact with infected animals. The virus can be passed through the urine for periods of up to one year. Dogs of any age are susceptible to the disease. The incubation period is from six to nine days, and the signs are fever, loss of appetite, congested mucous membranes, and pain in the region of the liver. Mortality is about 10%, and about 25% of the survivors develop a temporary corneal opacity (hepatitis blue eye). Treatment consists of the administration of intravenous fluids, antibiotics, and vitamins. Recent reports indicate that chronic infection may occur, leading to cirrhosis of the liver. Annual vaccination with a modified live virus will give permanent prevention.

Infeld, Leopold (lä'ōpôlt ĭn'fĕlt), 1898–1968, German theoretical physicist. He received his Ph.D. in 1921 from Jagiellonian Univ., Cracow, Poland. At Princeton from 1936 to 1938, he collaborated with Einstein in research involving the general theory of relativity and in writing the popular text *The Evolution of Physics.* From 1938 to 1950 he taught and did research on differential equations and relativistic cosmology at the University of Toronto. Returning to Poland in 1950, he directed the growth of its theoretical physics programs.

inferiority complex, term introduced into psychology by Alfred Adler and referring to a COMPLEX of ideas centered on real or imaginary handicaps and colored by feelings of discouragement. Adler believed that all children strive to compensate for feelings of inferiority arising from their small size and dependency. When compensation is unsuccessful, however, the individual develops a neurosis and may withdraw from reality and limit his social participation. Alternatively, he may develop a compensatory aggressiveness, like the bully among schoolchildren, with an underlying fear of his own weakness. Compensation is also used to overcome legitimate handicaps, as in the case of Demosthenes, who, according to tradition, compensated for a speech defect by becoming a great orator.

inferior planet, planet whose orbit lies inside that of the earth. There are two inferior planets, Mercury and Venus. They always seem to be close to the sun in the sky; the greatest ELONGATION of Mercury is 28°, and that of Venus, 47°. For this reason, neither can be seen for more than two or three hours after sunset or before sunrise.

infinitive: see MOOD.

infinity, in mathematics, that which is not finite; it is often indicated by the symbol ∞. A SEQUENCE of numbers, $a_1, a_2, a_3, \ldots$, is said to "approach infinity" if the numbers eventually become arbitrarily large, i.e., are larger than some number, N, that may be chosen at will to be a million, a billion, or any other large number (see LIMIT). The term INFINITY is used in a somewhat different sense to refer to a collection of objects that does not contain a finite number of objects. For example, there are infinitely many points on a line, and Euclid demonstrated that there are infinitely many prime numbers. The German mathematician Georg Cantor showed that there are different orders of infinity, the infinity of points on a line being of a greater order than that of prime numbers (see TRANSFINITE NUMBER). In geometry one may define a point at infinity, or ideal point, as the point of intersection of two parallel lines, and similarly the line at infinity is the locus of all such points; if homogeneous coordinates (x_1, x_2, x_3) are used, the line at infinity is the locus of all points $(x_1, x_2, 0)$, where x_1 and x_2 are not both zero. (Homogeneous coordinates are related to Cartesian coordinates by $x=x_1/x_3$ and $y=x_2/x_3$.)

inflammation, reaction of the body to injury or to infectious, allergic, or chemical irritation. The symptoms are redness, swelling, heat, and pain resulting from dilation of the blood vessels in the affected part with loss of plasma and leucocytes (white blood cells) into the tissues. Certain types of inflammation result in pus formation, as in an abscess. The leucocytes destroy harmful microorganisms and dead cells, preventing the spread of the irritation and permitting the injured tissue to repair itself.

inflation, in economics, persistent and relatively large increase in the general price level of goods and services. Its opposite is deflation, a process of generally declining prices. Inflation results from an increase in the amount of circulating currency beyond the needs of trade; an oversupply of currency is created, and, in accordance with the law of supply and demand, the value of money decreases, or, more accurately, the prices of goods and services increase. Deflation is brought about by the opposite condition. Inflation may be due to a large influx of bullion, such as took place in Europe after the discovery of America and at the end of the 19th cent. when new supplies of gold were found and exploited in South Africa. In modern times wars are the most common cause of inflation, as government b[illegible] the issuance of paper money, and a di[illegible] of consumer goods increase de[illegible] supply and thereby cause rising [illegible]timulates business and helps wages [illegible] increase in wages usually fails to match the increase in prices; hence, real wages diminish. Stockholders make gains—often illusory—from increased business profits, but bondholders lose because their fixed percentage return has less buying power. Deflation, which is characteristic of the downward movement of the business cycle, lowers prices and increases unemployment through the depression of business. An unusually steep or long-lasting rise in prices, sometimes called hyperinflation, may result in the eventual breakdown of an entire nation's economy. Notable examples are Germany (1923), where prices rose 2,500% in one month, and some contemporary Latin American nations, where prices have risen by as much as 50% a year since World War II. In the United States, price increases of less than about 2% or 3% are not considered indicative of inflation. During the early 1970s, however, prices rose by considerably higher percentages than that. The worldwide inflation of the 1970s was generally regarded as being caused by shortages of the available supply of crucial products, most especially petroleum. See L. V. Chandler, *Inflation in the United States, 1940–1948* (1951); Bent Hansen, *A Study in the Theory of Inflation* (tr. 1951); Thomas Wilson, *Inflation* (1961); G. L. Perry, *Unemployment, Money Wage Rates, and Inflation* (1966); A. M. Okun, *Inflation* (1970).

inflection, in grammar. In many languages, words or parts of words are arranged in formally similar sets consisting of a root, or base, and various affixes. Thus *walking, walks, walker* have in common the root *walk* and the affixes *-ing*, *-s*, and *-er*. An inflectional affix carries certain grammatical restrictions with it; for example, with the plural inflection *-s*, a change from singular to plural in the noun *tree/trees* requires a concommitant change in the verb form from singular to plural: "the tree is green," "the trees are green." Other examples of English inflectional suffixes are the verb tenses. Many languages have far more extensive inflection than English, e.g., Latin, Eskimo, Arabic. In Latin grammar the typical noun and adjective are inflected for CASE and NUMBER, and the adjective is additionally inflected for the GENDER of the noun. Latin verbs have overlapping categories of inflection: MOOD, VOICE, TENSE, person, and number. Noun inflection is called declension, and the inflection of verbs is called conjugation. To be distinguished from inflectional affixes are those of derivation. Derivation is the process of forming words from other words or roots by the addition of affixes that in themselves either have meaning or denote word function. Derivational affixes in English may be either prefixes—e.g., *de-press, un-common*—or suffixes—e.g., *work-er, re-tire-ment, happi-ness.* The name stem is given to a root together with its derivational affixes; thus in *racket-eer-s, racket* is the root, *racketeer* the stem, and *-s* the plural inflection. Beginning in the 19th cent., the modification of a root or base by the amount of inflection or derivation in a language was used as a basis for classification. An isolating language is one in which there are only roots, with no derivation or inflection, such as Chinese. On the other hand, inflected languages, e.g., English and Latin, use roots, stems, and affixes, but the amount of inflection is not as great as in agglutinative languages where roots and affixes are readily identifiable, e.g., Turkish *baba* 'father', *babam* 'my father', *babama* 'to my father'. The old belief that agglutinative languages were the most primitive and isolating languages the most civilized is no longer held, it being recognized that every language is just as expressive as any other and can develop new vocabulary to fit new situations. See ABLAUT; GRAMMAR; UMLAUT; ENGLISH LANGUAGE.

influenza, acute, highly contagious disease caused by a filtrable virus. It is difficult to diagnose in absence of an epidemic, since it resembles many common respiratory ailments. The disease usually begins abruptly with sudden fever, prostration, muscular aches and pains, and inflammation of the respiratory mucous membranes. Influenza is usually uncomplicated by secondary infections, but its more severe forms, bacterial pneumonia and bronchitis, are serious threats. Although sporadic cases do occur, epidemics of influenza, sometimes worldwide in scope, decimated large populations in former times (more than 20 million people in 1918). Since a number of different viruses can cause the disease, immunity to one type (which is incurred for a few years after having influenza) does not prevent susceptibility to another type. Temporary immunity to the disease can be conferred by injection with influenza virus vaccine. Treatment with antibiotics has greatly reduced the fatalities from secondary infections in epidemic influenza. The uncomplicated type of influenza requires only rest and treatment of its symptoms. Return to normal activity should be undertaken slowly since relapses are easily precipitated. The condition commonly known as grippe is difficult to differentiate from influenza.

information, in law: see INDICTMENT.

information theory, mathematical theory formulated principally by the American scientist Claude E. Shannon to explain aspects and problems of information and communication. In this theory, the term *information* is used in a special sense; it is a measure of the freedom of choice with which a message is selected from the set of all possible messages. Information is thus distinct from meaning, since it is entirely possible for a string of nonsense words and a meaningful sentence to be equivalent with respect to information content. Numerically, information is measured in bits (short for *binary digit*; see BINARY SYSTEM). One bit is equivalent to the choice between two equally likely choices. For example, if we know that a coin is to be tossed but are unable to see it as it falls, a message telling whether the coin came up heads or tails gives us one bit of information. When there are several equally likely choices, the number of bits is equal to the logarithm of the number of choices taken to the base two. For example, if a message specifies one of sixteen equally likely choices, it is said to contain four bits of information. When the various choices are not equally probable, the situation is more complex. Interestingly, the mathematical expression for information content closely resembles the expression for ENTROPY in thermodynamics. The greater the information in a message, the lower its randomness, or "noisiness," and hence the smaller its entropy. Since the information content is, in general, associated with a source that generates messages, it is often called the entropy of the source. Often, because of constraints such as grammar, a source does not use its full range of choice. A source that uses just 70% of its freedom of choice would be said to have a relative entropy of 0.7. The redundancy of such a source is defined as 100% minus the relative entropy, or, in this case, 30%. The redundancy of English is about 50%; i.e., about half of the elements used in writing or speaking are freely chosen, and the rest are required by the structure of the language. A message proceeds along some channel from the source to the receiver; information theory defines for any given channel a limiting capacity or rate at which it can carry information, expressed in bits per second. In general, it is necessary to process, or encode, information from a source before transmitting it through a given channel. For example, a human voice must be encoded before it can be transmitted by radio. An important theorem of information theory states that if a source with a given entropy feeds information to a channel with a given capacity, and if the source entropy is less than the channel capacity, a code exists for which the frequency of errors may be reduced as low as desired. If the channel capacity is less than the source entropy, no such code exists. The theory further shows that noise (see NOISE, ELECTRICAL), or random disturbance of the channel, creates uncertainty as to the correspondence between the received signal and the signal transmitted. The average uncertainty in the message when the signal is known is called the equivocation. It is shown that the net effect of noise is to reduce the information capacity of the channel. However, redundancy in a message, as distinguished from redundancy in a source, makes it more likely that the message can be reconstructed at the receiver without error. For example, if something is already known as a certainty, then all messages about it give no information and are 100% redundant, and the information is thus immune to any disturbances of the channel. Using various mathematical means, Shannon was able to define channel capacity for continuous signals, such as music and speech. While the theory is not specific in all respects, it proves the existence of optimum coding schemes without showing how to find them. For example, it succeeds remarkably in outlining the engineering requirements of communication systems and the limitations of such systems. See C. E. Shannon and Warren Weaver, *The Mathematical Theory of Communication* (1949).

infrared radiation, ELECTROMAGNETIC RADIATION having a wavelength in the range from c.75 × 10^{-6} cm to c.100,000 × 10^{-6} cm (0.000075–0.1 cm). Infrared rays thus occupy that part of the electromagnetic SPECTRUM with a frequency less than that of visible LIGHT and greater than that of most radio waves, although there is some overlap. The name infrared means "below the red," i.e., beyond the red, or lower-frequency (longer wavelength), end of the visible spectrum. Infrared radiation is thermal, or HEAT, radiation. It was first discovered in 1800 by Sir William Herschel, who was attempting to determine the part of the visible spectrum with the minimum associated heat in connection with astronomical observations he was making. In 1847, A. H. L. Fizeau and J. B. L. Foucault showed that infrared radiation has the same properties as visible light, being reflected, refracted, and capable of forming an INTERFERENCE pattern. Infrared radiation is produced by any object having a TEMPERATURE above absolute zero. There are many applications of infrared radiation. A number of these are analogous to similar uses of visible light. Thus, the spectrum of a substance in the infrared range can be used in chemical analysis much as the visible spectrum is used. Radiation at discrete wavelengths in the infrared range is characteristic of many molecules. The temperature of a distant object can also be determined by analysis of the infrared radiation from the object. Radiometers operating in the infrared range serve as the basis for many instruments, including heat-seeking devices in missiles and devices for spotting and photographing persons and objects in the dark or in fog. Medical uses of infrared radiation range from the simple heat lamp to the technique of thermal imaging, or THERMOGRAPHY. A thermograph of a person can show areas of the body where the temperature is much higher or lower than normal, thus indicating some medical problem. Thermography has also been used in industry and other applications. Some lasers produce infrared radiation. A recent development has been the expansion of research in infrared astronomy; infrared sensors are sent aloft in balloons, rockets, and satellites to study the infrared radiation reaching the earth from other parts of the solar system and beyond.

Inge, William (ĭnj), 1913-73, American playwright, b. Independence, Kansas, grad. Univ. of Kansas, 1935. He was a teacher and newspaper critic before he won recognition as a dramatist. Inge's plays portray sympathetically the aspirations and frustrations of small-town life in the Midwest. *Come Back, Little Sheba* (1950) established his reputation. It was followed by *Picnic* (1953; Pulitzer Prize), *Bus Stop* (1955), and *The Dark at the Top of the Stairs* (1957). After the unsuccessful production *A Loss of Roses* (1959) Inge's reputation as a dramatist declined; he turned to writing novels, notably *Good Luck, Miss Wyckoff* (1970). He died in 1973, apparently a suicide.

Inge, William Ralph (ĭng), 1860-1954, Anglican prelate and author. He was fellow of King's College, Cambridge (1886-88), fellow and tutor of Hertford College, Oxford (1889-1904), and vicar of a London parish (1905-7). He then became Lady Margaret professor of divinity and fellow of Jesus College, Cambridge. He was dean of St. Paul's Cathedral from 1911 to 1934. Well known for his originality of thought and for his pessimism, the latter earned him the title "the gloomy dean." His works include several on mysticism, a subject in which he was much interested. See *Christian Mysticism* (1897), *Personal Idealism and Mysticism* (1907), *Lay Thoughts of a Dean* (1926), *More Lay Thoughts of a Dean* (1931), *Mysticism in Religion* (1948), and *Diary of a Dean: St. Paul's 1911-1934* (1949). See also biography by Adam Fox (1960); study by R. M. Helm (1962).

Ingelow, Jean (ĭn'jəlō), 1820-97, English author. Her poems are characterized by religious introspection and an intimate knowledge of nature. Among her best-known poems are "High Tide on the Coast of Lincolnshire, 1571" and "Seven Times One." Of her novels, *Off the Skelligs* (1872) and *Sarah de Berenger* (1879) are the most noted. She also wrote the children's story *Mopsa the Fairy* (1869). See biography by Maureen Peters (1972).

Ingemann, Bernhard Severin (bĕrn'härt sĕv'ərēn ĭng'əmän), 1789-1862, Danish poet, playwright, and novelist. As teacher and director of Soro Academy, Ingemann adopted the folk high school principles of N. F. S. GRUNDTVIG. His novels, recalling Denmark's past greatness, were important in reviving national literary consciousness. The poems in *Holger Danske* (1837) became popular national songs, and the religious *Morning and Evening Songs* (1839) includes some of the finest lyric poetry in Danish.

Ingenhousz, Jan (yän ĭng'ənhous), 1730-99, Dutch scientist. He practiced medicine in Holland, England, and Vienna and was noted for his skillful inoculations against smallpox. He demonstrated respiration in plants and recorded his observations in *Experiments upon Vegetables* (1779).

Ingermanland (ĭng'gərmənlănd), or **Ingria** (ĭng'grēə), Finnish *Ingerinta*, historic region, NW European USSR, along the Neva River and on the east bank of the Gulf of Finland. Its name derives from the ancient Finnic inhabitants, the Ingers, some of whose descendants (about 93,000) still live in the Leningrad area and are called Ingrians or Leningrad Finns. In medieval times, the region was subject to Great Novgorod, with which it passed in 1478 to the grand duchy of Moscow. Conquered in the early 17th cent. by Sweden, it remained Swedish until Peter I of Russia captured it in 1702 and built his new capital of St. Petersburg (now Leningrad) there. The area was formally ceded to Russia by the Treaty of Nystad (1721), which ended the Northern War between Russia and Sweden.

Ingersoll, Charles Jared (ĭng'gərsôl), 1782-1862, American political leader and author, b. Philadelphia; son of Jared Ingersoll (1749-1822). In several influential publications, including *Inchiquin: The Jesuit's Letters on American Literature and Politics* (1810), he argued for more intellectual independence and national self-sufficiency. Admitted to the bar in 1802, Ingersoll served (1813-15) as a Jeffersonian in Congress and was (1815-29) U.S. district attorney for Pennsylvania. He returned to Congress (1841-49), where he was chairman of the Committee on Foreign Affairs and was influential in securing the annexation of Texas. Besides several plays, including *Julian: A Tragedy* (pub. 1831), he wrote a four-volume history of the War of 1812 (1845-52) and his recollections (1861). See biography by W. M. Meigs (1897, repr. 1970).

Ingersoll, Jared, 1722-81, American colonial official, b. Milford, Conn. He was made (1751) king's attorney in New Haven, and later he sailed (1758) for England as a colonial agent. From a second trip (1763) he returned (1765) with a commission to distribute stamps under the highly unpopular Stamp Act. A mob, led by John Durkee, forced Ingersoll to resign. He was later crown judge of the Philadelphia vice-admiralty court until, in the American Revolution, Loyalist-hunting colonials forced him to return to New Haven. His son, Jared Ingersoll, however, supported the Revolution. See biography by L. H. Gipson (1920, repr. 1971).

Ingersoll, Jared, 1749-1822, American jurist, b. New Haven, Conn.; son of Jared Ingersoll (1722-81) and father of Charles Jared Ingersoll. After studying law in England, he was admitted (1773) to the bar in Philadelphia and became a leading attorney; he later argued many important cases before the U.S. Supreme Court. He served (1780-81) in the Continental Congress and was (1787) a delegate to the Federal Constitutional Convention. In Pennsylvania he was attorney general (1790-99, 1811-17), U.S. district attorney (1800-1801), and presiding judge (1821-22) of the district court of Philadelphia co. In 1812 he was the unsuccessful candidate for Vice President, running on the antiwar Republican and Federalist ticket headed by De Witt Clinton. See Horace Binney, *The Leaders of the Old Bar of Philadelphia* (1859).

Ingersoll, Robert Green, 1833-99, American orator and lawyer, b. Dresden, N.Y. The son of a Congregational minister who settled eventually in Illinois, Ingersoll was admitted (1854) to the bar and became a court lawyer. He served in the Union army during the Civil War. Although previously a Democrat, he emerged from the war a Republican, and in 1876 he nominated James G. Blaine for President in his famous "plumed knight" speech. He served (1867-69) as attorney general of Illinois, but his antireligious beliefs prevented any further advance. Known as "the great agnostic," Ingersoll questioned the tenets of Christian belief in such lectures as "The Gods" (1872), "Some Mistakes of Moses" (1879), "Why I Am an Agnostic" (1896), and "Superstition" (1898), drawing large audiences through his eloquence and irreverent wit and provoking denunciations from the orthodox. One of the greatest orators of his day, Ingersoll was acclaimed by Henry Ward Beecher as the "most brilliant speaker of the English tongue of all the men on the globe." His lectures were widely read for a generation, and editions of his works still circulate; the Dresden edition (12 vol., 1900) has been reprinted several times. See his letters, ed. by E. I. Wakefield (1951, repr. 1974); biographies by C. H. Cramer (1952), O. P. Larson (1962), and D. D. Anderson (1972).

Ingersoll, town (1971 pop. 7,783), S Ont., Canada, on the Thames River, E of London. It has a large dairy-processing industry. Named for Thomas Ingersoll, father of the Canadian heroine Laura Secord, it was the birthplace of Aimée Semple McPherson.

Ingle, Richard, fl. 1642-53, English seaman and tobacco trader. Little is known of him. While the English civil war was in progress, he appeared (1645) with several ships off Maryland, and, armed with letters of marque from the lord high admiral under Parliament, he raided the colony and captured the capital, St. Mary's. Leonard Calvert, the proprietary governor and a royalist, fled to Virginia, but he returned the next year and reestablished his control. The proprietary government excluded Ingle from the pardon granted to the other rebels.

Inglewood, city (1970 pop. 89,985), Los Angeles co., S Calif., a residential and industrial suburb of Los Angeles, in an oil-producing area; founded 1873, inc. 1908. Its manufactures include machinery, aircraft parts, and electronic equipment. Northrop Institute of Technology and the Hollywood Park racetrack are in Inglewood.

Inglis, Charles (ĭng'glĭs, ĭng'gəlz), 1734-1816, Anglican clergyman in America, b. Ireland. He emigrated to America in 1755. While assistant rector (1765-77) of Trinity Church, New York City, he actively espoused England's position in the struggle with the colonies. He refused to omit the prayers for the king, and his *True Interest of America Impartially Stated* (1776) and other pamphlets as well as his letters to the press, which he signed Papinian, were strongly Loyalist. In 1777, Inglis became rector of Trinity, but he returned to England in 1783 when the British evacuated New York. In 1787 he was appointed the first bishop of Nova Scotia for the Church of England. See biography by R. U. Harris (1937).

Ingoldsby, Thomas: see BARHAM, RICHARD HARRIS.

Ingolstadt (ĭng'gôlshtät), city (1970 pop. 70,414), Bavaria, S West Germany, on the Danube River. It is a commercial and industrial center. Manufactures include engines, machinery, refined oil, textiles, and motor vehicles. Chartered about 1250, Ingolstadt was besieged (1632) by Gustavus II of Sweden during the Thirty Years War. The Univ. of Ingolstadt (founded 1472 and removed to Landshut in 1802 and then to Munich in 1826) was a stronghold of the Catholic Reformation; Joseph von Eck taught at the university from 1510 to 1543. The city's noteworthy buildings include the splendid Gothic Liebfrauenmünster (15th-16th cent.) and other churches.

Ingram, Arthur Foley Winnington (ĭng'grəm), 1858-1946, English prelate, bishop of London (1901-39). He was a lifelong leader in social work in London's East End. His many books include *What a Layman Should Believe* (1938) and *Fifty Years' Work in London* (1940). See biography by S. P. Carpenter (1949).

Ingres, Jean Auguste Dominique (zhäN ōgüst' dômēnēk' ăN'grə), 1780-1867, French painter, b. Montauban; son of a sculptor. He studied with J. L. David in Paris and in 1801 won the Prix de Rome. The French government could not afford to award the prize until 1806. In the Salon of that year Ingres exhibited his portrait of Madame Rivière (Louvre), an extraordinarily graceful and linear composition that marked him as an unparalleled draftsman. It also made clear his sensuality, which put him at odds with the strict neoclassicists of his day. This bizarre element in Ingres's work was made more disturbingly explicit in *Jupiter and Thetis* (1811; Musée Granet). For 18 years (1806-24) he lived in Italy, where he supported himself and his family by portraiture. Some of his pencil portraits of this period are considered among his finest productions (e.g., *Paganini,* 1819). Upon his return to Paris he was hailed the bulwark of Davidian classicism for his *Vow of Louis XIII* (cathedral, Montauban), although his true inspiration had always been Raphael. He lived in Paris until 1834, receiving many commissions and honors and returning to Rome as director of the Académie de France à Rome. There, during the remainder of his long life, he occupied a preeminent position as teacher and artist. After his death the Ingres Museum, housing a large collection of his paintings and drawings, was instituted in his native Montauban. His followers, the *Ingristes,* adopted his academicism but lacked his genius. Many later artists (e.g., Degas, Renoir, Puvis de Chavannes, and Picasso) have acknowledged their debt to him. The Louvre has a large collection of his work, ranging from rigidly academic compositions like *The Apotheosis of Homer* (1827) to the intimate, sensual nudes such as *Bather of Valpinçon* (1808) and *The Turkish Bath* (1852-63). Several of his paintings are in the Metropolitan Museum. There is a remarkable portrait of the comtesse d'Haussonville (1845) in the Frick Collection, New York City. See *Ingres Centennial Exhibition* (1967); studies by G. Wildenstein (2d ed. 1956) and R. Rosenblum (1967).

Ingria: see INGERMANLAND, USSR.

Ingul (ĕngo͞ol'), river, SW European USSR, in the Ukraine. Rising N of Kirovograd, it flows south c.210 mi (340 km) to empty into the Bug estuary, an inlet of the Black Sea, at Nikolayev.

Ingulets (ĕngo͞olyĕts'), river, c.340 mi (550 km) long, SW European USSR, in the Ukraine. Rising in the Kirovograd region, it flows through the Krivoy Rog iron district and then south to join the Dnepr River above Kherson.

Ingush: see CHECHEN-INGUSH AUTONOMOUS SOVIET SOCIALIST REPUBLIC.

Inhambane (ĭn"yəmbăn'ə), city (1960 pop. 22,108), SE Mozambique, on Inhambane Bay, an inlet of Mozambique Channel on the Indian Ocean. It is a port, a district capital, and the center of an important agricultural region. The bay was discovered in 1498 by Vasco da Gama, who claimed it for Portugal. Inhambane developed as a trade center, notably for slaves and ivory. Sugar and coconut products are significant exports.

inheritance, in biology: see HEREDITY.

inheritance, in law: see HEIR.

inheritance tax, assessment made on the portion of an estate received by an individual; it differs from an estate tax, which is a tax levied on an entire estate before it is distributed to individuals. The inheritance tax is usually progressive and is determined by the amount of property received by an individual. Strictly speaking, it is a tax on the right to receive the property; the estate tax can be characterized as a tax on the right to transmit the property. In the United States, inheritance taxes were levied by the Federal government during the Civil War period and again during the Spanish-American War. Since 1916, however, a progressive estate tax has been imposed. All states except Nevada and Vermont impose either an estate tax or an inheritance tax, some states employing both. See E. M. Wypyski, *Law of Inheritance* (rev. ed. 1973).

I-ning (ē-nĭng) or **Kuldja** (ko͞ol'jä'), city (1970 est. pop. 160,000), W Sinkiang Uigur Autonomous Region, China, on the Ili River in the Dzungarian basin. An old commercial center trading in tea and cattle, it is also an industrial city with manufactures of cotton and wool textiles and carpets. It has fruit orchards, and iron and coal are mined nearby. I-ning was seized by the Russians in 1871 but was restored to China in 1881. It became the capital of an autonomous district in 1954.

Inini: see FRENCH GUIANA.

initiation, the transition and attendant ceremonies, such as ordeals and rites, involved in passing from one state or status to another, often from childhood to adulthood. It was among the most important social institutions of early humans. The ordeal measures the initiate's worthiness to enter the new status. Initiation may mean the cessation of contact with those who have not been initiated. Seclusion, mutilation, symbolic representation of death and resurrection, the display of sacred objects, special instruction, and restrictions on the initiate are frequent attributes of the ceremonies. Many early societies had grade initiations. Their purpose was to induct the young person both into the full status of an adult and into the religion of the group.

initiative, the originating of a law or constitutional amendment by popular petition. It is intended to allow the electorate to initiate legislation independently of the legislature. This direct form of legislation, together with the REFERENDUM, was known in Greece and other early democracies. It is practiced in Switzerland. In the United States the initiative was recognized as early as 1777 in the first constitution of Georgia. It was subsequently adopted by a number of states and may apply also on local and city government levels. There are two kinds of initiative, direct and indirect. In both kinds of initiative a certain number of signatures (usually from 5% to 15% of the electorate in the district concerned) must appear on the petition that proposes the constitutional amendment or legislation. In direct initiative the proposed law is voted on in the next election, or in a special election, after a petition with the required number of signatures has been filed with state or local officials. In indirect initiative the petition goes directly to the legislature and reaches the people only if the legislature fails to enact it into law.

injection, introduction of a fluid into the body, usually by means of a needle and syringe. The material injected may be a test substance (as in determining allergic sensitivity or immunity to a disease), an anesthetic, a therapeutic drug, a nutrient (in cases where intravenous feeding is necessary), or blood or blood plasma (transfusion). An intracutaneous injection is the introduction of a small amount of fluid between the skin layers. A subcutaneous injection is directed to the tissues under the skin. When quicker absorption of a drug is required, injection is made into one of the muscles (intramuscular); even more rapid absorption is obtained by direct injection into a vein (intravenous). In certain emergencies involving the heart, such as cardiac arrest, a chamber of the musculature of the heart can be penetrated directly by injection (intracardiac). Anesthetics are sometimes injected into the spine (spinal injection). In an injection by means of a jet injector gun, the fluid penetrates through the skin by means of air pressure and there is no visible puncture mark.

injunction, formal written order of a court directing a certain party to perform or not to perform a certain act. The injunction, which developed as the main remedy of EQUITY, orders the defendant to perform his legal duty; it is especially used in cases where money DAMAGES cannot satisfy the plaintiff's claim. It is issued at the court's discretion to protect the plaintiff's personal or property rights from irreparable harm. Originally the courts granted only prohibitory injunctions, on the grounds that the performance of positive orders could not easily be compelled or supervised. However, the practice of making positive orders in negative guise (e.g., "Do not allow the wall to continue standing," meaning "Tear down the wall") gave place in the 19th cent. to a frank recognition of affirmative (or mandatory) injunctions, and they are now granted in very unusual circumstances. Injunctions granted while an action is pending are termed preliminary, or interlocutory, and are intended to protect the plaintiff's interest so that a judgment will be of use to him. If irreparable injury would result even before notice of a hearing could be served, the court may grant a temporary restraining order and schedule an early hearing on the motion for a preliminary injunction. A final or perpetual injunction is part of the final judgment of the court, made after all the evidence has been heard. Injunctions, like most remedies of an equitable nature, are usually granted by a judge sitting without a jury. If disobedience of the injunction is suspected, the judge may try the defendant for CONTEMPT. So long as the injunction is in effect the court may consider requests to terminate or modify it. Injunctions are granted in many circumstances, including some where courts of equity formerly refused to act. Examples of recent practices are the compelling of the performance of the terms of a contract and the ordering of a defendant personally to pay legal damages and spare the plaintiff from seeking execution of his JUDGMENT. An old and common injunction is that for abating a NUISANCE. The use of the injunction in labor disputes is a matter of great controversy. In the United States in the late 19th cent. employers were often granted injunctions against strikes or boycotts by alleging that the injury would be immediate, that the union was unable to pay damages, and that the purpose of the activity was illegal (e.g., unreasonably limiting the employer's freedom by requiring him to hire only union members). The power of Federal courts to enjoin union activity was greatly restricted by the Federal Anti-Injunction Act of 1932. Many states passed similar laws because certain union objectives formerly deemed illegal were made lawful. Subsequently, however, new legislation, notably the TAFT-HARTLEY LABOR ACT (1947), has restored to the courts some power over labor injunctions. Also, the Labor-Management Reporting and Disclosure Act of 1959 provides for the use of injunctions as an enforcement device to secure higher ethical standards within unions. See MANDAMUS.

ink, pigmented fluid used for writing and drawing, or a viscous compound used for printing, both of various colors but most frequently black. The oldest known variety, India ink or China ink, is still used in China and Japan for writing with small brushes instead of pens. India ink consists essentially of carbon black and water; various substances including glue and gum are used to stabilize suspension. Because of its rich blackness and permanence, India ink is used extensively by architects, engineers, and artists. In many early civilizations dyes obtained from plants, and sepia from the squid, octopus, and cuttlefish, were used as ink. The black and blue-black inks used today, composed of copperas (ferrous sulfate), gallic and tannic acids, and a preservative, were probably known as early as the 2d cent., the acids then being derived from oak or nut galls. Numerous master drawings made with ink containing the acids of gallnuts have been corroded by the ink itself. These inks, and also the colored inks used today, contain analine and other soluble dyes instead of holding their pigments in suspension; they are accordingly filterable and flow easily even through ball-point pens. Felt-tip markers contain organic compounds in solution. Fingerprint ink is a rapidly drying, pasty ink of permanent blackness. The glutinous inks used by printers owe their various viscosities to such ingredients as linseed oil, synthetics of the alkyd type, mineral oil, and petroleum fractions. Marking inks used to mark linen are composed of a salt of silver. Indelible or incorrodible ink is used for writing that is exposed to the weather or to strong acids or alkaline solutions. Fluorescent inks are used in printing maps to be read at night. Sympathetic inks are preparations used for writing that becomes visible only on the application of heat or a chemical. The liquid in the ink used in newspaper printing is absorbed into the paper, while in many other sorts of ink the liquid evaporates leaving the pigment above the paper surface.

Inkerman (ĭng'kərmən, Rus. ĕnkĭrmän'), eastern suburb of Sevastopol, S European USSR, in the Ukraine, in the Crimea. There in 1854 the French and British defeated the Russians in the Crimean War. Nearby are cave dwellings and a burial place (2d–4th cent.) and a 14th-century fortress.

Inkster, city (1970 pop. 38,595), Wayne co., SE Mich., a suburb of Dearborn, on the Rouge River; settled 1825 as Moulin Rouge, renamed 1863, inc. as a city 1964. The city's residents are primarily employed by nearby automotive plants.

Inland Sea, Jap. *Seto-naikai,* arm of the Pacific Ocean, c.3,670 sq mi (9,510 sq km), S Japan, between Honshu, Shikoku, and Kyushu islands. It is linked to the Sea of Japan by a narrow channel. The shallow sea is dotted with more than 950 islands, the largest of which is Awaji-shima. The shores of the Inland Sea are heavily populated and are part of Japan's most important industrial belt. Many industrial cities line the sea from the Osaka-Kobe complex on the east to the northern Kyushu industrial complex on the west. Many of Japan's greatest ports, including Osaka, Kobe, and Hiroshima are there. The Inland Sea is also famed for its scenic beauty and is the site of Inland Sea (Seto-naikai) National Park (255 sq mi/660 sq km; est. 1934) which includes some 600 islands and coastal segments.

inlaying, process of ornamenting a surface by setting into it material of different color or substance, usually in such a manner as to preserve a continuous plane. Inlay is employed in connection with a great variety of objects, both of major architectural character and of minor furnishing and decorative function, and makes use of a wide range of materials, such as wood, stone, ivory, glass, metal, mother-of-pearl, and tortoiseshell. The art is of ancient origin and has been continuously and widely employed. The use of the word *inlay* is now more generally restricted to the true process as applied to furniture and other objects of wood and as distinguished from parquetry and the veneered work of MARQUETRY. For stone or glass inlays, see MOSAIC; for metals, see NIELLO and DAMASCENING; and for special wood inlays, see INTARSIA.

Inman, Henry, 1801–46, American portrait, genre, and landscape painter, b. Yorkville, N.Y., studied with John Wesley Jarvis. He was a founder and first vice president of the National Academy of Design. He was highly esteemed as a portrait painter in the United States and in England. Among his distinguished sitters were Martin Van Buren and William C. Macready (Metropolitan Mus.); Wordsworth (Univ. of Pennsylvania); Fitz-Greene Halleck (N.Y. Historical Society); and Fanny Kemble (Brooklyn Mus., N.Y.). His landscapes and genre works include *Picnic in the Catskills* and *Rydal Falls, England* (Brooklyn Mus.).

Inn (ĭn), river, c.320 mi (515 km) long, rising near the Lake of Sils, SE Switzerland. It flows NE through the Engadine valley, then through W Austria, past Innsbruck and Solbad Hall (the head of navigation), and into SE West Germany. The Inn forms part of the West German–Austrian border before entering the Danube River at Passau. There are more than 20 hydroelectric power plants on the swift-flowing stream, and its water is also used in the production of chemicals.

inn, in Great Britain, any hotel, public house, tavern, or coffeehouse where lodging is provided. In American usage, the inn is generally a small rural lodging house for transients. Among the earliest public houses were empty huts placed at caravan stops in the Orient for the shelter of traders and travelers. To pilgrims, temples and religious houses gave rest and refreshment—a custom that still lingers in some Alpine hospices. The Romans maintained post stations on their great highways for the use of messengers of state and those especially privileged. For the accommodation of ordinary transients, *stabularia* were kept for man and beast. In the Middle Ages hospitality was observed as one of the Christian duties by the establishment of hospices in cities and by the entertainment of travelers at monasteries. Inns kept for profit appeared in Europe about the 15th cent. and gained a reputable standing in England, often being named for the powerful family on whose holdings they were established. They were usually built around a courtyard, approached by a wide, covered entry. In America, colonial inns similar to the English hostelries sprang up along the great turnpikes. See W. C. Firebaugh, *Inns of the Middle Ages* (1924); H. A. Monckton, *A History of the English Public House* (1969).

innate ideas, in philosophy, concepts present in the mind at birth as opposed to concepts arrived at through experience. The theory has been advanced at various times in the history of philosophy to secure a basis for certainty when the validity or adequacy of the observed functioning of the mind was in question. Plato, for example, asserted the inadequacy of knowledge arrived at through sense experience; the world apparent to sense was only a temporal, changing approximation of an eternal, unchanging reality. The next important occurrence of a doctrine of innate ideas, not directly based on Plato, is in the work of René Descartes. Among the ideas Descartes took to be innate were the existence of the self: *cogito ergo sum* [I think, therefore I am], the existence of God, and some logical propositions like, *from nothing comes nothing.* John Locke, objecting that the doctrine encouraged dogmatism and laziness in thinking, advanced the classic attack on innate ideas. He argued that if certain ideas were innate they would be universally held and used, which is not the case. In contemporary discussion the question of innate resources of the mind has been the subject of dispute between behavioral psychologist B. F. Skinner and linguistic theorist Noam Chomsky. Chomsky has pointed out that the learning of a language and linguistic performance cannot be adequately explained by the empirical behaviorist model.

Inner Hebrides, Scotland: see HEBRIDES, THE.

Inner Mongolian Autonomous Region, Mandarin *Nei Meng Ku Tzu-chih Ch'ü,* autonomous region (1967 est. pop. 13,000,000), c.164,000 sq mi (424,760 sq km), NE China. The capital is HU-HO-HAO-T'E (Huhehot). It is bounded on the N by the Mongolian People's Republic. Inner Mongolia is largely steppe country that becomes increasingly arid toward the Gobi Desert in the west. The climate is continental with cold dry winters and hot summers. Stockraising, mainly of sheep, goats, horses, and camels, is a major occupation; wool, hides, and skins are important exports. Rainfall is scanty, but irrigation makes agriculture possible, and in recent years much grazing land has been converted to raising spring wheat. The main farming areas are in the bend of the Huang Ho (Yellow River) and in the Hu-ho-hao-t'e plains. Principal crops are wheat, kaoliang, millet, oats, corn, linseed, soybeans, sugar beets, and rice. There are valuable mineral deposits (coal, lignite, iron ore, lead, zinc, and gold), as yet only partially exploited. A railway built in 1958, linking the USSR (through the Mongolian People's Republic) with Lan-chou in Kansu prov., passes through Hu-ho-hao-t'e and PAO-T'OU. The Peking-Ulan Bator road traverses the region. Considerable additional road and rail improvements have been made with the vigorous industrialization of Pao-t'ou. The Mongols of China are concentrated in the Inner Mongolian Autonomous Region, but there has been much Chinese immigration in the last two decades and the Mongols now comprise as little as 7% of the population. The Chinese live mostly in the farming areas. The traditionally nomadic Mongols are beginning to settle as their pastoral economy is collectivized. Livestock cooperatives and communes have been organized, and many herdsmen have been given permanent homes. The great steel mill in Pao-t'ou employs over 30,000 former nomads. Originally the southern part of MONGOLIA, Inner Mongolia was settled chiefly by the Tumet and Chahar tribes. From 1530 to 1583, Inner Mongolia was held by Anda (Altan Khan), chief of the Tumets, who harried N China and once besieged Peking. After his death, Likdan Khan of the Chahars became (c.1605) ruler, but in 1635 he was defeated by the Manchus, who soon annexed Inner Mongolia. Under Manchu rule S Mongolia became known as Inner Mongolia; N Mongolia, conquered by the Manchus at the end of the 17th cent., became known as Outer Mongolia. Until 1911, Inner Mongolia was only under nominal Chinese rule; however, Chinese settlers in the region soon forced the Mongol tribes into the steppe and arid parts of the region. After the Revolution of 1911, Inner Mongolia became an integral part of the Chinese Republic. In 1928 it was divided among the Chinese provinces of Ninghsia, Suiyuan, and Chahar. After the outbreak (1937) of the Sino-Japanese War, the Mongols of Suiyuan and Chahar established the Japanese-controlled state of Mengkiang or Meng-chiang, with its capital at Kweihwa. The Chinese Communists, after their conquest of Inner Mongolia in 1945, supported the traditional aspirations of the Mongols for autonomy, and in May, 1947, the Inner Mongolian Autonomous Region—with limited powers of self-government within the Communist state—was formally proclaimed. It was the first autonomous region established by the Communist government. From 1949 to 1956 the area of the region was expanded through the incorporation of the former province of Suiyuan and parts of the provinces of Liaopei, Jehol, Chahar, and Kansu. Extensive boundary changes since 1970, however, have considerably reduced the size of the province. The W Ala Shan desert region was given to Kansu and Ninghsia Autonomous Region, and the northeast corner, which bordered on the USSR, was divided between the Manchurian provinces. Hopeh prov. also received a section of Inner Mongolia. Hu-ho-hao-t'e has been the capital since 1952; from 1947 to 1950 the capital was at Ulan Hoto (now in Kirin prov.), and from 1950 to 1952 it was at CHANG-CHIA-K'OU (Kalgan; now in Hopeh prov.). Inner Mongolian Univ. is in Hu-ho-hao-t'e.

Inner Temple: see INNS OF COURT AND TEMPLE, THE.

Innes, James (ĭn'ĭs), 1754–98, American lawyer, b. Caroline co., Va. As commander of a Virginia regiment, he took part in many battles of the American Revolution. He was president of the board of war for Virginia (1779) and a member of the state legislature (1780–82, 1785–87). A noted lawyer, considered second only to Patrick Henry as an orator, Innes was chosen to make the final appeal for adoption of the Constitution in the Virginia ratifying convention (1788) and greatly impressed all those present. He defeated (1786) John Marshall for the office of attorney general of Virginia, but he declined an appointment as U.S. Attorney General. See study by Jane Carson (1965).

Innes, Michael, pseud. of **John Innes Mackintosh Stewart,** 1906–, British writer and scholar, b. near Edinburgh. Since 1969 he has been reader in English literature at Oxford. Under his own name he has written novels, short stories, and such critical studies as *Character and Motive in Shakespeare* (1949), *Rudyard Kipling* (1966), and *Thomas Hardy* (1971). As "Michael Innes" he has written detective stories featuring John Appleby, a gentleman turned policeman. These novels are excellent mysteries, erudite and witty, and a sensitive record of a changing civilization. They include *Seven Suspects* (1936), *A Comedy of Terrors* (1940), and *Open House* (1972).

Inness, George (ĭn'ĭs), 1825–94, American landscape painter, b. Newburgh, N.Y. His father intended Inness to be a grocer, but he showed artistic talent at an early age and was apprenticed to an engraver. In 1845 he opened a studio in New York City, devoting himself to painting, and two years later with a friend's aid was able to go to Rome. He made a subsequent visit to Rome in 1851, and in 1854 he and his wife went to Paris. On their return they settled in Medfield, Mass. There Inness painted many of his best-known canvases. In later life he enjoyed a high reputation, maintaining studios in New York City and in Montclair, N.J., where most of his last 20 years were spent. The early work of Inness is in the manner of the HUDSON RIVER SCHOOL. His panoramic *Peace and Plenty* (Metropolitan Mus.) is characteristic of this period. But in a short time he discovered his own personal style which became freer, more intimate, and richer in color. In his later works his subjects, covering a wide range of light effects, became a vehicle for the expression of a consistently romantic mood. Inness was a Swedenborgian and sought the mystical in nature. Among his principal works are *Rainbow after a Storm* and *Millpond* (Art Inst., Chicago); *Delaware Valley, Autumn Oaks,* and *Evening—Medfield, Mass.* (Metropolitan Mus.); *June* (1882; Brooklyn Mus., N.Y.); *Georgia Pines* and *Niagara* (National Gall. of Art, Washington, D.C.). Inness died in Scotland. See his *Life, Art and Letters,* introd. by E. Daingerfield (1969); study by Alfred Werner (1973).

innocence, in botany: see MADDER.

Innocent I, Saint, d. 417, pope (401–17), an Italian; successor of St. Anastasius I. A powerful champion of papal supremacy in the entire Church, he upheld St. JOHN CHRYSOSTOM and condemned Pelagius. He vainly tried to prevent the sack of Rome in 410 by the Visigoths under ALARIC I. St. Innocent was succeeded by St. Zosimus. Feast: July 28.

Innocent II, d. 1143, pope (1130–43), a Roman named Gregorio Papareschi; successor of Honorius II. He was created cardinal by Paschal II. On the death of HONORIUS II, a faction of the cardinals elected him pope. However, the others elected Cardinal Pietro Pierleoni as Anacletus II, and Innocent had to leave Rome. He was soon recognized in France at the instance of St. Bernard of Clairvaux, and in 1131, Holy Roman Emperor Lothair II, England, and Spain submitted to him. ROGER II of Sicily adhered to Anacletus. In 1137, Lothair attacked Rome, but Anacletus retained part of the city. On Anacletus' death (1138), an antipope Victor IV was elected, but he soon resigned. Innocent convened the Second LATERAN COUNCIL (1139). Innocent, at the behest of St. Bernard, condemned the teachings of Peter Abelard and of Arnold of Brescia. He was succeeded by Paschal II.

Innocent III, b. 1160 or 1161, d. 1216, pope (1198–1216), an Italian, b. Anagni, named Lotario di Segni; successor of Celestine III. He was of an important family, the counts of Segni, to which belonged also Gregory IX and Alexander IV. He was trained as a theologian and jurist, and under Celestine III, his uncle, he became (1190) a cardinal. At the time of his election as pope, Innocent seems already to have formed his theory, a most extreme ecclesiastico-political doctrine: that since things of the spirit take preeminence over things of the body, and since the church rules the spirit and earthly monarchs rule the body, earthly monarchs must be in all things in subjection to the pope; the doctrine that the sphere of the church was limited had no real place in Innocent's idea. He set out immediately after his election to realize his ideal of the pope as political, as well as ecclesiastical, ruler of the world. In imperial affairs he was constantly active. He acknowledged as king of Sicily the future Holy Roman Emperor FREDERICK II after Frederick's mother, the Empress CONSTANCE, had accepted papal suzerainty over Sicily and given up certain ecclesiastical privileges; on Constance's death, Innocent accepted Frederick as his ward, a trust he faithfully executed, as even his enemies admitted. In Germany the dispute between PHILIP OF SWABIA and OTTO IV was arbitrated by the pope in favor of Otto (1201). Later (1207–8) the pope favored Philip, but after Philip's murder, Innocent crowned Otto (1209) as emperor, only to excommunicate him (1210) and dictate the election of the papal ward, Frederick, as German king (1212). Frederick made elaborate promises (as had Otto) favorable to the Holy See. Innocent's relations with England proceeded to the same political end, but this was hastened by a purely ecclesiastical quarrel over the election of an archbishop of Canterbury. Innocent set aside the two rival claimants and procured the election of Stephen LANGTON; King JOHN, enraged at what he felt was unwarrantable interference by the pope and at the obduracy of the clergy in opposing the demands of the king, persecuted the church. As a result the pope laid England under the interdict, excommunicated John (1209), and even considered deposing him. The people and the barons supported the church and John had to submit; he received England and Ireland in fief from the pope, promising annual tribute to the Holy See. Subsequently the pope stood by John after the barons coerced him into granting the Magna Carta, for Innocent declared it null as a forcibly exacted promise and also as a vassal's promise made without his overlord's knowledge. PANDULF became Innocent's legate in England. Innocent was also the virtual overlord of Christian Spain, Scandinavia, Hungary, and the Latin East. Philip II of France remained independent of Innocent politically, but on a moral question, Philip's divorce, Innocent forced the king to bow to the canon law. The great failures of Innocent's policy were the Fourth Crusade (see CRUSADES) and the conduct of Italy. That crusade, proclaimed and blessed by Innocent, never went to the Holy Land, but attacked instead two Christian states, Zara and the Byzantine Empire. Innocent inveighed against the disobedience of the crusaders, but later accepted the fait accompli and tried to spread the Latin rite over the Latin Empire of Constantinople;

in spite of a new Latin patriarchate, these efforts were futile, and the schism of East and West was only exacerbated. In Italy, Innocent reclaimed the Patrimony of St. Peter (see PAPAL STATES), the duchy of Spoleto, the March of Ancona, and the Ravenna district; he was recognized as temporal overlord by Tuscany, but northern Italian cities were unruly and maintained their independence throughout Innocent's pontificate. Innocent initiated the Albigensian mission and the ALBIGENSIAN CRUSADE; when he heard of the misbehavior of the crusaders of Simon de MONTFORT, he protested in vain. He supported the Teutonic Knights in the incursions along the Baltic. Amid all his political activity Innocent was most energetic in the administration of the church. In this direction the triumph of his pontificate was the Fourth LATERAN COUNCIL (1215), one of the greatest of councils. His was the original impetus behind St. Dominic's mission, and he provided the first approbation of the institute of St. Francis. Innocent's interest in law was ever active; thus as pope he constantly held court, with a good name for impartiality. He wrote extensively; his tract *De contemptu mundi* [on the contempt of this world] was widely read in the Middle Ages. Innocent's theories of the papal monarchy had a profound effect, eventually damaging to the papacy, as when Boniface VIII attempted to use them. They are at variance with Roman Catholic doctrine, which teaches (with St. Thomas Aquinas) that the state has its proper sphere within which its rulers are as responsible to God for their conduct as the pope is for the conduct of the church. Innocent III was succeeded by Honorius III. See L. E. Elliott-Binns, *Innocent III* (1931, repr. 1968); C. E. Smith, *Innocent III, Church Defender* (1951, repr. 1971); S. R. Packard, *Europe and the Church under Innocent III* (rev. ed. 1968).

Innocent IV, d. 1254, pope (1243–54), a Genoese named Sinibaldo Fieschi; successor of Celestine IV. He was of a noble family. Although he had been a known imperialist, Innocent as pope quickly took up the papal struggle with Emperor FREDERICK II and the HOHENSTAUFEN. After a futile treaty he felt unsafe in Rome and fled to Lyons, where he convened the Council of Lyons (1245; see LYONS, FIRST COUNCIL OF). Frederick was condemned again and declared deposed, and Innocent supported Henry Raspe and, later, William II of Holland as pretenders to the imperium. He also tried to get an English or French prince to take Sicily as a fief, but Frederick was too strong. Frederick died as the pope was opening a crusade against him (1250). Innocent did not spare the other Hohenstaufen, CONRAD IV and MANFRED, but after finding them invincible in Sicily, he recognized CONRADIN as king of Sicily. Innocent was almost wholly occupied with his quarrel with the Hohenstaufen, and the taxes he levied to continue it made him unpopular with clergy and laity alike. He was succeeded by Alexander IV.

Innocent V, d. 1276, pope (1276), a Savoyard named Peter of Tarentaise; successor of GREGORY X. He was a Dominican and studied at Paris under St. Thomas Aquinas and St. Albertus Magnus. He became an eminent theologian and composed a standard commentary on Peter Lombard's *Sentences.* He was archbishop of Lyons (after 1272) and a leader in the council there in 1274. Innocent died five months after his election as pope and was succeeded by Adrian V. He was beatified in 1898.

Innocent VI, d. 1362, pope (1352–62), a Frenchman named Étienne Aubert; successor of Clement VI. He was a well-known jurist and was created cardinal in 1342. He lived at Avignon. He was one of the few reforming popes of his age, doing his best to eliminate venality from church administration. His major quarrel was with Holy Roman Emperor CHARLES IV over the Golden Bull. Innocent sent Cardinal de Albornoz into Italy to pacify the Papal States and liberated Cola di RIENZI to go with him. He was succeeded by Urban V.

Innocent VIII, 1432–92, pope (1484–92), a Genoese named Giovanni Battista Cibò; successor of Sixtus IV. He was made a cardinal in 1473. His close friend, Cardinal Giuliano della Rovere (later Pope Julius II), largely directed the papal affairs. Like his predecessors Innocent wished to stop the Turkish advance, but he succeeded by means other than the crusade he originally planned. Djem, brother and rival of Sultan BEYAZID II, was being held captive by Pierre d'AUBUSSON; the pope saw that if he held over the sultan the threat of supporting Djem's pretensions, Beyazid would come to terms. Beyazid (1490) agreed to leave Europe at peace if the pope kept Djem captive. Innocent VIII was not a man of bad character after he entered the clergy, although he was known as a nepotist and was attacked by Savonarola for his worldliness. He was succeeded by Alexander VI.

Innocent XI, 1611–89, pope (1676–89), an Italian named Benedetto Odescalchi, b. Como; successor of Clement X. He was elected because of his great saintliness and desire for reform. His election had been opposed by Louis XIV, with whom he had a long, bitter quarrel over GALLICANISM, begun in this phase with Louis's collection of the revenues of vacant benefices all over France. The Gallican statement of 1682 brought a papal condemnation; and when Louis revoked the Edict of Nantes, perhaps to gain papal favor, Innocent denounced the proceedings (1685). James II of England, Louis's ally, also excited Innocent's displeasure, but there is no proof of the allegation that Innocent supported the Protestant William III in his accession to the English throne. He was succeeded by Alexander VIII. Innocent was beatified in 1956.

Innocent XII, 1615–1700, pope (1691–1700), a Neapolitan named Antonio Pignatelli; successor of Alexander VIII. He was frequently employed by his predecessors as a nuncio, and Innocent XI created him cardinal. His election ended a five-month deadlock in the conclave. He showed himself a stern reformer, especially concerning nepotism, which he abolished. He brought Louis XIV over to his point of view on GALLICANISM, and he condemned certain of Fénelon's doctrines as quietistic. He was universally loved for his charity and piety. Clement XI succeeded him.

Innocents, Holy, children of Bethlehem killed by order of Herod the Great, who hoped to destroy the Infant Jesus. Mat. 2.16–18. Their feast (as martyrs), formerly called Childermas in the West, is Dec. 28.

Innoshima (ēn-nō'shĭmä), city (1970 pop. 41,729), Hiroshima prefecture, on Innoshima Island, Japan, on the Hiuchi Sea. It is a fishing and commercial port and an agricultural center.

Innsbruck (ĭns'bro͝ok), city (1971 pop. 115,200), capital of Tyrol prov., SW Austria, on the Inn River. A famous summer and winter resort, it is also an industrial, commercial, and transport center. Manufactures include textiles, metal products, processed food, and printed materials. Strategically located in the Eastern Alps, Innsbruck grew to early prominence as a transalpine trading post. It was established as a fortified town by 1180 and received city rights in the early 13th cent. It supplanted Merano as the capital of the Tyrol in 1420. The Tyrolese peasants, led by Andreas Hofer, made their heroic stand (1809) against French and Bavarian troops near Innsbruck; a monument in the city commemorates the event. The Hofkirche (built 1553–63), a Franciscan church, is an architectural gem; it contains a large monument to Emperor Maximilian I (d.1519), who often resided in Innsbruck. Equally famous is the Fürstenburg, a 15th-century castle, which has a balcony with a gilded copper roof (*Goldenes Dachl*). The Column of St. Anne (1706) is a landmark in Innsbruck's main thoroughfare, the Maria Theresienstrasse. The city has several museums, notably the Ferdinandeum; a botanical garden, which has a large collection of Alpine plants; and a university (founded 1677). The winter Olympic games were held in Innsbruck in 1964.

Inns of Court, collective name of the four legal societies in London that have the exclusive right of admission to the BAR. These societies—Lincoln's Inn, Gray's Inn, the Inner Temple, and the Middle Temple (see also TEMPLE, THE)—date from before the 14th cent. They take their name from the buildings where originally schools of law were held, apprentice lawyers gathering to learn from masters of law, much as in guild training. Today the societies are more like clubs, although they still control admission to the bar. The Inns of Chancery were lesser societies (preparatory colleges for law), dependent on the Inns of Court; their importance declined in the 18th cent., and they disappeared in the 19th cent. See W. B. Prest, *The Inns of Court under Elizabeth I and the Early Stuarts, 1590–1640* (1972).

Innuitians (ĭnyo͞oĭsh'ənz), mountain range, stretching c.800 mi (1,290 km) through the Arctic Archipelago, Northwest Territories, N Canada. Largely unexplored, the range runs NE from the Parry Islands to N Ellesmere Island, then south along the island's east coast. It rises to c.9,000 ft (2,740 m) on Ellesmere Island, where most of the range is covered by an ice cap. The Innuitians form the northern rim of the Canadian Shield.

Ino (ī'nō), in Greek mythology, daughter of Cadmus. She was the wife of ATHAMAS, to whom she bore Learchus and Melicertes. She plotted to kill her stepchildren, Phrixus and Helle, but their mother, Nephele, saved them with the help of a winged ram (see GOLDEN FLEECE). Later, when Athamas went mad and killed Learchus, Ino and Melicertes leaped into the sea to their deaths and were changed into sea deities, Leucothea and Palaemon.

inoculation, in medicine, introduction of a preparation into the tissues or fluids of the body for the purpose of preventing or curing certain diseases. The preparation is usually a weakened culture of the agent causing the disease, as in VACCINATION against smallpox; however, it may also be composed of ANTITOXINS, which provide immunity themselves, or TOXOIDS, which are proteins that stimulate the body to produce antitoxins (see IMMUNITY). Various forms of inoculation were used from ancient times in China, India, and Persia, but it remained for the English physician Edward Jenner in the late 18th cent. to demonstrate its feasibility to the Western world. The term *inoculation* is used also to refer to the introduction of certain substances into plant tissues or to the placement of microorganisms into culture media (for experimental or diagnostic purposes) or into the soil.

İnönü, İsmet (ĭsmĕt' ēnönü'), 1884–1973, Turkish statesman and soldier, president of Turkey (1938–50). He served in the Balkan Wars and World War I and became (1920) chief of staff to Mustafa Kemal, later known as Kemal ATATÜRK. He played an important part in the establishment of the Turkish republic and in Kemal's victory over the Greeks, and he represented Turkey at the Conference of Lausanne (see LAUSANNE, TREATY OF, 1922–23). As prime minister (1923–24, 1925–37) he ably seconded the reforms of Atatürk, whom he succeeded (1938) as president of the republic. İnönü instituted free general elections for the first time in 1950; his party was defeated, and he was succeeded by Celal Bayar. After a military coup (1960; see TURKEY) and the promulgation of a new constitution, İnönü's Republican People's party won a parliamentary plurality in the elections of 1961. He again became premier, heading successive coalition cabinets until 1965, when his government fell.

inositol (ĭnō'sĭtōl): see VITAMIN.

Inouye, Kaoru (kou'ro͞o ĭnō'ā), 1835–1915, Japanese statesman. He was a leader of the antiforeign movement in his native Choshu fief, and helped set fire to the British legation in Edo (now Tokyo) in 1862. He changed his views after study in England (1863) with Hirobuma Ito, and returned to urge Westernization and overthrow of the shogunate. After the Meiji restoration he was influential in reorganizing government finances on modern lines, especially in the reform of the land tax system. He was a friend and patron of the Mitsui financial house. As foreign minister (1885–87), he failed to negotiate a revision of the unequal treaties; this failure and his unpopular Westernizing influence forced him to resign. Later he served as home minister and as finance minister under Ito.

Inowrocław (ēnôvrôts'läf), Ger. *Hohensalza,* city (1970 pop. 54,817), N central Poland. It is an important railway and industrial center where agricultural machinery, glass, and bricks are produced. It is also a health resort, with saltwater springs. Rock salt is mined nearby. Chartered in 1267, Inowrocław passed to Prussia in 1772 and reverted to Poland in 1919.

inquest, in law, a body of men appointed by law to inquire into certain matters. The term also refers to the inquiry itself as well as to the findings of the inquiry. The most usual form of inquest today is that conducted by the CORONER to discover the cause of a death that was sudden, violent, or occurred in prison. This inquest is similar to the proceedings of a GRAND JURY. Witnesses are called, but a person suspected of guilt is not permitted to make a defense. Natural death, accidental death, suicide, and murder are among the possible findings. Criminal prosecution may follow a verdict of murder or culpable accident.

Inquisition (ĭn"kwĭzĭsh'ən), tribunal of the Roman Catholic Church established in the Middle Ages for the suppression of heresy. In the early Middle Ages investigation of heresy was a duty of the bishops. Alarmed especially by the spread of Albigensianism (see ALBIGENSES), the popes issued increasingly stringent instructions as to the methods for dealing with heretics. Finally, in 1233, Pope Gregory IX formally established the papal Inquisition, dispatching Dominican friars to S France to conduct inquests. When an inquisitor arrived in a district, a month of grace was allowed to all who wished to confess to heresy and to recant; these were given a light penance, which was intended to confirm their faith. After the period of grace, persons accused of heresy who had not abjured were brought to trial. The defendants were not given the names of their accusers, but they could name their enemies and thus nullify any testimony by these persons. After 1254 the accused had no right to counsel, but those found guilty could appeal to the pope. The trials were conducted secretly in the presence of a representative of the bishop and of a stipulated number of local laymen. Torture of the accused and his witnesses soon became customary and notorious, despite the long-standing papal condemnation of torture (e.g., by Nicholas I); Innocent IV ultimately permitted torture in cases of heresy. Most trials resulted in a verdict of guilty. The verdict and sentence of the inquisitor were enforced by the local ruler only; heresy was considered a civil as well as a spiritual offense. Burning at the stake was thought to be the fitting punishment for unrecanted heresy, probably through analogy with the Roman law on treason. However, the burning of heretics was not common in the Middle Ages; the usual punishments were penance, fine, and imprisonment. A verdict of guilty also meant the confiscation of property by the civil ruler, who might turn over part of it to the church. This practice led to graft, blackmail, and simony and also created suspicion of some of the inquests. Generally the inquisitors were eager to receive abjurations of heresy and to avoid trials; their purpose was to win back the heretics, rather than to burn them. The ecclesiastics were easily satisfied with assurances of goodwill—the sternest repressors were the secular rulers, who came to use the persecution of heresy as a weapon of state, as in the case of the suppression of the KNIGHTS TEMPLARS. The Inquisition was an emergency device and was employed mainly in S France, N Italy, and Germany. In 1542, Paul III assigned the medieval Inquisition to the Congregation of the Inquisition, or Holy Office. This institution, which became known as the Roman Inquisition, was intended to combat Protestantism, but it is perhaps best known historically for its condemnation of Galileo. After the Second Vatican Conference, it was replaced (1965) by the Congregation for the Doctrine of the Faith, which governs vigilance in matters of faith.

The Spanish Inquisition. The Spanish Inquisition was independent of the medieval Inquisition. It was established (1478) by Ferdinand and Isabella with the reluctant approval of Sixtus IV. One of the first and most notorious heads was Tomás de TORQUEMADA. It was entirely controlled by the Spanish kings, and the pope's only hold over it was in naming the inquisitor general. The popes were never reconciled to the institution, which they regarded as usurping a church prerogative. The purpose of the Spanish Inquisition was to discover and punish converted Jews (and later Muslims) who were insincere. However, soon no Spaniard could feel safe from it; thus, St. Ignatius of Loyola and St. Theresa of Ávila were investigated for heresy. The censorship policy even condemned books approved by the Holy See. The Spanish Inquisition was much harsher, more highly organized, and far freer with the death penalty than the medieval Inquisition; its *autos-da-fé* became notorious. The Spanish government tried to establish the Inquisition in all its dominions; but in the Spanish Netherlands the local officials did not cooperate, and the inquisitors were chased (1510) out of Naples, apparently with the pope's connivance. The Spanish Inquisition was finally abolished in 1834.

Bibliography. Unfortunately, many historical accounts of the Inquisitions are affected by religious bias, and much of the most recent research is available only in monographs and historical journals. The old standard scholarly (but anti-Catholic) works are those of Henry Charles LEA, who, however, did not properly distinguish between the different Inquisitions. Elphège Vacandard, *The Inquisition* (tr. 1908) approaches the subject from a Roman Catholic view. A. S. Tuberville, *Mediaeval Heresy and the Inquisition* (1920, repr. 1964) utilizes later research, as does the anti-Catholic G. G. Coulton, *Inquisition and Liberty* (1938, repr. 1968). For the Spanish Inquisition, see studies by A. S. Tuberville (1932, repr. 1968), Cecil Roth (1938, repr. 1964), H. A. F. Kamen (1965), R. E. Greenleaf (1969), and P. J. Hauber (1969).

insanity or **lunacy,** mental disorder of such severity as to render its victim incapable of managing his or her affairs or of conforming to social standards. The term *lunacy* [from Lat. *luna*=moon] has its basis in the ancient belief that the moon has the power to drive people insane; thus persons now thought of as mentally ill were once supposed to have become deranged by being exposed to the full moon. Carl Jung defined insanity as the condition in which the individual's unconscious controls his conscious mind. Legally the term insanity is used chiefly to denote mental aberrations or defects that may relieve a person from the legal consequences of his acts. Tests for insanity often try to ascertain whether a defendant can distinguish right from wrong or whether the defendant acted on an "irresistible impulse." The law distinguishes between present insanity, which renders a defendant incapable of understanding proceedings or making defenses, and past insanity, comprising those psychological states that excuse conduct ordinarily considered criminal and that make certain civil transactions invalid. The concepts of criminal and civil insanity differ to some degree from those of psychopathology (see PSYCHONEUROSIS), and there has been much medical criticism of the legal categories. The law of criminal insanity is designed to save from ordinary penal sanctions persons who are not responsible for their own acts and who could not have been deterred by any threatened punishment. In the United States the methods of determining insanity in criminal cases vary; decisions on insanity may be made by state mental health authorities, by the trial judge, by the regular jury, by a special jury, or by a commission composed of lawyers, physicians, and laymen. A lesser degree of mental aberration is required for civil insanity than for criminal insanity; in general, extreme deficiency of intelligence or a marked defect in reason may be sufficient. The legal presumption of civil sanity is strong in the case of a testator or one in the prime of life and weak in the case of one who is sick or old and decrepit. A harmless although insane person who is unable to carry on his affairs may be placed under guardianship on application to a court. Mentally ill persons termed lunatics by law (including the criminally insane) who are dangerous to themselves or others may be committed to institutions on the application of a close relative or of the public authorities. See R. C. Allen, ed., *Mental Impairment and Legal Incompetency* (1968); J. W. Polier, *The Rule of Law and the Role of Psychiatry* (1968); Herbert Fingarette, *The Meaning of Criminal Insanity* (1972).

inscription, WRITING on durable material. The art is called epigraphy. Modern inscriptions are made for permanent, monumental record, as on gravestones, cornerstones, and building fronts; they are often decorative and imitative of ancient (usually Roman) methods. The only current use of inscriptions that has no accepted substitute, the marking of graves, is also the oldest continuous use. The first writing was probably universally executed on hard materials, mainly stones (rough or hewn), clay (often marked when wet), metal, bone, and ivory. When light materials like paper were developed, it was possible to distinguish between writing for temporary use and permanent recording, and epigraphy became restricted. Outside Western history epigraphy was of importance in two independent civilizations—in the remarkable art of the MAYA, TOLTEC, and AZTEC cultures (see PRE-COLUMBIAN ART AND ARCHITECTURE), and in China. There is also the exotic mid-Pacific epigraphy of EASTER ISLAND. The earliest Chinese inscriptions are on bronze (c.1500 B.C.), and there are later writings on bone from N China. Dating from the classical period, before 200 B.C., are odes on great stone drums found in Shensi. The invention of paper (A.D. c.100) ended the role of epigraphy in China. The bilingual inscriptions near ORKHON contain minor Chinese texts as well as the oldest known Turkic material. The Hindus used palm leaves for writing early in their history, and their inscriptions do not record the older forms of their language. The most important are Prakrit inscriptions of ASOKA (3d cent. B.C.). The first Sanskrit inscriptions date from some centuries later. The course of Western epigraphy begins in Mesopotamia and on the Nile. The Mesopotamian writing, CUNEIFORM, was invented c.4000 B.C., probably by the Sumerians. It was created for writing on sun-dried brick. This combines durability with lightness and contrasts favorably with all other epigraphic materials in convenience of making and handling. It thus anticipates some of the merits of paper. (See BABYLONIA; ASSYRIA; HITTITES; ELAM. For notes on examples of epigraphic treasure-troves, see ERECH; LAGASH; NINEVEH; NIPPUR; SUSA; TEL EL AMARNA; BOĞAZKÖY.) An Eastern congener of Mesopotamian epigraphy is found in the seal inscriptions on faïence and ivory (c.3000 B.C.) at the archaeological sites of the INDUS VALLEY CIVILIZATION. Long after, in Persia, the Achaemenids revived cuneiform writing in an altered form; their chief monument is the BEHISTUN INSCRIPTIONS (c.500 B.C.) of Darius I. In EGYPT the HIEROGLYPHIC epigraphy had a parallel development. From the I dynasty (4th millennium B.C.) inscriptions of the Nile present a grand panorama of history, past the age of the PYRAMID to the XII dynasty, heyday of hieroglyphic writing, then to the New Empire, with the splendid rock inscriptions at THEBES. Egyptian epigraphy lost its vitality more from the development of papyrus than from the downfall of the kingdom. Its influences are found everywhere in the Arabian peninsula in inscriptions of the 1st millennium B.C.; examples are the MOABITE STONE, Phoenician stones and coins, inscriptions near Damascus, and the Himyaritic writing of Yemen (see SHEBA). In the Mediterranean, the earliest epigraphy of Greek culture appears in AEGEAN CIVILIZATION and MINOAN CIVILIZATION. In Cyprus there are inscriptions of many ages, cuneiform and Greek writing side by side. From the expansion of Greece through the course of Roman history, epigraphy flourished everywhere, and inscriptions are literally innumerable. Among the older Greek inscriptions are those on vases, coins, votive offerings, statues, and the like, besides accounts of expenditures in temples, annals (e.g., the Parian Chronicle on PÁROS), codes of laws (at GORTYNA), decrees, bookkeeping accounts, lists of citizens, ostraca (see OSTRACISM), and many graffiti (wall scribblings; see GRAFFITO). Greek influence was, of course, decisive in Italy, first in the inscriptions of the ETRUSCAN CIVILIZATION. There are also many inscriptions in Italic languages, notably the IGUVINE TABLES. Latin epigraphy began with religious documents, but by the end of the republic it was touching every phase of life. Contemporary with the late republic there was a Celtic epigraphy in Gaul, at first in Greek letters; but the chief Celtic inscriptions are in the OGHAM writings of the Christian era. The Germanic RUNES are another European alphabet used in inscriptions. Latin epigraphy extended in time far beyond the Roman Empire; the stoneworkers of Christianity adapted the old forms, first in the catacombs, then in churches. Modern monumental inscription is in the same tradition, but materially renovated by the neoclassicism of the Italian Renaissance. For the history and examples of epigraphy, see histories of appropriate cultures, countries, languages, literatures, and periods of art. See also CALLIGRAPHY.

insect, invertebrate animal of the class Insecta of the phylum ARTHROPODA. Like other arthropods, an insect has a hard outer covering, or exoskeleton, a segmented body, and jointed legs. Adult insects typically have wings and are the only flying invertebrates. The body of the typical adult insect is divided into three distinct parts, the head, thorax, and abdomen. The head bears three pairs of mouth parts, one pair of compound eyes, three simple eyes (ocelli), and one pair of jointed sensory antennae. The thorax is divided into three segments, each with a pair of jointed legs, and bears two pairs of wings. The abdomen has posterior appendages associated with reproduction. The exoskeleton is composed of a horny substance called chitin. Insects breathe through a complex network of air tubes (tracheae) that open to the outside through a series of small valved apertures (spiracles) along the sides of the body. In chewing insects the digestive system includes a muscular gizzard that is lacking in sucking insects. The simple circulatory system is composed of a tubular heart that pumps blood forward into the head, from which it diffuses through the tissues and back into the heart. The aquatic larvae of many insects breathe by means of external gills; some very primitive species breathe directly through the body wall. There are about 700,000 known insect species, three times as many as all other animal species together, and thousands of new ones are described each year. At present they are commonly classified in 27 orders. The largest order is that of the BEETLES (Coleoptera); next, in order of size, are the MOTHS and BUTTERFLIES (Lepidoptera), the WASPS, ANTS, and BEES (Hymenoptera), and the FLIES and MOSQUITOES (Diptera). Other major orders are the true BUGS (Hemiptera), the CICADAS, APHIDS, and SCALE INSECTS (Homoptera), and the roaches, MANTIDS, and GRASSHOPPERS (Orthoptera). Insects are found throughout the world except near the poles and pervade every habitat except the sea (although there is one marine species of water strider). Fossil records indicate that many species exist today in much the same form as they did 200 million years ago. Their enormous biological success is attributed to their small size, their high reproductive rate, and the remarkable adaptive abilities of the group as a whole, shown by the enormous variety in body structure and way of life. The mouthparts may be adapted to chewing, suck-

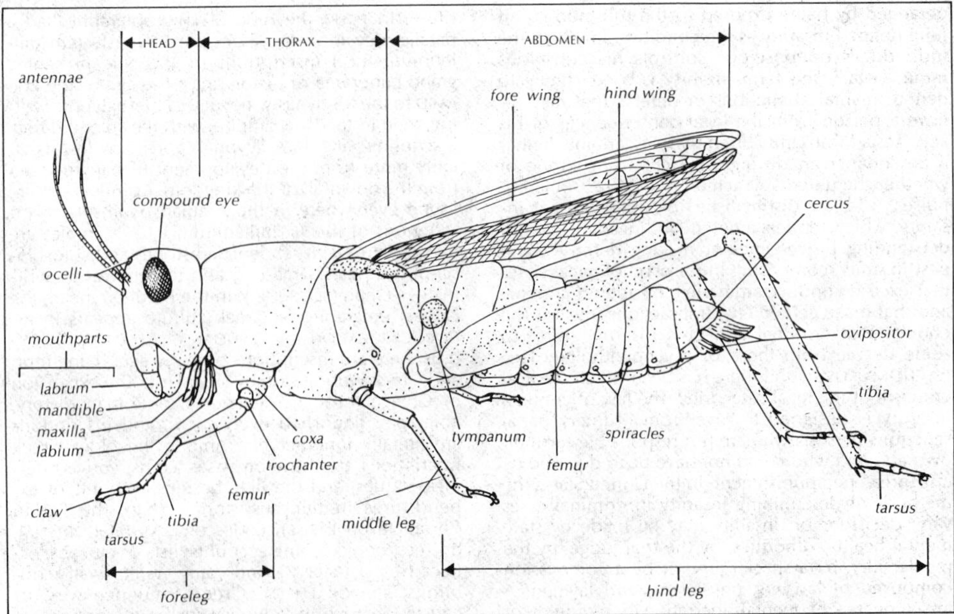

External anatomy of a female grasshopper, representative of the class Insecta

ing, piercing, or lapping and the legs for walking, running, jumping, burrowing, or swimming. Insects may feed on plants or decaying matter or prey upon other small animals (especially other insects) or parasitize larger ones; they may be omnivorous or highly specialized in their diets. They display a remarkable variety of adaptive shapes and colors that may serve either as camouflage or as warning (see MIMICRY). Some have stinging spines or hairs and blistering or noxious secretions, used for defense. A few species, notably the FIREFLIES, produce light, used as a signal in courtship, by a chemical reaction. The sexes are separate in insects, and reproduction is usually sexual, although in many insect groups eggs sometimes develop without fertilization by sperm (see PARTHENOGENESIS). In some insects, such as bees, unfertilized eggs become males and fertilized eggs females. In others, such as aphids, all-female generations are produced by parthenogenesis. Eggs are usually laid in a sheltered place; in a few insects they are retained and hatched internally. After hatching, the insect must molt periodically as it grows, since the rigid exoskeleton does not allow much expansion. A new, soft exoskeleton forms beneath the old one, and after each molt the insect undergoes a rapid expansion before its new covering hardens. The stages between molts are called instars; the final instar is the adult. In nearly all insects growth involves a metamorphosis, that is, a transformation in form and in way of life. Complete, or indirect, metamorphosis is characteristic of over 80% of all insect species and has four stages: egg, larva, pupa, and adult. The wingless, wormlike larva (in many species called a grub or a caterpillar) is completely unlike the adult, and its chief activities are eating and growing. Only the simple eyes are present, and the mouth is the chewing type, even in species whose adults have other kinds of mouthparts. After several molts the larva enters a quiescent stage called the pupa; the pupa does not eat and usually does not move, but within the exoskeleton a major transformation occurs that involves the reorganization of organ systems as well as the development of such adult external structures as wings and compound eyes. In some insects the pupa is enclosed in a protective case, called the cocoon, built by the larva just before pupation. When the transformation is complete the final molt occurs: the adult emerges, its wings fill with blood and expand, and the new exoskeleton hardens. The chief function of the adult is propagation; in some species it does not eat. Incomplete, or gradual, metamorphosis is seen in members of less advanced orders (such as locusts and their relatives and the true bugs). The larva, often called a nymph (or, if aquatic, a naiad) is usually similar in form to the adult, but lacks wings. The wings begin as external bumps on the larva and the adult emerges from the last molt without having undergone a pupal stage. In a few very primitive, wingless insects (such as the SILVERFISH) there is no metamorphosis. The insect emerges from the egg as a miniature adult and the only further changes are in size and in maturation of the reproductive organs. Plant-eating insects cause enormous damage to crops; any part of a plant is subject to attack by either the adult or the larva of some insect. Among the well known plant pests are the locust, ARMYWORM, aphid, CORN BORER, CODDLING MOTH, TENT CATERPILLAR, JAPANESE BEETLE, GYPSY MOTH, BAGWORM, and scale insect. Insect carriers of human diseases include the mosquito, HOUSEFLY, TSETSE FLY, and FLEA. On the other hand, many insects are valuable as predators on the harmful species, and some are important as scavengers and as aerators of the soil (see SCARAB BEETLE). Most important, many plants depend on insects as agents of pollination; in fact, flowering plants and insects evolved together. Insects are the source of useful products such as HONEY, beeswax, SILK, LAC, and COCHINEAL. They are a major source of food for many animals, and some are eaten by humans in many parts of the world. The FRUIT FLY has been the major experimental animal used in genetics. See F. E. Lutz, *Field Book of Insects of the United States and Canada* (rev. ed. 1948); P. P. and M. L. Larson, *Lives of Social Insects* (1968); D. J. Borror and D. M. DeLong, *An Introduction to the Study of Insects* (3d ed. 1971); E. O. Wilson, *The Insect Societies* (1971); L. A. Swan and C. S. Papp, *The Common Insects of North America* (1972).

insecticides, chemical, biological, or other agent used to destroy insect pests; generally the term is applied to chemical agents only. The modern use of chemical insecticides in the United States dates from 1867 when Paris green was used to control outbreaks of the Colorado potato beetle. The spectacular success of this application stimulated widespread experimentation, and within a decade Paris green and kerosene oil emulsion were being employed against a variety of chewing and sucking insects. In the early part of the 20th cent. fluorine compounds and plant-derived insecticides were developed. The use of insecticides in the United States had become sufficiently commonplace by the 1920s that concern over residues in foodstuffs began to arise; it was at this time that the need for regulation of insecticide usage was recognized. Insecticides used prior to the introduction of DDT were almost exclusively inorganic chemicals; the exceptions were plant derivatives, such as nicotine, the pyrethrins, and rotenone. The discovery in Europe in 1939 of the insecticidal value of DDT, a synthetic organic compound, was a revolutionary occurrence in the development of insecticides; this event led to the synthesis of thousands of organic chemicals, many of which have replaced earlier insecticides; over 400 chemical insecticidal agents are registered with the U.S. government. Chemical insecticides are generally the first line of defense in controlling insect outbreaks; they are used because they are immediately and highly effective, able to bring large insect populations under control, and can be employed as needed. Their use has contributed markedly to increased yields, improved quality, and greater efficiency of plant production, and has brought stability to agricultural enterprise. However, the use of insecticides has certain disadvantages: Insects may become resistant to them; chemical insecticides may disrupt the ecosystem with adverse effects; and health hazards may result because of residues remaining on treated material. Increasing awareness of these health problems has resulted in vigorous demands from governmental agencies for the development of insecticides that break down rapidly into nontoxic substances and act selectively, i.e., kill only certain harmful insects and nothing else. Chlorinated hydrocarbon insecticides, which account for the largest volume of chemical insecticides used annually, have fallen into disfavor because they are toxic to beneficial insects as well as to higher animals and to man and because they do not break down easily, becoming concentrated in animals high on food chains. Their use has been banned or restricted in many countries. The most common representative of this group is DDT; others include benzene hexachloride, lindane, aldrin, dieldrin, chlordane, heptachlor, endrin, and toxaphene. All chemicals of this group are powerful contact and stomach poisons. Organophosphate insecticides are of increasing interest because they break down into nontoxic substances more quickly than chlorinated hydrocarbons. Organophosphates are the largest and most versatile group of chemical insecticides in use at the present time. They kill through contact, ingestion, or fumigant action, attacking the nervous systems of insects. Included in this group are parathion, a pesticide with one of the highest mammalian toxicities, and Malathion, a compound with one of the lowest. Carbamate insecticides, which are esters of carbanilic acid, include some of the most promising chemical insecticides. They break down more quickly than organophosphates and are less hazardous to man. Carbamates act as contact poisons against insect larvae, nymphs, and adults. An example is sevin, or carbaryl, an N-methyl aromatic carbamate ester. Problems with chemical insecticides have led to increased interest in biological control agents. Microorganisms, such as viruses and bacteria, that are harmful to certain insects but not to other animals or man are sometimes used as biological control agents. In some instances the control agent has been a group of predator insects that is introduced in an area to prey on a particular insect pest. Large numbers of insects can be sterilized and then released to mate with normal insects. No offspring are produced by these matings, ultimately reducing the insect population. Biological control agents do not usually create any environmental pollutants. In many cases they are highly selective in action. However since many complex factors affect their action, biological control agents are not always effective. In many instances chemical insecticides must be used. See C. L. Metcalf and W. P. Flint, *Destructive and Useful Insects: Their Habits and Control* (3d ed. 1951); Rachel Carson, *Silent Spring* (1962); R. D. O'Brien, *Insecticides: Action and Metabolism* (1967).

insectivore (ĭnsĕk'təvōr"), term broadly given to any insect-eating animal or plant. More specifically, the term refers to mammals of the order Insectivora (see CHORDATA), including the SHREW, MOLE, HEDGEHOG, TENREC, and SOLENODON. Insectivores are small animals, ranging from 2 to 16 in. (5-40 cm) in length; they are generally quite active, and most of them are nocturnal. They feed on a variety of small animals, particularly worms and insects. Members of this group are thought to be closely related to the earliest placental mammals. The tenrecs have certain anatomical features in common with the more primitive pouched, or marsupial, mammals. The other groups of placental mammals, including the primates, the order to which man belongs, are thought to have evolved as radiations from a primitive insectivore stock. The tree-shrews were formerly classified as insectivores, but are now usually classified as primates; they represent a transitional form between the two groups. Primitive insectivores may have been arboreal, e.g., the tree shrew, but modern forms are ground or even underground dwellers; the mole is highly specialized for subterranean life. Insectivores are found in the Old and New Worlds from subarctic regions to the tropics, but there are none in Australia, New Guinea, New Zealand, or most of South America.

insectivorous plants: see BLADDERWORT; PITCHER PLANT; VENUS'S-FLYTRAP.

Inside Passage, natural, protected waterway, c.950 mi (1,530 km) long, threading through the Alexander Archipelago off the coast of British Columbia and SE Alaska. From Seattle, Wash., to Skagway, Alaska, or via Cross Sound to the Gulf of Alaska, the route uses channels and straits between islands and the mainland that afford protection from the storms and open waters of the Pacific Ocean. Snow-capped mountains, forests, waterfalls, glaciers, and deep, narrow channels give the Inside Passage great scenic beauty. It was known to Spanish, Russian, English, and American explorers. It is the route generally used by ships sailing between the continental United States and Alaska.

insomnia, abnormal wakefulness or inability to SLEEP. The condition may result from illness or physical discomfort, or it may be caused by stimulants such as coffee or drugs. However, frequently some psychological factor, such as worry or tension, is the cause. Mild insomnia may often be relieved by a soothing activity like reading or listening to soft music. Chronic or severe insomnia requires treatment of the underlying physical or psychological disorder. Sedatives and sleep-inducing drugs may be employed, but they should be taken under the supervision of a physician.

installment buying and selling, buying and selling of goods on credit, with the stipulation that payments shall be made at specified intervals in set amounts. The goods may be used by the buyer before or upon the first payment but legally belong to the seller until the last payment has been made. If the buyer defaults, the seller reclaims the goods, and all former payments are forfeit. The installment buyer pays a higher price, the difference covering interest on unpaid balances, insurance, and financing charges. Originating in Paris in the early 19th cent., the practice of retailing goods on the installment plan was first used in the United States to sell sewing machines, pianos, and household furnishings. After 1916, when manufacturers began to offer automobiles on the time-payment plan, installment selling rapidly came to include durable goods of every kind (household appliances, radios, oil burners), which otherwise would have been out of reach for the average income earner. Large merchandisers through various devices now make it possible for their customers to buy any type of goods on time (e.g., automobile tires, clothing). Long-term installment purchases are usually financed indirectly by firms specializing in that form of credit. Many banks offer personal loans to consumers that may be repaid in installments. Most states regulate installment transactions to prevent their becoming oppressive. Credit buying expands demand in periods of optimism, but when the purchaser's credit is exhausted it causes aggregate demand to decrease and may lead to a recession phase in the business cycle. See CREDIT CARD. See Adrian Rondileau, *Education for Installment Buying* (1944, repr. 1973); E. R. McAlister, *Retail Installment Credit* (1964); Neil Runcie, *The Economics of Installment Credit* (1969).

instinct, in psychology, term used generally to indicate an innate tendency to action, or pattern of behavior, elicited by specific stimuli and fulfilling vital needs of the organism. Examples of almost purely instinctive behavior are found in the behavior of many lower animals, in which activity (often quite complex) is performed that is not based upon past experience, e.g., reproductive and food-getting activity in insects. Most often instinctive behavior acts as an initiator or triggering mechanism to arouse the organism, and it is modified by learned behavior as well as innate regulatory mechanisms. For example, nest building by birds is a complex activity triggered by instinctive drives and modified by environmental conditions, such as the availability of materials and sites. In animal behavior, fixed patterns of instinctive behavior include fighting, courtship behavior, and escape; even these can usually be shown to be modified by experience (see ETHOLOGY). Relatively little is known about human drives; man's behavior is apparently highly modified and complicated by the socialization process and individual intelligence. Formerly the term *instinct* was used to include acts that are expressions of basic inner needs and are characteristic for any species, including man. This use of the term, implying a mystical force carrying an innate knowledge of an organism's goal, was used indiscriminately to describe many behavioral processes.

Institut de France (ăNstētü' də fräNs), cultural institution of the French state. Founded in 1795 by the Directory, it replaced five learned societies that had been suppressed in 1793 by the Convention. These were the FRENCH ACADEMY (governing language and literature; founded by Richelieu, granted letters patent 1635); the Académie royale de Peinture et de Sculpture (fine arts; founded 1648 by Charles Le Brun, reorganized 1663 by Colbert); the Académie royale des Inscriptions et Médailles (public inscriptions, medal design, etc.; founded 1663), renamed (1716) the Académie royale des Inscriptions et Belles-Lettres; the Académie royale des Sciences (founded 1666 by Colbert); and the Académie royale d'Architecture (organized 1671 by Colbert). The new organization was called at first Institut national des Sciences et des Arts; the name *Académie* was not used in the names of the sections because it was considered reactionary. After 1806 the title was changed to Institut de France. Originally the organization was divided into three classes (physical and mathematical sciences, moral and political sciences, literature and fine arts). In 1803 a decree of Napoleon I (a member since 1797) changed the division to four (physical and mathematical sciences, French language and literature, history and ancient literature, and fine arts), suppressing the second class (moral and political sciences) as subversive to the state. In 1816 there was another reorganization, based on the Institut of 1803, and the name *Académie* was again used in the names of the sections. In 1832, under the influence of Guizot, the second class of the Institut of 1795 was restored as a fifth academy. The Institut de France therefore finally came to be comprised of five academies—the French Academy, the Académie des Inscriptions et Belles-Lettres (history and archaeology), the Académie des Sciences, the Académie des Beaux-Arts, and the Académie des Sciences morales et politiques. Membership in one of the academies does not restrict an individual from being a member of any of the other academies. The academies are self-perpetuating, but the state has the right of veto over their elections. The awards and prizes given by the academies have encouraged endeavor in various fields.

Institute for Advanced Study, at Princeton, N.J.; chartered 1930, opened 1933. It differs from a university in that it offers no curriculum or examinations, and confers no degrees. Founded with a gift from Louis Bamberger and Mrs. Felix Fuld as a center for graduate study, it subsequently became a research center for advanced study in mathematics and the natural and social sciences. One of its first members was Albert Einstein.

Institutes: see CORPUS JURIS CIVILIS.

instrumental, in the grammar of certain languages (e.g., Russian), the CASE referring to means or instrument. The Latin ABLATIVE may in some instances be termed instrumental.

instrumentalism: see DEWEY, JOHN.

instrumentation, in music: see ORCHESTRA AND ORCHESTRATION.

instrument flight regulations: see AIR NAVIGATION.

instrument-landing system (ILS), ground-based radio system designed to provide an airplane pilot with precise guidance for the final approach in landing. The pilot flies his aircraft along a course delineated by the intersection of two radio beams—the localizer beam for guidance in the horizontal

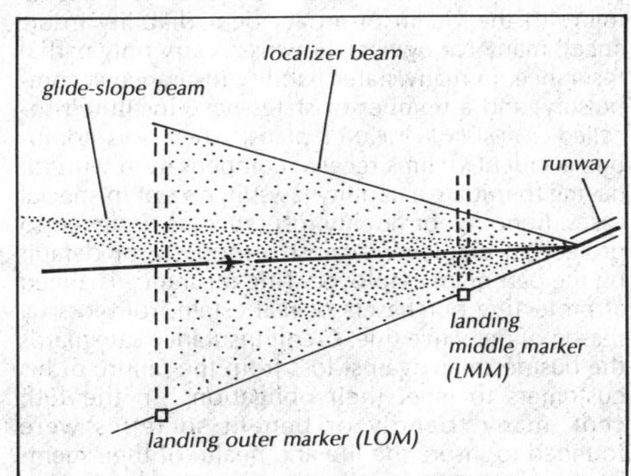

Instrument-landing system (ILS), the most common instrument-landing approach system, uses two beams to guide an airplane.

plane and the glide-slope beam for guidance in the vertical plane. These beams activate an indicator in the aircraft that contains a horizontal needle sensitive to deviations from the glide slope and a vertical needle sensitive to deviations from the localizer path. By keeping both needles centered, the pilot can guide his aircraft down to an altitude between 200 and 150 ft (61–46 m) above the approach end of the landing runway aligned with the runway center line. Limitations inherent in the system prevent it from being used safely at lower altitudes or in locations where the land beyond the approach end of the runway is not level. Also, false guidance can result from distortion of the radio beam by nearby buildings or mountains. Newer systems using microwave beams overcome most of these limitations. Radio marker beacons are also installed at several locations along the approach path to tell the pilot on the landing approach how far he is from the end of the runway. ILS is an approach rather than a landing system. It is called instrument low approach system (ILAS) by the U.S. military air forces. As a supplementary safety measure, especially in bad weather and for emergency landings, the ground-controlled approach (GCA) system is used. Precision radar indicates the location and movement of an aircraft to the ground controller at an airport, enabling him to direct the pilot by voice radio. Using GCA, a plane can be brought to a point from 50 to 100 ft (15–30 m) above the landing field while being guided along the center line of the runway. Techniques including computers and sophisticated guidance systems may well make "hands-off" landing approaches practicable in the future.

insulation (ĭn"səlā'shən, ĭn"syo͞o-), use of materials or devices to inhibit or prevent the CONDUCTION of heat or of electricity. Common heat insulators are asbestos, fur, feathers, fiberglass, cellulose fibers, stone, wood, and wool; all are poor conductors of heat. Industrial furnaces are built of brick, which conducts heat so slowly that a high temperature within is barely apparent in the temperature of the outer surface. Steam pipes and water pipes are commonly insulated with thick wrappings of asbestos pulp. Since insulators prevent the flow of heat in either direction, ice boxes are commonly constructed with double walls separated by an air space (air being a poor conductor) and lined with some insulating material. The use of double walls or hollow tiles in buildings prevents the entrance of heat and its escape. The very effective insulation in a vacuum bottle results almost entirely from the presence of a vacuum between the double walls of the inner flask. In the conduction of electricity from point to point, the conductor acts as a guide for the electric current and must be insulated at every point of contact with its supports to prevent escape, or leakage, of the current. Dry air is a good insulator, or DIELECTRIC, so that conductors used for long-distance transmission require insulating material only at their points of contact with the supporting steel structures. Glass and porcelain are commonly used, molded in bell-shaped forms or in rods made up of several segments. Underground conductors are insulated with dry cotton or pulp, rubber, and bitumen. In electrical apparatus, ebonite is widely used. Some other insulators are paraffin, sulfur, resin, and varnishes. Since wet materials can become conductors, insulation must often be waterproof. Ordinary household wires are commonly insulated by a thin rubber or plastic coating; the electric cables passing between house walls frequently have in addition a metal wrapping. Depending upon the application, the insulating material may also need to be resistant to various types of corrosion resulting from exposure to salt water, oils, or other influences.

insulin, HORMONE secreted by the β cells of the islets of Langerhans, specific groups of cells in the PANCREAS. Insufficiency of insulin in the body results in DIABETES. Canadians Frederick G. Banting and Charles H. Best were the first to obtain, from extracts of pancreas (1921–22), a preparation of insulin that could serve to replace a deficiency of the hormone in the human body. The complete amino acid sequence of the insulin molecule was described in the early 1950s; insulin was the first protein to be sequenced entirely. This pioneering work in protein chemistry was confirmed during the years from 1963 to 1966 when several groups reported the synthesis in their laboratories of biologically active insulin. The three-dimensional structure of the crystalline hormone was published in 1969. Insulin has been shown to be a protein consisting of two POLYPEPTIDE chains, one of 21 amino acid residues and the other of 30, joined by two disulfide bridges (see CYSTEINE). The two chains are originally synthesized in the β cells as part of one continuous polypeptide chain called proinsulin; a 32-amino acid sequence (the connecting peptide) is subsequently split out of the proinsulin molecule by an enzyme resembling TRYPSIN to yield active insulin. In general, insulin acts to reduce extracellular (including blood plasma) levels of GLUCOSE by interacting in some way yet unknown with various cell membranes. In adipose (fatty) tissue it facilitates the cellular uptake of glucose and its subsequent conversion to FATTY ACIDS, and it inhibits the breakdown of fatty acids to simpler compounds. In muscle it again facilitates the transport of glucose into cells and in addition stimulates its conversion to GLYCOGEN. It also increases protein synthesis in muscle. In the liver, insulin facilitates glucose CATABOLISM and its conversion to glycogen and inhibits its synthesis from simpler compounds.

Many, but not all, of the symptoms of diabetes can be controlled by the administration of insulin. The forms of insulin available in the early part of the 20th century had to be injected frequently because they were quick-acting. Later modifications gave the insulin solution a more prolonged action so that hypodermic injections could be made less frequently. In certain cases of mild diabetes, drugs such as tolbutamide and phenformin are useful; the former stimulates the secretion of insulin, but the mode of action of phenformin is unknown. Both can be taken orally. See GLUCAGON.

insulin shock: see HYPERINSULINISM.

Insull, Samuel, 1859–1938, American public utilities financier, b. London. He arrived in the United States in 1881 and was employed by Thomas A. Edison as a secretary. He later became prominent in the management of the Edison industrial holdings. By 1907 he overcame competing public utilities companies in Chicago and soon controlled the city's transit system. After numerous mergers he expanded his operations throughout Illinois and into neighboring states. He formed (1912) a mammoth interlocking directorate that operated over 300 steam plants, almost 200 hydroelectric generating plants, and numerous other power plants throughout the United States. Insull's public utilities empire, at its height worth more than $3 billion, collapsed in 1932. Insull went to Greece and later to Turkey. He was extradited (1934) to the United States, faced charges (1934–35) of using the mails to defraud investors and embezzlement, but he was acquitted. See study by Forrest McDonald (1962).

insurance or **assurance,** device for indemnifying or guaranteeing an individual against loss. Reimbursement is made from a fund to which many individuals exposed to the same risk have contributed certain specified amounts, called premiums. Payment for the loss, divided among many, does not fall heavily upon the actual loser. The essence of the contract of insurance, called a policy, is mutuality. The amount of the premium is determined by the operation of the law of averages as calculated by actuaries. Devices anticipating or resembling modern insurance seem to have been known from ancient times. In Babylonia traders were encouraged to assume the risks of the caravan trade through loans that were repaid (with interest) only after the goods had arrived safely—a practice resembling bottomry and given legal force in the Code of Hammurabi (c.2100 B.C.). The Phoenicians and the Greeks, apparently copying the practice from the Babylonians, applied it to their seaborne commerce. Loans on bottomry were common in the Roman Empire. The Romans, through burial clubs that provided funeral expenses for members and later payments to the survivors, seem also to have developed the germ of true life insurance. The construction of a crude mortality table (A.D. c.220) is ascribed to the jurist Ulpian. Insurancelike practices are traceable almost continuously from Roman times. With the growth of towns and trade in Europe, the medieval guilds undertook to protect their members from loss by fire and shipwreck and to ransom them from captivity by pirates as well as to provide decent burial and support in sickness and poverty. By the middle of the 14th cent., as evidenced by the earliest known insurance contract (Genoa, 1347), marine insurance was practically universal among the maritime nations of Europe. Insurance in the modern sense was brought from Lombardy to the Low Countries and England. The history of marine insurance is largely the history of Lloyd's, a London firm that had its inception at Lloyd's Coffee House, where merchants, shipowners, and underwriters met in the 17th cent. to transact business. Fire insurance arose in Germany in the 15th cent. as a communal undertaking. Life insurance, hampered by laws against usury and betting, developed in a later period. The first life insurance policy seems to have been issued in England in 1583. In 1693 the astronomer Edmund Halley constructed the first mortality table, based on the statistical laws of mortality and compound interest. The table, corrected (1756) by Joseph Dodson, made it possible to scale the premium rate to age; previously the rate had been the same for all ages. Insurance developed rapidly with the growth of British commerce in the 17th and 18th cent.; the complexity and multiple risks of civilized life in the 19th cent. gave it a further impetus. Prior to the formation of corporations devoted solely to the business of writing insurance, policies were signed by a number of individuals, each of whom wrote his name and the amount of risk he was assuming underneath the insurance proposal, hence the term *underwriter.* The first stock companies to engage in insurance were chartered in England in 1720; a little later (1735) the first insurance company in the American colonies was founded at Charleston, S.C. Fire insurance corporations were formed in New York City (1787) and in Philadelphia (1794). Almost from the beginning the companies were active in seeking means of preventing and extinguishing fires. The Presbyterian Synod of Philadelphia sponsored (1759) the first life insurance corporation in America—for the benefit of Presbyterian ministers and their dependents. After 1840, with the decline of religious prejudice against the practice, life insurance entered a boom period. In the 1830s the practice of classifying risks was begun. The New York fire of 1835 called attention to the need for adequate reserves to meet unexpectedly large losses; Massachusetts was the first state to require companies by law (1837) to maintain such reserves. The great Chicago fire (1871) emphasized the costly nature of fires in structurally dense modern cities. Reinsurance, whereby losses are distributed among many companies, was devised to meet such situations and is now common in other lines of insurance. Insurance against accidental injury was offered in 1845; travelers' insurance in 1864. The Workmen's Compensation Act of 1897 in England required employers to insure their employees against industrial accidents. Public liability insurance, fostered by legislation, made its appearance in the 1880s; it attained major importance with the advent of the automobile. Cab insurance (1895) and collision insurance (1899) originated in England. Burglary insurance, an American development, was first written in 1885. Corporate fidelity bonding goes back to 1840, and title and credit insurance were first offered in the 1890s. The 20th cent. saw the expansion of what has been called "inland marine" insurance, which covers a vast miscellany of items, including tourist baggage, express and parcel-post packages, motortruck cargoes, goods in transit, and even bridges and tunnels. Insurance may now be obtained against almost any conceivable risk; companies like Lloyd's will insure a dancer's legs, or a pianist's fingers, or an outdoor entertainment against loss from rain on a specified day. Fire insurance usually includes damage from lightning; other insurance against the elements includes hail, tornado, flood, and drought. Life insurance, originally conceived to protect a man's family when his death left them without income, has developed policies through which the amount paid in, augmented by compound interest, is paid back to the insured in a lump sum at the end of a term of years. Annuity policies, which pay the insured a yearly income after he attains a certain age, have also been developed. Complete automobile insurance includes not only insurance against fire and theft but also compensation for damage to the car and for personal injury to the victim of an accident (liability insurance); many car owners, however, carry only partial insurance. In many states liability insurance is compulsory, and a number of states have instituted so-called NO-FAULT INSURANCE plans, whereby automobile accident victims receive compensation without having to initiate a liability lawsuit, except in special cases. Bonding, or fidelity insurance, is designed to protect an employer against dishonesty or default on the part of an employee. Title insurance is aimed at protecting purchasers of real estate from loss by reason of defective title. Credit insurance safeguards the businessman against loss from the failure of his customers to meet their obligations. In the 19th cent. many friendly or benefit societies were founded to insure the life and health of their members, and many fraternal orders were originally created to provide low-cost, members-only insurance, the first fraternal group to provide such benefits being the Ancient Order of United Workmen (founded 1868). Fraternal orders continue to provide insurance coverage, as do most labor organizations. Many employers sponsor group insurance policies for their employees; such policies include not only life insurance, but sickness and accident benefits and old-age pensions, and the employees usually contribute a certain percentage of the premium. By investing premium payments in a wide range of revenue-producing projects, insurance companies have become major suppliers of capital, and they rank among the nation's largest institutional investors. Since the late 19th cent. there has been a growing tendency for the state to enter the field of insurance, especially with respect to safeguarding workers against sickness and disability, either temporary or permanent, destitute old age, and unemployment. Germany was the first in the field of so-called social insurance; by a series of laws (adopted 1883, 1884, and 1889) it provided protection against sickness, accident, disability, and old age. Most states in the United States have laws providing for workmen's compensation. An important feature of U.S. New Deal legislation was the Social Security Act of 1935 (see SOCIAL SECURITY), which provided for old-age assistance and old-age benefits; unemployment compensation; and aid to the blind and to mothers and children. The Federal government has also experimented with various types of crop insurance, a landmark in this field being the Federal Crop Insurance Act of 1938. In World War II the government provided life insurance for members of the armed forces; since then it has provided other forms of insurance such as pensions for veterans and for government employees. Since 1944 the supervision and regulation of insurance companies, previously an exclusive responsibility of the states, have become subject to regulation by Congress under the interstate commerce clause of the U.S. Constitution. Until the 1950s, most insurance companies in the United States were restricted to providing only one type of insurance. At that time, however, legislation was passed to permit fire and casualty companies to underwrite several classes of insurance. Since then many firms have expanded, many mergers have occurred, and the multiple-line companies have come to dominate the field. See HEALTH INSURANCE. See C. F. Trenerry, *The Origin and Early History of Insurance* (1926); A. H. Mowbray, *Insurance: Its Theory and Practice in the United States* (6th ed. 1969); D. W. Gregg and V. B. Lucas, eds., *Life and Health Insurance Handbook* (3d ed. 1973).

Insurgents, in U.S. history, the Republican Senators and Representatives who in 1909–10 rose against the Republican STANDPATTERS controlling Congress, to oppose the PAYNE-ALDRICH TARIFF and the dictatorial power of House speaker Joseph G. CANNON. Many—but by no means all—of them joined the PROGRESSIVE PARTY. See K. W. Hechler, *Insurgency* (1940, repr. 1970).

intaglio (ĭntăl'yō, –täl'–), design cut into stone or other material or etched or engraved in a metal plate, producing a concave, instead of a convex, effect. It is the reverse of a relief or CAMEO. The term also designates a gem so cut. Seals and signet rings usually bear intaglio designs, so that when stamped upon wax or other plastic substance the impression is in relief. See ENGRAVING; ETCHING; PRINTING.

intarsia (ĭntär'sēə) or **tarsia,** properly a form of wood INLAYING. The term is sometimes applied to inlays of other materials such as ivory and metal. It is differentiated from MARQUETRY by the basic veneering process of the latter. The term *intarsia* is specifically applied to a type of inlaying probably developed in Siena, Italy, in the 13th cent. and derived from Oriental inlays of ivory upon wood. This art was widely practiced in Italy from c.1400 to c.1600. The fashion for intarsia declined thereafter, although some works in this medium were still produced. Intarsia work was also practiced to a limited extent elsewhere in western Europe. Designs included pictorial scenes and conventionalized scrolls, arabesques, and geometric forms.

integer: see NUMBER; NUMBER THEORY.

integral calculus: see CALCULUS.

integrated circuit, electronic circuit or module packaged as a single unit, e.g., in a hermetically sealed case or a plastic capsule, with leads extending from it for input, output, and power supply connections, and for other connections that may be necessary when the device is put to use. Although there are several methods by which integrated circuits are fabricated, the method in which all the electronic devices used are formed by selective treatment (doping) of a single chip of SEMICONDUCTOR material has advantages that have allowed it to displace the other methods in almost all applications (see MICROELECTRONICS). Integrated circuits are categorized according to the number of transistors or other active circuit devices they contain; an active circuit device is one that receives power from a source other than its input signal. An ordinary integrated circuit (IC), of which the OPERATIONAL AMPLIFIER is an example, may contain up to several tens of such devices. A medium-scale integrated circuit (MSI), such as may be used as an FM stereo decoder, may contain from many tens to several hundred active circuit devices. A large-scale integrated circuit (LSI) may contain from several hundred to a few thousand; LSI circuits containing all the functions for an electronic desk calculator are in wide use. An extra-large-scale integrated circuit (ELSI) may contain a few thousand active circuit devices or more and are used in COMPUTERS as memory modules capable of storing thousands of bits of information.

integration, in U.S. history, the goal of an organized movement to break down the barriers of discrimination and segregation separating the NEGRO from the rest of American society. Segregation of blacks is peculiar neither to the American South nor to the United States (see APARTHEID).

Reconstruction to 1954. Segregation assumed its special form in the United States after the Southern states were defeated in the Civil War and slavery was abolished. BLACK CODES that restricted the rights of the newly freed slaves were enacted in the South in 1865-66. These were abolished during Reconstruction, but after Reconstruction white dominance was thoroughly reestablished in the South, partly by the terrorism of the Ku Klux Klan and other groups, but more by the persistence of social custom. Blacks were prevented from voting by devices such as the poll tax, unfair literacy tests, and, when necessary, intimidation. They were denied any equal share in community life. Toward the end of the 19th cent. segregation laws—the Jim Crow laws—were enacted to codify white dominance. Blacks were forced to attend separate schools and colleges, to occupy special sections in railway cars and buses, and to use separate public facilities; they were forbidden to sit with whites in most places of public amusement. These laws were upheld as regards railroad facilities by the case of *Plessy* vs. *Ferguson* (1896) in which the Supreme Court upheld the constitutionality of the so-called separate but equal accommodation. Legal validation of segregation was then extended to other public areas; in 1908 (*Berea College* vs. *Kentucky*) the Supreme Court held that a state could validly forbid a college, even a private institution, to teach whites and blacks at the same time and place. The period 1900 to 1920 brought full extension of segregation to all public transportation and education facilities, even to hospitals, churches, and jails. By the end of World War I, blacks and whites in the South were rigidly separated by law. The tide of opposition across the nation began to rise just before World War II and was given impetus by the activities of civil rights organizations. Blacks, enjoying a somewhat improved economic status, were in the 1930s more assertive of their rights. General opinion may have been influenced by the paradox of a nation urging war for democracy overseas while at the same time tolerating discrimination against a significant portion of its own population. There were many events in the 1940s that advanced integration. In 1941, President Franklin Delano Roosevelt created the FAIR EMPLOYMENT PRACTICES COMMITTEE (FEPC). Under the aegis of the FEPC, "no discrimination" clauses were included in most government contracts. In 1948, President Harry Truman issued a directive calling for an end to segregation in the armed forces. The Supreme Court had also begun to move away from the earlier opinions and toward a principle of racial equality. The court struck down state enforcement of restrictive covenants as well as racial barriers leading to unequal treatment in state professional schools and in interstate transportation. In these rulings, however, the court still ruled only on whether facilities provided for blacks and whites were equal, and not on whether the separation of the races itself was unconstitutional.

1954 to the Civil Rights Act of 1964. In 1954, the Supreme Court took a momentous step: In *Brown* vs. *Board of Education of Topeka* the court set aside a Kansas statute permitting cities of more than 15,000 population to maintain separate schools for blacks and whites and ruled instead that all segregation in public schools is "inherently unequal" and that all blacks barred from attending public schools with white pupils are denied equal protection of the law as guaranteed by the FOURTEENTH AMENDMENT. The doctrine was extended to state-supported colleges and universities in 1956. Meanwhile, in 1955 the court implemented its 1954 opinion by declaring that the Federal district courts would have jurisdiction over lawsuits to enforce the desegregation decision and asked that desegregation proceed "with all deliberate speed." At the time of the 1954 decision, laws in 17 Southern and border states (Delaware, Maryland, Virginia, West Virginia, Georgia, North Carolina, South Carolina, Florida, Tennessee, Kentucky, Alabama, Mississippi, Louisiana, Arkansas, Texas, Oklahoma, and Missouri) and the District of Columbia required that elementary schools be segregated. Four other states—Arizona, Kansas, New Mexico, and Wyoming—had laws permitting segregated schools, but Wyoming had never exercised the option, and the problem was not important in the other three. In the other states of the Union there was evidence of many instances of discrimination; these were not sanctioned by law. The struggle over desegregation now centered upon the school question. By the end of 1957 nine of the 17 states and the District of Columbia had begun integration of their school systems. Another five states had some integrated schools by 1961. The states mostly fell back on stop-gap measures or on pupil-placement laws, which assigned students to schools ostensibly on nonracial grounds. The first desegregated schools to open after the 1954 decision were in Milford, Del. Protests by white parents forced the schools to close, and the black students were expelled; however, court action restored integration within a few months. In 1957 a primary school in Nashville, Tenn., was destroyed by dynamite, and in 1958 the city's desegregated high school was blown up. More notable was the defiance in 1957 of Federal orders by Governor Orval FAUBUS of Arkansas, who called out the Arkansas National Guard to prevent integration in Little Rock. President Eisenhower responded by sending Federal troops to enforce the court order for integration. The governor failed in his intentions. The Little Rock schools opened peacefully on an integrated basis in 1960, but local sentiment remained firmly behind Faubus. In 1958 Virginia closed nine schools in four counties rather than have them integrated. However, Virginia and Federal courts ruled these moves illegal. A lame compromise of local option was adopted, but all counties except one accepted integration by 1959; the exception was Prince Edward county. In 1960 desegregation began in Louisiana; whites boycotted the integrated New Orleans public schools at first triumphantly, later with diminishing effectiveness. In 1961 two black students registered at the Univ. of Georgia but were suspended because of student disorders; they were later returned under a Federal judge's order. The school year 1961-62 was remarkably free of desegregation violence; after careful planning by officials the schools of Atlanta, Memphis, and Dallas were successfully integrated. However, violence erupted in Mississippi the next year, precipitating a serious crisis in Federal-state relations. Against the opposition of Gov. Ross R. Barnett, James H. Meredith, a black who was supported by Federal court orders, registered at the Univ. of Mississippi in 1962. A mob gathered and attacked the force of several hundred Federal marshals assigned to protect Meredith. Two persons were killed. The next day Federal troops occupied Oxford and restored order. Meredith became the first black to attend a public school in Mississippi with white students in accord with the 1954 court decision. In 1963 South Carolina's Clemson College became the first integrated public school in that state. Gov. George C. Wallace of Alabama stood in a doorway at the Univ. of Alabama in a symbolic attempt to block two black students from enrolling in 1963; the attempt failed. In the North attempts were also made to combat segregation. After a suit brought by black parents in 1960, the school system of New Rochelle, N.Y., was in 1961 ordered by a Federal judge to be desegregated. Similar suits followed in other cities. The fight over education overshadowed efforts to achieve integration in other areas, but moves against segregation in public transportation did gain wide notice. In 1955-56, Dr. Martin Luther KING, JR., led blacks in Montgomery, Ala., in a boycott against the municipal bus system after Rosa Parks, a black woman, refused to give up her seat to a white man and move to the segregated section of a bus. The boycott was brought to a successful conclusion when, on Nov. 13, 1956, the Supreme Court nullified the laws of Alabama and the ordinances of Montgomery that required segregation on buses. Mixed groups of whites and blacks, called freedom riders, in May, 1961, undertook a campaign to force integration in bus terminals and challenge segregation in local interstate travel facilities. The buses were attacked by mobs in Anniston, Ala., where one bus was destroyed by a fire bomb. There were riots in Birmingham and Montgomery when blacks attempted to use facilities previously reserved for whites; Federal marshals and national guardsmen were called out to restore order and escort the freedom riders to Mississippi. Many of them were arrested in Jackson, Miss., for infractions of the state's segregation laws, and a long series of court battles began. These protests led in 1961 to an Interstate Commerce Commission ban on segregation in all interstate transportation facilities. Passive resistance was undertaken by groups to eradicate discrimination in other fields. In 1960 black college students staged a sit-in at segregated public lunch counters in an effort to force desegregation; similar demonstrations were made in other cities. Other campaigns were waged with some success for the desegregation of beaches, restaurants, theaters, and libraries. Integration groups were also active in housing, particularly in the North; in 1957, New York City adopted the first law forbidding racial or religious discrimination in private rental housing. During the summer of 1963 thousands of blacks demonstrated in Birmingham, Ala., and were attacked by police using cattle prods and dogs. Nationwide revulsion to these attacks was expressed when over 200,000 people marched on Washington, D.C., and pressed for further civil rights legislation.

Civil Rights Movement to the Present. An attempt to deal with the increasing demands of blacks for equal rights came in 1964 when President Lyndon Baines Johnson asked for and received the most comprehensive civil rights act to date; the act specifically prohibited discrimination in voting, education, and the use of public facilities. For the first time since the Supreme Court ruled on segregation in public schools in 1954, the Federal government had a means of enforcing desegregation; Title VI of the act barred the use of Federal funds for segregated programs and schools. In 1964 only two Southern states (Tennessee and Texas) had more than 2% of their black students enrolled in integrated schools. Using Title VI, about 6% of the black students in the South were in integrated schools by the next year. Early in 1965 the Voting Rights Act was passed, but it did not prevent the rising tide of militance among blacks; Watts, a black slum in Los Angeles, erupted in violence, leaving 34 dead. The next year was marked by riots in practically all major U.S. cities as blacks began shifting to an independent course expressed in the concept of black power; the term originated with Stokely Carmichael, leader of the Student Nonviolent Coordinating Committee, an organization that dropped whites from membership the following year. Meanwhile, integration of Southern school districts was progressing; by 1967, 22% of the black students in the 17 southern and border states were in integrated schools. However, the continuing separation of blacks and whites in most areas was emphasized in 1968 when the National Advisory Commission on Civil Disorders (the Kerner Commission) issued a report that said, "our nation is moving toward two societies, one black, one white—separate and unequal." The assassination of Martin Luther King, Jr., that summer set off riots in 125 U.S. cities. The issue of segregated housing was faced in the Civil Rights Act of 1968 that contained a clause barring discrimination against blacks in the sale or rental of most housing. In May of that year the Supreme Court ruled that so-called freedom-of-choice plans in Southern school districts were inadequate because these plans did not desegregate as fast as other plans. In 1969 several school districts appealed to the Supreme Court to delay plans for desegregation; these requests were rejected and the districts were ordered to desegregate immediately. In the North new forms of de facto segregation had emerged whereby neighborhood schools were segregated not by law but in fact. While most blacks still favored integration, battles over community control of schools in black areas erupted; a notable example was the Ocean Hill-Brownsville school district in New York City. Although the U.S. armed forces had been integrated since 1948, violent racial outbursts began to occur between blacks and whites, especially in West Germany and Vietnam. Integration proponents received a setback in 1970; President Nixon announced that the desegregation of schools would be left to the courts and that his administration would de-emphasize strong desegregation procedures. Meanwhile a system of tax-exempt, segregated private schools had been developing in the South in the 1960s. Black college students were enrolling in previously white colleges at a greater rate; in 1964, 51% of black students had been in predominantly black colleges, but by 1971 only 34% were so. At the secondary and primary levels the South had begun to move ahead of the North. By the fall of 1972, 44% of the black students in the South were in predominantly white schools, while only 30% were in predominantly white schools in the North. The early 1970s were characterized by the controversial issue of busing as a tool to promote integration. An antibusing motorcade of over 3,000 drove from Richmond, Va., to Washington, D.C., and the higher education bill of 1972 contained three antibusing clauses. The Supreme Court continued, in the early 1970s, to back busing plans. The Boston busing plan caused widespread disturbances in the beginning of the 1974–75 school year, renewing the national debate concerning the validity of busing as a means of integration. By the mid-1970s only about 12% of black students in the United States still remained in completely segregated schools. See M. R. Konvitz, *A Century of Civil Rights* (1961, repr. 1967); T. B. Edwards, ed., *School Desegregation in the North* (1968); R. L. Green, *Racial Crisis in American Education* (1969); Betsy Fancher, *Voices from the South* (1970); C. V. Woodward, *The Strange Career of Jim Crow* (3d. rev. ed. 1974).

integumentary system: see SKIN.

intelligence, in psychology, the general mental ability involved in calculating, reasoning, perceiving relationships and analogies, learning quickly, storing and retrieving information, using language fluently, classifying, generalizing, and adjusting to new situations. Alfred Binet, the French psychologist, defined intelligence as the totality of mental processes involved in adapting to the environment. Although there remains a strong tendency to view intelligence as a purely intellectual or cognitive function, considerable evidence suggests that intelligence is an attribute of the entire personality that cannot be measured adequately in isolation. It is generally accepted that potential intelligence is related to heredity and that environment is a critical factor in determining the extent of its expression. Children reared in orphanages or other environments that are comparatively unstimulating tend to show retarded intellectual development as well as other deficits. The controversial Head Start program for preschool children represented an attempt to provide enriched learning environments to children from disadvantaged backgrounds. The concept of intelligence has proved to be so elusive that psychologists often prefer to define it as that which is measured by intelligence tests. While no consensus of opinion prevails about what such tests actually measure, their use in education has had great practical value in assigning children to suitable class groups and in predicting academic performance. Binet and Theodore Simon pioneered the first modern intelligence test in 1905, which was used to identify retarded children in the French school system. In 1916 the Binet-Simon Intelligence Scale was expanded and reworked by Lewis Terman at Stanford Univ., and later revisions called the Revised Stanford-Binet Intelligence Tests were published in 1937 and 1960. A highly successful series of tests designed by the psychologist David Wechsler are currently in wide use as diagnostic and evaluative instruments, including the Wechsler-Bellevue Intelligence Scale (1939), the Wechsler Intelligence Scale for Children (1949), and the Wechsler Adult Intelligence Scale (1955). All of these tests are administered to one individual at a time. The Army Alpha Test, which was first administered to nearly 2 million new recruits in World War I, and the Otis Group Intelligence Scale, were forerunners of many other group tests that, administered economically and quickly to large numbers, could be used in schools and industry; the California Test of Mental Maturity, the Kuhlmann-Anderson, and the College Entrance Examination, are other group tests. The work of Binet, Terman, and Wilhelm Stern opened the way for a method of classifying intelligence in terms of a standardized measure, with standardization obtained from having as many individuals as possible of various ages take the test. From the results thus obtained it is possible to determine the average number of questions answered, problems solved, and tasks completed by individuals of certain age. In an intelligence test of 100 questions, the average number answered correctly by 7 year olds might be 10; 9 year olds 15; 12 year olds 30; and so on. If then a child of 9 answers 30 questions correctly, he is classed with children of 12 and his mental age is said to be 12. The so-called intelligence quotient, or IQ, is a comparison between this mental age and his real or chronological age, in this case 9. It is computed by dividing the mental age, 12, by the chronological age, 9, and multiplying the result by 100 to eliminate the decimal point. Division of the mental age by the chronological age gives the quotient 1.33, and multiplication by 100 gives an IQ of 133, which is relatively high. As a child grows, the mental age and chronological age generally increase at a relatively equal pace so that the IQ varies to only a small extent. One criticism of intelligence tests is that it is difficult to insure that test items are equally meaningful or difficult for members of different social groups. However, their use is validated by the finding that whatever it is that is measured by the tests is closely associated in this society with career and academic achievement. There has been a decline in interest in pure intelligence tests since the 1920s and a corresponding increase in the number of mental tests that measure special aptitudes and personality factors (see PSYCHOLOGICAL TESTS). Investigation of the physiological basis of intelligence has revealed a positive correlation between intelligence and the size of the cortex of the brain. Animals in which the cortex has been removed show a loss of problem-solving ability roughly proportional to the amount of cortical destruction, and brain lesions in humans have also been found to correspond proportionally with deficits in abstract reasoning and symbolic functioning. See R. L. Thorndike and E. P. Hagen, *Measurement and Evaluation in Psychology and Education* (3d ed. 1969); L. J. Cronbach, *Essentials of Psychological Testing* (3d ed. 1970); J. D. Matarazzo, *Wechsler's Measurement and Appraisal of Adult Intelligence* (1972).

intendant (ĭntĕn'dənt), French administrative official who served as the chief royal representative in the provinces under the ancien régime. The intendants first gained importance under Cardinal Richelieu, Louis XIII's principal minister, in the early 17th cent.; he used them extensively to consolidate the country and undermine feudal authority. At first the intendant lacked power outside his specific commission from the king. Under Louis XIV's rule (1643–1715), however, the intendant became a vital permanent state official, appointed by the king. Granted full powers in the fields of justice, finance, and police in the provinces, the intendant often tried civil and criminal cases, suspended unsuitable judges, summoned special tribunals, regulated municipal government, stamped out banditry and smuggling, levied and collected taxes, and drew the militia by lot. Intendants were usually non-nobles, dependent upon royal favor for advancement. As faithful instruments of royal centralization they aroused the hostility of the local authorities, notably the parlements and the provincial governors. During the abortive revolution known as the Fronde (1648–53) the office was virtually abolished, but it was reinstated in 1653 after the rebellion had been crushed. Distributed throughout the realm, each *généralité* had one intendant by 1689; at the outbreak of the French Revolution (1789) there were 33 in France. The authority of the intendants was severely shaken in the provincial revolts of 1788. A symbol of royal absolutism, the office was abolished (Dec., 1789) by the Constituent Assembly early in the French Revolution.

Inter-American Conferences: see PAN-AMERICANISM.

Inter-American Highway, c.3,400 mi (5,470 km) long, section of the PAN AMERICAN HIGHWAY system from Nuevo Laredo, Mexico, to Panama City, Panama. Much of the highway prior to 1941 had been built by the countries concerned, but wartime necessity led the United States to appropriate funds to assist completion. Later work was done by each nation on its own. The highway includes alternate routes and makes use of previous local roads. The highway is virtually complete, and many sections have been upgraded and paved.

intercolumniation (ĭn"tərkəlŭm"nēā'shən), in classical architecture, the clear space between the edges of two adjacent columns, as measured at the lower portion of their shafts. Vitruvius compiled standard intercolumniations for the three orders, expressed in terms of the column diameter. In the great works of Greek architecture, spacings frequently varied within a single colonnade, being widest between the two center columns. The narrowest occurred at the corner columns, thus strengthening their effect. Renaissance architects employed a new type of intercolumniation with the use of columns in pairs, those of each pair almost touching.

intercontinental ballistic missile: see GUIDED MISSILE.

interdict (ĭn'tərdĭkt), ecclesiastical censure notably used in the Roman Catholic Church, especially in the Middle Ages. When a parish, state, or nation is placed under the interdict no public church ceremony may take place, only certain sacraments, especially baptism, may be administered, and the dead may not receive Christian burial. The interdict is used to sway public opinion and to force action. A famous example was the interdict placed upon England during the reign of King John by Innocent III in 1208.

interest, charge for the use of money, usually figured as a percentage of the principal and computed annually. Such charges have been made since ancient times, and they early fell into disrepute. In Greece, Solon forbade selling men into slavery for unpaid interest. The Jews and the Christian Church forbade interest charges, or usury, as it was called, among their own groups. The merchant princes of N Italy and elsewhere evaded such restrictions, even though the medieval churchmen considered money barren, or unable to produce wealth. Gradually the distinction was made between low interest rates and high ones, which came to be known, and condemned, as usury. England in 1545 removed the prohibition on interest charges and fixed a legal maximum interest; other countries followed. States of the United States fix a legal rate at which debts may be assessed if they have come due and remain unpaid, and fix the maximum rate allowed in a contract. Simple interest is computed annually on the principal. Compound interest, paid by some savings banks, computes the interest on the principal as well as on any previous interest that has been added to the principal. In Great Britain legal interest rates are not fixed by the government, but courts can determine whether a given rate is injurious. See J. M. Keynes, *General Theory of Employment, Interest, and Money* (1936); B. W. Dempsey, *Interest and Usury* (1948).

interference, in physics, the effect produced by the combination or superposition of two systems of WAVES, in which these waves reinforce, neutralize, or in other ways interfere with each other. Interference is observed in both sound waves and light waves. When, for example, two sound waves occur at the same time and are in the same phase, i.e., when the condensations of the two coincide and hence their rarefactions also, the waves reinforce each other and the sound becomes louder (see SOUND). This is known as constructive interference. On the other hand, two sound waves occurring simultaneously and having the same intensity neutralize each other if the rarefactions of the one coincide with the condensations of the other, i.e., if they are of opposite phase. This canceling is known as destructive interference. In this case, the result is silence. However, alternate reinforcement and neutralization (or weakening) take place when two sound waves differing slightly in frequency are superimposed. The audible result is a series of pulsations or, as these pulsations are called commonly, beats, caused by the alternate coincidence of first a condensation of the one wave with a condensation of the other and then a condensation with a rarefaction. The beat frequency is equal to the difference between the frequencies of the interfering sound waves. Light waves reinforce or neutralize each other in very much the same way (see LIGHT). If, for example, two light waves each of one color (monochromatic waves) of the same amplitude and of the same frequency are combined, the interference they exhibit is characterized by so-called fringes—a series of light bands (resulting from reinforcement) alternating with dark bands (caused by neutralization). Such a pattern is formed either by light passing through two narrow slits and being diffracted (see DIFFRACTION), or by light passing through a single slit. In the case of two slits, each slit acts as a light source, producing two sets of waves that may combine or cancel depending upon their phase relationship. In the case of a single slit, each point within the slit acts as a light source. The relative positions of light and dark lines depend upon the wavelength of the light, among other factors. Thus, if white light, which is made up of all colors, is used instead of monochromatic light, bands of color are formed because each color, or wavelength, is reinforced at a different position. This fact is utilized in the diffraction grating, which forms a SPECTRUM by diffraction and interference of a beam of light incident on it. Newton's rings also are the result of the interference of light. They are formed concentrically around the point of contact between a glass plate and a slightly convex lens set upon it or between two lenses pressed together; they consist of bright rings separated by dark ones when monochromatic light is used, or of alternate spectrum-colored and black rings when white light is used. The experiments of Thomas Young first illustrated interference and definitely pointed the way to a wave theory of light. A. J. Fresnel's experiments clearly demonstrated that the interference phenomena could be explained adequately only upon the basis of a wave theory. The determinations of the velocity of light as carried out by A. A. Michelson are based upon the interference of light waves. Various natural phenomena are the result of interference, e.g., the colors appearing in soap bubbles and the iridescence of mother-of-pearl and other substances. The thickness of a very thin film such as the soap-bubble wall

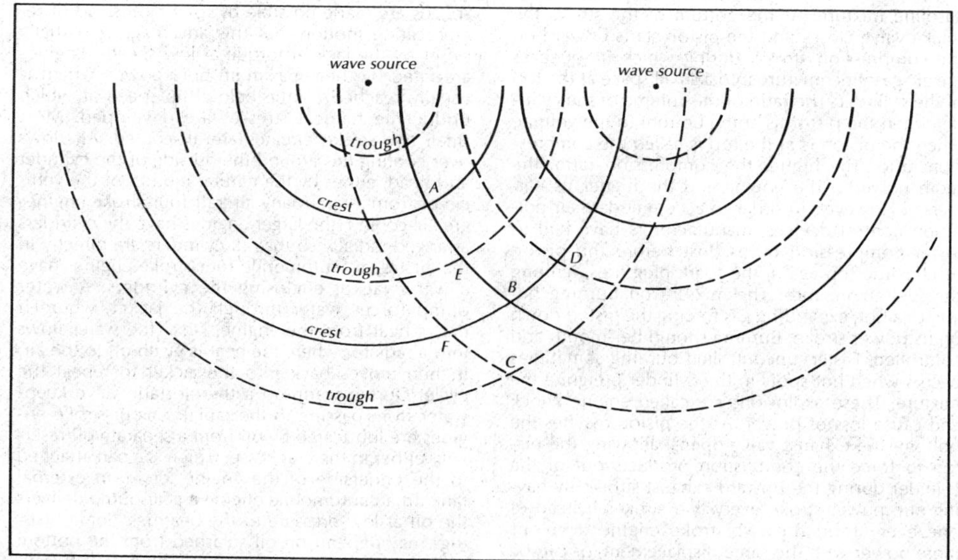

Constructive interference: Two crests or two troughs meet and combine (A, B, C). Destructive interference: A crest and a trough meet and cancel each other (D, E, F).

can be measured by an instrument called the **interferometer**. When the wavelength of the light is known, the interferometer indicates the thickness of the film by the interference patterns it forms. The reverse process, i.e., the measurement of the length of an unknown light wave, can also be carried out by the interferometer. The Michelson interferometer used in the Michelson-Morley experiment of 1887 had a half-silvered mirror to split an incident beam of light into two parts at right angles to one another. The two halves of the beam were then reflected off mirrors and rejoined. Any difference in the speed of light along the paths could be detected by the interference pattern. The failure of the experiment to detect any such difference threw doubt on the existence of the ETHER and thus paved the way for the special theory of RELATIVITY. Another type of interferometer divised by Michelson has been applied in measuring the diameters of certain stars. The radio interferometer consists of two or more radio telescopes separated by fairly large distances (necessary because radio waves are much longer than light waves) and is used to pinpoint and study various celestial sources of radiation in the radio range. See RADIO ASTRONOMY.

interferon: see IMMUNITY.

Interior, United States Department of the, Federal executive department established in 1849, delegated custodian of U.S. natural resources, and whose head, the Secretary of the Interior, has cabinet rank. Bureaus dealing with the department's responsibility for mineral resources include: the GEOLOGICAL SURVEY; the Bureau of Mines; and the Office of Oil and Gas. The last office is charged with ensuring the nation an adequate supply of fuel. During the energy crisis of 1973 several new offices were created to deal with energy conservation and development and to coordinate the gathering and analysis of energy data; these are the Office of Energy Conservation, the Office of Research and Development, and the Office of Energy Data and Analysis. The Bureau of Mines was established in 1910 to conserve and utilize American mineral resources and to promote safety in mining industries. The department's responsibility for water and power resources is handled primarily by the BUREAU OF RECLAMATION and various specific power administrations that operate projects generating electrical power and other energy and sell surplus power. The divisions of the department concerned with PUBLIC LAND management include the bureaus of INDIAN AFFAIRS, Land Management, and Outdoor Recreation. The Bureau of Land Management was formed in 1946 by merging the GENERAL LAND OFFICE with the Grazing Service. It manages and disposes of public land under programs designed to produce multiple use and sustained yield of resources while maintaining a quality environment. The Bureau of Outdoor Recreation was established (1962) to promote and develop effective programs for outdoor recreation. The U.S. Fish and Wildlife Service, reorganized in 1970, conducts its functions through the Bureau of Sport Fisheries and Wildlife; it is responsible for planning the best possible program for the use and enjoyment of sport fishing and wildlife resources by the people. To this end it runs fish hatcheries, manages animal populations, and regulates the natural environment. The National Park Service, established in 1916, acts as trustee for the recreation areas designated as NATIONAL PARKS AND MONUMENTS. It is charged with maintaining and preserving the areas for present and future enjoyment.

interior decoration, adornment of the interior of a building, public or domestic, comprising interior architecture, finishing, and furnishings. Oriental and classical cultures used the decorative arts to create elaborate interiors, and they originated forms extensively copied in later times. In Europe during the early medieval period few notable interiors were created except in Islamic Spain and in the Byzantine Empire. Simple movable and hanging objects were the chief furnishings of castles. In the late Middle Ages artistic resources were dedicated to the embellishment of churches and public buildings. With more settled conditions, Renaissance Italy, influenced by Greek and Roman styles, developed interiors of grandeur and magnificence; popes and nobles employed leading artists to decorate their palaces and villas. Italian forms spread to other countries. Spanish interiors displayed rich color, ornate furniture, decorated leather, and fine textiles. France was an early leader in setting styles, which changed with the sovereigns. Especially influential were the LOUIS PERIOD STYLES, RÉGENCE STYLE, DIRECTOIRE STYLE, and EMPIRE STYLE. England developed notably the ELIZABETHAN STYLE, the JACOBEAN STYLE, and the GEORGIAN STYLE; some 18th-century styles are known by the names of furniture designers such as CHIPPENDALE, SHERATON, and HEPPLEWHITE. Robert ADAM correlated interior and exterior architecture, furniture, and accessories. In America settlers used simple homemade furniture of native woods, homespun fabrics, and pewter. The style, known as Early Colonial, has been revived for re-creating early American interiors. The formal Late Colonial period used modified Georgian mansions and polished mahogany furniture of English type. Pennsylvania German decoration based on European provincial styles is also much reproduced. The 19th cent. was marked by a departure from old standards of craftsmanship; machine-made furnishings supplied the requirements of the growing middle classes. In the second half of the century William Morris and the Pre-Raphaelites instituted an ARTS AND CRAFTS movement that spread abroad and stimulated a reaction against ornate Victorian decoration. It resulted in a revival of earlier period styles, the simultaneous development of native provincial styles, and an attempt to create a new modern style. Contemporary styles are international in character. Designers and manufacturers are cooperating to produce low-cost furnishings scaled for small rooms, combining ease of upkeep and functionalism. Units permitting maximum use of wall space are designed on a modular system to allow flexible combinations. Synthetic materials are employed, and materials such as metals and glass are put to new uses. Lighting is emphasized, and arrangement is based on a correlation of scale, balance, comfort, pattern, and color. See FURNITURE; WALLPAPER; TEXTILES. See K. M. Ford and T. H. Creighton, *Designs for Living* (1955); Gerd and Ursula Hatje, *Design for Modern Living* (1962); Ian Grant, *Great Interiors* (1967); William Pahlmann, *The Pahlmann Book of Interior Design* (3d ed. 1968); Arnold Friedmann, *Interior Design* (1970); Robert Harling, *Modern Furniture and Decoration* (1971).

interjection, English PART OF SPEECH consisting of exclamatory words such as *oh, alas,* and *ouch.* They are marked by a feature of intonation that is usually shown in writing by an exclamation point (see PUNCTUATION). Many languages have classes like interjections.

Interlaken (ĭn'tərläkən), town (1970 pop. 4,735), Bern canton, central Switzerland, between the Lake of Brienz and the Lake of Thun. Interlaken is one of the largest resorts (mainly summer) in the Bernese Alps, and its yearly visitors far outnumber its permanent inhabitants. The region is famous for its magnificent view of the Jungfrau peak.

Interlingua, name of an artificial language introduced in 1951; also the name of a simplified form of Latin (sometimes called *Latino Sine Flexione,* or "Latin without inflection") introduced in the early 20th cent. See INTERNATIONAL LANGUAGE.

interlocking directorate, corporate structure in which an individual or group of individuals sit on the boards of directors of more than one business enterprise. The general tendency of interlocking directorates is toward cooperation between the corporations involved. Although such cooperation is frequently desirable from the point of view of the corporations as a means of improving operation and cutting costs, it becomes socially dangerous when used for the purpose of raising prices through monopolistic practices. The interlocking directorate has also been one of the chief means by which industrial power has been concentrated in the hands of a small group of men. Both the Sherman and the Clayton antitrust acts prohibit interlocking directorates when they tend to lessen competition. See TRUST.

interlude, development in the late 15th cent. of the English medieval morality play. Played between the acts of a long play, the interlude, treating intellectual rather than moral topics, often contained elements of satire or farce. The form developed in Italy as the intermedio and INTERMEZZO, in France as the entremet or intermede and as the entrée, which involved only dance. In Spain the entremés became an independent form as in the work of Cervantes. See E. K. Chambers, *The Medieval Stage* (1903); V. F. Hopper and G. B. Lahey, ed., *Medieval Mysteries, Moralities and Interludes* (1962).

intermediate range ballistic missile: see GUIDED MISSILE.

intermediate school: see SCHOOL.

intermezzo (ĭntərmĕt'sō, -mĕd'zō). **1** Any theatrical entertainment of a light nature performed between the divisions of a longer, more serious work. **2** In the 17th and 18th cent., a short independent comic scene with everyday characters was interpolated between acts of serious operas. In the 18th cent. it developed into opera buffa (see OPERA); a famous example is Pergolesi's *La serva padrona.* **3** In the 19th cent., a short independent piece having the character of an interlude, or a movement of such character in a larger work such as a symphony or sonata. It was a favorite form of Schumann and Brahms.

intermolecular forces, forces that are exerted by molecules on each other and that, in general, affect the macroscopic properties of the material of which the molecules are a part. Such forces may be either attractive or repulsive in nature. They are conveniently divided into two classes: short-range forces, which operate when the centers of the molecules are separated by 3 ANGSTROMS or less, and long-range forces, which operate at greater distances. Generally, if molecules do not tend to interact chemically, the short-range forces between them are repulsive. These forces arise from interactions of the electrons associated with the molecules and are also known as exchange forces. Molecules that interact chemically have attractive exchange forces; these are also known as valence forces. Mechanical rigidity of molecules and effects such as limited compressibility of matter arise from repulsive exchange forces. Long-range forces, or van der Waals forces as they are also called, are attractive and account for a wide range of physical phenomena, such as FRICTION, SURFACE TENSION, ADHESION AND COHESION of liquids and solids, VISCOSITY, and the discrepancies between the actual behavior of gases and that predicted by the ideal GAS LAW. Van der Waals forces arise in a number of ways, one being the tendency of electrically polarized molecules to become aligned. Quantum theory indicates also that in some cases the electrostatic fields associated with electrons in neighboring molecules constrain the electrons to move more or less in phase.

internal-combustion engine, one in which combustion of the fuel takes place in a confined space, producing expanding gases that are directly used to provide mechanical power. The most common internal-combustion engine is the piston-type gasoline engine used in most automobiles. In each cylinder a piston slides up and down. One end of a connecting rod is attached to the bottom of the piston by a joint; the other end of the rod clamps around a bearing on one of the throws, or convolutions, of a crankshaft; the reciprocating (up-and-down) motions of the piston rotate the crankshaft, which is connected by suitable gearing to the drive wheels of the automobile. The number of crankshaft revolutions per minute is called the engine speed. The top of the cylinder is closed by a metal cover (called the head) bolted onto it. Into a threaded aperture in the head is screwed the spark plug, which provides ignition. Two other openings in the cylinder are called ports: The intake port admits the air-gasoline mixture; the exhaust port lets out the products of combustion. A mushroom-shaped valve is held tightly over each port by a coil spring, and a camshaft rotating at one-half engine speed opens the valves in correct sequence. A pipe runs from each intake port to a carburetor, the pipes from all the cylinders joining to form a manifold; a similar manifold connects the exhaust ports with an exhaust pipe and noise muffler. The carburetor mixes air with gasoline in proportions of weight varying from 11 to 1 at the richest to a little over 16 to 1 at the leanest. The composition of the mixture is regulated by the throttle, an air valve in the intake manifold that varies the flow of fuel to the combustion chambers of the cylinders. The mixture is rich at idling speed (closed throttle) and at high speeds (wide-open throttle), and is lean at medium and slow speeds (partly open throttle). In most engines a single cycle of operation takes place over four strokes of a piston, made in two engine revolutions. When an engine has more than one cylinder the cycles are evenly staggered for smooth operation, but each cylinder will go through a full cycle in any two engine revolutions. In automobile engines, cylinders are commonly arranged in a single row (in-line) with the centerlines of the cylinders vertical, in a double row with the centerlines of opposite cylinders converging in a V (V-engine), or in two horizontal, opposed rows (opposed or pancake engine). When the piston is at the top of the cylinder at the beginning of the intake stroke, the intake valve opens and the descending piston draws in the air-gasoline mixture. At the bottom of the stroke the intake valve closes and the piston starts upward on the compression stroke, during which it squeezes the air-gasoline mixture into a small space at the top of the cylinder. The ratio of the volume of the cylinder when the piston is at the bottom to the volume when the piston is at the top is called the compression ratio. The higher the compression ratio, the more powerful the engine and the higher its efficiency. However, in order to accommodate air pollution control devices, manufacturers have had to lower compression ratios. Just before the piston reaches the top again, the spark plug fires, igniting the fuel-air mixture. The mixture on burning becomes a hot, expanding gas forcing the piston down on its power stroke. Burning should be smooth and controlled. Faster, uncontrolled burning sometimes occurs when hot spots in the cylinder preignite the mixture. These explosions are called engine knock and cause loss of power. As the piston reaches the bottom, the exhaust valve opens, allowing the piston to force the combustion products out of the cylinder during the upward exhaust stroke. By having one power stroke every two strokes instead of one every four, the two-stroke engine develops more power with the same displacement, or can be lighter and yet deliver the same power. The two-stroke engine is simpler mechanically than the four-stroke engine. For this reason it is used in lawn mowers, chain saws, small automobiles, motorcycles, and outboard marine engines. However, there are several disadvantages that restrict its use. Since there are twice as many power strokes during the operation of a two-stroke engine as there are during the operation of a four-stroke engine, the engine tends to heat up more, and thus is likely to have a shorter life. Also, in the two-stroke engine lubricating oil must be mixed with the fuel. This causes a very high level of pollution in its exhaust. The more recent Wankel engine, introduced by the German engineer Felix Wankel, has a disk that looks like a triangle with bulging sides rotating inside a cylinder shaped like a figure eight with a thick waist. Intake and exhaust are through ports in the flat sides of the cylinder. The spaces between the sides of the disk and the walls of the cylinder form combustion pockets. During a single rotation of the disk each pocket alternately grows smaller, then larger because of the contoured outline of the cylinder. This provides for compression and expansion. The engine runs on a four-stroke cycle. Its main advantage is that advanced pollution control devices are easier to design for it than for the conventional piston engine. Another advantage is that higher engine speeds are made possible by rotating instead of reciprocating motion, but this advantage is partially offset by the lack of torque at low speeds. Engines are rated by their maximum horsepower, which is usually reached a little below the speed at which undue mechanical stresses are developed. Most small two-stroke engines are air-cooled. Air flows over cooling fins around the outside of the cylinder and head, either by the natural motion of the vehicle or from a fan. Many aircraft four-stroke engines are air-cooled; the larger engines have the cylinders arranged radially so that all cylinders are directly in the airstream. Automobile four-stroke engines have a water jacket enclosing the cylinders. A water pump forces water through the jacket, where it draws heat from the engine. Next, the water flows into a radiator where the heat is given off to the air; it then moves back into the jacket to repeat the cycle. During warm-up a thermostatic valve keeps water from passing to the radiator. Four-stroke engines are lubricated by oil from a separate oil reservoir, either in the crankcase, which is a pan attached to the underside of the engine, or in an external tank. In an automobile engine a gear pump delivers the oil at low pressure to the bearings. Some bearings may depend on oil splashed from the bottom of the crankcase by the turning crankshaft. When an internal-combustion engine is operating, its untreated exhaust will contain pollutants such as unburned hydrocarbons, carbon monoxide, and nitrogen oxides. In order to meet U.S. government restrictions on such emissions, automobile manufacturers have had to make various modifications in the operation of their engines. For example, to reduce the emission of nitrogen oxides, one modification involves sending a certain proportion of the exhaust gases back into the air-gasoline mixture going into the engine. This cuts peak temperatures during combustion, lessening the amount of nitrogen oxides produced. In the stratified charge piston engine two separate air-gasoline mixtures are injected into the engine. A small, rich mixture that is easily ignited is used to ignite an exceptionally lean mixture that drives the piston. This results in much more efficient burning of the gasoline, thus reducing emissions. Another device, the catalytic converter, can be connected to the exhaust pipe; the gases are passed over bars or pellets coated with certain metals that promote chemical reactions reducing nitrogen oxides and burning hydrocarbons and carbon monoxide. The Dutch physicist Christiaan Huygens experimented (c.1680) with an internal-combustion engine that burned gunpowder. Not until 1859, when the French engineer J. J. Étienne Lenoir built a double-acting, spark-ignition gas engine, was there an internal-combustion engine that could run continuously under industrial conditions. The English inventor William Barnett had demonstrated (c.1838) the value of compressing the gas before its combustion. In 1862, Alphonse Beau de Roche, a French scientist, patented but did not build a four-stroke engine. In 1878 the German engineer Nikolaus A. Otto built a gas engine using the four-stroke cycle that still bears his name. George Brayton, a Boston engineer, built the first liquid-fuel engine (1873) and exhibited it at the Philadelphia Centennial Exposition (1876). It was a two-stroke kerosine engine. However, like previous engines, this oil engine was large and slow (engines of the period ran at a few hundred revolutions per minute). The German engineer Gottlieb Daimler combined many of the features of modern engines in his 1885 gas engine; it was small and fast, and had a vertical cylinder. Later in the same year he invented a carburetor and began using liquid fuel, soon substituting gasoline for the heavier petroleum oils, chiefly kerosine, used until then. In 1889 he introduced a four-stroke gasoline engine with mushroom-shaped valves and two cylinders arranged in a V. Because of its high power-to-weight ratio, this is the type of engine now widely used in airplanes, automobiles, motorcycles, tractors, and light trucks. It is also used in large trucks, buses, and other heavy vehicles, as is the DIESEL ENGINE, a type of internal-combustion engine used also to drive locomotives and electric generators, as well as tugboats, tankers, and other vessels. Other types of internal-combustion engine include the reaction engine (see JET PROPULSION; ROCKET) and the gas TURBINE. See E. F. Obert, *Internal Combustion Engine* (2d ed. 1950) and C. F. Taylor and E. S. Taylor, *The Internal-Combustion Engine* (1960).

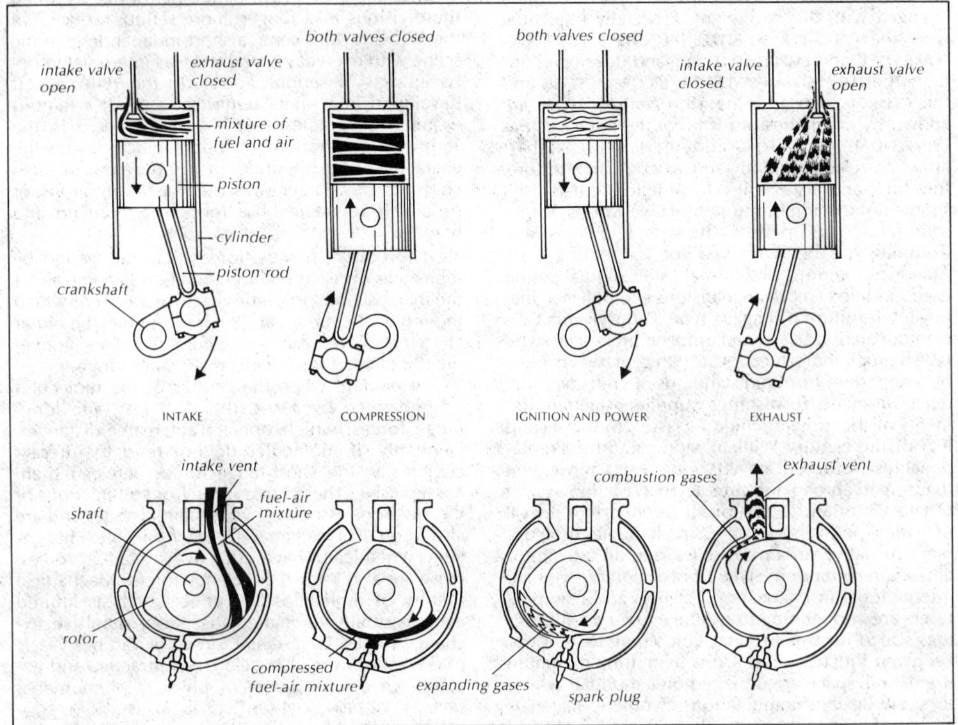

Internal-combustion engines: In the four-stroke reciprocating engine (above), a mixture of fuel and air is taken into the chamber on the down-stroke of the piston, is compressed on the up-stroke, is ignited and provides power on the next down-stroke, and finally is exhausted on the up-stroke. In the Wankel rotary engine (below), the same sequence is accomplished in a continuous motion as the volume varies between the triangular rotor and the specially shaped chamber.

internal medicine, branch of MEDICINE concerned with nonsurgical remedies for diseases of the internal organs. While the internist is trained to diagnose and treat all pathologies of the various internal organs and systems, he may specialize in a particular subbranch of the discipline, such as cardiology, the treatment of heart ailments, or gastroenterology, the treatment of diseases and disorders of the digestive system.

Internal Revenue Service (IRS), division of the U.S. Treasury Dept. that is responsible for the assessment and collection of most Federal taxes, except those relating to alcohol, tobacco, firearms, and explosives. Established in 1862, the IRS derives most of its revenues from the collection of corporate and individual INCOME TAX. In addition to its Washington, D.C., office, the IRS operates seven regional offices throughout the United States.

International, any of a succession of international socialist and Communist organizations of the 19th and 20th cent. The First International was founded in London in 1864 as the International Workingmen's Association. Karl MARX was a key figure in inspiring its creation and was later chosen as its leader. Its goal was to unite all workers for the purpose of achieving political power along the lines set down by Marx and Friedrich ENGELS in the *Communist Manifesto* (1848). Marx viewed the International as a vehicle for revolution, but it played only a minor role in the revolutionary COMMUNE OF PARIS (1871). Power struggles within the organization greatly weakened it, and the clash between Marx and the anarchist Mikhail BAKUNIN led to its complete disintegration (1876). By 1889, however, socialist parties had been founded in numerous European nations and the need for another International was felt. The Second, or Socialist, International, was founded in that year at a Paris congress, and it later set up permanent headquarters in Belgium, with Emile VANDERVELDE as its president. This International was predominantly political in character, and the German and Russian Social Democratic parties were its most important elements. Its early leaders included Engels, August BEBEL, Karl KAUTSKY, and Georgi Valentinovich PLEKHANOV. Despite the ideological schisms that plagued SOCIALISM during this period, the Second International did much to advance labor legislation and strengthen the democratic socialist movement. It failed, however, in what was perhaps its primary concern—the prevention of war. On the outbreak (1914) of World War I nearly all the socialist parties supported their individual governments, and the Second International collapsed. After the victory of COMMUNISM in the Russian Revolution (1917), a Third, or Communist, International was created (1919). Under the leadership of Vladimir Ilyich LENIN, this Communist International, or COMINTERN, hoped to foster world revolution. The Comintern was not generally acceptable to socialist labor groups, however, and was dissolved in 1943. After World War II, the Comintern was replaced (1947) by the Communist Information Bureau, or COMINFORM, which aided the seizure of power by the Communists in Czechoslovakia. Because of world political pressures the Cominform lost its influence and power after 1948 and became a vehicle for Soviet propaganda. It was disbanded in 1956. After World War I, the Second International was revived (1919) by moderate socialists, and a Vienna, or Two-and-a-Half, International was formed (1921) from splinter leftist groups that spurned both the Second International and the Comintern. In 1923 the Second and Vienna internationals merged to form the Labor and Socialist International, which lasted until the beginning of World War II. After the war this International was continued under the name of the Socialist International, and it exists today. Among its tenets are support for internationally integrated economic systems and civil rights and opposition to left-wing and right-wing totalitarianism and all forms of exploitation and enslavement. See G. M. Stekloff, *History of the First International* (tr. 1927, repr. 1968); James Joll, *The Second International, 1889–1914* (1955); M. M. Drachkovitch, ed., *The Revolutionary Internationals, 1864–1943* (1966); Julius Braunthal, *History of the International* (2 vol., 1967). See also bibliographies under COMMUNISM and SOCIALISM.

International Atomic Energy Agency: see ATOMIC ENERGY AGENCY, INTERNATIONAL.

International Bank for Reconstruction and Development, specialized agency of the United Nations, with headquarters at Washington, D.C.; also called the World Bank. Plans were laid at the Bretton Woods Conference (1944) for the formation of a world bank; it was formally organized in 1945, when 28 countries ratified the agreement. The capital, which may not exceed $24 billion, is divided into shares of $100,000. The bank may make loans to member nations and, under government guarantee, to private investors, for the purpose of facilitating productive investment, encouraging foreign trade, and discharging burdens of international debt. All members of the bank must also belong to the INTERNATIONAL MONETARY FUND. The bank, which by the early 1970s had 117 members, is self-sustaining and has maintained a profit on its lending activities. It is controlled by a board of governors, consisting of one representative of each member state. Each member of the board has 250 votes plus one vote for each share of stock. Ordinary affairs are conducted by the 20 executive directors, selected by the board. In 1972 five regional vice presidents were appointed to oversee the bank's operations in Asia, Latin America and the Caribbean, East Africa, West Africa, and (in one grouping) Europe, the Middle East, and North Africa. The bank also operates the Economic Development Institute, which offers training in economic development for officials of member countries. Closely affiliated with the bank is the International Finance Corporation, founded in 1956. An investment, rather than a lending, agency, it invests in private enterprises without government guarantee. Its 95 members subscribe to a capital of $100 million. In 1960 the bank organized the International Development Association to extend credit on easier terms to nations that cannot qualify for loans from the bank, mainly the developing countries. The group of institutions is collectively known as the World Bank Group. By 1972 they had made over 1,100 loans, credits, and investments, totaling over $22 billion. See the World Bank's publication, *World Bank Operations: Sectoral Programs and Policies* (1972); E. S. Mason and R. E. Asher, *The World Bank since Bretton Woods* (1973).

International Brotherhood of Teamsters, Chauffeurs, Warehousemen, and Helpers of America: see TEAMSTERS UNION.

International Civil Aviation Organization (ICAO), specialized agency of the United Nations, organized in 1947, with headquarters at Montreal. The objective of the ICAO, which in 1972 had 120 members, is to encourage the orderly growth of international civil aviation. Much work has been done in establishing uniform standards for aircraft markings, airworthiness, and licensing of pilots. The ICAO is governed by an assembly, which is composed of one representative of each member nation and meets at least once every three years, and a council of 27 members, which is in continual session. The council may act as arbiter between states in disputes regarding the interpretation of the Chicago Convention on International Civil Aviation of 1944 (see AIR, LAW OF THE). The ICAO also renders technical assistance to member nations, especially in the field of training. In the late 1960s and early 70s the ICAO was heavily engaged with the problem of aircraft hijacking.

International Court of Justice, principal judicial organ of the United Nations, established by chapter 14 of the UN Charter. It superseded the Permanent Court of International Justice (see WORLD COURT), and its statute for the most part repeats that of the former tribunal. The court consists of 15 judges; they are chosen by the General Assembly and the Security Council, voting independently, from a list of candidates nominated by government-appointed national groups of international law experts. No two judges may be from the same country. Nine judges constitute a quorum, and all questions are decided by a majority of the judges present. The permanent seat of the court is at The Hague, but it may hold hearings elsewhere. All states that are members of the United Nations are ipso facto members of the court, and other states may be permitted to adhere to the statute. If a member of the United Nations fails to comply with a judgment of the court, an appeal for assistance may be made to the Security Council. The court may render judgment in certain disputes between states, and with the authorization of the General Assembly it may deliver advisory opinions to any organ of the United Nations and its agencies. A dispute may be brought before the court by consent of the parties in the particular case or by virtue of an advance formal declaration of acceptance of the court's jurisdiction. Forty-six states (as of 1972) have made such declarations, some of them, however, imposing restrictive conditions on their acceptance. The United States has made a declaration that excludes all disputes concerning domestic matters from the court's jurisdiction and reserves to the U.S. government the right to determine what matters it will choose to regard as domestic. The court's competence between states, in any event, is limited to disputes concerning the interpretation of treaties, questions of international law, breaches of international obligation, and the amount of reparations due for such breaches. Much concern has been expressed about the small number of cases that nations have been willing to submit to it. Major opinions of the court have ruled that the General Assembly may not admit a state to the United Nations if the application is vetoed by one of the permanent members of the Security Council; that the United Nations is to be considered as an international legal person; that special United Nations assessments, such as those for the Congo (see ZAÏRE) and Middle East operations, are regular expenses of the United Nations and are binding on all members; and that the Republic of South Africa must withdraw from the territory of South West Africa. See Shabtai Rosenne, *The Law and Practice of the International Court* (2 vol., 1965); George Elian, *The International Court of Justice* (1971).

International Criminal Police Organization: see INTERPOL.

international date line, imaginary line on the earth's surface, generally following the 180° meridian of LONGITUDE, where, by international agreement, travelers change dates. Traveling eastward across the line, one subtracts one calendar day; traveling westward, one adds a day. The date line is necessary to avoid a confusion that would otherwise result. For example, if an airplane were to travel westward with the sun, 24 hr would elapse as it circled the globe, but it would still be the same day for those in the airplane while it would be one day later for those on the ground below them. The same problem would arise if two travelers journeyed in opposite directions to a point on the opposite side of the earth, 180° of longitude distant. The eastward traveler would set his clock ahead 1 hr for each 15° of longitude (see STANDARD TIME), so that his clock would gain a total of 12 hr; the westward traveler would set his clock back 1 hr for each 15°, resulting in a total loss of 12 hr. The two clocks would therefore differ by 24 hr, or one calendar day. The apparent paradox is resolved by requiring that the traveler crossing the date line change his date, thus bringing the travelers into agreement when they meet. The international date line does not follow the 180° meridian along its entire course but bends eastward around the eastern tip of Siberia, westward around the Aleutian Islands, and eastward again around various island groups in the South Pacific in order to avoid a time change in populated areas.

International Development Association: see INTERNATIONAL BANK FOR RECONSTRUCTION AND DEVELOPMENT.

International Finance Corporation: see INTERNATIONAL BANK FOR RECONSTRUCTION AND DEVELOPMENT.

International Geophysical Year (IGY), 18-month period from July, 1957, through Dec., 1958, designated for cooperative study of the earth and its cosmic environment by the scientists of 66 nations. Discoveries were made in the fields of cosmic ray research, climatology, oceanography, and the nature of the earth's atmosphere and magnetic field. Earth satellites (see SATELLITE, ARTIFICIAL) launched by the United States discovered the Van Allen radiation belts and the influx of charged solar particles believed responsible for the auroras. Cross-surface expeditions in the Antarctic led to the conclusion that in the eastern section it is actually composed of a continental region much smaller than was previously thought. Soundings of the world's oceans revealed much new information about the ocean floor and identified seismically active rifts along the summit of a 40,000-mi (64,400-km) chain of undersea mountains. These data led to the PLATE TECTONICS theory, used to explain movements of the earth's crust. The IGY was the largest and most important international scientific effort to that date; one of its many later ramifications was the setting aside of Antarctica as a nonmilitary region to be used for scientific purposes alone. See Sydney Chapman, *IGY: Year of Discovery* (1960); Walter Sullivan, *Assault on the Unknown* (1961); J. T. Wilson, *IGY: The Year of the New Moons* (1961).

international gold standard: see INTERNATIONAL MONETARY SYSTEM.

International Governmental Organizations, formed to deal with supranational problems through the cooperation of national governments. The period following World War II saw the development of many such organizations, especially regional associations designed to handle military or economic problems in a particular geographic area. Among the most important international organizations are the ARAB LEAGUE, BENELUX ECONOMIC UNION,

CENTRAL AMERICAN COMMON MARKET, CENTRAL TREATY ORGANIZATION, COMMON MARKET, COUNCIL FOR MUTUAL ECONOMIC ASSISTANCE, EUROPEAN COMMUNITY, EUROPEAN MONETARY AGREEMENT, EUROPEAN ORGANIZATION FOR NUCLEAR RESEARCH, LATIN AMERICAN FREE TRADE ASSOCIATION, NORDIC COUNCIL, NORTH ATLANTIC TREATY ORGANIZATION, ORGANIZATION OF AFRICAN UNITY, ORGANIZATION OF AMERICAN STATES, SOUTHEAST ASIA TREATY ORGANIZATION, and WARSAW TREATY ORGANIZATION. The charter of the United Nations recognizes the usefulness of such associations, and many of them have official connections with one or more of the specialized UN agencies. International governmental organizations operate in many fields; some examples are described below.

Economic Cooperation. The European Free Trade Association (EFTA) is a customs union and trading bloc, ratified in 1960 by Austria, Denmark, Great Britain, Norway, Portugal, Sweden, and Switzerland. Finland became an associate member in 1961, and Iceland joined in 1970. This group, known through the 1960s as the "outer seven" (as opposed to the "inner six" members of the Common Market), was organized largely on the initiative of Great Britain in an attempt to solve economic problems posed by the development of the Common Market. The EFTA agreement provided for gradual reduction of internal tariffs and quota restrictions between member states. Unlike the Common Market, EFTA did not propose to establish a single uniform tariff against the outside world. It began with two goals: to gain free trade among members and to seek a broader economic union with the rest of Western Europe. The first was accomplished in 1966, when most of the intra-EFTA tariffs were abolished. Negotiations toward the second goal began in 1961, when Great Britain sought entry into the Common Market. Its bid was rejected (1963) by France; however, later discussions succeeded, and in 1973 Denmark, Great Britain, and Ireland entered the Common Market. The same negotiations produced a new trade accord between the newly expanded Common Market and most of the remaining members of EFTA. The Organization for Economic Cooperation and Development (OECD) came into being in 1961, superseding the Organization for European Economic Cooperation, which had been founded in 1948. By the early 1970s its member nations included Austria, Belgium, Denmark, Finland, France, West Germany, Great Britain, Greece, Iceland, Ireland, Italy, Japan, Luxembourg, the Netherlands, Norway, Portugal, Spain, Sweden, Switzerland, Turkey, the United States, and Canada. Associated with certain OECD activities, in a special status, were Australia and Yugoslavia. The members are pledged to work together to promote their economies, to extend aid to underdeveloped nations, and to contribute to the expansion of world trade. Agencies operating under OECD include the Centre for Educational Research and Innovation, the Development Centre, the European Monetary Agreement, and the European Nuclear Energy Agency.

Political and Military Affairs. The Council of Europe was founded in 1949 to promote greater unity and to safeguard the political and cultural heritage of Europe. Its members at the beginning of 1972 included Austria, Belgium, Cyprus, Denmark, France, West Germany, Great Britain, Iceland, Ireland, Italy, Luxembourg, Malta, the Netherlands, Norway, Sweden, Switzerland, and Turkey. The conventions and treaties signed under the auspices of the Council of Europe deal with humanitarian, cultural, and social problems. In 1958 the council established a European Court of Human Rights to protect the rights of individuals in member nations against arbitrary government action. In 1966 the council reorganized in order to modernize its various activities. The Western European Union (WEU) became effective in 1955 as a defensive, economic, social, and cultural organization, consisting of Belgium, France, West Germany, Great Britain, Italy, Luxembourg, and the Netherlands. The WEU was created as a substitute solution embodied in the PARIS PACTS, after France had refused to ratify a treaty providing for a European Defense Community. Since Western military cooperation has been dominated by the North Atlantic Treaty Organization, and Western economic coordination by the Common Market, the primary function of the WEU has been to supervise the rearmament of Germany, as provided for under the Paris Pacts. In 1960 the WEU transferred its cultural and social activities to the Council of Europe. Between 1963 and 1970, WEU served as a regular forum for discussions between Great Britain and the Common Market countries concerning the entry of Great Britain into the Common Market.

Science and Technology. The Colombo Plan for Cooperative Economic Development in South and Southeast Asia came into force in 1951. The plan is a cooperative attempt to strengthen the economies of the nations of Southeast Asia. By the early 1970s there were 23 members. The original formulators of the plan were the nations of the British Commonwealth; the United States, which later joined the plan, became the largest donor. Assistance was given in the form of educational aid, training programs, loans, food supplies, equipment, and technical aid. Originally a seven-year program, the Colombo Plan has been several times extended.

Health and Sanitation. The Pan-American Health Organization was established in 1902 as the International Sanitary Bureau. In 1958 the present name was adopted. Its members include all the Latin American nations, Canada, and the United States. France, Great Britain, and the Netherlands are also associated with the organization on behalf of their departments and territories in the Western Hemisphere. The organization cooperates with members in developing public services, collects health statistics, and aids in the control of communicable diseases. The European Commission for the Control of Foot and Mouth Disease, founded in 1954, serves to advise its 21 member governments on the problems of controlling the disease and to purchase vaccine in emergency cases. It also carries out special research work on the disease.

International Grenfell Association, organization established in 1912 to aid the efforts of Sir Wilfred Thomason Grenfell (1865–1940), an English physician and missionary to the people of Labrador, Canada. The Association has helped to make possible the building of hospitals, orphanage boarding schools, agricultural stations, and other community enterprises in Canada.

International Labor Organization (ILO), specialized agency of the United Nations, with headquarters in Geneva. It was created in 1919 by the Versailles Treaty and affiliated with the League of Nations until 1945, when it voted to sever ties with the League. In 1946 it became an agency of the United Nations. Although not a member of the League, the United States joined the ILO in 1934. Through international action the ILO seeks to improve labor conditions, promote a higher standard of living, and further social justice. Promotion of international accord on such matters as regulation of hours of work, provision of adequate wages, protection of workers against occupational disease and injury, and protection of women and children and those who work outside their own countries accounts for much of its activities. The ILO consists of a general conference of representatives of the members (4 from each member state), a governing body of 48 people (24 representing governments, 12 employers, and 12 labor), and an International Labor Office controlled by the governing body. The ILO is financed by contributions from member states; in 1973 its membership stood at 123. In the course of its history the ILO has drafted more than 275 conventions and recommendations on international labor standards. It received the Nobel Peace Prize in 1969. See D. A. Morse, *The Origin and Evolution of the I.L.O. and Its Role in the World Community* (1969); C. W. Jenks, *Social Justice and the Law of Nations* (1970); A. E. Alcock, *History of the International Labour Organization* (1971).

International Ladies Garment Workers Union (ILGWU), U.S. labor union formed in 1900 by the amalgamation of seven local unions. At the turn of the century most of the workers in the garment industry were Jewish immigrants, whose attempts at organization were hampered by clashes between anarchists and socialists; this heritage of strife was carried over into the ILGWU, and in its early years many members were sympathetic to various radical movements. Despite these conflicts the union grew rapidly in its first years. However, the depression of 1903 and the open-shop campaign launched by the newly formed National Association of Manufacturers wiped out many hard-won gains. By 1908 it appeared as if the union might be merged with the United Garment Workers, then the American Federation of Labor (AFL) union of men's tailors. At that point the union launched two spectacular and successful mass strikes (1909–11) in the garment district of New York City. As a result of the strikes, the dress manufacturers agreed to deal with the ILGWU and its affiliates. That settlement also embodied the famous Protocol of Peace, which was proposed by Louis D. Brandeis and was based on the concept of perpetual economic peace in the union. Although that concept was in sharp contrast to the radical trade-union philosophy then prevailing among garment workers, it served as a model of cooperation between labor and management. The Communists' drive for control of the union during the 1920s was defeated by moderates under the leadership of David Dubinsky. Although the struggle seriously hurt the ILGWU, the union benefited by the labor policies of President Franklin Delano Roosevelt, and membership rose to 300,000 in 1942. In 1937 the ILGWU briefly joined the Congress of Industrial Organizations (CIO); it then temporarily became an independent union and finally rejoined the AFL in 1940. Under the presidency of David Dubinsky, the ILGWU grew into one of the nation's most powerful and progressive unions, with a wide range of member benefits. ILGWU gained the respect of the manufacturers by its willingness to assist employers in the industry with loans and technical assistance. Dubinsky retired in 1966. The following year a $1 million Dubinsky Foundation was established, with the goal of making grants to causes and institutions in line with ILGWU objectives. See L. L. Lorwin, *The Women's Garment Workers* (1924); Benjamin Stolberg, *Tailor's Progress* (1944); M. D. Danish, *The World of David Dubinsky* (1957).

international language, sometimes called universal language, a language intended to be used by people of different linguistic backgrounds to facilitate communication among them and, incidentally, to reduce the misunderstandings and antagonisms caused by language differences. An international language is usually intended not to supplant existing mother tongues but to play a secondary or auxiliary role as it furthers international communication. There are several kinds of international languages. These include artificial tongues; national languages used outside their national boundaries; and national languages used in a modified, usually greatly simplified form. An artificial tongue is an idiom that has not developed in a speech community like a natural language but has been constructed by human agents from various materials, such as devised signs, elements or modified elements taken from existing natural languages, and invented forms. It has been estimated that since the 17th cent. several hundred efforts have been made to create such artificial languages. Some philosophers of the 17th cent., among them Francis Bacon, René Descartes, and Gottfried Wilhelm Leibniz, proposed the construction of a so-called philosophical language that would consist of a system of communication based on classification according to logic rather than on human speech. It would therefore use signs to represent matters to be communicated. Several such systems were subsequently devised, but they turned out to be too difficult for most people to use and had, as well, the serious handicap of being unsuited to conversation. Another type of artificial language that has had more popular success is the kind formed from elements or modified elements of existing natural languages. The first artificial language of this kind to have some prominence was Volapük. Introduced in 1880, it was created by Johann Martin Schleyer, a Roman Catholic priest of German extraction. Schleyer worked out for Volapük an alphabet, a grammar, and a vocabulary based chiefly on Latin, the Romance languages, and the Germanic languages. Although Volapük had a great vogue at first, it rapidly lost ground when it proved to be difficult to learn and use. ESPERANTO, another artificial language, was invented by Dr. Ludwig L. Zamenhof of Poland, and was first presented to the public in 1887. It has enjoyed some recognition as an international language, often being used, for example, at international meetings and conferences. In fact, an estimated 8 million people are said to speak it. The vocabulary of Esperanto is formed by adding various affixes to individual roots and is derived chiefly from Latin, Greek, the Romance languages, and the Germanic languages. The grammar is based on that of European languages but is greatly simplified and regular. Esperanto has a phonetic spelling. It uses the symbols of the Roman alphabet, each one standing for only one sound. A simplified revision of Esperanto is Ido, short for Esperandido. Ido was introduced in 1907 by the French philosopher Louis Couturat, but it failed to replace Esperanto. Still another artificial language, known as INTERLINGUA, was created in 1951 by the International Auxiliary Language Association. Interlingua is derived from English and the Romance languages in both grammar and vocabulary. It has been used at medical and scientific meetings. Since so many artificial languages have their vocabulary and grammar based on those of the Indo-European tongues, speakers of non-Indo-European idioms find them difficult and even distasteful. Earlier it was said that a natural, national language used outside its national boundaries by other peoples could serve as an international language. Latin, for instance, was a universal language in Europe during the Middle Ages and the Renaissance. French was once known as the universal language of diplomacy, and English today is often said to fill such a role in world commerce. A modified, greatly simplified form of an existing national language has also been suggested as a possibility for an international language. One noteworthy example is *Latino Sine Flexione* ("Latin without inflection"), the brainchild of Giuseppe Peano, an Italian mathematician of the early 20th cent. Also called Interlingua, it is essentially a very simplified form of Latin. It too failed to gain widespread adoption, partly because its vocabulary was too extensive for the average man to master. More recently, Basic English, a dramatically simplified form of English, has been proposed as an international secondary tongue. Developed between 1925 and 1932 by the English scholar C. K. Ogden, it has a reduced vocabulary of 850 words and an uncomplicated grammar. The vocabulary is composed of 600 nouns, 150 adjectives, and 100 other words that include verbs, adverbs, prepositions, and pronouns. Basic English has several features that make it suitable as an international auxiliary tongue. It is easy to learn and adequate for satisfactory communication; in addition, it is a simplified form of a widely used, and therefore very familiar, world language. See Albert L. Guérard, *A Short History of the International Language Movement* (1922); C. K. Ogden, *Basic English* (9th ed. 1944); Marie Pei, *One Language for the World* (1958).

international law, body of rules considered legally binding in the relations between national states, also known as the law of nations. It is sometimes called public international law in contrast to private international law (or CONFLICT OF LAWS), which regulates private legal affairs affected by more than one jurisdiction. In content international law includes both the customary rules and usages to which states have given express or tacit assent and the provisions of ratified TREATIES and conventions. It does not include the usages of courtesy and good will that are termed "international comity," but some of these usages tend to assume the status of law. International law is directly and strongly influenced, although not made, by the writings of jurists and publicists, by instructions to diplomatic agents, by important conventions even when they are not ratified, and by arbitral awards. The decisions of the Permanent Court of International Justice (see WORLD COURT), of the INTERNATIONAL COURT OF JUSTICE, and of national courts, such as PRIZE courts, which decide questions of international law, are considered by some theorists to be a part of international law. In many modern states international law is by custom or statute regarded as part of national—or, as it is usually called, municipal—law, and the municipal courts will, if possible, interpret the municipal law so as to give effect to international law. Because there is no sovereign supernational body to enforce international law, some older theorists, including Hobbes, Pufendorf, and John Austin, have denied that it is true law. Nevertheless, international law is recognized as law in practice, and the sanctions for failing to comply, although often less direct, are similar to those of municipal law; they include the force of public opinion, self-help, intervention by third states, the sanctions of international organizations such as the League of Nations and the United Nations, and, in the last resort, war. National states are fundamentally the entities with which international law is concerned, although in certain cases municipal law may impose international duties upon private persons, e.g, the obligation to desist from PIRACY. New rights and duties have been imposed on individuals within the framework of international law by the decisions in the WAR CRIMES trials, by the GENOCIDE convention, and by the Declaration of Human Rights (see ECONOMIC AND SOCIAL COUNCIL). The nations of antiquity followed certain usages in their relations with one another, but they did not acknowledge any wholly uniform body of rules, although there were regular practices concerning aliens, asylum, and ambassadors. In the arbitration of their disputes the Greek city-states attained notable success. There was little scope for an international law in the period of ancient and medieval empires, and its modern beginnings coincide, therefore, with the rise of national states after the Middle Ages. Rules of maritime intercourse and rules respecting diplomatic agents (see DIPLOMATIC SERVICE) soon came into existence. At the beginning of the 17th cent. the great multitude of small independent states, which were finding international lawlessness intolerable, prepared the way for the favorable reception given to the *De jure belli ac pacis* [concerning the law of war and peace] (1625) of Hugo GROTIUS, the first comprehensive formulation of international law. Though not formally accepted by any nation, his opinions and observations were afterwards regularly consulted, and they often served as a basis for reaching agreement in international disputes. Among the principles that he enunciated and that form the basis of international law are the sovereignty and the legal equality of all states. Other important writers on international law were Cornelius van BYNKERSHOEK, Georg F. von MARTENS, Christian von WOLFF, and Emerich VATTEL. The later growth of international law came largely through treaties concluded among states accepted as members of the "family of nations," which first included the Christian states of Western Europe, then the states of the New World, and, finally, non-Christian states of the Orient and other parts of the world. The United States contributed much to the laws of NEUTRALITY and aided in securing recognition of the doctrine of freedom of the seas (see SEAS, FREEDOM OF THE). The provisions of international law were ignored in the Napoleonic period, but the Congress of Vienna (see VIENNA, CONGRESS OF) reestablished and added much, particularly in respect to international rivers and the classification and treatment of diplomatic agents. The Declaration of Paris (see PARIS, DECLARATION OF) abolished privateering, drew up rules of CONTRABAND, and stipulated rules of BLOCKADE. The Geneva Convention (1864) provided for more humane treatment of the wounded. The last quarter of the 19th cent. saw many international conventions concerning PRISONERS OF WAR, communication, collision and SALVAGE at sea, protection of migrating bird and sea life, and suppression of the white slave traffic. In the 20th cent. there were agreements concerning many subjects, including traffic in narcotics and aerial and radio communications. Resort to ARBITRATION of disputes became more frequent. The lawmaking conventions of the HAGUE CONFERENCES represent the chief development of international law before World War I. The Declaration of London (see LONDON, DECLARATION OF) contained a convention of prize law, which, although not ratified, is usually followed. At the Pan-American Congresses many lawmaking agreements affecting the Western Hemisphere have been signed. In World War I no strong nations remained on the sidelines to give effective backing to international law, and it was again endangered; many of its provisions were violated. New modes of warfare presented new problems in the laws of war, but attempts after the war to effect disarmament and to prohibit certain types of weapons (see WAR, LAWS OF) failed, as the outbreak and course of World War II showed. The end of hostilities in 1945 saw the world again faced with grave international problems including rectification of boundaries, care of refugees, and administration of the territory of the defeated enemy (see TRUSTEESHIP, TERRITORIAL). The inadequacy of the LEAGUE OF NATIONS and of such idealistic renunciations of war as the KELLOGG-BRIAND PACT led to the formation of the UNITED NATIONS as a body capable of compelling obedience to international law and maintaining peace. After World War II a notable advance in international law was the definition and punishment of war crimes. Attempts at a general codification of international law, however, proceeded slowly under the International Law Commission established in 1947 by the United Nations. The nuclear age and the space age have led to new developments in international law. The basis of SPACE LAW was developed in the 1960s under UN auspices. The 1963 limited test ban treaty (see DISARMAMENT, NUCLEAR) prohibited nuclear tests in the atmosphere, in outer space, and under water. The agreements of the Strategic Arms Limitation Talks, signed by the United States and the USSR in 1972, limited defensive and offensive weapon systems. See INTERNATIONAL RELATIONS. For a collection of texts by early writers, see J. B. Scott, ed., *Classics of International Law* (12 vol., 1911–27). For general treatises, see Henry Wheaton, *International Law* (1836, repr. 1972) and L F. L. Oppenheim, *International Law* (1905–6; 8th ed. 1955). See also Hersh Lauterpacht, *Function of Law in the International Community* (1933, repr. 1966); Philip C. Jessup, *A Modern Law of Nations* (1948, repr. 1968); Arthur Nussbaum, *A Concise History of the Law of Nations* (rev. ed. 1954); W. L. Gould, *An Introduction to International Law* (1957); J. L. Brierly, *The Law of Nations* (6th ed. 1963, ed. by H. Waldock); W. G. Friedmann, *The Changing Structure of International Law* (1964).

International Monetary Fund (IMF), specialized agency of the United Nations, established in 1945. It was planned at the Bretton Woods Conference (1944), and its headquarters are in Washington, D.C. There is close collaboration between it and the International Bank for Reconstruction and Development. The organization, using a fund of some $28 billion subscribed by the member nations, purchases foreign currencies on application from its members so as to discharge international indebtedness and stabilize exchange rates. To facilitate international trade and reduce inequities in exchange the fund has limited power to set the par value of currencies. Members are provided with technical assistance in making monetary transactions. The fund is ruled by a board of governors, with one representative from each nation. Each member has 250 votes plus one vote for each $100,000 of the nation's subscription quota. The board of governors elects an executive board of 20 representatives to conduct regular operations. In 1972 there were 124 members in the IMF, Rumania and Yugoslavia being the only Communist nations to belong to it. See studies by John Fleming (1964), Shigeo Horie (1964), and H. G. Grubel (1970).

international monetary system, rules and procedures by which different national currencies are exchanged for each other in world trade. The major need of such a system is to define a common standard of value for the world's currencies; for most of the period since the late 19th cent. gold, either directly or indirectly, has served as the standard. The first modern international monetary system was the international gold standard. Operating during the late 19th and early 20th cent., the gold standard provided for the free circulation between nations of gold coins of standard specification. Under the system, gold served as an instrument of exchange and the only standard of value; during the period of the international gold standard gold was, in effect, the international currency. The advantages of the system lay in its stabilizing influence. A nation that exported more than it imported would receive gold in payment of the balance; such an influx of gold lowered the value of the domestic currency and thus raised prices. Higher prices resulted in decreasing the demand for exports, an outflow of gold to pay for the now relatively cheap imports, and a return to the original price level (see BALANCE OF TRADE and BALANCE OF PAYMENTS). A major defect in such a system was its inherent lack of liquidity; the world's supply of money would necessarily be limited by the world's supply of gold. Moreover, any unusual increase in the supply of gold, such as the discovery of a rich lode, would cause prices to rise abruptly. Partly because of the liquidity problem and partly because of disruptions caused by World War I, the international gold standard broke down in 1914. During the 1920s it was replaced by the gold bullion standard, a variant of the basic system in which nations no longer mint gold coins but back their currencies with gold bullion and agree to buy and sell the bullion at a fixed price. However, the pressures of the Great Depression and economic nationalism proved too great for the modified system, and it too was abandoned in the 1930s. In the decades following World War II, international trade was conducted according to the gold-exchange standard. Under such a system, nations fix the value of their currencies not to gold but to some foreign currency, which is in turn fixed to and redeemable in gold. Most nations fixed their currencies to the U.S. dollar and retained dollar reserves in the United States, which was known as the "key currency" country. During the 1960s, as U.S. commitments abroad drew gold reserves from the nation, confidence in the dollar was weakened, leading some dollar-holding countries and speculators to seek to exchange their dollars for gold. A severe drain on U.S. gold reserves developed, and, in order to correct the situation, the so-called two-tier system was created in 1968. In the official tier, consisting of central bank gold traders, the value of gold was set by decree at $35 an ounce, and gold payments to non-central bankers were prohibited. In the free-market tier, consisting of all non-governmental gold traders, gold was completely demonitized, with its price set by supply and demand. Gold and the U.S. dollar remained the major reserve assets for the world's central banks, although SPECIAL DRAWING RIGHTS were created in the late 1960s as a new reserve currency. Despite such measures, the drain on U.S. gold reserves continued into the 1970s, and in 1971 the United States was forced to abandon gold convertibility. President Richard Nixon announced that it would no longer be possible for other governments automatically to convert dollars into gold or any other reserve currency. Moreover, the actions of 1971 left the world without a single, unified international monetary system. Gold, however, remained the nominal standard of value for the world's currencies; in 1973, following two devaluations (1971, 1973) of the dollar, the price of gold in the official tier was approximately $42 an ounce; its free-market price, however, was several times that amount. See R. A. Triffin, *Our International Monetary System* (1968); L. B. Yeager, *The International Monetary Mechanism* (1968); H. G. Grubel, *The International Monetary System* (1969).

International Red Cross: see RED CROSS.

International Refugee Organization (IRO), temporary agency of the United Nations, established in 1946. In arranging for the care and the repatriation or resettlement of Europeans made homeless by World War II, the organization brought to a conclusion part of the work of the UNITED NATIONS RELIEF AND REHABILITATION ADMINISTRATION. IRO terminated its work in 1952, having resettled c.1,000,000 persons. It was superseded by the Office of the UNITED NATIONS HIGH COMMISSIONER FOR REFUGEES. See L. W. Holborn, *The International Refugee Organization* (1956).

international relations, study of the relations among states and other political and economic units in the international system. Particular areas of study within the field of international relations include diplomacy and diplomatic history, INTERNATIONAL LAW, international organizations, international finance and economics, and communications, among others. In addition, increased attention has been paid in recent years to developing a more scientific understanding of the international system as a whole. Aspects of international relations have been studied as early as the time of the ancient Greek historian Thucydides. As a separate and definable discipline, however, it dates from the early 20th cent., when the first organized efforts were made to find alternatives to wars in nation-state international behavior. Two schools of thought quickly developed: One looks to strengthened international law and international organizations to preserve peace; the other emphasizes that nations will always use their power to achieve goals and sees the key to peace in a BALANCE OF POWER among competing states. With increased importance attached to a theoretical understanding of the whole international system, there has been a growing use of concepts and modes of analysis developed in the natural sciences in an attempt to improve the verifiability and applicability of theories. In many of the leading U.S. universities there are both research institutes and schools of international relations. See SECURITY; DIPLOMATIC SERVICE; UNITED NATIONS; EUROPEAN COMMUNITY. See Raymond Aron, *Peace and War* (tr. 1967); F. H. Hartmann, *The Relations of Nations* (3d ed. 1967); H. J. Morganthau, *Politics among Nations* (5th ed. 1972); F. S. Northedge and M. J. Grieve, *A Hundred Years of International Relations* (1971).

International style, in architecture, phase of the modern movement that emerged in the 1920s. New emphasis was given to a regularization of structure and a lightening of mass, often resulting in an austere framework surrounding great expanses of glass. Important examples are the BAUHAUS (1926) at Dessau by Gropius; the Barcelona pavilion (1929) by Miës van der Rohe; and the Villa Savoye (1929-31), Poissy, by Le Corbusier. In the United States exponents of the style were William Lescaze, George Howe, and Richard Neutra. See studies by Walters Art Gallery (1962) and H. R. Hitchcock (1932, repr. 1966).

International style, in painting: see GOTHIC ARCHITECTURE AND ART.

International System of Units, officially called the System International, or SI, system of units adopted by the 11th General Conference on Weights and Measures (1960). It is based on the METRIC SYSTEM. The basic units of length, mass, and time are those of the MKS SYSTEM of metric units: the METER, KILOGRAM, and SECOND. Other basic units are the AMPERE of electric current, the kelvin of temperature (a degree of temperature measured on the KELVIN TEMPERATURE SCALE), the candela, or CANDLE, of luminous intensity, and the MOLE, used to measure the amount of a substance present. All other units are derived from these basic units. See U.S. National Bureau of Standards, Spec. Pub. 330, *International System of Units* (1971).

International Telecommunication Union (ITU), specialized agency of the United Nations, with headquarters at Geneva. It was created in 1934 as a result of the merging of the International Telegraph Union (est. 1865; the first international governmental organization) and the International Radiotelegraph Union (est. 1906). The union functions under the International Telecommunication Convention, which was adopted in 1947 and revised in 1967. The goal of the organization is to extend and improve all forms of international telecommunication by allotting radio frequencies, by encouraging the establishment of low rates, and by perfecting communications in rescue operations. The ITU is governed by the plenipotentiary conference at which all members are represented; it normally meets once every four or five years. The conference elects an administrative council of 29 members. In 1970, ITU had 139 members. Conferences for the regulation of telecommunication in space have been among ITU's more recent activities.

internment, in international law, detention of the nationals or property of an enemy or a belligerent. A belligerent will intern enemy merchant ships or take them as PRIZE, and a neutral should intern both belligerent ships that fail to leave its ports within a specified time and belligerent troops that enter its territory. The practice of detaining persons considered dangerous during a war is often called internment, even though they may not be enemy nationals. In World War II the United States detained persons of Japanese ancestry in RELOCATION CENTERS. The Geneva Convention of 1949 on the Protection of Civilian Persons in Time of War provides for the unrestricted departure of enemy aliens from the territory of a belligerent at the outbreak of conflict, and the humane treatment of those aliens who choose to remain.

internuncio: see NUNCIO.

Interpol, acronym for the International Criminal Police Organization, a worldwide clearing house for police information. Conceived in 1914, Interpol was formally established in 1923 with headquarters at Vienna. In 1938 it was effectively disbanded by Hitler's *Anschluss* of Austria. After World War II the agency was reconstituted (1946) with headquarters in Paris. Its principal services are to provide member nations (more than 100) with information on the whereabouts of international criminals, to organize seminars on scientific crime detection, and to facilitate the apprehension of criminals (although it does not apprehend criminals directly). The organization claims to avoid those crimes that deal with political, military, religious, or racial matters. Interpol has been most successful with regard to counterfeiting, forgery, smuggling, and the narcotics trade. The United States became a member in 1938. See studies by A. J. Forrest (1955), Tom Tullett (1963), and Michael Fooner (1973).

interrogation point: see PUNCTUATION.

Interstate Commerce Commission (ICC), independent agency of the U.S. government established in 1887; it is charged with regulating the economics and services of specified carriers engaged in transportation between states. Surface transportation under the ICC's jurisdiction includes railroads, trucking companies, bus lines, freight forwarders, water carriers, oil pipelines, transportation brokers, and express agencies. The ICC, the first regulatory commission in U.S. history, was established as a result of mounting public indignation in the 1880's against railroad malpractices and abuses (see GRANGER MOVEMENT) and it originally had jurisdiction only over railroads. The ICC was designed chiefly to prevent railroads from charging exorbitant rates and from discriminatory practices (e.g., the REBATE); but until the presidential administration of Theodore ROOSEVELT, the effectiveness of the ICC was limited by the failure of Congress to provide it with the means to enforce the rate determinations it made, by a narrow interpretation of its powers by the Supreme Court, and by the vague and confusing language of its enabling act. The Hepburn Act (1906), however, extended the jurisdiction of the commission to include intraterritorial commerce, ferries, terminal facilities, bridges, and express, sleeping-car, and pipe-line (exclusive of those carrying water or gas) companies. This act, moreover, empowered the commission upon complaint and after a full hearing to reduce any rates adjudged unreasonable. The number of commissioners was increased from five to seven. The powers of the ICC were further amplified by the Mann-Elkins Act (1910), which put telegraph, telephone, wireless, and cable companies under the commission's jurisdiction and which allowed the board to fix rates without previous complaint. By authority of the Adamson-La Follette Valuation Act (1913), the ICC began a comprehensive evaluation of the property of common carrier companies to help the commission determine reasonable profits for the companies. The commission's control was enhanced by powers to investigate, halt, and indemnify violations of the Interstate Commerce Act, to inquire into the management of interstate transport companies, and to demand reports from them. These powers were augmented by decisions of the Supreme Court, whose broadening interpretation of the commerce clause of the Constitution extended Federal control of commerce. The Transportation Act of 1920 (also known as the Esch-Cummins Act) empowered the commission to fix rates that would yield "a fair return upon the aggregate value of the railway property of the country," to plan the consolidation of railroads into a small number of integrated systems, and to deal with labor disputes in interstate transportation. The number of members on the ICC was increased to 11. After World War I the lack of judicial interference with the operations of the ICC increased the commission's power and prestige. The Emergency Railroad Transportation Act of 1933 set up simpler rules for determining fair rates and repealed the recapture clause—also in the Transportation Act of 1920—which required a railroad to give the ICC one half of its net earnings in excess of 6 percent of valuation. The ICC's regulation of communication was transferred to the newly formed Federal Communications Commission in 1934. But the ICC's jurisdiction was extended to include buses and trucks (1935), water-borne carriers operating coastwise, intercoastally, and upon inland waters of the United States (1940), and freight forwarders (1942). In the 1950s and 1960s the ICC enforced U.S. Supreme Court rulings that required the desegregation of terminal passenger facilities. When the Dept. of Transportation was created in 1966 the safety functions of the ICC were transferred to it, but the ICC retained its rate-making and regulatory functions.

interstellar matter, matter in a GALAXY between the stars. Compared to the size of an entire galaxy, stars are virtually points, so that the region occupied by the interstellar matter constitutes nearly all the physical volume of a galaxy. Although the density of interstellar matter is far lower than in the best laboratory vacuum, the total mass contained between stars is an appreciable fraction of the mass of most galaxies. Interstellar matter is mostly gaseous, but about 1% exists in the form of tiny solid particles called interstellar grains. The grains are believed to be about 10^{-5}cm in size, elongated in shape, and aligned with the magnetic field; their composition is believed to be frozen water vapor and carbon dioxide. The grains are not distributed uniformly in space but are found in clumpy clouds. The clouds obscure the view of the galaxy in certain directions, particularly in the direction of the galactic center. They polarize and selectively scatter the starlight passing through them; blue light is scattered more than red light so that stars partially obscured by interstellar matter appear redder than their true color. Since the distances and intrinsic luminosities of many stars are estimated from analysis of their spectra, this effect has been responsible for errors in calculating the distances and luminosities of these stars. In the vicinity of bright stars the grains appear as glowing regions because of the intensity of the light they scatter; these regions are called reflection nebulas. Regions where the clouds are so thick that they obscure all starlight are called dark nebulas. The interstellar gas, which consists mostly of hydrogen and helium, is neutral at points far removed from any star (H I regions) but is highly ionized (the electrons are detached from their atoms) in the immediate vicinity of each star (H II regions). The gas is virtually transparent to visible light; there is weak optical absorption by certain trace atoms (sodium, calcium) and molecules (cyanogen, carbon hydride). However, within a short distance from a star, nearly all its ultraviolet light is absorbed; the energy from this light maintains the state of ionization in the circumstellar H II region, which is called the Strömgren sphere. If the ionized gas happens to be dense, it is also called an emission nebula because it is visible by the light emitted by the ions and electrons when they recombine. In addition to the spectra of hydrogen and helium (see SPECTRUM), some spectral lines not formed under ordinary laboratory conditions ("forbidden lines") are seen. The prominent green color of certain emission nebulas is due to a forbidden line of doubly ionized oxygen. In H I regions neutral hydrogen atoms absorb and emit radio waves with a wavelength of 21 cm, due to a reorientation of the proton spin in the magnetic field produced by the electron spin (see MAGNETIC RESONANCE). Besides atomic hydrogen, many molecules, including formaldehyde and water vapor, have been detected in the interstellar medium by the techniques of RADIO ASTRONOMY.

intertype, TYPE set by the Intertype machine. See PRINTING.

interval, in music, the difference in pitch between two tones. Intervals may be measured acoustically in terms of their vibration numbers. They are more generally named according to the number of steps they contain in the diatonic scale of the piano; e.g., from C to D is a second, C and D being the first two notes of the scale of C. The fourth, fifth, and octave are termed perfect intervals as they have a characteristic sonority quite unlike any other interval. An interval between two natural notes, neither note being a sharp or a flat, is a major interval; if it is reduced by a semitone, it becomes minor. If a perfect or a minor interval is made half a step smaller it is called diminished, and when half a step larger, augmented. An interval may also be expressed by means of the ratio of the frequencies of its two tones. For example, the octave may be expressed by the ratio 2:1 because its upper tone has a frequency twice that of its lower tone.

intestine, muscular hoselike portion of the gastrointestinal tract extending from the lower end of the stomach (pylorus) to the anal opening. In humans this fairly narrow (about 1 in./2.5 cm) tubelike structure winds compactly back and forth within the abdominal cavity for about 23 ft (7 m), and is known as the small intestine. It is not only an organ of digestion (for that part of the process not completed by the stomach) but is the chief organ of absorption. By contraction of its muscular walls (peristalsis) the food mass is propelled onward and, as it is carried along, it is subject to the digestive action of the secretions of the intestinal lining as well as to that of bile and pancreatic juice which enter the upper intestine (duodenum) from ducts leading from the liver and pancreas. Innumerable minute projections (villi) in the intestinal mucous lining absorb the altered food for distribution by the blood and lymphatic systems to the rest of the body. Food continues to pass into the middle (jejunum) and end (ileum) of the small intestines. The small intestine joins the large intestine (colon) at the cecum in the right lower abdominal cavity. Here, also, is the APPENDIX, a blind pouch projecting from the cecum. The large intestine is wider in diameter. Its direction as it leaves the cecum is upward (ascending colon), across the abdominal cavity (transverse colon) beneath the stomach, and then downward (descending colon) on the left side of the abdominal cavity, making a sharp turn in the left lower portion (sigmoid) to merge with the rectum. In all, the large intestine is about 5 ft (1.5 m) long. Bacteria, the indigestible residue of food, and mucus form the bulk of matter in the large intestine. The water content of the bulk is absorbed through the walls of the large intestine, and the solid matter is excreted through the rectum. See DIGESTIVE SYSTEM.

Inthanon (ĭn'tənôn"), peak, 8,512 ft (2,594 m), in the Thanon Tong Chai range, NW Thailand. It is the highest point in Thailand.

Intolerable Acts, name given by American patriots to five laws (including the QUEBEC ACT) adopted by Parliament in 1774, which limited the political and geographical freedom of the colonists. Four of these laws were passed to punish the people of Massachusetts for the BOSTON TEA PARTY. The Boston Port Bill closed the port until such time as the East India Company should be paid for the tea destroyed. Other acts changed the royal charter of Massachusetts; provided for the quartering of troops—the New York assembly had earlier (1767–69) been suspended for refusing to make provisions for British troops—in the colony without provincial consent; and gave royal officials in conflict with colonial authorities the right to trial in England. American opposition to these laws and to the Quebec Act was felt in all the colonies, since the actions taken against Massachusetts might be extended to any colony and the Quebec Act was considered a violation of the sea-to-sea grants of many colonial charters. The outcome was the First CONTINENTAL CONGRESS.

intoxication, condition of body tissue affected by a poisonous substance. Poisonous materials, or toxins, are to be found in heavy metals such as lead and mercury, in drugs, in chemicals such as alcohol and carbon tetrachloride, in gases such as carbon monoxide, and in radioactive materials. Toxins are also elaborated by the microorganisms that cause such diseases as diphtheria, tetanus, and botulism. The body itself may produce poisonous substances (autointoxication) in the course of such disorders as diabetes and in some infectious diseases. Which body tissues are affected depends on the type of toxin. Phosphorus, for example, affects the liver, poisonous mushrooms the nervous system and red blood cells. See ALCOHOLISM; LEAD POISONING; RADIATION SICKNESS.

Intracoastal Waterway, 2,455 mi (3,951 km) long, partly natural, partly man-made, providing sheltered passage for commercial and pleasure boats along the U.S. Atlantic coast from Trenton, N.J., on the Delaware River to Key West, S Fla., and along the Gulf of Mexico coast from the St. Marks River, NW Fla., to Brownsville, Texas, on the Rio Grande. Its total length is 3,100 mi (4,989 km), including its mainly open-water extensions N to Boston, Mass., and along the west coast of Florida. The toll-free waterway, authorized by Congress in 1919, is maintained by the Army Corps of Engineers at a minimum depth of 12 ft (4 m) for most of its length; some parts have 7-ft (2.1-m) and 9-ft (2.7-m) minimum depths. The waterway's main segments are the Chesapeake and Delaware Canal, the Albemarle and Chesapeake Canal, the Okeechobee Waterway, the New Orleans–Rigolets Cut, and the Port Arthur–Corpus Christi, Texas, channel. Plans to build a canal across N Florida to link the Atlantic and Gulf sections were blocked in 1971 by a presidential order to prevent potential environmental damage. Many miles of navigable waterways connect with the coastal system, including the Hudson River–New York State Barge Canal, the Savannah River, the Apalachicola River, and the entire Mississippi River system. The Intracoastal Waterway has great commercial importance; barges haul petroleum, petroleum products, foodstuffs, building materials, and manufactured goods.

intrauterine device (IUD): see BIRTH CONTROL.

introspection, looking inward at one's own mental processes. The psychoanalytic movement attributes this function to a postulated mental structure, the ego. In the raw experiencing of inner mental contents, as in SCHIZOPHRENIA or during intoxication with hallucinogenic drugs, the ego is weakened and overwhelmed and is unable to maintain sufficient distance for judgment or to censor or select thoughts and images. Introspection during psychoanalysis or during artistic creation involves a struggle against the force of repression and must be strongly motivated (see DEFENSE MECHANISM). Introspection as an experimental tool of psychology has also been valuable in elucidating the processes of learning, problem solving, and decision making.

introversion: see EXTROVERSION AND INTROVERSION.

intuition, in philosophy, way of knowing directly; immediate apprehension. The Greeks understood intuition to be the grasp of universal principles by the intelligence (nous), as distinguished from the fleeting impressions of the senses. The distinction used by the Greeks implied the superiority of intellectual intuitions over information received by the senses. Christian thinkers made a distinction between intuitive and discursive knowledge: God and angels know directly (intuitively) what men reach by reasoning. René Descartes insisted that there are not two faculties of intuition (the sensual and the intellectual) but only the faculty of intellect; sensual experience, although it appears necessary in practice, is not essential to knowledge. John Locke and others criticized Descartes's position, and under the influence of such criticism perception and the intellect came to be regarded as two separate, intuitive faculties, both necessary for genuine knowledge. Immanuel Kant took sense perception to be the paradigm of intuition, although pure intuitions of space and time were also basic to his system. Bertrand Russell formulated the conceptual-perceptual distinction as the difference between "knowledge by acquaintance" and "knowledge by description." Russell also postulated a faculty analogous to sensation that apprehended universals. The logical positivists felt it was unnecessary to posit such a faculty, and explained the apprehension of nonsensory intuitive (or noninferential) knowledge as the result of psychological conditioning in the learning of a language: To know that all events are caused is to have learned the usage of the terms *event* and *cause*. Critics have argued that such a position confuses the learning of a fact with the learning of a word. They have also observed that the learning of a language and linguistic performance cannot be adequately explained by such a behaviorist model. Psychological conditioning alone does not explain the creativity with which people use a language; some faculty, not dependent merely on experience, seems necessary. Since all knowledge that is not intuitive is assumed to be inferential, it has been suggested that certain kinds of knowledge, too complicated to be simply intuitive and yet not obviously inferential, must be logical constructs resting on unconscious inference. Advocates of the linguistic explanation of intuitive or noninferential knowledge have argued that such knowledge is based on social convention, just as a language is.

Inukai, Ki (Tsuyoshi) (kē ĭno͞o'kī; tso͞oyō'shē), 1855–1932, Japanese statesman. He became president of the Seiyukai party in 1929 and was prime minister from Jan. to May, 1932. His cabinet sanctioned the move of the Kwantung army into N Manchuria, and the formation of the puppet state of Manchukuo. His assassination in May, 1932, increased army power over the government and ended party cabinets until after World War II.

Inuvik (ĭn'o͞ovĭk), town (1971 pop. 2,669), Mackenzie dist., Northwest Territories, Canada, on the east channel of the Mackenzie River. It was built (1954–62) as a new townsite for AKLAVIK and was the first model town in the Canadian Arctic. Inuvik has an airport.

Inuyama (ēno͞oyä'mä), city (1970 pop. 50,594), Aichi prefecture, central Honshu, Japan, on the Kiso River. It is a former castle town and is now an industrial center where textiles, chemicals, and automobiles are produced.

Invalides, Hôtel des (ōtĕl' dāzăNvälēd'), celebrated landmark of Paris, France, built (1671–76) by Libéral BRUANT as a hospital for disabled veterans. One of the most imposing examples of French classical architecture, it now houses a military museum. It faces the vast Esplanade des Invalides and a monumental bridge, the Pont Alexandre III. Behind it, in the court of honor, is the church and **Dôme des Invalides** (1679–1706), the masterpiece of J. H. MANSART. Under the huge, yet seemingly weightless, dome are the tombs of Vauban, Turenne, Foch, and others. The remains of Napoleon I, brought (1840) in great pomp from St. Helena, were transferred there on completion of the crypt in 1861. They are in the center of the crypt, in a red granite sarcophagus, lighted by a circular opening in the dome.

invariance principles: see CONSERVATION LAWS.

Invercargill (ĭnvərkär'gĭl), city (1971 pop. 47,098), extreme S South Island, New Zealand, on the Waiopai River. It is an agricultural center with timber and food-processing industries. Bluff, on the Foveaux Strait, is its port.

Inverchapel of Loch Eck, Archibald John Kerr Clark Kerr, 1st Baron (kär, ĭn"vərchăp'əl, lŏkh ĕk), 1882–1951, British diplomat. He entered the diplomatic service in 1906 and served in numerous countries before being given (1938) the important post of ambassador to China during the Second Sino-Japanese War. In 1942 he was shifted to the ambassadorial post at Moscow, a position he held until 1946. In that year he went as special British envoy to Indonesia in an effort to end Dutch-Indonesian conflict. He was also made a baron in 1946 and served (1946–48) as ambassador to the United States.

Inver Grove Heights, village (1970 pop. 12,148), Dakota co., SE Minn. It is a residential suburb of St. Paul.

Inverness (ĭn"vərnĕs'), burgh (1971 pop. 34,870), county town of Inverness-shire, N Scotland, on the Moray Firth at the mouth of the Ness River. "Capital of the Highlands," it is a seaport and transportation center. There are diverse light industries, including printing, food processing, distilling, wool weaving, and shipbuilding. Electrical and mechanical products and automobile parts are manufactured. There is a herring fishery. Inverness holds an annual cattle and wool market. An ancient town, it is thought to have been a PICT stronghold. The castle, reputedly built by Malcolm III (late 11th cent.), was involved in many wars and was blown up by the JACOBITES in 1746. A new castle was built in 1835. Frequent invasions have destroyed most of the town's old buildings. Cromwell's Fort was demolished at the Restoration by Charles II. Inverness, a thriving tourist center, has a museum of Highland relics and hosts an annual Highland Gathering. In 1975, Inverness became part of the Highland region.

Inverness-shire (ĭn"vərnĕs' shĭr) county (1971 pop. 89,545), 4,211 sq mi (10,906 sq km), NW Scotland.

INVERNESS is the county town. Largest of the Scottish counties, Inverness-shire includes the islands of SKYE, the Saint Kilda group, and all the Outer Hebrides except Lewis (see HEBRIDES, THE). More than a third of its area is insular. The mainland is cut by the Great Glen Valley, a geological fault running from the Moray Firth to Loch Linnhe. The CALEDONIAN CANAL (build 1804-12) follows the glen through Lochs Ness, Oich, and Lochy. The county is mountainous and rugged. Fifty peaks rise above 3,000 ft (914 m), including BEN NEVIS, Great Britain's highest peak. The scenic splendor attracts many tourists and sportsmen. Sheep and cattle raising and fishing (herring and salmon) are the main occupations. Oats, barley, wheat, turnips, and potatoes are grown. Distilling and forestry are significant. Tweeds are manufactured on some of the Hebrides. There is some light industry at Inverness and aluminum works at Fort William and Foyers Falls. Inverness-shire has several hydroelectric plants. The county was first settled by PICTS and belonged to the independent province of Moray. It came under the Scottish crown in 1078 but was never fully controlled by the central government until the suppression of the Highland clans after 1746. It was a Catholic and JACOBITE stronghold in the wars of the 17th and 18th cent. The 5th earl of Montrose won a famous victory over the COVENANTERS at Inverlochy in 1645, and the Jacobite rising of 1745 was crushed at CULLODEN MOOR in 1746. In 1975 Inverness-shire was divided between the Highland and Western Isles regions.

invertebrate (ĭn″vûr'təbrət, –brāt″), any animal lacking a backbone. The invertebrates include the tunicates and amphioxi of phylum Chordata, as well as all animal phyla other than Chordata. The major invertebrate phyla include: the protozoans (PROTOZOA), sponges (PORIFERA), coelenterates (CNIDARIA), echinoderms (ECHINODERMATA), flatworms (PLATYHELMINTHES), roundworms (ASCHELMINTHES), segmented worms (ANNELIDA), mollusks (MOLLUSCA), and arthropods (ARTHROPODA). Invertebrates are tremendously diverse, ranging from microscopic protozoans to very large animals such as the giant squid. They are important as parasites and are essential elements of all ecological communities. See J. E. Smith et al., ed., *The Invertebrate Panorama* (1971); M. S. Gardiner, *The Biology of Invertebrates* (1972); P. A. Meglitsch, *Invertebrate Zoology* (2d ed. 1972).

investiture, in FEUDALISM, ceremony by which an overlord transferred a fief to his vassal or by which, in ecclesiastical law, an elected cleric received the pastoral ring and staff (the symbols of spiritual office) signifying the transfer of the office. After the oath of fealty, the lord "invested" the vassal with the fief, usually by giving him some symbol of the land or office transferred. The dispute over clerical investiture was one of the great struggles between church and state in the Middle Ages. The problem stemmed from the dual position of the important bishops and abbots, who were temporal as well as spiritual lords. Thus from early times both king and pope were concerned with clerical election and installation. When the struggle concerning investiture broke out (late 11th cent.), there was no general agreement as to the powers of the pope and the Holy Roman emperor in installing German bishops; it was only generally recognized that both had rights in the matter. Although *investiture* meant the ecclesiastical ceremony itself, it also more widely applied to the whole matter of election and installation. *Lay investiture* was the term used for investiture of clerics by the king or emperor, a layman. The right of a temporal prince to give spiritual power was claimed only by the extremists of the imperial party, but there was wide debate over canonical election, royal assent, and papal assent. Pope GREGORY VII and Holy Roman Emperor HENRY IV began the open struggle. The clerical reform movement generated the crisis; it was essential that the church have the power of selecting bishops if church reforms—abolition of SIMONY, clerical marriage, and political and economic abuse—were to be carried out. Holy Roman Emperor HENRY III (d. 1056) cooperated with the reform party, but in the minority of Henry IV, abuses were rife. The reform party came to feel that complete abolition of lay investiture was the necessary prerequisite for its goals. In 1075, Gregory forbade lay investiture, and the bitter struggle began in earnest. The encouragement of rebellious nobles in Germany and the excommunication of Henry IV were followed by steady warfare. Although only one phase of the contest, investiture was a crucial issue. Especially in such difficult times, the emperor needed power over the bishop-princes. The papacy also maintained its ground. After the death (1085) of Gregory VII, the argument took a new turn, and after the death (1106) of Henry IV the strain was lessened. However, Pope PASCHAL II, continuing the policy of his predecessors Gregory VII and URBAN II, condemned lay investiture, although he entered negotiations for settlement. Holy Roman Emperor HENRY V maintained the claims of his father and extended them ruthlessly. He made a vague settlement before his coronation, but at the last moment refused to surrender lay investiture; he seized the pope and forced him to surrender the church claims. Paschal later disavowed this forced agreement. The emperor and the antipopes he had set up effectively staved off settlement. Under Pope Gelasius II some progress was made, but it was not until 1122 that churchmen succeeded in bringing about an agreement in the Concordat of Worms (see WORMS, CONCORDAT OF) between Henry V and Pope CALIXTUS II. The compromise was a victory, although far from complete, for the church. The same problem recurred in struggles between the pope and other rulers. In France trouble between church and state centered in general on other issues (see INNOCENT III; PHILIP IV; GALLICANISM). In England, William I (William the Conqueror) came into conflict with the church, and William II embarked on a struggle over investiture. His abuse of power, particularly in keeping sees vacant, intensified the struggle that reached a climax in the long battle between King HENRY I and ANSELM. In 1107 a compromise provided that bishops and abbots should be invested by the church but should render homage to the king. Later trouble between church and state in England arose from other issues. See R. W. Carlyle and A. J. Carlyle, *A History of Medieval Political Theory in the West* (6 vol., 1903–36, repr. 1962); Gerd Tellenbach, *Church, State, and Christian Society at the Time of the Investiture Contest* (tr. 1940, repr. 1970); K. F. Morrison, *The Investiture Controversy* (1971). See also bibliography under HOLY ROMAN EMPIRE; MIDDLE AGES.

involutional psychotic reactions, psychotic reactions found only in certain people of the involutional, i.e., physically declining, period of life, from 40 to 60 years of age, who have had no previous psychotic history. The reaction tends to have a sudden onset and a prolonged course. Some cases are characterized chiefly by DEPRESSION and ANXIETY, and others chiefly by paranoid ideas. Incidence of the depressive type is two to three times greater in women than in men. Either type of the disorder is treated by electric shock therapy and phenothiazine drugs. See PSYCHOSIS; PARANOIA.

Io (ī'ō), in astronomy, one of the 12 known moons, or natural satellites, of JUPITER.

Io, in Greek mythology, daughter of Inachus, king of Argos. She was loved by Zeus, who, to protect her from Hera's jealousy, changed her into a white heifer. Hera, however, was not deceived; she claimed the heifer and sent Argus to guard it. When Hermes killed Argus, Hera tormented Io with a gadfly which drove her across Europe and through Asia, until she was finally allowed to rest in Egypt. There Zeus returned her to human form, and she bore his child Epaphus. Io has been identified with the Egyptian goddess Isis.

Ioánnina (yôä'nēnä), city (1971 pop. 40,130), capital of Ioánnina prefecture, NW Greece, in Epirus, on Lake Ioánnina. The chief city of Epirus, it is the commercial center for an agricultural region that produces cereals, fruits, and wine. Manufactures include textiles and gold and silver products. Founded c.527 by Justinian, Ioánnina became an important city in the 11th cent. It was taken (1081) by the Normans, and in 1204, Michael I, despot of Epirus, made it his capital. It was conquered by the Ottoman Turks in 1430. Ali Pasha made it (1788) the stronghold of his virtually independent state. Ioánnina passed to Greece in 1913 as a result of the First Balkan War. Long a center of Greek learning, it is today the seat of the Univ. of Ioánnina (1966). The city also appears as Janina, Jannina, or Yannina.

iodine (ī'ədīn, –dĭn) [Gr.,=violet], nonmetallic chemical element; symbol I; at. no. 53; at. wt. 126.9045; m. p. 113.5°C; b.p. 184.35°C; sp. gr. 4.93 at 20°C; valence −1, +1, +3, +5, or +7. Iodine is a dark-gray to purple-black, lustrous, solid element with a rhombic crystalline structure. It is the least active of the HALOGENS, which are found in group VIIa of the PERIODIC TABLE. It is normally diatomic, i.e., it has 2 iodine atoms in each molecule, in the solid, liquid, and vapor states. When heated it passes directly from the solid to the vapor state (sublimation), the vapor having an intense violet color and a characteristic irritating odor. Iodine is only slightly soluble in water but dissolves readily in a solution of sodium or potassium iodide. Tincture of iodine is a solution of iodine and potassium iodide in alcohol. Iodine also dissolves in carbon disulfide, carbon tetrachloride, and chloroform, giving a deep violet solution. Iodine forms many compounds. With hydrogen it forms hydrogen iodide, which in water solution becomes hydriodic acid. It forms compounds with certain nonmetals (e.g., carbon, nitrogen, phosphorus, and oxygen) and with most metals. Iodine is displaced from its compounds by the other halogens. The element is obtained from salt deposits, as from the saltpeter beds in Chile, where it occurs in small quantities as an iodate, and from the salt brines associated with some oil wells in California and Louisiana. It is also found as an iodide in the ash of certain seaweeds. Iodine may be prepared by displacement from its compounds with chlorine. Treating an iodide with manganese dioxide and sulfuric acid sublimes the iodine. Iodine is important in medical treatment; tincture of iodine and IODOFORM are widely used. Iodine is employed in the preparation of certain drugs and in the manufacture of some dyes. Silver iodide, a yellow salt, is used in photography; it is water insoluble and turns black when exposed to light. STARCH turns deep blue (almost black) in the presence of a small amount of iodine; this reaction serves as a test for either starch or iodine. Iodine in small amounts is essential to human nutrition; in the THYROID GLAND it becomes a part of the iodine-containing hormones. Goiter, a swelling of the thyroid, is often a symptom of inadequate iodine in the diet. Iodine has only one stable isotope, iodine-127; it is the only isotope of iodine occurring in nature, although 24 iodine isotopes are known. Iodine-131 is a radioactive isotope with a half-life of 8 days. It is used medically to diagnose abnormalities of the thyroid gland. It is also a component of fallout produced by nuclear explosions. Iodine was discovered in 1811 by Bernard Courtois.

iodoform (īō'dəfôrm″), CHI_3, yellow crystalline solid that has a penetrating odor. It melts at 119°C and is insoluble in water but soluble in ether or ethanol. Iodoform was formerly used as an antiseptic. It is produced when a methyl ketone, acetaldehyde, or an alcohol with the formula $RCHOHCH_3$ (where R is hydrogen or an alkyl or aryl group) is treated with sodium hydroxide and iodine.

Ion: see CREUSA **1.**

ion, atom or group of atoms having a net electric CHARGE. A neutral atom or group of atoms becomes an ion by gaining or losing one or more electrons or protons. Since the electron and proton have equal but opposite unit charges, the charge of an ion is always expressed as a whole number of unit charges and is either positive or negative. A simple ion consists of only one charged atom; a COMPLEX ION consists of an aggregate of atoms with a net charge. If an atom or group loses electrons or gains protons, it will have a net positive charge and is called a CATION. If an atom or group gains electrons or loses protons, it will have a net negative charge and is called an ANION. Since ordinary matter is electrically neutral, ions normally exist as groups of cations and anions such that the sum total of positive and negative charges is zero. In common table salt, or sodium chloride, NaCl, the sodium cations, Na^+, are neutralized by chlorine anions, Cl^-. In the salt sodium carbonate, Na_2CO_3, two sodium cations are needed to neutralize each carbonate anion, CO_3^{-2}, because its charge is twice that of the sodium ion. Ionization of neutral atoms can occur in several different ways. Compounds such as salts dissociate in SOLUTION into their ions, e.g., in solution sodium chloride exists as free Na^+ and Cl^- ions. Compounds that contain dissociable protons, or hydrogen ions, H^+, or basic ions such as hydroxide ion, OH^-, make acidic or basic solutions when they dissociate in water (see ACIDS AND BASES; DISSOCIATION). Substances that ionize in solution are called ELECTROLYTES; those that do not ionize, like sugar and alcohol, are called nonelectrolytes. Ions in solution conduct electricity. If a positive electrode, or anode, and a negative electrode, or cathode, are inserted into such a solution, the ions are attracted to the electrode of opposite charge, and simultaneous currents of ions arise in opposite directions to one another. Nonelectrolytes do not conduct electricity. Ionization can also be caused by the bombardment of matter with high-speed particles or other RADIATION. ULTRAVIOLET RADIATION and low-energy X RAYS excite molecules in the upper atmosphere sufficiently to cause them to lose electrons and become ionized, giving rise to several different layers of ions in the earth's atmosphere (see IONOSPHERE). A gas can be ionized by passing an electron current through it; the ionized gas then permits the passage of a much higher current. Heating to high temperatures also ionizes substances; certain salts yield ions in their melts as they do in solution. Ionization has many applications. Vapor lamps and fluorescent lamps take advantage of the light given off when positive ions recombine with electrons. Because of their electric charge the movement of ions can be controlled by electrostatic and magnetic fields. PARTICLE ACCELERATORS, or atom smashers, use both means to accelerate and aim electrons and hydrogen and helium ions. The mass spectrometer utilizes ionization to determine molecular weights and structures. High-energy electrons are used to ionize a molecule and break it up into fragment ions. The ratio of mass to charge for each fragment is determined by its behavior in electric and magnetic fields. The ratio of mass to charge of the parent ion gives the molecular weight directly, and the fragmentation pattern gives clues to the molecular structures. In ion-exchange reactions a specially prepared insoluble resin with attached dissociable ions is packed into a column. When a solution is passed through the column, ions from the solution are exchanged with ions on the resin (see CHROMATOGRAPHY). Water softeners use the mineral zeolite, a natural ion-exchange resin. Ion-permeable membranes allow some ions to pass through more readily than others; some membranes of the human nervous system are selectively permeable to the ions sodium and potassium. Engineers have developed experimental ion propulsion engines that propel rockets by ejecting high-speed ions; most other rocket engines eject combustion products. Although an ion engine does not develop enough thrust to launch a rocket into earth orbit, it is considered practical for propelling one through interplanetary space on long-distance trips, e.g., between the earth and Jupiter. If left running for long periods of time on such a trip, the ion engine would gradually accelerate the rocket to immense speeds.

Iona (īōn'ə) [from the Irish *Ioua*-island] or Icolmkill [Irish, -island of Columba of the church], island, 3.5 mi (5.6 km) long and 1.5 mi (2.4 km) wide, Argyllshire, NW Scotland, one of the Inner Hebrides. Separated from the island Mull by the Sound of Iona, it is hilly, with shell beaches. Farming and fishing are carried on, but tourism is the main industry. The island is famous as the early center of Celtic Christianity. St. Columba (see COLUMBA, ST.), with his companions, landed there from Ireland in 563. They founded a monastery, which was burned by the Danes in the 8th or 9th cent. Iona was the seat of a bishop from 838 to 1098. In 1203 a Benedictine monastery, of which there are remains, was established. The cathedral, formerly the Church of St. Mary, dates from the early 13th cent. There were many ancient crosses, of which several remain. The cemetery of St. Oran's Church contains the graves of many monarchs of Scotland, Ireland, Norway, and France. A group called the Iona Community (est. 1938), dedicated to reviving the spirit of Celtic Christianity, has restored many ancient buildings. Some members live on the island.

Ionesco, Eugène (ōzhĕn' yŏnĕs'kō), 1912–, French playwright, b. Rumania. Settling in France in 1938, he contributed to *Cahiers du Sud* and began writing avant-garde plays. His works stress the absurdity both of bourgeois values and of the way of life that they dictate. They express the futility of human endeavor in a universe ruled by chance. His play *La Cantatrice chauve* (1950; tr. *The Bald Soprano*, 1965) was suggested by the idiotic phrases in an English language textbook; it has become a classic of the theater of the absurd. Among Ionesco's other plays are *La Leçon* (1951), *Les Chaises* (1952), *Victimes du devoir* (1953), *Le Nouveau locataire* (1957), *Tueur sans gages* (1958), *Rhinocéros* (1959), *Photo du colonel* (1967), *Le roi se meurt* (1963), and *Jeux de massacre* (1970). He has written about the theater in *Notes and Counternotes* (1962, tr. 1964); a memoir, *Present Past, Past Present* (1968, tr. 1971); and the novel *The Hermit* (1974). His plays are all available in English translation. See studies by L. C. Pronko (1965), R. N. Coe (rev. ed. 1971), and Allan Lewis (1972).

Ionia (īō'nēə), ancient region of Asia Minor. It occupied a narrow coastal strip on the E Mediterranean (in present-day W Turkey) as well as the neighboring Aegean Islands, which now mainly belong to Greece. The region was of the utmost importance in ancient times, for it was there that Greek settlers established colonies before 1000 B.C. These colonists were called Ionians, and tradition says that they fled to Asia Minor from the mainland of Greece to escape from the conquering Dorians. Athens claimed to be the mother city of all the Ionian colonists, but modern scholars believe that the Ionians were actually a mixed group (mainly from Attica and Boeotia) and that after arrival they were further mixed by intermarriage with native groups such as the Carians. Nevertheless, they spoke the same distinctive form of Greek that was spoken in Attica and Évvoia, and in ancient times their culture was always distinguished from that of the Dorians and Aeolians. There came to be 12 important cities—Miletus, Myus, Priene, Sámos, Ephesus, Colophon, Lebedos, Teos, Erythrae, Khíos, Clazomenae, and Phocaea. A religious league (which reached its full power in the 8th cent. B.C.) was formed, with its center at the temple of Poseidon near Mycale. Smyrna, originally an Aeolian colony, later joined the league. The fertility of the region and its excellent harbors brought prosperity to the cities. Traders and colonists were sent into the Mediterranean as far west as Spain and up to the shores of the Black Sea. In the 7th cent. B.C. the cities were invaded by the Cimmerians, but they survived. In the same century Gyges, king of Lydia, invaded them; but it was not until the time of Croesus that their subjugation was completed. When Croesus was conquered (before 546 B.C.) by Cyrus the Great of Persia, the Greek cities came under Persian rule. That rule was not very exacting, but it was despotic in nature, and at the beginning of the 5th cent. B.C. the cities rose in revolt against Darius I. Although the revolt was easily put down, the Persians set out to punish the allies (Athens and Eretria) of the cities. The PERSIAN WARS resulted. Most of the Ionian cities thereby gained a brief freedom, but their fate continued to be subject to treaties with the Persians and changed as Persian fortunes waxed and waned. Alexander the Great easily took (c.335) all the Ionian cities in his power, and the Diadochi quarreled over them. The cities continued to be rich and important through the time of the Roman and Byzantine empires. It was only after the Turkish conquest in the 15th cent. A.D. that their culture was destroyed. In its favorable position between the civilizations to the west (e.g., the Greek Aegean) and to the east (e.g., Lydia and Phrygia), Ionia made an immense contribution to Greek art by supplying much of the Oriental influence in the 7th cent. B.C. See D. G. Hogarth, *Ionia and the East* (1909); Carl Roebuck, *Ionian Trade and Colonization* (1959); G. L. Huxley, *The Early Ionians* (1966, repr. 1972).

Ionian Islands (īō'nēən), chain of islands (1971 pop. 184,483), c.890 sq mi (2,310 sq km), W Greece, in the Ionian Sea, along the coasts of Epirus and the Peloponnesus. The group is made up of KÉRKIRA, PAXOÍ, LEVKÁS, KEFALLINÍA, ITHÁKI, ZÁKINTHOS, KÍTHIRA, and numerous islets. Largely mountainous, the islands reach their highest point at Mt. Ainos (c.5,340 ft/1,630 m) on Kefallinía. Fruits, olives, grains, and vegetables are grown, and sheep, goats, and hogs are raised. Industries include fishing, soapmaking, and boatbuilding. The islands had no unified history until the 10th cent. A.D., when they were made a province of the Byzantine Empire. Venice took the islands in the 14th and 15th cent. and held them until 1797, when the Treaty of Campo Formio, which ended the Venetian republic, gave the islands to France. In 1799 they were seized by a Russo-Turkish fleet and were constituted a republic under Russian protection. In 1807, by the Treaty of Tilsit, Russia returned the islands to France. From 1809 to 1814 the British navy occupied all the islands except Kérkira. In 1815 the Ionian Islands, known as the "United States of the Ionian Islands", were placed under British protection. The British ceded the islands to Greece in 1864 after considerable popular agitation on the islands.

Ionian school, pre-Socratic group of Greek philosophers of the 6th and 5th cent. B.C.; most of them were born in Ionia. Its members were primarily concerned with the origins of the universe—the forces that shaped it and the materials of which it is composed. THALES, his successor ANAXIMANDER, and ANAXIMENES were all from Miletus. Other prominent members included ANAXAGORAS, DIOGENES OF APOLLONIA, and Archelaus. It is also known as the Milesian school.

Ionian Sea, part of the Mediterranean Sea, S Europe, between Greece and S Italy. It is connected with the Adriatic Sea by the Strait of Otranto. The Gulf of Taranto and the Gulf of Corinth are its chief arms. The Ionian Islands lie in its eastern part. Kérkira and Pátrai (Greece) and Catania and Taranto (Italy) are the chief ports.

ionic bond: see CHEMICAL BOND.

Ionic order (īŏn'ĭk), one of the early ORDERS OF ARCHITECTURE. The spreading scroll-shaped CAPITAL is the distinctive feature of the Ionic order; it was primarily a product of Asia Minor, where early embryonic forms of this capital have been found. In the Ionian colonies of Greece on the southwestern shores of Asia Minor, the Ionic order had attained a full development in the 6th cent. B.C. In the 5th cent. B.C. it appeared in Greece proper, where the ERECHTHEUM embodies the one really complete example. Greek Ionic columns are of slender proportion, their height being generally about nine times the column's lower diameter; the order is always used with a base. A column shaft with 24 flutings seems to have been the most developed form. The spiral scrolls, or volutes, at either side of the cap run from front to rear, and an echinus molding with egg-and-dart ornamentation occupies the space between them. The entablature, usually about one quarter the height of the column, has an architrave generally divided into three bands, each projecting beyond the next; a frieze, often adorned with sculpture; and a cornice enriched with dentils, above which are a corona and a crowning cyma molding. A late and vigorously monumental development of the order took place in the Hellenistic temples of Asia Minor at the middle of the 4th cent. B.C. In employing this order the Romans used details that were not as fine. The temple of Saturn shows a variation of the four-cornered Ionic cap, which had been created in Greece for the corner columns of a portico. A cap of this type, with corner volutes, was developed by the Italian Renaissance architect Scamozzi into a design bearing his name; variations of it were widely used during the Renaissance and in subsequent periods, particularly the baroque. For the other Greek orders see DORIC ORDER; CORINTHIAN ORDER.

ionization: see ION.

ionization chamber, device for the detection and measurement of ionizing RADIATION. It consists basically of a sealed chamber containing a gas and two electrodes between which a voltage is maintained by an external circuit. When ionizing radiation, e.g., a PHOTON, enters the chamber (through a foil-covered window), it ionizes one or more gas molecules. The ions are attracted to the oppositely charged electrodes; their presence causes a momentary drop in the voltage, which is recorded by the external circuit. The observed voltage drop helps identify the radiation because it depends on the degree of ionization, which in turn depends on the charge, mass, and speed of the photon. See RADIOACTIVITY.

ionosphere (īŏn'əsfēr), series of concentric ionized layers forming part of the upper ATMOSPHERE of the earth. At about 400 mi (640 km) it merges with the magnetosphere, the region of the VAN ALLEN RADIATION BELTS. Fluctuations in the height of the layers and in the degree of ionization occur at different times of the day and night, at different seasons, and in different areas. It can generally be thought of as extending from about 50 to 400 mi (80–640 km) in height. Causes for some of the variations in characteristics are believed to include changes in the amount of ultraviolet radiation received from the sun and effects of the earth's magnetic field. Space probes are employed to explore the ionosphere and to ascertain the temperatures at various altitudes. The layers comprising the ionosphere are also known by letters of the alphabet—the D layer, the E layer (lying above the D layer), and the F layer (divided into the F-1 and F-2 layers and lying above the E layer). It is the ionosphere which, by reflecting radio waves back to the earth, makes possible long-distance wireless communication. Oliver Heaviside in England and A. E. Kennelly in the United States independently discovered the existence and effects of the ionosphere, which has been called the Kennelly-Heaviside layer.

Iorga, Nicolae (nē'kōlī yôr'gä), 1871–1940, Rumanian historian and statesman. A professor at the Univ. of Bucharest, he founded (1910) and later led the National Democratic party; after World War I he was president of the Rumanian national assembly. In 1931–32 he was premier of a coalition government under King Carol II. In Nov., 1940, Iorga was murdered by the IRON GUARD. His many fine historical works include detailed studies of Rumanian religion, education, and literature, *Geschichte des osmanischen Reiches* (5 vol., 1908–13), and *History of the Rumanians* (10 vol., 1935–39, in Rumanian). After 1965, Iorga's reputation as a great nationalist historian was acknowledged by the Rumanian Communists, who had hitherto played down his work. His name also appears spelled as Nicolas Jorga. See biography by M. M. Alexandrescu-Dersca Bulgaru (tr. 1972); study by W. O. Oldson (1973).

Ioshkar-Ola: see YOSHKAR-OLA, USSR.

Iowa (ī'əwə, ī'əwā), state (1970 pop., 2,825,041), 56,290 sq mi (145,791 sq km), N central United States, in the Midwest, admitted to the Union in 1846 as the 29th state. DES MOINES is the capital and largest city. Other major cities are CEDAR RAPIDS, DAVENPORT, and SIOUX CITY. Iowa is bordered on two sides by rivers; the Mississippi separates it on the E from Wisconsin and Illinois, and the Missouri and the Big Sioux separate it on the W from Nebraska and South Dakota. The state is bounded on the N by Minnesota and on the S by Missouri. Iowa is an area of rich, rolling plains, interrupted by many rivers. The terrain is low and gently sloping, except for the hills in the unglaciated area of NE Iowa, the steeply sloping bluffs on the banks of the Mississippi, and the moundlike bluffs on the banks of the Missouri. The rivers of the eastern two thirds of Iowa flow to the Mississippi; those of the west flow to the Missouri. The original woodlands, which included black walnut and hickory, were destroyed by lumbering in the 19th cent., and the present wooded sections are covered only with a second or third growth of timber. Typical of Iowa is the prairie. Covered a little more than a century ago with grass higher than the wheels of the pioneers' prairie schooners, or covered wagons, the prairies are now covered with fields of corn and other grains. The wild flowers that once blossomed among the prairie grass still brighten the roadsides; however, few areas of the original grassland remain, and prairie grass preserves have been established. The former habitat of wild turkeys, prairie chickens, and quail, Iowa now abounds with migratory geese and ducks and the imported ring-necked pheasant and European partridge, all of which are hunted in the autumn. The climate is continental—northwest winds drive the mercury down to below 0°F (−18°C) in winter, and in the summer hot air masses bring oppressive heat; violent thunderstorms, hail, and occasional droughts vex the farmer. In addition, floods have inflicted great losses of life and property on cities and countryside alike; therefore, flood control projects play a major role in Iowa. The average annual rainfall is 31 in. (78.7 cm), and, since most of this rain falls in summer, the soil is often washed away. Iowans have had to fight erosion with modern plowing and planting practices, control of water flow, and reforestation. Yet Iowa has some of the finest agricultural land in the world and 25% of the "grade A" farm land of the United States. The deep, porous soil yields corn and other grains in tremendous quantities, and the corn-fed hogs and cattle are nationally known. In 1972, Iowa led the nation in the production of corn, hogs, and pigs, and ranked second to Texas in the raising of cattle. In addition to corn, Iowa's other major crops are soybeans, hay, and oats. Iowans have used the rich earth and its bounty to gain the second highest total cash receipts of any state from farm marketing. Agriculture in Iowa also benefits the state's chief industry, food-processing, and in Sioux City and Cedar Rapids there are many factories that process farm products. Nonelectrical machinery, electronic equipment, and chemicals are among the other manufactures. Cement is the most important mineral product; others are stone, sand and gravel, and gypsum. Mineral production is small, however. In prehistoric times, the MOUND BUILDERS, a farming people, lived in the area of present-day Iowa. When white men first came to explore the region in the 17th cent., various Indian groups, including the IOWA INDIANS, from whom Iowa reputedly takes its name, occupied the land. The SAC AND FOX INDIANS also ranged over the land, but it was the belligerent SIOUX INDIANS who dominated the area. In 1673 the French explorers Father Jacques Marquette and Louis Jolliet traveled down the Mississippi River and touched upon the Iowa shores, as did Robert Cavelier, sieur de La Salle, in 1681–82. The areas surrounding the Des Moines and Mississippi rivers were profitable for fur traders, and a number of Iowa towns developed from trading posts. Late in the 18th cent. a French Canadian, Julien Dubuque, leased land from the Indians around the present-day city of Dubuque and opened lead mines there. After his death the Indians refused to permit other white men to work the mines, and U.S. troops under Lt. Jefferson Davis protected Indian rights to the land as late as 1830. However, the Indian hold was doomed after the United States acquired Iowa as part of the LOUISIANA PURCHASE of 1803. In 1832 the BLACK HAWK WAR broke out as Sac and Fox Indians, led by their chief, Black Hawk, fought to regain their former lands in Illinois along the Mississippi River. They were defeated by U.S. troops and were forced to leave the Illinois lands and cede to the United States much of their land along the river on the Iowa side. Within two decades after the Black Hawk War, all of the Indians' lands had been ceded to the whites. Meanwhile, a great rush of frontiersmen came to settle the prairies and take the mines. Slavery was prohibited in Iowa under the Missouri Compromise of 1820, which excluded it from the lands of the Louisiana Purchase north of lat. 36°30'N. Part of Missouri Territory prior to 1821, Iowa was subsequently part of Michigan Territory and Wisconsin Territory. By 1838, Iowa Territory was organized, with Burlington as the temporary capital. In the following year Iowa City became the capital. The Iowans quickly built a rural civilization like that of New England, where many of them had lived. Later, immigrants from Europe, notably Germans, Czechs, Dutch, and Scandinavians, brought their agricultural skills and their own customs to enrich Iowa's rural life, and a group of German Pietists established the AMANA CHURCH SOCIETY, a successful attempt at communal social organization. A system of public schools was set up in 1839, and successful efforts soon were made to establish colleges and universities. Iowa became a state in 1846, and Ansel Briggs was elected as the first governor. In 1857 the capital was moved from Iowa City to Des Moines. In that same year the state adopted its second constitution. Iowa prospered greatly with the beginning of railroad construction, and the rivalry between towns to get the lines was so fierce that the grant of big land tracts to railroad companies was curtailed by legislative act in 1857. Two years earlier the state's first railroad line was completed between Davenport and Muscatine along the eastern border. Before and during the Civil War, Iowans, generally owners of small, independent farms, were naturally sympathetic to the antislavery side in the contest over slavery, and many fought for the Union. The Underground Railroad, which helped many fugitive slaves escape to free states, was active in Iowa, and the abolitionist John Brown made his headquarters there for a time. Iowa's farmers prospered after the Civil War, but during the hard times that afflicted the country in the 1870s they found themselves burdened with debts. Feeling oppressed by the currency system, corporations, and high railroad and grain-storage rates, many of Iowa's farmers supported, along with other farmers of the West, the GRANGER MOVEMENT, the GREENBACK PARTY, and the POPULIST PARTY. The reform movements had some success in the state. Granger laws were enacted in 1874 and 1876 regulating railroad rates, but these laws were repealed in 1877 under pressure from the railroad companies. By the end of the 19th cent., times improved, and the agrarian movements declined. Since that time, except for the depression of the 1930s, Iowa's agricultural community has generally prospered, partly through advances in agricultural science, such as the improvement of corn by cross-pollination and selective breeding. In addition, farm units grew larger, and mechanization brought great increases in productivity. Organizations such as the Grange, the Farm Bureau, the 4-H clubs, and farmers' cooperatives have promoted improvements in Iowa's agriculture and, along with county fairs and the state fair, have also contributed to improvements of social life in the state. Much of Iowa's society may still resemble that depicted in the paintings of Grant Wood, an Iowan, but the state's growing industrial economy as well as other elements of modernization has altered this image. While on a visit to the United States in 1959, Nikita S. Khrushchev, then premier of the Soviet Union, was invited to a farm in Iowa to observe part of the U.S. farm economy. Among Iowa's colorful native sons were Buffalo Bill and Billy Sunday. Other public figures associated with the state are James Wilson, U.S. Secretary of Agriculture for 16 years (1897–1913), and the noted members of the Wallace family—Henry Wallace, Henry Cantwell Wallace, and Henry Agard Wallace. Herbert C. Hoover and Harry L. Hopkins were born in Iowa. Herbert Hoover National Historic Site, which contains Hoover's birthplace, childhood home, and grave, and the Herbert Hoover Presidential Library are at West Branch. Other places of interest in Iowa include the little town of Spillville, where the Czech composer Antonín Dvořák spent the summer of 1893 and composed part of his Symphony No. 9 in E Minor, Op. 95 (From the New World). The massacre (1857) at Spirit Lake of a white settlement by renegade Sioux is treated in MacKinlay Kantor's novel *Spirit Lake* (1961). Near Marquette is Effigy Mounds National Monument, site of Indian mounds built by the area's earliest inhabitants. Many state parks and forests provide recreational facilities. Iowa's present constitution was adopted in 1857. The governor is elected for a term of two years and may be reelected. The general assembly, or legislature, has a senate with 50 members elected for four-year terms and a house of representatives with 100 members elected for two-year terms. Iowa is represented in the U.S. Congress by two Senators and six Representatives. The state, which usually votes Republican, has eight electoral votes. Robert Ray, a Republican, was elected governor in 1968 and was reelected in 1970, 1972, and 1974. Among the educational institutions in Iowa are Iowa State Univ. of Science and Technology, at Ames; the Univ. of Iowa, at Iowa City; Grinnell College, at Grinnell; Cornell College, at Mount Vernon; Drake Univ., at Des Moines; Univ. of Northern Iowa, at Cedar Falls; and the Univ. of Dubuque, Loras College, and Clarke College, at Dubuque. See H. V. Hake, *Iowa Inside Out* (1968); H. M. Bowman, *The Administration of Iowa* (1969); J. E. McFarland, *A History of the Pioneer Era on the Iowa Prairies* (1969); William Houlette, *Iowa, the Pioneer Heritage* (1970); Harland Hahn, *Urban-Rural Conflict* (1971); G. S. Mills, *Rogues and Heroes from Iowa's Amazing Past* (1972); M. M. Rosenberg, *Iowa on the Eve of the Civil War* (1972); Federal Writers' Project, *Iowa: A Guide to the Hawkeye State* (1938, repr. 1973).

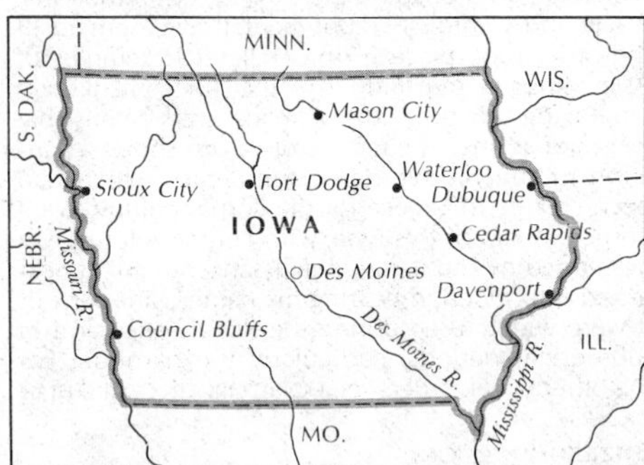

Iowa, river, 329 mi (529 km) long, rising in the lakes of N Iowa and flowing SE to the Mississippi River, SE Iowa; Cedar River (300 mi/483 km long) is its chief tributary. A power dam crosses the gorge at Iowa Falls. The Iowa River has an extensive flood-control system; Coralville Dam and reservoir, N of Iowa City, is the largest unit.

Iowa, University of, at Iowa City; state supported; coeducational; chartered 1847, opened 1855. It operates the Iowa Child Welfare Research Station, the Lakeside Laboratory for the biological sciences, and a hydraulic research institute, and it has a noted program in the creative arts.

Iowa City, city (1970 pop. 46,850), seat of Johnson co., E Iowa, on both sides of the Iowa River; founded 1839 as the capital of Iowa Territory, inc. 1853. Its manufactures include foam rubber, animal feed, dentifrices, toilet goods, coated paper, and food products. The city is the seat of the Univ. of Iowa (1855) and is a major center of medical treatment and research. The beautiful old stone capitol was begun in 1840, and the legislature sat there until the seat of government was moved to Des Moines in 1857. With the arrival of the railroad (1855), Iowa City became an important outfitting center for the westward trails. Today its activities center greatly around the university there. The library of the state historical society is in the city; nearby are the villages of the Amana Society, Coralville dam and reservoir, and the Herbert Hoover Presidential Library and Herbert Hoover's birthplace (in West Branch).

Iowa Indians, North American Indians, whose language belongs to the Siouan branch of the Hokan-Siouan linguistic stock (see AMERICAN INDIAN LANGUAGES); also called the Ioway. They, with the Missouri, the Omaha, the Oto, and the Ponca, are thought to have once formed part of the Winnebago people in their primal home N of the Great Lakes. Iowa culture was that of the Eastern Woodlands area with some Plains area traits. In 1700 the Iowa, separated from the parent nation, lived in Minnesota. Their population in 1760 was some 1,100. In 1804, according to Lewis and Clark, the Iowa lived on the Platte River and there were some 800, smallpox having reduced the population. In 1824 they ceded all their lands in Missouri and in 1836 were assigned a reservation in NE Kansas. Some of them later moved to central Oklahoma, and in 1890 land was allotted to them in severalty. In the early 1970s, Iowa Indians on reservations in Kansas and Oklahoma numbered some 250. See A. B. Skinner, *Ethnology of the Ioway Indians* (1926).

Iowa State University of Science and Technology, at Ames; land-grant with state and federal support; coeducational; chartered 1858, opened 1868 as an agricultural college; called Iowa State College of Agriculture and Mechanic Arts from 1896 to 1959. The Ames Laboratory of the U.S. Atomic Energy Commission is there.

ipecac (ĭp'ĭkăk), drug obtained from the dried roots of a creeping shrub, *Cephaelis* (or *Psychotria*) *ipecacuanha,* native to Brazil but cultivated in other tropical climates. There are three varieties of the root, brown, red, and gray, varying according to the age of the plant, its place of growth, or the method of drying. Emetine, the active principle of ipecac, is obtained from the bark of the root. It is a powerful poison that produces vomiting and is sometimes prescribed to relieve the stomach of some other poison. Ipecac is used as an expectorant in the treatment of bronchitis or croup, stimulating bronchial secretions to make coughing easier. Brazilian Indians used ipecac for centuries to treat amebic infections. Its use became more widespread in the 17th cent., and the pure substance emetine is still used in the treatment of amebic dysentery and amebic hepatitis, as well as some parasitic infestations. Ipecac must be used with great caution and only under medical supervision.

Iphedeiah (ĭf"ēdē'yə), chief Benjamite. 1 Chron. 8.25.

Iphicles (ĭf'əklēz"): see AMPHITRYON.

Iphigenia (ĭf"əjənī'ə), in Greek legend, daughter of Clytemnestra and Agamemnon. When the Greek ships were delayed by contrary winds at Aulis en route to the Trojan War, Calchas informed Agamemnon that Artemis demanded the sacrifice of his daughter Iphigenia. Agamemnon reluctantly agreed, and, despite Clytemnestra's protestations, Iphigenia nobly consented to die for the glory of Greece. Another legend contends that Artemis saved her life by substituting a hind at the altar and then carried her off to the land of the Taurians to serve as her high priestess. Years later Iphigenia had the opportunity of saving the life of her brother (Orestes), and she escaped with him to Greece. Euripides recounts both legends in his plays *Iphigenia in Aulis* and *Iphigenia in Tauris.*

I-pin or **Ipin** (both: ē-pĭn), city (1970 est. pop. 275,000), S Szechwan prov., China. It is a commercial and communications center at the junction of the Min and the Yangtze rivers, the last port for upriver traffic, and the gateway to Yünnan prov. The city was formerly called Suifu.

Ipiranga (ēpērăng'gə), stream flowing near the city of São Paulo, Brazil. On its banks the regent Pedro (later Emperor Pedro I) issued the *Grito do Ipiranga,* the declaration of the independence of Brazil from Portugal, on Sept. 7, 1822. The event is commemorated by a monument and a historical museum.

Ipoh (ē'pō), city (1971 pop. 247,689), capital of Perak state, Malaysia, central Malay Peninsula, in the Kinta River valley. A modern commercial town, it is the greatest tin-mining center of Malaysia. Nearby are rubber plantations and limestone quarries. The mine laborers and the population are mainly Chinese. The city has noted Chinese rock temples.

Ippolitov-Ivanov, Mikhail Mikhailovich (mēkhəyĕl' mēkhī'ləvĭch ēpəlyē'təf-ēvä'nəf), 1859–1935, Russian composer; pupil of Rimsky-Korsakov at the Moscow Conservatory. In 1882 he went to Tiflis, where he taught and conducted. In 1893, recommended by Tchaikovsky, he was made a professor at the Moscow Conservatory, of which he was director from 1906 to 1922. He also conducted opera in Moscow during and after this period. As a composer Ippolitov-Ivanov followed the aims of the Russian nationalist school. His work best-known outside of Russia is the suite *Caucasian Sketches* (1894).

Ipsambul: see ABU-SIMBEL.

Ipsus (ĭp'səs), small town, ancient Phrygia, Asia Minor. ANTIGONUS I, who had summoned his son Demetrius to his aid, was defeated and slain there by his rivals Seleucus and Lysimachus in 301 B.C. The battle of Ipsus resulted in the dissolution of Alexander's empire.

Ipswich (ĭp'swĭch), city (1971 pop. 61,514), Queensland, E Australia, a suburb of Brisbane. It is the principal coal-mining center of the state and has woolen mills and other industries.

Ipswich, county borough (1971 pop. 122,814), county town of East Suffolk, E England, on the Orwell estuary 12 mi (19 km) from its entry into the North Sea. A market and port, it exports barley, malt, and fertilizers and imports coal, petroleum, phosphates, grain, and timber. Agricultural machinery and construction vehicles are the chief manufactures of Ipswich, which also has fertilizer, cigarette, malting, milling, brewing, printing, and textile industries. Ipswich was a commercial center and pottery producer from the 7th to 12th cent. It reached the peak of its significance in the woolen trade in the 16th cent. Its port declined with the decline in wool trading but revived with new dock construction in the mid-19th cent. Vestiges of Roman habitation remain in Ipswich. It was an important ecclesiastical center in the 16th cent. and retains 12 old churches and several 15th- and 16th-century houses. Christchurch mansion (1548, now in part an art gallery), the public school (14th cent.), and Sparrowe's House (1567) are noteworthy. Wolsey's Gate is the only remnant of the college founded in the early 16th cent. by Cardinal Wolsey, who was born in Ipswich. In 1974, Ipswich became part of the new nonmetropolitan county of Suffolk.

Ipswich, town (1970 pop. 10,750), Essex co., NE Mass., on the Ipswich River and Ipswich Bay; inc. 1634. Ipswich clams are found there. Tourism and the production of electrical equipment are important. Crane's Beach, one of the country's most beautiful, is in Ipswich. Points of interest in the town, which retains its early colonial atmosphere, include Choate Bridge, the first stone bridge in the United States (1764), and many historic buildings, notably the John Whipple House (c.1640), with the Ipswich Historical Society collection. An air force radar experimental station is in Ipswich.

Iqbal, Muhammad (məhăm'ĭd ĭkhbäl'), 1873–1938, Indian Muslim poet, philosopher, and political leader. He studied at Government College, Lahore, Cambridge, and the Univ. of Munich, and then he taught philosophy at Government College and practiced law. He was elected (1927) to the Punjab provincial legislature and served (1930) as president of the Muslim League. At first a staunch advocate of Indian nationalism and Hindu-Muslim unity, he gradually came to adopt the concept of an independent homeland for India's Muslims. He is therefore regarded by many as the spiritual founder of Pakistan, where the anniversary of his death (April 21) is a national holiday. Iqbal was the foremost Muslim thinker of his period, and in his many volumes of poetry (written in Urdu and Persian) and essays, he urged a regeneration of Islam through the love of God and the active development of the self. He was a firm believer in freedom and the creative force that freedom can exert on men. His works include *The Secrets of the Self* (1915, tr. 1940), *A Message from the East* (1923, tr. 1971), *Javid-nama* (1934, tr. 1966), and *The Reconstruction of Religious Thought in Islam* (tr. 1934). See biographical studies by A. A. Beg (1961), Annemarie Schimmel (1963), and Hafeez Malik, ed. (1971).

Iquique (ēkē'kā), city (1970 pop. 64,900), capital of Tarapacá prov., N Chile. A port on the Pacific, it exports nitrates and iodine from the Atacama Desert. The city, founded in the 16th cent., was taken (1879) from Peru by Chile during the War of the Pacific (see PACIFIC, WAR OF THE). Since rain rarely falls, water must be brought from 60 mi (97 km) away. Rock and sand enclose the city on the landward side, and the harbor, although greatly improved, still suffers from Pacific storms. The city has fine beaches and excellent deep-sea fishing.

Iquitos (ēkē'tōs), city (1969 est. pop. 74,000), capital of Loreto dept., NE Peru, on the Amazon River, c.2,300 mi (3,700 km) from the Amazon's mouth. It is the farthest inland port of any considerable size in the world. With the boom in wild rubber at the beginning of the 20th cent. the city gained prominence, but it declined after the collapse of the market. Today coffee, cotton, timber, balata, and tagua nuts, as well as rubber, are exported. There is launch service some distance up the Marañón and Ucayali rivers and air service to the highlands, but the Andes mts. are so formidable a barrier to the transport of most commercial goods that Iquitos has been oriented toward the Atlantic rather than the Pacific. The city was founded in 1863.

Ir, in the Bible: see IRI.

Ir, chemical symbol of the element IRIDIUM.

Ira (ī'rə). **1** Chief officer of David. 2 Sam. 20.26. **2, 3** Two of David's guard. 2 Sam. 23.26,38; 1 Chron. 11.28,40; 27.9.

Irad (ī'răd), Enoch's son. Gen. 4.18.

Irak: see IRAQ.

Iráklion (ērä'klēôn) or **Candia** (kăn'dēə), city (1971 pop. 77,506), capital of Crete governorate and Iráklion prefecture, N Crete, Greece, a port on the Sea of Crete. It is the largest city on Crete and ships wine, olive oil, raisins, and almonds. Iráklion was founded (9th cent.) by the Muslim Saracens. In 961 it was conquered by the Byzantine emperor Nicephorus II, and in the 13th cent. it became a Venetian colony. The Venetians, who named the city Candia, fortified it and improved its port. In 1669 it was captured by the Ottoman Turks after a two-year siege. It was the capital of Crete until 1841, and in 1913 it passed to Greece. Iráklion has a museum of Minoan antiquities that were excavated at the site of ancient CNOSSUS, just outside the city. Among Iráklion's historic monuments are a cathedral, several mosques, and remains of Venetian walls and fortifications.

Irala, Domingo Martínez de (dōmēng'gō märtē'nās dā ērä'lä), d. 1556 or 1557, first governor of Paraguay. Of Basque origin, he accompanied Pedro de Mendoza on his expedition to La Plata in 1535. As the first governor in America elected by a free vote of the colonists, he founded in Asunción the first CABILDO in America. Under his administration, the city was a center for further colonization and a point of departure for Peru. From 1539, when he moved the inhabitants of BUENOS AIRES to Asunción, until his death (with a short interruption when CABEZA DE VACA was governor), he ruled forcefully. Churches and public buildings were erected, towns were established, and the Indians were subjugated and distributed among the colonists in encomiendas.

Iram (ī'răm), duke of Edom. Gen. 36.43; 1 Chron. 1.54.

Iran (ērän', īrăn'), kingdom (1971 est. pop. 30,000,000), 636,290 sq mi (1,648,000 sq km), SW Asia. The name of the kingdom was changed from Persia to Iran in 1935 by royal decree. TEHRAN is the capital. The second largest country of the Middle East, Iran is bordered on the N by the USSR and the Caspian Sea; on the E by Afghanistan and Pakistan; on the S by the Persian Gulf and the Gulf of Oman; and on the W by Turkey and Iraq. The Shatt al Arab forms part of the Iran-Iraq border. Physiographically, Iran lies within the Alpine-Himalayan mountain system and is composed of a vast central plateau rimmed by mountain ranges and limited lowland regions. Iran is subject to numerous and often severe earthquakes; since 1962 nearly 30,000 people have been killed and tens of thousands left homeless by five major series of earthquakes. The Iranian Plateau (alt. c.4,000 ft/1,200 m), which extends beyond the low ranges of E Iran into Afghanistan, is a region of interior drainage. It consists of a number of arid basins of salt and sand, such as those of DASHT-E KAVIR and Dasht-e Lut, and some marshlands, such as the area around Hamun-e Helmand along the Afghanistan border. The plateau is surrounded by high folded and volcanic mountain chains including the Kopet mts. in the northwest, the ELBURZ mts. (rising to 18,934 ft/5,771 m at Mt. Damavand, Iran's highest point) in the north, and the complex ZAGROS mts. in the west. Lake Rezaiyeh (the largest in the country) is in the Zagros of NW Iran. Narrow coastal plains are found along the shores of the Persian Gulf, Gulf of Oman, and the Caspian Sea; at the head of the Persian Gulf is the Iranian section of the Mesopotamian lowlands. Of the few perennial rivers in Iran, only the Kurun in the west is navigable for large craft; other major rivers are the Karkheh and the Safid Rud. The climate of Iran is continental, with hot summers and cold winters; the mountain regions of the north and west have a Mediterranean-type climate. Temperature and precipitation vary with elevation. Except for the Caspian littoral, which receives a well-distributed average annual rainfall of about 40 in. (102 cm), precipitation occurs mainly in the winter and decreases from northwest to southeast. Much of the precipitation in the mountains is in the form of snow. Meltwater is vital for Iran's water supply. The central portion of the plateau and the southern coastal plain (Makran) receive less than 5 in. (12.7 cm) of rain annually. Plant and animal life varies greatly, from virtual nonexistence in the deserts to a rich variety in the Caspian littoral. The northern slopes of the Elburz mts. are heavily wooded. The cutting of trees in Iran is rigidly controlled by the government, which also has a reforestation program. In the rivers entering the Caspian Sea are salmon, carp, trout, and pike; sturgeon are abundant in the Caspian Sea. Of the variety of natural resources found in Iran, petroleum (discovered in 1908 in Khuzistan) is by far the most important. Iran has at least 10% of the world's total petroleum reserves. The chief oil fields are found in the central and southwestern parts of the Zagros mts.; major oil fields are also found in N Iran and in the Persian Gulf. Other important minerals are coal, iron ore, copper, lead, salt, natural gas, manganese, and chromium. Among the precious and semiprecious stones are emeralds, topaz, sapphires, and turquoise. Domestic oil and gas, along with hydroelectric power facilities (such as the huge Muhammad Reza Shah Pahlevi Dam in W Iran), provide the country with power. Iran's central position has made it a crossroads of migration; the population is not homogeneous, although it has a Persian core. The migrant tribes of the mountains and highlands, including the Kurds, Lurs, Qashqai, and Bakhtiari, are the least racially mixed descendants of the original Iranians. In the northern provinces, Turkic and Tatar influences are evident; Arab strains predominate in the southeast. Islam entered the country in the 7th cent. A.D., and today it is the official religion; about 98% of Iranians are Muslims, mainly of the Shiite sect. The remainder, mostly Kurds and Arabs, are Sunnites. There are colonies of Zoroastrians (see ZOROASTRIANISM) at Yazd, Kerman, and other large towns. In addition to Armenian and Assyrian Christian sects, there are some Jews, Protestants, and Roman Catholics. Attempts have been made to suppress BABISM and its successor, BAHAISM, in Iran. Other religious movements, such as Mithraism (see under MITHRA) and MANICHAEISM, originated in Iran. The principal language of the country is Persian (Farsi), which is written in Arabic characters. Other languages are Turki and Armenian in the northwest, Kurdish in the western mountain regions, and Arabic along the Persian Gulf. Among the educated classes, English and French are spoken. Iran has a predominantly rural population, found mainly in agrarian villages, although there are nomadic and seminomadic pastoralists throughout the country. The annual population growth rate was around 2.8% in the early 1970s. Tehran is the largest city of Iran and is the political, cultural, commercial, and industrial center of the nation. ESFAHAN, MASHHAD, TABRIZ, RASHT, HAMADAN, ABADAN, SHIRAZ, and AHVAZ are other major cities. KHORRAMSHAHR, on the Shatt al Arab, is the country's chief general cargo port; BANDAR-E PAHLAVI is the chief Caspian port. A network of roads links the villages with the larger cities; most of the principal routes are paved. The Trans-Iranian RR links N Iran with the Persian Gulf; numerous branch lines connect with points east and west of the main line. Iran has a highly centralized education system. Its Education Corps has carried programs into the rural areas since 1962 and has been used as a model to counteract illiteracy in other parts of the world; in the early 1970s Iran's literacy rate approached 40%. There are universities at Tehran, Tabriz, Shiraz, Mashhad, Esfahan, and Ahvaz. Iran's gross national product has been increasing at a rapid rate. However, the inflation rate has been kept low. In 1970, per capita income was $341. Even though revenues from petroleum contribute some 80% of Iran's wealth, agriculture supports 75% of the population. A relatively high portion of Iran's area (some 12%), as compared with neighboring nations, is farmland. The main food-producing areas are in the Caspian littoral and in the valleys of the northwest. Wheat, the most important crop, is grown mainly in the west and northwest; rice is the major crop in the Caspian littoral. Barley, corn, cotton, tea, hemp, tobacco, sugar beets, fruits (including citrus), nuts, and dates are also grown. Sheep and goats are raised, and silkworms are bred. Cultivation of the opium poppy, whose output is controlled by the government, was prohibited in 1955, but resumed in 1969 pending the ban on its legal production in Turkey and Afghanistan. The principal obstacles to agricultural production are primitive farming methods, the overworked and underfertilized soil, poor seed, and the scarcity of water. About one-third of the cultivated land is irrigated; the construction of multipurpose dams and reservoirs along the rivers in the Zagros and Elburz mts. have increased the amount of water available for irrigation. Agricultural programs of modernization, mechanization, and crop and livestock improvement, and programs for the redistribution of land have been undertaken to increase agricultural production. The petroleum industry is the mainstay of Iran's economy, and the country's large oil revenues are used to stimulate industrial growth and diversification as well as to provide for better social conditions and to lure private and foreign investments. Petroleum production is concentrated in W Iran and major refineries are at Abadan (site of Iran's first refinery, built 1913), KERMANSHAH, and Tehran. Pipelines move oil from the fields to the refineries and to such exporting ports as Abadan, Bandar-e Mashur, and Khark island. Iran is a member of the Organization of Petroleum Exporting Countries (OPEC). Textiles are Iran's second most important industrial product; Tehran and Esfahan are the chief textile-producing centers. Other major industries are sugar refining, food processing, and the production of petrochemicals and machinery. There is an iron and steel plant at Esfahan and a fertilizer plant at Shiraz. The traditional handicrafts, such as carpet weaving, the manufacture of ceramics, and jewelry, are an important part of Iran's economy. Besides crude and refined petroleum, Iran's chief exports are cotton, carpets, and fruit; its chief imports are iron and steel, nonelectrical machinery, chemicals, and motor vehicles. Iran's chief trading partners are Japan, West Germany, the United States, and Great Britain. Iran is a constitutional monarchy with a parliamentary form of government. It is governed by the constitution of 1906, which has been supplemented and modified. The shah is the head of state and has autocratic powers; he appoints the prime minister, who is the head of government. The bicameral parliament is composed of the 200-seat Majlis, or national consultative assembly, whose members are popularly elected for four-year terms, and the 60-seat senate, whose members (half elected by the people and half appointed by the shah) serve six-year terms. The senate, which was authorized in the 1906 constitution, was not organized until 1949 and met for the first time in 1950. The shah has the right to dissolve one or both of the bodies. Iran's judicial system is similar to that of France; the supreme court is the nation's judicial body. Each province is governed by an appointed governor-general. The chief political parties are the Iran Novin party and the Mardom party. Iran has a long and rich history. For a detailed description of the Persian Empire, see PERSIA. Some of the world's most ancient settlements have been excavated in the Caspian littoral and on the Iranian plateau; village life began there c.4000 B.C. The Aryans came about 2000 B.C. and split into two main groups, the Medes and the Persians. The Persian Empire founded (c.550 B.C.) by Cyrus the Great was succeeded, after Greek and Parthian occupation, by the SASSANID in the early 3d cent. A.D. Their rule was weakened when Arab invaders took (636) the capital, Ctesiphon, and ended when the Arabs defeated the Sassanid armies at Nahavand in 641. The Arabs brought Islam to Persia, and it was in Persia that the Shiite sect was developed. The Turks began invading Iran in the 10th cent. and soon established several Turkish states. The Turks were followed by the Mongols, led by Jenghiz Khan in the 13th cent. and Tamerlane in the late 14th cent. The Safavid dynasty (1502–1736), founded by Shah ISMAIL, restored internal order in Iran and established the Shiite sect as the state religion; it reached its height during the reign (1587–1629) of Shah ABBAS I (Abbas the Great). He drove out the Portuguese, who had established colonies on the Persian Gulf early in the 16th cent. Shah Abbas also established trade relations with Great Britain and reorganized the army. Religious differences led to frequent wars with the Turks, whose interest in Iran was to continue well into the 20th cent. The fall of the Safavid dynasty was brought about by the Afghans, who overthrew the weak shah, Husein, in 1722. An interval of Afghan rule followed until NADIR SHAH expelled them and established (1736) the Afshar dynasty. He invaded India in 1738 and brought back fabulous wealth, including the legendary Peacock Throne and the Koh-i-noor diamond. Nadir Shah, a despotic ruler, was assassinated in 1747. The Afshar dynasty was followed by the Zand dynasty (1750–94), founded by Karim Kahn, best known as Vakil [regent], who established his capital at Shiraz and adorned that city with many fine buildings. His rule brought a period of peace and renewed prosperity. However, the country was soon again in turmoil, which lasted until the advent of Aga Muhammad Kahn, a detested ruler (assassinated 1797), who defeated the last ruler of the Zand dynasty and established the Kajar dynasty (1794–1925). This long period saw Iran steadily lose territory to neighboring countries and fall under the increasing pressure of European nations, particularly czarist Russia. Under FATH ALI SHAH (1797–1834) Persian claims in the entire Caucasian area were challenged by the Russians in a long struggle that ended with the Treaty of Gulistan (1813) and the Treaty of Turkamanchai (1828), by which Iran was forced to give up the Caucasian lands. Herat, the rice valley on the Hari Rud, which had been part of the ancient Persian Empire, was taken by the Afghans. A series of campaigns to reclaim it ended with the intervention of the British on behalf of Afghanistan and resulted in the recognition of Afghan independence by Iran in 1857. The discovery of oil in the early 1900s intensified the rivalry of Great Britain and Russia for power over the nation. Internally, the early 20th cent. saw the rise of the constitutional movement and a constitution establishing a parliament was accepted by the shah in 1906. Meanwhile, the British-Russian rivalry continued and in 1907 resulted in an Anglo-Russian agreement (annulled after World War I) that divided Iran into spheres of influence. The period preceding World War I was one of political and financial difficulty. In 1911, Morgan Shuster, an American financier, was engaged as financial adviser and treasurer general of Iran. Some reforms were made, but conflict with the Russians led to the failure and termination of the mission in 1912. During the war Iran was occupied by the British and Russians but remained neutral. After the war Iran was admitted to the League of Nations as an original member. In 1919,

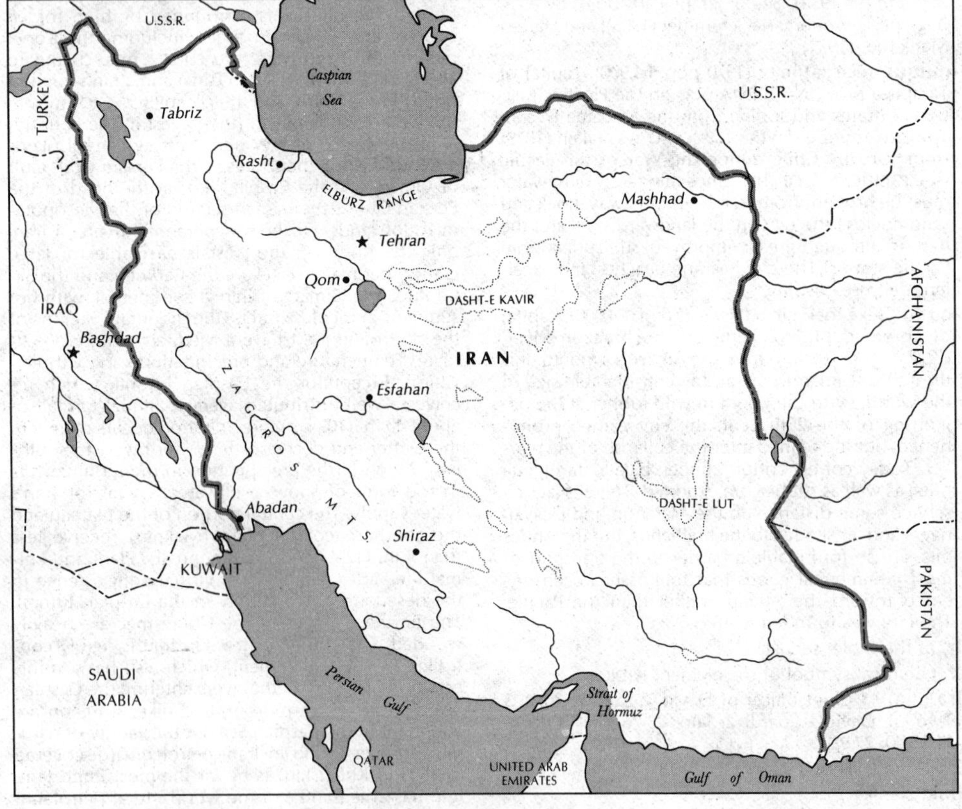

Iran made a trade agreement with Great Britain in which Britain formally reaffirmed Iran's independence but actually attempted to establish a complete protectorate over it. After Iranian recognition of the USSR in a treaty of 1921, the Soviet Union renounced czarist imperialistic policies toward Iran, canceled all debts and concessions, and withdrew occupation forces from Iranian territory. In 1921, Reza Khan, an army officer, effected a coup d'etat and established a military dictatorship. He was subsequently (1925) elected hereditary shah, thus ending the Kajar dynasty and founding the new Pahlevi dynasty. REZA SHAH PAHLEVI abolished the British treaty, reorganized the army, introduced many reforms, and encouraged the development of industry and education. In Aug., 1941, two months after the German invasion of the USSR, British and Soviet forces occupied Iran. On Sept. 16 the shah abdicated in favor of his son Muhammad REZA SHAH PAHLEVI. American troops later entered Iran to handle the delivery of war supplies to the USSR. At the Teheran Conference in 1943 the Teheran Declaration, signed by the United States, Great Britain, and the USSR, guaranteed the independence and territorial integrity of Iran. However, the USSR, dissatisfied with the refusal of the Iranian government to grant it oil concessions, fomented a revolt in the north which led to the establishment (Dec., 1945) of the People's Republic of Azerbaijan and the Kurdish People's Republic, headed by Soviet-controlled leaders. When Soviet troops remained in Iran following the expiration (Jan., 1946) of a wartime treaty that also allowed the presence of American and British troops, Iran protested to the United Nations. The Soviets finally withdrew (May, 1946) after receiving a promise of oil concessions from Iran subject to approval by the parliament. The Soviet-established governments in the north, lacking popular support, were deposed by Iranian troops late in 1946, and the parliament subsequently rejected the oil concessions. In 1951, the National Front movement, headed by Premier MUSSADEGH, a militant nationalist, forced the parliament to nationalize the oil industry and form the National Iranian Oil Company (NIOC). Although a British blockade lead to the virtual collapse of the oil industry and serious internal economic troubles, Mussadegh continued his nationalization policy. Openly opposed by the shah, Mussadegh was ousted in 1952 but quickly regained power. The shah fled Iran but returned when monarchist elements forced Mussadegh from office in Aug., 1953. In 1954, Iran allowed an international consortium of British, American, French, and Dutch oil companies to operate its oil facilities, with profits shared equally between Iran and the consortium. After 1953 a succession of premiers restored a measure of order to Iran; in 1957 martial law was ended after 16 years in force. Iran established closer relations with the West, joining the Baghdad Pact (later called the Central Treaty Organization), and receiving large amounts of military and economic aid from the United States until the late 1960s. Starting in the 1960s and continuing into the 1970s, the Iranian government, at the shah's initiative, undertook a broad program designed to improve economic and social conditions. Land reform was a major priority. In an effort to transform the feudal peasant-landlord agricultural system, the government purchased estates and sold the land to the people; it also distributed large tracts of crown land. In the Jan., 1963, referendum, the voters overwhelmingly approved the shah's extensive plan for further land redistribution, compulsory education, and a system of profit sharing in industry; the program was financed by the selling of government-owned factories to private investors. Within three years, 1.5 million former tenant farmers were plot owners. The shah, who held close reins on the government, slowly readied Iran for a more democratic political system. A new government-backed political party, the Iran Novin party, was introduced and won an overwhelming majority in the parliament in the 1963 and in subsequent elections. Women received the right to vote in national elections in 1963. However, the various reform programs and the continuing poor economic conditions alienated some of the major religious and political groups; there were riots in mid-1963. The general political instability was reflected by the assassination of Premier Hassan Ali Mansur and an unsuccessful attempt on the shah's life in Jan., 1965. Amir Abbas HOVEIDA succeeded as premier. In Oct., 1971, Iran commemorated the 2500th anniversary of the Persian Achaemenid Empire of Cyrus the Great with an elaborate celebration in the desert at Persepolis. Iran's pro-Western policies continued into the 1970s, although improved relations, especially in the economic sphere, were established with the Communist countries, including the USSR. However, relations with Iraq were strained for much of the late 1960s and early 1970s, and there were a number of armed clashes along the entire length of the border. In April, 1969, Iran voided the 1937 accord with Iraq on the control of the Shatt al Arab and demanded that the treaty, which had given Iraq virtual control of the river, be renegotiated. In 1971, Britain withdrew its military forces from the Persian Gulf. Concerned that Soviet-backed Arab nations might try to fill the power vacuum created by the British withdrawal, Iran increased its defense budget by almost 50%, and with the help of huge U.S. and British defense programs, emerged as the region's strongest military power. Although Iran renounced all claims to Bahrain in 1970, it took control (Nov., 1971) of three small islands at the mouth of the Persian Gulf. Iraq protested Iran's action by expelling thousands of Iranian nationals. In March, 1973, short of the end of the 25-year 1954 agreement with the international oil-producing consortium, the shah established the NIOC's full control over all aspects of Iran's oil industry, and the consortium agreed (May, 1973) to act merely in an advisory capacity in return for favorable long-term oil supply contracts. In the aftermath of the Arab-Israeli War of Oct., 1973, Iran, reluctant to use oil as a political weapon, did not participate in the oil embargo against the United States, Europe, and Japan. However, it used the situation to become a leader in the raising of oil prices in disregard of the Tehran Agreement of 1971. Iran utilized the revenue generated by price rises to bolster its position abroad as a creditor, to initiate domestic programs of modernization and economic development, and to increase its military power. See J. M. Upton, *The History of Modern Iran* (1961); D. N. Wilber, *Contemporary Iran* (1963); Peter Avery, *Modern Iran* (2d ed. 1967); H. H. Smith et al., *Area Handbook for Iran* (1971); Marvin Zonis, *The Political Elite of Iran* (1971); Yahya Armajani, *Iran* (1972); R. K. Ramazani, *The Persian Gulf: Iran's Role* (1972); R. E. Looney, *The Economic Development of Iran* (1973).

Iranian languages, group of languages belonging to the Indo-Iranian family of the Indo-European family of languages. See INDO-IRANIAN LANGUAGES.

Irapuato (ērāpwä'tō), city (1970 pop. 138,522), Guanajuato state, W central Mexico, on the Irapuato River. It is the commercial and communications center of the surrounding mining and agricultural (cereals and cattle) region. The fruits and flowers of Irapuato's luxurious gardens are famous throughout Mexico.

Iraq or **Irak** (both: ērāk', ĭrăk'), republic (1970 est. pop. 9,440,100), 167,924 sq mi (434,924 sq km), SW Asia. BAGHDAD is the capital. Iraq is bordered on the S by Kuwait, the Persian Gulf, a neutral zone, and Saudi Arabia, on the W by Jordan and Syria, on the N by Turkey, and on the E by Iran. The country's only outlet to the sea is a short stretch of coast on the northwestern end of the Persian Gulf. BASRA is the only port. Iraq is approximately coextensive with ancient MESOPOTAMIA. The southwest, part of the Syrian Desert, supports a small population of nomadic shepherds. In the rest of the country, life centers on the great southeast-flowing rivers, the Tigris and the Euphrates, which come together in the SHATT AL ARAB and form a delta with marshes and lakes at the head of the Persian Gulf; Hawr al Hammar is the largest lake. There is very little rainfall in Iraq except in the northeast, and all agriculture depends upon river water. The sandy soil and steady heat of the southeast enable a large date crop and much cotton to to be produced. The rivers often cause destructive floods, and numerous projects exist and are planned to prevent floods and to increase the amount of irrigated land. Farther upstream, as the elevation increases, rainfall becomes sufficient to grow diversified crops, including cereals and vegetables. In the mountainous north the economy shifts from agriculture to oil production, notably in the great fields near MOSUL and KIRKUK. The oil, which accounts for one quarter of the country's gross national product, is produced mainly by the Iraq Petroleum Company. The company was owned by an international group of shareholders until June, 1972, when it was nationalized by the Iraqi government. The oil is piped to Tripoli, Lebanon, and to Baniyas, Syria. Aside from petroleum, Iraq has a small, diversified industrial sector, including the production of textiles, cement, food products, leather goods, and a small amount of modern machinery. New industries have been started in electronics products, fertilizers, and refined sugar. The BAGHDAD RAILWAY, long an important means of communication, is declining in importance in favor of travel by road and air. There are

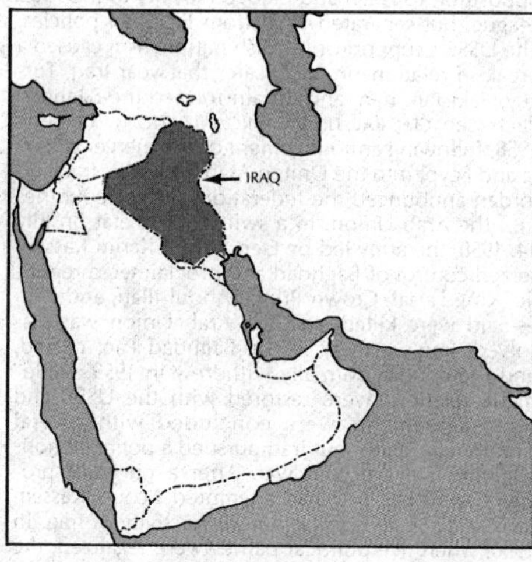

international airports at Baghdad and Basra, and a state-owned airline operates within Iraq and abroad. Most of the population of Iraq is Arabic-speaking and Muslim (Sunni and Shiite) in religion. In the hilly uplands of the northeast is Iraqi KURDISTAN, inhabited by restive Kurds; other large minorities of Iraq include Turks and Assyrians (Nestorian Christians). Most of the country's once large Jewish population emigrated to Israel. Iraq is a veritable treasure house of antiquities, and recent archaeological excavations have greatly expanded knowledge of the dawn of history. Prior to the Arab conquest in the 7th cent. A.D., Iraq had been the site of a number of flourishing civilizations, including the Sumerians (who developed one of the earliest known writing systems), the Akkadians, the Babylonians, and the Assyrians. The capital of the Abbasid caliphate was established at Baghdad in the 8th cent. and the city became a famous center for learning and the arts. Despite fierce resistance, Mesopotamia fell to the Ottoman Turks in the 16th cent., and passed under direct Turkish administration in the 19th cent., when it came to constitute the three Turkish provinces of Basra, Baghdad, and Mosul. In World War I the British invaded Iraq in their war against the Ottoman Empire; Britain declared then that it intended to return to Iraq some control of its own affairs. Nationalist elements, impatient over delay in gaining independence, revolted in 1920 but were suppressed by the British. Late that year the Treaty of Sèvres established Iraq as a mandate of the League of Nations under British administration, and in 1921 the country was made a kingdom headed by Faisal I, who had been recommended by Gertrude BELL. With strong reluctance an elected Iraqi assembly agreed in 1924 to a treaty with Great Britain providing for the maintenance of British military bases and for a British right of veto over legislation. By 1926 an Iraqi parliament and administration was governing the country. The treaty of 1930 provided for a 25-year alliance with Britain. The British mandate was terminated in 1932, and Iraq was admitted to the League of Nations. Meanwhile, the first oil concession had been granted in 1925, and in 1934 the export of oil began. Domestic politics were turbulent, with many factions contending for power. Late in 1936, the country experienced the first of seven military coups that were to take place in the next five years. In April, 1941, Rashid Ali al Ghailani, leader of an anti-British and pro-Axis military group, seized power and ousted Emir Abdul Illah, the pro-British regent for the child king, Faisal II (who had succeeded his father, Ghaza, ruler from Faisal I's death in 1933 to his own death in 1939). The British reinforced their garrisons by landing troops at Basra, and in May, al Ghailani, with some German and Italian support, opened hostilities. He was utterly defeated by June, and Emir Abdul Illah was recalled. On Jan. 16, 1943, Iraq declared war on the Axis countries. Anti-British sentiment was reasserted after the war, and in 1948 a British-sponsored modification of the treaty of 1930 was defeated by the Iraqi parliament because of animosity arising over the Palestine problem. Iraq, with other members of the ARAB LEAGUE, participated in 1948 in the unsuccessful war against Israel. Premier Nuri es-Said dissolved all political parties in 1954, and a new parliament was elected. A national development program, financed mostly by oil royalties, led to flood control measures, improvement of agricultural methods, and the building of a power industry. The United States extended technical aid, and after 1956, military assistance. In external affairs Iraq continued adamant opposition to Israel and pledged loyalty to the Arab League, but separated itself from Egyptian policies. The USSR's support of Kurdish nationalism caused a break in relations in 1955. Later that year Iraq, Turkey, Pakistan, Iran, and Britain formed the Baghdad Pact (see CENTRAL TREATY ORGANIZATION). In Feb., 1958, following announcement of the merger of Syria and Egypt into the United Arab Republic, Iraq and Jordan announced the federation of their countries into the Arab Union. In a swift coup d'etat on July 14, 1958, the army led by Gen. Abdul Karim Kassem seized control of Baghdad and proclaimed a republic. King Faisal, Crown Prince Abdul Illah, and Nuri es-Said were killed, and the Arab Union was dissolved. Iraq's activity in the Baghdad Pact ceased, and the country formally withdrew in 1959. Diplomatic relations were restored with the USSR and trade agreements were concluded with several Communist states, but Iraq pursued a policy of nonalignment in the cold war. After a purge of pro-Egyptian forces, who had attempted a coup, Kassem took steps to reduce Communist activity in Iraq. In 1960, when five political parties were legalized, the Communists were ignored. Relations with neighbors were strained when Iraq claimed sovereignty over Kuwait and over Iranian territory along the Shatt al Arab. In 1962 the chronic Kurdish problem flared up when tribes led by Mustafa al-Barzani revolted, demanded an autonomous Kurdistan, and gained control of much of N Iraq. A brief cease-fire was arranged in 1964 but fighting resumed. In June, 1966, a compromise was reached, but fighting broke out again in October, 1968. A new agreement was reached in March, 1970. The cease-fire lasted until March, 1974, when, following Iraq's rejection of the Kurdish bid for autonomy, fighting erupted between the Kurds and Iraqi troops. As of early 1975 the precise legal relationship of Kurdistan to Iraq had yet to be worked out. In Feb., 1963, Col. Abdul Salam Aref led a coup that overthrew the Kassem regime. Kassem and dozens of Communists were executed. The new regime was dominated by members of the Iraqi Ba'ath party, a socialist group whose goal was Arab unity. In Nov., 1963, however, the party's members in the governing council were expelled by an army coup engineered by Aref. In April, 1966, the president and two cabinet members died in a helicopter crash. The president's brother, Gen. Abdul Rahman Aref, assumed office. He was overthrown by a bloodless coup in July, 1968. Maj. Gen. Ahmad Hasan al-Bakr became president and began a purge of opponents. In 1969 espionage trials were begun, and more than 50 persons, including 9 Jews, were executed. The government accused Iran of complicity in an attempted coup in Jan., 1970. The Iraqi government was incensed when Iran occupied three islands in the Persian Gulf following Britain's withdrawal from the area in 1971; diplomatic relations were severed with both Iran (restored 1973) and Britain. Relations with the USSR improved, however, and in April, 1972, a 15-year friendship treaty was signed; the Communist party was legalized in 1972. In July, 1973, another coup was foiled, although one minister was killed and another wounded. The internal security chief was blamed, and he and 35 others were executed. Iraq took an active part in the 1973 Arab-Israeli War; it also participated in the oil boycott against nations supporting Israel. In early 1974, years of border conflicts with Iran culminated in heavy armed clashes along the entire length of their border. Following UN mediation, an accord was reached (June) between the two nations. Iraq is governed under a 1970 provisional constitution. The revolutionary council of 12 elects the president. Ministers are responsible to the president. See F. I. Qubain, *The Reconstruction of Iraq, 1950-1957* (1958); S. H. Longrigg and Frank Stoakes, *Iraq* (1959); K. M. Langley, *The Industrialization of Iraq* (1961); Georges Roux, *Ancient Iraq* (1965); Majid Khadduri, *Independent Iraq, 1932-1958* (1960) and *Republican Iraq* (1969); H. H. Smith et al., *Area Handbook for Iraq* (1969).

Irazú (ērăsōō'), active volcano, c.11,260 ft (3,430 m) high, central Costa Rica. It erupted in 1723, destroying Cartago, and in 1963, covering San José with ash. Vapor constantly rises from one of its craters. From the summit can be seen the Pacific Ocean, the Caribbean Sea, and Lake Nicaragua.

Irbil (ĭrbĭl'), town (1965 pop. 90,320), N Iraq. It is a commercial and administrative center. The ancient Sumerian and Assyrian city of Urbillum (Arbela) was on this site. Irbil is on an artificial mound surmounted by an old Turkish fort. The name is sometimes spelled Erbil.

IRBM: see GUIDED MISSILE.

Iredell, James (īr'dĕl), 1751-99, American jurist, b. Lewes, England. He emigrated (1767) to North Carolina, where he entered the customs service at Edenton and was made (1774) collector for the port. He was admitted to the bar in 1771, and after the outbreak of the American Revolution he helped to organize the North Carolina court system. He became (1777) a judge and later (1779-81) was attorney general. His strong support of the proposed U.S. Constitution helped procure its adoption by North Carolina. In 1790, Iredell was made an associate justice of the newly established U.S. Supreme Court. Among his notable opinions was his dissent in *Chisholm* vs. *Georgia* (1793) when the majority holding was that a state might be sued in the Federal courts without its consent. The Eleventh Amendment to the U.S. Constitution (adopted 1798) made that view the law of the land. See biography by G. J. McRee (1857, repr. 1949).

Ireland, John, 1838-1918, American Roman Catholic prelate, first archbishop of St. Paul, Minn. (1888-1918), b. Co. Kilkenny, Ireland. He emigrated to St. Paul in childhood. He was educated at French seminaries, was ordained (1861), and soon enlisted as a chaplain in the Civil War. He became prominent when he was cathedral pastor (1867-75) at St. Paul, as a strong advocate of total abstinence, opposing the liquor interests, and as an opponent of political corruption. In 1875 he was made coadjutor bishop of St. Paul and in 1884 bishop; in 1888 his see was made archiepiscopal. Bishop Ireland was an energetic spokesman for liberal American Catholicism. He gained many enemies by advocating state support and inspection of Catholic schools and by opposing the use of foreign languages in American Catholic churches, except in extreme need, and in parochial schools under any circumstances. He was in favor of Western settlement by immigrants, who could thereby escape the poverty of the Eastern urban environment. He continually made public statements on political matters, and he was a close personal friend of Presidents William McKinley and Theodore Roosevelt. See biography by J. H. Moynihan (1953).

Ireland, John, 1879-1962, English composer. Inspired by visits to the Channel Islands, he wrote music of a simple, rugged beauty. His many songs include the cycle *Songs of a Wayfarer* (1903) and *Sea Fever* (1913), to the poem by John Masefield. In addition to songs, chamber music, and piano pieces, Ireland wrote orchestral music, including *Symphonic Rhapsody* (1920-21), *Legend for Piano and Orchestra* (1933), and *London Overture* (1936); and a choral work, *These Things Shall Be* (1937).

Ireland, William Henry, 1777-1835, English forger of Shakespearean documents and manuscripts. Besides forging deeds and signatures relating to Shakespeare, Ireland fabricated two plays, *Vortigern and Rowena* (1796) and *Henry II* (both pub. 1799), as the works of Shakespeare. Edmond MALONE, however, exposed him, and Ireland later acknowledged the hoax.

Ireland, Irish *Eire* (âr'ə) [to it are related the poetic *Erin* and, perhaps, the Latin *Hibernia*], island, 32,598 sq mi (84,429 sq km), second largest of the British Isles. It lies west of the island of Great Britain, from which it is separated by the narrow North Channel, the Irish Sea (which attains a width of 130 mi/209 km), and St. George's Channel. More than a third the size of Britain, the island averages 140 mi (225 km) in width and 225 mi (362 km) in length. A large central plain extending to the Irish Sea between the Mourne Mts. in the north and the mountains of Wicklow in the south is roughly enclosed by a highland rim. The highlands of the north, west, and south, which rise to more than 3,000 ft (914 m), are generally barren, but the central plain is extremely fertile and the climate is temperate and moist, warmed by southwesterly winds. The rains, which are heaviest in the west (some areas have more than 80 in./203 cm annually), are responsible for the brilliant green grass of the "emerald isle," and for the large stretches of peat bog, a source of valuable fuel. The coastline is irregular, affording many natural harbors. Off the west coast are numerous small islands, including the ARAN ISLANDS, the BLASKET ISLANDS, ACHILL, and CLARE ISLAND. The interior is dotted with lakes (the most celebrated are the Lakes of KILLARNEY) and wide stretches of river called loughs. The SHANNON, the longest of Irish rivers, drains the western plain and widens into the beautiful loughs Allen, Ree, and Derg. The River Liffey empties into Dublin Bay, the Lee into Cork Harbour at Cobh, the Foyle into Lough Royle near Londonderry, and the Lagan into Belfast Lough. The island is divided into two major political units—Northern Ireland (see IRELAND, NORTHERN), which is joined with Great Britain in the United Kingdom, and the Republic of Ireland (see IRELAND, REPUBLIC OF). Of the 32 counties of Ireland, 26 lie in the Republic, and of the four historic provinces, three and part of the fourth are in the Republic.

Ireland to the English Conquest. The earliest known people in Ireland belonged to the groups that inhabited all of the British Isles in prehistoric times. In the several centuries preceding the birth of Christ a number of Celtic tribes invaded and conquered Ireland and established their distinctive culture (see CELT), although they do not seem to have come in great numbers. Ancient Irish legend tells of four successive peoples who invaded the country—the FIRBOLGS, the FOMORS, the TUATHA DE DANANN, and the MILESIANS. Oddly enough, the Romans, who occupied Britain for 400 years, never came to Ireland, and the Anglo-Saxon invaders of Britain, who largely replaced the Celtic population there, did not greatly affect Ireland. Until the raids of the Norsemen in the late 8th cent., Ireland remained relatively untouched by foreign incursions and enjoyed the golden age of its culture. The people, Celtic and non-Celtic alike, were organized into clans, or tribes, which in the early period owed allegiance to one of five provincial kings—of ULSTER, MUNSTER, CONNAUGHT, LEINSTER, and MEATH (now the northern part of Leinster). These kings nominally served the high king of all Ireland at Tara (in Meath). The clans fought constantly among themselves, but despite civil strife, literature and art were held in high respect. Each chief or king kept an official poet (Druid) who preserved the oral traditions of the people. The Gaelic language and culture were extended into Scotland by Irish emigrants in the 5th and 6th cent. Parts of Ireland had already been Christianized before the arrival of St. PATRICK in the 5th cent., but pagan tradition continued to appeal to the imagination of Irish poets even after the complete conversion of the country. The Celtic Christianity of Ireland produced many scholars and missionaries who traveled to England and the Continent, and it attracted students to Irish monasteries, until the 8th cent. perhaps the most brilliant of Europe. St. COLUMBA and St. COLUMBAN were among the most famous of Ireland's missionaries. All the arts flourished; Irish illuminated manuscripts were particularly noteworthy. The Book of Kells (see CEANANNUS MOR) is especially famous. The country did not develop a strong central government, however, and it was not united to meet the invasions of the Norsemen who settled on the shores of the island late in the 8th cent., establishing trading towns (including Dublin, Waterford, and Limerick) and creating new petty kingdoms. In 1014, at Clontarf, BRIAN BORU, who had become high king by conquest in 1002, broke the strength of the Norse invaders. There followed a period of 150 years during which Ireland was free from foreign interference but was torn by clan warfare. In the 12th cent., Pope Adrian IV granted overlordship of Ireland to Henry II of England. The English conquest of Ireland was begun by Richard de Clare, 2d earl of PEMBROKE, known as Strongbow, who intervened in behalf of a claimant to the throne of Leinster; in 1171, Henry himself went to Ireland, temporarily establishing his overlordship there. With this invasion commenced an Anglo-Irish struggle that continued for nearly 800 years.

Ireland and the English. The English established themselves in Dublin. Roughly a century of warfare ensued as Ireland was divided into English shires ruled from Dublin, the domains of feudal magnates who acknowledged English sovereignty, and the independent Irish kingdoms. Many Englishmen intermarried with the Irish and were assimilated into Irish society. In the late 13th cent. the English introduced a parliament in Ireland. In 1315, Edward BRUCE of Scotland invaded Ireland and was joined by many Irish kings. Although Bruce was killed in 1318, the English authority in Ireland was weakening, becoming limited to a small district around Dublin known as the Pale; the rest of the country fell into a struggle for power among the ruling Anglo-Irish families and Irish chieftains. English attention was diverted by the Hundred Years War with France (1337-1453) and the Wars of the Roses (1455-85). However, under Henry VII new interest in the island was aroused by Irish support for Lambert Simnel, a Yorkist pretender to the English throne. To crush this support, Henry sent to Ireland Sir Edward POYNINGS, who summoned an Irish Parliament at

Drogheda and forced it to pass the legislation known as Poynings' Law (1495). These acts provided that future Irish Parliaments and legislation receive prior approval from the English Privy Council. A free Irish Parliament was thus rendered impossible. The English Reformation under Henry VIII gave rise in England to increased fears of foreign, Catholic invasion; control of Ireland thus became even more imperative. Henry VIII put down a rebellion (1534–37), abolished the monasteries, confiscated lands, and established a Protestant "Church of Ireland" (1537). But since the vast majority of Irish remained Roman Catholic, the seeds of bitter religious contention were added to the already rancorous Anglo-Irish relations. The Irish rebelled three times during the reign of Elizabeth I and were brutally suppressed. Under James I, Ulster was settled by Scottish and English Protestants, and many of the Catholic inhabitants were driven off their lands; thus two sharply antagonistic communities were established. Another Irish rebellion, begun in 1641 in reaction to the hated rule of Charles I's deputy, Thomas Wentworth, earl of STRAFFORD, was crushed (1649–50) by Oliver Cromwell with the loss of hundreds of thousands of lives. More land was confiscated (and often given to absentee landlords), and more Protestants settled in Ireland. The intractable landlord-tenant problem that plagued Ireland in later centuries can be traced to the English confiscations of the 16th and 17th cent. Irish Catholics rallied to the cause of James II after his overthrow (1688) in England (see the GLORIOUS REVOLUTION), while the Protestants in Ulster enthusiastically supported William III. At the battle of the BOYNE (1690) near Dublin, James and his French allies were defeated by William. The English-controlled Irish Parliament passed harsh PENAL LAWS designed to keep the Catholic Irish powerless; political equality was also denied to Presbyterians. At the same time English trade policy depressed the economy of Protestant Ireland, causing many so-called Scotch-Irish to emigrate to America. A newly flourishing woolen industry was destroyed when export from Ireland was forbidden. During the American Revolution, fear of a French invasion of Ireland led Irish Protestants to form (1778–82) the Protestant Volunteer Army. The Protestants, led by Henry GRATTAN, and even supported by some Catholics, used their military strength to extract concessions for Ireland from Britain. Trade concessions were granted in 1779, and, with the repeal of Poynings' Law (1782), the Irish Parliament had its independence restored. But the Parliament was still chosen undemocratically and Catholics continued to be denied the right to hold political office. Another unsuccessful rebellion was staged in 1798 by Wolfe Tone, a Protestant who had formed the Society of UNITED IRISHMEN and who accepted French aid in the uprising. The reliance on French assistance revived anti-Catholic feeling among the Irish Protestants, who remembered French support of the Jacobite restoration. The rebellion convinced the British prime minister, William PITT, that the Irish problem could be solved by the adoption of three policies: abolition of the Irish Parliament, legislative union with Britain in a United Kingdom of Great Britain and Ireland, and CATHOLIC EMANCIPATION. The first two goals were achieved in 1800, but the opposition of George III and British Protestants prevented the enactment of the Catholic Emancipation Act until 1829, when it was accomplished largely through the efforts of the Irish leader, Daniel O'CONNELL.

Ireland under the Union. After 1829 the Irish representatives in the British Parliament attempted to maintain the Irish question as a major issue in British politics. O'Connell worked to repeal the union with Britain, which was felt to operate to Ireland's disadvantage, and to reform the government in Ireland. Towards the middle of the century, the IRISH LAND QUESTION grew increasingly urgent. But the Great Potato Famine (1845–49), one of the worst natural disasters in history, dwarfed political developments. During these years a blight ruined the potato crop, the staple food of the Irish population, and hundreds of thousands perished from hunger and disease. Many thousands of others emigrated; between 1847 and 1854 about 1,600,000 went to the United States. The population dropped from an estimated 8,500,000 in 1845 to 6,550,000 in 1851. Irish emigrants in America formed the secret FENIAN MOVEMENT, dedicated to Irish independence. In 1869 the British prime minister William Gladstone sponsored an act disestablishing the Protestant "Church of Ireland" and thereby removed one Irish grievance. In the 1870s, Irish politicians renewed efforts to achieve HOME RULE within the union, while in Britain Gladstone and others attempted to solve the Irish problem through land legislation and Home Rule. Gladstone twice submitted Home Rule bills (1886 and 1893) that failed. The proposals alarmed Protestant Ulster, which began to organize against Home Rule. In 1905, Arthur GRIFFITH founded SINN FEIN among Irish Catholics, but for the time being the dominant Irish nationalist group was the Home Rule party of John REDMOND. Home Rule was finally enacted in 1914, with the provision that Ulster could remain in the union for six more years, but the act was suspended for the duration of World War I and never went into effect. In both Ulster and Catholic Ireland volunteer military groups were formed. The Irish Republican Brotherhood, a descendent of the Fenians, organized a rebellion on Easter Sunday, 1916; although unsuccessful, the rising acquired great propaganda value when the British executed its leaders. Sinn Fein, linked in the Irish public's mind with the rising and aided by Britain's attempt to apply conscription to Ireland, scored a tremendous victory in the parliamentary elections of 1918. Its members refused to take their seats in Westminster, declared themselves the Dáil Éireann (Irish Assembly), and proclaimed an Irish Republic. The British outlawed both Sinn Fein and the Dáil, which went underground and engaged in guerrilla warfare (1919–21) against local Irish authorities representing the union. The British sent troops, the Black and Tans, who inflamed the situation further.

Partition. A new Home Rule bill was enacted in 1920, establishing separate parliaments for Ulster and Catholic Ireland. This was accepted by Ulster, and Northern Ireland was created. The plan was rejected by the Dáil, but in autumn 1921, Prime Minister Lloyd George negotiated with Griffith and Michael COLLINS of the Dáil a treaty granting Dominion status within the British Empire to Catholic Ireland. The Irish Free State was established in Jan., 1922. (See IRELAND, REPUBLIC OF and IRELAND, NORTHERN) See Richard Bagwell, *Ireland under the Tudors* (1890) and *Ireland under the Stuarts* (3 vol., 1890; repr. 1963); Robert Dunlop, *Ireland from the Earliest Times* (1922); Edmund Curtis, *A History of Ireland* (rev. ed. 1950); Joseph Rafferty, *Prehistoric Ireland* (1950); P. S. O'Hegarty, *History of Ireland under the Union* (1952); Nicholas Mansergh, *The Irish Question, 1840–1921* (1965); J. C. Beckett, *The Making of Modern Ireland, 1603–1921* (1966); Edward Norman, *A History of Modern Ireland* (1971); D. H. Akenson, *The United States and Ireland* (1973).

Ireland, Church of, Anglican church of both the Republic of Ireland and Northern Ireland. The Church of Ireland has always included only a small portion of the Irish population, and for that reason, it was disestablished by Gladstone's act of 1869. The church has a membership of about 500,000, with its main strength in Northern Ireland.

Ireland, National University of, founded 1908 to provide higher education for Irish Roman Catholics. It consists of three colleges: University College, Galway; University College, Cork; and University College, Dublin (not to be confused with the Univ. of Dublin; see DUBLIN, UNIV. OF). St. Patrick's College in Maynooth, a Roman Catholic seminary, is affiliated with the school.

Ireland, Northern, division of the United Kingdom of Great Britain and Northern Ireland (1971 pop. 1,527,593), 5,462 sq mi (14,147 sq km), NE Ireland. It is frequently called Ulster. The capital is BELFAST. It comprises the counties of ARMAGH, DOWN, ANTRIM, LONDONDERRY, TYRONE, and FERMANGH, six of the nine counties of the historic province of Ulster (see IRELAND). The land is mountainous and has few natural resources. Farming (livestock, dairy products, cereals) is the largest single occupation. Northern Ireland's fine linens are famous. Heavy industry is concentrated in and around Belfast, one of the chief ports of the British Isles. Shipbuilding and other engineering, food processing, and the manufacture of textiles are the leading industries; papermaking and furniture manufacturing are also important. Northern Ireland has 12 representatives in the British Parliament and possesses a large degree of self-government in domestic matters. The Ulster government is known as Stormont, from the hill where the Parliament building stands. About three fifths of the population are Protestant; one third are Catholic. English is the official language. Northern Ireland's relatively distinct history began in the early 17th cent., when, after the suppression of an Irish rebellion, much land was confiscated by the British crown and "planted" with Scottish and English settlers. Ulster took on a Protestant character as compared with the rest of Ireland; but there was no question of political separation until the late 19th cent. when William GLADSTONE presented (1886) his first proposal for HOME RULE for Ireland. Although the Irish of the north had their own grievances against the English, the largely Protestant population

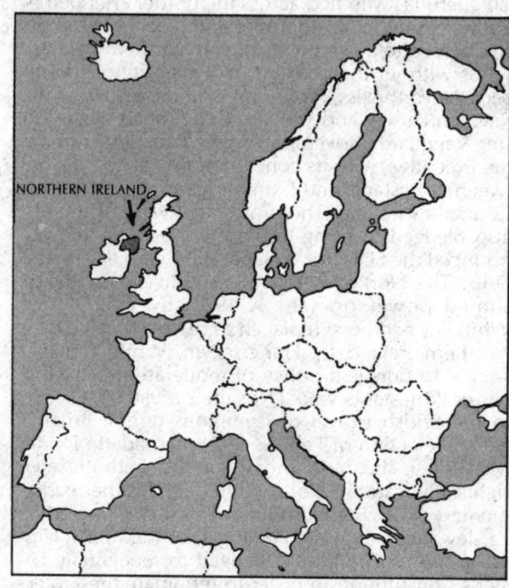

feared domination under Home Rule by the Catholic majority in the south. In addition, industrial Ulster was bound economically more to England than to the rest of Ireland. Successive schemes for Home Rule widened the rift, so that by the outbreak of World War I civil war in Ireland was an immediate danger. The Government of Ireland Act of 1920 attempted to solve the problem by enacting Home Rule separately for the two parts of Ireland, thus creating the province of Northern Ireland. However, the Irish Free State, now the Republic of Ireland (see IRELAND, REPUBLIC OF), which was established in 1922, refused to recognize the finality of the partition; and violence erupted frequently on both sides of the border. The late 1960s marked a new stage in the region's troubled history. The Catholic minority, which suffered economic and political discrimination, had grown steadily through immigration from the Republic. In 1968 civil rights protests by Catholics led to widespread violence. Prime Minister Terence O'Neill had sought to end anti-Catholic bias as part of his policy of fostering closer ties between Ulster and the Irish Republic, but opponents within his ruling Unionist party forced his resignation in April, 1969. His successor, James Chichester-Clark, was unable to restrain the growing unrest and in August called in British troops to help restore order. At the end of 1969 a split occurred in the IRISH REPUBLICAN ARMY (IRA), which is the illegal military arm of the Sinn Fein party in the Republic of Ireland; the new "provisional" wing of the IRA was made up of radical nationalists. Brian Faulkner became leader of the Unionist party and prime minister of Northern Ireland in March, 1971, and began a policy of imprisoning IRA and other militants. However, the IRA and the Ulster Defense Association, a Protestant terrorist group, continued and even intensified their activities. On March 30, 1972, the British prime minister, Edward Heath, suspended the Stormont government and appointed William Whitelaw secretary of state for Northern Ireland. Westminster's direct rule over the province was renewed in March, 1973. Two other important events occurred the same month. In a referendum held on March 8, an overwhelming majority of Ulster's citizens voted for union with the United Kingdom, with only a small number favoring union with the Irish Republic. On March 20, Britain published a White Paper outlining a new assembly, based on multiple parties and elected on the basis of proportional representation, that would replace the Stormont Parliament. In June elections, Faulkner's Unionist party won the largest number of seats (23) in the 78-member Assembly; in November it formed a coalition government with the Social Democratic and Labour party (SDLP), Ulster's major Catholic group, and the nonsectarian Alliance party. Representatives of these parties in turn formed an 11-man Northern Ireland Executive, with Faulkner as its head and SDLP leader Gerard Fitt as his deputy. While the Executive made decisions on most domestic issues and exercised day-to-day administration, London retained responsibility for security, foreign relations, justice, and some financial matters. Following the formation of this first coalition regime in Northern Ireland's history, Heath, Faulkner, and the Irish Republic's prime minister, Liam Cosgrave, agreed in Dec. 1973, to form a Council of Ireland as a consultative body to promote closer cooperation between Ulster and the Republic. Progress toward creation of the Council was to be contingent upon Dublin's taking steps to punish guerrillas who fled across the border after perpetrating crimes in Northern Ireland. The three leaders also agreed to make no change in Northern Ireland's status without the consent of a majority of its citizens. Nevertheless, Protestant extremists such as the Rev. Ian Paisley and William Craig (head of the Ulster Vanguard Movement) vowed to destroy both the Executive, with its concept of power-sharing between Protestants and Catholics, and the plans for a Council of Ireland. The provisional wing of the IRA also pledged to bring down the Executive and denounced the SDLP for collaboration with the Protestants. The Northern Ireland Executive officially assumed power on Jan. 1, 1974, by which time Whitelaw had been replaced as secretary of state for Northern Ireland by Francis Pym. While Faulkner sought to pursue a policy of moderation, hard-line Ulster Protestants won 11 of the province's 12 seats in the British House of Commons during Britain's general election of Feb. 28, 1974; Bernadette Devlin McAliskey, the best known of the Catholic civil rights advocates in Northern Ireland, lost her parliamentary seat. The hard-line Protestants (including Paisley and Craig), who emerged as the fourth largest group in Commons, pledged to renegotiate Ulster's Constitution in order to terminate the Protestant-Catholic coalition and halt progress toward a Council of Ireland. Faulkner's resignation as leader of the Unionist party because of opposition among party leaders to the proposed Council of Ireland represented another victory for the hard-line Protestants. Harry West, one of their new members of Commons, replaced Faulkner, who, however, remained as head of the Northern Ireland Executive. In March, 1974, the British named Merlyn Rees as the new secretary of state for Northern Ireland. The most dramatic attempt to upset Ulster's new governmental framework came in May, 1974, when militant Protestants, spearheaded by the Ulster Workers' Council, sponsored a general strike in the province. Under pressure from the 14-day strike the Northern Ireland Executive collapsed on May 28. The British government then took direct control of the province. Meanwhile, bombings and other terrorist activities had spread to Dublin and London. By early 1975, more than 1,100 people had perished in Northern Ireland's sectarian strife, and British troop strength in Ulster exceeded 16,000 men. The IRA declared a brief truce that lasted until mid-January, 1975. See Aodh Blacam, *The Black North* (1938); Thomas Wilson, ed., *Ulster under Home Rule* (1955); T. Q. Stewart, *The Ulster Crisis* (1967); Martin Wallace, *Northern Ireland: Fifty Years of Self-Government* (1971); C. C. O'Brien, *The States of Ireland* (1972).

Ireland, Republic of, country (1971 pop. 2,971,230), 27,136 sq mi (70,282 sq km). (For physical geography and history to 1922, see IRELAND.) From 1922 to 1937 the country was known as the **Irish Free State,** and from 1937 to 1949 as **Eire.** DUBLIN is the capital of the republic. Other urban areas are LIMERICK, CORK, DUN LAOGHAIRE, WATERFORD, GALWAY, and DUNDALK. The 26 counties of the republic are MONAGHAN, CAVAN, and DONEGAL (constituting part of the historic province of Ulster); LOUTH, MEATH, DUBLIN, KILDARE, WICKLOW, CARLOW, WEXFORD, KILKENNY, LAOIGHIS, OFFALY, WESTMEATH, and LONGFORD (comprising Leinster); TIPPERARY, WATERFORD, CORK, KERRY, LIMERICK, and CLARE (comprising Munster); and LEITRIM, ROSCOMMON, GALWAY, MAYO, and SLIGO (comprising Connaught). Agriculture is the primary economic activity, engaging about 70% of the land and 30% of the work force. The raising of dairy and beef cattle, sheep, pigs, and poultry is the chief enterprise. Among the leading crops are flax, oats, wheat, turnips, potatoes, sugar beets, and barley. The republic's industries, which are largely concentrated around Dublin, produce such items as linen and laces (for which Ireland is famous), food products, textiles, ships, iron products, and handicrafts. Around the free port of SHANNON are factories producing electronic equipment, chemicals, plastics, and textiles. The republic is governed (under the 1937 constitution) by a two-chamber legislature (the Dáil Eireann and the Seanad Éireann), and a prime minister and cabinet. The head of state, the president, is popularly elected. The Dáil, chosen by proportional representation, is the more powerful chamber. The main political parties are the Fianna Fáil, the Fine Gael, and the Labour party. Gaelic and English are the official languages, but English is the more widely used.

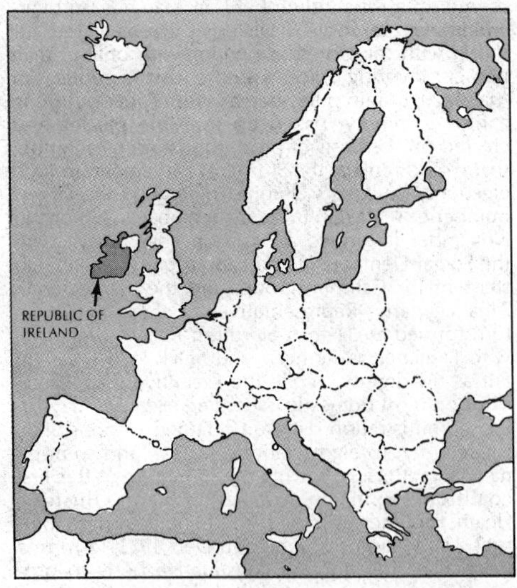

History. After the establishment by treaty with Great Britain of the Irish Free State (Jan., 1922), civil war broke out between supporters of the treaty and opponents, who refused to accept the partition of Ireland and the retention of any ties with Britain. The antitreaty forces, embodied in the IRISH REPUBLICAN ARMY (IRA) and led by Eamon DE VALERA, were defeated, although the IRA continued as a secret terrorist organization. William COSGRAVE became the first prime minister. De Valera and his followers, the Fianna Fáil party, agreed to take the oath of allegiance to the British crown and entered the Dáil in 1927. In 1932, De Valera became prime minister, and under his administration a new constitution was promulgated (1937), establishing the sovereign nation of Ireland, or Eire, within the British Commonwealth of Nations. De Valera's policies aimed at the political and economic independence and union of all of Ireland. The loyalty oath to the crown was abolished, and certain economic provisions of the 1921 treaty with England were repudiated, leading to an "economic war" (1932-38) with Britain. During World War II, Eire remained neutral and vigorously protested Allied military activity in Northern Ireland. The British were denied the use of Irish ports, and German and Japanese agents were allowed to operate in the country. However, great numbers of Irishmen volunteered to serve with the British armed forces. The people of Eire suffered relatively little hardship during the war and even profited from increased food exports. The postwar period brought a sharp rise in the cost of living and a decline in population, due in great part to steady emigration to Northern Ireland, Great Britain, and other countries. In 1948, Prime Minister Costello demanded total independence from Great Britain and reunification with the six counties of Northern Ireland. The Republic of Ireland was proclaimed on April 18, 1949. The country withdrew from the Commonwealth and formally claimed jurisdiction over the Ulster counties. It was admitted to the United Nations in 1955. Nothing came of the claim to Ulster, and during the 1950s and 60s the republic and Northern Ireland improved their economic relations. But the problem of Northern Ireland flared up again in the late 1960s with bitter fighting between the Protestant majority and Catholic minority there, aggravated by the actions of the IRA, which was headquartered in the republic. In 1973, Erskine H. Childers succeeded De Valera as president of Ireland, and Liam Cosgrave, at the head of a Fine Gael-Labour coalition, replaced John Lynch, a member of Fianna Fáil, as prime minister. In the same year the republic joined the COMMON MARKET. Childers died late in 1974 and was succeeded by Cearbhal O. Dalaigh. For bibliography, see under IRELAND.

Irenaeus, Saint (īrĭnē'əs), c.125–c.202, Greek theologian, bishop of Lyons, and Father of the Church. Born in Asia Minor, he was a disciple of St. Polycarp. Irenaeus went to Rome to plead for leniency toward the Montanists (see MONTANISM) and for those Eastern Christians who were threatened with excommunication because they did not observe the Roman date for Easter. He remained in the West and died in Gaul. He was the earliest Father of the Church to systematize Christian doctrine and is cited frequently by later theologians. Only two of his works survive—neither in the original Greek. *Against Heresies* establishes Christian doctrine against the Gnostics and incidentally supplies much information on Gnosticism. The *Epideixix* is a concise exposition of Christian doctrine (tr. by J. P. Smith *Proof of the Apostolic Preaching,* 1952). Feast: June 28.

Irene, c.750-803, Byzantine empress (797-802). At the death (780) of her husband, LEO IV, she became regent for her son, CONSTANTINE VI. Devoted to the Orthodox Church, she neglected the wars with the Arabs and Bulgars and bent most of her efforts to suppressing ICONOCLASM. The Second Council of Nicaea (see NICAEA, SECOND COUNCIL OF) decreed in 787 the restoration of images to the churches. Forced by the army to retire from the regency in 790, Irene was made joint ruler by Constantine in 792. Constantine's misconduct (encouraged by Irene, who thus sought to discredit him) led to his deposition in 797. Irene had her son blinded and ascended the throne. Because it left no emperor on the throne, her accession served as pretext for CHARLEMAGNE to be crowned emperor in 800. Irene was deposed in 802 and died in exile. NICEPHORUS I became emperor. See Charles Diehl, *Byzantine Portraits* (1906; tr. 1927).

Irene, in Greek mythology: see HORAE.

Ireton, Henry (ī'ərtən), 1611-51, English parliamentary general; son-in-law of Oliver Cromwell. He held various commands in the parliamentary army during the first civil war (see ENGLISH CIVIL WAR) and in 1646 married Cromwell's daughter Bridget. A conservative reformer and advocate of limited monarchy, he opposed the radical constitutional demands of the LEVELERS and drafted the peace settlement known as the Heads of the Proposals, presented to the king by the army in 1647. In 1648 he took the part of the army against Parliament, became a republican, and signed (1649) the death warrant of Charles I. Appointed (1650) lord deputy of Ireland, he sternly carried out Cromwell's policy of dispossessing the Irish and settling Englishmen there.

Iri (ī'rī) or **Ir** (ĭr), Benjamite. 1 Chron. 7.7,12.

Iri (ē'rē'), city (1970 est. pop. 87,000), SW South Korea. It is an agricultural center, where sake (rice wine) is brewed and rice is processed.

Irian Barat (ĭr'ēän bär'ät), **West Irian,** or **West New Guinea,** formerly Netherlands (or Dutch) New Guinea, province (1970 est. pop. 957,000), c.162,000 sq mi (419,580 sq km), Indonesia, comprising the western half of New Guinea and about 12 offshore islands. The capital is DJAJAPURA, formerly Sukarnapura or Hollandia. A rugged, densely forested region, with mountains rising to over 16,500 ft (5,029 m; highest in the nation), it is inhabited chiefly by primitive Papuans living in hundreds of tribes, each with its own language and customs; some still engage in cannibalism and headhunting. The coastal lowlands are swampy and cut by many rivers, including the Digul and the Mamberano, Indonesia'a largest. Subsistence farming is carried on (some of the highland tribes terrace and cultivate the mountains at 45° angles); taro, bananas, sugarcane, and sweet potatoes are the principal crops. Wild game is trapped, and there is fishing along the coast and the rivers. Magnetite has been found in the Star Mts., a region unexplored until 1959. There are deposits of oil in the west and nickel and cobalt on Waigeo island. The Dutch first visited the west coast of the island in 1606. They extended their rule along the coastal areas in the 18th cent., and in 1828 claimed possession of the coast west of the 141st meridian and in 1848 of the north coast W of Humboldt Bay. The Dutch claim to the western half of the island was recognized by Great Britain and Germany in treaties of 1885 and 1895. In World War II the northern coastal areas and offshore islands were occupied (1942) by the Japanese but retaken (1944) by the Allies, after which Hollandia became a staging base for operations in the Philippines. Following Indonesian independence (1949), the Dutch retained control of West New Guinea. Years of dispute over the territory culminated in the landing (early 1962) of Indonesian guerrillas and paratroopers there. The conflict ended in late 1962 when the Netherlands agreed to UN administration of West New Guinea and, after May 1, 1963, transfer of the territory to Indonesian control pending a plebiscite (to be held under UN supervision before 1970). The plebiscite was held in Aug., 1969; tribal leaders, voting as representatives of their people, chose to remain under Indonesian rule, and Indonesia then formally annexed the territory. The province was officially renamed Irian Joya in 1973. See Peter Matthiessen, *Under the Mountain Wall* (1962); Arend Lijphart, *The Trauma of Decolonization: The Dutch and West New Guinea* (1966); John Ryan, *The Hot Land* (1970); Peter Ryan, ed., *Encyclopedia of Papua and New Guinea* (3 vol., 1972).

Iriarte, Tomás de (tōmäs' dā ēryär'tā), 1750-91, Spanish poet and dramatist, b. Canary Islands. He spent most of his life in Madrid, where, like many of his contemporaries, he engaged in polemics, criticism, satire, and the translation of Latin and French works. Iriarte wrote several comedies of manners but is best known for his 76 *Fábulas literarias* [literary fables] (1782, tr. 1835), which earned him an international reputation as a wit and a moralist. Most of these deal with literary methods and style. The French fabulist Florian acknowledged a debt to Iriarte. See study by R. M. Cot (1972).

iridescence, exhibition of rainbowlike colors on a surface. It usually results from INTERFERENCE when light composed of different wavelengths is reflected from the superficial layers of organic or inorganic substances, e.g., minerals, mother-of-pearl, and the feathers of birds. Iridescence greatly enhances the value of certain gems.

iridium (ĭrĭd'ēəm), metallic chemical element; symbol Ir; at. no. 77; at. wt. 192.2; m.p. about 2450°C; b.p. above 4000°C; sp. gr. 22.55 at 20°C; valence +3 or +4. Iridium is a very hard, usually brittle, extremely corrosion-resistant silver-white metal with a face-centered cubic crystalline structure. It falls between platinum and osmium in group VIII of the PERIODIC TABLE. It is not certain whether osmium or iridium is the most dense element. Iridium is found uncombined in nature as the metal and in combination with osmium and platinum. It is obtained commercially from osmiridium, a by-product of platinum production. The metal is used in pivot bearings and in scientific and other special equipment, such as surgical tools. It is also used in making chemical crucibles. Iridium is used principally in alloys. An alloy with osmium is used to make fountain-pen nibs. Alloys with platinum are used in heavy-duty electrical contacts. An alloy of 10 parts iridium with 90 parts platinum is used in the international kilogram standard in Paris. Formerly the international meter standard was the distance between two marks on a bar made of that same alloy; it is now based on the wavelength of a line in the spectrum of an isotope of krypton. Iridium is chemically very unreactive. Pure iridium metal is not attacked by acids or acid mixtures, not even by aqua regia, which dissolves gold. Fluorine and chlorine attack it only at a red heat. It is oxidized slowly at high temperatures. It resists attack by fused bases and by most molten metals. Iridium was discovered in 1804 by Smithson Tennant; it is so named because of its various highly colored salts.

Irigoyen, Hipólito (ēpō'lētō ērēgō'yän), 1850?–1933, Argentine political leader, president of the republic (1916–22, 1928–30). In 1896 he became the leader of the Radicals, a bourgeois reform party. By propaganda, and sometimes by insurrection, he opposed the conservative regime. The electoral reform of Roque SÁENZ PEÑA enabled the Radicals in 1916 to replace the landowning oligarchy and to elect Irigoyen president. Ignoring congressional resolutions and public opinion, he maintained neutrality in World War I. Some reform measures were enacted during his administration but his efforts to increase Radical power led to forceful intervention in the provinces and produced much opposition. In 1922 he was succeeded by another Radical, Marcelo T. de ALVEAR. Irigoyen was swept back into the presidency in 1928 with great popular acclaim, but his second administration, in the midst of economic depression, was so unpopular that he was overthrown and the oligarchy was reinstated (Sept., 1930). See R. A. Potash, *The Army and Politics in Argentina* (Vol. I, 1969).

Irijah (īrī'jə), captain who detained Jeremiah on a false accusation in Jerusalem. Jer. 37.13,14.

Iris, river: see YEŞIL IRMAK.

iris: see EYE.

Iris (ī'rĭs), in Greek mythology, goddess of the rainbow; daughter of Electra and Thaumas. She was often represented as a messenger of Zeus and Hera.

iris, common name for members of the genus *Iris* of the Iridaceae, a family of perennial herbs that includes the crocuses, freesias, and gladioli. The family is characterized by thickened stem organs (bulbs, corms, and rhizomes) and by linear or sword-shaped leaves—small and grasslike in the crocuses and blue-eyed grasses. It is widely distributed over the world except in the coldest regions and is most abundant in S Africa and in tropical America. Almost all of the family's nearly 60 genera include commercially valuable ornamentals. The iris family is closely related to the lily and amaryllis families, differing from them in having three stamens rather than six. The cultivated irises (genus *Iris*), freesias (genus *Freesia*), and gladioli (genus *Gladiolus*) show a wide variety of colors in their large, usually perfumed blossoms; they are mostly hybrids of Old World species. The many species of wild iris are most common in temperate and subarctic regions of North America, where they are often called flags, or blue flags. The fleur-de-lis is thought to have been

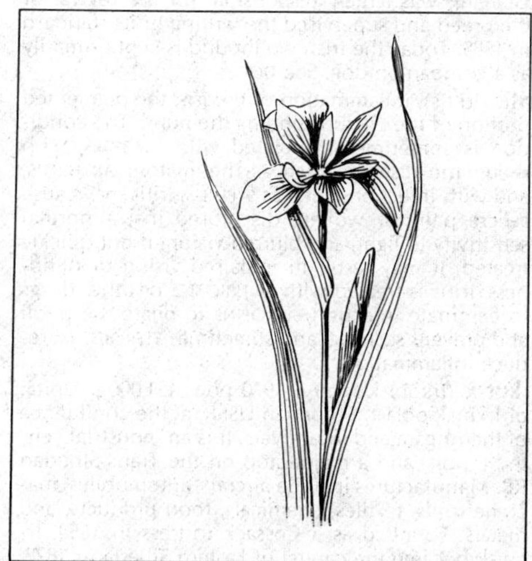

Red iris, Iris fulva

derived from the iris, and the flower of the Greek youth HYACINTH may have been an iris. Orrisroot, a violet-scented flavoring used in dentifrices, perfumes, and other products, is prepared from the powdered rhizomes of several European species of iris. The freesias, native to S Africa, characteristically bear their blossoms on a horizontal extension of the stem. The crocuses (genus *Crocus*), which usually bear a single yellow, purple, or white blossom, are native to the Mediterranean area and to SW Asia. One species, SAFFRON, is cultivated commercially for a yellow dye; the unrelated meadow saffron or autumn crocus and the wild crocus or pasqueflower belong to the lily and buttercup families respectively. Other members of the family found in the United States are the blue-eyed grasses (genus *Sisyrinchium*) with small clusters of blue, white, or purplish flowers, ranging from Canada to Patagonia, and the celestial lily (genus *Nemastylis*) with pairs of blue flowers, ranging from the Kansas prairies to Tennessee and Texas. Irises are classified in the division MAGNOLIOPHYTA, class Liliatae, order Liliales, family Iridaceae.

Irish elk: see ELK.

Irish Free State: see IRELAND; IRELAND, REPUBLIC OF.

Irish Land Question, name given in the 19th cent. to the problem of land ownership and agrarian distress in Ireland under British rule. As early as the 12th cent., Irish land was seized by invading Anglo-Normans. Confiscation was continued by England's Tudor monarchs, by James I, and by Oliver Cromwell, partly for spoils but largely to bring the rebellious country under English control. The long-term result was the creation of a class of absentee English landlords and of a rack-rented, impoverished Irish peasantry with attenuated tenant rights. In the 18th cent., under the PENAL LAWS, Roman Catholics—the vast majority of the Irish population—were prevented from acquiring land or from renting it at less than an exorbitant two thirds of the value of its produce. Tenants' improvements were thus discouraged since they meant higher rents. Eviction on short notice was also a problem. The securing (1829) of CATHOLIC EMANCIPATION brought into the British Parliament Irish Catholics who sympathized with the miserable tenantry, and the terrible Irish famine of the 1840s focused attention on the land question. In 1849, Parliament passed the Encumbered Estates Act, which provided for the sale of mortgaged estates. However, its liberal purpose was perverted by speculative purchasers who made the rents even more extortionate. The Irish Tenant Right League, established in 1850, demanded the "three F's"—fair rent, fixity of tenure, and freedom of sale. The violence of the FENIAN MOVEMENT, the extension of the franchise by the Reform Act of 1867, the movement for HOME RULE, and assistance from the Liberal party, headed by William GLADSTONE, furthered the cause of the tenant.

Approaches to a Solution. Gladstone's Land Act of 1870 protected the tenant from arbitrary eviction and provided some compensation for improvements. But a major agricultural depression beginning in the 1870s brought a new crisis. The National Land League, founded under the leadership of Michael DAVITT and Charles Stewart PARNELL, conducted a campaign of boycott and violence that influenced the passage of the Land Act of 1881, called the "Magna Carta" of the Irish farmer. It recognized the three F's and provided a land commission to fix a "fair rent." Thereafter land purchase by the tenant become the predominant issue. The Ashbourne Act of 1885 and supplementary acts of 1887 and 1891 provided a loan fund of many millions of pounds to tenants who wished to purchase their lands. Difficulties remained since the Anglo-Irish magistracy, which favored the landlords, did not satisfactorily implement the new laws. The Irish National League, an outgrowth of the suppressed National Land League, advocated withholding of rents from extortionate landlords. Its activities, too, were suppressed. In 1894 began the Irish Agricultural Organization Society, fostered by Sir Horace PLUNKETT, to encourage agricultural cooperation and improved farming methods; this led to the establishment (1899) of the Irish Dept. of Agriculture. The agitation of the United Irish League, under William O'BRIEN, demanding compulsory sales by landlords, led to the Wyndham Act of 1903 and the Amended Land Purchase Act of 1909. The Wyndham Act, which provided loans to tenants at reduced interest for the purchase of land and gave bonuses to landlords who sold, proved, in effect, a solution to the Irish Land Question. In 1907 the Evicted Tenants Act provided for the compulsory sale of land needed for evicted tenants. By 1921 two thirds of the land in Ireland had become the property of Irish tenants, and a compulsory law transferred the remaining portions soon after the establishment (1922) of the Irish Free State. See J. E. Pomfret, *The Struggle for Land in Ireland, 1800–1923* (1930, repr. 1969); N. D. Palmer, *The Irish Land League Crisis* (1940).

Irish language, also called Irish Gaelic, member of the Goidelic group of the Celtic subfamily of the Indo-European family of languages (see CELTIC LANGUAGES). The history of Irish as a literary language falls into three periods: Old Irish (7th–9th cent. A.D.), Middle Irish (10th–16th cent.), and Modern Irish (since the 16th cent.). In the medieval period a great Irish literature flourished. Grammatically, there are still four cases for the noun (nominative, genitive, dative, and vocative). In pronunciation the stress is on the first syllable. An acute accent is placed over a vowel to denote length, and a dot is placed over a consonant to indicate aspiration. The spelling currently used is not an accurate indication of present-day pronunciation. The alphabet employed today for Irish can be called a variant or a derivative of the Roman alphabet that took shape about the 8th cent. A.D. It has 18 letters: 13 consonants and 5 vowels. The oldest extant Irish texts are inscriptions written in the ogham script (see OGHAM). These texts date back to the 5th cent. A.D. or perhaps earlier and differ as much from the early literary Irish that follows them as Latin does from Old French. The government of Ireland is trying, thus far unsuccessfully, to revive Irish as the language of the country; the study of Irish is required in preparatory schools. See also IRISH LITERATURE. See Thomas F. O'Rahilly, *Irish Dialects Past and Present* (1932); Rudolf Thurneysen, *A Grammar of Old Irish* (1946–49, repr. 1961); Heinrich Wagner, *Linguistic Atlas and Survey of Irish Dialects* (4 vol., 1958–69).

Irish literary renaissance, late 19th- and early 20th-century movement that aimed at reviving ancient Irish folklore, legends, and traditions in new literary works. Essentially it was a rebirth of literature in Ireland as Irish literature rather than as a pale reflection of English literature. The movement, also called the Celtic renaissance, was in part the cultural aspect of a political movement that was concerned with self-government for Ireland. The revival produced some of the best plays of the 20th cent. in the dramas of J. M. Synge and Sean O'Casey and some of the greatest poetry in the works of W. B. Yeats. One of the movement's most impressive achievements was the establishment of the ABBEY THEATRE. Other important writers of the revival were Lady Gregory, G. W. Russell (pseud. A. E.), and James Stephens. James Joyce was influenced by the movement. See Una Ellis-Fermor, *The Irish Dramatic Movement* (2d ed. 1954, repr. 1967); Robert Hogan, *After the Irish Renaissance* (1967).

Irish literature: see GAELIC LITERATURE.

Irish moss: see SEAWEED.

Irish Republican Army, known as the IRA, nationalist organization devoted to the integration of Ireland as a complete and independent unit. Organized by Michael COLLINS from remnants of rebel units dispersed after the Easter Rebellion in 1916 (see IRELAND), it was composed of the more militant members of the Irish Volunteers, and it became the military wing of the SINN FEIN party. With the establishment of the Irish Free State in 1922, the IRA became the stronghold of intransigent opposition to Ireland's dominion status and to the separation of Northern Ireland. During the troubled early years of the Free State, the IRA was responsible for numerous bombings, raids and street battles on both sides of the Irish border. Popular and effective at first, its fortunes turned after Eamon De Valera, a former IRA supporter, took over the Free State government in 1932. Weakened by internal dissensions, by a loss of popular support because of its violence and its pro-German agitation during World War II, by the attainment of republican objectives in 1949, and by stern government measures against its lawless activities, the IRA declined swiftly. Eventually outlawed by both Irish governments, it became a secret organization. It perpetrated bombing attacks in Belfast, London, and on the Ulster border during the 1950s, particularly in 1956–57, but then became quiescent until the late 1960s. In 1969 the IRA split into two groups, the majority, or "officials," advocating a united socialist Ireland but disavowing terrorist activities, and the "provisionals," claiming terrorism as a necessary catalyst for unification. The "provisionals" then began a systematic terrorist campaign in Northern Ireland. British troops have been unable to contain their activities, and the number of casualties continued to rise through the mid-1970s. The violence contributed to the polarization between Roman Catholic and Protestant in Northern Ireland and exacerbated the acute political difficulties already existing there. The Dublin government, formerly fairly tolerant of the IRA, began in 1972 to imprison members of the militant wing. About the same time the IRA began to extend its activities with a series of bomb attacks in Great Britain. See J. B. Bell, *The Secret Army* (1970, repr. 1974).

Irish Sea, arm of the Atlantic Ocean, c.40,000 sq mi (103,600 sq km), 130 mi (209 km) long and up to c.140 mi (230 km) wide, lying between Ireland and Great Britain. It is connected with the Atlantic by the North Channel and (on the south) by St. George's Channel. Ireland is on its west shore, Scotland, England, and Wales on the east. The principal islands in the sea are the Isle of Man, Anglesey, and Holyhead. The chief ports are Dublin, Liverpool, and Barrow-in-Furness.

Irish setter, breed of large SPORTING DOG developed in Ireland in the 18th cent. It stands about 26 in. (66.0 cm) high at the shoulder and weighs between 50 and 70 lb (22.7–31.8 kg). Its moderately long, silky coat is flat or slightly wavy and forms fringes of longer hair, or feathers, on the ears, chest, belly, back of legs, and tail. The American variety is a solid chestnut red or mahogany color, while its Irish counterpart is often parti-colored—red and white. Although originally bred as a field hunter and still used in that capacity today, the striking appearance of the Irish setter has led many breeders to strive for bench-competition excellence rather than field ability. See DOG.

Irish terrier, a breed of hardy working TERRIER developed in the British Isles and believed to be one of the oldest terriers. It stands about 18 in. (46 cm) high at the shoulder and weighs from 25 to 27 lb (11–12 kg). The dense, wiry coat lies fairly close to the body and is usually solid red-wheaten, bright red, or golden red in color. Probably descended from the same wirehaired black-and-tan dog of Great Britain that produced most of the terriers, the Irish terrier was used to hunt small game and destroy vermin, both on land and in the water. Today it is principally raised as a show competitor and family pet. See DOG.

Irish water spaniel, breed of large SPORTING DOG developed in Ireland in the 19th cent. The tallest of the spaniels, it stands about 23 in. (58.4 cm) high at the shoulder and weighs between 45 and 65 lb (20.4–29.5 kg). Its dense, liver-colored coat is tightly curled and water-repellent. The tapering, smooth-coated tail and the topknot of long, loose curls that hang from a peak between the eyes are characteristic of the breed. A natural water dog with great endurance, the Irish water spaniel is often used to retrieve ducks. However, its coat, which may snag in heavy underbrush, makes it less suitable for hunting upland game. See DOG.

Irish wolfhound, breed of very large HOUND whose origins may be traced back many centuries in Ireland. The tallest of dogs, it stands about 34 in. (86.4 cm) high at the shoulder and weighs about 140 lb (63.5 kg). Its rough, wiry coat is usually gray in color. Originally bred as a hunter, the Irish wolfhound had become almost extinct by the mid-19th cent. as a result of the gradual disappearance of its natural quarry, the wolf and elk, and the depletion of its native Irish stock by exportation. A Scotsman, G. A. Graham, was largely responsible for the revival of the breed and supervised the writing of its standard in 1885. Today the Irish wolfhound is kept primarily as a companion dog. See DOG.

iritis (īrī'tĭs), inflammation of the iris, the pigmented portion of the EYE surrounding the pupil. The condition is sometimes associated with DIABETES, with rheumatic diseases such as rheumatoid ARTHRITIS, and with infections such as SYPHILIS. Iritis may cause severe pain, a swollen, discolored iris, abnormal sensitivity to light, and blurred vision. If not quickly treated, it may result in impaired vision or blindness. Iritis is treated with ANTIBIOTICS or other drugs to eliminate infection, ATROPINE to dilate the pupil and prevent scarring, and sometimes STEROIDS to reduce inflammation.

Irkutsk (ĭrkōōtsk'), city (1970 pop. 451,000), capital of Irkutsk oblast, S Siberian USSR, at the confluence of the Angara and Irkut rivers. It is an industrial center, a port, and a major stop on the Trans-Siberian RR. Manufactures include aircraft, automobiles, machine tools, textiles, chemicals, food products, and metals. Founded as a Cossack fortress in 1654, Irkutsk became the capital of Eastern Siberia in 1822. It has been a place of exile since the 18th cent. In the city are a university (founded 1918) and several agricultural, medical, and technical schools. A large hydroelectric station on the Angara River supplies the area with power.

Ir-nahash (ĭr-nā'hăsh), unidentified city, S Palestine. 1 Chron. 4.12.

Irnerius (ûr"nēr'ēəs), c.1055–c.1130, Italian jurist and founder of the law school (c.1088) at Bologna, which became the center of legal scholarship in Europe. Though little is known of his early life, it is generally agreed that he became a professor of rhetoric and dialectic at an early age. Later he turned to law. His interlinear glosses to the Corpus Juris are recognized as major contributions to the interpretation of Roman law. Attribution to him of other commentaries on philosophy and the theory of law is still much disputed.

Iron, Ralph: see SCHREINER, OLIVE.

Iron, unidentified city, in the mountains of N Palestine. Joshua 19.38.

iron, metallic chemical element; symbol Fe [Lat. *ferrum*]; at. no. 26; at. wt. 55.847; m.p. about 1535°C; b.p. about 2750°C; sp. gr. 7.87 at 20°C; valence +2, +3, +4, or +6. Iron is a lustrous, ductile, malleable, silver-gray metal (group VIII of the PERIODIC TABLE). It is known to exist in four distinct crystalline forms (see ALLOTROPY). The most common is the α-form, which is stable below about 770°C, and has a body-centered cubic crystalline structure; it is often called ferrite. Iron is attracted by a magnet and is itself easily magnetized (see MAGNETISM). It is a good conductor of heat and electricity. It is chemically active and forms two major series of chemical compounds, the bivalent iron (II), or ferrous, compounds and the trivalent iron (III), or ferric, compounds. It displaces hydrogen from hydrochloric or dilute sulfuric acid, but becomes passive (loses its normal chemical activity) when treated with cold nitric acid. Iron forms such compounds as oxides, hydroxides, halides, acetates, carbonates, sulfides, nitrates, sulfates, and a number of complex ions. Ferrous sulfate heptahydrate, $FeSO_4 \cdot 7H_2O$, sometimes called green vitriol, is a compound formed by the reaction of dilute sulfuric acid (formerly called oil of vitriol) with metallic iron; it is used in the manufacture of ink, in dyeing, and as a disinfectant. Ferric chloride hexahydrate, $FeCl_3 \cdot 6H_2O$, is a yellow-brown crystalline compound used as a MORDANT in dyeing and as an etching compound. Ferric oxide, Fe_2O_3, is a red-dish-brown powder used as a paint pigment and in abrasive rouges. Prussian blue, $KFe_2(CN)_6$, is a pigment containing the ferrocyanide complex ion. Iron rusts readily in moist air, forming a complex mixture of compounds that is mostly a ferrous-ferric oxide with the composition Fe_3O_4. Because iron is a component of hemoglobin, a red oxygen-carrying pigment of the red blood cells of vertebrates, iron compounds are important in nutrition; one cause of anemia is iron deficiency. Iron is an abundant element in the universe; it is found in many stars, including the sun. Iron is the fourth most abundant element in the earth's crust, of which it constitutes about 5% by weight, and is believed to be the major component of the earth's core. Iron is found distributed in the soil in low concentrations and is found dissolved in ground waters and the ocean to a limited extent. It is rarely found uncombined in nature except in meteorites, but iron ores and minerals are abundant and widely distributed. The principal ores of iron are HEMATITE (ferric oxide, Fe_2O_3) and LIMONITE (ferric oxide trihydrate, $Fe_2O_3 \cdot 3H_2O$). Other ores include SIDERITE (ferrous carbonate, $FeCO_3$), TACONITE (an iron silicate), and MAGNETITE (ferrous-ferric oxide, Fe_3O_4), which often occurs as a white sand. Iron PYRITE (iron disulfide, FeS_2) is a crystalline gold-colored mineral known as fool's gold. Chromite is a chromium ore that contains iron. Lodestone is a form of magnetite that exhibits natural magnetic properties. Iron is produced in the United States chiefly from oxide ores. For many years rich hematite ores were produced by open-pit mining in the Mesabi Range near Lake Superior. However, these ores have been largely depleted, and iron is now produced from low-grade ores that are treated to improve their quality; this process is called beneficiation. Iron ores are refined in the BLAST FURNACE. The product of the blast furnace is called pig iron and contains about 4% carbon and small amounts of manganese, silicon, phosphorus, and sulfur. About 95% of this iron is processed further to make STEEL, usually by the open-hearth process or the BESSEMER PROCESS. The balance is cast in sand molds into blocks called pigs. It is further processed in iron foundries (see CASTING AND FOUNDING). **Cast iron** is made when pig iron is remelted in small cupola furnaces (similar to the blast furnace in design and operation) and poured into molds to make castings. It usually contains 2% to 6% carbon. Scrap iron or steel is often added to vary the composition. Cast iron is used extensively to make machine parts, engine cylinder blocks, stoves, pipes, steam radiators, and many other products. Gray cast iron, or gray iron, is produced when the iron in the mold is cooled slowly. Part of the carbon separates out in plates in the form of graphite but remains physically mixed in the iron. Gray iron is brittle but soft and easily machined. White cast iron, or white iron, which is harder and more brittle, is made by cooling the molten iron rapidly. The carbon remains distributed throughout the iron as cementite (iron carbide, Fe_3C). A malleable cast iron can be made by annealing white iron castings in a special furnace. Some of the carbon separates from the cementite; it is much more finely divided than in gray iron. A ductile iron may be prepared by adding magnesium to the molten pig iron; when the iron is cast the carbon forms tiny spherical nodules around the magnesium. Ductile iron is strong, shock resistant, and easily machined. **Wrought iron** is commercially purified iron. In the Aston process, pig iron is refined in a Bessemer converter and then poured into molten iron silicate slag. The resulting semisolid mass is passed between rollers that squeeze out most of the slag. The wrought iron has a fibrous structure with threads of slag running through it; it is tough, malleable, ductile, corrosion resistant, and melts only at high temperatures. It is used to make rivets, bolts, pipes, chains, and anchors, and is also used for ornamental IRONWORK. For the history of iron, see IRON AGE. See W. H. Dennis, *Metallurgy of the Ferrous Metals* (1963) and *Foundations of Iron and Steel Metallurgy* (1967).

Iron Age, period in the development of industry that begins with the general use of iron and continues into modern times. In Asia, Egypt, and Europe it was preceded by the BRONZE AGE. It did not begin in the Americas until the coming of the Europeans. Iron beads were worn in Egypt as early as 4000 B.C., but these were of meteoric iron, evidently shaped by the rubbing process used in shaping implements of stone. The oldest known article of iron shaped by hammering is a dagger found in Egypt that was made before 1350 B.C. This dagger is believed not to have been made in Egypt but to be of HITTITE workmanship. The use of smelted iron ornaments and ceremonial weapons became common during the period extending from 1900 to 1400 B.C. About this time, the invention of tempering (see FORGING) was made by the Chalybes of the Hittite empire. It is possible that the Hittite kings kept ironworking techniques secret and restricted export of iron weapons. After the downfall of the Hittite empire in 1200 B.C., the great waves of migrants spreading through S Europe and the Middle East insured the rapid transmission of iron technology. In Europe knowledge of iron smelting was acquired in Greece and the Balkans, and somewhat later in N Italy (see ETRUSCAN CIVILIZATION; VILLANOVAN CULTURE) and central Europe. The Early Iron Age in central Europe, dating from c.800 B.C. to c.500 B.C., is known as the HALLSTADT period. Celtic migrations, beginning in the 5th cent. B.C., spread the use of iron into W Europe and to the British Isles. The Late Iron Age in

Europe, which is dated from this period, is called LA TÈNE. The casting of iron did not become technically useful until the Industrial Revolution. The people of the Iron Age developed the basic economic innovations of the Bronze Age and laid the foundations for feudal organization. They utilized the crops and domesticated animals introduced earlier from the Middle East. Ox-drawn plows and wheeled vehicles acquired a new importance and changed the agricultural patterns. For the first time man was able to exploit efficiently the temperate forests. Villages were fortified, warfare was conducted on horseback and in horse-drawn chariots, and alphabetic writing based on the Phoenician script became widespread. Distinctive art styles in metal, pottery, and stone characterized many Iron Age cultures. For the Iron Age in mythology, see AGE.

ironclad, mid-19th century wooden warship protected from gunfire by iron armor. The success of the ironclad when first employed by the French in the Crimean War sparked a naval armor and armaments race between France and Great Britain. Ironclads were later used by both sides in the U.S. Civil War, although only the Union navy had at its disposal sufficient industrial resources to build a sizable fleet. The armored ship became obsolete with the introduction (1870–90) of all-metal warship construction.

Iron Cross: see DECORATIONS, CIVIL AND MILITARY.

Iron Gate, Rum. *Porţile de Fier,* Serbo-Croatian *Gvozdena Vrata,* gorge of the Danube River, c.2 mi (3.2 km) long and c.550 ft (170 m) wide, on the Yugoslav-Rumanian border between Orşova and Turnu-Severin. There the river narrows and swiftly flows through a gap between the Carpathian and Balkan mts. Iron Gate, formerly an obstacle to shipping, was cleared of rock obstructions in the 1860s; the Sip Canal (opened 1896) permits large river craft to get past the gorge. Iron Gate is the site of one of Europe's largest hydroelectric power dams. The joint Yugoslav-Rumanian project (opened 1971) improves river navigation by impounding a large lake and will have an ultimate electricity generating capacity of 2,160,000 kw.

Iron Guard, Rumanian nationalistic, anti-Semitic, and antiparliamentary group, founded in 1924 by Corneliu Zelea CODREANU. Originally named the Legion of the Archangel Michael, it was organized on military lines and operated through terrorism. Its most notable victims were Premier Ion Duca, assassinated in 1933, and ex-Premier Nicolae Iorga, assassinated in 1940. Banned in 1933, the Iron Guard carried on as the All-for-the-Fatherland party. When King Carol II proclaimed his personal dictatorship in 1938, he had Codreanu and other leading Guardists imprisoned and eventually shot. Following the king's abduction in 1940, Marshall Ion ANTONESCU seized power with the help of the Iron Guard, but soon found himself in disagreement with it. He suppressed (1941) an Iron Guard rebellion, and Horia Sima, then leader of the Guard and vice premier, fled to Germany. With the collapse of the Axis Powers in World War II the Iron Guard disappeared from Rumanian politics.

iron lung, device used to maintain ARTIFICIAL RESPIRATION over an extended period of time. It is used primarily in cases of paralysis of the respiratory system, especially poliomyelitis, and of damage to the respiration control center of the brain. An iron lung is composed of a cylindrical steel drum, which encloses the entire body with only the head exposed. A rubber diaphragm makes the cylinder airtight without putting undue pressure on the neck. Pumps raise and lower the pressure within the chamber, forcing the lungs to expand and contract at the normal breathing rate. A number of problems can exist with the use of the iron lung machine, including the possibility of food or vomit being taken into the lungs. There is also the danger of serious skin ulcers with any patient who is immobilized for long periods of time. The iron lung is sometimes called the Drinker respirator after Philip Drinker, who invented it in 1928.

iron pyrites: see PYRITE.

Ironside, William Edmund Ironside, 1st **Baron,** 1880–1959, British general. After serving with distinction in the South African War and World War I, he was chosen (1918) to command the Allied forces at Archangel to aid Aleksandr KOLCHAK in fighting the Bolsheviks. After service in the Middle East, he became commandant of the staff college at Camberley. Other commands followed, including several years in India, and in 1938 Ironside became governor of Gibraltar. On the outbreak of World War II, he was recalled to England to be chief of the imperial general staff. In 1940 he was briefly chief of the home forces in England. He was made a field marshal in 1940 and created baron in 1941.

Ironton, industrial city (1970 pop. 15,030), seat of Lawrence co., S Ohio, on the Ohio River; inc. as a city 1865. Chemicals, dyes, metal pipes, power shovels, industrial tar, and iron products are manufactured, and there is some coal mining. Ironton was a great iron-producing center during the Civil War. From c.1900 to 1910 the city had the largest blast furnace in the world, Big Etna, with a capacity of 100 tons per day. However, the development of the northern iron-ore ranges and improved transportation by rail and on the Great Lakes left Ironton without a furnace by the end of World War I. Today the remains of many giant charcoal iron furnaces are local landmarks.

ironwood: see HORNBEAM.

ironwork, ornamental. The shaping of wrought IRON, used almost exclusively until the 16th cent., is primarily an art of the blacksmith, who must work with the metal while it is at the desired stage of heat and flexibility. Methods and tools used in modern hand-wrought work are similar to the early ones. However, much modern work is accomplished by mechanical means, with the pneumatic hammer and the acetylene or electric torch. A variety of stock pieces are currently available that the early smith had to fashion laboriously from crude ingots. Iron was used ornamentally in classical times. Because of rusting and the decay of the material, little survives of very early work. Door hinges, generally C- or S-shaped, still exist from the 12th cent. In the 13th cent. vine scrollwork on hinges and grilles replaced the earlier patterns. In succeeding periods, wrought-iron designs assumed the forms of other architectural decoration: Gothic tracery, plant forms, classical motifs, rococo broken curves, and delicate neoclassical work. In Spain the iron GRILLE attained a high development (see REJERÍA). In France in the mid-17th cent. a vogue developed for iron balconies, stair railings, and monumental fences and gateways, rich with scrollings and bold foliations. This style was transplanted to England c.1700 by Jean TIJOU. In American work of the 18th cent. simplicity and restrained ornamentation prevailed. Cast iron was rarely used prior to the 16th cent., when it came into demand for andirons and firebacks. For architectural embellishment and for garden furniture it became common in the early 19th cent. It was used extensively for fences and railings in the S United States. Since cast iron is cheaper and more rigid than wrought iron and is less affected by corrosion than any other cheap commercial iron, it has been widely used during the last three centuries. Modern sculptors who have worked in iron include Julio GONZÁLEZ, Picasso, and David SMITH. See G. K. Geerlings, *Wrought Iron in Architecture* (new ed. 1957); Fritz Kühn, *Wrought Iron* (2d ed. 1969).

irony, figure of speech in which what is stated is not what is meant. The user of irony assumes that his reader or listener understands the concealed meaning of his statement. Perhaps the simplest form of irony is rhetorical irony, when, for effect, a speaker says the direct opposite of what he means. Thus, in Shakespeare's *Julius Caesar,* when Mark Antony refers in his funeral oration to Brutus and his fellow assassins as "honorable men" he is really saying that they are totally dishonorable and not to be trusted. Dramatic irony occurs in a play when the audience knows facts of which the characters in the play are ignorant. The most sustained example of dramatic irony is undoubtedly Sophocles' *Oedipus Rex,* in which Oedipus searches to find the murderer of the former king of Thebes, only to discover that it is himself, a fact the audience has known all along.

Iroquoian (ĭrəkwoi'ən), branch of North American Indian languages belonging to the Hokan-Siouan linguistic family, or stock, of North and Central America. See AMERICAN INDIAN LANGUAGES.

Iroquois Confederacy or **Iroquois League** (ĭr'əkwoi), North American Indian confederation consisting of the Mohawk, Oneida, Onondaga, Cayuga, and Seneca Indians. They gave their name to the Iroquoian branch of the Hokan-Siouan linguistic stock (see AMERICAN INDIAN LANGUAGES), which included numerous other Indian groups of the E United States and E Canada. In the early 17th. cent. this confederacy of Five Nations (later to become six when the Tuscarora joined) inhabited New York state from the Hudson River N to the St. Lawrence River and W to the Genesee River; they numbered some 5,500. Their material culture was the most advanced of the Eastern Woodlands area, but they exhibited many traits peculiar to other areas, and this leads many authorities to believe that the Iroquois at some time in the distant past migrated from the lower Mississippi valley. They lived in palisaded villages; the men hunted deer and small game, and the women raised corn, squash, tobacco, and beans. Women held a high status in the society, and descent was matrilineal. Even before the formation of the confederation, the Iroquois families lived in the distinctive bark-covered rectangular structure known as the long house. When the prophet Deganawidah and his disciple HIAWATHA founded (c.1570) the confederacy (to eliminate incessant intertribal warfare and to end cannibalism), this dwelling became the symbol of the Five Nations. They thought of themselves metaphorically as dwelling in a large long house, which had a door on the eastern end, guarded by the Mohawk (in the extreme geographical east), and a door on the western end, guarded by the Seneca (in the extreme west). The Onondaga, keepers of the council fires and the wampum records, were between the Cayuga on the west and the Oneida on the east. The main Onondaga village served as the capital, or meeting place, of the federated council. Voting in the council was conducted by tribe, and a unanimous decision was necessary to wage war. Nevertheless, intertribal war was not unknown. The Iroquois were second to no other Indians N of Mexico in political organization, statecraft, and military prowess. In the mid-17th cent., at the height of their power, the Iroquois Confederacy, equipped with Dutch firearms, made its united force felt. It dispersed the Huron in 1649, the Tobacco Indians and the Neutral Nation in 1650, the Erie in 1656, the Conestoga in 1675, and the Illinois c.1700. Depleted by continual warfare, they increased the population by the wholesale adoption of alien tribes, so that by the end of the 17th cent. they numbered some 16,000. At this time they controlled the territory bounded by the Kennebec River, the Ottawa River, the Illinois River, and the Tennessee River. Their conquests were checked in the west by the Ojibwa, in the south by the Cherokee and the Catawba, and in the north by the French. Many historians argue that the hostility of the Iroquois toward the French was caused by Samuel Champlain when in 1609 he accompanied a Huron war party armed with French guns into Iroquois territory. In any case, the Iroquois, firm allies of the British, opposed the French at every step until the French lost control of Canada in 1763. The French, partly in the hope of winning over the Iroquois, sent missionaries to them. Isaac JOGUES, a notable Jesuit missionary, was killed by the Iroquois as a sorcerer in 1646, but the missionaries were somewhat successful, and a considerable number of the Mohawk withdrew from the confederacy and founded (c. 1670) a Catholic settlement. These Catholic Iroquois, called French Mohawks, took the part of the French against their former brethren. In the early 18th cent. the Five Nations became the Six Nations when the Oneida adopted (c.1722) the remnants of the Tuscarora Confederacy. British settlers had expelled (1711) the Tuscarora from North Carolina, and by 1712 they had moved to the North. The British, who had used the Six Nations as a buffer against the advance of the French from Canada in the FRENCH AND INDIAN WARS, attempted to retain their favor by accrediting various agents, notably Sir William JOHNSON (Johnson of the Mohawks). The American Revolution was disastrous for the Iroquois. The confederacy, as such, refused to take part in the conflict but allowed each tribe to decide for itself, and all the tribes, except the Oneida, joined the British. Samuel KIRKLAND, a Protestant missionary, was largely responsible for winning over the Oneida, who rallied to the side of the colonists after remaining neutral for two years. CORNPLANTER, RED JACKET, and Joseph BRANT (who was educated by Sir William Johnson) led the Iroquois who remained loyal to the British. Brant, the principal leader of the Iroquois troops, participated with the Tory Rangers of Walter BUTLER in raids in New York and Pennsylvania, particularly the Cherry Valley and Wyoming Valley massacres. Finally, the Continental Congress sent out a punitive expedition under John SULLIVAN, who in 1779 defeated Butler and his Iroquois allies. After the Revolution, Brant, in contrast to the other two chiefs, remained adamant in his hostility towards the United States. The Mohawk and the Cayuga, who were strong allies of the British, today live on reservations in Ontario, and most of the remaining Iroquois, except for the Oneida who live in Wisconsin, are in New York. The Iroquois in Canada and in the United States are either Christians or followers of HANDSOME LAKE, a Seneca prophet of the 18th cent. who was influenced by the Quakers. The total number of Iroquois in the United States and Canada is around 29,000. The Iroquois have been the subject of much study and literature. Early students included Cadwallader COLDEN and Lewis Henry MORGAN. See G. T. Hunt, *The Wars of the Iroquois* (1940, repr. 1960); F. G. Speck, *The Iroquois* (2d ed. 1955); J. V. Wright, *The Ontario Iroquois Tradition* (1966); Conference on Iroquois Research, *Iroquois Culture, History and Prehistory* (1967); A. F. C. Wallace, *The Death and Rebirth of the Seneca* (1969); Barbara Graymont, *The Iroquois in the American Revolution* (1972).

Iroquois League: see IROQUOIS CONFEDERACY.

Irpeel (ĭr'pēēl, ĭrpē'əl), unidentified city, SE Palestine. Joshua 18.27.

Irrawaddy (ĭrəwŏd'ē), chief river of Burma, c.1,000 mi (1,600 km) long, formed by the confluence of the Mali and Nmai rivers in N Burma. The combined stream flows south through gorges strewn with rapids past Myitkyina, Bhamo, Mandalay, Pakokku, and Pye; it receives the Chindwin River, its principal tributary, just below Mandalay. The vast Irrawaddy delta (c.200 mi/320 km wide), one of the world's great rice-producing regions, begins at Henzada, c.180 mi (290 km) from the Andaman Sea. On a mouth of the Irrawaddy is the port of Rangoon. The Irrawaddy is one of the great rivers of Asia and serves as the economic lifeline of Burma. It is navigable by steamers to Bhamo (c.650 mi/1,050 km upstream) and by launches up to Myitkyina. For many centuries it was Burma's principal communication route.

irredentism (ĭrĭden'tĭzəm), originally, the Italian nationalist movement for the annexation to Italy of territories—*Italia irredenta* [unredeemed Italy]—inhabited by an Italian majority but retained by Austria after 1866. These included the Trentino, Trieste, Istria, Fiume, and parts of Dalmatia. Agitation took place both inside Austria-Hungary and in Italy itself. The liberation of *Italia irredenta* was perhaps the strongest motive for the entry of Italy into World War I (see TRIPLE ALLIANCE AND TRIPLE ENTENTE). The Treaty of Versailles (1919) satisfied most of the irredentist claims. The term *irredentism* has, by extension, been applied to nationalist agitation in other countries, based on historical, ethnic, and geographical reasons, for the incorporation of territories under foreign rule. Irredentism is thus closely connected with NATIONALISM and with MINORITY problems.

irrigation, in agriculture, artificial watering of the land. Although used chiefly in regions receiving an annual rainfall of less than 20 in. (51 cm), it is also applied in areas of great rainfall to supply the high water requirement of certain crops, e.g., rice. There are more than 200 million acres (81 million hectares) of irrigated land in the world, half of which are in the Indian subcontinent and China. Irrigation must be correlated with provision for proper drainage in order to prevent excess leaching and waterlogging of the soil. Effective irrigation requires preliminary clearing, smoothing, and grading of land. Methods of applying water include free-flooding of entire areas from canals and ditches; check-flooding, in which water is guided over strips or checks of land between levees, or borders; the furrow method, in which water is run between rows of crops or trees at distances permitting lateral penetration to roots; the surface-pipe method, in which water is conducted through movable slip-joint pipes; and sprinkler systems. From prehistoric times water for irrigation has been obtained from rivers and smaller streams by primitive ditching. Early improvements included counterbalanced poles for raising attached water vessels and adaptations of the wheel and of a pump called the Archimedes' screw. The use of canals, dams, weirs, and reservoirs for the distribution, control, and storage of water was probably initiated in ancient Egypt. In modern times the use of pumps has facilitated the tapping of underground water as well as of surface water. Large-scale 20th-century irrigation is commonly a part of multipurpose water projects combining irrigation, water supply, the production of hydroelectric power, and flood control. Many regions, notably in China, Egypt, Mesopotamia, and India, have been under continuous irrigation from ancient times, and extensive areas are irrigated today in Pakistan, China, the United States, the USSR, Japan, and Mexico. In the area of the present United States, irrigation was practiced by Indians in the Southwest and by the Spanish, especially in California. Most of the arid and semiarid land in the United States lies west of the 100th meridian, and there irrigation is most extensive. Irrigation by individual or group initiative was early supplemented by commercial projects, and finally demands for water conservation led to water-rights legislation and to assistance by state and Federal governments. See J. D. Zimmerman, *Irrigation* (1966); L. M. Cantor, *A World Geography of Irrigation* (1970).

Ir-shemesh (ĭr-shē'mĕsh), the same as BETH-SHEMESH 2.

Irtysh (ĭrtĭsh'), river, c.2,650 mi (4,260 km) long, W Siberian USSR. It is the chief tributary of the Ob and one of the two major rivers of W Siberia. As the Kara-Irtysh, it rises in Sinkiang prov., China, in the Mongolian Altai mts., flows NW through Lake Zaysan (in Kazakhstan), and enters W Siberia. There it receives the Ishim and Tobol rivers, its chief tributaries. The Irtysh flows past Semipalatinsk, Omsk, and Tobolsk and joins the Ob near Khanty-Mansiysk. Major hydroelectric stations are at Ust-Kamenogorsk and Bakhtarminsk (1959). The river banks were occupied by Chinese, Kalmyks, and Mongols until the Russians arrived in the late 16th cent. The Russian conquest of the basin was completed by the early 19th cent.

Iru (ī'rōō), Caleb's eldest son. 1 Chron. 4.15.

Iruma (ērōō'mä), city (1970 pop. 65,369), Saitama prefecture, central Honshu, Japan, on the Iruma River. It is a residential and industrial suburb of Tokyo.

Irún (ērōōn'), town (1970 pop. 45,060), Guipúzcoa prov., N Spain, in the Basque Provinces near the French border, on the Bidassoa River near the Bay of Biscay. It is a commercial and manufacturing center with a large transit trade. Lead and iron mines are nearby. Irún was staunchly defended by the Loyalists in the civil war of 1936 to 1939.

Irvine, William (ûr'vĭn), 1741-1804, American soldier, b. Ireland. He studied medicine in Ireland and after 1764 practiced in Carlisle, Pa. He was called to service as colonel of a Pennsylvania regiment and later as brigadier general in the Continental Army in the Revolution. In 1781 he was given command of Fort Pitt and the Western frontier, serving until 1783. While acting as agent (1785) to select the free lands promised to Pennsylvania troops, he recommended that Pennsylvania purchase the Erie Triangle (see PENNSYLVANIA) from the United States. He was a member of the Continental Congress (1786-88), was sent (1793) as delegate to the 3d U.S. Congress, and was in command of Pennsylvania troops in the Whiskey Rebellion (1794).

Irvine, burgh (1971 pop. 23,011), Ayrshire, SW Scotland, on the Irvine River estuary. There are iron and brass foundries. Other products include chemicals, bottles, and hosiery. Formally an important port, Irvine now is engaged only in coastal trade. In 1975, Irvine became part of the Strathclyde region.

Irving, Edward, 1792-1834, Scottish preacher, under whose influence the CATHOLIC APOSTOLIC CHURCH was founded; its members have sometimes been called Irvingites. He was tutor to Jane Welsh, later the wife of Thomas Carlyle, and became the friend of Carlyle. After serving as assistant (1819-22) to Thomas CHALMERS in Glasgow, Irving was called to the Caledonian Church, London, where his oratory brought him great popularity; he and his congregation moved to the larger Regent Square Church in 1827. As his preaching began to emphasize the supernatural and the imminence of the second coming of Christ, criticism arose, especially over his views on the human nature of Christ. In 1832 he was debarred from the Regent Square Church; in 1833 he was deposed from the ministry of the Church of Scotland. Irving had, from 1826, been meeting with a group gathered together by Henry Drummond to study the prophecies of the Scriptures. From this "school of the prophets" was developed the Catholic Apostolic Church, of which Irving was an "angel." See biography by M. O. W. Oliphant (1864); H. C. Whitney, *Blinded Eagle* (1955).

Irving, Sir Henry, 1838-1905, English actor and manager, originally named John Henry Brodribb. He made his debut in 1856 and achieved fame in 1871 with his portrayal of Mathias in *The Bells*, a role which he often repeated. Irving was manager of the Lyceum Theatre, London, from 1878 to 1903. There, with Ellen Terry as his leading lady, he reigned as the dominant force of the English stage. He was a champion of the star system; his productions were artistic spectacles with emphasis on scenic detail. As an actor he was most successful in the "realistic" melodramas of the day. To him acting was movement; his realistic approach to creating a character led to the noted controversy with COQUELIN. His interpretations were frequently the butt of critics' scorn. In a production of *Othello* (1881) Irving alternated with Edwin Booth as Othello and Iago. His company toured the United States and was as well known there as in England. Irving was knighted in 1895, the first English actor to be so honored, and was buried in Westminster Abbey. See biographies by L. F. Austin (1884), Bram Stoker (1906), Gordon Craig (1930), and his grandson, Laurence Irving (1952).

Irving, Washington, 1783-1859, American author and diplomat, b. New York City. Irving was one of the first Americans to be recognized abroad as a man of letters, and he was a literary idol at home. While he studied law, he amused himself by writing for periodicals such essays on New York society and the theater as the *Letters of Jonathan Oldstyle, Gent.* (1802-3). From 1804 to 1806 his older brothers financed his tour of France and Italy. On his return he joined William Irving and J. K. Paulding in publishing *Salmagundi; or, The Whim-Whams and Opinions of Launcelot Langstaff & Others* (1807-8), a series of humorous and satirical essays. Under the pseudonym Diedrich Knickerbocker, he brought out in 1809 *A History of New York*, a satire that has been called the first great book of comic literature written by an American. Purporting to be a scholarly account of the Dutch occupation of the New World, the book is a burlesque of history books as well as a satire of politics in his own time. Irving went to England in 1815 to run the Liverpool branch of the family hardware business, but could not save it when the whole firm failed. Thereupon, with the encouragement of Walter Scott, Irving turned definitely to literature. The essays (including "Rip Van Winkle" and "The Legend of Sleepy Hollow") collected in *The Sketch Book of Geoffrey Crayon, Gent.* (London, 1820) appeared serially in New York in 1819-20; their enthusiastic reception made Irving the best-known figure in American literature both at home and abroad. *Bracebridge Hall* (1822), the next and inferior volume of essays, was well received, but his *Tales of a Traveller* (1824), written after visits to Germany and France, was a failure. Irving became a diplomatic attaché at the American embassy in Madrid in 1826. There he produced his biography of Columbus (1828), largely based on the work of the Spanish historian Navarrete; *The Conquest of Granada* (1829), a romantic narrative; and the soft, casually charming Spanish sketches of *The Alhambra* (1832). After a short period at the American legation in London, he returned to New York. In search of colorful material, he made a journey to the frontier and wrote about the American West in *A Tour of the Prairies* (1835). From records furnished by John Jacob Astor, he wrote *Astoria* (1836), with Pierre Irving, and *The Adventures of Captain Bonneville, U.S.A.* (1837). Irving established himself at his estate, Sunnyside, near Tarrytown, N.Y., until he was sent to Madrid as American minister to Spain (1842-46). Once more at Sunnyside, he wrote a biography of Goldsmith (1849) and the miscellaneous sketches called *Wolfert's Roost* (1855) and labored at his biography of George Washington (5 vol., 1855-59), which he completed just before his death. Irving was master of a graceful and unobtrusively sophisticated prose style. A gentle but effective satirist, he was the creator of a few widely loved essays and tales that have made his name endure. His journals were edited by W. P. Trent and G. S. Hellman, and *The Western Journals* by J. F. McDermott. See his life and letters by P. M. Irving (4 vol., 1864; repr. 1967); biography by S. T. Williams (2 vol., 1935; repr. 1971); studies by E. C. Wagenknecht (1962) and W. L. Hedges (1965 and 1974); bibliography by S. T. Williams and M. A. Edge (1936, repr. 1969).

Irving, city (1970 pop. 97,260), Dallas co., N Texas, a suburb of Dallas; inc. as a city 1952. Building supplies, chemicals, electronic equipment, snack foods, and tools are manufactured there. The Texas Stadium, home of the Dallas Cowboys professional football team; the Univ. of Dallas; and the Dallas-Fort Worth Regional Airport (opened 1974) are in Irving.

Irvington, town (1970 pop. 59,743), Essex co., NE N.J., an industrial suburb of Newark; settled 1692 as Camptown, renamed 1852, inc. 1898. Tools, castings, photographic equipment, paints, building materials, and plastic and paper products are among its manufactures.

Isaac I (Isaac Comnenus) (kŏmnē'nəs), c.1005-1061, Byzantine emperor (1057-59), first of the Comneni dynasty. Proclaimed emperor by the army, he deposed Michael VI, who had succeeded Theodora (reigned 1055-56), and sent him into a monastery. Although at first received with enthusiasm at Constantinople, Isaac soon lost popularity with the aristocracy and, because of his confiscation of ecclesiastic property, with the church and the patriarch Cerularius, who was exiled. In 1059, after an unsuccessful campaign against the Pechenegs, Isaac abdicated for reasons of health and retired to a monastery. Constantine X (Constantine Ducas) was his successor. After the reigns of ROMANUS IV, Michael VII, and Nicephorus III, the Comnenus dynasty returned to the throne with Isaac's nephew ALEXIUS I.

Isaac II (Isaac Angelus) (ăn'jələs), d. 1204, Byzantine emperor (1185–95, 1203–4). The great grandson of Alexius I, he was proclaimed emperor by the mob that had killed the unpopular Andronicus I. Isaac repulsed (1185) an invasion by the Normans under William II of Sicily but was unable to suppress the rebellious Bulgars. Corruption in public office continued during his reign. He was deposed and blinded in 1195 by his brother, who became emperor as ALEXIUS III, but Isaac's son (later Alexius IV) appealed to the Latins of the Fourth Crusade (see CRUSADES), and in 1203 father and son were restored as coemperors. Their overthrow (1204) by Alexius Ducas (ALEXIUS V) led to the storming of Constantinople by the Crusaders.

Isaac (ī'zək) [Heb., = laughter], only son of Abraham and Sarah. He married Rebecca, and their sons were Esau and Jacob. Ishmael was his half brother. As a supreme act of faith Abraham offered him at an early age as a sacrifice to God—a deed prevented by divine intervention. The Philistine king Abimelech gave him shelter in time of famine, and he grew rich in lands and possessions. Retiring and gentle, he lived the longest and led the least eventful life of any of the patriarchs. Before his death Rebecca caused him to bless Jacob in place of Esau. He was buried in the family tomb of Machpelah. Gen. 21–27, 35.29; 49.30,31; Mat. 8.11; Heb. 11.17; James 2.21. Some biblical scholars have questioned the historicity of Isaac.

Isaac, Heinrich (hīn'rĭkh ē'zäk), c.1450–1517, Flemish composer. Isaac, a prolific and versatile composer, traveled widely in Europe, serving at the courts of Lorenzo de' Medici and Emperor Maximilian I. Among his best-known works is the collection of his 58 four-part settings of the offices of the mass known as *Choralis Constantinus*, a major treasure of Gregorian liturgical music. He also wrote many motets, masses, hymns, and secular songs. See Alfred Einstein, *The Italian Madrigal* (3 vol., 1949, repr. 1971).

Isaacs, Sir Isaac Alfred, 1855–1948, Australian jurist and political leader. He sat in the colonial legislature (1892–1901), became solicitor general (1893), and served as attorney general (1894–99, 1900–1901). He was a framer of the commonwealth constitution and sat in the dominion Parliament (1901–6), becoming attorney general in 1905. He was for many years (1906–30) a high court justice and sat as chief justice (1930–31). His appointment (1931) as governor general was the first made by the British crown directly on the advice of a dominion ministry. The first native-born Australian to hold that office, he served until 1936.

Isaacs, Jorge (hôr'hā ē'säks), 1837–95, Colombian novelist. The son of a prosperous Englishman and a creole, Isaacs witnessed the ruin and premature death of his parents and the despoilment of his estate by civil war. He fled to Bogotá, where he won critical acclaim with a book of poems (*Poesiás*, 1864). His masterpiece, *María* (1867, tr. 1890), a melancholy romantic novel, won immediate success and was widely imitated. His finely drawn characters and colorful accounts of local customs are complemented by a masterful picture of the landscape of the Cauca valley. Isaacs was named consul to Chile and occupied several government posts, but died in poverty.

Isaacs, Rufus Daniel: see READING, RUFUS DANIEL ISAACS, 1ST MARQUESS OF.

Isabel, 1846–1921, princess imperial of Brazil; eldest daughter of PEDRO II. She acted as regent in her father's absence. Her marriage to the comte d'Eu added to her own unpopularity and probably contributed to the growing republican sentiment of her time. Along with her father, she is remembered for her espousal of the cause of emancipation. On May 13, 1888, she signed the law abolishing slavery, which alienated the large landholders and precipitated the downfall of the empire. When Pedro II was deposed and exiled (1889), Isabel followed him to Paris with her family and spent the remainder of her life there. See C. H. Haring, *Empire in Brazil* (1958).

Isabela (ĭzəbĕl'ə, Span. ēsäbä'lä), province (1970 est. pop. 670,000), NE Luzon, the Philippines. The capital is Ilagan. The fertile Cagayan River valley, which is in the central and eastern part of the province, is a leading tobacco- and cacao-producing region. The rugged Sierra Madre on the east is mineral rich; iron, nickel, and copper deposits, as well as the nation's major manganese mines are there.

Isabela (ēsäbä'lä), ruins of a town on the north shore of Hispaniola, in the Dominican Republic, at the base of Cape Isabela. Believed to have been founded by Columbus (c.1494), it was one of the first Spanish settlements in the New World.

Isabela, island, Ecuador: see GALÁPAGOS ISLANDS.

Isabella I or **Isabella the Catholic,** 1451–1504, Spanish queen of Castile and León (1474–1504), daughter of John II of Castile. In 1469 she married Ferdinand of Aragón (later King FERDINAND II of Aragón and Ferdinand V of Castile). At the death (1474) of her half brother HENRY IV of Castile, the succession to Castile was contested between Isabella and JUANA LA BELTRANEJA, who was supported by ALFONSO V of Portugal. The civil war ended with Isabella's victory in 1479, the year in which Ferdinand became king of Aragón. Isabella and Ferdinand, known as the Catholic kings, ruled Castile and Aragón jointly. Although the union of their crowns was personal rather than institutional, their reign in effect marked the beginning of the unified Spanish kingdom. Isabella's principal aim was to assert royal authority over the lawless Castilian nobility. To this end she revived the medieval HERMANDAD and confiscated the lands of many magnates. She also took over the administration of the holdings of the powerful religious military orders (by making Ferdinand their grand master) and established the INQUISITION under royal control. She was a prime mover in the expulsion (1492) of the Jews from Spain, the conquest (1492) of Granada, and the forced conversion of the Moors. She showed foresight in her patronage of Christopher COLUMBUS. The Catholic kings furthered learning and the arts and promoted great building activity. The style of the period is called *isabelino* after the queen; it combines Gothic, Mudejar, and Renaissance features. Isabella bequeathed Castile to her daughter JOANNA, with Ferdinand as regent. See biographies by I. L. Plunket (1915) and W. T. Walsh (1930); W. H. Prescott, *History of the Reign of Ferdinand and Isabella the Catholic* (3 vol., 1838; abr. ed. 1962); J. H. Mariéjol, *The Spain of Ferdinand and Isabella* (1892, tr. 1961); R. B. Merriman, *The Rise of the Spanish Empire,* Vol. II (1918, repr. 1962); J. H. Elliott, *Imperial Spain: 1469–1716* (1963).

Isabella II, 1830–1904, queen of Spain (1833–68), daughter of Ferdinand VII and of MARIA CHRISTINA. Her uncle, Don CARLOS, contested her succession under the SALIC LAW, and thus the Carlist Wars began (see CARLISTS). Isabella was under the regency of her mother until 1840, when ESPARTERO seized power. After his regency (1841–43) was overthrown, Isabella was declared of age. In 1846 the queen married her cousin, Francisco de Asís, and her sister, Luisa Fernanda, married a son of Louis Philippe of France, the duc de Montpensier. These Spanish marriages, which contravened earlier Anglo-French agreements about the choice of husbands for the two sisters, aroused the anger of England, who feared a Franco-Spanish rapprochement, and caused a temporary severance of the entente between England and France. Isabella's rule was one of party conflicts among moderates, progressives, and liberal unionists and of continuous cabinet changes. NARVÁEZ, Espartero, and O'DONNELL were among her premiers. Frequent rebellions culminated in 1868 in the insurrection led by Serrano and Juan Prim, and Isabella was deposed (see SPAIN). She spent the rest of her life in France. In 1870 she abdicated her rights in favor of her son, ALFONSO XII. See studies by P. D. Polnay (1962) and O. G. Boetzkes (1966).

Isabella, 1296–1358, queen consort of EDWARD II of England, daughter of Philip IV of France. She married Edward in 1308. Neglected and mistreated by her husband, Isabella nourished hatred for the royal favorites, the Despensers (see DESPENSER, HUGH LE), who were responsible (1324) for the confiscation of her estates. In 1325 she was sent to France to negotiate with her brother Charles IV over Gascony. Once there, she ignored royal orders to return to England with her son, the future EDWARD III. Becoming the mistress of Roger de MORTIMER, later 1st earl of March, she plotted with him to invade England. Their invasion in 1326 was successful. After Edward II was forced to abdicate and Edward III was enthroned early in 1327, Isabella and Mortimer caused the murder of Edward II and began a corrupt rule of England. Finally rebelling against the couple's flagrant misgovernment, Edward III seized power in 1330, had Mortimer executed, and made Isabella retire.

Isabel of Bavaria, 1371–1435, French queen, consort of CHARLES VI, daughter of the duke of Bavaria. After her marriage (1385) she was several times regent for her demented husband. Sympathizing with the enemies of France—the English and the Burgundians—in the Hundred Years War, she helped to bring about the Treaty of Troyes (1420), which disinherited her son (later Charles VII) in favor of Henry V of England.

Isabey, Jean Baptiste (zhäN bätēst' ēzäbā'), 1767–1855, French portrait painter and miniaturist. He was a pupil of J. L. David and was greatly influenced by Fragonard. His portraits are graceful and strongly individualized. Isabey prospered under all the changing regimes, portraying in turn Marie Antoinette, Mirabeau, David, Napoleon (Versailles), Josephine (National Gall., London), and Louis Philippe. He was one of the first painters to make lithographs. Much of his work, which constitutes a historical document of great interest, is in the Louvre. His son, **Eugène Louis Gabriel Isabey,** 1804–86, was a marine and genre painter who also made lithographs. He is well represented at the Louvre; the Metropolitan Museum has one of his paintings.

Isafjörður (ē'säfyör"thür), town (1970 pop. 2,680), NW Iceland, on the Isafjarðardjúp, an arm of the Denmark Strait. It is a fishing port and has refrigeration plants, shrimp and fish-meal factories, shipyards, and machine workshops. It was chartered in 1866.

Isahaya (ēsä'häyä), city (1970 pop. 65,621), Nagasaki prefecture, W Kyushu, Japan. It is an agricultural center and railway junction.

Isaiah (īzā'yə, īsā'-) or **Isaias** (īsā'yəs), book of the Old Testament, 23d in the order of the Authorized Version, the first and longest of the books of the Major Prophets. It is a collection of prophecies attributed to Isaiah, apparently a member of the nobility, in the kingdom of Judah. He received his call to prophesy in the year of King Uzziah's death (c.740 B.C.) and preached during the reigns of Jotham, Ahaz, and Hezekiah. His message was partly political; he urged King Hezekiah to recognize the power of Assyria, then at its height, and not to ally himself with Egypt, as a party of nobles urged. The book falls into two major sections of metrical prophecies (1–35 and 40–66), with a prose section between (36–39). The first set of poems treats the overthrow of the Assyrians, containing introduction (1–6), Messianic prophecies directed against Syria and Assyria (7–12), prophecies against many nations (13–27), finally prophecies affecting Israel and Judah, announcing destruction and subsequent redemption (28–35). The prose section (mainly identical with 2 Kings 18.13–20.19) falls into two parts, the first (36–37) telling of Sennacherib's unsuccessful siege of Jerusalem and his murder long after; the second (38–39) gives the sickness of Hezekiah, with recovery and reception of an embassy from Babylon and prophecy of captivity there. The second poetic section of the book (40–66) is a prophecy of redemption, falling, according to one mode of division, into three parts—delivery from captivity (40–48), redemption from sin (49–57), and the redeemed state of Israel (58–66). The book contains many of the most beautiful passages of the Bible; among them are prophecies interpreted by Christians as references to Christ (8–12; 40–42; 53); the most famous of such prophecies is the vision of the suffering servant (52.13; 53.12). Later biblical allusions are frequent, e.g., Ecclus. 48.25–28; Mat. 1.23; 4.15; 13.14. Esaias: Mat. 3.3. Many scholars would divide Isaiah into parts of diverse original authorship, assigning the second division of prophecies, Deutero-Isaiah (40–55), to exilic times and the third division (56–66) to postexilic times. Among the Dead Sea Scrolls are two manuscripts of the book of Isaiah; dating from the 2d–1st cent. B.C., they are pre-Masoretic texts. See G. A. F. Knight, *Isaiah* (1962); J. R. Rosenbloom, *The Dead Sea Isaiah Scrolls* (1970); J. W. Whedbee, *Isaiah and Wisdom* (1971).

Isaiah, Ascension of: see PSEUDEPIGRAPHA.

Isar (ē'zär), river, 160 mi (257 km) long, rising in the Tyrol, W Austria, and flowing NE through SE West Germany, past Munich, to the Danube River. There are more than 25 large hydroelectric plants below Munich.

Isauria (īsôr'ēə), ancient district of S Asia Minor, on the borders of Pisidia and Cilicia, N of the Taurus range, in present S central Turkey. It was a wild region inhabited by marauding bands. When the capital, Isaura or Isaura Vetus [old Isaura], a strongly fortified city at the foot of Mt. Taurus, was besieged by the Macedonian regent Perdiccas in the 4th cent. B.C., the Isaurians destroyed the town by fire rather than submit to capture. The Isaurians were partially checked (76-75 B.C.) by the Romans, but were not completely subdued until the arrival in the 11th cent. A.D. of the Seljuk Turks. The site contains ruins of the town and its fortifications.

Isca Dumnoniorum: see EXETER, England.

Iscah (ĭs'kə), niece of Abraham. Gen. 11.29.

Iscariot: see JUDAS ISCARIOT.

Ischia (ēs'kyä), volcanic island (1971 pop. 14,076), 18 sq mi (47 sq km), Campania, S Italy, in the Tyrrhenian Sea between the Gulf of Gaeta and the Bay of Naples. Known as the Emerald Isle, it is a health resort and a tourist center, celebrated for its warm mineral springs and for its scenery. Fishing and farming are also pursued, and wine, tiles, and pottery are made. Settled in the 8th cent. B.C., the island was abandoned several times because of volcanic eruptions (the last of which occurred in 1301). There was a severe earthquake in 1883. Monte Epomeo (2,585 ft/788 m) is the island's highest point. Ischia, the main town, has an imposing 15th-century castle, constructed on foundations built by the Greeks in the 5th cent. B.C.

Ischl: see BAD ISCHL, Austria.

Ise (ē'sä), city (1970 pop. 103,656), Mie prefecture, S Honshu, Japan, on Ise Bay. It is one of the foremost religious centers of Shinto, the site of the shrines of Ise. These three shrines, set deep in a forest, are said to have been built in 4 B.C. They exhibit an archaic style of architecture, completely without Chinese or Buddhist influence; until 1868 Buddhist priests and nuns were forbidden to enter the shrines. The Naigu, or Inner Shrine, is dedicated to Amaterasu-omikami, the "divine ancestress" of the imperial family, and still houses the Sacred Mirror, one of the three treasures that comprise the imperial regalia. Ise has a university and several museums of antiquities. It was called Uji-yamada until 1955.

Isère (ēzĕr'), department (1968 pop. 768,450), SE France, in DAUPHINÉ. GRENOBLE is the capital.

Iserlohn (ē"zərlōn'), city (1970 pop. 57,577), North Rhine-Westphalia, W West Germany. It is a commercial and industrial center. Its manufactures include metal goods, textiles, and electrical products. Iserlohn became an important town in the 13th cent. and was known for the manufacture of armor, chains, and needles. Until the 19th cent. it was the largest city in Westphalia.

Iseult: see TRISTRAM AND ISOLDE.

Iseyin (ēsā'äN), town (1969 est. pop. 110,000), SW Nigeria. The city, located in a tobacco-growing region, has an important traditional textile industry. Iseyin was the capital of a small YORUBA kingdom under the OYO empire. In 1893 it came under British control. A rebellion in 1916 against British-imposed taxes was quelled.

Isezaki (ēsā'zäkē), city (1970 pop. 91,277), Gumma prefecture, central Honshu, Japan. It is a center for weaving industries and a market for agricultural products. It was a castle town of the Sakai family during the Edo era.

Isfahan, Iran: see ESFAHAN.

Isfjorden (ēs"fyôr'dən) [Ice Fjord], inlet of the Greenland Sea and largest fjord of Spitsbergen island, Svalbard, Norway, 65 mi (105 km) long and from 8 to 20 mi (12.8-32 km) wide. It receives several glaciers. The mining towns of Longyearbyen, Grumantbyen, and Barentsburg are on the inlet.

Ishbah (ĭsh'bə), descendant of Judah. 1 Chron. 4.17.

Ishbak (ĭsh'băk), son of Abraham and Keturah. Gen. 25.2; 1 Chron. 1.32.

Ishbi-benob (ĭsh'bī-bē'nŏb), giant killed by Abishai. 2 Sam. 21.16,17.

Ish-bosheth (ĭsh-bō'shĕth, ĭsh-bŏsh'ĕth), son of Saul, and his would-be successor. 2 Sam. 2; 3; 4. Eshbaal: 1 Chron. 8.33; 9.39. For the relation between the names of this man, see BAAL.

Isherwood, Christopher (ish'ərwo͝od), 1904–, English author. After the appearance of his first novel, *All the Conspirators* (1928), Isherwood went to Germany. The four years he spent there furnished him with the material for what are probably his best novels, *The Last of Mr. Norris* (1935) and *Goodby to Berlin* (1939; reissued as *The Berlin Stories,* 1946); these books form the basis for John Van Druten's play, *I Am a Camera* (1951), and for the Broadway musical *Cabaret* (1966). The two Berlin novels, which attempt to report on the period of social and political unrest during the Nazi rise to power, illustrate Isherwood's general concern with the problem of the intellectual in a tyrannical society. A close friend of W. H. Auden, Isherwood collaborated with him on the dramas *The Dog beneath the Skin* (1935), *The Ascent of F6* (1936), and *On the Frontier* (1938), as well as on *Journey to a War* (1939), a book on China. In 1939, Isherwood emigrated to the United States. During the 1940s his interests also turned to Hinduism. Among his later works are the novels *Prater Violet* (1945), *The World in the Evening* (1954), *Down There on a Visit* (1962), *A Single Man* (1964), and *Essentials of Vedanta* (1969). See his study of his parents' lives, *Kathleen and Frank* (1971).

Ishi (ĭsh'ī). **1, 2** Judahites. 1 Chron. 2.31; 4.20. **3** Manassite. 1 Chron. 5.24. **4** Simeonite whose sons fought at Mt. Seir. 1 Chron. 4.42. **5** The name Ishi with the meaning "my husband" is a name of God in a prophecy. Hosea 2.16.

Ishiah (ĭshī'ə), chief of the tribe of Issachar. 1 Chron. 7.3.

Ishigaki (ēshē'gäkē), city (1970 pop. 36,554) Okinawa prefecture, Ryukyu Islands, Japan. It is an agricultural center where sake and dried tuna are produced.

Ishii, Kikujiro (kē"ko͞o"jērō', ĭshē'), 1865-1945, Japanese career diplomat. He entered the foreign ministry after graduating from Tokyo Univ. with a degree in English law. In 1907-8 he helped negotiate the gentlemen's agreement to exclude Japanese immigrants to the United States. He was ambassador to France (1912-14), foreign minister (1915-16), and ambassador to the United States (1918-19). In 1917 he negotiated the Lansing-Ishii agreement with the United States. He participated in many international diplomatic conferences. He was a member of the privy council.

Ishijah (ĭshī'jə), Israelite who married a foreign woman. Ezra 10.31.

Ishikari (ēshkä'rē), second largest river of Japan, c.225 mi (360 km) long, rising in the mountainous interior of Hokkaido and flowing generally southwest to Ishikari Bay near Otaru. It drains an extensive coal area and waters the Ishikari lowland, a fertile agricultural region.

Ishikawa (ēshē'käwä), prefecture (1970 pop. 1,002,-420), 1,619 sq mi (4,193 sq km), central Honshu, Japan. The capital is Kanazawa. There are wooded mountains in the interior and fertile plains along the coast. Lumber and raw silk are produced.

Ishim (ēshēm'), city (1970 pop. 56,000), W Siberian USSR, on the Ishim River and the Trans-Siberian RR. An agricultural center, it produces farm machinery and processes food. An old trading town known as Korkinsk, Ishim was renamed in 1782.

Ishim, river, c.1,130 mi (1,819 km) long, W Siberian USSR. It rises N of Karaganda in Kazakhstan, flows W past Atbasar, N past Petropavlovsk, and then joins the Irtysh River at Ust Ishim.

Ishimbay (ēshēmbī'), city (1970 pop. 54,000), Bashkir Autonomous Republic, E European USSR, on the Belaya River. Founded in 1932, Ishimbay developed around the first major oil field of the Volga-Ural region, formerly the leading Soviet oil area. Ishimbay's chief industries are oil refining and petrochemical production. The city is linked by natural gas pipeline with Shkapovo and Magnitogorsk.

Ishinomaki (ēshē'nōmäkē), city (1970 pop. 106,681), Miyagi prefecture, N Honshu, Japan, on Ishinomaki Bay. It is a commercial and fishing port and a center for marine product processing and paper manufacturing.

Ishma (ĭsh'mə), name appearing in the Judahite genealogy. 1 Chron. 4.3.

Ishmael (ĭsh'māēl). **1** Son of Abraham and Hagar and ancestor of 12 tribes in N Arabia. Through Sarah's jealousy he and his mother were sent into the desert; hence the name Ishmael came to be used as "outcast." He married an Egyptian, and had 12 sons and a daughter. He was the half brother of Isaac and the father-in-law of Esau. Gen. 16.4-16; 17.18-26; 21.8-21; 25.9,12-17; 28.9; 1 Chron. 1.29-30. The Muslims consider the Arabs the descendants of Ishmael, thus distinguishing themselves from the descendants of Isaac and Israel. The Bible does not make clear what peoples are indicated by the name Ishmaelites (or Ishmeelites), but the term generally refers to caravan traders. Gen. 37.25-28; 39.1; Judges 8.24; Ps. 83.6. **2** Descendant of Saul. 1 Chron. 8.38; 9.44. **3** Ancestor of the Zebediah of Jehoshaphat's court. 2 Chron. 19.11. **4** Ally of Jehoiada. 2 Chron. 23.1. **5** Priest separated from his foreign wife. Ezra 10.22. **6** Assassin of Gedaliah. 2 Kings 25.23-25; Jer. 40.7-16; 41.

Ishmaiah (ĭsh"māī'ə), ruler over the Zebulunites. 1 Chron. 27.19.

Ishmerai (ĭsh'mērā, ĭsh"mērā'ī), chief Benjamite. 1 Chron. 8.18.

Ishod (ī'shŏd), descendant of Manasseh. 1 Chron. 7.18.

Ishpan (ĭsh'păn), chief Benjamite. 1 Chron. 8.22.

Ishtar (ĭsh'tär), ancient fertility deity, the most widely worshiped goddess in Babylonian and Assyrian religion. She was worshiped under various names and forms. Most important as a mother goddess and as a goddess of love, Ishtar was the source of all the generative powers in nature and mankind. However, she was also a goddess of war and as such was capable of unremitting cruelty. Her cult spread throughout W Asia, and she became identified with various other earth goddesses (see GREAT MOTHER OF THE GODS). One of the most famous of the Babylonian legends related the trials of her descent into the underworld in search of her lover TAMMUZ and her triumphant return to earth. In Sumerian religion, where her cult probably originated, she was called Inanna or Innina.

Ishtob (ĭsh'tŏb): see TOB.

Ishuah (ĭsh'yo͞oə), son of Asher. Gen. 46.47. Isuah: 1 Chron. 7.30.

Ishuai (ĭsh'yo͞oī), the same as ISUI.

Ishui (ĭsh'yo͞oī), son of Saul. 1 Sam. 14.49.

Isidore of Seville, Saint, c.560-636, Spanish churchman and encyclopedist, bishop of Seville, Doctor of the Church. Born of a noble Hispano-Roman family from Cartagena, he spent his youth under the supervision of his brother St. Leander, powerful bishop of Seville, and may have helped the latter in the extirpation of Arianism among the Visigoths. During his own tenure of the bishopric (from c.600) Isidore wielded considerable ecclesiastical power; he presided at the second Council of Seville (619) and at the fourth national Council of Toledo (633). He is best known, however, for his voluminous writings. His most influential work is the *Etymologies* or *Origins*, an encyclopedic treatise that aims to set down all the knowledge of the time. It is a comprehensive work in plan, and it transmitted to scholars of the Middle Ages and the Renaissance a great measure of classical learning. It was, however, a completely derived work, unenlightened by firsthand observation, and sometimes faulty in its scholarship. His *Historia de Regibus Gothorum, Vandalorum et Suevorum* [history of the reigns of the Goths, Vandals, and Suevi] continues to be useful in studying the early history of Spain. He also wrote many treatises on theology, language, natural history, and other subjects. His great learning and defense of education before the rising tide of Gothic barbarism was important to the development of Spanish culture. Feast: April 4. See studies by Ernest Brehaut (1912) and Sister Patrick Mullins (1940).

Isidorus of Miletus (ĭzĭdôr'əs, mīlē'təs), name of two architects of the time of Justinian. The elder was associated with Anthemius of Tralles in rebuilding Hagia Sophia, A.D. 532-37; the younger rebuilt the church's dome after its destruction by earthquake, A.D. 553.

Isin (ĭs'ĭn), capital of an ancient Semitic kingdom of N Babylonia. The city became important after the third dynasty of Ur fell to the Elamites and the Amorites (c.2025 B.C.). The phase from c.2025-c.1763 B.C. is sometimes called the Isin-Larsa period. Many city-states vied with one another, but Isin and Larsa were the most powerful of these. Excavations have brought to light the law code of King Lipit-Ishtar of Isin. This code is one of several codes that predate the stele of Hammurabi.

isinglass (ī'zəngläs"), gelatinous semitransparent substance obtained by cleaning and drying the air bladders of the sturgeon, cod, hake, and other fishes. Isinglass is manufactured in the Soviet Union, the United States, Canada, Brazil, Indonesia, the West Indies, and the Philippines. It is used in the clarification of wines and beers, as a stiffening for jellies, in court plaster, and in glues and cements. The name isinglass is also commonly applied to thin sheets of mica and sometimes to a gelatinous substance obtained from certain seaweeds.

Isis: see THAMES, river, England.

Isis (ī'sĭs), nature goddess whose worship, originating in ancient Egypt, gradually extended throughout the lands of the Mediterranean world and became one of the chief religions of the Roman Empire. The worship of Isis, combined with that of her brother and husband OSIRIS and their son HORUS, was enormously resistant to the influence of early Christian teachings, and her mysteries, celebrating the death and resurrection of Osiris, were performed as late as the 6th cent. A.D. The functions of many goddesses were attributed to her, so that eventually she became the prototype of the beneficent mother goddess, the bringer of fertility and consolation to all. She was the daughter of the sky goddess Nut and the earth god Geb. Her symbol was a throne and later the cow, and she was frequently represented with a cow's head or cow's horns. Isis was also a goddess of magic, and legends tell of her ability to counteract evil by casting spells.

Iskandariyah, Al, Egypt: see ALEXANDRIA.

Iskander Bey: see SCANDERBEG.

İskenderun (ĭskĕn'dĕro͞on"), formerly **Alexandretta** (ăl"ĭgzăndrĕt'ə), city (1970 pop. 81,639), S Turkey, on the Gulf of Alexandretta, an inlet of the Mediterranean Sea. The principal Turkish port on the Mediterranean, it exports cotton, grain, fruit, wool, and hides. The city was founded by Alexander the Great to commemorate his victory over the Persians at ISSUS in 333 B.C. In A.D. 1515 the Ottoman Empire under Selim I, its ruler, captured the city. İskenderun was transferred (1920) to the French Syria League of Nations mandate as part of the sanjak of Alexandretta, but was returned to Turkey in 1939 (see ALEXANDRETTA, SANJAK OF).

Isker: see SIBIR, USSR.

Iskŭr (ĭs'kĕr), river, c.250 mi (400 km) long, rising in the Rhodope mts., W Bulgaria, and flowing generally NE past Sofia and through the Balkan mts. to the Danube River. The gorge of the Iskŭr is the chief pass through the Balkans.

Isla, José Francisco de (hōsā' fränthē'skō dā ē'slä), 1703–81, Spanish Jesuit preacher and writer. Enormously precocious, he took his law degree at 11. Isla's fame rests on the satricial novel *Historia del famoso predicador Fray Gerundio de Campazas* (1758, tr. 1772), which was banned by the Inquisition. In this account of the exploits of an ignorant preacher, he attacked the pedantry of pulpit eloquence. Isla's translation of Le Sage's picaresque novel *Gil Blas* is well known.

Islam (ĭslăm', ĭs'ləm) [Arab.,=submission to, or having peace with, God], the religion of which Muhammad was the prophet. An adherent of Islam is called a Muslim or Moslem [Arab.,=one who submits]. It was the latest to appear of the three great monotheistic religions (the others being Judaism and Christianity). Islam is the principal religion of much of Asia, including NW China, Indonesia, Malaya, Pakistan, Bangladesh, Afghanistan, Iran, Iraq, Syria, Jordan and the Arabian states, and Turkey, as well as part of the Philippines and Southeast Asia and much of Asian USSR. In Africa, Islam has been the only highly successful missionary faith (see ISLAM IN AFRICA). It is the religion prevailing in Egypt and in the rest of N Africa except Ethiopia; it is also well established in central Africa and along the east coast. In Europe, outside Russia, where Islam was the religion of the Crimea and of much of the lower Volga, the Ottoman Turks managed to establish (15th cent.) a foothold for Islam in the Balkans. The Americas are the only continents in which Islam has practically no adherents. Islam's most serious loss was suffered in SPAIN. The salient feature of Islam is its devotion to a book, the KORAN, believed to be the revelation of God to Muhammad; since the Koran is written in Arabic, this language is used in Islam all over the world; hence the common custom in Islam of referring to God as Allah, his name in Arabic. Although the Koran does not contain a systematic exposition of Muslim beliefs, there nevertheless has emerged a consistent body of doctrine, practical duties, rituals, and laws. The ethos of Islam is its attitude toward God; to his will Muslims submit; him they constantly praise and glorify; and in him alone they hope. He is awesome, transcendent, almighty, just, loving, merciful, and good. No creature may be compared to him, and to him alone do Muslims pray. Muslims ask intercession of the prophets and the saints, but they (the Shiites perhaps excepted) jealously preserve the distinction between Creator and creature. They seldom ask God for favors, limiting their prayer to thanksgiving and adoration. Associated with God are angels, generally represented as his messengers, who support his throne, guard the gates of hell, and serve as intermediaries. The chief angels are GABRIEL, MICHAEL, Azrael, and Uriel; devils are the evil jinn (see JINNI). According to Muslim teaching, God has made successive revelations to man through his prophets. Man has constantly fallen away from these prophets, and the merciful God has sent new ones; Muhammad is the last, and when the world falls away from Muhammad, that is, from Islam, the end of the world will come. The five principal early prophets are Adam, Noah, Abraham, Moses, and Jesus. Abraham was the Father of the Faithful, the first Muslim; Jesus was born of the Virgin Mary, did great miracles, and was not crucified, but was instead taken away by God, who left a shadow in his place (a common view among Gnostics and others), and Jesus, so one popular version goes, will return as the Mahdi at the end of the world to fight the Antichrist. Wherever the Koran differs from the Old and New Testaments, it is explained that the Jews and the Christians have corrupted or perverted the biblical text. Because of the close relationship acknowledged among Judaism, Christianity, and Islam, Jews and Christians have in principle been treated with special toleration in Muslim countries. It is commonly thought that Muhammad's ideas about Judaism and Christianity were derived not from reading but from converse with contemporary Arabian Jews and Christians who practiced their religion in a considerably corrupted form. The Muslim eschatology has affected believers much more than the orthodox account of history. In the course of time a rather elaborate account of what will happen at the Last Things has developed; but the final rewards have remained constant—there will be a judgment, and HEAVEN awaits the faithful and HELL the infidels. The ordinary pious Muslim does not distinguish faith from works: both are indispensable and mutually supplementary. There are five duties in Islam, the marks and the sine qua non of devotion. (1) Once in his life the believer must say with full understanding and absolute acceptance, "There is no god but God and Muhammad is his prophet." (2) Five times daily he must pray—at dawn, at noon, in midafternoon, at dusk, and after it has become dark. The prayers are set and are accompanied by traditional postures and preceded by ablutions; when he prays the Muslim covers his head, removes his shoes, and places a carpet under him; he prostrates himself continually. On Fridays the noonday prayer takes place in the MOSQUE, which exists for the meeting; set prayers are said, the Koran is read, and there is a sermon. The constantly recited prayer of Islam, used on all occasions, is Sura 1 of the Koran. It is singularly typical of the spirit of Islam: "In the name of God, the merciful, the compassionate. Praise be to God, the Lord of the worlds, the merciful, the compassionate, the ruler of the Judgment Day! Thee we serve and Thee we ask for aid. Guide us in the right path, the path of those to whom Thou art gracious; not of those with whom Thou art wroth; nor of those who err." When the Muslim prays, he faces Mecca, the direction of which is calculated in every Muslim settlement with the greatest exactness possible. (3) The Muslim must give alms generously; these are prescribed alms (e.g., so much of cattle, and so much of grain). He is also obliged to give some alms beyond the minimum. In places where Islam is the state religion the prescribed alms are often collected by the state. (4) The Muslim must keep the fast of RAMADAN; the physically weak, the sick, soldiers, and some others are exempted. (5) Once in his life the Muslim, if he can, must make the pilgrimage (Hajj) to Mecca. This, probably the greatest pilgrimage in the world, is made at a certain time of year, in the month (see CALENDAR) set apart for it. The importance of the pilgrimage can hardly be overestimated; it unites Islam as nothing else has ever done; at Mecca the Javanese meets the African from Senegal and the mountaineer of Albania, all brought together by the same holy purpose. The jihad, or holy war, is still in theory a religious duty but not a fundamental one. There are injunctions against wine, the touching or eating of pork, gambling, usury, fraud, slander, and the making of images. Circumcision, although widely practiced, is not mentioned in the Koran. There is a remarkable community of feeling in Islam, even today, when Muslims are divided politically into many groups. Islam is, of course, founded in the Koran, the divine word, but so little of this is dogmatic or legalistic that, early in the history of Islam, Muslims found the Koran inadequate as an authority for the good life. This was especially true when Islam was making its first rapid spread and as new peoples submitted to it. Hence arose the Sunna, fundamental in Islam. The Sunna is the way, or example, of the Prophet, which supplements the Koran. The Sunna is made up of collections of Traditions (moral sayings and anecdotes) of Muhammad, sifted and collected with unflagging effort by men from the earliest times of Islam. These collections are by al-BUKHARI (d. 870), Muslim (d. 875), Abn Dawud (d. 888), An-Nasai (d. 915), At-Tirmidi (d. 892), and Ibn Maja (d. 886). The first two of these collections are undoubtedly more reliable than the others if the truth is desired about Muhammad. The last four admittedly made use of a pious fraud based on the theory that all religious truth was implicit in Muhammad's sayings, so that a salutary maxim might be regarded as having been said by the Prophet. The Sunna is almost as important to Islam as the Koran, for in it lie all the elaborations of Koranic teaching essential to the firm establishment of a world religion. There are serious disagreements in the Traditions, and interpretations of the Koran and the Sunna have varied so much as to be contradictions. This situation is resolved by reference to what has become perhaps the most important of all the sayings attributed to Muhammad, "My community will never agree in an error." The principle this expresses is called Ijma, the agreement of Islam, and according to it every Muslim knows that a belief entertained by the greater part of Muslims in history is infallibly true and that a practice (e.g., the cult of saints) allowed by most Muslims over a long period must be legitimate and good. The Koran, the Sunna, and the Ijma are thus the three foundations of Islam. It is Ijma which has given Islam its catholicity of view, its constant unity with its past, and its continuous flexibility. But while Ijma has given Muslims a voice of authority, they have been saved from internal intolerance and the evils of extreme sectarianism by constantly bearing in mind the Tradition, "The difference of opinion in my community is a divine mercy." Muslim sectarianism in general may be said to be virtually negligible, except for a fundamental division of Islam into SUNNI and SHIITES. The division arose over the CALIPHATE in the first centuries. It is a convention to treat Sunni Islam as the norm, because of the vast superiority of numbers of the Sunni and the fact recognized by all non-Shiites (both Muslims and others) that the Shiites have departed to a marked degree from the original Islam. All Muslims except Shiites regard as monstrous and blasphemous the fundamental Shiite principles that Ali was a vicegerent of God and that his successors are infallible and sinless. The Ijma and the toleration of Sunni Islam have preserved the Sunni from serious defections and variations; the WAHABIS are the only important modern separatist Sunni sect. The Shiites have fathered countless sects; among them are the ASSASSINS, the DRUSES, the FATIMIDS, the ISMAILIS, and the KARMATHIANS. That the Muslim world should have divided irreparably over the political question of the caliphate illustrates a characteristic of Islam, that every Muslim thinks of himself as living in a theocracy. Just as the Prophet ruled Medina, the true ruler of the Muslim state is the caliph, and in theory, at least, all Islam should be united under one political and religious ruler, the caliph. Muslim princes have usually ruled their states according to the theocratic ideal; a corresponding phenomenon in Europe is a close incorporation of church and state. In the Muslim state only Muslims are really citizens; they alone are allowed and obliged to serve in the army; their taxes go to the support of the religious officers, the IMAM and the muezzin (announcer of prayer), as well as of the state, and their courts have religious as well as civil jurisdiction (see MUFTI). Non-Muslims are in theory aliens who live under sufferance in Muslim states; they have their own organization and often their own courts; they are not allowed to serve in the army; and they must pay a special tax, besides the taxes to support the bureaus of their community. In modern times this system has sometimes broken down completely. This was notably true of Turkey, where Kemal Atatürk made a clean sweep of most of Muslim culture, going even so far as to order the use of Turkish instead of Arabic in the mosque. Among his changes was the adoption of revised foreign codes of law (the Swiss civil code and the Italian criminal code) to replace Muslim law. Although most Muslim countries have long since been forced to separate in practice the religious law from the civil law, the civil law is strongly Muslim in flavor, and Muslim jurists all follow the same general method. The religious law of Islam in theory governs the whole life of any individual, but in reality his relations with his neighbor are a matter of state regulation. Any demarcation between civil and religious law is, however, very difficult to make. The law plays a great part in Muslim life, and in this respect Islam has developed more similarities to Judaism than to Christianity. Islam does not recognize a priestly class, but religious and legal officers have acquired an authority similar to that of the clergy in Christian communities. The minutiae of legal prescriptions in the Koran and the Sunna, extending not only to ceremonies and things forbidden but also to such matters as divorce, have often needed interpretation when they were to be applied to cases. There are in Sunni Islam four different systems of interpretations of the law, which may be called the Four Rites of Muslim Law; each of them is equally orthodox and is so regarded by all Muslims. They all agree entirely on the bases of Islam, although they may disagree on interpretation. The teaching of any rite is, of course, considered to be in accord with Ijma. The nearest analogy to the rites is probably the liturgical rites of Christianity. The Four Rites of Muslim Law are the Hanafite, founded by ABU HANIFA, the most speculative and individual of the rites, held in most of Muslim Asia; the Malikite, founded by Malik ibn Anas (d. 795), followed in the western and northern parts of Africa; the Shafite of Ash-Shafi (d. 820), the rite of much of Egypt, East Africa, Arabia, and the East Indies; and the Hanbalite, founded by Ahmad ibn Hanbal (d.855), the most literalistic and narrow of all, now not held in any great area. In Muslim view the study of the law is all-important, but with it are grouped dogmatic theology and mysticism as sacred studies. Philosophy, as distinct from theology, has no place in Islam. In fact, Muslim thought is a distinct unity that shows historically three major tendencies—toward legalism, toward rationalism, and toward mysticism. These have been tempered by one another and held in check by the three great faits accomplis of Islam—Koran, Sunna, and Ijma. Typical of the disputes in Muslim theology are those over freedom of the will, over the relative value of justification by faith alone or by faith and works, and over the creation of the Koran. The most famous school of religious thought was that of the Mutazilites, who flourished in the 10th and 11th cent. under the ABBASID caliphate; they have the distinction of beginning the first oppression on theological grounds in Islam, under Caliph al-MAMUN. The Mutazilites were in general rationalistic, and they took the stand that predestination was dangerous to religion; from this their interests spread all through dogma, and they became famous as believers in the "created Koran." This dispute over the creation of the Koran has much in common with Neoplatonic disputes over the LOGOS and with Christian disputes over ARIANISM. By far the most important figure in Muslim thought is al-GHAZALI, who has been called the Thomas Aquinas of Islam. He owed his fame to his acceptance of mysticism as the key to religion after he had so long held rationalistic principles that his rationalistic method checked any extreme tendency toward mysticism, while his mysticism prevented any resort to legalism. His great *Restoration of the Sciences of Religion* is a compendium of Muslim thought, the authoritative guide to what is Ijma, and the theological work par excellence of Islam. Those who may be called Muslim philosophers, al-FARABI, al-KINDI, AVEMPACE, AVERROËS, and AVICENNA, have had less influence on Islam than on the philosophy of Europe. (For the great mystical tendency of Islam, see SUFISM.) The great period of Muslim thought and culture was the 9th to the 11th cent. (see ARABIC LITERATURE and ISLAMIC ART AND ARCHITECTURE); typical of the enlightenment and culture were the great universities—Damascus, Baghdad, Bukhara, Seville, Córdoba, and later Cairo (now the intellectual capital of Islam). The spread of Islam within the first century after the hegira (622), the official beginning of Islam, was phenomenal (see ARABS). Various reasons for the rapid growth have been given; one, probably not the most potent, is the idea that he who dies fighting for the faith goes to paradise. The appeal of Islam as a universal religion is based on its awesome simplicity; the definite promises and the comparatively easy rules have undoubtedly added to that appeal. The modern spread of Islam, notably in the East Indies and Africa, has received no momentum at all from political advantage. Beginning in the 19th cent. a movement of Pan-Islamism has arisen to unite the now politically disunited Islam into a spiritual unity. Despite its lack of political success, it remains potent as an ideal. See D. B. Macdonald, *Development of Muslim Theology, Jurisprudence, and Constitutional Theory* (1903, repr. 1965); Carl Brockelmann, *A History of the Islamic Peoples* (tr. 1947, repr. 1964); A. S. Tritton, *Islam* (1951, repr. 1957); H. A. R. Gibb, *Modern Trends in Islam* (1947, repr. 1972) and *Mohammedanism* (2d ed. 1953, repr. 1969); Reuben Levy, *The Social Structure of Islam* (1957); W. C. Smith, *Islam in Modern History* (1957); G. E. von Grunebaum, *Medieval Islam* (2d ed. 1953, repr. 1961) and *Islam* (1961); Fazlur Rahman, *Islam* (1966); P. K. Hitti, *History of the Arabs* (10th ed. 1970); P. M. Holt et al., ed., *Cambridge History of Islam* (2 vol., 1970).

Islamabad (ĭs'ləməbăd', ĭslăm'-), city (1972 est. pop. 235,000), capital of Pakistan, NE Pakistan, just NE of RAWALPINDI, the interim capital. Construction of Islamabad [city of Islam] as the capital, replacing Karachi, began in 1960. There are light manufacturing industries. Points of interest include Pakistan House, the home of the President; the national assembly building; the National Univ.; the Grand National Mosque; and the botanical gardens. The nearby Murree Hills serve as a summer resort as well as summer headquarters for many diplomatic missions. Also near the city are the historical ruins of Taxila.

Islamic art and architecture. In the century after the death (A.D. 632) of the prophet Muhammad, his Arab followers spread his teachings through Egypt and N Africa, as far west as Spain, and as far east as Sassanid Persia. Because of their rapid expansion and the paucity of the artistic heritage brought from the Arabic Peninsula, the Muslims derived their unique style from a synthesizing of the arts of the Byzantines, the Copts, the Romans, and the Sassanids. The great interior surface of the Mosque of Damascus (715) was covered with stone mosaics in the Byzantine technique. No human figures were depicted; but there were crowns, fantastic plants, realistic trees, and even empty towns. The 8th-century desert palace Khirbat al-Mafjar (in present-day Jordan) reveals a wealth of carved and molded stucco decoration, sculptured stone reliefs, and figural fresco paintings. In A.D. 750 the Abbassid dynasty moved the capital east to Baghdad, and immediately the Persian influence became stronger. From 836 to 892 the Abbassid rulers resided at Samarra. When the city was abandoned, everything of value, even the carved wooden doors and marble window grilles, was removed. However, in the extensive ruins of the city abstract floral stucco decorations and fresco and pottery fragments have been found. Among the ceramic types are unglazed wares, molded pieces with the lead glaze of Hellenistic tradition, and most famous, the lusterware fragments. In 9th-century Islam the technique of tin-glazed ware was perfected. Lusterware was imported into Egypt and later made there. The Great Mosque of Al Qayrawan (c.862) is decorated with square luster tiles set in a lozenge pattern around the pierced marble prayer niche. The 9th cent. also saw the development of metalwork in a distinctive and powerful style under the Umayyads in Egypt. Skilled craftsmanship can be seen in rock-crystal carving, a continuation of Sassanid art, using floral motifs that became increasingly abstract. From the 10th to the mid-13th cent. great strides were made in the arts that Western critics persist in regarding as "minor." Egypt became the center of these arts and of CALLIGRAPHY. There remain leaves from parchment Korans, written in firm, compact Kufic, often in gold. During this period calligraphy, bookbinding, papermaking, and illumination were developed and were held in highest esteem throughout Islam. The Kufic script was animated by floriated, interlaced, and anthropomorphic designs. Calligraphy was used in metalwork, on pottery, and on buildings. The sloping cursive script most commonly used today, Nastaliq, was developed in the 15th cent. Before the 13th cent. rugs, silks, linens, and brocades were produced throughout the Islamic world, but only fragments remain; the same is true of delicate and highly refined carvings in wood and ivory. Early in the 13th cent. a school of secular manuscript painting arose in the Baghdad area. The pictures may be divided into two types: those that illustrate scientific works, descending directly from late Hellenistic models, and those that illustrate anecdotal tales and whose miniatures are in the true spirit of caricature. In the middle of the 13th cent. the Mongol invasions devastated Iran and deeply scarred all Islam as far west as the Mediterranean Sea. However, after a period of acclimatization, the Chinese taste and artifacts imported by the Mongols revitalized the art of Iran, where book illustration reached great heights. Textiles and rugs of great beauty were again manufactured throughout Islam, and Syria and Iraq continued to manufacture fine black-and-turquoise pottery. Turkish ceramics reached their peak in the "İznik" ware of the 16th and 17th cent. Distinctive green tiles are frequently used in the decoration of Turkish architecture. In early Islamic architecture, the Dome of the Rock (691) in Jerusalem and the great Mosque of Damascus (begun c.705) used the Syrian cut-stone technique of building and popularized the use of the dome (see MOSQUE). In Iran few Islamic buildings erected before the 10th cent. are still standing. Sassanid building techniques, such as the squinch, were combined with the mosque form (see PERSIAN ART AND ARCHITECTURE). Sassanid influence is also strong in many Umayyad dynasty residential palaces, built mostly in Syria. The most famous is the 8th-century palace of Mshatta; much of its delicately carved stone facade is now in Berlin. In the middle of the 8th cent. the last of the Umayyads escaped to Spain and refounded his dynasty there. The great Mosque of Córdoba was begun in 785. Late in the 9th cent. the governor of Egypt, Ibn Tulun, initiated the high period of Egypto-Islamic art with the building of his famous mosque in Cairo. In the 10th cent. the Fatimids introduced into Egypt the decorative stalactite ceiling from Iran and placed emphasis on decorative flat moldings. The most important Fatimid buildings are the Cairo mosques of al-Azhar and al-Aqmar. The cruciform Mosque of Hasan in Cairo, built by a Mameluke sultan in 1536, still reflects Persian influence. The culture of Islamic Spain reached its apogee in MOORISH ART AND ARCHITECTURE. Faïence and lacy pierced-stone screens are the hallmarks of its decoration. The same style prevails in N Africa and is seen at its best in Fez, Morocco, where much highly carved wood is used. The Mudéjar style of Spain, employed throughout the 18th cent. and influential until much later, is based on this architecture. In India, a distinct style, preserved mainly in architecture, developed after the DELHI SULTANATE was established (1192). This art was of high quality and reflected Indian adaptation to Islam rule, until Mogul art replaced it in the 17th cent. (see MOGUL ART AND ARCHITECTURE). The square Char Minar of Hyderabad (1591) with large arches, arcades, and minarets is characteristic. In Turkey the mosque form was also derived from Persia, as was most Turkish art. The great Byzantine church of HAGIA SOPHIA was used as a mosque and it too greatly influenced Turkish architects. The most famous among these is Sinan, chief architect in the Ottoman court from 1539 until his death in 1588. He constructed or designed most of Sulayman I's buildings, the most noted of which is his mosque (c.1557) in İstanbul, where the sultan is buried. It has four minarets and stained-glass windows flanking the mihrab. The mosque (1614) of Sultan Ahmed I is distinguished by its dome lighted by numerous windows, with the wall surfaces covered by green and blue tiles. Fine and very ornate buildings were erected in Turkey until the middle of the 17th cent. In general, all Islamic art and architecture is the result of synthesis rather than origination. Decoration of the surface is the most important factor in every work, large and small. Curving and often interlaced lines, of which the ARABESQUE is a typical example, and brilliant colors characterize almost all of the finest production of a greatly varied and widely practiced style. See D. T. Rice, *Islamic Art* (1965); Ernst Kühnel, *Islamic Art and Architecture* (tr. 1966); K. A. C. Creswell, *Early Muslim Architecture* (2 vol., 2d ed. 1969).

Islam in Africa. When the Muslim Arabs, sweeping forth from Arabia in the 6th and 7th cent., brought ISLAM to the Middle East and to the littoral of North Africa, black Africa was initially protected from their invasions by the Sahara. Along the east coast of Africa, however, Islam spread quickly. Arab mariners had for many years journeyed there to buy slaves, and in the 9th–10th cent. the Arabs founded permanent colonies on the offshore islands, especially on Zanzibar. From there Arab traders penetrated the interior of Africa, but the acceptance of Islam was slow. Prior to the 19th cent. the greatest gains made by Islam were in the lands immediately south of the Sahara. The black population of this savanna region was constantly exposed to the incursions of the Muslim nomads from the north. The Islamization of W Africa began when the ALMORAVIDS invaded (1076) the ancient kingdom of GHANA, but only gradually did the black rulers of W Africa accept the new faith. Mansa Musa (1307–32) of Mali was among the first to make Islam the official religion of state. In the region of the E Sudan, Islamic penetration followed the route of the Nile. By about 1366, Makurra, the more northerly of the two Christian kingdoms of the E Sudan, had fallen to Muslim invaders from Upper Egypt. The other kingdom, Aloa, was captured (c.1504) by the Muslims. Of all the old Christian states of Africa only Ethiopia survived. Yet even that isolated land almost succumbed in the 16th cent. to the invasion of the Somali conqueror Ahmad Gran. In the late 18th and early 19th cent., Africa, like the rest of the Muslim world, was swept by a wave of religious reform. Conquerors, such as the FULANI and the army of HAJJ OMAR, greatly extended the area over which Islam held sway in W

Africa. The Muslim brotherhoods also gained many new converts (see SANUSI). Yet for all their efforts the Muslims were unable to penetrate the heavily forested parts of Africa before the European colonial powers established modern conditions of trade and transport. The Europeans unwittingly fostered the spread of Islam by adopting Muslim law rather than indigenous custom in the administration of some of their colonies. Islam in Africa has tended to become less rigid in practice than the traditional Sunni orthodoxy. There has been a tendency for the Muslims of Africa to accept more readily the claims of self-proclaimed MAHDIS. Islamic ethics have proved less difficult for Africans to accept than those of Christianity, and in the 20th cent. Islam has consistently gained more converts in Africa than has Christianity. Unlike Christianity, Islam does not labor under the burden of identification with European imperialism. See J. S. Trimingham, *Islam in the Sudan* (2d ed. 1949, repr. 1965), *Islam in Ethiopia* (1952, repr. 1965), *Islam in West Africa* (1959), *Islam in East Africa* (1964), and *The Influence of Islam on Africa* (1968); James and Lewis Kritzeck, ed., *Islam in Africa* (1969).

island, relatively small body of land surrounded entirely by water. (As the oceans form a continuous mass of water on the earth's surface, all continents are islands in the strict sense of the word.) The largest islands of the earth are, in descending order of size, Greenland, New Guinea, Borneo, Madagascar, Baffin Island, Sumatra, Honshu (largest of the islands of Japan), and Great Britain. Depending on their origin, islands are either continental or oceanic. Continental islands are created by the submergence of coastal highlands of which only the summits remain above water or by the sea breaking through an isthmus or peninsula. Typical continental islands are Great Britain, the Japanese archipelago, and Sicily. In all three cases submarine banks indicate the former coherence with the mainland. Oceanic islands can result from the ascending of the ocean floor above water through volcanic action or other earth movements. In areas of seismic activity, especially on or near midocean ridges, the sudden and spectacular creation of an island by upswelling lava can occasionally be witnessed, as when the island of Surtsey appeared along the Mid-Atlantic Ridge S of Iceland in 1963. Oceanic islands that result from coral growth are called atolls (see CORAL REEF). They are always low and occur only in tropical ocean areas. Oceanic islands are characterized by a poor fauna, consisting mostly of a few kinds of sea birds and insects. Vegetation is more abundant, as seeds are carried from remote lands by air, water currents, and birds.

Island No. 10, island (no longer extant) in the Mississippi River, between NW Tenn. and SE Mo.; site of an important western campaign of the Civil War. With the advance of Union Gen. U. S. Grant up the Tennessee River, all Confederate positions, except New Madrid and Island No. 10, were abandoned. After the fall of New Madrid on March 14, 1862, Union troops dug a canal through the swamps to allow their supply barges to bypass the heavily fortified island. After many attempts, Union gunboats finally succeeded in passing the island, and reduced its shore batteries. The large Confederate garrison surrendered without a battle on April 7, after the Union troops seized the only escape route.

Islay (ī'lā, ī'lə), island (1971 pop. 3,825), 240 sq mi (622 sq km), Argyllshire, W central Scotland, southernmost of the Inner Hebrides. Bowmore is the ancient capital, but Port Ellen (founded 1844) is the main town. The land is fertile, with large livestock and dairy farms and vast fields of peat. Oats and potatoes are the main crops, and cheese is made. Distilling and tourism are important. Memorials to victims of the sinkings (1918) of the *Tuscania* and the *Otranto* are on the island.

Île-aux-Coudres (ēl-ō-ko͞o'drə), island, c.6 mi (9.7 km) long and 2.5 mi (4 km) wide, in the St. Lawrence River, SE Que., Canada. It was named by Jacques Cartier in 1535 for the hazelnuts growing there. The first Roman Catholic Mass in Canada was celebrated on the island the same year. Because it preserves traditional Quebec rural life, the island is a tourist attraction.

Isle La Motte (īl lə mŏt), island and town (1970 pop. 262), 6 mi (9.7 km) long and 2 mi (3.2 km) wide, in Lake Champlain, NW Vt. The French chose the island as the site for Fort Ste Anne (built 1666), the first white settlement in Vermont. It remained garrisoned for some time but was abandoned long before permanent settlement began c.1788. Black marble is quarried on the island.

Isle Royale National Park, 539,341 acres (218,271 hectares), comprising about 200 islands, in Lake Superior, NW Mich.; est. 1940. Isle Royale, 210 sq mi (544 sq km), is the largest island in Lake Superior; Greenstone Ridge extends along its entire length. Glaciated, the island has many lakes, streams, and inlets and remains a roadless, forested wilderness. Its abundant wildlife includes squirrels, beaver, fox, moose, and many kinds of birds. In prehistoric times, the island's copper was mined by Indians; artifacts from that period have been found. The French, lured by the fur trade, named the island in 1671. Isle Royale originally became U.S. territory in 1783 and was ceded to the United States by the Chippewa Indians in 1843. It was mined for copper from 1843 to 1899 by Americans; large areas of forest were burned to expose the ore and to build settlements. In the early 1900s the island was a popular vacation retreat.

Isles of the Blest: see FORTUNATE ISLES.

Isleta (īslĕt'ə), pueblo (1970 pop. 1,080), Bernalillo co., central N.Mex., on the east bank of the Rio Grande. It is a tourist attraction. According to many experts, the pueblo stands on the site it occupied when discovered in 1540. It was the seat of the Franciscan mission of San Antonio de Isleta from c.1621 until the Pueblo revolt of 1680. The Spanish captured the pueblo in 1681, and most of the captives were ultimately settled at present-day Ysleta, Texas. In the early 18th cent., when N Isleta was either rebuilt or repeopled, it became the mission of San Agustín de Isleta (today the principal feast of these Indians is that of St. Augustine, Aug. 28). The Indians are mainly farmers and are perhaps the most prosperous of all the Pueblo Indians. The language of Isleta is Tanoan.

islets of Langerhans: see PANCREAS.

Islington, borough (1971 pop. 184,392) of Greater London, SE England. The borough was created in 1965 by the merger of the metropolitan boroughs of Islington and Finsbury. Islington, in the north, is mostly residential, while Finsbury, in the south, is highly industrialized. Industries include special and electrical engineering, printing, clockmaking, and brewing; clothing, furniture, and scientific, surgical, and optical instruments are manufactured. Finsbury also has an important wholesale trade in industrial equipment and supplies. Pentonville Prison and Holloway Gaol for women are in Islington. Bunhill Fields in Finsbury contains the graves of several literary figures. John Wesley's chapel and house and the Sadler's Wells Theatre, former home of the Royal Ballet, are also in Finsbury.

Ismachiah (ĭz"məkī'ə), overseer under Hezekiah. 2 Chron. 31.13.

Ismaiah (ĭs"māī'ə), one of David's mighty men. 1 Chron. 12.4.

Ismail (ĭsmäēl'), 1486–1524, shah of Persia (1502–24), founder of the Safavid dynasty. He restored Persia to the position of a sovereign state for the first time since the Arab invasion of Persia. Ismail established the Shiite form of Islam as the state religion; this gained him the animosity of the Uzbeks and the Ottoman Turks, who were Sunni Muslims. He warred on the Uzbeks successfully in 1510, and Selim I attacked him in 1514, thus initiating a long series of border wars between the Ottoman Turks and the Persians.

Ismail, 1646?–1727, sultan of Morocco (1672–1727). He organized corps of Sudanese Negroes to subdue the revolts that followed his accession. He attacked Christian strongholds in Morocco, regaining Larache and Arzila. Encouraging trade with Europe, Ismail signed a commercial treaty with France (1682) and corresponded with Louis XIV. At Meknes he built a lavish new capital.

Ismailia (ĭzmāəlē'ə) or **Al Ismailiyah** (äl ĭsmălē'yə), city (1970 est. pop. 167,500), capital of Ismailia governorate, NE Egypt. It is the seat of the Suez Canal administration, as well as an important commercial and rail center. Ismailia was founded in 1863 by Ferdinand de LESSEPS, who used it as his base of operations during the construction of the canal. The city was named after Ismail, then khedive of Egypt. After Israeli forces shelled Ismailia in the wake of the 1967 Arab-Israeli War, part of the city's civilian population was evacuated. In the 1973 war Israeli ground forces pushed to within the city's outskirts.

Ismailis (ĭsmäēl'ēz), sect of Muslim Shiites that holds Ismail, the son of Jafar as-Sadiq, as its IMAM. When the sixth imam of the Shiites, Jafar as-Sadiq (d. 765), disinherited his eldest son, Ismail, and thus deprived him of the imamate, a schism occurred. The majority of Shiites accepted Musa al-Kazim, the younger son of Jafar, as seventh imam, but there were those who remained faithful to Ismail and soon evolved the belief that Ismail was endowed with an infallible gift of revelation; this remains a basic tenet of the Ismailis. The sect was given to great secrecy, and until the 13th cent. it practiced terrorism; the Karmathians, the Assassins, and the Fatimids are closely related to the Ismaili sect. The family of the AGA KHAN traces its descent from the imam Ismail.

Ismail Pasha, 1830–95, ruler of Egypt (1863–79), son of Ibrahim Pasha. He succeeded his uncle Said Pasha as ruler. Ismail used the Egyptian cotton crop, enormously enhanced in value by the American Civil War, to obtain credits for grandiose schemes, including irrigation projects, schools, palaces, the construction of the Suez Canal, and the extension of Egyptian rule in the Sudan. Much of the money was wasted, and the country was seriously involved in debt. In 1875, Ismail was forced to sell to Great Britain his stockholdings (some 44%) in the Suez Canal, and in 1876 he was obliged to place the finances of Egypt under the control of a debt commission that represented the French and British bondholders. His attempt to throw off foreign control in 1879 was answered by the Ottoman sultan's deposing him in favor of his son Tewfik Pasha. In 1866, Ismail received the title khedive (viceroy), which his successors also enjoyed. See studies by Pierre Crabitès (1933), M. F. Shukri (1937), and Mary Rowlatt (1962).

Ismay, Hastings Lionel Ismay, 1st **Baron,** 1887–1965, British general, known as "Pug" Ismay. He served in India and, during World War I, in Africa. During World War II he held simultaneously the posts of chief of staff to Winston Churchill and deputy secretary to the war cabinet. In 1946 he retired from the army and received a peerage. In 1951 he was appointed secretary of state for commonwealth relations. He resigned the following year to become secretary general to the North Atlantic Treaty Organization, remaining in that post until 1957. See his memoirs (1960, repr. 1974); biography by Ronald Wingate (1970).

Ismene (ĭsmē'nē), in Greek legend, daughter of Oedipus and sister of Antigone.

Isna (ĭs'nə) or **Esna** (ĕs'–), town (1966 pop. 27,400), central Egypt, on the Nile River. It is the center for an agricultural area that is irrigated by the Nile. Isna's manufactures include cotton fabrics and ceramics. The Ptolemaic temple (with Roman additions) to the ram-headed deity Khnum is the town's outstanding monument. Nearby is a Coptic Christian monastery, said to have been founded in the 4th cent. to commemorate those martyred by Diocletian, but now believed to date from the 10th or 11th cent.

isobar (ī'səbär") or **isobaric line** (ī"səbăr'ĭk), line drawn on a weather map through points of equal atmospheric pressure. Isobars are used to define cyclones (low-pressure regions) and anticyclones (high-pressure regions). Weather maps are designed to depict the horizontal pressure distribution across an area of land, but atmospheric pressure also varies vertically, i.e., with altitude. In order to eliminate any consideration of the vertical variations of pressure, the barometer readings at all stations are reduced to their corresponding sea-level pressures before the isobars are drawn.

isobutane (ī"səbyo͞o'tān): see BUTANE.

isobutyric acid (ī"səbyo͞otĕr'ĭk): see BUTYRIC ACID.

Isocrates (īsŏk'rətēz), 436–338 B.C., one of the Ten Attic Orators. He was a pupil of Socrates and of the Sophists. Perhaps the greatest teacher in Greek history, he taught every younger orator of his time. He did not deliver his speeches, but either wrote for litigants (six such speeches survive) or wrote discourses to be read (15 of which remain) dealing mainly with politics and education. *Panegyricus* (in which he urges Hellenic unity against Persia) is his most celebrated oration. Isocrates committed suicide (according to tradition) after the defeat of Athens by Philip II of Macedon at Chaeronea.

isogamy (īsŏg'əmē), in biology, a condition in which the sexual cells, or gametes, are of the same form and size and are usually indistinguishable from each other. Many ALGAE and some FUNGI have isogamous gametes. In spite of their apparent morphological similarity, however, isogametes may be quite different in their behavior and physiology, thus indicating that some physiological differentiation exists.

Isolde: see TRISTRAM AND ISOLDE.

isoleucine (ī"səlo͞o'sēn), organic compound, one of the 22 α-AMINO ACIDS commonly found in animal proteins. Only the L-stereoisomer appears in mammalian protein. It is one of several essential amino acids needed in the diet; human beings cannot synthesize it from simpler metabolites. Young adults need about 20 mg of this amino acid per day per kg (or about 8 mg per lb) of body weight. Isoleucine can be degraded into simpler compounds by the enzymes of the body. In a rare, inherited disorder

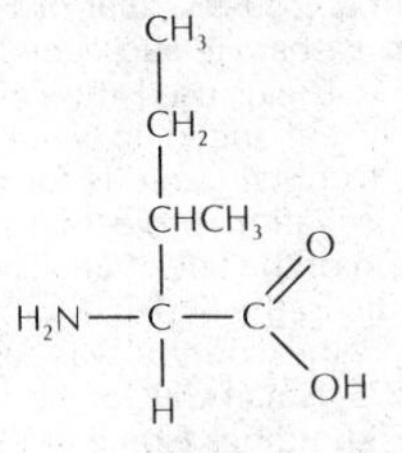

```
        CH3
        |
        CH2
        |
        CHCH3   O
        |      //
 H2N—C—C
        |      \
        H       OH
```

isoleucine

called maple syrup urine disease, a nonfunctional enzyme in the common pathway of isoleucine, LEUCINE, and VALINE degradation causes the buildup of certain metabolites in the urine, resulting in the characteristic odor from which the disease derives its name. Once isoleucine is incorporated into protein, it contributes to the structure of protein by the tendency of its side chain (composed only of carbon and hydrogen) to seek an environment consisting of similar side chains, like those of leucine, valine, TRYPTOPHAN, and PHENYLALANINE, and to exclude water. This hydrophobic property is analogous to that which prevents oil from dissolving in water. The tendency for these hydrophobic residues to associate with one another is evidently quite important in determining the bending and folding (tertiary structure) of the peptide chain characteristically seen in every protein. Isoleucine was isolated from beet sugar molasses in 1904.

isomer (ī'səmər), in chemistry, one of two or more compounds having the same molecular FORMULA but different structures (arrangements of atoms in the molecule). Isomerism is the occurrence of such compounds. Isomers have the same number of atoms of each element in them and the same atomic weight but differ in other properties. For example, there are two compounds with the molecular formula C_2H_6O. One is ethanol, CH_3CH_2OH, a colorless liquid alcohol; the other is dimethyl ether, CH_3OCH_3, a colorless gaseous ether. Ethanol and dimethyl ether are called structural isomers because they differ in the way the atoms are joined together in their molecules:

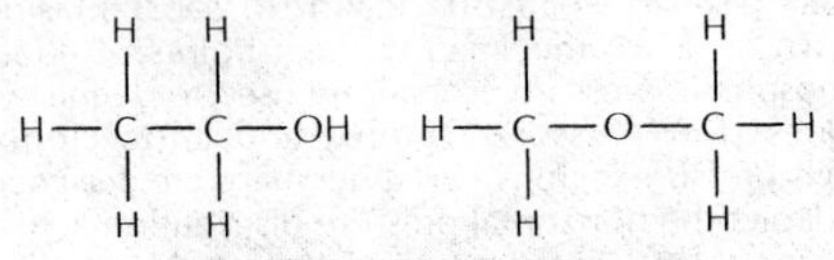

```
   H  H              H        H
   |  |              |        |
H—C—C—OH         H—C—O—C—H
   |  |              |        |
   H  H              H        H
```

ethanol *dimethyl ether*

Chain isomers occur among the ALKANES. There are two chain isomers of butane, C_4H_{10}. In n-butane, $CH_3CH_2CH_2CH_3$, the carbon atoms are joined in a so-called straight, or unbranched, chain. In isobutane, $CH_3CH(CH_3)_2$, the carbon atoms are joined in a branched chain; the isobutane molecule can be visualized as a carbon atom bonded to one hydrogen atom and to three methyl (CH_3) groups. Position isomers occur among substituted alkanes and other compounds. For example, 1-propanol, $CH_3CH_2CH_2OH$, and 2-propanol, $CH_3CH(OH)CH_3$, are position isomers, as are 1-butene, $CH_2{=}CHCH_2CH_3$, and 2-butene, $CH_3CH{=}CHCH_3$. Position isomers have similar chemical properties since they differ only in the location of the FUNCTIONAL GROUP (e.g., the OH in an alcohol or the double bond in an ALKENE). Functional group isomers, on the other hand, have very different chemical properties because differences in their structure give rise to different functional groups. Ethanol and dimethyl ether are functional group isomers. Stereoisomerism is different from the kinds of isomerism discussed above; it occurs when two or more molecules have the same basic arrangement of atoms in their molecules but differ in the way the atoms are arranged in space. There are two types of stereoisomerism. The first type, geometric isomerism, may occur when a compound contains a double bond or some other feature that gives the molecule a certain amount of structural rigidity. Geometric isomers differ in physical properties such as melting point and boiling point. For example, there are two geometric isomers of 2-butene, $CH_3CH{=}CHCH_3$:

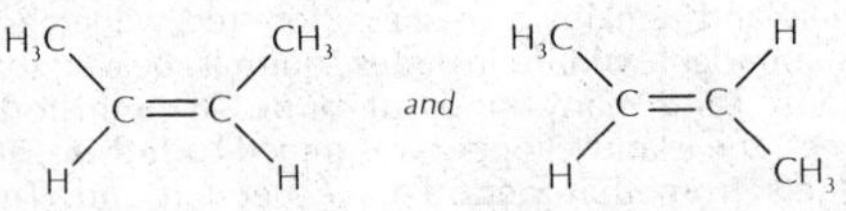

```
H3C       CH3          H3C       H
   \     /                \     /
    C=C         and        C=C
   /     \                /     \
  H       H              H       CH3
```

cis-2-butene trans-*2-butene*

The prefix *cis-* means "same side" and *trans-* means "opposite side"; they are used when the groups on either side of the double bond are identical or closely related, e.g., methyl and ethyl. *Syn-* and *anti-* have similar meanings but are used when the groups are not identical or closely related. The second type of stereoisomerism is optical isomerism. When plane-polarized light is passed through an optical isomer it is rotated into a different plane of polarization. Optical isomers exhibit this optical activity in varying degrees. Optical isomers of a given compound are often identical in all physical properties except the direction in which they rotate light. The molecules of optical isomers are asymmetrical. The simplest optical isomers have a single "asymmetrical carbon atom" in their molecules. An asymmetrical carbon atom has four different atoms or radicals bonded to it, arranged approximately at the corners of a tetrahedron centered on the carbon atom. For example, there are two optical isomers of lactic acid:

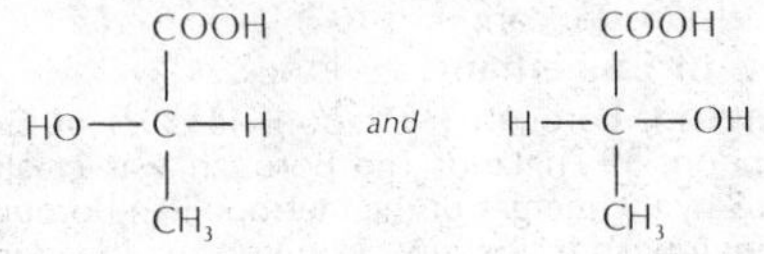

```
      COOH                 COOH
       |                    |
 HO—C—H       and      H—C—OH
       |                    |
      CH3                  CH3
```

d-*lactic acid* l-*lactic acid*

The atom and radical to either side of the carbon atom are visualized as being above the plane of the paper, the central carbon atom in the plane of the paper, and the radicals above and below the central carbon atom below the plane of the paper. Thus it is seen that the two molecules are mirror images of each other and, each being asymmetrical, cannot be superposed on each other. The *d-* and *l-* prefixes stand for *dextro* (right) and *levo* (left). Two optical isomers, such as these, whose molecules are asymmetrical and are mirror images of each other, are called enantiomorphs. When equal amounts of *d-* and *l-*enantiomorphs are mixed, the mixture has no effect on polarized light; such a mixture is called racemic. When there is more than one asymmetrical carbon atom, there may be more than two optical isomers. For example, tartaric acid has two asymmetrical carbon atoms and three optical isomers:

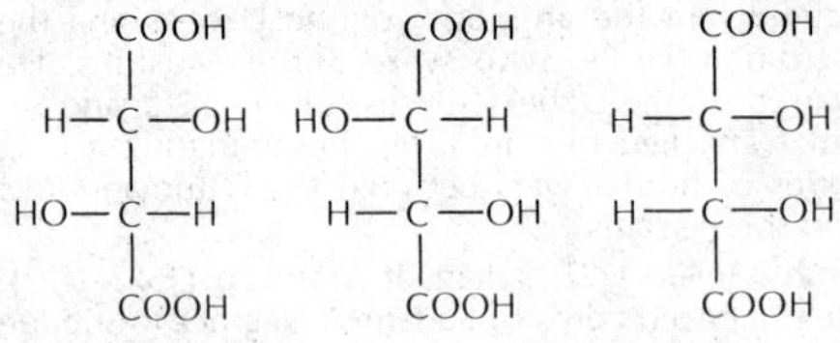

```
     COOH          COOH          COOH
      |             |             |
  H—C—OH      HO—C—H        H—C—OH
      |             |             |
 HO—C—H        H—C—OH       H—C—OH
      |             |             |
     COOH          COOH          COOH
```

d-*tartaric acid* l-*tartaric acid* meso-*tartaric acid*

The *d-* and *l-*tartaric acids are enantiomorphs; each molecule is asymmetrical and is the mirror image of the other. There are two asymmetrical carbon atoms in *meso-*tartaric acid, but the molecule is symmetrical and does not exhibit optical activity; the optical activity is internally compensated, the effect of one asymmetrical carbon atom balancing the effect of the other. A pair of optical isomers such as *d-*tartaric acid and *meso-*tartaric acid, which are not enantiomorphs, are called diastereoisomers. Molecular dissymmetry in optical isomers may come from some source other than an asymmetrical carbon atom, e.g., structural rigidity resulting from double bonds or ring structures within a molecule. Stereoisomers are important in metabolism; in many cases only one of several isomeric forms of a compound can take part in biochemical reactions. For example, there are 16 stereoisomers of a simple sugar whose molecular formula is $C_6H_{12}O_6$. Of these, only *d-*glucose is readily utilized in human metabolism. Isomerism was first recognized by J. J. Berzelius in 1827. Early work with stereoisomers was carried out by Louis Pasteur, who separated racemic acid into its two optically active tartaric acid components by crystallization (1848). Pasteur's results were given theoretical basis by J. H. Van't Hoff and independently by J. A. le Bel (1864). See TAUTOMER.

isomorphism (ī"səmôr'fĭzəm), of minerals, similarity of crystal structure between two or more distinct substances. Sodium nitrate and calcium sulfate are isomorphous, as are the sulfates of barium, strontium, and lead. Crystals of isomorphous substances are almost identical. The substances sometimes crystallize together in a solid solution. Isomorphous substances usually have similar chemical formulas, and the polarizability and ratio of anion and cation radii are generally comparable (see ION). Isomorphism was discovered (c.1820) by Eilhard Mitscherlich, who stated the principle that isomorphous substances have similar chemical formulas; this principle was used by J. J. Berzelius in determining chemical formulas and combining weights. See POLYMORPHISM; MINERAL; CRYSTAL.

isoniazid (ī"sōnī'əzĭd), drug used to treat TUBERCULOSIS. Also known as isonicotinic acid hydrazide, isoniazid is the most effective antituberculosis drug currently available. The drug inhibits or kills the tubercle bacilli that cause the disease. It is usually given together with some other antituberculosis drug such as STREPTOMYCIN or aminosalicylic acid to prevent emergence of drug resistant organisms (see DRUG RESISTANCE). To prevent development of tuberculosis in individuals who have a positive reaction to a tuberculin skin test, isoniazid is given alone. Side effects are seen only with very high doses.

Isonzo (ēzôn'tsō), river, 87 mi (140 km) long, rising in the Julian Alps, NW Yugoslavia, and flowing S through Yugoslavia, then SW through NE Italy before emptying into the Gulf of Trieste. At the entrance to the Venetian plain, the Isonzo valley was the scene of many battles during World Wars I and II. After World War II, the part of the valley above Gorizia, Italy, was given to Yugoslavia, where the river is known as the Soča.

isopleth, line drawn on a map through all points of equal value of some measurable quantity. In many meteorologic, oceanographic, or geologic studies some physical or chemical property is examined that varies from place to place on a map. Isopleths showing the quantity of the property being studied can be drawn on the map to highlight regional trends of high or low abundance of that property. For example, topographic maps showing CONTOURS of equal elevation are probably the most common type of isopleth maps. Relief "highs" (hills) are shown by concentric contour isopleths, and depressions such as volcanic craters are shown by concentric contours with hachures pointing toward the center of the depression. Isopleths are drawn on weather maps to indicate lines of equal air pressure (isobars) and equal temperature (isotherms). Isobaths are lines connecting points of equal depth in lakes and oceans. Isopach maps show distribution of thickness of a given rock unit. Gravity maps are drawn showing isogals (lines of equal gravitational acceleration). Variations in the strength of the earth's magnetic field are shown by isogams (after gamma, the common unit for measuring magnetic strength).

isopod (ī'səpŏd"), common name for crustaceans belonging to the order Isopoda and in the same subclass as lobsters and crayfish. Isopods are characterized by their flattened bodies, lack of a carapace, and gills located on the abdominal appendages. About 4,000 species are known. Most are aquatic; they are bottom-dwellers or are associated with water plants in freshwater or marine habitats. Some live under rocks on the shore, and some are terrestrial, living inconspicuously in surface litter or under logs. These, the pill bugs, or sow bugs, are the only large group of terrestrial crustaceans. Some isopods roll up like armadillos when disturbed. Some are parasitic, living on other crustaceans or in the mouths or on the gills of fishes. Most isopods are small, less than ½ in. (1.27 cm) long, but *Bathynomus gigantea,* a deep sea species, may be over 1 ft (30 cm) long. Isopods are classified in the phylum ARTHROPODA, class Crustacea, order Isopoda.

isoprene or **2-methyl-1,3-butadiene** (ī'səprēn, byo͞o"tədī'ēn), colorless liquid organic compound. It is a hydrocarbon, and is insoluble in water but soluble in many organic solvents; it boils at 34°C. The isoprene molecule contains two double bonds. It is readily polymerized by the use of special catalysts; large numbers of isoprene molecules join together to form a single large, threadlike polyisoprene molecule. Isoprene polymers also occur naturally. The natural rubber caoutchouc is *cis*-1,4-polyisoprene, and *trans*-1,4-polyisoprene is present in the natural rubbers balata and gutta-percha. (The *cis* and *trans* polyisoprenes are structural isomers.)

isopropanol, isopropyl alcohol, or **2-propanol** (ī″səprō′pənōl, ī″səprō′pĭl), $(CH_3)_2CHOH$, a colorless liquid that is miscible with water. It melts at −89°C and boils at 82.3°C. It is poisonous if taken internally. It is a major component of rubbing alcohols. Isopropanol is a secondary ALCOHOL. It is one of the cheapest alcohols and has replaced ethanol for many uses because of its similar solvent properties. Isopropanol is made commercially by dissolving propylene gas in sulfuric acid and then hydrolyzing the sulfate ester that is formed; the propylene is a by-product of petroleum refining. Isopropanol was formerly obtained largely by catalytic reduction of ACETONE; oxidation of isopropanol is now the major source of acetone.

isopropyl alcohol: see ISOPROPANOL.

isostasy (īsŏs′təsē): see CONTINENT.

isotherm, line drawn on a map of a particular region of the earth's surface connecting points of equal temperature; each point reflects one temperature reading or an average of several readings over a period of time. The relative spacing of the isothermal lines indicates a temperature gradient, i.e., the amount of temperature change over a given distance.

isotope (ī′sətōp), in chemistry and physics, one of two or more atoms having the same atomic number but differing in ATOMIC WEIGHT and mass number. The concept of isotope was introduced by F. Soddy in explaining aspects of radioactivity; the first stable isotope (of neon) was discovered by J. J. Thomson. The nuclei of isotopes contain identical numbers of protons, equal to the atomic number of the atom, and thus represent the same chemical element, but do not have the same number of neutrons. Thus isotopes of a given element have identical chemical properties but slightly different physical properties

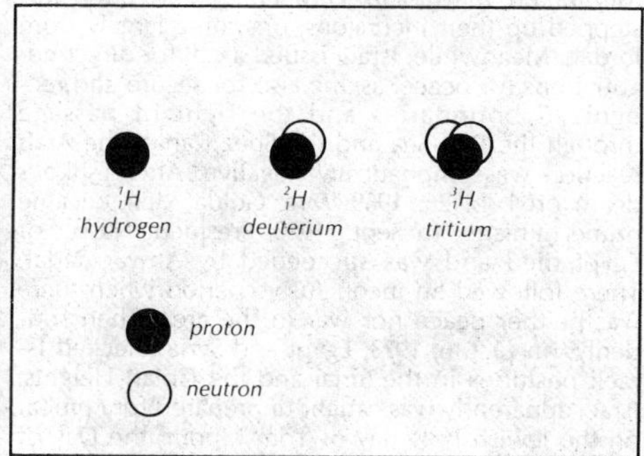

Isotopes of hydrogen

and very different half-lives, if they are radioactive (see HALF-LIFE). For most elements, both stable and radioactive isotopes are known. RADIOACTIVE ISOTOPES of many common elements, such as carbon and phosphorus, are used as tracers in medical, biological, and industrial research. Their radioactive nature makes it possible to follow the substances in their paths through a plant or animal body and through many chemical and mechanical processes; thus a more exact knowledge of the processes under investigation can be obtained. The very slow and regular transmutations of certain radioactive substances, notably carbon-14, make them useful as "nuclear clocks" for DATING archaeological and geological samples. By taking advantage of the slight differences in their physical properties, the isotopes may be separated. The MASS SPECTROGRAPH uses the slight difference in mass to separate different isotopes of the same element. Depending on their nuclear properties, the isotopes thus separated have important applications in nuclear energy. For example, the highly fissionable isotope uranium-235 must be separated from the more plentiful isotope uranium-238 before it can be used in a NUCLEAR REACTOR or ATOMIC BOMB.

Ispah (ĭs′pə), chief Benjamite. 1 Chron. 8.16.

Ispahan: see ESFAHAN, Iran.

İsparta (ĭspär′tä), city (1970 pop. 51,107), capital of İsparta prov., W central Turkey. It is a manufacturing center producing cotton, carpets, and attar of roses. A picturesque city, it was severely damaged by an earthquake in 1889.

Israel (ĭz′rēəl, ĭz′rāəl) [as understood by Hebrews, = striven with God], in the Bible, name given JACOB as eponymous ancestor of the Hebrews, the chosen people of God. The 12 tribes of Israel were named for 10 sons of Jacob (Reuben, Simeon, Judah, Zebulun, Issachar, Dan, Gad, Asher, Naphtali, and Benjamin) and the two sons of Jacob's son Joseph (Ephraim and Manasseh); the 13th tribe, Levi (the third of Jacob's sons), was set apart and had no one portion of its own. After the break in the Hebrew kingdom under REHOBOAM the northern kingdom, consisting of all but the tribes of Judah and Benjamin and a number of Levites, was called Israel, while the southern kingdom, composed of these latter elements, was known as Judah.

Israel (ĭz′rēəl), republic (1972 pop. 3,164,000), 7,992 sq mi (20,700 sq km), SW Asia, on the Mediterranean Sea. The area figure used above is based on the armistice agreements of 1949 and does not include the Syrian, Egyptian, and Jordanian territories occupied by Israel in its 1967 and 1973 wars with the Arabs. The capital of Israel is JERUSALEM; other important cities include TEL AVIV-JAFFA, HAIFA, ASHQELON, and ELAT. The country is a narrow, irregularly shaped strip of land bounded on the N by Lebanon, on the E by Syria and Jordan, on the W by the Mediterranean Sea, on the SW by Egypt, and on the S by the Gulf of Aqaba (an arm of the Red Sea). Israel has four principal regions: the plain along the Mediterranean coast; the mountains, which are east of this coastal plain; the NEGEV, which comprises the southern half of the country; and the portion of Israel that forms part of the Jordan Valley, in turn a part of the GREAT RIFT VALLEY. North of the Negev, Israel enjoys a Mediterranean climate, with long, hot, dry summers and short, cool, rainy winters. This northern half of the country has a limited but adequate supply of water, except in times of drought. The Negev, however, is a semiarid region, having less than 10 in. (25 cm) of rainfall a year. Because Israel is plagued by a shortage of water, Israeli scientists have worked with American scientists on the desalination of seawater. Success in developing an inexpensive process of desalinating seawater would help to solve Israel's problem of chronic water shortage and would make it possible to provide for increased development and a larger population. The most important river in Israel is the Jordan. Other, smaller, rivers are the Yarkon, the Kishon, and the Yarmuk. In the southern part of the country are many wadis, or riverbeds, that are dry except in the brief rainy season. Other bodies of water include the Sea of Galilee and the Dead Sea (part of which belongs to neighboring Jordan). The waters of the Dead Sea have about eight times as much salt as the ocean. The draining in 1957 of Lake Hula, located in Northern Israel, served to increase both the farming area and the number of fish ponds in the region. The highest point in Israel is Mt. Meron (3,692 ft/1,125 m) near Zefat. The lowest point is the surface of the Dead Sea, which is 1,292 ft (394 m) below sea level and which is also the lowest point on earth. As the result of an intensive reforestation program, more than 100 million trees have been planted since 1948, the year the state of Israel came into being. This article deals with the events in Israel from 1948 to the present. For the earlier history of the region, see PALESTINE. The economy of Israel is based on both state and private ownership and operation. Despite adverse conditions, agriculture in Israel has been developed to a degree that compares favorably with the agriculture of advanced countries. In 1948, Israel produced only 30% of the food it needed; by the early 1970s it produced enough fruits and vegetables, poultry and eggs, and milk and dairy products to meet all domestic needs, although much of the grain required was still imported. The area of land under cultivation has been greatly increased since the founding of the state in 1948, and extensive irrigation has been provided to develop farm land and compensate for the shortage of water. Close to 500,000 acres (200,000 hectares) are now irrigated as compared with 75,000 acres (30,000 hectares) in 1948. The chief crop and most important product of Israel is citrus fruit, 95% of which is exported. In addition, flowers (such as carnations and gladioli), noncitrus fruits (such as melons, bananas, and peaches), and vegetables (such as eggplants and tomatoes) are exported to Europe, especially as out-of-season crops in the winter. Other sizable crops are sugar beets, peanuts, cotton, sisal, and several rushes of the species *Juncus* (which are a source of cellulose used in the manufacture of paper). Agricultural exports add up to roughly one fifth of the total commodity exports. Most of the land (apart from the land belonging to non-Jews) is held in trust for the people of Israel by the state and the Jewish National Fund. The latter was set up in 1901 to buy land in Palestine for Jews to cultivate. The state and the Fund lease the land to kibbutzim, which are communal agricultural settlements; to moshavim, which are cooperative agricultural communities;

and to other agricultural villages. In the kibbutz, members receive all the necessities of life (housing, food, clothing, medical care, education, recreation, vacations, and spending money) instead of wages in return for their labor. Married couples are assigned living quarters and eat in a community dining hall, but their children usually live in separate dormitories, where they are cared for by a professional staff, although leisure time is shared with their parents. In the moshav, each family unit has its own home and cultivates its own plot of land, but the members own farming equipment collectively and market their crops as a group. The Israelis have also made great strides in developing their industry since 1948, despite a comparative scarcity of raw materials, many of which have to be imported. The owners of industry in Israel include individuals, the government, the Histadrut (or General Federation of Labor), and other public organizations. Israel encourages foreign investment in its industry by low rates of taxation and by permitting the withdrawal abroad of most of the profits. The major industries include the cutting and polishing of diamonds, the manufacture of chemical fertilizers from the potash obtained from the Dead Sea and from the phosphates found in the Negev, the mining of copper at Timna near the southern port of Elat (on the Gulf of Aqaba), and the manufacture of textiles. The Dead Sea has other minerals of commercial value, such as magnesium and bromine. Building construction has become a very large industry, partly because of the need to provide homes for the tremendous number of immigrants who have come to Israel since 1948 (close to 1.5 million persons) and partly because of the desire on the part of the government to build up the state as rapidly as possible to the level of the industrially developed nations. There are also a number of light industries, with a wide variety of goods produced. These include processed foods, precision instruments, shoes, ready-made clothes, and plastic products of various kinds. Diamonds are the largest industrial export, followed by chemical fertilizers, chemicals, pharmaceuticals, textiles, fashion goods, tires, and copper. The leading imports are machinery, rough diamonds, crude oil, and wheat. Although Israel still imports more than it exports, the balance of trade is far more favorable now than it was in the early years of the state. Israel's chief trading partners are the United States and the Common Market countries of Europe, especially Great Britain and West Germany. Israel also trades with countries in Asia, Africa, and South America. The Israeli government owns El Al, which is Israel's international airline. Shipping has also grown markedly. Since the 1967 war, Israel has been attempting to provide for its defense needs domestically. There are two nuclear reactors, one near Tel Aviv and another near Dimona in the Negev, where scientists are doing research on such peacetime uses of atomic energy as the production of electricity and the desalination of seawater. Another growing industry in Israel is tourism, which has proved a valuable source of revenue. Jews from all over the world are attracted to Israel, the first Jewish state in 2,000 years, where the holy places of the Jewish religion are located. Many Christian and Muslim pilgrims also come to visit the holy places of their respective religions. The standard of living in Israel is high for a Middle Eastern nation and is comparable to the standard of living prevailing in Western Europe, although it is below that of the United States. In 1972 the per capita gross national product (GNP) was $2,200, as compared with a per capita GNP of $859 in 1950. The standard of living of the Arabs in Israel (who, with other non-Jews, make up around 15% of the population) has improved markedly since 1948. The government of Israel consists of a legislature called the Knesset, a president, a prime minister, and the cabinet. The Knesset has a single chamber with 120 seats and is elected for four years by universal adult suffrage according to a system of proportional representation. If circumstances warrant it, the Knesset can call for new elections before its term is up. The president is elected for five years by the Knesset. He forms a new government by selecting a member of the Knesset to serve as prime minister after consulting with the representatives of the political parties in the Knesset. The prime minister, in turn, appoints a cabinet, which must be approved by the Knesset; both the prime minister and the cabinet are responsible to the Knesset. Israel has more than a dozen political parties. The largest is the Israel Labor party, which was formed in 1968 by the merger of the three older Labor parties (Mapai, established in 1930; Achdut Avoda, dating from 1944; and Rafi, founded in 1965). The United Workers' party (Mapam), a leftist Zionist Socialist organization, joined with the Israel Labor party in recent years to fashion a political bloc called the Labor Alignment. Another bloc, center-rightist in policy, is Likud, consisting of Gahal (composed of the Herut Movement and the Israel Liberal party), the Free Center party, and other factions. Three religious parties form a smaller bloc, and among the remaining parties are the Independent Liberal party and two Communist organizations. In Israel the Arab minority has the same political rights as the Jewish majority, including the right to vote. Arab members have been elected to the Knesset. In addition, Arabs in Israel have their own schools in which the language of instruction is Arabic. Education at the primary level is free and compulsory for everyone. Hebrew and Arabic are both official languages of Israel. The state of Israel is the culmination of some 60 years of activity in ZIONISM. Following World War I, Great Britain received (1922) Palestine as a mandate from the League of Nations. The struggle by Jews for a Jewish state in Palestine had begun in the late 19th cent.; the militant opposition of the Arabs to such a state and the inability of the British to solve the problem led eventually to a session of the General Assembly of the United Nations in April, 1947, which established the United Nations Special Committee on Palestine (UNSCOP). In August UNSCOP reported a plan to divide Palestine into a Jewish state, an Arab state, and a small internationally administered zone including Jerusalem. The necessary two-thirds majority of the General Assembly, led by the United States and the USSR, adopted the UNSCOP recommendations on Nov. 29, 1947. Great Britain abstained, and the Arabs left the meeting, asserting their intention to resist. As the British began to withdraw early in 1948, Arabs and Jews prepared for war. On May 14, 1948, when the British high commissioner for Palestine departed, the state of Israel was proclaimed at Tel Aviv. On the same day it received the de facto recognition of the United States (on May 17 the USSR extended de jure recognition). The Arab states of Lebanon, Syria, Jordan, Egypt, and Iraq invaded Israel with their regular armies on May 14, 1948. The Jews were prepared, however, and the flight of most Palestinian Arabs from Jewish territory facilitated defense. On May 28, the Jews surrendered the Old City of Jerusalem to the Arab Legion of Jordan but held on in the New City. After delays, on June 11 there went into effect a four-week truce. Israeli territory was intact, and the Jews had gained footholds elsewhere. Fighting resumed on July 9, with the Jews gaining territory on all fronts except in Jerusalem. On July 18, a second cease-fire was concluded on order of the UN Security Council. Not until late Jan., 1949, were armistice agreements reached. In this war of independence, Israel had lost none of its own territory and had increased its holdings by about one-half. There seemed little likelihood of a new Arab state, for Jordan annexed the area adjoining its territory and Egypt was occupying the southwest coastal strip. Israel quickly developed its governmental structure. A state council with Chaim WEIZMANN as president and David BEN-GURION as prime minister functioned at Tel Aviv. In Jan., 1949, there were elections for the Knesset, and the Mapai (moderate socialist) and the religious parties formed a government. Ben-Gurion (Mapai) became prime minister, and Chaim Weizmann was elected national president. In the opposition the major elements were the left-wing socialist Mapam and the conservative Herut (the former Irgun Zvai Leumi), who insisted that Israel should take Jordan. Minor opposition groups included Communists and an Arab party. The elected government received recognition by Great Britain and de jure recognition from the United States. On May 11, 1949, Israel was admitted to the United Nations. The Israeli claim to Jerusalem was strengthened by the removal (Dec. 14, 1949) of the capital to that city. Since the Lausanne Conference of 1949, Israel has offered to take back a limited number of Arab refugees and to discuss financial compensation. After 1950, attempting to reach some sort of economic stability within, Israel also met the hostility of Arab nations without. The ever-expanding Arab economic boycott hampered its growth, and continuous attacks by Arab border marauders threatened its security. One major aim of the government was to gather in all Jews who wished to immigrate to Israel. This led to the 1950 Law of the Return, which provided for free and automatic citizenship for all immigrant Jews. David Ben-Gurion, although his pro-Western policies often met with opposition, continued to be the chief figure in the coalition government that administered Israel. Although he was forced to resign four times, on each occasion he was chosen again to head the government. Border incidents with Egypt, Syria, and Jordan continued, and bloody attacks and reprisals were sharply condemned by the United Nations but recurred. Trouble in the Gaza area reached new heights in 1955 and 1956 despite UN intervention. On Oct. 29, 1956, provoked by fierce Arab threats of invasion, Israel made a preemptive attack on Egyptian territory and within a few days conquered the Gaza Strip and the Sinai peninsula, while Britain and France invaded the area of the Suez Canal. Israel eventually yielded to strong pressure from the United States, the USSR, and the United Nations and removed its troops from Sinai in Nov., 1956, and from Gaza by March, 1957, as UN forces were sent to the Sinai and Gaza to keep peace between Egypt and Israel. Through this war Israel succeeded in gaining the use of the Red Sea, which gave it access to East Africa and East Asia and which was to increase its commerce considerably. After 1957, despite occasional border clashes with Jordan and Syria, Israel's foreign relations improved. Trade relations were developed with African and Asian countries, and economic relations with Western Europe also improved. In 1957, despite strong left-wing opposition, Ben-Gurion's government supported the Eisenhower doctrine of economic and military aid to Middle Eastern nations threatened by Soviet-directed Communism. By 1962, despite warning by the USSR and Egypt, most of the new nations of Africa had signed aid agreements with Israel. About this time Israel also became the scene of the celebrated trial of Adolf EICHMANN. In 1963, Ben-Gurion resigned as prime minister and was succeeded in that office by Levi ESHKOL. Eshkol had to cope with increased guerrilla incursions into Israel from Syria and the shelling of Israeli villages by the Syrian army from the Golan Heights. In May, 1967, Egyptian President Nasser mobilized the Egyptian army in Sinai. He next demanded that the UN Emergency Force withdraw from the Israel-Egyptian border, where it had been stationed since 1956. The secretary general of the UN acceded to Nasser's demand. Nasser then blockaded the Israeli port of Elat (on the Gulf of Aqaba) by closing the Strait of Tiran. Israel appealed to the Security Council, arguing that it had the right of passage in the Gulf of Aqaba, which is an international waterway. The Arab states got strong support from the USSR, but the Western powers remained relatively neutral. Gen. Moshe Dayan, who was credited with the success of Israel's war with Egypt in 1956, was appointed minister of defense. On June 5, 1967, Israel launched preemptive attacks against Egypt, Jordan, and Syria. In six days Israel occupied the Gaza Strip and the Sinai peninsula of Egypt, the Golan Heights of Syria, and the West Bank and Arab sector of Jerusalem (both under Jordanian rule), thereby giving the conflict the name of the Six-Day War. Cease-fires were obtained on all three fronts by the UN Security Council. The USSR tried unsuccessfully to get either the Security Council or the General Assembly, which met in special session, to require that Israel withdraw unconditionally from the territories occupied. Israel unified the Arab and Israeli sectors of Jerusalem and ignored the UN resolution that asked Israel not to alter the status of that city's Arab sector. On Nov. 22, 1967, the Security Council adopted a resolution calling for the withdrawal of Israeli forces from the Arab territories occupied in the war, the right of all states to live in peace within secure and recognized boundaries, freedom of navigation through international waterways in the area, and a just settlement of the Arab refugee problem. On Aug. 28, 1967, Arab leaders (except for Syria) met in Khartoum. They decided upon a policy of no peace, no negotiations, and no recognition of Israel; at the same time they supported the rights of the Palestinian Arabs. Israel continued to occupy the Arab territory taken in the Six-Day War. Arab guerrillas stepped up their incursions, operating largely from Jordan. Meanwhile, Israel issued a call for direct negotiations for peace, asking also for secure and recognized boundaries and the right of passage through the Red Sea and the Suez Canal. The Arab reaction was emphatically negative. After Eshkol's death on Feb. 26, 1969, Mrs. Golda Meir became prime minister. In Sept., 1970, President Nasser of Egypt died and was succeeded by Anwar Sadat. There followed an inconclusive period when there was neither peace nor war in the area. Then suddenly, on Oct. 6, 1973, Egypt and Syria attacked Israeli positions in the Sinai and the Golan Heights. Israel apparently was caught unprepared for combat on the Jewish holy day of Yom Kippur, the Day of Atonement. Other Arab states sent contingents of soldiers to aid in the attack on Israel; among these states was Jordan, although Jordan did not attack Israel directly across their common border. Egypt succeeded in sending troops in force across the Suez Canal to the east bank before being halted by the Israelis, who toward the end of the fighting managed to send their own troops across the Suez Canal to the west bank, encircle Egypt's Third Army on the east bank, and drive the Syrians even further back toward Damascus. A cease-fire was called for by the UN Security Council on Oct. 22 and again on Oct. 23 and went into effect shortly thereafter. In an attempt to lessen American support for Israel, the Arab nations subsequently ordered a cutback on oil exports and put an embargo on oil shipments to the United States. On Dec. 21, 1973, the first Arab-Israeli peace conference opened in Geneva, Switzerland, under UN auspices. An agreement to disengage Israeli and Egyptian forces was reached in Jan., 1974, largely through the mediation of U.S. Secretary of State Henry Kissinger. Israeli troops withdrew several miles into the Sinai, a UN buffer zone was established, and Egyptian forces reoccupied the east bank of the Suez Canal and a small, adjoining strip of land in the Sinai. A similar agreement between Israel and Syria was achieved in May, 1974, again through the efforts of Kissinger. Under its terms Israeli forces evacuated the Syrian lands captured in the 1973 war (while continuing to hold most of the territory conquered in 1967) and a UN buffer zone was created. Following this agreement, U.S. President Richard M. Nixon visited Israel and four Arab countries in an effort to promote the settlements. In the course of the disengagement negotiations, the Israelis had held a national election, the outcome of which was a setback to Mrs. Meir's Labor party. After several unsuccessful attempts to form a working coalition, she resigned and was succeeded (June 3,

1974) by Yitzhak RABIN, a former general and ambassador to the United States. Rabin was able to form a narrow majority coalition (61 of the 120 seats) in the Knesset, consisting of the Labor Alignment, the Independent Liberals, and the Civil Rights Movement (a small party formed in the early 1970s). The Rabin government was faced with the immediate problem of increased terrorist attacks by Palestinian commandos within the borders of Israel and with the long-range questions concerning the return of occupied territories and the recognition of the Palestinians. See Jorge García-Granados, *The Birth of Israel* (1948); N. de M. Bentwich, *Israel Resurgent* (1960); David Ben-Gurion, *Israel: Years of Challenge* (1965); Christopher Sykes, *Cross Roads to Israel* (1965); F. H. Gervasi, *The Case for Israel* (1967); David Horowitz, *The Economics of Israel* (1967); Meyer Levin, *The Story of Israel* (1967); Terence Prittie, *Israel: Miracle in the Desert* (rev. ed. 1968); Winston Burdett, *Encounter with the Middle East* (1969); Edwin Samuel, *The Structure of Society in Israel* (1969); H. H. Smith et al., *Area Handbook for Israel* (1970); Amos Elon, *The Israelis: Founders and Sons* (1971); Yehuda Karmon, *Israel: A Regional Geography* (1971); Ephraim Orni and Elisha Efrat, *Geography of Israel* (3d ed. 1971); Michael Brecher, *The Foreign Policy System of Israel* (1972); I. T. Naamani, *Israel: A Profile* (1972); A. S. Eban, *My Country: The Story of Modern Israel* (1973).

Israeli-Arab Wars: see ARAB-ISRAELI WARS.

Israëls, Jozef (yō'zəf ĕs'räĕls), 1824–1911, Dutch genre painter. In Amsterdam he painted somber and moving scenes from the life of the Dutch fishermen and peasantry, for which he soon became famous. After 1870 he lived at The Hague. His dramatic use of silvery-gray light is expressive of the melancholy character of his themes. Israëls was equally proficient in oil and watercolor and was an accomplished etcher. Among his best-known works are *The Zandvoort Fisherman, Toilers of the Sea,* and *David Singing before Saul* (all: Amsterdam) and *Expectation* (Metropolitan Mus.). His son, **Isaäc Israëls,** 1865–1934, a painter of the social life of his day, was greatly influenced in style by the impressionists. Representative works are at The Hague.

Issachar (ĭs'əkər), son of Jacob and Leah and the ancestor of one of the 12 tribes. The territory allotted to the tribe of Issachar extended along the west bank of the Jordan. Gen. 30.18; 46.13; 49.14; Num. 1.29; 2.5; Deut. 27.12; 33.18; Joshua 19.17; 1 Chron. 7.1–5.

Isserles, Moses ben Israel (ĭs'ərlĕs), c.1525–1572, Polish rabbi, annotator, and philosopher, known as Remah. He is best known for his halakic works, particularly for his criticism of, and Ashkenazic additions to, the code of Joseph ben Ephraim CARO. It was because of Isserles's additions that Caro's code was eventually accepted as authoritative by the Ashkenazic Jews.

Isshiah (ĭshī'ə). **1** See JESHAIAH **3**. **2** Levite of David's time. 1 Chron. 24.25. Jesiah: 1 Chron. 23.20.

Issus (ĭs'əs), ancient town of SE Asia Minor, now in Turkey, 5 mi (8 km) NW of Dörtyol. Located near the head of a gulf (the modern Gulf of İskenderun), Issus was on a narrow strip of land backed by high mountains. Nearby is the pass known as the Cilician Gates. Issus was the scene of three historic battles. In 333 B.C., Alexander there defeated the forces of Darius III of Persia. There in A.D. 194, Septimius Severus conquered Pescennius Niger, a claimant to the throne of the Roman empire. In 622 the Byzantine emperor Heraclius won at Issus the first of a series of battles in which the west regained territory formerly lost to the Persians. There is a famous Roman mosaic of the battle in the Naples museum.

Issyk-Kul (ēsĭk'-kōōl), lake, E Central Asian USSR, in the Kirghiz Republic, in the Ala-Tau mts. At an altitude of c.5,300 ft (1,620 m) and with an area of c.2,400 sq mi (6,220 sq km), it is one of the largest mountain lakes in the world. It reaches a depth of 2,303 ft (702 m), is slightly saline, and is ice free in winter.

Issy-les-Moulineaux (ēsē'-lā-mōōlēnō'), suburb SW of Paris (1968 pop. 51,666), Hauts-de-Seine dept., N central France. It is an industrial center where metals, aeronautical equipment, chemicals, cartridges, and beer are manufactured. The major heliport of Paris and a Catholic theology school are in Issy-les-Moulineaux.

Istakhr (ĭstä'kər), old town, S Iran. Built largely from the ruins of ancient Persepolis, 3 mi (4.8 km) away, it was a capital of the Sassanid dynasty. Istakhr stubbornly resisted (640–49) the Arabs but soon afterward lost its importance to Shiraz. The name also appears as Stakhr.

İstanbul (ĭs"tănbōōl', ĭstan'bōōl), city (1970 pop. 2,247,630), capital of İstanbul prov., NW Turkey, on both sides of the Bosporus at its entrance into the Sea of Marmara. Its name was officially changed from Constantinople to İstanbul in 1930; before A.D. 330 it was known as Byzantium. One of the great historic cities of the world, İstanbul is the chief city and seaport of Turkey as well as its commercial and financial center. Tobacco is processed, and textiles, glass, shoes, and cement are manufactured. The city is visited by many tourists and is a summer resort. (For the history of the city, see BYZANTIUM and CONSTANTINOPLE.) İstanbul is the seat of İstanbul Univ. (founded 1453 as a theological school; completely reorganized 1933), a technical university, and Univ. of the Bosporus (formerly Robert College). It is the see of the patriarch of the Greek Orthodox Church, of a Latin-rite patriarch of the Roman Catholic Church, and of a patriarch of the Armenian Church. The European part of İstanbul is the terminus of an international rail service (formerly called the Orient Express), and at Haydarpaşa station, on the Asian side, begins the Baghdad Railway. The part of İstanbul corresponding to historic Constantinople is situated entirely on the European side. It rises on both sides of the Golden Horn, an inlet of the Bosporus, on one of the finest sites of the world, and like Rome is built on seven hills. Several miles of its ancient moated and turreted walls are still standing. Outside the walls and N of the Golden Horn are the commercial quarter of Galata, originally a Genoese settlement; the quarter of Beyoğlu (formerly Pera), which under the Ottoman sultans was reserved for foreigners and their embassies; and Hasköy, the Jewish quarter. The Golden Horn is crossed by two bridges, the famous Galata bridge and the modern Atatürk bridge. The former leads into the historic quarter of Stambul, the ancient core of the city, abutting on the Bosporus and the Sea of Marmara. The quarter of Phanar in the northwest, near the former site of the palace of Blachernae of the Byzantine emperors, contains the see of the Greek Orthodox Church and is inhabited mainly by Greeks. Some of the palace walls are still standing. The present administrative districts of İstanbul include Fatih and Eminönü on the European side and Kadiköy (ancient Chalcedon) and Üsküdar (Scutari) on the Asian side. The chief monument surviving from Byzantine times is the HAGIA SOPHIA, one of the world's noblest works of architecture. Originally a church, it was converted into a mosque after the Ottoman conquest in 1453 and is now a museum. Excavations on the sites of the former Byzantine palaces have brought to light fine works of art, and İstanbul has many monuments of the Byzantine past. The city was destroyed (1509) by an earthquake and was rebuilt by Sultan Beyazid II. Turkish culture reached its height in the 16th cent. and from that period date most of its magnificent mosques, notably those of Beyazid II, Sulayman I, and Ahmed I. They all reflect the influence of the Hagia Sophia—yet are distinctly Turkish—and give the skyline of İstanbul its unique character, a succession of perfectly proportioned domes broken by minarets. In the gardens by the Bosporus stand the buildings of the Seraglio, the former palace of the Ottoman sultans, now a museum. The Seraglio, begun by Muhammad II in 1462, consists of many buildings and kiosks, grouped into three courts, the last of which contained the treasury, the harem, and the private apartments of the ruler. In the 19th cent. the sultans shifted (1853) their residence to the Dolma Bahçe Palace and the Yıldız Kiosk, N of Beyoğlu on the Bosporus. The environs of İstanbul, particularly the villas, gardens, castles, and small communities along the Bosporus, are famed for their beauty. Always a cosmopolitan city, İstanbul has preserved much of its international and polyglot character and contains sizeable foreign minorities. In 1973 the European and Asian sections of the city were linked by the opening of the Bosporus Bridge, one of the world's longest (3,524 ft/1,074 m) suspension bridges.

Isthmian games (ĭs'mēən), athletic events organized c.581 B.C. They were held at Corinth in the spring of the first and third years of the OLYMPIAD, and they honored Palaemon as well as Poseidon. The contests were generally like the OLYMPIC GAMES, but they were conducted on a smaller scale; the many added amusements and the convenient journey from Athens made the Isthmian games popular. The victor's prize was a crown of wild celery, but after Corinth was destroyed (146 B.C.) by the Romans and restored (44 B.C.) by Julius Caesar, the Isthmian games were reestablished for a time with a crown of fir as the victor's prize.

isthmus (ĭs'məs), narrow neck of land connecting two larger land areas. Since it commands the only land route between two large areas and is on two seas, an isthmus has great strategical and commercial importance and is a favorable situation for a city. In modern times many isthmuses have been cut through by canals to eliminate the necessity of land transport. The most important isthmuses are the Isthmus of Panama, connecting Central and South America, and the Isthmus of Suez, joining Asia and Africa. Canals were dug through both of these. The Isthmus of Corinth between the Morea peninsula and central Greece also has a canal.

Istria (ĭs'trēə), Serbo-Croatian *Istra,* mountainous peninsula c.1,500 sq mi (3,900 sq km), NW Yugoslavia, projecting into the N Adriatic between the gulfs of Trieste and Fiume. A section of the northwestern portion, including the city of Trieste, belongs to Italy. The area is thickly forested and is predominantly agricultural. PULA is the chief city and a shipbuilding center. The population is Yugoslav and Italian. Istria was inhabited by Illyrian tribes when it passed (2d cent. B.C.) to Rome. It remained under nominal Byzantine rule until the 8th cent. A.D. By that time, Slavs had settled in the rural areas and Italians in the cities. By the 15th cent. Austria and Venice had absorbed, respectively, the northeastern and southwestern parts of the region. The Treaty of Campo Formio (1797) and the Congress of Vienna (1815) added the Venetian part ot Austria. In 1919 all Istria passed to Italy, but the Italian peace treaty of 1947 gave most of it to Yugoslavia. The northwestern section passed to Trieste (1954).

Isuah (ĭs'yōōə), the same as ISHUAH.

Isui (ĭs'yōōī), son of Asher. Gen. 46.17. Jesui: Num. 26.44. Ishuai: 1 Chron. 7.30.

Itabuna (ētəbōō'nə), city (1970 pop. 113,409), Bahia state, E Brazil, on the Itabuna River. It is a cacao-producing center and has a well-developed cattle industry.

Itagaki, Taisuke (tī'sōōkē ētä'gäkē), 1837–1919, Japanese statesman. After taking part in the MEIJI RESTORATION, he became (1869) a councillor of state. A samurai of Tosa, he opposed domination of the government by the Choshu and Satsuma clans and demanded representative institutions. He and others advocated war with Korea in 1873, and, unsuccessful, they withdrew from the government. The next year he helped launch a campaign for an elective assembly that led to the establishment of a senate in 1875 and, in 1878, of prefectural assemblies, with advisory powers only. Convinced that organized political action was the only way to force constitutional reform, Itagaki founded (1877) the RISSHISHA [Society of Independence], which was severely critical of the government. In 1881, Itagaki set up the Jiyuto [Liberal] party, a forerunner of the Seiyukai. He was home minister under Hirobumi Ito and in 1898 was associated with Shige nobu Okuma in an attempt to form a party government.

Italian architecture properly includes the several styles employed in Italy after the Roman period. ROMANESQUE ARCHITECTURE (12th cent.) reveals the first use of the groined VAULT with projecting ribs; it shows also the development of a type of BASILICA having side galleries. It was developed especially in Lombardy and is superbly exemplified in Sant' Ambrogio, Milan. There are two regional forms of Italian Romanesque—Tuscan (including Florentine) and southern. The cathedral of Pisa (1063–1118), with its campanile (the "leaning tower"), admirably displays the Tuscan characteristics, chief of which is the decorative use of tier upon tier of columns. Tuscan architects of the period also made a specialty of using variegated marbles and followed the antique style in this rather closely; while the Romanesque of the south, as in the cathedral of Monreale, is characterized by its rich mosaics and delicate carvings, which show Byzantine, Saracenic, and Norman influences. Gothic architecture was not greatly developed in Italy; a notable exception is the cathedral of Milan, built in part by foreign architects. The Church of St. Francis in Assisi (begun 1228) and the cathedral at Siena (begun 1269), among others, also have Gothic elements—the ribbed vault and the pointed arch (see GOTHIC ARCHITECTURE AND ART). However, the Italians largely adhered to the native tradition of building in terms of simple basilican proportions with massive walls, a practice that was carried into the Renaissance. In the 15th cent. there began a conscious revival of classical antiquity (see RENAISSANCE ART AND ARCHITECTURE). Brunelleschi emulated the ancient Romans in his masterly construction (1420–34) of the dome of the Florentine cathedral, and Michelozzo used antique elements in the courtyard of the Medici Palace, Florence (begun

1444). Alberti borrowed freely from a Roman triumphal arch in his design (1450s) for the exterior of the Tempio Malatestiano in Rimini. Bramante, Antonio da Sangallo, Peruzzi, and Raphael made Rome the center of exciting architectural developments in the first half of the 16th cent., when St. Peter's was the most important project under way. Vignola did significant work in Rome in the latter part of the 16th cent., while in N Italy the formal classicism of Palladio was a potent factor in the spreading of Renaissance architecture throughout Europe. The monumental work of Michelangelo reflected elements of MANNERISM and his influence extended into the BAROQUE period. The beginning of the 17th cent. ushered in the drama of the baroque with Maderno's nave and facade for St. Peter's, to which a magnificent colonnaded plaza was added, designed by Bernini, the foremost genius of the period. Other outstanding architects of the century included Borromini, Cortona, and Rainaldi. After their deaths, Carlo Fontana became the most influential architect in Italy, transmitting the ideas of the great baroque masters to many of the most important architects of Europe. Italy, however, no longer possessed the undisputed leadership in European architecture, although in the 18th cent. Piedmont in N Italy produced remarkable designers, such as Guarini, Juvarra, and Vittone. Nineteenth-century Italian architecture, such as Giuseppe Sacconi's Victor Emmanuel monument, shows a decline in quality and increased pomposity. In the 20th cent. Italy has followed the trends of MODERN ARCHITECTURE; its outstanding practitioners include Pier Luigi Nervi, Giuseppe Terragni, and Gio Ponti. See Rudolf Wittkower, *Art and Architecture in Italy, 1600 to 1750* (1958) and *Architectural Principles in the Age of Humanism* (3d ed. 1962); C. L. V. Meeks, *Italian Architecture, 1750-1914* (1966); T. W. West, *A History of Architecture in Italy* (1968).

Italian art. In Italy art has engendered great public interest and involvement, resulting in the consistent production of monumental and spectacular works. In addition, Italian art has nearly always been closely allied with the intellectual and/or religious currents of its day, while retaining its own remarkable past as a continual source of inspiration. Throughout the Middle Ages, Italian art consisted primarily of architectural decorations (frescoes and mosaics). Byzantine art in Italy was a highly formal and refined decoration with a standardized calligraphy and an admirable use of color and gold. Until the 13th cent., art in Italy was almost entirely regional, affected by external European and Eastern currents. After c.1250 the art of the various regions developed characteristics in common, so that a certain unity as well as great originality is observable. Major painters, including Guido of Siena, Cimabue, and Duccio di Buoninsegna, while retaining many of the Byzantine conventions, introduced a new naturalism and a more direct appeal to human emotion. The same spirit is seen in the powerful sculpture of Nicola Pisano. He made use of elements from classical antiquity, as did Pietro Cavallini in his fresco paintings in Rome. But it is with Giotto di Bondone, a contemporary of Dante, that the new painting first takes on life and warmth. His style, perfected c.1300, determined the future course of art in Italy. His figures abandon prescribed gestures and cryptic silence. They walk and speak and express joy and sorrow. A new idealism and belief in human dignity find expression in his simple and compelling frescoes in Padua and Florence. His immediate followers, Taddeo Gaddi, Bernardo Daddi, Giottino, and others spread his teachings and technique. Simultaneously, art flourished in 14th-century Siena, following the example set by Duccio and developing a more Gothic manner. Among the superb artists of the Sienese school were the painters Simone Martini and the brothers Pietro and Ambrogio Lorenzetti and the sculptors Giovanni Pisano and Arnolfo di Cambio. The Black Death (1348) severely curtailed artistic productivity for the next two generations. Apocalyptic frescoes were created during this time by Andrea Orcagna in Florence and by Francesco Traini in Pisa. The pessimistic content of this art was superseded in the early 15th cent. by an elegant manner known as the International style (see GOTHIC ARCHITECTURE AND ART), manifest in the works of Lorenzo Monaco, Gentile da Fabriano, Masolino da Panicale, and to a certain extent Pisanello. In the second decade of the 15th cent., Italy—primarily Florence—took the lead in the formation of an art that was to affect Europe profoundly for more than 500 years (see RENAISSANCE ART AND ARCHITECTURE). Political stability was established in several regions and powerful ruling families produced the patrons of art that made the artistic flowering possible. Donatello, Brunelleschi, and Alberti were among the first to look consciously toward classical antiquity as a model for their work. They, with Masaccio, whose style recalls Giotto's monumentality, began to devise the optical system of PERSPECTIVE. They also set a high artistic standard that was emulated by succeeding generations. In the first half of the 15th cent. the sculptor Lorenzo Ghiberti embellished the Florentine baptistery with his splendid bronze doors, winning the commission in competition against another great sculptor, Jacopo della Quercia of Siena. Other sculptors, such as Desiderio da Settignano, Antonio Rossellino, and Bertoldo di Giovanni, carried the tradition established by Donatello through to Michelangelo, while the workshop of the Della Robbias during the 15th cent. produced a great quantity of superb terra-cotta relief sculptures. The Tuscan painters, including Fra Angelico and Fra Filippo Lippi, created works of exquisite color. Paolo Uccello and Andrea del Castagno contributed refinements to the understanding of the laws of perspective. Domenico Veneziano and Piero della Francesca were attracted to Florence, while Florentine artists such as Donatello and Fra Filippo Lippi ventured into N Italy. By the second half of the *quattrocento,* schools in N Italy began to flourish. Squarcione was the teacher of many painters, among them Carlo Crivelli and the powerful master Andrea Mantegna, who painted magnificent frescoes for churches and palaces in Padua and Mantua. His father-in-law, Jacopo Bellini, a superb draftsman, had two sons, Gentile and Giovanni Bellini, who continued his Venetian workshop. Gentile painted detailed and delightful scenes of Venice, as did Carpaccio. Giovanni Bellini initiated a century of Venetian greatness with the richness of color for which Venice became famous. The Vivarini family produced paintings notable for a bright, translucent color. Antonello da Messina, a Sicilian who was briefly in Venice, was one of the first Italians to use the medium of oil painting, with remarkable effect. The impact of Mantegna's style was felt in Ferrara in the paintings of Cosimo Tura, Francesco del Cossa, and Ercole de' Roberti. In Siena during the 15th cent. the major artists included Sassetta, Giovanni di Paolo, Francesco di Giorgio, and the sculptor Vecchietta. The last half of the *quattrocento* in Florence saw the rise of a group of painters celebrated for their lyrical style—Botticelli, Filippino Lippi, and Baldovinetti—as well as the more austere masters Signorelli and Antonio Pollaiuolo. Perugino and particularly Melozzo da Forlì were among the notable painters of Umbria. Benozzo Gozzoli and Ghirlandaio decorated Florence with exquisite narrative frescoes. The Florentine sculptor Verrocchio infused his works with a fresh vitality and sense of drama. But in the years around the turn of the 16th cent. the works of these artists were reduced in significance as the figures of the High Renaissance emerged. Michelangelo, Leonardo da Vinci, and Raphael vied with one another in Florence and in Rome to create a perfect art. Raphael's idealized Madonnas and portraits and his Vatican frescoes exerted a tremendous influence over European artists. Whereas his works have come down to us fully realized, the schemes of Michelangelo and Leonardo remain largely on paper. Leonardo has left only a small group of magnificent easel paintings and one grand but deteriorated fresco, *The Last Supper* in Milan. His unparalleled, incredibly versatile genius is most clearly revealed in his notebooks, replete with extraordinary plans of all varieties. Michelangelo's magnificent ceiling and *Last Judgment* for the Sistine Chapel of the Vatican are the only monumental projects in painting, sculpture, or architecture that materialized according to his plans; most of his sculptural masterpieces are fragments of vast designs that were never executed in their entirety. In the early 16th cent. some of the grandeur of the High Renaissance artists was echoed in the works of Andrea del Sarto, Sebastiano del Piombo, and Fra Bartolommeo, but other followers of the great masters in Rome, in Florence, and elsewhere developed a complex, bizarre style in their own right known as MANNERISM. Among these were the painters Pontormo, Giulio Romano, Parmigianino, Il Rosso, Primaticcio, and later Bronzino and Vasari, as well as the sculptors Giovanni Bologna, Bandinelli, Ammanati, Buontalenti, and Benvenuto Cellini. But the mannerist style declined by the second half of the 16th cent. into a rather dry academism, seen in the works of the Zuccari family. Venice was comparatively unaffected by the elegant, tortuous forms of mannerism. At the beginning of the 16th cent. two superlative Venetian masters, the mysterious, short-lived Giorgione and the long-lived, prolific Titian, continued the tradition established by Giovanni Bellini of sumptuous, poetic coloring. They created sensuous figures whose contours melted into luminous, atmospheric landscapes. Their stylistic effects influenced the works of Palma Vecchio, Pordenone, the Bassano family, the Ferrarese Dosso Dossi, and the lavish banquet scenes of Paolo Veronese. Only Tintoretto veered away from the harmonious canvases that were typical of the Venetians. He created instead twisted, dramatic, elongated forms, related to those of the mannerists but more vigorously conceived. In Parma, Correggio decorated church vaults with lively figures floating softly on clouds—a scheme that was to have a profound influence on baroque ceiling paintings. In the early 17th cent. Rome became the center of a renewal of Italian dominance in the arts. The stormy chiaroscuro paintings of Caravaggio and the robust, illusionistic paintings of the Bolognese Carracci family gave rise to the BAROQUE. Domenichino, Francesco Albani, and later Andrea Sacchi were among those who carried out the classical implications in the art of the Carracci. On the other hand, Guido Reni, Guercino, Gentileschi, Lanfranco, and later Pietro da Cortona and Padre Pozzo, while thoroughly trained in a classical-allegorical mode, were at first inclined to paint dynamic compositions full of gesticulating figures in a manner closer to that of Caravaggio. The towering virtuoso of baroque exuberance and grandeur in sculpture and architecture was Bernini. Toward 1640 many of the painters leaned toward the classical style that had been brought to the fore in Rome by the French expatriate Nicolas Poussin. The sculptors Alessandro Algardi and the Fleming François Duquenoy also tended toward the classical. Notable late baroque artists include the Genoese Gaulli and the Neapolitans Luca Giordano and Francesco Solimena. The leading lights of the 18th cent. came from Venice. Among them were the brilliant exponent of the ROCOCO style, Tiepolo; the architectural painters Guardi, Canaletto, Piazzetta, and Bellotto; and the engraver of Roman antiquities, Piranesi. Fantastic landscape was brought into vogue in the works of Castiglione and Magnasco, who both worked in Naples. During the late 18th and 19th cent. Italy continued to serve as a training school for the artists of the world but tended to rest on her laurels. In the mid-19th cent. the group known as the MACCHIAIOLI gave new life to landscape and GENRE subjects. Early in the 20th cent. the exponents of FUTURISM developed a dynamic vision of the modern world while Chirico expressed a strange metaphysical quietude and Modigliani joined the SCHOOL OF PARIS. Gifted contemporary artists include the sculptors Giacomo Manzù, Marino Marini, and the still-life painter Giorgio Morandi. In the second half of the 20th cent. Italian designers have profoundly influenced international styles with their imaginative and ingenious functional works. See articles on individual artists, e.g., MASACCIO. See also ITALIAN ARCHITECTURE. See Anthony Blunt, *Artistic Theory in Italy, 1450-1600* (1940, repr. 1956); Walter Friedlaender, *Mannerism and Anti-Mannerism in Italian Painting* (1957, repr. 1965); Rudolf Wittkower, *Art and Architecture in Italy, 1600-1750* (2d ed. 1965); John White, *Art and Architecture in Italy, 1250-1400* (1966); Charles Seymour, Jr., *Sculpture in Italy, 1400-1500* (1966); S. J. Freedberg, *Painting in Italy, 1500-1600* (1970); John Pope-Hennessy, *An Introduction to Italian Sculpture* (3 vol., 2d ed. 1971).

Italian East Africa, former federation of the Italian colonies of Eritrea and Italian Somaliland and the kingdom of Ethiopia. The federation was formed (1936) to consolidate the administration of the three areas. During the federation's existence, efforts were made to construct road systems and to establish new industries and agricultural plantations. Resistance to Italian rule was particularly strong in Ethiopia, and when British forces invaded the federation in Jan., 1941, they received widespread support. By Dec., 1942, the Italians had been totally defeated. Ethiopia was restored its independence; Eritrea was placed under Ethiopian control in 1952; and Italian Somaliland, after a period as a UN trusteeship, became part of Somalia in 1960.

Italian greyhound, breed of sleek, active TOY DOG that stands from 6 to 10 in. (15.2-25.4 cm) high at the shoulder and weighs from 7 to 10 lb (3.2-4.5 kg). Its short, thin coat is glossy and may be any shade of red, fawn, blue, cream, or white. Although the belief that it was raised as a pet in ancient Rome and Pompeii is difficult to document, it is certain that it was a distinct breed and a favorite of the court in southern Europe by the Middle Ages. It was introduced into England more than three centuries ago, where it was brought to refinement. Although a relatively rare breed today, the Italian greyhound's striking appearance and extremely tractable disposition make it a desirable house pet. See DOG.

Italian language, member of the Romance group of the Italic subfamily of the Indo-European family of languages (see ROMANCE LANGUAGES). The official language of Italy and San Marino, and one of the official languages of Switzerland, Italian is spoken by about 55 million people in Italy, 20,000 in San Marino, 400,000 in Switzerland, another 1.3 million in other European countries, and approximately 5 million in North and South America. Historically, Italian is a daughter language of Latin (see LATIN LANGUAGE). It is not known exactly when Italian could be distinguished from its parent tongue; however, no text in Italian is recorded before the 10th cent. A.D. The idiom of Florence, one of the Tuscan dialects of Italian, became dominant from the end of the 13th cent. to the middle of the 14th cent., largely owing to the growing prestige of the city of Florence and the literary works written in the Florentine dialect during that period. These literary works included Dante's *Divine Comedy* and the vernacular writings of Petrarch and Boccaccio. Thus, although Italian had (and still has) a great many dialects, it was the culturally important idiom of Florence that in time gave rise to modern standard Italian. The dialect of the Italian capital, Rome, also has influenced modern standard Italian. Actually, the Italian language did not change too much after the 14th cent., so that modern educated Italians are still able to read Dante with comparatively little difficulty. More widespread education and the mass media have greatly aided the spread of standard Italian throughout Italy. The Roman alphabet is used for Italian. The employment of diacritics is limited to the grave accent (`), which sometimes serves to make clear where the stress of a word is to fall (as in *caffè*="coffee") or distinguishes between homonyms (as with *ne*="of it" or "of them," but *ne . . . nè*="neither. . . nor"). The pronunciation of the language follows the spelling very closely. Italian is often described both as the language of art and music and as the language best suited to singing. Since the Renaissance its general cultural importance has been considerable. See C. H. Grandgent, *From Latin to Italian* (1927); M. A. Pei, *The Italian Language* (1941); Ernst Pulgram, *The Tongues of Italy: Prehistory and History* (1958); Bruno Migliorini, *The Italian Language* (tr. 1966).

Italian literature. Italian vernacular literature, as distinct from works in Latin and French, began to take shape in the 13th cent. with the imitation of Provençal lyric poetry at the court of Frederick II in Sicily. The Sicilians are credited with inventing the SONNET, which became the most widely used form of Italian poetry and later flourished throughout Europe. The Sicilian style was dominant in the north until c.1260, when Guido Guinizelli, a Bolognese poet and jurist, moved from the Provençal conception of COURTLY LOVE to a more mystical and philosophical spirituality. The poets who took Guinizelli as their model originated the "sweet new style" (*dolce stil novo*). The group included Guido Cavalcanti, Cino da Pistoia, Lapo Gianni, and Dino Frescobaldi. Also one of the group was Dante, whose youthful *Vita nuova,* part prose and part poetry, recounts the poet's love for Beatrice in terms of the transcendental view of love typical of the *stil novo.* Dante's other works, of which the *Divine Comedy* is a masterpiece of world literature, go beyond the themes and manner of *stil novo* and embrace the whole of contemporary knowledge and experience. Dante invented the difficult terza rima (iambic tercets) for his epic journey through Hell, Purgatory, and Paradise. The 13th cent. also produced folk poetry, doctrinal poetry, imitations of the chansons de geste in various dialects, and a magnificent flowering of religious poetry in the *laudi* of Jacopone da Todi and in the *Hymn to Created Things* of St. Francis of Assisi. *Laudi* in dialogue form represent the beginning of dramatic literature, the *sacre rappresentazioni.* Prose works included translations from the Latin and French as well as collections of tales, anecdotes, and witty sayings. The two great writers of the 14th cent., Petrarch and Boccaccio, sought out and imitated the works of antiquity and cultivated their own artistic personalities. Petrarch achieved fame through his collection of poems, the *Canzoniere,* in which he gave Provençal and *stil novo* themes a peculiarly intimate and personal expression. Petrarch's poetry served as the model for European lyricism until the Romantic period. Equally influential was Boccaccio's *Decameron,* a collection of 100 novellas within a framework, which founded the short-story genre. Giovanni Sercambi and Franco Sacchetti in the 14th cent. and Matteo Bandello and Agnolo Firenzuola in the 16th cent. were among the numerous writers who continued the tradition of vivid, realistic, and often licentious storytelling in prose. The Tuscan vernacular that had been established by Dante, Petrarch, and Boccaccio was inhibited by a strong return to Latin in the 15th cent. After the sterile century that followed the Black Death (1348), the humanists, with a few exceptions, wrote in Latin. In the circle of Lorenzo de' Medici, however, the vernacular was used in popular, Petrarchan, and pastoral poetry, and in a return to medieval subject matter. Luigi Pulci's grotesque *Morgante* (c.1480) recounts the adventures of Orlando (Charlemagne's Roland) and other paladins with great comic verve. Boiardo's *Orlando innamorato* (3 parts, 1483–1544) adds Breton subject matter to the Carolingian and introduces motifs from classical mythology and contemporary society. But the great masterpiece of Italian Renaissance poetry is Ariosto's *Orlando furioso* (1516, rev. 1521 and 1536), in which varied and improbable adventures are worked into an aesthetic whole. The great lyric poet Tasso in *Gerusalemme liberata* (1580) wrote a chivalric Christian epic, making use of the same form (ottava rima), with attention to the Aristotelian canons of unity. Other Renaissance genres brought to a high level of perfection by outstanding writers were the pastoral poems (Politian, Tasso, and Guarini); the pastoral romance (Sannazaro); the Petrarchan lyric (Bembo, Michelangelo, Gaspara Stampa); imitations of classical tragedy (Trissino) and classical comedy (Machiavelli); dialogues in the Platonic manner (Castiglione's *The Courtier*); treatises on a variety of topics (Leonardo's *Della pittura;* Alberti's *Della famiglia;* Bembo's *Prose della volgar lingua,* which established the principle of linguistic purism for Italian literature; and Machiavelli's *The Prince*); biographical and autobiographical writings (Vasari, Machiavelli, and Cellini); and history (Guicciardini and Machiavelli). In the early 17th cent. philosophic and scientific prose (Campanella, Galileo) continued and surpassed the achievements of Giordano Bruno. But the new literary style, *secentismo,* or *marinismo* (from Giambattista Marino), aimed at dazzling the reader by the opulent use of rhetorical devices. At the end of the century the Arcadians began a movement to restore simplicity and classical restraint to poetry, as in Metastasio's heroic melodramas. The mock-heroic epic (Tassoni), the opera, and commedia dell'arte were minor genres cultivated in the 17th cent. The renewal of Italian culture in the 18th cent. produced major works of journalism (Gaspare Gozzi, Giuseppe Baretti, and the Milanese *Caffè*), philosophical and historical erudition (Vico, Muratori, and Tiraboschi), and translations from classical antiquity and from contemporary European writers. The outstanding Italian representatives of the Enlightenment were Carlo Goldoni, whose comedies of character drew upon contemporary life, Vittorio Alfieri, whose classical tragedies exalted freedom, and Giuseppe Parini, whose satirical poetry attacked the social abuses of the privileged. The Napoleonic period was both classical and romantic. The poetry of Vincenzo Monti typifies the first direction, and the work of Ugo Foscolo belongs to the second. A distinguishing feature of Italian romanticism was its political involvement in the struggle for Italian independence, the RISORGIMENTO: Poems, historical novels, and political works, such as Giuseppe Mazzini's, attest to this. Alessandro Manzoni's literary conversion included the rejection of classical mythology in favor of Christian subject matter, and of classical tragedy for Romantic drama. His historical novel, *I promessi sposi* (1825–27), which introduced the genre to Italy, combined social and psychological realism with Roman Catholic doctrine and established a new Italian linguistic norm and prose style. Giacomo Leopardi rejected the program of romanticism but wrote lyric poetry in which the romantic themes of despair predominate. In the second half of the 19th cent. Francesco de Sanctis, literary critic and historian, laid the theoretical and aesthetic foundations of modern Italian criticism, later elaborated by the philosopher Benedetto Croce. Giosuè Carducci brought to poetry a virility and classicism long absent. But Pascoli and D'Annunzio had a more lasting influence. Gabriele D'Annunzio, poet, novelist, and dramatist, employed sensuous, musical, and precious language. Giovanni Pascoli is Italy's great symbolist poet of the subconscious. The naturalistic, the irrational, and the decadent are also revealed in the work of the playwright and novelist Luigi Pirandello. Pirandello's prose roots are in Sicilian verismo, the impersonal, objective regionalism of Verga's works. Major 20th-century novelists of note are Italo Svevo, Alberto Moravia, Giuseppe di Lampedusa, Ignazio Silone, Elio Vittorini, Cesare Pavese, Italo Calvino, Pier Paolo Pasolini, and Carlo Gadda: Their work is variously marked by psychological analysis, social consciousness, and formal and linguistic experimentation. The outstanding poets are Giuseppe Ungaretti, Eugenio Montale, Umberto Saba, and Salvatore Quasimodo. See articles on individual writers, e.g., DANTE. See J. H. Whitfield, *A Short History of Italian Literature* (1964); Francesco de Sanctis, *History of Italian Literature* (tr., 2 vol., 1968); Eugenio Donadoni, *A History of Italian Literature* (tr. 1969); Cesare Foligno; *Epochs of Italian Literature* (1920, repr. 1970); P. M. Riccio, *Italian Authors of Today* (1970); J. A. Molinaro, ed., *Petrarch to Pirandello* (1973).

Italian pointer: see SPINONE ITALIANO.

Italian Somaliland: see SOMALI DEMOCRATIC REPUBLIC.

Italian Wars, 1494–1559, efforts by the great European powers to control the small independent states of Italy. Renaissance ITALY was split into numerous rival states, most of which sought foreign alliances to increase their individual power. It thus became prey to the national states that had begun to emerge in Europe. Foremost among those were France and Spain, whose prolonged struggle for supremacy in Italy was to end Italian liberties for more than three centuries. The wars began when, in 1494, CHARLES VIII of France invaded Italy and seized (1495) Naples without effort, only to be forced to retreat by a coalition of Spain, the Holy Roman emperor, the pope, Venice, and Milan. His successor, LOUIS XII, prepared a new invasion by diplomatically isolating his first objective, Milan, then ruled by Ludovico SFORZA. In 1499 the French, under Gian Giacomo TRIVULZIO, occupied Milan and Genoa. In 1500, Louis tackled his next objective, Naples, by agreeing to its conquest and partition with Ferdinand V of Spain and by securing the consent of Pope ALEXANDER VI. Alexander's son, Cesare BORGIA, who held a French command, himself had a huge territorial stake in the scheme. Naples was occupied in 1501, but disagreement between the Spanish and the French flared into open warfare in 1502. Defeated by Gonzalo Fernández de Córdoba at Cerignola and at the Garigliano (1503), Louis XII consented to the Treaties of Blois (1504–5), keeping Milan and Genoa but pledging Naples to Spain. Trouble began again when Pope JULIUS II formed (1508) an alliance against Venice with France, Spain, and Holy Roman Emperor MAXIMILIAN I (see CAMBRAI, LEAGUE OF). However, shortly after the French victory over the Venetians at Agnadello (1509), Julius made peace with Venice and began to form the HOLY LEAGUE (1510) in order to expel the French "barbarians" from Italy. The French, although they lost their ablest commander, Gaston de FOIX, in 1512, held their own until the Swiss cantons decided to intervene. The Swiss stormed Milan (1512), which they nominally restored to the Sforzas, routed the French at Novara (1513), and controlled Lombardy until they were defeated in turn by Louis's successor, Francis I, at MARIGNANO (1515). By the peace of Noyon (1516), Naples remained in Spanish hands and Milan was returned to France. However, the rivalry between FRANCIS I and CHARLES V, king of Spain and (after 1519) Holy Roman emperor, reopened warfare in 1521. Defeated at La Bicocca (1522) and captured at Pavia (1525), Francis signed the Treaty of Madrid (1526), by which he renounced his Italian claims and ceded Burgundy. This he repudiated, as soon as he was liberated, by forming the League of Cognac with Pope CLEMENT VII, Henry VIII of England, Venice, and Florence. To punish the pope, Charles V sent Charles de BOURBON against Rome, which was sacked for a full week (May, 1527). The French, under the vicomte de LAUTREC, seized Genoa with the aid of Andrea DORIA (July), and they were advancing to rescue the pope when Clement submitted to the emperor's terms. Lautrec, assisted by the Genoese fleet, laid siege to Naples instead, but a quarrel between Francis and Doria led (1528) to the defection of the fleet, the loss of Genoa, and, after Lautrec's death, the abandonment of the siege. The war ended (1529) with the Treaty of Cambrai (see CAMBRAI, TREATY OF) and the renunciation of Francis's claims in Italy. Francis's two subsequent wars, which, excepting the inconclusive victory of Ceresole (1544), were fought outside Italy, ended in failure. Francis died (1547), having renounced Naples (for the third time) in the Treaty of CRÉPY. Complete Spanish supremacy in Italy was obtained by the Treaty of CATEAU-CAMBRÉSIS (1559), which gave the Two Sicilies and MILAN to PHILIP II. The wars, though ruinous to Italy, had helped to spread the Italian

Renaissance in Western Europe. From the military viewpoint, they signified the passing of chivalry, which found its last great representative in the seigneur de BAYARD. The use of Swiss and German mercenaries was characteristic of the wars, and artillery passed its first major test. See F. L. Taylor, *Art of War in Italy, 1494 to 1529* (1921).

italic: see TYPE.

Italic languages, subfamily of the Indo-European family of languages that may be divided into two groups. The first group consists of the ancient Italic languages and dialects that were once spoken in Italy. The most important of these were Latin, Faliscan, Oscan, and Umbrian; Latin was the only one to survive antiquity (see LATIN LANGUAGE). From Latin are derived the ROMANCE LANGUAGES, which in turn comprise the second (or medieval and modern) group of the Italic subfamily; they include Catalan, French, Italian, Portuguese, Provençal, Rhaeto-Romanic, Rumanian, and Spanish. The ancient Italic languages, with the exception of Latin, are now preserved chiefly in inscriptions, although occasional references in ancient authors and a number of proper and place names furnish added evidence. Latin, however, is amply recorded in numerous literary works as well as in inscriptions. The earliest existing inscription in an Italic language is in Latin and goes back to the 5th or 6th cent. B.C. At first the use of Latin was limited to Rome and the area around it, but the Romans spread their language throughout Italy and eventually over their vast empire. Faliscan, which is closely related to Latin, was once prevalent in an area in S Etruria, which is N of Rome. It is thought that people speaking Latin and Faliscan first entered and settled in Italy before or about 1000 B.C. and that the speakers of Oscan and Umbrian probably arrived somewhat later. Umbrian, which was current in the region of Umbria in central Italy NE of Rome, was superseded by Latin in time. Oscan was spoken in central and S Italy and NE Sicily. It too was finally absorbed by Latin. In general, the texts and records of the ancient Italic languages, including Latin, are written in alphabets that can be traced back to the Greek alphabet, often by way of the Etruscan alphabet. See INDO-EUROPEAN. See Joshua Whatmough, *The Foundations of Italy* (1937); R. S. Conway, *The Italic Dialects* (2 vol., 1897, repr. 1967).

Italy, Ital. *Italia,* republic (1973 est. pop. 55,300,000), 116,303 sq mi (301,225 sq km), S Europe, bordering on France in the northwest, the Ligurian Sea and the Tyrrhenian Sea in the west, the Ionian Sea in the south, the Adriatic Sea in the east, Yugoslavia in the northeast, and Austria and Switzerland in the north. The country includes the large Mediterranean islands of SICILY and SARDINIA and several small islands, notably ELBA, CAPRI, ISCHIA, and the LIPARI ISLANDS. Vatican City (see under VATICAN) and SAN MARINO are two independent enclaves on the Italian mainland. ROME is Italy's capital and largest city; other important cities include MILAN, NAPLES, TURIN, GENOA, PALERMO, BOLOGNA, FLORENCE, CATANIA, VENICE, BARI, TRIESTE, MESSINA, VERONA, PADUA, CAGLIARI, TARANTO, BRESCIA, and LEGHORN. The country is divided into 20 regions, which are subdivided into a total of 94 provinces. The great majority of the population speaks Italian (including several dialects); there are small German-, French-, and Slavic-speaking minorities. Almost all Italians are Roman Catholic. About 75% of Italy is mountainous or hilly, and roughly 20% of the country is forested. There are narrow strips of low-lying land along the Adriatic coast and parts of the Tyrrhenian coast. Northern Italy, made up largely of a vast plain that is contained by the Alps in the north and drained by the Po River and its tributaries, comprises the regions of LIGURIA, PIEDMONT, Valle d'Aosta (see AOSTA, VALLE D'), LOMBARDY, TRENTINO-ALTO ADIGE, VENETIA, FRIULI-VENEZIA GIULIA, and part of EMILIA-ROMAGNA (which extends into central Italy). It is the richest part of the country, with the best farmland, the chief port (Genoa), and the largest industrial centers. Northern Italy also has a flourishing tourist trade on the Italian Riviera, in the Alps (including the Dolomites), on the shores of its beautiful lakes (Lago Maggiore, Lake Como, and Lake Garda), and in Venice. Gran Paradiso (13,323 ft/4,061 m), the highest peak wholly situated within Italy, rises in Valle d'Aosta. The Italian peninsula, bootlike in shape and traversed in its entire length by the Apennines (which continue on into Sicily), comprises central Italy (MARCHE, TUSCANY, UMBRIA, and LATIUM regions) and southern Italy (CAMPANIA, BASILICATA, ABRUZZI, MOLISE, CALABRIA, and APULIA regions). Central Italy contains great historic and cultural centers such as Rome, Florence, PISA, SIENA, PERUGIA, ASSISI, URBINO, Bologna, RAVENNA, RIMINI, FERRARA, and PARMA. The major cities of S Italy, generally the poorest and least developed part of the country, include Naples, Bari, BRINDISI, FOGGIA, and Taranto. Except for the Po and Adige, Italy has only short rivers, among which the Arno and the Tiber are the best known. Most of Italy enjoys a Mediterranean climate; however, that of Sicily is subtropical, and in the Alps there are long and severe winters. The country has great scenic beauty—the majestic Alps in the north, the soft and undulating hills of Umbria and Tuscany, and the romantically rugged landscape of the S Apennines. The Bay of Naples, dominated by Mt. Vesuvius, is one of the world's most famous sights. Italy began to industrialize late in comparison to other European nations, and until World War II was largely an agricultural country. However, after 1950 industry was developed rapidly so that by the early 1970s it contributed about 40% of the annual national product and agriculture only about 11%. The principal farm products are wheat, sugar beets, maize, potatoes, tomatoes, citrus fruit, olives, and livestock (especially cattle, pigs, sheep, and goats). In addition, much wine is produced from grapes grown throughout the country. Industry is centered in the north, particularly in the "golden triangle" of Milan-Turin-Genoa. The chief manufactures of the country include iron and steel, refined petroleum, chemicals, textiles, motor vehicles, and machinery. There is a small fishing industry. Italy has only limited mineral resources; the chief minerals produced are petroleum (especially in Sicily), lignite, iron ore, iron pyrites, bauxite, sulfur, and mercury. There are also large deposits of natural gas (methane). Much hydroelectricity is generated, and there are several nuclear power stations in the country. In order to further the economic development of the south, the *Cassa per il mezzogiorno* (Southern Italy Development Fund) was founded in 1950; it has since allocated considerable funds, especially for improving the economic infrastructure of the region. Italy has a large foreign trade, facilitated by its sizable commercial shipping fleet. The leading exports are machinery, motor vehicles, food products, and textiles; the main imports are food and food products, minerals (especially petroleum), machinery, and chemicals. Tourism is a major source of foreign exchange. The chief trade partners are West Germany, France, and the United States. Italy is a member of the European Economic Community (Common Market). There are numerous universities in Italy, including ones at Bari, Bologna, Genoa, Milan, Naples, Padua, Palermo, and Rome. The following generalized outline of the highly complex history of Italy can be supplemented by the articles on individual cities and regions and by such general articles as ETRUSCAN CIVILIZATION; PAPACY; ITALIAN ART; ITALIAN LITERATURE; and RENAISSANCE.

Ancient Italy and the Barbarian Invasions. Little is known of Italian history before the 5th cent. B.C., except for the regions (S Italy and Sicily) where the Greeks had established colonies (see MAGNA GRAECIA). The earliest known inhabitants seem to have been of Ligurian stock. The Etruscans, coming probably from Asia Minor, established themselves in central Italy before 800 B.C. They reduced the indigenous population to servile status and established a prosperous empire with a complex culture. In the 4th cent. B.C., the Celts (called Gauls by Roman historians) invaded Italy and drove the Etruscans from the Po valley. In the south, the Etruscan advance was checked about the same time by the Samnites (see SAMNIUM), who had adapted the civilization of their Greek neighbors and who in the 4th cent. B.C. drove the Etruscans out of Campania. The Latins, living along the coast of Latium, had not been fully subjected to the Etruscans; they and their neighbors, the SABINES, were the ancestors of the Romans. The history of Italy from the 5th cent. B.C. to the 5th cent. A.D. is largely that of the growth of Rome and of the Roman Empire, of which Italy was the core. Augustus divided Italy into 11 administrative regions (Latium and Campania, Apulia and Calabria, Lucania and Bruttium, Samnium, Picenum, Umbria, Etruria, Cispadane Gaul, Liguria, Venetia and Istria, Transpadane Gaul). By that time, at the beginning of the Christian era, all of Italy had been thoroughly latinized, Roman citizenship was extended to all free Italians, an excellent system of roads had been built, and Italy, made tax exempt, shared fully in the wealth of Rome. Never since has Italy known an equal degree of prosperity or as long a period of peace. Christianity spread rapidly. Like the rest of the Roman Empire, Italy in the early 5th cent. A.D. began to be invaded by successive waves of barbarian tribes—the Germanic VISIGOTHS, the HUNS, and the Germanic Heruli and OSTROGOTHS. The deposition (476) of Romulus Augustulus, the last Roman emperor of the West, and the assumption by ODOACER of the rule over Italy is commonly regarded as the end of the Roman Empire. The Eastern emperors, residing at Constantinople (see BYZANTINE EMPIRE), never renounced their claim to Italy and to succession to the West. On the urging of Zeno, the Eastern emperor, the Ostrogoth THEODORIC THE GREAT invaded Italy, took (493) Ravenna (which had replaced Rome as capital), killed Odoacer, and began a long and beneficent rule over Italy. Roman institutions were maintained with the help of scholars and administrators such as Boethius and Cassiodorus. After Theodoric's death (526), the murder (535) of the Gothic queen, AMALASUNTHA, was followed by the reconquest of Italy by Emperor JUSTINIAN I of the East and his generals, BELISARIUS and NARSES. Except, however, in the exarchate of Ravenna, the PENTAPOLIS and the coast of S Italy, Byzantine rule was soon displaced by that of the LOMBARDS, who under ALBOIN established (569) a new kingdom. The papacy emerged as the chief bulwark of Latin civilization. GREGORY I (reigned 590-604), without assistance from Byzantium, succeeded in saving Rome and the Patrimony of St. Peter from the Lombard conquest, thus laying the basis for the creation of the PAPAL STATES. At the same time, he effectively freed Rome from allegiance to the Byzantine conquerors. The Lombards warded off Byzantine efforts at reconquest and in 751 took Ravenna; their advance on Rome resulted in the appeal of Pope Stephen II to PEPIN THE SHORT, ruler of the Franks, who expelled the Lombards from the exarchate of Ravenna and from the Pentapolis, which he donated (754) to the pope. Pepin's intervention was followed by that of his son CHARLEMAGNE, who defeated the Lombard king, Desiderius, was crowned king of the Lombards, confirmed his father's donation to the papacy, and in 800 was crowned emperor of the West at Rome. These events shaped much of the later history of Italy and of the papacy. Among the direct results were the claim of later emperors to Italy and the temporal power of the popes.

Medieval Italy. In the divisions (9th cent.) of the Carolingian empire (see VERDUN, TREATY OF; MERSEN, TREATY OF), Italy passed to the successive emperors LOTHAIR I, LOUIS II, and CHARLES II; however, their control was largely nominal. Under CARLOMAN (d. 880) and Emperor CHARLES III (reigned 881-87), local power became increasingly strong in Italy. Emperor ARNULF (reigned 896-99) failed to reassert authority. From 888 to 962 Italy was nominally ruled by a series of weak kings and emperors including Guy of Spoleto, Berengar I of Friuli, Louis III of Burgundy, and BERENGAR II of Ivrea. The petty nobles were constantly feuding, and by the end of the period the papacy had sunk to its lowest point of degradation. The Magyars plundered N Italy, and in the south the Arabs seized (917) Sicily and raided the mainland. In 961, heeding an appeal by the pope for protection against Berengar II, the German king OTTO I invaded Italy. In 962 he was crowned emperor by the pope. This union of Italy and Germany marked the beginning of the HOLY ROMAN EMPIRE. Although the Alps had never prevented invaders from entering Italy, they did prevent the emperors from exercising effective control there. Again and again the emperors and German kings crossed the Alps to assert their authority; each time their authority virtually vanished when they left Italy. At best, their power was limited to the territories north of the Papal States. The popes, by exerting their influence and by arranging alliances with other powers, were important in frustrating imperial control. Apulia and Calabria, after being briefly held again by the Byzantines, were conquered (11th cent.) by the Normans under ROBERT GUISCARD and his successors, who also wrested Sicily from the Arabs and established the Norman kingdom of Sicily. In central and N Italy, the prevailing chaos was increased by the conflict between the emperors and the popes over INVESTITURE and by the contested succession to Tuscany after the death (1115) of Countess MATILDA. Because the many petty lords were independent of imperial authority and because the cities gradually gained control over these lords, FEUDALISM did not gain a firm foothold in central and N Italy. However, in the south the Norman kings and their successors, the HOHENSTAUFEN and ANGEVIN dynasties, firmly entrenched the feudal system, the worst features of which were later perpetuated by the Spanish rulers of Naples and Sicily. Thus, the great difference in social and economic structure between N and S Italy, which continued well into the 20th cent., can be traced back to the 11th cent. The characteristic development in central and N Italy was the rise of the city (see COMMUNE and CITY-STATE), beginning in the 10th cent. The rise was partly political in origin—the burghers were drawing together to protect

Bern
LIECHTENSTEIN
Innsbruck
SWITZERLAND
AUSTRIA
HUNGARY
A L P S
ALPS
Bolzano
TRENTINO ALTO-ADIGE
Lake Lugano
Lake Como
Aosta
VALLE D'AOSTA
Lake Maggiore
Como
Trent
Belluno
FRIULI-VENEZIA GIULIA
Udine
FRANCE
Lake Garda
VENETO
Milan
Brescia
Verona
Trieste
PIEDMONT
LOMBARDY
Venice
Turin
Po R.
Cremona
Mantua
Padua
Parma
Po R.
Ferrara
YUGOSLAVIA
LIGURIA
Modena
Genoa
Bologna
EMILIA-ROMAGNA
A P E N N I N E S
Ravenna
La Spezia
Rimini
SAN MARINO
LIGURIAN SEA
Pisa
Arno R.
Florence
Leghorn (Livorno)
Ancona
Arezzo
Siena
MARCHE
TUSCANY
Perugia
ADRIATIC SEA
ELBA
UMBRIA
CORSICA
Tiber R.
L'Aquila
Ajaccio
LATIUM
ABRUZZI
VATICAN CITY
Rome
ITALY
MOLISE
Campobasso
APULIA
PONTINE ISLANDS
Bari
Sassari
CAMPANIA
Naples
Salerno
ISCHIA
Potenza
CAPRI
TYRRHENIAN SEA
BASILICATA
Taranto
SARDINIA
Gulf of Taranto
Cagliari
CALABRIA
Catanzaro
LIPARI ISLANDS
Palermo
Messina
Reggio di Calabria
EGADI ISLANDS
Strait of Messina
IONIAN SEA
SICILY
MEDITERRANEAN SEA
Catania
Agrigento
Tunis
Syracuse
PANTELLERIA
TUNISIA
ALGERIA
Malta Channel
MALTA
Valletta

themselves from the nobles—and partly economic—contact with the Muslim world was making the Italian merchants the middlemen and the Italian cities the entrepôts of Western Europe. The survival of Roman institutions and the example of the commune of Rome facilitated the process. To protect their commerce and their industries (particularly the wool industry) cities grouped together in leagues, which often were at war with each other. The leagues were particularly strong in Lombardy. The attempt by Emperor FREDERICK I to impose imperial authority on some cities led to the formation of the LOMBARD LEAGUE, which defeated the emperor in 1176. Rivalry among the cities, however, prevented the formation of any union strong enough to consolidate even a part of Italy. In the 13th cent. the struggle between Emperor FREDERICK II and the papacy divided the cities and nobles into two strong parties, the GUELPHS AND GHIBELLINES. Their fratricidal warfare continued long after the death (1250) of Frederick, which marked the virtual demise of imperial rule in Italy and the ascendancy of the papacy. In 1268, Frederick's grandson, Conradin, was executed at Naples, thus ending Hohenstaufen aspirations. The factional strife led to the rise of despots in some cities. These despots, who were of noble or bourgeois origin, were generally factional leaders, who, having obtained the magistracy, made it hereditary. Some of them managed to restore order in the cities. In many cities, however, the republican institutions were upheld with little interruption. In other cities, dynasties were established and invested (14th and 15th cent.) with titles by the emperors, who still claimed suzerainty over N Italy. The most powerful princes (e.g., the VISCONTI and SFORZA of Milan, the GONZAGA of Mantua, the ESTE of Ferrara, and the dukes of SAVOY) and the most powerful republics (e.g., Florence, Venice, and Genoa) tended to increase their territories at the expense of weaker neighbors. The cities in the Papal States passed under local tyrants during the Babylonian captivity of the popes at Avignon (1309–78) and during the Great Schism (1378–1417). By the end of the 15th cent. Italy had fallen into the following chief component parts: in the south, the kingdoms of Sicily and Naples, torn by the rival claims of the French Angevin dynasty and the Spanish house of Aragón; in central Italy, the Papal States, the republics of Siena, Florence, and Lucca, and the cities of Bologna, Forlì, Rimini, and Faenza (only nominally subject to the pope); in the north, the duchies of Ferrara and Modena, Mantua, Milan, and Savoy. The two great merchant republics, Venice and Genoa, with their far-flung possessions, colonies, and outposts, were distinct in character and outlook from the rest of Italy. Constant warfare among these many states resulted in political turmoil, but did little to diminish their wealth or to hinder their cultural output. The wars were generally fought in a desultory manner by hired bands led by professional commanders (see CONDOTTIERE). Compared to the Black Death, the plague that ravaged Italy in 1348, the local wars did little harm. Material prosperity had been furthered considerably by the Crusades; by the expanding trade with the Middle East; and by the rise of great banking firms, notably in Genoa, in Lucca, and in Florence (where the MEDICI rose from bankers to dukes). The prosperity facilitated the great cultural flowering of the Italian Renaissance, which permanently changed the civilization of Western Europe.

Political Disintegration and Rebirth. The Renaissance reached its peak in the late 15th cent. Meanwhile, Italy's political independence was threatened by the growing nations of France, Spain, and Austria. Quarrels among Italian states invited foreign intervention. The invasion (1494) of Italy by CHARLES VIII of France marked the beginning of the ITALIAN WARS, which ended in 1559 with most of Italy subjected to Spanish rule or influence. Early in the wars, in which France and Spain were the main contenders for supremacy in Italy, several Italian statesmen, notably MACHIAVELLI, came to the belief that only unity could save Italy from foreign domination. Pope JULIUS II consolidated the Papal States, but his HOLY LEAGUE, devised (1510) to drive out the French, failed to create a wider Italian unity. After 1519 the Italian Wars became part of the European struggle between FRANCIS I of France and Emperor CHARLES V. By the Treaty of CATEAU-CAMBRÉSIS (1559), Spain gained the kingdoms of Sicily and Naples and the duchy of Milan. Foreign domination continued with the War of the SPANISH SUCCESSION (1701–14; see also UTRECHT, PEACE OF) and the War of the POLISH SUCCESSION (1733–35). By 1748, Naples, Sicily, and the duchies of Parma and Piacenza had passed to branches of the Spanish Bourbons, and the duchies of Milan, Mantua, Tuscany, and Modena to Austria. Remaining independent were the Papal States, the declining republics of Venice, Genoa, and Lucca, and the kingdom of Sardinia (see SARDINIA, KINGDOM OF), created in 1720 by the union of Piedmont, Savoy, and Sardinia under the house of Savoy. These centuries of political weakness were also a period of economic decline. The center of European trade shifted away from the Mediterranean, and commerce and industry suffered from the mercantilist policies of the European states. Taxes rose under Spanish rule, the amount of land under cultivation declined, the population decreased, and brigandage increased. Nevertheless, Italy continued to have considerable influence on European culture, especially in architecture and music. Yet to subsequent generations in Italy (especially in the 19th cent.), preoccupied with the concepts of national independence and political power, the political condition of 18th-century Italy represented national degradation. The French Revolution rekindled Italian national aspirations, and the FRENCH REVOLUTIONARY WARS swept away the political institutions of 18th-century Italy. General Bonaparte (later NAPOLEON I), who defeated Sardinian and Austrian armies in his Italian campaign of 1796–97, was at first acclaimed by most Italians. Napoleon redrew the Italian map several times. Extensive land reforms were carried out, especially in N Italy. The Cispadane and Transpadane republics, established in 1796, were united (1797) as the CISALPINE REPUBLIC, recognized in the Treaty of CAMPO FORMIO (1797). In 1802 the Cisalpine Republic, comprising Lombardy and Emilia-Romagna, was renamed the Italian Republic; in 1805 it became the kingdom of Italy (enlarged by the addition of Venetia), with Napoleon as king and Eugène de BEAUHARNAIS as viceroy. From 1795 to 1812, Savoy, Piedmont, Liguria, Tuscany, Parma, and the Papal States were annexed by France. In 1806, Joseph BONAPARTE was made king of Naples; he was replaced in 1808 by Joachim MURAT, Napoleon's brother-in-law. Sardinia remained under the house of Savoy and Sicily under the Bourbons. Napoleon's failure to unite Italy and to give it self-government disappointed Italian patriots, some of whom formed secret revolutionary societies such as the CARBONARI, which later played a vital role in Italian unification. The Congress of Vienna (1814–15) generally restored the pre-Napoleonic status quo and the old ruling families. However, Venetia was united with Lombardy as the Lombardo-Venetian kingdom under the Austrian crown, and Liguria passed to Sardinia. Naples and Sicily were united (1816) as the kingdom of the TWO SICILIES. Austrian influence became paramount in Italy. Nevertheless, the efforts of Metternich and of the Holy Alliance (e.g., in quelling insurrections in Naples and in Palermo) could not suppress the nationalist movement. The RISORGIMENTO, as the movement for unification was called, included three groups: the radicals, led by MAZZINI, who sought to create a republic; the moderate liberals, who regarded the house of Savoy as the agency for unification; and the Roman Catholic conservatives, who desired a confederation under the presidency of the pope. In 1848–49, there were several short-lived revolutionary outbreaks, notably in Naples, Venice, Tuscany, Rome, and the kingdom of Sardinia (whose new liberal constitution survived). Unification was ultimately achieved under the house of Savoy, largely through the efforts of CAVOUR, GARIBALDI, and VICTOR EMMANUEL II, who became king of Italy in 1861. At that time, the kingdom of Italy did not include Venetia, Rome, and part of the Papal States. By siding against Austria in the AUSTRO-PRUSSIAN WAR of 1866, Italy obtained Venetia. To NAPOLEON III of France, who had helped Sardinia defeat Austria in 1859, Sardinia had ceded Nice and Savoy. The protectorate of Napoleon III over the Papal States delayed the Italian annexation of the city of Rome until 1870. Relations between the Italian government and the papacy, which refused to concede the loss of its temporal power, remained a major problem until 1929, when the LATERAN TREATY made the pope sovereign within Vatican City. After 1870, Austria still retained areas with largely Italian populations (e.g., S Tyrol and Trieste); Italian agitation for their annexation (see IRREDENTISM) went unfulfilled until World War I.

1861 to World War II. From 1861 until the Fascist dictatorship (1922–43) of Benito Mussolini, Italy was governed under the liberal constitution adopted by Sardinia in 1848. The reigns of Victor Emmanuel II (1861–78) and HUMBERT I (1878–1900), and the first half of the reign of VICTOR EMMANUEL III (1900–46) were marked by moderate social and political reforms and by some industrial expansion in N Italy (mainly in the 20th cent.). Periodic social unrest was caused by the dislocations attending industrialization and by occasional economic depression. In the underdeveloped south, rapid population growth led to mass emigration, both to the industrial centers of N Italy and to the Americas. The outstanding statesmen of the pre-Fascist period were Agostino DEPRETIS, Francesco CRISPI, and Giovanni GIOLITTI. Colonial expansion was emphasized under Crispi, but was otherwise sporadic. A severe setback to Italian colonial aspirations was the establishment (1881) of a French protectorate over TUNISIA; it was an important motive for the conclusion (1882) of Italy's alliance with Germany and Austria (see TRIPLE ALLIANCE AND TRIPLE ENTENTE). Later, Italy acquired part of Somaliland in 1889 and Eritrea (now part of Ethiopia) in 1890, but further advances in NE Africa were checked by the Ethiopian victory (1896) at Aduwa. Libya and the Dodecanese were conquered in the Italo-Turkish War (1911–12). In World War I, Italy at first remained neutral. After the Allies offered substantial territorial rewards, Italy denounced the Triple Alliance and entered (1915) the war on the Allied side. Although the Italians initially suffered serious reverses, they won (1918) a great victory at VITTORIO VENETO, which was followed by the surrender of Austria-Hungary. At the Paris Peace Conference, Italy obtained S Tyrol, Trieste, Istria, part of Carniola, and several of the Dalmatian islands. Italian possession of the Dodecanese was confirmed. However, these terms granted far less than the Allies had secretly promised in 1915. Italian discontent was evident in the seizure (1919) of Fiume (see RIJEKA) by a nationalist band led by Gabriel D'ANNUNZIO. Within Italy, political and social unrest increased, furthering the growth of Fascism. The Fascist leader (Ital. *Il Duce*) MUSSOLINI, promising the restoration of social order and of political greatness, directed (Oct. 27, 1922) a successful march on Rome and was made premier by the king. Granted dictatorial powers, Mussolini quashed opposition to the state (especially that of socialists and Communists), regimented the press and the schools, imposed controls on industry and labor, and created a CORPORATIVE STATE controlled by the Fascist party and the militia. The Fascist economic program as a whole was a failure, but some programs of lasting value (e.g., the draining of the Pontine marshes and the construction of a network of superhighways) were undertaken. The problems caused by an increasing population were aggravated by drastic immigration restrictions in the United States and by the economic depression of the 1930s. Mussolini followed an aggressive foreign policy, and after 1935 he turned increasingly to militarist and imperialist solutions to Italy's problems. Italy conquered ETHIOPIA in 1935–36, easily overcoming the ineffective sanctions imposed by the League of Nations (from which Italy withdrew in 1937). At the same time, Italy drew closer to Nazi Germany and to Japan; in 1936, Italy formed an entente with Germany (see AXIS). Italy intervened on the Insurgent side in the Spanish civil war (1936–39), and in 1939 it seized ALBANIA. At the outbreak of World War II, Italy assumed a neutral stance friendly to Germany, but in June, 1940, it declared war on collapsing France and on Great Britain. In 1940, Italian forces were active in North Africa (see NORTH AFRICA, CAMPAIGNS IN) and attacked Greece; however, they were unsuccessful until German troops came to their aid in early 1941. Later in 1941, Italy declared war on the Soviet Union and on the United States. Soon Italy suffered major reverses, and by July, 1943, it had lost its African possessions, its army was shattered, Sicily was falling to U.S. troops, and Italian cities (especially ports) were being bombed by the Allies. In July, 1943, discontent among Italians culminated in the rebellion of the Fascist grand council against Mussolini, Mussolini's dismissal by Victor Emmanuel III, the appointment of BADOGLIO as premier, and the dissolution of the Fascist party. In September, 1943, Italy surrendered unconditionally to the Allies, while German forces quickly occupied N and central Italy. Aided by the Germans, Mussolini escaped from prison and established a puppet republic in N Italy. Meanwhile, the Badoglio government declared war on Germany, and Italy was recognized by the Allies as a cobelligerent. The Allied Italian campaign was a slow, grueling, and costly struggle (see CASSINO; ANZIO). The fall of Rome (July, 1944) was followed by a stalemate. In April, 1945, partisans captured and summarily executed Mussolini. In May, 1945, the Germans surrendered. After the war, Italy's borders were established by the peace treaty of 1947, which assigned several small Alpine districts (see BRIGUE AND TENDE) to France; the Dodecanese to Greece; and Trieste, Istria, most of Venezia Giulia, and several Adriatic islands to Yugoslavia and to the Free Territory of Trieste. In 1954, Trieste and its environs were returned to Italy. As a result of the war, Italy also lost effective control over its holdings of Libya, Eritrea, and Italian Somaliland.

Postwar Italy. In 1944 the unpopular Badoglio cabinet had resigned, and thereafter various coalition cabinets followed each other until Dec., 1945, when Alcide DE GASPERI, a Christian Democrat, became premier. De Gasperi remained an important influence on Italian politics until his death in 1954. In May, 1946, Victor Emmanuel abdicated, having previously transferred his powers to his son, HUMBERT II. After a month's rule, Humbert was exiled when the Italians in a plebiscite voted by a small majority to make the country a republic. A new republican constitution went into effect on Jan. 1, 1948. Enrico de Nicola was provisional president of Italy from 1946 to 1948; he was followed as president by Luigi Einaudi, Giovanni Gronchi (1955), Antonio Segni (1962), Giuseppe Saragat (1964), and Giovanni Leone (1971). The Christian Democrats, Communists, and Socialists emerged from the war as the chief parties. The split of the Socialists into the majority Socialists (the left wing) and the minority Social Democrats (the right wing) enabled the Christian Democrats to maintain power at the head of successive coalition governments with the Social Democrats (until 1959) and other center parties and to exclude the Communists from the government. However, the Communists dominated the local politics of Tuscany, Umbria, and Emilia-Romagna. In 1962, Premier Amintore FANFANI, a Christian Democrat, formed a center-left coalition with a cabinet that again included the Social Democrats, as well as the parliamentary support of the Socialist party, led by Pietro Nenni. However, Fanfani's government fell after general elections in 1963, and, in a manner characteristic of the 1960s and early 1970s, there was considerable uncertainty before Aldo Moro, also a Christian Democrat, was able to form a center-left coalition in late 1963. The Moro government fell in 1964 and in 1966, but on each occasion was reformed after a brief hiatus. However, following the general elections of May, 1968, the Moro government fell again and a government crisis began that was only ended in Dec., 1968, when Mariano Rumor, a Christian Democrat, formed a coalition government with Socialist support. In 1969–70, Rumor's government fell twice, but each time it was reconstructed after a period of uncertainty. However, after Rumor's coalition fell for a third time in July, 1970, he was replaced (Aug., 1970) as premier by Emilio Colombo, a Christian Democrat. Colombo resigned in Jan., 1972. After a long period of crisis, Giulio Andreotti, also a Christian Democrat, formed a new coalition government in June, 1972; for the first time in 10 years, the government had a center-right, rather than a center-left, character. But this combination also did not last long and was replaced (July, 1973) by a slightly left of center coalition headed by Rumor. In March, 1974, Rumor resigned, but after a short interim period he formed another center-left cabinet, the 36th government since the fall of Mussolini in 1943. Despite the pervasive political instability, Italy's economy, particularly the industrial sector, expanded dramatically after 1950. Beginning in the late 1960s, there was considerable industrial unrest in the country as workers demanded higher wages to offset inflation, better social services, and increased opportunities for education. In mid-1974, Italy faced its worst economic crisis in thirty years. An austerity program was initiated in July in an attempt to reduce the soaring inflation rate and the overwhelming foreign trade deficit. In international affairs, Italy was firmly tied to the West, joining the North Atlantic Treaty Organization at its inception in 1949. It was admitted to the United Nations in 1955. In 1971 a treaty between Austria and Italy granting increased autonomy to the German-speaking province of Bolzano in Trentino-Alto Adige was signed and ratified. In late 1966, N and central Italy suffered severe flooding; there was considerable damage to art treasures and libraries, especially in Florence. After much controversy, a bill legalizing divorce was passed in 1970.

Government. Under the 1948 constitution, legislative power is vested in a bicameral parliament consisting of the 630-member chamber of deputies, which is popularly elected, and the senate, made up of 315 members elected by region, plus 5 life members nominated by the president of Italy and all living former presidents. The chamber is the more important body. The council of ministers, led by the premier, is the country's executive; it must have the confidence of parliament. The head of state is the president, chosen in a joint session by parliament. The country's 20 regions also have parliaments and governments with limited powers.

Bibliography. Among general histories of Italy are Vernon Bartlett, *Introduction to Italy* (1967); Muriel Grindrod, *Italy* (1968); Great Britain, Naval Intelligence Division, *Italy* (4 vol., 1944–45, repr. 1969–); Peter Gunn, *A Concise History of Italy* (1972). A bibliography of the early period and the barbarian invasions is listed under ROME. For the medieval period, see D. P. Waley, *The Italian City-Republics* (1969); J. K. Hyde, *Society and Politics in Medieval Italy* (1973). For the Renaissance, see bibliography under RENAISSANCE. For the modern period, see Benedetto Croce, *History of Italy, 1871–1915* (tr. 1929, repr. 1963); Norman Kogan, *A Political History of Postwar Italy* (1966); Giuseppe Mammarella, *Italy after Fascism: A Political History, 1943–1965* (rev. and enl. ed. 1966); Bolton King, *A History of Italian Unity* (2 vol., 1924, repr. 1967); S. B. Clough and Salvatore Saladino, *A History of Modern Italy* (1968); Denis Mack Smith, *Italy, A Modern History* (rev. and enl. ed. 1969); F. R. Willis, *Italy Chooses Europe* (1971); J. C. Adams, *The Government of Republican Italy* (3d ed. 1972); S. J. Woolf, ed., *The Rebirth of Italy, 1943–50* (1972).

Itami (ētä'mē), city (1970 pop. 155,763), Hyogo prefecture, S Honshu, Japan, on the Muko River and Osaka Bay. It is a residential suburb of Osaka and the site of Osaka International Airport.

Itasca, Lake (ītăs'kə), shallow lake, 2 sq mi (5.2 sq km), in a pine-wooded swampy region, NW Minn. Henry R. Schoolcraft identified it (1832) as the source of the Mississippi. Later geographers consider the source to be above the lake. In 1891 the region was included in a state park, which has a historical and natural history museum.

Iténez: see GUAPORÉ.

Ithaca, Greece: see ITHÁKI.

Ithaca (ĭth'əkə), city (1970 pop. 26,226), seat of Tompkins co., S central N.Y., at the southern end of Cayuga Lake, in the Finger Lakes region; settled 1789, inc. as a city 1888. It is important chiefly as an educational center, the seat of Cornell Univ. and of Ithaca College. It is also a major producer of salt in the state, and, with access to the New York State Barge Canal, it is an inland shipping point. A state hospital is in Ithaca. The city is situated on hills above the lake and is traversed by creeks that cut deep, scenic gorges.

Ithai (ī''thā'ī, ĭthā'ī), variant of ITTAI **2.**

Itháki (ēthä'kē) or **Ithaca** (ĭth'əkə), island (1971 pop. 4,156), c.37 sq mi (96 sq km), W Greece, one of the IONIAN ISLANDS. It is mountainous, rising to c.2,650 ft (810 m) at Mt. Anoyi, and has little arable land. The chief products are olive oil, currants, and wine. The main town is Itháki (1971 pop. 2,293), located on the island's east coast. The island is traditionally celebrated as the home of ODYSSEUS. Cyclopean walls and remains of a Corinthian colony (c.8th cent. B.C.) have been found. In 1953, Itháki was devastated by tidal waves.

Ithamar (ĭth'əmär), son of Aaron. Ex. 6.23; 28.1; 38.21; Lev. 10.6; 1 Chron. 24.3; Ezra 8.2.

Ithiel (ĭth'ĭēl, ĭthī'-). **1** Benjamite. Neh. 11.7. **2** See UCAL.

Ithmah (ĭth'mə), Moabite member of David's guard. 1 Chron. 11.46.

Ithnan (ĭth'năn), unidentified town, S Palestine, perhaps to be read Hazor-ithnan and identified with HAZOR **1.** Joshua 15.23.

Ithra (ĭth'rə), variant of JETHER **2.**

Ithran (ĭth'răn). **1** Descendant of Asher. 1 Chron. 7.37. He is probably the same as Jether in verse 38. **2** Chief of the Horites. Gen. 36.26.

Ithream (ĭth'rēəm), son of David. 2 Sam. 3.5; 1 Chron. 3.3.

Ithrite (ĭth'rīt), family name of two of David's guard. 2 Sam. 23.38; 1 Chron. 11.40.

Ito, Hirobumi (hērō'bōōmē ē'tō), 1841–1909, Japanese statesman, the outstanding figure in the modernization of Japan. As a young Choshu samurai, he was a xenophobe. In 1863 he visited Europe, studied science in England, and became convinced of the necessity of adopting Western ways. After the MEIJI RESTORATION, Ito served in the ministries of foreign affairs, finance, and industry. He was a member of the mission sent abroad (1871) under Prince Iwakura to revise the unequal treaties with the Western powers and study Western technology. In 1873, Ito became a member of the ruling council and worked to modernize Japan and solidify the power of the oligarchs. By 1881 he forced Shigenobu OKUMA to resign and thus became the foremost political power in Japan. In 1882 he headed the mission sent abroad to study foreign governments. Returning, he established a cabinet and civil service (1885) and a privy council (1888), which he headed. He supervised (1883–89) the drafting of the constitution of 1889 and was intimate adviser to the emperor. In 1885 he negotiated the Li-Ito Convention, which postponed war with China over Korea. As prime minister (1892–96) he supported the Sino-Japanese War and negotiated the Treaty of Shimonoseki. After the war he became a supporter of party government, opposing Prince YAMAGATA. He was the first president of the Seiyukai party. Again prime minister (1898, 1900–1901), he tried to negotiate a peaceful settlement with Russia, but, failing, was forced to increase military appropriations. From 1901 to 1913 the premiership alternated between his protégé, Kammoche Saionji, and Taro Katsura, a follower of Yamagata. In 1905, Ito forced an agreement making Korea a virtual protectorate of Japan and became (1906) resident general there. His assassination (1909) by a Korean fanatic served as a pretext for annexation.

Ito, city (1970 pop. 63,003), Shizuoka prefecture, central Honshu, Japan, on the Izu Peninsula and the Sagami Sea. It is a port and hot spring resort.

Itsuku-shima (ētsōōkōō'-shĭm'ä), sacred island, 12 sq mi (31 sq km), in the Inland Sea, Japan, SW of Hiroshima. It is the site of an ancient Shinto shrine, famous for its magical beauty. It is also known for a 9th-century Buddhist temple, a pagoda (built 1407), a 16th-century hall built by Hideyoshi, and a huge torii (1875). Miya-jima, or Shrine Isle, is another name for the island.

Ittah-kazin (ĭt'ə-kā'zĭn), unidentified place, N Palestine. Joshua 19.13.

Ittai (ĭt'āī, ĭtā'ī). **1** Gittite follower of David. He stood by David in Absalom's revolt. 2 Sam. 15.19–22; 18.2,5,12. **2** Benjamite, one of David's mighty men. 2 Sam. 23.29. Ithai: 1 Chron. 11.31.

Ituraea (ĭtyōōrē'ə), ancient country on the northern border of Palestine. Jetur, the son of Ishmael, was its founder. Ancient geographers are not agreed as to the exact limits of the country. The inhabitants were Arabians with their capital at Chalchis and their religious center at Heliopolis (Baalbek). Ituraea was conquered in 105 B.C. by Aristobulus, king of Judaea, who annexed it to Judaea and converted many of the inhabitants to Judaism. Later, after a brief period of independence, the country was subdued by Pompey. It remained thereafter chiefly in Roman hands, being united (A.D. c.50) to the Roman province of Syria. Many Ituraeans served in the armies of Rome and were renowned for their skill as horsemen and archers.

Iturbi, José (hōsā' ētōōr'bē), 1895–, Spanish-American pianist, b. Valencia, Spain. Iturbi studied at the Valencia and Paris conservatories on scholarship. His worldwide concert tours were brilliantly successful. He excelled as an interpreter of Spanish music. In New York City in 1929 he made his American debut; he made his first appearance as a conductor in Mexico City in 1933. He was conductor of the Rochester (N.Y.) Philharmonic Orchestra from 1936 to 1944. Iturbi appeared as an actor-performer in several filmed musicals of the 1940s.

Iturbide, Agustín de (ägōōstēn' dā ētōōrbē'thā), 1783–1824, Mexican revolutionist, emperor of Mexico (1822–23). An officer in the royalist army, he was sympathetic to independence but took no part in the separatist movement led by Miguel Hidalgo y Costilla, and in fact helped to suppress the peasant revolt. His forces were instrumental in checking MORELOS Y PAVÓN. In 1820 he was commissioned by Viceroy APODACA to lead royalist troops against Vicente GUERRERO. Iturbide undertook the command with the intention of overthrowing the viceroyalty and establishing Mexican independence. After Guerrero had inflicted minor defeats on his troops, Iturbide opened negotiations with the insurgent leader, and the result was the Plan of IGUALA (1821). Iturbide's army swept the country. The new viceroy, O'DONOJÚ, capitulated to their demands in the Treaty of CÓRDOBA (1821). The independence of Mexico was assured, but without the social reforms advocated by Hidalgo; instead of a new liberal state, Iturbide had ushered in a new conservative one. He headed a provisional government which in time became dictatorial. When no Bourbon prince could be found to accept the crown of Mexico and Spain repudiated the Treaty of Córdoba, his soldiers proclaimed him emperor as Agustín I. Congress, hostile but intimidated, ratified the proclamation (1822). It was not long before a revolution was in the field, with SANTA ANNA and GUADALUPE VICTORIA as its principal leaders. In 1823, Iturbide was forced to abdicate and go into exile in Europe. Congress decreed him a traitor and an outlaw, forbidding his reentry into Mexico. Iturbide, ignorant of the decree, sailed back to Mexico in 1824. He was captured, tried by the Congress of Tamaulipas, and shot. Iturbide has been regarded by conservatives as the champion of Mexican independence, rather than Hidalgo or Morelos y Pavón. In 1838 a conservative government placed his body in the Cathedral of Mexico. See biography by W. S. Robertson (1968).

Iturrigaray, José de (hōsā' thā ētōō'rēgärä'ē), 1742–1815, Spanish colonial administrator, viceroy of New Spain (1803–8). During his rule, all of Spanish America was disturbed by the Napoleonic invasion of Spain and the abdication of Ferdinand VII. A quasi-separatist movement arose among the creoles of Mexico, and Iturrigaray lent his ear to their schemes. The Spanish-born officials of the viceroyalty resisted the liberal creoles and, suspecting Iturrigaray, deposed him (Sept. 15, 1808), confiscated his fortune, and shipped him to Spain. The separatist spirit of the creoles burst forth two years later in the uprising of Miguel Hidalgo y Costilla.

Ituzaingó, battle of (ē"tōōsīn-gō'), fought in S Uruguay, Feb. 20, 1827. A combined Argentine-Uruguayan force under Carlos María de Alvear decisively defeated Brazil. The United Provinces of La Plata (Argentina) and Brazil had both claimed Uruguay. In the peace treaty that followed (1828), an independent Uruguay was created as a buffer state.

Itys (ī'tĭs) or **Itylus** (ĭt'ələs): see PHILOMELA; AËDON.

Itzá (ētsä'), Maya Indians of Yucatán (Mexico) and PETÉN (Guatemala). Probable founders of CHICHÉN ITZÁ, which they occupied at various times from c.514 to 1194, they moved (1450?) S from Campeche to Lake Petén. Here, in spite of sporadic attempts by the Spanish to convert or subdue them after the visit of Cortés in 1525, the Itzá (the last strong, independent Mayan tribe) remained until driven from their capital, Tayasal, in 1697.

Itzamna (ētsäm' nä), chief deity of the Maya. Son of Hunab Ku, the creator, he was believed to be lord of the heavens, day, and night. Thought by the Maya to have been the inventor of writing and books, Itzamna was, by extension, creator of the calendar and chronology. He was a benevolent deity.

Itzehoe (ĭt'səhō), city (1970 pop. 36,176), Schleswig-Holstein, N West Germany, on the Stör River. It is a commercial center; manufactures include cement and machinery. Itzehoe was founded c.810 by Charlemagne and is one of the oldest cities in Schleswig-Holstein. It passed to Prussia in 1866.

Iulis, ancient Greece: see KÉA.

Ivah (ī'və), unidentified city of Mesopotamia, perhaps the same as AVA. 2 Kings 18.34; 19.13; Isa. 37.13.

Ivan II or **Ivan Asen** (ē'vän ä'sən), d. 1241, czar of Bulgaria (1218–41). On the death (1207) of his father, Kaloyan, founder of the second Bulgarian empire, the throne was usurped by Ivan's cousin Boril. Ivan fled to the duchy of Galich and secured its aid. Returning in 1218, he captured Trnovo, had Boril blinded, and was crowned czar. Under Ivan II the Bulgarian empire reached its zenith, becoming the strongest power in the Balkans; he added Macedonia, Epirus, and much of Albania and Serbia to his lands. He campaigned (1235) with JOHN III of Nicaea against the Latin Empire of Constantinople, but later helped the Latins oppose John. Ivan's generally mild conduct and sincere faith endeared him even to his foes. He restored the autonomy of the Bulgarian church, established a central administration, and encouraged the settlement of Ragusan merchants. For his repudiation (1232) of the union with Rome and his support of the heretic Bogomils, he was excommunicated (1236) by Pope Gregory IX. Ivan II was succeeded by his sons Kaliman I, who reigned 1241–46, and Michael, who reigned 1246–57. With Michael's death the direct Asen line became extinct.

Ivan III or **Ivan the Great,** 1440–1505, grand duke of Moscow (1462–1505), creator of the consolidated Muscovite (Russian) state. He subjugated (1478) Great NOVGOROD, asserted his sway over Vyatka, Tver, Yaroslavl, Rostov, and other territories, and checked the eastward expansion of Lithuania, from which he gained some former Russian lands. In 1480 he freed Muscovy from allegiance to the Tatars of the GOLDEN HORDE. To prevent insurrection in annexed territories, Ivan transplanted their ruling classes to Old Muscovy and replaced them with loyal Muscovites. Prudence and wisdom were said to be his dominant traits. He established autocratic government and took as his second wife Sophia, niece of the last Byzantine emperor. The two-headed eagle of Byzantium was added to the arms of Muscovy, Sophia introduced customs of the Byzantine court, and the idea of Moscow as a "third Rome" (successor to the might of Rome and the Byzantine Empire) became popular in official circles. Laws were codified, foreign artisans were introduced, and Italian architects erected churches, palaces, and fortifications. Ivan was succeeded by his son, Vasily III.

Ivan IV or **Ivan the Terrible,** 1530–84, grand duke of Moscow (1533–84), first to assume formally the title of czar. He succeeded his father VASILY III, who died in 1533, under the regency of his mother. When she died (1538), the regency alternated among several feuding boyar families. Boyar rule ended only in 1546, when Ivan announced his intention of becoming czar. He was crowned in 1547. As czar, Ivan attempted to establish czarist autocracy at the expense of boyar power. In the early years of his reign, he reduced the arbitrary powers of the boyar provincial governors, transferring their functions to locally elected officials. The former boyars' council was replaced by a "chosen council" consisting of members who owed their status to the czar. In 1566, Ivan summoned what was probably the first general council of the realm *(Zemsky Sobor),* composed of representatives of different social ranks, including merchants and lower nobility. After reorganizing the army, Ivan conquered Kazan (1552) and Astrakhan (1556), thereby inaugurating Russia's eastward expansion. The conquest of Siberia by the Cossack YERMAK took place late in his reign (1581–83). Ivan also began trade with England via the White Sea in the mid-1550s. To improve his access to the Baltic Sea, he undertook (1558) a campaign against Livonia. In the resulting war with Poland and Sweden, he was at first successful but was later defeated by Stephen BATHORY, king of Poland and Lithuania. The peace treaties (1582, 1583) forced the czar to renounce his territorial gains and cede additional territory to Sweden. In his later years, Ivan's character, always stern, grew tyrannical. Apart from the reverses of the war, the change has been attributed to humiliations at the hands of the boyars during his childhood; a serious illness (1553) and resistance at that time to his efforts to secure the succession of his infant son; the death of his wife, Anastasia Romanov (1560), whom historians credit with exercising a moderating influence; and the defection to Poland of his favorite, Prince Andrew Kurbsky (1564). Suspecting conspiracies everywhere, he acted ruthlessly to consolidate his power. In 1565 he set aside an extensive personal domain, the *oprichnina,* under his direct control. He established a special corps *(oprichniki),* responsible to him alone, to whom he granted part of this domain at will. With the help of this corps, he diminished the political influence of the boyars and forcibly confiscated their lands in a reign of terror. Many boyars were executed or exiled. He formally abolished the *oprichnina* in 1572, although in effect it continued until 1575. Fits of rage alternated with periods of repentance and prayer; in one of his rages he killed (1581) his son and heir, Ivan. Although the exact number of his wives is uncertain, Ivan probably married seven times, ridding himself of unwanted wives by forcing them to take the veil or arranging for their murder. Despite his cruelty, he was a man of intelligence and learning. Printing was introduced into Russia during his reign, and his correspondence with the mutinous Prince Kurbsky reveals literary talent. Two sons, FEODOR I and DMITRI, survived the czar, but after his death his favorite, Boris GODUNOV, gained power. See biographies by Stephen Graham (1933, repr. 1968), Hans von Eckhardt (tr. 1949), and Ian Grey (1964); J. L. I. Fennell, ed., *The Correspondence between Prince A. M. Kurbsky and Tsar Ivan IV of Russia, 1564–1579* (1955).

Ivan V, 1666–96, czar of Russia (1682–96), son of Czar Alexis by his first wife. Ivan was retarded, and on the death of his elder brother, Feodor III, his succession was widely opposed by the supporters of his half brother, PETER I (Peter the Great). However, Ivan and Peter jointly succeeded under the regency of Ivan's sister SOPHIA ALEKSEYEVNA. After the overthrow (1689) of Sophia's regency, Ivan was excluded from state affairs and Peter assumed control. Ivan's elder daughter, Catherine, was the grandmother of Ivan VI; his younger daughter, Anna, became czarina of Russia in 1730. See C. B. O'Brien, *Russia under Two Tsars* (1952).

Ivan VI, 1740–64, czar of Russia (1740–41), great-grandson of Ivan V. He was the son of Prince Anthony Ulric of Brunswick-Wolfenbüttel and of ANNA LEOPOLDOVNA. An infant, he succeeded his great-aunt, Czarina Anna, on the Russian throne under the unpopular regency of his mother. In 1741, ELIZABETH, daughter of Peter I (Peter the Great), overthrew Anna Leopoldovna's regime and became czarina. Ivan grew up in solitary confinement. An attempt by a young officer to liberate him and make him czar resulted in his murder in the fortress of Schlüsselburg, according to standing instructions given by Czarina Catherine II.

Ivan Asen: see IVAN II, czar of Bulgaria.

Ivano-Frankovsk (ĭvä'nô-fräng'kôfsk), formerly **Stanislav** (stənyĭsläf'), city (1970 pop. 105,000), capital of Ivano-Frankovsk oblast, extreme SW European USSR, in Ukraine, on the Bystritsa River. It is a rail junction and industrial center situated in a fertile agricultural zone of the Carpathian foothills. The city has oil refineries, railroad repair shops, engineering and food processing plants, and factories that produce farm machinery, metal goods, leather footwear, furniture, cement, clothing, and other items. Oil fields are nearby. An old Ukrainian settlement, Stanislav was chartered in 1662 and, despite Tatar and Turkish raids, flourished as a trade center in the 17th and 18th cent. It became the bishopric of the Ukrainian Catholic Uniate Church in 1850. It passed to Austria in 1772 and to Poland in 1919 and was incorporated into the Ukraine in 1939. The city and oblast were renamed in 1962 in honor of the Ukrainian poet and writer Ivan Franko. Landmarks include a wooden church (1601), a Catholic Uniate cathedral, and an 18th-century palace.

Ivanov, Lev (lyĕf ēvä'nôf), 1834–1901, Russian dancer, teacher, choreographer, and ballet-master. Ivanov was assistant to chief ballet-master Marius PETIPA at the Imperial St. Petersburg Theatres and was instrumental in the development of the classic romantic ballet in Russia. When Petipa fell ill, Ivanov created the choreography for *The Nutcracker* (1892) to the music of Tchaikovsky. After Tchaikovsky's death, the previously unsuccessful *Swan Lake* (1877) was revised with choreography by Petipa and Ivanov, each doing alternate acts in varying styles. His other major works include revivals or stagings of *La Fille Mal Gardée, The Enchanted Forest, The Magic Flute,* and *Cinderella.* Ivanov sought a closer relationship of dance and music, thereby influencing the work of later choreographers, including Michel FOKINE.

Ivanov, Vsevolod Vyacheslavovich (fəsyĕ'vələt vyĕ"chĭslä'vəvĭch), 1895–1963, Russian short-story writer, novelist, and dramatist, b. Siberia. Ivanov had an adventurous early life as a sailor, circus performer, fakir, and partisan fighter. His talent for vivid description and ironic point of view was discovered and encouraged by Gorky. The novel *Armoured Train 14-69* (1922, tr. 1933), based on an episode of Soviet expansion in Siberia, is considered the most important of his many works. A long, semi-autobiographical novel, *The Adventures of a Fakir,* was translated in abridged form in 1935. His later work includes *Saga of the Sergeant* (tr. 1952).

Ivanovo (ēvä'nəvə), city (1970 pop. 419,000), capital of Ivanovo oblast, central European USSR, in the Moscow industrial region. A great Soviet textile center, the city was the historic center of Russia's cotton-milling industry. From the 1880s it was a center of labor unrest. During the revolution of 1905, 60,000 workers went on strike and formed one of the first soviets of workers' representatives. After six weeks the strike was crushed. The city was called Ivano-Voznesensk until 1932.

Ivan the Great: see IVAN III.

Ivan the Terrible: see IVAN IV.

Ives, Charles, 1874–1954, American composer and organist, b. Danbury, Conn., grad. Yale, 1898; pupil of Dudley Buck and Horatio Parker. He was organist (1893–1904) in churches in Connecticut, New Jersey, and New York. In the insurance business from 1898 to 1930, Ives was at the same time composing music that was advanced in style, anticipating some of the innovations of Schoenberg and Stravinsky, but not influencing the trend of music because most of his works were not published. They were little known until 1939, when performance of his second piano sonata, *Concord* (1909–15), won him wide recognition. In 1947 his Third Symphony was awarded the Pulitzer Prize. His works include symphonies, orchestral suites, sonatas, organ pieces, choral works, a great deal of chamber music, and about 150 songs. He often used American folk music in compositions evoking the spirit of various aspects of American life such as revival meetings and brass-band parades. See his *Essays before a Sonata* (new ed. 1962) and his *Memos,* ed. by J. E. Kirkpatrick (1972); biography by Henry and Sidney Cowell (rev. ed. 1969); Vivian

Perlis, *Charles Ives Remembered* (1974); R. S. Perry, *Charles Ives and the American Mind* (1974).

Ives, Frederic Eugene, 1856–1937, American inventor, b. Litchfield, Conn. A pioneer in the development of orthochromatic and trichromatic photography and of photoengraving, he followed an earlier suggestion by James Clerk Maxwell and produced in 1881 the first set of trichromatic plates. In 1878 he devised the first practical halftone process of photoengraving, developing it in 1886 to the process which came into general use. Among his other inventions are the short-tube, single-objective binocular microscope; the parallax stereogram; and a process for moving pictures in natural colors. His son **Herbert Eugene Ives,** 1882–1953, inventor and physicist, b. Philadelphia, was active in the development of television. He demonstrated the transmission via telephone wires of black-and-white pictures in 1924 and of color pictures in 1929. He made a number of important contributions to color science and invented the first practical artificial-daylight lamp.

Ives, James Merritt: see CURRIER & IVES.

Ivigtut (ē'vĭgto͝ot), town (1969 pop. 75), SW Greenland, on the Arsuk Fjord. The world's largest known cryolite deposit was discovered there in 1806. Mined since 1864, the deposit has been recently exhausted; stockpiled cryolite has been exported since 1969.

Iviza: see IBIZA.

Ivo of Chartres, Saint (ī'vō, shär'trə), c.1040–c.1116, French churchman, bishop of Chartres (after 1090). He was fearlessly outspoken and was briefly imprisoned for opposing the irregular second marriage of King PHILIP I of France. He worked to obtain a compromise in the imperial struggle over investitures. His principal fame was for his knowledge of CANON LAW. His *Decretum* and *Panormia,* collections of canons, were perhaps the most extensive until supplanted by the work of GRATIAN. Feast: May 24.

ivory, type of dentin present only in the tusks of the ELEPHANT. In commerce, ivory is classified as live (from recently killed animals) and dead (tusks long stored or on the ground for extended periods and lacking the resilience of live ivory). Ivory may be of a soft or hard variety; the former type is more moist, cracks less easily than the brittle hard ivory, and is easier to work. Green, or guinea, ivory denotes certain types of ivory obtained from a wide belt in north central Africa, from the east to the west coasts. Ivory is obtained mainly from Africa, where elephant tusks are larger than they are in Asia, the second major source, and much dead ivory has been taken from remains of extinct mammoths found in Canada, Alaska, and Siberia. African tusks of about 55 lb (25 kg) each are common, although tusks of more than 200 lb (91 kg) have been recorded. At various periods in Africa native peoples, Arabs, and European colonial powers have dominated the trade in ivory. Zanzibar, Antwerp, and London have been major centers of ivory commerce. Europe, the United States, and India are major importers. In the West, soft ivory, obtainable primarily from the eastern half of Africa, is in greater demand than the hard variety from W Africa. Commercial uses of ivory include the manufacture of piano and organ keys, billiard balls, handles, and minor objects of decorative value. In modern industry, ivory is used in the manufacture of electrical appliances, including specialized electrical equipment for airplanes and radar. Large surfaces suitable for veneer are obtained by cutting spiral sheets around the tusk. Ivory is prized for its close-grained texture, adhesive hardness, mellow color, and pleasing smoothness. It may be painted or bleached, and is an excellent material for carving. Its use in art dates back to prehistoric times, when representations of animals were incised on tusks. Objects in ivory were created in ancient Egypt, Assyria, Crete, Mycenae, Greece, and Italy, and there are many Biblical references to its use at least from the time of Solomon. Large Greek statues, such as the Athena of PHIDIAS, were made in gold and ivory (chryselephantine), and the Romans made lavish use of ivory in furniture, implements of war, and decorative items. A considerable number of diptychs and panels in ivory, given as gifts primarily by Roman consuls, still exist. Ivory plaques, diptychs, boxes, liturgical objects, book covers, and small statues were made in great numbers from early Christian times until c.1400, but the production of these objects declined thereafter. Ivory carving was practiced both in W Europe and in the Byzantine Empire. In India, ivory carving and turning has been done from ancient times. In China and Japan ivory has been used for inlay and small objects, especially for statues and carvings of small size and great precision and beauty of detail. In the last few centuries in Europe and North America, ivory has been employed to decorate furniture, for small statues, and occasionally as a surface for miniature painting. The diminishing number of elephants, to a large extent the result of wholesale slaughter for tusks, and the resulting increased cost of ivory have encouraged the making of imitations. Natural substitutes (e.g., TAGUA, or vegetable ivory) or near equivalents have long been used. In the past, the tooth structure of many other animals, such as the hippopotamus, walrus, narwhal, sperm whale, and wild boar, was also called ivory. See O. Beigbeder, *Ivory* (1965); M. Carra, *Ivories of the West* (1970).

ivory-billed woodpecker, common name for the largest of the North American woodpeckers, *Campephilus principalis.* Believed since 1952 to be nearing extinction, the last known members of this species were reported from the deepest forests of NW Florida and central Louisiana. A shiny blue-black in color with extensive white markings on its wings and neck, this bird is distinguished by its pure white bill and by a prominent top crest, red in the male and black in the female. A true WOODPECKER, it has a strong and straight chisellike bill and a long, mobile, hard-tipped, sticky tongue. It measures from 18 to 20 in. (46–51 cm) in length, with short legs and feet ending in large, curved claws. The ivory-bill deposits from three to five glossy white eggs per clutch in an unlined hole, preferably drilled in a cyprus tree. Of its reproductive habits little more than this is known. The disappearance of the ivory-bills may be blamed on the cutting and eventual disappearance of the trees in which they lived. It is thought that a few ivory-bills are surviving today in the forests of the Gulf Coast of North America and in Cuba. Ivory-billed woodpeckers are classified in the phylum CHORDATA, subphylum Vertebrata, class Aves, order Piciformes, family Picidae.

Ivory Coast, Fr. *Côte d'Ivoire,* independent republic (1973 est. pop. 4,585,000), 124,503 sq mi (322,463 sq km), W Africa, on the Gulf of Guinea of the Atlantic Ocean. The capital and chief port is ABIDJAN. The Ivory Coast is bordered by Liberia and Guinea on the west, by Mali and Upper Volta on the north, and by Ghana on the east. The country consists of a coastal lowland in the south, a densely forested plateau in the interior, and a region of high savannas in the north. Rainfall is heavy, especially along the

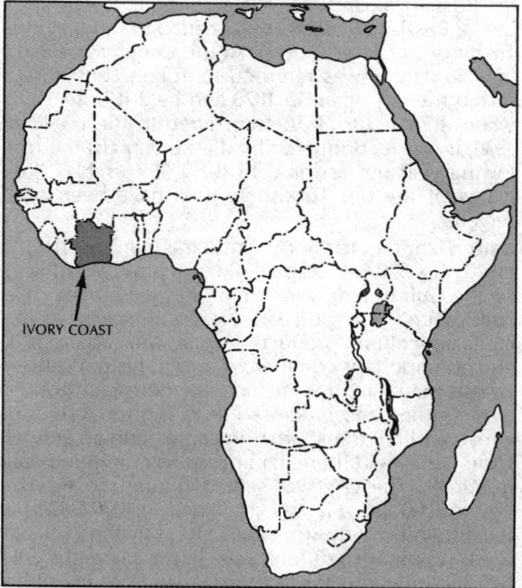

coast. Among the major ethnic groups in the Ivory Coast are the Agni, Baoulé, and Senufo tribes. The population is about 65% animist, 23% Muslim, and 12% Christian. French is the official language, and French personnel play an important role in the economy. The wealthiest member of what was formerly French West Africa, the Ivory Coast has enjoyed a high economic growth rate since independence. Despite steady industrialization during the 1960s, the country is still predominantly agricultural. The Ivory Coast is one of the world's largest coffee producers. Cotton, cocoa, bananas, pineapples, and palm kernels are raised for export. Mahogany and other hardwood forests provide timber, which is also a valuable export. Livestock is raised in the savannas. Fishing and the canning of tuna are also important occupations. Among the country's industries are the production of flour, palm oil, petroleum, textiles, cigarettes, and the assembly of motor vehicles and bicycles. France is the chief trading partner of the Ivory Coast, which belongs to the French franc zone and is an associate member of the European Common Market. In precolonial times the Ivory Coast was dominated by native kingdoms. The Portuguese established trading settlements along the coast in the 16th cent., and other Europeans later joined the burgeoning trade in slaves and ivory. In 1842 a French military mission imposed a protectorate over the coastal zone. After 1870, France undertook a systematic conquest; although a protectorate over the entire country was proclaimed in 1893, strong resistance by native tribes delayed French occupation of the interior. The Ivory Coast was incorporated into the Federation of French West Africa, and several thousand troops from the Ivory Coast fought with the French during World War I; but effective French control over the area was not established until after the war. Vichy forces held the Ivory Coast during World War II, but many Ivorians left to join the Free French forces in the Gold Coast. As the desire for independence mounted, Félix HOUPHOUËT-BOIGNY, a planter and founder of the federation-wide Rassemblement Démocratique Africain (RDA), formed (1946) the nationalist Parti Démocratique de la Côte d'Ivoire (PDCI). In the French constitutional referendum of 1958, the Ivory Coast chose autonomy within the French Community. The following year Houphouët-Boigny played an instrumental role in the formation of the Council of the Entente, a customs union with Dahomey, Nigeria, and Upper Volta (Togo joined later). In 1960 the Ivory Coast withdrew from the French Community and declared itself independent. The new republic joined the Organization of African Unity in 1963. The Ivory Coast is a one-party state. Houphouët-Boigny has headed the government as well as the PDCI since independence. As president of the republic, he is elected for a five-year term by universal adult suffrage. The national assembly is elected concurrently on a single slate. Despite student and worker unrest, Houphouët-Boigny's leadership has not been seriously challenged. In 1966 a treaty signed at Abidjan provided for a new West African customs union (superseding the Council of the Entente), including Mauritania and Senegal as well as the old council members. The Ivory Coast was one of the few African states to recognize Biafra during the Nigerian civil war (1967–70); this action, as well as Houphouët-Boigny's advocacy of dialogue with white-ruled South Africa, estranged the country somewhat from many other African states. See Immanuel Wallerstein, *Road to Independence: Ghana and the Ivory Coast* (1964); Aristide R. Zolberg, *One-Party Government in the Ivory Coast* (rev. ed. 1969); Christian P. Potholm, *Four African Political Systems* (1970); Philip Foster and Aristide R. Zolberg, ed., *Ghana and the Ivory Coast: Perspectives in Modernization* (1971).

ivory nut: see TAGUA.

Ivrea (ēvrĕ'ä), city (1971 pop. 29,358), Piedmont, NW Italy, on the Dora Baltea River. It is a commercial and industrial center. Manufactures include typewriters and calculating machines, textiles, and silverware. A Roman town (*Eporedia*), it was later the capital of a Lombard duchy and then the seat of a marquisate. BERENGAR II, one of its rulers, was briefly king of Italy (mid-10th cent.). Ivrea passed to the house of Savoy in the 14th cent. The city is dominated by a picturesque castle (14th cent.), which has four red brick towers.

Ivry-sur-Seine (ēvrē'-sür-sĕn), industrial and commercial suburb SE of Paris (1968 pop. 60,616), Val-de-Marne dept., N central France. Its port, on the Seine River, deals in wholesale trade in fuel, timber, barrels, and foodstuffs. Its manufactures include chemicals, metals, pharmaceuticals, and oils. There are churches dating from the 13th, 16th, and 17th cent. A thermal-power station is in the town.

ivy, name applied loosely to any trailing or CLIMBING PLANT, particularly cultivated forms, but more properly a designation for *Hedera helix,* the so-called English ivy, and some related species of the family Araliaceae (GINSENG family). Native to Europe and temperate Asia, English ivy is a woody evergreen vine, usually sterile, whose berries contain the poisonous principle hederin. Grown in numerous varieties, it is the most popular house and wall vine. The Boston, or Japanese, ivy (*Parthenocissus tricuspidata,* of Japan and China) and the American ivy, or VIRGINIA CREEPER (*P. quinquefolia,* of North America), are similar species of the family Vitaceae (GRAPE family). Both are sometimes called AMPELOPSIS, a name usually reserved for another related genus. Kenilworth ivy, *Cymbalaria muralis,* of the family Scrophulariaceae (FIGWORT family) is common to old ruins in Europe; it is often cultivated as a ground cover. Ivy was sacred to Bacchus and was associated with various pagan religions. It was formerly hung as a tavern sign in England. Ivy is classified in the division MAGNOLIOPHYTA, class Magnoliopsida. The ginseng family ivies are in the order Umbellales, the grape family ivies in the order Rhamnales, and the figwort family ivies in the order Scrophulariales.

Iwaki (ēwä'kē), city (1970 pop. 327,164), Fukushima prefecture, NE Honshu, Japan, on the Iwaki River. It is a major coal-mining center, railway hub, and industrial city where machinery, chemicals, and chemical fertilizers are produced.

Iwakuni (ēwä'ko͞onē), city (1970 pop. 106,116), Yamaguchi prefecture, SW Honshu, Japan, on the Aki Sea. It is an important industrial center with petroleum refineries and rayon, chemical fiber, paper pulp, and metal machine-tool industries. Iwakuni castle (1603) is an important historical site.

Iwakura, Tomomi, Prince (tōmō'mē ēwä'ko͞orä), 1825–83, Japanese statesman. A court noble, he supported the Meiji restoration and became a minister of state (1871–83). In 1871 he headed a mission to Europe and the United States that failed to secure abolition of the unequal treaties but brought back much useful information on foreign institutions and technology. He returned to Japan in 1873 to forestall the threat of war with Korea. From 1873 until his death Iwakura, a conservative, was a leader of the peace party.

Iwasa Matabei: see MATABEI, IWASA.

Iwata (ēwä'tä), city (1970 pop. 63,002), Shizuoka prefecture, central Honshu, Japan, on the estuary of the Tenryu River. It is an agricultural and industrial center.

Iwatsuki (ēwä'tso͞okē), city (1970 pop. 56,449), Saitama prefecture, central Honshu, Japan, on the Edo River. It is an industrial center where textiles and dolls are manufactured.

Iwo (ē'wō), city (1969 est. pop. 189,000), SW Nigeria. It is the trade center for a farm region specializing in cacao. A coffee plantation is located nearby. Iwo was the capital of a YORUBA kingdom (founded in the 17th cent.) that grew rapidly in the 19th cent. by taking in refugees during the Yoruba civil wars.

Iwo Jima (ē'wō jē'mə, ē'wô), Jap. *Io-jima,* volcanic island, c.8 sq mi (21 sq km), W Pacific, largest and most important of the VOLCANO ISLANDS. Mt. Suribachi, 546 ft (166 m) high, on the south side of the island, is an extinct volcano. The main industries are sulfur mining and sugar refining. During World War II the island, site of a Japanese air base, was taken (Feb.–March, 1945), at great cost by U.S. forces. Iwo Jima was formerly called Sulphur Island.

IWW: see INDUSTRIAL WORKERS OF THE WORLD.

Ixelles (ēksĕl'), Flemish *Elsene,* city (1970 pop. 86,450), Brabant prov., central Belgium, an industrial suburb of Brussels.

Ixion (ĭk'sēən), in Greek mythology, king of the Lapithes. Ixion murdered his father-in-law to avoid paying a price for his bride. When no one on earth would purify him, Zeus took Ixion to Olympus and purified him. While there Ixion attempted to seduce Hera, but Zeus created a phantom of her and by it Ixion became the father of the centaur monsters. As punishment for his impious act, Ixion was chained eternally to a revolving, fiery wheel in Tartarus.

Ixtacalco (ēstäkäl'kō), city (1970 pop. 474,700), Federal District, S central Mexico. It is an industrial center adjacent to Mexico City. Several historic landmarks have been preserved.

Ixtacihuatl, Ixtaccihuatl, or **Iztaccihuatl** (all: ēs"täsē'wätəl) [Aztec, = white woman], dormant volcano, 17,342 ft (5,286 m) high, central Mexico, on the border between Puebla and Mexico state. Irregular in outline, and snow-capped, it is also popularly known as the Sleeping Woman.

Ixtapalapa (ēstäpälä'pä), city (1970 pop. 533,569), Federal District, S central Mexico. It is a commercial and industrial center. Ixtapalapa was founded on the site of an important pre-Columbian Indian city.

Iyeyasu: see IEYASU.

Izabal (ēsäbäl'), lake, c.30 mi (48 km) long and 15 mi (24 km) wide, E Guatemala, largest lake in the country. Known also as the Golfo Dulce, it drains to the Caribbean Sea through the Golfete Dulce, a small adjacent lake, and the Rio Dulce, a broad tropical river. In Spanish colonial times Lake Izabal was the scene of lively trading between the seacoast and the highlands, and the small town of Izabal on its south shore was a thriving port, constantly subjected to raids in the 17th cent. by English and Dutch buccaneers. Today shipping is negligible, although Lívingston, at the mouth of the Rio Dulce, is of some importance. Nearby are many pre-Columbian ruins, the most outstanding being at Quiriguá.

Izalco (ēsäl'kō), volcano, 7,828 ft (2,386 m) high, W El Salvador. Constantly active and still increasing in height, it is sometimes called the Lighthouse of the Pacific. There have been severe eruptions. The crater was first studied in 1956 by a French expedition.

Izard, Ralph (ĭz'ərd), 1742–1804, American diplomat and legislator, b. near Charleston, S.C. After an education in England, he returned (1764) to South Carolina but in 1771 again went to London. Because of his sympathy with the colonial cause, Izard moved (1776) to Paris. Appointed (1777) commissioner to Tuscany by the Continental Congress, he was not received by that government, but he felt that, as an American diplomat, he should take part in American negotiations with France and thus won the enmity of Benjamin Franklin. Izard's connection with the De Lanceys, New York Loyalists, led to accusations that he was a Tory; however, his sincere devotion to the patriot cause was demonstrated, and after his return (1779) to America he served (1782–84) in the Continental Congress. A Federalist, he strongly supported the Constitution and was (1789–95) Senator from South Carolina. See his *Correspondence, 1774–1804* (1844).

Izehar (ĭz'ēhär) or **Izhar** (ĭz'här), grandson of Levi. 1 Chron. 6.2,18,38; 23.12,18; Ex. 6.18,21; Num. 3.19. Amminadab: 1 Chron. 6.22.

Izhevsk (ēzhĭfsk'), city (1970 pop. 422,000), capital of Udmurt Autonomous SSR, E European USSR. A major steel-milling and metallurgical center, Izhevsk has ironworks dating back to 1760.

Izmail (ēzməēl'), city (1967 est. pop. 63,000), SW European USSR, in the Ukraine, on an arm of the Danube delta and near the Rumanian border. It is a rail junction, river port, commercial center, and the naval base of the Soviet Danube flotilla. Orchards and vineyards surround the city. Izmail's industries include food and fish processing, winemaking, auto and ship repair, and the manufacture of bricks and tiles. First known in the 16th cent., the city was a Turkish fortress and capital of a Turkish sanjak. Russian forces took the city twice (1770, 1790) during the Russo-Turkish Wars of Catherine II. Recaptured by the Russians in 1809, it was ceded to them by the Treaty of Bucharest (1812). At the Congress of Paris in 1856, Izmail was returned to Turkey; but Russia seized the city again in 1878 and held it until 1918, when Rumania took it. Transferred to the USSR in 1940, it was reconquered by the Rumanians the following year but restored to the USSR in 1947. Remains of the old Turkish fortress have been preserved.

İzmir (ĭzmĭr'), formerly **Smyrna** (smûr'nə), city (1970 pop. 520,686), capital of İzmir prov., W Turkey, on the Gulf of İzmir, an arm of the Aegean Sea. The largest Turkish seaport after İstanbul, its exports include agricultural products, cotton, and carpets. It is also an important commercial and industrial center, whose manufactures include paper, metal goods, dyes, textiles, and processed food and tobacco. It is a road and rail transportation center, and an annual trade fair is held there. İzmir prov. is rich in mineral resources. The city was settled during the Bronze Age (c.3000 B.C.). It was colonized (c.1000 B.C.) by Ionians and was destroyed (627 B.C.) by the Lydians. It was rebuilt on a different site in the early 4th cent. B.C. by Antigonus I, was enlarged and beautified by Lysimachus, and became one of the largest and most prosperous cities of Asia Minor. Its wealth and splendor increased under Roman rule. The city had a sizeable Jewish colony, was an early center of Christianity, and was one of the Seven Churches in Asia (Rev. 2–8). It was pillaged by the Arabs in the 7th cent., fell to the Seljuk Turks in the 11th cent., was recaptured for Byzantium by Emperor Alexius I during the First Crusade, and formed part of the empire of Nicaea from 1204 to 1261, when the Byzantine Empire was restored. Also in 1261 the Genoese obtained trading privileges there, which they retained until the city fell (c.1329) to the Seljuk Turks. The Knights Hospitalers captured the city in 1344, restored Genoese privileges, and held the city until 1402, when it was captured and sacked by Tamerlane. The Mongols were succeeded in 1424 by the Ottoman Turks. A Greek Orthodox archiepiscopal see, the city retained a large Greek population and remained a center of Greek culture and the chief Mediterranean port of Asia Minor. After the collapse of the Ottoman Empire in World War I, the city was occupied (1919) by Greek forces. The Treaty of Sevres (1920) assigned İzmir and its hinterland to temporary Greek administration, but fighting soon erupted between Greek and Turkish forces. İzmir fell to the Turks in Sept., 1922, and a few days later was destroyed by fire. Thousands of Greek civilian refugees fled from the city. The Treaty of Lausanne (1923) restored İzmir to Turkey. A separate convention between Greece and Turkey provided for the exchange of their minorities, which was carried out under League of Nations supervision. Thus the population of İzmir became predominately Turkish. The city suffered greatly from severe earthquakes in 1928 and 1939. By the 1970s, however, it was a thriving, modern city. It is the site of Ege Univ. and several museums and was probably the birthplace of the poet Homer.

İzmit (ĭzmĕt') or **Kocaeli** (kō"jäĕl'ē), city (1970 pop. 123,016), capital of Kocaeli prov., NW Turkey, a port on the Bay of İzmit, at the eastern end of the Sea of Marmara. It is the center of a rich tobacco- and olive-growing region. Manufactures of the city include beer and paper and paper products. Founded c.712 B.C., the city became famous after Nicomedus I of Bithynia rebuilt it in 264 B.C. as his capital, NICOMEDIA.

Iznik: see NICAEA.

Izrahiah (ĭz"rəhī'ə), chief man of Issachar. 1 Chron. 7.3.

Izrahite (ĭz'rəhīt), patronymic: see ZERAH **1.**

Izri (ĭz'rī), temple musician. 1 Chron. 25.11. In verse 3 he is called Zeri.

Izumi (ēzo͞o'mē), city (1970 pop. 95,987), Osaka prefecture, S Honshu, Japan. It is a residential and commercial suburb of Osaka, with numerous textile mills.

Izumiotsu (ēzo͞omē'ōtso͞o), city (1970 pop. 59,437), Osaka prefecture, S Honshu, Japan, on Osaka Bay. It is a commercial port with chemical and textile industries.

Izumisano (ēzo͞omē'sänō), city (1970 pop. 77,000), Osaka prefecture, S Honshu, Japan, on Osaka Bay. It is a fishing and commercial port.

Izumo (ēzo͞o'mō), city (1970 pop. 69,708), Shimane prefecture, SW Honshu, Japan, on the Hii River. It is an important commercial, agricultural, and stock-raising center.

Izu-shichito (ē'zo͞o-shēchē'tō), island group, extending c.300 mi (480 km) S of Tokyo Bay, Japan. O-shima is the largest of these volcanic islands, which are now tourist attractions. The islands were formerly used for penal settlements. They are also called the Seven Isles of Izu.

Izvolsky, Aleksandr Petrovich (əlyĭksän'dər pētrô'-vĭch ēzvôl'skē), 1856–1919, Russian diplomat instrumental in fostering the Triple Entente with France and Great Britain. He rose in the diplomatic service and in 1906 was appointed foreign minister by Czar Nicholas II. In 1907 he reached an agreement with Great Britain ending the rivalry between the two powers in the Middle East: Persia was divided into three zones, one Russian, one British, with a neutral zone between; Afghanistan was recognized as being under British protection; and Tibet was declared neutral. This agreement, in conjunction with the Franco-Russian alliance formed in the 1890s and the Anglo-French accord in 1904, marked the emergence of the Triple Entente. In 1908, Izvolsky attempted to open the Dardanelles to Russian warships through an agreement with the Austro-Hungarian foreign minister AEHRENTHAL. In return for Russian acceptance of Austrian annexation of Bosnia and Hercegovina, Austria agreed to support the opening of the straits. Austria failed to keep its part of the pact, and Izvolsky suffered a humiliating diplomatic defeat. Appointed (1910) ambassador to France, he endeavored to strengthen Franco-Russian ties. After the Russian Revolution he remained in France. See his memoirs (tr. 1920).

J

J, 10th letter of the ALPHABET, a Western European medieval development of *I,* with which it was formerly quite interchangeable in writing. It is pronounced as a consonant in English and often as a *y* in other languages, as in the Hebrew *hallelujah.*

Jaakobah (jā″əkō′bə), prince of the family of Simeon. 1 Chron. 4.36.

Jaala or **Jaalah** (both: jā′ălə), post-Exilic family. Ezra 2.56; Neh. 7.58.

Jaalam (jā-ā′ləm, jā′əlăm), son of Esau. Gen. 36.5,14, 18; 1 Chron. 1.35.

Jaanai (jā′ānī, jā-ā′-), chief Gadite. 1 Chron. 5.12.

Jaare-oregim (jāăr′ē-ōr′ĕgĭm), father of David's man Elhanan. 2 Sam. 21.19. Jair: 1 Chron. 20.5.

Jaasau (jā′əsô), Jew who married a foreign wife. Ezra 10.37.

Jaasiel (jā-ā′sēēl), ruler of Benjamin. 1 Chron. 27.21. See JASIEL.

Jaazaniah (jā″ăzənī′ə). **1** Head of a number of idolatrous priests whom Ezekiel saw in a vision. Ezek. 8.11. **2** Captain active in the politics of Palestine at the time of the fall of Jerusalem. 2 Kings 25.23. Jezaniah: Jer. 40.8. Azariah: Jer. 43.2. **3** Rechabite. Jer. 35.3. **4** Prince. Ezek. 11.1.

Jaazer (jā-ā′zər), variant of JAZER.

Jaaziah (jā″əzī′ə), descendant of Merari. 1 Chron. 24.26,27.

Jaaziel (jā-ā′zēēl), Levite. 1 Chron. 15.18. Aziel: 1 Chron. 15.20.

Jabal (jā′bəl), son of Lamech. Gen. 4.19,20.

Jabal ad Duruz (jăbäl′ äd dōōrōōz′), mountain, c.5,900 ft (1,800 m), S Syria, highest point of the Druses mts.

Jabalpur (jŭb″əlpôr′), city (1971 pop. 533,751), Madhya Pradesh state, central India, on the Narmada River. It is a district administrative center and an important rail junction and military post. Manufactures include weapons, ammunition, and cigarettes. Jabalpur Univ. is in the city.

Jabal Shammar (jă′bäl shă′mər), former emirate, N Saudi Arabia. Its capital was at Hail. In 1921, Ibn Saud conquered the forces of the emir, Ibn Rashid, and annexed the territory to his kingdom of Nejd.

Jabbar, Kareem Abdul (kərēm′ ăb′dōōl jəbär′), 1947–, American basketball player, b. New York City. The towering Jabbar (7 ft 1⅜ in./217 cm) joined the Milwaukee Bucks of the National Basketball Association after brilliant accomplishments as a high school and college basketball star. He led the Univ. of California at Los Angeles to three consecutive National Collegiate Athletic Association basketball championships (1967–69). Originally named Ferdinand Lewis (Lew) Alcindor, he adopted his Muslim name in 1970. Jabbar led the Bucks to the championship in the 1970–71 season. In his first five years in professional basketball (1969–74), he was voted most valuable player three times and scored well over 10,000 points.

Jabbok, river, Jordan: see ZARQA.

Jabesh-gilead (jā′bĕsh-gĭl′ēăd), city of Gilead. After the affair at Gibeah, wives were provided for the Benjamites by sacking Jabesh. Later, Saul saved Jabesh, and at his death the grateful city buried him. Judges 21; 1 Sam. 11; 31.11; 2 Sam. 2.4.

Jabez (jā′bĭz). **1** Judahite. 1 Chron. 4.9,10. **2** Unidentified place, S Palestine. 1 Chron. 2.55.

Jabin (jā′bĭn), name of two kings of Hazor. Joshua 11.1; Judges 4.2.

Jabir (jā′bĭr) or **Geber** (jē′bər), fl. 8th cent., Arab alchemist and physician, originally named Jabir ibn Hayyan. He is believed to have lived at Kufa and at Baghdad. A great number of works on alchemy, many of them unpublished, have been attributed to him, but scholars disagree as to their authenticity. Recent studies indicate that many of the extant works in Arabic were written in the 9th and 10th cent. by later Arab alchemists and issued under Jabir's name. The works influenced the development of medieval alchemy and indicate the use of laboratory experiments. They perpetuated the theory that metals are composed of mercury and sulfur and can be transmuted into gold. In the early 14th cent. a Spanish alchemist wrote under the Latinized form of the name, Geber; his works are considered the clearest expression of alchemical thought to appear before the 16th cent. Several of the Arabic works were translated by E. J. Holmyard and published in 1928.

jabiru: see STORK.

Jablonec nad Nisou (yä′blônĕts nät nĭ′sôōō), Ger. *Gablonz,* city (1970 pop. 34,218), N Czechoslovakia, in Bohemia, on the Lausitzer Neisse. The glassware center of Czechoslovakia, it also has industries that manufacture automobile equipment, textiles, plastics, and buttons and costume jewelry. The city has a 14th-century Gothic church.

Jabneel (jăb′nēĕl) [Heb.,=God causes to build]. **1** Place, NE Palestine. Joshua 19.33. **2** See JAMNIA.

Jabneh (jăb′nē), variant of JAMNIA.

Jabotinsky, Vladimir (yăb″ətĭn′skē), 1880–1940, Jewish Zionist leader, b. Russia. A fiery orator and an accomplished writer in several languages, he was a militant Zionist and a persistent advocate of Jewish self-defense against pogroms in Russia. He formed the first Jewish self-defense unit in Palestine during the clashes with the Arabs in 1920; this brought him into open conflict with the British. He strongly condemned the official policy of the Zionist organization, charging it with weakness and appeasement of the British in Palestine. In 1925 he founded the Zionist Revisionist organization, which advocated large-scale Jewish immigration into Palestine and the creation of a Jewish state on both sides of the Jordan River. At the beginning of World War II he worked for the creation of a Jewish army. He was the author of several books, including *The Story of the Jewish Legion* (tr. 1945). See biography by Joseph B. Schechtman (2 vol., 1956–61).

Jaca (hä′kä), town (1970 pop. 11,134), Huesca prov., NE Spain, in Aragón, in the Pyrenees (alt. c.2,700 ft/820 m), near the French border on the Aragón River. A communications center and an episcopal see, it is a processing center for lumber and for the farm products of the fertile Aragón valley. After its recapture from the Moors it was (11th cent.) the cradle of the Aragonese kingdom. Huesca, taken in 1097, replaced it as the capital. Jaca has ancient walls and towers and a Romanesque cathedral (11th–15th cent.).

jaçana (jəkăn′ə, jəkän′ə), common name for members of the Jacanidae, a family of tropical and subtropical wading birds. Jaçanas, also called lily-trotters and lotus-birds, have long toes and toenails that enable them to walk delicately on floating vegetation as they search for insects and mollusks. Like certain of the related plovers, jaçanas have defensive spurs on the angles of their wings. The American jaçana (10 in./25 cm long), *Jacana spinosa,* is cinnamon red with striking yellow-green wing patches. The female jaçana is slightly larger than the male, but has similar coloration. It lays about 4 eggs per clutch, which is incubated by the male for three to four weeks. Jaçanas are excellent swimmers and divers and build their nests to float on water. They are classified in the phylum CHORDATA, subphylum Vertebrata, class Aves, order Charadriiformes, family Jacanidae.

jacaranda (jăk″ərăn′də): see BIGNONIA.

Jachan (jā′kăn), chief of the house of Gad. 1 Chron. 5.13.

Jachin (jā′kĭn). **1** Son of Simeon. Gen. 46.10; Ex. 6.15; Num. 26.12. Jarib: 1 Chron. 4.24. **2** Chief priest. 1 Chron. 9.10; 24.17; Neh. 11.10.

Jachin and Boaz (bō′ăz), two pillars in front of Solomon's Temple, probably symbolic of God's presence. 1 Kings 7.21; 2 Chron. 3.17.

Jáchymov (yä′khĭmôf), Ger. *Joachimsthal,* town, W Czechoslovakia, in Bohemia, in the Erzgebirge [ore mountains]. A major pitchblende-mining center of Europe, the city also produces iron, uranium, radium, lead, zinc, nickel, and cobalt. It is also a noted health resort, with thermal radioactive springs. Jáchymov was the main center of silver mining in Europe after the 16th cent., but its present output is negligible. The word *Thaler,* from which *dollar* is derived, is an abbreviation of *Joachimsthaler,* the name of a coin first struck there in the 16th cent.

jacinth (jā′sĭnth): see HYACINTH, in mineralogy.

jack: see POMPANO; TUNA.

jack, mechanical device used to multiply a relatively small applied force so that it can lift and support heavy loads, or sometimes, move massive objects into a desired position. The lever jack, often used in lifting automobiles, has a lever combined with a ratchet; the lever is used to lift the load a small distance and the ratchet prevents the load from falling back while the lever is reset so that the process can be repeated. In the screw jack the load is moved or lifted by the turning of a screw; the pitch of the screw threads is arranged so that friction is sufficient to hold the load in place when the torque applied to the screw is released. In yet another form of jack a hydraulic device is used. See HYDRAULIC MACHINE.

jackal, name for several Old World carnivorous mammals of the genus *Canis,* which also includes the DOG and the WOLF. Some authorities classify jackals in a separate genus (*Thos*). Jackals are found in Africa and S Asia, where they inhabit deserts, grasslands, and brush country. They are similar in size and behavior to the North American prairie wolf, or COYOTE, and like the coyote, they howl in the early evening. Although renowned as scavengers, jackals also hunt small animals. Secretive animals, they forage by night and spend the day in holes or hidden in grass or brush. The black-backed jackal, *Canis mesomelas,* the simenian jackal, *C. simensis,* and the side-striped jackal, *C. adustus,* are all found in Africa, and are generally solitary animals. The golden, or Asiatic, jackal, *C. aureus,* is found in S Asia and N Africa; golden jackals are more social than the African jackals and usually hunt in small packs. Jackals are classified in the phylum CHORDATA, subphylum Vertebrata, class Mammalia, order Carnivora, family Canidae.

jackass: see ASS.

jack-in-the-pulpit: see ARUM.

Jackman, Wilbur Samuel, 1855–1907, American educator, b. Mechanicstown, Ohio, grad. Harvard, 1884. Jackman was a leader of the nature study movement in elementary schools. He taught (after 1889) at the Cook County Normal School in Chicago and, beginning with *Nature Study for the Common Schools* (1891), wrote texts and manuals. He was appointed dean of the new college of education in the Univ. of Chicago in 1901, but resigned in 1904 to become principal of the University Elementary School and to edit the *Elementary School Teacher.*

jack-o'-lantern, common name for the MUSHROOM species *Clitocybe illudens.*

jackrabbit, popular name for several HARES of W North America, characterized by very long legs and ears. Jackrabbits are powerful jumpers and fast runners. In normal progress leaps are alternated with running steps; when pursued the hare runs fast and close to the ground. Jackrabbits are found W of the Great Lakes and the Mississippi River, from S Canada to Central America. They are brownish gray above and white below. The white-tailed jackrabbit (*Lepus townsendi*) is the most northerly species and ranges from plains to high mountains. It has an entirely white tail, and its coat turns white or light gray in winter. It averages 20 in. (51 cm) in length, with ears 5 to 6 in. (12.7–15.3 cm) long. It is closely related to the varying hare and the arctic hare. The black-tailed jackrabbit (*L. californicus*) found on the plains and in arid regions from the NW United States to Mexico, is slightly smaller, with longer ears; its tail is black above. The antelope jackrabbit (*L. alleni*) of Mexico and the extreme SW United States is a large, heavy hare with white sides and ears up to 8 in. (20.3 cm) long. It has been known to leap as high as 5 ft (1.5 m) and as far as 22 ft (6.7 m). Jackrabbits are classified in the phylum CHORDATA, subphylum Vertebrata, class Mammalia, order Lagomorpha, family Leporidae.

jackscrew: see SCREW.

Jackson, Abraham Valentine Williams, 1862–1937, American Orientalist, b. New York City. From 1895 to 1935 he taught at Columbia. His particular interest was Persia, and he became a great authority on ancient Persian religion, language, and literature as well as the modern Parsis.

Jackson, Andrew, 1767–1845, 7th President of the United States (1829–37), b. Waxhaw settlement on the border of South Carolina and North Carolina (both states claim him). A child of the backwoods, he was left an orphan at 14. His long military career began in 1781, when he fought against the British in a skirmish at Hanging Rock. He and his brother were captured and imprisoned at Camden, S.C. After studying law at Salisbury, N.C., he was admitted to the bar in 1787 and practiced in the vicinity until he was appointed solicitor for the western district of North Carolina (now Tennessee). In 1788 he moved west to Nashville. He was prosperous in his law practice and in land speculation until the Panic of 1795 struck, leaving him with little more than his estate, the HERMITAGE, on which he lived as a cotton planter during the intervals of his political career and where he is buried. Jackson married Rachel Donelson before she had secured a legal divorce from her first husband, and though the ceremony was later repeated, his enemies made capital of the circumstance. He rose in politics, was a member of the convention that drafted the Tennessee Constitution, and was elected (1796) as the sole member from the new state in the U. S. House of Representatives. The next year when his political chief, William Blount, was expelled from the Senate, Jackson resigned and, to vindicate his party, ran for the vacant seat. He won, but in 1798 he resigned. From 1798 to 1804 he served notably as judge of the Tennessee superior court. In the War of 1812 he defeated the Creek warriors at Horseshoe Bend (March, 1814) after a strenuous campaign and won the rank of major general in the U.S. army. He was given command of an expedition to defend New Orleans against the British. The decisive victory gained there over seasoned British troops under Gen. Edward Pakenham, though it came after peace had already been signed in Europe, made Jackson the one great military hero of the War of 1812. In 1818 he was sent to take reprisals against the Seminole, who were raiding settlements near the Florida border, but, misinterpreting orders, he crossed the boundary line, captured Pensacola, and executed two British subjects as punishment for their stirring up the Indians. He thus involved the United States in serious trouble with both Spain and Great Britain. John Q. Adams, then Secretary of State, was the only cabinet member to defend him, but the conduct of Old Hickory, as Jackson was called by his admirers, pleased the people of the West. He moved on to the national scene as the standard-bearer of one wing of the old Republican party. The greatest popular hero of his time, a man of action, and an expansionist, he became associated with the movement toward increased popular participation in government. He was regarded by many as the symbol of the democratic feelings of the time, and later generations were to speak of Jacksonian democracy. Although in broadest terms this movement often attacked citadels of privilege or monopoly and sought to broaden opportunities in many areas of life, there has been much dispute among historians over its essential social nature. At one time it was characterized as being rooted in the democratic nature of the frontier. Later historians pointed to the workingmen of the Eastern cities as the defining element in the Jacksonian political coalition. More recently the older interpretations have been challenged by those seeing the age as one that primarily offered new opportunities to the middle class—an era of liberal capitalism. Jackson had appeal for the farmer, for the artisan, for the small businessman; he was viewed with suspicion and fear by men of established position, who considered him a dangerous upstart. He rode on a wave of popularity that almost took him ino the presidency in the election of 1824. The vote was split with Henry CLAY and John Quincy ADAMS, and when the election was decided in the House of Representatives, Clay threw his influence to Adams, and Adams became President. By the time of the election of 1828, Jackson's cause was more assured. John C. CALHOUN, who was the candidate for Vice President with Jackson, brought most of William H. Crawford's former following to Jackson, while Martin VAN BUREN and the Albany Regency swung liberal-controlled New York state to him. The result was a sweeping victory; Jackson polled four times the popular vote that he had received in 1824. His inauguration brought the "rabble" into the White House, to the distaste of the established families. There was a strong element of personalism in the rule of the hotheaded Jackson, and the KITCHEN CABINET—a small group of favorite advisers—was powerful. Vigorous publicity and violent journalistic attacks on anti-Jacksonians were ably handled by such men as the elder Francis P. BLAIR, Duff GREEN, and Amos KENDALL. Party loyalty was intense, and party members were rewarded with government posts in what came to be known as the SPOILS SYSTEM. Personal relationships were of utmost importance, and the social slights suffered by the wife of Secretary of War John H. Eaton (see O'NEILL, MARGARET) helped to break up the cabinet. Calhoun's antagonism was more fundamental, however. Calhoun and the South generally felt threatened by the protective tariff that favored the industrial East, and Calhoun evolved the doctrine of NULLIFICATION and resigned from the vice presidency. Jackson stood firmly for the Union and had the force bill of 1833 (see FORCE BILL) passed to coerce South Carolina into accepting the Federal tariff, but a compromise tariff was rushed through and the affair ended. Jackson, on the other hand, took the part of Georgia in its insistence on states' rights and the privilege of ousting the Cherokee; he refused to aid in enforcing the Supreme Court's decision against Georgia, and the Indians were removed. More important than the estrangement of Calhoun was Jackson's long fight against the BANK OF THE UNITED STATES. Although its charter did not expire until 1836, Henry Clay succeeded in having a bill to recharter it passed in 1832, thus bringing the issue into the 1832 presidential election. Jackson vetoed the measure, and the powerful interests of the bank were joined with the other opponents of Jackson in a bitter struggle with the antibank Jacksonians. Jackson in the election of 1832 triumphed over Clay. His second administration—more bitterly resented by his enemies than the first—was dominated by the bank issue. Jackson promptly removed the funds from the bank and put them in chosen state banks (the "pet banks"). Secretary of Treasury Louis MCLANE refused to make the transfer as did his successor W. J. DUANE, but Roger B. TANEY agreed with Jackson's views and made the transfer (see also INDEPENDENT TREASURY SYSTEM). Jackson was a firm believer in a specie basis for currency, and the Specie Circular in 1836, which stipulated that all public lands must be paid for in specie, broke the speculation boom in Western lands, cast suspicion on many of the bank notes in circulation, and hastened the Panic of 1837. The panic, which had some of its roots in earlier crop failures and in overextended speculation, was a factor in the administration of Martin Van Buren, who was Jackson's choice and successful candidate for the presidency in 1836. Jackson retired to the Hermitage and lived out his life there, still despised as a high-handed and capricious dictator by his enemies and revered as a forceful democratic leader by his followers. Although he was known as a frontiersman, Jackson was personally dignified, courteous, and gentlemanly—with a devotion to the "gentleman's code" that led him to fight several duels. See biographies by Marquis James (2 vol., 1933–37, repr. 1968), Harold Syrett (1953, repr. 1971), J. W. Ward (1955, repr. 1962), and R. V. Remini (1966, repr. 1969); A. M. Schlesinger, Jr., *The Age of Jackson* (1945); G. G. Van Deusen, *The Jacksonian Era* (1959, repr. 1963); R. V. Remini, *Andrew Jackson and the Bank War* (1967); R. V. Remini, ed., *The Age of Jackson* (1972).

Jackson, Claiborne Fox, 1806–62, governor of Missouri, b. Fleming co., Ky. In 1822 he moved to Missouri, where he practiced law. Speaker of the state legislature (1844–46), he later was a leader of the proslavery Democrats who eventually defeated Sen. Thomas H. BENTON. Elected governor in 1860, Jackson recommended the calling of the state convention that voted against both secession and coercion of the South (1861). He attempted to arm the state militia from the Federal arsenal in St. Louis but was frustrated by Francis P. BLAIR and Nathaniel LYON. Lincoln's request for troops was refused by Jackson, who characterized the Union cause as an "unholy crusade." Upon Lyon's seizure of Camp Jackson, the governor called for volunteers but was forced to withdraw with them to SW Missouri. When the convention, assuming constituent powers, deposed the state government, Jackson, at Neosho, convened an ineffective rump legislature (1862).

Jackson, Frederick George, 1860–1938, British arctic explorer. He explored (1893–94) the tundra in arctic Russia and in Lapland, and he commanded (1894–97) the Jackson-Harmsworth expedition that explored Franz Josef Land. Jackson proved that Franz Josef Land was an archipelago, not a continent as had been suspected. His chance encounter (1896) with Fridtjof Nansen and F. H. Johansen, who were returning by sledge from their attempted journey to the North Pole, probably saved the lives of these two explorers. In later years Jackson became a well-known African traveler. His writings include *The Great Frozen Land* (1895) and *A Thousand Days in the Arctic* (1899).

Jackson, Frederick John Foakes-: see FOAKES-JACKSON, FREDERICK JOHN.

Jackson, Glenda, 1938–, English actress. Jackson's first starring role was as Charlotte Corday in *Marat/Sade* (1966) for the ROYAL SHAKESPEARE COMPANY. Her strong performance in the film *Women in Love* (1969) won her an Academy Award. Jackson's other major films include *Sunday Bloody Sunday* (1972), *A Touch of Class* (1973), and *The Maids* (1974). In 1971 she played Elizabeth I in a critically acclaimed television series.

Jackson, Helen (Fiske) Hunt, 1830–85, American writer whose pseudonym was H. H., b. Amherst, Mass. She was a lifelong friend of Emily Dickinson. In 1863, encouraged by T. W. Higginson, Jackson began writing for periodicals. She is the author of poetry, novels, children's stories, and travel sketches. In 1881 she published *A Century of Dishonor*, a historical account of the government's injustice to American Indians. This book led to her appointment (1882) as government investigator of the Mission Indians of California. She subsequently wrote *Ramona* (1884), her famous romance, which presented even more emphatically the plight of the Indians.

Jackson, Mahalia (məhăl'yə), 1911–72, American gospel singer and civil rights worker, b. New Orleans, La. She sang in church choirs during her childhood. Moving to Chicago in 1927, she worked at various menial jobs and sang in churches and revival meetings, attracting attention for her vigorous and joyful gospel style. As her reputation grew she made numerous recordings, and she was afforded national recognition with her Carnegie Hall debut in 1950. Jackson toured abroad and appeared on radio and at jazz festivals, refusing to sing the blues in favor of her more hopeful devotional songs. At Newport in 1958 she sang in Duke Ellington's *Black, Brown and Beige*. Deeply committed to the civil rights movement, she was closely associated with the work of Dr. Martin Luther King, Jr. See her autobiography (1966); biography by Jesse Jackson (1974).

Jackson, Robert Houghwout (hou'ət), 1892–1954, Associate Justice of the U.S. Supreme Court (1941–54), b. Spring Creek, Pa. Despite the fact that he did not have a law degree, he was admitted to the bar (1913) after a brief period of study at Albany law school. In 1934 he was appointed general counsel of the Bureau of Internal Revenue. From 1936 to 1938 he served as Assistant Attorney General in charge of the antitrust division. A strong advocate of New Deal policies, Jackson became (1938) U.S. Solicitor General and argued many Supreme Court cases involving constitutional law. In 1940 he became U.S. Attorney General, and in 1941 President Franklin D. Roosevelt appointed him to the Supreme Court. There his opinions continued to reflect his opposition to monopolies. He went on leave (1945–46) from the bench to be U.S. chief counsel at the Nuremberg war crimes trial. His feud with Justice Hugo L. Black probably eliminated him from consideration for Chief Justice when Harlan Stone died. An advocate of judicial restraint, he remained a firm defender of civil liberties. Known for his eloquent literary style, he defended freedom of religion with particular distinction. He wrote *The Struggle for Judicial Supremacy* (1940), *The Case Against the Nazi War Criminals* (1945), and *The Supreme Court in the American System of Government* (1955). See biography (1958) and study (1961) by E. C. Gerhart.

Jackson, Samuel Macauley, 1851–1912, American Presbyterian clergyman and encyclopedist, b. New York City. He was associate editor in the preparation of the original *Schaff-Herzog Encyclopedia* (1884) and editor in chief of the greatly enlarged *New Schaff-Herzog Encyclopedia of Religious Knowledge* (13 vol., 1908–14). He also edited the *Concise Dictionary of Religious Knowledge* (rev. ed. 1891) and the "American Church History" series (13 vol., 1893–97). Jackson was religious editor of several encyclopedias and dictionaries. He wrote a standard biography of Huldreich Zwingli (1901), part of the "Heroes of the Reformation" series, which he sponsored. He was long the moving spirit of the American Society of Church History and edited its papers.

Jackson, Sheldon, 1834–1909, American missionary and educator, b. Montgomery co., N.Y., grad. Union College, 1855, and Princeton Theological Seminary, 1858. After an active career as a Presbyterian home missionary in Minnesota and Wisconsin and (after 1870) as missionary superintendent in the Rocky Mt. area, he went to Alaska in 1884 as superintendent of missions, having already established missions and schools in that territory. In 1885 he became the first Federal superintendent of public instruction for Alaska, with the task of organizing a free school system for Indian, Eskimo, and white children. He succeeded in the next 20 years through work and travel in bringing school facilities to all corners of Alaska. He urged the introduction and raising of reindeer in the territory to supplement the dwindling food resources and in 1892, with government aid, brought the first reindeer into Alaska from Siberia. He aided in organizing the territorial government and in establishing mail routes. He was active in Alaskan politics as the moving spirit in the "missionary" party. He wrote numerous governmental and religious reports and *Difficulties at Sitka in 1885* (1886). See biography by J. A. Lazell (1960).

Jackson, Shirley, 1919–65, American writer, b. San Francisco. She is best known for her stories and novels of horror and the occult, rendered more terrifying because they are set against realistic, everyday backgrounds. Her works include *The Lottery* (1949), *We Have Always Lived in the Castle* (1953), and *The Haunting of Hill House* (1959). She was married to the critic Stanley Edgar Hyman. *The Magic of Shirley Jackson* (1966) and *Come Along With Me* (1968) are posthumous collections of her works.

Jackson, Stonewall (Thomas Jonathan Jackson), 1824–63, Confederate general, b. Clarksburg, Va. (now W. Va.), grad. West Point, 1846. He served with distinction under Winfield Scott in the Mexican War and from 1851 to 1861 taught at the Virginia Military Institute. He resigned from the army in Feb., 1852. At the beginning of the Civil War, Jackson, practically unknown, was made a colonel of Virginia troops and sent to command at Harpers Ferry. After J. E. JOHNSTON superseded him there in May, 1861, Jackson was given a brigade in Johnston's army and made a Confederate brigadier general. At the first battle of BULL RUN, he and his brigade earned their sobriquet by standing (in the words of Gen. Barnard Bee) "like a stone wall." He was promoted to major general, and in November, Johnston assigned him to command in the Shenandoah valley. Jackson's attack on James Shields's division at Kernstown on March 23, 1862, was repulsed but forced the retention of Union troops in the valley. In April, Robert E. LEE suggested that Jackson fall upon Nathaniel P. Banks's force in the lower valley, hoping that Irvin McDowell's army would thereby be diverted from joining George McClellan before Richmond (see PENINSULAR CAMPAIGN). Jackson's renowned Valley campaign resulted. He first defeated part of John C. Frémont's force at McDowell (c.25 mi/40 km W of Staunton) on May 8, 1862, and then, returning to the Shenandoah, routed Banks at Front Royal and Winchester (May 23–25) and drove him across the Potomac. The Federal administration, fearing that Jackson would now advance on Washington, sent Shields from McDowell's army to join Frémont, advancing from the west, in cutting off Jackson. Stonewall, however, retreated rapidly to the head of the valley and on June 8–9 defeated his pursuers at Cross Keys and PORT REPUBLIC. With the diversion a complete success, Jackson joined Lee in the SEVEN DAYS BATTLES. After the brilliance of the Shenandoah campaign, his service in that week of fighting was disappointing. But he soon redeemed himself. The speedy turning movement executed by his "foot cavalry" against Pope late in Aug., 1862, at the battle of Cedar Mt. set the stage for the crushing victory at the second battle of Bull Run, and in the ANTIETAM CAMPAIGN he marched promptly to Lee's aid after he had captured the Harpers Ferry garrison. When Lee reorganized the Army of Northern Virginia after Antietam, he made Jackson commander of the 2d Corps, and Stonewall was promoted to lieutenant general. He ably commanded the Confederate right in the battle of FREDERICKSBURG in December. In the battle of CHANCELLORSVILLE, Lee and Jackson repeated the tactics of second Bull Run. Jackson's turning movement completely crumbled Hooker's right (May 2, 1863). Pressing on in the darkness, Stonewall Jackson was mortally wounded by the fire of his own men. His death was a severe blow to the Southern cause. Jackson was a tactician of first rank and, though a strict disciplinarian, had the affection of his men. His devout Calvinism, fighting ability, and arresting personal quirks make him one of the most interesting figures of the war. He was Lee's ablest and most trusted lieutenant. See biographies by G. F. R. Henderson (1898, new ed. 1961), Burke Davis (1954, repr. 1961), Lenoir Chambers (1959), R. B. Cook (4th ed. 1963), and J. M. Selby (1968); H. K. Douglas, *I Rode with Stonewall* (1940).

Jackson, William Henry, 1843–1942, American artist and pioneer photographer of the West, b. Keeseville, N.Y. After serving with the Union army in the Civil War he traveled overland to California (1866–67), part of the way on a Mormon wagon train, and then settled in Omaha, Neb. (1868). Engaged in photography after 1858, Jackson devoted himself to recording the scenic grandeur and historic sites of the West. He photographed the building of the Union Pacific RR, the mining booms at Cripple Creek and Leadville, and the cliff dwellings at Mesa Verde. His photographic series on the Yellowstone region was instrumental in having the area set aside in 1872 as the first national park. In 1924, Jackson moved to Washington, D.C., began painting, and at the age of 93 executed a series of murals on the Old West for the new Dept. of the Interior Building. See his autobiography (1940) and his diaries, ed. by L. R. and A. W. Hafen (1959); C. S. Jackson, *Picture Maker of the Old West* (1947).

Jackson. **1** City (1970 pop. 45,484), seat of Jackson co., S Mich., on the Grand River; inc. 1857. It is an industrial and commercial center in a farm region. Several automobile models were pioneered in Jackson in the early 20th cent., and today the city's chief manufactures are a great variety of automobile and aircraft parts and accessories. Food products, tires, electronic equipment, sheet-metal items, and metal toys are also made. The Republican party was founded in Jackson on July 6, 1854; a tablet marks the site. A junior college is in the city. Nearby are Spring Arbor College and a state prison. **2** City (1970 pop. 153,968), state capital and seat of Hinds co., W central Miss., on the Pearl River; inc. 1833. It is the state's largest city and geographic center, with major rail, warehouse, and distributing operations. Industries include the production of oil and natural gas, food processing, and the manufacture of lumber, metal, glass, and wood products. The site of the city, a trading post known as Le Fleur's Bluff near the Natchez Trace, was chosen and laid out as the state capital in 1821 and named for Andrew Jackson. The first U.S. law giving property rights to married women was passed there in 1839. During the Civil War, Jackson was a military center for the VICKSBURG CAMPAIGN and was largely destroyed by Sherman's forces in 1863. The old capitol (1839) is preserved as a museum; the new capitol was completed in 1903. Among the many points of interest are the governor's mansion (erected 1839); city hall, which was used as a hospital during the Civil War; a 220-acre (89-hectare) scale model of the Mississippi River flood control system; Mynelle's gardens; a state wildlife museum; an art gallery; a notable Confederate monument; and many antebellum homes. Belhaven College, Jackson State College, the Univ. of Mississippi Medical Center, and several state institutions for the physically and mentally handicapped are there. Nearby are Tougaloo College and Mississippi College. During the 1960s Jackson was the scene of considerable racial unrest. In May, 1970, demonstrations at the predominantly black Jackson State College resulted in the death of two students. **3** City (1970 pop. 39,996), seat of Madison co., W Tenn., on the South Fork of the Forked Deer River; inc. 1823. It is a processing and rail shipping point for an extensive farm area. The city has railroad shops and industries producing a great variety of manufactures. The town was founded by a nephew of Andrew Jackson. It is the seat of Lane College, Lambuth College, Union Univ., and a junior college. Nearby are the West Tennessee Agricultural Experiment Station of the Univ. of Tennessee and a state park with Indian mounds. Casey Jones is buried in Jackson; his home and the Casey Jones railroad museum are of interest.

Jackson, Port, or **Sydney Harbour,** inlet of the Pacific Ocean, 22 sq mi (57 sq km), 12 mi (19 km) long and 1.5 mi (2.4 km) wide at its mouth, New South Wales, Australia, forming Australia's finest harbor. The Parramatta River forms its western arm. Sydney on the south shore is connected with its northern suburbs by Sydney Harbour Bridge (1932), the second longest steel-arch bridge in the world, with an arch span of 1,650 ft (503 m). In the inlet is Cockatoo Island, which has large shipyards.

Jackson College: see TUFTS UNIV.

Jackson Hole, fertile Rocky Mt. valley, c.50 mi (80 km) long and 6 to 8 mi (9.6–12.8 km) wide, NW Wyo., in Grand Teton National Park. Jackson Lake, 39 sq mi (101 sq km), a natural lake through which the Snake River flows, was dammed in 1916 to control the river's flow. The valley has been popular with hunters and trappers from the time U.S. trapper David Jackson, for whom it was named, wintered there in 1828–29. In the late 1880s, Jackson Hole was settled; two homesteads have been restored as historic sites. Jackson Hole Wildlife Park, 1,500 acres (607 hectares), est. 1948, is the winter home of the largest elk herd in North America. Many animals and birds inhabit the area, including the bald eagle and the rare trumpeter swan.

Jacksonville. **1** City (1970 pop. 19,832), Pulaski co., central Ark., inc. 1941. The nearby Little Rock Air Force Base, a tactical air command installation, is important to the city's economy. **2** City (1970 pop. 528,865), coextensive (since 1968) with Duval co., NE Fla., on the St. Johns River near its mouth on the Atlantic Ocean; inc. 1832. The largest city in the state and the second largest U.S. city in area (c.830 sq mi/2,150 sq km), it is a great rail, air, and highway focal point and a busy port of entry, with ship repair yards and extensive freight-handling facilities. Lumber, phosphate, paper, and wood pulp are the principal exports; automobiles and coffee are the major imports. The city is a leading manufacturing center, with lumber, paper, chemicals, food products, and cigars the principal products. Jacksonville is one of the most important Southern centers of commerce, finance, and insurance on the Atlantic coast. It is also a major East Coast center of U.S. navy operations; three important naval installations are in the area, including a naval air training station and the large base at the mouth of the St. Johns River. Jacksonville is also a tourist resort, with ocean beaches, fishing and yachting facilities, and inland hunting areas. It was settled in 1816 by Lewis Hogan. Named for Andrew Jackson, first territorial governor of Florida, the city was laid out in 1822. The Seminole War and the Civil War (in which much of the city was destroyed) interrupted its growth, but with the development of a good deepwater harbor and railroads in the late 19th cent., industry and commerce increased. A fire in 1901 destroyed a large part of the city; it was quickly rebuilt. Educational facilities include Jacksonville Univ., Edward Walters College, Jones College, and a junior college. The city has a symphony orchestra, a municipal zoo, and several museums and art galleries. It is the home of the enormous Gator Bowl. Points of interest include the Confederate monument in Hemming Park and nearby Fort Caroline National Memorial (see NATIONAL PARKS AND MONUMENTS, table). Jacksonville has an international airport. **3** City (1970 pop. 20,553), seat of Morgan co., W central Ill.; laid out 1825, inc. 1867. Its industries include bookbinding and the manufacture of clothing, plastics, phonograph records, and metal products. It is the seat of Illinois College, MacMurray College, a state mental hospital, and schools for the deaf and blind. Stephen A. Douglas and William Jennings Bryan lived there. Jacksonville was a station on the Underground Railroad. **4** City (1970 pop. 16,289), seat of Onslow co., E N.C., on the New River; settled c.1757. It is a trade center in a farm area, with sawmills and plants making clothing, mobile homes, food products, and farm equipment. It is also a summer resort. Camp Lejeune, a U.S. marine corps training base, is adjacent to the city, and Petersburg Point, a marine air station, is to the south. A junior college is in the city, and a state park is nearby.

Jackson Whites, name applied to a racially mixed (black, white, and Indian) group of people living in the Ramapo Mts. along the New Jersey–New York state line. The origins of these people have for years been surrounded by myth and legend, e.g., that they are descended from a mixture of the Tuscarora Indians, Hessian deserters, women kidnapped in England by a man named Jackson, and runaway slaves. Recent research suggests that the origin of these people is to be found among remnants of the Algonquin Indians, early white settlers (mainly British and Dutch), and free, landholding Negroes who pioneered the Hackensack River valley before migrating to the Ramapo Mts. in the early 19th cent. The term Jackson Whites probably developed as a result of the continued joint reference to the mountain people as Jacks (an 18th-century term for freed slaves or blacks in general) and Whites, i.e., it became Jackson Whites by elision.

Jacob (jā'kəb). **1** Ancestor of the Hebrews, the younger of the twin sons of Isaac and Rebecca. The older was Esau. Jacob got his brother's birthright by a bargain (a mess of pottage) and, with his mother's help, received the blessing that the dying Isaac had intended for Esau. His brother was so enraged at this that Jacob was forced to flee to his uncle, Laban, in Padanaram. On his way, at Bethel, he had a vision of angels ascending and descending the ladder to heaven. After serving the crafty Laban for 20 years Jacob started back to the land of his fathers with his two wives, Leah and Rachel, his many sons, and rich possessions. On the banks of the Jabbok he wrestled with an angel and received the name of ISRAEL. Later, in the days of famine, he migrated with his family to Egypt and was reunited with his son Joseph. There in the land of Goshen he died, but they buried him in the family burying ground of Machpelah. His sons were the ancestors of the 12 tribes of Israel. Gen. 25-50; Hosea 12.2-4,12; Mal. 1.2; Acts 7.12-16; Heb. 11.20,21. Some biblical scholars have questioned the historicity of Jacob. **2** Father of Joseph. Mat. 1.15,16.

Jacob, François, 1920-, French biologist, educated at the Sorbonne. His medical studies were interrupted by World War II. He joined the Free French Forces and fought in Africa and during the liberation of Paris. In 1950 he joined the Pasteur Institute, and in 1964 he became professor at the Collège de France. He shared the 1965 Nobel Prize in Physiology and Medicine with André Lwoff and Jacques Monod for discoveries concerning genes, the tiny structures in cells that determine hereditary characteristics and control production of enzymes and other proteins. Jacob and Monod coined the term *messenger RNA.* Jacob's writings include *The Logic of Life: A History of Heredity* (1974).

Jacob, Max (mäks zhäkôb'), 1876-1944, French writer and painter, b. Brittany, of a Jewish family. His dream-inspired verse, plays, and novels bridged and gave impetus to the symbolist and surrealist schools. His conversion (1914) to Roman Catholicism had great impact on his work. Among Jacob's novels are *Saint Matorel* (1911) and *Filibuth; ou La Montre en or* (1922); his verse, usually light and ironic, includes *Fond de l'eau* (1927) and *Rivages* (1932). Prose and poetry are combined in his *Défense de Tartufe* (1919) and the play *Le Siège de Jérusalem: drame céleste* (1912-14). His critical study, *Art poétique* (1922), had wide influence. One-man shows of Jacob's paintings were held in New York in 1930 and 1938. He died in a Nazi concentration camp. See study of his paintings by Gerald Kamber (1971).

Jacobean style (jăkəbē'ən), an early phase of English Renaissance architecture and decoration. It formed a transition between the Elizabethan and the pure Renaissance style later introduced by Inigo JONES. The reign of James I (1603-25), who was a disciple of the new scholarship, saw the first decisive adoption of Renaissance motifs, in a free form communicated to England through German and Flemish carvers rather than directly from Italy. Although the general lines of Elizabethan design remained, there was a more consistent and unified application of formal design, both in plan and elevation. Gothic influence did not cease completely; it lingered both in the building of the court and in the houses of the lesser gentry. Much use was made of columns and pilasters, round-arch arcades, and flat roofs with openwork parapets. These and other classical elements appeared in a free and fanciful vernacular rather than with any true classical purity. With them were mixed the prismatic rustications and the ornamental detail composed of scrolls, straps, and lozenges also characteristic of Elizabethan design. The style influenced furniture design and other decorative arts. Increase of wealth and the abundant construction of colleges, hospitals, almshouses, and manors encouraged innovations. Jacobean buildings of note are Hatfield House, Hertford; Knole House, Kent; and HOLLAND HOUSE by John Thorpe. See M. Whiffen, *An Introduction to Elizabethan and Jacobean Architecture* (1952).

Jacobi, Abraham (jəkō'bē), 1830-1919, American pediatrician, founder of pediatrics in the United States, b. Westphalia, Germany, M.D. Bonn, 1851. He was imprisoned for participating in the Revolution of 1848, but he escaped and in 1853 came to the United States. He was renowned as a lecturer on pediatrics and as professor of children's diseases at New York Medical College (where in 1860 he opened the first children's clinic in the country) and at Columbia (1870-1902). He was a founder and editor of the *American Journal of Obstetrics* and author of numerous works. Mary Putnam Jacobi, a physician and the first woman student at L'École de Médicine, Paris, was his wife.

Jacobi, Carl Gustav Jacob (kärl go͞os'täf yä'kôp yäkô'bē), 1804-51, German mathematician. He was an outstanding teacher and was professor of mathematics at Königsberg (1827-42) and lectured at Berlin from 1844. One of the greatest algorists of all time, he is noted for his work on elliptic functions, described in his *Fundamenta Nova Theoriae Functionum Ellipticarum* (1829), and on determinants, the theory of numbers, differential equations, and dynamics. His brother, **Moritz Hermann Jacobi** (1801-74), was a physicist and engineer who was the more famous of the two during their lifetimes. He was known for his supposed discovery (1837) of galvanoplastics, but his reputation faded when his ideas were later shown to be mistaken.

Jacobi, Friedrich Heinrich, 1743-1819, German philosopher. Although educated for commerce, he early gave up business and became in 1770 a member of the council for the duchies of Berg and Jülich. A brilliant personality, he attracted to his home near Düsseldorf a notable literary and philosophic circle. His later years were spent in Holstein and in Munich, where he was appointed (1807) president of the newly founded Academy of Sciences. His collected works were published in 1812-25. Among them are *Briefe über die Lehre des Spinoza* (1785) and *David Hume über den Glauben; oder, Idealismus und Realismus* (1787). Jacobi criticized both Kant and Spinoza, arguing that philosophy cannot maintain distinct realms of existence and that it must be consistent and consider everything in the same cause and effect sequence. If this is done, however, then the originality and individuality of our experiences are lost. Jacobi's solution involved a unity and consistency based entirely on faith. He felt that even immediate sense perception is miraculous. Reason, then, must be restricted to its immediate material, and the ultimate reality is to be intuitively sensed. See A. W. Crawford, *The Philosophy of F. H. Jacobi* (1905).

Jacobins (jăk'əbĭnz), political club of the FRENCH REVOLUTION. Formed in 1789 by the Breton deputies to the States-General, it was reconstituted as the Society of Friends of the Constitution after the revolutionary National Assembly moved (Oct., 1789) to Paris. The club derived its popular name from the monastery of the Jacobins (Parisian name of Dominicans), where the members met. Their chief purpose was to concert their activity and to secure support for the group from elements outside the Assembly. Patriotic societies were formed in most French cities in affiliation with the Parisian club. The members were, for the most part, bourgeois and at first included such moderates as Honoré de Mirabeau. The Jacobins exercised through their journals considerable pressure on the Legislative Assembly, in which they and the FEUILLANTS were (1791-92) the chief parties. They sought to limit the powers of the king, and many of them had republican tendencies. The group split on the issue of war against Europe, which the majority, the GIRONDISTS, sought. The minority, connected with the democratic, lower-class organizations in Paris, opposed foreign war and insisted on reform. This group of the Jacobins grew more radical, adopted republican ideas, and advocated universal manhood suffrage, popular education, and separation of church and state, although it adhered to orthodox economic principles. In the National Convention, which proclaimed the French republic, the Jacobins and other extremist opponents of the Girondists, notably the CORDELIERS, sat in the raised seats and were called the MOUNTAIN. Their leaders—Maximilien ROBESPIERRE and Louis de SAINT-JUST, among others—relied mainly on the strength of the Paris commune and the Parisian working class; the Girondists drew their strength from the provinces. After the fall of the Girondists (June, 1793), for which the Jacobins were largely responsible, the Jacobins instituted the REIGN OF TERROR. Under Robespierre, who came to dominate the government, the Terror was used not only against counterrevolutionaries, but also against former allies of the Jacobins, such as the Cordeliers and the Dantonists (followers of Georges DANTON). The fall of Robespierre on 9 Thermidor (July 27, 1794) meant the fall of the Jacobins, but their spirit lived on in revolutionary doctrine. The party reappeared in the DIRECTORY and in altered form much later in the Revolution of 1848. See Crane Brinton, *The Jacobins* (1930, repr. 1961); Isser Woloch, *Jacobin Legacy: The Democratic Movement under the Directory* (1970); M. L. Kennedy, *The Jacobin Club of Marseilles* (1973).

Jacobite Church (jăk'əbīt), Christian church of Syria, Iraq, and India, recognizing the Syrian Orthodox patriarch of Antioch as its spiritual head, regarded by Roman Catholics and Eastern Orthodox as heretical. It was founded (6th cent.) as a Monophysite church in Syria by Jacob Baradaeus, greatly helped by Empress Theodora. It is thus analogous in position to the Coptic Church, the Monophysite church of Egypt. For many centuries the Jacobites were under Muslim dominion. Most Jacobites live in Iraq, while their patriarch resides at Damascus. They resemble other Eastern Christians in custom; their rite is the Antiochene or West Syrian; the liturgical language is Syriac. Since the 17th cent. there has been constant contact with Rome; as a result there is a community in communion with the pope having practices and rite in common with the Jacobites. These "Syrian Catholics" number about as many as the Jacobites; their head, another patriarch of Antioch, lives at Beirut. They have a separate church organization from the Melchites, Maronites, and Chaldean Catholics, which are other communities of Syria and Iraq in communion with Rome. In Malabar, India, there is a Christian sect of "Malabar Jacobites"; this group came into existence in the 17th cent., when the bulk of the Malabar Christians left the Roman communion and established relations with the Jacobite patriarch. They now use the Antiochene rite, with some differences. They are divided into two disputing jurisdictional parties, and there is a quasi-Protestant group of "Reformed Jacobites." In the 20th cent. a large number of Malabar Jacobites entered into communion with the pope, retaining their liturgy and practices. These "Malankarese Catholics" are ecclesiastically separate from both the Syrian Catholics, whose rite they share, and from the "Syro-Malabar Catholics" (Chaldean rite), who represent the Malabar Christians who did not leave the Roman communion when the Malabar Jacobites did. See Donald Attwater, *The Christian Churches of the East* (1947-48).

Jacobites (jăk'əbīts), adherents of the exiled branch of the house of STUART who sought to restore JAMES II and his descendants to the English and Scottish thrones after the GLORIOUS REVOLUTION of 1688. They take their name from the Latin form (*Jacobus*) of the name James. When WILLIAM III and MARY II ascended the throne after the flight of James II to France, strong Stuart partisans remained to offer rebellion. However, the death (1689) of John Graham, Viscount DUNDEE, at Killiecrankie ended armed resistance in Scotland, and William III quashed Jacobite hopes in Ireland by his victory over James's forces at the battle of the BOYNE (1690). Thereafter the exiled English court in France became a center of intrigue for men like Henry ST. JOHN, Viscount Bolingbroke, and others like him who were out of favor in London. At home many Roman Catholics, high churchmen, and extreme Tories adhered to the Stuart cause. At the death (1701) of James II his son James Francis Edward STUART, the Old Pretender, was recognized as James III by the courts of France and Spain and proclaimed by the Jacobites. An invasion of Scotland in 1708 by the new claimant proved totally abortive. Each subsequent attempt also failed, and in each the Jacobites were the dupes of French or Spanish policy. After the death (1714) of Queen Anne and the accession of the Hanoverian George I, there was the rising known by its date as "the '15." Led by the incompetent John Erskine, 6th earl of MAR, it ended in the disastrous battles of Preston and Sheriffmuir. The Old Pretender, discredited by failure, retired first to Avignon and finally to Rome. Spain supported another Jacobite invasion of Scotland in 1719. After its failure hope lay dormant until the Old Pretender's son Charles Edward STUART (the Young Pretender or Bonnie Prince Charlie) reached manhood. Acting on the assumption that renewed French hostility toward England would bring support for a Jacobite invasion, the prince rashly sailed for Scotland, raised the clans in what was called "the '45," and won an initial victory at Prestonpans in Sept., 1745. An advance into England stalled at Derby for lack of support from English Jacobites and French allies. Despite Charles's objections, his council of war voted to retreat, an action skillfully managed by Lord George MURRAY. Disaster followed for the Jacobites at the battle of Culloden Moor (1746). Charles escaped to France, and Stuart hopes were extinguished, although a claimant to the throne lived on until 1807, in the person of Henry STUART, Cardinal York. Theoretical justification for the Stuart claim was found in the writings of the NONJURORS, who maintained the principles of hereditary succession and the divine right of kings. But the Stuarts' continued adherence to Roman Catholicism, the rash and incompetent leadership of their military ventures, and the duplicity of foreign courts had cost the Jacobite cause much support. Jacobite sympathies lingered, particularly in Scotland and Ireland, where Jacobitism had been practically synonymous with national discontent, but the movement ceased to be a serious political force. Jacobite activities gave rise to much ballad literature and were the theme of such later literary works as Sir Walter Scott's *Rob Roy, Waverley,* and *Redgauntlet,* William Thackeray's *Henry Esmond,* and R. L. Stevenson's *Kidnapped.* See studies by G. P. Insh (1952), G. H. Jones (1954), Sir Charles Petrie (rev. ed. 1959), and J. C. M. Baynes (1970); J. Prebble, *Culloden* (1961).

Jacobs, Helen Hull, 1908–, American tennis player, b. Globe, Ariz. She won wide recognition on the courts by taking the U.S. women's singles title for four consecutive years (1932–35) and by beating Alice Marble for the British women's singles crown in 1936. She was (1943–45) an officer in the Waves in World War II. She wrote *Modern Tennis* (1933) and *Beyond the Game* (1936).

Jacobs, Joseph, 1854–1916, Jewish writer, historian and folklorist, b. Australia. He lived in England until 1900, when he went to the United States to edit a revision of *The Jewish Encyclopedia.* He was later a teacher at the Jewish Theological Seminary in New York City and editor of the *American Hebrew.* His major contributions to Jewish history include *Jews of Angevin England* (1893), *An Inquiry into the Sources of the History of the Jews in Spain* (1894), and *Jewish Contributions to Civilization* (1919), an incomplete fragment. His *Story of Geographical Discovery* (1899) went through a number of editions. From 1889 to 1900 he edited *Folk-Lore,* the journal of the Folk-Lore Society. He compiled several collections of fairy tales and edited scholarly editions of Aesop's fables (1889) and the *Thousand and One Nights* (6 vol., 1896).

Jacobs, William Wymark, 1863–1943, English author. His humorous sea stories were first collected in *Many Cargoes* (1896). Of his several horror stories, the most famous is "The Monkey's Paw."

Jacobsen, Arne (är'nə yä'kōpsən), 1902–71, Danish architect and designer. Attentive to detail, Jacobsen suited his buildings to the surrounding landscape. He chiefly designed private housing, particularly in Søholm. The Bellevue seaside resort (1930–35) and Copenhagen's Jespersen (1955) and Scandinavian Airlines (1959–60) buildings are among his best-known works. Professor of architecture at the Royal Danish Academy after 1955, Jacobsen also designed cutlery, furniture, and textile and wallpaper patterns.

Jacobsen, Jens Peter (yĕns pä'tər yä'kōpsən), 1847–85, Danish writer. His great historical romance *Marie Grubbe* (1876, tr. 1925) deals with spiritual degeneration in 17th-century Denmark. Jacobsen's other works include *Nils Lyhne* (1880, tr. 1919), a semiautobiographical work about a dreamer unable to cope with the realities of his life, and a volume of poems. Jacobsen created a curt prose that had great influence on naturalistic style, both in Denmark and abroad. He translated Darwin's *Origin of Species* and *Descent of Man* into Danish. See Alrik Gustafson, *Six Scandinavian Novelists* (1940).

Jacob's ladder: see PHLOX.

Jacobus da Varagine (jəkō'bəs dä väräj'ĭnē), c.1230–1298, Italian hagiographer, b. Varazze (then Voraggio), near Savona; also known as Jacobus de Voragine. He became a Dominican in 1244, was provincial of Lombardy, and after 1292 was archbishop of Genoa. Noted for his piety and great charity, he was beatified in 1816 and is revered as a saint in Genoa and Savona. He is remembered chiefly as the compiler of *The Golden Legend* (see GOLDEN LEGEND, THE).

Jacopone da Todi (yäkōpō'nā dä tô'dē), 1230?–1306, Italian religious poet, whose name was originally Jacopo Benedetti. After the sudden death of his wife, he renounced (c.1268) his career as an advocate, gave his goods to the poor, and after 10 years of penance became a Franciscan tertiary. Jacopone was excommunicated and imprisoned (1298) for signing a manifesto against Pope Boniface VIII. After his release, he retired to a hermitage. He wrote many ardent, mystical poems and is probably the author of the hymn *Stabat Mater Dolorosa.* The spiritual value of poverty is frequently the theme of his poetry. See Evelyn Underhill, *Jacopone da Todi, Poet and Mystic* (with selections, 1919); Helen White, *A Watch in the Night* (1933).

Jacquard, Joseph Marie (zhôzĕf' märē' zhäkär'), 1752–1834, French inventor, whose loom is of the greatest importance in modern mechanical figure weaving. After several years of experimentation, he received a bronze medal for his model exhibited at the Industrial Exposition at Paris (1801). In 1806 his perfected loom was bought by the state and declared public property, and he was granted an annuity of 3,000 francs and a royalty on all looms sold. The Jacquard LOOM, the first machine to weave in patterns, has had countless adaptations in modern textile industry.

Jacqueline (1401–36), countess of Hainaut, Holland, and Zeeland (1417–28). The daughter and heiress of William IV, duke of Bavaria and count of Hainaut, Holland, and Zeeland, and of Margaret of Burgundy, Jacqueline was passed over for the succession to the counties on her father's death in 1417 in favor of her uncle, John of Bavaria. Jacqueline married a cousin, John IV, duke of Brabant, nephew of Philip the Good of Burgundy, but found him useless in helping her recover her inheritance and soon left him. She sought refuge in England, where, although her previous marriage had been dubiously annulled, she married (c.1422) Humphrey, duke of Gloucester, the brother of King Henry V. A subsequent invasion of Hainaut (1424–25) proved unsuccessful, and Jacqueline was abandoned by Humphrey and obliged to make peace with Duke Philip the Good of Burgundy, who sought to avenge her repudiation of John IV. Imprisoned at Ghent, she escaped but submitted after a struggle. The treaty of Delft (1428) recognized her as nominal countess and Philip as her administrator and heir. Four years later she attempted in vain to incite a rebellion in Holland against Philip, after which she abdicated her countships in Philip's favor in 1433.

Jacquerie (zhäk"ərē') [Fr.,=collection of *Jacques,* which is, like *Jacques Bonhomme,* a nickname for the French peasant], 1358, revolt of the French peasantry. The uprising was provoked by the depressed economic condition of the Hundred Years War, by the pillaging of the *écorcheurs,* and by the extortionate demands of the nobles. Beginning around Beauvais, north of Paris, the revolt spread over a wide area; castles were demolished, provisions stolen, and other violent acts committed. The leader, Guillaume Karle (or Cale), was captured and beheaded by Charles II of Navarre, and the mob was easily dispersed. The nobles took revenge by massacring thousands of the insurgents.

Jada (jā'də), Jerahmeelite. 1 Chron. 2.28,32.

Jadau (jā'dô), Jew who married a foreign wife. Ezra 10.43.

Jaddua (jădyōō'ə). **1** High priest after the Exile. Neh. 12.11,22. **2** Signer of the Covenant. Neh. 10.21.

jade, common name for either of two minerals used as gems. The rarer variety of jade is jadeite, a sodium aluminum silicate, $NaAl(SiO_3)_2$, usually white or green in color; the green variety is the more valuable. The commoner and less costly variety of jade is nephrite, a calcium magnesium iron silicate of varying composition, white to dark green in color. Jade has been prized by the Chinese and Japanese as the most precious of all gems. The Chinese in particular are known for the objets d'art they carve from it, and they traditionally associated it with the five cardinal virtues: charity, modesty, courage, justice, and wisdom; they also attributed healing powers to it. It was much used for implements by primitive people, especially in Mexico, Switzerland, France, Greece, Egypt, Asia Minor, and New Zealand. Jadeite is found in Upper Burma, in Japan, and in Guatemala; nephrite in New Zealand, Turkistan, Siberia, China, Silesia, Wyoming, California, and British Columbia. See J. L. Kraft, *Adventure in Jade* (1947); S. C. Nott, *Chinese Jade throughout the Ages* (2d ed. 1962); Richard Gump, *Jade* (1962); J. M. Hartman, *Chinese Jade of Five Centuries* (1969); Geoffrey Wills, *Jade of the East* (1972).

jadeite: see JADE.

Jadida, El: see AL-JADIDA, Morocco.

Jadon (jā'dŏn), worker on the wall at Jerusalem. Neh. 3.7.

Jadotville, Zaïre: see LIKASI.

Jadwiga (yädvē'gä), 1374–99, Polish queen (1384–99), daughter of LOUIS I of Hungary and Poland. To satisfy Polish demands for autonomy at Louis's death, she reigned in Poland and her sister reigned in Hungary. Jadwiga married (1386) Jagiello, grand duke of Lithuania (see LADISLAUS II), in order to unite Poland and Lithuania and to convert the Lithuanians to Christianity. They ruled jointly, and after she died without children he ruled alone. Jadwiga restored (1387) to Poland the regions of Lvov and Galich that her father had given to Hungarian governors. She founded (1397) a theological college in Kraków and effected the restoration of the Univ. of Kraków. She is nationally venerated as a saint. See Charlotte Kellogg, *Jadwiga, Queen of Poland* (1936).

jaeger (yā'gər), common name for several members of the family Stercorariidae, member of a family of hawklike sea birds closely related to the gull and the tern. The skua is also a member of this family. Jaegers and skuas are stocky, powerfully muscled birds with long, pointed wings, long tails, strong, hooked bills, and sharp, curved talons. They are tireless, wide-ranging flyers of the open seas. Their piratical habits give them the names robber gull and sea hawk. Jaegers and skuas rob the food of their smaller relatives, teasing and harassing them until they drop their prey. They also feed on the eggs of colonial sea birds, especially those of penguins. The skua (*Catharacta skua*) is the largest and darkest of the family, a denizen of the N Atlantic, though it breeds south to the antarctic. Of the three jaegers (*Stercorarius* species), all of northern oceans, the largest is the pomarine jaeger (also called jiddy hawk), the most common the parasitic jaeger, and the most graceful the long-tailed jaeger. All these birds are mostly blackish-brown above and white below, with a gilding of the head and neck in the older birds. Jaegers are classified in the phylum CHORDATA, subphylum Vertebrata, class Aves, order Charadriiformes, family Stercorariidae.

Jael (jāl), heroine of the time of Deborah. She murdered Sisera, her guest. Judges 4; 5.

Jaén (hään'), city (1970 pop. 78,156), capital of Jaén prov., S Spain, in Andalusia. It is a marketing and distribution center for a fertile area producing olive oil and wine. Nearby lead mines are believed to be among the richest in Europe; iron and copper are also exploited. Once the seat of a small Moorish kingdom, Jaén was conquered by Ferdinand III of Castile in 1246. There are remains of a Moorish castle and walls; an imposing cathedral (16th–18th cent.); and several palaces.

Jaffa (jăf'ə, yä'fä), Heb. *Yafo,* part of TEL AVIV-JAFFA, W central Israel, on the Mediterranean Sea. Originally a Phoenician city, Jaffa has been historically important largely because of its port (which was closed in 1965, when the port of Ashdod was completed). It was captured by Egypt in 1472 B.C. and made a provincial capital. In 701 B.C. the city was besieged by Sennacherib, king of Assyria. It was often held by Philistia, and not until after the Captivity in Babylon (6th cent. B.C.) did it become Hebrew territory. The Bible relates that Jonah set forth from there for Tarshish and that St. Peter restored Dorcas to life in Jaffa. Alexander the Great took Jaffa in the late 4th cent. B.C. The city changed hands frequently in the fighting between the Maccabees and the Syrians (2d and 1st cent. B.C.) and was destroyed by Vespasian in A.D. 68. The rebuilt city of Jaffa was conquered by the Arabs in 636. The Crusaders took it in 1126, Saladin recaptured it in 1187, and Richard I retook the city in 1191. In 1196 the Arabs again captured Jaffa, and in the 16th cent. the city, then in decline, was annexed by the Ottoman Empire. In the late 17th cent. Jaffa began to develop again as a seaport. It was captured by Napoleon in 1799. In World War I British troops took Jaffa, which became part of the British-administered PALESTINE mandate (1922–48). In 1947 and 1948 there was sharp fighting between Jaffa, which was largely inhabited by Arabs, and the adjoining all-Jewish city of Tel Aviv. The Arabs in Jaffa surrendered on the day (May 14, 1948) that the state of Israel was proclaimed. Most of the Arab population soon left. In 1950 the city was incorporated into Tel Aviv. Jaffa is mentioned in the Bible (2 Chron. 2.16) as marking the boundary of the tribe of Dan and is the Japho of Joshua 19.46. In the Apocrypha it is often spelled Joppe, but the usual Bible spelling is Joppa.

Jaffna (jăf'nə), peninsula, northernmost part of Sri Lanka (Ceylon), separated from India by Palk Strait. The peninsula is densely inhabited, largely by Tamil-speaking people. There are remains of ancient Tamil culture and of Portuguese and Dutch occupations of the 17th–18th cent. Tobacco, rice, coconuts, palmyra palm, and vegetables are grown, and fishing is an important occupation. The main industries are salt, cement, chemical, and tobacco production; cottage industries include textile weaving and gold filigree work. There is trade in elephants, peppers, and other commodities.

Jaffna moss: see AGAR.

Jagan, Cheddi (chĕd'ē jä'gän), 1918–, prime minister of British Guiana (1961–64), which later became Guyana. Of East Indian descent, he was trained as a dentist. In 1950 he founded, with Forbes BURNHAM, the country's first formal political party, and he was chief minister from April to Oct., 1953, when, in the wake of strikes and riots, the British authorities suspended the constitution and established an interim government. Jagan launched a civil disobedience campaign and was jailed (April-Sept., 1954) for violating an order restricting him to Georgetown. His extreme leftist views caused a rift with Burnham, who formed his own party in 1955. In 1957 elections, Jagan's party received a plurality, and he was named minister of trade and industry; his U.S.-born wife became minister of labor, health, and housing. In 1961, Jagan became prime minister. He attempted to impose a rigid austerity program, vigorously pushed social and economic reform, and worked for independence. Jagan's party led in the 1964 elections, but Burnham became prime minister after forming a coalition with a small third party. Jagan subsequently led the opposition to Burnham.

Jagannath, India: see PURI.

Jagatai (jăgətī'), d. 1242, Mongol conqueror; son of Jenghiz Khan. He led large armies on his father's campaigns of conquest. When the empire was divided in 1227 among Jenghiz Khan's three living sons and a grandson, Jagatai was rewarded with vast territories that correspond to present-day Turkistan and Afghanistan. He held this domain, a key area in the Mongol empire, as a satrapy under the rule of his brother Ogadai, who, although younger than Jagatai, had become grand khan. After Ogadai's death in 1241, dissension erupted between the Ogadai and Jagatai lines, and a third branch, which had descended from Jenghiz Khan's youngest son, Tule, dominated the Mongol empire. In the early 14th cent. Jagatai's descendants, the **Jagataids**, divided his khanate into two sections, the western region with its capital at Samarkand, and the eastern region, centering around Kashgar. Often at war with one another, the two domains were reunited by TAMERLANE (Timur), who may have been related to the family ruling the western region. The name Jagatai is sometimes spelled Chagatai or Djagatai.

Jagello: see JAGIELLO.

Jägerndorf: see KRNOV, Czechoslovakia.

Jaggard, William, c.1568-1623, London printer and publisher. Although it seems that he had previously pirated some of Shakespeare's works, he was chosen by the editors John Heming and Henry Condell as publisher of the First Folio edition of Shakespeare's plays. He died before the work was completed. To this book, undertaken after Jaggard became blind, are due the preservation of 18 of the plays and the correction of many textual errors in the plays printed in earlier editions, in quarto. See E. E. Willoughby, *A Printer of Shakespeare* (1934, repr. 1969).

Jagiello (yägyĕ'lō) or **Jagello** (yägĕ'lō), dynasty that ruled POLAND and LITHUANIA from 1386 to 1572, Hungary from 1440 to 1444 and again from 1490 to 1526, and Bohemia from 1471 to 1526. It took its name from Ladislaus Jagiello, grand duke of Lithuania, who became (1386) king of Poland as LADISLAUS II when he married Queen JADWIGA. His successors were LADISLAUS III (1434-44; as Uladislaus I also king of Hungary); CASIMIR IV (1447-92); John I (1492-1501); Alexander I (1501-5); SIGISMUND I (1506-48); and SIGISMUND II (1548-72), last ruler of the line. A son of Casimir IV became king of Bohemia (1471) as Ladislaus II and king of Hungary (1490) as ULADISLAUS II; his son was LOUIS II of Bohemia and Hungary (1516-26). The female line of Jagiello merged with the Swedish house of Vasa through the marriage of Catherine, sister of Sigismund II, with John III of Sweden; their son was king of Sweden and of Poland (see SIGISMUND III). Under Jagiello rule Poland reached its golden age.

jaguar (jăg'wär), large New World carnivore of the CAT family, *Panthera onca.* Jaguars range from the SW United States to S central Argentina. They have deep yellow or tawny coats marked with black rings, or rosettes, and spots. In all individuals at least some of the rings surround spots. This feature distinguishes the jaguar from the Old World LEOPARD, which has similar markings, but never has rosettes with internal spots. The jaguar is also shorter-limbed and stockier than the leopard. An adult male jaguar is up to 7 ft (2.2 m) long, including the 2½-ft (76-cm) tail, stands about 2½ ft (76 cm) high at the shoulder and weighs about 200 lb (90 kg). Jaguars are very adaptable animals. They are primarily forest dwellers but may be found on the South American pampas, or even in rocky semidesert areas of Mexico and the United States. They are the best tree climbers of all the big cats and in some regions live an almost entirely arboreal existence for months at a time when the forest floor is flooded. They are also good swimmers and sometimes catch fish for food. Jaguars hunt deer, agouti, capybara, and especially peccaries. They are retiring animals, not particularly inclined to attack people, but a jaguar may launch an attack or even stalk a human being if threatened. In Mexico the jaguar is known as *el tigre,* "the tiger," although true tigers are found only in Asia. Jaguars are classified in the phylum CHORDATA, subphylum Vertebrata, class Mammalia, order Carnivora, family Felidae.

Jagur (jā'gər), unidentified town, S Palestine. Joshua 15.21.

Jah (yä), abbreviation of one of the reconstructions (Jahveh, Jahweh) of the ancient Hebrew ineffable name of GOD.

Jahangir or **Jehangir** (both: jəhän"gēr'), 1569-1627, Mogul emperor of India (1605-27), son of Akbar. An indolent and pleasure-loving man, he nonetheless continued his father's policy of expansion. The Rajput principality of Mewar (Udaipur) capitulated in 1614. In the Deccan, Ahmadnagar was taken in 1616 and half of its kingdom annexed. In the northwest, however, the Persian ruler, Shah Abbas, retook (1622) Kandahar. In 1611, Jahangir married a Persian widow, Nur Jahan, and she and her relatives soon dominated politics, while Jahangir devoted himself to cultivation of the arts, especially miniature painting, and to drinking. He welcomed foreign visitors to his court, granting trading privileges first to the Portuguese and then to the British East India Company. Civil strife and court intrigues marked the last years of Jahangir's reign. Shah Jahan, his son, succeeded him. See Beni Prasad, *History of Jahangir* (1922).

Jahath (jā'hăth). **1** Descendant of Gershom. 1 Chron. 6.20,43. **2** Chief of a Gershonite family. 1 Chron. 23.10. **3** Descendant of Judah. 1 Chron. 4.2. **4** Levite. 1 Chron. 24.22. **5** Temple overseer. 2 Chron. 34.12.

Jahaz (jā'həz), **Jahaza** (jəhā'zə), **Jahazah** (jəhā'zə), or **Jahzah** (jä'zə), unidentified town, E of the Dead Sea. Israel's defeat there of the Amorites is recorded on the Moabite stone. Num. 21.23; Deut. 2.32; Joshua 13.18; 21.36; Judges 11.20; 1 Chron. 6.78; Isa. 15.4; Jer. 48.21,34.

Jahaziah (jā"həzī'ə), one associated with Ezra in the expulsion of the foreign wives. Ezra 10.15.

Jahaziel (jəhā'zēĕl, jā"hāzī'əl, jāhăz'ēĕl). **1** Man who joined David at Ziklag. 1 Chron. 12.4. **2** One who inspired Jehoshaphat to oppose the invading Ammonites. 2 Chron. 20.14. **3** Priest before the Ark. 1 Chron. 16.6. **4** Kohathite Levite. 1 Chron. 23.19; 24.23. **5** Head of a family that returned from the Exile. Ezra 8.5.

Jahdai (jä'dāī), Calebite. 1 Chron. 2.47.

Jahdiel (jä'dīĕl), head of a Manassite family. 1 Chron. 5.24.

Jahdo (jä'dō), one of the tribe of Gad. 1 Chron. 5.14.

Jahleel (jä'lēĕl), founder of a Zebulonite family. Gen. 46.14; Num. 26.26.

Jahmai (jä'māī, jämä'ī), head of the house of Tola. 1 Chron. 7.2.

Jahn, Friedrich Ludwig (frē'drĭkh lo͞ot'vĭkh yän), 1778-1852, German patriot. A high school teacher in Berlin, he was active in efforts to free Germany from Napoleonic rule. He organized the TURNVEREIN, a gymnastic association, to build strength and fellowship among young people of all classes. The gymnastic groups Jahn fostered became centers for nationalism and for the movement to unify Germany. After serving (1813-15) in the war against Napoleon, Jahn continued his work until his political agitation caused his imprisonment (1819-25). Jahn, who also was influential in the organization of the BURSCHENSCHAFT movement, was a delegate to the FRANKFURT PARLIAMENT in 1848.

Jahnn, Hans Henny (häns hĕn'ē yän), 1894-1959, German novelist, dramatist, music publisher, and organ builder. Jahnn's early dramas, including *Pastor Ephraim Magnus* (1919) and *Medea* (1926), were laden with sexual-pathological images. Among his later novels, of greater substance, are *Thomas Chatterhorn* (1955) and a trilogy, *Fluss ohne Ufer* [shoreless river] (1949-50; tr. Vol. I, *The Ship,* 1961), which explores the dangers of delving into the secrets of creation. Jahnn also published 17th-century organ music and gained an international reputation as a builder and renovator of organs.

Jahve, Jahveh, or **Jahweh** (yä'vā,-wā), modern reconstructions of the ancient Hebrew ineffable name of GOD.

Jahzah (jä'zə), variant of JAHAZ.

Jahzeel (jä'zēĕl), Naphtalite. Num. 26.48. Jahziel: 1 Chron. 7.13.

Jahzerah (jä'zērə), the same as AHASAI.

Jahziel (jä'zēĕl), variant of JAHZEEL.

jai alai (hī'lī"), handball-like game of Spanish Basque origin, now also popular in Latin America and Florida. It is also called pelota. Jai alai is played on a three-walled court, called a *cancha,* with a hard rubber ball that must be hurled against the front wall with the *cesta,* a wicker basket attached to the player's arm. The *cancha* is usually about 175 ft (53 m) long, 55 ft (17 m) wide, and 40 ft (12 m) high. Spectators sit behind a wire fence on the fourth side of the court. To their right is the front wall, or *frontis.* The object is to hurl the ball against the front wall in such a way that it cannot be returned. The ball may hit the side or rear wall before striking the *frontis;* it may not hit the spectators' fence. Jai alai is one of the fastest of all games. It is played as either singles or doubles with scoring similar to that of handball. The first player or team to reach the required number of points (usually 6 or 7 in singles and as high as 25 in doubles) wins. Betting on games is popular and gambling is legal at the Florida jai alai courts.

jail: see PRISON.

Jailolo: see HALMAHERA, Indonesia.

Jaime. For Spanish rulers thus named, see JAMES.

Jainism (jī'nĭzəm) [i.e., the religion of Jina], religious system of India practiced by about 2,000,000 persons. Jainism, AJIVIKA, and BUDDHISM arose in the 6th cent. B.C. as protests against the overdeveloped ritualism of HINDUISM, particularly its sacrificial cults, and the authority of the Veda. Jaina tradition teaches that a succession of 24 tirthankaras (saints) originated the religion. The last, Vardhamana, called Mahavira [the great hero] and Jina [the victor], seems to be historical. He preached a rigid asceticism and solicitude for all life as a means of escaping the cycle of rebirth, or the TRANSMIGRATION OF SOULS. Thus released from the rule of KARMA, the total consequences of past acts, the soul attains NIRVANA, and hence salvation. Mahavira organized a brotherhood of monks, who took vows of celibacy, nudity, self-mortification, and fasting. Since the 1st cent. A.D., when a schism developed over the issue of nudity, there have been two great divisions of Jains, the Digambaras [space-clothed, i.e., naked] and the Svetambaras [white-clothed]. Jainists, then as now, accumulate merit through charity, through good works, and in occasional monastic retreat. Early Jainism, arising in NE India, quickly spread west, and according to tradition CHANDRAGUPTA, the founder of the Maurya empire, was converted to the sect, as were several kings of Gujarat. The Jaina canon, however, is preserved in an ancient dialect of NE India (see PRAKRIT LITERATURE). As Jainism grew and prospered, reverence for Mahavira and for other teachers, historical and legendary, passed into adoration; many beautiful temples were built and cult images set up. However, as time passed, the line between Hindu and Jain became more and more unclear. Soon Hindu gods such as Rama and Krishna were drawn into the Jaina pantheon, and Hindu Brahmans began to preside at Jaina death and marriage ceremonies and temple worship. The caste system, which primitive Jainism had rejected, also became part of later Jaina doctrine. Modern Jainists, eschewing any occupation that even remotely endangers animal life, are engaged largely in commerce and finance. Among them are many of India's most prominent industrialists and bankers as well as several important political leaders. A distinctive form of charity among Jains is the establishment of asylums for diseased and decrepit animals. See M. S. Stevenson, *The Heart of Jainism* (1915, repr. 1970); M. L. Mehta, *Jaina Philosophy* (1970); Subramania Gopalan, *Outlines of Jainism* (1973).

Jaipur (jī'po͝or), former native state, W India. It is now part of Rajasthan state. The region of Jaipur is mostly level, and, despite light rainfall, fair crops of maize, millet, and cotton are raised. Salt is mined and cotton and woolen cloth and metal products are manufactured. Jaipur was founded in the 12th cent. by the Kachwaha clan of the RAJPUTS. It became (c.1550) a feudatory of the MOGUL empire. In 1818, Great Britain exacted a treaty providing for an annual tribute. **Jaipur,** city (1971 pop. 613,144), capital of Rajasthan, was founded in 1728. Known as the pink city from the color of its houses, it is a transportation junction and a commercial center. It is enclosed by a crenellated wall 20 ft (6 m) high. An unusual feature for an Indian city of this size is the system of wide, regular streets. The grounds of the former maharaja's palace occupy one seventh of the municipal area. Among Jaipur's famed art products are jewelry, enamels, and muslins. Rajasthan Univ. is there. Jaipur has a large banking business. The deserted city of Amber, which was the capital of Jaipur state until 1728, is 5 mi (8 km) from Jaipur. The palace there is a fine example of Rajput architecture.

Jair (jā'ər). **1** Manassite. Num. 32.41; Deut. 3.14. **2** Judge of Israel. Judges 10.3. **3** Mordecai's father. Esther 2.5. **4** See JAARE-OREGIM. See also HAVOTH-JAIR.

Jairus (jāī'rəs) [Gr. form of JAIR], prominent Jew whose daughter was raised from the dead by Jesus. Mat. 9.18–26; Mark 5.22–43; Luke 8.41–56.

Jaisalmer (jəsäl'mər), former principality, Rajasthan state, NW India. Its terrain is largely a sandy waste. Jaisalmer was brought under the Mogul empire by Akbar in 1570. It became a British protectorate in 1818. In 1949 the region was incorporated in Rajasthan state.

Jaja (jä'jə), fl. 1869–1887, Nigerian merchant prince. A former slave, he became an important trader in Bonny in the 1860s as a middleman between the coastal markets and the Nigerian interior. In 1869 he founded his own state at Opobo on the Gulf of Guinea. From there he controlled supplies of palm oil and opposed the efforts of British firms to penetrate the interior. The traders persuaded the British vice consul, Henry Hamilton (Sir Harry) Johnston, to act against Jaja, who was seized in 1887 and then deported to the West Indies.

Jakan (jā'kən), the same as AKAN.

Jakarta: see DJAKARTA, Indonesia.

Jakeh (jā'kĕ), father of Agur. Prov. 30.1.

Jakim (jā'kĭm). **1** Chief priest in David's reign. 1 Chron. 24.12. **2** Chief Benjamite. 1 Chron. 8.19.

Jakobshavn (yäkôps-houn'), town (1969 pop. 2,544), Jakobshavn dist. (1969 pop. 2,992), W Greenland, on Disko Bay. Founded in 1741, it is a sealing and fishing port.

Jalalabad (jəlä"läbäd', jəläl'əbăd), city (1969 pop. 48,919), capital of Nangarhar prov., E Afghanistan, near the KHYBER PASS. The city dominates the entrances to the Laghman and Kunar valleys and is a leading center for trade with India and Pakistan. Oranges, rice, and sugarcane grow in the fertile surrounding area, and the city has cane-processing and sugar-refining as well as papermaking industries. Jalalabad has long been both a military center and a winter resort. The site of the city belonged to the ancient Greco-Buddhist center of GANDHARA. Babur, founder of the Mogul empire of India, chose the site for the modern city, which was built c.1570 by his grandson, Akbar. During the First Afghan War, British troops held (1842) Jalalabad against a determined Afghan siege. Pathan tribesmen constitute most of the population. The city has a university and medical school.

Jalapa de Enriquez (hälä'pä thā änrē'kās), city (1970 pop. 127,081), capital of Veracruz state, E central Mexico, on the slopes of the Sierra Madre Oriental. It is located in a rich agricultural region of fertile valleys. Its cool climate and the proximity of colorful Indian villages and of scenic Mt. Orizaba also make Jalapa a popular resort. The site of a pre-Columbian city, Jalapa was captured by Cortés in 1519. It was an important commercial center during the Spanish colonial era, but declined in the late 18th cent., after which it served as an important military base. The local museum has an excellent archaeological collection, notably a group of colossal Olmec heads, which are displayed in the open air.

Jalgaon (jäl'goun), town (1971 pop. 106,739), Maharashtra state, W central India. It is the center of a cotton-growing district.

Jalisco (hälē'skō), state (1970 pop. 3,322,750), 31,152 sq mi (80,684 sq km), W Mexico, bounded on the west by the Pacific. GUADALAJARA is the capital. Jalisco is dominated by the southern end of the Sierra Madre Occidental and the western extremity of the chain of volcanic mountains extending across central Mexico. The hot, tropical plains of the coast are broken by spurs of the Sierra, and most of the eastern part of the state lies within the central plateau. In the central part of Jalisco is an intermontane basin containing Lake Chapala; it is drained by the Lerma-Santiago system. Because of the variety of climate, landform, and elevation, nearly every kind of fruit and vegetable grows somewhere in Jalisco. Maize and wheat from the central plateau make it known as the "granary of Mexico"; rice and wheat are grown in the south; and the mountains yield timber and minerals (silver, iron, tin, cinnabar, and some gold.) The raising of livestock and the production of textiles and food products are also important. Although Jalisco was explored as early as 1522, serious conquest of the area, later included in NUEVA GALICIA, was not undertaken until 1529 by Nuno de GUZMÁN. Shortly before the War of the Reform (1858–61), Jalisco became a leading state in the great liberal revolution heralded by the Plan of AYUTLA. It was occupied by the French in the wars of intervention but was recaptured in 1866. In 1884 the territory of NAYARIT was separated from Jalisco. The state has two universities and a technological institute.

Jalon (jā'lŏn), descendant of Judah. 1 Chron. 4.17.

Jalpaiguri (jəlpī'go͝orē), town (1971 pop. 55,345), West Bengal state, NE India, on the Tista River. It is the administrative center for a district that produces tea, rice, jute, tobacco, timber, and medicinal herbs.

Jaluit (jä'lo͞oĭt), atoll (1970 pop. 492), c.40 mi (60 km) long and c.20 mi (30 km) wide, central Pacific, one of the Ralik Chain in the U.S. MARSHALL ISLANDS. It comprises some 85 islets, of which Jaluit Island (4 sq mi/10.4 sq km) is the largest. In World War II it was the headquarters of the Japanese admiralty for the Marshall Islands. U.S. forces captured the atoll in 1944. Jaluit is a seaport and trade center for the Marshalls.

jam: see JELLY AND JAM.

Jamaica (jəmā'kə), republic (1973 est. pop. 2,000,000), 4,232 sq mi (10,962 sq km), coextensive with the island of Jamaica, West Indies, S of Cuba and W of Haiti. Jamaica is the largest island in the Caribbean after Cuba and Hispaniola. The capital is KINGSTON; other important cities are SPANISH TOWN and MONTEGO BAY. Although largely a limestone plateau more than 3,000 ft (914 m) above sea level, Jamaica has a mountainous backbone that extends across the island from the west and rises to the Blue Mts. in the east; Blue Mt. (7,402 ft/2,256 m) is the highest point. Rainfall is heavy in this region (where there are extensive timber reserves) but diminishes westward across the plateau, which is a rugged area deeply dissected by streams and underlain by subterranean rivers. The heart of the plateau, known as the Cockpits, is used mostly for livestock grazing. A narrow plain along the northern coast and several

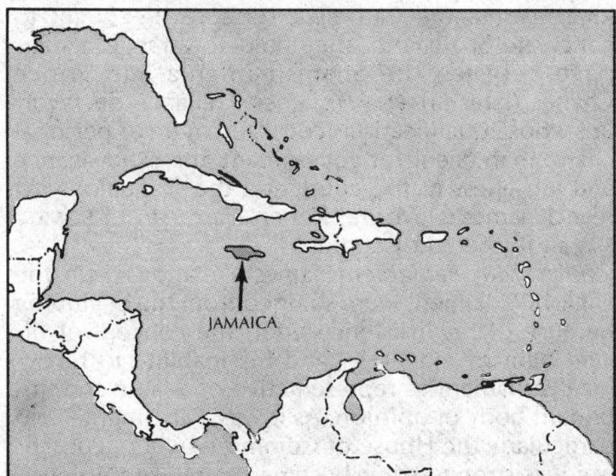

larger plains near the south shore are Jamaica's major agricultural zones. The north coast also has fine beaches and is the focus of the tourist industry. The Rio Grande and the Black River are the country's chief waterways, but neither is navigable for long distances. The coastal bands widened by broad river valleys, as well as the mountain slopes, support the bulk of Jamaica's export crops: the famed Blue Mt. coffee, sugarcane, from which rum and molasses are also made, bananas, ginger, citrus fruits, cocoa, pimento, and tobacco. Most of these crops are grown on large plantations. Small peasant farms produce some ginger, bananas, and sugarcane for export but mainly raise such subsistence crops as yams, breadfruit, and cassava. Mining is a major source of wealth; since large, easily accessible deposits of bauxite were discovered in 1942, Jamaica has become one of the world's leading suppliers of this ore. Along with the alumina made from it, bauxite accounts for about half of Jamaica's foreign exchange. Tourism is the second biggest earner of exchange. Clothing constitutes the chief export item of the manufacturing sector. Jamaica's other industries (mainly concentrated in the Kingston area) include oil refining, tobacco processing, flour milling, and the production of cement, textiles, and processed foods. Since the late 1960s industry has generated a greater share of the national income than agriculture, which, however, still employs the largest percentage of the work force. The United States, Great Britain, and Canada, Jamaica's top trading partners, also provide much-needed capital for economic development. About 75% of the population is rural, but migration to the cities continues; the greatest urban concentration is around Kingston. People of African descent predominate in Jamaica. The small upper class is mainly white. Afro-Europeans and such Middle Eastern and Asian groups as Lebanese, Syrians, Chinese, and Indians, make up the rest of the population. Although English is the official language, most Jamaicans speak a patois, creole English. The chief religion is Protestantism. Discovered by Christopher Columbus in 1494, Jamaica was conquered and settled in 1509 by Spaniards under a license from Columbus's son. Spanish exploitation decimated the native Arawaks. The island remained Spanish until 1655, when Admiral William Penn and Robert Venables captured it; it was formally ceded to England in 1670, but the local white population obtained a degree of autonomy. Jamaica prospered from the wealth brought by buccaneers, notably Sir Henry MORGAN, to Port Royal, the capital; in 1692, however, the city sank into the sea during an earthquake, and Spanish Town became the new capital. A huge, mostly Negro, slave population grew up around the sugarcane plantations in the 18th cent., when Jamaica was a leading world sugar producer. Freed slaves and runaways, sometimes aided by the MAROONS (slaves who had escaped to remote areas after Spain lost control of Jamaica), collaborated in fomenting frequent rebellions against the white colonials. The sugar industry declined in the 19th cent., partly because of the abolition of slavery in 1833 (effective 1838) and partly because of the elimination in 1846 of the imperial preference tariff for colonial products entering the British market. Economic hardship was the prime motive behind the Morant Bay rebellion by freedmen in 1865. The British ruthlessly quelled the uprising and also forced the frightened white legislature to surrender its powers; Jamaica became a crown colony. Poverty and economic decline led many Negroes to seek temporary work in neighboring Caribbean areas and in the United States; many left the island permanently. Indians were imported to meet the labor shortage on the plantations after the Negro slaves were freed, and agriculture was diversified to lessen dependence on sugar exports. A new constitution in 1884 marked the initial revival of local autonomy for Jamaica. Despite labor and other reforms, Negro riots recurred, notably those of 1938, which were caused mainly by unemployment and resentment against British racial policies. Jamaican blacks had been considerably influenced by the theories of black nationalism promulgated by the American expatriate Marcus Garvey. A royal commission investigating the 1938 riots recommended an increase of economic development funds and a faster restoration of representative government for Jamaica. In 1944 universal adult suffrage was introduced, and a new constitution provided for a popularly elected house of representatives. By 1958, Jamaica became a key member of the British-sponsored West Indies Federation (see under WEST INDIES). The fact that Jamaica received only one third of the representation in the federation, despite its having more than half the land area and population of the grouping, bred resentment; a campaign by the nationalist labor leader Sir Alexander Bustamante led to a 1961 decision, by popular referendum, to withdraw from the federation. The following year Jamaica won complete independence from Great Britain and became a member of the Commonwealth of Nations and the United Nations. It joined the Caribbean Free Trade Association in 1968. In March, 1974, Jamaica became one of the seven charter members of the International Association of Producers of Bauxite and later announced large increases in bauxite taxes and royalties. The country has a two-party system: the Jamaica Labor Party (JLP) favors private enterprise, while the People's National Party (PNP) advocates moderate socialism. Bustamante, leader of the JLP, became the first prime minister of independent Jamaica. The party continued in power under Donald B. Sangster after the 1967 elections; he died in office and was succeeded by Hugh Shearer. In 1972 the PNP won an impressive victory, and Michael Manley became prime minister. The prime minister and his cabinet are responsible to the bicameral Parliament. See M. M. Carley, *Jamaica* (1963); R. W. Palmer, *The Jamaican Economy* (1968); Edward Brathwaite, *The Development of Creole Society in Jamaica, 1770–1820* (1971); Frank Cundall, *Historic Jamaica* (1915, repr. 1971), S. J. Hurwitz and E. F. Hurwitz, *Jamaica: A Historical Portrait* (1971); R. M. Nettleford, *Identity, Race and Protest in Jamaica* (1972).

Jamaica Bay, c.20 sq mi (50 sq km), SW Long Island, SE N.Y., separated from the Atlantic Ocean by Rockaway Peninsula; the Rockaway Inlet links it to the sea. The shallow bay has many islands, and its shores are generally marshy. There is a minimum of water movement, and pollution is a problem. Nearly all of the bay is in New York City; since 1950 much of the adjacent area has been reclaimed for housing. John F. Kennedy International Airport extends into the bay. Part of Gateway National Recreation Area, the bay is used for boating and fishing and is a wildlife refuge.

Jambi: see DJAMBI, Indonesia.

Jamblichus: see IAMBLICHUS.

Jambol: see YAMBOL, Bulgaria.

Jambres: see JANNES AND JAMBRES.

James, Saint, d. A.D. c.43, one of the Twelve Disciples, called St. James the Greater. He was the son of Zebedee and the brother of St. John; these brothers were the Boanerges, or Sons of Thunder. St. James was killed by Herod Agrippa I. Mark 3.17; 5.37; 9.2; 10.35–45; 14.33; Mat. 20.20–29; Acts 12.1–2. Veneration of St. James has been widespread, especially in Spain (where he is called Santiago); the shrine of the apostle at Compostela, Spain, is one of the most celebrated of Europe. Feast: July 25.

James, Saint, one of the Twelve Disciples, called St. James the Less or St. James the Little. He was the son of Alphaeus; his mother, Mary, was one of those at the cross and tomb (Mat. 10.3; 27.56; Mark 15.40; 16.1; Acts 1.13). The Western Church identifies him with Saint James, "the Lord's brother" (see separate article). Feast (with St. Philip): May 1.

James, Saint, the "brother" of Jesus Christ. The Gospels make several references to the brothers of Jesus (Mat. 12.46; 13.55; Mark 6.3; John 2.12), and St. Paul speaks of "James the Lord's brother" (Gal. 1.19). However, since belief in the perpetual virginity of Mary precludes a blood relationship between Jesus and James, it has been posited that they were stepbrothers (assuming a previous marriage for Joseph) or cousins. The latter hypothesis, which is favored by the Roman Catholic Church, identifies James with St. James the Less. The James whom Paul calls "the Lord's brother" witnessed the Resurrection and became a leader of the church in Jerusalem, by tradition the first bishop there. He apparently opposed the imposition of Jewish Law on gentile Christians but believed that Jewish Christians should continue to observe it. (Acts 12.17; 15.13–21; 21.18; Gal. 2.9,12.) He is probably the James of the epistle of that name. Some scholars believe that he wrote it himself, others that it was written at a later date under his name. The Jewish historian Josephus records that James was stoned to death at the instigation of the priests A.D. c.62.

James I (James the Conqueror), 1208–76, king of Aragón and count of Barcelona (1213–76), son and successor of Peter II. After a minority disturbed by private wars among the nobles, James soon consolidated royal power and tried to create a new nobility dependent on him. He seized the Balearic Islands (1229–35) and Valencia (1238) from the Moors and helped Castile to recover control of Murcia after a Moorish rebellion (1266). A crusade to Palestine (1269) was unsuccessful. By the Treaty of Corbeil (1258) with Louis IX of France, James gave up several claims in S France, while the French king renounced his rights in Catalonia, derived from Charlemagne. James's own chronicle of his reign has been translated into English. He was succeeded in Aragón by his son Peter III. Another son became king of Majorca as James I. See biographies by C. R. Beazley (1890) and F. D. Swift (1894).

James II, c.1260–1327, king of Aragón and count of Barcelona (1291–1327), king of Sicily (1285–95). He succeeded his father, Peter III, in Sicily and his brother, Alfonso III, in Aragón. James defended Sicily against the claims of CHARLES II of Naples until 1295, when he relinquished the island in exchange for the title to Sardinia and Corsica. (Sardinia was annexed in 1323–24, but he did not take Corsica.) James later supported Charles against the former's own brother, who had been proclaimed king of Sicily as FREDERICK II. James was succeeded in Aragón by his son Alfonso IV.

James I, 1566–1625, king of England (1603–25) and, as James VI, of Scotland (1567–1625). The son of Lord Darnley and MARY QUEEN OF SCOTS, he succeeded to the Scottish throne on the forced abdication of his mother. He was placed in the care of John Erskine, 1st earl of MAR, and later of Mar's brother, Sir Alexander Erskine. The young king progressed in his studies under various teachers, notably George BUCHANAN, and acquired a taste for learning and theological debate. During James's minority, Scotland was ruled by a series of regents—the earls of MURRAY, LENNOX, Mar, and MORTON. The king was the creature of successive combinations of the nobility and clergy in a complicated struggle between the remnants of his mother's Catholic party, which favored an alliance with France, and the Protestant faction, which wished an alliance with England. In 1582, James was seized by William Ruthven, earl of Gowrie (see RUTHVEN, family), and other Protestant adherents. He escaped in 1583 and began his personal rule, though influenced by his favorite, James STUART, earl of Arran. James considered an alliance with his mother's French relatives, the GUISE, but in 1586, to improve his prospects of succeeding to the English throne, he allied himself with Elizabeth I. This caused a break with his mother's party, and he accepted her execution in 1587 calmly. James, by clever politics and armed force, succeeded in subduing the feudal Scottish baronage, in establishing royal authority, and in asserting the superiority of the state over the Presbyterian Church. In 1589, against the wishes of Elizabeth, James married ANNE OF DENMARK. He succeeded in 1603 to the English crown by virtue of his descent from MARGARET TUDOR, daughter of Henry VII.

King of England. Although at first welcomed in England, James brought to his new kingdom little understanding of its Parliament or its changing political, social, and religious conditions. On his arrival in England, the king was presented with the Millenary Petition, a plea for the accommodation of Puritans within the Established Church. However, at the Hampton Court Conference (1604), called to consider the petition, James displayed an uncompromising anti-Puritan attitude, which aroused great distrust. (This conference commissioned the translation of the BIBLE that resulted in the Authorized, or King James, Version.) James's inconsistent policy toward English Roman Catholics angered both Catholic and Protestant alike. The GUNPOWDER PLOT (1605), which sprang from Catholic anger at the reimposition of fines and penalties that James had earlier relaxed, led to greater harshness toward Catholics and prevented any cordial relations thereafter. Yet the suspicion arose that the king favored the Catholics, because he sought to conciliate Spain and attempted to arrange a marriage between the Spanish infanta and Prince Charles (later CHARLES I). James's reliance on favorites whose qualifications consisted more of personal charm than talent for government, the extravagance and looseness of the court, and the scandalous career of James's favorite, Robert Carr, earl of SOMERSET, all furthered discontent.

Conflict with Parliament. James's relations with the English Parliament were strained from the beginning because of his insistence upon the concept of divine right of monarchy and his inability to recognize Parliament as representative of a large and important body of opinion. As it was, Parliament—and particularly the House of Commons, where Puritanism was strong—soon became the rallying point of the forces opposing the crown. The Commons blocked (1607) James's cherished project of a union with Scotland. They also complained bitterly about James's methods of raising revenue by imposing new customs duties and selling monopolies. The Great Contract of 1610, a compromise whereby James would relinquish some of his feudal rights in return for a yearly income, did not come to fruition. In 1611, James dissolved Parliament and except for the Addled Parliament of 1614, which produced no legislation, ruled without one until 1621. After the death (1612) of his capable minister, Robert Cecil, earl of SALISBURY, the king exercised the royal prerogative with even less restraint and entered into battle with the courts of common law, whose position was strongly defended by Sir Edward COKE. After the fall of Somerset, George Villiers, later 1st duke of BUCKINGHAM, rose to favor and by 1619 was in complete possession of the king's confidence. At the Parliament of 1621, called in order to raise money for the cause of the German Protestants and James's son-in-law, FREDERICK THE WINTER KING, in the Thirty Years War, James was forced to abolish certain monopolies that had been abused by their holders. This Parliament also impeached the lord chancellor, Francis BACON. It was dissolved by James for asserting its right to debate foreign policy. The unpopular Spanish policy was pursued until the 1623 expedition of Prince Charles and Buckingham to Spain to facilitate the marriage arrangements ended in failure. A marriage treaty with France was concluded in 1624, and James was unable to prevent Parliament from voting a subsidy for war against Spain. James left to his son, Charles I, a foreign war and events leading up to the ENGLISH CIVIL WAR. During James's reign occurred the beginnings of English colonization in North America (Jamestown was founded in 1607) and the plantation of Scottish settlers in Ulster. The king was active as an author. He produced several youthful essays on literary theory, poetry, and numerous political works. Two other important writings are his *True Law of Free Monarchy* (1598), an assertion of the concept of divine right of kings, and BASILIKON DORON (1599), a treatise on the art of government. His political works have been edited by C. H. McIlwain (1918, repr. 1965). See biographies by D. H. Willson (1956, repr. 1967) and David Mathew (1967); Godfrey Davies, *The Early Stuarts* (2d ed. 1959); J. P. Kenyon, *The Stuarts* (1958); G. P. V. Akrigg, *Jacobean Pageant* (1962, repr. 1967).

James II, 1633–1701, king of England, Scotland, and Ireland (1685–88); second son of Charles I, brother and successor of CHARLES II. As the young duke of York he was surrendered (1646) to the parliamentary forces at the end of the first civil war, but he escaped (1648) to the Continent and served in the French (1652–55) and Spanish (1658) armies. At the Restoration (1660) he returned to England, married Anne Hyde, daughter of the 1st earl of Clarendon, and was made lord high admiral, in which capacity he served (1665, 1672) in the DUTCH WARS. Charles II granted him sweeping proprietary rights in America, and the captured Dutch settlement New Amsterdam was renamed (1664) New York in his honor. James was converted to Roman Catholicism probably in 1668—a step that was to have grave consequences. After his resignation (1673) as admiral because of the TEST ACT and his marriage (1673) to the staunchly Catholic MARY OF MODENA (his first wife having died in 1671), he became increasingly unpopular in England. James consented to the marriage (1677) of his daughter Mary (later MARY II) to the Protestant prince of Orange (later WILLIAM III), and the couple became the heirs presumptive, after James, to the English throne. In the anti-Catholic hysteria that accompanied the false accusations of Titus OATES about the Popish Plot (1678), efforts were made by the so-called WHIGS to exclude James from the succession. Charles stood by his brother, preventing passage of the Exclusion Bill, but sent him out of the country. After a period as commissioner (1680–82) in Scotland, James returned to England, and particularly after the RYE HOUSE PLOT (1683) his fortunes rose a little. When Charles died in 1685, James succeeded peacefully to the throne. An uprising led by the duke of MONMOUTH was crushed (1685), but the severe reprisals of the Bloody Assizes under Baron JEFFREYS OF WEM added to the animosity toward James. The king favored autocratic methods, proroguing the hostile Parliament (1685), reviving the old ecclesiastical court of high commission, and interfering with the courts and with local town and county government. His principal object was to fill positions of authority and influence with Roman Catholics, and to this end he issued two declarations of indulgence (1687, 1688), suspending the laws against Catholics and dissenters. Defiance and dislike of him grew, fed by the trial (1688) of seven bishops who had refused to read his second declaration. The birth of a son, who would have succeeded instead of the Protestant William and Mary, helped to bring the opposition to a head. William of Orange was invited to England by Whig and TORY leaders. The unpopular, autocratic, and Catholic king had few loyal followers and was unable to defend himself. He fled, was captured, and was allowed to escape to France, and William and Mary took the throne. The so-called GLORIOUS REVOLUTION had succeeded. James made an effort to restore himself by crossing over to Ireland in 1689 and raising his standard there, but the effort failed dismally in the battle of the BOYNE (1690). Other projects for restoration failed, and James's supporter, Louis XIV, recognized William III in the Treaty of Ryswick (1697). The cause of James's son and grandson was upheld later by the JACOBITES long after James had died in inglorious exile. See his early memoirs (tr. 1962); biographies by Hilaire Belloc (1928, repr. 1971), F. G. Turner (1948), and Vincent Buranelli (1962); David Ogg, *England in the Reigns of James II and William III* (1955, repr. 1969); J. P. Kenyon, *The Stuarts* (1958, repr. 1966).

James I, 1243–1311, king of Majorca (1276–1311), count of Roussillon and Cerdagne, lord of Montpellier, son of James I of Aragón. In 1278 he was forced to become a vassal of his brother, Peter III of Aragón. Having supported the French crusade against Peter, he was expelled (1285) from his territories by Peter's son, Alfonso III, but was restored 10 years later as the vassal of James II of Aragón. He was succeeded by his son Sancho IV (reigned 1311–24).

James II, 1315–49, king of Majorca (1324–49), count of Roussillon and Cerdagne, lord of Montpellier;

grandson of James I, nephew and successor of Sancho IV. In 1329 he declared himself a vassal of the Aragonese crown. Accusing James of illegal acts, Peter IV of Aragón invaded and conquered Majorca (1343) and Roussillon (1344) and annexed them to Aragón. James tried to recover his kingdom, but was defeated and killed in battle on Majorca. His son, James III, tried unsuccessfully to recover the kingdom in 1375.

James I, 1394–1437, king of Scotland (1406–37), son and successor of Robert III. King Robert feared for the safety of James because the king's brother, Robert STUART, 1st duke of Albany, who was virtual ruler of the realm, stood next in line of succession after the young prince. Albany had already been suspected of complicity in the death of James's older brother, David Stuart, duke of Rothesay. Accordingly, in 1406 the king sent James to France for safety, but the prince was captured on the way by the English and held prisoner until 1424. So, although James technically succeeded his father in 1406, the regent Albany ruled until his own death and was succeeded by his son, and the king's ransom was arranged only at the insistence of Archibald DOUGLAS, 4th earl of Douglas, and other nobles. The king had been well educated by his captors, Henry IV and Henry V of England, who had treated him as a royal guest. Shortly before his return to Scotland in 1424, James married Joan Beaufort, daughter of the earl of Somerset. *The Kingis Quair* [the king's book] (rev. ed. by W. W. Skeat, 1911), the story of his captivity and his romance with Joan, is usually considered to have been written by him. It and other poems attributed to him would establish him as one of the leading poets in the Chaucerian tradition. James was crowned at Scone and set about governing energetically. He asserted his authority over the nobility, ruthlessly exterminating members of the Albany family and a number of other barons and reducing the Highland clans to order. He also achieved important financial and judicial reforms and sought to remodel the Scottish Parliament, which he convened annually, along English lines. His plans for including burghers in the Parliament and improving commerce and the army were opposed by his militantly feudal nobles, and his vindictiveness, cupidity, and quick temper understandably diminished his popularity. He was assassinated by a group of nobles, one of whom, the earl of Atholl, probably hoped to claim the throne. However, James was succeeded by his son, James II. See biographies by E. W. M. Balfour-Melville (1936) and John Norton-Smith (1971).

James II, 1430–60, king of Scotland (1437–60), son and successor of James I. During his minority successive earls of Douglas vied for power with factions led by Sir William Crichton and Sir Alexander Livingstone. The power of the Douglases was temporarily broken (1440) by the judicial murder of William DOUGLAS, the 6th earl, but the king later allied himself with William DOUGLAS, the 8th earl, to overthrow Crichton and Livingstone. By 1450, James ruled in his own right. When in 1452 the king discovered Douglas in a conspiracy, James called him to Stirling, charged him with betrayal, and stabbed him. After the resulting rebellion, the king attainted James DOUGLAS, the 9th earl, and seized the Douglas lands. During his reign James improved the courts of justice and regulated the coinage. A Lancastrian partisan in the Wars of the ROSES, he invaded England and was accidentally killed at the siege of Roxburgh. His son James III succeeded him.

James III, 1452–88, king of Scotland (1460–88), son and successor of James II. During his minority he was under the care of his mother, Mary of Guelders, and her adviser, James Kennedy, bishop of St. Andrews. After their deaths, James was seized (1466) by the Boyd family, who ruled Scotland until 1469. In that year James married Margaret, daughter of the Danish king, and began to rule personally. He was a cultivated prince but lacked the force needed in so turbulent a period. James quarreled with and imprisoned (1479) his brother, Alexander STUART, duke of Albany, but Alexander escaped to France. In 1482, Albany, aided by the English, invaded Scotland. James moved to resist, but Archibald DOUGLAS, 5th earl of Angus, nominally one of his supporters, headed a group that hanged certain of James's favorites and briefly held the king prisoner. A period of peace followed, but in 1488 the nobles rebelled again, this time with the support of James's son, the future James IV. They defeated and murdered the king at Sauchieburn.

James IV, 1473–1513, king of Scotland (1488–1513), son and successor of James III. He was an able and popular king, and his reign was one of stability and progress for Scotland. After suppressing an insurrection of discontented nobles early in his reign, he set about restoring order, improving administrative and judicial procedure in the kingdom, and encouraging manufacturing and shipbuilding. A conflict with Henry VII of England over James's support of Perkin WARBECK, pretender to the English throne, ended with the conclusion of a seven-year truce in 1497. In 1503, James married Henry's daughter, MARGARET TUDOR. This marriage was to bring the Stuart line to the English throne in 1603. When Henry VIII ascended (1509) the English throne, relations between Scotland and England deteriorated. In 1512, Louis XII of France, already at war with England, urged and secured a renewal of his alliance with the Scottish king. In 1513, James, against the counsel of his advisers, invaded England, where at the battle of FLODDEN he was killed and the Scottish aristocracy was almost annihilated. See biography by R. L. Mackie (1958, repr. 1964).

James V, 1512–42, king of Scotland (1513–42), son and successor of James IV. His mother, MARGARET TUDOR, held the regency until her marriage in 1514 to Archibald DOUGLAS, 6th earl of Angus, when she lost it to John STUART, duke of Albany. The factions of Albany, Angus, and the queen mother struggled for control until Angus seized (1526) the young king. In 1528, James escaped, and Angus fled to England. James began to ally himself with France against his uncle, HENRY VIII of England. In 1537 he married Madeleine, daughter of Francis I of France, and after her death in the same year he married (1538) MARY OF GUISE. James rejected Henry's attempts to win his support for the English religious policy, and in 1542 war broke out between the two countries. James's nobles gave him little support, and his army was routed at Solway Moss in 1542. He died shortly thereafter and was succeeded by his infant daughter, MARY QUEEN OF SCOTS.

James VI, king of Scotland: see JAMES I, king of England.

James, kinsman of St. Jude. Luke 6.16. The original does not specify the relationship.

James, Henry, 1811–82, American student of religion and social problems, b. Albany, N.Y.; father of the philosopher William James and of the novelist Henry James. He rebelled against the strict Calvinist theology of his family and of Princeton Theological Seminary, to which he was sent, and sought a personal solution. Swedenborgian teachings opened for him a way and provided the framework for his own thought as expressed in *Substance and Shadow; or, Morality and Religion in Their Relation to Life* (1863), *Society the Redeemed Form of Man, and the Earnest of God's Omnipotence in Human Nature* (1879), and other books. He later developed a social philosophy based upon the principles of Charles Fourier. He was a close friend of many literary figures, including Ralph Waldo Emerson and Thomas Carlyle. See Austin Warren, *The Elder Henry James* (1934, repr. 1970); F. O. Matthiessen, *The James Family* (1947, repr. 1961).

James, Henry, 1843–1916, American novelist and critic, b. New York City. A master of the psychological novel, James was an innovator in technique and one of the most distinctive prose stylists in English. He was the son of Henry James, Sr., a Swedenborgian theologian, and the brother of William James, the philosopher. Educated privately by tutors in Europe and the United States, he entered Harvard law school in 1862. Encouraged by William Dean Howells and other members of the Cambridge literary circle in the 1860s, James wrote critical articles and reviews for the *Atlantic Monthly,* a periodical in which several of his novels later appeared in serial form. He made several trips to Europe, and while there he became associated with such notable literary figures as Turgenev and Flaubert. In 1876 he settled permanently in London and became a British subject in 1915. Having never married, he devoted himself to literature and travel, gradually assuming the role of detached spectator and analyst of life. In his early novels, including *Roderick Hudson* (1876), *The American* (1877), *Daisy Miller* (1879), and *The Portrait of a Lady* (1881), as well as some of his later work, James contrasts the sophisticated, though somewhat staid, Europeans with the innocent, eager, though often brash, Americans. In the novels of his middle period, *The Bostonians* (1886), *The Princess Casamassima* (1886), and *The Tragic Muse* (1890), he turned his attention from the international theme to reformers, revolutionaries, and political aspirants. During and after an unsuccessful six-year attempt (1889–95) to win recognition as a playwright, James wrote a series of short, powerful novels, including *The Aspern Papers* (1888), *What Maisie Knew* (1897), *The Spoils of Poynton* (1897), *The Turn of the Screw* (1898), and *The Sacred Fount* (1901). In his last and perhaps his greatest novels, *The Wings of the Dove* (1902), *The Ambassadors* (1903), and *The Golden Bowl* (1904), all marked by a return to the international theme, James reached his highest development in the portrayal of the intricate subtleties of character and in the use of a complex, convoluted style to express delicate nuances of thought. Perhaps more than any previous writer, James refined the technique of narrating a novel from the point of view of a character, thereby laying the foundations of modern STREAM OF CONSCIOUSNESS fiction. The series of critical prefaces he wrote for the reissue of his novels (beginning in 1907) won him a reputation as a superb technician. He is also famous for his finely wrought short stories, including "The Beast in the Jungle" and "The Real Thing," which are masterpieces of the genre. In addition to fiction and literary criticism, James wrote several books on travel and three autobiographical works. See his notebooks, ed. by F. O. Matthiessen and K. B. Murdock (1947); his plays, ed. by Leon Edel (1949); biographies by Leon Edel (5 vol., 1953–71) and F. W. Dupee (1951, repr. 1973); studies by F. O. Matthiessen (1944), J. W. Beach (rev. ed. 1954), Sallie Sears (1968), Peter Buitenhuis (1970), and Oscar Cargill (1961, repr. 1971).

James, Jesse, 1847–82, American outlaw, b. Clay co., Mo. At the age of 15 he joined the Confederate guerrilla band led by William QUANTRILL and participated in the civil warfare in Kansas and Missouri. In 1866, Jesse and his brother Frank became the leaders of a band of outlaws whose trail of robberies and murders led through most of the central states. At first they robbed only banks, but in 1873 they began to rob trains. The beginning of their downfall came in 1876 when, after killing two people and failing to secure any money in an attempted bank robbery at Northfield, Minn., they lost several members of the gang, including the Younger brothers, three of their most trusted followers, who were captured and imprisoned (see YOUNGER, COLE). The James brothers escaped and were quiet until 1879, when they robbed another train. The reward offered by Gov. Thomas T. Crittenden of Missouri for the capture of the James brothers, dead or alive, tempted one of the gang, Robert Ford, who caught Jesse (then living under the name of Thomas Howard) off guard and killed him. Frank James surrendered but was twice acquitted and lived out his life peacefully on his farm near Excelsior Springs, Mo. The melodramatic style of the exploits of the James gang attracted wide public admiration, giving rise to a number of legends, the famous song "The Ballad of Jesse James," and much popular literature. See biography by Robertus Love (1926); Homer Croy, *Jesse James Was My Neighbor* (1949, repr. 1962); C. W. Breihan, *The Complete and Authentic Life of Jesse James* (1953, repr. 1970); J. L. James, *Jesse James and the Lost Cause* (1961); W. A. Settle, *Jesse James was his Name* (1966).

James, Thomas, 1593?–1635?, English navigator and explorer (1631) of James Bay. Financed by Bristol merchants, he sailed in command of the *Henrietta Maria* in the spring of 1631 to find the NORTHWEST PASSAGE to the East. Having explored James Bay (the south extension of Hudson Bay), which was named for him, he wintered on Charlton Island, and in the summer of 1632 continued his attempt to find the passage, a quest that Luke Fox was also undertaking independently (1631). Upon his return to England, James wrote his *Strange and Dangerous Voyage* (1633), which was later to have a strong influence on the poet Samuel Taylor Coleridge. See R. B. Bodilly, *The Voyage of Captain Thomas James* (1928); C. M. MacInnes, *Captain Thomas James and the North West Passage* (1967).

James, Thomas, 1782–1847, American fur trader and pioneer, b. Maryland. He accompanied the 1809 expedition of the Missouri Fur Company up the Missouri River. He left the expedition at the Mandan Indian villages (in the vicinity of Bismarck, N. Dak.) and returned to St. Louis, where he became a merchant. With Robert McKnight he led an early expedition (1821–23) over the Santa Fe Trail. Later he settled in S Illinois. He is chiefly remembered for his valuable account of his early expedition, *Three Years among the Indians and Mexicans* (1846, ed. by W. B. Douglas, 1916).

James, William, 1842–1910, American philosopher, b. New York City, M.D. Harvard, 1869; son of the Swedenborgian theologian Henry James and brother of the novelist Henry James. In 1872 he joined the Harvard faculty as lecturer on anatomy and physiology, continuing to teach until 1907, after 1880 in the department of psychology and philosophy. In 1890 he published his brilliant and epoch-making *Principles of Psychology,* in which the seeds of his philosophy are already discernible. James's fascinating style and his broad culture and cosmopolitan outlook made him the most influential American thinker of his day. His philosophy has three principal aspects—his voluntarism, his pragmatism, and his "radical empiricism." He construes consciousness as essentially active, selective, interested, teleological. We "carve out" our world from "the jointless continuity of space." Will and interest are thus primary; knowledge is instrumental. The true is "only the expedient in our way of thinking." Ideas do not reproduce objects, but prepare for, or lead the way to, them. The function of an idea is to indicate "what conceivable effects of a practical kind the object may involve—what sensations we are to expect from it and what reactions we must prepare." This theory of knowledge James called PRAGMATISM, a term already used by Charles S. PEIRCE. James's "radical empiricism" is a philosophy of "pure experience," which rejects all transcendent principles and finds experience organized by means of "conjunctive relations" that are as much a matter of direct experience as things themselves. Moreover, James regards consciousness as only one type of conjunctive relation within experience, not as an entity above, or distinct from, its experience. James's other philosophical writings include *The Will to Believe* (1897), *The Varieties of Religious Experience* (1902), *Pragmatism* (1907), *A Pluralistic Universe* (1909), *The Meaning of Truth* (1909), *Some Problems in Philosophy* (1911), and *Essays in Radical Empiricism* (1912). See his letters (ed. by his son Henry James, 1920); biographies by E. C. Moore (1965) and G. W. Allen (1967); studies by B. P. Brennan (1968), John Wild (1969), and P. K. Dooley (1974); R. B. Perry, *The Thought and Character of William James* (2 vol. 1935, abr. ed. 1948) and *In the Spirit of William James* (1938, repr. 1958).

James. 1 Unnavigable river, 710 mi (1,143 km) long, rising in central N.Dak. and flowing across S.Dak. to the Missouri River at Yankton, S.Dak. Jamestown Dam on the river is an irrigation and flood control unit of the MISSOURI RIVER BASIN PROJECT of the U.S. Bureau of Reclamation. **2** River, 340 mi (547 km) long, formed in W central Va. by the union of the Jackson and Cowpasture rivers and winding E across Va. to enter Chesapeake Bay through Hampton Roads. One of Virginia's chief rivers, it is navigable for large ships to Richmond, c.100 mi (160 km) upstream; Norfolk, Newport News, and Portsmouth are large ports at its mouth. The James's upper course flows through scenic gorges in the Blue Ridge Mts. and the Piedmont; waterfalls and rapids provide power. English colonists founded Jamestown on the lower river in 1607. During the Civil War, Union forces used the river in vain attempts to capture Richmond (see PENINSULAR CAMPAIGN; SEVEN DAYS BATTLES).

James, epistle of the New Testament, the 20th book in the usual order, traditionally classified among the Catholic, or General, Epistles. The James of its ascription (1.1) is traditionally St. James the Less. The content is not very orderly, for the work, practical in stress, gives many diverse admonitions, some recurrent. It opens with a section on temptation (1.2–18; cf. 5.7–11), then goes on to two general ethical principles, "be doers of the word, not hearers only" (1.19–27) and "faith without works is dead" (2.14–26; cf. Heb. 11.17–40). The rest consists of specific points—human respect (2.1–13), bridling the tongue (1.26; 3.1–18; 5.12), living in harmony (4.1–17), the wickedness of the rich (2.2–7; 5.1–6), the efficacy of prayer (5.13–18), saving sinners (5.19–20). The scriptural authority cited for the anointing of the sick is here (5.14–15). Scholars differ widely on the origin and date of this epistle. It was one of the later books to be accepted as canonical. Martin Luther rejected it because it seems to deny his interpretation of justification by faith.

James, Protevangelium of: see PSEUDEPIGRAPHA.

James Bay, shallow southern arm of Hudson Bay, c.300 mi (480 km) long and 140 mi (230 km) wide, E central Canada, in the Northwest Territories between Ont. and Que. Numerous rivers flow into the bay. Of its many islands, the largest is Akimiski (898 sq mi/2,326 sq km). The bay was discovered (1610) by Henry Hudson but was named for Capt. Thomas James, an Englishman who explored much of it in 1631. An early fur-trading post established by Groseilliers and Radisson became (1670) Rupert House, the first post established there by the Hudson's Bay Company. Other important posts on James Bay are Fort Albany, Fort George, and Eastmain. The shores of the bay and some of its islands are wildlife reserves.

James Francis Edward Stuart: see STUART, JAMES FRANCIS EDWARD.

James Island: see CHARLESTON, S.C.

Jameson, Anna Brownell (Murphy), 1794–1860, English essayist, b. Dublin. The diary of her travels on the Continent as governess to a wealthy family was later published as *The Diary of an Ennuyée* (1826). Jameson's works—especially *Shakespeare's Heroines* (1932)—were popular in her day, but only *Sacred and Legendary Art* (1848–60; ed. by E. M. Hurll, 1896) had lasting currency.

Jameson, John Franklin, 1859–1937, American historian, b. Somerville, Mass. After teaching at Johns Hopkins, Brown, and the Univ. of Chicago he was director (1905–28) of the department of historical research of the Carnegie Institution, Washington, D.C., and from 1928 to his death he was chief of the division of manuscripts in the Library of Congress. As chairman of the committee of management of the *Dictionary of American Biography* he was largely responsible for the inauguration and completion of that monumental work. In these and other undertakings, Jameson exercised much influence in American historical scholarship. He wrote *Willem Usselinx, Founder of the Dutch and Swedish West India Companies* (1887), *The History of Historical Writing in America* (1891), *Dictionary of United States History* (1894, rev. ed. 1931), and *The American Revolution Considered as a Social Movement* (1926) and edited *Correspondence of John C. Calhoun* (1900, repr. 1969) and *Original Narratives of Early American History* (19 vol., 1906–17).

Jameson, Sir Leander Starr, 1853–1917, British colonial administrator and statesman in South Africa. He went to Kimberley (1878) as a physician, became associated with Cecil Rhodes in his colonizing ventures, and was appointed (1891) administrator of Mashonaland. On December 29, 1895, he led a band of volunteers on the famous Jameson Raid into the Boer colony of Transvaal in an effort to support a brewing rebellion by foreign settlers (mainly British), and to further Rhodes's ambition for a united South Africa. The raid was premature. Jameson was captured within a few days and turned over by President Kruger to the British to be punished for his unauthorized venture. He was returned to London for trial and sentenced to imprisonment for 15 months. On his release he returned to South Africa, served in the Cape Colony Parliament (1900–1902), and was premier (1904–8). He played an important role in the South African National Convention (1908–9), which achieved the union of the South African colonies. See Jean Van der Poel, *The Jameson Raid* (1952); E. H. Pakenham, *Jameson's Raid* (1960).

Jameson, Storm (Margaret Storm Jameson), 1891–, English novelist and critic, b. Whitby, Yorkshire, grad. Leeds Univ., 1912. Descended from a shipbuilding family, she drew on her knowledge of that business for her first three novels, a family chronicle trilogy reprinted as *The Triumph of Time* (1932). Most of her novels treat ethical and moral problems. Among them are *Cousin Honoré* (1940), *The White Crow* (1968), and *There Will Be a Short Interval* (1973). See her autobiography (1969).

Jameson Raid: see JAMESON, SIR LEANDER STARR.

Jamestown. 1 City (1970 pop. 39,795), Chautauqua co., W N.Y., on Chautauqua Lake; founded c.1806, inc. as a city 1886. It is the business and financial center of a dairy, livestock, and vineyard area, and its chief industries are food processing and furniture making. Two insurance companies have their headquarters there. The city has a junior college. Nearby are Allegany State Park and the Chautauqua Institution, a cultural and recreational center on the lake. **2** City (1970 pop. 15,385), seat of Stutsman co., SE N.Dak., on the James River, in a farm area; settled 1872 when Fort Seward was established to protect railroad workers, inc. 1896. It is the trade center for an agricultural area. Jamestown College, a state home for crippled children, and a state mental hospital are in the city. Fort Seward State Monument and a restored frontier village are on the outskirts. **3** Former village, SE Va., first permanent English settlement in America; est. May 14, 1607, by the LONDON COMPANY on a marshy peninsula (now an island) in the James River and named for the reigning English monarch, James I. Disease, starvation, and Indian attacks wiped out most of the colony, but the London Company continually sent more men and supplies, and John Smith briefly provided efficient leadership (he returned to England in 1609 for treatment of an injury). After the severe winter of 1609–10 (the "starving time"), the survivors prepared to return to England but were stopped by the timely arrival of Lord De la Warr with supplies. John Rolfe cultivated the first tobacco there in 1612, introducing a successful source of livelihood, and in 1614 he assured peace with the Indians by marrying Pocahontas, daughter of the Indian chief Powhatan. In 1619 the first representative government in the New World met at Jamestown, and Jamestown remained the capital of Virginia throughout the 17th cent. The village was almost entirely destroyed during BACON'S REBELLION; it was partially rebuilt but fell into decay with the removal of the capital to Williamsburg (1698–1700). Of the 17th-cent. settlement, only the old church tower (built c.1639) and a few gravestones were visible when National Park Service excavations began in 1934. Except for the land owned by the Association for the Preservation of Virginia Antiquities, Jamestown Island is today the property of the U.S. government. It is included in Colonial National Historical Park (see NATIONAL PARKS AND MONUMENTS, table). A tercentenary celebration was held in 1907, and in 1957 the Jamestown Festival Park was built to commemorate the 350th anniversary. The park contains exhibit pavilions and replicas of the first fort, the three ships that brought the first settlers, and an Indian lodge. See J. L. Kibler, *Cradle of the Nation* (1931); report by the Celebration Commission, *The 350th Anniversary of Jamestown, 1607–1957* (1958).

Jamestown weed: see JIMSON WEED.

Jami (jä'mē), 1414–92, Persian poet, b. Jam, near Herat. His full name was Nur ad-Din Abd ar-Rahman Jami. His poetic influence was widespread. Nearly 100 works are attributed to him, of which some 40 are considered authentic. He was also known as a saint for his devotion to dervish teaching and to Sufi philosophy. Among his works is the collection of poems *Haft Aurang* [the seven thrones], including the allegory "Salaman and Absal" (tr. by Edward FitzGerald in the 19th cent.), and a version of the tale of Joseph and Potiphar's wife. His *Baharistan* [abode of spring] is a collection of short stories.

Jamin (jā'mĭn). **1** Simeonite, Gen. 46.10; 1 Chron. 4.24. **2** Hezronite. 1 Chron. 2.27. **3** Reader of the Law. Neh. 8.7.

Jamitzer, Wenzel: see JAMNITZER, WENZEL.

Jamlech (jăm'lĕk), chief of the tribe of Simeon. 1 Chron. 4.34.

Jammes, Francis (fräNsēs' zhäm), 1868–1938, French poet. He lived most of his life in the Pyrenees. Jammes is usually grouped with the symbolists, but he is distinguished from them by the simplicity and artlessness of his pastoral poetry. *De l'angélus de l'aube à l'angélus du soir* (1898) brought him wide acclaim. Later works, including *Clairières dans le ciel* (1906) and *Géorgiques Chrétiennes* (1911–12), are suffused with Catholic spirit. He also wrote charming stories about rustic people. See Amy Lowell, *Six French Poets* (1915).

Jammu (jŭ'mōō), town (1971 pop. 155,249), Jammu and Kashmir state, N India, on the Tawi River and in the Himalayan foothills. The former winter capital of Jammu and Kashmir state, it is strategically important as the southern terminus of a highway linking the Vale of Kashmir with the North Indian plain. Once the seat of a Rajput dynasty, Jammu became the nucleus of the dominions of Gulab Singh, founder of the last ruling house of Kashmir. On one bank of the river is Jammu's old Fort of Bahu; on the other bank is the maharaja's palace, which dominates the city.

Jammu and Kashmir: see KASHMIR.

Jamnagar (jäm'nəgər), city (1971 pop. 214,853), Gujarat state, W central India. A port on the Gulf of Kutch, which is an arm of the Arabian Sea, Jamnagar has naval and aeronautical schools. A radium institute is also in the city. Jamnagar is a district administrative center and is known for its silk, embroidery, and marble. There are cotton-textile mills.

Jamnia (jăm'nēə), biblical *Jabneel* (jăb'nēel, jăb'-nēl) and *Jabneh* (jăb'nə,-nē) [Heb.,=God causes to build], ancient city, central Israel. The modern name is Yibna. It was a central city of Philistia, and in the Bible there is a reference to its walls being destroyed by Uzziah. It was pillaged by Judas Maccabaeus and later rebuilt. In the last years before the sack of Jerusalem (A.D. 70) Jamnia became a great Jewish cultural center, and at the prayer of JOHANAN BEN ZAKKAI, Vespasian spared Jamnia and permitted Johanan to settle there as leader of the Jewish community after the fall of Jerusalem. The Great Sanhedrin was moved to Jamnia, and under Johanan's guidance the city became the capital of the Jews. With great care the ceremonial and practices of the cult were preserved in the academy at Jamnia, and Jewish scholarship continued as before. Except for a short period Jamnia remained the seat of the rulers of Judaism until the rising of BAR KOKBA. In the Middle Ages the Crusaders fortified the city. See Joshua 15.11; 2 Chron. 26.6.

Jamnitzer, Jamitzer, or **Gemniczer, Wenzel** (vĕn'tsəl yäm'nĭtsər, yä'mĭtsər, gĕm'nĭtsər), 1508–85, leading member of a German family of goldsmiths and engravers. Born in Vienna, he settled in Nuremberg where, as a leading craftsman of his day, he executed work for emperors and officials of the court and the church. Examples of his refined workmanship, showing the German adaptation of Italian mannerist forms, are to be seen in the Louvre and in the Victoria and Albert Museum. His gilt bronze nude *Spring* is in Vienna.

Jamshedpur (jŭm"shĕdpo͝or'), city (1971 pop. 355,783), Bihar state, E central India, at the confluence of the Subarnarekha and Kharkai rivers. A great steel-producing center, it is sometimes called the "Pittsburgh of India." It was built in the early 20th cent. and was named for Jamshedji Tata, founder of the Tata Iron and Steel Works. Nearby are extensive coal and iron deposits. The National Metallurgical Laboratory is in the city.

Jamuna, river, Bangladesh: see BRAHMAPUTRA.

Janáček, Leoš (lĕ'ôsh yä'nächĕk), 1854–1928, Czech composer, theorist, and collector of Slavic folk music. He studied in Prague and Leipzig and founded a music conservatory at Brno in 1881. His works include the operas *Jenufa* (1904), his best-known work; *Katia Kabanova* (1921), after Ostrovski's *Storm; The Makropulos Affair* (1926); and *From the House of the Dead* (1930), after a novel by Dostoyevsky. Also of note are Janáček's song cycle, *The Diary of One Who Vanished* (1916–19), and his *Glagolitic Festival Mass* (1926), with a text in Old Slavonic. See biographies by Hans Hollander (1963) and Jarosla Vogel (1963).

Janesville, city (1970 pop. 46,426), seat of Rock co., S central Wis., on the Rock River; inc. 1853. It is an industrial and commercial center in a grain, dairy farm, and tobacco area. Manufactures include fountain pens, automobile bodies, and electronic and electrical equipment. A state school for the blind is in Janesville. Points of interest include the 26-room Tallman House, where Lincoln spent a weekend in 1859; the Stone House (1842), of Greek Revival style; and the Milton House (1844), which is connected with a log cabin by a slave tunnel.

Janet: see CLOUET, FRANÇOIS, and CLOUET, JEAN.

Janet, Pierre (pyĕr zhänā'), 1859–1947, French physician and psychologist. As director (1890–98) of the laboratory of pathological psychology at Salpêtrière and as professor of experimental and comparative psychology at the Collège de France from 1902, he made important contributions to the knowledge of mental pathology and the origins of hysteria through the use of hypnosis. In 1904 he founded the *Journal de psychologie normal et pathologique,* to which he contributed numerous articles. Among his important works were *L'Automatisme psychologique* (1889), in which he founded automatic psychology, and *Les Obsessions et la psychasthénie* (1903), which contains the first description of psychasthenia. *Major Symptoms of Hysteria* (1907) contains lectures delivered at Harvard. He wrote also *Principles of Psychotherapy* (1924), *Psychological Healing* (1925), and *Cours sur l'amour et la haine* (1933).

Janiculum: see *Rome before Augustus* under ROME.

Janina, Greece: see IOÁNNINA.

Janissaries (jăn'ĭsâr"ēz) [from Turkish, = recruits], elite corps in the service of the Ottoman Empire (Turkey). It was composed of war captives and Christian youths pressed into service; all the recruits were converted to Islam and trained under the strictest discipline. It was originally organized by Sultan Murad I. The Janissaries gained great power in the Ottoman Empire and made and unmade sultans. By 1600, Muslims had begun to enter the corps, largely through bribery, and in the 17th cent. membership in the corps became largely hereditary, while the drafting of Christians gradually ceased. In 1826, Sultan MAHMUD II rid himself of the unruly (and by now inefficient) Janissaries by having them massacred in their barracks by his loyal SPAHIS.

Jan Mayen (yän mī'ən), island, c.145 sq mi (380 sq km), in the Arctic Ocean, c.300 mi (480 km) E of Scoresby Sound, E Greenland. It was annexed by Norway in 1929. The island is barren tundra land rising abruptly to Håkon VII Toppen (c.7,450 ft/2,270 m) on Mt. Beerenberg, an extinct volcano. Fog and stormy weather characterize the island. Except for a meteorological and wireless station, the island is uninhabited, but it is visited by sealers. It was discovered (1607) by Henry Hudson and named for Jan Jacobsz May, a Dutch whaler who landed there in 1614.

Janna (jăn'ə), name in the Gospel genealogy. Luke 3.24.

Jannequin, Clément (klāmäN' zhänəkăN'), French composer, fl. 16th cent. Jannequin is famous for his descriptive four-part chansons about birds, battles, hunts, and other subjects. He is thought to have been a disciple of Josquin des Prés. See Alfred Einstein, *The Italian Madrigal* (1949).

Jannes and Jambres (jăn'ēz, jăm'brēz), opponents of Moses. 2 Tim. 3.8. Tradition gave these names to Pharaoh's magicians. Ex. 7.11. One of the PSEUDEPIGRAPHA bears their name.

Janoah (jənō'ə), unidentified town, N Palestine, captured by Tiglath-pileser III. 2 Kings 15.29.

Janohah (jənō'hə), town, Palestine, SE of Shechem. Joshua 16.6,7.

Jansen, Cornelis (kôrnā'lĭs yän'sən), 1585–1638, Dutch Roman Catholic theologian. He studied at the Univ. of Louvain and became imbued with the idea of reforming Christian life along the lines of a return to St. Augustine. He established a close friendship with DUVERGIER DE HAURANNE, a fellow student, with whom he shared and developed many of his theological ideas. In 1630, Jansen became professor at Louvain, and in 1636 bishop of Ypres. Out of his life work, the posthumous *Augustinus* (1642, in Latin), arose the great movement called **Jansenism.** This was strictly a Roman Catholic movement, and it had no repercussions in the Protestant world. Its fundamental purpose was a return of people to greater personal holiness, hence the characteristically mystical turn of Jansenist writings. St. Augustine's teaching on grace was especially appealing to Jansen, who stressed the doctrine that the soul must be converted to God by the action of divine grace, without which conversion could not begin. Predestination was accepted in an extreme form and was so essential to Jansenism that its adherents were even referred to as Calvinists by their opponents. But Jansenism had no appeal to Protestants, for it held the necessity of the Roman Catholic Church for salvation and opposed justification by faith alone. Jansenism, however, came into conflict with the church for its predestinarianism, for its discouragement of frequent communion for the faithful, and for its attack on the Jesuits and the new casuistry, which the Jansenists thought was demoralizing the confessional. Jansenism took root in France, especially among the clergy. There it early became involved with GALLICANISM, and high officials of church and state often sided with Jansenists to thwart the Holy See. The second great Jansenist work was *De la fréquente communion* (1643) of Antoine ARNAULD, which stirred the opposition of Jesuits and Dominicans. In 1653, Pope Innocent X condemned five of Jansen's doctrines, and in 1656 Arnauld was expelled from the Sorbonne. Meanwhile, Blaise PASCAL, the greatest Jansenist, aroused a storm by his anti-Jesuit *Provincial Letters,* and there was persecution of the Jansenists for a while. Pasquier QUESNEL published late in the 17th cent. a vernacular New Testament with Jansenist notes, which was condemned by Pope Clement XI. The aged Louis XIV undertook to suppress Jansenism, and the bulls *Vineam Domini* (1705) and *Unigenitus* (1713) virtually put the Jansenists out of the church. (Gallicanism, however, prevented the legal registration of *Unigenitus* in France until 1730.) The convent of PORT-ROYAL, the greatest center of Jansenism, was closed, and most Jansenists fled France. Jansenism survived as a tendency within the church, especially in France, taking the form usually of extreme scruples with regard to communion. In the Netherlands an organization not in submission to the pope was set up. There are Jansenist bishops of Utrecht, Haarlem, and Deventer. The independent Jansenists recognize the Council of Trent and are, except for their special differences, like Roman Catholics. The first Old Catholic bishop was consecrated by Jansenists (see OLD CATHOLICS). See Nigel Abercrombie, *The Origins of Jansenism* (1936); Marc Escholier, *Port-Royal: The Drama of the Jansenists* (tr. 1968).

Janson, Nicolas: see JENSON, NICOLAS.

Janssen, Cornelis van Ceulen: see JANSSENS, CORNELIS VAN CEULEN.

Janssen, Pierre Jules César (pyĕr zhül sāzär' zhäN-sĕn'), 1824–1907, French astronomer. In 1857–58, in Peru, he worked on the determination of the magnetic equator; in Italy (1861–62, 1864) he observed the telluric lines in the solar spectrum; in the Azores (1867) he examined magnetic and topographical conditions; and in Japan (1874) and in Algeria (1882) he observed the transit of Venus. Janssen accompanied various solar eclipse expeditions, notably that to Guntur, India, in 1868, where he devised a new method of studying the solar prominences spectroscopically and discovered, almost simultaneously with J. N. Lockyer, the chemical constitution of the prominences. He was active in the establishment of the astrophysical observatory of Meudon (in Paris) and in 1876 became its director. There he gathered an important series of solar photographs included in his *Atlas de photographies solaires* (1904). He later became director of the observatory on Mont Blanc.

Janssens, Janssen, or **Jonson, Cornelis van Ceulen** (kôrnā'lĭs vän kö'lən yän'səns, -sən, -sôn), 1593–c.1662, Dutch portrait painter who worked in England. He was the fashionable portrait painter of the English court from 1618 until the advent of Van Dyck. In 1643 Janssens moved to Holland. His portraits, one of which is in the Metropolitan Museum, are in many famous English collections.

January: see MONTH.

Janum (jăn'ĭm), unidentified town, apparently near Hebron. Joshua 15.53.

Janus, in astronomy, one of the 10 known moons, or natural satellites, of SATURN.

Janus (jā'nəs), in Roman religion, god of beginnings. He was one of the principal Roman gods, the custodian of the universe. The first hour of the day, the first day of the month, the first month of the year (which bears his name) were sacred to him. His chief function was as guardian deity of gates and doors. The gates of his temple in the Roman Forum were closed in time of peace and opened in time of war. Janus was usually represented with two bearded heads placed back to back so that he might look in two directions at the same time. His principal festival was celebrated on the first day of the year.

Japan, Jap. *Nihon* or *Nippon,* country (1970 pop., including Okinawa, 104,665,171), 142,811 sq mi (369,881 sq km), occupying an archipelago off the coast of E Asia. The capital is TOKYO, the world's most populous city. Japan proper has four main islands which are, from north to south, HOKKAIDO, HONSHU (the largest island, where the capital and most major cities are located), SHIKOKU, and KYUSHU. There are also many smaller islands stretched in an arc between the Sea of Japan and the East China Sea and the Pacific proper. Honshu, Shikoku, and Kyushu enclose the Inland Sea. The general features of the four main islands are shapely mountains, sometimes snowcapped, the highest and most famous being the sacred FUJIYAMA; rushing short rivers; forested slopes; irregular and lovely lakes; and small, rich plains. Mountains, many of them volcanoes, cover two thirds of Japan's surface, hampering transportation and limiting agriculture. Less than 20% of the land is arable, and on the arable sections the population density is among the highest in the world. The climate ranges from chilly humid continental to humid subtropical. Rainfall is abundant, and typhoons and earthquakes are frequent. (For a more detailed description of geography, see separate articles on the individual islands.) Mineral resources are meager, except for coal, which is an important source of industrial energy. The rapid streams supply plentiful hydroelectric power. Imported oil, however, is the major source of energy. Some nuclear energy is also produced. The rivers are generally unsuited for navigation (only two, the Ishikari and the Shinano, are over 200 mi/322 km long), and railroads and ships along the coast are the chief means of transportation. High-speed train service, the fastest in the world, was inaugurated in 1964 between Tokyo and Osaka. Japan's farming population has been declining steadily and was less than 30% of the total population in the early 1970s. Arable land in Japan is intensively cultivated; farmers use irrigation, terracing, and multiple cropping to coax rich crops from the overworked soil. Rice and other cereals are the main crops; some vegetables and industrial crops, such as mulberry trees (for feeding silkworms), are also grown, and livestock is raised. Fishing is highly developed, and the annual catch is one of the biggest in the world; Japan's fishing fleet ranges all over the world. In the late 19th cent. Japan was rapidly and thoroughly industrialized. Textiles were a leading item, vast quantities of light manufactures were also produced, and, in the

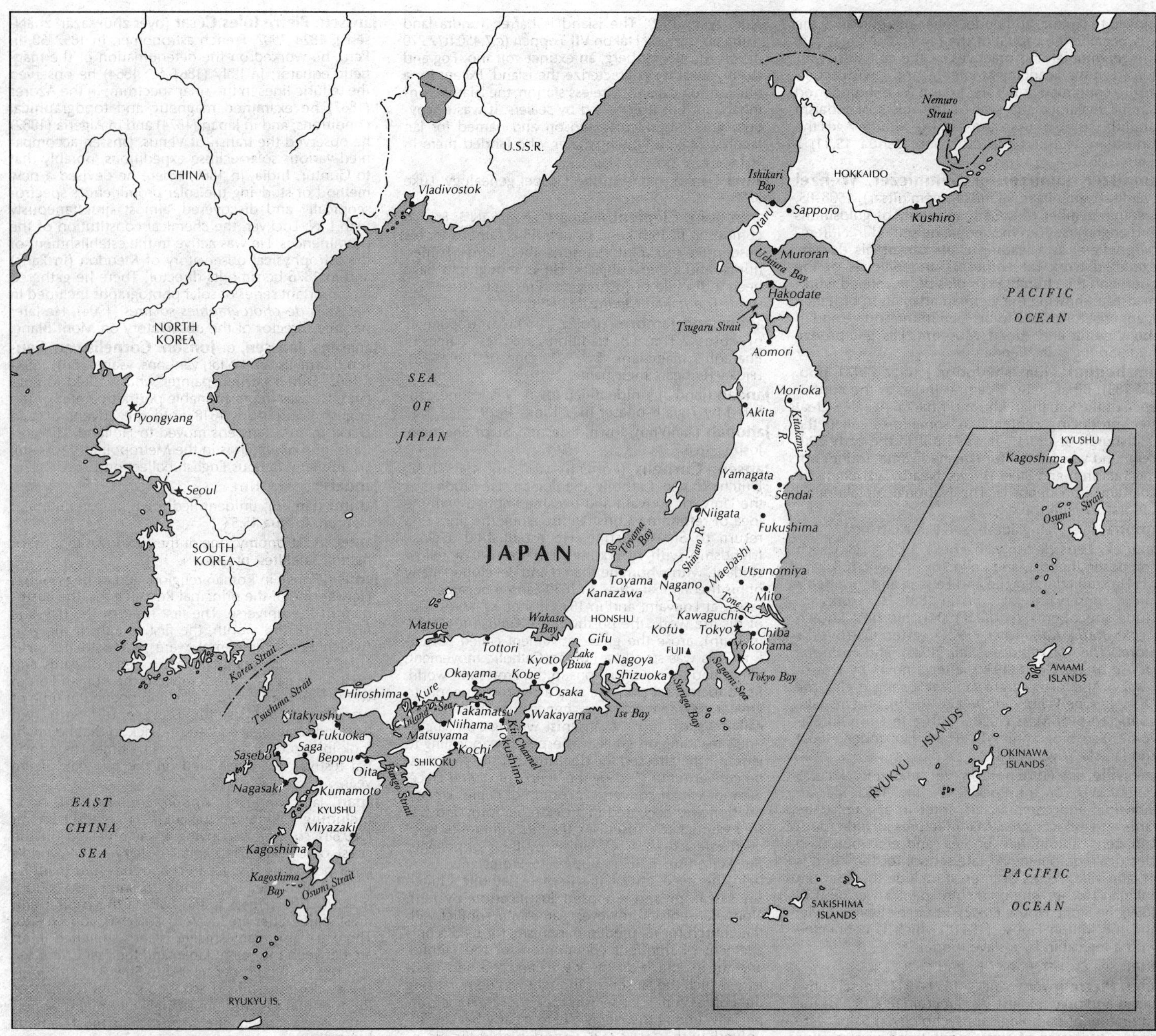

1920s and 1930s, heavy industries were greatly expanded, principally to support the military ambitions of the imperialists. Japan's economy collapsed after the defeat in World War II, and its merchant marine, one of the world's largest in the 1930s, was almost totally destroyed. In the late 1950s, however, the nation reemerged as a major industrial power. It is now the most industrialized country in Asia and the third greatest economic power in the world. Japanese industry is concentrated mainly in S Honshu and N Kyushu, with centers at Tokyo, YOKOHAMA, OSAKA, KOBE, and NAGOYA. In the 1950s and 1960s textiles became less important in Japanese industry while the production of heavy machinery expanded. Japan is the world's leading producer of ships and also ranks high in the production of cars and trucks, steel, and textiles. The manufacture of electronic equipment is also important. Japanese industry depends heavily on imported raw materials, which make up a large share of the country's imports. Japan receives all it needs of bauxite, phosphate, steel scrap, cotton, wool, and crude rubber, 99% of its crude oil, and 98% of its iron ore from imports. Exports are mainly manufactured goods, notably iron and steel, ships, and motor vehicles.

Japanese Society. The Japanese people are primarily the descendants of various peoples who migrated from Asia in prehistoric times; the dominant strain is N Asian or Mongoloid, with some Malay and Indonesian admixture. One of the earliest groups, the AINU, who still persist to some extent in Hokkaido, are physically somewhat similar to Caucasians. Non-Japanese, mostly Koreans, make up less than 1% of the population. Japan's principal religions are SHINTO and BUDDHISM. While the development of Shinto was radically altered by the influence of Buddhism, which was brought from China in the 6th cent., special varieties of Japanese Buddhism have developed in sects such as Jodo, Shingon, Nicheren, and Zen. Numerous cults formed after World War II and called the "new religions" have attracted many members. One of these, the Sokagakkai, a Buddhist sect, built up a large following in the 1950s and 1960s and became a strong social and political force. Less than 1% of the population are Christians. CONFUCIANISM has deeply affected Japanese thought and was part of the generally significant influence that Chinese culture wielded on the formation of Japanese civilization (see JAPANESE ARCHITECTURE; JAPANESE ART; JAPANESE LITERATURE). The family has long been the basic social unit in Japan. Family elders command much respect, and even in the 20th cent. many parents continued to select marriage partners for their children. The status of women improved after the end of World War II when they received the right to vote, but social customs still tend to restrict their freedom. The Japanese educational system, established during the Allied occupation after World War II, is modeled on the U.S. system. Nine years of schooling is compulsory. The two leading national universities are at Tokyo and Kyoto. The standard of living improved dramatically between the 1950s and the early 1970s, and the Japanese have the highest per capita income of all Asians. Programs for social welfare and health insurance exist but are financially limited. Trade unions, organized by enterprise rather than by occupation, represent about one third of all employed workers. The two largest unions are the General Council of Trade Unions and the General Council of Japan Labor Organization. Japanese traditional sports include judo; kendo, a kind of fencing; and suma, a stylized form of wrestling. Baseball, though not native to Japan, is also very popular.

Early History and the Shoguns. Japan's early history is lost in legend. The divine design of the empire—supposedly founded in 660 B.C. by the emperor Jimmu, a lineal descendant of the sun goddess and alleged ancestor of the present emperor—was held as official dogma until 1945. Actually, reliable records date back only to about A.D. 400. In the first centuries of the Christian era the country was inhabited by numerous clans or tribal kingdoms ruled by priest-chiefs. Contacts with Korea were close, and bronze and iron implements were probably introduced by invaders from Korea around the 1st cent. By the 5th cent. the Yamato clan, whose original home was apparently in Kyushu, had settled in the vicinity of modern Kyoto and had established a loose control over the other clans of central and W Japan, laying the foundation of the Japanese state. From the 6th to the 8th cent. the rapidly developing society gained much in the arts of civilization under the strong cultural influence of China, then flourishing in the splendor of the T'ang dynasty. Buddhism was introduced, and the Japanese upper classes assiduously studied Chinese language, literature, philosophy, art, science, and government, creating their own forms adapted from Chinese models. A partially successful attempt was made to set up a centralized, bureaucratic government like that of imperial China. The Yamato priest-chief assumed the dignity of an emperor, and an imposing capital city, modeled on the T'ang capital, was erected at Nara, to be succeeded by an equally imposing capital at Kyoto. By the 9th cent., however, the powerful Fujiwara family had established a firm control over the imperial court. The Fujiwara influence and the power of the Buddhist priesthood undermined the authority of the imperial government. Provincial gentry—particularly the great clans who opposed the Fujiwara—evaded imperial taxes and grew strong. A feudal system developed. Civil warfare was almost continuous in the 12th cent. The Minamoto family defeated their rivals, the Taira, and became masters of Japan. Their great leader, YORITOMO, took the title of SHOGUN, established his capital at Kamakura, and set up a military dictatorship. For the next 700 years Japan was ruled by warriors. The old civil administration was not abolished, but gradually decayed, and the imperial court at Kyoto fell into obscurity. The Minamoto soon gave way to the Hojo, who managed the Kamakura administration as regents for puppet shoguns, much as the Fujiwara had controlled the imperial court. In 1274 and again in 1281 the Mongols under Kublai Khan tried unsuccessfully to invade the country (see KAMIKAZE). In 1331 the emperor Daigo II attempted to restore imperial rule. He failed, but the revolt brought about the downfall of the Kamakura regime. The Ashikaga family took over the shogunate in 1338 and settled at Kyoto, but were unable to consolidate their power. The next 250 years were marked by civil wars, during which the feudal barons (the daimyo) and the Buddhist monasteries built up local domains and private armies. Nevertheless, in the midst of incessant wars there was a brisk development of manufacturing and trade, typified by the rise of Sakai (later Osaka) as a free city not subject to feudal control. This period saw the birth of a middle class. Extensive maritime commerce was carried on with the continent and with SE Asia; Japanese traders and pirates dominated Far Eastern waters until the arrival of the Europeans in the 16th cent.

Military Might and the Foreigners. The first European contact with Japan was made by Portuguese sailors in 1542. A small trade with the West developed. Christianity was introduced by St. FRANCIS XAVIER, who reached Japan in 1549. In the late 16th cent. three warriors, NOBUNAGA, HIDEYOSHI, and IEYASU, established military control over the whole country and succeeded one another in the dictatorship. Hideyoshi unsuccessfully invaded Korea in 1592 and 1596 in an effort to conquer China. After Hideyoshi's death, Ieyasu took the title of shogun, and his family ruled Japan for over 250 years. They set up at Yedo (later Tokyo) a centralized, efficient, but repressive system of feudal government (see TOKUGAWA). Stability and internal peace were secured, but social progress was stifled. Christianity was suppressed, and all intercourse with foreign countries was prohibited except for a Dutch trading post at Nagasaki. Tokugawa society was rigidly divided into the daimyo, SAMURAI, peasants, artisans, and merchants, in that order. The system was imbued with Confucian ideas of loyalty to superiors, and military virtues were cultivated by the ruling aristocracy (see BUSHIDO). Oppression of the peasants led to many sporadic uprisings. Yet despite feudal restrictions, production and trade expanded, the use of money and credit increased, flourishing cities grew up, and the rising merchant class acquired great wealth and economic power. Japan was in fact moving toward a capitalist system. By the middle of the 19th cent. the country was ripe for change. Most daimyo were in debt to the merchants, and discontent was rife among impoverished but ambitious samurai. The great clans of W Japan, notably Choshu and Satsuma, had long been impatient of Tokugawa control. In 1854 an American naval officer, Matthew C. PERRY, forced the opening of trade with the West. Japan was compelled to admit foreign merchants and to sign unequal treaties. Attacks on foreigners were answered by the bombardment of Kagoshima and Shimonoseki. Threatened from within and without, the shogunate collapsed. In 1867 a conspiracy engineered by the western clans and imperial court nobles forced the shogun's resignation. After brief fighting, in 1868 the boy emperor MEIJI was "restored" to power, and the imperial capital was transferred from Kyoto to Tokyo. This was the MEIJI RESTORATION.

Industries and Military Expansion. Although the Meiji restoration was originally inspired by anti-foreign sentiment, Japan's new rulers quickly realized the impossibility of expelling the foreigners. Instead they strove to strengthen Japan by adopting the techniques of Western civilization. Under the leadership of an exceptionally able group of statesmen (who were chiefly samurai of the western clans) Japan was rapidly transformed into a modern industrial state and a great military power. Feudalism was abolished in 1871. The defeat of the Satsuma rebellion in 1877 marked the end of opposition to the new regime. Emissaries were sent abroad to study Western military science, industrial technology, and political institutions. The administration was reorganized on Western lines. An efficient modern army and navy were created, and military conscription was introduced. Industrial development was actively fostered by the state, working in close cooperation with the great merchant houses. A new currency and banking system were established. New law codes were enacted. Primary education was made compulsory. In 1889 the emperor granted a constitution, modeled in part on that of Prussia. Supreme authority was vested in the emperor, who in practice was largely a figurehead controlled by the clan oligarchy. Subordinate organs of government included a privy council, a cabinet, and a diet consisting of a partially elected house of peers and a fully elected house of representatives. Universal manhood suffrage was not granted until 1925. After the Meiji restoration nationalistic feeling ran high. The old myths of imperial and racial divinity, rediscovered by scholars in the Tokugawa period, were revived, and the sentiment of loyalty to the emperor was actively propagated by the new government. Feudal glorification of the warrior and belief in the unique virtues of Japan's "Imperial Way" combined with the expansive drives of modern industrialism to produce a vigorous imperialism. At first concerned with defending Japanese independence against the Western powers, Japan soon joined them in the competition for an empire in the Orient. By 1899, Japan cast off the shackles of EXTRATERRITORIALITY, but not until 1911 was full tariff autonomy gained. The first SINO-JAPANESE WAR (1894–95) marked the real emergence of imperial Japan, with acquisition of Formosa and the Pescadores and also of the Liao-tung peninsula in Manchuria, which the great powers forced it to relinquish. An alliance with Great Britain in 1902 increased Japanese prestige, which reached a peak as a result of the RUSSO-JAPANESE WAR in 1904–5. Unexpectedly the Japanese smashed the might of Russia with speed and efficiency. The treaty of Portsmouth (see PORTSMOUTH, TREATY OF), ending the war, recognized Japan as a world power. A territorial foothold had been gained in Manchuria. In 1910, Japan was able to annex Korea. During World War I the Japanese secured the German interests in Shantung (later restored to China) and received the German-owned islands in the Pacific as mandates. In 1915, Japan presented the TWENTY-ONE DEMANDS designed to reduce China to a protectorate. The other world powers opposed the demands giving Japan policy control in Chinese affairs and prevented their execution, but China accepted the rest of the demands. In 1918, Japan took the lead in Allied military intervention in Siberia, and Japanese troops remained there until 1922. These moves, together with an intensive program of naval armament, led to some friction with the United States, which was temporarily adjusted by the Washington Conference of 1921–22 (see NAVAL CONFERENCES). During the next decade the expansionist drive abated in Japan, and liberal and democratic forces gained ground. The power of the diet increased, party cabinets were formed (see SEIYUKAI), and despite police repression, labor and peasant unions attained some strength. Liberal and radical ideas became popular among students and intelligentsia. Politics was dominated by big business (see ZAIBATSU), and businessmen were more interested in economic than in military expansion. Trade and industry, stimulated by World War I, continued to expand, though interrupted by the earthquake of 1923, which destroyed much of Tokyo and Yokohama. Agriculture, in contrast, remained depressed. Japan pursued a moderate policy toward China, relying chiefly on economic penetration and diplomacy to advance Japanese interests. This and other foreign policies pursued by the government displeased more extreme militarist and nationalist elements developing in Japan, some of whom disliked capitalism and advocated state socialism. Chief among these groups were the Kwantung army in Manchuria, young army and navy officers, and various organizations such as the Amur River Society, which included many prominent men. Militarist propaganda was aided by the depression of 1929, which ruined Japan's silk trade. In 1931 the Kwantung army precipitated an incident at Mukden (Shen-yang) and promptly overran all of Manchuria, which was detached from China and set up as the puppet state of Manchukuo. When the League of Nations criticized Japan's action, Japan withdrew from the organization. During the 1930s the military party gradually extended its control over the government, brought about an increase in armaments, and reached a working agreement with the zaibatsu. Military extremists instigated the assassination of Prime Minister Inukai in 1932 and an attempted coup d'etat in 1936. At the same time Japan was experiencing a great export boom, due largely to currency depreciation. From 1932 to 1937, Japan engaged in gradual economic and political penetration of N China. In July, 1937, after an incident at Peking, Japanese troops invaded the northern provinces. Chinese resistance led to full-scale though undeclared war (see SINO-JAPANESE WAR, SECOND). A puppet Chinese government was installed at Nanking in 1940. Meanwhile relations with the Soviet Union were tense and worsened after Japan and Germany joined together against the Soviet Union in the Anti-Comintern Pact of 1936 (see COMINTERN). In 1938 and 1939 armed clashes took place on the Manchurian border. Japan then stepped up an armament program, extended state control over industry through the National Mobilization Act (1938), and intensified police repression of dissident elements. In 1940 all political parties were dissolved and were replaced by the state-sponsored Imperial Rule Assistance Association. After World War II erupted (1939) in Europe, Japan signed a military alliance with Germany and Italy, sent troops to Indochina (1940), and announced the intention of creating a "Greater East Asia Co-Prosperity Sphere" under Japan's leadership. In April, 1941, a neutrality treaty with Russia was triumphantly concluded. In Oct., 1941, the militarists achieved complete control in Japan, when Gen. Hideki TOJO succeeded a civilian, Prince Fumimaro KONOYE, as prime minister. Unable to neutralize U.S. opposition to its actions in SE Asia, Japan opened hostilities against the United States and Great Britain on Dec. 7, 1941, by striking at Pearl Harbor, Singapore, and other Pacific possessions. The fortunes of war at first ran in favor of Japan, and by the end of 1942 the spread of Japanese military might over the Pacific to the doors of India and of Alaska was prodigious (see WORLD WAR II). Then the tide turned; territory was lost to the Allies island by island; warfare reached Japan itself with intensive bombing; and finally in 1945, following the explosion of atomic bombs by the United States over Hiroshima and Nagasaki, Japan surrendered on Aug. 14, the formal surrender being on the U.S. battleship *Missouri* in Tokyo Harbor on Sept. 2, 1945.

Surrender and Occupation. The surrender was unconditional, but the terms for Allied treatment of the conquered power had been laid down at the POTSDAM CONFERENCE. The empire was dissolved, and Japan was deprived of all territories it had seized by force. The Japanese Empire at its height had included the southern half of SAKHALIN, the KURILE ISLANDS, the RYUKYU ISLANDS, Formosa (see TAIWAN), the PESCADORES, KOREA, the BONIN ISLANDS, the Kwantung leased territory in Manchuria, and the island groups held as mandates from the League of Nations (the CAROLINE ISLANDS, MARSHALL ISLANDS, and MARIANAS ISLANDS). In the early years of the war, Japan had conquered vast new territories, including a large part of China, SE Asia, the Philippines, and the Dutch East Indies. With defeat, Japan was reduced to its size before the imperialist adventure began. The country was demilitarized, and steps were taken to bring forth "a peacefully inclined and responsible government." Industry was to be adequate for peacetime needs, but war-potential industries were forbidden. Until these conditions were fulfilled Japan was to be under Allied military occupation. The occupation began immediately under the command of Douglas MacArthur. A Far Eastern Commission, representing 11 Allied nations and an Allied council in Tokyo, was to supervise general policy. The commission, however, suffered from the general rising tension between the USSR and the Western nations and did not function effectively, leaving the U.S occupation forces in virtual control. The occupation force controlled Japan through the existing machinery of Japanese government. A new constitution was adopted in 1946 and went into effect in 1947; the emperor publicly disclaimed his divinity. The general conservative trend in politics was tempered by the elections of 1947, which made the Social Democratic party headed by Tetsu Katayama the dominant force in a two-party coalition government. In 1948 the Social Democrats slipped to a secondary position in the coalition, and in 1949 they lost power completely when the conservatives took full charge under Shigeru Yoshida. An attempt was made to break up the zaibatsu. Many of the militarist leaders and generals were tried as war criminals and in 1948 many were convicted. Economic revival proceeded slowly with much unemployment and a low level of production, which improved only gradually. In 1949, however, MacArthur loosened the bonds of military government, and many responsibilities were restored to local authorities. At

San Francisco in Sept., 1951, a peace treaty was signed between Japan and most of its opponents in World War II. India and Burma refused to attend the conference, and the USSR, Czechoslovakia, and Poland refused to sign the treaty. It nevertheless went into effect on April 28, 1952, and Japan again assumed full sovereignty. The elections in 1952 kept the conservative Liberal party and Premier Shigeru Yoshida in power. In Nov., 1954, the Japan Democratic party was founded. This new group attacked governmental corruption and advocated stable relations with the USSR and Communist China. In Dec., 1954, Yoshida resigned, and Ichiro Hatoyama, leader of the opposition, succeeded him. The Liberal and Japan Democratic parties merged in Nov., 1955, to become the Liberal Democratic party (LDP). Hatoyama resigned because of illness in Dec., 1956, and was succeeded by Tanzan Ishibashi of the LDP. Ishibashi was also forced to resign because of illness and was followed by his fellow party member Nobusuke Kishi in Feb., 1957. In the 1950s Japan signed peace treaties with Taiwan, India, Burma, the Philippines, and Indonesia. Reparations agreements were concluded with Burma, the Philippines, Indonesia, and South Vietnam, with reparations to be paid in the form of goods and services to stimulate Asian economic development. In 1951, Japan signed a security treaty with the United States, providing for U.S. defense of Japan against external attack and allowing the United States to station troops in the country. New security treaties with the United States were negotiated in 1960 and 1970. Many Japanese felt that military ties with the United States would draw them into another war. Student groups and labor unions, often led by Communists, demonstrated during the 1950s and 1960s against military alliances and nuclear testing. One such demonstration (June, 1960) forced U.S. President Eisenhower to cancel a scheduled trip to Japan. Prime Minister Kishi was forced to resign in 1960 following the diet's acceptance, under pressure, of the U.S.-Japanese security treaty. He was succeeded by Hayato Ikeda, also of the Liberal Democratic party. Ikeda led his party to two resounding victories in 1960 and 1963. He resigned in 1964 because of illness and was replaced by Eisaku Sato, also of the Liberal Democratic party. Sato overcame strong opposition to his policies and managed to keep himself and his party in firm control of the government. The Liberal Democratic party maintained its sizable strength in the diet in the 1967 and 1969 elections. Opposition to the government because of its U.S. ties abated somewhat in the early 1970s when the United States agreed to relinquish its control of the Ryukyu Islands, including Okinawa, which had come under U.S. administration after World War II. All of the Ryukyus formally reverted to Japanese control in 1972. In that same year, Sato resigned and was succeeded by Kakuei Tanaka, also a Liberal Democrat. In late 1974, Tanaka resigned and was replaced as prime minister by Takeo Miki, another Liberal Democrat.

Government and Politics. Government in Japan is based on the constitution drafted by the Allied occupation authorities and approved by the Japanese diet. It declares that the emperor is the symbolic head of state but that sovereignty rests with the people. The national diet has sole legislative power. Article nine disavows war as an instrument of national policy and forbids the maintenance of armed forces for offensive purposes. The constitution may be amended by a two-thirds vote in the diet followed by a majority vote in a national referendum. The diet is composed of the house of representatives, a body of 491 members elected for terms of four years, and the house of councillors, having 252 members elected for terms of six years. Executive power is vested in an 18-member cabinet appointed and headed by the prime minister, who is elected by the diet and is usually the leader of the majority party in that body. The diet may force the resignation of the prime minister through a vote of no confidence, and the cabinet may dissolve the house of representatives and call for new elections. The latter is often done, and house members rarely serve their full terms. A supreme court heads an independent judiciary. Japan is divided into 46 prefectures, each governed by a popularly elected governor and single-house legislature. Cities, towns, and villages elect their own mayors and assemblies. The Liberal-Democratic party has had control of the diet since 1955, when the party was formed. Relatively conservative, the LDP has supported the alliance with the United States and the mutual security pacts between the two countries. Most political parties in Japan are small and do not have broad, mass memberships. Their members are mainly professional politicians. The Socialist party, which opposes the security treaties with the United States, was the second largest party in the diet in 1974. The Democratic Socialist party, originally a splinter group from the Socialist party, favors the gradual phasing out of Japanese military dependence on U.S. defenses. Labor generally supports the Socialist or Democratic Socialist party. In 1967 a new political party, the Komeito, or Clean Government party, ran candidates for the house of representatives; it supports humanitarian programs and opposes Japanese military armament. The Communist party, which has steered independent of the Soviet and Chinese communist parties, became (Dec., 1972) the third most powerful party in the diet.

International Relations. Japan's postwar foreign policy was aimed at the maintenance and expansion of foreign markets, and in the late 1960s the country had a sizable trade surplus. The United States is its chief ally and trade partner. In the early 1970s, however, U.S.-Japanese relations became strained after the United States pressured Japan to revalue the yen and again when it opened communications with Communist China without prior consultation with Japan. Partly in response, the Tanaka government established (1972) diplomatic relations with Communist China and announced plans for negotiation of a peace treaty. Relations also became strained with South Korea and Taiwan. Japan did not sign a peace treaty with the USSR because of a dispute over territory in the Kuril Islands formerly held by Japan but occupied by the USSR after the war. The two countries did, however, sign (1956) a peace declaration and established fishing and trading agreements. Beginning in late 1973, when the Arab nations began a cutback in oil exports, Japan faced a grave economic situation that threatened to reduce power and industrial production. In addition, a high annual inflation rate (19% in 1973), a price freeze, and the instability of the yen on the international money markets slowed Japan's economy as it entered the mid-1970s. Although article nine of the constitution forbids the maintenance of armed forces, Japan has a sizable military capability for defensive warfare. See J. A. Murdoch, *A History of Japan* (3 vol., 1926; repr. 1964); G. J. Groot, *The Prehistory of Japan* (1951, repr. 1972); R. A. Scalapino, *Democracy and the Party Movement in Prewar Japan* (1953); D. M. Brown, *Nationalism in Japan* (1955); W. K. Bunce, ed., *Religions in Japan: Buddhism, Shinto, Christianity* (1955, repr. 1962); Herschel Webb, *An Introduction to Japan* (2d ed. 1957, repr. 1960); Nobutaka Ike, *Japanese Politics: An Introductory Survey* (1957); K. S. Latourette, *The History of Japan* (rev. ed. 1957); G. C. Allen, *Japan's Economic Recovery* (1958); G. B. Sansom, *A History of Japan* (3 vol., 1958–63); I. B. Taeuber, *The Population of Japan* (1958); Donald Keene, *Living Japan* (1959); Richard Storry, *A History of Modern Japan* (1960); J. M. Maki, *Government and Politics in Japan* (1962); A. E. Tiedemann, *Modern Japan* (rev. ed. 1962); G. C. Allen, *Japan's Economic Expansion* (1965); Shigeru Yoshida, *Japan's Decisive Century, 1867–1967* (1967); Richard Halloran, *Japan: Image and Realities* (1969); Hugh Borton, *Japan's Modern Century* (2d ed. 1970); E. O. Reischauer, *Japan: The Story of a Nation* (4th ed. 1970); F. C. Langdon, *Japan's Foreign Policy* (1973); R. H. P. Mason and J. G. Caiger, *A History of Japan* (1974).

Japan, Sea of, enclosed arm of the Pacific Ocean, c.405,000 sq mi (1,048,950 sq km), located between Japan and the Asian mainland, connecting with the East China Sea, the Pacific Ocean, and the Sea of Okhotsk through several straits. The shallower northern and southern portions of the sea are important fishing areas. The sea has depths of more than 10,000 ft (3,050 m). A branch of the warm Japan Current flows northeast through the sea, modifying the climate of the region; Vladivostok, the only ice-free port of the eastern USSR, is there.

Japan Current or **Kuroshio** (ko͝orōshē'ō)[Jap.,= black stream], warm ocean current of the Pacific Ocean, off E Asia. A northward flowing branch of the North Equatorial Current, it runs E of Taiwan and Japan; the Tsushima Current separates from the main current and flows into the Sea of Japan. At about lat. 35°N it divides to form an eastern branch flowing nearly to the Hawaiian Islands and a northern branch that skirts the coast of Asia and merges with the waters of the cold Oyashio Current to form the North Pacific Current. Dense fogs develop along the boundary between the Japan and Oyashio currents. Air moving over the warm Japan Current becomes more temperate and acts to moderate the climate of Taiwan and Japan.

Japanese, language of uncertain origin that is spoken by more than 100 million people, most of whom live in Japan. There are also many speakers of Japanese in the Ryukyu Islands, Korea, Taiwan, parts of the United States, and Brazil. Japanese appears to be unrelated to any other language; however, some scholars see a kinship with the Korean tongue because the grammars of the two are very similar. Some linguists also link both Japanese and Korean to the ALTAIC languages. Japanese exhibits a degree of agglutination. In an agglutinative language, different linguistic elements, each of which exists separately and has a fixed meaning, are often joined to form one word. Japanese lacks tones, but has a musical accent and usually stresses all syllables equally. There is no declension for nouns and pronouns, whose grammatical relationships are shown by particles that follow them. Verbs are inflected and generally are placed at the end of a sentence. Extensive use of honorific forms is especially characteristic of Japanese; varying constructions are used to indicate differences in the social status of the individual speaking, the individual addressed, and individual spoken about. In the 3d and 4th cent. A.D., the Japanese borrowed the Chinese writing system of ideographic characters. Since Chinese is not inflected and since Chinese writing is ideographic rather than phonetic, the Chinese characters do not completely fill the needs of the inflected Japanese language in the sphere of writing. In the 8th cent. A.D., two phonetic syllabaries, or *kana*, were therefore devised for the recording of the Japanese language. They are used along with the ideographic characters (or *kanji* characters) to indicate the syllables that form suffixes and particles. The direction of writing is usually from top to bottom in vertical columns and from right to left. In scientific texts horizontal writing from left to right is sometimes employed. The Roman alphabet has also been used increasingly to transcribe Japanese. Since several thousand characters and two sets of *kana* are necessary for reading Japanese literature and periodicals, a need for simplification was felt when universal literacy became a national goal. Thus, after World War II, many *kanji* characters were simplified, and the number generally used was limited to about 2,000. Through another reform, phonetic *kana* characters are now used to correspond more closely to modern pronunciation than previously was the case. The large number of its speakers and the high level of cultural, economic, and political development of the Japanese people make Japanese one of the leading languages of the world. See Patrick G. O'Neill and S. Yanada, *An Introduction to Written Japanese* (1963); Roy A. Miller, *The Japanese Language* (1967); Susumu Ono, *The Origins of the Japanese Language* (1970).

Japanese architecture. Evidence of prehistoric architecture in Japan has survived in the form of models of terra-cotta houses buried in tombs and by remains of pit houses of the Jomon, the neolithic people of Japan. The more highly developed religious architecture of China came to Japan with the introduction of Buddhism in the 6th cent. Late in the 7th cent. the great monastery of Horyu-ji, near Nara, was near completion. The gateway, temple, and pagoda remained practically untouched until the 20th cent., when they were faithfully restored. These buildings illustrate the first epoch of Japanese architecture (6th–8th cent.), which was characterized by gravity, frankness of construction, and simple, vital compositions, sparsely ornamented. Wood has always been the favorite material, and wood construction was brought to a structural and artistic culmination as complete as any of the great styles of masonry architecture. Interior wood columns receive the loads, while the thin exterior walls are of woodwork and plaster. As in Greek and Chinese architecture, little use is made of diagonal members, and the framing is almost exclusively a system of uprights and horizontals. Vitality and grace are contributed by the refined curvatures in the column outlines, in the shapes of rafters and brackets, and especially in the great overhanging roofs. Throughout the 8th cent., the Japanese continued to emulate the architects of China. The gigantic monastery of Todai-ji was begun in 745. A great hall was built to house the DAIBUTSU, in front of which stood twin pagodas, each seven stories high. A distinctly Japanese style of architecture was developed in the late Heian period (898–1185). The famous Phoenix Hall at Uji, near Kyoto, originally a nobleman's villa, was converted (c.1050) into a temple. It represents the apogee of Japanese design. Beautifully situated near a lotus lake, it has a new sense of airiness, with its open porch and lofty central roof. The emergence of Zen Buddhism coincided with a renewed interest in Chinese architecture during the 13th cent. The plan of the Japanese temple adhered to the symmetrical simplicity of Chinese design. The hall of worship contained a spacious chancel with a flat ceiling, usually painted with the Zen theme of dragons in clouds. By the mid-14th cent. Buddhist architecture tended toward eclecticism and an emphasis on rich sculptural adornment. Through the centuries Buddhist temples have varied little in general arrangement. In front of the main building, or *hon-den*, stands an imposing gateway. Accessory structures include the five-storied square PAGODA (often omitted), the drum tower, and the holy font protected by a shed. The Shinto temple, whose pre-Buddhist type is perpetuated, is a small and extremely simple structure, roofed with bark thatch and devoid of color adornment. Greatest importance was attached to the landscape setting, a forested and picturesque hillside being the favored location. This regard for a natural environment is also consistently reflected in secular building. In the Heian period complex building schemes, known as *shinden-zukuri*, were devised for the court nobles. A number of elegant rectangular houses were joined by long corridors that surrounded a landscaped garden and pond. During the Kamakura period (late 12th-14th cent.), the *shinden-zukuri* was modified for the samurai class, and clusters of separate buildings were united under one roof. During this period the standard for domestic architecture was set and has been maintained to the present day. The principal style of Japanese dwelling of the upper class is unexcelled for its refinement and simplicity. Interior posts form a supporting skeleton for the roof. The exterior walls usually consist of movable panels that slide in grooves. Wood panels (used at night or in rainy weather) alternate with screens of mounted rice paper (used in warm weather). The interior of the house is flexibly subdivided by screens (*shoji*) into a series of airy spaces. Important rooms are provided with a tokonoma, an alcove for the display of a flower arrangement and a few carefully chosen objects of art. Often a separate space is set aside for the tea ceremony, either incorporated within the house or constructed as a pavilion in the garden. An important development of the late 16th cent. arose as a result of feudal warfare. Fortified castles, of which one still exists at Himeji, were based on the European donjon and were erected on high bases formed of enormous stone blocks. In the Edo period (1615-1867) two particularly beautiful palaces were erected in and near Kyoto, both constructed on an asymmetrical and flexible plan. The Nijo palace is noted for its sumptuousness in terms of carved wood, black lacquer, gold decorations, and screen paintings. The Katsura palace is remarkable for its simplicity and elegance and its merging of outdoor and indoor spaces. Here Japanese taste is perhaps epitomized in the subtlety and delicacy of the landscaping, with an ingenious arrangement of rocks, pebbles, sand, plants, and water. The opening of Japan to the West in 1868 led to the adaptation of the European architectural tradition. After World War I the Japanese began to make their own original contributions to the development of the International style in modern architecture. Japanese architects incorporated Western technical innovations into buildings combining traditional and modern styles during the period following World War II. At first strongly influenced by Le Corbusier, Miës van der Rohe, and, to a lesser degree, Frank Lloyd Wright, major Japanese architects by the mid-1960s developed highly individual and imaginative visions that had worldwide following. Among the principal Japanese architects to gain international acclaim since 1950 are Kenzo TANGE, Sutemi Horiguchi, Kunio Maekawa, Togo Murano, Yoshiro Taniguchi, and Noriaki KUROKAWA. See A. L. Sadler, *A Short History of Japanese Architecture* (1941, repr. 1962); William Alex, *Japanese Architecture* (1963); Egon Tempel, *New Japanese Architecture* (1970); Ito Teiji, *Traditional Domestic Architecture of Japan* (1972); R. T. Paine and Alexander Soper, *The Art and Architecture of Japan* (1955, repr. 1973).

Japanese art. The earliest art of Japan, probably dating from the 3d and 2d millennia B.C., consisted of monochrome pottery in a cord pattern (*jomon*). This ware was gradually replaced by the art of the Yayoi culture, which produced bronze bells with simple designs, clay tomb figures (*haniwa*), and some painted burial chambers. The stylistic tradition of Japanese art was firmly established with the introduction of Buddhism in the 6th cent. The teaching of the arts progressed under Korean monks and craftsmen, who created Buddhist sculpture and pictures representing divinities, saints, and legendary figures. After the 6th cent. and throughout its history Japanese art has relied heavily on forms and techniques borrowed from China. Rare examples of wall paintings in the golden hall at Horyu-ji, near Nara (end of the 7th cent. to early 8th cent.) were based on Chinese models, reflecting the T'ang style of painting. During the Nara period (710-784) the traditional technical methods of Japanese painting were established. The work is executed upon thin or gauzelike silk or soft paper with Chinese ink and watercolors. It is then mounted on silk brocade or its paper imitation and rolled upon a rod when not on view. The hanging scroll is called *kakemono*. The long, narrow horizontal scroll (*emakimono*), unrolled in the hands, usually portrays a procession or progressive scenes. In the sculpture of the Nara period, clay figures and statues made in the dry-lacquer process (lacquer applied to a solid core of wood or lacquered cloths placed over some kind of armature) attained great popularity. Representations of Buddhist deities and saints in wood and bronze evolved in style from a general flatness in the works of Kuratsukuri-no-Tori (active c.600-630) to the more massive figures of the 8th and 9th cent., which reflect the style of the later T'ang dynasty in China. The Jogan period (794-897) witnessed the beginning of an indigenous style of art. KANAOKA (late 9th cent.) was the first major native painter. The Fujiwara period (898-1185) is marked by the crystallization of the *Yamato-e* tradition of painting (based on national rather than on Chinese taste). The famous illustrated scroll of the *Tale of the Genji*—with its rich color and dreamy, almost expressionless treatment of men and women—reflects the extreme sensitivity and overrefinement of the court during that period. The same delicacy of taste can be seen in the sculpture of Jocho (11th cent.). The school of Jocho was continued by Kokei, Unkei, and Kaikei of the Kamakura period (late 12th-14th cent.). Vigor and realism were restored to the medium, although after this time sculpture ceased to develop in style. In painting most of the fine *emakimono* that survive today are from the Kamakura period. These scrolls are often executed in continuous narrative form, with the same figures appearing many times against a unified background. This method of representation was used with utmost skill and imagination in superb scrolls such as the *Tales of the Heiji Insurrection* (13th cent., Mus. of Fine Arts, Boston). In this art form man occupied the most important role, whereas in Chinese painting he is the least significant part of nature. In the Kamakura period the country was governed by the military, who preferred strength to refinement, movement to dreamy atmosphere, and realism to formality. The new class created a demand for paintings and sculptures portraying officials, warriors, priests, and poets. Takanobu and his son Nobuzane were the most highly esteemed portrait painters of the age. Unkei was the principal Kamakura sculptor. The Muromachi period (1392-1568) ushered in a renaissance of Chinese-style ink painting. The Zen sect of Buddhism, which enjoyed a growing popularity in the early Kamakura period, received the continued support of the new rulers. Ink painting was accepted as a means of teaching Zen doctrine. Such priest-painters as Cho Densu, Josetsu, Shubun, and Sesshu are the most revered of Japanese landscapists. Their works are characterized by economy of execution, forceful brush strokes, and asymmetrical composition, with emphasis on unfilled space. Sculpture of the period began to lose its Buddhist inspiration. Architectural sculpture was on a par with the unprecedented grandeur and ostentation achieved in painted screens of the Momoyama period (1568-1615). At this time constant warfare created a need for many great fortresses. Their interiors were lavishly decorated with screens painted in strong, thick colors against a gold background. The KANO family of artists succeeded in fusing the technique of Chinese ink painting with the decorative quality of Japanese art. The school of painting started in the Edo period (1615-1867) by Koetsu and Sotatsu and continued by Korin and Kenzan represented a return to the native tradition of Japanese painting. *The Deer Scroll* (early 17th cent.; Seattle Art Mus.) by Koetsu and Sotatsu exemplifies the happy union of literature, calligraphy, and painting. A great demand for miniature sculptures in the form of ornamental buttons (*netsuke*) arose at this time and great masterpieces of carving were produced. Dutch engraving found its way to Japan in this period and influenced such painters as Okyo Maruyama, the leader of the naturalist school of painters, who worked from nature and created pictures with Western perspective. There arose a new type of art in the form of wood-block prints known as ukiyo-e (pictures of the fleeting or floating world), which appealed first to the taste of the lowest groups of feudal society. The color-print designers eventually won worldwide recognition and influenced Whistler and numerous other Western artists. Among the major ukiyo-e painters are Harunobu, Kiyonaga, Utamaro, Hokusai, and Hiroshige. Mid-19th-century contact with European culture had an enervating effect upon Japanese art. A few print designers attained distinction, but no masters appeared to equal their predecessors. In the 20th cent. the majority of painters and sculptors have been overwhelmingly influenced by Western styles. In lacquerware, ceramics, and textiles traditional forms have been retained and modern Japanese pottery is widely esteemed. See articles on individual artists, e.g., SESSHU. See R. T. Paine and Alexander Soper, *The Art and Architecture of Japan* (1955); James Michener, *Japanese Prints* (1959); J. E. Kidder, *Early Japanese Art* (1964) and *Japanese Temples* (1964); Kenji Toda, *Japanese Painting: A Brief History* (1965); Louis-Frédéric (pseud.), *Japan, Art and Civilization* (1971); Saburo Ienaga, *Painting in the Yamato Style* (1973).

Japanese beetle, common name for a destructive beetle, *Popillia japonica*, of the SCARAB BEETLE family. Accidentally imported to the United States from Japan, it was first discovered in New Jersey in 1916 and is now widespread in the northeastern states, where it is a serious pest of lawns, orchards, and gardens. The adult is about ½ in. (13 mm) long with a metallic-green head and thorax and reddish-brown wing covers. Metamorphosis is complete (see INSECT). The eggs are laid in the ground; the small white larvae, called grubs, feed on the roots of grasses, sometimes killing them, and hibernate during the winter. Pupation occurs in the spring, and the adult emerges in midsummer, feeding on and destroying leaves, flowers, and fruits. Many methods of control have been tried, especially those involving the insect's natural enemies—e.g., parasitic wasps and flies, some of them imported from Japan; bacteria that cause the "milky disease" of grubs; and certain parasitic nematodes. None, however, has been entirely successful in controlling the spread of the beetle. Japanese beetles are classified in the phylum ARTHROPODA, class Insecta, order Coleoptera, family Scarabaeidae. See bulletins of the U.S. Dept. of Agriculture.

Japanese flowering cherry, any of a variety of flowering CHERRY species native to the Far East.

Japanese literature. Although Japanese and Chinese are totally different languages, the Japanese borrowed and adapted Chinese ideographs early in the 8th cent. so that their spoken language could be written. Since, however, Japanese is better suited to phonetic transcription, the result is a language of extremely complicated linguistic construction. In 712 the new system of writing was used in the compilation of orally preserved poems and stories into the *Kojiki* [records of ancient matters], an account of the divine creation of Japan, its imperial family, and the rest of the world. Another historical work, the *Nihon-shoki* [chronicles of Japan] (721), was written in pure Chinese. The oldest anthology of Japanese verse, *Manyoshu* [collection of myriad leaves] (760), also written in Chinese, contains about 4,500 poems, many from much earlier times. A number of the poems in this collection are more varied in form and more passionate in statement than those written in later eras. The addition of two phonetic syllabaries (*kata-kana* and *hiragana*) during the Heian era (794-1185) opened the classic age, in which Japanese literature reached its first peak of development. Although classical Chinese still predominated in intellectual literary circles, literature in the native language gained increasing prestige. The poet Ki-no-Tsurayuki, in the preface to his travel journal *Tosa-Nikki* [Tosa diary] (936), apologized for writing in Japanese, but the book was widely read and respected. Much of Heian literature was written by women, foremost among whom was MURASAKI SHIKIBU. Her *Genji-Monogatari* [tale of Genji] (early 11th cent.) is ranked with the world's greatest novels. Sei Shonagon, another court lady of the time, wrote *Makura-no-soshi* [the pillow book], providing an excellent portrait of Heian aristocratic life, with its emphasis on elegance, always an important element of the Japanese aesthetic. The classic age closed in the 12th cent., followed by a period often called the dark age of Japanese letters, but during which Japanese drama—with its unique and rich heritage—developed its four forms; No (serious drama), Kyogen (short, simple comedies), Kabuki (popular drama), and *Ningyo-shibai* (marionette drama). The greatest writers of No plays were Kanami Kiyotsugu (1333-84) and his son Zeami Motokiyo

(1363-1443), who raised the No from its primitive origins to the highly purified art form that influenced such Western poets as W. B. Yeats and Ezra Pound. The *Heike-Monogatari* was one of several long narratives of the civil wars of the period. Establishment of the Tokugawa shogunate in 1603 brought an age of total cultural and physical isolation from other countries and a period of peace that lasted for more than 250 years. During this time the quality of Kabuki and *Ningyo-shibai* theater was much improved, largely due to the dramatist Monzaemon CHIKAMATSU. While Heian literature dealt mostly with the aristocracy, and Kamakura (1185–1333) and Muromachi (1333-1600) literatures dealt with the warrior class, the Tokugawa era was concerned with the bourgeoisie. Chikamatsu's plays are important in world literature as the first mature tragedies written about the common man. His contemporary Matsuo Basho (1648-94) was the greatest of haiku poets. The HAIKU, a 17-syllable poem, largely replaced the traditional tanka of 31 syllables. Buson Yosa (1716-81) and Issa Kabayashi (1763-1828) were also important haiku poets. The picaresque novel developed in Japan simultaneously with, but not influenced by, the rise of the genre in Europe. Saikaku Ihara (1642-93) was the foremost exponent of this form; his novel *Koshoku-ichida-onna* [the life of an amorous woman] presents a world of pleasure and eroticism that readers found appealing. The caliber of novel writing declined by the early 19th cent., not to be revivified until the dramatic opening of Japan to the West in 1858. The flood of translations from Western literature that followed induced the Japanese to give the novel a serious purpose. Shoyo Tsubouchi (1859-1935) had a great effect on the modern Japanese novel with his critical study *Shosetsushinzui* [the essence of the novel] (1885), in which he urged the use of colloquial speech rather than the special literary language that had been used by previous writers. *Ukigumo* [the drifting cloud] (1887-89), by Shimei Futabatei (1864-1909) was the first novel to be written in colloquial language. The "I novel," a type of extremely personal diary, was dominant for a time, followed by realistic and proletarian novels. Toson Shimazaki's *Hakai* [the broken commandment] (1906) deals with social problems, another example of European influence. Soseki Natsume (1867-1916), a major figure, was popular for *Wagahai-wa-neko-de-aru* [I am a cat] (1905) and *Botchan* (1906). Ryunosuke Akutagawa (1892-1907) is known for his unusual stories, notably "Rashomon." During World War II the military government suppressed literary expression. Kafu Nagai (1870-1959), with his talent for verbal portraiture, remained a popular figure during this time nevertheless. The immense public demand for fiction in postwar Japan has been fed by the prolific output of its writers, most of whom have faced the problem of reconciling Japanese tradition with Western influence. Possibly the most successful in combining these elements was Yasunari KAWABATA, who won the Nobel Prize for Literature in 1968. In the mid-20th cent. Japanese writers have attracted international attention and admiration. Junichiro TANIZAKI, Yukio MISHIMA, Kobo Abe, Shohei Ooka, the prewar writers Osamu Dazai and Ogai Mori, together with writers of earlier times, are among those whose works are available in English translation. Although modern Japanese poetry and drama have not kept pace with the development of novels and short stories, Japanese literature is now recognized as a major branch of world literature. See also ORIENTAL DRAMA. See Donald Keene, *Japanese Literature* (1955), and (ed.) *Anthology of Japanese Literature from the Earliest Era to the Mid-Nineteenth Century* (1955) and *Modern Japanese Literature: An Anthology* (1956); R. H. Brower and Earl Miner, *Japanese Court Poetry* (1961); Geoffrey Bownas and Anthony Thwaite, ed., *The Penguin Book of Japanese Verse* (1964); W. G. Aston, *A History of Japanese Literature* (1899, repr. 1966); A. M. Janeira, *Japanese and Western Literature* (1970); E. O. Reischauer and J. K. Yamagiwa, *Translations from Early Japanese Literature* (2d ed. 1972); Yukio Mishima and Geoffrey Bownas, ed. *New Writing in Japan* (1973); Harry Guest et al., ed., *Post-War Japanese Poetry* (1973).

Japanese music, musical culture of a highly eclectic nature. It has borrowed musical instruments, scales, and styles from many neighboring areas. The indigenous music present before A.D. 453 consisted of chanted poems (*reyei* and *imayo*), traditional war and social songs (*kume-uta* and *saibara*), and the *kagura*, solemn Shinto temple music. All were recitations on a few notes. The importation of foreign music, particularly from China, began in the 5th cent. and continued into the 12th cent. The ancient ceremonial music imported from China, which the Japanese called *gagaku*, no longer exists in China but has been preserved almost intact since the 5th cent. by a continuing tradition of performance in the imperial court of Japan. It is orchestral music using the *sho* (a mouth organ, the Chinese SHENG), the *shakuhachi* (a long flute), and the *hichiriki* (a small oboe). The cantillations of the Buddhist religion came to Japan by way of Korea in the 6th cent. and were followed in the 7th cent. by the *bugaku* of Indian origin, a ceremonial dance with music. In the 9th and 10th cent. many instruments, including the *biwa* (a four-stringed bass lute used for accompaniment) and the KOTO (a long zither with 13 silk strings, used both as a solo instrument and in ensemble), were introduced from China. Midway between sacred and secular is the music of the No drama, dating from the 14th cent. It is restrained vocal recitative, *utai*, using very small intervals, Oriental ornamentation (e.g., sliding, tremolo, vibrato), and accompaniment by flute and drums. Popular secular music in Japan began in the 16th cent. with the introduction from China of the samisen, a three-stringed plucked instrument resembling a guitar, used for accompanying songs. Later secular music also included operalike creations and many varieties of *kumi* (chamber music for ensemble, voice, and koto) and koto solo (often sets of melodic variations on a short theme, or *damono*). *Hogaku* is the name for folk and popular music heard at open-air festivals. The Japanese use two basic types of scale, both pentatonic. The first, used in sacred music and common to the whole Far East, has two modes—*ryo*, the male mode, and *ritsu*, the female mode. The more frequently used scale, found also in Indonesia and S India, emphasizes semitones and exists in three modes, all used freely within the same composition—*hirajoshi*, the most important, roughly represented on the piano by the series ABCEFA; *kumoijoshi*, second in importance, approximated by EFABCE; and *iwato*, approximated by BCEFAB. Japanese music is of uneven phrase length, and the fourth is a particularly important interval. Ornamentation depends on the type and purpose of the piece. The rhythm is almost invariably in duple meter, with ternary or irregular passages occurring rarely. However, the independent drum rhythms, when these are present, tend to obscure the basic beat to Western ears. The music is primarily monophonic, although heterophony occurs in orchestral music and in pieces for voice and koto. The Meiji restoration saw the importation of Western music to Japan, beginning with the brass band. In the 1880s, Western music was introduced into the schools, and in 1887 the Academy of Music was established in Tokyo. Later, symphony orchestras were formed, and Western music became an integral part of the cultural life of Japan. Notable contemporary Japanese composers include Yasushi Akutagawa, Kan Ishii, and Akira Miyoshi. Seiji OZAWA, a conductor of international reputation, was born in Japan. See W. P. Malm, *Japanese Music and Musical Instruments* (1959); Hisao Tanabe, *Japanese Music* (rev. ed. 1959); Shigeo Kishibe, *The Traditional Music of Japan* (1966); Eta Harich-Schneider, *A History of Japanese Music* (1973).

Japanese quince: see QUINCE.

Japanese spaniel, breed of dainty, alert TOY DOG probably originating in ancient China and developed in Japan over many centuries. It stands about 9 in. (22.9 cm) high at the shoulder and weighs about 7 lb (3.2 kg). Its long, profuse coat is straight and silky and is usually black and white or any of various shades of red and white. Traditionally given as the gift of emperors, the Japanese spaniel was introduced into the West by Commodore Matthew Perry in the mid-19th cent. Today it is a popular house pet. See DOG.

japanning, method of varnishing a surface, such as wood, metal, or glass, to obtain a durable, lustrous finish. The term is derived from a process popular in England, France, the Netherlands, and Spain in the 17th cent. that imitated the Oriental lacquer work known as Japan ware. Japanning varnishes usually have a resin base and are colored by mineral and other pigments. Several coats of varnish are applied to the desired surface, the successive layers being heat-dried. Luster and hardness are attained by polishing each coat. Japanning has been applied to furniture, screens, and such small objects as trays and snuff-boxes.

Japheth (jā'fĕth), son of Noah and ancestor of those who were to occupy the isles of the Gentiles. This has been supposed to mean the Mediterranean lands of Europe and Asia Minor. Gen. 5.32; 6.10; 9.27; 10.1-5.

Japhia (jəfī'ə). **1** King of Lachish slain by Joshua. Joshua 10.3. **2** Son of David. 2 Sam. 5.15; 1 Chron. 3.7. **3** Town, N central Palestine, the present-day Yafa (Israel). Remains of an ancient synagogue were found there. Joshua 19.12.

Japhlet (jăf'lĕt), descendant of Asher. 1 Chron. 7.32,33.

Japhleti (jăflē'tī), clan, in a region between Ataroth-adar and lower BETH-HORON, probably in the vicinity of the present-day Ramallah (Jordan). It was either of Canaanite origin or of the tribe of Asher. Joshua 16.3.

Japho: see JAFFA, Israel.

japonica (jəpŏn'əkə): see QUINCE; CAMELLIA.

Japurá (zhəpōōrä'), river, c.1,300 mi (2,090 km) long, rising as the Caquetá in the Andes, SW Colombia. It flows SE into Brazil, where it is called the Japurá, and enters the Amazon through a network of channels. It is navigable in Brazil.

Jaques-Dalcroze, Émile (āmēl' zhäk-dälkrōz'), 1865-1950, Swiss educator and composer, b. Vienna, studied at the Geneva Conservatory, at the Paris Conservatory with Léo Delibes, and in Vienna with Anton Bruckner. From 1892 to 1909 he taught at the Geneva Conservatory, where he developed his system of EURYTHMICS as an aid to his own teaching. After successful demonstrations of his method he established (1910-14) the Jaques-Dalcroze School at Hellerau, near Dresden. In 1915 the Institut Jaques-Dalcroze was opened at Geneva. Jaques-Dalcroze also composed music and wrote several books, including an autobiography (1942).

Jarah (jā'rə), descendant of Saul. 1 Chron. 9.42. Jehoadah: 1 Chron. 8.36.

Jarbah: see JERBA, Tunisia.

Jareb (jâr'ĭb), Assyrian king, perhaps a symbolic name. Hosea 5.13; 10.6.

Jared (jâr'ĭd), father of Enoch. Gen. 5.15-20; Luke 3.37. Jered: 1 Chron. 1.2.

Jaresiah (jărēsī'ə), chief man of Benjamin. 1 Chron. 8.27.

jargon, pejorative term applied to speech or writing that is considered meaningless, unintelligible, or ugly. In one sense the term is applied to the special language of a profession, which may be unnecessarily complicated, e.g., "medical jargon." Jargon can also mean clumsy language that is hard to understand, synonymous with gibberish or gobbledygook, or a mixture of languages that serves different people (see LINGUA FRANCA).

Jarha (jär'hə), Egyptian slave to whom Sheshan gave his daughter. 1 Chron. 2.34,35.

Jarib (jâr'ĭb). **1** The same as JACHIN **1**. **2** Companion of Ezra. Ezra 8.16. **3** One who had a foreign wife. Ezra 10.18.

Jarmo: see MESOPOTAMIA.

Jarmuth (jär'məth). **1** City, SW Palestine. It allied itself against Gibeon and was defeated by Joshua. Joshua 10; 12; 15.35; Neh. 11.29. **2** See REMETH.

Jarnac (zhärnäk'), town (1968 pop. 4,831), Charente dept., in the Cognac region, on the Charente River. At Jarnac in 1569 French Catholics under the duke of Anjou (later Henry III) defeated the Huguenots, whose leader, Louis I, Prince of Condé, was killed.

Jaroah (jərō'ə), chief Gadite. 1 Chron. 5.14.

Jarosław (yärô'släf), town (1970 pop. 29,100), SE Poland, on the San River. Primarily an agricultural and trading center, it has food processing plants and flour mills. The town was founded by Yaroslav the Wise, duke of Kiev, in the 11th cent. It passed to Poland in 1382. Despite continuous Tatar raids, it developed as an important trade center in the 15th and 16th cent. It passed to Austria in 1772 and was restored to Poland in 1919.

Jaroszewicz, Piotr (pyô'tər yärôsh'ĕvĭch), 1909-, Polish political leader. A schoolmaster, he lived during World War II in the Soviet Union, where he joined the Polish army in 1943. In the postwar years he held several important positions in Poland and from 1952 to 1970 was vice premier. He became premier in 1970 following Józef Cyrankiewicz's resignation in the wake of serious rioting over inflation. He also became a full member of the politburo.

Jarrell, Randall, 1914-65, American poet and critic, b. Nashville, Tenn., grad. Vanderbilt Univ. (B.A., 1935; M.A., 1938). His poetry, reflecting an unusually sensitive and tragic view of life, includes *Blood for a Stranger* (1942), *Little Friend, Little Friend* (1945), *Losses* (1948), *The Seven-League Crutches* (1951), and *The Woman at the Washington Zoo* (1960). In 1953 his critical essays were collected and published as *Poetry and the Age*. Jarrell's other works include several delightful children's books; *Pictures from an Institution* (1954), a satirical novel set in a progressive women's college; and *A Sad Heart at the Supermarket* (1962), a collection of essays and fables. See Robert Lowell, Peter Taylor, and Robert Penn Warren, ed., *Randall Jarrell 1914–1965* (1967).

Jarring, Gunnar (gŭn'är yär'ĭng), 1907–, Swedish diplomat. He entered diplomatic service during World War II and was minister to India (1948–51), Ceylon (1950–51), and Iran, Iraq, and Pakistan (1951–52). In 1956, he became Sweden's ambassador and permanent delegate to the United Nations. He later served as ambassador to the United States (1958–64) and ambassador to the Soviet Union (1964–). Appointed (1967) special envoy to the UN Secretary General on the Middle East crisis, he held extensive but largely unsuccessful talks with Arab and Israeli leaders.

Jarrow, municipal borough (1971 pop. 28,779), Durham, NE England, on the Tyne estuary. Industries include the manufacture of iron and steel products and shipbuilding and repairing. The port exports coal. St. Paul's Church and an adjacent Benedictine monastery (now in ruins) were both founded in the 7th cent. The Venerable Bede lived, worked, and died in the monastery. In 1974, Jarrow became part of the new metropolitan county of Tyne and Wear.

Jarry, Alfred (älfrĕd' zhärē'), 1873–1907, French author. He was well known in Paris for his eccentric and dissolute behavior and for his insistence on the superiority of hallucinations over rational intelligence. His most famous work is the satirical farce *Ubu Roi* [Ubu the king] (1896, tr. 1961), with a repulsive and cowardly hero based on one of his old schoolteachers. He also wrote surrealistic verse stories, which, although witty, are also blasphemous and scatological. They include *Les Minutes de sable mémorial* [the moments of a monument in sand] (1894), *César-Antéchrist* [Caesar-Antichrist] (1895, tr. 1972), *L'Amour en visites* [love on visits] (1898), *L'Amour absolu* [absolute love] (1899), and *Le Surmale* (1902), as well as another play, *Ubu enchaîné* [Ubu in chains] (1902). See his *Ubu Plays* (tr. 1969).

Jarves, James Jackson (jär'vĭs), 1818–88, American art critic and art collector, b. Boston. He spent some years in Honolulu, where he founded and edited a weekly newspaper, the *Polynesia*; it became the official organ of the Hawaiian government. Jarves settled in Florence in 1852 and served (1880–82) as U.S. vice consul. His writings include *History of the Hawaiian or Sandwich Islands* (1843), several European travel books, and a number of works on art. Through his writings and exhibitions of his early Italian paintings, he did much to influence the artistic taste of the American public. His collection of paintings is at the Yale School of Fine Arts and at the Cleveland Museum of Art; the Metropolitan Museum has his collection of Venetian glass. See catalogs of his collections by Russell Sturgis, Jr. (1868), Osvald Sirén (1916), and Stella Rubinstein (1917); biography by Francis Steegmuller (1951).

Jarvis Island, island, 1.7 sq mi (4.4 sq km), central Pacific, one of the LINE ISLANDS, just south of the equator and c.1,300 mi (2,090 km) S of Honolulu. Known to British and American mariners, it was claimed in 1856 by the United States along with HOWLAND ISLAND and BAKER ISLAND but was annexed by Great Britain in 1889. American colonists were brought to Jarvis in 1935; the following year the island was placed under the U.S. Dept. of the Interior. Jarvis, on the air route from Hawaii to New Zealand, is now uninhabited.

Jashar or **Jasher, Book of** (both: jăsh'ər), lost Hebrew work, apparently a collection of songs celebrating national events. Fragments appear in Joshua 10.13; 2 Sam. 1.18.

Jashen (jā'shən), father of some of David's men. 2 Sam. 23.32. Hashem the Gizonite: 1 Chron. 11.34. The term *Gizonite* is obscure.

Jashobeam (jăshō'bēəm), one of David's mighty men. 1 Chron. 11.11; 12.6; 27.2.

Jashub (jā'shəb). **1** Son of Issachar. Num. 26.24; 1 Chron. 7.1. Job: Gen. 46.13. **2** Jew who had a foreign wife. Ezra 10.29.

Jashubi-lehem (jăsh'yo͞obī-lē'hĕm), obscure name in a genealogy. 1 Chron. 4.22.

Jasiel (jăs'ēĕl), one of David's mighty men. 1 Chron. 11.47. He is perhaps the same as JAASIEL.

jasmine (jăs'mĭn, jăz-) or **jessamine** (jĕs'əmĭn), any plant of the genus *Jasminum* of the family Oleaceae (OLIVE family). The genus includes shrubs and clambering plants, chiefly of Old World tropical and subtropical regions but cultivated elsewhere, outdoors in mild climates and in greenhouses farther north. The blossoms, mostly white or yellow, are usually very fragrant, some being used for scenting tea; the oil is utilized in perfumery. The common jasmine (*J. officinale*) has white flowers and glossy deciduous leaves. Both names are often given to other plants, such as Cape jasmine (see MADDER) and Carolina jasmine (see LOGANIA). Jasmine is classified in the division MAGNOLIOPHYTA, class Magnoliopsida, order Scrophulariales, family Oleaceae.

Jason. **1** St. Paul's host at Thessalonica. Acts 17.5–9. **2** Companion of Paul at Corinth, perhaps the same as **1.** Rom. 16.21.

Jason, in Greek mythology, son of Aeson. When Pelias usurped the throne of Iolcus and killed (or imprisoned) Aeson and most of his descendants, Jason was smuggled off to the centaur Chiron, who reared him secretly on Mt. Pelion. Later Pelias promised Jason his rightful kingdom if he would bring the GOLDEN FLEECE to Boeotia. Jason assembled Greece's bravest heroes and together they sailed in the *Argo* in quest of the fleece. On their journey the Argonauts were seduced by beautiful women, attacked by unfriendly warriors, buffeted by storms, and challenged by monstrous creatures. Finally the blind prophet Phineus told them how to make their way safely to Colchis, where the Golden Fleece was kept. When they arrived there, King Aeëtes demanded that before Jason take the fleece he yoke together two fire-breathing bulls, plough the field of Ares, and sow it with dragon's teeth obtained from CADMUS. Aeëtes' daughter MEDEA fell in love with Jason and gave him magical protection that allowed him to complete the tasks. In return Jason swore an oath of fidelity and promised to take her with him to Greece. When Aeëtes still refused to relinquish the fleece, Medea revealed its hiding place and drugged the guardian dragon. The Argonauts then fled Colchis with the fleece, pursued by Aeëtes. But Medea killed and cut to pieces his son Absyrtus, scattering the parts of his body in the sea. Aeëtes stopped to retrieve them. In another version, Absyrtus led the pursuit and, when Medea tricked him into an ambush, was killed by Jason. Jason and Medea stopped to be purified of the murder by Circe at Aeaea, and there they were married. When they returned to Iolcus they found that Pelias had continued his tyrannical rule. Medea persuaded Pelias that he could be rejuvenated by having pieces of his body boiled in a magical brew. She then convinced his daughters that they should perform the task of cutting up their father. Pelias was thus murdered by his innocent daughters. Jason seized the city, but he and Medea were expelled by Acastus, the son of Pelias. They sailed on to Orchomenses in Boeotia, where they hung the fleece in a temple. Then they went to Corinth. There Medea had rights to the throne, and Jason reigned for many years. But he forgot his oath and tried to divorce Medea so that he could marry Creusa, daughter of King Creon. In revenge, Medea, by magic and trickery, burned to death both the father and daughter. Because Jason had broken his oath of fidelity, the gods caused him to wander homeless for many years. As an old man he returned to Corinth, where, resting in the shadow of the *Argo,* he was killed when the prow toppled over on him. The story of Jason and Medea appears frequently in literature, most notably in Euripides.

Jason of Cyrene (sīrē'nē), 2d cent. B.C., Jewish historian. He wrote a history of the Maccabean uprising, used as the basis of 2 Maccabees.

Jasper, William, c.1750–79, American Revolutionary soldier, b. South Carolina (possibly near Georgetown). He joined William Moultrie's regiment early in the Revolution (1775), was made sergeant, and was ordered to Fort Sullivan (now Fort Moultrie) in Charleston harbor. There he bravely rehoisted the flag over the fort in the face of British gunfire (1776). He later distinguished himself as a scout before he was killed in the attack on Savannah.

Jasper, city (1970 pop. 10,798), seat of Walker co., NW central Ala., in a coal-mining area; inc. 1889. The city's industries produce coal, lumber, and textiles.

jasper, opaque, impure cryptocrystalline QUARTZ, usually red, but also yellow, green, and grayish blue. It is used as a gem. Ribbon jasper has the colors in stripes.

Jasper National Park, 4,200 sq mi (10,878 sq km), W Alta., Canada, in the Canadian Rocky Mts.; est. 1907. It is the second largest of the Canadian scenic national parks and contains many high peaks, glaciers, lakes, hot springs, and streams. It is a game reserve and a popular recreation area, with mountain climbing and excellent fishing. The park was named for Jasper Hawes, agent of the North West Company fur-trading post established (1813) on the Athabasca River. Jasper, a resort town, is the park headquarters and is a station on the Canadian National Railways system.

Jaspers, Karl (kärl yäs'pərs), 1883–1969, German philosopher and psychopathologist, b. Oldenburg. After receiving his medical degree (1909) he became (1914) lecturer in psychology and in 1922 professor of philosophy at the Univ. of Heidelberg. One of the leading figures in contemporary philosophy, he is generally placed within the orbit of existentialism. Jaspers, however, rejected this classification, as it tends to place him within a school. Nevertheless his basic philosophic concern was with the concrete individual, and he believed that genuine philosophy must spring from a man's individual existence and address itself to other individuals to help them gain a true understanding of their existence. The basic concept of his philosophy is the "encompassing," an essentially religious concept, intended to suggest the all-embracing transcendent reality within which human existence is enclosed. Although this idea is not in the realm of scientific thought, it is not an irrational concept, since Jaspers believed that the study of science is a necessary preparatory stage to grasping the "encompassing." Thus, while maintaining the value of science, Jaspers was profoundly aware of its limitations and believed that abstract sociological and psychological theories cause the individual to lose sight of his freedom and concrete situation. His works include *Psychologie der Weltanschauungen* (1919), *Die geistige Situation der Zeit* (1931; tr. *Man in the Modern Age,* 1933), *Reason and Existenz* (1935, tr. 1956), *Existenzphilosophie* (1938), *The Question of German Guilt* (tr. 1947), and *Philosophie und Welt* (1958). See C. F. Wallraff, *Karl Jaspers: An Introduction to His Philosophy* (1970); Sebastian Samay, *Reason Revisited: The Philosophy of Karl Jaspers* (1971); O. O. Schrag, *Existence, Existenz, and Transcendence: An Introduction to the Philosophy of Karl Jaspers* (1971).

jasper ware, kind of WEDGWOOD pottery in green, blue, lilac, and other colors, with characteristic Greek reliefs and designs.

Jassy, Rumania: see IAŞI.

Jastrow, Marcus, 1829–1903, American rabbi and Talmudic scholar, b. Poland. He was a rabbi (1866–92) in Philadelphia, editor of the Talmud material of *The Jewish Encyclopedia,* and author of *Dictionary of the Targumim, the Talmud Babli and Yerushalmi, and the Midrashic Literature* (1903).

Jászberény (yäs'bĕrānyə), town (1970 pop. 29,785), central Hungary, on the Zagyva River, a tributary of the Tisza. Attila the Hun was reputedly buried at Jászberény.

Jataka: see PALI LITERATURE.

Jathniel (jăth'nēĕl), doorkeeper of the tabernacle. 1 Chron. 26.2.

Játiva (hä'tēvä), town (1970 pop. 21,578), Valencia prov., E Spain, in Valencia. The town is a processing and distribution center for farm products. Its famous linen industry dates back to Roman times; knitted goods, bicycles, and toys are among other manufactures. Játiva was liberated from the Moors by James I of Aragón in the 13th cent. There are many fine public and private buildings, notably the well-preserved Spanish-Moorish castle, a former Mozarabic church, and the Gothic collegiate church (15th cent.). Játiva was long the residence of the Borgia, or Borja, family. Popes Calixtus III and Alexander VI were born there, as was the painter Jusepe Ribera.

Jattir (jăt'ər), town, S Palestine, the modern Horbat Yattir (Israel), S of Hebron. Joshua 15.48; 21.14; 1 Sam. 30.27; 1 Chron. 6.57.

jaundice (jôn'dĭs, jän'-), abnormal condition in which the body fluids and tissues, particularly the skin and eyes, take on a yellowish color as a result of an excess of bilirubin. During the normal breakdown of old erythrocytes (red blood cells), their hemoglobin is converted into bilirubin. Normally the bilirubin is removed from the bloodstream by the LIVER and eliminated from the body in the BILE, which passes from the liver into the intestines. There are several conditions that may interrupt the elimination of bilirubin from the blood and cause jaundice. Hemolytic jaundice is caused by excessive disintegration of erythrocytes; it occurs in hemolytic and other types of anemia and in some infectious diseases like malaria. Another type of jaundice results from obstruction in or about the liver; usually a stone or stricture of the bile duct blocks the passage of bile from the liver into the intestines. A third type of jaundice occurs when the liver cells are damaged by diseases such as hepatitis or cirrhosis of the liver; the damaged liver is unable to remove bilirubin from the blood. Treatment of jaundice is directed to the underlying cause. Many instances of obstructive jaundice may require surgery.

Jaunpur (jounpo͝or'), town (1971 pop. 76,040), Uttar Pradesh state, NE India, on the Gomati River. Now a district administrative center and market town where perfume is made, Jaunpur was in the 15th cent. a brilliant center of Muslim learning and architecture. Of the many buildings from this period the great Atala Devi Masjid mosque (completed 1408) is the most notable.

Jauregg, Julius Wagner: see WAGNER-JAUREGG.

Jaurès, Jean (zhäN zhōrĕs'), 1859–1914, French Socialist leader and historian. A brilliant student and teacher, he entered the chamber of deputies in 1885 and subsequently became a Socialist. In his Socialist journals, notably *Humanité,* he denounced nationalism and upheld socialism and world peace. Jaurès saw socialism as the economic equivalent of political democracy; he believed that economic equality would come as the result of peaceful revolution. He sought to reconcile Marxian materialism and his own idealistic beliefs and emphasized the importance of individual rights and initiative. As leader of the Socialists, he opposed Boulanger, defended Dreyfus, and worked for the separation of church and state. He was active in the formation (1905) of the unified French Socialist party, and he attempted to preserve party harmony. In 1914, Jaurès advocated arbitration instead of war and declared that capitalist nations, including France, were responsible for the war crisis. He was assassinated by a fanatical patriot in July, 1914. His *Histoire socialiste de la Révolution française* (new ed. by Albert Mathiez, 8 vol., 1922–24), an economic interpretation of the French Revolution, strikes a balance between the materialistic approach of Marx and the dramatic history of Michelet. See biographies by J. H. Jackson (1943) and Harvey Goldberg (1962).

Java (jä'və), island (1970 est. pop. 78,201,000), c.51,000 sq mi (132,090 sq km), Indonesia, S of Borneo, from which it is separated by the Java Sea, and SE of Sumatra across Sunda Strait. Although Java is the fifth largest island of Indonesia, constituting only one seventh of the country's total area, it contains two thirds of the country's population; it is one of the most densely populated regions in the world. For centuries it has been the cultural, political, and economic center of the area. In Java are the republic's capital and largest city, DJAKARTA (formerly called Batavia), and the second and third largest cities, SURABAJA and BANDUNG. Tanjungpriok is the chief port, and JOGJAKARTA and SURAKARTA are cultural centers. A chain of volcanic mountains, most of them densely forested with teak, palms, and other woods, traverses the length of the island from east to west; Mt. Semeru rises to 12,060 ft (3,676 m). There are almost 2 million acres of planted teak forests, and although Java contains only about 3% of the country's forest land, it accounts for much of its timber production. The climate is warm and humid, and the volcanic soil is exceptionally fertile. There are elaborate irrigation systems, supplied by the island's numerous short, turbulent rivers. Most of Indonesia's sugarcane and kapok are grown in Java. Rubber, tea, coffee, tobacco, cacao, and cinchona are produced in highland plantations. While rice is the chief small-farm crop, other food crops are also grown. Cattle are raised in the east. In the northeast are important oil fields, and tin, gold, silver, coal, manganese, phosphate, and sulfur are also mined. Most of the country's manufacturing establishments are in Java; industry is centered chiefly in Djakarta and Surabaja, but Bandung is a noted textile center. Found mostly in the interior are such animals as tigers and leopards; birds of brilliant plumage are numerous. Java was a home of early man (see MAN, PREHISTORIC); there in 1891 were found the fossilized remains of the so-called Java man, or *Pithecanthropus erectus.* The typically Malayan inhabitants of the island comprise the Javanese (the most numerous), the Sudanese, and the Madurese. Numerous Chinese and Arabs live in the cities. Like Bali, Java is known for its highly developed arts. There is a rich literature, and the *wayang,* or shadow play, employing puppets and musical accompaniment, is an important dramatic form. Java has many state and private institutions of higher learning; most are in Djakarta, but Bandung, Bogor, Jogjakarta, and Surabaja all have several universities. Early in the Christian era Indians began colonizing Java, and by the 7th cent. "Indianized" kingdoms were dominant in both Java and Sumatra. The Sailendra dynasty (760–860 in Java) unified the Sumatran and Javan kingdoms and built in Java the magnificent Buddhist temple BOROBUDUR. From the 10th to the 15th cent., E Java was the center of Hindu-Javanese culture. The high point of Javanese history was the rise of the powerful Hindu-Javanese state of Majapahit (founded 1293), which extended its rule over much of Indonesia and the Malay Peninsula. Islam, which had been introduced in the 13th cent., peacefully spread its influence, and the new Muslim state of Mataram emerged in the 16th cent. Following the Portuguese, the Dutch arrived in 1596, and in 1619 the Dutch East India Company established its chief post in Batavia, thence gradually absorbing the native states into which the once powerful Javanese empire had disintegrated. Between 1811 and 1815, Java was briefly under British rule headed by Sir Thomas S. Raffles, who instituted certain reforms. The Dutch ignored these when they returned to power, resorting to a system of enforced labor, which, along with harsh methods of exploitation, led to a native uprising (1825–30) under Prince Diponegoro; the Dutch subsequently adopted a more humane approach. In the early phase of World War II, Java was left open to Japanese invasion by the disastrous Allied defeat in the battle of the Java Sea in Feb., 1942; Java was occupied by the Japanese until the end of the war. After the war the island was the scene of much fighting between Dutch and Indonesian forces; in 1946 the Dutch occupied many of the key cities, and the republic's capital was moved to Jogjakarta. Java now constitutes three provinces of Indonesia—West, Central, and East Java—as well as the autonomous districts of Jogjakarta and Djakarta. See Clifford Geertz, *The Religion of Java* (1960); Clive Day, *The Dutch in Java* (1904, repr. 1966); B. R. Anderson, *Java in a Time of Revolution* (1972).

Java man: see HOMO ERECTUS.

Javan (jā'văn). **1** Japheth's son, eponymous ancestor of the Greeks. Gen. 10.2,4; 1 Chron. 1.5,7; Isa. 66.19; Ezek. 27.13. **2** Unidentified place engaged in trade with Tyre, perhaps a Greek colony. Ezek. 27.19.

Javanese music, one of the richest and most distinctive of Oriental musical cultures. It was and is of enormous importance in religious, political, and entertainment functions. It possesses two separate tonal systems—*pélog* and *sléndro* or *salendro. Pélog* contains seven tones, only five of which are used in a given composition. The intervals of *pélog* are unequal, and the smaller ones approximate the semitone of Western music. *Sléndro* is a division of the octave into five roughly equal intervals. It was believed by the Javanese to be the older system, but contemporary musicologists find evidence that *sléndro* was derived from *pélog. Sléndro* is associated with that which is masculine, and *pélog* with that which is feminine. The Javanese *gamelan,* an orchestra of tuned percussion instruments, primarily of bronze, flourishes today in Bali, where it was introduced in the 15th cent. by Hindus escaping from the Muslim invasion of Java. The term *gamelan* includes percussion orchestras of varying function, style, size, and composition. The set of instruments known collectively as *gamelan* increase in value with age and with the concomitant stabilization of its individual sound. A complete double set, or *sapangkon,* half tuned to *pélog* and half to *sléndro,* may number as many as 80 separate instruments. They are played two ways: according to a subtle, flowing, quiet manner associated with singing and gentle dancing, and according to a powerful, louder manner associated with heroic dance. A fixed melody is the basis for complex vocal and instrumental improvisation. The archaic *gamelan,* no longer heard widely in Java, is best studied in BALINESE MUSIC. See Jaap Kunst, *Music in Java* (2 vol., 1949); D. A. Lentz, *The Gamelan Music of Java and Bali* (1965).

Javari (zhəvərē'), Span. *Yavarí,* river, c.500 mi (805 km) long, rising in the Cerro de Canchyuaya, E Peru. It flows northeast, forming part of the boundary between Brazil and Peru, before entering the Amazon near Tabatinga. It is navigable for most of its length.

javelina: see PECCARY.

Javelle water or **Javel water** (both: zhəvĕl') [Fr. *eau de Javelle*], aqueous solution of sodium or potassium hypochlorite. It was originally made near the French town of Javelle (now part of Paris) and was the first chemical bleach, a use first demonstrated by C. L. Berthollet in 1785. It was produced by passing chlorine gas through a water solution of potash (POTASSIUM CARBONATE). After the invention of BLEACHING POWDER Javelle water was sometimes produced by reacting the bleaching powder with potash or soda ash (SODIUM CARBONATE). Now usually sodium hypochlorite solution, it is used in BLEACHING and as a disinfectant.

Jawara, Sir Dauda Kairaba (dou'də kīrä'bə jä-wär'ə), 1924–, president of Gambia (1970–). Trained as a veterinarian, he became active in politics in 1960, when he was chosen leader of the People's Progressive party. He entered the government as minister of education (1960–61) and served as first minister (1962–70). In 1970, Gambia became a republic with Jawara as president. He was knighted in 1966.

Jawlensky, Aleksey von (əlyĭksyā' vôn youlĕn'skē), 1864–1941, Russian painter. He went to Munich in 1896 and met Kandinsky, with whom he was associated in avant-garde groups. A hint of folk art and a sense of religious meditation distinguish his landscapes and later portraits. After 1916, Jawlensky concentrated on abstract representations of the human head. His *Fir Tree* and many other works are in the Pasadena Art Museum, California.

Jaxartes: see SYR DARYA, river, USSR.

Jay, John, 1745–1829, American statesman, first Chief Justice of the United States, b. New York City, grad. King's College (now Columbia Univ.), 1764. He was admitted (1768) to the bar and for a time was a partner of Robert R. Livingston. His marriage to Sarah, daughter of William Livingston, allied him with that influential family. In pre-Revolutionary activities he reflected the views of the conservative colonial merchant, opposing British actions but not favoring independence. Once the Declaration of Independence was proclaimed, however, he energetically supported the patriot cause. As a delegate to the First and Second Continental Congresses he urged a moderate policy, served on various committees, drafted correspondence, and wrote a famous address to the people of Great Britain. Returning to the provincial congress of New York, he guided the drafting (1777) of the first New York state constitution. Jay was appointed (1777) chief justice of New York but left that post to become (Dec., 1778) president of the Continental Congress. In 1779 he was sent as minister plenipotentiary to Spain, where he secured some financial aid, but failed to win recognition for the colonial cause. He was appointed (1781) one of the commissioners to negotiate peace with Great Britain and joined Benjamin FRANKLIN in Paris. Jay declined further diplomatic appointments in Europe and returned to America to find that Congress had appointed him Secretary of Foreign Affairs, a post he held (1784–89) for the duration of the government under the Articles of Confederation. Although he was able to secure minor treaties, he found it impossible under the Articles of Confederation to make progress in the settlement of major disputes with Great Britain and Spain, a situation that caused him to become one of the strongest advocates of a more powerful central government. He contributed five papers to *The Federalist,* dealing chiefly with the Constitution in relation to foreign affairs. Under the new government Jay became (1789–95) the first Chief Justice of the United States. He concurred in Justice James Wilson's opinion in *Chisholm* vs. *Georgia,* which led to the passing of the Eleventh Amendment. When the still-unsettled controversies with Great Britain threatened to involve the United States in war, Jay was drafted for a mission to England in 1794, where he concluded what is known as JAY'S TREATY. After having unsuccessfully opposed George CLINTON for governor of New York in 1792, Jay was elected and served (1795–1801) two terms. He declined reelection and also renomination to the U.S. Supreme Court and retired to his farm at Bedford in Westchester co. for the remaining 28 years of his life. Publication of the definitive edition of Jay's papers, under the editorship of Richard B. Morris, will be achieved in the 1970s. See H. P. Johnston, ed., *Correspondence and Public Papers of John Jay* (4 vol., 1890–93, repr. 1970); biographies by George Pellew (1890, repr. 1972), Frank Monaghan (1935, repr. 1972), and D. L. Smith (1968); Richard B. Morris, *John Jay, the Nation and the Court* (1967).

Jay, William, 1789–1858, American jurist and reformer, b. New York City; son of John Jay (1745–1829). For most of the period from 1818 to 1843 he served as judge of the county court of Westchester co., N.Y. An active abolitionist, Jay helped establish (1833) the New York City Anti-Slavery Society, was a strong opponent of the African colonization plan as a solution to slavery, and wrote vigorous pamphlets and articles, which were collected in his *Miscellaneous Writings on Slavery* (1853). He was a founder (1816) of the American Bible Society and president (1848–58) of the American Peace Society. His writings include a two-volume life of his father (1833). See study by Bayard Tuckerman (1893, repr. 1969).

jay, common name for a number of birds of the family Corvidae (crows and jays), found in Europe, Asia, and the Americas. The best-known representatives in America are the BLUE JAY, *Cyanocitta cristata,* and the Canada jay. The Canada jay is gray, about 12 in. (30 cm) long, with a white throat and forehead and black nape; it has no crest. Found in northern coniferous forests and swamps, it is known for its habit of stealing bright objects, and is called locally camp robber, whisky jack, and moose bird. The common jay is of wide distribution and is hunted for game in England and Europe. The female lays from five to seven eggs per clutch, and the male helps incubate them. The Florida, or scrub, jay has blue markings and no crest. The European jay is fawn-colored, with a black and white crest and wings of black, white, and blue. Jays are classified in the phylum CHORDATA, subphylum Vertebrata, class Aves, order Passeriformes, family Corvidae.

Jayhawkers, term applied to free-state guerrilla fighters opposed to the proslavery "border ruffians" during the struggle over Kansas in the years prior to the Civil War. Later, during the war, it was the nickname of the Seventh Kansas Cavalry, commanded by Colonel Charles R. Jennison. The origin of the word is uncertain, but it is believed to signify a bird that worries its prey. Today Kansans are sometimes called Jayhawkers. See S. Z. Starr, *Jennison's Jayhawkers* (1974).

Jay's Treaty, concluded in 1794 between the United States and Great Britain to settle difficulties arising mainly out of violations of the Treaty of Paris of 1783 and to regulate commerce and navigation. War threatened when the British admiralty ordered the seizure of American vessels trading with the French West Indies. To avert further difficulties, George Washington in April, 1794, named Chief Justice John Jay as envoy extraordinary for the negotiation of a treaty. The principal American objects were to secure surrender of the posts in the Old Northwest, to obtain compensation for losses and damages resulting from seizure of American vessels and provisions as contraband of war and for the impressment of American seamen, and to remove the restrictions on American commerce, especially on the British West Indies trade. Jay, arriving in England in June, was received favorably, and the treaty was signed on Nov. 19, 1794, by Jay and Lord GRENVILLE. It provided for British evacuation of the Northwestern posts by June 1, 1796, allowing settlers the option of becoming Americans or remaining British citizens, with full protection of property guaranteed. It referred settlement of the northwest and northeast boundaries and the questions of debts and compensations to mixed commissions; provided for unrestricted navigation of the Mississippi and free trade between the North American territories of the two countries; granted equal privileges to American and British vessels in Great Britain and the East Indies, but placed severe and humiliating restrictions upon American trade with the British West Indies; and permitted admission of British vessels to American ports on terms of the most-favored nation. No discrimination in duties was to be made, and articles provided for EXTRADITION of criminals and defined contraband material. Indemnity for those Americans whose Negro slaves were carried off by Britain's evacuating armies was not allowed; protection to American seamen against impressment was not guaranteed; and no recognition of the principles of international maritime law was secured. The treaty, which owed much to the influence of Alexander Hamilton, caused a storm of indignation in America. Jay was denounced and burned in effigy, Hamilton was stoned while speaking in its defense, and the treaty was called a complete surrender of American rights. It was submitted to the U.S. Senate, in special session, on June 8, 1795, and on June 24, after stormy debate, it was ratified with a special reservation on the clause relative to trade with the West Indies. It was signed by Washington. When the treaty was proclaimed as law, after the exchange of ratifications at London in 1796, the U.S. House of Representatives called upon the President for papers relating to the negotiation. In a special message Washington refused to comply with the request of the House. After lengthy debate the House passed a resolution, by three votes, declaring it expedient to pass laws making the treaty effective, and an act was finally passed (April 30, 1796) making appropriations for carrying the treaty into effect. See studies by S. F. Bemis (1923, rev. ed. 1962) and J. A. Combs (1970).

Jazer (jā'zər) or **Jaazer** (jā-ā'-), ancient city E of the Jordan River, probably about 10 mi (16.1 km) N of Hisban (Jordan). It was assigned to Gad. Num. 21.32; 32.1,3; Joshua 13.25; 21.39; 2 Sam. 24.5; 1 Chron. 26.31; Isa. 16.8; Jer. 48.32; 1 Mac. 5.8.

Jaziz (jā'zīz), shepherd of David. 1 Chron. 27.31.

jazz, the most significant form of musical expression of American black culture and America's outstanding contribution to the art of music. Jazz developed in the latter part of the 19th cent. from black work songs, field shouts, sorrow songs, hymns, and AMERICAN NEGRO SPIRITUALS whose harmonic, rhythmic, and melodic elements were predominantly African. Because of its spontaneous, emotional, and improvisational character, and because it is basically of black origin and association, jazz has yet to be accorded the degree of recognition it deserves. European audiences are far more receptive to jazz, and thus many American jazz musicians have become expatriates. At the outset, jazz was slow to win acceptance in the general public not only because of its racial origin but also because it suggested loose morals and general low life; however, it gained a wide audience when white orchestras adapted or imitated it, and became legitimate entertainment in the late 1930s when Benny GOODMAN led racially mixed groups in concerts at Carnegie Hall. Jazz, like athletics, has weakened racism to some degree and has forced acceptance of black Americans on the basis of their outstanding artistic abilities, although an enormous compromise was required of black musicians in terms of the music that white audiences would tolerate and understand. Show tunes became common vehicles for performance, and, while the results were exquisite, rhythmic and harmonic developments were impeded until the mid-1940s. Jazz is generally thought to have begun in New Orleans, spreading to Chicago, Kansas City, New York City, and the West Coast. The blues, vocal and instrumental, was and is a vital component of jazz, which includes, roughly in order of appearance: ragtime; New Orleans or Dixieland jazz; swing; bop, or bebop; progressive, or cool jazz; neobop, or hard-bop; third stream; mainstream modern; Latin-jazz; jazz-rock; and avant-garde jazz. All these styles are current except bebop, whose characteristics have become the material of modern jazz.

Blues. The blues, the heart of jazz, is a musical form now standardized as 12 bars, based on the tonic, dominant, and subdominant chords. The "blue notes" are the flatted third and seventh. A statement is made in the first four bars, repeated (sometimes with slight variation) in the next four, and answered or commented upon in the last four. In vocal blues the lyrics are earthy and direct and are mostly concerned with basic human problems—love and sex, poverty, and death. The tempo may vary, and the mood ranges from total despair to cynicism and satire. W. C. HANDY, basing his songs on traditional blues, greatly increased the popularity of the idiom. Important vocal blues stylists include Blind Lemon Jefferson, Huddie LEDBETTER (Leadbelly), Lightnin' Sam Hopkins, Robert Johnson, Gertrude (Ma) Rainey, Bertha (Chippie) Hill, Bessie SMITH, Billie HOLIDAY, and Dinah Washington.

Ragtime. The earliest form of jazz to exert a wide appeal, ragtime was basically a piano style emphasizing syncopation and polyrhythm. Scott JOPLIN was a major composer and performer of ragtime. From about 1893 to the beginning of World War I this music was popularized through sheet music and player-piano rolls. In the early 1970s, ragtime, particularly Joplin's works, had a popular revival.

New Orleans Jazz. New Orleans, or Dixieland, jazz is played by small bands usually made up of cornet or trumpet, clarinet, trombone, and a rhythm section that includes bass, drums, guitar, and sometimes piano. When the band marched, as it often did in the early days, the piano and bass were omitted and a tuba was used. The three lead instruments provide a contrapuntal melody above the steady beat of the rhythm, and individualities of intonation and phrasing, with frequent use of vibrato and glissando, give the music its warm and highly personal quality. The music ranged from funeral dirges to the exuberant songs of the Mardi Gras. The pioneer black New Orleans jazz band of Buddy Bolden was formed in the 1890s. The Original Dixieland Jazz Band and the New Orleans Rhythm Kings, both of them white bands, successfully introduced jazz to the northern United States. The closing in 1917 of the notorious Storyville district of New Orleans produced an exodus of jazz musicians. Many went to Chicago, where the New Orleans style survived in the bands of KING OLIVER, and later in the music of Louis ARMSTRONG, Jelly Roll MORTON, and Johnny Dodds. Fate Marable, who had played on Mississippi riverboats since 1910, now began to organize riverboat jam sessions with outstanding musicians. Meanwhile, distinctive styles developed in many cities, evolved by younger musicians who stressed a single melodic line rather than the New Orleans counterpoint. Bix BEIDERBECKE, a cornetist and trumpeter and a major Chicago-style musician, was influential in developing more complex melodic lines. Jazz spread to Kansas City, Los Angeles, and New York City.

Swing. Originating in Kansas City and Harlem in the late 1920s and becoming a national craze, swing was marked by the substitution of orchestration for improvisation. The average big band had about 15 members (five reeds, five brass, piano, bass, and drums) and could generate overwhelming volume or evince the most subtle articulations. The bands of Duke ELLINGTON and Count BASIE were, and remain, the finest practitioners of this idiom, while those of Fletcher HENDERSON, Jimmy Lunceford, Benny Goodman, Artie Shaw, Glenn Miller, Tommy Dorsey, and Harry James were also outstanding. The music was often written to showcase soloists who were be supported by the ensemble.

Bop. The vigor of the music notwithstanding, a revolt against the confining nature of the harmony, melody, and rhythm of swing arose in Kansas City and Harlem in the late 1930s and reached fruition in the mid-40s. The new music, called "bebop" or "rebop" (later shortened to "bop"), was rejected at first by many critics. Bop was characterized by the flatted fifth, a more elaborate rhythmic structure, and a harmonic rather than melodic focus. Charlie PARKER, Dizzy GILLESPIE, Thelonius MONK, Kenny Clarke, and Charlie Christian were major influences in the new music, which became the basis for modern jazz. The influence of two swing musicians, the tenor saxophonist Lester YOUNG and the drummer Jo Jones, was of paramount importance in influencing the harmonic and rhythmic direction of bop.

Progressive Jazz. After beginning in New York City, progressive, or cool, jazz developed primarily on the West Coast in the late 1940s and early 50s. Intense yet ironically relaxed tonal sonorities are the major characteristic of this jazz form, while the melodic line is less convoluted than in bop. Lester Young's style was fundamental to the music of the cool saxophonists Lee Konitz, Warne Marsh, and Stan Getz. Miles DAVIS played an important part in the early stages, and the influence of virtuoso pianist Lennie Tristano was all-pervasive. The music was accepted more gracefully by the public and critics than bop, and the pianist Dave BRUBECK became its most widely known performer.

Later Trends. By the mid-1950s a form of neo-bop, or hard-bop, had arisen on the East Coast. John COLTRANE, Sonny Rollins, Horace Silver, Art Blakey, and Max Roach led various small groups that represent an idiom marked by crackling, explosive, uncompromising intensity. About the same period, a number of outstanding musician-composers, including Charles Mingus, John Lewis, and Gunther Schuller, produced "third stream" jazz, essentially a blend of classical music and jazz. Jazz has also been successfully combined with Afro-Latin music, as in the music of Candido, Machito, Eddie Palmieri, and Mongo Santamaria. In the last half of the 1950s there were three major trends in contemporary jazz. First, a general modern jazz form had developed in the period since World War II, which can be called "mainstream," best exemplified by the music of Gerry Mulligan's various bands. Second, a number of instruments that either had never been used seriously in jazz, such as the flute, oboe, and flügelhorn, or had been unpopular, such as the soprano saxophone, were used to bring new instrumental voices into the music. Third, avant-garde leaders such as John Coltrane, Ornette Coleman, Eric Dolphy, Pharaoh Sanders, Archie Shepp, Cecil Taylor, and Rahsaan Roland Kirk continued to explore new harmonic, melodic, and rhythmic relationships. The new jazz is often atonal, and traditional melodic instruments often assume rhythmic-percussive roles and vice versa. In the late 1960s many jazz musicians, such as Miles Davis, Wayne Shorter, Larry Coryell, and Gary Burton, investigated the connections between rock and jazz. One of the most striking conceptions in the idiom is that of Mahavishnu John McLaughlin. Jazz artists in America have suffered much and received little. In many cases the misery of their lives and public indifference have driven them to find relief in drugs and alcohol. Despite hardships they have produced a richly varied art form in which improvisation and experimentation are imperative; jazz promises continued growth in directions as yet unforseeable. See L. G. Feather, *The Book of Jazz* (rev. ed. 1965); Gunther Schuller, *Early Jazz* (1968); Albert McCarthy et al., *Jazz on Record: The First Fifty Years* (1969); Martin Williams,

Where's the Melody (rev. ed. 1969) and *The Jazz Tradition* (1970); Frank Kofsky, *Black Nationalism and the Revolution in Music* (1970); Donald Kennington, *The Literature of Jazz* (1971); L. G. Feather, ed., *The New Edition of the Encyclopedia of Jazz* (1972); Hughes Panassié, *The Real Jazz* (1960, repr. 1973). For blues see Charles Keil, *Urban Blues* (1966); Paul Oliver, *Aspects of the Blues Tradition* (1970). For ragtime see W. J. Schafer and Johannes Riedel, *The Art of Ragtime* (1974).

Jean, 1921–, grand duke of Luxembourg (1964–); son of Charlotte, grand duchess of Luxembourg, and Felix, prince of Bourbon-Parma. He fought with Great Britain's Irish Guards in World War II. In 1953, Jean married Princess Josephine Charlotte, daughter of Leopold III, former king of Belgium. Jean was made deputy to his mother in 1961, virtually assuming the powers of head of state. In 1964 he became grand duke.

Jean de Meun (zhäN də möN), d. 1305, French poet, also known as Jean Chopinel (or Clopinel) of Meung-sur-Loire. He wrote the second part of the ROMAN DE LA ROSE and made translations from Latin, including the letters of Abelard to Heloise. Called by some the Voltaire of the Middle Ages, Jean de Meun was a man of encyclopedic knowledge, a fearless thinker, and a satirical writer.

Jeanne d'Albret (zhän dälbrā'), 1528–72, queen of Navarre (1555–72), daughter of Henri d'Albret and Margaret of Navarre, and mother of King Henry IV of France (Henry III of Navarre). She became queen of Navarre on her father's death. Unlike her consort, Antoine de BOURBON, whom she married in 1548, she remained one of the staunchest leaders of the French Protestants and one of the bitterest foes of the house of GUISE. See biography by N. L. Roelker (1968).

Jeanne d'Arc: see JOAN OF ARC.

Jeanneret, Charles Édouard: see LE CORBUSIER.

Jeannette (jənĕt'), city (1970 pop. 15,209), Westmoreland co., SW Pa., part of the greater Pittsburgh industrial area; laid out 1888, inc. as a city 1937. Its glassworks date from 1889.

Jean Paul: see RICHTER, JOHANN PAUL FRIEDRICH.

Jeans, Sir James Hopwood, 1887–1946, English mathematician, physicist, and astronomer. He was professor of applied mathematics at Princeton Univ. (1905–9), later lectured at Cambridge (1910–12) and Oxford (1922), and was research associate at Mt. Wilson Observatory (1923–44). He was knighted in 1928. He devoted himself to mathematical physics and contributed to the dynamical theory of gases and the mathematical theory of electricity and magnetism. Going on to astrophysics and cosmogony, he solved the problem of the behavior of rotating masses of compressible fluids. He was then able to explain the behavior of certain nebulae, discuss the origins of binary stars, and describe the evolution of gaseous stars. These ideas are presented in *Problems of Cosmogony and Stellar Dynamics* (1919). With Harold A. Jeffreys he developed the tidal hypothesis of the origin of the earth. In 1929, Jeans abandoned research and became one of the most outstanding popularizers of science and the philosophy of science. His later works include *The Universe around Us* (1929), *The Mysterious Universe* (1930), and *The Growth of Physical Science* (1947). See biography by E. A. Milne (1952).

Jearim, Mount (jē'ərĭm), the same as CHESALON.

Jeaterai (jēăt'ərā", jē"ătərā'ī), Gershonite Levite. 1 Chron. 6.21. See ETHNI.

Jebail: see BYBLOS.

Jebba (jĕb'ä), town, W Nigeria, the head of navigation on the Niger River. It is a port as well as a rail and road center. Paper is manufactured in the city. Jebba was conquered by the British in 1897 and served as the temporary capital of the Protectorate of Northern Nigeria from 1900 to 1902. The railroad reached Jebba in 1909, and in 1916 one of the few bridges across the Niger was built there.

Jebel Aulia (jĕb'əl' ou'lēə), Arab. *Jabal al Awliya*, village, N central Sudan. Nearby is a large dam (completed in 1937) that is used to control the flow of the Nile and that helps the Aswan Dam to store water for summer cultivation in parts of Egypt.

Jebel Shammar: see JABAL SHAMMAR, Saudi Arabia.

Jeberechiah (jĕ"bĕrĕkī'ə), father of ZECHARIAH 7.

Jebus (jē'bəs), **Jebusi** (jĕb'yo͞osī), and **Jebusite** (jĕb'yo͞osīt), name of a tribe mentioned in the Bible as the inhabitants of Jerusalem before the Jews. They were apparently absorbed by their conquerors. Gen. 10.16; 15.21; Ex. 3.8; 34.11; Num. 13.29; Joshua 9.1; 11.3; 15.8; 18.16,28; Judges 1.21; 19.10,11; 2 Sam. 5.6; 1 Kings 9.20; 1 Chron. 11.4,5; 2 Chron. 8.7; Ezra 9.1.

Jecamiah (jĕkəmī'ə), descendant of David. 1 Chron. 3.18.

Jecholiah (jĕkōlī'ə), wife of King Amaziah. 2 Kings 15.2. Jecoliah: 2 Chron. 26.3.

Jechonias (jĕkōnī'əs): see JEHOIACHIN.

Jecoliah (jĕkōlī'ə), variant of JECHOLIAH.

Jeconiah (jĕkōnī'ə): see JEHOIACHIN.

Jedaiah (jēdā'yə, jĕd"āī'ə). **1** Simeonite chief. 1 Chron. 4.37. **2** Worker on the wall. Neh. 3.10. **3** Chief priest. 1 Chron. 24.7. **4** Priestly exile. Zech. 6.10,14.

Jedburgh (jĕd'bərə), burgh (1971 pop. 3,874), county town of Roxburghshire, SE Scotland, on the Jed River. The manufacture of rayon is the main industry. Jedburgh also has a tannery and woolen mills. The red sandstone ruins of an abbey founded in 1118 are notable. In 1975, Jedburgh became part of the Borders region.

Jedda: see JIDDA, Saudi Arabia.

Jediael (jēdī'āĕl). **1** Benjamite. 1 Chron. 7.6,11. **2** Doorkeeper. 1 Chron. 26.1,2. **3** One of David's guard. 1 Chron. 11.45; 12.20.

Jedidah (jēdī'də), wife of Amon of Judah. 2 Kings 22.1.

Jedidiah (jĕdĭdī'ə) [Heb.,=beloved of God], auspicious name that Nathan bestowed on the baby Solomon. 2 Sam. 12.24,25.

Jeduthun (jēdyo͞o'thən), Levite associated with the temple worship. 1 Chron. 9.16; 16.38; 25.3; 2 Chron. 29.14. It is not known why the name appears in the titles of Pss. 39; 62; 77.

jeep, small, durable automotive vehicle intended for heavy-duty applications and sometimes provided with the capability of delivering driving power to all four wheels. The last feature allows superior performance on slippery surfaces such as those formed by ice or mud. The earliest jeeps were used by U.S. military services during World War II.

Jeezer (jē-ē'zər), the same as ABIEZER.

Jefferies, Richard, 1848–87, English author. A naturalist, he wrote several books about the English countryside. He first achieved recognition with the sketches *The Gamekeeper at Home* (1878). His novels include *Wood Magic* (1881) and *Bevis* (1882). See his autobiography, *Story of My Heart* (1883).

Jeffers, Robinson, 1887–1962, American poet and dramatist, b. Pittsburgh, grad. Occidental College, 1905. From 1914 until his death Jeffers lived on an isolated section of the rocky California coast, finding his inspiration in its stern beauty. For Jeffers the world, viewed pantheistically, was marred only by man, a doomed and inverted animal. He frequently used Greek myth to illustrate man's tortured mind, his diseased introspection, and his alienation from nature. Jeffer's poetry is virile, intense, and rich in elemental power. Among his volumes of poetry are *Tamar and Other Poems* (1924), *Roan Stallion* (1925), *The Woman at Point Sur* (1927), *Cawdor* (1928), *Dear Judas* (1929), *Give Your Heart to the Hawks* (1933), *Such Counsels You Gave to Me* (1937), *The Double Axe & Other Poems* (1948), and *Hungerfield and Other Poems* (1954). His adaptations of Greek tragedy—*Medea* (1947), *The Tower Beyond Tragedy* (pub. 1924; produced 1950), and *The Cretan Woman* (1954)—brought him wide recognition. See his letters, ed. by A. N. Ridgway (1968); biography by M. B. Bennett (1966); studies by M. C. Monjian (1958, repr. 1970), A. B. Coffin (1971), and R. J. Brophy (1973).

Jefferson, Joseph, 1829–1905, American actor. He was the foremost of an old and distinguished family of English and American actors. Jefferson spent the first 20 years of his life as a strolling player. His fame came with his creation of the role of Rip Van Winkle in a dramatization of Washington Irving's story, first in 1859 and later in 1865 as revised by Dion Boucicault. He performed the second version almost exclusively until 1880. He infused the character with human tenderness and dignity and heightened the "fairy-tale" elements of the play. Almost as famous was his interpretation of Bob Acres in *The Rivals,* a part he played hundreds of times. He was one of the first star actors in America to establish his own road company, the earlier practice being to depend for support on local stock companies. Jefferson was a painter of merit and was a member of the American Academy of Arts and Letters. In 1893 he succeeded Edwin Booth as president of the Players' Club, thus becoming the recognized dean of his profession. He retired in 1904. See his autobiography, ed. by A. S. Downer (1964); biography by Gladys Malvern (1945); William Winter, *The Jeffersons* (1881, repr. 1969).

Jefferson, Thomas, 1743–1826, 3d President of the United States (1801–9), author of the Declaration of Independence, and apostle of agrarian democracy. He was born on April 13, 1743, at "Shadwell," in Goochland (now in Albemarle) co., Va. The vicinity, which at that time was considered a Western outpost, was to remain his lifelong home, and from boyhood he absorbed the democratic views of his Western countrymen. After graduating from the College of William and Mary (1762), he studied law under George WYTHE. In the colonial house of burgesses he was (1769–75) a leader of the patriot faction. He helped to form, and became a member of, the Virginia Committee of Correspondence, and in his paper *A Summary View of the Rights of British America* (1774), prepared for the First Virginia Convention, he brilliantly expounded the view that Parliament had no authority in the colonies and that the only bond with England was that of voluntary allegiance to the king. Although never effective as a public speaker, he won a reputation as a draftsman of resolutions and addresses. A delegate to the Second Continental Congress (1775–76), he served as a member of the committee to draft the DECLARATION OF INDEPENDENCE. That historic document, except for minor alterations by John Adams and Benjamin Franklin and others made on the floor of Congress, was wholly the work of Jefferson. In spirit it reflects his debt to English political theorists, particularly John Locke, and to French and other continental philosophers. Jefferson returned to the Virginia legislature in the hope of being able to translate his ideals into reality in the establishment of a new state government. He urged the abolition of entail and primogeniture to prevent the continuance of an aristocracy of wealth and birth; both practices were abolished, although primogeniture existed until 1785. His bill for establishing religious freedom, grounded in the belief that the opinions of man cannot be coerced, was not successful until 1786, when James MADISON was able to carry part of the Jeffersonian program through to completion. In 1779, Jefferson succeeded Patrick Henry as governor of Virginia. He served through the trying last years of the American Revolution when Virginia was invaded by the British, and, hampered by lack of financial and military resources, he experienced great difficulty. His conduct as governor was investigated in 1781, but he was completely vindicated. In 1783–84 he was again in the Continental Congress, where he drafted a plan for a decimal system of coinage based on the dollar and drew up a proposed ordinance for the government of the Northwest Territory, which, although not then adopted, was the basis for the very important ORDINANCE OF 1787. In 1785 he succeeded Franklin as minister to France, remaining to witness the beginning in 1789 of the French Revolution, to which he gave his sympathetic interest. On the other hand, his unsuccessful attempt, with John Adams, to negotiate a trade treaty with England left him convinced of that country's essential selfishness. On his return he became (1790) Secretary of State. Though absent when the Constitution was drafted and adopted, Jefferson gave his support to a stronger central government and to the Constitution, particularly with the addition of the Bill of Rights. He failed to realize the power that conservative spokesmen had attained in his absence, and he did not seem to be aware at first of the threat to agrarian interests posed by the measures advocated by Alexander HAMILTON. He would call himself neither a Federalist nor an Anti-Federalist and was anxious to secure unity and cooperation in the new government. Jefferson did not begin to differ with Hamilton until they clashed as to the best method to persuade England to release the Northwest forts, which the British still held in violation of the Treaty of Paris of 1783. Jefferson favored the application of economic pressure by forbidding imports from England, but Hamilton objected, fearing that the resulting loss of revenue would endanger his plans for the nation's financial structure. Jefferson next opposed Hamilton by declaring against his Bank of the United States scheme on the ground that the Constitution did not specifically authorize it, rejecting the doctrine of "implied powers," invoked by Hamilton's supporters. In both these encounters Hamilton, to Jefferson's chagrin, emerged the victor. Fearing a return to monarchist ideals, if not to actual monarchy, Jefferson became virtual leader of the Anti-Federalist forces. He drew closer to himself a group of like-minded men who began to call themselves Republicans—a group to which the present DEMOCRATIC PARTY traces its origin. An organization was developed, and the *National Gazette,* edited by Philip Freneau, was established

(1791) to disseminate Republican sentiments. Jefferson and Hamilton, from being suspicious of each other, became openly antagonistic, and President George Washington was unable to reconcile them. In 1793, Jefferson left the cabinet. Later he bitterly criticized JAY'S TREATY, which compromised the issues with Great Britain in ways outlined by Hamilton. Jefferson's party was able to elect him Vice President in 1796, when that office was still filled by the person who ran second in the presidential race. He took little part in the administration but presided over the Senate and wrote *A Manual of Parliamentary Practice* (1801). His followers kept up their agitation and under Jefferson's skillful direction extended the party's following both territorially and numerically, while the Federalists drifted into dissension. The passage of the ALIEN AND SEDITION ACTS immensely stimulated newspaper discussion, and Jefferson drafted, in protest against these laws, the Kentucky Resolutions (see KENTUCKY AND VIRGINIA RESOLUTIONS), the first statement of the STATES' RIGHTS interpretation of the Constitution. The Republicans triumphed easily at the polls in what is sometimes called "the Revolution of 1800." Aaron Burr, however, who had been slated for the office of Vice President, was found to have tied Jefferson for President, and the choice was automatically left to the House of Representatives. Jefferson was elected after a long deadlock, largely because Hamilton advised the Federalists to support Jefferson as less dangerous than Burr. Jefferson was the first President inaugurated in Washington, a city he had helped to plan (and where the THOMAS JEFFERSON MEMORIAL was dedicated in 1943). He instituted a republican simplicity in the new capital, cut expenditures in all branches of government, replaced Federalist appointees with Republicans, and sought to curb the powers of the judiciary, where he felt that the Federalists were attempting to entrench their philosophy. He believed that the Federal government should be concerned mostly with foreign affairs, leaving the states and local governments free to administer local matters. Despite his contention that the Constitution must be interpreted strictly, he pushed through the LOUISIANA PURCHASE, even though such an action was nowhere expressly authorized. His eager interest in the West and in exploration had already led him to plan and organize the LEWIS AND CLARK EXPEDITION. He held that West Florida was included in the Louisiana Purchase, but his attempts to secure Spanish recognition of this caused rifts in the party and made him the butt of sarcastic attacks by John Randolph in Congress. During his second administration, however, the chief difficulties resulted from attacks on the neutral shipping of the United States by the warring powers of Britain and Napoleonic France. Jefferson placed his faith in diplomacy backed by economic pressure as represented first by the Nonimportation Act (1806) and then by the EMBARGO ACT OF 1807. To enforce them, unfortunately, meant the impoverishment of classes that had supported him and the infringement of that individual liberty he cherished. Shortly before he left office a rebellious people forced him to yield in his aims, although he maintained that the embargo had not been in effect long enough to achieve its objective. After 1809, Jefferson lived in retirement at his beloved MONTICELLO, although he often advised his successors, James Madison and James MONROE. One of his cherished ambitions was attained when he was able to bring about the founding of the Univ. of Virginia (see VIRGINIA, UNIVERSITY OF). President of the American Philosophical Society (1797–1815), the learned Jefferson was a scientist, an architect, and a philosopher-statesman, vitally interested in literature, the arts, and every phase of human activity. He had complete faith that a people enlightened by education, which must be kept free, could under democratic-republican institutions govern themselves better than under any other system. A 52-volume definitive edition of Jefferson's complete works is being published by Princeton Univ. Press under the editorial supervision of Julian P. Boyd. The projected multivolume *Jefferson and His Time* (Vols. I–IV, 1948–70) by Dumas Malone will doubtless be the definitive biography. See Jefferson's *Autobiography* (new ed., 1959), and a selection of his writings in *Jefferson Himself,* ed. by Bernard Mayo (1942); biographies by Gilbert Chinard (1929, repr. 1957), Nathan Schachner (1951), A. J. Nock (1956, repr. 1960), and F. M. Brodie (1974). See also Claude G. Bowers, *Jefferson and Hamilton* (1925, repr. 1966), *Jefferson in Power* (1936, repr. 1967), and *The Young Jefferson 1743–1789* (1945); Karl Lehmann, *Thomas Jefferson, American Humanist* (1947); Marie Kimball, *Jefferson* (3 vol., 1943–50); L. W. Levy, *Jefferson and Civil Liberties* (1963, repr. 1974); L. S. Kaplan, *Jefferson and France* (1967); Merrill Peterson, *The Jeffersonian Image in the American Mind* (1960), *Thomas Jefferson: A Profile* (1967), and *Thomas Jefferson and the New Nation* (1970).

Jefferson, Territory of, in U.S. history, region that roughly encompassed the present-day state of Colorado, although extending 2° farther south and 1° farther north, organized by its inhabitants (1859–61), but never given congressional sanction. After a great increase in emigration in the 1850s, settlers in Arapahoe co., Kansas Territory, felt the need to be closer to the seat of government. They met in convention in Denver on Aug. 1, 1859, to discuss alternatives to the region's status. The 166 delegates present debated the benefits of reorganization as a state or as a territory and submitted the question on Sept. 5 to the public, which voted overwhelmingly for territorial status. Subsequently, Beverly D. Williams was sent as a representative to Congress, which, however, refused his petition. Nevertheless, the constitution of the Territory of Jefferson was adopted on Oct. 24, and the first session of its legislature met on Nov. 7. Robert W. Steele was elected provisional governor. Although illegal, the new government coexisted peacefully with the official county institutions. Laws were passed regarding taxation, and the franchise was denied Indians and blacks. On Feb. 28, 1861, Congress passed the Organic Act, which created the Territory of Colorado. The provisional government quickly dismantled, and William Gilpin replaced Steele as governor.

Jefferson, city (1970 pop. 25,432), Fairfax co., N Va. It is a suburb of Washington, D.C.

Jefferson, Mount, N.H.: see PRESIDENTIAL RANGE.

Jefferson City, city (1970 pop. 32,407), state capital and seat of Cole co., central Mo., on the south bank of the Missouri River, near the mouth of the Osage; inc. 1825. The state government is the major employer, but the city, with rail and river facilities, is also the commercial and processing center of an agricultural area. The city has printing and publishing houses; other industries produce shoes, clothing, electrical appliances, and steel products. It was a small river village when it was chosen (1821) for the state capital; the legislature moved there from St. Charles in 1826. Because of divided loyalties and the difficulties of holding the state in the Union, Jefferson City was occupied by Federal troops during the Civil War. The Italian-Renaissance capitol of Carthage marble (completed 1917) contains murals by Thomas Hart Benton and N. C. Wyeth, and is the site of the Missouri state museum. In the city are Lincoln Univ., a junior college, the state penitentiary, and a national cemetery.

Jefferson Heights, uninc. town (1970 pop. 16,489), Jefferson parish, SW La., a suburb of New Orleans.

Jefferson Memorial: see THOMAS JEFFERSON MEMORIAL.

Jefferson National Expansion Memorial National Historic Site: see SAINT LOUIS, Mo.

Jeffersonville, city (1970 pop. 20,008), seat of Clark co., S Ind., at the falls of the Ohio River opposite Louisville, Ky. (with which it is connected by a bridge); inc. 1817. Its shipbuilding industry dates from the 19th cent.; kitchen cabinets are also made there. Jeffersonville was founded (1802) on the site of Fort Steuben (originally Fort Finney) by veterans of George Rogers Clark's northwest expedition, who were given the land in gratitude for their services. The town was built according to plans made by Thomas Jefferson, after whom it is named. It served (1813–16) as temporary capital of Indiana Territory. Mineral springs once attracted many visitors to Jeffersonville; today the city is the seat of Indiana Univ. Southeast and contains a steamboat museum.

Jeffords, Thomas, 1832–1914, American pioneer, b. Chautauqua co., N.Y. He went to Arizona in 1862 as a U.S. army scout and messenger and later became a stage driver. In 1866–67, he controlled mail service between Fort Bowie and Tucson. A number of his men were killed by Apaches, and he decided to meet with their chief, COCHISE. He won the Indians' respect by riding into their camp alone. A strong friendship developed between Jeffords and the chief, and it halted for a short period the Chiricahua Apaches' warfare against the whites. As Jeffords was the only white man whom Cochise trusted, Gen. O. O. Howard, the Indian Commissioner, used him as an agent in a treaty (1872). Cochise agreed to live on a reservation only if Jeffords were the Indian agent. Jeffords consented, and during the four years that he was the Indian agent, trouble with the warlike Chiricahua Apache virtually subsided.

Jeffrey, Francis, Lord Jeffrey, 1773–1850, Scottish critic and judge. He was a founder and editor of the *Edinburgh Review,* which printed his critical essays. See his *Contributions to the Edinburgh Review* (4 vol., 1844).

Jeffreys of Wem, George Jeffreys, 1st **Baron,** 1645?–1689, English judge under Charles II and JAMES II. A notoriously cruel judge, he presided over many of the trials connected with the Popish Plot (see OATES, TITUS) and was responsible for the judicial murder of Algernon SIDNEY and for the brutal trials of Richard BAXTER and many others. He was created baron in 1685 and was soon sent to W England to punish those concerned in the rebellion of the duke of MONMOUTH. In the resulting Bloody Assizes he caused nearly 200 persons to be hanged, some 800 transported, and many more imprisoned or whipped. James II made him lord chancellor later that year. When James fled the country in 1688, Jeffreys was imprisoned and died in the Tower of London. See biography by P. J. Helm (1967); study by G. W. Keeton (1966).

Jeffries, James J., 1875–1953, American boxer, b. Carroll, Fairfield co., Ohio. He began boxing in 1896, and in 1899 he won the heavyweight championship from Robert Fitzsimmons at Coney Island in New York City. He retired undefeated in 1905, but returned to the ring in 1910, when he was defeated by Jack Johnson at Reno, Nev.

Jegar-sahadutha: see GALEED.

Jehaleleel (jēhăl'ēlēl), descendant of Judah. 1 Chron. 4.16.

Jehalelel (jēhăl'ĕlĕl), Levite. 2 Chron. 29.12

Jehangir: see JAHANGIR.

Jehannet: see CLOUET, FRANÇOIS, and CLOUET, JEAN.

Jehdeiah (jĕdē'yə). **1** Descendant of Moses. 1 Chron. 24.20. **2** One in charge of David's asses. 1 Chron. 27.30.

Jehezekel (jēhĕz'əkĕl), chief priest. 1 Chron. 24.16.

Jehiah (jēhī'ə), doorkeeper. 1 Chron. 15.24.

Jehiel (jēhī'əl). **1** Ancestor of Saul. 1 Chron. 9.35. **2** One of David's mighty men. 1 Chron. 11.44. **3** Musician of David. 1 Chron. 15.18; 16.5. **4** Son of Jehoshaphat. 2 Chron. 21.2. **5** Levite under David. 1 Chron. 23.8; 29.8. Jehieli: 1 Chron. 26.21. **6** Tutor of David's sons. 1 Chron. 27.32. **7** Levite under Hezekiah. 2 Chron. 31.13. **8** Leader under Josiah. 2 Chron. 35.8. **9** Father of a postexilic family. Ezra 8.9. **10** Father of one who had a foreign wife. Ezra 10.2. **11, 12** Men who had foreign wives. Ezra 10.21,26.

Jehieli (jēhī'ēlī), variant of JEHIEL **5.**

Jehizkiah (jēhĭzkī'ə), one of the leaders under Pekah, in the northern kingdom, who insisted on restoring the captives from Judah. 2 Chron. 28.12.

Jehlam, river, Kashmir: see JHELUM.

Jehoadah (jēhō'ədä), the same as JARAH.

Jehoaddan (jēhōăd'ăn), mother of King Amaziah of Judah. 2 Kings 14.2; 2 Chron. 25.1.

Jehoahaz (jēhō'əhăz) or **Joahaz** (jō'əhăz). **1** King of Israel, son and successor of Jehu. Under Jehoahaz, the kingdom of Israel was at its lowest. 2 Kings 13.1–9; 14.1. **2** King of Judah. After the death in battle of his father, Josiah, he was made king at Jerusalem; but the Pharaoh Necho removed Jehoahaz to Egypt and substituted Jehoiakim, his brother, in his place. 2 Kings 23.30–35; 2 Chron. 36. Shallum: 1 Chron. 3.15; Jer. 22.11. **3** In 2 Chron. 21.17 and 25.23 AHAZIAH **2** is meant. **4** Father of a recorder. 2 Chron. 34.8.

Jehoash (jēhō'ăsh) or **Joash** (jō'ăsh). **1** King of Israel, son and successor of Jehoahaz. He was generally successful in a war with Damascus, and he conquered Amaziah of Judah. He was succeeded by his son Jeroboam II. 2 Kings 13; 14. **2** King of Judah, son of AHAZIAH **2.** When his father was murdered and his grandmother Athaliah seized the power and massacred the royal family, Jehoash, a baby, was saved by his aunt and uncle, Jehosheba and Jehoiada (see JEHOIADA **1**). He was dominated by his guardians when he became king six years later. He was responsible for religious reforms against Baal worship. After a long reign he was assassinated. 2 Kings 11; 12. **3** Gideon's father. Judges 6.11. **4** One of Ahab's sons. 1 Kings 22.26. **5** Judahite. 1 Chron. 4.22. **6** Benjamite. 1 Chron. 7.8. **7** One who joined David at Ziklag. 1 Chron. 12.3. **8** One of David's officers. 1 Chron. 27.28.

Jehohanan (jēhōhā'năn). **1** Officer of Jehoshaphat. 2 Chron. 17.15. **2** Father of an officer of Jehoiada. 2 Chron. 23.1. **3** Korahite porter. 1 Chron. 26.3. **4** Husband of a foreign wife. Ezra 10.28. **5, 6** Postexilic priests. Neh. 12.13,42.

Jehoiachin (jēhoi'əkĭn), King of Judah. He was king for a few months after the death of his father, JEHOIAKIM. He was carried away by Nebuchadnezzar to Babylon and imprisoned. On the death of Nebuchadnezzar he was freed and given honorable treatment. 2 Kings 24.6–16; 25.27–30. Jeconiah: 1 Chron. 3.16,17; Esther 2.6; Jer. 24.1; 27.20; 28.4; 29.2. Jechonias: Mat. 1.11,12. Coniah: Jer. 22.24,28; 37.1.

Jehoiada (jēhoi'ədə). **1** High priest. He married Jehosheba, a princess of Judah, and together they saved the infant Jehoash. They led the conspiracy against Athaliah that put Jehoash on the throne (see JEHOASH **2**). Jehoiada was buried with the kings of Judah. His son was Zechariah the martyr. 2 Kings 11; 12; 2 Chron. 22–24. **2** Priest and ally of David, father of Solomon's general Benaiah. 2 Sam. 8.18; 1 Chron. 12.27; 27.5. At one point he is apparently called Benaiah's son. 1 Chron. 27.34. **3** Priest. Jer. 29.26. **4** Worker on the wall of Jerusalem. Neh. 3.6. **5** Priest who held office in Nehemiah's regime. Neh. 12.10.

Jehoiakim (jēhoi'əkĭm), King of Judah, son of Josiah. On Josiah's death his son Jehoahaz became king. The Pharaoh Necho dethroned him and set up another of Josiah's sons, Eliakim, who took the name Jehoiakim. Jeremiah tried to arouse the king from his ways, but Jehoiakim had the book of Jeremiah's prophecies burned. Nebuchadnezzar took the hegemony of the West at Carchemish, but three years later the king of Judah revolted. Jehoiakim died just before Nebuchadnezzar took the city. He left a son, Jehoiachin. 2 Kings 23.34; 24.6–16; 25.27–30; Jer. 36.

Jehoiarib (jēhoi'ərĭb), the same as JOIARIB **2.**

Jehol (jəhōl', -hōl'), Mandarin *Je-ho,* former province (c.44,000 sq mi/114,000 sq km), NE China. Ch'eng-te was the capital. In 1955, Jehol was divided between the Inner Mongolian Autonomous Region and the provinces of Hopeh and Liaoning. The Tsungling is one of the ranges of this largely hilly and mountainous region, which is crossed by swift, unnavigable rivers. Jehol was the traditional gateway to Mongolia and from time to time was overrun by Tatars, Huns, and Khitan Mongols. It was the seat (10th–12th cent.) of the Liao (Khitan) empire. Conquered by the Manchus in the 17th cent., Jehol became an imperial pastureland. It was taken by the Japanese early in 1933 and included in Manchukuo; it was not restored to China until the end of World War II. From 1945 to 1955 it retained its provincial status but was administered as part of Manchuria.

Jehol: see CH'ENG-TE, China.

Jehonadab (jēhŏn'ədăb), the same as JONADAB.

Jehonathan (jēhŏn'əthən). **1** Levite. 2 Chron. 17.8. **2** Officer under David. 1 Chron. 27.25. **3** High priest. Neh. 12.18. **4** Teaching Levite. 2 Chron. 17.8.

Jehoram (jēhō'rəm) or **Joram** (jō'rəm). **1** King of Israel, brother and successor of AHAZIAH **1.** He compelled Jehoshaphat of Judah to help him put down a revolt in Moab. Jehoram was wounded in an attack on Ramoth-gilead and retired to Jezreel. JEHU, whom Elisha had earlier anointed king of Israel, put Jehoram to death and took the throne. This was the end of the house of Ahab in Israel. 2 Kings 1.17; 3.6. **2** King of Judah, son and successor of Jehoshaphat. His wife was the notorious ATHALIAH **1.** The Bible says that he followed her family in the worship of Baal. He was succeeded by his son AHAZIAH **2.** 2 Kings 8.16–24; 2 Chron. 21–22.1. **3** Priest. 2 Chron. 17.8.

Jehoshabeath (jēhōshăb'ēăth): see JEHOSHEBA.

Jehoshaphat (jēhŏsh'əfăt), **Josaphat** (jŏs'-), or **Joshaphat** (jŏsh'-). **1** King of Judah, son and successor of ASA **1.** He continued his father's reforms. He was an ally of Ahab, who was king of Israel, and his successors, and he was the first king of Judah to make a treaty with the kingdom of Israel. He was succeeded by his son, JEHORAM **2.** 1 Kings 22; 2 Kings 3; 2 Chron. 17–21. **2** Recorder under David and Solomon. 2 Sam. 8.16; 1 Kings 4.3. **3** One of Solomon's officers. 1 Kings 4.17. **4** Priest. 1 Chron. 15.24. **5** Father of King Jehu. 2 Kings 9.2, 14. The **Valley of Jehoshaphat,** mentioned in Joel 3 as a place of judgment, has been identified by tradition with the northern extension of the vale of Kidron to the E of Jerusalem.

Jehosheba (jēhŏsh'ēbə), daughter of King Jehoram of Judah and aunt of King JEHOASH. She married the high priest Jehoiada. 2 Kings 11.2. Jehoshabeath: 2 Chron. 22.11.

Jehoshua and **Jehoshuah** (jəhŏsh'o͞oə), variants of JOSHUA.

Jehovah (jəhō'və, jē-), modern reconstruction of the ancient Hebrew ineffable name of GOD.

Jehovah-jireh (jəhō'və-jī'rē), Abraham's name for the spot where the angel prevented the sacrifice of Isaac. Gen. 22.14.

Jehovah-nissi (jəhō'və-nĭs'ī), name Moses gave to the altar commemorating the victory over the Amalekites. Ex. 17.15.

Jehovah-shalom (jəhō'və-shā'lŏm), name Gideon gave to his altar in Ophrah after an angel appeared to him. Judges 6.24.

Jehovah's Witnesses, sect originating in the United States at the end of the 19th cent., organized by Charles Taze RUSSELL, whose doctrine centers on the second coming of Christ. The Witnesses believe that the event has already commenced; they also believe the battle of Armageddon is imminent and that it will be followed by a millennial period when repentant sinners will have a second chance for salvation. The Witnesses base their teaching on the Bible. They have no churches but meet in buildings that are always named Kingdom Hall. There are no official ministers because all Jehovah's Witnesses are considered ministers of the gospel. The views of the sect are circulated in *The Watchtower, Awake!,* and other publications and by the zealous house-to-house canvassing carried on by its members. Since their beginning, the Witnesses have been the subject of harassment virtually everywhere that they have been active. Regarding governments as the work of Satan, the Witnesses refuse to bear arms in war or participate in the affairs of government. Their refusal to salute the flag brought about a controversy that resulted in a decision in their favor by the U.S. Supreme Court in 1943. The Witnesses insist upon a rigid moral code and refuse blood transfusions. Before 1931, Jehovah's Witnesses were called Russellites; abroad the movement is usually known as the International Bible Students Association. It is active in almost every country in the world. See studies by H. H. Stroup (1945, repr. 1967), Royston Pike (1954), Marley Cole (1957), W. J. Whalen (1962), and W. C. Stevenson (1967).

Jehozabad (jēhŏz'əbăd). **1** One of the murderers of Joash. 2 Kings 12.21; 2 Chron. 24.26. **2** Captain in Jehoshaphat's army. 2 Chron. 17.18. **3** Porter. 1 Chron. 26.4.

Jehozadak (jēhŏz'ədăk), the same as JOZADAK.

Jehu (jē'hyo͞o). **1** King of Israel. He was anointed king by ELISHA, who led the revolt against the house of Ahab. Jehu murdered King JEHORAM of Israel and King AHAZIAH of Judah and the rest of the house of Ahab. Jehu's rapid chariot driving has become proverbial. To receive protection from Assyria, Jehu paid tribute to Shalmaneser III, an event depicted on the black obelisk in the British Museum. His son Jehoahaz succeeded him. 2 Kings 9. **2** Prophet under Kings Baasha and Jehoshaphat. 1 Kings 16; 2 Chron. 19. **3** Descendant of Judah. 1 Chron. 2.38. **4** Simeonite. 1 Chron. 4.35. **5** One of those who joined David at Ziklag. 1 Chron. 12.3.

Jehubbah (jēhŭb'ə), Asherite. 1 Chron. 7.34.

Jehucal (jē'hyo͞okăl", jēhyo͞o'kəl), Zedekiah's messenger to Jeremiah. Jer. 37.3. Jucal: Jer. 38.1.

Jehud (jē'həd), town, SW Palestine, the present-day Yehud (Israel), E of Jaffa. Joshua 19.45.

Jehudi (jēhyo͞o'dī), officer of Jehoiakim's court. Jer. 36.14,21,23.

Jehudijah (jēhyo͞odī'jə), wife of a Judahite. 1 Chron. 4.18.

Jehush (jē'hŭsh"), descendant of Saul. 1 Chron. 8.39.

Jeiel (jēī'ĕl). **1** Levite under David. 1 Chron. 15.18. **2** Musician of David. 1 Chron. 15.21; 16.5. **3** Ancestor of JAHAZIEL **2.** **4** Scribe of Uzziah. 2 Chron. 26.11. **5** Levite of Hezekiah. 2 Chron. 29.13. **6** Levite of Josiah. 2 Chron. 35.9. **7** Companion of Ezra. Ezra 8.13. **8** Husband of a foreign wife. Ezra 10.43. **9** Reubenite. 1 Chron. 5.7.

jejunum: see INTESTINE.

Jekabzeel (jēkăb'zēēl), variant of KABZEEL.

Jekameam (jĕkəmē'əm), Kohathite Levite. 1 Chron. 23.19; 24.23.

Jekamiah (jĕkəmī'ə), descendant of Judah. 1 Chron. 2.41.

Jekuthiel (jēkyo͞o'thēēl), Judahite. 1 Chron. 4.18.

Jelenia Góra (yĕlĕ'nyä go͞o'rä), Ger. *Hirschberg,* city (1970 pop. 55,720), SW Poland. It is an industrial and commercial center known especially for its woolen textiles. Chartered in 1312, the city passed to Bohemia in 1368 and to Prussia in 1741.

Jelgava: see YELGAVA, USSR.

Jellachich de Buzim, Joseph, Count (yĕ'lăchĭch, bo͞o'zĭm, -zhĭm), 1801–59, Austrian general, a Croatian nobleman. He was governor of Croatia when the REVOLUTION OF 1848 broke out in Hungary, and he commanded an army against the revolutionists. His purpose was to separate CROATIA from Hungary, and he was backed by the Austrian government. After the fall (1849) of the Hungarian revolutionary government of KOSSUTH, Jellachich was again governor of Croatia, which remained a part of Hungary.

Jellicoe, John Rushworth Jellicoe, 1st **Earl,** 1859–1935, British admiral. Crowning a naval career begun in 1872, he served (1914–16) as commander in chief of the Grand Fleet in World War I. His tactics at the inconclusive battle of JUTLAND won him some praise and much censure. As first sea lord (1916–17) he opposed the introduction of convoys to combat the German submarine campaign and was dismissed by Lloyd George. He was (1920–24) governor general of New Zealand, and became an earl in 1925. He wrote *The Grand Fleet, 1914–16* (1919) and *The Crisis of the Naval War* (1921).

jelly and jam, gelatinous, sweet food prepared by preserving fresh fruits. Since most fresh fruits contain about 80% water and from 10% to 15% sugar, they are subject to fermentation. They may be preserved by adding sugar and reducing the water content. Almost any fresh fruit can be made into jam by mashing or slicing it fine, adding an approximately equal amount of sugar, and simmering until it reaches the proper concentration or gel at 218° to 222°F (103°–105°C). Preserves differ from jam in that the fruit retains its form. For jelly, only those fruits may successfully be used that contain a sufficient amount of PECTIN (the chief gelling substance) and acid. Among these are plums, apples, grapes, and quinces and such berries as currants, gooseberries, raspberries, blackberries, and cranberries. Pectin or GELATIN may be added to other fruits, such as peaches and strawberries, but the results do not equal the natural jellies. Jelly is made by extracting the juice of fresh, sound, barely ripe fruit, combining with sugar, and cooking. Excess heating dissipates the flavor and may hydrolyze the pectin. Too little sugar yields a tough jelly; too much, a sticky one. Too much acid may cause separation of liquid. The manufacture of jams and jellies is now largely commercial.

jellyfish, common name for the free-swimming stage (see POLYP AND MEDUSA), of certain invertebrate animals of the phylum CNIDARIA (the coelenterates). The body of a jellyfish is shaped like a bell or umbrella, with a clear, jellylike material filling most of the space between the upper and lower surfaces. A mouth is located in the center of the undersurface and tentacles dangle from the bell margin. Many jellyfish are colored, with pink or orange internal structures visible through the colorless or delicately tinted bell, and all are exquisitely designed; they are among the most beautiful of animal types. Typically, jellyfish catch their prey with the aid of stinging cells located in the tentacles; many jellyfish can cause irritating or even dangerous stings to humans. Food is carried by the tentacles to the mouth, then is moved into the stomach and is distributed to the body through radial canals. Jellyfish move up and down by contracting and relaxing the bell, using muscles that circle the bell margin; they are carried horizontally by waves and currents. Jellyfish of the class Hydrozoa are small, ranging from 1/8 in. (0.32 cm) to several inches in diameter, and usually have four tentacles. They have several (often four) unbranched radial canals and simple sense organs. In this group the polyp, or attached stage, is often larger and more conspicuous than the medusa. Jellyfish of the class Scyphozoa, sometimes called true jellyfish, are larger and often have numerous tentacles; they have branched radial canals and complex sense organs. In this group the medusa is the prominent form and the polyp is reduced to a small larval stage. Scyphozoan jellyfish are commonly 3/4 in. to 16 in. (2–40 cm) in diameter; *Aurelia,* the flattened jellyfish common along North American coasts, may be as much as 1 ft (30 cm) across. One species of *Cyanea* found in cold northern seas may reach 6 ft (1.8 m) across and have tentacles over 100 ft (30 m) long. Tiny *Craspedacusta,* a hydrozoan jellyfish less than 1 in. (2.5 cm) long, occurs in freshwater lakes and ponds, but all other jellyfish are marine, living in ocean depths as well as along the coasts. The hydrozoan *Physalia,* or Portuguese man-of-war, is actually a large colony of modified individuals, some medusalike and some polyplike; a large gas-filled sac acts as a float for the colony. The tentacles of such a colony may extend 60 ft (18 m) into the water and can cause severe injuries to swimmers. *Physalia* is usually bright blue, sometimes with tints of pink and orange. The purple sail, *Velella,* a floating colony 1 to 3 in. (2.5-7.5 cm) across, may be blue or purple. Jellyfish are classified in the phylum Cnidaria, classes Hydrozoa and Scyphozoa.

Jemappes (zhəmäp'), town (1970 pop. 12,455), Hainaut prov., S Belgium. It is a coal-mining center of the Borinage region. Manufactures include iron and steel. At Jemappes in 1792 the French under Dumouriez defeated the Austrians under Duke Albert of Saxe-Teschen in one of the first important battles of the French Revolutionary Wars. The victory opened the way to Brussels for the French.

Jemez (hā'mās), pueblo (1970 pop. 1,197), Sandoval co., central N.Mex., on the East Fork of the Jemez River. In the 16th cent. there were several Jemez pueblos, but by 1622 there were only two. One of the remaining pueblos was abandoned prior to the Pueblo revolt of 1680. The other took a prominent part in the revolt; the Jemez Indians attacked the Spanish repeatedly and even made war on those neighbors who remained loyal to the Spanish. In 1694 the pueblo was stormed and captured by the Spanish. Although the Jemez promised to remain at peace, they revolted (1696) and killed the missionaries. Expecting a Spanish attack, they fled into Navaho country, where they remained for several years. Finally some of the Indians returned and built (c.1700) the present village. The inhabitants are PUEBLO INDIANS of the Tonoan linguistic stock. Their principal feast is on Nov. 12, for San Diego (St. Didacus). See E. W. Parsons, *The Pueblo of Jemez* (1925).

Jemima (jēmī'mə), first daughter born to Job after his affliction. Job 42.14.

Jemison, Mary, 1743-1833, American frontierswoman. She was born at sea while her parents were en route from Ireland to America. In W Pennsylvania she was captured (1758) by a FRENCH AND INDIAN WAR party, taken to Fort Duquesne, and given to two Seneca women, who adopted her. She was married twice (to a Delaware and to a Seneca) and bore eight children. Known as the White Woman of the Genesee, Mary Jemison refused to leave the Senecas, and in 1817 New York confirmed her possession of a tract of land (given her in 1797) on the Genesee River. Her story is told in a classic tale of "Indian-capture," J. E. Seaver's *Narrative of the Life of Mrs. Mary Jemison* (1824; latest ed., 1967).

Jemuel (jēmyo͞o'əl), first son of Simeon. Gen. 46.10; Ex. 6.15. Nemuel: Num. 26.12; 1 Chron. 4.24.

Jena (yā'nä), city (1970 pop. 88,346), Gera district, S East Germany, on the Saale River. Manufactures of this industrial center include pharmaceuticals, glass, and optical and precision instruments (the Zeiss works, partly removed after 1945 by the Soviet occupation forces). Jena was known in the 9th cent. and was chartered in the 13th cent. The city passed to the house of Wettin in the 14th cent. and in 1485 passed to its Ernestine line. In 1806, Napoleon I decisively defeated the Prussians at Jena. The Univ. of Jena was founded in 1557-58 and reached its height in the late 18th and early 19th cent. At that time the dramatist Friedrich von Schiller, the philosophers Hegel, Fichte, and Schelling, and the poet August Wilhelm von Schlegel taught there. Schiller wrote the Wallenstein trilogy and Goethe wrote *Hermann und Dorothea* at Jena. Noteworthy structures in the city include the Church of St. Michael (13th cent.), a 15th-century city hall, and parts of the city's medieval fortifications.

Jena, University of, at Jena, East Germany; founded 1548 as an academy, became a university 10 years later. The school gained an international reputation in the 18th cent. when Friedrich Hegel, Johann Fichte, and Friedrich Schiller taught there. In 1934 the university's official name became the Friedrich Schiller University of Jena. It includes sections of Marxism-Leninism, physics of instrument construction, instrument technology, mathematics, chemistry, biology, philosophy and history, literature and art, languages, education, physical education, and medicine (including dentistry); faculties of theology (Protestant) and law; and institutes of classical studies and archaeology and history of medicine and natural science.

Jenghiz Khan or **Genghis Khan** (both: jĕng'gĭz, -'gĭs kän), Mandarin *Ch'eng-chi-ssu-han,* 1167?-1227, Mongol conqueror, originally named Temujin. He succeeded his father, Yekusai, as chieftain of a Mongol tribe and then fought to become ruler of a Mongol confederacy. After subjugating many tribes of Mongolia and establishing his capital at Karakorum, Temu-jin held (1206) a great meeting, the khuriltai, at which he accepted leadership of the Mongols and assumed his title. He promulgated a code of conduct and reorganized his armies. He attacked (1213) the Jurchen-ruled Chin empire of N China and by 1215 had occupied most of its territory, including the capital, Yenching (now Peking). From

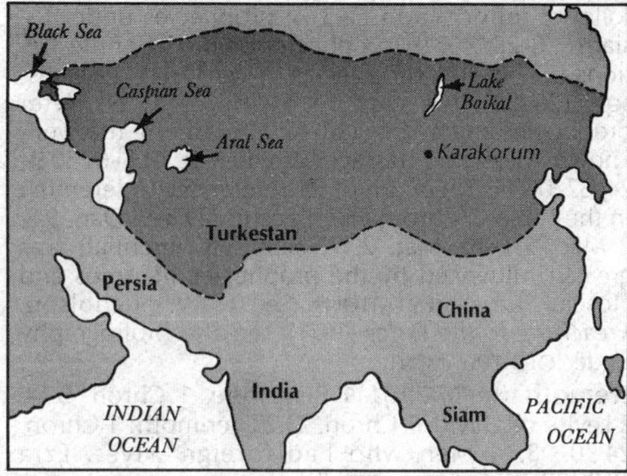

Empire of Jenghiz Khan (1227)

1218 to 1224 he conquered Turkistan, Transoxania, and Afghanistan and raided Persia and E Europe to the Dnepr River. Jenghiz Khan ruled one of the greatest land empires the world has ever known. He died while campaigning against the Jurchen, and his vast domains were divided among his sons and grandsons. His wars were marked by ruthless carnage, but Jenghiz Khan was a brilliant ruler and military leader. Tamerlane was said to be descended from him. See biographies by Harold Lamb (1927, repr. 1960), B. J. Vladimirtsov (1930, repr. 1969), Ralph Fox (1936, repr. 1962), René Grousset (tr. 1967), and R. P. Lister (1969); H. D. Martin, *The Rise of Chingis Khan and His Conquest of North China* (1950, repr. 1971).

Jenkins, John, 1728-85, American pioneer, b. probably Connecticut. In 1753, Jenkins explored the WYOMING VALLEY for the proposed Susquehanna Company. A settlement (1762) under his leadership was destroyed by the Indians, and in 1769, leading another group to the region, he founded Kingston. Jenkins lived there until the Wyoming Valley massacre (1778), then fled to Orange co., N.Y. After his retirement his son **John Jenkins** (1751-1827), b. New London, Conn., took his place as leader of the Connecticut settlers. During the American Revolution he took part in Gen. John Sullivan's punitive expedition against the Indians who had committed the Wyoming massacre. After the war Jenkins defended the Connecticut settlers in the Pennamite Wars and against Indian attacks. In 1786 he laid out the town of Athens, Pa.

Jenkins, Roy (Harris), 1920-, British politician. He entered the House of Commons in 1948 as a Labour member and soon became one of the most formidable debaters in Parliament. When the Labour party returned to power in 1964, he became minister of aviation. As home secretary from 1965 to 1967 he worked for broader laws against racial discrimination and played a large part in liberalizing the laws on abortion and homosexual activity. As chancellor of the exchequer from 1967 to 1970 he instituted a program of austerity in an effort to solve Britain's financial crisis. In 1971, in defiance of the Labour party majority, he supported Britain's entry into the Common Market. He subsequently (1972) resigned as deputy leader of the party but became (1974) home secretary in Harold Wilson's Labour government. He has written several books, including a biography of the Liberal leader Herbert Asquith.

Jenkinson, Robert Banks: see LIVERPOOL, ROBERT BANKS JENKINSON, 2D EARL OF.

Jenkins's Ear, War of, 1739-41, struggle between England and Spain. It grew out of the commercial rivalry of the two powers and led into the larger War of the AUSTRIAN SUCCESSION. The incident that gave the name to the war occurred in 1731 when Robert Jenkins, master of the ship *Rebecca,* claimed he had had his ear cut off by Spanish coast guards. English smuggling and resentment at exclusion from the Spanish colonial trade caused the war, but Jenkins's story in the House of Commons, reinforced by the showing of his ear, had tremendous propaganda effect and forced the reluctant Sir Robert WALPOLE to declare war. The hostilities with Spain up to 1741 were marked only by the naval engagements of Admiral Edward Vernon in the West Indies.

Jenks, Jeremiah Whipple, 1856-1929, American economist, b. St. Clair, Mich., grad. Univ. of Michigan, 1878 , Ph.D. Univ. of Halle, 1885. He was professor of political economy (1891-1912) at Cornell and from 1912 was professor of government at New York Univ. Interested especially in the political aspects of economic problems, he served frequently on government boards and commissions and made many reports on trust, currency, labor, and immigration problems. Out of these experiences came his authoritative books *The Trust Problem* (1900; 5th ed. 1929) and *The Immigration Problem* (with W. J. Lauck, 1911; 6th ed. 1925). As a financial expert he advised the governments of Mexico, Nicaragua, China, and Germany. He also wrote *Principles of Politics* (1909) and *Governmental Action for Social Welfare* (1910).

Jenné: see DJENNÉ, Mali.

Jenner, Edward, 1749-1823, English physician; pupil of John Hunter. His invaluable experiments beginning in 1796 with the vaccination of eight-year-old James Phipps proved that cowpox provided immunity against smallpox. His discovery was instrumental in ridding many areas of the world of a dread disease and laid the foundations of modern immunology as a science. See W. R. Le Fanu, *A Bio-bibliography of Edward Jenner, 1749-1823* (1951).

Jenney, William Le Baron, 1832-1907, American engineer and architect, b. Fairhaven, Mass. He studied at Harvard Scientific School and the École des Beaux-Arts. Later he learned engineering, constructed a railroad in Panama before the Civil War, and was chief engineer on General Sherman's staff in Georgia. The Home Insurance Building, 10 stories high, which he designed and built in Chicago (1883; since demolished), was the first in which both the floors and the exterior masonry walls were borne by a skeleton framework of metal. Although this structural system did not receive clear architectural expression, technically Jenney's building has come to be known as the first skyscraper.

Jennings, Herbert Spencer, 1868-1947, American zoologist, b. Tonica, Ill., B.S. Univ. of Michigan, 1893, Ph.D. Harvard, 1896. He was professor of zoology at Johns Hopkins (1906-10) and did research on genetics (especially heredity and variation in microorganisms) and on animal behavior there from 1910 to 1938 and from 1939 at the Univ. of California. His demonstration that physical and chemical stimuli produce responses in lower animals disproved the current belief that their behavior was controlled by will and intelligence. His works include *Behavior of the Lower Organisms* (1906), *The Biological Basis of Human Nature* (1930); and *Genetics* (1935).

Jennings, Sarah, duchess of Marlborough: see MARLBOROUGH, SARAH CHURCHILL, DUCHESS OF.

Jennings. 1 City (1970 pop. 11,783), seat of Jefferson Davis parish, SW La., on the Mermentau River; inc. 1888. **2** City (1970 pop. 19,379), St. Louis co., E Mo., a residential suburb adjacent to St. Louis; settled 1870, inc. 1946.

jenny: see ASS.

Jennys, family of American painters, fl. 1770-1810. Little is known of the Jennys family. William Jennys and his son Richard painted portraits in Massachusetts and Connecticut. These are classed as primitives in style, yet they exhibit sophisticated psychological understanding of the sitters. William Jennys's portraits of the Bacon family (1795) are in the Rockefeller Folk Art Collection, Williamsburg, Va.

Jensen, Johannes Vilhelm (yōhän'əs vĭl'hĕlm yĕn'sən), 1873-1950, Danish writer. As a young man he studied medicine; his interest in biology and anthropology is obvious throughout his works. Jensen created a distinctive literary form in his "myths," brief prose tales with an element of the essay. Selections have been translated as *The Waving Rye* (1959). His works, numbering more than 60 volumes, include essays, travel books, and lyrical poems. His epic novel cycle *The Long Journey* (6 vol., 1908-22; tr., 3 vol., 1923-24), a fantasy based on Darwinian theory, traces the story of man from primitive times to the age of Columbus. Jensen was awarded the 1944 Nobel Prize in Literature.

Jenson or **Janson, Nicolas** (both: nēkôlä' zhäN-sôN'), d. c.1480, Venetian printer, b. France. Jenson studied printing with Gutenberg at Mainz for three years. He was one of the first to design roman type, which was far superior in beauty and alignment of characters to that of JOHN OF SPEYER. He started publishing under his own name and with his own type in 1470 in Venice, producing numerous celebrated and beautiful editions. His roman type of 1470 furnished inspiration for Garamond, Caslon, William Morris, Bruce Rogers, and other masters. After his death, his type was used by the Aldine Press.

jeopardy, in law, condition of a person charged with a crime and thus in danger of punishment. At COMMON LAW a defendant could be exposed to jeopardy for the same offense only once; exposing a person twice is known as double jeopardy. Double jeopardy is prohibited in Federal and state courts by the Fifth and Fourteenth Amendments to the U.S. Constitution. The concept refers to an offense, not to an act giving rise to an offense; therefore, it is possible to try a person for multiple violations arising from a single act (e.g., assault, attempted murder, and carrying a deadly weapon). Jeopardy does not exist until the JURY is sworn in, or, if there is no jury, until evidence is introduced. The prohibition of double jeopardy does not preclude a second trial if the first court lacked jurisdiction (authority), if there was error in the proceedings, or if the jury could not reach a verdict. A similar principle, known as res judicata, operates in civil suits. It holds that once a civil case has been finally decided on the merits the same parties can not litigate it again.

Jephthae (jĕf'thē), Greek form of Jephthah.

Jephthah (jĕf'thə), son of Gilead and a judge of Israel. He vowed if victorious over his enemies to sacrifice the first of his household to greet him upon his return. His daughter and only child was the price of this vow. Judges 11;12. Jephthae: Heb. 11.32.

Jephunneh (jēfŭn'ē). **1** Father of Caleb. Num. 13.6. **2** Asherite. 1 Chron. 7.38.

Jequié (zhəkyĕ'), city (1970 pop. 100,411), Bahia state, E Brazil, on the Contas River. Cacao production and cattle breeding are the principal economic activities.

Jerah (jē'rə), descendant of Shem. Gen. 10.26; 1 Chron. 1.20.

Jerahmeel (jērä'mēĕl). **1** Descendant of Judah. 1 Chron. 2.9,25; 1 Sam. 27.10. **2** Levite. 1 Chron. 24.29. **3** Prince commanded by Jehoiakim to imprison Jeremiah. Jer. 36.26.

Jerash (jĕr'ăsh), ancient city: see GERASA.

Jerba (jĕr'bə) or **Jarbah** (jär'-), island (1966 pop. 62,445), 197 sq mi (510 sq km), SE Tunisia, in the Mediterranean Sea. Fruits are grown on the island, once identified as the land of the lotus eaters. It has extensive Roman remains.

jerboa (jərbō'ə), name for the small, jumping RODENTS of the family Dipodidae, found in arid parts of Asia, N Africa, and SE Europe. Jerboas have extremely long hind feet and short forelegs; they always walk upright or hop like kangaroos. A jerboa can hop faster than a person can run, and a single leap may carry it more than 6 ft (1.8 m). Jerboas have long silky fur, buff colored above and pale below; members of most species have a black face mask and tail tuft. They have large eyes and long ears. The combined head and body length is between 2 and 8 in. (5-20 cm), depending on the species; the tail is usually somewhat longer than the body. When the animal sits, the tail is used as a prop. Solitary, nocturnal animals, with a low tolerance for heat, jerboas spend the day in individual burrows with plugged entrances. In the northern parts of their range they hibernate; some jerboas of the true deserts aestivate. They feed on plant matter, especially seeds, and insects. They do not drink, but survive on water obtained from food or produced by their own metabolism. The similar appearing KANGAROO RAT and JUMPING MOUSE of North America are not of the same family as the jerboa. There are about 25 jerboa species, 22 of them in Asia. They are classified in 10 genera of the phylum CHORDATA, subphylum Vertebrata, class Mammalia, order Rodentia, family Dipodidae.

Jered (jē'rĕd). **1** Variant of JARED. **2** Judahite. 1 Chron. 4.18.

Jeremai (jĕrĕmā'ī), husband of a foreigner. Ezra 10.33.

Jeremiah (jĕrĭmī'ə). **1** Prophet of the book of JEREMIAH. **2** Father-in-law of Josiah. 2 Kings 23.31; Jer. 52.1. **3** Rechabite contemporary with Jeremiah the prophet. Jer. 35.3. **4, 5, 6** Three who joined David at Ziklag. 1 Chron. 12.4,10,13. **7** Manassite. 1 Chron. 5.24. **8, 9** Priests. Neh. 10.2; 12.1,12,34.

Jeremiah or **Jeremias** (jĕrĭmī'əs), book of the Old Testament, 24th in the order of the Authorized Version (AV), 2d of the books of the Major Prophets. It tells of the career of Jeremiah, a prophet who preached (c.628-586 B.C.) in Jerusalem under King Josiah and his successors. His message was a summons to moral reform, personal and social, backed by threats of doom. Jeremiah realistically opposed resistance to Babylon, and his insistence on unpalatable truths brought him to prison and the stocks. When Jerusalem fell to Babylon (586 B.C.), Jeremiah was allowed to stay with the Jews who remained; they took him to Egypt, where he continued prophesying. The prophecies of the book were arranged by the prophet's secretary, BARUCH. They are not in strict chronological order, and there are important differences in texts; thus there is good reason for believing that chapters 46-51 (AV) belong with chapter 25. One analysis of the book would be as follows: introduction (1-3.5); prophecies under Josiah (3.6-25; 4-24); prophecies against Gentile nations (25; 46-51); prophecies under Josiah's successors (26-38); the capture of the city (39); later prophecies and events (40-45; 52). Among the well-known Messianic passages are 14.8-9; 23.5-6; 30.9-24; 32.37-44. There are other references to Jeremiah in the Bible: 2 Chron. 35.25; Ecclus. 49.8-9; Dan. 9.2; 2 Mac. 2.1-10; Mat. 2.17; Heb. 8.8. Jeremiah was greatly influenced by the prophecies of Amos and Hosea. See LAMENTATIONS. See E. W. Nicholson, *Preaching to the Exiles* (1971); see also bibliography under OLD TESTAMENT.

Jeremoth (jĕr'ĭmōth). **1** Benjamite. 1 Chron. 8.14. **2** Levite of David. 1 Chron. 23.23. Jerimoth: 1 Chron. 24.30. **3, 4** Men who had foreign wives. Ezra 10.26,27. **5** See JERIMOTH **5.**

Jeremy (jĕr'ĭmē), English form of JEREMIAH. The **Epistle of Jeremy** is a title given to the sixth chapter of Baruch.

Jerez de la Frontera (hārāth dā lä frōntä'rä), city (1970 pop. 149,867), Cádiz prov., SW Spain, in Andalusia. Jerez is an important commercial center noted for its sherry and cognac. Its horses of mixed Spanish, Arab, and English blood are world famous. Captured by the Moors in 711, the city was recovered by Alfonso X of Castile in 1264. Of interest are its Gothic churches and an 11th-century Arabian alcazar.

Jeriah (jērī'ə), Kohathite Levite. 1 Chron. 23.19; 24.23. Jerijah: 1 Chron. 26.31.

Jeribai (jĕr'ĭbā), soldier of David. 1 Chron. 11.46.

Jericho (jĕr'ĭkō) [Heb.,=fragrant, or city of the moon god], ancient city, Palestine, in the Jordan valley N of the Dead Sea. The modern Ariha, Jordan, lies near the ancient site. Jericho was captured from the Canaanites by Joshua, according to the biblical account in Joshua 6, and was destroyed, an event several times repeated in its history. One of its conquerors was Herod the Great, who sacked and rebuilt it. Later it fell to the Muslims. Deut. 34.3; Joshua 18.21; 2 Sam. 10.5; 1 Kings 16.34; 2 Kings 2.4; 25.5; Jer. 39.5; 52.8; 1 Mac. 9.50; Mat. 20.29; Luke 10.30. Excavations of the mound of Tell es Sultan, the original site, were begun early in the 20th cent. and have revealed the oldest known settlement in the world, dating perhaps from c.8000 B.C. Because the town of Joshua was destroyed by erosion, scholars have been unable to fix the date of the conquest of Palestine but generally place it between 1400 B.C. and 1250 B.C. At the nearby site of Herodian Jericho, 2 mi (3.2 km) S of Tell es Sultan, a Hellenistic fortress and the palace of Herod have been excavated. See John Garstang and J. B. E. Garstang, *The Story of Jericho* (1948); K. M. Kenyon, *Digging Up Jericho* (1958) and *Excavations at Jericho,* Vol. 1 (1960).

Jericho, uninc. residential town (1970 pop. 14,010), Nassau co., SE N.Y., on Long Island.

Jeriel (jērī'ĕl, jĕr'ēĕl), chief Issacharite. 1 Chron. 7.2.

Jerijah (jērī'jə), variant of JERIAH.

Jerimoth (jĕr'ĭmōth). **1** Benjamite. 1 Chron. 7.7,8. **2** One who joined David at Ziklag. 1 Chron. 12.5. **3** Officer of David. 1 Chron. 27.19. **4** Son of David. 2 Chron. 11.18. **5** Levite of David. 1 Chron. 25.4. Jeremoth: 1 Chron. 25.22. **6** Levite of Hezekiah. 2 Chron. 31.13. **7** See JEREMOTH **2.**

Jerioth (jē'rĭōth), woman named in a genealogy. 1 Chron. 2.18.

Jeritza, Maria (yərĭt'sə), 1887–, Austrian-American soprano. b. Brünn (now Brno). After Jeritza's debut as Elsa in *Lohengrin* at Olmütz in 1910, she was a member (1912-35) of the Vienna State Opera. She created the title role in the opera *Ariadne* by Richard Strauss. Jeritza sang (1921-32) at the Metropolitan Opera, New York City, where her Tosca was renowned. See her autobiography (1924).

Jeroboam I (jĕrəbō'əm), first king of the northern kingdom of Israel. He was an Ephraimite and led a revolt against Solomon, inspired probably by the restlessness of N Palestine under southern rule. Jeroboam fled to Egypt when the plot failed but returned on the accession of Solomon's son, REHOBOAM. When the new king would not satisfy the northerners, Jeroboam led a secession, leaving the house of David only Judah and some of the area of Benjamin. Jeroboam became notorious for fostering idolatry in his kingdom of Israel. His capital was first in Shechem and later at Tirzah. Jeroboam was succeeded by his son Nadab. 1 Kings 11.26-14.20; 2 Chron. 10; 13.

Jeroboam II, king of Israel, son of Jehoash, whom he succeeded. His reign was marked by increasing prosperity and expansion northward, but also by corruption. Amos and Hosea appeared under Jeroboam. 2 Kings 14.16,23-29.

Jeroham (jērō'hăm). **1** Samuel's grandfather. 1 Sam. 1.1; 1 Chron. 6.27. **2** Priest. 1 Chron. 9.12; Neh. 11.12. **3** Father of a chief Danite. 1 Chron. 27.22. **4, 5** Benjamites. 1 Chron. 8.27; 9.8. **6** One of David's men. 1 Chron. 12.7. **7** Father of a captain of Jehoiada. 2 Chron. 23.1.

Jerome, Saint (jərōm', jĕr'əm), c.347-420?, Christian scholar, Father of the Church, Doctor of the Church. He was born in Stridon on the border of Dalmatia and Pannonia of Christian parents (although he was not baptized until 366); his Roman name was Sophronius Eusebius Hieronymus. He studied in Rome (c.359-363) under Aelius Donatus. After further study at Trier and Aquileia, he journeyed to the East. At Antioch, in 375, he experienced a vision in which Christ reproved him for his pagan studies. Renouncing his classical scholarship, he fled to the desert to live as an ascetic and to devote himself to scriptural studies, for which he learned Hebrew. In 378 he returned to Antioch, was ordained there the following year, and then went to Constantinople to study under St. Gregory Nazianzen. In 382, Jerome returned to Rome with Gregory, when Pope DAMASUS I asked them to help settle some Eastern problems; Jerome remained as papal secretary. He was acclaimed for his exposition of Scripture, and Damasus requested him to begin on a new version of the Bible. Jerome was spiritual adviser to a number of noble ladies leading conventual lives, among whom the most eminent was St. Paula. Jerome's outspoken criticism of the secular clergy, however, caused antagonism, and when Damasus died he returned East. From 386 to his death, Jerome worked in the monastery that Paula established for him in Bethlehem. There he did the bulk of revision of his Latin translations of the Bible. He also wrote commentaries on Ecclesiastes and the epistles of St. Paul, translated Origen's homilies, revised part of the Latin version of the Septuagint, and translated from the Hebrew Isaiah and other prophets, Psalms, Kings, and Job. Jerome's texts were the basis of the VULGATE. In 393 he wrote *De viris illustribus* [concerning illustrious men], biographies of 130 Christian writers. Other works include *Adversus Jovinianum* [against Jovinian], which praises virginity; a dialogue against the Pelagians; panegyrics on deceased friends (e.g., St. Paula); and brilliantly written letters, of which over 100 remain, which furnish a rare account of his time. His correspondence with St. Augustine, with whom he sometimes quarreled, is of particular interest. St. Jerome was involved in many theological and scholarly controversies, even with a long-established friend such as Rufinus. Collections of patristic literature have translations of many of his works. St. Jerome is buried in the Church of St. Mary Major in Rome. Feast: Sept. 30. See his letters (ed. by James Duff, 1942); Paul Monceaux, *St. Jerome: the Early Years* (tr. 1933); D. S. Wiesen, *St. Jerome as a Satirist* (1964).

Jerome, Jerome Klapka, 1859-1927, English humorist and playwright. His *Idle Thoughts of an Idle Fellow* (1886) and *Three Men in a Boat* (1889) gave him his reputation for genial humor. Of his dramatic works, *The Passing of the Third Floor Back* (1907), a contemporary morality play, was the most famous. See study by R. M. Favrot (1973).

Jerome, William Travers, 1859-1934, American lawyer, b. New York City. Prominent in the cause of reform, he served (1894-95) on the Lexow commission to investigate political corruption and managed (1894) the successful campaign of William L. Strong for reform mayor of New York City. He helped frame the legislation that created the court of special sessions (1894) and became (1895) justice of that court. As district attorney (1901-9) of New York co., Jerome led a continuous and independent campaign against crime and political corruption. Frequently he led surprise raids in person, notably the one against the gambling house of Richard CANFIELD. Jerome was the prosecutor in the trial of Harry K. Thaw for the murder of Stanford WHITE. See biography by Richard O'Connor (1963).

Jerome of Prague, c.1370-1416, Bohemian religious reformer. During his studies at Prague and at Oxford, Jerome was influenced by the doctrinal views of John WYCLIF. He continued to study and travel widely abroad, in constant conflict with the authorities. In 1407 he returned to Prague, where he joined forces with John HUSS in advocating Bohemian control of the Univ. of Prague and in opposing the papal bulls against Lancelot of Naples. When Huss was summoned before the Council of Constance (see CONSTANCE, COUNCIL OF), Jerome went there to defend him in 1415. Arrested while attempting to escape from the hostile churchmen, Jerome was brought back to Constance and imprisoned. After the burning of Huss, Jerome recanted his defenses of Huss and Wyclif, but his sincerity was doubted and he was not released. In 1416 he withdrew his recantation and was burned as a heretic.

Jerrold, Douglas William (jĕr'əld), 1803–57, English humorist and playwright. His plays *Blackeyed Susan* (1829) and *Time Works Wonders* (1845) were highly successful. Jerrold is best known, however, for his contributions to *Punch,* collected as *Punch's Letters to His Son* (1843) and *Mrs. Caudle's Curtain Lectures* (1846). From 1852 until his death he edited *Lloyd's Weekly Newspaper.* See study by R. M. Kelly (1972). His son, **William Blanchard Jerrold,** 1826–84, succeeded his father as editor of *Lloyd's* and was the author of plays, novels, and biographies of his father (1859) and George Cruikshank (1882).

Jersey, island (1971 pop. 72,532), 45 sq mi (117 sq km), in the English Channel, largest of the CHANNEL ISLANDS, which are dependencies of the British Crown. It is 15 mi (24 km) from the Normandy coast of France and SE of Guernsey. SAINT HELIER, the capital, is on St. Aubin's Bay. The mild climate (plants requiring subtropical conditions grow without protection), the moderate rainfall (30–35 in./76–89 cm), and the scenery have contributed to make Jersey, like other Channel Islands, a vacation resort. The soil is generally good, and large quantities of vegetables (especially potatoes, tomatoes, and broccoli) and fruits are raised; cattle raising and dairying (Jersey cattle) are important. The inhabitants are mostly of Norman descent; English, French (the official language), and a Norman dialect are spoken.

Jersey cattle, breed of dairy cattle native to the island of Jersey in the English Channel. Jerseys, smallest of the dairy breeds, are usually a shade of fawn or cream, although darker shades are common. The lighter colors are attributed to Norman ancestors, while the darker cattle are thought to have decended from breeds native to Brittany. Jerseys are adaptable to many environments and are now found throughout the world. They were first brought to the United States c.1850; among the dairy breeds they now rank second in number to HOLSTEIN-FRIESIAN CATTLE. Their milk has the highest butterfat content of any dairy breed, and when they are crossed with native stock or other breeds they usually transmit good milking qualities.

Jersey City, city (1970 pop. 260,545), seat of Hudson co., NE N.J., a port on a peninsula formed by the Hudson and Hackensack rivers and Upper New York Bay, opposite lower Manhattan; settled before 1650, inc. as Jersey City 1836. The second largest city in the state and its second most important commercial and industrial center (surpassed only by Newark), it is a port of entry and a great shipping and manufacturing center. With 11 mi (17.7 km) of waterfront and one of the world's densest concentration of railheads, it is a major transportation terminal point and distribution center. It has railroad shops, oil refineries, warehouses, and more than 600 plants manufacturing a great variety of products. The area was acquired by Michiel Pauw c.1629 as the patroonship of Pavonia. The Dutch soon set up the trading posts of Paulus Hook, Communipaw, and Horsimus. In 1674 the site came permanently under British rule. The fort at Paulus Hook was captured by Light-Horse Harry Lee under Washington's plan, Aug. 19, 1779. Bergen, nearby, was a stockaded Dutch village dating from before 1620 and had New Jersey's first municipal government, church (Dutch Reformed), and school (1662). Its site is marked today by Bergen Square. Jersey City was consolidated with Bergen and Hudson City in 1869 after various changes of title and boundaries. The town of Greenville was added in 1873. The city's industrial growth began in the 1840s with the arrival of the railroad and the improvement of its water transport system. In 1916, Jersey City docks were the scene of the Black Tom explosion that caused widespread property damage and was attributed to German saboteurs. The city was the birthplace and center of many of the political operations of Frank Hague. It has a modern medical center and is the seat of Jersey City State College and St. Peter's College. Of interest is J. E. Fraser's statue of Lincoln (1929) in Lincoln Park.

Jerubbaal (jĕr'əbāl): see GIDEON.

Jerubbesheth (jērŭb'ēshĕth): see GIDEON.

Jeruel (jēr''yo͞o'ĕl), unidentified wilderness, W of the Dead Sea. 2 Chron. 20.16.

Jerusalem, Heb. *Yerushalayim,* Arab. *Al Quds,* city (1972 pop. 304,500), capital of Israel. It is situated on a ridge 2,500 ft (760 m) high that lies W of the Dead Sea and the Jordan River. Jerusalem is an administrative, religious, and cultural center. Construction and tourism are the city's major industries. Manufactures include cut and polished diamonds, plastics, and shoes. The city is served by road, rail, and air transport. Jerusalem is the holy city for Jews, Christians, and Muslims. Often under the name of Zion, it figures familiarly in Jewish and Christian literature as a symbol of the capital of the Messiah. The eastern part of Jerusalem is the Old City, a quadrangular area built on two hills and surrounded by a wall completed in 1542 by Sulayman I. Within the wall are four quarters. The Muslim quarter, in the east, contains a sacred enclosure, the Haram esh-Sherif, within which, built on the old Mt. Moriah, are the Dome of the Rock (completed 691), or Mosque of Omar, and the Mosque of al-Aksa. In 1969 portions of al-Aksa were badly damaged by fire. The wall of the Haram incorporates the only extant piece of the Temple of Solomon; this, the western wall, or Wailing Wall, is a holy place for Jews. Nearby and SW of the Haram is the Jewish quarter, with several famous old synagogues. Largely destroyed in previous Arab-Israeli fighting, it was recaptured in 1967 by the Israelis, who began to rebuild and renovate it. To the W of the Jewish quarter is the Armenian quarter, site of the Gulbenkian Library. The Christian quarter occupies the northern and northwestern parts of the Old City. Its greatest monument is the Church of the Holy Sepulcher. Through the area runs the Via Dolorosa, where Jesus is said to have carried his cross. The New City, extending W and SW of the Old City, has largely developed since the 19th cent. It is the site of several educational institutions, as well as the Knesset (the Israeli parliament) and other government buildings. To the east of the Old City is the Valley of the Kidron, across which lie the Garden of Gethsemane and the Mount of Olives. To the north is Mt. Scopus, a Jewish intellectual center, which is the site of the Hadassah Medical Center and other branches of the Hebrew Univ. and the Jewish National Library. From 1948 to 1967, Mt. Scopus was an Israeli enclave in Arab territory. To the W and S of the Old City runs the Valley of Hinnom; this meets the Kidron near the pool of Siloam, which is next to the site of the original city of Jerusalem, now partly excavated and called the City of David (see OPHEL). Jerusalem's churches and shrines are innumerable. The traditional identifications vary in reliability from certainty (such as Gethsemane) to pious supposition (such as the Tomb of the Virgin). The most famous and most difficult identification is that of Calvary. Excavations have been made in Jerusalem since 1835, and after 1967 the Israelis increased this activity, uncovering remains of the Herodian period and ruins of a Muslim structure of the 7th or 8th cent. Despite the incomplete archaeological work, it is evident that Jerusalem was occupied as far back as the 4th millenium B.C. In the late Bronze Age (2000–1550 B.C.) it was a Jebusite (Canaanite) stronghold. DAVID captured it (c.1000 B.C.) from the Jebusites and walled the city. After SOLOMON built the Temple on Mt. Moriah in the 10th cent. B.C., Jerusalem became the spiritual and political capital of the Hebrews. In 586 B.C. it fell to the Babylonians, and the Temple was destroyed. The city was restored to Hebrew rule later in the 6th cent. B.C. by CYRUS THE GREAT, king of Persia. The Temple was rebuilt (538–515 B.C.; known as the Second Temple) by ZERUBBABEL, a governor of Jerusalem under the Persians. In the mid-5th cent. B.C., EZRA reinvigorated the Jewish community in Jerusalem. The city was the capital of the MACCABEES in the 2d and 1st cent. B.C. After Jerusalem had been taken for the Romans by POMPEY, it became the capital of the HEROD dynasty, which ruled under the aegis of Rome. The Roman emperor TITUS ruined the city and destroyed the Temple (A.D. 70) in order to punish and discourage the Jews. After the revolt of BAR KOKBA (132–35), HADRIAN rebuilt the city as a pagan shrine called Aelia Capitolina but forbade the Jews to live on the site. With the imperial toleration of Christianity (from 313), Jerusalem underwent a revival, greatly aided by St. Helena, who sponsored much building in the early 4th cent. Since that time Jerusalem has been a world pilgrimage spot. The Muslims, who believe that the city was visited by MUHAMMAD, treated Jerusalem well after they captured it in 637, making it their chief shrine after Mecca. From 688 to 691 the Dome of the Rock mosque was constructed. In the 11th cent. the FATIMIDS began to hinder Christian pilgrims; their destruction of the Church of the Holy Sepulcher helped bring on the CRUSADES. Jerusalem was conquered by the Crusaders in 1099 and for most of the 12th cent. was the capital of the Latin Kingdom of Jerusalem. In 1187, Muslims under SALADIN recaptured the city. Thereafter, under Mameluke and then Ottoman rule, Jerusalem was rebuilt and restored (especially by SULAYMAN I); but by the late 16th cent. it was declining as a commercial and religious center. In the early 19th cent. Jerusalem began to revive. The flow of Christian pilgrims increased, and churches, hospices, and other institutions were built. Jewish immigration accelerated (especially from the time of the Egyptian occupation of Jerusalem by MUHAMMAD ALI in 1832–41), and by 1900, Jews made up the largest community in the city. In 1917, during World War I, Jerusalem was captured by British forces under Gen. Edmund ALLENBY. After the war it was made the capital of the British-held League of Nations PALESTINE mandate (1922–48). As the end of the mandate approached, Arabs and Jews both sought to hold sole possession of the city. Christian opinion for the most part was strongly in favor of creating a free city safe for all religions. This view prevailed in the United Nations, which, in partitioning Palestine into Arab and Jewish states, declared that Jerusalem and its environs (including Bethlehem) would be an internationally-administered enclave in the projected Arab state. Even before the partition went into effect (May 14, 1948), fighting between Jews and Arabs broke out in the city. On May 28, the Jews in the Old City surrendered. The New City remained in Jewish hands. The Old City and all areas held by the Arab Legion were annexed by Jordan in Apr., 1949. Israel responded by announcing in Nov., 1949, that it would retain the area it held. On Dec. 14, 1949, the New City of Jerusalem was made the capital of Israel. In the Arab-Israeli War of 1967, Israeli forces took the Old City. Late in June of that year the Israeli government formally annexed the Old City and placed all of Jerusalem under a unified administration. Israel transferred many Arabs out of the Old City but promised access to the holy places there to people of all religions. Jerusalem is the seat of Hebrew Univ., the British School of Archaeology, the Dominican Fathers' Convent of St. Étienne, with the attached Bible School and French Archaeological School, the American College, the Greek Catholic Seminary of St. Anne, the Pontifical Biblical Institute, the Swedish Theological Institute, the Near East School of Archaeology, the Rubin Academy of Music, the Israel Academy of Sciences and Humanities, and the Israel Museum. See L. H. Cust, *Jerusalem* (1924); James Baikie, *Ancient Jerusalem* (1930); J. J. Simons, *Jerusalem in the Old Testament* (1952); A. N. Williams, *The Holy City* (1954); Michael Avi-Yonah, ed., *Jerusalem: The Saga of the Holy City* (1954); Teddy Kollek and Moshe Perlman, *Jerusalem: Sacred History of Mankind* (1968).

Jerusalem, Latin Kingdom of, feudal state created by leaders of the First Crusade (see CRUSADES) in the areas they had wrested from the Muslims in Syria and Palestine. In 1099, after their capture of Jerusalem, the Crusaders chose GODFREY OF BOUILLON king; he declined the title, preferring that of defender of the Holy Sepulcher, but with his election the kingdom may be said to have begun. His brother and successor, BALDWIN I, took the royal title. He and his successors were nominal overlords of the principality of Antioch and the counties of Edessa and Tripoli, which, with the royal domain of Jerusalem, constituted the great fiefs of the kingdom. Jerusalem itself contained the counties of Jaffa and Ashqelon, the lordships of Krak, Montreal, and Sidon, and the principality of Galilee. Coming into existence during the height of FEUDALISM, the kingdom was based on the purest forms of feudal theory. The kingship was elective, and the Assizes of Jerusalem, the law of the country, reflected the ideal feudal law. In practice, however, irregularities soon appeared, and the kings actually were chosen on dynastic considerations. The great feudal lords rarely felt bound to their overlord in the chronic struggles of the Latins among themselves and with the Mamelukes of Egypt, the Seljuk Turks, and the Byzantine emperors. The rise of the great military orders, the KNIGHTS TEMPLARS, the KNIGHTS HOSPITALERS, and the TEUTONIC KNIGHTS, as well as the intrusion of new Crusaders further undermined the royal authority. Edessa, captured by the Seljuks in 1144, was the first Latin state to fall to the infidel. The subsequent Crusades did not halt the Muslim advance, and in 1187 Jerusalem itself fell to Sultan SALADIN after his victory at Hattin. What remained of the Latin state was virtually destroyed by the complete rout of the Christians in the battle of Gaza (1244). The Crusades of Louis IX of France and Edward I of England were failures, and in 1291 Akko, the last Christian stronghold, fell. The kings of Jerusalem of the house of Bouillon were Baldwin I (reigned 1100–1118) and Baldwin II (reigned 1118–31). The crown then passed to the ANGEVIN dynasty, beginning (1131) with Fulk and ending (1186) with Baldwin V. Although it became an empty title, the kingship of Jerusalem continued nominally until the 20th cent. On Baldwin V's death the title passed to Guy of Lusignan and then to the successive husbands of Isabella, daughter of Amalric I: Conrad, marquis of Montferrat; Henry, count of Champagne; and Amalric II, king of Cyprus. In 1210, John of Brienne received the title, which passed (1225) to his son-in-law, Holy Roman Emperor Frederick II. After Frederick's death (1250) the title was held by various families who had a claim, notably the kings of Cyprus, the Angevins, and the houses of Lorraine and Savoy. The struggles of the Latin nobles of Jerusalem against the SARACENS have furnished the material for many chivalrous romances in subsequent ages, particularly for the poets of Renaissance Italy. See studies by D. C. Munro (1966), W. B. Stevenson (1968), Aharon Ben-Ami (1969), Meron Benvinistre (1970), and J. S. C. Riley-Smith (1973).

Jerusalem artichoke, tuberous-rooted perennial (*Helianthus tuberosus*) of the family Compositae (COMPOSITE family), native to North America, where it was early cultivated by the Indians. In this particular case the name Jerusalem is a corruption of *girasole* [turning toward the sun], the Italian name for SUNFLOWER, of which this plant is one species. The edible tubers are somewhat potatolike, but the carbohydrate present is inulin rather than starch, and the flavor resembles that of artichokes. Jerusalem artichoke is more favored as a food plant in Europe (where it was introduced in 1616) and China than in North America, where it is most frequently grown as stock feed. The inulin is valuable also as a source of fructose for diabetics. Jerusalem artichokes are classified in the division MAGNOLIOPHYTA, class Magnoliopsida, order Asterales, family Compositae.

Jerusalem cherry: see NIGHTSHADE.

Jerusalem thorn, name for various plants, particularly the CHRIST'S-THORN.

Jerusha or **Jerushah** (both: jērōō'shə), mother of King Jotham of Judah. 2 Kings 15.33; 2 Chron. 27.1.

Jervis, John, earl of St. Vincent (jär'vĭs, jûr'-), 1735–1823, British admiral. His most famous action as commander of the Mediterranean fleet was his defeat in 1797 of 27 Spanish ships off Cape St. Vincent with only 15 vessels. The victory was partly due to an unauthorized attack by Horatio NELSON and might have been more complete had Jervis realized the weakness of the enemy. However, it helped to reduce British concern at a time when a French invasion of Britain was threatened. Jervis received a peerage and pension. As first lord of the admiralty (1801–6), Jervis was especially concerned with the restoration of discipline and with problems of health and hygiene. He returned (1806–7) to a sea command until his health failed. See biographies by W. V. Anson (1913), O. A. Sherrard (1933), and W. M. James (1950).

Jervis Bay (jär'vĭs), sheltered inlet of the Pacific Ocean, 10 mi (16.1 km) long and 6 mi (9.7 km) wide, SE Australia. In 1915 the harbor and part of the coast were transferred to the federal government by New South Wales. Jervis Bay, connected by rail with Canberra, 85 mi (137 km) inland, then became the port of the landlocked Australian Capital Territory. The area around the bay is a popular summer resort.

Jesaiah (jēsā'yə). **1** Descendant of Zerubbabel. 1 Chron. 3.21. **2** Benjamite ancestor of Sallu. Neh. 11.7.

Jeshaiah (jēshā'yə). **1** Chief singer. 1 Chron. 25.3,15. **2** Tribal chief accompanying Ezra. Ezra 8.7. **3** Descendant of Moses. 1 Chron. 26.25. Isshiah: 1 Chron. 24.21. **4** Merarite who returned with Ezra. Ezra 8.19.

Jeshanah (jĕsh'ənə, jēshā'nə), unidentified town, probably N of Jerusalem. 2 Chron. 13.19.

Jesharelah (jĕshərē'lə), the same as ASARELAH.

Jeshebeab (jēshĕb'ēăb), chief priest of David. 1 Chron. 24.13.

Jesher (jē'shər), Caleb's son. 1 Chron. 2.18.

Jeshimon (jĕsh'ĭmŏn), desert, the Wilderness of Judah, between the hill country and the Dead Sea. Num. 21.20; 23.28; 1 Sam. 23.19,24; 26.1,3.

Jeshishai (jēshĭsh'ā), ancestor of Gadites of Gilead. 1 Chron. 5.14.

Jeshohaiah (jĕshōhā'yə), chief of a Simeonite family. 1 Chron. 4.36.

Jeshua or **Jeshuah** (both: jĕsh'yōōə) [Heb.,=God helps]. **1** See JOSHUA. **2** See JOSHUA **2.** **3** Head of a postexilic family. Ezra 2.6; Neh. 7.11. **4** Priestly family. 1 Chron. 24.11; Ezra 2.36; Neh. 7.39. **5** Head of a Levitical family. Ezra 2.40; 3.9; Neh. 10.9; 12.8. **6** Levite. 2 Chron. 31.15. **7** Unidentified town, S Palestine. Neh. 11.26.

Jeshurun (jĕshyōō'rən), affectionate name for Israel. Deut. 32.15; 33.5,26. Jesurun: Isa. 44.2.

Jesiah (jēsī'ə). **1** Ally of David at Ziklag. 1 Chron. 12.6. **2** See ISSHIAH.

Jesimiel (jĭsĭm'ēəl), Simeonite chief. 1 Chron. 4.36.

Jespersen, Otto (ŏ'tō yĕs'pərsən), 1860–1943, Danish philologist. Professor of English language and literature at the Univ. of Copenhagen and later rector there, Jespersen first earned a reputation for brilliant work in phonetics and later wrote widely used books on the English language and linguistics in general, notably *The Growth and Structure of the English Language* (1905), *A Modern English Grammar on Historical Principles* (in parts, 1909–31), *Language* (1922), *Philosophy of Grammar* (1924), and *Analytic Syntax* (1937).

jessamine: see JASMINE.

Jesse (jĕs'ē), in the Bible, the descendant of Rahab, the grandson of Boaz and Ruth and the father of David. He is therefore in the Gospel genealogy. Ruth 4.17–22; 1 Sam. 16.1–22; 17.12,58; 1 Chron. 2.12,13; Isa. 11.1,10; Mat. 1.5,6; Luke 3.32. Because Jesse was ancestor of the House of David, a custom of medieval artists was to represent the genealogy of Jesus as beginning from him: hence the Jesse window (as at Chartres, France, and at Wells, England), a favorite device in stained glass; hence also the epithet of the Virgin: Jesse's Root.

Jesselton: see KOTA KINABALU, Malaysia.

Jessore (jĕsōr'), city (1961 est. pop. 46,400), SW Bangladesh, on the Bhairab River. Modern Jessore, a market town for rice and sugar, also has rice and oilseed mills and celluloid and plastics industries. Michael Madhusudan College, an affiliate of Rajshahi Univ., is in the city.

Jessup, Philip Caryl, 1897–, American authority on international law, b. New York City, grad. Hamilton College, 1919, LL.B. Yale, 1924, Ph.D. Columbia, 1927. He was admitted (1925) to the bar, and from 1925 to 1961 he taught international law and diplomacy at Columbia. He served (1943) in the foreign relief and rehabilitation office in the Dept. of State and later was (1943–44) assistant secretary general of the United Nations Relief and Rehabilitation Administration and a delegate (1944) at the Bretton Woods monetary conference. Then he served (1948) in the UN General Assembly. He became (1948) U.S. delegate on the UN Security Council and took a leading part in the UN debate on the Berlin blockade. He was appointed a delegate to the UN General Assembly in 1951 and an alternate delegate in 1952. He resigned (Jan., 1953) and returned to his teaching duties at Columbia. He was later (1961–70) a judge of the International Court of Justice at The Hague. His works include a biography of Elihu Root (2 vol., 1938), *A Modern Law of Nations* (1948), *Controls for Outer Space* (1959), *The Price of International Justice* (1971), and *The Birth of Nations* (1974).

Jesui (jĕs'yōōī), the same as ISUI.

Jesuit: see JESUS, SOCIETY OF.

Jesuit Estates Act, law adopted in 1888 by the Quebec legislature, partly to indemnify the Society of Jesus for Jesuit property confiscated by the British during the period after the suppression (1773) of the society by Pope Clement XIV. The act caused a violent controversy in Canada, and Protestants generally demanded that it be disallowed; the federal government finally decided not to interfere with provincial legislation, and the act was allowed to stand.

Jesuit Relations, annual reports and narratives written by French Jesuit missionaries at their stations in New France (America) between 1632 and 1673. They are invaluable as historical sources for French exploration and Indian relations and also as a record of the various Indian tribes of the region before the influence of settlers and missionaries had changed them. Published originally in Paris in annual volumes, they were translated and edited by R. G. Thwaites (73 vol., 1896–1901). See bibliography by J. C. McCoy, *Jesuit Relations of Canada, 1632–1673* (1937, repr. 1973).

Jesurun (jĕsyōō'rən), variant of JESHURUN.

Jesus or **Jesus Christ,** in the beliefs of CHRISTIANITY, the Son of God, the second person of the TRINITY. According to traditional Christian interpretation, Jesus was God made man, wholly divine, wholly human; he was born to MARY, a virgin, and died to make ATONEMENT to God for man's sin; his resurrection from the dead provides man's hope for salvation. Christians believe that Jesus fulfilled Hebrew prophecies of the MESSIAH. The name *Jesus* is Greek for the Hebrew *Joshua,* a name meaning *Savior; Christ* is a Greek translation of the Hebrew *Messiah,* meaning *Anointed.* The primary sources for the life of Jesus are the four Gospels of Matthew, Mark, Luke, and John and the epistles of the NEW TESTAMENT (see the articles on the separate books, e.g., MATTHEW, GOSPEL ACCORDING TO SAINT; JOHN, epistles). The first three Gospels are chronological biographies, the last a biography in essay form; hence the first three harmonize, with variation of detail, while the fourth uses an order suitable to its purpose. There are many contradictions between one Gospel and another, the most important bearing on chronological issues such as the date of the Last Supper, which the first three place on the first day of Passover, while John places it before the feast. The epistles, mostly written contemporaneously with the Gospels, add very few other details. There are brief references to Jesus in non-Christian writers of the period, especially in Tacitus, Suetonius, Pliny the Younger, and Josephus (perhaps interpolated). The interest of these writers, however, was not in Jesus but in the Christians. Second-century Christian writers furnish material, some undoubtedly reliable. The apocryphal Gospels and the traditional sayings of Jesus are quite unreliable, although some, such as the Gospel of Thomas, shed light on the development of the Gospel tradition (see PSEUDEPIGRAPHA and AGRAPHA OF JESUS). The study of the historicity of Jesus was until the end of the 19th cent. impeded by two facts: his followers assumed his historicity and regarded study of it as superfluous; others assumed the Gospels to be a tissue of myth and refused to apply to the study of his life such scientific historical methods as were applied to the study of Muhammad. According to the Gospels, Jesus was born of Mary, wife of Joseph, a carpenter of Nazareth, Galilee, who had brought his wife to Bethlehem, his ancestral home, for the Roman tax-census. The Christian era is computed according to a 6th-century reckoning to begin with Jesus' birth, A.D. 1. The date is placed several years too late, for Jesus was probably born between 8 B.C. and 4 B.C. The month and day are unknown; CHRISTMAS (Dec. 25) was set as the feast several centuries later. According to the Gospels, wonderful events surrounded the birth of Jesus, particularly its annunciation to Mary by an angel (Mat. 1.18–25; Luke 1.26–56). In accordance with Jewish law Jesus was circumcised, his mother purified, and he was confirmed at the end of his boyhood (Luke 2.21–52). Jesus lived at a critical period in Jewish history. The Jews were restive under Roman rule as administered by the corrupt house of HEROD; the Temple and the religion were under the control of a party allied with the Herodians; and the provincials of Galilee and Judaea, always eager for the Messiah, looked for an immediate deliverance from Roman control. Some time before A.D. 30 an ascetic preacher drew attention in the Jordan valley by his call to repentance to prepare for the Messiah. This was JOHN THE BAPTIST. Among those he baptized was his cousin Jesus. Jesus went from his baptism into solitude, thence to emerge on a three-year mission. He was about 30 at this time. (Mat. 3; 4; Mark 1; Luke 3; 4; John 1.) Jesus went about as a wandering rabbi, accompanied by a small band of disciples (see APOSTLE) depending for their few needs largely on the charity of the people. The first and principal part of Jesus' mission was spent in Galilee. He apparently made a sensation in the country; the Gospels describe him as performing miracles of healing. His uncompromising demands on his hearers, repeated attacks on Pharisees and scribes, and his obvious preference for the company of social outcasts and the oppressed increased the popular enthusiasm. At the end of three years he set out with his disciples for Jerusalem for the Passover. Jesus' arrival there before the Passover was apparently marked by an outburst of messianic enthusiasm, and a day or so later, Jesus created a scene in the Temple by ousting the money-changers. The clique in power, whom he consistently upbraided, now felt they had to deal not only with a revolutionary preacher, but a violent reformer as well. So they induced one of his companions, JUDAS ISCARIOT, to betray him. Jesus ate a farewell supper (the Last Supper) with his disciples and went out of the city to pray in the garden of Gethsemane. There he was arrested. He was rushed to trial before the ecclesiastical court of the Sanhedrin. Jesus' claims to be the Messiah and the Son of God were taken as grounds to convict him of blasphemy, a crime in Jewish law worthy of death. The Roman governor, PONTIUS PILATE, who alone could order a man's death, tried to evade action, but he then yielded to the demand of Jewish authorities and delivered Jesus to be crucified. A sign was placed on the cross reading, "The King of the Jews." On the third day after his death, according to the Gospels, some women going to his tomb found it opened and the body of Jesus gone. An angel at the tomb told them that he had risen from the dead. Soon they saw him and talked with him, and his disciples (and others) met him as well. (Mat. 28; Mark 16; Luke 24; John 20; 21; 1 Cor. 15.3–8.) The Gospels end at this point, but the book of Acts tells how, 40 days after the Resurrection, he ascended into heaven in the sight of his disciples. The Christian calendar revolves around the life of Jesus; his principal feasts are (in the Western Church) the Annunciation (March 25), Christmas (Dec. 25) with its preparation in ADVENT, the Circumcision (Jan. 1), the EPIPHANY (Jan. 6), CANDLEMAS (Feb. 2), and the Transfiguration (Aug. 6). The EASTER cycle of movable feasts and fasts begins with LENT, which ends in HOLY WEEK; after Easter comes the Ascension. Sunday is the Christian weekly memorial of the Resurrection, and among Roman Catholics and Orthodox Eastern, Friday commemorates the Crucifixion. The original source for the life of Jesus is the New Testament; biblical archaeology and studies of early Palestine have uncovered nothing unequivocally related to Jesus himself. Biographies repeat the Bible stories from particular points of view; Ernest Renan's *Life of Jesus* (1864) is rationalistic and skeptical, Giovanni Papini's biography (1921) is sentimentally pious; Albert Schweitzer's *Quest of the Historical Jesus* (1906, tr. 1910) is brilliantly selective and makes use of the knowledge of early Palestine.

Jesus in Art. No documented portraits of Jesus have survived. In EARLY CHRISTIAN ART AND ARCHITECTURE he was symbolized by a monogram, a fish, or a lamb, or was represented as the Good Shepherd. In the 4th cent. Jesus was depicted as an idealized, beardless youth, but this figuration was gradually altered to that of a bearded ascetic, particularly in BYZANTINE ART (see also ICON). In medieval art he was represented as Judge or Ruler, or as the Infant Jesus, usually with the Madonna.

Jesus. 1 Son of Sirach, author of ECCLESIASTICUS. 2 or **Jesus Justus,** converted Jew in Rome. Col. 4.11. 3 Hero of the book of JOSHUA.

Jesus, Society of, religious order of the Roman Catholic Church. Its members are called Jesuits. St. IGNATIUS OF LOYOLA, its founder, named it *Compañía de Jesús* [Span.,=(military) company of Jesus]; in Latin it is *Societas Jesu* (abbr. S.J.). The largest single religious order, it is characterized by a highly disciplined organization, especially devoted to the pope and ruled by its general, who lives in Rome. Jesuits have no choral office; like the secular clergy they are under obligation to individually recite the divine office each day. They have no distinctive habit. In principle they may accept no ecclesiastical office or honor. Jesuit training is famous and may last for more than 15 years. The novice spends two years in spiritual training, after which he takes the simple vows of the regulars—chastity, poverty, and obedience. Then as a scholastic he spends 13 years and sometimes longer in study and teaching, completed by an additional year of spiritual training. Toward the end of this period he is ordained and becomes a coadjutor. He may then take a fourth vow of special obedience to the pope and become professed. The society had its beginnings in the little band of six who together with St. Ignatius took vows of poverty and chastity while students at Paris. Their first plan was to work for the conversion of Muslims. Unable to go to the Holy Land because of the Turkish wars, they went to Rome and received ordination. Their constitution was approved by Pope Paul III (1540), and St. Ignatius was made (1541) general. The order then immediately began to expand. The society has distinguished itself in three principal fields: foreign missions, schools, and studies in the sciences and humanities. One of the most brilliant of all foreign missionaries was St. FRANCIS XAVIER (see also MISSIONS); his work in the East was continued by a host of Jesuits. The mission in Japan was wiped out by persecution in the early 17th cent., but when Japan was reopened to the West in the 19th cent. a number of Christians were found there, descendants of these martyrs. The most distinguished early figures of the Chinese mission were Fathers Matteo Ricci, Adam Schall, and Ferdinand Verbiest in the 17th cent.; a characteristic of their mission was their popularity at court, where they were revered as men of wisdom and science. There were persecutions and martyrdoms, but the original Jesuit foundation became the nucleus of the Roman Catholic Church in that country. The Indian mission began under the aegis of the Portuguese in Goa, whence it spread over the country; one of the most remarkable Jesuits in this mission was Robert de' Nobili, who, after arduous asceticism and study, won recognition as an equal of the Brahmans. The Jesuits worked all over Latin America; among their number was St. PETER CLAVER. The most remarkable missions were in Paraguay. In French North America the Jesuits came frequently into rivalry with the government and the other clergy; their missions among the Huron were especially successful, and they made headway among the Iroquois. The "Black-Robes," as the Indians called them, traveled as far afield as Oregon. Some of these Jesuits died as martyrs for their faith (c.1640); six of them have been canonized together, with two of their lay helpers, as the Jesuit Martyrs of North America (feast: Sept. 26). The JESUIT RELATIONS is a firsthand account of Jesuit work in New France. The suppression of the order in Canada in 1791 and its later readmission as a teaching order led to the JESUIT ESTATES ACT. In Europe the Jesuits were a major force in the Catholic Reformation. They sought to reclaim Protestant Europe for the church and to raise the spiritual tone of the Catholic countries. They enjoyed considerable success in W and S Germany, France, Hungary, and Poland. In nearly every important city the Jesuits established schools and colleges, and for 150 years they were leaders in European education. One of their boldest efforts was the English mission of 1580, distinguished by Saint Edmund CAMPION. Another celebrated English Jesuit was Robert Southwell. The Jesuits eventually became the object of criticism from vested ecclesiastical interests in every Catholic state. The Gallican party in France, being antipapal, was naturally anti-Jesuit. The polemics of Blaise Pascal and the Jansenists against Jesuit casuistry and alleged laxity in confessional practice were damaging. Through their loyalty to papal policies, the Jesuits were drawn into the struggle between the papacy and the Bourbon monarchies. Before the middle of the 18th cent. a combination of publicists (including Voltaire) and the absolute monarchs of Catholic Europe undertook to destroy them. In 1759 the Jesuits were expelled from Portugal and its colonies, France suppressed them in 1764, and in 1767 the Spanish dominions were closed to them. Pope Clement XIII denounced these acts, but, in 1773, CLEMENT XIV, under the coercion of the Bourbon monarchs and of some of his own cardinals, dissolved the order, and the Society of Jesus ceased to exist in the Catholic world. Frederick the Great and Catherine the Great refused to publish the brief suppressing them, and the Jesuits continued to exist in Prussia and Russia, especially as educators. As the 18th cent. drew to a close Catholic Europe, especially Italy, began to ask for restoration of the Jesuits, and, in 1814, Pius VII reestablished them as a world order. Today the society numbers over 31,000 members; in the United States, where there were approximately 5,000 Jesuits in 1973, there are many Jesuit schools and colleges (e.g., Georgetown, Fordham, and St. Louis universities). The order has a tradition of learning and science; e.g., the BOLLANDISTS are Jesuits, and Jesuits have made a specialty of the study of earthquakes. Pierre TEILHARD DE CHARDIN is the most famous Jesuit scientist of this century. Among the great organizers and theologians of the order are St. FRANCIS BORGIA, Claudio AQUAVIVA, Saint Robert BELLARMINE, Luis MOLINA, and Francisco SUÁREZ. See T. A. Hughes, *History of the Society of Jesus in North America* (3 vol., 1907–17, repr. 1970); T. J. Campbell, *The Jesuits, 1534–1921* (1921, repr. 1971); James Brodrick, *Origin of the Jesuits* (1940, repr. 1971) and *Progress of the Jesuits* (1947); Theodore Maynard, *Saint Ignatius and the Jesuits* (1956); T. J. M. Burke, ed., *Beyond All Horizons* (1957); Christopher Hollis, *History of the Jesuits* (1968); W. V. Baugert, *A History of the Society of Jesus* (1972).

Jesus Island or **Île-Jésus,** Que., Canada: see LAVAL.

Jesus Justus: see JESUS 2.

jet, black variety of lignite. Compact and homogeneous, it takes a good polish and is easily made into beads and other ornaments. The chief source of the world's supply is Yorkshire, England, although commercially valuable deposits exist in several countries, notably the United States, Spain, France, and Germany. Imitations of jet include anthracite, black glass, and black quartz.

Jether (jē'thər). 1 Eldest of Gideon's sons. He was killed by his brother Abimelech. Judges 8.20; 9. 2 Husband of David's sister Abigail. 1 Kings 2.5,32; 1 Chron. 2.17. Ithra: 2 Sam. 17.25. 3, 4 Judahites. 1 Chron. 2.32; 4.17. 5 Descendant of Asher. 1 Chron. 7.38. See ITHRAN 1.

Jetheth (jē'thĕth), duke of Edom and descendant of Esau. Gen. 36.40; 1 Chron. 1.51.

Jethlah (jĕth'lə), unidentified town of Dan, NW of Jerusalem. Joshua 19.42.

Jethou: see CHANNEL ISLANDS.

Jethro (jĕth'rō), Midianite priest of the peninsula of Sinai who was the companion and father-in-law of Moses. Ex. 2.21; 3.1; 4.18; 18. Reuel: Ex. 2.18. Raguel: Num. 10.29. Hobab: Judges 4.11. Hobab is given once as the name of a brother-in-law of Moses. Num. 10.29.

jet propulsion, propulsion of a body by a force developed in reaction to the ejection of a high-speed jet of gas. In the combustion chamber of a jet propulsion engine the combustion of a fuel mixture generates expanding gases, which escape through an orifice to form the jet. Newton's third law of motion requires that the force which causes the high-speed motion of the jet of gas have a reaction force that is equal in magnitude and oppositely directed to push on the jet propulsion engine. Hence the term "reaction motor" is often applied to jet-propulsion engines. The first reaction engine, the aeolipile, was constructed by the inventor Heron of Alexandria. Developments through the centuries have resulted in two general types of reaction machines, the true ROCKET and the airstream engine, commonly known as the jet engine. Unlike a jet engine, a rocket engine carries with it chemicals that enable it to burn its fuel without drawing air from an outside source. Thus a rocket can operate in outer space, where there is no atmosphere. Fritz von Opel, a German automobile manufacturer, made the first flight entirely by rocket power in 1939. The American R. H. GODDARD did much of the important pioneer work in modern rocket development. The

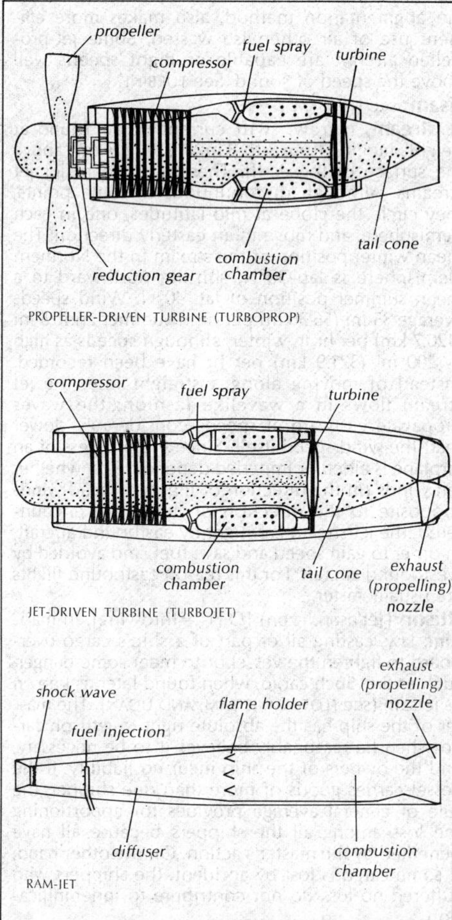

Types of jet engines: In the propeller-driven turbine a stream of high-velocity gases provides the power to drive the turbine and turn the propeller. In the jet-driven turbine the stream of gases is ejected through exhaust nozzles to provide propulsion. In the ram-jet the forward motion of the engine at high speeds compresses the entering air so that a separate compressor is not necessary.

second category of jet-propulsion motor, the jet engine, is a development of the late 18th-century gas turbine engines, which directed the combustion gases against the blades of a turbine wheel. Not until 1908 was it suggested that an aircraft could be driven by jet propulsion. René Lorin, a French engineer, proposed using the reciprocating engine to compress air, mix it with fuel, and thus propel the aircraft by the pulses of hot gas produced by combustion of the mixture. In 1939 the English engineer Frank WHITTLE developed a jet engine that powered a full-sized aircraft, and a year later Secundo Campini in Italy flew for 10 min with a thermal jet engine. Both of their machines had the four basic parts of a jet engine—compressor, turbine, combustion chamber, and propelling nozzles. Air is compressed and led through chambers where its volume is increased by the heat of fuel combustion. On emergence it spins the compression rotors, which act on the inflow of air. Intermittent duct jet propulsion does not operate with a continuous blast, as does the thermal jet, but proceeds by a series of pulses, or intermittent explosions. The ram-jet, or continuous duct, engine relies on its own forward motion to compress the air that enters it. It can be used only as an auxiliary power supply because its action commences only after sufficient speed has been attained. Jet-propelled aircraft have almost completely replaced propeller-driven types in all cases where high speed is desirable, as in long-range commercial airliners. Thrust-augmentation methods used to increase, at given moments, the effective driving force of jet engines are the afterburner, the water-injection, and air bleed-off methods. The afterburner method uses the exhaust gases from the engine for additional combustion with resulting higher compression; however, it consumes large amounts of fuel. The introduction of water into the air-compressor inlet also increases the thrust but can be used only at take-off because of the high water consumption. The air bleed-off, sometimes called the fan augmentation method, also makes more efficient use of air otherwise wasted. Some jet-propelled aircraft are capable of flight speeds well above the speed of sound. See TURBINE.

jetsam: see FLOTSAM.

jet stream, narrow, swift current of air found at heights ranging from 7 to 8 mi (11.3–12.9 km) above the surface of the earth. There are two major jet streams. Although discontinuous at some points, they circle the globe at mid-latitudes, one in each hemisphere, and move in an easterly direction. The mean winter position of the stream in the Northern Hemisphere is lat. 30°N, shifting northward to a mean summer position of lat. 40°N. Wind speeds average 35 mi (56.3 km) per hr in summer and 75 mi (120.7 km) per hr in winter, although speeds as high as 200 mi (321.9 km) per hr have been recorded. Instead of moving along a straight line, the jet stream flows in a wavelike fashion; the waves propagate eastward at speeds considerably slower than the wind speed itself. Since the progress of an airplane is aided or impeded depending on whether tail winds (in the direction of flight) or head winds (opposite to the direction of flight) are encountered, the jet stream is sought by eastbound aircraft, in order to gain speed and save fuel, and avoided by westbound aircraft. For this reason eastbound flights are usually faster.

jettison (jĕt'əsən, –zən) [O.Fr.,=throwing], in maritime law, casting all or part of a ship's cargo overboard to lighten the vessel or to meet some danger, such as fire. Such cargo, when found later, is known as jetsam (see FLOTSAM, JETSAM, AND LIGAN). The master of the ship has the absolute right to jettison cargo when he reasonably believes it to be necessary, and the owners of the ship incur no liability. If the vessel carries goods of more than one shipper, the rule of general average provides for apportioning the loss among all the shippers because all have benefited by the master's action. On the other hand, if some cargo is lost by accident, the shippers who suffered no loss do not contribute to indemnification.

jetty: see COAST PROTECTION.

Jetur (jē'tər), son of Ishmael, eponymous founder of Ituraea. 1 Chron. 1.31.

Jeuel (jo͞o'ĕl), chief of Judah. 1 Chron. 9.6.

Jeush (jē'əsh). **1** Son of Esau. Gen. 36.5,14,18; 1 Chron. 1.35. **2** Head of a Benjamite family. 1 Chron. 7.10. **3** Gershonite Levite. 1 Chron. 23.10,11. **4** Son of Rehoboam and Abihail. 2 Chron. 11.18,19.

Jeux Floraux, Académie des (äkädāmē' dā jö flôrō') [Fr.,=academy of floral games], one of the oldest known literary societies. It was founded (c.1323) at Toulouse, France, by seven troubadours to uphold the traditions of courtly lyricism. It promulgated (c.1355) a code of poetry known as the laws of love. With the decay of troubadour tradition, its literary contest (established 1324 and held in modern times in Toulouse on May 3) began to change. In place of LANGUE D'OC, French became, after 1539, the sole language of contributions. The society received its present title from Louis XIV in 1694. The group supported romanticism; 19th-century winners of its traditional golden flower included Chateaubriand and Hugo. In 1895, on the urging of Frédéric Mistral, *langue d'oc* was readmitted on a par with French in its contests.

Jeuz (jē'əz), chief Benjamite. 1 Chron. 8.10.

Jevons, William Stanley (jĕv'ənz), 1835–82, English economist and logician. After working in Australia as assayer to the mint, he taught at Owens College, Manchester, and University College, London. His major contribution to economics was his theory of utility; Jevons held that value was determined by utility, and he demonstrated the relationship in mathematical terms. *The Theory of Political Economy* (1871) was his chief theoretical work. His practical application of economics in *The Coal Question* (1865) influenced government action. His several texts include *Pure Logic* (1863) and *The Principles of Science* (1874). See his *Letters and Journal* (ed. by his wife, 1886); study by E. W. Eckard (1940).

Jewel Cave National Monument: see NATIONAL PARKS AND MONUMENTS (table).

jewelry, personal adornments worn for ornament or utility, to show rank or wealth, or to follow superstitious custom or fashion. The most universal forms are the necklace, bracelet, RING, PIN, and EARRING. Its use antedates clothing, and it has been made of a variety of materials including berries, nuts, seeds, perforated stones, feathers, hair, teeth, bone, shells, ivory, and metals. Although bronze and silver have been used by primitive peoples and in modern handwrought jewelry, gold has been the preferred metal. Jewelry has been decorated by engraving, embossing, etching, and filigree, and by application of enamel, mosaic, GEMS, semiprecious stones, and glass. The art reached an elaborate development in the Orient with its wealth of precious stones and pearls. Egyptian relics show a rare craftsmanship. The jewelry is largely emblematic, very colorful, and displays lotus flower and scarab motifs. Beads were used extensively, as in broad collars, and were often used for bartering. Armlets and anklets were also worn. The Greeks were highly expert goldsmiths and preferred exquisitely wrought ornaments of metal unadorned with color. After 400 B.C. precious stones were set in gold; later the cameo was used. Roman jewelry, although based on Greek and Etruscan forms, was massive and valued rather for precious stones and cameos than for artistic settings. Ropes of pearls were especially prized. Byzantine jewelry, influenced by the East and lavish in color and design, was of composite Greek and Roman styles. Jewelry of the Middle Ages was massive; large brooches and girdles predominated. Amber was worn as a protection against evil spirits. After 1300 glass beads were used. The Renaissance brought a transformation in the art of the jeweler; noted artists and architects often designed or even rendered pieces of jewelry. Jewelry was splendid with enamel and precious stones; heavy gold link chains, jeweled collars, and the necklace with pendant were worn by both men and women. Jewelry, worn to excess, became overcrowded with stones, to the neglect of the design and setting. By the late 17th cent. the goldsmith and enameler gave way before the lapidary and mounter. A process of making imitation pearls was first discovered in 1680; thereafter, ropes of pearls became highly popular for women. In the late 18th cent. the fashion for decorative buttons, watches, and snuff boxes almost superseded the wearing of jewelry. After 1800 the bracelet, which had dwindled (c.1500) in importance with the ruffed and cuffed long sleeve, was again in favor. The 19th cent. also saw the revival of the cameo and the introduction of the watch and chain and sets of jewelry. With the introduction of factory-made ornaments, artistry of workmanship declined. In the 20th cent. platinum became popular for settings; costume jewelry, which followed the rapidly changing fashions in dress, was introduced (by Gabrielle Chanel), as was the wristwatch. There was a renewal of enthusiasm for handwrought pieces during the craft revival of the 1960s in the United States. See Frances Rogers and Alice Beard, *5,000 Years of Gems and Jewelry* (1940); Graham Hughes, *Modern Jewelry: 1890–1963* (1963); Joan Evans, *A History of Jewelry: 1100–1870* (2d ed. 1970); Anita Mason, *An Illustrated Dictionary of Jewellery* (1974).

jewelweed, common name for the Balsaminaceae, a family of widely distributed annual and perennial herbs. The principal genus is *Impatiens,* so named because of the sudden bursting of the seed capsules when touched. It is found in tropical and north temperate regions and is especially abundant in the mountains of India and Sri Lanka (Ceylon). A few species are commonly cultivated as ornamentals, e.g., the garden balsam (*I. balsamina*). *I. noli-me-tangere,* ranging from Europe to Japan, is the species most often called touch-me-not. The native American species (two in the East and three in the far West) are known as jewelweeds, snapweeds, and touch-me-nots, the names being used interchangeably and sometimes applied to the whole genus. They grow in damp, shady places. The orange or yellow flowers dangle from the branches and have spurs filled with nectar that attracts bumblebees and hummingbirds. The orange sap is a traditional remedy for poison ivy and has also been used as a dye. Water on the leaves produces a silvery sheen that gives these plants the local name silverleaf. The jewelweed family is classified in the division MAGNOLIOPHYTA, class Magnoliopsida, order Geraniales.

Jewett, Charles Coffin (jo͞o'ĭt), 1816–68, American librarian, b. Lebanon, Maine. Jewett prepared his first catalog of books as librarian of Andover Theological Seminary. He was appointed librarian of Brown Univ. in 1841, where he rearranged and cataloged that library by subjects. In 1848 he became librarian of the Smithsonian Institution. There he published a survey of U.S. libraries and started mechanical duplication of individual catalog entries. As superintendent of the Boston Public Library from 1858 to 1865, Jewett worked out catalog rules which were adopted internationally.

Jewett, Sarah Orne, 1849–1909, American novelist and short-story writer, b. South Berwick, Maine. As a child she accompanied her father, a physician, on his country visits and became well acquainted with the countryside and its people. Her studies of small-town New England life are perceptive, sympathetic, and gently humorous. After contributing to periodicals, she published her first collection of stories and sketches, *Deephaven,* in 1877. It was followed by such collections as *The King of Folly Island* (1888) and her masterpiece, *The Country of the Pointed Firs* (1896). Her novels include *The Marsh Island* (1885) and *The Tory Lover* (1901); her best-known novel, *A Country Doctor* (1884), relates the conflicts of a woman physician. See her letters (ed. by Richard Cary, rev. ed. 1967); biography by F. O. Matthiessen (1929, repr. 1965); studies by Richard Cary (1962) and Richard Cary, ed. (1973).

jewfish: see GROUPER.

Jewish Autonomous Oblast or **Birobidzhan** (bērōbējän'), autonomous region (1970 pop. 173,000), c.13,800 sq mi (35,700 sq km), Khabarovsk Kray, Far Eastern USSR, in the basins of the Biro and Bidzhan rivers, tributaries of the Amur. The capital is Birobidzhan. The region is bounded on the south by Mongolia and on the north by the Bureya and Khingan mts., which yield gold, tin, iron ore, and graphite. Mining, agriculture (chiefly carried on in the Amur plain), lumbering, and light manufacturing are the major economic activities. Formed in 1928 to give Soviet Jews a home territory and to increase settlement along the vulnerable borders of the Soviet Far East, the region was raised to the status of an autonomous oblast in 1934. Russians and Ukrainians outnumber the Jewish inhabitants, however, and the harsh climate has discouraged settlement. Despite some remaining Yiddish influences, Jewish cultural activity in the oblast has declined since an anti-Semitic campaign launched in the late years of Stalin's rule.

Jewish literature: see HEBREW LITERATURE; Yiddish language.

Jewish liturgical music. The Bible and the Talmud record that spontaneous music making was common among the ancient Jews on all important occasions, religious and secular. Hebrew music was both instrumental and vocal. Singing was marked by responsorial and antiphonal forms, and singing and dancing were accompanied by instruments. The first instruments mentioned in the Bible are the kinnor, evidently a lyre similar to the KITHARA and the *ugab,* possibly a vertical flute. Other instruments, more of ceremonial than of musical value, included the *hasosra,* a trumpet, and the *shofar,* a ram's or goat's horn, the least musical of all and the only one still in use. When the kingdom of Israel was established, music was developed systematically. The part played by music in the Temple was essential and highly developed. New instruments were the nevel, a harp; the *halil,* possibly a double oboe; the asor, a 10-stringed instrument probably like a psaltery; and the *magrepha,* an instrument of powerful sound, used to signal the beginning of the service. Various types of cymbals originally used in the Temple were prohibited after its restoration. Ritual music was at first only cantillation, i.e., recitative chanting, of the prose books of the Bible; later the prayers and biblical poetry were chanted, presumably in a modal system similar to the ragas of Hindu music or the *maqamat* of Arab music, i.e., melodies with improvisations. After the destruction of Jerusalem under Roman rule in A.D. 70, much of the chant was preserved among congregations of Oriental Jews and remains intact today, but the instrumental music was lost when the dispersed peoples, as an act of mourning, ceased playing instruments. A system of mnemonic hand signs for traditional chant had been developed in the Temple, and this after the Dispersion became the base for the development of a system of notation. In the 9th cent., Aaron ben Asher of Tiberias perfected the *te'amim,* or *neginoth,* a system of accent signs. His notation superseded all other systems and influenced the development of the earliest Christian neumes, which became a precise system while the *te'amim* retained their vague character (see MUSICAL NOTATION). With the growth in importance of the synagogue came the rise of the chazan, or CANTOR. Among the Sephardic Jews in Arab-dominated Spain, Arab music had great influence and was introduced into the synagogue. Later the Ashkenazim (Jewish communities that had their original European base in Germany) accepted some of the melodic forms of German folk song and Italian court song; this adaptation was more or less successfully opposed by traditionalists who reintroduced elements from the song of the Oriental Jews. The post-Renaissance cantors developed a distinct type of coloratura, which was popular in 17th-century Europe. In the early 19th cent., instruments were introduced into some German synagogues, and other changes resulted from adaptations of Christian music. In the reform movement of the 19th cent., the cantor was eliminated, the organ was employed, and Jewish hymns were written in the vernacular and often set to tunes of Protestant hymns. Reaction against this movement brought a more moderate reform in which the Viennese cantor Salomon Sulzer (1804-90) was an outstanding figure. Sulzer aimed to restore the traditional cantillation, but without improvisation, and to make use of new music composed for the synagogue. He used the organ and included hymns in the vernacular. Sulzer's compositions, together with those of Louis Lewandowski (1821-94), another great reformer and the leading cantor of his day in Berlin, formed the basis of much modern synagogue music. In Eastern Europe, Hasidic influence was felt from the late 18th cent. Two major Eastern European composers of traditional music were the Russian cantors Eliezer Gerowitch (1844-1914) and David Nowakowsky (1849-1921). In the United States, the reform synagogues make extensive use of hymns, mixed choirs and soloists, and organ compositions. There is a cantor in modern orthodox and conservative services but the organ is used only in some conservative services. Several 20th-century musicians, notably Ernest BLOCH and Gershon Ephros, have composed new works for the reformed and traditional services, respectively. See Eric Werner, *The Sacred Bridge* (1959); A. Z. Idelsohn, *Jewish Music in its Historical Development* (1967); A. M. Rothmüller, *The Music of the Jews* (tr. 1954, rev. ed. 1967); Alfred Sendrey, *Music in Ancient Israel* (1969).

Jews [from Judah], originally descendants of Judah, the fourth son of Jacob, whose tribe, along with that of his half brother Benjamin, made up the kingdom of Judah; the term later came to designate followers of the religion JUDAISM. Before World War II the Jewish population, scattered over the world, amounted to about 16 million; it is estimated that some 6 million Jews perished in massacres during the war. There were about 14 million Jews in the world in the early 1970s, with 7 million in the Americas, 4 million in Europe and 3 million in Africa and Asia. The nations with the largest Jewish populations were the United States (about 5.8 million), the Soviet Union (about 3 million), and Israel (about 2.8 million). HEBREW, the national language of Israel, is rapidly becoming the common language of usage between the Jews of many nations replacing YIDDISH and Ladino (see SEPHARDIM). In the Bible, Jewish history begins with the patriarchs Abraham, Isaac, and Jacob, who considered Canaan (an area comprising present-day Israel and parts of Egypt and Jordan) their home. Their history continues in Goshen, NE Egypt, where they settled as agriculturists many centuries before the Christian era. Under Ramses II the Jews were severely persecuted, and finally Moses led them out of Egypt; at Mt. Sinai he delivered to them the Ten Commandments. Many years of wandering in desert wildernesses followed before the Jews conquered Canaan. Their enemies at this time were the Philistines, and the Jews, who had been divided under tribal leaders called judges, came to see the need for union; Saul became the first king. Initially successful against the Philistines, he was finally defeated at Gilboa. David, of the tribe of Judah, ruled, conquered the enemies of the Jews, expanded his territory across the Jordan River, and brought prosperity and peace to his people. The reign of his son Solomon, who built the first TEMPLE, was the last before a period of disruption, caused partly by Solomon's system of heavy taxation. The tribes of the north united under Jeroboam, previously one of Solomon's officers, and formed the kingdom of Israel; those of the south, led by Solomon's son Rehoboam, formed the smaller but more strongly united kingdom of Judah. The two kingdoms were constantly threatened during much of the following two centuries (935 B.C.–725 B.C.) as powerful states emerged to the east and west. In 722 B.C., Sargon II captured Samaria, capital of Israel, and most of the Israelites (the LOST TRIBES) were exiled. Judah passed under Assyrian domination, then under Egyptian, and in 586 B.C., under Babylonian, when the Temple was destroyed and the people were exiled until their return was permitted by CYRUS THE GREAT (538 B.C.). The rebuilding of the Temple was completed in 516 B.C. The Jews remained a strong religious group during the period of Hellenism, but regained political independence only under the MACCABEES. Strife between the PHARISEES and the SADDUCEES ended in Roman intervention and complete dominance, and Jerusalem was eventually destroyed in A.D. 70. A rebellion, led by BAR KOKBA against the Romans in the 2d cent. A.D., ended in defeat. As political aspirations subsided, Jewish life was increasingly led by scholars and rabbis. Its center remained in the Middle East until, following the organization of new kingdoms upon the ruins of the Roman Empire, Jews migrated to Western Europe and began to play an important part in its intellectual and economic life. From the 9th to the 12th cent. they enjoyed a golden age of literary efflorescence, particularly in Spain. From the time of the Crusades date the persecutions that persisted until the 18th cent. During this period the ownership of land and most occupations other than petty trading and moneylending were forbidden to them; the GHETTO came into existence. The Jews, who had earlier been an agricultural people became an urban population. In 1290 the Jews were expelled from England; in 1392 from France; in 1492 from Spain, under TORQUEMADA; in 1497 from Portugal. Many of the exiles perished; others found asylum in the Netherlands and in the Turkish possessions. The German Jews fled to Poland, but there too they were subjected to persecution. When a country suffered economically or in war, its Jews were likely to be the scapegoat. Their helplessness and their staunch religious faith gave rise to several messianic movements; one of the most important was led by SABBATAI ZEVI. The rise of capitalism provided the conditions for Jews to improve their economic lot throughout Europe, and the revolutionary sentiments at the end of the 18th cent. also contributed toward a more liberal attitude by many governments. Modern political emancipation of the Jews began with the American and French revolutions. In Germany and Austria emancipation of the Jews was proclaimed after the Revolution of 1848. In Russia, birthplace of the POGROM, equal rights were granted them shortly before the Bolsheviks took power in 1917; Soviet Russia established an autonomous Jewish state in remote Birobidzhan (see JEWISH AUTONOMOUS OBLAST, USSR), although Judaism, along with all other religions, was proscribed until 1936. In the late 1940s anti-Semitism again surfaced in the Soviet Union. In Rumania, Jews gained equal rights only at the end of World War I. The gradual emancipation of the Jews brought forth two opposed movements: cultural assimilation, first propounded by Moses MENDELSSOHN, and ZIONISM, founded by Theodor HERZL in 1896. A wave of persecution that had started in Russia after the assassination (1881) of Alexander II and moved westward to France temporarily abated. Then, beginning in 1933, with the rise to power in Germany of the Nazis, persecution of Jews became increasingly widespread and violent; their property was confiscated and thousands were driven into exile (see ANTI-SEMITISM; HOLOCAUST). After the Nazi concentration camps, massacres, and population displacements in World War II, great numbers of Jews sought refuge in Palestine. With the establishment of a Jewish state (see ISRAEL) in 1948, the Jews finally had a homeland that welcomed the immigration of Jews from other countries. Since then, Arab-Jewish relations have been marked by hostility, erupting in the Arab-Israeli Wars of 1956, 1967, and 1973. Jews have been in what is now the United States since 1654 and were prominent in its early history. However, it was not until the period c.1880 to 1922 that the great influx of European Jews, some 2.5 million, took place. A second, continuing, influx has taken place since the 1930s due to persecutions in various nations of Europe and Asia. See Heinrich Graetz, *History of the Jews* (6 vol., 1926; repr. 1956); Poul Borchsenius, *The History of the Jews* (1965); Ruth Gay, *Jews in America* (1965); A. L. Sachar, *A History of the Jews* (5th ed. 1965); E. H. Flannery, *Anguish of the Jews* (1966); Charles Raddock, *Portrait of a People* (2d ed. 1967); Abba Eban, *My People* (1968); Cecil Roth, *The Jewish Contribution to Civilization* (3d ed. 1956) and *A Short History of the Jewish People* (rev. ed. 1969); S. W. Baron, *A Social and Religious History of the Jews* (14 vol., 1952-1969); Louis Finkelstein, ed., *The Jews* (3 vol., 4th ed. 1970-71).

Jewsbury, Geraldine Endsor, 1812-80, English novelist. She is remembered as much for her friendship with the Carlyles and other literary people as for her novels, which include *Zoe* (1845) and *The Sorrows of Gentility* (1856). See biography by Susanne Howe (1935).

jew's-harp or **jews'-harp,** musical instrument of ancient lineage composed of a small metal frame containing a flexible metal tongue. The frame is held between the teeth and the metal tongue is plucked with the fingers. Each jew's-harp can produce only one tone, the quality of which may be varied by modifying the shape of the mouth to emphasize different harmonics of the tone. The musical possibilities may be increased by the use of additional tongues, giving additional tones, and in the early 19th cent., particularly in Germany, jew's-harps were made with as many as 16 tongues. The instrument bears no traceable relationship to the Jewish people. It has also been called jaw's-harp, jew's-trump or jews'-trump.

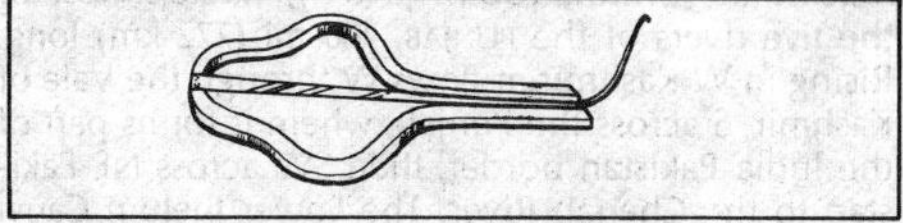

Jew's-harp

Jex-Blake, Sophia, 1840-1912, English physician, active in opening the medical profession to women in England. A graduate of Queen's College, London, she began (1866) her medical studies in the United States and continued them in Edinburgh, but she met much opposition there and was unable to obtain a degree. She carried the battle to Parliament, which finally passed a law enabling the medical schools to give degrees to women. Jex-Blake was influential in founding medical schools for women in London and Edinburgh. See her *Medical Women* (1886, repr. 1970); biography by Margaret Todd (1918).

Jezaniah (jē"zənī'ə), the same as JAAZANIAH **3.**

Jezebel (jĕz'əbĕl), Phoenician princess who was the wife of King Ahab and the mother of Ahaziah, Jehoram, and Athaliah. She encouraged idolatrous worship of Baal and persecuted the prophets. Jezebel was the bitter foe of ELIJAH. Elijah's prophecy of Jezebel's doom was fulfilled when Jehu triumphed over the house of Ahab, and Jezebel, defiant to the last, was thrown from her window and killed; her body was eaten by dogs. 1 Kings 16.31; 21; 2 Kings 9.1-10, 30-37. In the Apocalypse the name is applied to a false prophetess of Thyatira. It is probably used symbolically for a wicked woman. Rev. 2.20.

Jezer (jē'zər), son of Naphtali. Gen. 46.24; Num. 26.49; 1 Chron. 7.13.

Jeziah (jēzī'ə), Jew who had a foreign wife. Ezra 10.25.

Jeziel (jē'zēəl), ally of David at Ziklag. 1 Chron. 12.3.

Jezliah (jĕzlī'ə), Benjamite. 1 Chron. 8.18.

Jezoar (jēzō'ər), Judahite. 1 Chron. 4.7.

Jezrahiah (jĕzrəhī'ə), singer at the dedication of the wall. Neh. 12.42.

Jezreel (jĕz'rēĕl) [Heb., = God sows]. **1** Ancient city, Palestine, in the plain of ESDRAELON, halfway from Megiddo to the Jordan. It was a residence of King Ahab, whose family is therefore called the house of Jezreel. 1 Sam. 29; 2 Sam. 2.9; 1 Kings 21.1. The name is used for Israel in a pun in Hosea 2.22. It was later used for the whole valley. **2** Town of Judah. Joshua 15.56; 1 Sam. 27.3; 30.5. **3** Symbolic name for a son of Hosea. Hosea 1.4. **4** Judahite. 1 Chron. 4.3.

Jhang-Maghiana (jəng-məgyä'nə), twin cities (1972 metropolitan area est. pop. 127,000) c.2 mi (3.2 km) apart, central Pakistan, on the Chenab River. Metaled roads link the two cities, and a government college is halfway between them. Jhang has a government center that supplies blankets to the army and to hospitals. Maghiana, where many refugee weavers from India settled after the subcontinent's partition in 1947, is an important wool collection center. In the center of Jhang is the temple of Lal Nath, who founded the city in the late 17th cent.

Jhansi (jän'sē), city (1971 pop. 173,255), Uttar Pradesh state, N central India. An agricultural market and small industrial center, it has iron and steel mills and manufactures brassware. The city grew around a fort built in 1613 by the RAJPUTS and strengthened in 1742 by the MAHRATTAS. It reverted to Great Britain in 1853, when the ruling prince died without heirs. British residents in Jhansi were massacred during the INDIAN MUTINY (1857).

Jhelum (jā'lo͝om), town (1961 pop. 52,585), NE Pakistan, on the Jhelum River. It is an important market for timber, and has sawmills and plywood, textile, cigarette, and glass industries. An army supply corps training center and two colleges are also in the town. The area's history dates back at least to the 3d cent. B.C. Old Jhelum stood on the left bank of the river; boatmen crossed the river (c.1532) and founded the new town on the right bank. It became an important trade center owing its prosperity to the waterborne salt trade.

Jhelum or **Jehlam** (both: jā'ləm), westernmost of the five rivers of the PUNJAB, 480 mi (772 km) long. Rising in W Kashmir, it flows W through the Vale of Kashmir, S across the Punjab, where it forms part of the India-Pakistan border, then SW across NE Pakistan to the Chenab River. The Lower Jhelum Canal (opened 1901) and the Upper Jhelum Canal (1915) irrigate extensive areas of Pakistani Punjab. The Jhelum was crossed in 326 B.C. by Alexander the Great, who defeated the Indian king Porus. The river's ancient name was Hydaspes.

Jibsam (jĭb'săm), Issacharite. 1 Chron. 7.2.

Jibuti: see DJIBOUTI, French Territory of the Afars and the Issas.

Jidda (jĭ'də) or **Jedda** (jĕ–), city (1965 est. pop. 194,000), Hejaz, W Saudi Arabia, on the Red Sea. Jidda is the port of MECCA (c.45 mi/72 km to the east) and annually receives a hugh influx of pilgrims, mainly from Africa, Indonesia, and Pakistan. Unlike Mecca, Jidda has always accepted visitors of all religions. The diverse local population includes a large admixture of Negroes, Persians, and Indians. There are few exports, but many goods are imported to support the pilgrims. Several government ministries are in the city. Jidda was ruled by the Turks until 1916, when it became part of the independent HEJAZ. In 1925 it was conquered by Ibn Saud. The city, modernized in recent decades, is surrounded by a wall. There are many houses built of coral and embellished with ornate woodwork. Outside the wall was the reputed tomb of Eve, which was demolished in 1927. Present Jidda is not more than three centuries old, but Old Jidda, c.12 mi (19 km) south of the modern city, was founded c.646 by the caliph Uthman.

Jidlaph (jĭd'lăf), son of Abraham's brother, Nahor. Gen. 22.22.

jig, dance of English origin that is performed also in Ireland and Scotland. It is usually a lively dance, performed by one or more persons, with quick and irregular steps. When the jig was introduced to the United States, it was often danced in minstrel shows. In instrumental music the *gigue,* the successor to the jig, was used by Bach and Handel in their suites.

jigger: see CHIGOE.

jihad: see ISLAM.

Jih-k'a-tse (jŭr-kä-dzŭ) or **Shigatse** (shēgät'sē), town, S central Tibet Autonomous Region, China. It is in the center of a small, heavily populated alluvial plain near the Tsangpo (Brahmaputra) River. The second (after Lhasa) most important trade center in Tibet, it is on the ancient caravan route (now a modern highway) from Lhasa to Nepal, W Tibet, Kashmir, and Sinkiang (China). Jih-k'a-tse was the traditional seat of the Panchen Lama (see TIBETAN BUDDHISM), who ruled about 4,000 monks in the lamasery of Tashi Lumpo (founded 1446), west of the town. Jih-k'a-tse also has a large 17th-century fort. Other spellings of the name are Zhigatse and Zhikatse.

Jihlava (yĕkh'lävä), Ger. *Iglau,* city (1970 pop. 40,920), W central Czechoslovakia, in Moravia, on the Jihlava River. Jihlava is a railway junction and has industries manufacturing linen and woolen cloth, machinery, footwear, and tobacco. Chartered in 1227, it was the site of the signing (1436) of the Compactata—the Magna Carta of the HUSSITES. The city has two medieval churches and a 16th-century town hall.

Jima or **Jimma** (both: jĭm'ä), city (1968 est. pop. 30,580), capital of Kefa (Kaffa) prov., SW Ethiopia. It is the commercial center for a coffee-producing region. An agricultural school is located there.

Jim Crow laws, in U.S. history, statutes enacted by Southern states and muncipalities, beginning in the 1880s, that legalized segregation between blacks and whites. The name is believed to be derived from a character in a popular minstrel song. The Supreme Court ruling in 1896 in Plessy v. Ferguson that separate facilities for whites and blacks were constitutional encouraged the passage of discriminatory laws that wiped out the gains made by Negroes during Reconstruction. Railways and streetcars, public waiting rooms, restaurants, boarding houses, theaters, and public parks were segregated; separate schools, hospitals, and other public institutions, generally of inferior quality, were designated for Negroes. By World War I, even places of employment were segregated, and it was not until after World War II that an assault on Jim Crow in the South began to make headway. In 1950 the Supreme Court ruled that the Univ. of Texas must admit a Negro, Herman Sweatt, to the law school, on the grounds that the state did not provide equal education for him. This was followed (1954) by the Supreme Court decision in Brown v. Board of Education of Topeka, Kansas, declaring separate facilities by race to be unconstitutional. Negroes in the South used legal suits, mass sit-ins, and boycotts to hasten desegregation. A march on Washington by over 200,000 in 1963 dramatized the movement to end Jim Crow. Southern whites often responded with violence, and federal troops were needed to preserve order and protect Negroes, notably at Little Rock, Ark. (1957), Oxford, Miss. (1962), and Selma, Ala. (1965). The Civil Rights Act of 1964, the Voting Rights Act of 1965, and the Fair Housing Act of 1968 finally ended the legal sanctions to Jim Crow. See CIVIL RIGHTS; INTEGRATION; NEGRO. See C. Vann Woodward, *The Strange Career of Jim Crow* (1966).

Jiménez, Juan Ramón (hwän rämōn' hēmā'nāth), 1881–1958, Spanish lyric poet, b. Andalusia, studied at the Univ. of Seville. In his youth Jiménez was influenced by the French symbolists; he wrote the romantic *Almas de violeta* in 1900. He later turned to greater simplicity of style in *Diario de un poeta recién casado* [diary of a recently married poet]. Later collections include *Unidad* (1925), *Sucesión* (1932), and *Presente* (1935). During the civil war he left Spain and lived for many years in the United States, Cuba, and, finally, Puerto Rico. Jiménez wrote some 32 volumes of poetry. The Nobel Prize in Literature was awarded to him in 1956. For English translations see *Juan Ramón Jiménez: Fifty Spanish Poems* (1951), *Platero and I* (1956), and *Selected Writings* (1957). See studies by P. R. Olson (1967) and H. T. Young (1967).

Jiménez de Cisneros, Francisco (fränthēs'kō hēmā'nāth dā thēsnā'rōs), 1436–1517, Spanish prelate and statesman, cardinal of the Roman Catholic Church. An austere Franciscan, he was appointed (1492) confessor to Queen Isabella I and later became (1495) archbishop of Toledo. He undertook the forcible conversion of the Moors in Granada, thus provoking a Moorish uprising (1500–1502). After acting (1506–7) as regent of Castile until the return of Ferdinand II from Italy, he was made inquisitor general and cardinal. He financed and personally led the expedition (1509) that captured Oran, in Africa. On Ferdinand's death (1516) he again assumed the regency pending the arrival of Charles I (later Holy Roman Emperor Charles V) from Flanders. When Charles arrived, he dismissed Jiménez peremptorily on the advice of his Flemish counselors, but the cardinal died before learning of his fall. Jiménez founded (1508) the Univ. of Alcalá de Henares and had the Polyglot Bible compiled at his expense. He enacted clerical reforms, eliminating many abuses and introducing better education of the churchmen. His name also appears as Ximénez and Ximenes.

Jiménez de Quesada, Gonzalo (gōnthä'lō hēmā'nĕth dā kāsä'thä), c.1499–1579, Spanish conquistador in Colombia. Chief magistrate of Santa Marta, he arrived there in 1535 or 1536 and was commissioned to explore the MAGDALENA in search of EL DORADO. He set out in 1536, and after incredible hardships he defeated the CHIBCHA and founded (1538) BOGOTÁ as capital of the New Kingdom of Granada (see NEW GRANADA). A hard taskmaster but an able leader, Quesada wavered between humane and brutal treatment of the Indians. He obtained fabulous amounts of emeralds and gold. Meeting FEDERMANN and BENALCÁZAR, who claimed the same territory, Quesada persuaded them to return with him to Spain, where settlement could be made. There he was ignored until 1550, when he was appointed marshal of New Granada and councilor of Bogotá for life. In 1569, still seeking El Dorado, he led a lavishly equipped expedition to the confluence of the Guaviare and Orinoco; he and what remained of his company returned wasted and penniless after three years. Still later, suffering from a skin disease and carried on a litter, Quesada put down an Indian revolt. Some think that he was the model for Cervantes's Don Quixote. His own account of his conquests has been lost, but excerpts copied by others from the original survive. See studies by A. F. Bandelier (1893, repr. 1962), C. R. Markham (1912, repr. 1971), Germán Arciniegas (tr. 1942, repr. 1968), and R. B. C. Graham (1922, repr. 1973).

Jimna or **Jimnah** (both: jĭm'nə), son of Asher. Num. 26.44; Gen. 46.17. Imnah: 1 Chron. 7.30.

Jimson weed or **Jamestown weed,** large, coarse annual plant (*Datura stramonium*) of the family Solanaceae (NIGHTSHADE family), considered a native of the American tropics but long widely distributed and often weedy. This and other species of the genus contain a narcotic poison, stramonium, similar to that of the related belladonna, that has been used by many peoples for various purposes, e.g., as a medicine (now chiefly inhaled for the relief of asthma or applied externally as a painkiller) and in the past as a poison and an instrument for obtaining prophetic dreams or messages in various cults (suggested as possibly the medium of priests at the Delphian oracle). The amusing antics of soldiers in colonial Virginia who ate Jimson weed have been recorded for history. Stramonium, comprised of several alkaloids (e.g., SCOPOLAMINE, ATROPINE, and hyoscyamine), may also be obtained from some other species of *Datura.* Jimson weed is classified in the division MAGNOLIOPHYTA, class Magnoliopsida, order Polemoniales, family Solanaceae.

jingle shell: see MUSSEL.

jingoism (jĭng'gōĭzəm), advocacy of a policy of aggressive nationalism. The term was first used in connection with certain British politicians who sought to bring England into the Russo-Turkish War (1877–78) on the side of the Turks. It apparently derived from a popular song of the period: "We don't want to fight, but, by jingo, if we do. . . ."

Jinja (jĭn'jə), city (1969 pop. 47,300), SE Uganda, on the Victoria Nile River, near Victoria Nyanza. It is an industrial city and the commercial and processing center for a region where cotton, sugarcane, maize, and groundnuts are grown. Manufactures include refined copper, metal goods, forest products, textiles, soap, and processed food. It is connected by rail with Mombasa on the Indian Ocean. Jinja was founded in 1901 as a trading post; with the development of the nearby Owen Falls hydroelectric project, it became (1950s) a major industrial center.

Jinnah, Muhammad Ali (məhäm'əd älē' jĭn'ə), 1876–1948, founder of Pakistan, b. Karachi. After his admission to the bar in England, he returned to India to practice law. Early in his career he was a fervent supporter of the INDIAN NATIONAL CONGRESS and an advocate of Hindu-Muslim unity. He was a member of the legislative council of the viceroy from 1910 to 1919. He joined the MUSLIM LEAGUE in 1913 and was elected its president in 1916 and 1920. He played a major role in negotiating the so-called Lucknow Pact (1916) between the League and the Congress, in which the latter conceded that Muslims should have a separate communal electorate to insure them adequate legislative representation. Hindu-Muslim cooperation soon broke down, however, and the Congress reversed its position on separate electorates. Finally totally disillusioned with the Congress, Jinnah resigned from that organization in 1930. From 1934 until his death he headed the Muslim League and guided its struggle for an independent Pakistan, a state that would include the predominantly Muslim areas of India. He supported the British during World War II while the Congress was under ban. The claim of Jinnah that the Muslim League represented the Muslims of India was substantiated in 1946, when in the elections for the Indian constituent assembly, the League won all the seats assigned to the Muslim electorate. Jinnah's firm stand and the widespread Hindu-Muslim riots forced the Congress to accept establishment of the separate state of Pakistan, and in Aug., 1947, India was partitioned. Jinnah was appointed the first governor general of the dominion of Pakistan and elected president of its constituent assembly. He was called Quaid-i-Azam [great leader] by his followers. See Hector Bolitho, *Jinnah* (1954).

jinni (jĭnē'), feminine **jinniyah** (jĭnēyä'), plural **jinn** (jĭn), in Arabic and Islamic folklore, spirit or demon endowed with supernatural power. In ancient belief the jinn were associated with the destructive forces of nature. In Islamic tradition they were corporeal spirits similar to men in appearance but having certain supernatural powers, especially those of changing in size and shape. Capable of both good and evil, the jinn were popular in literatures of the Near East, notably in the stories of the *Thousand and One Nights.* The term *genie* is the English form and is sometimes confused with the Roman genius.

Jiphtah (jĭf'tə), unidentified town, SW Palestine. Joshua 15.43.

Jiphthah-el (jĭf'thə-ēl), unidentified town, Palestine. Joshua 19.14,27.

Jipijapa (hēpēhä'pä), city (1962 est. pop. 13,400), W Ecuador, on the equatorial lowlands. A few miles inland from the Pacific, Jipijapa is famous for the manufacture of high-grade Panama hats, made from the jipijapa plant. It is also the trade center for an agricultural region.

Jirja (jĭr'jä) or **Girga** (gĭr'-), town (1966 pop. 44,300), central Egypt, on the Nile. It is noted for its pottery. The town is the seat of a Coptic bishop and derives its name from the old Mara Girgis Coptic monastery, which was dedicated to St. George. A Roman Catholic monastery, said to be the oldest in Egypt, is in Jirja. Nearby is the ancient city of Abydos.

jiujitsu or **jiujutsu** (jo͞ojĭt'so͞o): see JUDO.

Jívaro (hē'värō), linguistic stock of South American Indians, Ecuador. The peoples, N of the Marañón River and E of the Andes, engage in farming, hunting, fishing, and weaving. They have a patrilineal society, with some 15 to 20 people, the family group, living in each huge, isolated communal house. Though not unique to the Jívaro, head shrinking, accompanied by elaborate ceremony, made them famous, but the practice has virtually disappeared. The Jívaro long resisted government and missionary efforts to subdue them. See V. W. Von Hagen, *Off With Their Heads* (1937); Jirí Hanzelka and Miroslav Zikmund, *Amazon Headhunters* (tr. 1964); M. J. Harner, *The Jívaro* (1972).

Jizah, Al (äl jē'zō) or **Giza** (gē'zə), city (1966 pop. 345,261), capital of Al Jizah governorate, N Egypt, surburb of Cairo. It is a manufacturing and agricultural trade center. Products include cotton textiles, cigarettes, and footwear. It is also a resort, as well as the seat of Egypt's motion-picture industry. The Univ. of Cairo and a research center for schistosomiasis are located there. Nearby are the Great SPHINX, the pyramid of KHUFU (Cheops), and the tombs of Khufu's mother and daughter. The city is also known as Gizeh.

Joab (jō'ăb). **1** Son of David's sister Zeruiah and commander of his uncle's armies. A trusted and skillful administrator, he was often vindictive and cruel, as in his killing of Abner, Absalom, and Amasa. David's dying curse on Joab is remarkable. 1 Kings 2.5,6. For his support of Adonijah, Solomon had him put to death. 2 Sam. 2.12–32; 3.22–31; 8.16; 10.7–14; 11; 12.26; 14; 18; 19.1,5–7,13; 20.7–23; 24.1–9; 1 Kings 1.7; 2.28–34. **2** Chief craftsman of the valley of Charashim. 1 Chron. 4.14. **3** Family returned from exile. Ezra 2.6; 8.9; Neh. 7.11.

Joachim, Saint (jō'əkĭm), in tradition, the father of the Virgin and husband of St. ANNE; there is no mention of him in the Bible. His cult is ancient in the East, but modern in the Western Church. Feast: Aug. 16.

Joachim, Joseph (yō'sĕf yō'äkhĭm), 1831–1907, Hungarian violinist; friend of Mendelssohn, Brahms, and Schumann. In his long career his performances of violin masterpieces came to be accepted as models. Joachim was concertmaster under Liszt at Weimar, 1849–53; later he became (1868) musical director of the Berlin Hochschule. The Joachim quartet, which he founded in 1869, presented the conservative quartet repertory of the 19th cent. in definitive interpretations. He composed cadenzas for the violin concertos of Beethoven and Brahms.

Joachim of Floris (jō'əkĭm), c.1132–1202, Italian Cistercian monk. He was abbot of Corazzo, Italy, but withdrew into solitude. He left scriptural commentaries prophesying a new age. In his "Age of the Spirit" the hierarchy of the church would be unnecessary and infidels would unite with Christians. Joachim's works had a vogue in the 13th and the 14th cent.; many, especially religious zealots like the Franciscan spirituals, acclaimed him as a prophet. Dante places him in Paradise. One of Joachim's works was condemned as heretical. See study by Marjorie Reeves (1972).

Joachimsthal: see JÁCHYMOV, Czechoslovakia.

Joad, Cyril Edwin Mitchinson, 1891–1953, English philosopher. He became head of the department of philosophy at Birbeck College, Univ. of London, in 1930. As a rationalist, he was a successful lecturer and writer, his works including *Common Sense Ethics* (1920), *Matter, Life, and Value* (1929), and *Return to Philosophy* (1936). After his conversion to religion he wrote *Good and Evil* (1943) and *The Recovery of Belief* (1953).

Joah (jō'ä). **1, 2** Keepers of records. 2 Kings 18; Isa. 36; 2 Chron. 34.8. **3, 4** Gershonites. 1 Chron. 6.21; 2 Chron. 29.12. **5** Korahite doorkeeper. 1 Chron. 26.4.

Joahaz (jō'əhăz): see JEHOAHAZ.

Joanes, Vicente: see MACIP, VICENTE JUAN.

Joanna I, 1326–82, queen of Naples (1343–81), countess of Provence. She was the granddaughter of King Robert of Naples, whom she succeeded with her husband, Andrew of Hungary. The murder (1345) of Andrew at the queen's behest brought the wrath of Andrew's brother, LOUIS I of Hungary. Louis twice invaded Naples; each time Joanna fled, and in 1352 she made peace with Hungary. Joanna married twice more but remained childless and adopted young Charles of Durazzo (later CHARLES III of Naples) as her heir. When Pope Urban VI, angered by Joanna's support of the antipope Clement VII, urged Charles to dethrone her, she disinherited Charles in favor of Louis of Anjou (see LOUIS I, king of Naples). Charles conquered (1381) Naples, imprisoned the queen, and was granted the kingdom by the pope. Joanna died by Charles's orders. Her successive adoptions caused chronic warfare between the two claimants (continued by their heirs); thus began the decline of French hegemony in Italy.

Joanna II, 1371–1435, queen of Naples (1414–35), sister and successor of LANCELOT. The intrigues of her favorites kept her court in turmoil. Her second husband, James of Bourbon, tried to seize power but was imprisoned in 1416. Threatened (1420) by the ANGEVIN claimant to Naples, LOUIS III, Joanna asked the aid of ALFONSO V of Aragón in expelling Louis; she adopted (1421) Alfonso as her heir. After Alfonso attempted to take over Naples she transferred (1423) the adoption to Louis. Louis died (1434) after regaining most of Naples, and Joanna adopted his brother RENÉ. Joanna II was the last Angevin to reign in Naples; at her death Alfonso seized power, and René's claim was never secured.

Joanna (Joanna the Mad), 1479–1555, Spanish queen of Castile and León (1504–55), daughter of Ferdinand II and Isabella I. She succeeded to Castile and León at the death of her mother. Ferdinand II briefly assumed the regency until he was replaced by Joanna's ambitious husband, PHILIP I. After Philip's death (1506), Ferdinand again assumed the rule, for Joanna had by this time become quite insane. At Ferdinand's death (1516) Joanna's elder son, Charles (later Holy Roman Emperor CHARLES V), was proclaimed joint ruler of Castile with his mother. Joanna spent the rest of her life in the castle of Tordesillas. The pretence that she was not actually insane was sometimes used by the discontented, including Juan de PADILLA, to justify revolts against the "foreign" ruler, Charles. See Townsend Miller, *The Castles and the Crown* (1963).

Joanna, in the Bible. **1** Wife of Herod's steward Chuza. She was a follower of Jesus and was one who found the tomb empty. Luke 8.3; 24.10. **2** Ancestor of St. Joseph. Luke 3.27.

Joan of Arc, Fr. *Jeanne D'Arc* (zhän därk), 1412?–31, French saint and national heroine, called the Maid of Orléans; daughter of a farmer of Domrémy on the border of Champagne and Lorraine. At a young age she began to hear "voices"—those of St. Michael, St. Catherine, and St. Margaret. When she was about 16, the voices exhorted her to bear aid to the dauphin, later King CHARLES VII, then kept from the throne by the English in the HUNDRED YEARS WAR. Joan won the aid of Robert de Baudricourt, captain of the dauphin's forces in Vaucouleurs, in obtaining an interview with the dauphin. She made the journey in male attire, with six companions. Meeting the dauphin at Chinon castle, she conquered his skepticism as to her divine mission. She was examined by theologians at Poitiers, and afterwards she was furnished with troops by Charles. Her leadership provided spirit and morale more than military prowess. In May, 1429, she succeeded in raising the siege of Orléans, and in June she took other English posts on the Loire and defeated the English at Patay. After considerable persuasion the dauphin agreed to be crowned at Rheims; Joan stood near him at his coronation. This was the pinnacle of her fortunes. In Sept., 1429, Joan unsuccessfully besieged Paris. The following spring she went to relieve Compiègne, but she was captured by the Burgundians and sold to the English, who were eager to destroy her influence by putting her to death. Charles VII made no attempt to secure her freedom. In order to escape responsibility, the English turned her over to the ecclesiastical court at Rouen. She was tried for heresy and witchcraft before Pierre CAUCHON and other French clerics who supported the English. Probably her most serious crime was the claim of direct inspiration from God; in the eyes of the court this refusal to accept the church hierarchy constituted heresy. Throughout the lengthy trial and imprisonment she bravely fought her inquisitors. Only at the end of the trial, when Joan was sentenced to be turned over to a secular court, did she recant. She was condemned to life imprisonment. Shortly afterward, however, she retracted her abjuration, was turned over to the secular court as a relapsed heretic, and was burned at the stake (May 30, 1431) in Rouen. Charles VII made tardy recognition of her services by a rehabilitation trial that annulled the proceedings of the original trial in 1456. Joan was beatified in 1909 and canonized in 1920. Feast: May 30. Her career lent itself to numerous legends, and she has been represented in many paintings and statues. In literature and music she appears notably, though not always accurately, in works by many eminent writers and composers. Among her biographies, the best known is that of Jules Michelet (tr. 1957). See also biographies by Andrew Lang (1908) and Vita Sackville-West (1936); translations of the trial records by W. P. Barrett (1932 ed.) and W. S. Scott (1950) ; Régine Pernoud, *The Retrial of Joan of Arc* (tr. 1955) and *Joan of Arc by Herself and Her Witnesses* (tr. 1966); C. W. Lightbody, *The Judgements of Joan* (1961); Henri Guillemin, *Joan, Maid of Orleans* (1973).

Joan of Kent, 1328–85, English noblewoman; daughter of Edmund of Woodstock, earl of Kent, youngest son of Edward I. She early gained wide note for her beauty and charm, though the appellation Fair Maid of Kent, by which she became known, was probably not contemporary. Her marriage to the earl of Salisbury was annulled on the grounds of a precontract with Sir Thomas Holland, whom she then married. Upon the death of her brother in 1352 she became countess of Kent in her own right. In 1361, after Holland's death, she married Edward the Black Prince, by whom she had two sons, Edward (1365–70) and Richard (later Richard II). In 1378 she was instrumental in halting proceedings against John WYCLIF, though there is insufficient evidence to determine if she accepted his doctrines. As long as she lived, she was probably the principal influence on her son Richard II.

João Pessoa (zhwouN pəsô'ə), city (1970 pop. 197,398), capital of Paraíba state, NE Brazil, at the confluence of the Sanhauá and Paraíba do Norte rivers. Cotton, sugar, and minerals are exported through its port, Cabedelo. Industries in the city produce tobacco, shoes, and cement. The city was established in the late 16th cent. and named (1585) Filipea, in honor of Philip II of Spain and Portugal. During the brief Dutch occupation (17th cent.) it was called Frederickstadt, and, after its reconquest by the Portuguese, Paraíba. Its present name was acquired in 1930, in honor of the state governor who was assassinated in Recife during the VARGAS revolution. João Pessoa is the site of a state university. The city's Franciscan convent and church are excellent examples of colonial architecture. Nearby are several resort areas.

Joash (jō'ăsh): see JEHOASH.

Joatham (jō'əthəm): see JOTHAM.

Job (jōb), book of the Old Testament, in the 18th place in the Authorized Version. It is based on a folktale and is of unknown authorship and date, although many scholars assign it to a time between

600 B.C. and 400 B.C. The book is in a dialogue or dramatic form, all in verse except for the opening and close. The subject is the problem of good and evil in the world: "Why do the just suffer and the wicked flourish?" In the prologue (1-2) Satan obtains God's permission to test Job, whom God regards as "a perfect and an upright man"; accordingly, all that Job has is destroyed, and he is physically afflicted. The main part of the book (3-31) consists of speeches by Job and three friends who come to "comfort" him: Job speaks, then each of the three speaks in turn, with Job replying each time; there are three such cycles of discussion, although the third is incomplete. The friends insist alike that Job cannot really be just, as he claims to be, and Job reiterates his innocence of wrong. The sequence changes with the appearance of a fourth speaker, Elihu (32-37), who accuses Job of arrogant pride. He in turn is followed by God himself, who speaks out of a storm (38-41) to convince Job of his ignorance and rebuke him for his questioning. The epilogue (42) tells how God rebukes the friends for their accusations and how happiness is restored to Job. The ethical problem is not explicitly resolved. The author did not intend to solve the paradox of the righteous man's suffering, but rather to criticize a philosophy that associated sin with the sufferer. The texts are imperfect, and there may be serious losses, misplacements, or even additions to the original. The book contains many eloquent passages; among them are Job's declaration of faith in the "redeemer" (19) and his speech on wisdom (28) and God's discourse on animals (39-41). Job is mentioned elsewhere in the Bible: Ezek. 14.12-23; James 5.11. The Job of Gen. 46.13 is the same as JASHUB **1.** See studies by Robert Gordis (1965) and J. D. Levenson (1972); see also bibliography under OLD TESTAMENT.

Jobab (jō'băb). **1** Descendant of Shem. Gen. 10.29; 1 Chron. 1.23. **2** King of Edom. Gen. 36.33,34. **3** Chief defeated by Joshua. Joshua 11.1. **4, 5** Benjamites. 1 Chron. 8.9,18.

Job Corps, U.S. Government program to provide basic education for the most disadvantaged youths between the ages of 16 and 21. Established by the Economic Opportunity Act of 1964, its goal is to prepare these youths "for the responsibility of citizenship and to increase their employability." The Job Corps is administered by the Dept. of Labor, which works in conjunction with other Federal agencies in providing training. For example, the Forest Service maintains 20 Job Corps Conservation Centers on national forest land where youths receive vocational training. Job Corps recruiting is done primarily through state employment services. Enrollees spend from six months to two year in the program.

Jobert, Michel (mĕshĕl' zhôbĕr'), 1921–, French diplomat, b. Morocco (then a French colony). He served for many years as a government official before joining (1963) Georges Pompidou's staff during Pompidou's premiership. After Pompidou's election as president (1969), Jobert was his adviser on foreign affairs. A skillful negotiator, he helped bring about Great Britain's entry into the European Economic Community in 1973. He was French foreign minister from April, 1973, to May, 1974.

Job's-tears, tall tropical plant of the family Gramineae (GRASS family), *Coix lacrymajobi,* native to E Asia and Malaya but elsewhere cultivated in gardens as an annual and naturalized in the S United States. The mature grains are enveloped by very hard, pearly white, oval structures which are used as beads for making rosaries, necklaces, and other objects. Some varieties are harvested for cereal food and are used medicinally in parts of the Orient. Job's-tears is classified in the division MAGNOLIOPHYTA, class Liliatae, order Cyperales, family Gramineae.

Jocasta (jōkăs'tə): see OEDIPUS.

Jocelin de Brakelond (jŏs'lĭn də brăk'lŏnd), fl. 1200, English chronicler, a monk of Bury St. Edmunds. His chronicle of St. Edmund's Abbey, covering the years 1173-1202, is written in a simple, vigorous style and is remarkable for its vivid pictures of monastic life and characters, particularly of the abbot Samson. Carlyle used it as the basis for the second part of his *Past and Present.* See edition by G. J. McFadden (1952).

Jochebed (jŏk'ēbĕd), mother of Moses. Ex. 6.20; Num. 26.59.

Jochumsson, Matthías (mät'tēäs yŏk'kŭms-sŏn), 1835-1920, Icelandic playwright, poet, and translator. Although Jochumsson was the founder of the modern drama in Iceland, with poetic plays such as *Útilegumennirnir* [the outlaws] (1864), he is best known as a lyric poet. After graduating from theological school he traveled abroad, returning to Iceland to work as a translator of Shakespeare, Byron, and Ibsen. His autobiography, *Sögukaflar af sjálfum mér* [stories from my life], was published in 1922. Jochumsson also composed hymns, including the Icelandic national hymn.

Jodelle, Estienne (ātyĕn' zhôdĕl'), 1532-73, French poet of the Pléiade (see under PLEIAD). He was the author of *Cléopatre captive* (1553), the first French tragedy that departed from medieval drama. His other plays were a comedy, *Eugène* (1552), and *Didon se sacrifiant* (1558), another tragedy.

Jodhpur (jŏd'po͝or) or **Marwar** (mär'wär), city and former principality, Rajasthan state, NW India. Except for the eastern section, it is largely an arid wasteland suitable only for the raising of camels. Gypsum and salt are mined, and cotton is raised. The state was founded in the 13th cent. by the Rahtor clan of RAJPUTS and was later a vassal of the MOGUL empire. The British brought it under their control in 1818, and in 1949 it was merged with the state of Rajasthan. **Jodhpur,** city (1971 pop. 318,894), capital of the former state and now a district administrative center, was founded in 1459. It is surrounded by a wall nearly 6 mi (9.7 km) long. Jodhpur is an important marketplace for wool. Its manufactures include textiles and electrical and leather goods. Towering above the city on a rock 400 ft (122 m) high is an old fortress housing several palaces and the treasury of the maharaja, which contains a famous gem collection. The Indian air force maintains a training center at Jodhpur.

Jodrell Bank Experimental Station (jŏd'rəl), observatory for RADIO ASTRONOMY located at Jodrell Bank, Macclesfield, Cheshire, England; its official name is the Nuffield Radio Astronomy Observatory. It was founded in 1945 and is administered by the Univ. of Manchester. The principal antennas are a fully steerable, altazimuth-mounted parabolic dish 250 ft (76 m) in diameter and a second altazimuth paraboloid measuring 125 ft (38 m) by 84 ft (26 m). In addition, the facility has a 50-ft (15 m) altazimuth paraboloid and a 50-ft polar-axis paraboloid. Research programs include studies of galactic structure, angular sizes and structure of radio sources, polarization of radio sources, quasars, pulsars, molecules in interstellar space, and lunar radar.

Joed (jō'ĕd), descendant of Benjamin. Neh. 11.7.

Joel (jō'əl). **1** Prophet of the book of JOEL. **2** Simeonite. 1 Chron. 4.35. **3** Reubenite. 1 Chron. 5.4,8. **4** Gadite. 1 Chron. 5.12. **5** Issacharite. 1 Chron. 7.3. **6** Manassite. 1 Chron. 27.20. **7, 8, 9** Levites. 1 Chron. 15.7, 11,17; 23.8; 26.22; 2 Chron. 29.12. **10** See IGAL. **11, 12** Men who returned from the Exile. Ezra 10.43; Neh. 11.9. **13** Ancestor of Samuel. 1 Chron. 6.36. Shaul: 1 Chron. 6.24. **14** Son of Samuel. 1 Sam. 8.2; 1 Chron. 6.33. Vashni: 1 Chron. 6.28.

Joel, book of the Old Testament, 29th in the order of the Authorized Version, 2d of the books of the Minor Prophets. It is the preaching of an otherwise unknown prophet, dated variously from the 9th to the 3d cent. B.C. It gives an account of a plague of locusts, divinely sent (1-2.17); the people, on repentance, will be rewarded with present (2.18-27) as well as future blessings, this being a Messianic prophecy (2.28-3.21). Peter used Joel as a text in his Pentecost sermon. Acts 2. See Mariano DiGangi, *The Book of Joel* (1970); G. W. Ahlström, *Joel and the Temple of Jerusalem* (1971).

Joelah (jōē'lə), warrior with David at Ziklag. 1 Chron. 12.7.

Joensuu (yô'ĕnso͞o), city (1970 pop. 36,281), capital of Pohjois-Karjala prov., SE Finland. It is the trade center of the forest region of NE Karelia, has plywood mills, and is an important lake port. It was chartered in 1848. The modern city hall was designed by Eliel Saarinen.

joe-pye weed (jō-pī'), name for a tall North American plant (*Eupatorium purpureum*) of the family Compositae (COMPOSITE family), having small, usually pinkish-purple blossoms in large terminal clusters. The name comes from that of an Indian who reputedly effected many cures with the herb. An infusion of the leaves and roots was formerly, and is sometimes yet, employed as a diuretic and an astringent among other things. It is also called gravelroot, trumpetweed, and purple BONESET or thoroughwort. Two related species, *E. maculatum* and *verticillatum,* are also called joe-pye weed. Joe-pye weed is classified in the division MAGNOLIOPHYTA, class Magnoliopsida, order Asterales, family Compositae.

Joezer (jōē'zər), one of David's captains. 1 Chron. 12.6.

Joffe, Abram (əbräm' yô'fyə), 1880-1960, Soviet scientist, b. Ukraine, grad. St. Petersburg (now Leningrad) Technological Institute, 1902. From 1902 to 1906 he worked in Munich as an assistant to W. C. Roentgen. In 1932, Joffe became director of the Leningrad Physico-Agronomy Institute. As a member of the Soviet Academy of Science, he helped found (1951) the Physico-Technical Institute of the academy. He is best known for his work on semiconductors, for his research on thermoelectric generators, and for his inventions in radio and aerodynamics, including a dynamo of a new type and a powerful accumulator for storing energy.

Joffre, Joseph Jacques Césaire (zhôzĕf' zhäk sāzĕr' zhô'frə), 1852-1931, marshal of France. He began his career as a military engineer in the French colonies and was appointed French commander in chief in 1911. Like other members of the French general staff, he underestimated German strength at the outbreak of World War I, but his operations helped achieve an orderly French retreat. He deserves partial credit for the victory of the Marne (1914) in which he took advantage of an opportunity to counterattack. After the Germans nearly captured Verdun (1916) Joffre was made chief military adviser to the government, a powerless post from which he soon resigned. He was replaced by Gen. Robert Georges Nivelle as commander in chief. Joffre later served as chairman of the Allied War Council. See his memoirs (tr. 1932).

Joffrey Ballet: see ROBERT JOFFREY BALLET.

Jogbehah (jŏg'bēhä), town, E of the Jordan River, NW of Amman (Jordan). Num. 32.35; Judges 8.11.

Jogjakarta (jōg"yəkär'tə, jōk"-) or **Djokjakarta** (jōk"-), city (1961 pop. 312,698), S Java, Indonesia, at the foot of volcanic Mt. Merapi, capital of the autonomous district of Jogjakarta, a former sultanate. It is the cultural center of Java, known for its artistic life, particularly its drama and dance festivals and handicraft industries. It is also the trade hub of a major rice-producing region, and there is some manufacturing. Tourism is important; the magnificent BOROBUDUR temple is in the area. The vast walled palace (18th cent.) of the sultan of Jogjakarta was the provisional capital (1949-50) of the republic of Indonesia; part of it now houses Gadjah Mada Univ. Also in the city are the Islamic Univ. of Indonesia and several colleges. The town was founded (1749) by a sultan in an area which had been the center of previous cultures. It was the focus of the revolt against the Dutch (1825-30) and was the stronghold of the Indonesian independence movement from 1946 to 1950.

Jogli (jŏg'lī), chief Danite. Num. 34.22.

Jogues, Isaac (Saint Isaac Jogues) (ēzäk' zhôg), 1607-46, French Jesuit missionary and martyr in the New World; one of the Jesuit Martyrs of North America. He arrived in Quebec in 1636, and immediately was sent to Christianize the Huron Indians on Georgian Bay. In 1641 he journeyed N to Sault Ste Marie, which he named. On his return from a journey to Quebec in 1642, the party was captured by the Iroquois; several were killed, and the rest were subjected to cruel tortures. Jogues was held captive until July, 1643, when he was ransomed by the Dutch and brought to New Amsterdam; from there he embarked for France. Later he returned to Canada. In April, 1646, he was sent among the Mohawks as an ambassador of peace. He discovered Lake George, which he named Lac du St. Sacrement. In May, 1646, he returned to Quebec to make plans for establishing a mission among the Mohawks. On his return, accompanied by Father Jean Lalande, he was met by a hostile band of Mohawks near the present Auriesville, N.Y., where both priests were murdered. Feast: Sept. 26 or (among the Jesuits) March 16. See G. D. Kittler, *Saint in the Wilderness* (1964).

Joha (jō'hə). **1** Son of BERIAH **3.** 1 Chron. 8.16. **2** One of David's guard. 1 Chron. 11.45.

Johanan (jōhā'năn) [short form of JEHOHANAN]. **1** Captain who led in the rescue of the captives of Ishmael. Jer. 40.8-43; 2 Kings 25.23. **2** Descendant of David. 1 Chron. 3.24. **3, 4** Two of David's men. 1 Chron. 12.4,12. **5** Chief priest. Neh. 12.22,23; Ezra 10.6. Jonathan: Neh. 12.11. **6** Son of King Josiah. 1 Chron. 3.15. **7** Father of AZARIAH **6.** **8** Father of AZARIAH **19.** **9** Head of a family in the return from the Exile. Ezra 8.12. **10** Son of TOBIAH **1.** Neh. 6.18.

Johanan ben Zakkai (jōhăn'ən bĕn zăk'āī), leader of the Pharisees of Jerusalem before the destruction of the Temple in A.D. 70, afterward founder of the academy of Jabneh (see JAMNIA). He emphasized the study of the Torah as the primary religious duty for which man was created. After A.D. 70 he taught that deeds of loving kindness might replace sacrifice in achieving atonement. His success at Jabneh assured the continuation of Judaism.

Johannesburg (jōhăn'ĭsbörg", yōhä'nəsbörkh"), city (1970 metropolitan pop. 1,407,963), Transvaal, NE South Africa, on the southern slopes of the WITWATERSRAND at an altitude of 5,750 ft (1,753 m). Johannesburg is the largest city in South Africa, the center of its important gold-mining industry, its manufacturing and commercial center, and the hub of its transportation network. Gold mining is the sprawling city's chief industry. Manufactures include cut diamonds, industrial chemicals, plastics, cement, electrical and mining equipment, paper and paper products, glass, food products, and beer. South Africa's main stock exchange (founded 1887) is in the city. Jan Smuts International Airport is nearby. Johannesburg was founded as a mining settlement in 1886, when gold was found on the Witwatersrand; by 1900 the city had a population of c.100,000. Johannesburg's large black African population provides labor for the mines. Today most black Africans live in a group of townships (known collectively as Soweto) southwest of the city. Rand Afrikaans Univ. (1966), the Univ. of the Witwatersrand (1922), and Witwatersrand College for Advanced Technical Education (1925) are in Johannesburg, which also houses several museums, an art gallery, a planetarium, a zoo, a bird sanctuary, and numerous parks. Jan Smuts House is in the city. Nearby is Kyalami Circuit, where international motor races are held.

Johannes von Saaz (Johannes von Tepl) (yōhän'əs fən zäts, tĕp'əl), c.1350-c.1414, Bohemian humanist and writer. Johannes is best known for his powerful work *Der Ackermann aus Böhmen* (tr. *Death and the Plowman*) (c.1400), a dialogue between Death and a recently widowed farmer. Among the first prose works in Modern High German, it is characterized by medieval style and form but it embodies Renaissance spirit in its defense of mankind.

Johannes von Tepl: see JOHANNES VON SAAZ.

Johannisberg (yōhä'nĭsbĕrkh), village, Hesse, central West Germany, near the Rhine River. A health resort, it is also noted for its magnificent wine.

John, Saint, one of the Twelve Disciples, traditional author of the fourth Gospel, three epistles, and the Revelation (see JOHN, GOSPEL ACCORDING TO SAINT; JOHN, epistles; REVELATION). He and his brother, St. James (the Greater), were sons of Zebedee. Jesus called them Boanerges or Sons of Thunder (Mark 3.17). The two brothers, together with Peter, were the three apostles closest to Jesus; they witnessed the Transfiguration and accompanied Jesus to Gethsemane (Mat. 17.1-13; 26.36-46; Mark 9.2-13; 14.33-45). John is thought to have been the disciple "whom Jesus loved"; to his care Jesus, in his dying moments, committed the Virgin Mary (John 13.23; 19.26; 21.20-23). He is mentioned occasionally in Acts (3,4; 8.14-25), and St. Paul refers to him (Gal. 2.9); inferences may also be drawn from the books bearing his name. According to 2d-century authorities John died at an advanced age at Ephesus (A.D. c.100), where he had chiefly lived except for a visit to Rome and a period of exile on Patmos (Rev. 1.9). However, many scholars believe that St. John the apostle and St. John of Ephesus were two different persons. He is variously called St. John the Evangelist, because of the Gospel; St. John the Divine (i.e., theologian), because of the theological interest of the books; and the Beloved Disciple. His symbol as evangelist is an eagle. Feast: Dec. 27; the Feast of St. John before the Latin Gate, commemorating the dedication of a Roman basilica to him on the traditional site of his miraculous escape from martyrdom: May 6.

John VIII, d. 882, pope (872-82), a Roman; successor of Adrian II. John strenuously opposed the activities of St. IGNATIUS OF CONSTANTINOPLE in Bulgaria. When Ignatius died, John recognized PHOTIUS as patriarch and called the council (879-80) that momentarily reconciled the differences between East and West. John was deeply involved in imperial politics. He crowned CHARLES II (Charles the Bald) emperor and excommunicated the future Pope Formosus for opposition to his policy. When Charles II lost his power, John favored Charles the Fat, who became emperor as Charles III. The pope had to bribe the Saracens to keep them from entering Rome. He did much to root out corruption in the church in Rome, and, except for Nicholas I, he was the strongest pope of the 9th cent. He was assassinated by his own relatives. Marinus I succeeded him.

John XII, c.937-964, pope (955-64), a Roman (count of Tusculum) named Octavian; successor of Agapetus II and predecessor of either Leo VIII or Benedict V. His father, Alberic, secured John's election before the latter was 20 years old. John's life was notoriously immoral and his pontificate a disgrace. He called on OTTO I to help him against Berengar II of Italy. John crowned (962) Otto the first German emperor, and the two, in the famous *Privilegium Ottonis,* pledged loyalty to each other. Disliking the emperor's new influence in papal affairs, John sided with Berengar's party against Otto. In retaliation, Otto invaded Rome and called a synod that deposed John and elected Leo VIII as pope. John was restored by Roman insurrectionists shortly before he was mysteriously murdered. Scholars differ on the legitimacy of Leo VIII's reign, as they do on the brief pontificate of Benedict V, elected upon John's death and deposed by Otto shortly thereafter again in favor of Leo. Leo died in 965.

John XXI, d. 1277, pope (1276-77), a Portuguese named Pedro Giuliano; successor of Adrian V. Known generally as Peter of Spain (Petrus Hispanus), he is the only Portuguese pope. Peter's reputation as a scholastic philosopher was widespread, and he was the reputed author of an extensively used book on logic. Nine months after his election the ceiling of his library at Viterbo fell and killed him. John was actually the 20th canonical pope named John, but through chronological errors he called himself John XXI; this numbering is usually maintained. He was succeeded by Nicholas III.

John XXII, 1244-1334, pope (1316-34), a Frenchman (b. Cahors) named Jacques Duèse; successor of Clement V. Formerly, he was often called John XXI. He reigned at Avignon. John was celebrated as a canon jurist under Boniface VIII, whom he supported. After the death of Clement there was a period of more than two years before the conclave could agree. Before John's election a contest had begun in the empire between LOUIS IV and his rival, Frederick of Austria. John was neutral at first; then in 1323, when Louis had won and became Holy Roman emperor, pope and emperor began a serious quarrel. This was partly provoked by John's extreme claims of authority over the empire and partly by Louis's support of the radical Franciscans, whom John XXII condemned for their insistence on evangelical poverty. Louis was assisted by Marsilius of Padua, who published his theories in 1324, and later by William of Ockham. The emperor invaded Italy and set up (1328) as an antipope Pietro Rainalducci (as Nicholas V). The project was a fiasco, but Louis silenced the papal claims. In John's last years he advanced a theory concerning the vision of God in heaven; the novelty he proposed (that this vision will begin only after the Last Judgment) was everywhere denied and scorned by theologians, and John abandoned it. He was an excellent administrator and did much efficient reorganizing. He was succeeded by Benedict XII.

John XXIII, antipope: see COSSA, BALDASSARRE.

John XXIII, 1881-1963, pope (1958-63), an Italian (b. Sotto il Monte, near Bergamo) named Angelo Giuseppe Roncalli; successor of Pius XII. He was of peasant stock. Educated at Bergamo and the Seminario Romano (called the Apollinare), Rome, he was ordained in 1904. While secretary to the bishop of Bergamo (1904-14) he wrote scholarly works, among them a life of St. Charles Borromeo (completed in 5 vol., 1936-52). Called up for service in World War I, he was first in the medical corps and was later a chaplain. After the war he held posts in Rome and reorganized the Society for the Propagation of the Faith. In 1925 he was made archbishop and sent as Vatican diplomatic representative to Bulgaria. Later he was representative in Turkey and Greece, and in 1944 he was named papal nuncio to France. There he acted as mediator between the conservative churchmen and the more socially "radical" clergy; he gained popularity. In 1953 he was made cardinal and the patriarch of Venice. He was elected pope Oct. 28, 1958. As pope, he put reforms into practice: He laid stress on his own pastoral duties as well as those of other bishops and the lesser clergy; he was active in promoting social reforms for workers, the poor, orphans, and the outcast; he advanced cooperation with other religions (among his innumerable visitors were many Protestant leaders, the head of the Greek Orthodox Church, the archbishop of Canterbury, and a Shinto high priest). In April, 1959, he forbade Roman Catholics to vote for parties supporting Communism, but his encyclical *Mater et Magistra*—a vigorous social document issued July 14, 1961, just 30 years after Pius XI's *Quadragesimo Anno*—advocated social reform, assistance to underdeveloped countries, a living wage for all workers, and support for all socialist measures that promised real benefit to society. Pope John XXIII almost doubled the number of cardinals, making the college the largest in history. On Jan. 25, 1959, he quietly announced the intention of calling an ecumenical council to consider measures for renewal of the church in the modern world, promotion of diversity within the encasing unity of the church, and the reforms that had been earnestly promoted by the ecumenical movement and the liturgical movement (see LITURGY). The convening of the council on Oct. 11, 1962, was the high point of his reign (see VATICAN COUNCIL, SECOND). His heartiness, his overflowing love for humanity individually and collectively, and his freshness of approach to ecclesiastical affairs made John one of the best-loved popes of modern times. He was succeeded by Paul VI. In 1965 the process of beatification of John XXIII was begun. See his memoirs, *Journal of a Soul* (tr. 1964) and *Letters to his Family* (1970); biographies by Meriol Trevor (1967) and Lawrence Elliott (1973).

John I (John Tzimisces)(tsĭmĭs'ēz), c.925-976, Byzantine emperor (969-76). Of a noble Armenian family, he was the leading general of Emperor NICEPHORUS II, but fell from favor in 969. With the aid of the emperor's wife, Theophano, he had Nicephorus murdered and himself proclaimed emperor. John gained the favor of the patriarch of Constantinople by revoking his predecessor's anticlerical legislation. He regained E Bulgaria from the Russians and extended Byzantine power in the east at the expense of the Arabs. He was succeeded by Basil II.

John II (John Comnenus)(kŏmnē'nəs), 1088-1143, Byzantine emperor (1118-43), son and successor of Alexius I. He was crowned despite the intrigues of his sister, ANNA COMNENA, and of his mother, Irene. His attempts to cancel the commercial privileges granted the Venetians by Alexius were unsuccessful, but his campaigns against the Magyars, Serbs, and Pechenegs were victorious. He successfully defied Roger II of Sicily, made an alliance with Emperor Conrad III to check growing Norman power, and conquered Cilicia from the Armenians. He died while preparing to fight the Latin prince of Antioch. John II was respected for his lofty character and for leniency toward his adversaries. He was succeeded by his son Manuel I.

John III (John Ducas Vatatzes) (do͞o'kəs vətăt'zēz), d. 1254, Byzantine emperor of Nicaea (1222-54), successor and son-in-law of Theodore I. He extended his territory in Asia Minor and the Aegean islands but failed (1235) to take Constantinople from the Latins, although he was aided by IVAN II of Bulgaria. Subsequently Ivan, the Cumans, and the Latins of Constantinople allied themselves against John, who held his own. John joined the Turks against the Mongol invaders. He annexed Salonica (Thessaloníki) in 1246 and reduced the despotat of Epirus to vassalage, thus nearly recovering the territories of the Byzantine Empire. He maintained close relations with the German emperor, Frederick II, whose daughter he married. During his reign the empire flourished. He was succeeded by his son Theodore II.

John IV (John Lascaris)(lăs'kərĭs), b. c.1250, d. after 1273, Byzantine emperor of Nicaea (1258-61), son and successor (under a regency) of Theodore II and last of the Lascarids. Michael Palaeologus (later MICHAEL VIII) overthrew the regency and in 1259 was crowned coemperor. He postponed John's coronation and in 1261 had the boy blinded and imprisoned. It is possible that John escaped from his fortress and went (c.1273) to the court of Charles of Anjou.

John V (John Palaeologus) (pālēŏl'əgəs), 1332-91, Byzantine emperor (1341-91), son and successor of Andronicus III. Forced to fight John VI (John Cantacuzene), who usurped the throne during his minority, he came into power in 1354. In his reign the Ottoman Turks took Adrianople and Philippolis, conquered Serbia, and exacted tribute from the emperor. John vainly tried to heal the schism between East and West in order to secure Western aid against the Turks. He professed (1369) the Roman Catholic faith at Rome; while returning to Constantinople he was briefly imprisoned for debt in Venice. In 1371 he recognized the suzerainty of the Ottoman sultan Murad I. Deposed (1376) by his son Andronicus IV, he was restored in 1379. In 1390 his grandnephew, John VII, briefly usurped the throne. John V was succeeded by his son Manuel II.

John VI (John Cantacuzene) (kăn"təkyo͞ozēn'), c.1292-1383, Byzantine emperor (1347-54). He was chief minister under Andronicus III, after whose death he proclaimed himself emperor and made war on the rightful heir, John V. He was aided by the Ottoman Turks. The war allowed STEPHEN DUSHAN to build his Serbian empire. John's reign briefly quieted civil and religious strife within the empire. In 1354 he abdicated in favor of John V and retired to a monastery, where he wrote a history of the period 1320–56. A defender of the mystical theory known as Hesychasm, he was instrumental in its acceptance by the Orthodox Eastern Church.

John VII (John Palaeologus) (pā″lēŏl′əgəs), c.1370–1408, Byzantine emperor, grandson of John V. Backed by the sultan Bayazid I, he usurped (1390) the throne from John V but was dethroned by his uncle, Manuel II, six months later. He again ruled (1394–1403) as coemperor when Manuel II went to the West to seek aid against the Turks.

John VIII (John Palaeologus), 1390–1448, Byzantine emperor (1425–48), son and successor of Manuel II. When he acceded, the Byzantine Empire had been reduced by the Turks to the city of Constantinople. John sought in vain to secure Western aid by agreeing at the Council of Florence (1439) to the union of the Eastern and Western churches. His brother, Constantine XI, succeeded him in 1449 and was the last Byzantine emperor.

John I, 1350–95, king of Aragón and count of Barcelona (1387–95), son and successor of Peter IV. During his reign Aragón lost (1388) the duchy of Athens. An enthusiastic patron of learning and an imitator of French customs, he held one of the most brilliant courts of the time. He was succeeded by his brother, Martin I.

John II, 1397–1479, king of Aragón and Sicily (1458–79), king of Navarre (1425–79), count of Barcelona. He succeeded his brother, Alfonso V, in Aragón, Catalonia, and Sicily and became king of Navarre through his marriage with Blanche, heiress of that kingdom. After Blanche's death (1442) Navarre was ruled by their son, CHARLES OF VIANA, but conflict between father and son plunged Navarre into civil war, and Charles fled to Italy. In 1461 a Catalan uprising forced John to recognize Charles as heir, but Charles died in the same year. John was expelled from Catalonia, and René of Anjou was chosen count of Barcelona. Only in 1472 did John succeed in pacifying Catalonia. At John's death Navarre passed to the house of FOIX through the marriage of John's daughter Leonor; Aragón, Catalonia, and Sicily passed to his son, Ferdinand II, who as Ferdinand V also became king of Castile.

John, 1167–1216, king of England (1199–1216), son of HENRY II and ELEANOR OF AQUITAINE. The king's youngest son, John was left out of Henry's original division of territory among his sons and was nicknamed John Lackland. He was, however, his father's favorite, and despite the opposition of his brothers (whose rebellion of 1173–74 was provoked by Henry's plans for John), he later received scattered possessions in England and France and the lordship of Ireland. His brief expedition to Ireland in 1185 was badly mismanaged. John deserted his dying father in 1189 and joined the rebellion of his brother Richard, who succeeded to the throne as RICHARD I in the same year. The new king generously conferred lands and titles on John. After Richard's departure on the Third Crusade, John led a rebellion against the chancellor, William of LONGCHAMP, had himself acknowledged (1191) temporary ruler and heir to the throne, and conspired with PHILIP II of France to supplant Richard on the throne. This plot was successfully thwarted by those loyal to Richard, including the queen mother, Eleanor of Aquitaine. Richard pardoned John's treachery. On Richard's death, John ascended the English throne to the exclusion of his nephew, ARTHUR I of Brittany. The supporters of Arthur, aided by King Philip, began a formidable revolt in France. At this time John alienated public opinion in England by divorcing his first wife, Isabel of Gloucester, and made enemies in France by marrying Isabel of Angoulême, who had been betrothed to Hugh de Lusignan. In 1202, Arthur was defeated and captured, and it is thought that John murdered him in 1203. Philip continued the war and gradually gained ground until by 1206 he was in control of Normandy, Anjou, Brittany, Maine, and Touraine. John had lost all his French dominions except Aquitaine and a part of Poitou. The death (1205) of John's chancellor, Hubert WALTER, archbishop of Canterbury, not only removed a moderating influence on the king but precipitated a crisis with the English church. John refused (1206) to accept the election of Stephen LANGTON as Walter's successor at Canterbury, and as a result Pope INNOCENT III placed (1208) England under interdict and excommunicated (1209) the king. The quarrel continued until 1213 when John, threatened by the danger of a French invasion and by increasing disaffection among the English barons, surrendered his kingdom to the pope and received it back as a papal fief. Submission improved John's situation greatly. Now backed by the pope, he formed an expedition to wage war on Philip in Poitou. However, while John was at La Rochelle, his allies, Holy Roman Emperor OTTO IV (his nephew) and the count of Flanders, were decisively beaten by Philip at Bouvines in 1214. John had resorted to all means to secure men and money for his Poitou campaign, and after returning home he attempted to collect SCUTAGE from the barons who had refused to aid him on the expedition. Abuses of feudal customs and extortion of money from the barons and the towns, not only by John but by Henry II and Richard I, had aroused intense opposition, which increased in John's unfortunate reign. The barons now rose in overwhelming force against the king, and John in capitulation set his seal on the MAGNA CARTA at Runnymede in June, 1215. Thus, the most famous document of English constitutional history was the fruit not of popular but of baronial force. John, supported by the pope, gathered forces and renewed the struggle with the barons, who sought the aid of Prince Louis of France (later LOUIS VIII). In the midst of this campaign John died, and his son, Henry III, was left to carry on the royal cause. John, though often cruel and treacherous, was an excellent administrator, much concerned with rendering justice among his subjects. The basic cause of his conflicts with the barons was not that he was an innovator in trying to wield an absolute royal power, but that in so doing he ignored and contravened the traditional feudal relationship between the crown and the nobility. The modern bitter and hostile picture of John is primarily the work of subsequent chroniclers, mainly ROGER OF WENDOVER and MATTHEW OF PARIS. John is the central character of one of Shakespeare's plays. See biographies by Kate Margate (1902, repr. 1970), John T. Appleby (1958), W. L. Warren (1961), J. C. Holt (1963), and Alan Lloyd (1972); A. L. Poole, *From Domesday Book to Magna Carta, 1087–1216* (2d ed. 1955).

John I or **John the Posthumous,** 1316, king of France, posthumous son of King Louis X. He lived only five days and was succeeded by his uncle, Philip V. According to legend, a dying child was substituted for John, who was then brought up by a merchant in Siena.

John II (John the Good), 1319–64, king of France (1350–64), son and successor of King Philip VI. An inept ruler, he began his reign by executing the constable of France (whose office he gave to his favorite, Charles de La Cerda) and by appointing dishonest and unpopular advisers. Because of a general economic crisis, he subsequently debased the coinage for the expenses of the Hundred Years War between France and England. His quarrels with his ambitious son-in-law, CHARLES II of Navarre, lasted throughout his reign. John was captured (1356) by the English at the battle of Poitiers. During his captivity, the dauphin (later King CHARLES V) acted as regent and dealt with several rebellions, such as the JACQUERIE. In 1360, by the Treaty of BRÉTIGNY, John was released in exchange for a ransom and hostages. In 1364 one of the hostages escaped, and John saved his honor by returning to England, where he died.

John I (John Zapolya) (zä′pôlyŏ), 1487–1540, king of Hungary (1526–40), voivode [governor] of Transylvania (1511–26). He was born John Zapolya, the son of Stephen ZAPOLYA. The leader of the antiforeign party of the Hungarian nobles, he secured a decree at the diet of 1505 by which no foreign ruler would be chosen king of Hungary after the death of the ruling king, ULADISLAUS II. To strengthen his own candidacy for the crown he sought to marry the king's daughter, Anna, but his suit was rejected and he was removed from the court through his appointment as voivode of Transylvania. He ruthlessly crushed a peasant uprising in 1514. His anger at the marriage of Anna to Ferdinand of Austria (later Holy Roman Emperor FERDINAND I) probably motivated his failure to assist Uladislaus' son, King Louis II of Hungary, at the battle of MOHACS (1526). Louis II was killed in the battle. John was crowned king by the Hungarian nobles, but Ferdinand claimed the crown on the basis of his marriage with Anna as well as previous agreements. In 1527, Ferdinand defeated John and was crowned by John's opponents. John retired to his stronghold in the Carpathians. In 1529 the Turks began to overrun Hungary. John now descended upon and defeated Ferdinand's army and, after surrendering the crown to Sultan Sulayman I, was confirmed king by the sultan, who exercised real control. The struggle between John and Ferdinand ended in 1538, when John, who was then childless, agreed that the crown should pass to Ferdinand after his death. John set aside the agreement when, a few months before his death, a son, John Sigismund (John II), was born.

John II (John Sigismund Zapolya), 1540–71, king of Hungary and prince of Transylvania, son of John I. Through his mother, Isabel (daughter of Sigismund I of Poland), he was related to the Jagiello dynasty. As an infant, he was crowned king of Hungary on his father's death (1540). Sultan SULAYMAN I, on the pretext of protecting John's interests, invaded (1541) Hungary and took the capital, Buda, which remained in Turkish hands for 150 years. John and Isabel received the principality of Transylvania under Turkish suzerainty, but actual power was held by John's guardian, the monk George Martinuzzi, who sought to restore a unified Hungary. In 1551, Martinuzzi procured the deposition of John and Isabel and reunited Transylvania with Hungary, recognizing Ferdinand of Austria and Bohemia (later Holy Roman Emperor FERDINAND I) as king. Martinuzzi, made prince-primate and a cardinal, soon fell out with Ferdinand, who had him assassinated. On the pressure of Sulayman I the diet of Transylvania recalled (1556) John and Isabel, and when Ferdinand made peace (1562) with Sulayman, he also recognized John as ruler of Transylvania. Thus Hungary remained split into three states—an Austrian part, a Turkish part, and Transylvania. It was under John II that the Transylvanian diet adopted (1564) Calvinism as the state religion. John was succeeded as prince of Transylvania by Stephen Bathory.

John II (John Casimir), 1609–72, king of Poland (1648–68), son of Sigismund III. He was elected to succeed his brother, Ladislaus IV. The turbulent period of his reign is known in Polish history as the Deluge. The uprising of the Cossacks under CHMIELNICKI, supported by the khan of Crimea, had begun under his predecessor. John II defeated (1651) the allied Cossack, Tatar, and Turkish forces, but in 1654 the Cossacks accepted Russian suzerainty over the UKRAINE, and Czar Alexis promptly invaded Poland. In 1655, CHARLES X of Sweden nearly overran Poland and was checked only by the successful Polish defense of CZESTOCHOWA, which inspired the Poles to renewed resistance. George II Rákóczy, prince of Transylvania, attacked Poland from the south but was defeated. FREDERICK WILLIAM of Brandenburg (the Great Elector), originally a Swedish ally, joined (1657) the Polish side in the struggle; in return John recognized his full sovereignty over East Prussia. The fighting in the west was concluded in 1660 (see OLIVA, PEACE OF). War with Russia ended only in 1667, with the cession of the eastern part of Ukraine to the czar. During John's reign the *liberum veto* (by which any deputy could dissolve the diet and annul its decisions) was greatly abused. The king and his French consort, Louise Marie de Gonzague (widow of Ladislaus IV), were childless; their efforts to nominate a successor evoked several rebellions of the nobles. A year after the death (1667) of his queen, who had exerted much influence over him, John abdicated and retired to an abbey at Nevers, France. Michael Wisniowiecki was elected his successor; disorder continued during his reign (1668–73), which was followed by that of John III.

John III (John Sobieski), (sôbyĕ′skē), 1624–96, king of Poland (1674–96), champion of Christian Europe against the Turks. Born to an ancient noble family, he was appointed (1668) commander of the Polish army. He defeated (1673) the Turks at Khotin shortly after the death of King Michael, and in 1674 he was elected to succeed Michael. John's plans to recover East Prussia led him to conclude alliances with France (1675) and Sweden (1677) against Frederick William of Brandenburg (the Great Elector). However, the emphasis of his foreign policy changed when Sultan Muhammad IV and the Hungarians under Thököly advanced against Austria. Realizing the danger to all Europe, John allied (1683) with Holy Roman Emperor Leopold I and, leading combined imperial and Polish forces, raised the siege of VIENNA and defeated the much larger Turkish army under Kara Mustapha. Despite Leopold's ungrateful reception, John continued his campaign and pursued the Turks into Hungary. In 1684 he formed a Holy League with the pope, the emperor, and Venice. In 1686 he made a treaty with Russia that confirmed Russian suzerainty in E Ukraine. However, John's attempts (1684–91) to secure access to the Black Sea by wresting Moldavia and Walachia from the Ottoman Empire were unsuccessful. His loss of military prestige encouraged the nobles to oppose him at home. John's death, followed by the choice of the elector of Saxony as King Augustus II of Poland, marked the virtual end of Polish independence.

John I (John the Great), 1357?-1433, king of Portugal (1385-1433), illegitimate son of Peter I. He was made (1364) grand master of the Knights of Aviz and exercised his influence in opposition to Leonor Teles, the queen of his half brother, FERDINAND I. After Ferdinand's death (1383), his widow and her lover, the conde de Ourém, set up a regency in the name of Ferdinand's daughter Beatrice, wife of John I of Castile. This provoked a popular national revolt, led by John of Aviz, who murdered Ourém, and Nun' Álvares PEREIRA. The Castilians invaded (1384) Portugal, but their forces were decimated by the plague while they laid siege to Lisbon. John was elected king in 1385, and in the same year a great victory over the Castilians at Aljubarrota assured Portuguese independence (though peace was not finally concluded until 1411). John's position was strengthened by an alliance with England, sealed by a treaty (1386) and by John's marriage (1387) to Philippa, daughter of JOHN OF GAUNT. The reign of John the Great was one of the most glorious in medieval Portuguese history. His popularity was heightened by his administrative reforms. His sons, Duarte, Peter, Henry the Navigator, John, and Ferdinand, were important in inaugurating the era of Portuguese colonial and maritime expansion. Ceuta in N Africa was conquered from the Moors in 1415. John was succeeded by his son Duarte.

John II (John the Perfect), 1455-95, king of Portugal (1481-95), son and successor of Alfonso V. He was an astute politician and statesman and a patron of Renaissance art and learning. He reduced the power of the feudal nobility and had his chief opponent, the duke of BRAGANZA, executed for treason. John maintained peace with Spain and signed (1494) the Treaty of TORDESILLAS, setting bounds for Spanish and Portuguese colonial expansion. Supporting Portuguese exploration, he sent land expeditions to India and Ethiopia in search of Prester John and sent a vessel N past North Cape. John refused to help Columbus, whom he thought a dreamer, but he encouraged the search for an eastern sea route to India. Diogo Cão discovered (1484) the Congo, and Bartholomew Diaz rounded (1488) the Cape of Good Hope during his reign. John's son Alfonso predeceased him, so he was succeeded by his cousin and brother-in-law, Manuel I.

John III (John the Fortunate), 1502-57, king of Portugal (1521-57), son of MANUEL I. His reign saw the Portuguese empire at its apogee. The great Asiatic possessions were extended by further conquest, and systematic colonization of Brazil was begun. However, in Portugal itself decadence had set in with the decline of both agriculture and the population. Portugal's African exploits were abandoned, but many Negro slaves were brought into the country. The Inquisition was introduced (1536) by John, who was devoted to the clerical party. The court was corrupt, though the king was not. Literature flourished early in his reign, but Portugal was falling into the stagnation that characterized the disastrous reign of Sebastian, who succeeded him.

John IV, 1604-56, king of Portugal (1640-56). He succeeded as duke of BRAGANZA in 1630. Descended from Manuel I and in illegitimate line from John I, he had the strongest claim to the Portuguese throne when a revolution was planned to cast off the rule of Philip IV of Spain. In 1640 the revolution was successfully carried out, and John became king of independent Portugal. John's policy was to secure foreign alliances, especially with France, in order to consolidate his position against Spain (which did not recognize Portuguese independence until 1668). During his reign the Dutch were expelled (1654) from Brazil, where they had seized territory during the period of Spanish rule. John was unwarlike himself and was devoted to hunting, music, and the arts. The first king of the Braganza line, he was succeeded by his son Alfonso VI. His daughter Catherine married Charles II of England.

John V (John the Magnanimous), 1689-1750, king of Portugal (1706-50), son and successor of Peter II. Before his accession the Methuen Treaty (1703) with England had brought Portugal into the War of the SPANISH SUCCESSION, but after a major defeat at Almansa (1707), the Portuguese played little part in the fighting. After the war, John sought to maintain Portugal's alliance with England and to keep peace, except in giving assistance (1716-17) to the Venetians against the Turks. Enriched by gold from Brazil, John was a patron of arts and letters, had a sumptuous court, and erected beautiful buildings in Lisbon. However, his wealth also made him independent of the Cortes, so he ruled with increasing absolutism. He has been criticized for subservience to the church, from which he drew most of his ministers, especially in later years. John was succeeded by his son Joseph.

John VI, 1769-1826, king of Portugal (1816-26), son of Maria I and Peter III. When his mother became insane, John assumed the reins of government (1792), although he did not formally become regent until 1799. He joined the coalition against revolutionary France, adopted a repressive policy in Portugal, and sought the friendship of England. The English alliance made Napoleon I an inveterate enemy of Portugal. French and Spanish forces in 1801 quickly defeated Portugal and forced on John the humiliating Treaty of Badajoz (1801). John was completely submissive to Napoleon, but nonetheless in 1807 the French again marched against Portugal. John and the royal family fled (1807) Lisbon and arrived (1808) in Brazil, where John set up his court. After the British defeated the French in Portugal, they set up a regency to rule the country. John, however, remained in Brazil even after succeeding as king on his mother's death (1816). It was only after the overthrow of the regency in Portugal by revolution (1820) and the proclamation of a liberal constitution that John was persuaded by the British to return (1821) to Portugal. He left his son Pedro (PEDRO I) as regent of Brazil. After accepting the constitution, he took advantage of every opportunity to modify it. He put down temporarily an absolutist revolt headed by his wife, Queen Carlota Joaquina, and his son Dom MIGUEL and in 1825 recognized Brazilian independence (proclaimed in 1822). On his death John left the regency of Portugal to his daughter Isabel, who recognized Pedro as Peter IV of Portugal.

John I, 1358-90, Spanish king of Castile and León (1379-90), son and successor of Henry II. He tried unsuccessfully to unite the Portuguese and Castilian crowns but was twice defeated by the Portuguese, notably in the battle of Aljubarrota (1385). He defended his crown against JOHN OF GAUNT and married his son Henry to John of Gaunt's daughter. Henry succeeded him as Henry III.

John II, 1405-54, Spanish king of Castile and León (1406-54), son and successor of Henry III. He was little interested in government, which he entrusted to his favorite Alvaro de LUNA. Literature, particularly poetry, flourished at his court, which was also celebrated for tournaments and brilliant festivals. John was succeeded by his son Henry IV.

John, in the Bible. **1** See JOHN, SAINT. **2** See JOHN THE BAPTIST. **3** See MARK, SAINT. **4** One of the high priest's family. Acts 4.6. There are also several persons named John in the books of the Maccabees. See MACCABEES and 1 Mac. 9.36-38; 13.53; 16.2; 2 Mac. 4.11; 11.17.

John, Augustus Edwin, 1879-1961, British painter and etcher, b. Wales. John studied at the Slade School, London. A leading portrait painter, he had many important sitters, among them Elizabeth II, Lloyd George, G. B. Shaw, T. E. Lawrence, Sean O'Casey, and Dylan Thomas. His portraits show vigorous characterization without flattery. His celebrated *Smiling Woman* is a portrait of his wife (1910; Tate Gall., London). John's etchings include several self-portraits as well as portraits of W. B. Yeats, Jacob Epstein, and James Joyce. See his autobiographical *Chiaroscuro* (1952); studies by T. W. Earp (1934) and John Rothenstein (1945). John's sister **Gwen John** (1876-1939) was a student of Whistler and a painter in the Pre-Raphaelite manner.

John, three epistles of the New Testament, the 23d, 24th, and 25th books in the usual order. By universal tradition they are ascribed to St. John, the disciple. This authorship is necessarily denied by the many critics who do not admit St. John to be the writer of the Gospel, for First John was certainly written by the man who wrote the Gospel, and Second and Third John are widely agreed to be by the same author also. The date of First John is about that of the Gospel; nothing can be said of the dates of the other two. These epistles are traditionally classed with the Catholic, or General, Epistles, but they were apparently addressed to definite churches or persons. First John is a homily on the blending of mystical and practical religion, intended for persons long Christian. A division of the book gives: prologue (1.1-4); God is light (1.5-2.28); God is righteous (2.29-4.6); God is love (4.7-5.12); epilogue (5.13-21). The necessity of good works to reveal the Christian heart is reiterated, e.g., 2.3-5; 3.24; 4.7-11,20. There is an allusion to the gnostic error of denying Jesus' historicity (4.2-3). Second John, in 13 verses, is the shortest book of the Bible. The author refers to himself as elder (presbyter or priest) and is addressing some "elect lady," probably an allegorical title, perhaps for a particular church. The letter warns against false teachers who deny the historicity of Jesus. Third John, in 14 verses, has the same author; it is addressed to a Gaius, of an unidentified church. It protests against the failure of the leader of the church to receive teaching missionaries.

John, Gospel according to Saint, fourth book of the New Testament. This life of Jesus is clearly set off from the other three Gospels (see SYNOPTIC GOSPELS), although it is probable that John knew and used both Mark and Luke as sources. The aim of the evangelist seems to be twofold—to show that Jesus is the vital force in the world now and forever and that he lived on earth in order to reveal himself to men in the flesh. These two ideas are, for the evangelist, complementary, and one of the artistic beauties of the Gospel is the way Jesus' acts as a human being introduce discourses upon his mystical nature. The Gospel opens with a philosophical prologue (1.1-18), in which Jesus is identified with the Word (or LOGOS). The author adopted this term from contemporary metaphysicians who used it to designate the link between God and man. Hence "the Word was made flesh" (1.14) is the explicit classical statement of the Incarnation. The book falls into two main sections, the ministry of Jesus (1.19-12.50) and the Passion and Resurrection (13-21). The first portion is a series of selected incidents from the ministry of Christ. The last part consists of a long account of the Last Supper (13-17), the Passion proper (18-19), and the Resurrection (20-21). The traditional date of composition is A.D. c.100; according to 20th-century scholarship it was composed probably between A.D. 95 and 115. The ascription to St. JOHN is very ancient, but it has been questioned by modern critics. Most scholars agree that 7.53-8.11 was not part of the Gospel as first composed; otherwise the book is usually considered to have been written almost exactly as it stands. The influence of the Gospel of St. John in Christianity has been tremendous. The unique position of Jesus Christ in Christian theology as God and man, which involves the dogmas of the Trinity, the Incarnation, and the Atonement, is first enunciated in this Gospel. See E. F. Scott, *The Fourth Gospel* (2d ed. 1930); C. H. Dodd, *The Interpretation of the Fourth Gospel* (1953, repr. 1960); J. L. Martyn, *History and Theology in the Fourth Gospel* (1968).

John Baptist de la Salle, Saint, 1651-1719, French educator, founder of the Christian Brothers, b. Rheims. He became a priest and canon of the cathedral. He spent his life teaching children of the poor. In 1684 (having resigned his canonry) he formed of his assistants a new order, the Christian Brothers. In 1685 to train his teachers, St. John Baptist founded at Rheims what is called the first normal school. He was a careful pedagogical thinker and ranks as one of the distinguished educators of modern times. His name in French is Jean Baptiste de la Salle. Feast: May 15. See W. J. Battersby, *De la Salle* (3 vol., 1945-52).

John Birch Society, ultraconservative, anti-Communist organization in the United States. It was founded in Dec., 1958, by manufacturer Robert Welch and named after John Birch, an American intelligence officer killed by Communists in China (Aug., 1945). The most prominent of the extreme right-wing groups active in the United States, the society was founded to fight subversive Communism within the United States. Its other objectives include the abolition of the graduated income tax, the repeal of social security legislation, the impeachment of various high government officials, and the end to bussing for the purpose of integrating the public schools. These objectives, together with charges made by Welch in his book, *The Politician*, to the effect that Dwight D. Eisenhower and John Foster Dulles had actively aided the so-called Communist conspiracy, tend to discredit the organization. See Richard Vahan, *The Truth about the John Birch Society* (1962); J. A. Broyles, *The John Birch Society* (1964); B. R. Epstein and Arnold Foster, *Radical Right* (1967).

John Bosco, Saint, 1815-88, Italian priest, b. Piedmont. As a priest at Turin he was very successful in work with boys. He founded (1841) the Salesian order (i.e., order of St. Francis of Sales) for this work and for foreign missions. Later he founded an order of women, Daughters of Mary Auxiliatrix, for similar work among girls. These orders have become very large. He was canonized in 1934. Feast: Jan. 31. See Henri Ghéon, *The Secret of Saint John Bosco* (1936).

John Bull: see ARBUTHNOT, JOHN.

John Carter Brown Library: see BROWN, JOHN CARTER.

John Chrysostom, Saint (krĭs'əstəm, krĭsŏs'-) [Gr.,=golden-mouth], c.347-407, Doctor of the Church, greatest of the Greek Fathers. He was born in Antioch and studied Greek classics there. As a young man he became an anchorite monk (374), a deacon (c.381) and a priest (386). Under Flavian of Antioch he preached brilliantly in the cathedral for 12 years, winning wide recognition. In 398 he was suddenly made patriarch of Constantinople, where he soon gained the admiration of the people by his eloquence, his ascetic life, and his charity. His attempts to reform the clergy, however, alienated many monks and priests, and the court of the Roman emperor of the East came to resent his denunciation of their ways. He lost favor when he demanded mercy for the dishonored EUTROPIUS and when he refused to condemn without a hearing certain monks accused of heresy. Empress Eudoxia and Theophilus, bishop of Alexandria, succeeded in having St. John condemned (403) by an illegal synod on false charges. The indignation of the people was reinforced by an opportune earthquake, and the superstitious Eudoxia had St. John recalled. He continued to attack the immorality of the court, and Emperor Arcadius exiled him to Cucusus in Armenia. There he continued to exert influence through his letters, and Arcadius moved him to a more isolated spot on the Black Sea. St. John, already ill, died from the rigors of the journey. Although not a formal polemicist, John Chrysostom influenced Christian thought notably. He wrote brilliant homilies, interpreting the Bible literally and historically rather than allegorically. His treatise on the priesthood (381) has always been popular. His sermons and writings, remarkable for their purity of Greek style, afford an invaluable picture of 4th-century life. His influence was already great in his own day, and the pope withdrew (406-16) from communion with Constantinople because of his banishment. In 438, St. John's body was returned to Constantinople, and Emperor Theodosius II did penance for his parents' offenses. John Chrysostom was not the author of the liturgy that bears his name. In 1909, Pope Pius X declared him patron of preachers. Feasts: in the Eastern Church, Sept. 14, Nov. 13, and Jan. 27; in the Western Church, Jan. 27. See studies by W. R. W. Stephens (3d ed. 1883; Anglican) and Donald Attwater (1939; Roman Catholic).

John Climax, Saint [Gr.,=ladder], d. c.649, Syrian hermit of Mt. Sinai. Little is known of his life, but his guide to the spiritual life in 30 steps, *The Ladder of Paradise,* was widely read in the Middle Ages. He is also known as John Climacus or John Scholasticus. Feast: March 30.

John Crerar Library: see CRERAR, JOHN.

John Damascene, Saint: see JOHN OF DAMASCUS, SAINT.

John Day, river, 281 mi (452 km) long, rising in several branches in the Strawberry Mts., NE Oregon, and flowing W, then N to the Columbia River. Unnavigable, the river is used to irrigate vegetable farms.

John Day Dam, 219 ft (67 m) high and 5,640 ft (1,719 m) long, on the Columbia River between Oregon and Wash.; one of the world's largest hydroelectric generating plants. Built between 1959 and 1968 by the U.S. Army Corps of Engineers, the dam will have an ultimate generating capacity of 2,700,000 kw. The dam's reservoir regulates navigation upstream; locks provide ship passage from The Dalles Dam reservoir to McNary Dam (see COLUMBIA BASIN PROJECT).

John Dory: see ROCKFISH.

John D. Rockefeller, Jr., Memorial Parkway, Wyo.: see NATIONAL PARKS AND MONUMENTS (table).

John Fisher, Saint: see FISHER, JOHN.

John Fitzgerald Kennedy National Historic Site: see NATIONAL PARKS AND MONUMENTS (table).

John Frederick I, 1503-54, elector (1532-47) and duke (1547-54) of Saxony; last elector of the Ernestine branch of the house of WETTIN. Like his father, John the Steadfast, whom he succeeded, John Frederick was a devout Lutheran. A leader of the SCHMALKALDIC LEAGUE, he vacillated in loyalty to Holy Roman Emperor CHARLES V, but he was thrown into opposition when Charles undertook the Schmalkaldic War to crush the independence of the imperial states in Germany and to restore Christian unity. Captured (1547) in the battle of Mühlberg, John Frederick was forced to renounce the electorate in favor of his cousin and enemy, MAURICE, duke of Saxony. He retained only a remnant of his lands and the title of duke. He refused to abandon his religious beliefs during subsequent imprisonment (1547-52).

John George, 1585-1656, elector of Saxony (1611-56). A drunkard, he nonetheless ruled the leading German Protestant state during the THIRTY YEARS WAR. He vacillated in his policy between support of the Holy Roman Empire against the Lutheran princes and aid to his fellow Lutherans. He backed (1620) Holy Roman Emperor FERDINAND II against Protestant rebels in Bohemia under FREDERICK THE WINTER KING, and in return was promised Lusatia. After Frederick's defeat, however, he opposed the transfer (1623) of the Palatinate to Duke MAXIMILIAN I of Bavaria. The Edict of Restitution (1629), abrogating Protestant rights, increased his opposition to imperial policy. John George joined the Swedes against the emperor, and the Saxon army invaded Bohemia. The Saxons were driven back by the imperial general WALLENSTEIN, who turned on Saxony (1632) and devastated it. In 1635, John George deserted the Swedish alliance and concluded the Peace of Prague with Ferdinand II, which confirmed his possession of Lusatia. War continued and Saxony was repeatedly destroyed by opposing armies. In 1645, John George signed an armistice with the Swedes. After the war, the Holy Roman emperor made him titular leader of the Protestant estates.

John Henry, legendary American Negro famous for his strength, celebrated in ballads and tales. In the most popular version of the story, John Henry tries to outwork a steam drill with only his hammer and steel bit. Although he succeeds in beating the machine, he dies of the strain. His legend originated c.1870 among the miners drilling the Big Bend Tunnel of the Chesapeake & Ohio Railway in West Virginia and may have some historical basis.

John Hyrcanus: see MACCABEES, Jewish family.

John Jay College of Criminal Justice of the City University of New York; est. 1964 as the College of Police Science, opened 1965. Its present name was adopted in 1966. The school offers a basic college curriculum, but its emphasis is on both undergraduate and graduate training in the field of criminal justice. The majority of its students are police and law enforcement officers; however, the college is open to civilian students. See NEW YORK, CITY UNIVERSITY OF.

John Mark: see MARK, ST.

John Maurice of Nassau, 1604-79, Dutch general and colonial administrator, a prince of the house of Nassau-Siegen; grandnephew of William the Silent. The Dutch West India Company appointed him (1636) governor-general of its newly acquired possessions in Brazil. He conquered NE Brazil from the Portuguese and, in order to insure the supply of slave labor, seized several Portuguese strongholds on the Guinea coast of Africa. An able administrator, John Maurice made broad plans for the development of Brazil. He built up the state of Pernambuco and rebuilt the city of Recife. However, the directors of the company criticized his expenses, while John Maurice was opposed to undertaking the new hostilities that they ordered. On his request he was recalled in 1643. He subsequently held commands in Europe in the Thirty Years War, governed, after 1647, Cleves, Mark, and Ravensberg for the elector of Brandenburg, and in 1652 was made a prince of the Holy Roman Empire; he also was made grand master of the Knights Hospitalers. Despite his advanced age, he won new distinction in the Dutch Wars. After his retirement in 1675 he lived at Cleves. His residence at The Hague is the celebrated Mauritshuis.

John Muir National Historic Site: see NATIONAL PARKS AND MONUMENTS (table).

Johnny Appleseed: see CHAPMAN, JOHN.

Johnny-jump-up: see VIOLET.

John of Austria, 1545-78, Spanish admiral and general; illegitimate son of Holy Roman Emperor Charles V. He was acknowledged in his father's will and was recognized by his half brother, Philip II of Spain. In 1569 he fought against the Morisco rebels in Granada. As admiral of the Holy League, formed against the Turks by Pope Pius V, Spain, and Venice, he won the famous naval victory of LEPANTO (1571). He later took Tunis and served as governor-general in Italy. In 1576 he was sent by Philip as governor-general to the Netherlands, then in rebellion against Spain under the leadership of WILLIAM THE SILENT. John was forced to make concessions but then resumed hostilities. His victorious general, Alessandro FARNESE, succeeded him as governor-general on his death. See Sir William Stirling-Maxwell, *Don John of Austria* (1883).

John of Austria, 1629-79, Spanish general and statesman; illegitimate son of Philip IV. He helped put down Masaniello's revolt (1647) in Naples, was viceroy of Sicily (1648-51), and fought (1651-52) against the rebels in Catalonia. In 1656, while France was at war with Spain (see FRONDE), he was appointed governor of the Spanish Netherlands. He was defeated by Turenne at the battle of the DUNES (1658) and recalled. His campaign (1661-64) for the reconquest of Portugal also failed. During the minority of CHARLES II, he overthrew the regency of the queen-mother Mariana and seized power (1677). His government lost Franche-Comté to France by the peace of Nijmegen (1678).

John of Brienne (brēĕn'), c.1170-1237, French crusader. He was a count and in 1210 married Mary, titular queen of Jerusalem. Mary died in 1212, and their daughter, Yolande (1212-28), succeeded to the title under John's regency. John played a conspicuous part in the Fifth Crusade (see CRUSADES), capturing Damietta in 1219, and in 1222 he went to Europe in search of support. He arranged the marriage (1225) between Yolande and Holy Roman Emperor FREDERICK II, who promptly claimed the crown of Jerusalem. John, claiming the title for himself, joined with a papal army in invading (1229) Frederick's kingdom in S Italy, while Frederick was absent on crusade. In 1228, John was chosen regent during the minority of BALDWIN II, Latin emperor of Constantinople (see CONSTANTINOPLE, LATIN EMPIRE OF), and he became coemperor in 1231. He successfully defended (1236) Constantinople against the joint forces of Emperor John III of Nicaea and Czar Ivan II of Bulgaria.

John of Damascus, Saint, or **Saint John Damascene** (dăm'əsēn), c.675-c.749, Syrian theologian, Father of the Church and Doctor of the Church. He was brought up at the court of the caliph in Damascus, where his father was an official, and he was educated by a Sicilian monk. John inherited his father's office but resigned it (c.726) and entered a monastery in Palestine. His life was spent largely in fighting with his pen for orthodoxy against ICONOCLASM. His fame rests on his theological masterpiece, *The Fountain of Wisdom,* a Greek work in three parts—a theological study of Aristotle's categories; a history of heresies, based on Epiphanius and Theodoret, with supplementary material on iconoclasm and Islam; and a formal exposition of the Christian faith (*De fide orthodoxa,* tr. by F. N. Chase, 1958). This last work was extensively used by the scholastics and is still a prime source for the dogmatic opinions of the principal Eastern Fathers. John also wrote hymns and regulated the choral parts of the Byzantine liturgy. He stimulated the production of Byzantine painting. The elegance of his Greek brought him the epithet Chrysorrhoas [gold-pouring]. His name appears also as John Damascenus. Feast: in Western calendars, March 27. See F. P. Cassidy, *Molders of the Medieval Mind* (1944).

John of Ephesus (ĕf'əsəs), c.505-c.585, Syrian Monophysite historian, bishop of Ephesus. He became a leader of the Monophysites (see MONOPHYSITISM), and Byzantine Emperor Justinian, whose favor he enjoyed, set him over the Monophysite community in Constantinople. John suffered greatly in the persecution of his sect after 571. His *Ecclesiastical History* makes an unusual effort to avoid prejudice. It is especially valuable for the events of the 6th cent. He is also called John of Asia.

John of Gaunt [Mid. Eng. *Gaunt*=Ghent, his birthplace], 1340-99, duke of Lancaster; fourth son of EDWARD III of England. He married (1359) Blanche, heiress of Lancaster, and through her became earl (1361) and duke (1362) of Lancaster. The Lancaster holdings made him the wealthiest and one of the most influential nobles in England. He served under his brother, EDWARD THE BLACK PRINCE, in the Hundred Years War and went (1367) on his campaign to aid PETER THE CRUEL of Castile. After the death of Blanche he married (1371) Peter's daughter, Constance, and thus gained a claim to the Castilian throne. When the Black Prince became ill during the French campaign of 1370-71, John took chief command. In 1373 he led his army from Calais to Bordeaux, but the expedition accomplished little. After a truce was reached (1375) he returned to England, where he allied himself with the corrupt court party led by Alice Perrers, mistress of the aging Edward III. For a short time John of Gaunt in effect ruled England. His party was temporarily dislodged from power by the Good Parliament of 1376, but John was soon able to restore his friends and assembled a hand-picked Parliament in 1377. Hostility to the strong clerical party, led by WILLIAM OF WYKEHAM, caused him to support the movement of John WYCLIF. After the accession (1377) of his nephew, RICHARD II, John remained the most powerful figure in the government, but he devoted himself primarily to military matters. In 1386, allied with John I of Portugal, who married one of his daughters, he led an expedition to make good his Castilian claims against John I of Castile. John of Gaunt finally agreed to peace in 1388, transferred his claims to his daughter by Constance of Castile, and married her to the future Henry III of Castile. He returned to England in 1389, was made duke of Aquitaine, and helped to restore peace between Richard II and the hostile barons led by Thomas of Woodstock, duke of GLOUCESTER. In 1396, John of Gaunt married Catherine Swynford, many years his mistress, and had his children by her, under the name of Beaufort, declared legitimate. He died soon after the king had exiled his eldest son, the duke of Hereford (later HENRY IV, first of the royal line of Lancaster). Another royal line, the Tudor, was descended from him and Catherine Swynford. John is also remembered as the patron of the poet Geoffrey Chaucer. See biography by Sydney Armitage-Smith (1904, repr. 1964); James R. Hulbert, *Chaucer's Official Life* (1912, repr. 1970).

John of Hollywood: see SACROBOSCO, JOHANNES DE.

John of Lancaster, duke of Bedford: see BEDFORD, JOHN OF LANCASTER, DUKE OF.

John of Leiden, c.1509–1536, Dutch ANABAPTIST leader. His original name was Beuckelszoon, Beuckelzoon, Bockelszoon, Bockelson, Beukels, or Buckholdt. John of Leiden was attracted to the extreme left of the early Reformation movement through the influence of Thomas MÜNZER. In 1533 he joined the Anabaptists and, as a follower of Johann Matthyszoon (Matthiesen) moved to Münster. There in 1534 the Anabaptists took up arms and deposed the civil and religious authorities of the town. After Matthyszoon's death in the siege, John of Leiden assumed leadership and set up a theocracy in the new Zion. Soon John declared himself "king," with Bernard Knipperdollinck second in command; during his brief and arbitrary rule general lawlessness prevailed, polygamy was legalized, and property communized. When the siege to recover the town, led by the expelled prince bishop, was successful in 1535, the leaders of the new "kingdom of Zion" were barbarously tortured and in the following year executed. See E. Belfort Bax, *Rise and Fall of the Anabaptists* (1903, repr. 1966).

John of Luxemburg, 1296–1346, king of Bohemia (1310–46). The son of Holy Roman Emperor HENRY VII, he married Elizabeth, sister of Wenceslaus III of Bohemia, and in 1310 he was chosen king of Bohemia, which had been in virtual anarchy since Wenceslaus's death (1306). As a condition of his accession John was forced to issue a charter guaranteeing the rights of the nobility and clergy. Perhaps disappointed that he was not elected to succeed his father, John spent much of his time in foreign wars. During his reign he extended Bohemian control to upper Lusatia and Silesia. He supported the Teutonic Knights in their wars against Lithuania. As a result of his campaigns he ruled parts of Lombardy and Tyrol briefly. He died fighting on the side of the French at CRÉCY though he had become blind. He was succeeded by his son, who later became Holy Roman emperor as Charles IV.

John of Nepomuk, Saint (nā'pōmo͝ok), d. 1393, patron saint of Bohemia, a martyr. He is also called John Nepomucen. He was vicar general of Bohemia under King Wenceslaus IV (later Holy Roman Emperor Wenceslaus). When the king wished uncanonically to convert an abbey into a cathedral, St. John opposed him, in spite of torture. The king had him drowned in the Moldau. An earlier story, since disproved, attributes his drowning to his refusal to disclose the confessional secrets of the queen. Feast: May 16.

John of Procida (prō'chĕdä), c.1225–c.1302, Italian conspirator, lord of the island of Procida. He was an ardent supporter of the Hohenstaufen cause in Sicily and attempted to secure the island for MANFRED and CONRADIN against the claims of Charles of Anjou, who was given Sicily by the pope. After Manfred's defeat and Conradin's execution (1268) by Charles, John went into exile at the court of Manfred's son-in-law, PETER III of Aragón. Peter sent him to seek the aid of the Byzantine emperor, Michael VIII, for a projected invasion of Sicily. John probably also secretly visited Sicily, preparing the great uprising of the SICILIAN VESPERS (1282) against Charles, which ultimately brought Peter to the Sicilian throne. In 1283, John was made chancellor of Sicily.

John of Salisbury (sôlz'bərē), c.1110–1180, English scholastic philosopher, b. Salisbury. He studied in France at Paris and Chartres under Abelard and other famous teachers. He was secretary to Theobald, archbishop of Canterbury, and friend and secretary to St. Thomas à Becket, of whom he wrote a biography. From 1176 to 1180, John was bishop of Chartres. His two main works are the *Polycraticus,* a treatise on the principles of government, and the *Metalogicus,* which presents a picture of the intellectual life and the scholastic controversies of the age. He was well acquainted with the Latin classics, and the influence of Platonism on his writing is considerable. He was one of the originators of moderate REALISM as a solution to the controversy with nominalism. See two selections from the *Polycraticus—The Statesman's Book of John of Salisbury* (tr. by John Dickinson, 1927, repr. 1963) and *Frivolities of Courtiers* (tr. by J. P. Pike, 1938, repr. 1972); *The Pontificalis Historia of John of Salisbury* (ed. by Marjorie Chibnall, 1956); C. C. J. Webb, *John of Salisbury* (1931, repr. 1971).

John of Speyer (spī'ər), d. 1470, first printer in Venice, b. Bavaria. He designed and patented the first type purely roman in character. It appears in Cicero's *Epistulae ad familiares* and Pliny's *Historia naturalis,* both printed in 1469. On his death his patent on the roman design expired; Nicolas JENSON was enabled to print with roman type in 1470.

John of the Cross, Saint, Span. *Juan de la Cruz,* 1542–91, Spanish mystic and poet, Doctor of the Church. His name was originally Juan de Yepes. He was a founder of the Discalced Carmelites and a close friend of St. Teresa of Ávila, who guided him in his spiritual life. Because of his ardor in pursuing St. Teresa's reforms he antagonized the hierarchy. In 1577 he was imprisoned in Toledo and was subjected to physical and mental tortures. It was in his prison cell that St. John wrote his famous *Spiritual Canticle* and began his *Songs of the Soul.* These poems—a blend of exquisite lyricism and profound mystical thought—are among the finest creations of the Golden Age of Spanish literature. St. John is regarded by many as Spain's finest lyric poet. After an escape (1578) considered by many to be miraculous, he went to Andalusia, where his last years were spent in a constant struggle against his opponents and in the creation of masterly prose treatises on mystical theology, notably *The Dark Night of the Soul* and *The Ascent of Mount Carmel.* Feast: Nov. 24. See translation of his complete works by E. A. Peers (3 vol., 1953) and of his poems by J. F. Nims (1959); E. A. Peers, *The Spirit of Flame* (1943); Robert Sencourt, *Carmelite and Poet* (1944); Léon Cristiani, *St. John of the Cross* (tr. 1962); Gerald Brenan, *St. John of the Cross* (1973).

Johns, Jasper, 1930–, American artist, b. Augusta, Ga. Influenced by Marcel DUCHAMP in the mid-1950s, Johns attempted to transform common objects into art by placing them in an art context. His flags and target images executed from 1954 to 1959 heralded the POP ART movement. Johns based his painting technique on the informal brushwork and texture of ABSTRACT EXPRESSIONISM, attaching literal elements such as rulers and brooms to the canvas. His bronze castings, such as *Beer Cans* (1960), are also derived from common objects.

John Scotus: see DUNS SCOTUS, JOHN; ERIGENA, JOHN SCOTUS.

Johns Hopkins University, mainly at Baltimore, Md. Johns HOPKINS in 1867 had a group of his associates incorporated as the trustees of a university and a hospital, endowing each with $3.5 million. Daniel C. GILMAN became the first president in 1875, modeled the new school after European universities rather than American colleges, and emphasized graduate research rather than collegiate instruction. When it opened in 1876, Johns Hopkins was considered an experiment, but it was an immediate success. It was extremely influential, and the organizers of such schools as Clark Univ. and the Univ. of Chicago took many of their ideas from the plan of Johns Hopkins. The first American university press was opened at Johns Hopkins in 1878. In 1889, Johns Hopkins Hospital was completed, and in 1893 the famous medical school opened. Today the university includes undergraduate and graduate schools of arts and sciences, schools of engineering, medicine, hygiene and public health, McCoy College (adult education), and the school of advanced international studies (at Washington, D.C.), which has foreign study centers at Bologna, Italy; Rangoon, Burma; and Jogjakarta, Indonesia. The extensive facilities at Baltimore include a nuclear physics laboratory with an electrostatic accelerator. The university operates an applied physics laboratory at Silver Spring, Md.; and the Chesapeake Bay Institute for oceanographic research at Annapolis, Md. Johns Hopkins has a noted library system that houses a number of important manuscript collections and documents. See history by J. C. French (1946).

Johnson, Alexander Bryan, 1786–1867, American philosopher and semanticist, b. Gosport, England. He emigrated (1801) to the United States and eventually became a wealthy banker in Utica, N.Y. Johnson anticipated many of the concerns of logical positivism and modern linguistic philosophy, but his views were ignored in his lifetime and were lost sight of for nearly a century. He held that a statement meant, for a speaker, whatever evidence he adduced or could adduce in its support: Language does not explain the world, rather the world explains language. He showed that many philosophical problems were the result of projecting distinctions of language onto nature, resulting in confusion. In addition to his philosophical works he wrote on politics, economics, and banking. His books included *The Philosophy of Human Knowledge; or A Treatise on Language* (1828), *Religion in its Relation to Present Life* (1841), *The Philosophical Emperor* (1841), and *The Meaning of Words* (1854). See *Centennial Conference on the Life and Works of Alexander Bryan Johnson,* ed. by C. L. Todd and R. T. Blackwood (1969).

Johnson, Allen, 1870–1931, American historian, b. Lowell, Mass. He was professor of history at Iowa (now Grinnell) College (1898–1905), Bowdoin College (1905–10), and Yale (1910–26). He achieved a notable success in editing the "Chronicles of America" (50 vol., 1918–21), a series both scholarly in material and popular in style, to which he contributed *Jefferson and His Colleagues* (Vol. XV, 1921). This success was partly responsible for his being selected as editor in chief of the *Dictionary of American Biography,* published under the auspices of the American Council of Learned Societies. Six volumes appeared before his death, setting the style and standard for the remainder of the enterprise. Among his other works are *Union and Democracy* (1915) and *The Historian and Historical Evidence* (1926, repr. 1965).

Johnson, Andrew, 1808–75, 17th President of the United States (1865–69), b. Raleigh, N.C. His father died when Johnson was 3, and at 14 he was apprenticed to a tailor. In 1826 the family moved to E Tennessee, and Andrew soon had his own tailor shop at Greeneville. A man of no formal schooling but of great perseverance and strength of character, he was greatly aided by his wife, Eliza McCardle, whom he married in 1827; she taught him to write and improved his reading and spelling. He prospered at his trade, and the tailor shop became the favored meeting place of other craftsmen, laborers, and small farmers interested in discussing public affairs. The best debater in the community, Johnson became the leader of his group in opposition to the slaveholding aristocracy. From 1830 onward he was almost continuously in public office, being alderman (1828–30) and mayor (1830–33) of Greeneville, state representative (1835–37, 1839–41), state senator (1841–43), Congressman (1843–53), governor of Tennessee (1853–57), and U.S. Senator (1857–62). As U.S. Representative and Senator, Johnson was principally interested in securing legislation to make land in the West available to homesteaders. He voted with other Southern legislators on questions concerning slavery, but after Tennessee seceded (June 8, 1861), he remained in the Senate, the only Southerner there. He vigorously supported Abraham Lincoln's administration, and in March, 1862, the President appointed him military governor of Tennessee with the rank of brigadier general of volunteers. His ability in filling this difficult position and the fact that he was a Southerner and a war Democrat made him an ideal choice as running mate to Lincoln on the successful Union ticket in 1864. On April 15, 1865, the day after Lincoln's assassination, he took the oath of office as President. Johnson's RECONSTRUCTION program (and he insisted that Reconstruction was an executive, not a legislative, function) was based on the theory that the Southern states had never been out of the Union. He therefore restored civil government in the ex-Confederate states as soon as it was feasible. Because he was not prepared to grant equal civil rights to Negroes and because he did not press for the wholesale disqualification for office of Confederate leaders, he was roundly denounced by the radical Republicans who, led by Thaddeus STEVENS, set out to undo Johnson's work on the convening of the 39th Congress in Dec., 1865. In April, 1866, Congress passed the Civil Rights

Act over Johnson's veto, and his political power began to decline sharply. The remainder of his administration saw one humiliation after another. His "swing around the circle" in the congressional elections of 1866 was unsuccessful. Baited by mobs organized by the radicals and slandered by the press, he struck out at his enemies in such harsh terms that he did his own cause much harm. On March 2, 1867, the radicals passed over his veto the First Reconstruction Act and the TENURE OF OFFICE ACT. When Johnson insisted upon his intention to force out of office his Secretary of War, Edwin M. STANTON, whom he rightly suspected of conspiring with the congressional leaders, the radical Republicans sought to remove the President. Their first attempt failed (Dec., 1867), but on Feb. 24, 1868, the House passed a resolution of impeachment against him even before it adopted (March 2-3) 11 articles detailing the reasons for it. Most important of the charges, which were purely political, was that he had violated the Tenure of Office Act in the Stanton affair. On March 5 the Senate, with Chief Justice Salmon P. Chase presiding, was organized as a court to hear the charges. The President himself did not appear. In spite of the terrific pressure brought to bear on several Senators, the court narrowly failed to convict; the vote, on the 11th article (May 16) and on the second and third articles (May 26), was 35 to 19, one short of the constitutional two thirds required for removal. Although the problems of Reconstruction dominated Johnson's administration, there were important achievements in foreign relations, notably the purchase (1867) of Alaska, negotiated by Secretary of State William H. SEWARD. Johnson's name figured in the balloting at the Democratic convention of 1868, but he did not actively seek the nomination. In 1875, on his third attempt to resume public office, he was returned to the Senate from Tennessee, but died a few months after taking his seat. Publication of his papers, ed. by L. P. Graf and R. W. Haskins, was begun in 1967. See biography by R. W. Winston (1928, repr. 1969); D. M. Dewitt, *The Impeachment and Trial of Andrew Johnson* (1903, repr. 1967); H. K. Beale, *The Critical Year* (1930, new introd. 1958); G. F. Milton, *The Age of Hate* (1930, repr. 1965); Milton Lomask, *Andrew Johnson: President on Trial* (1960, repr. 1973); E. L. McKitrick, *Andrew Johnson and Reconstruction* (1960) and *Andrew Johnson, A Profile* (1969, repr. 1972); M. L. Benedict, *The Impeachment and Trial of Andrew Johnson* (1973).

Johnson, Cave, 1793-1866, American political leader, b. Robertson co., Tenn. He practiced law in his native state and served (1829-37, 1839-45) in the U.S. House of Representatives. Johnson gave active support to James K. Polk in the presidential campaign of 1844 and served (1845-49) as Postmaster General in Polk's cabinet, introducing postage stamps in the U.S. postal system. He later became (1853) a circuit judge in Tennessee. During the Civil War he opposed secession but afterwards supported the Confederacy.

Johnson, Eastman, 1824-1906, American portrait and genre painter, b. Lovell, Maine. He studied with a lithographer in Boston and later in Düsseldorf, then for almost four years at The Hague, where he was greatly influenced by the 17th-century Dutch masters. In 1855 Johnson returned to the United States and in 1860 settled in New York City. His fame rests primarily upon his skillfully executed genre pictures, such as *Old Kentucky Home* (N.Y. Public Lib.) and *Corn Husking at Nantucket* (Metropolitan Mus.). After 1885, however, he devoted himself to portraiture. Among his sitters were Presidents Hayes, Cleveland, and Harrison, as well as Cornelius Vanderbilt, Emerson, and Longfellow. See study by Patricia Hills (1972).

Johnson, Edward, 1881-1959, Canadian tenor and operatic manager, b. Guelph, Ont. After singing light opera and oratorio in New York from 1907, he went to Italy, where he sang operatic roles, using the name Eduardo di Giovanni, in many theaters, including Milan's La Scala (1913-18). In 1920 he joined the Chicago Opera Company and in 1922, the Metropolitan, where he created the leading tenor roles in Deems Taylor's *King's Henchman* (1927) and *Peter Ibbetson* (1931). In 1935 he became general manager of the Metropolitan Opera, retiring in 1950. He was succeeded by Rudolf Bing.

Johnson, Emily Pauline, 1862-1913, Canadian poet, b. near Brantford, Ont.; daughter of an Indian chief and his English wife. Although she had little formal training, Johnson's early poems praising Indian life were highly popular in recitals, and in 1892 she began a series of successful tours through the United States and England. Her poems, noted for their passion and dramatic intensity, appeared in *White Wampum* (1895), *Canadian Born* (1903), and *Flint and Feather* (1913), her collected poems. She also published a volume of tales of the Indians of the Pacific Northwest entitled *Legends of Vancouver* (1911).

Johnson, Emory Richard, 1864-1950, American economist, b. Waupun, Wis., Ph.D. Univ. of Pennsylvannia, 1893. He joined the faculty of the Univ. of Pennsylvania in 1893 and was dean of its Wharton School of Finance and Commerce from 1919 to 1933. He served on several government commissions as a transportation expert and wrote many books on the subject, including *Elements of Transportation* (1909), *Government Regulation of Transportation* (1938), and *Transport Facilities, Services, and Policies* (1947).

Johnson, Eyvind (ü'vīnt), 1900-, Swedish novelist and short-story writer. After working as a laborer in the north of Sweden, Johnson moved to Stockholm in 1919 and began to write. He is best known outside Sweden for his cycle of four autobiographical novels entitled *Romanen om Olov* [the novel about Olov] (1934-37), which is noted for its extraordinary psychological penetration. Of his relatively few works translated into English the most celebrated is the novel *Return to Ithaca* (tr. 1952), concerning ancient and modern Greek culture. Johnson has written more than 40 works, including the novels *Grupp Krilon* (1941), *Krilon själv* (1943), and *Livsdagen lang* (1964) and the collection of short stories *Sju liv* (1944). Considered one of the foremost Swedish writers of the 20th cent., Johnson shared the 1974 Nobel Prize in Literature with his countryman Harry Martinson.

Johnson, Guy, c.1740-1788, Loyalist leader in colonial New York, b. Ireland. He emigrated to America as a boy and married (1763) a daughter of Sir William Johnson, whom he succeeded as superintendent of Indian affairs in 1774. He had served in the French and Indian War and had acted as a deputy of Sir William after 1762. In the American Revolution he helped to keep most of the Iroquois loyal to the British. He made his headquarters (1779-81) at Niagara and with his deputy, John BUTLER, directed Loyalist raids against the patriot frontier settlements. He was succeeded as superintendent of Indian affairs by Sir John JOHNSON in 1782.

Johnson, Herschel Vespasian, 1812-80, U.S. political leader, b. Burke co., Ga. Admitted to the bar in 1834, he filled (1848-49) an unexpired Senate term before serving as circuit court judge (1849-53) and Democratic governor of Georgia (1853-57). A proponent of both states' rights and unionism, Johnson in 1860 ran unsuccessfully for the vice presidency with Stephen A. Douglas against Abraham Lincoln. Although he opposed secession, Johnson later served (1862-65) in the Confederate senate, where he refused to support conscription and the suspension of the writ of habeas corpus. Johnson was president of the 1865 Georgia constitutional convention and was elected (1866) to the U.S. Senate, but he was not allowed to take his seat. He was again a circuit court judge from 1873 until his death. See biography by P. S. Flippin (1931).

Johnson, Hiram Warren, 1866-1945, American political leader, U.S. Senator from California (1917-45), b. Sacramento, Calif. His role as attorney in the successful prosecution of Abe RUEF, political boss of San Francisco, led to his election (1910) as governor of California. Johnson broke the political domination of the Southern Pacific RR in California and secured the enactment of much reform legislation. A founder of the Progressive party, he was Theodore Roosevelt's running mate on the unsuccessful Progressive ticket of 1912. He was reelected governor in 1914. In 1916, Johnson refused to support Charles E. Hughes, the Republican presidential candidate, and Hughes lost California and the election to Woodrow Wilson. Johnson himself was elected U.S. Senator on the Progressive ticket and, reelected four times, served in the Senate until his death. In 1920 he was a leading contestant for the Republican presidential nomination, but after Warren G. Harding was nominated, Johnson declined offers of the vice-presidential nomination. Although he at first supported the Hoover administration, he later became its bitter opponent, and in 1932 he gave Franklin D. Roosevelt strong support. Johnson had been a stubborn opponent of the League of Nations, and he remained one of the most consistent of the isolationists in Congress. See study by S. C. Olin, Jr. (1968).

Johnson, Hugh Samuel, 1882-1942, American army officer, government administrator, b. Fort Scott, Kansas. After graduation (1903) from West Point, he entered the U.S. army as a second lieutenant. In World War I he formulated (1917) plans for selective service in the U.S. army, administered the draft, and served on the War Industries Board. Johnson resigned (1919) from the army as brigadier general and became a business executive. He was summoned (1933) to Washington, D.C., to help formulate the National Industrial Recovery Act, and after its passage he served (1933-34) as head of the NATIONAL RECOVERY ADMINISTRATION.

Johnson, Jack (John Arthur Johnson), 1878-1946, American boxer, b. Galveston, Texas. He defeated (1908) Tommy Burns at Sydney, Australia, and claimed the world's heavyweight championship. Responding to popular urging, James J. JEFFRIES came out of retirement to fight Johnson. Johnson won (1910) at Reno, Nev., and became the first Negro heavyweight boxing champion. He lost his title (1915) to Jess Willard in Havana, Cuba.

Johnson, James Weldon, 1871-1938, American author, b. Jacksonville, Fla., educated at Atlanta Univ. (B.A, 1894) and at Columbia. Johnson was the first Negro to be admitted to the Florida bar and later was American consul (1906-12), first in Venezuela and then in Nicaragua. In 1930 he became a professor at Fisk Univ., and in 1934 a visiting professor at New York Univ. He helped found and was secretary (1916-30) of the National Association for the Advancement of Colored People. His novel *Autobiography of an Ex-Coloured Man* (1912), published anonymously, caused a great stir and was republished under his name in 1927. Among his other works are *God's Trombones* (1927), Negro sermons in verse, and *Black Manhattan* (1930). He wrote songs with his brother, John Rosamond JOHNSON. See his autobiography, *Along This Way* (1933, repr. 1973); study by Eugene Levy (1973).

Johnson, Sir John, 1742-1830, Loyalist leader in the American Revolution, b. Mohawk valley, N.Y.; son of Sir William Johnson. He fought against the Indians in Pontiac's Conspiracy and was one of his father's chief lieutenants. For his services he was knighted in 1765. In the Revolution, like his brother-in-law, Guy Johnson, he set out to organize the settlers and Indians of the Mohawk region against the Revolutionaries. The plan failed, and he fled to Montreal. In the Saratoga campaign (1777) he served with Barry St. Leger and led a detachment at Oriskany. Later he led several raids on the Mohawk and Schoharie valleys. After the Revolution, he moved to Canada and in 1782 succeeded Guy Johnson as superintendent of Indian affairs.

Johnson, John Albert, 1861-1909, American political leader, governor of Minnesota, b. St. Peter, Minn. The son of poor parents, he left school early and worked at various trades until 1887, when he became editor and half owner of the St. Peter *Herald*, a Democratic journal. His editorials brought him into public notice, and in 1898 he was elected state senator. In 1904 he was elected governor on the Democratic ticket in a Republican state that gave Theodore Roosevelt a two-to-one majority that year. Johnson's victory won him national fame, increased by his reelections in 1906 and 1908. His progressive administration, gracious personality, and talent for speaking made him one of Minnesota's most popular governors. See biography by W. G. Helmes (1949).

Johnson, John Rosamond, 1873-1954, American composer and singer, b. Jacksonville, Fla., studied at Atlanta Univ. and the New England Conservatory of Music, Boston. After a career in music halls and light opera in England and on the Continent, Johnson toured Europe and the United States giving programs of Negro spirituals. He composed several hundred songs, including *Lift Every Voice and Sing*, for which his brother, James Weldon Johnson, wrote the words; it has been called the Negro national anthem. He edited several collections of American Negro songs and spirituals.

Johnson, Lady Bird, 1912-, b. Karnack, Texas, originally named Claudia Alta Taylor. She married (1934) Lyndon B. Johnson and played an active role in his political career. As first lady (1963-69) she sponsored environmental causes and national beautification projects. A successful businesswoman, she bought (1943) a debt-ridden radio station in Austin, Texas, and built it into a multimillion dollar broadcasting company. She also owns and manages extensive ranching lands in Texas. She is the author of *A White House Diary* (1970). See biographies by M. D. Smith (1964) and G. L. Hall (1967).

Johnson, Lionel Pigot, 1867-1902, English poet and critic, b. Broadstairs, Kent, educated at Oxford. He lived an ascetic, scholarly life in London, converting to Roman Catholicism in 1891. His keen interest in the IRISH LITERARY RENAISSANCE is reflected in many of his poems. As a whole Johnson's poetry is spare and austere, often spiritual in content and rather medieval in outlook. His works include *Poems* (1895) and *Ireland and Other Poems* (1897), and a critical work, *The Art of Thomas Hardy* (1894). An alcoholic, Johnson died at 35 of a fractured skull, the result of a fall. An autopsy revealed that his body had never developed beyond the age of 15. See his complete poems, ed. by Iain Fletcher (1953); his essays and critical papers, ed. by Thomas Whittemore (1912, repr. 1968).

Johnson, Lyndon Baines, 1908-73, 36th President of the United States (1963-69), b. near Stonewall, Texas. Born into a farming family, he graduated (1930) from Southwest Texas State Teachers College (now Southwest Texas State Univ.), in San Marcos. He taught in a Houston high school before becoming (1932) secretary to a Texas Congressman in Washington. In 1934 he married Claudia Alta Taylor (nicknamed Lady Bird) and they had two daughters, Lynda Bird and Luci Baines. A staunch New Dealer, Johnson gained the friendship of the influential Sam Rayburn, at whose behest President Franklin Delano Roosevelt made him (1935) director in Texas of the National Youth Administration. In 1937, Johnson won election to a vacant congressional seat, and he was consistently reelected to the House through 1946. Despite Roosevelt's support, however, he was defeated in a special election to the Senate in 1941. He served (1941-42) in the navy, returning to Washington when President Roosevelt recalled all Congressmen from active service. In 1948, Johnson was elected U.S. Senator from Texas after winning the Democratic primary by a mere 87 votes. A strong advocate of military preparedness, he persuaded the Armed Services Committee to set up (1950) the Preparedness Investigating Subcommittee, of which he became chairman. Rising rapidly in the Senate hierarchy, Johnson became (1951) Democratic whip and then (1953) floor leader. As majority leader after the 1954 elections he wielded great power, exhibiting unusual skill in marshaling support for President Eisenhower's programs. He suffered a serious heart attack in 1955 but recovered to continue his senatorial command. Johnson lost the 1960 Democratic presidential nomination to John F. Kennedy, but accepted Kennedy's offer of the vice-presidential nomination. Elected with Kennedy, he energetically supported the President's programs, serving as an American emissary to nations throughout the world and as chairman of the National Aeronautics and Space Council and of the President's Committee on Equal Employment Opportunities. After Kennedy's assassination on Nov. 22, 1963, Johnson was immediately sworn in as President, and he announced that he would strive to carry through the late President's programs. Congress responded to Johnson's skillful prodding by enacting an $11 billion tax cut (Jan., 1964) and a sweeping Civil Rights Act (July, 1964). In May, 1964, Johnson called for a nationwide war against poverty and outlined a vast program of economic and social welfare legislation designed to create what he termed the Great Society. Elected (Nov., 1964) for a full term in a landslide victory over Senator Barry Goldwater, he pushed hard for his domestic program. The 89th Congress (1965-66) witnessed more major legislative action than any since the New Deal. A medicare bill, providing free medical care to the aged under Social Security, was enacted; Federal aid to education at all levels was greatly expanded; the Voting Rights Act of 1965 provided new safeguards for Negro voters; more money went to the antipoverty programs; and a Dept. of Transportation and Dept. of Housing and Urban Development were added to the Cabinet. Johnson's domestic achievements were soon obscured by foreign affairs, however. When North Vietnam attacked (Aug., 1964) American destroyers, Congress passed the Gulf of Tonkin resolution, giving the President authority to take any action necessary to protect American troops. Convinced that South Vietnam was about to fall to Communist forces, Johnson began (Feb., 1965) the bombing of North Vietnam. Within three years he increased American forces in South Vietnam from 20,000 to over 500,000. Johnson's actions eventually aroused widespread opposition in Congress and among the public, and a vigorous antiwar movement developed. As the cost of the war shot up, Congress scuttled many of Johnson's domestic programs. Large-scale riots in the Negro ghettos of major American cities further darkened his presidency, and by the beginning of 1968 he was under sharp attack from all sides. After Senators Eugene McCarthy and Robert Kennedy began campaigns for the Democratic nomination, Johnson announced (March, 1968) that he would not run for reelection. At the same time he called a partial halt to the bombing of North Vietnam; two months later peace talks began in Paris. When Johnson retired from office (Jan., 1969), he left the nation bitterly divided by the war. He retired to Texas, where he died on Jan. 22, 1973. See his memoirs, *The Vantage Point* (1971); biographies by Harry Provence (1964), E. F. Goldman (1969), Louis Heren (1970), G. E. Reedy (1970), and Richard Harwood and Haynes Johnson (1973).

Johnson, Martin Elmer, 1884-1937, American explorer and author, b. Rockford, Ill. He left home at 14 to work his way to Europe on a cattle boat, returning as a stowaway. He then joined the crew of Jack London's round-the-world cruise on the *Snark,* and was the only member of the party to complete the trip. His interest in photographing wildlife and native tribes seen on this voyage led him to make several trips for this purpose to the South Sea Islands and Borneo before undertaking (1921) the African expeditions for which he is best known. His films include *Simba, Congorilla,* and *Baboona,* as well as the film of vanishing wildlife in Africa that was made (1924-29) for the American Museum of Natural History. He was killed in an airplane crash in the United States. His wife, **Osa Helen (Leighty) Johnson,** 1894-1953, accompanied him on all his expeditions and was coauthor of *Cannibal Land* (1917), *Camera Trails in Africa* (1924), *Safari* (1928, repr. 1972), and *Lion* (1929). She also wrote *I Married Adventure* (1940) and *Bride in the Solomons* (1944).

Johnson, Pamela Hansford: see under SNOW, C. P.

Johnson, Philip Cortelyou, 1906-, American architect, museum curator, and historian, b. Cleveland. After studying the new European architecture, Johnson wrote (with H.R. Hitchcock) *The International Style: Architecture since 1922* (1932). As chairman of the department of architecture at the Museum of Modern Art (1932-34; 1945-54), he became an important advocate of the new architecture in America. He founded his own firm in 1953. Johnson's sumptuous, glass-walled house in New Canann, Conn. (1949), reveals the influence of MIËS VAN DER ROHE, with whom he collaborated on the Seagram Building in New York City (1958). His later works include the Munson-Williams-Proctor Institute, Utica, N. Y. (1960), the New York State Theater (1964) at LINCOLN CENTER FOR THE PERFORMING ARTS, the Investors Diversified Services Project in Minneapolis (1973), and the addition to the Boston Public Library (1973). He is the author of *Miës van der Rohe* (1947). See studies by J. M. Jacobus, Jr. (1962), and Charles Noble (1972).

Johnson, Reverdy, 1796-1876, American lawyer and statesman, b. Annapolis, Md. Admitted to the bar in 1816, he served in the Maryland legislature (1821-28) and the U.S. Senate (1845-49) and was attorney general under President Taylor. Johnson won a reputation as one of the ablest constitutional lawyers of the period. His constitutional argument as counsel for the defense in the DRED SCOTT CASE is known to have greatly influenced the Supreme Court, particularly Chief Justice Roger Taney. A Whig and then a conservative Democrat, Johnson was sympathetic with the South but was absolutely opposed to secession and used his influence to keep Maryland in the Union. He played an important role in the unsuccessful defense of Mary E. SURRATT, alleged accomplice of John Wilkes Booth. In his second term in the U.S. Senate (1863-68), he supported President Andrew Johnson's Reconstruction program, and his opposition to the impeachment of Johnson influenced other senators in voting for the President's acquittal. In 1868 he was appointed minister to Great Britain, where he negotiated the Johnson-Clarendon Treaty to settle the ALABAMA CLAIMS; the treaty was rejected by the U.S. Senate largely for party reasons, and Johnson was recalled in 1869. See biography by B.C. Steiner (1914, repr. 1970).

Johnson, Richard Mentor, 1780-1850, Vice President of the United States (1837-41), b. Kentucky, on the site of present Louisville. Admitted (1802) to the bar, he became prominent in state politics as a Jeffersonian Republican and sat (1804-7) in the Kentucky legislature. He served (1807-1819) in the U.S. House of Representatives and commanded a regiment of Kentucky riflemen in the War of 1812, in which he served under William Henry Harrison in the Canadian campaign. At the battle of the Thames (1813), Johnson was severely wounded in action, and he is said to have killed Tecumseh. He resigned (1819) from the House to fill an unexpired term in the U.S. Senate, where he served until 1829. Again (1829-37) in the House, Johnson supported President Jackson's administration and pushed the bill (1832) abolishing imprisonment for debt. Backed by Jackson, Johnson was nominated (1836) for Vice President on the Democratic ticket with Martin Van Buren. None of the vice presidential candidates received a majority of the electoral vote, so the election was decided by the U.S. Senate, which gave the office to Johnson. He was defeated (1840) in his bid for reelection by the Whig candidate, John Tyler. See biography by L. H. Meyer (1932).

Johnson, Richard W., 1827-97, Union general in the Civil War, b. Livingston co., Ky., grad. West Point, 1849. Before the Civil War he served principally on the frontier. Johnson, made a brigadier general of volunteers in Oct., 1861, served as a division commander in the Armies of the Ohio and the Cumberland. He fought at Shiloh and Murfreesboro and in the Chattanooga and Atlanta campaigns. After his service at the battle of Nashville in Dec., 1864, he was brevetted major general. Following his retirement from the army in 1867 Johnson taught military science at the Univ. of Missouri and the Univ. of Minnesota.

Johnson, Rossiter, 1840-1931, American editor, b. Rochester, N.Y. He was associate editor (1873-77) of the *American Cyclopaedia,* editor (1883-1902) of the *Annual Cyclopedia,* and managing editor (1886-89) of the *Cyclopedia of American Biography.* He originated and edited the "Little Classics" (18 vol., 1875-80) and was editor in chief of "The World's Great Books" (40 vol., 1898-1901). He also lectured widely and wrote a variety of books.

Johnson, Samuel, 1696-1772, American clergyman, educator, and philosopher, b. Guilford, Conn., grad. Collegiate School (now Yale), 1714; father of William Samuel Johnson. He became a Congregationalist minister, but in 1722 joined the Church of England. In 1724 he opened the first Anglican church in Connecticut at Stratford, remaining its minister until 1754, when he became the first president of an Anglican institution, King's College (now Columbia), in New York City. He resigned in 1763 to return to Stratford. A friend and correspondent of the English philosopher George Berkeley, Johnson became the principal exponent in America of Berkeleian idealism. His chief work was *Ethica* (1746), republished in an enlarged edition by Benjamin Franklin as *Elementa Philosophica* (1752). See Herbert Schneider and Carol Schneider, ed., *Samuel Johnson . . . His Career and His Writings* (4 vol., 1929, repr. 1972); study by J. J. Ellis (1973).

Johnson, Samuel, 1709-84, English author, b. Lichfield. The leading literary scholar and critic of his time, Johnson helped to shape and define the Augustan Age. But he was equally celebrated for his brilliant and witty conversation. His rather gross appearance and manners were viewed tolerantly, if not with a certain admiration. The son of a bookseller, Johnson excelled at school in spite of illness (he suffered the effects of scrofula throughout his life) and poverty. He entered Oxford in 1728 but was forced to leave after a year for lack of funds. He sustained himself as a bookseller and schoolmaster for the next six years, during which he continued his wide reading and published some translations. In 1735 he married Elizabeth Porter, a widow 20 years his senior, and remained devoted to her until her death in 1752. He settled in London in 1737 and began his literary career in earnest. He wrote at first primarily for Edward Cave's *Gentleman's Magazine*—poetry and prose on subjects literary and political. His poem "London," published anonymously in 1738, was praised by Pope and won Johnson recognition in literary circles. His *Life of Savage* (1744) is a bitter portrait of corruption in London and the miseries endured by writers. Also of note are *The Vanity of Human Wishes* (1749) and his essays in the periodical *The Rambler* (1750-52). Johnson's first work of lasting importance, and the one that permanently established his reputation in his own time, was his *Dictionary of the English Language* (1755), the first comprehensive lexicographical work on English ever undertaken. *Rasselas,* a moral romance, appeared in 1759, and *The Idler,* a collection of his essays, in 1761. Although Johnson enjoyed great literary acclaim, he remained close to poverty until a government pension was granted him in 1762. The following year was marked by his meeting with James BOSWELL, whose famous biography presents Johnson in exhaustive and fascinating detail, recreating his conversations verbatim. In 1764, Johnson and Joshua Reynolds founded "The Club" (known later as The Literary Club): Its membership included

Oliver Goldsmith, Edmund Burke, David Garrick, and Boswell. The brilliance of this intellectual elite was, reportedly, dazzling, and Dr. Johnson (he had received a degree in 1764) was its leading light. His witty remarks are remembered to this day. He was a master not only of the aphorism—e.g., his definition of angling as "a stick and a string, with a worm on one end and a fool on the other"—but also of the quick, unexpected retort, as when, while listening with displeasure to a violinist, he was told that the feat being performed was very difficult: "Difficult," replied Johnson, "I wish it had been impossible!" In 1765, Johnson met Henry and Hester THRALE, whose friendship and hospitality he enjoyed until Thrale's death and Mrs. Thrale's remarriage. In that same year Johnson's long-heralded edition of Shakespeare appeared. Its editorial principles served as a model for future editions, and its preface and critical notes are still highly valued. In the 1770s, Johnson wrote a series of Tory pamphlets. His political conservatism was based upon a profound skepticism as to the perfectibility of human nature. Although personally generous and compassionate, he held that a strict social order is necessary to save man from himself. In 1773 he toured the Hebrides with Boswell and published his account of the tour in 1775. Johnson's *Lives of the Poets* (1779-1781), his last major work, comprises ten small volumes of acute criticism, characterized, as is all of Johnson's work, by both classical values and sensitive perception. Dr. Johnson, as he is universally known, was England's first full-dress man of letters, and his mind and personality helped to create the traditions that have guided English taste and criticism. Besides the classic biography by Boswell, see biographies by J. W. Krutch (1944), J. L. Clifford (1955), Sir John Hawkins (1787; ed. by Bertram Davis, 1961), and Donald Greene (1970); critical studies by W. J. Bate (1955), R. B. Schwartz (1971), and Peter Quennell (1973); J. L. Clifford, Johnsonian Studies, 1887-1950 (1951; supplement, 1962); J. L. Clifford and D. J. Greene, *A Survey and Bibliography of Critical Studies* (1970).

Johnson, Thomas, 1732-1819, American political leader, b. Calvert co., Md. A lawyer, he served (1762-73) in the Maryland colonial assembly, where he became prominent in the fight against the Stamp Act (1765). He was a member (1774-77) of the Continental Congress, and he nominated (1775) George Washington as commander in chief of the Continental army. Johnson served as governor of Maryland (1777-79) and helped bring about Maryland's adoption of the Constitution. He served briefly (1791-93) as Associate Justice of the U.S. Supreme Court. See biography by E. S. Delaplane (1927).

Johnson, Tom Loftin, 1854-1911, American municipal reformer, mayor of Cleveland (1901-10), b. Georgetown, Ky. He acquired a substantial fortune from streetcar and steel interests, and, deeply influenced in the 1880s by the writings of Henry GEORGE, he devoted himself to reform. After two terms (1891-95) as a Democratic member of the U.S. House of Representatives, he became (1901) mayor of Cleveland, serving four terms. He fought strenuous battles for municipal reform against political bosses (especially Mark Hanna) and business interests. Although his plans for municipal ownership of public utilities were not realized, he helped create civic consciousness in Cleveland, initiated sanitary measures, and improved facilities to help the city's poor. Cleveland, in the time of Johnson's mayoralty, was called "the best governed city in the United States." See his autobiography (1911); biography by Carl Lorenz (1911).

Johnson, Uwe (ü'vā yôn'zôn), 1934-, German novelist. Johnson's works explore the complex effects on the average man of divided modern Germany, both halves of which he sees as zones of moral poverty. His best-known novels include *Mutmassungen über Jakob* (1959; tr. *Speculations about Jacob,* 1963) and *Das dritte Buch über Achim* (1961; tr. *The Third Book about Achim,* 1966). In the latter, as in *Zwei Ansichten* (1965; tr. *Two Views,* 1966), and *Absence* (tr. 1970), Johnson leaves to the reader any analysis of the problems he describes. See biography by Mark Boulby (1974).

Johnson, Walter Perry, 1887-1946, American baseball player, b. Humboldt, Kansas. He began playing with the Washington Senators of the American League in 1907. A right-handed pitcher, he won 416 games while losing 278 before he retired from active play in 1927. The numerous records he established include the greatest number of shutouts (113), the greatest number of strike-outs (3,510), and the most consecutive scoreless innings pitched (56). The "Big Train," as he was often called, later managed the Newark team (1928) of the International League and the Senators (1929-32) and the Cleveland Indians (1933-35) of the American League. He was elected to the National Baseball Hall of Fame in 1936. See biography by R. L. Treat (1948).

Johnson, Sir William, 1715-74, British colonial leader in America, b. Co. Meath, Ireland. He settled (1738) in the Mohawk valley, became a merchant, and gained great power among the Mohawk Indians and the other Iroquois. He had large landed properties, founded (1762) Johnstown, N.Y., and lived in baronial splendor at Johnson Hall. Because of his influence over the Indians, he was a key figure in the French and Indian Wars, first becoming prominent in King George's War. At the Albany Congress (1754) he helped formulate British Indian policy, and he was made (1755) superintendent of Iroquois affairs. In the French and Indian War, although his expedition against Crown Point did not capture that fort, he soundly defeated (1755) the French under Baron Dieskau at Lake George and built Fort William Henry. Johnson was rewarded with a baronetcy. In 1759 he captured Niagara, and in 1760 he served with Gen. Jeffrey Amherst in the capture of Montreal. He had been appointed general superintendent of Indian affairs N of the Ohio in 1756, and after the Peace of Paris (1763) his office was of great significance in the vast new areas gained from France. His chief lieutenants were George CROGHAN; Johnson's son-in-law, Guy JOHNSON; his son, Sir John JOHNSON; and Daniel Claus. Although Pontiac's Rebellion and British economy measures prevented him from establishing the centralized control over Indians and fur traders that he desired, he did much to further British rule in the formerly French territories. He presided at the council of FORT STANWIX (1768). His papers have been edited by the New York State Division of Archives (13 vol., 1921-62). See biographies by Arthur Pound and Richard Day (1930, repr. 1971) and J. T. Flexner (1959).

Johnson, William Samuel, 1727-1819, American political leader and president of Columbia College (1787-1800), b. Stratford, Conn. A lawyer in Connecticut, he soon became a leading figure in the colony, serving as a member of the lower house and in the governor's council. Although conservative in his views, he was sent (1765) as a delegate to the Stamp Act Congress. From 1767 to 1771 he was an agent of Connecticut in England and after his return was a judge of the superior court (1772-73). Because of his opposition to political independence of the colonies, he declined to serve when elected as a delegate to the Continental Congress (1774) and soon retired from politics. He was called from retirement to represent (1785-87) Connecticut in the Confederation Congress and at the Federal Constitutional Convention (1787), in which he took a prominent part in the debate on represention. He served (1787-1800) as president of the newly reorganized Columbia College, formerly King's College, of which his father, Samuel Johnson (1696-1772), had been president. He was elected U. S. Senator from Connecticut in 1789, but retired in 1791. See biographies by E. E. Beardsley (1876) and G. C. Groce, Jr. (1937).

Johnson City. 1 Village (1970 pop. 18,025), Broome co., S N.Y., in a tri-city area including Endicott and Binghamton; inc. 1892. It is noted for its Endicott-Johnson shoes. Originally called Lestershire, the area remained rural until a shoe company built a factory there in 1890. The name was changed in 1916. **2** City (1970 pop. 33,770), Washington co., NE Tenn., in a mountainous region; settled before 1800, inc. 1869. It is an important burley tobacco and dairy market and a railroad center. East Tennessee State Univ. and a large veterans hospital are there. The oldest church in the state (built 1782) is in Johnson City, and nearby is Rocky Mount historic shrine, a log cabin (built 1770) that served (1790-92) as the first capitol of the territory south of the Ohio River. Four Tennessee Valley Authority lakes in the area offer recreation. **3** City (1970 pop. 767), seat of Blanco co., central Texas. It is the site of the "LBJ Ranch," known as the Texas White House when Lyndon B. Johnson was President. The Lyndon B. Johnson National Historic Site includes the former President's boyhood home in the town and his birthplace 13 mi (21 km) to the west.

Johnson grass: see SORGHUM.

Johnston, Albert Sidney, 1803-62, Confederate general, b. Washington, Ky. After serving in the Black Hawk War, he resigned (1834) from the U.S. army and went to Texas where he enlisted (1835) in the revolutionary army. Johnston became its commander in 1837 and served as Texas secretary of war, 1838-40. In the Mexican War, he commanded a regiment of volunteers and saw action at Monterrey. Reentering the U.S. army in 1849, Johnston served on the Texas frontier, was commander of the Dept. of Texas (1856-58), led the expedition against the Mormons (1857), and commanded the Dept. of Utah (1858-60). When Texas seceded from the Union in April, 1861, Johnston, commanding the Dept. of the Pacific, again resigned his commission in the U.S. army and was soon made general in charge of Confederate operations in the West. Union victories, especially at Fort Donelson (Feb., 1862), forced him to withdraw from the line of defense he had established in 1861. He concentrated an army at Corinth, Miss., and on April 6, 1862, attacked Ulysses S. Grant at Shiloh (see SHILOH, BATTLE OF). Johnston was killed at the height of battle, and the Confederacy lost one of its ablest generals. See biography by his son W. P. Johnston (1878, repr. 1964).

Johnston, Alexander Keith, 1804-71, Scottish cartographer and geographer royal of Scotland. He issued many notable atlases, maps, and gazetteers, including *The National Atlas of Historical, Commercial, and Political Geography* (1843), *The Physical Atlas of Natural Phenomena* (1848), *The Dictionary of Geography* (1850; known as *Johnston's Gazetteer*), and *The Royal Atlas of Modern Geography* (1861). A son, **Alexander Keith Johnston,** 1844-79, carried on the work of the map-publishing house founded by his father. He assisted (1873-75) in a survey of Paraguay and died in Africa while leading an expedition of the Royal Geographical Society to Lake Nyasa.

Johnston, Gabriel, 1699-1752, colonial governor of North Carolina (1734-52). An efficient and popular Scot, he nevertheless had constant difficulties with the assembly over quitrents and other financial matters and several times dissolved that body. During his administration numerous land grants to immigrants were issued, free schools were established, and Wilmington was developed.

Johnston, Sir Harry Hamilton, 1858-1927, British explorer and colonial official. His early interest in the natural sciences was combined with his concern for the political problems of colonial Africa. He began his first trip to sub-Saharan Africa in 1882 and in 1883 encountered Henry Morton Stanley in the Congo Basin. In 1884 he made an expedition to Mt. Kilimanjaro that uncovered valuable scientific data and strengthened Britain's political hold in East Africa. Johnston entered the foreign service in 1885; he served in colonial administrative positions in many parts of Africa and established a British protectorate over Nyasaland (present-day Malawi). After his retirement (1902) he continued his naturalist studies. He was knighted in 1896.

Johnston, Joseph Eggleston, 1807-91, Confederate general, b. Prince Edward co., Va., grad. West Point, 1829. He served against the Seminole Indians in Florida and with distinction under Winfield Scott in the Mexican War. Johnston was quartermaster general with the rank of brigadier general when he resigned (April, 1861) to fight for the Confederacy. In May he was made a brigadier general and assigned to command at Harpers Ferry. He evaded the Union army under Gen. Robert Patterson and marched to the aid of General Beauregard at BULL RUN, where his part in the Confederate victory won him a generalcy and the command of the Army of Northern Virginia (July). Johnston opposed General McClellan in the PENINSULAR CAMPAIGN until he was wounded at Fair Oaks in May, 1862. Upon resuming service in November, he was assigned to command the Dept. of the West. Although it seems certain that President Davis intended him to give orders to John Clifford PEMBERTON at Vicksburg and Braxton BRAGG in Tennessee, Johnston chose to interpret his position as merely nominal. When he finally did take command in the VICKSBURG CAMPAIGN, it was too late to save Pemberton. Johnston, placed in command of the Army of the Tennessee (Dec., 1863), adopted the policy of strategic retreat against William Tecumseh SHERMAN in the ATLANTA CAMPAIGN—a policy that did not suit Davis, who appointed John Bell HOOD to succeed him. He was restored to command in Feb., 1865, by Lee, now commander in chief. He obstructed General Sherman's advance through North Carolina, but upon hearing of Lee's surrender to General Grant, he capitulated to Sherman on April 26. After the war Johnston served (1879-81) in the House of Representatives from Richmond, Va., and by appointment of President Cleveland, was (1885-91) Federal commissioner of railroads. Cautious as he was, Johnston was not a brilliant offensive commander but was probably the peer of Lee in defensive generalship. Davis's hostility to Johnston was widely known and seriously disrupted Confederate military organization. See Johnston's *Narrative of Military Operations* (1874; new ed. 1959, repr. 1969); biographies by R. M. Hughes (1893) and G. E. Govan and J. W. Livingood (1956).

Johnston, Mary, 1870-1936, American novelist, b. Buchanan, Va. Her books combine romance with history. She is chiefly remembered for *To Have and to Hold* (1900), a story of colonial Virginia, and its successor, *Audrey* (1902). Her other novels include two Civil War stories, *The Long Roll* (1911) and *Cease Firing* (1912); *The Great Valley* (1926); and *Miss Delicia Allen* (1932).

Johnston, Richard Malcolm, 1822-98, American author, b. Hancock co., Ga., grad. Mercer Univ., 1841. He is known for his stories and sketches of rural Georgia, of which the collection *Dukesborough Tales* (1871) is best known. See his autobiography (1900).

Johnston, Samuel, 1733-1816, political leader in the American Revolution, b. Dundee, Scotland. He emigrated as a child to North Carolina, where his uncle, Gabriel JOHNSTON, was royal governor. After being admitted to the bar, he was a member of the colonial assembly (1759-75) and of its standing Committee of Correspondence after 1773. He was elected to the four provincial congresses (1774-76), presiding at the third and at the fourth, which passed the Halifax Resolves declaring for independence of the colonies; served in the new state senate; and represented North Carolina in the Continental Congress (1780-82). Johnston was governor of North Carolina (1787-89) and presided over the convention that rejected the Federal Constitution (1788) and over the one (1789) at which North Carolina finally ratified it. He was one of the state's first U.S. Senators (1789-93), a judge of the superior court (1800-1803), and one of the first trustees of the Univ. of North Carolina.

Johnston, town (1970 pop. 22,037), Providence co., N central R.I., a suburb of Providence; inc. 1759. Among its manufactures are jewelry, textiles, and fabricated metals. Johnston is the home of several insurance companies. Its many historic landmarks include the Clemence-Irons House (c.1680).

Johnstone (jŏn'stən), burgh (1971 pop. 22,629), Renfrewshire, W Scotland. There are flax and cotton mills and engineering works. Chemicals, machine tools, and shoelaces are manufactured. In 1975, Johnstone became part of the Strathclyde region.

Johnston Island, central Pacific, c.3,000 ft (910 m) long and c.600 ft (180 m) wide, c.700 mi (1,130 km) SW of Honolulu. It was discovered by the British in 1807 and claimed by the United States in 1858. A bird reservation for years, the island became a U.S. naval base in 1941. In 1962 the United States conducted a series of nuclear tests in the area.

Johnstown. 1 City (1970 pop. 10,045), seat of Fulton co., E central N.Y.; founded 1772, inc. 1895. Its leather glove industry began in 1800. Knitted goods, boats, gelatin, and chemicals are also made. Johnson Hall, built by the city's founder, Sir William Johnson, houses many of his relics. Other notable old buildings include the county courthouse (1774) and Fort Johnstown (1771), now the county jail. The last Revolutionary battle in New York was fought in Johnstown on Oct. 25, 1781. Elizabeth Cady Stanton was born in the city. A junior college is there. **2** Industrial city (1970 pop. 42,476), Cambria co., SW Pa., on the Conemaugh River at the mouth of Stony Creek; settled 1770, inc. as a city 1936. Situated in a beautiful mountain region, it is a center of heavy industry. Manufactures include iron, steel, coal products, refractories, chemicals, wearing apparel, and mining, telegraph, railroad, and industrial equipment. Branches of U.S. Steel and Bethlehem Steel are there. In 1834 the Pennsylvania Canal and the Portage RR were joined in Johnstown. The first Kelly pneumatic converter for the transformation of crude iron into steel was built there in 1862. The city expanded with the rapid growth of iron and steel industries after the Civil War. On May 31, 1889, the dam across the river c.12 mi (19 km) above the city broke as a result of heavy rains, and the city was flooded, with the loss of about 2,200 lives. Flooding occurred again in 1936, but the river has since been channeled (completed 1943) for flood prevention. The Univ. of Pittsburgh at Johnstown and a state rehabilitation center are in the city. Johnstown Flood National Memorial and Allegheny Portage Railroad National Historic Site are nearby (see NATIONAL PARKS AND MONUMENTS, table). See D. G. McCullough, *The Johnstown Flood* (1968).

Johnstown Flood National Memorial: see JOHNSTOWN **2**; NATIONAL PARKS AND MONUMENTS (table).

John the Baptist, Saint, d. A.D. c.28-30, Jewish prophet, the forerunner of Jesus. He was the son of Zacharias and Elizabeth, who was a kinswoman of the Virgin Mary, and his birth was miraculously foretold. After spending some time in the desert, he received a divine call to preach repentance to the people of the Jordan valley in preparation for the Messiah. He baptized his followers, and he baptized Jesus, whom he recognized as the Son of God. John's vigorous preaching and great popularity enraged the aristocracy, and he offended Herodias, wife of HEROD, by rebuking her publicly. At her instigation and at the direct request of her daughter SALOME he was beheaded. (Mat. 11.1-19; 17.11-13; Mark 6.14-29; Luke 1.5-80; 3.1-20; John 1.15-36.) John is also mentioned by the Jewish historian Josephus. Christians have always venerated St. John the Baptist as high among the saints; he is the only saint besides the Virgin Mary whose birthday is celebrated: June 24. The feast of his beheading is Aug. 29. See Carl Kraeling, *Saint John the Baptist* (1951).

John the Fearless, 1371-1419, duke of Burgundy (1404-19); son of PHILIP THE BOLD. He fought against the Turks at NIKOPOL in 1396 and was a prisoner for a year until he was ransomed. He continued his father's feud with Louis, duc d'ORLÉANS, brother of King Charles VI, and became popular by advocating governmental reforms. In 1407 he had Louis assassinated; he was forced to leave Paris but later returned and obtained control of the French government. Rivalry between his party and the supporters of Orléans led to open civil war in 1411 (see ARMAGNACS AND BURGUNDIANS). In 1413, John was again forced to flee Paris as a result of a reaction against the violence of his supporters, the CABOCHIENS. He did not aid the government, now under Armagnac control, against the English invaders under King Henry V, and in 1418 he took advantage of French defeats to seize Paris and the king. John negotiated both with Henry V and with the dauphin (later King Charles VII), who now led the Armagnacs. At a meeting in Montereau with the dauphin, John was assassinated (1419). He was succeeded by his son, Philip the Good.

John the Posthumous: see JOHN I, king of France.

Johor or **Johore** (jōhôr', jə-), state (1971 pop. 1,273,-900), 7,360 sq mi (19,062 sq km), at the southern extremity of the Malay Peninsula, Malaysia, opposite Singapore. It is largely covered with rain forests and swamps. The principal rivers and communication routes are the Muar and the Johor; the capital is JOHOR BAHARU, across the strait from Singapore. The Chinese and the Malays are the two largest groups in the population, and there is a significant Indian minority. Johor has extensive rubber plantations; other agricultural products are rice, copra, pineapples, gambier, and palm products. Tin and bauxite are mined. After the fall of Malacca (Melaka) to the Portuguese (1511), the former sultan of Malacca continued to rule over Johor and the Riau Archipelago. In the 18th cent. the Bugis, a Malay people from Celebes, became dominant in Johor. In 1819 a British-installed sultan granted the site of Singapore to the British East India Company and became for practical purposes an independent ruler. Thereafter relations with Great Britain were friendly; Johor remained one of the most peaceful of the Malay states. In 1885, Johor and Great Britain established formal treaty relations, and in 1914 Johor became a British protectorate. Until 1948, when it entered the Federation of Malaya, Johor was classified as one of the Unfederated Malay States. See MALAYSIA, FEDERATION OF.

Johor Baharu (bəhär'ōō), **Johore Bharu,** or **Johore Bahru** (both: bär'ōō), city (1971 pop. 135,936), capital of Johor, Malaysia, S Malay Peninsula, opposite Singapore. The city is connected with Singapore by a stone causeway across the narrow Johore Strait. It is a trade center for rubber and tropical produce. The seat of the sultan of Johor is in Johor Baharu; his residence, Bakit Serene, contains priceless art treasures. The population of the city is mainly Chinese.

Johore Strait, arm of the Singapore Strait, c.40 mi (60 km) long and from 1 to 3 mi (1.6-4.8 km) wide, between Singapore Island and the Malay Peninsula. The eastern part of the strait has a deep channel leading to a port on N Singapore. A causeway (3,443 ft/1,049 m long; opened 1924) connects Johor Baharu, Malaysia, and Woodland, Singapore.

Joiada (joi'ədə), high priest. Neh. 12.10,11,22.

Joiakim (joi'əkĭm) [short for JEHOIAKIM], high priest. Neh. 12.10.

Joiarib (joi'ərĭb). **1** Exile returned from Babylon. Ezra 8.16. **2** Chief priest. Neh. 11.10; 12.6,19. Jehoiarib: 1 Chron. 9.10; 24.7. **3** Judahite. Neh. 11.5.

joinery, craft of assembling exposed woodwork in the interiors of buildings. Where CARPENTRY refers to the rougher, simpler, and primarily structural elements of wood assembling, joinery has to do with difficult surfaces and curvatures, such as those of spiral stairs, with complex intersections of members or moldings, and with the handling of the finer qualities and varieties of woods. The joiner's skill and art thus approach those of the cabinetmaker. One must have an extensive knowledge of geometrical relations and projections, in addition to being manually proficient. In modern woodworking, however, the hand processes of the joiner have, to a large degree, been superseded by mechanical means.

joint, in anatomy, juncture between two bones. Some joints are immovable, e.g., those that connect the bones of the skull, which are separated merely by short, tough fibers of cartilage. The movable joints are found for the most part in the limbs. Hinge joints provide a forward and backward motion as at the elbow and knee. Pivot joints permit rotary movement, like the turning of the head from side to side. Ball-and-socket joints, like those at the hip and shoulder, allow the greatest range of movement, as the rounded end of one bone fits into the hollow or socket of another bone, separated by elastic cartilage. Further ease of movement is assured by a lubricating liquid, the synovial fluid, supplied by the synovial membrane that lines movable joints. In addition, some joints contain a cushioning, fluid-filled sac, called a BURSA. Holding the joints in place are strong LIGAMENTS fastened to the bones above and below the joint. Joints are subject to SPRAINS and dislocations as well as to infections and disorders caused by diseases such as ARTHRITIS.

joint, in geology, fracture in rocks along which no appreciable movement has occurred (see FAULT). Most rocks are jointed, but the origin of these joints is not always clear. Nearly vertical joints that result from shrinkage during cooling are commonly found in igneous rocks. The prismatic joints of the Palisades of New Jersey and Devil's Tower, Wyoming, are examples of joints caused by contraction during the cooling of fine-grained igneous rock masses. Deep-seated igneous rocks often have joints approximately parallel to the surface, suggesting that they formed by expansion of the rock mass as overlying rocks were eroded away. Some joints in sedimentary rocks may have formed as the result of contraction during compaction and drying of the sediment. In some cases, jointing of the rock may result from the action of the same forces that cause FOLDS and faults. In relatively undisturbed sedimentary rocks, such joints are often in two vertical sets perpendicular to one another. Commonly, streams develop along zones of weakness caused by joints in rocks, and thus the regional pattern of joint orientation often exerts a strong control on the development of drainage patterns.

Joint Chiefs of Staff, U.S. statutory agency, created in 1949 within the Dept. of Defense, whose members are the principal military advisers to the President, the National Security Council, and the Secretary of Defense. Its four permanent members are the chairman; the chief of staff, U.S. army; the chief of naval operations; and the chief of staff, U.S. air force. The commandant of the U.S. Marine Corps attends meetings regularly and sits as a coequal with the other members when they are considering matters that directly concern the corps.

joint stock company: see CHARTERED COMPANIES.

Joinville, Jean, sire de (zhăN sĕr də zhwăNvēl'), 1224?-1317?, French chronicler, biographer of LOUIS IX of France (St. Louis). As seneschal (governor) of Champagne, Joinville was a close adviser to Louis, whom he accompanied (1248-54) on the Seventh Crusade. He opposed and refused to take part in the Eighth Crusade. His memoir of St. Louis, dictated between 1304 and 1309 for the instruction of Louis X, is an invaluable record of the king, of feudal France, and of the Seventh Crusade. It is written in a simple, delightful style, with moving reverence for the saintly and chivalrous king, with a sharp eye for graphic and psychological detail, and with occasional sly humor. Filled with digressions and personal recollections, it is less the work of a historian than that of a wise, experienced gentleman. There are several English translations of Joinville's memoirs, notably those by Sir Frank Marzials (1908), Joan Evans (1938), and René Hague (1955).

Jókai, Mór (mōr yō'koi), 1825–1904, Hungarian romantic novelist and journalist. Jókai was a fervent nationalist who, after the Hungarian defeat in 1848, became a fugitive from the Austrians. He was later a member (1861–97) of the Hungarian parliament. Often compared to both Dickens and Scott, Jókai was an enormously prolific and popular writer. His novels, national in character, often earthy and humorous in style, have been translated into 25 languages. Among them are *An Hungarian Nabob* (1853–54, tr. 1898) and *Black Diamonds* (1870, tr. 1896).

Jokdeam (jŏk'dēăm, jŏkdē'ăm), unidentified town, S Palestine. Joshua 15.56. Jorkeam: 1 Chron. 2.44.

Jokim (jō'kĭm), son of Shelah the Judahite. 1 Chron. 4.22.

Jokmeam (jŏk'mēăm). **1** Unidentified Levitical town of Ephraim, in central Palestine. 1 Chron. 6.68. Kibzaim: Joshua 21.22. **2** Town, in Solomon's 5th district. 1 Kings 4.12. Some scholars correct the text to read Jokneam, but this interpretation is doubtful.

Jokneam (jŏk'nēăm), Canaanite royal city, later a Levitical city of Zebulun, SW of Mt. Carmel (in present-day Israel). Joshua 12.22; 19.11; 21.34.

Jokshan (jŏk'shăn), son of Abraham. Gen. 25.2,3; 1 Chron. 1.32.

Joktan (jŏk'tăn), descendant of Shem. Gen. 10.25–30.

Joktheel (jŏk'thēĕl, -thēl). **1** Unidentified city, SW Palestine. Joshua 15.38. **2** City of Edom. 2 Kings 14.7. See also SELA.

Jökulsá (yö'külsou), name of several Icelandic rivers formed by glaciers. The best known is the Jökulsá á Fjöllum, which rises on the north slope of the Vatnajökull in SE Iceland and flows c.130 mi (210 km) N into the Axarfjörður, forming the Dettifoss c.30 mi (50 km) from its mouth.

Jokyakarta: see JOGJAKARTA, Indonesia.

Joliet, Louis: see JOLLIET, LOUIS.

Joliet (jō'lēĕt"), city (1970 pop. 78,887), seat of Will co., NE Ill., on the Des Plaines River; inc. 1857. It is an important river port and an industrial and railroad center, with limestone quarries and coal mines in the area. Earth-moving equipment; wire, radio and television parts; wallpaper; chemicals; and paper and metal products are made in the city. The state penitentiary is there. Joliet is the seat of the College of St. Francis and a junior college.

Joliette (zhôlyĕt'), city (1971 pop. 20,127), S Que., Canada, on L'Assomption River, NE of Montreal. Its industries include steel, paper, and textile manufacturing, tobacco processing, and limestone quarrying. The Séminaire de Joliette, affiliated with the Univ. of Montreal, is there.

Joliot-Curie (zhôlyō'-kürē'), French scientists who were husband and wife. **Frédéric Joliot-Curie**(frādārēk'), 1900–1958, formerly Frédéric Joliot, and **Irène Joliot-Curie** (ērĕn'), 1897–1956, daughter of Pierre and Marie Curie, were married in 1926. Both were assistants at the Radium Institute in Paris, of which Irène, succeeding her mother, was director in 1932. Together the Joliot-Curies continued the work of the Curies on radioactivity. For their artificial production of radioactive substances, by bombarding certain elements with alpha particles, they shared the 1935 Nobel Prize in Chemistry. In 1940 they collaborated on research on the chain reaction in nuclear fission. In 1946 they helped to organize the French atomic energy commission, and in the same year Frédéric was appointed chairman of the commission. He was forced to resign in 1950, however, because of his Communist activities, and in 1951 Irène was also dropped from the commission because of her Communist affiliations. In 1947, Irène became a professor and the director of the radium laboratory at the Sorbonne. In 1956, Frédéric was a member of the French Communist party's Central Committee, and in the same year he was appointed to the chair of nuclear physics at the Univ. of Paris.

Jolliet or **Joliet, Louis** (both: jō'lēĕt", jō"lēĕt', Fr. lwē zhôlyā'), 1645–1700, French explorer, joint discoverer with Jacques MARQUETTE of the upper Mississippi River, b. Quebec prov., Canada. After a year's study of hydrography in France and some years as a trader and trapper on the Great Lakes, Jolliet was appointed (1672) as leader of an expedition in search of the Mississippi. He and Father Marquette, with five voyageurs, set out from St. Ignace in May, 1673, went to Green Bay, ascended the Fox River, portaged (at the site of Portage, Wis.) to the Wisconsin River, and descended to the Mississippi. The group followed the west bank south until they passed the mouth of the Arkansas River; then, having convinced themselves that the river emptied into the Gulf of Mexico, they ascended its eastern bank. They came to the Illinois River, ascended it, and, on the site of modern Chicago, portaged to the Chicago River, and again reached Lake Michigan. Marquette remained in the West while Jolliet went east to make his report, but in the Lachine Rapids, near Montreal, Jolliet's canoe overturned and his records were lost. His brief narrative, written from memory, is in essential agreement with Marquette's, the chief source account of the journey. Jolliet was rewarded with the gift of Anticosti Island in the Gulf of St. Lawrence, which was, however, seized by the British while Jolliet was absent on explorations in Labrador and around Hudson Bay. In 1697 he was made royal professor of hydrography and given a small seigniory near Quebec. See biographies by Jean Delanglez (1948) and V. L. S. Eifert (1961); M. S. Scanlon, *Trails of the French Explorers* (1956).

Jolo (hō'lō, hōlō'), island (345 sq mi/894 sq km), SULU ARCHIPELAGO, the Philippines. The seaport city, Jolo (1969 est. pop. 46,800), on the northwest coast of the island, is the capital of Sulu prov., the trading and shipping hub of the archipelago, and a Muslim center. An ancient walled city, it was once a pirate base and served as the residence of a sultan until the sultanate was abolished in 1940. The city was almost completely destroyed in 1974 when fighting erupted between government forces and Muslim insurgents who were seeking to establish a secessionist state. After the battle, the rebels withdrew into the island's interior to fight a war of attrition.

Jolson, Al, 1888–1950, American entertainer, whose original name was Asa Yoelson, b. Russia. He emigrated to the United States c.1895. The son of a rabbi, Jolson first planned to become a cantor but soon turned to the stage. After his New York City debut in 1899, he worked in circuses, in minstrel shows, and in vaudeville; in 1909 in San Francisco he first sang "Mammy" in black face, and his style brought him fame and many imitators. The first of his many Broadway appearances was in *La Belle Paree* (1911); his film work began with *The Jazz Singer* (1927), the first major film with sound and a landmark in the history of motion pictures. After 1932 he had his own radio show. Among the songs he made famous were "April Showers," "Swanee," "Sonny-Boy," and "Mammy." See Harry Jolson, *Mistah Jolson* (1951); Michael Freedland, *Jolson* (1972).

Jomini, Antoine Henri (äNtwän' äNrē' zhômēnē'), 1779–1869, Swiss general and military writer. He organized (1799) the militia of the Helvetic Republic and after 1804 served as staff officer in the French army. In Aug., 1813, after a clash with Marshal Berthier, he defected to the enemy, joining the Russian army, in which a commission had previously been arranged. He rose to high rank in Russia, becoming a celebrated authority on strategy. His works include a study of the campaigns of Frederick the Great, *Traité des grandes opérations militaires* (5 vol., 1804–10; tr. *Treatise on Grand Military Operations*); *Histoire critique et militaire des guerres de la Révolution* (1819–24), on the French Revolutionary Wars; and the influential *Précis de l'art de la guerre* (1836; tr. *The Art of War,* 1862), which he wrote while military tutor to the future Czar Alexander II. Jomini emphasized the capture of major points and the importance of superior numbers, and he advocated the employment of speed and maneuver rather than battle whenever possible.

Jommelli, Niccolò (nēk-kōlô' yōm-mĕl'lē), 1714–74, Italian opera composer of the Neapolitan school. His earliest works, such as *L'errore amoroso* (1737) and *Ezio* (1741), were very successful. He produced operas in Vienna (1749–50). While he was choir director (1751–54) at St. Peter's in Rome, he composed church music. Jommelli was musical director (1754–69) to the duke of Württemberg at Stuttgart. After his return to Naples his last operas, such as *Armida abbandonata* (1770) and *Ifigenia in Tauride* (1771), were rejected by the public as too learned and too German. Despite an attack of apoplexy in 1773, he was still able, in his last year, to compose a Miserere that is considered his masterpiece. In his operas he introduced *recitativo accompagnato* and anticipated many of the reforms of Gluck.

Jona, variant of JONAH. See also BAR-JONA.

Jonadab (jō'nədăb). **1** Nephew of David. 2 Sam. 13.3,32–36. **2** Founder of the Rechabites and a companion of Jehu. Jer. 35. Jehonadab: 2 Kings 10.15–23.

Jonah (jō'nə), **Jonas** (jō'nəs), or **Jona,** book of the Old Testament, 32d in the order of the Authorized Version, 5th of the books of the Minor Prophets. It tells of the career of a Hebrew prophet sent to reform Nineveh; he is specifically dated (2 Kings 14.25) as living under Jeroboam II (reigned c.793–c.753 B.C.) of Israel. His story is famous: to avoid the divine mission he sails for Tarshish but is thrown overboard by the crew because his disobedience has brought down a storm on the ship. Swallowed by a "great fish," he is vomited up on shore after three days. Now willing, he preaches his mission so successfully that God is moved by the people's repentance and revokes the doom Jonah had foretold. The prophet, irritated by the divine change of heart, sulks, but he is shown by an example how God's mercy prevails. Allusions to the story are frequent in the Bible: Mat. 12.39–41; 16.4; Luke 11.29–30; Tobit 14.4. Jonah's coming forth from the fish or whale after being swallowed is famous as a prefiguration of the Resurrection of Christ. See study by R. H. Bowers (1971); see also bibliography under OLD TESTAMENT.

Jonan (jō'nən), ancestor of Joseph. Luke 3.30.

Jonas (jō'nəs), Greek form of Hebrew JONAH. For the father of St. Peter, see BAR-JONA.

Jonas, Franz (fränts yō'näs), 1899–1974, Austrian Socialist politician. Jonas was mayor of Vienna (1951–65) and a member of parliament (1962–65). In 1965 he was elected president, and in 1971 he was reelected, defeating Kurt Waldheim.

Jonas, Justus (yo͝os'to͝os yō'näs), 1493–1555, German Protestant reformer. In 1521, Jonas, then a professor at the Univ. of Erfurt, accompanied Martin Luther to the Diet of Worms. During an intimate friendship Jonas assisted Luther with the translation of the Bible. He also translated the Latin works of Luther and Melanchthon into German. He was present at Luther's death and preached his funeral sermon.

Jonathan (jŏn'əthən) [short for JEHONATHAN]. **1** Saul's son and David's friend, killed at the battle of Mt. Gilboa. 1 Sam. 13; 14.18–20; 20.16–18; 31.1,2. **2** David's nephew. 2 Sam. 21.21. This is probably the Jonathan called David's uncle in the translations of 1 Chron. 27.32. **3** Courtier under David. 2 Sam. 15; 17.17,20; 1 Kings 1.42. **4** One of David's men. 2 Sam. 23.32; 1 Chron. 11.34. **5** Official under David. 1 Chron. 27.25. **6** Levite. 2 Chron. 17.8. **7** Jerahmeelite. 1 Chron. 2.32,33. **8** Israelite in the return to Jerusalem. Ezra 8.6. **9** Priest involved with the foreign marriages. Ezra 10.15. **10** The same as JOHANAN **5.** **11** Priest. Neh. 12.14. **12** Levite. Neh. 12.35. **13** Scribe in whose house Jeremiah was imprisoned. Jer. 37.15; 38.26. **14** Captain under Gedaliah. Jer. 40.8. **15** One of the MACCABEES. 1 Mac. 9–13; 2 Mac. 8.22.

Jonathan, Joseph Leabua (lēä'bwä), 1914–, prime minister of Lesotho (1965–). He worked in South African mines (1933–37), returned to Basutoland, and later became active in politics (1952). A founder of the Basutoland National party (1959), he led it from its inception and worked for independence from South Africa. He became prime minister (1965) under a constitution that preceded Basutoland's independence as Lesotho in 1966. In 1970, when it appeared that he had lost the national election, he seized additional powers and suspended the constitution.

Jonath-elem-rechokim: see AIJELETH SHAHAR.

Jones, Anson, 1798–1858, last president of the Texas republic (1844–46), b. near Great Barrington, Mass. He studied medicine and after an itinerant business and medical career went (1833) to Texas and became a doctor. He joined the revolutionary forces in the war against Mexico and was present at the battle of San Jacinto (1836). Entering politics, Jones was a member of the Texas congress, was appointed (1838) by President Sam Houston as minister to the United States, was dismissed (1839) by President Mirabeau B. Lamar, and served as a senator. His appointment as secretary of state in the second Houston administration (1841–44) prepared the way for his election as president in 1844. Following the annexation of Texas, Jones resigned (1846) his authority to the new governor of the state. He committed suicide in 1858. See biography by Herbert Gambrell (1948).

Jones, Casey, 1864–1900, American locomotive engineer celebrated in ballad and song, probably b. Jordan, Fulton co., Ky. His real name was John Luther Jones, but at the age of 17 he went to Cayce, Ky., and there he was employed as a telegraph operator; from the name of the town he was given the nickname "Casey." In 1888 he entered the service of the Illinois Central RR as a locomotive fireman and soon (1890) was promoted to engineer. He was famous among railroad men for his boast that he always brought his train in on schedule and for his peculiar skill with a locomotive whistle. Given the "crack" assignment of driving the *Cannon Ball* express from Memphis, Tenn., to Canton, Miss.—a particularly dangerous run on which several accidents had occurred—Casey Jones was determined to bring the overdue train in on time but met with disaster. On the morning of April 30, 1900, confronted with a stationary freight train a few feet ahead of his speeding locomotive at Vaughan, Miss., he ordered his fireman to jump. He applied the brakes, and although the *Cannon Ball* crashed and Jones was killed, the passengers were saved. A fellow railroad worker, Wallace Saunders, soon composed a popular ballad about him; one version of it, *Casey Jones,* was published by T. Lawrence Siebert and Eddie Newton. Monuments commemorating Jones stand at Cayce, Ky., and Jackson, Tenn. He was buried at Jackson, Tenn. See biography by F. J. Lee (1939).

Jones, Davy: see DAVY JONES.

Jones, Sir Edward Burne-: see BURNE-JONES.

Jones, Ernest, 1879–1958, British psychoanalyst, b. Wales, M.D. Univ. of London, 1903. He taught (1910–13) at the Univ. of Toronto and was director (1908–13) of the Ontario Clinic for Nervous Diseases. In 1913 he returned to England, where he founded (1925) the London clinic for Psycho-Analysis and served as its director until 1935. Jones was instrumental in introducing the study of psychoanalysis into England and the United States. He is considered an authoritative biographer of Freud, whom he visited several times in Vienna; he also accompanied Freud on trips to Austria and the United States. His writings include *The Life and Work of Sigmund Freud* (3 vol., 1953–57) and *Free Associations: Memories of a Psychoanalyst* (1959).

Jones, Ernest Charles, 1819–69, English agitator, lawyer, journalist, and poet. He was a prominent leader of the more militant wing of the Chartists (see CHARTISM). After imprisonment for sedition (1848–50), he edited a radical journal and later practiced as a lawyer. *The Battle Day and Other Poems* (1855) and his other labor verse have more literary merit than his sensational novels. See his writings and speeches (ed. by John Saville, 1952).

Jones, Henry: see CAVENDISH.

Jones, Henry Arthur, 1851–1929, English playwright. His reputation was first established with the melodrama *The Silver King* (with Henry Herman; 1882). Strongly influenced by the great Norwegian playwright Henrik Ibsen, Jones turned to writing dramas of social and moral criticism. He was the author of over 60 plays, of which *The Middleman* (1889), *Michael and His Lost Angel* (1896), *The Liars* (1897), and *Mrs. Dane's Defense* (1900) are among the most important. His critical works include *The Renascence of the English Drama* (1895) and *The Theatre of Ideas* (1915).

Jones, Howard Mumford, 1892–, American man of letters, b. Saginaw, Mich., grad. Univ. of Wisconsin, 1914. A noted scholar and critic, he wrote on various phases of American literature and culture. He was professor of English and later of humanities at Harvard from 1930 to 1962. Among his works are *Ideas in America* (1944), *The Bright Medusa* (1952), *American Humanism* (1957), and *O Strange New World* (1964; Pulitzer Prize), a study of American culture from the 15th to the 19th cent. His *Education and World Tragedy* (1946) concerns the problems of higher education. His other writings include plays; translations of Heine; and a biography of Thomas Moore, *The Harp That Once—* (1937).

Jones, Inigo, 1573–1652, one of England's first great architects. Son of a London clothmaker, he was enabled to travel in Europe before 1603 to study paintings, perhaps at the expense of the earl of Rutland. On a second trip to Italy (1613–14) he thoroughly studied the remains of Roman architecture and the Renaissance buildings by Palladio. At the English courts of both James I and Charles I he designed settings for elaborate MASQUES, some of which he wrote. Besides performing various architectural services for the crown, he was also sponsored by the earl of Arundel. After renewed visits to Italy, Jones became (1615) king's surveyor of the works. In 1616 he began work on the Queen's House, Greenwich, the first English design to embody Palladian principles. He then built (1619–22) the royal banqueting hall in Whitehall, London, again adapting the classical proportions and use of architectural elements he had learned in Italy. He also made designs for St. Paul's church, Covent Garden, with its square (1631–38). He built other houses in London and in the country; especially outstanding is his advisory work (1649–53) on Wilton House, Wiltshire. Making a clean break from the prevailing Jacobean style, he achieved a magnificent coherence of design. The work of Inigo Jones marked a starting point for the classical architecture of the late Renaissance and Georgian periods in England. See study by Stephen Orgel and Roy Strong (2 vol., 1973).

Jones, James, 1921–, American novelist, b. Robinson, Ill. Written in the tradition of NATURALISM, his novels often celebrate the endurance of man. *From Here to Eternity* (1951), his best-known work, is a powerful story of army life in Hawaii immediately before the attack on Pearl Harbor. His other novels include *Some Came Running* (1957), *The Thin Red Line* (1962), and *A Touch of Danger* (1973). *Viet Journal* (1974) is an account of his trip to Vietnam.

Jones, James Earl, 1931–, American actor, b. Tate co., Miss. Jones achieved Broadway stardom with his powerful portrayal of the fighter Jack Johnson in *The Great White Hope* (1968). He made his stage debut at the Univ. of Michigan, and appeared thereafter for seven years with the New York Shakespeare Festival in *Macbeth* (1962), *Othello* (1963), and *King Lear* (1973), among many others. In 1973 he played Hickey in *The Iceman Cometh* and in 1974 Lenny in *Of Mice and Men,* both in New York.

Jones, Jesse Holman, 1874–1956, U.S. Secretary of Commerce (1940–45), b. Robertson co., Tenn. A lumber magnate, banker, and millionaire of Houston, Texas, Jones was appointed (1932) by President Hoover as a member of the RECONSTRUCTION FINANCE CORPORATION (RFC). He became (1933) its chairman under Franklin Delano Roosevelt, and, with the merging of the RFC with other Federal agencies, he was appointed (1939) Federal loan administrator. Jones's performance in the RFC won such high praise that, after his appointment (1940) as Secretary of Commerce, Congress transferred the RFC from the Federal Loan Administration to the Department of Commerce. His close ties with the business community made him indispensable to the Roosevelt administration, and during World War II he was one of the most powerful men in Washington, D.C. He retired from government service in 1945. See his *Fifty Billion Dollars* (1951); biography by B. N. Timmons (1956).

Jones, John Paul, 1747–92, American naval hero, b. near Kirkcudbright, Scotland. His name was originally simply John Paul. He went to sea when he was 12, and his youth was adventure-filled. He was chief mate on a slave ship in 1766 but, disgusted with the work, soon quit. In 1769 he obtained command of the *John,* a merchantman that he captained until 1770. In 1773, while Jones was in command of the *Betsy* off Tobago, members of his crew mutinied and he killed one of the sailors in self-defense. To avoid trial he fled, and in 1775 he was in Philadelphia, with the Jones added to his name. Joseph Hewes of Edenton, N.C., obtained for him a commission in the Continental navy. In 1777, Jones was given command of the *Ranger,* fresh from the Portsmouth shipyard. He sailed to France, then daringly took the war to the very shores of the British Isles on raids and in 1778 captured the *Drake,* a British warship. It was, however, only after long delay that he was given another ship, an old French merchantman, which he rebuilt and named the *Bon Homme Richard* ("Poor Richard"), to honor Benjamin Franklin. He set out with a small fleet but was disappointed in the hope of meeting a British fleet returning from the Baltic until the projected cruise was nearly finished. On Sept. 23, 1779, he did encounter the British merchantmen, convoyed by the frigate *Serapis* and a smaller warship. Despite the superiority of the *Serapis,* Jones did not hesitate. He sailed close in, to cut the advantage of the *Serapis,* and finally in the battle lashed the *Bon Homme Richard* to the British ship. The battle, which began at sunset and ended more than three and a half hours later by moonlight, was one of the most memorable in naval history. Both ships were heavily damaged. The *Serapis* was afire in at least 12 different places. The hull of the *Bon Homme Richard* was pierced, her decks were ripped, her hold was filling with water, and fires were destroying her, unchecked; yet when the British captain asked if Jones was ready to surrender, the answer came proudly, "Sir, I have not yet begun to fight." When the *Serapis* surrendered, Jones and his men boarded her while his own vessel sank. He was much honored in France for the victory but received little recognition in the United States. After the Revolution he was sent to Europe to collect the prize money due the United States. In 1788 he was asked by Catherine the Great to join the Russian navy; he accepted on the condition that he become a rear admiral. His command against the Turks in the Black Sea was successful, but political intrigue prevented his getting due credit. In 1789 he was discharged from the Russian navy and returned to Paris. There in the midst of the French Revolution he died, without receiving the commission that Jefferson had procured for him to negotiate with the dey of Algiers concerning American prisoners. Although he is today generally considered the greatest of American naval heroes and the founder of the American naval tradition, his grave was forgotten until the ambassador to France, Horace E. Porter, discovered it in 1905 after the expenditure of much of his own time and money. The remains were removed to Annapolis and since 1913 have been enshrined in a crypt at the U.S. Naval Academy. See his memoirs (1830, repr. 1972); Anna De Koven, *Life and Letters of John Paul Jones* (1913); F. A. Golder, *John Paul Jones in Russia* (1927); Lincoln Lorenz, *John Paul Jones* (1943, repr. 1969); Gerald W. Johnson, *The First Captain* (1947); Samuel Eliot Morison, *John Paul Jones* (1959, repr. 1964).

Jones, LeRoi, also known as **Imamu Baraka,** (ēmä'mo͞o bərä'kə), 1934–, American author and political activist, b. Newark, N.J. His writings express the violent hatred of a black man for all aspects of white society. Among his plays are *Dutchman, The Toilet,* and *The Slave* (all 1964). His other works include poems, essays, stories, and a novel, *The System of Dante's Hell* (1965). Jones has been active in black politics in Newark, and in 1972 he was one of the leaders of the National Black Political Caucus.

Jones, Mary Harris, 1830–1930, American labor agitator, called Mother Jones, b. Ireland. For many years interested in the labor movement, she became active in it after the death of her husband and children in 1867. She won fame as an effective speaker, always appearing at the scene of any major strike. In 1936 the Progressive Miners of America erected a memorial on her grave in Mt. Olive, Ill. Her autobiography (ed. by M. F. Parton, 1925, repr. 1969) contains some factual inaccuracies. See biography by Dale Fetherling (1974).

Jones, Robert Edmond, 1887–1954, American scene designer, b. Milton, N.H. With his design in 1915 for *The Man Who Married a Dumb Wife,* a new era of scene design began in the United States. His use of color and dramatic lighting enhanced his imaginative sets. Some of Jones's most notable designs were for *Macbeth, Richard III, Hamlet* (for John Barrymore), and *The Green Pastures.* After work with the Washington Square Players, he joined Kenneth Macgowan at the Greenwich Village Theatre; working in conjunction with the Provincetown Players, he created sets for the plays of Eugene O'Neill. Jones did the designing for the early three-color-process film *La Cucaracha* (1933). He wrote *Drawings for the Theatre* (1925), *The Dramatic Imagination* (1941), and, with Kenneth Macgowan, *Continental Stagecraft* (1922). See *The Theatre of Robert Edmond Jones* (ed. by Ralph Pendleton, 1958).

Jones, Robert Tyre, Jr. (Bobby Jones), 1902–71, American golfer, b. Atlanta, Ga. A lawyer, he became a golf devotee. Jones won the National Open (1923, 1926, 1929), the National Amateur (1924–25, 1927–28), and the British Open (1926–27). The first golfer to win the National and the British Open tournaments in the same year (1926), Jones became the only player ever to make the grand slam in golf—winning the National Open, the National Amateur, the British Open, and the British Amateur championships in 1930. He then retired from tournament play. See his *Down the Fairway* (1927; with O. B. Keeler); *Golf Is My Game* (1960); *Bobby Jones on Golf* (1966); *Bobby Jones on the Basic Golf Swing* (1969); O.B. Keeler, *The Bobby Jones Story* (1953).

Jones, Rufus Matthew, 1863–1948, American minister of the Society of Friends, educator, and author, b. South China, Maine. He taught philosophy and ethics at Haverford College, Pa., from 1893 to 1934. One of the founders of the noted American Friends Service Committee (1917), he was its chairman until 1928 and thereafter honorary chairman. His many books, mainly on the Quakers and on mysticism, include *Quakerism, a Religion of Life* (1908), *The Quakers in the American Colonies* (1911), *The New Quest* (1928), *George Fox, Seeker and Friend* (1930), *Radiant Life* (1944), and *The Luminous Trail* (1947). See anthology of his writings ed. by H. E. Fosdick (1951); biographies by David Hinshaw (1951, repr. 1970) and E. J. G. Vining (1958).

Jones, Samuel Milton, 1846–1904, American political reformer, known as "Golden Rule" Jones, b. Wales. He was brought to America as a child and worked in the oil fields of Pennsylvania and Ohio. He invented improvements in oil-drilling machinery, and after the oil trust refused to handle these inventions, Jones manufactured them himself—very successfully—in Toledo, Ohio. He was noted for his advanced program of employee-management relations. Elected (1897) mayor of Toledo on the Republican ticket, he put into operation a comprehensive program of municipal reform. When refused renomination in 1899, he ran as an independent and overwhelmingly defeated both political machines. He was reelected in 1901 and 1903 and died in office. During his administration he established civil service and instituted the eight-hour day and minimum wages for city employees. See his autobiography, *The New Right* (1899).

Jones, Thomas ap Catesby, 1789–1858, American naval officer, b. Westmoreland co., Va. He joined the navy in 1805 and helped suppress piracy and the slave trade in the Gulf of Mexico (1808–12). In the War of 1812 he made a desperate and unsuccessful effort to halt the fleet carrying the British army to New Orleans from crossing Lake Borgne (1814). In 1826 he made a visit to Hawaii that increased U.S. prestige in those islands. In 1842, acting upon a rumor that the United States and Mexico were at war, he captured Monterey, Calif. For this action he was removed from command but not otherwise censured.

Jones, Sir William, 1746–94, English philologist and jurist. Jones was celebrated for his understanding of jurisprudence and of Oriental languages. He published an *Essay on the Law of Bailments* (1781), widely used in America as well as in England. For 11 years he was a supreme court judge in Calcutta. Jones founded the Asiatic Society of Bengal at Calcutta. Through the Society, as well as through his publications, he had a great influence on literature, Oriental study, and philology in Western Europe. Jones was the first to suggest that Sanskrit originated from the same source as Latin and Greek, thus laying the foundation for modern comparative philology. See his letters, ed. by Garland Cannon (2 vol., 1970).

Jones Beach, state park, 2,413 acres (977 hectares), on an offshore bar, SW Long Island, SE N.Y., in Nassau co.; est. 1929. It is noted for its wide, white sand beaches, outdoor marine theater, and varied recreational facilities.

Jonesboro, city (1970 pop. 27,050), a seat of Craighead co., NE Ark., on Crowley's Ridge; founded 1859, inc. 1883. It is the trade, distributing, and industrial center for a large farm area. Arkansas State Univ. is there, and a state park is nearby. Parts of the city were devastated by tornadoes in May, 1973.

Jong, Petrus Josef Sietse de: see DE JONG, PETRUS JOSEF SIETSE.

Jongkind, Johann Barthold (yōhän' bär'tôlt yông'kĭnt), 1819–91, Dutch landscape painter and etcher. He studied in Paris with Isabey. Jongkind's work was a transition between the Barbizon school and the impressionists, and he notably influenced the latter group. He painted chiefly in France, though many of his scenes are Dutch. He was a fine watercolorist and one of the foremost etchers of the 19th cent. In these media he achieved a fresh rendering of atmospheric effects, especially in his marine scenes. Jongkind is represented in the Rijks Museum and in the Louvre.

jongleurs (zhông-glör'), itinerant entertainers of the Middle Ages in France and Norman England. Their repertoire included dancing, conjuring, acrobatics, the feats of the modern juggler, singing, and storytelling. Many were skilled in playing musical instruments. The jongleurs were often collaborators or assistants of TROUBADOURS or TROUVÈRES.

Jönköping (yön'chö"pĭng), city (1970 pop. 96,944), capital of Jönköping co., S Sweden, at the southern end of Lake Vättern. It is a commercial and industrial center. The safety match was developed there, and the city has large match factories (founded 1844). Other manufactures include machinery, paper, textiles, and airplanes. Jönköping was chartered in 1284 by Magnus I. Gustavus Adolphus gave (1620) it special privileges after its citizens had burned the city to prevent the Danes from sacking it. Jönköping's modern prosperity began in the 19th cent. with the opening of the Göta Canal and the coming of the railroad.

Jonquière (zhôNkyĕr'), city (1971 pop. 28,430), S Que., Canada, on the Saguenay River, adjacent to its twin city, Kénogami, W of Chicoutimi. Its chief industries produce paper and pulp. Jonquière has a college and a school of technology.

jonquil: see AMARYLLIS.

Jonson, Ben, 1572–1637, English dramatist and poet, b. Westminster, London. The high-spirited buoyancy of Jonson's plays and the brilliance of his language have earned him a reputation as one of the great playwrights in English literature. After a brief term at bricklaying, his stepfather's trade, and after military service in Flanders, he began working for Philip Henslowe as an actor and playwright. In 1598 he was tried for killing another actor in a duel but escaped execution by claiming right of clergy (that he could read and write). His first important play, *Every Man in His Humour,* was produced in 1598, with Shakespeare in the cast. In 1599 its companion piece, *Every Man out of His Humour,* was produced. In *The Poetaster* (1601) Jonson satirized several of his fellow playwrights, particularly Dekker and Marston, who were writing at that time for a rival company of child actors. He collaborated with Chapman and Marston on the comedy *Eastward Ho!* (1604). A passage in the play derogatory to the Scots offended James I, and the three playwrights spent a brief time in prison. Jonson's great period, both artistically and financially, began in 1606 with the production of *Volpone.* This was followed by his three other comic masterpieces, *Epicoene* (1609), *The Alchemist* (1610), and *Bartholomew Fair* (1614). Jonson became a favorite of James I and wrote many excellent masques for the court. He was the author of two Roman tragedies, *Sejanus* (1603) and *Catiline* (1611). With the unsuccessful production of *The Devil Is an Ass* in 1616 Jonson's good fortune declined rapidly. His final plays were failures, and with the accession of Charles I in 1625 his value at court was less appreciated. His plays, written along classical lines, are marked by a pungent and uncompromising satire, by a liveliness of action, and by numerous HUMOR characters, whose single passion or oddity overshadows all their other traits. He was a moralist who sought to improve the ways of men by portraying human foibles and passions in exaggeration and distortion. Jonson's nondramatic poetry includes *Epigrams* (1616); *The Forrest* (1616), notable for the two beautiful songs: "Drink to me only with thine eyes" and "Come, my Celia, let us prove"; and *Underwoods* (1640). His principal prose work *Timber or Discoveries* (1640) is a collection of notes and reflections on miscellaneous subjects. Jonson exerted a strong influence over his contemporaries. Although arrogant and contentious, he was a boon companion, and his followers, sometimes called the "sons of Ben," loved to gather with him in the London taverns. Examples of his conversation were recorded in *Conversations with Ben Jonson* by Drummond of Hawthornden. See Jonson's works (11 vol., 1925–52); biography by Marchette Chute (1953); studies by E. B. Partridge (1958), J. A. Barish (1960), Wesley Trimpi (1962), G. B. Jackson (1969), J. G. Nichols (1970), J. B. Bamborough (1970), J. A. Bryant (1973), and W. D. Wolf (1973).

Jonson, Cornelis van Ceulen: see JANSSENS, CORNELIS VAN CEULEN.

Jónsson, Einar (ā'när yōn'sôn), 1874–1954, Icelandic sculptor and painter. His subjects were drawn from Nordic mythology, Icelandic folklore, and the Bible. His statue of the explorer Thorfinn Karlsefni is in Fairmount Park, Philadelphia. In Reykjavik, Iceland, there is a museum of his work.

Joos of Ghent: see JUSTUS OF GHENT.

Jooss, Kurt (ko͝ort yōs), 1901–, German dancer, producer, and choreographer. Jooss was a student of Rudolf von Laban and was influenced by Émile Jaques-Dalcroze. *The Green Table* (1932), his most famous ballet, was an expressionistic view of the origins of war. Leaving Germany after the rise of Hitler, he worked in England with his Ballets Jooss and toured in many European and American cities, returning to Germany after the war. His group was disbanded in 1962; Jooss continued to perform with other Western European companies. His ballets, including *Chronica, The Big City, A Spring Tale,* and *Pandora,* have influenced the development of psychological themes in ballet. See A. V. Coton, *The New Ballet: Kurt Jooss and his Work* (1946).

Joplin, Scott, 1868–1917, American ragtime pianist and composer, b. Texarkana, Texas. Self-taught, Joplin left home in his early teens to seek his fortune in music. From 1885 to 1893 he lived in St. Louis, playing in saloons and bordellos. In 1894 he moved to Sedalia, Mo., and played second cornet in a local band. For the next two years Joplin toured with a vocal ensemble he had formed and made his first efforts at composing ragtime. When the group disbanded (1896), he returned to Sedalia, where he stayed about four years. During this time he studied music at George Smith College, an educational institution for blacks sponsored by the Methodist Church. In 1899 he published the "Maple Leaf Rag," and its success was instantaneous. However, his next two major efforts, a folk ballet titled *Rag Time Dance* (1902) and a ragtime opera called *A Guest of Honor* (never published) were failures. Joplin continued to write ragtime music and moved (1909) to New York City, where he had considerable success until 1915, when at his own expense he produced a second ragtime opera, *Treemonisha* (1911), that failed to gain recognition. This failure and the declining interest in ragtime is thought to have affected his personality, which became moody and temperamental. In 1916 he was confined to the Manhattan State Hospital, where he died the following year. Joplin's rags were highly innovative, characterized by a lyricism and suppleness that elevated ragtime from honky-tonk piano music to a serious art form. Some of his compositions are "The Entertainer" (1902), "Rose Leaf Rag" (1907), "Gladiolus Rag" (1908), "Fig Leaf Rag" (1908), and "Magnetic Rag" (1914). A revival of interest in ragtime occurred in the 1970s. Several of Joplin's rags were used as background music for the Hollywood film *The Sting* (1973), and a Joplin Festival was held at Sedalia in 1974. See Rudi Blesh and Harriet Janis, *They All Played Ragtime* (rev. ed. 1966).

Joplin (jŏp'lĭn), city (1970 pop. 39,256), Jasper and Newton counties, SW Mo., at the edge of the Ozarks; settled c.1839, inc. 1873. It is a railroad center, the shipping and processing point of a grain and livestock region with dairy and fruit farms, and the industrial center of a lead and zinc area. The city has a mineral museum and is the seat of Missouri Southern State College.

Joppa: see JAFFA, Israel.

Jorah (jō'rə), the same as HARIPH.

Jorai (jō'rāī, jōrā'ī), Gileadite. 1 Chron. 5.13.

Joram (jō'rəm). **1, 2** Kings of Israel and Judah: see JEHORAM **1, 2. 3** Son of Toi, king of Hamath, sent to congratulate David on the defeat of Hadadezer. 2 Sam. 8.9–10. Hadoram: 1 Chron. 18.10. **4** Levite. 1 Chron. 26.25.

Jordaens, Jacob (yä'kôp yôr'däns), 1593–1678, Flemish baroque painter, b. Antwerp. After the deaths of Rubens and Van Dyck, by whom he was influenced, he became the leading Flemish painter of his day and worked in Antwerp nearly all his life. Like Rubens, Jordaens produced portraits and religious and allegorical paintings, often expressing a joy of life. In early works (c.1612–25), such as *The Artist's Family* (Hermitage, Leningrad) and *Allegory of Fertility* (Brussels), he reveals the influence of Caravaggio in his firm modeling and realistically treated surface. Works executed c.1625–35 show increased grandeur and richness (*Triumph of Bacchus;* Kassel), and in the next years Rubens and Van Dyck influences are especially clear. In the last 25 years of his life, Jordaens stressed increasingly the classicist elements in baroque art, moving from the energetic *Triumph of Prince Frederik Hendrik of Orange* (The Hague) to the more rigidly composed *Christ and the Doctors* (Mainz). Examples of his work may be seen in many of the major museums of Europe and the United States. See study by Max Rooses (tr. 1908).

Jordan, Camille (kämē'yə zhôrdäN'), 1771–1821, French writer and political figure. A moderate supporter of the French Revolution, he fled France during the REIGN OF TERROR and again after the coup d'etat of Sept. 4, 1797. He befriended Johann von Goethe, J. C. F. von Schiller, and Johann von Herder. Returning to France after Napoleon Bonaparte (later Emperor Napoleon I) came to power, he wrote (1802) the widely read pamphlet, *Vrai sens du vote national* [the true meaning of the national vote], directed against Napoleon. After the Bourbon restoration Jordan was elected (1816) to the chamber of deputies.

Jordan, David Starr, 1851–1931, American scientist and educator, b. Gainesville, N.Y., M.S. Cornell, 1872, M.D. Indiana Medical College, 1875, and studied under Louis Agassiz at Penikese Island. He taught (1875–79) at Butler Univ. and in 1879 became professor of zoology and head of the department of natural science at Indiana Univ.; there he was president from 1885 to 1891. He served as the first president (1891–1913) of Stanford Univ. and as chancellor (1913–16). A prolific writer and a popular speaker, he was active as director (1910–14) of the World Peace Foundation and president (1915) of the World Peace Congress. Peace and international arbitration were the subjects of his books *The Human Harvest* (1907) and *War and Waste* (1913). As a leading ichthyologist Jordan served on international commissions for fisheries and as assistant (1877–91, 1894–1909) to the U.S. Fish Commission. His earliest important work, *A Manual of the Vertebrate Animals of Northern United States* (1876), went through many editions. He also wrote *The Fishes of North and Middle America* (4 vol., 1896–1900), *A Guide to the Study of Fishes* (2 vol., 1905), *Your Family Tree* (with S. L. Kimball, 1929), and *Trend of the American University* (1929). See his autobiographical *Days* *of a Man* (2 vol., 1922); biography by H. A. Moran (1969).

Jordan, officially Hashemite Kingdom of Jordan, formerly Transjordan, kingdom (1970 est. pop. 2,348,000), 37,737 sq mi (97,740 sq km), SW Asia, bordering on Israel in the west, on Syria in the north, on Iraq in the northeast, and on Saudi Arabia in the east and south. AMMAN is the country's capital and largest city; other cities include Zarqa, HEBRON, Irbid, the Old City of JERUSALEM, and NABLUS. In the Arab-Israeli War of 1967, Israel captured and occupied all of Jordan located W of the Jordan River and the Dead Sea (the area known collectively as the West Bank), which comprises about 2,165 sq mi (5,607 sq km) and includes Hebron, JERICHO, the Old City of Jerusalem, and Nablus. Jordan falls into three main geographical regions. East Jordan, which encompasses about 92% of the country's land area, is made up of a section (average elevation: 2,500 ft/760 m) of the Arabian Plateau that in the northeast includes part of the Syrian Desert. In the western

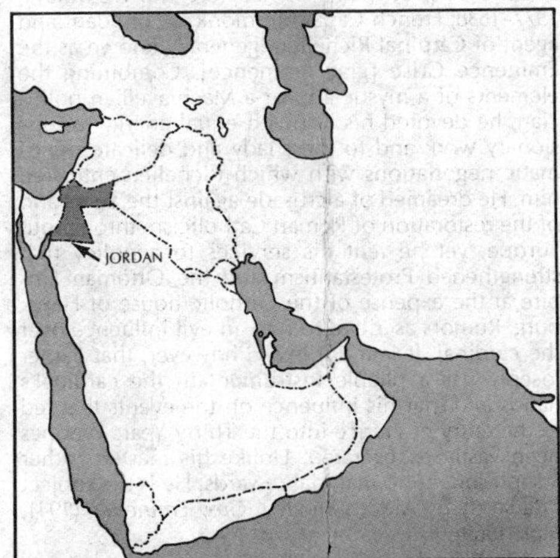

part of the plateau are the Jordanian Highlands, which include Jabal Ramm (5,755 ft/1,754 m), Jordan's loftiest point. Central Jordan is made up of a segment of the Great Rift Valley (which continues southward into Africa) and includes the Jordan River, the Dead Sea, and the Arabah (a dry riverbed). West Jordan, which is part of historic Palestine, is composed of the hilly regions of SAMARIA (in the north) and JUDAEA (in the south). Samaria has abundant fertile soil, and Judaea is largely stony and barren. The inhabitants of Jordan are mostly of Arab descent; however, the Palestinians are also descended from the people who lived in Palestine before the Arab conquest (7th cent.), whereas the inhabitants of E Jordan (many of whom belong to BEDOUIN tribes) are of purer Arab ancestry. There are small minorities of Armenians and Circassians. Arabic, the official language, is spoken by virtually everyone. About 90% of the people are Sunni Muslims. There are approximately 100,000 Christians, about half of whom are Greek Orthodox. Jordan's economy is largely agricultural. Only about 10% of the country's land is arable, and farm output is further limited by the small size of most farms, inefficient methods of tilling the soil, inadequate irrigation, and the dislocations caused by the Arab-Israeli Wars. The principal crops are wheat, barley, lentils, tomatoes, eggplants, citrus fruits, and grapes. Many Jordanians support themselves by raising sheep and goats. Manufactures are largely limited to basic items such as foodstuffs, beverages, clothing, construction materials (especially cement), soap, dairy products, and cigarettes. Numerous artisans make items of leather, wood, and metal. Phosphate rock and potash are the only minerals produced in significant quantities. Jordan's transportation system is limited to a small network of all-weather roads and a narrow-gauge railroad (formerly part of the Hejaz RR) that enters Jordan from Syria and runs through Amman and into S Jordan. Aqaba is the country's only seaport. The annual cost of Jordan's imports usually far exceeds its earnings from exports. The principal imports are foodstuffs, textiles, machinery, iron and steel, and chemicals; the main exports are phosphates and tomatoes. Jordan's leading trade partners are the United States, Saudi Arabia, Lebanon, and Syria. The history section of this article is primarily concerned with the region E of the Jordan River; for the history of the area to the west see PALESTINE. The region of present-day Jordan roughly corresponds to the biblical lands of AMMON, BASHAN, EDOM, and MOAB. The area was conquered by the Seleucids in the 4th cent. B.C. and was part of the Nabatean empire, whose capital was Petra, from the 1st cent. B.C. to the mid-1st cent. A.D., when it was captured by the Romans under Pompey. In the period between the 6th and 7th cent. it was the scene of considerable fighting between the Byzantine Empire and Persia. In the early 7th cent. the region was invaded by the Muslim Arabs, and after the Crusaders captured Jerusalem in 1099, it became part of the Latin Kingdom of Jerusalem. In 1516 the Ottoman Turks gained control of what is now Jordan, and it remained part of the Ottoman Empire until the 20th cent. After the fall of the Ottoman Empire in World War I the region came under (1919) the government of Faisal I centered at Damascus. When Faisal was defeated by the French, Transjordan (as Jordan was then known) was made (1920) part of the British League of Nations mandate of Palestine. In 1921, ABDULLAH ibn Husain, a member of the Hashemite dynasty and the brother of Faisal, was made head of Transjordan, which was administered separately from Palestine and was specifically exempted from being part of a Jewish national home. A Jordanian army, called the Arab Legion, was created by the British largely through the work of Sir John Bagot GLUBB. In a treaty signed with Great Britain in 1928, Transjordan became a constitutional state ruled by a king (to be hereditary in the family of Abdullah). The country supported the Allies in World War II, and, by a treaty with Great Britain signed in 1946, it became (May 25) independent as the Hashemite Kingdom of Transjordan. By an agreement signed in 1948, Britain guaranteed Transjordan an annual military subsidy. Abdullah opposed Zionist aims, and when Palestine was partitioned and the state of ISRAEL was established in 1948, Transjordan, like other members of the ARAB LEAGUE, sent forces to fight Israel (see ARAB-ISRAELI WARS). The troops of the Arab Legion were unsuccessful against the Israeli forces, but they did gain control of most of that part of W central Palestine that the United Nations had designated as Arab territory. In April, 1949, the country's name was changed to Jordan, thus reflecting its acquisition of land W of the Jordan River. In Dec., 1949, Jordan concluded an armistice with Israel, and early in 1950, it formally annexed the West Bank, a move that was deeply resented by other Arab states, which favored the establishment of an independent state of Palestine. The annexation of the West Bank increased Jordan's population by about 450,000 persons, many of them homeless refugees from Israel. In 1951, Abdullah was assassinated in Jerusalem by a Palestinian and was succeeded by his son Talal. Talal, however, was mentally ill, and in 1952 parliament replaced him with his son HUSSEIN I. In 1953 and 1954 border clashes with Israel threatened a renewal of major hostilities, and Jordan received promises of aid from other Arab countries. After a series of anti-Western riots in Jordan, Hussein early in 1956 dismissed Glubb as commander of the Arab Legion, and following the Suez crisis later in the year, he ended Jordan's treaty relationship with Great Britain. In Feb., 1958, Jordan and Iraq formed the Arab Federation as a countermove to the newly formed United Arab Republic (UAR); however, the federation was short-lived; Hussein dissolved it in August, following the July revolution in Iraq that toppled the monarchy there. At the time of the Iraqi revolution, the UAR called for the overthrow of the governments in Jordan and Lebanon. To stabilize politics in these countries, the British sent troops to Jordan, and the United States dispatched forces to Lebanon (in both cases at the request of the governments involved). Tensions were soon reduced, and by early November the troops had been withdrawn. However, for the next few years Jordan remained on poor terms with Iraq and the UAR. The terrorist killing in 1960 of Jordan's prime minister, Hazza Majali, was alleged to have been directed from Syria. In 1961, Hussein was among the first to recognize Syria after it withdrew from the UAR. Following the establishment in 1963 of a revolutionary Jordanian government-in-exile in Damascus, a state of emergency was declared in Jordan. The crisis ended only after the United States and Great Britain announced their support of Hussein and the U.S. 6th Fleet was placed on alert. In the mid-1960s, Jordanian politics were calm, Jordan's economy expanded as its international trade increased, and Jordan was on good terms with Egypt. In 1966 relations with Syria deteriorated, and there were serious border clashes with Israel. Following Egypt's declaration in 1967 of a blockade of Israeli shipping in the Gulf of Aqaba, Hussein signed a mutual defense pact with President Gamal Abdal Nasser of Egypt. In the brief Arab-Israeli War in June, Jordanian forces were routed by Israel, and Jordan lost the West Bank. In 1968–69 there were clashes along the frontier with Israel, but of greater significance was the growing hostility between the Jordanian government and the Palestinian guerrilla organizations (notably Al Fatah, the Palestine Liberation Organization, and the Popular Front for the Liberation of Palestine) operating in Jordan. The guerrillas sought to establish an independent Palestinian state, a goal that conflicted with Hussein's intention of reestablishing Jordan's control over the West Bank. There was major fighting between the guerrillas and the Jordanian army in Nov., 1968, and in Sept., 1970, the country was engulfed in a bloody 10-day civil war, which ended when other Arab countries (especially Egypt) arranged a cease fire. In July, 1971, the army carried out a successful offensive that destroyed the guerrillas' bases in Jordan. In Nov., 1971, Prime Minister Wasfi al-Tal was assassinated in Cairo by members of the "Black September" Palestinian guerrilla organization, which took its name from the month of the civil war in Jordan. In 1972, Hussein proposed the creation of the United Arab Kingdom, a federal state including the West Bank with the rest of Jordan and having two capitals (Amman and Jerusalem) but one army. Predicated on Israel's withdrawal from the West Bank, the proposal was rejected by the other Arab states (and Israel) and Egypt broke off diplomatic relations (reestablished in 1973) because of the plan. Hussein was mildly wounded in an assassination attempt by a Palestinian in Dec., 1972. Jordan played a minor role in the Arab-Israeli War of Oct., 1973, sending a small number of troops to fight on the Syrian front.

Government. Under the 1952 constitution as amended, the most powerful political and military figure in the country is the king. He appoints a cabinet (headed by a prime minister), which is responsible to the bicameral parliament that consists of a 30-member senate (appointed by the king) and a 60-member house of representatives (popularly elected to 4-year terms). See Sir John Bagot Glubb, *The Story of the Arab Legion* (1952) and *Syria, Lebanon, and Jordan* (1967); F. G. Peake, *A History of Jordan and its Tribes* (1958); Raphael Patai, *The Kingdom of Jordan* (1958); P. J. Vatikiotis, *Politics and the Military in Jordan: A Study of the Arab Legion, 1921–57* (1967); H. C. Reese et al., *Area Handbook for the Hashemite Kingdom of Jordan* (1969); N. H. Aruri, *Jordan: A Study in Political Development, 1921–1965* (1972); Sir Charles Johnston, *The Brink of Jordan* (1972).

Jordan, river, c.200 mi (320 km) long, formed in the Hula basin, N Israel, by the confluence of three headwater streams and meandering S through the Sea of Galilee to the Dead Sea; longest and most important river of Palestine. It flows through the northern section of the Jordan trough, a part of the Great Rift Valley; between the Sea of Galilee and the Dead Sea, the Jordan valley is called the Ghor. The Jordan is fed by many small streams; the Yarmuk River is its largest tributary. Deep and turbulent during the rainy season, the Jordan is reduced to a sluggish, shallow stream during the summer. As it nears the Dead Sea, its salinity increases. Although the river is not navigable, its waters are potentially very valuable for irrigation. Plans for the integrated development of the water of the entire Jordan basin collapsed in 1953 because of Arab-Israeli enmity. Individual mutually harmful schemes have been initiated, e.g., Israel's National Water Carrier Project, which uses the Sea of Galilee as a reservoir, and Jordan's East Ghor project, which diverts water from the Yarmuk River. Irrigation projects in Syria and Lebanon divert water from the Jordan's headstreams. The Jordan, scene of Christ's baptism, is frequently mentioned in the Bible. The southern half of the river formerly flowed through Jordan, but after the 1967 Arab-Israeli War this part of the river became a section of the defacto Israel-Jordan border.

Jordan, river, 60 mi (97 km) long, draining Utah Lake N into Great Salt Lake, N central Utah; it passes through Salt Lake City. Fed by numerous streams flowing off the Wasatch Range, the Jordan is used for irrigation and forms the heart of the Utah Oasis. Mormons settled along its banks in the mid-1800s.

Jordanes (jôrdā'nēz), fl. 6th cent., historian of the Ostrogoths. Born in the lower Danube region, he entered the priesthood and lived much of his life at Ravenna. His *History of the Goths*, an abridgment of the lost work of CASSIODORUS, is the only source for Ostrogothic history. It is one of the few works written in Vulgar Latin.

Jorga, Nicolas: see IORGA, NICOLAE.

Jørgensen, Jens Johannes (yĕns yōhä'nəs yör'gən-sən), 1866–1956, Danish poet and religious writer. He reacted against the naturalism of Georg Brandes and, in such works as *Poems* (1898), turned to symbolism and emotion. Jørgensen's conversion (1896) to Roman Catholicism is described in his autobiography (7 vol., 1916–28; tr., 2 vol., 1928–29). Among his works are *Saint Francis of Assisi* (1907, tr. 1912) and *Saint Catherine of Siena* (1915, tr. 1938). *Flowers and Fruit* (1907) and *The Brig Marie of Svendborg* (1926) are collections of his poems.

Jorim (jôr'ĭm), ancestor of Joseph. Luke 3.29.

Jorkoam (jôrkō'əm), descendant of Caleb. 1 Chron. 2.44.

Jos (jôs), city (1969 est. pop. 105,000), central Nigeria, on the Jos Plateau. It is a mining center for tin ore, which is processed in the city, and a collection point for hides and skins and for market-garden produce to be sent to Lagos. It is also a resort. Jos was developed in the early 20th cent. by the British as an administrative center and mining town. The railroad reached here in 1927. The Jos Museum includes a collection of neolithic Nok TERRA-COTTA figurines (see AFRICAN ART). The UNESCO School for Museum Technicians is attached to the museum.

Josabad (jō'zəbăd), officer of David. 1 Chron. 12.4.

Josaphat (jŏs'əfăt), in the Bible: see JEHOSHAPHAT.

Josaphat, in literature: see BARLAAM AND JOSAPHAT.

Jose (jō'zē), in the Gospel genealogy. Luke 3.29.

Josedech (jŏs'ədĕk), variant of JOZADAK.

Joselito (hōsālē'tō), 1895–1920, Spanish matador, b. Seville as José Gómez. A prodigy, he appeared first as a torero in 1908 and later toured Spain as one of a child-bullfighting group known as the Niños Sevillanos. His rivalry with Juan BELMONTE between 1914 and 1920 is known as the Golden Age of Bullfighting. It ended with Joselito's fatal goring at Talavera de la Reina on May 16, 1920, in a corrida in which both matadors appeared. Joselito and Belmonte are considered the two greatest matadors of all time.

Joseph, Saint, husband of the Virgin, a carpenter, a descendant of the house of David. He was apparently dead at the time of the Passion, for his last appearance in the Gospels is at the finding of the 12-year-old Jesus in the temple (Luke 2.42–50). As the foster father of Jesus and the chaste spouse of Mary, St. Joseph is highly honored by Orthodox and Roman Catholics. The latter regard him as patron of the Church. Feast: March 19; another feast, the Solemnity of St. Joseph: third Wednesday after Easter.

Joseph I, 1678–1711, Holy Roman emperor (1705–11), king of Hungary (1687–1711) and of Bohemia (1705–11), son and successor of Leopold I. Joseph became Holy Roman emperor in the midst of the War of the SPANISH SUCCESSION and died before it ended. He vigorously supported the claim of his brother (who succeeded him as CHARLES VI) to the Spanish throne. During his reign Hungary was in revolt under Francis II RÁKÓCZY, but by 1711 the rebellion had been quelled. Joseph made some attempts at internal reform. A musician and an admirer of art, he encouraged cultural life in Vienna.

Joseph II, 1741–90, Holy Roman emperor (1765–90), king of Bohemia and Hungary (1780–90), son of MARIA THERESA and Holy Roman Emperor FRANCIS I, whom he succeeded. He was the first emperor of the house of Hapsburg-Lorraine. From the death of his father (1765) to the death of his mother (1780) he ruled the Hapsburg lands jointly with his mother but had little authority. After his mother's death Joseph instituted far-reaching reforms that were more the result of Joseph's personal philosophy and principles than of the philosophy of ENLIGHTENMENT. As a young man he was profoundly impressed by the subhuman conditions of the peasantry that he saw while touring the provinces. He was impatient with the slowness of Maria Theresa's reforms. On her death, he was ready with a full revolutionary program. He contemplated nothing less than the abolition of hereditary and ecclesiastic privileges and the creation of a centralized and unified state administered by a civil service based on merit and loyalty rather than birth. He planned a series of fiscal, penal, civil, and social laws that would have established some measure of social equality and security for the masses. A strong exponent of absolutism, he used despotic means to push through his reforms over all opposition in order to consolidate them during his lifetime. Although Joseph was a faithful Roman Catholic he instituted a series of religious reforms aimed at making German Catholicism independent of Rome. Joseph's main piece of legislation was the abolition (1781) of serfdom and feudal dues; he also enabled tenants to acquire their own lands from the nobles for moderate fees and allowed peasants to marry whom they wished and to change their domicile. He forbade religious orders to obey foreign superiors, suppressed all contemplative orders, and even sought to interfere with the training of priests. A personal visit (1782) of Pope PIUS VI to Vienna did not halt these measures. The Patent of Tolerance (1781) provided for extensive, although not absolute, freedom of worship. In judicial affairs Joseph liberalized the civil and criminal law codes, abolishing torture altogether and removing the death penalty. In fiscal matters Joseph was influenced by the PHYSIOCRATS. He ordered a general reassessment of land preparatory to the imposition of a single land tax. This reform met widespread opposition. Still more unpopular, however, was his attempt to abrogate local governments, customs, and privileges in his far-flung and multilingual dominions, which he divided into 13 circles centrally administered from Vienna. He even sought to impose German as the sole official language; a multilingual administration seemed irrational to him. Revolts broke out in Hungary and in the Austrian Netherlands (see NETHERLANDS, AUSTRIAN AND SPANISH); these were subsequently halted during the reign of LEOPOLD II, Joseph's brother and successor, who rescinded Joseph's reforms in these lands. Joseph founded numerous hospitals, insane asylums, poorhouses, and orphanages; he opened parks and gardens to the public; and he legislated to provide free food and medicine for the indigent. Most of Joseph's reforms did not outlive him. His failure to make them permanent was largely caused by his lack of diplomacy, by his untimely death, by the reaction produced by the French Revolution, and by his unsuccessful foreign policy. Moreover, his scattered and varied lands offered poor conditions for reform. His plan to annex Bavaria to Austria and thus to consolidate his state was frustrated in the War of the BAVARIAN SUCCESSION (1778–79); his project to exchange the Austrian Netherlands for Bavaria was thwarted (1785) by King Frederick II of Prussia, who formed the *Fürstenbund* [princes' league] for that purpose. Joseph allied himself with Czarina CATHERINE II of Russia (whom he accompanied incognito on her Crimean journey), hoping to share in the spoils of the Ottoman Empire (Turkey). Austria joined Russia in the war of 1787–92 against Turkey but was unsuccessful. Obsessed with his social responsibility, Joseph found only occasional time to interest himself in any but the utilitarian arts. With the exception of the pliable KAUNITZ, Joseph's ministers found it difficult to collaborate with him. Joseph was hated and ridiculed by the clergy and nobles, but he was the idol of the common people. Judgments on Joseph II vary widely, but it is certain that he left a socially freer state on his death than he had found on his accession. See Saul K. Padover, *The Revolutionary Emperor, Joseph II* (rev. ed. 1967); P. P. Bernard, *Joseph II* (1968).

Joseph, 1714–77, king of Portugal (1750–77), son and successor of John V. His reign was dominated by his minister, the marquês de POMBAL. Joseph was succeeded at his death by his daughter, Maria I, and Peter III.

Joseph. 1 One of the early heroes of the Bible, the favored son of Jacob and Rachel, sold as a boy into slavery by his brothers who were jealous of Joseph's dreams and of his coat of many colors given him by Jacob. In Egypt, Joseph, after gaining a position of authority in the household of his master, Potiphar, was imprisoned on the false accusations of Potiphar's wife. He was released after interpreting Pharaoh's dream of the lean and fat kine. Pharaoh renamed him Zaphnath-paaneah and took him into favor. Joseph's recognition of his brothers in the famine years when he was governor over Egypt is a famous scene of literature. His wife was Asenath, an Egyptian, and their sons Manasseh and Ephraim were ancestors of 2 of the 12 tribes of Israel. Gen. 30; 37; 39–50. The story has been retold and reworked, as in Joseph and Asenath, among the PSEUDEPIGRAPHA, and in the works of Thomas MANN. **2** Issacharite. Num. 13.7. **3** Asaphite. 1 Chron. 25.2,9. **4** One who had a foreign wife. Ezra 10.42. **5** Priest. Neh. 12.14. **6, 7, 8** Ancestors of St. Joseph. Luke 3.24,26,30. See JOSES; BARNABAS.

Joseph (Chief Joseph), c.1840–1904, chief of a group of NEZ PERCÉ INDIANS. On his father's death in 1871, Joseph became leader of one of the groups that refused to leave the land ceded to the United States by the fraudulently obtained treaty of 1863. Faced with forcible removal (1877), Joseph and the other nontreaty chiefs prepared to leave peacefully for the reservation. Misinformed about the intentions of the Nez Percés, Gen. Oliver Otis HOWARD ordered an attack, which the Indians repulsed. Pursued by the U.S. army, the warriors, with many women and children, began a masterly retreat to Canada of more than 1,000 mi (1,609 km). The Indians won several engagements, notably one at Big Hole, Montana, but 30 mi (48 km) short of the Canadian border they were overtaken by troops under Gen. Nelson A. MILES and forced to surrender. The whites had assumed that Joseph, spokesman for the Indians in peacetime, was responsible for their outstanding strategy and tactics, which actually had been agreed upon in council by all the chiefs. He became, however, a symbol of the heroic, fighting retreat of the Nez Percés. He was taken to Fort Leavenworth, then spent the remainder of his life on the Colville Indian Reservation in the state of Washington and strove to improve the conditions of his people. In 1903 he made a ceremonial visit to Washington, D.C. See biographies by O. O. Howard (1881, repr. 1972), H. A. Howard (1941, repr. 1965), and M. D. Beal (1963, repr. 1973).

Joseph, Father (François Leclerc du Tremblay), 1577–1638, French Capuchin monk, a confidant and agent of Cardinal Richelieu, generally known as the Éminence Grise [gray eminence]. Combining the elements of a mystic and of a Machiavellian politician, he devoted his life with equal energy to missionary work and to the shady and delicate diplomatic negotiations with which Richelieu entrusted him. He dreamed of a crusade against the Turks and of the restoration of Roman Catholicism throughout Europe, yet he lent his services to a policy that strengthened Protestantism and the Ottoman Empire at the expense of the Catholic house of Hapsburg. Rumors ascribed to him an evil influence over the cardinal. It is more likely, however, that Father Joseph was a pliable instrument in the cardinal's hands and that his influence on the events that led to the entry of France into the Thirty Years War has been vastly exaggerated. Unlike his master, Father Joseph sought no material rewards. He is the subject of a study by Aldous Huxley, *Grey Eminence* (1941, repr. 1969).

Joseph Barsabas, Saint (bär'səbəs), surnamed Justus, Matthias' competitor for the place among the disciples left vacant by Judas Iscariot. Lots were drawn, and Matthias won. Acts 1.23. Feast: July 20.

Josephine, 1763–1814, empress of the French (1804–9) as the consort of NAPOLEON I. Born Marie Josèphe Rose Tascher de La Pagerie, in Martinique, she was married in 1779 to Alexandre de Beauharnais. Two children were born, Eugène (later viceroy of Italy) and Hortense (later queen of Holland). Josephine's husband was guillotined during the French Revolution, in 1794, but she escaped with brief imprisonment. In 1796 she was married, by a civil ceremony, to Napoleon Bonaparte, whom she had met through Paul BARRAS. Before Napoleon became emperor, they were remarried in a religious ceremony. Josephine took a prominent part in the social life of the time. Napoleon had the marriage annulled in 1809 because of her alleged sterility, so that he might marry Marie Louise, daughter of the Austrian emperor Francis I (formerly Holy Roman Emperor Francis II). Thereafter Josephine lived in retirement at Malmaison. See biographies by R. M. Wilson (1930) and André Castelot (tr. 1967); studies by Frédéric MASSON.

Joseph of Arimathea, Saint (âr"ĭməthē'ə), wealthy man, probably a member of the Sanhedrin, who gave the body of Jesus a decent burial. (Mat. 27.57–61; Mark 15.42–47; Luke 23.50–56; John 19.38–42.) The Christian Church has always honored him. The stories connecting him with the Holy GRAIL and with the founding of GLASTONBURY are probably literary fictions of the Middle Ages and have never received the approval of the church. Feast: March 17.

Joseph of Exeter, fl. c.1190, English poet who wrote in Latin. He is best known for *De Bello Trojano* (c.1184), an epic poem in six books, written in the style of Vergil. His adventures in the Third Crusade were recounted in *Antiocheis,* most of which is lost. He lived much of his life in France.

Josephus, Flavius (flā'vēəs jōsē'fəs), A.D. 37–A.D. 95?, Jewish historian and soldier, b. Jerusalem. Having studied the tenets of the three main sects of Judaism—Essenes, Sadducees, and Pharisees—he became a Pharisee. At the beginning of the war between the Romans and Jews, he was made governor of Galilee. He displayed valor and shrewdness in the war, but when the stronghold he defended was taken, he won the favor of the Roman general Vespasian (Titus Flavius Vespasianus) and took his name, Flavius. The conduct of Josephus toward the Roman conquerors has been both criticized and defended; however, our knowledge of his conduct is based on his own writings. It is as a historian of the Jews that Josephus is renowned. He wrote *The Jewish War;* the famous *Antiquities of the Jews,* a history of the race from creation to the war with Rome; *Against Apion,* an exalted defense of the Jews; and his autobiography, or apologia. His complete works have appeared in English editions. See H. St. John Thackeray, *Josephus: The Man and the Historian* (1929, rev. ed. 1968); F. J. Foakes Jackson, *Josephus and the Jews* (1930); R. J. H. Shutt, *Studies in Josephus* (1961); G. A. Williamson, *The World of Josephus* (1965).

Joses (jō'sēz) [Gr. form of Heb. JOSEPH]. **1** Kinsman of Jesus. Mark 6.3; Mat. 13.55. **2** Brother of St. JAMES (the Less); same as **1,** if the traditional interpretation is accepted. Mat. 27.56; Mark 15.40,47. **3** See BARNABAS, SAINT.

Josetsu (jō"sā'tso͞o), fl. 1425, Japanese landscape painter, teacher, and priest. His work shows the formal characteristics of Chinese *suiboku-ga* (black-and-white) painting. He worked in Kyoto, where SHUBUN was his pupil.

Joshah (jō'shə), Simeonite chief. 1 Chron 4.34.

Joshaphat (jŏsh'əfăt): see JEHOSHAPHAT.

Joshaviah (jŏshəvī'ə), one of David's guard. 1 Chron. 11.46.

Joshbekashah (jôshbĕk'əshä), Hemanite temple musician. 1 Chron. 25.4, 24.

Joshua (jŏsh'o͞oə, -əwə). **1** Central figure of the book of JOSHUA. **2** High priest associated with Zerubbabel in rebuilding the Temple. Hag. 1; 2; Zech. 3; 6.11. Jeshua: Ezra 3.2; 4.3; 10.18; Neh. 12.26. Jesus: Ecclus. 49.12. **3** Owner of the field where the Ark of the Covenant stood. 1 Sam. 6.14. **4** Governor of Jerusalem. 2 Kings 23.8.

Joshua (jŏsh'o͞oə) or **Josue** (jŏs'yo͞oē), book of the Old Testament, the sixth in the order of the Authorized Version (AV). It is a historical sequel to Deuteronomy, telling of the occupation of Palestine by the Hebrews. The chief figure of the book is Joshua, Moses' successor as leader of Israel. He appears in Moses' lifetime in increasingly important positions, as a warrior (Ex. 17.9, 14), as the assistant to Moses (Ex. 24.13; 33.11), as one of the spies (Num. 13; 14), and finally as Moses' designated successor (Deut. 31.1–8, 14–23; 32.44). The Book of Joshua may be divided into three sections: first, the conquest of the Promised Land (1–12), including the divine appointment of Joshua (1.1–9), the dry crossing of the Jordan River (3), the fall of Jericho (6), and the battle where the sun and moon stood still (10); second, the allotment of the land to the people by tribes (13–22), mainly lists of names, but including an account of how the tribes east of the Jordan acquitted themselves of the charge of setting up a sanctuary of their own (22); and, third, the farewell sermon of Joshua and his death (23–24). Joshua's name appears variously in AV: Jehoshua (Num. 13.16); Jehoshuah (1 Chron. 7.27); Jeshua (Neh. 8.17); Jesus (Acts 7.45; Heb. 4.8). He is also called Hoshea (Deut. 32.44) and Oshea (Num. 13.8, 16), both variants of Hosea. He is one of the great heroes of biblical history. Ecclus. 46.1–6; 1 Mac 2.55. For critical views of the composition of Joshua see study by J. A. Soggin (tr. 1972); see also bibliography under OLD TESTAMENT.

Joshua tree: see YUCCA.

Joshua Tree National Monument: see NATIONAL PARKS AND MONUMENTS (table).

Josiah (jōsī'ə) or **Josias** (jōsī'əs). **1** King of Judah, son and successor of Amon. The great event of his reign came in its 18th year, when the book of the law, apparently DEUTERONOMY, was found in the Temple. Josiah had it read publicly, and a reform movement began, led by the young king. The basis of the reforms, which extended to the northern kingdom of Israel, was the removal of all outlying religious centers so as to concentrate everything in worship at Jerusalem. When the pharaoh Necho set out to help the Assyrians in Haran, Josiah opposed him and fell, at Megiddo. He was succeeded by his son Jehoahaz. 2 Kings 22–23; 2 Chron. 34–35. **2** Man at whose house the prophet Zechariah was to crown the high priest. Zech. 6.10–11.

Josibiah (jŏsĭbī'ə), father of Jehu the Simeonite. 1 Chron. 4.35.

Jósika, Miklós, Baron (bä'rōn mĭk'lōsh yō'shĭkō), 1794–1865, Hungarian novelist and patriot. The originator of the Hungarian historical novel, he was often superficial and inaccurate, but was nevertheless responsible for a renewed interest in Hungary's history. His many novels include *Abafi* (1836) and *Az utolsó Bátory* (1840). Forced to flee abroad after his part in the unsuccessful revolution of 1848–49, he directed the central office of Polish émigrés in Brussels.

Josiphiah (jŏsĭfī'ə), father of one who returned with Ezra. Ezra 8.10.

Jos Plateau (jôs), region, c.3,000 sq mi (7,770 sq km), alt. c.4,200 ft (1,280 m), central Nigeria, W Africa. The plateau, composed mainly of granite, slopes gently to the north and is covered by grasslands; the Gongola River rises there. The region has one of the higher population densities in Nigeria and is freer from disease than the surrounding lowlands. Tin is mined and processed on the plateau, and farming and grazing are important. The town of Jos is the region's chief center. In the 19th cent. the plateau was a refuge for non-Islamic tribes fleeing from the Islamic Fulani people.

Josquin Desprez or **Des Prés** (both: zhōs'kăN dāprā'), c.1440–1521, Flemish composer, b. Hainaut, regarded by his contemporaries as the greatest of his age. Luther spoke highly of Desprez who may have instructed Erasmus in music. He was in Milan from 1459 to 1479, and he sang in the papal choir intermittently from 1486 to 1494. After brief service under the duke of Ferrara, he ended his days as provost of the Collegiate Church of Condé. His earlier works exhibit a preoccupation with contrapuntal skills, while his later works are more chordal. He wrote Masses and miscellaneous Italian pieces, but he was particularly noted for his chansons and motets.

Jostedalsbreen (yô'stədälsbrā"ən), largest glacier of the European mainland, 315 sq mi (816 sq km), Sogn og Fjordane co., SW Norway. Located W of the Jotunheimen mts., between Nordfjord and Sognafjord, the glacier is 60 mi (97 km) long and 15 mi (24 km) wide, with its head c.6,700 ft (2,040 m) above sea level. It has many tributary glaciers.

Josue (jŏs'yo͞oē), variant of JOSHUA.

Jotbah (jŏt'bə), unidentified place, probably in S Palestine. 2 Kings 21.19.

Jotbath (jŏt'bəth) or **Jotbathah** (-bəthə), unidentified desert place. Num. 33.33; Deut. 10.7.

Jotham (jō'thəm). **1** The only one of Gideon's sons not killed by Abimelech; noted for his parable of the trees electing the bramble to be their king. Judges 9.5–21. **2** King of Judah, son of Uzziah. He was a contemporary of Isaiah, Hosea, and Micah. 2 Kings 15.5,32–38. Joatham: Mat. 1.9. **3** Descendant of Caleb. 1 Chron. 2.47.

Jotunheimen (yō'to͝onhāmən), mountain group, S central Norway; highest of Scandinavia. It culminates in Galdhøpiggen (8,098 ft/2,468 m high) and Glittertinden (8,104 ft/2,470 m). The Jostedalsbreen, a huge glacier, is to the west. Sparsely inhabited, the region is used for summer pasture. In Norse mythology, it was the home of the giants, the Jotun.

Joubert, Joseph (zhôzĕf' zho͞obĕr'), 1754–1824, French moralist. His *Pensées* (of which there are many English translations) rank with those of La Rochefoucauld in their finished style but have a greater range, including ethics, politics, theology, and literature.

Joubert, Petrus Jacobus (pā'tro͞os yäkō'bo͞os yo͞obĕr'), 1831–1900, Boer general and politician. With Paul Kruger and Martinus Wessel Pretorius he governed the Transvaal from 1880 to 1883. In 1881 he defeated the British twice before routing them at Majuba Hill. Joubert ran for president against Kruger in 1883, 1893, and 1898. At the outbreak of the South African War he directed the siege of Ladysmith until ill health forced him to retire.

Jouett, Matthew Harris, 1787–1827, American painter, b. Mercer co., Ky., studied in Boston with Gilbert Stuart. He was the first prominent painter in the West. Among his more than 300 portraits are one of Lafayette in the state capitol at Frankfort, Ky., and one of John Grimes in the Metropolitan Museum. James Edward Jouett was his son.

Jouffroy, Théodore Simon (tāôdôr' sēmôN' zho͞ofrwä'), 1796–1842, French philosopher. He was professor at the Collège de France and librarian at the Univ. of Paris. His translations of Thomas Reid and Dugald Stewart spread the influence of the Scottish school of philosophy. His writings stressed the distinction between psychology and physiology. He was influenced by Victor Cousin. His works include *Cours de droit naturel* (1835), *Mélanges philosophiques* (1833), and *Cours d'esthétique* (1843).

Jouhaux, Léon (lāôN' zho͞o-ō'), 1879–1954, French Socialist labor leader. He headed the Confédération générale du Travail from 1909 to 1947, when he resigned in protest against its alliance with Communist interests. In 1949 he helped found the anti-Communist International Confederation of Free Trade Unions. Long prominent in the International Labor Organization and active in the service of peace, Jouhaux received the 1951 Nobel Peace Prize. His works include studies on labor and on disarmament.

Joule, James Prescott (jo͞ol, joul), 1818–89, English physicist. His scientific researches began in his youth when he invented an electromagnetic engine. Joule made valuable contributions to the fields of heat, electricity, and thermodynamics. His work established the mechanical theory of HEAT, and he was the first to determine the relationship between heat energy and mechanical energy (the mechanical equivalent of heat). Joule discovered the first law of THERMODYNAMICS, which is a form of the law of conservation of energy (see CONSERVATION LAWS). He was one of the great experimental scientists of the 19th cent. The electrical unit of work is named for him.

joule (jo͞ol, joul), abbr. J, unit of WORK or ENERGY in the MKS SYSTEM of units, which is based on the METRIC SYSTEM; it is the work done or energy expended by a force of 1 newton acting through a distance of 1 meter. The joule is named for James P. Joule.

Joule's law: see THERMOELECTRICITY.

Jourdan, Jean Baptiste (zhäN bätēst' zho͞ordäN'), 1762–1833, marshal of France. He fought in the American Revolution, and in the French Revolutionary Wars he commanded the Army of the North to Wattignies (1793), won a decisive victory at Fleurus (1794), and led the army of Sambre-et-Meuse into Cologne (1794). He sponsored the law of general conscription (1796) that bore his name. Although initially opposed to the coup d'etat of 18 Brumaire (1799), he served Napoleon as ambassador to the Cisalpine Republic (1801) and was made councilor of state (1802) and marshal of France (1804). After Napoleon's fall, he rallied to the Bourbons, who later made him a peer.

journalism, the collection and periodical publication of news. It includes writing for, editing, and managing such media as the NEWSPAPER and the PERIODICAL. Journalism dates at least from the *Acta Diurna* of Rome (a series of public announcements that can be considered the prototype of the modern newspaper), but it was not until the 15th cent. that the invention of printing made possible its rapid growth. Modern journalism, however, began in the latter years of the 18th cent. Up to that time journalistic enterprise had been hampered by government control, which the American and French Revolutions and the political freedom they fostered helped to break. Until the institution of freedom of speech and of the press, journalism had generally served as the handmaiden of politics or business. Even in the 19th cent. journalists, despite their increased liberties in England and America, were largely controlled by political parties. The advance of universal education, growing popular support of newspapers and periodicals, and new inventions such as the typewriter and linotype helped to extend the prestige and independence of journalism. Enterprising editors in the American newspaper field in the mid-19th cent. influenced other journalistic media (e.g., the muckraking magazine and the independent periodical). In the 20th cent. journalism has undergone profound changes. The personal power of the journalist declined in the face of tremendous technological advances, the growth of the NEWS AGENCY, vast strides in reporting techniques, heavier dependence on advertisement, and the development of other mass media such as radio, television, and motion pictures. However, interest in major political events, the two world wars, and a marked spirit of internationalism led to a great expansion of facilities. Journalism has tended to become more standardized, impersonalized, and sensationalized in England and in the United States and has expanded considerably beyond its original methods of publishing the news in printed form. Joseph Pulitzer, W. R. Hearst, Henry Luce, and Joseph Patterson have been influential names in the style development of contemporary American journalism. Radio and television have become an important and controversial aspect of journalism because they can render events as they actually occur; the psychological effect of the American landing on the coast of Normandy on June 6, 1944, was undoubtedly augmented by the fact that the event was broadcast on radio. Television has had an even stronger impact. Indeed, it has been noted that television not only reports events, it also, by its very presence, influences the course and outcome of these events. There has been controversy about television coverage of numerous events, including the Army-McCarthy hearings, the assassination of President Kennedy, occurrences in the

Vietnam War, the Democratic and Republican conventions of 1968 and 1972, and the hearings of the Senate Select Committee on 1972 Campaign Activities. The importance of journalism has been testified to by the establishment of schools of journalism at most of the world's leading universities. The earliest in the United States was established at the Univ. of Wisconsin (1905). Other early schools were the Univ. of Missouri (1908) and Columbia Univ. school of journalism, which was endowed in 1903 but which did not open until 1912. See F. L. Mott, *News in America* (1952) and *American Journalism* (3d ed. 1962); John Hohenberg, *The New Front Page* (1966); A. K. MacDougall, ed., *The Press* (1972); R. A. Rutland, *The Newsmongers* (1973).

joust: see TOURNAMENT.

Jouvenel, Henry de (äNrē' də zhōōvənĕl'), 1876–1935, French statesman and journalist. Although from an early age influential in politics, he refused to join a party, claiming that existing groups only pandered to the masses. He advocated a modified form of syndicalism. Long editor of the *Matin,* Jouvenel was elected (1921) to the senate, where he generally aligned himself with the left. He was minister of public instruction in 1924 and a delegate to the League of Nations in 1922 and in 1924. As French high commissioner (1925-26) in Syria he employed stern methods to quell a rebellion. Ambassador to Italy in early 1933, he labored to bring Benito Mussolini into the French camp. In 1912, Jouvenel married the French novelist Colette; they were later divorced. See Rudolph Binion, *Defeated Leaders* (1960).

Jouvenet, Jean Baptiste (zhäN bätēst' zhōōvənā'), 1644–1717, French painter, one of a family of painters. He worked in Paris in the studio of Charles Le Brun, whose manner he acquired and whose favor at court he shared. He is best known for his religious paintings; the most important are the series of four canvases for St. Martin des Champs, including the *Miraculous Draught of Fishes* (1706; Louvre). These later works are characterized by a baroque force, with naturalistic details.

Jouvet, Louis (lwē zhōōvā'), 1887-1951, French actor, producer, and director. A member of Copeau's Théâtre du Vieux Colombier after 1913, he left in 1922 to organize his own theater. He was director of the Comédie des Champs Élysées (1924-34) and from 1934 of the Athénée in Paris. He was the first to produce and act in many of the plays of Giraudoux. Jouvet also created highly original décors and stage lighting.

Jove: see JUPITER.

Jovellanos, Gaspar Melchor de (gäspär' mĕlchôr' dā hōvĕlyä'nōs), 1744–1811, Spanish statesman and writer. Jovellanos's poetry is philosophical and reflective; his best-known poem is *Epístola de Fabio a Anfriso* [epistle from Fabio to Anfriso]. His personal integrity put him at odds with church and state, and he was imprisoned for seven years (1801-8). In his prose writing he appealed for prison reform. Jovellanos's report on agrarian law and his memoir in defense of the Central Junta at the time of the French invasion in 1808 had a wide influence. A firsthand view of Jovellanos's life and times is afforded by his diary, covering the years from 1790 to 1801.

Jovian (Flavius Claudius Jovianus) (jō'vēən), c.331-364, Roman emperor (363-64). The commander of the imperial guard under JULIAN THE APOSTATE in his Persian campaign, Jovian was proclaimed emperor by the soldiers when Julian was killed. He made a humiliating peace with SHAPUR II of Persia. He returned Christianity to the privileged position it had enjoyed before Julian, and he restored his friend St. Athanasius to the episcopal see of Constantinople. After a reign of only eight months Jovian died and was succeeded by the joint emperors Valentinian I and Valens.

Jovian planets, the planets JUPITER, SATURN, URANUS, and NEPTUNE. They are all larger and more massive than the earth. Uranus has a radius about 4 times that of the earth and is about 15 times as massive, while Jupiter has a radius about 11 times that of the earth and is about 318 times as massive. However, they are all much less dense than the earth. Since they rotate faster, they are more flattened at the poles than are the TERRESTRIAL PLANETS.

Jowett, Benjamin (jou'ĕt), 1817-93, English educator and Greek scholar, b. London. Jowett was a Church of England clergyman, master of Balliol College, Oxford (1870-93), and vice chancellor of Oxford. His influence on his pupils was profound. Jowett's translation of the dialogues of Plato (1871) is an outstanding work both of English literature and of classical scholarship. See biography by G. C. Faber (1957).

Joyce, James, 1882-1941, Irish novelist. Probably the most significant British writer of the 20th century, Joyce was a master of language, exploiting its total resources. His novel *Ulysses,* which is among the great works of world literature, utilizes many radical literary techniques and forms. The effect of Joyce on other 20th-century writers is incalculable. Born one of ten children in a Dublin suburb, Joyce was educated at Jesuit schools—Clongowes Wood College in Clane (1888-91), Belvedere College in Dublin (1893-99)—and was graduated from University College in Dublin (1899-1902). Although a brilliant student, he paid little attention to his official studies; instead, repelled by the narrow orthodoxy of Catholicism, he abandoned his religion and led a dissolute life. In 1902 he lived briefly in Paris, returning to the Continent in 1904 with Nora Barnacle, the girl who would eventually become his wife. For the next 25 years Joyce, Nora, and their children (George, b. 1905, and Lucia Anna, b. 1907) lived at various times in Paris, Trieste, and Zürich. Joyce returned to Ireland twice: in 1909 in a futile attempt to start a chain of motion picture theaters in Dublin, and in 1912 to arrange for the publication of *Dubliners.* The book was published there but subsequently burned by the printers because the names of actual persons, places, and institutions were mentioned. It was finally published in England in 1914. Joyce and his family spent the years of World War I in Zürich, where he worked on his novel *A Portrait of the Artist as a Young Man.* It first appeared in *The Egoist,* a periodical edited by Harriet Shaw Weaver, and was published in book form in 1916. In 1917, Joyce contracted glaucoma and for the rest of his life endured pain, periods of near blindness, and innumerable operations. During these years he lived mainly on money donated by patrons, notably Harriet Shaw Weaver. His great novel *Ulysses,* written between 1914 and 1921, was published in parts in *The Little Review* and *The Egoist,* but Joyce encountered much opposition to publishing the novel in book form because charges of obscenity were leveled against it. It was finally published in Paris by Shakespeare & Company, a bookstore owned by an American, Sylvia Beach. Its publication was banned in the United States until 1933. From 1922 until 1939 Joyce worked on *Finnegans Wake* (1939). In 1931 he married Nora. Although she was unintellectual and rather uninterested in his work, their union was a happy one, marred only by the progressive insanity of their daughter. Joyce died in Zürich in 1941 after an operation for a malignant duodenal ulcer. With each of Joyce's four major works there is an increase in the profundity of his vision and the complexity of his literary technique, particularly his experiments with language. His first book, *Dubliners,* is a linked collection of 15 short stories treating the squalid lives of various Dublin residents. The stories often center on moments of spiritual insight, which Joyce called epiphanies. *A Portrait of the Artist as a Young Man* is a fairly realistic, highly autobiographical account of the adolescence and youth of Stephen Dedalus, who comes to realize that before he can be a true artist he must rid himself of the stultifying effects of the religion, politics, and essential bigotry of Ireland. *Ulysses* recreates the events of one day in Dublin, June 16, 1904, centering on the activities of a Jewish advertising-space salesman, Leopold Bloom, his wife Molly, and the aforementioned Stephen Dedalus, now a teacher. The fundamental design of *Ulysses* is based on Homer's *Odyssey.* Each of the novel's major characters has a counterpart in the *Odyssey,* and the novel's theme is Bloom's search for a son and Stephen's for a father. Each incident in the novel parallels one in the epic and is also associated with an hour of the day, color, art, and part of the body. Attempting to recreate the total life of his characters—the surface life and the inner life—Joyce mingles realistic descriptions with verbal representations of his characters' most intimate and random thoughts, for which he utilized the stream of consciousness technique. Interspersed throughout the work are historical, literary, religious, and geographical allusions, evocative patterns of words, word games, and many-sided puns, all of which imbue the ordinary events of the novel with the significance of those in an epic. *Ulysses* is a complex book, intricate in structure and proceeding on several levels of meaning. Yet it is also an extraordinarily satisfying book, a celebration of life unparalleled in its humor, characterization, and tragic irony. Joyce's last work, *Finnegans Wake,* is the book of night to supplement the day of *Ulysses.* Although appearing at times to present the dreams of a Dublin publican, the novel also seems to represent a universal consciousness. In order to present this new reality Joyce manipulated and disoriented language, pushing it to the furthest limits of comprehensibility and then beyond. Because of its complexity, *Finnegans Wake* is seldom read and is probably, despite much scholarly treatment, not thoroughly understood. The canon of Joyce's works includes volumes of poems, *Chamber Music* (1907), *Pomes Penyeach* (1927), and *Collected Poems* (1937); *Exiles* (1918), a play in the manner of Ibsen; and part of an early version of *A Portrait of the Artist as a Young Man* called *Stephen Hero* (1944). In June, 1962, a Joyce museum, containing pictures, papers, and first editions of Joyce's books, was dedicated in Dublin. Selections from his work appear in *The Portable James Joyce* (ed. by Harry Levin, 1947). See his letters (Vol. I ed. by Stuart Gilbert, 1957; Vol. II and III ed. by Richard Ellman, 1966); biographies by Richard Ellman (1959) and C. G. Anderson (1968); studies by Anthony Burgess (1965); R. M. Adams (1962 and 1966), John Gross (1970), A. Walton Litz (1961, 1966 and 1972) and Richard Ellman (1974); Don Gifford and R. J. Seidman, *Notes For Joyce: An Annotation of James Joyce's Ulysses* (1974); bibliography by J. J. Slocum and Herbert Cohoon (1953, repr. 1972).

Joyce, William, 1906-46, British Nazi propagandist, b. Brooklyn, N.Y., called Lord Haw-Haw. Taken to England as a child, Joyce became involved there in the fascist movement. He went to Germany just before the outbreak of World War II and throughout the war broadcast German propaganda in English from Berlin. He was captured by British soldiers in Germany in 1945. Despite his American birth, he was adjudged subject to British jurisdiction because he held a British passport. He was convicted of treason and hanged. See biography by J. A. Cole (1964); Rebecca West, *The New Meaning of Treason* (rev. ed. 1967).

Jozabad (jō'zəbăd). **1, 2** Two of David's captains. 1 Chron. 12.20. **3, 4** Important Levites. 2 Chron. 31.13; 35.9. **5** Man who had married a foreigner. Ezra 10.22. **6, 7, 8, 9** Levites in the return from the Exile. Ezra 8.33; 10.23; Neh. 8.7; 11.16. These four may be identical.

Jozachar (jōz'əkär), murderer of Joash. 2 Kings 12.20,21. Zabad: 2 Chron. 24.26.

Jozadak (jō'zədăk), one in the high priests' line who probably never held office, because he was carried away to Babylon. Ezra 3.2; 10.18; Neh. 12.26. Jehozadak: 1 Chron. 6.14,15. Josedech: Hag. 1.1; Zech. 6.11.

József, Attila (ä'tĭlä yō'zhĕf), 1905–37, Hungarian poet. Born in Budapest of a poor family, József had to support himself from the age of seven with menial jobs; he was never able to earn a living from his writing. He was dismissed from the Univ. of Szeged for publishing a poem that was considered blasphemous. After two years abroad he returned to Budapest, where he joined the illegal Communist Party. After suffering periodic struggles with schizophrenia, he committed suicide. His poetry, known abroad only after his death, deals with proletarian life, based largely on his personal experiences.

Juana, Spanish queen of Castile: see JOANNA.

Juana Inés de la Cruz (hwä'nä ēnās' dā lä krōōs), 1651-95, Spanish American poet, b. Mexico. She is considered the greatest lyric poet of the colonial period. A beautiful and intellectually precocious girl, Sor Juana was a favorite at the viceregal court before entering a convent at the age of 16. Forced to study outside the university, she devoted herself to amassing a fine library. Her classical erudition and her scientific curiosity led to reprimands from her convent superiors. The bishop of Puebla published one of her studies but criticized her for neglecting religious duties. Sor Juana answered the bishop's objections to the education of women in a spirited autobiographical letter (1691) that became a classic. Her spontaneous and original lyric poetry won enduring fame. *Primer sueño,* one of her major poetic works, nearly 1,000 lines long, is the metaphoric interpretation of a dream and of awakening. Sor Juana sold her books and devoted her last years to the spiritual life. She died trying to help the convent victims of an epidemic.

Juana la Beltraneja (hwä'nä lä bĕltrănā'hä), 1462-1530, Castilian princess; daughter of Juana of Portugal, queen of HENRY IV of Castile. Her paternity was generally attributed to the court favorite Beltrán de la Cueva, whence her name. Juana was recognized as legitimate heiress to the throne by the Cortes of Castile, but later Henry IV designated as successor first his half brother Alfonso (d.1468) and then his half sister Isabella (later ISABELLA I). In 1470, Henry recognized Juana again, but when he died (1474) Isabella seized the throne. Juana's partisans called upon Alfonso V of Portugal for help and arranged his marriage to the young princess. After five years of struggle Alfonso was decisively defeated at Toro (1476), and Isabella was recognized (1479) as queen of Castile. Juana retired to a convent in Portugal.

Juan Carlos (hwän kär'lōs), 1938– , prince of Asturias and Francisco Franco's designated successor as Spanish chief of state, b. Rome. The son of Don Juan de Borbón y Battenberg, count of Barcelona, and Doña María de las Mercedes de Borbón y Orleans and the grandson of Alfonso XIII, the last Spanish king, he was educated in Switzerland and in Spain. As part of his grooming by Franco as a possible successor, he graduated from Spain's three military academies and received commissions in the army, navy, and air force; he also did graduate work at the Univ. of Madrid and served apprenticeships in many government departments. In 1962 he married Princess Sophia of Greece, by whom he had three children. In 1969 he was designated heir to the Spanish throne and Franco's successor. Two years later Juan Carlos was empowered to act as head of state in case of the dictator's illness or absence. A law passed in 1972 provided for his coronation and proclamation as chief of state within eight days of Franco's death. From July 19 to Sept. 2, 1974, Juan Carlos served as provisional head of state while Franco was severely ill.

Juan de Fuca Strait (wän də fyo͞o'kə), inlet of the Pacific Ocean, 100 mi (161 km) long and 11 to 17 mi (18–27 km) wide, between Vancouver Island, British Columbia, and Washington state, linking the Strait of Georgia and Puget Sound with the Pacific; forms part of the U.S.-Canada border. Victoria, British Columbia, the strait's largest city, is located at its eastern end; ferries connect it with the U.S. mainland. Discovered by the English captain Charles W. Barkley in 1787, the strait was named for a sailor, Juan de Fuca, who reputedly had discovered it for Spain in 1592.

Juanes, Juan de: see MACIP, VICENTE JUAN.

Juan Fernández (hwän fārnän'dās), group of small islands, S Pacific, c.400 mi (640 km) W of Valparaiso, Chile. They belong to Chile and are administered as a part of Valparaiso prov. The two principal islands are Más a Tierra and Más Afuera. Volcanic in origin, they have a pleasant climate and are rugged and heavily wooded. The chief occupation is lobster fishing. Discovered by an obscure Spanish navigator in 1563, the islands achieved fame with the publication of Daniel Defoe's *Robinson Crusoe* (1719), generally acknowledged to have been inspired by the confinement on Más a Tierra (1704–9) of Alexander SELKIRK, a Scottish sailor. Occupied by the Spanish in 1750, the islands passed to Chile when it won independence. In the 19th cent. Más a Tierra was used as a penal colony.

Juan Manuel, Infante de Castile (hwän mänwĕl', ēnfän'tā thā kästē'lā), 1282–1349?, Spanish nobleman, soldier, and writer; nephew of Alfonso X (called the Wise). Juan Manuel was a wealthy and powerful prince. His masterpiece is the *Libro del Conde Lucanor* (1323–35, tr. 1868), a collection of 50 didactic tales that were source material for several major writers, including Boccaccio, Chaucer, and Calderón. See study by H. T. Sturcken (1974).

Juárez, Benito (bānē'tō hwä'rās), 1806–72, Mexican liberal statesman and national hero, an Indian. Revered by Mexicans as one of their greatest political figures, Juárez, with great moral courage and honesty, upheld the civil law and opposed the privileges of the clericals and the army. A lawyer, he was governor of Oaxaca from 1847 to 1852. In 1853 he was imprisoned for his opposition to SANTA ANNA. After a period of exile in the United States, Juárez was a chief figure in drawing up the Plan of AYUTLA and in the subsequent revolution that overthrew Santa Anna. Juárez became minister of justice in the new government and issued the Ley Juárez, which, with the Ley Lerdo (see LERDO DE TEJADA, MIGUEL), attacked the privileges of the church and the army. The conservatives rose against the liberal constitution of 1857. When COMONFORT resigned, Juárez became acting president. He showed his mettle as a high-minded leader of the liberal revolution, which transferred political power from the creoles to the mestizos and forged Mexico's national consciousness. Forced to flee to Guanajuato, then to Guadalajara, and finally to Veracruz with his government, he resisted the conservatives, and ultimately the liberals were successful in the War of the Reform (1858–61). After establishing the government in the capital, Juárez was immediately faced with new difficulties. The intervention of France, Spain, and Great Britain because of unpaid debts to their nationals was followed by the French attempt to establish a Mexican empire (1864–67) under MAXIMILIAN. Juárez, with the adherence of such notable Mexicans as Ignacio Manuel ALTAMIRANO, continued gallant resistance to the French soldiers and moved his capital to El Paso del Norte (later renamed Juárez city). The Mexican people rallied to Juárez, and the empire fell. Reelected in 1867, he instituted the program of reform in full force, but political divisions among the liberals hampered real accomplishments, and by his political maneuvers Juárez somewhat tarnished the glory gained by his defense of Mexico. He was again elected in 1871. An insurrection against him by Porfirio DÍAZ was being suppressed when Juárez died. See biography by U. R. Burke (1894); Ralph Roeder, *Juárez and His Mexico* (1947, repr. 1968); studies by W. V. Scholes (1969) and I. E. Cadenhead, Jr. (1973).

Juárez, city (1970 pop. 436,054) Chihuahua state, N Mexico, on the Rio Grande opposite El Paso, Texas. Connected with the United States by three international bridges, it is a shipping point and highway and rail terminus. It is also the commercial and processing center for the surrounding cotton-growing area. Except for the river valley, under intense cultivation southeast of the city, Juárez is hemmed in by desert. It is a straggling town with the nondescript air of most Mexican-American border settlements. Developing (1659) as the focal point for Spanish colonial expansion to the north, it was originally called El Paso del Norte and included settlements on both sides of the river, until they were split by the Treaty of Guadalupe Hidalgo (1848), which ended the Mexican War. In 1888 the name of the Mexican town was changed to honor Benito Juárez, who made it his capital when exiled from central Mexico. The city was captured by Pascual Orozco and Francisco Villa in the early days of the revolution in 1910.

Juárez Celman, Miguel (mēgĕl' hwä'rās sĕl'män), 1844–1909, president of Argentina (1886–90). After political service in the province of Córdoba, he became president for a six-year term. Speculation, flagrant under his predecessor Julio A. ROCA, now reached its height, and the administration was notorious for corruption. Political opposition to his government increased after he left his party. A revolt in July, 1890, was suppressed, but Juárez Celman was forced to resign (Aug., 1890). He was succeeded by Carlos Pellegrini.

Juba I, c.85 B.C.–46 B.C., king of Numidia. He joined Pompey's party and in 49 B.C. routed Caesar's legate, Curio. He fought on the side of Metellus SCIPIO and took his life after Caesar's victory at Thapsus. Despite his defeat, his son, **Juba II,** d. c.20 A.D., was educated in Rome and reinstated as king, probably first in Numidia, then in Mauretania (c.25 B.C.). Augustus gave to him in marriage Cleopatra Selene, the daughter of Antony and Cleopatra. Highly learned, Juba II wrote lengthy historical and geographical works.

Juba (jo͞o'bä), city, S Sudan, a port on the White Nile. It is the southern terminus of river traffic in the Sudan, and it is also a highway hub, with roads radiating into Uganda, Kenya, and Zaïre. At a conference in Juba in 1947, representatives of the northern and southern parts of Sudan agreed to unify the country, thus dashing Britain's hopes of adding the south to Uganda. As the administrative capital of S Sudan, Juba became the spearhead of southern resistance to alleged northern dominance of the country. Beginning with a mutiny of southern troops at Juba in 1955, southern unrest led to a Sudanese civil war that was not settled until 1969.

Juba, Ital. *Giuba,* river, c.1,000 mi (1,610 km) long, formed at the Ethiopia-Somali Republic border, E Africa, by the confluence of the Daua and Ganale Doria rivers, both of which rise in the highlands of S Ethiopia. The Juba River meanders S through SW Somali Republic to the Indian Ocean near Kismayu. It is navigable for shallow craft to Bardero. The only perennial river of the Somali Republic, the Juba has flood seasons in both spring and autumn. The valley is part of the nation's chief agricultural region, and the river is extensively used for irrigation.

Jubal (jo͞o'băl), son of Lamech and originator of musical instruments. Gen. 4.21.

jubilee (jo͞o'bĭlē) [Hebrew], in the Bible, a year when slaves were manumitted, debts were forgiven, and a general sabbatical year was observed. It occurred once in 50 years, as prescribed by Lev. 25.8–55. In the Roman Catholic Church the name is applied to a holy year when special privileges are given by the church for pilgrimage to Rome and an unusual jubilee indulgence is announced. The first holy year was celebrated in 1300. In 1343 the pope proclaimed that holy years would recur at 50-year intervals, and in 1470 the interval was reduced to 25 years. The most recent holy year proclaimed was 1975. On occasion an extraordinary jubilee is declared, such as that to celebrate the 50th anniversary of Pope Pius XI's ordination (1929) and that celebrating the conclusion of the Second Vatican Council (1966).

Jubilees, Book of: see PSEUDEPIGRAPHA.

Jucal (jo͞o'kəl), variant of JEHUCAL.

Juchitán (ho͞ochētän'), town (1970 pop. 27,907), Oaxaca state, S Mexico. Located on a vast expanse of flat, fertile plain only slightly above sea level, the old town, largely Indian in population, rivals Tehuantepec (20 mi/ 32 km to the east) as the cultural center of the ZAPOTEC. It is linked to Veracruz and the Guatemala border by railroad and is on the Inter-American Highway.

Juda (jo͞o'də) [variant of JUDAH]. **1** See JUDAH **1.** **2** See JUDE, SAINT. **3, 4** Ancestors of St. Joseph. Luke 3.26,30.

Judaea or **Judea** (both: jo͞odē'ə) [Lat. from JUDAH], Greco-Roman name for S Palestine. It varied in size in different periods. In the time of Christ it was both part of the province of Syria and a kingdom ruled by the Herods. It was the southernmost of the Roman divisions of Palestine, the others being Galilee, Samaria, and Peraea. Idumaea was S of Judaea. A strip of Samaria lay between Judaea and the Mediterranean.

Judah I, 135?–220?, leader of the Palestinian Jews, called *ha-Nasi* [prince] and Rabbi. He was redactor of the MISHNA and president of the Sanhedrin.

Judah (jo͞o'də). **1** Fourth son of Jacob and Leah and the eponymous ancestor of one of the 12 tribes of Israel. Judah is a distinctive figure, a leader in the family counsels. With Reuben he interceded for Joseph's life, and he was the spokesman for his brothers before Joseph in Egypt. In the exodus his tribe was in the lead, and it settled in the rich land of S Palestine, extending c.45 mi (72 m) north and south, from the Dead Sea to the Mediterranean. Within its borders was Jerusalem. It gave its name to the Kingdom of Judah. The royal and Messianic family of David was of the tribe of Judah. Gen. 29.35; 35.23; 37.26; 38; 43.3; 44.14; 46.12,28; 49.8; Num. 2.3; 10.14; 13.6; 26.22; Joshua 15.1; 1 Chron. 2–5. Juda: Luke 3.33; Heb. 7.14; Rev. 5.5; 7.5. Judas: Mat. 1.2. **2** Levitical family. Neh. 12.8. **3** Levite. Ezra 10.23. **4** Overseer. Neh. 11.9. **5** Priest's son. Neh. 12.36. **6** The same as HODAVIAH **3.**

Judah, Theodore Dehone, 1826–63, American railroad builder, b. Bridgeport, Conn. He built the Niagara Gorge RR and did canal work before going (1854) to lay out a railroad near Sacramento, Calif. There he promoted the idea of a railroad across the mountains eastward from the Central Valley and interested a number of men in the scheme. The Central Pacific RR was formed, with Judah as chief engineer. He became dissatisfied with his associates and was on his way to the East to obtain capital and support when he died. See biography by Helen Hinckley (1969).

Judah, the southern of the two kingdoms remaining after the division of the kingdom of the JEWS that occurred under REHOBOAM. The northern kingdom, Israel, was continually at war with Judah. In the Bible the southern kingdom is regarded as usually more loyal to God than the northern kingdom was. Judah's capital was Jerusalem and its dynasty was the house of David. It lasted from 931 B.C. to 586 B.C.

Judah ha-Levi or **Judah Halevy** (both: hä"lē'vī), c.1075–1141, Jewish rabbi, poet, and philosopher, b. Tudela, Spain. His poems—secular, religious, and nationalist—are filled with a serene and lofty spirit. In his great philosophic work, *Sefer ha-Kuzari,* he emphasized the superiority of religious truths, arrived at through intuition, over philosophical and speculative truths, arrived at through logic and reason. In this work he developed a philosophy of history wherein he explains the force of the "divine influence" at work in the world, known first by the patriarchs (Abraham, Isaac, and Jacob), through them by the Jewish people, and ultimately, through the martyrdom of the Jews, by all mankind. See *The Kuzari* (tr. by Hartwig Hirschfeld, 1964).

Judaism, broadly defined, the religious beliefs and practices and the way of life of the JEWS. The term itself is of predominantly modern usage; it is not used in the Bible or in Rabbinic literature and only rarely in the literature of the medieval period. The term closest to *Judaism* (Heb. *Yahadut*) in the Rabbinic literature is *Yehudit,* which refers to a specific law, custom, or practice; the word TORAH is employed when referring to what is now subsumed under the name Judaism. Today, the two terms are used interchangeably, although *Torah* usually connotes the divinely revealed teachings, while *Judaism* includes also the totality of human interpretation and practice. Thus, one may speak of "secular Judaism," referring to an adherence to values expressed by Judaism but removed from their religious context. The history of Judaism predates the period to which the term itself actually refers, in that Judaism formally applies to the post-Second Temple period, while its antecedents are to be found in the biblical "religion of Israel." The Bible is no longer considered a homogeneous work; the many traditions represented in it demonstrate variance and growth. While the historicity of the patriarchs' existence and of MOSES as the giver of all laws is under question, certain dominant themes can be seen developing in this early period that have importance for later Judaism. Central to these is the notion of monotheism, which most scholars believe to have been the outgrowth of a process that began with polytheism, progressed to henotheism (the worship of one god without denying the existence of others), and ended in the belief in a single Lord of the universe, uniquely different from all His creatures (Deut. 6.4). He is compassionate toward His creation, and in turn man is to love and fear (i.e., stand in awe of) Him. Because God is holy He demands that His people be holy, righteous, and just, a kingdom of priests (Ex. 19.6) to assist in the fulfillment of His designs for mankind and the world (Isa. 43.10). Israel's chosenness consists of this special designation and the task that accompanies it. God promises the land of Canaan to Israel as their homeland, the place in which the Temple will be built and sacrificial worship of God carried out (Deut. 12.11). The holy days consisted of the Sabbath, Passover, Shavuot, and Sukkoth; and circumcision, dietary laws, and laws pertaining to dress, agriculture, and social justice characterized the structure of the biblical religion. Three types of leaders existed during this period: the priest (*kohen*), who officiated in the Temple and executed the laws; the prophet (*navi*), to whom was revealed God's messages to His people; and the sage (*hacham*), who taught practical wisdom and proper behavior. There was developing already in this early period a belief in the ultimate coming of God's kingdom on earth, a time of peace and justice (Isa. 2.1–4). To this was added, after the destruction (586 B.C.) of the First Temple and the Babylonian captivity (which many saw as the consequence of idolatry and which may have been responsible for the final stage of the development from polytheism to monotheism), the expectation of national restoration under the leadership of a descendant of the Davidic house, the MESSIAH. It was during this post-exilic period (not later than the 5th cent. B.C.) that a compilation of earlier texts and oral traditions was made, forming the core of the Pentateuch, the Five Books of Moses (to which 19 others were later added to form the Hebrew Bible or OLD TESTAMENT, canonized perhaps as late as the 2d cent. A.D.). Attributed to Moses (although some scholars believe its legal portions were formulated by EZRA), these books were studied publicly, and were accompanied by expositions and explanations in which the Oral Law, as distinct from the Written Law (the Torah text), is rooted. While it is widely held that the PHARISEES further developed the Oral Law, in opposition to the literalness of the SADDUCEES, it is inconceivable that the latter group could have administered the biblical laws without reinterpreting them in accordance with a changing world, or in the face of a lack of specificity in the text. The Babylonian exile had exposed the Israelites to new ideas, and it is to that period that the notions of identifiable angels (such as Michael and Raphael), of the personification of evil (Satan), and of the resurrection of the dead (Dan. 12.2) can probably be traced. The conquests of Alexander the Great once again brought the Jews into contact with new ideas, most significantly that of the immortality of the soul. Conflict arose within the community of Israel concerning the level of Hellenization acceptable, out of which came the revolt of the MACCABEES against the Seleucid rulers of Syria and their Judean sympathizers. The resulting martyrdom of many gave added impetus to the belief in collective resurrection of the dead and the immortality of the soul after the body's death. Basically contradictory, these concepts were wed in such a way that while the body awaited its resurrection, the soul was seen as living on in another realm. This new development in no way supplanted the earlier notion of earthly reward; life on earth, however, was viewed by many as preparatory for the next. As the conditions of life deteriorated, apocalyptic beliefs grew—national catastrophe and the Messianic kingdom were seen as imminent events. Some groups (see ESSENES; QUMRAN) fled into the desert to lead righteous lives in anticipation, others followed claimants to the mantle of Messiah (most notably Jesus), while still others became adherents of one of the numerous mystery religions of the period. Out of these numerous ingredients came both Christianity and classical, or rabbinic, Judaism. Developing over a period of five centuries (until A.D. c.500), rabbinic Judaism was characterized by the replacement of the Temple by the SYNAGOGUE (the Second Temple was destroyed in A.D. 70), of the now defunct priesthood by the RABBI, and of the sacrificial ceremony by the prayer service and study. Basic to these changes was the development of the Oral Law (see MISHNA; TALMUD) and the MIDRASH, which, as outgrowths of the biblical religion, centered on the relationships between God, His Torah, and His people, Israel. Emphasis was placed upon study of the Torah (in its broadest sense) as the most important religious act, leading to an understanding of the proper way of life; upon the growing need for national restoration in the face of continued Exile from the Promised Land; and upon the function of this world as preparatory for the World to Come (*Olam ha-Bah*), while not devaluing the importance of life in this world. Significantly, a place in the World to Come could be achieved by persons of all nations. During the medieval period, these trends continued and were basic to the several important codifications of the legal material and to the many biblical and talmudic commentaries that were composed at this time (most notably by RASHI and MAIMONIDES). Two new developments arose in the medieval period. Built upon earlier mystical commentaries of biblical passages, the CABALA flowered during the Middle Ages under the impetus of ideas external to Judaism, predominant among them Neoplatonism, and due to the needs of a persecuted people for redemption. A Jewish philosophy developed in answer to the questions raised by the exposure to Greek thought as distilled through the Islamic philosophers' natural philosophy and metaphysics. Central to these issues was the conflict between reason and revelation: whether revelation was necessary if all could be ascertained through reason, or whether reason was imperfect and revelation was God's assisting man to know the truth. Biblical anthropomorphism had to be dealt with by the rationalists. Maimonides posited the untraditional notion of negative attributes, which tended to depersonalize God. He argued that one can say nothing positive about the personal nature of God, which is beyond human comprehension; one can only indicate what He is not (thus, the statement that God is wise says only that God is not ignorant, not how wise He actually is). The cabalists, taking a more comprehensive view, retained the idea that the totality of God's nature is ultimately beyond human grasp ("Ein Sof" [Heb., literally,= without end] as the "Nothing"), yet, in keeping with tradition, held to a vision of a personal God who exists as the active, creative, and sustaining force within the cosmos ("Ein Sof" as the "Everything"). While the Jewish Middle Ages is usually defined by scholars as extending at least into the 18th cent. (and by some into the 19th cent. to the 1807 convening by Napoleon I of the "French Sanhedrin" to map out the role of the Jews after their emancipation within his empire), there was a Jewish counterpart to the general European Renaissance of the 15th–16th cent. While being influenced by the period (as demonstrated by Judah ABRAVANEL), the Jews of N Italy, S France, and the Levant also came under Sephardic, and particularly under Marrano, influence, which forced them to reevaluate their traditions (see SEPHARDIM). Marrano skepticism, the result of living in two worlds, tended to be a liberalizing influence. Yet, as the victims of years of persecution, the Marranos harbored hopes that added fuel to the fires of Messianism. Both tendencies were present in the community of Amsterdam (and to a degree in Hamburg) that was established by the Marranos at the end of the 16th cent. and flourished as a creative entity (helping to establish the Jewish communities in New Amsterdam and London) until the collapse of the Messianic hope that had been centered on SABBATAI ZEVI. While the reaction to this episode led to a stiffening of rabbinic traditions wherever Sabbatianism had caught on, the spirit of skepticism and the renewed Messianism could not be extinguished. Both elements would add much to the future of the Reform movement (one of whose major centers was Hamburg) and Zionism (two of whose lights, Yehudah Alkalai and Theodor Herzl, claimed Sephardic Marrano descent). The 18th cent. produced both the great traditionalist rabbinic figure ELIJAH BEN SOLOMON and the untraditional figures of BAAL-SHEM-TOV, the founder of HASIDISM (which Elijah himself fought against), and Moses MENDELSSOHN, the spiritual progenitor of later reformers whom Elijah's spiritual descendants repeatedly condemned. The events of the early decades of the 19th cent., subsumed under the name of the Emancipation, brought most Western Jews and their Judaism into contact with modernity, resulting in more than one serious conflict. Particularly acute for many was the problem of maintaining claims of distinctiveness, of being "chosen," while at the same time wishing to participate in the general society. In addition, how were they to maintain Jewish traditions when the non-Jewish world demanded their abandonment, threatening otherwise to label Jews as antisocial or unassimilable. As the century progressed these problems, first dealt with by the Reform leaders of Germany (most notably Abraham GEIGER), were met head-on in Eastern Europe, giving rise to the Haskalah movement whose members (e.g., Nachman KROCHMAL) sought to revitalize Jewish life by recreating it along the lines of the best in European culture. Finally, in reaction both to the needs of a persecuted people and to the nationalistic desires growing in the late 19th cent., ZIONISM promised a return to the Holy Land. This again created problems for the traditionalists whose religious ideas and religiously oriented life-style were rooted in the Diaspora. For many Jews still unanswered is the question of whether a full Jewish life is possible in Exile, or whether residing in Zion is essential. Theologically, Zionism posed the problem of whether man can work for the Messianic return or whether this would be counter to another traditional belief that saw man awaiting the divine intervention. Today, traditionalists of both camps can be found in residence in the state of Israel, due in part to the necessities of emigration occasioned by the Holocaust of the Nazi era. Ultimately, it was the halakah (the law) over which the religion of the Jews divided beginning in the 19th cent. and continuing to the present. The Orthodox hold both the written law (the Scriptures) and the Oral Laws (the commentaries on the legal portions of the Scriptures) as authoritative, derived from God, while the Reform see them as neither derived from God nor authoritative in any absolute sense, but binding only in their ethical content. While Orthodox Jews maintain the traditional rituals of Ashkenazic Jewry [German Jews and their descendants], the Reform Jews continue to perform only those rituals that they believe can promote and enhance a Jewish, God-oriented life. The "historical school," or Conservative movement, attempts to formulate a middle position, maintaining most of the traditional rituals, but recognizing the need to make changes in accordance with overriding contemporary considerations. Conservative Jews believe that the history of Judaism proves their basic assumptions: that tradition and change have always gone hand in hand and that what is central to Judaism and has remained constant throughout the centuries is the people of Israel (and their needs), not the rigidified fundamentalism of Orthodoxy nor the abandonment of the traditions and uniqueness of the Jewish people by Reform. All three positions have softened to an extent in recent years, the more moderate elements in each group having expressed more tolerance toward the others, but the lines between them remain distinct. Also part of contemporary Judaism are the several Sephardic traditions maintained in Israel, France, Canada, and the United States by immigrants from the Near East and North Africa and by European Sephardim in Europe and the Americas; the several Hasidic groups in Israel and the United States predominantly; the religious and secular Zionists in Israel and the Diaspora; the unorganized secular Jews who maintain an atheist's or agnostic's adherence to Jewish values and culture; and those unorganized Jews who seek a religious life outside the synagogue, where they can no longer find fulfillment. These many positions represent the most recent attempts at defining the "essence of Judaism," a process that has been continuous throughout the ages, variously emphasizing one of the three major components of Judaism (God, Torah, Israel) over the remaining two. Among the most important holy days in Judaism are the SABBATH, ROSH HA-SHANAH, Yom Kippur (see ATONEMENT, DAY OF), Sukkoth (see TABERNACLES, FEAST OF), PASSOVER, SHAVUOT, HANUKKAH, and

PURIM. See Kaufmann Kohler, *Jewish Theology Systematically and Historically Considered* (1918, repr. 1968); W. R. Smith, *Lectures on the Religion of the Semites* (1927, repr. 1956); G. F. Moore, *Judaism in the First Centuries of the Christian Era* (3 vol., 1927-30, repr. 1958); Hayyim Schauss, *Guide to Jewish Holy Days* (1938, repr. 1966); Leo Baeck, *The Essence of Judaism* (1948, repr. 1961); Louis Finkelstein, *The Beliefs and Practices of Judaism* (2d ed. 1952); S. W. Baron, *A Social and Religious History of the Jews* (15 vol., 1952-73); Gershom Scholem, *Major Trends in Jewish Mysticism* (3d ed. 1954, repr. 1961); M. M. Kaplan, *Judaism as a Civilization* (2d ed. 1957, repr. 1967); J. B. Agus, *The Evolution of Jewish Thought* (1959, repr. 1973); John Bright, *A History of Israel* (1959); Isidore Epstein, *Judaism, A Historical Presentation* (1959); Yehezkel Kaufmann, *The Religion of Israel* (tr. 1960); Jacob Katz, *Tradition and Crisis* (tr. 1961); J. L. Blau, *The Story of Jewish Philosophy* (1962), *Modern Varieties of Judaism* (1966), and, ed., *Reform Judaism: A Historical Perspective* (1973); Martin Buber, *On Judaism* (1967); M. A. Meyer, *The Origins of the Modern Jew* (1967); Jacob Neusner, *There We Sat Down* (1972); Nathan Glazer, *American Judaism* (2d ed. 1973).

Judas, in the Bible. **1** See JUDE, SAINT. **2** Judas Maccabeus: see MACCABEES. **3** See JUDAS ISCARIOT. **4** See JUDAH (of which Judas is the Greek form) **1.** **5** Owner of a house in Damascus where St. Paul went after his conversion. Acts 9.11. **6** See JUDAS BARSABAS. **7** "Brother" of Jesus. Matt. 13.55; Mark 6.3.

Judas Barsabas (bär'səbəs), missionary apostle. Acts 15.22-33.

Judas Iscariot (ĭskâr'ēət), Jesus' betrayer, one of the Twelve Disciples, said to have been their treasurer. Judas went to the chief priests and offered to betray Jesus, for which he was paid the sum of 30 pieces of silver. After the Last Supper he led an armed band to Gethsemane and there identified Jesus to the soldiers by kissing him. Later he repented and killed himself. The blood money went to buy a potter's field, ACELDAMA. Mat. 26.14-16, 20-25, 47-49; 27.3-10; Mark 14.10,11,43-45; Luke 22.3-6; John 6.71; 12.4-6; 13.26-30; 18.1-5; Acts 1.16-20. The name Iscariot may be a corruption of *sicarius* (Lat.,=murderer), indicating that Judas, or his father (who was also called Iscariot), belonged to a radical anti-Roman Jewish sect, the Sicarii. This possibility would support the theory that Judas betrayed Jesus out of disappointment and anger that Jesus was not the political Messiah he looked for.

Judas Maccabeus: see MACCABEES, Jewish family.

Judas of Galilee, fl. A.D. 6, a leader of the Zealots, a radical revolutionary Jewish sect. He raised an insurrection against the taxation census of Cyrenius (A.D. 6) on the grounds that no one but God was Israel's master, and he was killed. Acts 5.37.

Judas tree: see REDBUD.

Judd, Donald, 1928–, American artist, b. Excelsior Springs, Mo. Judd's sculpture, allied with the minimalist school of the late 1960s (see MODERN ART), has the appearance of industrial fabrication. He uses a variety of rectangular forms fashioned from painted wood, polychrome, or steel. Examples of his work are in the Whitney Museum, New York City.

Judd, Gerrit Parmele, 1803-73, missionary and statesman, b. Paris, N.Y. He arrived in Hawaii as a medical missionary. He ended his mission service in 1842 and became a Hawaiian government official under King Kamehameha III, playing a leading role in establishing the constitution of the Hawaiian monarchy and gaining recognition of Hawaii as a sovereign nation.

Judd, Orange, 1822-92, American agricultural editor and publisher, b. near Niagara Falls, N.Y., grad. Wesleyan Univ., 1847. At Wesleyan he built (1871) the Orange Judd Hall of Natural Science and secured through his gifts the establishment of the first agricultural experiment station in the country. He became in 1853 joint editor and owner of the *American Agriculturist,* which he made into one of the leading farm papers of the country.

Jude, Saint, or **Saint Judas** [Jude is an English form to distinguish him from Judas Iscariot], one of the Twelve Disciples, also called Lebbaeus and Thaddaeus. He is thought to have been the brother of St. James the Less. It does not seem likely that he was the Judas called the brother of Jesus (Mat. 13.55; Mark 6.3) or the author of the epistle of St. Jude. (Mat. 10.3; Mark 3.18; Luke 6.16; John 14.22; Acts 1.13.) According to Western tradition he suffered martyrdom in Persia with St. SIMON, with whom he shares a feast: Oct. 28.

Jude, epistle of the New Testament, the next to last book of the Bible. The Jude who wrote it has been identified since ancient times with St. Jude the apostle; but most modern scholars deny the identity and date the letter as late as A.D. 100. It is called a Catholic (or General) Epistle, but it is clearly intended for a particular audience (3), which it warns against some heresy that led to immorality (4,8,10). The dangers are shown from Old Testament examples (5-11). The book contains references to Jewish apocryphal books, Enoch (14-15) and the Assumption of Moses (9). It ends with a doxology (24-25). Jude has a close literary relationship with Second PETER.

Judea (jo͞odē'ə): see JUDAEA.

Judenburg (yo͞o'dənbo͝orkh), city (1971 pop. 11,300), Styria prov., S central Austria, on the Mur River. It is an industrial city and winter sports center. Originally a settlement along a Roman road, Judenburg was settled by Jewish merchants in the 11th cent. and became an important regional commercial center. It has a Romanesque church and a 15th-century bell tower.

Judge, William Quan, 1851-96, American theosophist, b. Ireland. He emigrated as a boy to the United States. Becoming interested in theosophy, he associated himself with Madame BLAVATSKY and others in 1875 in founding the Theosophical Society, and he edited and published (1886-96) its organ, the *Path.* After a schism in the society, he became president (1894) of the American section of the Theosophical Society. He wrote *The Ocean of Theosophy* (14th ed. 1937).

Judges, book of the Old Testament, seventh in the order of the Authorized Version. It is the sequel of Joshua in the biblical history, telling of the Hebrews in the Promised Land from Joshua's death until, but not including, the time of Samuel. The religious interpretation is stated in an introduction (2.6-3.4): the book is an account of Israel's successive apostasies from God and their consequences, first, punishment at the hands of a foreign nation, then, delivery from it by God, who raises up a leader. The leaders are called judges; they are primarily military leaders, the heads of tribes. The chronology of the book is impossible to untangle, partly because of occasional failure to give the length of time between the judges. The book consists mainly of lengthy accounts of a few judges: Deborah with Barak (4-5), Gideon (6-8), Gideon's usurping son Abimelech (9-10), Jephthah (11-12), and Samson (13-16). The other judges receive less attention, some a bare mention: Othniel, Ehud, and Shamgar (3) before Deborah; Tola and Jair (10) before Jephthah; and Ibzan, Elon and Abdon (12) before Samson. The opening chapter of the book is out of order, for it belongs to the period of Joshua; the closing chapters contain two appended stories of violence, one laid in Dan (17-18), the other in Benjamin (19-21). For critical views of the composition and for bibliography, see OLD TESTAMENT.

judgment, decision of a court of law respecting the issues before it. The term ordinarily is not applied to the DECREE (order) of courts of EQUITY. The outstanding characteristic of a legal judgment in contrast to an equitable decree is its finality and fixity; thus, except for error justifying an APPEAL, the judgment may not be reconsidered (see JEOPARDY). The judgment, which in most cases of consequence follows the VERDICT of a JURY, is the determination of the judge that the defendant is guilty or innocent of the alleged offense. If the judgment is one of criminal guilt, the court proceeds to impose SENTENCE. In civil cases, when judgment is for the plaintiff, the court usually awards a sum as DAMAGES. The damages thereupon constitute a debt that takes priority over all other obligations of the defendant except taxes and previous judgments. If the debtor fails to pay, the sheriff, to execute the judgment, will seize and sell first his personal property and then his realty. The sheriff may also garnish monies owed to the defendant, e.g., his wages (see GARNISHMENT). Certain property of the debtor is exempt from seizure, including clothing, equipment needed to carry on his trade or profession, and the family homestead. In some jurisdictions a defendant who willfully refuses to pay a judgment may be punished for a CONTEMPT of court. A judgment rendered by the courts of one state is entitled to recognition by the courts of all other states.

Judgment Day or **Doomsday,** central point of Christian eschatology. The origin of Christian belief in the Last Judgment lies in the New Testament, from which comes the doctrine that this world will come to an end, the dead will be raised up in the general RESURRECTION, and Christ will come in glory to judge the living and the dead; then the sinners shall be cast into HELL, and the righteous shall live in HEAVEN forever. (Mat. 24.3-25.46; Luke 21.5-36; 1 Cor. 15; 1 Thess. 4.13-5.3.) There is no generally accepted teaching among Christians as to when the Second Coming shall take place, but many individuals have ventured to prophesy its date. Those who lay stress on the end of the world are called chiliasts, millenarians, or, specifically, ADVENTISTS. According to many, the book of REVELATION (the Apocalypse) gives notions of the end of the world. See ANTICHRIST; ARMAGEDDON; MILLENNIUM; APOCALYPSE.

Judith [Heb.,=Jewess], biblical book included in the Old Testament of the Western canon and Septuagint, but not included in the Hebrew Bible and placed in the Apocrypha in the Authorized Version. It tells of an attack on the Jews by an army led by Nebuchadnezzar's general Holofernes. Bethulia, a besieged Jewish city, is about to surrender when Judith, a Jewish widow of great beauty and devotion, enters the enemy camp, gains the favor of Holofernes, and murders him. Judith returns to the city with his head, and the Jews rout the armies. The story is informed with a spirit of God's interest in His people, and Judith is pictured as a woman of great self-sacrifice and nobility. The texts of Judith are in great confusion. The book was written probably by a Palestinian before 100 B.C., but some scholars date it in a later period. By identifying Nebuchadnezzar as the king of Assyria (he was king of Babylon), the author appears to be giving notice that the book is not historical. However, there are historical parallels for the invasion. Another Judith, a wife of Esau, is named in Gen. 26.34. For bibliography, see OLD TESTAMENT.

judo, sport of Japanese origin that makes use of the principles of jujitsu, a weaponless system of self-defense. Jujitsu was developed over a period of 2,000 years by Buddhist monks in China, Japan, and Tibet as a system of defense that could be used against armed marauders and yet would not be in conflict with their religion. Judo was created (1882) by Jigoro Kano, a Japanese jujitsu expert, who modified or dropped many holds that were too dangerous to be used in sport. It depends for success upon the skill of using an opponent's weight and strength against him, thus enabling a weak or light individual to overcome a physically superior opponent. A method of applying pressure to sensitive parts of an opponent's body, usually by means of blows with the side of the hand, is also used. This art, known in judo as *atemi,* has been separately developed and is known as karate. A judo match begins with a ceremonial bow, after which each player grasps the other by the collar and sleeve of his jacket, or *gi.* A point is scored when a player forcefully throws the other onto his back, when one is held down for 30 seconds, when one is caught in a judo "choke," or when a player is forced to submit because of a twisted elbow joint. Proficiency in judo is indicated by the color of a player's belt; white indicates a beginner, black an expert. There is a wide range of color in between. Jujitsu, the unmodified form of judo, has been taught to military and police forces. In 1953 judo was recognized in the United States as a sport by the Amateur Athletic Union, and annual championships are now held. Numerous schools throughout the world now teach judo. See Eric Dominy, *Judo, Techniques and Tactics* (1969); G. R. Gleeson, *Better Judo* (1972).

Judson, Adoniram (ădənī'rəm), 1788-1850, American Baptist missionary, b. Malden, Mass. At Andover Theological Seminary, he became the leader of a missionary movement out of which grew the American Board of Commissioners for Foreign Missions. As a Congregational minister, Judson sailed (1812) for India. After conversion to the Baptist faith, he went (1813) to Burma, where he remained for 30 years. In 1845 he visited the United States, and on his return to Moulmein (1846) he completed and published (1849) his *Dictionary, English and Burmese.* He had also translated the Bible into Burmese. The Judson Memorial Church in New York City is named for him. See biographies by his son Edward Judson (1883), S. R. Warburton (1937), and Courtney Anderson (1956); V. E. Robinson, *The Judsons of Burma* (1966).

Judson, Edward Zane Carroll: see BUNTLINE, NED.

Jugendstil: see ART NOUVEAU.

Juggernaut, India: see PURI.

Jugoslavia: see YUGOSLAVIA.

Jugurtha (jo͞ogûr'thə), c.156-104 B.C., king of Numidia, a grandson of MASINISSA. On the death of Micipsa (118 B.C.), the royal power devolved upon his two sons and upon his adopted son Jugurtha. The latter ousted the other two heirs and united Numidia under his rule. In the process, however, some Italians were murdered, leading Rome to invade Numidia; peace was reestablished in 111 B.C. Jugurtha, on a visit to Rome to explain his acts, ordered a rival murdered. War was resumed, and the Romans under Quintus Caecilius Metellus Numidicus gained some notable successes. Under a new commander, Caius MARIUS, the Romans continued to apply pressure on Jugurtha, who was being supported by his father-in-law, Bocchus, king of Mauretania. Jugurtha was captured (106 B.C.) when Bocchus betrayed him, and he was put to death in prison in Rome.

Juilliard School, The (jo͞ol'yärd), in New York City; school of music, drama, and dance; coeducational; est. 1905 as the Institute of Musical Art, chartered 1926 as the Juilliard School of Music with two separate units—the Juilliard Graduate School (1924) and Institute of Musical Art. These were amalgamated into a single school in 1946. In 1968 the dance department became a separate division, and a division of drama was created. In 1969 the school moved to the Lincoln Center for the Performing Arts and adopted its present name.

Juiz de Fora (zhwēzh dĭ fô'rə), city (1970 pop. 238,052), Minas Gerais state, SE Brazil. It is an industrial and commercial city with more than half of the labor force engaged in textile production. Foodstuffs are also produced. The city, founded at the end of the 18th cent., grew rapidly because of its strategic location on the road to Rio de Janeiro. In the 19th cent., coffee cultivation was the main economic activity. The first railroad in Brazil was constructed (1861) between Juiz de Fora and Petrópolis.

jujitsu: see JUDO.

jujube (jo͞o'jo͞ob): see BUCKTHORN.

jujutsu: see JUDO.

Jujuy (ho͞ohwē'), city (1960 pop. 44,188), capital of Jujuy prov., NW Argentina, on the Bermejo River. In the scenic foothill region of the E Andes, it is the center of an agricultural, mining, and cattle-raising area. It was in Jujuy that Manuel Belgrano, the patriot general, created the first Argentine national flag. Juan Lavalle, after a futile attempt to depose the caudillo Juan Manuel de Rosas, was killed in Jujuy in 1841. There are interesting Indian ruins nearby. Jujuy is also known as San Salvador de Jujuy.

Jukes: see DUGDALE, RICHARD LOUIS.

julep (jo͞olĭp) or **mint julep,** alcoholic beverage of the S United States. Its basis is properly bourbon whiskey, which is combined with water, sugar, crushed ice, and mint leaves.

Julia, feminine name in the Julian gens. **1** Died 54 B.C., daughter of Julius CAESAR and wife of POMPEY. By her grace and tact she maintained the bond between her father and her husband. After her death the two statesmen became open enemies. **2** 39 B.C.–A.D. 14, daughter of Augustus and wife, in turn, of Marcus Claudius Marcellus (d. 23 B.C.), Marcus Vipsanius Agrippa, and Tiberius. Her infidelities caused her banishment by Augustus to Pandataria Island in the Tyrrhenian Sea. Soon after Tiberius became emperor, she died of starvation. **3** 18 B.C.–A.D. 28, daughter of Julia and Agrippa (see above); wife of Lucius Aemilius Paullus. Because of her licentious conduct, she was banished by Augustus to the island of Tremerus off the coast of Apulia, where she died.

Julia, Christian at Rome. Rom. 16.15.

Julian, George Washington, 1817–99, American abolitionist, U.S. Representative from Indiana (1849–51, 1861–71), b. Wayne co., Ind. Elected to the Indiana legislature as a Whig in 1845, he later became prominent in the Free-Soil party and in 1849 was sent to Congress by a coalition of Free-Soilers and Democrats. There he continued his radical antislavery activities. In 1852 the Free-Soil party nominated him for Vice President on the ticket with John P. Hale. He joined the Republican party at the time of its formation and in 1861 returned to Congress, where he became chairman of the committee on public lands and a member of the committees on the conduct of the war, on Reconstruction, and on the impeachment of President Andrew Johnson. In 1872 he joined the Liberal Republican party and after its demise was associated with the Democratic party. From 1885 to 1889 he was surveyor general of New Mexico by appointment of President Cleveland. Among his writings are *Speeches on Political Questions* (1872); *Political Recollections, 1840 to 1872* (1884); *Later Speeches on Political Questions, with Select Controversial Papers,* by his daughter, Grace J. Clarke (1889); and a biography of his father-in-law, Joshua R. Giddings (1892). See biography by P. W. Riddleberger (1966).

Juliana, 1909–, queen of the Netherlands (1948–). She succeeded on the abdication of her mother, Queen WILHELMINA. She was married (1937) to Prince Bernhard of Lippe-Biesterfeld, to whom she bore four daughters. The eldest, Princess Beatrix (b. 1938), is the heiress apparent.

Julian Alps, mountain range, NE Italy and NW Yugoslavia, between the Carnic Alps and the Dinaric Alps, rising to 9,396 ft (2,864 m) in Triglav, the highest peak in Yugoslavia. The forested, glacier-scoured region is a popular resort area.

Juliana of Norwich (nôr'ĭch), d. c.1443, English religious writer, an anchoress, or hermit, of Norwich called Mother (or Dame) Juliana or Julian. Her work, completed c.1393, *Revelations of Divine Love,* is an expression of mystical fervor in the form of 16 visions of Jesus. Dominant ideas are the great love of God for men and the detestable character of human sin. She is considered one of the greatest English mystics. See edition of her book by George Tyrell, S.J. (1920); study by P. F. Chambers (1955)

Julian Day calendar, system of astronomical dating that allows the difference between two dates to be calculated more easily than conventional civil calendars. The Julian Period begins on Jan 1, 4713 B.C., and dates have been numbered in consecutive order since then, regardless of the various changes made in civil calendars based on changing definitions of the year. The Julian Day number for Jan. 1, 1976, is 2,442,779, for Jan. 1, 1977, is 2,443,145, for Jan. 1, 1980, is 2,444,240, and so on. The Julian Day is from noon, Greenwich mean time, on the given date to noon of the following date.

Julianehåb (yo͞olyä'nəhôp''), town (1969 pop. 2,703), in Julianehåb dist. (1969 pop. 3,213), SW Greenland. It is a fishing port with canneries. Sheep are raised in the surrounding region.

Julian the Apostate (Flavius Claudius Julianus), 331?–363, Roman emperor (361–63), nephew of Constantine I; successor of Constantius II. He was given an education that combined Christian and Neoplatonic ideas. He and his half brother Gallus were sent (c.341) to Cappadocia. When Gallus was appointed Caesar (351), Julian was brought back to Constantinople. After Gallus had been put to death, Julian was called from the quiet of a scholar's life and made (355) Caesar. Sent to Gaul, he was unexpectedly successful in combating the Franks and the Alemanni and was popular with his soldiers. When Constantius, fearing Julian, ordered him (360) to send soldiers to assist in a campaign against the Persians, Julian obeyed, but his soldiers mutinied and proclaimed him augustus. He accepted the title, but Constantius refused to yield the western provinces to him. Before the two could meet in battle to decide the claim, Constantius died, naming Julian as his successor. Sometime in the course of his studies, Julian abandoned Christianity. Although as emperor he issued an edict of religious toleration, he did try unsuccessfully to restore paganism; the result was much confusion since Christianity was rent by the quarrel over Arianism. His short reign was just, and he was responsible for far-reaching legislation. During a campaign against the Persians, he was killed in a skirmish. He was succeeded by JOVIAN. Julian was a writer of some merit, and his works have been translated into English by W. C. Wright (3 vols., 1913–24). See study by Giuseppe Ricciotti (tr. 1960).

Jülich (yü'lĭkh), former duchy, West Germany, between Cologne and Aachen. The town of Jülich was the capital. At first a county, Jülich was raised to a duchy in 1356, and in 1423 it was united with the county of BERG. After the extinction of the Jülich line, both Jülich and Berg passed (1521) to Duke John III of Cleves (see CLEVES, DUCHY OF). The struggle that broke out in 1609 for the succession to the territories of the dukes of Cleves ended in 1666. Jülich and Berg passed to the Palatinate-Neuburg branch of the Bavarian house of Wittelsbach and the rest to the electors of Brandenburg. Occupied by the French from 1794 to 1814, the territory was assigned (1815) to Prussia at the Congress of Vienna.

Jülich, town (1970 pop. 19,439), North Rhine-Westphalia, W West Germany. It has some light industry and is the seat of a nuclear research center. Originally a Roman settlement known as Juliacum, Jülich was chartered in the mid-13th cent. and served as the capital of the former duchy of Jülich. The town was almost totally destroyed in World War II.

Julier (yo͞ol'yər), pass, 7,504 ft (2,287 m) high, Grisons canton, SE Switzerland, connecting the Upper Engadine Valley to the Oberhalbstein Valley. Used since ancient times, it is crossed by the Julier Road (built 1820–40).

Julius I, Saint, pope (337–52), a Roman; successor of St. Marcus. In the controversy over ARIANISM, when both sides appealed to him for support, he convened a synod at Rome (340), at which were present St. ATHANASIUS, Marcellus of Ancyra, and many other Catholic exiles from the East. The Arians of the East seem to have evaded his invitation. The principal result of the entire incident was a letter from the pope to the Arians, questioning their sincerity in the matter of the council, acquitting Athanasius of every charge, and chiding the Arians for not appealing to the pope at the beginning, since, he said, he had the principal see and the appellate jurisdiction over the whole church. As an early example of the papal claims the letter is remarkable. He was succeeded by Liberius. Feast: April 12.

Julius II, 1443–1513, pope (1503–13), an Italian named Giuliano della Rovere, b. Savona; successor of Pius III. His uncle Sixtus IV gave him many offices and created him cardinal. Innocent VIII, successor to Sixtus IV, was entirely under Cardinal della Rovere's influence, and it was in reaction to the cardinal's power that the rest of the cardinals elected (1492) his bitter enemy, Rodrigo Borgia, as Pope ALEXANDER VI. Giuliano went into voluntary exile and had little to do with ecclesiastical affairs until Alexander's death (1503). Pius III succeeded for less than a month, and Giuliano succeeded him. Pope Julius showed himself first of all a warrior, and he ably completed the work, begun by his enemy Cesare Borgia, of restoring the Papal States to the church. Having joined the League of Cambrai, he was at war with Venice until 1509 and won back Ravenna, Rimini, and Faenza. He then formed (1510) the anti-French HOLY LEAGUE. The resultant struggle was a draw (see ITALIAN WARS). In 1512 he assembled the Fifth LATERAN COUNCIL, which condemned the Gallicanism of the church in France and abolished simony in the college of cardinals. Julius was a great patron of art, and Raphael (who painted his portrait), Michelangelo, and Bramante enjoyed his favor. He laid the cornerstone of St. Peter's. Worldly as Julius was, he was one of the first to suppress nepotism and to try, albeit feebly, to break the hold of Renaissance corruption on Rome. He was succeeded by Leo X.

Julius, centurion in whose charge Paul was sent to Rome. Acts 27.1.

Julius Caesar: see CAESAR, JULIUS.

Jullian, Camille (kämē'yə zhülyäN'), 1859–1933, French historian. His monumental *Histoire de la Gaule* (8 vol., 1908–26) combines scholarly erudition with colorful style and remains the most authoritative work on Gaul from 600 B.C. to the end of Roman rule. A disciple of FUSTEL DE COULANGES, Jullian also prepared the revision of Fustel's study of medieval institutions.

Jullundur (jŭl'əndər), city (1971 pop. 296,103), Punjab state, NW India. It has flour and silk mills. Jullundur was the capital of Punjab from the time of India's independence (1947) until Chandigarh was built in 1953.

July: see MONTH.

July Revolution, revolt in France in July, 1830, against the government of King CHARLES X. The attempt of the ultraroyalists under Charles to return to the ancien régime provoked the opposition of the middle classes, who wanted more voice in the government. The banker, Jacques LAFFITTE, was typical of the bourgeois who supported liberal journalists, such as Adolphe THIERS, in opposing the government. Liberal opposition reached its peak when Charles called on the reactionary and unpopular Jules Armand de POLIGNAC to form a new ministry (Aug., 1829). When the chamber of deputies registered its disapproval, Charles dissolved the chamber. New elections (July, 1830) returned an even stronger opposition majority. Charles and Polignac responded with the July Ordinances, which established rigid press control, dissolved the new chamber, and reduced the electorate. Insurrection developed, and street barricades and fighting cleared Paris of royal troops. Charles X was forced to flee and abdicated in favor of his grandson, Henri, conte de CHAMBORD. Henri was set aside and, although there was a movement for a republic, the duc d'Orléans was proclaimed (July 31) king of the French as LOUIS PHILIPPE. His reign was known as the July Monarchy. See study by D. H. Pinkney (1972).

Jumel Mansion (jo͞omĕl', zho͞o-), historic house, New York City. The sturdy Georgian mansion was completed in 1766 by Roger Morris, one of the city's wealthy merchants. In the American Revolution it served as headquarters of George Washington and Sir Henry Clinton, American and British commanders in chief. After the war it was used as a tavern. It was purchased (1810) by a rich wine merchant, Stephen Jumel (d. 1832), for his wife, Eliza Brown Jumel (1775–1865). After Jumel's death she married (1833) Aaron Burr, wrangled with him over family finances, and procured (1834) a divorce. When she died, the mansion passed to members of her family. In 1903 it was purchased by the city. By 1945 it was completely restored and opened to the public under the auspices of the Daughters of the American Revolution. See W. H. Shelton, *The Jumel Mansion* (1916).

Jumet (zhümā'), city (1970 pop. 28,029), Hainaut prov., S Belgium. Manufactures include metal products, glass, and beer.

Jumna (jŭm'nə) or **Yamuna** (yä'mənə), river, c.850 mi (1,370 km) long, rising in the Himalayas, N India, and flowing generally SE, through the Siwalik Range, past Delhi, to the Ganges River at Allahabad, Uttar Pradesh state; the Chambal and Betwa rivers are its main tributaries. The Jumna's confluence with the Ganges is sacred to Hindus; Allahabad is a major pilgrimage center. Along the Jumna's banks are many historic monuments including the TAJ MAHAL at Agra. Formerly an important trade artery, the Jumna is now the source of irrigation for Uttar Pradesh and Punjab states. The East Jumna, West Jumna, and Agra are the major canals on the river.

jumping bean: see SPURGE.

jumping mouse, RODENT slightly larger than the common mouse, found in North America and N Asia, also called the kangaroo mouse. Its long hind legs and tail enable it to leap distances up to 12 ft (3.7 m). Jumping mice have gray to brown fur and are white underneath. They can scurry as well as leap and are good swimmers. Solitary, nocturnal animals, they are found in marshes and on stream banks in coniferous and deciduous forests of both coasts of North America, and also in fields and pastures. Two genera, *Zapus* and *Napaeozapus,* are North American, ranging from the Arctic Circle S to New Mexico and Tennessee; a related genus, with one species, *Eozapus setchuanus,* the Szechuan jumping mouse, is native to China. Jumping mice feed on a diet of grass seeds, fruit, and insect larvae. They gain weight in autumn and hibernate in fur-lined burrows during winter. Litters, containing from three to six young, are born in late spring. Jumping mice are classified in the phylum CHORDATA, subphylum Vertebrata, class Mammalia, order Rodentia, family Zapodidae.

Junagadh (jo͞o'nəgäd") or **Junagarh** (-gär"), former principality, Kathiawar peninsula, W India, on the Arabian Sea. The region of Junagadh became a district of Gujarat state in 1960. Grains, cotton, and tobacco are grown there, and the fishing industry is important. Junagadh was wrested from the MOGUL empire in the mid-18th cent. by Sher Kahn Babi, a Muslim freebooter who established a dynasty that was later supported by the British. In 1947 the Muslim ruler ceded his state to Pakistan, although the population was overwhelmingly Hindu. He was forced to flee when Indian forces invaded the state. The town of **Junagadh** (1971 pop. 95,945) was formerly the state capital and is now a district administrative center. It is also a market for gold and silver embroidery, perfume, and copper and brass vessels. The town has ancient Buddhist caves and RAJPUT forts, as well as a modern college. Nearby is the Girnar forest, the only place in Asia where lions are found.

junco or **snowbird,** common name for a bird of the family Fringillidae (FINCH family). Juncos are small seed-eaters with white underparts and gray (sometimes also brown) backs. They travel in flocks, seeking weed seeds in fields. The slate-colored junco is common in the East; there are a number of Western juncos. Juncos belong to the genus *Junco* and are classified in the phylum CHORDATA, subphylum Vertebrata, class Aves, order Passeriformes, family Fringillidae.

Junction City, city (1970 pop. 19,018), seat of Geary co., NE Kansas, at the confluence of the Republican and Smoky Hill rivers; inc. 1859. The rail and trade center of an agricultural and dairy area, it grew as the supply point for nearby FORT RILEY. Limestone quarries are near the city.

Jundiaí (zho͞ondyī'), city (1970 pop. 169,096), São Paulo state, S Brazil, on the Jundiaí River. It is an agricultural and industrial center. Among its products are textiles, ceramics, furniture, soap, wines, foodstuffs, brushes, shoes, paper, matches, chemicals, and agricultural tools. The city was established in the 17th cent.

June, Jennie: see CROLY, JANE CUNNINGHAM.

June: see MONTH.

Juneau, Solomon Laurent (jo͞onō', jo͞o'nō), 1793–1856, French Canadian fur trader and founder of Milwaukee, Wis., b. near Montreal. In 1818, as an agent of the American Fur Company, he moved to their new post at Milwaukee. He amassed a fortune in independent trade, acquired large tracts of land there, and was revered by the Indians. He became an American citizen in 1831. He surveyed the town site, built the first store and first tavern, became Milwaukee's first postmaster (1835) and first president of the village (1837). His fortune was reduced by the Panic of 1837, but he remained a leading citizen of Milwaukee, becoming its first mayor in 1846.

Juneau (jo͞o'nō), city (1970 pop. 13,556), state capital, SE Alaska, in the Alaska Panhandle; settled by gold miners 1880, inc. 1900. A port on Gastineau Channel, Juneau is a trade center for the Panhandle area, with an ice-free harbor, a seaplane base, and an airport. The state and Federal government is the major employer. Salmon and halibut fishing, lumbering, and tourism are also important economic activities. Joseph Juneau and a partner discovered gold nearby in 1880, and the city developed as a gold rush town. It was officially designated as capital of the Territory of Alaska in 1900 but did not function as such until the government offices were moved from Sitka in 1906. In 1959 it became state capital with the admission of Alaska to the Union. Juneau lies at the foot of two spectacular peaks, Mt. Juneau and Mt. Roberts. Douglas Island lies across the channel. The huge boxlike Federal Building dominates the skyline. The Alaska Historical Library and Museum are in the city. A junior college (a unit of the Univ. of Alaska) serves the area. In 1970 the municipal boundaries were extended, making Juneau the largest city in area in the United States, at 3,108 sq mi (8,050 sq km). Glacier Bay National Monument is to the northwest. In 1974, Alaskans voted to move the state capital away from Juneau.

June beetle or **May beetle,** a blackish or mahogany-colored beetle of the SCARAB BEETLE family, widely distributed in North America and especially abundant in the NE United States and the adjacent parts of Canada. It is also known as June bug, although true bugs belong to a different insect order. The adults, which may swarm in great numbers in early summer and are attracted to lights, feed by night on the foliage of deciduous trees and hide during the day. The eggs are laid in the soil, where the larvae, called white grubs, remain for two or three years, eating the roots and other underground parts of grasses, grains, and trees. The grubs cause great destruction to lawns and fir trees. Many birds and small mammals, such as skunks and pigs, root out the grubs and eat them. The insects pupate underground in the fall and emerge as adults the following spring. June beetles are sometimes called cockchafers, a name used primarily for some of their close relatives in the Old World. They are closely allied to the leaf chafers, including the rose chafer. June beetles are classified in the phylum ARTHROPODA, class Insecta, order Coleoptera, family Scarabaeidae.

Juneberry: see SHADBUSH.

June bug, name for JUNE BEETLE and MAYFLY.

June Days, in French history, name usually given to the insurrection of workingmen in June, 1848. The working classes had played an important role in the FEBRUARY REVOLUTION of 1848, but with the triumph of the bourgeois, their hopes for economic and social reform were ignored. Their increasing unrest was due to continued economic crisis and rising unemployment and to the inadequacy of the national workshops, which, although proposed by Louis BLANC, were never organized as he planned them. Instead of providing work, the workshops became a system of registering the unemployed for a meager dole. When a decree of June 21 abolished the workshops, dispersing the workers to the army and to the provinces, the workingmen rose in revolt. There were four days (June 23–26) of violent fighting in the barricaded streets of Paris. General CAVAIGNAC was given dictatorial powers and used harsh measures to suppress the insurrection. The June Days further alienated the lower classes from the revolution.

Jung, Carl Gustav (kärl go͝os'täf yo͝ong), 1875–1961, Swiss psychiatrist, the founder of analytical psychology, studied at Basel (1895–1900) and Zürich (M.D., 1902). After work at the University Psychiatric Clinic in Zürich, he studied (1902) under Eugen Bleuler at the Burghölzli Clinic. He wrote valuable papers, but more important was a book on the psychology of dementia praecox (1906). In 1907 he met Sigmund Freud, whose work had impressed him. Jung edited the *Jahrbuch für psychologische und psychopathologische Forschungen* and was made (1911) president of the international psychoanalytic society. However, a formal break with Freud came when Jung's revolutionary work appeared as *Wandlungen und Symbole der Libido* (1912; tr. *Psychology of the Unconscious,* 1916; rev. ed. 1952; tr. *Symbols of Transformation,* 1956). Jungian psychology is based on psychic totality and psychic energism; he postulated two dimensions in the unconscious—the personal (repressed events of a person's life) and the archetypes of a collective unconscious. His *Psychologische Typen* (1921, tr. 1923) elucidated EXTROVERSION AND INTROVERSION. Other major concepts are those of anima/animus and of synchronicity, the coincidence of causally unrelated events having identical or similar meaning. To Jung, the most important and lifelong task imposed upon any person is fulfillment through the process of individuation, achievement of harmony of conscious and unconscious, which makes a person one and whole. Among Jung's many works are *Two Essays on Analytical Psychology* (tr. 1953); *Psychology and Alchemy* (tr. 1953); *Modern Man in Search of a Soul* (1933); *The Structure and Dynamics of the Psyche* (tr. 1960); *Psychology and Religion: West and East* (tr. 1958). Publication of the definitive edition of Jung's works in English translation was begun in 1953. See the autobiographical *Memories, Dreams, Reflections* (recorded and ed. by Aniela Jaffe, 1963); his letters, ed. by Gerhard Adler (Vol. I, 1973); his correspondence with Sigmund Freud, ed. by William McGuire (1974); studies by Jolande Jacobi (6th rev. ed. 1961), A. M. Dry (1962), Antonio Moreno (1970), and E. A. Bennet (1966, repr. 1972); C. S. Hall and V. J. Nordby, *A Primer of Jungian Psychology* (1973).

Jungaria: see DZUNGARIA, China.

Jungbunzlau: see MLADÁ BOLESLAV, Czechoslovakia.

Jünger, Ernst (ĕrnst yüng'ər), 1895–, German writer. Jünger's early war novels were based on arduous army experience. They glorified war and its sacrifice as the greatest physical and mental stimulants. Among these works are *Storm of Steel* (1920, tr. 1929), *Feuer und Blut* (1924), and *Copse 125* (1925, tr. 1930). Later he opposed Hitler and rejected his own militarism in a mystical plea for peace, expressed in his diaries of the war years, *On the Marble Cliffs* (1939, tr. 1947), *Gärten und Strassen* (1942), and *Heliopolis* (1949). Jünger's later works include *The Glass Bees* (1957, tr. 1961). See study by J. P. Stern (1953).

Jungfrau (yo͝ong'frou), peak, 13,642 ft (4,158 m) high, S central Switzerland, in the Bernese Alps. It was first ascended in 1811. Aletsch Glacier is on the south side. The **Jungfraujoch** (-yôkh") is a mountain saddle 11,333 ft (3,454 m) high, the highest point in Europe reached by rail. It has a scientific institute and is popular with tourists. A meteorological station is on the nearby Sphinx summit, 11,723 ft (3,573 m) high. The region is noted for its scenery and winter sports.

Jungius, Joachim (yō'äkhĭm yo͝ong'ēo͞os), 1587–1657, German mathematician, logician, and systematizer of natural history. In 1608 he made his inaugural dissertation at the University of Giessen, proclaiming in it the doctrine, endorsed by progressive 17th-century scientists, that science must be based on mathematics. A practicing physician as well as a professor of mathematics, he subsequently elaborated an empirical philosophy of science, a morphological system of botany, and a corpuscular chemistry that assumed the conservation of mass. Difficulties with religious authorities forced Jungius to refrain from publishing many of his later works.

jungle [Hindustani *jangal*=desert, forest; from Skt. *jangala*=wasteland, uncultivated land], densest form of tropical FOREST (usually second growth or later) found throughout tropical lowland regions. Jungle is characterized by high humidity and resultant abundance (both in numbers and variety) of flora and concomitantly of fauna. *Jungle* is not a strict ecological term and is often applied to any impenetrable thicket or tangled mass of vegetation.

jungle cat: see LYNX.

jungle fowl, common name for small, terrestrial wild fowl comprising four species in the genus *Gallus.* Most important of these is the red jungle fowl, which Charles Darwin determined to be the ancestor of all domesticated fowl. It is the only wild fowl that can crossbreed fertilely with domesticated species. It is yellow-headed with a red comb and wattles, and its multicolored plumage resembles a jester's costume. The female is slightly smaller and less brightly colored than its mate. Jungle fowl are found in large numbers from India through S China and the Malayan archipelago, where they inhabit thickly wooded areas. They feed on a diet of seeds, buds, fruit, and insects. The polygamous males are highly aggressive (the modern game cock is thought to be the domestic form closest to the ancestral species) and they take no part in nest building, incubation, or the care of the young. From archaeological evidence, it would seem that the jungle fowl was first domesticated in India as much as 5,200 years ago, and that by the 6th cent. B.C. it had entered Europe. The jungle fowl is classified in the phylum CHORDATA, subphylum Vertebrata, class Aves, order Galliformes, family Phasianidae.

Junia (jo͞o'nēə), man or woman early converted to Christianity. Rom. 16.7.

Junín (ho͞onēn'), city (1970 pop. 69,731), Buenos Aires prov., E Argentina, on the Salado River. It is a busy commercial center for an agricultural and livestock area. There are important railroad repair shops. Junín began as a frontier fort (est. 1827) during the struggle against the Indians of Pampa.

Junín, village (1961 est. pop. 5,000), W central Peru, in the Andes. In the vicinity on Aug. 6, 1824, Simón BOLÍVAR, aided by Antonio José de SUCRE, defeated the Spanish general, José Canterac, in the first important battle leading to Peruvian independence.

junior college: see COMMUNITY COLLEGE.

junior high school: see SCHOOL.

juniper, any tree or shrub of the genus *Juniperus,* aromatic evergreens of the family Cupressaceae (CYPRESS family), widely distributed over the north temperate zone. Many are valuable as a source of lumber and oil. The small fleshy cones are berrylike in appearance. The so-called common juniper (*J. communis*) is found throughout the genus range and is also much cultivated in different varieties, e.g., dwarf and pyramidal. Its fruits are the juniper berries used for flavoring gin and other beverages and sometimes in cooking. The juniper most common in North America is usually called red cedar (*J. virginiana*) and is found over most of the E United States. Its fragrant, insect-repellent wood, closegrained but brittle, is much used for chests, closets, posts, woodenware, and pencils, for which uses the large forests of these trees have been depleted. Oil of red cedar is used in medicine, perfumery, and microscopy. Other trees are sometimes called red cedar. Western juniper, *J. occidentalis,* of the W United States (not to be confused with the western ARBORVITAE, although both are also called western red cedar) has edible fruits. Indians also used the fruits of other Western species as food and the bark for fiber. Junipers have been used for incense in the Orient and by the Plains Indians in religious ceremonies. Juniper is classified in the division Pinophyta, class Pinopsida, order Coniferales, family Cupressaceae.

Junius, English political author, known only by the signature Junius, which he signed to various letters written to the London *Public Advertiser* from Jan., 1769, to Jan., 1772, attacking George III and his ministers. The letters, centering on John WILKES and the controversy over the Middlesex election, were written by a passionate opponent of the government familiar with secret government matters. Junius used scandal and invective rather than argument as his major tools of attack. The letters were reprinted by the publisher of the *Advertiser* in 1772, and a new edition, with additional letters, appeared in 1812. Although the identity of Junius has never been definitely established, the political beliefs, handwriting, and life of Sir Philip FRANCIS have led many to ascribe the authorship to him. Arguments have also been offered in favor of the authorship of Lord SHELBURNE and of Laughlin Macleane, British army surgeon and secretary to Shelburne.

Junius, Franciscus, 1589–1677, French philologist; son of Franciscus Junius (1545–1602), French Huguenot theologian. The younger Franciscus Junius was born in Heidelberg and lived chiefly in Holland and England. He was a pioneer in the study of Gothic and Anglo-Saxon. A unique manuscript of Anglo-Saxon poems formerly attributed to CÆDMON was owned and edited by him and is known as the Junius Manuscript (Bodleian Lib., Oxford). For a modern edition, see G. P. Krapp, *The Junius Manuscript* (1931).

Junkceylon: see PHUKET, Thailand.

Juno (jo͞o'nō), in astronomy, 3d ASTEROID to be discovered. It was found in 1804 by C. Harding. It has a diameter of c.120 mi (190 km). Its average distance from the sun is 2.67 ASTRONOMICAL UNITS, and its orbital period is 1,594 days.

Juno, in Roman religion, wife and sister of Jupiter. In early Roman times she, like the Greek Hera (with whom she was later identified), was goddess and protector of women, concerned especially with their sexual life. In later religion she became, however, the great goddess of the state and was worshiped, in conjunction with Jupiter and Minerva, at the temple on the Capitol.

Junot, Andoche (äNdôsh' zhünō'), 1771–1813, French general. Having served under Napoleon Bonaparte in Italy and Egypt, he became ambassador to Portugal (1804–5) and commanded the French invasion of that country in 1807, thus opening the PENINSULAR WAR. Appointed governor general of Portugal, he was forced to evacuate after his defeat by Arthur Wellesley (later the duke of Wellington) in 1808. He also served in Spain, Germany, and Russia. Napoleon created him duke of Abrantès, under which name his wife, Laure Junot, duchesse d'Abrantès, is generally known. Near the end of his life he became insane, and he may have committed suicide.

Jupiter, in astronomy, 5th planet from the sun and largest planet of the solar system. Jupiter's orbit lies beyond the ASTEROID belt at a mean distance of c.483 million mi (773 million km) from the sun; its period of revolution is c.11.9 years. In order from the sun it is the first of the Jovian planets (Jupiter, Saturn, Uranus, and Neptune), very large, massive planets of relatively low density, having rapid rotation and a thick, opaque atmosphere. Jupiter has a diameter of c.88,700 mi (142,000 km), nearly 11 times that of the earth, and its volume is more than 1,300 times greater than the earth's. Its mass is 318 times that of the earth and about 2½ times the mass of all other planets combined. The heavy atmosphere of Jupiter, which blocks any possible observation of its surface, is composed mainly of hydrogen, helium, methane, and ammonia. It appears to be divided into a number of light and dark bands parallel to its equator and shows a range of complex features, most notably the Great Red Spot, located in its southern hemisphere and measuring c.30,000 mi long by 10,000 mi wide (48,000 by 16,000 km). The Spot is taken by some as evidence of solid surface features beneath the atmosphere. Others think that because of its low density a definite surface might not exist. One theory pictures a gradual transition from the outer ammonia clouds to a thick layer of frozen gases and finally to a liquid or solid hydrogen mantle. The Spot and other markings of the atmosphere also provide evidence for Jupiter's rapid rotation, which has a period of about 9 hr 55 min. This rotation causes a polar flattening of over 6%. The temperature of the visible surface of its atmosphere is about −190°F (−124°C), yet Jupiter radiates about four times as much heat energy as it receives from the sun, suggesting higher temperatures deeper within the atmosphere. This energy is thought to be due in part to a slow contraction of the planet. Jupiter is also characterized by intense nonthermal radio emissions; in the 15-m range it is the strongest radio source in the sky. Twelve natural satellites are known to orbit Jupiter. The four largest—Io, Europa, Ganymede, and Callisto (also designated I, II, III, and IV)—were discovered by Galileo in 1610, shortly after he invented the telescope, and are known as the Galilean satellites. Ganymede is the largest satellite in the solar system; with a diameter exceeding 3,000 mi (4,800 km), it is larger than the planet Mercury. Satellite V, discovered by E. E. Barnard in 1892, is closest to Jupiter and has a diameter of c.100 mi (160 km). The seven remaining satellites orbit at greater distances from the planet, and none is larger than c.50 mi (80 km) in diameter. The outer four satellites—VIII, IX, XI, and XII—located from 14 million to 16 million mi from Jupiter (22 million–26 million km), have RETROGRADE MOTION, i.e., motion opposite to that of the planet's rotation, and may be captured asteroids.

Jupiter, in Roman religion, the supreme god, also called Jove. Originally a sky deity associated with rain and agriculture, he developed into the great father god, prime protector of the state, concerned, like the Greek Zeus (with whom he is identified), with all aspects of life. At his temple on the Capitol, triumphant generals honored him with their spoils and magistrates paid homage to him with sacrifices. Jupiter was the son of Saturn and Ops and the brother and husband of Juno.

Jura (zhürä'), department (1968 pop. 233,547), E France, in FRANCHE-COMTÉ. It borders on Switzerland. LONS-LE-SAUNIER is the capital.

Jura (jo͝or'ə, Fr. zhürä', Ger. yo͞o'rä), mountain range, part of the Alpine system, E France and NW Switzerland, occupying parts of the French region of Franche-Comté and the Swiss cantons of Vaud, Neuchâtel, Bern, Solothurn, and Basel. It extends in narrow, parallel ridges c 160 mi (260 km) from the Rhine River at Basel to the Rhône River SW of Geneva; Crêt de la Neige (5,652 ft/1,723 m), in France, is the highest peak. The Jura's rounded crests and summits are covered with dense pine forests and good pasture lands. The region is drained by the Doubs, the Ain, the Loué, and smaller streams. Major cities include La Chaux-de-Fonds, Neuchâtel, and Biel, Switzerland, and Besançon, France. Hydroelectric plants in the Jura supply power to pulp and paper, textile, and woodworking industries. Important watch industries, particularly in the Swiss towns of Le Locle, La Chaux-de-Fonds, and Grenchen, are also there. Export products from the French Jura include brierwood (for pipes), plastics, and cheese. The Jura mts. are a popular year-round resort region. Composed of sandstone and limestone and rich in fossils, the Jura gives its name to the JURASSIC PERIOD. The mountains N of the Lake of Constance in SW West Germany are called the Swabian Jura.

Jura, island, Great Britain: see HEBRIDES, THE.

Jurassic period (jərăs'ĭk) [from the Jura mts.], second period of the MESOZOIC ERA of geologic time. In the Jurassic period, E North America was mostly elevated and subject to erosion, which reduced the Appalachian region to a peneplain. Before the end of the period, the Appalachian borderland began to founder as the Atlantic Ocean continued to widen. The Pacific border of North America, from California to Alaska, was submerged for most of the period. In the Early Jurassic, large areas of Arizona, Colorado, and Utah were apparently desert, and the sand was later consolidated into the white and pinkish Glen Canyon and Navaho sandstones, which now enhance the scenic beauty of the district. During the Upper Jurassic the Logan Sea entered this area from the north. In its various advances and retreats, this body of water covered large areas of Montana, Idaho, Wyoming, Colorado, and Utah, depositing sandstone, shale, limestone, and some gypsum. The retreat of the Logan Sea toward the end of the period was followed, probably in the Upper Jurassic but possibly in the Lower Cretaceous Period, by the deposition of the Morrison continental series of clays and sandstones, noted for its richness in fossil dinosaurs. The close of the Jurassic in North America was marked by widespread folding along the western border of the continent, accompanied by the intrusion of lava as the eastern edge of the plate that carries the Pacific Ocean was thrust beneath the westward drifting plate that carries the North American continent. In this disturbance the Sierra Nevada, Klamaths, Cascades, Coast Ranges, and coastal mountains of Canada and Alaska were formed. The history of the European Jurassic is very well known, the system being one of the most complete on the Continent. Studies of oxygen isotopes, the extent of land flora, and marine fossils indicate that climates during Jurassic times were mild—perhaps 15°F (8°C) warmer than those of today. No glaciers existed during this period. The plant life of the Jurassic was dominated by the cycads, but conifers, ginkgoes, horsetails, and ferns were also abundant. Of the marine invertebrates, the most important were the ammonites. The dominant animals on land, in the sea, and in the air were the reptiles. Dinosaurs, more numerous and more extraordinary than those of the Triassic period, were the chief land animals; crocodiles, ichthyosaurs, and plesiosaurs ruled the sea; while the air was inhabited by the pterodactyls and relatives. Mammals, making their first appearance, were few and small but undoubtedly became well established during the Jurassic period. The Jurassic saw the appearance of the first bird, Archaeopteryx. See GEOLOGIC ERAS (table).

Jurieu, Pierre (pyĕr zhüryö'), 1637–1713, French Calvinist theologian. He was (1674–81) professor at Sedan. In 1681 in an attempt to preserve Huguenot liberties he published anonymously *La Politique du clergé de France;* his authorship soon became known, and he left France. From 1681 he was pastor of the Walloon Church in Rotterdam, writing in behalf of the French Reformed Church and giving aid to exiles from France after the revocation of the Edict of Nantes. His controversial works, often bitter and aggressive, were directed against such contemporaries as Antoine Arnauld, Bishop Bossuet, Archbishop Fénelon, and Pierre Bayle. Important writings are the *Pastoral Letters Addressed to the Faithful in France* (1686, tr. 1689) and *Critical History of Dogmas and Cults* (1704, tr. 1705). See G. H. Dodge, *The Political Theory of the Huguenots of the Dispersion* (1947).

jurisprudence (jŏŏr″ĭsprōōd′əns), study of the nature and the origin and development of LAW. It is variously regarded as a branch of ethics or of sociology. Many of the major systematic philosophers (e.g., Aristotle, St. Thomas Aquinas, and Kant) have expounded jurisprudential theories. Before the 19th cent. most jurisprudents adhered to NATURAL LAW, which maintained that sound legal doctrine was derivable only from a supposed law of nature established by divine ordinance. The natural-law school did not deny that the details of legal regulation depended upon the will of the sovereign. However, the positivist, or analytical, school, which first became important in the late 18th cent., insisted that law was entirely a matter of sovereign decree, distinct from morality and theology. Among important 19th-century trends was the view, represented by SAVIGNY, that a people's legal system expressed the national spirit. In the mid-19th cent. many jurisprudents attempted to avoid what they felt were theoretical preconceptions and to demonstrate a uniform evolution from primitive times to modern industrialized society. Other thinkers were skeptical of evolutionary explanations and sought the basic principles underlying all systems of law in various fields, including economics and psychology. Among the more important legal thinkers in the United States have been Learned HAND, Oliver Wendell HOLMES, and Roscoe POUND. See Jerome Hall, ed., *Readings in Jurisprudence* (1938); W. S. Carpenter, *Foundations of Modern Jurisprudence* (1958); Denis Lloyd, *Introduction to Jurisprudence* (3d ed. 1972).

Jurjan: see GORGAN, town, Iran.

Jurong Industrial Estate: see SINGAPORE.

Juruá (zhōōrwä′), river, c.1,500 mi (2,410 km) long, rising in the Cerros de Canchyuaya, E Peru. It flows in a winding course generally NE through Acre and Amazonas states, W Brazil, to the Amazon River E of Fonte Boa. One of the Amazon's longer tributaries, it is navigable along one third of its course and was important for transport during the wild-rubber boom.

jury, body convened to make decisions of fact in legal proceedings. Historians do not agree on the origin of the English jury. Although some authorities trace it to Anglo-Saxon or even more remote Germanic times, most believe that it was brought to England by the Normans. The first jurors were not triers of fact in legal disputes but were persons acquainted with the situation in question who spoke out of personal knowledge. Thus, in compiling the DOMESDAY BOOK inquests of neighbors were convened to furnish information on property holdings. In the enforcement of criminal justice the earliest function of the jury (mid-12th cent.) appears to have been the presentation of accusations, and it was only later that jurors were convened to answer on oath the question of guilt. These early jury trials, while supplanting the ORDEAL and other irrational procedures, were not themselves satisfactory, because they depended entirely on the unsupported oath of the jurors. A verdict could not be overturned except by attaint, that is, by summoning a second jury to give its sworn verdict on the question as to whether the first jury had committed perjury. By the 16th cent. the jury was used in civil as well as criminal cases, and the practice of calling witnesses was well developed. However, not until the mid-18th cent. were methods other than the attaint available to set aside an improper verdict. To Englishmen and other peoples who have adopted the English common-law system trial by jury became a cherished protection against the possibility of judicial and administrative tyranny. Among the abuses recited in the American Declaration of Independence is "depriving us in many cases, of the benefits of Trial by Jury." The Sixth and Seventh Amendments to the U.S. Constitution, reflecting this concern, require a jury in Federal trials in criminal prosecutions and in civil suits at common law where the damages sought exceed $20; the traditional exemption of cases in EQUITY was left unchanged. The merger of law and equity has led to the development of various tests to determine if a case can be tried before a jury. In 1967 the U.S. Supreme Court held that the Fourteenth Amendment guaranteed the right to a jury in state criminal trials. Most U.S. states preserve jury trials for a variety of civil cases. Great Britain has limited the use of civil juries to cases in which community attitudes are especially important (e.g., defamation and fraud). In most criminal cases the charge is first considered by a GRAND JURY with 12 to 23 members. It hears witnesses against the accused, and if 12 jurors believe that there is sufficient evidence to prosecute, an INDICTMENT or the like is presented. The jury sitting at the trial proper is called a petit (or petty) jury from its smaller size (usually 12 members). The selection of a jury is essentially alike in civil and in criminal cases. The venire, a panel of prospective jurors living in the district where the trial is to be held, is summoned for examination. Counsel for the parties may first challenge the array, that is, object that the venire as a whole was improperly chosen or is for some reason unfit. The challenges to the poll (the veniremen taken individually) that follow are designed to secure as jurors unbiased persons without special knowledge of the matters in issue. Included are challenges for principal cause, i.e., some grounds such as relationship to a party that requires dismissal of the venireman; challenges to the favor, i.e., suspicion of unfitness on which the judge rules; and a limited number of peremptory challenges. Once selected, the jury (usually with several alternates) takes an oath to act fairly and without preconceptions. At the close of the evidence and after the summations of counsel the judge instructs the jury concerning the VERDICT. The value of juries in civil trials is disputed. Opponents of juries argue that they are ineffective, irrational, and cause delay; proponents argue that juries bring community standards to bear, can modify the effects of harsh laws, and are a protection against incompetent judges. Outside of the English-speaking countries there is generally less recourse to the jury and less care in the selection of jurors. See A. T. Vanderbilt, *Judges and Jurors: Their Functions, Qualifications, and Selection* (1956); P. A. Devlin, *Trial by Jury* (1956).

Jushab-hesed (jōōshăb′-hēsĕd″), son of Zerubbabel. 1 Chron. 3.20.

Jusserand, Jean Jules (zhäN zhül zhüsəräN′), 1855–1932, French diplomat and author, b. Lyon. After service in London, Constantinople, and Copenhagen, he was ambassador to the United States (1902–25). A close friend of every U.S. President during the period, he did much to promote friendly Franco-American relations and to win the United States to the Allied side in World War I. Jusserand was also a noted scholar; his works include *English Wayfaring Life in the Middle Ages* (tr. 1889), *Shakespeare in France* (1898), a life of Ronsard (1913), and *With Americans of Past and Present Days* (1916), the first work on U.S. history to be awarded a Pulitzer Prize. See his reminiscences, *What Me Befell* (1933).

Jussieu (zhüsyö′), name of a French family of distinguished botanists. **Antoine de Jussieu,** 1686–1758, was director of the Jardin des Plantes, Paris. He edited Jacques Barrelier's posthumously published *Plantae per Galliam, Hispaniam et Italiam observatae* (1714) and the third edition (1719) of J. P. de Tournefort's *Institutiones rei herbariae.* **Bernard de Jussieu,** 1699–1777?, brother of Antoine, was director of the gardens at the Trianon, Versailles; there he arranged the plants according to his new system of classification, which he never published. He revised (1725) Tournefort's *Histoire des plantes qui naissent aux environs de Paris.* Another brother, **Joseph de Jussieu,** 1704–79, accompanied La Condamine to South America, where he remained until c.1771. He introduced into Europe many plants, including the heliotrope. A nephew, **Antoine Laurent de Jussieu,** 1748–1836, assisted Bernard de Jussieu, whose system of classification by natural affinities he elaborated in *Genera plantarum* (1789), which influenced later systems of classification. He was professor at the Museum of Natural History, Paris, and organized its botanical collection. His son, **Adrien de Jussieu,** 1797–1853, also professor of botany at the museum, wrote a standard text, *Cours élémentaire de botanique* (1842–44).

Justice, United States Department of, Federal executive department established in 1870 and charged with providing the means for enforcing Federal laws, furnishing legal counsel in Federal cases, and construing the laws under which other Federal executive departments act. The department is headed by the U.S. Attorney General, the chief U.S. law officer and an original cabinet member. Before the formation of the Dept. of Justice the Attorney General had represented the government in legal matters and given legal advice to the executive branch under the authority of the Judiciary Act of 1789, but he had had no executive department to assist him. Because of the mounting responsibilities of the Attorney General and because of the growing need for uniformity in the administration of law, a department was created. The act of 1870 also set up the office of Solicitor General to represent the government in Supreme Court cases. The Dept. of Justice comprises eight specialized divisions (the Antitrust Division, the Civil Division, the Criminal Division, the Land and Natural Resources Division, the Tax Division, the Civil Rights Division, the Administrative Division, and the division responsible for enforcing Federal narcotics laws). The Justice Dept. also comprises the FEDERAL BUREAU OF INVESTIGATION, the Immigration and Naturalization Service, the Bureau of Prisons, the Drug Enforcement Administration, the Law Enforcement Assistance Administration, the Board of Immigration Appeals, and the Board of Parole.

justice of the peace, official presiding over a type of POLICE COURT. In some states of the United States the justices, who are usually elected, have jurisdiction over petty civil and criminal cases as well as having such duties as the issuing of search warrants and the performance of marriage services. The justice of the peace was formerly of greater importance than he is at present. The establishment of the office throughout England in 1360 represented a further extension of royal authority to local government, especially to rural areas. The justices, selected from the gentry, enjoyed extensive administrative and police authority, and they had judicial power over most crimes. The office was established also in the American colonies, but by the latter part of the 19th cent. it had been relegated to a much less central role, especially in administrative areas, in both England and the United States.

Justin I, c.450–527, Byzantine emperor (518–27); successor of Anastasius I. He was chief of the imperial guard and became emperor when Anastasius died. Justin persecuted the Monophysites and maintained close relations with the Western church. An uneducated man, he entrusted the government largely to his nephew, who eventually succeeded him as JUSTINIAN I. See Alexander Vasiliev, *Justin the First* (1950).

Justin II, d. 578, Byzantine emperor (565–78), nephew and successor of Justinian I. He allied himself with the Turks and resumed the wars with Persia. During his reign Slavs and Avars attacked the empire, and Italy was invaded by the Lombards under ALBOIN. He severely persecuted the Monophysites. Subject to fits of insanity, he adopted (574) the general Tiberius as his son. Tiberius was made Caesar and exercised power until he succeeded Justin (578) on the latter's death. Tiberius was in turn succeeded (582) by Maurice.

Justin (Marcus Junianus Justinus), fl. 3d cent., Roman historian. He made a collection of excerpts from TROGUS, which gives many facts not recounted elsewhere.

Justinian I, 483–565, Byzantine emperor (527–65), nephew and successor of JUSTIN I. He was responsible for much imperial policy during his uncle's reign. Soon after becoming emperor, Justinian instituted major administrative changes and tried to increase state revenues at the expense of his subjects. Justinian's fiscal policies, the discontent of the Monophysites at his orthodoxy, and the loyalty of the populace to the family of Anastasius I produced the Nika riot (532), which would have cost Justinian his throne but for the firmness of his wife, Empress THEODORA, and the aid of his great generals, BELISARIUS and NARSES (see BLUES AND GREENS). Justinian, through Belisarius and Narses, recovered Africa from the Vandals (533–48) and Italy from the Ostrogoths (535–54). He was less successful in fighting the Persians and was unable to prevent the raids of the Slavs and the Bulgars. Justinian's policy of caesaropapism (i.e., the supremacy of the emperor over the church) included not only matters of organization, but also matters of dogma. In 553, seeking to reconcile the Monophysites to the church, he called a council (see CONSTANTINOPLE, SECOND COUNCIL OF) but accomplished nothing and finally tended to drift into heresy himself. Justinian's greatest accomplishment was the codification of Roman law, commonly called the CORPUS JURIS CIVILIS, executed under his direction by TRIBONIAN. It gave unity to the centralized state and greatly influenced all subsequent legal history. Justinian erected many public works, of which the church of HAGIA SOPHIA is the most notable. He was succeeded by his nephew, Justin II. The writings of PROCOPIUS are the main source of information on Justinian's reign. See Charles Diehl, *Justinien et la civilisation byzantine au VIe siècle* (1901, repr. 1969); W. G. Holmes, *The Age of Justinian and Theodora* (1912); J. W. Barker, *Justinian and the Later Roman Empire* (1966); Robert Browning, *Justinian and Theodora* (1971).

Justinian II (Justinian Rhinotmetus), 669–711, Byzantine emperor (685–95, 705–11), son and successor of Constantine IV. He unsuccessfully warred against the Persians. His extravagance and despotism and his ministers' extortions caused a revolution (695). Justinian had his nose cut off; hence he was given the epithet Rhinotmetus [Gr., = with the cut-off nose]. He was then exiled. Restored (705) with the help of the Bulgars, he was deposed and beheaded. A series of usurpers occupied the throne from 711. In 717 Leo III established a new dynasty. See study by Constance Head (1972).

Justin Martyr, Saint, A.D. c.100–c.165, Christian apologist, called also Justin the Philosopher. Born in Samaria of pagan parents, he studied philosophy, and after his conversion in Ephesus to Christianity at about the age of 38, he went from place to place trying to convert men of learning by philosophical argument. He opened a school of Christian philosophy at Rome, where he and some disciples were finally martyred under Marcus Aurelius. Of his writings (in Greek), only two undisputed works remain, the *Apology* (with an appendix called the *Second Apology*) and the *Dialogue*. The *Apology* is a learned defense of Christians against charges of atheism and sedition in the Roman state; it contains an exposition of Christian ethics and invaluable records of the customs and practices of 2d-century Christianity. The *Dialogue* sets forth in the form of an argument with Trypho (or Tryphon) the Jew a philosophic defense of Christian beliefs, particularly with reference to Jewish writings; it has references to the Gospels that have been of much interest to students of the Bible. Feast: April 14.

Justin Morgan, 1792–1821, American horse, the foundation sire of the Justin Morgan breed of horses. Originally called "Figure," the stallion was renamed for his first owner, Justin Morgan (1747–97), after both owner and horse were dead. The horse—small, weighing about 800 lb (363 kg), of tremendous endurance, and with a delicate head, heavy shoulders, and a short neck—was bought and sold many times. The Morgan breed preceded the Hambletonian strain as the favored type of trotting horses in America.

Justo, Agustín Pedro (ägo͞ostēn' pä'thrō ho͞os'tō), 1876–1943, president of Argentina (1932–38). An army general, he rose to prominence (1922) as minister of war under Marcelo Torcuato de Alvear and later participated in the conservative revolution that overthrew Hipólito Irigoyen (1930). As president he became a leading exponent of Pan-Americanism and the League of Nations; together with his foreign minister, Carlos SAAVEDRA LAMAS, he was instrumental in ending the Chaco War. In World War II, Justo supported the Allied cause and was, in the face of much pro-Axis sentiment in Argentine political circles, the chief advocate of the United Nations in Argentina. When Brazil declared war on the Axis he requested and received the rank of honorary general in the Brazilian army.

Justus. 1 Surname of JOSEPH BARSABAS. **2** or **Titus Justus,** Corinthian host of St. Paul. Acts 18.7. **3** Jesus Justus: see JESUS **2.**

Justus of Ghent, fl. c.1460–c.1480, Flemish religious and portrait painter, now generally identified with Joos van Wassenhove; also known as Jodocus or Joos of Ghent. His simple, quiet style provides a clear link between Flemish and Italian art. In 1460 he was admitted to the painters' guild in Antwerp, and in 1464 he was at Ghent, where he remained until his departure (c.1469) for Italy and the court of Federigo da Montefeltro, duke of Urbino. His Flemish works are the *Adoration of the Magi* (Metropolitan Mus.) and the *Calvary* (St. Bavo, Ghent); the *Communion of the Apostles* (Urbino) is his only certain Italian work, although he surely worked on a series of panels of poets and philosophers (Urbino and Louvre). His Flemish technical achievements interested the Italians, who must also have recognized affinities to their own art in Justus's graceful yet monumental figures and rhythmically arranged forms.

Justus of Tiberia, fl. 1st cent. A.D., Jewish historian. Friendly to Rome, he opposed the Jewish war against the Romans and fled to Beirut where he became the private secretary of Agrippa II. He is mainly known for his lost *History of the Jewish War*, written from a different point of view than the work of the same title by his rival Josephus. Justus' book is known to us through its mention by Josephus and the early Fathers of the Church.

jute (jo͞ot), name for any plant of the genus *Corchorus*, tropical annuals of the family Tiliaceae (LINDEN family), and for its fiber. Many species yield fiber, but the chief sources of commercial jute are two Indian species (*C. capsularis* and *C. olitorius*), grown primarily in the Ganges and Brahmaputra valleys. Although jute adapts well to loamy soil in any hot and humid region, cultivation and harvesting require abundant cheap labor, and India remains the unrivaled world producer as well as the chief fiber processor. Calcutta is the main center. Europe and the United States import large quantities of jute fiber and cloth; Dundee, Scotland, is also a major jute-textile manufacturer. The fiber strands in the bark are 6 to 10 ft long (2–3 m) and are separated from the woody stalk centers by retting. The fiber deteriorates quickly and, because of its uneven diameter and comparatively low cellulose content, is relatively weak. However, because of its low cost and the ease of dyeing and spinning, jute is the principal coarse fiber in commercial production and use. About 90% is spun into yarn for fabrics; the better qualities supply burlap and the poorer grades are used for baling and sacking (e.g., gunny sacks). It is also used for twine, rope, carpet and linoleum backing, and insulation. The discarded lower ends, called jute butts, are used for paper manufacture. The plant, cultivated in India from remote times, has been known to Western commerce only since about 1830. Jute is classified in the division MAGNOLIOPHYTA, class Magnoliopsida, order Malvales, family Tiliaceae.

Jutes: see ANGLO-SAXONS.

Jutland (jŭt'lənd), Dan. *Jylland*, Ger. *Jütland*, peninsula, c.250 mi (400 km) long and up to 110 mi (177 km) wide, N Europe, comprising continental Denmark and N Schleswig-Holstein state, West Germany. It is bounded by the Skagerrak in the north, the North Sea in the west, the Kattegat and Lille Baelt in the east, and the Eider River in the south. The term usually is applied only to the Danish territory. Danish Jutland, including adjacent islands, has an area of 11,441 sq mi (29,632 sq km) and contains about half the population of Denmark. The Limfjørd strait cuts across N Jutland. A glacial ridge extending through central Jutland divides the peninsula into two sections. Western Jutland is windswept and sandy and has poor soil. Its coast is marshy, with many lagoons, and Esbjerg is the only good port. The east coast of Jutland is fertile and densely populated. Dairying and livestock raising are the main occupations of E Jutland; Århus and Ålborg are the chief ports. The peninsula has many lakes and is traversed by the Gudenå, Denmark's principal river. Yding Skovhøj, the highest point (568 ft/173 m) in Denmark, is in E Jutland. Sønderjylland (South Jutland) is the name applied in Denmark to the northern part of the former duchy of Schleswig, including the towns of Åbenrå, Haderslev, and Sønderborg. Jutland was known to the ancients as the Cimbric Peninsula (Lat. *Chersonesus Cimbrica*). In 1916, off the coast of W Jutland, British and German fleets engaged in the largest naval battle of World War I.

Jutland, battle of, only major engagement between the British and German fleets in World War I. On May 31, 1916, a German squadron under Admiral Hipper met a British squadron under Admiral Beatty, c.60 mi (100 km) west of the coast of Jutland. The German high seas fleet, under Admiral Scheer, approached later in the day, and Beatty turned north to join the main body of the British grand fleet under Admiral Jellicoe. Although outnumbered in the ensuing engagement, the Germans displayed brilliant naval tactics, and the encounter ended only when fog and darkness permitted their escape to their home base. The tactics employed by Jellicoe and the heavy losses of the British navy in the battle caused one of the great controversies of the war. The battle is known in Germany as the battle of the Skagerrak. See studies by H. H. Frost (1934, repr. 1970), Donald Macintyre (1958), and J. J. C. Irving (1966).

Juttah (jŭt'ə), city, S Palestine, the present-day Yattah (Jordan), S of Hebron. Joshua 15.55; 21.16.

Juvarra, Filippo (fēlēp'pō yo͞ovär'rä), 1678–1736, Italian architect of the late baroque and early rococo periods. Trained in the studio of Carlo Fontana in Rome, he entered (1714) the service of Victor Amadeus II of Savoy and was soon appointed first architect to the king. Juvarra acquired an unparalleled reputation throughout Europe. In 1719 he was in Portugal planning the palace at Mafra for King John V, after which he traveled to London and Paris. He died in Madrid, where he had gone (1735) to design a royal palace for Philip V. The main body of his work, however, is in Piedmont, where he planned many royal residences and churches. Among them are the Palazzo Madama, Turin; the castle at Stupinigi; and the churches of the Superga near Turin and of the Carmine, Turin. Drawing mainly from Italian and German Renaissance and baroque works, Juvarra integrated a variety of elements, achieving unity and grandeur of design. See R. Pommer, *Eighteenth Century Architecture in Piedmont* (1967).

Juvenal (Decimus Junius Juvenalis) (jo͞o'vənəl), fl. 1st to 2d cent. A.D., Roman satirical poet. His verse established a model for the satire of indignation, in contrast to the less harsh satire of ridicule of Horace. Little is known about his life except that during much of it he was desperately poor. A tradition tells that as a youth he was banished from court for satirizing an imperial favorite; later his work reveals a deep hatred for the Emperor Domitian. He is known chiefly for his 16 satires, which contain a vivid representation of life in Rome under the empire. They were probably written in the years between A.D. 100 and A.D. 128. The biting tone of his diatribes has seldom been equaled. From the stern point of view of the older Roman standards he powerfully denounces the lax and luxurious society, the brutal tyranny, the affectations and immorality of women, and the criminal excesses of Romans as he saw them, especially in his earlier years. The rhetorical form of his verse is finished, exact, and epigrammatic, furnishing many sayings that have become familiar through quotation. See translations by Rolfe Humphries (1958), G. G. Ramsay (rev ed. 1961), and Jerome Mazzaro (1965); studies by I. G. Scott (1927), Gilbert Highet (1955, repr. 1961), and W. S. Anderson (1964).

juvenile delinquency, legal term for behavior of children and adolescents that in adults would be judged criminal under law. In the United States definitions and age limits of juveniles vary, the maximum age being set at 14 years in some states and as high as 21 years in others. The 16- to 20-year age group, considered adult in many places, has one of the highest incidences of serious crime. A high proportion of adult criminals have a background of early delinquency. Theft is the most common offense by children; more serious property crimes and rape are most frequently committed in later youth. The causes of such behavior, like those of crime in general, are found in a complex of psychological, social, and economic factors. Clinical studies have uncovered emotional maladjustments, usually arising from disorganized family situations, in many delinquents. Other studies have indicated that there are persisting patterns of delinquency in poverty neighborhoods regardless of changing occupants; here the GANG, a source of much delinquency, is strong. Not until the development, after 1899, of the juvenile court was judgment of youthful offenders effectively separated from that of adults. The system emphasizes informal procedure and correction rather than punishment. In some states psychiatric clinics are attached, and there has been a tendency to handle cases in public welfare agencies outside the court. Juvenile correctional institutions have been separated from regular prisons since the early 19th cent. and although most are inadequate, some have developed intensive rehabilitation programs, providing vocational training and psychiatric treatment. The English BORSTAL SYSTEM for youth is notable. The parole system, foster homes, child guidance clinics, and public juvenile protective agencies have contributed to the correction of delinquent and maladjusted children. Especially important for prevention is action by community groups to provide essential facilities for the well-being of children. On an international level, delinquency rates are highest in the more economically and technologically advanced countries. See W. C. Kvaraceus, *Juvenile Delinquency* (1964); T. C. N. Gibbens, ed., *Cultural Factors in Delinquency* (1966); Travis Hirschi, *Causes of Delinquency* (1969); Sheldon and Eleanor Glueck, *Toward a Typology of Juvenile Offenders* (1970); Sol Rubin, *Crime and Juvenile Delinquency* (3d ed., 1970); LaMar Empey, *Explaining Delinquency* (1971); W. C. Reckless, *The Prevention of Delinquency* (1972).

juvenile literature: see CHILDREN'S LITERATURE.

Jylland: see JUTLAND, peninsula, Denmark.

Jyväskylä (yü'väskü"lä), city (1970 pop. 57,370), capital of Keski-Suomi prov., S central Finland. Situated on Lake Päijänne, it is an important port. Paper and wood products are made. There is an arts festival held in July. The city was chartered in 1837 and was the site (1858) of the first Finnish-language secondary school.

K

K, 11th letter of the ALPHABET. It is a usual symbol for a voiceless velar stop, as in the English *cook.* It corresponds to Greek kappa. In chemistry K is the symbol for the element POTASSIUM.

K2, peak, Kashmir: see GODWIN-AUSTEN, MOUNT.

Kaaba or **Caaba** (both: kä'bə, kä'əbə), in ISLAM, the most sacred sanctuary, the center of the Muslim world and the chief goal of pilgrimage. It is a small building in the Great Mosque of MECCA nearly cubic in shape, built to enclose the Black Stone, which is the most venerated Muslim object. The Kaaba was a pagan holy place before Muhammad, and many legends surround its origin. Around the Kaaba is a road along which pilgrims perform the *tawaf,* or sevenfold circuit of the sanctuary, an old pagan ritual. The Kaaba stone, worn hollow by centuries of ritual kissing, is held together by a wide silver band. Its custody is keenly sought after in the Islamic world; in the 5th cent. it passed to the KURAISH, in the 10th cent. the KARMATHIANS carried it away, and in 1932 an Afghan attempted to steal it. Nonbelievers are forbidden to approach it. The Kaaba is the place toward which Muslims face when praying.

Kabalevsky, Dmitri (dəmē'trē kä"bəlĕf'skē), 1904–, Soviet composer. Kabalevsky studied at the Scriabin Music School and the Moscow Conservatory, where he became a professor of composition. His music is melodic and harmonically conservative. His large output includes the opera *Colas Breugnon* (1938); *The Commedians* suite (1940); a Requiem (1963); concertos for piano, for violin, and for cello; orchestral and choral symphonies; and piano and chamber works. His music often reflects the influence of folk tradition.

Kabardino-Balkar Autonomous Soviet Socialist Republic (kăb"ərdē'nō-bălkâr'), autonomous republic (1970 pop. 589,000), c.4,800 sq mi (12,400 sq km), SE European USSR, in the northern part of the Caucasus mts. NALCHIK is the capital. The area is a largely unsettled, roadless mountain wilderness. The population—Kabardins, Balkars, Russians, and Ukrainians—is concentrated in the narrow gorges of the streams flowing into the Terek River. The Kabardins speak a Caucasian language and are Muslims (Sunnites); the Balkars speak a Turkic language. Livestock and poultry are raised, and wheat, corn, hemp, and fruit are grown. Much of the republic's industry is related to agricultural processing. Lumbering, metallurgy, and mining are also important. The Kabardins were known in the 9th cent. They occupied the land in the foothills of the central Caucasus between the 13th and 15th cent. It is not known when the Balkars settled. They were formed from the Black Bulgars, the Alans, and the Cumans. The Kabardin area became a Muscovite protectorate in 1557. Its annexation by Russia began with the treaty of Kuchuk Kainarji (1774) and was completed in 1827. The area was organized as an oblast in 1922 and became an autonomous republic in 1936. In 1943 the Balkars, accused of collaborating with the Germans, were deported, and their area, the upper Baksan valley, was ceded to the Georgian SSR. The area was then renamed Kabardinian Autonomous SSR. In 1956 the Balkars were returned, and in 1957 the area assumed its old name.

kabbalah: see CABALA.

Kabeiroi (käbē'rē, kəbī'rī), in ancient religion of the Middle East, nature deities of obscure origin, possibly Phoenician. They were connected with several fertility cults, particularly at Lemnos and at Samothrace, where important mysteries were celebrated. According to one legend they were also patrons of navigation. In Greek religion they were associated with Hephaestus, Hermes, and Demeter and were similar to the Corybantes, Curetes, and Dactyls, who were attendants to the Gods.

Kabir (kəbēr'), 1440–1518, Indian mystic and poet. A Muslim by birth, he was a weaver in Benares (Varanasi) and early in life became the disciple of the famous Hindu saint Ramananda. Kabir opposed caste practices, ritual, image-worship, and all forms of religious sectarianism; he taught the brotherhood of Hindu and Muslim under one God. Because of his anti-institutional ideas he was subject to persecution and banished from Benares c.1495. Thereafter he traveled from one N Indian city to another and died at Maghar near Gorakhpur. His songs in Hindi show the fusion of Muslim and Hindu devotional traditions. See *Poems of Kabir,* tr. by Rabindranath Tagore, 1972; I. A. Ezekiel, *Kabir, the Great Mystic* (1966).

kabuki (käbo͞o'kē): see ORIENTAL DRAMA.

Kabul (kä'bo͝ol, kəbo͝ol'), city (1971 pop. 318,094), capital of Afghanistan and its largest city and economic and cultural center, E Afghanistan, on the Kabul River. It is strategically located in a high narrow valley, wedged between two mountain ranges that command the main approaches to the KHYBER PASS. A paved road links Kabul with the USSR border. The city's chief products are woolen and cotton cloth, beet sugar, ordnance, textiles, plastics, leather goods, furniture, glass, matches, soap, and machinery. Kabul's history dates back more than 3,000 years, although the city has been destroyed and rebuilt on several different sites. Conquered by Arabs in the 7th cent., it was overshadowed by Ghazni and Herat until Babur made it the capital (1504–26) of the Mogul empire. It remained under Mogul rule until its capture (1738) by Nadir Shah of Persia. It succeeded KANDAHAR as Afghanistan's capital in 1773. During the Afghan Wars a British army took (1839) Kabul. In 1842 the withdrawing British troops were ambushed and almost annihilated after the Afghans had promised them safe conduct; in retaliation another British force partly burned Kabul. The British again occupied the city in 1879, after their resident and his staff were massacred there. Kabul's old section, with its narrow, crooked streets, contains extensive bazaars; the modern section has administrative and commercial buildings. An educational center, Kabul has a university (est. 1931), numerous colleges, and a fine museum. Also in the city are Babur's tomb and gardens; the mausoleum of Nadir Shah; the Minar-i-Istiklal (column of independence), built in 1919 after the Third Afghan War; the tomb of Timur Shah (reigned 1773–93); and several important mosques. The fort of Bala Hissar, destroyed by the British in 1879 to avenge the death of their envoy in Kabul, is now a military college. The royal palace and an ancient citadel stand outside the present city.

Kabwe (kăb'wā), formerly **Broken Hill,** city (1972 est. pop., with suburbs, 83,000), central Zambia. It is a lead and zinc mining center.

Kabyles (kəbīlz'), tribal people, predominantly agricultural, of North Africa, whose center is the rugged Kabylia region of Algeria. Of uncertain origin, they form one of the larger divisions of the BERBERS. Known for their fierce resistance to the successive conquerors of the region, they were slow to adopt the Muslim religion and Arabic speech and in Great Kabylia (the central and southern region of Algeria) they still retain their vernacular.

Kabzeel (kăb'zēĕl), unidentified city, extreme S Palestine. Joshua 15.21; 2 Sam. 23.20; 1 Chron. 11.22. Jekabzeel: Neh. 11.25.

kachina, spirit of the invisible life forces of the Pueblo Indians of North America. The kachinas, or kachinam, are impersonated by elaborately costumed masked male members of the tribes who visit Pueblo villages the first half of the year. In a variety of ceremonies, they dance, sing, bring gifts to the children, and sometimes administer public scoldings. Although not worshiped, kachinas are greatly revered, and one of their main purposes is to bring rain for the spring crops. The term *kachina* also applies to cottonwood dolls made by the Hopi and Zuni that are exquisitely carved and dressed like the dancers. Originally intended to instruct the children about the hundreds of kachina spirits, the finer carvings have become collector's items. The name is also spelled katchina.

Kachin State (kəchĭn'), state (1969 est. pop. 687,000), 33,903 sq mi (87,809 sq km), extreme N Burma. It is a mountainous region bounded on the NW by India and on the N and E by China and traversed by tributaries of the Irrawaddy River. MYITKYINA, the capital, and BHAMO are the chief towns. Rice and sugarcane are grown, jade and amber mined, and timber and bamboo cut. The state is sparsely populated; Jinghpaw-speaking Kachins constitute the largest group. They maintain the tribal forms of organization under chiefs, practice shifting cultivation, and are mostly animists. The territory was never subject to the Burman kings, and after the establishment of British rule it was governed by the British directly, not as part of Burma. Antigovernment insurgents have been active in Kachin State since Burma achieved independence in 1948.

Kádár, János (yä'nôsh kä'där), 1912–, Hungarian Communist leader. In 1932 he joined the then illegal Communist party and held high government and party posts from 1942, becoming home secretary in 1948, when the Communist party took control in Hungary. In 1951, Kádár was accused of pro-Titoism and imprisoned until 1954. After his release he quickly regained power, becoming a member of the party's central committee in July, 1956, and first secretary of the party (the Socialist Workers' party from Sept., 1956) in October. In the Hungarian revolution of 1956, Kádár at first aligned himself with the rebels and joined the cabinet of Imre NAGY. However, in November he formed a countergovernment with Soviet support, and Soviet troops crushed the revolt. In 1958 he tried and executed Nagy and other leaders of the revolt. Kádár resigned as premier in 1958 but resumed that post from 1961 to 1965. In 1962 he carried out a drastic purge of former Stalinists. In the early 1960s, Kádár permitted limited domestic liberalization but adopted a strong pro-Moscow policy during the 1968 Soviet invasion of Czechoslovakia. See his selected speeches and articles, *Socialist Construction in Hungary* (tr. 1962) and *On the Road to Socialism* (tr. 1965); William Shawcross, *Crime and Compromise* (1974).

Kadesh (kā'dĕsh), ancient city of Syria, on the Orontes River. There Ramses II fought (c.1300 B.C.) the Hittites in a great battle that ended in a truce.

Kadesh (kā'dĕsh) or **Kadesh-barnea** (-bärnē'ə), oasis in the desert S of Palestine, mentioned frequently in the Bible, notably as a limit of Edom. Another biblical name is En-mishpat. Gen. 14.7; 16.14; Num. 20; 32.8; Deut. 1.46; 2.14.

Kadmiel (kăd'mēĕl), family that returned with Zerubbabel. Ezra 2.40; 3.9; Neh. 7.43; 9.4,5; 10.9; 12.8,24.

Kadmonites (kăd'mənīts), unidentified tribe, whose land was promised to Abraham's descendants. Gen. 15.19.

Kadoma (kädō'mä), city (1970 pop. 141,041), Osaka prefecture, Honshu, Japan, on the Furu River. It is an industrial and residential suburb of Osaka, with mechanical and textile industries.

Kaduna (kä"do͞onä'), town (1969 est. pop. 174,000), N Nigeria. A leading commercial and industrial center of N Nigeria, Kaduna has cotton textile, beverage, and furniture factories. It is also a rail and road junction and the trade center for the surrounding agricultural area. Cotton, peanuts, sorghum, and ginger are shipped. The city was founded by the British in 1913 and became the capital of Nigeria's Northern Region in 1917. Training colleges for teachers, police, and the military and a technical institute are in Kaduna.

Kael, Pauline (kāl), 1919–, American motion picture critic, b. Petaluma, Calif. Possessed of an extensive knowledge of the technical aspects of movie-making, Kael is noted for her perceptive and tough-minded film criticism. She became movie critic for the *New Yorker* magazine in 1968. Her books, mostly collections of reviews, include *I Lost It at the Movies* (1965), *Kiss Kiss Bang Bang* (1968), *The Citizen Kane Book* (1971), and *Deeper into Movies* (1973).

Kaesong or **Kaisong** (both: kä'sŭng'), Jap. *Kaijo,* city (1966 est. pop. 265,000), S North Korea. A long-time commercial center, it is important chiefly for its exports of ginseng, a valuable medicinal root. There is also active trade in rice, barley, and wheat. Fine porcelain is made in the city, and there is some heavy industry. In the 10th cent. Wang, founder of the Koryo dynasty, made Kaesong his capital; the city, then called Songdo, remained Korea's capital until 1392, when the Yi dynasty moved the capital to Seoul. Intersected by the 38th parallel, Kaesong served as the main contact point between North and South Korea from 1945 to 1951 and passed from United Nations to North Korean forces several times during the Korean War. The armistice talks, first held at Kaesong, were later transferred to PANMUNJOM. Historic landmarks include the tombs of several Korean kings, the old city walls, and the remains of a royal palace from the Koryo period.

Kaffa: see FEODOSIYA, USSR.

kaffir or **kaffir corn:** see SORGHUM.

Kaffraria (kəfrăr'ēə), former name for a region in the Transkei, E South Africa. Founded in 1848 as the dependency of British Kaffraria, it was added to Cape Colony in 1865.

Kafiristan, Afghanistan: see NURISTAN.

Kafirs or **Kaffirs** (both: kăf'ərz) [Arabic,=infidel], name applied by European settlers to the Xhosa branch of the Bantu-speaking people of S Africa. Originally used only for the inhabitants of the Transkeian Territories (then called Kaffraria), the name came to be commonly employed as a derogatory term for all Negro Africans. The South African government encourages use of the term *Bantu* rather than Kafir or native.

Kafka, Franz (fränts kăf'kä), 1883–1924, German novelist and short-story writer, b. Prague, Czechoslovakia. Of a middle-class Jewish family, he studied law and then obtained a position in the workmen's-compensation division of the Austrian government. His slow and conscientious methods made it impractical for him to gain a living by writing, and most of his works were published posthumously, including his symbolic novels *Der Prozess* (1925, tr. *The Trial,* 1937), *Das Schloss* (1926, tr. *The Castle,* 1930), and *Amerika* (1927, tr. 1938). In prose that is remarkable for its clarity and precision, Kafka presents a world which is at once real and dreamlike and in which modern man, burdened with guilt, isolation, and anxiety, makes a futile search for personal salvation. Important stories appearing during his lifetime were "Das Urteil" (1913, tr. "The Judgment," 1945), *Die Verwandlung* (1915, tr. *The Metamorphosis,* 1937), "Ein Landarzt" (1919, tr. "A Country Doctor," 1945), *In der Strafkolonie* (1920, tr. "In the Penal Colony," 1941), and "Ein Hungerkünstler" (1922, tr. "A Hunger Artist," 1938). See his diaries ed. by M. Brod (tr. 1948–49); his letters to Felice Bauer, ed. by Erich Heller and Jürgen Born (tr. 1973); biographies by Max Brod (new ed. 1964) and Gustav Janouch (rev. ed. 1971); studies by W. H. Sokel (1966), R. M. Albérès (1968),Wilhelm Emrich (1968), Martin Greenburg (1968), Anthony Thorlby (1972), and R. D. Gray (1973).

Kafue (käfōō'ä), river, c.600 mi (970 km) long, rising along the Zambia-Zaïre border, S central Africa, near Lubumbashi, and meandering through central Zambia to the Zambezi River. It provides water to Zambia's copperbelt. The lower Kafue valley is fertile. The river has a good hydroelectricity-generating potential, especially at Kafue Gorge.

Kafue National Park, c.8,650 sq mi (22,400 sq km), S central Zambia, S Africa; est. 1950. It is a haven for the animal and bird life of a diverse region that includes desert, grasslands, forests, and marshes.

Kaga (kä'gä), city (1970 pop. 56,514), Ishikawa prefecture, W Honshu, Japan. It is an agricultural market, hot spring resort, and industrial center with mechanical and textile industries.

Kagawa (kägä'wä), prefecture (1970 pop. 907,897), N Shikoku, Japan. TAKAMATSU is the capital. It is an agricultural region (rice, barley) with a mountainous and forested interior. The coast has fishing ports and salt-producing centers.

Kagera (kägä'rə), river, c.250 mi (400 km) long, formed on the Rwanda-Tanzania border, E central Africa, by the confluence of the Nyaburongo and Ruvubu rivers. The Kagera's headwaters, which rise in the highlands of Rwanda and Burundi, are the remotest sources of the Nile. The Kagera flows north and east, forming part of Tanzania's borders with Rwanda and Uganda, before emptying into Victoria Nyanza. There is a small hydroelectric plant at Kikagati, Uganda.

Kagoshima (kä"gō'shĭmä), city (1970 pop. 403,309), capital of Kagoshima prefecture, extreme S Kyushu, Japan, on Satsuma Peninsula and Kagoshima Bay. An important port, it has a navy yard. The city's industries produce Satsuma porcelain ware, silk and cotton clothing, tinware, and wood products. Kagoshima is the site (since 1961) of a major Japanese rocket base. It is the seat of two universities and is historically important as the castle town of the Shimazu family and as the birthplace of Takamori Saigo, Toshimichi Okubo, and Heihachiro Togo. The center of the Satsuma Rebellion, the city was destroyed in 1877. In 1914 it suffered damage from the eruption of a volcano on Sakurajima, an island in the bay, and it was bombed (1945) in World War II. It was at Kagoshima that St. Francis Xavier landed in 1549. Kagoshima prefecture (1970 pop. 1,729,010), 3,515 sq mi (9,104 sq km), is largely mountainous, with gold, silver, iron, and copper mines. There is some subtropical vegetation.

kagu (kä'gōō), common name for a long-legged, heronlike bird, *Rhynochetos jubatus.* It has a loose, gray plumage with darker bandings; broad, rounded wings marked with white, black, and red; and a striking orange-red bill and feet. About the size of domestic fowl, the kagu has a large head endowed with a long erectile topcrest. Once abundant on the islands of the Coral Sea, the shy, nocturnal kagu is now close to extinction, and may only be found in the remotest mountains of New Caledonia in the South Pacific. Like the dodo, the kagu suffered greatly from the ravages of domestic animals, especially pigs and dogs. A forest-floor dweller, it lives on a diet of insects and snails. It is practically flightless, but is a rapid runner with a curious manner of progress; it moves in short spurts, then stands motionless before moving on again. Its courtship behavior consists of a wild, skipping dance. The female lays a single, pale brown, rust-streaked egg, depositing it in a ground nest of leaves and twigs. Both sexes share in the incubation. Kagus are classified in the phylum CHORDATA, subphylum Vertebrata, class Aves, order Gruiformes, family Rhynochetidae.

Kahn, Albert (kän), 1869–1942, American architect, designer of factories, b. Germany. He organized a large office in Detroit that applied the techniques of mass production to architecture, and he designed a great number of factories, war plants, and naval bases. Kahn was a pioneer in the use of reinforced concrete and steel. From 1928 to 1932 he was in charge of the industrial building program in the USSR. See George Nelson, *Industrial Architecture of Albert Kahn, Inc.* (1939).

Kahn, Julius, 1861–1924, American legislator, b. Germany. He arrived (1866) in California as a child. He studied law in San Francisco, was elected (1892) to the state legislature, and was admitted (1894) to the bar. Kahn served (1899–1903, 1905–24) in the U.S. House of Representatives and became noted chiefly as an advocate of military preparedness. He helped draft and secure the passage of the National Defense Act of 1915, the Selective Draft Act of 1917, and the National Defense Act of 1920. His wife, **Florence Prag Kahn,** 1868–1948, succeeded him in Congress and served until 1937.

Kahn, Louis Isadore, 1901–74, American architect, b. Estonia. From the 1920s through World War II, Kahn worked on numerous housing projects including Carver Court (1944), in Coatesville, Pa. He also planned the Yale Univ. Art Gallery and the American Federation of Labor Medical Building, Philadelphia. Kahn was widely acclaimed for his design of the Richards Medical Research Laboratories at the Univ. of Pennsylvania (1958–60). In this work he arrived at a new and dynamic integration of formal and functional elements, ingeniously relating mechanical services to the total architecture. His notable later designs include the Olivetti-Underwood Corp. factory (1969) at Harrisburg, Pa., and the Kimbell Art Museum, Fort Worth, Texas. He exerted a wide influence as professor at the Univ. of Pennsylvania and at Yale. See his notebooks and drawings, ed. by R. S. Wurman and Eugene Feldman (1962); study by Vincent Scully, Jr. (1962).

Kahn, Otto Hermann, 1867–1934, American banker and patron of the arts, born and educated in Germany. He emigrated to the United States in 1893 and in 1897 joined the banking firm of Kuhn, Loeb & Company in New York City. He was closely associated with E. H. Harriman in the reorganization of the Union Pacific and other railroads and had a part in numerous international finance organizations. Among the many theatrical and musical groups he helped underwrite were the Russian ballet and the Paris Conservatory orchestra in their American appearances. From 1903 he was active on the board of the Metropolitan Opera Company; in 1908 he brought, from Milan, Giulio Gatti-Casazza as director and Arturo Toscanini as principal conductor, launching the company on one of its most successful periods. A collection of his writings and speeches was published as *Of Many Things* (1926). See biography by M. J. Matz (1963).

Kahoolawe (kähō'ōlä'vä, -wä, kähō'lä'-), uninhabited island, 45 sq mi (117 sq km), central Hawaii; separated from Maui island to the NE by Alalakeiki Channel. The island, low and unfertile, has served as a prison and as a military target range.

Kaieteur Falls (kīətōōr'), waterfall, 741 ft (226 m) high, in the Potaro River, W Guyana. It plunges over an escarpment of the Guiana Highlands. One of the most impressive falls in South America, it is included in a national park.

K'ai-feng or **Kaifeng** (both: kī-fŭng), city (1970 est. pop. 330,000), NE Honan prov., China, on the Lunghai RR. It is a commercial, agricultural, and industrial center. Manufactures include agricultural machinery, motor vehicles, electrical and electronic equipment, fertilizer, chemicals, and processed foods. The Huang Ho (Yellow River), just to the north, has frequently flooded the city. K'ai-feng has often been a major center of Chinese political and cultural life. Founded in the 3d cent. B.C., it was, as Pienliang, capital of the Five Dynasties (906–59) and then capital of the northern Sung dynasty (960–1127). Zoroastrians worshipped there, and in the 12th cent. a Jewish colony was established. The city fell to the Mongols in the 13th cent. K'ai-feng was the provincial capital until superseded (1954) by Cheng-chou.

Kaigetsudo (kīgĕt'sōōdō), school of Japanese artists painting in the ukiyo-e style (see JAPANESE ART). Kaigetsudo was founded by Kaigetsudo Ando in the early 18th cent. Characterized by broad lines, majestic poses, restrained color, and boldly designed costumes, Kaigetsudo paintings depicted the life of courtesans. These works reflect the rise of the mercantile classes and their enthusiasms. Principally painters, the Kaigetsudo artists are better known in the West for their prints, which had a wider distribution.

Kai Islands or **Kei Islands** (both: kī), island group (c.550 sq mi/ 1,420 sq km), E Indonesia, SE of Ceram, in the Banda Sea, in the Moluccas. It is densely forested with valuable timber; the people are skilled boat builders. The chief island is Great Kai. The group is sometimes called the Key Islands.

kail: see KALE.

Kailas (kīläs'), peak, c.22,280 ft (6,790 m) high, SW Tibet (China), highest point of the Kailas Range, in the Himalayas. It is near the sources of the Sutlej, Indus, and Brahmaputra rivers. The dwelling place of the Hindu god Shiva, Kailas is the goal of pilgrimages. The pilgrim road that girdles the mountain reaches 18,000 ft (5,486 m).

Kailasa, India: see ELLORA.

Kailua (käēlōō'ə), uninc. city (1970 pop. 33,783), Honolulu co., Hawaii, on the southeastern coast of Oahu, on Kailua Bay. An agricultural experiment station is in Kailua, and a U.S. marine corps air station is nearby.

Kain (kān): see KENITES.

Kainan (kīnäN'), city (1970 pop. 53,370), Wakayama prefecture, S Honshu, Japan, on the Kii Sound. It is a port, railway junction, and industrial center with spinning, textile, and print-dyeing industries.

Kairouan: see AL QAYRAWAN, Tunisia.

Kaisaria, Turkey: see KAYSERI.

Kaiser, Georg (gā'ôrkh kī'zər), 1878–1945, German expressionist playwright. His early plays dealt with the erotic and the psychological. In maturity Kaiser turned to social themes, glorifying the ideal of sacrifice for the mass interest and attacking the brutality of the machine age. Among his many dramas are *The Citizens of Calais* (1914, tr. 1946), *From Morn to Midnight* (1916, tr. 1920), and the trilogy *The Corals* (1917, tr. 1929), *Gas* (1918, tr. 1924), and *Gas II* (1920). See studies by B. J. Kenworthy (1957) and Ernst Schürer (1972).

Kaiser, Henry John, 1882–1967, American industrialist, b. Sprout Brook, N.Y. He organized his first construction company in 1913, soon entered the road-paving business, and by 1930 was a leader in the field. In 1931 he was named chairman of the executive committee of the company formed to build Hoover Dam. He also participated in the construction of Bonneville, Grand Coulee, and Shasta dams and the San Francisco–Oakland Bridge. During World War II he and his corporations made exceptional contributions to the war effort, producing ships, planes, and military vehicles in vast numbers. From 1945 until his death he served as chairman of Kaiser Industries, an enterprise involving steel, aluminum, and home building. His effort to become an automobile manufacturer after World War II was not successful.

Kaiserslautern (kī"zərslou'tərn), city (1970 pop. 99,617), Rhineland-Palatinate, W West Germany, on the Lauter River. It is a commercial, industrial, and cultural center. There are ironworks, textile mills, and sewing-machine, furniture, and automobile factories. Charlemagne built a castle in Kaiserslautern that was later enlarged (1153-58) by Emperor Frederick I (Barbarossa); some ruins of the castle remain today. The city was repeatedly devastated by warring armies, notably by the Spanish (1635) in the Thirty Years War. During the French Revolutionary Wars the Prussians defeated (1793) the French there. Kaiserslautern has a noted early Gothic collegiate church (13th-14th cent.) and an art gallery. It is the seat of part of the Univ. of Trier and Kaiserslautern (founded 1970).

Kaiser Wilhelm Canal: see KIEL CANAL.

Kaiser-Wilhelmsland: see PAPUA NEW GUINEA.

Kaizuka (kīzo͞o'kä), city (1970 pop. 73,265), Osaka prefecture, S Honshu, Japan, on Osaka Bay. It is a commercial port and industrial center where textiles and flour are produced.

Kajaani (kä'yänē), Swed. *Kajana,* city (1970 pop. 19,677), Oulu prov., central Finland, on the Kajaaninjoki River. Forest products (including paper goods and cellulose) and sports equipment are manufactured. The city is also a road, rail, and water transportation center. Kajaani was chartered in 1651. The Kajaneborg fortress, around which the city grew, was taken by the Russians in 1716. Restored in 1937, the fortress is today a tourist attraction.

Kakamigahara (käkä"mēgähä'rä), city (1970 pop. 78,107), Gifu prefecture, central Honshu, Japan. It is an agricultural and commercial center.

Kakhetia (kəkhĕt'yēə), historic region, SE European USSR, in Georgia. TELAVI is the chief town. Kakhetia was an independent kingdom from the 8th cent. until 1010, when it became part of Georgia. Again independent between 1468 and 1762, it then became part of the East Georgian kingdom that was joined with Russia in 1801.

Kakinada (kəkĭnä'də) or **Cocanada** (kōkənä'də), town (1971 pop. 164,172), Andhra Pradesh state, SE India, on the Godavari River delta. Formerly an important port on the Bay of Bengal, it is now a district administrative center and a market for sugarcane, oilseed, cotton, rice, jute, and iron ore.

Kakogawa (käkō'gäwä), city (1970 pop. 127,112), Hyogo prefecture, S Honshu, Japan, on the Kako River. It is an industrial center where woolen and rubber goods and chemical fertilizers are produced.

Kalahari (kä"lähä'rē), arid plateau region, c.100,000 sq mi (259,000 sq km), in Botswana, South West Africa, and the Republic of South Africa. The Kalahari, covered largely by reddish sand, lies between the Orange and Zambezi rivers and is studded with dry lake beds. Yearly rainfall varies from 5 in. (12.7 cm) in the southwest, where there are active sand dunes, to 20 in. (50.8 cm) in the northeast. Grass grows throughout the Kalahari in the rainy season, and some parts also support low thorn scrub and forest. Grazing and a little agriculture are possible in certain areas. Many game animals live in the Kalahari. Its human inhabitants are mainly SAN, who are nomadic hunters, and KHOIKHOI, who are hunters and farmers.

Kalahari Gemsbok National Park, c.8,030 sq mi (20,800 sq km), SW Botswana and N Cape Prov., Republic of South Africa, S Africa; est. 1931. One of Africa's largest game reserves, it is a sanctuary for the animals and birds of the Kalahari desert.

Kalakh: see CALAH.

Kalámai (kälä'mā) or **Kalamata** (käləmä'tə, kăl-), city (1971 pop. 39,133), capital of Messinia prefecture, S Greece, in the Peloponnesus; a port on the Gulf of Messinia. It is an agricultural trade center and ships olive oil and fruits. Silk and flour are manufactured. The city developed after c.1205, when it became a fief of the Villehardouin family. It later came under the rule of Venice and (1459-1821) the Ottoman Turks. It was destroyed (1825) by Ibrahim Pasha during the Greek War of Independence.

Kalamata, Greece: see KALÁMAI.

Kalamazoo (kăl"əməzo͞o'), city (1970 pop. 85,555), seat of Kalamazoo co., SW Mich., on the Kalamazoo River at its confluence with Portage Creek; inc. 1838. It is an industrial and commercial center in a fertile farm area that produces celery, peppermint, and fruit. Kalamazoo has a large paper industry, as well as many other industries. The city is the seat of Western Michigan Univ., Kalamazoo College, a junior college, and a state mental hospital. It has a natural history museum, an art institute, and a symphony orchestra.

kalang: see FRUIT BAT.

Kalanianole, Honah Kuhio, 1871-1922, delegate to U.S. Congress from the Territory of Hawaii. He was educated in Hawaii, the United States, and England and held minor posts in the Hawaiian monarchy before it was overthrown in 1893; he served as a delegate to the U.S. Congress from 1902 until his death. His great achievement was gaining the adoption of the Hawaiian Homes Commission Act, which preserved land for the native Hawaiians.

Kalávrita (kəlä'vrĭtə), ancient *Cynaetha,* town (1971 pop. 1,948), central Greece, in the Peloponnesus. It is chiefly a summer resort. At the nearby monastery of Hagia Laura (founded 961) the Greeks first rallied (1821) in the War of Independence. The monastery of Megaspelaion, said to date from the 4th cent., is in a vaulted cave just northeast of the town.

Kalb, Johann (Ger. yō'hän kälp), 1721-80, American general in the Revolution, known generally as Baron de Kalb, b. Hüttendorf, Germany. He assumed his title for military reasons and as Jean de Kalb served France in the War of the Austrian Succession and the Seven Years War. He again served France in 1768 as a secret agent in the English colonies in America. Silas DEANE offered (1776) commissions to Kalb, Lafayette, and other European soldiers of fortune, which the Continental Congress at first refused to honor. Finally Kalb was made general and was with Washington at Valley Forge. In 1780 he was made second in command to Horatio Gates in the CAROLINA CAMPAIGN, and he died (Aug. 19, 1780) from wounds received in the battle of Camden.

Kalckreuth, Leopold Karl Walter, Graf von (lā'ōpôlt kärl väl'tər gräf fən kälk'roit), 1855-1928, German painter and graphic artist. He taught at the Weimar and Karlsruhe academies and directed the Stuttgart Academy (1900-1905). Although noted for his somber early paintings of peasant women, he later abandoned naturalism for symbolist art.

kale, borecole (bôr'kōl), and **collards,** common names for nonheading, hardy types of CABBAGE (var. *acephala* and sometimes others), with thick stems and curly leaves, belonging to the family Cruciferae (MUSTARD family). They are grown for greens and, in Europe, for fodder. In the Channel Islands a tall fodder variety, known as Jersey kale, Jersey cabbage, or cow cabbage, grows to more than 7 ft (2.1 m). Kale (or kail) is a cool-weather crop—frost improves the flavor. In the United States the principal commercial growing regions are in Virginia and on Long Island. Kale is closest in form to the wild cabbage. In Scotland the word *kale* is used for cabbages of any kind. Sea kale is a European herb of the genus *Crambe* (also of the mustard family), found along the northern coasts and often used as a potherb. Kale, borecale, and collards are all classified in the division MAGNOLIOPHYTA, class Magnoliopsida, order Capparales, family Cruciferae.

kaleidoscope (kəlī'dəskōp), device consisting of a tube through which changing symmetrical patterns can be viewed. At one end of the tube is an eyepiece; at the other end colored chips of glass are loosely sandwiched between two glass disks. Between the ends of the tube are two rectangular plane mirrors. The long edge of one of the two mirrors lies against the long edge of the other at an angle, their intersection lying close to the axis of the tube. The glass chips form patterns where they lie, and these patterns change as the chips fall into new positions when the tube rotates. Each pattern undergoes multiple reflections in the mirrors in such a way as to produce a resulting symmetrical pattern that can be seen through the eyepiece. Invention of the device is credited to the Scottish physicist Sir David Brewster.

Kalemi (kälä'mē), formerly **Albertville** (ălbĕrvēl'), city (1967 est. pop. 87,000), Shaba region, SE Zaïre, on Lake Tanganyika at the mouth of the Lukuga River. It is a commercial center and a rail-steamer transfer point, handling goods moving between Zaïre and Tanzania. Manufactures include textiles and cement. The city was founded in 1892 by Belgians as a military post in their campaign against Arab traders.

Kalends: see CALENDAR.

Kalevala (kä'lĕvä"lä), Finnish national epic. It is a compilation of folk verses, dealing mainly with the extraordinary deeds of three semidivine brothers whose abode was in mythical Kaleva, land of the heroes. The epic was once thought to date from the first millennium B.C. and to reveal primitive Finnish life, but it is now thought that parts were created in the Middle Ages and perhaps later. Although known to scholars as early as 1733, the verses were largely ignored until the 19th cent., when, under the impetus of the romantic movement, they were collected by two Finnish physicians, Zakarias Topelius, who published the first fragments in 1822, and Elias LÖNNROT, who gave the cycle its present form. From the miscellaneous episodes chanted to him by the rune singers Lönnrot created a poetic whole, editing the material and sometimes writing transitional verses himself. A collection of 25 runes (about 12,000 lines) was published in 1835; a second edition containing 50 runes (nearly 23,000 lines) was published in 1849. The epic is rich in mythology, magic, enigma, and folklore; its expeditions are reminiscent of the *Odyssey,* with underlying themes of love, egoism, and the struggles of spirit against matter and man against nature. Its effect on Finnish art in all its branches has been great. The eight-syllable trochaic line of the *Kalevala* was imitated by Longfellow in *Hiawatha.* See tr. by W. F. Kirby (1907, new ed. 1956) and F. P. Magoun (1963).

Kalgan: see CHANG-CHIA-KOU, China.

Kalgoorlie (kălgo͝or'lē), town (1971 pop. 9,170), Western Australia, SW Australia. It is the chief mining town of the state and the center of the East Coolgardie Goldfield. Gold was found at nearby Coolgardie in 1892; nickel is also mined. The Western Australia School of Mines (1902) was transferred (1903) from Coolgardie to Kalgoorlie.

Kali (kä'lē) [Hindi, = the Black One], important goddess in popular Hinduism and TANTRA. Known also as Durga [the Inaccessible] and as Chandi [the Fierce], Kali is associated with disease, death, and destruction. As Parvati she is the consort of SHIVA. Although often represented as a terrifying figure, garlanded with skulls and bearing a bloody sword in one of her many arms, she is worshiped lovingly by many as the Divine Mother. Her cult, popular among many lower castes in India, especially in Bengal, frequently includes animal sacrifice. Kali was patroness of the THUGS.

Kalidasa (kä"lĭdä'sə), fl. 5th cent.?, Indian dramatist and poet. He is regarded as the greatest figure in classical Sanskrit literature. Except that he was retained by the Gupta court, no facts concerning his life are known. His three surviving plays are *Sakuntala* (or *Shakuntala*), *Vikramorvasi,* and *Malavikagnimitra.* These court dramas in verse (*nataka*) relate fanciful or mythological tales of profound romantic love intensified and matured by adversity. *Sakuntala,* which is generally considered his masterpiece, tells of a maiden, Sakuntala, whom King Dushyanta marries. The king is bewitched so that he forgets his bride until a ring he gave her is discovered in the body of a fish. In Kalidasa's two epics, *Raghuvansa* and *Kumarasambhava,* delicate descriptions of nature are mingled with battle scenes. The other poems of Kalidasa are shorter and almost purely lyrical. *Meghaduta* [cloud messenger] is a description of the regions of India crossed by a cloud traveling between a tree spirit and his wife. *Ritusamhara* describes the course of pastoral love through the six seasons into which Indians divided the year. See A. W. Ryder, *Shakuntala and Other Writings by Kalidasa* (1959); studies by M. B. Harris (1936) and K. Krishnamoorthy (1972).

Kalimantan: see BORNEO.

Kálimnos (kä'lēmnôs), mountainous island (1971 pop. 13,281), 41 sq mi (106 sq km), SE Greece, one of the DODECANESE, 11 mi (18 km) off the coast of Asia Minor. A sponge-fishing center, it also produces figs, olives, citrus fruits, and almonds. The main town is Kálimnos, on the southeastern shore of the island.

Kalinin, Mikhail Ivanovich (mēkhəyēl' ēvä'nəvĭch kəlyē'nyĭn), 1875-1946, Russian revolutionary. Of the working class, he was active in revolutionary affairs from his youth. He became the first chairman of the central executive committee of the USSR (now chairman of the presidium), or titular head of state (1919-46), and was a member (1925-46) of the politburo.

Kalinin, formerly **Tver,** city (1970 pop. 345,000), capital of Kalinin oblast, central European USSR, at the confluence of the Volga and Tver rivers. A major port on the upper Volga as well as an industrial center, it has industries producing linen textiles, heavy machinery, and rolling stock. The city grew around a fort established in the late 12th cent. It was early an important trade center, and from the mid-13th cent. until the late 14th cent. it was the seat of a powerful principality that rivaled Moscow. It was subjugated (1475-85) by Ivan III, grand duke of Moscow. Tver was renamed (1931) for M. I. Kalinin. There are a cathedral and castle, both from the 17th cent., in Kalinin.

Kaliningrad (kəlyē″nyĭn-grät′), formerly **Königsberg,** city (1970 pop. 297,000), capital of Kaliningrad oblast, W European USSR, on the Pregolya River near its mouth on the Vislinski Zalev, which empties into the Gulf of Kaliningrad on the Baltic Sea. A major ice-free Baltic seaport and naval base, and an important industrial and commercial center, Kaliningrad has industries that produce ships, machinery, food products, metals, automobile parts, and textiles. The city has an institute of oceanography and botanical and zoological gardens. The city was founded (1255) as a fortress of the Teutonic Knights by King Ottocar II of Bohemia, for whom it is supposedly named. It joined (1340) the Hanseatic League and became (1457) the seat of the grand master of the Teutonic Order after the knights lost Marienburg to Poland. It was the residence of the dukes of Prussia from 1525 until the union (1618) of Prussia and Brandenburg and became (1701) the coronation city of the kings of Prussia. The Univ. of Königsberg (founded 1544) reached its greatest fame when Kant (who was born and lived his entire life at Königsberg) taught there. The university building, the old castle, the 14th-century cathedral, and most of the old city were severely damaged by Soviet troops in World War II. As part of the northern section of East Prussia, the city was transferred to the USSR in 1945. The new Soviet city (named Kaliningrad for Mikhail Kalinin in 1946) was laid out after 1945 in the former residential suburbs of Königsberg; its population is almost entirely Russian.

Kalisch, Isidor (ēzēdôr′ kä′lĭsh, kä′-), 1816–86, Jewish rabbi and author, b. Prussia. Forced to leave Germany because of his liberal political views, he emigrated to the United States in 1849 and served as rabbi in various American cities. He is chiefly known for his place in the polemical controversy of the day over Reform Judaism, of which he was a leader. He wrote several books on Judaism.

Kalisch: see KALISZ, Poland.

Kalispel Indians: see PEND D'OREILLE INDIANS.

Kalispell (kăl′ĭspĕl″, -pĕl′), city (1970 pop. 10,526), seat of Flathead co., NW Mont., at the head of Flathead Lake near Glacier National Park; inc. 1892. It is the tourist and trade center of a rich agricultural, fruit, and timber region. The headquarters of the Flathead National Forest are in Kalispell. Hungry Horse Dam and a state park are nearby. A junior college is in the city.

Kalisz (kä′lēsh), Ger. *Kalisch,* city (1970 pop. 81,227), central Poland. An industrial center, it has industries producing textiles, machinery, metals, and chemicals. One of the oldest Polish towns, it has been identified as the Slavic settlement of Calissia mentioned in the 2d cent. A.D. by Ptolemy. It flourished as a trade center from the 13th cent. At Kalisz Casimir III signed (1343) the treaty with the Teutonic Knights by which he conceded his rule over East Pomerania. The city passed to Prussia in 1793, was transferred to Russia in 1815, and was restored to Poland in 1919. In a treaty signed (1813) at Kalisz, Prussia and Russia formed an alliance against Napoleon I.

kalium, Latin name for POTASSIUM.

Kalkbrenner, Friedrich Wilhelm Michael (frē′drĭkh vĭl′hĕlm mĭkh′äēl kälk′brĕnər), 1785–1849, German-French pianist and composer, son of the composer Christian Kalkbrenner (1755–1806). Kalkbrenner studied with his father and in 1798 enrolled in the Paris Conservatory. He was highly influential as a piano teacher, particularly in octave, left-hand, and pedal technique. His many compositions for the piano include four concertos.

Kallai (kălā′ī), priest of Joiakim. Neh. 12.20.

Kallio, Kyösti (kü′ōstē käl′lyō), 1873–1940, Finnish political leader. Of peasant background, he entered politics and was a vocal advocate of Finnish independence from Russia. Minister of agriculture in the newly independent government (1917–20, 1921–22), he was instrumental in inaugurating land redistribution. He served a number of times as prime minister (1922–24, 1925–26, 1929–30, and 1936–37) and was president of Finland from 1937 to Nov., 1940. Illness and strain brought on by the Finnish-Russian War of 1939–40 led to his resignation.

Kalmar (käl′mär), city (1970 pop. 34,680), capital of Kalmar co., SE Sweden, on the Kalmarsund (an arm of the Baltic Sea) opposite Öland Island. It is a commercial, industrial, and tourist center and is connected by ferry with Öland. Manufactures include matches, glass, processed food, and ships. It has been an important trade center since the 8th cent. The KALMAR UNION was negotiated there in 1397. Kalmar has a 12th-century castle, the Kalmarnahus, which withstood numerous sieges in the Danish-Swedish wars of the 16th–17th cent. The name is also spelled Calmar.

Kalmar Union, combination of the three crowns of Denmark, Sweden, and Norway, effected at Kalmar, Sweden, by Queen MARGARET I in 1397. Because the kingship was elective in all three countries, the union could not be maintained by inheritance. Nationalist forces used the election procedure to modify terms of the union. Margaret's successors controlled Sweden only for brief periods; the accession (1523) of GUSTAVUS I as king of Sweden dissolved the union. The union of Denmark and Norway lasted, however, until 1814.

Kalmyk Autonomous Soviet Socialist Republic (kăl′mĭk), autonomous republic (1970 pop. 268,000), c.29,400 sq mi (76,150 sq km), SE European USSR, on the Caspian Sea. Elista is the capital. Lying mostly in the vast depression of the N Caspian lowland, the republic is largely a steppe and desert area. There are salt lakes but no permanent waterways. Stock raising (horses, cattle, sheep, goats, and some pigs and camels) is by far the leading economic activity, and fishing is important. Irrigation has made limited agriculture possible; winter wheat, maize, and fodder crops are grown. Industry revolves primarily around the processing of agricultural products, fish, and minerals. The population is primarily Russian and Kalmyk. A seminomadic branch of the Oirat Mongols, the Kalmyks migrated from Chinese Turkistan to the steppe W of the Volga's mouth in the mid-17th cent. They became allies of the Russians and were charged by Peter I with guarding the eastern frontier of the Russian Empire. Under Catherine II, however, the Kalmyks became vassals. In 1771 about 300,000 Kalmyks E of the Volga set out to return to China but were decimated en route by Russian, Kazakh, and Kirghiz attacks. The Kalmyks W of the Volga remained in Russia, where they retained their Lamaist Buddhist religion and their seminomadic life. The word *Kalmyk* in Turkish means "remnant," referring to those who stayed behind. The Kalmyk Autonomous Oblast was established in 1920; it became an autonomous republic in 1936. During World War II, Kalmyk units fought the Russians in collaboration with the Germans. As a result, the Kalmyks were deported to Siberia in 1943, and their republic was dissolved. In 1956, Nikita Khrushchev denounced the deportation as a Stalinist crime, and the following year about 6,000 Kalmyks were returned. The Kalmyk Autonomous SSR was officially reestablished in 1958.

Kalocsa (kŏ′lôchŏ), town (1970 pop. 16,004), S Hungary, near the Danube River. It is an agricultural center and is famed for its embroidery. Created a bishopric by St. Stephen, it became the seat of an archbishop in 1260. The town has a Roman Catholic academy, a cathedral, and an archiepiscopal palace (built in 1786).

Kaluga (kəlo͞o′gə), city (1970 pop. 211,000), capital of Kaluga oblast, central European USSR, on the Oka River. It is a river port and an industrial center producing machinery, electrical equipment, and textiles. Known since 1389 as a Muscovite outpost, Kaluga was the scene of the murder (1610) of the second false DMITRI.

Kalundborg (kä′lo͝onbôr), city (1970 com. pop. 19,216), Vestsjaelland co., central Denmark, a port on the Kalundborg Fjord, an arm of the Store Baelt. It is a commercial, industrial, and communications center. Manufactures include chemicals and machinery. Founded c.1170, the city has a 12th-century church laid out in the form of a Greek cross. The novelist Sigrid Undset (1882–1949) was born in Kalundborg.

kalunite: see ALUM.

Kama (kä′mə), river, c.1,260 mi (2,030 km) long, E European USSR, the chief left tributary of the Volga. It rises in the foothills of the central Urals and flows N, then E, and then SW past Perm, Sarapul, and Chistopol to join the Volga below Kazan. The Vyatka is its principal tributary. The Kama is an important transportation artery. There is a large hydroelectric station at Perm.

Kamakura (kämä′ko͝orä), city (1970 pop. 139,253), Kanagawa prefecture, central Honshu, Japan, on Sagami Bay and at the base of the Miura Peninsula. It is a resort and residential area but is chiefly noted as a religious center, the site of more than 80 shrines and temples. Kamakura is especially famous for its *daibutsu* [Jap., = great Buddha], a 42-ft-high (12.8-m) bronze figure of Buddha, cast in 1252, and for a 30-ft-high (9.1-m) gilt and camphor statue of Kannon, the goddess of mercy. Kamakura was splendid as the seat of YORITOMO and his descendants (1192–1333); under the Ashikaga Shogunate (1333–1573) it was the government headquarters of eastern Japan. An earthquake in 1923 severely damaged the city.

Kamarhati (kämärhä′tē), city (1971 pop. 169,222), West Bengal state, NE India. It is a suburb of Calcutta.

Kamban, Guðmundur (gvüth′müntür käm′bän), 1888–1945, Icelandic dramatist and novelist. Many of Kamban's plays, among them *Hadda-Padda* (1914, tr. 1917), were produced in Denmark. His spirited and erudite historical novels, based upon the Icelandic sagas, include *Skalholt* (4 vol., 1930–32; tr. of Vol. I and II, *The Virgin of Skalholt,* 1935) and *I See a Wondrous Land* (1936, tr. 1938).

Kamchatka (kămchăt′kə), peninsula, 104,200 sq mi (269,878 sq km), Far Eastern USSR, separating the Sea of Okhotsk in the west from the Bering Sea and the Pacific Ocean in the east. Extending from lat. 51°N to lat. 61°N, it is 750 mi (1,207 km) long and terminates in the south in Cape Lopatka, beyond which lie the Kuril Islands. Petropavlovsk-Kamchatski is the chief city. There are many rivers and lakes, and the eastern shore is deeply indented by gulfs and bays. The peninsula's central valley, drained by the Kamchatka River, is enclosed by two parallel volcanic ranges that extend north-south; there are about 20 active volcanoes, the only active ones in the USSR. The highest point is Klyuchevskaya Sopka (15,600 ft/4,755 m), itself an active volcano. Kamchatka is covered with mountain vegetation, except in the central valley and on the west coast, which has peat marshes and tundralike moss. The climate is cold and humid. There are numerous forests, mineral springs, and geysers. Kamchatka's mineral resources include oil, coal, gold, mica, pyrites, sulfur, and tufa. Fishing, sealing, hunting, and lumbering are the main occupations. As a Soviet fishing area (notably for crabs, which are exported worldwide), Kamchatka is surpassed only by the Caspian Sea region. Fur trapping on the peninsula yields most of the furs of the Soviet Far East. Cattle breeding is carried on in the south and farming (rye, oats, potatoes, vegetables) in the Kamchatka valley and around Petropavlovsk-Kamchatski. Reindeer are also raised on the peninsula. Industries include fish processing, shipbuilding, and woodworking. The majority of the population is Russian, with large minorities of Koryak peoples. The Russian explorer Atlasov discovered Kamchatka in 1697. Its exploration and development continued in the early 18th cent. under Czar Peter I. Russian conquest was complete by 1732. Heavy Russian colonization occurred in the early 19th cent. From 1926 to 1938, Kamchatka formed part of the Far Eastern Territory.

kame (kām), low, steep, rounded hill or ridge of layered sand and gravel drift, developed from glacial deposits. Kames were probably formed by streams of melting glacial ice that deposited mud and sand along the ice front. The subsequent retreat of the glacier left them as more or less isolated hills and ridges, ranging in height from a few feet to 100 ft (30 m) or more. Kames generally occur in clusters and are situated directly behind a mass of rock and soil called a terminal MORAINE. They are common in the glaciated valleys of the Scottish Lowlands, where the name originated.

Kamehameha (kämā′hämā′hä), dynasty of Hawaiian monarchs. **Kamehameha I** (Kamehameha the Great), c.1738–1819, was king of the island of Hawaii after 1790. Through conquest he became (1810) ruler of all the Hawaiian islands, which were previously governed by warring chiefs. Law and order were established for the first time, and the islands became prosperous. Although he was cordial to the traders who visited the islands and encouraged the introduction of their technology, he also insisted on the preservation of the ancient customs and religious beliefs of Hawaii. See biographies by H. H. Gowen (1919) and J. T. Pole (1959). His son, **Kamehameha II,** 1797–1824, succeeded to the throne in 1819. During his short reign, American missionaries were admitted to the islands for the first time. Upon his death in London during a ceremonial visit, his younger brother, **Kamehameha III,** 1814–54, became (1824) king. His mother, Kaahumanu, who served as regent during his minority, encouraged the spread of Christianity in the islands. American traders entered the islands in large numbers, and there was a growing danger of filibustering expeditions and even annexation from the United States. Under these pressures, Kamehameha III gave in to Western influences. Hawaii was converted from semifeudalism into a constitutional monarchy. A constitution adopted in 1840 provided for religious freedom, representative government, and an independent judiciary; a later constitution (1852) granted suffrage to all adult males. His son, **Kamehameha IV,** 1834–63, attempted to resist American influence during his reign (1854–63) but without much success. When his brother, **Kamehameha V,** 1831–72, became (1863) king, he tried to restore the old tribal ways. The constitution of 1852 was abrogated, and he proclaimed a new one that restored power to the monarch, weakened the legislature, and restricted suffrage. Under his reign, the influence of American missionaries waned rapidly. He died without an heir, however, and the legislature chose his successor, thus bringing to an end the Kamehameha dynasty.

Kamenets-Podolski (käm'mĭnyĭts-pədôl'skē), city (1969 est. pop. 69,000), SW European USSR, in the Ukraine. It is a rail terminus and has industries that produce foodstuffs, tobacco, machinery, machine tools, and automobile parts. Kamenets-Podolski was part of the duchy of Galich-Volhynia from the 12th to the 14th cent., when it passed to Poland. It came under Russian control in 1793. Historic landmarks include the fortress (15th–16th cent.), which is now a museum, and some cathedrals and monasteries dating from the 14th cent.

Kamenev, Lev Borisovich (lyĕf bərē'səvĭch kä'mĭnyĭf), 1883–1936, Soviet Communist leader. His original name was Rosenfeld. He joined (1901) the Social Democratic party and sided with the Bolshevik wing when the party split (1903). Banished (1915) to Siberia for his revolutionary activities, he returned after the February Revolution of 1917 and became a member of the first Politburo of the Communist party. On Lenin's death (1924), Kamenev, STALIN, and ZINOVIEV formed a triumvirate of successors and excluded TROTSKY, Kamenev's brother-in-law, from power. In 1925 the Stalinist majority in the party defeated Kamenev and Zinoviev, who joined (1926) Trotsky's opposition. Kamenev was expelled from the party in 1927, but he recanted, was readmitted, and held minor offices. He was arrested late in 1934 on charges of complicity in the murder of KIROV and was sentenced to imprisonment. In 1936 he, Zinoviev, and 14 others were tried for treason in the first big public purge trial. They confessed and were executed.

Kamensk-Shakhtinskiy (kä'myĭnsk-shäkh'tyĭnskē), city (1970 pop. 68,000), SE European USSR, on the Donets River. A mining center of the Donets coal basin, the city is also an important producer of artificial fibers. Kamensk-Shakhtinskiy was founded in 1817.

Kamerlingh Onnes, Heike (hī'kə kä'mərlĭng ôn'əs), 1853–1926, Dutch physicist. He was, from 1882, professor of physics at the Univ. of Leiden. He made important studies of the properties of helium and, in attempting to solidify it, produced a temperature within one degree of absolute zero. In the course of his low temperature experiments, he discovered the property of SUPERCONDUCTIVITY in certain metals. For these researches he received the 1913 Nobel Prize in Physics.

Kamerun: see CAMEROONS.

Kames, Henry Home, Lord (hyo͞om), 1696–1782, Scottish judge and philosopher. A man of broad interests and a wide-ranging intellect, his works included dissertations on Scottish law, agriculture, and problems of moral and aesthetic philosophy. Among his writings were *Introduction to the Art of Thinking* (1761) and *Elements of Criticism* (1762). See studies by W. C. Lehmann (1971) and I. S. Ross (1972).

kamikaze (kä''məkä'zē) [Jap.,=divine wind], the typhoon that destroyed Kublai Khan's fleet, foiling his invasion of Japan in 1281. In World War II the term was used for a Japanese suicide air force, composed of fliers who crashed their bomb-laden planes into their targets, usually ships. The kamikaze was first used extensively at Leyte Gulf and was especially active at Okinawa.

Kamina (kämē'nä), city (1967 est. pop. 115,000), Shaba region, S Zaïre. It is an administrative and transportation center. A major military airfield is located there. Kamina was used by the Belgians as a center for interventionist actions in the early months of Zaïre's independence (1960). It later served as a center for UN operations during the crisis caused by the secession (1960–63) of Katanga.

Kaministikwia (kəmĭn''ĭstĭk'wēə), river, c.60 mi (100 km) long, rising in Dog Lake, W Ont., Canada, and flowing S, then E into Lake Superior at Thunder Bay. In fur trade days it was the chief alternate to the Grand Portage–Pigeon River route into the northwest. After 1783, when the Pigeon River formed part of the U.S. boundary, it became the main route used by the North West Company to Fort William, their western headquarters at the mouth of the river. Kakabeka Falls (130 ft/40 m high), W of Fort William, is used to generate hydroelectricity.

Kamloops (kăm'lo͞ops), city (1971 pop. 26,168), S British Columbia, Canada, at the junction of the North Thompson and South Thompson rivers. A trading post was first established on the site in 1812. A village grew up at the time of the Cariboo gold rush (1860), and in 1885 the main line of the Canadian Pacific reached Kamloops. It is now a tourist and supply center for an extensive lumbering, mining, and farming district.

Kammersee, lake, Austria: see SALZKAMMERGUT.

Kampala (kämpä'lä), city (1969 pop. 331,889), capital of Uganda, on Victoria Nyanza. It is Uganda's largest city and its administrative, communications, economic, and transportation center. Manufactures include processed foods, beverages, shoes, enamelware, furniture, and machine parts. It is linked by railroad with Kasese, a mining center in SW Uganda, and with Mombasa, Kenya, on the Indian Ocean coast. Steamers on Victoria Nyanza link the city with ports in Kenya and Tanzania. An international airport is nearby, at ENTEBBE. Kampala grew up around a fort constructed (1890) by Capt. Frederick LUGARD for the British East Africa Company. In 1962, Kampala replaced Entebbe as the capital of Uganda. Despite its proximity (20 mi/32 km) to the equator, the city has a moderate climate, largely because of its altitude (c.4,000 ft/1,220 m). The city is built on and around six hills and has modern government and commercial quarters as well as wide avenues that fan out toward the surrounding suburbs. Kampala is the seat of the East African Development Bank and Makerere Univ.

Kampen (käm'pən), town (1971 pop. 29,087), Overijssel prov., central Netherlands, on the IJssel River, near the IJsselmeer. It is a trade and industrial center. Kampen was first mentioned in the 13th cent., and in the 15th cent. it was a member of the Hanseatic League. Notable structures in the town include the 14th-century town hall and several churches and buildings dating from the 14th and 15th cent. Two theological schools are there.

Kamperduin, Netherlands: see CAMPERDOWN.

Kampot (kämpôt') town, capital of Kampot prov., S Cambodia, on the Gulf of Siam. It is a seaport on the Phnom Penh–Kompong Som RR and the center of the Cambodian pepper culture. A cement plant is located nearby.

Kan (gän), river, c.550 mi (885 km) long, flowing north through the plain of central Kiangsi prov., SE China, past Nan-ch'ang to P'o-yang lake. Despite many rapids, it is navigable for junks below Kan-chou and for steamers up to Nan-ch'ang. The lower Kan valley is fertile; rice and tea are the main crops.

Kanagawa (känä'gäwä), prefecture (1970 pop. 5,472,247), E central Honshu, Japan. Yokohama is the capital. Other important cities include Kawasaki, Yokosuka, and Kamakura (a religious center). The urban belt of the eastern part of the prefecture merges with Tokyo to the north.

Kanah (kā'nə). **1** Unidentified town, N Palestine. Joshua 19.28. **2** River, central Palestine. Joshua 16.8; 17.9.

Kanalit, mts.: see CERAUNIAN MOUNTAINS, Albania.

Kananga (kənäng'gə), formerly **Luluabourg** (lo͞olwäbo͞or'), city (1971 est. pop. 483,400), capital of Kasai-Occidental prov., S central Zaïre, on the Lulua River. It is the commercial and transportation center of an agricultural region where cotton is grown. The city was founded in 1884 by the German explorer Hermann von Wissmann. In 1895, Batetela troops stationed there revolted after their chief was executed by authorities of the Belgian-run Independent State of the Congo. At first successful, the mutineers were finally defeated in 1901. Kananga grew rapidly in the early 20th cent. with the coming of the railroad. Many Luba tribesmen settled there and became economically dominant over the indigenous Lulua people. After Zaïre (then called the Democratic Republic of the Congo) achieved independence (1960), there were violent clashes between the Luba and Lulua, and many Luba fled to the short-lived (1960–61) Mining State of South KASAI. In 1961–62, the city was held by rebel troops from Equateur prov., who were loyal to Antoine Gizenga.

Kanaoka (känä'ōkä), fl. 2d half of 9th cent., Japanese landscape and figure painter, founder of the Kose school of painting. None of his works survives, but tradition says that he was the first Japanese painter to paint Japanese subject matter. He is also known as Kose no Kanaoka.

Kanarak: see KONARAK.

Kanarese (känərēz'), Dravidian language of India. See DRAVIDIAN LANGUAGES.

Kanaris, Constantine (känä'rĭs), 1790–1877, Greek patriot, admiral, and politician. He distinguished himself in the Greek War of Independence, notably at Tenedos, where he destroyed (1822) the flagship of the Turkish admiral. Kanaris served several terms as minister of the navy and as premier in 1848–49, and he became increasingly active in political life. In 1862 he was a leader in the revolution that ousted King Otto and put George I on the Greek throne. Under George I, he was premier in 1864–65 and in 1877. The name also appears as Canaris.

Kanatha: see DECAPOLIS.

Kanawha (kənô'wə), principal river of W.Va., 97 mi (156 km) long, formed by the confluence of the New and Gauley rivers, S central W.Va., and flowing NW to the Ohio River at Point Pleasant; Charleston, W.Va., is the largest city on the river. The Kanawha flows through a rich coal, natural-gas, and salt-brine region; its valley is one of the world's largest chemical-manufacturing centers. There are navigation locks and power dams on the river; its tributaries have flood-control works.

Kanazawa (kä''nä'zäwä), city (1970 pop. 361,373), capital of Ishikawa prefecture, central Honshu, Japan, on the Sea of Japan. It produces cotton and silk textiles, machinery, rolling stock, iron, and fine porcelain and lacquer ware. The city, built on the site of the old village of Yamazaki, was the seat of the Maeda clan (16th–19th cent.) and gradually became an industrial center. Kenrokuran Park (rebuilt 17th cent.), with its splendid landscape gardens and a famous No theatre and school, is in Kanazawa.

Kanchenjunga, Kanchanjanga (both: kän''chənjo͝ong'gə, kăn'chĕnjŭng'gə), or **Kinchinjunga** (kĭn''chənjo͝ong'gə), mountain, on the Sikkim-Nepal border, E Himalayas; geologically regarded as the main axis of the Himalayan range. The third-highest mountain in the world, it has five peaks, of which the tallest is 28,208 ft (8,598 m). In 1955 a British expedition under Charles Evans climbed the mountain, but in deference to the wishes of Sikkimese authorities the party stopped a few yards short of the summit.

Kanchi or **Kancheepuram,** India: see KANCHIPURAM.

Kanchipuram (kŭn'chēpo͝orəm), formerly Conjeeveram, city (1971 pop. 110,505), Tamil Nadu state, S India. Sacred to Hindus, it is known as the "golden city" and the "Benares of the south." Several temples in the Dravidian style survive from the period when it was the capital of the Pallava empire (3d–8th cent.) of S India and Sri Lanka and a center of Brahmanical and Buddhist culture. The city was captured (8th cent.) by the Chalukya dynasty and subsequently passed to the Chola (11th–13th cent.), to the Vijayanagar (early 15th cent.), and to the Orissa (late 15th cent.) kingdoms. After 1481 it fell to several different Muslim sultanates. A base of French power in India, it was captured by Robert Clive in 1758. Its ancient name was Kanchi. The patterns and texture of its saris are famous.

Kan-chou or **Kanchow** (both: gän-jō), city, SW Kiangsi prov., China, on the Kan River. It is a large transportation, distribution, and commercial center. Fertilizer is manufactured in the city, and tungsten mines are nearby. The city was formerly known as Kanhsien.

Kanchow: see KAN-CHOU, China.

Kandahar (kăn''dəhär'), city (1971 pop. 133,795), capital of Kandahar prov., S Afghanistan. The country's second largest city and chief trade center, Kandahar is a market for sheep, wool, cotton, food grains, fresh and dried fruit, and tobacco. It has an international airport and is linked by road with the USSR border. Woolen cloth, felt, and silk are manufactured. The surrounding irrigated region produces fine fruits, especially grapes, and the city has plants for canning, drying, and packing fruit. Kandahar may have been founded by Alexander the Great (4th cent. B.C.). India and Persia long fought over the city, which was strategically located on the trade routes of central Asia. It was conquered by Arabs in the 7th cent. and by the Turkic Ghaznivids in the 10th cent. Jenghiz Khan sacked it in the 12th cent., after which it became a major city of the Karts (Mongol clients) until their defeat by Tamerlane in 1383. Babur, founder of the Mogul empire of India, took Kandahar in the 16th cent. It was later contested by the Persians and by the rulers of emerging

Afghanistan, who made it the capital (1748–73) of their newly independent kingdom. British forces occupied Kandahar during the First Afghan War (1839–42). The British again held the city from 1879 to 1881, when they finally recognized Abd ar-Rahman as emir of Afghanistan. The old city, sections of whose mud wall still survive, was laid out by Ahmad Shah (1724–73) and is dominated by his octangular, domed mausoleum. There are also numerous mosques (one said to contain the Prophet Muhammad's cloak) and bazaars. Modern Kandahar adjoins the old city. It has a technical college. Together with Peshawar, Pakistan, Kandahar is the principal city of the Pathan people.

Kandalaksha (kəndəläk'shə), Finnish *Kannanlahti*, city (1970 pop. 43,000), NW European USSR, on the Kandalaksha Bay of the White Sea. It is a seaport and has aluminum plants and hydroelectric stations. A settlement at the present site was known to the Vikings.

Kandinsky, Wassily (kăndĭn'skē, Rus. vəsē'lyē kəndyēn'skē), 1866–1944, Russian abstract painter and theorist. Usually regarded as the originator of abstract art, Kandinsky abandoned a legal career for painting at 30 when he moved to Munich. In subsequent trips to Paris he came into contact with the art of Gauguin, the neo-impressionists, and the fauves. He then developed his ideas concerning the power of pure color and nonrepresentational painting. His first work in this mode was completed in 1910, the year in which he wrote an important theoretical study, *Concerning the Spiritual in Art* (1912, tr. 1947). In this work he examines the psychological effects of color with analogies between music and art. He exhibited with the BRÜCKE group, and with Franz Marc and others he founded the BLAUE REITER group. In 1915, Kandinsky returned to Moscow, where he taught and directed artistic activities. During the early 1920s his style evolved from riotous bursts of color in his "Improvisations" to more precise, geometrically arranged compositions. In 1921 he returned to Germany and the next year joined the BAUHAUS faculty. In 1926 he wrote *Point and Line to Plane* (tr. 1947), which includes an analysis of geometric forms in art. At the outset of World War II, he went to France, where he spent the rest of his life. Kandinsky is well represented in the Solomon R. Guggenheim Museum, New York City, and the Pasadena Art Museum, California. See his *Reminiscences* (1913; tr. in *Modern Artists on Art*, ed. by R. L. Herbert, 1964); biographies by Will Grohmann (tr. 1958) and Jacques Lassaigne (1964); study by Paul Overy (1969).

Kandy (kăn'dē), city (1970 pop. 91,942), capital of Central prov., Sri Lanka (Ceylon), on the Kandy Plateau. It is a mountain resort and the market center for an area producing tea, rubber, rice, and cacao. The main part of the city overlooks a scenic artificial lake built by the last king of Kandy in 1806. Near the lake is the Temple of the Tooth, said to house one of Buddha's teeth. This sacred relic, brought to Ceylon in the 4th cent. (reputedly by a princess who hid it in her hair), may have been destroyed (1560) by the Portuguese. The relic, which has made Kandy a pilgrimage and tourist attraction, is honored in the annual *Esala Perahera* pageant. Kandy is noted for such local handicrafts as reed and lacquer work and silver and brassware. Although the city's history dates back to the 5th cent. B.C., it did not become the capital of the Sinhalese kings until 1592. It was temporarily occupied by the Portuguese (16th cent.) and the Dutch (18th cent.); but, as a stronghold, it remained free until 1815, when the British captured it and exiled the last king to India. A palace, an art museum, and an Oriental library are remains of the royal period. In the suburb of Peradeniya is the Univ. of Sri Lanka (1942) and the famous botanical gardens, noted especially for their orchids.

Kane, Elisha Kent, 1820–57, American physician and arctic explorer, b. Philadelphia. Seeking adventure after medical school, Kane entered naval service and before he was 30 had seen many parts of the world and had served in the Mexican War. As senior medical officer he sailed (1850) on the first Grinnell expedition in search of the lost Franklin party. Kane's *U.S. Grinnell Expedition in Search of Sir John Franklin* (1853; repr. in part as *Adrift in the Arctic Ice Pack*, 1915) stirred such interest that he was able to organize and lead the second Grinnell expedition (1853–55). This expedition, of which I. I. HAYES was medical officer, passed northward through Smith Sound at the head of Baffin Bay, discovered and explored Kane Basin, and discovered Kennedy Channel beyond. Several sledging journeys were undertaken, on one of which a record of lat. 80°10'N was achieved. Humboldt Glacier was sighted, and scientific observations resulted in valuable new information on the arctic regions. Frozen in at Rensselaer Bay, the party abandoned ship, and Kane led a difficult retreat by land to Upernavik, Greenland. Kane's expedition had contributed more knowledge of Greenland than that of anyone before him. His health, never robust, was weakened by the rigors of his adventurous life, and he lived only long enough to complete his narrative of the second expedition, *Arctic Explorations* (1856), which had a tremendous sale. The spiritualist Margaret Fox claimed after his death that she had been his wife. Kane's *Love Life of Dr. Kane* (1866) contains many of his letters to Margaret Fox. See studies by Jeannette Mirsky (1954, repr. 1971), Oscar M. Villarejo (1965), and G. W. Corner (1972).

Kane, John, 1860–1934, American primitive painter, b. Scotland. He came to Pittsburgh at the age of 19, and worked for years as a day laborer, painting in his spare time. His paintings exhibit a delight in precise pattern and a sturdy disregard for academic conventions. Examples of his work are *Across the Strip* (Phillips Memorial Gall., Washington, D.C.) and his striking self-portrait (1929; Mus. of Modern Art, New York City). See his autobiography (1938).

Kane, Paul, 1810–71, Canadian painter, b. Ireland. Kane went to Toronto as a child. He studied art in the United States (1836–41) and in Europe (1841–45). After his return to Canada (1845) he made an extended journey into the Hudson's Bay Company territories of W Canada, traveling by snowshoe, horseback, and canoe to paint the Indians of the region. He returned to E Canada in 1848. Most of the paintings resulting from his journey are in the Royal Ontario Museum, Toronto, and in the Parliament buildings, Ottawa. His account of his journey appeared as *Wanderings of an Artist among the Indians of North America* (1859; new ed. with title *Paul Kane's Frontier*, incl. biography and catalog by J. R. Harper, 1971).

Kane Basin, 110 mi (177 km) long, part of the channel between NW Greenland and E Ellesmere Island. The Humboldt Glacier flows into the basin. It is named for the U.S. explorer Elisha K. Kane.

Kanellopoulos, Panayotis (pänäyô'tēs känälō'-pōōlōs), 1902–, Greek writer and political leader. A professor of sociology at the Univ. of Athens, he was active in World War II in the resistance and in the government-in-exile, in which he served as deputy premier and war minister. He held the premiership for a brief period in 1945. In the government of Constantine Karamanlis he was (1959–63) deputy premier, and he became leader of the National Radical Union after Karamanlis's electoral defeat and voluntary exile in 1963. In April, 1967, King Constantine II appointed him head of the caretaker cabinet charged with preparations for the May, 1967, elections; his rightist cabinet was soon toppled by George Papadopoulos in the coup of April 21, 1967. An outspoken opponent of authoritarianism, Kanellopoulos was subjected to arrest and house detention under the junta. After the junta was overthrown in 1974, he declined to serve in the new Karamanlis government or to take part in the elections. Kanellopoulos is the author of books, poems, and dramas in the fields of sociology and cultural philosophy.

Kanem (känēm'), former empire in Africa in the areas near Lake Chad that are now part of Chad and N Nigeria. The empire began in the 9th cent., when the Sefawa migrated to the area from the Sahara. The rulers eventually embraced Islam and extended their control to neighboring BORNU. After attacks by the Bulalas forced the rulers of Kanem to shift their capital to Bornu (c.1380), Bornu gradually emerged as the center of a revitalized empire of which Kanem became a protectorate.

Kaneohe (kä'nāōhā), uninc. city (1970 pop. 29,903), Honolulu co., Hawaii, on the east coast of Oahu, on Kaneohe Bay. Once the site of a pineapple plantation and cannery, it is now a lovely residential seaside community. A state mental hospital and a missile-tracking station are there. The U.S. Kaneohe Marine Corps Air Base is nearby; it was attacked by the Japanese on Dec. 7, 1941. Many ancient fishponds built by Hawaiian chiefs are in the area.

Kaneohe Bay, Hawaii, on the east coast of Oahu, protected by coral reefs and dotted with islands. The shores of the bay are rimmed with ancient fishponds built by the Hawaiian chiefs. A U.S. marine corps air base is there.

Kangar (käng"är'), town (1970 pop. 8,757), capital of Perlis state, Malaysia, central Malay Peninsula, on the Perlis River. It is a port and the center of a rice-growing region.

kangaroo, name for a variety of hopping MARSUPIALS, or pouched mammals, of the family Macropodidae, found in Australia, Tasmania, and New Guinea. The term is applied especially to the large kangaroos of the genus *Macropus*. Kangaroos have powerful hind legs designed for leaping, long feet, short forelimbs, and long muscular tails. The hind legs are also used to deliver blows at enemies when the animal is cornered; the feet are sharply clawed. The tail serves as a balance when the animal leaps and as a prop when it stands; the usual posture is bipedal. The handlike forepaws are used for grasping. As in most marsupials, females have a pouch surrounding the teats. Kangaroos feed on grass and other vegetation; they are the chief grazers of the Australian plains. Day-active animals, they move about in herds called mobs and sleep on the ground at night. Males are called boomers, females flyers; the young are called joeys. The single young is born in an immature state after a gestation period of about 40 days and is suckled in the mother's pouch for about six months. After it begins to graze it returns frequently to the pouch for shelter and transport until it is too large to be carried. The largest kangaroo, and largest of all marsupials, is the great red kangaroo, *M. rufus*, which inhabits the inland plains of Australia. Males of this species may be over 7 ft (210 cm) tall and weigh over 200 lbs (90 kg). They are bright maroon in color, with white faces and underparts. Females, called blue flyers, are blue-gray; smaller and faster than the males, they may achieve speeds of 30 mi (48 km) per hr. The great gray kangaroo, *M. canguru*, is almost as large; it is found in open forest areas of E and W Australia and in Tasmania. A related kangaroo, *M. robustus*, is known as the wallaroo and inhabits rocky hills throughout most of the continent. Smaller, but quite similar in appearance and behavior, are members of the kangaroo family called wallabies and pademelons, of which there are many species, classified in several genera. Some of these are plains dwellers, others live among rocks or in scrub country; most are about the size of a rabbit. Of similar size are the tree and rat kangaroos. Tree kangaroos, species of the genus *Dendrolagus*, are the only arboreal members of the family. Found in the rain forests of New Guinea and N Australia, they climb well and can leap from branch to branch. Rat kangaroos are omnivorous animals of ratlike appearance. They feed largely on roots and fungi; members of many species live in burrows. They are classified in several genera and are distributed throughout the Australian region. Because many types of kangaroo have valuable hides, and because they compete with domestic livestock for grazing land, kangaroos have been extensively hunted and are now extremely reduced in numbers. They are classified in the phylum CHORDATA, subphylum Vertebrata, class Mammalia, order Marsupialia, family Macropodidae.

Kangaroo Island, small island, South Australia, S Australia, at the entrance to Gulf St. Vincent. It is 90 mi (145 km) long and 34 mi (55 km) wide. The chief products are barley, sheep, salt, gypsum, and eucalyptus oil. At its west end is Flinders Chase, a large reservation for native flora and fauna. There are many summer resorts. Kingscote (1971 pop. 2,665) is the principal settlement.

kangaroo mouse: see KANGAROO RAT.

kangaroo rat, small, jumping desert rodent, genus *Dipodomys*, related to the POCKET MOUSE. There are about 20 kangaroo rat species, found throughout the arid regions of Mexico and the S and W United States. Kangaroo rats have large, mouselike heads with big eyes, external fur-lined cheek pouches for food storage, and extremely long, tufted tails. In many species the tail is longer than the combined head and body length. The total length, including the tail, is 10 to 15 in. (25–37.5 cm), depending on the species. The front limbs are very short and the back limbs extremely long and stiltlike. The animal moves by long leaps, like a kangaroo, using its tail for balance and as a rudder for turning at high speeds. Kangaroo rats have long silky fur, pale brown above and white beneath, with black and white tail tufts and black face markings. Solitary, nocturnal creatures, they live in burrows by day and forage at night for seeds, grass, and tubers. Active hoarders, they sometimes dry their food in shallow pits just below the surface of the ground, then dig it up and store it in their burrows. Like a number of other desert animals, the kangaroo rat has physiological mechanisms for conserving the water that it obtains from food or produces metabollically, so that it does not need to drink. A related genus, *Microdipodops*, is called the kangaroo mouse, or dwarf kangaroo rat. It is about 6 in. (15 cm) in total length and is found in the Great Basin of the W United States. Kangaroo rats are classified in the phylum CHORDATA, subphylum Vertebrata, class Mammalia, order Rodentia, family Heteromyidae.

K'ang Hsi (käng shē), 1654–1722, 2d emperor of the Ch'ing dynasty of China (1661–1722). He extended Manchu control and promoted learning in the arts and sciences. K'ang Hsi conquered the feudatories of S China (1673–81), took Taiwan (1683), established China's first diplomatic relations with Russia (1689), and pushed the Ölöds from Outer Mongolia (1697). Repeated tax reductions, attention to water conservation, and imperial tours of inspection earned him a reputation for benevolence. Under his patronage, a Ming history, two monumental dictionaries, and a literary encyclopedia were completed. He employed Jesuit missionaries to map the empire and to teach mathematics and astronomy. See study by J. D. Spence (1974).

Kanghwa or **Kanghoa** (both: käng'hwä'), island, 163 sq mi (422 sq km), off SW South Korea, in the Yellow Sea. Farming and fishing are important occupations. Kanghwa was briefly the site of the Korean capital in the 13th cent. It was early fortified as an outer defense for Seoul and was stormed by the French in 1866 and by the Americans in 1871.

Kangnung (käng'no͝ong'), city (1970 est. pop. 74,500), NE South Korea, a port on the Sea of Japan. It is also an agricultural center and is famed for its beautiful scenery.

Kang Teh: see PU YI, HENRY.

K'ang-ting or **Kangting** (both: käng-dĭng), city, W Szechwan prov., China, in the Kan-tzu Tibetan Autonomous Region. It is a transportation center on the main road from Ch'eng-tu to Lhasa, Tibet. Until 1950 it was the capital of Sikang prov.

Kangwon (käng'wŭn'), province (1970 pop. 1,873,908), N South Korea. CHUNCHON is the capital. The 38th parallel that divided Korea after World War II ran through Kangwon, but after the Korean War truce of 1953 much of the province returned from North to South Korean rule. Mining, farming, and fishing are chief economic activities in the province.

K'ang Yu-wei (käng yo͞o-wē), 1858–1927, Chinese philosopher and reform movement leader. He was a leading philosopher of the new text school of Confucianism, which regarded Confucius as a utopian political reformer. K'ang first gained fame in 1895 when he sent a memorial to the emperor unsuccessfully urging continuation of the war with Japan, rejection of the Treaty of Shimonoseki, and adoption of extensive administrative reforms. That same year with LIANG CH'I-CH'AO he founded a reform newspaper and a reform organization, but both were quickly suppressed (1896). Enthusiasm for his ideas spread, however, and several provincial reform associations were founded (1896–97). Again confronted with foreign pressure for concessions, Emperor KUANG HSU (1898) summoned K'ang to Peking and asked him to draw up reform plans. In a series of decrees known as the "hundred days' reform," the emperor changed the civil service examination system to include essays on current affairs, established Peking Univ. as well as western-style provincial schools, abolished many sinecure posts, and revised administrative regulations. Backed by conservative officials, Dowager Empress TZ'U HSI imprisoned the emperor and rescinded most of the reforms. K'ang fled to Japan and spent the years before the 1911 revolution working for constitutional monarchy. He and Liang were bitterly opposed to the T'ung-meng-hui, an anti-Manchu revolutionary party founded in 1905 under the leadership of SUN YAT-SEN. After the revolution, K'ang remained in opposition to the republican government, participating (1917) in an unsuccessful attempt to restore the last Ch'ing emperor, PU YI. See M. E. Cameron, *The Reform Movement in China, 1898–1912* (1931, repr. 1963); biography ed. and tr. by Lo Jung-pang (1967).

Kanhsien: see KAN-CHOU, China.

Kaniapiskau (kănyəpĭs'kō''), river, c.575 mi (930 km) long, issuing from Kaniapiskau Lake, NE Que., Canada. It flows generally NW past Fort Mackenzie to the Koksoak River, which then flows NE to Ungava Bay at Fort Chimo. The river's lower course drains part of the iron belt of N Quebec. An alternate spelling is Caniapiscau.

Kanin (kä'nyĭn), peninsula, N European USSR, projecting into the Barents Sea between the White Sea (in the west) and Chesha (Cheshskaya) Bay (in the east). Its northernmost cape is called Kanin Nos. The native Nentsy (Samoyed) people engage in fishing, hunting, and reindeer raising.

Kanishka (kənĭsh'kə), fl. A.D. c.120, king of GANDHARA. He was the most powerful and renowned ruler of the Kushan dynasty, one of the five tribes of the Yüeh-chih who had divided (1st cent. B.C.) Bactria among them. Earlier Kushan kings had extended their dominion into N India, and Kanishka ruled over an empire that stretched from the Pamirs to Bengal. His capital was at Peshawar. A patron of Buddhism, he built many Buddhist monuments, helped found the Gandharan school of sculpture, and encouraged the spread of Buddhism to central Asia.

Kankakee (kăngkəkē'), city (1970 pop. 30,944), seat of Kankakee co., E Ill., on the Kankakee River; inc. 1855. It is an industrial and shipping center for a farm area. Kankakee's varied manufactures include ranges, water heaters, furniture, tractors, farm and garden equipment, biochemicals, and pharmaceuticals. Limestone quarries are nearby. A state mental hospital, a state park, Olivet Nazarene College, and a junior college are in the city.

Kankan (känkän', käNkäN'), city (1964 est. pop. 50,000), E Guinea, a port on the Milo River, a tributary of the Niger. It is the commercial center for a farm area where rice, sesame, maize, tomatoes, oranges, mangoes, and pineapples are grown. Diamonds are mined, and the national diamond exchange is there. Bricks and fruit juices are made in Kankan, which also has a tomato canning factory and a sawmill. The city is connected by rail with Conakry. Kankan was probably founded in the 18th cent. as a trade center that linked the Sudan region with the forest belt and the Atlantic coast. SAMORY began (c.1866) his career as a military leader and empire builder in the Kankan district, and in 1873 took Kankan itself. The French occupied the city in 1891. Kankan has a polytechnic institute and a center for research on rice cultivation.

Kanko: see HAMHUNG, North Korea.

Kannanlahti: see KANDALAKSHA, USSR.

Kannapolis (kənăp'əlĭs), uninc. city (1970 pop. 36,293), Cabarrus and Rowan counties, W central N.C.; founded c.1905. It is a planned company town owned by Cannon Mills, known for its production of household linens.

Kannauj (kənouj'), town (1971 pop. 28,189), Uttar Pradesh state, N central India, on the Ganges River. It is a market center for food grains, oilseed, fruit, perfume, and rose water. An ancient town, Kannauj was a brilliant cultural center and the capital of Harsha's empire in the 7th cent. In the 9th cent. it became the capital of the Pratihara empire. During that period, it was famous for its poets. Kannauj declined after being conquered by Turkish tribes under Mahmud of Ghazni in 1018.

Kano (kä'nō), family or school of Japanese painters. **Kano Masanobu,** c.1434–c.1530, the forerunner of the school, was attached to the shogun Yoshimasa's court. He painted landscapes, birds, and figure pieces, chiefly in ink with occasional touches of pale tints. His work is Japanese in spirit, reflecting the influence of Chinese art in technique and style. Only a few of his works survive. His son, **Kano Motonobu,** c.1476–1559, was the actual founder of the school and one of the foremost artists of Japan. Into Chinese-style ink painting he introduced heavily stressed outlines and bold decorative patterns. His screen paintings served well as architectural decorations and appealed to the tastes of the warrior class. Many of his screen paintings are still preserved in temples of Kyoto. **Kano Eitoku,** 1543–90, grandson of Motonobu, painted screens with landscapes and figures and decorated the interiors of the royal palaces. His art differs from that of the earlier Kano painters; it is less precise and is characterized by energy, ease, and inventiveness. His screen paintings were done in brilliant colors against a ground of gold leaf. He had many pupils and imitators, but most of his own work has perished. **Kano Tanyu,** 1602–74, first known as Morinobu, was the grandson of Eitoku and was called the reviver of the Kano school. He was appointed official painter of the Tokugawa government (1621) and established a school of his own. He became one of the most vigorous and versatile of Japanese painters. He worked in both Edo and Kyoto, decorating castles and royal palaces. Although much of his work has since disappeared, some screen paintings are still preserved at Nijo Castle in Kyoto and at Nagoya Castle. His *Confucius and Disciples* is at the Museum of Fine Arts, Boston. See S. E. Lee, *A History of Far Eastern Art* (1964).

Kano (kä'nō), city (1971 est. pop. 357,000), N Nigeria. It is the trade and shipping center for an agricultural region where cotton, cattle, and about half of Nigeria's groundnuts are raised. Kano is the major industrial center of N Nigeria; peanut flour and oil, cotton textiles, steel furniture, processed meat, concrete blocks, shoes, and soap are the chief manufactures. The city has long been known for its leatherwork; its tanned goatskins were sent (from about 15th cent.) to N Africa and were known in Europe as morocco leather. One of the seven HAUSA city-states, Kano's written history dates back to A.D. 999, when the city was already several hundred years old. It was a cultural, handicraft, and commercial center, with wide trade contacts in W and N Africa. In the early 16th cent. Kano accepted Islam, and c.1600 it was temporarily held by the Muslim state of BORNU. Kano reached the height of its power in the 17th and 18th cent. In 1809 it was conquered by the FULANI, but it soon regained its leading commercial position. In 1903 a British force under Frederick LUGARD captured the city. In Kano are Abdullahi Bayero College (1960; part of Ahmadu Bello Univ., Zari); Gidan Makama Museum, with examples of local art; and the palace of the emir, the former ruler of the Kano city-state.

Kanonji (känōn'jē), city (1970 pop. 43,162), Kagawa prefecture, E Shikoku, Japan, on the Hiuchi Sea. It is a religious center and agricultural market noted for its Kanonji (Buddhist) Temple.

Kanoya (känō'yä), city (1970 pop. 66,995), Kagoshima prefecture, S Kyushu, Japan, on the Osumi Peninsula. It is an agricultural market with a silk-rayon weaving industry.

Kanpur (kän'po͝or), city (1971 pop. 1,151,975), Uttar Pradesh state, N central India, on the Ganges River. A major industrial center, it produces chemicals, textiles, leather goods, and food products. It is also a transportation hub. An agricultural college is nearby. Kanpur was a village until its cession to the British in 1801 by the Nawab of Oudh. During the INDIAN MUTINY (1857), Nana Sahib, whose claim to a pension had been rejected, slaughtered the entire British garrison, including women and children.

Kansa Indians (kăn'sô), people whose language belongs to the Siouan branch of the Hokan-Siouan linguistic stock (see AMERICAN INDIAN LANGUAGES), also known as the Kansas or Kaw Indians. Closely related to the OSAGE INDIANS, from whom they separated probably not long before the settlers met them, they shared the typical Plains culture and began farming only after the buffalo had disappeared from the Plains. They were at the mouth of the Kansas River when traders reached them, but had moved westward to the mouth of the Saline River by 1815, when the United States made its first treaty with them. By treaties of 1825 and 1846, the Kansa Indians ceded most of their lands and accepted a reservation on the Neosho River at Council Grove, where they lived until 1873. They were then placed on a new reservation in Oklahoma, next to the Osage tribe. Their lands were allotted to them on an individual basis rather than to the whole tribe. See W. E. Unrau, *The Kansa Indians* (1971).

Kansas, state (1970 pop. 2,249,071), 82,264 sq mi (213,064 sq km), central United States, admitted to the Union in 1861 as the 34th state. TOPEKA is the capital; other major cities are WICHITA (the largest city in the state) and KANSAS CITY (adjoining Kansas City, Mo.). Almost rectangular in shape, Kansas is bounded on the N by Nebraska, on the E by Missouri (the Missouri River forms the boundary for a short distance), on the S by Oklahoma, and on the W by Colorado. The geographical center of the United States (exclusive of Alaska and Hawaii) is located in Kansas between Smith Center and Lebanon. Part of the GREAT PLAINS, Kansas is famous for its seemingly endless fields of ripe golden wheat. The land rises more than 3,000 ft (914 m) from the eastern alluvial prairies of Kansas to its western semiarid high plains, which stretch toward the foothills of the Rocky Mts. The rise is so gradual, however, that

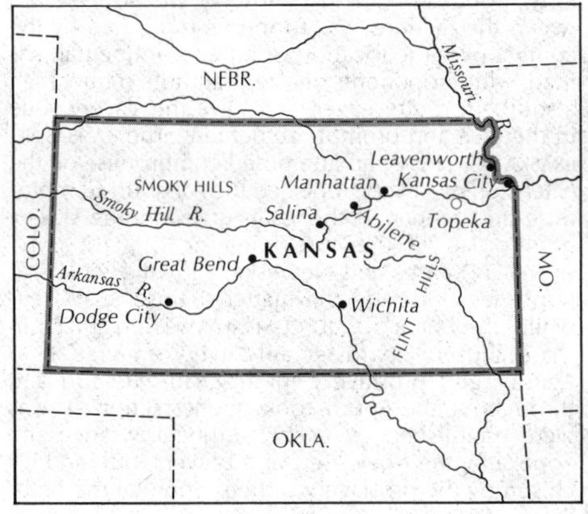

it is imperceptible, although the terrains of the east and the west are markedly different. The state is drained by the Kansas and Arkansas rivers, both of which generally run from west to east. The average annual rainfall of 27 in. (69 cm) is not evenly distributed: the eastern prairies receive up to 40 in. (102 cm) of rain, while the western plains average 17 in. (43 cm). Occasional dust storms plague farmers and ranchers in the west. The climate is continental, with wide extremes—cold winters with blizzards and hot summers with tornadoes. Floods also wreak havoc in the state; hence, flood-control projects, such as dams, reservoirs, and levees, are a major undertaking. Kansas was once primarily an agricultural state, but manufacturing has surpassed agriculture as a source of income. However, farming is still important to the state's economy, and Kansas is the nation's leading producer of wheat and second largest producer of sorghum for grain. Corn and hay are also major crops. Cattle and calves are raised on the state's abundant grazing lands and constitute the single most-valuable agricultural item. Meat-packing and dairy industries are major economic activities, and the Kansas City stockyards are among the nation's largest. Food processing ranked as the state's third largest industry in the early 1970s. The two leading industries are the manufacture of transportation equipment and of chemicals. Wichita is a leader in the aircraft industry, especially in the production of private planes. Other important manufactured items are petroleum and coal products and nonelectrical machinery. The state is a major producer of crude petroleum and has large reserves of natural gas and helium. Kansas was once a great shallow sea, and salt deposits in commercially profitable quantities still remain. When the Spanish explorer Francisco Vásquez de Coronado visited (1541) the Kansas area in his search for Quivira, a fabled kingdom of riches, the area was occupied by various Plains Indian tribes, notably the Kansa Indians, the Wichita Indians, and the Pawnee Indians. Another Spanish explorer, Juan de Oñate, penetrated the region in 1601. A result of Spanish entry into the region was the introduction of the horse, which revolutionized the life of the Plains Indians. While not actually exploring the Kansas area, Robert Cavelier, sieur de La Salle, claimed (c.1682) for France all territory drained by the Mississippi River, including Kansas. French traders were active among the Indians during most of the 18th cent. By the Treaty of Paris of 1763 (see PARIS, TREATY OF) ending the French and Indian Wars, France ceded the territory of W Louisiana (including Kansas) to Spain. In 1800, Spain secretly retroceded the territory to France, from whom the United States acquired it in the Louisiana Purchase in 1803. The region was little known, however, and subsequent explorations to include Kansas were the Lewis and Clark expedition (1803-6), the Arkansas River journey of Zebulon M. Pike in 1806, and the scientific expedition of Stephen H. Long in 1819. Most of the territory that eventually became Kansas was in an area known as the "Great American Desert," considered unsuitable for white settlement because of its apparent barrenness. In the 1830s the region was designated permanent Indian country, and northern and eastern tribes were relocated there (see INDIAN TERRITORY). Forts were constructed for frontier defense and for the protection of the growing trade along the Santa Fe Trail, which crossed Kansas. Fort Leavenworth was established in 1827, Fort Scott in 1842, and Fort Riley in 1853. Kansas, at this time mainly a region to be crossed on the way to California and Oregon, was organized as a territory in 1854. Its settlement, however, was spurred not so much by natural westward expansion as by the determination of both proslavery and antislavery factions to achieve a majority population in the territory. The struggle between the factions was further complicated by the conflict over the location of a transcontinental railroad, with proponents of a central route (rather than a southern route) eager to resolve the slavery issue in the area and promote settlement. The KANSAS-NEBRASKA ACT (1854), an attempted compromise on the extension of slavery, repealed the Missouri Compromise and reopened the issue of extending slavery north of lat. 36°30′ by providing for SQUATTER SOVEREIGNTY in Kansas and Nebraska, allowing settlers of territories to decide the matter themselves. Meanwhile, the EMIGRANT AID COMPANY was organized in Massachusetts to foster antislavery emigration to Kansas, and proslavery interests in Missouri and throughout the South took counteraction. Towns were established by each faction—Lawrence and Topeka by the free staters and Leavenworth and Atchison by the proslavery settlers. Soon all the problems attendant upon organizing a territory for statehood became subsidiary to the single issue of slavery. The first elections in 1854 and 1855 were won by the proslavery group; armed Missourians intimidated voters and election officials and stuffed the ballot boxes. Andrew H. Reeder was appointed the first territorial governor in 1854. The first territorial legislature ousted (1855) all free-state members, secured the removal of Gov. Reeder, moved the capital to Lecompton, and adopted proslavery statutes. In retaliation the abolitionists set up a rival government at Topeka in Oct., 1855. Violence soon came to the territory. The murder of a free-state man in Nov., 1855, led to the so-called Wakarusa War, a bloodless series of encounters along the Wakarusa River. The intervention of the new governor, Wilson Shannon, kept proslavery men from attacking Lawrence. However, civil war ultimately turned the territory into "bleeding Kansas." On May 21, 1856, proslavery groups and armed Missourians known as "Border Ruffians" raided Lawrence. A few days later a band led by the abolitionist crusader John Brown murdered five proslavery men in the Pottawatomie massacre. Guerrilla warfare between free-state men called Jayhawkers and proslavery bands—both sides abetted by desperadoes and opportunists—terrorized the land. After a new governor, John W. Geary, persuaded a large group of "Border Ruffians" to return to Missouri, the violence subsided. The Lecompton legislature met in 1857 to make preparations for convening a constitutional convention. Gov. Geary resigned after it became clear that free elections would not be held to approve a new constitution. Robert J. Walker was appointed governor, and a convention held at Lecompton drafted a constitution. Only that part of the resulting proslavery constitution dealing with slavery was submitted to the electorate, and the question was drafted to favor the proslavery group. Free-state men refused to participate in the election with the result that the constitution was overwhelmingly approved. Despite the dubious validity of the Lecompton constitution, President Buchanan recommended (1858) that Congress accept it and approve statehood for the territory. Instead, Congress returned it for another territorial vote. The proslavery group boycotted the election, and the constitution was rejected. Lawrence became de facto capital of the troubled territory until after the Wyandotte Constitution (framed in 1859 and totally forbidding slavery) was accepted by Congress. The Kansas conflict and the issue of statehood for the territory became a national issue and figured in the 1860 Republican party platform. Kansas became a state in 1861, with the capital at Topeka. Charles Robinson was the first governor and James H. Lane, an active free-stater during the 1850s, one of the U.S. Senators. In the Civil War, Kansas fought with the North and suffered the highest rate of fatal casualties of any state in the Union. Further hardships developed as Kansas was scourged by Indian raids in the west and border warfare in the east, climaxed by the burning of Lawrence in 1863 by the Confederate William C. Quantrill and his guerrilla band. With peace came the development of the prairie lands. The construction of railroads made cowtowns such as ABILENE and DODGE CITY, with their cowboys, saloons, and frontier marshals, the shipping point for large herds of cattle driven overland from Texas. The buffalo herds disappeared (today some buffalo roam in state parks and game preserves), and cattle took their place. Pioneer homesteaders, adjusting to life on the timberless prairie and living in sod houses, suffered privation. In 1874, Mennonite emigrants from Russia brought the Turkey Red variety of winter wheat to Kansas. This wheat was instrumental in making Kansas the Wheat State as winter wheat replaced spring wheat on an ever-increasing scale. Corn, too, soon became a major money crop. Agricultural production was periodically disrupted by national depressions and natural disasters. Repeated and prolonged droughts accompanied by dust storms, occasional grasshopper invasions, and floods caused severe economic dislocation. Mortgages often weighed heavily on farmers, and discontent was expressed in farmer support of radical farm organizations and third-party movements, such as the GRANGER MOVEMENT, GREENBACK PARTY, and POPULIST PARTY. Tax relief, better regulation of interest rates, and curbs on the power of railroads were sought by these organizations. Twice in the 1890s, Populist-Democrats were elected to the governorship. As conditions improved, Kansas returned largely to its allegiance to the Republican party and gained a reputation as a conservative stronghold with a bent for moral reform, indicated in the state's strong support of prohibition; laws against the sale of liquor remained on the books in Kansas from 1880 to 1949. Over the years improved agricultural methods and machines increased crop yield. Irrigation proved practicable in some areas, and winter wheat and alfalfa could be cultivated in dry regions. Wheat production greatly expanded during World War I, but the end of the war brought financial difficulties. During the 1920s and 30s, Kansas was faced with labor unrest and the economic hardships of the depression. As part of the Dust Bowl, Kansas sustained serious land erosion during the long drought of the 1930s. Erosion led to the implementation of conservation and reclamation projects, particularly in the northern and western parts of the state. In 1924 an effort of the Ku Klux Klan to gain political control was fought by William Allen White, editor of the Emporia *Gazette*, who supported many liberal causes. Alfred M. Landon, elected governor in 1932, was one of the few Republican candidates in the country to win election in the midst of the sweeping Democratic victory that year. He was nominated as the Republican presidential candidate in 1936. During World War II agriculture thrived and industry expanded rapidly. The food-processing industry grew substantially, the cement industry enjoyed a major revival, and the aircraft industry boomed. After the war agricultural prosperity once again declined when the state was hit by a severe drought and grasshopper invasion in 1948. Prosperity returned briefly during the Korean War, but afterwards farm surpluses and insufficient world markets combined to make the state's tremendous agricultural ability part of the national "farm problem." Kansas has become increasingly industrialized and urbanized, however, and industrial production has surpassed farm production in economic importance. Flood damage in the state, especially after a major flood in 1951, spurred the construction of dams (such as the Tuttle Creek, Milford, and Wilson dams) on major Kansas rivers, and their reservoirs have vastly increased water recreational facilities for Kansans. Points of historical interest in Kansas include the boyhood home of Dwight D. Eisenhower and the Eisenhower Library in Abilene. In Medicine Lodge is the home of Carry Nation, who, at the turn of the century, became convinced of her divine appointment to destroy the saloons; her home there is now a museum. Fort Leavenworth is the site of a large Federal penitentiary. Government in Kansas is based on the constitution of 1859, adopted just before Kansas attained statehood. An elected governor heads the executive and serves a term of two years. The legislature has a house of representatives and a senate, with the 125 members of the house elected for two-year terms and the 40 members of the senate elected for four-year terms. Kansas is represented in the U.S. Congress by five Representatives and two Senators and has seven electoral votes in presidential elections. Although Kansas has long been a Republican stronghold, a Democrat, Robert Docking, was elected governor in 1966 and was reelected in 1968, 1970, and 1972. In 1974, Robert F. Bennett, a Republican, was elected governor. Institutions of higher learning include the Univ. of Kansas, at Lawrence; Kansas State Univ., at Manhattan; Wichita State Univ., at Wichita; and Washburn Univ. of Topeka, at Topeka. See Paul Gates, *Fifty Million Acres: Conflicts over Kansas Land Policy, 1854-1890* (1954); W. F. Zornow, *Kansas: a History of the Jayhawk State* (1957); A. E. Castel, *A Frontier State at War: Kansas, 1861-1865* (1958); R. S. Brownlee, *Gray Ghosts of the Confederacy* (1960); R. W. Baughman, *Kansas in Maps* (1961); W. T. Nugent, *The Tolerant Populists: Kansas Populism and Nativism* (1963); J. R. Cook, *The Border and the Buffalo* (1967); Federal Writers' Project, *Kansas: a Guide to the Sunflower State* (1939, repr. 1973).

Kansas or **Kaw,** river, 170 mi (274 km) long, formed by the junction of the Smoky Hill and Republican rivers in NE Kansas and flowing E to the Missouri River at Kansas City; the system drains parts of Kansas, Nebraska, and Colorado. Heavy floods (especially in 1951) on the Kansas and its tributaries caused great damage in this primarily agricultural region. Since 1954 numerous dams, reservoirs, and levees have been built.

Kansas, University of, mainly at Lawrence; coeducational; state supported; chartered 1864, opened 1866 with aid from the philanthropist Amos A. Lawrence. Its school of medicine is partly at Kansas City. The university's library collections and the Dyche Museum of Natural History are noteworthy.

Kansas City, two adjacent cities of the same name, one (1970 pop. 168,213), seat of Wyandotte co., NE Kansas (inc. 1859), the other (1970 pop. 507,187),

Clay, Jackson, and Platte counties, NW Mo. (inc. 1850). They are at the junction of the Missouri and Kansas (or Kaw) rivers and together form a large commercial, industrial, and cultural center. They are a port of entry, the focus of many transportation lines, and a huge market for wheat, hay, poultry, and seed. Both cities have large stockyards, grain elevators, food-processing establishments (especially for meat-packing and flour milling), oil refineries, steel mills, soap and farm-machinery factories, automobile-assembly plants, and railroad shops. The area was the starting place of many Western expeditions; the Santa Fe and Oregon trails passed through there. Several historic settlements of the early 19th cent. (including Westport) were predecessors to the present-day cities. Kansas City, Kansas, is the seat of two junior colleges, two theological seminaries, the Univ. of Kansas Medical Center, and a state school for the blind (est. 1868). It has an agricultural hall of fame, a Shawnee mission (1839), and several museums. A 19th-century Indian cemetery there is being incorporated into a unique center city mall. Kansas City Mo., with its fine parks and residential districts, is the site of the noted Nelson Art Gallery and the Atkins Museum of Fine Arts. Among its educational institutions are the Univ. of Missouri-Kansas City, Avila College, Park College, Rockhurst College, Kansas City Art Institute, a college of osteopathy and surgery, a conservatory of music, two junior colleges, and a number of theological schools. The city has a philharmonic orchestra and several theaters. The Kansas City *Star* is nationally known; it was founded (1880) by William Rockhill Nelson and headed by him until 1915. Extensive flood damage in 1951 led to several river-control projects in the region. Richards-Gebaur Air Force Base is to the south. See J. H. McDowell, *Building a City: A Detailed History of Kansas City, Kansas* (1969).

Kansas-Nebraska Act, bill that became law on May 30, 1854, by which the U.S. Congress established the territories of Kansas and Nebraska. By 1854 the organization of the vast Platte and Kansas river countries W of Iowa and Missouri was overdue. As an isolated issue territorial organization of this area was no problem. It was, however, irrevocably bound to the bitter sectional controversy over the extension of slavery into the territories and was further complicated by conflict over the location of the projected TRANS-CONTINENTAL RAILROAD. Under no circumstances did proslavery Congressmen want a free territory (Kansas) W of Missouri. Because the West was expanding rapidly, territorial organization, despite these difficulties, could no longer be postponed. Four attempts to organize a single territory for this area had already been defeated in Congress, largely because of Southern opposition to the MISSOURI COMPROMISE. Although the last of these attempts to organize the area had nearly been successful, Stephen A. DOUGLAS, chairman of the Senate Committee on Territories, decided to offer territorial legislation making concessions to the South. Douglas's motives have remained largely a matter of speculation. Various historians have emphasized Douglas's desire for the Presidency, his wish to cement the bonds of the Democratic party, his interest in expansion and railroad building, or his desire to activate the unimpressive Pierce administration. The bill he reported in Jan., 1854, contained the provision that the question of slavery should be left to the decision of the territorial settlers themselves. This was the famous principle that Douglas now called "popular sovereignty" (see SQUATTER SOVEREIGNTY), though actually it had been enunciated four years earlier in the COMPROMISE OF 1850. In its final form Douglas's bill provided for the creation of two new territories—Kansas and Nebraska—instead of one. The obvious inference—at least to Missourians—was that the first would be slave, the second free. The Kansas-Nebraska Act flatly contradicted the provisions of the Missouri Compromise (under which slavery would have been barred from both territories); indeed, an amendment was added specifically repealing that compromise. This aspect of the bill in particular enraged the antislavery forces, but after three months of bitter debate in Congress, Douglas, backed by President Pierce and the Southerners, saw it adopted. Its effects were anything but reassuring to those who had hoped for a peaceful solution. The squatter sovereignty provision caused both proslavery and antislavery forces to marshal strength and exert full pressure to determine the "popular" decision in Kansas in their own favor, using groups such as the EMIGRANT AID COMPANY. The result was the tragedy of "bleeding" Kansas. Northerners and Southerners were aroused to such passions that sectional division reached a point that precluded reconciliation. A new political organization, the REPUBLICAN PARTY, was founded by opponents of the bill, and the United States was propelled toward the Civil War. See P. O. Ray, *The Repeal of the Missouri Compromise* (1909, repr. 1965).

Kansas State University, at Manhattan; coeducational; land-grant and state supported; chartered and opened 1863.

Kansu or **Kan-su** (both: kăn'so͞o, gän'so͞o'), province (1968 est. pop. 13,000,000), NW China. The capital is LAN-CHOU. Kansu is bordered by the Mongolian People's Republic on the north. Its mountains include part of the Nan Shan range and an extension of the Kunlun. The loess soil is very fertile, but rainfall is inadequate and irrigation and land reclamation programs have had to be developed. Winter wheat, kaoliang, millet, corn, rice, cotton, and tobacco are grown, especially in the Huang Ho (Yellow River) and Wei River valleys. Large state farms have been established in the province. Livestock (cows, sheep, goats, horses, and camels) are raised in the mountainous areas. Kansu's mineral resources include coal, copper, gold, and large deposits of iron ore and oil; two important oil fields are in the province. Lan-chou is a flourishing industrial center, with one of the largest oil refineries in the country, and Yu-men is an oil center; other towns are developing rapidly. Roads and railways have been extensively improved. Lan-chou is an important transportation hub; the Lan-chou-Sinkiang RR crosses the province, and the Lan-chou-Peking RR has a connection through Mongolia to the USSR. Long isolated from the center of Chinese power, the Kansu area has traditionally been independent of all but the strongest central governments. After the 13th cent., Muslim strength grew, and fierce Muslim rebellions often plagued the central government. Today the province's strategic importance is enhanced by its control of communications into Sinkiang, Mongolia, and the USSR. Although Mandarin Chinese comprise most of the population, there are 11 major minorities, of which Muslims and Mongols are the largest. Kansu's boundaries have been changed several times in recent years. The former province of Ninghsia was joined to it in 1954, then detached in 1958 and reconstituted as an autonomous region. In the 1969-70 redistricting, Kansu received a portion of W Inner Mongolian Autonomous Region.

Kant, Immanuel (ĭmăn'o͞oĕl känt), 1724–1804, German metaphysician, one of the greatest figures in philosophy, b. Königsberg (now Kaliningrad, USSR), where he was educated. He tutored in several families and after 1755 lectured at the Univ. of Königsberg in philosophy and various sciences. He became professor of logic and metaphysics in 1770 and achieved wide renown through his writings and teachings. His early work, reflecting his studies of Christian Wolff and G. W. Leibniz, was followed by a period of great development culminating in the *Kritik der reinen Vernunft* (1781, tr. *Critique of Pure Reason*). This work inaugurated his so-called "critical period"—the period of his major writings. The more important among these writings were *Prolegomena zu einer jeden künftigen Metaphysik* (1783, tr. *Prolegomena to Any Future Metaphysics*), *Grundlegung zur Metaphysik der Sitten* (1785, tr. *Foundations of the Metaphysics of Morals*), *Kritik der praktischen Vernunft* (1788, tr. *Critique of Practical Reason*), and *Kritik der Urteilskraft* (1790, tr. *Critique of Judgment*). His *Religion innerhalb der Grenzen der blossen Vernunft* (1793, tr. *Religion within the Limits of Reason Alone*) provoked a government order to desist from further publications on religion. According to Kant, his reading of David Hume awakened him from his dogmatic slumber and set him on the road to becoming the "critical philosopher," whose position can be seen as a synthesis of the Leibniz-Wolffian rationalism and the Humean skepticism. Kant termed his basic insight into the nature of knowledge "the Copernican revolution in philosophy." Instead of assuming that our ideas, to be true, must conform to an external reality independent of our knowing, Kant proposed that objective reality is known only insofar as it conforms to the essential structure of the knowing mind. He maintained that objects of experience—phenomena—may be known, but that things lying beyond the realm of possible experience—noumena, or things-in-themselves—are unknowable, although their existence is a necessary presupposition. Phenomena that can be perceived in the pure forms of sensibility, space, and time must, if they are to be understood, possess the characteristics that constitute our categories of understanding. Those categories, which include causality and substance, are the source of the structure of phenomenal experience. The scientist, therefore, may be sure that the natural events he observes are knowable in terms of the categories. Man's field of knowledge, thus emancipated from Humean skepticism, is nevertheless limited to the world of phenomena. All theoretical attempts to know things-in-themselves are bound to fail. This inevitable failure is the theme of the portion of the *Critique of Pure Reason* entitled the "Transcendental Dialectic." Here Kant shows that the three great problems of metaphysics—God, freedom, and immortality—are insoluble by speculative thought. Their existence can be neither affirmed nor denied on theoretical grounds, nor can they be scientifically demonstrated, but Kant shows the necessity of their existence in his moral philosophy. Kant's ethics centers in his categorical imperative (or moral law)—"Act as if the maxim from which you act were to become through your will a universal law." This law has its source in the autonomy of a rational being, and it is the formula for an absolutely good will. However, since man is a member of two worlds, the sensible and the intelligible, he does not infallibly act in accordance with this law but on the contrary almost always acts according to inclination. Thus what is objectively necessary, i.e., to will in conformity to the law, is subjectively contingent; and for this reason the moral law confronts man as an "ought." In the *Critique of Practical Reason* Kant went on to state that morality requires the belief in the existence of God, freedom, and immortality, because without their existence there can be no morality. In the *Critique of Judgment* Kant applied his critical method to aesthetic and teleological judgments. The chief purpose of this work was to find a bridge between the sensible and the intelligible worlds, sharply distinguished in his theoretical and practical philosophy. This bridge is found in the concepts of beauty and purposiveness that suggest at least the possibility of an ultimate union of the two realms. The results of Kant's work are incalculable. In addition to being the impetus to the development of German idealism by J. G. Fichte, F. W. Schelling, and G. W. F. Hegel, Kant's philosophy has influenced almost every area of thought. Among the major outgrowths of Kant's influence was the Neo-Kantianism of the late 19th cent. This movement had many branches in Germany, France, and Italy; the two chief ones were the Marburg school, founded by Hermann Cohen and including Ernst Cassirer, and the Heidelberg school, led by Wilhelm Windelband and Heinrich Rickert. The Marburg school was primarily concerned with the application of Kantian insights to the understanding of the physical sciences, and the Heidelberg school with the application of Kant to the historical and cultural sciences. Closely connected with the latter group was the social philosopher Wilhelm Dilthey. Kant influenced English thought through the philosophy of Sir William Hamilton and T. H. Green, and some Kantian ideas are found in the pragmatism of William James and John Dewey. In theology, Kant's influence can be seen in the writings of Friedrich Schleiermacher and Albrecht Ritschl; his ideas in biology were developed by Hans Driesch, and in Gestalt psychology by Wolfgang Köhler. All of Kant's important works have been translated into English. See Lucien Goldmann, *Immanuel Kant* (1945, tr. 1972); H. W. Cassirer, *A Commentary on Kant's Critique of Judgment* (1938, repr. 1970) and *Kant's First Critique* (1954); John Kemp, *The Philosophy of Kant* (1968); L. W. Beck, *Studies in the Philosophy of Kant* (1965) and (ed.) *Kant Studies Today* (1969).

Kantara, El: see QANTARAH, AL, town, Egypt.

Kantrowitz, Adrian, 1918–, American surgeon. The son of a physician, Kantrowitz received his M.D. from Western Reserve Univ. (1943), returning after World War II to study cardiovascular physiology under Carl John Wiggers. He devised (with Alan Lerrick) a plastic heart valve (1954), a heart-lung machine (1958), an internal pacemaker (1961–62), and (with Tetsuzo Akutsu) an auxiliary left ventricle (1964). In 1966 he performed the first implantation of a partial mechanical heart in a human, and on Dec. 6, 1967, the second human cardiac transplant. He also published pioneer motion pictures taken inside the living heart.

Kanuma (kăno͞o'mä), city (1970 pop. 77,746), Tochigi prefecture, central Honshu, Japan. It is an industrial center where brooms, hemp yarn and rope, and wood fittings are produced.

Kanye (kän'yə), town (1971 pop. 10,664), SE Botswana. It is a commercial and administrative center. Asbestos is mined nearby.

Kao-hsiung or **Kaohiung** (both: gou-shyōōng), city (1971 est. pop. 845,900), S Taiwan. It is the second largest city of Taiwan, the leading port in the southern part of the island, and a major industrial center. The leading industries produce sugar, petroleum products, cement, aluminum, wood and paper products, fertilizers, metals, and machinery; shipbuilding is also carried on. The city grew up from a small fishing village and was developed as a manufacturing center and port by the Japanese, who occupied Taiwan in 1895. Kao-hsiung has an important naval base.

Kaolack (kou'läk), city (1969 est. pop. 95,000), W Senegal, a port on the Saloum River. Lying in a farm area, Kaolack is a major peanut marketing and exporting center and has a large peanut oil factory. Brewing, leather tanning, cotton ginning, and fish processing are also important industries. Salt is produced from nearby salines. The city is on the railroad from Dakar to the Niger River in Mali. Kaolack is the center of the Sufi Muslim Tijaniyya brotherhood, whose mosque is on the city's outskirts.

kaoliang (kä"ōlēäng'): see SORGHUM.

kaolin (kā'əlĭn): see CHINA CLAY.

kaolinite (kā'əlĭnīt), clay mineral crystallizing in the monoclinic system and forming the chief constituent of CHINA CLAY and kaolin. It is a hydrous aluminum silicate commonly formed by the weathering and decomposition of rocks containing aluminum silicate compounds; feldspar is a chief source. Kaolinite has the same chemical composition as dickite and nacrite (both of which are also clay or kaolin minerals) but differs from them in origin, in optical properties, in reaction to heat, and in certain other physical properties. Kaolinite is the basic raw material for ceramics, and large quantities are also used in the manufacture of coated paper.

Kao Tsu: see LIU PANG.

Kapilavastu (kä"pĭləvä'stōō), ancient town, S Nepal. According to legend, the Buddha, whose father ruled the state of Kapilavastu, passed his early years there and was born nearby.

Kapitza, Peter (kä'pĕtsə), 1894–, Russian physicist, educated at the polytechnic institute of Petrograd (now Leningrad) and at Cambridge. He developed equipment (for a laboratory at Cambridge) capable of producing very powerful magnetic fields for his experiments in LOW TEMPERATURE PHYSICS. In 1934, Kapitza returned to the USSR, and the equipment he designed was bought by the Soviet government. Kapitza was made director of the Institute for Physical Problems of the Academy of Sciences of the USSR. In 1938 he discovered the SUPERFLUIDITY of liquid helium. He resigned as head of the Institute for Physical Problems in 1946, but returned as director in 1955 and also became editor of the *Journal of Theoretical and Experimental Physics.* He has been an outspoken advocate of open scientific thought in the USSR.

Kaplan, Mordecai Menahem, 1881–, American rabbi, educator, and philosopher, b. Lithuania, grad. College of the City of New York, 1900, M.A. Columbia, 1902. He went to the United States when he was eight years old. In 1909 he became principal and in 1931 dean of the Teachers Institute of the Jewish Theological Seminary of America. In 1922 he founded the Society for the Advancement of Judaism. He is best known, however, as the originator and leader of the Reconstructionist movement (see JUDAISM). Among his many books are *Judaism as a Civilization* (enl. ed. 1957), *The Meaning of God in Modern Jewish Religion* (1937), *The Future of the American Jew* (1948), *Judaism without Supernaturalism* (1958), *The Greater Judaism in the Making* (1960), *The Religion of Ethical Nationhood* (1970), *And If Not Now When? Toward a Reconstitution of the Jewish People* (1973). See Ira Eisenstein and Eugene Kohn, ed., *Mordecai M. Kaplan: An Evaluation* (1952).

kapok (kā'pŏk, kăp'ək), name for a tropical tree of the family Bombacaceae (BOMBAX family) and for the fiber (floss) obtained from the seeds in the ripened pods. The floss has been important in commerce since the 1890s; the chief source is *Ceiba pentandra,* the kapok (or silk-cotton) tree, cultivated in Java, Ceylon, the Philippines, and other parts of the Far East and in Africa, where it was introduced from its native America. The floss is removed by hand from the pods, dried, freed from seeds and dust, and baled for export. The lustrous, yellowish floss is light, fluffy, resilient, and resistant to water and decay. It is used as a stuffing, especially for life preservers, bedding, and upholstery, and for insulation against sound and heat. The seed kernels contain about 25% fatty oil used for soap or refined as edible oil. The residual cake is valuable as a fertilizer and as livestock fodder. Kapok is classified in the division MAGNOLIOPHYTA, class Magnoliopsida, order Malvales, family Bombacaceae.

Kaposvár (kō'pôshvär), city (1970 pop. 58,099), SW Hungary, on the Kapos River. It is a road and rail junction, a market for agricultural goods and livestock, and an industrial center. Landmarks include an 18th-century church, a 19th-century town hall, and the ruins of an old castle.

Kapp, Wolfgang (vôlf'gäng käp), 1858–1922, German right-wing politician. In 1920 he led the uprising known as the Kapp putsch, an armed revolt in Berlin aimed at restoring the German monarchy. He seized the Berlin government, but a general strike broke his power. Kapp fled to Sweden, returned (1922) to Germany, and died while awaiting trial for treason.

Kapteyn, Jacobus Cornelius (yäkō'bəs kôrnā'lēəs käptīn'), 1851–1922, Dutch astronomer. He was an authority on the Milky Way, of which he made notable statistical studies; he constructed a model of the galaxy known as the "Kapteyn universe." He computed the positions of the stars of the Southern Hemisphere photographed by Sir David Gill and in 1904 announced the discovery of two streams of stars moving in opposite directions in the plane of the Milky Way.

Kapuas (kä'pōōäs), river, c.710 mi (1,140 km) long, rising in the mountains of central Borneo and flowing SW through W Kalimantan, Indonesia, to the South China Sea near Pontianak. Its valley is intensively cultivated; rice is the chief crop. The river is navigable for c.560 mi (900 km).

Kapuskasing (kăpəskā'sĭng), town (1971 pop. 12,834), central Ont., Canada, on the Kapuskasing River, N of Timmins. It has lumbering and pulp and paper mills. A federal experimental farm is nearby.

Kara (kä'rə), river, c.140 mi (230 km) long, NE European and NW Siberian USSR. It flows N from the N Urals into the Kara Sea, forming part of the traditional border between European and Asian Russia. It is navigable in its lower course.

Karabakh: see NAGORNO-KARABAKH, USSR.

Kara-Bogaz-Gol (kä'rə-bəgäz'-gôl), shallow bay, c.7,000 sq mi (18,100 sq km), Central Asian USSR, in Turkmenistan. An arm of the Caspian Sea, it acts as a natural evaporating basin, drawing off the water of the Caspian and depositing salts along its shores. The town of **Kara-Bogaz-Gol** is a Caspian seaport at the entrance of the bay and produces chemicals, sulfates, and mirabilite.

Karabük (kärä'bük), city (1970 pop. 64,770), N Turkey. It was built in the 1930s as the seat of the iron and steel industry of Turkey. Nearby are the Zonguldak coal fields.

Karachay-Cherkess Autonomous Oblast (kärächī'-chĕrkĕs'), administrative division (1970 pop. 345,000), c.5,500 sq mi (14,200 sq km), Stavropol Kray, SE European USSR, in the Greater Caucasus, along the upper Kuban River. CHERKESSK is the capital. The oblast consists of lowland steppe in the north and the Caucasian foothills in the south. Grains, fruits, and vegetables are grown and livestock is raised. The oblast has coal, lead, zinc, copper, and gold mines. Industrial products include building materials, foodstuffs, and machinery. Though there are Cherkess, the overwhelming majority of the population are Karachay, Turkic-speaking Muslims who arrived in the region in the 14th cent. In the 16th cent. they became vassals of Kabardinian princes, then passed (1733) to Turkish suzerainty, and in 1828 were conquered by the Russians. The region was included (1921) in the Mountain People's Republic, but in 1922 it became the Karachay-Cherkess Autonomous Oblast. In 1924 it was divided into the Karachay Autonomous Oblast and the Cherkess National Okrug; the latter became an autonomous oblast in 1928 (see CIRCASSIA). In 1943 the Karachay, accused of collaborating with the Germans in World War II, were deported to Siberia and their autonomous oblast was abolished. However, the Karachay-Cherkess Autonomous Oblast was reestablished in 1957, when the "rehabilitation" of deported peoples was decreed.

Karachi (kərä'chē), city (1972 est. pop. 3,469,000), largest city and former capital of Pakistan, SE Pakistan, on the Arabian Sea near the Indus River delta. The capital of Sind prov., it is Pakistan's chief seaport and industrial center, as well as a transportation, commercial, and financial hub and a military headquarters. It has a large automobile assembly plant, an oil refinery, a steel mill, shipbuilding and repair and railroad yards, jute and textile factories, printing and publishing plants, food processing plants, and chemical and engineering works. Filmmaking and fishing are also important. Karachi airport, one of the busiest in Asia, is a major link in international air routes. An old settlement, Karachi was developed as a port and trading center by Hindu merchants in the early 18th cent. In 1843 it passed to the British, who made it the seat of the Sind government and a military center. Steady improvements in harbor facilities made Karachi a leading Indian port by the late 19th cent., while agricultural development of the hinterland gave it a large export trade in wheat and cotton. Karachi served as Pakistan's capital from 1947, when the country gained independence, until 1959, when Rawalpindi became the interim capital pending completion of Islamabad. In Karachi are a university and several other educational institutions; the national museum, with a fine archaeological collection; and the tomb of Muhammad Ali JINNAH, founder of Pakistan. Karachi's port was bombed and shelled during the 1971 India-Pakistan War.

Karadjordje: see KARAGEORGE.

Karadjordjević or **Karageorgevich** (both: kărəjôr'jəvĭch), Serbian dynasty, descended from Karageorge (Karadjordje). Its ruling members were ALEXANDER, prince of Serbia, and kings PETER I, ALEXANDER, and PETER II, of Yugoslavia. It was long involved in a feud with the OBRENOVIĆ dynasty. The Karadjordjević dynasty lost the throne in 1945 when Yugoslavia became a federal republic.

Karadžić, Vuk Stefanović (vōōk stĕfä'nôvich kä'räjĭch), 1787–1864, Serbian philologist and folklorist, of Moldavian descent. During his lifetime Karadžić published 10 volumes of Serbian folk poetry. He inaugurated language reforms and adopted the Serbian vernacular. His introduction of phonetic spelling and invention of new letters to complete the Cyrillic alphabet were major contributions to Serbian linguistics. Among his most important lexicographical works are a grammar of vernacular Serbian (1814) and a Serbian dictionary (1818). In 1847 he translated the New Testament into Serbian for the British and Foreign Bible Society.

Karafuto: see SAKHALIN, USSR.

Karaganda (kä'rəgəndä'), city (1970 pop. 522,000), capital of Karaganda oblast, Central Asian USSR, in Kazakhstan, on the Trans-Kazakhstan RR. It consists of about 50 coal-mining settlements scattered around the central part of the city, and it is a leading industrial and cultural center of Kazakhstan. Its industries include iron and steel foundries, flour mills, food and beverage plants, ship repair yards, and factories that produce mining equipment, building materials, machinery, and footwear. Karaganda was founded in 1857 as a copper-mining settlement. The Karaganda coal basin, developed in the late 1920s, is one of the USSR's largest producers of bituminous coal. Near the city is the gigantic Novo-Karaganda power station.

Karageorge (kăr'əjôrj', kä"räjôr'jā), 1768?–1817, Serbian patriot. Born George Petrović, he was known as Karageorge, or Black George. He led the Serbs in their insurrection (1804) against the Turks, took (1806) Belgrade, where the Turkish population was massacred, and was proclaimed (1808) hereditary chief of the Serbs. He fought with Russia against Turkey (1809–12). Abandoned by the Russians when peace was signed, he fled to Austria. On his return to Serbia he was murdered, probably at the instigation of Miloš Obrenović (see MILOŠ). Although an illiterate peasant, Karageorge showed great military ability. The name also appears as Karadjordje, and the dynasty descended from him is known as Karadjordjević.

Karageorgevich: see KARADJORDJEVIĆ.

Kara Irtysh: see IRTYSH, river, USSR.

Karaites (kâr'əīts), Jewish schismatic sect, reputedly founded (8th cent.) in Persia by ANAN BEN DAVID and originally known as Ananites. Its adherents were called Karaites after the 9th cent. The Karaites attacked the Talmudic interpretation of the Bible, rejecting the oral law and interpreting the Bible literally, and they developed their own commentaries, which were in many respects more rigorous and ascetic than the Talmudic interpretations. In the 10th cent. they produced a splendid literature in both Arabic and Hebrew. The sect declined after the 12th cent., but remnants are still extant, notably in the Crimea and Israel. The name is also spelled Caraites. See *Karaite Anthology* (ed. and tr. by Leon Nemoy, 1952), Zvi Ankori, *Karaites in Byzantium: The Formative Years, 970–1100* (1957, repr. 1968); Philip Birnbaum, ed., *Karaite Studies* (1971).

Karaj (käräj'), city (1966 pop. 44,243), Tehran prov., N Iran, on the Karaj River. It is an agricultural market and a transportation center. Chemicals are manufactured there.

Karajan, Herbert von (käräyän'), 1908–, Austrian conductor. Karajan began his conducting career in 1927. After World War II his reputation spread through Europe to the United States. He toured with various orchestras (notably the Berlin Philharmonic) and participated in many of Europe's music festivals. He is musical director of the Berlin Philharmonic and was artistic director of the Vienna State Opera (1956–64). Karajan is especially noted for his numerous recordings.

Kara-Kalpak Autonomous Soviet Socialist Republic (kä"rəkŭlpäk'), autonomous republic (1970 pop. 702,000), c.61,000 sq mi (158,000 sq km), Central Asian USSR, on the Amu Darya River. NUKUS is the capital. The republic comprises parts of the Ustyurt plateau, the Kyzyl-Kum desert, and the Amu Darya delta on the Aral Sea. The republic is the USSR's chief producer of alfalfa; other crops are cotton, rice, corn, and jute. Livestock raising (notably cattle and Karakul sheep) and silkworm breeding are widespread. There are many light industries. The population, concentrated in the delta, consists mostly of Kara-Kalpak (Turkic-speaking Muslims), Kazakhs, Uzbek, Turkomans, Russians, and Tatars. The Kara-Kalpak, known since the 16th cent., when they lived along the lower and middle courses of the Syr Darya River, were partly subjected by the Kazakhs. In the 18th cent. they migrated to their present homeland and in the 19th cent. came under the rule of the khanate of Khiva. The khanate passed under Russian control at the end of the 19th cent. and under Bolshevik control by 1920. The Kara-Kalpak Autonomous Oblast was formed in 1925 within the Kazakh Autonomous Republic. It became an autonomous republic itself in 1932 and was transferred to the Uzbek SSR in 1936.

Karakorum (kä"rəkō'rəm), ruined city, central Mongolian People's Republic, near the Orkhon River, SW of Ulan Bator. The area around Karakorum had been inhabited by nomadic Turkic tribes from the 1st cent. A.D., but the city itself was not laid out until c.1220, when Jenghiz Khan, founder of the Mongol empire, established his residence there. As capital of the MONGOLS, Karakorum was visited (c.1247) by a papal mission under Giovanni Carpini. The city was abandoned (and later destroyed) after Kublai Khan, grandson of Jenghiz, transferred (1267) the Mongol capital to Khanbaliq (modern Peking). The noted Lamaist monastery of Erdeni Dzu was built near Karakorum in 1586. The ruins of the ancient Mongol city were discovered in 1889 by N. M. Yadrinstev, a Russian explorer, who also uncovered the Orkhon Inscriptions (see under ORKHON). Karakorum is also the name of a nearby site, which in the 8th and 9th cent. was the capital of the UIGURS.

Karakorum, mountain system, extending c.300 mi (480 km), between the Indus and Yarkand rivers, N Kashmir, S central Asia; SE extension of the Hindu Kush. Karakorum's main range has some of the world's highest peaks, including Mt. Godwin-Austen (28,250 ft/8,611 m), the second-tallest peak in the world. Karakorum also has several of the world's largest glaciers. Its southern slopes are the watershed for many tributaries of the Indus River. The mountains, the greatest barrier between India and central Asia, are crossed above the perpetual snow line by two natural routes; **Karakorum Pass** (alt. 18,290 ft/5,575 m), the chief pass of the system, is on the main Kashmir-China route.

Kara-Kul (kä"rə-kōōl), mountain lake, c.140 sq mi (360 sq km), Gorno-Badakhshan Autonomous Oblast, Central Asian USSR, in the Pamir, near the Chinese border. It is c.12,840 ft (3,900 m) above sea level, and its greatest depth is 780 ft (240 m).

Karakul sheep (kăr'əkəl), breed native to central Asia. The newborn lambs usually have tightly curled black fur and are skinned before they are three days old to provide the commercial lambskin for which the sheep are raised. The finest pelts are often obtained from unborn lambs. A large percentage of this lambskin is classified as Persian lamb, though it may also be called karakul, broadtail, krimmer, or astrakhan, according to the quality and tightness of the curl. The lambs grow rapidly and produce good meat but are seldom raised for this purpose. The grown sheep are medium-sized and broad-tailed; their wool is a mixture of coarse and fine fibers, varying in color from black to shades of tan and gray, and is used in making carpeting and other heavy fabrics. Karakul sheep are raised in several countries of Asia, Europe, Africa, and the Americas. In the United States they are raised on a small scale, chiefly in Texas.

Kara-Kum (kär"ə-kōōm'), two deserts, S USSR. The Caspian Kara-Kum, the larger desert (c.115,000 sq mi/297,900 sq km), is W of the Amu Darya River and includes most of the Turkmen Republic. The Murghab and Tedzhen rivers flow out of the Hindu Kush Mts. to the south and empty into the desert, providing water for irrigation. The oases of Mary (Merv) and Tedzhen are noted for cotton growing. The Kara-Kum Canal, one of the largest irrigation projects in the Soviet Union, carries water from the Amu Darya at Kelif westward across the desert to Mary and ultimately to Ashkhabad, a distance of c.500 mi (800 km). The canal water permits irrigated agriculture (mainly cotton) and industry to flourish along the southern margin of the desert. The Trans-Caspian RR, a leading transportation artery of Soviet Central Asia, crosses the desert from Krasnovodsk, on the Caspian Sea, to Ashkhabad, Mary, Bukhara, and Tashkent. Natural gas deposits have been discovered at Darvaza and Mary. The Aral Kara-Kum desert (c.15,440 sq mi/40,000 sq km) lies NE of the Aral Sea in the Kazakh Republic.

Karamai (kärämī'), Mandarin *K'o-la-ma-i*, city, N Sinkiang Uigur Autonomous Region, China, in the Dzungarian basin. Since the discovery (1955) there of one of the largest oil fields in China, it has grown into an oil-producing and refining center.

Karaman (kärämän'), town (1970 pop. 35,049), S central Turkey, at the northern foot of the Taurus mts. The ancient Laranda, Karaman was renamed after the chieftain of a Turkic tribe who conquered the city c.1250 and set up the independent Muslim state of Karamania, which at one time comprised most of Asia Minor. A successor state of the Seljuk empire, Karamania existed until its final subjugation by the Ottoman Turks in the late 15th cent. Karaman has retained ruins of the Karamanid castle and of two fine mosques.

Karamanlis, Constantine (kôn'stäntēn kärämänlīs'), 1907–, Greek political leader, b. Macedonia. Elected to parliament in 1936, he held various cabinet posts from 1946 to 1955. After the death of Marshal Papagos, Karamanlis was named (1955) premier. He held that post from Oct., 1955, to June, 1963, except for brief intervals from March to May, 1958, and from Sept. to Nov., 1961, while his right-wing National Radical Union, founded in 1956, continued to gain majorities in the general elections. A partisan of the North Atlantic Treaty Organization, Karamanlis reached (1959) agreement with Great Britain and Turkey over Cyprus. In 1959 he announced a five-year plan (1960–64) for the Greek economy, emphasizing improvement of agricultural and industrial production. After his cabinet fell in 1963, Karamanlis went into exile abroad. He was a vocal opponent of the military junta that seized power in Greece in 1967. In July, 1974, the junta fell, following a disastrous military venture in Cyprus. Karamanlis returned as premier. He scheduled parliamentary elections in Nov., 1974, and his party, the New Democratic party, won a substantial majority. His name also appears as Caramanlis.

Kara Mustafa: see MUSTAFA.

Karamzin, Nikolai Mikhailovich (nyĭkəlī' mĕkhī'ləvĭch kərəmzēn'), 1766–1826, Russian historian and writer. *Letters of a Russian Traveler, 1789–90* (1792, abr. tr. 1957), dealing with a journey to Western Europe, brought a cosmopolitan awareness into Russian writing. Karamzin made the Russian literary language more polished, elegant, and rhythmic. These reforms were important for later writers, especially Pushkin. Karamzin's sentimental story of a betrayed peasant girl, "Poor Lisa" (1792), forecast the novel of social protest. His greatest work, an 11-volume *History of the Russian State* (1818–24), was a widely read dramatic account of the political actions of the Russian princes up to 1613. He believed in a strong monarchic state, but criticized 18th-century rulers in his vigorous *Memoir on Ancient and Modern Russia,* written in 1810–11 (1914, tr. 1959). See his *Selected Prose* (tr. 1969); studies by H. M. Nebel (1967) and A. G. Cross (1971).

Kara Sea, Rus. *Karskoye More*, shallow section of the Arctic Ocean, off N USSR, between Severnaya Zemlya and Novaya Zemlya. It is no deeper than 650 ft (198 m). It receives the Ob, the Yenisei, the Pyasina, and the Taimyra rivers, and is important as a fishing ground. Its main ports are Novyy Port and Dikson, but the ice-locked sea is navigable only during August and September. Ice floes menaced its early navigators and added to the difficulties of the Northeast Passage.

karate: see JUDO.

Karatsu (kärä'tsōō), city (1970 pop. 74,223), Saga prefecture, NW Kyushu, Japan, on Karatsu Bay. It is a summer resort and fishing port important historically as Japan's ancient communications point with Korea.

Karbala (kär'bələ), city (1965 pop. 83,301), provincial capital, central Iraq, at the edge of the Syrian Desert. The city's trade is in religious objects, hides, wool, and dates. Karbala is the site of the tomb of the Shiite leader Husein, who was killed in the city in 680, and is second only to Mecca in being a holy place visited by Shiite pilgrims. The tomb, with a gilded dome and three minarets, is the most notable building; it was destroyed by the Wahabis in 1801 but was quickly restored by contributions from Persians and other Shiite Muslims. Iranian pilgrims to Mecca usually begin their journey at Karbala, and many pious Muslims bring the bones of their dead for burial there.

Karcag (kŏr'tsŏg), city (1970 pop. 24,631), E Hungary. A road and rail junction, Karcag is an important communications point.

Kardelj, Edvard (ĕd'värt kär'dĕlyə), 1910–, Yugoslavian politician. A Slovenian schoolteacher, he early joined the Yugoslav Communist party. In 1940 he became a politburo member. He was important in the underground in World War II and was vice premier of Josip Broz Tito's provisional government, a position that he continued to hold after the formal establishment of the Yugoslav Communist state in 1945. He later served as minister of foreign affairs (1948–53), vice chairman of the federal executive council (1953–63), and president of the federal parliament (1963–67). A leading ideologist, Kardelj helped in carrying out Yugoslavia's break with the USSR in 1948 and in adapting the official ideology to the new independent course.

Kareah (kārē'ə), father of JOHANAN **1.** Jer. 40.8. Careah: 2 Kings 25.23.

Karelia: see KARELIAN AUTONOMOUS SOVIET SOCIALIST REPUBLIC.

Karelian Autonomous Soviet Socialist Republic (kərē'lyən) or **Karelia** (kərē'lyēə), autonomous region (1970 pop. 714,000), c.66,540 sq mi (172,300 sq km), NW European USSR, extending from the Finnish border in the west to the White Sea in the east and from the Kola Peninsula in the north to Lakes Ladoga and Onega (Europe's largest freshwater bodies) in the south. PETROZAVODSK is the capital. A glaciated plateau, Karelia is covered by about 50,000 lakes and by coniferous forests; fishing and lumbering are major industries. Agriculture, generally hampered by cold climate and poor soil, is possible only in the south, where some grains, potatoes, fodder grasses, and vegetables are grown; dairy farming and livestock raising are also carried on. Karelia has valuable deposits of iron ore, magnetite, lead, zinc, copper, titanium, marble, and pyrite. Power for industry is supplied by the republic's many short, rapid rivers. Besides lumbering and related industries, Karelia has shipbuilding and repair yards, food-processing plants, ironworks, and factories that produce machinery, aluminum, building materials, and textiles. The republic is crossed by the Murmansk RR and by the Baltic-White Sea Canal, which is both commercially and strategically important. Russians constitute a majority of the population, the rest of which consists mainly of Karelians, Finns, and Lapps, who are very closely related and have an identical written language. The Karelians, a major division of the Finns, were first mentioned in the 9th cent. and formed a strong medieval state. Karelia, properly speaking the region N and E of Lake Onega, was conquered in the 12th–13th cent. by the Swedes, who took the west, and by Novgorod, which took the east. The eastern part was taken from Russia by Sweden in 1617 but restored in 1721 by the Treaty of Nystad. The western part shared the history of Finland until 1940. It was from oral traditions among the Karelians that the Finnish national epic, the *Kalevala*, was compiled in the 19th cent. by Elias Lönnrot. The Karelian area of the Russian Empire was economically backward and was often a place of exile for political prisoners. In 1920 an autonomous oblast, known as the Karelian Workers' Commune, was set up in E Karelia; in 1923 it was made into the Karelian Autonomous SSR, which, after the Soviet-Finnish War of 1939–40, incorporated most of the territory ceded by Finland to the USSR. In March, 1940, the region's status was raised to that of a constituent republic, called the Karelo-Finnish SSR. During World War II, the Finns (allies of the Axis powers) occupied most of Karelia; but it was returned to the USSR in 1944. Karelia reverted to the status of an autonomous republic in 1956.

Karelian Isthmus, land bridge, NW European USSR, connecting Russia and Finland. Situated between the Gulf of Finland in the west and Lake Ladoga in the east, it is 25 to 70 mi (40–113 km) wide and 90 mi (145 km) long. LENINGRAD and VYBORG (Viipuri) are its chief cities. Originally part of the Grand Duchy of Sweden, the isthmus passed to Russia in 1721, and—except for its southernmost section—became part of Finland in 1917. The Mannerheim Line, which crossed the isthmus, was breached in 1940 by the Russians, who occupied the area. It was briefly held (1941–44) by Finnish and German units during World War II. The isthmus was formally ceded to the USSR in 1944, and more than 400,000 of its Finnish residents moved into Finland.

Karelo-Finnish Soviet Socialist Republic: see KARELIAN AUTONOMOUS SOVIET SOCIALIST REPUBLIC.

Karenni State: see KAYAH STATE, Burma.

Karens (kərĕnz'), members of a Thai-Chinese cultural group, one of the most important minorities in Burma, living in the KAYAH STATE, Tenasserim, and the Irrawaddy delta. They form 11% of the Burmese population. The Karen hill tribes have tended to remain animistic, but among those settled in the plains there are about 300,000 Christians and over a million Buddhists. The Karens speak the Karen languages, probably of the Sino-Tibetan family. They are mostly farmers, but Karen tribesmen were superior soldiers in the military units raised in Burma under British rule. A major unifying element among the Karens is a strong opposition to Burmese political domination. Their revolt (1948–49) against the union government aimed at separation from Burma. They scored important successes, and the government was forced to grant the Karenni State (later Kayah State) a large measure of autonomy.

Karfiol, Bernard (kär'fēōl), 1886–1952, American painter, b. Budapest of American parents; educated in Brooklyn, N.Y. He studied at the National Academy of Design in New York City and at Julian's in Paris. From 1908 to 1913 he taught and painted in New York. From 1917, Karfiol's work was widely exhibited and received many awards. It is characterized by tenderness, simplicity, sensuous form, and harmonious color. Perhaps best known as a painter of nudes, Karfiol was also an admirable landscape and portrait painter. Many of his scenes were inspired by the landscape of Maine. *Fishing Village* and *Seated Nude* (both: Mus. of Modern Art, New York City) are characteristic works. Karfiol is represented in many leading American galleries. See study by J. P. Slusser (1931).

Kariba Dam (kärē'bä), hydroelectric project, in Kariba gorge of the ZAMBEZI River, on the Zambia-Rhodesia border, S central Africa; built 1955–59. One of the world's largest dams, it is 420 ft (128 m) high and 1,900 ft (579 m) long. Kariba Lake, the dam's vast man-made reservoir, extends c.175 mi (280 km) and has a maximum width of 20 mi (32 km). The creation of the lake forced resettlement of about 50,000 Africans living along the Zambezi. In 1960–61, Operation Noah captured and removed the animals threatened by the lake's rising waters. The Kariba project supplies electricity to the COPPERBELT in Zambia and to parts of Rhodesia.

Karikal, India: see FRENCH INDIA.

Karim Khan (kärēm' khän), d. 1779, ruler of Persia (1750–79), founder of the Zand dynasty. He emerged victorious from a contest for power and ruled under the title Vakil [representative]. His rule was one of tranquility, and he made Shiraz, his capital, beautiful with buildings including the Mosque of Vakil and the Bazaar of Vakil. A few northern tribes were left almost independent. One of them was the Kajars (or Qajars), and from them was to come AGA MUHAMMAD KHAN, who overthrew (1794) Lutf Ali Khan, the last ruler of the Zand dynasty.

Karisimbi, mountain, Africa: see VIRUNGA.

Kariya (kärē'yä), city (1970 pop. 87,671), Aichi prefecture, central Honshu, Japan. It is an industrial center with textile, mechanical, and food-processing industries.

Karkaa (kärkā'ə), unidentified place, S Palestine. Joshua 15.3.

Karkheh (kär'kĕ), ancient *Choaspes,* river, c.350 mi (560 km) long, rising in the Zagros mts., W Iran, and flowing S into the Khuzistan lowland, where it forms a swamp bordering the Tigris River. An ancient storage dam on the river at Shush made Khuzistan one of the most prosperous agricultural regions of Asia until the system fell into disrepair and the irrigated area reverted to desert. The area is now being reclaimed as part of the Khuzistan project.

Karkonosze: see KRKONOŠE, mountains.

Karkor, place, in Gilead. Judges 8.10.

Karl. For German and Swedish kings thus named, see CHARLES.

Karlfeldt, Erik Axel (ā'rĭk äk'səl kärl'fĕlt), 1864–1931, Swedish lyric poet. Little known outside Sweden, his work was greatly loved in his native land. Themes of nature, love, and peasant life predominate in *Songs of the Wilderness and of Love* (1895), *Fridolin's Ballads* (1898), and other collections. He was posthumously awarded the 1931 Nobel Prize in Literature, which he had refused in his lifetime. Selected poems were translated as *Arcadia Borealis* (1938).

Karli (kär'lē), village, Maharashtra state, W India. Nearby are Buddhist caves that may have been excavated as early as the 2d cent. B.C. The most famous of them measures 124 ft by 45 ft (38 m by 14 m) and is India's largest cave temple. Its ancient shrine, columns, and ornamentation survive in part.

Karl-Marx-Stadt (kärl-märks-shtät), formerly **Chemnitz** (kĕm'nĭts), city (1970 pop. 299,312), capital of Karl-Marx-Stadt district, S East Germany, on the Chemnitz River. It is a major industrial center and a road and rail junction. Manufactures include machine tools, machinery, chemicals, optical instruments, furniture, and textiles. Nearby is a large open-pit lignite mine. Of Wendish origin, the city was chartered in 1143, when it was also granted a linen-weaving monopoly. It grew as a trade center, was devastated in the Thirty Years War (1618–48), and recovered its prosperity after the introduction (late 17th cent.) of cotton milling. Noteworthy buildings of the city include the Renaissance-style city hall and a late-Gothic church, the Stadtkirche. The city was renamed Karl-Marx-Stadt in 1953.

Karl Marx University: see LEIPZIG, UNIV. OF.

Karloff, Boris, 1887–1969, Anglo-American actor, b. Dulwich, England; his original name was William Pratt. A distinguished character actor with a superb speaking voice, Karloff was famous for his monster roles in Hollywood horror films, notably *Frankenstein* (1931). His other movies include *The Ghoul* (1933), *The Bride of Frankenstein* (1935), *Isle of the Dead* (1945), and *Targets* (1968).

Karlovci, Sremski: see KARLOWITZ, TREATY OF.

Karlovy Vary (kär'lôvĭ vä'rĭ), Ger. *Karlsbad,* city (1970 pop. 43,708), NW Czechoslovakia, in Bohemia, at the confluence of the Teplá and Ohře rivers. A famous health resort, Karlovy Vary is one of the best-known spas of Europe; its hot mineral water is taken particularly for digestive diseases. The medicinal springs, known for centuries, attracted European aristocrats until World War I. Karlovy Vary is also noted for its china, glass, and porcelain industries, and bricks are produced in quantity. The city was chartered in the 14th cent. by Emperor Charles IV, who is said to have discovered its springs. In recent years, Karlovy Vary has hosted conferences of Soviet and East European Communist leaders.

Karlowitz, Treaty of (kär'lōvĭts), 1699, peace treaty signed at Sremski Karlovci (Ger. *Karlowitz*), N Serbia, Yugoslavia. It was concluded between the Ottoman Empire (Turkey) on the one side and Austria, Poland, and Venice on the other. The preceding war (1683–97) had resulted in the Turkish defeat in 1697, thereby forcing Turkey to consent to the treaty. All Hungary (including Transylvania but not the Banat of Temesvar), Croatia, and Slavonia were ceded to Austria by Turkey. Podolia passed to Poland, and the Peloponnesus and most of Dalmatia passed to Venice. Russia, also at war with Turkey, captured Azov in 1696 and concluded a separate peace treaty with Turkey in 1700. The Venetian gains were lost again at the Treaty of PASSAROWITZ (1718). The Treaty of Karlowitz, which crowned the successful campaign of Prince Eugene of Savoy, marked the beginning of the Ottoman Empire's disintegration.

Karlsbad: see KARLOVY VARY, Czechoslovakia.

Karlsefni, Thorfinn: see THORFINN KARLSEFNI.

Karlshamm (kärls-hä'mən, kärls'hä"-), city (1970 pop. 13,121), Blekinge co., SE Sweden, a busy port on the Baltic Sea; chartered 1664. It is the seat of a large fishing fleet and has a major concentrated food factory.

Karlskoga (kärl'skōō"gä), city (1970 pop. 36,963), Örebro co., S Sweden; chartered 1940. An industrial center, it is the seat of the Bofors iron and armaments works and has other industries that manufacture steel, machines, explosives, chemicals, and clothing.

Karlskrona (kärlskrōō'nä), city (1970 pop. 34,145), capital of Blekinge co., SE Sweden, on the Baltic Sea. It is a seaport and fishing center with a large modern port. The city has been the headquarters of the Swedish navy since 1679 and has many service-connected industries. Manufactures include metal goods, canned food, and porcelain. A naval museum is in the city. A variant spelling is Carlscrona.

Karlsruhe (kärls'rōōə), city (1970 pop. 259,245), Baden-Württemberg, SW West Germany, on the northern fringes of the Black Forest, connected by canal with a port on the nearby Rhine River. It is a transportation, industrial, and cultural center and is the seat of the federal constitutional court and the federal court of justice. Manufactures include textiles, jewelry, pharmaceuticals, machinery, and refined oil. Karlsruhe was founded in 1715 by Karl Wilhelm, margrave of Baden-Durlach, to replace nearby Durlach (incorporated into Karlsruhe in 1938) as the margravial residence. After 1771 it was the capital of the duchy (later grand duchy and, after 1919, state) of Baden. The old part of Karlsruhe, badly damaged in World War II, was laid out as a vast semicircle with the streets converging radially upon the ducal palace (1752–85; restored after 1945). The city has a university (founded as a technical academy in 1825), a school of fine arts, a school of music, a center for atomic research, well-known theaters and art galleries, and a large conference center, the Schwarzwaldhalle (1953–54). It is sometimes spelled Carlsruhe.

Karlstad (kärl'städ), city (1970 pop. 64,458), capital of Värmland co., S Sweden, on Lake Vänern. It has ironworks and machine shops and other industries that manufacture forest products and heavy machinery. Known as Thingvalla (or Tingvalla) in the Middle Ages, it was chartered by Charles IX as Karlstad in 1584. A fire in 1865 destroyed much of the city. The treaty that severed the union of Norway and Sweden was negotiated and signed there in 1905.

Karlstadt, Reformation leader: see CARLSTADT.

karma or **karman** (kär'mə, kär'mən) [Skt.,=action, work, or ritual], basic concept common to HINDUISM, BUDDHISM, and JAINISM. The doctrine of karma states that one's state in this life is a result of actions (both physical and mental) in past incarnations, and action in this life can determine one's destiny in future incarnations. Karma is a natural, impersonal law of moral cause and effect and has no connection with the idea of a supreme power that decrees punishment or forgiveness of sins. Karmic law is universally applicable, and only those who have attained liberation from rebirth, called *mukti* (or *moksha*) or NIRVANA, can transcend it. *Karma yoga* (see YOGA), the spiritual discipline of detachment from the results of action, is a famous teaching of the BHAGAVAD-GITA.

Karman, Theodor von, 1881–1963, American aeronautical engineer, b. Hungary, grad. Royal Technical Univ., Budapest (1902) and Univ. of Göttingen (Ph.D., 1908). From 1909 to 1912 he served as director of the aeronautical institute at the Univ. of Aachen. He came to the United States in 1930, was naturalized in 1936, and was on the staff of the California Institute of Technology from 1930 to 1949. He made many contributions to the field of aerodynamics and is known especially for his mathematical formulas called the von Karman theory of vortex streets. These formulas are used in the calculation of the resistance by air to objects (e.g., aircraft, rockets) moving through it. His writings include *Aerodynamics* (1954) and his autobiography, *Wind and Beyond* (with Lee Edson, publ. posthumously, 1967).

Karmathians or **Carmathians** (kärmā'thēənz), a Muslim sect of the 9th and 10th cent., similar to the ASSASSIN sect. They were part of a movement for social reform which spread widely through Islam from the 9th to the 12th cent. They were organized according to initiation and illumination, like other similar sects of the period. Although heretical, their doctrine had a great influence on Islamic philosophy and remnants of it are today found in the religion of the Druses. The chief importance of the Karmathians came with their establishment of an independent communist community in lower Mesopotamia before 900. They were the source of rebellions in Khorasan and Syria, and after 900 they conquered all of Yemen. In spite of the efforts of the Abbasid caliph at Baghdad, the Karmathians continued their career until (c.930) they created a sensation that rocked Islam by carrying away the Black Stone from the Kaaba at Mecca. Ten years later the Karmathians returned the stone. They were in constant touch with the founders of Fatimid rule in Egypt, alternately at war or peace with them. They ceased to be a political power after 1000.

Karnak (kär'năk), village, central Egypt, on the Nile. It is 1 mi (1.6 km) E of LUXOR and occupies part of the site of THEBES. Remains of the pharaohs abound at Karnak. Most notable is the Great Temple of Amon. Although there was an older foundation, the temple was largely conceived and accomplished in the XVIII dynasty, and it is often considered the finest example of New Empire religious architecture. The temple grounds extend about 1,000 ft (300 m). The western half comprises a vast court and the great hypostyle hall (388 ft by 170 ft/118 m by 52 m), with 134 columns arranged in 16 rows. The eastern half is a complex of halls and shrines, many of the Middle Empire. There are smaller temples at Karnak dedicated to Mut and to Khensu, wife and son respectively of AMON.

Karnal (kərnälʹ), town (1971 pop. 92,835), Haryana state, N central India. The town's name is derived from Karna, the rival of Arjuna in the Sanskrit MAHABHARATA epic. It is on the Delhi-Ambala railroad. Karnal is a market for rice, wheat, and maize, a cattle-breeding center, and the site of the National Dairy Research Institute. The British occupied the town in 1805.

Karnataka (kärnäʹtəkə), formerly **Mysore** (mīsôrʹ), state (1971 pop. 29,263,334), 74,122 sq mi (191,976 sq km), SW India, bordering on the Arabian Sea. The capital is BANGALORE. The Cauvery, the Tunga, and the Badhra rivers, are used for both power and irrigation. Coffee is the major crop, but cotton, millet, sugarcane, rice, and fodder are also grown. The state has the most valuable sandalwood forests in India. Karnataka produces nearly all of India's gold and chromite and has considerable deposits of iron ore and manganese. There is an excellent road and railway system, and the state has many industries. Steel and steel products, automobiles, and airplanes are among the manufactures. The population is Hindu and speaks Kannada (Kanarese). The linguistic uniformity of the state and its excellent education system contribute to one of India's highest literacy rates. The region was part of the empire of the Mauryas (c.325–185 B.C.). From the 3d to the 11th cent. it was ruled by the Gangas and Chalukyas. In 1313 it was conquered by the DELHI SULTANATE, but it was soon lost to the Vijayanagar kingdom. In the late 18th cent. the Muslim leaders HAIDER ALI and his son, TIPPOO SAHIB, conquered the Hindu rulers of Karnataka. They fought the British but were finally defeated in 1799. The British restored the Old Hindu dynasty and thereafter provided protection. The state acceded to the Indian Union in 1947 and in 1956 its area was doubled. Karnataka is governed by a chief minister and cabinet responsible to a bicameral legislature (with one elected house) and by a governor appointed by the president of India. The name was officially changed from Mysore to Karnataka in 1973.

Karo, Joseph ben Ephraim: see CARO, JOSEPH BEN EPHRAIM.

Karolostadt, Reformation leader: see CARLSTADT.

Károlyi, Count Julius (käʹrôlyĭ), 1871–1946?, Hungarian politician; cousin of Michael Károlyi. He became premier and finance minister in 1931. He resigned in 1932 after failing to satisfy either the nationalist right or the liberal left. Julius Gombos succeeded him.

Károlyi, Count Michael, 1875–1955, Hungarian politician, of an ancient noble family. A liberal, he organized (1918) a national council for Hungary after the dissolution of the Austro-Hungarian Monarchy and was made premier. His attempt to strike a balance between the extreme right and left undermined his position. A republic was set up and in Jan., 1919, Károlyi was elected provisional president, apparently in order to remove him from active control. Forced in the end to choose between the conservatives and the Communists, he surrendered the government to the Communists. The dictatorship of Bela KUN was set up in March, 1919. Károlyi left Hungary when Kun's regime collapsed. He returned from England to Hungary after World War II and was appointed (1947) Hungarian ambassador to France. In 1949 he resigned because of disagreement with the policy of his government. He remained in France until his death. His memoirs appeared in English in 1956.

Kárpathos (kärʹpäthôs), Ital. *Scarpanto*, Lat. *Carpathus*, island (1971 pop. 5,420), c.110 sq mi (280 sq km), SE Greece, in the Aegean Sea, one of the DODECANESE. It is mountainous, rising to c.4,000 ft (1,220 m).

Karpaty: see CARPATHIANS.

Karpinsky, Alexander Petrovich (əlyĭksänʹdər pētrôʹvĭch kärpĕnʹskē), 1846–1936, Soviet geologist. From 1869 to 1885 he was at the Mining Institute, St. Petersburg (now Leningrad), as student and teacher. He was imperial director (1885–1916) of mining research and in 1886 was elected to what is now known as the Soviet Academy of Sciences, of which he was president from 1916 until his death. Karpinsky was noted for his prolific research on various geological subjects, especially paleontology, mineralogy, and petrology. His work was chiefly in the Urals, and he completed the first geological map of European Russia; it appeared in *Outline of the Geological History of European Russia* (1883–94). At the time of the Soviet revolution he was influential in preserving much scientific equipment and many invaluable records and also in securing for the Academy of Sciences an important role in the new regime.

Karroo (kəro͞oʹ, kä–), the semiarid plateaus of W Cape Prov., Republic of South Africa. The Little Karroo is located N of the Cape Ranges and extends c.200 mi (320 km) from east to west at an altitude of from 1,000 to 2,000 ft (305–610 m). It is separated from the Great Karroo (c.300 mi/480 km long; alt. 2,000–3,000 ft/610–915 m) by the Zwartberg Mts. The Karroo, where irrigated, is very fertile. Livestock grazing is important there, and citrus fruits and grains are raised. The name is also applied to the low scrub vegetation found in semiarid regions and also to a system of rocks laid down over central and southern Africa during the late Paleozoic and early Mesozoic eras.

Kars (kärs), city (1970 pop. 53,473), capital of Kars prov., E Turkey, in Armenia, on the Kars River, near the Soviet border. Its manufactures include textiles, carpets, and food products. An old fortified city, well situated in the mountains, Kars was the capital of an Armenian state in the 9th and 10th cent. It was destroyed by Tamerlane in 1386 and was captured and rebuilt by the Ottoman Turks in the 16th cent. In 1828, 1855, and 1877 the city was occupied by Russia and together with the surrounding region was ceded to Russia by the Congress of Berlin in 1878. By a peace treaty (1921) between the nationalist Turkish government of Kemal Atatürk and the USSR, Kars and Ardahan were returned to Turkey. Kars has an 11th-century Armenian church.

Karsavina, Tamara (təmäʹrə Kərsäʹvyĭnə), 1885–, Russian prima ballerina. Karsavina was trained in the Imperial Theatre School and the Maryinsky Theatre in St. Petersburg, making her debut at the latter in 1902. At its inception in 1909 she joined the Diaghilev Ballets Russes in Paris and was considered the greatest ballerina to perform with the company. Partner to Nijinsky, she created principal roles in many works, including *Les Sylphides, Petrouchka, Firebird, Le Spectre de la rose, Daphnis and Chloë*, and *The Three-Cornered Hat*. She danced with the company until 1929 and was a leading exponent of Michael Fokine's dance theories. In the 1940s she coached the Sadler's Wells company. Her books include her reminiscences, *Theatre Street* (1931), *Classical Ballet: The Flow of Movement* (1962), and *Ballet Technique* (1968).

Karshi (kərshēʹ), city (1970 pop. 71,000), S Central Asian USSR, in Uzbekistan, on the Kashka-Darya River. It is the center of a fertile oasis that produces wheat, cotton, and silk. Karshi was founded in the 14th cent. and has a 16th-century mosque and mausoleum.

Karst (kärst), Ital. *Carso*, Serbo-Croatian *Kras*, limestone plateau, in the Dinaric Alps, NW Yugoslavia, N of Istria and extending c.50 mi (80 km) SE from the lower Isonzo valley. It is characterized by deep gullies, caves, sinkholes, and underground drainage—all the result of carbonation-solution. The best-known caves are at Postojna. The barren nature of the plateau deters human settlement. Rough pasture or forest covers much of the surface, and there is little arable land. The term *karst* is used to describe any area where similar geological formations are found.

Kartah (kärʹtə), unidentified city, N central Palestine. Joshua 21.34.

Kartan (kärʹtăn), the same as KIRJATHAIM **1**.

Karun (käro͞onʹ), river, c.450 mi (720 km) long, rising in the Zagros mts., W Iran, and flowing S to the Shatt al Arab on the Iraqi border. The Karun is navigable to Ahvaz for shallow draft vessels; rapids prevent further upstream passage except during high water in April and May. The river was opened to foreign trade in 1888; but since the construction of a rail line during World War II between the river port of Khorramshahr, Ahvaz, and the main Iranian system, this route has lost importance. At Shushtar there is a dam designed to irrigate an area of 500 sq mi (1,295 sq km); it is surmounted by a magnificent bridge (no longer in use), probably built in the 3rd cent. for Shapur I of Persia by captured Roman soldiers.

Karun, Lake, Egypt: see MOERIS.

Karur (kəro͞orʹ), city (1971 pop. 65,246), Tamil Nadu state, S central India. Milled rice, cotton fabrics, and brassware are the city's chief products. According to Hindu legend, Brahma began the work of creation in Karur, which is referred to as the "place of the sacred cow." Upon the dissolution of the Hindu VIJAYANAGAR empire in 1565, Karur fell to the Naik kings of Madurai. The British occupied the city in 1760.

Karviná (kärʹvĭnä), Ger. *Karwin*, city (1970 pop. 76,215), N central Czechoslovakia, in Moravia, near the Polish border. It is an industrial center of the Ostrava-Karviná coal-mining region. Formerly in Austria, the city became (after 1918) an object of dispute between Poland and Czechoslovakia; after World War I a conference of Allied ambassadors awarded (1920) it to Czechoslovakia despite Polish claims. The city was seized by Poland in Oct., 1938, but was restored to Czechoslovakia in 1945.

Karyai, Greece: see ATHOS.

Kasai (käsīʹ), former province, c.124,000 sq mi (321,160 sq km), S central Zaïre. Luluabourg (present Kananga) was the capital. Between the Kasai and the Sankuru rivers the Kuba kingdom of the Shongo people existed from the early 17th cent. In the south of the province were the constantly warring Luba and Bena Lulua peoples. This ethnic conflict was partly responsible for the secession (Aug., 1960) of the Baluba-dominated Mining State of South Kasai, headed by Albert Kalonji, who proclaimed himself king of South Kasai. The central government reestablished control over the whole of Kasai in Dec., 1961. In 1967 the province was divided into two regions, Kasai-Oriental (capital, Mbuji-Mayi) and Kasai-Occidental (capital, Kananga).

Kasai or **Kassai,** river, c.1,100 mi (1,800 km) long, rising in central Angola, S central Africa, flowing E, N, and NW through W Zaïre to the Congo (Zaïre) River; it forms part of the Angola-Zaïre border. The Kasai, navigable for c.475 mi (760 km) above its mouth, is an important trade artery. Its tributaries include many navigable streams (some of which are rich in alluvial diamonds).

Kasan: see KAZAN, USSR.

Kasavubu, Joseph (käsʺəvo͞oʹbo͞o, käʹsə–), 1917?–1969, African political leader, president of the Republic of the Congo (now Zaïre) from 1960 to 1965. He studied for the Roman Catholic priesthood but did not complete his training. Later, he became active in the nationalist movement while teaching school and working for the Belgian government in the Congo. In 1946 he asserted that the Congolese were the legitimate owners of the country and that the Belgians, as intruders, had to leave. In 1955 he became president of Abako, a cultural association of the Bakongo tribe. Under his leadership Abako became a powerful political organization. Briefly imprisoned in 1959 for inciting violence, he later attended (1960) the conference at Brussels that led to independence for the Congo. He became (1960) the Congo's first head of state. There ensued a struggle for power between him and Patrice LUMUMBA, the premier, in which each attempted to dismiss the other. Lumumba was ousted by Kasavubu with the aid of General MOBUTU SESE SEKO. In 1965, Mobutu deposed Kasavubu, who retired from politics.

Kasbek, Mount: see KAZBEK, MOUNT, USSR.

Kasbin, Iran: see QAZVIN.

Kaschau: see KOŠICE, Czechoslovakia.

Kashan (kăshänʹ), city (1966 pop. 58,468), Tehran prov., central Iran. The city has long been noted for its silk textiles, carpets, ceramics, copperware, and rose water. The Ardebil carpet and celebrated porcelain tiles were made there in the Safavid period. The present city is also a transportation center. Kashan is one of Iran's loveliest cities; the skyline is dominated by a 13th-century minaret that is 150 ft (45 m) high. Sialk, a prehistoric site, is nearby. The well-known rose fields of Qamsar, or Kamsar, are nearby.

Kashgar (kăshʹgärʹ), Mandarin *K'a-shih*, city (1970 est. pop. 175,000), SW Sinkiang Uigur Autonomous Region, China, on the Kashgar River (a tributary of the Tarim). It is the hub of an important commercial district, the western terminus of the main road of the province, and a center for caravan trade with India, Afghanistan, and the USSR. Cotton and wool cloth, rugs, and gold and silver jewelry are manufactured. From Kashgar a mountain pass provides a route to Samarkand and thence to the Middle East. The city, predominantly Uigur in ethnic composition, first came under Chinese rule in the period of the Han dynasty (206 B.C.–A.D. 221). Romans traded there in the 6th cent. When Kashgar was the capital of the Uigur Turks (750–840), it was also a center of

Manichaeism. Visited by Marco Polo in 1275, Kashgar was soon after conquered by Jenghiz Khan. From the 15th to the 17th cent. it was ruled by hereditary Khojar (Muslim) kings. The city passed definitively to China in 1760, but since then there have been uprisings and periods of contested control.

Kashing: see CHIA-HSING, China.

Kashiwazaki (kăshēwä'zäkē), city (1970 pop. 73,569), Niigata prefecture, central Honshu, Japan, on the Japan Sea. It is an agricultural center and a resort with hot springs.

Kashka-Darya (kəshkä'-dəryä'), river, c.200 mi (320 km) long, Central Asian USSR. It is the basis of a wide network of irrigation canals near the towns of Kitab and Kashi.

Kashmir, officially **Jammu and Kashmir** (kăshmēr', kăsh'mēr; jŭ'mo͞o), former princely state, c.86,000 sq mi (222,800 sq km), NW India and NE Pakistan. The region is administered in two sections: the Indian state of Jammu and Kashmir (1971 pop. 4,615,176), c.54,000 sq mi (139,900 sq km), with its capital at SRINAGAR, the historic capital of the state; and the Pakistani-controlled Azad Kashmir, c.32,000 sq mi (82,900 sq km), with MUZAFFARABAD as its capital. Kashmir is bordered on the W by Pakistan, on the S by India, and on the N and E by China. One of the most beautiful regions of the East, Kashmir is covered with lofty, rugged mountains, including sections of the Himalayan and Karakorum ranges. Rivers, including the Indus, run through relatively narrow but heavily populated valleys. The valley of the Jhelum River, the celebrated Vale of Kashmir, is the most populous area and the economic heart of the region; it produces abundant crops of wheat and rice. The handicraft industry, particularly the making of woolen cloth and shawls (cashmeres), for which the state was renowned, has declined. In the late 14th cent., after years of Buddhist and Hindu rule, Kashmir was conquered by Muslims who converted most of the population to Islam. It became part of the Mogul empire in 1586, but by 1751 the local ruler was independent. After a century of disorder the British pacified Kashmir in 1846 and installed a Hindu prince as ruler of the predominantly Muslim region. When India was partitioned in 1947, a Muslim revolt, supported by tribesmen from Pakistan, flared up against the state government of Kashmir. The Hindu ruler fled to Delhi and there signed an agreement that placed Kashmir under the dominion of India. Indian troops were flown to Srinagar to engage the rebels. Pakistan, backing the rebels, later dispatched troops to oppose the Indian forces. The fighting was ended by a UN cease-fire in 1949, but the region was divided between India and Pakistan along the cease-fire line. A constituent assembly in Indian Kashmir voted in 1953 for incorporation into India, but this move was delayed by continued Pakistani-Indian disagreement and disapproval by the United Nations of annexation without a plebiscite. In 1955 an outbreak of fighting ended in an agreement between India and Pakistan to keep their respective forces in Kashmir 6 mi (10 km) apart. A new vote by the assembly in Indian Kashmir in 1956 led to the integration of Kashmir as an Indian state; Azad Kashmir remained, however, under the control of Pakistan. India refused to consider subsequent Pakistani protests and UN resolutions calling for a plebiscite. The situation was further complicated in 1959, when Chinese troops occupied the district of Ladakh and neighboring areas. China, rejecting Indian protests, held the territory. Indian-Pakistani relations became more inflamed in 1963 when a Sino-Pakistani agreement defined the Chinese border with Pakistani Kashmir. Serious fighting between India and Pakistan broke out again in Aug., 1965. A UN cease-fire took effect in September. In Jan., 1966, President Ayub Khan of Pakistan and Prime Minister Lal Bahadur Shastri of India met at Tashkent in the Soviet Union at the invitation of the Soviet government and an agreement was reached providing for the mutual withdrawal of troops to the positions held before the latest outbreak of fighting. In the Dec., 1971, war between India and Pakistan, however, there was further fighting in Kashmir in which India made some gains. In Dec., 1972, a new cease-fire line along the positions held at the end of the 1971 war was agreed to by India and Pakistan.

Kashmiri (kăshmē'rē), language belonging to the Dardic group of the Indo-Iranian subfamily of the Indo-European family of languages. See INDO-IRANIAN LANGUAGES.

Kasimir. For Polish rulers thus named, see CASIMIR.

Kaskaskia (kăskăs'kēə), village (1970 pop. 79), Randolph co., SE Ill., on Kaskaskia island in the Mississippi River where it is joined by the Kaskaskia River. It is now relatively unpopulated, mainly because it was inundated by the Mississippi toward the close of the 19th cent., but Kaskaskia's past is deeply rooted in the history of the region. The settlement was established by Jesuit missionaries in 1703 (four years after the founding of Cahokia) and named for the Kaskaskia Indians, a tribe of the Illinois, who inhabited the area. In time an agricultural community grew up on the fertile bottomlands surrounding the village, and traders made it a center of operations. The French built a fort there in 1721 and occupied it until 1755; it was destroyed when Kaskaskia was taken over by the British in 1763. In 1778, during the American Revolution, George Rogers Clark, with a company of Virginia militia, took possession of the village for the United States, and a period of turbulence followed the departure of Clark's troops in 1780. Kaskaskia declined for two decades, then thrived as the capital of Illinois Territory (1809–18) and state capital (1818–20). The first Illinois newspaper was started there in 1814. The community again declined after the capital of Illinois was shifted (1820) to Vandalia, and periodic floods discouraged further growth. Fort Kaskaskia State Park was set aside in 1927 across the Mississippi River near Chester, Ill.

Kasprowicz, Jan (yän käsprô'vēch), 1860–1926, Polish poet. His writings progressed from social revolt (e.g., *From a Peasant's Field,* 1891) to poems of spiritual struggle and philosophical intensity. Among his later works are *To a Dying World* (1902), *Ballad of the Sunflower* (1908), and *The Book of the Poor* (1916). Highly regarded by his contemporaries, Kasprowicz was also renowned for his translations of English, French, German, and Italian classics.

Kassa: see KOŠICE, Czechoslovakia.

Kassala (käsä'lä, kăs'əlä), city (1969 est. pop. 81,000), NE Sudan. It is a cotton market and rail transport center and has extensive fruit gardens. Founded in 1840 as a military camp for the troops of Muhammad Ali during his conquest of Sudan, Kassala was captured by the Mahdists in 1885 and by the Italians in 1894. Restored to Egyptian sovereignty in 1897, it became part of the Anglo-Egyptian Sudan.

Kassel (käs'əl), city (1970 pop. 214,156), Hesse, E West Germany, on the Fulda River. It is an industrial, rail, and cultural center. Manufactures include machinery, chemicals, textiles, optical and precision instruments, locomotives, and motor vehicles. Kassel was mentioned in 913 and was chartered in 1198. It became (1567) the capital of the landgraviate of Hesse-Kassel (raised to an electorate in 1803). Kassel also was the capital of the kingdom of Westphalia (1807–13) under Jérôme Bonaparte. After Electoral Hesse and Nassau passed (1866) to Prussia and were united as the province of Hesse-Nassau, Kassel was made the capital. As a center of German airplane and tank production in World War II, Kassel was severely damaged by Allied air raids. Many historic buildings were destroyed, but after 1945 much of the city's former beauty was restored. Kassel has several important museums. International exhibits ("Documenta") of modern art are periodically held in the city. A former spelling is Cassel.

Kassem, Abdul Karim (äbdo͝ol' kärēm' kässēm'), 1914–63, Iraqi general and politician. A graduate (1934) of the Iraqi military academy, he attended the army staff college. His outstanding bravery, shown in campaigns against the Kurds and in the Palestinian war of 1948, won him many military decorations. He organized the military coup d'etat that in July, 1958, overthrew the Iraqi monarchy and established Kassem as premier of the new republic. An Arab nationalist, he quelled a pro-Communist uprising in 1959. After this, Kassem's power and influence steadily deteriorated. He was overthrown and executed by military and civilian members of the BA'ATH PARTY in Feb., 1963.

Kasserine Pass, gap, 2 mi (3.2 km) wide, central Tunisia, in the Grand Dorsal chain (an extension of the Atlas Mts.). A key point in the Allied offensive in Tunisia in World War II, the pass was the scene of an Axis breakthrough (Feb. 20, 1943), but it was retaken with very heavy losses by U.S. forces on Feb. 25. See NORTH AFRICA, CAMPAIGNS IN.

Kassites or **Cassites,** ancient people, probably of Indo-European origin. They were first mentioned in historical texts as occupying the W Iranian plateau. In the 18th cent. B.C. they swept down on BABYLONIA, conquered the region, and ruled there until the 12th cent. B.C., when they returned to the Iranian plateau. They remained more or less independent until the beginning of the Christian era, when they disappeared from history.

Kastamonu (kä"stämōno͞o'), city (1970 pop. 29,303), capital of Kastamonu prov., N Turkey. It is a manufacturing center, noted for its textiles and copper utensils, and is the chief city of a region rich in minerals. Kastamonu was captured by the Ottoman Turks in 1393, was taken by Tamerlane in 1403, and was regained by the Ottomans in 1460.

Kastoría (kästôrē'ə), city (1971 pop. 15,407), capital of Kastoría prefecture, N Greece, in Macedonia, on a peninsula extending into Lake Kastoría. It is a market for farm produce, and it has fisheries. In the 17th and 18th cent. it was a major fur-trade center. In the city are many little Byzantine churches and palatial homes.

Kástron (kä'strôn), town (1971 pop. 3,982), E Greece, on Límnos island, in the Aegean Sea. It is a seaport trading in local produce. In ancient times it was known as Myrina. Today it is also called Kastro or Castro.

Kasugai (käso͞o'gī), city (1970 pop. 161,835), Aichi prefecture, central Honshu, Japan. It is a suburb of Nagoya and the site of silk and textile industries.

Katahdin (kətä'dĭn), mountain, 5,267 ft (1,605 m) high, between branches of the Penobscot River in N central Maine; highest point in Maine. The peak and the beautifully wooded, lake-dotted territory surrounding it constitute Baxter State Park, the gift of Gov. Percival P. Baxter in 1931. Katahdin mt. is the northern terminus of the Appalachian Trail.

Katanga: see SHABA, province, Zaïre.

Katar: see QATAR.

Katayama, Tetsu (tĕt'so͞o kätäyä'mä), 1887–, Japanese statesman. Active as a youth in the Japanese labor movement, he was a founder (1926) of the Social Democratic party. When the party was suppressed by the police, he helped organize (1931) its successor, the Social Mass party. He was forced to retire from prewar politics because of his opposition to the invasion of Manchuria (1931–32) and continuation of the second Sino-Japanese War (1937–45). After World War II he reentered politics as president of the Socialist party and was prime minister (1947–48) of a coalition cabinet.

Katayev, Valentin Petrovich (vəlyĭntyēn' pētrô'vĭch kətī'əf), 1897–, Russian novelist, short-story writer, and playwright. Katayev's novels portray almost the entire range of Soviet life, from the period of the New Economic Policy (*The Embezzlers,* 1927, tr. 1929) through the first Five-Year Plan (*Time, Forward!,* 1932, tr. 1933) to World War II (*The Wife,* 1944, tr. 1946). In *Peace Is Where the Tempests Blow* (1936, tr. 1937) he described a pleasant childhood in Odessa against the background of the Revolution of 1905. Katayev's comedies became very popular, especially *Squaring the Circle* (1929, tr. 1934), a farce about Soviet marriage and housing conditions. His later works include *The Holy Well* (tr. 1967) and a volume of reminiscences, *Grass of Oblivion* (1967, tr. 1970). His younger brother, Yevgeny, used the surname Petrov in collaborating with Ilya ILF.

Kateríni (kätərē'nē), city (1971 pop. 28,808), capital of Piería prefecture, N Greece, in Macedonia. It is the commercial center for a productive tobacco-growing region.

Katharine or **Katherine.** For some persons so named, see CATHERINE.

Katharine of Aragón, 1485–1536, first queen consort of HENRY VIII of England; daughter of Ferdinand II of Aragón and Isabella of Castile. In 1501 she was married to Arthur, eldest son of Henry VII. He died in 1502, and the marriage of Katharine to his brother, Henry, was projected. A papal dispensation was obtained, but the marriage was delayed by diplomatic wrangling between Henry VII and Ferdinand and did not take place until the prince had ascended (1509) the throne as Henry VIII. As governor of the realm during Henry's expedition to the Continent in 1513, she organized the successful defense against Scottish invasion that ended in the English victory at Flodden. Only one of Katharine's six children survived infancy (see MARY I), and Henry was disappointed at her failure to produce a male heir. The English alliance with Katharine's nephew, Holy Roman Emperor CHARLES V, wavered and fell in 1525, and her political importance declined. Finally, Henry became strongly infatuated with Anne BOLEYN. In 1527, with the help of Cardinal Thomas WOLSEY, Henry began the attempt to have his marriage annulled. This move precipitated the chain of events that ended in the English Reformation. Katharine steadfastly refused to acknowledge the invalidity of the marriage or to retire to a convent. In 1529 at a trial conducted by cardinals CAMPEGGIO and Wolsey, she appealed vainly to Henry, denied the jurisdiction of the court because it was under pressure by the king, and withdrew. Pope CLEMENT

VII recalled the hearing to Rome, in effect denying the divorce. Henry then proceeded on his own; after his secret marriage to Anne Boleyn in 1533, a court presided over by Thomas CRANMER pronounced the former marriage invalid. Katharine refused to accept the decision. The pope's formal declaration for her in 1534 came too late. She was separated from her daughter, Mary, never visited by Henry, and confined with few attendants at various inferior estates. Katharine nevertheless refused, despite all threats and mistreatment, to take the title of princess dowager or to acknowledge the Act of Succession and the Act of Supremacy. Her great popularity with the common people of England never waned throughout the long period of her misfortunes. She died after a prolonged illness. See Albert Du Boys, *Catherine of Aragon and the Sources of the English Reformation* (1881, repr. 1968); biographies by Garrett Mattingly (1941, repr. 1960) and Mary M. Luke (1967).

Kathiawar (kä'tēəwär''), peninsula, c.25,000 sq mi (64,750 sq km), W India, between the Gulf of Kutch and the Gulf of Cambay. Almost all of Kathiawar is included in Gujarat state; a small area is part of Goa, Damar, and Diu. The region, mostly level, produces much cotton and has stone quarries and cement and chemical industries. Bhavnagar is the chief port. Under British rule the region contained numerous princely states.

Katmai National Monument (kăt'mī), 2,792,137 acres (1,129,978 hectares), at the northern end of the Alaska Peninsula, S Alaska; has the second largest area in the U.S. National Park System; est. 1918. Mt. Katmai and Novarupta volcanoes and the Valley of the Ten Thousand Smokes are located in this dying volcanic region, which is the site of one of the greatest eruptions in history, that of Novarupta in 1912. All plant and animal life in the area was destroyed by the ash and lava, although no persons were reported killed. Kodiak Island, 100 mi (160 km) to the southeast, was covered with c.1 ft (.3 m) of ash. As lava beneath Mt. Katmai drained W to Novarupta, its top collapsed, forming a crater, 8 mi (12.8 km) in circumference and 3,700 ft (1,128 m) deep, in which a lake has formed. The Valley of the Ten Thousand Smokes (72 sq mi/186 sq km) has countless holes and cracks through which hot gases passed to the surface; all but a few are now extinct. The region is inaccessible except to specially equipped expeditions. The national monument also includes glacier-covered peaks and crater lakes. Moose and brown bear thrive in the area.

Katmandu (kätmändōō'), city (1971 pop. 332,982), capital of Nepal, central Nepal, c.4,500 ft (1,370 m) above sea level, in a fertile valley of the E Himalayas. It is the administrative, business, and commercial center of Nepal, and lies astride an ancient trade and pilgrim route from India to Tibet, China, and Mongolia. The Buddha was reputedly born near the city. Originally ruled by the Newars, Katmandu became independent in the 15th cent. and was captured in 1768 by the Gurkhas, who made it their capital. The Gurkhas timed their invasion to coincide with the annual Indra Jatra festival (in honor of the goddess Devi), knowing that the people of Katmandu would be engrossed in the celebration and unlikely to offer resistance. In the late 18th cent. the city became the seat of a British resident. Landmarks include the elaborate royal palace, several pagoda-shaped temples, and many Sanskrit libraries. Katmandu also has a number of colleges.

Kato, Komei (Takaaki) (kō'mā kä'tō, täkä-ä'kē), 1860-1926, Japanese statesman. He entered the foreign ministry after graduating from Tokyo Univ. He served (1909) as ambassador to Great Britain. He was foreign minister (1914-15), but his presentation of the Twenty-one Demands to China forced his resignation. Later he organized and headed the conservative Kenseikai party. During his term (1924-25) as prime minister his cabinet was called "the Mitsubishi government," because he and his foreign minister, SHIDEHARA, were both connected by marriage with the Mitsubishi interests. His administration reduced army strength and government expenditures, initiated universal military training, increased military instruction on all educational levels, sponsored the manhood-suffrage law, and favored the Peace Preservation Law, penalizing political heterodoxy.

Kato, Tomosaburo (tōmōs''ä''bōōrō', kä'tō), 1861-1923, Japanese admiral. He was naval chief of staff (1894-95) and chief assistant to Admiral Togo in the Russo-Japanese War. As navy minister from 1915 to 1923, he directed Japanese naval operations in World War I and the naval expansion thereafter. At the Washington Conference (1921-22) he accepted the principle of naval limitation. He was prime minister (1922-23).

Katona, József (yō'zhĕf kŏ'tônŏ), 1791-1830, Hungarian dramatist. His classic tragedy *Bánk Bán* (1821) was among the first important works in Magyar. It was set to music by Francis Erkel (1810-93) and became Hungary's most popular opera. The work is remarkable for its portrayal of emotional conflict.

Katowice (kätôvē'tsĕ), Ger. *Kattowitz,* city (1970 pop. 303,264), S Poland. One of the chief mining and industrial centers of Poland, it has industries producing heavy machinery and chemicals; mines in the region yield coal, iron, zinc, and lead. The city was chartered in 1865 and passed from Germany to Poland in 1921. Katowice is also an important educational and cultural center.

Katrine, Loch (lŏkh kăt'rĭn), lake, 8 mi (12.9 km) long and 1 mi (1.6 km) wide, Perthshire, central Scotland. Its beauty is celebrated in Sir Walter Scott's *Lady of the Lake.* When Loch Katrine became Glasgow's main source of water, the lake was enlarged (1859), and the Silver Strand of Scott's poem disappeared. Glen Gyle, at the head of the lake, is Rob Roy's birthplace.

Katrineholm (kä''trēnəhôlm'), city (1970 pop. 22,045), Södermanland co., S Sweden; chartered 1917. It is a commercial, industrial, and transportation center. The city has one of Europe's largest dairies and other industries thát manufacture ball bearings, automobile bodies, furniture, and machinery.

Katsina (kätsē'nə, kăt'sīnə), city (1969 est. pop. 105,000), N Nigeria, near the Niger frontier. The city, surrounded by a wall 13 mi (21 km) long, is the trade center for an agricultural region where guinea corn and millet are grown for home consumption, and groundnuts, cotton, and hides are produced commercially. Leather handicrafts are made in Katsina. In the 17th and 18th cent. it was the largest of the seven HAUSA city-states and the cultural and commercial center of Hausaland. In 1807, Katsina was conquered by the FULANI and lost its preeminent position among Hausa cities to KANO. The city is the site of Katsina Training College and Gobaru Tower mosque.

Katsura, Taro (tärō' kät'sōōrä), 1847-1913, Japanese statesman. A Choshu clansman, and a protégé of Aritomo YAMAGATA, he served as war minister, then (1901-6) as prime minister. During that administration, with the Anglo-Japanese Alliance in 1902 and the defeat (1904-5) of Russia, Japan emerged as the major power in the Far East and gained effective control over Korea. In the Taft-Katsura agreement of 1905, the United States recognized that control. In 1906, Katsura resigned because of public dissatisfaction with the Portsmouth Treaty. As prime minister again (1908-11), he annexed Korea and engaged in a struggle with the Diet over expansion of the military budget. His reappointment as prime minister in 1912 came after the overthrow of Kimmochi SAIONJI for failure to approve increased army spending, and was widely interpreted as an example of GENRO manipulation. The major parliamentary parties united in opposition, organized mass demonstrations, and passed a nonconfidence motion. Katsura lost support of the genro when he attempted to form a new party and sought imperial intervention to rescind the nonconfidence motion. He was forced to resign.

Katsuta (kätsōō'tä), city (1970 pop. 66,754), Ibaraki prefecture, central Honshu, Japan, on the Naka River. It is a commercial center with mechanical, automotive, and electronics industries.

Kattath (kăt'tăth), unidentified city, N central Palestine. Joshua 19.15.

Kattegat (kăt'ĭgăt''), strait, c.140 mi (230 km) long and from 40 to 100 mi (60-160 km) wide, between Sweden and Denmark. It is connected with the North Sea through the Skagerrak, which begins at the northern tip of Jutland, and with the Baltic Sea by way of the Øresund, Store Baelt, and Lille Baelt. Göteborg (Sweden) and Århus (Denmark) are the chief ports.

Kattowitz: see KATOWICE, Poland.

Katun (kətōōn'), river, c.415 mi (670 km) long, Altai Kray, S Siberian USSR. It rises in the Katun Alps and flows generally north to join the Biya, with which it forms the Ob River. The Katun is partly navigable.

katydid, common name of certain large, singing, winged INSECTS belonging to the long-horned GRASSHOPPER family (Tettigoniidae) in the order Orthoptera. Katydids are green or, occasionally, pink and range in size from 1¼ to 5 in. (3-12.5 cm) long. Katydids are nocturnal and arboreal; they sing in the evening. The males have song-producing, or stridulating, organs located on their front wings. The females chirp in response to the shrill song of the males, which supposedly sounds like "katy did, katy didn't," hence the name. The song serves a function in courtship, which occurs in late summer. The female lays eggs in the ground or in plant tissue; the eggs hatch in spring. Newly hatched katydids resemble the adults except for their smaller size and lack of wings. Katydids are common in the E United States and are also found in the tropics. They are classified in the phylum ARTHROPODA, class Insecta, order Orthoptera, suborder Ensifera, family Tettigoniidae.

Katyn (kətĭn'), village, W central European USSR. It was occupied by the Germans in Aug., 1941, during World War II. In 1943 the German government announced that the mass grave of some 4,250 Polish officers had been found in a forest near Katyn and accused the Soviets of having massacred them. The officers had been captured during the Soviet invasion of Poland in 1939. The Soviet government denied the German charges and asserted that the Poles, war prisoners, had been captured and executed by invading German units in 1941. The Soviets refused to permit an investigation by the International Red Cross. In 1944, a Soviet investigating commission alleged that the Germans killed the officers. In 1951-52, a U.S. Congressional investigation charged that the Soviets had executed the Poles. See J. K. Zawodny, *Death in the Forest* (1972).

Katzenbach, Nicholas deBelleville (kăt'sənbăk), 1922-, U.S. Attorney General (1965-66), b. Philadelphia. He served (1950-56) as adviser in the office of the general counsel to the Secretary of the Air Force and was on the law faculties of Yale (1952-56) and the Univ. of Chicago (1956-60). In 1961 he joined the Justice Department as Assistant Attorney General in charge of the Office of Legal Counsel. As Deputy Attorney General (1962-64) he played an important role in the enforcement of desegregation at the universities of Mississippi and Alabama, and he helped draft the Civil Rights Act of 1964. When Robert F. Kennedy resigned as Attorney General in Sept., 1964, President Lyndon B. Johnson named him acting Attorney General. In Feb., 1965, he was confirmed as Attorney General. He succeeded George Ball as Undersecretary of State in 1966. He resigned in 1968 to become vice president of IBM Corp.

Katzimo, New Mexico: see ENCHANTED MESA.

Kauai (kou''wī'), circular island (1970 pop. 29,524), 549 sq mi (1,422 sq km), 32 mi (52 km) in diameter, N Hawaii, separated from Oahu island to the southeast by Kauai Channel. Lihue (1970 pop. 3,124) is the largest town and Nawiliwili Harbor the chief port. Geologically, Kauai is the oldest of the Hawaiian Islands. It was formed by now extinct volcanoes; Kawaikini (5,170 ft/1,576 m high) and Waialeale (5,080 ft/1,548 m high) are the tallest peaks. High annual rainfall has eroded deep valleys in Kauai's central mountain mass. Waimea Canyon (2,000-3,000 ft/610-915 m deep; c.10 mi/16 km long) resembles a miniature Grand Canyon. The northeastern slopes of Waialeale, one of the wettest spots on earth, receive an annual average rainfall of 450 in. (1,143 cm). An independent kingdom when visited by English Capt. James Cook in 1778, Kauai became part of the Kingdom of Hawaii in 1810. The first major attempt at agricultural development in Hawaii took place there with the establishment of a sugar plantation in 1835. Most of the island's people live along the coast. Agriculture is the main industry, with sugarcane, rice, and pineapples the chief crops; ranching and tourism are also important.

Kauffmann, Angelica (äng-gä'lēkä kouf'män), 1741-1807, Swiss neoclassical painter and graphic artist. From her youth she was known for her artistic, musical, and linguistic abilities. She went to England, where she enjoyed success as a fashionable portrait painter and decorator. A protégée of Sir Joshua Reynolds, Kauffman was one of the original members of the Royal Academy. She often decorated houses designed by the ADAM brothers. After her marriage in 1781 to the Venetian painter Antonio Zucchi, she lived in Italy, where she flourished in artistic and literary circles. Reynolds, Winckelmann, Goethe, and Garrick commissioned her to paint their portraits. Representative works include *Religion* (National Gall., London); *Self-Portrait* (Staatliche Museen, Berlin); and the etchings of *L'Allegra* and *La Pensierosa.* The British Museum has a collection of her drawings and prints. See study by Lady Victoria Manners and G. C. Williamson (1924).

Kaufman, George S. (kôf'mən), 1889-1961, American dramatist and journalist, b. Pittsburgh. As a drama critic for various New York newspapers he was influential in raising the standards of criticism in the theater. He collaborated on more than 40 plays, many of them tremendously successful, which varied in mood from the rowdy farces of his early days to his later more sophisticated comedies. His collaboration with Marc Connelly produced such plays as *Merton of the Movies* (1922) and *Beggar on Horseback* (1924) and was followed by collaborations with Ring Lardner—*June Moon* (1929)—and Edna Ferber—*The Royal Family* (1927), *Dinner at Eight* (1932), and *Stage Door* (1936). In 1932, Kaufman won the Pulitzer Prize for the musical *Of Thee I Sing* (1931), written with Morrie Ryskind, to a score by George Gershwin. Some of his most famous plays were done in collaboration with Moss Hart, notably *Once in a Lifetime* (1930), *Merrily We Roll Along* (1934), *You Can't Take It with You* (1936; Pulitzer Prize), and *The Man Who Came to Dinner* (1939). Among his later works are *The Late George Apley* (with J. P. Marquand, 1944) and *The Solid Gold Cadillac* (with Howard Teichmann, 1954). Kaufman directed several successful plays including *The Front Page* (1928), *My Sister Eileen* (1940), and *Guys and Dolls* (1950). See biographies by Howard Teichmann (1972) and Scott Meredith (1974).

Kaufmann Peak: see LENIN PEAK, USSR.

Kaukauna (kôkô'nə), industrial city (1970 pop. 11,292), Outagamie co., E Wis., on the Fox River; settled 1793, inc. 1885. The city has a large paper plant; dairy items, foundry products, machine tools, and farm equipment are also manufactured. A fur-trading post was established on the site by Pierre Grignon in 1760. The Grignon mansion, built 1836–39 on the first land deeded in Wisconsin, has been restored. Outagamie County Teachers College is in Kaukauna.

Kaunas (kou'näs), Pol. *Kowno,* Rus. *Kovno,* city (1967 est. pop. 284,000), W European USSR, in Lithuania, on the Neman River. It is a river port and an industrial center with industries producing machinery, iron and steel, chemicals, plastics, and textiles. Probably founded as a fortress at the end of the 10th cent., Kaunas was a medieval trading center and a Lithuanian stronghold against the Teutonic Knights. It passed to a united Lithuanian-Polish state in 1569 and to Russia in the third partition of Poland (1795). Although strongly fortified by the Russians, it was captured (1915) by the Germans in World War I. From 1918 to 1940, Kaunas was the provisional capital of Lithuania—Vilnius (which Lithuania claimed as its rightful capital) being held by Poland until 1939 and by Russia in 1939–40. Kaunas was occupied by German forces from 1941 to 1944. During the German occupation the Jews of Kaunas (about 30% of the prewar population) were virtually exterminated. Before evacuating at the approach of Soviet troops the Germans destroyed much of the city. Nearby are a 16th-century town hall, the ruins of a castle (14th–15th cent.), the Vytautus church (15th cent.), and a noted 17th-century monastery. The city has a university (founded 1922), a polytechnical institute (founded 1950), a medical institute (founded 1951), and several museums.

Kaunda, Kenneth (koun'də), 1924–, African political leader, president of Zambia (1964–), b. Northern Rhodesia (now Zambia). Kaunda entered the nationalist movement after working as a teacher and welfare officer. He opposed (1953) the formation of the Federation of Rhodesia and Nyasaland. His party was banned in 1959, and Kaunda was imprisoned, but in 1960 he was released and became head of a new independence party, the United National Independence party (UNIP). In 1962 he rejected a constitution proposed by Great Britain for Northern Rhodesia, charging that it would perpetuate white supremacy. Nevertheless, he took part in elections that October, and after winning a parliamentary seat, formed a coalition government. He continued to press for dissolution of the federation, which eventually came about in Dec., 1963, and the following year, when Zambia gained its independence, Kaunda became its first president. He was reelected in 1968 and 1973. In 1969, he nationalized Zambia's copper mines. Faced with increasing tribal dissension, Kaunda, in 1972, pushed through a bill making the UNIP the only political party in Zambia. In foreign affairs, Kaunda became increasingly uncompromising toward the white-supremacist government of neighboring Rhodesia. Kaunda has written several books, including *Black Government,* (with C. M. Morris, 1960), *Zambia Shall be Free* (an autobiography, 1962), and *Humanism in Africa and a Guide to Its Implementation* (1967). See biography by R. S. Hall (1965).

Kaunitz, Wenzel Anton, Fürst von (vĕn'tsəl än'tôn fürst fən kou'nĭts), 1711–94, Austrian statesman. He distinguished himself as a negotiator of the Treaty of Aix-la-Chapelle (1748) and was (1750–53) ambassador to Paris. From 1753 until his retirement in 1792 he served the Hapsburg rulers, Maria Theresa, Joseph II, and Leopold II, as chancellor and foreign minister. Reversing 300 years of Hapsburg diplomacy, Kaunitz recognized Prussia rather than France as the chief enemy of Austria and was responsible for the coalition that led to the SEVEN YEARS WAR. Through Kaunitz, Austria shared in the first partition of Poland (1772). Kaunitz did not agree with all of the reforms of Joseph II, but he helped Joseph centralize the administration. Kaunitz is regarded as one of the most astute statesmen of the 18th cent.

Kautsky, Karl Johann (kärl yō'hän kout'skē), 1854–1938, German-Austrian socialist, b. Prague. A leading figure in the effort to spread Marxist doctrine in Germany, he was the principal deviser of the Erfurt Program, which set the German Social Democratic party on an orthodox Marxist path and established him as a dominant figure in the Second INTERNATIONAL. He was a consistent opponent of Eduard BERNSTEIN and other socialists who advocated revision of Marxist doctrines. After initial hesitation he opposed the Social Democratic party's support of the German effort in World War I and helped form, with Hugo HAASE, the Independent Social Democratic party. Soon after the Bolshevik Revolution (1917) in Russia, he condemned it as undemocratic and non-Marxian. Kautsky wrote a great amount of socialist and other literature and edited the German documents on the origin of World War I (4 vol., 1919). Among his translated works are *The Economic Doctrines of Karl Marx* (tr. 1925), *Ethics and the Materialist Conception of History* (tr. 1907), and *Bolshevism at a Deadlock* (tr. 1931).

kava or **kavakava** (kä'vəkä"və): see PEPPER.

Kaválla or **Cavala** (both: kävä'lä), city (1971 pop. 46,234), capital of Kaválla prefecture, NE Greece, in Macedonia; a port on the Gulf of Kaválla, an inlet of the Aegean Sea. Surrounded by a rich tobacco-growing hinterland, it is a leading Greek city for processing and exporting tobacco. Fish and manganese are also shipped, and flour is manufactured. Known as Neapolis in ancient times, the city was the landing place of St. Paul on his way to Philippi, the ancient site of which is nearby. Kaválla was held by the Ottoman Turks from 1387 to 1913, when it passed to Greece.

Kaveri, river, India: see CAUVERY.

Kaverin, Veniamin Aleksandrovich (vĕnyəmēn' əlyĭksän'drəvĭch kəvyĕ'rĭn), 1902–, Russian novelist and short-story writer. He was a member of the literary group that called itself the Serapion Brothers, and he expounded that circle's creed of the artistic independence of politics in the story *The Unknown Artist* (1931, tr. 1947). Later Kaverin turned to a more conventional style. A long novel, *The Fulfillment of Desires* (1934–35, tr. *The Larger View,* 1938), deals with the adjustment of the intellectual to Soviet society. His later work includes *Open Book* (1953, tr. 1957). See study by Donald Piper (1970).

Kavir Buzurg, Iran: see DASHT-E KAVIR.

Kaw, river: see KANSAS, river.

Kawabata, Yasunari (yäsōōnä'rē käwä'bätä), 1899–1972, Japanese novelist. His first major work, *The Izu Dancer,* was published in 1925. He came to be a leader of the school of Japanese writers that propounded a lyrical and impressionistic style, in opposition to the proletarian literature of the 1920s. Kawabata's melancholy novels often treat, in a delicate, oblique fashion, sexual relationships between men and women. For example, *Snow Country* (tr. 1956), probably his best-known work in the West, depicts the affair of an aging geisha and an insensitive Tokyo businessman. All Kawabata's works are distinguished by a masterful, and frequently arresting, use of imagery. Among his works in English translation are the novels *Thousand Cranes* (tr. 1959), *The Sound of the Mountain* (tr. 1970), and *The Lake* (tr. 1974), and the volume of short stories, *The House of the Sleeping Beauties and Other Stories* (tr. 1969). In 1968, Kawabata became the first Japanese author to receive the Nobel Prize in literature. Four years later, in declining health and probably depressed by the suicide of his friend Yukio Mishima, he committed suicide. See his Nobel Prize speech, *Japan the Beautiful and Myself* (tr. 1969).

Kawagoe (käwä'gōä), city (1970 pop. 171,038), Saitama prefecture, central Honshu, Japan. Silk textiles are manufactured in the city. Kawagoe is the site of Kitain Temple (built 830), famed for its images of the 500 disciples of Buddha.

Kawaguchi (käwä'gōōchē), city (1970 pop. 305,887), Saitama prefecture, central Honshu, Japan, on the Ajikawa and Kizagawa rivers. A Tokyo suburb, it has ironworks and textile mills.

Kawanishi (käwä'nēshē), city (1970 pop. 87,127), Hyogo prefecture, central Honshu, Japan, on the Ina River. It is an agricultural and commercial center and the site of a hat-manufacturing industry.

Kawartha Lakes (kəwôr'thə), group of 14 lakes, in a region c.50 mi (80 km) long and c.25 mi (40 km) wide, S Ont., Canada, near the towns of Lindsay and Peterborough. Balsam is the largest lake. They are popular as summer resorts. Many of the lakes form part of the Trent Canal system.

Kawasaki (käwä'säkē), city (1970 pop. 973,251), Kanagawa prefecture, central Honshu, Japan, on Tokyo Bay. Located in the Tokyo-Yokohama industrial area, it has steel mills, shipyards, oil refineries, engineering works, and factories that produce motors, electrical machinery and parts, petrochemicals, and cement. Heigenji Temple, dedicated to Kobo-Daishi, is in Kawasaki.

Kaw Indians: see KANSAS INDIANS.

Kay, John, 1704–64, English inventor. He patented in 1733 the fly shuttle, operated by pulling a cord that drove the shuttle to either side, freeing one hand of the weaver to press home the weft. Workers in the weaving industry who regarded Kay's invention as a threat to their jobs mobbed Kay and destroyed his model. Various factory owners duplicated his device but managed not to pay him a royalty. Kay went to France, resumed his work, and tried unsuccessfully to win recognition in England. Although he was the inventor of one of the most important principles of modern mechanical weaving, he died in poverty.

Kay, Ulysses, 1917–, American composer, b. Tucson, Ariz. He graduated from the Univ. of Arizona in 1938 and studied for several years at the Eastman School of Music and at Yale Univ. During World War II he served in the navy. He has won many awards and fellowships, including a Fulbright scholarship and a Rosenwald fellowship. Kay is one of the foremost black composers of serious neoclassical music. He has written several operas, choral works, and chamber and orchestra pieces. His works include *Of New Horizons* (1944), a piece for orchestra; *Jeremiah* (1945), a cantata; and *The Juggler of Our Lady* (1956), a one-act opera.

Kayah State (kəyä') or **Karenni State** (kərĕn'ē), state (1969 est. pop. 113,000), 4,506 sq mi (11,671 sq km), E Burma, on the Thai border. Loikaw is the capital. The terrain is mountainous and is traversed by the Salween, the principal river. The inhabitants of the state are Karens. In the south are the Mawchi mines, an important source of tungsten. Rice and vegetables are grown, and the forests yield teak. Under the 1947 Burmese constitution the Karenni State was constituted from the three states that had treaty relationships with the British crown. The name was changed to Kayah State in 1952.

kayak (kī'ăk), Eskimo canoe, originally made of sealskin stretched over a framework of whalebone or driftwood. It is completely covered except for the opening in which the paddler sits. Since the paddler wears a waterproof skin shirt which is laced to the boat, he can turn all the way over without sinking. The kayak is propelled by a double-bladed paddle and is primarily a hunting canoe. Because of its maneuverability in ice-infested waters, it is still in use over a great extent of the Arctic. The kayak is also popular today as a sporting boat. See also CANOE.

Kaye, Nora (Nora Koreff), 1920–, American ballerina, b. New York City. Kaye studied with Michel Fokine and Antony Tudor. She joined the Ballet Theatre in 1940 and scored a major triumph in 1942 in *Pillar of Fire.* Noted for her astounding versatility, she has performed in works ranging from *Giselle* and *Swan Lake* to the comic *Gala Performance* and *Age of Anxiety.*

Kayes (kāz), town (1970 est. pop. 30,000), W Mali, a port on the Senegal River. It is the administrative and commercial center for a region where peanuts and gum arabic are produced. The town has tanneries. Kayes is at the upper limit of navigation on the Senegal.

Kayibanda, Grégoire (grāgwär' kēbän'dä), 1924–, political leader in Rwanda. A member of the Hutu tribe, he worked as a journalist and later founded the Ruanda (now Rwanda) Cooperative Movement (1952), the Hutu Social Movement (1957), and the Democratic Republican Movement (1959). In 1961 he became president of Rwanda. He was overthrown in a bloodless army coup just before the 1973 elections.

Kayser, Heinrich Gustav Johannes (hīn'rĭkh gōōs'täf yōhän'əs kī'zər), 1853–1940, German physicist. He was professor at Bonn from 1894 to 1920. He is known for his work in sound and, in association with C. D. T. Runge, in SPECTRUM analysis. He wrote a handbook of spectroscopy (1901–12) and a treatise on the electron theory (1905). In his later years he was widely respected as the dean of European spectroscopists.

Kayseri (kī'sĕrē''), city (1970 pop. 167,696), capital of Kayseri prov., central Turkey, at the foot of Mt. Erciyas. It is an important commercial center and has textile mills, sugar refineries, and cement factories. Carpets are made there. The ancient CAESAREA MAZACA, it was taken by the Seljuk Turks in the mid-11th cent., briefly held (1097) by the Crusaders, and captured (1243) by the Mongols. The city was occupied by the Mamelukes of Egypt in 1419. Sultan Selim I incorporated Kayseri into the Ottoman Empire in 1515. The city has numerous historical remains. Nearby is Kanesh, an archaeological site that dates back to the 3d millennium B.C.

Kazakh Soviet Socialist Republic (käzäk', Rus. kə-) or **Kazakhstan** (kä''zäkstän', Rus. kəzəkhstän'), constituent republic (1970 pop. 12,850,000), c.1,050,000 sq mi (2,719,500 sq km), S USSR. It borders on Siberia in the north, China in the east, the Kirghiz, Uzbek, and Turkmen republics in the south, and the Caspian Sea in the west. ALMA-ATA, the capital, Chimkent, Semipalatinsk, Aktyubinsk, Tselinograd, and Ust-Kamenogorsk are the major cities. It is the second largest constituent republic after the Russian Soviet Federated Socialist Republic (RSFSR) and the third largest in population after the RSFSR and the Ukraine. Kazakhstan is a vast flatland, bordered by a high mountain belt in the southeast. It extends nearly 2,000 mi (3,200 km) from the lower Volga and the Caspian Sea in the west to the Altai mts. in the east, comprising N Central Asian and SW Siberian USSR. It is largely lowland in the north and west (W Siberian, Caspian, and Turan lowlands), hilly in the center (Kazakh Hills), and mountainous in the south and east (Tien Shan and Altai ranges). Kazakhstan is a region of inland drainage; the Syr Darya, the Ili, the Chu, and other rivers drain into the Aral Sea and Lake Balkhash. Most of the region is desert or has limited and irregular rainfall; however, dry farming along the northern borders of Kazakhstan has been expanding at a considerable rate since cultivation began in 1954. As a result of the cultivation of these virgin lands, the Tselinny Kray (Virgin Lands Territory) was established in 1961. Kazakhstan produces much of the USSR's wool and cattle and a very great part of its wheat. The Kazakh Plateau covers the core of the region, and has important mineral resources. Coal is mined at Karaganda and Ekibatuz, and there are major oil fields at Emba, at the northern tip of the Caspian. Well over half the copper, lead, zinc, nickel, chromium, and silver mined in the USSR is from this area; in northern and central Kazakhstan there are huge iron ore deposits. The Irtysh hydroelectric stations are a major source of power. The republic's industries are located along the margins of the region: Agricultural and mining machinery is manufactured, and Temir-Tau is the iron and steel center. Superphosphate fertilizers, phosphorus acids, artificial fibers, synthetic rubber, textiles, and medicines are among the many products. The population of Kazakhstan consists of Kazakhs, Russians, Ukrainians, Uzbeks, Belorussians, and Uigurs. The Kazakhs, who make up about one third of the population, speak a Turkic language and are Muslims. The original Turkic tribes were conquered by the Mongols in the 13th cent. and ruled by various khanates until the Russian conquest (1730–1840). In 1916 the Kazakhs rebelled against Russian domination and were in the process of establishing a Western-style state at the time of the 1917 Bolshevik Revolution. Organized as the Kirghiz Autonomous SSR in 1920, it was renamed the Kazakh Autonomous SSR in 1925 and became a constituent republic in 1936. The culture of the Kazakh nomads featured the Central Asian epics, ritual songs, and legends. The 19th cent. saw the growth of the Kazakh intelligentsia. A written literature strongly influenced by Russian culture was then developed. The republic is the site of the Kazakh State Univ. (founded 1934) and the Kazakh Academy of Sciences (founded 1946).

Kazan, Elia (īlī'ə, ēl'yə kəzăn', -zän'), 1909–, American stage and film director, producer, writer, actor, b. Turkey, as Elia Kazanjoglous. Emigrating to the United States in 1913, Kazan began his acting career with the New York Group Theatre in the 1930s. He became a founding member and director of the Actors' Studio. Kazan's outstanding stage productions include *The Skin of Our Teeth* (1942), *All My Sons* (1947), *A Streetcar Named Desire* (1947; film version, 1951), *Death of a Salesman* (1948), and *Tea and Sympathy* (1953). Among his major films are *A Tree Grows in Brooklyn* (1944), *Gentlemen's Agreement* (1947), *On the Waterfront* (1954), *East of Eden* (1955), *A Face in the Crowd* (1957), and *Wild River* (1960). He directed the films *America, America* (1963) and *The Arrangement* (1969) from his own novels.

Kazan (kəzän', -zăn', Rus. kəzä'nyə), city (1970 pop. 869,000), capital of the Tatar Autonomous Soviet Socialist Republic, E European USSR, on the Volga. It is a major historic, cultural, industrial, and commercial center. Manufactures include aircraft, machines and machine tools, chemicals, explosives, electrical equipment, building materials, food products, and furs. Kazan's port and shipyards on the Volga make it an important water transport center. Founded in 1401, Kazan became the capital of a powerful, independent Tatar khanate (1445), which emerged from the empire of the Golden Horde. The khanate was conquered and the city sacked in 1552 by Ivan IV. It became the capital of the Volga region in 1708 and was an outpost (18th cent.) of Russian colonization in the east. It was burned by Pugachev in 1774 and was rebuilt by Catherine II. Little remains of the Muslim period except the Suyumbeka tower in the impressive 16th-century kremlin. Lenin and Tolstoy studied at the Univ. of Kazan (founded 1804). The city also has a branch of the Soviet Academy of Sciences, an ancient cathedral, and several monasteries and mosques. The name is sometimes spelled Kasan.

Kazanlik (kä''zänlĭk'), town (1968 est. pop. 48,800), central Bulgaria, in the Kazanlik valley, a region famous for its rose fields. Kazanlik developed in the 17th cent. as a manufacturing center for attar of roses. Other manufactures include textiles and musical instruments.

Kazan-retto: see VOLCANO ISLANDS.

Kazantzakis, Nikos (nē'kôs kä''zändzä'kēs), 1883?–1957, Greek writer, b. Crete. After obtaining a law degree he studied philosophy under Henri Bergson in Paris and traveled widely in Europe and Asia. Although attracted to Communism early in life, he later grew disillusioned with revolutionary materialism and rationalism. From 1919 to 1927 he directed the Greek ministry of public welfare, and as minister of state (1945–46) he vainly tried to reconcile the factions of left and right. Of an intensely poetic and religious nature, Kazantzakis was torn between the active and the contemplative, between the sensual and the ascetic, and between nihilism and commitment. A tendency toward hero worship is revealed in his interpretative works on Bergson and Nietzsche. His most ambitious work, *The Odyssey, a Modern Sequel* (1938, tr. 1958), a verse tale, begins where Homer's *Odyssey* ends; the new adventures of Odysseus are used to explore the world views of Jesus, Buddha, Lenin, Nietzsche, and others. He presents the human struggle for spiritual freedom and philosophic maturity, showing particular enthusiasm for heroic pessimism and for nihilism. *Zorba the Greek* (1946, tr. 1952) reflects an enormous exuberance for life, and *Christ Recrucified* (1938, tr. *The Greek Passion,* 1953) is a darker tale of good and evil in which a modern man reenacts a Christlike destiny. Other works include *The Last Temptation of Christ* (1951, tr. 1960) and *The Poor Man of God* (1953, tr. *Saint Francis,* 1962). He also translated many classics into Greek. See biography by Helen Kazantzakis (1968); study by Pandelis Prevelakis (1958, tr. 1961).

Kazbek, Mount (kŏzbĕk', Rus. kəzbyĕk'), peak, 16,541 ft (5,042 m) high, SE European USSR, in Georgia, in the Greater Caucasus. An extinct volcano, it rises above the Daryal gorge and the Georgian Military Road. Its glaciers give rise to the Terek River. Mt. Kazbek was first scaled in 1868. An alternate spelling is Kasbek.

Kaz Dağı (käz däŭ'), anc. Ida Mts., range, NW Turkey, SE of the location of ancient Troy. Mt. Gargarus (5,797 ft/1,767 m) is the highest point. The mountain was dedicated in ancient times to the worship of Cybele who was therefore sometimes called Idae Mater.

Kazerun (kä''zĕrōōn'), city (1971 est. pop. 42,000), Fars prov., SW Iran. It is an agricultural trade center.

Kazimierz: For Polish rulers thus named, see CASIMIR.

Kazin, Alfred (kā'zĭn), 1915–, American critic, b. Brooklyn, N.Y., grad. College of the City of New York (B.S., 1935) and Columbia (M.A., 1938). His first book, *On Native Grounds* (1942), is a study of American prose literature starting with William Dean Howells. Kazin's later writings include *The Inmost Leaf* (1955) and *Contemporaries* (1962), and *Bright Book of Life* (1973), which carries his analysis of American literature up to 1972. *Walker in the City* (1951) is a lyrical reminiscence of his childhood in the Jewish immigrant section of Brooklyn; *Starting Out in the Thirties* (1965) recalls his young manhood.

Kazinczy, Ferencz (fĕ'rĕnts kŏ'zĭntsē), 1759–1831, Hungarian author and critic. The influence of Kazinczy's works made him a leading reformer of the Hungarian language. He was imprisoned (1794–1801) for revolutionary activity. His didactic verse (e.g., *Poetai Berke,* 1813) and works of biography brought him renown. Kazinczy's translations of Shakespeare and major European authors greatly benefited Hungarian literature. His voluminous correspondence is of great historical value.

Kazvin, Iran: see QAZVIN.

Kéa (kā'ä) or **Keos** (kā'ôs, kē'ŏs), Lat. *Ceos,* island (1971 pop. 1,666), c.61 sq mi (160 sq km), SE Greece, in the Aegean Sea; one of the Cyclades. Fruits, barley, and silk are produced. Kéa (1971 pop. 693), the main town, is situated on the site of ancient Iulis. The poets Bacchylides and Simonides were born on the island. Under Ottoman rule it was a pirates' haven.

kea: see PARROT.

Kealakekua Bay (kā'əläkākōō'ə), on the Kona (west) coast of the island of Hawaii. Capt. James Cook, who discovered the islands in 1776, stopped there on his second voyage to Hawaii and was killed during a beach fight with the natives on Feb. 14, 1779. A monument to him stands on the shore.

Kean, Edmund, 1787?–1833, English actor. Kean's acting expressed the ideal of the romantic temperament. With his energy and violent emotions, he brought about a radical change in the prevailing classical style of the period. His parentage is uncertain, although evidence favors Aaron Kean, a surveyor's clerk, and Ann Carey, one of a company of strolling players. He served an apprenticeship with groups of provincial and strolling players and in 1814 appeared at Drury Lane as Shylock, a triumph that is a landmark in the history of the theater. He further increased his reputation with portrayals of Richard III, Iago, Othello, Macbeth, Barabbas, and Sir Giles Overreach. In the United States in 1820–21 Kean had many triumphs, but a broken engagement in Boston ruined his popularity there. His personal life was as stormy as his career. In 1822 a suit against him for adultery resulted in Kean's separation from his wife and son and hastened the disintegration of his reputation. In 1825 he again visited the United States and in some measure retrieved his reputation. After his return to England in 1826 his health and dramatic powers declined. A small man with a wild spirit and a gruff voice, he was lauded for his facial mobility; according to Coleridge he had the power to reveal Shakespeare by "flashes of lightning." See biographies by H. N. Hillebrand (1933) and M. W. Disher (1950). His son, **Charles John Kean,** 1811?–1868, went on the stage against his father's wishes and proved best in melodrama. At his father's last appearance in 1833 he played Iago to his father's Othello at Covent Garden. He is best known for his spectacular and historically accurate productions of Shakespeare and contemporary works, especially Byron's *Sardanapalus,* at the Princess Theatre (1851–59). He often played opposite his wife **Ellen Tree Kean,** 1808–80, a noted comedienne, whom he married in 1842. See the letters of Charles and Ellen Kean, ed. by J. M. D. Hardwick (1954).

Kearney, Denis (kär'nē), 1847–1907, American political agitator, b. Co. Cork, Ireland. He was a sailor and then a San Francisco drayman. When California suffered a depression in 1877, Kearney began addressing the workingmen and the unemployed in vacant San Francisco sand lots. He denounced the Central Pacific RR monopoly, political and economic abuses, and particularly Chinese labor, ending many of his speeches with the words, "The Chinese must go." His inflammatory harangues attracted many followers, and after organizing the Workingmen's Party of California—often called the "Sand-Lotters"—he led in the 1870s in driving Orientals from their factories, in burning their laundries, and in threatening violence to those who employed Chinese workers. The party united with the Granger organization and sent a large number of delegates to the California constitutional convention of 1878, where their influence brought about many new laws. The state judicial system was reformed, a railroad commission was established, and home rule was set up in San Francisco. The Chinese were forbidden to hold property and to engage in specified occupations. The provisions denying the Chinese civil liberties were later voided by the courts. Kearney went East to popularize the Workingmen's party, but, gaining little success, he dropped back into obscurity after 1884.

Kearney, city (1970 pop. 19,181), seat of Buffalo co., S central Nebr., on the Platte River; inc. 1873. It is a commercial, industrial, and transportation center in an agricultural area. Farm and irrigation equipment are among its many products. Fort Kearny (named for Gen. Stephen W. Kearny), established nearby in 1848 to protect the Oregon Trail, was abandoned in 1871. The site is now a state park. A state college and a museum are in the city.

Kearns (kûrnz), uninc. town (1970 pop. 17,071), Salt Lake co., N Utah, a suburb of Salt Lake City. There are dairy farms in the area, and sugar beets are grown.

Kearny, Lawrence (kär'nē), 1789–1868, American naval officer, b. Perth Amboy, N.J.; cousin of Stephen Watts Kearny. He became a midshipman in 1807, served in the War of 1812, and later saw action in the Caribbean and Mediterranean against pirates. As commander (1840–43) of the East India squadron, he opened negotiations that resulted in the signing of a commercial treaty between China and the United States in 1844. On his way home he stopped at the Hawaiian Islands and protested the proposed cession of the islands to Great Britain. See biography by C. S. Alden (1937).

Kearny, Philip, 1814–62, Union general in the American Civil War, b. New York City; nephew of Stephen Watts Kearny. After studying law he joined (1837) the army. One of three officers sent to study the French cavalry service (1839), he served (1840) with the French in Algeria. In the Mexican War, Kearny lost an arm at Churubusco. He resigned from the army in 1851 to travel and in 1859 fought again with the French in the war for Italian liberation. Upon the outbreak of the Civil War he was appointed brigadier general of volunteers and given command of the 1st New Jersey Brigade. Kearny fought in the Peninsular campaign and at the second battle of Bull Run. While reconnoitering at Chantilly, he unknowingly entered the enemy's lines and was killed (Sept., 1862). Kearny was noted for his courage and dash and was idolized by his men. Kearny, N.J., was named for him. See biography by Irving Werstein (1962).

Kearny, Stephen Watts, 1794–1848, American general in the Mexican War, b. Newark, N.J. At the beginning of the Mexican War he was made commander of the Army of the West with the rank (June, 1846) of brigadier general. With about 1,600 men he marched over the Santa Fe Trail to New Mexico, entered the city of Santa Fe without opposition, and organized a civil government for the territory. On his way to join the forces of Commodore Robert F. STOCKTON in California he was besieged at San Pasqual, where he was wounded and suffered casualties of a third of his command before being rescued by relief forces from Stockton. After several skirmishes the combined forces reached Los Angeles and occupied the town. A dispute arose between Kearny and Stockton as to the chief command, and Col. John C. FRÉMONT, appointed civil governor of California by Stockton, refused to obey Kearny's orders. When orders from Washington sustained Kearny, he had Frémont court-martialed. Kearny was military governor of the territory until the end of May, 1847. Afterward he went to Mexico, where he was governor of Veracruz and then of Mexico City for brief periods in 1848. Fort Kearney, erected in 1848 on the Platte River in what is now Nebraska, was named for Kearny but misspelled.

Kearny (kär'nē), town (1970 pop. 37,585), Hudson co., NE N.J.; inc. 1899. The town is the site of shipyards (greatly enlarged in 1941) and dry docks. Its chief product is communications equipment. Kearny contains much of the tidal wastelands between the Passaic and the Hackensack rivers that is being reclaimed for industrial and recreational purposes.

Kearsarge (kēr'särj"), Union ship in the Civil War. See CONFEDERATE CRUISERS.

Keaton, Buster (Joseph Francis Keaton), 1895–1966, American movie actor, b. Piqua, Kans. Considered one of the greatest comic actors in film history, Keaton was featured in many silent comedies as a deadpan hero who survived against incredible odds. Among these movies are *The Navigator* (1924), *The General* (1926), and *Steamboat Bill Junior* (1927). He made a comeback as a supporting actor in such films as *Sunset Boulevard* (1959), *Limelight* (1952), and *A Funny Thing Happened on the Way to the Forum* (1966).

Keats, John, 1795–1821, English poet, b. London. He is considered one of the greatest of English poets. The son of a livery stable keeper, Keats attended school at Enfield, where he became the friend of Charles Cowden Clarke, the headmaster's son, who encouraged his early learning. Apprenticed to a surgeon (1811), Keats came to know Leigh Hunt and his literary circle, and in 1816 he gave up surgery to write poetry. His first volume of poems appeared in 1817. It included "I stood tip-toe upon a little hill," "Sleep and Poetry," and the famous sonnet "On First Looking into Chapman's Homer." *Endymion,* a long poem, was published in 1818. Although faulty in structure, it is nevertheless full of rich imagery and color. Keats returned from a walking tour in the Highlands to find himself attacked in *Blackwood's Magazine*—an article berated him for belonging to Leigh Hunt's "Cockney school" of poetry—and in the *Quarterly Review.* The critical assaults of 1818 mark a turning point in Keats's life; he was forced to examine his work more carefully, and as a result the influence of Hunt was diminished. However, these attacks did not contribute to Keats's decline in health and his early death, as Shelley maintained in his elegy "Adonais." Keats's passionate love for Fanny Brawne seems to have begun in 1818. Fanny's letters to Keats's sister show that her critics' contention that she was a cruel flirt was not true. Only Keats's failing health prevented their marriage. He had contracted tuberculosis, probably from nursing his brother Tom, who died in 1818. With his friend, the artist Joseph Severn, Keats sailed for Italy shortly after the publication of *Lamia, Isabella, The Eve of St. Agnes, and Other Poems* (1820), which contains most of his important work and is probably the greatest single volume of poetry published in England in the 19th cent. He died in Rome in Feb., 1821, at the age of 25. In spite of his tragically brief career, Keats is one of the most important English poets. He is also among the most personally appealing. Noble, generous, and sympathetic, he was capable not only of passionate love but also of warm, steadfast friendship. Keats is ranked, with Shelley and Byron, as one of the three great Romantic poets. Such poems as "Ode to a Nightingale," "Ode on a Grecian Urn," "To Autumn," and "Ode on Melancholy" are unequaled for dignity, melody, and richness of sensuous imagery. All of Keats's poetry is filled with a mysterious and elevating sense of beauty and joy. His posthumous pieces include "La Belle Dame sans Merci," in its way as great an evocation of romantic medievalism as "The Eve of St. Agnes." Among his sonnets, familiar ones are "When I have fears that I may cease to be" and "Bright star! would I were as steadfast as thou art." "Lines on the Mermaid Tavern," "Fancy," and "Bards of Passion and of Mirth" are delightful short poems. Some of Keats's finest work is in the unfinished epic "Hyperion." In recent years critical attention has focused on Keats's philosophy, which involves not abstract thought but rather absolute receptivity to experience. This attitude is indicated in his celebrated term "negative capability"—"to let the mind be a thoroughfare for all thought." Keats's letters (ed. by H. E. Rollins, 1958) vividly reveal his character, opinions, and feelings. See his poetical works, ed. by H. W. Garrod (2d ed. 1958); his autobiography, ed. by E. V. Weller (1933); biographies by Aileen Ward (1963), W. J. Bate (1963) and Robert Gittings (1968); studies by W. J. Bate (1945) and Morris Dickstein (1971).

Keble, John (kē'bəl), 1792–1866, English clergyman and poet. His career (1807–11) at Corpus Christi College, Oxford, was one of unusual distinction. Made fellow of Oriel College in 1811 and ordained in 1816, he became tutor and examiner, but resigned in 1823 to become his father's curate. He based the doctrine and devotion of his important poetical work *The Christian Year* (1827) on the Book of Common Prayer. It sold 150 editions in 50 years and led to a professorship of poetry at Oxford (1831–41). Alarmed at the suppression of 10 bishoprics in Ireland, Keble preached (1833) a sermon that he called "National Apostasy." J. H. Newman later called this the beginning of the OXFORD MOVEMENT. From 1836 he held the living of Hursley, Hampshire. His works include an edition of Richard Hooker's works (1836), a life of Bishop Wilson (1863), the Oxford Psalter (1839) and *Lyra Innocentium: Thoughts in Verse on Children* (1846). Among his poems are the well-known hymns *Red o'er the Forest, New Every Morning is Thy Love,* and *Sun of My Soul.* See biographies by J. T. Coleridge (1869) and Walter Lock (1892); study by G. Battiscombe (1964).

Kebnekaise (kĕb'nəkī"sə) [Lappish,=kettle top], mountain peak, 6,965 ft (2,123 m) high, Norrbotten prov., N Sweden; highest in Sweden. There are 16 small glaciers on the slopes.

Kechua: see QUECHUA; AMERICAN INDIAN LANGUAGES.

Kecskemét (kĕch'kĕmāt), city (1970 pop. 77,484), central Hungary, in a fruit-growing region. It is a county administrative center, a road and rail hub, and a manufacturing city whose industries produce food products, alcoholic beverages, textiles, and furniture. Known since the 4th cent., the city has several churches, a museum, and a law school with a large library. The Hungarian dramatist Joseph Katona was born in Kecskemét.

Kedah (kĕ'də, kā'dä), state (1971 pop. 955,374), 3,660 sq mi (9,479 sq km), central Malay Peninsula, Malaysia, on the Strait of Malacca. It is bordered on the N and NE by Thailand. The capital and chief city is ALOR SETAR; Sungai Patani is an important town. Along the coast are wide alluvial plains where rice is grown. South Kedah has rubber plantations, and tin is mined in the hills of the interior. Generally level, Kedah has on its east border a mountain range that rises to 6,600 ft (2,012 m). Several islands are also included in the state; Langkawi off the northwest coast is the largest. The majority of the inhabitants of Kedah are Malays; there are also many Chinese, Indians working on the rubber plantations, and small groups of aborigines. Kedah was the center of the early Hinduized kingdom of Langkasuka, according to Arab and Chinese reports of the 6th–8th cent. During the Sri Vijaya domination of the Malay Peninsula (8th–13th cent.), it was an important naval base and the terminus of transpeninsular trade routes. During the 15th cent. it fell under the domination of Malacca (see MELAKA) but maintained substantial independence and a profitable trade with India and Indonesia. At this time most of the inhabitants were converted to Islam. After the fall of Malacca (1511), Kedah was fought over by the Portuguese, Dutch, Bugis, Minangkabau, and Siamese. By ceding PINANG (1786) and Province Wellesley (1800) to the British, the sultan of Kedah embittered his relations with the Siamese court, which was not appeased by his subsequent conquest of PERAK for Siam. A bloody Siamese invasion (1821) drove him into exile until 1842; upon his return PERLIS was created as a separate state. In 1909, Siam transferred sovereignty over Kedah to Great Britain. Before the establishment of the Federation of Malaya (1948), Kedah was classed as one of the Unfederated Malay States. See MALAYSIA, FEDERATION OF.

Kedar (kē'dər), powerful nomadic tribe, descendants of the second son of Ishmael, living NW of the Sinai peninsula, E of Palestine. Gen. 25.13; Ps. 120.5; Cant. 1.5; Isa. 21.16; 42.11; 60.7; Jer. 2.10; 49.28; Ezek. 27.21.

Kedemah (kĕd'ēmə, kē'dēmə), son of Ishmael. Gen. 25.15; 1 Chron. 1.31.

Kedemoth (kĕd'əmōth, kē'dē-), unidentified town E of the Dead Sea. Deut. 2.26; Joshua 13.18; 21.37; 1 Chron. 6.79.

Kedesh (kēdĕsh). **1** Town, S Judah. Joshua 15.23. **2** See KISHION. **3** or **Kedesh-naphtali,** city, extreme N Palestine, NW of Lake Huleh. Joshua 12.22; 19.37; 20.7; 21.32; Judges 4.6–11; 2 Kings 15.29; 1 Chron. 6.76.

Keeler, James Edward, 1857–1900, American astronomer, b. La Salle, Ill. At the age of 21 he went on the Naval Observatory expedition to Colorado to observe the solar eclipse of July, 1878. In 1886 he became an assistant and in 1888 full astronomer at Lick Observatory, Mt. Hamilton, Calif. He was director of the Allegheny Observatory from 1891 to 1898. In the course of his examination of the spectra of the heavenly bodies, he furnished confirmation for Clerk Maxwell's theory that the rings of Saturn are composed of meteoric particles. In 1898, Keeler returned to Lick Observatory as director, and there, working with the Crossley reflector, he observed and photographed vast numbers of nebulas whose existence had never before been suspected, arriving at the conclusion that the spiral nebula is the normal type. He contributed memoirs to the Royal Astronomical Society of England and many papers to the *Astrophysical Journal,* of which he was coeditor. He wrote *Spectroscopic Observations of Nebulae* (1894).

Keeling Islands: see COCOS ISLANDS.

Keelung: see CHI-LUNG, Taiwan.

Keene, Charles Samuel, 1823–91, English pen-and-ink artist and caricaturist. In 1851 he began his long association with *Punch,* where the bulk of his work appeared. His drawings ranged from interesting vignettes of the contemporary scene to tidy landscapes and interiors. See studies by Joseph Pennell (1897) and Derek Hudson (1947).

Keene, Laura, c.1826–1873, Anglo-American actress-manager, b. England. She played with Mme Vestris at the Lyceum, London. She emigrated to the United States in 1852 and became manager (1855) of Laura Keene's Varieties Theater, New York City. In 1856 she opened Laura Keene's Theater (later the Olympic) and successfully produced and acted in many foreign and American plays until 1863. Her most famous production was Tom Taylor's *Our American Cousin,* which she gave at Ford's Theater, Washington, when Lincoln was shot there in 1865.

Keene, city (1970 pop. 20,467), seat of Cheshire co., SW N.H., on the Ashuelot River; settled 1736, inc. as a city 1873. It is a trade and manufacturing center in a farming and resort area. The city is the seat of Keene State College. A state park is to the north, and Mt. Monadnock, a popular ski site, is to the east.

Keeshond (kās'hŏnd) (pl. Keeshonden), breed of medium-sized NONSPORTING DOG raised in Holland for several hundred years and introduced into England in the year 1900. It stands about 18 in. (46 cm) high at the shoulder and weighs from 32 to 40 lb (14.5–18.1 kg). Its weather-resistant double coat consists of a thick, downy underlayer and an abundant, straight, harsh topcoat that stands out from the body. The undercoat is gray or cream-colored, and the outer hairs are black-tipped. Undoubtedly of Arctic origin, the Keeshond is related to the Norwegian elkhound, the Samoyed, the chow chow, and, most closely, the Pomeranian. In Holland it was so common a sight in the barges on the Dutch canals that it was first registered in England under the name "Dutch barge dog." The Keeshond is raised as a pet and watchdog. See DOG.

Keetmanshoop (kēt'mäns-ho͝op''), town (1970 pop. 10,297), S South West Africa. It is the trade center for a region where karakul sheep are raised. Keetmanshoop was founded in 1866 as a German missionary station.

Keewatin (kēwä'tĭn, -wā'-), administrative district (228,160 sq mi/590,934 sq km), Northwest Territories, Canada, N of Manitoba and W of Hudson Bay. Its boundaries, set in 1920, include all of Hudson and James bays and all of the mainland of the Northwest Territories E of long. 102°W, except for the Boothia and Melville peninsulas.

Keewatin: see PRECAMBRIAN ERA.

Kefallinía (kĕfälēnē'ä) or **Cephalonia** (sĕfəlō'nyə), island (1971 pop. 31,787), c.300 sq mi (780 sq km), W Greece, the largest of the IONIAN ISLANDS. It has an irregular coastline and is largely mountainous, rising to c.5,340 ft (1,630 m) at Mt. Ainos, which in ancient times was crowned by a temple to Zeus. Argostolion, a port, is the island's main town and ships local products such as fruit and wine. Sheep raising and fishing are important occupations on the island. Kefallinía was an ally of Athens in the Peloponnesian War and later was a member of the Aetolian League. The island was taken by Rome in 189 B.C. After the division of the Roman Empire (A.D. 395), it was held by the Byzantine Empire until its occupation (1126) by Venice. It subsequently was ruled by several Italian families, was seized by the Ottoman Turks (1479), and was ceded (1499) to Venice, which held it until the Treaty of Campo Formio (1797). Its subsequent history is that of the Ionian Islands. In 1953 the island was devastated by earthquakes of such force that Mt. Ainos was split.

Kefauver, Carey Estes (kēfôvər), 1903–63, U.S. Senator from Tennessee (1949–63), b. Madisonville, Tenn., known as Estes Kefauver. He became a Chattanooga lawyer and in 1938 was elected to the U.S. House of Representatives, where he served until he entered the Senate in 1949. His victory in the senatorial race was conspicuous because it ended "Boss" Edward H. Crump's domination of Tennessee politics. As chairman of the Senate crime investigating committee in 1950 and 1951, Kefauver attracted nationwide publicity. *Crime in America* (1951) was Kefauver's own book on the results of this investigation. Reelected to the Senate in 1954, he won the Democratic party's nomination for Vice President in 1956, but, with Adlai Stevenson, was defeated in the Eisenhower landslide. A supporter of civil rights legislation, Kefauver won (1960) reelection after overcoming the active opposition of a staunch segregationist in Tennessee's Democratic primary. He was a principal sponsor of a law enacted in 1962 to protect the public from harmful and ineffective pharmaceuticals. See biography by J. B. Gorman (1971).

Keflavík (kĕp'lävēk''), town (1970 pop. 5,663), SW Iceland, on the Faxaflói, W of Reykjavík. It is a major fishing port, best known for its large international airport, which was built by the United States during World War II; in 1951 the United States was granted the right to use it as a military base.

Kehelathah (kē''hēlā'thə), unidentified desert encampment. Num. 33.22,23.

Keighley (kēth'lē), municipal borough (1971 pop. 55,263), West Riding of Yorkshire, N central England, at the junction of the Aire and Worth rivers. The Leeds and Liverpool Canal connects Keighley with Liverpool and Hull. Keighley's products include woolen, silk, and rayon goods; spinning machinery and looms; and sewing and washing machines. In 1938, Keighley absorbed nearby Haworth, home of the Brontë family and site of a Brontë museum. In 1974, Keighley became part of the new metropolitan county of West Yorkshire.

Keihin: see YOKOHAMA, Japan.

Kei Islands: see KAI ISLANDS, Indonesia.

Keijo: see SEOUL, South Korea.

Keilah (kēī'lə), town, SW Palestine. David rescued it from the Philistines and lived there until the treachery of its inhabitants caused him to leave. Joshua 15.44; 1 Sam. 23.1–13; Neh. 3.17.

Keita, Modibo (mōdē'bō kā'tä), 1915–, African political leader in the Republic of Mali. He studied in France and taught in the French Sudan (later the Republic of Mali) before becoming active in nationalist politics in 1946. He represented the French Sudan in the French national assembly from 1956 to 1958. A strong supporter of African unity, Keita promoted the Mali Federation, formed in 1959, and after the federation was dissolved (1960) he was elected the first president of the Republic of Mali. He ruled until 1968, when he was ousted by an army coup.

Keitel, Wilhelm (vĭl'hĕlm kī'təl), 1882–1946, German general. A supporter of Hitler, he became (1938) chief of staff of the supreme command of the armed forces, a new post that marked the German army's subjection to Hitler. On May 8, 1945, Keitel ratified in Berlin the unconditional surrender of Germany. He was convicted at the Nuremberg war-crimes trial and hanged.

Keith, Sir Arthur, 1866–1955, British anatomist, b. Aberdeen, Scotland, educated at the Univ. of Aberdeen, University College, London, and the Univ. of Leipzig. He became conservator of the museum and professor at the Royal College of Surgeons (1908), then professor of physiology at the Royal Institution, London (1917–23). From 1933 he carried out research on tuberculosis as master of the Buckston Browne Research Farm at Downe, Kent. He also applied his knowledge of anatomy to an influential study of human origins, reconstructing prehistoric man based on fossil remains from Europe and N Africa. His writings include *Human Embryology and Morphology* (1902, 6th ed. 1949), *The Antiquity of Man* (1915, 2d ed. 1925), and *A New Theory of Evolution* (1948). See his autobiography (1950).

Keith, George, c.1638–1716, Scottish preacher. Joining the Quakers c.1663, he was closely associated with Robert Barclay, George Fox, and other influential Friends. Shortly after his arrival in America (1684) he became the leader of a separate faction known as Christian Quakers, for which he was denounced by William Penn in 1692. Keith returned to England where, in 1700, he was ordained a priest in the Anglican Church. He was again in America (1702–4), preaching and baptizing. His journeys in the colonies are recorded in his *Journal of Travels from New Hampshire to Caratuck* (1706). See biography by E. W. Kirby (1942).

Keith, George, 1693?–1778, Scottish Jacobite, 10th earl marischal [marshal] of Scotland. He took part in the Jacobite uprising of 1715 and after its failure escaped to the Continent. A leader of the Spanish expedition to Scotland (1719) in behalf of the Old Pretender, he again escaped. Later he joined his brother James Francis Edward Keith in Prussia and rose high in the favor of Frederick the Great, who appointed him ambassador to Paris (1751), governor of Neuchâtel (1752), and ambassador to Spain (1758). Although pardoned by George II of Britain, he spent most of the remainder of his life in Prussia. See biography by E. E. Cuthell (1915).

Keith, George Keith Elphinstone, Viscount 1746–1823, British admiral. After serving as a captain in the American Revolution and early French Revolutionary Wars, he was appointed (1795) vice admiral. He suppressed the mutinies at Nore and Spithead (1797) and commanded the Mediterranean fleet (1798–1801), the North Sea fleet (1803–7), and the Channel fleet (1812–15), receiving Napoleon's surrender after Waterloo. Not a military tactician, he won no notable battles but was a skilled administrator and commander.

Keith, James Francis Edward, 1696–1758, Scottish field marshal of Prussia; brother of George Keith, 10th earl marischal [marshal] of Scotland. He participated in the Jacobite uprising of 1715 and in the abortive invasion of 1719 with his brother. Escaping to the Continent, he first entered the Spanish service and then went to Russia, where he gained honor in both civil and military offices. Later he went to Prussia and became close friends with Frederick the Great, who made him a field marshal (1747). Keith entered the circle of Europe's leading intellectuals and rendered great service to Prussia in the early part of the Seven Years War. He was killed in the battle of Hochkirch. See Peter Wilding, *Adventurers in the Eighteenth Century* (1937).

Keith, Minor Cooper, 1848–1929, American magnate, a founder of the United Fruit Company, b. Brooklyn, N.Y. In the face of incredible hardships he built (1871–90) a railroad from the port of Limón, which he founded on the Caribbean, to San José, capital of Costa Rica. Banana plantations that he started experimentally near Limón in 1873 prospered, and he established the first steamship service to bring these bananas to the United States. He gained control of other plantations in Panama and Colombia and dominated the banana trade. In 1899 he combined his plantation interests with those of the Boston Fruit Company in the West Indies to form the United Fruit Company. He returned to railroad building, organized (1912) the International Railways of Central America, and completed an 800-mi (1,287-km) railway system, but died before realizing his dream of a line from Guatemala to the Panama Canal. His work profoundly altered the economic life of Central American countries. See Watt Stewart, *Keith and Costa Rica* (1964).

Keith, William, 1838–1911, American painter, b. Scotland. In 1851 he came to New York City, where he learned wood engraving and did illustrations for *Harper's Weekly.* He moved to San Francisco in 1860 and later turned to painting, studying in Düsseldorf in 1870 and in Munich in the 1880s. His Western landscapes evolved from early mountain epics to later intimate natural scenes. The Keith Memorial Gallery of the Oakland Art Museum is devoted entirely to his work. His *By the Creek, Sonoma* is in the Corcoran Gallery of Art, Washington, D.C. See Brother Cornelius, *Keith, Old Master of California* (2 vol., 1942, 1956).

Keizer (kī'zər), uninc. town (1970 pop. 11,405), Marion co., NW Oregon, a suburb of Salem.

Kejimkujik National Park, 140 sq mi (363 sq km), S central N.S., Canada, near Maitland Bridge; est. 1968. The park has a rolling landscape with numerous lakes and streams. Micmac Indian petroglyphs are found there.

Kekkonen, Urho Kaleva (o͞or'hô kä'lävä kĕ'kōnĕn), 1900–, president of Finland (1956–). The leading spokesman of the Center party (known as the Agrarian party until 1965), he held various cabinet posts from 1936 and was prime minister from 1950 to 1956. He succeeded Juho Paasikivi as president in 1956. His reelection in 1962 and 1968 affirmed his policy of maintaining friendly neutrality with the USSR. In 1973 the Finnish parliament voted to extend his term, which was to expire in March, 1974, for four years.

Kekulé von Stradonitz, Friedrich August (frē'-drĭkh ou'go͞ost kā'ko͞olā fən shträ'dōnĭts), 1829–96, German organic chemist. He was professor at Ghent (1858–65) and at Bonn from 1865. He made studies of various carbon compounds, especially BENZENE, for the molecular structure of which he developed the ring theory. This theory is of fundamental importance to modern chemistry.

Kelaiah (kēlā'yə) or **Kelita** (kēlī'tə), Levite active in the return to Palestine. Ezra 10.23; Neh. 8.7; 10.10. The texts could refer to different persons.

Kelantan (kəlăn'tən, kəlän''tän'), state (1971 pop. 680,626), 5,780 sq mi (14,970 sq km), central Malay Peninsula, Malaysia, on the South China Sea. It is bordered on the N by Thailand. The capital is KOTA BAHARU. It is drained by the Kelantan River (c.150 mi/240 km long), which flows into the South China Sea. Rice, the most important commercial crop, is grown on the wide coastal plains; other products are rubber and copra. Tin, gold, manganese, and iron are mined on a small scale in the hills of the interior. The people are mainly Malay, but there is a small Chinese minority. Kelantan was ruled by Sri Vijaya until the 13th cent.; it fell under the sway of Malacca (see MELAKA) in the 15th cent. After the fall of Malacca (1511), conflict among many powers resulted eventually in the establishment by Siam of sovereignty over the area (early 19th cent.). Kelantan became a protectorate of Great Britain in 1909. Before the establishment of the Federation of Malaya (1948), Kelantan was classed as one of the Unfederated Malay States. See MALAYSIA, FEDERATION OF.

Kelita (kēlī'tə): see KELAIAH.

Keller, Gottfried (gôt'frēt), 1819-90, Swiss novelist, poet, and short-story writer. His vital, realistic, and purposeful fiction gives him a high place among 19th-century authors. Chief among his works is the "educational" novel *Der grüne Heinrich* (1854-55; tr. *Green Henry,* 1960), which he later revised. It is considered one of the outstanding works of the 19th cent. A number of short stories are included in *People of Seldwyla* (1856-74; tr. 1929); among them is the highly regarded tale which was the basis of Delius's opera *A Village Romeo and Juliet.* See J. M. Lindsay, *Gottfried Keller: Life and Works* (Am. ed. 1969).

Keller, Helen Adams, 1880-1968, American author and lecturer, blind and deaf from the age of two, b. Tuscumbia, Ala. In 1887 she was put under the charge of Anne Sullivan (see MACY, ANNE SULLIVAN), who was her teacher and companion. As a pupil Helen Keller made rapid progress and was graduated from Radcliffe in 1904 with honors. She lectured all over America and in Europe and Asia, raising funds for the training of the blind and promoting other social causes. Her books include *The Story of My Life* (1903), *The World I Live In* (1908), *Helen Keller's Journal, 1936-1937* (1938), *Let Us Have Faith* (1940), and *The Open Door* (1957). See biography by Margery Weiner (1970).

Kellermann, François Christophe (fräNswä' krĕstôf' kĕlĕrmän'), 1735-1820, marshal of France, b. Strasbourg. He served in the Seven Years War and won renown in the FRENCH REVOLUTIONARY WARS when he and General Dumouriez stopped the Prussians at VALMY (1792). In the Reign of Terror, he was accused of treason and imprisoned (1793-94), but was not convicted. Napoleon made him senator (1799) and duke of Valmy (1808). Rallying (1814) to Louis XVIII, Kellermann was raised to the peerage.

Kelley, Abby: see FOSTER, ABBY KELLEY.

Kelley, Edgar Stillman, 1857-1944, American composer and critic, b. Sparta, Wis., studied in Chicago and at the Stuttgart Conservatory. After his return to the United States he played the organ in Oakland, Calif., and in San Francisco and served as music critic of the San Francisco *Examiner.* He taught (1901-2) at Yale, replacing Horatio Parker, and afterward in Berlin until 1910, when he became dean of the composition department of the Cincinnati Conservatory. Among his works are an operetta, *Puritania* (1892); an orchestral suite, *Aladdin* (1915), based on Chinese music heard in San Francisco; two symphonies, *Gulliver* (1913-36) and *New England* (1914); incidental music to the play *Ben Hur* (1899); and an oratorio, *The Pilgrim's Progress* (1918). His writings include *Chopin the Composer* (1913).

Kelley, Florence, 1859-1932, American social worker and reformer, b. Philadelphia, grad. Cornell, 1882, and Northwestern Univ. law school, 1894. Married in 1884 to a Polish doctor, Lazare Wishnieweski, she divorced him six years later and became a Hull House resident. A confirmed socialist and active in many reforms, Kelley devoted most of her energies toward securing protective labor legislation, especially for women and children. From 1899 she served for many years as director of the National Consumer's League, which strove for industrial reform through consumer activity. Her writings include *Ethical Gains through Legislation* (1905) and *Modern Industry* (1914). See Josephine Goldmark, *Impatient Crusader* (1953); D. R. Blumberg, *Florence Kelley* (1966).

Kelley, Hall Jackson, 1790-1874, American propagandist for the settlement of Oregon, b. Northwood, N.H. A schoolmaster in Boston (1818-23) and later a railroad surveyor in Maine, he founded (1829) a society to promote American settlement in the disputed Columbia River country and wrote appeals to prospective colonists. He secured the aid of Nathaniel J. WYETH, but plans for a joint expedition to the West were delayed, and Wyeth went alone. In 1833, Kelley went to New Orleans, sailed to Veracruz, and crossed Mexico to California, where he met the trader Ewing Young. The two arrived in the Oregon country in 1834. A sick and discouraged man, Kelley was sheltered at Fort Vancouver by Dr. John MCLOUGHLIN until the spring of 1835, when he returned to Boston. He subsequently wrote a "memoir" on Oregon, which was presented to Congress by Caleb Cushing. See biography by Fred W. Powell (1917); Fred W. Powell, ed., *Hall J. Kelley on Oregon* (1932).

Kelley, Oliver Hudson, 1826-1913, American agriculturist, b. Boston. He was a founder of the National Grange of the Patrons of Husbandry, the central influence in the GRANGER MOVEMENT of the 1870s. Kelley took up land on the Minnesota frontier in 1849 and farmed until, in 1864, he became connected with the U.S. Bureau of Agriculture, traveling in the West and South to report on agricultural conditions. At this time he conceived the idea of the Grange as a social and fraternal organization of farmers, and in 1867 he and six others secured the charter and Kelley became secretary. After 1873 the leadership passed to others, and Kelley resigned as secretary in 1878. He wrote *Origin and Progress of the Order of the Patrons of Husbandry* (1875).

Kelley, William Darrah (dâr'ə), 1814-90, American legislator, b. Philadelphia. He was admitted (1841) to the bar and served (1847-56) as judge of the court of common pleas for Philadelphia. Originally a Democrat and a believer in free trade, he joined the Republican party when it was founded, because of its antislavery stand. The depression of 1857 and his fear that goods produced by low-paid foreign labor would flood the country converted him to protectionism. He was elected to Congress in 1860 and was continuously reelected for the rest of his life. As a staunch radical, he supported Negro suffrage and military reconstruction in the South. He served on the Committee on Ways and Means for 20 years. His sincerity and financial disinterestedness were never questioned, but his constant emphasis on protection as a cure-all and his frequent mention of Pennsylvania's iron industry led his colleagues to call him "Pig Iron" Kelley. He was an advocate of currency inflation for the sake of labor and the farmer. He published a number of books, including *Speeches, Addresses, and Letters on Industrial and Financial Questions* (1872), *Letters from Europe* (1879), and *The Old South and the New* (1888).

Kellogg, Clara Louise, 1842-1916, American operatic soprano, b. Sumterville, S.C. She made her debut in 1861 in New York City and in 1863 sang Marguerite in the first New York performance of Gounod's *Faust.* From 1873 to 1876 she toured the United States with her own company, producing opera in English.

Kellogg, Edward, 1790-1858, American economist, b. Norwalk, Conn. He advocated a financial scheme to abolish interest, which was often usurious at the time he wrote. Kellogg devised a system of financial control whereby the government would issue legal tender notes and then lend them on the security of real estate at a low rate of interest. At the same time the government would issue at the same rate of interest bonds that could be exchanged freely for the notes. By that system Kellogg hoped to keep the interest rate close to the estimated rate of accumulation of wealth in the United States. His pamphlet *Currency: The Evil and the Remedy* (1844) was circulated with Horace Greeley's aid; it was revised under the title *Labor and Other Capital* (1849) and went into many editions after Kellogg's death as *A New Monetary System;* the 1883 edition includes a biographical sketch by his daughter. Kellogg's views were favored by agrarian and labor organizations and led to the formation of a number of political parties (e.g., the Greenbacks, the Populists) whose aim was a national economy and currency not manipulable by banking and financial interests.

Kellogg, Frank Billings, 1856-1937, American lawyer, U.S. Senator (1917-23), and cabinet member, b. Potsdam, N.Y. As a child, he moved to Olmstead co., Minn. He later studied law and held several municipal posts. He entered private law practice in St. Paul, Minn., where he became an outstanding corporation lawyer and gained stature in the Republican party. Appointed (1904) special counsel to the U.S. Attorney General, Kellogg played an important role in antitrust prosecution, particularly in the dissolution of the General Paper and the Standard Oil companies. As special counsel to the Interstate Commerce Commission, he was active in the investigation of the railroads controlled by Edward H. Harriman. Elected U.S. Senator, he was one of the few Republicans who supported the League of Nations, although he believed minor changes were needed to permit U.S. entry. After serving (1924-25) as ambassador to Great Britain, he succeeded (1925) Charles E. Hughes as Secretary of State. He bettered relations with Mexico and helped to settle the TACNA-ARICA CONTROVERSY between Chile and Peru. Largely for his successful promotion of the KELLOGG-BRIAND PACT, he was awarded the 1929 Nobel Peace Prize. He resigned his cabinet post in 1929 and afterward served (1930-35) as a judge of the Permanent Court of International Justice. He established a foundation for the study of international relations at Carleton College in Minnesota. See biography by David Bryn-Jones (1937); L. E. Ellis, *Frank B. Kellogg and American Foreign Relations, 1925-1929* (1961).

Kellogg, Vernon Lyman, 1867-1937, American zoologist, b. Emporia, Kansas, B.A. Univ. of Kansas, 1889. He was professor (1894-1920) of entomology at Stanford Univ. He served (1915-16) as director in Brussels of the American Commission for Relief in Belgium and later held other positions with the American Relief Administration in Europe. From 1919 to 1931 he was permanent secretary of the National Research Council. He worked in insect taxonomy and in economic entomology and was also known for his interpretations of science for the layman.

Kellogg-Briand Pact (-brēäN'), agreement, signed Aug. 27, 1928, condemning "recourse to war for the solution of international controversies." It is more properly known as the Pact of Paris. In June, 1927, Aristide BRIAND, foreign minister of France, proposed to the U.S. government a treaty outlawing war between the two countries. Frank B. KELLOGG, the U.S. Secretary of State, returned a proposal for a general pact against war, and after prolonged negotiations the Pact of Paris was signed by 15 nations—Australia, Belgium, Canada, Czechoslovakia, France, Germany, Great Britain, India, the Irish Free State, Italy, Japan, New Zealand, Poland, South Africa, and the United States. The contracting parties agreed that settlement of all conflicts, no matter of what origin or nature, that might arise among them should be sought only by pacific means and that war was to be renounced as an instrument of national policy. Although 62 nations ultimately ratified the pact, its effectiveness was vitiated by its failure to provide measures of enforcement. The Kellogg-Briand Pact was given an unenthusiastic reception by many countries. The U.S. Senate, ratifying the treaty with only one dissenting vote, still insisted that there must be no curtailment of America's right of self-defense and that the United States was not compelled to take action against countries that broke the treaty. The pact never made a meaningful contribution to international order, although it was invoked in 1929 with some success, when China and the USSR reached a tense moment over possession of the Chinese Eastern RR in Manchuria. Ultimately, however, the pact proved to be meaningless, especially with the practice of waging undeclared wars in the 1930s (e.g., the Japanese invasion of Manchuria in 1931, the Italian invasion of Ethiopia in 1935, and the German occupation of Austria in 1938). See R. H. Ferrell, *Peace in Their Time* (1952, repr. 1968).

Kellogg Foundation, philanthropic institution established (1930) at Battle Creek, Mich., by food manufacturer W. K. Kellogg (1860-1951). Kellogg eventually gave the institution a total of $47 million, and by 1972 its endowment had increased to more than $490 million. After World War II the foundation broadened its interests, formerly restricted to Michigan, to include support of projects throughout the world, with an emphasis on activities in the Western Hemisphere. The foundation has concentrated on the application of knowledge rather than on basic research. Its major interests have been in the fields of agriculture, health, and education.

Kells, Republic of Ireland: see CEANANNUS MOR.

Kelly, Ellsworth, 1923-, American painter, b. Newburgh, New York. Kelly paints flat color areas usually having sharp contours and geometric shapes. *Atlantic* (1956) and *Green Blue Red* (1964) are in the Whitney Museum, New York City. The Walker Art Center, Minneapolis, Minnesota, owns *Blue Red Green* (1962).

Kelly, Gene, 1912-, American dancer, choreographer, and movie actor and director, b. Pittsburgh. Kelly first gained fame in the Broadway musical *Pal Joey* (1941). His best-known work has been in motion pictures, where he excelled in a novel combination of camera and dance techniques in such films as *On the Town* (1949), *An American in Paris* (1951), *Singin' in the Rain* (1952), and *Invitation to the Dance* (1956). A skillful and expressive performer, he has appeared in such film musicals as *Anchors Aweigh* (1945), *Take Me Out to the Ballgame* (1949), and *Brigadoon* (1954). He has also played dramatic film roles, as in *Inherit the Wind* (1960), and has directed several movies, including *The Happy Road* (1950) and *Hello Dolly* (1969).

Kelly, George, 1887-1974, American playwright, b. Philadelphia. He began his career as a vaudevillian, as both an actor and skit writer. His best-known plays, penetrating satires on American middle-class life, include *The Torch-Bearers* (1922), *The Show-off* (1924), *Craig's Wife* (1925; Pulitzer Prize), and *The Deep Mrs. Sykes* (1945).

Kelly, Hugh, 1739–77, English dramatist, b. Killarney. His first and best-known play, the sentimental comedy *False Delicacy,* was produced by Garrick in 1768 and was extremely popular in its time.

Kelly, John, 1822–86, American politician, boss of TAMMANY Hall, b. New York City. He entered politics at an early age. At first he opposed Tammany Hall, but later (1853) joined the organization and became city alderman. He served (1855–58) in Congress and was (1859–61, 1865–67) sheriff of New York County. After the exposure of William M. Tweed, Kelly, by then popularly known as "Honest John," reorganized the Tammany machine. By 1874 he held control of the organization and carried on continuous warfare with the faction of Samuel J. Tilden, who originally had cooperated with him in reorganizing Tammany. Kelly's refusal to back Tilden's candidate for governor, Lucius Robinson, and his decision to run for governor himself as an independent helped bring about the election (1879) of Alonzo Cornell. While he was head of Tammany, Kelly was able to determine the course of New York City elections, and he himself was city comptroller from 1876 to 1880. Upon retirement (1884) he yielded his political control to one of his lieutenants, Richard CROKER. See M. R. Werner, *Tammany Hall* (1932, repr. 1968).

Kelmscott Press, printing establishment in London. There William MORRIS led the 19th-century revival of the art and craft of making books (see ARTS AND CRAFTS). The first book made by the press was *The Story of the Glittering Plain* (1891), by William Morris. The masterpiece of the press was *The Works of Geoffrey Chaucer* (1896), a folio with illustrations by Sir Edward Burne-Jones and decorative designs and typeface by William Morris. After the death of Morris, in 1896, the press completed some work that he had planned, but no new work was undertaken. The final publication of the press was *A Note by William Morris on His Aims in Founding the Kelmscott Press* (1898). The three types designed by Morris and used by the press were the Golden type, named for *The Golden Legend* (1892); the Troy type, named for *The Recuyell of the Historyes of Troye* (1892); and the Chaucer type, named for the *Chaucer.* The Chaucer type is smaller than the Troy type; otherwise they are the same. The type designs were influenced directly by printers of the 15th cent. The enormous achievement of the press owes much to the art of Burne-Jones and to the inspiration and guidance of the master printer Emery Walker. It gave to the making of books new dignity and raised the level of printing craftsmanship, profoundly influencing book-design quality. See ASHENDENE PRESS; VALE PRESS; DOVES PRESS. See M. J. Perry, *A Chronological List of the Books Printed at the Kelmscott Press* (1928); Temple Scott, *A Bibliography of the Works of William Morris* (1877, repr. 1971).

Kelowna (kĭlō'nə), city (1971 pop. 19,412), S British Columbia, Canada, on Okanagan Lake. It is a tourist resort and serves as a trade center for a fruit-growing and lumbering area.

kelp: see SEAWEED.

kelpfish: see BLENNY.

Kelsey, Henry, c.1670–1729, English fur trader and explorer in Canada. He entered the service of the Hudson's Bay Company in 1684. He was sent (1689) inland to secure Indian trade and later (1691–92) made his much disputed journey into W Canada; some say he went southwest, but evidence points to his being west of Churchill in the region of Reindeer Lake. He was present when York Factory was surrendered to the sieur d'Iberville in 1694 and in 1697. He then served the company in a number of different posts. He returned to the Hudson's Bay region (1714) and served as second in command (1714–17), as governor of York (1717–18), and as governor of all the company's forts in the region (1718–22). He was replaced as governor in 1722 and returned to England. In 1719 he commanded an expedition to explore the northwest coast of Hudson Bay. See A. G. Doughty and Chester Martin, ed., *The Kelsey Papers* (1929).

Kelso, city (1970 pop. 10,296), seat of Cowlitz co., SW Wash., on the Cowlitz River near the Columbia, in a rich farm area; inc. 1889. Boatbuilding, meat-packing, and the manufacture of cement are the major industries. Settled in 1847, Kelso was an important stopping place for early steamboat travel along the Cowlitz River.

Kelt: see CELT.

Keltie, Sir John Scott, 1840–1927, Scottish geographer. He was inspector of geographical education for the Royal Geographic Society, librarian, and secretary of the society. In 1880 he became editor of *The Statesman's Yearbook,* and in 1925 joint editor of the *Geographical Journal.* His works include *A History of the Scottish Highlands and Clans* (1874), *Report on Geographic Education* (1886), *The Partition of Africa* (1894), *Applied Geography* (new ed. 1908), and *History of Geography* (with O. J. R. Howarth, 1914).

Kelvin, William Thomson, 1st Baron, 1824–1907, British mathematician and physicist, b. Belfast. He was professor of natural philosophy at the Univ. of Glasgow (1846–99). He is known especially for his work on heat and electricity. In THERMODYNAMICS his work of coordinating the theories of heat held by various leading scientists of his time established firmly the law of the conservation of energy as proposed by Joule. He introduced the Kelvin scale, or absolute scale, of TEMPERATURE. He also discovered the Thomson effect in THERMOELECTRICITY. The importance of the discoveries and improvements that he made in connection with the transmission of messages by submarine cables led to his establishment as a leading authority in this field. He invented the reflecting galvanometer and the siphon recorder, an instrument by which telegraphic messages are recorded in ink fed from a siphon. See biographies by S. P. Thompson (1910) and A. G. King (1925). His brother, **James Thomson,** 1822–92, an engineer, was professor at Queen's College, Belfast, from 1857 to 1873. He is known for his studies of the variation in melting point with pressure as well as for his research in hydraulics.

kelvin, abbr. K, official name in the INTERNATIONAL SYSTEM OF UNITS (SI) for the degree of temperature as measured on the KELVIN TEMPERATURE SCALE.

Kelvin temperature scale, a TEMPERATURE scale based on the properties of gases. It is found experimentally that all gases, when their temperature is reduced, contract at such a rate that their volume would be zero at a temperature of −273.15°C (degrees Celsius). The Kelvin scale is defined so that 0°K (degrees Kelvin) corresponds to this theoretical lowest temperature. The Kelvin degree is the same size as the Celsius degree (see CELSIUS TEMPERATURE SCALE); hence the two reference temperatures, the freezing point of water (0°C), and the boiling point of water (100°C), correspond to 273.15°K and 373.15°K, respectively. Because the Kelvin scale begins at the lowest possible temperature, it is known as an absolute scale; thus 0°K can be called absolute zero. The Kelvin scale is used only by scientists. Another absolute scale, the Rankine scale, is used by some engineers. It also begins at absolute zero but has degrees the same size as those of the FAHRENHEIT TEMPERATURE SCALE.

Kem (kĕm), river, c.240 mi (390 km) long, Karelian Autonomous Republic, NW European USSR. It rises SE of Kuusamo, Finland, and flows E into the White Sea. The first hydroelectric station along the Kem went into operation in 1967 at Putkinsk; others are planned.

Kemal Pasha, Mustafa: see ATATÜRK, KEMAL.

Kemano Dam: see NECHAKO, river, Canada.

Kemble, Roger, 1721–1802, English actor and manager. During his years as the leader of a traveling company, he married (1753) Sarah Wood, an actress, who bore him 12 children. They thus founded one of the most distinguished families of actors ever to grace the English stage. Five of the children became famous. See Percy Fitzgerald, *The Kembles* (1871); Stephen Kemble, *The Kemble Papers* (New-York Historical Society Collections, 1885). The best known of the children was Sarah Kemble (see SIDDONS, SARAH KEMBLE). The eldest son, **John Philip Kemble,** 1757–1823, was educated for the priesthood, but instead went on the stage and in 1783 made his London debut as Hamlet, in which role he was painted by Sir Thomas Lawrence. A stately, formal actor, suited only for tragedy, his best role was Coriolanus, which was also his farewell performance in 1817. At the Drury Lane from 1783 to 1803, he became manager in 1788 and often played opposite Mrs. Siddons. He managed Covent Garden (1803–8) and, when it was destroyed by fire, built a new one, opening it in 1809. Because of a heavy financial loss, he increased prices, setting off the Old Prices Riots which forced a compromise agreement. See biography by Herschel Baker (1942). His brother **George Stephen Kemble,** 1758–1822, lived always in his shadow. He gave up chemistry when his sister Sarah became famous and returned to the stage, achieving success in roles such as Falstaff. He managed at various times a provincial company, a theater in Edinburgh, where he introduced John Philip Kemble and Mrs. Siddons to the public, and a company in Ireland. His younger brother, **Charles Kemble,** 1775–1854, was most successful in comedy. He first appeared as Malcolm in *Macbeth* in 1794 with John Philip Kemble and Mrs. Siddons in the lead roles. He was poetic rather than emotional, and Romeo was considered his best role. He assumed (1822) the management of Covent Garden in 1822, but he had little financial success until the stage debut of his eldest daughter, Fanny, with whom he successfully toured the United States (1832–34). He retired in 1840. See biography by Jane Williamson (1970). His sister, **Elizabeth Kemble,** 1761–1836, married an actor, Charles Whitlock, in 1785 and, taking as her stage name Mrs. Whitlock, she attained considerable popularity during a visit to the United States in 1792. She retired in 1807 **Fanny Kemble** (Frances Anne Kemble), 1809–93, elder daughter of Charles Kemble, made her debut as Juliet in 1829 under her father's management at Covent Garden. Her success was great and immediate, and her stature as an actress grew in both comedy and tragedy. She was the original Julia in *The Hunchback,* written for her by Sheridan Knowles. She received extravagant praise on her American tour in 1832. In 1834 she married Pierce Butler of Philadelphia, went with him to an estate in Georgia, but later divorced him. During the Civil War she lived in England, writing against slavery for the London *Times.* Her *Journal of a Residence on a Georgia Plantation in 1838–1839* (1863, ed. by John A. Scott, 1961) and *Records of a Later Life* (1882) are much-used sources. See biographies by L. S. Driver (1933), Robert Rushmore (1970), and Constance Wright (1972). **Adelaide Kemble,** 1814–79, second daughter of Charles Kemble, was an opera singer. She studied in Italy and appeared with success in Germany and France (1837–38) and at Covent Garden (1841–42). In 1843 she married Edward Sartoris. She wrote *A Week in a French Country House* (1867).

Kemerovo (kĕm'ərō''vō), city (1970 pop. 385,000), capital of Kemerovo oblast, central Siberian USSR, on the Tom River and on a branch of the Trans-Siberian RR. It is a coal-mining center of the Kuznetsk Basin, with important chemical and synthetic fiber industries. Founded as Shcheglova in 1720, the city was renamed Kemerovo in 1863.

Kemi (kĕ'mē), city (1970 pop. 28,984), Lappi prov., W central Finland, on the Gulf of Bothnia at the mouth of the Kemijoki River. An old trading post, it was chartered in 1869. Kemi is a port and has large sawmills and pulp mills and a power station.

Kemijoki (kĕ'mēyôkē), longest river of Finland, c.345 mi (560 km) long, rising near Sokosti peak, NE Finland. It flows generally SW to Kemijärvi lake, then W into the Gulf of Bothnia at Kemi. With its many tributaries, the Kemijoki drains most of N Finland. It is an important logging route.

Kemnitz, Martin: see CHEMNITZ, MARTIN.

Kempe, Margery (kĕmp), d. 1438 or afterward, English religious writer, b. King's Lynn. She was the wife of a prominent citizen and the mother of 14 children. Her autobiography, *The Book of Margery Kempe* (complete ed. 1940; ed. with modern spelling 1944), was known only in small excerpts until 1934, when the whole was discovered. She was a religious enthusiast whose loud weeping in church and reproof of her neighbors kept her in public disfavor. She traveled abroad as a pilgrim, and her work has rich details of the everyday life of her time. The narrative is occasionally interrupted with visions, prayers, and meditations, many of them of great beauty. The book may be the earliest autobiography in English. See MYSTICISM. See biographies by Martin Thornton (1961) and L. Collis (1964); study by R. K. Stone (1970).

Kempener, Pieter de (pē'tər də kĕm'pənər), c.1503–1580, Flemish painter, b. Brussels. He studied and painted for 10 years in Italy and about 1537 settled in Seville, Spain, where he was known as Pedro Campaña. For churches in Seville he painted religious pictures remarkable for the strong chiaroscuro and naturalistic detail that influenced the school of Seville. The development toward mannerism can be seen in the agitated movements and elongated figures of his masterpiece *The Descent from the Cross* in the Seville Cathedral. On his return to Brussels (1563) he became chief engineer to the duque de Alba and director of the tapestry works.

Kempenfelt, Richard: see ROYAL GEORGE.

Kempenland (kĕm'pənländ), Fr. *Campine,* region, Limburg and Antwerp provs., NE Belgium, and North Brabant prov., S Netherlands. It is a coal-mining and manufacturing area. Once covered by moors and marshes, it has been partially reclaimed. Hasselt and Turnhout are the main cities.

Kemper, Reuben, d. 1827, American adventurer, b. Virginia. With his brothers Nathan and Samuel he settled c.1800 in Feliciana, just above Baton Rouge, in West Florida, then Spanish territory. Expelled from their land by the Spanish authorities, they crossed the border into Mississippi Territory, where they organized a small force and declared West Florida independent of Spain. An attempt to take Baton Rouge in 1804 failed. The three were kidnapped in 1805 but were rescued by a U.S. force as they were being taken down the Mississippi River to Baton Rouge by the Spanish. Other forays were climaxed in 1810 by Reuben's attempt to occupy Mobile. He failed and was arrested and detained by U.S. authorities while the Spanish dispersed the rest of his band. See I. J. Cox, *The West Florida Controversy* (1918, repr. 1967).

Kempis, Thomas à: see THOMAS À KEMPIS.

Kempten (kĕmp'tən), city (1970 pop. 44,910), Bavaria, S West Germany, on the Iller River, in the Allgäu. It is the center of a dairying region. Among the city's manufactures are textiles, paper, and machinery. Of Celtic origin, Kempten became a flourishing Roman colony called Cambodunum. A free imperial city from the late 13th cent., it was sacked (1632) by the Swedes in the Thirty Years War. Kempten passed to Bavaria in 1803. The city is rich in historic architecture.

Kemuel (kĕmyōō'ĕl). **1** Father of Aram. Gen. 22.21. **2** Ephraimite prince. Num. 34.24. **3** Levite prince. 1 Chron. 27.17.

Ken, Thomas, 1637-1711, English prelate and hymn writer, prominent among the nonjuring bishops. He became chaplain to Charles II in 1680 and was nominated by that monarch to the bishopric of Bath and Wells in 1684. Under James II, Ken refused to publish the Declaration of Indulgence in accordance with the king's order; for this he was sent to the Tower with six other bishops in 1688. On the accession of William of Orange (William III) Bishop Ken would not take the oath of allegiance to him after having given it to the Stuarts, and in 1691 his see was taken from him as a nonjuror. Most noted of his hymns is the doxology, "Praise God from whom all blessings flow." See biographies by E. H. Plumptre (1888), F. A. Clarke (1896), and H. A. L. Rice (1958).

Kenai Peninsula (kē'nī), S Alaska, jutting c.150 mi (240 km) into the Gulf of Alaska, between Prince William Sound and Cook Inlet. The Kenai Mts., c.7,000 ft (2,130 m) high, occupy most of the peninsula. The coastal climate is mild, with abundant rainfall and a growing season adequate for many crops. There are forest, mineral, and fishing resources in the east and, in the western section, good farmland. The Alaska RR crosses the peninsula from Seward (1970 pop. 1,587), the largest town.

Kenan (kē'nən), son of Enos. 1 Chron. 1.2. Cainan: Gen. 5.9-14; Luke 3.37.

Kenath (kē'năth), town, ancient Palestine, E of the Jordan. It was captured and renamed by Nobah after himself. It was later the Kanata of the Decapolis. Num. 32.42; 1 Chron. 2.23.

Kenaz (kē'năz). **1** Edomite. Gen. 36.15,42; 1 Chron. 1.36. **2** Kinsman of Caleb. 1 Chron. 4.13,15; Judges 1.13. One of these was the eponym of the Kenezites. Num. 32.12; Joshua 14.6-14; 15.17.

Kendal, Ehrengard Melusina von der Schulenburg, duchess of: see SCHULENBURG, EHRENGARD.

Kendal, Dame Madge (kĕn'dəl), 1849-1935, English actress, whose maiden name was Margaret Robertson. She was the 22d child of an actor-manager and the sister of T. W. Robertson, the dramatist. After early performances in juvenile roles, she made her debut (1865) as Ophelia at the Haymarket Theatre, London, and became prominent in both comedy and tragedy. She married William Kendal in 1869 and thereafter co-starred with him in productions of Shakespeare and contemporary comedies, touring the United States in 1889. Kendal was made Dame of the British Empire in 1927. See her *Dramatic Opinions* (1890) and *Dame Madge Kendal by Herself* (1933). Her husband, **William Kendal,** 1843-1917, whose original name was William Hunter Grimston, became a favorite in romantic roles after 1861, though his talent was never equal to that of his wife. In partnership with John Hare, the Kendals managed the St. James Theatre (1879-88). They both retired in 1908. See T. E. Pemberton, *The Kendals* (1900).

Kendall, Amos, 1789-1869, American journalist and statesman, b. Dunstable, Middlesex co., Mass. He edited (1816-29) at Frankfort, Ky., the *Argus of Western America,* one of the most influential Western papers of the day. At first a supporter of Henry Clay, he shifted allegiance to Andrew JACKSON and helped to build Jackson's political strength. In 1829 he went to Washington, D.C., and was appointed by President Jackson fourth auditor of the Treasury. His real importance was as one of the ablest and most influential members of the Kitchen Cabinet—a group of intimate advisers to President Jackson. He helped draft many of Jackson's more important state papers, was chief counselor to Jackson in the controversy over rechartering the Bank of the United States, and vigorously defended administration policies in the newspapers. He was appointed (1835) U.S. Postmaster General by Jackson, and he remained at the post under President Van Buren, thoroughly reorganizing a badly managed department. He became (1845) business manager for Samuel F. B. Morse and played an important role in the development of telegraph service. Kendall opposed secession and urged vigorous prosecution of the war against the South, although he was often critical of President Lincoln's policies. See his autobiography, ed. by his son-in-law, William Stickney (1872, repr. 1949).

Kendall, Edward Calvin, 1886-1972, American biochemist, b. South Norwalk, Conn., grad. Columbia (B.S., 1908; Ph.D., 1910). At St. Luke's Hospital, New York City, he did research on the thyroid gland (1911-14). He became (1914) head of the biochemistry section at the Mayo Clinic and was (1921-51) professor of physiological chemistry at the Mayo Foundation (affiliated with the Univ. of Minnesota). After 1952 he was professor of chemistry at Princeton. He shared with Philip S. Hench and Tadeus Reichstein the 1950 Nobel Prize in Physiology and Medicine for his work on the hormones of the adrenal gland cortex. Kendall isolated and identified a series of compounds from the adrenal gland cortex, prepared cortisone by partial synthesis (with Merck & Co., Inc.), and with P. S. Hench, H. F. Polley, and C. H. Slocumb, investigated the effects of cortisone and of adrenocorticotropic hormone (ACTH) on rheumatoid arthritis. Other contributions include the isolation of thyroxine (1914) and the crystallization of glutathione and establishment of its chemical structure.

Kendall, George Wilkins, 1809-67, American journalist, b. near Amherst, N.H. After a succession of journalistic jobs, he was a partner in founding (1837) the New Orleans *Picayune.* In 1841 he joined the disastrous Texan expedition to Santa Fe, sponsored by the president of Texas, Mirabeau Lamar, in the hope of winning the allegiance of the New Mexico area to the republic of Texas. The surviving members, including Kendall, were marched to Mexico City and imprisoned. After his release Kendall wrote *Narrative of the Texan Santa Fe Expedition* (1844). He was an exponent of war with Mexico, and, when hostilities began, he served first under Gen. Zachary Taylor and then as aide to Gen. William Worth in Gen. Winfield Scott's campaigns. He sent back to his paper, by private express, narrative accounts that became famous and were widely copied, thus earning him a reputation as the first of the modern war correspondents. He also wrote *The War between the United States and Mexico* (1851).

Kendrick, John, c.1740-1794, American sea captain, b. Massachusetts. During part of the American Revolution he commanded privateers. As commander of an expedition composed of the *Columbia* and *Washington,* he explored (1788-89) the Pacific Northwest Coast in the neighborhood of Nootka Sound, managing to avoid conflict with the Spanish who were there at the time. Robert Gray, later discoverer of the Columbia River, sailed with him. Kendrick also visited Japan, becoming the first to fly the American flag in a port of that country.

Keneh: see QINA, Egypt.

Kenilworth (kĕn'əlwûrth''), urban district (1971 pop. 20,121), Warwickshire, central England. A market town, it is famous for the ruins of Kenilworth Castle, celebrated in Sir Walter Scott's novel *Kenilworth* and founded c.1120 by Geoffrey de Clinton. In the 13th cent. the castle became the property of Simon de Montfort. In the castle's Great Hall, Edward II was forced to relinquish his crown in 1327. The castle then passed by marriage to John of Gaunt, who made many alterations in the buildings. It became royal property through John's son, Henry IV, until Queen Elizabeth I presented it to Robert Dudley, earl of Leicester. The castle was donated to the government in 1937. Also in Kenilworth are ruins of an Augustinian priory founded c.1122.

Kenilworth ivy, an IVY of the FIGWORT family.

Kenites (kĕn'īts), wilderness nomadic tribe friendly to the Jews. They came with the Jews into Palestine and made the south of the country their home up to the time of David. Moses' father-in-law was a Kenite, and so was the husband of Jael. Gen. 15.19; Num. 24.21; Judges 1.16; 4.11,17; 1 Sam. 15.6; 27.10; 30.29; 1 Chron. 2.55.

Kenitra (kənē'trə), city (1970 est. pop. 130,000), NW Morocco, on the Sebou River. It is a busy port exporting agricultural products. The city was built by the French and called by them Port Lyautey. American troops landed there in Nov., 1942, during World War II.

Kenmore, village (1970 pop. 20,980), Erie co., NW N.Y., a residential suburb adjacent to Buffalo; inc. 1899. Agnes B. McKirdy lived there.

Kennan, George, 1845-1924, American authority on Siberia, b. Norwalk, Ohio. In 1864 he made the first of his journeys to the Far East as an engineer. His articles on Siberia, for many years almost the sole authoritative source of information on that region, were published as *Tent Life in Siberia* (1870) and *Siberia and the Exile System* (2 vol., 1891).

Kennan, George Frost, 1904-, U.S. diplomat and historian, b. Milwaukee, Wis., grad. Princeton, 1925. After 1927 he served in various diplomatic posts in Europe, including Hamburg, Riga, Berlin, Prague, and Moscow. In 1947 he was on the policy-planning staff of the Dept. of State; later (1949-50) he was one of the chief advisers to Secretary of State Dean Acheson. He was appointed ambassador to the USSR in 1952, but was recalled at the demand of the Soviet government because of comments he made on the isolation of diplomats in Moscow and the campaign that Soviet propagandists were conducting against the United States. Retiring from the diplomatic service in 1953, he joined the Institute for Advanced Study at Princeton, N.J., and in 1956 became professor at its school of historical studies. He served (1961-63) as U.S. ambassador to Yugoslavia. Kennan, who had helped formulate the Truman administration's policy of "containment" of the USSR, eventually became an advocate of withdrawal of U.S. forces from Western Europe and of Soviet forces from the satellite countries. His works include *Soviet-American Relations, 1917-1920* (2 vol., 1956-58), *American Diplomacy, 1900-1950* (1951), *Realities of American Foreign Policy* (1954), *Russia and the West under Lenin and Stalin* (1961), and *Democracy and the Student Left* (1968). See his memoirs (2 vol., 1967-72).

Kennebec (kĕn'əbĕk), river, 164 mi (264 km) long, rising in Moosehead Lake, NW Maine, and flowing S to the Atlantic; the Androscoggin River is its chief tributary. French explorer Samuel de Champlain explored it in 1604 and 1605; in 1607 English colonist George Popham established a short-lived colony, Fort St. George, at its mouth. Trading posts were established shortly after 1625. In 1775, American Gen. Benedict Arnold's expedition went up the Kennebec en route to Quebec. Lumber and, in the 19th cent., ice were shipped down the river to the coast, and shipbuilding flourished along its banks. Villages such as Augusta and Waterville, established near power sites, became industrial centers.

Kennebunk (kĕnəbŭngk'), town (1970 pop. 5,646), York co., S Maine; inc. 1820. The first settlement (c.1650) grew as a trading and, later, a shipbuilding and shipping center. The Wedding Cake House at Kennebunk is known for its scroll-saw architecture.

Kennebunkport (kĕn''ĭbŭngkpôrt', kĕn''ĭbŭngk'-pôrt), town (1970 pop. 2,160), York co., S Maine, on the Atlantic coast; settled 1629, inc. 1653. The early town, called Arundel, appears in Kenneth Roberts's books; the name was changed in 1821. The town is a summer resort, especially for authors, artists, and actors.

Kennedy, Charles Rann, 1871-1950, Anglo-American dramatist, b. Derby, England. He became a U.S. citizen in 1917. His plays, concerned with moral problems, include *The Servant in the House* (1908), *Winterfeast* (1908), and *The Terrible Meek* (1912).

Kennedy, Edward Moore, 1932-, U.S. Senator (1962-), brother of John Fitzgerald and Robert Francis Kennedy, b. Boston, Mass. Ted Kennedy served (1961-62) as an assistant district attorney in Massachusetts before being elected (1962) as a Democrat to the U.S. Senate. After the assassination of his brother, Robert, in June, 1968, he became the acknowledged leader of Senate liberals and served (1969-71) as assistant majority leader. His political future was marred somewhat by his involvement in the Chappaquiddick incident (July, 1969), in which Mary Jo Kopechne, a passenger in the car he was driving, drowned when the car crashed and fell into a creek. Kennedy's reputation survived, however, and he continued to advocate such liberal reforms as a national health insurance program and tax reform. He was considered a leading Democratic presidential candidate, but in Sept., 1974, announced that he would not run for President in 1976. Kennedy is the author of *Decisions for a Decade* (1968) and *In Critical Condition* (1972). See biographies by W. H. Honan (1972) and Burton Hersh (1972).

Kennedy, John Fitzgerald, 1917-63, 35th President of the United States (1961-63), b. Brookline, Mass.; son of Joseph P. Kennedy. While an undergraduate at Harvard (1936-40) he served briefly in London as secretary to his father, who was then ambassador there. His Harvard honors thesis on the British failure to judge adequately the threat of Nazi Germany was published as *Why England Slept* (1940). Enlisting in the navy in Sept., 1941, he became commander of a PT boat in the Pacific in World War II. In action off the Solomon Islands (Aug., 1943), his boat was sheared in two and sunk, and Kennedy was credited with saving the life of at least one of his crew. After the war he was briefly a journalist. As Congressman from Massachusetts (1947-53), he consistently supported the domestic programs of the Truman administration but criticized its China policy. In 1952, despite the Eisenhower landslide, he defeated Henry Cabot Lodge for a seat in the U.S. Senate, where he served on the Labor and Public Welfare Committee and on the Foreign Relations Committee. In 1953, Kennedy married Jacqueline Lee Bouvier. While recuperating in 1955 from a serious operation to repair a spinal injury, he wrote *Profiles in Courage* (1956), brief portraits of American political leaders who have defied public opinion to vote according to their consciences; for this work he received the Pulitzer Prize. Although Kennedy narrowly lost the Democratic vice-presidential nomination in 1956, his overwhelming reelection as Senator in 1958 helped him toward the goal of presidential candidacy. In 1960 he entered and won seven presidential primaries and won the Democratic nomination on the first ballot. He selected Lyndon Baines JOHNSON as his vice-presidential candidate. In the campaign that followed, Kennedy engaged in a series of televised debates with his Republican opponent, Richard M. NIXON. Defeating Nixon by a narrow popular margin, Kennedy became at 43 the youngest man ever elected President and the first Roman Catholic President. Soon after his eloquent inaugural address (" . . . Ask not what your country can do for you—ask what you can do for your country"), Kennedy set out his domestic program, known as the New Frontier: tax reform, federal aid to education, medical care for the aged under social security, enlargement of civil rights through executive action, aid to depressed areas, and an accelerated space program. He was almost immediately, however, caught up in foreign affairs crises. The first (April, 1961) was the abortive BAY OF PIGS INVASION of Cuba by Cuban exiles trained and aided by the Central Intelligence Agency. Although the planning had been done under the Eisenhower administration, Kennedy had approved the invasion and was widely criticized for it. In June, 1961, the President met in Vienna with Soviet Premier Khrushchev. Hopes of a thaw in the cold war were dashed by Khrushchev's threat that the USSR would conclude a peace treaty with East Germany and thus cut off Western access to West Berlin. In the period of tension that followed, the United States increased its military strength while the East Germans erected the Berlin Wall. The danger of a confrontation between the United States and the USSR subsided for a time. But in Oct., 1962, U.S. reconnaissance planes discovered the existence of Soviet missile bases in Cuba. President Kennedy immediately ordered a blockade to prevent further weapons from reaching Cuba and demanded the removal of installations already there. After a brief interval of extreme tension when the world appeared to be on the brink of nuclear warfare, the USSR complied with U.S. demands. Kennedy won much praise for his stance in the Cuban crisis, but some have criticized him for what they felt was unnecessary "brinkmanship." The following year (Aug., 1963) tension with the USSR was eased by the conclusion of a nuclear test ban treaty that prohibited the atmospheric testing of nuclear weapons. In Southeast Asia, however, the Kennedy administration perceived a growing Communist threat to the South Vietnamese government. It steadily increased the number of U.S. military "advisers" in South Vietnam (from 685 to about 16,000) and for the first time placed U.S. troops in combat situations there. As disaffection in South Vietnam grew, moreover, the United States involved itself in local political maneuvering and finally connived at the overthrow (Oct., 1963) of the corrupt South Vietnamese dictator, Ngo Dinh Diem (see VIETNAM WAR). Within the Western Hemisphere, Kennedy established (1961) the ALLIANCE FOR PROGRESS, which provided economic assistance to the Latin American countries. He also initiated the PEACE CORPS program, which sent U.S. volunteers to work in the developing countries. Many of Kennedy's proposed domestic reforms were either killed or not acted upon by Congress. In the area of civil rights the administration pressed hard to achieve INTEGRATION in the South; it assigned Federal marshals to protect the Freedom Ride demonstrations and used Federal troops in Mississippi (1962) and a federalized National Guard in Alabama (1963) to quell disturbances resulting from enforced school desegregation. In June, 1963, the President proposed extensive civil rights legislation, but this, like his tax reform program, was not enacted until after his death. On Nov. 22, 1963, President Kennedy was shot while riding in an open car in Dallas, Texas. He died half an hour later and was succeeded as President by Lyndon Johnson. The WARREN COMMISSION, appointed by Johnson to investigate the murder, concluded that it was the work of a single assassin, Lee Harvey OSWALD. Kennedy's death shocked a nation grown accustomed to his eloquence and his idealistic concern for social justice and international accord. Many felt that had he not been killed at the age of 46 he would have gone on to achieve real greatness as a President. Kennedy was buried in Arlington National Cemetery. See biographies by J. M. Burns (1960) and Victor Lasky (1963); T. H. White, *The Making of the President, 1960* (1961); T. C. Sorenson, *Kennedy* (1965); A. M. Schlesinger, Jr., *A Thousand Days* (1965); Pierre Salinger, *With Kennedy* (1966); Tom Wicker, *JFK and LBJ* (1968); Earl Latham, ed., *J. F. Kennedy and Presidential Power* (1972).

Kennedy, Joseph Patrick, 1888-1969, U.S. ambassador to Great Britain (1937-40), b. Boston, grad. Harvard, 1912, father of John F. Kennedy, Robert F. Kennedy, and Edward M. Kennedy. He engaged in banking, shipbuilding, investment banking, and motion-picture distribution before he served (1934-35) as chairman of the Securities and Exchange Commission. He was (1936-37) head of the U.S. Maritime Commission until his appointment as ambassador. In London he supported the overtures of the Chamberlain government to Hitler and was generally noninterventionist. He resigned as ambassador in November, 1940. In his later years he continued to be successful in business (notably real estate) and devoted considerable time to philanthropic activities, especially the Joseph P. Kennedy, Jr., Memorial Foundation, dedicated to a son killed in World War II. He wrote *I'm for Roosevelt* (1936). See J. F. Dinneen, *The Kennedy Family* (1960) and biographies by R. J. Whalen (1964) and D. E. Koskoff (1974).

Kennedy, Robert Francis, 1925-68, American politician, U.S. Attorney General (1961-64), b. Brookline, Mass., younger brother of President John F. Kennedy. A graduate of Harvard (1948) and the Univ. of Virginia law school (1951), he managed John F. Kennedy's successful campaign for the U.S. Senate in 1952. From 1953 to 1956 he was counsel to the Senate subcommittee chaired by Sen. Joseph R. McCarthy. He then became (1957) chief counsel to the Senate subcommittee investigating labor rackets and there gained a reputation by exposing corruption in the Teamsters union. In 1960 he was manager of his older brother's presidential campaign. His inclusion in President Kennedy's cabinet gave rise to charges of nepotism, but he proved a vigorous Attorney General, especially in prosecuting cases relating to civil rights. He was also his brother's closest adviser. After John Kennedy's assassination, Robert Kennedy continued for a time to serve in President Lyndon Johnson's cabinet, but in 1964 he resigned to run for election as Senator from New York. Despite criticism that he was a carpetbagger from Massachusetts, he won the election. In the Senate he was a vigorous advocate of social reform and became identified particularly as a spokesman for the rights of the minorities. Although Kennedy had supported his brother's intensification of American aid to the South Vietnamese government, he became increasingly critical of Johnson's escalation of the Vietnam War and by 1968 was advocating that the Viet Cong be included in a South Vietnamese coalition government. Urged to run against President Johnson for the Democratic nomination in 1968, Kennedy appeared reluctant until Sen. Eugene McCarthy's showing in the New Hampshire Democratic primary convinced him that a challenge to Johnson could be successful. He announced his candidacy on March 16, 1968. Although Johnson withdrew (March 31) from the race, the administration's standard passed to Vice President Hubert Humphrey, while Senator McCarthy retained the support of many opponents of the Vietnam War, who accused Kennedy of opportunism. Kennedy conducted an energetic campaign and won a series of primary victories, culminating in the one in California on June 4. At the end of that day he gave a victory speech to his supporters in the Ambassador Hotel in Los Angeles, and then, while leaving by a rear exit, was shot. He died a day later (June 6, 1968). The gunman, Sirhan Bishara Sirhan, was captured at the scene of the crime and later convicted of first degree murder. Like his brother John F. Kennedy, Robert Kennedy was buried in Arlington National Cemetery. He wrote *The Enemy Within* (1960), *Thirteen Days: A Memoir of the Cuban Missile Crisis* (1969), and *To Seek a Newer World* (1969). See Penn Kimball, *Bobby Kennedy and the New Politics* (1968); David Halberstam, *The Unfinished Odyssey of Robert Kennedy* (1968); Douglas Ross, ed., *Robert Kennedy: Apostle of Change* (1968); Jack Newfield, *Robert Kennedy: A Memoir* (1969); Jules Witcover, *Eighty-Five Days* (1969); Victor Navasky, *Kennedy Justice* (1971).

Kennedy, Mount, 13,095 ft (3,991 m) high, SW Yukon Territory, Canada, in the St. Elias Mts. near the Alaskan border. It was named in honor of U.S. President John F. Kennedy in 1965. Although discovered in 1935, the mountain was climbed for the first time in 1965 by a team that included Robert F. Kennedy, the President's brother.

Kennelly, Arthur Edwin (kĕn'əlē), 1861-1939, American electrical engineer, b. Bombay, India, educated at University College School, London. He was Edison's chief electrical assistant (1887-94) and was later professor at Harvard (1902-30) and at the Massachusetts Institute of Technology (1913-24). Much of his research was on electromagnetism and alternating currents. In 1902 he advanced the theory, also proposed by Oliver Heaviside, that a layer of ionized air in the upper atmosphere might deflect downward electromagnetic waves. The theory was demonstrated as fact, and the deflecting layer is variously called the Heaviside layer or the Kennelly-Heaviside layer (see IONOSPHERE).

Kenner, city (1970 pop. 29,858), Jefferson parish, SE La., a suburb of New Orleans; inc. 1952. New Orleans International Airport is within the city limits, and a racetrack is nearby.

Kennesaw Mountain National Battlefield Park: see NATIONAL PARKS AND MONUMENTS (table).

Kenneth I ((Kenneth mac Alpin), d. 858, traditional founder of the kingdom of Scotland. He succeeded his father, Alpin, as king of Dalriada (the kingdom of the Gaelic Scots in W Scotland) and c.843 obtained the Pictish throne, thus establishing the nucleus of the kingdom of Scotland. Because of continual depredations by the Danes from the Irish coast, Kenneth moved his capital eastward to Scone.

Kenneth II, d. 995, Scottish king (971-995). The son of Malcolm I (reigned 943-54), he became king of the united Picts and Scots in 971 and immediately led a savage raid on the British in Northumbria. He is later listed, however, as submitting to the Anglo-Saxon king Edgar c.973 and being granted by him the land between the Tweed and Forth rivers. This is the earliest mention of the Tweed as the border between England and Scotland. Kenneth's reign also saw consolidation of his kingdom in the central area north of the Tay River. He was murdered as a result of a conflict with the mormaor (high steward) of Argyll.

Kennewick, city (1970 pop. 15,212), Benton co., SE Wash., on the Columbia River near the influx of the Snake River, in an irrigated farm and vineyard region; inc. 1904. Food processing is the chief industry. The Atomic Energy Commission's nearby Hanford Works (established during World War II) is a major employer.

Kennicott, Benjamin, 1718-83, English clergyman and biblical scholar. His long career at Oxford was one of devotion to learning. He was rector of Culham, Oxfordshire, from 1753 to 1783. With the aim of preparing an improved Hebrew text of the Old Testament, he secured the assistance of other scholars in the study of Hebrew manuscripts. Besides the many printed editions, 615 Hebrew manuscripts and 16 manuscripts of the Samaritan Pentateuch were collated to produce his edition, the *Vetus testamentum Hebraicum cum variis lectionibus* (1776-80).

Kenny, Elizabeth, 1886–1952, Australian nurse, b. New South Wales, grad. St. Ursula's College, Australia, 1902. She became "Sister" Kenny as a first lieutenant nurse (1914–18) in the Australian army. While caring for poliomyelitis victims in her homeland, she developed a method using hot, moist applications in conjunction with passive exercise. She came to the United States in 1940 to demonstrate her techniques, which were used extensively with good results. She was coauthor with John F. Pohl of *The Kenny Concept of Infantile Paralysis and Its Treatment* (1942); with Martha Ostenso she wrote the autobiographical *And They Shall Walk* (1943). See biography by H. J. Levine (1954).

Kénogami (kānŏg'əmē), city (1971 pop. 10,970), SE Que., Canada, on the Saguenay River, adjacent to its twin city, Jonquière. It has pulp and paper mills and a hydroelectric station.

Kenora (kənô'rə), town (1971 pop. 10,952), W Ont., Canada, at the north end of the Lake of the Woods. There are fish-processing plants and lumber, flour, pulp, and paper mills in the town. Kenora contains an airport and serves as a base for fishing, hunting, and canoe trips.

Kenosha (kĭnō'shə), industrial city (1970 pop. 78,805), seat of Kenosha co., SE Wis., a port of entry on Lake Michigan; inc. 1850. Clothing, automobiles, electronic equipment, and metal products are among its many manufactures. The first public school in the state was begun there in 1849. A historical and art museum and the county courthouse (containing the county historical museum) are part of the civic center. Also in the city are Carthage College, a technical institute, and a library designed by Daniel Burnham.

Kenrick, Francis Patrick, 1797–1863, American Roman Catholic churchman, b. Dublin, Ireland, educated in Rome. In 1821 he was ordained priest and went to America to teach in the college at Bardstown, Ky. In 1829 he was made bishop coadjutor of Philadelphia. His charitable work in the cholera epidemic in 1832 and his courageous dignity in the anti-Catholic riots of 1844 won him considerable admiration. He was made archbishop of Baltimore and apostolic delegate in 1851. He wrote many works on the Bible. His brother, **Peter Richard Kenrick,** 1806–96, was also an American Roman Catholic churchman and was also born in Dublin. He was educated at Maynooth. Called by his brother in 1833 to be pastor of the Philadelphia cathedral and vicar general of the diocese, he was sent in 1841 at the request of the bishop of St. Louis to be coadjutor there. In 1843 he became bishop and in 1847 archbishop. At the First Vatican Council (1870) he at first opposed the enunciation of papal infallibility as a dogma. See J. J. O'Shea, *The Two Kenricks* (1904).

Kensett, John Frederick, 1818–72, American landscape painter, of the Hudson River school, b. Cheshire, Conn. He began painting while working as an engraver and in 1840 went to England to study. He spent some time in Paris and in Düsseldorf before going (1845) to Rome, where he became a popular member of the American art colony and perfected his technique. After a few years he returned to the United States and in 1848 became a member of the National Academy of Design. His delicately colored, poetic landscapes brought him fame and wealth. The Metropolitan Museum has several of his paintings. There are others in the Corcoran Gallery and the New York Public Library.

Kensico Reservoir (kĕn'zĭkō), c.4 sq mi (10 sq km), SE N.Y., N of White Plains, formed by Kensico Dam (completed 1915) on the Bronx River. A principal unit in the New York City water supply system, the reservoir receives water from sources in the Catskill Mts. and from the Delaware River.

Kensington, England: see KENSINGTON AND CHELSEA.

Kensington and Chelsea, borough (1971 pop. 184,392) of Greater London, SE England. It was created in 1965 by the merger of the metropolitan London boroughs of Kensington and Chelsea. Kensington is a largely residential district with fashionable shopping streets. Portobello Road is a well-known street market. The area has undergone extensive urban renewal and now contains blocks of large, tall flats. A large park, Kensington Gardens, adjoins Hyde Park. The gardens originally were the grounds of Kensington Palace (Nottingham House), partially built by Christopher Wren, which was the home of William and Mary, Queen Anne, and George I and George II. HOLLAND HOUSE was the residence of the Fox family and, for a time, of William Penn. South Kensington is a center of colleges and museums; it is the site of the natural history section of the BRITISH MUSEUM, the VICTORIA AND ALBERT MUSEUM, the Science Museum, the Royal College of Art, and the Royal College of Science, among others. Albert Hall, a concert hall, is also there. Chelsea is a literary and artistic quarter. Sir Thomas More, D. G. Rossetti, James Whistler, Charles Dickens, and many others were associated with it. Thomas Carlyle's house is there. Chelsea Old Church, part of which dates from the 13th cent., includes the Chapel of Sir Thomas More (1528). The church, as well as the Royal Hospital for Soldiers built (1682–92) by Christopher Wren, was badly damaged in World War II.

Kensington Rune Stone, much-disputed stone found (1898) on a farm near Kensington, Minn., SW of Alexandria. Inscribed on the stone in RUNES is an account of a party of Norse explorers, 14 days' journey from the sea, who camped nearby in 1362 and lost 10 of their men, presumably to Indians. Archaeological and philological disputes have been waged over the authenticity of the stone, with no definite conclusions having been reached. Most scholars argue that the stone is a hoax, i.e., that it is of more recent origin than the 14th cent., though some accept it with the corroborative archaeological evidence. See VINLAND. See Erik Wahlgren, *The Kensington Rune Stone: A Mystery Solved* (1958); H. R. Holand, *Norse Discoveries and Explorations in America, 982–1362* (1940, repr. 1969); T. C. Blegen, *The Kensington Rune Stone* (1968).

Kent, Edward Augustus, duke of, 1767–1820, fourth son of George III of Great Britain and father of Queen Victoria. Most of his mature life was spent in military service at Gibraltar, in Canada, and in the West Indies. He was married (1818) to Victoria Mary Louise of Saxe-Coburg.

Kent, George Edward Alexander Edmund, duke of, 1902–42, fourth son of George V of Great Britain. He traveled extensively as "salesman of the empire." A member of the Royal Air Force after 1940, he was killed on active service in a plane crash in Scotland. Three children were born of his marriage (1934) to Princess Marina (1906–68) of Greece: Prince Edward (b. 1935), who succeeded him as duke of Kent, Princess Alexandra (b. 1936), and Prince Michael (b. 1942).

Kent, James, 1763–1847, American jurist, b. near Brewster, N.Y. He was admitted to the bar in 1785 and began practice in Poughkeepsie, N. Y. Active in the Federalist party, he served several terms in the New York legislature. In 1793, Kent moved to New York City, where his reputation for learning established him as first professor of law at Columbia College. His lectures (1794–98) were not especially well received, and he welcomed the appointment in 1798 as a judge of the state supreme court. He was made chief judge in 1804, and from 1814 until his statutory retirement in 1823 he presided over the state court of chancery. Kent's written opinions as chancellor were instrumental in reviving EQUITY, which had largely lapsed in the United States after the American Revolution. He refashioned many of the doctrines in that area by combining concepts from English chancery jurisprudence with the principles of Roman law. After his retirement he again (1824–26) was professor of law at Columbia, but found the delivery of lectures tedious and soon resigned. He vastly expanded the material of his courses to prepare his *Commentaries on American Law* (4 vol., 1826–30), a systematic treatment of international law, American constitutional law, the sources of state law, and the law of personal rights and of property. It was enthusiastically received by the legal profession and in Kent's lifetime went through six editions. See *Memoirs and Letters of James Kent* by his great-grandson, William Kent (1898, repr. 1970); study by J. T. Horton (1939, repr. 1969).

Kent, Rockwell, 1882–1971, American painter, muralist, wood engraver, lithographer, and writer, b. Tarrytown, N.Y. Kent studied with Robert Henri. He lived in Labrador, Alaska, Greenland, and Tierra del Fuego and painted vigorous, exotic landscapes during his travels. His graphic art and his painting are notable for their stark, powerful style. Among his major works are *Winter* (Metropolitan Mus.), *Down to the Sea* (Brooklyn Mus.), and *Toilers of the Sea* (Art Inst., Chicago). He is the author of *Wilderness* (1921), *Voyaging Southward from the Strait of Magellan* (1924), *Salamina* (1935), *Greenland Journal* (1962), and the autobiographical *This Is My Own* (1940).

Kent, William, 1685–1748, English landscape gardener, architect, and painter. A very minor painter, Kent made ceiling decorations for Kensington Palace. He greatly influenced landscape gardening by changing the prevailing artificial style to one based more closely on nature, as in the gardens at Rousham. As an architect, he followed Neo-Palladian tenets and adhered to strictly symmetrical planning, especially in his masterpiece, Holkham Hall, Norfolk (begun 1734). In London he planned the treasury building (1734) and the Horse Guards building (erected posthumously, 1750–58). See study by Margaret Jourdain (1948).

Kent, county (1971 pop. 1,396,030), 1,525 sq mi (3,950 sq km), SE England. It lies between the Thames estuary and the Strait of Dover. The county town is MAIDSTONE. The Isle of SHEPPEY is separated from the north coast by the narrow Swale channel. The chalky North Downs cross the county from east to west, and to the south lie the fertile Weald and ROMNEY MARSH. The Medway, the Stour, and the Darent are the chief rivers. The region, largely agricultural, is a market-gardening center. Crops include fruit, grain, and hops. Sheep and cattle grazing, fishing, and dairying are also important. One of London's "Home Counties," Kent is becoming increasingly important industrially because of the encroachment of the London urban area into its western portion. Paper, pottery, tile and brick, cement, beer, malt, and chemicals are manufactured, and there is shipbuilding and oil refining. Kent has some coal deposits. Because of its strategic location on the path to the Continent through Dover, Kent has been important throughout English history. Julius Caesar landed at Kent in 55 B.C. Roman roads crossed the county. Kent was one of the seven Anglo-Saxon kingdoms. In the Middle Ages many religious houses were established in the old kingdom of Kent, and CANTERBURY became the goal of numerous pilgrims such as Chaucer described in the *Canterbury Tales.* The region was intimately associated with the rebellions of Wat Tyler, Jack Cade, and Sir Thomas Wyatt. The coast was heavily fortified during the two World Wars. In 1974, Kent was reorganized as a nonmetropolitan county.

Kent. 1 Industrial city (1970 pop. 28,183), Portage co., NE Ohio; settled in 1805 as Franklin Mills, combined with Carthage and renamed as Kent 1863, inc. as a city 1920. Electric motors, compressors, drilling rigs, fasteners, and locks are made there. The city is the seat of Kent State Univ. **2** City (1970 pop. 16,275), King co., W central Wash., near Puget Sound; inc. 1890. Formerly a farm area, Kent is now rapidly urbanizing. It has a large aerospace industry. Food is processed, and electrical supplies and chemical products are made.

Kent, kingdom of, one of the kingdoms of Anglo-Saxon England. It was settled in the mid-5th cent. by aggressive bands of people called Jutes (see ANGLO-SAXONS). Historians are in dispute over the authenticity of the traditional belief that HENGIST AND HORSA landed in 449 to defend the Britons against the Picts and whether Hengist and his son Aesc subsequently turned against their employer, VORTIGERN. The Jutes, at any rate, soon overcame the British inhabitants and established a kingdom that comprised essentially the same area as the modern county of Kent. ÆTHELBERT of Kent established his hegemony over England S of the Humber River, received St. Augustine of Canterbury's first mission to England in 597, and became a Christian. During the following century, Kent was periodically subjugated and divided by Wessex and Mercia and finally became a Mercian province under OFFA. A Kentish revolt after Offa's death in 796 was put down. Conquered by Egbert of Wessex in 825, Kent was forced to acknowledge the overlordship of Wessex and became part of that kingdom. Although it suffered heavily from Danish raids, it remained one of the most advanced areas in pre-Norman England because of the archbishopric of Canterbury and because of its steady intercourse with the Continent. The metalwork and jewelry of Kent were distinctive and beautiful. See J. E. A. Jolliffe, *Pre-Feudal England: the Jutes* (1933, repr. 1963); F. M. Stenton, *Anglo-Saxon England* (3d ed., 1971).

Kent, Maid of: see BARTON, ELIZABETH.

Kenton, Simon, 1755–1836, American frontiersman, b. probably Fauquier co., Va. In 1771, believing he had killed a man, he fled westward, assuming the name Simon Butler. He settled in Boonesboro, Ky., in 1775 and defended the settlement against frequent Indian attacks; in one of these encounters he saved Daniel Boone's life. During the American Revolution he accompanied (1778) George Rogers Clark on his expedition to Kaskaskia and Vincennes and helped Boone in the raid on Chillicothe. He was later captured by the Indians, who brought him to the British in Detroit, but he escaped (1779) and again joined Clark as a scout. Learning that the man he thought he had killed was alive, he resumed his original name, and eventually settled (1799) in Ohio. Kenton was elected a brigadier general of militia in 1804 and served in the War of 1812 at the battle of the Thames. See biography by Edna Kenton (1930, repr. 1971); Patricia Jahns, *The Violent Years: Simon Kenton and the Ohio-Kentucky Frontier* (1962).

Kent's Cavern or **Kent's Hole,** limestone cave, Devonshire, SW England, near Torquay. The floor is composed of several strata, with remains indicating the prehistoric coexistence there of man and now extinct animals. The Rev. J. McEnery explored (1825–29) the cave and put forth the coexistence theory. The cave was extensively explored from 1865 to 1880.

Kent State University, mainly at Kent, Ohio; coeducational; founded 1910 as a normal school, became Kent State College in 1929, gained university status in 1935. The university's schools include the Honors Experimental College (begun in 1961 as an honors program, became in 1970 a separate college). The university maintains two-year branches at Ashtabula, East Liverpool, Geauga County, Salem, Stark County, Trumbull County, and Tuscarawas County.

Kentucky (kəntŭk'ē, kĭn-), state (1970 pop. 3,219,311), 40,395 sq mi (104,623 sq km), S central United States, admitted as the 15th state of the Union in 1792. FRANKFORT is the capital, LOUISVILLE the largest city. The northern boundary is formed by the erratic course of the Ohio River, separating Kentucky from Ohio, Indiana, and Illinois. The river runs generally SW below Covington, in the north, until it joins the Mississippi River, which forms the western border with Missouri. At the southwest tip of the state about 5 sq mi (13 sq km) of Kentucky territory, created by a double hairpin turn in the Mississippi River, protrudes N from Tennessee into Missouri and is entirely separate from Kentucky. Tennessee borders Kentucky in a straight line on the south. In the east, the boundary with West Virginia is formed by the Big Sandy River and its tributary, the Tug Fork, while the Virginia border runs through the

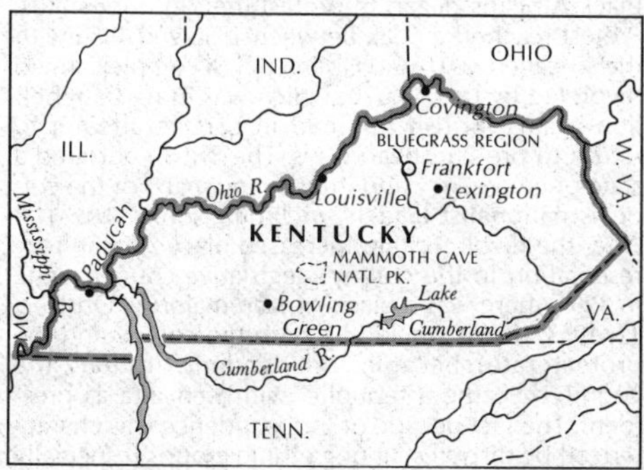

Cumberland Mts., part of the Appalachian Mt. chain. Many rapid creeks in the mountains feed the Kentucky, the Cumberland, and the Licking rivers, which together with the Tennessee and the Ohio are the chief rivers of the state. The Kentucky Dam on the Tennessee River near Paducah, is a major part of the Tennessee Valley Authority system. From elevations of about 2,000 ft (610 m) on the Cumberland Plateau in the southeast, where Black Mt. (4,145 ft/1,263 m) marks the state's highest point, Kentucky slopes to elevations of less than 800 ft (244 m) along the western rim. The narrow valleys and sharp ridges of the mountain region are noted for forests of giant hardwoods and scented pine and for springtime blooms of laurel, magnolia, rhododendron, and dogwood. To the west, the plateau breaks in a series of escarpments, bordering a narrow plains region interrupted by many single conical peaks called knobs. Surrounded by the knobs region on the south, west, and east and extending as far west as Louisville is the BLUEGRASS country, the heart and trademark of the state. To the south and west lie the rolling plains and rocky hillsides of the Pennyroyal, a section that takes its name from a species of mint that grows abundantly in the area. There underground streams have washed through limestone to form miles of subterranean passages, some of the notable ones being in Mammoth Cave National Park. Northwest Kentucky is generally rough, rolling terrain, with scattered but important coal deposits. The isolated far-western region, bounded by the Mississippi, Ohio, and Tennessee rivers, is referred to as the Purchase, or Jackson Purchase (for Andrew Jackson, who was a prominent member of the commission that bought it from the Chickasaw Indians in 1818). Consisting of flood plains and rolling uplands, it is the largest migratory bird route in the United States. Little remains of Kentucky's great forests that once spread over three quarters of the state and were renowned for their size and density. Kentucky's climate is generally mild, with few extremes of heat and cold. The state is noted for the distilling of Bourbon whiskey and for the breeding of thoroughbred racehorses. In 1973 the state was also the country's largest grower of tobacco after North Carolina. Tobacco has long been the state's chief crop, and it is also the chief farm product, followed by cattle, dairy products, and hogs. Hay, corn, and soybeans are other major crops raised in the state. Kentucky's economy, traditionally based on agriculture, now derives by far the greatest share of its income from industry. Even Lexington, long known as one of the world's largest loose-leaf tobacco markets, has become industrialized. The state's chief industries manufacture electrical equipment, food products, nonelectrical machinery, chemicals, and fabricated and primary metals. Kentucky is one of the country's major producers of coal, the state's most valuable mineral. Other mineral products include stone, petroleum, and natural gas. When the Eastern seaboard of North America was being colonized in the 1600s, Kentucky was part of the inaccessible country beyond the mountains. After Robert Cavelier, sieur de La Salle, claimed all regions drained by the Mississippi and its tributaries for France, British interest in the area quickened. The first major expedition to the Tennessee region was led by Dr. Thomas Walker, who explored the eastern mountain region in 1750 for the Loyal Land Company. Walker was soon followed by hunters and scouts including Christopher Gist. Further exploration was interrupted by the French and Indian War (1754–63) between the French and British for control of North America, and PONTIAC'S REBELLION, an Indian uprising (1763–66), but, with the British victorious in both, settlers soon began to enter Kentucky. They came in defiance of a royal proclamation of 1763, which forbade settlement W of the Appalachians. Daniel Boone, the famous American frontiersman, first came to Kentucky in 1767; he returned in 1769 and spent two years in the area. A surveying party under James Harrod established the first permanent settlement at Harrodsburg in 1774, and the next year Daniel Boone, as agent for Richard Henderson and the Transylvania Company, a colonizing group of which Henderson was a member, blazed the WILDERNESS ROAD from Tennessee into the Kentucky region and founded Boonesboro. Title to this land was challenged by Virginia, whose legislature voided (1778) the Transylvania Company's claims, although individual settlers were confirmed in their grants. Meanwhile, Kentucky was made (1776) a county of Virginia, and new settlers came through the Cumberland Gap and over the Wilderness Road or down the Ohio River. These early pioneers of Kentucky and Tennessee were constantly in conflict with Indians. The white population nevertheless increased, and many Kentuckians, feeling that Virginia had failed to give them adequate protection, worked for statehood in a series of conventions held at Danville (1784–91). Others, observing the weaknesses of the U.S. government, considered forming an independent nation. Since trade down the Mississippi and out of Spanish-held New Orleans was indispensable to Kentucky's economic development, an alliance with Spain was contemplated, and U.S. Gen. James Wilkinson, who lived in Kentucky at the time, worked toward that end. However, in 1792 a constitution was finally framed and accepted, and in the same year the Commonwealth of Kentucky (its official designation) was admitted to the Union, the first state W of the Appalachians. Isaac Shelby was elected the first governor, and Frankfort was chosen capital. Indian troubles in Kentucky were virtually ended with U.S. Gen. Anthony Wayne's victory over the Indians at the battle of Fallen Timbers in 1794. In 1795, Pinckney's Treaty between the United States and Spain granted Americans the right to navigate the Mississippi, a right soon completely assured by the Louisiana Purchase of 1803. Enactment by the Federal government of the ALIEN AND SEDITION ACTS (1798) promptly provoked a sharp protest in Kentucky (see KENTUCKY AND VIRGINIA RESOLUTIONS). The state grew fast as trade and shipping centers developed and river traffic down the Ohio and Mississippi increased. The War of 1812 spurred economic prosperity in Kentucky, but financial difficulties after the war threatened many with ruin. The state responded to the situation by chartering in 1818 a number of new banks that were allowed to issue their own currency. These banks soon collapsed, and the state legislature passed measures for the relief of the banks' creditors. However, the relief measures were subsequently declared unconstitutional by a state court. The legislature then repealed legislation that had established the offending court and set up a new one. The state became divided between prorelief and antirelief factions, and the issue also figured in the division of the state politically between followers of the Tennesseean Andrew Jackson, then rising to national political prominence, and supporters of the Whig Party of Henry Clay, who was a leader in Kentucky politics for almost half a century. In the first half of the 19th cent., Kentucky was primarily a state of small farms rather than large plantations and was not adaptable to extensive use of slave labor. Slavery thus declined after 1830, and for 17 years, beginning in 1833, the importation of slaves into the state was forbidden. In 1850, however, the legislature repealed this restriction, and Kentucky, where slave trading had begun to develop quietly in the 1840s, was converted into a huge slave market for the lower south. Antislavery agitation had begun in the state in the late 18th cent. within the churches, and abolitionists such as James G. Birney and Cassius M. Clay labored vigorously in Kentucky for emancipation before the Civil War. Soon Kentucky, like other border states, was torn by conflict over the slavery issue. In addition to the radical antislavery element and the aggressive proslavery faction, there was also in the state a conciliatory group, in which John J. Crittenden, then U.S. Senator, was most conspicuous, that strove to preserve the Union at all costs. At the outbreak of the Civil War, Kentucky attempted to remain neutral. Gov. Beriah Magoffin refused to sanction President Lincoln's call for volunteers, but his warnings to both the Union and the Confederacy not to invade were ignored. A native son, Gen. Albert S. Johnston, and his Confederate forces invaded and occupied part of S Kentucky, including Columbus and Bowling Green. The state legislature voted (Sept., 1861) to oust the Confederates and Ulysses S. Grant crossed the Ohio and took Paducah. Johnston was forced to abandon his Kentucky positions completely, and the state was secured for the Union. After battles in Mill Springs, Richmond, and Perryville in 1862, there was no major fighting in the state, although the Confederate cavalryman John Hunt Morgan occasionally led raids into the state, and guerrilla warfare was constant. For Kentucky it was truly a civil war as neighbors, friends, and even families became bitterly divided in their loyalties. Over 30,000 Kentuckians fought for the Confederacy, while about 64,000 served in the Union ranks. After the war many in the state opposed federal Reconstruction policies, and Kentucky refused to ratify the Thirteenth and Fourteenth amendments to the U.S. Constitution. As in the South, an overwhelming majority of Kentuckians supported the Democratic party in the period of readjustment after the war, in many ways as bitter as the war itself. After the Civil War industrial and commercial recovery was aided by increased railroad construction, but farmers were plagued by the liabilities of the one-crop (tobacco) system. After the turn of the century, the depressed price of tobacco gave rise to a feud between buyers and growers, resulting in the Black Patch War. Night riders terrorized buyers and growers in an effort to stage an effective boycott against monopolistic practices of buyers. For more than a year general lawlessness prevailed until the state militia forced an agreement in 1908. Coal mining, which began on a large scale in the 1870s, was well established in mountainous E Kentucky by the early 20th cent. The mines boomed during World War I, but after the war, when demand for coal lessened and production fell off, intense labor troubles developed. The attempt of the United Mine Workers of America (U.M.W.) to organize the coal industry in Harlan co. in the 1930s resulted in outbreaks of violence, drawing national attention to "bloody" Harlan, and in 1937 a U.S. Senate subcommittee began an investigation into allegations that workers' civil rights were being violated. Further violence ensued, and it was not until 1939 that the U.M.W. was finally recognized as a bargaining agent for most of the state's miners. Labor disputes and strikes have persisted in the state; some are still accompanied by violence. After World War I improvements of the state's highways were made, and a much-needed reorganization of the state government was carried out in the 1920s and 30s. Since World War II, construction of turnpikes, extensive development of state parks, and a marked rise in tourism have all contributed to the development of the state. Tourist attractions include the famous Kentucky Derby at Churchill Downs in Louisville and the celebrated horse farms surrounding Lexington in the heart of the bluegrass region.

The Abraham Lincoln Birthplace National Historic Site and Cumberland Gap National Historic Park are historic landmarks. At Fort Knox is the U.S. Depository. Kentucky is renowned for its former family feuds, such as the notorious Hatfield-McCoy affair in the early 19th cent. Kentucky's state constitution was adopted in 1891. The governor of the state is elected for a term of four years. The general assembly, or legislature, is bicameral with a senate of 38 members and a house of representatives of 100 members. State senators are elected to serve for terms of four years and representatives, for two years. Kentucky is represented in the U.S. Congress by seven Representatives and two Senators and has nine electoral votes in presidential elections. Wendell H. Ford, a Democrat, was elected governor in 1971. Upon his election (1974) to the U.S. Senate, he was succeeded by Lt. Gov. Julian Carroll. The Democratic party has long been dominant in Kentucky politics, but Republicans have been making significant inroads into Democratic strength in the state. A public school system was established in the state in the mid-19th cent. Except for a disturbance in Sturgis in 1956, compliance in Kentucky with the 1954 Supreme Court decision on the INTEGRATION of public schools has been general and without extreme resistance. Institutions of higher learning include the Univ. of Kentucky and Transylvania Univ., at Lexington; the Univ. of Louisville, at Louisville; Kentucky Wesleyan College, at Owensboro; Union College, at Barbourville, and Kentucky State Univ., at Frankfort. An excellent bibliography of Kentucky is J. Winston Coleman, Jr., *A Bibliography of Kentucky History* (1949). See F. G. Davenport, *Ante-bellum Kentucky: A Social History, 1800–1860* (1943); J. W. Coleman, *Historic Kentucky* (1967); T. D. Clark, *A History of Kentucky* (4th ed. 1961) and *Kentucky, Land of Contrast* (1968); Federal Writers' Project, *Kentucky: A Guide to the Bluegrass State* (1939, repr. 1973).

Kentucky, river, 259 mi (417 km) long, formed by the junction of the North Fork and the Middle Fork rivers, central Ky., and flowing NW to the Ohio River at Carrollton. Frankfort, Ky., is the river's largest city. The river is navigable for its entire length by means of locks. The Kentucky's upper course flows through a coal-mining district and the middle course through a deep gorge before entering the fertile bluegrass region.

Kentucky, University of, mainly at Lexington; coeducational; land-grant and state supported; opened 1865 as part of Kentucky Univ. (see TRANSYLVANIA UNIV.), became a state agricultural and mechanical college in 1878, and a university in 1908. It has several extension centers throughout the state.

Kentucky and Virginia Resolutions, in U.S. history, resolutions passed in opposition to the ALIEN AND SEDITION ACTS, which were enacted by the Federalists in 1798. The Jeffersonian Republicans first replied in the Kentucky Resolutions, adopted by the Kentucky legislature in Nov., 1798. Written by Thomas Jefferson himself, they were a severe attack on the Federalists' broad interpretation of the Constitution, which would have extended the powers of the national government over the states. The resolutions declared that the Constitution merely established a compact between the states and that the Federal government had no right to exercise powers not specifically delegated to it under the terms of the compact; should the Federal government assume such powers, its acts under them would be unauthoritative and therefore void. It was the right of the states and not the Federal government to decide as to the constitutionality of such acts. A further resolution, adopted in Feb., 1799, provided a means by which the states could enforce their decisions by formal nullification of the objectionable laws. A similar set of resolutions was adopted in Virginia in Dec., 1798, but these Virginia Resolutions, written by James Madison, were a somewhat milder expression of the strict construction of the Constitution and the compact theory of the Union. The resolutions were submitted to the other states for approval with no real result; their chief importance lies in the fact that they were later considered to be the first notable statements of the STATES' RIGHTS theory of government, a theory that opened the way for the NULLIFICATION controversy and ultimately for SECESSION. See E. D. Warfield, *The Kentucky Resolutions of 1798* (1887, repr. 1969); John C. Miller, *Crisis in Freedom* (1951, repr. 1964).

Kentucky saddler: see AMERICAN SADDLE HORSE.

Kentville, town (1971 pop. 5,198), W N.S., Canada, on the Cornwallis River, NW of Halifax. It is a tourist and trade center in the Annapolis valley, a fruit-growing region.

Kenya (kĕn'yə, kēn'-), republic (1969 pop. 10,942,708), 224,960 sq mi (582,646 sq km), E Africa. NAIROBI is the capital; other cities include MOMBASA (the chief port), NAKURU, KISUMU, Thika, and Eldoret. Kenya is bordered by the Somali Democratic Republic on the east, the Indian Ocean on the southeast, Tanzania on the south, Victoria Nyanza (Lake Victoria) on the southwest, Uganda on the west, the Sudan on the northwest, and Ethiopia on the north. The country, which lies astride the equator, is made up of several geographical regions. The first is a narrow, dry coastal strip that is low lying except for the Taita Hills in the south. The second, an inland region of bush-covered plains, constitutes most of the country's land area. In the northwest, straddling Lake Rudolf and the Kulal Mts., are high-lying scrublands. In the southwest are the fertile grasslands, and forests of the Kenya highlands. In the west is the Great Rift Valley, an irregular depression that cuts through W Kenya from north to south in two branches. It is also the location of some of the country's highest mountains, including Mt. Kenya

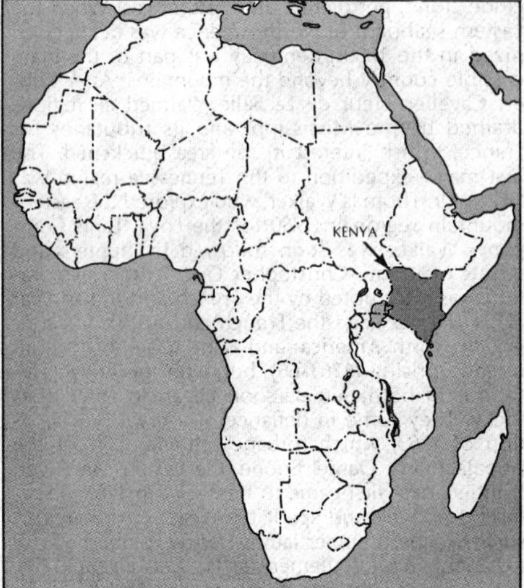

(17,058 ft/5,199 m). Kenya's main rivers are the Tana and the Althi. Except for the temperate highlands, the country's climate is hot and dry. Black Africans make up about 97% of the population; they are divided into about 40 ethnic groups, of which the Bantu-speaking Kikuyu, Kamba, Gusii, and Luhya and the Nilotic-speaking Luo are predominant. Persons of Indian, Pakistani, Goanese, and European descent live in the interior, and there are some Arabs along the coast. The official language of Kenya is Swahili, which replaced English in 1974. Most of the population follows traditional religious beliefs, but about 30% are Christian and about 6% Muslim. The great majority of Kenyans are engaged in farming, largely of the subsistence type, but industry is growing. Coffee, tea, sisal, pyrethrum, maize, and wheat are grown in the highlands, mainly on small African-owned farms formed by dividing some of the large, formerly European-owned estates. Coconuts, cashew nuts, cotton, sugarcane, sisal, and maize are grown in the lower-lying areas. Much of the country remains grassland, where large numbers of cattle are pastured. Kenya's leading manufactures include refined petroleum, processed food, cement, textiles, leather goods, and metal products. The chief minerals produced are limestone, soda ash, gold, and salt. Kenya attracts many tourists, largely lured by its varied wildlife, which is protected in the expansive Tsavo National Park (8,034 sq mi/20,808 sq km) in the southeast. Kenya's chief exports are coffee, tea, pyrethrum, and sisal; the leading imports are petroleum and petroleum products, chemicals, and machinery; trade is mainly with Great Britain, West Germany, and the United States. In 1967, Kenya formed the East African Economic Community with Tanzania and Uganda.

History. During the 1950s and 60s, the anthropologist L. S. B. Leakey discovered in N Tanzania the remains of men who lived c.2 million years ago. These persons, perhaps the earliest men on earth, most likely also inhabited S Kenya. In the Kenya highlands, the existence of farming and domestic herds can be dated to c.1000 B.C. Trade between the Kenya coast and Arabia was brisk by A.D. 100. Arabs settled on the coast by the 8th cent., and they soon established several autonomous city-states (including Mombasa, Malindi, and Pate). Around the year 1000, ironworking reached the interior of Kenya, at about the same time that the first Bantu-speaking people arrived there. The Portuguese first visited the Kenya coast in 1498, and by the end of the 16th cent. they controlled much of it, including Mombasa. However, in 1729, the Portuguese were permanently expelled from Mombasa and were replaced as the leading power on the coast by two Arab dynasties: the Busaidi dynasty, based first at Masqat (in Oman) and from 1832 on Zanzibar, and the Mazrui dynasty, based at Mombasa. The Busaidi wrested Mombasa from the Mazrui in 1837. From the early 19th cent. there was long-distance caravan trading between Mombasa and Victoria Nyanza. Beginning in the mid-19th cent., European explorers (especially John Ludwig Krapf and Joseph THOMSON) mapped parts of the interior. The British and German governments agreed upon spheres of influence in E Africa in 1886, with most of present-day Kenya passing to the British. In 1887, a British association received concessionary rights to the Kenya coast from the sultan of Zanzibar. The association in 1888 was given a royal charter as the Imperial British East Africa Company, but severe financial difficulties soon led to its takeover by the British government, which established the East Africa Protectorate in 1895. A railroad was built (1895–1901) from Mombasa to Kisumu on Victoria Nyanza in order to facilitate trade with the interior and with Uganda. In 1903, the first settlers of European descent established themselves as large-scale farmers in the highlands by taking land from the Kikuyu, Masai, and others. At the same time, Indian merchants moved inland from the coast. In 1920, the territory was renamed and its administration changed; the interior became Kenya Colony and a coastal strip (10 mi/16 km wide) was constituted the Protectorate of Kenya. From the 1920s to the 40s, European settlers controlled the government and owned extensive farmlands; Indians maintained small trade establishments and were lower-level government employees; and black Africans grew cash crops such as coffee and cotton on a small scale, were subsistence farmers, or were laborers in the towns (especially Nairobi). In the 1920s, black Africans began to protest their inferior status. Protest reached a peak between 1952 and 1956 with the so-called MAU-MAU Emergency, a complex armed revolt led by the Kikuyu, which was in part a rebellion against British rule and in part an attempt to return to pre-European ways. The British declared a state of emergency and imprisoned many of the colony's nationalist leaders, including Jomo KENYATTA. After the revolt, Britain increased black African representation in the colony's legislative council until, in 1961, there was a black African majority. On Dec. 12, 1963, Kenya (including both the colony and the protectorate) became independent. In 1964 the country became a republic, with Kenyatta as president. The first decade of independence was characterized by disputes among ethnic groups (especially between the Kikuyu and the Luo), by economic growth and diversification, and by the end of European predominance. Many Europeans (who numbered about 55,000 in 1962) and Asians voluntarily left the country. Boundary disputes with the Somali Democratic Republic resulted in sporadic fighting (1963–68). In 1969, Tom MBOYA, a leading government official and a possible successor to Kenyatta, was assassinated. More than 70% of the country was affected by the sub-Saharan drought of the early 1970s.

Government. Kenya is run by a president, who is assisted by a vice president and a cabinet. There is a unicameral legislature. The only legal political party is the Kikuyu-dominated Kenya African National Union. See R. A. Oliver et al., ed., *History of East Africa* (2 vol., 1963–65); C. G. Rosberg and J. C. Nottingham, *The Myth of 'Mau Mau': Nationalism in Kenya* (1966); J. S. Roberts, *A Land Full of People* (1967); M. P. K. Sorenson, *The Origins of European Settlement in Kenya* (1969); C. J. Gertzel, *The Politics of Independent Kenya* (1970).

Kenya, Mount, extinct volcano, central Kenya, just south of the equator. Its highest peak, Batian, reaches 17,058 ft (5,199 m), making Mt. Kenya the highest mountain in Africa after Kilimanjaro. In the heart of Kikuyu country, Mt. Kenya was a focal point during the "Mau Mau" disturbances (1952–56). The Kikuyu people cultivate Mt. Kenya's fertile lower slopes. From 5,000 to 15,000 ft (1,524–4,572 m) are dense woodlands inhabited by elephants, buffalo, and leopards. Snow-capped Mt. Kenya has several glaciers in its uppermost regions.

Kenyatta, Jomo (jō'mō kĕnyä'tə), 1893?–, African political leader, first president of Kenya (1964–). One of the earliest and best-known African nationalist leaders, he was a member of the Kikuyu tribe.

As secretary of the Kikuyu Central Association (1928), he campaigned for land reform and political rights for Africans. In 1930 he went to Europe; in England he collaborated with other nationalist African students and was (1946) cofounder with Kwame Nkrumah of the Pan-African Federation. Returning (1946) to Kenya, he became president of the Kenya African Union and greatly influenced Kenya's young Africans. In 1953, following the MAU MAU uprising, Kenyatta was imprisoned by the British as one of its instigators and then exiled (1959) to a remote desert outpost. Still in exile, Kenyatta was elected president of the newly founded (1960) Kenya African National Union. Released in 1961, he participated in negotiations with the British government for a new constitution for Kenya, which became independent in 1963. It became a republic, with Kenyatta as president, in 1964. He had an influential voice throughout Africa. Kenyatta was intolerant of dissent in Kenya, outlawing opposition parties in 1969. He wrote *Facing Mount Kenya* (1938) and *Suffering Without Bitterness* (1968). See biographies by George Delf (1961), Richard Cox (1965), and Jeremy Murray-Brown (1972).

Kenyon, William Squire, 1869–1933, U.S. Senator (1911–22) from Iowa, b. Elyria, Ohio. He practiced law at Fort Dodge, Iowa, was county prosecutor, and became a state district court judge before serving (1910–11) as assistant to the U.S. Attorney General. He was elected to the U.S. Senate in 1911 and served there until 1922. Kenyon immediately joined the Republican insurgents, backed much progressive legislation, was the co-author of the Webb-Kenyon Act (1913) prohibiting the shipment of intoxicating beverages in interstate commerce, and was the first leader of the Senate farm bloc. Kenyon later served (1922–33) as judge of the U.S. Circuit Court of Appeals and was (1929–30) a member of the Wickersham Commission (see WICKERSHAM, GEORGE WOODWARD).

Kenyon College, at Gambier, Ohio, near Mt. Vernon; Episcopal; coeducational; chartered and opened 1824. It was founded by Philander CHASE as a theological seminary with some undergraduate work, assumed its present name in 1891, and today comprises Kenyon College and the Divinity School of Kenyon College. The College publishes a noted literary quarterly, the *Kenyon Review.*

Keokuk (kē'əkək), c.1780–1848, American Indian, chief of the Sac and Fox Indians, b. near present-day Rock Island, Ill. When Black Hawk supported the British in the War of 1812, Keokuk refused to join him, thereby gaining recognition and support from the U.S. government. After Black Hawk's defeat, in 1832, Keokuk's people were given a large tract of land in SE Iowa. Keokuk visited Washington D.C., in 1833 and 1837. His grave and a statue of him are at Keokuk, Iowa. See biography by Myna Lockwood (1943).

Keokuk, city (1970 pop. 14,631), seat of Lee co., extreme SE Iowa, on the Mississippi River at the foot of the Des Moines River rapids and in a farm area; inc. 1847. A gravity dam (built 1910–13) and a power plant on the Mississippi furnish hydroelectric power for Keokuk's industries, which include food processing and packaging (turkeys, dairy items, grain products) and the manufacture of sponge rubber goods, trucks, corrugated cartons, and a great variety of metals and metal products. The first cabin was erected there in 1820, and a trading post was founded in 1829 and named for Keokuk, a Sac Indian chief (who is buried beneath an impressive statue in the city's Rand Park). Heavy river traffic brought quick prosperity. Because of its location at the foot of the treacherous Des Moines River rapids, Keokuk was a natural rest stop for boats ascending the Mississippi. Often boats were unloaded at Keokuk and their cargoes hauled overland past the rapids, where they were then reloaded for the rest of the journey. During the Civil War five army hospitals were located in Keokuk; the wounded who did not survive were buried in the national cemetery (1861) there. In 1877 the U.S. government completed a ship canal (9 mi/14.5 km long) around the rapids. Tourist attractions include Keokuk Dam (which forms a lake that extends to Burlington; its lock is the largest on the Mississippi), the Unknown Soldier Monument in the national cemetery, and many old homes. Mark Twain worked as a printer in Keokuk, and mementos of his stay are preserved. The city also contains a junior college.

Keos, Greece: see KÉA.

Kepler, Johannes (yōhä'nəs kĕp'lər), 1571–1630, German astronomer. From his student days at the Univ. of Tübingen, he was influenced by the Copernican teachings. From 1593 to 1598 he was professor of mathematics at Graz and while there wrote his *Mysterium cosmographicum* (1596). This work opened the way to friendly intercourse with Galileo and Tycho Brahe, and in 1600 Kepler became Tycho's assistant in his observatory near Prague. On Tycho's death (1601) Kepler succeeded him as court mathematician to Holy Roman Emperor Rudolf II. In 1609 he published the results of Tycho's calculations of the orbit of Mars. In this celebrated work were stated the first two of what became known as Kepler's laws (see separate article). In 1612, becoming mathematician to the states of Upper Austria, he moved to Linz. He wrote an epitome of the astronomy of Copernicus in 1618, and in 1619 *De cometis* and *Harmonice mundi* (in which was announced the third of Kepler's laws). In 1626, Kepler moved to Ulm. After his death his manuscript writings, bought by Catherine II of Russia, were placed in the observatory of Pulkovo. See biographies by Max Caspar (tr. 1959, repr. 1962) and Angus Armitage (1966); Arthur Beer, ed., *Kepler: Four Hundred Years* (1974).

Kepler's laws, three mathematical statements that accurately describe the revolutions of the planets around the sun. The first law states that the shape of each planet's orbit is an ELLIPSE with the sun at one focus. The sun is thus off-center in the ellipse and the planet's distance from the sun varies as the planet moves through one orbit. The second law specifies quantitatively how the speed of a planet increases as its distance from the sun decreases. If an imaginary line is drawn from the sun to the planet, the line will sweep out areas in space that are shaped like pie slices. The second law states that the area swept out in equal periods of time is the same at all points in the orbit. When the planet is far from the sun and moving slowly, the pie slice will be long and narrow; when the planet is near the sun and moving fast, the pie slice will be short and fat. The third law establishes a relation between the average distance of the planet from the sun (the semimajor axis of the ellipse) and the time to complete one revolution around the sun (the period): the ratio of the cube of the semimajor axis to the square of the period is the same for all the planets including the earth. Kepler's first and second laws were published in 1609 in *Commentaries on the Motions of Mars.* Mars was the planet whose motions were in greatest disagreement with existing theories. Kepler relied on the astronomical observations of Tycho Brahe, which were much more accurate than any earlier work. The third law appeared in 1619 in *Harmony of the Worlds.* Kepler's laws opened the way for the development of celestial mechanics, i.e., the application of the laws of physics to the motions of heavenly bodies. His work shows the hallmarks of great scientific theories: simplicity and universality. Earlier theories of planetary motion, such as the geocentric PTOLEMAIC SYSTEM and the heliocentric COPERNICAN SYSTEM, had allowed only perfect circles as orbits and were therefore compelled to combine many circular motions to reproduce the variations in the planets' motions. Kepler eliminated the epicycles and deferents that had made each planet a special case. His laws apply in generality to all the planets. Kepler believed that the sun did not sit passively at the center of the solar system but that through some mysterious power or "virtue" actually compelled the planets to hold to their orbits. Because the planets moved slower when they were farther from the sun, this power must diminish with increasing distance. The idea that the planets were controlled by the sun was developed by Isaac Newton in his laws of MOTION and law of GRAVITATION. Newton assumed that the sun continuously exerts a force on each planet pulling the planet toward the sun. He calculated that elliptical orbits would result if the force varied inversely as the square of the distance from the sun (i.e., when the distance doubles, the force becomes four times weaker). His law of universal gravitation predicts that the planets exert small forces on each other although subject to the dominant force of the sun. These small additional forces explain most of the small departures from Kepler's laws revealed by later, more accurate observations.

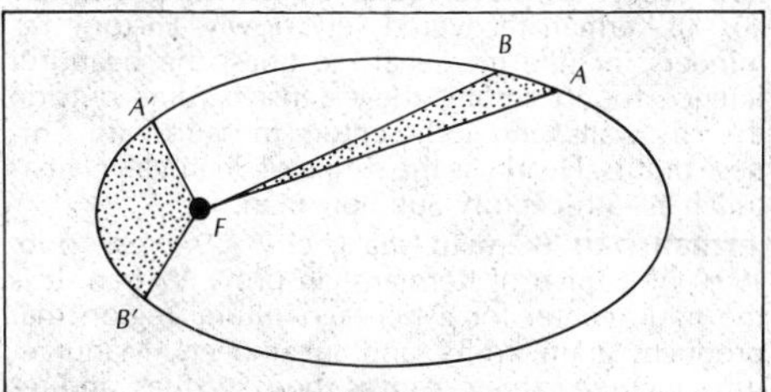

Schematic representation of Kepler's second law: The areas ABF and A′B′F are equal and are swept out in equal intervals of time by a planet orbiting around the sun (at F).

Keppel, Arnold Joost van: see ALBEMARLE, ARNOLD JOOST VAN KEPPEL, 1ST EARL OF.

Keppel Harbor: see SINGAPORE.

Keppler, Joseph, 1838–94, American cartoonist, b. Vienna. Emigrating to America in 1867, he established with Adolph Schwarzmann in St. Louis a humorous German periodical, *Puck* (1871). Upon its failure, Keppler joined the staff of *Frank Leslie's Illustrated Newspaper* in New York City and in 1876 started a second *Puck,* followed in 1877 by the English edition. Both magazines became famous for their political cartoons, which espoused the cause of the national Democratic party. Keppler's cartoons were skillfully drawn and notable for their penetrating satire. He was the first in the United States to apply color lithography to caricature.

Ker, Robert, earl of Somerset: see SOMERSET, ROBERT CARR, EARL OF.

Kerala (kä'rälä, kərä'lə), state (1971 pop. 21,280,397), 15,003 sq mi (38,858 sq km), SW India, on the Arabian Sea. TRIVANDRUM is the capital. The most densely populated Indian state, Kerala was created in 1956 from the Malayalam-speaking former princely states of Cochin and Travancore and Malayalam-speaking areas formerly in Madras state (now Tamil Nadu). About 60% of the population is Hindu; Christians and Muslims each make up about 20% of the remaining inhabitants. Although Kerala has the highest literacy rate in India, it suffers from economic underdevelopment and unemployment. In 1957, India's first Communist state administration was elected in Kerala, and a Communist coalition was again elected in 1967 and 1970. Maoist Naxalite groups are active in the state. Kerala takes its name from the ancient Tamil kingdom of Kerala (Chera), which traded with the Phoenicians, Greeks, and Romans. The state is governed by a chief minister responsible to an elected unicameral legislature and by a governor appointed by the president of India.

keratin (kĕr'ətĭn), any one of a class of fibrous PROTEIN molecules that serve as structural units for various living tissues. The keratins are the major protein components of hair, wool, nails, horn, hoofs, and the quills of feathers. These proteins generally contain large quantities of the sulfur-containing AMINO ACIDS, particulary cystine (see CYSTEINE); human hair is approximately 14% cystine in composition. The formation of a covalent chemical bond between two atoms of sulfur, called a disulfide bridge, on separate polypeptide chains of keratin allows for the cross-linkage of these molecules and results in a fairly rigid aggregation of the constituent proteins. This phenomenon is seen to be consistent with the physiological role of the keratins, which provide a tough, fibrous matrix for the tissues in which they are found. The keratins have been of particular interest to biochemists concerned with the three-dimensional geometry of proteins.

Kerbela: see KARBALA, Iraq.

Kerch (kyĕrch), city (1970 pop. 128,000), SE European USSR, in the Crimea. It lies on the Kerch Strait of the Black Sea and at the eastern end of the Kerch Peninsula, a land strip between the Sea of Azov and the Black Sea. A seaport and major industrial center, it has iron and steel mills, machine, chemical, and coking plants, shipyards, fisheries, and canneries. Iron ore, vanadium, and natural gas are extracted nearby. The city was founded as Panticapaeum (6th cent. B.C.) by Greek colonists from Miletus and was the forerunner of all Milesian cities in the area. It was a large trade center and a terraced mountain city with self-government. It became (5th cent. B.C. to 4th cent. A.D.) the capital of the European part of the Kingdom of Bosporus (see CRIMEA). It was conquered (c.110 B.C.) by Mithridates VI of Pontus, then passed under Roman and Byzantine rule, and was taken by Novogorod in the 9th cent. and called Korchev. Later (13th cent.) it became a Genoese trade center called Cherkio and was conquered (1475) by the Crimean Tatars, who called it Cherzeti. It was captured (1771) by the Russians in the first Russo-Turkish War (1768–74), and the Treaty of Kuchuk Kainarji (1774) formally gave it to Russia. Under Russia, Kerch was a military port and then became (1820) a commercial port. There are ruins of the ancient acropolis on top of the steep hill of Mithridates. Archaeological remains, discovered in catacombs and burial mounds near the city, are in the archaeological museum (founded 1826), which is famous for its Greco-Scythian antiquities. The Church of St. John the Baptist dates from the 8th cent. The city has a marine fishery and oceanography research institute.

Kerch Strait, shallow channel, c.25 mi (40 km) long, S European USSR, connecting the Sea of Azov with the Black Sea and separating the Crimea in the west from the Taman peninsula in the east. Its northern end, opening into the Sea of Azov, is narrowed to a width of from 2 to 3 mi (3.2–4.8 km) by the narrow Chuska landspit; the southern end, opening into the Black Sea, is c.9 mi (14 km) wide. Its arm, the Taman Gulf, penetrates east into the Taman peninsula. The city of Kerch lies near the middle of the strait, on the Crimean side, in Ukraine. Kerch Strait was the Cimmerian Bosporus of the ancients; it is also known by its Tatar name, Yenikale.

Keren-Happuch (kĕr′ən-hăp′ək), Job's third daughter after his affliction. Job 42.14.

Kerensky, Aleksandr Feodorovich (kərĕn′skē, Rus. əlyĭksän′dər fyô′dərəvĭch kâ′rĭnskē), 1881–1970, Russian revolutionary. A lawyer, he was elected to the fourth Duma in 1912 as a representative of the moderate Labor party. He joined the Socialist Revolutionary party after the February Revolution of 1917 that overthrew the czarist government and became minister of justice, then war minister in the provisional government of Prince Lvov. He succeeded (July, 1917) Lvov as premier. Kerensky's insistence on remaining in World War I, his failure to deal with urgent economic problems (particularly land distribution), and his moderation enabled the Bolsheviks to overthrow his government later in 1917. Kerensky fled to Paris, where he continued as an active propagandist against the Soviet regime. In 1940 he fled to the United States; later he continued to travel and lecture. Among his writings are *The Prelude to Bolshevism* (1919) and *The Catastrophe* (1927).

Kerguelen (kûr′gəlĕn, Fr. kĕrgālĕn′), subantarctic island of volcanic origin, 1,318 sq mi (3,414 sq km), in the S Indian Ocean, c.3,300 mi (5,310 km) SE of the southern tip of Africa; largest of the 300 Kerguelen Islands (total area c.2,700 sq mi/7,000 sq km), part of the French Southern and Antarctic Territories. Kerguelen Island rises in the south to Mt. Rose (6,120 ft/1,865 m), and Cook Glacier covers its western third. Glacial lakes, peat marshes, lignite, and guano deposits are found on the island; it also has seals, rabbits, wild hogs, and wild dogs. The island, famous for the native Kerguelen cabbage, is used mainly as a research station and a seal-hunting and whaling base. Kerguelen was discovered in 1772 by the French navigator Yves Joseph de Kerguélen-Trémarec, who named it Desolation Island. It has belonged to France since 1893.

Kerintji (kərĭn′chē), peak, 12,467 ft (3,800 m) high, in the Pegunungan Barisan, W central Sumatra, Indonesia. It is Sumatra's highest point.

Kerioth (kĕr′ēŏth). **1** Unidentified town, E of the Jordan in Moab. Jer. 48.24,41. Kirioth: Amos 2.2. **2** Unidentified town, S Palestine. In AV what had been one name is given as two: "Kerioth and Hezron." Another name was Hazor. Joshua 15.25.

Kérkira (kĕr′kērä) or **Corfu** (kôr′fo͞o), Lat. *Corcyra* (kôrsī′rə), city (1971 pop. 28,630), capital of Kérkira prefecture, NW Greece, the only city on Kérkira island, a port on the channel that separates the island from the mainland. Olive oil, wine, and citrus fruits are shipped from Kérkira, and textiles are manufactured there. It is also a commercial and tourist center and has been the summer home of the Greek royal family. A Venetian fortress (c.1550) and the Church of St. Spyridon, containing the tomb of the patron saint of the island, are among Kérkira's historic buildings.

Kérkira or **Corfu** Lat. *Corcyra,* island (1971 pop. 89,578), 229 sq mi (593 sq km), NW Greece, in the Ionian Sea, the second largest of the IONIAN ISLANDS, separated by a narrow channel from the Albanian and Greek coasts. Though rising 2,980 ft (910 m) at Mt. Pantokrator in the northeast, Kérkira is largely a fertile lowland producing olive oil, figs, wine, and citrus fruit. Livestock raising (poultry, hogs, and sheep) and fishing are important sources of livelihood. Commerce and tourism are centered in Kérkira city, the capital. The island has been identified with Scheria, the island of the Phaeacians in Homer's *Odyssey.* It was settled c.730 B.C. by Corinthian colonists and shared with Corinth in the founding of Epidamnus on the mainland but became the competitor of Corinth in the Adriatic Sea. The two rivals fought the first recorded (by Thucydides) naval battle in 665 B.C. In 435 B.C., Kérkira (then Corcyra) made war on Corinth over the control of Epidamnus, and in 433 it concluded an alliance (often renewed) with Athens; this alliance helped to precipitate (431) the PELOPONNESIAN WAR. The island passed under Roman rule in 229 B.C. and in A.D. 336 became part of the Byzantine Empire. It was seized from the Byzantines by the Normans of Sicily in the 1080s and 1150s, by Venice (1206), and later by Epirus (1214–59) and the Angevins of Naples. In 1386 the Venetians obtained a hold that ended only with the fall of the Venetian republic in 1797. Under Venetian rule, the island had successfully resisted two celebrated Turkish sieges (1537, 1716). The island was under the protection of Great Britain from 1815 to 1864, when it was ceded to Greece. It was occupied (1916) by the French in World War I, and in 1917 the union of Serbia, Croatia, and Slovenia was concluded there. In 1923, after Italian officers trying to establish the Greek-Albanian border were slain in Greece, Kérkira was bombarded and temporarily occupied in retaliation by Italian forces.

Kerkrade (kĕrk′rä″də), city (1971 pop. 47,753), Limburg prov., SE Netherlands, on the West German border. It is one of Europe's oldest coal-mining centers; coal mining began there in the 12th cent.

Kermadec Islands (kərmăd′ĕk), uninhabited volcanic group (c.13 sq mi/34 sq km), South Pacific, a dependency of New Zealand. Sunday Island, the largest, is mountainous and fertile. The group was annexed to New Zealand in 1887.

Kerman (kĕrmän′), city (1971 est. pop. 88,000), capital of Kerman prov., E central Iran. It is noted for making and exporting carpets. Cotton textiles and goats-wool shawls are also manufactured. Kerman was under the Seljuk Turks in the 11th and 12th cent., but remained virtually independent, conquering Oman and Fars. Marco Polo visited (late 13th cent.) and described the city. Kerman changed hands many times in ensuing years, prospering under the Safavid dynasty (16th cent.) and suffering under the Afghans (17th cent.). In 1794 its greatest disaster occurred: Aga Muhammad Khan, shah of Persia, ravaged the city by selling 20,000 of its inhabitants into slavery and by blinding another 20,000. Kerman recovered very slowly. Historic reminders include medieval mosques, the beautiful faïence found among the extensive ruins outside the city walls, and 16th-century mosaics with Chinese motifs. Nearby is the shrine of Shah Vali Namatullah, a 15th-century Sufi holy man.

Kermanshah (kĕrmän″shä′), city (1971 est. pop. 190,000), capital of Kermanshah prov., W Iran. It is the trade center for a rich agricultural region that produces grain, fruits, and sugar beets. Manufactures include carpets, canvas shoes, textiles, and refined petroleum. The city has numerous caravansaries that are crowded semiannually with Shiite pilgrims to Karbala, Iraq. Kermanshah was founded by the Sassanids in the 4th cent. A.D. and became a secondary royal residence. It was captured by the Arabs in the 7th cent.; Harun ar-Rashid spent his summers there. It was later a frontier fortress against the Ottoman Turks, who occupied it a number of times including the period from 1915 to 1917. Nearby are the famed BEHISTUN INSCRIPTIONS and notable Sassanian rock reliefs.

kermes (kûr′mēz), brilliant red natural dye extracted from the bodies of the adult females of a scale insect parasitic upon oak trees; the females are large and similar in appearance to galls. A very ancient dye, kermes has largely been replaced by cochineal and artificial dyes.

Kern, Jerome (kûrn), 1885–1945, American composer of musicals, b. New York City. After studying in New Jersey and New York he studied composition in Germany and England. His first success was the operetta *The Red Petticoat* (1912). Among the numerous musicals that followed were *The Girl from Utah* (1914), *Leave It to Jane* (1917), *Sally* (1920), *Sunny* (1925), *The Cat and the Fiddle* (1931), and *Roberta* (1933). After 1931 he wrote scores for many films, including versions of several of his stage successes. His outstanding work is *Show Boat* (1927), for which Oscar Hammerstein II wrote an adaptation of Edna Ferber's novel. Kern's many famous songs include "Ol' Man River," from *Show Boat,* and "Smoke Gets in Your Eyes," from *Roberta.* He also wrote an orchestral work, *A Portrait of Mark Twain* (1942). See biography by David Ewen (1960).

Kern, river, 155 mi (249 km) long, rising in the S Sierra Nevada Mts., E Calif., and flowing south, then southwest to a reservoir in the extreme southern part of the San Joaquin valley. The river, one of California's important power-generating streams, has Isabella Dam as its chief facility. Kern River is the southern terminus of the Friant-Kern Canal, constructed between 1945 and 1951 to bring the waters of the San Joaquin River to the region (see CENTRAL VALLEY PROJECT); irrigated agriculture (alfalfa, fruit, and cotton) and cattle grazing are practiced. U.S. explorer John Frémont named the river in honor of Edward M. Kern, the topographer of his third expedition. Gold was discovered along the river in 1853. The canyon of the upper Kern in Sequoia National Park is noted for its beauty.

Keros (kē′rŏs), family that returned from Babylon. Ezra 2.44; Neh. 7.47.

kerosine, colorless, thin mineral oil whose density is between 0.75 and 0.85 grams per cubic centimeter. A mixture of hydrocarbons, it is commonly obtained in the fractional distillation of petroleum as the portion boiling off between 150°C and 275°C (302°F–527°F). Kerosine has been recovered from other substances, notably coal (hence another name, coal oil), oil shale, and wood. At one time kerosine was the most important refinery product because of its use in lamps. Now it is most noted for its use as a carrier in insecticide sprays and as a fuel in jet engines.

Kerouac, Jack (John Kerouac) (kĕr′o͞oăk″), 1922–69, American novelist, b. Lowell, Mass., educated at Columbia. One of the leaders of the BEAT GENERATION, he was the author of *On the Road* (1957), the novel considered to be the testament of the beat movement. Kerouac's writings reflect a frenetic, restless pursuit of new sensation and experience. Among his works are the novels *The Subterraneans* (1958), *The Dharma Bums* (1958), *Big Sur* (1962), and *Desolation Angels* (1965); a volume of poetry, *Mexico City Blues* (1959); and a volume describing Kerouac's dreams, *Book of Dreams* (1961). See biography by Ann Charters (1973).

Kéroualle, Louise Renée de: see PORTSMOUTH, LOUISE RENÉE DE KÉROUALLE, DUCHESS OF.

Kerr, Archibald John Kerr Clark: see INVERCHAPEL OF LOCH ECK, ARCHIBALD JOHN KERR CLARK KERR, 1ST BARON.

Kerr, Clark, 1911–, American educational reformer, b. Reading, Pa., grad. Swarthmore (B.A., 1932), and the Univ. of California at Berkeley (Ph.D., 1939). He was a professor of industrial relations at Berkeley from 1945 until 1952 when he was named chancellor. In 1958 he was named president of the Univ. of California, a post he held until 1967, when he became director of the Carnegie Fund Study on the Future of Higher Education. His writings include *The Uses of the University* (1963).

Kerr, Philip Henry: see LOTHIAN, PHILIP HENRY KERR, 11TH MARQUESS OF.

Kerr, Walter Francis (kûr), 1913–, American drama critic and playwright, b. Evanston, Ill. He became drama critic for the New York *Herald Tribune* in 1951 and for the New York *Times* in 1966. Kerr believes that great theater must be popular theater, and his influential reviews have often aroused controversy. Among his plays are *Murder in Reverse* (1935) and the musical *Goldilocks* (1958), written with Jean Kerr. His other works include *How Not To Write A Play* (1956) and *Tragedy and Comedy* (1967). His wife is **Jean Collins Kerr,** 1923–, author and playwright, b. Scranton, Pa. Her plays, all comedies, include *Mary, Mary* (1961), *Poor Richard* (1964), and *Finishing Touches* (1973). She has also written amusing autobiographical works about her family, notably *Please Don't Eat the Daisies* (1957) and *The Snake Has All the Lines* (1960).

Kerrville (kûr′vĭl), city (1970 pop. 12,672), seat of Kerr co., S central Texas, on the Guadalupe River; settled 1846, inc. 1942. It is a vacation and health resort in the cool hill country on the edge of the Edwards Plateau. A military junior college and a number of art galleries are there. A state park is nearby.

Kerry, county (1971 pop. 112,941), 1,815 sq mi (4,701 sq km), SW Republic of Ireland. The county town is TRALEE. Kerry consists of a series of mountainous peninsulas that extend into the Atlantic. The shore line is deeply indented by Dingle Bay, Tralee Bay, and the Kenmare River. Carrantuohill (3,414 ft/1,041 m), in the mountains known as Macgillycuddy's Reeks, is the highest point in Ireland. The streams are short and precipitous, and there are many bogs. The Lakes of KILLARNEY are a popular tourist attraction. Farming (oats and potatoes), sheep and cattle raising, and dairying are the chief occupations. Peat is sold commercially. Footwear is made in Tralee and Killarney. There are many well-preserved dolmens, stone forts, round towers, castles, and abbeys. Irish Gaelic is still spoken by many of the inhabitants of Kerry.

Kerry blue terrier, breed of large, sturdy TERRIER perfected in Ireland more than 100 years ago. It stands from 17 to 19 in. (43.2–48.3 cm) high at the shoulder and weighs from 30 to 40 lb (13.6–18.2 kg). Its dense coat is soft and wavy, never harsh, and may be any shade of blue-gray or gray-blue. A truly all-purpose working terrier, the Kerry blue was used to hunt small game, destroy vermin, retrieve on land and water, and herd sheep and cattle. Today it is a popular house pet and show competitor. See DOG.

Kerulen (kĕr'o͞olĕn) or **Herelen** (hĕr'əlĕn), river, 785 mi (1,263 km) long, E Mongolian People's Republic, rising in the Kentei Mts., NE of Ulan Bator, and flowing S, then E to Hu-lun Lake, Heilungkiang prov., NE China. A road from Ulan Bator to Choybalsan, a railhead linked to the Trans-Siberian RR, follows the river.

Kesennuma (kāsän-no͞o'mä), city (1970 pop. 63,265), Miyagi prefecture, NE Honshu, Japan, on Kesennuma Bay. It is a fishing port.

Kesselring, Albert (äl'bĕrt kĕs'əlrĭng), 1885–1960, German field marshal. An artillery staff officer in World War I, he later joined the air force and rapidly rose in rank during the Hitler regime. In World War II, he commanded air operations in Poland, on the Western Front, in central Russia, and in the Mediterranean area. Late in 1943, Kesselring was made supreme commander in Italy, and in March, 1945, he replaced Rundstedt as commander in chief in the West. He was convicted of war crimes by a British tribunal in 1947, but his death sentence was commuted to life imprisonment. Freed by an act of clemency in 1952, he was elected (1953) president of the Stahlhelm, a veterans' organization in West Germany. See his memoirs (1953; tr. 1953, repr. 1970).

Kesten, Hermann (hĕr'män kĕst'ən), 1900–, German-American novelist, essayist, publisher, and dramatist. In Amsterdam, Kesten was director (1933–40) of the German-language publishing house Allert de Lange. He is well known for his attacks on Nazism, as in *Die Zwillinge von Nürnberg* (1946; tr. *The Twins of Nuremberg,* 1947). Kesten often uses a historical format for his works of social criticism, which include *Josef sucht die Freiheit* (1927; tr. *Joseph Breaks Free,* 1930); *Der Scharlatan* [the charlatan] (1932); and *Die Kinder von Gernica* (1939; tr. *The Children of Guernica,* 1939). His essay collection, *Ein Optimist* (tr. *The Optimist*) appeared in 1970.

Kesteven, Parts of: see LINCOLNSHIRE.

Ket (kĕ'tyə), river, c.845 mi (1,360 km) long, W central Siberian USSR. It rises in central Siberia, just N of Krasnoyarsk, and flows NW and W into the Ob. The Ket is navigable c.410 mi (660 km). It is connected with the Kas (a tributary of the Yenisei) by the Ob-Yenisei canal system.

ketch, fore-and-aft-rigged sailing vessel with a mainmast forward carrying a mainsail and jibs. It has a mizzenmast aft, stepped forward of the rudder post. In the United States, ketch-rigged vessels are widely used today as yachts. The term was formerly applied to a two-masted square-rigged vessel with the mainmast stepped amidship. Widely employed in offshore fishing by the Americans until about 1700, the ketch was also used until the mid-19th cent. as a warship in European navies.

Ketchikan (kĕ'chĭkăn"), city (1970 pop. 6,994), SE Alaska, a port of entry on Revillagigedo Island in the Alexander Archipelago. A supply point for miners in the gold rush of the 1890s, it has become a center of Alaska's fishing (especially salmon but also halibut) and pulp industries and a tourist hub. Its excellent ice-free harbor on Tongass Narrows makes it an important port on the Inside Passage and a distribution point for a large area.

Ketchwayo: see CETEWAYO.

ketone (kē'tōn), any of a class of organic compounds that contain the CARBONYL GROUP, C=O, and in which the carbonyl group is bonded only to carbon atoms. The general formula for a ketone is RCOR′, where R and R′ are alkyl or aryl groups. The simplest ketone, where R and R′ are methyl groups, is ACETONE; this is one of the most important ketones used in industry. Low-molecular-weight ketones are used chiefly as solvents. Ketones may be prepared by several methods, including the oxidation of secondary alcohols and the destructive distillation of certain salts of organic acids. Ketones are related to the ALDEHYDES but are less active chemically.

$$R-\overset{\overset{\displaystyle O}{\|}}{C}-R'$$

general formula

$$H-\underset{\underset{\displaystyle H}{|}}{\overset{\overset{\displaystyle H}{|}}{C}}-\overset{\overset{\displaystyle O}{\|}}{C}-\underset{\underset{\displaystyle H}{|}}{\overset{\overset{\displaystyle H}{|}}{C}}-H$$

acetone (dimethyl ketone)

Ketones

Kett or **Ket, Robert,** d. 1549, English rebel. He led an agrarian revolt in 1549 as a protest against the enclosure of common land for sheep grazing. With 16,000 men he blockaded Norwich, but was defeated and executed.

Kettering, municipal borough (1971 pop. 42,628), Northamptonshire, central England. It is a center for the manufacture of shoes, other leather products, and textiles. There are also iron mining and smelting, engineering, and cardboard and brush-making industries.

Kettering, city (1970 pop. 71,864), Montgomery co., SW Ohio, a suburb of Dayton; settled c.1812, inc. 1952. Among Kettering's many manufactures are shock absorbers, electric motors, and tool and die products. The city is the seat of the Kettering College of Medical Arts and a defense electronics center, a supply facility for the U.S. armed forces.

kettle, oval depression found in glacial MORAINES, which are landforms made up of rock debris. When a glacier melts and draws away from an area, a block of ice may break off and be covered by earth and rock. As the block melts, the ground above it subsides, forming a kettle. Kettles may be deeper than 100 ft (30 m) in depth and more than 1 mi (1.6 km) in diameter. Pitted outwash plains contain many kettles.

kettledrum, in music, percussion instrument consisting of a hemispherical metal vessel over which a membrane is stretched, played with soft-headed wooden drumsticks. Of ancient origin, it appeared early in Europe, copied from the Saracens. These early kettledrums were small and appeared in pairs, often hung about the player's waist. The kettledrum was introduced into the opera orchestra by Lully in the 17th cent. and was commonly used to express joy or triumph in the music of the baroque period. Unique among Western percussion instruments, it can be tuned to definite pitches by adjusting the tension of the head. Usually there are two or more in the modern orchestra, the tuning of which varies. Berlioz used eight pairs in his *Requiem.* Several improved methods of tuning were developed in the 19th cent.; common today is a single pedal capable of giving the instrument a full chromatic range of over an octave. Kettledrums are also called timpani. See DRUM.

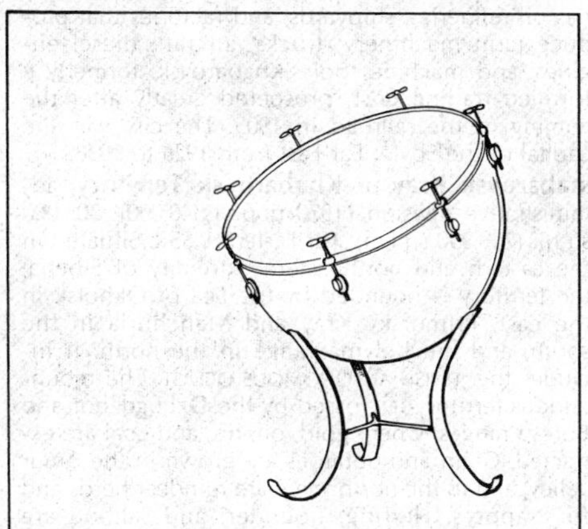

Kettledrum

Kettle Rapids Dam: see NELSON, river, Canada.

Keturah (kĕtyo͞o'rə), mother of six sons of Abraham. Gen. 25.1; 1 Chron. 1.32.

Keuka Lake (kyo͞o'kə), 18 mi (29 km) long and .5 to 2 mi (.8–3 km) wide, W central N.Y., one of the FINGER LAKES; drains NE into Seneca Lake. Penn Yan at its northern end and Hammondsport at its southern end are trade centers for the surrounding resort, grape-growing, and wine-making region.

Kewanee (kĭwä'nē), industrial city (1970 pop. 15,762), Henry co., NW Ill., in a farm and livestock area; inc. 1855. Its manufactures include gloves, trailers and trucks, boilers, steel doors and windows, farm machinery, foundry equipment, valves, and pipe fittings. The city holds an annual "Hog Capital Festival." A junior college is there.

Keweenaw (kē'wĭnô), peninsula, 60 mi (97 km) long, projecting NE from the W Upper Peninsula, NW Mich., into Lake Superior. Portage Lake and a connecting ship canal cut across the middle of the peninsula, converting its upper portion into an island and creating an important waterway. The canal is crossed by a bridge with one of the heaviest lift spans in the world. The peninsula has the richest and longest-mined copper deposits in the United States. Tourism and lumbering are also important.

Kew Gardens (kyo͞o), Surrey, S England, on the Thames just W of London; Royal Botanic Gardens is the official name. The gardens were founded by the dowager princess of Wales in 1761 and consisted of about 9 acres (3.6 hectares). In 1841 they were presented to the nation as a royal gift. They now cover 288 acres (117 hectares) and contain thousands of species of plants, four museums, and laboratories and hothouses. The Chinese Pagoda, c.165 ft (50 m) high, was designed by William Chambers in 1761; it is still a famous landmark. Near the main entrance is Kew Palace, a red-brick mansion, once the home of George III and Queen Charlotte.

Key, David McKendree, 1824–1900, American politician and jurist, b. Greene co., Tenn. He practiced law in Chattanooga, Tenn., from 1853 to 1870, except during the Civil War, when he was an officer in the Confederate army. He served in the U.S. Senate (1875–77) to complete Andrew Johnson's term. In 1877, President Hayes chose Key to be his Postmaster General, an action that provoked sharp criticism from Republicans, who felt that the presence of an ex-Confederate in the cabinet violated party principles. From 1880 to 1894, Key served as U.S. judge for the eastern and middle districts of Tennessee.

Key, Ellen (kā), 1849–1926, Swedish author and feminist. Believing that women are primarily fitted for motherhood, she advocated political and educational equality to prepare them for this role but deplored feminist claims to equality in competitive occupations. Her ideas influenced social legislation in many countries. Among her best-known works published in English are *Love and Marriage* (1911, repr. with critical and biographical notes by Havelock Ellis, 1931), *The Century of the Child* (1909), *The Woman Movement* (1912), *The Younger Generation* (1914), and *War, Peace, and the Future* (1916). See biographies by John Landquist (1909) and L. S. Nyström (1913).

Key, Francis Scott (kē), 1779–1843, American poet, author of the STAR-SPANGLED BANNER, b. present Carroll co., Md. A lawyer, he was U.S. attorney for the District of Columbia (1833–41). His works include *The Power of Literature and Its Connection with Religion* (1834) and the posthumous collection *Poems* (1857), which contains several hymns.

key, in mechanics: see LOCK AND KEY.

key. 1 In music, term used to indicate the SCALE from which the tonal material of a given composition is derived. To say, for example, that a composition is in the key of C major means that it uses as its basic tonal material the tones of the C major scale and that its harmony employs the chords built on the tones of that scale. C is then the keynote, and the C major triad, or the notes CEG, the tonic chord of the composition. In addition to the seven tones of the C major scale, however, the remaining five tones of the chromatic scale may appear as auxiliary tones, and chords may be borrowed from other keys. MODULATION to another key may take place, but if there is a return to the original key the whole composition is said to be in the key of C. At the beginning of a composition, its key is usually indicated by a key signature (see MUSICAL NOTATION). A term usually used synonymously with key is TONALITY. Absence of a feeling of key is called ATONALITY. The concept of keynotes was developed during the 16th cent. and has been to some extent abandoned, temporarily at least, in the 20th cent. Polytonality, the employment of two or more keys simultaneously, has been used by some 20th-century composers. **2** Also in music, in reference to musical instruments the term *key* refers to a lever depressed by the player's finger or, in the case of the pedal keyboard of the organ, his foot. In woodwind instruments the keys control covers on the holes that shorten the vibrating column of air. In brass winds they control the valves that lower the pitch of the instrument by lengthening the tube.

Keyes, Roger John Brownlow Keyes, 1st **Baron** (kēz), 1872–1945, British admiral. In World War I he achieved his greatest fame as commander of the Dover patrol when he raided Zeebrugge and Ostend in Belgium (April 23, 1918) to cripple the last German submarine campaign in the English Channel. He became admiral of the fleet in 1930 and retired in 1935, but he was recalled to active duty in World War II. As director of combined operations (1940–41) he influenced the early developments in amphibious warfare. From 1934 to 1943 he served as a Conservative member of Parliament, and in 1943 he was raised to the peerage as Baron Keyes of Zeebrugge and Dover.

Key Islands: see KAI ISLANDS, Indonesia.

Key Largo, narrow island, c.30 mi (48 km) long, off S Fla., largest of the FLORIDA KEYS.

Keynes, John Maynard, Baron Keynes of Tilton (kānz), 1883–1946, English economist and monetary expert, studied at Cambridge. He served (1906–8) in the India Office of the civil service, where he was concerned with problems of Indian currency. In 1919 he became principal British treasury representative at the peace conference ending World War I, but he resigned in protest against what he considered the inequitable and unworkable economic provisions of the Versailles Treaty. His *Economic Consequences of the Peace* (1919) vividly presented his views and won him world fame. Keynes criticized the Versailles Treaty from the viewpoint of a classical economist, unfavorably contrasting the economic nationalism inherent in the treaty with the relatively free pre-1914 economy based on gold and low tariffs. He foresaw that German economic weakness stemming from the Versailles provisions would involve the whole of Europe in ruin. Keynes's departure from classical concepts of free economy dates from 1929, when he endorsed David Lloyd George's campaign pledge to promote employment by a program of government spending on public works. Keynes came to believe that such a program would increase national purchasing power as well as promote employment in complementary industries. Instead of simply relying on the free economy to solve most economic problems, Keynes advocated active government intervention in the market. For the sake of full employment Keynes also abridged his classical belief in international free trade. In the world depression of the 1930s, Keynes's theories influenced governments in several nations to adopt spending programs, such as those embodied in the New Deal, aimed at maintaining a high level of national income. Today Keynesian economics stands as the most influential economic formulation of the 20th cent.; Keynes's ideas appeal to both practical politicians and theoretical economists with equal force, perhaps because he attacked the real problems of national employment and income while still remaining faithful to the requirements of rigorous economic thought. His ideas, based on large-scale government economic planning, are best expressed in his chief work, *The General Theory of Employment, Interest, and Money* (1936). In the years following 1936, Keynes contributed little to economic theory, spending most of his time in public service. During World War II he was a consultant to the chancellor of the exchequer and a director of the Bank of England. He was raised to the peerage in 1942. At Bretton Woods (1944) he influenced proposals for the establishment of a world bank to stimulate the development of underdeveloped areas. Although he favored a planned economy and wide control of the economic life by democratic public-service corporations, he never wavered in his faith in the capitalist system. In Keynesian theory, government action is designed to influence the market, not to eliminate it. Other works by Keynes include the *Tract on Monetary Reform* (1923) and the *Treatise on Money* (1930). An edition of his complete works was begun in 1971. See biography by R. F. Harrod (1951, repr. 1969); S. E. Harris, *John Maynard Keynes* (1955) and *The New Economics* (1960); L. R. Klein, *The Keynesian Revolution* (2d ed. 1966).

Keyser, Thomas de, c.1596–1667, Dutch portrait and figure painter of Amsterdam. He was the outstanding practitioner in his field prior to Rembrandt. De Keyser's work is distinguished for its clear, warm color, masterly characterization, and strong light and shade. Among his best-known paintings are *Burgomasters of Amsterdam* (The Hague) and the portrait of Constantijn Huygens and *Merchant and His Clerk* (both: National Gall., London).

Keyserling, Eduard, Graf von (ā'dōōärt gräf fən kī'sərlĭng), 1855–1918, German novelist. A member of an old and aristocratic family in the Baltic province of Courland, he depicts with delicate precision the life of his social class. Several of his novels have been translated—*Beate und Mareile* (1903, tr. *The Curse of the Tarniffs,* 1928), *Dumala* (1908, tr. *Man of God,* 1930), and *Wellen* (1911, tr. *Tides,* 1929).

Key West, city (1970 pop. 29,312), seat of Monroe co., S Fla., on an island at the southwestern extremity of the FLORIDA KEYS; inc. 1828. About 150 mi (240 km) from Miami (but only 90 mi/145 km from Cuba), it is the southernmost city of the continental United States. It is a port of entry; a winter and fishing resort, with a tropical climate; a shrimping and fishing center; and artists' colony; and a key military point. Its military installations include a major U.S. naval air station, a naval base, and a U.S. Coast Guard base (at Fort Taylor, built 1844–46). Early Spanish sailors called the site Cayo Hueso (Bone Island), because of the human bones they found there. Key West became a center for ship salvaging, cigar manufacturing, sponge gathering, and fishing. A railroad (completed 1912) serving those industries linked the Keys with the mainland. It was abandoned after being damaged by a hurricane in 1935 and was replaced by a 123-mi (198-km) highway (completed in 1938). After a severe decline in industry, the Federal government took over (1934) the bankrupt city. Places of interest include a sponge pier, an aquarium, a lighthouse (1846; replacing one built in 1825), and two Civil War forts. There is a junior college in the city. John James Audubon and Winslow Homer painted in Key West, and the city, with its heterogeneous population, of Cuban, Spanish, Negro, and English descent, has been used as a setting in the works of Hemingway, who lived there at one time. Hemingway's home (built 1851) is now a museum. See Federal Writers' Project, *A Guide to Key West* (2d ed. 1950); W. C. Maloney, *A Sketch of the History of Key West, Florida* (1968).

Kezia (kēzī'ə), second daughter of Job after his affliction. Job 42.14.

Keziz (kē'zĭz), valley, in the vicinity of Jericho. Joshua 18.21.

KGB: see SECRET POLICE.

Khabarovsk (khəbä'rəfsk, khəbərôfsk'), city (1970 pop. 436,000), capital of Khabarovsk Kray, Far Eastern USSR, on the Amur River near its junction with the Ussuri. An industrial center and a major transportation point on the Trans-Siberian RR, the city has oil refineries, shipyards, and factories that produce farm machinery, trucks, aircraft, diesel engines, and machine tools. Khabarovsk, formerly a fortified trading post, prospered greatly after the coming of the railroad in 1905. The city was the capital of the Soviet Far East from 1926 to 1938.

Khabarovsk Kray or **Khabarovsk Territory,** administrative division (1970 pop. 1,346,000), 305,000 sq mi (789,950 sq km), Far Eastern USSR. Situated in the eastern and northeastern extremity of Siberia, the territory is bounded by the Sea of Okhotsk in the east, Primorsky Kray and Manchuria in the south, and the Kolyma range in the north. It includes the JEWISH AUTONOMOUS OBLAST. The mountainous territory is crossed by the Dzhugdzhur and Bureya ranges, where gold, oil, tin, and coal are extracted. Grain and potatoes are grown in the Amur valley, and in the north there are reindeer herds and fur trappers. Herring, flounder, and salmon are caught along the coast. Major cities are the capital, Khabarovsk, the industrial center Komsomolsk-on-Amur, and the ports Sovetskaya Gavan and Nikolayevsk-on-Amur; 75 percent of the total population (Russians, Ukrainians, Byelorussians, Jews, Tatars, and Yakuts) is concentrated in the cities. The territory was founded in 1938 and reorganized in 1953 and 1957. For history, see SOVIET FAR EAST.

Khabur (khäbōōr'), river, c.200 mi (320 km) long, rising in SE Turkey, and flowing generally south through NE Syria to enter the Euphrates River, near Dayr az Zawr. The Khabur River project, begun in the 1960s, seeks, by the construction of a series of dams and a drainage scheme, to remove salt from the soil and to bring c.250,000 acres (101,200 hectares) of land under cultivation. In ancient times the Khabur was known as the Habor; along its banks in Gozan the Israelite captives from Samaria were settled in the 8th cent. B.C. (2 Kings 17.6; 18.11).

Khachaturian, Aram Ilich (ərām' ĭlyēch' khä"chətōōryän'), 1903–, Russian composer of Armenian parentage. Khachaturian graduated from the Moscow Conservatory in 1934. He first studied the cello and c.1926 began to compose. His music, colorful and energetic, uses Armenian and Oriental folk idioms. His piano concerto (1935), violin concerto (1940), the ballet *Gayané* (1942), containing the popular *Sabre Dance,* and the orchestral suite *Masquerade* (1944) are especially popular. Despite official Soviet criticism of his "modernistic" style, he continues to create works of harmonic complexity. His name also appears in English as Khatchatourian.

Khafre (khä'frä) or **Chephren** (kĕf'rĕn), fl. 2565 B.C., king of ancient Egypt, of the IV dynasty, and builder of the second pyramid at Gizeh. His face is perhaps that represented on the Sphinx. An obscure king, Dedefre, may have come between Khufu and Khafre in the dynasty.

Khair ad-Din: see BARBAROSSA.

Khairpur (khīr'pōōr), city (1961 pop. 34,144), SE Pakistan, in Sind prov. It trades in wheat, cotton, tobacco, and dates. Manufactures include textiles, armaments, and pharmaceuticals. The city was the capital of the former princely state of Khairpur, which was founded in 1783 and merged into Pakistan in 1955. It is a cultural center with fine historic buildings, notably the Faiz Palace, and with several educational facilities.

Khakass Autonomous Oblast (khəkäs'), administrative division (1970 pop. 446,000) 23,900 sq mi (61,900 sq km), S central Siberian USSR, in Krasnoyarsk Kray. ABAKAN (the capital) and Chernogorsk (a coal-mining center) are the major cities. The oblast, largely consisting of black-earth steppe, is bounded by the upper Yenisei River on the east and by the wooded Kuznetsk Ala-Tau and Sayan ranges on the west and south, respectively. The Abakan (a tributary of the Yenisei) and Chulym rivers drain the area. Railroads are the chief mode of transportation. The oblast's swift-flowing rivers provide hydroelectric power, and many of the numerous lakes are sources of therapeutic mineral waters. Mining, forestry, and food processing are the main industries. Gold, coal, iron ore, barite, copper, lead, and molybdenum are mined, and gypsum, limestone, marble, and other building stones are quarried. The forests of the taiga zone yield lumber and wood products. Logs are floated down the Abakan River to sawmills located in the capital. Although the oblast's population is primarily Russian (with some Ukrainians), there is a large Khakass minority. The Khakass are an ancient Turkic-Mongol nationality that inhabited the S Yenisei valley for many centuries. Formerly nomadic herdsmen, they are now mostly settled in farming, hunting, or livestock-breeding collectives. They speak a Turkic language and are Orthodox Christians. The region, known for mining and trade from the 8th to the 11th cent., came under Russian control in the 17th cent. Numerous Russian settlers were attracted by copper mining in the 18th cent. The Khakass sided with counterrevolutionary forces during the Russian civil war. The autonomous oblast was formed in 1930.

khaki (kăk'ē, kä'kē) [Hindi,=dust-colored], closely twilled cloth of linen or cotton, dyed a dust color. It was first used (1848) for uniforms for the English regiment of Sir Harry Burnett Lumsden in India and later became the official color for British army uniforms, as well as for those of other countries. It became popular for hunting and outdoor wear, as in the uniforms of groups such as the Boy Scouts and for heavy working clothes.

Khalid (khä'lēd) (Khalid ibn al-Walid), d. 642, Arab warrior. He assisted the Meccans in attacking (625) Muhammad and the inhabitants of Medina after the battle of Badr. Khalid and the Meccans were victorious in the battle of Ohud but did not follow up their victory. In 629, Khalid accepted Islam. He became the chief Muslim general in the conquest of Syria, Egypt, Iraq, and Persia. Muhammad gave him the title "The Sword of God."

Khalkidhikí (khälkēthēkē') or **Chalcidice** (kălsĭd'ĭsē), peninsula (1971 pop. 75,582), NE Greece, projecting into the Aegean Sea from SE Macedonia. Its southern extremity terminates in three peninsulas: Kassandra (anc. Gr. *Pallene*) in the west, Sithonia in the center, and ATHOS in the east. The region is largely mountainous, dry, and agricultural. Olive oil, wine, wheat, and tobacco are produced; magnesite is mined. In antiquity the peninsula was famous for its timber. OLYNTHUS and POTIDAEA were the chief towns in antiquity; Poliyiros is today the leading town and an administrative center. The peninsula was named for KHALKÍS, which established colonies there in the 8th and 7th cent. B.C. In the 4th cent. B.C. the peninsula was conquered by Philip II of Macedon, and in the 2d cent. B.C. by Rome. The subsequent history of Khalkidhikí is essentially that of THESSALONÍKI.

Khalkís (khälkēs') or **Chalcis** (kăl'sĭs), city (1971 pop. 36,300), capital of Évvoia (Euboea) prefecture, E Greece, on the island of ÉVVOIA. Connected to the mainland by a bridge, the city is a trade center for local products, including wine, cotton, and citrus fruits. Soap and cement are manufactured. The chief city of ancient Euboea, Khalkís was settled by the Ionians and early became a commercial and colonizing center. It established (8th-7th cent. B.C.) colonies on KHALKIDHIKÍ and in Sicily. The city was subdued by Athens (c.506 B.C.) and led the revolt of Euboea against Athens in 446 B.C. Again defeated, it came under Athenian rule until 411 B.C. In 338 B.C. it passed to Macedonia. Aristotle died there (322 B.C.). In succeeding centuries the city was used as a base for invading Greece. In the Middle Ages it was named Negropont by the Venetians, who occupied it in 1209. It passed to the Ottoman Turks in 1470 and in 1830 became part of Greece. A diamond-shaped Venetian citadel is there.

Khama (kä'mə), d. 1923?, chief of the Bamangwato people of Bechuanaland (now Botswana) from 1875 until his death; grandfather of Sir Seretse Khama. To counter threats from neighboring Africans and from the Boers of S Africa, he and other chiefs arranged (1885) for Great Britain to make Bechuanaland a protectorate. Despite the opposition of many British imperialists wishing to undermine the chief's authority, this status was confirmed when Khama made a journey to England in 1895. Khama's firm leadership eliminated much of the internal dissension that had divided his people.

Khama, Sir Seretse (sĕrĕt'sä kä'mä), 1921–, president of Botswana (1966–); grandson of Chief Khama. After studying in England he returned to Bechuanaland (now Botswana) but was banished (1950) in a dispute with the British government over his succession to the chieftaincy of the Bamangwato tribe. He renounced (1956) his claim, returned, and launched the Bechuanaland Democratic party. He served (1965–66) as prime minister; when Bechuanaland became independent as Botswana, he assumed the presidency. He was knighted in 1966.

Khanabad (khän'äbäd), city (1967 est. pop. 30,000), NE Afghanistan, near the USSR border. It is a market town for wool and silk.

Khanaqin (khän'äkēn), town (1965 pop. 23,527), E Iraq, on a tributary of the Diyala. It is located in an oil-producing region and has an oil refinery.

Khandwa (kŭnd'və), town (1971 pop. 85,513), Madhya Pradesh state, central India. Khandwa is a district administrative center and a market for cotton, timber, and grain. There are cotton gins and oilseed mills. The town is believed by some authorities to be the city of Kognabanda mentioned by the ancient Hellenistic geographer Ptolemy. During the 12th cent. it was a center of JAINISM. Two colleges in the town are affiliated with Sagar Univ.

Khangai (khän'gī'), massive mountain range, W central Mongolian People's Republic, extending from east to west for c.500 mi (800 km); rises to c.13,000 ft (3,960 m). Many rivers, notably the Orkhon and the Selenga, rise on the range's wooded slopes.

Khaniá (khänyä') or **Canea** (kənē'ə), ancient Gr. *Cydonia* (sīdō'nēə), city (1971 pop. 40,564), capital of Khaniá prefecture, NW Crete, Greece, a port on the Gulf of Khaniá, an arm of the Sea of Crete. Olives, citrus fruits, and wine are shipped. One of the oldest Cretan cities, it was conquered in 69 B.C. by the Romans and in A.D. 826 fell under Arab rule. Reconquered (961) by the Byzantine Empire, it became (13th cent.) a Venetian colony. The Ottoman Empire took the city in 1645. It was the capital of Crete from 1841 to the mid-20th cent. The city has a synagogue, a mosque, and several churches. Among its historic sites are medieval fortifications and an old Venetian arsenal.

Khanty-Mansi National Okrug (khŭntē'-mŭnsē'), administrative division (1970 pop. 272,000), 201,969 sq mi (523,100 sq km), W Siberian USSR. Khanty-Mansisk is the capital. The region, mostly forest and swamp with numerous lakes and peat bogs, is drained by the lower Irtysh and the Ob rivers, which are also important transportation arteries. Although the territory is about the size of France, it is very sparsely populated; the largest concentrations of people are in the Ob and Irtysh valleys. Lumbering, fishing, fur farming and trading, and reindeer breeding are the okrug's chief occupations. Cattle, horses, hogs, and reindeer are raised on state and collective farms. Some grain and vegetables are grown in the south, and fish processing is carried on. Oil and natural gas production is increasingly important, notably at Berezovo, where large natural gas fields have been developed. Lumbering is hampered by the okrug's great distance from markets. Russians comprise the majority of the okrug's population, but there are large minorities of Khanty (Ostyaks) and Mansi (Yugra or Voguls), both of whom belong to the Finno-Ugric linguistic family. Some Komi and Nentsy people also inhabit the region. The Khanty, who were under the control of the Siberian Tatars, opposed Russian conquest and rule from the 16th through the 18th cent. The Mansi have been in the area since the 11th cent.; they, too, resisted Muscovite domination. The okrug, formed in 1930, was known until 1940 as the Ostyak-Vogul National Okrug.

Kharagpur (käräg'pər), city (1971 pop. 161,911), West Bengal state, E central India. It is an industrial city and has a scientific-research center.

Kharbin: see HARBIN, China.

Kharga: see KHARIJAH, AL, Egypt.

Kharijah, Al (äl khär'ēnjä) or **Kharga** (khär'gə), large oasis, S central Egypt, in the Libyan (Western) Desert. Populated chiefly by Bedouins and Berbers, the irrigated oasis produces cereals, vegetables, dates, citrus fruits, and alfalfa. Cattle and poultry are also raised. Al Kharijah, the chief settlement, is a rail terminus. The oasis was prosperous in ancient times, and there are ruins of temples built by the Achaemenids of ancient Persia and by the Romans.

Khark (khärk), island, c.4 mi (6 km) long and c.2 mi (3 km) wide, SW Iran, in the Persian Gulf. Site of one of the world's largest deep-water oil ports, it is linked to the mainland by a 25-mi (40-km) pipeline. The name is also spelled Kharg.

Kharkov (khär'kəf), city (1970 pop. 1,223,000), capital of Kharkov oblast, S European USSR, in the Ukraine, at the confluence of the Kharkov, Lopan, and Udy rivers in the upper Donets valley. The USSR's sixth largest city, Kharkov is also one of the country's main rail junctions and economic and cultural centers. Proximity to the iron mines of KRIVOY ROG and the coal of the DONETS BASIN has provided the basis for engineering industries that produce a wide variety of other heavy metal items. Kharkov's industries also include food and tobacco processing, printing, and the manufacture of chemicals. Founded in 1656 as a military strongpoint to defend Moscow's southern border, it became an important frontier headquarters of the Ukrainian Cossacks. They kept the city loyal to the czar during the Cossack uprisings of the late 17th cent., and, as a result, Kharkov received more autonomy than most other Ukrainian cities. Developing as an intellectual and commercial center, Kharkov became the site of large annual trade fairs, which were held from the second half of the 18th cent. until the Russian Revolution. Russia's annexation of the Crimea in 1783 and colonization of the steppes further stimulated Kharkov's economic growth. The coal and metallurgical industries developed after the 1860s, and railroads were built in the late 19th cent. Kharkov also became an important center of the 19th-century Ukrainian national and literary movements. The city became the capital of the Ukraine in 1919 but was superseded by Kiev in 1934. Kharkov's landmarks include the cathedral of the Protectoress (1686), the cathedral of the Assumption (1771), and a bell tower that was built to celebrate Napoleon's defeat in 1812. The university dates from 1805, and there are numerous scientific research institutes. Heavy fighting raged in Kharkov during World War II.

Khartoum (kärto͞om'), city (1969 est. pop. 231,000), capital of the Sudan, a port at the confluence of the Blue Nile and White Nile rivers. Khartoum is the Sudan's second largest city and its administrative center. Food, beverages, cotton, gum, and oil seeds are processed in the city. Manufactures include cotton textiles, knitwear, glass, and tiles. Khartoum is a railroad hub and is connected by road to the heart of the adjacent cotton-growing region. The city also has an international airport. Founded in 1821 as an Egyptian army camp, Khartoum developed as a trade center and slave market. In the war between Great Britain and the forces of the MAHDI, Gen. Charles GORDON was killed there (1885) after resisting a long siege, which was one of the most notable events in British imperial history and during which the city was severely damaged. Khartoum was retaken by H. H. KITCHENER in 1898 and rebuilt. An educational center, Khartoum is the site of the Univ. of Khartoum (founded 1903 as Gordon Memorial College), a branch of the Univ. of Cairo, and Khartoum Polytechnic. The city's Sudan Museum has important archaeological holdings. Bridges link Khartoum with Khartoum North and Omdurman.

Khaskovo, or **Haskovo,** city (1968 est. pop. 68,000), S Bulgaria, in an agricultural region noted for its tobacco. The city has one of Bulgaria's largest cigarette factories.

Khatanga (khətän'gə), river, Krasnoyarsk Kray, N central Siberian USSR, formed by the union of the Kotui and the Kheta rivers. From the Kotui it is c.715 mi (1,150 km) long and flows north through the central Siberian Plateau past Khatanga village and NE into the Khatanga Gulf of the Laptev Sea, forming the southeastern border of the Taymyr peninsula. The river is navigable.

Khatchatourian, Aram Ilich: see KHACHATURIAN.

Khatti: see HITTITES.

Khayr ad-Din: see BARBAROSSA.

Khayyam, Omar: see OMAR KHAYYAM.

Khazars (khä'zärz), ancient Turkic people who appeared in TRANSCAUCASIA in the 2d cent. A.D. and subsequently settled in the lower Volga region. They emerged as a force in the 7th cent. and rose to great power. The Khazar empire extended (8th-10th cent.) from the northern shores of the Black Sea and the Caspian Sea to the Urals and as far westward as Kiev. The Khazars conquered the Volga Bulgars and the Crimea, levied tribute from the eastern Slavs, and warred with the Arabs, Persians, and Armenians. In the 10th cent. they entered into friendly relations with the Byzantine Empire, which attempted to use them in the struggle against the Arabs. In the 8th cent. the Khazar nobility embraced Judaism. Cyril and Methodius subsequently made some Christian converts among them. Religious tolerance was complete in the Khazar empire, which reached a relatively high degree of civilization. Itil, its capital in the Volga delta, was a great commercial center. The Khazar empire fell when Sviatoslav, duke of Kiev, defeated its army in 965. The Khazars (or Chazars) are believed by some to have been the ancestors of many East European Jews.

Kherson (khĕrsôn'), city (1970 pop. 261,000), capital of Kherson oblast, S European USSR, in the Ukraine, on the Dnepr River near its mouth on the Black Sea. It is a rail junction and a sea and river port, exporting grain, timber, and manganese ore and importing oil from the Caucasus. Kherson has one of the Ukraine's largest cotton textile mills; the city's other industries include shipbuilding and food processing. Kherson was founded in 1778 by Potemkin as a naval station, fortress, and shipbuilding center. Its name derives from its location on the probable site of the Greek colony Chersonesus Heracleotica. The city became the administrative center for Russia's newly acquired holdings along the Black Sea. By the late 19th cent. it was an important export center. The dredging of a deepwater canal along an arm of the Dnepr to the sea in 1901 further stimulated Kherson's growth as a port. The city's importance was enhanced still more with the building of the DNEPROGES power station in 1932 and the development of navigation on the Dnepr. Kherson's landmarks include the fortress with earthen ramparts and stone gates and the 18th-century cathedral that contains Potemkin's tomb.

Khibinogorsk: see KIROVSK, USSR.

Khingan, Great (khĭn'gän', shĭng'än'), Mandarin *Ta-hsing-an*, mountain range, Heilungkiang, Kirin, and Liaoning prov., NE China, extending c.750 mi (1,210 km) from the Amur River S to the Liao River; the highest point is 5,657 ft (1,724 m). The range forms the eastern edge of the Mongolian Plateau. Heavily forested, it has some of China's richest timber resources. The **Lesser Khingan,** Mandarin *Hsiao-hsing-an*, Heilungkiang prov., is a continuation of the Bureya range in the Siberian USSR. It extends c.400 mi (640 km) NE from the Sungari River and is linked to the Great Khingan by the I-lo-hu-li range, N Heilungkiang prov.

Khíos (khē'ôs) or **Chios** (kī'ŏs), island (1971 pop. 52,487), c.350 sq mi (910 sq km), E Greece, in the Aegean Sea, just W of Asia Minor. It is mountainous and is famous for its scenic beauty and good climate. The highest point is Mt. Elias (c.4,160 ft/1,270 m). The island produces olives, figs, and mastic and has marble quarries, lignite deposits, and sulfur springs. Sheep and goats are raised. Khíos was colonized by Ionians and later held (494–479 B.C.) by the Persians. In 479 B.C. it recovered its independence and joined the DELIAN LEAGUE. It rebelled several times against Athenian ascendancy in the league. The island was on good terms with Rome, maintaining its independence until the reign of Vespasian (1st cent. A.D.). It became part of the Byzantine Empire and later passed (1204) to the Latin emperors of Constantinople and then (1261) to the Genoese. The Ottoman Turks conquered the island in 1566 and held it until the First Balkan War (1912), when it was taken by Greece. A rebellion against Turkish rule resulted (1822) in a ruthless massacre of the population. Khíos claims to be the birthplace of Homer. **Khíos,** a seaport (1971 pop. 24,084), is the island's chief town and the capital of Khíos prefecture.

Khiva (khē'və, khēvä'), city (1967 est. pop. 22,000), Central Asian USSR, in Uzbekistan, in the Khiva oasis and on the Amu Darya River. Industries include metalworking, cotton and silk spinning, wood carving, and carpetmaking. The city, in existence by the 6th cent., was the capital of the Khorezm kingdom in the 7th and 8th cent. From the late 16th until the early 20th cent., Khiva was the capital of the khanate of the same name. The city was a significant trade and handicraft center in the late 18th and early 19th cent. It passed to Russia in 1873. It served as the capital of the Khorezm Soviet People's Republic from 1920 to 1923 and of the Khorezm SSR in 1923 and 1924. The ancient quarter of the city has been set aside to preserve such landmarks as an 18th-century fort, the khan's palace (now a museum), and a 19th-century mausoleum and minaret.

Khiva, khanate of, former state of central Asia, based on the Khiva (Khorezm) oasis along the Amu Darya River. The khanate lay S of the Aral Sea and included large areas of the Kyzyl-Kum and Kara-Kum deserts. Founded c.1511 as part of the Khorezm state, Khiva rose in the late 16th cent. as a Muslim Uzbek state. It flourished in the early 19th cent. but was conquered by Russia in 1873; the khans subsequently continued to rule under Russian protection. Khiva's economy was based on agriculture, livestock breeding, brigandage, and handicrafts. The territory comprised the Khorezm Soviet People's Republic from 1920 to 1924, when the area was divided between the Uzbek SSR and the Turkmen SSR. For earlier history, see KHOREZM.

Khlesl, Melchior: see KLESL, MELCHIOR.

Khmelnitsky, Bohdan: see CHMIELNICKI, BOHDAN.

Khmelnitsky (khmĕlnēt'skē), city (1970 pop. 113,000), capital of Khmelnitsky oblast, SW European USSR, in the Ukraine, on the Southern Bug River. It is a rail terminus and highway hub and has metal forges, food-processing (notably sugar-refining) plants, and factories that produce machine tools, equipment for power stations, reinforced concrete items, clothing, and footwear. Known since the 15th cent., the city was a fortress by the late 16th cent. and became part of Russia in 1795. Formerly called Proskurov, it was renamed in 1954 on the 300th anniversary of a treaty between the Russians and the Cossacks led by Bohdan Chmielnicki (Khmelnitsky).

Khmer Empire, ancient kingdom of SE Asia. In the 6th cent. the Cambodians, or Khmers, established an empire roughly corresponding to modern CAMBODIA and LAOS. Divided during the 8th cent., it was reunited under the rule of Jayavarman II in the early 9th cent.; the capital was established in the area of ANGKOR by the king Yasovarman I (889-900). The Angkor period (889-1434), the golden age of Khmer civilization, saw the empire at its greatest extent; it held sway over the valleys of the lower Menam (in present-day Thailand) and the lower Mekong (present-day Cambodia and South Vietnam), as well as N into Laos. The Khmer civilization was largely formed by Indian influences. Buddhism flourished side by side with the worship of Shiva and of other Hindu gods, while both religions coalesced with the cult of the deified king. In the Angkor period many Indian scholars, artists, and religious teachers were attracted to the Khmer court, and Sanskrit literature flourished with royal patronage. The great achievement of the Khmers was in architecture and sculpture. The earliest known Khmer monuments, isolated towers of brick probably date from the 7th cent. Small temples set on stepped pyramids next appeared. The development of covered galleries led gradually to a great elaboration of plan. Brick was largely abandoned in favor of stone. Khmer architecture reached its height with the construction of Angkor Wat by Suryavarman II (1113-50) and Angkor Thom by Jayavarman VII (1181-c.1218). Sculpture, which also prospered at Angkor, showed a steady development from relative naturalism to a more conventionalized technique. Bas-reliefs, lacking in the earliest monuments, came to overshadow in importance statues in the round; in the later stages of Khmer art hardly a wall was left bare of bas-reliefs, which conveyed in the richness of their detail and vitality a vivid picture of Khmer life. The Khmers fought repeated wars against the Annamese and the Chams; in the early 12th cent. they invaded Champa, but, in 1177, Angkor was sacked by the Chams. After the founding of Ayuthia (c.1350), Cambodia was subjected to repeated invasions from Thailand, and the Khmer power declined. In 1434, after the Thai captured Angkor, the capital was transferred to Phnom Penh; this event marks the end of the brilliance of the Khmer civilization. See L. P. Briggs, *The Ancient Khmer Empire* (1951); John Audric, *Angkor and the Khmer Empire* (1972).

Khmer Republic: see CAMBODIA.

Khmer Rouge (ro͞ozh), name given to native Cambodian Communists. Khmer Rouge soldiers, aided by North Vietnamese and Viet Cong troops, began a large-scale insurgency against government forces in 1970, quickly gaining control over more than two thirds of the total land area of Cambodia and maintaining a fairly steady siege of the capital city of Phnom Penh. The strength of the Khmer Rouge rose dramatically from around 3,000 in 1970 to more than 30,000 in 1973, enabling most of the North Vietnamese and Viet Cong troops to withdraw and leave the fighting to the native Communists.

Khodzhent: see LENINABAD, USSR.

Khoi, Iran: see KHVOY.

Khoikhoi (koi'koi"), people numbering about 39,000 mainly in South West Africa and in NW Cape Prov., Republic of South Africa. The Khoikhoi have been called Hottentots by whites in South Africa. In language and in physical type the Khoikhoi appear to be related to the SAN (Bushmen), i.e., they speak a variation of the Khoisan, or Click, language (see AFRICAN LANGUAGES); they are generally much lighter in complexion than the neighboring Bantu. A pastoral people, inhabiting the coast of the Cape of Good Hope in historic times, the Khoikhoi were the first native people to come into contact (mid-17th cent.) with the Dutch settlers. As the Dutch took over land for farms, the Khoikhoi were dispossessed, exterminated, or enslaved, and their numbers dwindled. They were formerly divided into 10 clans, each ruled by a headman and councillors elected by universal male suffrage. The Khoikhoi have largely disappeared as a group, except for the Namas (see NAMAQUALAND) of SW Africa, who still live as pastoral nomads. Most Khoikhoi have settled in villages, living as farmers and laborers. See Isaac Schapera, *The Khoisan Peoples of South Africa* (1930, repr. 1965); Peggy Heap, *The Story of Hottentots Holland* (1970).

Khokand: see KOKAND, USSR.

Kholmogory (khŭl"məgô'rē), village, NW European USSR, SE of Arkhangelsk and at the mouth of the Northern Dvina River. Known since 1355, Kholmogory was a major trade center for Novgorod merchants in the 15th and 16th cent. and became a shipping and cattle raising center in the 18th cent. Its significance declined with the rise of Arkhangelsk.

Khoper (khəpyôr'), river, c.625 mi (1,010 km) long, S European USSR. It rises SW of Penza and flows SW, then S into the Don. It is partly navigable.

Khorasan (khôräsän'), province (1966 pop. 2,497,-381), c.125,000 sq mi (323,750 sq km), NE Iran. Mashhad is the capital and chief city; other cities include Sabzevar, Bojnurd, and Neyshabur. It is mainly mountainous and arid. Products include agricultural goods, refined sugar, textiles, carpets, turquoises, opium, and wool. Khorasan was occupied by the Arabs in the mid-7th cent., and it was there that Abu Muslim began (8th cent.) his campaign against the Umayyads. The province contributed to the military power of the early Abbasid caliphs. Khorasan was devastated by the Oghuz Turks in 1153 and 1157 and by the Mongols from 1220 to 1222. In 1383 the province was invaded by Tamerlane. It is also known as Khurasan.

Khorezm (khərĕz'əm) or **Khwarazm** (khwäräz'əm), ancient and medieval state of central Asia, situated in and around the basin of the lower Amu Darya River; now an oblast, NW Uzbek Republic, USSR. Khorezm is one of the oldest centers of civilization in central Asia. It was a part of the Achaemenid empire of Cyrus the Great in the 6th cent. B.C. and became independent in the 4th cent. B.C. It was later inhabited by Persians who adhered to Zoroastrianism and used Aramaic script. Khorezm was conquered by the Arabs in the 7th cent. and was converted to Islam. In 995 the country was united under the emirs of N Khorezm, whose capital URGENCH became a major seat of Arabic learning. The capital was a center of agriculture and trade and the residence of the ruling shahs. In the late 12th cent., Khorezm gained independence from the Seljuk Turks, the successors to the Arabs. With independence it expanded its rule, and at the height of its power in the early 13th cent. ruled from the Caspian Sea to Bukhara and Samarkand. It was conquered in 1221 by Jenghiz Khan and was included in the Golden Horde. The development of caravan trade by the Mongols was profitable to Khorezm. In the late 14th cent., Khorezm, along with its vast irrigation system, was destroyed by Tamerlane. A century of struggle over Khorezm between the Timurids, the descendants of Tamerlane, and the Golden Horde was followed by the Uzbek conquest in the early 16th cent. Khorezm became an independent Uzbek state and was known as the khanate of Khiva after Khiva became the capital. There are ruins of ancient forts, one of which dates back to the 6th cent. B.C.

Khorog (khərôk'), city (1970 pop. 12,000), capital of Gorno-Badakhshan Autonomous Oblast, Central Asian USSR, in Tadzhikistan, in the Pamir. Khorog has shoe factories and metal-working plants, and building materials are produced.

Khorramabad (khōräm"äbäd'), city (1971 est. pop. 62,000), capital of Luristan governorate, Khuzistan prov., W Iran. It is the trade center of a mountainous region where fruit, grain, and wool are produced.

Khorramshahr (khōräm"shä'hər), city (1971 est. pop. 90,000), Khuzistan prov., SW Iran, at the confluence of the Karun River and the Shatt al Arab, near the Persian Gulf. It is a busy port. Its development dates to the late 19th cent., when steam navigation on the Karun was started. The city was known as Muhammerah until the mid-1920s, when Reza Shah took it out of the hands of a semi-independent local sheikh and placed it under the control of the central government.

Khorsabad (khôrsäbäd'), village, NE Iraq, near the Tigris River and 12 mi (20 km) NE of Mosul. It is built on the site of Dur Sharrukin, an Assyrian city (founded 8th cent. B.C. by Sargon), which covered 1 sq mi (2.6 sq km). Its mounds were excavated by P. E. Botta in 1842 and in 1851, and statues of Sargon and of huge, winged bulls that guarded the gates of the royal palace were taken to the Louvre. In 1932 there were discovered hundreds of cuneiform tablets in the Elamite language and a list of kings ruling from c.2200 B.C. to 730 B.C.

Khortitsa: see ZAPOROZHYE, USSR.

Khosru I (Khosru Nushirvan) (khŏsro͞o'; no͞oshĭr-vän'), d. 579, king of Persia (531-79), greatest of the Sassanid or Sassanian monarchs. He is also known as Chosroes I. He succeeded his father, Kavadh I, but before becoming king, Khosru was responsible for a great massacre (c.528) of the communistic Mazdakites. He extended Persian rule E to the Indus River with the capture (560) of Bactria, W across Arabia by establishing (570) at least nominal rule over Yemen, and north and northwest by taking part of Armenia and Caucasia from the Byzantine Empire. He fought against Belisarius and the other generals of Justinian I and against Justin II. Khosru is revered by the Persians as a just though despotic ruler who encouraged learning, stimulated commerce, rebuilt cities, and set up a reformed system of taxation.

Khosru II (Khosru Parviz) (pärvēz'), d. 628, king of Persia of the Sassanid, or Sassanian, dynasty; grandson of Khosru I. He is also called Chosroes II. He succeeded his father Hormizd, or Hormoz, in 590, but he was opposed by the usurper Bahram Chukin, and forced to flee to the Byzantine Empire. Emperor Maurice aided him in overthrowing Bahram, but Khosru had to cede practically all of Armenia. When Maurice was murdered by the tyrant Phocas, Khosru declared a war of revenge against his murderer and conquered much Byzantine territory until he was finally defeated by Heraclius I. Khosru was murdered by his son and successor, Kauadh II Shiruya.

Khotan: see HO-T'IEN, China.

Khotin (khətyēn'), city, SW European USSR, in the Ukraine, on the Dnestr River. It lies in Bessarabia in an agricultural district and has agricultural and food-processing industries. Located on the site of an ancient fortified Slavic settlement, the city is named for Kotizon, a 3d-century Dacian chief. It was included in Kievan Russia in the 10th cent. and later became part of the Galich and Galich-Volhynian duchies. Khotin developed into an important trade and craft center and in the 13th cent. was the site of a Genoese trading colony. The city was included in the Hungarian and Moldavian states in the 14th and 15th cent. Its strategic location at an important Dnestr River crossing caused the city to change hands frequently from the 16th to 18th cent. Seized by Russia in 1739, Khotin was incorporated into the Russian Empire in 1812 as part of Bessarabia. The city was under Rumanian rule from 1918 to 1940 and under German occupation from 1941 to 1944. Khotin has remains of an imposing fortified castle that was built (13th cent.) by the Genoese, enlarged (14th-15th cent.) by the Moldavians, and restored (18th cent.) by the Turks.

Khrushchev, Nikita Sergeyevich (nyĭkē'tə syĭrgā'-yəvĭch khro͞oschôf'), 1894-1971, Soviet Communist leader, premier of the USSR (1958-64), and first secretary of the Communist party of the Soviet Union (1953-64). Of a peasant family, he worked in the plants and mines of Ukraine, joined the Communist party in 1918, and in 1929 was sent to Moscow for further study. He became a member of the central committee of the Communist party of the Soviet Union (CPSU) in 1934 and first secretary of the powerful Moscow city and oblast party organization in 1935. Made first secretary of the Ukrainian Communist party in 1938, he carried out Stalin's ruthless purge of its ranks. As a full member of the politburo, the ruling body of the central committee of the CPSU after 1939, Khrushchev was one of Stalin's close associates. In World War II he served on the military councils of several fronts. He was recalled from Ukraine to his Moscow post in 1949. After the death of STALIN on March 5, 1953, a "collective leadership" replaced the single ruler of the USSR; from the ensuing struggle for power Khrushchev emerged victorious. He replaced MALENKOV as first secretary of the party in Sept., 1953, and, in 1955, Malenkov resigned as premier and was succeeded by BULGANIN, a change clearly leaving Khrushchev with the advantage. In 1954 he initiated the virgin lands program to increase grain production and headed a delegation to Communist China. At the 20th All-Union Party Congress (1956), Khrushchev delivered a "secret" report on "The Personality Cult and Its Consequences," bitterly denouncing the rule, policies, and personality of Stalin. The program of destalinization, which had already begun, was supported and continued by Khrushchev. Legality of procedure was restored, the secret police became less of a threat, concentration camps and many forced labor camps were closed, and some greater degree of meaningful public controversy was permitted. The new atmosphere of relative freedom constituted a great change from the days of Stalin. Destalinization had, however, repercussions in other Communist countries, creating unrest that exploded in the Polish defiance of the USSR in 1956 and in the quickly quelled Hungarian revolution of the same year. These events and the abandonment of the sixth FIVE-YEAR PLAN weakened Khrushchev's position, but he gained strength in 1957 with his program for decentralization of industry. In 1957 a faction headed by Malenkov, MOLOTOV, and Kaganovich tried in vain to remove Khrushchev from leadership; they were instead removed from important posts, as, soon after, was ZHUKOV, who had supported Khrushchev against them. Khrushchev replaced Bulganin as premier in March, 1958, becoming undisputed leader of both state and party. Jovial in manner, often deliberately uncouth, he showed himself capable of alternating belligerence with camaraderie. He soon was known throughout the world as a leader of great shrewdness, fully attuned to the realities of the international scene. In foreign affairs Khrushchev's announced policy, opposite to that of Stalin, was one of "peaceful coexistence" in the COLD WAR. He toured the United States in 1959 and met with President Eisenhower at Camp David, Md., thus helping to improve the tense international relations created by his threats (1958) to sign a separate peace with East Germany. In 1960, however, Khrushchev cancelled the Paris summit conference after a U.S. reconnaissance plane was shot down over the USSR. In the fall of 1960 he headed the Soviet delegation to the UN General Assembly, where he raged against UN interference in the Republic of the Congo (now Zaïre). Khrushchev's policies at home and abroad involved him in an increasingly bitter struggle with Communist China, which continued to adhere strongly to a bellicose Stalinist ideology. International tension was created by Khrushchev's adamant stand over BERLIN, but was lessened somewhat by his withdrawal of Soviet missiles from CUBA in 1962 and by small compromises in the Soviet proposals for disarmament. In Oct., 1964, Khrushchev was removed from power. Repeated failures in agricultural production as well as Khrushchev's retreat in the Cuban missile crisis and the rift with Communist China had intensified the opposition to him. He lived in obscurity outside Moscow until his death in 1971. See UNION OF SOVIET SOCIALIST REPUBLICS. See biographies by George Paloczi-Horvath (1960), Lazar Pistrak (1961), Edward Crankshaw (1966), and Mark Frankland (1969); Strobe Talbott, ed., *Khrushchev Remembers* (2 vol., tr. 1970 and 1974).

Khufu (kho͞o'fo͞o) or **Cheops** (kē'ŏps), fl. c.2680 B.C., king of ancient Egypt, founder of the IV dynasty. He was king for 23 years and was famous as the builder of the greatest PYRAMID at Gizeh.

Khulna (ko͝ol'nə), town (1961 est. pop. 128,000), SW Bangladesh, near the Ganges delta. It is a river port and the trade and processing center for the products of the Sundarbans, a swampy, forested region. Agricultural products, especially rice and jute, are processed, and there is some textile manufacturing and shipbuilding. Khulna is also an educational center.

Khurasan, Iran: see KHORASAN.

Khuzistan (kho͞ozēstän'), province (1966 pop. 1,578,-079), c.24,000 sq mi (62,160 sq km), SW Iran, bordering on Iraq in the west and the Persian Gulf in the south. Its major cities include Ahvaz (the capital), Khorramshahr, Dezful, and Abadeh. Khuzistan has large petroleum deposits and major oil refineries. Mountainous in the east, it has a hot climate; agricultural products include dates, citrus fruit, rice, and vegetables. Dams on the Dez River in the northern part of the province provide water for irrigation and hydroelectricity. Khuzistan was the biblical Elam, called Susiana in classical times. The area was conquered (7th cent.) by the Arabs and invaded (13th cent.) by the Mongols; it passed to Tamerlane in the 14th cent. About half the population today is made up of Shiite Muslims. The province was formerly called Arabistan.

Khvoy (khvō'ē), city (1971 est. pop. 51,000), West Azerbaijan prov., NW Iran. It is the trade center for a fertile farm region. Because of its strategic location near Turkey and the Soviet Union, control of the city has frequently been in dispute. Khvoy was attacked by Russia in 1827, occupied by Turkey in 1911, and held by the Soviet Union during World War II. Nearby, in 1514, Selim I, an Ottoman sultan, defeated Shah Ismail of Persia at the battle of Chaldiran. The city is also known as Khoi.

Khwarazm: see KHOREZM.

Khyber Pass (kī'bər), narrow, steep-sided pass, 28 mi (45 km) long, winding through the Safed Koh Mts., on the Pakistan-Afghanistan border; highest point is 3,500 ft (1,067 m). It links the cities of Peshawar, Pakistan, and Kabul, Afghanistan. For centuries a trade and invasion route from central Asia, the Khyber Pass was one of the principal approaches of the armies of ALEXANDER THE GREAT, TAMERLANE, BABUR, MAHMUD OF GHAZNI, and NADIR SHAH in their invasions of India. The pass was also important in the Afghan Wars fought by the British in the 19th cent. The Khyber Pass is now traversed by a modern road, an old caravan route, and a railroad (built 1920–25), which passes through 34 tunnels and over 92 bridges and culverts. Pakistan controls the entire pass.

Kiakhta: see KYAKHTA, USSR.

Kialing, river, China: see CHIA-LING.

Kiamusze: see CHIA-MU-SSU, China.

Kian: see CHI'AN, China.

kiang: see ASS.

Kiangsi (kyăng'sē', jēäng'sē'), Mandarin *Chiang-hsi,* province (1968 est. pop. 22,000,000), c.66,000 sq mi (170,940 sq km), SE China. NAN-CH'ANG is the capital. The largely hilly and mountainous surface is drained by many rivers; the longest is the navigable Kan, which flows NE to P'o-yang lake. In Kiangsi's fertile soil and mild climate agriculture flourishes; the growing season is 9 to 11 months long, and more than 30% of the area is cultivated. Kiangsi is one of China's leading rice producers; other food crops include wheat, sweet potatoes, barley, and corn. Commerical crops are cotton, oil-bearing plants (rapeseed, sesame, soybeans, and peanuts), ramie, tea, sugarcane, tobacco, and oranges. Ten percent of the province is forested, and a lumbering industry has developed. Tung and mulberry trees are grown; a large, integrated silk complex is at Nan-ch'ang. Fish culture is important. Kiangsi is China's main source of tungsten; it also has high-grade coking coal (near P'ing-hsiang) and kaolin, which supplies the ancient porcelain industry of Ching-te-chen. Uranium is mined at Ch'üan-nan, and manganese, tin, and antimony are also found. Cities, such as Nan-ch'ang, Chiu-chiang, Kan-chou, and Fu-chou, are generally situated along the Kan River or on the province's two main railroads. The population in the north consists of largely Chinese who speak the Kan (Kiangsi) variety of Mandarin, while in the south, adjoining Kwangtung, there is a large Hakka minority. Kiangsi, linked with Kwangtung by the Meiling Pass, has been for centuries China's main north-south corridor for migration and communication. Traditionally known as Kan, Kiangsi was ruled by the Chou dynasty (722–481 B.C.); it received its present name only under the Southern Sung dynasty (A.D. 1127–1280). The province, whose present boundaries date from the Ming dynasty, passed under Manchu rule in 1650. The Chinese Communist movement began (1927) in Kiangsi; the province was a stronghold for the Communists until they were dislodged in 1934. The famous LONG MARCH began from Kiangsi. Following World War II, during which Kiangsi was largely free of Japanese forces, the province passed (1949) to the Communists.

Kiangsu (kyăng'so͞o, jēäng'so͞o'), Mandarin *Chiang-su,* province (1968 est. pop. 47,000,000), c.41,000 sq mi (106,190 sq km), E China, on the Yellow Sea. NANKING is the capital. Kiangsu consists largely of the alluvial plain of the Yangtze River and includes much of its delta; in elevation it rarely rises above sea level. The fairly warm climate, moderate rainfall, and fertile soil make Kiangsu one of the richest agricultural regions of China and one of the most densely populated. The province straddles two agricultural zones, with wheat, millet, koaliang, corn, soybeans, and peanuts cultivated in the north and rice, tea, sugarcane, and barley raised in the south. Cotton is grown along the coast (north and south) in the saline soil, which is not suited for other crops. Tea is planted in the western hills, and some experimenting with oak trees for silk culture has been initiated. Intensive land reclamation has been accomplished, with extensive dikes and the use of the raised-field system. Fish are abundant in the many lakes (of which T'ai is the most famous), in the streams and canals, and off the Yangtze delta; Kiangsu, which is known to the Chinese as "the land of rice and fish," is rich in marine products. It is also a major salt-producing area. Kiangsu is bisected by the Yangtze, which can be navigated by steamers up to 15,000 tons, and by a portion of the Grand Canal. Its first-class roads and extensive railroad system, including the busiest railway in China, the Shanghai-Nanking line, make for excellent communications. Perhaps the most prosperous province in China, Kiangsu is deficient only in timber and minerals. A major part of China's foreign trade clears through the port of SHANGHAI into Kiangsu. Shanghai, one of the world's great seaports and the chief manufacturing center of China, is in Kiangsu prov. but is administered directly by the central government. Nanking has been developed into an industrial center, with a great variety of manufactures. SU-CHOU, WU-HSI, and CHEN-CHIANG are known for their silk. Textile, food-processing, cement, and fertilizer industries are found throughout the province. Kiangsu was originally part of the Wu kingdom, and the name Wu is still its traditional name. Kiangsu received its present name, derived from Kiangning (Nanking) and Su-chou (Soochow), in 1667, when it was formed from the old Kiangnan prov. The gateway to central China, Kiangsu became the main scene of European commercial activity after the Treaty of Nanking (1842). The capture of Kiangsu in 1937 was an important phase of Japan's effort to conquer all China (see SINO-JAPANESE WAR, SECOND). Liberated by the Chinese Nationalists in 1945, Kiangsu fell to the Communists in 1949. For a time Kiangsu was administered as two regional units, North and South Kiangsu, but in 1952 the province was reunited. Many archaeological sites have been excavated in Kiangsu since 1956.

Kiangtu: see YANG-CHOU, China.

Kiaochow (kyou'chou', jēou'jō'), Mandarin *Chia-chou,* former German territory, area c.200 sq mi (520 sq km), along the southern coast of Shantung prov., China. Its administrative center was the city of Ch'ing-tao. Germany leased Kiaochow in 1898 for 99 years, but in 1914 Japan seized it. Through agreements reached at the Washington Conference in 1922, Kiaochow was returned to China.

Kiating: see LO-SHAN, China.

kibbutz: see COLLECTIVE FARM.

Kibo, peak, Africa: see KILIMANJARO.

Kibroth-hattaavah (kĭb'rŏth-hătā'āvə), unidentified desert camp. There the Israelites were punished with a plague. Num. 11.34; 33.16; Deut. 9.22.

Kibzaim (kĭb'zāĭm, kĭbzā'-): see JOKMEAM.

Kickapoo Indians (kĭk'əpo͞o), North American Indians, whose language belongs to the Algonquian branch of the Algonquian-Wakashan linguistic stock (see AMERICAN INDIAN LANGUAGES) and who in the late 17th cent. occupied SW Wisconsin. They were closely related to the SAC AND FOX INDIANS. The culture of the Kickapoo Indians was essentially that of the Eastern Woodlands area, but they also hunted buffalo, one of the few traits that the Kickapoo adopted from their neighbors in the Plains area. After the allied Kickapoo, Ojibwa, Ottawa, Potawatomi, and Sac and Fox tribes massacred (c.1769) the ILLINOIS INDIANS, they partitioned the Illinois territory. The Kickapoo, numbering about 3,000, moved south to central Illinois. Later they split in two; the Vermilion group settled on the Vermilion River, a tributary of the Wabash, and the Prairie group on the Sangamon River. The Kickapoo, a power in the region, sided with the British in the American Revolution and in the War of 1812, when they aided the Shawnee chief Tecumseh. By the Treaty of Edwardsville (1819) the Kickapoo ceded all their lands in Illinois to the United States. They were prevented from entering Missouri, which had been set aside for them, because that region was occupied by the hostile Osage Indians. Kanakuk, a prophet, exhorted the Kickapoo to remain where they were, promising that if they avoided liquor and infractions of the white man's law, they would inherit a land of plenty. His pleas were futile, and the Kickapoo, after aiding the Sac and Fox in the Black Hawk War, were forced to leave Illinois. The Kickapoo moved first to Missouri and then to Kansas. A large group, dissatisfied with conditions on the reservation, went (c.1852) to Mexico, where they became known as the Mexican Kickapoo. After the U.S. Civil War, the Mexican Kickapoo proved so constant an annoyance to border settlements that the United States made efforts to induce them to return. The negotiations were successful, and a number returned to settle (1873-74) on a reservation in Oklahoma. The remaining Mexican Kickapoo are settled on a reservation in Chihuahua, Mexico. The Kickapoo living on reservations in Kansas and Oklahoma number some 1,000. See R. E. Ritzenthaler, *The Mexican Kickapoo Indians* (1956, repr. 1970); A. M. Gibson, *The Kickapoos* (1963).

Kicking Horse, river of SE British Columbia, Canada, rising in the Rocky Mts., and flowing SW and NW to Golden, where it enters the Columbia River. Its course is rapid, with several high falls. **Kicking Horse Pass,** 5,339 ft (1,627 m) high, NW of Lake Louise, in Banff National Park, connects the Bow River with the Kicking Horse and is one of the principal rail and highway passes over the Continental Divide.

Kid, Thomas: see KYD, THOMAS.

Kidd, Benjamin, 1858-1916, English social philosopher. His most noted work, *Social Evolution* (1894), sets forth his doctrine of the constant strife between individual and public interest. His works also include *Control of the Tropics* (1898) and *The Principles of Western Civilization* (1902).

Kidd, William, 1645?-1701, British privateer and pirate, known as Captain Kidd. He went to sea in his youth and later settled in New York, where he married and owned property. In 1691 he was rewarded for his services against French privateers. While in London in 1695 he was commissioned by the earl of Bellomont, recently appointed governor of New York, as a privateer to defend English ships from pirates in the Red Sea and the Indian Ocean. In 1696, Kidd set sail for New York and from there to Madagascar. Disease, mutiny, and failure to take prizes apparently caused him to turn pirate. Returning (1699) to the West Indies with his richest prize, the Armenian *Quedagh Merchant*, he learned of piracy charges against him. He sailed to New York to clear himself by claiming that the vessels he had attacked were lawful prizes. He was arrested and taken to London, where in 1701 he was tried on five charges of piracy and one of murder. The trial was complicated by the fact that four Whig peers who had backed him were politically embarrassed by his career. He was convicted and hanged. The barbaric cruelty and buried treasure of Captain Kidd are unsubstantiated bits of the legends about him. The Kidd legend has often been referred to in literature, for instance in Edgar Allen Poe's *Gold Bug* and Robert Louis Stevenson's *Treasure Island.* See D. C. Seitz, ed., *The Tryal of Captain William Kidd* (1935); biographies by W. H. Bonner (1947) and D. M. Hinrichs (1955).

Kidder, Alfred Vincent, 1885-1963, American archaeologist, b. Marquette, Mich., grad. Harvard (B.A. 1908; Ph.D. 1914). From 1915 to 1929 he conducted excavations at Pecos, N.Mex., for the Phillips Academy, Andover, Mass. This research is considered to have laid the foundation for modern archaeological field methods. In the late 1920s he started the Pecos conferences for archaeologists and ethnologists. As an associate in charge of archaeological investigations (1927-29) and as chairman of the division of historical research (1929-50) at the Carnegie Institution, he conducted a broad-scale research program in the Guatemalan highlands which established the framework of Mayan stratigraphy. In 1939 he became honorary curator of Southwestern American archaeology at the Peabody Museum, Harvard. His writings include *Introduction to the Study of Southwestern Archaeology* (1924), regarded as the first comprehensive archaeological study of a New World area; *The Pottery of Pecos* (2 vol., 1931-36); *The Artifacts of Pecos* (1932); and *Pecos, New Mexico: Archaeological Notes* (1958). See biography by R. B. Woodbury (1973).

Kidderminster, municipal borough (1971 pop. 47,255), Worcestershire, W central England. It is a market town. Kidderminster carpets have been produced since 1735; other industries include spinning, dyeing, metal forging, and the production of beet sugar. In 1974, Kidderminster became part of the new nonmetropolitan county of Hereford and Worcester.

Kiddush (kĭd'əsh) [Heb.,=sanctification], Jewish ceremonial blessing indicating the beginning of the Sabbath or any other Hebrew festival. Kiddush is also said at mealtime and consists of a prayer of benediction over the occasion and the wine or bread.

kidnapping, in law, the unlawful and willful taking away of a person by force, threat, or deceit with intent to cause him to be detained against his will. Kidnapping is usually done for RANSOM but may be for political or other purposes. A parent whose legal rights to custody of a child have been taken away can be guilty of the crime if he takes his own child. Consent of the kidnapped person is a defense, unless he was legally incompetent at the time (e.g., a minor or an insane person). The crime differs from abduction, in that the intent of sexual intercourse is not required, and from false imprisonment, in which there is no attempt to abduct. Under English common law it was only a MISDEMEANOR, but in most states of the United States it is punishable by death or life imprisonment if there are no extenuating circumstances. The kidnapping and murder of the son of Charles A. Lindbergh in 1932 stirred public sentiment and led to a Federal statute prescribing very severe penalties for persons transporting the victims of kidnapping across state or national boundaries. The practice of kidnapping, in the wider and not strictly legal sense, has been known since the beginnings of man's history. It was common as a method for procuring slaves, and it has been prominent as a more or less systematic means for groups of brigands and revolutionary bands to obtain money through ransom. In the 1970s, kidnapping became a common tactic of revolutionary groups. Public officials, businessmen, and diplomats were held for ransom or as hostages whose safe release was dependent on the freeing of political prisoners.

kidney, artificial, mechanical device capable of assuming the functions ordinarily performed by the kidneys. In treating cases of kidney failure a tube is inserted into an artery in the patient's arm, and the blood is channeled through a cellophane tube immersed in a bath containing all the normal blood chemicals except urea and other metabolic waste products. When the blood flows through the tube the poisonous wastes pass out through the cellophane and into the bath because of the difference in concentration of the solutions on either side of the cellophane membrane. The purified blood is returned to the body through a vein in the arm. This process of blood purification, called hemodialysis (see DIALYSIS), is usually repeated twice a week and requires several hours to complete.

kidneys: see URINARY SYSTEM.

Kidron (kĭd'rŏn) or **Cedron** (sē'-), brook or field, the present-day Qidron (Jordan), E of Jerusalem between the city and the Mount of Olives. 2 Sam. 15.23; 1 Kings 2.37; 2 Kings 23.4, 6,12; John 18.1. See also JEHOSHAPHAT.

Kieft, Willem (vĭl'əm kĕft), 1597-1647, Dutch director general of NEW NETHERLAND. Arriving in New Amsterdam in 1638 to succeed Wouter VAN TWILLER, Kieft immediately assumed absolute control. His arbitrary rule and tactless handling of the Indians resulted in almost continuous Indian warfare during his administration. He was replaced by Peter STUYVESANT (1647) and was lost at sea on his way to Holland.

Kiel (kēl), city (1970 pop. 271,719), capital of Schleswig-Holstein, N West Germany, on Kiel Bay, an arm of the Baltic Sea. Situated at the head of the Kiel Canal, the city was Germany's chief naval base from 1871 to 1945, when the naval installations were dismantled. Kiel is now a shipping and industrial center, with large shipyards and factories that manufacture textiles, processed foods, and printed materials. Chartered in 1242, Kiel joined the Hanseatic League in 1284. It became the residence of the dukes of Holstein. Kiel passed to Denmark in 1773; with Holstein it was annexed by Prussia in 1866. The sailors' mutiny that began at Kiel at the end of World War I touched off a socialist revolution in Germany. In World War II the city suffered severe damage from Allied air attacks. The city is the seat of a university (founded 1665) and several museums. The sailing and yachting events of the 1972 Olympic summer games were held there.

Kiel Canal, artificial waterway, 61 mi (98 km) long, in Schleswig-Holstein, N West Germany, connecting the North Sea with the Baltic Sea. At sea level, the canal extends from Kiel on the Baltic to Brunsbüttelkoog at the mouth of the Elbe River. Locks at each end of the canal minimize tidal variation. Built (1887-95) to facilitate movement of the German fleet, the Kiel Canal was widened and deepened from 1905 to 1914. Large oceangoing ships can pass through the canal. Because of its great military and commercial importance the canal was internationalized by the Treaty of Versailles (1919). Hitler repudiated its international status in 1936. The canal is also known as the Kaiser Wilhelm Canal, for William II of Germany, and as the North Sea-Baltic Canal (Ger. *Nord-Ostsee-Kanal*).

Kielce (kyĕl'tsĕ), city (1970 pop. 126,000), S central Poland. It is a railway junction and manufacturing center where metals, agricultural machinery, and chemicals are produced. It also has marble quarries. Founded in 1173, Kielce obtained municipal rights in the 14th cent. It belonged to the bishops of Kraków until 1789. The city passed to Austria in 1795 and to Russia in 1815 and reverted to Poland in 1919. Its most notable buildings are a 12th-century cathedral and a 17th-century palace.

Kielland, Alexander Lange (äləksän'dər läng'ə khĕl'län), 1849-1906, Norwegian novelist, short-story writer, and playwright. Two early volumes of short stories—*Tales of Two Countries* (1879, tr. 1891) and *Norse Tales and Sketches* (1897)—placed him among the important realists. His witty and ironic novels, written with the purpose of social reform, include *Skipper Worse* (1882, tr. 1885). His writing was greatly influenced by George BRANDES.

Kierkegaard, Søren (sö'rən kyĕr'kəgôr), 1813-55, Danish philosopher and religious thinker. Kierkegaard's outwardly uneventful life in Copenhagen contrasted with his intensive inner examination of self and society, which resulted in many diversified and profound writings; their dominant theme is that "truth is subjectivity." Kierkegaard argued that in religion the important thing is not truth as objective fact but rather the individual's relationship to it. Thus it is not enough to believe the Christian doctrine; one must also live it. He attacked what he felt to be the sterile metaphysics of G. W. Hegel and the worldliness of the Danish church. His writings fall into two categories—the aesthetic and the religious. The aesthetic works, which include *Either/Or* (1843), *Philosophical Fragments* (1844), *Stages on Life's Way* (1845), and *The Concluding Unscientific Postscript* (1846), were all published under pseudonyms and interpret human existence through the eyes of various poetically delineated characters. In those works Kierkegaard developed an "existential dialectic" in opposition to the Hegelian dialectic, and described the various stages of existence as the aesthetic, the ethical, and the religious. As the individual advances through these stages he becomes increasingly more aware of his relationship to God. This awareness leads to despair as the individual realizes the antithesis between temporal existence and eternal truth. The specifically religious writings include *Works of Love* (1847) and *Training in Christianity* (1850). Kierkegaard also kept an extensive journal that contains many of his deepest insights. Although practically unknown outside of Denmark during the 19th cent., he later exerted a tremendous influence upon both contemporary Protestant theology and the philosophic movement known as EXISTENTIALISM. His major works have been translated into English. See James Collins, *The Mind of Kierkegaard* (1953, repr. 1965); P. P. Rohde, *Søren Kierkegaard* (1963); Louis Mackey, *Kierkegaard* (1971).

kieselguhr (kē'zəlgo͝or"): see DIATOM.

Kiev (kē'ĕf, Rus. kē'yəf), Ukrainian *Kyyiv,* Rus. *Kiyev,* city (1970 pop. 1,632,000), capital of the Ukrainian Soviet Socialist Republic and of Kiev oblast, SW European USSR, a port on the Dnepr River. The largest city of the Ukraine and the third largest of the USSR, Kiev is a leading industrial, commercial, and cultural center. Food processing (notably the processing of beet sugar), metallurgy, and the manufacture of machinery, machine tools, rolling stock, chemicals, building materials, and textiles are the major industries. Known to Russians as the "mother of cities," Kiev is one of the oldest towns in Europe. It probably existed as a commercial center as early as the 5th cent. A Slavic settlement on the great trade route between Scandinavia and Constantinople, Kiev was tributary to the Khazars when the VARANGIANS under Oleg established themselves there in 882. Under Oleg's successors it became the capital of medieval

Kievan Russia (the first Russian state) and was a leading European cultural and commercial center. It was also an early seat of Russian Christianity. The city reached its apogee in the 11th cent., but by the late 12th cent. it had begun to decline. From 1240, when it was devastated by the Mongols, until the 14th cent., the city paid tribute to the Golden Horde. Kiev then passed under the control of Lithuania, which in 1569 was united with Poland. With the establishment of the Kievan Academy in 1632, the city became a center of Ukrainian learning and scholarship. In 1648, when the Ukrainian Cossacks under Bohdan Chmielnicki rose against Poland, Kiev became for a brief period the center of a Ukrainian state. After the Ukraine's union with Russia in 1654, however, the city was acquired (1686) by Moscow. In Jan., 1918, Kiev became the capital of the newly proclaimed Ukrainian republic; but in the ensuing civil war (1918–20), it was occupied in succession by German, White Russian, Polish, and Soviet troops. In 1934 the capital of the Ukrainian SSR was transferred from Kharkov to Kiev. German forces held the city during World War II and massacred thousands of its inhabitants, including 50,000 Jews. Postwar reconstruction of the heavily damaged city was not completed until c.1960. Lying amid hills along the Dnepr and filled with gardens and parks, Kiev is one of Europe's most beautiful cities, as well as a treasury of medieval art and architecture. Its most outstanding buildings include the Tithes Church, the ruins of the Golden Gate (11th cent.), and the 11th-century Cathedral of St. Sophia (now a museum), which was modeled on Hagia Sophia in Constantinople and contains splendid mosaics, frescoes, and icons. The Uspensky Cathedral, virtually destroyed during World War II, has been fully restored. The celebrated Lavra cave monastery (11th cent.) is now a museum and a sacred place of pilgrimage. The St. Vladimir Cathedral (9th cent.) is famed for its murals. Among the city's educational and cultural institutions are the Univ. of Kiev (1833) and the Ukrainian Academy of Sciences (1918).

Kievan Russia (kē'ĕfən), medieval state of the Eastern Slavs. It was the earliest predecessor of the present-day Union of Soviet Socialist Republics. Flourishing from the 10th to the 13th cent., it included nearly all of present-day UKRAINE and BELORUSSIA and part of NW European USSR, extending as far N as Novgorod and Vladimir. According to the Russian

Kievan Russia (c.1000)

Primary Chronicle, a medieval history, the Varangian RURIK established himself at Novgorod c.862 and founded a dynasty. His successor, OLEG (d. c.912), shifted his attention to the south, seized Kiev (c.879), and established the new Kievan state. The Varangians were also known as *Rus* or *Rhos*; it is possible that this name was early extended to the Slavs of the Kievan state, which became known as Kievan Rus. Other theories trace the name *Rus* to a Slavic origin. Oleg united the Eastern Slavs and freed them from the suzerainty of the KHAZARS. His successors were IGOR (reigned 912–45) and Igor's widow, St. Olga, who was regent until about 962. Under Olga's son, SVIATOSLAV (d. 972), the Khazars were crushed, and Kievan power was extended to the lower Volga and N Caucasus. Christianity was introduced by VLADIMIR I (reigned 980–1015), who adopted (c.989) Greek Orthodoxy from the Byzantines. The reign (1019–54) of Vladimir's son, YAROSLAV the Wise, represented the political and cultural apex of Kievan Russia. After his death the state was divided into principalities ruled by his sons; this soon led to civil strife. A last effort for unity was made by VLADIMIR II (reigned 1113–25), but the perpetual princely strife and the devastating raids of the nomadic CUMANS soon ended the supremacy of Kiev. In the middle of the 12th cent. a number of local centers of power developed: Galich in the west, Novgorod in the north, Vladimir-Suzdal (see VLADIMIR) in the northwest, and Kiev in the south. In 1169, Kiev was sacked and pillaged by the armies of Andrei Bogolubsky of Suzdal, and the final blow to the Kievan state came with the Mongol invasion (1237–40). The economy of the Kievan state was based on agriculture and on extensive trade with Byzantium, the Orient, and Scandinavia. Culture, as well as religion, was drawn from Byzantium; CHURCH SLAVONIC was the literary and liturgical language of the state. According to Soviet and some Western scholars the history of the Kievan state is the common heritage of modern Russians, Ukrainians, and Belorussians, although their existence as separate peoples has been traced as far back as the 12th cent. See S. H. Cross, ed., *The Russian Primary Chronicle* (tr. 1953, repr. 1973); George Vernadsky, *Kievan Russia* (vol. II of *A History of Russia,* 2d ed. 1973).

Kigali (kēgä'lē), town (1970 est. pop. 60,000), capital of Kigali prefecture and of Rwanda, central Rwanda. It is the country's main administrative and economic center. The town has an international airport. Iron ore (cassiterite) is mined nearby.

Kigoma-Ujiji (kēgō'mä'-o͞ojē'jē), municipality (1967 pop. 21,369), capital of Kigoma prov., W Tanzania, a port on Lake Tanganyika. It is the terminus of the railroad from Dar es Salaam (completed 1914) and is connected by ship with Zaïre and Burundi. There are fisheries. Ujiji and Kigoma were important settlements of Arab and Swahili ivory and slave traders between c.1850 and c.1890. The explorer Henry M. Stanley successfully ended his search for David Livingstone at Ujiji on Nov. 10, 1871. The region was occupied by the Germans in the 1890s. Kigoma and Ujiji were combined into a single municipality in the 1960s.

Kikuyu (kĭko͞o'yo͞o), Bantu-speaking people, numbering over 1.5 million, forming the largest tribal group in Kenya. The Kikuyu live in the highlands NE of Nairobi. Before the British conquest they were the most influential people in the country. During the 1950s, under the leadership of Jomo KENYATTA, the Kikuyu fought the British colonialists in what was known as the Mau Mau Emergency. Although the Kikuyu traditionally lived in separate family homesteads, most were moved into villages during the rebellion. After the removal of the colonists, a large number chose to remain in the villages. The Kikuyu economy centers mainly around agriculture, with little or no hunting or fishing. See H. E. Lambert, *Kikuyu Social and Political Institutions* (1956, repr. 1965); R. M. Gatheru, *Child of Two Worlds* (1964, repr. 1972).

Kilauea (kē'läwā'ə), crater, 3,646 ft (1,111 m) deep, central Hawaii island, Hawaii, on the southeastern slope of Mauna Loa in HAWAII VOLCANOES NATIONAL PARK. One of the largest active craters in the world, Kilauea has a circumference of c.8 mi (13 km) and is surrounded by a wall of volcanic rock 200 to 500 ft (61–152 m) high. In its floor is Halemaumau, a fiery pit. The usual level of the lake of molten lava is c.740 ft (230 m) below the pit's rim.

Kildare, James Fitzgerald, 20th **earl of** (kĭldâr'), 1722–73, Irish nobleman. He sat in the Irish House of Commons from 1741 until 1744, when he succeeded as earl of Kildare. He was created Viscount Leinster (in the English peerage) in 1747 and duke of Leinster in 1766. He emerged as a popular hero when he successfully opposed attempts to divert surplus Irish revenues to the British crown. He became lord deputy of Ireland in 1756.

Kildare, Thomas Fitzgerald, 10th **earl of,** 1513–37, Irish nobleman, called Silken Thomas. When his father, the 9th earl and lord deputy of Ireland, was summoned to London on charges of maladministration in 1534, Thomas became vice deputy. The same year, hearing the rumor that his father had been executed (he actually died later in the Tower of London), he renounced his allegiance to King Henry VIII and rose in rebellion. Thomas was excommunicated for the murder of his enemy, the archbishop of Dublin. The rebellion was crushed the following year, and Thomas eventually surrendered and was hanged in London with five of his uncles.

Kildare, county (1971 pop. 71,522), 654 sq mi (1,694 sq km), E central Republic of Ireland. The county town is Naas, the ancient seat of the kings of Leinster. The region is a flat plain, containing the greater portion of the Bog of Allen and the CURRAGH. The principal rivers are the Liffey, the Greese, and the Barrow. Agriculture is the chief occupation; the breeding of racehorses is significant. The county is named for the oak (*Cill Dara*) under which St. Bridget constructed her cell. There are many pre-Christian and early Christian remains.

Kilham, Alexander (kĭl'əm), 1762–98, English Methodist minister, founder of the Methodist New Connection. He took a leading part in Methodist affairs after the death of John Wesley, advocating separation from the Church of England (see METHODISM). He supported the right of preachers to administer the Lord's Supper and sought to have powers of church government distributed between clerical and lay members. For a series of pamphlets that he wrote, he was brought to trial at the conference of 1796 and expelled from the connection. In 1798 he and three other preachers formed the Methodist New Connection, the first group of Methodists to break away.

Kilimanjaro (kĭl"ĭmənjä'rō), highest mountain of Africa, NE Tanzania. An extinct volcano, it rises in two snow-capped peaks, Kibo (19,340 ft/5,895 m) and Mawenzi (17,564 ft/5,354 m), which are joined by a broad saddle (alt. c.15,000 ft/4,600 m). Coffee and plantains are the chief crops raised on Kilimanjaro's intensively cultivated lower southern slopes.

Kilindini: see MOMBASA, Kenya.

Kilkenny (kĭlkĕn'ē), county (1971 pop. 61,811), 796 sq mi (2,062 sq km), S Republic of Ireland. The county town is KILKENNY. It is mainly a rolling plain, part of the central plain of Ireland, with low hills to the south. The principal rivers are the Suir, the Nore, and the Barrow. Grains and vegetables are grown, and livestock is raised. There are food-processing and brewing industries. In the northeast is a large anthracite coal field. Castlecomer is the coal-mining center. Kilkenny is roughly coextensive with the ancient kingdom of OSSORY. It is rich in antiquities.

Kilkenny, urban district (1971 pop. 10,292), county town of Co. Kilkenny, S Republic of Ireland, on the Nore River. The districts of Irishtown and Englishtown, separated by a stream, were legally united in 1843. Strife between the inhabitants of the two districts, to the near destruction of both, may have given rise to the stories of the Kilkenny cats, who ate each other up. A third district is High Town. Kilkenny was the seat of the kings of OSSORY. The first earl of Pembroke founded a castle in the 12th cent. (restored c.1835) overlooking the Nore. Parliaments and assemblies were held in the 14th, 16th, and 17th cent. Among noted pupils at the Protestant school of Kilkenny were Swift, Bishop Berkeley, and Congreve. In Irishtown is the great Cathedral of St. Canice (13th cent.), the seat of the Protestant dioceses of the United Dioceses of Ossory, Ferns, and Leighlin. The Roman Catholic Cathedral of St. Mary (seat of the diocese of Ossory), a round tower, and remains of Dominican and Franciscan monasteries (mostly 13th cent.) are noteworthy. The Statute of Kilkenny (1366) forbade the English settlers from marrying the Irish inhabitants, speaking Irish, or wearing Irish dress.

Killarney, urban district (1971 pop. 7,179), Co. Kerry, SW Republic of Ireland. The town, which has footwear and other industries, is a tourist center for the three Lakes of Killarney. They occupy a wooded valley stretching south between the mountains. Lough Leane or Lower Lake is the largest; it has about 30 islands. The largest island is the "sweet Innisfallen" of Thomas Moore's poem. On the island are the ruins of an abbey founded c.600 by St. Finian. There the Annals of Innisfallen, an important historical document, were written (11th–14th cent.). The ruins of the 15th-century Muckross Abbey lie on the shore of Muckross Lake (Middle Lake or Lough Torc), which has picturesque waterfalls and limestone caves. Upper Lake is the third lake. In the town is the cathedral of the diocese of Kerry, designed by A. W. N. Pugin.

killdeer, common North American shorebird related to the PLOVER and the SANDPIPER. It is about 10 in. (25 cm) in length and its plumage is grayish brown with a double black band across a white breast. Its simple nest is a depression in the soil or gravel. The killdeer is classified in the phylum CHORDATA, subphylum Vertebrata, class Aves, order Charadriiformes, family Charadriidae.

Killeen (kĭlēn'), city (1970 pop. 35,507), Bell co., central Texas, in a ranching and cotton region; inc. 1893.

The city has some varied light manufacturing, but adjacent Fort Hood is the major source of employment. Founded in 1882 and named for a Santa Fe RR official, Killeen remained a small farming and ranching village until the establishment (1942) of Camp Hood. The camp's redesignation (1950) as a fort with a permanent status spurred a great population growth in the city. A junior college is in Killeen, and nearby Belton and Stillhouse Hollow lakes provide recreational facilities.

killer whale, or **grampus,** a large, rapacious marine mammal, *Orcinus orca,* of the DOLPHIN family. Male killer whales may reach a length of 30 ft (9 m) and females half that length. The killer whale is black above, with a sharply contrasting white oval patch around each eye; its belly is white with white markings projecting up along the animal's sides. It has a high, triangular dorsal fin midway between head and tail, and broad, paddle-shaped flippers. The killer whale is worldwide in distribution. It is a swift and ferocious animal, armed with more than four dozen sharp teeth, and is the only cetacean (see WHALE) that feeds regularly on birds or mammals. Killer whales eat seals, sea birds, and fish, and in packs they will even attack larger whales. The female gives birth to a single calf, up to 7 ft (2.1 m) long, following a gestation period of approximately one year. Females mature in 6 to 7 years, males in 12. They are classified in the phylum CHORDATA, subphylum Vertebrata, class Mammalia, order Cetacea, family Delphinidae.

Killiecrankie, Pass of (kĭlĭkrăng'ke), wooded pass, Tayside region, central Scotland, through which the river Garry flows, near Pitlochry. There Jacobite Highlanders defeated (1689) a large government force under Hugh MacKay and the Jacobite leader, Viscount Dundee, was killed.

killifish, northern representative, especially the genus *Fundulus,* of the Cyprinodontidae or toothed minnows, a family that includes also the topminnows and many popular aquarium fishes (e.g., the guppy or rainbow fish, *Lebistes reticulatus)* among its brightly colored tropical species. Most North American toothed minnows are oviparous, i.e., bearing young hatched from eggs, and some are quite colorful; however, the tropical viviparous species (i.e., bearing live young) are preferred for aquariums, since they are easier to raise. Killifishes average from 2 to 4 in. (5-10 cm) in length and have compressed bodies, small mouths with projecting lower jaws, unforked tails, and large scales. They live in ponds, streams, ditches, and salt marshes throughout the United States and feed on insect larvae, crustaceans, and small water plants. The banded killifish is found in the Mississippi basin; the common killifish (5 in./12.5 cm) is an eastern species. Guppies can survive temperatures of up to 100°F (38°C) as can certain topminnows of the W United States. The greenish-gray female guppy (1½ in./3.75 cm) produces from 12 to 25 live offspring every few weeks; in captivity they must be separated from the cannibalistic adults. The rainbow colors of the male guppy (1 in./2.5 cm) are marked with black spots and bars. Like the guppy, the 2-in. (5-cm) *Gambusia,* a topminnow of the S Atlantic and the Gulf, bears live young and is important in controlling mosquitoes, on whose larvae both the guppy and the minnow feed. Killifishes are classified in the phylum CHORDATA, subphylum Vertebrata, class Osteichthyes, order Cyprinodontiformes, family Cyprinodontidae.

Killigrew, Thomas, 1612-83, English dramatist and theater manager, b. London. Before the closing of the theaters by the Puritans in 1642, he wrote several tragicomedies, including *The Prisoners* and *Claracilla.* His most popular play was the coarse comedy, *The Parson's Wedding* (1637). In 1647 he followed Prince Charles into exile and at the Restoration was rewarded by being made groom of the bedchamber to Charles II and chamberlain to the queen. Charles granted to Killigrew and to Sir William D'Avenant exclusive patents in 1660 to build two new theaters and to form companies of players. Killigrew was first to establish his company, the King's Servants, at Gibbon's tennis court, Vere St.; three years later he moved to his new building, the Theatre Royal, in Drury Lane. He produced garbled versions of Shakespeare, the plays of Dryden and Aphra Behn, and his own plays. See study by A. B. Harbage (1930, repr. 1967).

Killingly (kĭl'ĭng-lē), town (1970 pop. 13,573), Windham co., NE Conn., on the Quinebaug River and the R.I. border, in a farm area; settled 1693, inc. 1708. Once a great textile town, it still has some textile manufactures.

Killingworth, rural town (1970 pop. 2,435), S Conn., bordered on the W by the Hammonasset River and on the S by Clinton; organized c.1667. It has 18th-century houses, a noted church (1817), and Ely House, in which Longfellow supposedly wrote "The Birds of Killingworth."

Kill Van Kull (kĭl văn kŭl), channel, 4 mi (6.4 km) long and .5 mi (.8 km) wide, connecting Upper New York Bay with Newark Bay, between Bayonne, N.J., and Staten Island, N.Y. It is the main route for ships docking at Port Elizabeth and Port Newark, N.J. Bayonne Bridge (1931; 1,652 ft/504 m long), the world's longest steel-arch bridge, spans the channel.

Killy, Jean-Claude (zhäN-klōd kēlē'), 1943–, French skier. He grew up at his father's ski resort and began skiing at the age of 3. At 18 he was a senior member of the French national team. A daring athlete with superb reflexes, Killy has reached speeds of more than 80 mi (129 km) per hr. The dominant male in the sport from 1966 to 1968, Killy won the triple Olympic crown (downhill, slalom, and giant slalom) in the 1968 Winter Olympics, the second person ever to do so. A World Cup winner in 1966-67 and 1967-68, he also led the French team to world championships in those years. In 1968, Killy retired to race automobiles and pursue commercial ventures, but he returned in 1972, becoming a professional skier.

Kilmainham (kĭlmān'əm), suburb of Dublin, Co. Dublin, E Republic of Ireland. The commander of the British forces in Ireland had his headquarters there. Parnell was imprisoned there until he agreed (1882) to the "Kilmainham Treaty" with the English government (see PARNELL, Charles Stewart).

Kilmarnock (kĭlmär'nək), burgh (1971 pop. 48,785), Ayrshire, SW Scotland. An industrial town in a mining region, it has industries that manufacture carpets, hosiery, farm and hydraulic machinery, whiskey, and shoes. Its textile industry (bonnets) dates from 1603. Robert Burns's first poems were published there in 1786; the Burns Monument has a museum. In 1975, Kilmarnock became part of the Strathclyde region.

Kilmer, Joyce, 1886-1918, American poet, b. New Brunswick, N.J., educated at Rutgers College and Columbia (B.A., 1908). He is known chiefly for his poem "Trees," in *Trees and Other Poems* (1914).

kiln (kĭl, kĭln), furnace for firing pottery and enamels, for making brick, charcoal, lime, and cement, for roasting ores, and for drying various substances (e.g., lumber, chemicals). Kilns may be updraft or downdraft; round, conical, annular, or rectangular; arranged for intermittent or continuous firing; and of the muffle (double-wall) or direct-contact type, as required. Rotary kilns are much used in continuous processes, including cement manufacturing and the drying of granular materials. They consist of long tubes lying almost horizontally that are rotated slowly as heat is applied to the material being treated inside the tubes. The fuel used may be electricity, oil, gas, or coal. The temperature of firing and the length of time required depend on the design of the kiln and the type of material being fired.

kilogram, abbr. kg, fundamental unit of mass in the METRIC SYSTEM, defined as the mass of the International Prototype Kilogram, a platinum-iridium cylinder kept at Sèvres, France, near Paris. Copies of this standard are deposited at bureaus of standards throughout the world, and other units of mass are defined in terms of it. When the metric system was originally devised, the kilogram was defined so that 1,000 cubic centimeters (1 cubic decimeter) of pure water has a mass of exactly 1 kilogram.

kilowatt: see WATT.

Kilpatrick, William Heard, 1871-1965, American philosopher, b. White Plains, Ga., grad. Mercer College, 1891, Ph.D. Columbia, 1912, and studied at Johns Hopkins Univ. He taught at Teachers College, Columbia, from 1909, becoming professor of the philosophy of education in 1918; he retired in 1938. Acclaimed as the great popularizer of the philosophy of John DEWEY, Kilpatrick rejected organized subjects; his child-centered emphasis, however, represented a sharp divergence from the position of Dewey. Among his writings are *Source Book in the Philosophy of Education* (1923), *Foundations of Method* (1925), and *Education and the Social Crisis* (1932).

Kilung: see CHI-LUNG, Taiwan.

Kimball, Fiske (Sidney Fiske Kimball), 1888-1955, American architect and writer, b. Newton, Mass. He was professor of architecture and fine arts at the Univ. of Michigan (1912-19) and of art and architecture at the Univ. of Virginia (1919-23) and was in charge of the fine arts department, New York Univ. (1923-25). From 1925 until his retirement in 1955 he was director of the Philadelphia Museum of Art and was responsible for the acquisition of many important collections. Much of his architectural work consisted of the restoration of old houses, e.g., of Monticello, the Jefferson home, near Charlottesville, and Stratford, the seat of the Lees, both in Virginia. With G. H. Edgell he wrote *A History of Architecture* (1918). He was also the author of *Domestic Architecture of the American Colonies* (1922), *American Architecture* (1928), and *The Creation of the Rococo* (1943).

Kimball, Sumner Increase, 1834-1923, organizer of the U.S. Life-Saving Service, b. Lebanon, Maine. A lawyer, he became (1871) head of the revenue marine service of the Treasury Dept., and his investigations into shipwrecks along the Atlantic coast led to a reorganization of LIFESAVING methods. Kimball commanded the Life-Saving Service from its inception in 1878 until it became part of the U.S. coast guard in 1915. He wrote *Organization and Methods of the U.S. Life Saving Service* (1889) and *Joshua James, Life Saver* (1909).

Kimball, William Wirt, 1848-1930, American naval officer, b. Paris, Maine, grad. Annapolis, 1869. One of the first to serve on torpedo boats, he did much in the 1880s to develop magazine and machine guns, and he designed armored cars. In the '90s he did important work in the development of the submarine, and in the Spanish-American War, having organized the navy's first torpedo-boat flotilla, he commanded the Atlantic torpedo-boat flotilla. Kimball was made rear admiral in 1908, and in 1909 he commanded the expeditionary forces sent to Nicaragua. He retired from active duty in 1910.

Kimberley (kĭm'bərlē), town (1971 pop. 7,641), SE British Columbia, Canada. At an elevation of more than 3,000 ft (914 m), it is the site of the Sullivan mine, where large quantities of silver, lead, and zinc are mined.

Kimberley (kĭm'bərlē), city (1970 pop. 113,681), Cape Prov., central South Africa. The city is primarily a diamond-mining center, although textiles, construction materials, and machinery are manufactured. The city is also an important railroad junction. Kimberley was founded in 1871 when diamonds were discovered on a nearby farm. The De Beers Consolidated Mines, organized by Cecil RHODES, assumed control of the diamond fields in 1888. In 1899-1900, during the SOUTH AFRICAN WAR, the city was besieged by BOER forces. Northern Cape Technical College, Alexander McGregor Memorial Museum, and the Duggan-Cronin Bantu Gallery are in Kimberley.

Kimberley, geographical area, c.139,000 sq mi (360,010 sq km), Western Australia, NW Australia. The Kimberley Goldfield was the site (1882) of the first major Western Australian gold strike. Little gold was mined after 1900.

kimberlite: see DIAMOND.

Kimhi (kĭm'hē) or **Kimchi** (kĭm'khē), family of Jewish scholars and grammarians in Spain and France. **Joseph ben Isaac Kimhi,** 1105?-1170?, besides writing a Bible commentary, making numerous translations, and writing poems of merit, introduced the long and short divisions of Hebrew vowels (increasing their number from 7 to 10) and elaborated the passive verb forms. He is the author of what may be the first European Jewish anti-Christian polemic, *Sefer Ha-Berit.* **Moses Kimhi,** d. 1190?, son of Joseph, wrote *The Paths of Knowledge,* a grammatical textbook, which is a mine of philological information and which was heavily used by the 16th cent. Christian Hebraists. **David Kimhi,** known as Redak, 1160?-1235?, another son, wrote *Mikhlol* [completeness], long the leading Hebrew grammar, *The Book of Roots,* a dictionary of the Bible, and *The Pen of the Scribe,* a manual of punctuation. His learned and lucid commentaries on the Old Testament were included in the standard editions of the Hebrew Bible. The Latin translations of his commentaries greatly influenced Christian translators of the Bible.

Kim Il Sung (kēm ēl sŏŏng), 1912–, North Korean political leader, chief of state of the Democratic People's Republic of Korea (1948–); originally named Kim Sung Chu. While fighting Japanese occupation forces in the 1930s, he renamed himself Kim Il Sung after a famous Korean guerrilla leader of the early 20th cent. He was trained in Moscow before World War II, and in 1945 he became chairman of the Soviet-sponsored People's Committee of North Korea. In 1948, when the People's Republic was established, he became its first premier. Between 1950 and 1953 he led his nation in the KOREAN WAR. In 1972 he relinquished the premiership, but retained his position as North Korea's leader by assuming the presidency under a revised constitution. Under his rule, North Korea increased its military forces, embarked on a program of industrialization, and maintained close relations with both Communist China and the Soviet Union.

Kinabalu or **Kinibalu, Mount** (both: kĭn″əbəlo͞o′), peak, 13,455 ft (4,101 m) high, N Sabah, Malaysia, NE of Kota Kinabalu; highest peak on Borneo.

Kinah (kī′nə), unidentified town, extreme S Palestine. Joshua 15.22.

Kincardine (kĭnkär′dĭn, kĭng-), town (1971 pop. 3,239), S Ont., Canada, on Lake Huron, W of Walkerton. It is a resort, with knitting and woolen mills and a furniture factory. Just to the north is Douglas Point, the site of a nuclear power plant.

Kincardineshire (kĭngkär′dĭnshĭr), county (1971 pop. 26,050), 379 sq mi (982 sq km), E Scotland; sometimes called the Mearns. STONEHAVEN is the county town. The Grampian mountains, which extend into the county, rise to 2,555 ft (779 m) at Mt. Battock and slope to a fertile lowland between the Dee and the North Esk rivers behind the rocky coast. Pastoral agriculture (sheep and dairy and beef cattle) is more important than cultivation (oats, barley, and potatoes). Fishing is pursued from North Sea ports. Woolens, whiskey, and leather goods are made at Stonehaven; Johnshaven and Inverbervie have flax-spinning factories. Kincardineshire, long inhabited by Picts, was occupied briefly by the Romans. Remains of their forts and of Pictish castles are found in the county. Dunnottar Castle was a seat of the earls marischal of Scotland. In 1975, Kincardineshire became part of the Grampian region.

Kinchinjunga: see KANCHENJUNGA.

kindergarten (Ger., = garden of children), system of preschool education. Friedrich FROEBEL designed (1837) the kindergarten to provide an educational situation less formal than that of the elementary school but one in which children's creative play instincts would be organized constructively. Through the use of songs, stories, games, simple manual materials, and group activities for which the furnishings of a kindergarten are adapted, children develop habits of cooperation and application, and the transition from home to school is thought to be made less formidable. The theory implicit in the kindergarten system, that education develops through expression and social cooperation, has greatly influenced elementary education and PARENT EDUCATION, especially in the United States, where kindergartens are generally a part of public school systems. The first kindergarten in America was founded (1856) at Watertown, Wis., by Margaretta Schurz, wife of Carl Schurz. It was followed by a school opened (1861) by Elizabeth Peabody in Boston and by a public kindergarten established (1873) in St. Louis by Susan Blow. See also NURSERY SCHOOL. See J. C. Foster and N.E. Headley, *Education in the Kindergarten* (4th ed., 1965); Helen Peterson, *Kindergarten: the Key to Child Growth* (1958); H. F. Robison, *New Directions in the Kindergarten* (1965); Clancy Goode, *World of Kindergarten* (1970).

Kinderhook (kĭn′dərho͝ok″), village (1970 pop. 1,233), Columbia co., SE N.Y.; settled before the Revolution, inc. 1838. Richard Upjohn designed St. Paul's Church (1851) there. Martin Van Buren was born and is buried in Kinderhook; the Van Buren homestead, "Lindenwald," is south of the village. The House of History, maintained by the county historical society, occupies an early 19th-century mansion.

Kindi, al- (Abu Yusuf Yakub ibn Ishak al-Kindi) (ä′-bo͞o yo͞oso͞of′ yăko͞ob′ ĭb′ən ĕshäk′ ăl-kĭn′dē), 9th cent. Arab philosopher, b. Basra, Iraq. He studied at Basra and at Baghdad and is noted as one of the earliest scholars in the Middle East to become thoroughly versed in the writings of Aristotle. In his own teachings al-Kindi undertook to demonstrate the essential harmony between the views of Plato and those of Aristotle. His philosophical ideas show some elements of NEOPLATONISM. He is regarded as one of the Peripatetics in Islam, and, as one of the earliest of the Muslim philosophers of Arabic descent, he has been called "the philosopher of the Arabs." He emphasized the righteousness as well as the unity of God and considered that the Creator revealing Himself in prophecy was a reasonable truth and the highest form of knowledge. In his doctrine of manifold intelligence, he defined four types of reason. Besides his translations and commentaries on Aristotle's works, he produced over 250 treatises on a great variety of subjects; although only a few on medicine and astrology are extant, in the 1940s 24 of his hitherto unknown philosophical works were found. Al-Kindi was well known to the Christian scholars of the Middle Ages. He wrote strongly in opposition to alchemy and some kinds of belief in miracles. Al-Kindi's library was confiscated later in his life by the caliph al-Mutawakkil, who looked upon philosophy with suspicion.

Kindia (kĭn′dyə), town (1964 est. pop. 25,000), W Guinea. It is the trade center for an area where bananas, manioc, rice, fruits, and vegetables are grown and bauxite is mined. The bottling of tonic water and the manufacture of soap are carried on in the town, and wood is processed for use in furniture factories outside Conakry. Kindia has a fruit research center.

kinematics: see DYNAMICS.

Kineshma (kē′nyĭshmə), city (1970 pop. 96,000), N central European USSR, on the Volga River. A river port and a rail terminus, it is an old textile center with sawmills and chemical plants.

kinetic art, term referring to sculptured works that include motion as a significant dimension. The form was pioneered by Marcel DUCHAMP, Naum GABO, and Alexander CALDER. Kinetic art is either nonmechanical, e.g., Calder's MOBILES, or mechanical, e.g., works by Gabo and Jean TINGUELY. The latter sort of kineticism developed in response to an increasingly technological culture.

kinetic-molecular theory of gases, physical theory that explains the behavior of gases on the basis of the following assumptions: (1) Any gas is composed of a very large number of very tiny particles called molecules; (2) The molecules are very far apart compared to their sizes, so that they can be considered as points; (3) The molecules exert no forces on one another except during rare collisions, and these collisions are perfectly elastic, i.e., they take place within a negligible span of time and in accordance with the laws of mechanics. A gas corresponding to these assumptions is called an *ideal gas;* as the temperature of a real gas is lowered, or its pressure is raised, its behavior no longer resembles that of an ideal gas because one or more of the assumptions of the theory is no longer valid. The analysis of the behavior of an ideal gas according to the laws of mechanics leads to the general gas law, or ideal gas law: The product of the pressure and volume of an ideal gas is directly proportional to its absolute temperature, or $PV = kT$ (see GAS LAWS). Boyle's law, Charles's law, and Gay-Lussac's law, which are special cases of the general gas law, may also be easily derived. The theory further shows that the absolute temperature is directly proportional to the average kinetic energy of the molecules, thus providing an interpretation of the nature of temperature in general in terms of the detailed structure of matter (see TEMPERATURE; KELVIN TEMPERATURE SCALE). Pressure is seen to be the result of large numbers of collisions between the molecules and the walls of the container in which the gas is held. See THERMODYNAMICS.

kinetics: see DYNAMICS.

kinetin, one of a group of chemically similar plant hormones, the cytokinins, that promote cell division. In some instances kinetin acts together with another hormone, indoleacetic acid, or AUXIN; in other cases it acts in opposition to auxin.

King, Billie Jean, 1943–, American tennis player, b. Long Beach, Calif. Her original name was Billie Jean Moffitt. She began playing tennis at age 11 and enjoyed success from age 15 when she won the S California championship in her age group. In 1961 (and again in 1962, 1965, 1967, 1968, 1971, and 1972) she won the women's doubles title at Wimbledon and the singles title in 1966, 1967, 1968, 1972, and 1973. She was the U.S. Lawn Tennis women's singles champion in 1967, 1971, 1972, and 1974. In 1973 she defeated Bobby RIGGS in a "battle of the sexes." An aggressive hard-hitting competitor, she turned professional in 1968. Very active in the women's rights movement, particularly in the area of equality of wages, she began publishing (1974) with her husband Larry King, a magazine, *Womensport.* See her autobiography written with Kim Chapin (1974).

King, Charles Bird, 1785–1862, American portrait painter, b. Newport, R.I. He studied under Edward Savage and with Benjamin West in London. His work, executed in Washington, D.C., included Indian portraits for a 3-volume work on the tribes of North America, still lifes, and portraits of eminent Americans. His portraits of Henry Clay and John C. Calhoun are in the Corcoran Gallery, Washington, D.C.

King, Ernest Joseph, 1878–1956, American admiral, commander in chief of the U.S. fleet (1941–45), b. Lorain, Ohio. A graduate of Annapolis, he distinguished himself in many branches of naval service, including the submarine and air arms. In World War I he was assistant chief of staff to Admiral Henry T. Mayo, commander of the Atlantic Fleet. King himself commanded (Feb.–Dec., 1941) the Atlantic Fleet and then became commander of the U.S. naval forces. King also became (March, 1942) chief of naval operations and directed the naval strategy that took the U.S. fleet into Japanese waters. He was made (1944) admiral of the fleet ("five-star admiral") and retired from the navy a year later. See his autobiographical *Fleet Admiral King: A Naval Record* (with W. M. Whitehill, 1952).

King, Henry, 1592–1669, English poet. He became bishop of Chichester in 1642. Elegies constitute nearly half his work, his most notable being "The Exequy," written on the death of his young wife. However, he is chiefly remembered for his love poem "Tell me no more how fair she is." See his poems, ed. by Margaret Crum (1965); Ronald Berman, *Henry King & the Seventeenth Century* (1964).

King, Henry Churchill, 1858–1934, American theologian and educator, b. Hillsdale, Mich. At Oberlin from 1884, he taught in succession mathematics, philosophy, and theology. He was president of the college from 1902 to 1927. Prominent in the councils of the Congregational Church, he was moderator (1919–21) of its National Council and chairman (1921–27) of the Congregational Foundation for Education. Among his many books are *Rational Living* (1905), *The Ethics of Jesus* (1910), *Fundamental Questions* (1917), and *Seeing Life Whole* (1923). See study by Ronald Berman (1964).

King, James Gore: see KING, RUFUS.

King, John Alsop: see KING, RUFUS.

King, Martin Luther, Jr., 1929–68, American clergyman and civil rights leader, b. Atlanta, Ga., grad. Morehouse College (B.A., 1948), Crozer Theological Seminary (B.D., 1951), Boston Univ. (Ph.D., 1955). The son of the pastor of the Ebenezer Baptist Church in Atlanta, King was ordained in 1947 and became (1954) minister of a Baptist church in Montgomery, Ala. He led the boycott (1955–56) by Montgomery blacks against the segregated city bus lines, and he attained national prominence by advocating a policy of passive resistance to segregation. In 1956, he gained a major victory and prestige as a civil rights leader when the Montgomery buses began to operate on a desegregated basis. After the Montgomery success, King organized the Southern Christian Leadership Conference, which gave him a base to pursue further civil rights activities, first in the South and later nation-wide. His philosophy of nonviolent resistance led to his arrest on numerous occasions in the 1950s and 60s. He organized (1963) the massive March on Washington, which brought more than 200,000 people together. In 1964 he was awarded the Nobel Peace Prize. King's leadership in the civil rights movement was challenged in the mid-1960s as others grew more militant. However, King's interests widened from civil rights to criticism of the Vietnam War and to a deeper concern for poverty. His plans for a Poor People's March to Washington were interrupted (1968) for a trip to Memphis, Tenn., in support of striking sanitation workers. On April 4, 1968, he was shot and killed by an assassin's bullet on the balcony of the motel where he was staying. James Earl Ray was later convicted of his murder. See his *Stride Toward Freedom* (1958), *Why We Can't Wait* (1964), and *Where Do We Go From Here: Chaos or Community?* (1967). See biographies by W. R. Miller (1968), C. E. Lincoln, ed. (1970), D. L. Lewis (1971), J. A. Bishop (1971), L. G. Davis (1969, repr. 1973), K. L. Smith and I. G. Zepp, Jr. (1974); Coretta King, *My Life With Martin Luther King, Jr.* (1969).

King, Rufus, 1755–1827, American political leader, b. Scarboro, Maine (then a district of Massachusetts). He served briefly in the American Revolution and practiced law in Massachusetts before serving (1783–85) as a member of the Massachusetts General Court. He was (1784–87) a delegate to the Continental Congress, where he helped draft the Ordinance of 1787 and was chiefly responsible for the exclusion of slavery from the Northwest Territory. At the Federal Constitutional Convention (1787), he was an effective supporter of a strong central government and helped to secure Massachusetts's ratification of the Constitution. Moving to New York City, King was elected to the state assembly and was chosen (1789) as one of New York's first two U.S. Senators. He strongly supported Alexander Hamilton's financial measures and later defended Jay's Treaty. As minister to Great Britain (1796–1803) he reconciled many differences between the two countries and proved himself an able diplomat. He was the unsuccessful Federalist party candidate for Vice President in 1804 and 1808 and for President in 1816. From 1813 to 1825 he again served as U.S. Senator. Although at first an opponent of the War of 1812, he later came to support the administration's war measures. King opposed the Missouri Compromise and advocated solving the slavery problem by emancipating and colonizing the Negroes outside the country on the proceeds of the sale of public lands. In 1824 he declined reelection but was again minister to Great Britain (1825-26). Charles King (1789-1867) was his son. See Charles King, ed., *The Life and Correspondence of Rufus King* (6 vol., 1894-1900, repr. 1971); biography by E. H. Brush (1926); study by Robert Ernst (1968).

King, William, 1650-1729, Irish clergyman and author. He was made archbishop of Dublin in 1702. An ardent believer in the rights of the Church of Ireland, he published in 1691 his *State of the Protestants in Ireland under the late King James's Government.* His chief work is *De origine mali* (1702, tr. 1730).

King, William, 1663-1712, English poet. He supported the Tory and High Church party. He is noted for his humorous and satirical writings, which include *Dialogues of the Dead* (attacks against Richard Bentley, pub. 1699) and *Miscellanies in Prose and Verse* (1709).

King, William Lyon Mackenzie, 1874-1950, Canadian political leader, b. Kitchener, Ont.; grandson of William Lyon Mackenzie. An expert on labor questions, he served in Wilfrid Laurier's Liberal administration as deputy minister of labor (1900-1908) and minister of labor (1909-1911) and was editor (1900-1908) of the *Labour Gazette.* He first served in the House of Commons from 1909 to 1911, and during World War I he was engaged (1914-1917) in investigating industrial relations in the United States. Chosen in 1919 to succeed Laurier as leader of the Liberal party, Mackenzie King led the opposition in Parliament until 1921, when he became prime minister, a post he filled, except for a brief interval in 1926, until 1930. Leader of the opposition during Richard Bedford Bennett's government (1930-35), he afterward again served (1935-48) as prime minister. Called upon to guide Canadian affairs during World War II, King enunciated his position in *Canada at Britain's Side* (1941) and *Canada and the Fight for Freedom* (1944). In 1940 he concluded with President Franklin Delano Roosevelt the Ogdensburg Agreement and in 1941, the Hyde Park Declaration; by these Canada and the United States agreed to create a permanent joint board of defense and to cooperate in the production of defense materials. King served as chairman of the Canadian delegation at the conference (1945) in San Francisco to draft the Charter of the United Nations and at the Paris Conference of 1946. With President Harry Truman and Prime Minister Clement Attlee of Great Britain, he signed in 1945 the Washington declaration on atomic energy. See biography by R. M. Dawson (Vol. I, 1958) and H. B. Neatby (Vol. II, 1963); J. W. Pickersgill and D. F. Forster, *The Mackenzie King Record* (4 vol., 1960-70).

King, William Rufus Devane, 1786-1853, U.S. Senator from Alabama (1819-44, 1848-52), b. Sampson co., N.C. A Democratic Congressman from North Carolina (1811-16), he settled (1818) in Alabama and became one of its first Senators. King resigned in 1844 to become minister to France; he successfully urged France to refrain from joining England in a protest against U.S. annexation of Texas. Later he again entered (1848) the Senate. Elected (1852) Vice President under Franklin Pierce, he died in Alabama soon after taking the oath of office.

King Arthur: see ARTHURIAN LEGEND.

kingbird: see FLYCATCHER.

King Charles Land: see KONG KARLS LAND.

king crab: see HORSESHOE CRAB.

king crow: see DRONGO.

king devil: see HAWKWEED.

kingdom, in taxonomy: see CLASSIFICATION.

kingfish, common name for several fishes, among them the CROAKER and POMPANO.

kingfisher, common name for members of the family Alcedinidae, essentially tropical and subtropical land birds, with affinities to trogons and swifts and related to the hornbill. Kingfishers have chunky bodies, short necks and tails, large heads with erectile crests, and strong, long beaks. Most kingfishers are carnivorous. The family is divided into two subfamilies, the fishing and the forest kingfishers, the American species being in the former category. The common eastern American belted kingfisher, *Megaceryle alcyon,* perches above the banks of freshwater streams and dives for small fish, crustaceans, reptiles, amphibians, and aquatic insects, returning to its perch to eat. It is 12 to 14 in. (30-35 cm) long, blue-gray above and white beneath; the female has chestnut breast markings. The Texas kingfisher is green above, has no crest, and is smaller (8 in./20 cm). Of the forest kingfishers, the best known is the Australian kookaburra, *Dacelo gigas,* famous for its laughing cry and valued as a destroyer of harmful snakes and lizards. The related (family Todidae) colorful West Indian tody is insectivorous. The genus *Halcyon,* of the forest kingfishers, is the largest group, comprising some 33 species. Fishing kingfishers nest in deep burrows dug out along streams. The burrows may extend up to 10 ft (300 cm) vertically, and from five to eight eggs are laid in the chamber rounded out at the end of the tunnel. Both male and female share the incubation duties. Many forest kingfishers nest in the same fashion as the fishing kingfishers, but some, e.g., the kookaburra, never go near the water and nest in trees. Kingfishers are classified in the phylum CHORDATA, subphylum Vertebrata, class Aves, order Coraciiformes, family Alcedinidae.

King George's War: see FRENCH AND INDIAN WARS.

King Horn, probably the earliest English-language romance, written c.1250 and containing about 1,500 lines. It is anonymous and is based on an earlier work in French. Emphasizing action and adventure, the poem relates the story of a heroic Scottish prince's successful fight to regain his kingdom after his expulsion by invaders. See edition ed. by Joseph Hall (1901); W. H. French, *Essays on King Horn* (1940).

Kingisepp, town: see SAREMA, USSR.

Kingisepp (kēn"gĭsyĕp'), city, NW European USSR, SW of Leningrad, near the Estonian border, on the Luga River. A river port, it has leather and shoe industries. The site was settled in the 9th cent., and the fortress of Yam was founded there in 1384 as a frontier post of Novgorod. The fortress was taken by Sweden in 1585 and passed to Russia in 1703, when it was renamed Yamburg. In 1922 it was renamed for an Estonian Communist leader.

Kingis Quair, The: see JAMES I, king of Scotland.

kinglet, common name for members of a subfamily of five species of Old and New World warblers, similar to the thrushes and the Old World flycatchers. Kinglets are small birds (4 in./10 cm) with soft, fluffy, olive or grayish green plumage and bright crown patches. Their distribution is circumpolar in the conifer belt. The two American species, the ruby-crowned and golden-crowned kinglets, breed in Canada and winter in Mexico. Similar are the Old World goldcrest and the European firecrest. They are active, insectivorous birds, traveling in loose bands together with nuthatches, woodpeckers, creepers, and titmice. Their hanging nests are purse-shaped. In the same order as the kinglets are the gnatwrens of Central and South America and the gnatcatchers, both of the family Polioptilidae, found from the N United States to Argentina. These dainty, slender birds are colored in soft grays and have thin, pointed bills; they feed on small insects. The blue-gray gnatcatcher of the United States and Mexico is typical of the group. Kinglets are classified in the phylum CHORDATA, subphylum Vertebrata, class Aves, order Passeriformes, family Sylviidae.

Kingman Reef, uninhabited reef, less than 1 sq mi (2.6 sq km), central Pacific, one of the LINE ISLANDS, 1,075 mi (1,730 km) SW of Honolulu. It was discovered by Americans in 1798 and annexed by the United States in 1922. Formerly an airport on the route from Honolulu to Pago Pago, Kingman Reef is now under the jurisdiction of the U.S. navy.

King Philip's War, 1675-76, the most devastating Indian war in New England. The war is named for King Philip, the son of MASSASOIT and chief of the WAMPANOAG INDIANS. His Indian name was Metacom, Metacomet, or Pometacom. Upon the death (1662) of his brother, Alexander (Wamsutta), whom the Indians suspected the English of murdering, Philip became sachem and maintained peace with the colonists for a number of years. However, hostility developed over the steady succession of land sales forced on the Indians by their growing dependence on English goods. Suspicious of Philip, the English colonists in 1671 questioned and fined him and demanded that the Wampanoag surrender their arms, which they did. In 1675 a Christian Indian who had been acting as an informer to the English was murdered, probably at Philip's instigation. Three Wampanoags were tried for the murder and executed. Incensed by this act, the Indians in June, 1675, made a sudden raid on the border settlement of Swansea. Other raids followed; towns were burned and many whites—men, women, and children—were slain. Unable to draw the Indians into a major battle, the colonists resorted to similar methods of warfare in retaliation and antagonized other tribes. The Wampanoag were joined by the Nipmuck and by the NARRAGANSETT INDIANS (after the latter were attacked by the colonists), and soon all the New England colonies were involved in the war. Philip's cause began to decline after he made a long journey west in an unsuccessful attempt to secure aid from the Mohawk. In 1676 the Narragansett were completely defeated and their chief, Canonchet, was killed in April of that year; the Wampanoag and Nipmuck were gradually subdued. Philip's wife and son were captured, and he was killed (Aug., 1676) by an Indian in the service of Capt. Benjamin Church after his hiding place at Mt. Hope (Bristol, R.I.) was betrayed. His body was drawn and quartered and his head exposed on a pole in Plymouth. The war, which was extremely costly to the colonists in men and money, resulted in the virtual extermination of tribal Indian life in S New England and the disappearance of the fur trade. The New England Confederation then had the way completely clear for white settlement. See G. M. Bodge, *Soldiers in King Philip's War* (1891, 3d ed. 1906, repr. 1967); G. W. Ellis and J. E. Morris, *King Philip's War* (1906); J. T. Adams, *The Founding of New England* (1921, repr. 1963); D. E. Leach, *Flintlock and Tomahawk* (1958, repr. 1966).

King Ranch, 1,000,000 acres (404,700 hectares), S Texas, SW of Corpus Christi with headquarters at Kingsville, Texas; one of the largest ranches in the world. Larger than the state of Rhode Island, it has several divisions, of which the best known is Santa Gertrudis, the "home" ranch. The Santa Gertrudis, the only true cattle breed developed in North America, was developed there. Thoroughbred racehorses are also raised on the ranch. The ranch was founded in 1853 by Richard King, a steamboat captain. After King's death, the giant holdings were managed by his son-in-law, Robert Kleberg; later, Kleberg's son succeeded to the management. The property was divided in 1935, but the central ranches are still large enough to resemble a semifeudal domain. Profits from oil and natural-gas rights and farming have been added to income gained from the great beef herds, which total more than 50,000 head.

Kings, county, N.Y.: see BROOKLYN, borough.

Kings, river, 125 mi (201 km) long, rising in three forks in the Sierra Nevada, E Calif., and flowing SW to Tulare Lake in the San Joaquin valley. Its middle and southern forks flow through the great gorges of Kings Canyon National Park (see NATIONAL PARKS AND MONUMENTS, table). Part of the Central Valley project, the Kings River has been linked with the San Joaquin River; Pine Flat Dam (completed 1954) impounds a huge reservoir used for flood control, irrigation, and river regulation.

Kings, books of the Old Testament, originally a single work in the Hebrew canon, called First and Second Kings in the Authorized Version, where they occupy the 11th and 12th place, and called Third and Fourth Kings in the Greek versions and the Western canon (the books of Samuel are called First and Second Kings in this enumeration). They continue the historical narrative of First and Second Samuel from the death of David until the destruction of the southern Hebrew kingdom (Judah), i.e., roughly from 1000 B.C. to 560 B.C. The major divisions of the history are as follows: first, the reign of Solomon (1 Kings 1-11), including the end of David's reign (1 Kings 1-2) and a lengthy account of the Temple (1 Kings 5-8); second, a synchronizing parallel account of the two Hebrew kingdoms (1 Kings 12 to 2 Kings 17), beginning with the division between Rehoboam and Jeroboam (1 Kings 12-14) and including as its major single portion the rise and fall of the house of Ahab of Israel, with which is woven the careers of the prophets Elijah and Elisha (1 Kings 17 to 2 Kings 9); and, third, the end of the southern kingdom (2 Kings 18-25). Although the books of Kings continue Samuel, they differ in having more frequent condemnation and praise of actions. The events of Kings are told with a different point of view in Chronicles. A noteworthy feature is the constant allusion to books containing historical data left out of Kings. The books of Kings have a persistent note of catastrophe caused by the sins of the Jews. See John Gray, *I & II Kings: A Commentary* (1963).

Kings Bay, Spitsbergen: see KONGSFJORDEN.

Kings Canyon National Park: see NATIONAL PARKS AND MONUMENTS (table); SEQUOIA NATIONAL PARK.

King's College, former name of COLUMBIA UNIV.

King's College, University of: see DALHOUSIE UNIV.

King's County, Republic of Ireland: see OFFALY.

Kingsley, Charles, 1819–75, English author and clergyman. Ordained in 1842, he became vicar of Eversley in Hampshire in 1844. From 1848 to 1852 he published tracts advocating CHRISTIAN SOCIALISM. These views were embodied in his first two novels, *Alton Locke* (1850) and *Yeast* (1851), both of which deal with contemporary social problems. In his subsequent novels, including *Hypatia* (1853), *Westward Ho!* (1855), and *Hereward the Wake* (1866), he used historical settings to communicate his ideas. A statement denigrating the Roman Catholic clergy, made by Kingsley in an article, started a controversy with John Henry NEWMAN that resulted in Newman's famous *Apologia*. In 1859, Kingsley was made chaplain to Queen Victoria. From 1860 to 1869 he was professor of modern history at Cambridge and in 1873 was appointed canon of Westminster. Several collections of his sermons were published during his lifetime. Included among his other notable work is the well-known children's book *The Water Babies* (1863). See *Letters and Memories* (ed. by his wife, 2 vol., 1877 repr. 1973); biographies by M. F. Thorp (1937, repr. 1969) and Una Pope-Hennessy (1948, repr. 1973).

King's Lynn, municipal borough (1971 pop. 30,102), Norfolk, E England, on the Great Ouse River near its influx into The Wash. The town's large harbor serves foreign as well as coastal trade and is the base for a fishing fleet. A farm market, it is also a center of fertilizer production, canning, flour milling, beet-sugar refining, shipbuilding, and metalworking. King's Lynn dates from Saxon times. Red Mount Chapel was visited by pilgrims in the 15th and 16th cent. The two market places are interesting for their ancient buildings and for the fairs that are still held. There is a Norman church and other old buildings. King's Lynn was the birthplace of the novelist Fanny Burney and the mystic Margery Kempe.

Kings Mountain National Military Park: see NATIONAL PARKS AND MONUMENTS (table).

king snake, name for a number of species of the genus *Lampropeltis*, nonvenomous, egg-laying, constricting SNAKES of North America which show much variation in color and markings. The common king snake, or chain snake, (*Lampropeltis getulus*), of the E United States is usually about 3 to 5 ft (90–150 cm) long and black or brown with yellow and white rings or bands that form a chainlike pattern. It eats rodents, birds, and snakes. It is immune to the venom of the rattlesnake and the copperhead, which it kills by constriction. The scarlet king snake (*L. doliata*), has a pattern of black, red, and yellow bands similar to that of the unrelated coral snake. Other less brightly marked varieties of the same species are called milk snakes, because they are reputed by legend to milk cows. King snakes are valuable destroyers of rodents. They are classified in the phylum CHORDATA, subphylum Vertebrata, class Reptilia, order Squamata, family Colubridae.

Kings Peak, Utah: see UINTA MOUNTAINS.

Kingsport, city (1970 pop. 31,938), Hawkins and Sullivan counties, NE Tenn., on the Holston River near the Va. line; inc. 1917. Industries include bookbinding and the manufacture of film, textiles, and plastics. The city, which is encircled by mountains, stands on the site of forts Robinson (1761) and Patrick Henry (1775) on the old Wilderness Road.

Kingston, city (1971 pop. 59,047), S Ont., Canada, on Lake Ontario, near the head of the St. Lawrence River and at the end of Rideau Canal from Ottawa. Kingston has probably the best harbor on the lake. Industries include the manufacture of locomotives, textiles, aluminum products, synthetic yarn, and ceramics. On the site stood FORT FRONTENAC, of great importance in the French and Indian War. The present city was founded by United Empire Loyalists in 1783 and prospered during the War of 1812 as the Canadian naval base for operations against the Americans. From 1841 to 1844 it served as the capital of Canada. Fort Henry, built during the War of 1812 and rebuilt from 1832 to 1836, is now a museum. Kingston is the seat of Queen's Univ. (1842), of the Royal Military College, and of Anglican and Roman Catholic bishoprics and cathedrals. In 1953 the village of Portsmouth was joined to Kingston.

Kingston, city (1970 pop. 111,879), capital and largest city of Jamaica, SE Jamaica. The country's chief port, it has one of the finest harbors in the West Indies and exports sugar, rum, molasses, and bananas. The city's industries include tourism, food processing, and oil refining. Kingston was founded in 1693 on a deep, landlocked harbor. The former capital, Port Royal, at the tip of the long, narrow peninsula forming the harbor, was inundated after an earthquake in 1692; the capital was then moved to Spanish Town and, in 1872, to Kingston. After fire destroyed the new Port Royal in 1703, Kingston became Jamaica's leading commercial city. It has suffered from severe hurricanes and was leveled by an earthquake in 1907. Kingston is famed for its lively calypsos and its relics of buccaneering days. In the suburb of Mona are the University College of the West Indies and the Royal Botanical Gardens, noted especially for their orchids.

Kingston. 1 City (1970 pop. 25,544), seat of Ulster co., SE N.Y., on the Hudson River at the mouth of Rondout Creek; inc. as a village 1805, and as a city through the union (1872) of Kingston and Rondout. The eastern gateway to the Catskill-Shawangunk vacationland and the center of an expanding industrial region, it has plants making electronic computers, farm machinery, and apparel. Fur trading posts were built there between 1611 and 1615. The first permanent settlement (called Wiltwyck) was established in 1652. Kingston served as the first capital of New York state until it was burned by the British in Oct., 1777. Its growth in the early 19th cent. was stimulated by the Delaware and Hudson Canal. Among notable landmarks are many old Dutch stone houses; the senate house (1676), meeting place of the first New York state legislature and now a museum; the old Dutch church (1659) and cemetery (1661); the burial place of James Clinton; and nearby "Slabsides," former cottage of John Burroughs. To the west is Ashokan Reservoir. **2** Borough (1970 pop. 18,325), Luzerne co., NE Pa., on the Susquehanna River opposite Wilkes-Barre; settled 1769, inc. 1857. Although chiefly residential, it has railroad shops and varied manufactures. It was devastated by a flood in June, 1972.

Kingston upon Hull: see HULL, England.

Kingston upon Thames, borough (1971 pop. 140,210) of Greater London, SE England. The borough was created in 1965 by the merger of the municipal boroughs of Kingston upon Thames, Malden and Coombe, and Surbiton. Mainly residential, it has light-engineering works and manufactures electronic equipment. In the 10th cent. several Anglo-Saxon kings were crowned at Kingston upon Thames; the stone believed to have been used during the coronations is preserved in the market place. Kingston College of Further Education and Kingston Polytechnic are in the borough. Kingston Grammar School was founded in 1561.

Kingstown, borough, Republic of Ireland: see DÚN LAOGHAIRE.

Kingstown, town (1970 pop. 17,258), capital of St. Vincent, British West Indies. The chief port of entry, it is also a popular winter resort.

Kingsville, city (1970 pop. 28,915), seat of Kleberg co., S Texas; inc. 1911. It is headquarters of the gigantic KING RANCH, part of which is nearby. The city is a processing center for a farm, oil, and gas area. Large petrochemical and gas plants are in the vicinity. Kingsville is the seat of Texas Arts and Industries (A&I) Univ.

Kingswood, urban district (1971 pop. 30,269), Gloucestershire, SW England. A residential suburb of Bristol, Kingswood has a footwear industry. It is noted for its open-air chapel, which marks the site of Methodist open-air sermons on Hanham Mount by John Wesley and George Whitefield in the 18th cent. In 1974, Kingswood became part of the new nonmetropolitan county of Avon.

King William Island, part of the Arctic Archipelago, in the Arctic Ocean, central Northwest Territories, Canada, between Boothia Peninsula and Victoria Island. The island was discovered (1831) by Sir James C. Ross, who also explored the northern coast. In 1837, Thomas Simpson of the Hudson's Bay Company traced the southern coast. The ships of the expedition of Sir John Franklin were wrecked off the west coast, and the island was further explored by searchers for Franklin, notably John Rae and Sir Francis L. McClintock. Roald Amundsen wintered there in 1903–4 while on his way through the Northwest Passage. See P. F. Cooper, *Island of the Lost* (1961).

King William's War: see FRENCH AND INDIAN WARS.

Kinhwa: see CHIN-HUA, China.

Kinibalu, Mount: see KINABALU, MOUNT, Malaysia.

kinkajou (kĭng'kəjo͞o"), nocturnal, arboreal mammal, *Potos flavus,* found from Mexico to Brazil and related to the RACCOON. It has a long, slender body with soft, short, woolly hair of any of various shades of brown or yellow. Its tail is prehensile and is used to grasp branches when the animal climbs. The kinkajou spends most of its time in trees. It eats small animals, fruits, and honey and is sometimes called honey-bear, a name also applied to a true BEAR of SE Asia. Kinkajous are classified in the phylum CHORDATA, subphylum Vertebrata, class Mammalia, order Carnivora, family Procyonidae.

Kinnarodden: see NORDKYN, CAPE, Norway.

Kinneret, Lake: see GALILEE, SEA OF.

Kino, Eusebio Francisco (āo͞osā'byō fränsēs'kō kē'-nō), c.1644–1711, missionary explorer in the American Southwest, b. Segno, in the Tyrol. He was in 1669 admitted to the Jesuit order. A distinguished mathematician, he observed the comet of 1680–81 at Cádiz, publishing his results in his *Exposición astronómica de el* [sic] *cometa* (1681). He arrived as a missionary in New Spain in 1681 and was appointed royal cosmographer to accompany the expedition to colonize Lower California. When the settlement in S California was abandoned, he went to Pimería Alta (now N Sonora and S Arizona), where he labored as a missionary, explorer, and colonizer until his death. He made more than 50 journeys from his base, the mission of Nuestra Señora de los Dolores in Sonora, frequently with only Indian guides as companions. He established agriculture at the missions he founded and brought in cattle, horses, and sheep; he distributed cattle and seed grain among the Indian tribes. In 1701–2 he made two expeditions down the Colorado, on the second reaching the head of the Gulf and proving anew that California was not an island. He was the first to map Pimería Alta on the basis of actual exploration, and his map, published in 1705, and many times reproduced, remained the basis for maps of the region until the 19th cent. His valuable historical and autobiographical chronicle, *Favores celestiales,* was edited by H. E. Bolton as *Kino's Historical Memoir of Pimería Alta* (1919, repr. 1948). See E. J. Burros, *Kino and the Cartography of Northwestern New Spain* (1965); F. J. Smith, J. L. Kessell, and F. J. Fox, *Father Kino in Arizona* (1966).

Kinorhyncha (kĭn"ərĭng'kə), class of organisms belonging to the phylum ASCHELMINTHES.

Kinross, burgh (1971 pop. 2,418), county town of Kinross-shire, E Scotland, on Loch Leven. It is a market town. Kinross House, in the style of an Italian Renaissance mansion, was built for James II of England (then duke of York) in 1685. In 1975, Kinross became part of the Tayside region.

Kinross-shire (kĭnrŏs'shĭr), county (1971 pop. 6,422), 81 sq mi (210 sq km), E Scotland. KINROSS is the county town. The central plain is sheltered by hills to the east and the northwest. Loch Leven lies in SE Kinross-shire. There are stock and dairy farms, and oats and barley are grown. Wool and linen weaving are other industries. Mary Queen of Scots was imprisoned in Loch Leven Castle for 11 months (1567–68).In 1975, Kinross-shire became part of the Tayside region.

Kinsale (kĭnsāl'), urban district (1971 pop. 1,628), Co. Cork, S Republic of Ireland, on the Bandon River estuary. It is a fishing port and seaside resort. Kinsale was an Anglo-Norman settlement. In 1601, Kinsale was held for 10 weeks by a Spanish force. Charles Fort, built in 1677, was several times the object of siege and was burned by Irish nationalists in 1922. James II landed at Kinsale in 1689. The town surrendered to the English under the duke of Marlborough in 1690. St. Multose Church dates from the 12th cent.

Kinsey, Alfred Charles, 1894–1956, American biologist, b. Hoboken, N.J., grad. Bowdoin (B.S., 1916), Harvard (D.Sc., 1920). He was associated with the Univ. of Indiana from 1920, becoming professor of zoology in 1929. His early work dealt with the life cycle, evolution, geographic distribution, and speciation of the gall wasp. He is most widely known for his later extensive studies of human sexual behavior. His program of research on this subject received financial support from the National Research Council, the Rockefeller Foundation, and the Univ. of Indiana. Kinsey and his assistants interviewed many thousands of individuals in all parts of the country. Their findings met with considerable popular response when they were presented in *Sexual Behavior of the Human Male* (1948) and *Sexual Behavior of the Human Female* (1953). Kinsey's program of studies is continuing at the Institute for Sex Research, Inc., Bloomington, Ind.

Kinshasa (kēn'shäsə), formerly **Leopoldville,** city (1970 pop. 1,323,039), capital of Zaïre, W Zaïre, a port on Stanley (Malebo) Pool of the Congo River. It is Zaïre's largest city and its administrative, communications, and commercial center. Major industries are food and beverage processing, tanning, construction, ship repairing, and the manufacture of chemicals, mineral oils, textiles, and cement. A transportation hub, Kinshasa is the terminus of the railroad from MATADI and of navigation on the Congo River from Kisangani; the international airport is a major link for African air traffic with Europe and the Americas. There is motorboat service to BRAZZAVILLE, Congo Republic, on the opposite bank of Stanley Pool. Kinshasa was founded in 1881 by Henry M. Stanley, the Anglo-American explorer, who named it Leopoldville after his patron, Leopold II, king of the Belgians. In 1898 the rail link with Matadi was completed, and in 1926 the city succeeded Boma as the capital of the Belgian Congo (see ZAÏRE). Its main growth occurred after 1945. A major anti-Belgian rebellion that took place there in Jan., 1959, started the country on the road to independence (June, 1960). In 1966 the city's name was changed from Leopoldville to Kinshasa, the name of one of the African villages that occupied the site in 1881. Modern Kinshasa is an educational and cultural center and is the seat of Lovanium Univ. of Kinshasa (1954), which has an archaeological museum, the National School of Law and Administration, a telecommunications school, a research center for tropical medicine, and a museum of Africana. Historical buildings in the city include the chapel of the American Baptist Missionary Society (1891) and a Roman Catholic cathedral (1914). There is a large stadium (seating capacity about 70,000). An international trade fair is held annually in July.

kinship, relationship by blood or marriage between persons; also, in anthropology and sociology, a system of rules, based on such relationships, governing descent, inheritance, marriage, extramarital sexual relations, and sometimes residence. All societies recognize consanguineal and affinitive ties between individuals, but there is great divergence in the manner of reckoning descent and relationship. Kinship patterns are so specific and elaborate that they constitute an important and independent field of anthropological and sociological investigation. In many societies the concept of kinship extends beyond FAMILY ties, which vary in breadth and inclusiveness, to less precisely defined groupings such as the CLAN, where consanguinity is often hypothetical if not actually mythological. As a rule, however, these groups maintain INCEST rules as strict as those for close biological relatives. See Robin Fox, *Kinship and Marriage* (1967); Ira Buchler and H. A. Selby, *Kinship and Social Organization* (1968); Bernard Farber, *Comparative Kinship Systems* (1968); J. R. Goody, *Comparative Studies in Kinship* (1969).

Kinston, city (1970 pop. 23,020), seat of Lenoir co., E N.C., on the Neuse River; settled c.1740, inc. 1849. It is a market for bright leaf tobacco and an industrial city where lumber, textiles, and fertilizers are produced. A junior college is in Kinston.

Kintyre (kĭntīr'), peninsula, 42 mi (68 km) long and 10 mi (16 km) wide, Argyllshire, W Scotland, joined to the mainland at the isthmus of Tarbert between East Loch Tarbert and West Loch Tarbert. The Mull of Kintyre, at the southwestern tip, is 13 mi (21 km) from Ireland. The terrain is hilly and uncultivated. Campbeltown is the main town.

Kioga: see KYOGA, lake, Africa.

Kiowa Indians (kī'əwə), North American Indians, whose language is thought to form a branch of the Aztec-Tanoan linguistic stock (see AMERICAN INDIAN LANGUAGES). The Kiowa, a nomadic people of the Plains area, had several distinctive traits, including a pictographic calendar and the worship of a stone image, the *taimay*. In the 17th cent. they occupied W Montana, but by about 1700 they had moved to an area SE of the Yellowstone River. Here they came into contact with the Crow Indians, who gave the Kiowa permission to settle in the Black Hills. While living there, they acquired (c.1710) the horse, probably from the Crow. Their trade was mainly with the Arikara, the Mandan, and the Hidatsa. After the invading Cheyenne and the Sioux drove the Kiowa from the Black Hills, they were forced to move south to Comanche territory; in 1790, after a bloody war, the Kiowa reached a permanent peace with the Comanche. According to Lewis and Clark, the Kiowa were on the North Platte River in 1805, but not much later they occupied the Arkansas River region. Later the Kiowa, who allied themselves with the Comanche, raided as far south as Durango, Mexico, attacking Mexicans, Texans, and Indians, principally the Navaho and the Osage. In 1837 the Kiowa were forced to sign their first treaty, providing for the passage of Americans through Kiowa-Comanche land; the presence of settlers in increased numbers accelerated hostilities. After 1840, when the Kiowa made peace with the Cheyenne, four groups—the Kiowa, the Cheyenne, the Comanche, and the Apache—combined to fight the eastern Indians, who had migrated to Indian Territory. This caused more hostility between the Indians and the U.S. government, and U.S. forces finally defeated the confederacy and imposed the Treaty of Medicine Lodge (1867). This confederated the Kiowa, the Comanche, and the Apache and provided that they should settle in Oklahoma. However, parts of the Kiowa remained hostile until the mid-1870s. Oncoming settlers, unaware of treaty rights, caused friction with the Kiowa, resulting in a series of minor outbreaks. In 1874 the Kiowa were involved in a serious conflict, which was suppressed by the U.S. army. American soldiers killed the horses of the Kiowa, and the government deported the Kiowa leaders to Florida. By 1879 most of them were settled on their present reservation in Oklahoma, where they number about 2,000. The **Kiowa Apache,** a small group of North American Indians traditionally associated with the Kiowa from the earliest times, now live with them on their reservation. The Kiowa Apache retain their own language. See R. H. Lowie, *Societies of the Kiowa* (1916); A. L. Marriott, *Kiowa Years* (1968); M. P. Mayhall, *The Kiowas* (rev. ed., 1972).

Kipawa: see TÉMISCAMING, Que., Canada.

Kipchaks: see CUMANS.

Kipling, Rudyard, 1865-1936, English author, b. Bombay, India. Educated in England, Kipling returned to India in 1882 and worked as an editor on a Lahore paper. His early poems were collected in *Departmental Ditties* (1886), *Barrack-Room Ballads* (1892), and other volumes. His first short stories of Anglo-Indian life appeared in *Plain Tales from the Hills* (1888) and *Soldiers Three* (1888). In 1889 he returned to London, where his novel *The Light That Failed* (1890) appeared. Kipling's masterful stories and poems interpreted India in all its heat, strife, and ennui. His romantic imperialism and his characterization of the true Englishman as brave, conscientious, and self-reliant did much to enhance his popularity. These views are reflected in such well-known poems as "The White Man's Burden," "Loot," "Mandalay," "Gunga Din," and *Recessional* (1897). In London in 1892, Kipling married Caroline Balestier, an American, and lived in Vermont for four years. There he wrote children's stories, *The Jungle Book* (1894) and *Second Jungle Book* (1895), *Kim* (1901), *Just So Stories* (1902), and *Captains Courageous* (1897). Returning to England in 1900, he lived in Sussex, the setting of *Puck of Pook's Hill* (1906). Other works include *Stalky and Co.* (1899) and his famous poem "If" (1910). England's first Nobel Prize winner in literature (1907), he was buried in Westminster Abbey. See his *Something of Myself* (1937); biographies by C. E. Carrington (1955) and J. I. M. Stewart (1966); studies by J. M. S. Tompkins (2d ed. 1965), Bonamy Dobrée (1967), and V. A. Shashane (1973).

Kipnis, Alexander, 1891-, Russian-American operatic bass. He studied conducting at the Warsaw Conservatory and voice in Berlin. He made his operatic debut (1915) in Hamburg. Imprisoned by the Germans in World War I as an enemy alien, he was freed and permitted to sing in Wiesbaden. From 1922 to 1925 he was the principal bass of the Berlin Opera Company. He appeared with the Chicago Opera Company (1924-32) and toured extensively. His debut at the Metropolitan Opera House (1940) was as Gurnemanz in *Parsifal*. He is noted for his performance of the role of Boris Godunov.

Kir (kûr). **1** Unidentified land to which Tiglath-pileser III banished the Syrians, credited by Amos as the original home of the Aramaeans. 2 Kings 16.9; Isa. 22.6; Amos 1.5; 9.7. **2** Place in Moab, identified with Kir-haraseth, Kir-hareseth, Kir-haresh, and Kir-heres. 2 Kings 3.25; Isa. 15.1; 16.7, 11; Jer. 48.31, 36.

Kirby, William, 1817-1906, Canadian author, b. England. He was a journalist and civil servant. Besides volumes of verse and tales, he wrote *The Golden Dog* (1877), also published as *Le Chien d'or* (1884), a popular romance of 17th-century Quebec.

Kirby-Smith, Edmund: see SMITH, EDMUND KIRBY.

Kircher, Athanasius (ätänä'zēo͞os kĭrkh'ər), 1601?-1680, German Jesuit archaeologist, mathematician, biologist, and physicist. He was interested in all branches of science, especially in subterranean phenomena (volcanic forces in particular), in the deciphering of hieroglyphics, and in linguistic relations. At first professor of ethics and mathematics at the Univ. of Würzburg, he later became (1635) professor of physics, mathematics, and Oriental languages at the College of Rome, resigning in 1643 to devote himself to archaeological research. His studies with the microscope led him to the belief, which he was possibly the first to hold, that disease and putrefaction were caused by the presence of invisible living bodies. He also perfected the aeolian harp. His remarkable collection of antiquities became the nucleus of the Museum Kircherianum of the College of Rome. His writings filled 44 folio volumes and included an autobiography.

Kirchhoff, Gustav Robert (go͞os'täf rō'bĕrt kĭrkh'hôf), 1824-87, German physicist. He served as professor of physics at the universities of Breslau (1850-54), Heidelberg (1854-74), and Berlin (from 1875). He is known especially for his work with the SPECTROSCOPE in association with R. W. Bunsen, with whom he discovered the elements cesium and rubidium, and for his explanation of the Fraunhofer lines in the solar SPECTRUM. He also did important research in electricity (he formulated KIRCHHOFF'S LAWS) and thermodynamics.

Kirchhoff's laws [for Gustav R. Kirchhoff], pair of laws stating general restrictions on the current and voltage in an electric network or CIRCUIT. The first of these states that at any given instant the sum of the voltages around any closed path, or loop, in the network is zero. The second states that at any junction of paths, or node, in a network the sum of the currents arriving at any instant is equal to the sum of the currents flowing away.

Kirchner, Ernst Ludwig (ĕrnst lo͝ot'vĭkh kĭrkh'nər), 1880-1938, German expressionist painter and graphic artist. He studied art in Munich and was greatly impressed by the neo-impressionists. Kirchner studied Oceanic and other primitive sculpture at the Dresden Museum of Ethnology in 1904. This art was of great importance for him and for the movement known as the BRÜCKE, which he co-founded the following year. Also inspired by late Gothic woodcuts and the art of Edvard Munch, Van Gogh, and the Fauves, Kirchner merged their expressive forces into powerful and original creations. With startling contrasts of pure color and aggressive forms, Kirchner explored the world of night cafés and the streets of metropolitan Berlin. His savagely executed woodcuts are among the outstanding works in this medium produced in the 20th cent. and are among the most powerful creations of the expressionist vision. He suffered an emotional breakdown in 1914 and moved to a sanatorium in Davos, Switzerland, after World War I. In the next few years, his art became less tortured and more abstract. In 1938, following the Nazi condemnation of "degenerate art," including some 600 of Kirchner's works, the artist, in failing health, committed suicide. Characteristic works are the portrait of Erich Heckel and his wife (Smith College Mus.); *The Street* (1913; Mus. of Modern Art, New York City); and the illustrations for *Peter Schlemihl* (1916). See biographical study by D. E. Gordon (1968).

Kirchner, Leon, 1919-, American composer, b. Brooklyn, N.Y. Kirchner studied at the Univ. of California at Berkeley with Ernest Bloch, Arnold Schoenberg, and Roger Sessions. He became professor of music at Harvard in 1961. Although he uses many of the most modern techniques of composition, including electronics, he is a self-proclaimed romantic. Among his works are two piano concertos (1953 and 1963); three string quartets (1949, 1958, and 1967), the third for strings and tape; and the opera *Lily*, in progress in 1974.

Kirghiz Soviet Socialist Republic (kĭrgēz', kûr'gēz, Rus. kĭrgēs'), **Kirghizia** (kĭrgē'zhə), or **Kirghizstan** (kĭrgēstän'), constituent republic (1970 pop. 2,933,000), c.76,600 sq mi (198,400 sq km), Central Asian USSR. It borders on China in the southeast and on the Kazakh SSR, the Uzbek SSR, and the Tadzhik SSR in the north, west, and southwest. FRUNZE, the capital, and Osh are the chief cities. Kirghizia is a mountainous country in the Tien Shan and Pamir systems, rising to 24,409 ft (7,440 m) at Pobeda Peak on the Chinese border. It has rich pasturage for goats, sheep, cattle, and horses. Over 80% of the cultivated area is irrigated. Cotton, sugar beets, tobacco, fruit, and grapes are grown; sericulture is carried on; and grain crops are cultivated in the nonirrigated areas. There are coal, antimony, lead, tungsten, mercury, uranium, petroleum, and natural gas deposits. Industries include food processing, sugar refining, nonferrous metallurgy, and the manufacture of agricultural machinery, textiles, and building materials. The Kirghiz, a Muslim, Turkic-speaking pastoral people with definite Mongol strains, constitute about one half of the population; the rest are Russians, Uzbeks, and Ukrainians. Formerly known as

Kara [black] Kirghiz to distinguish them from the Kazakhs (at one time called Kirghiz), the Kirghiz migrated to Kirghizia from the region of the upper Yenisei, where they had lived from the 7th to the 17th cent. The area came under the rule of the Kokand khanate in the 19th cent. and was gradually annexed by Russia between 1855 and 1876. The nomadic Kirghiz resisted conscription into the czarist army in 1916 and fought the establishment of Bolshevik control from 1917 to 1921. As a result of war devastation, there was a famine in 1921–22 in which over 500,000 Kirghiz died. The area was formed into the Kara-Kirghiz Autonomous Oblast within the Russian Soviet Federated Socialist Republic in 1924, an autonomous republic in 1926, and a constituent republic in 1936. The Kirghiz state university was established in 1951 and the Kirghiz Academy of Sciences in 1954. The republic's cultural life stresses epic poems, tales, and folk songs, and the Kirghiz have traditionally excelled in wood carving, rug weaving, and jewelry making.

Kir-haraseth, Kir-hareseth, Kir-haresh, and **Kir-heres:** see KIR **2.**

Kiriathaim (kĭr'ēăthā'ĭm), town of Moab. Jer. 48.1,23; Ezek. 25.9. Kirjathaim: Num. 32.37; Joshua 13.19.

Kirin (kē'rĭn'), Mandarin *Chi-lin* [propitious forest], province (1968 est. pop. 17,000,000), NE China; one of the original Manchurian provinces. The capital is CH'ANG-CH'UN. It is bordered by the USSR on the northeast, by North Korea on the southeast, and by the Inner Mongolian Autonomous Region on the west. Kirin, crossed by the Sungari River and forming part of the fertile alluvial Manchurian plain, enjoys great agricultural prosperity; soybeans, wheat, upland rice, sweet potatoes, and beans are grown. Mountains in the east rise to more than 9,000 ft (2,740 m). Vast timberlands, among the best in China, are exploited, and iron, coal, gold, and lead are extracted. The province has a good network of railroads, including the line between Shen-yang, Ch'ang-ch'un, and Harbin, and its branches. The population, mainly Chinese, is concentrated in the industrial cities of CH'ANG-CH'UN, CHI-LIN, SSU-P'ING, and LIAO-YÜAN. Near the North Korean border is the Yenpien Korean autonomous region (est. 1952), which has a large Korean population. Kirin Univ. is in CH'ANG-CH'UN.

Kirin, city: see CHI-LIN, China.

Kirioth (kĭr'ēŏth), the same as KERIOTH **1.**

Kirjath (kûr'jăth), the same as KIRJATH-JEARIM.

Kirjathaim (kərjəthā'ĭm). **1** Town, N Palestine. 1 Chron. 6.76. Kartan: Joshua 21.32. **2** See KIRIATHAIM.

Kirjath-arba: see HEBRON, Jordan.

Kirjath-arim (kûr'jăth-ā'rĭm) and **Kirjath-baal** (-bā'əl), alternative names of KIRJATH-JEARIM.

Kirjath-huzoth (kûr'jăth-hyōō'zŏth), unidentified place, E of the Dead Sea. Num. 22.39.

Kirjath-jearim (kûr'jăth-jē'ərĭm), ancient fortress and holy place, Palestine, W of Jerusalem. Joshua 9.17; 1 Sam. 6.21; 1 Chron. 2.50, 52; 13.5, 6; 2 Chron. 1.4; Neh. 7.29. Kirjath: Joshua 18.28. Kirjath-arim: Ezra 2.25. Kirjath-baal: Joshua 15.60; Judges 18.12. Baalah: Joshua 15.9, 10. Baale of Judah: 2 Sam. 6.2.

Kirjath-sannah (kûr'jăth-săn'ə) and **Kirjath-sepher** (-sē'fər), alternative names of DEBIR **2.**

Kirk, Grayson Louis, 1903–, American educator, b. Jeffersonville, Ohio, grad. Miami Univ., 1924, Ph.D. Univ. of Wisconsin, 1930. He taught at Wisconsin from 1929 to 1940, when he became associate professor of government at Columbia. In 1942 he became full professor of government and in 1947 professor of international relations. After 1959 Kirk served as Bryce Professor of History of International Relations. In 1953 he succeeded Dwight D. Eisenhower as president of Columbia, a post he held until 1968. He is the author of *Philippine Independence* (1936), *Contemporary International Politics* (with W. R. Sharp, 1940), and *The Study of International Relations in American Colleges and Universities* (1947).

Kirk, Norman Eric, 1923–74, New Zealand political leader. A Labour party member, he rose in New Zealand politics, entering Parliament in 1957, and becoming vice president (1963) and then president (1964) of the Labor party. In the Nov., 1972, elections Kirk's party gained a parliamentary majority and he assumed the posts of prime minister and foreign minister. He was a supporter of increased social security, housing, and welfare benefits.

Kirkaldy of Grange, Sir William (kərkôl'dē), d. 1573, Scottish soldier and politician. Associated with his father in the murder of Cardinal BEATON in 1546, he was captured by the French in 1547 and held prisoner in France until 1550, when he escaped to become a secret agent of England in France. On the accession of Mary I to the English throne in 1553 he entered the service of the king of France. Pardoned for his part in the murder of Beaton, he returned to Scotland in 1557 and became a prominent Protestant leader. He opposed the marriage of MARY QUEEN OF SCOTS to Lord Darnley and was implicated in the assassination of Rizzio. After Mary's marriage to Lord Bothwell, Kirkaldy was the leader to whom the queen surrendered at Carberry Hill in 1567. While she was a prisoner in England, Kirkaldy shifted his allegiance to Mary's supporters and held Edinburgh castle for her, bringing upon himself the denunciation of his former friend, John Knox, and of other Presbyterian leaders. In 1573 he was forced to surrender the castle to an Anglo-Scottish force and was hanged.

Kirkcaldy (kərkô'dē, -kôl'-), burgh (1971 pop. 50,338), Fife, E Scotland, on the Firth of Forth. It is composed of seven villages, including Dysart, strung along the shore, giving rise to the name "Lang Toun." It is one of the largest producers of linoleum and oilcloth in Great Britain. Other industries include textile printing and the manufacture of farm machinery. The port is engaged in coastal trade. The city is the birthplace of Adam Smith.

Kirkcudbright (kûrkōō'brē), burgh (1971 pop. 2,506), county town of Kirkcudbrightshire, SW Scotland, at the head of the Dee estuary. It has granaries and creameries and is a market town and artists' colony. There are traces of an ancient wall and moat and of a McClellan clan castle (1582). In 1975, Kirkcudbright became part of the Strathclyde region.

Kirkcudbrightshire (kûrkōō'brēshĭr), county (1971 pop. 27,450), 897 sq mi (2,323 sq km), SW Scotland, in the GALLOWAY district. KIRKCUDBRIGHT is the county town. The land is mountainous, sloping to a rugged coastline along the Solway Firth. The Cree, the Dee (the western border), and the Urr are the main rivers. Stock raising and dairy farming are the main occupations; oats, barley, and turnips are also grown. There is a forestry industry. The county has a number of ruined abbeys and castles. In 1975, Kirkcudbrightshire became part of the Strathclyde region.

Kirke, Sir David (kûrk), 1597–1655?, English merchant adventurer, b. France. In 1627 he and his brothers Lewis and Thomas sailed in a fleet outfitted by their father, Gervase Kirke, and Sir William Alexander (later earl of Stirling) on a royal patent to expel the French settlements in Canada and establish a monopoly of trade in Nova Scotia. Near Newfoundland they seized a fleet of French vessels. They then attacked the French stations in Nova Scotia and went back to England with captives and spoils. In 1629, David returned and forced Samuel de CHAMPLAIN to surrender Quebec. Meanwhile Charles I had made peace with France and all French possessions taken after April 24, 1629, had to be restored. Knighted in 1633, Sir David went to Newfoundland in 1638 as governor and colonizer. Royalist in sympathy during the English civil war, he was deprived of his governorship after the execution of the king. A portion of his properties was restored to him shortly before his death. See Henry Kirke, *First English Conquest of Canada* (1871).

Kirkenes (kēr'kənĕs), town, Finnmark co., NE Norway, a port on the Varangerfjord, near the Soviet border. It is the processing and shipping center of an iron ore mining region. It was severely damaged in World War II.

Kirkintilloch (kûrkĭntĭl'ŏkh), burgh (1971 pop. 25,185), Dumbartonshire, W Scotland, on the Forth and Clyde Canal. An engineering center, the burgh has factories that produce mining machinery and valves. The electrical power system of S Scotland is controlled from Kirkintilloch. Chartered in the 13th cent., the burgh is located on the line of the Roman Antonine wall. In 1975, Kirkintilloch became part of the Strathclyde region.

Kirkland, Samuel, 1741–1808, American missionary to the Oneida Indians, b. Norwich, Conn. He made a trip among the Oneida in 1764. In 1766 he went among them again and lived with them according to their customs, preached to them, and became their valued counselor. Kirkland kept the Oneida loyal to the colonists throughout the American Revolution; after the war he assisted in making treaties of peace with the Iroquois and in working out plans for their welfare. He again (1790–92) pacified the Six Nations, when there was some danger of their joining the Ohio tribes in revolt. He realized one of his life's ambitions when (1793) he received—through the aid of Alexander Hamilton—a charter from New York state to found Hamilton Oneida Academy for the education of both white and Indian youths. Few Indians attended, however, and as Hamilton College it changed over to a regular curriculum.

Kirkland, city (1970 pop. 15,249), King co., W Wash., a suburb of Seattle on Lake Washington; inc. 1905. Furniture is the principal manufacture.

Kirkland Lake, mining town, E Ont., Canada. It is one of Canada's largest gold-mining centers. Gold was discovered there in 1911.

Kırklareli (kərklär'ĕlē''), city (1970 pop. 28,290), capital of Kırklareli prov., NW Turkey. It is a transportation hub and a trade center for butter and cheese. During the First Balkan War the Bulgarians defeated (1912) the Turks there. The city has numerous mosques and Greek churches. It was formerly known as Kırk-Kilise.

Kirksville, city (1970 pop. 15,560), seat of Adair co., N Mo.; inc. 1857. Among its manufactures are shoes, gloves, machinery, and hospital equipment. Andrew Taylor Still founded a school of osteopathy there in 1892; it is now the Kirksville College of Medicine. A state college and a state park are also in the city.

Kirkuk (kĭrkōōk'), city (1965 pop. 167,413), NE Iraq. It is the center of Iraq's oil industry and is connected by pipelines to ports on the Mediterranean Sea. It is also a market for the region's produce, including cereals, olives, fruits, and cotton. There is a small textile industry. Kirkuk is built on a mound containing the remains of a settlement dating back to 3000 B.C. The majority of the inhabitants are Kurds.

Kirkwall (kûrk'wôl, -wəl), burgh (1971 pop. 4,618), county town of Orkney, N Scotland, on the east coast of Mainland Island. It is the trading center of the Orkney Islands, with exports of eggs, fish, whiskey, cattle, and sheep. It is also a boatbuilding center. Kirkwall was founded sometime prior to 1046 (when it was mentioned in a saga) and became important as a port on the northern trade route to Scandinavia and the Baltic states. St. Magnus Cathedral dates from 1137, the bishop's palace from c.1200, and the earl's palace from 1600. The latter two are ruins.

Kirkwood, Samuel Jordan, 1813–94, American politician, b. Harford co., Md. Moving to Ohio in 1835, he served (1845–49) as prosecuting attorney for Richland co. and was a member (1850–51) of the Ohio constitutional convention. After settling in Iowa in 1855, he was elected (1856) to the state legislature and then to the governorship (1860–64). A thoroughgoing radical Republican, he successfully quelled internal dissension and supplied the Union Army with over 50 regiments of infantry and cavalry, partly fitted out with his own money. In 1866–67, Kirkwood filled out a term in the U.S. Senate. He was again governor (1876–77), U.S. Senator (1877–81), and Secretary of the Interior (1881–82). See biography by D. E. Clark (1917).

Kirkwood, city (1970 pop. 31,769), St. Louis co., E Mo., a suburb of St. Louis; inc. 1865. Lime, cement, and lumber products are made. A junior college is in the city.

Kirkwood's gaps, regions in the ASTEROID belt within which no asteroids are found; first observed (1886) by the astronomer D. Kirkwood. None of the asteroids has an orbital period close to ½, ⅓, or ⅖ that of Jupiter. It was at first believed that the orbits of these "missing" asteroids had been altered by a resonant gravitational PERTURBATION caused by Jupiter; recent calculations indicate that the gaps are probably due to mutual interactions of the asteroids themselves.

Kirov, Sergei Mironovich (syĭrgā' mērô'nəvĭch kē'rəf), 1888–1934, Russian Soviet leader. He fought in the civil war of 1918–20 and rose to power as one of Stalin's most trusted aides. A member of the Communist party Politburo from 1930, he was secretary of the party at Leningrad when he was assassinated, probably at Stalin's order. However, Stalin used Kirov's murder to institute the party purge and the treason trials of the late 1930s. Among those tried and executed were ZINOVIEV, KAMENEV, and RYKOV, who were charged with association with TROTSKY and counterrevolutionary conspiracy.

Kirov (kē'rəf), formerly **Vyatka** (vyät'kə), city (1970 pop. 332,000), capital of Kirov oblast, central European USSR, on the Vyatka River. It is a river port and an industrial center with sawmills and machine and metalworking plants. Founded in 1174 as Khlynov by Novgorod colonists, it was fortified against Votyak (Udmurt) and Cheremiss (Mari) attacks. It soon became the capital of an independent republic which was annexed to Moscow by Ivan III in 1489. Its location made for favorable trade conditions with Ustyug, the Volga region, and Archangelsk. In the 17th cent. it grew in importance because it was on the road from Moscow to Siberia. The city was renamed Vyatka in 1780. In the 19th cent. it was used as a place of political exile. The city was renamed in 1934 for S. M. Kirov. In Kirov are a 17th-century cathedral and a library (1837) founded by Alexander Herzen, who was an exile in the city.

Kirovabad (kē"rəvəbät'), city (1970 pop. 190,000), SE European USSR, in Azerbaijan, on the Gandzha River. The largest Azerbaijan industrial center after Baku, Kirovabad produces cotton and silk textiles, building materials, carpets, cottonseed oil, agricultural implements, copper sulfate, and wine. Formerly named Gandzha or Ganja, it was founded in the 6th cent., c.4 mi (6 km) east of the modern city, but was demolished by earthquake in 1139, after which the survivors settled on the present site. The medieval city was an important textile and wine center. It was destroyed by the Mongols in 1231 and recovered slowly. It was the seat of a khanate under Persian suzerainty from the 17th cent. until its conquest (1804) by the Russians, who named it Elisavetpol. It became Gandzha again after the Russian Revolution, but in 1935 it was renamed in honor of S. M. Kirov. Ancient Gandzha was the native city of the 12th-century poet, Nizami Gandzhevi, whose tomb still remains. There is also a 17th-century mosque.

Kirov Ballet, one of the two major ballet companies of the Soviet Union, the other being the BOLSHOI BALLET. It was originally the Imperial Russian Ballet, performing in St. Petersburg, now Leningrad. In 1889 it moved into the Maryinsky Theatre. Under the direction of Marius PETIPA the company premiered the Tchaikovsky ballets *Sleeping Beauty* (1890) and *Swan Lake* (1895). The company went into decline after the Russian Revolution in 1917. The great teacher and ballet mistress Agrippina Vaganova (1879–1951) helped perpetuate its traditions by training the company's principal dancers. Her work became the foundation of modern Soviet ballet instruction. In 1935 the company was renamed the Kirov Ballet. It is often regarded as the foremost European ballet company, maintaining strict classical traditions of elegance and beauty.

Kirovograd (kē"rəvəgrät'), city (1972 est. pop. 201,000), capital of Kirovograd oblast, S central European USSR, in the Ukraine, on the Ingul River. It is an agricultural trade center, with one of the USSR's largest farm machinery plants. Other industries include metallurgy, food processing, and the manufacture of building materials. Founded as a fortress in 1754, it was named Elisavetgrad for Empress Elizabeth. Between 1881 and 1919 it was the scene of several pogroms. It was renamed Zinovievsk in 1924, Kirovo in 1936, and Kirovograd in 1939.

Kirovsk (kē'rəfsk), city (1970 pop. 38,000), N European USSR, on the Kola Peninsula. The city is the center of a mining complex that produces apatite and nephelite, raw materials for the superphosphate and aluminum industries. It was founded in 1929 as Khibinogorsk.

kirsch or **kirschwasser** (kĭrsh, -väs'ər) [Ger.,= cherry water], a LIQUEUR made principally in France, Germany, and Switzerland from the pulp and crushed stones of the cherry, fermented, then distilled and sweetened. It is distilled in earthenware or paraffin-lined casks to prevent it from taking on the color imparted by wood.

Kırşehir (kŭr"shĕhĕr'), city (1970 pop. 32,580), capital of Kırşehir prov., central Turkey. It is noted for its carpets. Grains are grown nearby.

Kirshon, Vladimir Mikhailovich (vlədyē'mĭr mĕkhī'ləvĭch kĕrshôn'), 1902–38, Russian dramatist. He began his career with *Red Dust* (1927, tr. 1930), a play showing the degeneration of a revolutionist under the reconstruction program known as the New Economic Policy. His play *Bread* (1930, tr. 1934) deals with the struggle against private hoarding on collective farms. The majority of his plays concerned the social problems of the new order. Kirshon was expelled from the Communist party in 1937 because of his leading role in the suspect Russian Association of Proletarian Writers.

Kirstein, Lincoln, 1907–, American dance and theater executive and writer, b. Rochester, N.Y. Kirstein was cofounder of the American Ballet in 1934. In 1948 he helped establish the New York City Ballet, becoming its general director. Together with the choreographer George BALANCHINE he encouraged the development of a truly American style of dance. He is the author of many books including *Dance* (1935), a compendious history; *Ballet Alphabet* (1939); *The Classic Ballet, Basic Technique and Terminology* (with Muriel Stuart, 1952); *Movement and Metaphor* (1970); a history of the New York City Ballet (1973); and the definitive biography of Elie Nadelman (1973). Kirstein was instrumental in recovering for their owners works of art plundered by Nazi officials during World War II. As a producer he has worked with the Shakespeare Memorial Theater at Stratford, Conn., and for many years presented the 12th-century musical drama *The Play of Daniel* annually at Christmas in New York. Kirstein has also promoted cultural exchange programs between Japan and the United States.

Kirun: see CHI-LUNG, Taiwan.

Kiruna (kē'rünä), city (1970 pop. 25,034), Norrbotten co., N Sweden. The northernmost city in Sweden, it is the center of the Lapland iron-mining region. The ore, more than 70% pure, is shipped on the Lapland railroad (completed 1902) either to Narvik, Norway, an ice-free Atlantic port, or to Luleå, Sweden, on the Gulf of Bothnia. Kiruna became the most extensive city (c.5,500 sq mi/14,250sq km) in the world in 1948, when several distant mining villages were incorporated into it. The city is also a winter sports center and has a geophysical institute.

Kiryu (kĭryo͞o'), city (1970 pop. 133,141), Gumma prefecture, central Honshu, Japan. A major center of silk production since the 8th cent., it now manufactures rayon as well.

Kisangani (kēsangä'nē), formerly **Stanleyville,** city (1970 pop. 230,000), capital of Haut-Zaïre region, N central Zaïre, a port on the Congo River. The city is the terminus of steamer navigation on the Congo from Kinshasa and is a transportation center for NE Zaïre. It is on a short rail line (to Ubundi) that skirts the Stanley Falls. Manufactures include metal goods and beer, and cotton and rice are shipped from the city. Founded in 1883 by the explorer Henry M. Stanley and originally located on a nearby island in the river, the city, as Stanleyville, became the stronghold of Patrice Lumumba in the late 1950s. After the assassination of Lumumba in 1961, Antoine Gizenga set up a government there that rivaled the central government in Leopoldville (now Kinshasa). Gizenga's regime was quashed in 1962, but in 1964, 1966, and 1967 the city was the site of temporarily successful revolts against the central government. Kisangani has a university and a museum.

Kisarazu (kēsärä'zo͞o), city (1970 pop. 73,319), Chiba prefecture, E central Honshu, Japan, on Tokyo Bay. It is a residential and industrial suburb of Tokyo noted for its Shojoji (Buddhist) temple.

Kiselevsk (kēsĭ'lyôfsk"), city (1970 pop. 127,000), S Siberian USSR. It is a major coal-mining center in the Kuznetsk Basin and also manufactures mining machinery.

Kisfaludy, Károly (kä'roi kĭsh'fŏlo͝odē), 1788–1830, Hungarian dramatist, founder of the Hungarian national drama. Kisfaludy traveled abroad extensively and studied painting before he returned to Hungary and began his literary career. His *Tatars in Hungary* (1819) was the first genuinely dramatic Hungarian play and the first of the many successes by which he established the national drama and the Hungarian romantic movement. With his brother Sándor he was cofounder (1822), editor, and a major contributor of the vigorous, influential literary journal *Aurora.* Among his works are the comedies *The Suitors* and *The Rebels* and the tragedy *Irene.* His brother, the poet **Sándor Kisfaludy,** 1772–1844, is considered the first major romantic poet of Hungary. He is especially celebrated for his two volumes of love lyrics, *The Loves of Himfy* (1801, 1807).

Kish (kĭsh). **1** Father of Saul. 1 Sam. 9.1; 10.21. Cis: Acts 13.21. **2** Uncle of Saul. 1 Chron. 8.30; 9.36. **3** Ancestor of Mordecai. Esther 2.5. **4** Merarite. 1 Chron. 23.21; 24.29; 2 Chron. 29.12.

Kish, ancient city of Mesopotamia, in the Euphrates valley, 8 mi (12.9 km) E of Babylon and 12 mi (19 km) east of the modern city of Hillah, Iraq. It was occupied from very ancient times, and its remains go back as far as the protoliterate period in Mesopotamia. In the early 3d millennium B.C., Kish was a Semitic city. Although it was one of the provincial outposts of Sumerian civilization, it had a cultural style of its own. There is an excavated palace of Sargon I of Agade, a native of Kish, and a great temple built by Nebuchadnezzar and Nabonidus in the later Babylonian period. The site also yielded a complete sequence of pottery from the Sumerian period to that of Nebuchadnezzar.

Kishi (kĭsh'ī), Levite: see KUSHAIAH.

Kishi, Nobusuke (nōbo͞os'kā kē'shē), 1896–, Japanese statesman. The son of a minor official, he attended the law college of Tokyo Univ. He entered government service in 1920 and rose to high office in the ministry of commerce and industry. After 1935 he played a key role in the industrial development of MANCHUKUO. During World War II he was minister of commerce and industry in Hideki Tojo's cabinet; he was imprisoned for three years after the war. As secretary general of the postwar Democratic party, he was instrumental in uniting all conservative factions into the powerful Liberal Democratic party (1955). He became party president and prime minister in 1957, but widespread public agitation over the new UNITED STATES-JAPAN SECURITY TREATY forced Kishi to resign from both posts in 1960. He was succeeded by Hayato Ikeda. See Dan Kurzman, *Kishi and Japan* (1960).

Kishinev (kĭshĭnyĕf',-nĕf'), Rumanian *Chisinau,* city (1972 est. pop. 400,000), capital of the Moldavian Soviet Socialist Republic, SW European USSR, on the Byk River, a tributary of the Dnestr. Major industries include food and tobacco processing, metalworking, and the manufacture of building materials, machinery, plastics, rubber, and textiles. Founded in the early 15th cent. as a monastery town, Kishinev was taken in the 16th cent. by the Turks and in 1812 by the Russians, who made it the center of Bessarabia. Rumania held the city from 1918 to 1940, when it was seized by the USSR. The Jewish population, which formerly constituted about 40% of the total, was largely exterminated in World War II. Kishinev's educational and cultural facilities include a university (1945) and the Academy of Sciences of the Moldavian SSR.

Kishion (kĭsh'ēŏn), unidentified Levitical border town, W of the Sea of Galilee. Joshua 19.20. Kishon: Joshua 21.28. Kedesh: 1 Chron. 6.72.

Kishiwada (kēshēwä'dä), city (1970 pop. 162,022), Osaka prefecture, SW Honshu, Japan, on Osaka Bay. It is an industrial and residential suburb of Osaka.

Kishon (kī'shŏn) [Heb. *Qishon*=tortuous], intermittent river, c.45 mi (70 km) long, rising below Mt. Gilboa, N Israel, and flowing NW to the Mediterranean Sea near Haifa; only the lower 7-mi (11.3-km) section is a permanent stream. The defeat of Sisera and the slaying by Elijah of the prophets of Baal occurred on the river bank (Judges 4.7,13; 5.21; 1 Kings 18.40. Kison: Ps. 83.9). For Kishon, the town, see KISHION.

Kiska, island: see ALEUTIAN ISLANDS.

Kiskunfélegyháza (kĭsh'ko͝onfā'lĕdyəhä"zŏ), city (1970 pop. 34,127), S central Hungary. It is a road and rail junction; trade and industry are based on the agricultural products of the surrounding region.

Kislovodsk (kēsləvôtsk') [Rus.,=sour water], city (1970 pop. 90,000), S European USSR, in the N Caucasus mts. It is a famous health resort with mineral springs, sanatoriums, and a physico-therapeutical institute. Kislovodsk was founded in 1803.

Kismayu (kĭsmī'o͞o), town (1968 est. pop. 18,000), SW Somalia, on the Indian Ocean. It is the principal town and port of the Juba region. Kismayu was founded in 1872 by the sultan of Zanzibar, passed to Great Britain in 1887, and was held until 1924, when it was transferred to Italian control. The town has several mosques and a palace that was constructed by the sultan.

Kispest: see BUDAPEST, Hungary.

Kissidougou (kēsēdo͞o'go͞o), town (1961 est. pop. 12,000), S Guinea. It is a market town for an agricultural area that produces coffee, rice, palm products, kola nuts, and other crops. There are sawmills in the town, and diamonds are mined nearby.

Kissimmee, Lake, 55 sq mi (142 sq km), central Fla.; one of the largest freshwater lakes in Florida. The Kissimmee River, 140 mi (225 km) long, rises in small lakes and flows S through Lake Kissimmee to Lake Okeechobee. The lake and river region is a major U.S. cattle-raising area; truck crops and citrus fruits are also grown.

kissing bug: see ASSASSIN BUG.

Kissinger, Henry Alfred (kĭs'ənjər), 1923–, American political scientist and U.S. Secretary of State (1973–), b. Fürth, Germany. He emigrated to the United States in 1938 and later became (1943) a citizen. As a leading expert on international relations and nuclear defense policy, Kissinger taught (1957–69) at Harvard and served as a consultant to government agencies and private foundations. As President Nixon's assistant for national security affairs (1969–) and later as Secretary of State, he played a major role in formulating U.S. foreign policy. Kissinger helped initiate (1969) the Strategic Arms Limitation Talks (SALT) with the Soviet Union and arranged President Nixon's 1972 visit to the People's Republic of China. He supported U.S. disengagement from Vietnam and won (1973) the Nobel Peace Prize for negotiating the cease-fire with North Vietnam. His negotiating skill also led to a cease-fire between Israel and Egypt, and the disengagement of their troops after the 1973 Arab-Israeli War. Kissinger continued in office after Gerald R. Ford succeeded (1974) to the presidency. He is the author of many articles and books, including *Nuclear Weapons and Foreign Policy* (1957), *The Necessity for Choice* (1961), and *The Troubled Partnership* (1965). See biographies by David Landau (1972) and S. R. Graubard (1973); studies by C. R. Ashman (1972) and Bernard and Marvin Kalb (1974).

Kistna (kĭst'nə) or **Krishna** (krĭsh'nə), river, c.800 mi (1,290 km) long, rising in Maharashtra state, central India, in the Western Ghats, and flowing SE through Andhra Pradesh state to the Bay of Bengal. The river supplies water for irrigation. Its source is sacred to Hindus; the river is named for the god Krishna.

Kisumu (kēso͞o'mo͞o), city (1969 pop. 30,700), capital of Nyanza prov., SW Kenya, on Kavirondo Gulf (an arm of Victoria Nyanza). It is the principal lake port of Kenya and the commercial center of a prosperous farm region. Manufactures include refined sugar, frozen fish, textiles, and processed sisal. The railroad from Mombasa reached Kisumu in 1901. The city was formerly called Port Florence.

Kitab al-Aghani (kētäb' äl-ägänē') [Arabic,=book of songs], collection of poems in many volumes compiled by ABU AL-FARAJ ALI OF ESFAHAN. It contains poems from the oldest epoch of Arabic literature down to the 9th cent. The poems were put to music, but the musical signs are no longer readable. Because of the accompanying biographical annotations on the authors and composers, the work is an important historical source.

Kitai: see CH'I-T'AI, China.

Kitakyushu (kētä'kyo͞osho͞o), city (1970 pop. 1,042,-321), Fukuoka prefecture, N Kyushu, Japan, on the Shimonoseki Strait between the Inland Sea and the Korea Strait. It was formed in 1963 by the union of the cities of Kokura, Moji, Tobata, Wakamatsu, and Yawata (or Yahata), which are now wards of the city. Kitakyushu is one of Japan's most important manufacturing regions and one of its chief ports and railroad centers. It has a great variety of industries, the chief of which produce iron and steel (especially in Yawata ward), textiles, chemicals, machinery, ships, porcelain, and glass. Its ports (especially in Moji and Wakamatsu wards) receive raw materials and export manufactured goods. Kokura ward is the city's commercial and financial center. Tobata ward has a major coal-handling facility; a deep-sea fishing fleet is based there. There are several institutions of higher learning in Kitakyushu. The city is connected by tunnel and bridge with Shimonoseki on Honshu.

Kitami (kētä'mē), city (1970 pop. 82,727), Hokkaido prefecture, NE Hokkaido, Japan, on the Tokoro River. It is an agricultural market and a major center for the production of peppermint.

Kitasato, Shibasaburo (shĭbä'säbo͞orō kē'täsä'tō), 1852–1931, Japanese physician. He worked with Robert Koch in Germany (1885–91), and with Emil Behring he studied the tetanus bacillus and developed (1890) an antitoxin for diphtheria. After returning to Japan he founded an institute for the study of infectious diseases and became its director in 1891. His most noted contribution to bacteriology was the discovery (1894) of the infectious agent of bubonic plague, which he described simultaneously with Alexandre Yersin.

Kit-Cat Club, London political and literary club, active c.1700–1720. The membership of some four dozen included leading Whig politicians and London's best young writers. Among them were Charles Seymour, 6th duke of Somerset; Sir Robert Walpole; Thomas Pelham-Holles, duke of Newcastle; William Congreve; Joseph Addison; Sir Richard Steele; and Sir Godfrey KNELLER, who did portraits of the members. The club was the center of opposition during Queen Anne's Tory ministry (1710–14).

kitchen, separate room or other space set aside for the cooking or preparation of meals. When cooking first moved indoors, it was performed, with other domestic labors, in the common room, where the fire burned on the hearth, or—even earlier, before chimneys were known—on the floor in the center of the room. With the building of larger houses, the kitchen became a separate room. Little is known of the culinary arrangements of antiquity. Excavations at Pompeii show separate rooms fitted with the simple equipment still used in some Oriental cooking. A large brazier, or metal basket on legs, held burning charcoal over which a single basin could be simmered. In homes of wealthy Romans a bench of brick or masonry contained several holes, so that a number of dishes could be cooked at once. Water was kept in jars and heated in large caldrons. Although the peoples of N Europe used stoves from ancient times for heating, they cooked over open fires and baked in outdoor ovens. In the Middle Ages, many of the finest kitchens were in the monasteries; the kitchens were in separate buildings and were equipped for cooking, brewing, and baking on a large scale. In North American colonial and pioneer days the kitchen was large enough to accommodate the operations of spinning, weaving, sewing, knitting, and harness mending as well as cooking. Early American manor houses, especially in the South, usually had separate kitchens, often connected with the house by a covered way or porch. Many farmhouses, before the use of gas or electricity, had a separate summer kitchen, where canning or preserving and the preparation of meals for harvest workers could be carried on without heating the house. See Molly Harrison, *The Kitchen in History* (1973).

Kitchen Cabinet, in U.S. history, popular name for the group of intimate, unofficial advisers of President JACKSON. Early in his administration Jackson abandoned official cabinet meetings and used heads of departments solely to execute their departmental duties, while the policies of his administration were formed in meetings of the Kitchen Cabinet. The members of the informal cabinet included the elder Francis P. BLAIR, Duff GREEN, Isaac Hill, Amos KENDALL, and William B. Lewis. John H. EATON of the regular cabinet met with the group; Martin VAN BUREN also was taken into its confidence. Several members of the Kitchen Cabinet were able journalists, editors of influential regional newspapers. They continued to wield effective pens in defense of the administration measures after they came to Washington. Kendall—perhaps the ablest and most influential member—vigorously defended the policies of Andrew Jackson in the *Globe*, the administration journal edited by Francis P. Blair. Following the cabinet reorganization of 1831, the Kitchen Cabinet became less important.

Kitchener, Horatio Herbert Kitchener, 1st Earl, 1850–1916, British field marshal and statesman. Trained at the Royal Military Academy, Woolwich (1868–70), he had a brief period of service in the French army before being commissioned (1871) in the Royal Engineers. After duty in Palestine and Cyprus, he was attached (1883) to the Egyptian army, then being reorganized by the British. He took part (1884–85) in the unsuccessful attempt to relieve Charles George GORDON at Khartoum. He was then (1886–88) governor general of Eastern Sudan and helped (1889) turn back the last Mahdist invasion of Egypt. In 1892 he was made commander in chief of the Egyptian army and in 1896 began the reconquest of the Sudan, having prepared the way by a reorganization of the army and the construction of a railway along the Nile. A series of victories culminated (1898) in the battle of OMDURMAN and the reoccupation of Khartoum. He forestalled a French attempt to claim part of the Sudan (see FASHODA INCIDENT) in the same year and was made governor of the Sudan. In 1899, Kitchener was appointed chief of staff to Lord ROBERTS in the SOUTH AFRICAN WAR. He reorganized transport, led an unsuccessful attack on Paardeberg, and suppressed the Boer revolt near Priska. When Roberts returned to England late in 1900, believing the Boer resistance crushed, Kitchener was left to face continued guerrilla warfare. By a slow extension of fortified blockhouses, the use of concentration camps for civilians, and the systematic denudation of the farm lands—methods for which he was much criticized—Kitchener finally secured Boer submission (1902). He was created viscount and sent to India as commander in chief of British forces there. He redistributed the troops and gained greater administrative control of the army in the face of serious opposition from the viceroy Lord CURZON. He left India in 1909, was made field marshal, and served (1911–14) as consul general in Egypt. He was made an earl in 1914. At the outbreak of World War I, Kitchener was recalled to England as secretary of state for war. Virtually alone in his belief that the war would last a number of years, he planned and carried out a vast expansion of the army from 20 divisions in 1914 to 70 in 1916. However, his relations with the cabinet were strained. In 1915 when he was attacked by the newspapers of Lord NORTHCLIFFE for the shortage of shells, responsibility for munitions was taken away from him, and later in the same year he was stripped of control over strategy. He offered to resign, but his colleagues feared the effect on the British public, which still idolized him. In 1916, Kitchener embarked on a mission to Russia to encourage that flagging ally to continued resistance. His ship, the H.M.S. *Hampshire*, hit a German mine and sank off the Orkney Islands, and he was drowned. See biography by Philip Magnus (1958, repr. 1968).

Kitchener, city (1971 pop. 111,804), S Ont., Canada, in the Grand River valley. Settled largely by Mennonites from Pennsylvania in 1806, it was known as Berlin until 1916, when it was renamed in memory of Lord Kitchener. Its products include packaged meats, metal goods, and rubber products. The city of Waterloo adjoins Kitchener. Woodside National Historic Park commemorates the birthplace of W. L. McKenzie King.

kitchen midden, refuse heap left by a prehistoric settlement; kitchen middens have been found throughout the world. First studied (1848) in Denmark, middens are an important source of ecological and cultural information. Kitchen middens, sometimes known as shell mounds, usually date from the late MESOLITHIC period. Their contents include artifacts that can be dated, suggesting the mode of life and technology of ancient peoples. Analysis of animal remains can indicate the climate, season, length of occupation, hunting patterns, and the possible presence of domestication. Estimates of population density are derived from the size and depth of the middens and from the distribution of sites.

kite, in aviation, aircraft restrained by a towline and deriving its lift from the aerodynamic action of the wind flowing across it. Commonly the kite consists of a light framework upon which paper, silk, or other thin material is stretched. Kites having one plane surface require flexible tails for lateral and directional stability. Kite making has been popular in China and other Far Eastern countries for centuries. It is thought that the first use of kites to secure meteorological information was made by Alexander Wilson of Scotland, who in 1749 used them to carry thermometers aloft. In 1752, Benjamin Franklin used kites to study the lightning. The box kite was invented c.1893 by Lawrence Hargrave, an Australian, and was used effectively in meteorological and aerodynamic studies. The tetrahedral kite was used by Alexander Graham Bell for making experiments on problems of airplane construction. See Clive Hart, *Kites: An Historical Survey* (1967); Otto Piene, *More Sky* (1973).

kite, in zoology, common name for a bird of the family Accipitridae, which also includes the HAWK. Kites are found near water and marshes in warm parts of the world. They prey chiefly on reptiles, frogs, and insects. The swallow-tailed, white-tailed, and Mississippi kites are found in the Gulf states and in Central and South America. The Everglade kite, *Rostrhamus sociabilis,* feeds exclusively on a large freshwater snail. The common kite of England, now rare, was once a scavenger in the streets of London. Kites are classified in the phylum CHORDATA, subphylum Vertebrata, class Aves, order Falconiformes, family Accipitridae.

kithara (kĭth'ərə) or **cithara** (sĭth'-), musical instrument of the ancient Greeks. It was a plucked instrument, a larger and stronger form of the LYRE, used by professional musicians both for solo playing and for the accompaniment of poetry and song. It consisted of a relatively square wooden box that extended at one end into heavy arms. Originally it had 5 strings, but later there were 7 and finally 11 strings. These were stretched from the sound box across a bridge

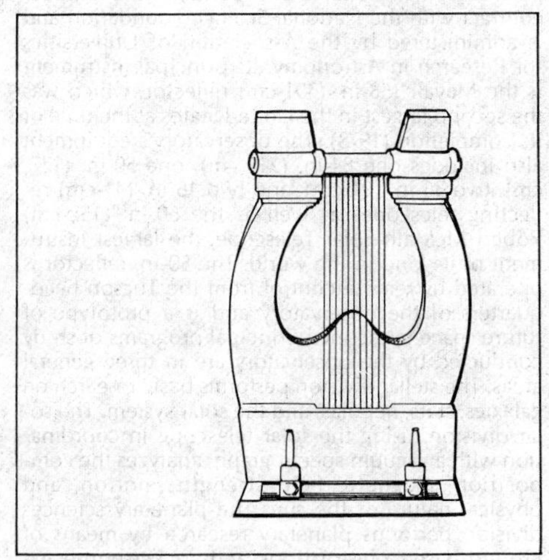

Kithara

and up to a crossbar fastened to the arms. Since the strings were of equal length, tuning was determined only by the thickness and tension of each string. Because of its size and weight, it rested against the body of the player and was held in position by a band. The player usually stood when performing.

Kíthira (kē'thērä) or **Cythera** (sĭthēr'ə), island (1971 pop. 3,961), c.109 sq mi (282 sq km), S Greece, in the Mediterranean Sea, southernmost of the IONIAN ISLANDS, off the S Peloponnesus. Mostly rocky with many streams, it produces wine, goat cheese, olives, corn, and flax. On the south shore is Kíthira (1971 pop. 349), the chief village, formerly called Kapsali. Ancient Kíthira was a center of the cult of Aphrodite. The island passed to Greece in 1864.

Kithlish (kĭth'lĭsh), unidentified town, SW Palestine. Joshua 15.40.

Kitimat (kĭt'ĭmăt), town (1971 pop. 11,803), W British Columbia, Canada, at the head of Douglas Channel. It is the site of a huge aluminum smelter (opened 1954). There are also pulp and paper mills. Kitimat has a deep-water anchorage.

Kitron (kĭt'rŏn), unidentified town, N central Palestine. Judges 1.30.

kitsch [Ger.,=trash], term most frequently applied since the early 20th cent. to works considered pretentious and tasteless. Exploitative commercial objects such as Mona Lisa scarves and abominable plaster reproductions of sculptural masterpieces are described as kitsch, as are works that claim artistic value but are weak, cheap, or sentimental. A museum of kitsch was opened in Stuttgart.

Kittatinny Mountain (kĭtətĭn'ē), ridge of the Appalachian system, extending across NW N.J. from Shawangunk Mt., SE N.Y., to Blue Mt., E Pa.; rises to High Point (1,803 ft/550 m), the highest peak in New Jersey. Kittatinny Mt. is a major resort and recreation area; the Appalachian Trail follows the ridge. The Delaware River cuts through the western part of the ridge forming Delaware Water Gap.

Kittery (kĭt'ərē), town (1970 pop. 11,028), York co., extreme SW Maine, at the mouth of the Piscataqua River opposite Portsmouth, N.H.; inc. 1647. Its economy centers around tourism and the Portsmouth Naval Shipyard, which is located on two islands (formerly part of Kittery and now Federal property) and connected with Kittery by two bridges. The oldest town in Maine (settled c.1623), it grew as a trading, fishing, lumber-shipping, and shipbuilding center. John Paul Jones's ship *Ranger* (built in 1777), and the *Kearsarge* of Civil War fame were both built in Kittery. There are several 18th-century houses in the town, and in the village of Kittery Point, a resort, is the William Pepperrell house (1682). William Whipple, a signer of the Declaration of Independence, was born in Kittery.

Kittikachorn, Thanom: see THANOM KITTIKACHORN.

Kittim or **Chittim** (both: kĭt'ĭm), biblical term for Cyprus, but often extended to include lands in general W of Syria. The name was originally used for the Phoenician port of CITIUM in Cyprus. Gen. 10.4; Num. 24.24; 1 Chron. 1.7; Isa. 23.1,12; Jer. 2.10; Ezek. 27.6; Dan. 11.30; 1 Mac. 1.1.

kittiwake: see GULL.

Kitt Peak, 6,875 ft (2,095 m) high, on the Papago Indian reservation in the Quinlan Mts., S Ariz., SW of Tucson. It is the site of KITT PEAK NATIONAL OBSERVATORY.

Kitt Peak National Observatory, astronomical OBSERVATORY located on the Papago Indian reservation near Tucson, Arizona; it was founded in 1960 under contract with the National Science Foundation and is administered by the Association of Universities for Research in Astronomy. Its principal instrument is the Mayall 158-in. (401-cm) reflector, which was the second largest in the United States at the time of its completion (1973). The observatory's equipment also includes one 84-in. (213-cm), one 50-in. (127-cm), two 36-in. (91-cm), and two 16-in. (41-cm) reflecting telescopes as well as the 60-in. (152-cm) Robert McMath Solar Telescope, the largest instrument of its kind in the world. The 50-in. reflector is operated by remote control from the Tucson headquarters of the observatory and is a prototype of future space telescopes. Principal programs of study conducted by the observatory are in three general areas. The stellar division performs basic research on galaxies, stars, nebulas, and the solar system. The solar division, using the solar telescope in coordination with a vacuum spectrograph, analyzes the composition, magnetic field strength, motion, and physical nature of the sun. The planetary sciences division performs planetary research by means of ground-based observations and rocket-borne experiments.

Kittredge, George Lyman, 1860–1941, American scholar, b. Boston. A member of the Harvard faculty (1888–1936), Kittredge was a noted authority on the English language, Shakespeare and Chaucer. His one-volume edition of the complete works of Shakespeare appeared in 1936. He began a more detailed edition of the separate plays in 1939, which was not completed. His books on English include *The Mother Tongue* (with Sarah Arnold; 1900).

Kitty Hawk or **Kittyhawk,** sandy peninsula, NE N.C., E of Albemarle Sound. Nearby is Kill Devil Hill, where the Wright brothers experimented successfully (1900–1903) with gliders and airplanes. Wright Brothers National Memorial (see NATIONAL PARKS AND MONUMENTS, table), commemorating their first successful flight, is there.

Kitwe (kē'twä), city (1972 est. pop., with suburbs, 251,600), N central Zambia, near Zaïre; founded 1936. It is the main commercial and industrial center of the COPPERBELT. Copper is mined, and food products, clothing, and plastics are manufactured there. The Zambia Institute of Technology is in Kitwe.

Kitzbühel (kĭts'bü"həl), town (1971 pop. 8,000), in Tyrol prov., W Austria, in the Kitzbühel Alps. It is a famous winter sports and resort center.

Kiukiang: see CHIU-CHIANG, China.

Kiungshan: see CH'IUNG-SHAN, China.

Kiuprili: see KÖPRÜLÜ.

kiva (kē'və), large, underground ceremonial chamber, peculiar to the ancient and modern PUEBLO INDIANS. The modern kiva probably evolved from the slab houses (i.e., storage pits and dwellings that were partly underground and lined with stone slabs set on edge) of their cultural ancestors, the BASKET MAKERS. A modern kiva is either a rectangular or a circular structure, with a timbered roof. It is entered through a hatchway by means of a ladder. The floor is made of smooth sandstone slabs, and the walls of fine masonry. There is a dais at one end, a fire pit in the center, and an opening in the floor at the other end. This orifice represents the entrance to the lower world and the place of emergence through which life came to this world. The walls also have a symbolic significance and are decorated with mythological figures. Women are traditionally restricted from entering a kiva. Men use the kiva for secret ceremonies, as a lounging place, and as a workshop where weaving is done.

Kivu (kē'vo͞o, kēvo͞o'), region (1970 pop. 3,361,883), c.89,000 sq mi (230,510 sq km), E Zaïre. It borders on Uganda, Rwanda, Burundi, and Lake Tanganyika on the east. Bukavu is the capital. Coffee, cotton, rice, and palm oil are produced, and some tin and gold are mined. The Ruwenzori mts. and Albert National Park, a vast game preserve, are in the region. Most of Kivu was controlled (1961–62) by the breakaway regime of Antoine Gizenga, which was centered at Kisangani (then Stanleyville). The central government reestablished control over Kivu in 1962, but rebel activity continued there in the later 1960s.

Kivu, lake, 1,042 sq mi (2,699 sq km), 55 mi (89 km) long, on the Zaïre-Rwanda border, E central Africa; highest lake in Africa (4,788 ft/1,459 m). It is drained by the Ruzizi River, which flows S into Lake Tanganyika. Lake Kivu is a tourist center.

Kiwanis International (kĭwä'nĭs), community service organization of business and professional men, founded in 1915 at Detroit, Mich. Local Kiwanis clubs meet weekly; their activities are carried on through committees that include agriculture and conservation, public affairs, business standards, support of churches, children's aid, and vocational guidance. Kiwanis sponsors Key Club International, a service organization for outstanding male high school students. Each local Kiwanis club has a voice in Kiwanis International, which is organized throughout the United States and Canada.

kiwi (kē'wē) or **apteryx** (ăp'tərĭks), common name for the smallest member of an order of primitive flightless birds related to the ostrich, the emu, and the cassowary. The kiwi, named by the Maoris for its shrill, piping call, is most closely related to the extinct MOA. It is the size of a large chicken and has short, stout legs and coarse, dark plumage that hides the rudimentary wings. It lacks wing and tail plumes and walks with a rolling gait. It is the only bird whose nostrils open at the tip of the bill, which is 6 in. (15 cm) long, slender, and curved. Kiwis hide during the day and forage at night for grubs and worms. Their eyesight is poor; the long, hairy bristles at the base of the bill are believed to have a tactile function which is thought to supplement their keen sense of smell in hunting. Kiwis nest in underground burrows, the male performing the incubational duties. The one or two chalky white eggs are 5 in. (12.5 cm) long, weigh almost 1 lb. (0.5 kg), and take from 75 to 80 days to hatch. The three living species of kiwi, genus *Apteryx,* have dwindled with the advance of agriculture and the introduction of predators such as cats, weasels, and stoats, but they are now rigidly protected by law. The kiwi is the symbol of New Zealand and appears on the seal, coins, stamps, and on various products of its homeland; overseas New Zealand troops are popularly called kiwis. Kiwis are classified in the phylum CHORDATA, subphylum Vertebrata, class Aves, order Apterygiformes, family Apterygidae.

Kiyonaga (kēyōnä'ga), 1752–1815, Japanese painter and designer of woodcuts of the Torii school. After working as a bookseller in Tokyo, he took lessons from the Torii master Kiyomitsu but created a more individual linear style. He is best known for his cuts of beautiful women and of warriors. He published (1771–1811) over 100 illustrated books. His unmannered, vivid style had wide appeal and won him many followers. See study by Seiichiro Takahashi (1956).

Kiyonobu I (Torii Kiyonobu I) (kēyōnō'bo͞o), 1664–1729, Japanese printmaker. Specializing in portraits of Kabuki actors, Kiyonobu I worked in the ukiyo-e print style (see JAPANESE ART), concentrating on intricate elements of costume design. Flat and vividly colorful, Kiyonobu's work was notable for its sweeping contour lines and for the boldness of its composition. Kiyonobu was closely allied with the world of theater and frequently painted the actors in their best-known roles. His son, Kiyonobu II, 1702–52, collaborated with him and helped perpetuate his style.

Kizel (kēzyĕl'), city (1970 pop. 54,000), E European USSR, on the Kizel River and on the western slopes of the Urals. It is a coal-mining and industrial center with coal-concentrating factories and plants that produce mining equipment, clothing, and food products. It was founded in the late 18th cent. when the coal mines of the Kizel basin were being developed.

Kizil: see KYZYL, USSR.

Kızıl Adalar (kəzŭl' ädälär') or **Princes Islands,** group of nine small islands (1970 pop. 15,244), c.4 sq mi (10.4 sq km), NW Turkey, in the Sea of Marmara, near İstanbul. The islands are a popular resort area. They were used as places of exile in Byzantine times. There are several old monasteries and churches. Büyük Island is the largest of the group.

Kızıl Irmak (kəzŭl' ərmäk'), anc. *Halys,* longest river of Turkey, c.715 mi (1,150 km) long, rising in the Kızıl Dağ, N central Turkey, and flowing in a wide arc SW, then N, and then NE into the Black Sea. It has an irregular volume and is not used for navigation. The river is an important source of hydroelectric power.

Kizil Kum, desert, USSR: see KYZYL-KUM.

Klabund (kläbo͝ont'), pseud. of **Alfred Henschke** (äl'frĕt hĕnsh'kə), 1890–1928, German poet, novelist, and dramatist. A skillful translator and adapter of Oriental literature, he wrote original poems in a Chinese style. His play *Kreidekreis* (1924, tr. *Circle of Chalk,* 1929), based on Chinese legend, was very popular. His novels include *Bracke* (1918, tr. *Brackie the Fool,* 1927) and *Pjotr* (1923, tr. *Peter the Czar,* 1925).

Kladno (kläd'nô), city (1970 pop. 58,069), NW Czechoslovakia, in Bohemia. An industrial center of the Kladno coal-mining region, it has large iron and steel plants, and manufactures chemicals and machinery. Known in 973, Kladno grew rapidly with the opening of its first coal mine in 1846.

Klagenfurt (klä'gənfo͝ort), city (1971 pop. 74,300), capital of Carinthia prov., S Austria, on the Glan River. Situated in a mountain lake region, it is a noted winter sports center. Manufactures include machinery, textiles, and leather goods. An annual timber fair is held there. Klagenfurt was chartered about the mid-13th cent. and became an episcopal see in the late 18th cent. The city has a cathedral (16th cent.), a theological seminary, and several museums.

Klaipeda: see KLAYPEDA, USSR.

Klamath (klăm'əth), river, c.265 mi (430 km) long, rising in Upper Klamath Lake in the Klamath Mts., SW Oregon and flowing generally SW across NW Calif. to the Pacific Ocean. Most of its course passes through national forests and wildlife refuges. The river is used for irrigation and power production. Klamath Falls is the largest city on the river.

Klamath Falls, city (1970 pop. 15,775), seat of Klamath co., SW Oregon, at the southern tip of Upper Klamath Lake; inc. 1905. It is the processing and distributing center of a lumber, livestock, and farm area, and is a resort center. There is some manufacturing. Klamath Falls was settled in 1867 as Linkville. The Klamath irrigation project (1900) and the coming of the railroad (1909) stimulated its growth from a hamlet to a thriving city. A junior college is in the city, and Crater Lake National Park, Lava Beds National Monument, and Klamath Indian Reservation are nearby.

Klamath Indians, North American Indians, who in the 19th cent. lived in SW Oregon. They speak a language of the Sahaptin-Chinook branch of the Penutian linguistic stock (see AMERICAN INDIAN LANGUAGES). The material for the first description of the Klamath was collected by Peter Skene Ogden, who visited them in 1829 and opened trade relations. They subsisted by hunting, fishing, and collecting roots and wokas, or water-lily seeds. The Klamath were peaceful toward the settlers but not toward the N California Indians. They raided those Indians periodically and carried off the women and children, keeping their captives as slaves or selling them to other Indians. By the treaty of 1864 with the United States, the practice of slavery was abolished and their land NE of Upper Klamath Lake in Oregon was set aside as the Klamath Indian Reservation. Today they are mostly farmers and number some 700. See Leslie Spier, *Klamath Ethnography* (1930); Theodore Stern, *The Klamath Tribe* (1965).

Klaproth, Martin Heinrich (mär'tēn hīn'rĭkh kläp'rōt), 1743-1817, German chemist. He is often referred to as the father of analytic chemistry. He recognized (1789) the presence of zirconium in the ore zirconia and of uranium in a precipitate of pitchblende. He also worked on other elements, including titanium and tellurium.

Klaus, Josef (yō'zĕf klous), 1910-, Austrian politician. He was drafted into the army and fought in World War II on the Axis side. Chosen leader (1963) of the business- and church-oriented People's party, Klaus tended to oppose compromises with the party's coalition partner, the Socialists. He became chancellor in 1964 and was succeeded in 1970 by the Socialist Bruno KREISKY.

Klaypeda (klī'pĕdä), formerly **Memel** (mā'məl), city (1970 pop. 140,000), NW European USSR, in Lithuania, on the Baltic Sea, at the entrance to the Kursky Zaliv. An ice-free seaport and an industrial center, it has shipyards and industries producing textiles, fertilizers, and wood products. One of the oldest cities of Lithuania, Klaypeda was the site of a settlement as early as the 7th cent. It was conquered and burned in 1252 by the Teutonic Knights, who built a fortress and named it Memelburg. The city was ceded (1629) by Prussia to Sweden but reverted to Prussia in 1635. In the Napoleonic Wars the city was (1807) the refuge and residence of Frederick William III of Prussia, who signed there the edict emancipating the serfs in his kingdom. From 1919 it shared the history of the MEMEL TERRITORY. The name also appears as Klaipeda.

Kléber, Jean Baptiste (zhäN bätēst' klābĕr'), 1753-1800, French general, b. Strasbourg. A trained architect, he attended military school in Munich and served in the Austrian army from 1777 to 1783. In 1789 he entered the French National Guard. He fought with distinction in the French Revolutionary Wars and crushed the 1793 royalist uprising in the Vendée. He accompanied Napoleon Bonaparte to Egypt in 1798. Left in command when Napoleon returned (1799) to France, Kléber defeated (March, 1800) the Turks at Heliopolis, near Cairo, and recaptured Cairo. He was assassinated (June) at Cairo by a Turkish fanatic.

Klebs, Edwin (klāps), 1834-1913, German-American pathologist, b. Prussia. He was an assistant of Rudolf Virchow and professor of pathology at Zürich (1872-92) and from 1896 at Rush Medical College, Chicago. He is known for his many original observations on the pathology of infectious diseases. He worked on tuberculosis, malaria, anthrax, and syphilis and described the diphtheria bacillus and typhoid bacillus although he did not demonstrate them to be the causes of these diseases. The diphtheria bacillus is also known as the Klebs-Löffler bacillus.

Klee, Paul (poul klā), 1879-1940, Swiss painter, graphic artist, and art theorist, b. near Bern. Klee's enormous production (more than 9,000 works) is unique in that it represents the successful combination of his sophisticated theories of abstraction with a very personal inventiveness that has the appearance of great innocence. The son of a music teacher, he was himself a musician, and musical analogies permeate his writing. He traveled through Europe, open to many artistic influences. The most important of these were the works of Blake, Beardsley, Goya, Ensor, and, especially, Cézanne. In 1911 he became associated with the BLAUE REITER group and later exhibited as one of the Blue Four. Klee's awakening to color occurred on a trip to Tunis in 1914, a year after he had met DELAUNAY and been made aware of new theories of color use. Thereafter his whimsical and fantastic images were rendered with a luminous and subtle color sense. Characteristic of his witty, often grotesque, pieces are *The Twittering Machine* (1922, Mus. of Modern Art, New York City) and *Fish Magic* (1925, Phila. Mus. of Art). Other works reveal the strong, rhythmic patterns of a relentless terror, as in *Revolutions of the Viaducts* (1937, Hamburg). World-famous by 1929, Klee taught at the BAUHAUS (1922-31) and at the Düsseldorf academy (1931-33) until the Nazis, who judged his work degenerate, forced him to resign. In his series of *Pedagogical Sketchbooks* (tr. 1944) and lecture notes entitled *The Thinking Eye* (tr. 1961), Klee sought to define his intuitive approach to artistic creation. His last ten years were spent in Switzerland, and nearly 2,600 of his works are in the Klee Foundation, Bern. See his notebooks, ed. by Jürg Spiller (Vol I, tr. 1961, Vol II, tr. 1974); his diaries, ed. by his son Felix Klee (tr. 1964); his life and work in documents, ed. by Felix Klee (tr. 1962); studies by Will Grohmann (1958 and 1967), Werner Haftmann (1968), and Christian Geelhaar (1973).

Klein, Christian Felix (krĭs'tēän fā'lĭks klīn), 1849-1925, German mathematician. He is noted for his work in geometry and on the theory of functions. His Erlangen program (1872) for unifying the diverse forms of geometry through the study of equivalence in transformation groups was influential, especially in the United States, for over 50 years. In his *Lectures on the Icosahedron and the Solution of Equations of the Fifth Degree* (1884, tr. 1888) he showed how the rotation groups of regular solids could be applied to the solution of difficult algebraic problems. Klein was professor of mathematics successively at the Univ. of Erlangen, the Technical Institute, Munich, and the universities of Leipzig and Göttingen, and was a prolific writer and lecturer on the theory, history, and teaching of mathematics. His works include *Famous Problems of Elementary Geometry* (1895; tr., 2d ed. 1930) and *Elementary Mathematics from an Advanced Standpoint* (2 vol., 1907-8; tr. 1932-40).

Kleist, Heinrich von (hīn'rĭkh fən klīst), 1777-1811, German dramatic poet. His writings rank high in German romantic literature. Kleist served (1792-99) in the army and led an unhappy life that ended in suicide. His comedies include *The Broken Pitcher* (1806, tr. 1961) and *Amphitryon* (1807), after Molière. Among his passionate tragedies is *Penthesilea* (1808). *Käthchen von Heilbronn* (1810) is a tale of chivalry; his masterpiece is *The Prince of Homburg* (1821, tr. 1956), a historical tragedy. Kleist's terse, dynamic style and his sense of conflict—between reason and feeling, divine law and human law—are also evident in his *Novellen*. Best known of these is *Michael Kohlhaas* (1808, tr. 1967). See studies by Walter Silz (1961) and J. Gearey (1968).

Klemperer, Otto (ô'tō klĕm'pərər), 1885-1973, German conductor, b. Breslau. Klemperer studied in Frankfurt and Berlin. Working first in Prague, he later conducted the Berlin State Opera (1927-33), introducing new works by Janáček, Schoenberg, Stravinsky, and Hindemith. With the rise of the Nazi regime, he went to the United States where he conducted the Los Angeles Philharmonic (1933-40). Klemperer was celebrated for his interpretations of Beethoven, Mahler, and Richard Strauss. In 1938 he directed the reorganization of the Pittsburgh Orchestra. In 1946 he returned to Europe where he conducted in Budapest, Germany, and England. See his *Minor Recollections* (1964).

Klenze, Leo von (lā'ō fən klĕn'tsə), 1784-1864, German architect and landscape and portrait painter. He was court architect to Jérôme Bonaparte of Westphalia and to Louis I of Bavaria, for whom he built many structures in the Italian Renaissance and neo-Greek styles. His chief works in Munich were the Glyptothek (1816-30), the Pinakothek, and the Odeon (1828). In 1839 he began additions to the Hermitage in Leningrad.

kleptomania (klĕp"təmā'nēə) [Gr.,=craze for stealing], irresistible compulsion to steal, motivated by neurotic impulse rather than material need. No specific cause is known. The condition is considered generally as the result of some underlying emotional disturbance rather than as a form of neurosis in itself. Legally kleptomania is not classified as insanity, and the individual is held responsible except when complete lack of control over his actions can be definitely established.

Klerksdorp (klĕrks'dôrp), town (1970 pop. 70,710), Transvaal, NE Republic of South Africa, on the Schoonspruit River. The town, which has grain elevators, lumberyards, and food-processing and beverage-making industries, is the mining and processing center for major gold and uranium deposits and is also the distribution center for neighboring farms. There are rail and road connections with Cape Town and Johannesburg. Klerksdorp was founded in 1837 by BOER farmers and, with POTCHEFSTROM, was one of the first European towns founded in the Transvaal. Gold mining began in 1886 but declined in the late 1890s. Heavy fighting occurred in the area during the SOUTH AFRICAN WAR (1899-1902). Gold mining revived in 1932, and the town underwent an economic revival, which accelerated after World War II. Klerksdorp has a training school for nurses.

Klesl or **Khlesl, Melchior** (both: mĕl'khyôr klā'səl), 1552-1630, Austrian politician, cardinal of the Roman Catholic Church. The son of a Protestant baker, he was converted to Catholicism by the Jesuits and became chancellor of the Univ. of Vienna. Made (1581) an official of the bishop of Passau and then (1598) bishop of Vienna, he led the campaign to drive Protestantism from Lower Austria. Later, however, as adviser to Archduke (after 1612, Holy Roman Emperor) MATTHIAS, he concluded that only a policy of compromise would preserve intact the Hapsburg domains. In 1615 he was created cardinal. Archduke Ferdinand (later Holy Roman Emperor FERDINAND II), attributing the emperor's delay in putting down the Prague insurrection (the prelude to the THIRTY YEARS WAR) to Klesl's influence, had him imprisoned (1618). Later released (1622) and transferred to Rome, he returned to Vienna as bishop in 1627.

Kleve, city and former duchy, West Germany: see CLEVES.

Klikitat Indians (klĭk'ĭtăt"), North American Indians whose language belongs to the Sahaptin-Chinook branch of the Penutian linguistic stock (see AMERICAN INDIAN LANGUAGES), inhabiting S central Washington in the early 19th cent. Lewis and Clark visited (1805) them and estimated their population to be some 700. They were energetic traders, acting as middlemen between the Indians of the coast and those of the interior. By the Yakima treaty (1855) they ceded their territory to the United States, and most of them went to live on the Yakima Reservation, where they have lost their identity as a tribe. See C. O. Bunnell, *Legends of the Klikitats* (1933).

Klimt, Gustav (go͝os'täf klĭmt), 1862-1918, Austrian painter. He cofounded the Vienna Secession group, an alliance against 19th-century eclecticism in art, and in 1897 became its first president. In the following decade Klimt became the foremost painter of ART NOUVEAU in Vienna. He created many murals for public buildings, e.g., the frieze for the Palais Stoclet, Brussels (1908). Klimt achieved his greatest fame as a portrait and landscape painter of exotic and erotic sensibility. Delineating symbolic themes with extravagant rhythms, Klimt was the quintessential exponent of art nouveau. The Museum of Modern Art, New York City, has examples of his work. See his catalogue raisonné by Fritz Novotny and Johannes Dobai (tr. 1969).

Kline, Franz, 1910-62, American painter, b. Wilkes-Barre, Pa. He studied (1937-38) in England, then settled in New York City. From the early 1950s, Kline exhibited large canvases of dynamically painted black-and-white grids. His works often recall Chinese calligraphy but he himself denied Oriental influence. His subsequent works, sometimes with notes of bright color, established his reputation as an important figure in the movement known as ABSTRACT EXPRESSIONISM. See memoir by Fielding Dawson (1967).

Klinger, Friedrich Maximilian von (frē'drĭkh mäk"sēmē'lyän fən klĭng'ər), 1752-1831, German dramatist. A friend of the young Goethe, he was a playwright for a theatrical troupe and later an army officer. His early work typified the STURM UND DRANG period, so named after his play *Wirrwarr; oder, Sturm und Drang* [confusion; or, storm and stress] (1776); his later plays, influenced by Schiller and Iffland, are more reserved in tone. Klinger's other works include the play *The Twins* (1776) and the novel *Faust's Life, Deeds, and Journey to Hell* (1791, tr. 1825).

Klinger, Max (mäks), 1857-1920, German painter, sculptor, and etcher. Before 1886 he produced cycles of original and somewhat morbidly imaginative etchings, such as *Deliverances of Sacrificial Victims Told in Ovid* and *Brahms-Phantasie.* From 1886 to 1894 Klinger devoted himself primarily to painting, usually on a grandiose scale. Among his paintings are *Judgment of Paris* and *Christ on Olympus* (both: Vienna). After 1894 he worked predominantly in sculpture, his most successful medium. Notable examples are *Salome, Cassandra,* and the dramatic polychromed statue of Beethoven (all: Leipzig) and the bust of Nietzsche (Weimar).

klipspringer: see ANTELOPE.

Kłodzko (klôts'kô), Ger. *Glatz,* town (1970 pop. 26,100), SW Poland. It is a commercial center with textile mills, metalworks, slate quarries, and sugar refineries. Founded in the 10th cent., it was capital of a county created in 1462. It was seized by Frederick II of Prussia in the War of the Austrian Succession and was formally ceded to Prussia in 1745.

Klondike (klŏn'dīk), region of YUKON TERRITORY, NW Canada, just E of the Alaska border. It lies around Klondike River, a small stream that enters the Yukon River from the east at Dawson. The discovery in 1896 of rich placer gold deposits in Bonanza (Rabbit) Creek, a tributary of the Klondike, caused the Klondike stampede of 1897-98. News of the discovery reached the United States in July, 1897, and within a month thousands of people were rushing north. Most landed at Skagway at the head of Lynn Canal and crossed by Chilkoot or White Pass to the upper Yukon, which they descended to Dawson. Others went in by the Copper River Trail or over the Teslin Trail by Stikine River and Teslin Lake, and some by the all-Canadian Ashcroft and Edmonton trails. The rush continued by these passes all the following winter. The other main access route was up the Yukon River, c.1,600 mi (2,575 km), by steamer. Many of those using this route late in 1897 were caught by winter ice below Fort Yukon and had to be rescued. With unexpected thousands in the region a food famine threatened, and supplies were commandeered and rationed. The number in the Klondike in 1898 was c.25,000. Thousands of others who did not find claims drifted down the Yukon and found placer gold in Alaskan streams, notably at Nome, to which there was a new rush. Others went back to the United States. Gold is still mined in the area. The hardships of the trails and the color of Klondike days are described in many personal narratives; among the best are W. B. Haskell's *Two Years in the Klondike* (1898) and James Wickersham's *Old Yukon* (1938). See Pierre Berton, *Klondike, the Last Great Gold Rush, 1896-99* (rev. ed. 1972).

Kloos, Willem (vĭl'əm klōs), 1859-1938, Dutch poet and critic. In 1885 he founded the progressive literary journal *De Nieuwe Gids* [the new guide]. His personal anger against prevailing modes of literary expression is vented in the sonnets in *Verzen* (1894), notable for the fresh imagery and metaphor they introduced to Dutch poetry. Unlike some of his literary associates, Kloos never developed social concerns and remained primarily a literary reformer.

Klopstock, Friedrich Gottlieb (frē'drĭkh gôt'lēp klôp'shtôk), 1724-1803, German poet, important for his influence upon Goethe, the GÖTTINGEN poets, and the STURM UND DRANG movement. His epic *Messias* (4 vol., 1748-73, tr. *The Messiah*) created a literary storm when it first appeared in the *Bremen Beitrage.* The poem has the merit of being the first major modern work by a distinctively German poet, but the poem as a whole is weak, for Klopstock's genius was lyrical rather than epic. His rhapsodic, musical *Odes* (1747-80) strongly influenced German song composition. Gluck, C. P. E. Bach, Beethoven, Schubert, Mahler, and many others set them to music. Klopstock also wrote a trilogy of dramas on the Germanic hero *Hermann* (1769, 1784, 1787).

Klosterneuburg (klôs"tərnoi'bŏŏrkh), city (1971 pop. 21,900), Lower Austria prov., NE Austria, on the Danube River and the north slope of the Wienerwald, near Vienna. Klosterneuburg was formed in 1938 through the merger of seven towns. It is the site of a wealthy Augustinian monastery (consecrated 1136), the oldest in Austria. The monastery has an extensive library, enormous wine cellars, and the famous Verduner Altar (1181) by Nicholaus of Verdun.

Kloster-Zeven, Convention of (klôs'tər-tsā'fən), 1757. Early in the Seven Years War the English army, under the command of the duke of CUMBERLAND, was defeated by the French at Hastenbeck. Cumberland capitulated at the former Benedictine abbey near Zeven (a small town, formerly in Hanover, NE of Bremen) and allowed the French to occupy Hanover. The convention was disavowed by the English government, and Cumberland was dismissed.

Kluane National Park (klo͞oän'), c.8,500 sq mi (22,000 sq km), SW Yukon Territory, Canada, between Kluane Lake and the British Columbia and Alaska borders; est. 1972. Located in the St. Elias Mts., the park contains some of Canada's highest mountains (including Mt. Logan, the nation's highest peak) and one of the world's largest nonpolar systems of ice fields. There is a great variety of wildlife.

Kluckhohn, Clyde Kay Maben (klŭck'hōn), 1905-1960, American anthropologist, b. LeMars, Iowa, grad. Univ. of Wisconsin, 1928, M.A. Oxford, 1932, Ph.D. Harvard, 1936. He taught at the Univ. of New Mexico (1932-34) and at Harvard (1935-60). Kluckhohn is known primarily for his studies of the Navaho Indians and of personality and culture. His other works include an introduction to anthropology, *Mirror for Man* (1949) and *Culture: A Critical Review of Concepts and Definitions* (1952). See W. W. Taylor et al., ed., *Culture and Life* (1973).

klystron (klīs'trŏn, klīs'-), vacuum tube used in electronic circuits that operate at frequencies from about 200 megahertz to about 30,000 megahertz. A stream of electrons directed and focused by a series of electrodes is made to pass through one or more cavity resonators (spaces enclosed by electrically conducting surfaces). Signal voltages applied to the input cavity resonator modify the speed of the electrons, speeding some up and slowing others down. The output cavity resonator slows the electrons, causing them to emit radiation that constitutes the output signal. Klystrons may be adjusted to provide amplification or oscillation. Unlike the conventional electron tube, the output of the klystron is not measured by the electron flow in the cathode-anode circuit but by the high frequency currents produced in its resonant cavities. Klystrons are widely used in microwave radar and communications equipment and in linear accelerators for nuclear physics experiments.

Klyuchevsky, Vasily Osipovich (vəsē'lyē ô'sĭpəvĭch klyo͞ochĕv'skē), 1841-1911, Russian historian. Interpreting history from a sociological viewpoint, he emphasized geographic and economic conditions as the determining factors of social change. Klyuchevsky considered colonization a distinctive feature of Russian development and an important factor in the rise of a strong central state. Among his many writings, noted for scrupulous research and documentation, is his *Course of Russian History* (5 vol., 1902-21; tr. *A History of Russia,* 5 vol., 1960).

Knapp, Seaman Asahel, 1833-1911, agriculturist and teacher, b. Schroon Lake, N.Y., grad. Union College, Schenectady, 1856. He went to Iowa in 1866 and began publication in 1872 at Cedar Rapids of the *Western Stock Journal and Farmer.* In 1879 he became professor of agriculture and manager of the Iowa State College farm, and from 1884 to 1886 he was president of the college. He resigned to conduct in Louisiana farm demonstration work, an innovative method of instruction which he introduced, consisting of practical demonstrations on individual farms. Later, under James Wilson as Secretary of Agriculture, Knapp was employed by the department as a special agent to promote better farming methods in the South—particularly in the growing and handling of rice, for which he was sent to the Orient to study techniques there. His greatest work was the demonstration of methods of fighting the boll weevil. This led to the development in the Dept. of Agriculture of the Farmers Cooperative Demonstration Work division, which he headed. See biography by J. C. Bailey (1945). He was succeeded by his son, **Bradford Knapp,** 1870-1938, b. Vinton, Iowa, grad. Vanderbilt Univ., 1892, who after his father's death was director of the Farmers Cooperative Demonstration Work division until the department was reorganized in 1914; until 1920 he headed the extension work in the South. He served as president at Oklahoma Agricultural and Mechanical College (1923-28), at Alabama Polytechnic Institute (1928-32), and at Texas Technological College (from 1932). He wrote *Safe Farming* (1919).

kneecap (patella), saucer-shaped bone at the front of the knee joint; it protects the ends of the femur, or thighbone, and the tibia, the large bone of the foreleg. The kneecap is embedded in the tendon tissue of the quadriceps femoris, a large thigh muscle. As the leg bends and straightens, the kneecap glides up and down in a groove of the femur. Dislocation of the kneecap is a common athletic injury, occurring when stress on the powerful extensor muscles that straighten the leg pulls the kneecap to one side. See SKELETON.

Kneller, Sir Godfrey (nĕl'ər) or **Gottfried von Kniller** (gôt'frēt fən knĭl'ər), 1646-1723, English portrait painter, b. Germany. After study in Amsterdam, Rome, and Venice, he settled in England in 1675, achieving success in fashionable circles and at court, where he was named principal painter in 1688. Serving under the monarchs from Charles II to George I, Kneller and the factory of painters in his employ mass-produced such works as *Ten Beauties of the Court* (Hampton Court), *The Duchess of Portsmouth* (Goodwood, Sussex), and *Charles Beauclerk* (Metropolitan Mus.). From 1702 to 1717 he executed 42 portraits of the members of the KIT-CAT CLUB (National Portrait Gall., London), which are among his best works. His facile and standardized paintings are sometimes careless of execution. Kneller became the director, in 1711, of the first Academy of Painting in London and strongly influenced the subsequent generation of English portraitists.

Knickerbocker (nĭk'ərbŏk"ər), term used almost synonymously with the adjective "Dutch" in respect to Dutch families and customs and the Dutch region of early New York state. *A History of New York* (1809), written by Washington Irving under the pseudonym Diedrich Knickerbocker, popularized the term. There was an actual Knickerbocker family that came from Holland c.1674 and lived chiefly in Albany co.

knife: see CUTLERY.

Knight, Charles, 1874-1953, American artist, b. New York City. Knight painted and sculpted animal subjects. He is best known for his murals at the American Museum of Natural History, New York City. These depict scenes of prehistoric life based on information from fossil remains. His books include *Before the Dawn of History* (1935) and *Prehistoric Man* (1949).

Knight, George Wilson, 1897-, English writer and critic, grad. Oxford (B.A., 1923; M.A., 1925). He has written numerous books and essays on English literature, including *The Wheel of Fire* (1930), *The Imperial Theme* (1931), *The Crown of Life* (1946), *The Golden Labyrinth* (1962), and *Neglected Powers: Essays on 19th and 20th Century Literature* (1971), as well as studies of Byron, Milton, and Shakespeare. In addition he has written plays, poems, and an autobiography.

Knight, Sarah Kemble, 1666-1727, American teacher, b. Boston. She was known as Madam Knight in connection with her writing school and her work as a recorder of public documents. Her famous *Private Journal of a Journey from Boston to New York in the Year 1704* (1825) is a source of information on colonial customs and conditions, especially of inns. In later life she herself maintained an inn near New London, Conn.

knight. 1 In ancient history, as in Athens and Rome, a noble of the second class who in military service had to furnish his own mount and equipment. In Roman society, the knights (Latin *equites*) ranked below the senatorial class and above ordinary citizens. A knight forfeited his status if his fortune sank below the assessed value of 400,000 sesterces (about $16,000). **2** In medieval history, an armed and mounted warrior belonging to the nobility. The incessant private warfare that characterized early medieval times brought about a permanent military class, and by the 10th cent. the institution of knighthood was well established. The knight was essentially a military officer, although with the growth of FEUDALISM the term tended to assume a position not only in the ranks of nobility but also in the ranks of landholders. The knight generally held his lands by military tenure; thus knight service was a military service, usually 40 days a year, normally expected by an overlord in exchange for each fief held by a knight. All military service was measured in terms of knight service, and a vassal might owe any number of knight services. Although all true nobles of military age were necessarily knights, knighthood had to be earned. In the late Middle Ages the son of a noble would serve first as page, then as squire, before being made a knight. Knighthood was conferred by the overlord with the accolade (a blow, usually with the flat of the sword, on the neck or shoulder); the ceremony was preceded, especially in the later period of feudalism, by the religious ceremony of the vigil before an altar. A knight fighting under another's banner was called a knight bachelor; a knight fighting under his own banner was a knight banneret. Knights were ordinarily accompanied in battle by personal attendants (squires, pages) and by vassals (see YEOMAN) and servants. Military tenure was generally subject to the law of PRIMOGENITURE, which resulted in a class of landless knights; at the time of the Crusades those landless knights formed the great military orders of knighthood, which were religious as well as military bodies. Important among these were the KNIGHTS TEMPLARS, KNIGHTS HOSPITALERS, TEUTONIC KNIGHTS, LIVONIAN BROTHERS OF THE SWORD, Knights of CALATRAVA, and Knights of AVIZ. Secular orders, patterned loosely on the religious ones, but not limited to landless knights, also grew up, principally as honorary establishments by the kings or great nobles. Examples in England were the Order of the Garter and in Burgundy the Order of the Golden Fleece. The most important of these orders have survived and many more have been added (e.g., the orders of the Bath, of Victoria, and of the British Empire in Great Britain and the Legion of Honor in France; see DECORATIONS, CIVIL AND MILITARY). As the feudal system disintegrated, knight service was with growing frequency commuted into cash payments. In England the payment was known as SCUTAGE. Many landowners found the duties of knighthood too onerous for their meager resources and contented themselves with the rank of squire. This was particularly true in England, where gentlemen landowners are still termed squires. The military value of a cavalry consisting of heavily armored knights lessened with the rise of the infantry, artillery, and mercenary armies. In Germany, where the institution of knighthood persisted somewhat longer than in Britain and France, knighthood in its feudal meaning may be said to have come to an end in the early 16th cent. with the defeat of Franz von SICKINGEN. The title knight (Ger. *Ritter*, Fr. *chevalier*) was later used as a noble title in Germany and France. In the French hierarchy of nobles the title chevalier was borne by a younger son of a duke, marquis, or count. In modern Britain, knighthood is not a title of nobility, but is conferred by the royal sovereign (upon recommendation of the government) on commoners or nobles for civil or military achievements. A knight is addressed with the title Sir (e.g., Sir John); a woman, if knighted in her own right, is addressed as Dame.

knighthood: see CHIVALRY; COURTLY LOVE.

knight service: see KNIGHT 2.

Knights Hospitalers, members of the military and religious Order of the Hospital of St. John of Jerusalem, sometimes called the Knights of St. John and the Knights of Jerusalem. Early in the 11th cent. the increasing number of pilgrimages to the holy city of Jerusalem led some Italian merchants to obtain from the city's Muslim rulers the right to maintain a Latin-rite church there. In connection with this church a hospital for ill or infirm pilgrims was established. When the Crusaders took Jerusalem, the master of the hospital was Gerard de Martignes, who created a separate order, the Friars of the Hospital of St. John of Jerusalem. In 1113, Pope Paschal II recognized the order.

The Knights in the Holy Land. The object of the order was to aid the pilgrims, and it soon became apparent that military protection was necessary. Gerard's successor, Raymond du Puy, reconstituted the order as a military one. The members were divided into three classes—the knights of justice, who had to be of noble birth and had to be knights already; the chaplains, who served the spiritual needs of the establishment; and the serving brothers, who merely carried out orders given them. Besides these, there were the honorary members called donats, who contributed estates and funds to the order. The Hospitalers obtained a great income through gifts, and the necessity of caring for their estates led to the formation of subsidiary establishments all over Europe, the preceptories. The knights took part in the major crusading campaigns, notably the capture (1154) of Ascalon. When Jerusalem fell (1187) to the Muslims, the Hospitalers established themselves at Margat and then (1189) at Acre. The subsequent period was marked by rivalry with the KNIGHTS TEMPLARS and by military failure. Meanwhile, the hospital work of the order went on. In 1291 the knights were driven from the Holy Land by the fall of Acre and established themselves in Cyprus. They continued to combat the Muslims but now by sea rather than by land; the Hospitalers became the principal agents of convoys for pilgrims. Cyprus, however, was not the ideal place for the establishment, and the grand master, William de Villaret, planned the conquest of Rhodes from the Saracens, a conquest achieved by his brother and successor, Fulk (or Foulques) de Villaret in a special crusade (1308–10).

On the Island of Rhodes. The order grew stronger on Rhodes. They had received some benefit from the dissolution of the Knights Templars, and the wealth of their grand priories all over Europe had greatly increased. To some extent, at least, the change was accompanied by a decline in moral standards. The Knights of Rhodes, as they came to be known, maintained their reputation as fighting men. In 1344 the knights, with the Genoese, retook Smyrna and held it for a short time. In 1365, in conjunction with the king of Cyprus, they captured Alexandria, which, however, they were unable to retain. The island of Rhodes was an important strategic point, and the Turks on their advance after the capture of Constantinople determined to take it. A heroic episode in medieval military history was the successful defense of Rhodes by the grand master, Pierre (later Cardinal) d'Aubusson, against the forces sent by Sultan Muhammad II. But the knights could not summon the means to resist indefinitely, and in 1522 the grand master Philippe de L'Isle Adam was forced to capitulate. The knights wandered homeless until in 1530 Holy Roman Emperor Charles V conferred upon them the sovereignty of the island of Malta.

The Knights of Malta. The island became the fixed home of the order and gave its name to the knights. Under Jean de La Valette they built the great fortifications and defended Malta against the Turks in 1565. Meanwhile, the Protestant Reformation had dealt a severe blow to the order. It refused to yield to Henry VIII in England, and the English branch was suppressed. In Malta the order continued to live in fear of the Turks. The city of Valetta was built, and, as in Rhodes, the rule of the order was beneficial. The battle of Lepanto (1571) checked the Turks in the Mediterranean and a time of relative quiet began. The hospital at Malta was the equal of any in Europe, and the knights continued their charitable work. There was some reorganization of the order, and admission became more and more a test of nobility of birth. The order received its death blow when Napoleon Bonaparte on his Egyptian campaign took Malta (1798). The knights were compelled to leave. They chose Czar Paul of Russia as grand master by an illegal election, which was later validated. Many of the knights went to St. Petersburg. Thus a Roman Catholic order, with the permission of the pope, passed under the rule of an Orthodox emperor. The order was practically at an end. Admiral Nelson took Malta, and although by earlier agreement the island was to be returned to the knights, it was by the Congress of Vienna permanently ceded to Great Britain. After Paul's death there was a period of some indecision and deliberation. The pope named Tommasi as grand master; in 1802 he became the last regular head of the order, which moved to Catania. After 1805 the knights had no regular head and the fraternity continued but had little more than nominal existence in Catania, then Ferrara, then Rome. In 1879 the pope restored the office of grand master, but the reconstructed order that resulted has little relation to the old Knights of Malta. It is a charitable organization especially devoted to the care of the sick and the wounded. It expanded considerably, and in 1926 an association was founded in the United States. The reestablishment of the grand priory in conjunction with the efforts of some French Hospitalers who had attempted to revive the order in France took place in 1827, but the reconstituted order had no organic connection with the old order. The symbol of the Order of St. John came to be a white cross worn on a black robe; thus the Hospitalers were the Knights of the White Cross, in contradistinction to the Templars, the Knights of the Red Cross. The Maltese cross (see CROSS) has been used by various secret organizations, which have been falsely alleged to have a connection with the Knights of St. John. See E. J. King, *The Knights Hospitallers in the Holy Land* (1931); E. E. Hume, *Medical Work of the Knights Hospitallers* (1940); Roger Peyrefitte, *Knights of Malta* (tr. 1959); Roderigo Cavaliero, *The Last of the Crusaders* (1960, repr. 1963); C. E. Engel, *Knights of Malta* (1963); Ernie Bradford, *The Shield and the Sword* (1973).

Knights of Columbus, American Roman Catholic society for men, founded (1882) at New Haven, Conn. (where its headquarters are still located). Its objects are to encourage fraternity and benevolence among its members, to promote tolerance, to encourage civic loyalty, and to protect the interests of the Roman Catholic Church.

Knights of Jerusalem: see KNIGHTS HOSPITALERS.

Knights of Labor, American labor organization, started by Philadelphia tailors in 1869, led by Uriah S. Stephens. It became a body of national scope and importance in 1878 and grew more rapidly after 1881, when its earlier secrecy was abandoned. Organized on an industrial basis, with women, Negro workers (after 1883), and employers welcomed, excluding only bankers, lawyers, gamblers, and stockholders, the Knights of Labor aided various groups in strikes and boycotts, winning important strikes on the Union Pacific in 1884 and on the Wabash RR in 1885. But failure in the Missouri Pacific strike in 1886 and the HAYMARKET SQUARE RIOT (for which it was, although not responsible, condemned by the press) caused a loss of prestige and strengthened factional disputes between the craft unionists and the advocates of all-inclusive unionism. With the motto "an injury to one is the concern of all," the Knights of Labor attempted through educational means to further its aims—an 8-hour day, abolition of child and convict labor, equal pay for equal work, elimination of private banks, cooperation—which, like its methods, were highly idealistic. The organization reached its apex in 1886, when under Terence V. Powderly its membership reached a total of 702,000. Among the causes of its downfall were factional disputes, too much centralization with a resulting autocracy from top to bottom, mismanagement, drainage of financial resources through unsuccessful strikes, and the emergence of the American Federation of Labor. By 1890 its membership had dropped to 100,000, and in 1900 it was practically extinct. See T. V. Powderly, *Thirty Years of Labor* (1889, repr. 1967); N. J. Ware, *The Labor Movement in the United States, 1860–1895* (1929, repr. 1964).

Knights of Malta and **Knights of Rhodes:** see KNIGHTS HOSPITALERS.

Knights of Saint Crispin, union of shoemakers, organized in 1867 by Newell Daniels of Milwaukee in protest against the increasing industrialization of the shoe industry, which was replacing the skilled workers with new unskilled factory labor. As a result of a series of successful strikes, it became for a time the largest trade union in the country, with a membership of from 40,000 to 50,000. Interference in politics, corruption among its officers, the combination of employers against it, and the financial crisis of 1873 caused its downfall. By 1878 it was defunct, many of its members having joined the KNIGHTS OF LABOR, in which they became the largest trade element. See D. D. Lescohier, *The Knights of St. Crispin, 1867–1874* (1910, repr. 1969).

Knights of Saint John of Jerusalem: see KNIGHTS HOSPITALERS.

Knights of the Golden Circle, secret order of Southern sympathizers in the North during the Civil War. Its members were known as COPPERHEADS. Dr. George W. L. Bickley, a Virginian who had moved to Ohio, organized the first "castle," or local branch, in Cincinnati in 1854 and soon took the order to the South, where it was enthusiastically received. Its principal object was to provide a force to colonize the northern part of Mexico and thus extend proslavery interests, and the Knights became especially active in Texas. Secession and the outbreak of the Civil War prompted a shift in its aims from filibustering in Mexico to support of the new Southern government. Appealing to the South's friends in the North, the order soon spread to Kentucky, Indiana, Ohio, Illinois, and Missouri. Its membership in these states, where it became strongest, was largely composed of Peace Democrats, who felt that the Civil War was a mistake and that the increasing power of the Federal government was leading toward tyranny. They did not, however, at this time engage in any treasonable activity. In late 1863 the Knights of the Golden Circle was reorganized as the Order of American Knights and again, early in 1864, as the Order of the Sons of Liberty, with Clement L. VALLANDIGHAM, most prominent of the Copperheads, as its supreme commander. Membership in the Sons of Liberty was perhaps between 200,000 and 300,000 in 1864, when it reached its maximum. Only a minority of this membership was radical enough—in some localities—to discourage enlistments, resist the draft, and shield deserters. Numerous peace meetings were held. A few extreme agitators, some of them encouraged by Southern money, talked of a revolt in the Old Northwest, which, if brought about, would end the war. Southern newspapers wishfully reported stories of widespread disaffection, and John Hunt Morgan's raid (1863) into Kentucky, Indiana, and Ohio was undertaken in the expectation that the disaffected element would rally to his standard. Gov. Oliver P. Morton of Indiana and Gen. Henry B. Carrington effectively curbed the Sons of Liberty in that state in the fall of 1864. With mounting Union victories late in 1864, the order's agitation for a negotiated peace lost appeal, and it soon dissolved. See Wood Gray, *The Hidden Civil War* (1942); G. F. Milton, *Abraham Lincoln and the Fifth Column* (1942, repr. 1962); F. L. Klement, *The Copperheads in the Middle West* (1960); R. O. Curry, *A House Divided* (1964).

Knights of the Sword: see LIVONIAN BROTHERS OF THE SWORD.

Knights of the White Camellia: see KU KLUX KLAN.

Knights Templars: see FREEMASONRY.

Knights Templars, in medieval history, members of the military and religious order of the Poor Knights of Christ, called the Knights of the Temple of Solomon from their house in Jerusalem. Like the Knights Hospitalers and the Teutonic Knights, the Templars were formed during the CRUSADES. They originally had a purely military function. Founded when Hugh de Payens and eight other knights joined together c.1118 to protect pilgrims, the order grew rapidly. St. Bernard of Clairvaux drew up its rules, and it was recognized at the Council of Troyes (1128) and confirmed by Pope Honorius III. The Templars received gifts of estates and money, and the organization soon became one of the most powerful in Europe. By combining monastic privilege with chivalrous adventure, they attracted many nobles. The order, organized under a grand master and general council, had its headquarters at Jerusalem. It was directly responsible only to the pope and thus was free from the control of the secular crusading leaders. As Crusaders the knights were important both in fighting the Muslims (notably at Gaza in 1244 and later at Damietta, during the Fifth Crusade) and in the internal struggles of the Latin Kingdom of Jerusalem (see JERUSALEM, LATIN KINGDOM OF). Although the Knights of the White Cross (the Hospitalers) were at first probably larger and richer, the Templars, who wore the red cross on a white ground, were greater warriors. In the later crusades the deadly rivalry of the three orders helped weaken the Crusaders' chances of success. When Jerusalem fell to the Muslims (1187), the Templars operated from Acre; after its fall (1291) the order retreated to Cyprus. By that time the Templars had ceased to be primarily a fighting organization and had become the leading money-handlers of Europe. From the beginning the knights aroused opposition because of their special privileges, their freedom from secular control, and their great military and financial strength. As their banking role increased—they served such kings as Henry II of England and Louis IX of France—and their landholdings grew, they aroused the hostility, fear, and jealousy of secular rulers and of the secular clergy as well. When the Crusades failed, the Hospitalers became a naval patrol in the East, but the Templars grew more worldly, more decadent, and more hated. In 1307, Philip IV of France, who needed money for his Flemish war and was unable to obtain it elsewhere, began a persecution of the Templars. With the aid of Pope Clement V, the king had members of the order arrested and their possessions confiscated. By 1308 the persecutions were in full process. The knights were put on trial and were tortured to extract confessions of sacrilegious practices. The pope at first opposed the trials but soon reversed his position, and at the Council of Vienne (1311–12) he dissolved the order by papal bull. The Templars were completely destroyed by 1314. Much of their property, theoretically designated for the Hospitalers, was acquired by secular rulers. The leaders of the order, including the last grand master, Jacques de Molay, were tried by ecclesiastic judges and sentenced to life imprisonment, but after denouncing their confessions they were burned at the stake (1314) as lapsed heretics by civil authorities. It is impossible to evaluate fairly the Templars and their fate; the injustices of their final treatment have led some to consider them blameless, yet the charges against them were not entirely unfounded. The literature on the Templars is vast. A defense of the order is C. G. Addison, *The History of the Knights Templars* (rev. ed. 1912). See also the studies by E. J. Martin (1928), G. A. Campbell (1937), Edith Simon (1959), and T. W. Parker (1963).

Kniller, Gottfried von: see KNELLER, SIR GODFREY.

knitting, construction of a fabric made of interlocking loops of yarn by means of needles. Knitting, allied in origin to weaving and to the netting and knotting of fishnets and snares, was apparently unknown in Europe before the 15th cent., when it began to be practiced in Italy and Spain. The Scots claimed its invention and also its introduction into France. Hand-knitting needles are of bone, wood, steel, ivory, or celluloid. Two needles with heads are required for flat or selvage work; three or more, pointed at both ends, for tubular work such as hose; and for larger tubular work, a circular needle. The first knitting machine, invented in England in 1589 by William Lee, was refused a patent by Queen Elizabeth on the grounds that it would curtail the work of hand knitters. Lee's machine, marketed in France, was the forerunner of the warp and circular frames used after 1790; these in turn developed into the two modern types of power machines, the warp and the weft. The springbeard needle of Lee's frame was supplemented in 1847 by Matthew Townsend's latch needle, commonly used for coarse work. In 1864, William Cotton patented a machine by which garments and the heels and toes of hosiery might be shaped. Automatic machines were first introduced in 1889. In weft knitting, which includes hand knitting, the fabric is constructed in horizontal courses with one continuous yarn. The basic stitches are the plain (or jersey), purl, and rib. Either flatbed or circular machines may be used. The warp, or chainloom, machine, generally flatbed, builds vertical chains, or wales, each having a separate yarn. The wales are tied together by zigzagging the yarns from needle to needle in the basic tricot or milanese stitches or variants of these. The warp-knit fabric is run-resistant but less elastic than the weft. See Barbara Abbey, *The Complete Book of Knitting* (1972).

Knob Lake: see SCHEFFERVILLE, Que., Canada.

Knolles or **Knollys, Sir Robert** (both: nōlz), d. 1407, English military commander in the Hundred Years War. He became a leader of a company of mercenaries, fought against Bertrand DU GUESCLIN, whom he captured in 1359, and assisted EDWARD THE BLACK PRINCE in his Spanish campaign, especially at Nájera (1367). Continuing to fight throughout France, either for the English or for his own plunder, he ravaged Normandy and the Loire valley. In 1381 he helped to disperse the Peasants' Revolt in England.

Knopf, Alfred A., 1892–, American publisher, b. New York City. After working (1912–14) for the Doubleday, Page Publishing Company, he founded (1915) his own firm (Alfred A. Knopf, Inc.), which remained independent until 1960, when the company was sold by Knopf to Random House, Inc.; the Knopf imprint remained in existence. Knopf emphasized translations of great contemporary European literature, at that time neglected by American publishers, and specialized in producing books that were outstanding for fine printing, binding, and design. His colophon, the borzoi, became synonymous with beauty and taste in book design and high standards in the selection of books for publication.

Knossos: see CNOSSUS.

knot, any fastening made with cord or rope, including such forms as the hitch, splice, tie, and bend. The art of tying knots, known to sailors as marlinespike seamanship, was used in building bridges and rigging ships by the early Egyptians, Phoenicians, Persians, and Greeks; it reached a high stage of development among the seafaring peoples of the West in the 19th cent. The kinds of knots used by sailors are innumerable, but almost any navigator of small pleasure craft will find four secure knots sufficient: the reef, or square, knot (for securing the ends of two lines); the bowline (for forming a loop); the half hitch (for forming a loop); and the eye splice (for any permanent loop, frequently formed around a metal lining called a thimble). In marine speed measurement, a knot is equal to one nautical mile per hour, a nautical mile being 6,076.1 ft (1,852.0 m). In architecture, an ornament of leaves, flowers, or the like on a projecting piece is called a knot. In heraldry, a knot is an ornamental design representing the interlacing of cordage.

Knowles, James Sheridan (nōlz), 1784–1862, Anglo-Irish dramatist; cousin of Richard Brinsley Sheridan. Although he was one of the leading playwrights of his time, his works are seldom produced today. His chief plays, which are noted for their professional, workmanlike construction, include the tragedies *Virginius* (1820) and *William Tell* (1825) and the comedies *The Hunchback* (1832) and *The Beggar of Bethnal Green* (1834). In 1845, Knowles became a Baptist minister.

Knowles, John, 1926–, American writer, b. Fairmont, W.Va., grad. Yale, 1949. He is best known for his first novel, *A Separate Peace* (1960), in which a boy in a New England prep school during World War II learns about love and hate, conflict and death, war and peace. Knowles's other novels include *Morning in Antibes* (1962), *The Paragon* (1971), and *Spreading Fires* (1974).

Know-Nothing movement, in U.S. history. The increasing rate of immigration in the 1840s encouraged nativism. In Eastern cities where Roman Catholic immigrants especially had concentrated and were welcomed by the Democrats, local nativistic societies were formed to combat "foreign" influences and to uphold the "American" view. The American Republican party, formed (1843) in New York, spread into neighboring states as the Native American party, which became a national party at its Philadelphia convention in 1845. The movement was temporarily eclipsed by the Mexican War and the debates over slavery. When the slavery issue was temporarily quieted by the Compromise of 1850 nativism again came to the fore. Many secret orders grew up, of which the Order of United Americans and the Order of the Star-spangled Banner came to be the most important. These organizations baffled political managers of the older parties, since efforts to learn something of the leaders or designs of the movement were futile; all their inquiries of supposed members were met with a statement to the effect that they knew nothing. Hence members were called Know-Nothings, although there was never a political organization bearing the name. Efforts were concentrated on electing only native Americans to office and on agitating for a 25-year residence qualification for citizenship. Growing rapidly, the Know-Nothings allied themselves with the group of Whigs who followed Millard Fillmore and almost captured New York state in the 1854 election, while they did sweep the polls in Massachusetts and Delaware and had local successes in other states. The disintegration of the Whig party aided them in their strides towards national influence. In 1854 they looked towards extension into the South, and in the following year they openly assumed the name American party and cast aside much of their characteristic secrecy. In June, 1855, a crisis developed; at a meeting of the national council in Philadelphia, Southerners seized control and adopted a resolution calling for the maintenance of slavery. The slavery issue, after the passage of the Kansas-Nebraska Act, again came to the front, and this time the slavery issue split apart the Know-Nothing movement as it had the Whigs. The antislavery men went into the newly organized Republican party. Millard Fillmore, the American party candidate for President in 1856, polled a small vote and won only the state of Maryland. The national strength of the Know-Nothing movement thus was broken. See R. A. Billington, *The Protestant Crusade, 1800–1860* (1938, repr. 1964); W. D. Overdyke, *The Know-Nothing Party in the South* (1950, repr. 1968); Carleton Beals, *Brass-Knuckle Crusade* (1960).

Knox, Frank (William Franklin Knox), 1874–1944, U.S. Secretary of the Navy (1940–44), b. Boston. He joined the Rough Riders in the Spanish-American War and also served in World War I. Knox was general manager (1928–31) of the Hearst papers and after 1931 owner of the Chicago *Daily News*. A strong opponent of the New Deal, he was the unsuccessful Republican candidate for Vice President in 1936. In 1940, President Franklin Delano Roosevelt, seeking to create national unity in defense preparations, made Knox Secretary of the Navy. He died in office and was succeeded by James V. Forrestal.

Knox, Henry, 1750–1806, American Revolutionary officer, b. Boston. He volunteered for service and went, in 1775, to Ticonderoga to retrieve the captured cannon and mortar there for use in the siege of Boston. The fortification of Dorchester Heights with this artillery compelled the evacuation of Boston by the British. From that time he was a trusted companion of George Washington. The artillery, under his charge, took a conspicuous part in the battles of Princeton, Brandywine, Germantown, Monmouth, and Yorktown. He commanded at West Point (1782–84) and was a founder (1783) of the Society of the Cincinnati. Knox was Secretary of War both under the Articles of Confederation and under the Constitution (1785–94). A conservative, he attempted to raise a force to oppose Shay's Rebellion, and he favored a strong Federal government. See biography by North Callahan (1958).

Knox, John, 1514?–1572, Scottish religious reformer, founder of Scottish PRESBYTERIANISM. Little is recorded of his life before 1545. He probably attended St. Andrews Univ., where he may have become acquainted with some of the new Protestant heresies. He entered the Roman Catholic priesthood, however, and from 1540 to 1544 was engaged as an ecclesiastical notary and as a private tutor. By late 1545 he had attached himself closely to the reformer George WISHART. When, after Wishart's execution (1546), a group of Protestant conspirators took revenge by murdering Cardinal David BEATON, Knox, now definitely a Protestant, took refuge with them in St. Andrews Castle and preached in the parish church. Attacked by both Scottish and French forces, the castle was eventually surrendered (1547), and Knox served 19 months in the French galleys before his release (1549) through the efforts of the English government of Edward VI. Knox spent the next few years in England, preaching in Berwick and

Newcastle as a licensed minister of the crown and serving briefly as a royal chaplain. He helped to prepare the second Book of Common Prayer, but he declined a bishopric in the newly established Church of England. Shortly after the accession (1553) of the Catholic Mary I to the English throne, Knox went into exile on the Continent, living chiefly in Geneva and Frankfurt. In Geneva he consulted with John CALVIN on questions of church doctrine and civil authority. Meanwhile, through his frequent letters, he exerted considerable influence among Protestants in England and Scotland; in his "Faithful Admonition" pamphlet of 1554 he began to urge the duty of the righteous to overthrow "ungodly" monarchs. In 1555-56 he visited Scotland, preaching in private and counseling the Protestant congregations. After his return to Geneva, where he served (1556-58) as pastor to the English congregation, he wrote the *First Blast of the Trumpet against the Monstrous Regiment* [i.e., regimen] *of Women.* That fiery tract was directed against the Catholic MARY OF GUISE, regent of Scotland, and Queen Mary of England, but it also alienated the Protestant Elizabeth I, who succeeded to the English throne in 1558. *The Scottish Reformation.* In 1557 the Scottish Protestant nobles signed their First Covenant, banding together to form the group known as the lords of the congregation (see SCOTLAND, CHURCH OF). When, in 1559, Mary of Guise moved against the Protestants, the lords of the congregation took up arms and invited Knox back from Geneva to lead them. Aided by England and by the regent's death in 1560, the reformers forced the withdrawal of the French troops that had come to Mary's aid and won their freedom as well as dominance for the new religion. Under Knox's direction, a confession of faith (basically Calvinist) was drawn up (1560) and passed by the Scottish Parliament, which also passed laws abolishing the authority of the pope and condemning all creeds and practices of the old religion. The Book of Discipline, however, which provided an organizational structure for the new church, failed to get adequate approval from the nobles in 1561. When MARY QUEEN OF SCOTS arrived from France to assume her crown in the same year, many Protestant lords deserted Knox and his cause, and some even joined the queen. From his pulpit and in personal debates with Mary on questions of theology and the loyalty owed by the subject to his monarch, Knox stubbornly defied Mary's authority and thundered against her religion. The queen's marriage to Lord Darnley, her suspected complicity in his murder, and her hasty marriage to James Hepburn, earl of Bothwell, stirred the Protestant lords to revolt. Mary was forced to abdicate (1567) in favor of her young son, James VI. All the acts of 1560 were then confirmed, thereby establishing Presbyterianism as the official religion. Despite the ill-health of his last years, Knox continued to be an outspoken preacher until his death. It has been said of Knox that "rarely has any country produced a stronger will." His single-minded zeal made him the outstanding leader of the Scottish Reformation and an important influence on the Protestant movements in England and on the Continent, but the same quality tended to close his mind to divergent views. His *History of the Reformation in Scotland,* finished in 1564 but published in 1584 after his death, is a striking record of that conflict, but includes a number of misstatements and omissions resulting from his strong bias. The standard edition of his works is that edited by David Laing (6 vol., 1846-64, repr. 1967). See biographies by P. Hume Brown (1895), E. S. C. Percy (1937, repr. 1965), Geddes MacGregor (1957), J. G. Ridley (1968), and W. S. Reid (1974); J. S. McEwen, *The Faith of John Knox* (1961); S. W. Reid, *Trumpeter of God* (1974).

Knox, Philander Chase, 1853-1921, U.S. cabinet member, b. Brownsville, Pa. He built up a fortune as a corporation lawyer in Pittsburgh. He was Attorney General (1901-4) in the cabinets of Presidents William McKinley and Theodore Roosevelt. He was prominently identified with trust prosecutions, but failed to dissolve any significant organizations, except that of the Northern Securities Company, a railroad holding corporation. He served as U. S. Senator by appointment (1904-5) and was elected for the succeeding full term, but resigned in 1909 to become Secretary of State under President Taft. Continuing the policies of his predecessors, John Hay and Elihu Root, Knox sought to protect financial interests abroad, particularly in Latin America and China—a policy that became known as "dollar diplomacy." Knox returned to the Senate in 1917 and allied himself with those who fought ratification of the Treaty of Versailles and participation in the League of Nations. See S. F. Bemis, ed., *The American Secretaries of State,* Vol. IX (1929, repr. 1963).

Knox, Ronald, 1888-1957, English theologian and author. He attended Eton and then Balliol College, Oxford, and in 1910 was ordained as an Anglican minister. Doctrinal preferences, however, led to his Roman Catholic ordination (1919) and appointment as Catholic chaplain at Oxford (1926). While chaplain, Knox wrote several detective novels until appointed to produce a new English Bible (complete ed. 1955). Other works include *Spiritual Aeneid* (1918), a defense of his adoption of Catholicism, and *Enthusiasm* (1950), a history of Christian sectarianism.

Knox, Fort: see FORT KNOX.

Knox College, at Galesburg, Ill.; coeducational; chartered 1837, opened 1841 with funds from George W. GALE; called Knox Manual Labor College until 1857. In 1930 it absorbed Lombard College (chartered 1851, opened 1852). The college was the scene of a Lincoln-Douglas debate in 1858.

Knoxville, city (1970 pop. 174,587), seat of Knox co., E Tenn., on the Tennessee River; inc. 1876. A port of entry, it is a major trade and shipping center for a farm, bituminous-coal, and marble area. Its industries include meat packing, tobacco marketing, and the manufacture of seat belts, plastics, textiles, and marble, wood, and metal products. Tourism is also important. The city is surrounded by mountains and lakes, and the Great Smoky Mts. National Park and several state parks are nearby. A house was built on this site c.1785, followed by a fort and then a town, named for Gen. Henry Knox. Knoxville was the capital of the Territory of the United States South of the River Ohio from 1792 to 1796 and twice (1796-1812, 1817-18) served as the state capital. During the Civil War the area was torn by divided loyalties. Federals under Gen. A. E. Burnside occupied the city in Sept., 1863, and successfully withstood a Confederate siege (Nov.-Dec., 1863) led by Gen. James Longstreet, after which the Confederates had no influence in the area. The Univ. of Tennessee at Knoxville and Knoxville College are there. Knoxville is headquarters of the TENNESSEE VALLEY AUTHORITY, and Norris Dam, from which the city procures its power, is nearby. Points of interest include the graves of John Sevier and William Blount, the Blount Mansion (1792), a replica of the old fort, Chisholm's Tavern (1792), and many other old buildings.

Knudsen, William Signius (no͝od'sən), 1879-1948, American industrialist and U.S. government official, b. Copenhagen, Denmark. He emigrated to the United States at age 20, worked in various factories, and became production manager in the Ford Motor Company during World War I. Employed (1922) by the General Motors Corp., Knudsen became (1937) president. From 1940 to 1945, during World War II, he served successively as director of industrial production for the National Defense Commission, the Office of Production Management, and, as lieutenant general in the U.S. army, for the War Dept. See biography by Norman Beasley (1947).

Knut: see CANUTE.

Knutson, Paul: see PAUL KNUTSON.

Knyphausen, Wilhelm, Baron von (vĭl'hĕlm bärôn' fən kənüp'houzən), 1716-1800, German general in British service in the American Revolution. He served in the army of Frederick the Great before coming to America with the Hessian troops in 1776. Knyphausen distinguished himself in the battles at White Plains, Brandywine, Germantown, and Monmouth. He commanded (1779-80) New York in the absence of Sir Henry Clinton.

Koa (kō'ə), obscure name associated with the Assyrians. Ezek. 23.23.

koala (kōä'lə), arboreal MARSUPIAL, or pouched mammal, *Phascolarctos cinereus,* native to Australia. Although it is sometimes called koala bear, or Australian bear, and is somewhat bearlike in appearance, it is not related to true bears. Once abundant, it is now found in much-reduced numbers in Queensland, Victoria, and New South Wales. It has thick grayish fur, a tailless body 2 to 2½ ft (60-75 cm) long, a protuberant, curved, black nose, and large furry ears. The five sharply clawed toes on each foot enable it to grasp and climb. A slow-moving, nocturnal animal, the koala has perhaps the most specialized diet of any living mammal; it feeds on leaves and shoots of a particular stage of maturation from particular species of eucalyptus. The single cub is about ¾ in (1.9 cm) long at birth and is nursed in the mother's pouch, from which it emerges for the first time when about six months old. Until it is about eight months old it continues to ride in the pouch, and until about a year of age it is carried on its mother's back or in her arms. The harmless and defenseless koala has been ruthlessly hunted, chiefly for fur but also for food; disease and the clearing of the eucalyptus forests have also taken a heavy toll. Protective measures have been adopted to prevent its extinction. The koala is classified in the phylum CHORDATA, subphylum Vertebrata, class Mammalia, order Marsupialia, family Phalangeridae.

koan (kō'än) [Jap.,=public case; Chin. *kung-ar*], a subject for meditation in ZEN BUDDHISM, usually one of the sayings of a great Zen master of the past. In the formative period of Zen in China, masters tested the enlightenment of their students and of one another through statements and dialogue that expressed spiritual intuition in nonrational, paradoxical language. In later generations records of such conversations began to be used in teaching, and the first collections of subjects, or koans, were made in the 11th cent. Koan practice was transmitted to Japan as a part of Zen in the 13th cent., and it remains one of the main practices of the Rinzai sect. The most famous koan collections are the *Wu-men-kuan* (Jap. *Mu-mon-kan*) or "Gateless Gate" and the *Pi-yen-lu* (Jap. *Heki-gan-roku*) or "Blue Cliff Records." An example of a well-known koan is: "What is the sound of one hand clapping?" See Isshu Miura and R. F. Sasaki, *Zen Dust* (1966); G. M. Kubose, *Zen Koans* (1973).

kob: see MARSH ANTELOPE.

Kobe (kō'bā), city (1970 pop. 1,288,754), capital of Hyogo prefecture, S Honshu, Japan, on Osaka Bay. One of the leading Japanese ports, it is also a major industrial center and railway hub. It has shipbuilding yards, vehicle factories, iron and steel mills, sugar refineries, and chemical, rubber, and food-processing plants. A cultural center, Kobe has seven colleges and universities and many temples and shrines. Since 1878 the city has included Hyogo (formerly Hiogo), an ancient port that was prominent during the Ashikaga period (14th-16th cent.) and regained importance after it was reopened to foreign trade in 1868. Kobe was heavily bombed during World War II but has since been rebuilt and enlarged.

København, Denmark: see COPENHAGEN.

Koberger, Anton (än'tōn kō'bĕr"gŭr), c.1445-1513, German printer. He established in 1470 the first printery in Nuremberg. In 1483 he produced a German Bible and in 1484 the first book printed in the Hungarian language. Koberger was primarily a publisher. He had agencies in many cities, employed traveling salesmen, and issued one of the first advertising circulars.

Koblenz (kō'blĕnts), Eng. *Coblenz,* city (1970 pop. 119,423), Rhineland-Palatinate, W West Germany, at the confluence of the Rhine and the Moselle (Ger. *Mosel*) rivers. Its manufactures include machines, furniture, pianos, textiles, and printed materials. It is an important trade center for Rhine and Moselle wines. The city was founded (9 B.C.) as Castrum ad Confluentes by Drusus. It was prominent in Carolingian times as a residence of the Frankish kings and as a meeting place for churchmen. Koblenz was held by the archbishops of Trier from 1018 to the late 18th cent. In 1794 it was occupied by French troops and in 1798 was annexed by France and made the capital of the Rhine and Moselle department. The city passed to Prussia in 1815. After World War I it was occupied by Allied troops from 1919 to 1929. Noteworthy buildings in Koblenz include the Church of St. Castor (founded 836; rebuilt c.1200), the fortress of EHRENBREITSTEIN, and an 18th-century castle. Part of the West German state archives are located in the city.

Kobo-Daishi: see KUKAI.

Koch, Johannes: see COCCEIUS, JOHANNES.

Koch, Kenneth (kŏch), 1925-, American poet, novelist, and playwright, b. Cincinnati, Ohio. Since studying at Harvard and Columbia he has been associated with the Artist's Theatre and *Locus Solus* magazine. Koch's "antisymbolic" poetic style contains witty juxtapositions and dislocations of words. His works include *Poems* (1953); *Ko, or a Season on Earth* (1959), a novel in verse; *Bertha and Other Plays* (1966); *Wishes, Lies, and Dreams: Teaching Children to Write Poetry* (1970) and *Rose, Where Did You Get That Red?: Teaching Great Poetry to Children* (1973).

Koch, Lauge (lou'gə kôk), 1892-1964, Danish geologist and explorer, noted for his scientific work in Greenland. He accompanied Knud Rasmussen's second Thule expedition (1916-18) as geologist and cartographer and was chief of a notable expedition (1920-23) to N Greenland during which he completed the mapping of the Greenland coast and gave for the first time the geological picture of the northern portion of the island. Thereafter Koch was almost continuously in Greenland, as leader of Danish expeditions. In 1938 his air photographs over N Greenland proved the much-sought Peary Channel to be only a fjord.

Koch, Robert (rō'bĕrt kôkh), 1843–1910, German bacteriologist. He studied at Göttingen under Jacob Henle. As a country practitioner in Wollstein, Posen, he devoted much time to microscopic studies of bacteria, for which he devised not only a method of staining with aniline dyes but also techniques of bacteriological culture still in general use. He established the bacterial cause of many infectious diseases and discovered the microorganisms causing anthrax (1876), wound infections (1878), tuberculosis (1882), conjunctivitis (1883), Asiatic cholera (1884), and other diseases. He was professor at the Univ. of Berlin from 1885 to 1891 and head of the Institute for Infectious Diseases (founded for him) from 1891 to 1904. In the course of his bacteriological investigations for the British and German governments he traveled to South Africa, India, Egypt, and other countries and made valuable studies of sleeping sickness, malaria, bubonic plague, rinderpest, and other diseases. For his work in developing tuberculin as a test for tuberculosis he received the 1905 Nobel Prize in Physiology and Medicine.

Kochanowski, Jan (yän kôkhänôf'skē), 1530–84, esteemed as the greatest poet of the Polish Renaissance. Kochanowski assimilated the poetic traditions of Italy and France and created new rhythmic patterns, expressive phrases, and syntactic structures that were integrated into the Polish literary language. His philosophical, erotic, and patriotic lyrics lifted Polish literature out of its provincialism and brought it into the mainstream of the European Renaissance. His works include *Trifles* (1584), short poems on many subjects; *Laments*, elegies upon the death of his daughter; an epic, *The Standard*; and a tragedy, *The Dismissal of the Greek Envoys* (1578). Of special note is his Polish version of the Psalms. Much of his work is available in English translation.

Kocher, Emil Theodor (ā'mĭl tā'ōdôr kôkh'ər), 1841–1917, Swiss surgeon, M.D. Univ. of Bern, 1865. He was professor of surgery at Bern (1872–1911). For his work on the physiology, pathology, and surgery of the thyroid gland—which he was the first (1876) to excise in cases of goiter—he received the 1909 Nobel Prize in Medicine. He was a skilled surgeon and a pioneer in the application of asepsis. His works include a textbook on operative surgery (1894).

Kochi (kō'chē), city (1970 pop. 240,321), capital of Kochi prefecture, S Shikoku, Japan. From its port, Urado, the city exports dried bonito, ornamental coral, cement, and paper. Kochi prefecture (1970 pop. 786,690), 2,743 sq mi (7,104 sq km), is a mountainous region with fertile coastal plains.

Ko-chiu or **Kokiu** (both: gô-jēōō), town, S Yünnan prov., China. Site of the country's largest tin reserves, it is the great tin-mining center of China, with smelters and concentrating plants. Iron is also found there, and chemicals are produced.

Kock, Hieronymus: see COCK, HIERONYMUS.

Kodaira (kōdī'rä), city (1970 pop. 137,373), Tokyo Metropolis, central Honshu, Japan. It is a suburb of Tokyo.

Kodály, Zoltán (zôl'tän kō'dī), 1882–1967, Hungarian composer and collector of folk music. In 1906 he began to teach at the Budapest Hochschule, of which he became assistant director in 1919. He lectured (1931–33) at the Univ. of Budapest. Kodály did much to raise the standards of music education in Hungary. With Bartók he collected thousands of Hungarian folk songs and dances, and the influence of this interest is strong in his compositions, which have a romantic style. Among his best-known works are the opera *Háry János* (1926, orchestral suite 1927), the *Psalmus Hungaricus* (1923) and *Missa Brevis* (1945) for chorus and orchestra, and orchestral dances.

Kodiak Island, 5,363 sq mi (13,890 sq km), c.100 mi (160 km) long and 10–60 mi (16–96 km) wide, off S Alaska, separated from the Alaska Peninsula by Shelikof Strait. Alaska's largest island, Kodiak is mountainous and heavily forested in the north and east; the native grasses in the south offer good pasturage for cattle and sheep. The island has many ice-free, deeply penetrating bays that provide sheltered anchorages and transportation routes. The Kodiak bear and the Kodiak king crab are native to the island. Most of the island is a national wildlife refuge. In 1912 the eruption of Mt. Katmai on the mainland blanketed the island with volcanic ash, causing widespread destruction and loss of life (see KATMAI NATIONAL MONUMENT). Discovered in 1763 by Russian fur trader Stepan Glotov, the island was the scene of the first permanent Russian settlement in Alaska, founded by Grigori Shelekhov, a fur trader, on Three Saints Bay in 1784. The settlement was moved to Kodiak village in 1792 and became the center of Russian fur trading. Kodiak is the island's chief town. Salmon fishing is now the main occupation, and the Karluk River is famous for its salmon run. Fish canning, fox breeding, and grazing are also important. A U.S. naval base is there.

Kodok (kō'dŏk), formerly **Fashoda** (fəshō'də), town, SE Sudan, on the White Nile. In 1898 it was the scene of the Fashoda Incident, which brought Britain and France to the brink of war and resulted, in 1899, in an Anglo-French agreement establishing the frontier between the Sudan and the French Congo along the watershed between the Congo and Nile basins. The formation of an Anglo-French entente in 1904 prompted the British to change the town's name in hopes of obliterating the memory of the incident.

Koechlin, Charles (shärl kāklăN'), 1867–1950, French composer. Koechlin studied composition with Massenet and Fauré. He composed in all forms and many styles, but his music is rarely performed. Koechlin was also active as a teacher and music theorist, and wrote books about Fauré and Debussy, for some of whose works he did orchestration.

Koelreuter, Joseph Gottlieb: see KÖLREUTER.

Koerber, Ernest von (fən kör'bər), 1850–1919, Austro-Hungarian prime minister. A career civil servant, he became prime minister (1900–1904) and made a vigorous but vain attempt to reconcile the national factions of the monarchy by liberal, parliamentary methods. His second tenure, after the assassination (1916) of Count STÜRGKH, was brief because of differences with the new emperor, Charles I.

Koestler, Arthur (kĕst'lər), 1905–, English writer, b. Budapest of Hungarian parents. He became a Communist in 1931 but left the party at the time of the Stalin purge trials of the 1930s. While a correspondent in the Spanish civil war, he was captured by Franco's forces and imprisoned; *Spanish Testament* (1937) relates his experiences. Released in 1937, he edited an anti-Nazi and anti-Soviet French weekly and served in the French foreign legion (1939–40). After the German invasion he was interned in a concentration camp. He escaped from France in 1940 and joined the British army. Koestler combines a brilliant journalistic style with an understanding of the great movements of his times and a participant's sense of commitment. His greatest influence has been as spokesman of the ex-Communist left. *Darkness at Noon* (1941), his most important novel, vividly describes the purge of an old Bolshevik for "deviationist" belief in the individual. Other novels include *Thieves in the Night* (1946), a powerful description of the Arab-Israeli struggle, *The Age of Longing* (1951), and *The Call Girls: A Tragicomedy* (1973). His later essays and studies are often philosophic, examining the nature of art, science, and man himself. They include "The Yogi and the Commissar" (1945), a famous essay in *The God That Failed* (ed. by R. H. Crossman, 1951), *The Lotus and the Robot* (1960), *The Ghost in the Machine* (1968), *The Case of the Midwife Toad* (1971), and *The Roots of Coincidence* (1972). See his autobiography in 2 vol., *Arrow in the Blue* (1952) and *The Invisible Writing* (1954); study by Wolfe Mays (1973).

Koffka, Kurt (kôf'kə, Ger. kōōrt kôf'kä), 1886–1941, American psychologist, b. Germany, Ph.D. Univ. of Berlin, 1908. Before settling permanently in the United States in 1928 as a professor at Smith, he taught at Cornell and at the Univ. of Wisconsin. With Max Wertheimer and Wolfgang Köhler he is credited with developing the theories that gave rise to the school of GESTALT psychology. His book *Growth of the Mind* (1924) was considered responsible for awakening much interest in Gestalt concepts. See his *Principles of Gestalt Psychology* (1935).

Koforidua (kōfōrēdōō'ä), town (1970 pop. 44,768), capital of the Eastern region, S Ghana. It is the commercial center for a region producing palm oil, cassava, and corn; it also serves as a road and rail center. Fruit juice is made in the town. Koforidua was founded (c.1875) by refugees from ASHANTI. It is also called New Juaben.

Kofu (kō'fōō), city (1970 pop. 182,604), capital of Yamanashi prefecture, central Honshu, Japan. It is an industrial center, with manufactures of silk textiles and crystal ware, as well as a collection point for silk cocoons and raw silk. In the 16th cent. Kofu was the castle town of the Takeda family. Yamanashi prefecture (1970 pop. 762,029), 1,724 sq mi (4,465 sq km), is a major production area for raw silk and grapes.

Koganei (kōgä'nā), city (1970 pop. 94,448), Tokyo Metropolis, central Honshu, Japan. It is a suburb of Tokyo.

Kohala (kōhä'lə), peninsula, Hawaii, on the northern tip of the island of Hawaii. The region is rich in relics of ancient Hawaii, such as burial caves and *heiau* (temples). Kamehameha I was born near the village of Kapaau-Halaula. The Kohala Mts. there rise to 5,489 ft (1,673 m).

Kohat (kō'hät), town (1961 pop. 49,854), N Pakistan, on the Kohat Toi River. The town, enclosed by a wall with 14 gates, is noted for its cotton fabrics and sarongs. Kohat contains a 19th-century British fort built on the site of an old Sikh fortress.

Kohath (kō'hăth), founder of a family of the Levites. It comprised four groups, the Amramites, Izeharites, Hebronites, and Uzzielites. Gen. 46.11; Num. 3.19,27,29,30; 4; 7.9; 10.21; Joshua 21; 1 Chron. 6; 9.32; 15.5; 26; 2 Chron. 20.19; 29.12; 34.12.

Koh-i-noor: see DIAMOND.

Kohler, Kaufmann (kouf'mən kō'lər), 1843–1926, American rabbi, scholar, and leader in Reform Judaism, b. Bavaria. He emigrated to the United States in 1869 and served with congregations in Detroit and Chicago before becoming (1879) rabbi of Temple Beth-El in New York City. From 1903 to 1921 he was president of the Hebrew Union College in Cincinnati. He called the conference (1885) at which the Pittsburgh Platform of Reformed Judaism was adopted. One of the editors of *The Jewish Encyclopedia*, he also wrote *Backwards or Forwards: Lectures on Reform Judaism* (1885), *Jewish Theology Systematically and Historically Considered* (1918), *Heaven and Hell in Comparative Religion* (1923), and the *Origins of the Synagogue and the Church* (1929). His *Studies, Addresses, and Personal Papers* (1931) contains a short autobiography. See R. J. Marx, *Kaufmann Kohler as Reformer* (1951).

Köhler, Wolfgang (kö'lər), 1887–1967, American psychologist, b. Estonia, Ph.D. Univ. of Berlin, 1909. From 1913 to 1920 he was director of a research station on Tenerife, Canary Islands. Later he served as both professor of psychology and director of the Psychology Institute, Berlin. He came to the United States in 1934, where he became professor of psychology at Swarthmore College. Köhler is best known for his experiments with problem-solving in apes at Tenerife and the influence of his writings in the founding of the school of GESTALT psychology. His writings include *Gestalt Psychology* (rev. ed. 1947) and *The Mentality of Apes* (rev. ed. 1948). See his selected papers, ed. by Mary Henle (1971).

Kohler, village (1970 pop. 1,738), Sheboygan co., E Wis., on the Sheboygan River; inc. 1912. The Kohler plumbing-fixtures plant there has been the scene of some of the longest and most bitter labor disputes in U.S. history. The last strike began in 1954 and ended in 1962.

kohlrabi (kōl'rä'bē) [Ger. partly from Ital.,=turnip cabbage], plant (*Brassica caulorapa*, sometimes classified as var. *caulorapa* of the CABBAGE species) of the family Cruciferae (MUSTARD family), with an edible turniplike, swollen stem. It is a cool-weather plant grown more in Europe, where some varieties are used for fodder, than in America. The flavor is more delicate than that of some of the other cabbage plants. Kohlrabi is classified in the division MAGNOLIOPHYTA, class Magnoliopsida, order Capparales, family Cruciferae.

Koiso, Kuniaki (kōōnēä'kē koi'sō), 1880–1950, Japanese general. He was chief of staff of the Kwantung army, commander in chief in Korea, and governor-general of Korea before he replaced Tojo as prime minister in July, 1944. He resigned in April, 1945, after Iwo Jima, the Philippines, and Okinawa were lost. Sentenced (1948) to life imprisonment as a war criminal, he died in a U.S. army hospital.

Kokand or **Khokand** (kəkänt'), city (1972 est. pop. 139,000), Central Asian USSR, in Uzbekistan, in the Fergana Valley. It is a center for the manufacture of fertilizers, chemicals, machinery, and cotton and food products. Important since the 10th cent., Kokand became the capital of an Uzbek khanate which became independent of the emirate of Bukhara in the middle of the 18th cent. and flowered in the 1820s and '30s. Kokand was taken by the Russians in 1876 and became part of Russian Turkistan. It was the capital (1917–18) of the anti-Bolshevik autonomous government of Turkistan.

Koken, Johannes: see COCCEIUS, JOHANNES.

Kokiu: see KO-CHIU, China.

Kokkola (kōk'kōlä), Swed. *Gamlakarleby*, city (1970 pop. 20,932), Vaasa prov., W Finland, on the Gulf of Bothnia. It is a port with steel, engineering, and lumber industries. It was chartered in 1620.

Kokomo (kō'kəmō), city (1970 pop. 44,042), seat of Howard co., N central Ind., on Wildcat Creek; inc. 1865. Radios, automobile parts, and metal products are manufactured there. The first commercially built automobile was invented and tested in Kokomo in 1894 by Elwood Haynes. Points of interest include the Elwood Haynes Museum. Indiana Univ. has a campus at Kokomo, and Grissom Air Force Base is nearby.

Koko Nor or **Kuku Nor** (both: kōkō nōr), Chin. *Ch'ing Hai* or *Tsinghai* [blue sea], salt lake, c.1,625 sq mi (4,210 sq km), in the Tibetan highlands, NE Tsinghai prov., China; one of the largest lakes in China. At an altitude of 10,515 ft (3,205 m), it is shallow and brackish and of little economic value.

Kokoschka, Oskar (ôs'kär kōkôsh'kä), 1886–, Austrian expressionist painter and writer. After teaching at the art academy in Dresden (1920–24), Kokoschka traveled extensively in Europe and N Africa before moving to London in 1938. In 1937 his works in German galleries were removed by the Nazi regime. After World War II he lived in Switzerland and established an international summer school in Salzburg. Kokoschka was influenced by the elegant work of Klimt, but soon developed his own expressionist style. His early portraits emphasize psychological tension (e.g., the portrait of Hans Tietze and his wife, 1909; Mus. of Modern Art, New York City). The same restless, energetic draftsmanship is revealed in his expressionist landscapes and his striking posters and lithographs. His landscapes include *Jerusalem* (Detroit Inst. of Arts) and *View of Prague* (Phillips Memorial Gall., Washington, D.C.). See his volume of watercolors, drawings, and writings (1962); reproductions of his work, comp. by Bernhard Bultmann (1961), Ludwig Goldscheider (1963), E. G. Rathenau (1970), and Jan Tomeš (1972); biography by Edith Hoffmann (1947).

Kokubunji (kōkōō'bōōnjē), city (1970 pop. 81,259), Tokyo Metropolis, central Honshu, Japan. It is a suburb of Tokyo and is noted for its Kokubunji (Buddhist) temple founded in 1588.

Kokura: see KITAKYUSHU, Japan.

kola: see COLA.

Kolaiah (kōlā'yə). **1** Benjamite family in Jerusalem. Neh. 11.7. **2** Father of Ahab, a false prophet. Jer. 29.21.

Kola Peninsula (kō'lə, Rus. kô'lə), peninsula, c.50,000 sq mi (129,500 sq km), NW European USSR, in Murmansk oblast. Forming an eastern extension of the Scandinavian peninsula, it lies between the Barents Sea to the north and the White Sea to the south. In the northeastern part are tundras; the southwestern area is forested. The peninsula has rich mineral deposits in the Khibiny mts., which rise to c.4,000 ft (1,220 m). Hydroelectric plants have been built along the Tuloma, Voronya, and Niva rivers. The port of MURMANSK and the mining center of KIROVSK are the major cities of the peninsula. Along the coasts and in the mining centers, the population is primarily Russian; in the interior are Lapps, who subsist largely on reindeer raising. Near Murmansk is the ancient town of Kola founded in 1264 by Slavs from Novgorod.

Kolar (kōlär'), city (1971 pop. 43,345), Karnataka state, SW India. Founded in the late 19th cent., it is the center of the Indian gold-mining industry. The first hydroelectric project in S India was built in 1902 to provide electricity for the gold fields.

Kolarovgrad: see SHUMEN, Bulgaria.

Kolas, Jakub (yä'kōōb kō'läs), 1882–1956, Belorussian poet and novelist, whose original name was Konstantin Mitskevich. With Janka Kupala, he was a leading figure in Belorussian national and literary life. Among his many works are novels concerned with moral themes, such as *Through Life* (1926), with collectivism, and with war themes, among them *The Fisherman's Hut* (1949). Kolas is best known for his stirring patriotic poems, including *New Earth* (1923).

Kolbe, Georg (gā'ôrkh kôl'bə), 1877–1947, German sculptor. Kolbe studied painting and after meeting Rodin turned to sculpture, working in Berlin from 1903 until his death. He is best known for his impressionist figure studies, many of which are in American museums. During the Nazi regime, Kolbe turned to works of a more aggressive nature, producing idealized figures of warriors and athletes.

Kolberg: see KOŁOBRZEG, Poland.

Kolchak, Aleksandr Vasilyevich (əlyĭksän'dər vəsē'lyəvĭch kəlchäk'), 1874–1920, Russian admiral, leader of the anti-Bolshevik forces in W Siberia during the civil war (1918–20). He distinguished himself in the Russo-Japanese War, and in World War I he commanded the Black Sea fleet. After the October Revolution of 1917, Kolchak became (Oct., 1918) minister of war in an anti-Bolshevik government set up in Omsk, Siberia. In November he carried out a coup d'etat against the Socialist Revolutionaries in the government and assumed dictatorship over Siberia. At first successful against the Bolshevik forces, he was recognized by the Allies as well as by General DENIKIN as representing the provisional Russian government. However, his great offensive of 1919 (in which he intended to join the British forces and the Russian counterrevolutionaries on the coast of the White Sea) collapsed rapidly and exposed Denikin's army in S Russia. Kolchak retreated to Irkutsk, lost most of his following (especially the Czechs, who controlled the Trans-Siberian RR) and was betrayed to the Bolsheviks, who shot him. Before his death, he recognized Denikin as head of all anti-Bolshevik forces in Russia. His defeat left all Siberia in Bolshevik control, except the Far Eastern portion, which was controlled by Japanese intervention troops.

Kölcsey, Ferenc (fĕ'rĕnts köl'chĕĭ), 1790–1838, Hungarian writer and orator. A student of the Enlightenment, he aided his friend Krasiński in a reform of the Hungarian language, investigated Hungarian literary history, and introduced the critical essay. As a member of parliament (1832–36), he spoke eloquently to urge freedom for the serfs. His prose and poetry are somber and elaborately classical in style; they reveal a strong moral sense. Kölcsey wrote the Hungarian national hymn (1823).

Kolding (kôl'dĭng), city (1970 com. pop. 52,510), Vejle co., S central Denmark, a port on Kolding Fjord, an arm of the Lille Baelt. It is a commercial, industrial, and fishing center. Of note in the city are Koldinghus, a royal castle built in 1248 that now houses a historical museum, and the oldest stone church (built in the 13th cent.) in Denmark.

Kolguyev (kəlgōō'yĭf), island, 1,350 sq mi (3,497 sq km), off NE European USSR, in the Barents Sea, E of the Kanin peninsula and 50 mi (80 km) from the mainland. It is a part of the NENETS NATIONAL OKRUG, Archangelsk oblast, and is inhabited mainly by Nentsy (Samoyedes). It is a tundra region, and the Nentsy engage in fishing, seal hunting, reindeer raising, and trapping. Burgino is the major settlement.

Kolhapur (kōləpōōr'), former princely state, 3,219 sq mi (8,337 sq km), Maharashtra state, SW India. Largely agricultural, the region produces cotton and textiles. It also has large bauxite deposits. A center of the MAHRATTAS, Kolhapur was an important state of the Deccan. It was transferred to Maharashtra state in 1960. The city of **Kolhapur** (1971 pop. 259,068) was the capital of the former state. It occupies the site of an ancient Buddhist center. There are many Buddhist remains, notably a stupa, or shrine (3rd cent. B.C.), with inscriptions in characters of the Asoka period.

Kolín (kô'lēn), city (1970 pop. 26,769), N central Czechoslovakia, in Bohemia, on the Elbe (Labe) River. It is a river port and manufactures railroad cars, chemicals, light machinery, and metal products. The city also has a petroleum refinery and a hydroelectric station. Founded in the 13th cent., Kolín grew rapidly after the construction (19th cent.) of the Vienna-Prague railway. The 13th-century Church of St. Bartholomew is noted for its Gothic choir.

kolkhoz: see COLLECTIVE FARM.

Kollár, Jan (yän kō'lär), 1793–1852, Slovak poet who wrote in Czech. An Evangelist minister, he was an ardent proponent of Pan-Slavism. He promoted his ideas in a famous essay on Slavonic cultural unity (1836) and in his best-known poem, *The Daughter of Slava* (1821–24). Kollár is regarded as the greatest poet of the Czech revival.

Kölliker, Albert von (äl'bĕrt fən kö'lĭkər), 1817–1905, Swiss physiologist and histologist. He was professor of physiology and of microscopic and comparative anatomy at Würzburg from 1847. His researches and texts on histology and embryology and his recognition of Schwann's cell theory were pioneer contributions toward understanding the function of spermatozoa and of spontaneous variation in evolution. He also wrote numerous memoirs on his findings and an autobiography (1899).

Kollontai, Aleksandra Mikhailovna (əlyĭksän'drə mēkhī'ləvnə kələntī'), 1872–1952, Russian revolutionary, diplomat, and novelist, whose maiden name was Aleksandra M. Domontovich. The daughter of a general, she early rebelled against her society. Although she married an officer of the czarist army, she was active in revolutionary circles and in 1908 was forced to flee abroad. She visited the United States in 1916 and edited, with Bukharin, the Communist daily *Novy Mir* [new world] in New York City. In 1917 she returned to Russia to take part in the Bolshevik Revolution. In 1920 she became people's commissar for social welfare. She was a leader of the "Workers' Opposition" that opposed party and government control of trade unions; this position was defeated by Lenin in 1921. Kollontai joined the people's commissariat for foreign affairs and became (1923) minister to Norway—the first woman to hold that diplomatic rank. After several ministerial appointments she became (1930) minister to Sweden and remained there until 1945. She was raised to ambassadorial rank in 1943 and was instrumental in conducting the Soviet-Finnish armistice negotiations of 1944. Known as a proponent of free love, she wrote extensively on this and on other social questions. See her autobiography (tr. 1971); biography by Isabel de Palencia (1947).

Kollwitz, Käthe Schmidt (kā'tə shmĭt kôl'vĭts), 1867–1945, German graphic artist and sculptor. She first gained a reputation with her illustrations for Hauptmann's *Weavers* and Zola's *Germinal*. Kollwitz became known for her superb woodcuts and lithographs. An ardent socialist and pacifist, she produced stark and anguished portrayals of misery and hunger such as *Death and the Mother* (1934, Phila. Mus. of Art). These powerful images convey her compassion for the poor. In 1932 she was director of the department of graphic arts at the Berlin Academy, but the advent of the Nazi party ended her public career in Germany. See her diary and letters (1955); her prints and drawings, ed. by Carl Zigrosser (2d ed. 1969); study by Otto Nagel (tr. 1971).

Kolmar, France: see COLMAR.

Köln, West Germany: see COLOGNE.

Kol Nidre: see ATONEMENT, DAY OF.

Kołobrzeg (kôlôb'zhĕk) or **Kolberg,** town (1970 pop. 25,400), NW Poland, on the Baltic Sea at the mouth of the Prośnica River. It is a seaport, seaside resort, and rail junction. A salt-trading center in the Middle Ages, it was chartered in 1255. It was besieged three times by the Russians in the Seven Years War before it fell in 1761. Kołobrzeg was virtually obliterated during World War II.

Kolokotronis, Theodore (kôlôkôtrô'nyēs), 1770–1843, Greek patriot and general. A leader in the Greek War of Independence against Ottoman rule in the 1820s, he was instrumental in the capture of Trípolis, Návplion, Corinth, Pátrai, and Árgos. In 1823 he was appointed commander-in-chief of forces in the Peloponnesus. A supporter of Count CAPO D'ISTRIA, Kolokotronis was one of the leading pro-Russian advocates. He opposed the regency of Bavarian ministers during the minority of King Otto I and was charged with treason, but he was pardoned in 1835. Kolokotronis is the hero of numerous folk songs. See his *Memoirs from the Greek War of Independence, 1821–1833* (tr., new and enl. ed. 1969).

Kolomna (kəlôm'nə), city (1970 pop. 136,000), central European USSR, at the confluence of the Moskva and Oka rivers. Locomotives and machine tools are produced. Known in 1177, the city became a Muscovite outpost in 1301 and has been an industrial center since 1863. Remains of the towers of Kolomna's 16th-century kremlin are still standing.

Kolomyya (kələmī'yə), Ger. *Kolomea*, Pol. *Kołomyja*, city (1967 est. pop. 39,000), SW European USSR, in the Ukraine, on the Prut River and in the Carpathian foothills. It is a rail junction and agricultural trade center. Industries include food processing, woodworking, oil refining, and the manufacture of building materials, farm machinery, and textiles. First mentioned in 1240, Kolomyya was then a Ukrainian settlement in the Galich-Volhynian principality. It passed in the 14th cent. to the Poles, who fortified it. Kolomyya was taken by Austria during the Polish partition of 1772 and became part of the newly independent republic of Ukraine in 1918 but reverted to Poland in 1920. It was incorporated into the Ukrainian Soviet Socialist Republic in 1939.

Kolozsvár, Rumania: see CLUJ.

Kölreuter or **Koelreuter, Joseph Gottlieb** (both: yō'zĕf gôt'lēp köl'roi"tər), 1733–1806, German botanist. In 1764 he became professor of natural history and director of the botanical gardens at Karlsruhe. He experimented with hybridization of plants, studied their fertilization and development, and pointed out the importance of insects and of wind in the pollination of flowers.

Koltsov, Aleksey Vasilyevich (əlyĭksyä' vəsē'lyəvĭch kəltsôf'), 1809-42, Russian poet. Although he had little formal education, he taught himself by studying great works of literature. He was encouraged by the critic Belinsky, and became well known for his fresh, unsophisticated lyrics on themes of peasant life published as *Stikhotvoreniya* [poetry-making] (1835).

Kolwezi (kōlwĕz'ē), city (1968 est. pop. 71,000), Shaba region, SE Zaïre. It is a center for copper and cobalt mining. There are copper-ore concentration plants, a zinc refinery, and a brewery.

Kolyma (kŏlĭmä', kōlē'mə, Rus. kəlĭ'mə), river, c.1,500 mi (2,410 km) long, rising in several headstreams in the Kolyma and Cherskogo ranges, Far Eastern USSR. It flows generally N to the Arctic Ocean at Nizhniye Kresty. It is navigable (June-October) for c.1,000 mi (1,610 km). Its upper course crosses the rich **Kolyma Gold Fields,** which supply much of the gold for Soviet foreign trade. Gold mining was begun in the 1930s, and both the fields and the surrounding area were developed with the use of forced labor. The **Kolyma Range** (or Gyda Range), E of the Kolyma River, extends NE from Magadan and rises to c.6,000 ft (1,830 m).

Komaki (kōmä'kē), city (1970 pop. 77,996), Aichi prefecture, Honshu, Japan, on the Nobi Plain. It is a suburb of Nagoya and an agricultural market.

Komandorski Islands (kŏməndôr'skē) or **Commander Islands,** Rus. *Komandorskiye Ostrova,* group of treeless islands, off E Kamchatka Peninsula, E Far Eastern USSR, in SW Bering Sea. They consist of Bering Island, Medny Island, and two islets. These hilly, foggy islands often have earthquakes. Their inhabitants, Russians and Aleuts, are engaged in fishing, hunting, and whaling. The largest village is Nikolskoye on Bering Island.

Komárno (kô'märnô) or **Komárom** (kô'märôm), Ger. *Komorn,* city of Czechoslovakia and Hungary, on both sides of the Danube, at its confluence with the Nitra and Váh rivers. Komárno (1970 pop. 27,031) is located on the left bank and belongs to Czechoslovakia. It is a shipbuilding center and has flour mills and machinery and textile plants. Hungarian Komárom (1968 est. pop. 26,800), on the right bank, has lumber yards, sawmills, and textile plants. Both parts of the city have port installations. The site of Komárno was fortified by the Romans. It became a free city in 1331. Later a part of the AUSTRO-HUNGARIAN MONARCHY, it was partitioned in 1920 between Hungary and Czechoslovakia.

Komatsu (kōmä'tso͞o), city (1970 pop. 95,684), Ishikawa prefecture, central Honshu, Japan. It is a flourishing market town noted for its production of silk, rayon, and pottery.

Komeito: see SOKA GAKKAI.

Komi (kō'mē, kô'-), Finnic people of the northeastern part of the European USSR. There are two traditional branches of the Komi—Zyrians and Permyaks. The Zyrians are now officially called Komi and make up over half of the population. The Permyaks are now called Komi-Permyaks. Both speak a Finno-Permian language. The Komi live in the Komi ASSR and the Komi-Permyaks live in the Komi-Permyak National Okrug, both administrative divisions of the Russian SFSR. There are about 370,000 Komi (both groups) in the USSR. Traditionally they have been Orthodox Christians since the 14th cent. The enlightener of the Komi and a saint of the Orthodox Eastern Church was Stephen of Perm (1340-96). He constructed an alphabet for the Komi and translated some parts of the Bible into their language.

Komi Autonomous Soviet Socialist Republic, autonomous region (1970 pop. 965,000), c.160,000 sq mi (414,400 sq km), NE European USSR. SYKTYVKAR is the capital. The region is a wooded lowland, stretching across the Pechora and the Vychegda river basins and the upper reaches of the Mezen River. The northern part is permanently frozen, wooded tundra. Mining is the most important economic activity. There are major coal fields in the Pechora basin, yielding heating and coking coal. Along the Ukhta River there are important oil fields. Leningrad receives most of its coal and oil from the region. Syktyvkar, the capital, is a major lumber center; Vorkuta is a coal-mining center; and there is extensive lumbering, stock raising, fishing, and hunting. Komi, Russians, and Ukrainians constitute the population. The Komi, formerly called Zyrians, speak a Finno-Ugric language and adhere to the Russian Orthodox religion. The area underwent a spectacular economic advance after the opening (1942) of the Kotlas-Vorkuta RR to transport the area's coal and oil. The area belonged to the Novgorod Republic from the 13th cent. The Zyrian Autonomous Oblast was constituted in 1921; it became an autonomous republic in 1936.

Komi-Permyak National Okrug (kô'mē-pĭrmyäk'), administrative division (1970 pop. 212,000), 12,664 sq mi (32,800 sq km), E central European USSR, in the basin of the upper Kama River. The terrain is slightly hilly and heavily forested and is drained by the Kama and its tributaries. The navigable Kama is also the area's chief transportation artery. Lumbering is the major industry of the okrug. Among the crops grown are rye, oats, spring wheat, and flax. The territory is the oldest and most populous of the USSR's national okrugs. The Komi and the Permyaks, both Finno-Ugric peoples, make up around 75% of the population; the rest are mostly Russians. The okrug was established in 1925.

Komodo dragon: see LIZARD.

komondor (kŏm'əndôr") (pl. komondorok), breed of large, powerful WORKING DOG recognized as a distinct breed in Hungary since the 9th cent. It stands from 23½ to 31½ in. (60-80 cm) high at the shoulder and weighs from 75 to 90 lb (34.0-40.8 kg). Its long, smooth, dense coat is white and shaggy, tending to tangle. The ancestral home of the komondor is stated by many authorities to be Tibet, although others have traced its origin to the Russian Steppes, from whence it was thought to have been brought into Europe with the migration of Huns. Recently, however, evidence has come to light that strongly suggests that the komondor was the guard dog used by Sumerian shepherds in the Tigris-Euphrates valley 7,000 to 8,000 years ago. Whatever its origins, it is one of the oldest European breeds of dogs, the guardian of herds and homes for centuries. Today it is raised for show competition and as a watchdog and pet. See DOG.

Komorn: see KOMÁRNO.

Komotau: see CHOMUTOV, Czechoslovakia.

Komotiní (kômətĭnē'), city (1971 pop. 28,896), capital of Rodhópi prefecture, NE Greece, in Thrace. It is the commercial center for a region that produces grains, silk, and tobacco. The city has a sizable Muslim minority.

Kompong Cham (käm'pông' chäm), city (1967 est. pop. 31,000), capital of Kompong Cham prov., SE Cambodia, a port on the Mekong River. The third largest city in Cambodia, it has a large textile factory, built with aid from the People's Republic of China. In Sept., 1973, it was the scene of heavy fighting as government forces, reinforced and supplied via the Mekong River, withstood a massive attack by the Khmer Rouge. A technical university is located in the city.

Kompong Som (käm'pông' sôm), formerly **Sihanoukville,** city and seaport (1962 pop. 6,578), located in, but politically independent of Kampot prov., S Cambodia, on the Gulf of Siam. Although a new city (completed 1960), it is the principal deep-water port and commercial outlet of Cambodia. The city and port were built on mud flats, with French aid, and grew with the construction of a highway and railroad to Phnom Penh. The docks and warehouses have been greatly expanded with U.S. aid. The country's only oil refinery, located there, was destroyed (1971) by insurgent Khmer Rouge troops. Kompong Som has an international airport.

Komsomolsk (kəmsəmôlsk') or **Komsomolsk-on-Amur** (-ämo͝or'), Rus. *Komsomolsk-na-Amure,* city (1970 pop. 218,000), Khabarovsk Kray, S Far Eastern USSR, on the Amur River. It is a manufacturing center producing steel, refined oil, and wood products. Tin mines are nearby. The city was founded (1932) by the Komsomol (the Communist youth organization).

Kona (kō'nə), district, along the western coast of the island of Hawaii. It is Hawaii's coffee belt and the only coffee-producing area in the United States. The Kona coast, with fine deep-sea fishing offshore, is a favorite tourist spot. On Kealakelua Bay stands a monument to English explorer Capt. James Cook, killed there by natives in 1779. Kailua Bay to the north was the landing site in 1820 of the first U.S. missionaries to Hawaii.

Konakry: see CONAKRY, Guinea.

Konarak (kōnä'rək, kō'nərək), Hindu temple of the sun god, Orissa state, E India. Built during the reign of Narasimha I (1238-64), it is made of red sandstone and is called the Black Pagoda in contrast to the whitewashed temples of nearby Puri. Although Konarak is partially ruined, enormous wheels carved in high relief about the base have survived, suggesting the chariot of the sun god. Many of the carvings are erotic. Another form of the name is Kanarak.

Kondouriotis, Paul (kôndo͝oryô'tĭs), 1857-1935, Greek admiral and statesman. He became a national hero through his victories over the Turkish fleet in the Greco-Turkish War of 1897 and in the Balkan Wars of 1912-13. He was regent after the death (1920) of King Alexander and again after the departure (1923) of King George II from Greece. In 1924 he was elected provisional president of the newly formed Greek republic. Early in 1926 General PANGALOS compelled Kondouriotis to resign, but in August, General Kondylis overthrew Pangalos and recalled Kondouriotis. A new constitution was promulgated. Kondouriotis sought to resign several times during the premierships of ZAÏMIS (1926-28) and VENIZELOS, and in 1929 his resignation was final. Zaïmis succeeded him as president. The name also appears as Koundouriotis.

Kondylis, George (kônthē'lĭs), 1879-1936, Greek general and statesman. He fought in the Balkan Wars and at Salonica (now Thessaloníki) in World War I. Entering politics in the turbulent postwar years, he served (1924-25) as minister of war and of the interior in the republican government. He overthrew the dictatorship of General PANGALOS in 1926 and served briefly as premier. After 1933 he suddenly switched to the royalist camp. As minister of war (1932-35) under Panayoti TSALDARIS, he suppressed (1935) the Cretan uprising in favor of Eleutherios VENIZELOS; in Oct., 1935, he ousted Tsaldaris in a coup d'etat, became premier in his place, and induced the parliament to recall King GEORGE II, who, however, soon dismissed him. The name also appears as Condylis.

Konev, Ivan Stepanovich (ēvän' styĭpä'nəvĭch kô'nyĭf), 1897-1973, Russian field marshal. In World War II he reconquered (1944-45) the Ukraine and S Poland from the Germans, took Silesia, and participated in the conquest of Czechoslovakia and the capture of Berlin. He became (1945) military governor of the Soviet occupation zone in Austria and (1946) commander in chief of Soviet ground forces. From 1955 to 1960 he commanded the unified military forces set up by the Warsaw Treaty. In 1961-62 he headed Soviet forces in East Germany.

Kong Karls Land (kông kärls län) or **King Charles Land,** island group, 128 sq mi (332 sq km), in the Barents Sea, part of the Norwegian possession of Svalbard, W of Spitsbergen. It includes Kongsøya, Svenskøya, and Abeløya islands.

Kongo, kingdom of the, former state of W central Africa, founded in the 14th cent. In the 15th cent. the kingdom stretched from the Congo (Zaïre) River in the north to the Loje River in the south and from the Atlantic Ocean in the west to beyond the Kwango River in the east. Several smaller autonomous states to the south and east paid tribute to it. The Kongo was ruled by the *manikongo,* or king, and was divided into six provinces, each administered by a governor appointed by the *manikongo.* In 1482, Diogo Cão, a Portuguese explorer, visited the kingdom, and the reigning *manikongo,* Nzinga Nkuwu, was favorably impressed with Portuguese culture. In 1491, Portuguese missionaries, soldiers, and artisans were welcomed at Mbanza, the capital of the kingdom. The missionaries soon gained converts, including Nzinga Nkuwu (who took the name João I), and the soldiers helped the *manikongo* defeat an internal rebellion. The next *manikongo,* Afonso I (reigned 1505-43), was raised as a Christian and attempted to convert the kingdom to Christianity and European ways. However, the Portuguese residents in the Kongo were primarily interested in increasing their private fortunes (especially through capturing black Africans and selling them into slavery), and, despite the attempts of King Manuel I of Portugal to channel the efforts of his subjects into constructive projects, the continued rapaciousness of the Portuguese played a major part in weakening the kingdom and reducing the hold of the capital (renamed São Salvador) over the provinces. After the death of Afonso, the Kongo declined rapidly and suffered major civil wars. The Portuguese shifted their interest southward to the Ndongo kingdom and helped the Ndongo defeat the Kongo in 1556. However, in 1569 the Portuguese aided the Kongo by helping to repel an invasion from the east by a LUNDA ethnic group. The slave trade, which undermined the social structure of the Kongo, continued to weaken the authority of the *manikongo.* In 1641, Manikongo Garcia II allied himself with the Dutch in an attempt to control Portuguese slave traders, but in 1665 a Portuguese force decisively defeated the army of the Kongo and from that time onward the *manikon-*

go was little more than a vassal of Portugal. The kingdom disintegrated into a number of small states, all controlled to varying degrees by the Portuguese. The area of the Kongo was incorporated mostly into Angola and partly into the Independent State of the Congo (now ZAÏRE) in the late 19th cent.

kongoni: see HARTEBEEST.

Kongsberg (kôngs'bĕr), city (1970 pop. 18,497), Buskerud co., SE Norway, on the Lågen River. It is a commercial, industrial, and winter sports center and has a hydroelectric power plant. Formerly a silver-mining center, Kongsberg has old mines and a great church (1761) that are tourist attractions.

Kongsfjorden (kôngs"fyôr'dən) [Kings Bay], inlet of the Arctic Ocean, 14 mi (23 km) long, NW Spitsbergen, Svalbard. Ny-Ålesund is on the inlet. The scenic fjord is often visited by tourist vessels.

Königgrätz: see HRADEC KRÁLOVÉ; SADOVÁ, Czechoslovakia.

Königinhof: see DVŮR KRÁLOVÉ NAD LABEM, Czechoslovakia.

König Rother (kön'ĭk rōt'ər), earliest heroic minstrel epic from the precourtly period of Middle High German literature. Written in Bavaria in popular verse style by an unknown Rhenish poet (c.1140–50), the epic has a fairy-tale quality. It recounts King Rother's adventurous quest to the Orient for his bride, portraying with sympathy the lord-vassal relationship. See *King Rother* (tr. 1962).

Königsberg: see KALININGRAD, USSR.

Königshütte: see CHORZÓW, Poland.

Königsmark, Countess Maria Aurora (märē'ä ourō͞o'rä kö'nĭksmärk), 1666–1728, Swedish noblewoman; sister of Count Philipp Christoph Königsmark. She went to Dresden in search of her missing brother and there became the mistress of Augustus II of Poland and Saxony. Their son, Maurice, was the famous Marshal de SAXE. In her last years she was abbess coadjutor at Quedlinburg.

Königsmark, Count Philipp Christoph (fē'lĭp krĭs'tôf), d. 1694?, Swedish nobleman, an officer in the service of Hanover. Accused of having an affair with SOPHIA DOROTHEA, wife of Elector George Louis (later George I of England), the count disappeared in 1694. It is believed that he was killed by order of the elector.

konimeter or **coniometer** (both: kōnĭm'ətər), instrument for determining the concentration of dust in air, e.g., in a mine or mill. A measured volume of air is passed over a plate to which dust particles adhere; the particles are later counted under a microscope. Other methods, now more widely used, involve the collection (by filtration or precipitation) of dust from a large volume of air and the subsequent weighing of the dust.

Koninck or **Coningh, Philips de** (fē'lĭps də kō'nĭngk, kō'nĭng), 1619–88, Dutch landscape and portrait painter. His panoramic landscapes, rich and warm in tone, suggest dramatic atmosphere and space. They are among the best in the Dutch landscape tradition. A number of his drawings have been preserved. Koninck's paintings include *Entrance to a Forest* and *Landscape* (both: Rijks Mus.), *Landscape with Hunting Party* (National Gall., London), and a landscape in the Metropolitan Museum.

Koninksloo, Gillis van: see CONINXLOO, GILLIS VAN.

Köniz (kö'nĭts), town (1970 pop. 32,505), Bern canton, W central Switzerland. It is a suburb of Bern. The Romanesque-Gothic church, founded in the 10th cent. by Rudolph II of Burgundy, has noteworthy 14th-century stained glass and frescoes.

Konotop (kŏnətŏp'), city (1969 est. pop. 62,000), central European USSR, in Ukraine, on the Ezuch River. It is a rail junction and agricultural center, with food-processing plants, railroad repair shops, an electromechanics industry, and factories that produce clothing and mining equipment. Konotop was founded in 1634 by the Poles, who made it a fortress. It was ruled briefly by the Ukrainian hetman Chmielnicki and his successor and later became a Polish district center.

Konoye, Fumimaro (fō͞o"mēmärō' kōnoyä'), 1891–1945, Japanese statesman. A scion of the ancient Fujiwara noble family and protégé of Kimmichi Saionji, he was president of the house of peers from 1933 to 1937. In June, 1937, he accepted the premiership. A former liberal, he now favored increased armament and centralized government control. Following the outbreak of war with China in July, 1937, he pressed Chiang Kai-shek to establish autonomous demilitarized regions in N China and to recognize the puppet state of MANCHUKUO. The National Mobilization Law was passed in March, 1938, and in November, Konoye proclaimed Japan's aim of a "new order in East Asia." He resigned in Jan., 1939, and became president of the privy council and minister without portfolio. Recalled to the premiership in July, 1940, he concluded an alliance with the Axis and founded (Oct., 1940) the Imperial Rule Assistance Association to replace the political parties. Having failed to reach an agreement with the United States, he resigned in Oct., 1941, to be followed by Hideki Tojo. In July, 1945, he was chosen as a peace envoy to Moscow and later became vice premier in the first postwar cabinet and head of the constitutional drafting committee. He was listed for trial as a war criminal but committed suicide in Dec., 1945.

Konstantinovka (kənstəntyē'nəfkə), Ukr. *Kostyantyniwka,* city (1970 pop. 105,000), S central European USSR, in the Donets Basin of the Ukraine. It is a zinc-refining and superphosphate-producing center.

Konstanz, West Germany: see CONSTANCE.

Kon Tiki: see HEYERDAHL, THOR.

Konya (kōn'yä), city (1970 pop. 200,760), capital of Konya prov., S central Turkey. It is the trade center of a rich agricultural and livestock-raising region. Manufactures include cement, carpets, and leather, cotton, and silk goods. As the ancient ICONIUM, the city was important in Roman times, but it reached its peak after the victory (1071) of Alp Arslan over the Byzantines at Manzikert, which resulted in the establishment (1099) of the sultanate of Iconium or Rum (so called after Rome), a powerful state of the Seljuk Turks. In the late 13th cent. the Seljuks of Iconium were defeated by the Mongols, and their territories subsequently passed to Karamania (see KARAMAN). In the 15th cent. the whole region was annexed to the Ottoman Empire by Sultan Muhammad II, the conqueror of Constantinople. Konya lost its political importance but remained a religious center as the chief seat of the whirling dervishes, whose order was founded there in the 13th cent. by the poet and mystic Celaleddin Rumi. The tomb of the founder, several medieval mosques, and the old city walls have been preserved. In 1832 an Egyptian army under Ibrahim Pasha completely routed the Turks at Konya. The Armenian population of the town, once very numerous, was largely deported during World War I. Konya prov., the largest in Turkey, has important mineral resources and produces much opium.

Koo, Vi Kuiyuin Wellington (vē jün wĕl'ĭngtən kō͞o), Mandarin *Ku Wei-chün,* 1887–, Chinese Nationalist diplomat, b. Shanghai. Koo was educated at Columbia (B.A., 1908; M.A., 1909; Ph.D., 1912), where he specialized in international law. In 1912, Wellington Koo was secretary to Yüan Shih-kai, president of China. He was ambassador to France (1936–41), Great Britain (1941–46), and the United States (1946–56). He served as delegate to the Paris Peace Conference (1919) and then was a representative on the Council of the League of Nations. At various times he was minister of foreign affairs and prime minister. He headed the Chinese delegation to the San Francisco conference which founded (1945) the United Nations. From 1957 to 1967 he served on the International Court of Justice at The Hague.

Kook, Abraham Isaac, 1864–1935, Jewish scholar and philosopher, b. Latvia. He settled (1904) in Palestine, where he became the chief rabbi of the Ashkenazi community in 1921. He was one of the first Orthodox rabbis to apply his Talmudic learning to current problems. He attempted to show that Palestine and Zionism were an integral part of Judaism: that those secularist Jews who worked to build up the Jewish homeland were unknowingly doing God's work, which one day would become evident to them; and that the present condition of nationalism was a necessary step on the way to universalism, as nations are the organizational units in which man will be educated for the fulfillment of this idea. He was the author of several books on Judaism. See biography by J. B. Agus (2d ed. 1972); S. H. Bergman, *Faith and Reason* (tr. 1963).

kookaburra (ko͝ok'əbûr"ə), common name for a squat, long-tailed Australian kingfisher, *Dacelo navaguinae.* It is one of the largest birds of the family Alcedinidae (kingfisher family). Because of its loud, maniacal-sounding call, it is also known as the laughing jackass, or jackass kingfisher. The kookaburra has dull plumage and is about the size of a raven. Like many forest kingfishers, it does not fish at all, but rather feeds mainly on a diet of snakes, which it picks up by the head and drops from great heights in order to kill before consuming them. It also feeds on lizards, young birds, and large insects. Today, the kookaburra is often found in the vicinity of human settlements, using its large, hooked bill to scavenge for scraps. It is chiefly a solitary, nonmigratory bird. The kookaburra lays its pure white eggs in a burrow carved out of a termite nest. Both sexes participate in the incubation and care of their virtually helpless young. Kookaburras are classified in the phylum CHORDATA, subphylum Vertebrata, class Aves, order Coraciiformes, family Alcedinidae. See study by V. A. Parry (1972).

Koolau Range (kō'əlou"), mountain chain, extending northwest-southeast, E Oahu island, Hawaii; rises to 3,105 ft (946 m) in Konahuanui. It is cut by two scenic passes, Nuuanu Pali and Waimanalo Pali, which shorten the route between E and W Oahu.

Kootenai (ko͞o'tĭnā), river, 407 mi (655 km) long, rising in the Rocky Mts., SE British Columbia, Canada. It flows S into NW Montana, NW through N Idaho, then N into Canada. There it flows through Kootenay Lake (64 mi/103 km long; 191 sq mi/495 sq km), an expansion of the river, before joining the Columbia River at Castlegar. The river is used to generate hydroelectricity. The Canadian name is spelled Kootenay.

Kootenai Indians (ko͞ot'ənā"), group of North American Indians, who in the 18th cent. occupied the so-called Kootenai country (i.e., N Montana, N Idaho, and SE British Columbia). Their language is thought by some scholars to form a branch of the Algonquian-Wakashan linguistic stock, although others argue that it has not been definitely related to any known linguistic family (see AMERICAN INDIAN LANGUAGES). The Upper Kootenai lived near the headwaters of the Columbia River, and the Lower Kootenai lived on the Lower Kootenai River. According to tradition the Kootenai once lived E of the Rocky Mts., but they were driven westward by their enemies the Blackfoot Indians. Kootenai culture was essentially that of the Plateau area, but after the advent of the horse the Kootenai adopted many Plains area traits including a seasonal buffalo hunt. Contact with whites began early in the 19th cent., when the North West Company established Rocky Mountain House on the upper Saskatchewan River. In 1807 the same company opened the first trading post in Kootenai country. Today a group of the Kootenai live with the Salish Indians on the Flathead Reservation in NW Montana, where together they number some 2,800. The name is sometimes spelled Kootenay or Kutenai. See H. H. Turney-High, *Ethnography of the Kutenai* (1941, repr. 1974); O. W. Johnson, *Flathead and Kootenay* (1969).

Kootenay Lake, Canada: see KOOTENAI, river.

Kootenay National Park, 543 sq mi (1,406 sq km), SE British Columbia, Canada; est. 1920. In the Rocky Mts. near Kootenay Lake, it contains high peaks, glaciers, deep canyons, and hot springs. The Banff-Windermere Highway crosses the park.

Kooweskoowe: see ROSS, JOHN.

Köpenick (kö'pənĭk), district of East Berlin, E central East Germany, at the confluence of the Spree and Dahme rivers. It is an industrial center and a tourist spot, with forests and large lakes. Köpenick was the scene of the trial (1730) of Crown Prince Frederick (later FREDERICK II), who had attempted to escape from Prussia to England. In 1906, Wilhelm Voight, a shoemaker dressed as an army captain, imprisoned the mayor of Köpenick (then an independent town), an episode dramatized (1931) by Carl Zuckmayer in *Der Hauptmann von Köpenick.*

Koper (kô'pĕr), Ital. *Capodistria,* town (1971 pop. 35,407), NW Yugoslavia, in Slovenia, on the Istrian peninsula in the Gulf of Trieste. It is a fishing port and has small shipyards. From 1278 until 1797 the town was the capital of ISTRIA under Venetian rule. The Treaty of Campo Formio, which dissolved the republic of Venice, transferred Koper to Austria. The town passed to Italy after World War I and became part of the Free Territory of Trieste in 1947. In 1954, Koper was annexed to Yugoslavia. It preserves the aspect of a Venetian town, with a Romanesque cathedral and campanile, a Gothic loggia, and a pinnacled town hall.

Köping (chö'pĭng"), city (1970 pop. 21,740), Västmanland co., S central Sweden, at the western end of Lake Mälaren. It is an important lake port and a commercial and industrial center. Manufactures include machinery, textiles, and cement. It was the site of the strong Köpingshus fortress, destroyed in 1434.

Kopp, Hermann Franz Moritz (hĕr'män fräntz mō'rĭts kôp), 1817–92, German physical chemist and historian of chemistry. His research concerned the connection between the physical properties and the chemical structure of compounds. He continued

Jöns Berzelius's annual reports on developments in chemistry, broadening their scope to include related sciences. Kopp is perhaps best known for his *Geschichte der Chemie* [history of chemistry] (4 vol., 1843–47).

Köprülü (köprülü'), family of humble Albanian origin, several members of which served as grand vizier (chief executive officer) in the Ottoman Empire (Turkey). The name is also spelled Kiuprili, Koprili, and Kuprili. **Mehmed Köprülü**, 1583–1661, became grand vizier of MUHAMMAD IV in 1656. He gained complete authority and control and displayed remarkable statesmanship and efficiency. He reorganized the Ottoman fleet, conquered (1658) Transylvania, restored internal order (by executing dissidents), reformed the finances, and built forts along the Don and Dnepr rivers. During his vizierate the Ottoman Empire regained some of its former prestige and vitality. He was succeeded as vizier by his son **Ahmed Köprülü**, 1635–76. An able statesman and soldier, he took (1669) the last Venetian stronghold in Crete, but he was severely defeated (1664) by MONTECUCCOLI at Szentgotthárd in Hungary and suffered reverses in his campaigns against John III of Poland. Ahmed, who died from overindulgence, was succeeded as vizier by Kara Mustafa, his brother-in-law. Ahmed's brother, **Mustafa Köprülü,** 1637–91, became vizier in 1689, at a time when the Austrians and their allies were advancing victoriously into the Ottoman Empire. He continued his predecessors' administrative and fiscal reforms and improved the status of the Christian subjects. He drove the Austrians from Serbia but was killed in the battle of Slankamen. His cousin, **Hüseyin Köprülü,** d. 1702, became vizier after the Turkish defeat at Senta in 1697. Recognizing the exhaustion of Turkey, he negotiated a humiliating peace (see KARLOWITZ, TREATY OF). He too was a reformer and patronized the arts and letters. Mustafa Köprülü's son, **Numan Köprülü,** d.1719, was vizier in 1710–11. Another son, **Abdullah Köprülü,** d. 1735, was acting vizier from 1723 until his death.

Korah (kō'rə). **1** Levite leader, with Dathan and Abiram, of the unsuccessful revolt in the desert against Moses that ended by the rebels' being consumed by fire and earthquake. Num. 16; 26.9–11. Core: Jude 11. **2** Son of Esau. Gen. 36.5,14,18. **3** Another descendant of Esau. Gen. 36.16. **4** Descendant of Caleb. 1 Chron. 2.43. **5** Levitical family, perhaps descended from **1,** that had duties as doorkeepers and singers. Ex. 6.24; 1 Chron. 9.19,31; 2 Chron. 20.19; titles of Pss. 42; 44–49; 84; 85; 87; 88. Kore: 1 Chron. 26.19.

Koran or **Quran** (kōrăn', -rän') [Arab.,=reading, lection], the sacred book of Islam. According to Islamic belief, it was revealed by God to the Prophet MUHAMMAD in separate revelations over the major portion of the Prophet's life at Mecca and at Medina. The canonical text was established A.H. 30 (A.D. 651–52), under the caliph UTHMAN, by Arabic editors, who used for their basis a collection made by Zaid ibn Thabit, the Prophet's secretary. The caliph had all collections destroyed save Zaid's and thus made the new edition unique. The revelations are divided into 114 suras (chapters), but many of the suras include several revelations. The arrangement of the suras is mechanical: the first (Fatihah) is a short exultation in God, the rest are graded generally by length, from longest to shortest. It is thus impossible to tell from the book the chronological order of revelations; generally, however, the shorter suras, more electric and fervent than the rest, are the earlier, while many of the longer suras (and all of those revealed at Medina) are later. The Koran is in classical Arabic; that is to say, the Arabic of the Koran is the classic language. The Koran is undoubtedly the most influential book in the world after the Bible. Muslims memorize much or all of it, and Islam considers all science but a commentary on the Koran. It is probably true that the Koran accounts for the remarkable unity of Islam, one of the most widespread religions. Many Muslims believe it a sacrilege to translate the Koran, but despite their objections translations have been made. See A. J. Arberry, *The Koran Interpreted* (2 vol., 1955, repr. 1969); Izutsu Toshihiko, *God and Man in the Koran* (1964); Richard Bell, *Introduction to the Quran* (2d ed. 1970).

Korat: see NAKHON RATCHASIMA, Thailand.

Korçë (kôr'chə), city (1970 pop. 43,300), capital of Korçë prov., SE Albania, near the Greek border. Located in an agricultural region, it is a commercial and industrial center producing leather, tobacco and glass products, and knitwear. There are lignite, copper, and iron ore deposits nearby. Korçë is the seat of a Greek Orthodox metropolitan. Known in 1280, it was destroyed (1440) by the Turks but developed again after the 16th cent. Ever since Albania gained independence in the Balkan Wars, Korçë has been claimed by Greece. Greek troops occupied it in 1912–13 during the Balkan Wars and again early in World War I. From 1916 to 1920 it was occupied and administered by the French, and in World War II it was held (Nov., 1940–April, 1941) by the Greeks. Korçë has a large 15th-century mosque and several modern government buildings. It is also known as Korça and Koritsa.

Korčula (kôr'cho͞olä), Ital. *Curzola,* island (1971 pop. 20,176), 105 sq mi (272 sq km), in the Adriatic Sea, off Dalmatia, W Yugoslavia. It is covered with pine forests, pastures, and vineyards. Most of the inhabitants are sailors, farmers, or fishermen. The island was colonized by the Greeks in the 4th cent. B.C. The chief town Korčula, has retained its fine medieval cathedral and fortifications. According to some sources, Marco Polo was born there.

Kordofan (kôrdōfăn'), province (1969 est. pop. 2,400,000), central Sudan. AL UBAYYID is the capital. The terrain, generally level in the north, rises in the south to the Nuba Mts. Kordofan's economy is agricultural, with millet as the staple crop. The government has sponsored many irrigation projects. Conquered for Egypt in 1821, Kordofan was under Turco-Egyptian rule until 1882, when the Mahdi fomented revolt. With the defeat of Mahdist forces in 1898, Kordofan became part of Anglo-Egyptian Sudan.

Kore (kō'rē). **1** Family of temple doorkeepers. 1 Chron. 9.19. **2** Levite under Hezekiah. 2 Chron. 31.14. **3** See KORAH **5.**

Kore, in Greek religion: see PERSEPHONE.

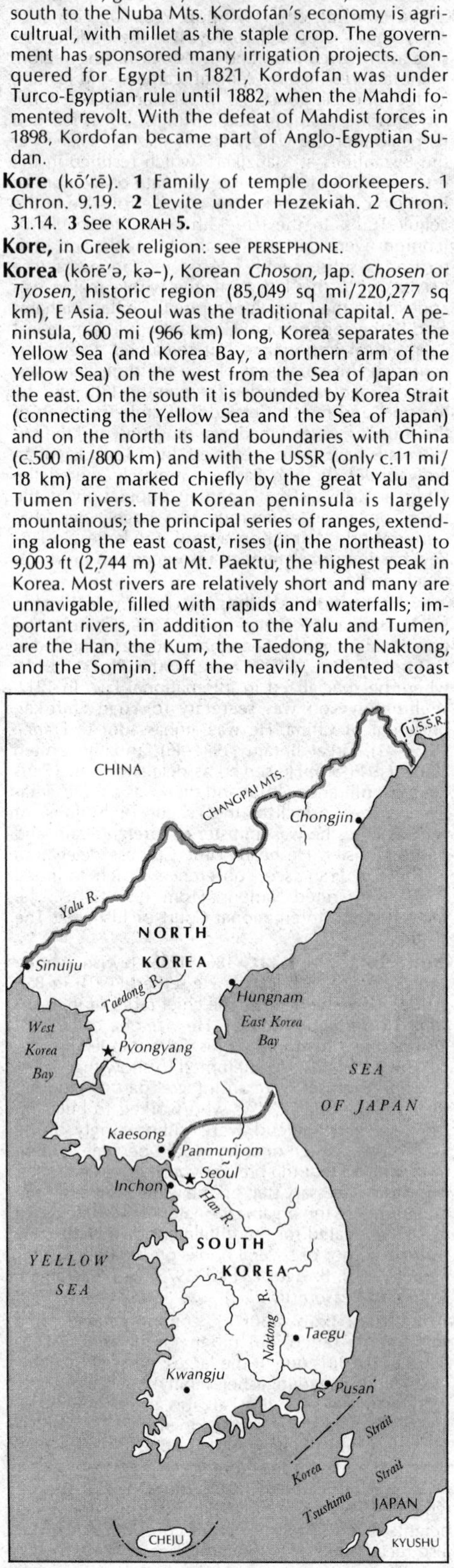

Korea (kôrē'ə, kə-), Korean *Choson,* Jap. *Chosen* or *Tyosen,* historic region (85,049 sq mi/220,277 sq km), E Asia. Seoul was the traditional capital. A peninsula, 600 mi (966 km) long, Korea separates the Yellow Sea (and Korea Bay, a northern arm of the Yellow Sea) on the west from the Sea of Japan on the east. On the south it is bounded by Korea Strait (connecting the Yellow Sea and the Sea of Japan) and on the north its land boundaries with China (c.500 mi/800 km) and with the USSR (only c.11 mi/18 km) are marked chiefly by the great Yalu and Tumen rivers. The Korean peninsula is largely mountainous; the principal series of ranges, extending along the east coast, rises (in the northeast) to 9,003 ft (2,744 m) at Mt. Paektu, the highest peak in Korea. Most rivers are relatively short and many are unnavigable, filled with rapids and waterfalls; important rivers, in addition to the Yalu and Tumen, are the Han, the Kum, the Taedong, the Naktong, and the Somjin. Off the heavily indented coast (c.5,400 mi/8,690 km long) lie some 3,420 islands, most of them rocky and uninhabited (of the inhabited islands, about half have a population of less than 100); the main island group is in the Korean Archipelago in the Yellow Sea. The climate of Korea ranges from dry and extremely cold winters in the north to almost tropical conditions in parts of the south. The country once had large timber resources. Most of the remaining stands are in the north, where, despite excessive cutting during the Japanese occupation (1910–45), timber remains an important resource. Predominant trees are larch, oak, alder, pine, spruce, and fir. Intensive government conservation and reforestation programs have increased the supply, and timber occasionally appears on North Korean export lists. The south, on the other hand, is largely deforested—the result of illegal cutting after 1945 and damage during the Korean War (1950–53). Some forests remain, especially in the west central area of South Korea, and a government reforestation program has been initiated, but the dense population and extensive agriculture continue to encroach upon the small reserves and considerable timber has to be imported. Korea has great mineral wealth, most of it (80% to 90%) concentrated in the north. Of the peninsula's five major minerals—gold, iron ore, coal, tungsten, and graphite—only the tungsten and amorphous graphite are found principally in the south. South Korea has only 10% of the peninsula's rich coal and iron deposits. Its minerals are widely scattered, and mining operations are generally small-scaled, although tungsten is an important export item. In the north, modern mining methods have been instituted, and minerals and metals account for about 15% of the export revenue. North Korea is especially rich in iron and coal and has some 300 different kinds of minerals; in 1970 it ranked first among world producers of graphite and was among the world's top 10 in deposits and production of gold, tungsten, magnesite, zinc, barites, magnatite, molybdenum, limestone, mica, and fluorite. Other important minerals include copper, kaolin, lead, nickel, silver, and manganese. Because of the mountainous and rocky terrain, only about 20% of Korean land is arable. Rice is the chief crop, with wet paddy fields constituting about half of the farmland. Paddies are found along the coasts, in claimed tidal areas, and in river valleys. Barley, wheat, corn, soybeans, and grain sorghums are also extensively cultivated, especially in the uplands; other crops include cotton, tobacco, fruits, potatoes, beans, and sweet potatoes. Before the country was divided (1945), the colder and less fertile north depended heavily upon the south for food. Agricultural self-sufficiency has now become a major goal of the North Korean government, and the establishment of highly mechanized state farms has been a step in that direction. Both governments have recently expanded irrigation facilities; numerous dams are being constructed, and land reclamation projects are in progress. Livestock plays a minor role in Korean agriculture, especially in the north, where the steep and often barren hills are unsuitable for large-scale grazing. In the south, cattle are used largely as beasts of burden, and while chickens and rabbits are raised, relatively little meat is eaten. Fish remains the chief source of protein in the Korean diet. The fishing waters off Korea are among the best in the world; the long coastline and numerous islands, inlets, and reefs provide excellent fishing grounds, and the presence of both a warm and a cold current attracts a great variety of species—cuttlefish, anchovy, yellow corvina, hairtail, saury, pollack, flatfish, cod, sandfish, herring, and mackerel. Octopus and shrimp are also caught, and seaweed is valuable; agar (a seaweed product) is an important export item. Deep-sea fishing is expanding, and Korean ships now range into the Atlantic and Arctic Oceans. Almost all of the deep-sea catch (consisting largely of tuna) is canned and exported. The Korean economy was shattered by the war of 1950 to 1953. Postwar reconstruction was abetted by enormous amounts of foreign aid (in the north, from Communist countries and in the south, chiefly from the United States) and intensive government economic development programs. The greatest industrial advances were made during the 1960s; in that decade the south experienced an 85% increase in productivity and a 250% rise in per capita gross national product. The north has changed from a predominantly agricultural society (in 1946) to an industrial one; 70% of its national product is now derived from manufacturing and mining. Major North Korean products include iron, steel, and other metals, machinery, textiles (synthetics, wool, cotton, silk), and chemicals. In the south the traditional consumer goods industries (textiles, garments, food-processing) are still dominant, but heavy industry has been established and a great variety of products are now manufactured; these include electrical and electronic equipment, chemicals, ceramic goods, and plywood (made from imported lumber; in 1972 South Korea was the world's leading plywood exporter). The industrialization of both north and south has been accompanied by improved transportation. By the end of the Korean War the rail system had been destroyed, and paved highways were almost nonexistent. The railroads have been extensively rebuilt, and the South Korean government has completed a series of superhighways connecting Seoul with numerous major cities. There is domestic air service, and international airports are located at both Seoul and Pyongyang. Educational facilities have expanded enormously. South Korea has some 200 institutions of higher learning, about one half of which are in Seoul; these include colleges and universities, graduate schools, junior colleges, and other specialized institutions. The emphasis in North Korea has been on specialized and technical education. There are many technical colleges, and the major university, Kim Il Sung, is on the outskirts of Pyongyang. Most Koreans are Confucianists or Buddhists, although the people tend to be eclectic in their religious practices. Korean Confucianism, for example, has developed into more of an ethical system than a religion, and its influence is wide and pervasive. Of the various indigenous religions, Chon-do-gyo (a native mixture of Buddhism, Confucianism, and Taoism) is the most influential. South Korea has a large number of practicing Christians; the Christian religion was introduced by missionaries in the late 19th cent. and had a particular appeal during the years of Japanese occupation. The North Korean government has actively suppressed religion as contrary to Marxist belief.

History. Chinese and Japanese influences have been strong throughout Korean history, but the Koreans, descended from Tungusic tribal peoples, are a distinct racial and cultural group. The documented history of Korea begins in the 12th cent. B.C., when a Chinese scholar, Ki-tze (Kija), founded a colony at Pyongyang. After 100 B.C. the Chinese colony of Lolang, established near Pyongyang, exerted a strong cultural influence on the Korean tribes settled in the peninsula. The kingdom of Koguryo, the first native Korean state, arose in the north near the Yalu River in the 1st cent. A.D., and by the 4th cent. it had conquered Lolang. In the south, two kingdoms emerged, that of Paekche (A.D. c.250) and the powerful kingdom of Silla (A.D. c.350). With Chinese support, the kingdom of Silla conquered Koguryo and Paekche in the 7th cent. and unified the peninsula. Under Silla rule, Korea prospered and the arts flourished; Buddhism, which had entered Korea in the 4th cent., became dominant in this period. In 935 the Silla dynasty was peacefully overthrown by Wang Kon, who established the Koryo dynasty (the name was selected as an abbreviated form of Koguryo). During the Koryo period, literature was cultivated, and although Buddhism remained the state religion, Confucianism—introduced from China during the Silla years—controlled the pattern of government. In 1231, Mongol forces invaded from China, initiating a war that was waged intermittently for some 30 years. Peace came when the Koryo kings accepted Mongol rule, and a long period of Koryo-Mongol alliance followed. In 1392, Yi Songgye, with the aid of the Ming dynasty (which had replaced the Mongols in China) seized the throne. The Yi dynasty, which was to rule until 1910, built a new capital at Seoul and established Confucianism as the official religion. Early in the Yi period (mid-15th cent.) an efficient Korean phonetic alphabet as well as printing with movable metal type were developed. In 1592 an invasion of the Japanese conqueror Hideyoshi was driven back by the Yi dynasty with Chinese help, but only after six years of great devastation and suffering. Manchu invasions in the first half of the 17th cent. resulted in Korea being made (1637) a vassal of the Manchu dynasty. Korea attempted to close its frontiers and became so isolated from other foreign contact as to be called the Hermit Kingdom. All non-Chinese influences were excluded until 1876, when Japan forced a commercial treaty with Korea. To offset the Japanese influence, trade agreements were also concluded (1880s) with the United States and the countries of Europe. Japan's control was tightened after the First SINO-JAPANESE WAR (1894–95) and the RUSSO-JAPANESE WAR (1904–5), when Japanese troops moved through Korea to attack Manchuria. These troops were never withdrawn, and in 1905 Japan declared a virtual protectorate over Korea and in 1910 formally annexed the country. The Japanese instituted vast social and economic changes, building modern industries and railroads, but their rule (1910–45) was harsh and exploitative. Sporadic Korean attempts to overthrow the Japanese were unsuccessful, and after 1919 a provisional Korean government, under Syngman Rhee, was established at Shanghai. In World War II, at the Cairo Conference (1943), the United States, Great Britain, and China promised Korea independence. At the end of the war Korea was arbitrarily divided into two zones as a temporary expedient; Soviet troops were north and Americans south of the line of lat. 38°N. The Soviet Union thwarted all UN efforts to hold elections and reunite the country under one government. When relations between the Soviet Union and the United States worsened, trade between the two zones ceased; great economic hardship resulted, since the regions were economically interdependent, industry and trade being concentrated in the north and agriculture in the south. In 1948 two separate regimes were formally established—the Republic of Korea in the south, and the Democratic People's Republic under Communist rule in the north. By mid-1949 all Soviet and American troops were withdrawn, and two rival Korean governments were in operation, each eager to unify the country under its own rule. In June, 1950, the North Korean army launched a surprise attack against South Korea, initiating the KOREAN WAR, and with it, severe hardship, loss of life, and enormous devastation. After the war the boundary was stabilized along a line running from the Han estuary northeast across the 38th parallel, with a "no-man's land," 1.24 mi (2 km) wide and occupying a total of 487 sq mi (1,261 sq km), on either side of the boundary. Throughout the 1950s and 60s an uneasy truce prevailed; thousands of soldiers were poised on each side of the demilitarized zone, and there were occasional shooting incidents. In 1971 negotiations between North and South Korea provided the first hope for peaceful reunification of the peninsula; in Nov., 1972, an agreement was reached for the establishment of joint machinery to work toward unification. The difficulty of real concessions being made by both sides persisted, however, and Korea remained divided. **North Korea,** or Democratic People's Republic of Korea (1973 est. pop. 14,900,000), 46,540 sq mi (120,538 sq km), founded on May 1, 1948, has its capital at PYONGYANG, the largest city. After the Korean War, the Communist government of North Korea, under the leadership of KIM IL SUNG, used the region's rich mineral and power resources as the basis for an ambitious program of industrialization and rehabilitation. With Chinese and Soviet aid, railroads, industrial plants, and power facilities were rebuilt. Farms were collectivized, and industries were nationalized. In a series of three-year, five-year, seven-year, and six-year economic development plans, the coal, iron, and steel industries were greatly expanded, new industries were introduced, and the mechanization of agriculture was pushed. A serious population loss, resulting from the exodus of several million people to the south, was somewhat offset by Chinese colonists and Koreans from Manchuria and Japan. North Korea has maintained close relations with the Soviet Union and Communist China (military aid treaties were signed with both countries in 1961), but has sought to retain a degree of independence; the Sino-Soviet rift has facilitated this. Relations with the United States have remained uncompromisingly hostile, as dramatized by the seizure (1968) of the U.S. intelligence ship *Pueblo* and the imprisonment of its crew for 11 months, and the shooting down of an American plane in 1969. North Korea, although nominally a republic governed by a representative assembly, is actually ruled by the Communist party (known in Korea as the Korea Workers' Party). All governmental institutions are controlled by Kim Il Sung, who has been premier since the country's inception in 1948. **South Korea,** or Republic of Korea (1973 est. pop. 33,400,000), 38,022 sq mi (98,477 sq km), formally proclaimed on Aug. 15, 1948, has its capital at SEOUL, the largest city. PUSAN, the second largest city, is the country's chief port, with an excellent natural harbor near the delta of the Naktong River. Other important cities are TAEGU and INCHON. Syngman RHEE was elected first president in 1948. Traditionally the agricultural region of the Korean peninsula, South Korea faced severe economic problems after partition. Attempts to establish an adequate industrial base were hampered by limited resources and an acute lack of power, most of which, prior to 1948, had been supplied by the north. War damage and the flood of refugees from North Korea further intensified the economic problem. The country depended upon foreign aid, chiefly from the United States, and the economy was characterized by runaway inflation, highly unfavorable trade balances, and mass unemployment. The increasingly authoritarian rule of President Syngman Rhee, with government corruption and injustice, added to the discontent of the people. The elections of March, 1960, in which Rhee won a fourth term, were marked by widespread violence, police brutality, and accusations by Rhee's opponents of government fraud. A student protest march on April 19, 1960, in which 125 students were shot down by the police, triggered a wave of uprisings across the country. The government capitulated, and Rhee resigned and went into exile. A Second Republic of Korea, under the leadership of Dr. John M. Chang (Chang Myun), was unable to correct the economic problems or maintain order, and in May, 1961, the South Korean armed forces seized power in a bloodless coup. A military junta under Gen. Park Chung Hee established firm control over civil freedoms, the press, and the economy, somewhat relaxing restrictions as its power solidified. General Park was elected president in 1963, reelected in 1967, and, following a constitutional amendment permitting a third term, again in 1971. His government was remarkably successful in fighting graft and corruption and in reviving the economy. Successive five-year economic development plans, first launched in 1962, brought dramatic changes. Between 1962 and 1972 manufacturing was established as a leading economic sector and exports increased at an average annual rate of 41%. In Oct., 1972, President Park proclaimed martial law and dissolved the national assembly, asserting that such measures were necessary to improve South Korea's position in the reunification talks with North Korea. Constitutional changes greatly increasing the presidential power were approved by a national referendum in Nov., 1972; these provided for the election of the president for six-year terms by a national conference for unification consisting of 2,000 to 5,000 delegates chosen by popular vote in small administrative units. In Dec., 1972, President Park was elected to a new six-year term by such a conference. In Aug., 1974, a Korean resident in Japan unsuccessfully attempted to assassinate Park in Seoul; Park's wife was fatally wounded by the assassin. See K. G. Clare et al., *Area Handbook for the Republic of Korea* (1969); Rinn-Sup Shinn et al., *Area Handbook for North Korea* (1969); Pow-Key Sohn et al., *The History of Korea* (1970); B. Y. Choy, *Korea: A History* (1971); D. C. Cole, *Korean Development* (1971); Yung-hwan Jo, comp., *Korea's Response to the West* (1971); Se-Jin Kim, *The Politics of Military Revolution in Korea* (1971); P. M. Bartz, *South Korea* (1972); U-gun Hang, *The History of Korea* (tr. 1972); W. E. Henthorn, *A History of Korea* (1972); R. A. Scalapino and Chong-Sik Lee, *Communism in Korea* (2 vol., 1973).

Korean, language of uncertain relationship. It is thought by some scholars to be akin to Japanese, by others to be a member of the Altaic subfamily of the Ural-Altaic family of languages (see URALIC AND ALTAIC LANGUAGES), and by still others to be unrelated to any known language. The Korean tongue is spoken by about 36 million people in Korea (27 million in South Korea and 9 million in North Korea) and by nearly 1 million others in Japan. Unlike Chinese, Korean does not use tones to make semantic distinctions. Its syntax, however, is similar to that of Chinese, while its morphology resembles that of Japanese. Korean is an agglutinative language in which different linguistic elements, each of which exists separately and has a fixed meaning, are often joined to form one word. A distinctive feature of Korean is the use of a number of different forms to indicate the respective social positions of the speaker, the individual spoken to, and the individual spoken about. The literature in the language dates from the 7th cent. A.D. Once written in Chinese characters, modern Korean has its own phonetic alphabet, called Hankul (or *onmun*), which was devised in the 15th cent. See Edward W. Wagner, *Elementary Written Korean* (3 vol., 1963–71); S. E. Martin et al, *Beginning Korean* (1969).

Korean War, conflict between Communist and non-Communist forces in Korea from June 25, 1950, to July 27, 1953. At the end of World War II, Korea was divided at the 38th parallel into Soviet (North Korean) and U.S. (South Korean) zones of occupation. In 1948 rival governments were established: The Republic of Korea was proclaimed in the South and the People's Democratic Republic of Korea in the North. Relations between them became increasingly strained, and on June 25, 1950, North Korean forces invaded South Korea. The United Nations quickly condemned the invasion as an act of aggression, demanded the withdrawal of North Korean troops from the South, and called upon its members to aid South Korea. On June 30, U.S. President Truman authorized the use of American land, sea, and air forces in Korea; a week later, the United Nations placed the forces of 15 other member nations under U.S. command, and Truman appointed Gen. Douglas MACARTHUR supreme commander. In the first weeks of the conflict the North Korean forces met little resistance and advanced rapidly. By Sept. 10 they had driven the South Korean army and a few American troops to the Pusan area at the southeast tip of Korea. A counteroffensive began on Sept. 15, when UN forces made a daring landing at Inchon on the west coast. North Korean forces fell back and MacArthur received orders to pursue them into North Korea. On Oct. 19, the North Korean capital of Pyongyang was captured; by Nov. 24, North Korean forces were driven almost to the Yalu River, which marked the border of Communist China. As MacArthur prepared for a final offensive, the Chinese Communists joined with the North Koreans to launch (Nov. 26) a successful counterattack. The troops were forced back, and in Jan., 1951, the Communists again advanced into the South, capturing Seoul, the South Korean capital. After months of heavy fighting, the center of the conflict was returned to the 38th parallel, where it remained for the rest of the war. MacArthur, however, wished to mount another invasion of North Korea. When a letter of his was read in Congress, urging a full-scale war against Communism, Truman removed (April 10, 1951) MacArthur from command and installed Gen. Matthew B. RIDGWAY as commander-in-chief. Ridgway began (July 10, 1951) truce negotiations with the North Koreans and Chinese, while small unit actions, bitter but indecisive, continued to take place. Negotiations broke down in Oct., 1952, over repatriation of prisoners of war, but were resumed the following April. After much difficulty, an armistice agreement was signed (July 27, 1953). Casualties in the war were heavy. U.S. losses were placed at over 54,000 dead and 103,000 wounded, while North and South Korean casualties were each at least 10 times as high. See John Miller, Jr., *Korea, 1951–53* (1956); Robert Leckie, *Conflict: The History of the Korean War, 1950–53* (1962); David Rees, *Korea: The Limited War* (1964, repr. 1970); H. J. Middleton, *The Compact History of the Korean War* (1965); M. B. Ridgway, *The Korean War* (1967); L. C. Gardener, ed., *The Korean War* (1972).

Koreish: see KURAISH.

Korhogo (kôrhō'gō), town (1967 est. pop. 30,000), N Ivory Coast. It is an administrative and processing center for a mountainous region where cotton, kapok, rice, millet, groundnuts, maize, and yams are grown and sheep and goats are raised. Diamonds are mined in the area. Korhogo was on an important precolonial trade route to the Atlantic coast.

Korin, Ogata (ōgä'tä kō'rēn), 1658–1716, Japanese decorator and painter. He is renowned for his lacquer work and paintings on screens, decorated with bold designs and striking color contrasts, and his masterful compositional use of empty space. These works show the influence of two earlier artists, Koetsu and Sotatsu, but he departed from conventions, creating his own nearly abstract style. Korin also excelled as a teacher. See study by Doanda Randall (1960).

Kórinthos, Greece: see CORINTH.

Koritsa: see KORÇË, Albania.

Koriyama (kōrē'yämä), city (1970 pop. 241,673), Fukushima prefecture, N Honshu, Japan, on the Abukuma River. It is a major commercial and communications center with industries producing textiles, electrical appliances, and food products.

Körmendi, Ferenc (fĕ'rĕnts kör'mĕndē), 1900–1972, Hungarian novelist. His *Escape to Life* (1932) won the international novel competition of 1932. Among his translated novels are *The Happy Generation* (1934, tr. 1945) and *That One Mistake* (1938, tr. 1947).

Kornberg, Arthur, 1918–, American biochemist, b. Brooklyn, grad. College of the City of New York (B.S., 1937) and Univ. of Rochester (M.D., 1941). In 1942 he joined the U.S. Public Health Service and became (1951) medical director. He was a staff member (1942–52) of the National Institutes of Health, Bethesda, Md. He taught at Washington Univ., St. Louis, and became chairman (1959) of the department of biochemistry at Stanford. Kornberg shared the 1959 Nobel Prize in Physiology and Medicine with Severo Ochoa for their work in the discovery of the mechanisms in the biological synthesis of deoxyribonucleic acid (DNA) and ribonucleic acid (RNA).

Kornilov, Lavr Georgyevich (lä'vər gēyôr'gyĭvĭch kərnyē'ləf), 1870–1918, Russian general, anti-Bolshevik commander during the civil war (1918–20). He fought in the Russo-Japanese War, and in World War I he was captured (1915) by the Austrians and escaped (1916). After the February Revolution of 1917, he was made commander in chief by Kerensky and proceeded to restore discipline among the troops. Conservative elements rallied to Kornilov, who hoped to reconstruct the provisional government on more conservative lines. In Sept., 1917 (Aug., 1917, O.S.) he sent troops to Petrograd (now Leningrad) to carry out these plans. Kerensky—who feared that Kornilov planned to establish a military dictatorship—dismissed Kornilov and, upon Kornilov's refusal to accept dismissal, arrested him and his assistants, including Denikin. Shortly after the October Revolution of 1917, Kornilov escaped from Petrograd and joined M. V. ALEKSEYEV in S Russia. Their volunteer army was greatly weakened by the virtual defection of the Don Cossacks early in 1918; under Kornilov's leadership the army fell back to the Kuban region. He was killed while attacking Ekaterinodar (now Krasnodar) and was succeeded by Denikin as anti-Bolshevik commander in the south.

Korolenko, Vladimir Galaktionovich (vlədyē'mĭr gələktyô'nəvĭch kərəlyĕn'kə), 1853–1921, Russian short-story writer and publicist. A member of a Populist circle, he was arrested in 1879 and exiled to Siberia until 1885. There he wrote many of his lyrical tales, notable for their descriptions of desolate nature. His most famous story, "Makar's Dream" (1885, tr. 1954 in *Korolenko's Siberia*), describes a dying peasant's dream of heaven. After 1895, Korolenko devoted himself to liberal journalism. Greatly honored in Russia by 1903, he welcomed the revolution but later opposed the Bolshevik regime. See his autobiography, ed. by Neil Parsons (1972).

Körös or **Harmás Körös** (här'mŏsh kö'rösh) [Hung.,=triple Körös], Rum. *Criş,* river, c.345 mi (560 km) long, formed in E Hungary by the junction of three headstreams that rise in Transylvania, NW Rumania. It meanders west through farmland to the Tisza River at Csongrád. The Körös is used for irrigation.

korrigum: see DAMALISK.

Korsør (kôrsör'), city (1970 com. pop. 19,864), Vestsjaelland co., S central Denmark, a seaport on the Store Baelt. In the city are fisheries and factories producing glass and processed food.

Kortrijk (kôrt'rĭk), Fr. *Courtrai,* city (1970 pop. 44,961), West Flanders prov., SW Belgium, on the Leie River. It is an important linen and textile-manufacturing center. Kortrijk was one of the earliest (14th cent.) and most important cloth-manufacturing towns of medieval Flanders. In 1302, Flemish burghers defeated French knights there in the first BATTLE OF THE SPURS. The Church of Notre Dame (13th cent.) in the city contains Anthony Van Dyck's *Elevation of the Cross* (1631). The Gothic city hall dates from the 16th cent.

Koruk, Algerian corsair: see BARBAROSSA.

Koryak National Okrug: see KAMCHATKA, peninsula, USSR.

Korzybski, Alfred Habdank (kôrzĭb'skē), 1879–1950, Polish-American linguist, b. Warsaw. In his system, which he called General Semantics, Korzybski aimed at a distinction between the word and the object it describes and between the individual objects all described by the same word, insisting also that the effect of time be taken into consideration. In 1949, Korzybski lectured at Yale on his system; he wrote two books describing it (1921 and 1933). See Kelly Thurman, *Semantics* (1960).

Kós (kŏs, kôs), Lat. *Cos,* island (1971 pop. 16,650), 111 sq mi (287 sq km), SE Greece, in the Aegean Sea; 2d largest of the DODECANESE, near the Bodrum peninsula of Turkey. Although it rises to c.2,870 ft (875 m) in the southeast, the island is mostly low-lying. Fishing and sponge diving are important occupations. Grain, tobacco, olive oil, and wine are produced, and cattle, horses, and goats are raised. Kós has mineral deposits and several sulfur springs. The island's main town is Kós (1971 pop. 7,828), situated on the northeast shore. In ancient times the island was controlled in turn by Athens, Macedon, Syria, and Egypt. A cultural center, it was the site of a school of medicine founded in the 5th cent. B.C. by Hippocrates. Kós later enjoyed great prosperity as a result of its alliance with the Ptolemaic dynasty of Egypt, which valued the island as a naval base. The island became part of modern Greece in 1947. It is called Coos in Acts 21.1.

Kosala (kō'sələ), ancient Indian kingdom, corresponding roughly in area with the region of OUDH. Its capital was Ajodhya. It was a powerful state in the 6th cent. B.C. but was weakened by a series of wars with the neighboring kingdom of Magadha and finally (4th cent. B.C.) absorbed by it. Kosala was the setting of much Sanskrit epic literature including the RAMAYANA. Buddha and Mahavira, founder of Jainism, taught in the kingdom.

Kosciusko, Thaddeus (kŏs"ēŭs'kō), Pol. *Tadeusz Andrzej Bonawentura Kościuszko,* 1746–1817, Polish general. Trained in military academies in Warsaw and Paris, he offered his services to the colonists in the American Revolution because of his commitment to the ideal of liberty. Arriving in America in 1777, he took part in the Saratoga campaign and advised Horatio Gates to fortify Bemis Heights. Later he fortified (1778) West Point and fought (1780) with distinction under Gen. Nathanael Greene in the Carolina campaign. After his return to Poland he became a champion of Polish independence. He fought (1792–93) in the campaign that resulted in the second partition (1793) of Poland (see POLAND, PARTITIONS OF). In 1794 he issued a call at Kraków for a national uprising and led the Polish forces against both Russians and Prussians in a gallant but unsuccessful rebellion that ended with the final partition of Poland. He was imprisoned, and after being freed (1796) went to the United States and later (1798) to France, where after the fall of Napoleon he pleaded with Alexander I of Russia for Polish independence. He died in Solothurn, Switzerland, and is buried in Kraków. His devotion to liberty and Polish independence have made him one of the great Polish heroes. See Miecislaus Haiman, *Kosciuszko in the American Revolution* (1943, repr. 1972) and *Kosciuszko, Leader and Exile* (1946).

Kosciusko, Mount (kŏzēŭ'skō), 7,316 ft (2,230 m) high, SE New South Wales, Australia, in the Australian Alps; highest peak of Australia. Winter sports are held on its slopes.

Kose no Kanaoka: see KANAOKA.

kosher [Heb.,=proper, i.e., fit for use], term used in rabbinic literature to mean what is ritually correct, but most widely applied to food that is in accordance with the Jewish dietary laws based on Old Testament passages (primarily Lev. 11 and Deut. 14). Kosher meat is the flesh of animals that both chew the cud and have cloven hoofs (as the cow and sheep); the animal must have been slaughtered with a skillful stroke by a specially trained and highly learned and pious Jew; the meat must be carefully inspected, and, unless cooked by broiling, it must be salted and soaked to remove all traces of blood. Kosher fishes are those that have scales and fins. The rules that apply to the slaughter and preparation of fowl are the same as those for the slaughter of animals. The cooking and eating of milk products with, or immediately after, meats or meat products is unkosher; even the use of the same kitchen and table utensils and towels is forbidden. The cleansing of newly acquired utensils and the preparation of articles for Passover use are also called koshering. The antithesis of kosher is *tref* [from Heb.,=animal torn by wild beasts]. The origins and motivations for the dietary laws and customs have been variously given as hygienic, aesthetic, folkloric, ethical, and psychological. Reform Judaism does not require observance of the kosher laws.

Koshigaya (kōshē'gäyä), city (1970 pop. 139,168), Saitama prefecture, central Honshu, Japan, on the Motoara River. It is a suburb of Tokyo and is noted for its peach orchards.

Koshtan-Tau (kəshtän"-tou', kôsh"tän-), peak, c.16,880 ft (5,150 m) high, Kabardino-Balkar Autonomous SSR, S European USSR, in the central Greater Caucasus.

Košice (kô'shĭtsĕ), Ger. *Kaschau,* Hung. *Kassa,* city (1970 pop. 145,027), E Czechoslovakia, in Slovakia. It is a major industrial center and transportation hub and a market for the surrounding agricultural area. The city's industries include food processing, brewing and distilling, printing, and the manufacture of machinery, cement, and ceramics. A petroleum refinery and a modern iron and steel center are nearby. Originally a fortress town, Košice was chartered in 1241 and became an important trade center during the Middle Ages. It was frequently occupied by Austrian, Hungarian, and Turkish forces. By the Treaty of Trianon (1920) the city passed from Hungary to Czechoslovakia. Košice's most notable historic buildings are the Gothic Cathedral of St. Elizabeth (14th–15th cent.), the 14th-century Franciscan monastery and church, and an 18th-century town hall. The city also has a university and several cultural institutions.

Kosinski, Jerzy (jûr'zē kəzĭn'skē), 1933–, Polish-American writer, b. Łódź, Poland. He learned English after emigrating to the United States in 1957. His best-known work is *The Painted Bird* (1965), a novel depicting the nightmarish wanderings of a young boy among the brutal peasants of a nameless country during World War II. The horrors of war and the violation of a human being are rendered in language of remarkable beauty. Kosinski's other novels, *Steps* (1968), *Being There* (1971), and *The Devil Tree* (1973), echo the theme of character disintegration through cruelty and revenge. He also writes under the name Joseph Novak.

Köslin: see KOSZALIN, Poland.

Kosseir: see QUSAYR, AL, Egypt.

Kossel, Albrecht (äl'brĕkht kôs'əl), 1853–1927, German physiologist. He was professor at Heidelberg from 1901. He specialized in the physiological chemistry of the cell and its nucleus and of proteins, including nucleins. He discovered the purine adenine and the pyrimidine thymine. For this work he received the 1910 Nobel Prize in Physiology and Medicine. He wrote *Protamines and Histones* (tr. 1928).

Kossovo or **Kossovo-Metohija** (kô'sôvô-mĕtô'khēä), Serbo-Croatian *Kosovo i Metohija* and *Kosmet*, autonomous region, 4,126 sq mi (10,686 sq km), SE Yugoslavia, in Serbia. PRIŠTINA is the chief city. The largely mountainous region includes the fertile valleys of Kossovo and Metohija and is drained by the Southern Morava River. Agriculture, stock raising, forestry, and lead and silver mining are the major occupations. Kossovo's population is mainly Albanian, Serbian, and Montenegrin. Settled by the Slavs in the 7th cent., the region passed to Bulgaria in the 9th cent. and to Serbia in the 12th cent. From the battle of Kossovo in 1389 until the Balkan War of 1913, it was under Turkish rule. Partitioned in 1913 between Serbia and Montenegro, it was incorporated into Yugoslavia after World War I. Following World War II, Kossovo became an autonomous region within Serbia. At **Kossovo Field,** Serbo-Croatian *Kosovo Polje*, in 1389, the Turks under Sultan Murad I defeated Serbia and its Bosnian, Montenegrin, Bulgarian, and other allies. Before the battle Milosh Obilich, a Serb, posing as a deserter, was taken into the tent of Murad, whom he stabbed to death; he was immediately slain, as was Prince Lazar of Serbia after being captured. The battle of Kossovo Field (the name means "field of the black birds") broke the power of Serbia and Bulgaria, which soon passed under Ottoman rule. The battle figures prominently in Serbian poetry. In another battle on the site in 1448, Sultan Murad II defeated an army led by John Hunyadi.

Kossuth, Louis (kŏsōōth'), Hung. *Kossuth Lajos,* 1802–94, Hungarian revolutionary hero. Born of a Protestant family and a lawyer by training, he entered politics as a member of the diet and soon won a large following. His liberal and nationalist program did not avoid the possibility of dissolving the union of the Hungarian and Austrian crowns. He was arrested in 1837, but popular pressure forced the Metternich regime to release him in 1840. Kossuth, a fiery orator, was one of the principal figures of the Hungarian revolution of March, 1848. When, in April, Hungary was granted a separate government, Kossuth became finance minister. He continued and intensified his anti-Austrian agitation. His principles were liberal, but his nationalism was opposed to the fulfillment of the national aspirations of the Slavic, Rumanian, and German minorities in Hungary and was particularly resented in Croatia. When the Austrian government, supported by the *ban* [governor] of Croatia, Count JELLACHICH DE BUZIM, prepared to move against Hungary, Kossuth became head of the Hungarian government of national defense. His government withdrew to Debrecen before the advance of the Austrians under Alfred WINDISCHGRÄTZ. In April, 1849, the Hungarian parliament declared Hungary an independent republic and Kossuth became president. The Hungarians won several victories, but in 1849, Russian troops intervened in favor of Austria, and Kossuth was obliged to resign the government to General GÖRGEY. The Hungarian surrender at Vilagos marked the end of the republic. Kossuth fled to Turkey. He visited England and the United States and received ovations as a champion of liberty. Kossuth lived in exile in England and (after 1865) in Italy. He was dissatisfied with the *Ausgleich* [compromise] of 1867, by which the AUSTRO-HUNGARIAN MONARCHY was created, and he refused an offer of amnesty in 1890. After his death at Turin, Italy, his body was returned to Budapest and buried in state. See biographies by Otto Zarek (tr. 1937, repr. 1970), Endre Sebestyen (1950), and P. C. Headley (1971); F. A. Pulszky, *White, Red, Black* (2 vol., 1853, repr. 1970).

Kostelanetz, André (än'drā kŏs"təlä'nĭts), 1901–, American pianist and conductor, b. St. Petersburg (now Leningrad), Russia. After studying at the St. Petersburg Conservatory of Music, he emigrated to the United States in 1922 and became a citizen in 1928. As a conductor Kostelanetz concentrates on popular and semiclassical works and on simplified versions of famous symphonies. He became popular while appearing regularly on radio and has made many records. He is conductor of the annual Promenade Concerts at Avery Fisher Hall at Lincoln Center in New York City.

Koster or **Coster, Laurens Janszoon** (lou'rəns yän'sōn kôs'tər), c.1370–c.1440, Dutch sexton of a church in Haarlem, one of the men to whom has been ascribed the invention of printing with movable types. His name was Laurens Janszoon, but he is known by his office, as Koster or Coster [sexton]. The evidence that his printing with movable type preceded Gutenberg's is inconclusive.

Kostroma (kəstrəmä'), city (1970 pop. 223,000), capital of Kostroma oblast, E European USSR, on the Volga at the mouth of the Kostroma River. It is a major linen-milling center. Metallurgy, ship repair, and the production of machinery, plywood, and footwear are also important. Founded in 1152, it was the capital of a principality in the 13th and 14th cent. It became an important commercial center after it was annexed by Moscow in 1364. At Kostroma in 1613, Michael Romanov was elected czar. Among the ancient buildings of Kostroma are the Ipatyev monastery (16th cent.) and the Uspensky Cathedral (c.1250).

Kosygin, Alexei Nikolayevich (əlyĭksyā' nyĭkəlī'əvĭch kəsē'gĭn), 1904–, Soviet political leader. A member of the Communist party from 1927, he joined its central committee in 1939. In the 1940s, as an aide to Joseph Stalin, he became recognized as an expert in economics and industry. He held various other government and party posts before becoming (1960) first deputy chairman of the USSR council of ministers. In 1964 he succeeded Nikita Khrushchev as premier, sharing overall power with Leonid BREZHNEV, general secretary of the Communist party. By the late 1960s, however, his importance in the party and government hierarchy had diminished in relation to that of Brezhnev, although Kosygin continued as premier. In this post he introduced various economic measures designed to reform and modernize Soviet agriculture, industry, and trade.

Koszalin (kôshä'lēn), Ger. *Köslin,* city (1970 pop. 64,400), NW Poland, near the Baltic Sea. Its industries produce canned fish, metal products, and chemicals. It was founded in 1188, prospered from the 14th to the 16th cent., but suffered greatly in the Thirty Years War. There is a 14th-century Gothic cathedral in Koszalin. The city was transferred from Germany to Poland by the Potsdam Conference (1945).

Kota (kō'tə), city (1971 pop. 213,005), Rajasthan state, NW India, on the Chambal River. Kota, enclosed by a massive wall, is a district administrative center and a market for sugarcane, oilseed, and building stone. The city has an airport. The Mathureshi temple is the most famous of Kota's many temples.

Kota Baharu (kōt'ə bəhär'ōō) or **Kota Bahru** (bär'ōō), city (1971 pop. 55,052), capital of Kelantan state, Malaysia, central Malay Peninsula, on the South China Sea at the mouth of the Kelantan River. It is a modern city with an important power station. It was seized by Japan (Dec. 10, 1941) early in the campaign against Singapore during World War II.

Kota Kinabalu (kĭn"əbəlōō'), formerly **Jesselton,** town (1971 pop. 41,830), capital of Sabah, Malaysia, in N Borneo and on a small inlet of the South China Sea. It is the chief port of the state and is connected by road and rail with the interior. Rubber is exported. It was founded in 1899 and in 1947 replaced SANDAKAN as the capital of what was then British North Borneo.

Kotelny Island (kōtĕl'nē), largest island of the Anjou group of the NEW SIBERIAN ISLANDS, c.100 mi (160 km) long and c.60 mi (100 km) wide, off N Siberian USSR. The island was discovered in 1773 by Ivan Lyakhov, a Russian merchant. Polar foxes and deer inhabit the island.

Köthen (kö'tən), city (1970 pop. 36,587), Halle district, central East Germany. There are lignite mines, sugar refineries, textile mills, and chemical factories in the city. Known in 1115, Köthen was from 1603 to 1847 the residence of the dukes of Anhalt-Köthen, at whose court Johann Sebastian Bach was musical director from 1717 to 1723. A former spelling was Cöthen.

Kotka (kōt'kä), city (1970 pop. 34,349), Kymi prov., SE Finland, on the Gulf of Finland. It is a major export center for paper, pulp, and timber, and it has chemical industries. It was chartered in 1878.

koto (kō'tō), a Japanese string instrument related in structure to the ZITHER. It consists of an elongated rectangular wooden body, strung lengthwise with 7 to 13 silk strings. The uniformly long strings are tuned to one of several standard tunings by wooden bridges. The koto is placed horizontally on the floor with the player seated behind it, and it is plucked with the fingernails or with a plectum. The instrument flourished in Japanese art music from the 17th cent. until the middle of the 19th cent., when European music began to overshadow indigenous music in popularity.

Koto

Kotor (kô'tôr), Ital. *Cattaro,* town (1971 pop. 32,439), SW Yugoslavia, in Montenegro, on the Bay of Kotor, an inlet of the Adriatic. It is a seaport and a tourist center. The town was colonized by Greeks (3d cent. B.C.) and later belonged to the Roman and Byzantine empires. In 1797 it passed to Austria and became an important naval base; in 1918 it was transferred to Yugoslavia. It has a medieval fort and town walls and a 16th-century cathedral.

Kottbus: see COTTBUS, East Germany.

Kotzebue, August von (ou'gōōst fən kôt'səbōō), 1761–1819, German dramatist and politician. He wrote some 200 plays, including *Menschenhass und Reue* (1789, tr. *The Stranger,* 1798), *Die Spanier in Peru; oder, Rollas Tod* (1795, tr. *Rolla,* 1797), and *Die beiden Klingsberg* (1801, tr. *Father and Son,* 1914). Kotzebue was a gifted, though superficial, playwright; his comedies and operatic librettos remained popular throughout the 19th cent. Among those who set his librettos to music were Beethoven, Schubert, and C. M. von Weber. After a stay in Russia, Kotzebue returned to Germany as an agent of Czar Alexander I. He was detested for his reactionary propaganda; his assassination at Mannheim by a student led to the suppression of German student organizations (see BURSCHENSCHAFT) through the Carlsbad Decrees.

Kotzebue, Otto von (ô'tō), 1787–1846, Russian naval officer and explorer; son of A. F. F. von Kotzebue. He accompanied A. J. von Krusenstern on his circumnavigation (1803–6) and himself commanded two voyages around the world (1815–18, 1823–26). He discovered some 400 islands in the South Seas, checked the location of others, and gathered new information on the Pacific coast of Siberia. He sailed N through Bering Strait, explored the northwest coast of Alaska hoping to find a Northwest Passage, and in 1816 discovered and explored Kotzebue Sound. Scientists accompanying his expeditions made valuable reports on ethnography and natural history. Kotzebue's own narratives were translated into English as *A Voyage of Discovery* (3 vol., 1821) and *A New Voyage round the World* (2 vol., 1830, repr. 1967).

Kotzebue (kŏt'səbyōō), city (1970 pop. 1,696), NW Alaska, on Kotzebue Sound at the tip of Baldwin Peninsula; inc. 1958. It has one of the largest settlements of Eskimos in Alaska. A regional trade center, Kotzebue has a tourist industry. The city, set on a tundra, began in the 18th cent. as an Eskimo trading post for arctic Alaska and part of Siberia.

Koublai Khan: see KUBLAI KHAN.

Kouchibouguac National Park (kōō"shēbəkwăk'), 87 sq mi (225 sq km), on Kouchibouguac Bay, E N.B., Canada, near Richibuct; est. 1969. The park's scenic features include lagoons, bays, and offshore sandbars.

Koufax, Sanford (Sandy Koufax), 1935–, American baseball player, b. New York City. He played (1955–66) with the Dodgers, remaining on the team when the franchise was moved from Brooklyn, N.Y., to Los Angeles. He three times received the Cy Young Award for his outstanding pitching (1963, 1965, 1966). A left-hander with overwhelming speed and a brilliant curve, Koufax struck out 2,396 batters between 1955 and 1966 before being forced into premature retirement with an arm ailment. He was elected to the Baseball Hall of Fame in 1972.

koumiss (kōō'mĭs): see FERMENTED MILK.

Koundouritis, Paul: see KONDOURIOTIS, PAUL.

kouprey: see GAUR.

Koussevitzky, Serge (Sergei Aleksandrovich Koussevitzky) (sĕrzh ko͞osəvĭt'skē; syĭrgā' əlyĭksän'drəvĭch ko͞osyĭvēt'skē), 1874–1951, Russian-American conductor, studied in Moscow. He began his career as a double bass player, but in 1908 he made his debut as a conductor in Berlin. In 1910 he and his wife, Natalie, formed an orchestra that Koussevitzky conducted until 1918. In 1917 he was made conductor of the State Symphony Orchestra in Petrograd. Leaving Russia in 1920, he made Paris the center of his activity until he came to the United States in 1924, becoming a citizen in 1941. He was conductor (1924–49) of the Boston Symphony Orchestra and also directed (from 1936) the Berkshire Symphonic Festivals, today known as the Berkshire Festival. A champion of modern music, he repeatedly commissioned and performed new works by American composers, such as Aaron Copland, Samuel Barber, and William Schuman. See biographies by Moses Smith (1947) and Arthur Lourié (1931, repr. 1969); study by H. Leichtentritt (1946).

Kovalevsky, Sonya or **Sophie,** 1850–91, Russian mathematician. She studied at the universities of Heidelberg and Berlin (under K. T. Weierstrass) and in 1874 received a Ph.D in absentia from the Univ. of Göttingen for her remarkable thesis on partial differential equations. From 1884 she taught at the Univ. of Stockholm. In 1888 she won the Bordin Prize of the French Academy of Sciences for a memoir on the rotation of a solid body about a fixed point. Her childhood reminiscences, published in 1890, were translated as *Sonya Kovalevsky: Her Recollections of Childhood* (1895), with a biographical study by Anna Leffler Edgren. See biography by P. Ia. Polubarinova-Kochina (1957).

Kovel (kō'vəl, Rus. kô'vĭl), Pol. *Kowel,* city (1967 est. pop. 31,000), W European USSR, in the Ukraine, on the Tura River. A rail junction and agriculture center, it has food and peat processing plants, railroad shops, and sewing, flax, and woodworking industries. First mentioned in the 14th cent., Kovel belonged to Lithuania and passed to Poland when the two states were united in 1569. The city was taken by Russia during the third partition of Poland in 1795. It was again under Polish rule from 1921 to 1945, when it reverted to the USSR.

Kovno: see KAUNAS, USSR.

Kovrov (kərôf'), city (1970 pop. 123,000), central European USSR, on the Klyazma River. Kovrov is an industrial center that produces excavating machines, linen textiles, and machine tools.

Kowait: see KUWAIT.

Kowel: see KOVEL, USSR.

Kowloon: see HONG KONG.

Koxinga (kōksĭng'gə), Mandarin *Kuo-hsing-yeh* [lord of the imperial surname], 1624–62, Chinese general, whose original name was Chêng Ch'êng-kung. From 1646 to 1660 he led many unsuccessful campaigns of Ming dynasty loyalists against the invading Ch'ing dynasty. Koxinga captured (1661) part of TAIWAN (Formosa) from the Dutch. The population of the southern coast of China was evacuated (1662) to facilitate the defense against his raids. After the death of his son Chêng Ching, Taiwan fell to the Ch'ing (1683).

Koya (kō'yä), peak, 2,858 ft (871 m) high, S Honshu, Japan. On its summit is a Buddhist monastery, founded in 816. The monastery has 120 temples and is visited by more than a million pilgrims annually. The peak is also known as Koyasan.

Koz, priestly family. Ezra 2.61; Neh. 3.4,21; 7.63. Hakkoz: 1 Chron. 24.10.

Kozhikode, India: see CALICUT.

Kozlov, Frol Romanovich (frōl rəmä'nəvĭch kŏz'lôf), 1908–65, Soviet Communist leader. Early in his career he joined the Communist party and rose in the party organization. Kozlov reached prominence as a close ally of Khrushchev and became (1957) a full member of the presidium. In 1960 he was made secretary of the party central committee. He suffered a stroke in 1963 and resigned his posts in Nov., 1964, after Khrushchev's removal.

Kozlov: see MICHURINSK, USSR.

Kr, chemical symbol of the element KRYPTON.

Kra, Isthmus of (krä), narrow neck of the Malay Peninsula, c.40 mi (60 km) wide, SW Thailand, between the Bay of Bengal and the Gulf of Siam. It has long been the proposed site of a ship canal that would bypass the congested Straits of Malacca.

Kraepelin, Emil (krĕpəlēn'), 1856–1926, German psychiatrist, educated at Würzburg (M.D., 1878). He also studied under Wilhelm Wundt in Leipzig. He was appointed professor of psychiatry at the Univ. of Dorpat, Heidelberg (1891) and at Munich (1903), where he also directed a clinic. He investigated (1883–92) the influence of fatigue and alcohol upon physical functions. He also classified mental diseases according to their cause, symptomatology, course, final stage, and pathological anatomical findings. He established the clinical pictures of dementia praecox (schizophrenia) in 1893 and of manic-depressive psychosis in 1899. He was concerned only with diagnostic classification and did not accept the theory of unconscious mental activity postulated by psychoanalysts. He contributed little toward understanding mental disorders, but he brought clarity into psychiatric thought and helped introduce scientific methods of investigation. His major work is his *Textbook of Psychiatry* (9th ed. 1927).

Krafft, Adam: see KRAFT, ADAM.

Krafft-Ebing, Richard von (rĭkh'ärt fən kräft-ā'bĭng), 1840–1902, German physician and neurologist. Professor of psychiatry at Strasbourg (1872), Graz (1873), and Vienna (1889), he was recognized as an authority on deviant sexual behavior and its medicolegal aspects. His most noted work is *Psychopathia sexualis* (1886, tr. 1892).

Kraft or **Krafft, Adam** (both: ä'däm kräft), c.1455–1509, German sculptor of Nuremberg. He moved from an ornamental late Gothic style toward clarity, symmetry, and a powerful use of rounded, organically constructed figures. His decorations for the Schreyer family tomb (c.1490) in the Church of St. Sebald in Nuremberg and his openwork tabernacle (1493–96) for the Church of St. Lawrence typify his earlier style. His later manner may be seen in his *Stations of the Cross* (1505–8; Nuremberg). Kraft was notably adept at blending architectural and sculptural forms.

Krag, Jens Otto (yĕns ô'tō kräkh), 1914–, Danish political leader. A Social Democrat, he entered parliament in 1947 and played a leading role in shaping Denmark's postwar economic policies. He served as minister of commerce, industry, and shipping (1947–50), minister of economy and labor (1953–57), and minister of external economic affairs (1957–58). Minister of Foreign Affairs (1958–62,1966–67), he was twice prime minister (1962–68, 1971–72). In 1972 his goal of Common Market membership for Denmark was realized when his government won a resounding victory in a referendum on the issue; one day later Krag resigned the premiership for personal reasons.

Krak: see AL KARAK, Jordan.

Krakatoa (krākətō'ə, krä-) or **Krakatau** (kräkätou'), volcanic island, c.5 sq mi (13 sq km), W Indonesia, in Sunda Strait between Java and Sumatra; rising to 2,667 ft (813 m). A terrific volcanic explosion in 1883 blew up most of the island and altered the configuration of the strait; the accompanying tsunami caused great destruction and loss of life along the nearby coasts of Java and Sumatra. The explosion is classed as one of the largest volcanic eruptions in modern times; so great was the outpouring of ashes and lava that new islands were formed and debris was scattered across the Indian Ocean as far as Madagascar. Since then there have been lesser eruptions.

Kraków (krä'kou, Pol. krä'ko͞of), Ger. *Krakau,* city (1970 pop. 583,444), S Poland, on the Vistula. A river port and industrial center, it has varied manufactures including metals, machinery, electrical equipment, and chemicals. One of E Europe's largest iron and steel plants is in the city. Founded c.700 and made a bishopric c.1000, Kraków became (1320) the residence of the kings of Poland. The Kraków fire (1595) caused the transfer (1596) of the royal residence to Warsaw, but the kings were still crowned and buried in Kraków until the 18th cent. The city passed to Austria in the third partition of Poland (1795) and was included (1809) in the grand duchy of Warsaw. In 1815 the Congress of Vienna made the city and its vicinity into the republic of Kraków, a protectorate of Russia, Prussia, and Austria, and in 1846 it was included in Austria. The city reverted to Poland in 1919. Kraków has many historic landmarks and national relics. Its university (known sometimes as the Jagiellonian Univ.), founded in 1364 by Casimir the Great, has long been a leading European center of learning; Copernicus was one of its students. The city has some 50 old churches, many of which contain works of art. Standing on a hill, the Wawel, are the royal castle (rebuilt 16th cent. in Italian Renaissance style) and the Gothic cathedral (rebuilt in the 14th cent.), which contains the tombs of great Poles. The Rynek [market] square is noted for the Church of Our Lady (13th cent.), which has carvings by Veit Stoss; the 14th-century cloth hall; and the remaining tower of the 14th-century town hall.

Kramař, Charles or **Karel** (kä'rĕl krä'märsh), 1860–1937, Czechoslovakian political leader. Elected (1891) to the Austrian parliament, Kramař soon became leader of the liberal nationalist Young Czech party. An ardent Slavophile, he called (1898) for an alliance of Austria-Hungary and Russia against the Germans, whom he regarded as the implacable enemy of all Slavs. He publicly advocated Czech autonomy within the Austrian Empire but privately favored an independent Czech state within a Russian-led Slavic federation. In World War I he led the resistance movement of the Czech nationalists at home, while Thomas G. MASARYK and Eduard BENEŠ led it abroad. He received a death sentence (1916) for treason, but the sentence was commuted to life imprisonment. An amnesty (1917) brought about his release. On October 28, 1918, Kramař led a bloodless coup in Prague, making Czech independence from Austria a reality. He was (1918–19) the first premier of the new state under President Masaryk, but was forced to resign as a result of his opposition to land reform and other progressive measures. After 1919 he led a rightist minority against Masaryk and Beneš.

Kramatorsk (krəmətôrsk'), city (1970 pop. 150,000), S central European USSR, in the Donets Basin of the Ukraine. It is an iron and steel center with factories that produce equipment for coal-mining and chemical industries.

Kramer, Jack (John Albert Kramer), 1921–, American tennis player, b. Las Vegas, Nev. He excelled at tennis while still in high school. Kramer and Frederick (Ted) Schroeder won the U.S. national doubles championship in 1940 and again in 1941. While serving (1942–46) in the U.S. coast guard in World War II, Kramer continued to play tournament tennis, and in 1943 (with Frank Parker) he again won the national doubles title. In 1946–47 he led the U.S. teams that won the Davis Cup, and he also won the national singles title, the national doubles (with Ted Schroeder), the British singles, and the British doubles (with Bob Falkenburg). After turning professional (1947), he took the U.S. professional singles (1948), the world professional singles (1949), and (with Robert Riggs) the world professional doubles (1949) championships. He began promoting professional tennis tournaments in 1952, retiring in 1954 to continue these activities.

Kranach, Lucas: see CRANACH, LUCAS.

Krapp, George Philip, 1872–1934, American scholar, b. Cincinnati. Krapp joined the faculty of Columbia Univ. in 1897, was professor of English at the Univ. of Cincinnati (1908–10) and at Columbia (1910–34). An authority on Anglo-Saxon, he was the first editor of the "Anglo-Saxon Poetic Records," an edition of the existing body of Anglo-Saxon poetry. Besides his authoritative works *Modern English: Its Growth and Present Use* (1909) and *The English Language in America* (1925), Krapp wrote books on English language and literature, speech improvement, and grammar.

Krasicki, Ignacy (ēgnä'tsē kräsēts'kē), 1735–1801, Polish satirist. He is noted for the poems *Myszeis,* an allegory on political disorder, and *Monachomachia,* a witty inspection of monastic life, as well as for his novels, prose satires (e.g., *Satyry,* 1779), and fables. Krasicki enjoyed the favor of both Stanislaus II and Frederick the Great. Six years before his death he was made archbishop of Gniezo.

Krasiński, Zygmunt, Count (zĭg'mo͞ont kräsēn'yəskē), 1812–59, Polish romantic poet. An ardent patriot and Slavophile, he lived much of his life abroad. His majestic works, often set in classical antiquity, include *The Undivine Comedy* (1833, tr. 1875), an allegory of the tragic history of Poland entitled *Iridion* (1835, tr. 1927), *Dawn* (1843), and *The Psalms of the Future* (1845–48). His works transcend nationalist themes in their philosophical concern with the plight of modern man.

Krasnodar (krəs"nədär'), city (1970 pop. 465,000), capital of Krasnodar Kray, SE European USSR, on the Kuban River. A river port and railroad junction, it has petroleum refineries and machinery, metalworking, textile, chemical, and food-processing plants. Founded in 1794 by Zaporozhe (Black Sea) Cossacks upon orders from Catherine II, it was organized as their administrative center and called Ekaterinodar (Yekaterinodar). It served as a military center protecting Russia's Caucasian frontier. After 1918 it was the capital of the Kuban-Black Sea Soviet Republic and was renamed in 1920.

Krasnodar Kray or **Krasnodar Territory,** administrative division (1970 pop. 4,511,000), 32,317 sq mi (83,701 sq km), SE European USSR, extending E from the Sea of Azov and the Black Sea into the KUBAN steppe and straddling the northwestern end of the Greater Caucasus. Krasnodar is the capital. The territory includes the ADYGE AUTONOMOUS OBLAST. The main agricultural section is in the Kuban steppe and along the lower Kuban River. Most of the area has high quality black soil. The territory is one of the USSR's principal tobacco-growing regions. The subtropical Black Sea littoral produces fruit, tea, and wine and is dotted with health resorts, of which Sochi is the best known. There are petroleum, gas, machinery, cement, and lumber industries. Krasnodar, Maikop, and Armavir are the chief industrial centers; Tuapse is the main port. More than 90% of the population is Russian and Ukrainian; their dialect is a mixture of the two languages. The rest of the population is Adyge or Circassian. The area N of the Kuban belonged to the Crimean Khanate and was annexed by Russia in 1783. The Kuban Cossacks, who settled there, gradually displaced the native nomadic Nogay Tatars. The Black Sea littoral was ceded to Russia by Turkey in the Treaty of Adrianople (1829). The remainder, known as CIRCASSIA, was annexed in 1864. Krasnodar Kray was formed in 1937.

Krasnovodsk (krəsnəvôtsk'), city (1970 pop. 64,800), S Central Asian USSR, in the Turkmen Republic, on the Krasnovodsk Gulf of the Caspian Sea. It is the western terminus of oil and natural gas pipelines and of the Trans-Caspian RR, which links the Caspian region with central Asia. It is also a transshipment point for agricultural produce. The city was founded in 1869.

Krasnoyarsk (krəsnəyärsk'), city (1972 est. pop. 688,000), capital of Krasnoyarsk Kray, W Siberian USSR, on the Yenisei River. A major river port and rail center, it has industries producing heavy equipment for the Trans-Siberian RR, building and mining equipment, and farm and shipbuilding machinery. There are also plants producing cement, aluminum, and textiles. One of the world's largest hydroelectric plants is on the Yenisei at Krasnoyarsk. Founded in 1628 as the Cossack outpost of Krasny Yar, it grew rapidly after the discovery of gold and the construction of the Trans-Siberian RR (late 19th cent.). Krasnoyarsk is the seat of the Siberian Institute of Forestry.

Krasnoyarsk Kray or **Krasnoyarsk Territory,** administrative division (1970 pop. 2,962,000), c.928,000 sq mi (2,403,520 sq km), central Siberian USSR, extending from the Sayan Mts. and the Minusinsk basin in the south across the Siberian wooded steppe, taiga, and tundra to the Arctic Ocean. The territory stretches along the entire course of the Yenisei, comprising parts of the West Siberian lowland on the left bank and the central Siberian Plateau on the right bank. The Yenisei and its tributaries are important transportation routes and electric power sources. The Trans-Siberian RR crosses the southern section of the territory. There are deposits of brown coal, graphite, iron ore, manganese, gold, copper, nickel, aluminum, uranium, and mica. In the north is an extensive lumber industry. Grain is grown, cattle and reindeer are raised, and fur trapping is carried on. Krasnoyarsk, the capital, and Kansk, Achinsk, Norilsk, Minusinsk, and Igarka are the chief cities. The territory includes Krasnoyarsk proper (S and E of the Yenisei), the Khakass Autonomous Oblast (in the southwest), the Evenki National Okrug (in the east central section), and the Taymyr National Okrug and Peninsula (N of the Arctic Circle). The southern part of the territory contains 90% of the population, which includes Russians, Ukrainians, Belorussians, Khakass, Tatars, Evenki, Yakuts, and Nenets. The territory was organized in 1934. During Stalin's rule and after, the area was the site of labor camps.

Krasnoye Selo (kräs'nəyə syĭlô'), city (1969 est. pop. 22,000), NW European USSR. It is a rail terminus and has industries producing paper and plastics. Krasnoye Selo was a favorite summer resort of St. Petersburg before the Russian Revolution. Nearby are two of the former summer palaces.

Kraszewski, Józef Ignacy (yo͞o'zĕf ēgnä'tsē kräshĕf'skē), 1812-87, Polish writer. He was imprisoned for political activities in Lithuania and in Germany. Wandering in exile through Europe, he died in Geneva. A large part of Kraszewski's nearly 600-volume output (much of it in English translation) consists of historical novels in the manner of Gogol. His most important work is the epic *Anafielas* (1839-43), a trilogy concerning Lithuanian history.

Kraus, Karl (kärl krous), 1874-1936, Austrian essayist and poet, b. Bohemia. His satirical review the *Fackel* lashed out at hypocrisy, intellectual corruption, and the machine age. His voluminous works include *Worte in Versen* (9 vol., 1916-30, partial tr. *Poems,* 1930); *Die letzten Tage der Menschheit* (1919, tr. *The Last Days of Mankind,* 1974), a monumental drama of World War I; and volumes of essays, aphorisms, and epigrams.

Krauskopf, Joseph (krous'kŏpf), 1858-1923, American rabbi and humanitarian, b. Prussia. He went to the United States in 1872, enrolling (1875) in the first class of the Hebrew Union College, Cincinnati, and receiving ordination in 1883. From 1887 until his death he was rabbi of the Congregation Keneseth Israel, Philadelphia, which flourished under his leadership. He was founder and president of the National Farm School at Doylestown, Pa., which opened in 1897, and he studied agricultural conditions in Russia. Krauskopf was a leader of charitable activities and reform movements in Philadelphia and Pennsylvania and a leading spokesman for his people. His writings include *Evolution and Judaism* (1887). See biography by W. W. Blood (1973).

Krautheimer, Richard (krout'hīmər), 1897-, American art historian, b. Germany. In 1935, Krautheimer began teaching in American universities, becoming professor of fine arts at New York Univ. in 1952. He is an authority on Christian and Byzantine architecture, compiler of *The Early Christian Basilicas of Rome* (1937-) and author of *Early Christian and Byzantine Architecture* (1965). His biography of Lorenzo Ghiberti (1956) and his *Studies in Early Christian, Medieval, and Renaissance Art* (1969) are widely acclaimed.

Kravchinski, Sergei Mikhailovich: see STEPNIAK, S.

kray (krī) [Rus.,=edge], administrative and territorial unit of the USSR. There are six krays, or territories, within the Russian Soviet Federated Socialist Republic (RSFSR), the largest of the country's 15 constituent republics. They are: ALTAI KRAY, KRASNODAR KRAY, KRASNOYARSK KRAY, PRIMORSKY KRAY, STAVROPOL KRAY, and KHABAROVSK KRAY. Historically, these areas were frontier zones at the edges of the Russian Empire and were gradually annexed by Moscow. The only kray outside the RSFSR is TSELINNY KRAY (Virgin Lands Territory), which was formed in 1960 in the Kazakh Republic.

Krebs, Sir Hans Adolf, 1900-, English biochemist, b. Germany, M.D. Univ. of Hamburg, 1925. He taught at Cambridge and at the Univ. of Sheffield and after 1954 was professor of biochemistry at Oxford. In 1939 he became an English citizen. He received the 1953 Nobel Prize in Physiology and Medicine, awarded jointly to him and to F. A. Lipmann, for his studies of intermediary metabolism. These studies included the elucidation of the cycle of chemical reactions called the citric acid, or Krebs, cycle, which has proved to be the major source of energy in living organisms.

Krebs cycle: see CITRIC ACID CYCLE.

Krefeld (krā'fĕlt), city (1970 pop. 222,250), North Rhine-Westphalia, W West Germany, a port on the Rhine River. It is the center of the West German silk and velvet industry. Other manufactures include quality steels, machinery, and dyes. Krefeld was chartered in 1373 and was an important linen-weaving center until it passed (1702) to Prussia. The silk industry, encouraged by a monopoly given to the city by Frederick II of Prussia, soon replaced linen weaving; and in the 20th cent. the manufacture of artificial silk became important. The city was heavily damaged in World War II. In 1929 the neighboring town of Uerdingen was incorporated into Krefeld. A former spelling is Crefeld.

Krehbiel, Henry Edward (krā'bēl), 1854-1923, American music critic, b. Ann Arbor, Mich. In 1880 he became music critic of the New York *Tribune.* He championed the music of Wagner, Brahms, and Tchaikovsky when it was little known in the United States. Krehbiel wrote many books on music and edited the English version of A. W. Thayer's biography of Beethoven, which appeared in 1921.

Kreisky, Bruno (bro͞o'nō krĭ'skē), 1911-, Austrian Socialist politician. He served as a diplomat and foreign affairs minister (1959-66). His goal of Austrian independence and neutrality was realized in a treaty in 1955 that he helped negotiate. Elected chairman of the Socialist party in 1967, he led the Socialists to victory in 1970 but failed to gain a majority of the seats in parliament. After the People's party under Josef KLAUS refused to continue the long-standing coalition, Kreisky became chancellor and formed a minority government, the first single-party government in Austria since World War II.

Kreisler, Fritz (krīs'lər), 1875-1962, Austrian-American violinist, studied at the conservatories of Vienna and Paris. He first appeared in the United States in 1888. After studying medicine, then art, Kreisler returned to the violin, making a sensationally successful appearance in Berlin in 1899. In 1901 he played again in the United States and afterward was perhaps the most popular violinist in the country. He served briefly in the Austrian army in World War I; in 1939 he became a French citizen and in 1943 a U.S. citizen. He composed the operettas *Apple Blossoms* (1919) and *Sissy* (1933) and numerous famous violin pieces, including *Caprice Viennois, Tambourin chinois,* and *Polichinelle Sérénade.* In 1935 he revealed that a number of the pieces he had published as compositions of old masters were actually his own. See biography by L. P. Lochner (1950).

Kremenchug (krĕmĭncho͞ok'), city (1970 pop. 148,000), S central European USSR, in the Ukraine, on the Dnepr River. It is the center of an industrial complex based on a hydroelectric plant; construction of the plant created the large Kremenchug Reservoir nearby. Kremenchug was founded in 1571 as a fortress.

Kremenets (krĕmĭnyĕts'), Pol. *Krzemieniec,* city (1967 est. pop. 20,000), W European USSR, in the Ukraine. It is a rail terminus, highway hub, and agriculture trade center. Food and tobacco processing and the manufacture of milling machinery, tiles, cement, and hats are important industries. Founded in the 11th cent., Kremenets was part of the Kievan duchy and in the 13th cent. became a fortified city of Galich-Volhynia. After the Polish-Lithuanian union in 1569, it served as a royal residence. The city passed to Russia during the third partition of Poland in 1795. It was again under Polish rule from 1919 to 1945, when it reverted to the USSR.

Kremer, Gerhard: see MERCATOR, GERARDUS.

kremlin (krĕm'lĭn), Rus. *kreml,* citadel or walled center of several Russian cities. During the Middle Ages, the kremlin served as an administrative and religious center and offered protection against military attacks. Thus a kremlin constituted a city in itself, containing palaces, government buildings, churches, marketplaces, and munitions stockpiles. Famous kremlins still preserved include those of Moscow, Astrakhan, Gorky, Kazan, Novgorod, and Pskov. That of Moscow is known simply as the **Kremlin.** Triangular and surrounded by crenellated walls, it occupies 90 acres (36.4 hectares) in the historic core of Moscow. It is bounded on the south by the Moscow River and Kremlin quay, on the east by Red Square with Lenin's tomb, the Moscow Historical Museum, and St. Basil's Cathedral, and on the west and south by the old Alexander Gardens. The Kremlin's walls, built in the 15th cent., are topped on each side by seven towers (20 towers altogether); among these is the Spasskaya [of the Savior], with famous chimes, above the main gate. In the center of the Kremlin is Cathedral Square, with the Uspenski [Assumption] Cathedral (late 15th cent. but containing rare icons of the 12th and 14th cent.), which was used for czarist state occasions, for the crowning of czars, and for the burial of church patriarchs; the Blagoveschenski [Annunciation] Cathedral (15th-16th cent.), which served as the private chapel for the czars' families; the Arkhangelski Cathedral (14th-17th cent.), which contains tombs of the czars; and the separate bell tower of Ivan the Great, c.266 ft (81 m) high, the golden cupola of which dominates the crosses, cupolas, and roofs of the other buildings. On a pedestal adjoining the bell tower is the Czar Bell (cast in 1735), the world's largest bell, with a height of 20 ft (6.1 m) and a weight of 200 tons. The Czar Cannon, located nearby, was cast in 1586 and weighs 40 tons. Along the Kremlin walls are large palaces, including the 15th-century Granovitaya Palata (the throne and banquet hall of the czars); the 19th-century Oruzheinaya Palata (Armory), built as a museum for crowns, scepters, thrones, costumes, and armor; and the 19th-century Grand Palace (Rus. *Bolshoi Dvorets*), rebuilt under the Communist regime and now housing the Supreme Soviet (parliament) of the USSR. The Kremlin's architectural history may be divided into the three periods of the wooden Kremlin (founded in the 13th cent.), the Italian Renaissance Kremlin, and the modern Kremlin started by Catherine the Great in the 18th cent. The Kremlin is almost the only part of Moscow that has escaped all of the city's numerous fires, including that of 1812, when Napoleon's headquarters were in Moscow. It suffered minor damage during the 1917 Bolshevik Revolution. The Kremlin was the residence of the czars until Peter the Great transferred the capital to St. Petersburg (see LENINGRAD) in 1712. Since 1918, when the capital was moved back to Moscow, the Kremlin has been the USSR's political and administrative center.

Křenek, Ernst (krĕ'nĕk, Czech kerzhĕ'nĕk), 1900–, Austrian-American composer, b. Vienna. Křenek was born to Czech parents. He studied in Vienna and Berlin, and in the early 1920s he composed chamber music, a violin concerto (1924), and two operas, in a neoclassical style. In 1925 he became conductor at the opera house in Kassel. His jazz opera *Johnny Strikes Up* (1926), about a Negro band leader, was extremely successful and has been translated into many languages. He returned to Vienna in 1928, and after a brief period of neo-Romanticism, during which he wrote the opera *Leben des Orest* (1930) and a Schubertian song cycle, he gradually adopted the 12-tone technique (see SERIAL MUSIC) originated by Arnold Schoenberg. His opera *Karl V* (1933) is entirely in the 12-tone system. In 1937, Křenek moved to the United States, where he taught and composed chamber, orchestral, and choral music and wrote the opera *Tarquin* (1940) and the chamber opera *Dark Waters* (1950). He wrote *Eleven Transparencies* (1956) for orchestra and electronic music. Křenek is also known as lecturer, pianist, and the author of *Studies in Counterpoint* (1940), *Self-Analysis* (1950), excerpts from an unpublished autobiography, and *Exploring* Music (tr. 1966).

Kresge Foundation, fund established (1924) by retail chain store owner Sebastian S. Kresge (1867–1966) as a broad-purpose philanthropic institution. The foundation describes its policy as "to favor grants providing for the maintenance, expansion, or perpetuation of existing organizations over grants which look to the establishment or initiating of new organizations or experimental projects." Prior to the middle 1960s the foundation gave most of its support to colleges and universities, hospitals, religious institutions, and child welfare agencies in Michigan and the Northeast. Since then, however, there has been a wider geographic distribution of grants and a decrease in support to religious programs. Most assistance goes to the construction and maintenance of buildings or other major capital equipment. Given an initial endowment of $1.3 million, in 1972 the foundation had assets totaling $887 million.

Kresilas: see CRESILAS.

Kretschmer, Ernest, 1888–1964, German psychiatrist, educated at Tübingen, Hamburg, and Munich (M.D., 1913). He served as director of the neurological clinic of the Univ. of Marburg (1926–46) and in 1946 became the director of the neurological clinic of the Univ. of Tübingen. He emphasized the morphological-physiological-psychological unity of the individual, correlating body types and personality characteristics. He maintained that a person's temperamental reaction tendencies are a reflection of his physical make-up. His theories have not found general acceptance.

Kreuger, Ivar (ē'vär krōō'gər), 1880–1932, Swedish financier. After studying engineering in Stockholm and engaging in construction enterprises in the United States, he returned to Sweden and organized the firm of Kreuger and Toll. In 1913 he began to form a TRUST to control all aspects of the production of matches in Sweden, and later throughout the world; it eventually became a huge international finance agency. Speculation and fraudulent practices during the 1920s wrecked the trust and led to Kreuger's suicide. Much of his money was obtained from U.S. backers. See studies by Allen Churchill (1957) and Robert Shaplen (1960).

Kreutzer, Rodolphe (kroit'sər, Fr. rôdôlf' krötzĕr'), 1766–1831, French composer and violinist. He was professor of violin at the Paris Conservatory from its founding in 1795 until 1826 and was one of the authors of the violin method taught there. Although he composed some 40 operas and numerous concertos and sonatas, he is remembered for his 40 études for the violin, which remain unsurpassed. Beethoven's *Kreutzer Sonata* is dedicated to him.

Kreuzlingen (kroits'lĭng"ən), town (1970 pop. 15,760), Thurgau canton, NE Switzerland, on the Lake of Constance. The town is contiguous with the German city of Constance. It is an industrial center with the oldest aluminum rolling mill in Switzerland. Foodstuffs, chemicals, and motor vehicles are also manufactured. The Augustinian monastery, founded in the 13th cent. and now a school, has a noted baroque church.

Kreymborg, Alfred (krām'bôrg), 1883–1966, American poet and anthologist, b. New York City. Originally one of the IMAGISTS, he wrote poems collected in *Mushrooms* (1916), *Manhattan Men* (1929), *Selected Poems* (1945), and *Man and Shadow* (1946). He chronicled American poetry in such works as the critical history *Our Singing Strength* (1929, 1934) and the anthology *Lyric America* (1930). His puppet plays were also popular. See his autobiography, *Troubadour* (1925).

Krieghoff, Cornelius (krēg'hŏf), 1812–72, Canadian painter, b. Düsseldorf, Germany. He traveled widely and took part in the Seminole Indian wars in Florida as a member of the U.S. army. Commissioned by the War Dept. to make paintings from many sketches done in these wars, he worked at Rochester, N.Y., and then moved to Canada, working first at Toronto, then at Montreal, and in 1853 at Quebec. He had a keen sense of the picturesque in French-Canadian life, and his numerous pictures are much sought after. See biography by C. M. Barbeau (1934).

Kriemhild: see NIBELUNGEN.

Kriens (krēĕns'), town (1970 pop. 20,409), Lucerne canton, central Switzerland, at the foot of Mt. Pilatus. It is a suburb of Lucerne.

Krilenko, Nikolai Vasilyevich: see KRYLENKO.

krill: see CRUSTACEAN.

Krio, Cape (krēō'), Turk. *Deveboynu Burnu,* promontory, SW Turkey, on the Aegean Sea, on Reşadiye Peninsula north of the island of Rhodes. Ancient CNIDUS was situated there.

Krishna (krĭsh'nə) [Sanskrit, = black], one of the most popular deities in Hinduism, the eighth avatar, or incarnation of VISHNU. Krishna appears in the MAHABHARATA epic as a prince of the Yadava tribe and the friend and counselor of the Pandava princes. His divinity is proclaimed in several places in the epic, particularly in the BHAGAVAD-GITA. Krishna's childhood and youth are described in the *Harivamsa* (a supplement to the *Mahabharata*), the *Vishnu Purana,* and the *Bhagavata Purana,* the last being one of the most important texts of the Bhakti, or devotional, movement. As a young boy Krishna is the foster child of cowherds and shows his divine nature by conquering demons. As a youth he is the lover of the *gopis* (milkmaids), playing his flute and dancing with them by moonlight. The play of Krishna and the *gopis* is regarded in Hinduism as an image of the soul's relationship with God. The love of Krishna and Radha, his favorite *gopi,* is celebrated in a great genre of Sanskrit and Bengali love poetry. See W. G. Archer, *The Loves of Krishna in Indian Painting and Poetry* (1953, repr. 1960); Milton Singer, ed., *Krishna: Myths, Rites and Attitudes* (1965).

Krishna, river: see KISTNA.

Krishnagar (krĭsh'nəgər), town (1971 pop. 86,354), West Bengal state, E central India, on the Jalangi River. It is a district administrative center. The main products of the area are rice, jute, sugar, ceramics, and plywood. Krishnagar was the residence of the rajas of the former princely state of Nadia.

Krishna Menon, Vengalil Krishnan (vĕngä'lēl krĭsh'nən krĭsh'nə mĕn'ĭn), 1897–1974, Indian diplomat. He was educated at the Presidency College and the Law College of Madras and at the London School of Economics and University College, London. During his long stay (1924–47) in England he joined the Labour party, was admitted (1934) to the English bar, and served (1934–47) as borough councilor of St. Pancras, London. As secretary (1929–47) of the India League and also as a journalist, he worked hard for Indian self-government and became closely associated with Jawaharlal Nehru. After Indian independence (1947), Krishna Menon served as high commissioner for India in Great Britain (1947–52) and as Indian delegate to the United Nations (1952–62), where he was an outspoken critic of the United States and a staunch supporter of mainland China. In 1957 he was appointed minister of defense, but in 1962, following the Chinese invasion of India's northern frontiers, he was severely criticized for India's lack of military preparedness and was relieved of office. In 1967 he lost his seat in the national legislature, where he had served since 1953, but he was reelected in 1969. See biography by T. J. S. George (1964); study by Michael Brecher (1968).

Krishnamurti, Jiddu (jĭd'ōō krĭsh"nəmōōr'tē), 1895–, Indian religious figure. Annie BESANT met him in 1909 and proclaimed that he was an incarnation of Maitreya, the messianic Buddha. In 1929, following a two-year tour of England and America with Annie Besant, Krishnamurti repudiated these claims and dissolved the World Order of the Star, a religious organization that he had founded in 1911. He retained some connection with the theosophical movement, however, and continued an active career of lecturing and writing. He finally settled in Ojai, Calif., where from 1969 he headed the Krishnamurti Foundation. His writings include *The Songs of Life* (1931), *Commentaries on Living* (1956–60), *Freedom from the Known* (1969), *The Urgency of Change* (1970), and *The Awakening of Intelligence* (1974). See Emily Lutyens, *Candles in the Sun* (1957); L. S. R. Vas, *The Mind of J. Krishnamurti* (1971).

Kristiania: see OSLO, Norway.

Kristiansand (krĭstyänsän'), city (1970 pop. 56,914), capital of Vest-Agder co., S Norway, a commercial and passenger port on the Skagerrak. Manufactures include ships, textiles, canned fish, and beer. The city was founded (1641) by Christian IV and became an episcopal see in 1682. Its Christiansholm Fortress (1662–72) now houses a restaurant. The Varodden Bridge (1956), one of the largest suspension bridges in N Europe, spans the nearby Randesund.

Kristianstad (krĭstyän'städ), city (1970 pop. 43,799), capital of Kristianstad co., SE Sweden, on the Helgaän River. Its nearby seaport, Åhus, is on the Baltic Sea. Kristianstad is a commercial and industrial center, located in a fertile agricultural region. Manufactures include textiles, machinery, and processed food. Founded (1614) by Christian IV of Denmark, Kristianstad changed hands frequently, but passed definitively to Sweden in 1678. A church built (12th cent.) by Archbishop Absalon is nearby.

Kristiansund (krĭstyänsōōn'), city (1970 pop. 18,508), Møre og Romsdal co., W Norway, a port on the Atlantic Ocean. It is the site of a large trawler fleet and has industries that produce ships and fish and forest products. Chartered in 1742, Kristiansund was destroyed (1940) by bombardment in World War II and has since been rebuilt on three islands enclosing the harbor.

Kristinehamn (krĭ"stĭnəhä'mən), city (1970 pop. 21,403), Värmland co., S central Sweden, a port on Lake Vänern. The city was first chartered in 1582 as Bro. It was rechartered in 1642 by Queen Christina and renamed Kristinehamn.

Kritios: see CRITIUS.

Krivoy Rog (krēvoi' rôk'), city (1972 est. pop. 600,000), SW European USSR, in the Ukraine, at the confluence of the Ingulets and Saksagan rivers. It is a rail junction, an industrial center, and a metallurgical and coking center of one of the world's richest iron-mining regions. Burial mounds in the area indicate that Scythians inhabited it and used the iron deposits. Founded in the 17th cent. by Zaporozhe Cossacks, the city received its name (Crooked Horn) because of the shape of the iron-mining area. Krivoy Rog's industrial growth dates from 1881, when French, Belgian, and other foreign interests founded a mining syndicate. The city has mining and pedagogical institutes.

Krk (kûrk), Ital. *Veglia,* island (1971 pop. 13,078), 157 sq mi (407 sq km), in the Adriatic, off the Dalmatian coast, NW Yugoslavia. The largest of Yugoslav islands in the Adriatic, it has several small seaside resorts. The chief town, Krk, has retained its medieval walls and castle and has a 13th-century Roman Catholic cathedral.

Krkonoše (kŭr'kônôshĕ), Ger. *Riesengebirge,* Pol. *Karkonosze,* highest range of the Sudetes, extending c.25 mi (40 km) along the border of N Czechoslovakia and SW Poland. Its highest peak, Sněžka (Ger. *Schneekoppe,* Pol. *Śnieżka*), rises to 5,258 ft (1,603 m). Paper and textile mills, which use the range's waterpower, are found on both sides of the border. Coal is mined near Zacléř, Czechoslovakia. There are numerous resorts and spas in the mountains; the most notable is Janské Lázně, Czechoslovakia. A national park (est. 1963) straddles the international border. The Labe (Elbe) River rises in the Krkonoše.

Krnov (kûr'nôf), Ger. *Jägerndorf,* city (1970 pop. 22,496), N Czechoslovakia, in Moravia, on the Opava River, near the Polish border. An industrial center, it manufactures machinery, textiles (especially woolens), and musical instruments (notably organs). The city was founded in 1221 and served as the capital of an independent duchy from 1377 to 1523. Krnov has an 18th-century castle and several fine churches and abbeys.

Krochmal, Nachman Kohen (näkh'män kō'hĕn krôkh'mäl), 1785–1840, Jewish secular historian and writer, b. Galicia. He was a leader in the movement of the Jewish enlightenment, a founder of the Conservative movement in Judaism, and a pioneer of modern Jewish scholarship. He applied his synthesis of religion and philosophy to the writing and teaching of Jewish history. His most important work, *Guide to the Perplexed of Our Age,* in Hebrew, was published posthumously in 1851.

Krock, Arthur, 1886–1974, American journalist, b. Glasgow, Ky. He left Princeton to take up reporting and worked in Louisville and Washington. In 1927 he joined the New York *Times,* becoming Washington correspondent in 1932. Krock's pungent and controversial columns generally espoused a conservative viewpoint. He was the only man to win four Pulitzer awards, two prizes (1935, 1938), a special commendation, and a special citation. His books include *Sixty Years On The Firing Line* (1968), *In the Nation: 1932-1966* (1969), *The Consent of the Governed and Other Deceits* (1971), and *Myself When Young: Growing Up in the 1890's* (1973).

Kroeber, Alfred Louis (krō'bər), 1876-1960, American anthropologist, b. Hoboken, N.J., Ph.D. Columbia, 1901. He taught (1901-46) at the Univ. of California and was director (1925-46) of the anthropological museum there. An authority on the Indians of North and South America, he participated in many expeditions in the Southwest and in Mexico and Peru. Like his teacher Franz BOAS, Kroeber upheld the tradition of broad scholarship, and he was a major figure in the founding of the modern science of anthropology. He set forth clearly the relationship of culture patterns to the individual and presented a new concept of society as the interaction of groups and persons. Kroeber wrote many influential articles, and his books include *Anthropology* (1923, rev. ed. 1948), *Configurations of Culture Growth* (1944), *The Nature of Culture* (1952), and *Style and Civilization* (1957). See biographies by his wife Theodora Kroeber (1970) and J. H. Steward (1973).

Krogh, Schack August Steenberg (shäk ou'go͝ost stān'bĕrg krôkh), 1874-1949, Danish physiologist. He taught at the Univ. of Copenhagen (1916-45) and studied respiration, circulation, and the effect of an exclusive meat diet on the Eskimo and of deep-sea conditions on living organisms. For his discovery of the regulation of the vasomotor mechanism of the capillaries he received the 1920 Nobel Prize in Physiology and Medicine. His writings include *The Anatomy and Physiology of Capillaries* (1922, rev. ed. 1959), *Osmotic Regulation in Aquatic Animals* (1939), and *Comparative Physiology of Respiratory Mechanisms* (1941).

Krohg, Christian (krĭs'tyän krōg), 1852-1925, Norwegian genre and portrait painter and author. After studying on the continent, Krohg returned to Norway in 1878 and became a well-known advocate of impressionism. He later taught in Paris and in 1909 became director of the Oslo Academy. In *The Struggle for Existence* (4 vol., 1920-21) he advocated the social mission of the arts.

Krolewska Huta: see CHORZÓW, Poland.

Kroll, Leon (krōl), 1884-1974, American painter and lithographer, b. New York City. Kroll studied in New York with J. H. Twachtman and later in Paris. He returned to New York, where he became a well-known teacher. His oils are characterized by clarity, strong color, and attention to modeling of forms. Kroll's work is represented in major galleries throughout the United States. His many murals include one for the Worcester War Memorial and one for the Justice Dept., Washington, D.C.

Kroměříž (krô'myĕrzhēsh), Ger. *Kremsier,* city (1970 pop. 22,308), central Czechoslovakia, in Moravia, on the Morava River. An agricultural center, it manufactures farm machinery and machine tools and has sugar refineries. Kroměříž was chartered in 1290 and served as the residence of the bishops of Olmütz. It was also the site of a meeting (Nov., 1848-March, 1849) of the first Austrian constituent parliament (see AUSTRIA). Among the city's present-day landmarks is an 18th-century palace with a large library and a ceremonial hall.

Kronborg castle: see HELSINGØR, Denmark.

Kronecker, Leopold (lā'ōpôlt krō'nĕk"ər), 1823-91, German mathematician. After making a fortune in business he devoted his attention to mathematics and became professor at the Univ. of Berlin in 1883. Noted as an algebraist, he was a pioneer in the field of algebraic numbers and in formulating the relationship between the theory of numbers, the theory of equations, and elliptic functions.

Kronos: see CRONUS.

Kronshtadt (krənshtät'), city, NW European USSR, on the small island of Kotlin in the Gulf of Finland, c.15 mi (20 km) from Leningrad. It is the chief naval base for the Soviet Baltic fleet. The harbor is icebound for several months each year. It was founded (1703) by Peter I as a port and a fortress to protect the site of St. Petersburg, and it was the commercial harbor of St. Petersburg until the 1880s. The port lost its commercial value after the development of St. Petersburg. The visit (1891) of a French naval squadron to Kronshtadt was followed by a Franco-Russian military agreement heralding the formation of the Triple Entente of France, England, and Russia. Mutinies of the naval garrison took place in 1825 and 1882 and played a part in the revolutions of 1905 and 1917 (see RUSSIAN REVOLUTION). A revolt of the sailors in March, 1921, was instrumental in establishing Lenin's NEW ECONOMIC POLICY. The general unrest among peasants and workers touched off this mutiny of the naval garrison that had been loyal to the Bolsheviks during the revolution. This was the climax of the anti-Bolshevik unrest in the country. In World War II, Kronshtadt played a major role in the defense of Leningrad against the Germans. It is also spelled Cronstadt.

Kroonstad (kro͞on'stät), town (1970 pop. 50,898), Orange Free State, E central South Africa, on the Vals River. It is an agricultural and industrial center. There is a grain elevator, and grain is shipped from the town. Kroonstad is also an important rail junction and has large marshaling yards. The town's chief industries are clothing manufacture and mineral processing, and the production of machine parts. Kroonstad was founded in 1855. Its growth was stimulated by the discovery of gold in the region in the late 19th cent. After the fall of BLOEMFONTEIN during the SOUTH AFRICAN WAR, it was (March 13-May 11, 1900) the capital of the ORANGE FREE STATE. Kroonstad Technical College is in the town.

Kropotkin, Piotr Alekseyevich, Prince (pyô'tər əlyĭksyā'ĭvĭch krəpôt'kĭn), 1842-1921, Russian anarchist. He came from a wealthy princely family and as a boy was a page to the czar. Repelled by court life, he obtained permission to serve as an army officer in Siberia, where his explorations and scientific observations established his reputation as a geographer. After returning to European Russia, he became an adherent of the Bakuninist faction of the NARODNIKI and engaged in clandestine propaganda activities until arrested in 1874. Two years later he escaped to Western Europe, where he worked with various anarchist groups until his imprisonment in France (1883). Pardoned in 1886, partly as the result of the popular clamor for his release, he moved to England and spent the next 30 years mainly as a scholar and writer developing a coherent anarchist theory. In his most famous book, *Mutual Aid* (1902), he attacked T. H. Huxley and other Social Darwinists for their picture of nature and human society as essentially competitive. He insisted that cooperation and mutual aid were the norms in both the natural and social worlds. From this perspective he developed a theory of social organization—in *Fields, Factories and Workshops* (1898) and elsewhere—that was based upon communes of producers linked with each other through common custom and free contract. Returning to Russia following the February Revolution of 1917, he attempted to engender support for a continued Russian effort in World War I and to combat the rising influence of Bolshevism. Following the Bolshevik triumph in the October Revolution (1917), he retired from active politics. Consistently nonviolent in his anarchist beliefs, Kropotkin, as both thinker and man, was admired and acclaimed by many far removed from anarchist circles. See his *Memoirs of a Revolutionist* (1899, repr. 1968); biography by George Woodcock and Ivan Avakumović (1950, repr. 1971); J. W. Hulse, *Revolutionists in London* (1970); Paul Avrich, ed., *The Anarchists in the Russian Revolution* (1973).

Krüdener, Juliana, Baroness von (fən krüd'ənər), 1764-1824, Russian novelist and mystic. Born a Livonian aristocrat, she married a Russian diplomat. She left her husband (1801) for the pleasures of literary and social life in Paris and Switzerland. There Krüdener wrote a sentimental, largely autobiographical novel, *Valérie* (1804), which became a literary sensation. Converted to Moravian pietism, she devoted herself to preaching her faith and for a time held enormous influence over Alexander I of Russia. She claimed to have inspired the formation of the Holy Alliance of Russia, Austria, and Prussia. See E. J. Knapton, *The Lady of the Holy Alliance* (1939).

Kruger, Paul (Stephanas Johannes Paulus) (kro͞o'gər, Afrikaans stäfä'nəs yōhä'nəs pou'ləs krügər), 1825-1904, South African Transvaal statesman, known as Oom Paul. As a child he accompanied (1836) his family northward from the Cape Colony in the Great Trek that was eventually to cross the Vaal River and establish the Dutch-speaking republic of Transvaal (1852). Kruger's life was closely tied to the development of the country; he was a pioneer, soldier, farmer, and politician. The Transvaal was annexed by Great Britain in 1877. Kruger at first cooperated with the British but shortly thereafter was dismissed because of his demands for retrocession. He was one of the triumvirate (with Piet Joubert and Martinius Pretorius) who negotiated the Pretoria agreement with the British (1881) granting the Boers independence. Kruger was elected president in 1883 and reelected in 1888, 1893, and 1898. His policy was one of continual resistance to the British, who came to be personified in South Africa by Cecil RHODES. Colonization of Rhodesia N of the Transvaal and the increasing importance of gold mining merely brought much greater resistance on Kruger's part to Rhodes's dream of a unified South Africa. In the 1890s, Kruger adopted a stringent policy against the enfranchisement of the Uitlanders who were settling in the Transvaal. The Jameson Raid (see JAMESON, SIR LEANDER STARR) into the Transvaal (Dec., 1895), undertaken with Rhodes's knowledge, created an international crisis. The Kaiser congratulated Kruger (in the "Kruger telegram") for the successful repulsion of the British, with the implication that Germany had a right to interfere in the Transvaal. The message caused great indignation in England. Kruger fought in the early stages of the SOUTH AFRICAN WAR, but in 1900 he went to Europe on a Dutch cruiser in a vain effort to enlist aid for his country. He died an exile in Switzerland. See his memoirs (tr. 1902, repr. 1969); biography by Manfred Nathan (1941); studies by J. S. Marais (1962), D. M. Schreuder (1969), and C. T. Gordan (1970).

Kruger National Park, game reserve, c.8,000 sq mi (20,720 sq km), Transvaal, NE Republic of South Africa. One of the world's largest wildlife sanctuaries, it has almost every species of game in southern Africa. In its rivers are found hippopotamuses and crocodiles; everywhere countless varieties of birds can be seen. Tourists driving along the park's extensive (c.1,200-mi/1,930-km) road system can observe the animals at close quarters. The park was originally founded as the Sabi Game Reserve (1898) by S. J. P. Kruger; it was enlarged and made a national park in 1926.

Krugersdorp (kro͞o'gərzdôp), city (1970 pop. 91,202) Transvaal, NE South Africa. The chief industrial city of the W Witwatersrand, Krugersdorp is the center for a region where gold, manganese, asbestos, lime, and uranium are mined. The city has uranium extraction plants. It also serves as the trade center for the surrounding farming area. Founded in 1887, it was named for Paul Kruger, president of the Transvaal republic. The Paardekraal monument marks the spot where in 1880 BOERS pledged themselves to end British rule in the Transvaal. Nearby are the Sterkfontein Caves (an important archaeological site), Kromdei Paleontological Reserve, and Krugersdorp Game Reserve. The city has a technical college.

Krupp (kro͝op), family of German armament manufacturers. The family settled in Essen in the 16th cent. The core of the great Krupp industrial empire was started by **Friedrich Krupp,** 1787-1826, who built a small steel plant c.1810. His son, **Alfred Krupp,** 1812-87, known as the "Cannon King," introduced new methods for producing large quantities of cast steel. After the Franco-Prussian War he specialized more and more in armaments and acquired mines all over Germany. Under his son, **Friedrich Alfred Krupp** (Fritz Krupp), 1854-1902, who was interested in the financial rather than the technical aspects of the enterprise, the Krupp family vastly extended its operations. His daughter, Bertha Krupp (after whom the Big Berthas were named), married Gustav von Bohlen und Halbach, who assumed the name **Gustav Krupp von Bohlen und Halbach,** 1870-1950. He took over the management of the firm, which had become a public company in 1903. After 1933 the Krupp works became the center of German rearmament. In 1943, by a special order from Hitler, the company was again converted into a family holding and **Alfried Krupp von Bohlen und Halbach,** 1907-1967, son of Gustav and Bertha, took over the management. After Germany's defeat, he was tried as a war criminal and sentenced (1948) to imprisonment for 12 years. In 1951 he was released, and in 1953 he resumed control of the firm with the stipulation that he sell his major interests in iron, steel, and coal. The condition was not fulfilled, however. Shortly before his death in July, 1967, the firm's indebtedness caused Alfried to announce that the Krupp concern would become a public corporation. His son **Arndt von Bohlen and Halbach,** 1938-, relinquished his inheritance rights, and in 1968 the Krupp family ceased to control the firm. See Gert von Klass, *Krupps: The Story of an Industrial Empire* (1953, tr. 1954); Norbert Mühlen, *The Incredible Krupps* (1959); William Manchester, *The Arms of Krupp, 1587-1968* (1968).

Krusenstern, Adam Johann von (ä'däm yō'hän fən kro͞o'zənshtĕrn), 1770—1846, Russian navigator. From 1803 to 1806 he circumnavigated the globe. Although the voyage was undertaken to stimulate the fur trade of the Pacific coast and to revive trade with China and Japan, its real contribution was to the knowledge of the hydrography of the N Pacific coast of America. Krusenstern was director (1827–42) of the royal naval academy and was promoted to the rank of admiral. He wrote an account of his voyage (3 vol. and atlas, 1809–13; tr. 1813).

Krusenstjerna, Agnes von (äng'nās vôn kro͞osĕnshĕr'nä), 1894–1940, Swedish novelist. Krusenstjerna's works reflect the aristocratic and emotionally disturbed background from which she came. She frequently portrayed the degeneracy of the society from which she separated herself. Her works include the controversial novel cycles *Tony-böckerna* [the Tony books] (1922–26) and *Fröknarna von Pahlen* [the Misses von Pahlen] (1930–35). In these novels she presented for the first time in Swedish literature a candid picture of sexual problems. Her works are outstanding for the skill and psychological acuity of her writing.

Kruševac (kro͞o'shĕväts), town (1971 pop. 117,926), E Yugoslavia, in Serbia. A commercial center, it has chemical and munitions industries. The seat of the kings of Serbia until 1389, it has retained the ruins of a medieval castle.

Krušné Hory: see ERZGEBIRGE.

Krutch, Joseph Wood (kro͞och), 1893–1970, American author, editor, and teacher, b. Knoxville, Tenn., grad. Univ. of Tennessee, 1915, Ph.D. Columbia, 1923. He was on the editorial staff of the *Nation,* primarily as drama critic, from 1924 to 1952. From 1937 to 1953 he held a professorship at Columbia. Highly regarded as both a social and literary critic, Krutch is the author of such works as *Comedy and Conscience after the Restoration* (1924), *Edgar Allan Poe: A Study in Genius* (1926), *The Modern Temper* (1929), *The American Drama since 1918* (1939), *Samuel Johnson* (1944), *Henry David Thoreau* (1948), *The Measure of Man* (1954), and *Human Nature and the Human Condition* (1959). After he moved to Arizona, he turned also to the study of nature; his books in this field include *The Twelve Seasons* (1949), *The Desert Year* (1952), and *The Voice of the Desert: A Naturalist's Interpretation* (1955). See his autobiography, *More Lives than One* (1962); *A Krutch Omnibus: Forty Years of Social and Literary Criticism* (1970); *The Best Nature Writings of Joseph Wood Krutch* (1970).

Krylenko or **Krilenko, Nikolai Vasilyevich** (both: nyĭkəlī' vəsē'lyəvĭch krĭlyĕn'kō), 1885–1938, Russian revolutionary and jurist. In Nov., 1917, Trotsky promoted him from ensign to commander in chief of the Russian forces for the purpose of opening peace negotiations with the Central Powers. Krylenko resigned in 1918 and later became public prosecutor and commissar of justice. He was tried (1938) in the party purge trials instituted by Stalin and was executed.

Krylov, Ivan Andreyevich (ēvän' əndrā'əvĭch krĭlôf'), 1768–1844, Russian fabulist. Some of his more than 200 fables were adapted from Aesop and La Fontaine, but most were original. A moralist, Krylov used popular language to satirize human weaknesses, social customs, and political events. His works won him international renown. See translations by Bernard Pares (1926); *Russian Fables of Ivan Krylov* (tr. by Walter Morison, 1942); study by N. L. Stepanov (1973).

Krym: see CRIMEA, USSR.

kryolite: see CRYOLITE.

krypton (krĭp'tŏn) [Gr.,=hidden], gaseous chemical element; symbol Kr; at. no. 36; at. wt. 83.80; m. p. −156.6°C; b. p. −152.3°C; density 3.73 grams per liter at STP (see separate article); valence usually 0. Krypton is a colorless, odorless, tasteless gas. It is one of the so-called INERT GASES found in group 0 of the PERIODIC TABLE. It is a rare gas present in air at a concentration of about one part per million. Naturally occuring krypton is a mixture of six stable isotopes. It is produced commercially by fractional distillation of liquid air. Krypton is used to fill electric lamp bulbs and various electronic devices. Fluorescent lamps are filled with a mixture of krypton and argon. Krypton is also used in tungsten-filament photographic projection lamps and in very high-powered electric arc lights used at airports. A mixture of stable and unstable isotopes of krypton is produced by slow neutron fission of uranium in nuclear reactors. Krypton-85 (half-life about 10 years) is the most stable of the 17 radioactive isotopes known; it makes up about 5% by volume of the krypton produced in the nuclear reactor. It is used to detect leaks in sealed containers, to excite phosphors in light sources with no external source of energy, and in medicine to detect abnormal heart openings. Although krypton does not generally form chemical compounds in the normal sense, gram quantities of krypton difluoride have been prepared and several other compounds have been reported. Krypton has characteristic green and orange lines in its spectrum. In 1960 the meter was defined by international agreement as exactly 1,650,763.73 times the wavelength (in a vacuum) of the orange-red line in the emission spectrum of krypton-86 (see WEIGHTS AND MEASURES). Krypton was discovered in 1898 by William RAMSAY and W. M. Travers in residue from the evaporation of a sample of liquid air from which oxygen and nitrogen had been removed.

Kuala Lumpur (kwä'lə lo͝om'po͝or), city (1971 pop. 451,278), capital of the Federation of Malaysia, S Malay Peninsula, at the confluence of the Klang and Gombak rivers. The chief inland city of Malaysia, Kuala Lumpur is the commercial center of a tin-mining and rubber-growing district and is a transportation hub. It was founded in 1857 by Chinese tin miners and superseded Klang in 1880 as the capital of Selangor. In 1896 it became the capital of the Federated Malay States (see MALAYSIA). Among the notable structures is the modern parliament building in Moorish style. The population is about two-thirds Chinese.

Kuala Terengganu (tərĕng-gä'no͞o) or **Kuala Trengganu** (trĕng-), city (1971 pop. 53,353), capital of Terengganu state, Malaysia, central Malay Peninsula, on the South China Sea at the mouth of the Terengganu River. It is a port and has a weaving industry. The residence of the sultan of Terengganu is in the city.

Kuang Hsü (gwäng shü), 1871–1908, emperor of China (1875–1908). Although he was not in the direct line of succession, he was appointed to the throne by his aunt, the dowager empress and regent, TZ'U HSI. He began his rule in 1889. In 1898, during the "hundred days of reform," he rebelled against her domination and issued many decrees modernizing the political and social structure of China. His aunt thereupon resumed the regency and kept him imprisoned for the remainder of his life while she ruled China in a conservative manner.

Kuang Wu Ti: see LIU HSIU.

Kuban (ko͞obăn', -bän', Rus. ko͞obä'nyə), river, c.570 mi (920 km) long, rising in the Greater Caucasus on the western slopes of Mt. Elbrus, S European USSR, and flowing north in a wide arc past Karachayevsk, Cherkessk, and Armavir, then W past Krasnodar, entering the Sea of Azov through two arms. Its upper course is precipitous and leads through several gorges; it then meanders slowly through the Kuban Steppe, a rich black-earth area and one of the major grain and sugar-beet districts of the USSR. The last 150 mi (240 km) are navigable. Russia annexed the khanate of Crimea, of which the Kuban area was a part, in 1783. Now mainly within the KRASNODAR KRAY, the Kuban region was from about the mid-18th cent. to 1920 the territory of the **Kuban Cossacks.** After Catherine II defeated (1775) the ZAPOROZHYE Cossacks in the Ukraine, some of them emigrated to Turkey, but in 1787 they were allowed to return and settle along the Black Sea between the Dnepr and the Bug rivers. Then known as the Black Sea Cossacks, they were in 1792 resettled in the Kuban region. Though they lost much of their freedom and their rights were restricted, they were granted local self-government in return for military service. In 1860 they were renamed the Kuban Cossacks, while defending the Kuban region from hostile Circassian mountaineers to the south. After the Bolshevik Revolution of 1917, the Kuban Cossacks proclaimed an independent republic and fought against the Bolsheviks. After the civil war of 1918–20 the Soviet regime abolished their government, and their traditional privileges were abrogated.

Kubelík, Jan (yän ko͞o'bəlĭk), 1880–1940, Czech violinist. Kubelík studied with Otakar Ševčik at the Prague Conservatory. He made his debut in Vienna in 1898 and was thereafter acclaimed for his great virtuosity and dramatic power by critics in England, on the Continent, and in the United States, where he first appeared in 1901. Kubelík composed six violin concertos, a symphony, and some chamber music. He performed very little after World War I. His son, **Rafael Kubelík,** 1914–, b. Býchory, Czechoslovakia, was conductor of the Chicago Symphony (1950–53) and later director of the Covent Garden Opera in London. He also composed the opera *Veronika* (1947), as well as symphonic and instrumental works.

Kubitschek, Juscelino (zho͞osəlē'no͞o ko͞o'bəchĕk), 1902–, president of Brazil (1956–61). A surgeon who served as mayor of Belohorizonte and governor of Minas Gerais, he was elected president in 1955. He launched an immense public works program, borrowing heavily to construct buildings, highways, hydroelectric projects, and the new capital city, Brasília. He offered enormous incentives to industry, and the country's productive capacity soared. The huge deficit spending, however, sparked an inflationary spiral, and the national debt reached almost $4 billion. Kubitschek was succeeded in office by Janio Quadros. In 1964, after a military takeover in Brazil, Kubitschek was deprived of his political rights and went into exile temporarily.

Kublai Khan (ko͞o'blī kän), 1215?–1294, Mongol emperor, founder of the Yüan dynasty of China. From 1251 to 1259 he led military campaigns in S China. He succeeded (1260) his brother Mangu as khan of the empire that their grandfather JENGHIZ KHAN had founded. The empire reached its greatest territorial extent with Kublai's final defeat (1279) of the Sung dynasty of China; however, his campaigns against Japan (see KAMIKAZE), SE Asia, and Indonesia failed. Kublai's rule was nominal except in Mongolia and China. He recruited men of all nations for his civil service, but only Mongolians were permitted to hold the highest government posts. He promoted economic prosperity by rebuilding the Grand Canal, repairing public granaries, and extending highways. He fostered Chinese scholarship and arts. Although he favored Buddhism, other religions (except Taoism) were tolerated. Kublai encouraged foreign commerce, and his magnificent capital at Cambuluc (now Peking) was visited by several Europeans, notably Marco Polo, who described it. It is perhaps this city which figures in Coleridge's poem *Kubla Khan.* Kublai's name is also spelled Kubilai, Koublai, and Kubla.

Kuching (ko͞o'chĭng), city (1971 pop. 63,491), capital of Sarawak, Malaysia, in W Borneo and on the Sarawak River. It is the largest city in the state and a river port. Sago flour and pepper are exported. It was founded in 1839 by James BROOKE. In the city are Anglican and Roman Catholic cathedrals and a museum of Borneo folklore. The population is about two-thirds Chinese.

Kuchuk Kainarji, Treaty of (ko͞ocho͞ok' kīnär'jē, Turk. küchük' kī''närjä'), 1774, peace treaty signed at the end of the first of the Russo-Turkish Wars undertaken by Catherine II of Russia against Sultan Mustafa III of the Ottoman Empire (Turkey). It was signed at the village of Kuchuk Kainarji, now Kaynardzha, NE Bulgaria, in the Dobruja, near the Danube and SE of Silistra. The treaty ceded Kerch and several other Black Sea ports in the Crimea to Russia and declared the rest of the khanate of Crimea independent. Russian trading ships were allowed to navigate in Turkish waters. Moldavia and Walachia were restored to the suzerainty of the sultan, but Russia obtained the right of intervening with the Sublime Porte (the sultan's court) on behalf of those two principalities. Russia furthermore acquired certain rights of representation on behalf of the Greek Orthodox subjects of the sultan. By a separate treaty (1775) Turkey ceded Bukovina to Austria. The Treaty of Kuchuk Kainarji facilitated the eventual Russian annexation (1783) of the Crimea and was the basis of the later claims of Russia as protector of the Christians in the Ottoman Empire. The Russian ascendancy over Turkey, of which the treaty was a symptom, made the EASTERN QUESTION acute. Varied spellings include the forms Kutchuk and Kainardji.

Küçük Menderes, river, Turkey: see SCAMANDER.

Kudalur, India: see CUDDALORE.

Kudrun: see GUDRUN.

kudu (ko͞o'do͞o), short-haired African ANTELOPE, genus *Strepsiceros.* The greater kudu, *Strepsiceros strepsiceros,* has a reddish brown coat with thin vertical white stripes on its sides. It is among the largest of the antelopes; males may reach a shoulder height of 5 ft (150 cm) and a weight of 500 lb (230 kg). The male has widely spread spiral horns with up to three full twists, sometimes exceeding 5 ft in length; it has a long throat fringe and a white chevron on the muzzle. Females are smaller and hornless, without a beard or nose markings. The greater kudu inhabits hilly brush country of E and S Africa, ranging to altitudes above the treeline. Members of this species are always found near water and are excellent swimmers. Kudus are primarily browsers, feeding on leaves and young shoots, but they may graze as well. Females and their young travel in small bands; males are solitary and join the band only during the mating season. The lesser kudu, *S. imberbia,* reaches a shoulder height of about 3 ft (90 cm) and has more numerous stripes and no throat fringe; it inhabits desert and semidesert areas of eastern Africa. Kudus are classified in the phylum CHORDATA, subphylum Vertebrata, class Mammalia, order Artiodactyla, family Bovidae.

kudzu (ko͝od'zo͞o), plant of the family Leguminosae (PULSE family), native to Japan, and introduced in the United States c.1876 as a decorative vine now widely grown in the South. It is for use as a cover crop, for pasturage and hay, and for controlling soil erosion. Kudzu *(Pueraria thunbergiana)* has a woody stem, broad leaves, and clusters of large purple flowers. In the Orient it is cultivated for its edible tubers and hemplike fiber. Kudzu is classified in the division MAGNOLIOPHYTA, class Magnoliopsida, order Rosales, family Leguminosae.

Kuei-lin or **Kweilin** (both: gwā-lĭn'), city (1970 est. pop. 235,000), N Kwangsi Chuang Autonomous Region, S China, on the Kuei River. It is a transportation center, with connections by rail, river, and road. Paper products are manufactured in the city. The country's second largest tin mine is nearby, and tungsten, manganese, and antimony are also found in the area. Kuei-lin is known for its beautiful karst scenery, often pictured by Chinese landscape painters. A U.S. air force base was there during World War II. Kuei-lin was once capital of Kwangsi prov.

Kuei-yang or **Kweiyang** (both:gwā-yäng), city (1970 est. pop. 1,500,000), capital of Kweichow prov., SW China. On the main road from K'un-ming to Chungking, it is also a rail (since 1959) and industrial center. Textiles, chemical fertilizers, machine tools, petroleum products, cement, and paper are among its manufactures. Important coal fields are nearby. Kuei-yang's institutions of higher learning include Kweichow Univ.

Kufa (ko͞o'fə), former Mesopotamian city, near the Euphrates River, c.110 mi (177 km) S of Baghdad. Founded in 638, it soon rivaled Basra (Al Basrah) in size. The Arab governor of Iraq resided there until 702. For a time Kufa was the seat of the Abbasid caliphate, and Ali, the fourth caliph, was murdered there. Celebrated as a major seat of Arab learning, it was also a continual source of political and religious unrest. The city was repeatedly plundered by the Karmathians in the 10th cent. and lost its importance. It is now an uninhabited ruin surrounded by desert.

Kufstein (ko͞of'shtīn), city (1971 pop. 12,800), in Tyrol prov., W Austria, on the Inn River, near the West German border. It is a summer and winter resort. Manufactures include skis and chemicals. The fortress of Geroldseck, rebuilt by Emperor Maximilian I in the 16th cent. on 12th-century foundations, contains a modern organ famous for its great size and power.

Kuhlau, Friedrich (frē'drĭkh ko͞o'lou), 1786–1832, Danish composer, b. Germany. Kuhlau went to Denmark in 1810 to avoid Napoleon's conscription. Despite the loss in childhood of one eye, he became a flutist and pianist and a favorite of the Danish court. He composed a great deal of incidental music, many works for the flute, and a number of piano pieces that are often studied by beginners.

Kühlmann, Richard von (rĭkh'ärt fən kül'män), 1873–1948, German diplomat. Appointed foreign secretary in Aug., 1917, he led the delegation that negotiated (March, 1918) the Treaty of Brest-Litovsk, which removed Russia from World War I. In July, 1918, army leaders forced his removal from office for publicly declaring that the war could not be ended by military action alone and without recourse to diplomacy.

Kuhn, Bowie (bo͞o'ē kyo͞on), 1926–, American commissioner of baseball, b. Takoma Park, Md. A lawyer, he was (1950–69) legal counsel for baseball club owners before his election as baseball commissioner in 1969. He soon became known as the most vigorous and imaginative commissioner since Kenesaw Mountain Landis.

Kuhn, Richard (rĭkh'ärt ko͞on), 1900–1967, Austrian chemist, director of the Kaiser Wilhelm Institute, Heidelberg. For his research on the carotinoids (he prepared eight of them in pure form) and on vitamins (he isolated riboflavin, or B_2) he was awarded the 1938 Nobel Prize in Chemistry. A Nazi decree prevented his acceptance of the award until after World War II. Kuhn also isolated vitamin B_6.

Kuhn, Walt, 1880–1949, American painter, b. New York City. At the age of 19 he worked as a cartoonist in San Francisco, contributing later to *Life* magazine. After travel and study in Europe he devoted himself largely to oil painting. In 1913, in cooperation with his friend Arthur B. Davies, he was instrumental in assembling the famous Armory Show. He is best known for his bold and brilliant interpretive portraits and figure studies of circus and backstage types, of which *Blue Clown* (Whitney Mus., New York City) is a characteristic example. He is represented in the galleries of Andover, Mass.; Brooklyn, N.Y.; Denver; Los Angeles; San Francisco; Washington, D.C.; and Dublin, Ireland.

Kuhnau, Johann (yō'hän ko͞o'nou), 1660–1722, German musician. Kuhnau was J. S. Bach's predecessor as organist and cantor at St. Thomas Church in Leipzig. He wrote various treatises on music and composed the first harpsichord sonatas.

Kukai or **Kobo-Daishi** (ko͞o'kī, kō'bō-dī'shē), 774–835, Japanese priest, scholar, and artist, founder of the Shingon or "True Word" sect of Buddhism. Of aristocratic birth, he studied the Chinese classics as a young man, but left the university and became a wandering ascetic, eventually making a commitment to Buddhism. He was (804–806) a member of a Japanese embassy to T'ang China, where he studied the Buddhist TANTRA. He returned to Japan with many scriptures and art objects and was honored by the emperor. In 816 he founded the Kongobuji monastery on Mt. Koya, S of Kyoto. Kukai is famous as a calligrapher and is said to have invented (on the model of Sanskrit) hiragana, the syllabary in which, in combination with Chinese characters, Japanese is written. Mt. Koya is still a center of pilgrimage, and there is a folk belief that Kukai, who is buried there, is not dead but in deep meditation and will one day rise again. See collection of his major works ed. by Yoshito Hakeda (1972).

Ku K'ai-chih (go͞o kī-jûr), c.344–c.406, Chinese painter, one of the most eminent painters before the T'ang dynasty. He was especially noted for his portraits but also painted landscapes. None of his works survive today, but his genius can be surmised from ancient writings and from presumed copies of his works. *The Admonitions of the Instructress to Court Ladies* (British Mus.)—the oldest-known Chinese scroll—is thought to be a 7th-century copy of his painting. Another such scroll (early 12th cent.?), *The Nymph of the Lo River,* is at the Freer Gallery, Washington, D.C. These scrolls supply valuable information on paintings of the archaic period in China.

Kukawa (ko͞o'käwä") or **Kuka** (ko͞o'kä), town, NE Nigeria. It is in a farming and salt-mining region. Kukawa was founded in 1814 by Muhammad al-Kanemi of the state of BORNU. The capital and chief commercial center of Bornu, Kukawa was also the southern terminus of a trans-Saharan caravan route to TRIPOLI, Libya. In 1893, Kukawa was conquered and destroyed by forces under Rabih, a Sudanese slave trader. It was rebuilt by the British in 1902 as a garrison town.

Ku Klux Klan (kyo͞o klŭks klăn, ko͞o"), designation mainly given to two distinct secret societies that played a part in American history, although other less important groups have also used the name. The first Ku Klux Klan was an organization that thrived in the South during the RECONSTRUCTION period following the Civil War. The second was a nationwide organization that flourished after World War I. Subsequent groups calling themselves the Ku Klux Klan sprang up in much of the South after World War II and in response to civil rights activity during the 1960s. The original Ku Klux Klan was organized by ex-Confederate elements to oppose the Reconstruction policies of the radical Republican Congress and to maintain "white supremacy." After the Civil War, when local government in the South was weak or nonexistent and there were fears of black outrages and even of an insurrection, informal vigilante organizations or armed patrols were formed in almost all communities. These were linked together in societies, such as the Men of Justice, the Pale Faces, the Constitutional Union Guards, the White Brotherhood, and the Order of the White Rose. The Ku Klux Klan was the best known of these, and in time it absorbed many of the smaller organizations. It was organized at Pulaski, Tenn., in May, 1866. Its strange disguises, its silent parades, its midnight rides, its mysterious language and commands, were found to be most effective in playing upon fears and superstitions. The riders muffled their horses' feet and covered the horses with white robes. They themselves, dressed in flowing white sheets, their faces covered with white masks, and with skulls at their saddle horns, posed as spirits of the Confederate dead returned from the battlefields. Although the Klan was often able to achieve its aims by terror alone, whippings and lynchings were also used; not only against the blacks but also against the carpetbaggers and scalawags. A general organization of the local Klans was effected in April, 1867, at Nashville, Tenn. Gen. N. B. FORREST, the famous Confederate cavalry leader, was made Grand Wizard of the Empire and was assisted by ten Genii. Each state constituted a Realm under a Grand Dragon with eight Hydras as a staff; several counties formed a Dominion controlled by a Grand Titan and six Furies; a county was a Province ruled by a Grand Giant and four Night Hawks; the local Den was governed by a Grand Cyclops with two Night Hawks as aides. The individual members were called Ghouls. Control over local Dens was not as complete as this organization would seem to indicate, and reckless and even lawless local leaders sometimes committed acts that the leaders could not countenance. General Forrest, in Jan., 1869, seemingly under some apprehension as to the use of its power, ordered the disbandment of the Klan and resigned as Grand Wizard. Local organizations continued, some of them for many years. The Klan was particularly effective in systematically keeping black people away from the polls, so that the ex-Confederates gained political control in many states. Congress in 1870 and 1871 passed legislation to combat the Klan (see FORCE BILL). The Klan was especially strong in the mountain and Piedmont areas. In the Lower South the Knights of the White Camellia were dominant. That order, founded (1867) in Louisiana, is reputed to have had even more members than the Ku Klux Klan, but its membership was more conservative and its actions less spectacular. It had a similar divisional organization, with headquarters in New Orleans. The second Ku Klux Klan was founded in 1915 by William J. Simmons, an ex-minister and promoter of fraternal orders; its first meeting was held on Stone Mt., Ga. The new Klan had a wider program than its forerunner, for it added to "white supremacy" an intense nativism and anti-Catholicism (it was also anti-Semitic) closely related to that of the Know-Nothing movement of the middle 19th cent. Consequently its appeal was not sectional, and, aided after 1920 by the activities of professional promoters Elizabeth Tyler and Edward Y. Clarke, it spread rapidly throughout the North as well as the South. It furnished an outlet for the militant patriotism aroused by World War I, and it stressed fundamentalism in religion. Professing itself nonpolitical, the Klan nevertheless controlled politics in many communities and in 1922, 1924, and 1926 elected many state officials and a number of Congressmen. Texas, Oklahoma, Indiana, Oregon, and Maine were particularly under its influence. Its power in the Midwest was broken during the late 1920s when David C. Stephenson, a major Klan leader there, was convicted of second degree murder, and evidence of corruption came out that led to the indictment of the governor of Indiana and the mayor of Indianapolis, both supporters of the Klan. The Klan frequently took extralegal measures, especially against those whom it considered its enemies. As was the case with the earlier Klan, some of these measures, whether authorized by the central organization or not, were extreme. At its peak in the mid-1920s its membership was estimated at 4 million to 5 million. Although the actual figures were probably much smaller, the Klan nevertheless declined with amazing rapidity to an estimated 30,000 by 1930. The Klan spirit, however, was a factor in breaking the Democratic hold on the South in 1928, when Alfred E. Smith, a Roman Catholic, was that party's presidential candidate. Its collapse thereafter was largely due to state laws that forbade masks and eliminated the secret element, to the bad publicity the organization received through its thugs and swindlers, and apparently from the declining interest of the members. With the depression of the 1930s, dues-paying membership of the Klan shrank to almost nothing. Meanwhile, many of its leaders had done extremely well financially from the dues and the sale of Klan paraphernalia. After World War II, Dr. Samuel Green of Georgia led a concerted attempt to revive the Klan, but it failed dismally as the organization splintered and as state after state specifically barred the order. Southern civil rights activities during the 1960s gave the Klan a new impetus and led to revivals of scattered Klan organizations. The most notable of these were Mississippi's White Knights of the Ku Klux Klan, led by Robert Shelton. The newly revived Klan groups were responsible for violent attacks against blacks and civil rights workers in cities throughout the South, including Jacksonville and St. Augustine, Fla., Birmingham and Montgomery, Ala., and Meridian, Miss. In spite of its efforts, the new Klan was not strong, and by the end of the decade its power and membership had declined to practically nothing. A. W. Tourgée's *Fool's Errand* (1880) and Thomas Dixon's *Clansman* (1905), on which D. W. Griffith based his famous film *The Birth of a Nation,* were two popular novels about the original Klan. For other works on the Reconstruction era Ku Klux Klan see W. L. Fleming's edition (1905) of J. C. Lester and D. L. Wilson, *Ku Klux Klan;* S. F. Horn, *Invisible Empire: The Story of the Ku Klux Klan, 1866–1871* (1939, repr. 1973). The structure of the Klan after World War I is discussed in J. M. Mecklin, *The Ku Klux Klan* (1924); A. S. Rice, *The Ku Klux Klan in American Politics* (1962). David Lowe's *Ku Klux Klan: The Invisible Empire* (1967) deals with the final period of Klan activity, as does David M. Chalmer's *Hooded Americanism* (1968), which also discusses the first and second Klans.

Kükong: see SHAO-KUAN, China.

Kukulcán: see QUETZALCOATL.

Kulakov, Feodor (fyô'dər kōō'läkôf), 1918–, Soviet political leader. A member of the Communist party after 1940, Kulakov held various agricultural management positions before becoming deputy minister of agriculture (1955–59) and then minister of grain products (1959–60) for the Russian Soviet Federated Socialist Republic. He headed the agriculture department of the Communist party central committee from 1964 to 1965. He was made a member of the party's central committee in 1961, one of its secretaries in 1965, and a politburo member in 1971.

kulan: see ASS.

Kuldiga (kōōl'dĭgä), Ger. *Goldingen*, town, W European USSR, in Latvia. Founded in 1244, Kuldiga was a residence of the dukes of Courland and still retains a medieval character. The city has two 17th-century churches.

Kuldja: see I-NING, China.

Kulikovo, battle of (kōōlyĭkô'və), 1380, victory of Grand Duke DMITRI DONSKOI of Moscow over Khan Mamai of the Golden Horde. The battle was fought on a plain by the Don near the present village of Kurkino, RSFSR, SE of Tula. Although the victory was the first Russian defeat of the Tatars, it did not eliminate Mongol rule, which endured for another century.

Kulm: see CHEŁMNO, Poland.

Kulmbach, Hans von (häns fən kōōlm'bäkh), c.1480–1522, German painter and graphic artist. His real name was Hans Süss. In general his work reveals the influence of Dürer, but he had little of the master's power. Von Kulmbach worked chiefly in Nuremberg, although he probably spent several years in Cracow as court painter. His masterpiece is the Tucher altarpiece for the Church of St. Sebald in Nuremberg. He also executed portraits and designs for painted glass.

Kulmbach, town (1970 pop. 23,647), Bavaria, E central West Germany, on the White Main River. It has breweries, textile and paper mills, and canneries. Known in 1035, Kulmbach became (1340) the residence of the margraves of Kulmbach (later known as the margraves of Bayreuth) of the house of Hohenzollern. In 1791 the town passed to Prussia, in 1807 it was taken by France, and in 1810 it was annexed by Bavaria and made part of Upper Franconia. On a nearby hill is the fortress (now a museum) of Plassenburg (12th cent.; rebuilt in Renaissance style 1560–70), which served as a prison from 1808 to the early 20th cent.

Kulturkampf (kōōltōōr'kämpf") [Ger.,=conflict of cultures], the conflict between the German government under BISMARCK and the Roman Catholic Church. The promulgation (1870) of the dogma of the INFALLIBILITY of the pope in matters of faith and morals within the church sparked the conflict; it implied that the pope was the defender of the church against incursions by states. The German bishops and most lay Catholics supported this dogma. Bismarck, who was anxious to strengthen the central power of the new German Empire, feared the strongly organized church, which found its political voice in the Catholic Center party (organized 1870). The Center party received additional support from particularists in Bavaria and from other disaffected minorities such as the suppressed Poles in Prussia and the Guelph party of HANOVER, which refused to recognize Hanover's annexation (1866) by Prussia. In his opposition to the church, Bismarck found himself in alliance with the liberals, the traditional opponents of the church. The struggle was initiated by the abolition (July, 1871) of the Catholic department in the Prussian ministry of culture. Feelings grew stronger when Bismarck gave support to the small group of churchmen led by DÖLLINGER who refused to accept the dogma of papal infallibility. In 1872, Bismarck gave the state direct control of the schools in Prussia and obtained the expulsion of the Jesuits, first from Prussia and then from Germany as a whole. The May Laws (of May, 1873) restricted the disciplinary powers of the church, placed the education of the clergy under state supervision, and provided for the punishment of those who refused to cooperate. Next, civil ceremonies became obligatory for marriages in Germany. The church resisted these laws, and many clerics were imprisoned or removed from office for their refusal to comply. Meanwhile, the Center party increased its strength significantly. After its large gains in the Reichstag elections of 1878, Bismarck began to moderate his policy, influenced also by the alienation of the liberals through his protective tariff policies. The death of Pope PIUS IX (1878) aided the gradual resolution of the conflict. Many of the antichurch laws were repealed or fell into disuse. In 1887 a modus vivendi was reached with Pope LEO XIII. In evaluating the Kulturkampf in Germany it is important to remember that the church was at odds with a number of European states during this period. See L. P. Walace, *The Papacy and European Diplomacy, 1869–1878* (1948); see also bibliography under BISMARCK, OTTO VON.

Kulun, Chinese name of ULAN BATOR.

Kum, Iran: see QOM.

Kumamoto (kōōmä'mōtō), city (1970 pop. 439,886), capital of Kumamoto prefecture, W Kyushu, Japan. An agricultural market town, it has manufactures of bamboo ware and pottery. It was an important castle town in the 17th cent.; one of its castles (built 1651) still stands. There are also two universities and several shrines in the city. Kumamoto prefecture (1970 pop. 1,700,079), 2,872 sq mi (7,438 sq km), is noted for the Aso-san volcanic peaks and for its many islands.

Kumanovo (kōō'mänôvô), town (1971 pop. 113,382), S Yugoslavia, in Macedonia. It is the center of a tobacco-growing region. The Serbs won a decisive victory over the Turks at Kumanovo in 1912.

Kumans: see CUMANS.

Kumarajiva (kōōmär'əjīvə), 344–413, Buddhist scholar and missionary, b. Kucha, in what is now Sinkiang prov., China. When his mother, a Kuchean princess, became a nun, he followed her into monastic life at the age of seven. He grew up in centers of Hinayana BUDDHISM, but he was converted to Mahayana Buddhism in his teens and became a specialist in MADHYAMIKA philosophy. In 383, Chinese forces seized Kucha and carried Kumarajiva off to China. From 401 he was at the Ch'in court in the capital Chang-an (the modern Sian), where he taught and translated Buddhist scriptures into Chinese. More than 100 translations are attributed to him. Of these only about 24 can be authenticated, but they include some of the most important titles in the Chinese Buddhist canon. Kumarajiva's career had an epoch-making influence on Chinese Buddhist thought, not only because he made available important texts that were previously unknown, but also because he did much to clarify Buddhist terminology and philosophical concepts. He and his disciples established the Chinese branch of the Madhyamika, known as the San-lun, or "Three Treatises" school.

Kumasi (kōōmä'sē, -mä'-), city (1970 pop. 234,274), capital of the Ashanti Region, central Ghana. The second largest city in Ghana, it is a commercial and transportation center in a cocoa-producing region, and it has a large central market. Kumasi was founded c.1700 as the capital of the Ashanti confederacy. A fort built by the British in 1897 is of interest. A university of science and technology and other schools are in the city.

Kumbakonam (kōōmbəkō'nəm), town (1971 pop. 112,971), Tamil Nadu state, SE India, on the Cauvery River. Its district, in the richest part of the river delta, has one of the highest population densities in India. The area is known for its betel vines. Manufactures include brassware, textiles, and jewelry. The town is a Brahmanic cultural center. The many Hindu temples along the river are visited by pilgrims every 12 years.

Kumbum (kōōm'bōōm'), large lamasery at Huang-ch'ang, NE Tsinghai prov., China, c.12 mi (20 km) SW of Hsi-ning. Long a renowned pilgrimage center, it stands on the spot where Tsong-kha-pa (b.1417), the great Tibetan reformer of Lamaism (see TIBETAN BUDDHISM), is said to have been born. Its Living Buddha became (1952) the 10th Panchen Lama of Tibet. The lamasery is sometimes spelled Gumbum.

Kumgang San (kōōm'gäng' sän), mountain range, SE North Korea, rising to 5,374 ft (1,638 m). There are scenic ravines and caverns and many ancient Buddhist temples. The range is also known as the Diamond Mts.

kumiss (kōō'mĭs): see FERMENTED MILK.

kümmel (kĭm'əl, Ger. küm'əl), sweet LIQUEUR, popular in the Baltic states and produced chiefly in Latvia. Cumin and caraway seeds give the predominating flavor. A fine variety is Allasch kümmel, made in Allasch near Riga, now part of the Soviet Union.

kumquat (kŭm'kwŏt), ornamental shrub of the genus *Fortunella* of the family Rutaceae (RUE family), closely related to the orange and other CITRUS FRUITS. It has evergreen leaves, sweet-scented white flowers, and small, orange-yellow edible fruits which are eaten fresh or in preserves. Three or four types of the kumquat, which is probably native to China, are cultivated as house and hedge plants in the Gulf states and in California. They are much hardier than most oranges. The kumquat is also called kinkan. Kumquats are classified in the division MAGNOLIOPHYTA, class Magnoliopsida, order Sapindales, family Rutaceae.

Kun, Béla (bā'lō kōōn), 1886–1939?, Hungarian Communist. A prisoner of war in Russia after 1915, he embraced Bolshevism. After the outbreak of the Russian Revolution in 1917 he was sent to Hungary as a propagandist. In 1919, Count Michael Károlyi and his government resigned and the Communists and Social Democrats formed a coalition government under Kun. Kun set up a dictatorship of the proletariat; nationalized banks, large businesses and estates, and all private property above a certain minimum; and ruthlessly put down all opposition. He raised a Red Army and overran Slovakia. The allies forced Kun to evacuate Slovakia, and a counterrevolution broke out. Kun was at first victorious over the counterrevolutionists, but he was defeated by a Rumanian army of intervention and was forced to flee to Vienna. Kun's Red Terror was followed by a White Terror. Nicholas HORTHY DE NAGYBANYA became regent of Hungary. Kun, after being held at an insane asylum in Vienna, went (1920) to Soviet Russia. He reappeared (1928) in Vienna and was briefly imprisoned but was allowed to return to the USSR. There he took an active part in the Comintern until he was accused of anti-Stalinism in the Communist party purges of the 1930s. It is usually thought that he died in prison or in exile in Siberia. In the late 1950s and 1960s his reputation was restored in the USSR. See Oszkár Jászi, *Revolution and Counter-Revolution in Hungary* (1924); R. L. Tőkés, *Béla Kun and the Hungarian Soviet Republic* (1967).

kundalini: see YOGA.

Küng, Hans (häns küng), 1928–, Swiss Roman Catholic theologian and author. Ordained in 1954, he became (1960) professor of fundamental theology at Tübingen Univ. and later served (1962–65) as adviser to the Second Vatican Council. Having consistently criticized papal authority, he became the first major Roman Catholic theologian to reject the doctrine of papal infallibility in his book *Infallible? An Inquiry* (tr. 1971). His other works include *The Council in Action* (tr. 1963), *Structures of the Church* (tr. 1966), *Truthfulness: the Future of the Church* (tr. 1968), and *Why Priests?* (tr. 1972).

Kungälv (kŭng'ĕlv"), town (1970 pop. 11,500), Göteborg och Bohus co., SW Sweden, on the Götaälv River. Founded in the 10th cent., Kungälv was one of the chief cities of medieval Norway, known as Konghelle and mentioned in the sagas. The town was plundered (1135) by Wends, seized (1368) by Hansa merchants, and ceded (1658) to Sweden.

Kungei Ala-Tau, mountains, Asia: see ALA-TAU.

K'ung Hsiang-hsi (kōōng shyäng-shē), 1881–1967, Chinese banker and political leader, educated at Oberlin and at Yale. He deemed himself a direct descendant of Confucius in the 75th generation. Throughout his career he supported Sun Yat-sen and Chiang Kai-shek. His first important position was minister of industry and commerce (1928–31). After 1931 he belonged to the central executive committee of the Kuomintang. He was minister of finance (1933–44), and governor of the Bank of China (1933–45). One of China's wealthiest and most powerful men, he was married to Soong Ai-ling (see SOONG, family). K'ung Hsiang-hsi, also known as H. H. Kung, retired in 1945. After the fall of the Nationalist government (1949) he went to live in the United States.

Kunié, New Caledonia: see PINES, ISLE OF.

Kunigunde, Saint: see HENRY II, Holy Roman emperor.

Kunitz, Stanley (kyōō'nĭts), 1905–, American writer and editor, b. Worcester, Mass. He has taught poetry at many colleges and universities. His volumes of poetry, complex and metaphysical, include *Intellectual Things* (1930), *Selected Poems, 1928–1958* (1958; Pulitzer Prize), and *The Testing Tree* (1971). Kunitz is also known as the editor (with Howard Haycraft) of such reference books as *American Authors 1600–1900* (1938), *Twentieth Century Authors* (1942), and *British Authors Before 1800* (1952).

Kuniyoshi, Yasuo (yäsōō-ō' kōōn"ēyō'shē), 1892?–1953, American painter, b. Okayama, Japan. He came to the United States in 1906 and studied art in Los Angeles and at the Art Students League in New York City. He visited Europe in 1925 and in 1928. Kuniyoshi's work has been described as Oriental in spirit but Western in technique, with an inclination toward somber color. His paintings, drawings, and prints are rich in symbolism and fantasy. They are best seen in the galleries of New York City. Kuniyoshi was long a popular teacher at the Art Students League. See monograph by Atsuo Imaizumi and Lloyd Goodrich (1954).

Kunlun (ko͞on'lo͞on'), great mountain system of central Asia, between the Himalayas and the Tien Shan, extending c.1,000 mi (1,610 km) E from the Pamir mts., along the Tibet-Sinkiang prov. border of W China and into Tsinghai prov., where it branches into the mountain ranges of central China; it rises to 25,340 ft (7,724 m) in Ulugh Mus Tagh (Wu-lu-k'o Mu-shih), NE Tibet. The Kunlun's main branches are the A-erh-chin Shan-Mo (Altyn Tagh) and Nan Shan in the north; the Min Shan in the south; and the Tsinling Shan in the east. The Kunlun system acts as a natural barrier between N Tibet and the Tarim basin of Sinkiang; streams rising on the northern slope of the Kunlun disappear into the basin's desert sands. Great sections of the system are inaccessible and uninhabited; there is a very small nomad population, and yaks are the beasts of burden in the high mountain passes.

K'un-ming or **Kunming** (both: ko͞o-mĭng), city (1970 est. pop. 1,700,000), capital of Yünnan prov., S China, on the northern shore of Tien Ch'ih. It is a major administrative, commercial, and cultural center of S China and leading transportation hub (air, road, rail), with rail connections to North Vietnam. Coal is mined, and the city has an iron and steel complex. Other manufactures include phosphorus, chemicals, machinery, textiles, paper, and cement. K'un-ming has long been noted for its scenic beauty and equable climate. It consists of an old walled city, a modern commercial suburb, and a residential and university section. Although it was often the seat of kings in ancient times, K'un-ming's modern prosperity dates only from 1910, when the railroad from Hanoi was built. In World War II, K'un-ming was important as the Chinese terminus of the Burma Road. The city has an astronomical observatory, and its institutions of higher learning include Yünnan Univ. and a medical college. On the outskirts is a famed bronze temple, dating from the Ming dynasty. K'un-ming was formerly called Yünnanfu.

Kunsan (ko͞on'sän'), Jap. *Gunzan*, city (1970 est. pop. 112,500), SW South Korea, on the Yellow Sea at the Kum River estuary. It is a major port, especially for rice shipments, and is a commercial center for the rice grown in the Kum basin. Rice processing, fishing and fish processing, shipbuilding, and the production of salt, rubber, and alcohol are the chief industries. The city is also an important railroad hub. Originally a poor fishing village, Kunsan gained importance with the development of its port, which was opened to foreign trade in 1899. The Japanese, who ruled Korea from 1910 to 1945, further developed the city and port.

Kunya-Urgench: see URGENCH, ancient city, USSR.

Kuomintang (kwō'mĭntăng', ko͞o'ō-), [Chin.,=national people's party]. SUNG CHIAO-JEN organized this party in 1912 under the nominal leadership of SUN YAT-SEN to succeed the Revolutionary Alliance. The original Kuomintang program called for parliamentary democracy and moderate socialism. In 1913, Yüan Shih-kai, the president of China, suppressed the Kuomintang although it held a majority in the first national assembly. Under Sun Yat-sen, the party established unrecognized revolutionary governments at Canton in 1918 and 1921 and even sent a delegation to the Versailles Peace Conference. Sun accepted aid from the USSR, and after 1922 many Comintern agents, notably Michael Borodin and V. K. Blücher, helped reorganize the Kuomintang. At the party congress in 1924 at Canton, a coalition including Communists adopted Sun's political theory, which included the Three People's Principles (San Min Chu I), namely, nationalism, democracy, and a guaranteed livelihood. Sun thought that Chinese national reconstruction must follow a progression of stages: military government, tutelage under the Kuomintang, and popular sovereignty. In 1926, Kuomintang general CHIANG KAI-SHEK launched the NORTHERN EXPEDITION advancing N from Canton against the Peking government. After halting temporarily in 1927, when the Communists were purged and the civil war between the two factions began, Kuomintang forces finally captured Peking in 1928. The Kuomintang government at Nanking received diplomatic recognition in 1928 and began the period of tutelage. After several Kuomintang military campaigns, the Communists were forced (1934–35) to withdraw from their bases in S and central China and establish new strongholds in the northwest. The Kuomintang, except for the period between 1937 and 1940, continued to war against the Communists, greatly weakening its military capacity against the Japanese. Although plagued by bureaucratic inefficiency and corruption, it controlled the Chinese government absolutely until 1947, when it permitted some participation by minor liberal parties. Full-scale civil war, further complicated by inflation, characterized the years from 1945 to 1949. The power of the Kuomintang steadily declined, and by the end of 1949 the Communists controlled the mainland. Since then the Kuomintang, forced from the mainland, has governed TAIWAN. See G. T. Yu, *Party Politics in Republican China: The Kuomintang, 1912–1924* (1966); Hsieh Jan-chih, ed., *The Kuomintang* (1970).

Kuopio (ko͞o'ôpēō), city (1970 pop. 64,744), capital of Kuopio prov., central Finland, on Lake Kallavesi. Situated in a large forest region, its industries are based on timber. It is at the head of the Saimaa lake system and is a tourist and inland-navigation center. Kuopio was chartered in 1782. There are several colleges in the city.

Kupala, Janka (yäng'kä ko͞opä'lä), 1888–1942, Belorussian poet and writer, whose original name was Ivan Lutsevich. Kupala was a major figure of the Belorussian national and cultural revival. His prerevolutionary works, which stress national liberation, include the novel *Along the Path of Life* (1913), a collection of verse entitled *Heritage* (1922), and the drama *Ravaged Nest* (1919). Hostility toward Communism is evident in his poetry written between 1918 and 1928 and in the allegorical comedy *The Natives* (1922). Kupala's works after 1930 are of slight literary value.

Kupka, Frank or **František** (frän'tyĭshĕk ko͞op'kä), 1871–1957, Czech painter, etcher, and illustrator. Kupka illustrated works by Reclus and Leconte de Lisle and an edition of Aristophanes' *Lysistrata.* In 1911 he joined the ORPHISM movement led by DELAUNAY. He was one of the first painters to explore pure geometric abstraction. His decorative style was affected by the "machine esthetic" of the 1920s. Kupka is well represented in the Musée national d'Art moderne, Paris, and in the National Gallery, Prague.

Kuprili: see KÖPRÜLÜ.

Kuprin, Aleksandr Ivanovich (əlyĭksän'dər ēvä'nəvĭch ko͞o'prĭn), 1870–1938, Russian novelist and short-story writer. Kuprin was an army officer for several years before he resigned to pursue a writing career. He won fame with *The Duel* (1905, tr. 1916), a novel of protest against the Russian military system. In 1909, *The Pit* (tr. 1922), his novel dealing with prostitution in Odessa, created a sensation. Kuprin left Russia after the revolution but returned in 1937. Some of his best short stories of action and adventure appear in English in the collections *The River of Life* (1916) and *The Bracelet of Garnets* (1917).

Kura (ko͝orä'), ancient *Cyrus*, river, c.950 mi (1,530 km) long, the chief river of Georgian SSR and Azerbaijan SSR, S European USSR. It rises in NE Turkey, NW of Kars, and flows NE into the USSR, then SE, parallel to the Caucasus Mts., to the Caspian Sea. There are hydroelectric plants on the river near Tbilisi and Mingechaur; the extensive reservoir at Mingechaur is also used for irrigation. The lower Kura River, joined by the Araks River, its chief tributary, flows through an irrigated plain that extends into NW Iran. Cotton is the chief crop of the region, which lies partly below sea level. The Kura is navigable c.300 mi (480 km) upstream.

Kuraish (ko͝orĭsh'), ancient Bedouin tribe near Mecca to which Muhammad belonged. At one time camel drivers and caravan guides, they became, after acquiring custody of the KAABA (5th cent.), one of the most powerful tribes in central Arabia and the chief family of Mecca. They were at first bitter opponents of Muhammad but became his devoted followers when Muhammad retained the Kaaba, a source of pilgrim revenue, as a sanctuary of Islam. The great founders of the Umayyad, Abbasid, and Fatimid dynasties were of Kuraish origin. The modern Hashemite rulers of Jordan, the former Imam of Yemen, and the king of Morocco claim to be the descendants of Muhammad's tribe. The name also appears as Quraysh or Koreish.

Kurayoshi (ko͝orä'yōshē), city (1970 pop. 49,629), Tottori prefecture, W Honshu, Japan, on the Tenjin River. It is an agricultural and communications center with a textile industry.

Kurdistan (kûr'dĭstăn", ko͝ordĭstän'), an extensive plateau and mountain region in SW Asia (c.74,000 sq mi/191,660 sq km), inhabited mainly by Kurds and including parts of E Turkey, NE Iraq, NW Iran and smaller sections of NE Syria and Soviet Armenia. The region lies astride the Zagros mts. (Iran) and the eastern extension of the Taurus mts. (Turkey) and extends in the south across the Mesopotamian plain. Kurdistan includes the upper reaches of the Tigris and Euphrates rivers. There are an estimated 4 million Kurds in Turkey, 2 million in Iran, and 2 million in Iraq. In Turkey they dwell near the Iranian frontier around Lake Van, as well as in the vicinity of Diyarbakır and Erzurum. The Kurds in Iran live principally in Azerbaijan and Khurasan, with some in Fars. In Iraq the Kurds live mostly in the vicinity of Mosul, Kirkuk, and Sulaimaniyah. Ethnically close to the Iranians, the Kurds were traditionally nomadic herdsmen who are now mostly seminomadic or sedentary. Railroads have not penetrated far into Kurdistan; much transportation between Kurdish villages is by mule, donkey, ox, or pony. The majority of Kurds are devout Sunnite Muslims. Kurdish dialects belong to the northwestern branch of the Iranian languages. The Kurds have traditionally resisted subjugation by other nations. Commonly identified with the ancient Corduene, which was inhabited by the Carduchi (mentioned in Xenophon), Kurdistan was conquered by the Arabs and converted to Islam in the 7th cent. The region was held by the Seljuk Turks in the 11th cent., by the Mongols from the 13th to 15th cent., and then by the Ottoman Empire. Having struggled for centuries to free themselves from Ottoman rule, the Kurds were encouraged by the Turkish defeat in World War I and by U.S. President Woodrow Wilson's plea for self-determination for non-Turkish nationalities in the empire. The Kurds brought their claims for independence to the Paris Peace Conference in 1919. The Treaty of Sèvres (1920), which liquidated the Ottoman Empire, provided for the creation of an autonomous Kurdish state. Because of Turkey's military revival under Kemal Atatürk, however, the Treaty of Lausanne (1923), which superseded Sèvres, failed to mention Kurdistan. Revolts by the Kurds of Turkey in 1925 and 1930 were forcibly quelled, and manifestations of Kurdish nationalism there are still suppressed. The Kurds in Iran also rebelled during the 1920s, and at the end of World War II a Soviet-backed Kurdish "republic" existed briefly. Agitation among Iraq's Kurds for a unified and autonomous Kurdistan led in the 1960s to prolonged warfare between Iraqi troops and the Kurds under Gen. Mustafa al-Barzani. In 1970, Iraq finally promised local self-rule to the Kurds, with the city of Irbil as the capital of the Kurdish area. The Kurds refused to accept the terms of the agreement, however contending that the president of Iraq would retain real authority and demanding that Kirkuk, an important oil center, be included in the autonomous Kurdish region. In 1974 the Iraqi government sought to impose its plan for limited autonomy in Kurdistan. It was rejected by the Kurds, and heavy fighting erupted and continued throughout the year. Despite their lack of political unity throughout history, the Kurds, as individuals and in small groups, have had a lasting impact on developments in SW Asia. Saladin, who gained fame during the Crusades, is perhaps the most famous of all Kurds. See studies by Arfa Hassan (1966), Thomas Bois (tr. 1966), and Edgar O'Balliance (1973).

Kurds: see KURDISTAN.

Kure (ko͞o'rā), city (1970 pop. 234,184), Hiroshima prefecture, SW Honshu, Japan, on Hiroshima Bay. It is a major naval base and port, with shipbuilding yards. Steel, pulp, files, machinery, and tools are manufactured in Kure.

Kure Island or **Curé Island** (both: ko͞o'rā), formerly **Ocean Island,** circular atoll, c.15 mi (24 km) in circumference, in the NW part of the Hawaiian group, c.50 mi (80 km) NW of Midway Island. Kure is uninhabited but has a large variety of sea birds. The island was annexed in 1886 by the Kingdom of Hawaii and was worked for guano.

Kurgan (ko͝orgän'), city (1970 pop. 244,000), capital of Kurgan oblast, W Siberian USSR, on the Tobol River. Kurgan is the important junction of the western branches of the Trans-Siberian RR. Its factories produce agricultural and road-building equipment, machine tools, and food products. Kurgan was founded in the 17th cent. There are many ancient burial mounds (Turkic *Kurgan*) in the area.

Kuril Islands (ko͞o'rēl, ko͞or'ĭl) or **Kuriles,** Jap. *Chishima-Retto*, Rus. *Kurilskiye Ostrova*, island chain, c.6,020 sq mi (15,590 sq km), Sakhalin oblast, E USSR. They stretch c.775 mi (1,250 km) between S Kamchatka Peninsula and NE Hokkaido, Japan, and separate the Sea of Okhotsk from the Pacific Ocean. There are 30 large and numerous small islands; Iturup is the largest. Atlasova volcano (7,674 ft/2,339 m) on Atlasova Island is the highest point of the chain. The islands are mainly of volcanic origin. Active volcanoes are present and earthquakes are frequent. The low temperature, high humidity, and persistent fog make the islands unpleasant for human habitation. There are, however, communities engaged in sulfur mining, hunting, and fishing. In the 18th cent. both Russia and Japan penetrated the islands. In 1875, Japan gave up Sakhalin in return for Russian withdrawal from the Kuriles, and the Japanese held the islands until the end of World War II. The Yalta Conference ceded the islands to the USSR, and Soviet forces occupied the chain in Sept., 1945. Japan has challenged the Soviet right to the Kuriles, and failure to resolve the impasse has been a major obstacle to the signing of a peace treaty between Japan and the USSR.

Kurland: see COURLAND, USSR.

Kurnool (kərno͞ol'), town (1971 pop. 136,682), Andhra Pradesh state, S central India, at the confluence of the Tungabhadra and Hindri rivers. Formerly the state capital, Kurnool is now a district administrative center and a market for grain, hides, and cotton. There are ruins of a fort built by the Hindu Vijayanagar kings in the 16th cent. The town was overrun by Muslims in 1565 and was ceded to the British by the Nizam of Hyderabad in 1800. Kurnool is a center of pilgrimage and is surrounded by hill resorts.

Kurokawa, Noriaki (nôrēä'kē ko͞orō'käwä), 1934–, Japanese architect. Youngest of the group of architects known as the metabolists, who perceive architectural works as living organisms, Kurokawa plans for the growth or change of his buildings by addition or subtraction of modular units. The Takara Beautilion (1970, Osaka), the Toshiba IHI Pavilion, Hawaiian Dreamland (1966–67), and the Nitto Foods Co. plant in Sagae, Japan, are among his best-known designs.

Kuropatkin, Aleksey Nikolayevich (əlyĭksyā' nyĭkəlī'əvĭch ko͞oro͝opät'kĭn), 1848–1925, Russian general. He distinguished himself in the Russo-Turkish War of 1877–78. Made minister of war in 1898, he opposed the course that precipitated the Russo-Japanese War of 1904–5, but after its outbreak he took command of the troops in Manchuria. Kuropatkin resigned after the Russian defeat at Mukden. During World War I he was (1916–17) governor of Turkistan. See his book, *The Russian Army and the Japanese War* (tr. 1909).

Kurosawa, Akira (äkē'rä ko͞orō'säwä), 1910–, Japanese film director, scriptwriter, and producer, b. Tokyo. He is regarded as one of the world's great directors. His *Ikiru* (1952), a moving study of an elderly bureaucrat facing death by cancer, is an acknowledged classic. Among his other films are *Rashomon* (1950), about truth and illusion; *Seven Samurai* (1954), an epic adventure story; *Throne of Blood* (1957), an adaptation of *Macbeth;* and *Yojimbo* (1961), a rousing Japanese-style Western. See study by Donald Richie (1970).

Kuroshio, ocean current: see JAPAN CURRENT.

Kursk (ko͝orsk), city (1970 pop. 284,000), capital of Kursk oblast, central European USSR, at the confluence of the Tuskor and Seim rivers. An important rail junction, it has machine, chemical, and synthetic fiber plants. A large iron deposit is south of the city. Known since 1095, Kursk was destroyed by the Mongols in 1240 and was rebuilt as a Muscovite fortress in 1586. During World War II the Soviets won a major battle near Kursk in 1943.

Kursky Zaliv (ko͝or'skē zä'lĕv) or **Courland Lagoon** (ko͝or'lănd), lagoon, 56 mi (90 km) long and 28 mi (45 km) wide, W USSR, in the Lithuanian and Russian republics. It is separated from the Baltic Sea by Courland Spit, a sandspit c.60 mi (100 km) long and 1 to 2 mi (1.6–3.2 km) wide, which leaves only a narrow opening at the Klaypeda Channel in the north. The Neman River empties into the lagoon.

Kurume (ko͞oro͞o'mā), city (1970 pop. 194,178), Fukuoka prefecture, W Kyushu, Japan, on the Chikugo Plain. It is a commercial and agricultural center and manufactures rubber and cotton goods. Kurume, a former castle town, is now the seat of a medical college.

Kurunegala (ko͝or"o͞onā'gələ), town (1968 est. pop. 23,000), W central Sri Lanka (Ceylon). It is an important road junction and the administrative and commercial center of a coconut, rice, and rubber plantation district. Overlooking the town is Elephant Hill, a stronghold in the 14th cent., when Kurunegala was the capital of a Sinhalese kingdom.

Kurusu, Saburo (sä"bo͞orō' ko͞oro͞o'so͞o), 1886–1954, Japanese career diplomat. As ambassador to Germany from 1939 to 1941, he signed the Berlin Pact (Sept., 1940). A special envoy to Washington, he and Admiral Nomura were negotiating when Pearl Harbor was bombed on Dec. 7, 1941. Interned in the United States from Dec., 1941 to June, 1942, he returned to Japan and became (1945) a professor at Tokyo Univ.

Kurzeme: see COURLAND, USSR.

Kusatsu (ko͞osä'tso͞o), town (1970 pop. 46,610), Gumma prefecture, central Honshu, Japan. As early as the 12th cent. its hot sulfur springs were known for their medicinal properties.

Kush: see CUSH.

Kushaiah (ko͞oshā'yə), Levite. 1 Chron. 15.17. Kishi: 1 Chron. 6.44.

Kushiro (ko͞oshē'rō), city (1970 pop. 191,946), SE Hokkaido, Japan, on the Pacific Ocean. The main port of E Hokkaido and the island's only ice-free trading port, it exports timber, fish, and coal. Kushiro is also a major base for fishermen. The city is the center of the huge Kushiro coal field, which extends far out to sea; mining is carried on in the sea. Industrialization has made Kushiro important in the production of marine products, dairy products, lumber, paper, pulp, and fertilizer. The city is traversed by the Kushiro River.

Kuskokwim (kŭs'kōkwĭm), river, c.800 mi (1,290 km) long, rising on the northwest slopes of the Alaska Range, central Alaska, and flowing SW to the Bering Sea. The river is a potential source for hydroelectric power production.

Küssnacht am Rigi (küs'näkht äm rē'gē), town (1970 pop. 7,956), Schwyz canton, central Switzerland, on the Lake of Lucerne. A small resort, it is known chiefly as the scene of the killing of Gessler by William TELL. A nearby 17th-century chapel commemorates the legendary exploit.

Kustanay (ko͞ostənī'), city (1970 pop. 124,000), capital of Kustanay oblast, NW Central Asian USSR, in Kazakhstan, on the Tobol River. It is an agricultural center and producer of chemical fibers. Rich iron deposits are nearby.

Kütahya (kütä'yä), city (1970 pop. 62,060), capital of Kütahya prov., W central Turkey. An agricultural market center, the city has been famous since the 16th cent. for the manufacture of ceramics. It has a hydroelectric plant. Known in ancient history as Cotyaeum, it was occupied by the Seljuk Turks soon after the battle of Manzikert (1071). In the 15th cent. it passed to the Ottomans. A former spelling is Kutaiah.

Kutaisi (ko͞otəē'sē), city (1970 pop. 161,000), SE European USSR, in Georgia, on the Rioni River. An industrial center, it has industries producing trucks, mining and transport equipment, textiles, chemicals, and food products. Industry is aided by a large hydroelectric station on the Rioni. Kutaisi was the capital of ancient Colchis (8th cent. B.C.), and the capital of Imeritia in the 13th, 15th, and 16th cent. A.D. It was taken by the Russians in 1810. There is some notable medieval architecture, including the ruins of the 11th-century St. George Cathedral.

Kutb Minar: see QUTB MINAR.

Kutch or **Cutch** (both: kŭch, ko͞och), district, 17,000 sq mi (44,030 sq km), Gujarat state, W India, bounded on the N by Pakistan. It is largely barren except for a fertile band along the Arabian Sea. There is some horse and camel breeding. Bhuj and Mandvi, a port, are the chief towns. Formerly a princely state, Kutch was established in the 14th cent. by RAJPUTS, was often invaded from Sind, and passed under British rule in 1815. Kutch was incorporated into Gujarat in 1960. The Rann of Kutch, a salt waste (9,000 sq mi/23,310 sq km) mainly in the N of the district, was the scene of Indo-Pakistani fighting in 1965.

Kutchin Indians (kŭch"ĭn'), group of North American Indians of the ATHABASCAN branch of the Nadene linguistic stock (see AMERICAN INDIAN LANGUAGES). They inhabit the Yukon valley in NW Canada and E Alaska and also the valley of the Peel River, a tributary of the Mackenzie. In prehistoric times the Kutchin subsisted as caribou hunters. They practiced polygamy, and they sometimes practiced infanticide on female children to prevent overpopulation. Sir Alexander Mackenzie was the first European to visit (1789) this area, and by c.1810 a trading post was established. The Kutchin are extremely hospitable, sometimes entertaining guests for weeks at a time. In the mid-19th cent. they numbered some 1,200; presently they number about 1,500. The Kutchin are also called the Loucheux. See Cornelius Osgood, *Contributions to the Ethnography of the Kutchin* (1936).

Kutchuk Kainardji or **Kutchuk Kainarji, Treaty of:** see KUCHUK KAINARJI, TREATY OF.

Kut-el-Amara: see AL KUT, Iraq.

Kutenai Indians: see KOOTENAI INDIANS.

Kutná Hora (ko͝ot'nä hô'rä), Ger. *Kuttenberg,* city (1970 pop. 18,097), NW Czechoslovakia, in Bohemia. Now an agricultural center, it was an important silver-mining center in the Middle Ages. Its famous mint largely created the power and greatness of the medieval kings of Bohemia. In 1409, Emperor Wenceslaus IV issued a decree at Kutná Hora that changed the status of the Univ. of Prague. In 1421–24, Kutná Hora was captured by the Hussites, recaptured by Emperor Sigismund, and captured again and burned by John Žižka. Till then a stronghold of Catholicism, it became for two centuries the center of Bohemian Protestantism. The city suffered again in the Thirty Years War (1618–48) and lost its importance after the silver mines closed in the 17th cent. Kutná Hora is rich in medieval architecture; the Church of St. Barbara (14th cent.) is a splendid example of Bohemian Gothic, and the Gothic Cathedral of St. James (14th cent.) has a tower 266 ft (81 m) high. The "Italian Court," begun in the 13th cent., is a palace once used both as a mint and as a residence of the kings of Bohemia.

Kuttenberg: see KUTNÁ HORA, Czechoslovakia.

Kutuzov, Mikhail Ilarionovich (mĕkhəyĕl' ēləryôn'əvĭch ko͞oto͞o'zəf), 1745–1813, Russian field marshal. He fought against the Polish Confederation of Bar (see BAR, CONFEDERATION OF) and served in the RUSSO-TURKISH WARS of 1768–74 and 1787–92, in which he lost an eye. He took part (1805) in the battle of Austerlitz, which was fought against his advice. In 1811–12 he again took command against the Turks and defeated them in a brilliant campaign that brought Bessarabia to Russia. In Aug., 1812, Kutuzov replaced BARCLAY DE TOLLY as commander in chief against the invading armies of NAPOLEON I. Kutuzov was expected to engage the French in battle and to abandon his predecessor's delaying tactics. The battle of BORODINO was the result; after that butchery, Kutuzov resumed Barclay's wise policy of retreat, which eventually led to Napoleon's ruin. He pursued Napoleon relentlessly after the retreat of the *Grande Armée* from Moscow (1812–13). He was created prince of Smolensk for a victory there late in 1812.

kuvasz (pl. kuvaszok), (ko͞ov'äs, ko͞o'väs), breed of powerful WORKING DOG perfected in Hungary over many centuries. The kuvasz may stand as high as 30 in. (76 cm) at the shoulder and weigh up to 120 lb (54 kg). Its double coat of fine underhairs and thick, medium-length, straight or slightly wavy outercoat is pure white in color. Although both Tibet and Turkey have been cited as the original home of the kuvasz, recently assimilated evidence seems to support the contention that it was one of the sheepherding dogs used in Mesopotamia more than 7,000 years ago. Whatever its origins, its history in Hungary is well attested to, as is its service there, for a period of hundreds of years, as a guard, shepherd, and hunting dog. Today it is also raised for show competition and as a pet. See DOG.

Kuwait (ko͞owīt', -wāt) or **Kowait** (kō'-), independent sheikhdom (1970 pop. 738,663), 6,177 sq mi (16,000 sq km), NE Arabian peninsula, at the head of the Persian Gulf. A low, sandy region, generally bar-

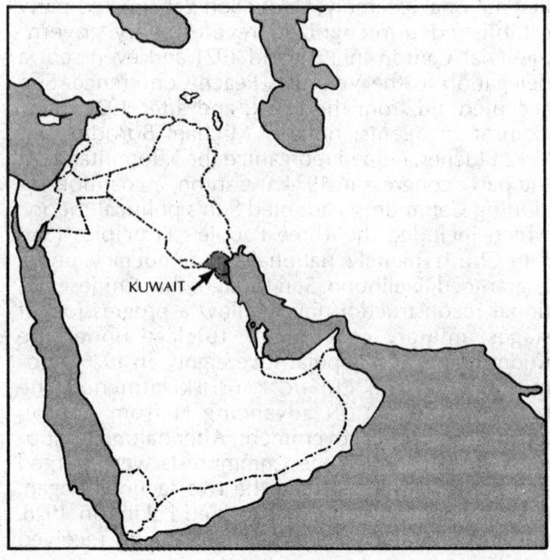

ren and sparsely settled, Kuwait is bounded by Saudi Arabia on the south and by Iraq on the north and west. It has a warm climate, dry inland and humid along the coast. The population is predominantly Arab. The capital is Al-Kuwait, or Kuwait (1970 pop. 80,008), a modern city; its port, Mina al-Ahmad, is a trade center with shipyards and oil refineries. Kuwait's traditional exports were pearls and hides, but since 1946 it has become a major petroleum producer. It is estimated that Kuwait possesses about one fifth of the world's oil reserves. The main concession for oil exploitation was held by a joint British-American firm until 1974 when Kuwait took control of most of the operations; it had previously retained a large part of the oil profits. Much of the profits have been devoted to the improvement of living conditions and education in the country. To provide against the possible future exhaustion of the oil reserves, the government in the 1960s launched a program of industrial diversification. Kuwait was settled by Arab tribes in the early 18th cent. The present ruling dynasty was founded by Sabah abu Abdullah (ruled 1756-72). In the late 18th and early 19th cent. the sheikhdom, nominally an Ottoman province, was frequently threatened by the WAHABIS. In 1897 the sheikh, fearing that the Turks intended to make their nominal authority effective, made Kuwait a British protectorate. By this the British prevented Kuwait from becoming linked to the German Berlin-to-Baghdad railroad. In June, 1961, the British ended their protectorate but supplied troops in July at the request of the sheikh when Iraq claimed sovereignty over Kuwait. A short time later the British troops were replaced by detachments from the Arab League. Kuwait joined the United Nations in 1963. It is a large donor of financial aid to the other Arab countries. Kuwait took part in the oil embargo against nations that had supported Israel during the 1973 war. The country is governed under a constitution promulgated in 1963. The sheikh and the council of ministers appointed by him constitute the executive. A 50-member national assembly is elected every four years by the male citizens. See John Daniels, *Kuwait Journey* (1971); H. V. Winstone and Zahra Freeth, *Kuwait: Prospects and Reality* (1972).

Kuwana (ko͞owä'nä), city (1970 pop. 81,015), Mie prefecture, S Honshu, Japan, on Ise Bay. It is an important port and industrial center with large metal and textile industries.

Kuybyshev (kwē'bĭshĕf, Rus. ko͞o'ēbĭshĭf), formerly **Samara** (səmâ'rə, Rus. səmä'rə), city (1970 pop. 1,047,000), capital of Kuybyshev oblast, E central European USSR, on the left bank of the Volga and at the mouth of the Samara River. It is a major river port and rail center (Moscow-Siberian line) and has important industries producing automobiles, aircraft, locomotives, machinery, ball bearings, synthetic rubber, chemicals, textiles, and petroleum. Grain and livestock are the chief exports. The gigantic Kuybyshev barrage and hydroelectric plant is a few miles upstream from the city. Founded in 1586 as a Muscovite stronghold for the defense of the Volga trade route and of Russia's eastern frontier, Samara was attacked by the Nogai Tatars (1615) and the Kalmyks (1644) and opened its gates to the Cossack rebels under Stenka Razin in 1670. It grew to be the chief grain center on the Volga and was the seat of immensely rich grain merchants. Its industrial expansion dates from the early 20th cent., when railroads to Siberia and central Asia were built. Samara was (1918) the seat of the anti-Bolshevik provisional government and constituent assembly of Russia. During World War II the central government of the USSR was transferred to Kuybyshev (1941-43) from Moscow. As a result, the population increased tremendously, and the city limits were greatly expanded. The city was renamed in 1935. Kuybyshev has a university.

Kuyp, family of Dutch painters: see CUYP.

Kuyper, Abraham (ä'brähäm koi'pər), 1837-1920, Dutch political figure and Calvinist theologian. After holding important pastorates, he became interested in politics and engaged in political and theological controversies. In 1886 he founded the Free Reformed Church. He edited an encyclopedia of sacred theology. Kuyper was first elected to the States-General in 1874 and served a number of terms. He was minister of the interior from 1901 to 1905.

Kuzbas, USSR: see KUZNETSK BASIN.

Kuznets, Simon, 1901-, American economist, b. Kharkov, Russia, grad. Columbia (B.S., 1923; M.A., 1924; Ph.D., 1926). He emigrated to the United States in 1922. After serving as a fellow on the Social Science Research Council (1925-27), he worked for the National Bureau of Economic Research (1927-63), where he became involved in the study of business cycles. Kuznets taught at the Univ. of Pennsylvania (1930-54) and Johns Hopkins Univ. (1954-60); he joined the faculty of Harvard in 1960. Generally credited with having developed the Gross National Product as a measure of economic output, Kuznets was awarded the Nobel Memorial Prize in Economics in 1971. The massive *National Income and Its Composition, 1919 to 1938* (1941) is considered his major work. A prolific writer, Kuznets has also written *National Income and Capital Formation* (1938), *National Product Since 1869* (1946), *Economic Growth of Nations* (1971), and numerous other books and scholarly articles.

Kuznetsk, Kemerovo Oblast, USSR: see NOVOKUZNETSK.

Kuznetsk Ala-Tau (ko͞oznyĕtsk' əlä'-tou), mountain range, S Siberian USSR, E of Novokuznetsk, rising to about 6,900 ft (2,100 m). Part of the great mountain system of central Asia, the range is composed mainly of metamorphic rocks and yields such minerals as iron, manganese, and gold.

Kuznetsk Basin, coal basin, c.10,000 sq mi (25,900 sq km), W Siberian USSR, between the Kuznetsk Ala-Tau and the Salair Ridge. Its abbreviated name is Kuzbas. With extensive coal deposits, particularly of high-grade coking coal, the Kuznetsk Basin is second only to the Donets Basin of the Ukraine in Soviet regional coal production. The main fields are around ANZHERO-SUDZHENSK, KEMEROVO, LENINSK-KUZNETSKI, KISELEVSK, and PROKOPYEVSK. The first iron-smelting works were founded in 1697. Coal deposits were discovered in 1721 and first mined in 1851. The area's industries grew rapidly in the late 19th cent., and new heavy industry was started from 1930 to 1932 when the Ural-Kuznetsk industrial combine was formed. With major plants at NOVOKUZNETSK, the Kuznetsk industrial region (c.27,000 sq mi/69,900 sq km) produces iron and steel, zinc, aluminum, heavy machinery, and chemicals. Ores were brought from E Siberia for processing, and during World War II the basin's industrial importance was surpassed only by that of the Urals.

Kwajalein (kwä'jälān, -lēn, -līn), coral atoll, 6.5 sq mi (16.8 sq km), central Pacific, in the Ralik Chain of the MARSHALL ISLANDS. The largest atoll of the Marshalls, Kwajalein, a group of 97 islets surrounding a lagoon, is a district headquarters of the U.S. Trust Territory of the PACIFIC ISLANDS. A large Japanese naval and air base was located there during World War II, and after the U.S. conquest of the Marshalls (1944) U.S. military bases were established. An antimissile missile installation under control of the U.S. navy is on Kwajalein.

Kwakiutl Indians (kwä'kēo͞o"təl), group of closely related North American Indians who inhabit N Vancouver Island and the adjacent mainland of British Columbia, Canada. They together with the Nootka Indians, their southern neighbors, make up the Wakashan branch of the Algonquian-Wakashan linguistic stock (see AMERICAN INDIAN LANGUAGES). Kwakiutl culture was typical of the Northwest Coast area (including the custom of POTLATCH). Their population before the coming of Europeans, was estimated to be some 15,000, but by the early 1970s it was reduced to less than 1,500. The ethnographer, Franz Boas, produced an enormous number of ethnographic studies on the Kwakiutl. See Franz Boas, *Kwakiutl Ethnography,* ed. by H. F. Codere (1966); R. P. Rohner and E. C. Rohner, *The Kwakiutl* (1970).

Kwangchowan: see CHAN-CHIANG, China.

Kwang Hsü: see KUANG HSÜ.

Kwangju (kwäng'jo͞o'), city (1970 est. pop. 503,000), capital of South Cholla prov., SW South Korea, in the Yongsan River lowland. A regional agricultural and commercial center built on the site of an ancient market, Kwangju has rice mills and industries that produce rayon and cotton textiles and beer. The city is also a railroad hub. In the hills around Kwangju are ancient tombs and temples.

Kwangsi Chuang Autonomous Region (kwăng'sē', gwäng'sē'), Mandarin *Kuang-si,* province (1968 est. pop. 24,000,000), c.85,000 sq mi (220,150 sq km), S China, bordering on North Vietnam. The capital is NAN-NING. Kwangsi is drained by the navigable Si River and its many tributaries. It is in the double-crop agricultural belt, but because of the hilly and mountainous terrain only about 10% to 15% of the land is cultivated. Rice is an important crop, and Kwangsi is a major sugarcane-producing area. Wheat, corn, vegetables, peanuts, tropical and subtropical fruit, sesame, rapeseed, jute, and tobacco are also grown, chiefly in the Si River plain. Forestry is centered around Liu-chou; timber and tung oil are valuable commodities. Kwangsi is a major producer of manganese ore and a significant source of fluorspar. The country's second largest tin mine is in NE Kwangsi, near Kuei-lin; tungsten and antimony are also found there. Uranium has been reported in the region. Kwangsi has oil refineries and fertilizer and cement plants. The region is well supplied with roads and railroads; a railway runs to North Vietnam. The Kwangsi Chuang Autonomous Region, which has a large non-Chinese minority, was created in 1958 from Kwangsi prov. Almost half of the population are Chuang; other tribes include the Yao and Miao. Many Chinese Muslims also live in Kwangsi.

Kwangtung (kwăng'to͝ong', gwäng'do͝ong'), Mandarin *Kuang-tung,* province (1968 est. pop. 40,000,000), c.89,400 sq mi (231,500 sq km), S China. The capital is CANTON. The province includes some 730 islands, of which HAINAN is the largest. On coastal islands and adjacent mainland territories are the British colony of Hong Kong and the Portuguese colony of Macao. The hilly coastline is the longest of any province (constituting almost one fourth of the country's total coastline); the only real breaks to the interior are at Shan-t'ou on the Han River delta and at Canton at the Pearl River delta. Inland transportation is good; before the 1950s water routes predominated, but now railroads have taken over the freighting. In the canals and off the coast there is considerable fishing. Between 15% and 20% of the province is under cultivation, primarily in the delta areas, which are among the most populous in China. There the climate is subtropical and the rainfall heavy most of the year. Two or three crops are generally harvested, but some grain must still be imported for local needs. Kwangtung is the country's leading producer of sugarcane and stands second in rice production and third in silk, although the silk industry is no longer as important as it once was. Other commercial crops include hemp, tobacco, tea, tropical and subtropical fruits, and peanuts. Kwangtung has tungsten, iron, manganese, titanium, tin, gold, and silver deposits, but they are little exploited. A uranium mine has begun operation in Weng-yüan. Shale oil deposits are found in the south, and there is offshore drilling for oil; the province has several oil refineries. There are also lumber and paper mills, and food-processing, cement, and fertilizer plants. The large handicraft industry, which once thrived on European trade, has dwindled. Canton is a great industrial center, with a wide range of manufactures. The Cantonese constitute the bulk of the population, which is non-Mandarin speaking. The people of Kwangtung are known around the world; one half of the overseas Chinese are from Kwangtung province. The region, originally settled by Miao, Li, and Yao tribes, continually attracted migrating groups from the north; some (notably the Hakka) retained their own languages. Kwangtung came under Chinese suzerainty during the unification under the Ch'in dynasty (c.211 B.C.), and was more firmly absorbed during the Han dynasty. Kwangtung was the main scene of China's early foreign contact, chiefly through Canton; there was trade with the west during the Roman Empire, trade with the Arabs during the T'ang dynasty, and European trade that originated during the 16th cent. with the Portuguese. Kwangtung has been a center of revolutionary activity; there the KUOMINTANG was formed (1912) under the leadership of Sun Yat-sen, and there Chiang Kai-shek began his drive (1920s) for the unification of the country.

Kwantung: see LIAONING, China.

kwashiorkor (kwăsh"ēôr'kôr), protein deficiency disorder of children. It is prevalent in overpopulated parts of the world where the diet consists mainly of starchy vegetables, particularly in sections of Africa, Central and South America, and S Asia. Such a diet, although adequate in calories, is deficient in certain amino acids, the constituents of PROTEINS vital for growth. The nursing infant gets the required amino acids from the mother's milk. But the weaned child, who receives neither milk nor meat, is likely to develop kwashiorkor. The most striking manifestations of the disease are a swollen and severely bloated abdomen, resulting from decreased albumin in the blood, and various skin changes resulting in a reddish discoloration of the hair and skin in black African children. Other symptoms include severe diarrhea, enlarged fatty liver, atrophy of muscles and glands, mental apathy, and generally retarded development. Kwashiorkor is treated by adding proteins to the diet, usually in the form of dried milk.

Kwazulu, Bantustan: see ZULULAND, South Africa.

Kweichow (kwā'chou', gwā'jō'), Mandarin *Kuei-chou,* province (1968 est. pop. 17,000,000), c.66,000 sq mi (170, 940 sq km), SW China. KUEI-YANG is the capital and chief city; TSUN-I and Tu-yün are important towns. Kweichow is almost entirely a high plateau, and its sheer limestone hills form some of the most spectacular karst scenery in the world. Kweichow has many deep river valleys, notably those of the Wu (the major river), the Ho, and the Yüan. The climate is mild and the rainfall adequate, but the soil is poor and there is little arable land. Rice is the major crop; the same amount of acreage is given to corn but with about half the yield. Soybeans, wheat, millet, barely, kaoliang, and beans are raised for food. Commerical crops include rapeseed, tobacco, tea, oakleaf silk, sugarcane, and indigo. Cotton is being developed. Kweichow has rich forests, and lumber, tung oil, lacquer, and paint are produced. Mineral resources include mercury, coal, iron, phosphorous, copper, manganese, and silver. With a limited railway system, few highways, and unnavigable rivers, communications are generally unsatisfactory. The province has two autonomous districts: one in the southeast, peopled by Miao (known for their embroideries) and T'ung; and another in the south, inhabited by Pu-i and Miao. Chinese settlement of the region began around 2,000 years ago, but it was only in the 10th cent. that it passed under the suzerainty of China. Kweichow became a province in the 17th cent. under the Ming dynasty, but the native Miaos were not completely subdued until about 1870. The traditional name of Kweichow is Kien or Ch'ien. Kweichow Univ. is in Kuei-yang.

Kweilin: see KUEI-LIN, China.

Kweisui: see HU-HO-HAO-T'E, China.

Kweiyang: see KUEI-YANG, China.

Kwinana, city (1971 pop. 12,208), Western Australia, SW Australia, a suburb of Perth. A new industrial city, Kwinana has oil refineries and steelworks.

Ky, Nguyen Cao (nəwĭn' kou kē), 1930–, premier (1965–67) and vice president (1967–71) of the Republic of (South) Vietnam. After receiving flight training from the French, he returned to Vietnam (1954) and held a series of commands in the South Vietnamese air force. After President Diem's overthrow (1963), Premier Duong Van Minh made Ky air force commander. Following a military coup led by Nguyen Van Thieu in 1965, Ky became premier and in the 1967 election was Thieu's vice-presidential running mate. Gradually alienated from Thieu, Ky intended to oppose him in the 1971 elections but was out-manuevered by Thieu and lost most of his political influence.

Kyakhta or **Kiakhta** (both: kyäkh'tə), city, Buryat Autonomous SSR, S Siberian USSR, near the Soviet-Mongolian border. Kyakhta is on the highway from Ulan-Ude to Ulan Bator and is a major transit point for Soviet-Mongolian trade. It has textile, lumber, and food-processing plants. Founded in 1728, it was a trading point between Russia and Western Europe and China; it was then a trading center between Russia and Outer Mongolia. Until 1935 it was called Troitskosavsk.

Kyd or **Kid, Thomas,** 1558–94, English dramatist, b. London. The son of a scrivener, he evidently followed his father's profession for a few years. In the 1580's he began writing plays. His literary fame rests on *The Spanish Tragedy* (c.1586), which initiated an important Elizabethan dramatic genre—the revenge tragedy. Popular throughout the 17th cent., *The Spanish Tragedy* is notable for its exciting action, splendid rhetoric, and complex delineation of character. Kyd is believed to be the author of an earlier version of *Hamlet,* which Shakespeare used as the basis of his play. In 1593, Kyd was accused of holding unorthodox religious and moral views; he was arrested and subjected to torture. Although he extricated himself by implicating his friend Christopher Marlowe, his reputation was severely marred, and he died in poverty the following year. See study by A. Freeman (1967).

Kyffhäuser (kĭf'hoizər), forested mountain, c.1,550 ft (470 m), Halle district, W East Germany. It is crowned by the two ruined castles of Rothenburg (7th cent.) and Kyffhausen (12th cent.) and by a huge monument to Emperor William I (erected 1896). According to legend, Emperor Frederick I (Frederick Barbarossa) sleeps bewitched in a limestone cave in the mountain, sitting at a stone table through which his beard has grown; there he awaits the time when he will go forth to restore German greatness. The legend, treated in poems by Uhland, Heine, and others, probably originally applied to Emperor Frederick II (reigned 1220–50).

Kyoga or **Kioga** (kyō'gä), lake, c.100 mi (160 km) long, formed by the Victoria Nile, S central Uganda, E Africa. It occupies part of the same depression as Victoria Nyanza, to which it was once joined. The shallow lake has large areas of papyrus swamp. Kyoga provides transportation for a large cotton-growing region.

kyogen: see ORIENTAL DRAMA.

Kyonggi (kyŭng'gē'), province (1970 pop. 3,361,730), NW South Korea. Agriculture dominates the economy; rice, wheat, barley, pulses, fruits, and vegetables are the chief crops. The northern part of the old Kyonggi prov. became part of North Korea after World War II.

Kyongsong: see SEOUL, South Korea.

Kyoto (kyō'tō), city (1970 pop. 1,418,933), capital of Kyoto prefecture, S Honshu, Japan, on the Kamo River. Yodo is its port. Kyoto is one of Japan's largest cities and an important industrial and cultural center. Industries include copper rolling, food processing, and the manufacture of electrical equipment, spinning and dyeing machinery, precision tools, chemicals, and cameras. The city is famous for its cloisonné, bronzes, damascene work, porcelain, and lacquer ware, and its renowned silk industry dates from 794. Founded in the 8th cent. as Uda and named Heian-kyo when it became Japan's capital in 794, the city was popularly called Miyako or Kyoto (sometimes Kioto). After 1192 it lost its political power to Tokyo; but since 1868, when the latter became the official capital, Kyoto has often been referred to as Saikyo [western capital]. For centuries it has been the cultural heart of Japan; it contains magnificent art treasures and is the seat of Kyoto Univ., Doshisha Univ. (founded in 1873 as an American mission college), and other higher educational institutions. Rich in historic interest, Kyoto is the site of the tombs of many famous Japanese; the old imperial palace as well as Nijd Castle (former palace of the shoguns), with their fine parks and gardens, are also in the city. In addition, Kyoto is a religious center, noted especially for its ancient Buddhist temples, its Heian shrine (a Shinto holy place), and its 59-ft (18-m) statue *(daibatsu)* of Buddha. Kyoto prefecture (1970 pop. 2,249,819), 1,784 sq mi (4,621 sq km), is centered principally in the region of the city of Kyoto.

kyphosis (kīfō'səs): see HUNCHBACK.

Kyrie eleison (kē'rēā ālā'ēsōn) [Gr.,=Lord, have mercy], in the Roman Catholic Church, prayer of the MASS coming after the introit, the only ordinary part of the traditional liturgy said not in Latin but in Greek. It has nine lines: "Lord have mercy (thrice), Christ have mercy (thrice), Lord have mercy (thrice)." As the first invariable hymn, the *Kyrie* is often the first piece in a musical Mass. An English version is used in the Anglican liturgy and in the reformed Roman Catholic vernacular liturgy. The phrase *Kyrie eleison* used by itself is, of course, common in the Eastern rites, but without the phrase *Christe eleison.* The corresponding prayer in the Russian Orthodox church is often called a Kyrie.

Kyushu (kyo͞o'sho͞o), island (1970 pop. 12,072,169), c.13,760 sq mi (35,640 sq km), S Japan. It is the third largest, southernmost, and most densely populated of the major islands of Japan. It is separated from Shikoku by the Bungo Strait and from Honshu by the Shimonoseki Strait; a railroad tunnel under the strait links Kyushu with Honshu. Mainly of volcanic origin, the island has a mountainous interior rising to 5,886 ft (1,794 m) in Kuju-san; Aso-san, Japan's largest active volcano, is on Kyushu, and there are many hot springs. The Chikugo (88 mi/142 km long), the island's longest river, waters an extensive rice-growing area in the northwest. Kyushu has a subtropical climate and receives much precipitation. Rice, tea, tobacco, sweet potatoes, fruits, wheat, and soybeans are major crops. Coal, zinc, and copper are mined in Kyushu, and raw silk is extensively produced. The island is noted for its porcelain (Satsuma and Hizen ware). The famous Imari ware was manufactured at the ancient town of Arita. Heavy industry is concentrated in N Kyushu, near Japan's oldest coal field; Kitakyushu, Fukuoka, and Omuta are major industrial centers. Nagasaki, the chief port of Kyushu, was the first Japanese port to receive Western trade. There are four national parks on the island.

Kyustendil (kyo͞ostĕndĕl'), city (1968 est. pop. 42,000), SW Bulgaria, near the Yugoslav border. Famous for its mineral springs used to heat hothouses, Kyustendil is a market city for fruit and other agricultural produce. There are varied light industries. The city's history dates to Roman times. It was the capital of an independent Bulgarian principality when the Turks took it in the 14th cent. The city remained under Turkish rule until 1878, when it became part of Bulgaria.

Kyzyl or **Kizil** (both: kĭzĭl'), city (1970 pop. 52,500), capital of Tuva Autonomous Republic, S Siberian USSR, on the Yenisei River. It services motor transport and has brickyards, sawmills, furniture factories, and food-processing plants. Founded in 1914, the city was called Belotsarsk until 1917 and Khem-Beldyr until 1926. It has a language, history, and literature research institute (founded in 1953).

Kyzyl-Kum or **Kizil Kum** (both: kəzŭl' ko͝om) [Turk.,=red sand], desert, c.115,000 sq mi (297,900 sq km), Central Asian USSR, in Kazakhstan and Uzbekistan. This vast region SE of the Aral Sea between the Amu Darya and Syr Darya rivers consists mainly of rocky areas covered by sparse vegetation and shifting sand dunes. Cotton, rice, and wheat are grown in river valleys and irrigated oases. Seminomadic tribesmen raise Karakul sheep and camels. Important gold deposits have been discovered in the desert.

L

L, 12th letter of the ALPHABET. It is a usual symbol for a lateral consonant, as in the English *lateral.* The Greek correspondent is lambda. L is the Roman numeral for 50.

La. For names beginning thus and not listed here, see second element; e.g., for La Ceiba, see CEIBA, LA.

La, chemical symbol of the element LANTHANUM.

Laadah (lā'ədə), Judah's grandson. 1 Chron. 4.21.

Laadan (lā'ədăn). **1** Ancestor of Joshua. 1 Chron. 7.26,27. **2** See LIBNI **1.**

Laaland: see LOLLAND, Denmark.

Laar, Pieter van: see LAER, PIETER VAN.

Labadie, Jean de, or **Jean de la Badie** (both: zhäN də lä bädē'), 1610–74, French mystic, founder of the Labadists, a quietist sect. He had been a Roman Catholic priest, but c.1650 he embraced Protestantism. He was a minister in Geneva (1659–66), then in Holland (until 1670). There under his leadership his congregation at Middelburg became a religious community dedicated to simple living, holding goods and children in common. The Dutch authorities found him too independent of the ecclesiastical discipline, and the community moved to Westphalia in 1670 and later to Altona. By 1732 the movement had died. Labadists settled in Maryland (1684), but the community failed before 1730.

Laban (lā'băn). **1** Father of Leah and Rachel and uncle of Jacob. The NUZI tablets contain the stories of Laban and Jacob. Gen. 24.29–60; 29–31. **2** Unidentified place in the desert. Deut. 1.1.

Labat, Jean Baptiste (zhäN bätēst' läbä'), 1663–1738, French Dominican missionary. Sent to the West Indies, he explored the islands, founded (1703) the city of Basse-Terre, and defended Guadeloupe against the English. Labat did valuable botanical research and wrote extensively about his travels.

Labé, Louise (lwēz läbā'), c.1520–1566, French poet. Her elegies and sonnets, in *Oeuvres* (1555), are love poems notable for their passion and honesty. She was nicknamed "La Belle Cordière."

Labé (läbā'), town (1961 est. pop. 11,609), W central Guinea, in the Fouta Jallon. It is the market center for a farm region where citrus fruit, bananas, vegetables, and rice are grown and cattle are raised. Labé was incorporated in the Mali empire in the early 13th cent. From the 16th to the 18th cent., after the decline of Mali, it was of commercial and political importance and served as a center of Islam. The FULANI settled there in the second half of the 18th cent., displacing the original inhabitants. Labé is today a leading center of Islam in Guinea.

Labe, river: see ELBE.

Labiche, Eugène Marin (özhĕn' märăN' läbēsh'), 1815–88, French playwright. His *Chapeau de paille d'Italie* (1851) was the first of many successful farcical comedies. Best-known is *Le Voyage de M. Perrichon* (with Édouard Martin, 1860).

Labille-Guiard, Adélaïde (ädālăēd' läbē'yə-gēär'), 1749–1803, French painter. Labille-Guiard was a painter of the French nobility before the Revolution and survived to paint the citizens of the Directory. Emerging from the 18th-century tradition of powdered wigs and shimmering satins, she captured informal moments in the lives of her subjects, frequently depicting them interrupted from some pastime. Her self-portrait (1785) is at the Metropolitan Museum of Art.

La Boétie, Étienne de (ātyĕn' də lä bôăsē'), 1530–63, French judge and writer. He served with Montaigne in the Bordeaux parlement and is immortalized in Montaigne's essay on friendship. La Boétie's writings include a few sonnets, translations from the classics, and an essay attacking absolute monarchy, *Discours sur la servitude volontaire; ou Contr'un* (tr. 1735, 1942).

labor: see BIRTH.

labor, term used both for the effort of performing a task and for the workers engaged in the activity. In ancient times most work was done by slaves (see SLAVERY). In the feudal period agricultural labor was in the main performed by the SERF. In medieval towns, however, the skilled artisans of the craft GUILDS became influential citizens. Many manual labor jobs were eliminated with the introduction of machinery (mid-18th cent.), thus creating a labor surplus (see INDUSTRIAL REVOLUTION). With increased competition for jobs and consequent decreasing wages, a form of labor contract came into use in Great Britain and its colonies, called indenture, by which people could hire themselves out for a certain number of years either for a lump sum of money or to pay off a debt. This practice disappeared by the end of the 19th cent. From the last quarter of the 19th cent. the condition of most manual labor has improved slowly in industrial countries through organization (see UNION, LABOR), permitting collective bargaining with employers and successful pressure on governments for protective legislation. In fact, the term *labor* is today most frequently used to signify organized labor. For labor disputes, see STRIKE. See also CHILD LABOR, MIGRANT LABOR, PEONAGE. See J. R. Commons et al., *History of Labour in the United States* (4 vol., 1918–35, repr. 1966); G. D. H. Cole, *A Short History of the British Working-Class Movement* (new ed. 1960); N. J. Ware, *Labor in Modern Industrial Society* (1935, repr. 1968); Alfred Kuhn, *Labor: Institutions and Economics* (rev. ed. 1967); M. W. Jernegan, *The Laboring and Dependent Classes in Colonial America* (1961); A. A. Paradis, *The Labor Reference Book* (1972).

labor, division of: see DIVISION OF LABOR.

labor, hours of. Until the Industrial Revolution the usual workday was from dawn to dusk and varied from 8 to 14 hr, depending upon the season and, during the Middle Ages, upon guild regulations. With the establishment of the factory system in the 18th and early 19th cent., the workday became longer, typically from 14 to 15 hr. In the early 19th cent., British trade unionists and other social reformers called for a decrease in the hours of labor without a decrease in pay. Factory apprentices won a 12-hour day in 1802, as did miners in 1833. In 1848 a 10-hour workday was legally established. In the United States, the Federal government introduced a 10-hour day among its employees in 1840, but few private businesses followed its example until after the Civil War. In the 1860s the U.S. labor movement began to demand an 8-hour day. The 8-hour movement was marked by strikes and violence; the most famous incident was the HAYMARKET SQUARE RIOT of 1886. In Great Britain the 9-hour day was enacted into law in 1874. As a result of labor shortages in Australia, the 8-hour day was established in the 1850s, well in advance of Great Britain, the United States, or continental Europe. Although labor unions in France and Germany agitated for the 8-hour day in the latter part of the 19th cent., they were unsuccessful. During the early part of the 20th cent., U.S. labor unions continued to press for the 8-hour day, but it was not until World War I that it became a common practice. In 1919, British workers in a wide variety of jobs won a 48-hour work week; in the same year France and Germany enacted 8-hour workday laws. The most significant wage and hour legislation in the United States was enacted during the New Deal period of the 1930s, when an 8-hour day and a 40-hour week were mandated for employees of firms holding government contracts and when, by the Fair Labor Standards Act of 1938, the work week was set at 44 hours (later reduced to 40 hours) for workers employed by firms engaged in interstate commerce. Besides the United States, the 40-hour week is now firmly established in Great Britain, Canada, Australia, and France. In other European countries, as well as in Latin America and the Soviet Union, the 48-hour week is more common. The 35-hour work week is becoming quite common for office workers in the United States. In the early 1970s labor unions began to press for a 4-day work week, and some companies, even without union pressure, began to institute the 4-day week. In some cases the number of hours is reduced to 32, whereas in others it has remained at 40 (i.e., four 10-hour days a week).

Labor, United States Department of, Federal executive department established in 1913 and charged with administering and enforcing statutes that promote the welfare of U.S. wage earners, improve their working conditions, and advance their opportunities for profitable employment. Before gaining separate cabinet status in 1913, labor had been represented by various Federal agencies. The first such agency was established in 1884 as the Bureau of Labor within the Dept. of the Interior. In 1888 an independent department was created, but in 1903 labor was placed in the new Dept. of Commerce and Labor, which was reorganized as two cabinet-level departments in 1913. The Dept. of Labor has six major specialized divisions: Bureau of International Labor Affairs; MANPOWER ADMINISTRATION; Labor-Management Services Administration; Bureau of Labor Statistics; Employment Standards Administration; and Occupational Safety and Health Administration. The Bureau of International Labor Affairs deals with the interaction among U.S. foreign policy, foreign labor developments, and U.S. labor developments. The Labor-Management Services Administration enforces Federal laws pertaining to union activities and union-related employer activities. The Bureau of Labor Statistics, a direct descendent of the 1884 Bureau of Labor, gathers data in the field of labor economics. The agencies of the Employment Standards Administration administer Federal labor legislation and the administration conducts research to support their programs. Agencies and the legislation they administer include: Wage and Hour Division, minimum wage and fringe benefits; Office of Workmen's Compensation Programs and Office of Federal Employees Compensation, workmen's compensation for job-related injuries; and Office of Federal Contract Compliance, executive order prohibiting discrimination in employment in federally involved contracts. The Women's Bureau encourages better utilization of women in the economy. The Occupational Safety and Health Administration is responsible for ensuring the best possible U.S. working conditions in terms of safety and health.

Labor Day, holiday celebrated in the United States and Canada on the first Monday in September to honor the laborer. It was inaugurated by the Knights of Labor in 1882 and made a national holiday by the U.S. Congress in 1894. In most other countries—and among the leftists in the United States and Canada—May Day (May 1) is celebrated instead.

labor law, legislation dealing with human beings in their capacity as workers or wage earners. The Industrial Revolution, by introducing the machine and factory production, created a class of workers dependent on wages as their source of income. The terms of the labor contract, working conditions, and the relations between workers and employers early became matters of public concern. In England, Parliament was averse to legislating on these subjects because of the prevailing policy of LAISSEZ FAIRE. The earliest factory law (1802) dealt with the health, safety, and morals of children employed in textile mills, and subsequent laws regulated their hours and working conditions. An act of 1833 provided for inspection to enforce the law. Young mine workers were first protected in 1842, women in 1844. Although labor unions were legalized in 1825, agreements among their members to seek better hours and wages were punishable as conspiracy under the common law until they were legalized by acts of Parliament in 1871 and 1906. In the United States early legislation was aimed at improving conditions of employment and at making places of work safer and more healthful. As in Great Britain, labor organizing was discouraged by the common law doctrine of conspiracy; the Massachusetts supreme court abolished the doctrine in 1842, and the decision was followed in most of the other states. Indenture and the importing of contract labor were prohibited, and immigration has been restricted from time to time to minimize competition in the labor market. Night work and work in hazardous occupations have been prohibited to women and children. Legal minimums have been set for wages in certain occupations (see MINIMUM WAGE), and other laws require rest periods and sanitary conveniences in industry and fix the minimum age at which children may be employed. Sweatshop labor and child labor were discouraged through laws regulating interstate commerce. The working conditions of railway employees and seamen were standardized. Employees of the Federal government were early granted an 8-hr day, and by the Wages and Hours Act of 1938 Congress established minimum hours and wages in many basic industries. A number of laws have provided for workmen's compensation, old-age pensions, and a system of old-age insurance. Congress exempted (1916) unions from the antitrust laws, and the use of injunctions in labor disputes, begun in 1877, was outlawed by Congress in 1932, although the use of injunctions was later reestablished by law. The National Labor Relations Act of 1935 established the right of workers to organize and required employers to accept collective bargaining as a ruling principle in industry. In 1938 the Fair Labor Standards Act provided for minimum wages and overtime payments for workers in interstate commerce. During World War II a no-strike pledge by union leaders insured labor peace, but the widespread outbreak of strikes after the war resulted in a strong movement for more restrictive labor legislation. This led to the TAFT-HARTLEY ACT, which was passed over the veto of President Truman in 1947. Incorporating the guarantees of collective bargaining found in the National Labor Relations Act, it declared illegal such union practices as secondary boycotts and the closed shop. It also gave the President the power to secure an injunction to postpone for 80 days any strike that might affect the national security. Under the act, officers of unions were required to file affidavits that they were not members of the Communist party. Later the Federal Mediation and Conciliation Service was established as an independent agency. Congressional investigations of labor-management corruption led to the passage of the LANDRUM-GRIFFIN ACT in 1959. It guaranteed freedom of speech and of assembly for union members, and it provided for the regular election of union officers by secret ballot and for periodic and detailed financial reports by unions. See H. A. Millis and E. C. Brown, *From the Wagner Act to Taft-Hartley* (1950, repr. 1961); C. O. Gregory, *Labor and the Law* (2d rev. ed. 1961); U.S. Bureau of Labor Standards, *The Growth of Labor Law in the United States* (1967); S. J. Mueller, *Labor Law and Legislation* (4th ed. 1968); Philip Selznick, *Law, Society, and Industrial Justice* (1969); S. I. Schlossberg, *Organizing and the Law* (1971).

Labor-Management Reporting and Disclosure Act: see LANDRUM-GRIFFIN ACT.

Labor Relations Act: see NATIONAL LABOR RELATIONS BOARD; TAFT-HARTLEY LABOR ACT.

labor union: see UNION, LABOR.

Labouchere, Henry du Pré (lă"bōōshâr'), 1831–1912, British politician and journalist. Following diplomatic service (1854–64), he sat in the House of Commons (1880–1906) as a Radical. He was a supporter of William Gladstone and an anti-imperialist. He founded (1877) and edited *Truth,* a magazine devoted to the exposure of social fraud. See Hesketh Pearson, *Labby* (1937); study by R. J. Hind (1972).

La Bourdonnais, Bertrand François, comte Mahé de (bĕrtrăN' frăNswă', kôNt măā' də lä bōōrdônā'), 1699–1753, French naval officer. He entered the service of the French India Company and in 1724 distinguished himself in the capture of Mahé (named in his honor). Governor of Île de France and Île de Bourbon (later Mauritius and Réunion; 1735–46), he was placed (1740) in command of the French fleet in India. He relieved Mahé (1741), and after the outbreak of hostilities with Great Britian captured (1746) Madras, but he quarreled with Joseph François DUPLEIX and was removed (1746) from his governorship. On his return to France he was imprisoned (1748) in the Bastille on charges of poor administration and embezzlement. In 1751 he was tried and acquitted, largely through pressure of popular opinion.

Labour party, British political party. The Labour party was founded in 1900 after several generations of preparatory trade union politics made possible by the Reform Bills of 1867 and 1884, which enfranchised urban workers. Although the Labour Representation League, organized in 1869, elected parliamentary representatives, they were absorbed into the Liberal party. A Marxist organization, the Social Democratic Federation, was founded by H. M. HYNDMAN in 1881; but more important for the history of the Labour party was the founding of the FABIAN SOCIETY (1883) and the Independent Labour party (ILP; 1893). With the help of the Fabian Society and the Trades Union Congress, the ILP in 1900 set up the Labour Representation Committee, renamed the Labour party in 1906. The new party elected 29 members to Parliament in 1906; in the two elections of 1910 it elected 40 and 42. Its strength lay in the industrial North and in Welsh mining areas; the evolutionary socialism espoused by the Fabians was the dominant ideology. At the outbreak of World War I, Ramsay MACDONALD led a pacifist wing of the party, but the majority of the party supported the war effort, and the party's leader, Arthur HENDERSON, served in the wartime coalition governments. Until 1918 the party was distinctly a federation of trade unions and socialist groups and had no individual members. After the war economic depression, the growing political consciousness of the working classes, and the split in the Liberal party gave Labour a national following. In 1918, Labour withdrew completely from the coalition, and in 1922 it became the second largest party in the House of Commons and thus the official opposition. In 1924 the party formed its first ministry, with MacDonald as prime minister. As Labour was a minority in Parliament and depended on Liberal support, the enactment of legislation proved difficult, and the government's domestic program of unemployment relief and housing differed little from that of its Conservative predecessor. Effective primarily in foreign affairs, the ministry recognized the USSR. The party was turned out of office in Oct., 1924, in an election marked by Conservative exploitation of the Zinoviev letter (see under ZINOVIEV, GREGORI). In 1929, Labour formed another minority ministry. MacDonald and Philip SNOWDEN reacted to the severe depression with conservative economic policies that involved reducing unemployment relief. When the majority of the cabinet refused to accede, MacDonald formed (1931) a coalition government, but he and the Labour leaders who joined him were expelled from the party. Heavily defeated in the election of 1931, the Labour party moved slightly to the left, advocating nationalization of major industries and more progressive taxation. In the next few years Labour found new leaders in Clement Attlee (later Earl ATTLEE), Herbert MORRISON, and Ernest BEVIN. In the early 1930s the party passed anti-war resolutions and advocated collective security through the League of Nations, but it favored aid to the republican government in the Spanish civil war and eventually came to accept rearmament against the threat from Nazi Germany. After the outbreak of World War II, Labour agreed to join Winston Churchill's coalition government; Bevin as minister of labor and Attlee as deputy prime minister, together with other Labour ministers, took charge of domestic affairs during the war years. In 1945 the party won an overwhelming electoral victory, and Attlee became prime minister in Labour's first majority government. The new government nationalized the Bank of England, the fuel and power industries (coal, electricity, gas, and atomic energy), transportation, and most of the iron and steel industry. It also enacted a comprehensive social security system, which included a national health service. In the areas of colonial and foreign policy, it granted independence to India and Pakistan, Burma, and Ceylon, and allied itself with the United States in a strong anti-Communist posture. Faced with postwar shortages and the problems of reconstruction, Attlee's government encountered severe financial difficulties, despite American assistance. Rationing continued to be a necessity, economic recovery was slow, and the cost of rearmament increased the strains on the economy. The government barely maintained its majority in the general elections of 1950, and the following year it was defeated by the Conservatives. During the long period of opposition that followed (the Conservatives were returned to power in 1955 and in 1959), the Labour party argued and almost split on questions of disarmament, aid to developing countries, and furtherance of socialism at home. When Attlee and other elder leaders retired and Hugh GAITSKELL became party leader, Aneurin BEVAN, leading the left wing of the party, unsuccessfully contested Gaitskell's position. Although Bevan was soon reconciled with the party leadership, his supporters continued to urge a policy of diplomatic neutralism and unilateral disarmament, in addition to a strong socialist program. The party's right-wing, on the other hand, argued that prosperity had diminished the appeal of socialism to the average worker and that the party should adopt a broader, more pragmatic program. As Gaitskell consolidated his position as leader in the early 1960s the party achieved a new solidarity, and Harold WILSON, who became leader on Gaitskell's death in 1963, was able to lead the party to victory in 1964. He was prime minister until the Conservative party returned to power in 1970. Wilson's administration was marked by a continued decline in Britain's international political and economic position, which gave little opportunity for social innovation. After 1970, the Labour party, in opposition, again found it difficult to present a united front. The reversal of the party's position on Britain's entry into the Common Market, after having earlier supported it, and a renewed call for further nationalization of industry were indications of a greater left-wing militancy within the party. The party returned to power as a result of the elections of Feb., 1974, but as a minority government. Mr. Wilson's second administration began renegotiation of the terms of Britain's membership in the Common Market and announced plans for large-scale nationalization. Despite continuing economic difficulties it called new elections in Oct., 1974, and won a small majority. See studies by C. F. Brand (1964) and Henry Pelling (4th ed. 1972); G. D. H. Cole, *History of the Labour Party from 1914* (1948); R. T. McKenzie, *British Political Parties* (1955); R. E. Dowse, *Left in the Centre: The Independent Labour Party, 1893–1940* (1966); W. T. Rodgers and Bernard Donoughue, *The People into Parliament* (1966); Harold Wilson, *The Labour Government 1964–1970* (1971).

Labrador: see LABRADOR-UNGAVA; NEWFOUNDLAND, Canada.

labradorite (lăb'rədôrīt", lăbrədôr'īt), variety of plagioclase FELDSPAR.

Labrador retriever, breed of large SPORTING DOG whose origins are obscure but whose immediate ancestors were developed in Newfoundland and brought to England in the early 1800s. It stands about 23 in. (58.4 cm) high at the shoulder and weighs between 60 and 75 lb (27.2–34.1 kg). The dense, short coat is flat and oily, providing great resistance to cold weather and icy water. Its color may be black, chocolate, or yellow. The Labrador retriever is widely used to hunt both waterfowl and upland game birds; its loyal and gentle disposition has made it very popular as a companion dog. See DOG.

Labrador-Ungava, peninsular region of E Canada, c.550,000 sq mi (1,424,500 sq km), bounded on the W by Hudson Bay, on the N by Hudson Strait and Ungava Bay, on the E by the Atlantic Ocean, and on the S by the St. Lawrence River. It is almost completely unpopulated. The western four fifths of the peninsula belongs to Nouveau Québec (Ungava) and Saguenay counties of Québec prov. The eastern fifth, called simply Labrador, is part of Newfoundland. The region south of Ungava Bay, originally a possession of the Hudson's Bay Company, was made a part of the Northwest Territories in 1869, and later (1895) became a separate district. In 1912 it was added to Québec prov., but in 1927 the eastern coast was awarded to Newfoundland by the British Privy Council. The northern part of the region is a cold, barren tundra; the southern part is covered by coniferous forests. Geologically part of the Canadian Shield, the glaciated peninsula has many lakes and streams. There are vast and largely untapped mineral, hydroelectric, and timber resources on the peninsula. Since the mid-1950s the region's development has been aided by the construction of new ports and railheads at Sept-Îles and Port Cartier on the St. Lawrence River, which provide outlets for rich, new iron ore mines in the interior; asbestos, titanium, and copper are also mined. The largest hydroelectric facility is at Churchill Falls.

La Brea (lə brā'ə), area, S Calif., formerly in Rancho La Brea. The La Brea asphalt pits, which yielded prehistoric animal and plant remains, are in Hancock Park, Los Angeles. The first fossils were found in 1875; since 1906 the pits have been extensively explored.

Labrouste, Henri (äNrē' läbrōōst'), 1801–75, French architect. He was among the first to make effective architectural use of metal construction, as in his treatment of the reading room of the Bibliothèque Ste Geneviève (1843–50), Paris, in which the ceiling domes were supported upon an exposed iron framework. Labrouste also made extensive alterations on the Bibliothèque nationale.

La Bruyère, Jean de (zhäN də lä brüyĕr'), 1645–96, French writer. He lived (1684–96) as tutor in the house of the prince de Condé. His great work, *Les Caractères de Théophraste, traduits du grec; avec Les Caractères ou les mœurs de ce siècle,* appeared in 1688 and subsequently in revised and augmented editions until the ninth (1696). The first, and least, part of this work is a translation of Theophrastus; the balance is a series of random character sketches, maxims, and literary discussions, written in a terse, ironic style. La Bruyère's strong moral views on the contemporary economy, on the widespread poverty, and on the idle life of the nobility gained lasting attention. He was less a reformer than a detached observer. A defender of classical writers in the "quarrel of the ancients and moderns," he was admitted to the French Academy in 1693.

Labuan (ləbo͞o'ən, lä"bo͞oän'), island, 38 sq mi (98 sq km), part of Sabah, Malaysia, off N Borneo, in the South China Sea. Coconuts, rubber, and rice are the main products. Victoria (est. pop. 4,000), the chief town, has a fine harbor and an airport and is the shipping center for much of N Borneo. Labuan was ceded to Great Britain by the sultan of Brunei in 1846 and became a crown colony in 1848. It was included in the STRAITS SETTLEMENTS in 1906 and in 1946 was joined to British North Borneo, which became SABAH in 1963.

laburnum (ləbûr'nəm) or **golden chain,** small tree *(Laburnum anagyroides)* of the family Leguminosae (PULSE family) with decorative dark green leaves and sprays of bright yellow flowers. It is native to Europe, where, as in America, it is widely grown for ornament. The leaves and seeds are poisonous to cattle. The durable and hard heartwood takes a high polish; it is used in cabinetwork for inlays. The laburnum is also called the bean tree. Laburnum is classified in the division MAGNOLIOPHYTA, class Magnoliopsida, order Rosales, family Leguminosae.

labyrinth (lăb'ərĭnth), intricate building of chambers and passages, often constructed so as to perplex and confuse a person inside. In Egypt, Amenemhet III of the XII dynasty built himself a funeral temple in the

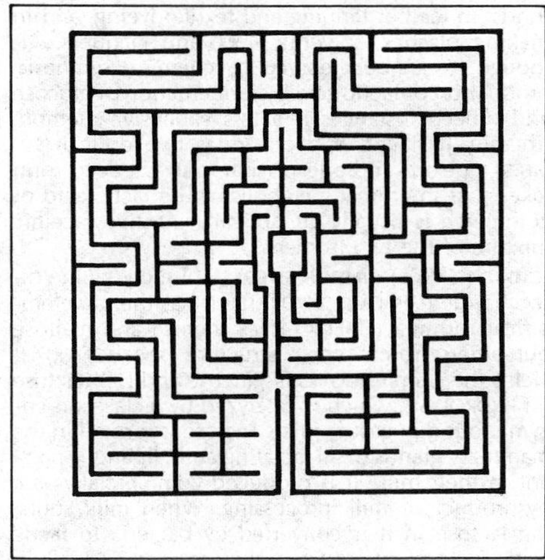

Labyrinth

form of a great labyrinth near Lake Moeris. More celebrated was a labyrinth in Crete built, according to Greek myth, by DAEDALUS to house the Minotaur (see MINOS).

labyrinth fish: see BETTA; CLIMBING PERCH; GOURAMI.

lac, resinous exudation from the bodies of females of a species of scale insect (*Tachardia lacca*), of the same family as the cochineal insect, from which SHELLAC is prepared. India is the chief source of shellac, although some is obtained from other areas in Southeast Asia. The insects feed on the sap of the twigs of certain tropical trees, some of which are cultivated for this purpose. The resinous secretion hardens upon exposure to air and forms a protective incrustation around the female and young, which are thus held fast to the twigs. The twigs are scraped to remove the incrustation; this crude lac material is known as stick lac. If the stick lac is crushed, the wood splinters and other foreign materials removed, and the red coloring matter produced by the insects dissolved out, the residue when dried is seed lac. Seed lac is melted, filtered, and stretched into thin sheets, which are broken into flakes when cool. Orange-colored shellac is made from these flakes by dissolving them in alcohol. White shellac is made from bleached lac.

Lacaille, Nicolas Louis de (nēkôlä' lwē də läkä'yə), 1713–62, French astronomer. As a result of his success in making meridional measurements in France under the patronage of the duke of Bourbon he was elected to the French Academy. He also became professor of mathematics at the Collège Mazarin, where he established an observatory in 1746. He was at the head of an astronomical expedition (1750–54) to the Cape of Good Hope. There he made observations of 10,000 southern stars, recording their positions; made the first measurement of an arc of the meridian of South Africa; and determined the lunar and solar parallax. Among his works are *Astronomiae fundamenta* (1757), *Tables solaires* (1758), *Coelum australe stelliferum* (1763), and *Journal historique du voyage fait au cap de Bonne-Esperance* (1763).

La Calprenède, Gautier de Costes, sieur de (gōtyā' də kôst syör də lä kälprənĕd'), 1609?–1663, French novelist and dramatist. His best-known works were *Cassandre* (10 vol., 1642) and *Cléopâtre* (12 vol., 1647), romances esteemed in their time for their austere morality and lofty sentiment.

Laccadive, Minicoy, and Amindivi Islands (lăk'ədīv, mĭn'ĭkoi, ămĭndē'vī), island group (1971 pop. 31,798), 11 sq mi (28 sq km), SW India, in the Arabian Sea off the coast of Kerala state. The capital of this group of 26 islands (10 are inhabited) is Kavaratti Island. Minicoy is the largest island. The population, mainly Muslim, engages in fishing and copra production. Malayalam is the main language except on Minicoy, where Mahl is spoken. The islands compose the Union Territory of Lakshadweep, which is administered by the home minister in the central government of India with an appointed local advisory council.

lace, patterned openwork fabric made by plaiting, knotting, looping, or twisting. The finest lace is made from linen thread. Handmade laces include needlepoint and bobbin lace, tatting, CROCHET WORK, and some fabrics made by netting and darning. Lace was developed prior to the 16th cent. from the drawn work, cutwork, and lacis (darning on squares of net) of the embroiderers' craft. With drawn work, more and more threads were removed until the ground vanished altogether. A design was executed and its principal line supported the complete pattern. The first of such laces, reticella, originated in Venice and was based on geometric forms. Later, as laceworkers sought relief from the restrictions of symmetrical design, the illogical but beautiful designs of *punto in aria* (literally, a stitch in the air) were first created. The richest, most sumptuous of these needlepoint laces was the Venetian raised point of the 17th cent. The vogue for lace began c.1540, and pattern books began to appear. Early reticella designs usually included pointed or scalloped edges. By the time of Charles I lace was used extravagantly for both costume and interior decorating; by 1643 lacemaking had become an established industry. In France patterns became increasingly more detailed and delicate; the light, flowery *point de France* was used for every conceivable decorative purpose. Later the laces of Alençon, Argentan, and Valencienne exemplified French style and design. The making of bobbin, pillow, or bone lace, which is mentioned as early as 1495, passed from Italy to Flanders, reaching its height of production there in the 18th cent. Laces, often named for their location of origination, are of many types. Valenciennes is a fine, diamond-meshed lace much used for trimmings and ruffles. Mechlin is of similar type, but filmier; torchon is a simple, loose lace, made and used by peasants all over Europe; Honiton, one of the fine English laces, has a net foundation with appliqués of delicate, handmade braid. Brussels is a rich lace of several varieties. Duchesse has exquisite patterns with much raised work. Maltese is coarse and heavy, usually made of silk. Chantilly is a delicate mesh with ornate patterns, originally made of the yellowish undyed silk called blonde, later often dyed black. *Point d'Espagne* is lace of gold or silver thread. A number of laces fall outside a strict classification. Guipure has a heavy pattern formed by a braid with a less valuable core covered with fine silk, gold, or silver thread. Limerick lace is tambour work on net. Renaissance or Battenberg lace is of heavy tape formed into a pattern and filled in with lace stitches. Carrickmacross is cutwork lace. So-called English point or *point d'Angleterre* is Flemish point, at one time smuggled into England and renamed. *Filet* is a combination of knotting and darning, reminiscent of the earliest lace forms attempted. Cutwork, or various combinations of early lace forms with EMBROIDERY, also formed an important step in lacemaking. The better-known knotted laces are tatting and MACRAMÉ; macramé evolved from the early Italian *punto a groppo.* Crocheted lace reached its finest development in Ireland. Knitted laces, for which many intricate patterns survive, have been mainly of peasant use. The chief modern centers of lacemaking are France, Belgium, England, Ireland, and Italy. Machine-made lace first appeared c.1760, and by 1813 a bobbinet machine was perfected. After 1832 cotton thread somewhat replaced linen. In the 20th cent. many lace patterns have been revived and modified, and called Cluny lace. See Marian Powys, *Lace and Lace-Making* (1953).

Lacedaemon, Greece: see LACONIA.

Lacépède, Bernard Germain Étienne de la Ville, comte de (bĕrnär' zhĕrmăN' ātyĕn' də lä vēl kôNt də läsāpĕd'), 1756–1825, French naturalist. As a youth he showed considerable talent in both music and physics and won the favor of BUFFON, whose work in animal classification he was encouraged to continue. Buffon secured him a position at the Jardin du Roi (later the Jardin des Plantes). His best-known works deal with the oviparous quadrupeds, reptiles, fishes, and whales; they are frequently printed with Buffon's works, which they supplement. Lacépède was active in politics and was exiled during the Reign of Terror. After his return he gave up scientific work for a political career and held several state offices.

La Ceppède, Jean de (zhäN də lä sĕpĕd'), 1550–1622, French poet and magistrate. In 1608 he was appointed president of the Court of the Exchequer of Provence. After centuries of oblivion, he is again receiving recognition for his *Théorèmes spirituels* (c.1621), a two-volume collection of sacred sonnets notable for their anticipatory use of symbolism.

La Chaise, François d'Aix de (fräNswä' dāks də lä shĕz), 1624–1709, French Jesuit, confessor of Louis XIV after 1675. His influence at court was considerable. The great cemetery in NE Paris called Père-Lachaise is named for him.

Lachaise, Gaston, 1882–1935, American sculptor, b. Paris. After studying in Paris, he emigrated to the United States in 1906. For 12 years he worked in Boston and New York City, chiefly for the sculptors H. H. Kitson and Paul Manship, who employed him to execute details on some of their commissions. Lachaise made decorations in New York for the Telephone and Telegraph Building, the RCA Building, and the International Building at Rockefeller Center. Perhaps his most famous works, however, are single figures, such as his *Standing Woman* (Mus. of Modern Art, New York City), which has monumental charm and extraordinary vitality. See study by Hilton Kramer et al. (1967).

Lachesis (lăch'ĭsĭs): see FATES.

Lachine (ləshēn'), city (1971 pop. 44,423), S Que., Canada, on Montreal island, at the east end of Lake St. Louis just SW of Montreal. Its industries include iron and steel foundries and the manufacture of tires, wire, and tiles. Lachine was first settled in 1675 and in 1689 was the scene of a massacre by the Iroquois Indians. The city is the southwest terminal of the **Lachine Canal,** connecting Lake St. Louis with the St. Lawrence River at Montreal. Constructed between 1821 and 1825 (later enlarged) to bypass the Lachine Rapids of the St. Lawrence, the canal has been superseded by the St. Lawrence Seaway canals.

Lachish (lā'kĭsh), ancient city, S Palestine (present-day Israel), SW of Jerusalem. It is mentioned in the Tell-el-Amarna letters and was one of the Amorite cities allied against the Gibeonites and destroyed by Joshua. Rehoboam fortified it, and Amaziah was murdered there. It was besieged (701 B.C.) by Sennacherib. Later, Micah denounced it. Excavations were begun in 1935; they show that Lachish had been populated since c.3200 B.C. and was a thriving community as early as the 17th cent. B.C. The finds include 21 ostraca, or potsherds, written in ink. They were written (c.589 B.C.) in Hebrew by local commanders to their officers when Lachish was being threatened by the Babylonians under Nebuchadnezzar. The letters are of great linguistic and historic value. Lachish is frequently mentioned in the Bible (Joshua 10; 15.39; 2 Kings 14.19; 18.14, 17; 19.8; 2 Chron. 11.9; Neh. 11.30; Micah 1.13).

Lachute (ləsho͞ot'), town (1971 pop. 11,813), S Que., Canada, on the North River, W of Montreal. It is at the foot of the Laurentian Mts. Textiles and lumber, wood, and paper products are made.

Lackawanna (lăkəwä'nə), city (1970 pop. 28,657), Erie co., W N.Y., on Lake Erie; inc. 1909. Lackawanna is one of the major steelmaking centers in the United States. Its commercial and cultural life centers around nearby Buffalo. The spectacular Basilica of Our Lady of Victory there is a Roman Catholic shrine.

Lackawanna, river, 35 mi (56 km) long, rising in NE Pa. and flowing southwest to join the Susquehanna River near Pittston. It crosses the chief anthracite-coal region of the state, passing the cities of Scranton, Dunmore, Dickson City, and Carbondale.

Lackland Air Force Base, U.S. military installation, 6,835 acres (2,766 hectares), S Texas, W of San Antonio; est. 1941. It is a major air force training center.

Laclede, Pierre (pyĕr läklĕd'), c.1724–1778, French pioneer in the United States. His surname was Liguest, but he adopted the name Pierre Laclede. He went to New Orleans in 1755 and was a member of the fur-trading firm that received (1762) a monopoly of the fur trade of the Missouri region. Accompanied by his stepson René Auguste CHOUTEAU, he led a party up the Mississippi River to found a trading post. Since the region east of the river was transferred to Great Britain in 1763, Laclede established (1764) his post on the west bank. It was the beginning of the city of St. Louis.

Laclos, Pierre Ambroise François Choderlos de (pyĕr äNbrwäz' fräNswä' shôdĕrlō' də läklō'), 1741–1803, French novelist and general, known as Choderlos de Laclos. He is best known for *Les Liaisons dangereuses* (1782; tr. *Dangerous Connections,* 1784, and *Dangerous Acquaintances,* 1924), a novel of cynical seduction whose savage tone contrasted with the vogue for high moral sentiment established by Rousseau. Laclos was also the author of *Poésies fugitives* (1782) and collaborated on *Galerie des États Généraux* (1789). He commanded troops both under the Directory and under Napoleon.

Lacolle (läkôl'), village (1971 pop. 1,254), S Que., Canada, S of Montreal and near the U.S. border. During the War of 1812, an invading American army was defeated in the area by the British on March 30, 1814.

Lacombe, Albert (älbĕr' läkôNb'), 1827–1916, French Canadian Roman Catholic missionary. He studied at Assumption College in Quebec prov. before he joined the Oblate order and was ordained (1849). Lacombe was one of the first Roman Catholic missionaries sent (1850) to the Canadian Northwest. There he served the Indians and was known as the Apostle of the Cree and the Blackfoot. He translated the New Testament into Cree and also wrote a grammar (1874) and dictionary (1874) of the Cree language. See biography by Katherine Hughes (1911).

La Condamine, Charles Marie de (shärl märē' də lä kôNdämēn'), 1701–74, French traveler and mathematical geographer. He was one of a group sent to Peru in 1735 to measure the length of an arc of one degree of the meridian at the equator. While in South America he made the first scientific exploration of the Amazon region. His journal was published in 1751.

Laconia (ləkō'nēə) or **Lacedaemon** (lăsədē'mən), ancient region, S Peloponnesus, Greece, bounded on the W by Messenia and on the N by Arcadia and Argolis. On the Eurotas (now Evrotás), the principal river, stood SPARTA, the capital. Sparta dominated the region, despite the existence of many other towns, until the rise of the second ACHAEAN LEAGUE in the 3d and 2d cent. B.C. Laconia (now Lakonías) is today a nome of Greece.

Laconia, city (1970 pop. 14,888), seat of Belknap co., central N.H., near lakes Winnisquam and Winnipesaukee and on the Winnipesaukee River; settled c.1761, inc. as a city 1893. It is a popular summer and winter resort and the industrial and trade center of a lake resort and farming region.

Lacordaire, Jean Baptiste Henri (zhäN bätēst' äNrē' läkôrdĕr'), 1802–61, French Roman Catholic preacher and liberal. Ordained in 1827, he came under the influence of LAMENNAIS and collaborated with him on *Avenir,* a journal advocating ULTRAMONTANISM, complete freedom of the church from the state, and a wide program of democratic reform. After papal condemnation of the journal, Lacordaire submitted. He became known as one of the greatest Catholic preachers; his sermons at Notre-Dame in Paris were the literary and social sensation of the day. He entered the Dominican order and was responsible for the revival of that order in France. Always a liberal, Lacordaire greeted the revolution of 1848 with enthusiasm and sat for a time as a deputy on the left. The coup d'etat of Napoleon III sent him into voluntary exile after he had attacked the government unsparingly. In 1861 he was elected to the French Academy. See biography by L. C. Sheppard (1964).

Lacoste, René (rənā' läkôst'), 1905–, French tennis player. He won the French singles championship (1925, 1927, and 1929), the British singles championship (1925, 1928), and the U.S. singles championship (1926, 1927). He was a member of the French team that won the Davis cup in 1927 and in 1928. He wrote *Lacoste on Tennis* (1928).

lacquer, solution of film-forming materials, natural or synthetic, usually applied as an ornamental or protective coating. Quick-drying synthetic lacquers are used to coat automobiles, furniture, textiles, paper, and metalware. The lacquer formula may be varied to impart durability, hardness, gloss, or imperviousness to water. Nitrocellulose (pyroxylin) lacquers are the most widely employed. Slower-drying natural lacquers contain oleoresins obtained from the juice of trees, especially of *Rhus vernicifera,* a sumac of SE Asia. Lacquer work was one of the earliest industrial arts of the Orient. It was highly developed in India; the Chinese inlaid lacquer work with ivory, jade, coral, or abalone and were unrivaled in making articles carved from it. The art spread to Korea, then to Japan, where it took new forms, notably gold lacquer work. Fine Oriental ware may have more than 40 coats, each being dried and smoothed with a whetstone before application of the next. The ware may be decorated in color, gold, or silver and enhanced by modeled reliefs, engraving, or carving. Buddhist monasteries encouraged the art and now preserve some of the oldest pieces extant; in the temple of Horyu-ji, near Nara, Japan, is a Chinese-made sword scabbard of the 8th cent. Notable lacquer artists include Ogata KORIN (17th cent.) and Shibata Yeshin (19th cent.). In the 17th cent., Western European imitations were popularized as JAPANNING and carried to great perfection in France in the *vernis Martin* developed by the Martin brothers under Louis XV. Commercial production of lacquer work in the 19th cent. resulted in a decline in quality. See Tomio Yoshino, *Japanese Lacquer Ware* (1959); A. C. Newell, *Coloring, Finishing and Painting Wood* (rev. ed. 1961); K. Herberts, *Oriental Lacquer: Art and Technique* (1962).

lacrimal gland: see TEARS.

La Crosse (lə krôs), city (1970 pop. 51,153), seat of La Crosse co., W Wis., at the foot of high bluffs on the Mississippi, where the La Crosse and Black rivers meet; inc. 1856. Air-conditioning systems, rubber footwear, welling equipment, clothing, metal products, and vending machines are made in La Crosse. A French fur-trading post was there in the late 18th cent., and later the city had a thriving lumber industry. The Univ. of Wisconsin at La Crosse, Viterbo College, Western Wisconsin Technical Institute, and a U.S. fish hatchery and experimental farm are in La Crosse. The city also has a zoo, an aquarium, a historical museum, and a wildlife project.

lacrosse (ləkrôs'), soccerlike ball and goal game usually played outdoors. It is played by two teams of 10 players each on a field 60 to 70 yd (54.86 to 64.01 m) wide by 110 yd (100.58 m) long. Two goals face each other 80 yd (73.15 m) apart; each cone-shaped goal is 6 ft (1.8 m) square at the mouth and 7 ft (2.13 m) deep. The ball, about 8 in. (20 cm) in circumference and about 5 oz (.14 kg) in weight, is made of hard rubber. The stick, or crosse—from which the game gets its name because of its resemblance to a bishop's crosier—consists of a handle and an adjustable, pocketlike meshwork head in which the ball is received, carried, and passed. Teams direct their play toward advancing the ball so that it can be hurled with the crosse or kicked into the opponent's goal (each goal counting one point) and toward defending their own goal. The team scoring the most points wins. Only the goalkeeper may touch the ball with his hands, and no field man may enter the crease—the 18 ft x 12 ft (5.49 m x 3.66 m) area surrounding the goal. Lacrosse is a game of rough physical contact; personal and technical fouls are penalized by disqualification or by temporary suspensions (as in ice hockey) that leave the penalized team with a player handicap. A referee and a judge are the officials. A game is divided into four quarters of 15 min each; two overtime periods of 5 min each are played in the event of a tie. The game was developed as a war-training exercise by North American Indians. Called "baggataway," it was a violent game with few fixed rules. It was adopted and named lacrosse by French settlers, and it became increasingly popular. In 1856 the Montreal Lacrosse Club was organized, and four years later the rules of the game were standardized. After the Canadian Parliament adopted (1867) lacrosse as the national game of Canada, the National Lacrosse Association (now the Canadian Lacrosse Association) was established as the governing body of the sport. Lacrosse has attracted a wide following of amateurs since that time, and the game was played professionally in Canada by 12-man teams between 1920 and 1932. Lacrosse was introduced into the United States in the 1870s. It is now a popular college, secondary school, and club game in the eastern United States in the spring. It is particularly popular in Maryland. The U.S. Intercollegiate Lacrosse Association supervises college play. Lacrosse is also popular in Great Britain and Australia. Women's lacrosse, developed in England in the early 1900s, is less rough than the men's game. See A. M. Weyand and M. R. Roberts, *The Lacrosse Story* (1965); P. E. Hartman, *Lacrosse Fundamentals* (1968).

La Cruz, Ramón de: see CRUZ, RAMÓN DE LA.

Lactantius, Lucius Caelius Firmianus (lo͞o'shəs sē'lēəs fûrmēā'nəs lăktăn'shəs), c.260–340 A.D., Christian author and apologist, b. Africa. He taught rhetoric at Diocletian's school in Nicomedia and during the persecutions was converted to Christianity. Later (c.316) he was Latin tutor at Trier to Crispus, Constantine's son. His works, which were influenced by Cicero and Seneca, were sincere, well-written expositions of Christian doctrine, but some of his theological details have been pronounced erroneous. Among his works are *The Divine Institutions* (*Divinae institutiones*), the *Epitome,* and *On God's Wrath* (*De ira Dei*). *On the Death of the Persecutors* (*De mortibus persecutorum*), telling of the horrible end of such emperors as Nero, Domitian, and Decius, is a chief source for the history of the persecutions. The poem *On the Phoenix* (*De ave pheoenice*), a source of Cynewulf's *Christ,* is possibly by Lactantius. See *Excerpts from the Works of Lactantius,* tr. by W. Fletcher (1972).

lactic acid, $CH_3CHOHCO_2H$, a colorless liquid organic acid. It is miscible with water or ethanol. Lactic acid is a fermentation product of lactose (milk sugar); it is present in sour milk, koumiss, leban, yogurt, and cottage cheese. The protein in milk is coagulated (curdled) by lactic acid. Lactic acid is produced in the muscles during intense activity. Calcium lactate, a soluble lactic acid salt, is used as a source of calcium in the diet. Lactic acid is produced commercially for use in pharmaceuticals and foods, in leather tanning and textile dyeing, and in making plastics, solvents, inks, and lacquers. Although it can be prepared by chemical synthesis, production of lactic acid by fermentation of glucose and other substances is a less expensive method. Chemically, lactic acid occurs as two optical ISOMERS, a dextro and a levo form; only the levo form takes part in animal metabolism. The lactic acid of commerce is usually an optically inactive racemic mixture of the two isomers.

lactose (lăk'tōs) or **milk sugar,** white crystalline disaccharide (see CARBOHYDRATE). It has the same empirical formula ($C_{12}H_{22}O_{11}$) as sucrose and maltose but differs from both in structure (see ISOMER). It yields the simple SUGARS D-glucose and D-galactose on HYDROLYSIS, which is catalyzed by lactase, an enzyme found in gastric juice. Lactose is formed in the mammary glands of all lactating animals and is present in their milk. It is produced commercially as a by-product of milk processing. When milk sours, the lactose in it is converted by bacteria to lactic acid. Lactose differs from sucrose (cane sugar) in several ways: it is not so sweet-tasting, is not found in plants, is not fermented by ordinary yeast, and does react with Fehling's solution.

La Cueva, Juan de: see CUEVA, JUAN DE LA.

Ladakh (lədäk'), region (1971 pop. 105,001), 45,762 sq mi (118,524 sq km), E Kashmir, on the border of China. LEH is the chief town. Although allied ethnologically and geographically with Tibet, the region has a predominantly Muslim population. It was nominally a dependency of Tibet, but after 1531 it was invaded periodically by Muslims from Kashmir. It was annexed to Kashmir in the mid-19th cent. The region is now claimed by China, which in 1962 occupied part of the area despite Indian opposition.

Ladd, Edwin Fremont, 1859–1925, American chemist and political leader, b. Somerset co., Maine. From 1890 to 1916 he was dean of the School of Chemistry and Pharmacy at the North Dakota Agricultural College (now North Dakota State Univ. of Agriculture and Applied Science) and later (1916–21) was president of the college. He served (1902–21) as food commissioner of North Dakota; his campaign against adulterated food products and his efforts to protect the farmers from speculators and distributors brought him national prominence. With the support of the Nonpartisan League, he was elected (1920) to the U.S. Senate and thereafter was associated with the farm bloc. For his support of Robert M. La Follette in the presidential campaign of 1924 he was expelled from the Republican party.

Ladd, George Trumbull, 1842–1921, American philosopher, b. Painesville, Ohio, grad. Western Reserve Univ., 1864, and Andover Theological Seminary, 1869. He taught at Yale from 1881 until his retirement in 1906. Greatly influenced by Hermann

Lotze, he worked primarily in experimental psychology, a new science to the United States. He was the founder of the psychology laboratory at Yale. Among his books are *Elements of Physiological Psychology* (1887, rev. ed. 1911), *Philosophy of Mind* (1895), and *Knowledge, Life, and Reality* (1909). See biography by E. S. Mills (1969).

Ladd, William, 1778–1841, American pacifist, b. Exeter, N.H., grad. Harvard, 1797. He commanded sailing vessels until the outbreak of the War of 1812, when he retired to a farm in Maine. In 1820 he began to write and speak against war, and in 1828 he founded the American Peace Society, of which he was president until his death. His *Essay on a Congress of Nations* (1840; ed. with introduction by J. B. Scott, 1916) proposed a world organization involving both a congress of nations and an international court of arbitration. In popularizing this plan Ladd had the help of Elihu BURRITT. See M. E. Curti, *The American Peace Crusade, 1850–1860* (1929); study by Georg Schwarzenberger (1935).

Ladd-Franklin, Christine, 1847–1930, American scientist, b. Windsor, Conn., grad. Vassar 1869. She was the first woman student to enter Johns Hopkins (1878), her special studies being directed toward logic and the theory of color. She studied in Göttingen (1891–92) and worked in Helmholtz's laboratory, developing the theory of color vision that bears her name and that is described in *Colour and Colour Theories* (1929), a collection of her papers.

Ladies' Peace: see CAMBRAI, TREATY OF.

ladies'-tresses: see ORCHID.

Ladin: see RHAETO-ROMANIC.

Ladino: see SEPHARDIM.

Ladislas. For rulers thus named, see LADISLAUS; LANCELOT; ULADISLAUS.

Ladislaus I, king of Bohemia: see LADISLAUS V, king of Hungary.

Ladislaus II, king of Bohemia: see ULADISLAUS II, king of Hungary.

Ladislaus I or **Saint Ladislaus,** 1040–95, king of Hungary (1077–95). He supported Pope Gregory VII against Holy Roman Emperor Henry IV, but rejected Gregory's suggestion that he swear fealty to the papacy. At the invitation of his sister, the widowed queen of Croatia, he invaded and conquered that country in 1091. He successfully fought the CUMANS, compelling those whose lives he spared to turn Christian and to settle in designated regions. He modified the Hungarian criminal code and issued laws safeguarding private property. In Hungarian tradition he is the model of chivalry and valor. He secured the canonization of St. Stephen and was canonized himself in 1198. Feast: June 27.

Ladislaus IV, 1262–90, king of Hungary (1272–90), son and successor of Stephen V. Ladislaus became unpopular by favoring the CUMANS, from whom he was descended through his mother. During his reign, much of it while he was a minor, the magnates and lower nobility were able to establish their power constitutionally, at the expense of the monarchy. There were several revolts against the king, and he was finally slain by the once-favored Cumans. He died heirless; his successor, Andrew III (reigned 1290–1301), who issued from another branch of the Arpad dynasty, was succeeded as king of Hungary by King Wenceslaus III of Bohemia.

Ladislaus V or **Ladislaus Posthumus,** 1440–57, king of Hungary (1444–57) and, as Ladislaus I, king of Bohemia (1453–57). Ladislaus, duke of Austria by birth as the posthumous son of Albert of Hapsburg, duke of Austria and German king (see ALBERT II), was recognized (1443) as king of Bohemia by the majority of the Bohemian diet but was only crowned in 1453. He was elected king of Hungary after the death (1444) of LADISLAUS III of Poland. However, his guardian and second cousin, Holy Roman Emperor FREDERICK III, at whose court Ladislaus grew up, refused to surrender the boy and thus enable him to take his rightful place as king of Bohemia and of Hungary. In 1451 the Austrians rebelled and demanded that Frederick release their young duke; he was released in 1452 as the unofficial ward of his powerful uncle, Ulrich, count of Cilli, but Ladislaus governed none of his realms. GEORGE OF PODEBRAD was regent in Bohemia, John HUNYADI in Hungary. After the death (1456) of Hunyadi, Ulrich became regent of Hungary. He and the king were captured by Hunyadi's son Ladislaus, and Ulrich was killed. Freed shortly afterward, the king had Ladislaus Hunyadi executed in 1457 and then fled to Prague, where he died, probably by poisoning. He was succeeded in Austria by his Hapsburg relatives, in Bohemia by George of Podebrad, and in Hungary by MATTHIAS CORVINUS.

Ladislaus, king of Naples: see LANCELOT.

Ladislaus I, 1260–1333, duke (1306–20) and later king (1320–33) of Poland; called Ladislaus the Short. He restored the Polish kingdom, which had been partitioned since 1138 (see PIAST). In his conflict with Brandenburg over Danzig and Pomerania, he invoked the aid of the TEUTONIC KNIGHTS, who instead proceeded to take the territories for themselves. His son and successor was Casimir III.

Ladislaus II or **Ladislaus Jagiello** (yägyĕ'lō), 1350?–1434, king of Poland (1386–1434), grand duke of Lithuania (1378–1401), founder of the JAGIELLO dynasty. Leaguing with Poland against the menacing TEUTONIC KNIGHTS, he acceded to the Polish throne by marrying Queen JADWIGA. Baptized at this time, he agreed to convert Lithuania to Christianity. The union of Poland and Lithuania continued after he delegated (1401) a cousin as grand duke. Jagiello's victory over the Teutonic Knights at Tannenberg (1410) resulted in the First Peace of TORUN in 1411. His son by a later wife, Ladislaus III, succeeded him as Polish king.

Ladislaus III, 1424–44, king of Poland (1434–44) and, as Uladislaus I, king of Hungary (1440–44), son of Ladislaus II. He led two crusades against the Turks; the first (1443) was highly successful, but the second ended with his defeat and death in the heroic battle of VARNA. In 1447 his younger brother was elected to succeed him as Casimir IV.

Ladislaus IV, 1595–1648, king of Poland (1632–48), son and successor of Sigismund III. His reign was marked by struggles with his subjects and wars with the Swedes, the Russians, and the Turks. Ladislaus in his later years vainly sought to establish authority over the nobles. The Cossack revolt, under Chmielnicki, broke out just before his death. He was succeeded by his brother, JOHN II.

Ladislaus Herman, 1040–1102, duke of Poland (1079–1102), brother and successor of BOLESLAUS II. His rule was one of weakness and decline. At his death the kingdom passed to his two sons, Zbigniew and BOLESLAUS III.

Ladoga, Lake (lä'dōgə, Rus. lä'dəgə), Finnish *Laatokka,* Rus. *Ladozhskoye Ozero,* c.7,000 sq mi (18,100 sq km), NW European USSR, in Karelia, NE of Leningrad. The largest lake in Europe, it is c.130 mi (210 km) long and c.80 mi (130 km) wide and has a maximum depth of 738 ft (225 m). Located on the heavily glaciated Baltic Shield, the lake has shores that are low and marshy in the south, rocky and indented in the north. It is subject to autumn storms and freezes every year for two months in the north and four months in the south. Chief among the many rivers that feed the lake are the Svir, descending from Lake Onega; the Vuoska, which forms the outlet of the Saimaa lake system of Finland; and the Volkhov, coming from Lake Ilmen. The main outlet is the Neva, which flows W into the Gulf of Finland at Leningrad. The fortress at Petrokrepost commands the Neva's exit from the lake. Among the many islands in the northern part of the lake is Valaam (Finnish *Valama* or *Valamo*), with a famous Russian monastery dating from the 12th cent. or earlier. Until the Finnish-Russian War of 1939–40, the northern part of the lake belonged to Finland; cession of the Finnish shore to the USSR was confirmed by the peace treaty of 1947. During the defense of Leningrad against the Germans in World War II, the frozen Lake Ladoga was the lifeline by which Leningrad was supplied in the winters from 1941 to 1943. Because of the difficulties of navigation, the southern shore of Lake Ladoga is paralleled by the **Ladoga Canals,** c.100 mi (160 km) long, connecting the Svir and Neva rivers and forming part of the Mariinsk System (see VOLGA-BALTIC WATERWAY) and the Baltic-White Sea Canal System.

Ladrones Islands: see MARIANAS ISLANDS.

Ladue (lədo͞o', -dyo͞o'), city (1970 pop. 10,491), St. Louis co., E Mo., a suburb of St. Louis; inc. 1936. Pharmaceuticals are produced in Ladue.

ladybird beetle or **ladybug,** member of a cosmopolitan BEETLE family with over 4,000 species, including 350 species in the United States. Ladybird beetles are mostly under ¼ in. (6 mm) long and are nearly hemispherical in shape, with very short legs. They are usually red or yellow with black spots, or black with red or yellow spots, the common species differing only in the number of spots. They have a bitter taste, and their bright coloration is thought to serve as a warning to predators. The name is believed to date from the Middle Ages, when these beneficial beetles were dedicated to the Virgin. Nearly all ladybird beetles, both larvae and adults, are predators on destructive, plant-eating insects. The eggs are laid on plants infested with aphids or scale insects, on which the larvae feed until they pupate in the remains of the last larval skin. The adults gather in large numbers in the fall, prior to winter hibernation, and are often collected at that time by farmers for use in pest control. The first outstanding demonstration of pest control by use of natural enemies occurred in the United States in 1889, when Australian ladybird beetles (*Rhodolia cardinalis*) were imported to wipe out the cottony-cushion scale, an insect that had accidentally been imported from Australia to California and there became a threat to citrus orchards. The Mexican bean beetle (*Epilachna varivestis*), which has spread through E North America, and the squash beetle (*E. borealis*) are the only North American ladybird beetles considered destructive. They are yellowish with black spots; adults and larvae feed on plants. Ladybird beetles are classified in the phylum ARTHROPODA, class Insecta, order Coleoptera, family Coccinellidae.

Lady Day or **Annunciation:** see MARY.

ladyfish: see BONEFISH.

Lady of the Lake, in ARTHURIAN LEGEND, a misty, supernatural figure endowed with magic powers, who gave the sword EXCALIBUR to King Arthur. She inhabited a castle in an underwater kingdom. According to one legend she kidnapped the infant Launcelot and brought him to her castle where he lived until manhood. She has been identified variously with Morgan le Fay and Vivien. The poem *The Lady of the Lake,* by Sir Walter Scott, is based on a totally different legend.

Ladysmith, town (1970 est. pop. 27,000), Natal, E South Africa. The town has railroad yards and food-processing, textile, and tire factories. It is the distribution center for the surrounding agricultural and coal-mining region. Ladysmith was founded in 1851 by BOERS who had been persuaded by British governor Sir Harry Smith to remain in Natal rather than join the TREK to other areas. The town, named for Smith's wife, grew after a railroad to Durban was opened in 1886. During the SOUTH AFRICAN WAR, Sir George White's British forces at Ladysmith were under siege by Boers from Nov., 1899, to Feb., 1900, when British reinforcements arrived. Nearby battlefields associated with the siege include Wagon Hill, Nicholson's Nek, and Spioen Kop.

lady's-slipper, a wild ORCHID; the name is sometimes applied also to impatiens.

Lae (lä'ē, lī), town (1970 est. pop. 24,300), Papua New Guinea, on NE New Guinea island, at the head of the Huon Gulf. Lae is an important administrative and commercial center of Papua New Guinea. Founded in 1927 to serve air transport into the Morobe gold fields in the mountainous interior, Lae has retained its importance as a transportation center.

Laeken (lä'kən), part of Brussels, Brabant prov., central Belgium. The palace built there (early 19th cent.) by Napoleon I is used today as a Belgian royal residence.

Lael (lā'ĕl), father of a Gershonite. Num. 3.24.

Laelius, Caius (kā'əs lē'lēəs), d. c.160 B.C., Roman general, consul in 190 B.C. He was the intimate friend and companion of SCIPIO AFRICANUS MAJOR from youth, and he held command under him in numerous campaigns. His son **Caius Laelius Sapiens,** b. c.186 B.C., consul in 140 B.C., was famous for his friendship with Scipio Africanus Minor. Cicero named one of his great works *Laelius; sive, De amicitia* [Laelius; or, on friendship].

Laënnec, René Théophile Hyacinthe (rənā' tāôfēl' yäsaNt' läänĕk'), 1781–1826, French physician. While connected with the Necker Hospital in Paris he invented the stethoscope, which he described, together with the symptoms he had noted through its use, in his classic book *De l'auscultation médiate* (2 vol. 1819; tr. 1821). His method of auscultation for detecting diseases of the chest, together with the procedure of percussion developed by Leopold Auenbrugger, form the basis of the modern diagnostic technique. See study by Roger Kervran (1960).

Laer or **Laar, Pieter van** (both: pē'tər vän lär), c.1592–1642, Dutch landscape and genre painter and etcher. In 1625 he went to Rome, where he stayed until 1639. He was nicknamed Il Bamboccio [puppet] because his body was deformed. The influence of Caravaggio is apparent in the genre scenes of peasant life that Laer and his followers created. The paintings themselves came to be called Bambocciantí by hostile critics. The name survived, but it lost its derogative sense as aesthetic tastes changed. Laer's *The Halt* (Metropolitan Mus.) and *Water Carrier* (National Gall., Rome) are characteristic paintings of this type. He produced 18 notable etchings of landscapes and animals.

Laertes (lāûr'tēz): see ODYSSEUS.

Laërtius, Diogenes: see DIOGENES LAËRTIUS.

La Farge, John (lə färzh), 1835–1910, American artist and writer, b. New York City. He studied with William Morris Hunt in Newport, R.I., and with Couture in Paris. La Farge began his career as a painter of landscapes and figure compositions. Commissioned (1876) to decorate Trinity Church, Boston, he thereafter engaged primarily in mural painting and the manufacture and design of stained glass. An eclectic artist and a man of the widest culture, friend of Henry Adams and Henry James, La Farge did much to create a sound tradition of the fine arts in the United States. His murals in Trinity Church and the Church of the Ascension, New York City, set a standard for the art unsurpassed in the United States. A lifelong Roman Catholic, he did much of his best work for churches. His splendid windows may be seen in the churches of Buffalo, N.Y., and Worcester, Mass., and in the chapels of Harvard and Columbia universities. La Farge worked in many media. His watercolors and drawings are well known, particularly those commemorating his visit to the South Seas in 1886. His easel paintings are in many leading American museums. His writings and lectures on art are distinguished for their urbanity and judgment. Among them are *Considerations on Painting* (1895), *An Artist's Letters from Japan* (1897), *The Higher Life in Art* (1908), and *Reminiscences of the South Seas* (1912). See study by Royal Cortissoz (1911, repr. 1971).

La Farge, Oliver (lä färzh), 1901–1963, American writer and anthropologist, b. New York City, grad. Harvard (B.A., 1924; M.A., 1929). He conducted three archaeological expeditions to Arizona and ethnological expeditions to Guatemala and Mexico. La Farge used his field experience to authenticate his reflective stories of Indian habit and character. *Laughing Boy* (1929), a novel of Navaho life, won him the Pulitzer Prize in 1929. Other works are *The Sparks Fly Upward* (1931), *The Enemy Gods* (1937), and the stories *All the Young Men* (1935). *Santa Fe* recounts the history of that city. See his autobiographical *Raw Material* (1945); biographies by Everett Gillis (1967), D'Arcy McNickle (1971), and T. M. Pearce (1972).

Lafargue, Paul (pôl läfärg'), 1842–1911, French socialist, b. Cuba; son-in-law of Karl Marx. With Jules Guesde he helped found a Marxist socialist party in France. His many writings, which were influential in other countries, include *The Religion of Capital* (1887, tr. 1894) and *The Evolution of Property from Savagery to Civilization* (1891, tr. 1894).

Lafayette, or **La Fayette, Marie Joseph Paul Yves Roch Gilbert du Motier, marquis de** (märē' zhôzĕf' pôl ēv rôk zhēlbĕr' dü môtyā' märkē' də läfāĕt'), 1757–1834, French general and political leader. He was born of a distinguished family and early entered the army. Enthusiastic over the news of the American Revolution, he evaded all obstacles set in his way by the officially neutral French government and left France to join George Washington's army. He arrived (1777) in Philadelphia, where Congress appointed him a major general. He quickly won the close friendship of Washington, was wounded at Brandywine, shared the hardships of Valley Forge, and obtained a divisional command. After a trip to France (1779–80), where he negotiated for French aid, he distinguished himself in the YORKTOWN CAMPAIGN. Returning to France in 1782, Lafayette was a member of the Assembly of Notables (1787) and the States-General (1789). Elected vice president of the National Assembly, he was made commander of the militia (later named the National Guard) the day after the fall of the Bastille (July, 1789). In this key position he sought to exploit his immense popularity and to maintain order by acting as moderator between the contending factions. However, he did not have the confidence of the court, and he lost all influence and popularity when he gave the order to fire into a crowd that had gathered (July 17, 1791) on the Champs de Mars to draft a petition for dethronement of the king. He took command (1792) of the army of the center, formed in preparation for war against Austria. After a brief visit to Paris (June, 1792), when he attempted to defend the monarchy, he returned to the front. He was, however, relieved of his command and ordered to return to Paris. Lafayette left his army, fled (Aug., 1792) across the border, and was captured and imprisoned in Austria. Finally liberated (1797) by Napoleon, he returned (1799) to France, where he lived in retirement during the First Empire. As member of the chamber of deputies in the Restoration, he joined the liberal party. In 1824–25 he visited the United States, where he was given an unparalleled welcome. Lafayette took part in the July Revolution (1830) as a leader of the moderates. His prestige was largely responsible for the installation of Louis Philippe as king of the French. Lafayette's unswerving courage, integrity, and idealism made him a popular symbol of the bond between France and the United States. His direct descendants, the Chambrun family, are honorary U.S. citizens. The modern French flag was created by Lafayette in July, 1789, by combining the royal white with the blue and red of Paris. See biographies by Joseph Delteil (tr. 1928), Brand Whitlock (1929), Constance Wright (1957), and Louis Gottschalk (5 vol., 1935–69). See also S. W. Jackson, *La Fayette: A Bibliography* (1930).

La Fayette, Marie Madeleine Pioche de La Vergne, comtesse de (märē' mädəlĕn' pyôsh də lä vĕr'nyə, kôtĕs'), 1634–92, French novelist of the classical period, whose chief and only surviving work, *La Princesse de Clèves* (1678), is the first great French novel. The psychological realism of this story of a woman's renunciation of an illicit love, treated with chaste simplicity and quiet wit, has given the novel enduring appeal. Mme de La Fayette's friendship with the duc de LA ROCHEFOUCAULD has led to the unfounded theory that he appears in her novel as the unhappy lover. See Martin Turnell, *The Novel in France* (1958).

Lafayette (lä"fēĕt', lăf"ēĕt'). **1** City (1970 pop. 20,484), Contra Costa co., NW Calif., a residential suburb in the San Francisco-Oakland area; settled 1848, inc. 1968. **2** City (1970 pop. 44,955), seat of Tippecanoe co., W central Ind., on the Wabash River; inc. 1853. A manufacturing city in a grain, livestock, and dairy area, it has railroad shops, meat-packing houses, and plants making aluminum and rubber goods. It is the seat of Purdue Univ. The nearby site of the battle of TIPPECANOE (Nov., 1811) is a state memorial. Also of interest is the rebuilt blockhouse of Fort Ouiatenon (1717). **3** City (1970 pop. 68,908), seat of Lafayette parish, S central La., on the Vermilion River (which is linked to the Intracoastal Waterway); settled 1770s by Acadians, inc. 1836. It is a commercial, shipping, and medical center for an area producing sugarcane, rice, cotton, dairy cattle, livestock, and petroleum. Manufactures include building materials, electrical appliances, auto parts, furniture, and metal products. The Heymann Oil Center there is headquarters for several hundred oil companies. The city retains a colorful Cajun atmosphere. Of interest are St. John's Cathedral (1916), a Carmelite monastery, a planetarium, a museum, and the Art Center for Southwestern Louisiana. Lafayette is the seat of the Univ. of Southwestern Louisiana and the scene of an annual Mardi Gras. Evangeline Downs racetrack is nearby.

Lafayette College, at Easton, Pa.; United Presbyterian; coeducational; chartered 1826, opened 1832. The school concentrates on liberal arts and engineering.

Lafayette Escadrille (ĕskədrĭl'), small group of American volunteer aviators in World War I, created (April, 1916) as Escadrille Américaine in the French air service. It was renamed the Lafayette Escadrille in December of the same year, and the outfit saw much frontline action and suffered heavy casualties. In Jan., 1918, the Lafayette Escadrille was reorganized in the U.S. army as the 103d Pursuit Squadron. See E. C. Parson's *The Great Adventure* (1937, repr. 1972 under the title *I Flew with the Lafayette Escadrille);* study by H. M. Mason (1964).

Laffite, Jean (zhäN läfēt'), c.1780–1826?, leader of a band of privateers and smugglers. The name is often spelled Lafitte. He and his men began operating (1810) off the Baratarian coast S of New Orleans and, after 1817, from the island site of the present city of Galveston, Texas. His ships, commissioned by several of the Latin American nations in revolt against Spain, preyed on Spanish commerce. The booty (including slaves) was brought from Barataria Bay through bayous to New Orleans, where it was disposed of chiefly through the agency of Pierre Laffite, a brother. In Sept., 1814, a U.S. naval force raided their establishment at Barataria and their ships. Laffite, a few days before, had refused a British offer of money and land and a commission in the royal navy as an inducement to aid the British in their attempt on New Orleans. Instead Laffite turned his information over to the Americans and offered his services to them in return for the pardon of his men. Gen. Andrew Jackson accepted their help, and many of the Baratarians participated with credit in the battle of New Orleans and were subsequently pardoned by President Madison. Laffite returned to his old life, moving his base of operations to the disputed Texas area, where he gathered about him almost a thousand followers. He was unmolested until several members of his colony attacked (1820) American property, whereupon the U.S. government again dispatched a naval force against him. Laffite with his closest followers departed (1821) peaceably. His final end is not certainly known; fragmentary evidence suggests that he died in Mexico in 1826. In his lifetime he was regarded as a romantic figure, and after his death legend heightened his fame. See biographies by J. H. Ingraham (1836, repr. 1970) and Lyle Saxon (1930).

Laffitte, Jacques (zhäk läfēt'), 1767–1844, French banker and politician. He rose from poverty to become one of the wealthiest and most influential men in France. He was director (1809) and later governor (1814–19) of the Bank of France. Elected a deputy in 1816, he opposed changes in the electoral laws during the reign of Louis XVIII and was removed as governor of the bank. Thrown into the opposition, he brought all his influence to bear and, particularly by encouraging journalists such as Adolphe Thiers, helped to effect the JULY REVOLUTION of 1830 and put Louis Philippe on the throne. He was made premier by the new king, but his policy failed to satisfy any of the parties, and his support of the Polish and Italian revolutionaries annoyed the king. He resigned in 1831, by then having lost most of his fortune.

Lafitte, Jean: see LAFFITE, JEAN.

La Follette, Robert Marion (ləfŏl'ĭt), 1855–1925, American political leader, U.S. Senator from Wisconsin (1906–25), b. Primrose, Wis. Admitted (1880) to the Wisconsin bar, he practiced in Madison, Wis., and was district attorney (1880–84) of Dane co. As U.S. Representative (1885–91), he generally followed the traditionally conservative policies of the Republican party. After a political conflict that led to his break with the state Republican leaders, La Follette began to formulate a detailed reform program and, appealing directly to the people, to build a broad constituency. He unsuccessfully sought the Republican gubernatorial nomination in 1896 and 1898 and finally won it in 1900. As governor of Wisconsin (1901–6) he secured a direct primary law, tax reform legislation, railroad rate control, and other measures that became collectively known as the Wisconsin Idea. In 1906 he entered the U.S. Senate and served until his death. At odds with the conservative leadership of President Taft, La Follette helped found (1911) the National Progressive Republican League; its aim was to wrest the Republican presidential nomination from Taft in 1912 and secure it for La Follette. When Theodore Roosevelt announced his candidacy for the nomination, however, many of La Follette's supporters switched to Roosevelt, who eventually ran on the PROGRESSIVE PARTY ticket. In the Senate, La Follette generally supported the reform measures of President Wilson's administration, championing Federal railroad regulation, sponsoring (1915) the act that elevated and regulated conditions of maritime employment, and advocating (1913) passage of the Seventeenth Amendment to the U.S. Constitution. He broke with the Wilson administration, however, when he resisted the increasing tendency to side with the Allies; he led the resistance to arming merchant ships and voted against the U.S. declaration of war. He afterwards supported war legislation, but made every effort to place the financial burden on the rich. From 1919 to 1925 he was one of the most powerful men in the Senate. He opposed the League of Nations and the Permanent Court of International Justice (the World Court) and fought the U.S. postwar deflation policy. In 1924 he ran for President on the Progressive ticket and polled 5 million votes. The strain of the campaign sapped his strength, and he died the following summer. His wife, **Belle Case La Follette,** 1859–1931, b. Juneau co., Wis., obtained a law degree, worked for woman suffrage, engaged in journalism, and ably advised her husband throughout his life. Their older son, **Robert Marion La Follette, Jr.,** 1895–1953, b. Madison, Wis., assisted (1919–1925) his father as secretary, then succeeded him in the U.S. Senate and served there until 1947, when he was defeated in the Wisconsin primaries. "Young Bob," as he was known, also championed tax reform and backed New Deal legislation until the passage of the 1938 naval expansion bill. Another son, **Philip Fox La Follette,** 1897–1965, b. Madison, Wis., served (1931–33, 1935–39) as governor of Wisconsin. See the elder Robert La Follette's autobiography (1913, new ed. 1960); E. N. Doan, *The La Follettes and the Wiscon-*

sin Idea (1947); Robert S. Maxwell, *La Follette and the Rise of the Progressives in Wisconsin* (1956) and (ed.), *La Follette* (1969); Donald Young, ed., *Adventures in Politics: The Memoirs of Philip La Follette* (1970).

La Fontaine, Henri (äNrē' läfôNtĕn'), 1854–1943, Belgian jurist and statesman. A senator from 1894 to 1936, he headed the International Peace Bureau from 1907 and was awarded the 1913 Nobel Peace Prize. His writings on international law were extensive.

La Fontaine, Jean de (zhäN də), 1621–95, French poet, whose celebrated fables place him among the masters of world literature. He was born at Château-Thierry to a bourgeois family. A restless dilettante as a youth, he settled at last in Paris. His marriage (1647) terminated in 1658, and from 1673 to 1693 he lived in the household of Mme de La Sablière, one of his several patrons. La Fontaine's masterpiece is the collection of *Fables choisies, mises en vers* [selected fables versified] (1668–94), comprising 12 books of some 230 fables drawn largely from Aesop. Each fable is a short tale of beasts behaving like men; each serves as a comment on human behavior. Although their charm and simple facade have made them popular with children, many are sophisticated satires and serious commentaries on French society. Their wit, acumen, and brilliance of verse and narrative have assured their worldwide success; they ran into 37 editions before La Fontaine's death. Among his other works are *Contes et nouvelles en vers* (4 vol., 1664–74, tr. *Tales and Novels in Verse,* 1934), humorous and often ribald verse tales drawn from Boccaccio, Ariosto, and others. He also wrote comedies and librettos for opera, poems on classical themes, and long original poems, notably the *Élégie aux nymphes de Vaux* (1671), a complaint on the disgrace (1661) of his patron Fouquet. See English translations of the fables by Joseph Auslander and Jacques Le Clercq (1930), Edward Marsh (1933), and Marianne Moore (1954); biography by A. E. Mackay (1973); studies by Margaret O. Guiton (1961) and Philip A. Wadsworth (1952, repr. 1970).

LaFontaine, Sir Louis Hippolyte, 1807–64, Canadian political leader, b. Lower Canada (now Quebec). A lawyer, he entered (1830) the Legislative Assembly of Lower Canada and supported Louis Joseph Papineau in his opposition to the British administration but did not approve of the rebellion of 1837. After the rebellion, with Papineau in exile, LaFontaine became the accepted leader of the French Canadians and of the Reform party in Lower Canada. Sir Charles Bagot, as governor general, recognized the powerful coalition formed by the French Canadians and the moderate reformers of Upper Canada led by Robert BALDWIN and called into existence in 1842 the first Baldwin-LaFontaine ministry. When Bagot died, the ministry soon found itself in opposition to Sir Charles METCALFE, his successor, on the issue of responsible government and resigned in 1843. With the triumph of the Reform party in 1847, the new governor general, the 8th earl of ELGIN, called into existence the second Baldwin-LaFontaine administration, notable for its reforms and its achievement of genuine responsible government. The test of the latter was the Rebellion Losses Bill (1849), brought in by LaFontaine, to compensate persons in Lower Canada who had suffered property loss during the rebellion of 1837. It was denounced as a "rebel measure" but was upheld by Lord Elgin at the cost of personal violence to himself. LaFontaine resigned in 1851; from 1853 until his death he served with distinction as chief justice of Lower Canada. He was made a baronet in 1854. See S. B. Leacock, *Mackenzie, Baldwin, LaFontaine, Hincks* (rev. ed. 1926).

Laforet, Carmen (kär'mān läfōrĕt'), 1921–, Spanish writer, b. Barcelona. Her autobiographical first novel, *Nada* [nothing] (1944), describes the spiritual desolation of a country emerging from civil war. Her other works, noted for their sensitivity and accuracy of observation, include *La isla y los demonios* [the island and the devils] (1952), *La mujer nueva* [the new woman] (1955), *Grand Canary* (tr. 1961), and *La niña y otros relatos* [the little girl and other stories] (1970).

Laforgue, Jules (zhül läfôrg'), 1860–87, French symbolist poet. He was one of the first French poets to write in free verse. The revolutionary form of *Les Complaintes* (1885) and *Derniers Vers* (1890) influenced later French poets as well as such foreign poets as T. S. Eliot and Ezra Pound.

Lafosse, or **La Fosse, Charles de** (shärl də lä fôs), 1636–1716, French painter. A pupil of Le Brun, he was more influenced by Veronese and Correggio, whose works he saw when he was in Italy (1658–63). His most classical work was done in the late 1670s, while he assisted Le Brun at the Tuileries and at Versailles, where he was responsible for the Salon d'Apollon. His inclination toward spirited movement and Venetian color is evident in his later work. He was the first notable French artist to use Rubens's works for inspiration. Lafosse was commissioned by Louis XIV in 1688 to paint mythological scenes for the Trianon. A major achievement is his fresco of *St. Louis Presenting His Sword to Christ* (1700–02) for the dome of the Hôtel des Invalides, Paris.

Lagan (lăg'ən), river, c.40 mi (60 km) long, rising in Slieve Croob, Co. Down, SE Northern Ireland. It flows NW, then NE past Lisburn to Belfast Lough at Belfast. The port of Belfast and its shipbuilding yards are located at the Lagan's mouth; a canal joins the river to Lough Neagh.

Lagarde, Paul Anton de (pōl äNtôN' də lägärd'), 1827–91, German Orientalist. Lagarde was one of the most important biblical critics and Oriental philologists of his century. His work included studies in Iranian, Syriac, Greek, Arabic, and Aramaic, but perhaps his best-known contributions were to the criticism of the biblical text. See study by R. W. Lougee (1962).

Lagash (lā'găsh) or **Shirpurla** (shĭrpo͝or'lə), ancient city of SUMER, S Mesopotamia. Lagash was flourishing by c.2400 B.C., but traces of habitation go back at least to the 4th millennium B.C. After the fall of Akkad (2180 B.C.), when the rest of Mesopotamia was in a state of chaos, Lagash was able to maintain peace and prosperity under its ruler Gudea. Excavations begun on the site in 1877 revealed the beautiful sculptures of Gudea, which had been dedicated to the city's patron goddess, Ningirsu. Thousands of inscribed tablets were also found at the site.

Lagerkvist, Pär Fabian (pâr fä'bēän lä'gərkvĭst), 1891–1974, Swedish poet, dramatist, and novelist. Lagerkvist is considered one of the most significant figures of modern Swedish literature. His central concern is the soul of man, his main theme the problem of good and evil. With the short novel *The Hangman* (1933, tr. 1936) and the play *The Man Without A Soul* (1936, tr. 1944) he became a major spokesman against totalitarianism. *Midsummer Dream in a Workhouse* (1941, tr. 1953) and *Let Man Live* (1949, tr. 1951) are experimental dramas. Of his novels, *The Dwarf* (1944, tr. 1945) deals with man's destructiveness, while *Barabbas* (1950, tr. 1951), *The Sibyl* (1956, tr. 1958), and *The Death of Ahasuerus* (1960, tr. 1962) concern man's search for God. Lagerkvist's verse, marked by simple diction and imagery, includes *Songs of the Heart* (1926) and *Evening Land* (1953). He received the 1951 Nobel Prize in Literature. See his autobiographical *Guest of Reality* (1925); studies by Winston Weathers (1968) and R. D. Spector (1973); bibliography by Anders Ryberg (1964).

Lagerlöf, Selma (sĕl'mä lä'gərlöv), 1858–1940, Swedish novelist. Her native Värmland is the background for many of her excellent stories, which deal with peasant life. Novels include *The Story of Gösta Berling* (1891, tr. 1898), a romantic tale of a renegade priest, lyrical in style; *Jerusalem* (1901, tr. 1901–2); and a trilogy (1925–28) which was published in English as *The Ring of the Lowenskolds* (1931). Her works are often based on legends and sagas, and possess the descriptive strength and flow of epic poetry. The short stories of *The Wonderful Adventures of Nils* (1906, tr. 1907) are classics of children's literature. She received the 1909 Nobel Prize in Literature and was the first woman to be thus honored. See biographies by H. A. Larsen (1936) and W. A. Berendsohn (1968).

Laghouat (lägwät'), town (1966 pop. 26,553), N Algeria, an oasis on the north edge of the Sahara Desert. It is an important administrative and military center and marketplace and is known for rug and tapestry weaving. There are natural gas deposits in the region. The town has a meteorological station. Laghouat traces its history at least to the 11th cent. It paid tribute to Morocco in the 17th cent. The Turks captured Laghouat in 1786, and the French conquered the city in 1852.

Lagoon Islands: see ELLICE ISLANDS.

Lagoon Nebula, bright, diffuse NEBULA in the southern constellation Sagittarius; cataloged as M8 or NGC 6526. It is visible to the naked eye and has an angular area larger than that of the full moon. The central parts are extremely bright, and some stars can be seen embedded in the nebulosity. Because of the nebula's large size, light from its stars cannot illuminate all of the associated interstellar gas and dust. Thus, parts of it appear blacker than the surrounding sky.

Lagos (lā'gŏs, lä'gôs), city (1971 est. pop. 1,112,000), capital of Nigeria, SW Nigeria, on the Gulf of Guinea. It comprises four islands (Lagos, Iddo, Ikoyi, and Victoria) and four mainland sections (Ebute-Metta, Apapa, Yaba, and Suru-Lere) that are interconnected by causeways and bridges. Lagos is Nigeria's largest city, its administrative and economic center, and its chief port. Industries include railroad repair, motor vehicle assembly, food processing, and the manufacture of metal products, textiles, beverages, chemicals, pharmaceuticals, soap, and furniture. The city is a road and rail terminus and has an international airport. An old Yoruba town, Lagos, beginning in the 15th cent., grew as a trade center and seaport. From the 1820s until it became a British colony, Lagos was a notorious center of the slave trade. Britain annexed the city in 1861, both to tap the trade in palm products and other goods with the interior and to suppress the slave trade. In 1906, Lagos was joined with the British protectorate of Southern Nigeria, and, in 1914, when Southern and Northern Nigeria were amalgamated, it became part of the small coastal Colony of Nigeria. In 1954 most of the colony was merged with the rest of Nigeria, but Lagos was made a separate federal territory. From the late 19th cent. to independence in 1960, Lagos was the center of the Nigerian nationalist movement. The Univ. of Lagos (1962), the College of Technology (1948), the National Museum, and a large sports stadium are in Lagos, which is also the seat of Anglican and Roman Catholic bishops.

Lagos (lä'go͞osh), city (1970 municipal pop. 16,610), Faro dist., S Portugal, in Algarve, on the Atlantic Ocean. The excellent harbor shelters much coastwise trade and an important sardine and tuna fishing fleet. Sancho I with the help of bands of Crusaders captured (1189) the city from the Moors; in 1191 it was recaptured by the Moors but was soon (c.1250) restored to the Portuguese. Lagos was a starting port for Portuguese navigators in the time of Prince Henry the Navigator, who was first buried at Lagos. The disastrous expedition of King Sebastian set out from there. The city was severely damaged in the 1755 earthquake. Off Lagos, in 1759, the British under Admiral Boscawen defeated the French.

Lagrange, Joseph Louis, Comte (zhôzĕf' lwē kôNt lägräNzh'), 1736–1813, French mathematician and astronomer, b. Turin, of French and Italian descent. Before the age of 20 he was professor of geometry at the royal artillery school at Turin. With his pupils he organized (1759) a society from which the Turin Academy of Sciences developed. Among his early successes were his method of solving isoperimetrical problems, on which the calculus of variations is based in part; his researches on the nature and propagation of sound and on the vibration of strings; and his studies on the libration of the moon and on the satellites of Jupiter. On the recommendation of Euler and D'Alembert, Frederick the Great invited him (1766) to succeed Euler as director of mathematics at the Berlin Academy of Sciences. The memoirs of the academy were enriched by his distinguished treatises, and during this time he wrote his chief work, *Mécanique analytique,* a treatment of mechanics based solely on algebra and the calculus and containing not a single diagram or geometric explanation. This was published (1788) in Paris, where he had been called by Louis XVI in 1787. In 1793 he became president of the commission on weights and measures; he was influential in causing the adoption of the decimal base for the metric system. A professor at the École polytechnique from 1797, he developed the use in teaching of the analytic method that he so skillfully employed in his research. He wrote *Théorie des fonctions analytiques* (1797) and *Leçons sur le calcul des fonctions* (1806), both based on his lectures. Under Napoleon, Lagrange was made senator and count; he is buried in the Panthéon. His contributions to the development of mathematics also include the application of differential calculus to the theory of probabilities and notable work on the solution of equations. In astronomy he is known for his calculations of the motions of planets.

La Grange (lə grānj). **1** City (1970 pop. 23,301), seat of Troupe co., W central Ga., inc. 1828. It is an industrial center that has retained its charm as a residential city, containing a number of classic revival houses. La Grange College is in the city. **2** Village (1970 pop. 16,773), Cook co., NE Ill., a suburb of Chicago; settled 1830s, inc. 1879. It is primarily residential.

La Grange Park, village (1970 pop. 15,626), Cook co., NE Ill., a suburb of Chicago; inc. 1892. Its main industry is the manufacture of pens.

La Granja, Spain: see SAN ILDEFONSO.

La Guaira (lä gwī'rä), city, federal district, N Venezuela, on the Caribbean Sea NW of Caracas. It is the principal international port of Venezuela; cacao, coffee, and tobacco are the chief exports. La Guaira is also a seaside resort. Founded in the 16th cent. as an outlet for Caracas, the city was sacked by English pirates in 1743. During the war for independence (19th cent.) La Guaira's dungeons held many noted political prisoners.

La Guajira (lä gwähē'rä), peninsula, c.100 mi (160 km) long, N Colombia, extending into the Caribbean Sea. Punta Gallinas, at the tip, is the northernmost point of South America. On the sparsely populated peninsula are outliers of the Cordillera Oriental, surrounded by hot, arid plains. Salt and pearls are found along the shoreline.

LaGuardia, Fiorello Henry (fēərĕl'ō, ləgwär'dēə), 1882–1947, U.S. public official, Congressman, and mayor of New York City (1934–45), b. New York City. He spent his early years in Arizona with his father, an army bandmaster who had come from Italy to the United States. LaGuardia went to Europe while still a youth, and was employed by the U.S. consulates in Hungary, Trieste, and Fiume. Returning to New York City, he studied law while working (1907–10) in the U.S. immigration service, and was admitted (1910) to the bar. He ran for Congress on the Republican ticket unsuccessfully in 1914, but won in 1916 after a vigorous campaign against the Tammany machine. In Congress he joined in the successful fight for the liberalization of the House rules. He commanded (1917) U.S. air forces on the Italian-Austrian front in World War I. LaGuardia was president (1920–21) of the New York City board of aldermen and returned (1923–33) to the House of Representatives, where he fought for numerous labor reforms and sponsored the Norris-LaGuardia Act, which prohibited injunctions in labor disputes. With the backing of Samuel SEABURY (1873–1958), LaGuardia successfully ran (1933) for mayor of New York City on the Fusion ticket. As mayor he executed a vast program of reform. He reduced political corruption, forwarded the modernizing and beautification of New York City, brought about the adoption (1938) of a new city charter, introduced slum clearance projects, and improved health and sanitary conditions. "The Little Flower" (from his first name) was reelected mayor of New York City for three consecutive terms, but chose not to run in 1945. LaGuardia served (1946) as director of the UN Relief and Rehabilitation Administration. His courage, enthusiasm, and energy made him a nationally known figure. See his autobiography (ed. by M. L. Werner, 1948, repr. 1961); biography by Arthur Mann (2 vol., 1959–65, repr. 1969); Ernest Cuneo, *Life with Fiorello* (1955); Howard Zinn, *LaGuardia in Congress* (1959, repr. 1969).

Laguna (ləgo͞o'nə), pueblo, Valencia co., central N.Mex.; established on its present site 1699. Its inhabitants are Pueblo Indians of the Keresan linguistic stock. Most of them farm in outlying areas, and the pueblo is used essentially for ceremonial purposes. The principal feast is that of San José (St. Joseph) on March 19.

Laguna, La (lä lägo͞o'nä), city (1970 pop. 79,963), on Teneriffe island, Canary Islands. The center of a fertile farm area producing cereals, grapes, fruits, and vegetables, it is also a tourist resort. The Univ. of San Fernando is there.

Laguna Beach (ləgo͞o'nə), city (1970 pop. 14,550), Orange co., S Calif., on the Pacific coast; founded 1887, inc. 1927. It is a residential and resort city with a noted art colony and many cultural attractions.

Laguna District [Span.,=lake], irrigated area in E Durango and W Coahuila states, N central Mexico. Originally a 900,000-acre (364,200-hectare) tract, consisting of large estates, the land was reapportioned (1936) under President Lázaro Cárdenas and distributed to Mexican farmers on the EJIDO system. It was a successful experiment in agrarian reform until 1952, when a severe drought scorched more than half the district, turning 200,000 acres (80,940 hectares) of wheat and cotton fields into a dust bowl and obliging the government to take emergency measures to avert a famine. Settlement has continued there, but on a greatly reduced scale; water for irrigation comes from wells and from dams on the Nazas and Aguanaval rivers.

La Habana (lä häbä'nä, hävä'–), province (1970 pop. 2,305,241), W Cuba. HAVANA is the capital. The province has coastal plains in the north and south, as well as fine beaches, and there are some low mountains in the north. Included in the province is the Isle of Pines (see PINES, ISLE OF). The Almendares and the Jaruco are the main rivers. La Habana is the smallest but the most industrialized Cuban province. The majority of the population and industry is concentrated in and around Havana. Tobacco, sugarcane, and vegetables are the principal crops of the province, and food processing is the leading industry. Tourism was economically important until the United States and Cuba severed relations in 1960.

La Habra (lə hăb'rə), city (1970 pop. 41,350), Orange co., S Calif.; inc. 1925. A suburb of Los Angeles, La Habra is a distribution center for an area where citrus fruits, avocados, and vegetables are grown and oil is produced. The city has an oil research center. La Habra was settled in the 1860s by Basque sheepherders.

Lahad (lā'hăd), Zorathite family. 1 Chron. 4.2.

Lahaina (ləhī'nə), city (1970 pop. 3,718), Maui co., on the west coast of Maui Island, Hawaii, in a sugarcane and pineapple region. It was the scene of the first white settlement in the islands and served as capital from 1810 until the seat of government was moved (1845) to Honolulu. Hawaii's first newspaper was printed in Lahaina, and the island's first school, Lahainaluna School, was established there in 1831. A whaling port in the mid-19th cent., Lahaina was also an important anchorage for the U.S. Pacific Fleet in the 20th cent.

Lahai-roi (lāhā'-roi) or **Beer-lahai-roi** (bē'ər–), well, probably near Kadesh-barnea. Gen. 16.14; 24.62; 25.11.

La Halle, Adam de: see ADAM DE LA HALLE.

La Harpe, Frédéric César de (frādārēk' sāzär' də lä ärp), 1754–1838, Swiss statesman. He went (1782) to St. Petersburg, Russia, where he became the tutor of the future Czar Alexander I, in whom he attempted to instill liberal and democratic ideals. After the outbreak of the French Revolution, La Harpe returned to Switzerland. Failing initially to stir up a revolution in his native VAUD against the Bernese authorities, he went to Paris and obtained the intervention of the Directory. After the establishment (1798) of the HELVETIC REPUBLIC with the help of French arms, La Harpe was one of its directors, but in 1800 the conservatives, backed by Napoleon Bonaparte, ousted him as a Jacobin. La Harpe retired to Paris. When the allies entered Paris in 1814, Czar Alexander gave him the rank of a Russian general. La Harpe represented Vaud and Ticino at the Congress of Vienna (1814–15), where with the help of the czar he secured recognition of the two cantons as sovereign members of the Swiss Confederation.

La Harpe, Jean François de (zhäN fräNswä' də), 1739–1803, French critic. He was the author of the monumental *Cours de littérature ancienne et moderne,* lectures he delivered after his appointment (1786) at a lycée in Paris. His judgments on the classical period especially have been borne out by time. He also wrote plays, commentaries (notably on Racine), and critical essays.

La Hire (lä ēr), c.1390–c.1443, French commander in the Hundred Years War, whose real name was Étienne de Vignoles or Vignolles. He entered (1418) the service of the dauphin (later King Charles VII) and was a loyal companion of Joan of Arc, with whom he helped to defeat (1429) the English at Orléans and Patay. For a time La Hire ravaged N France at the head of a marauding band of soldiers, but in 1437 he resumed the fight against the English.

La Hire or **La Hyre, Laurent de** (both: lōräN' də), 1606–56, French painter. He produced many portraits and historical paintings, a few romantic landscapes, important decorative works for Richelieu, Pierre Séguier, and others, and tapestry designs for the Gobelins. His tasteful paintings reflect the influence of Vouet, Poussin, and Claude. His *Pope Nicolas V before St. Francis* (1630) and *St. Peter Healing the Sick* are both in the Louvre.

Lahmam (lä'măm), unidentified town, S central Palestine. Joshua 15.40.

Lahmi (lä'mī), giant brother of Goliath killed by Elhanan. 1 Chron. 20.5.

Lahontan, Lake (ləhŏn'tən), extinct lake of W Nev. and NE Calif. It was formed by heavy precipitation caused by the Pleistocene glaciers and with Lake BONNEVILLE occupied a part of the Great Basin region. Lake Lahontan vanished shortly after the Pleistocene epoch, but Pyramid, Winnemucca, and Walker lakes and Carson Sink are its remnants. The area, especially Lovelock Cave, Nev., is rich in Pleistocene fossils.

Lahore (ləhôr'), city (1972 est. pop. 2,148,000), capital of Punjab prov., E central Pakistan, on the Ravi River. It is the second largest city of Pakistan. A railway center near the Indo-Pakistani border, Lahore is a banking and commercial city that markets the products of the surrounding fertile agricultural area. Its diverse industries include motion picture production, food processing, engineering, metalworking, sawmilling, and the manufacture of textiles, chemicals, pharmaceuticals, iron and steel, electrical goods, rubber and leather items, farm implements, sewing machines, surgical instruments, bicycles, carpets, glass, and matches. Handicrafts, especially gold and silver work, also flourish. According to Hindu legend, Lahore was founded by Loh, or Lava, son of Rama, the hero of the Sanskrit epic *Ramayana.* In 1036 it was conquered from a Brahman dynasty by the Muslim Turkish Ghaznivids, who made it the capital of their empire in 1106. It passed in 1186 to the Ghori sultans, also from Afghanistan. India's first Muslim emperor, Kutb-ud-din Aibak, was crowned in Lahore in 1206 and is buried there. The city, which suffered Mongol raids in the 13th and 14th cent., entered the period of its greatest glory in the 16th cent., when it became one of the capitals of the Mogul empire. Lahore declined after the reign of Aurangzeb; it was annexed in 1767 by the Sikhs, who, under Ranjit Singh, made it their capital. It passed to the British in 1849. When Pakistan won independence in 1947, Lahore became the capital of its West Punjab; from 1955 to 1970 it was the capital of the entire province of West Pakistan, composed of all provinces in the western wing; and upon the province's dissolution it became the capital of Punjab prov. The architectural remains of the Mogul period, although imperfectly preserved, are among the most splendid of Mogul art. Especially notable are the palace and mausoleum of emperor Jahangir and the Shalimar gardens, just outside the city; only three sections of the gardens remain of the original seven that had symbolized the divisions of the Islamic paradise. Other landmarks include the Pearl and Golden mosques, the tomb of Ranjit Singh, and the Wazir Khan mosque, which contains the finest known examples of *khashi,* or inlaid pottery. Lahore's museum of Indian antiquities, which figures in Rudyard Kipling's *Kim,* is among the most noted in the East. The city's educational facilities include the Univ. of the Punjab (1882), Pakistan's oldest university; several affiliated colleges; and a university of engineering and technology. Lahore also has an atomic research institute.

Lahr, Bert, 1895–1967, American comic actor, b. New York City, originally named Irving Lahrheim. Lahr first performed in burlesque and vaudeville, where he became known for his morose facial expression. After his Broadway debut in *Harry Delmar's Revels* (1927), he appeared in numerous Broadway shows, in films, and on television. His performance in *Waiting for Godot* in 1956 is considered the high point of his career, but he is probably best remembered as the Cowardly Lion in the film *The Wizard of Oz* (1939). See biography by his son John Lahr (1969).

Lahti (lä'tē, läkh'–), city (1970 pop. 89,349), Häme prov., S central Finland. Connected with the southern end of the Päijänne lake system, it is an important lake port as well as a transportation center. It has many large factories and is a center of the Finnish wood-products industry. The city was chartered in 1905. Many Karelians came to Lahti after the Finnish-Soviet armistice of 1944. The city hall (1912) was designed by Eliel Saarinen.

La Huerta, Adolfo de: see HUERTA, ADOLFO DE LA.

La Hyre, Laurent de: see LA HIRE, LAURENT DE.

Laibach: see LJUBLJANA, Yugoslavia.

Laibach, Congress of (lī'bäkh), conference of European powers in 1821, held in what is now Ljubljana, Yugoslavia. The chief powers at the congress were Russia, Austria, Prussia, France, and Great Britain. The meeting was convened to complete discussions begun at the Congress of Troppau (see TROPPAU, CONGRESS OF). The congress caused the breach between Great Britain and the three conservative powers of Austria, Prussia, and Russia (popularly called the Holy Alliance) to widen. FERDINAND I of the Two Sicilies was present upon invitation, and the chief action of the congress was the sanctioning of the suppression by Austrian forces of uprisings in Naples and Piedmont.

Laidler, Harry Wellington (lād'lər), 1884–1970, American economist and Socialist leader, b. Brooklyn, N.Y., grad. Wesleyan Univ., 1907, Brooklyn Law School, 1910, Ph.D. Columbia, 1914. A founder (1905) and secretary (1910–21) of the Intercollegiate Socialist Society, he was also executive director (1921–57) of its successor organization, the League for Industrial Democracy. From 1920 a director of the National Bureau of Economic Research, he served twice as president (1930–32, 1948–49). Laidler was the Socialist candidate for numerous public offices and served (1940–41) on the New York City council. His writings include *Boycotts and the Labor Struggle* (1914), *A History of Socialist Thought* (1927), *Concentration of Control in American Industry* (1931), *Social-Economic Movements* (1944), and *The History of Socialism* (1968).

Lainez, Diego (dēä'gō lĭnĕth'), 1512–65, Spanish theologian, leader of the Catholic Reformation; general of the Society of Jesus. He was one of the small band that formed the original Society of Jesus under St. IGNATIUS OF LOYOLA. At the Council of Trent (see TRENT, COUNCIL OF) he was papal theologian and made a sensation by his brilliant expositions of doctrine; his words were incorporated exactly in some of the canons. At St. Ignatius's death (1556) he was vicar general of the Jesuits, and in 1558 he was made general. The next year he avoided being made pope only by secretly leaving Rome. He represented the church in disputation with the Calvinists in the Colloquy of Poissy (1561). The name also appears as Laynez.

Laird, Melvin Robert, 1922–, American politician, U.S. Secretary of Defense (1969–73), b. Omaha, Nebr. After serving (1942–46) in the navy during World War II, he entered politics as a Republican and was (1946–52) a state senator in Wisconsin. As a member (1953–69) of the U.S. House of Representatives, he served on the appropriations committee where he actively supported a large military budget and a strong nuclear defense posture. Laird became Secretary of Defense in President Nixon's cabinet and presided over the shift from a conscripted to an all-volunteer army. He supported (1970) the invasion of Cambodia and approved the strategy of bombing North Vietnam to force a peace settlement. After his resignation as secretary, he served (1973) briefly as counsellor to the President for domestic affairs. Laird is the author of *A House Divided* (1962) and editor of *Republican Papers* (1968). See M. R. Laird, et al., *The Nixon Doctrine* (1972).

Lairesse, Gerard de (gä'rärt də lārĕs'), 1641–1711, Flemish painter of allegorical and religious subjects, b. Liège. Most of his life was spent in Holland, where he achieved great success in decorating the homes and palaces of Amsterdam with allegorical themes in a classical style. His books on the principles of drawing and painting, dictated after he became blind, were illustrated with his own etchings. They were translated into English, French, and German. Among his best-known paintings are *Revolution* and *Mars, Venus, and Cupid* (Rijks Mus.) and *Cleopatra Landing at Tarsus* (Louvre).

Laish (lā'ĭsh), original name of DAN **2.**

laissez faire (lĕs"ā fâr') [Fr.,=leave alone], in economics and politics, doctrine that an economic system functions best when there is no interference by government. It is based on the belief that the natural economic order tends, when undisturbed by artificial stimulus or regulation, to secure the maximum well-being for the individual and therefore for the community as a whole. Historically, laissez faire was a reaction against MERCANTILISM, a system of commercial controls in which industry and trade, especially foreign trade, were merely seen as means of strengthening the state. Navigation laws, trade monopolies, taxes, and paternalistic regulations of all kinds bore heavily upon the rising class of merchants in the period of European colonial expansion. It was on behalf of this class that the French physiocrats, pioneer economists in the 18th cent., first formulated the principles of laissez faire. With the physiocrats, state noninterference became a cardinal teaching; they especially opposed the taxation of commercial pursuits. Opposition to mercantilism and state paternalism also motivated Adam Smith, father of classical economics, whose name more than any other is connected with British laissez-faire doctrines. Smith believed that individual welfare rather than national power was the correct goal; he thus advocated that trade should be free of government restrictions. When individuals were free to pursue self-interest, the "invisible hand" of rivalry or competition would become more effective than the state as a regulator of economic life. Smith did not believe in laissez faire in an absolute sense; he found a place for government in public works, such as canals and docks to facilitate trade, and in the regulation of foreign commerce to protect certain home industries. In the hands of Jeremy Bentham the doctrine of laissez faire became a philosophy of individualism and of utilitarian ethics, and John Stuart Mill brought it to what was probably its highest point. The strong individualism of the theory naturally appealed to the factory owners and merchants of the Industrial Revolution, whose attempts to transform society along capitalistic lines were often hampered by old laws and the opposition of the landed interests. The so-called Manchester school of economics, especially Richard Cobden and John Bright, popularized the doctrines of free trade and laissez faire, which from being radical doctrines were becoming the accepted theory of classical economics. Cobden and Bright, both successful businessmen, brought laissez faire into the arena of politics: they secured the repeal of the corn laws—mercantilist import duties that raised the price of food needed by the industrial workers—and they opposed even the minimal provisions of the factory acts that Parliament had passed in order to regulate such abuses as long hours and woman and child labor. Laissez-faire principles were nowhere embodied fully in legislation. Governments, at the very least, continued to levy tariffs as a means of protecting domestic manufacturers. As the system of capitalist enterprise evolved in the 19th cent., more and more businessmen found it to their interest to combine with their competitors in huge trusts or cartels in order to control prices and production. Competition, which had been expected to regulate the market, seemed instead to be encouraging monopoly. The principle of state noninterference was discarded; indeed, during the 20th cent. the state was often called upon to restore and preserve freedom of competition where it appeared to be in danger of disappearing. Agreements in restraint of trade, and practices of "unfair" competition, were outlawed. Thus the practice of laissez faire was modified. The theory, however, was not abandoned; it became a tenet of the conservative opponents of socialism. "Big business," which had done so much to destroy the self-regulation of the laissez-faire system, was itself defended against governmental regulation. It was credited with lowering consumer prices by eliminating the high costs of competition. In that way, the emphasis in laissez-faire theory was shifted from competition to the importance of profit as an incentive to production and of individual initiative as necessary to economic progress. See J. W. McConnell, *Basic Teachings of the Great Economists* (1943); F. W. Hirst, ed., *Free Trade and Other Fundamental Doctrines of the Manchester School* (1903, repr. 1968); A. W. Coats, ed., *The Classical Economists and Economic Policy* (1971).

Laius (lā'əs): see OEDIPUS.

La Jolla (lə hoi'yə) [Sp.,=the jewel], resort on the Pacific Ocean, S Calif., an uninc. district within the confines of San Diego; founded 1869. The beautiful ocean beaches and sea-washed caves attract visitors and year-round residents. The Scripps Institution of Oceanography and the Univ. of California at San Diego are located in La Jolla.

Lake, Kirsopp, 1872–1946, noted English biblical scholar. He was curate of St. Mary the Virgin (Oxford) until 1904, when he became a professor at the Univ. of Leiden (until 1913). After 1914 he was at Harvard, first as professor of early Christian literature, from 1919 to 1932 as professor of ecclesiastical history, and from 1932 to 1937 as professor of history. Lake was also interested in archaeology and participated in many expeditions. He periodically visited Mt. Sinai, Mt. Athos, and other centers of ancient culture, and in Greece he did valuable research work on old manuscripts. Among his many publications are *Early Days of Monasticism on Mt. Athos* (1909), *The Beginnings of Christianity* (5 vol., 1920–32), and *Immortality and the Modern Mind* (1922).

lake, body of standing water occupying a hollow in the earth's surface. Ponds are generally small, shallow lakes, although no clear size criterion exists to differentiate them. The primary source of lake water is precipitation that may enter the depression directly as runoff, or by underground springs. Although lakes are usually thought to be freshwater bodies, many lakes, especially in arid regions, become quite salty because a high rate of evaporation concentrates inflowing salts. The Caspian Sea, Dead Sea, and Great Salt Lake are among the greatest of the world's salt lakes. The Great Lakes of the United States and Canada are the world's largest system of freshwater lakes. Lake Superior alone is the world's largest freshwater lake with an area of 31,820 sq mi (82,414 sq km). The Caspian Sea is the largest lake in the world, with an area of c.144,000 sq mi (372,960 sq km). Lake Baykal in the USSR contains the second greatest volume of water and is one of the world's deepest lake at 5,714 ft (1,742 m). Lake Titicaca in the Andes Mts. of South America is the world's highest large lake at 12,500 ft (3,800 m) above sea level; the Dead Sea is the lowest at 1,292 ft (394 m) below sea level. Lakes are not evenly distributed on the earth's surface; most are located in high latitudes and mountainous regions. Canada alone contains nearly 50% of the world's lakes. Most modern lakes were formed as a result of glacial action of the Pleistocene ice sheets. In some areas, as exemplified by the Great Lakes, basins were carved into bedrock by the erosive action of the advancing ice mass. Lake basins are also formed by glacial moraine deposits that dam preexisting stream valleys. Small lakes and ponds often form in kettles, which are small depressions found in moraine deposits caused by the melting of blocks of stagnant ice trapped within the moraine deposit. Volcanic action creates lake basins when lava flows block stream valleys. Calderas, created by the collapse of volcanic craters, also develop basins where lakes can form. In humid climates, where extensive limestone deposits underlie the region, groundwater seeping through the rocks can dissolve great volumes of the limestone, forming caves that often contain underground lakes. Eventually the roofs of these caves collapse, leaving deep, oval-shaped lake basins. Tectonic activity in the earth's crust forms lake basins in many ways. For example, faulting generates RIFT VALLEYS that fill with lake water. Gentle downwarping of the earth's crust can form structural basins that trap runoff, and uplift of ridges of rock can cut off an arm of the sea. OXBOW LAKES are formed in abandoned stream channels in floodplains of meandering rivers with gentle gradients. Deposition of sediment along a shoreline can completely cut off bays, forming coastal lagoons. Man often forms lakes by building dams across river valleys for flood control, hydroelectric generation, or recreational purposes. Lakes are transient features on the earth's surface, and generally will disappear in a short period of geologic time by a combination of processes, e.g., erosion of an outlet, climatic changes that bring drier conditions, and eutrophication. The latter process is the filling of a lake basin by deposition of organic and inorganic sediment that eventually results in the lake becoming a swamp or bog, and eventually a meadow. Human activity has greatly increased the rates of eutrophication. Urban and suburban land construction activities result in increased discharge of soil debris into streams draining into lakes, filling them. Discharge of nutrient-rich sewage effluent and fertilizer into streams and lakes results in increased growth of aquatic plants, and a concomitant decrease in oxygen levels. The plant material is thus incompletely oxidized and eventually chokes the lake basin.

lake, in dyeing, an insoluble PIGMENT formed by the reaction between an organic dye and a MORDANT. The color of a lake depends upon the mordant as well as the dye used. Generally, lakes are not as colorfast as many inorganic dyes, but their colors are more brilliant.

Lake Charles, city (1970 pop. 77,998), seat of Calcasieu parish, SW La.; inc. 1867. It is located on Lake Charles at the mouth of the Calcasieu River in a rice, timber, oil, and natural-gas region. The city is a leading producer of petrochemicals. Other industries include the manufacture of rubber and tires, plastics, and aluminum, the refining of petroleum, and aircraft maintenance. Lake Charles is an important deepwater port and port of entry. A 30-mi (48-km) long channel connects it with the Gulf of Mexico. Petroleum products, chemicals, rice, and cotton are shipped. McNeese State Univ. and Sowela Technical Institute are in the city.

Lake Chelan National Recreation Area: see NATIONAL PARKS AND MONUMENTS (table).

Lake City, city (1970 pop. 10,575), seat of Columbia co., N Fla.; inc. 1921. It was founded in the 1830s as a military post. Lake City is located in a farm and cattle area and produces tobacco, lumber, and naval stores.

Lake District, region of mountains and lakes, c.30 mi (50 km) in diameter, NW England. It includes the Cumbrian Mts. and part of the Furness peninsula. There are 15 lakes, among them Ullswater, Windermere, Derwentwater, and Bassenthwaite; several beautiful falls; and some of England's highest peaks—Scafell Pike (3,210 ft/978 m), Scafell, and Helvellyn. Numerous ancient relics remain, such as the stone circle near Keswick, and there are ruins of old castles and churches and remains of Roman occupation. This scenic district is a favorite resort of artists and writers. William Wordsworth, Samuel Taylor Coleridge, and Robert Southey were known as the Lake Poets. Many writers lived in the district. Herwick sheep, native to the region, are raised there. Tourism is a major source of income. Lake

District National Park (c.80,000 acres/32,370 hectares) was established there in 1951.

lake dwelling, prehistoric habitation built over the shallow waters of a lake shore or a marsh, usually erected on pile-supported platforms, but sometimes on artificial mounds. Such a site afforded easy access to a varied food supply by the availability of fish, marsh fowl, and good crop lands. Africa, Asia, and South America have had lake-dwelling peoples; pile dwellings were also found in the lagoons of Pacific islands. In Europe, remains of Bronze Age lake dwellings were discovered in Britain, Ireland (where they are called *crannogs*), and central Europe. The lake dwellings of Neolithic Switzerland have been reinterpreted as lakeside villages constructed during periods of low water level; sometimes houses were built even on dry lake beds.

Lake Forest, city (1970 pop. 15,642), Lake co., NE Ill., a residential suburb of Chicago, on Lake Michigan; inc. 1861. It is the seat of Lake Forest College and Barat College.

Lake George, village (1970 pop. 1,046), seat of Warren co., E N.Y.; inc. 1903. Situated on the southern tip of Lake George in the foothills of the Adirondack Mts., it is a year-round tourist and sports center. Vestiges of Fort William Henry, built by Sir William Johnson, and of Fort George, begun by Jeffrey Amherst, are in the village.

Lakehead University, at Thunder Bay, Ont., Canada; founded 1946 as Lakehead Technical Institute. It achieved university status in 1965. It has faculties of arts, science, and education, and schools of business administration, engineering, forestry, library technology, nursing, and physical and health education.

Lakehurst, borough (1970 pop. 2,641), Ocean co., E central N.J.; inc. 1921. It is important as the site of the Lakehurst Naval Air Station (est. 1919), which until 1962 accommodated dirigibles. The *Shenandoah* (1923) was the first airship to use the station, and transatlantic airships made it their U.S. terminal from 1924. The burning of the *Hindenburg,* which took 36 lives, occurred there (May 6, 1937) as the hydrogen-filled zeppelin was being moored.

Lake Jackson, city (1970 pop. 13,376), Brazoria co., SE Texas, on a branch of the Brazos River, near the Gulf of Mexico; founded 1941. It is mainly residential.

Lakeland, resort city (1970 pop. 41,550), Polk co., central Fla., in the highland region; inc. 1885. It is an important processing and shipping center for a citrus-fruit region and is a retail trade center serving a large area. It has many diverse manufactures. The Florida Citrus Commission, other state citrus organizations, and the Florida Phosphate Council have their headquarters in Lakeland. Points of interest include Florida Southern College, South-Eastern Bible College, a Hindu temple, and Lake Mirror. The Orange Cup regatta is held on nearby Lake Hollingsworth every February.

Lakeland terrier, breed of strong working TERRIER developed in the 18th and 19th cent. in the Lake District of England. It stands about 14 in. (35.6 cm) high at the shoulder and weighs about 17 lb (7.7 kg). Its short, dense coat is harsh and wiry and usually blue or black marked with tan, bluish black, red, grizzle, or wheaten. The Lakeland was originally bred to follow to ground and kill foxes that preyed upon the Lake District's livestock. To this end, it was common practice on the part of fox hunters to include several of these fearless terriers in their hound packs. Today, the Lakeland is chiefly raised as a pet. See DOG.

Lake Mead National Recreation Area: see NATIONAL PARKS AND MONUMENTS (table).

Lake Meredith National Recreation Area, Texas: see NATIONAL PARKS AND MONUMENTS (table).

Lake of the Woods, 1,485 sq mi (3,846 sq km), c.70 mi (110 km) long, on the U.S.-Canada border in the pine forest region of N Minn., SE Man., and SW Ont. More than two thirds of the lake is in Canada. A remnant of former glacial Lake Agassiz, it is fed by the Rainy River and drained to the northwest by the Winnipeg River. It has a very irregular shoreline and approximately 14,000 islands. Lake of the Woods separates the Northwest Angle, the northernmost land of the conterminous United States, from the rest of Minnesota. Abundant in fish and game, the region is a resort area.

Lake Placid, village (1970 pop. 2,731), Essex co., NE N.Y.; settled 1850, inc. 1900. In the Adirondack Mts. at an altitude of 1,800 ft (549 m), the village surrounds Mirror Lake. It is a famous resort and sports center. The 1932 Winter Olympics and the 1969 World Bobsled Championships were held in the village. Lake Placid has a summer theater and music festival and a figure-skating school. There is a large center for the study of cells and tissue cultures. The farm and burial place of the abolitionist John Brown are nearby.

Lake Success, village (1970 pop. 3,254), Nassau co., SE N.Y., on NW Long Island; settled c.1730, inc. 1926. A residential suburb of New York City, Lake Success was the temporary home of the United Nations from 1946 to 1950.

Lakeview, uninc. town (1970 pop. 11,391), Calhoun co., S central Mich., a suburb of Battle Creek.

Lakewood. 1 City (1970 pop. 82,973), Los Angeles co., S Calif., a residential and industrial suburb of Long Beach; inc. 1954. **2** City (1970 pop. 92,787), Jefferson co., N central Colo., a suburb of Denver; inc. 1969. **3** Township (1970 pop. 17,874), Ocean co., E central N.J., on the Metedeconk River, a health resort in a pine forest and lake region, near the Atlantic coast; settled 1800, inc. 1892. It has poultry farms and plants making a variety of products. It was the site of early ironworks. Georgian Court College is in the town, and the former Rockefeller estate (now a state reserve), a naval air station, and a parachuting center are nearby. **4** City (1970 pop. 70,173), Cuyahoga co., NE Ohio, a suburb of Cleveland, on Lake Erie; inc. 1911. It has many varied industries. The city was settled as East Rockport and renamed in 1889.

Lake Worth, city (1970 pop. 23,714), Palm Beach co., SE Fla., on Lake Worth (a lagoon); inc. 1913. It is a resort center popular for its bathing and fishing facilities. Sports equipment, tents and awnings, clothing, and food products are among its manufactures. A junior college is in Lake Worth.

Lakshadweep, union territory, India: see LACCADIVE, MINICOY, AND AMINDIVI ISLANDS.

Lakshmi: see HINDUISM.

Lakum (lā'kəm), unidentified town, N Palestine. Joshua 19.33.

Lalande, Jean (Saint John Lalande) (zhäN läläNd'), d. 1646, French Jesuit missionary in Canada and New York, one of the Jesuit Martyrs of North America. He came to the New World in 1644. He accompanied (1646) Father Isaac JOGUES on his mission to the Mohawk Indians and was martyred with him. Feast: Sept. 26 or (among the Jesuits) March 16.

Lalande, Joseph Jérôme Lefrançais de (zhôzĕf' zhārōm' ləfräNsā' də), 1732-1807, French astronomer. Under the direction of the French Academy of Science, he went to Berlin in 1751 to make observations on the parallax of the moon for comparison with those that Nicolas Lacaille was making at the Cape of Good Hope. In spite of his youth, he was admitted to the Berlin Academy. In 1760 he became professor of astronomy in the Collège de France, holding the post for 46 years. In 1768 he became director of the Paris Observatory. The Lalande Prize, which he established in 1802, is awarded for the outstanding achievement in astronomy each year. His works include *Traité d'astronomie* (1764); *Histoire céleste française* (1801), including a catalog of over 47,000 stars; and *Bibliographie astronomique* (1802).

Lalemant, Charles (shärl lälmäN'), 1587-1674, French Jesuit missionary in North America; brother of Jérôme Lalemant and uncle of Gabriel Lalemant. He arrived in Quebec in 1625 and acted as novice master and superior. His account, the earliest of the JESUIT RELATIONS, is valuable. He was noted as a mystic. In 1639 he returned to France, where he acted as forwarding agent for the Canadian missions.

Lalemant, Gabriel (Saint Gabriel Lalemant) (gäbrēĕl'), 1610-49, French Jesuit missionary in North America, nephew of Charles Lalemant and Jérôme Lalemant, one of the Jesuit Martyrs of North America. He entered the order in 1630 and was sent to Quebec in 1646. He was assistant to Jean de BRÉBEUF at a mission among the Huron Indians when a band of Iroquois took the village and tortured the priests to death. Feast: Sept. 26 or (among the Jesuits) March 16.

Lalemant, Jérôme (zhārōm'), 1593-1673, French Jesuit missionary in North America, brother of Charles Lalemant and uncle of Gabriel Lalemant. He was an active missionary among the Huron Indians (1638-45) and then was director (1645-56) of all Jesuit missions in Canada. He returned to France but went again (1659-73) to Canada, where he was again the director of missions and served as vicar general to Bishop LAVAL.

Lalitpur, Nepal: see PATAN.

Lally, Thomas Arthur, baron de Tollendal, comte de (tômä' ärtür' bärôN də tôläNdäl' kôNt də lälē'), 1702-66, French general; son of an Irish Jacobite resident in France. As commander of a French expedition to India at the beginning of the Seven Years War, he failed to take Madras (1758-59) and had to surrender to the English at Pondicherry. This defeat put an end to the French empire in India. Taken prisoner and than paroled, Lally returned to France to answer charges of treason. After imprisonment for more than two years, he was tried, and although the procedure of the trial was universally criticized, he was executed. With the help of such notables as Voltaire, he was later vindicated.

Lalo, Édouard Victor Antoine (ādwär' vēktôr' äNtwän' lälō'), 1823-92, French composer. Lalo's opera, *Le Roi d'Ys* (1888), *Symphonie espagnole* for violin and orchestra (1875), and ballet, *Namouna* (1882), gained him wide renown in his time.

lama: see TIBETAN BUDDHISM.

Lamaism: see TIBETAN BUDDHISM.

La Malbaie (lä mälbā') or **Murray Bay,** village, S central Que., Canada, at the confluence of the Malbaie (or Murray) River with the St. Lawrence. It is a well-known resort in dairy-farming country.

Lamar, Joseph Rucker, 1857-1916, American jurist, b. Elbert co., Ga. He was admitted to the Georgia bar in 1878, served (1886-89) in the state legislature, and compiled *The Code of the State of Georgia* (1896). He served (1904-6) on the state supreme court and was Associate Justice of the U.S. Supreme Court (1911-16). See biography by his wife, C. P. Lamar (1926).

Lamar, Lucius Quintus Cincinnatus, 1825-93, American statesman, b. Putnam co., Ga. He practiced law in Oxford, Miss., and sat (1857-60) as a Democrat in Congress. Although he at first opposed secession, Lamar drafted the Mississippi ordinance of secession. In Nov., 1862, he was appointed Confederate commissioner to Russia but was recalled from Paris before reaching Russia. He returned to the Army of Northern Virginia, in which he had previously served as lieutenant colonel of a Mississippi regiment, as a judge advocate. After the Civil War he resumed his practice at Oxford and taught at the Univ. of Mississippi. He was a U.S. Representative (1873-77), Senator (1877-85), and Secretary of the Interior in President Cleveland's cabinet from 1885 to 1888, when he resigned to serve (1888-93) as Associate Justice of the Supreme Court. His efforts after the war to restore friendly relations between North and South brought him into particular prominence. See biographies by Edward Mayes (1896) and J. B. Murphy (1973).

Lamar, Mirabeau Buonaparte, 1798-1859, president of the Texas republic (1838-41), b. Warren co., Ga. He went to Texas (1835), joined the revolutionaries, and took part in the battle of San Jacinto (1836). He held a number of offices in Texas before becoming president. During his term he secured foreign recognition of Texas independence and laid the basis for the system of public education in Texas. Lamar did not favor annexation to the United States at this time and planned to make the new republic self-sufficient, but his various ventures (including filibustering expeditions to New Mexico) disarranged the republic's finances. In 1841 he was replaced by Sam Houston. Lamar later came to favor annexation, served in the Mexican War, and was U.S. minister to Nicaragua and Costa Rica (1858-59). He published a number of romantic lyrics in *Verse Memorials* (1857). See biographies by H. P. Gambrell (1934) and Philip Graham (1938).

Lamarck, Jean Baptiste Pierre Antoine de Monet, chevalier de (zhäN bätēst' pyĕr äNtwän'də mônā', shəvälyā' də lämärk'), 1744-1829, French naturalist. He is noted for his study and classification of invertebrates and for his introduction of evolutionary theories. After varied careers he turned his attention to botany, and recognition of his skill followed upon publication of *Flore françoise* (3 vol., 1778). He was elected to the Academy of Sciences, and, aided by Buffon, he traveled over Europe, under the title of royal botanist, visiting museums and collecting material for the museum of the academy. From 1793 he was professor of zoology at the Museum of Natural History. His ideas concerning the origin of species were first made public in his *Système des animaux sans vertèbres* (1801). He introduced the terms *biology* and *Invertebrata* and suggested the invertebrate classes Infusoria, Annelida, Crustacea, Arachnida, and Tunicata. He is also considered the founder of invertebrate paleontology. His later works were *Philosophie zoologique* (2 vol., 1809; tr. *Zoological Philosophy,* 1963) and *Histoire naturelle des animaux sans vertèbres* (7 vol. in 8, 1815-22). Blindness and poverty marred his later years. **Lamarck's theory of evolution,** or Lamarckism, asserts that all life forms have arisen by a continuous process of gradual modification throughout geologic history. To explain this process he cited the then generally accepted theory of ACQUIRED CHARACTERISTICS, which held that new traits in an organism develop because of a need created by the environment and that they are transmitted to its offspring. Although the latter hypothesis was disputed during Lamarck's lifetime by Cuvier and others and was rejected altogether as the principles of HEREDITY were established, Lamarck's theory of evolution was an important forerunner of the work of Charles Darwin, who recognized a modified influence of environment in evolutionary processes. See studies by A. S. Packard (1901), Edmond Perrier (1925), and H. G. Cannon (1960).

La Marmora (lä mär'mōrä), distinguished Italian noble family. Its best-known member was **Alfonso Ferrero, marchese della Marmora,** 1804–78, general and political leader. He fought for Sardinia against Austria in the wars of 1848–49 and 1859, completely reorganized the Sardinian army, and led (1855–56) the Sardinian expeditionary force in the Crimean War. He was twice premier (1859, 1865–66). His conduct of Italian operations in the Austro-Prussian War (1866) was unsatisfactory, and he resigned after the Italian rout at Custozza.

La Marque (lə märk), city (1970 pop. 16,131), Galveston co., SE Texas, in an agricultural and oil area; settled c.1860, inc. 1953. Originally a farm settlement, it later became a railroad shipping point between Houston and Galveston. Today it is primarily a residential suburb for workers in Texas City and other nearby industrial centers.

Lamartine, Alphonse Marie Louis de (älfôNs' märē' lwē də lämärtēn'), 1790–1869, French poet, novelist, and statesman. After a trip to Italy and a brief period in the army, Lamartine began to write and achieved immediate success with his first publication, *Méditations poétiques* (1820). This group of 24 poems, including the famous "Le Lac," expressed his own feelings—religious, melancholic, or amorous—as he came in contact with nature and the land. He drew from tradition, from Ronsard as well as from the 18th cent., while adding something new in the form of a very personal lyricism expressed in a verse that was intended to be musical. This musicality was developed in *Harmonies* (1830). His religious orthodoxy becomes a kind of pantheism in *Jocelyn* (1836) and *La Chute d'un ange* (1838). In politics, Lamartine held aloof from all parties; his idealism made him embrace the principles of democracy, social justice, and international peace. His *Histoire des Girondins* (1847), a glorification of the GIRONDISTS, was immensely popular, and after the FEBRUARY REVOLUTION of 1848 Lamartine briefly headed the provisional government and was a member of the executive committee that replaced it. His moderation soon cost him the support of both the right and the left wings of the revolutionists. He competed unsuccessfully for the presidency with Louis Napoleon Bonaparte (later Napoleon III). Lamartine left politics and devoted himself entirely to writing, spending much of the remainder of his life in a hopeless effort to repay the fantastic debts he had accumulated in his youth. His later prose works include the novel *Graziella* (1849, tr. 1876) and *Les Confidences* (1852). See studies by H. Remsen Whitehouse (1918) and C. M. Lombard (1973).

La Maurice National Park, 210 sq mi (544 sq km), S Que., Canada, near Trois-Rivières; est. 1970. It is in a heavily wooded part of the Laurentian Mts.

Lamb, Lady Caroline: see under MELBOURNE, WILLIAM LAMB, 2D VISCOUNT.

Lamb, Charles, 1775–1834, English essayist, b. London. He went to school at Christ's Hospital, where his lifelong friendship with Coleridge began. Lamb was a clerk at the India House from 1792 to 1825. In 1796 his sister Mary Ann Lamb (1764–1847) in a fit of temporary insanity attacked and wounded their father and stabbed and killed their mother. Lamb had himself declared her guardian to save her from permanent commitment to an asylum, and after 1799 they lived together. Mary was an intelligent and affectionate companion, but the shadow of her madness continued to plague their lives. They collaborated on several books for children, publishing in 1807 their famous *Tales from Shakespeare.* Lamb wrote four plays, none of which were successful. However, his dramatic essays, *Specimens of English Dramatic Poets* (1808), established his reputation as a critic and did much in reviving the popularity of Elizabethan drama. From 1800 on he wrote intermittently for periodicals, the major contribution being the famous *Essays of Elia* (*London Magazine,* 1820–25), which were collected in 1823 and 1833. The essays cover a variety of subjects and maintain throughout an intimate and familiar tone. Lamb's style is peculiarly his own. His close-knit, subtle organization, his self-revealing observations on life, and his humor, fantasy, and pathos combine to make him one of the great masters of the English essay. Lamb was a gifted conversationalist and was friendly with most of the major literary figures of his time. See his *Life, Letters and Writings,* ed. by Percy Fitzgerald (1895, repr. 1971); biography by Alfred Ainger (1901, repr. 1970); studies by Edmund Blunden (1954; 1933, repr. 1967).

Lamb, John, 1735–1800, American Revolutionary leader, b. New York City. Prior to the Revolution he was a leader of the Sons of Liberty in New York and helped form the New York committee of correspondence to coordinate anti-British activity. With Isaac SEARS he led (1775) a mob that seized the New York customhouse and another that captured the British arms at Turtle Bay in Manhattan. Lamb served in the Quebec campaign and in later battles. In 1784, he became collector of customs in New York City. Later he was one of the leaders of the opposition to the Federal Constitution in New York.

Lamb, William: see MELBOURNE, WILLIAM LAMB, 2D VISCOUNT.

lamb: see MUTTON; SHEEP.

Lambaesis: see TAZOULT, Algeria.

Lamballe, Marie Thérèse Louise de Savoie-Carignan, princesse de (märē' tārĕz' lwēz də sävwä-kärēnyäN', präNsĕs' də läNbäl'), 1749–92, devoted friend and favorite of Queen MARIE ANTOINETTE of France. Extremely unpopular, she was killed by a mob during the French Revolution in the September massacres (1792), and her head was displayed on a pike under the queen's windows.

Lambaréné (lämbärĕnā'), town (1970 est. pop. 18,000), W Gabon, on the Ogooué River. It is a river port and trade center. The famous mission hospital founded by Albert SCHWEITZER is there.

Lambert, Johann Heinrich (yō'hän hīn'rĭkh läm'-bĕrt), 1728–77, German-French philosopher and scientist, b. Alsace. He developed many basic concepts in mathematics, including that of the hyperbolic functions in trigonometry. In physics he achieved valuable results in work on the measurement of the intensity of light (the metric unit of brightness in the cgs system is named for him), degrees of heat, and humidity. In his philosophical work *Neues Organon* (1764) he pointed out the importance of beginning with experience and using the analytical method to investigate any theory of knowledge. His correspondence with Kant is of great philosophical significance. His other important books are *Photometria* (1760) and *Pyrometrie* (1779).

Lambert, John, 1619–83, English parliamentary general. He fought in the first civil war (1642–46) and assisted Henry IRETON in drawing up the Heads of the Proposals in 1647. In 1648 he commanded the Army of the North against the Scots in the second civil war and later took part in the Scottish campaigns of 1650–51 and the defeat of Charles II at Worcester. He played a leading role in drafting the Instrument of Government (1653), by which Oliver CROMWELL became protector, but broke with Cromwell over the latter's acceptance of the Humble Petition and Advice. At the fall of Richard CROMWELL (1659) Lambert defeated a royalist uprising in Cheshire and assisted in dissolving the Rump Parliament. When Gen. George MONCK marched south to restore Parliament, Lambert attempted to meet him, but his army deserted him. After the Restoration (1660), he was tried for treason and banished to the island of Guernsey.

Lambèse: see TAZOULT, Algeria.

Lambeth, borough (1971 pop. 302,616) of Greater London, SE England, on the Thames River. The borough was created in 1965 by the merger of the metropolitan borough of Lambeth with part of the metropolitan borough of Wandsworth. It is largely residential but is important as an area of governmental and commercial offices, including the headquarters of the Greater London Council. The borough is also a major transportation hub with several railroad stations, including Waterloo, London's largest. Lambeth is connected to Westminster borough across the Thames by five bridges. The National Theatre (the Old Vic), the National Film Theatre, and the Royal Festival Hall are in Lambeth, as are the Imperial War Museum, Morley College, and eight hospitals, two of which (St. Thomas's and King's College hospitals) have medical schools.

Lambeth Conference, decennial convocation at Lambeth Palace, London, that brings together all the bishops in the ANGLICAN COMMUNION. It meets at the invitation of the archbishop of Canterbury and is the principal instrument of international Anglican life, although it has no legislative authority over the national churches. The first convocation was held in 1867, the tenth in 1968.

Lamb of God: see AGNUS DEI.

lamb's-quarters: see GOOSEFOOT.

Lambton, John George: see DURHAM, JOHN GEORGE LAMBTON, 1ST EARL OF.

Lamech (lā'mĕk). **1** Descendant of Cain and therefore accursed. He was the father of Jabal, Jubal, and Tubal-cain. Gen. 4.18–24. **2** Descendant of Seth and father of Noah. Gen. 5.25–31.

Lamennais or **La Mennais, Félicité Robert de** (fālēsētā' rōbĕr' də lämənā'), 1782–1854, French Roman Catholic apologist and liberal, b. Saint-Malo. He was largely self-educated by wide, indiscriminate reading. He was converted (1804) to active Catholicism and resolved to serve the church. In 1817 he was ordained and began a brilliant campaign against Gallicanism and anti-Christian philosophy. He soon became the most celebrated French cleric of his day and was for many years the most open advocate of ULTRAMONTANISM in France. He felt that the church could have no real liberty under a royal government and that free speech and a free press were necessary. He and his friends MONTALEMBERT and LACORDAIRE founded (1830) the journal *Avenir.* His work created a sensation, and he was soon embroiled with the conservative, royalistic Gallicans among the clergy. In 1831 he went to Rome to submit his quarrel to the pope, Gregory XVI, only to be condemned in the encyclical *Mirari vos.* He retired for two years and appeared in public as a non-Christian. His *Paroles d'un croyant* (1834) was the greatest work of this period. He died excommunicate. Paradoxically, Lamennais probably did more than any other church figure to break down Gallicanism and to open the way for the universal acceptance of the papal authority by French Catholics. See studies by A. R. Vidler (1954), W. G. Roe (1966), and P. N. Stearns (1967).

Lamentations, book of the Old Testament, placed in the Authorized Version immediately after Jeremiah, to whose author it has been ascribed since ancient times. It is a series of five poems mourning the destruction of Jerusalem by Babylon. The first four poems are an alphabetical acrostic, the third having three verses to the letter, instead of one; the fifth is a prayer. Scholars generally—including those who deny the traditional authorship—would place four of the poems in the years soon after the fall of the city (586 B.C.); the fifth may be a little later. See studies by Bertil Albrektson (1963) and D. R. Hillers (1972); see also bibliography under OLD TESTAMENT.

La Mesa (lə mā'sə), city (1970 pop. 39,178), San Diego co., S Calif., a suburb of San Diego; inc. 1912. It is a retail-trade center for an area of truck and poultry farms.

Lamesa (ləmē'sə), city (1970 pop. 11,559), seat of Dawson co., NW Texas, in the Llano Estacado; inc. 1917. Lamesa is a processing and shipping center for an irrigated area where cattle and poultry are raised and cotton, grains, black-eyed peas, and soybeans are grown. The city processes cottonseed oil and manufactures furniture and mattresses.

La Mettrie, Julien Offray de (zhülyăN' ôfrā' də lä mĕtrē'), 1709–51, French physician and philosopher. On the basis of personal observation he claimed that psychical activity is purely the result of the organic construction of the brain and nervous system and developed this theory in *Histoire naturelle de l'âme* (1745). The protest against his atheistic materialism was so strong that La Mettrie had to leave the country. He further alienated the public with *L'Homme machine* (1748), the final development of his mechanical explanation of man and the world. He lived in Berlin under the protection of his patron Frederick the Great. His ethics, purely hedonistic, are set forth in *L'Art de jouir* (1751).

Lamía (lämē'ä, lä'mēə), city (1971 pop. 37,872), capital of Fthiótis prefecture, E central Greece. It is a transportation hub and an agricultural center. Founded about the 5th cent. B.C., it was the chief city of the small region of Malis and developed as an ally of Athens. It gave its name to the Lamian War (323–322 B.C.), waged by the confederate Greeks against Antipater, the Macedonian general, who took refuge in the city and was besieged there for several months. Antipater conquered (322 B.C.) the confederates at Crannon, near Lárisa. Lamía was known as Zituni from the 10th to the 19th cent.

Lamia (lā′mēə), in Greek mythology, grief-crazed woman whose name was used to frighten children. Her own children were killed by Hera, who was jealous of Zeus' love for her; thereafter Lamia, out of envy for happy mothers, stole and killed the children of others. In later legend, the name Lamia was also used for a woman who lured a youth to his destruction.

laminated wood: see PLYWOOD.

laminitis (lăm″ənī′tĭs), also called founder, inflammation of the lamina, the innermost layer of the hoof wall in horses, ponies, and donkeys. Although the condition usually affects only the front feet, it may involve all four feet. Both acute and chronic forms occur. The laminae become inflamed because of congestion of blood and accumulation of toxins in the hoof region resulting from any of several causes, e.g., consumption of large quantities of grain; ingestion of large amounts of cold water by overheated horses; concussion during fast, hard road work; and toxemia following pneumonia or infection of the uterus. The signs of acute laminitis appear rapidly and include sweating, a rise in temperature to as high as 106°F (62°C), a pounding pulse in the digital artery to the involved hoof, an expression of anxiety, and a stance with the legs forward of their natural position so as to reduce the pain of weight bearing. Chronic laminitis is characterized by a shifting or rotation of the bone and other anatomical distortions in the hoof. The disease is treated by eliminating the causative factors, administering drugs for the acute form, and trimming hooves and fitting corrective horseshoes for the chronic form.

La Mirada (lä mĭrä′də), city (1970 pop. 30,808), Los Angeles co., S Calif.; inc. 1960. La Mirada derives from the Spanish for "the view," referring to the panoramic view of the surrounding valleys from atop the city's hills. La Mirada was the original site of California's olive industry. Biola College is in the city.

Lamizana, Sangoulé (säng-go͞olā′ lämēzä′nä), 1916–, president of Upper Volta (1967–). He served in the French army in World War II and in Indochina before he became Upper Volta's chief of staff (1961). He overthrew Maurice Yameogo in a bloodless coup in 1966 and assumed the titles of president of the republic and president of the council of ministers in 1967.

Lammermuir Hills (lăm′ərmyo͝or′, lăm′ərmyo͝or), range of hills, Lothian and Borders regions, SE Scotland. Meikle Says Law (1,749 ft/533 m) is the highest point. Sheep are grazed in the hills.

Lamont, Johann von (yō′hän fən lä′mônt), 1805–79, Scottish-German astronomer and magnetician, b. Scotland. In 1817 he went to Ratisbon to study at the seminary. He remained in Germany to work in the new observatory at Bogenhausen. Lamont became its director in 1835 and professor of astronomy at the Univ. of Munich in 1852. His most important work was in the field of terrestrial magnetism; he made (1849–58) magnetic surveys in Bavaria, France, Spain, N Germany, and Denmark. In 1850 he announced the theory of the magnetic decennial period and in 1862 the discovery of earth currents. In astronomy he cataloged 34,674 stars, measured nebulas and clusters, and made studies of Uranus. Lamont is the author of *Handbuch des erdmagnetismus* (1849).

Lamont, Thomas William (ləmŏnt′), 1870–1948, American banker, b. Claverack, N.Y., grad. Harvard, 1892. Lamont entered (1903) the banking business in New York City and by 1911 was a partner of J. P. Morgan & Company. In the 1920s and the 1930s, Lamont was sent on special missions to several countries—e.g., China, Japan, Mexico, and Egypt—to help transact loans and to advise on financial matters. He served on the U.S. commission to the Paris Peace Conference and was (1933) a U.S. delegate to the World Economic Conference. After the reorganization (1940) of J. P. Morgan & Company, Lamont became (1943) chairman of the board of directors. His many philanthropies included gifts of $2 million to Harvard and $500,000 for the restoration of the Canterbury Cathedral after World War II. He recounted the story of his youth in *My Boyhood in a Parsonage* (1946).

Lamoricière, Christophe Léon Louis Juchault de (krĕstôf′ lāôN′ lwē zhüshō′ də lämôresyĕr′), 1806–65, French general. Important in the conquest of Algeria, he distinguished himself at the head of his celebrated Zouaves and received (1847) the submission of Abd al-Kadir. He was active in French politics after the February Revolution of 1848, but his opposition to Napoleon III led to his banishment (1852). In 1860, as commander of the papal army, he was routed by a superior Piedmontese force.

La Motte-Fouqué, Friedrich Heinrich Karl, Baron de: see FOUQUÉ.

lamp, originally a vessel for holding oil or some combustible substance that could be burned through a wick for illumination; the term has been extended to other lighting devices. Stones, shells, and other objects of suitable shape were used for burning oil in the Paleolithic period. In Egypt and the Middle East saucerlike terra-cotta lamps were early known. In Greece torches were supplemented in the 6th cent. B.C. with pottery and metal lamps. The Greeks often used a cylindrical spout for the wick. The Romans used a superior closed type of lamp, often with multiple spouts. The float-wick lamp, in which the wick is supported above the oil, was probably of Egyptian origin; it survived in the West chiefly as a sanctuary lamp. The seven-branched candlestick of the Hebrews is believed to have been a support for a group of float-wick lamps. Its symbolical descendant is the eight-branched Hanukkah lamp, usually of the spouted saucer type. There was little improvement in the design of lamps from ancient times to the 18th cent. The Betty lamp of the North American colonists and pioneers was a spouted saucer lamp with a lid. Lamps were smoky because the center of the round wick received too little air for complete combustion. Flat wicks, introduced late in the 18th cent., made less smoke, but the light was somewhat dim. At about the same time a circular wick with an open center was invented by Aimé Argand, a Swiss chemist, who also introduced the glass lamp chimney. One- and two-burner lamps were common from the late 18th cent., and these often burned whale oil. Kerosine, used from the mid-19th cent., almost entirely superseded other oils for lamps; the kerosine lamp is still used for lighting where gas and electricity (the most common form of energy for lamps in industrialized countries) are not available and in many safety, signal, and hurricane lamps. In literature and art the lamp has often symbolized learning or knowledge; in religious ritual, honor to the divine. For the development of the electric lamp, see LIGHTING. See F. W. Robins, *The Story of the Lamp* (1939, repr. 1970); Thamér Szentléky, *Ancient Lamps* (tr. 1969).

lampblack: see CARBON BLACK.

Lampedusa, Giuseppe di (jo͞ozĕp′pā dē lämpädo͞o′zä), 1896–1957, Italian novelist. A wealthy Sicilian prince, Lampedusa drew on his family's history for his internationally acclaimed work, *Il gattopardo,* published posthumously in 1958 (tr. *The Leopard,* 1960). In urbane, elegant style, Lampedusa depicts the demise of an old, aristocratic society that came about with the unification of Italy. Lampedusa based much of his novel on Sicilian history as well as on autobiography. His only other work, *Racconti* (tr. *Two Stories and a Memory,* 1962) appeared in 1961. His name also appears as Giuseppe Tomasi di Lampedusa.

Lampedusa, island, 8 sq mi (20.7 sq km), S Sicily, Italy, in the Mediterranean Sea between Malta and Tunisia, the largest of the Pelagie Islands. Il Porto is the only town of the island. Sponge and sardine fishing are the main occupations. Lampedusa was settled in the 18th cent. In World War II, it was bombed by the Allies. There is a penal colony on the island.

Lampman, Archibald, 1861–99, Canadian poet, b. Ontario. A post office employee all his life, he was a noted nature poet. His work appeared in *Among the Millet* (1888), *Lyrics of Earth* (1893), and *Alcyone* (1899). Collections of his poems include volumes by D. C. Scott (1900, 1947) and E. K. Brown (1943).

Lamprecht, Karl (kärl läm′prĕkht), 1856–1915, German historian. Opposing the notion of heroes in history, he advocated a history based on broad social, cultural, and psychological trends. His chief works are *Die kulturhistorische Methode* (1900) and a monumental multivolume history of Germany (1891–1913). Several of his lectures have been translated as *What Is History?* (1905).

lamprey, name for several primitive marine and freshwater fishes of the order Cyclostomata, or jawless fishes (see CYCLOSTOME). As in the other member of the order, the HAGFISH, the adult lamprey retains the NOTOCHORD, the supporting structure that in higher vertebrates is found only in the embryo. It lacks a sympathetic nervous system, a spleen, and scales. Most adult lampreys are parasitic, sucking the blood of other fishes. The horny teeth, set in the circular, jawless mouth, attach to the prey and the lamprey feeds as it is carried along. Lampreys have an anticoagulant in the saliva that keeps the blood of the victim fluid. Some freshwater lampreys eat flesh as well as blood. Lampreys resemble eels in external appearance and, although not related to the true eels, are sometimes called lamprey eels. When not attached to prey, they swim with undulating movements. The marine lampreys normally migrate into fresh water to spawn, and some populations have become landlocked in fresh water. The Atlantic lamprey, *Petromyzon marinus,* found on both sides of the Atlantic, has become well established in the Great Lakes, where it is considered a serious pest by the fishing industry. The sexes are separate in lampreys and fertilization is external. The parents die shortly after the eggs are deposited in a nest. The larvae, called ammocoetes, are about 1/4 in. (6 mm) long. They are transparent, eyeless filter-feeders and live in muddy river bottoms, eating particles of organic matter. At about five years of age they metamorphose into the adult, parasitic form. Ammocoetes larvae are used in zoology courses to demonstrate a theoretically primitive vertebrate construction. In some species the adult does not feed and remains the size of the larva. There are 7 genera and about 25 species of lampreys, with 13 species in the United States. Lampreys are classified in the phylum CHORDATA, subphylum Vertebrata, class Agnatha, order Cyclostomata, family Petromyzontidae.

Lampsacus (lămp′səkəs), ancient Greek city of NW Asia Minor, on the Hellespont (now Dardanelles) opposite Callipolis (now Gallipoli). It was colonized in the 7th cent. B.C. by Greeks from Phocaea. Artaxerxes I assigned the city to THEMISTOCLES. After the battle of MYCALE (479 B.C.) the citizens joined with the Athenians, and the city continued to flourish under the Greeks and the Romans. It was the seat of the cult of Priapus.

lamp shell, common name for organisms of the phylum BRACHIOPODA.

Lamy, Jean Baptiste (zhäN bätēst′ lämē′), 1814–88, Roman Catholic archbishop in the U.S. Southwest, b. France. He was ordained in 1838 and, after doing missionary work in S Ohio, was sent to New Mexico in 1850 as vicar apostolic. In 1852 he was responsible for the establishment of the first school for teaching English in Santa Fe, and he brought from France and the eastern states nuns and priests to establish other schools. Created bishop in 1853 and archbishop in 1875, he worked tirelessly until 1885 in his vast region, which included, in addition to present-day New Mexico, most of Arizona and parts of Utah, Nevada, and Colorado. Willa Cather's novel *Death Comes for the Archbishop* (1927) is based on his career.

Lanai (lənī′), island (1970 pop. 2,204), 141 sq mi (365 sq km), central Hawaii, W of Maui island across the Auau Channel; Mt. Lanaihale (3,370 ft/1,027 m) is the island's highest point. For many years the island was used for sugarcane raising and cattle grazing. The entire island was purchased in 1922 by a pineapple company and developed as a pineapple-growing center. The company also built Lanai City (1970 pop. 2,122) and Kaumalapau port.

Lanark (lăn′ərk, -ärk), burgh (1971 pop. 8,701), county town of Lanarkshire, S central Scotland, on the Clyde River. It has cattle markets and textile mills. There are hydroelectric power stations at the Falls of Clyde, just S of Lanark. Sir William Wallace's first act of rebellion (1297) was the murder of the English sheriff of Lanark and the burning of the town. Robert Owen conducted industrial and social experiments at the nearby New Lanark mills, founded by his father-in-law, David Dale, in 1785. In 1975, Lanark became part of the Strathclyde region.

Lanarkshire (lă′nərkshĭr, lă′närk-), county (1971 pop. 627,217), 898 sq mi (2,326 sq km), central Scotland. The county town is LANARK, but the administrative offices are in HAMILTON. The region, which includes the valley of the Clyde and is sometimes referred to as Clydesdale, has a varied terrain, rising from the level valley in the north to more than 2,000 ft (609 m) in the mountainous southern portion. Lanarkshire is Scotland's most populous and most highly industrialized county. In the north is the great port and industrial center of GLASGOW; in and near this city are extensive shipyards, engineering works, brick factories, textile plants, and various other factories. In the heart of the Clyde industrial belt is the great steel capital of MOTHERWELL AND WISHAW (which now utilizes imported ores). After World War II the Lanarkshire coal industry began a shift to the Lothians and Fife, but coal is still mined. The central part of the county is an undulating agricultural region. Oats, wheat, potatoes, turnips, and market produce for Glasgow are raised. Clydesdale work horses, cattle, and sheep are bred, and dairying is important. At Langside, Mary Queen of Scots was defeated (1568). In 1975, Lanarkshire became part of the Strathclyde region.

Lancashire (lăng'kəshĭr, -shər), county (1971 pop. 5,106,123), 1,878 sq mi (4,864 sq km), N England, on the Irish Sea. The county town is LANCASTER. The northwestern portion of the county is part of the picturesque LAKE DISTRICT; in the west and south are lowlands (the Lancashire plain) and occasional moors, with rich deposits of coal, slate, and sandstone. The principal rivers are the Mersey (which forms much of the county's southern border), the Lune, the Wyre, and the Ribble. The coastline is low and much broken by estuaries. Morecambe Bay separates FURNESS from the rest of the county. Lancashire is the most populous county of England, and its two great cities, MANCHESTER and the famous port of LIVERPOOL, are the heart of one of the great industrial regions of the world. The chief manufactures are heavy iron and steel products, textiles, paper, chemicals, rubber goods, and glass. There are large shipyards, notably at Liverpool and BARROW-IN-FURNESS. Throughout the 19th cent. Manchester was the greatest cotton-manufacturing center in the world. Vegetables and dairy products are also important in the county's economy. Lancashire in Anglo-Saxon times was part of the kingdom of NORTHUMBRIA. In 1351 it was made a county palatine, and in 1399 the palatine rights were vested in the king; to the present time a minister of the monarch has the title chancellor of the duchy of Lancaster. Lancashire's economic growth began in medieval times with the introduction of the woolen industry. The process was accelerated by the Industrial Revolution, and the population increased rapidly in the 19th and early 20th cent. In 1974, Lancashire was reorganized as a nonmetropolitan county.

Lancaster, Edmund Crouchback, earl of: see LANCASTER, HOUSE OF.

Lancaster, Henry, earl of: see LANCASTER, HOUSE OF.

Lancaster, John of, duke of Bedford: see BEDFORD, JOHN OF LANCASTER, DUKE OF.

Lancaster, John of Gaunt, duke of: see JOHN OF GAUNT.

Lancaster, Joseph, 1778–1838, English educator. In 1801 he founded a free elementary school, using a type of MONITORIAL SYSTEM for which he acknowledged his debt to Andrew BELL. The Royal Lancasterian Society was later established (1808) to direct the school. However, Lancaster, embittered by controversy with the society and with Bell, whose system had the support of the established church—Lancaster was a Quaker—went to the United States in 1818 to lecture. His efforts to establish a school at Baltimore were ended by his failing health. He moved to Venezuela, and later to Canada and New York City, to promote his educational ideas. Although Lancaster's ideas were generally well received during those journeys, he was unable to establish another school outside of England. His writings on his system include *Report of Joseph Lancaster's Progress from 1798* (1810) and *The Lancasterian System of Education* (1821). See study ed. by C. F. Kaestle (1973).

Lancaster, Thomas, earl of: see LANCASTER, HOUSE OF.

Lancaster (lăng'kəstər), municipal borough (1971 pop. 49,525), county town of Lancashire, NW England, on the Lune River. The city's products include furniture, textiles, farm machinery, linoleum, soap, and flour. Lancaster Castle occupies the site of a Roman station. It has a Norman keep and tower (built 1170) with a turret called John o' Gaunt's Chair. St. Mary's Church dates mostly from the 15th cent.

Lancaster. **1** Uninc. city (1970 pop. 30,948), Los Angeles co., S Calif., in Antelope Valley and in the Mojave Desert; laid out 1894. It is a trade center for an irrigated farming area. An Indian museum there has prehistoric artifacts. A junior college is in the city, and nearby are a state park and Edwards Air Force Base. **2** Village (1970 pop. 13,365), Erie co., W N.Y.; inc. 1849. Its industries include lumber mills, dairy farms, and stone quarries. **3** City (1970 pop. 32,911), seat of Fairfield co., S central Ohio, on the Hocking River, in a livestock and dairy area; founded 1800 by Ebenezer Zane, inc. as a village 1831. Its manufactures include glassware, shoes, and automotive parts. The birthplace of the brothers Gen. William T. Sherman and Senator John Sherman has been preserved. In the area are many covered bridges and an Indian mound in the form of a cross. **4** City (1970 pop. 57,690), seat of Lancaster co., SE Pa., on the Conestoga River, in the heart of the Pennsylvania Dutch country; inc. as a city 1818. It is the commercial center for one of the most productive agricultural counties in the United States. Chief products are tobacco, small grains, and livestock. Lancaster has a huge farmers' market and one of the largest stockyards east of Chicago. Manufactures include linoleum, watches, radio tubes, cigars, razors, tools, and metal products. It is the seat of Franklin and Marshall College and of a theological seminary. The area was settled by German Mennonites c.1709, and the famous Conestoga wagon was developed there shortly thereafter. The borough of Lancaster was laid out in 1730 and was one of the first inland cities in the country. A munitions center during the Revolution, it was briefly (1777) a meeting place of the Continental Congress and served as capital of the state for more than 10 years before 1812. It was the western terminus of the Lancaster Turnpike. Robert Fulton was born near there, and Thaddeus Stevens practiced law in the city. Points of interest include Wheatland, the home of James Buchanan (built in 1828; a national shrine since 1962); homes of several Revolutionary War patriots; and the Fulton Opera House (1854), one of the oldest continuously operating theaters in the country and now a historic monument. **5** City (1970 pop. 10,522), Dallas co., in NE Texas, in a blackland farming area; settled 1846, inc. 1886. Clothing is made in the city.

Lancaster, house of (lăng'kəstər), royal family of England. The line was founded by the second son of Henry III, **Edmund Crouchback,** 1245–96, who was created earl of Lancaster in 1267. Earlier (1254) the prince had been made titular king of Sicily when the pope offered that crown to Henry III in order to keep Sicily and the Holy Roman Empire separated. However, the English barons refused financial support for the Sicilian wars, and the title was withdrawn (1258). Later Edmund fought for his brother, Edward I, in Wales and Gascony. His nickname "Crouchback," or crossed back, refers only to the fact that he went on crusade to Palestine in 1271 and, hence, was entitled to wear the cross. Edmund's son **Thomas, earl of Lancaster,** 1277?–1322, led the baronial opposition to his cousin EDWARD II. He was one of the lords ordainers and from 1314 to 1318 was virtual ruler of England. He tried unsuccessfully to drive the Despensers (see DESPENSER, HUGH LE) from England, was defeated at the battle of Boroughbridge, and was beheaded for treason. Thomas's brother, **Henry, earl of Lancaster,** 1281?–1345, was chief adviser to the young EDWARD III in getting rid of the dominance of the queen mother, Isabella, and her paramour, Roger de Mortimer, 1st earl of March. His son, **Henry, duke of Lancaster,** 1299?–1361, was made duke in 1351 for his excellent service as a military commander in the early part of the Hundred Years War. When he died without male heirs, his daughter Blanche married the fourth son of Edward III, JOHN OF GAUNT, who inherited the Lancaster lands in her right, and was made duke of Lancaster in 1362. His son Henry deposed (1399) Richard II and ascended the throne as HENRY IV. In order to appear legitimate, Henry devised the fiction that his ancestor Edmund Crouchback had actually been Henry III's elder son but had been disinherited because he was a hunchback. Later Lancastrian kings were HENRY V and HENRY VI. The latter was deposed by the house of YORK in the course of the long dynastic struggle known as the Wars of the ROSES. However, through the Beauforts, the legitimated descendants of John of Gaunt and Catherine Swynford, the Lancastrian claims passed to the house of TUDOR. See K. B. McFarlane, "The Lancastrian Kings," *Cambridge Medieval History,* Vol. VIII (1936); R. Somerville, *History of the Duchy of Lancaster,* Vol. I (1953).

Lancaster Sound, arm of Baffin Bay, c.200 mi (320 km) long and 40 mi (60 km) wide, E Franklin dist., Northwest Territories, Canada. It extends west between Devon and Baffin islands and is part of the shortest water route across N Canada to the Beaufort Sea. It was discovered in 1616 by William Baffin, the English explorer.

lance: see SPEAR.

lancelet, name for small, fishlike lower chordate (see CHORDATA), also called amphioxus; it shows many affinities with the vertebrates. There are about 30 lancelet species, most belonging to the genus *Branchiostoma* (formerly *Amphioxus*). Lancelets are usually about 1 in. (2.5 cm) long, with transparent bodies tapered at both ends. There is no distinct head and no paired fins. Lancelets are filter feeders and live in shallow marine waters; they can swim through water or wet sand, but are usually found buried in the sand with only the mouth end projecting. Small food particles enter the pharynx through the mouth and are filtered out as the water exits through the gill slits. Respiration probably occurs mostly through the skin. The use of the gill slits for feeding rather than respiration is characteristic of the lower chordates (see TUNICATE). The lancelet has a dorsal notochord, or stiffening rod, extending from tip to tail, that gives it its characteristic pointed shape. It retains the notochord as the major skeletal support throughout life; in vertebrates the notochord is surrounded and usually replaced by a vertebral column during embryonic development. In the lancelet there is a nerve cord above the notochord, but no brain and no eyes. A ventral blood vessel carries the colorless blood; there is no heart. It is thought that vertebrates evolved from ancestors similar to lancelets. The larva of the LAMPREY, the most primitive living vertebrate, resembles a lancelet in many respects. Lancelets are classified in the phylum CHORDATA, subphylum Cephalochordata.

Lancelot (lăn'sələt, -lŏt) or **Ladislaus** (lăd'ĭslôs, -ləs), c.1376–1414, king of Naples (1386–1414), son and successor of Charles III. Almost his entire reign was consumed by his struggle with the ANGEVIN rival king of Naples, LOUIS II, and with Louis's ally, the antipope John XXIII (see COSSA, BALDASSARRE). Fortunes shifted repeatedly, but at his death Lancelot was able to transfer his kingdom to his sister, Joanna II. Lancelot occupied Rome several times and in 1413 ordered it sacked.

Lancelot, Sir: see LAUNCELOT, SIR.

Lan-chou or **Lanchow** (both: län-jō), city (1970 est. pop. 1,500,000), capital of Kansu prov., W China, on the Huang Ho (Yellow River) at its confluence with the Wei. It is a rail, highway, and air hub and the junction point to remote Sinkiang in extreme NW China. Lan-chou is linked by rail to Peking and to the Mongolian People's Republic and the USSR. It is on the highway to Tibet. A rapidly growing industrial city, it receives its power from a nearby hydroelectric facility and from the coal that is mined in the area. It has one of the largest oil refineries in the country, a gas-diffusion plant for processing plutonium, textile mills, and petrochemical, plastic, chemical fertilizer, and machine manufactures. An old walled city, Lan-chou was the scene (1936) of a successful Chinese Communist revolt. It is the seat of an oil research institute, Lan-chou Univ., and numerous technical colleges.

Lanchow: see LAN-CHOU, China.

Lanciani, Rodolfo Amadeo (rōdôl'fō ämädĕ'ō länchä'nē), 1847?–1929, Italian archaeologist. He was an authority on the ancient topography of Ostia and Rome and discovered many important Roman antiquities. Lanciani was made director of excavations (1875) and professor of Roman topography at the Univ. of Rome (1878). Among his works in English are *Wanderings in the Roman Campagna* (1909) and *Ancient and Modern Rome* (1925).

Lancret, Nicolas (nēkôlä' läNkrā'), 1690–1743, French rococo painter. He studied in Gillot's studio, together with WATTEAU whose themes and manner he popularized. His favorite subjects were festivities, genre, and theatrical scenes, of which he painted a vast number in a pleasing, though somewhat stilted, style. His work is charming, but not equal to Watteau's in color, grace, or poetic quality. Examples are in the Louvre (e.g., *The Music Lesson,* 1743) and in the National Gallery, London.

land, in law, any ground, soil, or earth regarded as the subject of ownership, including trees, water, buildings added by man, the air above, and the earth below. Private ownership of land does not exist in groups that live by hunting, fishing, or herding; e.g., in pre-Columbian times in America, the Indian tribe owned the land, and each tribesman had equal access to it and equal rights to its use. In simple agricultural groups, as in early Europe, the VILLAGE community made an annual allotment of land to individuals for cultivation. Similar allotments were made under the MANORIAL SYSTEM. A communal form of rural landholding persisted in Russia into the 20th cent. and still exists in India. The modern sovereign state asserts dominion over all property within its territorial limits, including the land, and by the right of eminent domain (see PUBLIC OWNERSHIP) can seize privately owned land for public use, with the proviso that the owner be justly compensated. In the Soviet Union ownership of all land is vested in the nation outright, individuals and organizations being granted provisional rights to its use. Widely distributed private ownership of farmland has been regarded in Western countries as socially—if not always economically—advantageous. The concentration of landholding in a few hands has frequently led to political unrest and social upheaval, as in Latin America, Spain, Italy, the Middle

East, and parts of Asia. In economics the term *land* is used to designate one of the main factors of production; it is another name for nature or natural resources. But few natural resources are free; farmland, for instance, is almost valueless without cultivation. In order to extract crops, minerals, and energy from the land, labor and capital must be applied. In economic theories of value, the share assigned to land as a factor in production is called RENT. See PUBLIC LAND; TENURE; PROPERTY. See A. W. Griswold, *Farming and Democracy* (1948); Graham Hallett, *The Economics of Agricultural Land Tenure* (1960); R. E. Megarry and H. W. R. Wade, *The Law of Real Property* (3d ed. 1966).

Landau, Lev Davidovich (lyĕf dəvē'dəvĭch ləndou'), 1908–68, Soviet physicist, b. Baku, Azerbaijan. A child prodigy in mathematics, he entered Baku Univ. at 14; at 21 he received a doctorate from the Univ. of Leningrad. In 1934 he worked with Niels Bohr in Copenhagen. In 1937 he became head of the theoretical department of the USSR Academy of Sciences. A key figure in Soviet space technology, he helped make the first Soviet atomic bomb. For his contributions to low-temperature physics he was voted the Fritz London Award at the 1960 International Congress of Physics, held in Toronto. For his pioneering studies on gases, especially his development of a mathematical theory of SUPERFLUIDITY that accounts for the properties of liquid helium II at a temperature below −455.73°F (−270.96°C), he received the 1962 Nobel Prize in Physics.

Landau, Mark Aleksandrovich: see ALDANOV, MARK.

Lander, Richard Lemon, 1804–34, English explorer. He accompanied Clapperton to the Niger River in 1827 and brought back Clapperton's journal, which was published (1829) with an account of Lander's return to the coast. Accompanied by his brother John Lander (1807–39), he led an expedition (1830–31) to determine the course of the lower Niger and discovered that the river emptied into the Bight of Benin. The brothers published their combined journals (3 vol., 1832). Richard Lander died of wounds received on a trading expedition to the Niger (1832–34); an account of the trip was published by survivors, Macgregor Laird and R. A. K. Oldfield.

Landes (läNd), region, SW France. It is a vast, flat, nearly triangular tract of sand and marshland, stretching along the Atlantic coast for more than 100 mi (160 km) between the Adour River and the Médoc region and reaching inland as far as 40 mi (60 km). It thus covers most of Landes dept. and part of Gironde dept. and converges on Nérac (Lot-et-Garonne). Formerly, sheep grazing was the only occupation in this insalubrious region, but much of the land has been reclaimed through drainage and the planting of pine forests. Agriculture is progressing and lumber and resins are important products. The chief towns are Mont-de-Marsan, Dax, and Arcachon, a popular resort.

Landes, department (1968 pop. 277,381), SW France, in GASCONY, on the Atlantic coast. Mont-de-Marsan is the capital.

land-grant colleges and universities, U.S. institutions benefiting from the provisions of the Morrill Act (1862), which gave to the states Federal lands for the establishment of colleges offering programs in agriculture, engineering, and home economics, as well as in the traditional academic subjects. Because of the act's stress on the practical arts, the land-grant system has come to include practically all of the nation's agricultural colleges and a large number of its engineering schools; in 1973 there were 70 land-grant colleges. Another provision of the Morrill Act called for the establishment of a military training program, now part of the Reserve Officers' Training Corps (ROTC), at every land-grant college. Although the act itself did not stipulate that the training be compulsory, nearly every state had made it so by the 1920s. After World War II, however, ROTC was generally put on an elective basis. The Hatch Act (1887) expanded the land-grant program by providing Federal funds for research and experiment stations; the Smith-Lever Act (1914) granted Federal support for extension work in agriculture and home economics. See Earle D. Ross, *Democracy's College* (1942); Allan Nevins, *The State Universities and Democracy* (1962); Herman R. Allen, *Open Door to Learning* (1963).

Landini, Francesco (fränchās'kō ländē'nē), 1325–97, Italian composer. Although Landini was blinded from smallpox in childhood, he learned to play the lute, guitar, flute, and organ. His organ playing was highly regarded. He was a celebrated master of the Florentine *ars nova* style. Among his works are madrigals, cacce, and ballate. His name was also spelled Landino.

Landis, James McCauley, 1899–1964, American lawyer and public official, b. Tokyo, Japan, of American parents. At first a law clerk (1925) to Associate Justice Louis Brandeis, Landis taught (1926–34) at Harvard law school. He was appointed (1933) by President Franklin Delano Roosevelt to the Federal Trade Commission; he then served (1934–37) on the Securities and Exchange Commission, becoming its chairman in 1935. After a period (1937–46) as dean of the Harvard law school, he served (1946–47) as chairman of the Civil Aeronautics Board. In 1961 he was a special assistant to President Kennedy. With Felix Frankfurter he wrote *The Business of the Supreme Court* (1927). His books also include *Cases on Labor Law* (1934) and *The Administrative Process* (1938).

Landis, Kenesaw Mountain, 1866–1944, American jurist and commissioner of baseball (1921–44), b. Millville, Butler co., Ohio, grad. Union College of Law (now Northwestern Univ. law school), 1891. He practiced law in Chicago after 1891, the year he was admitted to the bar, and later served (1905–22) as a U.S. district judge in N Illinois. In 1907 he imposed a $29,240,000 fine on the Standard Oil Company of Indiana in a rebate case. Though it was reversed by a higher court, the decision won him wide acclaim. In 1917 he sentenced William D. HAYWOOD, American labor leader, to a 20-year prison term, and although the decision was later reversed by the U.S. Supreme Court, Landis sentenced Victor Berger and six other Socialists for sedition (impeding the war effort). After organized baseball was confronted (1920) with the "Black Sox" scandal, a committee of baseball executives appointed (1921) Landis—who had presided at the case in which the newly organized Federal League brought suit against the National and American leagues for violating the Sherman Anti-Trust Act—to the new post of baseball commissioner. Landis immediately barred from organized baseball the eight Chicago White Sox players charged with bribery in the 1919 world series. The strict discipline he imposed on players and managements did much to restore public faith in professional baseball. See biography by J. G. T. Spink (1947).

Land League: see IRISH LAND QUESTION.

Landon, Alfred Mossman, 1887–, U.S. politician, b. West Middlesex, Pa. He was a banker and oil operator before he ran for public office. Landon served (1933–37) as governor of Kansas and gained a national reputation by his economic administration. As Republican candidate for President in 1936, running against Franklin Delano Roosevelt, he carried only Maine and Vermont. See biography by Donald R. McCoy (1966).

Landor, Walter Savage, 1775–1864, English poet and essayist, educated at Oxford. After a quarrel with his father, he went to live in Wales, where he wrote the epic poem *Gebir* (1798). The middle and most productive years of his life were spent in Italy. There he wrote the greater portion of his voluminous prose work *Imaginary Conversations* (1824–53), consisting of nearly 150 dialogues between notables both ancient and modern. Landor's verse ranges from the epic to the epigrammatic, including many lyrics of great simplicity and intensity. His other works include *Pericles and Aspasia* (1836), *Hellenics* (1847), and *Heroic Idylls* (1863). See his complete works (ed. by T. E. Welby and Stephen Wheeler, 16 vol., 1927–36); biographies by R. H. Super (1954) and Malcolm Elwin (1970); bibliography by R. H. Super (1954).

Landowska, Wanda (vän'dä ländôf'skä), 1877–1959, Polish-French harpsichordist and pianist, studied at the Warsaw Conservatory. She taught piano (1900–1912) at the Schola Cantorum, Paris, and harpsichord (1912–19) at the Berlin Hochschule. At Saint-Leu-la-Forêt, near Paris, she established her École de Musique ancienne and there, between 1919 and 1940, gave many concerts of early music. In 1940 she came to the United States, settling in Lakeville, Conn., where she taught and made recordings. Largely responsible for the revival of interest in the harpsichord and its music, she was the teacher of many noted contemporary harpsichordists. Manuel de Falla and Francis Poulenc wrote (1926 and 1929) the first 20th-century harpsichord concertos for her. With her husband, Henry Lew, she wrote *Music of the Past* (tr. 1923). See Wanda Landowska, *Landowska on Music* (1969), ed. by D. Restout and R. Hawkins.

Land process, single-step photographic process invented by Edwin H. Land; it is used in cameras and film marketed under the trade name Polaroid. The black-and-white process was first demonstrated in 1947 and marketed the following year, and the color process was marketed in 1963. The following are common to both processes: a light-sensitive negative material on a base of paper or plastic; a light-insensitive positive material (the receiving sheet), usually on a paper base; a sealed container of processing reagent (the pod) for each picture, attached to either the positive or the negative; and a reagent spreader system consisting either of a pair of closely spaced rollers (usually of steel) or of nonrotating spreader bars. After exposure, equal lengths of negative and receiving sheet are drawn between the rollers or spreader bars, thus bursting the pod and spreading a layer of viscous processing reagent between the negative and the receiving sheet to form a thin, tightly sealed sandwich. Processing takes place either inside or outside the camera, depending on the camera type. See PHOTOGRAPHIC PROCESSING.

Landrum-Griffin Act, 1959, passed by the U.S. Congress, officially known as the Labor-Management Reporting and Disclosure Act. It resulted from hearings of the Senate committee on improper activities in the fields of labor and management, which uncovered evidence of collusion between dishonest employers and union officials, the use of violence by certain segments of labor leadership, and the diversion and misuse of labor union funds by high-ranking officials. The act provided for the regulation of internal union affairs, including the regulation and control of union funds. Former members of the Communist party and former convicts are prevented from holding a union office for a period of five years after resigning their Communist party membership or being released from prison. Union members are protected against abuses by a bill of rights that includes guarantees of freedom of speech and periodic secret elections. Secondary boycotting and organizational and recognition picketing (i.e., picketing of companies where a rival union is already recognized) are severely restricted by the act. In the field of arbitration, an amendment to the Taft-Hartley Labor Act (1947) written into this 1959 act authorized states to process cases that fall outside the province of the National Labor Relations Board. Organized labor has, in general, opposed the act for strengthening what they consider the anti-labor provisions of the Taft-Hartley Labor Act.

Landsberg am Lech (länts'bĕrk äm lĕkh) or **Landsberg,** town (1970 pop. 14,205), Bavaria, S West Germany, on the Lech River. Textiles, metal goods, and paper are manufactured. Its fortress served as a political prison; Adolf Hitler wrote *Mein Kampf* while imprisoned there in 1923–24, and numerous convicted Nazi war criminals were held there after 1945.

Landsberg an der Warthe: see GORZÓW WIELKOPOLSKI, Poland.

landscape gardening: see GARDEN.

landscape painting. The concept of landscape grew very slowly. Nature was viewed as isolated objects long before it was appreciated as scene or environment. As a result landscape painting as an independent art was a late development in the West. Many scenes, from the Hellenistic pastoral paintings of antiquity to the religious works of the 16th cent. A.D., contained expansive landscape backgrounds, but they were usually subordinated within a narrative context. In Renaissance Italy the study of PERSPECTIVE gave rise to a careful rendering of scenery according to conventional formulas. Giorgione and the Venetian painters excelled at pastoral vistas that recalled scenes from classical literature. Flemish works enhanced by meticulous landscape detail became popular in Italy and encouraged PATINIR and others to cater to this taste. ALTDORFER, the Danube painter of the early 16th cent., created some of the first works devoted entirely to landscape. During and after the Reformation the use of religious subject matter was restricted and numerous artists in the north became specialists in the landscape genre at which, when painting backgrounds of religious works, they had become proficient. These artists, among whom Pieter BRUEGEL, the elder, was most notable, were devoted to fantastic scenes painted according to established convention in tones of brown for the foreground, green for the middle ground, and blue for the background panorama. In Rome, Dutch artists, led by CONINXLOO, initiated the concept of the ideal landscape. CLAUDE LORRAIN was supreme master of this genre. His serene pastoral works and the heroic compositions of POUSSIN contrasted with the concurrent Dutch tendency toward realism. The great 17th-century Dutch landscape masters from van GOYEN to RUISDAEL, HOBBEMA, and REMBRANDT transformed into paint what they saw in the Dutch countryside (see DUTCH ART). The Rococo saw a revival of ideal pastoral scenes in the works of WATTEAU and GAINSBOROUGH. England produced the major late 18th-century landscape masters: GIRTIN, the visionary TURNER, and CONSTABLE, who greatly influenced the French Romantics. In addition, Constable's work served as inspiration to the BARBIZON SCHOOL in France, whose members returned to the serene pastoral mood. In Germany, C. D. FRIEDRICH sustained the poetic tradition of landscape, as did the luminists of the American HUDSON RIVER SCHOOL. Turner's exploration of the atmospheric effects of light interested MONET, whose PLEIN-AIR works, forming the basis of IMPRESSIONISM, elevated landscape to the highest position in artists' esteem that it had yet held. It became a principal source material of POSTIMPRESSIONISM. The exponents of SURREALISM revealed the fearful power of imaginary landscape. The 20th-century artists working in the abstract idiom have employed both landscape and still life as basic sources. In China landscape art reached extraordinary perfection as early as the 8th cent. and engaged the highest talents during the T'ang, Sung, and Ming dynasties. The prominence accorded landscape in both Chinese and Japanese art reflects the mystical esteem for nature characteristic of the Oriental religions. See C. L. Hind, *Landscape Painting from Giotto to the Present Day* (1923); Sir Kenneth Clark, *Landscape into Art* (1949, repr. 1961); Marco Valsecchi, *Landscape Painting in the 19th Century* (tr. 1969); Zoltan Szabo, *Landscape Painting in Watercolor* (1971).

Landseer, Sir Edwin Henry (lăn'sēr), 1802–73, English animal painter. The best known of all animal painters, he is especially remembered for his sentimental, humanized paintings of dogs. He was an infant prodigy and one of the most prolific and famous artists of his period. Innumerable engravings were made of such works as *The Stag at Bay* and *Dignity and Impudence.* Landseer rendered his great talent insipid by pandering to a taste that favored dainty, saccharine morality paintings. His work had enormous significance in popularizing the anthropomorphic concept of animals. See study by James Manson (1902).

Lands End, promontory, Cornwall, SW England, forming the westernmost extremity of the English mainland. Of wave-carved granite, it has cliffs c.60 ft (20 m) high. Offshore are reefs and rocky islets, on one of which is Longships Lighthouse.

Landshut (länts'ho͝ot), city (1970 pop. 52,417), Bavaria, SE West Germany, on the Isar River. Once the capital of Lower Bavaria, it is now a transportation and industrial center. Manufactures include glass, ceramics, chemicals, and machinery. Founded in 1204, Landshut became the residence of the dukes of Bavaria-Landshut in 1255. The city suffered heavily in the Thirty Years War (1618–48). From 1802 to 1826 it was the seat of the Bavarian university (now at Munich). A 13th-century castle, Burg Trausnitz, overlooks the city.

Landskrona (länskro͞o'nä), city (1970 pop. 30,110), Malmöhus co., SW Sweden, a seaport on the Øresund. It is a commercial and industrial center. Manufactures include refined sugar, metal goods, rubber, and textiles. Chartered in 1413, Landskrona was devastated in the Danish-Swedish wars of the 16th–17th cent. In 1677 the Swedes won a naval victory over the Danes off Landskrona. The city was largely rebuilt in the mid-18th cent. The nearby town of Ven, the residence of the 16th-century astronomer Tycho Brahe, was annexed by Landskrona in 1959.

landslide, rapid slipping of a mass of earth or rock from a higher elevation to a lower level under the influence of gravity and water lubrication. More specifically, rockslides are the rapid downhill movement of large masses of rock with little or no hydraulic flow. In 1903, 35 million cubic yards (27 million cubic meters) of limestone slid down Turtle Mountain in Alberta, Canada, partly destroying the town of Frank and killing 70 inhabitants. Rockslides triggered by an earthquake in Montana in 1959 caused an entire mountainside to slide into the Madison River gorge, killing 27 people in its path, damming the gorge, and forming a new lake. In humid climates, water-saturated soil or clay on a slope may slide downhill over a period of several hours. Earthflows of this type are usually not serious threats to life because of their slow movement, yet they can cause blockage of roads and do extensive damage to property. Mudflows are more spectacular streams of mud that pour down canyons in mountainous regions where there is little vegetation to protect hillsides from erosion during severe thunderstorms. The runoff from the storm becomes a thin mud slurry that funnels down the canyons until it thickens and stops. Even boulders may be carried by the mudflow, which can engulf houses and bridges. Man has triggered a number of tragic earthflows and mudflows that have caused great damage and loss of life. Particularly in Los Angeles co., California, extensive real estate development carried out on hillsides has resulted in widespread mudflows when winter rains have saturated the over-steepened embankments of soil. These mudflows have pushed houses, automobiles, and people down the slope and engulfed houses on the valley floor below. Brush fires, a common problem in this area during the dry spell, often contribute to the inability of the soil to retain moisture. In some areas, slow-moving earthflows have been initiated by the lubrication of certain types of underlying clays by septic tank effluent.

landsmaal: see NORWEGIAN LANGUAGE.

Landsteiner, Karl (kärl länt'shtīnər), 1868–1943, American medical research worker, b. Vienna, M.D. Univ. of Vienna, 1891. In 1922 he came to the United States to join the staff of the Rockefeller Institute (now Rockefeller Univ.). He later became a citizen. For his discovery of human BLOOD GROUPS he won the 1930 Nobel Prize in Physiology and Medicine. As a result of his research in immunology and the chemistry of antigens and serological reactions, he made valuable contributions in hemolysis and in methods of studying poliomyelitis. In 1940 he identified, in collaboration with A. S. Wiener, the RH FACTOR.

land tax, impost levied upon real property. It is sometimes called a real estate tax, especially when assessed against both improved and unimproved land. Probably the earliest direct tax and formerly the chief source of government revenue, it was known in ancient China and Egypt. Until modern times, European countries depended on it almost exclusively. In the United States the land tax (including the tax on improved property) has been the chief method of collecting local revenue, accounting for some 25% of all state and local government receipts. The tax may be assessed on the sale value of the property, although a fairer method is classification of the land according to its productiveness. The argument against the land tax is that it raises the cost of agricultural production by discouraging attempts to increase the productivity of land through additional capital investment. For special theories of land tax, see PHYSIOCRATS; SINGLE TAX. See R. T. Ely and E. W. Morehouse, *Elements of Land Taxation* (1924); Harry Brown et al., ed., *Land-Value Taxation Around the World* (1955); H. P. Wald, *Taxation of Agricultural Land in Underdeveloped Economies* (1959).

land tenure: see TENURE, in law.

land use, exploitation of land for agricultural, industrial, residential, recreational, or other purposes. Historically a laissez-faire attitude toward land use has prevailed in the United States. The philosophy has been that in general the landowner may use his holdings as he sees fit. Hence land has been exploited at will for economic gain regardless of other considerations. To the pioneers and later Americans, land seemed a limitless commodity capable of supporting any and all human activities. But in recent decades, increasing population and industrial expansion have generated urban sprawl, with thousands of square miles of open space being taken over annually for housing, commercial facilities, and industrial plants. As a result congestion and widespread POLLUTION, along with depletion of water and mineral resources and destruction of wilderness and wildlife habitats, have become increasingly severe. Since such environmental problems arise largely from the way land is used, traditional land-use policy has come under challenge. Zoning regulations are one example of legalistic limitations on land use. Another is the common law concept of nuisance, which places limits and responsibilities on the rights of ownership. On such grounds, pressure for land-use reform sharply intensified during the 1960s and 1970s. It is argued that as accessible land grows scarcer, its function becomes more critical; therefore choice of that function should no longer be dictated by private profit or local convenience. Moreover, local laws and zoning regulations have proved inadequate to settle major land-use questions involving such geographical regions that cut across local boundaries as wetlands, shorelines, and flood plains, and such large-scale facilities as strip mines, sewer systems, power plants, and highways. As a consequence, environmentalists have gone to court to prevent or resite the construction of projects that would cause pollution, destroy ecologically important areas, or otherwise degrade the environment. Land-use court battles have been waged over the siting of jetports, petroleum refineries, offshore tanker depots and drilling rigs, nuclear power stations, high-voltage transmission lines, dams, and even shopping centers and housing developments. Legislative action has also been sought, with considerable success. Although varying in scope and stringency, land-use laws are now in force in most of the United States. The National Environmental Policy Act (NEPA) requires that Federal agencies file statements assessing the environmental impact of proposed projects. This requirement, along with other legislation empowering citizens to sue industry and government for failure to comply with AIR POLLUTION and WATER POLLUTION standards, has had a profound effect on land-use decisions. Agencies such as the Army Corps of Engineers, the Federal Power Commission, and the Atomic Energy Commission must now subject their land-use proposals to the Environmental Protection Agency and therefore to public scrutiny. Pending Federal legislation would further encourage state land-use planning. It would implement what has been called a new land ethic aimed at preserving space and beauty, conserving resources, and protecting the environment for the public benefit. See also ENVIRONMENTALISM. See F. P. Bosselman and David Callies, *The Quiet Revolution in Land Use Control* (1972), U.S. Council on Environmental Quality, *Environmental Quality, Annual Report* (4th, 1973).

Landy, John (John Michael Landy), 1930–, Australian athlete. Landy, the second man to run the mile (1,605 m) in less than 4 min (Roger Bannister was the first), set a world's record of 3 min 58 sec in June, 1954; the mark stood until July, 1957. Landy was later a schoolteacher until 1959 and also served with the Australian national parks authority.

Lane, FitzHugh, 1804–65, American painter, b. Gloucester, Mass. A painter of ships and coastal panoramas, Lane is most notable as a precursor of American LUMINISM. He illuminated his canvases with warm, glowing yellow and pink skies reflected in water. The resulting paintings project a shimmering density that expresses profound serenity. *Owl's Head, Penobscot Bay, Maine* (1862; Mus. of Fine Arts, Boston) is a characteristic work.

Lane, Franklin Knight, 1864–1921, U.S. Secretary of the Interior (1913–20), b. near Charlottetown, P.E.I., Canada. Raised in California, he later studied law and practiced in San Francisco, where he entered Democratic politics and served as city and county attorney. His unsuccessful campaigns for governor of California (1902) and mayor of San Francisco (1903) won national attention, and in 1905, President Theodore Roosevelt appointed him to the Interstate Commerce Commission, on which he sat until 1913, serving briefly as chairman in 1913. As Secretary of the Interior under President Wilson, he was a conservationist, and he also sought to increase the independence of the Indians. He promoted self-government in Alaska and sponsored the Alaska RR from Seward to Fairbanks to tap the interior. See his letters (ed. by his wife, Anne W. Lane, and L. H. Wall, 1922).

Lane, James Henry, 1814–66, American politician, called the "liberator of Kansas." He was probably born in Lawrenceburg, Ind., where he practiced law. Lane commanded an Indiana regiment in the Mexican War and was lieutenant governor (1849–53) and Congressman (1853–55). Having voted for the Kansas-Nebraska Act (1854), he moved to Kansas, where he soon joined the free-state forces and united their several factions. He was president of the convention at Topeka (1855) that framed a free-state constitution and set up a state government, with himself as Senator-elect. After the Senate refused to admit Kansas under this constitution, Lane traveled throughout the Old Northwest, encouraging antislavery men to emigrate to Kansas. He led the free-state militia in subsequent armed clashes with proslavery troops and directed the campaign by which his party won control of the territorial legislature. When Kansas was granted statehood (1861), Lane was chosen one of its first Senators. A friend and supporter of Abraham Lincoln, he aided the Union cause both in the Senate and in the army. Lane supported President Andrew Johnson's Reconstruction policy, thus losing political support in Kansas. Depressed by this and other events, he shot himself. See biographical study by K. E. Bailes (1962).

Lane, Joseph, 1801–81, American general in the Mexican War and territorial governor of Oregon, b. Buncombe co., N.C. In the Mexican War he commanded a brigade under Gen. Zachary Taylor at Buena Vista, later received a brevet major generalship for his gallantry in action, and emerged one of the heroes of the war. In 1848 he was commissioned governor of the newly organized Oregon Territory and superintendent of Indian affairs there. Arriving in March, 1849, he traveled through the territory settling matters between the Indians and the whites. He prepared for Congress one of the most complete reports on record of the Indians of the region. After resigning as governor in 1850, he became territorial delegate to the U.S. Congress (1851–59) and later served (1859–61) as one of Oregon's first U.S. Senators. In 1853 he led the settlers against the Rogue Indians, defeated them, and concluded a peace treaty. See study by J. E. Hendrickson (1967).

Lane, Sir Ralph, c.1530–1603, leader of the first attempted English settlement in America, on ROANOKE ISLAND, N.C. Sent by Sir Walter RALEIGH, the expedition of over 100 colonists left England in April, 1585, in a fleet of seven ships commanded by Sir Richard Grenville. The group landed on Roanoke in August but returned to England with Sir Francis DRAKE in the summer of 1586. Lane's account of the settlement appeared in Richard Hakluyt's *The Principal Navigations . . . of the English Nation* (1589).

Lane, Ralph Norman Angell: see ANGELL, SIR NORMAN.

Lanfranc (lăn'frăngk), d. 1089, Italian churchman and theologian, archbishop of Canterbury (1070–89), b. Pavia. At first educated in civil law, he was an able advocate. He then turned to theology and became a pupil of BERENGAR OF TOURS. After teaching in Avranches, in Normandy, he went to Bec (c.1040), where he founded an illustrious school and became prior (c.1043). Among his pupils were St. ANSELM and Pope Alexander II. In 1049, Berengar impugned Lanfranc's orthodoxy, and Lanfranc, successfully clearing himself, attacked Berengar in turn. Some 10 years later Lanfranc wrote the treatise *De Corpore et Sanguine Domine* [concerning the Body and Blood of the Lord], which, though ineffective as a rebuttal of Berengar's writings on the Eucharist, became a medieval classic. He was closely associated with Duke William of Normandy (later WILLIAM I of England) and probably helped secure papal recognition of the duke's marriage and the papal blessing for the conquest of England. In 1070, William replaced STIGAND as archbishop with Lanfranc, who accepted only on the direct command of the pope. Thereafter king and archbishop worked closely together in matters of both church and state. Lanfranc was one of the reform party of the church (led by GREGORY VII). He replaced English abbots and bishops with Normans (a course often denounced but quite essential to any reform), reduced the archbishop of York to subjection to Canterbury, legislated against clerical marriage and concubinage, built churches, reformed ecclesiastical finance, established ecclesiastical courts, strengthened the monasteries, and removed the bishoprics from small towns to important cities. Occasional friction between church and state caused no quarrels until the reign of WILLIAM II. Lanfranc had favored young William, and crowned him, but the archbishop was deeply displeased by the king's arbitrary actions, and trouble was averted only by Lanfranc's death. See A. J. MacDonald, *Lanfranc* (2d ed. 1944).

Lanfranco, Giovanni (jōvän'nē länfräng'kō), 1582–1647, Italian painter. Lanfranco is considered one of the foremost artists of the High Baroque. He was trained by the CARRACCI and worked primarily in Rome and Naples, where he executed numerous decorative plans for churches and palaces. Lanfranco greatly extended the scope of the ILLUSIONISM that he had studied in the works of Correggio and the Carracci. His remarkable *trompe l'oeil* designs, characterized by piercing shafts of light illuminating boldly foreshortened, cloud-borne figures that recede into infinite celestial distances, were endlessly imitated throughout Europe. Among his greatest works are the ceiling of the Casino Borghese (1616) and the dome of San Andrea della Valle (1621–25), both in Rome, and the magnificent ceiling of the Chapel of San Gennaro in Naples Cathedral (1641). The brilliant, translucent quality of his later works is displayed by his apse painting for San Carlo ai Catinari (Rome, 1646), his last work.

Lang, Andrew, 1844–1912, English scholar and man of letters, b. Scotland. His poetry, much of it written in the forms of ballades, triolets, and rondeaux, appeared in such volumes as his *Ballads in Blue China* (2 vol., 1880–81). Lang was one of the first to apply anthropological findings to the study of myth and folklore; his best work in this field was *Myth, Literature, and Religion* (1887, rev. ed. 1899). He is known for his prose translations of the *Odyssey* (with S. H. Butcher, 1879), and the *Iliad* (with Walter Leaf and Ernest Myers, 1883), and for his defense of the unity of Homer in *The World of Homer* (1910). With his wife, Leonora Blanche Lang, he translated and adapted traditional stories for children, published in his *Blue Fairy Book* (1889) and others. Lang also wrote literary and art criticism, a biography of J. G. Lockhart (1896), and several works on Scottish history, culminating in his *History of Scotland* (4 vol., 1900–1907). His poetical works were edited (1923) by his wife. See biography by R. L. Green (1946, repr. 1973).

Lang, Cosmo Gordon, 1864–1945, English churchman, archbishop of York (1908–28), archbishop of Canterbury (1928–42), b. Aberdeen, Scotland. From 1901 to 1908, while suffragan bishop of Stepney, London, and canon of St. Paul's Cathedral, he attempted to improve slum conditions and attracted wide attention. He was an acknowledged leader in the House of Lords and supported in Parliament the proposed revision (1928) of the Book of Common Prayer. With Stanley Baldwin he was instrumental in securing the abdication of Edward VIII, and he crowned George VI as king in 1937. Shortly after his resignation as archbishop in 1942, Lang was created Baron Lang of Lambeth. See biography by J. G. Lockhart (1949).

Lang, Fritz, 1890–, German-American film director, b. Vienna. The best known of his early silent films are the fantasies *Destiny* (1921) and *Metropolis* (1926). Lang gained worldwide acclaim with *M* (1933), a study of a child molester and murderer. He fled Nazi Germany to avoid collaborating with the government. His Hollywood works, most of them melodramatic thrillers, include *Fury* (1936), *You Only Live Once* (1937), *Manhunt* (1941), *Hangmen Also Die* (1943), *Ministry of Fear* (1944), *The Big Heat* (1953), and *Beyond a Reasonable Doubt* (1956). See studies by Peter Bogdanovich (1967) and P. M. Jensen (1969).

Lang, Pearl, 1922–, American dancer and choreographer, b. Chicago. Lang was a soloist with Martha Graham's company (1942–52) before forming her own company in 1952. As a dancer and choreographer she is noted for her range of dramatic expression in such works as *Rites* (1953) and *Falls the Shadow Between* (1957). Lang has appeared in Broadway musicals, including *Carousel* and *Finian's Rainbow*. She has taught at the Yale Univ. School of Drama and the Juilliard School of Music.

Langdell, Christopher Columbus, 1826–1906, American teacher of law, b. New Boston, N.H. He practiced in New York City from 1854 to 1870, when he was appointed Dane professor of law at Harvard; in 1875 he became dean of Harvard law school. Together with J. B. AMES, who succeeded him as dean in 1895, he revised the curriculum of the school. Langdell is especially famed for the introduction of the "case method" in the study of law. In his view the principles of law are best learned by inductive study of the actual legal situations (the cases) in which they occur. Much opposition was expressed by conservative teachers who believed that an abstract formulation of the law was the essential need of the student. Langdell's theory was first adopted at Harvard, then at Columbia law school, and in time gained almost universal acceptance. Langdell prepared casebooks in the fields of contracts, equity, and sales.

Langdon, John, 1741–1819, American political leader, b. Portsmouth, N.H. A prosperous merchant, Langdon was active in pre-Revolutionary activities. In 1775 he became a delegate to the Continental Congress, and in Nov., 1775, he accompanied Robert R. Livingston and Robert Treat Paine on an unsuccessful mission to win Canada to the patriot cause. In the Saratoga campaign (1777) he financed the New Hampshire militia under Gen. John Stark in the expedition against General Burgoyne, and he saw action himself at Bennington and Saratoga. After the war he was (1785–86, 1788–89) president (governor) of New Hampshire. Langdon was a delegate to the U.S. Constitutional Convention, and it was largely through his efforts that New Hampshire ratified the Constitution as the ninth state, thus making the instrument effective. As U.S. Senator (1789–1801) he aligned himself more and more with the Jeffersonians, but he declined national offices. Langdon was governor of New Hampshire from 1805 to 1809 and from 1810 to 1812. See biography by L. S. Mayo (1937, repr. 1970).

Lange, Christian Louis (krĭs'tyän lo͞o'ē läng'ə), 1869–1938, Norwegian pacifist. In his youth he joined the Young Norway movement and worked for the separation of Norway from Sweden. He taught in the Norwegian Nobel Institute, represented his country at the Hague Conference of 1907 and at the League of Nations, and was secretary (1909–33) of the Interparliamentary Union. Lange shared the 1921 Nobel Peace Prize with Hjalmar Branting.

Lange, Dorothea, 1895–1965, American photographer, b. Hoboken, N.J. From 1916 until 1932, Lange operated a portrait studio. During the Depression she took her camera into the streets of San Francisco where she began to make exceptionally powerful images of people, which speak of the time and the world in which they were made; among the best known of these is *White Angel Breadline* (1933). Her famous portrait *Migrant Mother* (1936) was made as part of a report commissioned by the state of California, investigating the way of life of migrant laborers. Lange's photographs emphasized the workers' essential dignity and pride, surviving an environment of starkest poverty. The report, which resulted in the establishment of state-built camps for the migrants, was made in collaboration with Paul Taylor, professor of economics at the Univ. of California, whom Lange married. From 1935 to 1942 she worked in the Farm Security Administration, documenting rural America. Her photographs were reproduced in thousands of magazines and newspapers, helping to create a national awareness of the farmers' plight and profoundly influencing American photojournalism by their simplicity and directness. At the outbreak of war with Japan, Lange documented the mass evacuation of Japanese-Americans to concentration camps. In 1945 she covered the United Nations Conference in San Francisco, and collapsed from overwork. She did not photograph again until 1951, when she began to travel, producing photo-essays for *Life* magazine, e.g., "Three Mormon Towns" (1954) and "The Irish Country People" (1955). Lange's books include *An American Exodus* (with Paul Taylor; 1939) and *The American Country Woman* (1966). See catalog of her exhibition at the Museum of Modern Art, New York City (1966).

Lange, Friedrich Albert (frē'drĭkh äl'bĕrt läng'ə), 1828–75, German neo-Kantian philosopher. Accepting the materialistic method of investigating phenomena, he rejected its concept of nature. He regarded consciousness as subjective experience, not merely the effect of matter, and submitted that speculative and idealistic concepts should be supported in their relations to the values of human existence. He is celebrated for his *Geschichte des Materialismus und Kritik seiner Bedeutung in der Gegenwart* (1866; tr. *A History of Materialism*, 3d ed. 1950).

Langeland (läng'əlän), narrow island (1965 pop. 17,745), 110 sq mi (285 sq km), S Denmark, between Fyn and Lolland. Rudkøbing is the main town; other towns include Bagenkop and Lohals. The island is largely agricultural, and grain is the chief product.

Langensalza, Bad (bät läng"ənzäl'tsä), town (1970 pop. 16,951), Erfurt district, SW East Germany, on the Unstrut River. It is an industrial and horticultural center. Manufactures include textiles, paper, processed food, and beer. Bad Langensalza was an early seat (13th cent.) of the Teutonic Knights. The town was annexed (14th cent.) by the house of WETTIN, passing to its Albertine line in 1485. Bad Langensalza was annexed by Prussia in 1815, and in 1866 the Prussians defeated the Hanoverians there in a battle during the Austro-Prussian War. The town has retained parts of its medieval walls and a 13th-century castle.

Langer, Susanne (Knauth), 1895–, American philosopher, b. New York City, grad. Radcliffe (B.A., 1920; Ph.D., 1926). After holding various teaching posts, she was a lecturer (1945–50) at Columbia and was then professor of philosophy at Connecticut College from 1954 to 1962, when she became an emeritus professor. A student of Alfred North Whitehead, she wrote extensively on aesthetics and other subjects. In her chief work, *Philosophy in a New Key: A Study in the Symbolism of Reason, Rite and Art* (1942), she attempted to give art the claim to meaning that science was given through Whitehead's analysis of symbolic modes. She made an important distinction between discursive and nondiscursive symbols: The former are found in scientific and ordinary language, the latter in art. Among her other works are *The Practice of Philosophy* (1930), *Feeling and Form* (1953), *An Introduction to Symbolic Logic* (2d ed. 1953), *Problems of Art* (1957), *Philosophical Sketches* (1962), and *Mind: An Essay on Human Feeling* (2 vol., 1967–72).

Langer, William Leonard, 1896–, American historian, b. Boston. He received his Ph.D. from Harvard in 1923 and began teaching there in 1927. Langer served in U.S. intelligence in World War II and as assistant to the Secretary of State in 1946. A leading authority in the field of diplomatic history, he wrote extensively on the diplomatic climate preceding World Wars I and II. His many works include *The Diplomacy of Imperialism* (1935, 2d ed. 1951), *European Alliances and Alignments* (1939, 2d ed. 1950), *Our Vichy Gamble* (1947), and, with S. E. Gleason, *The Challenge to Isolation* (2 vol., 1952). Langer also edited *An Encyclopedia of World History* (5th ed., rev. and enl., 1972) and the valuable series *The Rise of Modern Europe* (1934–), an analytic synthesis. He was one of the first to urge that historians make fuller use of related disciplines, especially of psychology.

Langevin, Sir Hector Louis (ĕktôr' lwē läNzhəvăN'), 1826–1906, Canadian legislator, b. Quebec. A lawyer, he served in the Legislative Assembly (1857–67) and its successor, the House of Commons (1867–74, 1878–96). He was solicitor general (1964–66) for Lower Canada and postmaster (1866–67) before confederation. He succeeded Georges Étienne Cartier in 1873 as leader of the French Canadian Conservative party. After the Conservatives returned to power in 1878, he was postmaster general (1878–79) and minister of public works (1879–91). There were charges of corruption (1891) in Langevin's public works department; although acquitted of complicity, he was found guilty of negligence in office and was forced to resign. He was knighted in 1881.

Langevin, Paul (pōl), 1872–1946, French physicist and chemist. He was professor of experimental physics at the Collège de France from 1909 and at the École municipale de Physique et de Chimie, Paris, from 1904 (director from 1929); dismissed by the Vichy government in 1940, he resumed his posts in 1944. He is noted for his work on the electron theory of magnetism and for his research on sound devices for submarine detection.

Langham, Simon, d. 1376, English prelate and statesman, cardinal of the Roman Catholic Church. He ruled the abbey of Westminster with such skill that Edward III appointed (1360) him treasurer and chancellor (1363). Created bishop of Ely in 1362, Langham rose to be archbishop of Canterbury (1366). His acceptance of the red hat without royal permission led to a breach with Edward, and Langham resigned (1368). He went to Avignon, where he held office at the court of Pope Gregory XI.

Langlade, Charles Michel de (shärl mēshĕl' də), 1729–1800, pioneer in present-day Wisconsin and soldier, b. Mackinac region, now in Mich.; son of a trader, Augustin Langlade, who established the settlement of Green Bay, Wis., and an Ottawa Indian woman. In the French and Indian Wars, as an ally of the French, he led the Indian force that helped defeat the British army under Gen. Edward Braddock near Fort Duquesne (1755). Langlade defeated Robert Rogers's Rangers on Lake Champlain (1757), and served in the Quebec campaign under the French General Montcalm (1759). After surrendering the fort at Mackinac to the British, he became a British citizen. In 1763 he warned the British western posts of Pontiac's Rebellion. In the American Revolution he led a force of Indians to General Burgoyne's assistance, but the Indians deserted upon being reprimanded for a murder. He also fought in the West against George Rogers Clark. After the war he retired to his trading post at Green Bay, Wis.; he became known as the father of Wisconsin.

Langland, William, c.1332–c.1400, putative author of *Piers Plowman.* He was born probably at Ledbury near the Welsh marshes and may have gone to school at Great Malvern Priory. Although he took minor orders he never became a priest. Later in London he apparently eked out his living by singing masses and copying documents. His great work, *Piers Plowman,* or, more precisely, *The Vision of William concerning Piers the Plowman,* is an allegorical poem in unrhymed alliterative verse, regarded as the greatest Middle English poem prior to Chaucer. It is both a social satire and a vision of the simple Christian life. The poem consists of three dream visions: (1) in which Holy Church and Lady Meed (representing the temptation of riches) woo the dreamer; (2) in which Piers leads a crowd of penitants in search of St. Truth; and (3) the vision of Do-well (the practice of the virtues), Do-bet (in which Piers becomes the Good Samaritan practicing charity), and Do-best (in which the simple plowman is identified with Christ himself). The 47 extant manuscripts of the poem fall into three groups: the A-text (2,567 lines, c.1362); the B-text, which greatly expands the third vision (7,242 lines, c.1376–77); the C-text, a revision of B (7,357 lines, between 1393 and 1398). Most scholars now believe that at least the A- and B-texts are the work of William Langland, whose biography has been deduced from passages in the poem. However, some still hold that the poem is the work of two or even five authors. The popularity of the poem is attested to by the large number of surviving manuscripts and by its many imitators. The 19th-century edition of W. W. Skeat (new ed. 1954) is still standard; the best modern versions are those of Donald Attwater (1930) and H. W. Wells (1935). See studies by E. T. Donaldson (1955; and 1949, repr. 1966), M. W. Bloomfield (1962), and E. D. Kirk (1972); critical writings, ed. by S. S. Hussey (1969).

Langley, Samuel Pierpont, 1834–1906, American scientist, b. Roxbury, Mass., received only a high school education but continued his studies in science in Boston libraries. He became, in 1866, professor of physics at the Western Univ. of Pennsylvania (now the Univ. of Pittsburgh) and director of the Allegheny Observatory there. He did much to popularize astronomy; his book *The New Astronomy* (1888) was widely read. He invented the bolometer, a highly sensitive instrument for recording variations in heat radiation, and with it measured the distribution of heat in the solar and lunar spectra. In 1887, Langley became secretary of the Smithsonian Institution and established the Astrophysical Observatory and the National Zoological Park there. He continued his study of the solar spectrum and made new determinations of the solar constant of radiation and, in 1904, announced his conclusion that this solar constant was a variable. He constructed power-driven model aircraft with specially designed light engines, which, in 1896, performed successfully in the air, thus proving to Langley's satisfaction and to the satisfaction of a few of his followers that mechanical flight was possible. Few others were convinced. Langley, assisted by Charles M. Manly, built a machine which in 1903 he twice attempted to launch on the Potomac. His failures brought him a tremendous amount of unmerited ridicule. He maintained that the failures were due to defects in the launching apparatus and not to the machine itself. In 1914, reconstructed and with a higher-powered engine, the machine was actually flown. Most of Langley's many papers are in the publications of the Smithsonian Institution. See C. D. Walcott, *Biographical Memoir* (1912); study by R. B. Meyer, ed. (1971).

Langley Air Force Base, U.S. military installation, 3,195 acres (1,293 hectares), SE Va., N of Hampton; est. 1916 and named for aviation pioneer Samuel P. Langley. The facility, the oldest continuously active air force base in the United States, is the headquarters of the Tactical Air Command and has air-defense missile units.

Langley Park, uninc. town (1970 pop. 11,564), Prince Georges co., W central Md., a suburb of Washington, D.C.

Langmuir, Irving (lăng'myo͝or), 1881–1957, American chemist, b. Brooklyn, N.Y. Associated (1909–50) with the research laboratory of the General Electric Company, he introduced atomic-hydrogen welding, invented a gas-filled tungsten lamp, and by his work on the high vacuum contributed greatly to the development of the radio vacuum tube. He extended the work of Gilbert Lewis on electron bonding, evolving the Lewis-Langmuir theory of atomic structure. In his research on surface tension and surface chemistry he developed a new technique (employing monolayers, i.e., layers of molecules one molecule thick) for the study of molecules, which has applications in research on microorganisms and toxins and in other studies contributing to advances in immunology. For his contributions in surface chemistry he received the 1932 Nobel Prize in Chemistry. It was Langmuir who discovered that the introduction of particles of dry ice and iodide into a cloud of low temperature containing sufficient moisture in tiny droplets triggered a chain reaction producing rain or snow, depending on the condition of the weather. See his works, ed. by C. G. Suits and H. E. Way (12 vol., 1960–62); study by Albert Rosenfeld (1966).

Langres (läN'grə), town (1968 pop. 11,835), Haute-Marne dept., NE France. It has an old and famous cutlery industry. An episcopal see since the 3d cent., Langres has preserved a large part of its ancient fortifications. Diderot, whose father was a cutler, was born there.

Langside, district of Glasgow, S central Scotland. At the battle of Langside (1568) the 1st earl of Murray defeated the forces of Mary Queen of Scots led by Archibald Campbell, 5th earl of Argyll. As a result Mary fled to England.

Langton, Stephen, c.1155–1228, English prelate, cardinal of the Roman Catholic Church. He was educated at Paris. Innocent III created him cardinal in 1206, and he became archbishop of Canterbury the following year. The opposition of King JOHN prevented his occupation of the see until 1213. He acted with the barons in securing the Magna Carta and opposed the papal legate, PANDULF. Because of his continued opposition to John after the reconciliation of pope and king, he was suspended as archbishop in 1215 but was restored after the accession of Henry III and continued his efforts to reform church and state. He was a learned and prolific writer, and the present chapter division of the Scriptures is derived from Langton. He probably composed the hymn *Veni, sancte spiritus.* See F. M. Powicke, *Stephen Langton* (1928, repr. 1965); study by P. B. Roberts (1968).

Langtry, Lillie, 1853–1929, English actress, b. Jersey, Channel Islands; known as the Jersey Lily. One of the first English women of elevated social rank to go on the stage, she made her debut at the Haymarket theater in 1881 after her husband, a diplomat, failed financially. Never considered a great actress, Langtry was noted for her great beauty and for her affair with Edward VII. Oscar Wilde wrote *Lady Windermere's Fan* for her. In 1899 she married Sir Hugo Gerald de Bathe. See her memoirs, *The Days I Knew* (1925); Pierre Sichel, *The Jersey Lily* (1958).

language, systematic communication by vocal symbols. It is a universal characteristic of the human species. Nothing is known of its origin, and scientists generally hold that it has been so long in use that the length of time WRITING is known to cover (7,900 years at most) is trifling in comparison. Just as languages spoken now by peoples of the most primitive cultures are as subtle and as intricate as those of the peoples of more complex civilizations, similarly the forms of languages known (or hypothetically reconstructed) from the earliest records show no trace of being more "primitive" than their modern forms. Because language is a cultural system, individual languages may classify objects and ideas in completely different fashions. For example, the sex or age of the speaker may determine the use of certain grammatical forms or avoidance of taboo words. Many languages divide the color spectrum into completely different and unequal units of color. Terms of address may vary according to the age, sex, and status of speaker and hearer. Every person belongs to a speech community (a group of people who speak the same language). There are between 3,000 and 4,000 speech communities, with numbers ranging from many millions of speakers down to a few dozen or even fewer. The following list probably includes (in approximate descending order) all languages spoken by groups of more than 50 million people: North Chinese vernacular (Mandarin), English, Hindustani, Spanish, Russian, German, Japanese, Malay (Bahasa Indonesia), Bengali, French, Portuguese, and Italian. Many persons speak more than one language. The language first learned is one's maternal or native language—figurative expressions—for language is in no sense inherited; it is learned behavior. When a person learns a second language very well, he is said to be bilingual. He may abandon his native language entirely, because he has moved from where it is spoken or because of politico-economic and cultural pressure (as among American Indians and speakers of the Celtic languages in Europe). Such abandonment may lead to the disappearance of languages. Individuals differ in speech, although usually not markedly within a small area. The differences between groups of speakers in the same speech community can, however, be considerable; the variations of a language constitute its DIALECTS. All languages are continuously changing. If there is a common direction of change, however, it has never been convincingly described. Various factors, especially the extended use of writing, have led to the development of a standard language in most of the major speech communities—a special official dialect of a language that is theoretically maintained unchanged. This is the school form of a language, and by a familiar fallacy it has been supposed to be the norm from which the everyday language deviated. Rather, the standard language is a development of some local dialect that has had prestige; thus the standard English of England is derived from London English and standard Italian from that of Tuscany. Use of the standard language is often a mark of polite behavior; thus in America using standard English, "good grammar," and approved pronunciation mark a man as cultivated. Ordinary speech may be affected by the standard language; thus, many forms of expression come to be considered substandard and are regarded as badges of ignorance or "bad grammar," such as *you was* in place of the standard *you were.* As in other fields of etiquette, there is variation; thus, *gotten* is acceptable in the United States but not in England. The literary standard may differ from the colloquial standard of educated people, and the jargon of a trade or school group may be unintelligible to outsiders; such linguistic variations in English are mainly a matter of vocabulary. An auxiliary language is a nonnative language adopted for specific use; such are the LINGUA FRANCA, PIDGIN, and INTERNATIONAL LANGUAGE. The differences between languages are not uniform. When languages resemble each other in a systematic way, they are held to be genetically related. Such relationships have been established in many cases, but always on the basis of the sounds of the languages and the way the sounds are grouped in systematic patterns; no certainty has been attained in comparing the fundamental grammatical structures of languages. Maximal groups of related languages are called families, or stocks. A language that cannot be assigned to an existing language is termed a language isolate. Languages of the Indo-European and Hamito-Semitic families have received vastly more attention than the others. These languages actually represent a very small part of the world linguistic spectrum; as a consequence, most generalized statements about language, grammar, and related matters made before 1920 are not valid as generalizations at all. No two authorities agree on all points of language classification and analysis, and knowledge of the languages of some isolated regions (e.g., Australia, New Guinea, and E Siberia) is still too scanty to permit proper classification. For general descriptive information see articles on individual languages, e.g., FRENCH LANGUAGE. See also CREOLE; DICTIONARY; ETYMOLOGY; GRAMMAR; INFLECTION; LINGUISTICS; PART OF SPEECH; PHONETICS; SEMANTICS; SIGN LANGUAGE; SLANG. See Leonard Bloomfield, *Language* (1933); Edward Sapir, *Language* (1921, repr. 1949); Dell Hymes, *Language in Culture and Society* (1964); S. I. Hayakawa, *Language in Thought and Action* (3d ed. 1972); Ronald W. Langacker, *Language and Its Structure* (2d ed. 1973).

language of signs: see SIGN LANGUAGE.

Languedoc (läNgdôk'), region and former province, S France, bounded by the foot of the Pyrenees, the upper Garonne River, the Auvergne Mts., the Rhône, and the Mediterranean. It comprises the departments of Aude, Gard, Hérault, Lozère, and Pyrénées Orientales. The Garonne plains, centering around Toulouse, the chief city, are fertile farming and wine-producing districts. The name was derived from the language of its inhabitants (see LANGUE D'OC AND LANGUE D'OÏL). It now generally refers to Lower Languedoc, an alluvial plain along the Mediterranean, with a warm climate; wine is the chief product, and Montpellier, Nîmes, Sète, Béziers, and Narbonne are the chief cities. Historic Carcassonne is also there. The Massif Central rises in the north and the east. Historically, Languedoc roughly corresponds to Narbonensis prov. of Roman Gaul; Lower Languedoc was the later Septimania. Its history from the Frankish conquest (completed 8th cent.) to its final incorporation into the French royal domain (1271) is largely that of the counts of TOULOUSE. Under the old regime the parlement of Languedoc sat at Toulouse; the provincial assembly retained importance until the French Revolution.

langue d'oc (läNg dôk) and **langue d'oïl** (dôē), names of the two principal groups of medieval French dialects. *Langue d'oc* (literally, "language of yes") was spoken south of a line running, roughly, from Bordeaux to Grenoble, whereas *langue d'oïl* (literally, "language of yes") was prevalent in central and N France. The two dialect groups were named after their respective words for "yes," *oc* having been the form of "yes" in the south and *oïl* (now *oui*) having been used for "yes" in the north. *Langue d'oc,* or PROVENÇAL, became the language employed by the TROUBADOURS of the south of France for their poems. Of the *langue d'oïl* dialects, that of the Paris region gradually supplanted all others as the standard idiom and developed into modern French. Both *langue d'oïl* and *langue d'oc* dialects persisted, however, in some rural areas as *patois,* or popular, provincial speech.

langur: see MONKEY.

Lanier, Sidney (lənēr'), 1842–81, American poet and musician, b. Macon, Ga., grad. Oglethorpe College 1860. His first work, the novel *Tiger-Lilies* (1867), was based on his experiences as a Confederate soldier in the Civil War. An accomplished musician, Lanier was first flutist of the Peabody Orchestra, Baltimore, in 1873. Following his appointment as lecturer on English literature at Johns Hopkins, his study of the interrelation of music and poetry was published as *The Science of English Verse* (1880). His *Poems* appeared in 1887. Lanier's poetry is marked by its melodic verse and extravagant conceits. Among his best-known poems are "Corn," "The Marshes of Glyn," and "Song of the Chattahoochee." See Centennial edition of his works (ed. by C. R. Anderson et al., 10 vol., 1945); biography by A. H. Starke (1933, repr. 1964); studies by E. W. Parks (1968) and Jack De Bellis (1972).

Lankester, Sir Edwin Ray (lăng'kəstər), 1847–1929, English zoologist. He was professor at University College, London (1874–90), and at Oxford (1891–98) and was director of the natural history department of the British Museum (1898–1907). He was a founder (1884) of the Marine Biological Association, which established an important station at Plymouth. Influential as teacher and writer on biological theories, comparative anatomy, and evolution, Lankester studied the protozoa, mollusca, and arthropoda. He was knighted in 1907.

Lannes, Jean (zhäN län), 1769–1809, marshal of France. He fought under Napoleon Bonaparte (later Napoleon I) in the Italian and Egyptian campaigns, supported his coup d'etat of 18 Brumaire, and distinguished himself at Montebello, Austerlitz, Jena, Friedland, and Saragossa. Napoleon considered Lannes one of his ablest generals and created him duke of Montebello. Lannes was killed in the battle of Essling.

lanolin, greasy, yellow substance extracted from wool. When purified, it is used as a base for ointments and creams, as a lubricant, and in finishing and preserving leather. It is also a constituent of some varnishes and paints. Chemically, lanolin is chiefly a mixture of cholesterol and the esters of several fatty acids. With water it forms an emulsion. As a waste product in wool processing, it is known also as wool wax, wool fat, or wool grease.

La Noue, François de (fräNswä' də lä nōō), 1531–91, French Protestant general in the Wars of Religion (see RELIGION, WARS OF). He fought at Jarnac (1569) and Moncontour (1569). In 1570 he lost his left arm in battle and had it replaced with an iron hook, whence he became known as *Bras-de-fer* [ironarm]. He took part in the Netherlands expedition sponsored by Gaspard de COLIGNY. His reputation for fairness led to his being sent by King Charles IX to negotiate (1572–73) with the defenders of La ROCHELLE. After the failure of these negotiations he gave up his commission and assumed the leadership of the Protestant forces in W France (1574–78). He fought for the Dutch Protestants against the Spanish, but was captured (1580) and held prisoner for five years. At this time he wrote *Discours politiques et militaires* (1587, tr. 1587). He fought under King HENRY IV at Arques and Ivry.

Lansbury, George (lănz'bərē), 1859–1940, British Labour party leader. During the 1880s he was influenced by Christian socialism, and he later joined (1892) the Social Democratic Federation. An active reformer, he campaigned constantly for the amelioration of the conditions of the poor, particularly the unemployed, and for woman suffrage. He was a member of the royal commission on the Poor Laws (1905–9) and signed the famous minority report. He helped to found the *Daily Herald* (1912), which he edited until 1922, when it became the official Labour party newspaper. A Labour member of Parliament (1910–12, 1922–40), he served as commissioner of works (1929–31) and as leader of the opposition (1931–35) against the National government of Ramsay MacDonald. A lifelong pacifist, he had defended conscientious objectors during World War I, and in 1935 he resigned as party leader on the issue of League of Nations sanctions against Italy, a move he thought would lead to war. He advocated unilateral disarmament by Great Britain during the 1930s, and in 1937 he visited Adolf Hitler and Benito Mussolini in an attempt to avoid war. See his autobiographical *Looking Backwards—and Forwards* (1935); biography by R. W. Postgate (1951).

Lansdale, borough (1970 pop. 18,451), Montgomery co., SE Pa.; inc. 1872. The Jenkins House there dates from 1702.

Lansdowne, Henry Charles Keith Petty Fitzmaurice, 5th **marquess of** (lănz'doun), 1845–1927, British statesman. He held various offices in William Gladstone's ministries but resigned (1880) because of the prime minister's Irish policy and in 1886 joined the Liberal Unionist defection from the LIBERAL PARTY. During his period as governor general of Canada (1883–88), a beginning was made in settling disputes over the North American fisheries, and the rebellion of Louis RIEL was suppressed. He was viceroy of India (1888–94) and secretary for war (1895–1900). As foreign secretary (1900–1905) he sought to end England's comparative diplomatic isolation by concluding an alliance with Japan (1902), the Anglo-French entente (1904; see TRIPLE ALLIANCE AND TRIPLE ENTENTE), and arbitration treaties with the United States. During World War I he was (1915–16) a member of the coalition government, and in 1917 he published in the *Daily Telegraph* a letter setting forth proposals for a negotiated peace. The letter was repudiated by the government. See biography by T. W. L. Newton (1929); D. Barker, *Prominent Edwardians* (1969).

Lansdowne, William Petty Fitzmaurice, 1st **marquess of:** see SHELBURNE, WILLIAM PETTY FITZMAURICE, 2D EARL OF.

Lansdowne. 1 Uninc. town (1970 pop. 16,976), Baltimore co., NE Md., a suburb of Baltimore. **2** Borough (1970 pop. 14,090), Delaware co., SE Pa., a residential suburb of Philadelphia; inc. 1893.

Lansing, John, 1754–1829?, American political leader and jurist, b. Albany, N.Y. He served as military secretary to Gen. Philip J. Schuyler in the American Revolution and later became a prominent lawyer. He was a member of the New York assembly (1780–88) and of the Continental Congress (1784–85) and was mayor of Albany (1786–90). In 1787 he was a delegate to the Federal Constitutional Convention but withdrew when that body began to draft a new constitution instead of revising the Articles of Confederation as it had been empowered to do. He was one of the leaders of the opposition in New York to the Constitution. He was a state supreme court justice (1790–1801), being appointed chief justice in 1798, and from 1801 to 1814 served as chancellor of New York. In 1829 he disappeared and was never found. His notes on the Federal Constitutional Convention were edited by J. R. Strayer in *Delegate from New York* (1939, repr. 1967).

Lansing, Robert, 1864–1928, U.S. Secretary of State (1915–20), b. Watertown, N.Y. An authority in the field of international law, he founded the *American Journal of International Law* in 1907 and remained an editor of it until his death. He served as counsel for the United States in several international disputes, and he became attached (1914) to the Dept. of State. President Wilson appointed him to succeed William Jennings Bryan as Secretary of State after the latter's resignation. Lansing was a strong, although not outspoken, advocate of U.S. participation in World War I on the side of the Allies. Because Wilson largely conducted foreign policy himself with his political confidant Edward M. House, Lansing had little influence in the negotiations that led to the declaration of war against Germany. In 1917, Lansing concluded with Kikujiro Ishii of Japan the Lansing-Ishii agreement, which gave U.S. recognition to Japan's special interests in China, while reaffirming the Open Door policy. Lansing, who was nominal head of the U.S. commission to the Paris Peace Conference, lost Wilson's confidence because he did not regard the Covenant of the League of Nations as essential to the peace treaty. The breach between the two was completed when Wilson learned that during Wilson's illness Lansing had on several occasions called the cabinet together for consultations. In Feb., 1920, at Wilson's request, Lansing resigned. He later returned to his law practice. His writings include *The Big Four and Others at the Peace Conference* (1921), *The Peace Negotiations* (1921), and *Notes on Sovereignty* (1921). *The War Memoirs of Robert Lansing* (1935) was published posthumously. See studies by D. M. Smith (1958, repr. 1972) and B. F. Beers (1962).

Lansing. 1 Village (1970 pop. 25,805), Cook co., NE Ill., a suburb of Chicago, near the Ind. line; inc. 1893. **2** City (1970 pop. 131,546), state capital, Clinton, Eaton, and Ingham counties, S Mich., on the Grand River at its confluence with the Red Cedar River; inc. 1859. Automobiles and automobile parts are the major manufactures. The city grew after it was made the state capital (1847), and industrial development came with the railroads (1870s) and the automobile industry (1897). The state capitol houses a museum, and the state office building contains the state library and the state historical office. The city has a junior college. Ray S. Baker was born there.

Lanston, Tolbert, 1844–1913, American inventor, b. Troy, Ohio. Lanston spent his youth on an Iowa farm and served in the military throughout the Civil War. For 22 years he was a clerk in the U.S. Pension Office, and during that time he studied law and gained admission to the bar. His first patents for his typesetting machine, the MONOTYPE, were granted in 1885. Lanston resigned his government position and worked for the rest of his life at perfecting and manufacturing his invention, which was marketed in 1897.

lantana (lăntā′nə): see VERVAIN.

lantern, device for shielding a light from wind and rain. The Romans used lanterns with sides of thin horn to shield oil lamps. The horn lantern was revived in the Middle Ages and furnished with candles. Perforated or openwork metal lanterns became common during the Renaissance but were largely replaced by the glass-shielded form. Paper or textile coverings, which are often collapsible, are widespread in the East. Openwork brass lanterns are used in the Middle East; clay lanterns are used in parts of Africa. In some modern lanterns liquefied petroleum gas is burned in a gas mantle.

lanthanide series, in chemistry, a series of RARE-EARTH METALS in group IIIb of the PERIODIC TABLE. Members of the series are often called lanthanides, although LANTHANUM (atomic number 57) is not always considered a member of the series. The series always includes the 14 elements with atomic numbers 58 through 71, which are (in order of increasing atomic number) CERIUM, PRASEODYMIUM, NEODYMIUM, PROMETHIUM, SAMARIUM, EUROPIUM, GADOLINIUM, TERBIUM, DYSPROSIUM, HOLMIUM, ERBIUM, THULIUM, YTTERBIUM, and LUTETIUM. All of the members of the series very closely resemble lanthanum and one another in their chemical and physical properties. Chemically, they are about as reactive as calcium. They all form trivalent compounds; some also form divalent or quadrivalent compounds. As the atomic number increases in this group of elements, the radius of the atom or trivalent ion decreases, a phenomenon known as the lanthanide contraction. As the nuclear charge increases, the attractive force on the electrons increases, but added electrons enter the 4*f* electron orbital (which is relatively deep inside the atom) and do not increase the atomic or ionic size.

lanthanum (lăn′thənəm) [Gr.,=to lie hidden], metallic chemical element; symbol La; at. no. 57; at. wt. 138.91; m.p. about 920°C; b.p. about 3460°C; sp. gr. 6.19 at 25°C; valence +3. Lanthanum is a soft, malleable, ductile, silver-white metal; at room temperature it has a hexagonal close-packed crystalline structure that is unstable at higher temperatures (see ALLOTROPY). Lanthanum is usually considered the first member of the LANTHANIDE SERIES, a group of elements with similar physical and chemical properties. It is one of the RARE-EARTH METALS of group IIIb of the PERIODIC TABLE. Lanthanum is a chemically active element. It oxidizes rapidly in air and reacts with water to form the hydroxide. It reacts readily with acids, with elemental boron, carbon, nitrogen, phosphorus, selenium, silicon, or sulfur, and with the halogens. The oxide and the boride are used in electronic vacuum tubes. The oxide is added to optical glass to increase its alkali resistance and refractive index. Although lanthanum is not found uncombined in nature, it occurs in the rare-earth minerals MONAZITE and bastnasite. Lanthanum may be prepared by reduction of lanthanum fluoride with calcium metal. Lanthanum may be used in making ductile cast IRON; alloyed with other metals, it is used in cigarette lighter flints. Natural lanthanum is a mixture of two stable isotopes. One radioactive by-product of the fission of plutonium, thorium, or uranium is a mixture of radioactive isotopes of lanthanum; 17 radioactive isotopes are known. Lanthanum was discovered in the form lanthanium oxide, called lanthana, in 1839 by C. G. Mosander.

Lan-ts'ang Chiang, river: see MEKONG.

Lanús (länōōs′), city (1970 pop. 449,824), Buenos Aires prov., E Argentina. An administrative center in the Greater Buenos Aires area, it is named for Anacarsis Lanús, a local landowner, merchant, and politician of the 19th cent.

Lanuvium (lənōō′vēəm), ancient city of Latium, Italy, c.20 mi (32 km) S of Rome, in the Alban Hills near the Appian Way. It was celebrated for its temple of Juno. The modern village is Lanuvio; there are ruins of a temple and Roman walls on the site.

Laocoön (lāŏk′ōōn), in Greek mythology, priest of Apollo who warned the Trojans not to touch the wooden horse made by the Greeks during the Trojan War. While he and his two sons were sacrificing to Poseidon at the seashore, two serpents came from the water and crushed them. The Trojans interpreted this event as a sign of the gods' disapproval of Laocoön's prophecy, and they brought the wooden horse into the city. Subsequent events vindicated Laocoön's judgment, however, since the horse was filled with Greeks, who waited until night and then sacked Troy. A magnificent Greek statue by Agesander, Athenodorus, and Polydorus, now in the Vatican, shows Laocoön and his sons in their death struggle.

Laodamia (lāŏd″əmī′ə): see PROTESILAUS.

Laodicea (lāŏd″ĭsē′ə), name of several Greek cities of Asia and Asia Minor built by the Seleucids in the 3d cent. B.C. The most important, Laodicea ad Lycum, was N of Colossae near the present Denizli. On the trade route from the East, the city prospered, particularly under Rome. It was early a Christian center, the seat of one of the Seven Churches in Asia (Col. 2.1; 4.16; Rev. 3.14). Extensive Roman ruins include theaters, an aqueduct, a gymnasium, and sarcophagi. Laodicea ad Mare, a seaport of Syria S of Antioch, flourished under the Romans. It is the modern Latakia.

Laoighis, Laois (both: lā′ĭsh), or **Leix** (lā′ĭsh, lāks), county (1971 pop. 45,349), 664 sq mi (1,720 sq km), central Republic of Ireland. The county town is Port Laoise (Maryborough). A part of the central plain of Ireland, Laoighis is generally level, except for the Slieve Bloom Mts. in the northwest. The Barrow and the Nore are the chief rivers. Agriculture (oats, barley, potatoes, and turnips) and dairy farming are the main occupations.

Laomedon (lāŏm′ĭdŏn), in Greek mythology, king of Troy. When Laomedon failed to pay Poseidon, Apollo, and King Aeacus for building the walls of Troy, Poseidon sent a sea monster to ravage the land. Total catastrophe could be averted only by the sacrifice of Laomedon's daughter, Hesione. Laomedon offered Hercules a pair of immortal horses if he would rescue his daughter. Hercules slew the sea monster and saved Hesione but Laomedon refused to give him the horses. In revenge, Hercules sacked Troy and killed Laomedon and all his sons except Priam, who became the new king of Troy.

Laon (läN), commercial town (1968 pop. 28,613), capital of Aisne dept., N France. It has forges, a printing plant, and factories that make heating equipment and metal goods. Situated on a rocky height c.300 ft (90 km) above the plain, it was fortified as early as Roman times. Laon was an episcopal see from the 5th cent. until the French Revolution. During the Middle Ages it was torn by bitter struggles against the bishops by the burghers, who ultimately succeeded (12th cent.) in obtaining recognition of their charter. Notable monuments include the vast Church of Notre Dame, St. Martin Church (both: 12th–13th cent.), and an octagonal chapel of the Templars (12th cent.).

Laos (lä′ōs), constitutional monarchy (1973 est. pop. 3,140,000), 91,428 sq mi (236,800 sq km), SE Asia. The administrative capital is VIENTIANE, the royal capital, LUANG PRABANG. A landlocked region, Laos is bordered by China on the north, by North and South Vietnam on the east, by Cambodia on the south, and by Thailand and Burma on the west. In general, the Mekong River, most of which flows in a broad valley, forms the boundaries with Burma and Thailand. For two stretches, however—one greater than 300 mi (480 km)—the Mekong flows entirely through the territory of Laos. Except for the Mekong lowlands and three major plateaus, the terrain of Laos is rugged, mountainous, and heavily forested; jagged crests in the north tower over 9,000 ft (2,740 m). Laos is one of the regions of SE Asia least touched by modern civilization. There are no railroads; roads and trails are limited; and use of the country's main communications artery, the Mekong River, is impeded by many falls and rapids. More than half of the population lives along the Mekong and its tributaries. Most are subsistence farmers, who even weave their own cloth. Rice is by far the chief crop; corn and vegetables are also grown. Commercial crops include coffee, tobacco, sugarcane, and cotton. Fish from the rivers supplement the diet. Forests cover about two thirds of the country; teak is cut and lac is extracted, but poor transportation and the lack of industry limit production. Although tin is mined, mineral resources are practically undeveloped. The principal exports of Laos are tin, timber, and coffee; since almost all manufactured items have to be imported, however, there is a continuing foreign trade deficit. About half the population is Lao, a people ethnically related to the Thai. Upland tribes include the many groups that constitute the Mountain Mon-Khmer, as well as the Meo, the Yao, and several Tibeto-Burman speaking peoples. There are also important minorities of Vietnamese and Chinese. The state religion is Hinayana Buddhism; although the mountain tribes are gener-

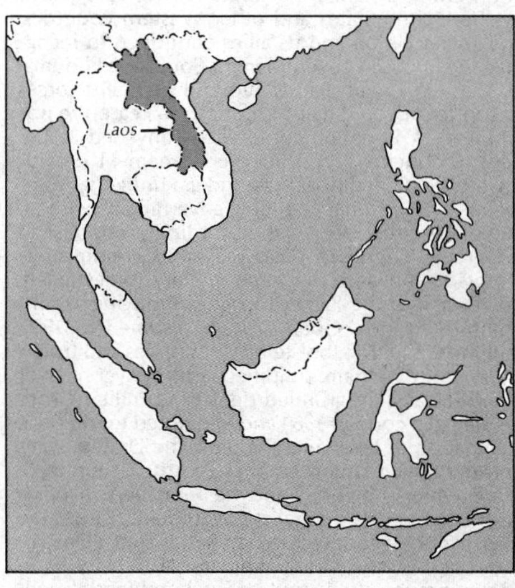

ally animists, some have adopted Buddhism. The Laotians are descendants of Thai tribes that were pushed southward from Yünnan, China, in the 13th cent. and gradually infiltrated the territory of the KHMER EMPIRE. In the mid-14th cent. a powerful kingdom called Lan Xang was founded in Laos by Fa Ngoun (1353–73), who is also credited with the introduction of Hinayana Buddhism and much of Khmer civilization into Laos. Lan Xang waged intermittent wars with the Khmer, Burmese, Vietnamese, and Thai, and by the 17th cent. it held sway over sections of Yünnan, China, of S Burma, of the Vietnamese and Cambodian plateaus, and large stretches of N Thailand. In 1707, however, internal dissensions brought about a split of Lan Xang into two kingdoms: Luang Prabang in upper (northern) Laos and Vientiane in lower (southern) Laos. During the next century the two states, constantly quarreling, were overrun by the armies of neighboring countries. In the early 19th cent. Siam was dominant over the two Laotian kingdoms, although Siamese claims were disputed by Annam. After French explorations in the late 19th cent. Siam was forced (1893) to recognize a French protectorate over Laos, which was incorporated into the union of INDOCHINA. During World War II, Laos was gradually occupied by the Japanese, who in 1945 persuaded the king of Luang Prabang to declare the country's independence. The French nevertheless reestablished (1946) dominion over Laos, recognizing the king as constitutional monarch of the entire country. The French granted an increasing measure of self-government, and in 1949 Laos became a semiautonomous state within the French Union. In 1951, a Communist Laotian nationalist movement, the Pathet Lao, was formed by Prince Souphanouvong in North Vietnam. In 1953, Pathet Lao guerrillas accompanied a VIET MINH invasion of Laos from Vietnam and established a government at Samneua in N Laos. That year Laos attained full sovereignty; admission into the United Nations came in 1955. The new country faced immediate civil war as Pathet Lao forces, supported by the Viet Minh, made incursions into central Laos, soon occupying sizable portions of the country. Agreements reached at the Geneva Conference of 1954 provided for the withdrawal of foreign troops and the establishment of the Pathet Lao in two northern provinces. An agreement between the royal forces and the Pathet Lao signed in 1957 provided for the reestablishment of government authority in the north, partial integration of Pathet Lao troops into the Laotian royal army, and Pathet Lao participation in the government. In 1959, however, the coalition government collapsed and hostilities were renewed. A succession of coups resulted (1960) in a three-way struggle for power between neutralist, rightist, and Communist forces. The neutralists were headed by Premier Souvanna Phouma, who remained in the administrative capital of Vientiane. The rightists were led by General Phoumi Nosavan, who controlled the bulk of the royal Laotian army; he proclaimed a pro-Western government under Prince Boun Oum. The Communist Pathet Lao rebels remained under the leadership of Prince Souphanouvong in the northern provinces. In Dec., 1960, General Phoumi captured Vientiane; Premier Souvanna Phouma fled to neighboring Cambodia while the Pathet Lao forces, allied with pro-neutralist Laotian troops (loyal to Souvanna Phouma), continued fighting in the north. The government of Boun Oum, installed in Vientiane, was recognized by the United States and other Western countries. The Soviet Union and its allies continued to recognize the deposed government of Souvanna Phouma. In May, 1961, with Pathet Lao and neutralist forces in control of about half the country, a cease-fire was arranged. A 14-nation conference convened in Geneva, producing (1962) another agreement providing for the neutrality of Laos under a unified government. A provisional coalition government, with all factions represented, was accordingly established under the premiership of Souvanna Phouma. Attempts to integrate the three military forces failed, however, and the Pathet Lao began moving against neutralist troops. Open warfare resumed in 1963, and the Pathet Lao, bolstered by supplies and troops from North Vietnam, solidified control over most of N and E Laos. Disgruntled right-wing military leaders staged a coup in 1964 and attempted to force the resignation of Souvanna Phouma; the United States and the Soviet Union emphasized their support of the premier, however, and he remained in office with a right-wing neutralist government. Pathet Lao guerrilla activity decreased after the start (1965) of U.S. bombings of North Vietnamese military bases and communications routes. The bombings also included attacks on what came to be known as the Ho Chi Minh Trail, a North Vietnamese supply route through E Laos. Communist pressure increased during 1969, and early in 1970 the Pathet Lao launched several major offensives. The number of North Vietnamese troops in Laos rose to some 67,000 that year, and North Vietnamese use of the Ho Chi Minh Trail increased greatly after a U.S.-South Vietnamese invasion of Cambodia in the spring of 1970 closed alternate routes. Early in 1971, South Vietnamese troops invaded Laotian territory in an unsuccessful attempt to cut the Ho Chi Minh trail. The attack drove the North Vietnamese deeper into Laos, and Laos became another battleground of the VIETNAM WAR, with heavy U.S. aerial bombardments. The United States extended enormous military and economic aid to the Laotian government and financed the use of Thai mercenary troops, whose numbers peaked to over 21,000 in 1972. The Pathet Lao, supported by North Vietnamese troops, scored major gains, consolidating their control over more than two thirds of Laotian territory (but over only one third of the population). Heavy fighting persisted until Feb., 1973, when a cease-fire was finally declared. A final agreement between the government and the Pathet Lao, concluded in Sept., 1973, provided for the formation of a coalition government under the premiership of Souvanna Phouma (inaugurated in April, 1974), the stationing of an equal number of government and Pathet Lao troops in the two capitals, and the withdrawal of all foreign troops and advisers. An abortive right-wing coup, staged one month before the agreement was announced, was quickly suppressed by government troops. The constitution of Laos, promulgated by the king in 1947 (after Franco-Laotian agreements provided for gradual independence), provides for a limited monarchy and parliamentary democracy. The supreme head of state is King Savang Vatthana, a direct descendant of the royal family of the ancient kingdom of Lan Xang; he succeeded to the throne in 1959 after the death of King Sisavang Vong. Executive power is exercised by the prime minister and a council of ministers. The legislature is composed of the king's council and a popularly elected national assembly. See Sisouk Na Champassak, *Storm over Laos* (1961); J. M. Halpern, *Economy and Society of Laos* (1964) and *Government, Politics and Social Structure in Laos* (1964); M. S. Viravong, *History of Laos* (tr. 1959, repr. 1964); Hugh Toye, *Laos: Buffer State or Battleground* (1968); P. F. Langer and J. J. Zasloff, *North Vietnam and the Pathet Lao* (1970); A. J. Dommen, *Conflict in Laos* (rev. ed. 1971); D. P. Whitaker et al., *Area Handbook for Laos* (1972); Marek Gdański, *Notes of a Witness: Laos and the Second Indochinese War* (1973).

Lao-tze or **Lao-tzu** (both: lou-dzŭ), b. c.604 B.C., Chinese philosopher, reputedly the founder of TAOISM. It is uncertain that Lao-tze [Chinese,=old person or old philosopher] is historical. Knowledge of him is derived from the history of Ssu-ma Ch'ien (1st cent. B.C.) and from legends. According to these his original name was Li Erh and he was the librarian of the Chou court. A meeting with his younger contemporary, Confucius, is reported. Lao-tze is traditionally deemed the author of the *Tao-te-ching*, but the text must have been composed several centuries after his supposed lifetime. This work and the figure of Lao-tze are central to Taoism. See studies by Max Kaltenmark (tr. 1969) and I. L. Harris (1972).

La Paz (lä päs), city (1971 est. pop. 850,000), W Bolivia, administrative capital (since 1898) and largest city of Bolivia. The legal capital is SUCRE. La Paz, the highest capital in the world, lies at an altitude of c.12,000 ft (3,660 m) and is crowded into a long, narrow valley cut by the La Paz River. The site, where there was an Inca village, was chosen by Alonso de Mendoza in 1548 because it offered a modicum of protection in winter from the wind and cold of the barren high plateau c.1,400 ft (430 m) above. Because of the narrowness of the valley, the city could not be laid out in the customary Spanish gridiron pattern. The Plaza Murillo, named after the independence leader Pedro Domingo Murillo, with the national palace, cathedral, and other buildings, is small; there are only a few broad, long avenues, and the streets ascend steeply on either side. Since the climate is generally cool and extreme variations in temperature are common, what flowers and trees there are must be carefully tended. La Paz's location on colonial trade routes made it the commercial and political focus of colonial life. It is an agricultural market and has light manufacturing industries. Its Univ. of San Andrés was founded in 1830. There are extraordinary tourist attractions in the region, notably the Andean peaks Illimani and Illampú, Lake Titicaca, the ruins of Tiahuanaco, and the adjacent tropical YUNGAS. The city's full name is La Paz de Ayacucho, after a Bolivian victory at Ayacucho, Peru, in the war for independence (1809–25).

La Paz, town (1970 pop. 43,722), capital of Baja California Sur state, NW Mexico. It is a fishing and pearling center located on a bay near the entrance to the Gulf of California. Maize, cotton, and cattle are raised in the surrounding area. Its warm, dry climate has made La Paz a winter resort. The city was captured in 1853 by the filibuster William Walker.

La Pérouse, Jean François de Galaup, comte de (zhäN fräNswä' də gälō' kôNt də lä pārōōz'), 1741–c.1788, French navigator. A naval captain, in 1785 he took command of a French government expedition that was to search for the Northwest Passage from the Pacific side and to explore along the coasts of America, China, and Siberia and in the South Seas. He reached Alaska, visited the Hawaiian Islands, Macao, and the Philippines, then went to Japan and Kamchatka, and discovered La Pérouse Strait in 1787. He touched at Samoa and the Friendly Islands. In 1788 he sailed from Botany Bay and was lost at sea. In 1826 the wrecks of what appeared to be his ships were discovered in the New Hebrides. La Pérouse's journals have appeared in French in several editions. See E. W. Allen, *The Vanishing Frenchman* (1959).

La Pérouse Strait (lä pərōōz') or **Soya Strait** (sō'yä), channel, 25 mi (40 km) wide, separating N Hokkaido island, Japan, from S Sakhalin island, USSR, and connecting the Sea of Japan on the west with the Sea of Okhotsk on the east.

Lapidoth (lăp'ĭdŏth), Deborah's husband. Judges 4.4.

lapis lazuli (lăp'ĭs lăz'ōōlē), gem, deep blue, violet, or greenish blue in color and usually flecked with yellow iron pyrites. It is composed of lazurite, a complex sodium aluminum silicate, mixed with other minerals, and is usually found in masses, rather than in crystals, in metamorphosed limestones. Sources of supply are Afghanistan, Chile, Siberia, Upper Burma, California, and Colorado. It was formerly made into vases and bowls and has been used from ancient times for beads and small ornaments. Once highly valued for grinding into a pigment (natural ultramarine), it has now been replaced for this purpose by artificial ultramarine. It was also extensively used in mosaics and was the "sapphire" of the ancients.

Laplace, Pierre Simon, marquis de (pyĕr sēmôN' märkē' də läpläs'), 1749–1827, French astronomer and mathematician. At 18 he went to Paris, proved his gift for mathematical analysis to Jean le Rond d'Alembert, and was made professor of mathematics in the École militaire of Paris. He had a seat in the senate (1799) and became its vice president and (1803) chancellor. He was elected to the French Academy in 1816. He investigated the variations of the moon's motions, especially as affected by the eccentricity of the earth's orbit; the inequalities in the motions of Jupiter and Saturn; the motion of the satellites of Jupiter; the aberration in the movements of comets; and the theory of the tides. With J. L. Lagrange he established beyond a doubt Newton's hypothesis of gravitation. The results of his researches were published in his famous *Mécanique céleste* (1799–1825, tr. by Nathaniel Bowditch, 1829–39). In the more popular work, *Exposition du système du monde* (1796), a summary of the history of astronomy is included. This work contains also a statement of the nebular hypothesis of the origin of the SOLAR SYSTEM. His *Théorie des attractions des sphéroides et de la figure des planètes* (1785) introduced "Laplace's coefficients" and the potential function, two means of applying analysis to physical problems. The *Théorie analytique des probabilités* (1812), a mathematical classic, was followed by *Essai philosophique sur les probabilités* (1814).

Lapland (lăp'lănd''), Finn. *Lappi*, Nor. *Lapland*, Swed. *Lappland*, vast region of N Europe, largely within the Arctic Circle. It includes the Norwegian provinces of Finnmark and Troms and part of Nordland; the Swedish historic province of Lappland; N Finland; and the Kola Peninsula of the USSR. Swedish Lappland is now included in Norrbotten and Västerbotten counties. Lapland is mountainous in N Norway and Sweden, reaching its highest point (6,965 ft/2,123 m) in Kebnekaise (Sweden), and consists largely of tundra in the northeast. There are also extensive forests and many lakes and rivers. The climate is arctic and the vegetation is generally sparse, except in the forested southern zone. Lapland is very rich in mineral resources, particularly in high-grade iron ore at Gällivare and Kiruna (Sweden), in copper at Sulitjelma (Norway), and in nickel and apatite in the USSR. Kirkenes and Narvik (both in Norway) are the chief maritime outlets for Scandinavian Lapland, and Murmansk is the port for Russian Lapland. The region abounds in sea and river fisheries and in aquatic and land fowl. Reindeer (c.350,000) are essential to the economy; there is a growing tourist industry in the region. The **Lapps** or **Laplanders,** who constitute the indigenous population, number about 31,500 and are concentrated mainly in Norway (about 22,000), where they are called Samme or Finns (hence the Finnmark). They speak a Finno-Ugric language. Largely nomadic, the majority of the Lapps follow their reindeer herds, wintering in the lowlands and summering in the western mountains. Their movements today are more restricted than in former times. Other Lapps are sea and river fishermen and hunters. Little is known of their early history; it is believed that they came from central Asia and were pushed to the northern extremity of Europe by the migrations of the Finns, Goths, and Slavs. They may have assumed their Finnic language in the last millennium B.C. Though mainly conquered by Sweden and Norway in the Middle Ages, the Lapps long resisted Christianization, which was completed only in the 18th cent. by Russian and Scandinavian missionaries. See J. O. Turi, *Turi's Book of Lapland* (1931, repr. 1966); Valerie Stalder, *Lapland* (1971).

La Plata (lä plä'tä), city (1970 pop. 408,300), capital of Buenos Aires prov., E central Argentina, 5 mi (8.1 km) inland from Ensenada, its port on the Río de la Plata. La Plata's chief function is that of provincial capital, but industrial growth has been steady, and large quantities of oil, grain, and refrigerated meat products are exported. La Plata is Argentina's main oil-refining center. Although the proximity of Buenos Aires has to some extent checked its development, La Plata is also a major cultural center, with fine museums and colleges and a national university. The city was founded in 1882, after Buenos Aires was federalized as the national capital. During the dictatorship of Juan Perón (1946–55) both city and province were renamed Eva Perón, in honor of his wife. The name La Plata was restored when Perón's regime was overthrown (1955).

La Plata, Río de: see PLATA, RÍO DE LA.

Lapointe, Ernest (läpwăNt'), 1876–1941, Canadian political leader, b. Quebec prov. A lawyer, he was from 1904 and 1941 a Liberal member of the Canadian House of Commons. After the death of Wilfrid Laurier in 1919, Lapointe was regarded as the leader of the French Canadian Liberal party. Appointed (1921) minister of marine and fisheries, he negotiated and signed (1923) with the United States a treaty concerning fisheries in the Pacific; this was the first treaty signed by a Canadian acting alone, with full powers from the king. A close friend and adviser of William Lyon Mackenzie King, Lapointe was powerful in the dominion government and was minister of justice from 1924 to 1930 and again from 1935 to 1941; he was also attorney general from 1935 to 1941. A delegate (1922) to the League of Nations, he attended the imperial conferences in London in 1926 and 1937 and firmly supported Canada's entry into World War II, although he opposed conscription.

Laporte, Roland (rōläN' läpôrt'), 1675–1704, a leader of the CAMISARDS, known as Roland. He was noted for his fearlessness, his knowledge of military tactics, and his ability at organizing guerrilla warfare. Unlike his colleague Jean CAVALIER, Roland refused (1704) to deal with Marshal Villars unless the Edict of Nantes (see NANTES, EDICT OF) was restored. Shortly afterward he was betrayed and died defending himself.

La Porte (lə pôrt), city (1970 pop. 22,140), seat of La Porte co., NW Ind.; inc. 1835. It is a manufacturing center in a fertile farmland on the edge of the Calumet industrial region. Seven lakes adjoin the city, which also has summer resort activities.

Lappeenranta (läp'pänrän"tä), Swed. *Villmanstrand,* city (1970 pop. 51,621), Kymi prov., SE Finland, on Lake Saimaa. It is an important trade and industrial center. There is a hydrotherapy center (est. 1824) in Lappeenranta. The city was chartered in 1649 and became an important border fortress after the Treaty of Nystad (1721).

Lapps: see LAPLAND.

Laptev Sea (läp'tyĭf), section of the Arctic Ocean, c.250,900 sq mi (649,800 sq km), N Siberian USSR, between the Taymyr Peninsula and the New Siberian Islands. It is shallow sea and is frozen for most of the year. The Lena River empties into it through an extensive delta; the sea also receives the Khatanga and Yana rivers. The Laptev Sea, part of the Northern Sea Route, is navigable only during August and September; Tiksi and Nordvik are the chief ports. Formerly called the Nordenskjöld Sea for the Swedish explorer Nils Adolf Nordenskjöld, it was renamed in honor of Khariton and Dmitri Laptev, two Russian arctic explorers of the second Bering expedition.

La Puente (lä pwĕn'tē), city (1970 pop. 31,092), Los Angeles co., S Calif., a residential suburb of Los Angeles; laid out 1841, inc. 1956.

lapwing, common name for some members of the family Charadriidae, which includes the PLOVERS. Lapwings are almost all inland or upland birds, found in all temperate and tropical regions except North America. The lapwing of Eurasia *(Vanellus vanellus),* called also green plover, or pewit, is a noisy and conspicuous bird distinguished by a strikingly upcurved, slender crest. Its back is an iridescent deep green, the crown and crest greenish black, the throat and upper breast black, the underparts white, and the tail coverts fawn. The lapwing has been much exploited in Europe for its flesh and eggs but is now protected by law. The name derives from the irregular lag of its wingbeats in flight. The "blacksmith" group of lapwings of Africa, with sharp spurs on the bend of the wings, are named for the metallic ring of their cries. Other lapwings of Africa, S Asia, and Malaya have prominent red or yellow wattles at the base of the bill, such as in the red-wattled lapwing, *Lobivanellus indica.* Lapwings nest on the ground in scooped-out shallow depressions lined with shells, pebbles, or vegetation; both sexes incubate and care for the young. Lapwings are classified in the phylum CHORDATA, subphylum Vertebrata, class Aves, order Charadriiformes, family Charadriidae.

L'Aquila or **L'Aquila degli Abruzzi** (lä'kwēlä dā'lyē äbrōōt'tsē), city (1971 pop. 61,128), capital of L'Aquila prov. and of Abruzzi, central Italy, on the Pescara River. It is an agricultural and industrial center. Manufactures include building materials, textiles, and electronic equipment. L'Aquila is situated at the foot of the Gran Sasso d'Italia mountain group and is a popular base for mountain climbing. Built around a castle (13th–16th cent.), it rose to importance in the 13th cent. and later became the second city of the kingdom of Naples. However, the city's influence declined during the wars of the 16th cent. Despite several devastating earthquakes L'Aquila has retained its medieval fortifications and a number of impressive old buildings, including St. Bernardino's Basilica (15th–16th cent.). There is a university in the city.

Larache (läräsh'), Arab. *Al Araish,* city (1960 pop. 30,763), N Morocco, on the Atlantic Ocean. Vegetables, cork, and timber are exported. The Phoenicians founded a trading post on the site, which was later captured by the Romans and called Lixus. Spain held the city twice (1610–91 and 1911–56).

Laramie (lâr'əmē), city (1970 pop. 23,143), seat of Albany co., SE Wyo., on the Laramie River; inc. 1874. It is a commercial and industrial center for a livestock and timber region. Tourism is an important economic activity; the city is surrounded by mountain ranges and many nearby ski, hunting, and fishing areas. It is the seat of the Univ. of Wyoming. Laramie was settled in 1868 with the arrival of the railroad and grew with the development of the surrounding ranch country and nearby mining enterprises. It is headquarters for the Medicine Bow National Forest. Nearby is the site of Fort Sanders, established in 1866 to protect the Overland Trail and workers on the Union Pacific RR.

Larbaud, Valery (välärē' lärbō'), 1881–1957, French novelist, poet, critic, and translator. A wealthy and cosmopolitan scholar and poet, Larbaud learned six languages and produced notable French translations of Coleridge's "Rime of the Ancient Mariner" and the works of such writers as Conrad, Hardy, and Joyce. He was particularly noted for his creation of the fictional character Archibaldo Olson Barnabooth, a wealthy young South American who travels through Europe searching for fulfillment. Larbaud's *Poèmes par un riche amateur* (1908) was attributed to Barnabooth as was his *Journal d'A. O. Barnabooth* (1913), in reality a novel splendid in its evocation of Europe. Larbaud's other works include the novel *Fermina Marquez* (1911); *Enfantines* (1918), short stories; *Amants, heureux amants* (1924), three short novels; and such critical works as *Ce Vice impuni la lecture* (1925).

larceny, in law, the unlawful taking and carrying away of the property of another, with intent to deprive the owner of its use or to appropriate it to the use of the perpetrator or of someone else. It is usually distinguished from EMBEZZLEMENT and false pretenses in that the actual taking of the property is accomplished unlawfully and without the victim's consent (see ROBBERY); along with the taking there must be a carrying-off. Statutes in some states of the United States enlarge the scope of larceny to include embezzlement and false pretenses. Grand larceny, usually a FELONY, is distinguished from petty larceny, usually a MISDEMEANOR, by the value of the property stolen.

larch, any tree of the genus *Larix,* conifers of the family Pinaceae (PINE family), which are unusual in that they are not evergreen. The various species are widely distributed in the Northern Hemisphere. Needles of the larches are mostly borne in characteristic radiating clusters. A western American larch *(L. occidentalis)* achieves a great height, and its lumber is used for interior construction, ties, posts, and cabinetmaking. The American, or black, larch *(L. laricina),* commonly called also tamarack and hackmatack, ranges from the Arctic Circle to cold swamps in more temperate regions of the NE United States and is cultivated elsewhere for its beauty. The wood of this species has been used in shipbuilding and for posts, ties, and poles. The European larch *(L. decidua)* has long been valued for its durable wood and as a source of Venice turpentine. This tree, the Japanese larch *(L. leptolepis),* and the Siberian larch *(L. sibirica)* are also cultivated for ornament. The related golden larch is *Pseudolarix amabilis.* Larch is classified in the division PINOPHYTA, class Pinopsida, order Coniferales, family Pinaceae.

lard, hog's fat melted and strained from the tissues, an important by-product of the meat-packing industry. The highest grade, leaf lard, is from the fat around the kidneys; the next best is from the back, and the poorest from the small intestines. Lard is classed by method of preparation as prime steam, rendered in a closed vessel into which steam is injected; neutral, melted at low temperature; kettle-rendered, heated with added water in steam-jacketed kettles; and dry-rendered, hashed, then heated in cookers equipped with agitators. Good lard melts quickly and is free from disagreeable odor. Pure lard (99% fat) is highly valued as a cooking oil because it smokes very little when heated.

Lardner, Ring (Ringgold Wilmer Lardner), 1885–1933, American humorist and short-story writer, b. Niles, Mich. He was a sports reporter in Chicago, St. Louis, and Boston from 1907 to 1919. His first collection of short stories, *You Know Me, Al* (1916) revealed his talent for the racy sports idiom he made famous. Among his other early volumes of short stories are *Gullible's Travels* (1917) and *Treat 'Em Rough* (1918). With the publication of *How to Write Short Stories (with Samples)* (1924), Lardner's reputation as a satirist was established. Usually cynical and pessimistic, his stories are peopled by ordinary characters—baseball players, stenographers, barbers—who are stunningly revealed, often through their own conversation, as being stupid, dull, and vicious. His later story collections include *What of It?* (1925) and *First and Last* (1934). With George S. Kaufman he collaborated on the comedy *June Moon* (produced 1929). See his *Best Short Stories* (1957); biography by Donald Elder (1956); study by Maxwell Geismar (1972).

Laredo (lərā'dō), city (1970 pop. 69,024), seat of Webb co., S Texas, on the Rio Grande; founded 1755, inc. 1852. It is the major port of entry on the U.S.-Mexican border, with a thriving export-import trade and a busy tourist industry. It is also a wholesale and retail center for a large area on both sides of the Rio Grande. Important to its economy are cattle ranching, irrigated farming, oil production, and mining and smelting. A wide variety of products are manufactured, including clothing, electronic equipment, ceramics, medical supplies, and leather goods. Laredo has close economic ties with its large sister city in Mexico—Nueva Laredo—with which it is linked by an international bridge. Laredo was founded by the Spanish and still retains a semi-Mexican flavor. It grew as a post on the road to San Antonio and other Texas cities. After the Texas Revolution its ownership remained in doubt until the southern boundary of Texas was definitively established by the Mexican War; during that period the city set up a "Republic of the Rio Grande" (the capitol building, erected in 1755, still stands). Laredo's growth was aided by the arrival of the railroads (1880s), the development of irrigated farming, the discovery of oil and natural gas, and the opening (1936) of an excellent highway to Mexico City. Laredo has an international airport. The former army post Fort McIntosh, founded in 1849 and intermittently rebuilt and used until 1946, now houses a junior college. An extension center of the Texas Arts and Industries Univ. is also in the city. Laredo Air Force Base, a large jet-pilot training center, is on the outskirts.

Larentia or **Larentina:** see ACCA LARENTIA.

lares (lâr'ēz), in Roman religion, guardian spirits. According to some they were ghosts of the dead, destructive spirits who frequented crossroads and had to be propitiated. Others say that the lares were farm deities, worshiped as fertility powers of the earth. The most common myth, however, identifies them as household gods, beneficent spirits of ancestors, worshiped in close connection with the PENATES.

Largillière, Nicolas de (nēkôlä' də lärzhēlyĕr'), 1656–1746, French portrait and history painter, b. Paris. He was brought up in Antwerp, and the influence of Rubens is evident in his vigorous and colorful style. Favored by Le Brun, he became a successful portrait painter in Paris and London. One of his best-known pictures is *The Painter and His Family* (Louvre). Examples of his work are to be seen in the National Portrait Gallery and the Wallace Collection, London, and in the Metropolitan Museum.

Largo, town (1970 pop. 22,031), Pinellas co., W Fla., on the Pinellas peninsula and the Gulf Coast, across the bay from Tampa; settled 1853, inc. 1905. It is a packing, canning, and shipping center in a citrus fruit area. Its beautiful beaches and many recreational facilities make it a popular resort spot.

Largo Caballero, Francisco (frănthēs'kō lär'gō käbälyā'rō), 1869–1946, Spanish Socialist leader and politician. A plasterer, he became a Socialist trade union leader. He collaborated with the dictatorship of Primo de Rivera (1923–30). After the overthrow of the monarchy he was minister of labor (1931–33). He promoted agitation against the rightist government of 1933 and helped stir rebellion in 1934. His radical propaganda early in 1936 is considered a chief factor in bringing the civil war of 1936–39. He was premier (1936–37) of a leftist coalition cabinet and fled to France in 1939. After four years of imprisonment by the Germans, he died in Paris.

lariat: see LASSO.

Larionov, Mikhail (mēkhəyĕl' lərĭyô'nôf), 1881–1964, Russian painter. Larionov, together with Natalya Goncherova, was the founder of Rayonism, one of the earliest movements in nonfigurative art. Settling in Paris in 1914, Larionov stopped painting in 1915 and designed sets for Diaghilev's Ballet Russe the same year.

Lárisa (lä'rēsä) or **Larissa** (lərĭs'ə), city (1971 pop. 72,336), capital of Lárisa prefecture, E Greece, in Thessaly on the Piniós River. It is an agricultural trade center and a transportation hub, linked by rail with the port of Vólos and with Thessaloníki and Athens. The chief city of ancient Thessaly, it was annexed (4th cent. B.C.) by Philip II of Macedon and in 196 B.C. became an ally of Rome. It was taken from the Byzantine Empire by Bulgaria and later was held by Serbia, with which it passed (15th cent.) under the rule of the Ottoman Turks. In the Greek War of Independence the city was (1821) the headquarters of Ali Pasha. Turkey ceded the city to Greece in 1881.

lark, common name for members of the large family Alaudidae, perching birds of terrestrial habits, chiefly of the Old World and best-known through the SKYLARK, *Alauda arvensis*. The horned larks belong to the one species native to North America, *Eremophila alpestris*. They vary in color and markings in different geographical areas but are generally protectively plumaged in mixed browns and grays above, with light underparts and with black and yellow or white about the head and throat. Dark feathers form the tufts on their heads. On the ground they run rather than hop. They have a melodious flight song. The prairie lark is a subspecies. The MEADOWLARK belongs to the family Icteridae. The 75 species of larks are fairly similar in their habits and appearance. They are found in meadows, plains, beaches, and other open areas. They are omnivorous. With the exception of the bush lark, genus *Mirafra*, larks lay their eggs (two to six per clutch) in open nests on the ground. Bush larks have domed nests. The female almost exclusively incubates the eggs for three to four weeks. Larks are classified in the phylum CHORDATA, subphylum Vertebrata, class Aves, order Passeriformes, family Alaudidae.

Larkana (lärkä'nə), town (1961 pop.48,008), S central Pakistan, on the Ghar canal. Famous for the quality of its rice, it is an important grain market and a trading center for silk and cotton goods. Brass and other metalware are manufactured. The city has two colleges affiliated with Sind Univ. Larkana, named for the Larak tribe that inhabited the neighboring area, is the birthplace of Pakistani Prime Minister Zulfikar Ali Bhutto. Remains of the ancient city of Mohenjo-Daro (see INDUS VALLEY CIVILIZATION) have been uncovered c.15 mi (24 km) S of Larkana.

Larkin, James, 1876-1947, Irish labor leader. The Irish Transport and General Workers' Union, which he organized and of which he was secretary, had as its goal the combining of all Irish industrial workers, skilled and unskilled, into one organization. After his activity in the general strike of 1913 he was tried by the British for sedition and jailed briefly. When World War I began, Larkin traveled to the United States to raise funds for the Irish to fight the British. His radical socialist manifestos and close association with the founders of the American Communist party resulted in a conviction (1920) for criminal anarchy. Pardoned in 1923 by the governor of New York, Alfred E. Smith, Larkin was deported to Ireland. There he organized (1924) the Workers' Union of Ireland and served in the Dáil Éireann (1937-38, 1943-44), on the Dublin Trades Council, and on the Dublin Corporation. See biographies by R. M. Fox (1957) and E. J. Larkin (1965).

Larkin, Oliver Waterman, 1896-1970, American art historian, b. Medford, Mass. Larkin taught at Smith from 1924 to 1964. His major work is *Art and Life in America* (1949; Pulitzer Prize in history, 1950). He is also the author of *Samuel F. B. Morse* (1954) and *Daumier, Man of His Time* (1966). Larkin has contributed many outstanding articles to the major art journals.

Larkin, Philip, 1922-, English poet. He graduated from St. John's College, Oxford (B.A., 1943; M.A., 1947) and was for many years librarian at the Univ. of Hull. With an eye for the ordinary and the mean, Larkin writes poetry of diminution, quietly exposing the weakness and pretensions of English life. His wit is subtle, delicate, and deadly. Among his volumes of poetry are *The North Ship* (1946), *The Less Deceived* (1955), *The Whitsun Weddings* (1964), and *High Windows* (1974). Larkin edited *The Oxford Book of Twentieth-Century English Verse* (1973). In addition, he has published novels, including *Jill* (1940) and *A Girl in Winter* (1947); and *All What Jazz: A Record Diary, 1961-1968* (1970), a collection of his critical pieces on jazz for the London *Daily Telegraph*.

Larkin, Thomas Oliver, 1802-58, American merchant and diplomatic agent, b. Charlestown, Mass. He settled (1832) in Monterey, Calif., where he became a successful merchant trading with Mexico and the Hawaiian Islands. As U.S. consul in California (1844-48) and confidential agent of the U.S. government (1846-48), he waged an extensive propaganda campaign in favor of American acquisition of California that helped to bring about the U.S. seizure of California in the Mexican War. He also served (1847-49) as navy agent and was a delegate to the state constitutional convention of 1849. See the collection of his papers, ed. by G. P. Hammond (10 vol., 1951-1964); biography by R. L. Underhill (2d ed. 1946).

Larkspur, city (1970 pop. 10,487), Marin co., W Calif., a residential suburb of San Francisco near Mt. Tamalpais; inc. 1908. Nearby Larkspur Canyon has a redwood grove.

larkspur or **delphinium,** any plant of the large north temperate genus *Delphinium* of the family Ranunculaceae (BUTTERCUP family), annual or perennial herbs, several popular for garden cultivation. The annuals are commonly referred to as larkspur and the perennials as delphinium. Blue is the most common color of the spurred flowers, borne in a spire above the deeply cut leaves. Most native North American larkspurs are poisonous to cattle; garden kinds are chiefly derived from Old World species. Larkspurs are classified in the division MAGNOLIOPHYTA, class Magnoliopsida, order Ranunculales, family Ranunculaceae.

Larnaca (lär'nəkə), town (1970 est. pop. 21,500), SE Cyprus, on Larnaca Bay. It is a port and district administrative center. Salt and umber are mined in the district. The modern section of the town occupies the site of ancient CITIUM. There is a tradition that St. Lazarus settled in Larnaca after his resurrection and became its first bishop. In the town is a fort built by the Turks in 1625.

Larne (lärn), municipal borough (1971 pop. 18,242), Co. Antrim, NE Northern Ireland, on an inlet of the North Channel. It is a seaport and a tourist center. Metal ores, beef, and potatoes are exported; among the industrial products are electrical equipment, paper, and linen. In 1315, Edward Bruce landed at Larne.

La Rochefoucauld, François, duc de (fräNswä', dük də lä rôshfo͞okō'), 1613-80, French writer. As head of an ancient family (in his youth he bore the title prince de Marcillac) he opposed Richelieu and was later active in both FRONDES. Wounded and disheartened, he made his peace (1652) and retired to his estates in Angoumois. Later he settled (c.1658) in Paris where he moved in the literary circle of Mme de Sablé, which included Mme de La Fayette, whose close friendship had an important influence on him. Although his *Mémoires* are interesting historically, La Rochefoucauld's place in French literature is assured by his moral maxims and reflective epigrams, which are marked by lucidity and polished brilliance. A collection was published in 1665 as *Réflexions ou sentences et maximes morales*. The fifth edition, which appeared in his lifetime, contained 504 maxims. La Rochefoucauld's philosophy derives from his pessimistic view that selfishness is the source of all human behavior—a famous maxim is "The virtues join with self-interest as the rivers join with the sea." Translations of the *Maximes* include that by Louis Kronenberger (1959).

La Rochefoucauld-Liancourt, François Alexandre Frédéric, duc de (äləksäN'drə frädärĕk' dük də lä rôshfo͞okō'-lyäNko͞or'), 1747-1827, French social reformer. Before the French Revolution he established a model farm, two factories, and a trade school on his estate, and in the Constituent Assembly he urged the necessity of public welfare. A royalist during the French Revolution, he was forced to flee to England in 1792. From there he traveled to the United States where he wrote *Voyage dans les États-Unis d'Amérique* (1799). Upon his return to France (1799), he resumed his philanthropic activities, working especially for health, educational, and economic reforms.

La Rochejaquelein or **La Rochejacquelin, Henri Du Vergier, comte de** (both: äNrē' dü vĕrzhyā' kôNt də lä rôshzhäkəläN'), 1772-94, French commander, leader of the counterrevolutionary army in the VENDÉE. His legendary gallantry and tactical abilities were of little avail against superior republican armies. He was killed in battle.

La Romana, city (1970 pop. 36,722), SE Dominican Republic, on the Caribbean Sea. It is a provincial capital and port.

Larra, Mariano José de (märyä'nō hōsā' thə lä'rä), 1809-37, Spanish satirist, b. Madrid. Using several pseudonyms, Larra wrote a series of satirical articles on Spanish politics and customs. These were published in his own periodical, *Pobrecito hablador* (1832-33). His best-known works are the novel *El doncel de don Enrique el doliente* [the page of Don Enrique the sorrowful] (1834), the drama *Macías* (1834), and *No más mostrador* [good-bye to the shop counter] (1831), an adaptation of a play by Scribe. Unhappy in love and an incurable melancholic, Larra committed suicide.

Larreta, Enrique Rodríguez (änrē'kä rôthrē'gāth lärrä'tä), 1875-1961, Argentine novelist. Larreta lived for many years in Spain and France. His fame rests on *La gloria de don Ramiro* (1908, tr. 1924), a historical novel of the days of Philip II. It is a classic of the polished *modernista* genre. Larreta's other novels include the gaucho story *Zogoibi* (1926) and *En la pampa* (1955).

Larsa (lär'sə), ancient city of S Babylonia, in modern Iraq, 30 mi (48 km) NW of An Nasiriyah. It was the biblical Ellasar (Gen. 14.1). When the last king of the third dynasty of Ur was overthrown (c.1950 B.C.) by the Elamites and Amorites, the cities of ISIN and Larsa were rivals for hegemony in MESOPOTAMIA. In 1763 B.C. Hammurabi defeated Larsa and succeeded in uniting Babylonia under his power. The city was dedicated to the sun god, Shamash. Temple libraries and important documents have been found in the ruins.

Larsen, Peter Laurentius, 1833-1915, American educator, b. Norway. He emigrated to the United States in 1857 as a Lutheran missionary. From 1859 to 1861 he was professor of theology at Concordia Seminary, St. Louis, but left that institution to become president of the new Luther College, established by the Norwegian Synod. Although he resigned from the presidency in 1902, he continued to teach there until 1913. Larsen was also a prominent theological leader and was for many years editor of the weekly *Evangelisk luthersk kirketidende* [Evangelical Lutheran Church times]. See biography by his daughter, Karen Larsen (1936).

Lars Porsena or **Lars Porsenna** (both: lärz pôr'sənə, pôrsĕn'ə) [Etruscan, *Lars*=lord], semilegendary king of Clusium (modern Chiusi) in Etruria, who marched against Rome to reinstate the exiled Tarquinius Priscus. It was said that the heroism of such Romans as Horatius and Scaevola moved him to grant honorable terms of peace and to withdraw. However, the Etruscan version identifies Lars Porsena with Mastarna, a legendary hero of Etruria, who conquered Rome and ruled over the city. According to this tradition, the Romans recovered their independence after Aruns, son of Porsena, was defeated at Aricia by the united forces of the Latin cities. Roman historians dated these events c.500 B.C.

Larsson, Carl (kärl lär'sôn), 1853-1919, Swedish painter and illustrator. He was a popular and imaginative illustrator and was equally successful as a watercolorist. In watercolor he painted exquisite interiors that influenced Swedish decorative arts. He is perhaps best known, however, for his historical mural decorations in fresco for the national museum and the opera house in Stockholm.

Lartigue, Jacques Henri (zhäk äNrē' lärtēg'), 1894-, French photographer. The first exhibition of Lartigue's work in 1962 revealed a remarkable personal use of the photographic medium. Presented with his first camera at seven, he illustrated a witty, sophisticated, and detailed diary with thousands of photographs. They form a moving and exuberant composite portrait of the family, friends, and lifetime of a man of the world. Lartigue's diary and photographs have been published as *Diary of a Century* (ed. by Richard Avedon, 1970).

larva, independent, immature animal that undergoes a profound change, or metamorphosis, to assume the typical adult form. Larvae occur in almost all of the animal phyla; because most are tiny or microscopic, they are rarely seen. They play diverse roles in the lives of animals. Motile larvae help to disseminate sessile, or sedentary, animals such as SPONGES, OYSTERS, BARNACLES, or scale insects. Larvae of parasites may be dispersed by penetrating the skin of new hosts; other parasite larvae live in intermediate hosts that are normally eaten by the final host, in which the adult parasites develop. The larvae of other parasites live in and are dispersed by intermediate hosts such as MOSQUITOES, GNATS, or LEECHES; when the blood meals are taken from the final host, the parasite larvae are introduced into the blood or skin. Parasitic infections can often be reduced by eliminating the larval hosts. Among VERTEBRATES a number of FISHES pass through larval stages; the larva of the EEL is interesting because it is flat and transparent. The tadpole, the familiar larva of the AMPHIBIAN, develops to a considerable size in the relatively hospitable aquatic environment before metamorphosis prepares it for an amphibious or terrestrial life as a FROG or TOAD. In some animals, especially INSECTS, larvae represent a special feeding stage in the life cycle. Some insects pass through more or less wormlike larval stages, enter the outwardly inactive, or pupal, form, and emerge from the pupal case as adults (see PUPA). Insect larvae feed voraciously, necessarily becoming larger than the adult, as considerable energy and material is needed for the profound changes made during pupation. For this reason, insect larvae often cause far more damage to stored crops and textiles than adult insects. Insect larvae generally have a thinner exoskeleton than the adult; many are white and soft. The characteristic FLY larvae are maggots, often developing in decaying plant or animal material. Mosquito larvae are the familiar aquatic wrigglers; they breathe air and are killed by a thin film of oil on the water that prevents contact with air. Maggots and wrigglers are legless, as are all larvae of the insect order Diptera. BEETLE larvae, including the whitish forms called grubs and the long brownish WIREWORMS, are quite diverse, but all are equipped with the six legs characteristic of adults. MOTHS and BUTTERFLIES have wormlike caterpillars as larvae, each equipped with the six legs characteristic of adults and false legs known as prolegs to support the long abdominal section. Some, like the milkweed worm (the larva of the monarch butterfly), are relatively naked, while other caterpillars are covered by hairy bristles, sometimes equipped with irritating chemicals that can cause intense itching. The young of the social insects (BEES, ANTS, and WASPS) are legless but otherwise grublike. Although all social insect larvae are ultimately dependent on the parent colony for food, they are considered true larvae because they pass through a pupal stage. Larval DOBSONFLIES, called hellgrammites, are much sought as bait by fishermen. The importance of larvae in the life cycle of insects varies greatly, as does the proportion of the life span spent in larval, pupal, and adult stages. In many insects, the adult life is relatively short, consisting mostly of mating and egg laying, while the larvae live for many months or, in some species, for several years.

Larvae: see LEMURES.

Larvik (lär'vēk), city (1970 pop. 10,221), Vestfold co., SE Norway, at the head of the Larviksfjord (an arm of the Skagerrak); chartered 1671. It is a shipping and whaling center. Tanum Church, a medieval stone structure, is nearby.

laryngitis, inflammation of the mucous membrane of the voice box, or LARYNX, usually accompanied by hoarseness, sore throat, and coughing. Acute laryngitis is often a secondary bacterial infection triggered by infecting agents causing such illnesses as colds, measles, whooping cough, or influenza. It may also result from straining the voice, drinking hot liquids, or exposure to irritating gases. In chronic laryngitis, inflammation of the mucous membrane of the larynx persists. When such a condition continues for long periods, the membrane becomes irreversibly thickened and the voice permanently changed. Laryngitis resulting from weakened laryngeal muscles is common in singers, teachers, and others who use the voice professionally.

larynx (lâr'ĭngks), organ of voice in mammals. A boxlike chamber about 2 in. (5 cm) high with walls of cartilage bound by muscles and membranes, the human larynx is an extension of the TRACHEA. In men part of the structure may protrude at the front of the neck, forming the so-called Adam's apple. Within the larynx lie the vocal cords, a pair of elastic folds in the lining of mucous membrane. During silent breathing the vocal cords rest along the larynx walls, leaving the air passage fully open (see RESPIRATORY SYSTEM). During speech the cords are stretched across the larynx; outgoing breath from the lungs is forced between the cords, causing them to vibrate and so produce voice. Various muscles adjust the tension of the cords as well as the space between them, thus varying the pitch and other qualities of the sounds produced. The more taut the cords, the higher the pitch. Since men's larynges are usually larger than women's, male vocal cords tend to be longer and the male voice therefore deeper. Growth may double the length of the vocal cords in the male adolescent; hence his dramatic "change of voice." Over the vocal cords extend parallel bands of protective tissue, the false vocal cords. Above them, at the opening of the larynx into the throat, hangs the epiglottis, a flap of cartilage that automatically seals off the air passage during swallowing so that food does not enter it.

La-sa: see LHASA, China.

La Salle, Jean Baptiste de: see JOHN BAPTIST DE LA SALLE, SAINT.

La Salle, Robert Cavelier, sieur de (rōbĕr' kävəlyā' syör də lä säl'), 1643–87, French explorer in North America. He entered a Jesuit novitiate as a boy but left the religious life to become one of the most celebrated explorers and builders of New France. In 1666 he went to Canada, where he developed a seigniory at Lachine. In 1673 the governor of New France, Frontenac, made him commandant of Fort Frontenac (see KINGSTON, Ont., Canada). After a visit to France, where he was granted a patent of nobility, La Salle began (1675) to develop the trade at the post. In 1677 he was in France again and obtained a patent to build forts, explore, and trade. When he returned, he brought with him Henri de TONTI, who was his lieutenant in later enterprises. In 1679 a blockhouse was built at the outlet of the Niagara River, and in August they set out across the Great Lakes in the *Griffon,* which Tonti had built. That first sailing vessel on the lakes took the adventuring traders to Green Bay; the party then went by land. The *Griffon* was lost a little later, probably in a storm. La Salle went along Lake Michigan, erected Fort Miami on the site of present St. Joseph, Mich., then continued to the Illinois River. On that stream Fort Creve Coeur was built. La Salle sent Michel ACO and Father HENNEPIN on an expedition to the upper Mississippi, while he himself went back to Fort Frontenac for supplies. After La Salle's departure Tonti was attacked by hostile Iroquois and was forced to flee the settlement. La Salle, returning, found the Illinois posts deserted. He set out to find Tonti and also organized (1681) an Indian federation of the Illinois, the Miami, and smaller tribes to fight the Iroquois. He was reunited with Tonti at Mackinac Island, and the two men with Father Zenobe Membré and a small party descended the Mississippi to its mouth, arriving April 9, 1682. La Salle took possession of the whole valley, calling the region Louisiana. Tonti went back to the Illinois and at Starved Rock began reconstruction of a village; La Salle joined him, and Fort St. Louis was completed (1682–83). La Salle was deprived of his authority by the new governor in 1683 and went to France, leaving Tonti in the Illinois country. Given power to colonize and to govern the region between Lake Michigan and the Gulf of Mexico, La Salle set out (1684) with four ships for the mouth of the Mississippi. He never reached it. With three of his ships La Salle reached the Gulf of Mexico; but because of the sandy sameness of the coastline he was unable to find the Mississippi. He and his men landed on the Texas shore, probably on Lavaca Bay. They made futile attempts to reach the Mississippi overland, and the men grew mutinous. On the third attempt the great explorer was murdered by his own men. Original narratives are translated in I. J. Cox, *The Journeys of René Robert Cavelier, Sieur da la Salle* (2 vol., 1922; repr. 1973). A classic account is Francis Parkman's *La Salle and the Discovery of the Great West* (1889, repr. 1968). See biographies by R. F. Lockridge (1931) and E. B. Osler (1967).

Lasalle (ləsăl') or **Ville Lasalle,** city (1971 pop. 72,912), S Que., Canada, SW of Montreal on the St. Lawrence River at the head of the Lachine Rapids. It is a suburb of Montreal.

La Salle, city (1970 pop. 10,736), La Salle co., N Ill., on the Illinois River, in an area where coal and other minerals are found; settled 1830, inc. 1852. It forms a tri-city unit with Peru and Oglesby. Manufactures include zinc products, cement, electrical and electronic equipment, steel items, clocks, and motors. The city developed as an important water transportation center after the opening of the Illinois and Michigan Canal in 1848. Nearby is Starved Rock State Park on the site of a fort begun in 1680 by Henri de Tonti and completed by La Salle and Tonti in 1682–83.

Lasca, Il: see GRAZZINI, ANTONIO FRANCESCO.

Lascaris (lăs'kərĭs), family name of the Greek emperors of Nicaea (see NICAEA, EMPIRE OF). The empire was founded in 1204 by THEODORE I, a son-in-law of Alexius III (Alexius Angelus). Theodore I was succeeded (1222) by his son-in-law, JOHN III (John Ducas Vatatzes). John's son THEODORE II (1254–58) assumed the family name Lascaris. He was succeeded by his son JOHN IV, who was forced (1259) to share his throne with Michael VIII, founder of the Palaeologus dynasty. John was deposed in 1261.

Lascaris, Constantine (kŏn'stəntēn lăs'kərĭs), d. 1501?, Greek grammarian. After the fall of Constantinople, Lascaris went to Italy and in Milan obtained the patronage of Francisco Sforza. His Greek grammar (1476) was the first book printed in Greek characters. He earned fame as a teacher of Greek and a leading proponent of the new learning of the Renaissance in Italy. His brother, **Andreas Joannes Lascaris** or **Janus Lascaris,** c.1445–1535, taught Greek in Florence, Paris, and Rome.

Las Casas, Bartolomé de (bärtōlōmā' dā läs kä'säs), 1474–1566, Spanish missionary and historian, called the apostle of the Indies. He went to Hispaniola with his father in 1502, and eight years later he was ordained a priest. In 1514 he began to work for the improvement of Indian conditions, especially for abolition of Indian slavery and of the forced labor of the ENCOMIENDA. He devoted the rest of his life to that cause, going to Spain to urge the government to action, converting uncivilized tribes, and striving to break the power of Spanish landholders over Indian laborers. He tried unsuccessfully to establish a model Indian colony (1520–21), went to Peru with a royal cedula prohibiting Indian enslavement, worked among the natives of Guatemala, and for a brief time (1544–47) was bishop of Chiapa. In his anxiety to help the Indians he endorsed the proposal to import Negro slaves, but repented his action almost immediately. Chiefly through his agency, humanitarian laws, called the New Laws, were adopted (1542) to protect the Indians in Spanish colonies, although later alterations, notably those of Pedro de la GASCA, rendered them almost ineffective. The writings of Las Casas contain good anthropological and historical material. He spent much of his time writing the monumental *Historia de las Indias* (1875–76); for selections in English translation, see *Tears of the Indians* (ed. by John Phillips, 1953) and *Devastation of the Indies* (1974). See biographies by H. R. Wagner (1967), and Juan Friede and Benjamin Keen, ed. (1971).

Las Cases, Emmanuel, comte de (ĕmänüĕl' kôNt də läs käz), 1766–1842, French historian. He accompanied Napoleon into exile to St. Helena, where the emperor dictated a part of his memoirs to him. His famous *Mémorial de Sainte-Hélène* (tr. 8 vol. in 4, 1823) is a primary source, although not always an accurate one, for Napoleon's last years and his judgment of himself. The *Mémorial* became something of a bible to Napoleon-worshipers.

Lascaux: see PALEOLITHIC ART.

Las Cruces (läs kro͞o'sĭs), city (1970 pop. 37,857), seat of Dona Ana co., SW N. Mex., on the Rio Grande, in a farm area irrigated by the Elephant Butte system; founded 1848, inc. 1907. Its economy is based chiefly upon agriculture and the nearby White Sands Missile Range, testing grounds for the first atomic bomb and now a major military and NASA testing site. The city also has textile and canning industries. The name, Spanish for "the crosses," refers to a massacre (1830) of some 40 travelers by Apache Indians on this site. New Mexico State Univ. is to the east. Nearby are the historic village of Mesilla, the picturesque Organ Mts., Fort Fillmore (1851), Fort Seldon (1865), and the Indian village Tortugas.

Lasea (lāsē'ə), ancient town of Crete, S of Candia. It was near the harbor called Fair Havens, where Paul landed (Acts 27.8). Some ruins remain.

laser [acronym for *l*ight *a*mplification by *s*timulated *e*mission of *r*adiation], device for the creation, amplification, and transmission of a narrow, intense beam of coherent LIGHT. The coherent light produced by a laser differs from ordinary light in that it is made up of waves all of the same wavelength and all in phase (i.e., in step with each other); ordinary light contains many different wavelengths and phase relations. The physical size of a laser depends on the materials used for light emission, on its power output, and on whether the light is emitted in pulses or as a steady beam. Lasers have been developed that are not much larger than a common flashlight. The light beam produced by most lasers is

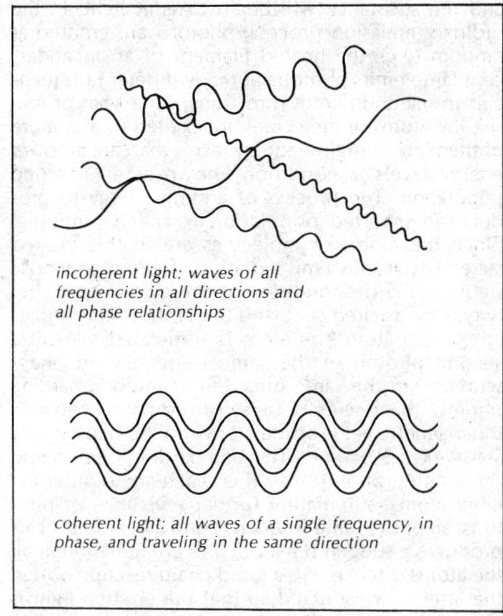

Ordinary light sources produce incoherent light, while a laser produces a beam of coherent light.

pencil-sized, and maintains its size and direction over very large distances; this sharply focused beam of coherent light is suitable for a wide variety of applications. Lasers have been used in industry for cutting and boring metals and other materials, and for inspecting optical equipment. In medicine, they have been used in surgical operations. Lasers have been used in several kinds of scientific research. The field of HOLOGRAPHY is based on the fact that actual wave-front patterns, captured in a photographic image of an object illuminated with laser light, can be reconstructed to produce a three-dimensional image of the object. Lasers have opened a new field of scientific research, nonlinear optics, which is concerned with the study of such phenomena as the frequency doubling of coherent light by certain crystals. One important result of laser research is the development of lasers that can be tuned to emit light over a range of frequencies, instead of producing light of only a single frequency. Work is being done to develop lasers for communication; in a manner similar to radio transmission, the transmitted light beam is modulated with a signal and is received and demodulated some distance away. Lasers have also been used in plasma physics and chemistry. The laser is sometimes referred to as an optical MASER; both the laser and the maser find theoretical basis for their operation in the quantum theory. ELECTROMAGNETIC RADIATION (e.g., light or microwaves) is emitted or absorbed by the atoms or molecules of a substance only at certain characteristic frequencies. According to the QUANTUM THEORY, the electromagnetic energy is transmitted in discrete amounts (i.e., in units or packets) called quanta. A quantum of electromagnetic energy is called a PHOTON. The energy carried by each photon is proportional to its frequency. An atom or molecule of a substance usually does not emit energy; it is then said to be in a low-energy or ground state. When an atom or molecule in the ground state absorbs a photon, it is raised to a higher energy, and is said to be excited. The substance spontaneously returns to a lower energy state by emitting a photon with a frequency proportional to the energy difference between the excited state and the lower state. In the simplest case, the substance will return directly to the ground state, emitting a single photon with the same frequency as the absorbed photon. However, when there are several possible energy levels between the excited state and the ground state, several photons may be emitted with frequencies proportional to the energy differences between successive levels. Under normal conditions, most atoms or molecules in a substance are in low energy states, and little energy is emitted. If energy is added to the substance, the atoms or molecules become excited, and the substance will begin to emit light. In the ordinary emission process, photons are emitted at random (e.g., the heated filament of an incandescent lamp emits photons of many different frequencies in many different directions). In a laser or maser, the atoms or molecules are excited so that more of them are at higher energy levels than are at lower energy levels, a condition known as an inverted population. The process of adding energy to produce an inverted population is called pumping. Once the atoms or molecules are in this excited state, they readily emit radiation. If a photon whose frequency corresponds to the energy difference between the excited state and the ground state strikes an excited atom, the atom is stimulated to emit a second photon of the same frequency, in phase with and in the same direction as the bombarding photon; this occurs because of resonance between the magnetic fields of the atom and the photon (see MAGNETIC RESONANCE). The bombarding photon and the emitted photon may then each strike other excited atoms, stimulating further emissions of photons, all of the same frequency and all in phase. This produces a sudden burst of coherent radiation as all the atoms discharge in a rapid chain reaction. Often the laser is constructed so that the emitted light is reflected between opposite ends of a resonant cavity; an intense, highly focused light beam passes out through one end, which is only partially reflecting. If the atoms are pumped back to an excited state as soon as they are discharged, a steady beam of coherent light is produced. Various materials have been used as the active media in lasers. The first laser, built in 1960, used a RUBY rod with polished ends; the chromium atoms embedded in the ruby's aluminum oxide crystal lattice were pumped to an excited state by a flash tube that, wrapped around the rod, saturated the rod with light of a frequency higher than that of the laser frequency (this method is called optical pumping). This first ruby laser produced intense pulses of red light. In many other optically pumped lasers, the basic element is a transparent, nonconducting crystal such as yttrium aluminum garnet (YAG). Another type of crystal laser uses a semiconductor diode as the element; pumping is done by passing a current through the crystal. In some lasers, a gas or liquid is used as the emitting medium. In one kind of gas laser the inverted population is achieved through collisional pumping, the gas molecules gaining energy from collisions with other molecules or with electrons released through current discharge. Some gas lasers make use of molecular dissociation to create the inverted population. See Stanley Leinwoll, *Understanding Lasers and Masers* (1965); Ronald Brown, *Lasers* (1968); F. T. Arecchi and E. O. Schulz-Dubois, *Laser Handbook* (1973).

La Serena (lä sārā'nä), city (1970 pop. 71,898), capital of Coquimbo prov., N central Chile, on the Elqui River. A commercial and agricultural center in a region of orchards and vineyards, it is a popular resort. La Serena was founded in 1544, destroyed by Indians in 1549, and sacked by the English in 1680. It was the site of Chile's declaration of independence in 1818. Often damaged by earthquakes, La Serena is a city of old-world charm, noted for its cathedral, fine buildings, and gardens.

Lasharon (lăshā'rŏn), probably the same as SHARON. Joshua 12.18.

Lashio (lăsh'yō, ləshyō'), town, Shan state, E central Burma. It is a trade center and the terminus of the railroad line from Mandalay. Lashio was famous in World War II as the starting point of the Burma Road.

Lashkar (ləsh'kər), city, Madhya Pradesh state, central India. Formerly the capital of Madhya Bharat state, it adjoins Gwalior town and is a modern commercial center and transportation hub. Victoria College, the palace of the maharaja of Gwalior, and a state museum are of interest.

Lasker, Emanuel (āmä'no͞oĕl), 1868–1941, German chess player. He won the world championship in 1894 when he defeated Wilhelm Steinitz and held it until he was defeated by José Raúl CAPABLANCA in 1921. Lasker studied the games of his opponents for their weaknesses and predilections in technique and played primarily against the temperament of his opponents. He was a master in closed positions. See his *Common Sense in Chess* (1896; rev. ed. by D. A. Mitchell, 1965), *Lasker's Manual of Chess* (1934), and *The Games of Emanuel Lasker, Chess Champion* (ed. by J. Gilchrist, 2 vol., 1955–58).

Laski, Harold Joseph (lăs'kē), 1893–1950, British political scientist, economist, author, and lecturer. A graduate of New College, Oxford, he taught at McGill University (1914–16) and Harvard (1916–20). In 1920 he joined the faculty of the London School of Economics and in 1926 became professor of political science there, a position he held for the rest of his life. A member (1922–36) of the executive committee of the FABIAN SOCIETY, Laski became a member of the Labour party executive committee in 1936 and was chairman of the party in 1945–46. He also held various official and semiofficial government posts. However, he is best known for his books on political science and for his speeches in Britain and the United States on political, social, and economic trends. Politically, Laski moved from an early belief in antistatist pluralism to the conviction that the state had to take the lead in socialist reform. His books include *Studies in the Problem of Sovereignty* (1917), *Authority in the Modern State* (1919), *Political Thought in England from Locke to Bentham* (1920), *Karl Marx* (1921), *Communism* (1927), *Democracy in Crisis* (1933), *The American Presidency* (1940), *Faith, Reason, and Civilisation* (1944), *The American Democracy* (1948), and *Liberty in the Modern State* (rev. ed. 1948). See *Holmes-Laski Letters* (2 vol.,1953); biography by Kingsley Martin (1953); Herbert Deane, *The Political Ideas of Harold Laski* (1955, repr. 1972).

Laski, John (lăs'kē), Pol. *Jan Łaski* (yän lăs'kē), Latin *Johannes Alasco,* 1499–1560, Polish Protestant reformer. A learned priest, he went in 1523 to Basel, where he was a close friend of Erasmus. After returning to Poland he rose to archbishop of Warsaw, but because of his Calvinistic views he had to leave. He became pastor of a Protestant church at Emden in 1542 and shortly after went to England, where in 1550 he was superintendent of the church for Protestant foreigners and had some influence on ecclesiastical affairs in the reign of Edward VI. On the accession of the Roman Catholic Queen Mary he fled to the Continent. In 1556 he was recalled to Poland, where he was secretary to King Sigismund II and was a leader in the Calvinistic Reformation. See biography by H. Dalton (tr. 1886).

Las Palmas: see PALMAS, LAS, Spain.

Lassalle, Ferdinand (fĕr'dēnänt läsäl'), 1825–64, German socialist. The son of a Jewish merchant, he studied at the universities of Breslau and Berlin, where he became a philosophical Hegelian. He gained wide recognition as an attorney in a lengthy and notorious divorce suit (1846–54). In this period he became acquainted with Karl Marx and, partly influenced by him, developed a theory of state socialism. In contrast to Marxian theory, Lassalle's theories emphasized the role of the state and nationalism. He argued that the state should make capital outlays to enable the workers to set up producers' cooperatives; he believed that the state could be forced to do this once universal suffrage was achieved. Lassalle's influence on German politics was great, particularly in introducing the workers as a third element in the contest between Otto von BISMARCK and the Prussian liberals. He played a key role in establishing (1863) the General German Workers' Association, the first workers' political party in Germany; this later developed (1875) into the Social Democratic party. Lassalle was killed in a duel over a love affair, which is the subject of George Meredith's novel *The Tragic Comedians.* His collected works were edited by Eduard Bernstein (12 vol., 1919–20). See biographies by Arnold Schirokauer (tr. 1931) and D. J. Footman (1947, repr. 1969).

Lassen Volcanic National Park, 106,934 acres (43,276 hectares), N Calif., at the southern tip of the Cascade Range; est. 1916. The park contains volcanic peaks, lava flows, vents, and hot springs. **Lassen Peak,** 10,457 ft (3,187 m) high, is the only active volcano in the United States excluding Alaska and Hawaii. It erupted in 1914 and was intermittently active until 1921. The peak was a prominent landmark in the mid-1800s for westward travelers to California.

Lasso, Orlando di (ōrlän'dō dē läs'sō), 1532–94, Dutch composer, b. Mons, also known as Orlandus Lassus or Roland de Lassus. Variously called the "Belgian Orpheus" and "Prince of Music" in his time, Lasso represents the culmination of Renaissance musical art. In childhood his voice was so beautiful that he was kidnapped three times for choirs. He was finally allowed by his parents to enter (1544) the service of Ferdinand Gonzaga, viceroy of Sicily. After his voice changed, he left (1549) the viceroy's entourage to live (1550–53) in Naples. He was choirmaster of St. John Lateran, Rome, from 1553 to 1554. The following year he went to Antwerp and there published his first books of madrigals. Offered a position by the duke of Bavaria, Lasso moved in 1556 to Munich, where he remained as court composer and director of music until his death. In 1570 he was raised to a hereditary rank of nobility by Emperor Maximilian II, and in 1574 he became one of the very few musicians to receive a papal knighthood. Lasso brought Flemish polyphony to its highest development in the Renaissance and distilled in his music the best elements of European music of his time. His more than 2,000 works in every form known to his day—masses, motets, French chansons, Italian madrigals, German lieder, and others—make him one of the most versatile and cosmopolitan composers in history. In contrast to the restrained mystical style of Palestrina, Lasso's music is vigorous, often passionate and earthy. Many of his love songs were set to poems by Petrarch and other poets. Undisputed master of the motet, he showed his skill at its richest in the *Magnum opus musicum* (pub. 1604), a selection of 516 sacred motets. His best-known works are his *Penitential Psalms of David* (c.1560; pub. 1584) and his last work, *Lagrime di San Pietro* (1594), completed three weeks before he died. See Alfred Einstein, *The Italian Madrigal* (1949); Gustave Reese, *Music in the Renaissance* (2d ed. 1961).

lasso (lăs'ō, lăso͞o'), light, strong rope, usually with a smooth, hard finish, made of a fine quality of hemp or nylon. It is used primarily for catching large animals such as cattle and horses. Horsehair or rawhide lassos were formerly common in America, but they have almost completely given way to the hemp and nylon ropes, which are far more efficient roping tools. The rope varies in length from 35 to 50 ft (11–15 m). At one end of the rope is a running knot or a metal ring by means of which a loop or noose is made. The loop is thrown, from as far away as 30 ft (9 m), around the horns or the feet of an animal and drawn tight. The lasso was invented by American Indians, who used it effectively in war against the Spanish invaders. In the W United States and in parts of Latin America the lasso is a part of the equipment of a cattle herder. To use it on horseback requires great skill of the rider and his horse—the pull of the captured animal may throw the rider's horse, or the horse or rider may become entangled in the rope. The lasso is often called a lariat; the term *lariat* is applied also to a rope used in picketing, or tethering, animals.

Lassus, Orlandus: see LASSO, ORLANDO DI.

Lassus, Roland de: see LASSO, ORLANDO DI.

Last Judgment: see JUDGMENT DAY.

Lastman, Pieter (pē'tər läst'män), 1583-1633, Dutch painter. During a stay in Rome, Lastman was influenced by Caravaggio's chiaroscuro technique and by the work of Elsheimer. In Holland he painted historical and biblical scenes remarkable for their vivid, realistic delineation of faces and gestures. Lastman was Rembrandt's teacher and thereby became an important link between the Italian and Dutch baroque styles.

Last Supper, repast taken by Jesus and his disciples on the eve of the passion (Mat. 26.17-30; Mark 14.12-26; Luke 22.7-39; John 13-17; 1 Cor. 11.23-29). At that time Jesus instituted the sacrament of the EUCHARIST. It has been a favorite subject of painting. Duccio di Buoninsegna's painting of this ceremony is now in the Academy of Fine Arts, Siena, and in Florence are the interpretations of Ghirlandaio (San Marco Mus. and refectory of Ognissanti), Andrea del Castagno for the Sant' Apollonia monastery (now in the Castagno Mus.), and Andrea del Sarto (San Salvi). The best known is a fresco by Leonardo da Vinci at Santa Maria delle Grazie, Milan. In the Church of San Giorgio Maggiore, Venice, is Tintoretto's dramatic composition. A version by Hans Holbein, the younger, is in Basel. Nicolas Poussin painted the subject for the royal chapel, Versailles (now in the Louvre).

Lasus (lā'səs), fl. 6th cent. B.C., Greek poet from the town of Hermione in Argolis. He is said to have been Pindar's teacher. Lasus contributed to the development of the DITHYRAMB.

Las Vegas (läs vā'gəs), city (1970 pop. 125,787), seat of Clark co., S Nev.; inc. 1911. Revenue from hotels, gambling, entertainment, and other tourist-oriented industries forms the backbone of Las Vegas's economy. Its nightclubs and casinos are world famous. The city is also the commercial hub of a ranching and mining area. In the 19th cent. Las Vegas was a watering place for travelers to S California. In 1855-57 the Mormons maintained a fort there, and in 1864 Fort Baker was built by the U.S. army. In 1867, Las Vegas was detached from the Arizona Territory and joined to Nevada. Its main growth began with the completion of a railroad in 1905. It is now the largest city in Nevada; during the 1960s its population nearly doubled. A branch of the Univ. of Nevada is there. Hoover Dam is nearby.

Las Villas (läs vē'yäs), province (1970 pop. 1,362,179), central Cuba. SANTA CLARA is the capital. The western part of the province (also including the Zapata peninsula) belongs to the Colon plain; the eastern section has mountain ranges. The northern coast is highly irregular, although there are a few good harbors. The BAY OF PIGS and CIENFUEGOS are among the indentations along the southern coast. The Sagua la Grande and the Damuji are the main rivers of the province. Its economy is based on cattle raising and the growing of sugarcane and tobacco. Mineral resources, chiefly copper and iron, have not been fully exploited.

László. For Hungarian rulers thus named, see LADISLAUS.

Latacunga (lätäko͞ong'gä), city (1970 est. pop. 17,300), capital of Cotopaxi prov., N central Ecuador. A town of the ancient Incas, it is in a high mountain basin between the E and W Andean cordilleras. It is a commercial center. Not far from Cotopaxi volcano, the city has suffered severe earthquakes.

Latakia (lătəkē'ə, lätə-), city (1960 pop. 67,799), capital of Latakia governorate, W Syria, on the Mediterranean Sea. It is Syria's leading port, exporting bitumen, asphalt, cereals, raw cotton, fruit, and the famous Latakia tobacco (cultivated since the 17th cent.). Industries include sponge fishing, vegetable-oil milling, and cotton ginning. Formerly the ancient Phoenician city of Ramitha, it was rebuilt (c.290 B.C.) by SELEUCUS I and later prospered as the Roman Laodicea ad Mare. Byzantines and Arabs fought over it from the 7th to 11th cent. A.D. The city was captured in 1098 by the Crusaders and flourished in the 12th cent. until after its capture in 1188 by Saladin. From the 16th cent. to World War I it was part of the Ottoman Empire. While Syria was under the French League of Nations mandate, Latakia was (1920-42) the capital of the territory of the Alawites. A deep-water port was completed in 1959.

Latané, John Holladay (lă'tənā), 1869-1932, American historian, b. Staunton, Va. He was professor of history at Washington and Lee Univ. (1902-13) and professor of American history and head of the department of history at Johns Hopkins Univ. (1913-30). He helped found the Walter Hines Page School of International Relations at Johns Hopkins in 1930 and was a member of its research staff. A champion of Woodrow Wilson and the League of Nations, he was an authority on diplomatic history. Among his books are *America as a World Power, 1897-1907* (1907, repr. 1971), *From Isolation to Leadership* (1918), *The United States and Latin America* (1920), and *A History of American Foreign Policy* (1927; 2d ed., rev. by David W. Wainhouse, 1941).

La Tène (lä tĕn), ancient Celtic site on Lake Neuchâtel, Switzerland, that gives its name to the cultures of the Late IRON AGE. It is characterized by an art style that drew upon Greek, Etruscan, and Scythian motifs and translated them into highly abstract designs in metal, pottery, and wood. The earliest phase of Tenian culture, from the 6th to the late 5th cent. B.C., which was the period of the first of the great Celtic (see CELT) migrations, spread from the middle Rhine region E into the Danube valley, S into Switzerland, and W and N into France, the Low Countries, Denmark, and the British Isles. It flourished until subjected to the advances of the Roman Empire. The Celtic peoples of the La Tène period borrowed much from older civilizations, including the Etruscan chariot, wood-working tools that enabled them to clear temperate forests for planting, and Greek agricultural implements such as the rotary millstone. Native coinage appeared in Gaul during the latter part of the period, along with the fortified townships eventually conquered by Julius Caesar. An exceptional example of late Tenian culture is found in the ancient lake dwellings of Glastonbury, S England.

latent heat, heat change associated with a change of state or phase (see STATES OF MATTER). Latent heat, also called heat of transformation, is the HEAT given up or absorbed by a unit mass of a substance as it changes from a solid to a liquid, from a liquid to a gas, or the reverse of either of these changes. It is called latent because it is not associated with a change in temperature. Each substance has a characteristic heat of fusion, associated with the solid-liquid transition, and a characteristic heat of vaporization, associated with the liquid-gas transition. The latent heat of fusion for ice is 80 calories per gram (see CALORIE). This amount of heat is absorbed by each gram of ice in melting or is given up by each gram of water in freezing. The latent heat of vaporization of steam is 540 calories per gram, absorbed during VAPORIZATION or given up during CONDENSATION. For a substance going directly from the solid to the gas state, or the reverse, the heat absorbed or given up is known as the latent heat of SUBLIMATION.

Lateran (lăt'ərən), name applied to a group of buildings of SE Rome facing the Piazza San Giovanni. They are on land once belonging to the Laterani; it was presented to the Church by Constantine. The Lateran basilica is the cathedral of Rome, the pope's church, the first-ranking church of the Roman Catholic Church. It is officially named the Basilica of the Savior, familiarly called St. John Lateran, from a monastery of St. John formerly nearby. The basilica, built perhaps before 311, was restored in the 5th and the 10th cent., rebuilt in the 14th and the 15th cent., and altered again in the 16th, the 17th, and the 18th cent.; the main facade was added in 1733-36. Much of the decoration dates from the Middle Ages and includes the mosaics of the apse, which are among the most celebrated. Frescoes by Gentile da Fabriano and Pisanello have disappeared. The Lateran baptistery, built probably in the 4th cent., was much restored. The Lateran palace, the papal residence until the 14th cent., survived, greatly changed, until the 16th cent., when it was demolished to make way for the much smaller present palace. It now contains the pontifical museum of Christian antiquities. The older palace was the scene of the five Lateran Councils, and the new one of the signing of the Lateran Treaty.

Lateran Council, First, 1123, 9th ecumenical council of the Roman Catholic Church, summoned by Pope CALIXTUS II to signal the end of the INVESTITURE controversy by confirming the Concordat of Worms (1122). It was held in the Lateran Palace, Rome, making it the first council to be held in the West. Its most important canons prohibited the marriage of certain classes of clerics.

Lateran Council, Second, 1139, 10th ecumenical council of the Roman Catholic Church, convened at the Lateran Palace, Rome, by Pope INNOCENT II to heal the wounds left by the schism of the antipope Anacletus II (d. 1138) and to condemn the theories of ARNOLD OF BRESCIA. Among the council's canons were prohibitions of clerical concubinage and marriage and of the use of bows and crossbows in fighting Christians; simony and usury were also condemned.

Lateran Council, Third, 1179, 11th ecumenical council of the Roman Catholic Church. It was convened at the Lateran Palace, Rome, by Pope Alexander III after the Peace of Venice (1178) had reconciled him with Holy Roman Emperor Frederick I. It was well attended and included an envoy from the Orthodox Greeks. The most important legislation was the first canon, which provided that the election of the pope was thereafter to be in the hands of the cardinals alone, two thirds being necessary for election. The council condemned usury, tournaments, and brigandage. The Albigenses and Waldenses were also condemned.

Lateran Council, Fourth, 1215, 12th ecumenical council of the Roman Catholic Church, convened at the Lateran Palace, Rome, by Pope INNOCENT III to crown the work of his pontificate. It was one of the most brilliant councils ever held, and its canons sum up Innocent's ideas for the church. They include a statement of faith with a definition of transubstantiation, confirmation of all kinds of previous disciplinary canons, regulations for the trials of ecclesiastics, arrangements for a new crusade, and many other important matters. This council established the precept of annual confession and communion at Easter time as the minimum requirement for church membership; this is the Easter duty, still binding on all Roman Catholics.

Lateran Council, Fifth, 1512-17, 18th ecumenical council of the Roman Catholic Church, convened by Pope JULIUS II and continued by his successor LEO X. Julius called the council to counter an attempt begun (1510) by Louis XII of France to revive the conciliar theory (i.e., that a council has supreme power, even over the pope) of a hundred years before (see SCHISM, GREAT) and thus precipitate a new schism. In this maneuver the council was a success. The Concordat of 1516, a papal settlement with France, was ratified there. Otherwise the council accomplished little; the reforming party had to wait until the Council of Trent. It did republish the bull of Julius (1503), which declared that simony invalidated a papal election—a signal reform. Interesting enactments of the council include a decree legalizing the charitable pawnshops the Franciscans had been establishing and another that set up a censorship of printed books.

Lateran Treaty, concordat between the Holy See and the kingdom of Italy signed in 1929 in the Lateran Palace, Rome, by Cardinal GASPARRI for PIUS XI and by Benito MUSSOLINI for Victor Emmanuel III. One of the important negotiators was Cardinal Pacelli, later Pope Pius XII. In 1871 the unity of Italy was perfected by restricting the papal sovereignty to a few buildings and awarding to Pius IX and his successors an annual indemnity for the lost Papal States. The Roman Catholic Church never recognized this arrangement and never accepted the indemnity, and the subsequent popes considered themselves prisoners in the Vatican. The problems involved were called the Roman Question, and they were solved by the treaty. It states that Roman Catholicism is the only state religion of Italy and that Italy recognizes the new state called Vatican City as fully sovereign and independent. Italy guarantees Vatican City public services and protection and recognizes as parts of it certain buildings not actually inside Vatican City. The Italian government will punish crimes committed within Vatican City, when so requested, and the Holy See will extradite to Italy persons accused of acts recognized by both parties as crimes. As to the reestablishment of the canon law in Italy, matrimony is a sacrament, and banns must be published; nullity of marriages is a question for the Church, while separations are adjudicated by the state. Religion is to be taught in primary and secondary schools, and the Holy See guarantees that Roman Catholic organizations will abstain from politics. The Italian government guarantees the inviolability of the pope. The Holy See, pursuant to its perpetual mission of peace, will remain apart from temporal competitions of other states and from international congresses for peace, unless a unanimous appeal is made to its mission; the Holy See will use its moral and spiritual power to prevent warfare when it sees fit. The Holy See announced in the treaty that it had its proper liberty, that the Roman Question was closed, and that it recognized the kingdom of Italy under the house of Savoy. The Lateran Treaty remained in effect after the monarchy was abolished at the end of World War II.

Lateur, Frank: see STREUVELS, STIJN.

latex, emulsion of a polymer (e.g., RUBBER) in water (see COLLOID). Natural latexes are produced by a number of plants, are usually white in color, and often contain, in addition to rubber, various gums, oils, and waxes. Balata, caoutchouc, chicle, and gutta-percha are produced from natural latexes. Synthetic latexes may be prepared in two ways; the polymer may be prepared as an emulsion (emulsion polymerization), or the dry, powdered polymer may be dispersed in water. Both natural and synthetic latexes are widely used, especially in the production of rubber goods. Latex paints, sometimes called rubber-base paints, consist of a latex colored by the addition of a pigment.

Latgale (lät'gälĕ) or **Latgallia** (lătgăl'ēə), region and former province, NW European USSR, in Latvia, N of the Western Dvina River. DAUGAVPILS was the chief city. The region was settled in the early Middle Ages by the Latgalians, who were closely akin to the Letts and spoke a Lettish dialect. Latgale shared the history of LIVONIA (of which it formed the southern part) until 1561, when it passed to Poland. Unlike the rest of Latvia, however, Latgale retained Roman Catholicism. The area was ceded to Russia during the Polish partition of 1772. In 1918 it became part of newly independent Latvia.

lathe (lāth), machine tool for holding and turning metal, wood, plastic, or other material against a cutting tool to form a cylindrical product or part. It also drills, bores, polishes, grinds, makes threads, and performs other operations. Its principal parts are the headstock (attached to the bed or base of the machine), which holds one end of the material in a rotating spur; the tailstock, which holds the other end, moves along the bed, and can be clamped in position at any point; the cutting tool; and the power feed, comprising the drive and its motive parts.

Lathrop, George Parsons (lā'thrəp), 1851-98, American author, b. near Honolulu; studied in Germany (1867-70). He was the husband of Rose Hawthorne Lathrop, the daughter of Nathaniel Hawthorne. Lathrop wrote *A Study of Hawthorne* (1876), edited the Riverside edition of Hawthorne's works (1883), and adapted Hawthorne's *Scarlet Letter* for Walter Damrosch's opera (1896). His other writings include poems, *Rose and Roof-tree* (1875); travel essays, *Spanish Vistas* (1883); and several novels. Lathrop and his wife were Roman Catholics, and after his death she became a nun.

Lathrop, Julia Clifford, 1858-1932, American social worker and administrator, b. Rockford, Ill., grad. Vassar, 1880. Associated with Jane Addams at Hull House in Chicago, she was active in civic work, aiding in founding (1899) the country's first juvenile court. From 1912 to 1921 she was head of the U.S. Children's Bureau. See biography by Jane Addams (1935).

Lathrop, Rose Hawthorne, 1851-1926, American nun, philanthropist, and writer; youngest daughter of Nathaniel Hawthorne. In 1871 she married George Parsons LATHROP. In 1891 she and her husband embraced Roman Catholicism. She chose as a mission the work of helping relieve the pain and discomfort of penniless sufferers from incurable cancer and went to live in New York City slums to be near them. She founded St. Rose's Free Home for Incurable Cancer in New York City, and in 1901 she established for the same purpose Rosary Hill Home at Hawthorne, N.Y., a place named after her. She took religious orders after her husband's death in 1898 and became Mother Mary Alphonsa Lathrop. She founded a community of sisters to perpetuate her work; they are Dominican tertiaries. Her literary works include *Along the Shore* (1888), verse; *A Story of Courage* (1894), an account, written with her husband, of the Visitation convent at Georgetown; and *Memories of Hawthorne* (1923). See Katherine Burton, *Sorrow Built a Bridge* (1937); A. T. Sheehan, *Rose Hawthorne; the Pilgrimage of Nathaniel's Daughter* (1959).

Latimer, Hugh, 1485?-1555, English bishop and Protestant martyr. Latimer was educated at Cambridge, entered the church, and came under the influence of the Reformation. He first became prominent by defending Henry VIII's divorce from Katharine of Aragón and in 1535 was made bishop of Worcester. His strong Protestant convictions led him to resign his see after the passage of Henry VIII's Six Articles (1539). He was kept in close confinement until the accession of Edward VI (1547), when he resumed preaching against the abuses of church and clergy in eloquent and vivid sermons. When the Roman Catholic Mary I came to the throne he declined to evade trial, refused to recant his Protestantism, and with Nicholas RIDLEY was burned at the stake as a martyr. See A. G. Chester, *Hugh Latimer, Apostle to the English* (1954).

Latina (lätē'nä), city (1971 pop. 78,227), capital of Latina prov., in Latium, central Italy, near the Tyrrhenian Sea. It is an industrial, commercial, and agricultural center. Manufactures include tires, chemicals, and processed food. It was the first community founded (1932) by Mussolini in the reclaimed Pontine Marshes and was known as Littoria until 1947. There is a nuclear power station in the city.

Latin America, the Spanish-speaking, Portuguese-speaking, and French-speaking countries (except Canada) of North America, South America, Central America, and the West Indies. The 20 republics are Argentina, Bolivia, Brazil, Chile, Colombia, Costa Rica, Cuba, Dominican Republic, Ecuador, El Salvador, Guatemala, Haiti, Honduras, Mexico, Nicaragua, Panama, Paraguay, Peru, Uruguay, and Venezuela. The term *Latin America* is also used to include Puerto Rico, the French West Indies, and other islands of the West Indies where a Romance tongue is spoken. Occasionally the term is used to include British Honduras, Guyana, French Guiana, and Surinam. See Germán Arciniegas, *Latin America: A Cultural History* (tr. 1968); Hubert Herring, *A History of Latin America* (3d ed. 1968); J. P. Cole, *Latin America: An Economic and Social Geography* (rev. ed. 1971); I. A. Leonard, *Colonial Travelers in Latin America* (1972); K. E. Webb, *Geography of Latin America: A Regional Analysis* (1972); R. J. Alexander, *Latin American Political Parties* (1973); H. M. Bailey and A. P. Nasatir, *Latin America: The Development of its Civilization* (3d ed. 1973).

Latin American Free Trade Association (LAFTA), organization formed in 1960 by Argentina, Brazil, Chile, Mexico, Paraguay, Peru, and Uruguay. Colombia and Ecuador became members later the same year, and Venezuela and Bolivia joined in the mid-1960s. Goals on tariff reductions proposed by LAFTA called for an average 8% annual decrease leading to total elimination of tariff barriers by 1973. In 1969 the deadline was extended until 1980. Trade between LAFTA members increased after 1961, but problems arose by the mid-1960s between the less developed countries and the more prosperous ones. At the conference of American presidents held in Punta del Este, Uruguay, in 1967, it was agreed that efforts would be made to create a comprehensive Latin American common market based on LAFTA and on the CENTRAL AMERICAN COMMON MARKET. Beginning in 1966, discussions were begun with the goal of forming a new association within LAFTA. These talks resulted in the creation of the Andean Group, composed of Bolivia, Chile, Colombia, Ecuador, and Peru. It was formally accepted as a subregional association within LAFTA in 1969.

Latin Empire of Constantinople: see CONSTANTINOPLE, LATIN EMPIRE OF.

Latini, Brunetto (brōōnĕt'tō lätē'nē), d. 1294?, Italian man of letters, a diplomat. He introduced French literature to Italy and wrote, in French, *Li livres dou tresor,* the first vernacular encyclopedia. It was an immediate success. Dante praised him in the *Divine Comedy.*

Latin Kingdom of Jerusalem: see JERUSALEM, LATIN KINGDOM OF.

Latin language, member of the Italic subfamily of the Indo-European family of languages. Latin was first encountered in ancient times as the language of Latium, the region of central Italy in which Rome was located (see ITALIC LANGUAGES). Roman conquests later spread Latin over Italy and the vast Roman Empire. Numerous documents, such as Latin inscriptions and literary works, furnish much information about the language, as do the comments of ancient scholars and various related dialects and languages. After the ancient Romans began to develop a literature (in the 3d cent. B.C.), a gap emerged between the literary, or classical, Latin and Vulgar Latin, which was the popular (spoken) form of the language. This division had become considerable by the beginning of the Roman Empire. It is especially from Vulgar Latin, carried by the soldiers and colonists of Rome throughout the Roman Empire, that the modern ROMANCE LANGUAGES are descended. Vulgar Latin differed from classical Latin in its increased use of prepositions, its less frequent employment of inflection, its greater regularity of word order, and, to some extent, in its vocabulary. Literary Latin was more formal and elegant stylistically. With the triumph of Christianity in the 4th cent. A.D., Vulgar Latin grew in literary significance, as evidenced by the Vulgate, St. Jerome's translation of the Bible into Vulgar Latin. The new religion stressed equality before God, and its advocates tried to reach as many in the empire as possible through the everyday speech of the common people. Classical Latin, distinguished by its formality and elegance, was greatly influenced in vocabulary, grammar, and style by Greek. By the end of the Roman Republic (1st cent. B.C.) classical Latin had become a suitable medium for the greatest poetry and prose of the day. Grammatically, classical Latin featured five declensions and six cases in its inflection of the noun; there was no definite article. Noun subclassifications included three genders (masculine, feminine, and neuter) and two numbers (singular and plural). Verbal inflection was highly developed, expressing tense, mood, voice, person, and number. Latin is written in the Roman alphabet, which was apparently derived from the Etruscan alphabet. The latter, in turn, was adapted from the Greek alphabet (see GREEK LANGUAGE). To this day, Latin survives as the official tongue of Vatican City and as the official language of communication of the Roman Catholic Church. Until recently, it was also the language of the Roman Catholic liturgy and is still so used under certain conditions. During the Middle Ages it flourished as the language of the universities, scholars, and writers. It was the language of diplomacy in Europe as late as the 17th cent. and was still widely used in scholarly writing in the 19th cent. Today, although the language is beginning to disappear from the school curriculum, Latin roots continue to serve as a major source for the derivation of new terms in the sciences and technologies. See C. D. Buck, *Comparative Grammar of Greek and Latin* (3d ed. 1948); Ernst Pulgram, *The Tongues of Italy: Prehistory and History* (1958); L. R. Palmer, *The Latin Language* (3d ed. 1961); A. M. Gessman, *The Tongue of the Romans* (1970).

Latin literature. Very little remains of the ritualistic songs and the native poetry of the Romans and Latins before the rise of a literature. The history of the Roman Empire is fundamental to the fabric of this literature: In the first three centuries of its development, the influence of captive Greece was all-pervasive. The close of the First Punic War (c.240 B.C.) marks the beginning of literary work in Rome with the plays of the slave LIVIUS ANDRONICUS, adapted from the Greek. The epic poet Gnaes Naevius also wrote dramas, but he was far surpassed by the greatest of Roman dramatists, PLAUTUS, a master of comedy. In his *Satires* ENNIUS introduced the hexameter into Latin; CATO THE ELDER opposed the hellenizing group, to which Ennius belonged, and wrote his works in as rude a Latin as possible. However, his efforts had little effect and the works of TERENCE and of the historian POLYBIUS reflect the increasing interest in Greek culture. The 1st cent. B.C., the last era of the Roman republic, produced some of the greatest figures in Latin literature—the statesmen and prose masters CICERO and Julius CAESAR, the poets LUCRETIUS and CATULLUS, the historian SALLUST, and the encyclopedist VARRO. In the 1st cent. A.D., VERGIL exemplifies a new atmosphere in the Augustan age, with his admiration of the new empire. The more sophisticated poet HORACE brought the Latin lyric to perfection. The elegy was cultivated by TIBULLUS, PROPERTIUS, and OVID. The notable historian of the age was LIVY. At the end of the century Latin literature in its classical form began to decline. The works of SENECA, LUCAN, PERSIUS, and STATIUS typify a period in which the masters, both Latin and Greek, were imitated. Among the most original poets were MARTIAL and JUVENAL, celebrated for their satiric writings. PETRONIUS, FRONTINUS, PLINY THE ELDER, Pliny the Younger (see under PLINY THE ELDER), and TACITUS were the chief writers of prose. QUINTILIAN brought classical literary criticism to its greatest development. In the 3d and 4th cent. the writings of AUSONIUS and Avienus treat a more varied subject matter, extending beyond classical studies to deal with everyday life and the world of nature. CLAUDIAN is considered the best of the late poets, and FRONTO and MARCUS AURELIUS, the chief prose writers. APELEIUS and AMMIANUS MARCELLINUS were exceptional in not following set canons of expression. The philological scholars of the empire were numerous. These included Aulus GELLIUS, Terentianus, MACROBIUS, Martianus CAPELLA, and PRISCIAN. As the classical inspiration died, an entirely new kind of Latin literature was growing up. This was formed in the writings of Christians. PRUDENTIUS attempted to build a Christian style on classical models, but failed. The LATIN LANGUAGE became the standard language of the West and by far the greater bulk of medieval literature as well as records, documents, and letters were written in Latin (see PATRISTIC LITERATURE; MEDIEVAL LATIN LITERATURE; ROMAN LAW). The literature of the RENAISSANCE represents a conscious attempt to recapture the classical spirit. Most learned men cultivated Latin, and many of them succeeded in writing a Latin style that stands comparison with classical Latin models. PETRARCH, BOCCACCIO, POGGIO BRACCIOLINI, POLIZIANO, PONTANO, and PIUS II were accomplished Latin writers. ERASMUS violently attacked the ubiquitous Ciceronianism of the time. Good Latin poets have been fewer since the Renaissance, but George BUCHANAN and John MILTON are among the exceptions. Among the great scholars whose major works were written in Latin were Thomas MORE, Baruch SPINOZA, Francis BACON, Gottfried Wilhelm von LEIBNIZ, and Isaac NEWTON. Latin literature, as such, in the 20th cent. is nearly dead, for its cultivation is limited to the ever-narrowing circles of classicists and to the Roman Catholic Church, which adds new matter to the liturgy only rarely and confines use of extraliturgical Latin to official, nonliterary documents. See Gilbert Highet, *The Classical Tradition* (1949); J. W. Duff, *A Literary History of Rome* (3d ed. 1960); H. J. Rose, *A Handbook of Latin Literature* (3d ed. 1961); Moses Hadas, *A History of Latin Literature* (1952, repr. 1964); F. O. Copley, *Latin Literature* (1969).

Latin Monetary Union. In 1865, France, Belgium, Italy, and Switzerland (joined in 1868 by Greece) agreed to regulate their national currencies on a uniform basis, thus making it freely interchangeable. Several other countries joined informally. The fluctuations of gold and silver created difficulties, and the union, further disrupted by World War I, was disbanded in 1927.

Latin Road: see ROMAN ROADS.

Latins, in ancient times, inhabitants of Latium, particularly of the great plain of Latium. They succeeded an earlier people, whom they probably absorbed. The Latins established themselves in many small settlements. Gradually increasing in size, these settlements were joined in religious confederations that later took on political significance. Rome early took a dominant place among the cities of Latium, but the Latins remained united against the Etruscans and the Samnites. Roman hegemony was definitely established by 338 B.C.; the smaller states were absorbed and the larger states made subject allies by Rome. The Latins, however, continued to have a special status, and in theory the social and political equality of the Latins continued. There was some rebellion, especially late in the 2d cent. B.C., but generally the Latins remained loyal to Rome. They were admitted to Roman citizenship in 90 B.C. at the time of the Social War.

Latin Way: see ROMAN ROADS.

latitude, angular distance of any point on the surface of the earth north or south of the equator. The equator is latitude 0°, and the North Pole and South Pole are latitudes 90°N and 90°S, respectively. The length of one degree of latitude averages about 69 mi (110 km); it increases slightly from the equator to the poles as a result of the earth's polar flattening. Latitude is commonly determined by means of a SEXTANT or other instrument that measures the angle between the horizon and the sun or another celestial body, such as the North Star (see POLARIS). The latitude is then found by means of tables that give the position of the sun and other bodies for that date and hour. An imaginary line on the earth's surface connecting all points equidistant from the equator (and thus at the same latitude) is called a parallel of latitude. On most globes and maps parallels are usually shown in multiples of 5°. Because of their special meanings, four fractional parallels are also shown. These are the Tropic of Cancer (23½°N) and the Tropic of Capricorn (23½°S), marking the farthest points north and south of the equator where the sun's rays fall vertically (see TROPICS), and the ARCTIC CIRCLE (66½°N) and the ANTARCTIC CIRCLE (66½°S), marking the farthest points north and south of the equator where the sun appears above the horizon each day of the year (see also MIDNIGHT SUN). Parallels of latitude and meridians of LONGITUDE together form a grid by which any point on the earth's surface can be specified. The term *latitude* is also used in various celestial coordinate systems (see ECLIPTIC COORDINATE SYSTEM).

Latium (lā'shēəm), Ital. *Lazio,* region (1971 pop. 4,754,484), 6,642 sq mi (17,203 sq km), central Italy, extending from the Apennines westward to the Tyrrhenian Sea. ROME is the capital of the region, which is divided into Frosinone, Latina, Rieti, Rome, and Viterbo provs. (named for their capitals). The region is mostly hilly and mountainous, with a narrow coastal plain, much of which has been reclaimed in the 20th cent. (see CAMPAGNA DI ROMA; PONTINE MARSHES). Agriculture forms the backbone of the regional economy; products include cereals, vegetables, grapes, olives, and fodder. Sheep and cattle are raised. Rome is Latium's main commercial and industrial center. Industry in the region has been spurred (mid-20th cent.) by the construction of hydroelectric facilities on the Aniene and Liri rivers and a nuclear power plant at Latina. Manufactures include chemicals, cement, textiles, and processed food. There is a large tourist industry, and fishing is pursued along the coast, especially at Civitavecchia, the region's chief port. In ancient times, Latium comprised a limited area E and S of the Tiber River that extended to the Alban Hills; only after it became part of Italy in 1870 did it approximately reach its present limits. In early Roman times Latium was inhabited by the Latins, the Etruscans (N of the Tiber River), and several Italic tribes. In the 3d cent. B.C., Rome subdued all of Latium. The fertile coastal plain became marshy, malaria-infested, and impoverished during the late Roman Empire and early Republic. After the fall of Rome, Latium was invaded in turn by the Visigoths, the Vandals, and the Lombards. From the 8th cent. the duchy of Rome, including most of modern Latium, belonged to the popes. Their authority was not always recognized in the towns, which were ruled at times as free communes or by local feudal lords. Except for the area S of Terracina, which belonged to the kingdom of Naples, Latium remained a part of the Papal States until 1870. In World War II, S Latium was the scene of bloody battles during the Allied drive on Rome (see CASSINO; ANZIO). There are universities at Rome, which is also the site of the Vatican.

Latona: see LETO.

La Tour, Georges de (zhôrzh də lä to͝or), 1593–1652, French painter. By 1618 he was settled at Lunéville, in his native Lorraine. He bore the title of painter to the king in 1639. La Tour painted religious and genre pictures, many of which show the influence of Dutch modifications of Caravaggio's style. La Tour's early works (1620s) include *The Fortune Teller* (Metropolitan Mus.) and *St. Jerome* (Stockholm), both minutely descriptive. A transitional painting, *Job and His Wife* (Épinal), is an early example of La Tour's nocturnal scenes, in which forms are dramatically illuminated by a candle or a hidden light source. In his later works (c.1640–1652), La Tour discarded extraneous detail and reduced figures to simple, sculptural forms rendered in warm colors. Characteristic later paintings are *Repentant St. Peter* (Cleveland Mus.), *Christ and St. Joseph in the Carpenter's Shop* (Louvre), *The Hurdy-Gurdy Player* (Nantes), and *St. Sebastian Mourned by St. Irene* (Berlin). His works were not well known until the early 20th cent. In 1974 the National Gallery of Art in Washington, D.C. purchased his *Magdalen of the Mirror* for an estimated $1.5 million. See study by S. M. M. Furness (1949).

La Tour, Maurice Quentin de (mōrēs' käNtăN'), 1704–88, French portraitist working in pastel. From 1737 to 1773 he exhibited at the Salon portraits of considerable technical virtuosity and psychological penetration. They brought him an immense and continuing popularity. Among his famous sitters were Louis XV, Mme de Pompadour, Voltaire, Rousseau, and Marshal de Saxe. Most of his work is in the Louvre and in the museum of his native Saint-Quentin. See biography by Adrian Bury (1973).

La Tour d'Auvergne, Théophile Malo Corret de (tāōfēl' mälō' kôrā' də lä to͞or dōvĕr'nyə), 1743–1800, French soldier. Although an aristocrat, he fought for the revolutionaries in the French Revolutionary Wars. He had left the army because of ill health when he was captured (1795) by a British corsair and was imprisoned until 1797. Although he had retired, he rejoined the army to serve in place of his youngest and only surviving son. La Tour d'Auvergne was noted for his bravery and modesty; when he refused promotion he was officially dubbed the "first grenadier of France." He was killed in battle. Until 1814 his name was still heard at roll call, and his comrades' response was "Dead on the field of honor!" La Tour d'Auvergne was also a scholar of Gallic antiquities and of Celtic languages (especially Breton).

La Trappe: see TRAPPISTS.

La Trémoille or **La Trimouille, Georges de** (zhôrzh də lä trāmoi'yə or trēmo͞o'yə), c.1385–1446, favorite of King Charles VII of France, sometime chamberlain to JOHN THE FEARLESS of Burgundy. He was captured by the English at Agincourt (1415) during the Hundred Years War. He later served as a mediator between John the Fearless and the dauphin, Charles VII. Having become Charles's favorite after the murder of Pierre de Giac (1427), he attempted to undermine the influence of Joan of Arc on the king. Overthrown (1433) by a coalition under Constable de Richemont (ARTHUR III of Brittany), he joined the PRAGUERIE (1440) but was later pardoned.

La Trémoille or **La Trimouille, Louis de** (lwē), 1460–1525, French general; grandson of Georges de La Trémoille. He commanded the army that attempted to secure Brittany for the French crown after the death (1488) of Duke FRANCIS II. He distinguished himself in the ITALIAN WARS, notably at Fornovo (1495), Marignano (1515), and Pavia (1525).

Latrobe, Benjamin Henry (Benjamin Henry Boneval Latrobe) (lətrōb'), 1764–1820, American architect, b. Yorkshire, England. He is considered the first professional architect in the United States. Latrobe received his training both in architecture and in engineering in England and Germany and then practiced successfully in London. After the death of his first wife he came to the United States, arriving in Norfolk in 1796. He practiced there and in Richmond until 1799, when he went to Philadelphia. In 1803, President Jefferson appointed him surveyor of public buildings. Besides building residences in Washington, Philadelphia, and other cities, Latrobe did much monumental work and introduced Greek forms, an important element of the classic revival. His design (1799) for the Bank of Pennsylvania in Philadelphia was modeled after a Greek Ionic temple. This building and his Roman Catholic cathedral in Baltimore (1805–18)—the first cathedral built in the United States—make a group expressive of the best monumental architecture of the time. Other works are St. John's Church in Washington, D.C. (1816) and the penitentiary in Richmond, Va. (1797–1800). His design for "Sedgeley" (1800), a residence near Philadelphia, is supposed to be the first executed example of the Gothic revival in the country. After the burning of the Capitol he was engaged, from 1815 to 1817, in rebuilding it. Latrobe's son Henry had been sent to New Orleans to construct the city's waterworks after his father's design, but he died of yellow fever in 1817. In 1818, Latrobe sailed to New Orleans to complete the project, bringing his family overland in 1820. He too died of yellow fever. See Latrobe's diary of his trips to New Orleans and his stay there, *Impressions respecting New Orleans* (ed. by Samuel Wilson, Jr., 1951); study by Talbot Hamlin (1955). His other sons were John H. B. LATROBE and **Benjamin Henry Latrobe,** 1806–78, an engineer, b. Philadelphia. He served (1847–75) as chief engineer of the Baltimore & Ohio RR, laying out the line between Washington and Baltimore, between Harpers Ferry and Cumberland, and over the mountains between Cumberland and Wheeling.

Latrobe, John Hazlehurst Boneval, 1803–91, American philanthropist, b. Philadelphia; son of Benjamin H. Latrobe. He studied law, and from 1828 until his death he was regularly retained as counsel for the Baltimore & Ohio RR, but he appeared in many independent cases. He was a founder of the Maryland Institute for the Promotion of Mechanic Arts and of the Maryland Historical Society. He was a prominent supporter of the African colonization of Liberia and in 1853 succeeded Henry Clay as president of the American Colonization Society. See biography by J. E. Semmes (1917).

Latrobe, industrial borough (1970 pop. 11,749), Westmoreland co., SW Pa., in the foothills of the Alleghenies; inc. 1854. Among its varied manufactures are steel, castings, beer, ceramics, forgings, carbides, and aluminum siding. St. Vincent College and a state hospital are there. A state park is nearby.

Latrocinium: see EUTYCHES.

Latter-Day Saints, Church of Jesus Christ of, name of the religious sect founded (1830) at Fayette, N.Y., by Joseph Smith. The headquarters are in Salt Lake City. Its members, now numbering about 3 million, are commonly called Mormons (for their history, see MORMONS). Their beliefs are based primarily on the Bible, on the Book of Mormon (a translation of inscriptions on tablets of gold revealed to Joseph SMITH), on revelations made to Smith and contained in the volume *Doctrine and Covenants,* on later revelations, and on *The Pearl of Great Price* (sayings attributed to Moses and Abraham). The Book of Mormon, ascribed to the prophet Mormon, recounts the early history of peoples in America from c.600 B.C. to A.D. c.420. In a further revelation, priesthood was conferred upon Smith and upon an associate, Oliver Cowdery. They then established their church on the basis of the priesthood of the two orders of Aaron and Melchizedek. The Aaronic priesthood (deacons, teachers, and priests), which includes every worthy male between the ages of 12 and 20, is primarily concerned with the temporal affairs of the church; that of Melchizedek (elders, seventies, and high priests) is concerned with the spiritual leadership. Both are represented in the Council of Twelve (the Apostles) and in the first presidency (the president and two counselors—three high priests vested with supreme authority). The territorial divisions of the Mormon settlements are wards and stakes. Each ward has a bishop and two counselors; five to ten wards compose a stake. Significant characteristics of the Mormon creed include the emphasis on revelation in the establishment of doctrines and rituals, the interdependence of temporal and spiritual life, tithing, and attention to community welfare. Mormons practice baptism for the dead; they believe that the deceased soul may receive the baptism necessary for salvation by proxy of a living believer. They also believe in "celestial marriage," whereby two individuals marry for all eternity. Mormons carry out a campaign of vigorous proselytizing which has, in the course of a century and a quarter, raised the church from a handful of followers to its present size. See Joseph Smith, *The Doctrine and Covenants of the Church of Jesus Christ of Latter-Day Saints* (1880 ed., repr. 1971); George Reynolds, *The Story of the Book of Mormon* (1957); R. R. Mullen, *The Latter-Day Saints* (1966).

Latter Day Saints, Reorganized Church of Jesus Christ of, a Mormon body that regards itself as the successor of the church founded by Joseph SMITH. They organized in 1852, with Joseph Smith, Jr. (son of the Mormon founder), as their first president, and since that time have been separate and distinct from the Church of Jesus Christ of Latter-Day Saints with its headquarters in Salt Lake City, Utah. The headquarters of the Reorganized Church were first at Plano, Ill., until 1881, then at Lamoni, Iowa, until 1904, and since 1904 in Independence, Mo. The doctrines of the church are derived from the Bible, the Book of Mormon, *The Pearl of Great Price* (sayings ascribed to Moses and Abraham), and the revelations made to Joseph Smith. Brigham Young and his position on polygamy are rejected. Unlike the Utah church, the Reorganized Church admits blacks into the priesthood. In the early 1970s there were about 160,000 members.

Lattimore, Owen, 1900–, American author and educator, b. Washington, D.C. He was educated (1915–19) at St. Bees School, Cumberland, England, and did graduate research (1928–29) at Harvard. From 1920 to 1926 he was engaged in business and newspaper work in China. Afterward he traveled and did research for various organizations in China, Manchuria, Mongolia, and Chinese Turkestan, writing such books as *Manchuria: Cradle of Conflict* (1932) and *The Mongols of Manchuria* (1934). He was (1938–50) director of the Page School of International Relations at Johns Hopkins. In 1950 he was accused by Senator Joseph McCarthy of being the Soviet Union's top espionage agent in the United States, but subsequent investigation cleared him of the charges. In 1952, Lattimore was indicted for perjury on seven counts by a Federal grand jury on the charge that he had lied when he told a Senate internal security subcommittee earlier in 1952 that he had not promoted Communism and Communist interests; by 1955 all charges against him had been dismissed. He was lecturer in history at Johns Hopkins until 1963. From 1963–70 he was professor of Chinese studies at Leeds Univ., England. Among his other books are *America and Asia* (1943), *The Situation in Asia* (1949), *Pivot of Asia* (1950), *Ordeal by Slander* (1950), *Studies in Asian Frontier History* (1962), and *Silks, Spices and Empire* (ed., with Eleanor Lattimore, 1968). See J. T. Flynn, *The Lattimore Story* (1953).

La Tuque (lä tük), town (1971 pop. 13,099), S Que., Canada, on the St. Maurice River, NW of Quebec. La Tuque, in a lumbering and farming region, was established as a trading post in the French period; it grew after the coming of the railroad in 1908. It is a pulp and paper center with a hydroelectric-power station.

Latvia (lăt'vēə), Latvian *Latvija,* constituent republic (1970 pop. 2,365,000), 24,590 sq mi (63,688 sq km), NW European USSR. It borders on Estonia in the north, Lithuania in the south, the Baltic Sea with the Gulf of Riga in the west, the Russian Republic in the east, and Belorussia in the southeast. RIGA (the capital), Liepaya, Daugavpils, Cesis, and Yelgava are the chief cities. Latvia falls into four historic regions: N of the Western Dvina River are Vidzeme and Latgale, which were parts of LIVONIA; S of the Dvina are Kurzeme and Zemgale, which belonged to the former duchy of COURLAND. Latvia is largely a fertile lowland, drained by the Western Dvina, the Venta, the Gauja, and the Lielupe. There are numerous lakes, and morainic hills rise to the east. Dairying and stock raising are extensively carried on. Latvia also has valuable timber resources. Machinery, metals, electrical equipment, and textiles are among the chief industrial products. Food and dairy processing, distilling, and shipbuilding are also important. The majority of the population consists of Letts and of the closely related Latgalians, both members of the Baltic language subfamily. About one quarter of the people are Russians, and there are Belorussian, Lithuanian, Polish, and Jewish minorities. The Letts (after whom the country is also called Lettland) were conquered and Christianized by the LIVONIAN BROTHERS OF THE SWORD in the 13th cent. Their country formed the southern part of Livonia until 1561, when Courland became a vassal duchy under Polish suzerainty and Livonia passed to Poland. In 1629, Sweden conquered Livonia (save Latgale), which it lost in turn to Russia in 1721. With the first (1772) and third (1795) partitions of Poland, Latgale and Courland also passed to Russia. The region had been dominated since the time of the Livonian Knights by German merchants, settled there by the Hanseatic League, and by a German landowning aristocracy, which reduced the Letts to servitude. Under the Russian regime these German "Baltic barons" retained their power, and German remained the official language until 1885, when it was replaced by Russian. Between 1817 and 1819 the serfs were emancipated, and in the middle of the 19th cent. a national revival began. By the end of the 19th cent. there was great agricultural and industrial prosperity. In the revolution of 1905 the Letts played a prominent role, and bloody reprisals were meted out. Latvia was devastated in World War I. However, the collapse of Russia and Germany made Latvian independence possible in 1918. Soviet troops and German volunteer bands were expelled. Peace with Russia followed in 1920. The Latvian constitution of 1920 provided for a democratic republic. The largest land holdings were expropriated. However, there was no political stability, and in 1934 the constituent assembly and the political parties were dissolved. In 1936, Karlis Ulmanis became a virtual dictator. Soviet pressure forced Latvia to grant (1939) the USSR several naval and military bases; a subsequent Latvian-German agreement provided for the transfer of the German minority to Germany. Soviet troops occupied Latvia in 1940, and subsequent elections held under Soviet auspices resulted in the absorption of Latvia into the USSR as a constituent republic. Occupied (1941–44) by German troops in World War II, it was reconquered by the Soviet Union. In the postwar years, the remaining estates were at first distributed to landless peasants, but soon almost all the land was collectivized. Latvia's resources and industry were nationalized, and a program of industrialization was pursued by the Soviet regime.

Latvian language: see LETTISH.

Laube, Heinrich (hīn'rĭkh lou'bə), 1806–84, German writer. Prominent in the liberal Young Germany movement, he wrote historical novels, among them the cycle *Der deutsche Krieg* [the German war] (9 vol., 1863–66). He was a successful theatrical manager; his popular plays include *Die Karlsschüler* (1847) and *Graf Essex* (1856).

Laud, William, 1573–1645, archbishop of Canterbury (1633–45). He studied at St. John's College, Oxford, and was ordained a priest in 1601. From the beginning Laud showed his hostility to Puritanism. He became president of St. John's College in 1611, dean of Gloucester in 1616, and bishop of London in 1628. Laud thought of the English church as a branch of the universal church, claimed apostolic succession for the bishops, and believed that the Anglican ritual should be strictly followed in all churches. To accomplish these ends, Laud, working closely with Charles I, tried to eliminate Puritans from important positions in the church. As chancellor of Oxford (from 1629) he carried out many reforms, strengthened moral and intellectual discipline, and stamped out Calvinism to make Oxford a royalist stronghold. In 1633, Laud became archbishop of Canterbury and continued on a larger scale his efforts to enforce High Church forms of worship. Through the courts of high commission and Star Chamber he persecuted and imprisoned many nonconformists, such as William PRYNNE. The tyranny of his courts and his identification of the episcopal form of church government with the absolutism of Charles brought about violent opposition not only from the Puritans but also from those who were jealous of the rights of Parliament. Supporting Charles and the earl of Strafford to the end, Laud was impeached (1640) by the Long Parliament. Found not guilty of treason by the House of Lords (1644), he was condemned to death by the Commons through a bill of attainder. See biographies by A. Duncan-Jones (1927) and Hugh Trevor-Roper (2d ed., 1962).

laudanum (lôd'ənəm), tincture, or alcoholic solution, of OPIUM, first compounded by Paracelsus in the 16th cent. Not then known to be addictive, the preparation was widely used up through the 19th cent. to treat a variety of disorders. Many literary and artistic figures, including Coleridge, Poe, Moussorgsky, and De Quincey, are known to have been addicted.

Lauder, Sir Harry (lô'dər), 1870–1950, Scottish baritone. His original name was MacLennan. Lauder was popular for his singing of ballads and comic songs, many of his own composition. During World War II he emerged from retirement to entertain the Allied soldiers. He was knighted in 1919.

Lauderdale, John Maitland, duke of (lô'dərdāl), 1616–82, Scottish statesman. He entered public life as a staunch Presbyterian and was one of the commissioners who signed the Solemn League and Covenant (1643; see ENGLISH CIVIL WAR). However, in the course of the Scottish dealings with Charles I that followed the end of the first civil war, he attached himself to the royalists. He gained the confidence of Charles II, whom he accompanied to Scotland (1650), was captured at the battle of Worcester, and was held prisoner until 1660. At the Restoration (1660) Charles II made him secretary of state for Scotland. After 1667 he was a member of the CABAL ministry and became all-powerful in Scotland. Made earl of March and duke of Lauderdale (in the Scottish peerage) in 1672, he was raised to the English peerage as earl of Guilford and made a privy councilor in 1674. His rule in Scotland was arbitrary and harsh, and his use of Highland troops to suppress the COVENANTERS in the southwest provoked an uprising in 1679. Despite attacks in Parliament, he kept his influence by intrigues until 1680, when his health broke. In 1682 he gave up all his offices. Although able, he was debauched, arrogant, and unscrupulous and one of the most unpopular statesmen of the period. See biography by W. C. Mackenzie (1923).

Laudonnière, René Goulaine de (rənā' gōōlĕn' də lōdônyĕr'), fl. 1562–82, French colonizer in Florida. After accompanying Jean RIBAUT on the first French expedition to Florida (1562), he led a second colonization attempt in 1564, establishing Fort Caroline (named for Charles IX of France) on the south bank of the St. Johns River near its mouth. The colonists soon incurred the enmity of the Indians, many refused to work, others took to piracy, and finally most of them mutinied. Fort Caroline was in desperate straits when the English privateer Sir John Hawkins appeared in Aug., 1565, and sold Laudonnière food and one of his ships. Laudonnière was prepared to sail for France when Ribaut arrived with supplies, reinforcements, and an order for Laudonnière to return to answer charges that had been brought against him. His departure was delayed by the appearance of the Spanish. Ribaut sailed to attack them at St. Augustine, but Pedro MENÉNDEZ DE AVILÉS attacked Fort Caroline by land and massacred most of those left there by Ribaut. Laudonnière, one of the few who escaped, finally reached France in Jan., 1566. His *Histoire notable de la Floride* (1586) was translated by Richard Hakluyt as *A Notable Historie Containing Foure Voyages Made by Certayne French Captaynes into Florida* (1587). See study by C. E. Bennett (1964).

Laue, Max von (mäks fən lou'ə), 1879–1960, German physicist, studied under Max Planck. From 1919 he was professor of theoretical physics at the Univ. of Berlin. He worked out a method for measuring X-ray wavelengths, in which a crystal (rock salt) is used, producing diffraction of the rays. For this work, which also made possible a closer study of crystal structure, he received the 1914 Nobel Prize in Physics.

Lauenburg (lou'ənbŏŏrkh), former duchy, NE West Germany, on the right bank of the lower Elbe. Lauenburg or Lauenburg an der Elbe (1970 pop. 11,319) was the chief town. The duchy belonged to a branch of the house of Saxony from the 12th to the late 17th cent., when it passed to the house of Hanover. Lauenburg was occupied by France from 1803 to 1813. The Congress of Vienna awarded (1815) it to Prussia and made it a member state of the German Confederation, but Prussia ceded it to the Danish crown in exchange for W Pomerania; this exchange, however, did not affect the membership of Lauenburg in the confederation. In the Danish War of 1864 the duchy was seized by Prussia and Austria, and Austria soon afterward ceded its rights to Prussia. Lauenburg was incorporated into the province of Schleswig-Holstein in 1876 and ceased to be a duchy in 1918.

laughing gas: see NITROUS OXIDE.

laughing jackass: see KOOKABURRA.

Laughlin, James Laurence (lŏf'lĭn), 1850-1933, American economist, b. Deerfield, Ohio, Ph.D. Harvard, 1876. He was a distinguished teacher, and as head of the department of political economy at the Univ. of Chicago (1892-1916) he gathered a group of brilliant men. A classicist and follower of John Stuart Mill in economic theory, he nevertheless encouraged such unorthodox thinkers as Thorstein Veblen and Wesley C. Mitchell. He edited (1892-1933) the *Journal of Political Economy.* Laughlin's chief interests were currency and monetary problems, and he served as adviser to various state and national governments. In 1894-95 he reorganized the monetary system of Santo Domingo. He later urged reform of the U.S. Federal Reserve Act. Important among his prolific writings is *A New Exposition of Money, Credit, and Prices* (1931).

Laughton, Charles, 1899-1962, Anglo-American actor, b. Scarborough, England. A large, versatile character actor, Laughton was successful both in films and on the stage. His best-known movies include *The Sign of the Cross* (1932), *The Private Life of Henry VIII* (1932), *Ruggles of Red Gap* (1935), *Mutiny on the Bounty* (1935), *Witness for the Prosecution* (1957), and *Advise and Consent* (1962). In 1951 he directed and starred in a dramatic reading of Shaw's *Don Juan in Hell.* See biography by his wife Elsa Lanchester (1938).

Launay, vicomte de: see GIRARDIN, DELPHINE GAY DE.

Launcelot, Sir, in ARTHURIAN LEGEND, bravest and most celebrated knight at the court of King Arthur. He was kidnapped as an infant by the mysterious LADY OF THE LAKE, from whom he received his education and took his title, Launcelot of the Lake. As a young man he went to the court of King Arthur, where he was knighted and became one of the most feared warriors in all Christendom. Launcelot was the lover of Guinevere, his sovereign's queen. He was also loved by Elaine (the daughter of King Pelles), by whom he was the father of Sir Galahad, and by Elaine, the Lily Maid of Astolat, who died for love of him. Launcelot's name sometimes appears as Lancelot. See study by J. L. Weston (1901, repr. 1972).

Launceston (lôn'sĕstən, lŏn'-), city (1971 pop. 35,001; urban agglomeration pop. 62,181), on Tasmania, SE Australia, where the North Esk and South Esk rivers join to form the Tamar estuary; founded 1806. Launceston is the second most populous city in Tasmania and the main port for trade with the Australian mainland. The principal exports are dairy products, flour, and lumber. There are woolen mills and brass works. The city has teacher-training and technical schools.

Laura, subject of the love poems of PETRARCH. She is thought to be Laura de Noves (1308?-1348), wife of Hugo de Sade, but this has not been proved.

Laurance, John, 1750-1810, American Revolutionary officer, b. near Falmouth, Cornwall, England; son-in-law of Alexander MacDougall. A lawyer, he was (1777-82) judge advocate general of the Continental Army and presided at the trial of Major John ANDRÉ. He served in the Continental Congress (1785-87), in the House of Representatives from New York (1789-93), and was U.S. Senator from New York (1796-1800).

Laurasia (lôrāzh'ə): see CONTINENTAL DRIFT.

Laurel. 1 Town (1970 pop. 10,525), Prince Georges co., W central Md., a residential suburb about halfway between Washington, D.C., and Baltimore; patented in the late 1600s, inc. 1870. The Washington, D.C. children's center and a large race track are there. In the area are two additional raceways, the Patuxent Wildlife Research Refuge, a large U.S. Dept. of Agriculture research installation, and U.S. Fort George G. Meade (est. 1917). **2** City (1970 pop. 24,145), seat of Jones co., SE Miss., on Tallahala Creek; inc. 1892. Industries include petroleum exploration and production and meat and poultry processing. The city was founded as the site of a saw mill in 1882. Oil was discovered in the vicinity in 1944. Nearby are a U.S. Indian reservation and a junior college.

laurel, common name for the Lauraceae, a family of forest trees and shrubs found mainly in tropical SE Asia but also abundant in tropical America. Most have aromatic bark and foliage and are evergreen; deciduous species are usually those that extend into temperate zones. The plants are important for aromatic oils and spices, edible fruits, and timber (e.g., from species of the largest genus, *Ocotea*). The true laurel—that of history and classical literature—is *Laurus nobilis,* called also bay and sweet bay. It is native to the Mediterranean, where to the ancients it symbolized victory and merit and was sacred to Apollo. The fragrant leaves are sold commercially as bay leaf, a seasoning. Many plants of the unrelated HEATH family are also called laurels in the United States because of their similarly dark and glossy but poisonous leaves; the cherry laurel is a species of

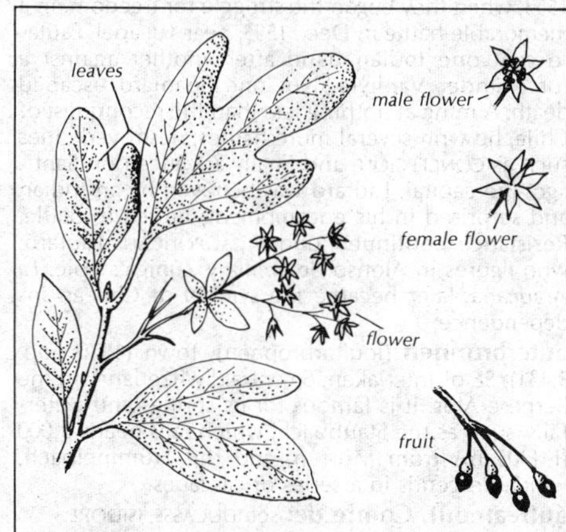

Sassafras, Sassafras albidum, *a member of the laurel family*

the ROSE family. A native American laurel is the evergreen California laurel (*Umbellaria californica*), also called pepperwood, bay-tree, and Oregon myrtle. It grows in California and Oregon and provides wood, medicinal leaves, and fruit kernels that were eaten by the Indians. *Lindera benzoin,* commonly called spicebush, benzoin, or wild allspice, is another fragrant species found in America; its powdered berries are sometimes used as a substitute for allspice. All other *Lindera* species are Asiatic. The red bay (*Persea borbonia*) of the southeast coastal plains has very strong, bright reddish-brown heartwood used in cabinetmaking and interior finishing. *P. americana,* the alligator pear, or avocado (from Sp. *aguacate*), has been cultivated in Mexico and Guatemala for centuries; it is now grown extensively in Florida and California for its nutritious oil-rich fruit and is used chiefly in salads. Sassafras (*Sassafras albidum*), a tree or shrub, was one of the first American plants to command the attention of European settlers, who exported it to the Old World as a high-priced panacea. Its aromatic bark is still occasionally used for medicinal tea, and its pulverized leaves for soup and condiments. Safrole, used in flavorings and medicinals, is obtained from oil of sassafras as well as from the camphor tree. The camphor tree, the cassia-bark tree, and the cinnamon tree all belong to the Asiatic genus *Cinnamomum* and are extensively cultivated for their aromatic bark (see CINNAMON and CAMPHOR). Many of the evergreen laurels are grown as hedges and, because of their handsome foliage, are used by florists. The laurel family is classified in the division MAGNOLIOPHYTA, class Magnoliopsida, order Magnoliales.

Laurel and Hardy, American film comedy team. Its members were Stan Laurel, 1890-1965, b. Ulverson, England, whose real name was Arthur Stanley Jefferson; and Oliver Hardy, 1892-1957, b. Atlanta, Ga. The thin Laurel and rotund Hardy were famous for their zany comic routines, often involving pantomime and the innovative use of props. Many of their best films were devised and directed by Laurel. Among their finest two-reelers are *Putting Pants on Philip* (1926), *The Hoosegow* (1930), and *Helpmates* (1931). Their best-known feature films include *Jailbirds* (1931), *Fra Diavolo* (1933), *Babes in Toyland* (1934), *Way Out West* (1937), *A Chump at Oxford* (1940), and *Saps at Sea* (1940). *Laurel and Hardy's Laughing Twenties* (1965) is a film compilation.

Laurence, Saint: see LAWRENCE, SAINT.

Laurence, Margaret (Jean Margaret Laurence), 1926-, Canadian novelist. Born in Manitoba, she has lived in Somaliland, Ghana, and England. Many of her early works have an African setting. Laurence is particularly concerned with character, and her writings usually focus on individuals. Among her novels are *This Side Jordan* (1960), *The Stone Angel* (1964), *A Jest of God* (1966), upon which the film *Rachel Rachel* (1968) was based, and *The Fire-Dwellers* (1969). In addition to short stories and children's books, Laurence has published works on African literature, notably *A Tree for Poverty* (1954), a collection of Somali folktales and poetry, and *Long Drums and Cannons: Nigerian Dramatists and Novelists* (1968), a critical evaluation.

Laurencin, Marie (märē' lōräNsăN'), 1885-1956, French painter and print maker. She studied under Carrière and was influenced by the fauvist and cubist movements. By 1918 Laurencin had developed her elegant, highly personal style, which became extremely popular and which altered very little subsequently. It is characterized by extreme simplification of form, flat and decorative surface, and delicate pastel colors (e.g., *The Assembly,* 1910). See study by Marcel Jouhandeau (1928).

Laurens, Henry, 1724-92, political leader in the American Revolution, b. Charleston, S.C. A wealthy merchant and planter, he was, in the years preceding the Revolution, an opponent of British colonial policy, although he disapproved of the radical policies of some colonists. Late in 1774 he was elected to the first provincial congress of South Carolina and was an active advocate of independence. He was later a member of the Continental Congress (1777-80) and its president (1777-78). In 1780, while en route to the Netherlands with the draft of a possible U.S.-Dutch treaty prepared by William LEE, Laurens was captured by the British and was imprisoned in the Tower of London and later exchanged (1782) for General Cornwallis; the treaty was used as a reason for war between Great Britain and the Netherlands. Laurens was a commissioner to negotiate the Treaty of Paris (1783) but arrived too late to take much part in the negotiations. Publication of his papers was begun in 1968. See biography by D. D. Wallace (1915, repr. 1967).

Laurens, John, 1754-82, American Revolutionary soldier, b. Charleston, S.C.; son of Henry Laurens. In 1777 he joined George Washington's staff as a volunteer aide-de-camp, fought at Brandywine and in subsequent battles, and was promoted (1779) to lieutenant colonel in recognition of his bravery and ability. The intemperate criticism of Washington by Charles LEE caused Laurens to challenge Lee and fight an inconclusive duel. Going to the South, Laurens was captured (1780) when the British took Charleston, but was soon exchanged. In 1781 he was sent on a special and successful mission to France to procure money, arms, and supplies. He showed conspicuous gallantry in the Yorktown campaign and drew up the terms for the surrender of General Cornwallis. He accompanied Nathanael Greene on a mopping-up campaign in the Carolinas and was killed in a minor skirmish. See his *Army Correspondence,* 1777-78 (1867, repr. 1969); biography by D. D. Wallace (1915, repr. 1967).

Laurens (lô'rənz), city (1970 pop. 10,298), seat of Laurens co., NW S.C.; inc. 1875. Textiles, glass, and related products are made, and grain is processed there. Three Revolutionary War battles were fought in the area.

Laurent, Auguste (ōgüst' lōräN'), 1808-53, French organic chemist. He devised a systematic nomenclature for organic chemistry. His studies on naphthalene and its chlorination products led him to propose a nucleus theory that foreshadowed modern structural chemistry; he proposed that the structural grouping of atoms within molecules determined how the molecules combined in organic reactions. This theory conflicted with the then current notion that the product of organic reactions depended solely on the electrical charge of the atoms involved. His theory greatly influenced the theory of types proposed by J. B. Dumas and C. F. Gerhardt.

Laurent, Robert (rōbâr' lôrĕnt'), 1890-1970, American sculptor, b. France. He emigrated to the United States in 1902 and later studied in Rome. Progressing from early decorative works, he developed a monumental, dignified figural style. His works are exhibited in many American museums. Among Laurent's sculptures in many media are *Goose Girl* (Radio City Music Hall, New York City), *Awakening* (Whitney Mus., New York City), and *Spanning the Continent* (Fairmount Park, Philadelphia). His *Spirit of Drama* and *Spirit of Music* are at Indiana Univ., where he taught (1942–60).

Laurentian Mountains (lôrĕn'shən) or **Laurentides,** S Que., Canada, N of the St. Lawrence and Ottawa rivers, rising to 3,150 ft (960 m) in Mt. Tremblant. The Gatineau, L'Assomption, Lièvre, Montmorency, and St. Maurice rivers rise in lakes in this region, which is a popular year-round recreational area, especially for Montreal and Ottawa. Mt. Tremblant Provincial Park is there.

Laurentian Plateau, Canada: see CANADIAN SHIELD.

Laurentian University, at Sudbury, Ont., Canada; nondenominational, bilingual, coeducational; founded 1960. It has a faculty of arts and science and schools of graduate studies, commerce and business administration, engineering, nursing, physical and health education, social work, and translating and interpreting.

Lauria, Roger of: see ROGER OF LORIA.

Laurier, Sir Wilfrid (lô'rēā, Fr. lōrya'), 1841–1919, Canadian prime minister. He studied law at McGill Univ. His premiership of Canada (1896–1911), the first to be held by a French Canadian, was the longest continuous term in the history of the dominion. From his first speech in the Quebec legislature, to which he was elected in 1871, his notable oratory was recognized. He served (1874–78) in the Canadian House of Commons, where he worked for moderate protection and for cooperation between the French and British in Canada, an objective which was his lifelong concern. He was briefly (1877–78) a minister in the cabinet of Alexander Mackenzie. Then, while the Conservative party was in power, he was prominent in the Liberal opposition in Parliament; in 1887 he succeeded Edward Blake as Liberal leader. As prime minister, he formed a strong administration and helped to build a national image for Canada. When in 1911 his party met defeat on the question of trade reciprocity with the United States, he resigned. The years of his ministry witnessed Canada's steady growth and progress. Ambitious for the development of the dominion, but within the framework of the empire, Laurier was committed to such policies as the development of the Western territories, building up railroads, tariff arrangements with the United States as well as Great Britain, and control by Canada of her own defenses. As leader of the Liberal opposition during World War I, he supported Great Britain, but opposed conscription and refused to form a coalition with the Conservative government of Canada in 1917. He was knighted in 1897. See biographies by O. D. Skelton (2 vol., abr. ed. 1965) and Barbara Robertson (1971); H. B. Neatby et al., *Imperial Relations in the Age of Laurier* (1969).

Laurium, Greece: see LÁVRION.

Lausanne (lōzän'), city (1970 pop. 137,383), capital of Vaud canton, W Switzerland, on the Lake of Geneva. An important rail junction and lake port (see OUCHY), it is the trade and commercial center of a rich agricultural region. Food and tobacco products are produced. Lausanne is also a well-known resort city and has been a meeting place of many international conferences. It is the seat of the Swiss federal court of appeal. Originally a Celtic settlement, it became a Roman military camp called *Lousanna.* An episcopal see since the late 6th cent., it was ruled by prince-bishops until 1536, when it was conquered by Bern and accepted the Reformation. Bernese rule ended in 1798, and Lausanne became (1803) the capital of the newly formed canton of VAUD. The scene of brilliant social life in the 18th cent., Lausanne was the residence of Gibbon, Rousseau, and Voltaire. Lausanne has the famous Gothic Cathedral of Notre Dame and several notable museums. The Univ. of Lausanne was founded as a Protestant school of theology in 1537 and became famous as a center of Calvinism. It was made a university in 1890.

Lausanne, Treaty of, 1922–23. The peace treaty (see SÈVRES, TREATY OF) imposed by the Allies on the Ottoman Empire (Turkey) after World War I had virtually destroyed Turkey as a national state. The treaty was not recognized by the nationalist government under Kemal Pasha (later known as ATATÜRK). After the nationalist victory over the Greeks and the overthrow of the sultan, Kemal's government was in a position to request a new peace treaty. Accordingly, the signatories of the Treaty of Sèvres and delegates of the USSR (excluded from the previous treaty) met at Lausanne, Switzerland. After lengthy negotiations a peace treaty was signed in 1923. Turkey recovered E Thrace, several Aegean islands, a strip along the Syrian border, the Smyrna district, and the internationalized Zone of the Straits, which, however, was to remain demilitarized and remain subject to an international convention (see DARDANELLES). Turkey recovered full sovereign rights over all its territory, and foreign zones of influence and capitulations (see OTTOMAN EMPIRE) were abolished. Outside the Zone of the Straits, no limitation was imposed on the Turkish military establishment. No reparations were exacted. In return, Turkey renounced all claims on former Turkish territories outside its new boundaries and undertook to guarantee the rights of its minorities. A separate agreement between Greece and Turkey provided for the compulsory exchange of minorities.

Lausanne Pact, 1932: see REPARATIONS.

Lausitz: see LUSATIA.

Lausitzer Neisse: see under NEISSE, river.

Lautaro (loutä'rō), c.1533–57, leader of the ARAUCANIAN INDIANS in their nearly successful attempt to reconquer S central Chile from the Spanish. He was captured by the Spanish conquistador, Pedro de VALDIVIA, but escaped and returned to his people in 1553, when they began the struggle for freedom. In a memorable battle in Dec., 1553, near Tucapel, Lautaro sent one Indian band after another against a force under Valdivia. Not one Spaniard escaped death. Aiming at nothing less than the reconquest of Chile, he won several more battles, destroyed cities such as CONCEPCIÓN, and finally advanced on Santiago, the capital. Lautaro was betrayed by an Indian and surprised in his encampment; he fell in battle. Resistance continued under CAUPOLICÁN. Lautaro, who figures in Alonso de Ercilla y Zúñiga's epic, *La Araucana,* later became the symbol of Chilean independence.

Lauterbrunnen (lou'tərbrŏŏnən), town (1970 pop. 3,431), SE of Interlaken, S central Switzerland, in the Bernese Alps. It is famous for its springs and waterfalls, such as the Staubbach, which falls nearly 1,000 ft (305 m) from Mürren, and the Trümmelbach, which descends in a series of cascades.

Lautréamont, Comte de: see DUCASSE, ISIDORE.

Lautrec, Henri de Toulouse-: see TOULOUSE-LAUTREC, HENRI DE.

Lautrec, Odet de Foix, vicomte de (ôdā' də fwä vēkôNt' də lōtrĕk'), 1485–1528, marshal of France. In the ITALIAN WARS he fought at Marignano (1515) and was subsequently governor of Milan. Defeated at La Bicocca (1522), he was forced to evacuate Italy. He recovered favor as governor of Languedoc and was made marshal in 1523. In 1527 he headed the French expedition to Italy and reconquered Milan but died of plague while besieging Naples.

Lauzon (lōzôN'), city (1971 pop. 12,809), S Que., Canada, on the St. Lawrence River adjoining Lévis and opposite Île d'Orléans. It was settled in 1647 and was named in 1867 for Jean de Lauzon, governor of New France, to whom the seigniory of Lauzon was granted in 1636. It is a shipbuilding center.

Lauzun, Antonin Nompar de Caumont, duc de (äNtônăN' nôNpär' də kōmôN' dük də lōzöN'), 1633–1723, French courtier and soldier. Mlle de MONTPENSIER sought him in marriage; the king consented to the match but forbade it three days later (1670). Shortly afterward (1671) Lauzun was imprisoned and was not freed until 1681. After his release he and Mlle de Montpensier were probably married, but they quarreled and separated in 1684. Lauzun brought the family of King James II of England to safety in France after the Glorious Revolution of 1688. In 1689–90 he commanded the unsuccessful Irish expedition to restore James. He was created duke in 1692.

lava (lä'və), molten ROCK erupted on the earth's surface by a VOLCANO or through a fissure in the earth's surface. It solidifies into igneous rock that is also called lava. Before reaching the earth's surface, the liquid rock, mixed with gases, is known as magma. Lavas are composed chiefly of silica and the oxides of aluminum, iron, magnesium, calcium, sodium, and potassium. Silica, with soda and potash, predominates in the light-colored, acid felsites; iron oxides, lime, and magnesia, in the dark-colored, basic BASALTS. Rock froth forms on the upper part of a lava flow if bubbles solidify before the gas can escape. Light-colored, glassy froth is PUMICE; dark, cindery or slaggy froth, of a coarser texture than pumice, forms what is known as scoriae. Lava flows which solidify as a mass of blocks and fragments with a rough surface are called block lava, or aa; those which solidify with a smooth, ropy, billowy surface are known as corded lava, or pahoehoe. Lava is sometimes poured out over wide regions through great fissures in the earth's surface, as in the Columbia River plateau of the NW United States, where it is spread over 30,000 sq mi (77,700 sq km) and is up to 5,000 ft (1,524 m) deep. Other such regions are found in the Deccan plateau of India, in E Brazil, and in Iceland. In most instances the reasons for the heat and liquidity of magma, its exact source, and the causes of its rise in the earth are not clearly known. However, the volcanic activity near Iceland and Icelandic fissure flows are related to the spreading of the Atlantic Ocean away from the underwater midocean ridge lying between the plates of the earth on which the North American and European continents rest. Other volcanic areas also lie along plate boundaries. See PLATE TECTONICS.

Lava Beds National Monument: see NATIONAL PARKS AND MONUMENTS (table).

Lavaca Bay: see MATAGORDA BAY.

Laval, François Xavier de (fräNswä' zävyā' də läväl'), 1623–1708, French prelate in Canada, first bishop of Quebec. Of noble family (his family name in full was Laval-Montmorency), he gave up his large patrimony to enter the church. The clergy of New France was under the archbishop of Rouen, and it was the desire of the Jesuits to be directly under the pope that caused Laval to be sent (1659) as vicar apostolic in New France. As such and later (1674–88) as first bishop of Quebec, he was the strongest figure of the Canadian church and one of the most powerful in the colony. His vigor—which continued undiminished into his old age—and his stubborn fight for what he considered the welfare of his people made the Quebec church the vital force of colonial life. He transformed education and founded a seminary that later formed the nucleus of Laval Univ. He fought bitterly with the royal governors, partly because they attempted to subordinate missionary effort to the state but more because he strongly opposed their policy of allowing the sale of alcohol to the Indians. Laval returned (1679) to France to protest against the actions of Frontenac and the so-called brandy parliament, and although he did not get government support, Frontenac was, nevertheless, recalled in 1682. Because of poor health Laval resigned as bishop and was succeeded by his former vicar general, Saint-Vallier. Laval testily disapproved of some of the new bishop's ways, but the church continued strong and Laval's influence continued; when Saint-Vallier was in Europe for long periods (1694–97, 1700–1708) Laval administered the see. Thus to the end of his life Laval had a hand in the building of New France. He appears as a principal character in Willa Cather's novel *Shadows on the Rock.* See biography by H. A. Scott (1926).

Laval, Pierre (pyĕr), 1883–1945, French politician. Elected (1914) to the chamber of deputies as a Socialist, he held various cabinet posts and in 1926 became a senator as an Independent, moving away from his leftist affiliations. In 1931–32 and 1935–36 he was premier and foreign minister. With Sir Samuel Hoare (later Viscount TEMPLEWOOD), he proposed (Dec., 1935) a settlement to halt the Italian conquest of Ethiopia; the plan, designed to appease Benito MUSSOLINI, would have given Italy much of Ethiopia. After the start of World War II and the fall of France in 1940, Laval reached new prominence. In the VICHY government under Marshal Pétain he became vice premier and foreign minister, but in Dec., 1940, he was dismissed and replaced by Admiral DARLAN, apparently on the suspicion that he was planning to overthrow Pétain. Entering the German-occupied part of France, Laval outspokenly advocated collaboration with Germany. Pétain reinstated Laval in April, 1942, and in November gave him dictatorial powers. Laval agreed to draft labor for Germany, authorized a French fascist militia, and instituted a rule of terror. After the Allied invasion of France he was taken (Aug., 1944) with the retreating Germans to Germany. He fled (May, 1945) to Spain, was expelled, and went to Austria. There he surrendered to American forces, who extradited him to France. Tried for treason, he was sentenced to death, and after an unsuccessful attempt at suicide he was executed. While the verdict may have been just, Laval's trial was conducted so poorly that it was denounced by many. Laval defended himself brilliantly and ascribed patriotic motives to his opportunist policies. His notes for his defense were edited by his daughter, Josée Laval, comtesse de Chambrun, and appeared in English in 1948. See biography by Hubert Cole (1963); David Thompson, *Two Frenchmen: Pierre Laval and Charles de Gaulle* (1951); Geoffrey Warner, *Pierre Laval and the Eclipse of France* (1968).

Laval, city (1971 pop. 228,010), coextensive with Île-Jésus (94 sq mi/243 sq km), S Que., Canada, between the Rivière des Mille Îles and the Rivière des Prairies, just NW of Montreal. The second largest city in Quebec, Laval was created in 1965, when 14 small communities on the island were amalgamated. It is a largely residential suburb of Montreal, with summer tourist facilities. The island was known as Montmagny Island until 1699, when it was granted to the Jesuits of Quebec and began to be settled.

Laval, town (1968 pop. 49,052), capital of Mayenne dept., NW France, in Maine. It has been noted for its linen products since the 14th cent. Among its other industrial products are sheet metal, shoes, and furniture. It was founded in the 9th cent. Laval was a center of the Chouans in the French Revolution.

Lavalle, Juan (hwän lävä'yä), 1797–1841, Argentine general, governor of Buenos Aires province (1828–29). He served (1816–24) in the War of Independence and (1826–28) in the war with Brazil. Returning to Buenos Aires, he led his troops in revolt (Dec. 1, 1828) against the governor, Manuel DORREGO, who fled. Lavalle was proclaimed governor. He pursued Dorrego, defeated him, and ordered his summary execution (Dec. 13, 1828). The Argentine provinces protested; a national convention pronounced the execution high treason. Forces commanded by Estanislao López, governor of Santa Fe, and Juan Manuel de ROSAS defeated Lavalle (April, 1829), who took refuge in Montevideo. Aided by Argentine exiles there and, for a time, by French officials, Lavalle organized an army in 1839 and, invading Argentina, campaigned against Rosas. The campaign was generally unsuccessful; Lavalle was decisively defeated by Manuel Oribe, an ally of Rosas, in 1841. He was killed in Jujuy when attempting to reach Bolivia.

Lavalleja, Juan Antonio (hwän äntō'nyō läväyä'hä), c.1786–1853, Uruguayan revolutionist. After serving under José Gervasio Artigas, Lavalleja was imprisoned for a short time by Brazil, then in control of Uruguay. Subsequently he led a small group—the Thirty-three Immortals—in a declaration of independence from Brazil in 1825. To secure support from Buenos Aires the declaration accepted the sovereignty of the United Provinces of La Plata (Argentina). After the victory of Ituzaingó (1827), Uruguay became (1828) an independent buffer state. Two bitter rivals sought the presidency in 1830—Lavalleja and Fructuoso RIVERA. Rivera ultimately won power, and the disgruntled Lavalleja twice (1832, 1834) revolted unsuccessfully. From exile in Buenos Aires he joined Manuel ORIBE against Rivera. A long civil war (1843–51) ensued during which two parties developed: the Blancos [whites], led by Lavalleja, and the Colorados [reds], led by Rivera. These rival factions have dominated Uruguayan politics to the present day. When it ended, Lavalleja was one of a triumvirate chosen (1853) to govern Uruguay, but he died before serving.

La Vallière, Louise Françoise de La Baume Le Blanc de (lwēz fräNswäz' də lä bōm lə bläN də lä välyěr'), 1644–1710, mistress of King Louis XIV of France. Maid of honor to Louis's sister-in-law, Henrietta of England, she became the king's mistress in 1661. She bore him four children, of whom two died in infancy. In 1667, by the same government act that legitimized her daughter, she was created duchess. She was replaced in the king's affections by Mme de Montespan. In 1674 she retired to a Carmelite convent and became celebrated for her piety. See biography by Joan Sanders (1959).

Laval-Montmorency, François Xavier de: see LAVAL, FRANÇOIS XAVIER DE.

Laval University, at Quebec, Que., Canada; Roman Catholic, coeducational, French language; chartered 1852, an outgrowth of a seminary established 1663 by Bishop Laval. In 1876 a branch was established in Montreal, which in 1919 became independent as the Univ. of Montreal. Laval has faculties of arts, law, medicine, theology, philosophy, agriculture, administrative and commercial sciences, education, forestry and geology, letters, sciences, and social sciences. It has schools of architecture, graduate studies, dentistry, fine arts, music, nursing, pharmacy, and social work.

Lavater, Johann Kaspar (yō'hän käs'pär lä'vätər, lävä'tər), 1741–1801, Swiss theologian and mystic. He wrote several books on metaphysics, but he is chiefly remembered for his work on physiognomy, the art of determining character from facial characteristics.

La Vega, city (1970 pop. 31,085), central Dominican Republic, on the Camú River. La Vega is a communications center near a religious sanctuary erected on the site of an important battle in the colonial period. The city was founded in 1495.

lavender, common name for any plant of the genus *Lavandula,* herbs or shrubby plants of the family Labiatae (MINT family), most of which are native to the Mediterranean region but naturalized elsewhere. The true lavender (*L. officinalis*) has grayish foliage and small blue or pale purplish flowers (white in one variety). It is popular for herb gardens and is cultivated commercially (chiefly in France and England) or, more commonly, gathered wild (in S Europe) for the fragrant flowers, valued for scenting linens and clothes and as the source of oil of lavender. The oil is distilled for use in perfumery, in toilet preparations (e.g., lavender water), and in medicine. Lavender is sometimes used as a flavoring. Spike lavender (*L. latifolia*), a broader-leaved, less fragrant species, yields spike-lavender oil, which is also used in perfumery and in varnishes and porcelain painting. Lavender is classified in the division MAGNOLIOPHYTA, class Magnoliopsida, order Lamiales, family Labiatae.

Laver, Rod (Rodney George Laver), 1938–, Australian tennis player. He left school at age 15 to pursue tennis and in 1962 became the first male grand-slam winner in tennis since Don Budge in 1938. Noted for his extraordinarily powerful serve, Laver turned professional in 1962. He won the grand slam again in 1969, the only person ever to do so twice. In 1971 he became the first professional tennis player to pass the $1 million mark in total earnings. He wrote, with Bud Collins, *Education of a Tennis Player* (1971).

Laveran, Charles Louis Alphonse (shärl lwē älfôNs' lävəräN'), 1845–1922, French physician. While an army surgeon in Algiers he discovered (1880) the parasite that causes MALARIA and wrote many treatises on the subject. He received the 1907 Nobel Prize in Physiology and Medicine for his work on protozoa in the causation of disease.

La Vérendrye, Pierre Gaultier de Varennes, sieur de: see VÉRENDRYE.

La Verne (lə vûrn), city (1970 pop. 12,965), Los Angeles co., S Calif., in a citrus-fruit area; inc. 1906. It is chiefly residential with some small industries. La Verne College and a water filtration plant that serves much of S California are there.

Lavigerie, Charles Martial Allemand (shärl märsēäl' älmäN' lävēzhərē'), 1825–92, French churchman, cardinal of the Roman Catholic Church, b. near Bayonne. He was ordained in 1849 and became prominent in the newly formed Écoles d'Orient. He was an authority on Islam. He was bishop of Nancy (1863–67), archbishop of Algiers (1867–92), and in 1884 he was named archbishop of the reestablished see of Carthage, a jurisdiction that included all of French Africa. His most successful efforts were directed toward African missions to Muslims, and he founded the White Fathers (the Society of Missionaries of Africa) for this work. He was a leader in the abolition of slavery in Africa. Cardinal Lavigerie created a sensation when (1890) he repudiated royalism and called on Catholics to support the Third Republic wholeheartedly.

Lavisse, Ernest (ěrněst' lävēs'), 1842–1922, French historian. He was for many years a professor at the Sorbonne. His early works deal chiefly with the history of Prussia, particularly Frederick the Great. His chief fame rests, however, on his brilliant editorship of several large collectively written works. With Alfred Rambaud he edited *Histoire générale du 4e siècle à nos jours* (12 vol., 1893–1901). Alone, he edited *Histoire de France depuis les origines jusqu'à la révolution* (9 vol. in 18, 1900–1911, repr. 1969) and *Histoire de France contemporaine* (10 vol., 1920–22). Some of the best volumes in all three collections are by Lavisse himself; among his distinguished collaborators were Aulard, Luchaire, Pirenne, and Seignobos. The volumes are a synthesis of political, cultural, economic, and social history, and they remain a model for similar undertakings.

Lavoisier, Antoine Laurent (äNtwän' lōräN' lävwäzyā'), 1743–94, French chemist and physicist, a founder of modern chemistry. He studied under eminent men of his day, won early recognition, and was admitted to the Academy of Sciences in 1768. Much of his work was the result of extending and coordinating the research of others; his concepts were largely evolved through his superior ability to organize and interpret and were substantiated by his own experiments. He was one of the first to introduce effective quantitative methods in the study of chemical reactions. He explained combustion and thereby discredited the phlogiston theory. He also described clearly the role of oxygen in the respiration of both animals and plants. His classification of substances is the basis of the modern distinction between chemical elements and compounds and of the system of chemical nomenclature. He also conducted experiments to establish the composition of water and of many organic compounds. Lavoisier worked as well to improve economic and social conditions in France, holding various government posts. He was appointed director of the gunpowder commission (1775), member of the committee on agriculture (1785), director of the Academy of Sciences (1785), member of the commission on weights and measures (1790), and commissioner of the treasury (1791). As one of the farmers general, however, charged with the collection of taxes, he was guillotined during the Reign of Terror. His works include *Traité élémentaire de chimie* (1789) and the posthumously published *Mémoires de chimie* (1805). See biographies by S. J. French (1941) and Douglas McKie (1952, repr. 1962); study by Henry Guerlac (1966).

La Voisin: see POISON AFFAIR.

Lavongai (lävông'ī), volcanic island, c.460 sq mi (1,190 sq km), in the BISMARCK ARCHIPELAGO, part of Papua New Guinea. Lavongai is mountainous and densely forested. There are several coconut plantations. Germany, which held the island from 1884 until World War I, called it Neu Hannover (New Hanover).

Lávrion (läv'rēōn) or **Laurium** (lôr'ēəm), town, E central Greece, in Attica; a port on the Aegean Sea. It is a mining, smelting, and shipping center for lead, manganese, cadmium, and silver ores. Silver was mined there from the 6th to the 2d cent. B.C. and was one of the chief sources of Athenian revenue in the 5th cent. B.C. The present town of Lávrion, formerly called Ergasteria, was founded in the 19th cent., when mining was resumed in the area.

Law, Andrew, 1749?–1821, American composer, b. Milford, Conn. He was a preacher in Philadelphia and Baltimore and, later, a singing teacher in New England. Opposed to the contrapuntal style of William BILLINGS, Law wrote rather simple hymn tunes. In his *Select Harmony* (1778), *Collection of Best Tunes and Anthems* (1779), and other compilations, he collected and arranged many tunes of other composers. He was among the first Americans to arrange hymns with the melody in the soprano instead of the tenor part. Law's teaching books were important in early American music education. One of the first American writers about music, he published *Essays on Music* in 1814.

Law, Andrew Bonar (bŏn'ər), 1858–1923, British statesman, b. Canada. He went to Scotland as a boy and in 1900, after a business career, was elected to Parliament as a Conservative. He soon became known as a spokesman for tariff reform. In 1911 he succeeded Arthur Balfour as leader of the Conservative party. Working closely with Sir Edward CARSON, he led the fierce opposition to Irish HOME RULE that carried Ireland to the brink of civil war. During World War I he was colonial secretary (1915–16) in Herbert Asquith's coalition cabinet and then (1916) became chancellor of the exchequer and leader of the House of Commons under David LLOYD GEORGE. He resigned party leadership in 1921, but in 1922 he returned to politics to lead the Conservative revolt against the continuation of the wartime coalition. He became (Oct., 1922) prime minister but had to resign the following May because of ill health. See biography by Robert Blake (1956).

Law, Edward: see ELLENBOROUGH, EDWARD LAW, 1ST EARL OF; ELLENBOROUGH, EDWARD LAW, 1ST BARON.

Law, John, 1671–1729, Scottish financier in France. After killing a man in a duel he fled to Amsterdam, where he studied banking. Returning to Scotland (1700), he proposed to Parliament plans for trade and revenue reforms and published *Money and Trade Considered* (1705). His ideas and a proposal for a national bank were rejected, and Law went to France. The finances of France were in critical condition at the death of King Louis XIV, and Law succeeded in winning the support of the regent, Philippe II, duc d'ORLÉANS, for a scheme that promised to reduce the public debt and stimulate French trade and industry. Law believed that credit and paper money, by encouraging investment, would regenerate the French economy. In 1716 the regent chartered Law's private Banque générale and authorized it to issue paper currency. In 1717, Law acquired the monopoly of commercial privileges in the French colony of Louisiana and organized the Compagnie d'Occident, or Mississippi Company, which was consolidated (1719) with the French East India Company and other organizations as the Compagnie des Indes. The Banque générale was made the royal bank in 1718, and its issues of notes were guaranteed by the state. Finally (1720), Law, made controller general of finances, merged the huge stock company with the royal bank and took over most of the public debt and the administration of revenue. A rash of speculation swept France. Numerous small investors bought stock, which soared to heights far beyond what could be expected in returns from the exploitation of the colonies (see MISSISSIPPI SCHEME) and from trade with the Far East. The bubble burst suddenly. Well-informed speculators sold their stock at huge profits, setting off a frenzy of selling that ruined thousands of investors. The system collapsed (1720), and Law left France in disgrace. He died in Venice, where he had supported himself by gambling. The dizzy speculation caused by Law's system greatly helped to discredit the regency and the idea of a national bank. Although the immediate results of Law's schemes were disastrous, colonial enterprise received a lasting stimulus. His monetary theories have found defenders among later economists. See biography by H. M. Hyde (rev. ed. 1969).

Law, William, 1686–1761, English clergyman, noted for his controversial, devotional, and mystical writings. One of the NONJURORS, Law was deprived of his fellowship in Emmanuel College, Cambridge, and lost all chances for advancement in the church. Unexcelled among the controversialists of his day, he was also a leading devotional writer. In the former role he wrote *Three Letters to the Bishop of Bangor* (1717–19) in the BANGORIAN CONTROVERSY, and *The Case of Reason* (1731), in reply to Matthew Tindal, the deist. In the field of devotional writings, few books have been given so high a place as his *Serious Call to a Devout and Holy Life* (1728). Its influence was acknowledged by John Wesley. In *The Spirit of Prayer* (1750) and *The Spirit of Love* (1754) is discernible the influence of Law's study of Jakob Boehme, the mystic. Law's collected works (9 vol., 1753–76) were edited by G. B. Morgan in 1892–93. See biography by J. H. Overton (1881); W. R. Inge, *Studies of English Mystics* (1906); Stephen Hobhouse, *William Law and Eighteenth Century Quakerism* (1927); J. B. Green, *John Wesley and William Law* (1945).

Law, the, in Judaism: see TORAH.

law, rules of conduct of any organized society, however simple or small, that are enforced by threat of punishment if they are violated. Law does not develop systematically until a state with a centralized police authority has appeared. For this development a written language is not required, but necessarily the earliest known legal codes are those of literate societies. Examples of early law systems are to be found in the code of HAMMURABI (Babylonia), the Laws of MANU (India), and the Mosaic code (Palestine). These codes show what would seem to be the universal tendency of the religious and ethical system of a society to produce a legal order to enforce its ethical and social mandates. In classical antiquity the first codes of law are those attributed to SOLON and to Lycurgus. The first in Roman history was the Law of the TWELVE TABLES, the prelude to the development of ROMAN LAW, a highly elaborate system that has had immeasurable influence on the growth of Western law. It was summarized in the CORPUS JURIS CIVILIS in the time of Justinian. Roman law developed the distinction between public law (in which the state is concerned directly, e.g., treason and taxation) and private law (concerned with disputes between persons, e.g., over contracts). The breakup of the Roman Empire under the pressure of the Germanic invasions brought the disruption of the Roman legal administration. Temporarily the codes of GERMANIC LAWS eclipsed Roman law in Western Europe. In the simpler Germanic codes the main distinctive element was the use of COMPOSITION for crimes, but most of the Germanic codes showed at least some Roman influence, and Roman law, together with the Bible, was the basis of CANON LAW, the legal system of the Roman Catholic Church, while Muslim law was derived from the KORAN and the traditional sayings of Muhammad, and later Hebrew law was based on the TALMUD. Feudal law also showed the effects of Roman law, although in theory it was based not upon any concept of the state but on personal relations (see FEUDALISM). The revival of trade in the commercial revolution, and in the Renaissance brought new developments in the law of the sea (see MARITIME LAW). The study of Roman law itself was also revived, notably at the Univ. of Bologna. It became the basis of most Continental law, as exemplified in the French Code Napoléon, the archetype of codes that govern the jurisdiction of CIVIL LAW. In England after the Norman Conquest the feudal law was ultimately replaced by the law of the royal courts, such as the king's bench. The royal courts developed COMMON LAW, i.e., judicial legislation as opposed to the law of the formally enacted STATUTE. Common law adhered excessively to precedent, and EQUITY, exercised by the king's chancery, appeared, with its reliance upon the dictates of conscience rather than upon precedent. The two systems became bitter rivals. In the early 17th cent. Francis Bacon championed equity, while such eminent jurists as Edward Coke upheld the common law. In the 18th cent. English jurisprudence stressed natural law (the theory that law must incorporate the NATURAL RIGHTS of man), and the highly influential work of Sir William BLACKSTONE exemplifies the theory. The work of Blackstone was the most important influence in U.S. law (except for Louisiana, Puerto Rico, and the Virgin Islands, where Continental civil law prevailed). Among those who helped to develop the American concept of law were James KENT and Joseph STORY; in constitutional law the most important figure was John MARSHALL. In the United States the distinctive feature is the coexistence of Federal and state law, for the U.S. Constitution limits the sphere in which Federal law is supreme. Modern law has a wide sweep and regulates many branches of conduct. See R. A. Wormser, *The Story of the Law and the Men Who Made It* (rev. ed. 1962); René David, *Major Legal Systems in the World Today* (tr. 1968).

Lawes, Henry, 1596–1662, English composer. Both he and his brother William were prominent musician-composers, and Henry served the royal family in various capacities until the civil war. As music tutor in the family of the Earl of Bridgewater, he became acquainted with the great poets of the time. He wrote the music for Milton's masque *Comus* (1634) and for Carew's *Coelum Britannicum* (1633). He is historically important because of his facility for setting the English language to music.

Lawes, Sir John Bennet (lôz), 1814–1900, English agriculturist. He founded the famous experimental farm at Rothamsted, where, with the English chemist Sir J. H. Gilbert, he experimented with plants and animals. He developed the fertilizing material called superphosphate, which marked the beginning of the chemical fertilizer business. In 1889 he established the Lawes Agricultural Trust for the continuation of the ROTHAMSTED EXPERIMENTAL STATION.

Lawes, Lewis Edward, 1883–1947, American penologist, b. Elmira, N.Y. As warden (1920–41) of Sing Sing Prison, a New York State Prison located at Ossining, N.Y., he carried out many reforms and was active in promoting prison reform, advocating vocational training for convicts and the abolition of capital punishment. *Twenty Thousand Years in Sing Sing* (1932) is the best known of his books.

law merchant: see COMMERCIAL LAW.

lawn, grass turf or greensward cultivated in private yard or public park. A good lawn, or green, has both beauty and usefulness; its maintenance for golf, tennis, baseball, and other sports is a costly and specialized procedure. It requires good soil, frequent watering and mowing, and occasional rolling and fertilizing. Weed pests, such as dandelions and crabgrass, are eliminated by root removal or by SPRAYING. Most lawn plants are types of CLOVER and, especially, of GRASS. Bluegrass, white clover, and a few types of fescue and bent grass are most often selected for temperate climates in the United States. Bermuda grass, rye grass, St. Augustine grass (*Stenotaphrum secundatum*), and carpet grass (*Axonopus affinus*) are planted in warmer regions. See U.S. Dept. of Agriculture bulletins; J. U. Crochett, *Lawns and Ground Covers* (1971).

lawn bowling: see BOWLS.

Lawndale, city (1970 pop. 24,825), Los Angeles co., S Calif., in the Centinela valley; inc. 1959.

lawn tennis: see TENNIS.

law of simple multiple proportions, in chemistry, the statement that when two or more elements form more than one compound, the ratio of the weights of one element that combine with a given weight of another element in the different compounds is a ratio of small whole numbers. For example, carbon and oxygen combine in carbon dioxide (CO_2) and carbon monoxide (CO). A sample of carbon dioxide containing 1 gram of carbon contains 2.66 grams of oxygen; a sample of carbon monoxide containing 1 gram of carbon contains 1.33 grams of oxygen. The ratio of the two weights of oxygen (2.66:1.33) is exactly 2:1. The law of simple multiple proportions can be regarded as an extension of the early law of definite composition, which states that the proportions by weight of the elements present in any pure compound are always the same. An even broader generalization is the law of combining (or equivalent) weights (also known as the law of reciprocal proportions), which states that the ratio in which two substances react with each other is the ratio, or some multiple of the ratio, of the weight of the same two substances reacting with a third substance. All three laws are elementary consequences of the atomic theory, as proposed by John Dalton (see ATOM; CHEMISTRY).

Lawrence or **Laurence, Saint,** d. 258, Roman deacon and martyr. According to legend he was roasted to death on a gridiron. The Latin Fathers praise him in their writings for his role in the conversion of Rome. One of the most venerated martyrs of the Roman Catholic Church, he is mentioned in the Canon of the Mass. Feast: Aug. 10.

Lawrence, Abbott, 1792–1855, American manufacturer and statesman, b. Groton, Mass. Apprenticed (1808) to his brother Amos, a Boston merchant, Abbott became (1814) a partner with Amos in the firm known as A. & A. Lawrence, importers of English manufactures. As agent for the cotton mills at Lowell, he became interested in manufacturing and took the lead in founding (1845) the textile city of Lawrence, Mass. (named for the family), and setting up the mills. He was a reluctant convert to the protective tariff, along with other New England merchants turned manufacturers. His public career included two terms in the U.S. Congress (1835–37, 1839–40), service on the Northeast Boundary Commission (1842), and minister to Great Britain (1849–52). Lawrence supported the work of Louis Agassiz and other scientists, giving $100,000 to Harvard to establish the Lawrence Scientific School. See biography by H. A. Hill (1884).

Lawrence, Amos Adams, 1814–86, American colonizer and philanthropist, b. Boston, grad. Harvard, 1835; nephew of Abbott Lawrence. A prosperous commission merchant and manufacturer of textiles, Lawrence gave liberally to abolitionist movements such as the EMIGRANT AID COMPANY. His interest in education led him to aid in the establishment of Lawrence College, Appleton, Wis., and a college at Lawrence, Kansas (the city was named for him), which became the nucleus of the Univ. of Kansas. Lawrence was also a generous benefactor of Harvard and of the Episcopal Theological School, Cambridge, Mass. See biography by his son, Bishop William Lawrence (1888, repr. 1971).

Lawrence, Charles, 1709–60, governor of Nova Scotia, b. England. A soldier, he accompanied his regiment to Nova Scotia in 1747 and later became lieutenant governor (1754–56) and governor (1756–60) of the province. It was mainly by his orders as governor that the Acadians were deported (see ACADIA). It was in his regime, but not with his approval, that the first elected assembly of Nova Scotia met (1758); it is the oldest representative body in Canada. He attained (1757) the rank of brigadier general and commanded (1759) a brigade at the siege of Louisburg.

Lawrence, D. H. (David Herbert Lawrence), 1885–1930, English author, one of the most original and controversial British writers of the 20th cent. The son of a Nottingham coal miner, Lawrence was a sickly child, devoted to his refined but domineering mother, who insisted upon his education. He graduated from the two-year teacher-training course at University College, Nottingham, in 1905, and became a schoolmaster in a London suburb. In 1909 some of his poems were published in the *English Review*, edited by Ford Madox Ford, who was also instrumental in the publication of Lawrence's first novel, *The White Peacock* (1911). Lawrence eloped to the Continent in 1912 with Frieda von Richthofen Weekley, a German noblewoman who was the wife of a Nottingham professor. He married her in 1914 after her divorce. During World War I the couple was forced to remain in England; Lawrence's outspoken opposition to the war and Frieda's German birth aroused suspicion that they were spies. In 1919 they left England, returning only for brief visits. Their subsequent nomadic existence was spent variously in Ceylon, Australia, the United States (New Mexico), and Mexico. Lawrence died at the age of 45 of tuberculosis; he had struggled with the disease for years. It was Lawrence's belief that industrialized Western culture dehumanized man, emphasizing his intellectual attributes to the exclusion of his natural or physical instincts. He thought, however, that this culture was in decline and that man would soon evolve out of his separateness into a new awareness of himself as a part of nature. One aspect of this "blood consciousness" would be an acceptance of his need for sexual fulfillment. His three great novels, *Sons and Lovers* (1913), *The Rainbow*

(1915), and *Women in Love* (1921), concern the consequences of trying to deny man's union with nature. After World War I, Lawrence was less optimistic about the decline of Western culture and began to believe that mankind must be reorganized under one superhuman leader. The novels that contain this theme—*Aaron's Rod* (1922), *Kangaroo* (1923), and *The Plumed Serpent* (1926)—have been called Fascist and are all considered failures. Lawrence's most famous and controversial novel is *Lady Chatterley's Lover* (1928), the story of an English noblewoman who finds love and sexual completion with her husband's gamekeeper. Because their lovemaking is described in intimate detail, the novel caused a sensation and was banned in England and the United States for many years. All of Lawrence's novels are written in a lyrical, sensuous prose style of almost biblical rhetoric. He had an extraordinary ability to convey a sense of specific time and place. Lawrence himself was a complex person, compelling, ruthless, and dominating, whose work undoubtedly reflects his own psychological maladjustments. Nonetheless, he was a genius who must be ranked as one of the primary molders of 20th-century fiction. Lawrence's works include volumes of stories, poems, and essays; plays, travel books such as *Etruscan Places* (1932), and volumes of literary criticism, notably *Studies in Classic American Literature* (1916). See the *Portable D. H. Lawrence*, ed. by D. Trilling (1947); his collected letters (ed. with introduction by H. T. Moore, 1962); biographies by Geoffrey Trease (1973) and H. T. Moore (rev. ed., 1974); studies by David Cavitch (1970), R. E. Pritchard (1972), Stephen Spender, ed. (1973), and Scott Sanders (1974).

Lawrence, Ernest Orlando, 1901-58, American physicist, b. Canton, S.Dak., grad. Univ. of South Dakota, 1922, Ph.D. Yale, 1925. Affiliated with the Univ. of California from 1928, he became professor in 1930 and director of the radiation laboratory in 1936. For his invention (1930) and development of the cyclotron (see PARTICLE ACCELERATOR) and his researches in atomic structure and transmutation he received the 1939 Nobel Prize in Physics. With the cyclotron he produced artificially radioactive elements and neutrons useful in nuclear, chemical, and biological research.

Lawrence, Gertrude, 1902?-1952, English actress and singer. Her original name was Alexandre Dagmar Lawrence-Klasen. Performing on the musical stage from childhood, Lawrence made her New York debut (1924) in *Charlot's Revue*, together with Beatrice Lillie. A childhood friend of Noel Coward, she appeared with him in his *Private Lives* (1931) and *Tonight at 8:30* (1936). Her charm and magnetic personality in *Susan and God* (1937) and in such musicals as *Lady in the Dark* (1941) and *The King and I* (1951) endeared her to the public. In 1950 she played Amanda in a film version of *The Glass Menagerie*. See her memoirs, *A Star Danced* (1945); biography by her husband, R. S. Aldrich (1955).

Lawrence, Sir Henry Montgomery, 1806-57, British general and administrator in India; brother of John Laird Mair Lawrence. Commissioned (1822) in the Bengal artillery, he fought in Burma (1824-26), against the Afghans (1842), and in the Sikh Wars (1845-49). In 1847, Lawrence became a British resident at Lahore and began to reorganize the Punjab. He continued that work after the annexation (1849) of the Punjab, becoming head of the board of administration for the province. Resigning because of policy differences with his brother, who was also on the board, Lawrence was posted to Rajputana (1853) and then Oudh (1856). He was killed defending besieged Lucknow during the Indian Mutiny. See biography by J. J. Innes (1898); Michael Edwardes, *The Necessary Hell* (1958).

Lawrence, Jacob, 1917-, American painter, b. Atlantic City, N.J. In Lawrence's work social themes are expressed in angular, richly decorative effects. He has executed many cycles of paintings, including the *Harlem, Migration of the Negro,* and *Coast Guard* series. His *War* series and *Tombstones* are in the Whitney Museum of American Art, New York City. Lawrence has taught at several major art schools in New York City.

Lawrence, James, 1781-1813, American naval hero, b. Burlington, N.J. He entered the navy in 1798 and saw his first important service in the Tripolitan War. In the War of 1812, as commander of the *Hornet,* he defeated and sank (1813) the British *Peacock.* He was promoted to captain and was given command of the *Chesapeake* at Boston. On his way out of Boston harbor he met, engaged, and was defeated by the British frigate *Shannon,* which had been blockading Boston. His words "Don't give up the ship!" shouted as he was carried from the deck, mortally wounded, became a popular naval battle cry. See biography by Albert Gleaves (1904); Peter Padfield, *Broke and the Shannon* (1968).

Lawrence, John Laird Mair Lawrence, 1st **Baron,** 1811-79, British colonial administrator in India; brother of Sir Henry Montgomery Lawrence. He went to India in 1829 and served with energy and intelligence in many administrative posts. In 1846, after the first Sikh War, he was made commissioner of the newly acquired Sikh territory and thus played an important part in the second Sikh War. After the total annexation (1849) of the Punjab, Lawrence and his brother Henry reorganized the province, creating a system of administration by which all government functions in each district were concentrated in the hands of a single official, the district commissioner. The Punjab remained quiet during the Indian Mutiny (1857-58), and Lawrence directed the British troops in the recapture of Delhi. He returned to England in 1859 but in 1863 was appointed viceroy of India. His governorship was marked by an expansion of public works programs. Lawrence was a vigorous opponent of the expansionist policies that led to the Afghan Wars. He was made a baron on his retirement in 1869. See studies by Dharm Pal (1952) and Michael Edwardes (1958).

Lawrence, Sir Thomas, 1769-1830, English portrait painter, b. Bristol. He began to draw when very young. In 1787, on his first visit to London, he met Sir Joshua Reynolds, who encouraged the development of his work. Lawrence studied for a short time at the Royal Academy. His reputation was established with the exhibition in 1790 of his portrait of Elizabeth Farren, the actress (Metropolitan Mus.). He soon won royal patronage, and after the deaths of Reynolds and Hoppner he became the fashionable portrait painter of his day. He succeeded Reynolds as painter in ordinary to the king, became an Academician, and was knighted in 1815. After the fall of Napoleon, Lawrence was sent by George IV to the conference at Aix-la-Chapelle to paint the dignitaries assembled there (portraits in Waterloo Gall., Windsor Castle, England). In Austria and Italy he made portraits of state and Church officials and, upon his return to England in 1820, he succeeded Benjamin West as president of the Royal Academy. Among the best of his portraits of children are the group *The Calmady Children* (Metropolitan Mus.), and the celebrated *Pinkie* (Henry E. Huntington Gall., San Marino, Calif.). A number of his works were hurriedly executed to alleviate financial pressure and were imperfectly finished. Among the best-known of his numerous works are portraits of Mrs. Siddons, Benjamin West, and Princess Lieven (National Gall., London) and those of George IV and Princess Caroline (National Portrait Gall., London). Examples of his portraiture are in the Metropolitan Museum and the Frick Collection, New York City, and in the Museum of Fine Arts, Boston. See catalog ed. by K. Garlick (1960); study by D. Goldring (1951).

Lawrence, Thomas Edward, 1888-1935, British adventurer, soldier, and scholar, known as Lawrence of Arabia. While a student at Oxford he went on a walking tour of Syria and in 1911 joined a British Museum archaeological expedition in Mesopotamia. He remained in the Middle East until 1914, learning colloquial Arabic and making exploratory trips and archaeological surveys. After the outbreak of World War I, Lawrence was attached to the intelligence section of the British army in Egypt. In 1916, he joined the Arab forces under Faisal al Husayn (FAISAL I) and became a leader in their revolt against Turkish domination. His use of small rapid assaults succeeded in tying down large Turkish armies with an Arab force of only a few thousand. After the war he was a delegate to the Paris Peace Conference, where he sought in vain to achieve independence for the Arabs. He became (1919) a research fellow at Oxford and served (1921-22) as Middle East adviser to the colonial office, working constantly to promote the formation of independent Arab states. Lawrence had meanwhile become something of a legendary figure, but in 1922 he enlisted, under the name of Ross, as a mechanic in the Royal Air Force. There have been many interpretations of his search for anonymity: his feeling that he had betrayed Arab hopes for independence or, conversely, the conviction that he had done everything possible for his Arab friends and could do no more; an almost pathological aversion to publicity; or emotional disturbances produced by his war experiences. When Lawrence's identity was discovered (1923), he went into the tank corps; in 1925 he rejoined the air force. He legally adopted (1927) the name T. E. Shaw. In Paris in 1919, Lawrence began to write a narrative of his Arabian adventures, but he lost most of the manuscript and had to rewrite the whole without his notes, which he had destroyed. The result was the celebrated *Seven Pillars of Wisdom,* which was privately printed and circulated in 1926 although not published commercially until 1935. An abridged version, *Revolt in the Desert,* appeared in 1927. *The Mint,* an account of his life in the Royal Air Force, written under the pseudonym J. H. Ross, was published in 1955. Other works are a translation of the *Odyssey* (1932), *Oriental Assembly* (papers, ed. by his brother, A. W. Lawrence, 1939), and his letters (ed. by David Garnett, 1938, new ed. 1964). See biographies by Robert Graves (1928), Flora Armitage (1955), B. H. Liddell Hart (new ed. 1964), P. Knightly and C. Simpson (1969), and Douglas Orgil (1973); A. W. Lawrence, ed., *T. E. Lawrence by His Friends* (1937) and *Letters to T. E. Lawrence* (1964); Frank Clements, *T. E. Lawrence: A Reader's Guide* (1973).

Lawrence, William Beach, 1800-1881, American political leader and jurist, b. New York City. He was appointed secretary of the legation in Great Britain in 1826 and was made (1827) chargé d'affaires. In 1829 he returned to New York City, where he practiced law. Lawrence moved to Rhode Island in 1850, was elected lieutenant governor in 1851, and was acting governor in 1852. Soon afterward he retired from politics to devote himself to writing on international law. His annotated edition of Henry Wheaton's *Elements of International Law* (1855) was long a standard work. From his service on an international commission to codify international law came his *Commentaire sur les éléments du droit international* [commentary on the elements of international law] (4 vol., 1868-80).

Lawrence. 1 Town (1970 pop. 16,646), Marion co., central Ind., a residential suburb of Indianapolis, on the West Fork of the White River. **2** City (1970 pop. 45,698), seat of Douglas co., NE Kansas, on the Kansas River; inc. 1858. Manufactures include farm chemicals and corrugated boxes. Major employers are the Univ. of Kansas and Haskell Institute (1884), the largest Indian school in the United States. Lawrence was founded in 1854 by the New England EMIGRANT AID COMPANY, with Charles Robinson as agent, and was named for Amos A. Lawrence. The political center of the Free Staters, it was actually, though not legally, capital for a short time after 1857. In 1856 there was a proslavery raid on the town that instigated the retaliatory Pottawatamie killings by John Brown. In 1863 the town was again sacked and burned, this time by William Quantrill. The Plymouth Congregational Church there was the first church built (1854) by white settlers in Kansas. **3** City (1970 pop. 66,915), a seat of Essex co., NE Mass., on the Merrimack River; settled 1655, set off from Andover and Methuen 1847, inc. as a city 1853. It is a port of entry. Textiles, textile machinery, leather goods, wearing apparel, electrical equipment, and rubber and paper products are manufactured. Boston capitalists laid out an industrial town there in 1845 and built a granite dam on the Merrimack River. They also built mills and workers' dwellings, which were soon crowded with laborers, mainly from Europe, and Lawrence became one of the world's greatest centers for woolen textiles. Several disastrous events have occurred there—the collapse and burning of the Pemberton Mill in 1860, when over 500 trapped workers were killed or injured; the tornado of 1890; and the labor strife of 1912, when the strikers (members of the International Workers of the World) finally won some of their demands. See M. B. Dorgan, *History of Lawrence, Massachusetts* (1924); D. B. Cole, *Immigrant City: Lawrence, Massachusetts, 1845-1921* (1963).

Lawrence Berkeley Laboratory and **Lawrence Livermore Laboratory,** nuclear science research centers run by the Univ. of California, located in Berkeley, Calif., and Livermore, Calif., respectively. They are named for their founder, physicist Ernest O. Lawrence, who organized the Berkeley laboratory in the early 1930s and the Livermore laboratory in 1952. They are administered by the Univ. of California with funds provided by the U.S. Atomic Energy Commission. Formerly these two laboratories were run as a single research center known as the Lawrence Radiation Laboratory at Berkeley and Livermore. At the Lawrence Berkeley Laboratory an international staff carries out fundamental research and graduate study in physics, nuclear chemistry, biology and medicine, chemical biodynamics, and inorganic materials. Since most of the work is centered around the study of atomic nuclei, the greatest portion of research involves the use of four major particle accelerators. In 1971 research was also formally instituted there in environmental problems. At the Lawrence Livermore Laboratory applied research is carried out on nuclear weaponry, peaceful uses of nuclear explosives, the effects of man-made radiation on living organisms, and controlled thermonuclear reactions. The laboratory maintains a test site for nuclear explosives near Las Vegas, Nev. Basic research, partly in support of the applied work, is conducted in chemistry, physics, biology, and computer sciences.

lawrencium, artificially produced radioactive chemical element; symbol Lr; at. no. 103; mass number of most stable isotope 256; m.p., b.p., and sp. gr. unknown; valence +3. Lawrencium is the last member of the ACTINIDE SERIES of elements found in group IIIb of the PERIODIC TABLE. Lawrencium was first prepared in 1961 (after three years of preliminary work) by A. Ghiorso, T. Sikkeland, A. E. Larsh, and R. M. Latimer at the Univ. of California at Berkeley; a sample of californium isotopes was bombarded with a beam of boron nuclei from the heavy-ion linear accelerator. The resulting isotope, believed to be lawrencium-257, had a half-life of less than 8 sec. The element was named for E. O. Lawrence, the inventor of the cyclotron. The symbol Lw was first used, but it was changed to Lr in 1963. The isotope lawrencium-256 is more stable (half-life 35 sec); it was first prepared in 1965 at the Dubna laboratories near Moscow in the Soviet Union by the reaction of oxygen-18 ions with americium-243. Chemical studies of lawrencium-256 show it to have a stable +3 valence state. Lawrencium-256 is a product of the radioactive decay of isotope 260 of element 105.

Lawrie, Lee (lō'rē), 1877–1963, American sculptor, b. Germany. Brought to America as an infant, he studied with Augustus Saint-Gaudens and Philip Martiny. Lawrie specialized in architectural sculpture. Among his works are decorations for the U.S. Military Academy at West Point, the state capitol at Lincoln, Nebr., and the Harkness Memorial Tower at Yale; the *Atlas* at Rockefeller Center, New York; and sculptures in the Church of St. Vincent Ferrer, St. Thomas Church, and the Chapel of the Intercession, New York City.

Lawson, Ernest, 1873–1939, American landscape painter, b. San Francisco. He studied art in Kansas City, in New York City under Twachtman and J. Alden Weir, and in Paris. On returning to New York he joined the independent artists' group called the EIGHT. His impressionist landscapes won him many awards, and he is represented in most leading American galleries. *High Bridge* (Whitney Mus., New York City) is a characteristic and fine example of his work. See monograph by Guy Pène du Bois (1932).

Lawson, John, d. 1711, English explorer of North Carolina. He came to the Carolinas in 1700 and within the next few years traveled approximately 1,000 mi (1,600 km) through previously unexplored parts. His detailed, lively description of the flora, the fauna, and the Indians, *A New Voyage to Carolina* (1709), was several times reissued as the *History of Carolina*. Lawson was one of the incorporators (1705) of Bath, N.C. He was made surveyor general of North Carolina in 1708 and was one of the founders of New Bern, N.C. He was captured and put to death in the Tuscarora Indian uprising of 1711. See F. L. Harriss, ed., *Lawson's History of North Carolina* (1937).

lawsuit: see PROCEDURE.

Lawton, city (1970 pop. 74,470), seat of Comanche co., SW Okla.; inc. 1901. It is a commercial and trade center for the surrounding cotton, wheat, and cattle area and for Fort Sill, a U.S. field artillery center. The fort is the largest local civilian employer. Lawton's industries produce mobile homes, horse trailers, clothing, mattresses, bedding, and processed foods. Cameron College is in the city. Nearby is a large limestone quarry and the Wichita Mts. Wildlife Refuge.

laxative, drug or other substance used to stimulate the action of the intestines in eliminating waste from the body. The term *laxative* usually refers to a mild-acting substance; substances of increasingly drastic action are known as cathartics, purgatives, hydrogogues, and drastics, respectively. Laxatives or cathartics fall into three general categories: irritants that stimulate the muscular action of the intestines (cascara, phenolphthalein, senna); compounds that increase the amount of bulk in the intestines either by withdrawing water from the body (salines such as Epsom salts, citrate of magnesia) or by increasing the bulk when combined with fluids (agar-agar, bran, the various cellulose substances); and lubricants such as mineral oil, which ease the passage of waste and counteract excessive drying of the intestinal contents. Frequent or regular use of cathartics may seriously disrupt the natural digestive processes. When food and even waste products are forced out of the intestinal tract too rapidly, the body is deprived of vital substances, including the nutrients absorbed in the small intestine and the water, vitamins, and minerals extracted from the waste matter in the large intestine. Vitamins A and D, which are soluble in oil, are removed from the body even when the least irritating laxative, mineral oil, is taken. In addition to disrupting digestive and nutritional processes, laxatives reinforce the condition they are intended to overcome. When the intestines are purged, it may be several days before they can fill again with sufficient waste to induce natural elimination. The person who is trying to establish "regularity" will resort again and again to the laxative, and thus the harm is perpetuated. The response to laxatives is soon lessened, so that larger and more frequent doses may become necessary. Daily elimination of intestinal wastes is desirable but not essential to life or health; natural elimination at longer intervals is preferable. Laxatives should be avoided especially when there is abdominal pain. An inflamed appendix may rupture after the use of a laxative. See CONSTIPATION.

Laxness Halldór Kiljan (häl'dōr kĭl'yän läkhs'nĕs), 1902–, Icelandic novelist, b. Reykjavík. Although Laxness was converted to Roman Catholicism briefly, *The Weaver of Cashmere* (1927) expressed his disillusionment with Christianity. His sympathies turned toward Socialism and Communism; these philosophies are reflected in his later novels. *Salka Valka* (1931–32, tr. 1936), *Independent People* (1934–35, tr. 1946), and *The Light of the World* (1937–40) deal with Icelandic peasant life and describe man's endless search for independence. Written in the great narrative tradition of the epics, his novels set a new style for modern Icelandic literature and were often the focus of bitter controversy. His later works include *Paradise Reclaimed* (tr. 1962). Laxness received the 1955 Nobel Prize in Literature. See biography by Peter Hallberg (tr. 1971).

Layamon (lā'əmən, -mŏn, lī'-), fl. c.1200, first prominent Middle English poet. He described himself as a humble priest attached to the church at Ernley (Arley Regis) near Radstone. His *Brut* is a chronicle in 32,341 short lines on the history of Britain, from the fall of Troy to the arrival of Brutus in Britain and continuing through the death of Cadwaladr. Layamon freely adapted the *Brut* of Wace and added material from other sources. His Anglo-Saxon narrative meter foreshadows the Middle English metrical system. This chronicle, important in the development of the ARTHURIAN LEGEND, gives one of the finest renderings of King Arthur as a national hero. It also contains the first mention of LEAR and CYMBELINE. See his *Brut*, ed. by G. L. Brook and R. F. Leslie (1963).

Layard, Sir Austen Henry (lā'ərd), 1817–94, English archaeologist and diplomat. Between 1842 and 1851 he explored and excavated in Mesopotamia, especially at Nineveh. In the period from 1852 to 1869 he held various government positions, including those of under secretary of foreign affairs and chief commissioner of works. Later he was minister to Spain (1869–77) and ambassador to Constantinople (1877–80). His fine collections are in the Assyrian section of the British Museum. Among his books are *Discoveries in the Ruins of Nineveh and Babylon* (1853) and his autobiography (1903). See biographies by Gordon Waterfield (1963) and N. B. Kubie (1964).

layering, horticultural practice of propagating a plant by rooting a branch before severing it from the mother plant. Typically the branch is bent and a section that has been slit or broken on the underside is covered with soil and held in place by means of stakes or pins. Trench layering induces new shoots from a length of buried branch. In mound, or stool, layering, the many shoots of a closely cropped young plant are heaped with soil. Air (or pot, or Chinese) layering is used when the branch cannot be bent to the ground; peat moss or some other suitable rooting medium is attached to a cut place on the branch. Layering is used mostly for multiplying plants not easily propagated from cuttings. Some plants propagate naturally by layering, e.g., raspberries, strawberries, and chrysanthemums. See bulletins of the U.S. Dept. of Agriculture; H. T. Hartmann, *Plant Propagation* (1968).

Laynez, Diego: see LAINEZ, DIEGO.

Layton, city (1970 pop. 13,603), Davis co., N Utah, between the Wasatch Range and Great Salt Lake. In an irrigated farm area served by the Weber basin project, it has a beet-sugar refinery, canning and packing plants, and a flour mill.

Lazarus (lăz'ərəs) [Gr., = Heb., ELEAZAR]. **1** Brother of Mary and Martha of Bethany who, after four days in the tomb, was brought back to life by Jesus. John 11.1–44; 12.1,2. **2** Beggar in the parable who lay suffering and neglected at the rich man's gate. After death the rich man, parching in hell, pleads in vain that Lazarus, now happy in heaven, be permitted to give him a cooling drink. Luke 16.19–25.

Lazarus, Emma, 1849–87, American poet and essayist, b. New York City. Her early verse includes *Admetus and Other Poems* (1871) and *The Spagnoletto* (1876), a poetic drama. Enraged by the Russian pogroms of the 1880s, she became an impassioned spokesman for Judaism, writing many essays and the book of poems, *Songs of a Semite* (1882), which contains her best work. Her sonnet about the Statue of Liberty, "The New Colossus," was engraved on the statue's pedestal. Her other work includes translations of Heine. See H. E. Jacob, *The World of Emma Lazarus* (1949).

l-dopa (ĕl-dō'pə), drug used to alleviate some of the symptoms of PARKINSONISM, particularly trembling, rigidity, and slow movements; the drug is also called levodopa. Parkinsonism results when the concentration of dopamine in the brain is depleted (see CATECHOLAMINE). Medical administration of dopamine itself is ineffective since that chemical apparently does not enter the brain from the blood. A metabolic precursor of dopamine, l-dopa does enter the brain via the bloodstream and is probably converted into dopamine there. Because there are many brain disorders with similar symptoms, many patients with Parkinsonism do not show any improvement when treated with the drug. Furthermore, virtually all patients on l-dopa experience side effects including nausea, loss of appetite, cardiac irregularities, and psychological changes.

Le. For names beginning thus, not listed here, see second element; e.g., for Le Havre, see HAVRE, LE.

Lea, Henry Charles (lē), 1825–1909, U.S. historian, b. Philadelphia. He was associated with the family publishing business for many years, but his real interest was in historical work. Working with primary sources, he produced a series of works on the Roman Catholic Church during the Middle Ages. Although he was attacked by the Catholic Church in the United States for his criticism of church policy, Lea's work was highly praised by Catholic and non-Catholic scholars in Europe, and he received many honors abroad. Perhaps best known among his works are his first, *Superstition and Force* (1866; reprints and additions, 1878–92), and *A History of the Inquisition of the Middle Ages* (3 vol., 1888), *A History of Auricular Confession and Indulgences in the Latin Church* (3 vol., 1896), *The Moriscos of Spain* (1901), and *The Inquisition of Spain* (4 vol., 1906–7). Recent scholarship has challenged some of Lea's work. However, where his great contribution was his originality and his profound influence in impressing on American historians the importance of direct study of sources. See biography by E. S. Bradley (1931); G. G. Coulton, *Sectarian History* (1937), a defense of Lea's scholarship.

Leach, Edmund Ronald, 1910–, British anthropologist, grad. Cambridge Univ. (B.A., 1932; M.A., 1938) and Univ. of London (Ph.D., 1947). He was (1957–72) university reader in social anthropology at Cambridge, and in 1972 he was appointed professor. In 1966 he became provost of Kings College. His major areas of study have been the kinship, structuralism, mythology, and social anthropology of South Asia. Among his writings are *Political Systems of Highland Burma (1954), Pul Eliya: A Village in Ceylon* (1961), *Rethinking Anthropology* (1961), *A Runaway World?* (1968), *Lévi-Strauss* (1970), and *Genesis as Myth* (1970).

leaching, method of extraction in which a solvent is passed through a mixture to remove some desired substance from it. A simple example is the passage of boiling water through ground coffee to dissolve and carry out the chemicals necessary for producing the beverage. Another example is the removal of sugar from sugar beets using water as the solvent. Leaching is also used to remove metals from their ores. In one procedure certain crushed ores of copper are placed into a series of tanks. As a solvent, such as sulfuric acid, is pumped into the first tank, it dissolves the copper from the ore. Eventually overflowing the first tank, the solution passes into the second, where more copper is dissolved. When this tank overflows, the process is repeated in the third tank and so on. The copper is ultimately removed from the solution by chemical or other treatment.

Leacock, Stephen Butler, 1869–1944, Canadian economist and humorist, b. England, grad. Univ. of Toronto (B.A., 1891), Univ. of Chicago (Ph.D., 1903). Head of the department of political science and economics (1908–36) at McGill Univ., he wrote standard works in his own field, in Canadian history, and in biography. He is best remembered, however, for his many volumes of humorous essays and stories, many of them genial satires, including *Literary Lapses* (1910), *Nonsense Novels* (1911), *Behind the Beyond* (1913), *Frenzied Fiction* (1918), *Winnowed Wisdom* (1926), *My Discovery of the West* (1937), and *How to Write* (1942). *Last Leaves* (1945) are posthumously published essays. See his autobiographical fragment, *The Boy I Left behind Me* (1946).

Lead (lĕd), city (1970 pop. 5,420), Lawrence co., W S. Dak., in the Black Hills; laid out 1876 after the discovery of gold there, inc. 1890. It is the site of the famous Homestake Mine, which has been in operation since 1877.

lead, metallic chemical element; symbol Pb [Lat. *plumbum*]; at. no. 82; at. wt. 207.19; m.p. 327.5°C; b.p. about 1744°C; sp. gr. 11.35 at 20°C; valence +2 or +4. Lead is a dense, relatively soft, malleable metal with low tensile strength. It is a poor conductor of electricity and heat. Lead has a face-centered cubic crystalline structure. It is below tin in group IVa of the PERIODIC TABLE. Although lead has a lustrous silver-blue appearance when freshly cut, it darkens upon exposure to moist air because of the rapid formation of an oxide film; the film protects the metal from further oxidation or corrosion. All lead compounds are poisonous (see LEAD POISONING). Lead resists reaction with cold concentrated sulfuric acid but reacts slowly with hydrochloric acid and readily with nitric acid. It has many commonly used compounds. Commercially important are tetraethyl lead, a gasoline antiknock compound, and the lead oxides, which have many uses. LITHARGE is lead monoxide, PbO; RED LEAD is lead tetroxide, Pb_3O_4; lead peroxide or dioxide, PbO_2, is used in matches, as a mordant in dyeing, and as an oxidizing agent. WHITE LEAD, $2PbCO_3 \cdot Pb(OH)_2$ (basic lead carbonate), is an important pigment used in paints, putty, and ceramics. Chrome yellow, $PbCrO_4$, is a bright yellow pigment. "Sublimed white lead," $PbSO_4 \cdot Pb(OH)_2$ (basic lead sulfate), is also used as a pigment. LEAD ACETATE (sugar of lead) is used as a mordant, and lead azide, $Pb(N_3)_2$, is employed as a detonator for explosives. Lead arsenate is used as an insecticide. The single most important commercial use of lead is in the manufacture of lead-acid storage batteries (see BATTERY, ELECTRIC). It is also used in alloys such as fusible metals, ANTIFRICTION METALS, SOLDER, and TYPE METAL. Shot lead is an alloy of lead, antimony, and arsenic. Lead foil is made with lead alloys. Lead is used for covering cables and as a lining for laboratory sinks, tanks, and the "chambers" in the lead-chamber process for the manufacture of sulfuric acid. It is used extensively in PLUMBING. Because it has excellent vibration-dampening characteristics, lead is often used to support heavy machinery and was used in the foundations of the Pan Am Building built over Grand Central Station in New York City. Lead is also employed as protective shielding against X rays and radiation from nuclear reactors. Although lead and most of its compounds are only slightly soluble in water, the use of lead pipe to carry drinking water is dangerous, since lead is a cumulative poison that is not excreted from the body. The "lead" of lead pencils does not contain lead; it is a mixture of graphite and clay. Although lead is seldom found uncombined in nature, its compounds are widely distributed throughout the world, principally in the ores GALENA, CERUSSITE, and ANGLESITE. Australia, the United States, Canada, and the Soviet Union are the chief producers of lead. In the United States galena (a lead sulfide ore) is mined in southern Missouri, with some ore coming from the western states. The ore is concentrated by the FLOTATION PROCESS and is then refined by electrolysis or by smelting. About one third of the lead used in the United States is so-called secondary lead, i.e., lead and lead alloys reclaimed chiefly from automobile batteries. The element has four naturally occurring stable isotopes, three of which result from the decay of naturally occurring radioactive elements (THORIUM and URANIUM). Since this decay takes place at a constant rate, it is possible to predict either the maximum age of a lead-containing rock or its composition at some earlier date, as long as the rock has not been chemically altered. There are 25 known radioactive isotopes of lead, some of which occur naturally in small amounts. One of the oldest metals used by man, lead was known to the ancient Egyptians and Babylonians. The Romans used it for pipes and in solder. It was one of the first metals mined in North America, where it was sought after especially for making shot.

lead acetate, chemical compound, a white crystalline substance with a sweetish taste. Like other lead compounds, it is very poisonous. Lead acetate is soluble in water and glycerin. With water it forms the trihydrate, $Pb(CH_3COO)_2 \cdot 3H_2O$, a colorless or white efflorescent monoclinic crystalline substance that is commonly known as sugar of lead, plumbous acetate, or Goulard's powder. Lead acetate is used as a mordant in textile printing and dyeing, as a drier in paints and varnishes, and in preparing other lead compounds. It is made by treating litharge (lead monoxide, PbO) with acetic acid.

Leadbelly: see LEDBETTER, HUDDIE.

lead chamber process: see SULFURIC ACID.

lead glance: see GALENA.

lead poisoning, intoxication of the system by organic compounds containing lead. These enter the body by respiration (of dust, fumes, or sprays) or by ingestion of food or other substances that contain lead. Lead poisoning, formerly a leading occupational hazard in industrialized countries, can be an acute episode but is usually a chronic, cumulative disease brought about by continuous exposure. Occupational risk occurs in a wide variety of situations, including inhalation of fumes from lead-containing gasolines, ingestion of foods taken from pottery finished with lead glaze, and exposure during the manufacture and the use of lead paints. A frequent cause among children is ingestion of paint chips containing lead. This source of lead poisoning is most prevalent in poverty areas where old, peeling lead-containing paint and plaster in run-down housing is common. Inadequately nourished or emotionally deprived children who resort to chewing inedible things (a condition known as pica) are most susceptible. The symptoms are the appearance of a blue line on the gums, weakness, anemia, colic, alternating constipation and diarrhea, and paralysis of the wrists and ankles. Massive exposure may lead to brain damage and death. "Deleading" the body may be accomplished by injections of various metal attracting (chelating) compounds; treatment of symptoms is also necessary. Persons who have been treated for lead poisoning should not be further exposed. The risk of lead poisoning in industry has been greatly reduced by precautionary measures and the issuance of protective equipment. The federal government has issued guidelines for the gradual reduction in the lead content of gasoline. Free diagnostic tests for determination of lead poisoning are available in some areas.

Leadville (lĕd'vĭl), mining city (1970 pop. 4,314), alt. c.10,200 ft (3,110 m), seat of Lake co., central Colo., near the headwaters of the Arkansas River, in the Rocky Mts.; inc. 1878. Some mining and smelting are still carried on (at nearby Climax are huge deposits of molybdenum), and farming, ranching, and the tourist trade have kept this famous city from becoming another ghost town. Rich placer gold deposits were discovered c.1860 in California Gulch. Oro City, the principal camp, flourished for about two years until the diggings were exhausted. The camps were virtually deserted until 1877, when the discovery of carbonates of lead with a high silver content again transformed Oro City into a boom town. By 1880, two years after its incorporation, Leadville had become one of the greatest silver camps in the world, with a lusty, heterogeneous population estimated at 40,000. In 1893, with the repeal of the Sherman Silver Act, silver mining collapsed; but in the late 1890s, with the discovery of gold nearby, Leadville revived again. In this district great fortunes were quickly made and often quickly lost. The spectacular history of Leadville is epitomized in the life of H. A. W. Tabor. Points of interest include the Tabor home, restored; the Matchless Mine, now a museum; and the Healy House–Dexter Cabin Museums. See G. F. Willison, *Here They Dug the Gold* (1946); D. L. Griswold and J. H. Griswold, *The Carbonate Camp Called Leadville* (1951).

leadwort, common name for the Plumbaginaceae, a family of perennial herbs and shrubs found in semiarid regions, especially of the Mediterranean area and Central Asia. Several species—e.g., thrift (genus *Armeria*), prickly thrift (genus *Acantholimon*), sea lavender (genus *Limonium*), and plumbago, or leadwort (genus *Plumbago*)—are cultivated in gardens for their papery globe-shaped flowers of various colors, which are also used in EVERLASTING bouquets. The common thrift, or sea pink, of W North America is *Armeria maritima.* The leadwort family is classified in the division MAGNOLIOPHYTA, class Magnoliopsida, order Plumbaginales.

leaf, chief food-manufacturing organ of a plant, a lateral outgrowth of the stem. The typical leaf consists of a stalk, the petiole, and a blade—the thin, flat, expanded portion (needlelike in most conifers) that is normally green in color because of the presence of the pigment chlorophyll. In many leaves small processes called stipules occur at the base of the stalk; sometimes the stipule is large (as in the Japanese quince) and, if green, also manufactures food. The leaf blade is veined with sap-conducting tubes (xylem and phloem) with thick-walled supporting cells. The blade consists of an upper and a lower layer of closely fitted epidermal cells, including specialized paired guard cells that control the size of tiny pores, or stomata, for gaseous exchange and the release of water vapor (see TRANSPIRATION). The upper epidermis is usually coated with a waterproof cuticle and contains fewer stomata than the underside. Between these two layers are large palisade and spongy cells, rich in chlorophyll for food manufacture (see PHOTOSYNTHESIS) and permeated with interconnecting air passages leading to the stomata. Leaves vary in size (up to 60 ft/18m long in some palms), shape, venation, color, and texture and are classified as simple (one blade) or compound (divided into leaflets). The blade margins may be entire (smooth and unindented), toothed

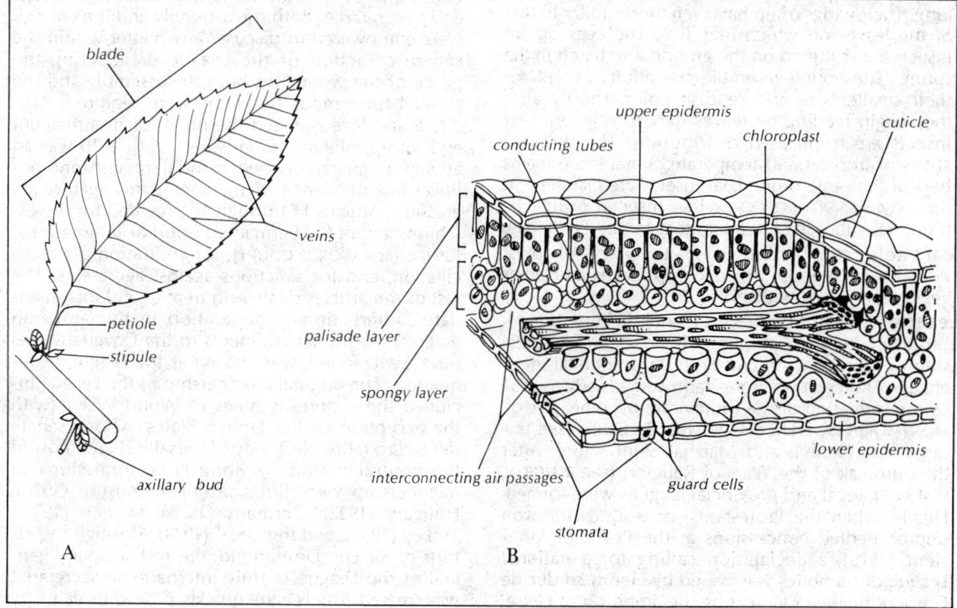

A. *General structure of a leaf*
B. *Microscopic cross section of the leaf blade*

(with small sharp or wavy indentations), or lobed (with large indentations, or sinuses). In monocotyledonous plants the veins are usually parallel; dicotyledons have leaves that are net-veined and may be pinnate (with one central vein, the midrib, and smaller branching veins) or palmate (with several large veins branching from the leaf base into the blade). Pigments besides chlorophyll that give a leaf its characteristic color are the carotinoids (orange-red and yellow), the anthocyanins (red, purple, and blue), and the tannins (brown). White results from the absence of pigments. In deciduous plants a layer of cells forms the abscission tissue at the base of the stalk in the autumn, cutting off the flow of sap; the unstable chlorophyll disintegrates and the remaining pigments are displayed. When these cells dry up completely, the leaf falls. Evergreen plants usually produce new leaves as soon as the old ones fall; the leaves of most conifers remain on the tree from 2 to 10 years (in some species up to 20 years). Leaves may be modified or specialized for protection (spines and bud scales), climbing (tendrils), trapping insects (as in pitcher plants), water storage (as in the succulents), or food storage (bulb scales and, in the embryo plantlet, cotyledons).

leafhopper, common name for small, wedge-shaped leaping insects, cosmopolitan in distribution, belonging to the family Cicadellidae, which comprises some 5,500 species of insects. Some are brightly colored and others are green to brown; they generally measure less than ¼ in. (6 mm) in length. Leafhoppers, and the family as a whole, attack a wide range of trees, shrubs, grasses, and forbs. However, the nymphs and adults frequently suck the sap of only one or a few kinds of plants. Besides stunting plant growth by causing loss of sap, some leafhoppers introduce a toxin into the plant as they feed; others introduce disease organisms. The potato leafhopper, *Empoasca fabae,* is a serious pest in the E United States. It causes a disease commonly known as hopperburn on potatoes and damages many other plants, including apples, beans, and clover. As a result of the potato leafhopper's attack, the leaf's conducting tissue is plugged; the plant leaves curl and begin to turn brown near the tip, and eventually the whole leaf appears blighted. As many as 5 to 6 million leafhoppers may be found per acre. Many leafhoppers have a single generation per year, but there may be several. They overwinter either in the adult or egg stage, depending on the species. Eggs are laid singly or a few at a time in stems and leaves. The adults overwinter only in the south; those migrating north each year cause much damage, but are usually killed by the frost. Other leafhopper pests include the beet leafhopper, which causes the beet disease known as curly top in the W United States; the grape leafhopper; the rose leafhopper; and the apple leafhopper. Leafhoppers are classified in the phylum ARTHROPODA, class Insecta, order Homoptera, family Cicadellidae.

leaf insect, common name given to herbivorous INSECTS of leaflike appearance forming a single family in the order Orthoptera. Leaf insects are green and have extremely flattened, irregularly shaped bodies, wings, and legs; they are usually about 4 in. (10 cm) long. Their wings often have venation similar to that of the leaves on which they live. The eggs of leaf insects are scattered on the ground and hatch in the spring. The young resemble the adults except for their smaller size and reddish color; shortly after they begin feeding on leaves they turn green. Leaf insects are tropical in distribution. The WALKING STICKS of tropical and temperate climates are members of the same order. Leaf insects are classified in the phylum ARTHROPODA, class Insecta, order Orthoptera, suborder Phasmatodea, family Phylliidae.

leaf mold, crumbly brown HUMUS typical of forest floors. It is composed of decayed leaves and other vegetation mixed with soil.

League or **Holy League,** in French history, organization of Roman Catholics, aimed at the suppression of Protestantism and Protestant political influence in France. It was foreshadowed as early as 1561 by the formation of the triumvirate of Anne, duc de MONTMORENCY; François, 2d duc de Guise (see under GUISE, family); and Marshal Saint-André. After the outbreak of the Wars of Religion (see RELIGION, WARS OF), local and provincial leagues were formed. Finally, when the Protestants, or HUGUENOTS, won unprecedented concessions at the Peace of Monsieur (1576), a declaration calling for a national League of Catholics was issued by Henri, 3d duc de Guise. King HENRY III, fearing the ambition of Guise, proclaimed himself its head. A Huguenot uprising soon followed. After a successful campaign that enabled him to withdraw some of his previous concessions to the Huguenots, Henry III dissolved (1577) the League. It was revived in 1585, soon after the Protestant Henry of Navarre (later King HENRY IV) had become the heir presumptive to the throne. Having taken up arms, Guise forced the king (July, 1585) to issue an edict for the conversion or exile of Protestants and the exclusion of Henry of Navarre from the succession. In the war that followed (the War of the Three Henrys), the League and the king were technically allied, but the League assumed the right to dictate, forcing the king to leave Paris (1588) and to renew his previous concessions. This dictation led Henry to order the assassination of Henri de Guise, who was succeeded at the head of the League by his brother Charles, duc de MAYENNE. After the accession (1589) of Henry IV, the League controlled all the large cities, including Paris, and had the active support of Philip II of Spain, who sent Alessandro FARNESE to Mayenne's aid. It split into two factions, however, over the question of Spanish interference, and it was weakened by Henry's military successes. Henry's victory at Ivry (1590), his abjuration of Protestantism (1593), and his entry into Paris (1594) brought the League's organized resistance to an end, and by 1598 the last important League member had submitted to Henry. For the Holy League in Italian history, see HOLY LEAGUE. See De Lamar Jensen, *Diplomacy and Dogmatism* (1964).

League City, city (1970 pop. 10,818), Galveston co., SE Texas; inc. 1961. The aeronautics industry is important; the NASA Lyndon B. Johnson Space Center is nearby. Other industries in League City produce petroleum and petroleum products and paints.

League of Arab States: see ARAB LEAGUE.

League of Nations, former international organization, established by the peace treaties that ended World War I. Like its successor, the United Nations, its purpose was the promotion of international peace and security. The League was a product of World War I in the sense that that conflict convinced most persons of the necessity of averting another such cataclysm. But its background lay in the visions of men like the duc de Sully and Immanuel Kant and in the later growth of formal international organizations like the International Telegraphic Union (1865) and the Universal Postal Union (1874). The Red Cross, the Hague Conferences, and the Permanent Court of Arbitration (Hague Tribunal) were also important stepping-stones toward international cooperation. At the close of World War I, such prominent figures as Jan Smuts, Lord Robert Cecil, and Léon Bourgeois advocated a society of nations. U.S. President Woodrow Wilson incorporated the proposal into the FOURTEEN POINTS and was the chief figure in the establishment of the League at the Paris Peace Conference in 1919. The basis of the League was the Covenant, which was included in the Treaty of Versailles and the other peace treaties. The Covenant consisted of 26 articles. Articles 1 through 7 concerned organization, providing for an assembly, composed of all member nations; a council, composed of the great powers (originally Great Britain, France, Italy, and Japan, later also Germany and the USSR) and of four other, nonpermanent members; and a secretariat. Both the assembly and the council were empowered to discuss "any matter within the sphere of action of the League or affecting the peace of the world." In both the assembly and the council unanimous decisions were required. Articles 8 and 9 recognized the need for disarmament and set up military commissions. Article 10 was an attempt to guarantee the territorial integrity and political independence of member states against aggression. Articles 11 through 17 provided for the establishment of the Permanent Court of International Justice (see WORLD COURT), for arbitration and conciliation, and for sanctions against aggressors. The rest of the articles dealt with treaties, colonial mandates, international cooperation in humanitarian enterprises, and amendments to the Covenant. Geneva, Switzerland, was chosen as the League headquarters. The original membership of the League included the victorious Allies of World War I (with the exception of the United States, whose Senate refused to ratify the Treaty of Versailles) and most of the neutral nations. Among later admissions to membership were Bulgaria (1920), Austria (1920), Hungary (1922), Germany (1926), Mexico (1931), Turkey (1932), and the USSR (1934). Through the efforts of Sir Eric Drummond, the first secretary general of the League, a truly international secretariat was created. The League quickly proved its value by settling the Swedish-Finnish dispute over the ALAND ISLANDS (1920–21), guaranteeing the security of Albania (1921), rescuing Austria from economic disaster, settling the division of Upper SILESIA (1922), and preventing the outbreak of war in the Balkans between Greece and Bulgaria (1925). In addition, the League extended considerable aid to refugees; it helped to suppress white slave and opium traffic; it did pioneering work in surveys of health; it extended financial aid to needy states; and it furthered international cooperation in labor relations and many other fields. However, the problem of bringing its political influence to bear, especially on the great powers, soon made itself felt. Poland refused to abide by the League decision in the VILNA dispute, and the League was forced to stand by powerlessly in the face of the French occupation of the Ruhr (1923) and Italy's occupation of Kérkira (1923). Failure to take action over the Japanese invasion of Manchuria (1931) was a blow to the League's prestige, especially when followed by Japan's withdrawal from the League (1933). Another serious failure was the inability of the League to stop the Chaco War (1932–35; see under CHACO) between Bolivia and Paraguay. In 1935 the League completed its successful 15-year administration of the Saar territory (see SAARLAND) by conducting a plebiscite under the supervision of an international military force. But even this success was not sufficient to offset the failure of the DISARMAMENT CONFERENCE, Germany's withdrawal from the League (1933), and Italy's successful attack on Ethiopia, in defiance of the League's economic sanctions (1935). In 1936, Adolf Hitler remilitarized the Rhineland and denounced the Treaty of Versailles; in 1938 he seized Austria. Faced by threats to international peace from all sides—the Spanish civil war, Japan's resumption of war against China (1937), and finally the appeasement of Hitler at Munich (1938), the League collapsed. German claims on Danzig (see GDAŃSK), where the League commissioner had been reduced to impotence, led to the outbreak of World War II. The last important act of the League came in Dec., 1939, when it expelled the USSR for its attack on Finland. In 1940 the League secretariat in Geneva was reduced to a skeleton staff; some of the technical services were removed to the United States and Canada. The allied INTERNATIONAL LABOR ORGANIZATION continued to function and eventually became affiliated with the United Nations. In 1946 the League dissolved itself, and its services and real estate (notably the Palais des Nations in Geneva) were transferred to the United Nations. The League's chief success lay in providing the first pattern of permanent international organization, a pattern on which much of the United Nations was modeled. Its failures were due as much to the indifference of the great powers, which preferred to reserve important matters for their own decisions, as to weaknesses of organization. See P. J. Noel Baker, *The League of Nations at Work* (1926); F. P. Walters, *A History of the League of Nations* (2 vol., 1952; repr. 1960); Walter Schiffer, *Legal Community of Mankind* (1954, repr. 1972); Byron Dexter, *The Years of Opportunity* (1967); George Scott, *The Rise and Fall of the League of Nations* (1974).

League of Women Voters, voluntary public service organization of U.S. citizens. Organized in 1920 in Chicago as an outgrowth of the National American Woman Suffrage Association, it had as its original nucleus the leaders of the latter organization. The league was organized to educate American women in the intelligent use of their newly won suffrage. At its founding the league was primarily concerned with the status and rights of women, but it later broadened its interests to encompass the improvement of the entire political, economic, and social structure of the nation. It has directed its educational and research campaigns to those ends on local, state, and national levels. Formerly limited to female membership, the league voted in 1974 to accept men as full members. With headquarters in Washington, D.C., the organization had 155,000 members in 1974.

Leah (lē'ə), Laban's elder, uglier daughter and Jacob's first wife. Gen. 29–30.

Leahy, Frank William (lā'hē), 1908–73, American football coach, b. O'Neill, Nebr. He was an assistant coach at Georgetown Univ. (1931–32), Michigan State College (1933), and Fordham Univ. (1934–38), and after his success as head coach (1939–41) at Boston College he was made (1941) athletic director and head coach at Notre Dame, his alma mater. Under Leahy, one of the leading exponents of the T formation in college football, Notre Dame regained the dominant position it had enjoyed in the days of his old coach, Knute Rockne. In four complete seasons through 1949, Notre Dame played 39 straight games without a defeat and with only two ties. Leahy retired from coaching after 1953; in the 13 years that he coached Notre Dame, his teams won 107 games, lost 13, and tied 9.

Leahy, William Daniel, 1875–1959, American naval officer and diplomat, b. Hampton, Iowa. He served in the Spanish-American War, in the Philippines, then in Nicaragua (1912), in Haiti (1916), in the Mexican expedition (1916), and in World War I. He later became chief of naval operations (1937) and governor of Puerto Rico (1939), and he served (1940–42) as ambassador to Vichy France. In 1942, he became chief of staff to President Franklin Delano Roosevelt, who made him (1944) an admiral of the fleet (five-star admiral). He continued as chief of staff under President Truman until 1949. He wrote *I Was There* (1950).

Leakey, Louis Seymour Bazett, 1903–72, British archaeologist and anthropologist in East Africa, b. Kabete, Kenya. His fossil discoveries in East Africa showed that humans were far older than had previously been suspected. Leakey, born of missionary parents, grew up among the Kikuyu people of Kenya. Educated at Cambridge Univ., he began his archaeological research in East Africa in 1924. Leakey was curator of the Coryndon Museum of Nairobi from 1945 to 1961, after which he did research and taught in Africa, England, and the United States. In 1959 Mary Leakey, his wife, discovered in Olduvai Gorge, Tanzania, a hominid fossil (*Zinjanthropus*) believed to be 1,750,000 years old. In 1961 Leakey unearthed there another fossil (*Homo Habilis*), which he believed to be a more direct ancestor of *Homo Sapiens*. The Leakeys' son, Richard Leakey, discovered yet another type of hominid skull near Lake Rudolf, Kenya, in 1972. This fossil, estimated to be 2.6 million years old, appeared to be an even more direct ancestor of man. See Louis Leakey's *The Stone Age Cultures of Kenya Colony* (1931); *Mau Mau and the Kikuyu* (1952); *Adam's Ancestors* (4th ed. 1953, repr. 1960); *Unveiling Man's Origins* (1969).

Leamington (lĕ'mĭngtən, lĕm'-), town (1971 pop. 10,435), S Ont., Canada, on Lake Erie. In a market-gardening area, it has large canneries.

Leamington, England: see ROYAL LEAMINGTON SPA.

Lean, David, 1908–, English film director, producer, and scriptwriter, b. Croyden, England. He was one of Britain's most accomplished film editors before he turned to directing. His films include *In Which We Serve* (1942), *Brief Encounter* (1946), *Great Expectations* (1946), *Oliver Twist* (1948), and *The Sound Barrier* (1951). Lean's later works have been lavish productions with historical backgrounds like *The Bridge on the River Kwai* (1957), *Lawrence of Arabia* (1962), *Dr. Zhivago* (1965), and *Ryan's Daughter* (1969).

Leander (lēăn'dər): see HERO, in Greek mythology.

leap year: see CALENDAR.

Lear (lēr), legendary English king, supposed descendant, through Locrine and Brut, of Aeneas of Troy. The story of Lear and his three daughters probably originated in early Celtic mythology. GEOFFREY OF MONMOUTH claimed to have translated the story from old English records, and succeeding historians and authors, including Holinshed and Spenser, perpetuated the legend. It is best known as the subject of one of Shakespeare's greatest tragedies, *King Lear.*

Lear, Edward, 1812–88, English humorist and artist. At the age of 19 he was employed as a draftsman by the London Zoological Society; the paintings of birds that he produced for *The Family of the Psittacidae* (1832) were among the first color plates of animals ever published in Great Britain. Lear is best known for his illustrated limericks and nonsense verse, which were collected in *A Book of Nonsense* (1846), *Nonsense Songs* (1871), *Laughable Lyrics* (1877), and others. He wrote several illustrated journals of his travels through S Europe. See biographies by Angus Davidson (1938, repr. 1968) and Vivien Noakes (1969).

Learchus: see ATHAMAS and INO.

learning, in psychology, the process by which a relatively lasting change in behavior occurs as a result of practice or past experience. Although learning is distinguished from behavioral changes arising from maturation, illness, fatigue, or motivation, it is not independent of these factors. Learning applies to motor skills, such as driving a car, to intellectual skills, such as reading, and to attitudes and values, such as prejudice; many learned behaviors are acquired in the absence of conscious awareness. There is evidence that neurotic symptoms and patterns of mental illness are also learned behavior. Learning occurs throughout life in animals, and learned behavior accounts for a large proportion of all behavior in the higher animals, especially in man. The scientific investigation of the learning process was begun at the end of the 19th cent. by Hermann Ebbinghaus in Germany, Ivan Pavlov in Russia, and Edward Thorndike in the United States. Three models are currently used to explain changes in learned behavior; two emphasize the establishment of relations between stimuli and responses, and the third emphasizes the establishment of cognitive structures, such as attitudes and rules. The first model, classical conditioning, was initially identified by Pavlov in the salivation reflex of dogs. Salivation is the innate reflex, or unconditioned response, to the presentation of food, the unconditioned stimulus. Pavlov showed that after successive trials in which a buzzer, the conditioned stimulus, was sounded either simultaneously with presentation of food or just before, the dog would eventually salivate at the sound of the buzzer alone. Learning is said to occur because salivation has been conditioned to a new stimulus that did not elicit it initially. The pairing of food with the buzzer acts to reinforce the buzzer as the prominent stimulus. In a second type of learning, known as operant, or instrumental, conditioning, learning takes place as the individual acts upon his environment; this type of learning is distinguished from classical conditioning in that the latter involves the innate reflexes of organisms. Thorndike found that cats and other animals will learn by a gradual trial-and-error process to escape from a puzzle box in order to get food that has been placed outside. Thorndike showed that a reward, especially an intermittently offered reward (in this experiment, the food outside the cage) is essential to reinforce this type of learning; discontinuing the use of reinforcement tends to extinguish the learned behavior. Punishment produces avoidance behavior, which appears to weaken learning but not curtail it; however, competing behaviors induced by punishment, such as fear or shame, may suppress it. In both types of conditioning, stimulus generalization occurs; i.e., the conditioned response may be elicited by stimuli similar to the original conditioned stimulus but not used in the original training. Stimulus generalization has enormous practical importance because it allows for the application of learned behaviors across different contexts. A third type of learning is referred to as insight learning. The GESTALT psychologist Wolfgang Köhler, working with chimpanzees, reported that slow trial-and-error responses are often replaced by a sudden understanding that grasps the interrelationships of a problem. Köhler viewed learning as the product of perceptual and cognitive processes rather than as response mechanisms. Learning theorists are divided by tradition between those who see learning as a process in which complex behavior chains are constructed through the formation of discrete habits (John B. Watson and B. F. Skinner), and those who focus on learning as a consequence of insight, expectation, or cognition (Köhler and Edward C. Tolman). See G. A. Kimble, ed., *Foundations of Conditioning and Learning* (1967); Wolfgang Köhler, *Gestalt Psychology* (new ed. 1970); Howard Rachlin, *Introduction to Modern Behaviorism* (1970); E. L. Thorndike, *The Fundamentals of Learning* (1932, repr. 1974).

Lease, Mary Elizabeth, 1853–1933, American agrarian reformer and temperance advocate, b. Ridgeway, Pa. The daughter of an Irish political refugee, she first gained recognition for a series of lectures (1885–87) on Ireland and the Irish. She had gone to Kansas as a young woman, was admitted to the bar, and became active in Populist politics in the campaign of 1890. Known during this period as Mary Ellen Lease, she was dubbed Mary Yellin Lease by her opponents because of her flamboyant oratorical style. Urging the popular election of Senators, the setting up of postal savings banks, government control of railroads, federal supervision of corporations, woman suffrage, free silver, prohibition, and other reforms, she gained lasting fame by advising the farmers "to raise less corn and more hell." In 1908 she became a lecturer for the New York department of education and in 1912 supported Theodore Roosevelt in the Bull Moose campaign.

leather, skin or hide of animals, cured by TANNING to prevent decay and to impart flexibility and toughness. Prehistoric and primitive peoples preserved pelts with grease and smoke and used them chiefly for shoes, garments, coverings, tents, and containers. Today pelts are prepared for tanning by dehairing, usually with lime, followed by fleshing and cleaning. After tanning, leather is generally treated with fats to assure pliability. The practice of shaving leather to the required thickness was abandoned early in the 18th cent. after the invention of a machine that split the tanned leather into a flesh layer and a grain (hair-side) layer; skivers are thin, soft grains used for linings and for covering firm surfaces. Characteristic grains may be brought out by rubbing, as in morocco leather (goatskin), or may be imitated by embossing. Finishes include glazing, a high glaze being achieved by rolling with glass cylinders; coloring with stains or dyes; enameling or lacquering as for patent leather; and sueding, buffing with emery or carborundum wheels to raise a nap, usually on the flesh side. Russia leather, originally vegetable-tanned calfskin dressed with birch oil that imparted a characteristic odor and often dyed red with brazilwood, is a term now covering a number of variants. Rawhide is similar to parchment and is untanned. Cordovan, or Spanish, leather, a soft, colored leather made at Córdoba during the Middle Ages and often richly modeled and gilded, is imitated for wall coverings, panels, and screens. Leather is much used in BOOKBINDING. Artificial leather, made since about 1850, was originally a strong fabric coated with a rubber composition or with a synthetic substance such as pyroxylin. Since World War II, materials made from VINYL POLYMERS have far outstripped the earlier artificial leathers in commercial importance.

leatherback, marine turtle, *Dermochelys coriacea,* found in tropical and subtropical waters around the world. The largest of all turtles, it may reach a length of 7½ ft (230 cm) and weigh 1200 lb (540 kg). Its shell, unlike that of most turtles, has no horny layer; the bone layer is covered with tough, leathery, black skin. Seven bony ridges running the length of the shell give this turtle its distinctive appearance. Highly pelagic turtles, leatherbacks have occasionally been seen as far N as Norway and as far S as New Zealand. They sometimes enter shallow coastal waters, but come ashore only to lay eggs. They are omnivorous feeders. Like other SEA TURTLES, the leatherback is declining in numbers as a result of hunting and egg harvesting. It is classified in the phylum CHORDATA, subphylum Vertebrata, class Reptilia, order Chelonia, family Dermochelidae.

leather jack: see POMPANO.

leaven (lĕv'ən), agent used to raise bread or other flour foods. Physical leavens include water vapor, which is released as steam at high temperatures (as in popovers), and air, which is incorporated by beating. Chemical leaven (baking powder and baking soda) and biological leavens (yeasts and certain bacteria) raise the mixture by the formation of carbon dioxide gas, which is expanded by heat. Some of the earliest leavens were barm, a yeast of fermenting malt liquor, and sourdough, a portion saved from a mass of dough as a starter for the next batch.

Leavenworth (lĕv'ənwûrth''), city (1970 pop. 25,147), seat of Leavenworth co., NE Kansas, on the Missouri River; inc. 1855. It is the commercial center of a farm and livestock region, with a flour mill, a shipyard, and plants that make automobile batteries and machinery. Nearby Fort Leavenworth, with its various institutions (including the Federal penitentiary, which is located on the grounds although operated by the Justice Dept.), is an important factor in the city's economy. Leavenworth is the oldest city in Kansas and was the first city in the state to be incorporated. It was settled (1854) near the fort by proslavery Missourians and flourished as a supply point on the westward travel routes. The state's first newspaper was printed there in 1854. A veterans' hospital, St. Mary College, and a state penitentiary are nearby.

Leavenworth, Fort: see FORT LEAVENWORTH.

Leavis, F. R. (Frank Raymond Leavis), 1895–, English critic and teacher. A controversial figure, Leavis is regarded as one of the most formidable literary critics of the 20th cent. His works of criticism, combining close textual analysis with moral principles of evaluation, include *New Bearings in English Poetry* (1932), *The Great Tradition* (1948), *The Common Pursuit* (1952), *D. H. Lawrence, Novelist* (1955), and *Anna Karenina and Other Essays* (1968). He was editor and cofounder of the influential quarterly *Scrutiny* from 1932 until its demise in 1953. From 1936 to 1962, Leavis was a fellow at Downing College, Cambridge. His views on education and society are expressed in such works as *Mass Civilization and Minority Culture* (1930), *Education and the University* (1943), and *English Literature in Our Time and the University* (1969). *Nor Shall My Sword: Discourses on Pluralism, Compassion and Social Hope* (1972) is a collection of lectures. Leavis's wife, **Q. D. Leavis**

(Queenie Dorothy Leavis), 1900–, is also a critic of note. Her best-known work is probably *Fiction and the Reading Public* (1932). With her husband she has published *Lectures in America* (1969) and *Dickens the Novelist* (1971).

Leawood, city (1970 pop. 10,349), Johnson co., NE Kansas, a residential suburb of Kansas City; inc. 1948.

Lebanon (lĕb'ənən), republic (1973 est. pop. 3,000,000), 4,015 sq mi (10,400 sq km), SW Asia, on the Mediterranean Sea. The capital is BEIRUT. The country faces the eastern shore of the Mediterranean and is bordered on the N and E by Syria and on the S by Israel. In addition to Beirut there are three ports, TRIPOLI in the north and Sidon (Saida) and Tyre (Sur) in the south. Much of the terrain is mountainous; the Lebanon Mts., which run parallel to the coast, reach their highest point at Qurnet as Sawda (10,131 ft/3,088 m); on the eastern border is the Anti-Lebanon range. Between the two mountain ranges lies the fertile valley of Al Biqa. The Orontes in the north and the Litani in the south are the main rivers. Lebanon is the distribution center for the Middle East, and commerce is its major industry. Two oil pipelines terminate in Lebanon, one from Iraq to Tripoli and one from Saudi Arabia to Sidon. Lebanon itself is largely agricultural. The main crops are citrus fruits, sugar beets, potatoes, and grapes; wheat is the most important grain. Cotton and tobacco are also

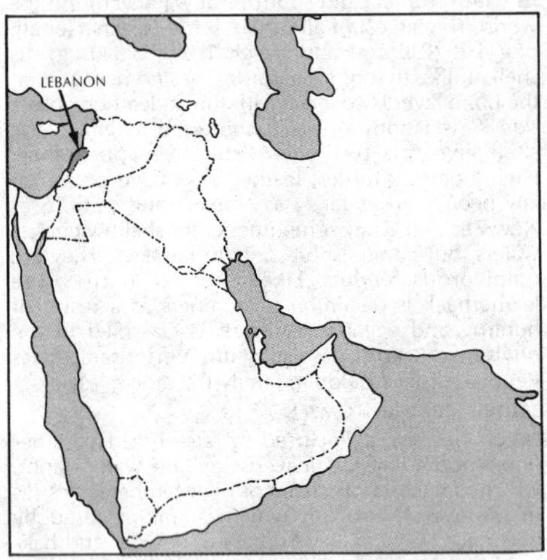

grown, and goats, sheep, and cattle are raised. The largest manufacturing industries are engaged in food processing and the production of textiles and tobacco products. Lebanon has few minerals. Not many of the famed cedars remain, although oak and pine are exploited. Tourism is important to the economy. The country exports fruit and vegetables, wool, cotton, and hides, largely to the other Arab countries; imports include grain, flour, and manufactured goods from Great Britain, West Germany, the United States, Switzerland, and France. Most Lebanese are Arabs, and Arabic is the official language. English and French are, however, widely spoken. About half the population is Muslim, and half Christian, and each is divided into different sects. Political life is profoundly affected by the country's religious diversity; political groups that are mainly Christian, especially of the MARONITE sect, generally favor an independent course for Lebanon, stressing its ties with Europe; the Muslims, however, favor closer ties with the surrounding Arab countries. Traditionally the president of Lebanon is a Christian, and the prime minister a Muslim. The sects are represented proportionally in the legislature, cabinet, and civil service. The country is governed under a 1926 constitution with later amendments. The legislature is the 99-member chamber of deputies, elected every four years. The president, who appoints the cabinet and wields real power, is elected for six years. In ancient times the area of Lebanon and Syria was occupied by the Canaanites, who founded the great Phoenician cities and later established a commercial maritime empire (see PHOENICIA). Lebanon's cities as well as its forests and iron and copper mines (since exhausted) attracted the successive dominant powers in the Middle East. The Phoenician cities occupied a favored position in the Persian Empire and were conquered by Alexander the Great. The region came under Roman dominion starting in 64 B.C. (there are notable Roman ruins at BAALBEK) and was Christianized before the Arab conquest in the 7th cent. By then the Maronites had established themselves—a cardinal fact in the history of Lebanon, which long remained predominantly Christian while Syria became Muslim. Later (11th cent.) the DRUSES settled in S Lebanon and in adjacent regions of Syria, and trouble between them and the Christians was to become a constant theme in regional history. The Crusaders (see CRUSADES) were active in Lebanon (late 11th cent.) and were aided by the Lebanese Christians. After the Crusaders, Lebanon was loosely ruled by the Mamelukes (c.1300). Invasions by Mongols and others contributed to the decline of trade until the reunification of the Middle East under the Ottoman Turks (early 16th cent.). Under Ottoman control, Lebanon had considerable autonomy, and powerful families ruled the country. Many western religious missions and businesses were established in the area in the 19th cent. Conflict among the religious communities, culminating in massacres of the Maronites by the Druses in 1860, led to intervention by France (1861), and the Ottoman sultan was forced to appoint a Christian governor for Lebanon. After World War I, Lebanon and Muslim areas not previously part of it became a French mandate known as Greater Lebanon. There was much discontent and, among the Muslims, a desire for independence within a wider Arab state. In 1926 the mandate was given a republican constitution. A treaty with France in 1936 provided for independence after a three-year transition period, but it was not ratified by France. In World War II the French Vichy government controlled Lebanon until a British-Free French force conquered (June-July, 1941) the Lebanese coast. The Free French proclaimed Lebanon an independent republic. Elections were held in 1943, and, after considerable controversy, Lebanon became independent on Jan. 1, 1945. In that year it became a member of the United Nations, and soon afterward all British and French troops were evacuated. As a member of the Arab League, Lebanon declared war on Israel in 1948 but took little part in the conflict. In 1952, after the election of Camille Chamoun as president, Lebanon formed closer ties with the West. In the spring of 1958 opposition to Chamoun's pro-Western policies and his acceptance of U.S. aid under the Eisenhower doctrine erupted in rioting in Tripoli, Beirut, and elsewhere. The rioting grew into full-scale rebellion, and Chamoun called in U.S. forces (July, 1958). Gen. Fouad Chehab, a nonpolitical personality, who had kept the army out of the civil strife, was elected to succeed Chamoun, and the rebellion ebbed. Chehab appointed Rashid Karameh, an opposition leader, prime minister. By the fall, U.S. forces, following a UN resolution, had left the country. Lebanon subsequently steered a course closer to that of the other Arab nations. The secession of Syria (1961) from the United Arab Republic revived once again the rift between pro-Western and pan-Arab elements in Lebanon. In 1962 a military coup was attempted in Beirut but was crushed. The insurgents had the support of the Popular Syrian party, which favored a "Greater Syria"—a merger of Syria, Lebanon, Jordan, and Iraq. Chehab's term ended without incident. He was succeeded in 1964 by Charles Helou; Suleiman Franjieh was elected in 1970. In Arab affairs Lebanon attempted to maintain a neutral position, particularly in the dispute between Egypt and Saudi Arabia. During the 1967 Arab-Israeli war, Lebanon gave verbal support to the Arab effort against Israel but did not become involved in any military action. Since then, however, Lebanon's position has become increasingly difficult because of the activities against Israel of Palestinian terrorists based in Lebanon. (There are a large number of Palestinian refugees in Lebanon; the United Nations Relief and Works Agency has registered 186,000.) Israel has repeatedly accused Lebanon of not doing enough to prevent the Palestinian commandos from operating against Israel from Lebanese soil. On Dec. 26, 1968, two Arab gunmen departed from Beirut to Athens, where they fired on an Israeli passenger airplane, killing one person. Two days later Israeli forces raided Beirut Airport and destroyed 13 airplanes in what was the first of a series of reprisals against Palestinian strongholds in Lebanon. In Oct., 1969, fighting broke out between the Lebanese army and the Palestinian commandos, after the government had threatened to limit the latter's activity. In 1970 there were several incursions by Israelis into Lebanese territory to strike at the guerrillas. After the suppression in 1970-71 of the guerrillas in Jordan, many of them moved into S Lebanon. Again in 1972 there was heavy fighting between the Lebanese army and the Palestinians. More anti-Israeli terrorist attacks occurred, including an attack (May, 1972) on travelers at Tel Aviv's Lod International Airport by mercenaries allegedly hired by the Lebanese-based Popular Front for the Liberation of Palestine, and the abduction and murder in Munich of 11 Israeli Olympic team members (Sept., 1972). Lebanon disclaimed responsibility, but the Israelis struck repeatedly across the border in search of terrorists; inevitably civilians were killed. In April, 1973, Israelis raided Beirut and killed three Palestinian leaders. The incident precipitated rioting and demonstrations in Lebanon and the resignation of the cabinet. In May, intense fighting erupted throughout the country between the Lebanese army and the Palestinians, including some Syria-based groups. The three-week-long conflict caused many casualties and precipitated the resignation of the government in June. Lebanon did not enter the Oct., 1973, Arab-Israeli war even though Israeli planes destroyed an important radar station near Beirut, nor did the Lebanese army interfere with Palestinian guerrillas operating in S Lebanon. Following the disengagement agreements between Israel and Egypt and Syria in early 1974, and the resulting stepped up anti-Israeli activities by the Palestinians, who adamantly opposed the agreements, Israel continued its attacks on Palestinian guerrilla bases in S Lebanon. See Kamal Salibi, *The Modern History of Lebanon* (1965); Philip Hitti, *Lebanon in History* (3d ed. 1967); Michael Suleiman, *Political Parties in Lebanon* (1967); I. F. Harik, *Politics and Change in a Traditional Society: Lebanon, 1711–1845* (1968); H. H. Smith et al., *Area Handbook for Lebanon* (1969); S. H. Longrigg, *Syria and Lebanon under French Mandate* (1958, repr. 1972); E. A. Salem, *Modernization without Revolution: Lebanon's Experience* (1973).

Lebanon. **1** City (1970 pop. 28,572), seat of Lebanon co., SE Pa., in the Pennsylvania Dutch farm country; founded 1753, inc. as a city 1868. It has steel and steel-fabricating industries. Lebanon was a flourishing town before 1790, and early 18th-century German religious groups are still represented there. The city has a historical museum. Horse shows are a local feature. Also in the area are the Cornwall Furnace (operated 1742–1883) and the Union Canal tunnel, a civil engineering landmark. **2** City (1970 pop. 12,492), seat of Wilson co., N central Tenn., in a timber and livestock area of the Cumberland River basin; inc. 1819. Steering gears, clocks, boots, luggage, and plastic products are manufactured. Points of interest include an early log meeting house, the law office of Sam Houston, and antebellum homes. A junior college and a military academy are there.

Lebanon, ancient *Libanus,* mountain range, c.100 mi (160 km) long, paralleling the Mediterranean Sea from S Lebanon N into Syria and rising steeply from the coast; Qurnet as Sawda (10,131 ft/3,088 m) is the highest peak. A great fault line, site of the fertile Al Biqa valley, separates the Lebanon from the Anti-Lebanon mts. to the east. The Litani River rises in the valley and flows west, through deep gorges in the Lebanon, to the Mediterranean. The mountains were famed in ancient times for the huge, old cedars that extended in a narrow strip for 85 mi (137 km) along the upper western slope of the range; however, these trees were depleted by long use as a building material and a fuel, and only 10 small isolated groves remain. Through history the Lebanon Mts. have provided refuge for persecuted minorities, such as the DRUSES and the MARONITES, who settled on the fertile middle slopes. Many springs, fed by the melting snow, exit from the mountainside and make extensive irrigation possible. Clusters of villages are found on the terraced slopes. The eastern slope has become a summer resort area.

Lebaoth, the same as BETH-LEBAOTH.

Lebbaeus (lĕbē'əs), apostle: see JUDE, SAINT.

Lebedev, Pyotr Nikolaevich (pyô'tə nyĭkəlī'əvĭch lā'byədyəf), 1866–1912, Russian physicist. The most noted Russian physicist of his time, he studied at Strasbourg and Berlin and was professor at Moscow Univ. He was the first to measure the pressure of light in a vacuum tube, confirming predictions based on Maxwell's equations. He was also the first to show that this pressure is twice as great for reflecting surfaces as for absorbing surfaces.

Le Bel, Joseph Achille (zhôsĕf' äshēl' ləbĕl), 1847–1930, French chemist. He was educated at the École polytechnique and carried out much of his research in his own private laboratory. He theorized (1874) that optical activity—the presence of two forms of the same organic molecule, one a mirror image of the other—is due to an asymmetric carbon atom bound to four different groups. For this contribution he is regarded as the cofounder of stereochemistry, with J. H. van't Hoff. His interests also included petrochemistry, cosmology, and biology.

Leblanc, Nicolas (nēkôlä' ləbläN'), 1742–1806, French chemist. He was appointed (1780) physician to Louis Philippe Joseph, duc d'Orléans, who later aided him in setting up a factory for producing soda ash from salt. Leblanc developed his process after a prize had been offered by the government for a commercial method of obtaining the soda. Leblanc's patents were confiscated in the Revolution, and, impoverished, he finally committed suicide.

Le Bon, Gustave (güstäv' lə bôN), 1841–1931, French psychologist and sociologist. He was the author of a number of works on social psychology, in which he expounded theories of national traits and racial superiority. His works include *Psychologie des foules* (1895; tr. *The Crowd: A Study of the Popular Mind,* 1897).

Lebonah (lēbō'nə), place, central Palestine, near Shiloh. Judges 21.19.

Lebrun, Albert (älbĕr' ləbröN'), 1871–1950, French statesman, last president of the Third Republic. Elected to the chamber of deputies in 1900, he later became a senator and held various cabinet posts. A moderate, he succeeded Paul Doumer as president in 1932 and was reelected in 1939. In July, 1940, the establishment of the Vichy government under Marshal Pétain deprived Lebrun of all authority. In 1944 he recognized Charles de Gaulle as provisional president of France.

Le Brun, Charles (shärl), 1619–90, French painter, decorator, and architect. He studied with Vouet and in Rome. Strongly influenced by Poussin, he returned in 1646 to Paris, where he gradually developed a more decorative form of classicism. He decorated the Hôtel Lambert and worked at Vaux-le-Vicomte with the architect Le Vau. His first royal commission (1661), the painting *The Family of Darius before Alexander,* established his favor with Louis XIV. With the support of Colbert, he became painter to the king in 1662. Le Brun controlled artistic production and theory in France for more than two decades. Appointed head of the Gobelins works in 1663, he was responsible for the design of royal furnishings. He supervised the work of a large corps of painters, sculptors, engravers, weavers, and other decorators. He was also director of the Académie royale, through which office he set the standard for the Grand Manner and imposed a stringent discipline upon artistic expression. Among his numerous achievements are the decorations at Versailles. In collaboration with J. H. Mansart, he designed several rooms there, including the Galerie des Glaces. Though not a highly original artist, Le Brun was a skilled administrator and was able to create an atmosphere of richness and splendor consonant with the age of Louis XIV.

Lebrun, Charles François (fräNswä'), 1739–1824, French statesman. A moderate member of the Constituent Assembly after the start of the French Revolution, he was imprisoned during the Reign of Terror. Following the coup d'etat of Napoleon Bonaparte (Nov. 1799), Lebrun served as third consul. In 1804 when Napoleon became emperor he made Lebrun arch-treasurer of the empire, and later duke of Piacenza. In 1810 he was appointed governor of Holland. Made (1814) a peer by King Louis XVIII, he supported Napoleon during the Hundred Days and was excluded from the house of peers from 1815 to 1819.

Lebrun, Élisabeth Vigée-: see VIGEE-LEBRUN.

Lecah (lē'kə), descendant of Judah. 1 Chron. 4.21.

Le Cap: see CAP-HAÏTIEN, Haiti.

Le Carré, John (lə kärā'), pseud. of **David John Moore Cornwell,** b. 1931–, English novelist, b. Poole, Dorset, grad. Oxford, 1956. He was a tutor at Eton College (1956–58) and in the British Foreign Service in Germany (1961–64). Le Carré's best-known novel is *The Spy Who Came In from the Cold* (1963), a bleak and terrifying study of cold-war espionage, that emphasizes the inhumanity and amorality of international intrigue. His other works include *A Call for the Dead* (1961), *A Small Town in Germany* (1968), and *Tinker, Tailor, Soldier, Spy* (1974).

Lecce (lĕt'chä), city (1971 pop. 82,175), capital of Lecce prov., Apulia region, S Italy. It is an industrial and agricultural center. Manufactures include ceramics, toys, food products, and wine. A Greek and later a Roman town, Lecce was from 1053 to 1463 a semi-independent county under various lords. In the 16th and 17th cent. culture and commerce flourished there. There are many fine churches and palaces built or restored in a characteristic baroque style. The city has a university (founded 1959).

Lech (lĕkh), river, c.175 mi (280 km) long, rising in Vorarlberg, W Austria, and flowing NE into S West Germany past Augsburg to the Danube River. The Wertach River is its chief tributary. There are about 20 hydroelectric stations on the river, of which Rain (105,000 kw capacity) is the largest. In 1632 Gustavus II of Sweden defeated the Count of Tilly near the mouth of the Lech.

Le Châtelier, Henri Louis (äNrē' lwē lə shätəlyā'), 1850–1936, French industrial chemist. He made many contributions to industrial chemistry, but is best known for his work on the structure of alloys and for his enunciation of LE CHÂTELIER'S PRINCIPLE. This fundamental contribution to chemical thermodynamics had been anticipated in part by J. W. Gibbs, whose work Le Châtelier helped to spread in France. Toward the end of his life he wrote on topics involving industrial efficiency and labor-management relations.

Le Châtelier's principle, chemical principle that states that if a system in equilibrium is disturbed by changes in determining factors, such as temperature, pressure, and concentration of components, the system will tend to shift its equilibrium position so as to counteract the effect of the disturbance (see CHEMICAL EQUILIBRIUM). For example, at a given temperature a covered beaker partly filled with water constitutes a system in which the liquid water is in equilibrium with the water vapor that forms above the surface of the liquid. While some molecules of liquid are absorbing heat and evaporating to become vapor, an equal number of vapor molecules are giving up heat and condensing to become liquid. If stress is put on the system by raising the temperature, then according to Le Châtelier's principle the rate of evaporation will exceed the rate of condensation until a new equilibrium is established. At the new equilibrium point a greater proportion of molecules will exist in the vapor phase. Le Châtelier's principle is evident in chemical systems, as in the COMMON-ION EFFECT and in BUFFER solutions (see also separate article on *p*H). Le Châtelier's principle can be used to encourage formation of a desired product in chemical reactions. In the HABER PROCESS for the industrial synthesis of ammonia, nitrogen gas and hydrogen gas react to form ammonia gas in the reaction $N_2+3H_2 \rightarrow 2NH_3$; the process is exothermic, i.e., one that gives off heat. Since four molecules—three of hydrogen and one of nitrogen—react to form two molecules of ammonia, the reactants have a higher gas pressure than the products. When the reaction is run under high external pressure, up to 1000 atmospheres, and relatively low temperature, about 500°C (932°F), the system favors formation of the substance that will result in a lower total number of molecules, i.e., the ammonia. Running the reaction at relatively low temperature causes it to go far to completion, although if the temperature is too much below 500°C the rate of reaction is too slow.

Lechfeld (lĕkh'fĕlt), plain near Augsburg, S West Germany, drained by the Lech River. There in 955, King (later Emperor) Otto I defeated the Magyars and stopped their expansion into central Europe.

lechwe: see MARSH ANTELOPE.

Lecky, William Edward Hartpole, 1838–1903, British historian, b. Ireland. His *History of the Rise and Influence of the Spirit of Rationalism in Europe* (1865) and his *History of European Morals from Augustus to Charlemagne* (1869) first won him a large public. His masterpiece is his *History of England in the Eighteenth Century* (8 vol., 1878–90), which places him high in the ranks of literary historians. The combination of social and political history made the work a lasting contribution to history, but his moderate liberal views, his rationalism, and his dislike of democratic reforms color the history considerably. Especially distinguished are those parts dealing with Ireland, with the American and French revolutions, and with the Wesleyan movement.

Leclair, Jean-Marie (zhäN-märē' ləklĕr), 1697–1764, French violinist and composer. Leclair studied in Italy, and his music was strongly influenced by Italian models, especially Vivaldi, although it has its own distinct character. He composed much violin music and an opera. Leclair was murdered, possibly by his estranged wife.

Leclerc, Charles Victor Emmanuel (shärl vĕktôr' ĕmänüĕl' ləklĕr'), 1772–1802, French general. He served under Napoleon Bonaparte in the Italian campaign, married (1797) Pauline BONAPARTE, and took part in Napoleon's coup d'etat of 18 Brumaire (1799). In 1801 he commanded the French expedition to Portugal. He then headed the force sent to subdue HAITI, where François Dominique TOUSSAINT L'OUVERTURE had established a virtually autonomous state. The French won several victories after severe fighting, and an agreement was reached. This was broken by Leclerc, who, acting on Napoleon's secret instructions, had Toussaint seized by trickery and deported to France. The natives, led by Jean Jacques DESSALINES and Henri CHRISTOPHE, rose in revolt and expelled the French, who were weakened by an epidemic of yellow fever. Leclerc died of the fever.

Leclerc, Jacques Philippe (zhäk fēlēp'), 1902–47, French general. His real name was Philippe, vicomte de Hauteclocque, but he adopted the name Leclerc in World War II. Commanding the Free French forces in French Equatorial Africa, he led (Dec., 1942–Jan., 1943) their spectacular march from Lake Chad to Tripoli, over c.1,500 mi (2,400 km); they entered Tripoli with the British 8th Army. Leclerc and his troops then took part in the Tunisian campaign. In 1944 he commanded the French 2d Armored Division; its nucleus was the veterans of his African campaign. Gen. Omar N. Bradley honored Leclerc by letting his division enter Paris first (Aug., 1944) to complete the liberation of the city. Leclerc subsequently took Strasbourg. He was made (1945) French commander in the Far East and accepted the Japanese surrender at Tokyo for France. He later commanded against the insurgents in Indochina. Made inspector general of the French forces in North Africa in 1946, he died a year later in a plane crash. He was posthumously created a marshal of France in 1952.

Le Clerc, Jean (zhäN), Latin *Johannes Clericus,* 1657–1736, Swiss Arminian theologian and biblical scholar. He preached in France and in London, then, drawn to the teachings of the Dutch Remonstrants, settled in Amsterdam, where he became professor in the Remonstrant Seminary. His biblical commentaries pointed the way to scientific criticism. Among his important works are *Bibliothèque universelle et historique* (1686–93), *Bibliothèque choisie* (1703–13), and *Bibliothèque ancienne et moderne* (1714–27). See REMONSTRANTS. See biography by S. A. Golden (1972).

Lecompton (ləkŏmp'tən), city (1970 pop. 434), Douglas co., NE Kansas, on the Kansas River; a residential suburb between Lawrence and Topeka. The pro-slavery **Lecompton Constitution** was formulated (Sept. 1857) in the city, and was ratified (Dec., 1857) after an election in which voters were given a choice only between limited or unlimited slavery; free state men refused to cast their ballots. President Buchanan urged Congress to admit Kansas as a slave state under the Lecompton Constitution, but Stephen A. Douglas and his followers broke with the pro-slavery Democrats, and the bill could not pass the House. At a subsequent election (Aug., 1858), Kansans decisively rejected the Lecompton Constitution. Kansas was later (1861) admitted as a free state.

Leconte de Lisle, Charles Marie (shärl märē' ləkôNt' də lēl), 1818–94, French poet. His first two books of poetry, *Poèmes antiques* (1852) and *Poèmes et poésies* (1855), were immediately successful. It was, however, *Poésies barbares* (1862; later enlarged as *Poèmes barbares,* 1872) that established him as the leading figure of the group later to be known as the PARNASSIANS. Anti-Christian and a pessimist, Leconte de Lisle saw death as the only existing reality and drew his inspiration from antiquity. Later works include *Les Erinnyes* (1872), a verse drama; and *Poèmes tragiques* (1884). He was elected to the French Academy. See studies by Irving Putter (1961) and I. H. Brown (1924, repr. 1966).

Lecoq de Boisbaudran, Paul Émile: see BOISBAUDRAN.

Le Corbusier (lə kôrbüzyā'), pseud. of **Charles Édouard Jeanneret** (shärl ādwär' zhänərā'), 1887–1965, French architect, b. Switzerland. His buildings and writings have had a revolutionary effect on the international development of modern architecture. In 1908 Le Corbusier worked with Auguste Perret, pioneer in the architectural use of reinforced concrete. He also worked and studied under Peter Behrens in Berlin. In 1915 a series of architectural sketches made evident his new and radical approach to the technical and aesthetic problems of building. In the following years he produced schemes for houses and apartments and for a city built on pillars, often drawing his inspiration from industrial forms, such as steamship construction. In 1921, in his "Citrohan" model for dwelling houses, he expressed a need for new construction methods, and in 1923, at Vaucresson, near Paris, the first building (a villa) embodying his principles was erected. He contributed articles to the review *Esprit nouveau,* which he had founded in 1920 with Amédée Ozenfant. Collected under the title *Vers une architecture* (1923, tr. from the 13th French ed., *Towards a*

New Architecture, 1927), they attained international circulation. Among Le Corbusier's better-known buildings are a workers' housing project at Pessac near Bordeaux, the Villa Savoye at Poissy, and the Swiss and Brazilian students' pavilions at Cité Universitaire, Paris. His competition-winning design (1927) for the palace of the League of Nations was later rejected on a technicality. In 1946 he was invited to join the international group of architects who designed the headquarters of the United Nations in New York City. After World War II, Le Corbusier's plan for a "vertical city" was in part realized in the Unité d'Habitation in Marseilles (1946–52). His most ambitious work was the design of the main buildings of the new capital of the Punjab, Chandigarh (begun 1951). Other major works are the massive sculptural forms of the chapel at Ronchamp (1950–55); the convent of La Tourette near Lyons (1955–60); and the Visual Arts Center, Harvard Univ. (1961–62). After 1940 Le Corbusier developed the *modulor* system of harmonious but not identical proportions; the system was devised to offer architectural individuality and yet serve the needs of modern mass production. See studies by P. Blake (1964) and M. Besset (1969); W. Boesiger, ed., *Le Corbusier* (1972).

Lecouvreur, Adrienne (ädrēĕn' ləkōōvrör'), 1692–1730, French actress. With Michel Baron she helped change the traditional acting techniques of the French stage. Her style was marked by natural speech and a simple manner. She made her debut at the Comédie Française in 1717 and for 13 years was the idol of the French people. Her love for Maurice de SAXE ended in tragedy; her mysterious death was ascribed to poisoning by her rival, the duchesse de Bouillon. The refusal by the Church to grant Lecouvreur a Christian burial resulted in a bitter poem by her friend Voltaire. She is the subject of a play bearing her name by Scribe and Legouvé and of the opera *Adriana Lecouvreur* by Francesco Cilea. See biography by Jac Richtman (1971).

Lecuona, Ernesto (ärnĕs'tō lākwō'nä), 1896–1963, Cuban composer and pianist, grad. National Conservatory of Music of Havana, 1913. He appeared as a pianist in Spain, France, and the United States. Lecuona is known for his *Rapsodia negra* (1943) as well as for his popular songs *Malagueña* and *Siboney.*

LED, light-emitting diode. See DIODE.

Leda (lē'də), in Greek mythology, daughter of Thestios, king of Aetolia, and wife of Tyndareus, king of Sparta. According to most legends, she was seduced by Zeus, who visited her in the form of a swan. She bore two eggs; from one issued Castor and Pollux, from the other Helen (and, in some myths, Clytemnestra). Castor and Clytemnestra, however, are usually said to be the offspring of Tyndareus.

Le Daim or **Le Dain, Olivier** (both: ôlēvyā' lə dăN), d. 1484, favorite of King Louis XI of France. His original surname was Necker. Beginning as the king's barber and valet, he gained great influence over Louis and became one of the most powerful and feared men in the country. Shortly after the death of Louis, Le Daim's enemies had him tried and hanged.

Ledbetter, Huddie (Leadbelly), 1888–1949, American singer, b. Mooringsport, La. While wandering through Louisiana and Texas, he earned a living by playing the guitar for dances. For a time he joined with Blind Lemon Jefferson, the blues singer, who influenced his future style. Leadbelly's blues and work songs are a survival of the earliest American Negro music (see JAZZ). He was jailed in 1918 for murder and put on a chain gang; he was pardoned in 1925 but was again put in jail for attempted murder (1930–34) and for assault (1939–40). The folklorist John A. Lomax discovered Leadbelly in prison and used his songs for a book, *Negro Folk Songs as Sung by Lead Belly* (1936). In the 1940s Leadbelly made numerous nightclub appearances, accompanying himself on his 12-string guitar; in 1949 he made a concert tour in France.

Lederberg, Joshua, 1925–, American geneticist, b. Montclair, N.J., grad. Columbia, 1944, Ph.D. Yale, 1948. He is known for his studies of the genetic mechanisms of bacteria. He shared with G. W. Beadle and E. L. Tatum the 1958 Nobel Prize in Physiology and Medicine for his studies establishing that sexual recombination occurs in bacteria. Lederberg showed that although bacteria reproduce only by dividing, they are able to effect sexual recombination by other processes that result in exchange of genetic material between different bacteria.

Ledóchowski, Count Mieczisław (myĕchĭs'läf lĕdōōkhôf'skē), 1822–1902, cardinal of the Roman Catholic Church, b. Russian Poland. He became (1865) archbishop of Gniezno and Poznań (then in Prussian Poland). When the Prussian government, opening the KULTURKAMPF, forbade the use of Polish in instruction in Poznań, Ledóchowski ignored the order and was jailed in 1874. In March the pope created him a cardinal, and in April the government declared him deposed. In 1875, Ledóchowski was released and banished and thereafter ruled his see from Rome. He resigned in 1885.

Ledo Road: see BURMA ROAD.

Ledoux, Claude Nicolas (klōd nēkôlä' lədōō'), 1736–1806, French architect. He built palaces and various public buildings, among them the tollhouses (*barrières*) around Paris (1784). His main work was the planning of an ideal city, "Chaux," for the salt mines of the Franche-Comté; it was never built. His fame and importance, however, rest chiefly on his treatise *L'architecture considérée sous le rapport de l'art, des moeurs et de la législation* (1804).

Ledru-Rollin, Alexandre Auguste (älĕksäN'drə ôgüst' lədrü'-rôlăN'), 1807–74, French politician. A lawyer, he first became known as a radical opponent to the accession (1830) of Louis Philippe and the defender of the journalists. He was elected (1841) to the chamber of deputies and was very active in the banquet campaign, which led to the FEBRUARY REVOLUTION of 1848. He became minister of the interior in the provisional government formed by Alphonse de LAMARTINE. Largely because of his pressure, universal suffrage was adopted in the elections to the Constituent Assembly. Ledru-Rollin, supported by Lamartine, was included (May, 1848) in the executive commission that replaced the provisional government, although many conservative republicans opposed him for favoring moderate social reform. After the JUNE DAYS the executive commission was dissolved. Ledru-Rollin was a candidate for president in the election of Dec., 1848, but was defeated by Louis Napoleon (later NAPOLEON III). In June, 1849, he attempted an insurrection against the government of Louis Napoleon, but his plans failed and he fled to England. During his long exile, he wrote numerous revolutionary pamphlets. At the fall of the Second Empire, he returned to France and was elected (1874) to the chamber of deputies. Ledru-Rollin was a powerful speaker. His speeches and pamphlets were collected in his *Discours politiques et écrits divers* (1879). See A. R. Calman, *Ledru-Rollin and the Second French Republic* (1922).

Le Duan (lā dwän), 1908–, Communist party leader in the Democratic Republic of (North) Vietnam. His early political activities led to imprisonment in the 1930s and 1940s under French colonial rule. Released in 1945 by the Viet Minh army, he rose rapidly in the Communist party hierarchy and was largely responsible for organizing Communist forces in the South after the French withdrawal from Vietnam in 1954. He became the party's first secretary in 1959. After Ho Chi Minh's death (1969), Le Duan tightened his hold on the party and emerged as the strongest of the small group that ruled North Vietnam.

Leduc (lədōōk'), town (1971 pop. 4,000), central Alta., Canada, S of Edmonton. It is the center of the Leduc oil field (discovered 1947). The town has oil refineries and grain elevators.

Ledyard, William (lĕd'yərd), 1738–81, American Revolutionary officer, b. Groton, Conn. In 1781, as commander of Fort Griswold (near Groton), he refused to surrender, despite threats of massacre if he should resist the overwhelming British force. After heroic defense, the fort fell and Ledyard and most of his 165 men were killed.

Ledyard, town (1970 pop. 14,837), New London co., SE Conn., on the Thames River; settled c.1653, inc. 1836. It is a farm center. The site of Fort Decatur is marked.

Lee, Ann, 1736–84, English religious visionary, founder of the SHAKERS in America. Born in Manchester, she worked there in the cotton factories and then became a cook. In 1762 she was married to Abraham Stanley, a blacksmith. In 1758 she had joined the "Shaking Quakers." Claiming revelation in a vision (c.1770) that the second coming of Christ was fulfilled in her, she became their accepted leader and was known as Ann the Word or Mother Ann. Although illiterate, she claimed the gift of tongues and the ability to discern spirits and work miracles. She was also convinced of the holiness of celibacy. In 1774 she led a band of eight to America, where, two years later, at Watervliet, N.Y., the first Shaker settlement in America was founded.

Lee, Arthur, 1740–92, American Revolutionary diplomat, b. Westmoreland co., Va.; brother of Francis L. Lee, Richard H. Lee, and William Lee. Educated in Great Britain, he returned to Virginia to practice medicine, but soon decided to study law and went (1768) to London. There, like William Lee, he became a partisan of John WILKES and a political pamphleteer. In 1770 he became agent for Massachusetts in London. After the outbreak of the American Revolution, he was made a commissioner for the Continental Congress to seek foreign aid. In 1777 he went to Spain, but was unable to obtain a formal treaty; he was also refused recognition at the Prussian court in Berlin. With Benjamin FRANKLIN and Silas DEANE he helped persuade Pierre de BEAUMARCHAIS to act as agent for supplying aid to the rebellious colonials. In Paris, however, he quarreled with Franklin and Deane, and his unfavorable reports to Congress resulted in the recall of Deane and a halt on payments to Beaumarchais. In 1779 he was recalled. He later served in the Continental Congress. See B. J. Hendrick, *The Lees of Virginia* (1935).

Lee, Charles, 1731–82, American Revolutionary army officer, b. Cheshire, England. He first came to America to serve in the French and Indian War and took part in General Braddock's disastrous campaign (1755), in the unsuccessful campaign against Ticonderoga (1758), and in the capture of Montreal (1760). His duties as a British officer later took him to Portugal under Gen. John Burgoyne (1762) and to Poland. In 1773 he went to Virginia to live and became a supporter of colonial independence. At the start of the American Revolution his military experience won him a commission as major general in the Continental army. After directing the fortification of New York City early in 1776, he went to Charleston, S.C., and received credit for the successful defense of that city, despite his having advised William Moultrie to abandon the fort that saved the city. Returning to New York, he repeatedly disregarded General Washington's command to cross the Hudson River in the retreat after the battle of White Plains, in the hope that he could win a personal success and replace Washington as commander in chief. When he did cross he was captured (Dec. 13, 1776) by the British at Basking Ridge, N.J. As a captive he gave Gen. William Howe a plan for defeating the Americans, but his treason was not discovered. Lee was exchanged and joined Washington at Valley Forge (1778). At the battle of Monmouth (1778) he ordered a retreat of his forces and thus prevented an American victory. The rout was stemmed only by Washington, Baron von Steuben, and Nathanael Greene. A court-martial resulted in a year's suspension from command for Lee, who continued to criticize Washington abusively. In 1780 he was finally dismissed from service. His papers have been published by the New-York Historical Society (1872–75). See biographies by J. R. Alden (1951) and S. W. Patterson (1958).

Lee, Fitzhugh, 1835–1905, Confederate cavalry general in the American Civil War, b. "Clermont," Fairfax co., Va.; nephew of Robert E. Lee. He campaigned against the Comanche Indians in Texas and was an instructor at West Point when Virginia seceded in May, 1861. He immediately resigned his commission to serve his state. In the Civil War, Lee was made a brigadier general (1862) for his part in the raid led by J. E. B. STUART around George B. McClellan's army, and he brilliantly covered the Confederate retreat in the Antietam campaign (1862). In a cavalry engagement at Kelly's Ford in March, 1863, his brigade opposed the superior Federal force under Gen. William W. Averell. His discovery of the weakness of Joseph Hooker's right led to Stonewall Jackson's successful flanking movement in the battle of CHANCELLORSVILLE (May, 1863). Lee was with Stuart in the Gettysburg and Wilderness campaigns (1863, 1864). He was promoted to major general in Sept., 1863. Sent to support Jubal A. EARLY in the Shenandoah Valley in Aug., 1864, Lee was wounded at Winchester and did not return to active service until Jan., 1865. He was chief of the cavalry corps of the Army of Northern Virginia in the last days of the war and covered the retreat to Appomattox. He was (1886–90) governor of Virginia, and in 1896 President Cleveland appointed him consul general at Havana. Lee won national approval by his conduct in the difficult period preceding the Spanish-American War, and in that conflict he was a major general of volunteers. He was military governor of Havana after the war and later commanded the Dept. of the Missouri. He wrote a biography of his uncle (1894). See D. S. Freeman, *Lee's Lieutenants* (3 vol., 1942–44).

Lee, Francis Lightfoot, 1734–97, political leader in the American Revolution, signer of the Declaration of Independence, b. Westmoreland co., Va.; brother of Arthur, Richard H., and William Lee. While a member of the house of burgesses (1758-76), he urged resistance to Great Britain in the disturbances leading to the Revolution. He served in the Continental Congress (1775-79) and the Virginia senate (1780-82), and later he supported the Federal Constitution. See B. J. Hendrick, *The Lees of Virginia* (1935).

Lee, George Washington Custis, 1832-1913, Confederate general in the American Civil War, b. Fort Monroe, Va.; eldest son of Robert E. Lee. He served in the Corps of Engineers until May, 1861, when he resigned to fight for the Confederacy. Aide-de-camp to President Jefferson Davis through most of the Civil War, he was promoted to major general in 1864. In the last days of the war, Lee commanded a brigade and was captured in the fighting at Sailor's Creek (April, 1865). He was professor of civil and military engineering at the Virginia Military Institute (1865-71) and, succeeding his father, president of Washington and Lee Univ. (1871-97).

Lee, Henry, 1756-1818, American Revolutionary soldier, known as Light-Horse Harry Lee, b. Prince William co., Va. He was a cousin of Arthur Lee, Francis L. Lee, Richard H. Lee, and William Lee and was the father of Robert E. Lee. As a cavalry commander he established an enviable record in the Revolution. He first gained wide notice for his capture of the fort at Paulus Hook (now in Jersey City), N.J., on Aug. 19, 1779. His service under Nathanael Greene after 1780 in the CAROLINA CAMPAIGN was notable for daring and brilliance and he distinguished himself at Guilford Courthouse and Eutaw Springs. After the war he was elected (1785) to Congress. He favored a stronger government and in 1788 was a leader in the struggle to have Virginia ratify the Constitution. He was (1791-94) governor of Virginia, and in 1794 he commanded the troops who suppressed the Whiskey Rebellion. A Federalist Congressman (1799-1801), he was author of the description of George Washington as "first in war, first in peace, and first in the hearts of his countrymen" in the resolutions on the first President's death. A poor business manager, Lee was imprisoned (1808-9) for debt. In 1812 he was severely injured when an angry mob dragged Alexander Hanson, Lee, and others from a jail where they had gone for protection after Hanson's Federalist newspaper had denounced President Madison and the War of 1812. He wrote *Memoirs of the War in the Southern Department* (1812, repr. 1869 with a biographical sketch by Robert E. Lee). See biographies by Thomas Boyd (1931) and N. B. Gerson (1966).

Lee, Jesse, 1758-1816, American Methodist clergyman, b. Virginia. He is known as the apostle of Methodism in New England where, from 1789 to 1798, his labors as an itinerant preacher over a wide area met with signal success. After serving (1797-1800) as assistant to Bishop Asbury, Lee was appointed presiding elder of the South District of Virginia in 1801. He served three terms as chaplain in the House of Representatives and one in the Senate. His *Short History of Methodism in America* (1810) is the first history of American Methodism. See his memoirs (1823, repr. 1969).

Lee, John Doyle, 1812-77, American Mormon leader, b. Kaskaskia, Ill. He joined (c.1837) the Mormon Church and became a bodyguard for Joseph Smith and later for Brigham Young. He was one of the first Mormon migrants to Utah and was active in helping to plant settlements there. Somewhat of a religious fanatic, Lee played an important part in the massacre of the non-Mormon emigrants at MOUNTAIN MEADOWS in 1857. He was finally brought to justice in 1875. The jury disagreed at his first trial, but a second trial found him guilty. He was sentenced to be shot at the scene of the massacre. While the case was being vainly appealed, he wrote *Mormonism Unveiled* (later republished as *The Mormon Menace*), a book blaming the Mormon Church for his crime. He was executed. See his journals (ed. by Charles Kelly, 1938); diaries (ed. by R. G. Cleland and Juanita Brooks, 1955); biography by Juanita Brooks (1961).

Lee, Light-Horse Harry: see LEE, HENRY.

Lee, Nathaniel, 1653-92, English dramatist. After failing as an actor, he turned to writing plays. Lee confined himself entirely to tragedy, turning often to the classical historians for the background of his plays. His most famous work, the blank-verse tragedy *The Rival Queens* (produced in 1677), deals with the jealousy between the wives of Alexander the Great. His plays, which were extremely popular in his time, are marked by bombast and extravagance.

Lee, Richard, 1613?-1664, American colonist, founder of the Lee family of Virginia. A member of the Coton branch of the Lees of Shropshire, England, he emigrated (c.1642) to Virginia, settling first in York co. and later in Northumberland co. A tobacco planter, Lee became wealthy and was an important figure in Virginia, being at various times justice, burgess, member of the council, attorney general, and secretary of state.

Lee, Richard Henry, 1732-94, political leader in the American Revolution, b. Westmoreland co., Va.; brother of Arthur Lee, Francis L. Lee, and William Lee. He served in the house of burgesses (1758-75), where he favored ending the slave trade. An opponent of the Stamp Act (1765), he was the leader in the formation of a nonimportation organization. To help unite colonial resistance further, he advocated, and helped to form, the intercolonial committees of correspondence. As a member (1774-79) of the Continental Congress, he was most active in promoting a nonimportation agreement. Lee was a member (with John Adams and Edward Rutledge) of the committee that placed George Washington in command of the Continental Army. He was also vigorous in arguing for independence and introduced the motion that led to the Declaration of Independence, which he later signed. Lee served again in the Continental Congress (1784-87). He opposed the Federal Constitution because he feared that it would destroy states' rights. As U.S. Senator from Virginia (1789-92) Lee was largely responsible for adoption of the first 10 amendments (the Bill of Rights) to the Constitution. See his letters, ed. by J. C. Ballagh (2 vol., 1911-14, repr. 1970); biography by O. P. Chitwood (1967).

Lee, Robert Edward, 1807-70, general in chief of the Confederate armies in the American Civil War, b. Jan. 19, 1807, at STRATFORD, Westmoreland co., Va.; son of Henry ("Light-Horse Harry") Lee. After graduating second in his class from West Point in 1829, he was commissioned in the Corps of Engineers. He married (1831) Mary Anne Randolph Custis, a great-granddaughter of Martha Washington, and Arlington House, her father's residence in Virginia, was their home until the Civil War (see ARLINGTON HOUSE NATIONAL MEMORIAL). In the Mexican War, Lee made a brilliant record as captain of engineers with Gen. Winfield Scott's army, winning three brevets; his reconnaissances on the advance to Mexico City were important to the American success. Lee was superintendent at West Point from 1852 to 1855, when he was made lieutenant colonel of the 2d Cavalry and sent to W Texas. He commanded the regiment from 1857 to 1861. While at Arlington House on an extended leave, he was called to lead the company of U.S. marines that captured John BROWN at Harpers Ferry in Oct., 1859. In Feb., 1861 (after the secession of the lower South), General Scott, with whom Lee was a great favorite, recalled him from Texas. Lee had no sympathy with either secession or slavery and, loving the Union and the army, deprecated the thought of sectional conflict. But in his tradition, loyalty to Virginia came first, and upon Virginia's secession he resigned (April 20, 1861) from the army. His resolve not to fight against the South had already led him to decline (April 18) the field command of the U.S. forces. On April 23 he assumed command of the military and naval forces of Virginia, which he organized thoroughly before they were absorbed by the Confederacy. Lee then became military adviser to President Jefferson Davis and was made a Confederate general. After the failure of his efforts to coordinate the activity of Confederate forces in the western part of Virginia (July-Oct., 1861), Lee organized the S Atlantic coast defenses. In March, 1862, Davis recalled him to Richmond. His plan to prevent reinforcements from reaching Gen. George B. MCCLELLAN, whose army was threatening Richmond, was brilliantly executed by T. J. (Stonewall) JACKSON in the Shenandoah Valley. When Joseph E. JOHNSTON was wounded at Fair Oaks in the PENINSULAR CAMPAIGN, Lee assumed command of the Army of Northern Virginia (June 1, 1862). His leadership of that army through the next three years has placed him among the world's great commanders. Lee immediately took the offensive, and after ending McClellan's threat to Richmond in the SEVEN DAYS BATTLES (June 26-July 2), he thoroughly defeated John POPE at the second battle of BULL RUN (Aug. 29-30). McClellan, however, checked him in his first Northern invasion, the ANTIETAM CAMPAIGN (Sept.). Advances by Ambrose E. BURNSIDE and Joseph HOOKER were brutally repulsed in the battles of Fredericksburg (Dec. 13; see FREDERICKSBURG, BATTLE OF) and CHANCELLORSVILLE (May 2-4, 1863), though in the latter victory Lee lost his ablest lieutenant, Stonewall Jackson. Lee's second invasion of the North resulted in the Confederate defeat in the GETTYSBURG CAMPAIGN (June-July). He sorely missed the services of Jackson, and some historians attribute his defeat at Gettysburg to the failures of his subordinates, particularly James LONGSTREET. Other authorities argue that Lee underestimated his opposition and failed to impose his will upon his subordinates. Lee assumed full blame for the defeat, but Davis refused to entertain his offer of resignation. After Gettysburg, Lee did not engage in any major campaign until May, 1864, when Ulysses S. GRANT moved against him. He repulsed Grant's direct assaults in the WILDERNESS CAMPAIGN (May-June), but was not strong enough to turn him back, and in July, 1864, Grant began the long siege of PETERSBURG. Lee's appointment as general in chief of all Confederate armies came (Feb., 1865) when the Confederacy had virtually collapsed. On April 2, the Army of the Potomac broke through the Petersburg defenses, and Lee's forces retreated. One week later Lee surrendered to Grant at APPOMATTOX COURTHOUSE. After the war Lee became president of Washington College (now Washington and Lee University) and made it one of the outstanding educational institutions of the South. Although President Andrew Johnson never granted him the official amnesty for which he applied, Lee nevertheless urged the people of the South to work for the restoration of peace and harmony in a united country. Many historians consider Robert E. Lee the greatest general of the Civil War, and it is generally agreed that his military genius, hampered though it was by lack of men and material, was a principal factor in keeping the Confederacy alive. Others point out, however, that he never developed a coordinated overall strategy, that he failed to provide an adequate supply system for his armies, and that he was reluctant to deal with difficult subordinates such as Longstreet. Of admirable personal character, Lee was idolized by his soldiers and the people of the South and soon won the admiration of the North. He has remained a Southern ideal and an American hero. The definitive biography, *R. E. Lee* (4 vol., 1934-37; abr. ed. 1961), is by Douglas Southall FREEMAN. See also biographies by Sir Frederick Maurice (1925), Gamaliel Bradford (rev. ed. 1927), E. S. Miers (1956), and Clifford Dowdey (1965); Capt. R. E. Lee, *Recollections and Letters of General Robert E. Lee* (2d ed. 1924; new ed., *My Father General Lee,* 1960); A. H. Burne, *Lee, Grant, and Sherman* (1939); S. F. Horn, ed., *The Robert E. Lee Reader* (1949); D. S. Freeman, ed., *Lee's Dispatches* (new ed. 1958); *The Wartime Papers of Robert E. Lee* (ed. by Clifford Dowdey, 1961); M. W. Fishwick, *Lee after the War* (1963).

Lee, Rooney: see LEE, WILLIAM HENRY FITZHUGH.

Lee or **Legh, Rowland** (both: lē), d. 1543, English bishop. Educated at Cambridge, he received preferments under the patronage of Cardinal Wolsey, who employed him in the suppression of the monasteries (1528-29). He was greatly esteemed by Henry VIII and is believed to have performed the ceremony of Henry's marriage to Anne Boleyn (1533). He was made (1534) bishop of Coventry and Lichfield and president of the council of the marches in Wales, where he proved to be an efficient administrator. He was one of the first bishops to take the oath of supremacy recognizing Henry as head of the church.

Lee, Sir Sidney, 1859-1926, English editor and author. He was editor (1891-1901) of the *Dictionary of National Biography* but is best known for his *Life of William Shakespeare* (1898, rev. ed. 1925), which was an enlargement of his work for the *Dictionary.* Lee was knighted in 1911.

Lee, Tsung-Dao (so͝ong-dä'ō lē), 1926-, American physicist, b. China, Ph.D. Univ. of Chicago, 1950. He was a member (1951-53) of the Institute for Advanced Study, Princeton; and professor of theoretical physics there (1960-63). He also served as professor at Columbia (1953-60, 1963-). Lee is known for his studies in statistical mechanics, elementary particles, and astrophysics. He shared with C. N. Yang the 1957 Nobel Prize in Physics for researches refuting the law of conservation of PARITY.

Lee, William, 1739-95, American Revolutionary diplomat, b. Westmoreland co., Va.; brother of Arthur Lee, Francis L. Lee, and Richard H. Lee. He opened a business house in London in 1768 and later was a political supporter of John Wilkes and became (1775) an alderman of London. He accepted appointment by the Continental Congress as an agent for the newly created United States, and later attempted unsuccessfully to obtain recognition from both Austria and Prussia. He and a Dutch merchant made a draft of a possible U.S.-Dutch commercial treaty. The draft, which had no official sanction at all, Lee sent back to America. A copy of it, seized by the British when they captured Henry LAURENS, was used as a cause for warfare between Great Britain and the Netherlands. See his *Letters* 1766–83, ed. by W. C. Ford (3 vol., 1891; repr. 1971); B. J. Hendrick, *The Lees of Virginia* (1935).

Lee, William Henry Fitzhugh, known as **Rooney Lee,** 1837–91, Confederate cavalry general in the American Civil War, b. Arlington House, near Alexandria, Va.; son of Robert E. Lee. He entered Harvard in 1854 but left in 1857 when he secured a commission in the infantry. After serving under Albert S. Johnston in the campaign against the Mormons, he resigned (1859) and lived at White House, his Virginia plantation, until the Civil War. Like his cousin Fitzhugh LEE, Rooney served in J. E. B. Stuart's cavalry. Wounded at Brandy Station in June, 1863, he was subsequently captured. Upon his exchange in March, 1864, he was promoted to major general and served until the end of the war. From 1887 to his death, Lee was a Democratic Representative in Congress. See D. S. Freeman, *Lee's Lieutenants* (3 vol., 1942–44).

leech, predacious or parasitic annelid worm of the class Hirudinea, characterized by a cylindrical or slightly flattened body with suckers at either end for attaching to prey. The leech, like other annelids, is segmented, but its numerous surface folds obscure the internal segments. In many forms the mouth has three small jaws equipped with sharp teeth. The digestive tract has lateral pouches that hold enough of the leech's staple food, blood, to last for months. The reproductive system is complex; leeches are hermaphroditic and cross-fertilizing. Nearly all leeches are aquatic, abounding in freshwater ponds in temperate regions. Some are permanent parasites of man, horses, cattle, fish, and mollusks, but most are merely predatory. The salivary secretions of the leech contain hirudin, an anticoagulant. Medicinal leeches, once used by physicians to bleed patients suffering from almost any ailment, are now used in some parts of the world chiefly in the treatment of bruises such as black eyes. Certain small leeches of the E Mediterranean region may enter the bodies of humans and animals through drinking water and lodge as parasites in the mouth or the respiratory passages. Leeches are classified in the phylum ANNELIDA, class Hirudinea.

leechee: see LITCHI.

Leeds, Thomas Osborne, 1st **duke of:** see DANBY, THOMAS OSBORNE, EARL OF.

Leeds, county borough (1971 pop. 494, 971), West Riding of Yorkshire, N central England, on the Aire River. It lies between one of England's leading manufacturing regions on the west and south and an agricultural region on the north and east. Leeds is a communications and regional-government center and an important junction of transportation routes, both rail and water; canal and river connect the city with both east and west coasts. Manufactures include woolen goods (produced since the 14th cent.) and clothing, for which Leeds is a center of wholesale trade; metal goods—locomotives, machinery, farm implements, and airplane parts; leather goods; chemicals; and glass. Extensive slum-clearance and rehousing schemes have been successfully carried out since 1920. Yorkshire College, founded in 1874, became in 1887 a constituent college of Victoria Univ. and in 1904 the independent Univ. of Leeds. Among the other educational institutions is a 16th-century grammar school. Leeds has a classical town hall (1858) in which triennial musical festivals are held; of interest also are St. Peter's Church, the Cathedral of St. Anne, St. John's Church, and the City Art Gallery. Kirkstall Abbey, founded in the 12th cent., is near the city. Joseph Priestley was pastor at Mill Hill Chapel. In 1974, Leeds became part of the new metropolitan county of West Yorkshire.

Leeds, University of, at Leeds, England; established 1884 by the amalgamation of Yorkshire College (1874) with the Leeds School of Medicine (1831). The school was known as Yorkshire College until 1904 when its present name was adopted. It has faculties of arts, economic and social studies, education, law, science, applied science, and medicine. The College of the Resurrection and St. John's College of Education are affiliated.

leek: see ONION.

Lee Kuan Yew (lē kwän yo͞o, yü), 1923–, prime minister of Singapore (1959–). Educated in England as a lawyer, he founded (1954) the moderately leftist People's Action party. Shortly afterward he entered the legislature and helped to write Singapore's constitution for internal self-government within the British Commonwealth. In 1959 he became Singapore's first prime minister; in 1963 he led Singapore into the Federation of Malaysia, but political problems caused it to withdraw in 1965. A republic was proclaimed with Lee Kuan Yew continuing as prime minister. Under him Singapore followed a program of regional cooperation within a general policy of nonalignment.

Lee of Fareham, Arthur Hamilton Lee, 1st **Viscount** (fâr'əm), 1868–1947, British politician. He was (1900–1918) a Conservative member of the House of Commons. During World War I, Lee was military secretary to David Lloyd George (1916) and director general of food production (1917–18). He was later minister of agriculture (1919–21), first lord of the admiralty (1921–22), and a delegate to the Washington Naval Conference (1921–22). He was raised to the peerage in 1918. In 1921 he presented Chequers, his estate, to the nation as a country residence for the prime minister.

Leerdam (lârdäm'), town (1970 pop. 13,282), South Holland prov., S central Netherlands. It is famous for its glassware and ceramics.

Leesburg, city (1970 pop. 11,869), Lake co., N central Fla., in a hill and lake region; inc. 1875. Leesburg, named for Evander Lee, its founder, is a processing and shipping center in a citrus-fruit and truck-farm area. Cattle raising and the manufacture of such items as crates, boxes, concrete products, fertilizer, athletic equipment, and mobile homes are also important.

Lee's Summit, city (1970 pop. 16,230), Jackson co., W Mo., in the Kansas City metropolitan area; inc. 1868. Along the route of several major highways, Lee's Summit is a trucking center. Its manufactures include communications equipment, tools, machinery, and plastics. Nearby Richards-Gebaur Air Force Base is economically important to the city. Lee's Summit has several higher-education facilities.

Leeuwarden (lā'vär"dən), Frisian *Ljouwert,* city (1971 pop. 88,644), capital of Friesland prov., N Netherlands. It is the center of an agricultural and dairying region and has a noted cattle market. Manufactures include food products, clothing, and artificial silk. Chartered in 1435, Leeuwarden was (16th–18th cent.) the center of a goldworking and silverworking industry. There are many structures dating from the 16th and 17th cent., notably the huge brick Oldehove Tower. The large Frisian Museum is there.

Leeuwenhoek, Antony van (än'tōnē vän lā'vənho͝ok"), 1632–1723, Dutch student of natural history and maker of microscopes, b. Delft. His use of lenses in examining cloth as a draper's apprentice probably led to his interest in lens making. He assembled over 247 microscopes, some of which magnified objects 270 times. In the course of his examination of innumerable microorganisms and tissue samples, he gave the first complete descriptions of bacteria, protozoa (which he called animalcules), spermatozoa, and striped muscle. He also observed the red blood cells in his detailed study of capillary circulation. He was elected to the Royal Society of England in recognition of his work. See his collected letters (Vol. I–VI, 1939–61); study by Clifford Dobell (1960).

Leeward Islands (lo͞o'ərd, yo͞o'-, lē'-), northern group of the Lesser Antilles in the West Indies, extending SE from Puerto Rico to the Windward Islands. The principal islands are the VIRGIN ISLANDS of the United States; the French island of GUADELOUPE and its dependencies; the Dutch islands of SAINT EUSTATIUS and SABA; the jointly owned (Dutch and French) SAINT MARTIN; and the British Leeward Islands, grouped into ANTIGUA, SAINT KITTS-NEVIS, MONTSERRAT, and the British Virgin Islands. Largely volcanic in origin, the Leeward Islands have lush, subtropical vegetation, rich soil, and abundant rainfall. The warm, delightful climate is tempered by the surrounding water so that there is little variation in temperature. Most of the islands have become popular winter resorts. Products for the most part are agricultural—fruits, vegetables, sugar, cotton, coffee, and tobacco. Although the population varies from island to island, in general blacks predominate; whites are of French or English descent. Columbus discovered the Leeward Islands in 1493, but settlement began only after the British arrived in the 17th cent. Sir Thomas Warner, sent to St. Kitts in 1623, was made governor general of the yet uncolonized neighboring islands (Nevis, Antigua, Montserrat, and Barbuda), and in the same year the Frenchman, Pierre Bélain d'Esnambuc, also established a colony on St. Kitts. By 1632, when the English had settled the neighboring islands, the sharp, three-way colonial conflict of England, France, and Spain had begun. The Spanish were forced from the struggle, but for nearly two centuries the islands were pawns in the Anglo-French worldwide wars. They changed hands with each fresh attack by British or French forces and were reshuffled in ownership whenever a new treaty was signed. Their final disposition did not come until the end of the Napoleonic Wars in 1815. Carleen O'Loughlin, *Economic and Political Change in the Leeward and Windward Islands* (1968); Ellis Gladwin, *Living in the Changing Caribbean* (1970).

Le Fanu, Joseph Sheridan (lĕ'fənyo͞o), 1814–73, Irish author. He spent his early career as a journalist. In 1863 he began to produce a series of stories that are noted for their reflections of Irish life and for their atmosphere of the supernatural and mysterious. His two best works are the novels *The House by the Churchyard* (1863) and *Uncle Silas* (1864). Other works include *In a Glass Darkly* (1872) and *The Purcell Papers* (1880), both collections of stories. See his ghost stories collected in *Best Ghost Stories,* ed. by E. F. Bleiler (1964); study by M. H. Begnal (1971).

Lefebvre, François Joseph (fräNswä' zhôzĕf' ləfĕ'-vrə), 1755–1820, marshal of France. He rose from the ranks in the French Revolutionary Wars and distinguished himself under Napoleon Bonaparte (later Emperor Napoleon I). He aided Napoleon in the coup d'etat of 18 BRUMAIRE and was later made (1803) duke of Danzig. His wife, who had been a washerwoman, caused some sensation through her unconventional manners and is the heroine of Victorien Sardou's play *Madame Sans-Gêne.*

Lefebvre, Georges (zhôrzh), 1874–1959, French historian, an authority on the French Revolutionary period. From 1937 to 1945 he held the chair of French Revolutionary history at the Sorbonne, and he founded the Institut d'histoire de la Révolution française. Lefebvre's mastery of statistical and quantitative research is evident in *Les Paysans du Nord pendant la Révolution française* (1924), and his brilliance as a stylist is demonstrated in *The Coming of the French Revolution* (1939, tr. 1947). Although influenced by Marxism, he was, like his model Jean Jaurès, predominantly an empiricist and a humanist; he saw in history a complex interaction of social, economic, and political phenomena. His *La Révolution française* (rev. ed. 1951) has been translated in two volumes as *The French Revolution* (1962–64) and *The French Revolution From 1793 to 1799* (1964). This study is considered the authoritative work on the subject. Another work is the judicious biography *Napoléon* (4th ed. 1953; tr., 2 vols., 1969).

Lefèvre d'Étaples, Jacques (zhäk ləfĕv'rə dātäp'lə), c.1450–1536, French theologian and humanist. A priest, he studied in Italy, where he was influenced by Neoplatonism. In 1507, he was made librarian at the abbey of Saint-Germain-des-Prés. He became famous for his commentary on the epistles of St. Paul (1512) and his edition of the works of the mystic, Nicholas of Cusa (1514). Caught up in the spirit of criticism of the abuses of the Roman Catholic Church, he became a leading figure of Christian humanism. Although advocating some of the ideas later integral to the Reformation, he believed, like Erasmus, in reform from within and refused to break with the church. Nevertheless, he was subjected to suspicion and persecution. In 1521, the Sorbonne condemned as heretical his book on the three Marys, but Francis I and his sister Margaret of Navarre prevented further action against him. Forced to seek refuge in Strasbourg in 1525, he returned the following year as tutor to the royal children and librarian in the château at Blois. His last years were spent at Nérac, under the protection of Margaret of Navarre. The Protestant reformer Guillaume FAREL was one of his pupils. Lefèvre d'Étaples translated the Bible into French (1523–30). He was also known as Jacobus Faber Stapulensis.

Lefkosha, Cyprus: see NICOSIA.

Lefort, François (fräNswä' ləfôr'), 1656–99, Swiss soldier of fortune in Russian service, b. Geneva. He was one of the early boon companions of PETER I (Peter the Great) and remained Peter's favorite until his death. A drunkard and libertine, Lefort nevertheless had great influence. Some believe that he advised Peter's attack on Azov, helping in its capture from Turkey (1696), and counseled Peter's apprenticeship abroad. Made a general and an admiral, Lefort helped to reorganize the Russian army and to create the Russian navy.

left, in politics, the more radical wing in any legislative body or party. The designation apparently originated in the French National Assembly of 1789, where the radicals were seated to the left of the presiding officer.

left-handedness: see HANDEDNESS.

leg, one of the paired limbs of an animal used for support of the body and for locomotion. Properly, the human leg is that portion of the extremity between the foot and the thigh. This section of the human leg contains two long bones, the tibia and the fibula. The upper end of the tibia joins with the lower end of the thighbone (femur) and forms a hinged joint. The kneecap (patella), a flat triangular-shaped bone, surrounds and protects this joint. The lower end of both tibia and fibula join with the talus, a bone in the foot, to form the ankle joint. The upper end of the femur, which is the longest bone in the body, forms a ball and socket joint where it meets the hipbone. In quadrupeds, both the hind and fore limbs are referred to as legs.

legacy, bequest by WILL of personal PROPERTY, similar in many respects to a GIFT *causa mortis.* A legacy ordinarily is distinguished from a devise, which transfers real property by will. The person who receives a legacy is called a legatee. Legacies are of various types. A specific legacy bequeaths a designated object, e.g., a named painting. A general legacy is a sum of money to be paid out of any assets of the estate. The residuary legacy is all of the deceased's personal property otherwise undistributed.

Le Gallienne, Eva (ləgăl'yən), 1899–, American actress, producer, director, and translator, b. London; daughter of Richard Le Gallienne. She made her debut in London in 1915 and in New York City the next year. She achieved distinction in 1921 in Molnar's *Liliom* and became known as an outstanding interpreter of Ibsen, whose works she translated. In 1926 she founded and directed the Civic Repertory Theatre in New York, the first professional group of its kind. In 1946 she was a cofounder, with Margaret Webster, of the American Repertory Theatre and produced numerous classic revivals. In 1968 she directed her translation of *The Cherry Orchard* on Broadway. See her autobiographies (1934 and 1953, repr. 1974).

Le Gallienne, Richard, 1866–1947, English man of letters. As literary critic and contributor to the *Yellow Book,* he was associated with the fin-de-siècle aesthetes of the 1890s before becoming a resident of the United States. His works include the poems *Volumes in Folio* (1889), the novel *Quest of the Golden Girl* (1896), and books of reminiscences, *The Romantic '90's* (1925) and *From a Paris Garret* (1936). His works were period pieces and not of lasting importance. He was the father of Eva Le Gallienne. See his life and letters, ed. by Richard Whittington-Egan and Geoffrey Smerdon (1960).

Legal Tender cases, lawsuits brought to the U.S. Supreme Court involving the constitutionality of the Legal Tender Act of 1862, which was passed to meet currency needs during the Civil War. The act authorized the issue of $150 million in "United States notes" (see GREENBACK) without any reserve or specie basis. The notes (about $450 million had been issued by the end of the war) depreciated in terms of gold and became the subject of controversy, particularly because debts contracted earlier could be paid in this cheaper currency. Many cases concerning the greenbacks were entered in the courts. The Supreme Court decided two of them in 1868 (*Lane County* vs. *Oregon* and *Bronson* vs. *Rodes*) without passing on the question of constitutionality. In *Hepburn* vs. *Griswold* (1870) the majority opinion, which was written by Chief Justice Samuel P. Chase, declared the act unconstitutional; but with changes in its membership, the court reversed its decision and, in *Knox* vs. *Lee* and *Parker* vs. *Davis* (1871), ruled that the act was valid. The constitutionality of the act was more widely sustained in *Juillard* vs. *Greenman* (1884).

Legaré, Hugh Swinton (ləgrē'), 1797–1843, American lawyer and public official, b. Charleston, S.C. He was admitted to the bar in 1822, served in the South Carolina legislature (1820–22, 1824–30), and was state attorney general (1830–32). He was a founder, editor (1828–32), and a chief contributor to the *Southern Review.* From 1832 to 1836 he was chargé d'affaires at Brussels. A strong opponent of NULLIFICATION, he was elected (1837) to Congress as a Union Democrat. When, on William Henry Harrison's death, John Tyler succeeded as President, Legaré became (1841) Attorney General. He also became (1843) Secretary of State ad interim after Daniel Webster's resignation, but he died two months later.

Legaspi, Miguel López de: see LÓPEZ DE LEGASPI.

Legaspi (ləgă'spē, lāgä'-), city (1970 est. pop. 84,700), capital of Albay prov., SE Luzon, the Philippines, on Albay Gulf. It is a large seaport and the southern terminus of the Manila railroad. Copra and hemp are shipped. Founded c.1639 as Albay, it was renamed Legaspi in 1925. In World War II it was the scene (Dec. 12, 1941) of a large Japanese landing, part of a pincers movement on Manila. Towering directly behind the city is the spectacular active volcano, Mt. Mayon. Its eruption in 1814 severely damaged the town and killed over 1,000 people.

legate (lĕg'ət) [from Lat. *legare*=to send], one sent as a representative of a state or of some high authority. In Roman history a legate was sent by the senate to the provinces as an envoy of the emperor. Sometime during the 12th cent. the word came into use to designate a papal ambassador. There are various types of papal legate, including the *legatus a latere,* a cardinal commissioned for a special confidential assignment as a representative of the pope; the nuncio or internuncio, who represents the Holy See, both temporally and ecclesiastically, in countries that exchange ambassadors with the Vatican (see NUNCIO, APOSTOLIC); and the apostolic delegate, a papal representative in a country, such as the United States, that does not exchange ambassadors with the Vatican.

legation: see DIPLOMATIC SERVICE; EXTRATERRITORIALITY.

Legendre, Adrien Marie (ädrēăN' märē' ləzhăN'-drə), 1752–1833, French mathematician. He is noted especially for his work on the theory of numbers, on which he wrote an essay (1798) containing the law of quadratic reciprocity as well as several supplements, all later incorporated in a definitive work, *Théorie des nombres* (1830). The results of his long study of elliptic integrals appeared in *Traité des fonctions elliptiques* (3 vol., 1825–32). He invented independently of C. F. Gauss, and was the first to state in print (1806), the method of least squares, and he collaborated in drawing up centesimal trigonometric tables. He taught at the École militaire, Paris, and at the École normale and was associated with the bureau of longitudes from 1812. His *Éléments de géométrie* (1794, tr. 1867) was an influential textbook.

Léger, Alexis Saint-Legér: see PERSE, ST.-JOHN.

Léger, Fernand (fĕrnăN' lāzhā'), 1881–1955, French painter. Léger first studied architecture, then he began to paint, studying briefly at the École des Beaux-Arts. He became known for his cubist paintings in 1910, and a modified cubism is apparent in much of his subsequent work. In works such as *The City* (1919; Phila. Mus. of Art), Léger celebrated the machine in a naïve, energetic style characterized by flat tones of pure color, black, white, and gray. He taught painting in Paris and New York City. Two of his mural designs were executed by a pupil at the United Nations, New York. Several of his paintings are in the Museum of Modern Art, New York City. See studies by Katharine Kuh (1953), R. L. Delevoy (tr. 1962), and Jean Casson and Jean Leymarie (1974).

Legh, Rowland: see LEE, ROWLAND.

Leghorn (lĕg'hôrn), Ital. *Livorno,* city (1971 pop. 173,774), capital of Livorno prov., Tuscany, central Italy, on the Ligurian Sea and on the Aurelian Way. It is a busy commercial, industrial, and tourist center and is one of the most important ports of Italy. Manufactures include refined petroleum, iron and steel, chemicals, and electrical equipment. The city has major shipyards and a fishing industry. A fortified castle in the Middle Ages, Leghorn was developed (16th cent.) into a flourishing city by the Medici. In 1590, Ferdinand I, grand duke of Tuscany, made it a free port and opened it to all religious and political refugees. The city was badly damaged in World War II. Points of interest include the cathedral (16th cent., restored after 1945) and the remains of the 17th-century city wall. The Italian naval academy is there.

Leghorn chicken, relatively small, white-colored breed of POULTRY that currently dominates the American egg-producing class. The bird, as bred today, produces a good number of chalk white eggs, a feature which has brought it to the forefront of modern commercial egg production. Although only the "single comb" variety is popular today, many other strains with large egg, better shell, better interior egg qualities, or other desirable traits, are retained as breeding stock.

legion, large unit of the Roman army. It came into prominence c.400 B.C. Originally it was a phalanx consisting of from 3,000 to 4,000 men in eight ranks. The first six ranks were called hoplites and were heavily armed. The last two were velites and were only lightly armed. Marcus Furius Camillus is traditionally regarded as the great organizer of the legion after the burning of Rome. Under Camillus the hoplites were divided into three groups: the hastati (youngest men), the principes, and the triarii (oldest). Within the legion was the cohort, consisting of one maniple of each of the three groups plus 120 velites and a cavalry unit about 30 strong. A legion was composed of 10 cohorts and comprised about 5,000 men. In Caesar's time each legion had a commander who was responsible to the Senate, 6 tribunes, a legate, a prefect, and some 60 centurions. Training was hard, with much difficult drilling to prepare the men especially in shock tactics and for rapid marches. The standard weapons were the spear (*pilum*) and (after Scipio Africanus Major conquered Spain) the short thrusting sword (*gladius*). The characteristic emblems of the legions were eagles inscribed SPQR [*Senatus Populusque Romanus*—the Senate and the people of Rome], and they carried the eagles in triumph over the far reaches of the empire for hundreds of years. Upon the legions rested to a large extent the glory of Rome. They were primarily heavy infantry and were vulnerable chiefly to quickly moving cavalry and archers (e.g., the defeat of Marcus Lucinius Crassus at Carrhae) and to guerrilla fighters (e.g., the famous defeat of Varus by the Germans). After the Germanic invasions had begun, the Roman army was increasingly staffed with Germans, and the legions, proving unable to match the barbarian horsemen, disappeared. See Henry M. D. Parker, *The Roman Legions* (1928, repr. 1958); Graham Webster, *The Roman Imperial Army of the First and Second Centuries* (1969).

Legion of Honor: see DECORATIONS, CIVIL AND MILITARY.

legislative apportionment, subdivision of a political body (e.g., a state or province) for the purpose of electing legislative representatives. In the United States, the Constitution requires that Congressional representatives be elected on the basis of population. State legislatures, not bound by the constitutional strictures, were apportioned according to considerations including population, as well as geographic size, special interests, and political divisions such as counties or towns. This often resulted in unrepresentative, minority control of the state legislature. The state legislatures were responsible for drawing up districts for the purpose of electing representatives to Congress. GERRYMANDERING often resulted. In some states legislatures did not redistrict, despite population shifts, for as many as sixty years. This was the case until 1962 when the U.S. Supreme Court ruled in BAKER VS. CARR that a voter could challenge legislative apportionment on the grounds that it violated the equal protection clause of the Fourteenth Amendment to the Constitution. Within nine months of the decision suits for reapportionment were brought in at least 34 states. In 1964, in *Reynolds* vs. *Sims,* the Supreme Court ruled that population, i.e., the one-person, one-vote principle, must be the primary consideration in apportionment plans for both houses of state legislatures.

legislature, representative assembly empowered to enact statute law. Generally the representatives who compose a legislature are constitutionally elected by a broad spectrum of the population. While rules of law have always been a concern for society, the use of legislatures for their establishment is a relatively modern phenomenon. In earlier times, human laws were considered part of the universal natural law, discoverable through the use of reason rather than made by the declaration of men. With the growth of belief in positive law, the increasing need in emerging modern society for adaptable law, and the decline of monarchial power, however, legislatures with law-making powers came about. One of the oldest legislatures (with the possible exception of the Icelandic ALTHING) is the English PARLIAMENT, which, although originally nonelective and advisory to the king, has evolved over the centuries to the point where it is now elected through universal suffrage and possesses the sovereign power of the state. In its early history, the English Parliament, like the STATES-GENERAL of France and the DIET of the Holy Roman Empire consisted of representatives chosen according to classes or estates (see ESTATE, in constitutional law). Out of the estates arose the typical bicameral system, in which an upper house represented the nobility and clergy and a lower house represented the bourgeoisie. The CONGRESS OF THE UNITED STATES is bicameral, but rather than being rooted in societal class differences, it is based upon principles of federalism. The founders of the American republic, in order to assure acceptance of the Constitution, gave each state equal REPRESENTATION in the Senate, as a gesture to the smaller states, and made membership in the House of Representatives dependent upon population size, thereby favoring the larger states. Most of the American state legislatures are also bicameral. Although the upper house assemblies of many countries are still nonelective or hereditary, they are generally much weaker than the popularly elected lower house and carry out only minor functions. Those states with unicameral legislatures include Czechoslovakia, Finland, and Israel. Two common types of legislature are those in which the executive and the legislative branches are clearly separated, as in the United States, and those in which members of the executive branch are chosen from the legislative membership, as in Great Britain. Respectively termed presidential and parliamentary systems, there are innumerable variations of the two forms. It should be noted that while popular assemblies of citizens, as in direct DEMOCRACY, are often called legislatures, the term should properly be applied only to those assemblies that perform a representative function. Some of the modern national legislatures are the Althing (Iceland), the CORTES (Spain), the Knesset (Israel), the DÁIL ÉIREANN (Ireland), the BUNDESTAG (West Germany), the FOLKETING (Denmark), the RIKSDAG (Sweden), the STORTING (Norway), and the Supreme Soviet (USSR). The term *parliament* is often applied to national legislatures without regard to the official designation. See Robert Luce, *Legislative Assemblies* (1924); Council of State Governments, *American Legislatures* (1959); W. Ivor Jennings, *Parliament* (2d ed. 1957, repr. 1969); J. B. Fordham, *The State Legislative Institution* (1959); J. C. Wahlke, ed., *Legislative Behavior* (1959); American Assembly, *State Legislatures in American Politics* (1966); George S. Blair, *American Legislatures: Structure and Process* (1967); W. H. Agor, ed., *Latin American Legislatures—Their Role and Influence* (1971).

legitimation, act of giving the status of legitimacy to a child whose parents were not married at the time the child was born. This is generally accomplished by the subsequent marriage of the parents. Under the common law, legitimation by this process was not allowed, although that rule came under the displeasure of the church. It was not until 1926 that a statute was passed in England allowing legitimation by subsequent marriage. In the United States, legitimation by subsequent marriage is the general rule. In some states there are, moreover, special judicial proceedings for the legitimation of a child. In other states one or both of the parents may adopt the child. See BASTARD.

Legnano (lānyä'nō), city (1971 pop. 47,635), Lombardy, NW Italy, near Milan. Manufactures of this important industrial center include chemicals, plastics, steel, and textiles. Near Legnano the LOMBARD LEAGUE defeated (1176) Emperor Frederick I.

Legnica (lĕgnē'tsä), Ger. *Liegnitz*, city (1970 pop. 75,843), SW Poland, on the Kaczawa River. A center of a vegetable-growing region, it also has manufactures of textiles, machinery, and chemicals. Chartered in 1252, it was until 1675 the capital of a duchy ruled by a branch of the PIAST dynasty. In the War of the Austrian Succession it was acquired (1742) by Prussia. The city was heavily damaged in World War II, but it has retained its 11th-century castle (rebuilt 1835), parts of its medieval walls and towers, and two churches (13th–14th cent.), one of which contains the tombs of the Piasts.

Legros, Alphonse (älfôNs' ləgrō'), 1837–1911, French etcher, painter, and sculptor. Legros's draftsmanship was similar to that of Ingres, but his approach was sentimental. He moved to England in 1863 and became a professor of fine arts at the Slade School of Art, London. Best known as a graphic artist, he depicted religious subjects, peasant scenes, and landscapes, which sometimes display a taste for the grotesque. His *Angelus* (1859) is in the Louvre.

Leguía, Augusto Bernardino (ougo͞os'tō bärnärdē'nō lāgē'ä), 1863–1932, president of Peru (1908–12, 1919–30). In his second administration Leguía promulgated a new constitution (1920), expanded and developed Lima, and considerably modernized his country, but increased the national debt and suppressed all opposition harshly. In 1929 the TACNA-ARICA CONTROVERSY with Chile, which had begun in 1883, was finally resolved, but Leguía was bitterly criticized for accepting the compromise. Coupled with the economic depression, his financial dealings, and his harsh rule, the reaction brought about his overthrow. He was charged with misappropriating government funds and imprisoned.

legume (lĕ'gyo͞om, lĭgyo͞om'), common name for any plant of the family Leguminosae, which is called also the PULSE, legume, pea, or bean family. The word is often used loosely in the plural for vegetables in general. Botanically, a legume is the characteristic fruit of the pulse family plants, called also leguminous plants. It is a POD which splits along two sides, with the seeds attached along one of the sutures. The family Leguminosae is classified in the division MAGNOLIOPHYTA, class Magnoliopsida, order Rosales.

Leh (lā), town (1971 pop. 5,506), E Kashmir, N India. It is the chief town of the Ladakh district in Indian-controlled Kashmir. It lies at an altitude of c.11,500 ft (3,500 m). Much of the trade between India and Tibet passed through Leh until 1959, when fighting broke out between India and China. The region around Leh was contested by India and China in the 1960s. The palace of the former rulers of W Tibet and a Lamaist monastery are in Leh.

Lehabim (lēhā'bĭm), African people, perhaps the same as the LUDIM. Gen. 10.13 (same as 1 Chron. 1.11).

Lehár, Franz (fränts lĕ'här), 1870–1948, Hungarian composer of operettas. After completing studies at the Prague Conservatory (1882–88), he began a career as a conductor of military bands and settled in Vienna. There, following the success of his first operetta, *Wiener Frauen* (1902), he devoted himself to composition. He endowed such works as *Der Graf von Luxemburg* (1909) and *Zigeunerliebe* (1910) with his engaging melodies, capturing the frivolous gaiety that pervaded Viennese life early in the century. *Die lustige Witwe* (*The Merry Widow,* 1905), his outstanding work, had international success.

Lehi, in the Bible: see RAMATH-LEHI.

Lehigh, river, 103 mi (166 km) long, rising in NE Pa. and flowing generally SE to the Delaware River at Easton. The river flows through a major industrial area. Rich anthracite-coal deposits are mined in the valley. Allentown and Bethlehem are the largest cities on the river.

Lehigh University, at Bethlehem, Pa.; undergraduate for men, graduate coeducational; chartered and opened 1866 by Asa Packer.

Lehman, Herbert Henry (lē'mən), 1878–1963, American political leader, b. New York City. At first an executive of a textile firm, he became (1908) a partner in the family banking house of Lehman Brothers. In World War I he was assistant director of purchase, storage, and traffic of the U.S. army. He was finance chairman of the Democratic National Committee in 1928, the year he was elected lieutenant governor of New York state. After serving another term as lieutenant governor, Lehman was elected (1932) governor of the state, succeeding Franklin Delano Roosevelt. He was reelected twice for two-year terms and in 1938 for a four-year term. In the course of Lehman's gubernatorial administrations, state income taxes were cut, a huge budgetary surplus was accumulated, and much liberal legislation was enacted. He refused to run again in 1942 and was appointed (1943) director of the United Nations Relief and Rehabilitation Administration. He resigned (1946) because of ill health. In a special senatorial election in 1949, he defeated John Foster Dulles to fill the unexpired term of Robert F. Wagner, Sr. Reelected in 1950, he was a leading liberal and an opponent of Senator Joseph R. McCarthy. Retiring from the Senate in 1956, he continued to be a leader of the reform faction in the New York Democratic party. See biography by Allan Nevins (1963).

Lehman Caves National Monument: see NATIONAL PARKS AND MONUMENTS (table).

Lehman College of the City University of New York; coeducational; founded 1931 as the Bronx campus of Hunter College. In 1968 it became a separate liberal arts college under the administration of the City University of New York (see NEW YORK, CITY UNIVERSITY OF). Residents of New York City are admitted to the baccalaureate program tuition free.

Lehmann, John, 1907–, English poet, editor, and publisher. Educated at Trinity College, Cambridge, he began working at Virginia and Leonard Woolf's Hogarth Press in 1931 and managed it from 1938 to 1946. In that year he founded a publishing house, John Lehmann, Ltd., which he directed until 1952. He also founded the *London Magazine* and edited it from 1952 to 1961. Lehmann is perhaps best remembered as the editor of *New Writing,* an English book-periodical that appeared (under various titles) about twice yearly between 1936 and 1946; it included work by writers considered too radical to be published elsewhere and came to be considered an important influence on 20th-century English literature. Lehmann also edited the paperback *Penguin New Writing* from 1946 to 1950. Among his works are the volumes of poetry *A Garden Revisited* (1931), *The Age of the Dragon* (1951), and *Collected Poems* (1961); and the study *A Nest of Tigers: The Sitwells in Their Time* (1969). Lehmann's sister, **Rosamond Lehmann,** b. 1905–, is also a writer. She is noted for her delicately crafted studies of women, particularly of young girls. Her first novel, *Dusty Answer* (1927), concerning a deep emotional attachment between two college girls, was highly successful. *Invitation to the Waltz* (1932) describes the launching of a young girl into society; *The Weather in the Streets* (1936) treats the same girl 10 years later, after an abortion and a divorce. Lehmann's other works include *The Gypsy's Baby and Other Stories* (1946) and the novel *The Echoing Grove* (1953). See her autobiographical *The Swan in the Evening: Fragments of an Inner Life* (1967).

Lehmann, Lilli (lā'män), 1848–1929, German operatic soprano. She made her debut in 1865 in Prague and in 1870 joined the Royal Opera, Berlin. Her stature as one of the greatest singers of her time was realized in London and in New York City where she was a member of the Metropolitan Opera Company (1885–90). Although she began her career as a coloratura, she became most famous as a Wagnerian singer. Her vast repertory of 170 roles also included Italian and French works. In addition, she was an outstanding interpreter of lieder and a great teacher, Geraldine Farrar being among her pupils. Her *Meine Gesangskunst* was translated by Richard Aldrich as *How to Sing* (1902, 3d ed. 1924). See her autobiography (tr. 1914).

Lehmann, Lotte (lā'mən, Ger. lā'män), 1888–, German-American soprano. Lehmann studied at the Berlin State Conservatory. She made her debut in Hamburg in 1909 and was a member of the Vienna State Opera (1914–38). After her North American debut (1930) in Chicago, she sang with the Metropolitan Opera (1934–45). She wrote *Eternal Flight* (tr. 1938), a novel; *Midway in My Song* (tr. 1938), her autobiography; and *More than Singing* (tr. 1945), on technique and repertoire.

Lehmbruck, Wilhelm (vĭl'hĕlm lām'bro͝ok), 1881–1919, German sculptor. He studied at Düsseldorf and went to Paris in 1910. Influenced at first by Rodin, Brancusi, and Maillol, he later arrived at his own highly individual style. His large, elongated figures express a dramatic poignancy. *Woman Kneeling* (Mus. of Modern Art, New York City) is generally regarded as his best work. Often considered the greatest German sculptor of the 20th cent., Lehmbruck committed suicide in Berlin at the age of 38. See study by Werner Hofmann (1958).

Leibl, Wilhelm (vĭl'hĕlm lī'bəl), 1844–1900, German genre and portrait painter. He studied in Munich where numerous painters came under his influence; the "Leibl group" shared his predilection for the realistic perfection of the old masters. He left Munich to paint the rural people of Bavaria, owing much in his technique to an understanding of Holbein's works. His most famous picture, *Three Women in Church* (1878–81; Hamburg), marks the height of meticulous naturalism but is also a subtly composed study.

Leibniz or **Leibnitz, Gottfried Wilhelm, Baron von** (both: gôt'frēt vĭl'hĕlm bärôn' fan lĭp'nĭts), 1646–1716, German philosopher and mathematician. Although known primarily as a philosopher, Leibniz's scholarship embraced the physical sciences, history, law, diplomacy, and logic. The recognition of his work in logic came quite late; manuscripts published in the 20th cent. mark him as the founder of symbolic logic. After studying at Leipzig, his native city, and at Jena, he became a doctor of law at Altdorf (1666). Constantly occupied with practical political concerns, Leibniz never accepted an academic position. He was (1666–73) in the diplomatic service of the elector of Mainz, who employed him on several political projects; one of these was a plan to persuade King Louis XIV of France to attack Egypt and thereby to divert his attention from Germany. While in Paris (1672–76) he came into contact with some of the foremost minds of Europe. About that time he developed, independently of Newton, the infinitesimal calculus. Leibniz's calculus was published in 1684, three years before Newton's, and his system of notation was universally adopted. From 1676 he was employed by the duke of Brunswick-Lüneburg (later the elector of Hanover), whom he served as privy councillor, librarian, and historian. This association brought him close to the elector of Brandenburg (soon to be king of Prussia), who was persuaded by Leibniz to establish a scientific academy at Berlin. In 1700 he became its first president. Leibniz's philosophical writings are occasional pieces, addressed to various people. The two published in his lifetime were *Essais de Théodicée sur la bonté de Dieu, la liberté de l'homme, et l'origine du mal* (1710) and *Monadology* (1714). It was largely these works that influenced Christian von WOLFF, whose popularization of the Leibnizian system became the standard academic philosophy in 18th-century Germany. Leibniz's major philosophical work, *Nouveaux Essais sur l'entendement humain* (1704), contains the views of Leibniz on points raised in Locke's *Essay Concerning Human Understanding.* Because of Locke's death, however, it was not published until 1765. The publication of *Nouveaux Essais* in 1765 was important because it revealed for the first time the "true Leibniz" as opposed to the popularized version of Wolff, and it had a decisive effect on Immanuel Kant and the whole German Enlightenment. Leibniz's philosophy is a consistent rationalism. The universe forms one context in which each occurrence can be seen in relation to every other. Since the universe is the result of a divine plan, Leibniz calls it the best of all possible worlds; for this he was satirized by Voltaire in *Candide.* Leibniz's assertion, however, does not imply an unqualified optimism, since evil is a necessary ingredient in even the best of all possible worlds. The ultimate constituents of the universe are monads or simple substances, each of which represents the universe from a different point of view. Being simple, monads are immaterial and thus cannot act. Apparent interaction is explained in terms of the principle of preestablished harmony. The principle of continuity as expressed in the phrase "nature makes no leaps" is another part of Leibniz's rationalism. The monads are arranged in an infinitely ascending scale, based on the distinctness with which each represents the universe. All monads have perception (consciousness), but only rational monads have apperception (self-consciousness). A basic distinction in Leibniz's logic is that between "truths of reason," or necessary propositions, whose principle is the law of noncontradiction, and "truths of fact," or contingent propositions, based on the principle of sufficient reason. The principle has its root in the divine intellect, and its most important expression is the law of causality. With the decline of interest in metaphysics in contemporary philosophy, recent studies have tended to emphasize Leibniz's significance in mathematics and logic. However, Leibniz's metaphysics have not been neglected but rather reinterpreted in light of his mathematical and logical works. See his political writings, ed. and tr. by Patrick Riley (1972); G. H. Parkinson, *Logic and Reality in Leibniz's Metaphysics* (1965); Hidé Ishiguro, *Leibniz's Philosophy of Logic and Language* (1972); L. E. Loemaker, *Struggle for Synthesis* (1972); Ivor Leclerc, comp., *The Philosophy of Leibniz and the Modern World* (1973).

Leicester, Robert Dudley, earl of (lĕs'tər), 1532?–1588, English courtier and favorite of Queen ELIZABETH I. A younger son of John Dudley, duke of NORTHUMBERLAND, he was early brought into the society of Edward VI and Princess (later Queen) Elizabeth. Knighted at an early age, Dudley married Amy ROBSART in 1549 and received preferment from the crown. Upon Edward's death (1553), he aided his father in the plot to place Lady Jane GREY upon the throne, was sent to the Tower of London, and condemned to death. He was later released, pardoned, and, after military service in France, restored to his rights (perhaps through the intervention of Mary I's husband, Philip II of Spain). On the accession of Elizabeth (1558), Dudley was made master of the horse and later a privy councillor. Within a year he was acknowledged as her favorite and as her most probable choice for a husband. His wife's mysterious death in 1560 darkened his reputation. He then proposed (1561) to Philip II to restore Roman Catholicism in England in return for Philip's endorsement of Dudley's marriage to Elizabeth. By 1563, Elizabeth seems to have realized the impracticality of marriage with Dudley, but her personal feeling toward him did not change, and he remained in a position of influence at court. She offered his hand to MARY QUEEN OF SCOTS and, to facilitate this scheme, created him earl of Leicester (1564), but the plan was halted by Mary's marriage to Lord Darnley. Leicester married secretly in 1573 and in 1578 (perhaps bigamously) wed the countess of Essex, an act that led to a temporary estrangement from Elizabeth. From about 1564, Leicester was leader at court of the Puritan party, which desired war with Spain. In 1585 he was named commander of an expedition to help the United Provinces of the Netherlands against Spain. His military efforts were undistinguished, and he enraged Elizabeth by accepting (1586) the title of governor of the Netherlands. He was finally recalled in 1587. Upon the approach of the Spanish Armada (1588), Leicester was appointed captain general of the armies. Leicester was a patron of letters and the drama. The first royal patent for actors was granted to his company. See Milton Waldman, *Elizabeth and Leicester* (1944, repr. 1969); Eleanor Rosenberg, *Leicester, Patron of Letters* (1955); R. C. Strong and J. A. Van Dorsten, *Leicester's Triumph* (1964).

Leicester, Simon de Montfort, earl of: see MONTFORT, SIMON DE.

Leicester, Thomas William Coke, earl of: see COKE, THOMAS WILLIAM.

Leicester (lĕs'tər), county borough (1971 pop. 283,549), county town of Leicestershire, central England. It is connected by canals with the Trent River and London and is a railway center. Leicester was of industrial importance as early as the 14th cent.; the making of hosiery and shoes are long-established industries. Other manufactures are chemicals, aniline dyes, textiles, textile and woodworking machinery, and light-metal products. Leicester was the Ratae Coritanorum, or Ratae, of the Romans, whose Fosse Way passes nearby. It was also a town of the ancient Britons and was one of the Five Boroughs of the Danes. Its antiquities include the Jewry Wall, a Roman structure 18 ft (5 m) high and 70 ft (21 m) long (near which extensive Roman remains have been found); remains of the ancient Norman castle in whose banquet hall county assizes are now held; and ruins of an abbey founded in 1143, in which Cardinal Wolsey died in 1530. Several of the churches (St. Nicholas, St. Mary de Castro, and All Saints) show Norman work, and Trinity Hospital is a 14th-century foundation. Richard III stayed in Leicester the night before he was killed in the battle of Bosworth Field; his body was brought back to Leicester for burial. The University College, now the Univ. of Leicester, was founded in 1918 and chartered as a university in 1957.

Leicester sheep (lĕs'tər), breed of sheep originated from native stock as mutton producers in Leicestershire, England, by the English livestock breeder Robert Bakewell (c.1755). English Leicesters have white faces and legs, broad backs, and thick flesh. They mature early and have heavy fleeces, the wool hanging in compact locks. Offspring of a cross of Merino ewes and English Leicester rams provide some of the choicest of all wools. The Border Leicester strain was developed in the border counties of England and Scotland by crossbreeding English Leicesters and Cheviots. Their heads are free of wool, their bodies square, and their carriage alert. Leicesters were first brought to the United States in colonial times and are bred in small numbers in parts of the N United States. In Canada Border Leicesters are more common than the English.

Leicestershire (lĕs'tərshĭr), county (1971 pop. 771,213), 832 sq mi (2,155 sq km), central England. The county town is LEICESTER. There is good farming land in the uplands of the east, while the west is devoted primarily to mining and industry. The hilly Charnwood Forest is in the northwest. The Soar and the Wreak are the principal rivers. Leicestershire is primarily an agricultural county (sheep, dairy cattle, wheat, and barley). Stilton cheese is a well-known dairy product of the region. Leicester is one of the great industrial cities of England and the center of the boot and shoe industry. LOUGHBOROUGH and HINCKLEY also have industrial concentrations, and there is an oilfield at Plungar. Melton Mowbray and Market Harborough are famous fox-hunting centers. Leicestershire was part of the Anglo-Saxon kingdom of MERCIA. At Bosworth Field, in 1485, Richard III was slain by the forces of Henry Tudor, who ascended the throne as Henry VII. In 1974, Leicestershire was reorganized as a new nonmetropolitan county.

Leichhardt, Friedrich Wilhelm Ludwig (frē'drĭkh vĭl'hĕlm lo͝od'vĭkh lĭkh'härt), 1813–1848?, Prussian explorer of Australia. He led (1844–45) an expedition from Moreton Bay to Port Essington and in 1848 set out from Moreton Bay to cross the central part of the continent east to west. After sending a message from Macpherson's Station, on the Cogoon River, he disappeared. No trace of him was ever discovered.

Leiden or **Leyden** (both: lī'dən), city (1971 pop. 100,135), South Holland prov., W Netherlands, on the Old Rhine (Oude Rijn) River. Its manufactures include textiles, medical equipment, machinery, and food products. The city is famous for its university (founded 1575), which is the oldest in the Netherlands. It was a center for the study of Protestant theology, classical and oriental languages, science, and medicine in the 17th and 18th cent. The university is today particularly noted for its departments of oriental studies, physics, and astronomy. The LEYDEN JAR was invented at the university, and Boerhaave taught there in the 18th cent. Dating from Roman times, Leiden has had an important textile industry since the 16th cent., when there was an influx of weavers from Flanders. The city took a prominent part in the revolt (late 16th cent.) of the Netherlands against Spanish rule. Besieged and reduced to starvation in 1574, it was saved from surrender when William the Silent ordered the flooding of the surrounding land by cutting the dikes, thus enabling the fleet of the Beggars of the Sea (see GUEUX) to sail to its relief across the countryside. Leiden became famous as a center of printing after the Elzevir family established its press there in 1580. The city was the home of many of the Pilgrims for about 10 years before they embarked (1620) for America. Leiden was the birthplace of the Anabaptist leader John of Leiden and of the painters Jan van Goyen, Jan Steen, Lucas van Leyden, and Rembrandt. The city has a 10th-century fortress; two old churches, the Pieterskerk (14th cent.) and the Hooglandsche Kerk (15th cent.); several museums; and many 17th-century houses.

Leiden, University of, at Leiden, the Netherlands; founded 1575 by William the Silent, Prince of Orange. It became a state institution in the 19th cent. It has faculties of theology, law, medicine, science, arts, social science, philosophy, and geography and prehistory.

Leidy, Joseph (lī'dē), 1823–91, American scientist, b. Philadelphia, grad. Univ. of Pennsylvania medical school. From 1853 he taught anatomy at his alma mater. He was also professor of natural history at Swarthmore College (1870–85) and served as chairman of the board of curators (1847–91) and president (1881–91) of the Academy of Natural Sciences of Philadelphia. He ranked among the foremost anatomists of the day, and his *Elementary Treatise on Human Anatomy* (1861) was long the best American textbook in the field. He studied the fossil beds in Nebraska and South Dakota and, later, in Wyoming and Oregon and classified the fossils collected by the F. V. Hayden survey. Three important monographs followed, *Ancient Fauna of Nebraska* (1853), *Extinct Mammalian Fauna of Dakota and Nebraska* (1869), and *Contributions to the Extinct Vertebrate Fauna of the Western Territories* (1873), all landmarks in American paleontology. He was the first to identify in the United States extinct species of the horse, camel, sloth, tiger, rhinoceros, and many other genera and species. His *Flora and Fauna within Living Animals* (1853) was epoch-making in the field of parasitology, and his *Fresh Water Rhizopods of North America* (1879), with his own notable drawings, is still one of the finest works in its field. See biography by W. S. W. Rauschenberger (1892).

Leif Ericsson (lēf ĕr'ĭksən), Old Norse *Leifr Eiriksson,* fl. A.D. 999–1000, Norse discoverer of America, b. probably in Iceland; son of ERIC THE RED. He spent his youth in Greenland and in 999 visited Norway, where he was converted to Christianity and commissioned by King Olaf I to carry the faith to Greenland. According to the "Saga of Eric the Red" in the collection of sagas known as *Hauksbok,* it was on the return voyage from Norway to Greenland in 1000 that Leif Ericsson, blown off his course, discovered hitherto unknown lands in which he found grapes, self-sown wheat, and a species of trees called "mausur." He landed, secured specimens, and continued to Greenland, where he was successful in introducing Christianity. In another version of the story, interpolated in the "Saga of Olaf Tryggvason" in the *Flateyjarbok,* Leif completed his mission to Greenland, set out from there c.1002 on a voyage to western lands, discovered several places, and settled for a winter in VINLAND. This account is much more detailed, but the account in the "Saga of Eric the Red" is more widely accepted. Many scholars believe that Leif Ericsson landed on some part of the North American coast, but there has been no agreement on the modern identity of Vinland. Various sites have been nominated, from Newfoundland to Virginia, with Nova Scotia and New England as favorites. For the sources, see A. M. Reeves, *The Finding of Wineland* (1895, repr. 1973). See also E. F. Gray, *Leif Eriksson* (1930, repr. 1972); Matthias Thordarson, *The Vinland Voyages* (1930); Edward Reman, *The Norse Discoveries and Explorations in America* (1949).

Leigh, Vivien: see OLIVIER, LAURENCE KERR, BARON OLIVIER OF BRIGHTON.

Leigh (lē), municipal borough (1971 pop. 46,117), Lancashire, NW England. There are coal mines, cotton and rayon mills, and metalworks. In 1974, Leigh became part of the new metropolitan county of Greater Manchester.

Leigh-Mallory, George Herbert: see MALLORY, GEORGE HERBERT LEIGH.

Leighton, Clare (lā'tən), 1899–, English print maker, writer, and illustrator. Leighton is best known for her fine woodcuts and engravings and is represented in leading print collections in England and America. She illustrated works by Hardy and the Brontës and wrote and illustrated *Wood-engraving and Woodcuts* (1932), *The Farmer's Year* (1933), *Southern Harvest* (1942), and other works.

Leighton, Frederick Leighton, Baron (lā'tən), 1830–96, English painter and sculptor. He studied in Florence. His first exhibited picture, which showed Cimabue's *Madonna* being carried through the streets of Florence, was purchased by Queen Victoria in 1855. Leighton was president of the Royal Academy from 1878 until his death. His popular pictures dealt with subjects taken from antiquity. See biography by Ernest Rhys (3d ed. 1900); M. H. Shackford, *The Brownings and Leighton* (1942); William Gaunt, *Victorian Olympus* (1952).

Leighton, Margaret, 1922–, English stage and film actress. After six years with the Birmingham Repertory Theatre, Leighton joined the Old Vic and had her first London stage experience in *Peer Gynt* (1944). Although noted for her portrayals of nervous, sensitive ladies, she has been seen in a wide range of roles, e.g., in *The Cocktail Party, Separate Tables, The Night of the Iguana, The Chinese Prime Minister,* and *The Lady from the Sea,* and in the films *The Waltz of the Toreadors* (1961) and *The Go-Between* (1971).

Leighton, Robert, 1611–84, Scottish prelate and classical scholar. After several years in France, where he seems to have developed an admiration for the Jansenists, he became (1641) a Presbyterian minister in Midlothian and signed the Covenant in 1643 (see COVENANTERS). A noted preacher, he was made principal of the Univ. of Edinburgh in 1653 and professor of divinity. With the Restoration, Charles II attempted to force episcopacy on the Church of Scotland, and the king persuaded Leighton to accept (1661) the bishopric of Dunblane. Leighton's attempts to find a basis for union between Presbyterianism and episcopacy led to accusations of treason by the Covenanters and to lukewarm feelings on the part of the Episcopal party. Temperamentally unfitted for his work and grieved by the government's persecution of the Covenanters, he tried to resign, only to be appointed (1670) archbishop of Glasgow. In 1674 he retired to private life. Leighton's collected writings, including many of his sermons, appeared posthumously in several editions. See study by E. A. Knox (1930).

Leinsdorf, Erich, 1912–, American conductor, b. Vienna. Leinsdorf studied at the Vienna state academy of music and in 1934 began his conducting career, serving as assistant to Bruno Walter and then to Toscanini at the Salzburg festival. He made his debut as an assistant conductor at the Metropolitan Opera in 1938, remaining there as Wagnerian conductor until 1943, when he was made conductor of the Cleveland Symphony Orchestra. He returned to the Metropolitan Opera (1944) for one season and then served (1945–54) as conductor of the Rochester (N.Y.) Symphony Orchestra. After one year with the New York City Opera Company, he again conducted at the Metropolitan Opera until 1962, when he became music director of the Boston Symphony Orchestra. He had enormous success in that position, from which he resigned in 1969.

Leinster (lĕn'stər, lĭn'-), province (1971 pop. 1,494,544), 7,580 sq mi (19,632 sq km), E Republic of Ireland, comprising the counties of CARLOW, DUBLIN, KILDARE, KILKENNY, LAOIGHIS, LONGFORD, LOUTH, MEATH, OFFALY, WESTMEATH, WEXFORD, and WICKLOW. Most populous and fertile of the Irish provinces, it contains the capital of Ireland, DUBLIN. Its wealth and accessibility made the ancient province subject to Danish and Anglo-Norman invasions.

Leipzig (lĭp'tsĭkh), city (1970 pop. 584,365), capital of Leipzig district, S central East Germany, at the confluence of the Pleisse, White Elster, and Parthe rivers. It is East Germany's second largest city and one of its chief industrial, commercial, and transportation centers. Manufactures include textiles, steel, machinery, chemicals, paper, toys, and motor vehicles. Important international trade and industrial fairs have been held in the city since the Middle Ages. Originally a Slavic settlement called Lipsk, Leipzig was chartered at the end of the 12th cent. and rapidly developed into a commercial center located at the intersection of important trade routes. A printing industry, which later became important, was started there c.1480. The city was the scene of the famous religious debate between Martin Luther, Carlstadt, and Johann Eck in 1519. In 1539 it accepted the Reformation. Three great battles of the Thirty Years War (two at BREITENFELD and one at LÜTZEN) were fought near Leipzig. The city was one of the leading cultural centers of Europe in the age of the philosopher and mathematician Leibnitz, who was born there in 1646, and of the composer Johann Sebastian Bach, who was cantor at the Church of St. Thomas from 1723 until his death. The Univ. of Leipzig (founded 1409; renamed Karl Marx Univ. in 1953) became one of the most important in Germany. In the 18th cent. Gottsched, Gellert, Schiller, and many others made Leipzig a literary center; the young Goethe studied there in 1765. The city's musical reputation reached its peak in the 19th and early 20th cent. Felix Mendelssohn, who died there in 1847, made the Gewandhaus concerts (begun in the 18th cent. in a former guildhouse and still continuing) internationally famous. Robert Schumann worked in Leipzig, Richard Wagner was born there in 1813, and the Leipzig Conservatory (founded by Mendelssohn in 1842–43) became one of the world's best-known musical academies. Until World War II, Leipzig was the center of the German book and music publishing industry, and the center of the European trade in furs and smoked foods. The city (including the book-trade quarter) was badly damaged in World War II. Noteworthy buildings include the Church of St. Thomas (late 15th cent.), which has housed the tomb of Bach since 1950; the Gewandhaus, built in 1884 to replace the earlier structure; the 13th-century Pauline Church; Auerbach's Keller (16th cent.), an inn in which a scene of Goethe's *Faust* is set; the old city hall (1558); the old stock exchange (1682); the Church of St. John (17th cent.); the large main railroad station; the former German supreme court building (which now houses an art museum); and the opera (1960). The house in which Richard Wagner was born is located on The Brühl, one of the main streets of the city. In addition to the univ., the city has institutes of applied radioactivity and stable isotopes. The **battle of Leipzig,** Oct. 16–19, 1813, also called the Battle of the Nations, was a decisive victory of the Austrian, Russian, and Prussian forces over Napoleon I. On Oct. 16 the Prussians under General Blücher defeated the French under Auguste de Marmont at Möckern, near Leipzig. A peace offer by the vastly outnumbered French army was rejected on the following day while the Allies closed in. On Oct. 18 the French were driven to the gates of Leipzig, and most of their Saxon and Württemberg auxiliaries (but not the king of Saxony himself) passed over to the enemy camp. Leipzig was stormed on Oct. 19, and Napoleon's forces began their flight across Germany and beyond the Rhine. It is estimated that 120,000 men (of both sides) were killed or wounded in the battle. Allied losses were heavier than those of the French. The battle is commemorated by a large monument in the city.

Leipzig, University of, at Leipzig, East Germany; founded 1409 when German scholars withdrew from Charles Univ. It was reorganized in 1946, and in 1953 its name was changed officially to Karl Marx Univ. It has faculties of economics and law; philosophy and history; culture, linguistics, and education; mathematics and natural sciences; medicine; and agronomy.

Leiria (lär'yə), town (1970 pop. 10,286), capital of Leiria dist., W central Portugal, in Beira Litoral. It is an agricultural trade center. There Alfonso I erected (beginning 1135) a castle on a cliff above the present city; it was taken and retaken in the wars with the Moors. In 1254, Alfonso III summoned to Leiria the first Cortes to have representatives of the towns. The first duke of Braganza, son of an illegitimate son of John I and a daughter of Nun' Álvares Pereira and ancestor of the Braganza royal line, was reared there. At Marinha Grande, near Leiria, is the national glass factory. One of the first printing presses in Portugal was opened in Leiria in 1466.

Leisler, Jacob (lĭs'lər), 1640–91, leader of an insurrection (1689–91) in colonial New York, b. Frankfurt, Germany. He emigrated to America in 1660 as a penniless soldier, married a wealthy widow, and became a trader in New York. The overthrow (1688) of the Roman Catholic James II and accession of William III and Mary II in England caused uprisings in the colonies, where many royal officials were suspected of being Roman Catholics, and fear of a Catholic French invasion prevailed. Leisler, a Protestant champion, in 1689 gained control of S New York with the aid of militia, proclaimed the new sovereigns, and was appointed commander in chief by his followers. The lieutenant governor, Francis NICHOLSON, fled the country and Leisler assumed his office upon seizure of letters from King William that he interpreted as authorization. The council at Albany eventually recognized his authority, although he was bitterly opposed by the rich and aristocratic faction. Leisler maintained power through military force and the suppression of opposition. Meanwhile, William commissioned Col. Henry Sloughter as governor, and troops were dispatched to New York under Major Richard Ingoldesby, who, arriving early in 1691, sided with the faction opposed to Leisler and demanded the surrender of the fort on Manhattan island. Leisler refused, and fighting broke out. On the arrival of Sloughter, Leisler surrendered, was tried as a traitor, and was hanged in May, 1691. Parliament, in 1695, on petition of the Leisler family, passed an act reversing the attainder and later voted an indemnity to his heirs. See H. L. Osgood, *The American Colonies in the Seventeenth Century,* Vol. III (1907, repr. 1957); Jerome Reich, *Leisler's Rebellion* (1953).

Leith (lēth), former burgh, Lothian region, SE Scotland, on the south shore of the Firth of Forth. It was incorporated into EDINBURGH in 1920. As a strategically located port, Leith was the object of contention in several struggles. It was sacked by the English in 1544 and 1547, and Mary of Guise held it for the Catholics against a siege by English and Scottish Protestants in 1559–60. Leith was burned in the Jacobite uprising of 1715.

Leitha (lī'tä), Hung. *Lajta,* river, 112 mi (180 km) long, formed in E Austria by the confluence of the Schwarza and Pitten rivers. It flows generally east to an arm of the Danube River near Mosonmagyaróvár, Hungary. The historic boundary between Austria and Hungary, it divided Cisleithania on the west from Transleithania on the east.

Leith Hill (lēth), 965 ft (294 m) high, Surrey, SE England; highest point of the North Downs. On the summit is a tower, with a view on clear days of London and the English Channel.

Leitrim (lē'trĭm), county (1971 pop. 28,313), 589 sq mi (1,526 sq km), N Republic of Ireland. The county town is CARRICK-ON-SHANNON. The county is divided into two parts by Lough Allen; the northern part is mountainous, the southern part level. Cattle and sheep raising and tillage are the chief occupations, but the soil is generally unproductive and the climate excessively moist. Coal is mined in the northern highlands. The population has declined by more than 100,000 in the past century.

Leix, Ireland: see LAOIGHIS.

Leixões (lā'shoiNsh), artificial seaport of OPORTO, NW Portugal. It was built in the late 19th cent.

Lejeune, Camp: see JACKSONVILLE, N.C.

Lek (lĕk), northern arm of the Rhine River, 40 mi (64 km) long, branching from the Neder Rijn (Lower Rhine), central Netherlands, and flowing W into the Nieuwe Maas (New Meuse) River. It is navigable for its entire length. Rotterdam, the chief city on the river, is connected with the North Sea by the Nieuwe Waterweg (canal).

Lekain (ləkăN'), 1728–78, French actor, whose original name was Henri Louis Cain. In 1750 he made his debut at the Comédie Française and became a protégé of Voltaire. Together with Mlle Clairon, he took steps to introduce simple, realistic acting and historically accurate costuming. Because of the low status accorded to actors of his time, Lekain served three prison terms, once because he declined to appear on stage with an actor who had disgraced the company. His memoirs were published in 1825.

Leland, Charles Godfrey (lē'lənd), pseud. **Hans Breitmann** (häns' brĭtmän), 1824–1903, American author, b. Philadelphia, grad. College of New Jersey (now Princeton), 1845, studied at Heidelberg, Munich, and Paris. While editor of *Graham's Magazine* in 1857, he printed in it his German dialect poem, "Hans Breitmann's Party," which became so popular that he wrote others. In 1869 he published *Hans Breitmann's Ballads.* He founded and edited the *Continental Monthly* in Boston in 1862 to further the Union cause. After other journalistic ventures he devoted himself to traveling and studying languages and folklore. Leland wrote more than 50 books, including *The English Gypsies* (1873), *Algonquin Legends* (1884), and *Legends of Florence* (1895–96). In the 1880s he also successfully introduced industrial and craft arts into American schools. See his memoirs (1893); E. R. Pennell, *Charles Godfrey Leland* (2 vol., 1906, repr. 1970).

Leland or **Leyland, John,** c.1506–1552, English antiquary. He was successively chaplain and librarian to Henry VIII. In 1533 he was appointed king's antiquarian, and in this capacity traveled through England, collecting a great mass of historical and geographical data for a proposed book to be entitled *History and Antiquities.* The work was never completed because he went insane in 1550. His notes, however, were invaluable to later scholars. See his *Itinerary* (ed. by Thomas Hearne, 9 vol., 1710–12) and *Collectanea* (ed. by Hearne, 6 vol., 1715); biography by Edward Burton (1896).

Lelong, Lucien: see under FASHION.

Lely, Sir Peter (lē'lē), 1618–80, Dutch portrait painter in England. His original name was Pieter van der Faes. He studied in Haarlem but worked in England from c.1643. After the death of Van Dyck he outshone his rivals and became court painter in 1661. Lely painted in turn the great figures of the court of Charles I, the Protectorate, and the Restoration. His portraits are colorful, elegant, and flattering. Examples of his work are to be seen in the National Portrait Gallery, London, and at Hampton Court. The Metropolitan Museum has several of his portraits, including those of Sir Henry Capel and Barbara Villiers. See study by R. B. Beckett (1951).

Lemaître, Frédérick (frādārĕk' ləmĕt'rə), 1800–1876, French actor, originally named Antoine Louis Prosper Lemaître. First known in pantomimes and melodramas, he gained fame (1823) for his creation of the part of Robert Macaire in *L'Auberge des Adrets.* Equally at home in comedy and tragedy, he was especially popular in the plays of Victor Hugo and other romantic dramatists. He wrote the play *Robert Macaire* (1834). His early years at the Funambules with DEBUREAU are described in the Marcel Carné film classic *Children of Paradise* (1944). See biography by Robert Baldick (1959).

Lemaître, Georges, Abbé (zhôrzh, äbā'), 1894–, Belgian astrophysicist and mathematician. He postulated the theory that the universe originated as a condensed primeval atom that exploded, producing the force by which the universe is still expanding.

Lemaître, Jules (zhül), 1853–1914, French literary critic and writer. He wrote plays; novels and stories in the manner of Anatole France; and biographies, notably *Jean Racine* (1908) and *Jean-Jacques Rousseau* (1907, tr. 1907). His boldly subjective critical essays in *Les Contemporains* (1885–99; partial tr., *Literary Impressions,* 1921) and *Impressions de théâtre* (1888; partial tr., *Theatrical Impressions,* 1924) reflect the contemporary reaction against "scientific" criticism.

Léman, Lac: see GENEVA, LAKE, Switzerland.

LeMay, Curtis Emerson, 1906–, U.S. general, b. Columbus, Ohio. Commissioned a second lieutenant in the U.S. army air corps in 1930, he advanced through grades and in World War II commanded a bomber group in Europe and later the 20th Air Force in the Pacific. After the war he served (1945–47) as deputy chief of air staff for research and development before commanding the U.S. air force in Europe. LeMay was appointed (1948) commander in chief of the strategic air command and in 1957 was also made vice chief of staff for the air force. In 1961, he became air force chief of staff, serving until his retirement in 1965. Chosen by George C. Wallace in 1968 as his running mate, he ran unsuccessfully for vice president on the American Independent party ticket.

Lemberg: see LVOV, USSR.

Lemercier, Jacques (zhäk ləmĕrsyā'), c.1585–1654, French architect, one of the group that evolved a classical mode of expression for French architecture. In Italy (c.1607–1614) he was strongly influenced by the architecture of Rome. With Cardinal Richelieu as his patron, Lemercier received his greatest opportunities as a designer of churches for the Jesuits. His chief remaining work is the church of the Sorbonne, Paris (1635), inspired by Giacomo della Porta's designs and containing a dome which furnished a model for that of the Church of the Invalides. It was built at Richelieu's order, as were Richelieu's Paris residence, later transformed into the Palais-Royal, and the entire town of Richelieu, an ambitious piece of 17th-century town planning. In Paris at the palace of the Louvre, Lemercier built the Pavillon de l'Horloge, and he superseded (c.1646) François Mansart in supervising the construction of the Church of Val-de-Grâce.

Lémery, Nicolas (nēkôlä' lāmərē'), 1645–1715, French chemist. He was a pharmacist and lecturer in Paris and was the author of a standard textbook in chemistry (1675) and of a treatise on antimony (1707).

lemma (lĕm'ə): see THEOREM.

lemming, name for several species of mouselike RODENTS related to the VOLES. All live in arctic or northern regions, inhabiting tundra or open meadows. They frequently nest in underground burrows, particularly in winter, although they do not hibernate. They feed on grasses and roots, and probably on insects. All are about 5 in. (13 cm) long, with stout bodies, thick fluffy fur, small ears, very short tails, and long claws. The brown to black Norway lemming, *Lemmus lemmus,* of Scandinavia, is the best known, because of its spectacular periodic swarming. Two or three times per decade, this species undergoes a population explosion of such proportions that the lemmings set out in all directions in search of food. They cross bodies of water by swimming and occasionally some reach and enter the ocean, where they drown. This behavior has given rise to folklore about lemmings committing mass suicide. Other species of the genus *Lemmus* are found in the northern portions of Eurasia and North America and sometimes exhibit similar swarmings. The snow, or collard, lemmings, *Dicrostonyx,* found in the arctic regions of Asia and North America, are pure white in winter and brown, gray, or reddish in summer; this color change is unique among rodents. They are also distinguished by the growth in winter of an extremely long two-pronged claw on the third and fourth finger of each forefoot; these claws may function in shoveling snow. Bog lemmings, members of the genus *Synaptus,* are found in marshy places in North America as far south as the N United States. The wood lemming, *Myopus schisticolor,* is found in N Eurasia. The steppe lemmings, members of the genus *Lagarus,* of S Russia and Mongolia, are properly classified as voles; the North American species of this genus, *Lagarus curtatus,* is found in the W United States and is known as the sagebrush vole. Lemmings are classified in the phylum CHORDATA, subphylum Vertebrata, class Mammalia, order Rodentia, family Cricetidae. See MOUSE.

lemming mouse: see VOLE.

Lemnitzer, Lyman Louis, 1899–, U.S. general, b. Honesdale, Pa., grad. West Point, 1920. He held both staff and command assignments in World War II, serving in the North African, Sicilian, and Italian campaigns. In the Korean War he commanded the 7th Infantry Division. Lemnitzer was afterwards deputy chief of staff for plans and research (1952–53) and commander of the U.S. and UN forces in the Far East (1955–57). He served as the army chief of staff (1959–60) and chairman of the joint chiefs of staff (1960–62) before succeeding (1963) General Norstad as commander of the North Atlantic Treaty Organization forces, a post that he held until 1969.

Le Moine, François: see LE MOYNE, FRANÇOIS.

Lemon, Mark, 1809–70, English editor and humorist. He was a founder of *Punch* in 1841 and one of its first editors. Besides contributing to periodicals, he wrote more than 60 plays, none of them memorable.

lemon, one of the CITRUS FRUITS, from a tree (*Citrus limon*) of the family Rutaceae (ORANGE family), probably native to India. A small tree (about 15 ft/5 m tall) with thorny branches and purple-edged white blossoms, it requires a mild, equable climate. The European crop is centered on the islands and coasts of the Mediterranean. In the United States, lemons are grown chiefly in California, especially in the southern seacoast areas, and in Florida. The trees are prolific, producing ripe fruit practically all the year. In the United States the fruit is cut from the tree while green, at a standard size, and the good lemons are placed in cool, dark rooms to ripen slowly; the skin grows yellow, thin, and pliable, and the quality of the fruit is better than when ripened on the tree. The imperfect fruit is manufactured into lemon oil, lemon juice, CITRIC ACID, pectin, and other useful products. Lemons have better preservative qualities than other citrus fruits and are thus more easily transported. The fruit is high in vitamin content (especially in ascorbic acid, or vitamin C) and has long been known as a preventive of scurvy. Lemons have a refreshing, acid flavor; they are in great demand for use in summer drinks, such as lemonade and punch, and are often preferred to vinegar as an ingredient in sauces and salad dressings. Lemon juice is the main source of citric acid, which is used by calico printers to keep the fabric clear of rusty stains from the machinery; it is also a domestic remedy for rust, ink, and mildew stains. Lemon oil, or the essential oil extracted from the skin, usually while green, is manufactured mostly in Italy and France. It is used in the making of flavoring extract (essential oil combined with alcohol), perfumes and cosmetics, and furniture polish. Lemon is classified in the division MAGNOLIOPHYTA, class Magnoliopsida, order Sapindales, family Rutaceae.

lemon balm: see BEE BALM.

Lemon Grove, uninc. town (1970 pop. 19,690), San Diego co., S Calif. It is residential and agricultural, with some small industries.

Lemonnier, Camille (kämē'yə ləmônyā'), 1844–1913, Belgian novelist and art critic. After abandoning law, Lemonnier published his first work, *Salon de Bruxelles* (1863), a collection of art essays. His novels, including his masterpiece, *Le Mâle* (1881), vividly describe rural life and reveal a pantheistic outlook. *L'Arche* (1894) is one of a trio of novels defending female individuality. His other works include the novels *Happo-Chair* (1886) and *Au Coeur frais de la forêt* (1900).

Lemonnier, Pierre Charles (pyĕr shärl ləmônyā'), 1715–99, French astronomer. For many years he was professor of physics at the Collège de France. He studied the moon and the influence of Saturn on the motion of Jupiter, determined the positions of many fixed stars, and made extensive researches in terrestrial magnetism and atmospheric electricity. He repeatedly saw Uranus and recorded it in his charts before it was recognized as a planet by Sir William Herschel (see under HERSCHEL, family). His brother **Louis Guillaume Lemonnier,** 1717–99, was a botanist and physicist. He was appointed by King Louis XV head of the botanical garden of the Trianon at Versailles and introduced many plants to French horticulture. His work in physics included the Leyden jar experiment, by which he established that water is one of the best electrical conductors and that the surface area, not the mass, of a conducting body determines its electrical charge. His research on electricity produced by storms confirmed the theories of Benjamin Franklin.

Le Moyne (lə mwän), Canadian family. It was founded by Charles le Moyne, sieur de LONGUEUIL, whose 11 sons were noted soldiers, explorers, and colonizers. The two most famous sons were the sieur d'IBERVILLE and the sieur de BIENVILLE.

Le Moyne, Le Moine, or **Lemoine, François** (all: fräNswä' ləmwän'), 1688–1737, French painter. After a stay in Venice in 1723, he developed a colorful, sumptuous manner based on the Venetian style. Le Moyne's masterpiece is his decoration of the Salon of Hercules at Versailles. Boucher was his pupil.

Lemoyne, Jean Baptiste (zhäN bäptēst'), 1704–78, French sculptor. Much of his work, including three equestrian statues of Louis XV, was destroyed in the French Revolution. His picturesque portrait busts of Voltaire, Fontenelle, and Mme de Pompadour are considered his best work. He was the teacher of Houdon, Pigalle, Falconet, and Pajou.

Lempa (lām'pä), river, c.200 mi (320 km) long, rising in Guatemala and flowing S through Honduras into El Salvador, then generally S to the Pacific Ocean. An important stream, it waters the fertile Lempa valley, largely within El Salvador, which supports a dense agricultural population.

Lemuel (lĕm'yōōəl), unknown king. Prov. 31.1.

lemur (lē'mər), name for prosimians, or lower PRIMATES, of two related families, found only on Madagascar and adjacent islands. Lemurs have monkeylike bodies and limbs, and most have bushy tails about as long as the body. They have pointed muzzles and large eyes. The fingers and toes have flat nails, except the second toe, which has a stout claw. Most lemurs lead an arboreal existence. The woolly lemurs (family Lemuridae) are agile animals with woolly coats. They vary in size from the lesser mouse lemur (*Microcebus murinus*), about 8 in. (20 cm) long including the tail, to some species of common woolly lemur (*Lemur*) that reach about 4 ft (120 cm) in length. They forage in trees and on the ground in large family groups and engage in social grooming. Most types are active both by day and by night. Their diet, which varies with the species, may include leaves, fruits, eggs, and insects and other small animals. Some build nests of leaves and branches in trees. The best-known species, the ring-tailed lemur (*Lemur catta*), is atypical, spending most of the time on the ground. Its fur is gray and its tail ringed with black and white stripes. Members of the other lemur family (Indriidae) are sometimes called silky lemurs. They are larger, slower-moving, strictly vegetarian animals; most have silky coats. One member of this family, the indri (*Indri indri*), has no tail. The AYE-AYE is closely related to the lemurs. The so-called FLYING LEMUR is not a primate, but a member of a different mammalian order. Lemurs are classified in the phylum CHORDATA, subphylum Vertebrata, class Mammalia, order Primates, families Lemuridae and Indriidae.

lemures (lĕm'ərās''), in Roman religion, vampirelike ghosts of the dead; also called larvae. To exorcise these malevolent spirits from the home, the Romans held rites, the Lemuria (May 9, 11, 13). The lemures were similar to the manes.

Lemus, José María (hōsā' märē'ä lā'mōōs), 1911–, president of El Salvador (1956–60). An army lieutenant colonel, he served as minister of interior (1949–55). As president, he pardoned political prisoners and attempted to continue the progressive programs of his predecessor President Osorio. A decline in the prices of coffee and cotton, however, brought strikes, political unrest, and violence. After an attempt was made to assassinate him, Lemus became increasingly harsh and dictatorial. He was deposed (Oct., 1960) by a leftist group and deported.

Lena (lē'nə, Rus. lyĕ'nə), river, easternmost of the great rivers of Siberia, c.2,670 mi (4,300 km) long, rising near Lake Baykal, SE Siberian USSR. It flows northeast, then north along the east side of the central Siberian uplands and parallels the Verkhoyansk Range, reaching a width of 8.5 mi (13.7 km). It empties through a c.250-mi- (400-km-) wide delta into the Arctic Ocean. It is navigable for 2,135 mi (3,436 km) upstream; at Yakutsk (915 mi/1,473 km upstream) it is ice free from June to October; at the delta from July to September. Coal, oil, and gold are found along the Lena and its tributaries (the Vitim and the Aldan). The Lena was first reached by the Russians in 1630.

Le Nain (lə năN), family of French painters consisting of three brothers: **Antoine Le Nain,** 1588?–1648, **Louis Le Nain,** 1593?–1648, and **Mathieu Le Nain,** 1607–77. They went to Paris from Laon c.1629 and were admitted to the Académie royale at the time of its foundation in 1648. It is believed that much of their work was done in collaboration. Antoine excelled in painting colorful miniatures of family scenes. Mathieu became painter to the city of Paris in 1633 and specialized in portraiture and in depicting the city militia. Louis is credited with the conception of the famous Le Nain genre scenes of peasant life. At a time when allegorical compositions in France were the rule, these pictures are unique in the choice of peasants as subject matter, treated sympathetically and realistically, and yet arranged in almost classical compositions. Among the paintings by the Le Nain brothers may be cited *The Forge* and *Peasants' Repast* (Louvre) and *Portrait Group* (National Gall., London).

Lenape: see DELAWARE INDIANS.

Lenard, Philipp Eduard Anton (fē'lĭp ā'dōōart än'tōn lā'närt), 1862–1947, German physicist, b. Bratislava. After serving as professor at the universities of Kiel (1898–1907) and Heidelberg (1896–98, 1907–31), he headed the Philipp Lenard Institute at Heidelberg. He was the first to cause cathode rays to pass from the interior of a vacuum tube through a thin metal window into the air, where they produce luminosity. For his research in this field he received the 1905 Nobel Prize in Physics. He is noted also for his work on the structure of the atom and for the discovery (1902), in connection with the photoelectric effect, that the velocity of electrons is independent of the intensity of the light that emits them.

Lenau, Nikolaus (nē'kōlous lā'nou), pseud. of **Nikolaus Niembsch Edler von Strehlenau** (nēmpsh ād'lər fən shtrā'lənou), 1802–50, Austrian romantic poet, b. Hungary. He is considered Austria's chief lyric poet. Pessimism and melancholy dominate his work, which includes three volumes of vivid poems of peasant life (1832, 1838, 1840); the epics *Savonarola* (1837) and *Die Albigenser* (1842); and the long lyric poem *Faust* (1836). Lenau's mind failed in 1844, and he spent his last years in an asylum. See study by Hugo Schmidt (1971).

Lenbach, Franz von (fränts fən lān'bäkh), 1836–1904, German portrait painter. He studied in Munich and Rome and from 1863 to 1868 worked as a copyist of old masters in Italy and Spain. His early work was in genre, but later he devoted himself to portraiture, in a style derivative of Titian and Rembrandt. Lenbach executed portraits of Bismarck, Emperor William I, Field Marshal von Moltke, Pope Leo XIII, Gladstone, Mommsen, Wagner, Liszt, and Johann Strauss. The Metropolitan Museum has *A Young Woman* and a portrait of Edwin Emerson.

Lenclos, Ninon de (nēnôN' də läNklō'), 1620–1705, French beauty and wit. Her real name was Anne de Lenclos. She numbered among her many lovers and friends such eminent men as the Great Condé, La Rochefoucauld, and Saint-Évremond. She gathered in her Paris salon a circle of wits and literary figures. See biography by E. H. Cohen (1970).

lend-lease, arrangement for the transfer of war supplies, including food, machinery, and services, to nations whose defense was considered vital to the defense of the United States in World War II. The Lend-Lease Act, passed (1941) by the U.S. Congress, gave the President power to sell, transfer, lend, or lease such war materials. The President was to set the terms for aid; repayment was to be "in kind or property, or any other direct or indirect benefit which the President deems satisfactory." Harry L. Hopkins was appointed (March, 1941) to administer lend-lease. He was replaced (July) by Edward R. Stettinius, Jr., who headed the Office of Lend-Lease Administration, set up in Oct., 1941. In Sept., 1943, lend-lease was incorporated into the Foreign Economic Administration under Leo T. Crowley. In Sept., 1945, it was transferred to the Dept. of State. Lend-lease was originally intended for China and countries of the British Empire. In Nov., 1941, the USSR was included, and by the end of the war practically all the allies of the United States had been declared eligible for lend-lease aid. Although not all requested or received it, lend-lease agreements were signed with numerous countries. In 1942, a reciprocal aid agreement of the United States with Great Britain, Australia, New Zealand, and the Free French was announced. Under its terms a "reverse lend-lease" was effected, whereby goods, services, shipping, and military installations were given to American forces overseas. Other nations in which U.S. forces were stationed subsequently adhered to the agreement. On Aug. 21, 1945, President Truman announced the end of lend-lease aid. Arrangements were made—notably with Great Britain and China—to continue shipments, on a cash or credit basis, of goods earmarked for them under lend-lease appropriations. Total lend-lease aid exceeded $50 billion, of which the British Commonwealth received some $31 billion and the USSR received over $11 billion. Within 15 years after the termination of lend-lease, settlements were made with most of the countries that had received aid, although a settlement with the USSR was not reached until 1972. See W. F. Kimball, *The Most Unsordid Act* (1969).

L'Enfant, Pierre Charles (pyĕr shärl läNfäN'), 1754–1825, American soldier, engineer, and architect. Born in France, he volunteered as a private in the American Revolution. He won Gen. Washington's attention with his design for the insignia of the Society of the Cincinnati. L'Enfant had remodeled the New York City city hall to serve as a temporary seat of Federal government when he was asked (1789) by Washington to submit plans for the capital city at Washington. His plans were presented in 1791, but he antagonized Congress and was opposed by Thomas Jefferson. In 1792 he was dismissed. He was offered in payment of his services 500 guineas and a lot in Washington, which he refused. In 1889, L'Enfant's plans were exhumed from the archives, and in 1901 the design of the capital was developed along the lines that he had laid down. L'Enfant's body was moved to the Arlington National Cemetery in 1909. See biography by H. L. Caemmerer (1950).

Lenglen, Suzanne (süzän' läNglĕn'), 1899–1938, French tennis player. She won the world hard-court singles and doubles titles in 1914. She was champion of French women's singles (1920–23, 1925–26) and one of the winners of women's doubles (1925–26); from 1919 to 1923 and again in 1925 she won the British women's singles crowns and was also a doubles champion. In 1920 she took the tennis honors of the Olympic games at Antwerp. She turned professional in 1926 and played in the United States in 1927. She wrote *Lawn Tennis* (1925), *Lawn Tennis for Girls* (1930), and *Tennis by Simple Exercises* (1937).

Lenin, Vladimir Ilyich (lĕn'ĭn, Rus. vlədyē'mĭr ĭlyēch' lyĕ'nĭn), 1870–1924, Russian revolutionary, the founder of Bolshevism and the major force behind the Soviet Revolution in Oct., 1917. Born Vladimir Ilyich Ulyanov, at Simbirsk (now called Ulyanovsk in his honor), he was the son of a school and civil service official and was drawn early to the revolutionary cause, especially when his brother, Aleksandr I. Ulyanov, was executed (1887) for his participation in a plot on the life of Alexander III. Lenin's law studies at the Univ. of Kazan were interrupted when he was banished for revolutionary activities. He completed his studies independently and practiced law briefly, but soon renounced his legal practice, turning entirely to the study of the teachings of Karl Marx and to propagandizing among the workers, particularly in St. Petersburg. He was exiled to Siberia in 1887, and when his exile ended (1900) he left Russia to continue his revolutionary activities abroad.

Theoretician and Revolutionary. In a pamphlet titled *What Is to Be Done?* (1902) he argued that only a disciplined party of professional revolutionaries could bring socialism to Russia. In 1903, at a meeting of the Russian Social Democratic Labor party held in London, the party split into two factions, the Bolsheviks, headed by Lenin, and the Mensheviks (see BOLSHEVISM AND MENSHEVISM). Lenin continued to be the chief exponent of Bolshevik thought in the long struggles for supremacy against PLEKHANOV, KAUTSKY, and other less radical Marxists. With the outbreak of revolution in 1905, Lenin returned to Russia. His view that the Bolsheviks should take part in the second Duma prevailed in 1907, but he left Russia again in the same year and subsequently engaged in complex theoretical disputes. Lenin was in Switzerland during the early years of World War I. In his view the war was an imperialist struggle; since imperialism was "the final stage of capitalism," it was a historical necessity that the war would bring opportunities for a revolution of the proletariat. Consequently, Lenin urged the proletariat to oppose the war by an international civil war against the capitalist class. After the outbreak of the RUSSIAN REVOLUTION of Feb., 1917, the German government allowed Lenin to cross Germany from Switzerland to Sweden in a sealed railway car; by thus aiding his return to Russia, the Germans hoped (correctly) to disrupt the Russian war effort. Lenin concluded that Russia was now ripe for a socialist revolution, arguing that the moderate provisional government represented the bourgeoisie whereas the soviets represented, in his words, a revolutionary democratic dictatorship of the proletariat and peasantry. In July, 1917, after an abortive mass uprising in Petrograd, Lenin was forced to flee to Finland. Although the Bolsheviks were represented only by a minority in the first all-Russian Soviet congress (June, 1917), they soon gained decisive power. In Nov., 1917 (October according to the Old Style), the Bolsheviks, led by Lenin, who had returned to Petrograd, overthrew Kerensky's weak and disorganized regime and established a Soviet government headed by the Council of People's Commissars.

Head of Government. Lenin became chairman of the council and virtual dictator; TROTSKY, STALIN, and RYKOV were the other chief members. The Bolsheviks (who became the Communist party) asserted that the October Revolution had established a proletarian dictatorship. In fact, Lenin had set up a dictatorship of the Communist party, controlling the hierarchy of local, regional, and central soviets. The new government's first acts were to propose an armistice with Germany and to abolish private ownership of land and distribute it among the peasants. Banks were nationalized, a supreme council was established to revive the dislocated economy, and workers' control over factory production was introduced. Atheism officially replaced doctrinal religion. All opposition was ruthlessly suppressed by the Cheka, or political police, under DZERZHINSKY. Lenin fulfilled his promise of peace by accepting the humiliating treaty of BREST-LITOVSK (March, 1918). However, civil war in Russia and a war with Poland prevented peace from coming to Russia until late 1920. In 1919, Lenin established the Third International, or COMINTERN, to further world revolution. The policy of "war Communism" prevailed until 1921. It brought extensive nationalization, food requisitioning, and control over industry. In 1921 in an attempt to boost the economy Lenin launched the NEW ECONOMIC POLICY (NEP), which allowed some private enterprise. By 1922, Lenin had eliminated all organized opposition and had silenced hostile factions within the party. He retained the post of chairman of the Council of People's Commissars and was a member of the ruling Politburo of the Communist party until his death.

Legacy. The strain of Lenin's labors had completely broken his health. He suffered a first stroke in 1922; a later stroke (1923) deprived him of speech. In a testament criticizing Stalin, written near the end of his life, he recommended Stalin's removal from the post of general secretary of the party. After his death (Jan. 21, 1924) this testament was suppressed, and Stalin emerged victorious in the contest for succession. Lenin's remains are in a mausoleum on Red Square. His speeches and writings are highly regarded by his successors and followers. Lenin's major contributions to Marxism were his analysis of imperialism (stressing, among other things, the importance of colonial areas as the breeding ground for revolution) and his concept of a revolutionary party as a highly disciplined unit. One of the greatest and most practical revolutionists of all times, Lenin combined mastery of theory with shrewd political instinct. Although he attacked any theoretical revisionism or gradualism, he supported the most opportunistic compromises to further the establishment of socialism. His voluminous writings and speeches are available in collected and selective English editions and in individual pamphlets. See *Memories of Lenin* (1930) by N. K. Krupskaya (Lenin's wife); biographies by L. Fischer (1964), D. Shub (1948, repr. 1967), L. Trotsky (1925, repr. 1971); B. D. Wolfe, *Three Who Made a Revolution* (4th ed. rev., 1964); studies by A. Meyer (1957, repr. 1962), S. T. Possony (1964), L. Shapiro (1967), and R. H. Theen (1973).

Leninabad (lyĕ″nyĭnəbät′), city (1970 pop. 103,000), capital of Leninabad oblast, Central Asian USSR, in Tadzhikistan, on the Syr Darya River at its exit from the Fergana Valley. It is the major Soviet center for silk production; other industries produce clothing, footwear, and food products. Leninabad, located on an ancient caravan route from China to the Mediterranean, was a famous town marking the farthest expansion of Alexander the Great. There he founded a new fortress called Alexandria Eskhat (the Outermost Alexandria). It was plundered (711) by the Arabs and later (1220) was razed by Jenghiz Khan. As part of the Kokand khanate (early 19th cent.), it was annexed (1866) by Russia. The city and surrounding area belonged to Uzbekistan from 1924 to 1929. Until 1936 it was known as Khodzhent. Leninabad is one of the oldest centers of Tadzhik decorative and applied arts.

Leninakan (lyĕ″nyĭnəkän′), city (1970 pop. 165,000), SE European USSR, in Armenia, near the Turkish border. It has textile and metalworking plants. The old craft of rug making is still practiced. Leninakan is the most important Armenian industrial center after YEREVAN. It was founded (1837) as Aleksandropol on the site of the Turkish fortress of Gumri and was renamed in 1924.

Leningrad (lĕn′ĭn-grăd, Rus. lyĕnyĭngrät′), city (1970 pop. 3,950,000), capital of Leningrad oblast, NW European USSR, at the head of the Gulf of Finland on both banks of the Neva River and on the islands of its delta. Leningrad's port is linked by deepwater canal with Kotlin Island, where the outer port and the KRONSHTADT naval base are located. The Soviet Union's second largest city and its former capital, Leningrad is a major seaport, rail junction, and industrial, cultural, and scientific center. Although the harbor is frozen for three or four months annually, icebreakers have prolonged the navigation season. The seaport is one of the world's largest, but it handles relatively little traffic because the volume of foreign trade for the USSR is small. The river port, one of the most important in the country, stands at the end of two artificial waterways, the Volga-Baltic and the White Sea-Baltic. A series of canals within the city carries considerable cargo. The city's diverse industries include shipbuilding, metallurgy, oil refining, printing, woodworking, food and tobacco processing, and the manufacture of machinery, electrical equipment, chemicals, pharmaceuticals, and textiles. Originally called St. Petersburg, the city was built by Peter I (Peter the Great), who sought a Russian outlet to the sea and a port for trade through the Baltic. The city was built in 1703 in what was then Ingermanland, an area conquered from Sweden during the Northern War. The fortress of Peter and Paul was erected to defend the projected new Russian capital, which was to be a modern city and a "window looking on Europe." Construction was carried out at tremendous human and material cost. The capital was moved from Moscow in 1712, although the land on which the city stood was not formally ceded to Russia until 1721. Italian and French architects planned the city for Peter and his successors, giving it the spacious, classical beauty which it has retained. St. Petersburg soon replaced Archangelsk as Russia's leading seaport and became an important commercial center. From the second half of the 18th cent. it was also the country's principal industrial center, at first for shipbuilding and engineering and later for textiles. In 1851 a rail link with Moscow was completed. One of the world's most brilliant capitals and cultural centers, St. Petersburg was immortalized in the great novels of Pushkin, Turgenev, Dostoyevsky, and Tolstoy. Its apex as an international center of literature, music, theater, and ballet and as the scene of lavish and reckless social life was reached in the late 19th and early 20th cent. Under the glittering surface, however, the seeds of social upheaval ripened, especially among the industrial workers. Secret revolutionary societies sprang up, and an attempt by St. Petersburg workers to petition the czar precipitated a revolution. The city was renamed Petrograd in 1914. The workers, soldiers, and sailors of Petrograd also spearheaded the revolutions of February and October, 1917. Although it lost much of its former glamor, the city remained the economic and cultural rival of Moscow, which replaced it as capital in 1918. Petrograd was renamed Leningrad in 1924. During World War II the city was cut off from the rest of the USSR by the fall of Schlüsselburg (now PETROKREPOST) to the Germans (Aug., 1941). It was besieged by German armies for more than two years, during which many thousands died of famine and disease. The city's main thoroughfare is the celebrated Nevsky Prospekt. On it are the high-spired admiralty building; the Winter Palace, built by Rastrelli; the HERMITAGE museum; the huge domed Cathedral of St. Isaac (1858); and the equestrian statue of Peter the Great, Falconet's masterpiece and the subject of Pushkin's poem "The Bronze Horsemen." The city's oldest building is the fortress of Peter and Paul (1703), which served as a political prison in imperial days. Among the baroque buildings of the early 18th cent. are the Alexander Nevsky monastery (1710), the Cathedral of Saint Peter and Saint Paul (1733), the Winter Palace (1762), and the Smolny convent (1764). Neoclassical buildings of the late 18th and early 19th cent. include the Academy of Arts (1772), the Marble Palace (1785), the Taurida Palace (1788), the cathedral of the Virgin of Kazan (1811), and the Exchange (1816). Leningrad also has a university (est. 1804); numerous theaters, museums, scientific and medical institutes; and libraries, including the Saltykov-Shchedrin Public Library (1795) and the Academy of Sciences library. Outside the city are PUSHKIN, with the Summer Palace, and the former imperial residence of Peterhof (now PETRODVORETS) and GATCHINA. A unique phenomenon of Leningrad is the prolonged twilight, or the "white nights," of June and July.

Leninogorsk (lyĕ″nyĭnəgôrsk′), city (1970 pop. 72,000), E Central Asian USSR, in Kazakhstan, in the Altai mts. It is a mining center in an area that is the chief source of Soviet zinc and lead. Silver, copper, and gold are also mined. The first mines were opened in the late 18th cent. Leninogorsk's metallurgical factories produce lead, copper, and zinc concentrates and cadmium. Until 1940 the city was known as Ridder.

Lenin Peak, 23,405 ft (7,134 m) high, on the border of Tadzhikistan and Kirghizia, Central Asian USSR. It is the highest point in the Trans-Alai range, and in the USSR its height is exceeded only by Mt. Communism and Pobeda Peak.

Leninsk-Kuznetski (lyĕ′nĭnsk-ko͞oznyĕt′skē), city (1970 pop. 128,000), S central Siberian USSR, on the Inya River. It is a coal center in the KUZNETSK BASIN. Founded in 1864 as a mining settlement called Kolchygino, it was renamed in 1925 and underwent rapid development in the 1930s.

Lenkoran (lyĕnkərän′yə), city (1970 pop. 36,000), SE European USSR, in the Azerbaijan Republic, near the Iranian border, on the Caspian Sea. It is a port and an important food-processing center for fish and tea. Its inhabitants are mostly Talysh, an Iranian-speaking people who are Shiah Muslims. Lenkoran, known since the 17th cent., was the capital of the Talysh khanate under Persia in the 18th cent. and was ceded to Russia by Persia in 1813. The **Lenkoran Lowland,** a coastal strip c.40 mi (60 km) long, has a humid, subtropical climate. Citrus fruit, tea, and rice are grown here, and there are fisheries.

Lennep, Jacob van (yä′kōp vän lĕn′ĕp), 1802–68, Dutch writer. He was state's attorney (1852) and served in the legislature (1853–56). He is best known for his historical novels influenced by Walter Scott, which include *The Adopted Son* (1833, tr. 1844) and *The Rose of Dekama* (1836, tr. 1847). He also wrote verse; translated Byron, Tennyson, and others; and wrote on Vondel, whose works he edited.

Lenni-Lenape: see DELAWARE INDIANS.

Lennox, Matthew Stuart or **Stewart,** 4th **earl of,** 1516–71, Scottish nobleman. Related to the royal family, being next in the line of succession to the throne after James HAMILTON, 2d earl of Arran, Lennox returned to Scotland in 1542, after service in France, to contest Arran's claim to be regent for the infant MARY QUEEN OF SCOTS. In 1544 he allied himself with Henry VIII of England, marrying Margaret Douglas, the daughter of Henry's sister MARGARET TUDOR and Archibald Douglas, 6th earl of Angus. He lived in England for the next 20 years and led several invasions of Scotland. Lennox and his wife, a woman of great ambition and ability, were in great favor in England until the accession (1558) of Elizabeth I, who did not trust them. They became leaders among the Catholic nobility and succeeded in marrying (1565) their son, Lord DARNLEY, to Mary Queen of Scots. After Darnley's murder (1567), Lennox formally accused the earl of BOTHWELL of the deed but failed to appear at his farcical trial. When Mary was imprisoned, Lennox again became prominent and, through Elizabeth's intervention, was chosen regent to succeed (1570) the 1st earl of Murray. Mary's party, led by the Hamiltons and William MAITLAND, at once declared war against him. Lennox was stabbed to death in a raid during this war. His surviving son, Charles, was created earl of Lennox and was the father of Arabella STUART.

Lennox, uninc. city (1970 pop. 16,121), Los Angeles co., S Calif., an industrial suburb of Los Angeles. Los Angeles International Airport is nearby.

Lennoxville, town (1971 pop. 3,859), S Que., Canada, at the confluence of the St. Francis and Massawippi rivers, SE of Sherbrooke. It is chiefly a residential town and is the seat of Bishop's Univ. (1843).

Lenoir (lənôr′), city (1970 pop. 14,705), seat of Caldwell co., W N.C.; inc. 1851. It is a resort in the eastern foothills of the Blue Ridge Mts. Furniture making is the main industry. Caldwell Community College and Technical Institute is in Lenoir.

Lenormand, Henri René (äNrē′ rənā′ lənôrmäN′), 1882–1951, French dramatist. His plays, Freudian in tone and theme and often heavily symbolic, include *Les Ratés* (1918, tr. *The Failures,* 1923), *Time Is a Dream* (1919, tr. 1923) and *Man and His Phantoms* (1924, tr. 1928).

Lenôtre or **Le Nôtre, André** (äNdrā′ lənō′trə), 1613–1700, French landscape architect. Lenôtre's first important design, the park of Vaux-le-Vicomte, attracted the attention of Louis XIV, who then entrusted to him the direction of nearly all the royal parks and gardens. He brought to full development that type of spacious formal garden, characterized by extensive unbroken vistas, that so accurately expressed the grandeur of his period. The gardens of the palace of Versailles are his most celebrated work. In 1664 he transformed the palace gardens of the Tuileries. He also designed parks for Saint-Cloud, Marly-le-Roi, Chantilly, Fontainebleau, and Saint-Germain-en-Laye. His principles in garden design dominated throughout Europe until the rise of the English school of informal and naturalistic gardens. See biography by Helen Fox (1962).

Lenox, James, 1800–1880, American bibliophile and philanthropist, b. New York City. Lenox was a founder of the Presbyterian Hospital, New York City. He amassed a fine collection of paintings and books which, as the Lenox Library, became part of the New York Public Library in 1895 and in 1913 was moved to the central library. The Frick Collection stands on the library's former Fifth Avenue site. See Henry Stevens, *Recollections of James Lenox and the Formation of His Library* (1886, new ed. by V. H. Paltsits, 1952).

Lens (läNs), city (1968 pop. 42,014), Pas-de-Calais dept., N France. Since the 19th cent. it has been one of the most important coal centers in N France. It is also a manufacturing center with metallurgical and textile industries. The victory there (1648) of the French under Louis II de Condé was the last important battle of the Thirty Years War. Lens was occupied and devastated by the Germans in both world wars.

lens, device for forming an IMAGE of an object by the REFRACTION of light. In its simplest form it is a disk of transparent substance, commonly glass, with its two surfaces curved or with one surface plane and the other curved. All rays of light passing through a lens are refracted (bent) except those that pass directly through a point called the optical center. Lenses are classified according to the way in which they bend the rays of light entering them. Parallel rays of light passing through converging lenses are bent toward one another; these lenses are thicker at the center than at the edges. Examples are the double convex lens (both surfaces curved outward as in the simple magnifying glass), the plano-convex (one flat and one convex surface), and the concavo-convex (one surface concave, the other convex). Diverging lenses bend parallel rays away from one another; they are thicker at the edges than at the center. Examples are the double concave lens (both surfaces curved inward), the plano-concave (one surface flat, the other concave), and the convexo-concave (one surface convex, the other concave). Generally each curved surface of a lens is made as a portion of a spherical surface. The center of the sphere is called the center of curvature of the surface; every point on the surface is equidistant to it, this distance being the radius of curvature. The line joining the two centers of curvature also passes through the optical center of the lens and is called the principal axis. Any other line through the optical center at an angle to the principal axis is called a secondary axis. In converging lenses all rays entering parallel to the principal axis are bent toward a point on the principal axis called the principal focus. The distance from the principal focus to the optical center of the lens is the focal length of the lens. It varies with different lenses, according to the curvature of the surfaces and index of refraction of the lens material. Conjugate points are two points on opposite sides of a lens in such position that rays from one, after passing through the lens, will converge at the other. Light rays are not always brought to a focus at one point; this condition of inexact focus is known as aberration and may be of two types: spherical, resulting from the shape of the lens, and chromatic, resulting from the fact that different colors are refracted by different amounts (see ABERRATION, in optics). The image formed by a diverging lens is always virtual, erect (upright), and smaller than the object and is located on the same side of the lens as the object. The image formed by a converging lens depends on the position of the object relative to the focal length of the lens and the center of curvature. If the object is beyond the center of curvature, the image is real, inverted, and smaller than the object. As the object is brought toward the lens, the size of the image grows, becoming as large as the object when the object is at the center of curvature and larger than the object as the object is brought closer. When the object is one focal length away from the lens, however, no image at all is formed; and when the object moves closer than this distance, the image becomes virtual, erect, and larger than the object, as when one uses a magnifying glass. Lenses are used singly or in groups in such instruments as cameras, projectors, microscopes, telescopes, and common field, opera, and reading glasses. The lens of the eye is known as a crystalline lens. Lenses have long been made of glass; a piece roughly approximating the desired size and shape of the lens is cut from a glass block and then ground and polished to the correct curvature. Great skill and accuracy are required in this process and also in mounting the lenses so that the principal axes of all the lenses fall on the same line. A number of transparent plastics that permit the lenses to be cast in a mold are used as substitutes for glass. See EYEGLASSES; TELESCOPE; MICROSCOPE.

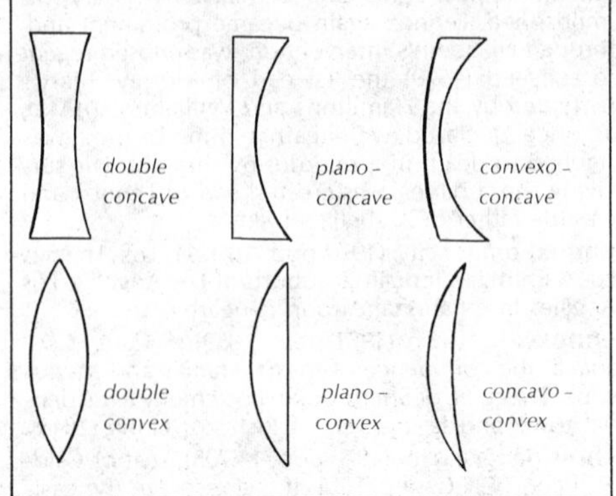

Lenses

Lent [from Old Eng. *lencten,*= spring], Latin *Quadragesima,* Christian period of FASTING and penitence preparatory to EASTER. Observance of Lent is as old as the 4th cent. In Eastern churches it is reckoned as the six weeks before Palm Sunday. In the West the penitential season begins liturgically with Septuagesima, the ninth Sunday before Easter; the next Sundays are Sexagesima and Quinquagesima. Lent begins on ASH WEDNESDAY, the 40th weekday before Easter. Of the Sundays in Lent the fifth is Passion Sunday and the last is Palm Sunday. The week preceding Easter is HOLY WEEK. Lent ends at midnight Holy Saturday. See SHROVE TUESDAY.

lentil, leguminous Old World annual plant (*Lens culinaris*) with whitish or pale blue flowers. Its pods contain two greenish brown or dark-colored seeds, also called lentils, which when fully ripe are ground into meal or used in soups and stews. Probably indigenous to SW Asia, and known to have been used as early as the Bronze Age, the lentil was introduced to Greece and Egypt before biblical times and was one of the first food plants cultivated in Europe. Esau sold his heritage for a mess of lentils—although the name in the Scriptures may have been applied to several plants. Lentils are unusually high in protein content and are much used for food in Europe, especially by the poor, and increasingly in the United States. Many varieties are cultivated, for the seeds as well as for forage. *Revalenta Arabica,* a lentil meal used in a sick person's diet, is an article of commerce. Lentil seeds, from their shape, gave their name to the magnifying lens. The gulfweed (see SEAWEED) is sometimes called sea lentil. Lentils are classified in the division MAGNOLIOPHYTA, class Magnoliopsida, order Rosales, family Leguminosae.

Lentulus (lĕn'tyo͞oləs), ancient Roman patrician family of the Cornelian gens. **Publius Cornelius Lentulus Sura,** d. 63 B.C., was notorious for his private life and was ejected from the senate because of it. He was quaestor (81) and twice praetor (75 and 63). He joined the conspiracy of CATILINE, who put him in charge of the operations in the city. By opening negotiations with the Allobrogian ambassadors, he spoiled the plot. He was arrested and strangled. **Publius Cornelius Lentulus Spinther,** d. after 49 B.C., was curule aedile (63), praetor (60), and consul (57). He was a consistent partisan of Cicero, who gave him charge of Publius Cornelius Lentulus Sura on the revelation of the Catiline conspiracy. As consul he was instrumental in procuring Cicero's recall, and he received Cilicia for his proconsulship. In 49, Lentulus Spinther took sides with Pompey against Caesar; he was executed after PHARSALA.

Lenya, Lotte (lôt'ə lĕn'yä), 1900–, Viennese singer and character actress, b. Caroline Blamauer. The widow of the composer Kurt WEILL, Lenya is still the foremost singer of his songs. She and Weill fled Germany in 1933 to work in the United States, where she appeared in *The Threepenny Opera* (as Jenny, a role she created in Berlin), *Brecht on Brecht, Mahagonny,* and *Cabaret.* Lenya has also made recordings and films (including *The Roman Spring of Mrs. Stone,* 1961, and *From Russia with Love,* 1963).

Lenz, Jakob Michael Reinhold (yä'kôp mĭkh'äĕl rīn'hôlt lĕnts), 1751–92, German writer. He was a friend of Goethe, whom he first imitated, then lampooned. A gifted poet, he wrote lyric poems; plays, including the comedies *Der Hofmeister* (1774) and *Die Soldaten* (1776); and critical works, notably *Anmerkungen übers Theater* [remarks on the theater] (1774). He is a principal representative of the STURM UND DRANG movement.

Lenz's law, physical law, discovered by the German scientist H. F. E. Lenz in 1834, that states that the ELECTROMOTIVE FORCE (emf) induced in a conductor moving perpendicular to a magnetic field tends to oppose that motion. When an electric MOTOR is in operation, the armature is turning in a magnetic field, and an emf is thus induced in it. Lenz's law requires that this emf, called back emf or counter emf, oppose the motion of the armature and also the original emf, causing the motor to operate. As a result, the speed of the motor changes in such a way that the energy supplied by the original voltage source less the energy required to overcome the back emf is always exactly equal to the sum of the energy used to drive the mechanism to which the motor is attached and the energy lost as heat within the motor. Lenz's law may thus be seen as a consequence of the law of conservation of energy (see CONSERVATION LAWS, in physics).

Leo I, Saint (Saint Leo the Great), c.400–461, pope (440–61), an Italian; successor of St. Sixtus III. A Doctor of the Church, he was one of the greatest pontiffs of the early years of the church. He waged a firm campaign against schism and heresy. With the aid of VALENTINIAN III, the Roman emperor of the West, he campaigned to eliminate Manichaeism from Italy. Later, asserting his authority over St. HILARY OF ARLES, he obtained an imperial rescript that effectively confirmed the authority of the pope over all his bishops. In the Nestorian-Monophysite controversy Leo was the leader in defending Catholic teaching. He wrote the celebrated *Tome of Leo,* a doctrinal letter defining the two natures and one person of Christ that was later adopted as ecumenical at Chalcedon (see CHALCEDON, COUNCIL OF), when the heresiarch Eutyches was condemned. He was also effective as a statesman and met (452) ATTILA the Hun to persuade him not to invade Rome. In 455 he similarly urged Gaiseric the Vandal to spare the lives of the Romans. St. Leo's letters and sermons reflect the many aspects of his career and personality, including his great personal influence for good, and are invaluable historical sources. His rhythmic prose style, called *cursus leonicus,* influenced ecclesiastical language for centuries. The celebrated *Leonian Sacramentary,* the oldest form of the Roman Missal, is probably not his work. He was succeeded by St. Hilary. Feast: April 11.

Leo III, Saint, d. 816, pope (795–816), a Roman; successor of Adrian I. He was attacked about the face and eyes by members of Adrian's family, who hoped to render him unfit for the papacy. Leo recovered and fled (799) to Charlemagne's protection at Paderborn. In 800, CHARLEMAGNE went to Rome and conducted a trial during which Leo successfully defended himself against charges of misconduct made by his enemies. On Christmas day, 800, Leo crowned Charlemagne emperor, the event that traditionally marks the beginning of the Holy Roman Empire. Leo's successor, Stephen IV, crowned Charlemagne's son, Louis the Pious, and thus was established the papal claim to the right to consecrate the emperor. In the East-West controversy over the Procession of the Holy Spirit, Leo declared that the *Filioque* of the CREED was dogmatically necessary but liturgically dispensable, and he recommended its omission in the name of East-West unity. Leo did much to beautify Christian Rome. He was sanctified in 1673. Feast: June 12.

Leo IV, Saint, d. 855, pope (847–55), a Roman; successor of Sergius II. He had seen the Saracen attack on Rome (846), and to prevent its recurrence he fortified the city and its suburbs. He built a wall around the Vatican, established and fortified the part of Rome still called the Leonine City, and rebuilt churches. He crowned Louis II Holy Roman emperor. Leo was succeeded by Benedict III. Feast: July 17.

Leo IX, Saint, 1002–54, pope (1049–54), a German named Bruno, b. Alsace; successor of Damasus II. A relative of Holy Roman Emperor Conrad II, he was educated at Toul and was made bishop there in 1027. As pope he traveled widely, vigorously combating clerical incontinency and simony. The chief figure in this reform program was Hildebrand (later Pope Gregory VII). The heresy of Berengar of Tours on the Real Presence and his quarrel with Lanfranc also occupied the attention of the pope and Hildebrand. St. Leo mediated questions presented by England, France, and Hungary. He added to the papal lands in Italy through an exchange with Emperor Henry III. He fought the Normans of S Italy, but was defeated (1053) at Civitella. The bitter feeling between East and West brought an attack (1053) on the pope by Michael Cerularius, the patriarch of Constantinople. This culminated in the excommunication of Michael and those in his communion by the papal legates (1054), an action that began the formal schism between East and West. The schism became definite in 1439. He was succeeded by Victor II. Feast: April 19.

Leo X, 1475–1521, pope (1513–21), a Florentine named Giovanni de' Medici; successor of Julius II. He was the son of Lorenzo de' Medici, was made a cardinal in his boyhood, and was head of his family before he was 30 (see MEDICI). Leo was not a competent ruler; he was a good, pious man, a dilettante of letters and art, but not greatly interested in the advancement of the church. His chief fame rests on his patronage of Raphael, on the continuation of St. Peter's by Bramante, and on his literary circle, including Cardinals Bembo and Bibbiena and many others. The Fifth LATERAN COUNCIL, called with the hope that it would effect reforms, failed to achieve anything. The Protestant Reformation began when Martin Luther posted (1517) his famous theses against the sale of indulgences, an activity practiced by Leo to provide income for his building program. Leo condemned the heresies and excommunicated the reformers, notably with the bull *Exsurge Domine* (1520), but he failed to deal effectively with the trouble. In politics he brought the papacy temporary hegemony in Italy by dexterity in diplomatic maneuvers. Leo granted Henry VIII of England the title Defender of the Faith (*Defensor Fidei*). He was succeeded by Adrian VI.

Leo XIII, 1810–1903, pope (1878–1903), an Italian (b. Carpineto, E of Rome) named Gioacchino Pecci; successor of Pius IX. Ordained in 1837, he earned an excellent reputation as archbishop of Perugia (1846–77), and was created cardinal in 1853. Leo's election brought a turn in the course of the PAPACY; he was abreast of the times and tried, especially by preaching to the whole church, in encyclical letters, to form Roman Catholic attitudes appropriate to living in the modern world. His influence was increased by the length of his reign; thus he was able to furnish the college of cardinals with an unusual number of excellent men (including John Henry Newman in 1879 and James Gibbons in 1886). By a combination of vigor and tact he ended the KULTUR-

KAMPF (1887). He tried repeatedly to bring French Roman Catholics to support the republic. In 1885 his encyclical *Immortale Dei* charted the course of Catholics as responsible citizens in modern secular, democratic states; he thus refuted both the French royalists' claim that they were especially good Catholics and the contention of French anti-Catholics that the church was committed to political reaction. The letter was a great vindication of Catholic democrats. With the anti-Catholic government of Italy there was no conciliation. Leo's program for society appeared in *Rerum novarum* (1891), an arraignment of capitalism that also showed the insufficiencies of Marxian socialism; it set up Catholic aims and ideals. (It was supplemented in *Quadragesimo Anno* [1931] of Pius XI and in *Mater et Magistra* [1961] of John XXIII.) Leo met the intellectual attack on Christianity by advancing Thomism, with its insistence that there can be no conflict between science and faith; to this end he wrote *Aeterni Patris* (1879), declaring the philosophy of St. Thomas Aquinas official and requiring its study; he also founded the institute of Thomistic philosophy at the Univ. of Louvain. He was profoundly interested in the advancement of learning. He opened the Vatican secret archives to all scholars, and he reminded Catholic historians that nothing but the whole truth must be found in their work. He encouraged Bible study and set up (1902) the permanent Biblical Commission. He sponsored a number of faculties and universities, including the Catholic Univ. at Washington, D.C. For sheer productivity Leo surpassed all his predecessors in modern times. He was succeeded by Pius X. See biography by K. K. Burton (1962); studies by L. P. Wallace (1966) and Joseph Watzlawik (1966); Étienne Gilson, ed., *The Church Speaks to the Modern World* (tr. 1954; containing nine encyclicals of Pope Leo XIII); E. T. Gargan, ed., *Leo XIII and the Modern World* (1961).

Leo I, d. 474, Byzantine or East Roman emperor (457–74). Chosen by the senate to succeed Marcian, he sought to counteract the preponderance of Germans in the Roman army by enlisting Isaurians. A naval expedition (468) against the Vandals of Africa failed through the incompetence or treachery of the commander, BASILISCUS, who delayed his attack until Gaiseric was able to attack him with fire ships. Leo I was succeeded by his grandson, Leo II, a child of six, who died in the year of his accession; Leo I's son-in-law, Zeno, then became emperor.

Leo III (Leo the Isaurian or Leo the Syrian), c.680–741, Byzantine emperor (717–41). He was probably born in N Syria (rather than in Isauria, as formerly thought). He held diplomatic and military posts before he deposed and succeeded Theodosius III. His accession ended the anarchy into which the empire had fallen since the reign of JUSTINIAN II. Leo defended Constantinople against the last Arab siege (717–18), and although he had to contend with Arab attacks in Asia Minor, he succeeded in ending serious Arab threats for nearly two centuries and reorganized the military provinces (*themes*) of the empire for greater efficiency. His civil code, the *Ecloga*, written in Greek rather than in Latin, was a practical handbook that had considerable influence in Byzantium. He is also credited with issuing military, maritime, and rural codes. Leo's attack (726) on devotion to holy images began the long struggle over ICONOCLASM. Riots and rebellions broke out in Greece while Byzantine rule in Italy (the exarchate of Ravenna and the Pentapolis) began to crumble. The popes Gregory II and Gregory III opposed Leo's iconoclasm and successfully defied his armed expeditions, thus virtually ending Byzantine suzerainty over Rome. Nevertheless, Leo left a revitalized empire to his son, Constantine V. The Isaurian, or Syrian, dynasty, which he founded, ruled the Byzantine Empire until 802.

Leo IV (Leo the Khazar), d. 780, Byzantine emperor (775–80), son and successor of Constantine V. He owed his nickname to his mother, a Khazar princess. Leo tempered the iconoclastic excesses of his father's reign. On his death his Athenian wife, Irene, became regent for their son, Constantine VI.

Leo V (Leo the Armenian), d. 820, Byzantine emperor (813–20), successor of Michael I. A former general, Leo successfully defended (813) Constantinople against the Bulgars and concluded a 30-year truce with them. Reviving ICONOCLASM, he deposed the patriarch NICEPHORUS in the synod of 815 and persecuted the orthodox party led by THEODORE OF STUDIUM. Leo was murdered by the supporters of his successor, Michael II.

Leo VI (Leo the Wise or Leo the Philosopher), 862?–912, Byzantine emperor (886–912), son and successor of Basil I. He added to the work of his father by the publication (887–93) of the *Basilica*, a modernization of the law of Justinian I and of canon law. Leo attempted to end the schism which had been provoked by the patriarch PHOTIUS, but the quarrel was renewed (906), partly over the issue of Leo's fourth marriage. During his reign, Leo was forced to pay tribute to the Bulgars after his defeat in 896. The Arabs completed the conquest of Sicily by taking Taormina in 902. They then sacked Salonica (906), and advanced in Asia Minor. Among Leo's edicts are the *Tactics*, for the army and navy, and the *Book of the Prefect*, on the duties of that officer, including his jurisdiction over the guilds of Constantinople. Leo was succeeded by his brother Alexander (reigned 912–13) and by his son Constantine VII.

Leo [Lat.,=the lion], northern CONSTELLATION lying S of Ursa Major and on the ECLIPTIC (apparent path of the sun through the heavens) between Cancer and Virgo; it is one of the constellations of the ZODIAC. The Egyptians, Babylonians, Arabs, and Greeks all represented this constellation as a lion; it may be the first constellation to be pictorially represented. The most famous star in Leo is REGULUS (Alpha Leonis). The western part of the constellation is a curved line known as the Sickle; it represents the lion's head. The main constellation terminates in Denebola (Beta Leonis), the Lion's Tail. The METEOR SHOWERS known as the Leonids appear to come from this constellation. Leo reaches its highest point in the evening sky in April.

Leo Africanus (ăfrĭkā'nəs), c.1465–1550, Moorish traveler in Africa and the Middle East. His arabic name was Al-Hassan ibn Muhammad. Captured by pirates, he was sent as a slave to Pope Leo X. He became a Christian, adopting the name Johannes Leo, and taught Arabic in Rome. There he wrote in Arabic a description of his journeys in Africa (issued in Italian in 1526), which was for many years the only known source on the Sudan. An English translation (1600) was reissued by the Hakluyt Society as *The History and Description of Africa* (3 vol., 1896, repr. 1963).

Leoben (lā'ōbən), city (1971 pop. 35,200), Styria prov., S central Austria, on the Mur River. An industrial center in a coal-mining region, it has large ironworks, textile mills, and breweries. An armistice between France and Austria, preliminary to the Treaty of CAMPO FORMIO, was signed (1797) at Leoben to conclude Napoleon I's victorious Italian campaign.

Leochares (lēŏk'ərēz), fl. 4th cent. B.C., Greek sculptor, probably an Athenian. Leochares was associated in the decoration of the Mausoleum at Halicarnassus. He is known to have made portraits, including a gold and ivory group of Philip, Alexander, and others, for Olympia. His *Lion Hunt of Alexander* was made with Lysippos after 321 B.C. A copy of his *Ganymede and the Eagle of Zeus* is in the Vatican. The *Apollo Belvedere* (Vatican) is sometimes attributed to him, and the *Diana of Versailles* (Louvre), conceived as a companion piece, also reflects his style.

Leominster (lĕm'ĭnstər), city (1970 pop. 32,939), Worcester co., N central Mass.; set off from Lancaster 1740, inc. as a city 1915. Plastics are made there. It was the birthplace of John Chapman (Johnny Appleseed).

León, Juan Ponce de: see PONCE DE LEÓN, JUAN.

León, Luis Ponce de (lōōēs' pōn'thā dā lāōn'), 1527?–1591, Spanish mystic and poet, an Augustinian monk. Fray Luis held various theological chairs at the Univ. of Salamanca. A noted Hebraist, he translated the Song of Songs and the Book of Job. His theological disputes with leading Dominicans and his translations caused him to be imprisoned for four years by the Inquisition. Of his exquisite lyric poetry, enhanced by a humanist familiarity with classical and Hebrew literature, only 23 poems survive. His work was not published until 1631. Fray Luis's prose works include *Los nombres de Cristo* (1583; tr. *The Names of Christ,* 1926) and *La perfecta casada* [the perfect wife] (1583). See biographies by James Fitzmaurice-Kelly (1921) and A. F. G. Bell (1925); studies by Manuel Durán (1971) and K. A. Kottman (1972).

León, region and former kingdom (1970 pop. 1,172,262), NW Spain, E of Portugal and Galicia. It includes the provinces of León, Salamanca, and Zamora, named after their chief cities. It is sparsely populated, and the climate is harsh; winters are long and cold, and the summers are extremely hot and often accompanied by drought. Northern León, which is crossed by the Cantabrian mts., has coal mines, forests, and mountain pastures; the rest of the region is a dry plateau drained by the Duero River and its tributaries; livestock are raised, and cereals, hops, and flax are grown. Industries are based on the processing of the agricultural and forest products; León has long been noted for its linen manufactures. Early in the Christian reconquest, the kings of Asturias gained control over León (8th–9th cent.); their territory, of which the city of León was made the capital in the 10th cent., became the kingdom of Asturias and León. The power of the kings also extended over Galicia and part of Castile, Navarre, and the Basque Province, but it was too weak to prevent the rise of the independent kingdoms of Navarre and Castile. León was conquered (1037) by Ferdinand I of Castile, on whose death (1065) the kingdoms again became separate. Reunited in 1072 under Alfonso VI, León and Castile were again separated in the 12th cent. and remained so until Ferdinand III accomplished the final reunion in 1230.

León, city (1970 pop. 453,976), Guanajuato state, central Mexico. It is located in a fertile river valley c.5,600 ft (1,700 m) high, but with a mild, temperate climate. Frequent floods, which in 1888 almost washed the city away, necessitated the building of a protective dam. León, on the main rail line between El Paso, Texas, and Mexico City, is a commercial, agricultural, and mining center. It is also one of Mexico's leading shoe manufacturers and has gained fame for the knives and iron goods produced by local artisans. The city's mines yield gold, copper, silver, lead, and tin. León was officially founded in 1577.

León, city (1970 est. pop. 90,897), W Nicaragua. It is the second largest city of the republic. León is the rail and commercial center between CORINTO and MANAGUA. It was founded in 1524 on Lake Managua by Francisco FERNÁNDEZ DE CÓRDOBA and moved westward to its present site in 1610 after a severe earthquake. In colonial times León was the political hub of Nicaragua. Center of the intellectuals and artisans, León became the stronghold of the liberal forces after independence from Spain (1821) and engaged in bitter rivalry with conservative GRANADA. Costly revolutions, in one of which León accepted aid from William WALKER, led to the founding of Managua (1855). The poet Rubén Darío is buried in the cathedral in León. Some of the city's Spanish colonial atmosphere survives.

León, city (1970 pop. 105,235), capital of León prov., NW Spain, at the foot of the Cantabrian mts. and at the confluence of the Bernesga and Torio rivers. It is an agricultural and commercial center. Dating from Roman times, it was reconquered from the Moors in 882 by Alfonso III of Asturias. Early in the 10th cent., León replaced Oviedo as the capital of the kingdom of Asturias, which became the kingdom of León. The city flourished in the 12th and 13th cent. but declined after the kings of León and Castile made Valladolid their favored residence. It still retains a medieval atmosphere, and its many historic monuments attract tourists. Most notable is the Spanish Gothic cathedral (13th–14th cent.).

Leonard, Benny, 1896–1947, American boxer, originally named Benjamin Leiner, b. New York City. Leonard, a master boxer and hard puncher, fought in 209 professional bouts, losing only 5. He was lightweight champion from 1917 until 1925, when he retired as undefeated champion. After a brief comeback in 1931–32, he became a boxing referee.

Leonard, William Ellery, 1876–1944, American poet, b. Plainfield, N.J., grad. Boston Univ., 1899, Ph.D. Columbia, 1904. For many years he was professor of English at the Univ. of Wisconsin. Of his numerous volumes of poetry the most famous is *Two Lives* (1922), a sonnet sequence relating the tragic story of his first marriage, which ended in his young wife's suicide. His psychological autobiography, *The Locomotive God* (1927), describes his distance phobia. Leonard wrote many scholarly works, notably translations of *Beowulf* and of the writings of Lucretius.

Leonardo da Pisa: see FIBONACCI, LEONARDO.

Leonardo da Vinci (də vĭn'chē, Ital. lāōnär'dō dä vēn'chē), 1452–1519, Italian painter, sculptor, architect, musician, engineer, and scientist, b. near Vinci, a hill village in Tuscany. He was the illegitimate son of a Florentine notary and a peasant girl. Presumably he passed his childhood with his father's family in Vinci, where he developed his enduring interest in nature. Early sources describe his beauty, charm of manner, and precocious display of artistic talent. In 1466 he moved to Florence, where he entered the workshop of Verrocchio and came into contact with such artists as Botticelli, Ghirlandaio, and Lorenzo di Credi. Early in his apprenticeship he painted an angel, and perhaps portions of the landscape, in Verrocchio's *Baptism of Christ* (Uffizi). In 1472 he was registered in the painters' guild. The culmination of Leonardo's art during his first period in Florence is the magnificent unfinished *Adoration of the Magi* (Uffizi) commissioned in 1481 by the monks of San Donato a Scopeto. In this work is revealed the integration of dramatic movement and chiaroscuro that characterizes the master's mature style. He went to Milan c.1482 and remained at the court of Ludovico Sforza for 16 years. In this time he composed the greater part of his *Trattato della pittura* and the extensive notebooks that demonstrate the marvelous versatility and penetration of his genius. As court artist he also organized elaborate festivals. Severe plagues in 1484 and 1485 drew his attention to problems of town planning, an interest which was revived during his last years in France. Many drawings of plans and elevations for domed churches reflect a concern with architectural problems that must have been stimulated by contact with Bramante during these years. He worked c.1488 on a model for the tambour and dome of the cathedral at Milan. In 1490 he was employed with Francesco di Giorgio as consulting engineer on the restoration of the cathedral at Pavia and later on the cathedral at Piacenza. In 1483, Leonardo, with his pupil Ambrogio de Predis, was commissioned to execute the famous *Madonna of the Rocks.* Two versions of the painting exist—one in the Louvre (1483–c.1486), another in the National Gallery, London (1483–1508). Leonardo's fresco of the *Last Supper* (Milan) was begun c.1495 and completed by 1498. This work is now badly damaged. Leonardo's own experiments with the fresco medium account in part for its disintegration, which was already noticed by 1517. Deterioration and repeated restorations have obliterated details and individual figures. Despite this, the composition and general disposition of the figures reveal a power of invention and a sublimity of spiritual content that mark the painting among the world's masterpieces. While at Ludovico's court, Leonardo also worked on an equestrian monument to the duke's father, Francesco Sforza. The work was never cast, and the model, admired by his contemporaries, perished during the French invasion of 1499. In 1511 he undertook a similar work with the commission of an equestrian monument for Gian Giacomo Trivulzio. This work was also never completed and known only through drawings related to the project. After the fall (1499) of Ludovico Sforza, Leonardo left Milan and, following brief sojourns in Mantua and Venice, returned to Florence in 1500. Here he engaged in much theoretical work in mathematics and pursued his anatomical studies at the hospital of Santa Maria Nuova. In 1502 he entered the service of Cesare Borgia as a military engineer. His engagement took him to central Italy to study swamp reclamation projects in Piombino and to tour the cities of Romagna. At Urbino he met Niccolò Machiavelli, who later became a close friend. By 1503 he was back in Florence, where he was commissioned to execute the fresco of the battle of Anghiari. This work, like its companion piece assigned to Michelangelo, was never completed, and the cartoons were subsequently destroyed. The work exerted enormous influence on later artists, however, and some impression of the original may be had from anonymous copies in the Uffizi and Casa Horne (Florence), from an engraving of 1558 of Lorenzo Zacchia, and from a drawing by Rubens (Louvre). From about this time dates the celebrated *Mona Lisa* (Louvre), the portrait of the wife of a Florentine merchant. In 1506, Leonardo returned to Milan, engaged by Charles d'Amboise in the name of the French king, Louis XII. Here he again served as architect and engineer. Gifted with a gargantuan curiosity concerning the physical world, he continued his scientific investigations, concerning himself with problems of geology, botany, hydraulics, and mechanics. In 1510–11 his interest in anatomy quickened considerably. At the same time he was active as painter and sculptor, had many pupils, and profoundly influenced the Milanese painters. A painting generally ascribed to this period is the *St. Anne, Mary, and the Child* (Louvre), a work which exemplifies Leonardo's handling of *sfumato*—misty, subtle transitions in tone. In 1513 he went to Rome, attracted by the patronage of the newly elected Medici pope, Leo X, and his brother Giuliano. Here he found the field dominated by Michelangelo and Raphael. The aging master was assigned to various architectural and engineering projects at the Vatican and received commissions for several paintings. It was perhaps in this period that he executed the enigmatic painting of the young *St. John the Baptist* (Louvre). Giuliano de'Medici left Rome in 1515 and died at Fiesole in the following year. It is conjectured that Leonardo left with him, attached to his household, and that soon afterward he accepted an invitation of Francis I of France to settle at the castle of Cloux, near Amboise. Here the old master was left entirely free to pursue his own researches until his death. Although there is no certain record of his last years, he seems to have been active with festival decoration and to have been interested in a canal project. Notes and drawings ascribed to this late period show his continued interest in natural philosophy and experimental science. The versatility and creative power of Leonardo mark him as a supreme example of Renaissance genius. He depicted in his drawings, with scientific precision and consummate artistry, subjects ranging from flying machines to caricatures; he also executed intricate anatomical studies of people, animals, and plants. The richness and originality of intellect expressed in his notebooks reveal one of the greatest minds of all time. In 1965 two previously lost notebooks were discovered in the National Library of Spain, Madrid. The first is a vast work concerning technological principles; the second is an intellectual diary spanning 14 years. They are published as *The Madrid Codices* (1974). See *Leonardo da Vinci: Life and Work, Paintings and Drawings,* ed. by Ludwig Goldschneider (8th ed., 1967); *The Notebooks of Leonardo da Vinci,* ed. by J. P. Richter (2 vol., 1970); *The Literary Works of Leonardo da Vinci,* ed. by J. P. Richter (3d ed., 1970); I. B. Hart, *The World of Leonardo da Vinci* (1962, repr. 1970); P. R. Ritchie-Calder, *Leonardo and the Age of the Eye* (1970); Carlo Pedretti, *Leonardo: a Study in Chronology and Style* (1973); Ladislao Reti, ed., *The Unknown Leonardo* (1974).

Leoncavallo, Ruggiero (rōōd-jâ'rō lā"ōnkävälˈlō), 1858–1919, Italian composer. The opera *Pagliacci* (1892), his one outstanding success, is a classic example of Italian *verismo,* or realism. Of his numerous other operas, only *Zaza* (1900) had moderate success.

Leoni, Leone (lāō'nā lāō'nē), 1509–90, Italian sculptor and medalist, called Leone Aretino. Entering the service of the emperor, Charles V, he devoted himself to making statues, busts, and reliefs for the imperial family. His *Charles V Repressing Violence* and other works are in the Prado. His son, **Pompeo Leoni,** c.1533–1608, who worked with him, continued in the imperial service. His most important works were kneeling bronze figures of Charles V and Philip II, with their families, for the sanctuary in the Escorial. He executed many fine tomb monuments with figures at prayer, including two effigies now in the Hispanic Society, New York City. See study by B. I. Proske (1956).

Leoni, Raúl (räōōl' lāō'nē), 1905–72, president of Venezuela (1964–69). As a student (1921) he was jailed for political activity and during the next 37 years was several times exiled. He returned to Caracas after the overthrow of President Pérez Jiménez in 1958, was elected to the senate, and became leader of the Democratic Action party. As president, he continued Rómulo Betancourt's social and economic reforms and launched an ambitious program to develop the interior. His succession by Rafael Caldera, a Social Christian, marked the first time in Venezuelan history that power was peacefully transferred to a member of an opposition party.

Leonidas (lēŏn'ĭdəs), d. 480 B.C., king of Sparta. He succeeded (c.491 B.C.) his half brother, Cleomenes I. When the Persians invaded Greece under Xerxes (480 B.C.), Leonidas with 300 Spartans and 5,000 auxiliaries was given the pass at Thermopylae to hold. There was treachery. Most of the Greeks got away, but the Spartans and 700 Thespians refused to flee and were killed. Herodotus immortalized the incident. See PERSIAN WARS.

Leonov, Leonid Maksimovich (lyāənyĕt' məksyĕm'-əvĭch lyāō'nəf), 1899–, Russian novelist and playwright. Leonov is a major figure in the development of psychological and social realism in the novel. His works are strongly influenced by Dostoyevsky in their complex style, psychological insight, and compassion for the downtrodden. His first long novel, *The Badgers* (1924, tr. 1947), is concerned with the deep cleavage between urban and rural life in the Soviet Union. His greatest novel, *The Thief* (1927, tr. 1931), treats the redemption of a former Red Army commissar who had become a bandit. Among Leonov's other novels are *Sot* (1931, tr. *Soviet River,* 1932), *Road to the Ocean* (1935, tr. 1944), *The Taking of Velikoshumsk* (1944, tr. *Chariot of Wrath,* 1946), and *Russian Forest* (1953). As a dramatist, Leonov is best known for *The Orchards of Polovchansk* (1936, tr. 1946 in *Seven Soviet Plays*), and *Invasion* (1942, tr. 1943 in *Four Soviet War Plays*). Leonov's work has received two Stalin prizes; he is among the most greatly honored of Soviet authors. See E. J. Simmons, *Russian Fiction and Soviet Ideology: Introduction to Fedin, Leonov, and Sholokhov* (1958); study by Nathan Rosen (1961).

Leontief, Wassily (lē'ŏntēf), 1906–, American economist, b. Russia, grad. Univ. of Berlin (Ph.D., 1928). The son of a Russian economist, he and his family left the Soviet Union in 1925 because of their opposition to the Bolshevik government. After serving as an adviser on railroad construction to the Chinese government (1929), he emigrated to the United States. He joined the faculty of Harvard in 1931, rising to the rank of professor in 1946. Since 1948 he has been director of Harvard's Economic Research Project. Leontief is best known for his development of the input-output method of economic analysis, used by most industrialized nations for planning and predicting economic progress. He was awarded (1973) the Nobel Memorial Prize in Economics.

Leontini (lēəntī'nī), ancient city, E Sicily, c.20 mi (32 km) S of Catania. It was (729 B.C.) a colony of Chalcidians from the island of Naxos and passed (5th cent. B.C.) under the rule of Syracuse. It was sacked (A.D. 848) by Saracens and destroyed (1693) by an earthquake. It was the legendary home of the Laestrygones, a group of giants encountered by Odysseus. The modern town occupying the site is Lentini.

leopard, large carnivore of the CAT family, *Panthera pardus,* widely distributed in Africa and Asia. It is commonly yellow, buff, or gray, patterned with black spots and rings. The rings, unlike those of the New World JAGUAR, never have spots inside them. Black leopards are commonly called panthers, a name sometimes used for all leopards. Black leopards are not a distinct species, but merely a color variant, and often occur in normally colored litters. On close inspection black leopards may be seen to have the typical spotting, which is obscured by the darkness of the background. The melanism, or excessive pigmentation, of black leopards is a mutation and does not breed true. Leopards are somewhat smaller than lions and tigers; the largest males are about 7 ft (2.3 m) long, including the 3-ft (90-cm) tail. They are essentially forest dwellers, but are found all over Africa outside of the deserts and in Asia from the southwest to Korea and Java. They are solitary, nocturnal, and good climbers; they hunt both on the ground and in trees. They prey on monkeys, birds, and other small animals, including domestic stock. Unlike lions and tigers, they are inclined to attack humans when hunting or when startled. A closely related species is the snow leopard, or ounce, *P. uncia,* which replaces ordinary leopards in the high mountains of Central Asia. It has long whitish fur and diffuse spotting. In summer, when the mountain animals on which it preys range to high pastures, the snow leopard may climb to an altitude of 13,000 ft (3,900 m). It usually hunts at dusk or at night. More distantly related is the clouded leopard, *Neofelis nebulosa,* of the forests of SE Asia. Its gray or yellowish coat is strikingly marked with black and brown; it has stripes on the face and tail, spots on the limbs, and rosettes on the body. Its tail is exceptionally long and heavy and is thickly furred. The clouded leopard is nocturnal and arboreal in its habits. Hunting leopard is a name for the CHEETAH. Leopards are classified in the phylum CHORDATA, subphylum Vertebrata, class Mammalia, order Carnivora, family Felidae.

Leopardi, Giacomo, Conte (jä'kōmō kôn'tā lāōpär'dē), 1798–1837, Italian poet and scholar. An invalid from early childhood, he led a life of suffering and frustration. Much of the time he was a virtual prisoner of his parents, who largely through mistrust of his ideas kept him without funds. He was a liberal and an agnostic at a time when independence of thought was dangerous in Italy. His poetry, deeply patriotic and contemptuous of the Italian rulers of his day, is lyrical, lofty in feeling, and profoundly pessimistic. Leopardi's fame rests primarily on the poems *Canti* [songs], written between 1816 and 1836. They include patriotic appeals (the RISORGIMENTO was under way), verses of melancholy, and idylls of love and nature. In later years he turned to political and social satire with such works in prose as *Palinodia* and *Paralipomeni* (both 1837). Other prose works include *Zibaldóne,* his notebooks from 1817 until his death, and the *Operette morali* (1826–27, tr. *Essays, Dialogues, and Thoughts,* 1893 and 1905). A complete edition of his works was issued in 1845 by his friend Antonio Raniero. Leopardi is considered the outstanding poet of Italy in the 19th cent. See English translation of his poems by G. L. Bickersteth (1923); biography by J. H. Whitfield (1954); study by G. S. Singh (1964).

leopard shark: see DOGFISH.

Leopold I, 1640–1705, Holy Roman emperor (1658–1705), king of Bohemia (1656–1705) and of Hungary (1655–1705), second son and successor of Ferdinand III. Upon his elder brother's death (1654), Leopold, who had been educated for the church, became Ferdinand's heir. During his reign the Holy Roman Empire was menaced by the Ottoman Empire (Turkey) in the east and by King Louis XIV of France in the west. The Turkish invasions of Hungary were temporarily checked by the imperial commander MONTECUCCULI, but by the Treaty of Vasvar (1664) the Turks kept their conquests and their suzerainty over Transylvania. In the west, Leopold joined the anti-French coalition in the third (1672–78) of the DUTCH WARS. A revolt in Hungary against Hapsburg rule reopened war with the Ottomans, who supported the rebel leader THÖKÖLY. The Turks besieged Vienna (1683), which Leopold saved with the aid of King John III of Poland and the imperial general Charles V of Lorraine. Other victories followed. However, Leopold's attempts to stop French aggression divided his energies and postponed the successful conclusion of war with the Turks. In 1686 he formed a defensive alliance against France known as the League of Augsburg. In 1688, Louis XIV invaded the Palatinate and war broke out (see GRAND ALLIANCE, WAR OF THE). The Treaty of RYSWICK with Louis XIV temporarily halted French expansion. In the east the triumph of EUGENE OF SAVOY over the Turks at Zenta (1697) led to the Treaty of KARLOWITZ by which Leopold obtained nearly all of Hungary. War with France over the succession to the Spanish throne ensued in 1701 (see SPANISH SUCCESSION, WAR OF THE). After Leopold's death the war continued under Joseph I, his son and successor. During Leopold's reign Vienna became a cultural center. His particular interest was music, and he was a fair composer.

Leopold II, 1747–92, Holy Roman emperor (1790–92), king of Bohemia and Hungary (1790–92), as Leopold I grand duke of Tuscany (1765–90), third son of Maria Theresa. Succeeding his father, Holy Roman Emperor Francis I, in Tuscany, Leopold reorganized the Tuscan government, abolished torture and the death penalty, equalized taxation, and sought to gain control over the church. When Leopold succeeded (1790) his brother JOSEPH II as emperor and as ruler of the Hapsburg lands, he took over a nearly disrupted state. To pacify his subjects in the Austrian Netherlands (see NETHERLANDS, AUSTRIAN AND SPANISH), in Hungary, and in Bohemia, he repealed most of Joseph's reforms. Unlike Joseph, he had himself crowned king at Pozsony in Hungary (now Bratislava) and at Prague in Bohemia; he was the last crowned king of Bohemia. Having reached an agreement (1790) with Frederick William II of Prussia, who wished to prevent Austrian expansion in the east and was about to side with the Ottoman Empire (Turkey) in its war against Russia and Austria, Leopold abandoned his alliance with the Russian czarina, Catherine II. He concluded a separate peace treaty at Sistova (1791) with Turkey by which the pre-war borders were substantially restored. Leopold's troops marched into the Austrian Netherlands and suppressed the Belgian insurrection in 1790. Although he hoped to avoid war with revolutionary France, Leopold instigated (1791) the Declaration of PILLNITZ, by which the emperor and the king of Prussia stated that if all other European powers would join them, they were prepared to restore Louis XVI to his lawful powers by force. Contrary to his expectations, this declaration was a basic cause of the outbreak of the French Revolutionary Wars a few weeks after Leopold's death. Leopold was succeeded by his son, Francis II. Leopold II is generally considered a ruler of outstanding diplomatic and administrative abilities.

Leopold I, 1790–1865, king of the Belgians (1831–65); youngest son of Francis Frederick, duke of Saxe-Coburg-Saalfeld. After serving as a page at the court of Napoleon I and as a general of the Russian army, he married (1816) Princess Charlotte, daughter of the English prince regent (later King George IV) and heiress presumptive to the English throne. After her death (1817) Leopold remained in England. In 1830 he rejected the throne of Greece, but in 1831 he accepted election as king of newly formed Belgium. Though his primary concern was with maintaining the unity and independence of his kingdom, his reign was notable for such improvements as the introduction of ministerial responsibility, a reformed electoral law, and a national bank. He married (1832) a daughter of King Louis Philippe of France, and he brought about the marriage of his niece Queen VICTORIA of England to his nephew Prince ALBERT. He was succeeded by his son, Leopold II. He was also the father of CARLOTTA, empress of Mexico.

Leopold II, 1835–1909, king of the Belgians (1865–1909), son and successor of Leopold I. His reign was one of industrial and colonial expansion. In 1876 he organized, with the help of H. M. STANLEY, the International Association for the Exploration and Civilization of the Congo. At a European conference on African affairs (Berlin, 1884–85), the Congo Free State was established under Leopold's personal rule (see ZAÏRE). Leopold proceeded to amass a huge personal fortune by exploiting the Congo directly and by leasing concessions. Forced labor was extorted from the natives, frequently by barbarous methods, until scandal compelled Leopold to turn over the Congo to the Belgian government (1908). In Belgium itself the Conservative Catholic party replaced (1880) the Liberals in power. Increasing social discontent and the rise of the Labor party forced the introduction (1893) of universal male suffrage, but labor unrest continued because of the appalling condition of industrial workers. Leopold's private life was as scandalous and dissolute as his public conduct. He was succeeded by his nephew, Albert I.

Leopold III, 1901–, king of the Belgians (1934–51), son and successor of Albert I. In 1936, Leopold announced a fundamental change in foreign policy; Belgium abandoned its military alliance with France in favor of a return to neutrality. Leopold and Queen Wilhelmina of the Netherlands vainly sought to mediate at the outbreak (1939) of World War II. In May, 1940, Germany—which in 1937 had guaranteed Belgian neutrality—invaded the Low Countries. Leopold led the Belgian army in resisting the invaders. After the defense became hopeless, Leopold, over the opposition of his cabinet, surrendered unconditionally (May 28), thus provoking accusations of treason. A prisoner of war at his castle at Laken, Leopold refused to exercise active rule under German tutelage. His first wife, Astrid, having been killed in an automobile accident while Leopold was at the wheel, he married (1941) a commoner, whom he later created princess of Réthy. Removed (1944) to Germany, Leopold was freed by Allied troops in 1945. His return to Belgium was a burning political issue. The Liberal and leftist parties accused him of cooperation with Nazi Germany and of fascist sympathies, and his main support came from the Catholic Conservatives. In 1945, Leopold was barred from returning without the permission of the parliament. He spent his exile mostly in Switzerland while his brother, Prince Charles, acted as regent. A referendum held in 1950 favored the king's return by a slight majority. However, Leopold's arrival in Belgium was followed by such unrest that he transferred the royal powers to his eldest son, BAUDOUIN. In July, 1951, Leopold formally abdicated.

Leopold I, 1676–1747, prince of Anhalt-Dessau (1693–1747). He served as field marshal in the Prussian army and was nicknamed "the Old Dessauer." As chief military adviser to King Frederick William I of Prussia, he reorganized the Prussian infantry, making it the best in Europe. A stern disciplinarian, Leopold was an able commander. He also helped introduce administrative reform in Prussia. In the War of the Austrian Succession (1740–48) his victory at Kesseldorf (1745) helped bring about the Treaty of Dresden between Prussia and Austria.

Leopold I, grand duke of Tuscany: see LEOPOLD II, Holy Roman emperor.

Leopold II, 1797–1870, grand duke of Tuscany (1824–59). Liberally inclined at first, he granted some reforms and undertook public works. In 1848 he approved a constitution and joined Sardinia in its war against Austria (see RISORGIMENTO). Refusing the demands of the extremists, however, Leopold left Tuscany in Feb., 1849, and returned several months later in the wake of Austrian troops. In 1852 he repealed the constitution, and in 1859 he was forced to abdicate in favor of his son, Ferdinand IV, who was deposed in 1860.

Leopold III or **Saint Leopold,** c.1073–1136, margrave of Austria (1095–1136). By his marriage (1106) with Agnes, widow of Duke Frederick I of Swabia (see HOHENSTAUFEN), he became the stepfather of German King Conrad III and the father of Otto of Freising and of Duke Henry II of Austria (see BABENBERG). He helped arrange the Concordat of Worms (1122), which ended the conflict over investiture. In 1125 he refused an offer of the imperial crown. The founder of numerous monasteries (of which Heiligenkreuz, Klosterneuburg, and Mariazell still exist), Leopold was canonized in 1485 and is the patron saint of Austria. Feast: November 15.

Leopoldville: see KINSHASA, Zaïre.

Leovigild (lēōv'ĭgĭld", lēō'-), d. 586, Visigothic king of Spain (568–86), brother and successor of Athanagild. He was joint ruler to 573 with his brother Liuva. He reorganized the administration and assumed a royal pomp that imitated that of the Byzantine court. Leovigild was constantly at war with the Byzantines in S Spain and the Suevi in the north. When these enemies supported the revolt of his son Hermenegild, who had converted from Arianism to Catholicism, he finally annexed (584–85) the kingdom of the Suevi. Hermenegild was put to death. At the end of Leovigild's reign the only non-Visigothic parts of Spain were two small territories of the Byzantine Empire. Leovigild made important additions to the Visigothic laws (see GERMANIC LAWS). His son Recared succeeded him.

Lepanto, battle of (lĭpăn'tō), Oct. 7, 1571, naval battle between the Christians and Turks fought at the mouth of the Gulf of Patras, off Lepanto, Greece. The fleet of the Holy League commanded by JOHN OF AUSTRIA (d. 1578) opposed the Turkish fleet under Uluç Ali Pasha. The allied fleet (about 200 galleys, not counting smaller ships) consisted mainly of Spanish, Venetian, and papal ships and of vessels sent by a number of Italian states. It carried approximately 30,000 fighting men and was about evenly matched with the Turkish fleet. The battle ended with the virtual destruction of the Turkish navy (except 40 galleys, with which Uluç Ali escaped). Approximately 15,000 Turks were slain or captured, some 10,000 Christian galley slaves were liberated, and much booty was taken. The victors, however, lost over 7,000 men. Among the allied wounded was Cervantes, who lost the use of his left arm. Lepanto was the first major Turkish defeat by the Christian powers, and it ended the myth of Turkish naval invincibility. It did not, however, affect Turkish supremacy on the land, and a new Turkish fleet was speedily built by Sokollu, grand vizier of Selim II. Nevertheless, the battle was decisive in the sense that a Turkish victory probably would have made the Ottoman Empire supreme in the Mediterranean.

Lepcis: see LEPTIS.

Lepidodendron (lĕp"ĭdōdĕn'drən) and **Sigillaria** (sĭjĭlâr'ēə), two principal genera of an extinct group of primitive vascular trees. They dominated the forests of the early CARBONIFEROUS PERIOD until the ferns gained ascendancy. Related to the CLUB MOSSES, they are sometimes called giant club mosses. The spore-bearing leaves formed cones. The tall, thick trunks, rarely branching, were crowned with a cluster of narrow leaves. The closely packed leaf scars left on the stems as the plants grew provide some of the most interesting and common fossils in shales and accompanying coal deposits. In *Lepidodendron* the leaf scars are diamond-shaped, and in *Sigillaria* they are arranged in vertical rows. The rhizomes, or root systems, of both genera, known as stigmaria, were thought to be distinct plants when their fossils were first discovered. Actually they served to support the trees and to produce new shoots. Lepidodendron and Sigillaria are classified in the division LYCOPODIOPHYTA, order Lepidodendrales.

Lepidus (lĕp'ĭdəs), family of the ancient Roman patrician gens Aemilia. **Marcus Aemilius Lepidus,** d. 77 B.C., was praetor of Sicily (81 B.C.). As consul (78 B.C.), he was bitterly opposed to the senatorial leader CATULUS (d. c.60 B.C.). When Lepidus was ostensibly on his way to his proconsulship in Gaul, he raised an army in N Italy. Pompey and Catulus defeated him, and he fled from Italy. His son, **Marcus Aemilius Lepidus,** d. 13 B.C., was praetor (49 B.C.) and consul (46 B.C.) with Caesar. He was appointed to Narbonese Gaul and Hither Spain. He supported ANTONY, who joined him in Gaul after the defeat at Mutina (modern Modena) in 43 B.C. They formed the Second Triumvirate with Octavian (AUGUSTUS). After the battle of Philippi (42 B.C.), Lepidus received the governorship of Africa, whence he returned (36 B.C.) to conquer Sicily. Octavian suspected him of trying to keep Sicily for himself and deprived him of his offices, except that of pontifex maximus.

Le Play, Pierre Guillaume Frédéric (pyĕr gēyōm' frādārēk' lə plā), 1806–82, French sociologist and economist. As an engineer he traveled through Europe, at the same time gathering data on the economic status of workers and making detailed studies to determine the relationships of the family and worker to the environment. His use of the social-survey method had a widespread influence on sociologists. Among his books are *Les Ouvriers europé-*

ens [the European workers] (1855), condensed and republished as *Réforme sociale en France* (1864), and *La Constitution de l'Angleterre* [the constitution of England] (1875). See biography by M. Z. Brooke (1970).

leprechaun (lĕp'rəkŏn), Irish fairy represented as a tiny old man. Leprechauns are mischievous and elusive creatures, said to possess buried crocks of gold, the location of which they will reveal if forced.

leprosy or **Hansen's disease,** chronic, mildly infectious malady capable of producing, when untreated, various deformities and mutilations. It is caused by the rod-shaped organism *Mycobacterium leprae,* first described by G. Armauer Hansen, a Norwegian physician, in 1874. The mode of transmission is not fully understood. The onset is intermittent and gradual, and symptoms of the disease may not appear until many years after exposure. In the tuberculoid form of the disease the skin lesions appear as light red or purplish spots, in the lepromatous type as yellow or brown infiltrated nodules (protuberances) that affect the mucous membranes of the eyes, nose, and throat. The former is the more benign type even though it is accompanied by nerve involvement. This leads to numbness (usually of the extremities), contractures, and ulceration. The diagnosis is established when the bacterium is isolated from the skin lesions or the mucous membrane of the nose. Duration and treatment of the disease depend upon its extent and character. Patients with nodular lesions are more difficult to treat and may succumb sooner; those with the neural type of lesion, despite possible mutilation and deformity, usually live longer and even experience spontaneous periods of subsidence of the malady. Sulfa drugs, sometimes coupled with streptomycin, have supplemented chaulmoogra oil in treatment; sulfones are the treatment of choice. In some cases therapy must be continued for at least 3 to 5 years before the disease can be arrested, and in the nodular type of leprosy treatment is effective in about 15% of the patients; in the neural type there is a much higher percentage of effective treatment. Diseases that probably included the malady now known as Hansen's disease are described as leprosy in the Bible; segregation and disinfection were advocated as methods of control (Lev. 13.14). Leprosy is believed to have existed in Egypt as long ago as 4000 B.C., and in India and Japan earlier than 1000 B.C. Infectious diseases from the East—all called leprosy—later spread over most of Europe and the British Isles, and the Crusades were a factor in disseminating them still farther, so that by the 13th cent. they had reached epidemic proportions. Leprosariums were eventually established in most countries for the care of those actually afflicted with leprosy. The disease still occurs in tropical and subtropical countries, especially where crowded and unsanitary conditions contribute to its spread, and even in the more developed countries it crops up from time to time. In the United States the disease is found mostly in Louisiana, Texas, Florida and occasionally in California. Infectious patients are cared for in the National Leprosarium, Carville, La.; many others receive outpatient treatment elsewhere.

Lepsius, Karl Richard (rĭkh'ärt lĕp'sēo͞os), 1810–84, German Egyptologist and philologist. He made an expedition (1842–45) to the Nile valley and the Sudan and as a result of his excavations and studies wrote *Denkmäler aus Ägypten und Äthiopien* [monuments from Egypt and Ethiopia] (12 vol., 1849–59), which remains an important archaeological work.

Leptis (lĕp'tĭs), ancient city of Libya, E of Tripoli. It was founded (c.600 B.C.) by Phoenicians from Sidon. Annexed (46 B.C.) to the Roman province of Africa, it flourished as an important port under the Romans, particularly during the reign of Septimius Severus (who had been born in Leptis). Some of the most impressive ruins of Roman Africa are there, including walls, baths, arches, temples, and forums. The city is also known as Lepcis. It is sometimes called Leptis Magna to distinguish it from another Leptis, S of Hadrumetum, in present Tunisia. See K. B. Matthews, Jr., *Cities in the Sand* (1957).

lepton (lĕp'tŏn") [Gr.,=light (i.e., lightweight)], class of ELEMENTARY PARTICLES that includes the ELECTRON and its ANTIPARTICLE, the MUON and its antiparticle, and the NEUTRINO and antineutrino associated with each of these particles. Leptons are the lightest class of particles having nonzero rest mass. From a technical point of view, they are defined by their behavior, being weakly interacting fermions, i.e., leptons can result from the slow decay of nuclear particles such as the neutron but do not experience a strong attraction toward the nuclear particles; they are described by the Fermi-Dirac statistics, which apply to all particles restricted by the Pauli EXCLUSION PRINCIPLE. This means that two identical leptons cannot occupy the same quantum state. However, one muon and one electron are allowed to occupy the same state. The muon was originally classed as a MESON because of its mass, about 200 times that of the electron, but the subsequent reclassification of particles on the basis of their behavior placed it with the electron in the lepton category. The electron and the muon are almost twins, except for their large mass difference; each is negatively charged, has a positively charged antiparticle, and has an associated neutrino and antineutrino. Separate laws govern the conservation of electron family number and of muon family number, the number being +1 for ordinary particles of either family and −1 for antiparticles (see CONSERVATION LAWS, in physics).

leptospirosis (lĕp"təspīrō'sĭs), febrile disease caused by bacteria of the genus *Leptospirae.* The disease occurs in dogs, cattle, pigs, sheep, goats, and horses and is transmissible to man. It is most common in areas where the climate is warm and humid, soils are alkaline, and there is abundant surface water. The source of infection in farm animals is usually through pastures, drinking water, or feed, when contaminated by infected urine. Infection may also occur as a result of contact with infected uterine discharges and aborted fetuses. Infected animals may pass the causative organism through the urine for as long as one year. Recovered animals can therefore act as carriers. In cattle, pigs, sheep, and goats, the disease is characterized by fever, depression, anemia, and abortion. Horses develop an ocular infection. In dogs the disease causes a severe kidney infection. Control of leptospirosis depends on the elimination of carrier animals, appropriate hygienic measures, and vaccination of susceptible animals.

Lerdo or **Ciudad Lerdo:** see TORREÓN.

Lerdo de Tejada, Miguel (mēgĕl' lĕr'thō dā tāhä'thä), d. 1861, Mexican liberal statesman, a leader of the Revolution of AYUTLA, cabinet member under Juan Álvarez. As minister under COMONFORT, he initiated the Ley Lerdo (1856), a law providing for the forced sale of all real property of the Roman Catholic Church. He helped draft the constitution of 1857 and later drew up a law nationalizing church property. His laws, disastrous failures in his day, were essential parts of the reforms of Benito JUÁREZ. His younger brother, **Sebastián Lerdo de Tejada,** 1820?–1889, also an important liberal in the Revolution of Ayutla, was for years a close associate of Juárez. He succeeded as provisional president after the death of Juárez (1872). A revolt under Porfirio DÍAZ, begun in 1871, was put down. The reform laws were incorporated in the constitution (1874). Order was restored for a time, but when, in 1876, Lerdo procured the consent of congress to his continuance in office, a new revolt began, again led by Porfirio Díaz. Lerdo's forces were defeated, and he fled to New York City, where he died. See biography by F. A. Knapp (1951, repr. 1968).

Lérida (lā'rēthä), city (1970 pop. 90,884), capital of Lérida prov., NE Spain, in Catalonia, on the Segre River. Lérida is the center of a fertile farm area and manufactures arms and chemicals. The ancient Ilerda, it was taken (49 B.C.) by Julius Caesar, who defeated Pompey's generals there. Lérida fell to the Moors in A.D. 714 and was liberated (1149) by Raymond Berengar IV of Barcelona. The university founded there (c.1300) by James II of Aragón was discontinued in 1717. Traditionally a strategic, fortified city, Lérida was a key defense point for Barcelona in the Spanish civil war; it fell (April, 1938) after a nine-month battle. The old section of the city is dominated by the castle, whose ramparts enclose a Romanesque cathedral.

Lérins (lārăNs'), group of four small islands, Alpes-Maritimes dept., SE France, in the Mediterranean Sea SE of Cannes. Sainte-Marguerite is the largest island. On Saint-Honorat is the oldest monastery in W Europe, founded (A.D. 400) by St. Honoratus.

Lerma, Francisco Gómez de Sandoval y Rojas, duque de (fränthēs'kō gō'māth dā sändōväl' ē rō'häs do͞o'kā dā lär'mä), 1553–1625, Spanish statesman, favorite of King PHILIP III. He became premier upon Philip's accession (1598) and controlled the government for 20 years. Lerma pursued a pacific foreign policy, ending (1604) the war with England and securing (1609) a 12-year truce in the Netherlands. Within Spain, however, he concentrated mainly on enriching himself. The most vigorous action taken by his administration was the expulsion (1609–14) of the Moriscos. In 1618, shortly after he had become a cardinal, he was ousted from power by his own son. After an inquiry ordered (1621) by Philip IV, Lerma was made to restore to the state part of his wealth.

Lerma (lār'mä), river, c.350 mi (560 km) long, rising in Mexico state, central Mexico. It flows NW and W through Guanajuato state to Lake Chapala, crossing the part of the central plateau known as the Anáhuac. The river draining the lake and flowing NW through Jalisco state to the Pacific Ocean is generally called the Rio Grande de Santiago (c.200 mi/320 km long) but it is considered a continuation of the Lerma. The river system is extensively used for irrigation and hydroelectric power.

Lermontov, Mikhail Yurevich (mēkhəyēl' yo͞or'yĭvĭch lyĕr'məntŭf), 1814–41, Russian poet and novelist. Given an extensive private education by his wealthy grandmother, Lermontov began writing poetry when he was 14. He first attracted public attention in 1837 with the inflammatory poem "On the Death of the Poet," written to protest the death of Pushkin in a duel. He was temporarily banished to the Caucasus, where he had recuperated from illness as a child. The stirring landscape became a prevailing element in his work. Of his early work, which was greatly influenced by Byron, only the lyric "The Angel" (1832) is equal to his later work. His poetic reputation, second in Russia only to Pushkin's, rests upon the lyric and narrative works of his last five years. *The Demon* (1829–41, tr. 1930), his narrative poem about the love of a fallen angel for a mortal, was used by Anton Rubinstein as the basis of an opera. *Mtsyri* (1840; tr. *The Circassian Boy,* 1875) reflects Lermontov's antireligious feeling and idealization of primitive life. His heroic poems include "Borodino" (1837) and "The Song of the Merchant Kalashnikov" (1837, tr. 1929). Lermontov's novel *A Hero of Our Time* (1840, tr. 1958) is partly autobiographical. It consists of five tales about Pechorin, a disenchanted and bored nobleman. The novel is considered a classic of Russian psychological realism. Lermontov, who had sought a position in fashionable society, became enormously critical of it. His caustic wit made him numerous enemies, and, like Pushkin, he was killed in a duel. See biography by Janko Lavrin (1959); study by John Mersereau (1962).

Lerner, Alan Jay, 1918–, American lyricist and librettist, b. New York City. After two years as a radio scriptwriter, Lerner began an association with the composer Frederick Loewe that resulted in several popular musicals, including *Brigadoon* (1947, film 1954), *Paint Your Wagon* (1951, film 1969), *Camelot* (1960, film 1967), and the Academy-Award-winning film *Gigi* (1958). Their highly successful *My Fair Lady* (1956, film 1964), an adaptation of Shaw's *Pygmalion,* ran for more than six years on Broadway and was translated into many languages. Lerner also wrote *Love Life* (1948) with Kurt Weill and the book for the film *An American in Paris* (1951).

Léros (lĕ'rôs, lē'rŏs), island (1971 pop. 8,494), c.20 sq mi (50 sq km), SE Greece, in the Aegean Sea; one of the DODECANESE.

Lerroux, Alejandro (älāhän'drō lāro͞o'), 1864–1949, Spanish politician. He first won prominence as a radical and virulently anticlerical demagogue in Barcelona. However, he gradually moved to the right politically. Under the second republic (1931–36) he held various cabinet positions and was several times premier from 1933 to 1935. In Oct., 1934, his government suppressed a miners' uprising in Asturias and a Catalan separatist revolt. A financial scandal forced his resignation in 1935. He fled to Portugal after the outbreak (1936) of civil war, but was allowed to return to Spain in 1947.

Lerwick (lûr'wĭk, lĕr'ĭk), burgh (1971 pop. 6,107), county town of Shetland, extreme N Scotland. On the southeastern coast of Mainland island, Lerwick has herring fishing and hosiery industries. It is the central market town of the Shetlands, dealing in produce, knitwear, cattle, and sheep. Lerwick grew up around a Dutch trading post in the 17th cent. Oliver Cromwell built a fort, named Fort Charlotte under George III, that is now a coast guard station. A Norse festival to celebrate the new year is held annually in January.

Les. For names beginning thus and not listed here, see second element; e.g., for Les Andelys, see ANDELYS, LES.

Le Sage, Alain René (älăN' rənā' ləsäzh'), 1668–1747, French novelist and dramatist. His masterpiece, *Gil Blas de Santillane* (1715–35, tr. by Tobias Smollett, *The Adventures of Gil Blas of Santillane,* 1749), is a rambling story in the style of Spanish picaresque romances, though unlike them in conception. It is instead strongly realistic, especially in its incidents; exact description of exterior and physical appearance suffices to show character and to imply moral judgment. *Gil Blas* was a major influence in the development of the realistic novel. Smollett drew heavily on it, especially in *Roderick Random.* Of Le Sage's lesser novels, *Le Diable boiteux* (1707, tr. *The Devil upon Two Sticks,* 1708) is an adaptation of a Spanish novel, and *Le Bachelier de Salamanque* (1736, tr. 1737) is an imitation of *Gil Blas.* Le Sage made his living by writing light pieces for the theaters of Paris; his best dramatic work is *Turcaret* (1709), a comedy of character, which bitterly satirizes tax farmers and the world of finance in general.

lesbianism: see HOMOSEXUALITY.

Lesbos (lĕz'bŏs) or **Lésvos** (lāz'vôs), island (1971 pop. 114,797), c.630 sq mi (1,630 sq km), E Greece, in the Aegean Sea near Turkey. A fertile island, it has vast olive groves and also produces wheat, wine, and citrus fruit. Sardines are caught. MITILÍNI is the island's chief town. Lesbos was a center of Bronze Age civilization and later (c.1000 B.C.) was settled by Aeolians. The island was a brilliant cultural center from the 7th to the 6th cent. B.C., when the poets Alcaeus and Sappho and the statesman Pittacus were active there. Aristotle and Epicurus lived on the island, and Theophrastus was born on Lesbos. Lesbos joined the Delian League and revolted unsuccessfully against Athens in 428–27 B.C. Later, Lesbos passed to Macedonia, Rome, and the Byzantine Empire. It was taken by the Ottoman Turks in 1462 and became part of Greece in 1913. The island is sometimes known as Mytilene, which is a variation of Mitilíni.

Les Cayes, Haiti: see AUX CAYES.

Lescaze, William (lĕskäz'), 1896–1969, American architect, born and trained in Switzerland. Emigrating to the United States in 1920, Lescaze became influential in introducing the new European architecture to America. His works emphasized prismatic simplicity, as in his plan for the Philadelphia Saving Fund Society Building (with George Howe, 1930–32) and the CBS studios in Hollywood (1938). His writings include *On Being an Architect* (1942).

Lescot, Pierre (pyĕr lĕskō'), c.1510–1578, French Renaissance architect. Appointed by Francis I to design a new royal palace in Paris, he built the earliest portions of what was later to become the vast palace of the Louvre. In this, as in other known works, the fine sculptural decorations were executed by Jean GOUJON. To Lescot is attributed the original design of the Hôtel Carnavalet in Paris, later altered by François Mansart. His work is marked by the correct use of classical detail. Instead of following the monumental style of the Italians, Lescot created a more decorative interpretation of antiquity, distinguishing himself as one of the founders of the French tradition of classicism.

Lesdiguières, François de Bonne, duc de (fräNswä' də bôn dük də lādēgyĕr'), 1543–1626, marshal and constable of France. He fought on the Huguenot (Protestant) side in the Wars of Religion and in 1575 became chief of the Huguenots of the Dauphiné. He supported Henry of Navarre (King HENRY IV) and in 1590 took Grenoble from the Catholic LEAGUE. He fought a series of campaigns against CHARLES EMMANUEL I of Savoy, and was made a marshal by Henry IV in 1609. After his abjuration of Protestantism (1622) he became constable of France under King Louis XIII. Upon his death Richelieu abolished the office of constable.

lese majesty or **leze majesty** (both: lēz mă'jĭstē) [Fr. *lèse majesté,* Lat. *laesae maiestatis (crimen)*= (crime of) violating majesty], offense against the dignity of the sovereign of a state or of a state itself. The offense as such first appeared in Rome but bore a decided resemblance to the crime against the people of Greek law. Although not defined with great exactness, lese majesty seems to have been considered originally as a violation of the fundamental laws of the Roman state, a crime against the Roman people. When the Roman Empire replaced the republic, the crime became an offense against the person of the emperor, but it still included cases that were more generally designated treason; all attempts to upset the state, as well as actions or words derogatory to, or dangerous to, the state were interpreted as offenses against the sovereign's person. This personality cult became the main element in the term lese majesty, which in time was applied especially to physical or verbal attack on the sovereign. The legislation against the crime passed into Germanic law, and feudal law heightened the personalization of the concept because of the personal nature of the feudal bond. In most modern states the specific crime of lese majesty is confounded with, and included in, the crime of TREASON. The decline of absolute monarchies hastened the disappearance of the crime, though it remained in German law until the fall of the German monarchy in 1918. In some modern countries, however, verbal attacks on the form of government, the head of the state, or public officials are made crimes analogous to lese majesty. See F. S. Lear, *Treason in Roman and Germanic Law* (1965).

Leshem (lē'shəm), original name of DAN **2.**

Leskov, Nikolai Semyonovich (nyĭkəlī' sĭmyô'nəvĭch lyĭskôf'), 1831–95, Russian short-story writer and novelist. Leskov was first a civil servant, then an agent for his uncle's business. Encouraged by his uncle he became a journalist and writer of narrative tales, told in a colorful, vital, and humorous style. An early story of sex and violence, "Lady Macbeth of the Mzinsk District" (1866, tr. in *The Sentry,* 1922), was used by Shostakovich as the basis of an opera (1934). *Cathedral Folk* (1872, tr. 1924) is a panoramic novel emphasizing the strengths of the provincial clergy and the faults of church bureaucracy. The brilliance of Leskov's narration transcended his frequent attempts to serve an idea. See translations of his tales by David Magarshack (1946) and W. B. Edgerton (1969).

Lesley, John: see LESLIE, JOHN.

Leslie, Alexander, 1st **earl of Leven:** see LEVEN ALEXANDER LESLIE, 1ST EARL OF.

Leslie, Charles Robert, 1794–1859, English painter and writer, b. London. Educated in the United States, he returned to England to study art and to work. He painted incidents from literature and also executed portraits, including one of Dr. John Wakefield Francis at the Metropolitan Museum. Leslie is probably best known for his writings which include *Memoirs of the Life of John Constable* (1843), *A Handbook for Young Painters* (1855), and *Autobiographical Recollections* (1860).

Leslie, David, d. 1682, Scottish military commander. After serving in the Swedish army, he was a major general under his uncle, Alexander Leslie, 1st earl of LEVEN, in the Scottish army that joined the forces of Oliver Cromwell in defeating the royalists at Marston Moor (1644). He defeated James Graham, earl of MONTROSE, at Philiphaugh in 1645. By 1650 he himself was supporting Charles II and as commander of the Scottish royalists was defeated by Oliver Cromwell at Dunbar (1650). After Charles's defeat at Worcester, Leslie was imprisoned (1651–60). He was created (1661) Baron Newark after the Restoration.

Leslie, Frank, 1821–80, American engraver and publisher, b. England. He learned his trade on the *Illustrated London News,* but in 1848 immigrated to New York City, where in 1855 he began publishing *Frank Leslie's Illustrated Newspaper.* His real name, Henry Carter, was discarded when his pseudonym, Frank Leslie, became widely known. He inaugurated a method for speedily illustrating current events by dividing his drawings into blocks that could be distributed among a number of engravers and afterwards reassembled. His profits and fame were greatest when, during the Civil War, his artists on the battlefields sent back illustrations. They now have great historical value. He became bankrupt in 1877. His second wife was **Miriam Florence (Folline) Leslie,** c.1836–1914, b. New Orleans. She became editor of *Frank Leslie's Lady's Journal* in 1871 and married Leslie in 1874. After his death Mrs. Leslie skillfully managed the business, bringing it out of debt. She leased it to a syndicate in 1895, but in 1898 was again obliged to take charge to save it. She wrote several books, including *Rents in Our Robes* (1888) and *Are Men Gay Deceivers* (1893). She was an ardent feminist and gave much of her fortune to that cause. See biography by M. B. Stern (1953).

Leslie or **Lesley, John,** 1527–96, Scottish bishop, historian, and statesman. After studying in France, he returned (c.1554) to Scotland, where he opposed the Reformation. He became ecclesiastical adviser to MARY QUEEN OF SCOTS and a member of her privy council and was appointed (1566) bishop of Ross. In 1569 he was made Mary's representative at the court of Elizabeth I of England, but he was arrested (1571) for complicity in the plot to marry the Scottish queen to Thomas Howard, 4th duke of NORFOLK. He was released after his full confession and fled to France and then to Rome. An able historian, he left valuable accounts of the Catholic view of the events of his time. His 10-volume Latin history of Scotland (1578) was translated by James Dalrymple (ed. by E. G. Cody, 1888–95).

Leslie, Miriam Florence (Folline): see LESLIE, FRANK.

Lesotho (ləsō'tō), formerly **Basutoland,** kingdom (1972 pop. 1,080,857), 11,720 sq mi (30,355 sq km), S Africa, enclave within the Republic of South Africa. MASERU is the capital. The Draksenberg range occupies the eastern part of the country; elevations vary

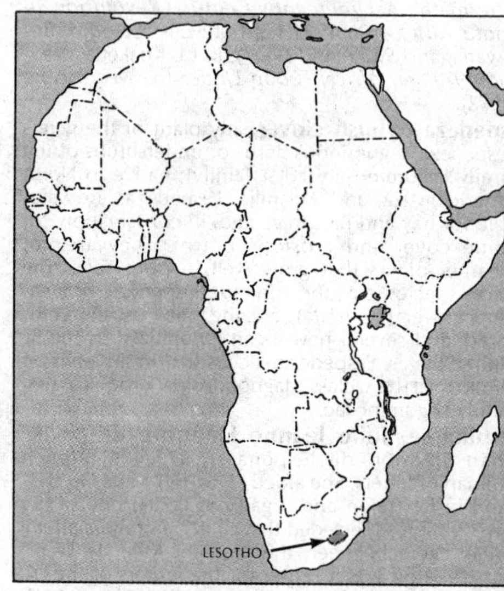

from more than 11,000 ft (3,353 m) along the eastern frontier to c.8,000 ft (2,440 m) further west. The rest of the kingdom is a heavily populated, rocky tableland with a dry climate. Only a small percentage of Lesotho's land is arable. Maize, sorghum, and wheat are extensively cultivated. Sheep are bred for wool, and cattle and Angora goats are raised. All land in Lesotho is held by the king in trust for the SOTHO nation and is apportioned on his behalf by local chiefs; non-Sotho may not hold land, and no land may be sold. Most of Lesotho's non-Africans, barred from owning land, engage in administrative, commercial, or missionary work. More than 100,000 Sotho are employed in South Africa's mines; their remittances provide an important source of revenue. Lesotho's mineral resources are limited to diamonds, which have been exploited on a large scale by foreign firms since the 1960s. The country has varied light industries. Lesotho uses the South African rand as currency and belongs to a customs union with South Africa, Botswana, and Swaziland. About 70% of the Sotho are Christian, and the country has one of the highest literacy rates in Africa. At Roma, near Maseru, is the Univ. of Botswana, Lesotho, and Swaziland. English is the official language of the kingdom, the chief indigenous tongue being Sesotho, a Bantu language. San (Bushmen), who were the region's earliest known inhabitants, were supplanted c.1800 by various Bantu-speaking peoples. The Sotho are made up of remnants of ethnic groups that were scattered during the disturbances accompanying the rise of the Zulu (1816–30). They were rallied c.1820 by Moshesh, a paramount chief who founded a dynasty in what is now Lesotho. Moshesh not only defended his people from Zulu raids but preserved their independence against Boer and British interlopers. He also welcomed Catholic and Protestant missionaries, who still play an important role in the kingdom. Following wars with the Boer-ruled Orange Free State in 1858 and 1865, Moshesh put the Sotho under British protection (1868). The protectorate was annexed to Cape Colony in 1871 without Sotho consent; but in 1884 it was placed under the direct control of Britain. A resident commissioner was established at Maseru, where he administered through Sotho chiefs. When the Union of South Africa was forged in 1910, Basutoland came under the jurisdiction of the British High Commissioner in South Africa. Provisions were made for the eventual incorporation of the territory into the Union; but Sotho opposition, especially after the rise of the Nationalist party with its apartheid policy, prevented annexation. In 1960 the British granted Basutoland a new constitution that paved the way to internal self-government. On Oct. 4, 1966, Basutoland became independent as Lesotho. Following general elections in early 1970, which the opposition Congress party apparently won, Prime Minister Leabua Jonathan declared a state of emergency and suspended the constitution; King Moshoeshoe II went into exile but returned at the end of the year. In 1973 an interim assembly began work on a new constitution, but the Congress party, led by Ntsu Mokhehle, refused to participate. In Jan., 1974, Chief Leabua Jonathan accused the Congress party of attempting to stage a coup d'etat, and in the months that followed hundreds of its members reportedly were killed. See J. D. Omer-Cooper, *Zulu Aftermath: A Nineteenth Century Revolution in Bantu Africa* (1966); Richard Stevens, *Lesotho, Botswana, and Swaziland* (1967); B. M. Khaketla, *Lesotho 1970: An African Coup Under the Microscope* (1972).

lespedeza or **bush clover,** any plant of the genus *Lespedeza,* leguminous herbs or undershrubs of the family Leguminosae (PULSE family); native to North America, Asia, and Australia. Lespedezas are valuable for hay and pasturage and, in conservation, for game cover and erosion control. They are hot weather plants that grow well in poor soils. The Asian species, e.g., the common lespedeza, or Japanese clover (*L. striata*), are the ones usually cultivated, and several have been naturalized in the SE United States. Lespedeza is classified in the division MAGNOLIOPHYTA, class Magnoliopsida, order Rosales, family Leguminosae.

Lespinasse, Julie Jeanne Éléonore de (zhülē' zhän ālāōnôr' də lĕspēnäs'), 1732–76, French woman of letters. She aided (1754–64) Mme Du Deffand in her salon and organized (1764) one of her own, which superseded that of her patroness after a break came between the women. Mlle de Lespinasse's salon was a center for the writers of the ENCYCLOPÉDIE. Her letters (written 1773–76, tr. 1901, 1929) to the comte de Guibert are celebrated as a chronicle of unhappy love. See biography by Janine Bouissounouse (tr. 1962).

Lesse (lĕs'ə), river, c.50 mi (80 km) long, rising in the Ardennes, SE Belgium, and flowing northwest to join the Meuse River near Dinant. It passes in its middle course through underground limestone caves.

Lesseps, Ferdinand Marie, vicomte de (fĕrdēnäN' märē' vēkôNt' də lĕsĕps'), 1805–94, French diplomat and engineer. He entered the consular service in 1825 and was minister to Spain (1848–49). Later, while serving in Egypt, he conceived the idea of a SUEZ CANAL, and in 1854 he obtained from Said Pasha, viceroy of Egypt, the concession for opening a passage through the Isthmus of Suez. He was the chief figure in organizing the canal company and raised, by popular subscription in France, over half the capital needed. He supervised the actual construction (1859–69) and achieved world renown when the venture proved successful. In 1878 he assumed the presidency of a French company formed to construct the PANAMA CANAL, and work was begun in 1881. Lack of funds forced the project into bankruptcy seven years later, amid charges of corruption. Lesseps was brought to trial for misappropriation of funds and, together with his son, was sentenced to prison by the French government. The sentence, however, was not carried out, and most objective observers, then and since, have held Lesseps to have been guilty only of negligence. See biography by C. R. L. Beatty (1956); study by John Pudney (1969).

Lesser Antilles: see WEST INDIES.

Lesser Slave Lake, 60 mi (97 km) long and from 3 to 10 mi (4.8–16 km) wide, central Alta., Canada, NW of Edmonton. It drains E into the Athabasca River by the Lesser Slave River. In addition to commercial fishing, there is lumbering and farming on its shores.

lesser wax moth: see BEE MOTH.

Lessing, Doris, 1919–, British novelist, b. Kermanshah, Persia. She was brought up on a farm in Rhodesia (formerly Southern Rhodesia) and in 1949 went to England, where her first novel, *The Grass is Singing* (1950), was published. Widely regarded as one of the major writers of the mid-20th cent., Lessing writes on a wide variety of themes—Rhodesia, women, Communism, cats. Although her work is always distinguished by energy and intelligence, it is uneven, often flawed. She is probably principally concerned with detailing the lives of intelligent women—their psychology, their politics, their work, their relationship to men and to their children, their change of vision as they age. In her later works she is interested in madness and its relation to an insane universe. Her novels include a series of five novels collectively entitled *The Children of Violence,* which concern an autobiographical character named Martha Quest; the series includes *Martha Quest* (1952), *Ripple from the Storm* (1958), and *The Four-Gated City* (1969). Among her other works are the novels *The Golden Notebook* (1962), *Briefing for a Descent into Hell* (1971), and *The Summer Before the Dark* (1973), and a collection of short pieces, *A Small Personal Voice* (1974).

Lessing, Gotthold Ephraim (gôt'hôlt ā'fräïm), 1729–81, German philosopher, dramatist, and critic, one of the most influential figures of the Enlightenment. He was connected with the theater in Berlin, where he produced some of his most famous works, and with the national theater in Hamburg. His series of critical essays, *Hamburgische Dramaturgie* (1767–69), attacked the French classical theater and claimed that it had failed to capture the true spirit of Aristotelian dramatic unities. From 1770 he was librarian at Wolfenbüttel, writing there *Zur Geschichte und Literatur* [on history and literature] (1773–77). Other significant critical works are *Literaturbriefe* [literary letters] (1759–65) and *Laokoon* (1766). Lessing differentiated between the poet as interpreter of time and the artist as interpreter of space; he found different aesthetic criteria applicable to each. His plays include *Miss Sara Sampson* (1755), *Minna von Barnhelm* (1763, tr. 1799), *Emilia Galotti* (1772, tr. 1909), and *Nathan the Wise* (1779, tr. 1781), which was partly the result of the numerous theological controversies into which he was drawn by his insistence on freedom of thought. A deist, Lessing took theology seriously. His *Erziehung des Menschengeschlechts* [education of the human race] (1780) applied to Enlightenment ideas of progress and evolution to religion. Lessing's introduction in Germany of English literature, especially of Shakespeare, was an important contribution. See studies by H. E. Allison (1966), A. F. Brown (1971), and H. B. Garland (1949, repr. 1973).

Le Sueur, Eustache (östäsh' lə süör'), 1616–55, French painter. He was a disciple of Vouet and a founding member of the Académie royale (1648). In his short life he painted many decorative works for apartments in the Louvre and for churches and convents. His work was greatly influenced by that of Poussin, whom he rivaled in popularity for a time. The Louvre contains his *St. Paul Preaching at Ephesus* and episodes from the *Life of St. Bruno.*

Lesueur or **Le Sueur, Jean François** (zhäN fräNswä'), 1760–1837, French composer. He was director of music (1786–88) at Notre-Dame de Paris. During the French Revolution his operas, such as *La Caverne* (1793) and *Paul et Virginie* (1794), were highly popular and imitated; their violence and sensationalism reflected the spirit of the time. On the founding of the Paris Conservatory (1795), he became an inspector of instruction, and later he was a professor of composition, his many distinguished students including Ambroise Thomas, Gounod, and Berlioz. He was composer to the court chapel under both Napoleon I and Louis XVIII.

Leszno (lĕsh'nô), Ger. *Lissa,* town (1970 pop. 33,890), SW Poland. A railway junction, it has industries producing synthetic fibers, chemicals, and carpets. There are lignite deposits in the vicinity. Chartered in 1547, it passed to Prussia in 1793 and again in 1815. It reverted to Poland in 1919. Leszno was a center of the Protestant Reformation of the 16th cent. and the chief seat of the Moravian Brethren in Poland. John Amos Comenius was a rector of the famous Moravian school here. The town has an 18th-century palace.

Letcher, John, 1813–84, American politician, b. Lexington, Va. He studied law and practiced at Lexington, where he also edited the Jacksonian Democrat *Valley Star.* In Congress (1851–59), he was known as "Honest John" because of his opposition to government extravagance. As governor (1860–64) of Virginia, Letcher opposed secession until the state was asked to supply its quota of troops for action against the South. Upon Virginia's secession, he turned the state's military forces and supplies over to the Confederacy, which he supported vigorously throughout his Civil War governorship. See biography by F. N. Boney (1966).

Letchworth, urban district (1971 pop. 30,884), Hertfordshire, E central England. It was the first GARDEN CITY, founded in 1903 by Sir Ebenezer Howard. The main industries are printing and the manufacture of printing machinery.

Le Tellier, Michel (mēshĕl' lə tĕlyā'), 1603–85, French statesman. A minister of state under Cardinal MAZARIN, he became war minister in 1643. He later shared his duties with his son, the marquis de LOUVOIS. At the time of his death he was chancellor of France.

Lethaby, William Richard (lĕth'əbē), 1857–1931, English architect. He was a founder and first principal (1893–1911) of the London County Council Central School of Arts and Crafts, and professor of design at the Royal College of Art. He was also an influential writer on architectural subjects. Besides his important books *Greek Buildings* (1908), *Mediaeval Art* (1912), and *Architecture* (1912), he contributed to many periodicals. See his *Form in Civilization* (with foreword by Lewis Mumford, 1957).

Lethbridge (lĕth'brĭj), city (1971 pop. 41,217), S Alta., Canada, on the Oldman River. Formerly a coal-mining center, Lethbridge is now a commercial center for an irrigated farming and ranching district. Industries include sugar refining, food processing, brewing, steel fabricating, and the manufacture of electronic equipment. There is a federal agricultural-research station. The Univ. of Lethbridge was founded in 1967.

Lethe (lē'thē), in Greek mythology, river of forgetfulness in Hades. The dead drank from Lethe upon their arrival in the underworld.

Leticia (lātē'sēä), town (1968 est. pop. 4,600), capital of Amazonas commissary, SE Colombia, on the upper Amazon. The Leticia region, a narrow strip of land extending S of the Putumayo River to the Amazon, was disputed, at times violently, between Colombia and Peru (1932–34). The region was awarded to Colombia by the League of Nations in 1934. Active U.S. participation by Secretary of State Henry Stimson with the League established a precedent, permitting interference by an international body in an area covered by the Monroe Doctrine.

Leto (lē'tō), in Greek mythology, daughter of the Titans Coeus and Phoebe and mother of Artemis and Apollo. When she conceived twins by Zeus, Hera sent the serpent Python after her and forbade all to give her rest or help. Finally Leto stopped on the island Delos and gave birth to Artemis and Apollo. The twins were devoted to their mother and assiduously protected her, as in the stories of NIOBE and PYTHON. In Rome, Leto was called Latona.

Leto, Giulio Pomponio: see POMPONIUS LAETUS, JULIUS.

letter: see ALPHABET.

lettering: see CALLIGRAPHY; TYPOGRAPHY.

Letteris, Meir ha-Levi (mīr hä-lā'vē lĕtär'ĭs), 1800–1871, Austrian-Jewish poet. He wrote about 30 volumes of prose and poetry. The poem called "Yonah Homiyah" [the plaintive dove] became very widely known and is still popular. He is also famous for his Hebrew version of *Faust* called *Ben Abuya.*

letter of credit: see CREDIT, LETTER OF.

letters, in literature, written messages, ranging from those addressed to the public and those sent from lover to lover, to business letters and thank-you notes. The common quality they share is a lively style, echoing the personality of the sender yet aimed at the mind and heart of the receiver. Their intimacy gives them an immediacy that touches general readers as well. Long, eloquent letters, or EPISTLES, were the favored means of communication in the ancient world. Those of Cicero and Horace, ranging in subject from political philosophy to literary criticism and social satire, served as models for the formal statement or manifesto. Although the epistles of Saint Paul and Saint Jerome are concerned with the Christian life of the spirit, they are patterned upon classical models. The writings of Cicero and Horace served as models once again for a revival of the epistle in the 18th cent., when John Dryden and Alexander Pope composed verse epistles and Thomas Jefferson drafted the Declaration of Independence. Two famous sets of letters vividly portray life in the Middle Ages. The passionate correspondence of Peter Abelard and his mistress, Héloise, poignantly suggests the cruelty of the supposedly civilized church in 12th-century France; the PASTON LETTERS reveal in detail the daily life of an English family in the 15th cent. The 18th cent. was a golden age of letters. Madame de Sévigné, Lady Mary Wortley Montagu, and Lord Chesterfield all entered into long, highly polished, and extremely readable correspondences with their respective children. Letter writing was so popular in England at this time that Samuel Richardson capitalized on the vogue by writing the first epistolary novels, *Pamela* (1740) and *Clarissa* (1747–48). Each was meant to serve as a guide for writing different kinds of letters as well as for designating correct female behavior under trying circumstances. Among British writers of the 19th cent., the best correspondents included John Keats, Lord Byron, Charles Dickens, and R. L. Stevenson. George Bernard Shaw wrote love letters to the actress Ellen Terry for three years before they met. Their eventual encounter was not a success, but the correspondence continued for 23 years. The particular ability of letters to convey with immediacy not only the emotions and tragedies of a past time but also the substance of daily life is well illustrated in *The Children of Pride: A True Story of Georgia and the Civil War* (1972, ed. by Robert Myers), a collection of letters written by a Georgia family from 1854–1868. Important to students of American literature are the letters of the editor Maxwell Perkins to such writers as Ernest Hemingway, F. Scott Fitzgerald, and Thomas Wolfe. Also illuminating, partly because of their very existence, are the letters of Groucho Marx to T. S. Eliot.

Lettish (lĕt′ĭsh), or Latvian, a language belonging to the Baltic subfamily of the Indo-European family of languages (see BALTIC LANGUAGES). The mother tongue of close to 2 million persons living chiefly in Latvia, Lettish first became that country's official language in 1918, the year in which Latvian independence was won. In the pronunciation of Lettish, stress is placed on the first syllable of a word. Grammatically, both nouns and verbs are highly inflected. Since 1922, Lettish has used the Roman alphabet (supplemented by several diacritical signs) for writing. The oldest surviving texts in Lettish date from the late 16th cent. See William K. Matthews, *Languages of the U.S.S.R.* (1951).

Lettland: see LATVIA, USSR.

Lettow-Vorbeck, Paul von (poul fən lĕt′ō-fôr′bĕk), 1870–1964, German general. In World War I he conducted a brilliant defense of German East Africa against vastly superior Allied power.

lettre de cachet (lĕ′trə də käshā′), formerly in French law, private, sealed document, issued as a communication from the king. Such a letter could order imprisonment or exile for an individual without recourse to courts of law. Of very early origin, the lettre de cachet came into common use in the 17th cent. as an instrument of the new monarchy. Although its actual use was restrained, the issuance to local officials of lettres de cachet with the space for the name left blank inspired great fear. The occasional invocation of them against leaders of opinion, including Voltaire, became a symbol of arbitrary royal power and tyranny. They were abolished by the Constituent Assembly in the French Revolution. Napoleon I briefly renewed use of the lettres de cachet.

lettuce, annual garden plant (*Lactuca sativa* and varieties) of the family Compositae (COMPOSITE family), probably native to the East Indies or Asia Minor, possibly as a derivative of the widespread weed called wild lettuce (*L. scariola*). *L. sativa* is not known anywhere in a wild state, having been in cultivation as a salad plant from antiquity. Three types of lettuce are planted: head, or cabbage, lettuce; the leaf, or loose, type; and Cos lettuce, or romaine. The first forms a tight, crisp, white head; the second has many more leaves and a less compact head, which is white toward its center only. Cos lettuce, or romaine, forms long, upright leaves, which, according to variety, may or may not have to be tied up to blanch and form a head. It is not as commonly planted, but is useful where summers are too hot for the other two varieties. Since lettuce has come into increased favor as a source of vitamins its culture has been greatly stimulated in the United States, and forcing it for winter use is becoming an extensive industry, especially near large cities. Much of the winter crop comes from Florida and California. The plant is generally eaten as a salad but may be cooked, as it often is in France. A narcotic from the thickened juice of some *Lactuca* species is used as an opium substitute. Among the many north temperate species is *L. canadensis*, the American wild lettuce. Lettuce is classified in the division MAGNOLIOPHYTA, class Magnoliopsida, order Asterales, family Compositae.

Letushim (lētōō′shĭm), eponymous ancestor of an Asiatic tribe. Gen. 25.3.

Leucas, Greece: see LEVKÁS.

Leuchtenburg, William Edward, 1922–, U.S. historian, b. Ridgewood, N.Y. He received his Ph.D. from Columbia in 1951 and taught at Smith College and Harvard before joining the Columbia faculty in 1952. He became a full professor in 1959 and DeWitt Clinton professor of history in 1971. A masterly synthesizer of historical scholarship for the general reader, he has written extensively on 20th-cent. American history, especially the New Deal era. His works include *The Perils of Prosperity, 1914–1932* (1958) and *Franklin D. Roosevelt and the New Deal* (1963). In addition he edited *Franklin D. Roosevelt: A Profile* (1967), *The New Deal: A Documentary History* (1968), and *The Unfinished Century* (1973).

leucine (lōō′sēn), organic compound, one of the 22 α-AMINO ACIDS commonly found in animal proteins. Only the L-stereoisomer appears in mammalian protein. It is one of several essential amino acids needed in the diet; the human body cannot synthesize it from simpler metabolites. Young adults need about 31 mg of this amino acid per day per kilogram (14 mg per lb) of body weight. Leucine can be degraded into simpler compounds by the enzymes of the body; an inherited defect in one of the enzymes involved in this process results in a rare disorder called maple syrup urine disease. Leucine contributes to the structure of proteins into which it has been incorporated by the tendency of its side chain to participate in hydrophobic interactions. It was isolated from cheese in an impure form in 1819 and from muscle and wool in the crystalline state in 1820. The compound was named leucine after the Greek word *leukos* [white], evidently because at that time the purification of a substance from nature to a white, crystalline state was considered noteworthy. The structure of leucine was established by laboratory synthesis in 1891. See ISOLEUCINE.

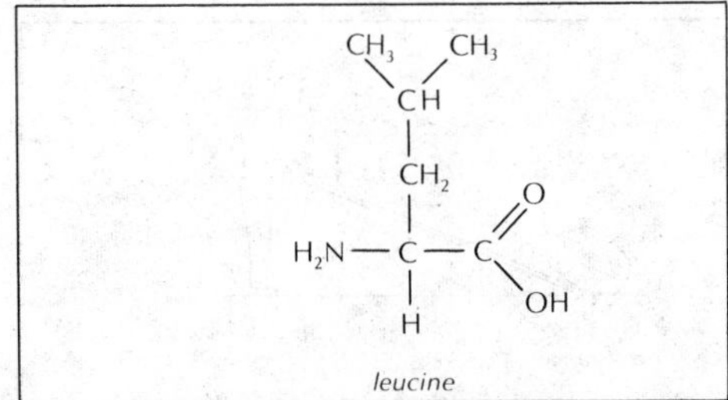

leucine

Leucippus (lōōsĭp′əs), 5th cent. B.C., Greek philosopher. Aristotle believed that Leucippus inspired the atomistic theory with which Democritus is identified. Little is known about Leucippus.

Leuckart, Karl Georg Friedrich Rudolf (kärl gā′ôrk frē′drĭkh rōō′dôlf loi′kärt), 1823–98, German zoologist, a founder of the science of parasitology. He made important discoveries in animal physiology and in comparative morphology and classification of invertebrates. His studies and writings on parasites, including worms and insects, were valuable.

leucoplast: see AMYLOPLAST.

Leucothea (lōōkŏth′ēə), in Greek mythology, sea deity. In some legends she was the deification of INO, the wife of Athmas; in others she was the deification of the sea nymph Halia, mother of Rhodos. The Romans identified Matuta with her.

Leuctra (lōōk′trə), village of ancient Greece, in Boeotia, 7 mi (11.3 km) SW of Thebes. There the Spartans were defeated (371 B.C.) by the Thebans under EPAMINONDAS. A brilliant tactical success, the battle also dealt a severe blow to Spartan hegemony.

leukemia (lōōkē′mēə), cancerous disorder of the blood-forming tissues (bone marrow, lymphatics, liver, spleen) characterized by excessive production of white cells and consequently a crowding-out of the other blood elements. The lymph nodes, liver, and spleen become enlarged, and anemia (because of the attrition of red cells) is always present. Leukemia can occur at any age. Its cause is not certain but a relationship to excessive exposure to X rays or other radioactive materials and to toxic chemicals has been noted. Symptoms include weakness, general ill feelings, and fever. Hemorrhaging may develop because blood-clotting elements are scarce. Leukemia occurs in both acute and chronic form. In the former, death supervenes rapidly; in the latter, life may be prolonged with treatment for many years. No cure is as yet known. Several types of leukemia exist, depending upon the kind of white cell that is being abnormally produced. X-ray treatment is useful in the chronic form of leukemia. In most forms of the disease drugs (corticosteroids) are administered that cause a temporary remission in the proliferation of white blood cells. Blood transfusions are given in many instances. Eventually, however, the proliferating white cells infiltrate the body tissues, and death ensues. See CANCER.

leukocyte (lōō′kəsīt″): see BLOOD.

Leummim (lēŭm′ĭm), unidentified tribal name. Gen. 25.3.

Leuna (loi′nä), city (1970 pop. 11,168), Halle district, S central East Germany. There, in 1916, the first synthetic nitrogen plant began to operate after the invention of the Haber process. The city grew as the center of the German synthetic chemical industry, and it is today the seat of the largest chemical works in East Germany. The city was badly damaged in World War II.

Leutze, Emanuel (loit′sə), 1816–68, American historical painter, b. Germany. In 1859 he settled in the United States, working in Washington, D.C., and New York City. His pictures are chiefly English and American historical episodes, memorable more for their patriotic than for their aesthetic value. The most famous example is *Washington Crossing the Delaware* (Metropolitan Mus.). For the Capitol at Washington, D. C., he painted a gigantic mural, *Westward the Course of Empire Takes Its Way*.

Levallois-Perret (ləvälwä′-pĕrā′), residential and industrial suburb of Paris (1968 pop. 59,212), Hauts-de-Seine dept., N central France, on the Seine River. Automobiles, electrical and radio equipment, and perfume are manufactured. The town also has foundries, distilleries, and food-processing plants.

Levant (ləvănt′) [Ital.,=east], collective name for the countries of the eastern shore of the Mediterranean from Egypt to, and including, Turkey. The divisions of the French mandate over Syria and Lebanon were called the Levant States, and the term is still sometimes applied to those two nations.

Levasseur, Émile (Pierre Émile Levasseur) (pyĕr āmēl′ lüväsör′), 1828–1911, French economist. He was noted especially for his historical approach to the study of economics. He studied at the École normale supérieure, Paris, and taught (1868–72) economic history at the Collège de France before becoming (1872) professor of geography, history, and economic statistics. His most famous works are histories of the French working class, *Histoire des classes ouvrières en France depuis la conquête de Jules César jusqu'à la révolution* (1859) and *Histoire des classes ouvrières en France depuis la révolution jusqu'à nos jours* (1867). He also wrote *La Question de l'or* [the question of gold] (1858), *La Population française* (3 vol., 1889–92), and *Histoire du commerce de la France* (1911–12).

Le Vau, Louis (lwē lə vō), 1612–70, French architect, involved in most of the important building projects for Louis XIV. He settled on the Île Saint-Louis, where he built his own house and the Hôtels Lambert and Lauzun. In 1655, Le Vau succeeded Jacques Lemercier as architect for the Louvre, on which he collaborated with Claude Perrault. He designed the palace of Versailles, where he worked with Lebrun, creating a nucleus later completed by J. H. Mansart. Among his other designs are the château of Vaux-le-Vicomte; the Collège des Quatre Nations, Paris, now the Institut de France; and the Church of St. Sulpice, Paris, the facade of which was later built by Servandoni.

levee (lĕv′ē) [Fr.,=raised], embankment built along a river to prevent flooding by high water. Levees are the oldest and the most extensively used method of FLOOD control. They are constructed by piling earth on a surface that has been cleared of vegetation and leveled. From a broad base the levee narrows to a flat crown, on which sandbags or some other temporary protection may be placed to contain unusually high waters. Levee surfaces are commonly protected from erosion by vegetation, notably Bermuda grass. A banquette, or low terrace of earth, is usually added on the land side of high levees to prevent loss of material from the slope through rain erosion. On the river side, plantings of willows, weighted brush matting, or concrete revetments protect those sections of levee that are exposed to strong waves or currents, while ditches or drainage tiles keep the foundation from becoming waterlogged. Levee systems require careful planning, with sections set back from the river to form a wider channel and with flood valley basins divided by cross levees to prevent inundation of large areas by a single break. The most extensive levee systems in the United States are along the Mississippi and Sacramento rivers and their tributaries. The dikes of Holland are a form of levee, and levee-type embankments are used along the Danube, Vistula, Po, and other European rivers.

level: see SPIRIT LEVEL.

Levelers or **Levellers,** English Puritan sect active at the time of the ENGLISH CIVIL WAR. The name was apparently applied to them in 1647, in derision of their beliefs in equality. The leader of the movement and its most indefatigable propagandist was John LILBURNE. The Levelers demanded fundamental constitutional reform—a written constitution, a single supreme representative body elected by universal manhood suffrage, proportional representation, and the abolition of monarchy and noble privilege. Their ideals, far in advance of their time, were those of complete religious and political equality. They were adept at the use of mass petitions and extensive pamphleteering to arouse the public. When the

Long Parliament did not respond to their ideas, they tried to build support in the ranks of the army, with some success. They identified themselves with the army's demands for arrears of pay, and Lilburne's pamphlet *The Case of the Army Truly Stated* was presented (1647) to Thomas Fairfax (later 3d Baron FAIRFAX OF CAMERON). An expanded version, *Foundations of Freedom; or, An Agreement of the People,* describing the whole Leveler program, was discussed at the Putney debates (Oct., 1647) between the elected army council and their commanding officers. The Leveler proposals were totally rejected by Gen. Henry IRETON as subversive of property interests. A later pamphlet, *England's New Chains,* published after the execution of Charles I, and several Leveler mutinies (1649) resulted in severe suppression of the Levelers by Oliver Cromwell, who had constantly opposed them. See T. C. Pease, *The Leveller Movement* (1916, repr. 1965); William Haller and Godfrey Davies, ed., *The Leveller Tracts, 1647-1653* (1944, repr. 1964); Joseph Frank, *The Levellers* (1955, repr. 1969); N. H. Brailsford, *The Levellers and the English Revolution* (1961); C. H. Shaw, *The Levellers* (1968).

leveling: see SURVEYING.

Levelland (lĕv'əlănd"), city (1970 pop. 11,445), seat of Hockley co., NW Texas, on the Llano Estacado; inc. 1926. The economy is based chiefly on oil, agriculture, and the manufacture of mobile homes. South Plains College is in Levelland. Reese Air Force Base is nearby.

Leven, Alexander Leslie, 1st **earl of** (lĕv'ən), 1580?-1661, Scottish general. He served in the Swedish army some 30 years, being knighted by Gustavus II and fighting in the Thirty Years War. Returning to Scotland in 1638, he led the army of the COVENANTERS in the BISHOPS' WARS. Charles I made him earl in 1641, hoping to gain his support. Nevertheless, following the conclusion of the Solemn League and Covenant between the Scots and the English Parliament (see ENGLISH CIVIL WAR), Leven led (1644) an army into England and took part in the defeat of the king at Marston Moor. When Charles surrendered to the Scottish army in 1646, Leven had charge of him until the royal prisoner was handed over to the English in 1647. Although Leven resigned actual command of the army to his nephew David Leslie before the Scottish Covenanters (by then royalists) were defeated (1650) at Dunbar, he was twice imprisoned briefly in the Tower of London.

Leven (lē'vən), burgh (1971 pop. 9,454), Fife, E Scotland, at the mouth of the Leven River on the Firth of Forth. It is a summer resort, famous for its golf links and beaches. It has steel and iron foundries and paper and jute mills.

Leven, Loch (lŏkh), lake, 3½ mi (5.6 km) long, Tayside region, E Scotland. Its several islands include Castle Island, with the ruins of the castle in which Mary Queen of Scots was imprisoned in 1567-68, and St. Serf's, with the ruins of an ancient priory. The Leven River, outlet of the lake, flows E through Fife to the Firth of Forth.

Levene, Sam (ləvēn'), 1905-, American actor, b. Russia. After working in the garment industry, Levene began his stage career in *Wall Street* (1927). His best-known performances include roles in *Three Men on a Horse, Guys and Dolls, The Sunshine Boys* (1973), and *Dreyfus in Rehearsal* (1974). Among his films are *Golden Boy* (1939) and *Sweet Smell of Success* (1957). Levene appeared on television in *The World of Sholom Aleichem.*

Lever, Charles James (lē'vər), 1806-72, Irish novelist. He began his career as a practicing physician. His early novels appeared periodically in the *Dublin University Magazine,* whose editorship he assumed in 1842. A prolific writer, Lever is best known for his farcical picaresque novels of Irish military life, notably *Harry Lorrequer* (1839) and *Charles O'Malley* (1841). In his later work he became more serious and his novels more carefully constructed, but he diminished in popularity.

lever, simple MACHINE consisting of a bar supported at some stationary point along its length and used to overcome resistance at a second point by application of force at a third point. The stationary point of a lever is known as its fulcrum. The lever is used for prying, as in the case of the crowbar, or for lifting. It has been found by experiment that two equal forces acting in opposite directions, i.e., clockwise and counterclockwise, and applied to a uniform lever at equal distances from the fulcrum counteract each other and establish a state of EQUILIBRIUM, or balance, in the lever. Experiment has also shown that two unequal forces when acting in opposite directions will bring about an equilibrium when the product of the magnitude of one force and its effort arm, or lever arm (the distance of its point of application from the fulcrum), is equal to the product of

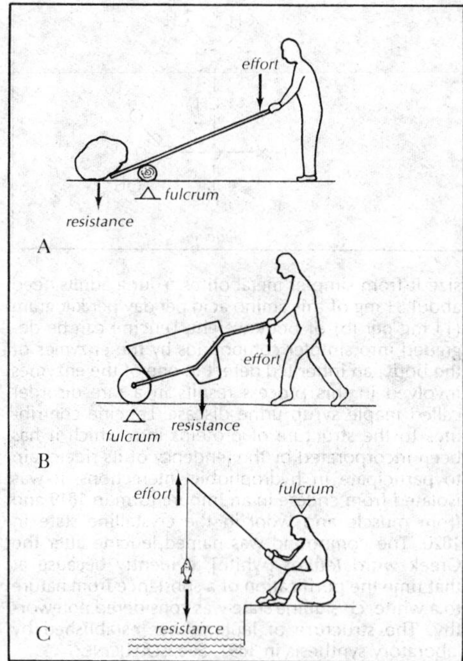

Classes of levers: A first-class lever (A), a second-class lever (B), and a third-class lever (C)

the magnitude of the other force and its effort arm. In physics the product of a force by its effort arm is called a MOMENT of the force; the general conclusion known as the principle of moments states that equilibrium is established when the sum of the moments of the forces acting in a clockwise direction is equal to the sum of the moments of the forces acting in a counterclockwise direction. It is possible, as a result, to overcome a very large force at a short distance from the fulcrum with a very small force at a great distance from the fulcrum. Archimedes is supposed to have boasted, having the lever in mind, that given a place to stand he could move the world. In the use of a small force to overcome a large one the lever finds its many common applications. For example, the fulcrum is the point upon which a crowbar rests when used to lift or to pry loose some object; the effort is applied at the end farther from the fulcrum and is relatively small. The distance from the operator's hands to the fulcrum is known as the lever arm, or effort arm; the object being pried loose is the resisting force, or resistance; the object's distance from the fulcrum is the resistance arm. Levers in which the fulcrum is located between the effort and the resistance, as in the crowbar and the beam balance, are known as first-class levers. The fulcrum may also be located at one end of the lever, with the effort applied at the other end and the resistance in between; this type of lever, illustrated by the wheelbarrow and the nutcracker, is known as a second-class lever. The final possibility, known as a third-class lever, has the effort applied between the fulcrum and the resistance and is illustrated by various types of tongs. Many other common tools, instruments, and appliances are applications of the principle of the lever. The human forearm is an application of the third-class lever, the elbow acting as the fulcrum, the weight held in the hand and being lifted as the resistance, and the pull of the muscles between the elbow and the hand as the effort. In a second-class lever, the effort arm is always longer than the resistance arm, so that a smaller effort moves a larger resistance, while in a third-class lever the reverse is always true, with the effort greater than the resistance. In a first-class lever, the effort may be either larger or smaller than the resistance, depending upon the location of the fulcrum. By the term *lever* is also meant a projecting piece that is moved to operate or adjust inner machinery, such as a lever moved to the right or left to switch electric current on or off or to adjust the size of the opening of a shutter in a camera.

Leverett, John (lĕv'ərĭt), 1616-79, American colonial governor, b. Boston, England. He went to Boston, Mass., with his father in 1633, but went back (1644) to England to serve in the parliamentary army in the English civil war. He returned (1648) to Massachusetts, served a term in the General Court, was appointed one of the commissioners sent to Maine to bring it under the jurisdiction of Massachusetts, and represented (1653-62) Massachusetts in England. On his return to Massachusetts he served in the General Court or the governor's council until 1671, when he was appointed deputy governor. He became governor in 1673 and continued to serve until his death. During his administration he successfully directed the colonial forces in King Philip's War (1675-76). His knighthood, c.1676, has not been definitely established.

Leverkusen (lā"fərko͞o'zən), city (1970 pop. 107,546), North Rhine-Westphalia, W West Germany, on the Rhine River. It is an industrial center and a road and rail junction. Manufactures include chemicals, machinery, and textiles. There is a noted chemical-research library in the city.

Leverrier, Urbain Jean Joseph (ürbăN' zhăN zhôzĕf' ləvĕryā'), 1811-77, French astronomer, discoverer of the planet Neptune. In considering the perturbations of Uranus, Leverrier made calculations indicating the presence of an unknown planet in an orbit outside that of Uranus. The same conclusion had been reached by the Englishman J. C. Adams a little earlier but had not been published, so Leverrier was initially given sole credit for the discovery of Neptune. Later both Adams and Leverrier were honored as responsible for the planet's discovery. In 1854, Leverrier became director of the Paris Observatory. His revision of the planetary theories was completed in 1875.

Levertov, Denise (lĕv'ərtôf), 1923-, Anglo-American poet, b. Ilford, Essex, England. She was educated in England and came to the United States when she married an American in 1948. Her poems are sparse and clear and hint at an intuitive order behind the apparent chaos in modern life. Collections of her work include *The Double Image* (1946), *Here and Now* (1957), *The Jacob's Ladder* (1961), *O Taste and See* (1964), *The Sorrow Dance* (1967), *Relearning the Alphabet* (1970), and *Footprints: Poems* (1972).

Leveson-Gower, Sir Francis: see ELLESMERE, FRANCIS EGERTON, 1ST EARL OF.

Leveson-Gower, Granville George: see GRANVILLE, GRANVILLE GEORGE LEVESON-GOWER, 2D EARL.

Levi (lē'vī). **1** Son of Jacob and Leah and eponymous ancestor of the Levites. His name appears infrequently—at his birth, when he and Simeon massacred the Shechemites out of revenge, when Jacob migrated to Egypt, and finally when he is named in the prophecy of his father. Gen. 29.34; 34; 46.11; 49.5-7. **2** See MATTHEW, SAINT. **3, 4** Names in the Gospel genealogy. Luke 3.24.29.

Levi, Carlo (kär'lō lā'vē), 1902-75, Italian writer and painter, noted as an anti-Fascist leader. After taking a medical degree, Levi devoted himself to painting, gaining international acclaim. His political activity in the 1920s resulted in his exile (1935-36) to the remote province of Lucania. His experiences there are described in *Cristo si è fermato a Eboli* (1945, tr. *Christ Stopped at Eboli,* 1947). While in France (1939-41) he wrote the essay *Of Fear and Freedom* (1946, tr. 1950). Levi's other works include *The Watch* (1948, tr. 1951) and *The Linden Trees* (tr. 1962), as well as studies of modern Italy, Sicily, and the USSR.

Levi, Edward Hirsch, 1911-, American educator, b. Chicago, grad. Univ. of Chicago and Yale Univ. law school. He has been a professor of law at the Univ. of Chicago (since 1945) and dean of the law school (1950-62). He was provost of the Univ. of Chicago from 1963 to 1968, when he became its president. Among his writings are *An Introduction to Legal Reasoning* (1949), *Four Talks on Legal Education* (1952), and *Point of View* (1969).

leviathan (lĕvī'əthən), aquatic monster, presumably the crocodile, the whale, or a dragon. It was a symbol of evil to be ultimately defeated by the power of good. Job 41; Pss. 74.14; 104.26; Isa. 27.1.

Levi ben Gershon: see GERSONIDES.

Levi-Civita, Tullio (to͞ol'lyō lā'vē-chē'vētä), 1873-1942, Italian mathematician. He taught at the universities of Padua (1898-1919) and Rome (1919-38) and was noted for his researches in pure geometry, hydrodynamics, celestial mechanics, and tensor analysis (see TENSOR), on which Einstein's work depended in part. He wrote *Simplified Presentation of Einstein's Unified Field Equations* (authorized tr. 1929).

Levine, Jack, 1915-, American painter, b. Boston. Levine began his career with the Federal Arts Project. His paintings treat social themes in a bitter, satirical vein. They are executed with diffused, prismatic textural effects. The persons he portrays are the essence of corruption, withered, distorted, yet glittering.

Among his most celebrated paintings are *Gangster Funeral* (Whitney Mus., New York City), *The Feast of Pure Reason* and *Election Night* (both: Mus. of Modern Art, New York City), *Welcome Home* (Brooklyn Mus.) and *The Trial* (Art Inst., Chicago).

levirate: see MARRIAGE.

Lévis, François Gaston, duc de (fräNswä' gästôN' dük də lāvēs'), 1720-87, French soldier. Entering the army in 1735, he distinguished himself in the War of the Austrian Succession. As second in command to General Montcalm, he was sent (1756) to Canada. After Montcalm's death, he was commander (1759-60) of the French troops in Canada. Lévis defeated the British at Ste Foy, near Quebec, but abandoned his siege of Quebec on the arrival of the British fleet. Later that year (1760) he was forced to surrender Montreal. After his return to France, he became lieutenant general (1761), marshal (1783), and duke (1784). H. R. Casgrain edited Lévis's papers (12 vol., 1889-96) and wrote *Montcalm et Lévis* (1891).

Lévis (lē'vĭs, Fr. lāvē'), city (1970 pop. 16,597), S Que., Canada, on the St. Lawrence River opposite Quebec. Settled in 1647, it was a base (1759) for Wolfe's siege of Quebec. Lévis is a port with shipbuilding and other industries.

Lévi-Strauss, Claude (klōd lā'vē-strous), 1908–, French anthropologist, b. Brussels, Belgium. He carried out research in Brazil from 1935 to 1939. From 1942 to 1945 he taught at the New School for Social Research, New York City, and in 1946-47 he was French cultural attaché in the United States. In 1948 he was appointed professor at the Institut d'Ethnologie, Univ. of Paris, and research associate at the National Science Research Fund, Paris. After 1959 he was professor of anthropology at the Collège de France. He is best known as the founder of structural anthropology, a theory that contends that history was shaped into a collective, fragmented structure comparable to preliterate mythology. He was elected to the French Academy in 1973. His works include *The Elementary Structures of Kinship* (1949, tr. 1962), *Race and History* (1952), *Structural Anthropology* (1958), *Totemism* (1962), *From Honey to Ashes* (1967), and *The Raw and the Cooked* (1969). See studies by E. N. Hayes, ed. (1970), E. R. Leach (1970), Octavio Paz (tr. 1970), and Howard Gardner (1972).

Levita, Elijah (ēlī'jə lēvī'tə) (Elya Bokher), c.1468-1549, German philologist, grammarian, and lexicographer who wrote in Hebrew. He spent most of his life in Italy, teaching Christian Hebraists. His works, including the grammatical treatise *Sefer ha-Bokher* (1518) and the Talmudic dictionary *Sefer ha-Tishbi* (1541), pioneered Hebrew and Yiddish linguistic research.

levitation (lĕvĭtā'shən), the raising of a human or other body in the air without mechanical aid. The idea is ancient; holy men, both pagan and Christian, were reputed to have had the power of becoming light at will and of moving through the air. It is a favorite manifestation in séances. It is also a popular conjuring trick, the illusion being produced by clever mechanical or lighting arrangements or other means.

Levites (lē'vīts), among the ancient Hebrews, a religious caste, descended from Levi, son of Jacob. They replaced the firstborn, who in ancient times served as priests. They alone of the tribes received no allotment of land; instead they received revenues from certain cities, and each city had its quota of Levites to support. The priests were of the family of AARON, within the tribe. With the unification of worship at Jerusalem, the Levites became temple servants with hereditary assignments. Later they became teachers of the Law. There were three divisions of Levites—Kohathites, Merarites, and Gershonites. They are mentioned frequently in the Old Testament, and Leviticus is named for them. Levitical cities were allotted to the Levites in the conquest of Canaan. Ex. 6.16; 32.26-28; 38.21; Num. 1; 3-5; 8; Deut. 18; Joshua 21; 1 Chron. 6; 9; 15; 23; 2 Chron. 17.8,9; 19.8-11; 20.19-21; 23; Ezra 7.24; 8.20. Anthropology presents many other cases of hereditary religious castes and consecrated families. In this light many of the biblical statements about the Levites are reinterpreted by critics.

Leviticus (lĭvĭt'əkəs), book of the Old Testament, 3d of the five books of the Law (the Pentateuch or Torah) ascribed by tradition to Moses. It is in essence a collection of liturgical legislation, introduced in the scriptural sequence immediately after the institution of public worship at the end of Exodus. There are laws on sacrifice (1-7); on the installation of the priests (8-10); on purity and impurity (11-16), including the dietary laws (11); and moral instructions (18-22) not contained in Exodus. There also are regulations on the jubilee year (25) and on vows (27). The only narrative incident of the book is the destruction of Aaron's sons Nadab and Abihu for violation of laws (10.1-2). See study by Martin Noth (1965). For critical views on the composition of Leviticus see OLD TESTAMENT.

Levittown, uninc. residential city (1970 pop. 65,440), Nassau co., SE N.Y., on Long Island; founded 1947 as a private, low-cost housing development for veterans and their families.

Levkás (lĕfkäs') or **Leucas** (lo͞o'kəs), mountainous island (1971 pop. 22,917), c.115 sq mi (300 sq km), W Greece, in the Ionian Sea; one of the IONIAN ISLANDS. Levkás (1971 pop. 6,818), the chief town and the capital of Levkás prefecture, is at the northern end of the island. Olive oil, currants, wine, and tobacco are produced. The island was colonized (7th cent. B.C.) by Corinthians, and Corinth and Levkás were allies in the Peloponnesian War. Levkás later was the capital of the Acarnanian League (3d cent. B.C.). The island was captured (1697) from the Ottoman Turks by Venice, which held it until 1797. There are ruins of Cyclopean walls and a temple to Apollo Leukates. Sappho is said, probably falsely, to have committed suicide by plunging into the sea from a cliff of the island. Levkás is also known as Santa Maura.

Levkosia, Cyprus: see NICOSIA.

levodopa: see L-DOPA.

levulose: see FRUCTOSE.

Lévy-Bruhl, Lucien (lāvē'-brül), 1857-1939, French philosopher, psychologist, and ethnologist. He was professor at the Sorbonne from 1899 and editor of the *Revue philosophique de la France et de l'étranger*. Particularly known for his research on the mentality of preliterate peoples, he wrote numerous studies, including *How Natives Think* (1910, tr. 1926), *Primitive Mentality* (1922, tr. 1923), and *Primitives and the Supernatural* (1931, tr. 1935). See biography by Jean Cazeneuve (1972).

Lewes, George Henry (lo͞o'ĭs), 1817-78, English critic and author. As editor of the *Leader* (1850-54) and of the *Fortnightly Review* (1865-66), Lewes distinguished himself as a critic. Influenced by Comte's POSITIVISM, he wrote *Biographical History of Philosophy* (4 vol., 1845-46), *Comte's Philosophy of the Sciences* (1853), *The Physiology of Common Life* (2 vol., 1859-60), and *Problems of Life and Mind* (5 vol., 1874-79). Lewes's plays and novels are forgotten but his most noted work, the *Life of Goethe* (1855), had a tremendous success. Few men in English literature have produced as much excellent material in such diverse areas. Having been separated from his wife some years earlier, in 1854 he began living with George Eliot (Mary Ann Evans), whose work he encouraged and influenced profoundly. See A. T. Kitchel, *George Lewes and George Eliot* (1933).

Lewes (lo͞o'ĭs,-ĭz), municipal borough (1971 pop. 14,015), county town of East Sussex, SE England. Lewes is a farm market with light manufactures. St. Pancras priory, now a ruin, was founded in the 11th cent. In 1264, Lewes was the scene of a victory by Simon de Montfort, earl of Leicester, over Henry III.

Lewin, Kurt, 1890-1947, American psychologist, b. Germany, Ph.D. Univ. of Berlin, 1914. He taught at the Univ. of Berlin before coming to the United States in 1932. He was professor (1935-44) of child psychology at the Univ. of Iowa and director (from 1944) of the research center for group dynamics at the Massachusetts Institute of Technology. Influenced by Gestalt psychology, he was concerned with problems of motivation of individuals and of groups as determined by the context of a given situation. His work opened up a new realm of psychological investigation. His writings include *A Dynamic Theory of Personality* (tr. 1935), *Principles of Topological Psychology* (1936), *The Conceptual Representation and Measurement of Psychological Forces* (1938), and *Resolving Social Conflicts* (1947).

Lewis. For rulers thus named, see LOUIS.

Lewis, Andrew, 1720?-1781, American soldier, b. Ireland. As a boy he emigrated with his family to America and settled near Staunton, Va. Later, he became a leading frontier Indian fighter. In 1754, at the beginning of the French and Indian War, he was with George Washington at the defeat at Fort Necessity. He led an unsuccessful expedition (the Sandy Creek expedition) against the Indians in the Ohio country in 1756. He is best remembered for his victory (1774) in Lord Dunmore's War over the Indians at Point Pleasant (now in West Virginia). In the American Revolution he was a brigadier general in the Continental Army.

Lewis, Cecil Day: see DAY LEWIS, CECIL.

Lewis, Clarence Irving, 1883-1964, American philosopher, b. Stoneham, Mass., grad. Harvard (B.A., 1906; Ph.D., 1910). After teaching (1911-20) at the Univ. of California, he was professor of philosophy at Harvard from 1920 to 1953, when he became professor emeritus. Lewis's importance as a philosopher lies in his combination of symbolic logic with an essentially pragmatic epistemology. After studying logic under Josiah Royce, he developed his own system of symbolic logic in opposition to the *Principia Mathematica* of Bertrand Russell and Alfred North Whitehead. However, he soon began investigations in the field of epistemology. In his main work, *Mind and the World-Order* (1929), he developed a position according to which the choice between logical (and thus philosophical) systems must be based on pragmatic grounds. His other works include *A Survey of Symbolic Logic* (1918), *Symbolic Logic* (with C. H. Langford, 1932), *An Analysis of Knowledge and Valuation* (1946), *Our Social Inheritance* (1957), and *The Ground and Nature of the Right* (1955). See his *Collected Papers*, ed. by J. D. Goheen and J. L. Mothershead (1970); J. R. Saydah, *The Ethical Theory of Clarence Irving Lewis* (1969).

Lewis, Clive Staples, 1898-1963, English author, b. Belfast, Ireland. A fellow and tutor of English at Magdalen College, Oxford, from 1925 to 1954, C. S. Lewis was noted equally for his literary scholarship and for his intellectual and witty expositions of Christian tenets. Among his most important works are *The Allegory of Love* (1936), an analysis of the literary evolution of romantic love during the Middle Ages; *The Screwtape Letters* (1942, rev. ed. 1961), an ironic treatment of the theme of salvation; and a history of *English Literature in the Sixteenth Century* (1954). He is also the author of *Out of the Silent Planet* (1938) and *That Hideous Strength* (1945), outer-planetary fantasies with deep Catholic and moral overtones; the "Chronicles of Narnia," a series of allegorical fantasies set in the mythical kingdom of Narnia, including *The Lion, the Witch and the Wardrobe* (1950) and *The Silver Chair* (1953); many works of literary criticism, including *Studies in Medieval and Renaissance Literature* (1966); and the autobiographical *Surprised by Joy* (1954). From 1954 until his death he was professor of Medieval and Renaissance English at Cambridge. See his *Selected Literary Essays* (1970) and *Narrative Poems* (1970), both ed. by Walter Hooper; his letters, ed. by his brother W. H. Lewis (1966); biographies by C. S. Kilby and Douglas Gilbert (1973), and R. L. Green and Walter Hooper (1974); study by K. A. Lindskoog (1973).

Lewis, Francis, 1713-1802?, political leader in the American Revolution, signer of the Declaration of Independence, b. Llandaff, Wales. As clothing contractor for British troops during the French and Indian War, he was captured (1756) at Oswego, and was sent to France. Lewis later returned to America and was a member of the Stamp Act Congress (1765) and the Continental Congress (1775-79).

Lewis, Sir George Cornewall, 1806-63, English statesman and man of letters. Entering Parliament as a Liberal in 1847, he served as chancellor of the exchequer (1855-58), home secretary (1859-61), and secretary of war (1861-63). While editor (1852-55) of the *Edinburgh Review*, he contributed many articles to the publication. He was the author of *An Essay on the Origin and Formation of the Romance Languages* (1835), *Enquiry into the Credibility of the Early Roman History* (1855), and *An Historical Survey of the Astronomy of the Ancients* (1862).

Lewis, Gilbert Newton, 1875-1946, American chemist, b. Weymouth, Mass., grad. Harvard (B.A., 1896; Ph.D., 1899). He taught at Harvard and at the Massachusetts Institute of Technology (1907-12) and from 1912 was professor of physical chemistry and dean of the college of chemistry, Univ. of California. His recognition of the importance of the electron pair bond led to a revision of the theory of valence. He also made special studies in thermodynamics, formulated the Lewis theory of ACIDS AND BASES, and with Harold C. Urey, a graduate student of his, discovered heavy water (1932). He wrote *Valence and the Structure of Atoms and Molecules* (1923).

Lewis, Jerry, 1926–, American comedian, b. Newark, N.J.; his original name was Joseph Levitch. Specializing in slapstick farce, Lewis usually plays idiotic yet pathetic characters, his portrayals replete with facial mugging and sight gags. During his partnership (1946-57) with the singer Dean Martin they made several movies, including *My Friend Irma* (1949) and *Partners* (1957). Among the many films Lewis has starred in—and often directed—are *Cinderfella*

(1960), *The Family Jewels* (1964), and *Hook, Line, and Sinker* (1969).

Lewis, John Llewellyn, 1880–1969, American labor leader, b. Lucas co., Iowa; son of a Welsh immigrant coal miner. He became a miner and after 1906 rose through the union ranks to become president (1920) of the UNITED MINE WORKERS OF AMERICA (UMW). Forceful and determined, Lewis fought vigorously to build up the union, won the loyalty of the miners, and thus consolidated his own power. He was one of the most important figures in the American Federation of Labor (AFL) until, moved by the desire to unionize the mass production industries, he split with the AFL and its leader, William Green. Taking several of the largest unions with him, Lewis founded (1935) a new organization, the Committee for Industrial Organization (CIO; see AMERICAN FEDERATION OF LABOR AND CONGRESS OF INDUSTRIAL ORGANIZATIONS). He had supported Franklin Delano Roosevelt for President in 1932 and had welcomed the New Deal, but coolness developed between Lewis and Roosevelt, and in 1940 Lewis supported Wendell Willkie for the presidency and staked his CIO presidency on Willkie's victory. Roosevelt won, and Lewis resigned. Increasing antagonism between him and Philip Murray, the new head of the CIO, led to a break, and in 1942 the UMW withdrew from the CIO. Lewis kept his own power. During World War II, Lewis was faced with the hostility of the War Labor Board and with unfavorable public sentiment because of the many strikes of the coal miners in the "no-strike" period. Although these strikes may have helped to pave the way for antistrike legislation, they did win the demands of the miners. The UMW was again joined (1946) to the AFL but split off (1947) once more in a dispute over means of combating the restrictive Taft-Hartley Act. Lewis's failure to obey a Federal court order to end a protracted coal strike led (1948) to a heavy fine for criminal contempt of court. In the 1950s Lewis discontinued his more aggressive tactics and followed a policy of accommodation with the depressed coal industry. He resigned as president of the UMW in 1960. See J. A. Wechsler, *Labor Baron* (1944, repr. 1972); Saul Alinsky, *John L. Lewis: An Unauthorized Biography* (1949, repr. 1970); D. F. Selvin, *The Thundering Voice of John L. Lewis* (1969).

Lewis, Matthew Gregory, 1775–1818, English author, b. London. In addition to his writing he pursued a diplomatic career and served for a time in Parliament. He was often called "Monk" Lewis from the title of his extravagant thriller *The Monk* (1796), the writing of which was influenced by the Gothic tales of Ann Radcliffe. The novel concerns a saintly Capuchin monk who is led into a life of depravity by a fiend-inspired woman. Charges of immorality and irreligion brought against Lewis by his critics caused a less offensive second edition to be published. Of his melodramatic plays the most famous is *The Castle Spectre* (1797). His ballads, notably *Alonzo the Brave and the Fair Imogene,* influenced Sir Walter Scott's early poetry. See biography by Louis F. Peck (1961); study by Montague Summers (1938, repr. 1964).

Lewis, Meriwether, 1774–1809, American explorer, one of the leaders of the LEWIS AND CLARK EXPEDITION, b. near Charlottesville, Va. He was a captain in the army and served in a number of Indian campaigns before becoming (1801) secretary to his friend President Jefferson. Selected to head the expedition for a land route to the Pacific ocean, he chose William CLARK as his associate. Upon that successful venture Lewis's fame rests. In 1807 he was made governor of Louisiana Territory, with headquarters at St. Louis. In 1809, while traveling to Washington to prepare the journals of the expedition for publication, he died suddenly—either by murder or suicide—in a lonely inn on the Natchez Trace. The cause of his death is still the subject of controversy. See biography by R. H. Dillon (1968); see also bibliography under LEWIS AND CLARK EXPEDITION.

Lewis, Morgan, 1754–1844, American army officer and governor of New York (1804–7), b. New York City; son of Francis Lewis. After serving in the American Revolution, he held a variety of state offices before becoming governor in 1804. Lewis was aided in his career by his marriage to a daughter of Robert R. Livingston. His term as governor was marred by factional rivalry, but he did much to encourage the growth of the public school system. Serving on the Niagara frontier in the War of 1812, he captured Fort George and commanded at the battles of Sackets Harbor and French Creek. He was a founder of New York Univ. See biography by his granddaughter, J. L. Delafield (2 vol., 1877).

Lewis, Oscar, 1914–70, American anthropologist, b. New York City, grad. City College of New York (B.S.S., 1936) and Columbia (Ph.D., 1940). He was a professor of anthropology at Washington Univ. (St. Louis) from 1946 to 1948 and after that at the Univ. of Illinois. His most important theory was that poverty creates an identifiable culture that transcends national differences. Among his writings were *Five Families* (1959), *The Children of Sánchez* (1961), *La Vida* (1966), and *Anthropological Essays* (1970).

Lewis, Sinclair, 1885–1951, American novelist, b. Sauk Centre, Minn., grad. Yale, 1908. Probably the greatest satirist of his era, Lewis wrote novels that present a devastating picture of middle-class American life in the 1920s. Although he ridiculed the values, the life-styles, and even the speech of his characters, there is affection behind the irony. Lewis began his career as a journalist, editor, and hack writer. With the publication of *Main Street* (1920), a merciless satire on life in a Midwestern small town, Lewis immediately became an important literary figure. His next novel, *Babbitt* (1922), considered by many critics to be his greatest work, is a portrait of an average American businessman, a Republican and a Rotarian, whose individuality has been erased by conformist values. *Arrowsmith* (1925; Pulitzer Prize, refused by Lewis) satirizes the medical profession, and *Elmer Gantry* (1927) attacks hypocritical religious revivalism. *Dodsworth* (1929), a more mellow work, is a sympathetic picture of a wealthy American businessman in Europe; it was successfully dramatized by Lewis and Sidney Howard in 1934. In 1930, Lewis became the first American to win the Nobel Prize for Literature. During his lifetime he published 22 novels. Among his later works are *It Can't Happen Here* (1935), *Cass Timberlane* (1945), *Kingsblood Royal* (1947), and *World So Wide* (1951). From 1928 to 1942 he was married to Dorothy Thompson (1894–1961), a distinguished newspaperwoman and foreign correspondent. See memoir by his first wife, G. H. Lewis (1955); biographies by Mark Shorer (1961), Vincent Sheean (1963), and Carl Van Doren (1933, repr. 1969); study by D. J. Dooley (1967).

Lewis, Wyndham (Percy Wyndham Lewis), 1886–1957, English author and painter, b. Maine. With Ezra Pound, he was cofounder and editor of *Blast* (1914–15), a magazine connected with VORTICISM. Lewis's paintings, however, were not limited to the cubism of the vorticists; he produced many conventional works that gained recognition. His paintings are in several museums, including the Tate Gallery, London, and the Museum of Modern Art, New York City. As an author, he is noted for his iconoclastic, quasi-philosophical novels and essays. Among his most important nonfiction works are *The Art of Being Ruled* (1926), *Time and Western Man* (1927), and *The Writer and the Absolute* (1952). His finest novels are generally judged to be *The Revenge for Love* (1937) and *Self-Condemned* (1954), but also of interest are *The Childermass* (1928; rev. and continued as *The Human Age,* 1955–56) and *The Apes of God* (1930). *Blasting and Bombardiering* (1937) and *Rude Assignment* (1950) are autobiographical. See his letters, ed. by W. K. Rose (1964); studies by W. H. Pritchard (1968) and R. T. Chapman (1973).

Lewis, Scotland: see LEWIS WITH HARRIS.

Lewis. 1 Early name of the SNAKE River. **2** River, c.95 mi (155 km) long, rising in the Cascade Range, SW Wash., and flowing SW to the Columbia River NW of Vancouver. Three privately owned dams furnish hydroelectric power (combined capacity 447,000 kw) and form a string of lakes along the river's middle course.

Lewis and Clark expedition, 1803–6, U.S. expedition that explored the territory of the LOUISIANA PURCHASE and the country beyond as far as the Pacific Ocean. Thomas Jefferson had long considered the project of a Western expedition, and as President he contemplated the matter in earnest and discussed it with his private secretary, Capt. Meriwether LEWIS. When Congress approved the plan in 1803 and appropriated money for it, Jefferson named Lewis to head it, and Lewis selected William CLARK as his associate in command. The purpose was to search out a land route to the Pacific, to strengthen American claims to Oregon territory, and to gather information about the Indians and the country of the Far West. Before the long march was begun, the Louisiana Purchase was made, increasing the need for a survey of the West. The men were gathered and in the winter of 1803–4 were trained in Illinois across the Mississippi from St. Louis, the starting point. In May, 1804, they set out up the Missouri, and the next winter was spent at the Mandan Indian villages (near present Bismarck, N.Dak.). In 1805 the hardest part of the journey was made. After reaching the Three Forks of the Missouri River (and naming the three branches after Jefferson, Madison, and Gallatin in loyalty to the administration), they followed the Jefferson as far as they could. Then their Indian woman guide, the remarkable SACAJAWEA, helped to obtain horses for them to continue across the high Rockies. They crossed the Continental Divide at Lemhi Pass and went over the Bitterroot Mts. through Lolo Pass. They had reached the land of westward-flowing rivers, and for part of their way they followed the Clearwater River down to the Snake River (long called the Lewis). The Snake took them to the Columbia River and they spent a miserable, rainy winter season in Fort Clatsop, a crude post they built on the Pacific coast. In the spring they started back across the continent. In July, 1806, the party split for a time in order to explore as much territory as possible. Lewis went with a group down the Marias River, while Clark and most of the men descended the Yellowstone River; they were reunited on the Missouri at the mouth of the Yellowstone on Aug. 12, 1806. The party arrived in St. Louis on Sept. 23, 1806, and were greeted with much acclaim. The importance of the well-planned, well-executed expedition (only one man had been lost) was enormous. Although it was not the first transcontinental crossing in the north (Alexander Mackenzie had preceded them in a remarkable voyage), it opened vast new territories to the United States. Its influence on the history of the West is incalculable. Its results matched the efficiency and capability of its leaders. Since the journey was under official auspices many records were kept. The first report of it to be published appeared in a message of President Jefferson in 1806. In 1807 the journal of Patrick Gass appeared; it was several times reissued before *The History of the Expedition under the Command of Captains Lewis and Clark* was published (ed. by Nicholas Biddle and Paul Allen, 2 vol., 1814; repr. 1966). This appeared in later editions by Elliott Coues (4 vol., 1893; repr. 1965) and J. B. McMaster (1904). R. G. Thwaites edited a full issue of *Original Journals of the Lewis and Clark Expedition* (8 vol., 1904–5; repr. 1969; abridged ed. by Bernard DeVoto, 1953, repr. 1963). There have been many studies and monographs on the expedition. See study by John Bakeless (1947, repr. 1962). See also *Letters of the Lewis and Clark Expedition* (ed. by D. D. Jackson, 1962); R. H. Dillon, *Meriwether Lewis: A Biography* (1968); P. R. Cutright, *Lewis and Clark, Pioneering Naturalists* (1969).

Lewisham (lo͞o'ĭs-həm), borough (1971 pop. 264,800) of Greater London, SE England, on the Thames. The borough was created in 1965 by the merger of the metropolitan boroughs of Lewisham and Deptford. It is mainly residential, but there is some light engineering. Deptford, which was noted in Elizabethan times for its cattle market and royal dockyard, trades in timber. The writer Christopher Marlowe was killed in a brawl at Deptford in 1593. Goldsmith's College, a faculty of the Univ. of London, is in the borough.

Lewis Hills, section of the Long Range, W Newfoundland island, Canada, S of the Bay of Islands. It rises to 2,672 ft (814 m), the highest point on the island.

lewisite (lo͞o'əsīt"), liquid chemical compound used as a POISON GAS. Like mustard gas and nitrogen mustard, it is a blistering agent; when inhaled, it is a powerful respiratory irritant. Lewisite penetrates ordinary clothing and can even penetrate rubber. Its absorption through the skin may be fatal. Chemically, lewisite is dichloro-2-chlorovinyl arsine, $ClCHCHAsCl_2$. It boils with decomposition at 190°C, and its vapor has a faint odor of geraniums. Lewisite is neutralized by reaction with British antilewisite (2, 3-dimercapto-1-propanol).

Lewisohn, Ludwig (lo͞o'ĭzōn), 1882–1955, American author, b. Berlin. After teaching German at Ohio State (1911–19), he was associate editor for the *Nation* (1920–24). His novels include *Don Juan* (1923), *The Island Within* (1928), *The Case of Mr. Crump* (1926), and *In a Summer Season* (1955). A prominent Zionist, Lewisohn often wrote on Jewish affairs. Besides making several notable translations from the German, he was a distinguished literary and drama critic; among his critical works are *The Creative Life* (1924) and *Cities and Men* (1927). He was one of the founding professors of Brandeis Univ. See his autobiographical works, *Upstream* (1922) and *Mid-Channel* (1929).

Lewiston. 1 City (1970 pop. 26,068), seat of Nez Perce co., NW Idaho, at the Wash. line and at the junction of the Snake and Clearwater rivers; founded 1861. It is the commercial and industrial center of a timber, grain, and livestock region that also has lime, clay, and silica deposits. The city has food-processing plants, a large pulp and paper mill, and factories making ammunition primers and concrete products. Lewis and Clark camped there in 1805. At nearby Lapwai, Henry H. Spalding established (1836) a mission and operated the first printing press in the Pacific Northwest. Lewiston grew as a supply and shipping center after gold was discovered on the Clearwater. It was the first capital (1863-64) of Idaho Territory and had the first newspaper, the *Golden Age* (1862), in Idaho. Lewis-Clark Normal School is in the city. **2** Industrial city (1970 pop. 41,779), Androscoggin co., SW Maine, on the Androscoggin River opposite Auburn; inc. 1795. A 50-ft (15-m) waterfall has supplied power for textile mills there since the early 19th cent. Now the second largest city in the state, Lewiston also has printing and poultry-hatching industries and plants making electrical equipment, Christmas-tree ornaments, and molybdenum and tungsten fine wire. Bates College, a junior college, and a beautiful cathedral are in Lewiston.

Lewistown, borough (1970 pop. 11,098), seat of Mifflin co., central Pa., on the Juniata River, in a beautiful farm and dairy area; inc. 1795. Many Amish live and farm in the surrounding area.

Lewis with Harris, island, 825 sq mi (2,137 sq km), largest and northernmost of the Outer Hebrides, NW Scotland, 24 mi (35 km) from the mainland across the Minch. The island is also called Lewis or the Lews. Harris has hilly terrain. Central Lewis is a vast, wet moor, uninhabited and unproductive. All the towns lie on the coast, and the bulk of the island's population is in Stornoway and the northern parish of Ness. Crofting, fishing, and stock raising are the main occupations. The thriving Harris tweed industry is centered in Stornoway, but utilizes home looms throughout the island. Gaelic is spoken. There is a prehistoric monument with large standing stones at Callanish in Lewis. In 1975, the island became part of the Western Isles island area.

Lewitt, Sol (ləwĭt'), 1928–, American artist, b. Hartford, Conn. Lewitt terms his work conceptual art, emphasizing the idea or concept as its most important aspect. His modular cubes and grid structures, wall drawings, and serial graphics reflect his study of mathematics. His work is represented in the Museum of Modern Art, New York City.

Lexan: see POLYCARBONATES.

lexicography, the applied study of the meaning, evolution, and function of the vocabulary units of a language for the purpose of compilation in book form—in short, the process of dictionary making. Early lexicography, practiced from the 7th cent. B.C. in Mesopotamia, Greece, and Rome, was reserved for abstruse words of specific disciplines. General lexicography originated in the 16th cent., and aspects of the modern DICTIONARY, such as etymology, developed during the 17th and 18th cent.

Lexington. 1 City (1970 pop. 108,137), seat of Fayette co., N central Ky., in the heart of the bluegrass region; inc. 1832. The outstanding center in the United States for the raising of thoroughbred horses, it is also an important market for tobacco and bluegrass seed and a railroad shipping point for E Kentucky's oil, coal, farm produce, and quarry products. Lexington has railroad shops, meat-packing plants, distilleries, and plants making electronic equipment, electric typewriters, and paper products. The city was named in 1775 by a group of hunters (including Simon Kenton) who were encamped on the site when they heard the news of the battle of Lexington. The city is the seat of the Univ. of Kentucky, Transylvania Univ., and two theological seminaries. Other places of interest are "Ashland," the home of Henry Clay (designed by Latrobe in 1806 and rebuilt with the original materials in the 1850s); "Hopemont," the home of John Hunt Morgan (1811); the Thomas Hart house (1794); the home of Mary Todd Lincoln; and the library, which has a file of the *Kentucky Gazette,* founded by John Bradford in 1787. Lexington cemetery contains the graves of Clay, Morgan, J. C. Breckinridge, and James Lane Allen. A U.S. hospital for the treatment of drug addicts, a U.S. veterans' hospital, and a state mental hospital are there. A national cemetery is nearby. See George W. Ranck, *History of Lexington, Kentucky* (1872, repr. 1971). **2** Town (1970 pop. 31, 886), Middlesex co., E Mass., a residential suburb of Boston; settled c.1640, inc. 1713. On April 19, 1775, the first battle of the Revolution was fought there (see LEXINGTON AND CONCORD, BATTLES OF). The site is marked by a monument on the triangular green, around which are several 17th-century buildings, including Buckman Tavern (1710), where the minutemen assembled; and an old burying ground. Other attractions include Monroe Tavern (1695), British headquarters during the battle; and the Hancock-Clarke House (1698), where John Hancock and Samuel Adams were awakened by Paul Revere's alarm. The first state normal school in the country was established there in 1839. The theologian and reformer Theodore Parker was born in Lexington. See F. S. Piper, *Lexington, the Birthplace of American Liberty* (11th ed. 1963). **3** City (1970 pop. 17,205), seat of Davidson co., central N.C., in the Yadkin valley; inc. 1827. Major industries are food processing and the manufacture of furniture and textiles. A junior college is there. **4** Town (1970 pop. 7,597), seat of Rockbridge co., W central Va., in the Shenandoah valley, in a beautiful farm area not far from Natural Bridge; laid out 1777, inc. 1841. It is the seat of Virginia Military Institute and Washington and Lee Univ. and the burial place of both Robert E. Lee and Stonewall Jackson. The Lee family crypt and museum is on the campus of Washington and Lee Univ. The home of Stonewall Jackson, who taught at the Virginia Military Institute, has many of his possessions; Jackson is buried in Lexington cemetery. The town was bombarded and partially burned by Gen. David Hunter in 1864.

Lexington and Concord, battles of, opening engagements of the AMERICAN REVOLUTION, April 19, 1775. After the passage (1774) of the INTOLERABLE ACTS by the British Parliament, unrest in the colonies increased. The British commander at Boston, Gen. Thomas GAGE, sought to avoid armed rebellion by sending a column of royal infantry from Boston to capture colonial military stores at Concord. News of his plan was dispatched to the countryside by Paul Revere, William Dawes, and Samuel Prescott. As the advance column under Major John PITCAIRN reached Lexington, they came upon a group of militia (the minutemen). After a brief exchange of shots in which several Americans were killed, the colonials withdrew, and the British continued to Concord. Here they destroyed some military supplies, fought another engagement, and began a harried withdrawal to Boston, which cost them over 200 casualties. See studies by Allen French (1925) and A. B. Tourtellot (1959, repr. 1963).

Leyden, Lucas van: see LUCAS VAN LEYDEN.

Leyden, Netherlands: see LEIDEN.

Leyden jar (lī'dən), form of CAPACITOR invented at the Univ. of Leiden in the 18th cent. It consists of a narrow-necked glass jar coated over part of its inner and outer surfaces with conductive metal foil; a conducting rod or wire passes through an insulating stopper in the neck of the jar and contacts the inner foil layer, which is separated from the outer layer by the glass wall. By modern standards, the Leyden jar is cumbersome and inefficient. It is rarely used except in laboratory demonstrations of capacitance.

Leyland, John: see LELAND, JOHN.

Leyte (lā'tē, -tā), island (1970 est. pop. 1,340,000), 2,785 sq mi (7,213 sq km), one of the Visayan Islands, the Philippines, between Luzon and Mindanao. A fertile agricultural land, it is the nation's leading producer of sweet potatoes and bananas and a major producer of corn and peanuts. It has commercial coconut plantations and extensive forest reserves; lumbering is an important industry. In World War II, Leyte was occupied by the Japanese in early 1942. It was the scene of the first main American landing (Oct. 20, 1944) in the campaign to recover the Philippines. That landing was followed by the battle of Leyte Gulf, the greatest naval-engagement of all time, in which American naval forces destroyed the Japanese fleet.

Leyton: see WALTHAM FOREST.

leze majesty: see LESE MAJESTY.

Lhasa or **La-sa** (lä-sŭ), city (1970 est. pop. 175,000), capital of Tibet Autonomous Region, SW China. It is on a tributary of the Tsangpo (Brahmaputra) River at an altitude of c.11,800 ft (3,600 m). Lhasa is the chief Tibetan trade center, connected by road with the Chinese provinces of Tsinghai, Szechwan, and Sinkiang Uigur Autonomous Region, and with India, Kashmir, and Nepal. Chemicals are manufactured, and copper and gold, which are mined nearby, are processed. Because of the remoteness of the city and the traditional hostility of the Tibetan clergy toward foreigners, Lhasa has long been called the Forbidden City. Prior to the Chinese occupation (1951) of Tibet, Lhasa was the center of Lamaism (see TIBETAN BUDDHISM), and about half its population were Lamaist monks. Lhasa has little noteworthy architecture, but there are impressive religious edifices. On a nearby hill, backed by lofty mountains in the distance, stands the magnificent Potala, the former palace of the Dalai Lama, a gigantic block of buildings nine stories high, whitewashed save for the central portion, which is red, and surmounted by gilded roofs and towers. It has reception rooms, chapels, and quarters for thousands of monks. A smaller palace of the Dalai Lama is set in the beautifully wooded grounds of Jewel Park. Near the city is the Drepung monastery, one of the largest in the world. The holiest temple in Lhasa, unimpressive from the outside, is the Jokang, which contains a jeweled image of the young Buddha. Several of the religious edifices were damaged during the Tibetan revolt (1959-60) against the Chinese. A modern highway bridge, made of reinforced concrete (c.2,400 ft/730 m long) crosses the river at Lhasa. The city's name also appears as Lassa. See Theos Bernard, *Penthouse of the Gods* (1939); Heinrich Harrer, *Seven Years in Tibet* (1953); Giuseppe Tucci, *To Lhasa and Beyond* (1956); Peter Fleming, *Bayonets to Lhasa* (1961); F. S. Chapman, *Lhasa* (1940, repr. 1972); L. A. Waddell, *Lhasa and its Mysteries* (3d ed. 1906, repr. 1972).

Lhasa apso (lä'sə ăp'sō), breed of small, alert NON-SPORTING DOG developed in Tibet many centuries ago. It stands about 11 in. (27.9 cm) high at the shoulder and weighs from 13 to 15 lb (5.9-6.8 kg). Its heavy, straight coat is long and very dense. It may be any of various colors or combinations of colors, although shades of gold are preferred. The Lhasa apso was raised in the lamaseries and villages outlying Lhasa, the ancient center of Lamaism. Specimens of the breed were traditionally given as gifts by the Dali Lamas to the Chinese emperors and other dignitaries. Today it is raised as a watchdog and pet. See DOG.

L'Hôpital or **L'Hospital, Michel de** (both: mēshĕl' də lōpētäl'), c.1505-1573, chancellor of France under CATHERINE DE' MEDICI. He was Catherine's chief collaborator in the policy of religious toleration that she followed during most of her early administration. He favored, although he did not originate, the Edict of Romorantin (1560), which deprived the secular courts of jurisdiction in cases involving religion, and he was responsible for the edicts granting liberty of conscience (1561) and restricted liberty of worship (1562). He withdrew from court during the first War of Religion (1562-63; see RELIGION, WARS OF), but subsequently returned to power and in 1566 was the author of important judicial reforms. After the outbreak (1567) of the second War of Religion he was forced out of office (1568) by Charles and Henri de GUISE. In his retirement he composed Latin poetry.

Li, chemical symbol of the element LITHIUM.

liana (lēä'nə) or **liane** (lēän'), name for any climbing plant that roots in the ground. The term is most often used for the woody vines that form a characteristic part of tropical rain-forest vegetation; they are sometimes also called bushropes or simply vines. Although lianas are found in every climate where there are trees to support them, they are most abundant and luxuriant in the tropics, where rapid growth to reach the light is of particular advantage in the dense vegetation. There they often ascend and descend more than one tree. Climbing palms have been measured at over 700 ft (210 m) long; a length of over 200 ft (60 m) is not unusual for many other types. Most plant families with tropical species include lianas. The distinction between true lianas and weak-stemmed trees or half-climbing shrubs cannot always be clearly drawn and depends largely on the age of the plant concerned.

Liang Ch'i-ch'ao (lēäng chē-chou), 1873-1929, Chinese reform leader. Liang was a disciple of K'ANG YU-WEI. Stunned by China's disastrous defeat by Japan (see SINO-JAPANESE WAR, FIRST), K'ang and Liang launched (1895) a movement for constitutional and educational reform. The movement received the backing of Emperor KUANG HSÜ in 1898, but the "hundred days' reform" was aborted by the Empress Dowager TZ'U HSI. Liang fled to Japan where he continued to promote gradualist reform and constitutional monarchy. Although his writings had a great influence on the constitutional movement within China, the large Chinese student community in Japan increasingly favored an anti-Manchu revolution as espoused by SUN YAT-SEN. Following the republican revolution of 1911, Liang returned to China and led the Progressive party in parliament, generally supporting the regimes of YÜAN SHIH-K'AI and TUAN CH'I-JUI and opposing the KUOMINTANG. See studies by J. R. Levenson (2d rev. ed. 1967) and Ch'ang Hao (1971).

Liao (lyou), principal river of NE China, c.900 mi (1,450 km) long, rising in Inner Mongolia and flowing east then south through the fertile Liao alluvial plain to the Gulf of Liaotung. The eastern branch, its main tributary, joins it at the Kirin-Liaoning prov. border. The shallow, silt-laden Liao is navigable for light junks c.400 mi (640 km) upstream. It was the main route into S Manchuria until the construction of the railroad in the early 20th cent. Through sedimentation, the Liao delta has steadily grown.

Liaoning or **Liao-ning** (both: lyou-nĭng), province (1968 est. pop. 28,000,000), c.89,000 sq mi (230,510 sq km), NE China, on the Po Hai and West Korea Bay. The capital is SHEN-YANG (Mukden). A part of Manchuria, it encompasses the Liaotung peninsula and the plain of the Liao River. Rainfall is adequate, but long, severe winters permit only one harvest annually. Soybeans are the major crop, and millet, kaoliang, wheat, rice, sweet potatoes, beans, cotton, fruit, and oakleaf silk (pongee silk) are also produced. Liaoning is China's most industrialized province. It is a major coal-producing area and contains more than half of China's iron ore reserves; there are large deposits of magnesite and smaller ones of copper, lead, and molybdenum. Shen-yang is the center of a vast heavy-industrial complex (metallurgy, machinery, chemicals, petroleum, and coal) that also embraces AN-SHAN, a major city for iron and steel; FU-SHUN, a coal and a shale oil producing center; and TA-LIEN, the chief commercial port of Manchuria. Important manufactures include aircraft, locomotives, tractors, and a wide range of heavy equipment. Liaoning is also the nation's leading producer of machine-made paper, and it has numerous brick and tile factories that utilize waste ash and slag. Along the coast, salt production and fishing are important; chief catches are prawns and yellow croakers. The Liao River, which crosses Liaoning, is navigable in its lower reaches, and an extensive rail net, including sections of the South Manchuria RR, connects the interior with the ports along the coast. The growth of railroads after 1900 spurred the development of the province; the Japanese concentrated heavy industry there, especially after 1931. The Supung Dam on the Yalu River, built by the Japanese, supplies power to Liaoning and North Korea. Liaoning's fine harbors were long coveted by Russia and Japan for their strategic positions. Japan acquired (1895) the Liaotung peninsula after the first Sino-Japanese War, but was forced by Russia, Germany, and France to return it to China that same year. In 1898 Russia received the southern portion of the Liaotung peninsula as a 25-year leasehold. After the Russo-Japanese War (1904-5), Japan took this territory (which it called Kwantung) and held it until the end of World War II, when approximately the same area was made the Port Arthur Naval Base District, under joint Soviet and Chinese operation. As the special municipality of Lü-ta, the district, which includes the cities of Lü-shun and Ta-lien, has been under sole Chinese administration since 1955. The eastern part of Jehol prov. became part of Liaoning in 1956, and in 1970 more than 30,000 sq mi (77,700 sq km) of territory from the Inner Mongolian Autonomous Region was added to Liaoning in the west. Liaoning Univ. is in Shen-yang.

Liaopei or **Liao-pei** (lēou-bā), former province (c.47,000 sq mi/121,700 sq km), NE China. The capital was Liao-yüan. It was one of nine provinces created in Manchuria in 1945 by the Chinese Nationalist government. However, since the Nationalists never gained effective control of Manchuria after World War II, the province existed only on paper. It was later divided between the Inner Mongolian Autonomous Region and the provinces of Heilungkiang, Kirin, and Liaoning.

Liaotung: see LIAONING, China.

Liao-yang or **Liaoyang** (both: lyou-yăng), city (1970 est. pop. 250,000), E Liaoning prov., China, on a tributary of the Hun River. It is a flourishing industrial city in the great Shen-yang (Mukden) urban complex. Iron and coal are mined, and there are textile and other light industries. One of the oldest cities of Manchuria, Liao-yang contains several Buddhist temples built in the 11th cent. In the Russo-Japanese War it was the site of a battle (Aug. 23-Sept. 3, 1904) in which the Russians were forced to retreat.

Liao-yüan or **Liaoyüan** (lyou-yüän), city, SW Kirin prov., China, on the railroad connecting Ch'ang-ch'un and Lü-ta. It is a coal-mining center with iron and steel works. It was the capital of Liaopei prov. from 1945 to 1949; from 1949 to 1954 it was part of Liaotung prov.

Liaquat Ali Khan (lēä'kət älē' kän), 1895-1951, first prime minister of Pakistan. He was educated at Aligarh Muslim Univ. and at Oxford and was admitted to the English bar in 1922. A year later he joined the Muslim League. He served (1926-40) in the United Provs. legislative council, and while there he became (1936) general secretary of the Muslim League; thereafter he was chief lieutenant to Muhammad Ali JINNAH. He represented the Muslim League in the Central Legislative Assembly of India from 1940 to 1946, when he was appointed to the interim Indian government organized by the British to prepare the way for India's independence. With the creation of Pakistan (Aug., 1947) he became prime minister of the new dominion. He was assassinated in 1951.

Liard (lē'ärd''), river, 755 mi (1,215 km) long, rising in the Pelly Mts., SE Yukon Territory, Canada, and flowing SE into N British Columbia, passing through the main range of the Rocky Mts., thence northeast through densely wooded country to the Mackenzie River at Fort Simpson, SW Mackenzie dist., Northwest Territories. It is navigable to Fort Liard, an old Hudson's Bay Company post, c.165 mi (270 km) from its mouth. The South Nahanni and Fort Nelson rivers are its chief tributaries. Part of its course is followed by the Alaska Highway.

Libanus: see LEBANON, mountain range.

Libau: see LIEPAYA, USSR.

Libby, Willard Frank, 1908-, American chemist, b. Grand Valley, Colo., grad. Univ. of California (B.S., 1931; Ph.D., 1933). He taught (1933-45) at the Univ. of California and was a chemist (1941-45) in the war research division at Columbia. From 1945 to 1954 he was with the Univ. of Chicago and was a member of the committee of reviewers for the Atomic Energy Commission (AEC); he was then (1954-59) an AEC commissioner. In 1959 he joined the faculty of the Univ. of California at Los Angeles. Libby was awarded the 1960 Nobel Prize in Chemistry for his development (c.1946) of radioactive carbon-14 DATING. He is the recipient of several other prizes, including the 1959 Albert Einstein award. Libby is the author of *Radiocarbon Dating* (1955).

Libby Prison, in Richmond, Va., a Confederate prison for captured Union officers in the American Civil War. It was previously a tobacco warehouse. Living conditions were extremely bad; the food, sometimes lacking altogether, was poor and sanitation practically nonexistent. Thousands died there. Except for Andersonville Prison, Ga., Libby Prison was the most notorious in the Confederacy. See F. A. Bartleson, *Letters from Libby Prison* (ed. by M. W. Peelle, 1956).

libel and **slander,** in law, types of defamation. At COMMON LAW, written defamation was libel and spoken defamation was slander. Today there are no clear definitions. Permanent forms of defamation, such as the written or pictorial, are usually called libel, while the spoken or gestured forms are called slander. The term libel is also often used if a wide audience for the defamation is possible. Courts have split over which category radio and television are in; today's statutes generally categorize defamation occurring in those media as slander. The offenses are alike in several respects. The defamation—essentially exposure to hatred, contempt, ridicule, or pecuniary loss—must directly affect the reputation of a living person. It must be published, i.e., revealed to someone besides the subject of the attack. It is no defense that the defendant merely repeated but did not originate the defamation. The plaintiff is required to prove the colloquium (circumstances of utterance showing that the statement was directed against him specifically) and, when necessary, the innuendo (the factors making an apparently innocent statement defamatory). The requirement of colloquium makes unactionable defamation of a large group, e.g., a racial or professional group. Generally truth is an absolute defense in a suit for defamation. A false defamatory statement may be privileged if the actor was a legislator, executive officer, or speaking in a court proceeding. Whether the charge is libel or slander is important. Any libel is deemed injurious and gives immediate ground for suit. However, only certain types of statements are slanderous per se and do not require proof of pecuniary damages; these are imputation of crime, of loathsome disease, of professional or occupational incapacity, or of unchastity in a woman. If the alleged slander falls into some other category, there may not be any recovery unless the pecuniary loss caused by the injury is proved. The award to the successful plaintiff in a suit for defamation will usually include punitive, as well as compensatory, DAMAGES if the defendant willfully lied or published the defamation repeatedly. For criminal, or seditious, libel, see PRESS, FREEDOM OF THE. See Philip Wittenberg, *Dangerous Words: A Guide to the Law of Libel* (1947); R. H. Phelps and E. D. Hamilton, *Libel* (1966, repr. 1969); A. B. Hanson, *Libel and Related Torts* (2 vol., 1969).

Liber (lī'bər), in Roman religion, god of fertility and wine. He was usually identified with Bacchus, the Greek Dionysus. His consort **Libera** was identified with Persephone or Ariadne. Liber and Libera had a famous cult on the Aventine Hill in Rome in connection with Ceres. The festival LIBERALIA was celebrated in their honor.

Liberal, city (1970 pop. 13,489), seat of Seward co., SW Kansas; founded 1888, inc. 1945. It is the trade center for a grazing and farm area. Beef processing and the cattle and feed-grain industries are important to the economy. Oil and natural gas are extracted, and helium is processed in the city. Aircraft, fabricated metals, and handling equipment are also manufactured in Liberal. The International Pancake Race between the housewives of Liberal and Olney, England, is held annually on Shrove Tuesday. Seward County Community College is in Liberal.

liberal arts, term originally used to designate the arts or studies suited to freemen. It was applied in the Middle Ages to seven branches of learning, the trivium of grammar, logic, and rhetoric, and the quadrivium of arithmetic, geometry, astronomy, and music. The study of the trivium led to the Bachelor of Arts degree, and the quadrivium to the Master of Arts. During the Renaissance, the term was interpreted more broadly to mean all of those studies that impart a general, as opposed to a vocational or specialized, education. This corresponds rather closely to the interpretation used in most undergraduate colleges today, although the curriculum of the latter is more flexible than that of the Renaissance university. See Mark Van Doren, *Liberal Education* (1959); Jacques Barzun, *The Teacher in America* (1945); Harvard Committee, *General Education in a Free Society* (1945); Thomas Woody, *Liberal Education for Free Men* (1951); A. W. Griswold, *Liberal Education and the Democratic Ideal* (1959, rev. ed. 1962); Carl Weinberg, *Humanistic Foundations of Education* (1972); writings of Robert Maynard HUTCHINS.

Liberale da Verona (lēbārä'lā dä värō'nä), b. c.1445, d. 1526 or 1529, Italian painter of the Veronese school, whose name was Liberale de Jacopo della Biava. He was employed at Monte Oliveto near Siena as a miniature painter and illustrator of liturgical books (some of which are now preserved at Chiusi), and in the Cathedral of Siena. Returning (c.1488) to Verona, he took up fresco and oil painting. His earlier paintings are executed in a meticulous and minute style, but his later works are more broadly treated, apparently under the influence of Mantegna. Notable examples are *Madonna with Saints,* his earliest known painting; *Adoration of the Magi* (cathedral, Verona); and a predella, with scenes of the *Nativity, Epiphany,* and *Death of the Virgin* (Episcopal Palace, Verona). See study by F. Zeri (1951).

Liberalia (lĭbərā'lēə), in Roman religion, festival of Liber and Libera. The rustic festival of great rejoicing and merrymaking was held on March 17. Roman youths generally first assumed the *toga virilis* (i.e., began dressing like adults) at this time.

liberalism, philosophy or movement that has as its aim the development of individual freedom. Because the concepts of liberty or freedom change in different historical periods the specific programs of liberalism also change. The final aim of liberalism, however, remains fixed, as does its characteristic belief not only in the essential goodness of man but also in his rationality. Because man functions primarily according to his rational intellect, he has the ability to recognize problems and solve them. This leads to systematic improvement in the human condition. Often opposed to liberalism is the doctrine of CONSERVATISM, which, simply stated, supports the maintenance of the status quo. Liberalism, which continually seeks what it considers to be improvement or progress, necessarily desires to change the existing order. Neither individualism nor the belief that freedom is a primary political good are immutable laws of history. Only in the Western world in the last several centuries have they assumed such importance as social factors that they could be blended into a political creed. Although Christianity had long taught the worth of the individual soul and the Renaissance had placed a value upon individualism in limited circles, it was not until the REFORMATION that the importance of independent individual thought and action were expressed in the teachings of Protestantism. At the same time, centralizing monarchs were destroying FEUDALISM and alongside the nobility arose the BOURGEOISIE, a new social class that demanded the right to function in society, especially commercially, without restriction. This process took several centuries, and it may be said that the first philosopher to offer a complete liberal doctrine of individual freedom was the Englishman John LOCKE (1689). From this period on the doctrines of classical liberalism were evolved. Classical liberalism stressed not only man's rationality but the importance of individual property rights, natural rights, the need for constitutional limitations on government, and, especially, freedom of the individual from any kind of external restraint. Classical liberalism drew upon the ideals of the ENLIGHTENMENT and the doctrines of liberty supported in the American and French Revolutions. The Enlightenment, also known as the Age of Reason, was characterized by a belief in the perfection of the natural order and a belief that natural laws should govern society. Logically it was reasoned that if the natural order produces perfection, then society should operate freely without interference from government. The writings of such men as Adam SMITH, David RICARDO, Jeremy BENTHAM, and John Stuart MILL mark the height of such thinking. In Great Britain and the United States the classic liberal program, including the principles of representative government, the protection of civil liberties, and LAISSEZ FAIRE economics, had been more or less effected by the mid-19th cent. The growth of industrial society, however, soon produced great inequalities in wealth and power, which led many persons, especially workers, to question the liberal creed. It was in reaction to the failure of liberalism to provide a good life for everyone that workers' movements and MARXISM arose. Because true liberalism is concerned with liberating the individual, however, its doctrines changed with the change in historical realities. By 1900, L. T. HOBHOUSE and T. H. GREEN began to look to the state to prevent oppression and to advance the welfare of all individuals. Liberal thought was soon stating that the government should be responsible for providing the minimum conditions necessary for decent individual existence. In the early 20th cent. in Great Britain and France and later in the United States, the welfare state came into existence, and social reform became an accepted governmental role. In the United States minimum wage laws, progressive taxation, and social security programs were all instituted, initially by the NEW DEAL, and today remain an integral part of modern democratic government. While these programs are also advocated by SOCIALISM, liberalism does not support the socialist goal of complete equality imposed by state control, and because it is still dedicated to the primacy of the individual, liberalism also strongly opposes COMMUNISM. Current liberal goals in the United States include INTEGRATION of the races, sexual equality, and the eradication of poverty. The classic works of liberalism include John Locke, *Second Treatise on Government* (1689); John Stuart Mill, *On Representative Government* (1862); L. T. Hobhouse, *Liberalism* (1911); John Dewey, *Liberalism and Social Action* (1935). See also Guido de Ruggiero, *The History of European Liberalism* (1927); Frederick Watkins, *The Political Tradition of the West* (1948); Harry K. Girvetz, *From Wealth to Welfare* (1950); Thomas P. Neill, *The Rise and Decline of Liberalism* (1953); George L. Cheery, *Early English Liberalism* (1962); Kenneth R. Minogue, *The Liberal Mind* (1963).

Liberal party, British political party. It was an outgrowth of the WHIG party that, after the REFORM BILL of 1832, joined with the bulk of enfranchised industrialists and business classes to form a political alliance that, over the next few decades, came to be called the Liberal party. Lord John RUSSELL is credited with originating the party's name, and his government of 1846 is sometimes described as the first Liberal ministry. Their distinguishing policies included free trade, low budgets, and religious liberty. Their anti-imperialism reflected confidence in Britain's economic supremacy. Most Liberals believed in the economic doctrines of LAISSEZ FAIRE and thought labor unions, factory acts, and substantial poor relief a threat to rapid industrialization. Much of the Liberal program was formulated by an important manufacturing middle-class element of the party known as the Radicals, who were strongly influenced by Jeremy BENTHAM. Whig peers like Lord MELBOURNE and Lord PALMERSTON, upholding the principle of aristocratic government, for 30 years prevented further franchise reforms. But Lord John Russell, William GLADSTONE, and John BRIGHT (one of the Radicals) fought stubbornly for electoral reforms, even though the newly enfranchised masses might then insist on labor legislation opposed by the party. These leaders provided the impetus for the Reform Bill that their Conservative opponents passed in 1867. The laissez-faire outlook and hegemony of the Liberal party were challenged in the last quarter of the 19th cent. When the party's program of electoral reform reached completion in 1884, Gladstone took up Irish HOME RULE as a new cause. However, during the long period of depression from 1873 to 1893, many businessmen began to demand closer imperial ties. Because of the Home Rule issue, a large segment of businessmen, led by Joseph CHAMBERLAIN, along with English owners of Irish land left the Liberal party in 1886 to form the Liberal-Unionists, who allied themselves with the Conservative party. In losing office, the divided Liberals became stronger advocates of labor legislation. They came to depend more heavily upon the support of special groups like the Irish, labor, and nonconformists. The party was once more victorious in 1892 and again, under Sir Henry CAMPBELL-BANNERMAN, in 1906. Herbert Asquith (see OXFORD AND ASQUITH, 1st EARL OF), a Liberal imperialist, became prime minister in 1908, to be followed by the flamboyant David LLOYD GEORGE during World War I. By 1914 the Liberal government had passed substantial welfare legislation but, unwilling to adopt a full socialist program, the Liberals began to lose support to the new LABOUR PARTY. The party's stubborn adherence to outmoded doctrines of free trade, arguments between the Lloyd George and Asquith factions of the party, long years of depression, the Irish problem, growing labor radicalism, and the rise of a working-class party all account for the rapid postwar decline of the Liberals. During the 1920s they were still a strong element in Parliament, and several, notably Sir John Simon (later 1st Viscount SIMON), were members of the National government of the 1930s. During the 30s, however, their parliamentary representation fell rapidly, and in no election between the end of World War II and 1974 did they return more than a handful of candidates. Nonetheless, in the early 1970s the party appeared to be gathering strength. Although it won only six seats (and 7% of the vote) in the 1970 general election, it gained an additional five in by-elections in 1972–73. In the general election of Feb., 1974, the Liberals won 19% of the national vote; in Oct., 1974, they won 18%. Despite these substantial votes, however, they returned only 14 members in February and 13 in October to the 635-member House of Commons. For this reason the Liberals favor electoral reform with the adoption of some form of proportional representation. The party also strongly supports the European Common Market and advocates a system of federal government for Great Britain with parliaments for Scotland and Wales. See Sir Henry Slesser, *A History of the Liberal Party* (1944); R. B. McCallum, *The Liberal Party from Earl Grey to Asquith* (1963); Trevor Wilson, *The Downfall of the Liberal Party, 1914–1935* (1966); R. I. Douglas, *The History of the Liberal Party, 1895–1970* (1971).

Liberal party, in U.S. history, political party formed in 1944 in New York City by a group of anti-Communist trade unionists and liberals who withdrew from the AMERICAN LABOR PARTY when that party became pro-Communist. Among those responsible for its creation was Reinhold NIEBUHR. The original party platform called for a strong United Nations, extended civil rights, and support of the American trade-union movement. Rather than attempting to elect its own candidates, as political parties usually do, the Liberal party generally seeks to influence the candidate choice of the major parties by promises of support or nonsupport. Although the party operates almost entirely in New York state, its endorsement of presidential candidates sometimes affects national politics. That the endorsement of the Liberal party can be important was evidenced in its first year of existence, when it was responsible for Franklin Delano Roosevelt's presidential victory in New York state. In the 1960 presidential election the party provided New York's margin of victory for John F. Kennedy. In state and local elections the party sometimes nominates its own candidates. In 1969, John Lindsay, having lost the Republican nomination, won reelection as mayor of New York City on the Liberal ticket; the Liberal party has also elected its own U.S. congressman, a president of the New York city council, and numerous other local officials. Although the Liberal party has generally supported Democratic candidates, it claims to stand for broader social and economic reforms than the Democratic party. At one time the Liberal party was criticized for having too close ties with the Democratic party. However, its support of the Republican mayoral candidate in 1965, John Lindsay, and its support of the Republican Senator Jacob Javits tended to quell such criticism. The Liberal vote declined somewhat in the late 1960s and early 1970s; in 1974 the party drew less than 5% of the vote.

Liberal Republican party, in U.S. history, organization formed in 1872 by Republicans discontented at the political corruption and the policies of President Grant's first administration. Other disaffected elements were drawn into the party. Among its leaders were Carl SCHURZ and B. Gratz BROWN, both of Missouri, who had defeated the regular Republicans in the state election of 1870, Horace GREELEY, Charles SUMNER, and Lyman TRUMBULL. The party convention, held at Cincinnati in May, passed over Charles Francis ADAMS (1807–86), David DAVIS, and others to nominate Greeley for President; Brown was named for Vice President. In their convention at Baltimore, the Democrats also accepted these candidates. The party program called for civil service reform and an end to the strong Reconstruction program of the radical Republicans; so as not to offend the party's divergent segments, it avoided adopting a position on the tariff question. Greeley's nomination was not popular with many of the party leaders, who supported him without enthusiasm, and Grant was easily reelected. See E. D. Ross, *The Liberal Republican Movement* (1919, repr. 1971).

Liberec (lĭ'bĕrĕts), Ger. *Reichenberg,* city (1970 pop. 72,752), N Czechoslovakia, in Bohemia, on the Lausitzer Neisse (Lužická Nisa) River and near the East German and Polish borders. The city is a textile center known especially for its woolens; textile machinery, electrical equipment, and automobiles are also produced there. Founded c.1350, Liberec has enjoyed prosperity since the 16th cent., when clothmaking was introduced; the first textile factories were built in the 18th cent. German troops occupied the city from 1938 to 1945 and expelled the Czech residents.

Liberia (lībēr'ēə) (New Lat.,=place of freedom), republic (1970 est. pop. 1,225,000), 43,000 sq mi (111,370 sq km), W Africa. Liberia fronts on the Atlantic Ocean for some 350 mi (560 km) and is bordered on the NW by Sierra Leone, on the N by Guinea, and on the E by the Ivory Coast. MONROVIA is the capital, main port, and commercial center. Other important towns include Buchanan and Harper, both ports. Liberia can be divided into three

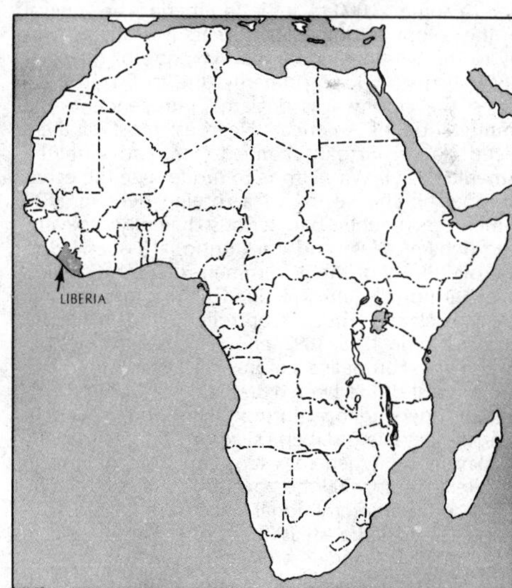

distinct topographical areas. First, a flat coastal plain of some 10 to 50 mi (16–80 km), with creeks, lagoons, and mangrove swamps; second, an area of broken, forested hills and mountain ranges, with altitudes from 600 to 1,200 ft (180–370 m), which covers most of the country; and third, an area of mountains in the northern highlands, with elevations reaching 4,540 ft (1,384 m) in the Nimba Mts. and 4,528 ft (1,380 m) in the Wutivi Mts. The six main rivers, which flow into the Atlantic, divide the country at right angles to the coast. Vegetation in much of the country is dense forest growth. The climate is tropical and humid, with a heavy rainfall, averaging 183 in. (465 cm) on the coast and some 88 in. (224 cm) in the southeastern interior. There are two rainy seasons and a dry, harmattan season in December and January. The majority of the population are members of some 28 tribes. Of these, the Vai and

Mandingo, largely Muslim peoples, and the Kru, Bassa, and Grebo peoples are the most numerous. Decentralized political organizations are common among the tribal peoples, with government-appointed chiefs directing most local affairs. The Poro, a men's organization with educational, legal, and religious functions, continues to be of importance, particularly among the Vai, Kpelle, and Gola peoples. Traditional religions and Islam are practiced by the majority of the population, and tribal languages are used extensively, although English is the official language. Far less numerous, but of great political importance, are the descendants of American settlers. These people, formerly called Americo-Liberians, are concentrated in the towns, where they provide the country's westernized leadership and, for the most part, are adherents of various Protestant sects. There are also a sizable Lebanese community of merchants as well as European and American technicians. Until the 1950s, Liberia's economy was almost totally dependent upon subsistence farming and the production of rubber. The American-owned Firestone plantation was the country's largest employer and held a concession on some one million acres (404,700 hectares) of land. With the discovery of high-grade iron ore, first at Bomi Hills, and then at Bong and Nimba, the production and export of minerals became the country's major cash-earning economic activity. Other important minerals include gold, diamonds, barite, and kyanite. Some three quarters of the population remain in the subsistence economy, producing such crops as rice, cassava, yams, and okra. Much of the rice, the main staple, is imported, but efforts are underway to develop intensive rice production and to establish fish farms. Rubber and timber, produced mainly on foreign concessions, are the main nonagricultural exports. Iron ore, rubber, and diamonds provide the bulk of the export earnings. Much of the country's industry is concentrated around Monrovia and is directed toward the production of consumer goods. Mineral processing plants are located near Buchanan and Bong. The government derives a sizable income from registering ships; low fees and lack of control over shipping operations have made the Liberian merchant marine one of the world's largest. Internal communications are poor, with few paved roads and only a few short, freight-carrying rail lines. Liberia was founded in 1821, when officials of the AMERICAN COLONIZATION SOCIETY were granted possession of Cape Mesurado by local De chiefs. American Negro settlers were landed in 1822, the first of some 15,000 to settle in Liberia. The survival of the colony during its early years was due primarily to the work of Jehudi ASHMUN, one of the society's agents. In 1847, primarily due to British pressures, the colony was declared independent. The immigration of American Negroes, most of them freed slaves, virtually came to an end with the American Civil War. Efforts to modernize the economy led to the raising of a foreign debt in 1871, which the republic had serious difficulty repaying. The debt problem and constitutional issues led to the overthrow of the government in 1871. Conflicts over territorial claims resulted in the loss of large areas of claimed, but uncontrolled, lands to Britain and France in 1885, 1892, and 1919, but rivalries between the Europeans colonizing West Africa and the interest of the United States helped preserve Liberian independence during this period. Nevertheless, the decline of Liberia's exports and its inability to pay its debts led to a large measure of foreign interference. In 1909 the government was bankrupt, and a series of international loans were floated. Firestone leased large areas for rubber production in 1926. In 1930 scandals broke out over the exportation of forced labor from Liberia, and a League of Nations investigation upheld the charges that slave trading had gone on with the connivance of the government. President King and his associates resigned, and international control of the republic was proposed. Under the leadership of presidents Edwin Barclay (1930–44) and William V. S. Tubman (1944–71), however, Liberia avoided such control. Under Tubman, new policies to open the country to international investment and to allow the tribal peoples a greater say in Liberian affairs were undertaken. The value of these new approaches was shown in the gradual improvement of roads, schools, and health standards, after the country's mineral wealth, particularly iron ore, began to be exploited, and in the decline of hostilities between native peoples and Americo-Liberians. Upon Tubman's death in 1971, Vice President W. R. Tolbert took charge, and in 1972 he was elected to the presidency. The Liberian constitution is modeled on that of the United States. A president, elected for an initial eight-year term, and eligible for succeeding four-year terms, provides strong executive leadership. Legislative authority is divided between a Senate and a House of Representatives. The True Whig Party has been in effective control of the government since the 1880s. See C. H. Huberich, *The Political and Legislative History of Liberia* (2 vol., 1947); P. J. Staudenraus, *The African Colonization Movement, 1816–1865* (1961); American University, Washington, D.C., *Area Handbook for Liberia* (1964); A. D. Henries, *The Liberian Nation: A Short History* (1966); C. M. Wilson, *Liberia* (1971).

Liberius (lībēr'ēəs), d. 366, pope (352–66), a Roman; successor of St. Julius I. At the beginning of his pontificate, the status of ATHANASIUS was still disputed, and Liberius requested Emperor CONSTANTIUS II to call the Council of Arles (353). Subdued by imperial favor toward ARIANISM, the papal legates signed against Athanasius, but Liberius refused to be coerced or bribed. He was banished to Thrace by Constantius, who set up an antipope, Felix II. In 358, Liberius was permitted to return to Rome after signing a vaguely worded creed and repudiating communion with Athanasius. Felix was forced to retire. After Constantius died, Liberius openly avowed his orthodox position and reasserted the primacy of Rome as arbiter in matters of faith.

Libertad, La (lä lēbärtäth'), town (1961 pop. 4,943), S El Salvador, on the Pacific Ocean. It is the port of entry for San Salvador, the capital, and is also a beach resort.

Liberty, city (1970 pop. 13,704), seat of Clay co., W central Mo., in a grain, tobacco, and livestock area; laid out 1822. It has railroad yards and grain elevators. William Jewell College is there.

liberty, term used to describe various types of individual freedom, such as religious liberty, political liberty, freedom of speech, right of self-defense, and others. It is also used as a general term for the sum of specific liberties. Fundamental perhaps is personal liberty, the freedom of a person to come and go as he pleases without unwarranted restraint. Like other freedoms, this one has a history that shows that liberty varies with time and place. In England prior to the Habeas Corpus Act (1679) a person could be seized and kept in prison indefinitely without trial or hearing. The common-law prohibition of conspiracy as dangerous to domestic peace and order was invoked far into the 19th cent. to limit the right of association in labor unions. Specifically political liberties, such as the general right to vote and to hold public office, were practically unknown before the 19th cent., when they were achieved by the liberal movement in England. The same is true of such civil liberties as freedom of speech and of the press. Freedom of conscience, the right of private judgment in religious matters, and the right to worship with groups of one's own choosing were nonexistent prior to the Protestant Reformation. Liberty has found philosophical expression in individualism and ANARCHISM (an extreme form of individualism) and in NATIONALISM. Such philosophers as John Locke and Jean Jacques Rousseau popularized the conception of the individual as having certain natural rights that could not be denied or taken away by society or by any external authority, rights that Thomas Jefferson spoke of in the Declaration of Independence as "unalienable" and that were embodied in the Bill of Rights of the Constitution. Rousseau especially thought of them as the rights possessed by people living in a "state of nature" and not surrendered, only modified, in the social contract by which they agreed to live together in society. Political scientists point out that even in a state of nature people are subject to the law of nature and that the rights enjoyed by them in society are historically acquired and not natural except in a strictly social sense. Liberties are acquired through the joining of like-minded individuals to gain special privileges for themselves. Thus, through Magna Carta the English barons in 1215 wrested from King John certain freedoms that in time they had to share with the rest of the people. The history of liberty in the later Middle Ages is that of numerous corporate groups, such as guilds of artisans and merchants, winning immunity from external control. By agreements with their feudal overlords these groups obtained release from certain feudal dues and bonds, gaining a limited freedom to carry on trade and manufacture, which forms the nucleus of the liberties extended to the bourgeoisie in the 19th cent. Some ethnic minorities, as in the Austro-Hungarian Monarchy, were able by a show of strength to gain legal status for their language and culture as well as assurance of some political rights. Freedom to follow the trade or profession of one's inclination, as of women to practice medicine, denied in most societies, was gained only in recent times. The feminist movement in the 19th and 20th cent. is a good example of the attempt to gain such rights. The acquired nature of rights—their dependence on conditions of time and place—also makes them peculiarly subject to danger of loss. Liberties have to be defended against encroachment, and sometimes populations have to submit to their temporary curtailment. In times of national danger some rights are suspended, as was the right of habeas corpus by President Abraham Lincoln in the American Civil War, and the struggle for rights not yet acquired may have to be discontinued. Philosophers have made a distinction between two types of liberty: freedom from external restraint and freedom for self-expression. Since medieval times liberty has been increased by the gradual but advancing removal of restraints once imposed by church and state, by custom and law; in the 20th cent. attention was turned to the creation of certain conditions regarded as necessary if individuals are to develop their fullest potential. The idea of equality, emphasized by the philosophers of the French Revolution, came to be closely associated with the idea of liberty in democratic societies—not equality based on a supposed equality of ability but equality of opportunity. Inequality, especially economic inequality, was held to be as great an obstacle to individual development as any form of external restraint. Therefore it was proposed that the state should seek to equalize as far as possible the conditions in such areas as education, health, and housing, thereby establishing economic and social security, and freedom from want and fear, so that every individual might have equal opportunity for self-realization. The right of national groups to be independent and sovereign has also come to be regarded as a principle of liberty. Since 1945, more than 50 former colonial areas have become independent states (see IMPERIALISM). The UN Commission on Human Rights has sought to promote the extension of political and cultural liberty throughout the world through treaties and covenants, the most important of which has been the Declaration of Human Rights. See J. S. Mill, *On Liberty* (1859, repr. 1972); Herbert Butterfield, *Liberty in the Modern World* (1952); Sidney Hook, *Political Power and Personal Freedom* (1959, repr. 1962); Horace Kallen, *A Study of Liberty* (1959, repr. 1973); M. R. Konvitz, ed., *Aspects of Liberty* (1958, repr. 1965) and *Expanding Liberties* (1967); J. M. Swomley, *Liberation Ethics* (1972).

Liberty, Statue of, colossal statue on Liberty Island in Upper New York Bay, commanding the entrance to New York City. The statue, originally known as *Liberty Enlightening the World,* was proposed by the French historian Édouard Laboulaye in 1865 to commemorate the alliance of France with the American colonies during the American Revolution. Funds were raised by the Franco-American Union (est. 1875), and the statue was designed by the French sculptor F. A. Bartholdi in the form of a woman with an uplifted arm holding a torch. The statue, 152 ft (46 m) high, was constructed of copper sheets, using Bartholdi's 9-ft (2.7-m) model. It was shipped to New York City in 1885, assembled, and dedicated in 1886. The base of the statue is an 11-pointed star, part of old Fort Wood; a 150-ft (45-m) pedestal, built through American funding, is made of concrete faced with granite. An elevator runs to the top of the pedestal, and steps within the statue lead to the crown. The Statue of Liberty became a national monument in 1924. The American Museum of Immigration is in its base. In 1965, Ellis Island, the entrance point of millions of immigrants to the United States, was added to the monument (see NATIONAL PARKS AND MONUMENTS, table).

Liberty Bell, historic relic in INDEPENDENCE HALL, Philadelphia. First hung in 1753, it bore the inscription, "Proclaim Liberty throughout all the Land unto all the Inhabitants Thereof" (Lev. 25.10); thus it was fitting that the bell was rung in July, 1776, to proclaim the Declaration of Independence. Taken to Allentown and hidden (1777–78) during the British occupation of Philadelphia, it was later brought back. In 1781 it was moved from the steeple to the brick tower. It was cracked in 1835 and again in 1846, and it rests on its original timbers as an exhibit. See Victor Rosewater, *The Liberty Bell* (1926); C. M. Boland, *Ring in the Jubilee* (1973).

Liberty Island, c.10 acres (4 hectares), in Upper New York Bay, SW of Manhattan island, SE N.Y.; part of Statue of Liberty National Monument. In the mid-1700s, John Bard, a physician, established New York

City's first quarantine station there. The Statue of Liberty was placed on the island in 1885, using star-shaped Fort Wood (built in 1841 for harbor defense) as a base. Formerly called Bedloe's Island, Liberty Island was renamed by Congress in 1956.

Liberty party, in U.S. history, an antislavery political organization founded in 1840. It was formed by those ABOLITIONISTS, under the leadership of James G. BIRNEY and Gerrit SMITH, who repudiated William Lloyd Garrison's nonpolitical stand. Birney, their presidential candidate in 1840, received a little more than 7,000 votes. Because of better local organization and the issue of the annexation of Texas, he polled more than 60,000 votes in 1844, drawing enough support away from Henry Clay in New York state to throw the presidency to James K. Polk. The party remained strong in local elections in 1846, but in 1848 it withdrew its nominee, John P. Hale, and united with antislavery Whigs and Democrats to form the stronger FREE-SOIL PARTY. See T. C. Smith, *The Liberty and Free Soil Parties in the Northwest* (1897; repr. 1967).

Libertyville, village (1970 pop. 11,684), Lake co., NE Ill., in a lake area; inc. 1882. Earth-moving equipment, outdoor rugs, and pressure hoses are made. Adlai E. Stevenson had a home there. A naval training station is nearby.

libido (lĭbē'dō, -bī'-) [Lat.,=lust], psychoanalytic term used by Sigmund Freud to identify instinctive energy with the sex instinct. For Freud, libido is the generalized sexual energy of which conscious activity is the expression. C. G. Jung used the term synonymously with instinctive energy in general. Many psychiatrists now feel that Freud overemphasized the concept of libido as the determinant of personality development and did not adequately emphasize the results of socializing forces. The term *drive* is often used instead of *libido* but without the sexual implications of the latter. See PSYCHOANALYSIS.

Libnah (lĭb'nə). **1** Unidentified place in the desert wanderings. Num. 33.20. **2** Canaanite city, SW Palestine, N of Lachish. It was captured by Joshua. Joshua 10.29; 12.15; 15.42; 21.13; 2 Kings 8.22; 19.8; 23.31; 24.18; 1 Chron. 6.57; 2 Chron. 21.10; Jer. 52.1.

Libni (lĭb'nī). **1** Founder of a Gershonite family. Ex. 6.17; Num. 3.18,21; 26.58; 1 Chron. 6.17,20. Laadan: 1 Chron. 23.7; 26.21. **2** Head of a Merarite family. 1 Chron. 6.29.

Libon (lī'bŏn), fl.5th cent. B.C., Greek architect. Within the sacred precincts of Altis at Olympia where the Greeks celebrated their Olympic games, he built the Doric temple to Zeus (completed c.456 B.C.).

Libra (lē'brə, lī'-) [Lat.,=the scales], southern CONSTELLATION lying on the ECLIPTIC (the sun's apparent path through the heavens) between Virgo and Scorpius; it is one of the constellations of the ZODIAC. Sometimes depicted as a pair of scales, it is also known as the Balance. The ancient Greeks represented it as the claws of the Scorpion (Scorpius). Zubenelschemal (Beta Librae), which lies between ARCTURUS and ANTARES, is the only star observable by the naked eye that has been reported to appear greenish. Libra reaches its highest point in the evening sky in late June.

library. The earliest known library was a collection of clay tablets in Babylonia in the 21st cent. B.C. Ancient Egyptian temple libraries are known through the Greek writers. Diodorus Siculus describes the library of Ramses III, c.1200 B.C. The extensively cataloged library of Assurbanipal (d. 626? B.C.) in Nineveh was the most noted before that at Alexandria. The temple at Jerusalem contained a sacred library. The first public library in Greece was established in 330 B.C., in order to preserve accurate examples of the work of the great dramatists. The most famous libraries of antiquity were those of ALEXANDRIA, founded by Ptolemy I. The library at PERGAMUM, founded or expanded by Eumenes II, rivaled those at Alexandria. The first Roman libraries were brought from Greece, Asia Minor, and Syria as a result of conquests in the 1st and 2d cent. B.C. Caius Asinius Pollio established (c.40 B.C.) the first public library in Rome, but the great public libraries of the Roman Empire were the Octavian (destroyed A.D. 80) and the Palatine (destroyed A.D. c.190) and the more important Ulpian library, founded during the reign of Trajan. In addition to these public collections, there were many fine private libraries by the time the Roman Republic was ended in 27 B.C. Of these there remain only fragments of one at Herculaneum. The early Christian libraries were in monasteries; the Benedictines amassed a fine collection at Monte Cassino. The Romans had brought book collections to the British Isles, but important early monastic libraries were founded in York, Wearmouth, Canterbury, and elsewhere in England and Ireland by Anglo-Saxon monks. Some of the finest manuscript ILLUMINATION was produced in these libraries. On the Continent, St. Columban and other missionaries founded monastic libraries in the 6th cent. In the 14th and 15th cent. Charles V of France, Lorenzo de' Medici, and Frederick, duke of Urbino, all formed fine libraries; part of the Urbino library is now in the Vatican Library. The Arabs in the 9th to 15th cent. collected and preserved many libraries. The Jews and the Byzantines also developed fine libraries during the medieval period. In the 15th cent. the Vatican Library, the oldest public library in Europe, was formed. In 1475, Platina, as its first librarian, made a catalog that included 2,527 volumes. In 1257 the Sorbonne library at Paris was founded, and in 1525 the erection of the Laurentian Library in Florence, designed by Michelangelo, was begun. Many of the great university libraries (e.g., Bologna, Prague, Oxford, and Heidelberg) were opened in the 14th cent. Among the chief modern libraries are the BIBLIOTHÈQUE NATIONALE and the Mazarine, Paris; the BRITISH MUSEUM, London; the Bodleian Library, Oxford; the VATICAN LIBRARY, Rome; the AMBROSIAN LIBRARY, Milan; the Laurentian, Florence; the Lenin Library, Moscow; the Huntington Library, San Marino, Calif.; the LIBRARY OF CONGRESS, Washington, D.C.; the NEW YORK PUBLIC LIBRARY; the libraries of Columbia, Harvard, Yale, Princeton, Chicago, and other major American universities; and the Newberry and John Crerar libraries, Chicago. In the United States a circulating library, the Library Company of Philadelphia, was chartered in 1732 on the initiative of Benjamin Franklin. A public library had, however, been opened in Boston as early as 1653 (see BOSTON PUBLIC LIBRARY). Other early subscription libraries included the Boston Athenaeum, the New York Society Library, and the Charleston (S.C.) Library Society. In 1833 the first tax-supported library in the country opened at Peterborough, N.H. The American Library Association was formed in 1876, and this organization spurred improvements in library methods and in the training of librarians. Libraries in the United States and Great Britain benefited greatly from the philanthropy of Andrew CARNEGIE, who gave more than $65 million for public library buildings in the United States alone and strengthened local interest by making the grants contingent upon public support. Among the innovations of the late 19th cent. were free public access to books (involving elaborate classification schemes) and branch libraries or deposit stations for books in many parts of cities; in the early 20th cent. traveling libraries, or "bookmobiles," began to take books to readers in rural or outlying areas. Modern libraries often publish lists of accessions and maintain a readers' advisory service. Interlibrary loan services, lecture series, public book reviews, and the maintenance of special juvenile collections are other important recent developments. Three widely used systems of book classification are the Dewey decimal system of Melvil DEWEY, the system of Charles Ammi CUTTER, and the Library of Congress system. Since the 1930s the public library systems have had several new technological tools at their disposal: microphotographic techniques, for copying, and computer data banks enabling them to store far more information and produce better indexes and catalogs than ever before. The architectural design of public libraries in the United States has placed the highest priority on functionalism. Outstanding examples of library construction include the central housing for collections in New York City (1911), Los Angeles (1926), and Baltimore (1932), and university buildings at Harvard (1915) and Columbia (1934). Modern buildings tend toward modular construction and smaller, separate housing for special collections. The major university libraries in the United States, working to meet the enormous and ever-increasing demand for research materials, spend nearly $2 million a year for books and related supplies such as binding materials. Such libraries receive private endowments as well as Federal and state support. Other libraries throughout the world operate on far smaller budgets, frequently with severe financial handicaps. There are several sorts of libraries in the United States and elsewhere that exist apart from the public systems. Three major categories of these are private libraries, usually housing special collections, e.g., the PIERPONT MORGAN LIBRARY in New York City of rare books in the humanities and the Folger Shakespeare Library in Washington, D.C. (see under FOLGER, HENRY CLAY); presidential libraries, which contain the papers of past presidents not held in the Library of Congress, e.g., the Rutherford B. Hayes Library, Fremont, Ohio, the Harry S. Truman Library, Independence, Mo., and the Lyndon B. Johnson Library at the Univ. of Texas; and industrial libraries formed by many corporations to house research works relevant to their business. See LIBRARY SCHOOL; CATALOG. The classic works on the history of libraries are Edward Edwards's *Memoirs of Libraries* (2 vol., 1859, repr. 1964) and *Libraries and Founders of Libraries* (1865, repr. 1968). See also E. A. Savage, *The Story of Libraries and Book-Collecting* (1909, repr. 1969); J. W. Thompson, *The Medieval Library* (1939, repr. 1967) and *Ancient Libraries* (1940, repr. 1962); Thelman Eaton, ed., *Contributions to American Library History* (1962); Raymond Irwin, *The English Library: Sources and History* (1966); A. R. A. Hobson, *Great Libraries* (1970); E. D. Johnson, *History of Libraries in the Western World* (2d ed. 1970); L. W. Dunlap, *Readings in Library History* (1972).

Library of Congress, national library of the United States, Washington, D.C., est. 1800. Thomas Jefferson while Vice President was a prime mover in the creation of the library, and he supported it strongly during his presidency. In 1814, when much of the collection was destroyed by fire, Jefferson offered his own fine library to the Congress. This formed the basis of the collection until 1851, when fire destroyed some 35,000 volumes. The growth of the library progressed slowly thereafter until the passage of the Copyright Act of 1870, which required the deposit in the library of all copyright material. The acquisition in 1866 of the Smithsonian Institution's collection of 44,000 volumes and the purchase of the Peter Force collection of Americana (60,000 volumes; 1867) and the Joseph M. Toner American and Medical Library (24,000 volumes; 1892) made it one of the world's great libraries. Intended primarily to serve the legislative branch of the government, it is now open to the public as a reference library and sends out many books by an interlibrary loan system. For a small fee the library sells duplicate catalog cards to smaller libraries for the books it adds to its collections. It provides other vital services to libraries through its bibliographic functions and its Copyright Office. Mainly supported by congressional appropriations, the library also has the income from gifts by foundations and individuals, administered by the Library of Congress Trust Fund Board. The collection has divisions of manuscripts, incunabula, maps, rare books, prints and photographs, music, aeronautics, and Orientalia. In 1966 the collection totaled over 55 million items on every conceivable subject and in a multitude of languages. The library is estimated to have 270 mi (435 km) of bookshelves. See studies by P. M. Angle (1958), Gene Gurney (1966), Monro McCloskey (1968), and C. A. Goodrum (1974).

library school. Librarians were trained by apprenticeship until the late 19th cent. The first school for training librarians was established by Melvil DEWEY at Columbia Univ. in 1887. The success of this institution combined with a shortage of librarians in a period of growth and expansion led to a proliferation of such schools, many of which were inadequate. With the formation of the Association of American Library Schools in 1915, standards of accreditation were established and maintained. A number of university schools of library service were established in the 1920s, many of them funded by the Carnegie Corporation of New York. In 1973, of 348 institutions offering training in librarianship, 60 were accredited by the American Library Association. These schools require a minimum of five years' study beyond the secondary level: The four years of undergraduate study constitute a general education in the humanities and natural and social sciences; the fifth year is in professional study at the graduate level and leads to a master's degree. The first school to confer the doctoral degree in library science was the Univ. of Chicago. Some of the schools are part of a university (as at Columbia and the Univ. of Illinois); others are at independent undergraduate institutions (e.g., Pratt Institute). In the 1960s and early 70s, U.S. graduate schools remained unable to meet the rising demand for librarians, particularly those with special knowledge of bibliographic methods and particular areas of study. According to the 1970 U.S. census figures, there are some 114,500 full-time professional librarians; nearly 6,800 received degrees from the 60 accredited schools in 1973. The first library school outside the United States and Canada was founded at the Univ. of London in 1917. In many underdeveloped countries university library schools have been established by grants from UNESCO and other sources, employing at the outset European- or American-trained staff. This staff is replaced as soon as possible with local personnel. Although the number of non-American library schools has steadily increased, many foreign librarians are still trained in the United States. See also LIBRARY. See *World Guide to Library Schools and Training Centers in Documentation*, pub. by UNESCO (1972).

libration (lībrā'shən): see MOON.

libretto (ləbrĕt'ō) [Ital.,=little book], the text of an opera or an oratorio. Although a play usually emphasizes an integrated plot, a libretto is most often a loose plot connecting a series of episodes. Characterization and emotion are suggested by the words of a libretto but are expressed by the music. The first major librettist was Ottavio Rinuccini, an Italian poet of the 16th cent. Outstanding in the 17th cent. was Philippe QUINAULT, and in the 18th cent. important librettists were the poet Pietro METASTASIO, many of whose 50 libretti were set numerous times by major composers, Ranieri di Calzabigi, and Lorenzo DA PONTE. The 19th-century librettists of note included Augustin Eugène SCRIBE, W. S. GILBERT, and the composers Arrigo BOITO and Richard WAGNER; prominent in the 20th cent. was Hugo von HOFMANNSTHAL.

Libreville (lēbrəvēl'), city (1972 est. pop. 55,000), capital of Gabon, a port on the Gabon River estuary, near the Gulf of Guinea. Primarily an administrative center, is is also a trade center for a lumbering region. The city was founded in 1843 as a French trading station. Freed slaves were sent there, and in 1848 it was named Libreville [Fr.,=freetown]. It was the chief port of French Equatorial Africa before the development (1934-46) of POINTE NOIRE, in the People's Republic of the Congo. Gabon's school of administration and school of law are in Libreville. An international airport is nearby.

Librium, trade name for chlordiazepoxide, a TRANQUILIZER and muscle relaxant. See PSYCHOPHARMACOLOGY.

Libya (lĭb'ēə), officially Libyan Arab Republic, republic (1973 est. pop. 2,100,000), 679,358 sq mi (1,759,540 sq km), N Africa, bordering on Algeria in the west, on Tunisia in the northwest, on the Mediterranean Sea in the north, on Egypt in the east, on Sudan in the southeast, and on Chad and Niger in the south. TRIPOLI is the capital of Libya; other cities include Ajdabiyah, AL BAYDA, Al Marj, BENGASI, DARNAH, MISRATAH, and TOBRUK. The country is divided into 10 administrative districts. Libya falls into three main

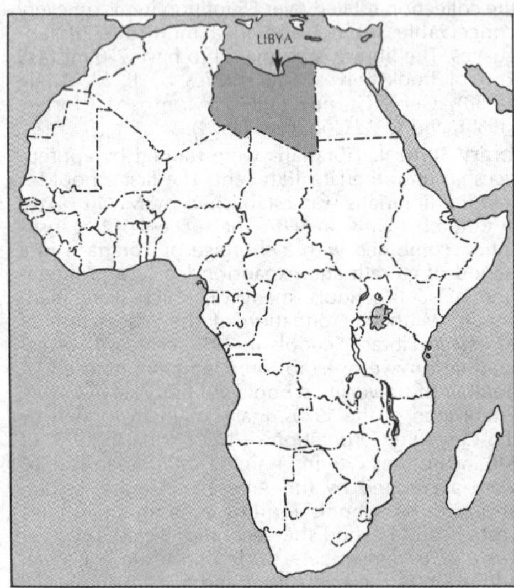

geographical regions—Tripolitania in the west, Fazzan in the southwest, and Cyrenaica in the east. Tripolitania in turn can be divided into three zones. In the north is a low-lying coastal plain called the Gefara, which, although mainly arid, has several irrigated areas. It also includes the city of Tripoli. South of the Gefara is a mountainous zone (highest altitude: c.2,500 ft/760 m) known as the Jabal; it is mostly arid and barren, but has scattered areas of cultivation. South of the Jabal is an upland plateau, largely desert, but crossed by a string of oases in the south. South of Tripolitania is the Fazzan region, which is largely made up of sandy desert but has a number of scattered oases. Cyrenaica is Libya's largest region. In the N along the Mediterranean is a narrow upland plateau (highest altitude: c.2,000 ft/610 m) called the Jabal al Akhdar, which includes the cities of Bengasi and Darnah. In the west the Jabal al Akhdar drops abruptly to the shore of the Gulf of Sidra, which deeply indents Libya's Mediterranean coastline, and in the east it falls gradually toward the Egyptian border, where there is another upland region. South of the Jabal al Akhdar is a vast region of sandy desert, which in the east includes part of the Libyan Desert. Cyrenaica is fringed in the southwest by the Tibesti Mts. (located mostly in Chad), which include Libya's loftiest point, Picco Bette (c.7,500 ft/2,290 m). The majority of the inhabitants of Libya are of almost pure Arab descent, most of their ancestors having come to the country from Arabia from the 9th to the 11th cent. There are scattered communities of Berbers, and in Fazzan many persons are of mixed Berber and black African descent. About 5% of the people live as pastoral nomads, mostly in Cyrenaica. Arabic is the official language. The great majority of the population are Muslim; the people of Tripolitania adhere almost exclusively to the Sunni branch, and the inhabitants of Cyrenaica belong mostly to the SANUSI brotherhood. Until the late 1950s, Libya was a very poor agricultural country whose prospects for economic development were extremely bleak. However, in 1958 petroleum was discovered in the region 200 to 300 mi (320-480 km) S and SE of the Gulf of Sidra, and from 1961, crude petroleum has been exported on an increasingly significant scale. Oil pipelines were built to five terminals on the Mediterranean—Qasr al Burayqah, As Sidar, Ras al Unuf, Marsa al Hariqah, and Az Zuwaytinah. Production of petroleum increased from 22 million metric tons in 1963 to 163 million metric tons in 1970 and 133 million metric tons in 1971. Libya was the world's seventh leading producer of petroleum in 1971, outdistanced only by the United States, the USSR, Saudi Arabia, Iran, Venezuela, and Kuwait. In the early 1970s, Libya's proved reserves were put at about 5.2 billion metric tons (30 billion barrels). Much of the oil has a low-sulfur content, which is desirable because it causes less pollution when burned. The petroleum was located and extracted by a large number of foreign firms (mostly headquartered in the United States, France, West Germany, and Great Britain), in contrast to other Middle East countries, where usually only a handful of firms held concessions to produce petroleum. As production increased, so did Libya's receipts of royalties and taxes, estimated at $2.1 billion annually at the start of the 1970s. The income increased markedly in 1972-73, when the Libyan government nationalized (with compensation) 51% ownership in most of the subsidiaries of foreign petroleum firms operating in the country. The remaining subsidiaries were completely nationalized. At the same time, the price of petroleum was raised dramatically, thus further increasing Libya's receipts. Much of the income was used to build up the cities, to improve transportation facilities, and to modernize agriculture. Relatively few Libyans (about 3,800 in 1969) were directly employed by the capital-intensive petroleum industry; many more persons migrated to the cities seeking to benefit indirectly from the country's new riches. This migration created an unemployment problem and spurred the government to invest greater sums in agricultural development in an attempt to make farming an attractive occupation. All phases of the petroleum industry are regulated by the Libyan National Oil Corporation (LINOCO), founded in 1970 as the successor to the Libyan General Petroleum Company (established in 1968). In 1962, Libya joined the Organization of Petroleum Exporting Countries (OPEC), and in the early 1970s it was a leading member of that group. In 1968, Libya became a charter member of the less-important Organization of Arab Petroleum Exporting Countries (OAPEC). Libya is in addition a major producer of natural gas (ranking 10th in the world in 1971) and has several large gas liquefication plants. Gypsum, salt, and limestone are also produced in significant quantities. Despite the petroleum boom, the majority of Libya's workers were still employed in agriculture in the early 1970s. Farming is severely limited by the small amount of fertile soil and by inadequate rainfall. It is estimated that only 8% of the country's land area is cultivable; most of this area is used for pasturing livestock, leaving very little land for raising crops. About two-thirds of the arable land is located in Tripolitania (largely in the Tripoli region), and most of the rest is situated in N Cyrenaica; Fazzan's tiny amount of cultivable land is limited to its oases, where dates are the main crop. Overall, Libya's chief agricultural products are wheat, barley, olives, dates, tobacco, citrus fruit, tomatoes, millet, maize, groundnuts, and almonds. Large numbers of sheep and goats are raised. Libya has little industry. The principal manufactures are refined petroleum, liquefied natural gas, construction materials (especially cement), and basic consumer items like processed food, beverages, clothing, footwear, soap, and cigarettes. Handicraftsmen produce woven goods and items of metal, leather, and wood. Libya's annual earnings from exports are usually much higher than the cost of its imports. Crude petroleum is by far the leading export; the main imports are machinery, foodstuffs, transport equipment, and manufactured consumer goods. The principal trade partners are Italy, West Germany, Great Britain, and France. Throughout most of its history the territory that constitutes modern Libya has been held by foreign powers. TRIPOLITANIA and CYRENAICA had divergent histories for most of the period up to their conquest by the Ottoman Empire in the mid-16th cent. FAZZAN was captured by the Ottomans only in 1842. The Ottomans gained control of most of N Africa in the 16th cent., dividing it into three regencies—Algeria, Tunisia, and Tripoli (which also included Cyrenaica). Ottoman rule in Tripoli was limited largely to the coastal region, where taxes were regularly collected. The Janissaries, professional soldiers of slave origins, became a military caste, wielding considerable influence over the Ottoman governor. From the early 1600s the Janissaries chose a leader, called the dey, who at times had as much power as the Ottoman governor sent from Constantinople. Numerous pirates who preyed on the shipping of Christian nations in the Mediterranean were based at Tripoli's ports. In 1711, Ahmad Karamanli, a Janissary, became dey, killed the Ottoman governor, and prevailed upon the Ottomans to name him governor. The post of governor remained hereditary in the Karamanli family until 1835. In the 18th cent. and during the Napoleonic Wars, the dey took in great revenues from the pirates and also extended the central government's control to much of the interior. During 1801-5 the United States and Tripoli fought a war precipitated by disagreements over the amount of tribute to be paid to the dey in order to gain immunity from raids by pirates (see TRIPOLITAN WAR). After 1815, England, France, and the kingdom of the Two Sicilies undertook a successful campaign against the pirates, which undermined the finances of the dey and thus facilitated the reestablishment of direct Ottoman rule in Tripoli in 1835. During the rest of the 19th cent., the Ottomans contributed little toward the political stability or the economic development of Tripoli. Beginning in the 1840s the Sanusi brotherhood gained many adherents, primarily in Cyrenaica but also in S Tripolitania and Fazzan. During the Turko-Italian War of 1911-12 Italy conquered N Tripoli, but by the Treaty of Ouchy, which ended the war, Turkey granted Tripoli autonomy. The Libyans continued to fight the Italians, but by 1914 Italy had occupied much of the country. However, Italy was forced to undertake a long series of wars of pacification (led for part of the time by Pietro BADOGLIO and Rodolfo GRAZIANI) against the Sanusi and their allies. Until the 1930s, when Italo BALBO was governor-general, little was done to develop the country. Under Balbo, roads, civic buildings, schools, and hospitals were constructed. In 1934 Tripolitania and Cyrenaica were formally united to form the colony of Libya; Fazzan was administered as part of Tripolitania. About 40,000 colonists were sent from Italy to the plateau regions of Libya at the end of the 1930s. In 1939, Libya was made an integral part of Italy, and Balbo reorganized the colonial administration and granted the Muslim population a limited form of citizenship. Libya became one of the main battlegrounds of North Africa after Italy entered World War II in June, 1940 (for military details, see NORTH AFRICA, CAMPAIGNS IN). After the Allied victory over the Axis in N Africa (1943), Libya was placed under an Anglo-French military government. When the Big Four (Great Britain, France, the United States, and the USSR) failed to reach agreement on the future of Libya as stipulated in the 1947 peace treaty with Italy, the United Nations was given (1949) jurisdiction. The United Nations decided that Libya should become independent by 1952, and on Dec. 24, 1951, the country in fact became independent as the United Kingdom of Libya, ruled by King Idris I (see under IDRISIDS), head of the Sanusi brotherhood. Libya was a federal state, divided into three semiautonomous provinces (Tripolitania, Cyrenaica, and Fazzan) and with a federal bicameral parliament. The king was the most important political leader. In 1953, Libya joined the ARAB LEAGUE, and in 1955, it was admitted into the United Nations. Libya signed treaties with Great Britain in 1953 and with the United States in 1954, allowing those countries to establish military bases in return for giving Libya annual subsidies. The 1950s in Libya were characterized by great poverty, the government's budget being balanced and minimal economic development being made possible only by the payments and loans received from various Western nations. In 1958, petroleum was discovered in the country, and by the early 1960s Libya was taking in growing revenues from the exploitation of that resource. Internal politics were characterized by considerable acrimony both among the three provinces and among individual politicians. In an effort to make administration more efficient, Libya was transformed (1963) by royal decree from a federal to a unitary state. The three provinces and their parliaments were abolished and in their place 10 administrative divisions were established. The council of ministers (headed by a prime minister), appointed by the king and answerable to parliament, became responsible for the overall administration of the country. The Anglo-Libyan treaty of 1953 was terminated by Libya in 1964, and most British troops were withdrawn from the country in early 1966. There were demonstrations in favor of the Arab cause during the Arab-Israeli war of June, 1967, but Libyan forces did not take part in the fighting; for a few months after the war Libya refused to sell petroleum to Great Britain, the United States, and West Germany because of their support of Israel. On Sept. 1, 1969, a group of army officers led by Col. Muammar al-QADDAFI (then 27 years old) staged a successful coup d'etat, ousting Idris, who was in Turkey at the time. The 1951 constitution was abrogated, and government was placed in the hands of a 12-member Revolutionary Command Council (RCC) headed by al-Qaddafi. The RCC appointed a cabinet headed by a prime minister, and al-Qaddafi served in that office from early 1970 to mid-1972, when he turned the post over to Abdul Salam Jallud as part of a move to increase civilian participation in government. Al-Qaddafi was also president of the RCC, the most important political and military office in the country, retaining that position after stepping down as prime minister. Al-Qaddafi pursued a policy of Arab nationalism and strict adherence to Islamic law; he also espoused socialist principles, but was strongly anti-Communist. He was particularly concerned with reducing Western influence in Libya. Coups aimed at deposing al-Qaddafi failed in Dec., 1969, and July, 1970. In 1970, the British were forced to evacuate their remaining bases in Libya, and the United States was required to abandon Wheelus Field, a U.S. air force base located near Tripoli. Under al-Qaddafi, Libya's foreign policy was generally reoriented away from N Africa and toward the heart of the Middle East. Close ties were established with Egypt, and in 1971 Libya joined with Egypt and Syria to form a loose alliance called the Federation of Arab Republics. However, al-Qaddafi also gave considerable support to President Idi Amin of Uganda, largely because Amin, who came to power in early 1971, was a Muslim. In early 1973, Libya launched an extensive "cultural revolution" designed to make life in the country more closely approximate socialist and Muslim principles. Largely as a result of extreme pressure applied on Egypt by al-Qaddafi, Libya and Egypt announced (Aug., 1973) that they would form a unified state in stages, but disagreements later held up the plan. Al-Qaddafi was a strong supporter of Palestinian guerrilla groups and an implacable foe of Israel. Libya contributed some men and matériel (especially aircraft) to the Arab side in the Arab-Israeli war of Oct., 1973, and al-Qaddafi was severely critical of Egypt for negotiating a cease-fire with Israel. After the war, Libya was a strong advocate of reducing sales of petroleum to nations that had supported Israel and was also a leading force in increasing the price of crude petroleum. See W. C. Askew, *Europe and Italy's Acquisition of Libya, 1911–1912* (1942); E. E. Evans-Pritchard, *The Sanusi of Cyrenaica* (1949, repr. 1963); Majid Khadduri, *Modern Libya: A Study in Political Development* (1963); J. L. Wright, *Libya* (1969); Adrian Pelt, *Libyan Independence and the United Nations: A Case of Planned Decolonization* (1970); M. O. Ansell and I. M. al-Arif, *The Libyan Revolution* (1972); J. A. Allan et al., ed., *Libya: Agriculture and Economic Development* (1973); R. F. Nyrop et al., *Area Handbook for Libya* (2d ed. 1973).

Libyan Desert, northeast part of the Sahara Desert, NE Africa, in SW Egypt, E Libya, and NW Sudan; called the Western Desert in Egypt. It is a region of sand dunes, stony plains, and rocky plateaus. There are few inhabitants and little traffic across it; Al Kufrah, Libya, is the chief oasis.

Licata (lĕkä'tä), city (1971 pop. 37,446), S Sicily, Italy, on the Mediterranean Sea at the mouth of the Salso River. Licata is a seaport, seaside resort, and commercial and industrial center. Sulfur and asphalt are shipped through its port. It was founded in the early 3d cent. B.C. as a refuge for the inhabitants of GELA after that city's destruction and was called Phintias after the tyrant of Acragas. Off nearby Cape Economus (now Poggio di Sant' Angelo), the Roman consul Regulus won (256 B.C.) a decisive battle in the first of the PUNIC WARS.

lice: see LOUSE.

license, in public law, permission by legal authority to engage in certain acts and also the document showing such permission. Some licenses are required for the protection of the public; they assure professional competence (e.g., physicians) or moral fitness (e.g., tavern keepers). Others are designed primarily to raise revenue or to keep a registry (e.g., automobile licenses). It is a crime to engage in a licensed activity without having first procured a license. In property law, a license is a right that the owner grants some other party to make use of his land. Such licenses are revocable at will if they are not part of a contract. They are personal and hence may not be sold; they expire on the death of the grantee. A license to cross another's land is an EASEMENT in gross. In PATENT law, a license is a written authority granted by the owner of a patent to another person, empowering the latter to make or use the patented article for a limited period or in a limited territory.

lichen (lī'kən), usually slow-growing plant of simple structure, composed of blue-green or green algae and of fungi living together in a symbiotic relationship. Lichens commonly grow on rocks, trees, fence posts, and similar objects. The body (thallus) of the lichen is made up of the filaments, or hyphae, of the fungus, usually a sac fungus (Ascomycete). Its typical greenish gray color is due to the combination of the chlorophyll of the algae with the colorless fungi, although sometimes the thallus may be red, orange, or brown. The fungi obtain food from the algal cells and, in turn, absorb and retain water that is partially used by the algae for photosynthesis. The fungi and algae usually reproduce simultaneously (see ALGAE; FUNGUS INFECTION). The fungi produce acids that disintegrate rock, giving the lichen a better hold and aiding weathering processes, which eventually turn rock into soil. Lichens can withstand great extremes of temperature and are found in arctic, antarctic, and tropical regions. They are often the pioneer forms of life—as in parts of Iceland and Greenland, where they are the predominant vegetation. Reindeer moss (*Cladonia rangiferina*) and Iceland moss (*Cetraria islandica*), both low, branching forms, provide food for large mammals and other animals in northern regions. Old-man's-beard (*Usnea barbata*) is a temperate species that hangs like Spanish moss from coniferous trees. Before the discovery of aniline dyes, lichens were much used for silk and wool dyes. The blue and purple dyes LITMUS and ARCHIL are still obtained from species of lichens. Others have been used in perfume manufacturing and brewing. The "manna" of the Bible is thought by some to have been a lichen found in Old World deserts and easily carried along by wind. See Vernon Alimadjian, *The Lichen Symbiosis* (1967); M. E. Hale, Jr., *The Biology of Lichens* (1970).

Lichfield, municipal borough (1971 pop. 22,672), Staffordshire, W central England. It is a market town with light industries, famous for its three-spired cathedral and its close associations with Dr. Samuel Johnson. The cathedral, dating from the 13th and 14th cent., replaced the original church built by St. Chad, who first founded the see in the 7th cent. It suffered considerable damage at the hands of the parliamentary forces during the English Civil War and was not completely restored until the 19th cent. The house where Dr. Johnson was born and lived is now a museum containing many relics of his life and works, and there is also a statue of him in the market square. At the grammar school (founded 1497) Johnson, Addison, and Garrick studied. In the 18th cent. a literary circle which included Erasmus Darwin, Thomas Day, and Anna Seward was known as the Lichfield group.

Lichnowsky, Karl Max, Fürst von (kärl mäks fürst fən lĭkhnôf'skē), 1860–1928, German diplomat, ambassador to London (1912–14). In a privately circulated pamphlet (1916) he asserted that his efforts to prevent the outbreak of World War I had not been supported by his government. The pamphlet, published in Jan., 1918, without his permission and widely distributed by the Allies, was the cause of his expulsion from the Prussian upper house. It was translated into English as *My Mission to London, 1912–1914.* See biography by E. F. Willis (1942).

Lichtenberg, Georg Christoph (gā'ôrkh krĭs'tôf lĭkh'tənbĕrk), 1742–99, German physicist and satirist. He taught at the Univ. of Göttingen, where his special field was electricity. Lichtenberg made several visits to England and was influenced by the satire of Swift and by the English theater. He satirized the pseudoscience of LAVATER and attacked the STURM UND DRANG writers. He also wrote witty commentaries on Hogarth's engravings.

Lichtenstein, Roy, 1923–, American painter, b. New York City. Lichtenstein derives his subject matter from popular sources such as comic strips. His paintings reflect modern typographic techniques and his commonplace imagery links him to the POP ART movement. Among his sophisticated and ironic works are *Flatten . . . sandfleas* (1962; Mus. of Modern Art, New York City) and *Preparedness* (1968; Guggenheim Mus., New York City).

Licinius (lĭsĭn'ēəs), Roman plebeian gens, of which several men were noteworthy. **Caius Licinius Calvus Stolo,** fl. 375 B.C., was tribune of the people with Lucius Sextius. Roman historians attributed to him a number of laws, but most of these were probably made at later dates. These laws, the **Licinian Rogations,** provided a strict limitation on the amount of public land that one person might hold and on the number of livestock that one could graze on the public land. They included also a strict regulation of the collection of debts, and, most significant politically, they ordained that one consul must be a plebeian. It is said that Licinius Stolo was later fined for violating his own law on the possession of public land. **Caius Licinius Macer,** d. 66 B.C., orator and historian, committed suicide after his conviction by Cicero under the law against bribery and extortion. His son, **Caius Licinius Macer Calvus,** 82 B.C.–c.47 B.C., poet and orator, was considered the peer of Catullus by the ancients. Only short fragments of his works remain.

Licinius, 250–325, Roman emperor. He became coemperor with Galerius, being given the rule of Illyricum (308); after the death of Galerius he added Greece and Thrace to his territories. He allied himself with Constantine I and defeated Maximin in 313, thus becoming sole ruler in the East. He subsequently quarreled with Constantine, who defeated him (314) and forced him to cede all his European territories except for Thrace. War was resumed in 324, and Constantine defeated Licinius at Adrianople and Chrysopolis. Licinius was imprisoned and eventually put to death.

Licking, river, c.320 mi (515 km) long, rising in E Ky. and flowing NW to the Ohio River opposite Cincinnati; the North and South Forks are its chief tributaries. The Licking was an important means of travel for Indians and pioneers and later a busy trade route. In 1780, at the river's mouth, George Rogers Clark's frontiersmen gathered for their march up the Little Miami; the battle of Blue Licks (1782) occurred in the Licking valley. Covington and Newport are at the mouth of the Licking.

Lick Observatory, astronomical OBSERVATORY located on Mt. Hamilton, Calif., near San Jose; it was founded through gifts made by James Lick in 1874–75 and came under the direction of the Univ. of California in 1888. The principal instrument is a 120-in. (305-cm) reflecting TELESCOPE that went into operation in 1959. Also at the observatory is a 36-in. (91.4-cm) refracting telescope (second largest in the world after the 40-in. (101.6-cm) refractor at Yerkes). Other equipment includes 36-in. and 22-in. (55.9-cm) reflectors, a 12-in. (30.5-cm) refractor, and a 20-in. (50.8-cm) twin astrographic telescope. Plans were proposed in 1974 to move some of the observatory's equipment to and erect new telescopes at a new location away from the increasing interference of reflected city lights from San Jose.

licorice (lĭk'ərĭs, -rĭsh), name for a European plant (*Glycyrrhiza glabra*) of the family Leguminosae (PULSE family) and for the sweet substance obtained from the root. Since early times the root has been used medicinally (for coughs and as a laxative); it is used also in brewing, for confectionery, and for flavoring (e.g., in some tobacco). The licorice plant, a perennial with blue pealike blossoms, is cultivated chiefly in the Near East. Another species, the wild licorice (*G. lepidota*), is native to North America; other plants of similar flavor may be called licorice. Licorice is classified in the division MAGNOLIOPHYTA, class Magnoliopsida, order Rosales, family Leguminosae.

Liddell, Henry George (lĭd'əl), 1811–98, English classical scholar. He was headmaster (1846–55) of Westminster School and dean (1855–91) of Christ Church, Oxford. Liddell is famous for his compilation of the *Greek-English Lexicon* (with Robert Scott, 1843). It was his daughter, Alice Liddell (d. 1934), for whom Lewis Carroll wrote *Alice in Wonderland.*

Liddell Hart, Basil Henry (lĭ'dəl härt), 1895–1970, English author and military strategist, b. Paris. His education at Cambridge was interrupted by World War I, in which he served (1914–18) and was twice wounded. Retiring from the army as a captain in 1927, he was military correspondent for the London *Daily Telegraph* (1925–35) and the London *Times* (1935–39). He was an early advocate of mechanized warfare, and his thinking had a profound effect upon the German high command prior to World War II. He also evolved a number of infantry tactics and training methods that were adopted by the British army. From 1937 to 1938 he was personal adviser to the British war minister, Leslie Hore-Belisha, and suggested a program of reorganization and reform that was partly instituted. He was knighted in 1966. Among his numerous books are *Sherman: Soldier, Realist, American* (1929), *The Future of Infantry* (1933), *A History of the World War, 1914–1918* (1934), *The German Generals Talk* (1948), *The Tanks* (1959), *Deterrent or Defence* (1961), and *A History of the Second World War* (1970). He edited *The Rommel Papers* (1953). See his memoirs (2 vol., 1965–66).

Liddesdale, William Douglas, Knight of (lĭdz'-dāl), 1300?–1353, Scottish nobleman. Called the Flower of Chivalry he was warden of the Western Marches and was given the lordship of Liddesdale by David II in 1342. He served as ambassador to the French court and fought against the English on the border until they took him prisoner near Durham (1346) and made him do homage to Edward III. He had murdered his rival, Sir Alexander Ramsay of Dalhousie, and was in turn murdered (for reasons that are not clear) by William Douglas, later 1st earl of Douglas and Mar, his godson, who inherited some of Liddesdale's lands.

Liddon, Henry Parry, 1829–90, English clergyman, a noted preacher and lecturer. As canon of St. Paul's Cathedral (1870–90) and Dean Ireland professor of exegesis at Oxford (1870–82), he exercised great influence, which he used chiefly for advancing the High Church movement in the Church of England. The most important of his popular sermons were the Bampton Lectures of 1866. Published as *The Divinity of Our Lord and Saviour Jesus Christ,* they have passed through many editions. His life of E. B. Pusey was completed and published after his death. See biographies by J. O. Johnston (1904) and G. W. E. Russell (1909); the centenary memoir (1929).

Lidice (lĭ'dyĭtsĕ), village, NW Czechoslovakia, in Bohemia. It is a mining settlement of the Kladno coal basin. In reprisal for the assassination of Reinhard HEYDRICH, the Germans "liquidated" (1942) Lidice by killing all the men, deporting all women and children, and razing the village to the ground. After World War II a new village was built near the site of old Lidice, which is now a national park and memorial.

Lidingö (lē'dĭng-ö"), city (1970 pop. 35,839), Stockholm co., SE Sweden, on Lidingö Island in the Baltic Sea; chartered 1926. It is a residential suburb of Stockholm and a resort.

Lidköping (lēd'chö"pĭng), city (1970 pop. 21,265), Skaraborg co., S Sweden, a port on Lake Vänern; chartered 1446. It has machine shops, match factories, and porcelain works. Nearby is Läckö castle (13th–17th cent.).

Lidman, Sara (sä'rä lēd'män), 1923–, Swedish writer. Her novels *The Tar Still* (1953), *Cloudberry Land* (1955), and *The Rain Bird* (1958, tr. 1962) treat rural life in N Sweden with warmth and spontaneity. Among her plays are *Job the Clockmaker's Daughter* (1954) and *Aina* (1956).

lidocaine: see XYLOCAINE.

Lido di Venezia (lē'dō dē vānĕ'tsyä), long, narrow, sandy island in Venetia, Italy, separating the lagoon of Venice from the Adriatic. It has a beautiful beach and is one of the most fashionable bathing resorts in Europe.

Lie, Jonas Lauritz Idemil (yō'näs lou'rĭts ē'dəmēl lē), 1833–1908, Norwegian novelist, poet, and playwright. His writing deals with family life in diverse settings. *The Pilot and His Wife* (1874, tr. 1876), the first of his several sea tales, was the first Norwegian novel to treat marriage realistically. *The Family at Gilje* (1883, tr. 1920) and *The Commodore's Daughters* (1886, tr. 1892) portray the social and intellectual restrictions on women of the educated classes. See Alrik Gustafson, *Six Scandinavian Novelists* (1940).

Lie, Marius Sophus (mä'rēo͞os sō'fo͞os lē), 1842–99, Norwegian mathematician. He is noted for his contributions to the theories of differential equations and continuous transformation groups. He was professor at the Univ. of Christiania and at Leipzig.

Lie, Trygve Halvdan (trüg'və hälv'dän lē), 1896–1968, Norwegian statesman, first secretary general of the United Nations. A lawyer and Labor party leader, he was Norwegian minister of justice (1935–39) and minister of trade and supply (1939–41). He became (1941) foreign minister of the government in exile. Elected (1946) secretary general of the United Nations, Lie took an active part in negotiations and incurred the enmity of the USSR by supporting UN action in the Korean War. In 1953 he was succeeded at the United Nations by Dag Hammarskjöld. In Norway, Lie was appointed (1955) governor of Oslo and of Akershus prov. He also served as minister of industries (1963–64) and minister of commerce (1965). He wrote *In the Cause of Peace* (1954). See his *Public Papers, 1946–1956,* ed. by A. W. Cordier and Wilder Foote (1969).

Lieber, Francis (lē'bər), 1798–1872, German-American political philosopher, b. Berlin. Ardently patriotic, he enlisted in the Prussian army and fought and was wounded at the battle of Waterloo. On his return to Germany he joined the TURNVEREIN movement. In the suppression of student organizations in 1819, Lieber became suspect for his liberal ideas and was harried by the police for the remainder of his life in Germany; he was twice imprisoned. Not permitted to attend a Prussian university, he obtained a degree at Jena. In 1826 he fled to England. He went to Boston in 1827 to teach Jahn's system of gymnastics. From his idea of translating the Brockhaus encyclopedia into English sprang the first edition of *The Encyclopaedia Americana* (13 vol., 1829–33), which he edited. Lieber was professor of history and political economy (1835–56) at South Carolina College (now Univ. of South Carolina). While there he wrote the books that established his reputation as a political philosopher—*A Manual of Political Ethics* (1838), *Essays on Property and Labor* (1841), and *On Civil Liberty and Self-Government* (1853). He taught at Columbia from 1856 until his death. During the Civil War, he prepared for the Union government *Instructions for the Government of Armies of the United States in the Field,* known in its final form as *General Order No. 100,* issued in 1863. It was the basis for later efforts to codify the international law of war. After the Civil War, Lieber joined the radical Republicans. See biography by Frank Freidel (1948, repr. 1968).

Lieber, Thomas: see ERASTUS, THOMAS.

Liebermann, Max (mäks), 1847–1935, German genre painter and etcher. He went to Paris in 1873, where he was impressed by the Barbizon painters. In Holland he was influenced by Frans Hals and Jozef Israëls. His style, as it developed, was close to impressionism. As leader of the Berlin secession group, he was instrumental in bringing French impressionism to Germany, where younger artists were already moving toward expressionism. Liebermann depicted the life of the working classes, landscapes, and outdoor group studies. In his last year he was forbidden by the Nazis to paint. Liebermann's *Ropewalk* is in the Metropolitan Museum.

Liebig, Justus, Baron von (yo͞os'to͞os bärōn' fən lē'-bĭkh), 1803–73, German chemist. As professor at Giessen (1824–52), he was among the first to establish a chemical teaching laboratory; there some of the leading chemists of the 19th cent. were trained. He was professor at Munich from 1852 to 1873. Liebig improved methods of organic analysis and investigated organic compounds such as uric acid. He discovered chloral and was one of the discoverers of chloroform. He made valuable contributions to agricultural chemistry. Liebig refuted the prevalent theory that plants derive their nourishment from humus and emphasized the importance to plants of the nitrogen and carbon dioxide of the air and of the mineral constituents of the soil; subsequently he did important work in the development of artificial fertilizers. His works include *Organic Chemistry in Its Applications to Agriculture and Physiology* (1840, tr. 1840). See F. R. Moulton, ed., *Liebig and after Liebig* (1942).

Liebknecht, Karl (kärl lēp'kənĕkht), 1871–1919, German socialist, leader of the SPARTACUS PARTY; son of WILHELM LIEBKNECHT. His antimilitaristic writings caused his conviction (1907) for high treason. Released from prison, Liebknecht entered the Prussian lower house in 1908 and the Reichstag in 1912. As a member of the extreme left wing of the Social Democratic party, he refused to support the government during World War I. In 1915 he and Rosa LUXEMBURG formed the Internationale, a revolutionary, antiwar socialist group. This group later became the Spartacus party. Imprisoned again for his antiwar activities, Liebknecht was released just before the proclamation of the German republic in Nov., 1918. With Rosa Luxemburg he opposed the moderate government formed by the Social Democrats and advocated its violent overthrow. Shortly afterward, the Spartacists were reconstituted as the German Communist party. In Jan., 1919, Liebknecht led an uprising against the government. After its failure he was arrested and killed while being taken to prison. See K. W. Meyer, *Karl Liebknecht* (1957).

Liebknecht, Wilhelm (vĭl'hĕlm), 1826–1900, German socialist leader and journalist. His participation in the revolution in Germany in 1848–49 forced him into exile and he lived in England until 1862. While there he became associated with Karl MARX. Although greatly influenced by Marx, he disagreed with him on many fundamental principles of socialism. Upon his return to Germany Liebknecht initially joined the socialist group founded by Ferdinand LASSALLE. Shortly afterward he broke with the Lassalleans because of doctrinal differences, and in 1869 with his disciple August BEBEL he formed the Social Democratic Labor party. For several years the two groups conflicted but in 1875 they merged as the Socialist Labor party. As a member of the North German Reichstag, Liebknecht, a confirmed pacifist, voted against extending war credits for the Franco-Prussian War (1870–71). He incurred the enmity of Otto von BISMARCK, was convicted of treason, and with Bebel spent two years in prison (1872–74). Elected to the Reichstag in 1874, he was a member at his death. He wrote many books on historical and social topics and edited several socialist newspapers.

Liebler, Thomas: see ERASTUS, THOMAS.

Liechtenstein (lĭkh'tənshtīn"), principality (1970 pop. 21,350), 61 sq mi (157 sq km), W central Europe. It is situated in the Alps between Austria and Switzerland and is bounded in the west by the Rhine River. VADUZ is the capital. Traditionally agricultural, it has been increasingly industrialized in recent years. Only a fraction of the population still engages in agriculture (dairying, wine production, and the raising of livestock and cereals). The leading manufactured products are machinery and other metal goods, ceramics, textiles, and foodstuffs. A large part of the production is exported. Tourism is an increasingly important industry. The country has no army and only a small police force (21 members as of 1970). Much revenue is derived from the sale of postage stamps and from the minimal taxes imposed on international corporations, which, because of the low taxes, are headquartered in Vaduz. The ruling prince, Francis Joseph II, acceded in 1938. The 1921 constitution, amended in 1972, establishes a parliament of 21 members, elected by male suffrage. Since 1919, Liechtenstein has been represented abroad through Switzerland. It adopted Swiss currency in 1921 and formed a customs union with Switzerland in 1924. Catholicism is the state religion and German is the national language. The Liechtenstein ruling house is an old Austrian family. The principality was created in 1719 by uniting the county of Vaduz with the barony of Schellenburg. The princes, vassals of the Holy Roman emperors, also owned huge estates (many times larger than their principality) in Austria and adjacent territories; they rarely visited their country but were active in the service of the Hapsburg monarchy. Liechtenstein became independent in 1866, after having been a member of the German Confederation from 1815 to 1866. The principality escaped the major upheavals of the 19th and 20th cent. A parliament-approved proposal granting women the right to vote was decisively defeated in two referendums (1971, 1973), thus making Liechtenstein the only Western European country to deny women suffrage. Liechtenstein is a member of the European Free Trade Association (EFTA). See Barbara Greene, *Liechtenstein* (new and enl. ed. 1967); Pierre Raton, *Liechtenstein: History and Institutions of the Principality* (1970).

lied and **lieder:** see SONG.

lie detector, instrument designed to record bodily changes resulting from the telling of a lie. Cesare Lombroso, in 1895, was the first to utilize such an instrument, but it was not until 1914 and 1915 that Vittorio Benussi, Harold Burtt, and, most importantly, William Marston produced devices establishing correlation of blood pressure and respiratory changes with lying. In 1921 an instrument capable of continuously recording blood pressure, respiration, and pulse rate was devised by John Larson. This was followed by the polygraph (1926) of Leonarde Keeler, a refinement of earlier detecting devices, and by the psychogalvanometer (1936) of Walter Summers, a machine that measures electrical changes occurring on the skin. A more recent innovation in lie detection is a device, developed in 1970, called the psychological stress evaluator, which operates by measuring voice frequencies from tape recordings. Although the lie detector is used in police work, the similarity of physical changes caused by emotional factors such as feelings of guilt to those caused by lies has made its evidence for the most part legally inacceptable. See John Reid, *Truth and Deception* (1966).

Liège (ly'ĕzh), Flemish *Luik,* Ger. *Lüttich,* province (1970 pop. 1,008,905), 1,526 sq mi (3,952 sq km), E Belgium, bordering on West Germany in the east. The chief cities are Liège (the capital), Verviers, Herstal, Huy, and Seraing. The province is French speaking (see WALLOONS) except in the eastern districts of Eupen and Malmédy, located near the West German border, where German prevails. Liège is part of the industrial Meuse valley and of the agricultural Ardennes plateau. The leading manufactures include steel, machinery, armaments, and textiles.

Liège, Flemish *Luik,* Ger. *Lüttich,* city (1970 pop. 145,573), capital of Liège prov., E Belgium, at the confluence of the Meuse and Ourthe rivers, near the Dutch and West German borders. Greater Liège includes the suburbs of Herstal, Ougrée, and Grivegnée. The commercial center of the industrial Meuse valley and itself a major industrial center, Liège is also an important transportation hub located on the Albert Canal and on the Liège-Maastricht Canal and at the center of a road and rail network connecting Belgium and West Germany. Manufactures include metal goods, armaments, motor vehicles, electrical and electronics equipment, chemicals, textiles, clothing, and furniture. A growing trade center by the 10th cent., Liège became the capital of the extensive prince-bishopric of Liège, which included most of modern Liège prov. and parts of Limburg and Namur provs. This ecclesiastical state, part of the Holy Roman Empire, lasted until 1792. Liège city, the strongly fortified key to the Meuse valley, suffered numerous sieges in its history. In the Middle Ages it was a leading cultural center and had important textile and metal industries. In the late Middle Ages, Liège was torn by bitter social strife. In the 14th cent. the workers (organized in guilds) won far-reaching concessions from the nobles and the wealthy bourgeoisie and began to take part in the government of the city. The episcopal functionaries were placed (1373) under the supervision of a tribunal of 22 persons, 14 of whom were burgesses. This Peace of the Twenty-Two remained, with interruptions, the basic guarantee of the constitutional liberty of the inhabitants of Liège until 1792. In 1465 the city became a protectorate of Burgundy, and in 1467, Charles the Bold, duke of Burgundy, abolished the citizens' communal liberties. The citizens of Liège, encouraged by Louis XI of France, rose in rebellion, but Charles forced Louis to assist him in suppressing the revolt and then sacked the city (1468). As an episcopal principality, Liège remained technically a sovereign member of the Holy Roman Empire after the Netherlands passed (1477) under Hapsburg rule (see NETHERLANDS, AUSTRIAN AND SPANISH); in fact, however, the prince-bishops were dependent on the Spanish kings and, after 1714, the emperors. Liège flourished under prince-bishop Erard de la Marck in the 16th cent. and became a center of arms manufacture. In 1792 the French under Dumouriez entered Liège. In the 19th cent. the city was a center of Walloon particularism (see WALLOONS), of rapid industrial growth, and of social unrest. In World War I its fortifications, reputed to be among the strongest in Europe, fell (1914) to the Germans after a 12-day siege. In World War II, Liège was again taken (May, 1940) by the Germans. It was liberated (May, 1944) by U.S. forces, but during the Battle of the Bulge (Dec., 1944–Jan., 1945) it suffered considerable destruction from German rockets. In the 1950s and 60s Liège was again a center of social and political unrest. Today Liège is a generally modern city that retains some historic buildings including a cathedral (founded 971), the Church of the Holy Cross (10th cent.), the Church of St. Denis (10th–11th cent.), and the 16th-century palace of justice (the former residence of the prince-bishops). The city is the cultural center of French-speaking Belgium and has a university (founded 1816). The composer César Franck was born there (1822).

Liegnitz: see LEGNICA, Poland.

lien, claim or charge held by one party, on property owned by a second party, as security for payment of some debt, obligation, or duty owed by that second party. A lien may arise by agreement between the parties or by operation of law from the relation of the parties or the circumstances of their dealings.

Liepaya (lēĕ'päyä), Ger. *Libau,* city (1969 est. pop. 88,000), W European USSR, in Latvia. An ice-free port on the Baltic Sea, it is located at the end of an isthmus separating the Baltic from Lake Liepaya. The city has a naval base as well as a commercial harbor. Liepaya is second only to Riga in size and industrial development among Latvian cities. Metallurgy is the leading industry; others include shipbuilding, food and fish processing, and sugar refining. Founded by the Teutonic Knights in 1263, the city was part of LIVONIA and later of the duchy of COURLAND, with which it passed to Russia in 1795. In the late 19th and early 20th cent. Liepaya acquired great commercial importance and became one of the main Russian emigration ports with a direct shipping line to the United States. The city was under German occupation during most of World War I. It was briefly the site of the provisional Latvian government when Bolshevik forces attacked Riga in 1918. Held by the Germans from 1941–45, Liepaya suffered heavy damage. After World War II it was annexed by the USSR along with the rest of Latvia. City landmarks include a residence of Peter the Great and the 18th-century Church of the Trinity. It is also spelled Liepaja.

Lieven, Dorothea, Princess (lē'vən), 1785–1857, Russian noblewoman; wife of the Russian ambassador to London (1812–34). After her husband's recall she settled in Paris. A brilliant personality, she was intimate with the great world of London and Paris, and her Paris salon acquired some note. Her friends included Metternich, Wellington, and Guizot. Her diary and much of her lively correspondence have been published in English. See biography by H. M. Hyde (1938).

Lièvre (lēā'vrə), river, c.200 mi (320 km) long, rising in Kempt Lake, S Que., Canada, and flowing generally SW into the Ottawa River near Buckingham. Parts of it are navigable. There are five hydroelectric plants along its course; two of the most important are at Masson and High Falls.

Lifar, Serge, 1905–, Russian dancer, choreographer, director, teacher, and dance historian, b. Kiev. Lifar studied briefly with Bronislava Nijinska, but he was primarily self-taught. In 1923 he joined the Diaghilev Ballets Russes in Paris, for which he became premier danseur in 1925. He created the title role in George Balanchine's *The Prodigal Son* (1929). Lifar choreographed and staged Stravinsky's *Le Renard* (1929), and after Diaghilev's death in 1930 he joined the Paris Grand Opéra as principal dancer and ballet-master (1930–44). Celebrated for having revolutionized the French ballet, he is best known for his ballets *Lucifer* (1948), *Phèdre* (1950), *Romeo and Juliet* (1955), and *Daphnis and Chloë* (1958). Lifar is the author of many books on the dance.

life. Although there is no universal agreement as to a definition of life, its biological manifestations are generally considered to be organization, metabolism, growth, irritability, adaptation, and reproduction. Organization is found in the basic living material, PROTOPLASM, in the basic living unit, the CELL, and in the organized groupings of cells into organs and organisms. Metabolism includes the conversion of nonliving material into protoplasm (synthesis) and the decomposition of organic matter (catalysis), producing energy. Growth in living matter is an increase in size of all parts, as distinguished from simple addition of material; it results from a higher rate of synthesis than catalysis. Irritability, or response to stimuli, takes many forms, from the contraction of a unicellular organism when touched to complex reactions involving all the senses of higher animals; in plants response is usually much different than in animals but is nonetheless present. Adaptation, the accommodation of a living organism to its present or to a new environment, is fundamental to the process of evolution and is determined by the individual's heredity. The division of one cell to form two new cells is reproduction; usually the term is applied to the production of a new individual (either asexually, from a single parent organism, or sexually, from two differing parent organisms), although strictly speaking it also describes the production of new cells in the process of growth. Protozoa perform, in a single cell, the same life functions as those carried on by the complex tissues and organs of man and other highly developed organisms. The attributes of life are inherent in such minute structures as viruses, bacteria, and genes just as they are in the whale and the giant sequoia. In seeking an understanding of life, scientists have, to a great extent, broken down the barriers that once separated the physical sciences from the biological sciences; a result of the growth of biochemistry, biophysics, and other interrelated fields of study has been a better understanding of the composition and functioning of living tissues of all kinds. Much of the history of biology and of philosophy as related to biology has been marked by a division of thought between vitalistic (or animistic) and mechanistic (or materialistic) concepts. In the most antithetic interpretations of these concepts the vitalistic school maintains that there is a vital force that distinguishes the living from the nonliving and the mechanistic school holds that there is no essential difference between the animate and inanimate and that all life can be explained by physical and chemical laws. Such diametrically opposed views have actually seldom been held by investigators of either school; elements of both are usually involved. The animistic school, largely predicated on the inexplicability of the basic phenomena of life, has been greatly overshadowed by the accumulating weight of scientific data. As more and more is learned of the minute details of the structure and composition of the substances that make up protoplasm and its inclusions (to the extent that some have been synthesized chemically), it has become increasingly apparent that living matter is made up of the same (and only those) elements found in inorganic material, except that they are differently organized. As to the origin of life, fundamental religious concepts center around special creation and belief in the infusion of life into inanimate substance by God or another superhuman entity. On the other hand, many scientists hypothesize that during an early geological period (perhaps 2 billion years ago) there gradually formed in the atmosphere increasingly complex organic substances composed of the available inorganic compounds and water, utilizing ultraviolet rays and electrical discharges as energy sources. At a certain stage they precipitated into the hydrosphere, the earth's original water sheath, to form a diffuse solution of "nutrient broth." Then in some way there were drawn together separate units and systems capable of continuing synthesis and catalysis, thus ensuring their continued existence through the capacity for self-renewal and self-reproduction. In 1953, S. L. Miller synthesized several of the most basic amino acids in a glass flask by introducing an electrical discharge into an atmosphere of water vapor and some simple compounds thought by geologists to have been present naturally at the time when life first developed on earth. The theory that life on earth came in a simple form from another planet has had small currency, although the recent discovery by Melvin Calvin of molecules resembling genetic material in meteors has given it some force. See J. B. S. Haldane, *What is Life?* (1947); Erwin Schrödinger, *What is Life?* (new ed. 1967); J. B. Bernal, *The Origin of Life* (1967); Alexander I. Oparin, *Genesis and Evolutionary Development of Life* (1968); Melvin Calvin, *Chemical Evolution* (1969); Robert Jastrow, *Red Giants and White Dwarfs* (1967, rev. ed. 1971); Ernest Borek, *The Sculpture of Life* (1973).

life insurance: see INSURANCE.

life preserver, contrivance, usually adjustable to fit the body, for buoying up persons in water, particularly in case of shipwreck. The most common type, generally considered the most reliable in spite of its clumsiness, is made of cork blocks sewed in canvas, with belts and shoulder straps; it is so contructed that the cork beneath the wearer's shoulders and around his body keeps him afloat. It should contain at least 6 lb (2.7 kg) of cork. Another common type, developed during World War II for fliers and called the Mae West (named for the actress because of its shape), is made of inflatable rubber, and constructed in such a way that the wearer's face is kept above the surface of the water even if he should be unconscious. Some life preservers have the form of pillows, vests, or mattresses; these are either inflatable or filled with buoyant material such as cork, fiber glass, or kapok pads. A familiar type is the life buoy, a ring of canvas-covered cork, which is fitted with a rope so that several persons may cling to it. Warships have large life rafts, often consisting of a frame supported by metal air chambers and able to support six men. The law of most countries requires that ships carry life preservers and that crew and passengers be drilled in their use.

Liffey (lĭf'ē), river, c.50 mi (80 km) long, rising in the Wicklow Mts., E Republic of Ireland, and flowing W,

NE, and then E through Dublin to Dublin Bay. There are three electric power stations on the river.

ligament (lĭg'əmənt), strong band of white fibrous CONNECTIVE TISSUE that joins bones to other bones or to cartilage in the joint areas. The bundles of collagenous fibers that form ligaments tend to be pliable, but not elastic. They therefore permit freedom of movement within a certain limited range while holding the attached bones firmly in place. For example, the ligaments at the knee limit the movement of the lower leg to a certain range. Other types of ligaments form fibrous sheets that support such internal organs as the kidneys and the spleen.

ligan (lī'gən): see FLOTSAM, JETSAM, AND LIGAN.

ligand (lĭg'ənd), charged or uncharged molecule with one or more unshared pairs of electrons that can attach to a central metallic ATOM or ION to form an aggregate known as a complex ion (see CHEMICAL BOND). Some ligands that share electrons with metals form very stable complexes. Some common bases that act as ligands are water and ammonia molecules and halide, hydroxide, acetate, cyanide, thiocyanate, and nitrite ANIONS. These ligands are monofunctional, i.e., they are attached by one unshared pair of electrons during complexing. Polyfunctional ligands, which bind to the metal ion with two or more pairs of electrons, are called chelates (see CHELATING AGENTS). Ethylenediamine-tetraacetate, a commonly used chelating compound, has six pairs of electrons to bind to metal ions. Electron-donating functional groups containing nitrogen, oxygen, sulfur, phosphorous, or carbon may act as ligands in complex biological systems. For example, in enzymes that need complexed metal ions to function, mercapto (sulfur-containing) groups and amino (nitrogen-containing) groups act as chelating agents; these groups fix the metal ion in a specific position. Other biologically important molecules, such as chlorophyll, vitamin B_{12}, and heme, also have nitrogen-containing groups that donate electrons and have a chelating function.

light, visible ELECTROMAGNETIC RADIATION. Of the entire electromagnetic SPECTRUM, the human eye is sensitive to only a tiny part, the part that is called light. The wavelengths of visible light range from about 3,500 or 4,000 ANGSTROMS to about 7,500 or 8,000 angstroms (1 angstrom = .00000001 cm). If white light, which contains all wavelengths, is separated, or dispersed, into a spectrum, each wavelength is seen to correspond to a different COLOR. In general, VISION is due to the stimulation of the optic nerves in the eye by light either directly from its source or indirectly after reflection from other objects. A luminous body, such as the sun, another star, or a light bulb, is thus distinguished from an illuminated body, such as the moon and most of the other objects one sees. The amount and type of light given off by a luminous body or reflected by an illuminated body is of concern to the branch of physics known as PHOTOMETRY (see also LIGHTING). Illuminated bodies not only reflect light, but sometimes also transmit it. Transparent objects, such as glass, air, and some liquids, allow light to pass through them. Translucent objects, such as tissue paper and certain types of glass, also allow light to pass through them but diffuse (scatter) it in the process, so that an observer cannot see a clear image of whatever lies on the other side of the object. Opaque objects do not allow light to pass through them at all. Some transparent and translucent objects allow only light of certain wavelengths to pass through them and thus appear colored. The colors of opaque objects are caused by selective reflection of certain wavelengths and absorption of others. The scientific study of the behavior of light is called OPTICS and covers REFLECTION of light by a MIRROR or other object, REFRACTION by a LENS or PRISM, DIFFRACTION of light as it passes by the edge of an opaque object, and INTERFERENCE patterns resulting from diffraction. Also studied is the POLARIZATION OF LIGHT. Any successful theory of the nature of light must be able to explain these and other optical phenomena. The earliest scientific theories of the nature of light were proposed around the end of the 17th cent. In 1690, Christiaan Huygens proposed a theory that explained light as a WAVE phenomenon. However, a rival theory was offered by Sir Isaac Newton in 1704. Newton, who had discovered the visible spectrum in 1666, held that light is composed of tiny particles, or corpuscles, emitted by luminous bodies. By combining this corpuscular theory with his laws of mechanics, he was able to explain many optical phenomena. For more than 100 years, Newton's corpuscular theory of light was favored over the wave theory, partly because of Newton's great prestige and partly because not enough experimental evidence existed to provide an adequate basis of comparison between the two theories. Finally, important experiments were done on the diffraction and interference of light by Thomas Young (1801) and A. J. Fresnel (1814–15) that could only be interpreted in terms of the wave theory. Moreover, the corpuscular theory predicted a form of the law of refraction that was exactly the reverse of observation. Polarization was still another phenomenon that could only be explained by the wave theory. Thus, in the 19th cent. the wave theory became the dominant theory of the nature of light. The wave theory received additional support from the electromagnetic theory of James Clerk Maxwell (1864), who showed that electric and magnetic fields were propagated together and that their speed was identical with the speed of light. It thus became clear that visible light is a form of electromagnetic radiation, constituting only a small part of the electromagnetic spectrum. Maxwell's theory was confirmed experimentally with the discovery of radio waves by Heinrich Hertz in 1886. With the acceptance of the electromagnetic theory of light, only two general problems remained. One of these was that of the luminiferous ETHER, a hypothetical medium suggested as the carrier of light waves just as air or water carries sound waves. The ether was assumed to have some very unusual properties, e.g., being massless but having high elasticity. A number of experiments performed to give evidence of the ether, most notably by A. A. Michelson in 1881 and by Michelson and E. W. Morley in 1887, failed to support the ether hypothesis. With the publication of the special theory of RELATIVITY in 1905 by Albert Einstein, the ether was shown to be unnecessary to the electromagnetic theory. The second main problem, and the more serious of the two, was the explanation of various phenomena, such as the PHOTOELECTRIC EFFECT, that involved the interaction of light with matter. Again the solution to the problem was proposed by Einstein, also in 1905. Einstein extended the QUANTUM THEORY of thermal radiation proposed by Max Planck in 1900 to cover not only vibrations of the source of radiation but also vibrations of the radiation itself. He thus suggested that light, and other forms of electromagnetic radiation as well, travel as tiny bundles of energy called light quanta, or PHOTONS. The energy of each photon is directly proportional to its frequency. With the development of the quantum theory of atomic and molecular structure by Niels Bohr and others, it became apparent that light and other forms of electromagnetic radiation are emitted and absorbed in connection with energy transitions of the particles of the substance radiating or absorbing the light. In these processes, the quantum, or particle, nature of light is more important than its wave nature. When the transmission of light is under consideration, however, the wave nature dominates over the particle nature. In 1924, Louis de Broglie showed that an analogous picture holds for particle behavior, with moving particles having certain wavelike properties that govern their motion, so that there exists a complementarity between particles and waves known as particle-wave duality (see also COMPLEMENTARITY PRINCIPLE). The quantum theory of light has successfully explained all aspects of the behavior of light. Another important question in the history of the study of light has been the determination of its speed and of the relationship of this speed to other physical phenomena. At one time it was thought that light travels with infinite speed; i.e., it is propagated instantaneously from its source to an observer. Olaus Rømer showed that it was finite, however, and in 1675 estimated its value from differences in the time of eclipse of certain of Jupiter's satellites when observed from different points in the earth's orbit. More accurate measurements were made during the 19th cent. by A. H. L. Fizeau (1849), using a toothed wheel to interrupt the light, and by J. B. L. Foucault (1850), using a rotating mirror. The most accurate measurements of this type were made by Michelson. Modern electronic methods have improved this accuracy, yielding a value of 299,792.8 km (c.186,000 mi) per sec for the speed of light in a vacuum, and less for its speed in other media. The theory of relativity predicts that the speed of light in a vacuum is the limiting velocity for material particles; no particle can be accelerated from rest to the speed of light, although they may approach it very closely. Particles moving at less than the speed of light in a vacuum but greater than that of light in some other medium will emit a faint blue light known as CHERENKOV RADIATION when they pass through the other medium. This phenomenon has been used in various applications. One of the most important modern applications of light has been the development of a source of coherent light—the LASER. Coherent light is light that is all of the same wavelength and phase. See W. L. Bragg, *The Universe of Light* (1959); John Rublowsky, *Light* (1964); A. C. S. Van Heel and C. H. F. Velzel, *What Is Light* (tr. 1968).

light-emitting diode: see DIODE.

lighter: see BARGE.

Lightfoot, Joseph Barber, 1828–89, English prelate and scholar. A fellow of Trinity College, Cambridge, he became Hulsean professor of divinity (1861) and Lady Margaret professor (1875). In 1871 he became a canon of St. Paul's, London; in 1879 he was consecrated bishop of Durham. He was learned in biblical and early Christian literature. From 1870 to 1880 he was one of the revisers of the King James Version of the Bible. He published commentaries (3 vol., 1865–75) on St. Paul's epistles to the Galatians, Philippians, Colossians, and Philemon. His editions of the Apostolic Fathers include *Clement of Rome* (1869) and *Ignatius and Polycarp* (1885). See *Lightfoot of Durham* (ed. by G. R. Eden and F. C. Macdonald, 1932).

light-gathering power, in astronomy, a measure of the ability of a TELESCOPE to collect light. It is directly related to the area of the lens or mirror that serves as the objective; the greater the area of the objective, the more light that can enter the telescope and be focused to form an image. For this reason, telescopes can often aid in detecting objects too dim to be observed with the unaided eye. The light-gathering power increases as the square of the diameter of the objective; a 200-in. telescope has an objective with a diameter 1,000 times that of a human eye with a pupil dilation of 1/5 in., so its light-gathering power is $1{,}000^2$, or 1,000,000, times as great.

light horse, any breed of HORSE that is used primarily for riding or for light work such as pulling buggies. Light horses have their origin in the Middle East and N Africa. All modern breeds of light horse trace their origins to the ARABIAN HORSE, usually through the THOROUGHBRED. Light horses are classified according to training, e.g., racers, trotters, riding horses, and cow horses. See also PONY, AMERICAN SADDLE HORSE, APPALOOSA, MORGAN, PALOMINO, PINTO, QUARTER HORSE, and STANDARDBRED.

lighthouse, towerlike structure erected to give guidance and warning to ships and aircraft by either visible or radioelectrical means. Lighthouses were long built to conform in structure to their geographical location. Where a good rock foundation existed, masonry tower lighthouses were preferred, circular in form, with a low center of gravity. Later, reinforced concrete was substituted for masonry. Openwork steel construction was chosen where it was necessary to drive in wooden or steel piles to obtain a firm foundation. Some lighthouses have been erected on foundations of cylinders or caissons. Until the beginning of the 19th cent., tallow candles, coal fires, and oil lamps were used as illuminating agents; coal gas followed, to be succeeded by acetylene. Electricity was used for the first time at South Foreland Light, England, in 1858. Other 19th-century innovations were rapidly revolving lights, the incandescent oil-vapor light, fog bells, whistles, sirens, diaphones (fog signals similar to sirens), and the Fresnel lens (used to focus the beam). In modern lighthouses there are three kinds of lighting systems: the catoptric system, in which rays of light are reflected from silvered mirrors to form a parallel beam visible at a distance; the dioptric, or refractive, system, in which the rays pass through optical glass and are refracted as they enter and emerge from it; and the catadioptric system, in which rays are both refracted and reflected. Increased use of radio beams and radar has made the conventional lighthouse obsolete. The first radio beacon for directing ships was built in New York in 1921; from 1934 remote control stations equipped with radio and sensing devices began to take the place of conventional lighthouses. Lamps, fog warnings, and signal beacons are now activated by radio; an electric eye starts a light when daylight fails, and foghorns are turned on automatically when moisture increases in the atmosphere. Also, attendants need no longer live within or adjacent to the tower; modern devices have enabled lighthouses to function virtually unmanned. Historically, lighthouses date back to ancient Egypt, where priests maintained the beacon fires. For about 1,500 years the lighthouse of PHAROS, built in the 3d cent. B.C., guided ships into the Nile; it was lighted by a wood fire and showed smoke by day and a glow by night. The Romans built famous lighthouses in Ostia, Ravenna, and Messina and on both sides of the English Channel. In the United States, the tower for the Boston Light on Little Brewster Island was built in 1716; the first structure of the Brant Point Light, Nantucket, was built in 1746; and Beavertail Light on Conanicut Island, Narragansett Bay, was erected in 1749. In 1789 the U.S. government took over the care of lighthouses from their former private owners. The government set up (1852) the Lighthouse Board, which was eventually superseded by the Lighthouse Service, established (1910) to supervise lighthouses and lightships (see LIGHTSHIP). In 1939 this service was transferred from the Dept. of Commerce to the U.S. coast guard. See H. C. Adamson, *Keepers of the Lights* (1955); D. A. Stevenson, *The World's Lighthouses before 1820* (1960); F. R. Holland, *America's Lighthouses: Their Illustrated History Since 1716* (1972).

lighting, light produced by artificial means to allow visibility in enclosures and at night. The earliest means of artificial lighting were the open fire, firebrands, and torches. The first LAMP was a dish of stone (later of clay, pottery, or metal) containing vegetable or animal oil and a wick. This was succeeded by the CANDLE, first made of wax and later also of tallow, and by the LANTERN, which is of early origin. The Argand burner was an improved oil lamp with a burner and a chimney, and this type of lamp was widely used after the Canadian geologist Abraham Gesner popularized the use of kerosine. Coal gas was first used as an illuminant in the late 18th cent. by the engineer William Murdock in England and by the engineer Philippe Lebon in Paris. It was used in London in 1802, in Baltimore in 1817, and in New York state in 1823. The invention of the BUNSEN BURNER by the German chemist Robert Wilhelm Bunsen and the invention of the WELSBACH MANTLE, a

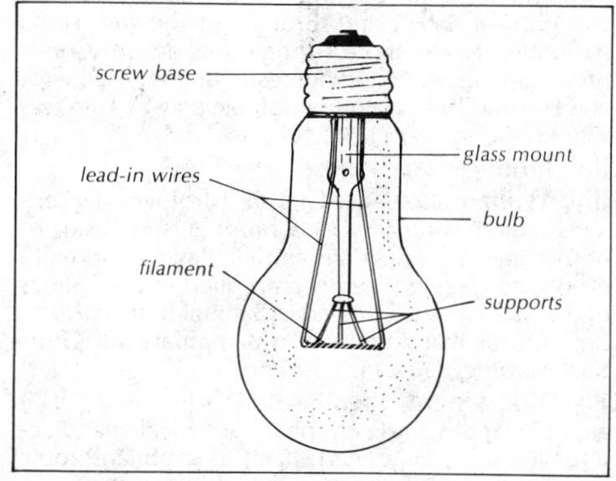

Incandescent lamp

device developed by the Austrian scientist Carl von Welsbach that gives off bright light when placed over a flame, greatly stimulated the use of gas for lighting purposes. The first development in electric lighting was the arc lamp, which was evolved from the carbon-arc lamp demonstrated in 1801 by Sir Humphry Davy, in which an electric current bridges a gap between two carbon rods and forms a bright discharge called an arc. Early lamps of this type were made with an open arc; later ones were enclosed in glass and thus made more practicable. Carbon-arc street lamps, first produced by the American scientist Charles F. Brush, were used in Cleveland in 1879 and soon came into wide use in other cities. The mercury-vapor electric lamp was devised by the American inventor Peter Cooper Hewitt in 1903. This type of lamp makes use of a pool of mercury liquid in a condition of high vacuum; when an electric current passes through the mercury it produces ionized vapor, which gives off a blue-green light. Modern improvements have given this lamp a much greater efficiency. The incandescent electric lamp, in which the current passes through a resistance filament (e.g., one of carbon and tungsten) enclosed in a vacuum tube, was developed by the American electrician Moses G. Farmer in 1858–59 but was not practicable. Sir Joseph Swan in England and Thomas Edison in the United States, working independently, developed lamps of this kind; the lamp patented by Edison in 1879 was the first widely marketed incandescent lamp and was the forerunner of the modern Mazda lamp that utilizes a filament of drawn tungsten hermetically sealed in a glass envelope. A gas-filled incandescent lamp was invented by the American chemist Irving Langmuir in 1913. The neon lamp, developed by the French physicist Georges Claude in 1911, has been largely used in commercial signs. The French physicist A. E. Becquerel constructed a fluorescent lamp and described (1867) the preparation of fluorescent tubes basically similar to those made today. Considerable progress in developing fluorescent lighting was

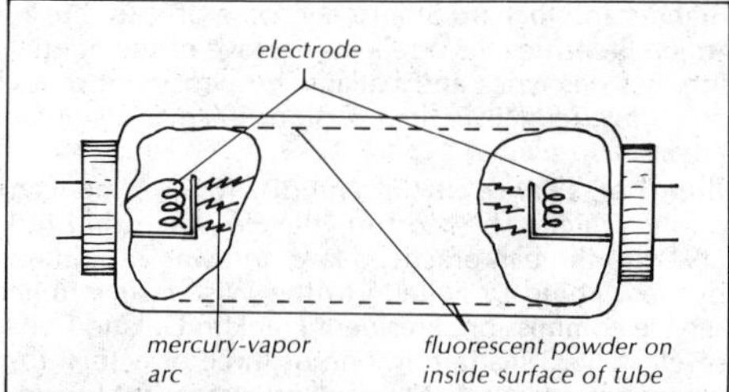

Basic fluorescent lamp

made in several European countries, and during the 1920s high-voltage fluorescent tubes were used in advertising signs. In the United States the first practical hot-cathode, low-voltage fluorescent lamp was marketed in 1938. This is the form of lamp still commonly used. It consists of a long, sealed glass tube with an electrode at each end; a small amount of mercury is contained within the tube. The inside surface of the tube is coated with a mixture of fluorescent powders. When an electric current is maintained through the lamp, the mercury becomes vaporized and gives off invisible ultraviolet radiation that is absorbed by the fluorescent coating. The coating then emits visible light. The design of the lamps varies somewhat according to use. Soon after the hot-cathode fluorescent lamp came into use the more general use of cold-cathode fluorescent tubing (previously used chiefly in outdoor advertising signs) was promoted, but it is employed less commonly than the hot-cathode lamps. Fluorescent lamps are widely used in factories, offices, stores, and public buildings because they produce far more light for the same expenditure of electricity than do incandescent lamps. However, to many observers the colors of objects illuminated by a fluorescent lamp often appear less true than they would appear if the objects were illuminated by an incandescent lamp. (By "true" colors is meant colors of objects illuminated by sunlight.) The effort to improve street and highway lighting continues. Sodium vapor lamps are used on some highways. For stage lighting, see SCENE DESIGN.

lightning, electrical discharge accompanied by THUNDER, commonly occurring during a THUNDERSTORM. The discharge may take place between one part of a cloud and another part, between one cloud and another, or between a cloud and the earth. Lightning may appear as a jagged streak (forked lightning), as a vast flash in the sky (sheet lightning), or, rarely, as a brilliant ball (ball lightning). Illumination from lightning flashes occurring near the horizon, often with clear sky overhead and with the accompanying thunder too distant to be audible, is referred to as heat lightning. Benjamin Franklin, in his kite experiment (1752), proved that lightning and electricity are identical. He invented the lightning rod, which is mounted on top of a building or other structure and attached to the ground by a cable. Both the rod and cable are made of materials that are good conductors of electricity. By virtue of its position and shape the rod attracts lightning discharges much more readily than the building on which it is mounted. When struck, the cable connected to it carries the discharge into the ground, preventing any damage to the building.

lightning bug: see FIREFLY.

light pen: see GRAPHIC TERMINAL.

lightship, moored vessel bearing lights and other signal devices to guide ships and warn of hazards to navigation. Lightships are generally stationed at points where a lighthouse cannot be erected; they are given distinctive features (e.g., high bows, special coloring) so as to be readily distinguishable from other vessels, and they have strong hulls, able to withstand consistent pressures. The first lightship in the United States was posted in 1820 (in the Elizabeth River, near Norfolk, Va.). Afterward, for a time, lightships proliferated; but their number has steadily decreased since the end of World War I. They are costly to man and maintain, and various engineering developments, such as the construction of large radio buoys, have helped to reduce the need for them. Shortly before World War II all U.S. lightships were placed under the control of the U.S. coast guard.

light-year, in astronomy, unit of length equal to the distance LIGHT travels in one SIDEREAL YEAR. It is 9.461 $\times 10^{12}$ km (about 6 million million mi). ALPHA CENTAURI and Proxima Centauri, the stars nearest our solar system, are about 4.3 light-years distant. See also PARSEC.

Ligne, Charles Joseph, prince de (shärl zhôzĕf′ prăNs də lē′nyə), 1735–1814, Austrian field marshal. He belonged to an ancient princely family of Hainaut, in the Austrian Netherlands (now Belgium). He held high military and diplomatic posts, was an adviser of Holy Roman Emperor Joseph II, and won the favor of Catherine II of Russia while on a mission at her court. Though deprived of most of his estates by the French and sunk to relative obscurity, he remained active in European affairs. Ligne was celebrated for his cosmopolitanism and wit; his most famous remark, a reference to the Congress of Vienna, was *Le congrès ne marche pas, il danse.* [The congress does not walk (i.e., make progress), but it dances.] His selected letters and memoirs (tr. 1927) mirror his personal charm, polished gaiety, and unpretentious wisdom.

lignin, a highly polymerized and complex chemical compound especially common in woody plants. The cellulose walls of the wood become impregnated with lignin, a process called lignification, which greatly increases the strength and hardness of the cell and gives the necessary rigidity to the tree. It is essential to woody plants in order that they stand erect.

lignite (lĭg′nīt) or **brown coal,** carbonaceous fuel intermediate between COAL and PEAT, brown or yellowish in color and woody in texture. It contains more moisture than coal and tends to dry and crumble when exposed to the air; the flame is long and smoky and the heating power low. It is found chiefly in geologically young formations in the United States, Canada, Germany, and elsewhere.

lignum vitae (lĭg′nəm vī′tē) [Lat.,=wood of life], tropical American evergreen tree of the genus *Guaiacum.* The hard, dense, and extremely durable wood, obtained chiefly from *G. officinale* and *G. sanctum,* is used for ship construction, butcher blocks, and other articles requiring strength and hardness. The trees are cultivated to some extent in Florida and California for ornament. They also yield guaiacum, a gum RESIN used in certain drugs. Various other hardwoods of Australasia (e.g., the acacia and eucalyptus) are also called lignum vitae. Lignum vitae is classified in several orders in the division MAGNOLIOPHYTA, class Magnoliopsida.

Ligny (lēnyē′), village (1969 est. pop. 2,000), Namur prov., central Belgium, near Namur. At Ligny, on June 16, 1815, Napoleon I of France defeated the Prussians under Blücher early in the WATERLOO CAMPAIGN.

Liguasan Marsh (lĭgwəsän′, lĭgwä′sän), extensive swamp region, c.25 mi (40 km) long and 20 mi (30 km) wide, along the Pulangi River, S central Mindanao, the Philippines. There are fertile rice-growing areas and mangrove forests in the marsh. A game refuge and bird sanctuary (c.170 sq mi/440 sq km) was established there in 1941.

Liguori, Alfonso Maria de′: see ALPHONSUS LIGUORI, SAINT.

Liguria (lĭgŏŏr′ēə, Ital. lēgōō′ryä), region (1971 pop. 1,848,539), 2,098 sq mi (5,434 sq km), NW Italy, extending along the Ligurian Sea and bordering France on the west. The generally mountainous region has a steep, narrow coastal strip that includes the beautiful Italian RIVIERA. In the interior, the Ligurian Alps rise in the west and the Ligurian Apennines in the east. GENOA is the capital of Liguria, which is divided into Genoa, Imperia, La Spezia, and Savona provs. (named for their capitals, all of which are seaports). Flowers (mostly for use in making perfume), olives, wine grapes, citrus fruit, mushrooms, and cereals are grown. Chestnuts are gathered in the mountains, where there are extensive pastures, timberland, and marble, slate, quartz, and limestone quarries. Fishing is pursued along the coast. Manufactures of the region include iron and steel, ships, machinery, textiles, chemicals, processed food, and forest products. Liguria derives its name from the ancient Ligurii, who occupied the Mediterranean coast from the Rhône River to the Arno River. In the 4th cent. the Ligurii were driven from the Alpine regions by Celtic immigrants, while Phoenicians, Greeks, and Carthaginians colonized the coast. In the 2d cent. B.C. the entire region was subdued by the Romans. Throughout the Middle Ages, Genoa struggled with local feudal lords (and at times with Venice) for control of the area. By the 16th cent. it controlled virtually all of present-day Liguria, and from that time until its annexation (1815) by the kingdom of Sardinia, Liguria shared the history of Genoa. There is a university at Genoa.

Ligurian Sea (lĭgyŏŏr'ēən), arm of the Mediterranean Sea, between the Ligurian coast (Italian Riviera) and the islands of Corsica and Elba; the Gulf of Genoa is its northernmost part. The sea receives the Arno River from the east. The ports of Genoa, La Spezia, and Livorno are on its rocky coast. The sea's northwest coast is noted for its favorable climate and scenic beauty.

Li Hung-chang (lē hŏŏng-jäng), 1823–1901, Chinese statesman and general. His first success was as a commander of forces fighting the Taiping Rebellion. As viceroy of the capital province of Chihli (1870–95), he controlled Chinese foreign affairs for the dowager empress Tz'u Hsi. Li was the chief negotiator of the Treaty of Shimonoseki (1895) which ended the First Sino-Japanese War. In 1896 he negotiated the treaty that granted Russia the right to build the Trans-Siberian RR across N Manchuria. He protected foreigners when he was viceroy of Canton during the Boxer Uprising (1900), and he was able to reduce the demands of the foreign powers for reparations. His moderately progressive internal policy included modernization of the army and railroad building.

Likasi (lĭkäs'ē), formerly **Jadotville** (zhädōvēl'), city (1970 pop. 146,394), Shaba region, SE Zaïre. It is a major industrial, mining, and transportation center. Copper and cobalt are mined and refined, and cement, chemicals, and beverages are manufactured.

Likhi (lĭk'hī), Manassite. 1 Chron. 7.19.

lilac, any plant of the genus *Syringa,* deciduous Old World shrubs or small trees of the family Oleaceae (OLIVE family), widely cultivated as ornamentals. Since colonial days, the common lilac has been in America one of the best loved of the flowering shrubs, meriting its favor by its cone-shaped masses of lavender or white flowers, its fragrance, and its ease of cultivation. A familiar shrub of American dooryards, it often marks the site of old farmhouses. Some cities (e.g., Rochester, N.Y.) have lilac festivals. The purple flower clusters are the floral emblem of New Hampshire. From this old-fashioned common lilac (*S. vulgaris*) and others, many hybrids have been developed with variations in form (such as double flowers) and in color (such as rosy pink and white). These hybrids, which may lack the fragrance of the common lilac, are often called French lilacs because much of the pioneer hybridizing was done in France. The most famous use of the lilac in poetry is Whitman's elegy on Lincoln, "When Lilacs Last in the Dooryard Bloom'd." The lilac should not be confused with the unrelated mock orange (of the SAXIFRAGE family), which is sometimes also called syringa; both plants are sometimes called pipe tree. Lilacs are classified in the division MAGNOLIOPHYTA, class Magnoliopsida, order Scrophulariales, family Oleaceae. See Donald Wyman, *Shrubs and Vines for American Gardens* (rev. ed., 1969).

Lilburne, John, 1614?–1657, English political leader and pamphleteer of the LEVELERS. He was tried before the court of the Star Chamber as early as 1638 for printing and distributing antiepiscopal works. Imprisoned from 1638 to 1640, he was released with the aid of Oliver Cromwell and in the course of the first civil war rose (1642–45) to be a lieutenant colonel in the parliamentary army. He resigned from the army because he refused to sign the Presbyterian Covenant required for admission to the New Model Army. Lilburne then became a pamphleteer and leader of a large following of common soldiers and artisans who hoped for a fundamental, democratic revision of the constitution and the social system. After 1646 he spent much of his life in prison or exile but continued his propaganda work even there. His pamphlet *England's Birthright* (1645) contained the principles that became the basis for the Leveler program later stated in *An Agreement of the People.* Lilburne protested the arbitrary rule of the Rump Parliament and, though no royalist, protested the tribunal that condemned Charles I to death. In 1649, Lilburne, with several of his associates, was tried for treason and acquitted. Under the Commonwealth, Lilburne was banished (1652), returned to England, and was again tried and acquitted (1653). Deemed dangerous, he was held in prison. In his last years he became a Quaker. See biographies by M. A. Gibb (1947) and Pauline Gregg (1961); see also bibliography under LEVELERS.

Liliencron, Detlev, Freiherr von (dĕt'lĕf frī'hĕr fən lē'lyənkrôn), 1844–1909, German lyric poet, b. Schleswig-Holstein. First a Prussian army officer and later a minor government official, he retired in 1885 to devote himself to writing. Liliencron was one of the first German lyric poets to break with the romantic tradition. His verse, varied, colorful, and humorous, is impressionistic rather than naturalistic. Brahms and Richard Strauss set some of it to music. *Adjutantenritte* (1883) reflects his love of the martial life. Besides lyrics and ballads, he wrote the mock epic *Poggfred* (1896; final version, 1906) and stories, novels, and plays.

Lilienthal, David Eli (lĭl'yənthôl), 1899–, American public official, b. Morton, Ill. He was admitted (1923) to the bar, practiced law, and was appointed by Gov. Philip La Follette to the Wisconsin public service commission. President Franklin Delano Roosevelt in 1933 made him one of three directors, together with Arthur E. Morgan and Harcourt Morgan, of the TENNESSEE VALLEY AUTHORITY (TVA). There were severe internal struggles as well as violent disputes with opponents of the TVA. As chairman (1941–46) of the TVA, he fought bitter battles with various competing private interests, and he insisted on nonpolitical administration. He was appointed chairman of the U.S. Atomic Energy Commission by President Truman, and in that office (1947–49) he was a pioneer in civilian control of the American atomic-energy program. He wrote *TVA, Democracy on the March* (1944, new ed. 1953), *This I Do Believe* (1949), *Big Business: A New Era* (1953), and *Change, Hope and the Bomb* (1963). See his journals (5 vol., 1964–71); biography by Willson Whitman (1948).

Lilienthal, Otto (ô'tō lē'lyəntäl), 1848–96, German aeronautical engineer, a pioneer in his experiments with GLIDERS. He made major developments in the glider based on his observations of birds and wrote a number of books on aviation. His brother, **Gustav Lilienthal,** 1849–1933, was associated with Otto in his flying experiments and continued them after his brother's death.

Lilith (lĭl'ĭth), Jewish female demon, originally probably the Assyrian storm demon Lilitu. In Talmudic tradition many evil attributes were given to this supposedly nocturnal creature. In Jewish folklore she is a vampirelike child-killer and the symbol of sensual lust. Of the various legends connected with her, the one making her Adam's first wife is the strongest. Lilith appears in the Walpurgis Night section of Goethe's *Faust* and is discussed in Bernard Shaw's *Back to Methuselah.* See Louis Ginzberg, *The Legends of the Jews,* vol. V (tr. 1956).

Liliuokalani (lēlēōō"ōkälä'nē), 1838–1917, last reigning queen of the Hawaiian Islands. She ascended the throne in 1891 upon the death of her brother, King Kalakaua. Her refusal to recognize the constitutional changes inaugurated in 1887 precipitated a revolt, fostered largely by sugar planters (mostly American residents of Hawaii), that led to her dethronement early in 1893 and the establishment of a provisional government. Failing in an attempt to regain the throne in 1895, she formally renounced her royal claims. Much of the remainder of her life was spent in the United States, where she unsuccessfully entered against the Federal government claims totaling $450,000 for property and other losses. The territorial legislature of Hawaii finally voted her an annual pension of $4,000 and permitted her to receive the income from a sugar plantation of 6,000 acres (2,428 hectares). She wrote many songs, including the popular "Aloha Oe," or "Farewell to Thee."

Lille (lēl), city (1968 pop. 194,948), capital of Nord dept., N France, near the Belgian border. It is a great commercial, cultural, and manufacturing center, long known for its textile products—notably lisle (the name is derived from an older spelling of the city's name). Intense industrial expansion in the 1960s led to the establishment (1967) of a metropolitan community uniting almost 90 towns with a total population of over 900,000; this is now France's richest economic region and one of the most important urban centers in Europe. Lille was the chief city of the county of Flanders, a brilliant residence of the 16th-century dukes of Burgundy, and (after 1668) the capital of French Flanders. Taken (1708) after a costly siege by Eugene of Savoy and the duke of Marlborough, it was restored to France in the Peace of Utrecht (1713). Among its principal buildings are the huge citadel, one of the finest works of Vauban; the old stock exchange (17th cent.); several fine churches; and the unfinished cathedral (begun 1854). Lille has a large university, transferred there from Douai in 1808, and one of the most important art museums in Europe; its paintings include many of the best works of the Flemish, Dutch, French, and Spanish masters.

Lille Baelt: see STORE BAELT, strait, Denmark.

Lillehammer (lĭ'ləhämər), town (1970 pop. 20,548), capital of Oppland co., S Norway, at the northern end of Lake Mjøsa. It is a commercial center for the fertile Gudbrandsdalen valley and is a popular summer and winter resort. Its open-air museum (founded 1887) features complete farms, peasant cottages, workshops, and handicrafts of the region.

Lillie, Beatrice (Lady Peel), 1898–, British comedienne, b. Toronto, Canada. Lillie first performed in London in 1914 and in New York in 1924. She won an international reputation for sophisticated wit and vivacity in revues, in radio, television, and films, and in her one-woman shows, with which she subsequently toured throughout the United States. Her films include *On Approval* (1943) and *Thoroughly Modern Millie* (1967). She married Sir Robert Peel in 1920. See her autobiography (1972).

Lillie, Frank Rattray, 1870–1947, American zoologist and educator, b. Toronto, B.A. Univ. of Toronto, 1891, Ph.D. Univ. of Chicago, 1894. He taught, conducted research, and was an administrator at the Univ. of Chicago from 1900. His embryological investigations reached into all aspects of cellular and embryonic development, including the role of the sex hormones. He is best known for his dedicated efforts in shaping the Marine Biological Laboratory and the Oceanographic Institute at Woods Hole, Mass. In addition to many scientific papers, he wrote *The Development of the Chick* (1908, 3d ed. 1952), a leading text in embryology, and *The Woods Hole Marine Biological Laboratory* (1944).

Lillo, George, 1693–1739, English dramatist. The son of a prosperous jeweller, he was for many years his father's partner in the trade. He is chiefly remembered as the author of *The London Merchant; or, The History of George Barnwell* (1731), the first prose domestic tragedy in English. Though the play was popular in England throughout the 18th cent., its influence was more strongly felt on the Continent, particularly in the domestic drama of Diderot and Lessing. The only other notable play by Lillo was *The Fatal Curiosity* (1736).

Lilly, John: see LYLY, JOHN.

Lilly, William, 1602–81, English astrologer. He enjoyed some popularity as a prophet and caster of horoscopes. He issued an annual almanac, foretold events, and was frequently embroiled in the politics of the day. He was satirized in Samuel Butler's *Hudibras.* Of his many books and pamphlets the *Christian Astrology* (1647) is best known.

Lilly Endowment, Inc., institution founded (1937) at Indianapolis, Ind., by pharmaceutical manufacturer Josiah K. Lilly (1861–1948) as a philanthropic foundation for "the promotion and support of religious, educational, or charitable purposes"; most of its work is confined to the Midwest. The foundation is especially interested in undertakings designed to foster the growth and development of Christian character. It provides aid to Protestant theological seminaries and other colleges and also supports a broad range of projects in Indianapolis. Its assets in 1973 were about $1,250,000,000.

Lilongwe (lēlông'gwā), city (1971 est. pop. 40,000), S central Malawi, in a fertile agricultural area. The capital of Malawi since 1966, it is an administrative and commercial center. The city was founded in 1947 as an agricultural marketing center. Banda College of Agriculture is in Lilongwe.

lily, common name for the Liliaceae, a plant family numbering several thousand species of over 200 genera, widely distributed over the earth and particularly abundant in warm temperate and tropical regions. Most species are perennial herbs characterized by bulbs (or other forms of enlarged underground stem) from which grow erect clusters of narrow, grasslike leaves or leafy stems. A few are woody and some are small trees. Evolutionarily, the lily family is probably the basic monocotyledonous stock, its ancestors having given rise to the majority of contemporary monocots, e.g., the orchids, the palms, the iris and amaryllis families, and possibly also the grasses. The relationships between plants of the modern lily family are not always clear, and some botanists subdivide the Liliaceae into several families or combine certain genera with those of other families to indicate a truer evolutionary relationship, e.g., the aloes with the agaves (amaryllis family) and similar forms. Many common wild flowers belong to the lily family, e.g., the ASPHODEL, BRODIEA, CAMASS, Canada mayflower (see MAYFLOWER), DOGTOOTH VIOLET, greenbrier (see SMILAX), LILY OF THE VALLEY, SOLOMON'S-SEAL, STAR-OF-BETHLEHEM, and TRILLIUM. Because of the showy blossoms characteristic of the family, many species, including several of the above, are cultivated as ornamentals. This is the chief economic value of the Liliaceae; over 160 genera are represented in American trade. Types of HYACINTH, lily, MEADOW SAFFRON, SQUILL, and TULIP constitute the bulk of the "Dutch bulb" trade. YUCCA and ALOE species are popular succulents; the latter is also a drug source. ASPARAGUS and plants of the ONION genus are the only liliaceous food plants of commercial importance. A small tropical tree was the original source of DRAGON'S BLOOD. The name lily is used chiefly for plants of the genus *Lilium* and related species but is applied also to plants of other families, e.g., the water lily, the calla lily, and, especially, the numerous species of the AMARYLLIS family whose blossoms closely resemble the true lilies in appearance. Familiar among North American species of *Lilium* are the wood lily (*L. philadelphicum*), Turk's-cap lily (*L. superbum*), and Canada, or wild yellow, lily (*L. canadense*) of the East and the leopard lily (*L. paradalinum*), Washington lily (*L. washingtonianum*), lemon lily (*L. parryi*), and Humboldt's lily (*L. humboldtii*) of the West. Widely cultivated and often naturalized Old World species are the Madonna lily (*L. candidum*) and the martagon lily (*L. martagon*), also called Turk's cap lily. The white trumpet lily (*L. longiflorum*) of Japan includes the Easter, or Bermuda, lily (var. *eximium*), which is the most popular greenhouse lily. The garden tiger lily is the Oriental species *L. tigrinum*, but many other lilies with spotted blossoms also bear the name. *Calochortus*, mariposa or mariposa lily, is a genus of W North America. The white-blossomed sego lily (*C. nuttallii*) is the state flower of Utah. The day lilies, genus *Hemerocallis* [Gr.,=beautiful for a day], native to Central Europe and Asia, are much cultivated and often found naturalized along roadsides. The name day lily is occasionally used for the Oriental plantain lily genus (*Hosta*) because it too has short-lived flowers. The glory, or climbing, lilies (genus *Gloriosa*) are plants of tropical Asia and Africa which climb by means of tendrillike leaf tips. In religion and art the lily symbolizes purity, and as the flower of the Resurrection and of the Virgin it is widely used at Easter. The lily of the Bible (Cant. 2.1) has been variously identified with the scarlet anemone, Madonna lily, and other plants; the "lilies of the field" (Mat. 6.28) probably means any wild flowers, perhaps the iris. Lilies are classified in the division MAGNOLIOPHYTA, class Liliatae, order Liliales, family Liliaceae. See F. F. Rockwell and others, *The Complete Book of Lilies* (1961); Carl Feldmaier, *Lilies* (1970).

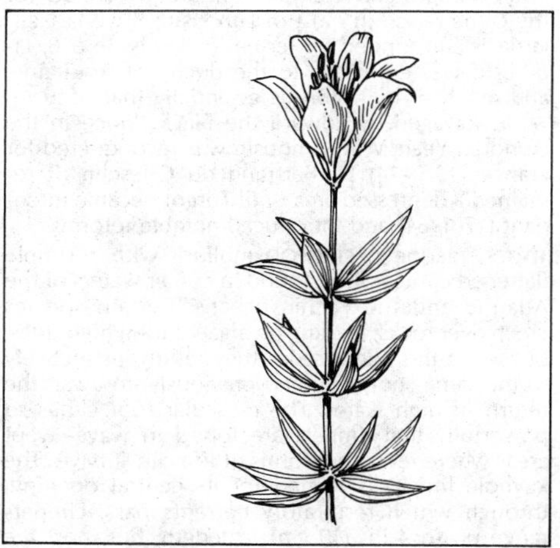

Wood lily, Lilium philadelphicum

Lilybaeum (lĭlĭbē'əm), ancient city of Sicily, on the extreme western coast. It is the modern MARSALA. It was founded (396 B.C.) by Carthage and became a stronghold. In the First Punic War it resisted a long Roman siege (250–242). Later Rome acquired Sicily by treaty, and Lilybaeum became a subject of the empire. The city was famous for its harbor.

lily of the valley, common name for either of the two species of *Convallaria*, spring-blooming perennials of the family Liliaceae (LILY family). *C. majalis*, the species usually in cultivation, is native to Eurasia; *C. montana*, a slightly larger plant, grows in the Appalachian mts. Lilies of the valley live in shady places and have delicate bell-shaped, fragrant white flowers growing on a stalk between two shiny leaves. The plant was long used medicinally for cardiac disorders and contains poisonous substances. It is a symbol of humility in religious painting. Lily of the valley is classified in the division MAGNOLIOPHYTA, class Liliatae, order Liliales, family Liliaceae.

Lima (lē'mə, Span. lē'mä), city (1970 est. pop. 2,541,300), W Peru, capital and largest city of Peru. Its port is CALLAO. The Lima urban area is Peru's economic center and the site of oil-refining and diversified manufacturing industries. The city was founded on Jan. 18, 1535, by Francisco Pizarro and is the second oldest capital city in South America. It was the capital of Spain's New World empire until the 19th cent. Its cultural supremacy on the continent was contested in colonial times only by Bogotá, Colombia, and in magnificence and political prestige Lima's only rival was Mexico City. It was named the City of Kings by Pizarro. Rebuilt several times, Lima reflects the architectural styles prevalent in various periods; much of the city is characterized by modern steel and concrete buildings. Although many streets are narrow and preserve a colonial atmosphere, spacious boulevards traverse the entire metropolitan area. Small squares, statues of national heroes, parks, and gardens are common. The focal point of the city's life is the central square, the Plaza de las Armas. It is dominated by the huge national palace and cathedral. The cathedral, begun by Pizarro and containing what are claimed to be his remains, was almost totally destroyed by earthquakes in 1687 and 1746, along with much of the city. Besides the palace, the cathedral, and numerous churches, including the monastery of Santa Rosa with the relics of St. Rose of Lima, notable public buildings include the National Library, founded in 1821 by José de San Martín, and the Univ. of San Marcos, founded in 1551. The library, which once contained priceless documents of the Spanish Conquest and rare European books, was looted by Chilean soldiers during Chile's occupation of Lima (1881–83) in the War of the Pacific. The university is one of the finest in South America. Lima has a uniformly cool climate and during the winter is subject to the fogs and heavy mists peculiar to Peru's southern desert coast. It almost never rains. Not far from the city are the pre-Incan ruins at PACHACAMAC.

Lima (lī'mə), city (1970 pop. 53,734), seat of Allen co., NW Ohio; settled 1831, inc. 1842. Located in a rich farm area, it is a processing and marketing center for grain, dairy, and meat products. Auto engines, school buses, electric signs and motors, cranes and power shovels, petroleum products, cigars, steel castings, machine tools, plastics, chemicals, and fertilizers are produced in the city. Lima, formerly a large oil producer (1885–1910), is still a pipeline and refinery center. Lima houses a symphony orchestra and a branch of Ohio State Univ.

lima bean: see BEAN.

Liman von Sanders, Otto (ô'tō lē'män fən zän'dərs), 1855–1929, German general. In 1913 he was made head of the German military mission to Constantinople to reorganize the army of the Ottoman Empire (Turkey). His appointment caused a diplomatic crisis between Germany and Russia, which suspected German designs on the Turkish capital. A compromise was reached when the Germans agreed that Liman become inspector general of the army, a post with less extensive authority. In World War I, Liman commanded Turkish armies in the GALLIPOLI CAMPAIGN (1915–16) and was given (1918) supreme command in Palestine, where he was defeated by Allenby and T. E. Lawrence. He wrote *Five Years in Turkey* (1920, tr. 1957).

Limassol (lēmäsôl'), city (1970 est. pop. 52,000), S Cyprus, on Akrotiri Bay. It is a district administrative center, a port, and a resort. Wine and agricultural goods are exported. Umber is mined in the district. At Limassol, in 1191, Richard I of England married Berengaria of Navarre.

limb darkening: see SUN.

Limbourg brothers (lăNbo͞or'), fl. 1380–1416, family of Franco-Flemish manuscript illuminators. The Limbourg brothers, Pol, Jan, and Herman, were trained as goldsmiths. They succeeded Jacquemart de HESDIN in 1411 as court painters to Jean, duc de Berry. Their masterpiece is the magnificent BOOK OF HOURS known as the *Très Riches Heures* (c.1415; Musée Condé, Chantilly). This is filled with exquisite illustrations of the daily life of the aristocracy and peasantry, including a series of calendar ILLUMINATIONS that are considered the finest extant examples of the International Gothic style (see GOTHIC ARCHITECTURE AND ART). The Limbourgs' influence upon Flemish painting, especially in landscape and GENRE subjects, was profound and extensive.

Limburg (lĭm'bûrg, Flemish lĭm'bûrkh), Fr. *Limbourg*, province (1970 pop. 652,547), 930 sq mi (2,409 sq km), NE Belgium, bordering on the Netherlands in the north. The chief cities are HASSELT (the capital), Tongeren, and Sint-Truiden. The province is bordered in the E by the Meuse River and is crossed by the Albert Canal. It is largely agricultural; dairy products, wheat, and sugar beets are the main items. Coal is mined in the CAMPINE region in the north. Most of Limburg was included in the prince-bishopric of Liège until 1792. It became (1815) part of the Dutch province of Limburg, which was divided between Belgium and the Netherlands in 1839. The province is largely Flemish speaking.

Limburg (lĭm'bûrg, Dutch lĭm'bûrkh), province (1971 pop. 1,012,400), c.850 sq mi (2,200 sq km), SE Netherlands, bordering on Belgium in the west and south and West Germany in the east. Maastricht, on the Meuse (Maas) River, is the province's capital and chief industrial center. Heerlen, Sittard, Roermond, and Venlo are other important cities in the province. Rich in historic antiquities, the province takes its name from the former duchy of Limburg, which comprised the southern part of the modern province, including Maastricht, and an eastern portion of modern Liège prov. in Belgium. The small town of Limbourg, E of Liège, was its capital. Founded in the 11th cent., the duchy was divided in the Peace of Westphalia (1648) between the United Netherlands (which received Maastricht) and the Spanish Netherlands. The duchy was united (1815) under the kingdom of the Netherlands. Limburg prov., as established in 1815, did not correspond to the borders of the old duchy. It was contested after the establishment (1831) of an independent Belgium. The Dutch-Belgian treaty of 1839 divided the territory, which was incorporated, respectively, with the Dutch and Belgian provinces of Limburg. There was some Belgian separatist feeling in the Netherlands' Limburg prov. in the 19th cent., and the province was not fully integrated into the Dutch national structure until the early 20th cent.

lime: see CALCIUM OXIDE.

lime, in botany, small shrublike tree (*Citrus aurantifolia*) of the family Rutaceae (RUE family), one of the citrus fruit trees, similar to the lemon but more spreading and irregular in growth. It is native to SE Asia and has been introduced into S Europe, the West Indies, Mexico, and Florida. Chief production is in tropical regions of the Old and New World; most American limes come from the West Indies or Mexico. The lime is the most susceptible to frost injury of all citrus fruits; this confines its commercial culture in the United States to the southernmost parts of Florida. Here some of the varieties often do well in sandy or rocky soils—conditions usually unfavorable to most citrus fruits. The bright green fruit is smaller than the lemon, more globular, more acid, and with a thinner rind. It has the vitamin value and other properties of the CITRUS FRUITS. The juice has long been known as a preventive against scurvy and is one of the main sources of CITRIC ACID. The name lime is also applied to the LINDEN and sometimes to a species of tupelo, or sour gum, known also as the Ogeechee lime. Limes are classified in the division MAGNOLIOPHYTA, class Magnoliopsida, order Sapindales, family Rutaceae.

limelight: see CALCIUM OXIDE.

Limerick (lĭm'ərĭk), county (1971 pop. 140,370), 1,037 sq mi (2,686 sq km), SW Republic of Ireland. LIMERICK, the county town, is the only town of notable size. The region is an agricultural plain lying S of the Shannon estuary. The Golden Vale in the eastern part of the county and the Shannon bank are especially fertile. Dairy farming and salmon fishing are the chief occupations. On the Shannon River above Limerick is an important hydroelectric plant. There are food-processing, wool, and paper industries. After the Anglo-Norman invasion and the organization of Limerick as a shire (c.1200) the district was controlled for many centuries by the earls of Desmond.

Limerick, county borough (1971 pop. 57,137), county town of Co. Limerick, SW Republic of Ireland, at the head of the Shannon estuary. The town is a port for small vessels. Industry includes salmon fishing, food processing, flour milling, and lacemaking. It was occupied by the Norsemen in the 9th cent., became the capital of Munster under Brian Boru (c.1000), was taken by the English toward the end of the 12th cent., and was James II's last stronghold in Ireland after the GLORIOUS REVOLUTION. There are three sections—English Town, the oldest, on King's Island; Irish Town to the south; and Newtown Pery, S of Irish Town, founded in 1769. Preserved in Limerick is the Treaty Stone on which was signed (1691) the treaty granting the Irish Catholics certain rights, chiefly the guarantee of political and religious liberty. The repeated violations of this treaty during the reigns of William III and Queen Anne caused Limerick to be called City of the Violated Treaty. There is a Protestant cathedral (12th cent.), a Roman Catholic cathedral, and the castle (begun 1210) of King John.

limerick, type of humorous verse. It is always short, often nonsensical, and sometimes ribald. Of unknown origin, the limerick is popular rather than literary and has even been used in advertising. The rhyme scheme of most limericks is usually *aabba*, as in the following example:

There was a young lady of Niger,
Who smiled as she rode on a tiger;
They returned from the ride
With the lady inside,
And the smile on the face of the tiger.

The most famous collection of limericks is Edward Lear's *Book of Nonsense* (1846). See Langford Reed, *The Complete Limerick Book* (1925); C. P. Aiken, *A Seizure of Limericks* (1964); V. B. Holland, *An Explosion of Limericks* (1967); W. S. Baring-Gould, *The Lure of the Limerick* (1967).

limestone, sedimentary rock wholly or in large part composed of calcium carbonate. It is ordinarily white but may be colored by impurities, iron oxide making it brown, yellow, or red and carbon making it blue, black, or gray. The texture varies from coarse to fine. Most limestones are formed by the deposition and consolidation of the skeletons of marine invertebrates; a few originate in chemical precipitation from solution. Limestone deposits are frequently of great thickness. The action of organic acids on underground deposits causes such formations as the Luray Caverns, the Carlsbad Caverns, and Mammoth Cave. Limestone is used as a flux in the extraction of iron, as an ingredient in Portland cement, as a source of lime (see CALCIUM OXIDE), as a building stone, and for ornamentation. Among the important varieties of limestone are MARL, CHALK, OOLITE, TRAVERTINE, DOLOMITE, and MARBLE.

lime-sulfur, mixture of calcium polysulfides formed by reacting (e.g., by boiling) calcium hydroxide (slaked lime) with sulfur. It is used as an insecticide and fungicide.

limewater: see CALCIUM HYDROXIDE.

Limfjørd (lēm'fyörd''), waterway, c.110 mi (180 km) long, cutting across N Jutland, Denmark, and connecting the North Sea with the Kattegat. It is very irregular in shape, forming Løgstør, a lagoon 15 mi (24 km) wide in its middle section; its maximum depth is c.50 ft (15 m). There are several islands, notably Mors. Before 1825, when the fjord cut through to the North Sea, its western part consisted of several freshwater lakes that drained eastward into the Kattegat. The Thyborøn Canal keeps the western entrance of Limfjørd open. Ålborg is the chief port on the waterway.

liming (līm'ĭng), application to the soil of calcium in various forms, generally as ground limestone, but also as marl, chalk, shells, or hydrated lime. Lime benefits soil by neutralizing acidity, improving texture, and increasing the activity of soil microorganisms. It enables bacteria on the roots of legumes, e.g., alfalfa and clover, to secure nitrogen from the air, making the soil richer in this essential element. It also increases the amount of available phosphorus in soils. The value of liming was recognized in ancient Rome, and it was extensively used in France and England during the Middle Ages. Approximately 25 million tons of ground limestone are applied annually to soils in the United States.

limit, in mathematics, value approached by a SEQUENCE or a FUNCTION under certain specified conditions. For example, the terms of the sequence $\frac{1}{2}$, $\frac{1}{4}$, $\frac{1}{8}$, $\frac{1}{16}$, . . . are obviously getting smaller and smaller; since, if enough terms are taken, one can make the last term as small, i.e., as close to zero, as one pleases, the limit of this sequence is said to be zero. Similarly, the sequence 3, 5, $3\frac{1}{2}$, $4\frac{1}{2}$, $3\frac{3}{4}$, $4\frac{1}{4}$, $3\frac{7}{8}$, $4\frac{1}{8}$, . . . is seen to approach 4 as a limit. However, the sequences 1, 2, 4, 8, 16, . . . and 1, 2, 1, 2, 1, 2, . . . do not have limits. Frequently a sequence is denoted by giving an expression for the *n*th term, s_n; e.g., the first example is denoted by $s_n = \frac{1}{2}^n$. The limit, *s*, of a sequence can then be expressed as $\lim_{n\to\infty} s_n = s$, or in the case of the example, $\lim_{n\to\infty} \frac{1}{2}^n = 0$ (read "the limit of $\frac{1}{2}^n$ as *n* approaches infinity is zero"). A sequence is a special case of a function. In many functions commonly encountered, the values of the independent variable (the domain) and those of the dependent variable (the range) may be any numbers, while for a sequence the domain is restricted to the positive integers, 1, 2, 3, ... The function $y = \frac{1}{2}^x$ resembles the sequence used as an example, but note that *x* can take on values other than 1, 2, 3, . . . ; thus we find not only $\lim_{x\to\infty} \frac{1}{2}^x = 0$ but also $\lim_{x\to -2} \frac{1}{2}^x = 4$. A more precise definition of the limit of a function is: The function $y = f(x)$ approaches a limit *L* as *x* approaches some number *a* if, for any positive number ε, there is a number δ such that $|f(x) - L| < \varepsilon$ if $0 < |x - a| < \delta$. Similarly, $f(x)$ has the limit *L* as *x* becomes infinite if for any positive ε there is a δ such that $|f(x) - L| < \varepsilon$ if $|x| > \delta$.

limner (lĭm'nər), the work of untrained, generally anonymous artists active in the English American colonies. Characteristic examples of their paintings show flat, awkward, often frontal figures in richly detailed costumes and landscape settings copied from European prints. The limner tradition extended well into the 19th cent.

limnology, the study of the ECOLOGY of freshwater habitats. See MARINE BIOLOGY.

Límnos (lēm'nôs) or **Lemnos** (lĕm'nŏs), island (1971 pop. 17,367), 186 sq mi (482 sq km), NE Greece, in the Aegean Sea near Turkey. It is largely mountainous, with areas of fertile lava soil. Fruits, wine, silk, and wheat are produced, sheep and goats are raised, and fish are caught. A medicinal earth, used in treating open wounds and snake bites, has been produced there since ancient times. Kástron and Moúdhros, a port, are the island's chief towns. In ancient Greece, the island, because of its volcanic origin, was sacred to Hephaestus. It became a colony of Athens c.500 B.C. After the fall (1204) of the Byzantine Empire, Límnos was captured by the Genoese, who held the island until 1464, when it passed to Venice. It was seized by the Ottoman Turks in 1479 and became part of Greece in 1913. Nearby are remains of a Bronze Age settlement.

Limoges (lēmôzh'), city (1968 pop. 135,917), capital of Haute-Vienne dept., W central France, on the Vienne River. It is famous for its ceramics industry, which uses the abundant kaolin in the area; the city's porcelain workshops employ more than 10,000 people. The shoe industry is also large. An ancient town, Limoges became (12th cent.) the seat of the viscounty of Limoges and (1589) the capital of Limousin prov. It was often visited by war, pestilence, and famine. Richard Coeur de Lion (Richard I of England) was killed in battle near Limoges (1199). In 1370, Edward the Black Prince burned the city and massacred its inhabitants. The famous Limoges enamel industry was fully developed by the 13th cent. and culminated in the work of Léonard Limousin, but it declined when Limoges was once more devastated in the Wars of Religion. Turgot, who was intendant from 1761 to 1764, brought back prosperity by introducing (1771) the china manufactures. Limoges has a cathedral (chiefly 13th–16th cent.), a notable ceramics museum, and an art gallery containing many works by Renoir, who was born there.

Limón (lēmōn'), city (1968 est. pop. 22,555), capital of Limón prov., Costa Rica, on the Caribbean Sea. The leading port of Costa Rica, it exports bananas, cacao, and timber. It is also a tourist resort. Limón was founded (1874) during the construction of the railroad to San José. Columbus may have visited the site on his 1502 voyage.

limonite (līm'ənīt) or **brown hematite** (hĕm'ətīt, hē'-), yellowish to dark brown mineral, a hydrated oxide of iron, $FeO(OH) \cdot nH_2O$, occurring commonly in deposits of secondary origin, i.e., those formed by the alteration of other minerals containing iron. Both iron rust and bog iron ore are limonite. It serves as a pigment (see OCHER) and as an ore of iron; it occurs naturally throughout the world.

Limousin or **Limosin, Léonard** (lāônär' lēmo͞ozăN', lēmôzăN'), c.1505–c.1577, French painter in enamel, most celebrated member of a family of Limoges enamel artists. His earliest authenticated works (1532) show both German and Italian influence. He was enameler and *valet de chambre* at the French court after 1548, and for Francis I and Henry II he executed plates, vases, goblets, medals, and exquisite portraits in enamel. They include plaques of the French kings, of Diane de Poitiers, of Luther, and of Calvin. His works are remarkable for their elegance, precise technique, and intense color. The art of Limousin is best studied in the Louvre, which owns many portraits and two celebrated votive tablets comprising 46 plaques. Fine examples of his art and the works of his shop are found in the Limoges Museum and the Cluny Museum, Paris. The Metropolitan Museum has several portrait plaques including those of the Huguenots François de Maurel and Claude Condinet, and of Francis I.

Limousin (lēmo͞ozăN'), region and former province, S central France, in the arid, hilly country W of the Auvergne Mts. It comprises the depts. of Corrèze, Creuse, and Haute-Vienne. Limoges, the historic capital, is the center of ceramics industries, for which the abundant kaolin of the region is used; both Limoges and Tulle are important markets for the cattle raised in most of Limousin; Brive-la-Gaillarde is surrounded by fertile lowlands. In 918, Limousin was enfeoffed to the duchy of Aquitaine, and much of its history is essentially that of AQUITAINE. Ravaged by Edward the Black Prince in the Hundred Years War, Limousin was reconquered for France (1370–74) by Bertrand du Guesclin. It remained a depressed area until Turgot became intendant (1761–64) and introduced notable reforms.

limpet, marine GASTROPOD mollusk with a simple flattened conical shell, found in cooler waters of the Atlantic and the Pacific oceans. Certain species creep over rocks, feeding on algae during high tides, but when the tide recedes they return instinctively to the same spot occupied previously, to await the return of high water. The muscular foot clings so powerfully that limpets are found in wave-swept areas where few other forms of life can survive. The keyhole limpet is named for its central opening, through which respiratory currents pass. Limpets range up to 4 in. (10 cm) in length, but most are smaller; there are several freshwater species. Limpets are classified in the phylum MOLLUSCA, class Gastropoda, order Archeogastropoda.

limpkin or **courlan** (ko͝or'lən), common terms for a long-legged nonmigratory marsh bird, considered the connecting evolutionary link between the crane and the rail. They have a cranelike skeletal structure, but their digestive system, as well as their nesting habits and behavior, is raillike. There is only one species, *Aramus quarauna,* which is divided into 5 subspecies, some found exclusively in South America and the others found from South Carolina and Florida to Argentina. Limpkins are large (28 in./70 cm) grayish-brown birds that feed on freshwater snails and mollusks. Their name derives from their limping flight, with legs dangling and wingbeats jerky; although weak and infrequent fliers they are good swimmers. Limpkins roost in trees and nest in marsh grass or low bushes. They lay four to eight eggs per clutch with both male and female incubating the young. They are noisy birds; their sad call gives them the name "crying bird." Because limpkins were considered good food birds, they were almost wiped out in Florida and Georgia. Today, they are protected and are regaining their former abundance. Limpkins are classified in the phylum CHORDATA, subphylum Vertebrata, class Aves, order Gruiformes, family Aramidae.

Limpopo (lĭmpō'pō), river, c.1,100 mi (1,770 km) long, rising in Transvaal prov., Republic of South Africa. It flows in a great arc, first north (forming part of the South Africa–Botswana border), then east (forming the South Africa–Rhodesia border), and finally southeast through Mozambique to the Indian Ocean. The upper Limpopo is also known as the Krokodil, or Crocodile. The river's main tributary, the Olifants, enters the Limpopo c.130 mi (210 km) from its mouth; below this point the Limpopo is permanently navigable. The lower Limpopo waters a fertile and heavily populated region.

Linacre or **Lynaker, Thomas** (both: lĭ'nəkər), 1460?–1524, English humanist and physician. He took the degree of doctor of medicine at the Univ. of Padua, returned to England c.1492, and became tutor to Prince Arthur and later physician to Henry VIII. He was interested in the humanistic revival, wrote a Latin grammar (c.1523) for Princess Mary (then a child), and included among his pupils Desiderius Erasmus and Sir Thomas More. Linacre translated many of Aristotle's and Galen's works into Latin and founded readerships in medicine at Oxford and Cambridge. He was the founder and first president of the Royal College of Physicians. See biography by Sir William Osler (1908).

Linares (lēnä'räs), city (1970 pop. 50,516), Jaén prov., S Spain, in Andalusia. The rich silver and lead mines nearby have brought prosperity to the city, which now has many metallurgical industries. Powder and dynamite are chief products.

Linchwan: see FU-CHOU, China.

Lincoln, Abraham, 1809–65, 16th President of the United States (1861–65). Born on Feb. 12, 1809, in a log cabin in backwoods Hardin co., Ky. (now Larue co.), he grew up on newly broken pioneer farms of the frontier. His father, Thomas Lincoln, was a migratory carpenter and farmer, nearly always poverty-stricken. Little is known of his mother, Nancy Hanks, who died in 1818, not long after the family had settled in the wilds of what is now Spencer co., Ind. Thomas Lincoln soon afterward married Sarah

Bush Johnston, a widow; she was a kind and affectionate stepmother to the boy. Abraham had almost no formal schooling—the scattered weeks of school attendance in Kentucky and Indiana amounted to less than a year; but he taught himself, reading and rereading a small stock of books. His first glimpse of the wider world came in a voyage downriver to New Orleans on a flatboat in 1828, but little is known of that journey. In 1830 the Lincolns moved once more, this time to Macon co., Ill. After another visit to New Orleans, the young Lincoln settled in 1837 in the village of New Salem, Ill., not far from Springfield. There he began by working in a store and managing a mill. By this time a tall (6 ft 4 in./190 cm), rawboned young man, he won much popularity among the inhabitants of the frontier town by his great strength and his flair for storytelling, but most of all by his strength of character. His sincerity and capability won respect that was strengthened by his ability to hold his own in the roughest society. He was chosen captain of a volunteer company gathered for the Black Hawk War (1832), but the company did not see battle. Returning to New Salem, Lincoln was a partner in a grocery store that failed, leaving him with a heavy burden of debt. He became a surveyor for a time, was village postmaster, and did various odd jobs, including rail splitting. All the while he sought to improve his education and studied law. The story of a brief love affair with Ann RUTLEDGE, which supposedly occurred at this time, is now discredited. In 1834, Lincoln was elected to the state legislature, in which he served four successive terms (until 1841) and achieved prominence as a Whig. In 1836 he obtained his license as an attorney, and the next year he moved to Springfield, where he became a law partner of John T. Stuart. Lincoln's practice steadily increased. That first partnership was succeeded by others, with Stephen T. Logan and then with William H. HERNDON, who was later to be Lincoln's biographer. Lincoln displayed great ability in law, a ready grasp of argument, and sincerity, color, and lucidity of speech. In 1842 he married Mary Todd (see LINCOLN, MARY TODD) after a troubled courtship. He continued his interest in politics and entered on the national scene by serving one term in Congress (1847–49). He remained obscure, however, and his attacks as a Whig on the motives behind the Mexican War (though he voted for war supplies) seemed unpatriotic to his constituents, so he lost popularity at home. Lincoln worked hard for the election of the Whig candidate, Zachary Taylor, in 1848, but when he was not rewarded with the office he desired—Commissioner of the General Land Office—he decided to retire from politics and return to the practice of law. The prairie lawyer emerged again into politics in 1854, when he was caught up in the rising quarrel over slavery. He stoutly opposed the policy of Stephen A. DOUGLAS and particularly the KANSAS-NEBRASKA ACT. In a speech at Springfield, repeated at Peoria, he attacked the compromises concerning the question of slavery in the territories and invoked the democratic ideals contained in the Declaration of Independence. In 1855 he sought to become a Senator but failed. He had already realized that his sentiments were leading him away from the Whigs and toward the new Republican party, and in 1856 he became a Republican. He quickly came to the fore in the party as a moderate opponent of slavery who could win both the abolitionists and the conservative Free-Staters, and at the Republican national convention of 1856 he was prominent as a possible vice presidential candidate. Two years later he was nominated by the Republican party to oppose Douglas in the Illinois senatorial race. Accepting the nomination (in a speech delivered at Springfield on June 16), Lincoln gave a ringing declaration in support of the Union: "A house divided against itself cannot stand." The campaign that followed was impressive. Lincoln challenged Douglas to a series of debates (seven were held), in which he delivered masterful addresses for the Union and for the democratic idea. He was not an abolitionist, but he regarded slavery as an injustice and an evil, and uncompromisingly opposed its extension. Though Douglas won the election, Lincoln had made his mark by the debates; he was now a potential presidential candidate. His first appearance in the East was in Feb., 1860, when he spoke at Cooper Union in New York City. He gained a large following in the antislavery states, but his nomination for President by the Republican convention in Chicago (May, 1860) was as much due to the opposition to William H. SEWARD, the leading contender, as to Lincoln's own appeal. He was nominated on the third ballot. In the election the Democratic party split; Lincoln was opposed by Douglas (Northern Democrat), John C. BRECKENRIDGE (Southern Democrat), and John BELL (Constitutional Unionist). Lincoln was elected with a minority of the popular vote. To the South, Lincoln's election was the signal for secession. All compromise plans, such as that proposed by John J. CRITTENDEN, failed, and by the time of Lincoln's inauguration seven states had seceded. The new President, determined to preserve the Union at all costs, condemned secession but promised that he would not initiate the use of force. After a slight delay, however, he did order the provisioning of FORT SUMTER, and the South chose to regard this as an act of war. On April 12, 1861, Fort Sumter was fired upon, and the CIVIL WAR began. Although various criticisms have been leveled against him, it is generally agreed that Lincoln attacked the vast problems of the war with vigor and surpassing skill. He immediately issued a summons to the militia (an act that precipitated the secession of four more Southern states), ordered a blockade of Confederate ports, and suspended habeas corpus. The last action provoked much criticism, but Lincoln adhered to it, ignoring the Supreme Court ruling against him in the Merryman Case (see MERRYMAN, EX PARTE). In the course of the war, Lincoln further extended his executive powers, but in general he exercised those powers with restraint. He was beset not only by the difficulties of the war, but by opposition from men on his own side. His cabinet was rent by internal jealousies and hatred; radical abolitionists condemned him as too mild; conservatives were gloomy over the prospects of success in the war. In the midst of all this strife, Lincoln continued his course, sometimes almost alone, with wisdom and patience. The progress of battle went against the North at first. Lincoln himself made some bad military decisions (e.g., in ordering the direct advance into Virginia that resulted in the Union defeat at the first battle of Bull Run), and he ran through a succession of commanders in chief before he found Ulysses S. GRANT. In the early stages of the war Lincoln revoked orders by John C. Frémont and David Hunter freeing the slaves in their military departments. However, the Union victory at Antietam gave him a position of strength from which to issue his own EMANCIPATION PROCLAMATION. The restoration and preservation of the Union was still the main tenet of Lincoln's war aims. The sorrows of war and its rigorous necessity afflicted him; he expressed both in one of the noblest public speeches ever made, the GETTYSBURG ADDRESS, made at the dedication of the soldiers' cemetery at Gettysburg in 1863. For a time Lincoln was threatened by the desertion of the Republican leaders as well as by a strong opposition party in the presidential election that loomed ahead in the dark days of 1864; but a turn for the better took place before the election, a turn brought about to some extent by a change of military fortune after Grant became commander and particularly after William T. Sherman took Atlanta. Lincoln was reelected over George B. MCCLELLAN by a great majority. His second inaugural address, delivered when the war was drawing to its close, was a plea for the new country that would arise from the ashes of the South. His own view was one of forgiveness, as shown in his memorable phrase "With malice toward none; with charity for all." He lived to see the end of the war, but he was to have no chance to implement his plans for RECONSTRUCTION. On the night of April 14, 1865, when attending a performance at Ford's Theater, he was shot by the actor John Wilkes BOOTH. The next morning Lincoln died. His death was an occasion for grief even among those who had been his opponents, and many considered him a martyr. As time passed he became more and more the object of adulation; a full-blown "Lincoln legend" appeared. Yet, even if his faults and mistakes are acknowledged, he stands out as a statesman of noble vision, great humanity, and remarkable political skill. It is not surprising that the Illinois "rail-splitter" is regarded as a foremost symbol of American democracy. Paintings, sculptures, and architectural works memorializing Lincoln are legion; the most famous shrines are his home and tomb in SPRINGFIELD, Ill., and the LINCOLN MEMORIAL in Washington, D.C. He has perhaps been more written about than any other American figure; not only innumerable biographies but novels, poems, plays, and many essays have been devoted to him. Lincoln's collected works have been edited by R. P. Basler (9 vol., 1953). See also D. C. Mearns, ed., *The Lincoln Papers* (1948). The standard bibliography is Jay Monaghan, *Lincoln Bibliography, 1839–1939* (2 vol., 1943–45); others are P. M. Angle, *A Shelf of Lincoln Books* (1946); Victor Searcher, *Lincoln Today* (1969). One of the most important early biographies was W. H. Herndon and J. W. Weid, *Herndon's Life of Lincoln* (3 vol., 1889; ed. by P. M. Angle, 1930, repr. 1965). J. G. Nicolay and John Hay wrote the monumental *Abraham Lincoln: A History* (10 vol., 1890, abbr. ed. 1966). Probably the most popular biography is Carl Sandburg, *Abraham Lincoln: The Prairie Years* (1926), and *Abraham Lincoln: The War Years* (4 vol., 1939); a one-volume condensation was published in 1954, repr. 1970. See also *The Lincoln Reader* (1947, repr. 1964, ed. by P. M. Angle) and biographies by A. J. Beveridge (2 vol., 1928, repr. 1971), B. P. Thomas (1952, repr. 1968), Stefan Lorant (1954, repr. 1961), and R. H. Luthin (1960). Almost the only work portraying Lincoln in a completely unfavorable light is Edgar Lee Masters, *Lincoln the Man* (1931). Preeminent among the special studies on Lincoln are those of James G. RANDALL. See also T. H. Williams, *Lincoln and the Radicals* (1941, repr. 1965); H. J. Carman and R. H. Luthin, *Lincoln and the Patronage* (1943, repr. 1964); F. H. Meserve and Carl Sandburg, *The Photographs of Abraham Lincoln* (1944); Jay Monaghan, *Diplomat in Carpet Slippers* (1945, repr. 1962); B. J. Hendrick, *Lincoln's War Cabinet* (1946, repr. 1965); B. P. Thomas, *Portrait for Posterity: Lincoln and His Biographers* (1947); W. B. Hesseltine, *Lincoln and the War Governors* (1948); *The Living Lincoln* (ed. by P. M. Angle and E. S. Miers, 1955); David Donald, *Lincoln Reconsidered* (2d ed. 1961, repr. 1966); D. E. Fehrenbacher, *Prelude to Greatness* (1962, repr. 1970) and *The Leadership of Abraham Lincoln* (1970).

Lincoln, Benjamin, 1733–1810, American Revolutionary soldier, b. Hingham, Mass. He served under Horatio Gates in the Saratoga campaign before becoming (1778) commander in the South. In 1779 he failed, in conjunction with a French fleet under Admiral d'Estaing, to take Savannah and was beaten back to Charleston, where he surrendered (1780) to an overwhelming force commanded by Sir Henry Clinton. Lincoln was exchanged in time for the Yorktown campaign and received General Cornwallis's sword at the surrender. From 1781 to 1783 he was Secretary of War. In 1787 he commanded the Massachusetts state militia that helped suppress SHAYS'S REBELLION.

Lincoln, John de la Pole, earl of: see POLE, family.

Lincoln, Levi, 1749–1820, American public official, b. Hingham, Mass., grad. Harvard, 1772. A lawyer, he held various local offices during the American Revolution and later became a Jeffersonian political leader. He served (1801–4) as U.S. Attorney General. He was subsequently lieutenant governor and governor of Massachusetts.

Lincoln, Mary Todd, 1818–82, wife of Abraham Lincoln, b. Lexington, Ky. Of a good Kentucky family, she was living with her sister, daughter-in-law of Gov. Ninian Edwards of Illinois, in Springfield, Ill., when she met and married (1842) Lincoln. Although they were very different in temperament and upbringing, their marriage was an affectionate one. The harsh portrayal of Mary Lincoln by William H. HERNDON is certainly exaggerated. Of the four sons she bore (Robert Todd, Edward Baker, William Wallace, and Thomas or "Tad"), only Robert Todd lived to manhood. The death of Willie in 1862 was a great sorrow to both Abraham and Mary Lincoln, and Tad's death in 1871 seems to have unsettled her mind (already affected by seeing her husband murdered at her side). She was adjudged insane (1875), but the decision was reversed a year later. See her letters, ed. by J. G. Turner and L. L. Turner (1972); biographies by R. P. Randall (1953), Carl Sandburg (new ed. 1972), and Ishbel Ross (1973).

Lincoln, Robert Todd, 1843–1926, American lawyer and public official, b. Springfield, Ill., son of Abraham Lincoln and Mary Todd Lincoln. He served on General Grant's staff and after the Civil War studied law. An able corporation lawyer, he chiefly served railroad interests and was (1897–1911) president of the Pullman Company. Of retiring disposition, he never ran for office but was Secretary of War (1881–85) and minister to Great Britain (1889–93). He denied access to those papers of his father that he owned to all except the authorized biographers, John G. Nicolay and John Hay, and left them to the Library of Congress on the condition that they be sealed until 21 years after his death. In 1947 the papers were made public.

Lincoln, county: see LINCOLNSHIRE.

Lincoln, county borough (1971 pop. 74,207), county town of Lincolnshire, E England, in the Parts of Kesteven, on the Witham river. Located at the junction of the Roman Fosse Way and Ermine Street, it is a center of road and rail transportation. Manufactures include heavy machinery, light-metal products, automobile parts, radios, and food products. Lincoln was an ancient British settlement, the Roman Lindum or Lindum Colonia, and was one of the Five Boroughs of the Danes. Lincoln Castle, begun by William I in 1068, was contested in the civil war between Matilda and Stephen (12th cent.). The town was burned in the 12th cent.; three parliaments were held in Lincoln in the 14th cent. Parliamentarians captured it in 1644. For centuries horse races and fairs have been held in Lincoln. The great Lincoln Cathedral, first built from 1075 to 1501, has a central tower 271 ft (83 m) high, containing the famous bell "Great Tom of Lincoln." One of the few extant copies of the Magna Carta is in the cathedral. In Lincoln are teacher-training, theological, art, and technical colleges.

Lincoln. 1 City (1970 pop. 17,582), seat of Logan co., central Ill., in a farm area; inc. 1865. It is a shipping and industrial center. The city was platted and promoted (1853) with the aid of Abraham Lincoln and named for him when he was still an unknown country lawyer. Lincoln practiced law there from 1847 to 1859, and buildings and places associated with him have been preserved or reconstructed. A junior college and a state school for the mentally retarded are in the city. 2 City (1970 pop. 149,518), state capital, and seat of Lancaster co., SE Nebr.; inc. 1869. It is the railroad, trade, and industrial center for a large grain and livestock area. Cattle are slaughtered and processed; railroad cars are built and repaired; and rubber products, candy, sports and industrial vehicles, and circuit breakers are among the manufactures. Many insurance companies have their home offices there. Founded in 1864 as Lancaster, the city was chosen as the site of the capital in 1867 and renamed. It is the seat of the Univ. of Nebraska, Union College, Nebraska Wesleyan Univ., and an adult education center. It has a planetarium, an art gallery and sculpture garden, and several parks. Many state institutions are there—the historical society and its museum, the penitentiary, a mental hospital, an orthopedic hospital, and the state fair. A veterans hospital is in the city. The state capitol, designed by B. G. Goodhue, with sculptures by Lee Lawrie, was completed in 1934. W. J. Bryan lived in Lincoln from 1887 to 1916, and his home is preserved. 3 Uninc. town (1970 pop. 11,215), Richland co., N central Ohio. It is mainly residential. 4 Town (1970 pop. 16,182), Providence co., NE R.I.; set off from Smithfield and inc. 1871. Once a textile town, its manufactures now include wire, tubing, metal parts, and thread. Limestone has been quarried there since colonial times. Many pre-Revolutionary houses and a state park are in the town.

Lincoln Boyhood National Memorial: see NATIONAL PARKS AND MONUMENTS (table).

Lincoln Center for the Performing Arts, in central Manhattan, New York City, between 62d and 66th streets west of Broadway. Lincoln Center is a complex of many buildings, including the Metropolitan Opera, Avery Fisher (formerly Philharmonic) Hall, New York State Theater, Juilliard School (including Alice Tully Hall for recitals and a chamber music hall), Vivian Beaumont Theater, Library-Museum of the Performing Arts, Guggenheim Bandshell in Damrosch Park, and several Fordham University buildings. The elegant fountain in the central plaza is controlled by a computer program. A nonprofit organization with municipal support, Lincoln Center is dedicated to the encouragement of new artists and to the presentation of internationally acclaimed performers. The project was constructed between 1959 and 1972. Among those selected to design the buildings were the architects W. K. Harrison, Eero Saarinen, Philip Johnson, and Max Abramowitz, and the stage designer Jo Mielziner.

Lincoln Home National Historic Site: see NATIONAL PARKS AND MONUMENTS (table).

Lincoln Memorial, monument, 164 acres (66 hectares), in Potomac Park, Washington, D.C.; built 1914–17. The building, designed by Henry Bacon and styled after a Greek temple, has 36 Doric columns representing the states of the Union at the time of Lincoln's death. Inside the building is a heroic statue of Lincoln by Daniel Chester French and two murals by Jules Guerin.

Lincoln Park, city (1970 pop. 52,984), Wayne co., SE Mich., a suburb adjacent to Detroit, on the Detroit River; inc. 1921. It is a residential community in a highly industrialized area.

Lincoln sheep, very large bodied, white-faced, hornless breed having coarse wool, developed in England. It has made considerable contributions to the American sheep industry in the parentage of other breeds and is widely raised in several countries of the Southern Hemisphere.

Lincolnshire (lĭng'kənshĭr), county (1971 pop. 808,384), 2,662 sq mi (6,895 sq km), E England, on the Humber estuary, the North Sea, and The Wash. It is divided into three administrative counties: the Parts of Holland, in the southeast, with its administrative seat at BOSTON; the Parts of Kesteven (kĕstē'vən), in the southwest, with its administrative seat at SLEAFORD; and the Parts of Lindsey, with its administrative seat at LINCOLN. The region is generally low and flat, with extensive marshes along the coast. It is crossed by many dikes and canals, some of which, notably the Foss Dyke, date back to Roman times. Lincolnshire is an important agricultural area. Potatoes, vegetables, and sugar beets are the chief crops. GRIMSBY is a great fishing port, and there are also engineering, steelmaking, and other industries in the county. Lincoln and Grimsby are the largest cities. In Anglo-Saxon times, Lincolnshire was variously under the control of Mercia and Northumberland. There are a large number of medieval churches and ecclesiastical remains. In 1974, Lincolnshire was reorganized as a nonmetropolitan county; the parts of Holland, Kesteven, and Lindsey were abolished as administrative counties, and a considerable area in the north was attached to the new nonmetropolitan county of Humberside.

Lincoln's Inn: see INNS OF COURT.

Lincoln University. 1 At Jefferson City, Mo.; coeducational; land-grant and state supported; founded 1866 as Lincoln Institute. The school was established for the education of freed slaves by members of the 62d and 65th U.S. Colored Regiments. Its present name was adopted in 1921. The university became open to all qualified students in 1954. 2 At Lincoln University, Pa.; primarily for men; chartered 1854 as the Ashmun Institute. Its present name was adopted in 1866. The school is the oldest college in the United States having as its original purpose the higher education of black students. Since 1866, however, it has been open to all qualified students.

Lincolnwood, village (1970 pop. 12,929), Cook co., NE Ill., a suburb of Chicago; settled in the 1840s, inc. 1911. It is chiefly residential.

lincomycin (lĭng"kōmī'sĭn), ANTIBIOTIC isolated from bacteria of the genus *Streptomyces.* Similar in activity to ERYTHROMYCIN, it is effective against most gram-positive organisms including staphylococci, some streptococci, and anaerobic bacteria of the genus *Clostridium* (see GRAM'S STAIN). Diarrhea and nausea are common side effects of the drug.

Lind, James, 1716–94, English naval surgeon. Considered the founder of naval hygiene in England, Lind observed on a ten-week cruise (1746) that 80 seamen of 350 came down with SCURVY. In his *Treatise of the Scurvy* (1753) he emphasized the preventive effect of ingesting fresh fruit or lemon juice, thus reviving a practice of Dutch and English seafarers of the 16th cent. However, it was not until 1795, and through the efforts of Sir Gilbert Blane (1749–1834), that lemon juice was officially ordered as part of naval rations by the Admiralty. Lind also improved sanitary conditions aboard ships of the line, advocated the distilling of seawater for drinking purposes on long journeys, and, through his writings on tropical diseases, helped prevent much unnecessary loss of life during British campaigns.

Lind, Jenny, 1820–87, Swedish soprano. She made her debut in 1838 as Agathe in Weber's *Der Freischütz.* She studied in Paris and sang in Germany, England, and Sweden. In 1849 she abandoned opera for concert and oratorio until 1870. Under the management of P. T. Barnum she toured (1850–52) the United States with great success. After her marriage to Otto Goldschmidt in 1852 she lived in Dresden and in London, where she taught at the Royal College of Music. Called "the Swedish nightingale," she was one of the greatest coloratura sopranos of her time, possessing a voice of remarkable range and quality.

lindane: see INSECTICIDE.

Lindau (lĭn'dou), town (1970 pop. 25,235), Bavaria, S West Germany, on an island in the Lake of Constance (Ger. *Bodensee*). Connected by bridges with the mainland, it is a picturesque summer resort and tourist center. Lindau was an imperial city from 1275 to 1803 and passed to Bavaria in 1805.

Lindbergh, Charles Augustus, 1859–1924, American Congressman (1907–17), b. Sweden. He was brought to Minnesota as an infant, and later practiced law in Little Falls, Minn. As a Republican member of the U.S. House of Representatives, he consistently attacked the methods of large industrial trusts and sponsored various reforms but incurred vilification by his denunciation of war propaganda and war profiteering. His outspoken book *Why Is Your Country at War?* (1917, repr. 1934) was suppressed and contributed to his defeat (1918) as candidate of the Nonpartisan League for the post of governor of Minnesota. He was the father of Charles Augustus Lindbergh, the aviator. See biography by B. L. Larson (1973).

Lindbergh, Charles Augustus, 1902–74, American aviator who made the first solo, nonstop transatlantic flight, b. Detroit; son of Charles A. Lindbergh (1859–1924). He left the Univ. of Wisconsin (1922) to study flying. After service as a flying cadet, he was commissioned (1925) in the air force reserve and later became an airmail pilot. On May 21, 1927, Lindbergh astounded the world by landing in Paris after a solo flight from New York across the Atlantic in *The Spirit of St. Louis.* Upon his return to the United States he received an unprecedented welcome, was promoted to colonel, and made a nationwide tour to foster popular interest in aviation. Lindbergh married (1929) Anne Morrow, the daughter of the U.S. ambassador to Mexico Dwight W. MORROW, and with her made several long flights. After the kidnapping and death of their son (see HAUPTMANN, BRUNO RICHARD) in 1932, the Lindberghs moved (1935) to England. In 1936, Lindbergh collaborated with Alexis CARREL on the invention of a perfusion pump called an artificial heart. After inspecting (1938) European air forces, Lindbergh became convinced of German air superiority; he favored a U.S. policy of isolationism with respect to the political and military struggle threatening in Europe. He returned (1939) to the United States and made antiwar speeches for the America First Committee. When these speeches were branded pro-Nazi, he resigned his reserve commission and quit the National Advisory Committee for Aeronautics. Upon U.S. entry into the war Lindbergh offered his services to the air force; he subsequently flew combat missions in the Pacific. In his later years he emerged as a spokesman on conservation issues. See his *We* (1927), *Of Flight and Life* (1948), *The Spirit of St. Louis* (1953; Pulitzer Prize), and *The Wartime Journals* (1970); biography by W. S. Ross (1968). His wife, **Anne Spencer Morrow Lindbergh,** 1906–, b. Englewood, N.J., grad. Smith College, 1927, is a writer. Her works include *North to the Orient* (1935) and *Listen! the Wind* (1938), both accounts of flights she made with her husband; *The Wave of the Future* (1940), a tract advocating isolationism; *Gift from the Sea* (1955), a poetic, highly personal study of the problems of women; *The Unicorn and Other Poems* (1956); a novel, *Dearly Beloved* (1962); and a volume of essays, *Earth Shine* (1969). See her diaries and letters, *Bring Me a Unicorn* (1972), *Hour of Gold, Hour of Lead* (1973), and *Locked Rooms and Open Doors* (1974).

Lindemann, Frederick Alexander (Viscount Cherwell), 1886–1957, British physicist and government official. He studied with W. H. Nernst and developed with him the Nernst-Lindemann theory of specific heat. His achievements also include the Lindemann melting-point formula and the Lindemann electrometer. During World War I he discovered how to recover an aircraft from an uncontrolled spin. Lindemann was scientific adviser to Winston Churchill during World War II, serving also as paymaster general from 1942 to 1945 and again from 1951 to 1953. He developed Clarendon Laboratory, Oxford, into a major research facility, and he was an important influence in the founding of the United Kingdom Atomic Energy Authority. See biographies by R. F. Harrod (1959) and Frederick Winston, 2d earl of Birkenhead (1961).

Linden, city (1970 pop. 41,409), Union co., NE N.J., in the New York metropolitan area; inc. 1925. During the first half of the 20th cent., Linden changed from an agricultural district to a city of diverse manufactures, chief among which are chemicals, petroleum products, and automobiles. The city, named for the linden trees in the vicinity, was part of Elizabeth until 1861.

linden, common name for the Tiliaceae, a family of chiefly woody shrubs and trees. Most genera are tropical, but the widespread genus *Tilia*, commonly called linden, or lime tree, in Europe and Asia and basswood in North America, is found throughout the north temperate zone. These deciduous trees are valued for ornament and shade. Their light, strong lumber, often called basswood, or whitewood, is variously employed, e.g., for woodenware, cheap furniture, excelsior, and for beehives and honeycomb frames. The nectar of the flowers is a commercial source of an excellent honey; the blossoms themselves are used for tea. Fiber was formerly made from the tough inner bark, or bast (hence the name basswood), which is still used for caning and wickerwork. The most important member of the family economically is the tropical genus *Corchorus,* from which JUTE is obtained. The linden family is classified in the division MAGNOLIOPHYTA, class Magnoliopsida, order Malvales.

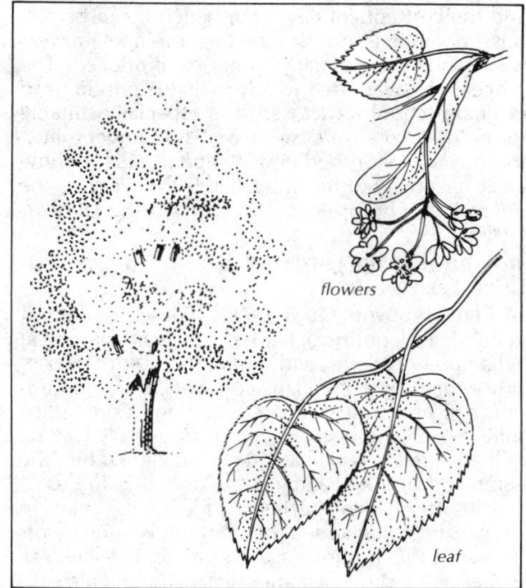

Linden, Tilia americana

Lindenhurst, village (1970 pop. 28,338), Suffolk co., SE N.Y., on S Long Island; inc. 1923. It is a residential area with some manufacturing.

Lindenwold, borough (1970 pop. 12,199), Camden co., SW N.J.; settled 1742, inc. 1929.

Lindesnes (lĭn'dəsnĕs) or **the Naze** (nāz), cape, in Vest-Agder co., southernmost point of the Norwegian mainland. An old lighthouse (1655) is there.

Lindisfarne, England: see HOLY ISLAND.

Lindley, John, 1799–1865, English botanist and horticulturist. He organized the first flower shows in England and was influential in preserving the Royal Gardens at Kew. In 1829 he was appointed the first professor of botany at the Univ. of London (later University College). Lindley wrote the botanical articles for the *Penny Cyclopaedia* and a major portion of those in Loudon's *Encyclopaedia of Plants.* He also wrote *The Fossil Flora of Great Britain* (with William Hutton, 1831–37), *The Theory of Horticulture* (1840), and *The Vegetable Kingdom* (1846).

Lindsay or **Lyndsay, Sir David** (both: lĭn'zē), c.1490–c.1555, Scottish poet. He was a courtier and diplomat by profession. As a writer he was a harsh satirist and moralist who directed most of his invective against the Roman Catholic Church. He never formally left the church, but his exposure of its abuses gives him a place second only to that of John Knox in bringing about the Scottish Reformation. Lindsay's verse is sometimes rich and elevated, sometimes coarsely realistic; his literary technique is frequently made secondary to satirical or didactic themes. In his *Testament and Complaynt of Our Soverane Lordis Papyngo* (1538) the king's parrot censures certain birds of prey—the clergy of the feathered world—for their hypocrisy and avarice. His long morality play, *Ane Pleasant Satyre of the Thrie Estaitis* (produced 1540), contains attacks on political abuses. Among Lindsay's other notable works are *The Dreme, The Historie and Testament of Squyer Meldrum,* and *The Monarchie.* See edition of his works by Douglas Hamer for the Scottish Texts Society (4 vol., 1931–36, repr. 1972).

Lindsay, John Vliet, 1921–, American politician, mayor of New York City (1966–74), b. New York City. He practiced law and then served (1955–57) as executive assistant to Attorney General Herbert Brownell. A liberal Republican, he was elected to the U.S. House of Representatives in 1958 and was reelected in 1960, 1962, and 1964. In 1965 he successfully ran for mayor of New York City on a Republican-Liberal ticket. An innovative and controversial mayor, he lost the Republican primary in June, 1969, to a conservative, "law-and-order" candidate but was reelected mayor as the candidate of the Liberal and Independent parties. In Aug., 1971, he announced his switch from the Republican to the Democratic party. In 1972, Lindsay entered several Democratic presidential primaries, but he withdrew from the running after finishing sixth in the Wisconsin primary. He did not run for reelection as mayor in 1973.

Lindsay, Norman, 1879–1969, Australian cartoonist. Born into an eminent family of Australian artists, Lindsay became chief cartoonist of the Sydney *Bulletin* in 1901. His vigorous illustrations include watercolors, lithographs, and etchings. His drawings have been collected in several volumes.

Lindsay, Vachel (Nicholas Vachel Lindsay) (vā'chəl), 1879–1931, American poet, b. Springfield, Ill., studied at Hiram College, the Art Institute of Chicago, and the New York School of Art. Lindsay made tours selling his poems and drawings, living as a modern-day troubadour. He was particularly effective when reading his own poems. His poetry at its best is virile and strong. It has a fine spoken music, often enhanced by jazz rhythms. Volumes of his poetry include *General William Booth Enters into Heaven* (1913), *The Congo* (1914), *The Chinese Nightingale* (1917), and *Collected Poems* (1938). Lindsay was plagued by poverty and illness in his later years, and the quality of his poetry declined. See his autobiographical *Adventures While Preaching the Gospel of Beauty* (1914) and *A Handy Guide for Beggars* (1916); his letters (ed. by A. J. Armstrong, 1940); biography by his friend E. L. Masters (1935, repr. 1969); studies by J. T. Flanagan, comp. (1970), and Ann Massa (1970).

Lindsay, town (1971 pop. 12,746), SE Ont., Canada, on the Scugog River, NE of Toronto. It is an industrial town, with woolen, flour, and lumber mills, in a scenic lake district.

Lindsey, Benjamin Barr (Ben Lindsey), 1869–1943, American judge and reformer, b. Jackson, Tenn. As judge of the juvenile court of Denver from 1900 to 1927, he founded the American juvenile court system, for which he won world recognition. He championed "companionate marriage" in a book (written with Wainwright Evans) that appeared in 1927. Other works include *The Beast* (with Harvey J. O'Higgins, 1910) and an autobiography, *The Dangerous Life* (with Rube Borough, 1931). See biography by C. E. Larsen (1972).

Lindsey, Parts of: see LINCOLNSHIRE.

Línea, La (lä lē'näā), city (1970 pop. 52,127), Cádiz prov., S Spain, on the Strait of Gibraltar. Situated on the Spanish border north of the neutral zone that separates the city from the British colony, La Línea is fortified and holds strategic importance. La Línea supplies the British colony with fresh fruits and vegetables, and many of its citizens are employed by the British.

linear accelerator: see PARTICLE ACCELERATOR.

linear programming, solution of a mathematical problem concerning maximum and minimum values of a first-degree (linear) algebraic expression, with variables subject to certain stated conditions (restraints). For example, the problem might be to find the maximum value of the expression $x+y$ subject to the restraints $x\geq0$, $y\geq0$, $2x+y\geq12$, $5x+8y\geq74$, and $x+6y\geq24$. The solution was set forth by the Russian mathematician L. V. Kantorovich in 1939 and was developed independently by the American George B. Dantzig, whose first work on the subject appeared in 1947. Linear programming is particularly important in military and industrial planning.

Line Islands or **Equatorial Islands,** coral group, 43 sq mi (111 sq km), central and S Pacific. Once valuable for their guano deposits, the islands now have coconut groves, airfields, and meteorological stations. The group includes FANNING ISLAND, CHRISTMAS ISLAND, and WASHINGTON ISLAND (which belong to the British GILBERT AND ELLICE ISLANDS colony) and KINGMAN REEF, PALMYRA, and JARVIS ISLAND (which belong to the United States). Both countries claim the rest of the islands: Malden, Starbuck, Caroline, Vostok, and Flint. The islands were uninhabited when discovered by American sailors in 1798, although a few show evidence of ancient Polynesian culture. The British government has conducted hydrogen bomb tests on Malden.

linen, fabric or yarn made from the fiber of FLAX, probably the first vegetable fiber known to man. Linens more than 3,500 years old have been recovered from Egyptian tombs. Phoenician traders marketed linen in Mediterranean ports. Worn by Egyptian, Greek, and Jewish priests as a symbol of purity, it also typified luxury as in the phrase "purple and fine linen." Flax was cultivated by the Romans and introduced by them into N Europe. The production of linen was encouraged by Charlemagne, and linen became the principal European textile of the Middle Ages. Flanders has been renowned from the 11th cent. for its creamy flax and fine thread. French Huguenots excelled in working flax and carried the art abroad, notably to Ireland, where Louis Crommelin established (c.1699) a manufactory at Lisburn, near Belfast. Ireland is still the largest producer of fine linen, with Belgium, Japan, and the Soviet Union producing somewhat lesser amounts. The first flax-spinning mill was opened in England in 1787, but only in 1812 was linen successfully woven with power looms. The industry suffered in relation to cotton because many textile inventions were not applicable to linen, the inelasticity of the fiber causing it to break readily under tension. Although linen exceeds cotton in coolness, luster, strength, and length of fiber, the expense of production limits its use. After the flax fiber is removed from the stems, it is delivered to the mills, where it is hackled to separate and straighten the fibers, overlapped on a spreadboard to form a continuous ribbon, drawn out through rollers, then wound from the roving frame on bobbins in a loosely twisted thread. For fine goods the thread is usually spun wet. Linen may be bleached in the yarn or in the piece. It is woven into fabrics ranging from heavy canvas to sheer handkerchief linen.

line spectrum: see SPECTRUM.

ling: see COD.

Lingelbach, Johannes (yōhä'nəs lĭng'əlbäkh"), 1622–74, Dutch genre and landscape painter, b. Frankfurt am Main. He first went to Amsterdam in 1637 and settled there about 16 years later after some years of study in Rome. Influenced by van Laer, he painted Italian landscapes, seaports, military subjects, and genre, with cool colors, good draftsmanship, and careful execution. He often inserted little figures in landscapes for Wynants, Hobbema, and other masters. *Battle Scene* and *Dance of the Peasants* are in the Metropolitan Museum.

Lingga Archipelago: see RIAU ARCHIPELAGO.

Linggajati: see TJIREBON, Indonesia.

lingua franca (lĭng'gwə frăng'kə), an auxiliary language, generally of a hybrid and partially developed nature, that is employed over an extensive area by people speaking different and mutually unintelligible tongues in order to communicate with one another. Such a language frequently is used primarily for commercial purposes. Examples are the several varieties of the hybrid pidgin English (see PIDGIN); Swahili, a native language of E Africa (see SWAHILI LANGUAGE); Chinook jargon, a lingua franca formerly used in the American Northwest that was a mixture of Chinook, other American Indian languages, English, and French; and a variety of Malay (called *bazaar Malay*), which served as a compromise language in the area of British Malaya, the Dutch East Indies, and neighboring regions (see MALAYO-POLYNESIAN LANGUAGES). The original lingua franca was a tongue actually called Lingua Franca (or Sabir) that was employed for commerce in the Mediterranean area during the Middle Ages. Now extinct, it had Italian as its base with an admixture of words from Spanish, French, Greek, and Arabic. The designation "Lingua Franca" [language of the Franks] came about because the Arabs in the medieval period used to refer to Western Europeans in general as "Franks." Occasionally the term *lingua franca* is applied to a fully established formal language; thus formerly it was said that French was the lingua franca of diplomacy. See Henry R. Kahane et al., *The Lingua Franca in the Levant* (1958); Robert A. Hall, Jr., *Pidgin and Creole Languages* (1966); Bernd Heine, *Status and Use of African Lingua Francas* (1970).

Linguetta: see CERAUNIAN MOUNTAINS, Albania.

linguistics, scientific study of LANGUAGE, covering the structure (GRAMMAR, PHONETICS, morphology) as well as the history of the relations of languages to each other and the cultural place of language in human behavior. Before the 19th cent., language was studied mainly as a field of philosophy. Among the philosophers interested in language was Wilhelm von HUMBOLDT, who considered language an activity that arises spontaneously from the human spirit; thus, he felt, languages are different just as the characteristics of individuals are different. In 1786 the great English scholar Sir William JONES suggested the possible affinity of Sanskrit and Persian with Greek and Latin, for the first time bringing to light genetic relations between languages. With Jones's revelation the school of comparative historical linguistics began. Through the comparison of language structures, such 19th-century European linguists as Jakob GRIMM, Rasmus RASK, Karl BRUGMANN, and Antoine Meillet, as well as the American William Dwight WHITNEY, did much to establish the existence of the Indo-European family of languages. In the 20th cent. the structural or descriptive linguistics school emerged. It dealt with languages at particular points in time (synchronic) rather than throughout their historical development (diachronic). The father of modern structural linguistics was Ferdinand de Saussure, who believed in language as a systematic structure serving as a link between thought and sound; he thought of language sounds as a series of linguistic signs that are purely arbitrary, as can be seen in the linguistic signs or words for *horse:* German *Pferd,* Turkish *at,* French *cheval,* and Russian *loshad'.* In America, structuralism was continued through the efforts of Franz BOAS and Edward SAPIR, who worked primarily with American Indian languages, and Leonard BLOOMFIELD, whose methodology required that nonlinguistic criteria must not enter a structural description. Rigorous procedures for determining language structure were developed by Kenneth Pike, Bernard Bloch, Charles Hockett, and others. One of the most recent schools of linguistic thought is transformational-generative grammar, which has received wide acclaim through the works of Noam CHOMSKY. Chomsky believes in a syntactic base of language (called deep structure), which consists of a series of phrase-structure rewrite rules, i.e., a series of (possibly universal) rules that generates the underlying phrase-structure of a sentence, and a series of rules (called transformations) that act upon the phrase-structure to form more complex sentences. The end result of a transformational-generative grammar is a surface structure that, after the addition of words and pronunciations, is identical to an actual sentence of a language. All languages have the same deep structure, but they differ from each other in surface structure because of the application of different rules for transformations, pronunciation, and word insertion. Another important distinction made in transformational-generative grammar is the difference between language competence (the subconscious control of a linguistic system) and language performance (the speaker's actual use of language). Although the first work done in transformational-generative grammar was syntactic, later studies have applied the theory to the phonological and semantic components of language. In contrast to theoretical schools of linguistics, workers in applied linguistics in the latter part of the 20th cent. have produced much work in the areas of foreign-language teaching and of bilingual education in the public schools (in the United States this has primarily involved Spanish and, in the Southwest, some American Indian languages in addition to English). See also Henry A. Gleason, *Introduction to Descriptive Linguistics* (rev. ed. 1961); Ferdinand de Saussure, *Course in General Linguistics* (tr. 1966); John Lyons, *Introduction to Theoretical Linguistics* (1968); Noam Chomsky, *Aspects of the Theory of Syntax* (1969); John T. Waterman, *Perspectives in Linguistics* (2d ed. 1971).

Lin-hsia or **Linsia** (both: lĭn-shēä), city, SE Kansu prov., China. The city is a gateway to the Tibetan areas near the Tsinghai and Szechwan borders. It trades in hides and wool.

Liniers, Jacques de, Span. *Santiago de Liniers y de Bremond* (säntēä'gō thä lēnēärs' ē thä brāmōnd'), 1753–1810, French officer in Spanish service, viceroy of Río de la Plata. After a military and naval career in Europe, he was transferred to the Río de la Plata (1788) as a Spanish naval officer. In 1806 he recaptured Buenos Aires from British forces under William Carr BERESFORD. The viceroy had fled, and Liniers was named commander in chief and lieutenant to the viceroy. When a second British invasion occurred the following year, Liniers called a junta of war, including Manuel BELGRANO, which deposed the viceroy (Feb. 10, 1807). Despite the rout of the creole army outside Buenos Aires, the hastily organized defenses of the city proved effective (July 5, 1807); the British general, John Whitelocke, surrendered. In May, 1808, the appointment of Liniers as viceroy became known; he served until Aug., 1809, though there were attempts by his political enemies to oust him. After retirement, he became involved in a counterrevolutionary plot and was executed.

liniment, liquid preparation rubbed on skin, used to relieve muscular aches and pains. It contains some substance that when rubbed over the affected part causes mild irritation and often brings more blood to the painful part. Most liniments contain camphor, oil of turpentine, oil of wintergreen, or ethyl alcohol. See SALICYLATE.

Linköping (lĭn'chö"pĭng), city (1970 pop. 91,112), capital of Östergötland co., S Sweden, near Lake Roxen. It is a commercial, industrial, and transportation center. Manufactures include motor vehicles, railroad cars, airplanes, electrical appliances, and processed food. An episcopal see since 1120, Linköping flourished in the Middle Ages as an intellectual and religious center. In 1598, SIGISMUND III, king of Sweden, was defeated by the future CHARLES IX at nearby Stangebrô and soon thereafter was formally deposed. Linköping has a splendid Romanesque cathedral (12th cent.; rebuilt 1230s), which has a 344-ft (105-m) spire. The city also has a 13th-century castle (restored 1931–32), a large library, and a university.

Linlithgow, Victor Alexander John Hope, 2d marquess of (lĭnlĭth'gō), 1887–1952, British statesman, viceroy of India. Linlithgow was civil lord of the admiralty (1922–24) and held numerous other public positions. As chairman of the committee on Indian constitutional reform (1933), he helped formulate the Government of India Act of 1935, and in 1936 he was appointed viceroy of India. In the first elections held (1937) under the act, the Indian National Congress party won in 7 of the 11 provinces, and Linlithgow persuaded its leaders to take office in spite of their reservations about certain aspects of the act. At the outbreak (1939) of World War II, however, the viceroy, without consulting the Indian parties, declared that India was at war with Germany, and the Congress provincial ministries resigned in protest. In 1942, when Congress mounted a massive civil disobedience campaign at a time when India was threatened by Japanese invasion, he interned the Congress leaders. Linlithgow was succeeded as viceroy in 1943 by Lord Wavell.

Linlithgow, burgh (1971 pop. 2,777), county town of West Lothian, central Scotland. Manufactures include chemicals, paper, whiskey, and soap. Linlithgow Palace, now a ruin, was a seat of Stuart kings and the birthplace of James V and Mary Queen of Scots. Begun in the 15th cent. by James I, it was occupied (1651–59) by Oliver Cromwell's forces and burned in 1746. The 1st earl of Murray, regent of Scotland, was murdered there in 1570. In 1975, Linlithgow became part of the Lothian region.

Linlithgowshire, county, Scotland: see WEST LOTHIAN.

Linnaeus, Carolus (kărō'ləs lĭnā'əs), 1707–78, Swedish botanist and taxonomist, considered the founder of the binomial system of nomenclature and the originator of modern scientific CLASSIFICATION of plants and animals. He studied botany and medicine and taught both at Uppsala. In *Systema naturae* (1735) he presented his classification of plants, animals, and minerals, and in *Genera plantarum* (1737) he explained his system for classifying plants largely on the basis of the number of stamens and pistils in the flower. Despite the admitted artificiality of his premise, the Linnaean system has remained the basis of modern taxonomy. *Species plantarum* (2 vol., 1753) described plants in terms of genera and species, and the 10th edition (1758) of *Systema naturae* applied this system to animals as well. These two works are therefore considered the basis of binomial nomenclature, although the early herbalists had used a binomial system before Linnaeus. Among the more than 180 works published in his lifetime were several books on the flora of Lapland and Sweden and the *Genera morborum* (1763), a classification of diseases. After Linnaeus' death his priceless botanical collection was removed to England (see HERBARIUM). Linnaeus was also known as Karl (or Carl) Linné (of which Carolus Linnaeus is a Latinized version); when he was ennobled in 1761 he formally adopted the name Karl von Linné. See biography by Wilfrid Blunt and W. T. Stearn (1971); studies by J. L. Larson (1971) and F. A. Stafleu (1971).

linoleum (lĭnō'lēəm), resilient floor or wall covering made of burlap, canvas, or felt, surfaced with a composition of wood flour, oxidized linseed oil, gums or other ingredients, and coloring matter. An English rubber manufacturer, Frederick Walton, patented linoleum in 1863. It replaced Kamptulicon, a costly rubber composition. In the manufacture of linoleum, linseed oil is exposed to the air in a succession of thin films until it is of a rubbery consistency, or it is thickened by heating until it becomes a spongy mass, after which it is ground, mixed with pulverized wood and other ingredients, and then applied to the foundation and rolled smooth. The final process is a thorough seasoning in drying rooms. In inlaid linoleum the pattern is built up from the base in the colors of the design and is therefore permanent. Linoleum is made in several thicknesses and in the form of tiles. It is sometimes surfaced with a durable pyroxylin lacquer. Although large amounts of linoleum are still produced, other materials such as vinyl are now more widely used as floor coverings.

linoleum block printing or **linocut,** 20th-century development in the art of relief cuts. The linoleum block consists of a thin layer of linoleum mounted on wood; in this the design to be printed is cut in the same manner as for a WOODCUT. The advantage of linoleum cuts lies in the softness of the material and the consequent ease with which it can be cut, but linoleum is not so suitable for fine lines as wood, nor can as many prints be produced. The process has been used widely in textile printing and in grade-school art classes. It is especially suitable for bold, decorative designs. Matisse's linocut illustrations for Montherlant's *Pasiphaë* (1944) show great sensitivity of handling. See E. W. Watson, *The Relief Print* (1945); Jane Elam, *Introducing Linocuts* (1969).

linotype (lĭn'ətīp"), TYPE set by the Linotype machine. See PRINTING.

Lin Piao (lĭn byou), 1908–1971, Chinese Communist general and political leader. Lin was trained at Whampoa Academy, and during the NORTHERN EXPEDITION he rose to company commander in the Kuomintang army. After the Kuomintang-Communist split in 1927, he became one of Chu Teh's leading military aides. His skill as a tactician earned him the command of a Red Army corps, and after the LONG MARCH, he headed the Red Academy at Yenan. In 1947–48 he commanded the Communist military offensive in the northeast against Chiang Kai-shek. Lin was appointed defense minister of the people's republic in 1959. In 1966 he displaced LIU SHAO-CH'I as the second-ranking member of the Chinese Communist party, a position that made him Mao Tsetung's heir apparent. A supporter of the Cultural Revolution (1966–69), Lin mysteriously died in an airplane crash in Mongolia (1971). His death, however, was not officially disclosed until 1972, when the Chinese press also reported on his alleged attempt to overthrow the government shortly before the crash.

linsang: see CIVET.

Lins do Rego, José (zhōōzĕ' lĕnz dô rĕ'gōō), 1901–57, Brazilian novelist. His fame rests largely on his "sugar cane cycle," dealing with social transformation in the Brazilian northeast. The first of the series, *Menino de engenho* [child of the sugar plantation] was published in 1932. *Fogo Morto* [dead fires] (1943) is considered his principal work. His autobiography, *Meus verdes anos* [my green years], appeared in 1956.

linseed, seed of the FLAX plant.

linseed cake, concentrated feed for livestock, prepared by pressing into cakes linseed from which most of the oil has been removed. The amount of oil remaining in the cake varies; the seed husks may or may not be removed. Linseed cake has a high protein value.

linseed oil, amber-colored, fatty oil extracted from the cotyledons and inner coats of the linseed. The raw oil extracted from the seeds by hydraulic pressure is pale in color and practically without taste or odor. When boiled or extracted by application of heat and pressure, it is darker and has a bitter taste and an unpleasant odor. Linseed oil has long been used as a drying oil in paints and varnish. It is also used in making linoleum, oilcloth, and certain inks.

Lin Sen (lĭn sŭn), 1868–1943, president of China (1932–43). He was an anti-Manchu revolutionary, overseas organizer for the Kuomintang, and parliamentarian. For a time after the death of Sun Yat-sen, he was in rightist opposition to Chiang Kai-shek. Politically Lin was unimportant, and his appointment to the essentially honorary office of president was a personal tribute. Lin's successor was Chiang Kai-shek.

Linsia: see LIN-HSIA, China.

lintel, in architecture, the horizontal member that spans an opening, such as a door or window, or that connects two columns. The post-and-lintel, or trabeated, system of construction, with spans limited to the length of available wood or stone beams, is the basis of the Egyptian and Greek styles of architecture, as contrasted with the later arched and vaulted, or arcuated, styles.

Linton, Ralph, 1893–1953, American anthropologist, b. Philadelphia, B.A. Swarthmore College, 1915, Ph.D. Harvard, 1925. He was (1922–28) assistant curator at the Field Museum, Chicago, then taught at the Univ. of Wisconsin (1928–37), at Columbia (1937–46), and at Yale (1946–53). His wide studies in the Americas, Africa, Madagascar, and the South Pacific produced insights into the process of acculturation and the complex of cultural-psychiatric relationships. Among his more general works are *The Study of Man* (1936), *The Science of Man in the World Crisis* (1945), *Most of the World* (1949), and

The Tree of Culture (1955). See biography by A. S. Linton and Charles Wagley (1971).

Linton, William James, 1812-97, Anglo-American wood engraver, author, and political reformer. In 1842 he began working as a wood engraver with John Orrin Smith and produced illustrations for the newly formed London *Illustrated News.* An ardent radical, he helped found the *Leader,* expounded the principles of Mazzini in the *Red Republican,* and started (1851) the *English Republic.* Later, he returned to wood engraving and in 1867 moved to the United States and set up a printing press in New Haven, Conn.; he continued the tradition of Thomas Bewick, advocating the use of the white as well as the black line. The best wood engraver of his day in England, he contributed more than any other to the regeneration of the art in America. His publications include *The Life of Thomas Paine* (1839), *Some Practical Hints on Wood-Engraving* (1879), *The History of Wood-Engraving in America* (1882), and *Memories* (1895). See biography by F. B. Smith (1973).

Linus, Saint (lī'nəs), d. A.D. 76?, pope (A.D. 67?-A.D. 76?), martyr, an Italian; successor of St. Peter and predecessor of St. Cletus (or Anacletus). Nothing is known of his life, but he has been (as early as 189) identified with the biblical Linus. He is mentioned in the canon of the Mass. Feast: Sept. 23.

Linus, Roman Christian. 2 Tim. 4.21. He is often identified with St. Linus.

Linus, in Greek mythology. **1** Son of Apollo and Psamathe of Argos. He was deserted by his mother on a hillside and devoured by dogs. When Psamathe's father learned what his daughter had done, he had her killed. For this double outrage, Apollo cursed Argos with a plague for which there could be no release until Psamathe and Linus were propitiated with prayers and songs of lamentation. The "Linus song," a lament derived from this legend, was sung at harvest time as a dirge for the dying vegetation. **2** Famous musician who taught Hercules. When Linus tried to punish Hercules, the latter killed him. Another legend says that Linus was killed by Apollo, who tolerated no rivals in music.

Lin-yü: see SHAN-HAI-KUAN, China.

Lin Yutang (lĭn yü'täng'), 1895–, Chinese-American writer, educated in mission schools in China and at Harvard, Ph.D. Univ. of Leipzig, 1923. Dr. Lin returned to China (1923) to teach at the Univ. of Peking. He returned again in 1943 and in 1954 but on both occasions found his concept of literature as an expression of the mind and spirit of the writer in conflict with the prevalent official Chinese view of literature as a vehicle for propaganda. Since c.1928 he has spent most of his time in the United States and written most of his many works in English. His books include *My Country and My People* (1935); *The Importance of Living* (1937); *A Leaf in the Storm* (1941), about war-torn China; *Between Tears and Laughter* (1943), a critical view of Western relations with China; and *The Pleasures of a Nonconformist* (1962). Among his novels are *Moment in Peking* (1939), *Chinatown Family* (1948), *Red Peony* (1961), and *The Flight of the Innocents* (1965). He has also translated, compiled, and edited many works, among them *The Chinese Theory of Art* (1968).

Linz (lĭnts), city (1971 pop. 202,900), capital of Upper Austria, NW Austria, a major port on the Danube River. It is a commercial and industrial center and a rail junction. Manufactures include iron and steel, machinery, and textiles. Originally a Roman settlement called Lentia, Linz was made a provincial capital of the Holy Roman Empire in the late 15th cent. The city has numerous historic structures, including the Romanesque Church of St. Martin (8th cent.); the baroque old cathedral (17th cent.), where the composer Anton Bruckner was organist (1856-68); the city hall (17th cent.); the baroque bishop's palace (1721-26); and the new neo-Gothic cathedral (19th-20th cent.). The Provincial Museum in Linz contains paintings, folk art, and Roman artifacts.

lion, large carnivore of the CAT family, *Panthera leo,* found in open country in Africa, with a few surviving in India. Lions have short-haired coats of tawny brown, with the tail ending in a dark tuft. Most males have black or tawny manes of varying length growing from the head, neck, and shoulders. The mane may be quite long and magnificent, giving the lion the imposing appearance that has led it to be known as king of the beasts in folklore. Grown males are about 9 ft (2.7 m) long including the 3-ft (90-cm) tail, stand about 3 ft (90 cm) at the shoulder, and weigh up to 400 lb (180 kg). Females are smaller and lack manes. The lion is anatomically very similar to the TIGER although it is different in habitat and way of life. Lions are the only cats that are social rather than solitary. They usually live in groups called prides, which vary in composition but may occasionally include as many as 30 individuals. They inhabit grasslands, scrubland, and semidesert areas, where they hunt antelope, zebra, and other large herbivorous animals, as well as domestic stock. Females do most of the hunting. Lions also eat carrion. They do not normally attack humans unless wounded or provoked; under unusual conditions they may become man-eaters, but even old and sick animals are more likely to subsist on rodents, insects, and other small prey. In early historic times lions ranged over Eurasia from E Europe to India and over all of Africa. They were eliminated from Europe and the Middle East by the beginning of the 2d cent. A.D. and from most of the rest of their range in recent times. They are now numerous only in central Africa. At the beginning of this century a few pairs remained in India and were preserved as tourist attractions in the Girnar forest of Gujarat state, in the northwest. This group had increased to 290 individuals in 1955, but in 1968 numbered only 177. In early Christian symbolism the lion represented Jesus and has also represented St. Mark. Lions are classified in the phylum CHORDATA, subphylum Vertebrata, class Mammalia, order Carnivora, family Felidae. For the constellation and sign of the zodiac see LEO. See the many books by Joy Adamson; M. H. Cowie, *The African Lion* (1966); J. Dominis, *The Cats of Africa* (1968); G. B. Schaller, *The Serengeti Lion* (1972).

Lion, Gulf of, Fr. *Golfe du Lion* (gôlf dü lyôN'), arm of the Mediterranean Sea, S France, extending from the French-Spanish border to Toulon. Its coastline includes many lagoons and the Rhône delta. Marseilles is the chief port on the gulf.

Lion, The, English name for LEO, a CONSTELLATION.

Lions International, organization of business and professional men, founded (1917) by Melvin Jones. The International Association of Lions Clubs (popularly known as Lions International) is devoted to meeting community needs either through its own efforts or in cooperation with other agencies. Its clubs throughout the world conduct activities in the following areas: agriculture, children and youth, citizenship and patriotism, civic improvements, community betterment, education, health and welfare, safety, sight conservation and the blind, and the United Nations. The official organ is the *Lion.*

Liotard, Jean Étienne (zhäN ātyĕn' lyôtär'), 1702–89, Swiss painter. He is best known for his portraits and drawings in pastel, but he also made portraits in oil, paintings on glass and porcelain, and engravings and enamels. He painted the portraits of Marie Antoinette, Francis I, and Maria Theresa. His work is best seen in Amsterdam and Geneva.

Lipari Islands (lĭp'ərē), formerly **Aeolian Islands** (ēō'lēən), Ital. *Isole Eolie,* volcanic island group (1971 pop. 10,043), 44 sq mi (114 sq km), Messina prov., NE Sicily, Italy, in the Tyrrhenian Sea. The group includes Lipari (14.5 sq mi/37.6 sq km), an exporter of pumice and the site of Lipari, the group's main town; Salina, where malmsey wine and currants are produced; Vulcano, the site in former times of the worship of the mythical fire god, with a high volcano that emits hot sulfurous vapors; Stromboli, with an active volcano (3,040 ft/927 m) that has several craters; Panarea; Filicudi; Alicudi; and 11 other islands. Fishing is an important occupation, and there is a growing tourist industry. The mythical residence of Aeolus, the wind god, for whom they were formerly named, the islands were colonized by the Greeks in the 6th cent. B.C. Under the Roman Empire and during the Fascist regime in Italy (20th cent.) the island group served as a place of exile for political prisoners.

lipase (lī'pās), any ENZYME capable of degrading LIPID molecules. The bulk of dietary lipids are from a class of organic compounds called triacylglycerols that are attacked by lipases to yield simple FATTY ACIDS and glycerol, molecules which are readily assimilated by the digestive process and transported to the blood from the stomach and small intestine. Gastric lipase, secreted by the stomach lining, has a *p*H value for optimal activity around neutrality and would appear, therefore, to be essentially inactive in the strongly acid environment of the stomach. It is suggested that this enzyme is more important for infant digestion since the gastric *p*H in infancy is much less acid than later in life. Most lipid digestion in the adult occurs in the upper loop of the small intestine and is accomplished by a lipase secreted by the pancreas.

Lipchitz, Jacques (zhäk lēpshēts'), 1891-1973, French sculptor, b. Lithuania. From 1909, Lipchitz studied in Paris; he became a member of the *Esprit Nouveau* group and was associated with the cubists. His vibrant skeletal constructions, which he originated in 1913, are unique in modern sculpture. In 1924 he began creating transparent sculptures, using the lost-wax technique. Allegories of struggle preoccupied him in the late 1930s, and he executed such works as *The Rape of Europa, Bull and Candor,* and *Prometheus.* Lipchitz lived in the United States in the early 1940s. Returning to France after World War II, he was commissioned in 1946 to design a font for the new church of Assy, Haute-Savoie. The bronze models for it, along with many of his works, were destroyed by fire in his New York studio in 1952, but the following year he resumed work on the Assy Madonna and on another sculpture, *The Spirit of Enterprise,* for Fairmount Park, Philadelphia. In 1955 he began producing his celebrated semi-automatics—masses of clay or plasticine, which he first molded under water, using only his sense of touch, before seeing the sculpture through to completion. Examples of his work are in the Museum of Modern Art, New York City and the Barnes Foundation, Merion, Pa. See his *My Life in Sculpture,* written with H. H. Arnason (1972).

Lipetsk (lyē'pyĭtsk), city (1970 pop. 290,000), capital of Lipetsk oblast, E central European USSR, on the Voronezh River. It is the center of an iron-ore-mining area. Industrial products include steel, silicates, tractors, food products, cement, and metal goods. The city has mineral springs and since the 18th cent. has been a health resort center. It was founded in the 13th cent., completely destroyed by the Tatars at the end of the 13th cent., and rebuilt (1707) by Peter the Great as a metallurgical center.

lipids, those natural products found in living systems that are insoluble in water but soluble in such organic solvents as diethyl ether, petroleum ether, chloroform, hot alcohol, benzene, carbon tetrachloride, and acetone. The definition excludes the mineral oils and other petroleum products obtained from fossil material. Major classes of lipids include the FATTY ACIDS, the glycerol-derived lipids (including the FATS AND OILS and the PHOSPHOLIPIDS), the sphingosine-derived lipids (including the ceramides, cerebrosides, gangliosides, and sphingomyelins), the STEROIDS and their derivatives, the terpenes and their derivatives, certain aromatic compounds, and long-chain alcohols and WAXES. Often lipids are found conjugated with proteins or carbohydrates, and the resulting substances are known as LIPOPROTEINS and lipopolysaccharides. The fat-soluble VITAMINS can be classified as lipids.

Lipmann, Fritz Albert, 1899–, American biochemist, b. Germany, grad. Univ. of Berlin (M.D., 1922; Ph.D., 1927). He emigrated to the United States in 1939 and became a citizen in 1944. In 1941 he became research chemist at Massachusetts General Hospital, Boston, and in 1949 professor of biochemistry at Harvard Univ. medical school. For his discovery of coenzyme A, a crucial intermediary in carbohydrate oxidation, he was awarded jointly with H. A. Krebs the 1953 Nobel Prize in Physiology and Medicine.

Li Po (lē pō, Chin. lē bô) or **Li Tai Po** (tī), c.700-762, Chinese poet of the T'ang dynasty. He was born in what is now Szechwan prov. Most authorities believe that he was a Taoist; his unconcern for worldly preferment and his love for retirement and wandering are expressive of both Taoism and the delicate romanticism typical of Chinese poets. An early period of patronage by the court was followed by banishment. Poor and homeless, the poet remained, as ever, a lighthearted winebibber. The traditional account of his death is that while drunk he attempted to kiss his reflection in a moonlit river, fell into the water, and drowned. Li Po was an extremely fecund and facile poet. He made no attempt to preserve his work, and most has been lost; the nearly 2,000 poems collected in the official recension in 1080 are believed to comprise only about one tenth of his output. His themes, largely traditional, are the grief of lovers separated by official duty or military service, the beauty of mountain and river scenery, and the surcease from melancholy and apparent wisdom to be found in wine. An exquisite choice of language and a sense of universal mystery are characteristic of his work. His name is also spelled Li Tai Peh. For anthologies containing selections from his work, see the bibliography of CHINESE LITERATURE. See Arthur Waley, *The Poetry and Career of Li Po* (1950); *Li Po and Tu Fu,* ed. and tr. by Arthur Cooper (1973).

lipoic acid: see COENZYME.

lipoma: see NEOPLASM.

lipoprotein (lĭp"əprō'tēn), any organic compound that is composed of both PROTEIN and the various fatty substances classed as LIPIDS, including FATTY ACIDS and STEROIDS such as CHOLESTEROL. The lipoprotein complex of proteins and steroids is usually provided by a weak, noncovalent interaction; proteins complexed with other lipids often do so by the formation of covalent chemical bonds. Current ideas regarding the structure of cellular membranes suggest that they are essentially lipoprotein in nature; the membrane is believed to be a continuous sheet of lipid molecules in close association with proteins that either face one side of the membrane or penetrate all the way through the membrane.

Lippe (lĭp'ə), former state, N central West Germany, between the Teutoburg Forest and the Weser River. It was incorporated in 1947 into the state of NORTH RHINE-WESTPHALIA. Detmold, the former capital, was the chief city. The region of Lippe was mainly agricultural. Originally included in the duchy of Saxony, Lippe became (12th cent.) a lordship under Bernhard I (1113–44). In 1529 it was raised to a county; from the various divisions of the county after the death (1613) of Simon VI, two counties emerged—Lippe, or Lippe-Detmold, and SCHAUMBURG-LIPPE. Lippe became a principality in 1720 and in 1815 joined the German Confederation. It sided with Prussia in the Austro-Prussian War (1866) and joined the German Empire in 1871. The succession to Lippe, contested in 1895, was finally resolved in 1905 with the accession of Count Leopold of Lippe-Biesterfeld, a collateral branch. After Leopold abdicated in 1918, Lippe joined the Weimar Republic. A local electoral victory (Jan., 1933) of the National Socialists in Lippe helped Adolf Hitler into power. A nephew of Leopold, Bernhard zu Lippe-Biesterfeld (b.1911) married Princess—later Queen—Juliana of the Netherlands in 1937.

Lippe, river, c.150 mi (240 km) long, rising in the Teutoburg Forest, W West Germany and flowing westward into the Rhine River. It is canalized to permit barge navigation. Water from the Lippe is used in the Ruhr canal system.

Lippi (lēp'pē), name of two celebrated Italian painters of the 15th cent. **Fra Filippo Lippi,** c.1406–1469, called Lippo Lippi, was one of the foremost Florentine painters of the early Renaissance. One of the best colorists and draftsmen of his day, Fra Filippo excelled in a graceful, narrative style. If his religious painting falls short of the sublime, it is always decorative and full of keen observation and human interest. An orphan, he spent much of his youth in the convent of the Carmelites. He may have studied directly under Masaccio, whose influence is evident in his early works. Temperamentally unsuited for the life of a monk, he left the convent c.1431. A few years later he executed an altarpiece (since lost) for the cathedral in Padua that distinctly influenced northern Italian painters. He was a highly popular artist in Florence and enjoyed the constant patronage of the Medici. In the 1450s he was at Prato, decorating the choir of the cathedral. These great frescoes, representing scenes from the lives of John the Baptist and St. Stephen, are Lippi's most important work. In 1467 he painted a series of frescoes from the life of the Virgin in the cathedral at Spoleto, where he is buried. These were completed after his death by Fra Diamante. Lippi is perhaps best known through his many easel paintings, among which are the famous *Coronation of the Virgin,* painted (1441) for the altar of the nuns of Sant' Ambrogio, and *Virgin Adoring the Christ Child* (Uffizi); *Madonna with Saints* (Louvre); *Annunciation* and *Vision of St. Bernard* (National Gall., London); *Coronation with Saints and Donors* (Palazzo Venezia, Rome); *Four Saints* (damaged) and *Madonna and Child with Angels* (both: Metropolitan Mus.). Among Fra Filippo's pupils were Botticelli and Il Pesellino. **Filippino Lippi,** c.1457–1504, son of Fra Filippo and Lucrezia Buti, was placed after his father's death with Fra Diamante and later studied under Botticelli. He soon became an accomplished painter, revealing the same mastery of color and line as his father and in 1480 was entrusted with the completion of Masaccio's frescoes in the Brancacci Chapel, Florence. He completed Masaccio's *Raising of the Dead Youth* and painted *Peter and Paul before Nero, Paul's Interview with Peter in Prison, Liberation of St. Peter,* and *Crucifixion of St. Peter,* adapting his style to that of Masaccio. His early works include the charming altarpiece, *Vision of St. Bernard* (Badia, Florence); the great altarpiece in the Nerli Chapel, Santo Spirito, Florence; and *Madonna Enthroned* (Uffizi). In 1488 he went to Rome where he painted a series of impressive frescoes in the Church of Santa Maria sopra Minerva. Returning to Florence, he executed many paintings, including the frescoes in Santa Trinita and the panel, *Adoration of the Magi* (Uffizi). In his last years he created the dramatic frescoes of the lives of St. John and St. Philip for the Strozzi Chapel in Santa Maria Novella, Florence. Greatly influenced by Botticelli, Filippino echoed his graceful expression and refinement of line. Examples of his art are in the National Gallery of Art, Washington, D.C.; the Metropolitan Museum; and the Cleveland Museum of Art. See B. Berenson, *The Drawings of the Florentine Painters* (3 vol., 1970); E. C. Strutt, *Fra Lippo Lippi* (1901, repr. 1971).

Lippmann, Walter, 1889–1974, American essayist and editor, b. New York City. He was associate editor of the *New Republic* in its early days (1914–17), but at the outbreak of World War I he left to become Assistant Secretary of War, later helping to prepare data for the peace conference. From 1921 to 1931 he was on the editorial staff of the New York *World,* serving as editor the last two years. In 1931 he began writing for the New York *Herald Tribune* a highly influential syndicated column, which moved to the Washington *Post* in 1962. He ceased writing a regular newspaper column in 1967. Lippmann's early books, written when he was a champion of liberalism, include *A Preface to Politics* (1913), *Public Opinion* (1922), and *A Preface to Morals* (1929). An early supporter of Franklin D. Roosevelt and the New Deal, Lippmann became disillusioned and condemned collectivism in *The Good Society* (1937). His political stance became one of moderate detachment, and he won distinction as a farsighted and incisive analyst of foreign policy. A special Pulitzer Prize citation (1958) praised his powers of news analysis, which he demonstrated in *U.S. War Aims* (1944), *The Cold War* (1947), *Isolation and Alliances* (1952), *The Communist World and Ours* (1959), and *Western Unity and the Common Market* (1962). See Marquis W. Childs and James B. Reston, ed., *Walter Lippmann and His Times* (1959); Edward W. Weeks, ed., *Conversations With Walter Lippmann* (1965); B. F. Wright, *Five Public Philosophies of Walter Lippmann* (1973).

Lippold, Richard, 1915–, American sculptor, engineer, and designer, b. Milwaukee. Until 1941, Lippold worked as an industrial designer; since then he has achieved startling effects in intricately arranged, precisely engineered constructions of suspended wire and sheet metal. In these works the play of light is an integral part of the sculpture. He has held teaching positions in various schools and colleges and was on the faculty of Hunter College, New York City (1952–67). Among his major works are *Aerial Act* (Wadsworth Atheneum, Hartford); *Sun* (Metropolitan Mus.), which contains more than 2 mi (3.2 km) of gold wire; and *Orpheus and Apollo* (Avery Fischer Hall, Lincoln Center, New York City). See catalog of exhibition in Willard Gallery, New York City (1962).

lip reading, method by which the deaf are able to read the speech of others from the movements of the lips and mouth. Lip reading is the medium of education in many schools for deaf children; it came into wide use after World War I in the rehabilitation of shell-shocked, or otherwise deafened, soldiers. See publications of the National Association of Hearing and Speech Agencies (formerly American Hearing Society); O. M. Wyatt, *Teach Yourself Lip-Reading* (1961, repr. 1969); Elizabeth Hazard, *Lipreading for the Oral Deaf and Hard-of-Hearing Person* (1971); Janet Jeffers, *Speechreading* (1971).

Lipsius, Justus (jŭs'təs lĭp'sēəs), 1547–1606, Flemish scholar, whose original name was Joest Lips. He was one of the most celebrated authorities of his day on Roman literature, history, and antiquities. Lipsius edited many works of Latin literature, his edition of Tacitus being particularly famous.

Lipton, Seymour, 1903–, American sculptor, b. New York City. Self-taught as a sculptor, Lipton worked directly in sheet metals and molten alloys, creating organically twisting forms with richly brazed textural effects. During the 1940s he sculpted heavy jagged shapes suggesting spiritual conflict. In the 1950s his work tended to more graceful forms evocative of plant and animal life. Representative works are *Jungle Bloom* (Yale Univ. Art Gall., New Haven) and *Sanctuary* (Mus. of Modern Art, New York City).

Lipton, Sir Thomas Johnstone, 1850–1931, Scottish merchant and yachting enthusiast. After spending several years in the United States he returned (1869) to his native Glasgow and opened a small grocery store. A pioneer in the art of publicity, he rapidly expanded his business and was a millionaire at the age of 30. He ran printing and paper works, set up several bacon-curing establishments in Chicago, and in 1889 acquired his own tea plantations in Ceylon. He was knighted in 1898 and was created a baronet in 1902. He made five attempts to win the America's Cup yachting trophy. His good sportsmanship endeared him to the American public, which gave him a gold cup after his last defeat in 1930. See his autobiography (1932); Alec Waugh, *The Lipton Story* (1950).

liquefaction, change of a substance from the solid or the gaseous state to the liquid state. Since the different states of matter correspond to different amounts of ENERGY of the molecules making up the substance, energy in the form of HEAT must either be supplied to a substance or be removed from the substance in order to change its state. Thus, changing a solid to a liquid or a liquid to a gas requires the addition of heat, while changing a gas to a liquid or a liquid to a solid requires the removal of heat. In the liquefaction of gases, extreme cooling is not necessary, for if a gas is held in a confined space and is subjected to high pressure, heat is given off as it undergoes COMPRESSION and it turns eventually to a liquid. Some cooling is, however, necessary; it was discovered by Thomas Andrews in 1869 that each gas has a definite TEMPERATURE, called its critical temperature, above which it cannot be liquefied, no matter what pressure is exerted upon it. A gas must, therefore, be cooled below its critical temperature before it can be liquefied. When a gas is compressed its molecules are forced closer together and, their vibratory motion being reduced, heat is given off. As compression proceeds, the speed of the molecules and the distances between them continue to decrease, until eventually the substance undergoes change of state and becomes liquid. Although before the 19th cent. a number of scientists had experimented in liquefying gases, Davy and Faraday are usually credited with being the first to achieve success. The production of liquefied gases in large quantities (and consequently their use in refrigeration) was made possible by the work of Z. F. Wroblewski and K. S. Olszewski, two Polish scientists. The work of Sir James Dewar is also important, especially in the liquefaction of air and its change to a solid. Heike Kamerlingh Onnes first liquefied helium. The critical temperature of helium is −267.9°C, only a few degrees above absolute zero (−273.15°C). The processes for the liquefaction of gases as developed by Linde and others form the basis for those used in modern REFRIGERATION. Liquefied gases are much used in low-temperature research; some, e.g., liquid oxygen, find use as rocket propellants. See LIQUID AIR; LOW-TEMPERATURE PHYSICS.

liquefied natural gas: see under NATURAL GAS.

liquefied petroleum gas or **LPG,** mixture of gases, chiefly propane and butane, produced commercially from petroleum and stored under pressure to keep it in a liquid state. The boiling point of liquefied petroleum gas varies from about −44°C to 0°C (−47°F to 32°F), so that the pressure required to liquefy it is considerable and the containers for it must be of heavy steel. When prepared as fuel, LPG is largely propane; common uses are for powering automotive vehicles, for cooking and heating, and sometimes for lighting in rural areas. LPG is an attractive fuel for internal-combustion engines, because it burns with little air pollution and little solid residue, it does not dilute lubricants, and it has a high octane rating. However, severely restricted supplies make its widespread use in this application impractical.

liqueur (lĭkûr'), strong alcoholic beverage made of nearly neutral spirits, flavored with herb mixtures, fruits, or other materials, and usually sweetened. The processes and ingredients are often strictly guarded trade secrets. The alcoholic content ranges from about 27% to 80% (for ABSINTHE). Fine liqueurs are distilled after flavoring matters have been macerated in spirits. In inferior liqueurs natural or artificial essential oils are added to strong spirits, filtered, and sweetened. Cordials are prepared by steeping in sweetened alcohol the fruit pulps or juices of such fruits as cherry, apricot, peach, and berry. Many famous liqueurs were originated by monks, notably BENEDICTINE and CHARTREUSE. Other liqueurs include anisette, CRÈME DE MENTHE, CURAÇAO, KIRSCH, KÜMMEL, and MARASCHINO.

liquid, one of the three states in which MATTER occurs, i.e., that state, as distinguished from solid and gas, in which a substance has a definite volume but no definite shape. Liquids, like gases, differ from solids in that they are fluids, that is, they flow into the shape of a containing vessel. The molecules (or atoms or ions) of a liquid, like those of a solid (and unlike those of a gas), are quite close together; however, while molecules in a solid are held in fixed positions by intermolecular forces, molecules in a liquid have too much thermal energy to be bound by these forces and move about freely within the liquid, although they cannot escape the liquid easily. A liquid changes at its BOILING POINT to a gas and at its freezing point, or MELTING POINT, to a solid. The boiling point is especially important because, since liquids change their states at different temperatures, those in a mixture can be separated from one another by raising the temperature of the mixture gradually so that each component in turn undergoes vaporization at its boiling point. This process is known as fractional distillation. Although the molecules of a liquid have greater cohesion than those of a gas, it is not sufficient to prevent some of those at the free surface of the liquid from bounding off (see EVAPORATION). On the other hand, the cohesive forces between the molecules at the surface of a mass of liquid and those within cause the free surface to act somewhat like a stretched elastic membrane; it tends to draw inward toward the center of the liquid mass, to draw the liquid into the shape of a sphere, thus exhibiting the phenomenon known as SURFACE TENSION. A liquid is said to "wet" a solid substance when the attractive force between the molecules of the liquid and those of the solid is great enough to hold the liquid's molecules at the solid surface. For example, water "wets" glass since its molecules cling to glass surfaces, whereas mercury does not since the adhesive force between its molecules and those of glass is not strong enough to hold them together. CAPILLARITY is an example of surface tension and adhesion acting at the same time. Liquids, like gases, exhibit the property of diffusion. When two miscible liquids are poured carefully into a container so that the denser one forms a separate layer on the bottom, each will diffuse slowly into the other until they are thoroughly mixed. In general, liquids show expansion upon heating, contraction upon cooling; water, however, does not follow the rule exactly. Liquids exert pressure upon the sides of a containing vessel and upon any body immersed in them, and pressure is transmitted through a liquid undiminished and in all directions. Liquids exert a buoyant force upon an immersed body equal to the weight of the liquid displaced by the body (see ARCHIMEDES' PRINCIPLE and SPECIFIC GRAVITY). Unlike gases, liquids are very nearly incompressible, and for that reason are useful in such devices as the hydraulic press. Liquids are useful as solvents. No one liquid can dissolve all substances; each takes into solution only certain specific substances.

liquid air, ordinary air that has been liquefied by compression and cooling to extremely low temperatures (see LIQUEFACTION). Its commercial preparation involves purification by washing to remove soluble impurities and by passage over calcium oxide (lime) to remove the carbon dioxide; compression, under a pressure of 200 atmospheres, or about 3,000 lb per sq in.; cooling, by passage through pipes immersed in cold water; treatment with sodium hydroxide to remove excess water; and rapid expansion, the expanding air passing back over the pipe from which it has just escaped absorbing so much heat that the air remaining in the pipe becomes liquid. Freshly liquefied air consists of 78.1% nitrogen, 21.0% oxygen, 0.9% argon, and very small amounts of rare gases and hydrogen in solution. Its boiling point is approximately −195°C. Because of fractional evaporation, its oxygen concentration and its boiling point increase with time. It must be kept in a specially designed container, the Dewar flask, because at ordinary temperatures it absorbs heat rapidly and reverts to the gaseous state. Liquid air is used commercially for freezing other substances and especially as an intermediate step in the production of nitrogen, oxygen, and argon and the other inert gases. As the temperature of liquid air rises, the nitrogen evaporates first at −195.8°C, the argon next at −185.7°C, and the oxygen last at −183°C. See LOW-TEMPERATURE PHYSICS.

liquid crystal, liquid whose component particles, atoms or molecules, tend to arrange themselves with a degree of order far exceeding that found in ordinary liquids and approaching that of solid crystals. As a result, liquid crystals have many of the optical properties of solid crystals. Moreover, since the order is not as firmly fixed as that of a solid crystal, it can be easily modified with corresponding changes in the optical properties. Thus, liquid crystals are extremely useful in producing visual displays such as those used on some digital clocks and electronic calculators. Some liquid crystals vary the color of the light that they reflect as their temperature changes. Since the colors reflected at any given temperature are quite specific, temperature can be measured by this means to an accuracy of 0.1°C.

liquor laws, legislation designed to restrict, regulate, or totally abolish the manufacture, sale, and use of alcoholic beverages. The passage of liquor laws has been prompted chiefly by the desire to prevent immoderate use of intoxicants, but sometimes also by the need to raise revenue. Direct taxation and license requirements are among the oldest methods of regulating the sale of liquor. With the license system the state can exercise extensive regulatory power by revoking permits upon violation of rules and by restricting licenses, although the system is vulnerable to political corruption. Licensing has been practiced most extensively and severely in Great Britain (especially since 1904), where regulation of the public house has resulted in the decrease of liquor consumption. Licenses are also used in the United States, and there are general regulatory provisions such as hours of closing and consumption privileges. National PROHIBITION of the manufacture and sale of liquor received its major test in the United States from 1919 to 1933. Many states have granted counties and municipalities a local option to restrict or abolish by vote the sale of liquor. Several states have monopolies of retail distribution, and a similar system prevails in most of Canada. Limitation of profits on the manufacture of liquors was begun in Sweden (1865) with the Goteborg licensing system, which restricts both production and consumption of alcoholic beverages. Norway and Finland have variations of this plan. A state monopoly of vodka manufacture was instituted (1894) in Russia for reasons of public finance and after a period of prohibition during World War I was restored by the Soviet Union. In France and other Latin countries where wine making is an important industry and where distilled liquors are less heavily consumed, few government restrictions have been imposed other than stringent labeling laws. Conditions are similar in Germany and other countries where malt liquors have wider use than spirits. See J. P. Bourke, *Liquor Laws* (1956).

Liri (lē'rē), river, 98 mi (158 km) long, rising in the Apennines, in Latium, central Italy, and flowing generally SE to the Tyrrhenian Sea. Below its junction with the Rapido River near Cassino it is called the Garigliano. There are hydroelectric stations along its course. In World War II the area around the river was the scene of heavy fighting between Allied and German troops.

Liriodendron: see MAGNOLIA.

Lisbon (lĭz'bən), Port. *Lisboa,* ancient *Olisipo,* city (1970 pop. 782,266), W Portugal, capital of Portugal, of Estremadura prov., and of Lisboa dist., on the Tagus River where it broadens to enter the Atlantic Ocean. Lisbon is Portugal's largest city and its cultural, administrative, commercial, and industrial hub. It has one of the best harbors in Europe, handling a large carrying trade. Agricultural and forest products and fish are exported. The city's industries include the production of textiles, chemicals, and steel; oil and sugar refining; and shipbuilding. A large transient and tourist trade is drawn to Lisbon, which is set on seven terraced hills. The Castelo de São Jorge, a fort that dominates the city, may have been built by the Romans on the site of the citadel of the early inhabitants, who traded with Phoenician and Carthaginian navigators. The Romans occupied the town in 205 B.C. It was conquered by the Moors in 714. The city's true importance dates, however, from 1147, when King Alfonso I, with the help of Crusaders, drove out the Moors. Alfonso III transferred (c.1260) his court there from Coimbra, and the city rose to great prosperity in the 16th cent. with the establishment of Portugal's empire in Africa and India. Although many of the old buildings were destroyed by earthquakes, particularly the disastrous earthquake of 1755, some of the medieval buildings remain. The old quarter, the picturesque and crowded Alfama, surrounds the 12th-century cathedral (rebuilt later). The new quarter, built by the marquês de Pombal after the great earthquake, centers about a large square, the Terreiro do Paço. Some of the well-known buildings in and near Lisbon are the Renaissance Monastery of São Vicente de Fora, with the tombs of the Braganza kings; the Church of St. Roque, with the fine Chapel of St. John (built by John V in the 18th cent.); and the magnificent monastery at Belém, on the north bank of the Tagus facing the sea, built by Manuel I to commemorate the discovery of the route to India by Vasco da Gama. Camões was born in Lisbon. The Univ. of Lisbon (originally founded 1292, but transferred to Coimbra in 1537), was reestablished in Lisbon in 1911. In 1966 the Salazar Bridge, one of the world's longest (3,323 ft/1,013 m) suspension bridges, was completed across the Tagus, linking Lisbon with the Setual Peninsula. See T. D. Kendrich, *The Lisbon Earthquake* (1957); David Wright and Patrick Swift, *Lisbon* (1971).

Lisburn (lĭz'bûrn", lĭs'-), municipal borough (1971 pop. 27,405), Co. Antrim, E Northern Ireland, on the Lagan River. Its chief industry, linen manufacture, was introduced by the Huguenots after the revocation of the Edict of Nantes (1685). In the city is a monument to Jeremy Taylor, who died there. Lisburn is the seat of the Roman Catholic bishop of Down and Connor and of the Protestant bishop of Connor. There is a technical school, located in the former home of Sir William Wallace.

Lisieux (lēzyö'), town (1968 pop. 25,233), Calvados dept., N France. It is one of the oldest towns in Normandy. Its modern importance dates from the canonization (1925) of St. Theresa, whose shrine there attracts many pilgrims. Lisieux has some small industries. Two thirds of the town was destroyed in World War II, but several beautiful old churches remain.

Lismore (lĭz'môr), city (1971 pop. 20,901), New South Wales, E Australia, on the North Arm of the Richmond River. An important industrial city, Lismore is a leading producer of butter. Its port is Ballina. There is a Roman Catholic cathedral in the city.

Lismore (lĭsmôr', lĭz-), rural district (1971 pop. 7,681), Co. Waterford, S Republic of Ireland, on the Blackwater River. It is a market town with a salmon fishing industry. In the 7th cent. St. Carthagh founded a monastery there. By the 8th cent. it was a famed center of learning. Lismore Castle, which has been restored, was built by Prince (later King) John in 1185. Robert Boyle was born in Lismore.

Lismore (lĭz'môr, lĭzmôr'), island, 9½ mi (15.3 km) long and 1½ mi (2.4 km) wide, Argyll dist., W Scotland, in Loch Linnhe. There are ruins of several old castles, one of which was a 9th-century viking fortress, another the residence of the bishops of Argyll. The present parish church was the choir of a 13th-century cathedral. The 16th-century **Book of the Dean of Lismore** is a volume of Scottish Gaelic and other verse, compiled by Dean James Macgregor and his brother Duncan. It is one of the oldest Scottish Gaelic collections.

Lissa: see LESZNO, Poland.

Lissitzky, Eliezer (El) Markovich (lyĭsyĕts'kē), 1890–1941, Russian painter, designer, teacher, and architect. Lissitzky studied at Darmstadt and later taught at the Moscow Academy of Arts, collaborating with avant-garde artists and architects. He left Russia and lived in Germany after Lenin issued an edict against the avant-garde. Before returning to the Soviet Union in 1928 he designed the Russian section of the Cologne Newspaper Exhibition, one of his many severely abstract, geometric exhibition designs. Lissitzky's writings about architecture include *Russia: The Reconstruction of Architecture in the Soviet Union* (1930). See biography by his wife, Sophie Lissitzky-Küppers (tr. 1968).

List, Friedrich (frē'drĭkh lĭst), 1789–1846, German economist. The first professor of economics at the Univ. of Tübingen, he was elected (1820) to the Württemberg legislature. For his advocacy of administrative reforms he was sentenced to imprisonment but was released on condition that he would emigrate to the United States. There he engaged in various enterprises, and in 1832 he was returned to Germany as U.S. consul at Leipzig. Insisting upon the necessity for a commercial association of German states and the full development of productive powers in those states, he became a ceaseless advocate of a customs union (ZOLLVEREIN). He urged a policy of economic protection for young industries and nations. His ideas were influential, and many of them were subsequently adopted by the U.S. government. List's most important work is *The National System of Political Economy* (1840, tr. 1904). See Margaret Hirst, *Life of Friedrich List and Selections from His Writings* (1909, repr. 1965).

Lister, Joseph Lister, 1st **Baron,** 1827–1912, English surgeon, educated at University College, London. He brought to surgery the principle of antisepsis, an outgrowth of Pasteur's theory that bacteria cause infection. In 1865, Lister proved the effectiveness of his methods, thus founding modern antiseptic surgery. Using carbolic acid as the antiseptic agent, he devised techniques of applying it that, when used in conjunction with his heat sterilization of instruments, brought about dramatic decreases in postoperative fatality. He developed absorbable ligatures and the drainage tube, both of which have come into general use for wounds and incisions. He was professor of clinical surgery at Edinburgh Univ. (1869-76) and at King's College, London (1877-93). See biographies by K. M. Walker (1956) and Laurence Farmer (1962).

lister: see PLOW.

Liston, Sonny (Charles Liston), 1932-1971, American boxer, b. Little Rock, Ark. While serving a sentence for robbery at the Missouri State Penitentiary, Liston became interested in boxing. In 1953 he began his professional fighting career. A hard-hitting heavyweight, he became (Sept., 1962) the world's heavyweight champion after a crushing first-round knockout of Floyd Patterson. He defended his championship in 1963, knocking out Patterson once again, before losing his title to Muhammad Ali in 1964. Losing his return match with Ali in 1965, Liston began a comeback in 1966. His lifetime record was 50 victories (39 knockouts) and 4 losses.

Liszt, Franz (fränts lĭst), 1811-86, Hungarian composer and pianist. Liszt was a revolutionary figure of romantic music and was acknowledged as the greatest pianist of his time. He made his debut at nine, going thereafter to Vienna to study with Czerny and Salieri. In Paris (1823-25) he knew all the principal artistic figures of the period and was influenced by Berlioz, Chopin, and Paganini. He lived with Mme d'Agoult (better known by her pen name, Daniel Stern) from 1833 to 1844, and they had three children; their daughter Cosima became the wife of Hans von Bülow and later of Wagner. As a piano virtuoso, Liszt enthralled his audiences with his expressive interpretations and grand style of playing, augmented with dramatic gestures. In 1848 he became musical director to the duke of Weimar. He resigned (1859) and two years later went to Rome, where he became an abbé (1865). During the years between 1880 and 1885, in Rome, Weimar, and Budapest, he taught most of the famous pianists of the succeeding generation. In his compositions he favored PROGRAM MUSIC over traditional musical forms. Liszt originated the symphonic poem, and although he wrote symphonies, such as the Faust Symphony (1854-57), most of his orchestral pieces, including *Les Préludes* and *Mazeppa* (both 1856), are symphonic poems. In his Sonata in B Minor (1853) he developed the technique of transformation of themes, later known as leitmotiv, which completely altered the concept of SONATA construction. This technique, together with his chromatic harmony, strongly influenced both Wagner and Richard Strauss. For the piano Liszt composed prolifically in addition to transcribing many works of other composers. His most outstanding works for the piano include *Années de pèlerinage* (1855-83), *Douze Études d'exécution transcendante* (final version, 1852), Six Paganini Études (final version, 1851), concertos in E Flat (1849-53) and A (1848-61), and 20 Hungarian Rhapsodies (of which he published 19). Some of his most popular pieces, including *Liebestraüme* (c.1850), are characterized by lyrical, romantic sentiment; many of his later compositions are somber in tone, full of dissonance and unusual harmonic effects that foreshadow 20th-century music. See his correspondence with Wagner, ed. by Francis Hueffer (2 vol., rev. ed. 1969); his letters, ed. by La Mara (2 vol., 1968); biographies by Sacheverell Sitwell (rev. ed. 1955) and Ernest Newman (1935, repr. 1970); study by Humphrey Searle (2d ed. 1966).

Li Ta-chao (lē dä-jou), 1888-1927, professor of history and librarian at Peking Univ., cofounder of the Chinese Communist party with CH'EN TU-HSIU. He was the first important Chinese intellectual to support the Bolshevik Revolution in Russia. A leader in the MAY FOURTH MOVEMENT (1919), he organized several Marxist study groups and helped found the Communist party in 1921. Although his populist, nationalistic view of the peasant role in the revolution was not favored by the early party, it deeply influenced his assistant, MAO TSE-TUNG. He was executed by the Manchurian general Chang Tso-lin. See M. J. Meisner, *Li Ta-chao and the Origins of Chinese Marxism* (1967).

Li Tai Po: see LI PO.

Li T'ang (lē täng), c.1050-1130, Chinese painter of the Sung dynasty. A leader of the academy founded by the Emperor Hui-tsung, he established a mode of painting that was widely followed in succeeding centuries. A master of village scenes, he also initiated a more intimate scale in landscape painting, with greater expanses of space and mist. A landscape attributed to him is in the Museum of Fine Arts, Boston.

Litani, river, Lebanon: see BIQA, AL.

litany (lĭt'ənē) [Gr.,=prayer], solemn prayer characterized by varying petitions with set responses. The term is mainly used for Christian forms. Litanies were developed in Christendom for use in processions. In the West there were traditionally four days for these processional litanies, the ROGATION DAYS. The Eastern liturgies make frequent use of litanies, recited by the deacon; the response is usually "Lord, have mercy." The KYRIE ELEISON is a relic of such a litany. In the Roman Catholic Church the one liturgical litany, the Litany of the Saints, dates from the 5th cent. substantially. Modeled after it are a number of nonliturgical (i.e., nonprescribed) litanies, of which the following are authorized: Litany of the Holy Name of Jesus (15th cent.), Litany of the Blessed Virgin Mary (or of Loreto; 16th cent.), Litany of the Sacred Heart, and Litany of St. Joseph. The litany in the Anglican Book of Common Prayer is much like the Litany of the Saints. Moravian and Lutheran liturgies also use litanies.

litchi (lē'chē), Chinese tree (*Litchi chinensis*) of the family Sapindaceae (soapberry family), having a small, aromatic, pulpy fruit in a thin, rough shell. It is the best-known Chinese fruit and a favorite with the Chinese, who use it fresh, dried, or preserved. In commerce it is usually seen dried, in which form it appears as a nut with a raisinlike center. The juicy pulp is also canned. The tree is now grown in other warm countries and to some extent in the United States in S Florida and California. Among variant spellings are leechee, lichee, and lychee. Litchis are classified in the division MAGNOLIOPHYTA, class Magnoliopsida, order Sapindales, family Sapindaceae.

liter, abbr. l, unit of volume in the METRIC SYSTEM, defined since 1964 as equal to 0.001 cubic meters, or 1 cubic decimeter. A cube that has each of its edges equal to 10 centimeters has a volume of 1 liter. The liter is equal to 1.057 liquid quarts, 0.908 dry quarts, and 61.024 cubic inches.

literary frauds, manuscripts that are presented to the public as works of famous authors but that are actually forgeries or imitations. Literary frauds are perpetrated for various reasons—occasionally to sell a manuscript or book for large sums, often to win recognition for an original work that would not attract attention by itself, sometimes simply as a joke. Although such hoaxes were evident in classical times and during the Middle Ages, it was in the 18th cent. that literary frauds flourished. A man who pretended to be a native of Formosa published a *Description of Formosa* (1704) with an autobiography; subsequently he confessed that he was George PSALMANAZAR and that he was born in France. In the 1760s James MACPHERSON wrote a group of poems that he claimed were translations of the 3d-century Celtic poet Ossian. Thomas CHATTERTON wrote poems in an imitation of 15th-century English that he claimed were transcriptions from a manuscript of a poet-priest of that period. William IRELAND falsely claimed to have found two lost plays of Shakespeare. The most famous 19th-century literary frauds were spurious first editions of such famous writers as Tennyson, Dickens, Matthew Arnold, Elizabeth Browning, and Kipling. They were long considered genuine and were not definitely proved forgeries until 1934. In 1939 the author of these forgeries was shown to be Thomas WISE, a noted book dealer. Perhaps the most interesting literary fraud of the 20th cent. was the "*Spectra* hoax." In 1916 the American poets Witter BYNNER and Arthur Davison Ficke published a book of parodies, *Spectra: A Book of Poetic Experiments,* satirizing such contemporary literary movements as the vorticists and the imagists. The book won acclaim from critics, however, and the Spectrists were publicly accepted as a valid literary school. Of more financial than literary interest was the Hughes hoax, which occurred in 1972 when a writer named Clifford Irving received some $750,000 from several publishers, including McGraw-Hill and *Life* magazine, after he convinced them that the reclusive billionaire Howard Hughes wished Irving to assist him in writing his autobiography. It soon transpired that Hughes had never even heard of Irving and had no intention of writing an autobiography; Irving was subsequently convicted of fraud and sent to prison.

literature. For the literature of England, see ENGLISH LITERATURE; for that of Germany, see GERMAN LITERATURE, and so forth. For the forms of literary art, see BIOGRAPHY, ESSAY, NOVEL, THEATER, LETTERS, and so forth; for its methods and purposes, see CRITICISM, STYLE, SATIRE, VERSIFICATION, FIGURE OF SPEECH. See also JOURNALISM.

litharge (lĭthärj'), yellow to brownish-red solid that is a by-product of lead refining; it is formed when crude lead is heated in air to oxidize metallic impurities. Litharge is used in the manufacture of optical glass, paints, enamels, varnish, ceramics, and rubber. A yellow powder of the same chemical composition and with the same uses is known as massicot. Chemically, litharge is the water-insoluble poisonous compound lead monoxide, PbO; it occurs naturally in silver-bearing lead ores.

Lithgow (lĭth'gō), town (1971 pop. 12,814), New South Wales, SE Australia, in the Blue Mts. It is a coal-mining center, with a small arms industry.

lithium (lĭth'ēəm) [Gr.,=stone], metallic chemical element; symbol Li; at. no. 3; at. wt. 6.941; m.p. about 179°C; b.p. about 1,317°C; sp. gr. .534 at 20°C; valence +1. Lithium is a soft, silver-white metal. It is one of the ALKALI METALS in group Ia of the PERIODIC TABLE. It is the least dense metal. Because it has high specific heat, it has found some use in cooling systems for nuclear reactors; such use is limited because lithium is very corrosive. Lithium metal is prepared by electrolysis of fused lithium chloride. Lithium reacts with water less readily than sodium. It burns in air with a brilliant white flame. Lithium forms many inorganic compounds, among them a hydride (LiH), a nitride (Li_3N), an oxide (lithia, Li_2O), a hydroxide (LiOH), a carbide (Li_2C_2), a carbonate (Li_2CO_3), and a phosphate (Li_3PO_4). When heated it reacts directly with the halogens to form halides. Lithium aluminum hydride ($LiAlH_4$) is an important reagent in organic chemistry. Lithium also forms numerous organic compounds. One compound of major importance is lithium stearate, produced by cooking tallow (or other animal fat) with lithium hydroxide; lithium stearate is used to transform oil into lithium-base lubricating greases, which have found extensive use in the automotive industry. Lithium carbonate is used in special glasses and ceramic glazes. Lithium chloride and bromide are used as brazing and welding fluxes; they are also used in air conditioning systems because they are very hygroscopic; i.e., they absorb moisture. Lithium hydroxide is used to increase the capacity of alkaline storage cells. Lithium compounds are used in the nuclear energy industry, in the preparation of plastics and synthetic rubber, and in the synthesis of vitamin A. Lithium is added in small amounts to magnesium, aluminum, or lead-base alloys; it is also used as a degasifier in iron, steel, and copper refining. In addition, lithium is used to scavenge small amounts of oxygen and nitrogen in electronic vacuum tubes. Trace amounts of lithium and its compounds color a flame bright red; they are used in pyrotechnics. Lithium in the salt form has recently come into use as a medical treatment for manic depression. Lithium is widely distributed in nature; it is found in the soil, in plants, in animals, and in the human body. It is also found in the sun. Lithium may be profitably extracted from ores containing as little as 1% lithium (measured as lithium oxide). Some commercially important minerals are lepidolite, petalite, spodumene, and amblygonite. Lithium is also produced from brines such as those in Searles Lake, Calif., and in the Great Salt Lake, Utah. Lithium was discovered in 1817 by J. A. Arfvedson.

lithography (lĭthŏg'rəfē), type of planographic or surface printing. It is distinguished from letter-press (relief) printing and from intaglio printing (in which the design is cut or etched into the plate). Lithography is used both as an art process and as a commercial PRINTING process. In commercial printing the term is used synonymously with offset printing. All planographic printing is based on chemical action, and lithography is based on the mutual antipathy of oil and water. As the name [from Gr.,=writing on stone] implies, a lithograph is printed from a stone (except in commercial processes, where grained metal or plastic plates are employed). The process was invented c.1796 by the playwright Aloys Senefelder, and the Bavarian limestone that he employed is still considered the best material for art lithography. The slab of stone is ground to a level surface, which may be of coarse or fine texture as desired. The drawing is made in reverse directly on the stone with a lithographic crayon or ink that contains soap or grease. The fatty acid of this material interacts with the lime of the stone to form an insoluble lime soap on the surface, which will accept the greasy printing ink and reject water. Accordingly, those parts of the stone that have been drawn upon have an affinity for ink. Sometimes the drawing is made on paper and transferred to a heated stone by pressure. This is known as a transfer lithograph and does not require the artist to reverse his drawing. Next, the surface of the stone untouched by grease is desensitized to it, and the portions drawn upon are fixed against spreading by treatment with a gum arabic and nitric acid solution. The grease has now penetrated the stone, and the drawing is washed off with turpentine and water. The stone is ready to be inked with a roller and printed, but it must be kept moist. The printing requires a special lithographic press with a sliding bed passing under a scraper. As a printing process lithography is probably the most unrestricted. It produces tones ranging from intense black to the most delicate gray and simulates with equal facility the effects of pencil, pen, crayon, or brush drawing. White lines are readily produced by scratching through the drawing on the stone. Several hundred fine proofs can be taken from a stone. The medium was exploited by many artists in the 19th cent., including Goya, Delacroix, Daumier, Gavarni, Manet, Degas, Bonnard, Whistler, and Toulouse-Lautrec, whose POSTERS are among the most celebrated lithographic masterworks. In the United States, A. B. Davies, George Bellows, Joseph Pennell, and Currier and Ives are among the many artists noted for their lithographs. For the commercial reproduction of art works, photolithography plays an increasingly important role. A photographic negative is exposed to light over a gelatin-covered paper. Wherever the light does not strike the gelatin, the latter remains soluble while the other parts are rendered insoluble. When the soluble portions are washed away, the pattern to be printed can be inked and transferred to the stone or plate. Color lithography and color photolithography require as many stones or plates as the number of colors employed. The commercial printing applications of the lithographic process are vast in scope and almost unlimited in number. See Joseph Pennell and Elizabeth Pennell, *Lithographs and Lithographers* (1915); V. Strauss, *Lithographers Manual* (2 vol. 1958); W. Weber, *A History of Lithography* (1966); F. H. Man, *Artists' Lithographs: A World History* (1970).

lithopone (lĭth'əpōn), brilliant white PIGMENT used chiefly for interior paints. It is a mixture of barium sulfate and zinc sulfide precipitated from a mixture of solutions of zinc sulfate and barium sulfide. This pigment has fair covering power, is inexpensive, is not poisonous, and does not darken with exposure to industrial gases, particularly hydrogen sulfide, a gas often present in the air of manufacturing cities.

lithosphere (lĭth'əsfēr''), brittle uppermost shell of the earth, broken into a number of so-called lithospheric plates. The lithosphere consists of the crust, the earth's thin outer layer of granitic and basaltic rocks, and the uppermost portion of the mantle, the layer beneath the crust, thought to be composed of ultrabasic rocks. The lithosphere rests on a soft layer called the ASTHENOSPHERE, over which the plates of the lithosphere glide. See PLATE TECTONICS.

Lithuania (lĭthōōā'nēə), Lithuanian *Lietuva,* constituent republic (1970 pop. 3,129,000), 25,174 sq mi (65,201 sq km), W European USSR. VILNIUS is the capital; other important cities are KAUNAS, KLAYPEDA (Memel), and SIAULAI. Lithuania borders on the Baltic Sea in the west, Latvia in the north, Belorussia in the east, Poland in the south, and Kaliningrad oblast (formerly East Prussia) in the southwest. Lithuania is a flatland, drained by the Nemen River. Dairy farming and stock raising are carried on extensively, and grains, flax, sugar beets, potatoes, and vegetables are grown. Primarily agricultural before 1940, Lithuania has since developed considerable industry, including food processing, shipbuilding, and the manufacture of textiles, machinery, metal products, chemicals, and electrical equipment. About 80% of the population is Lithuanian; there are Russian, Polish, Belorussian, Lettish, and Jewish minorities. The Lithuanians speak a Baltic language (see BALTS). The pagan Liths, or Lithuanians, may have settled along the Nemen as early as 1500 B.C. In the 13th cent. the LIVONIAN BROTHERS OF THE SWORD and the TEUTONIC KNIGHTS conquered the region now comprising Estonia, Latvia, and parts of Lithuania. To protect themselves against the Knights, who pressed them from the north and the south, the Lithuanians formed (13th cent.) a strong unified state. The grand dukes Gedimin (1316-41) and Olgerd (1345-77) expanded their territories at the expense of the neighboring Russian principalities, which were weakened by the Mongol invasion. Lithuania became one of the largest states of medieval Europe, including all Belorussia, a large part of the Ukraine, and sections of Great Russia; at its furthest extent it touched the Black Sea. Olgerd's son, Jagiello, became king of Poland in 1386 as LADISLAUS II by his marriage with JADWIGA, daughter of Louis I of Poland and Hungary. He accepted and introduced Christianity. The union between Lithuania and Poland had at first the character of an alliance between independent nations. WITOWT, a cousin of Ladislaus II, ruled Lithuania independently (1392-1430) and brought it to the height of its power and expansion. In 1410 the Polish-Lithuanian forces severely defeated the Teutonic Knights at TANNENBERG. However, with Witowt's death decline set in. The Belorussians, who had retained their Greek Orthodox faith, inclined toward the rising grand duchy of Moscow. In 1569, hard pressed by the Russians under Ivan IV, Lithuania fully merged with Poland by the Union of Lublin. The Lithuanian aristocracy and burghers became thoroughly Polonized, while the peasantry sank into servitude. By the three successive partitions of Poland (1772, 1793, 1795) Lithuania disappeared as a national unit and passed to Russia. A Lithuanian linguistic and cultural revival began in the 19th cent., inspired largely by the Roman Catholic clergy and accompanied by frequent anti-Russian uprisings. World War I and the consequent collapse of Russia and Germany made Lithuanian independence possible. Proclaimed (Feb., 1918) an independent kingdom under German protection, Lithuania became (Nov., 1918) an independent republic. It resisted attacks by Bolshevik troops and by volunteer bands of German adventurers, but in 1920 Vilnius was seized by Poland. Lithuania remained technically at war with Poland until 1927. In 1923, Lithuania seized the MEMEL TERRITORY. Internal politics were unstable. The virtual dictatorship (1926-29) of Augustine Voldemaras was succeeded (1929-39) by that of Antanas SMETONA, and an authoritarian constitution on corporative (fascist) lines became effective in 1938. Poland forced the official cession of Vilnius (1938), which, however, passed to Lithuania after the Soviet-German partition of Poland in 1939. A German ultimatum forced (1939) the restitution of Memel. In 1940 the USSR, which had obtained military bases in Lithuania, occupied the country. After a Soviet-sponsored "election," Lithuania became a constituent republic of the USSR. During the German occupation (1941-44) of Lithuania in World War II the considerable Jewish minority was largely exterminated. In 1944 the Communist government returned. The republic's educational and cultural institutions include universities at Vilnius and Kaunas and the Lithuanian Academy of Sciences. See A. E. Senn, *The Emergence of Modern Lithuania* (1959).

Lithuanian (lĭth''ōōā'nēən), a language belonging to the Baltic subfamily of the Indo-European family of languages (see BALTIC LANGUAGES). The official language of Lithuania since 1918, Lithuanian is spoken by approximately 2.5 million people there and by an additional half-million elsewhere in the world, chiefly in the Western Hemisphere. The importance of Lithuanian in linguistic studies stems from its designation as the most ancient of the living Indo-European languages. It is also the language closest to Proto-Indo-European, the ancestral tongue from which all the Indo-European languages evolved. Currently, Lithuanian uses a modified Roman alphabet for writing. See Alfred Senn, *The Lithuanian Language* (1942).

litmus, organic dye usually used in the laboratory as an indicator of acidity or alkalinity (see ACIDS AND BASES). Naturally pink in color, it turns blue in alkali solutions and red in acids. Commonly, paper is treated with the coloring matter to form so-called litmus paper. Litmus is extracted, chiefly in the Netherlands, from certain lichens (see ARCHIL), which are mashed, treated with potassium carbonate and ammonia, and allowed to ferment. The resulting product is mixed with various colorless substances, such as chalk or gypsum, and is sold in dark blue lumps, masses, or tablets. The active component of litmus, i.e., the part sensitive to acids or bases, is called erythrolitmin.

litotes (lī'tətēz''), figure of speech in which a statement is made by indicating the negative of its opposite, e.g., "not many" meaning "a few." A form of IRONY, litotes is meant to emphasize by understating. Its opposite is HYPERBOLE.

Li Tsung-jên (lē dzōōng-jŭn), 1890-1969, Chinese Nationalist general and political leader. For 25 years (1925-49) he was a leader of the military clique that ruled Kwangsi prov. The Kwangsi army was an important element in the NORTHERN EXPEDITION (1926-28) of the KUOMINTANG party, but the Kwangsi clique was not close to power in the Nanking government formed by CHIANG KAI-SHEK. Li led Nationalist forces in central China against the Japanese invaders (1937-45). In 1948 he was elected vice president after defeating Sun Fo, the personal choice of Chiang. Although serving as acting president following the resignation of Chiang in Jan., 1949, Li had little real power. Chiang retained the party leadership and controlled the Nationalist armies through trusted aides. When the Nationalist government moved to Taiwan in Dec., 1949, Li went instead to the United States. He returned to mainland China in 1965. See E. F. Carlson, *The Chinese Army* (1940); Edgar Snow, *The Battle for Asia* (1941).

Little, Lou, 1893-, American football coach, b. Leominster, Mass. He studied and played football at the Univ. of Pennsylvania (1915-19). He played professional football and coached at Georgetown Univ. (1924-29) before going to Columbia in 1930. He retired after the 1956 season. His record at Columbia included several notable upsets—the defeat (7-0) of Stanford in the 1934 Rose Bowl and the 1947 victory (21-20) over Army, Army's first defeat in 33 games since 1943. He became chairman of the Football Coaches Association Rules Committee in 1932 and exerted great influence on gridiron regulations. He was president of the association in 1939.

Little America, base for Antarctic exploring expeditions, Antarctica, on the Ross Ice Shelf, S of the Bay of Whales. Richard E. BYRD, a U.S. explorer, established and named Little America in 1929 and built bases on the same site in 1933-35 and 1939-41 for subsequent expeditions. Little America IV at Kainan Bay, 30 mi (48 km) to the east, was a U.S. station during the International Geophysical Year (1957-58).

Little Armenia: see CILICIA.

Little Belt: see STORE BAELT, strait, Denmark.

Little Bighorn, river, c.90 mi (145 km) long, rising in the Bighorn Mts., N Wyo., and flowing north to join the Bighorn River in S Mont. On June 25-26, 1876, Sioux and Cheyenne warriors defeated the forces of Col. George CUSTER in the Little Bighorn valley. Custer Battlefield National Monument occupies the site of the battle. The graves of those killed in the battle are located around a granite monument marking the spot of Custer's "last stand." See NATIONAL PARKS AND MONUMENTS (table).

Little Current, town (1971 pop. 1,565), S Ont., Canada, on N Manitoulin island, on North Channel of Lake Huron. A port and a popular yachting resort, it has rail connections with the mainland.

Little Dipper, familiar configuration of stars in the constellation Ursa Minor (see URSA MAJOR AND URSA MINOR).

Little Entente (äntänt'), loose alliance formed in 1920-21 by Czechoslovakia, Rumania, and Yugoslavia. Its specific purposes were the containment of Hungarian revisionism (of the terms of the World War I peace treaty) and the prevention of a restoration of the Hapsburgs. The three nations were drawn together by three bilateral treaties of defensive and economic alliance. This combination eventually became closely bound to France by financial and treaty obligations, and Poland sometimes cooperated with it but did not enter the alliance. Yugoslavia and Rumania were also members of the BALKAN ENTENTE, formed in 1934. The overall aims of the Little Entente and the Balkan Entente, taken together, were the preservation of the territorial status quo, established by the treaties of Versailles, Saint-Germain, Trianon, and Neuilly, against the efforts of Germany, Hungary, Italy, and Bulgaria to have those treaties revised; the prevention of ANSCHLUSS, or union, between Germany and Austria; and the encouragement of closer economic ties among its members. The Little Entente was successful in its aims until the rise of Hitler in Germany, when French prestige was gradually displaced by German economic penetration and political pressure. It began to break apart in 1936 and was effectively ended when Czechoslovakia lost its membership by the formation of the Munich Pact (1938).

Little Flower of Jesus: see THERESA, SAINT (Theresa of the Child Jesus).

little magazine, term used to designate certain magazines appearing since about 1912 that have generally had as their purpose the publication of art, literature, or social theory by little-known writers. They have been distinguished from the large commercial periodical and major scholarly reviews by their emphasis on experimentation in writing, their perilous nonprofit operation, their comparatively small audience drawn from the intelligentsia, and the fact that they have usually been short-lived. Prototypes of the 20th-century little magazine were *The Dial* (Boston, 1840-44), a transcendentalist review edited by Ralph Waldo Emerson and Margaret Fuller, and the English *Savoy* (1896), a manifesto in revolt against Victorian materialism. The little-magazine movement in this century began in 1912 with *Poetry: A Magazine of Verse* (Chicago, 1912-), edited by Harriet Monroe with Ezra Pound as the foreign editor. *Poetry* enjoyed a long period of success. During World War I a large number of other magazines appeared, the most notable of which were *Others* (1915–19), edited by Alfred Kreymborg; *The Little Review* (Chicago, San Francisco, New York, Paris, 1914–29), edited by Margaret Anderson; and *The Egoist* (London, 1914–19), edited by Dora Mardson (1914) and Harriet Shaw Weaver (1914–19), which voiced the theories and practices of the imagists. Among the many poets whose early reputations owed much to little magazines were T. S. Eliot, Robert Frost, Ezra Pound, Edgar Lee Masters, Hart Crane, and Wallace Stevens. *The Little Review* gave the first American publication (printed in serial installments) to James Joyce's *Ulysses.* As a result, the magazine was banned by court order and subsequently broken financially. Also appearing before 1920 and prefiguring much of the little-magazine movement of the 1930s were the proletarian or left-wing magazines. The first and most significant of these was *The Masses* (New York, 1911–17), guided principally by Max Eastman and Floyd Dell. After World War I the "new" literary magazine appeared. Noted examples of this type were the *Modern Review* (1922–24), edited by Firwoode Tarleton; *The Fugitive* (Nashville, Tenn., 1922–25), with a board of editors that included John Crowe Ransome, Allen Tate, Donald Davidson, and Robert Penn Warren; *Voices* (Boston, 1921–), edited by Harold Vinal; *Seccession* (1922–24), published in Vienna, Berlin, Brooklyn, and other places and edited by Gorham Munson; and *Broom* (1921–24), a rival of *Seccession,* edited by Harold Loeb and Alfred Kreymborg. Ezra Pound's *The Exile* (1927–28) was characterized by a strong disdain for the American mind. Also important were *This Quarter* (Paris, Milan, 1925–32), edited by Ernest J. Walsh and *The Enemy* (London, 1927–29), edited by Wyndham Lewis. Regional magazines also appeared at this time. The first of these was *The Midland* (Iowa City, 1915–33), edited by John T. Frederick, which celebrated the Midwest. Others were *The Frontier* (1920–39), which celebrated the Pacific Northwest; the *Southwest Review* (1924–), edited by J. B. Hubbell; *Double-Dealer* (New Orleans, 1921–26), edited by John McClure; and the *Prairie Schooner* (1927–). In the 1930s most of the important little magazines were connected with the left-wing movement, and while advocating certain reforms within the capitalist system, they also called for a new political system. The most significant among these magazines were *New Masses* (1926–48), which became increasingly associated with the Communist party (although one of its editors denied that it was financed by the party); the *Modern Quarterly* (1923–40); *The Anvil* (1933–35); *Blast* (1933–34); and *The Partisan Review* (1933–), which soon abandoned politics and turned to literary affairs. Some literary magazines also appeared. Notable among them were *transition* (Paris, 1927–38), established by Eugene Jolas; *New Verse* (London, 1933–39); and *Criterion* (London, 1922–39), edited by T. S. Eliot, which concentrated mainly on European writers. After 1940, the little magazines declined; postwar attempts to revive them failed as financing became increasingly difficult and as writers and poets turned to academic quarterlies and journals. In the late 1960s the underground press in combination with an avant-garde striving to articulate their rejection of established attitudes fostered a rebirth of little-magazine publishing. This movement has produced hundreds of new reviews, including the *New York Quarterly* (1969–), *Aphra, A Feminist Literary Magazine* (1969–), *The Little Magazine* (1966–), and *The New American Review* (now *The American Review,* 1967–). See Frederick Hoffman et al., *The Little Magazine* (1947); Rowena Ferguson, *Editing the Small Magazine* (1958); Reed Whittemore, ed., *Symposium on Little Magazines* (1966); Lee Ash, ed., *Union List of Little Magazines* (1956, repr. 1972).

Little Miami, river: see MIAMI, river.

Little Minch, strait: see MINCH, Scotland.

Little Missouri. 1 River, c.145 mi (230 km) long, rising in the Ouachita Mts., SW Ark., and flowing generally SE to join the Ouachita River N of Camden. North of Murfreesboro is Narrows Dam (1950; 25,500 kw capacity) impounding Lake Greeson. **2** River, c.560 mi (900 km) long, rising in NE Wyo. and flowing NE into Garrison Reservoir on the Missouri River, W N.Dak. It flows through Theodore Roosevelt National Memorial Park.

Little Red River, 105 mi (169 km) long, rising in the Boston Mts., NW Ark., and flowing SE to the White River. Greers Dam and reservoir (completed 1964) provide flood control and power (96,000 kw capacity).

Little Rock, city (1970 pop. 132,483), state capital and seat of Pulaski co., central Ark., on the Arkansas River; inc. 1831. It is a river port and the administrative, commercial, transportation, and cultural center of the state. The city's industries process agricultural products, fish, beef, poultry, and bauxite and timber. Its manufacturing industries are closely related with those of North Little Rock across the river. The settlement was a well-known river crossing when Arkansas Territory was established in 1819. It became territorial capital in 1821 and state capital when Arkansas entered the Union in 1836. In the Civil War the battle of Little Rock (1863) was fought there. The city became a center of world attention in 1957, when Federal troops were sent there to enforce a 1954 U.S. Supreme Court ruling against segregation in the public schools. Little Rock is the seat of Philander Smith College, Shorter College, Arkansas Baptist College, the Univ. of Arkansas at Little Rock, and several other branches of the university, including the law and medical schools. Of interest are the beautiful old statehouse (which served as capitol from 1836 to 1910) and several museums. The present capitol building was built in 1911. The city also contains a U.S. veterans hospital and several state institutions. Little Rock Air Force Base is in nearby Jacksonville.

Little Saint Bernard, pass: see SAINT BERNARD.

Little Sioux (so͞o), river, 221 mi (356 km) long, rising in SW Minn. and flowing generally SW across NW Iowa to the Missouri River S of Sioux City. Flowing through a rich agricultural area in the Corn Belt, the river is used extensively for irrigation. The Nepper watershed project, near Mapleton, Iowa, consisting of four dams, was completed in 1948. Serious floods in 1953 and 1954 led to programs for flood control and soil conservation.

Little Tennessee, river, c.135 mi (220 km) long, rising in the Blue Ridge, NE Ga., and flowing generally NW across SW N.C. and through E Tenn. to the Tennessee River opposite Lenoir City. On the river in North Carolina near the Tennessee line is Fontana Dam (480 ft/146 m high; 2,365 ft/721 m long; completed 1945), impounding Fontana Lake. It is part of the Tennessee Valley Authority (TVA) and is the highest dam E of the Rocky Mts. The dam provides flood control, river regulation, and hydroelectricity (202,500-kw capacity). Cheoah Dam in North Carolina, and Calderwood and Chilhowee dams in Tennessee are also part of the TVA.

Littleton, Sir Thomas, 1422?–1481, English jurist. He became a sergeant-at-law, i.e., a barrister, in the Court of Common Pleas in 1453 and a judge in 1466. He is best known for his *Tenures,* a short work in French on the types of estates in land in England. The work, one of the earliest printed books in England, was much admired for its concise and simple quality. In the much-expanded edition of Sir Edward Coke, the *Tenures* was the standard text on property law until the 19th cent. His name also occurs as Lyttelton or Lyttleton.

Littleton, city (1970 pop. 26,466), seat of Arapahoe co., N central Colo.; platted 1812, inc. 1890. It is a suburb S of Denver in an irrigated farm area. Its industries include petroleum research and aerospace firms as well as the manufacture of tires, precision castings, photographic equipment, and tow trucks. Arapahoe Community College and a thoroughbred racing track are in Littleton.

Little Turtle, c. 1752–1812, chief of the Miami Indians, born in a Miami village near present-day Fort Wayne, Ind. He was noted for his oratorical powers, military skill, and intelligence. He was a principal commander of the Indians in the defeat of Gen. Josiah Harmar on the Miami River in 1790 and of Gen. Arthur ST. CLAIR on the Wabash River in 1791. After several attacks on the forces of Gen. Anthony WAYNE, he counseled peace but was overruled. Consequently he was not in command at Fallen Timbers. He reluctantly signed the Treaty of Greenville (Ohio) in 1795, ceding a great part of Ohio to the whites, and he also signed several subsequent treaties. Later he refused to join Tecumseh's confederacy against the whites. He persuaded many of the Miami to turn to agriculture and appealed to the government to halt the liquor trade among his people. See biography by Calvin Young (1917).

littoral zone: see OCEAN.

Littoria: see LATINA, Italy.

Littré, Maximilien Paul Émile (mäksēmēlyăN' pōl āmēl' lĕtrā'), 1801–81, French lexicographer. Known as a positivist philosopher and as professor of history and geography at the École polytechnique, Littré is best remembered for his dictionary of the French language (5 vol., 1863–72), for his translation of Hippocrates, and for his works in medical history.

liturgy, form of public worship, particularly the form of rite or services prescribed by the various Christian churches. In the Western Church the principal service centered upon the Eucharistic sacrifice, but with the Protestant Reformation, the reformers generally rejected the idea of sacrifice and shifted toward the sermon as the focus of formal worship. They also adopted vernacular speech. The liturgy of the Roman Catholic, the Orthodox Eastern, and some other groups centers upon the MASS. In the ROMAN CATHOLIC CHURCH there are nine rites with distinctive liturgies (in various languages). The ORTHODOX EASTERN CHURCH has several liturgies. The ancient liturgies of the East are classified as Antiochene or Syrian (with modern liturgies in Greek, Old Slavonic, Rumanian, Armenian, Arabic, and Syriac) and Alexandrine or Egyptian (with liturgies in Coptic and Ethiopic). The liturgies that arose in the West are classified as either Gallican (including the Celtic, Mozarabic, and Ambrosian) or Roman, both using Latin. In the 8th cent. the Gallican was largely superseded by the Roman, which is the principal liturgy of the Roman Catholic Church today. The language was Latin until the vernacular liturgy was introduced following the Second Vatican Council. In a broader sense, liturgy includes the divine office (given in the breviary) and also services other than the Mass. In the 20th cent. there has been a movement, called the liturgical movement, for purification and renewal of liturgy. Most of its demands were met in the Roman Catholic Church by the liturgical reformation directed by the Second Vatican Council, including the use of vernacular languages in the Mass, participation of the laity in public prayer, and an emphasis on music and song. In the Protestant churches a similar liturgical movement has gained much ground, urging the formulation and reform of service and wider awareness of the value of form itself. See Romano Guardini, *The Spirit of Liturgy* (tr. 1930); Virgil Michel, *The Liturgy of the Church according to the Roman Rite* (1937); E. B. Koenker, *The Liturgical Renaissance in the Roman Catholic Church* (1954, repr. 1966); A. A. King, *Liturgies of the Past* (1959); Donald Attwater, *The Christian Churches of the East* (2 vol., rev. ed. 1961); Bard Thompson, *Liturgies of the Western Church* (1961); Theodor Klauser, *A Short History of the Western Liturgy* (tr. 1969).

Litvinov, Maxim Maximovich (məksyēm' mäksē'-məvĭch lyĭtvē'nəf), 1876–1951, Russian revolutionary and diplomat. A Jew, he changed his name from Wallach after joining the Social Democratic party. He became a member of the Bolshevik wing after the party split (1903). He took part in the Revolution of 1905 and subsequently spent years in exile in Great Britain and Switzerland. Imprisoned in England after the Bolshevik Revolution, he was released in exchange for the British consul general, Bruce Lockhart, who had been arrested in Moscow. As chief assistant to the commissar for foreign affairs, CHICHERIN, he assumed much of his superior's work, and in 1930 he succeeded Chicherin. He pursued a policy of collective security and cooperation with the great powers. In 1933 he obtained American recognition of the USSR, and in 1934, Russia entered the League of Nations, where Litvinov continued to promote a peace policy and called for joint action against the aggression of Germany, Italy, and Japan. His policy was abandoned by Stalin after the Munich Pact of 1938, when Great Britain and France capitulated to German demands in Czechoslovakia, and in May, 1939, he was replaced by Molotov as foreign commissar. In 1941, Litvinov was named ambassador to the United States, where he served until 1943.

Li Tzu-ch'eng (lē dzo͞o-chŭng), 1605–45, Chinese rebel leader who contributed to the fall of the MING dynasty. With the help of scholars he organized a government in S Shansi prov., proclaimed a new dynasty, and sought popular support by giving famine relief and spreading songs and stories lauding his heroic qualities. By 1643 he held much of Hupei, Honan, and Shensi provs., and in 1644 he captured Peking, finding the last Ming emperor dead by suicide. Advancing to Shanhaikwan, a strategic pass on the Great Wall, Li confronted the Ming general Wu San-kuei. Rather than surrender to a Chinese rebel leader, Wu preferred to collaborate with the Manchu. Li was driven from Peking, and within a year he was killed and his forces were crushed. The new Manchu CH'ING dynasty rewarded Wu with an independent satrapy in Yunnan and Kweichou provs.

Liu Chih-chi (lyo͞o jûr-jē), 661–721, Chinese T'ang dynasty historian. Drawing on experience gained while working on histories of the preceding dynasties, he wrote the first important Chinese work on historiography, the *Understanding of History* (*Shih-t'ung*). In a series of essays Liu discusses the origin, development, and relative merits of various forms of historical writing.

Liu-ch'iu: see RYUKYU ISLANDS.

Liu-chou or **Liuchow** (both: lyo͞o-jō), city, N central Kwangsi Chuang Autonomous Region, S China, on the Liu River. At the intersection of highways and three railroads, it is a manufacturing town with important paper and wood-product industries, a large integrated iron and steel complex, machine shops, chemical plants, textile mills, and food-processing establishments.

Liu Hsiu (lyo͞o shyo͞o), A.D. 6–A.D. 57, restorer of the HAN dynasty. As first emperor (A.D. 25–A.D. 57) of the Later, or Eastern, Han (A.D. 25–A.D. 200), he curbed the power of the imperial princes and recreated the centralized state administration of the Former, or Western, Han (206 B.C.–A.D. 8). Although only a distant relative of the last emperor of the Earlier Han, Liu Hsiu emerged victorious from the free-for-all that followed the downfall of the usurper WANG MANG. Liu Hsiu moved the capital eastward from Ch'ang-an, which had been destroyed by rebels, to Loyang. The new capital was nearer his large landholdings in E Honan prov. and was more easily supplied with grain than the old capital. Liu Hsiu is also known by his posthumous temple name, Kuang Wu Ti.

Liu-kiu Islands: see RYUKYU ISLANDS.

Liu Pang (lyo͞o bäng), Chinese emperor (206–195 B.C.), founder of the HAN dynasty. Liu was of peasant origin and had been a minor official before joining the free-for-all struggle that attended the collapse of the CH'IN dynasty. Threatened by internal dissension and nomadic incursions, Liu slowly consolidated power, but it was several decades before Han rule recreated the imperial system of the Ch'in. Liu is also known by his posthumous temple name, Kao Tsu [Chin.,=high progenitor].

Liu Shao-ch'i (lyo͞o shou-chē), 1898?–1973?, Chinese Communist political leader. Liu joined (1920) a Comintern organization in Shanghai, where he studied Russian. While in Moscow in 1921, he joined the Chinese Communist party. After he returned to China, his reputation as a labor organizer grew. He rose rapidly in the party hierarchy, was a member of the central committee in 1927, and in 1934 was promoted to the powerful politburo. Liu became the Communists' foremost expert on organization and party structure. In the 1950s and early 60s he played an important role in all aspects of public life, especially as chairman and head of state of the Chinese People's Republic (1959–68). Severely criticized during the early stages of the Cultural Revolution (1966–69) for his allegedly "revisionist" views, Liu was removed from power in 1968. Rumors of his death were confirmed in 1974.

Liutprand (lēo͞ot'prănd), d. 744, king of the Lombards (712–44). Under his rule the Lombard kingdom of Italy reached its zenith. The first Christian Lombard ruler, Liutprand strongly favored Roman law and institutions. His legislation anticipated the reforms of Charlemagne by protecting his subjects from denial of justice through special envoys authorized to administer justice and redress grievances. He curbed the powers of the local dukes and bishops, thus creating a centralized state, and he obtained the submission of the duchies of Spoleto and Benevento. In the north, he expanded his dominions at the expense of Bavaria. Liutprand died after attempting to bring Ravenna, which was under Byzantine rule, into his domain. After the brief reigns of Liutprand's nephew Hildeprand and of Ratchis, duke of Friuli, Liutprand's brother Aistulf acceded (749) and took Ravenna in 751.

Livadiya (lyĭvä'dyēə), town, SE European USSR, in the Ukraine, in the Crimea, on the Black Sea. It produces wine and is a noted health resort. Dating from medieval times, Livadiya became a summer residence of the Russian czars in 1861. The Livadiya palace, built in 1910–11, is now a sanatorium. It was the meeting place of U.S. President Franklin Delano Roosevelt, British Prime Minister Winston Churchill, and Soviet leader Joseph Stalin during the Yalta Conference in 1945.

live-forever: see STONECROP.

live oak: see OAK.

liver, largest glandular organ of the body, weighing about 3 lb (1.36 kg). It is reddish brown in color and is divided into four lobes of unequal size and shape. The liver lies on the right side of the abdominal cavity beneath the diaphragm. Blood is carried to the liver via two large vessels: The hepatic artery carries oxygen-rich blood from the aorta, and the portal vein carries blood containing digested food from the small intestine. These blood vessels subdivide in the liver repeatedly, terminating in minute capillaries. Each capillary leads to a lobule. Liver tissue is composed of thousands of lobules, and each lobule is made up of hepatic cells, the basic metabolic cells of the liver. It is thought that the liver performs more than 500 functions. It manufactures and secretes BILE, which is stored in the GALL BLADDER and released in the small intestine. Bile salts emulsify fats, a process that prepares the latter for digestion by the intestinal enzymes (see DIGESTIVE SYSTEM). The hepatic cells assimilate carbohydrates, fats, and proteins. They convert glucose to its stored form, glycogen, which is reconverted into glucose as the body requires it for energy. The ability of the liver to maintain the proper level of glucose in the blood is called its glucose buffer function. The end products of fat digestion, fatty acids, are used to synthesize cholesterol and other substances needed by the body. Excess carbohydrates and protein are also converted into fat by the liver. Digested proteins in the form of amino acids are broken down further in the liver in the process called deamination. Part of the amino acid molecule is converted into glycogen and other compounds. Urea, a waste product of protein breakdown, is produced by the liver, a process which removes poisonous ammonia from the body fluids. The liver is also capable of synthesizing certain amino acids (the so-called nonessential amino acids) from other amino acids in a process called transamination. Some essential components of blood are manufactured by the liver, including about 95% of the plasma proteins and the blood-clotting substances (fibrinogen, prothrombin, and other coagulation factors). The liver also filters harmful substances from the blood. Phagocytic cells in the liver, called Kupffer cells, remove large amounts of debris and bacteria that tend to be plentiful in the blood brought from the intestinal tract via the portal vein. In addition, the liver stores important vitamins and minerals, including vitamins A, D, K, and B_{12}.

liver fluke: see FLUKE.

Livermore, city (1970 pop. 37,703), Alameda co., W central Calif.; inc. 1876. The major sources of employment are wineries and the Livermore Radiation Laboratory of the Univ. of California, which conducts nuclear research.

Liverpool, Robert Banks Jenkinson, 2nd earl of, 1770–1828, English statesman. He was elected to Parliament as a Tory in 1790 and succeeded his father to the peerage in 1808. He served as foreign secretary (1801–3), home secretary (1804–6, 1807–9), and secretary for war and the colonies (1809–12) before becoming prime minister in 1812. His government ended the Napoleonic Wars, negotiated the peace settlement, and attempted to deal with the social and economic malaise that followed. His early domestic policy was typified by a strong conservatism in the face of changing social and economic conditions and by repressive legislation, including the periodic suspension of habeas corpus. His administration, initially thought of as weak, lasted for 15 years, in a large part due to his ability to work with colleagues more talented and ambitious than himself, allowing them broad responsibilities yet retaining the cohesion of the ministry. His cabinet included such disparate elements as Viscount Sidmouth, Lord Eldon, the duke of Wellington, Viscount Castlereagh, George Canning, and William Huskisson. During the 1820s government policy became increasingly liberal. The anti-trade union laws were repealed, and many trading restrictions were removed. In matters where Liverpool had had of necessity to remain politically equivocal, Catholic Emancipation and parliamentary reform, his administration gradually moved toward a more liberal position. He resigned because of ill health (1827). See biography by C. A. Petrie (1954); W. R. Brock, *Lord Liverpool and Liberal Toryism, 1820–1827* (2d ed. 1967).

Liverpool, county borough (1971 pop. 606,834), Lancashire, NW England, on the Mersey River near its mouth. It is one of Britain's greatest ports and largest cities and the country's major outlet for industrial exports. A large center for food processing (especially flour and sugar), Liverpool has a variety of industries, including the manufacture of electrical equipment, chemicals, and rubber. Its first wet dock was completed by 1715; today, Liverpool's vast docks are more than 7 mi (11.3 km) long. The city is connected by tunnel with Birkenhead across the Mersey. Liverpool was once famous for its pottery, and its textile industry was also prosperous; however, since World War II its cotton market has declined considerably. In 1207, King John granted Liverpool its first charter. In 1644, during the English Civil War, Liverpool surrendered to the royalists under Prince Rupert after several sieges. Air raids during World War II caused heavy damage and casualties. Liverpool Cathedral, designed by Sir George Gilbert Scott, was begun in 1904 but is still unfinished. It will be the largest in England. A Roman Catholic cathedral was consecrated in 1967. St. George's Hall is an imposing building in a group that includes libraries and art galleries. The Walker Gallery has a fine collection of Italian and Flemish paintings, as well as more modern works. The Univ. of Liverpool was incorporated in 1903. There is a separate school of tropical medicine. The statesman William Gladstone, the artist George Stubbs, and the members of the musical group the Beatles were born in Liverpool. In 1974, Liverpool became part of the new metropolitan county of Merseyside.

Liverpool, University of, at Liverpool, England; established 1903 by royal charter. It has faculties of arts, engineering science, law, medicine, science, social and environmental studies, and veterinary science. The Institute of Coastal Oceanography and Tides and a school of tropical medicine are affiliated.

liverwort, any plant of the class Marchantiopsida. Mosses and liverworts together comprise the division BRYOPHYTA, primitive green land plants (see MOSS; PLANT). In contrast to mosses, most liverworts grow prostrate and consist of a flattened, branching (but undifferentiated) green structure, the thallus; other liverworts produce leafy stems, which are flattened and usually prostrate. The ancients believed that liverworts could cure diseases of the liver. They are also called hepatics, and the unrelated flowering plant HEPATICA is frequently called liverwort. Liverworts are classified in the division Bryophyta, class Marchantiopsida.

livery companies, London trade GUILDS incorporated by royal charter, deriving their name from the assumption of distinctive dress (livery) by their members. Edward III granted the first charters in the 14th cent., and most of the existing companies had been incorporated by the 17th cent. Several, however, have been formed in the 20th cent., including the Scientific Instrument Makers and the Air Pilots and Navigators. Liverymen were not artisans or journeymen but rather the controlling elite of their trades. In addition to regulating conditions of apprenticeship and standards of work, they elected the local government of the City of London and had the sole power to confer on members the freedom of the city, a necessary prerequisite to the practice of any trade. They still elect the lord mayor of London. By the 18th cent. more competitive trade practices and early industrial expansion eroded the guilds' practical power over their trades, but they retained their roles as administrators of trusts and benefactors of educational institutions. The Mercers founded St. Paul's School as early as 1509, and to the present day the companies continue to endow colleges and scholarships, particularly in the field of technical education. There are currently 84 livery companies. Twelve of them, according to an order of precedence established by Henry VIII, are known as the great companies—the Mercers, Grocers, Drapers, Fishmongers, Goldsmiths, Skinners, Merchant Taylors, Haberdashers, Salters, Ironmongers, Vintners, and Clothworkers. See William Herbert, *The History of the Twelve Great Livery Companies of London* (1937, repr. 1968); W. F. Kahl, *The Development of London Livery Companies* (1960); George Unwin, *The Gilds and Companies of London* (4th ed. 1964).

Livia Drusilla (lĭv'ēə dro͞osĭl'ə), c.55 B.C.–A.D. 29, Roman matron; mother of the Roman emperor TIBERIUS. She first married Tiberius Claudius Nero. Tiberius was his son. In 38 B.C., AUGUSTUS forced her husband to divorce her so that he might marry her himself. Her son Drusus Senior (see DRUSUS), born soon after her remarriage, was not the son of Augustus but of her first husband. On the accession of her son Tiberius, Livia Drusilla attempted unsuccessfully to control the government. She was known for her dignity, intelligence, and ambition.

Livingston, family of American statesmen, diplomats, and jurists. **Robert R. Livingston,** 1654–1728, b. Roxburghshire, Scotland, was raised in Holland and immigrated to America in 1673 after his father died.

He made Albany, N.Y., his home, married (1679) Alida Van Rensselaer, and, mainly through trade with the Indians, rose quickly to a position of wealth and influence in New York. Through the influence of Gov. Thomas DONGAN, he secured (1686) a patent (later confirmed by royal charter) to shape his extensive land holdings, amounting to 160,000 acres, into Livingston Manor—in the present Dutchess and Columbia counties. Livingston and his brother-in-law, Peter Schuyler, were the leaders of the Albany opposition to the rebellion of Jacob LEISLER, and afterward Livingston found his estates and privileges so endangered by the Leislerian faction, that he twice had to go to England to defend them. He served as secretary of Indian affairs from 1695 until his death and had considerable influence on the Indian policy of the colony; the governors of New York in this period relied heavily on Livingston's advice and were careful to retain his favor. A representative (1709-11, 1716-25) in the New York provincial assembly, he was elected (1718) speaker and supported the legislative body in opposition to the royal control of the governor. See biography by L. H. Leder (1961). He had two sons, Robert and Philip. The younger Robert was the father of **Robert R. Livingston,** 1718-75, who became noted in New York as a Whig political leader, as a judge of the admiralty court (1759-63), and as a judge of the supreme court of the colony (1763-75); he was also a delegate to the Stamp Act Congress and chairman of the New York Committee of Correspondence. Five of his seven daughters made notable marriages, bringing into the family Gen. Richard Montgomery, Thomas Tillotson, Freeborn Garrettson, Morgan Lewis, and John Armstrong (1758-1843). His son, the younger **Robert R. Livingston,** 1746-1813, b. New York City, was admitted to the bar and became a law partner of John JAY. He was a member of the Continental Congress and a member of the committee to draft the Declaration of Independence, but he did not sign that document because the New York provincial congress had not authorized him to do so. He was the first secretary of the department of foreign affairs, a post created in 1781, and he issued the instructions for the commissioners to negotiate peace in France. He was (1777-1801) the first chancellor of the state of New York and an ardent New York supporter of the new Constitution of the United States. As chancellor, he administered the presidential oath to George Washington. One of the leading Federalists, he fell out with Alexander Hamilton and John Jay over the Federalist financial program and questions of patronage; after 1791 he was an ardent Jeffersonian. In 1801, Thomas Jefferson appointed Livingston minister to France, where he conducted the negotiations that resulted in the LOUISIANA PURCHASE. He held a monopoly on steamboat operations in New York waters, and his financing of the experiments of Robert FULTON resulted in the launching of the *Clermont,* the first American steamboat to be commercially successful. See biography by George Dangerfield (1960). A brother, **Edward Livingston,** 1764-1836, b. Livingston Manor, also established a reputation as a jurist and political figure. As a member (1795-1801) of the U.S. House of Representatives he opposed Jay's Treaty and the Alien and Sedition Acts. President Jefferson appointed him U.S. district attorney of New York in 1801, the same year that he became mayor of New York City. Because one of his clerks lost or misappropriated public funds, Livingston was forced to resign and to sell his property to pay off the debt. He then went to New Orleans. In the War of 1812 he became chairman of the committee on public defense and acted as aide-de-camp to Gen. Andrew Jackson. He was elected (1820) to the Louisiana legislature, and in 1821 was appointed to prepare a new code of laws and criminal procedure. Although the code was not adopted, its completeness and reasoned unity brought him international fame. He served again (1823-29) in the U.S. House of Representatives and then in the Senate (1829-31) before resigning to become Secretary of State under Andrew Jackson—for whom he wrote many important state papers, including the famous reply to the doctrine of nullification. As minister to France (1833-35), Livingston was unable to secure payment on American claims for spoliations resulting from the Napoleonic Wars. See biography by W. B. Hatcher (1940). Another line of Livingstons descended from Philip Livingston, son of Robert Livingston (1654-1728). Philip had six sons, three of whom gained distinction. The eldest of these three, **Peter Van Brugh Livingston,** 1710-92, b. Albany, N.Y., was on the Whig side in the bitter political contests preceding the American Revolution and was a strong opponent of the Stamp Act and other British taxation measures. He was president (1775) of the first provincial congress. He became (1748) an original trustee of the College of New Jersey (now Princeton). Another of these three brothers, **Philip Livingston,** 1716-78, b. Albany, N.Y., was a successful merchant and a leader in the protest against the Stamp Act and other British trade restrictions. Although he looked with disfavor upon radicalism and was not originally an advocate of independence, he nevertheless signed the Declaration of Independence and after that time remained an active member of the Continental Congress. He was generous with his large fortune and was a supporter of many philanthropies. He was one of the original promoters of King's College (now Columbia Univ.), established a professorship of divinity at Yale, and helped to found the New York Society Library. The third of these brothers, **William Livingston,** 1723-90, b. Albany, N.Y., fought actively in the American Revolution. He was admitted (1748) to the bar and became one of the leading lawyers of New York City. Together with the historian William Smith he prepared a digest of the laws (1691-1756) of provincial New York. He moved (1772) to New Jersey and was sent to the First and Second Continental Congresses, resigning in 1776 to command briefly the New Jersey militia. In the same year he was elected New Jersey's first governor, and he remained in this office for the rest of his life. His influence played a large part in the prompt ratification of the U.S. Constitution in New Jersey. His daughter married John Jay. His son, **Henry Brockholst Livingston,** 1757-1823, b. New York City, served in the American Revolution and went (1779) to Spain as private secretary to John Jay. On the return journey Livingston was captured (1782) by the British but was soon released. After he was admitted (1783) to the New York bar, he became an ardent Jeffersonian and wrote a number of newspaper articles opposing Jay's Treaty. In 1802 he was appointed a judge of the New York supreme court, and, in 1806, Jefferson appointed him Associate Justice of the U.S. Supreme Court. He remained on the Supreme Court bench until 1823. See E. B. Livingston, *The Livingstons of Livingston Manor* (1910).

Livingston, Edward: see under LIVINGSTON, family.

Livingston, Henry Brockholst: see under LIVINGSTON, family.

Livingston, Peter Van Brugh: see under LIVINGSTON, family.

Livingston, Philip: see under LIVINGSTON, family.

Livingston, Robert: see under LIVINGSTON, family.

Livingston, Robert R. (1718-75): see under LIVINGSTON, family.

Livingston, Robert R. (1746-1813): see under LIVINGSTON, family.

Livingston, William: see under LIVINGSTON, family.

Livingstone, David, 1813-73, Scottish missionary and explorer in Africa. From 1841 to 1852, while a medical missionary for the London Missionary Society in what is now Botswana, he crossed the Kalahari desert and reached (1849) Lake Ngami. He discovered the Zambezi River in 1851. Hoping to abolish the slave trade by opening Africa to Christian commerce and missionary stations, he traveled (1853) to Luanda on the west coast. Following the Zambezi River, he discovered Victoria Falls (1855) and reached the east coast at Quelimane, Portuguese East Africa, in 1856. His *Missionary Travels* (1857) in South Africa is an account of that journey. Appointed British consul at Quelimane, he was given command of an expedition (1857-63) to explore the Zambezi region. He returned to England (1864) and wrote with his brother Charles *The Zambezi and Its Tributaries* (1865). In 1866, Livingstone returned to Africa to seek the source of the Nile. He discovered lakes Mweru and Bangweula and in 1871 reached the Lualaba tributary of the Zaïre River. Sickness compelled his return to Ujiji on Lake Tanganyika, where H. M. STANLEY found him in 1871. Unable to persuade Livingstone to leave, Stanley joined him on a journey (1871-72) to the north end of Lake Tanganyika. In 1873, Livingstone died in the village of Chief Chitambo. Black African followers carried his body to the coast; it was sent to England and buried in Westminster Abbey. Livingstone's last journals were edited by Horace Waller (1874). See biographies by J. Simmons (1955, repr. 1962), G. Martelli (1970), and Tim Jeal (1973).

Livingstone, city (1972 est. pop., with suburbs, 52,000), S Zambia, on the Zambezi River, which forms the border with Rhodesia. It is an industrial, commercial, and transportation center. Manufactures include clothing, textiles, and food products. Founded in 1905, the city was named for David Livingstone, the Scots explorer. From 1911 to 1935 it served as capital of the British protectorate of Northern Rhodesia. Today it is the site of Livingstone Museum, which contains archaeological, ethnological, and historical materials, including letters and relics of Livingstone. Victoria Falls and a game reserve are nearby.

Living Theater: see DRAMA, WESTERN; BECK, JULIAN.

Livius Andronicus (lĭ'vēəs ăndrənī'kəs), fl. 3d cent. B.C., Roman poet, a Greek, b. Tarentum (Taranto). He was captured and made a slave at the fall of Tarentum and was freed by a noble of the Livian gens, hence his name. Later he became a teacher and an actor. He introduced Greek literature into Rome, translating the *Odyssey* and adapting Greek plays that he first produced in 240 B.C. Sometimes called the founder of Roman drama, he composed and acted in the first comedy and the first tragedy in Latin (both adopted from Greek models). Only fragments of his works remain.

Livonia (lĭvō'nēə), region and former Russian province, comprising present ESTONIA and parts of LATVIA (Vidzeme and LATGALE). It borders on the Baltic Sea and its arms, the Gulf of Riga and the Gulf of Finland, in the west and the north and extends E to Lake Chudskoye and the Narva. Livonia, also known as Livland, was named after the Livs, a Finnic tribe that inhabited the coast when, in the 13th cent., the LIVONIAN BROTHERS OF THE SWORD conquered the entire region. The knights formed a strong state and threatened Lithuania and Novgorod in the 13th and 14th cent. They reduced the native population to servility. The chief cities—notably RIGA, TARTU, and TALLINN—were Germanic in culture and were dominated by the Hanseatic League. After the dissolution (1561) of the Livonian Order, Livonia was contested by Poland, Russia, and Sweden. COURLAND, in the southwest, became a duchy under Polish suzerainty, and Latgale, in the southeast, became part of Poland. Vidzeme, in the center, passed first to Poland, then (1629) to Sweden, which also held the northern part (Estonia). The Swedish share was conquered (1710) in the NORTHERN WAR by Peter I of Russia, who kept it at the Peace of Nystad (1721). Latgale passed to Russia in 1772. In 1783, Livonia was constituted a Russian province, and in 1918 it was divided between Estonia and Latvia. In 1940, Estonia and Latvia were absorbed into the USSR as constituent republics.

Livonia (lĭvōn'yə), city (1970 pop. 110,109), Wayne co., SE Mich., a suburb of Detroit; founded 1835, inc. 1950. Among its manufactures are auto bodies and parts, tools and dies, and paints. The city is the seat of Madonna College and a junior college. The Detroit race track is there.

Livonian Brothers of the Sword or **Livonian Knights** (lĭvō'nēən), German military and religious order, founded in 1202 by Bishop Albert of Livonia for the purpose of conquest and Christianization in the Baltic lands. The knights were organized similarly to the older TEUTONIC KNIGHTS. Their habit was a white robe with a red cross and sword. They subdued the Livs, Ests, and Letts, whose territories, subsequently known as LIVONIA and COURLAND, became the domain of the order. In 1236 the knights were severely defeated by the Lithuanians at Siauliai; as a result they merged (1237) with the Teutonic Order, but they continued to form a separate state. Their defeat (1242) by ALEXANDER NEVSKY at Lake Peipus checked their eastward expansion. After the secularization (1525) of the Teutonic Order, they resumed independence. In 1558, Czar Ivan IV of Russia invaded their territories, which were eventually partitioned between Russia, Poland, and Sweden. In 1561 the knights were disbanded; their grand master became the first duke of Courland under Polish suzerainty. However, the knights retained their vast estates in the Baltics.

Livorno: see LEGHORN, Italy.

Livy (Titus Livius) (lĭv'ē), 59 B.C.-A.D. 17, Roman historian, b. Patavium (Padua), probably of noble family. He lived most of his life in Rome. The breadth of his education is apparent in his evident familiarity with the ancient Greek and Latin authors. His life work was the *History of Rome* from its founding in 753 B.C. The narrative comes to an end with Drusus (9 B.C.). Of the original 142 books of the work (published in sections) 35 are extant (Books I-X, XXI-XLV). There are fragments of some others, and all but two are known through epitomes. Livy gathered his material from the best sources at his command, chose what seemed to him most authentic and credible, and presented it with the enthusiasm of a patriot in the form of annals. While Livy's accuracy is often questionable, he has achieved and deserved a long popularity because of his vivid depictions, his freedom of expression, and his masterly style (developed from Cicero). W. M. Roberts's translation (1912-24) is one of the many English translations of Livy's history. See P. G. Walsh, *Livy: His Historical Aims and Method* (1961); T. A. Dorey, ed., *Livy* (1971).

Li Yüan-hung (lē yüän-hŏŏng), 1864-1928, president of China (1916-17, 1922-23). A brigade commander under the Ch'ing dynasty, Li was compelled by army rebels to become military governor of Hupei prov. in the republican revolution of 1911. Elected vice president (1912) of the new republican government, Li assumed the presidency (1916) on the death of YÜAN SHIH-K'AI but was soon overshadowed by TUAN CH'I-JUI, premier and leader of the Anfu WARLORD clique. He was restored as president (1922) by the rival Chihli military clique in an unsuccessful attempt to conciliate the KUOMINTANG party.

Lizard, The, peninsula, Cornwall, SW England. Its southern extremity (the southernmost point of Great Britain) is called Lizard Point or Lizard Head. The coast has colored serpentine rocks, small coves and bays, wave-hollowed caves, islets (e.g., Asparagus Island), and dangerous reefs. There are two lighthouses.

lizard, a REPTILE of the order Squamata, which also includes the SNAKE. Lizards form the suborder Sauria. They typically have four legs with five toes on each foot, although a few, such as the WORM LIZARD and the so-called GLASS SNAKE, are limbless, retaining only internal vestiges of legs. Lizards are further distinguished from snakes by having ear openings, movable eyelids, and less flexible jaws. As in snakes, there is a chemosensory organ opening in the roof of the mouth. The tongue, which may be short and wide, slender and forked, or highly extendible, conveys particles from the environment to this organ. The skin of the lizard is scaly and in most species is molted in irregular patches. Members of several lizard families, notably the CHAMELEONS, undergo color changes under the influence of environmental and emotional stimuli. Lizards range in size from species under 3 in. (7.6 cm) long to the 10-ft (3-m) Komodo dragon of SE Asia. There are over 3,000 lizard species distributed throughout the world (except for the Arctic), with the greatest number found in warm climates. Members of most species are carnivorous, feeding especially on insects, but some are herbivorous or omnivorous. Many are arboreal, and many terrestrial species are well adapted for climbing. They are often fast runners, some achieving speeds of over 15 mi (24 km) per hr. Some lizards are adapted for burrowing. Most can swim and a few lead a semiaquatic existence, among them the single marine species, an IGUANA of the Galapagos Islands. Gliding forms, the FLYING DRAGONS, are found in the forests of SE Asia. The GILA MONSTER and the related beaded lizard of the North American deserts are the only known poisonous lizards. Fertilization is internal in lizards; males have paired copulatory organs, characteristic of the order. In most species females lay eggs, which they bury in the ground, but in some the eggs are incubated in the oviducts and hatched as they are laid. In both types the young have a special temporary tooth for rupturing the shell. In a few species there is true viviparity, or live birth, with the young nourished by a simple placenta. The greatest number of species in the United States is found in the South and West. The majority are members of the iguana family, including the collared lizards, swifts, utas, HORNED LIZARDS (popularly known as horned toads), and the so-called American chameleon, or anole. These are day-active lizards commonly seen basking on rocks. Most are valuable destroyers of insects. Lizards are classified in the phylum CHORDATA, subphylum Vertebrata, class Reptilia, order Squamata, suborder Sauria. See also GECKO; MONITOR. See W. M. Milstead, ed., *Lizard Ecology* (1967); H. S. Fitch, *Reproductive Cycles of Lizards and Snakes* (1970); B. R. Headstrom, *Lizards as Pets* (1971).

Ljubljana (lyōō'blyänä), Ger. *Laibach,* city (1971 pop. 257,640), capital of Slovenia, NW Yugoslavia, on the Sava River. An industrial and transportation center, it has industries that manufacture machinery, optical instruments, textiles, and chemicals. It is a Roman Catholic archiepiscopal see and is the seat of the Slovene Academy of Arts and Sciences and a university (founded 1919). Known as Emona in Roman times, Ljubljana passed in 1277 to the Hapsburgs and became the chief city of the Austrian province of CARNIOLA. The city was held briefly by the French during the Napoleonic Wars; it passed to Yugoslavia in 1919 and was made the capital of Slovenia in 1946. Ljubljana was the center of the Slovene national movement in the 19th cent. It has a medieval fortress and several fine palaces and churches. For the international congress held there in 1821, see LAIBACH, CONGRESS OF.

llama (lä'mə), South American domesticated hoofed mammal, *Lama glama,* of the camel family, believed by some to be descended from the GUANACO. Smaller than the camel and lacking a hump, it somewhat resembles a large sheep with a long neck, camellike face, and long ears. It may be brown, white, black, or piebald. Llamas live in herds, owned by the Indians, on the high plains of the Andes mts. and can work at altitudes that most animals cannot tolerate. The llama carries loads of up to 100 lbs (45 kg) but is never ridden. Used as a pack animal since the days of the Incas, it is also valued for its flesh, wool, and milk. It is classified in the phylum CHORDATA, subphylum Vertebrata, class Mammalia, order Artiodactyla, family Camelidae. See also ALPACA; VICUÑA.

Llandaff (lăn'dăf''), suburb of Cardiff, Glamorganshire, S Wales, on the Taff River. According to tradition St. Teilo founded a church there in the late 6th or early 7th cent. The present cathedral, the oldest parts of which date from 1120, was restored in the 19th cent. and again after World War II. Llandaff has an Anglican theological college. In 1974, Llandaff became part of the new nonmetropolitan county of South Glamorgan.

Llandudno (lăndŭd'nō, -dĭd'nō), urban district (1971 pop. 19,009), Caernarvonshire, NW Wales, on a point of land jutting into the Irish Sea. Llandudno is a popular seaside resort with a mild climate. In 1974, Llandudno became part of the new nonmetropolitan county of Gwynedd.

Llanelli (lănĕl'ē, -ĕth'lē), municipal borough (1971 pop. 26,320), Carmarthenshire, S Wales, on the estuary of the Burry River. There are important tin-plate works and steelworks. Pottery and chemicals are also made. Coal is mined and was formerly exported from Llanelli. In 1974, Llanelli became part of the new nonmetropolitan county of Dyfed.

Llangollen (lăn-gō'lĭn, -thlĭn), urban district (1971 pop. 3,108), Denbighshire, NE Wales, at the head of the Vale of Llangollen on the Dee River. It is a resort for fishermen and tourists interested in the antiquities in the vicinity, which include the castle Dinas Bran (13th cent.), Eliseg's Pillar (a shaft of a cross dating probably from the 9th cent.), and Valle Crucis Abbey (1200). The Church of St. Collen (partly Norman) and a 14th-century bridge are noteworthy. The International Musical Eisteddfod has been held there since 1949. In 1974, Llangollen became part of the new nonmetropolitan county of Clwyd.

Llano Estacado (lä'nō ĕstəkä'dō) or **Staked Plain,** level, semi-arid, plateaulike region of the S Great Plains, c.40,000 sq mi (103,600 sq km), E N.Mex. and W Texas, between the Pecos River and the Cap Rock escarpment. The High Plains of the Texas Panhandle (c.4,000 ft/1,220 m high), centered around Amarillo, are usually distinguished from the somewhat lower South Plains (c.2,500 ft/760 m), centered around Lubbock, Texas. Both are wind-swept grasslands, formerly used for cattle ranching, now dotted with dry-land and irrigated farms and oil and natural-gas fields.

llanos (yä'nōs), Spanish American term for prairies, specifically those of the Orinoco River basin of N South America, in Venezuela and E Colombia. Shunned by man before the Spanish came, the llanos of the Orinoco are a vast, hot region of rolling savanna broken by low-lying mesas, scrub forest, and scattered palms. Elevation above sea level never reaches more than a few hundred feet. During the dry season (November to April) the land is sear, the grass brown, brittle, and inedible; during the rainy season much of the area is inundated. The region is subject to insect plagues. The sparsely populated llanos support a pastoral economy; cattle raising is dominant. With flood control and water storage projects in the region, sections of the llanos have been turned into fertile agricultural land. Oil has been found there. Ciudad Bolívar and San Fernando de Apure are the chief cities of the region. The llanero, an expert horseman comparable to the gaucho of the Argentine pampas, is of mixed Spanish, Indian, and black African stock. The llanero has played an important role in Venezuelan history as an ardent henchman of successive revolutionary caudillos, notably José Antonio PÁEZ.

Lleras Camargo, Alberto (älbār'tō lyä'räs kämär'gō), 1906-, president of Colombia (1945-46, 1958-62). A journalist, he entered politics as a Liberal, occupying many important government posts in the 1930s and 1940s. After his first short stint as president (1945-46), he served as director of the Pan American Union (1947-48) and as first secretary general of the Organization of American States (1948-54). He was instrumental in unseating the dictator Gustavo Rojas Pinilla (1957) and was the chief architect of the constitutional amendment (approved Dec., 1957) that provided for bipartisan Liberal-Conservative rule for a period of 12 years (later extended to 16 years). This plan, almost unique in the politics of the hemisphere, ended 10 years of bloody political strife that had cost approximately 200,000 lives. It also enabled Lleras, as president (1958-62), to stabilize the economy.

Lleras Restrepo, Carlos (kär'lōs lyä'räs rāstrā'pō), 1908-, president of Colombia (1966-70). The son of a well-known bacteriologist, he was a lawyer and economist who served in a number of government posts in the 1930s and 1940s. He served as leader of the Liberal party during the bloody civil war touched off by the assassination (1948) of Jorge Eliécer Gaitán. He became party leader again in 1961. As president, Lleras Restrepo won acclaim by sharply reducing the rate of inflation, diversifying the country's ailing one-crop (coffee) economy, restoring the balance of payments, and instituting a land reform program. After completing his term of office he remained politically active as head of the Liberal party. He wrote numerous books on social and economic problems.

Llewellyn, Richard (lōōĕl'ĭn), 1907-, Anglo-Welsh novelist. He is best known as the author of *How Green Was My Valley* (1939), a story of life in the S Wales mining areas, and *None but the Lonely Heart* (1943). His later novels include *Night is a Child* (1972) and *Bride of Israel, My Love* (1973).

Llewelyn ap Gruffydd (lōōĕl'ĭn äp grōō'fĭth, thlōōĕl'ĭn, grĭf'ĭth), d. 1282, Welsh prince, grandson of Llewelyn ap Iorwerth. He succeeded (1246) his uncle, David II, as ruler of North Wales and in 1247, with his brother Owen as coruler, did homage to Henry III of England, surrendering to him a large part of their territory. In 1256, having overthrown Owen, he launched a campaign to recover his lands. He soon won the allegiance of other Welsh princes and by 1263 controlled much of Wales. In the BARON'S WAR he was allied with Simon de Montfort, earl of Leicester, against Henry III. Montfort's downfall did not check Llewelyn's rise; by the Treaty of Montgomery (1267) he was recognized as prince of Wales—the first official English use of that title, although Llewelyn had assumed it in 1258. On the accession (1272) of Edward I, Llewelyn refused homage to the English king. In the English invasion of 1276 he lost all but a small portion of North Wales and submitted to Edward by the Treaty of Conway (1277). He was killed in a second rebellion in 1282. Llewelyn was the last independent ruler of Wales. The name also appears as Llewelyn ap Griffith.

Llewelyn ap Iorwerth (ēôr'wĕrth) (Llewelyn the Great), 1173-1240, Welsh prince; grandson of Owain Gwynedd. He first proved his capacity by wresting (1194) N Wales from his uncle David I and by taking (1199) the border fortress of Mold from the English. He was at first on good terms with King JOHN of England (whose illegitimate daughter Joan he married in 1206), but after 1210 he was attacked by the English king. He became a powerful ally of the English barons in their revolt against John, and his rights and those of the Welsh were recognized in the MAGNA CARTA (1215). Thereafter he set about establishing his power and destroying Norman castles in S Wales. Though he did homage (1218) to John's successor, Henry III, Llewelyn continued fighting against the English until 1234. Llewelyn's munificent patronage of the bards brought a renaissance of Welsh letters. He was an able soldier, a generous supporter of the church, and, above all, a zealous fighter for national unity. He was succeeded by his son David II.

Lloyd, David, c.1656-1731, political leader in colonial Pennsylvania, b. Wales. Having been commissioned attorney general of Pennsylvania by William Penn, Lloyd arrived in Philadelphia in 1686. He later became a member of the provincial assembly, acting as its speaker and serving in the provincial council on several occasions. After 1703, Lloyd assumed the leadership of the antiproprietary party and was in constant sharp conflict with James LOGAN. He served as chief justice of Pennsylvania from 1717 until his death. See biography by R. N. Lokken (1959).

Lloyd, Harold, 1893-1971, American movie actor, b. Burchard, Kans. Lloyd was famous for his comic portrayals of the wistful innocent with thick-lensed glasses who blunders in and out of hair-raising situations. He appeared in over 500 films, including many shorts, spanning both the silent and sound eras; among them were *Safety Last* (1923), *Girl Shy* (1924), *The Freshman* (1925), *Movie Crazy* (1932), and *Mad Wednesday* (1947).

Lloyd, Henry Demarest, 1847-1903, American reformer, b. New York City. He was on the editorial staff of the Chicago *Tribune* from 1872 to 1885 but resigned to study social problems. His *Wealth against Commonwealth* (1894) is an attack on monopolies, based especially on the methods of the Standard Oil Company. He traveled widely, writing about conditions in various countries and always supporting the causes of the underprivileged. See biography by C. A. Lloyd (1912); study by C. M. Destler (1963).

Lloyd, Seton Howard Frederick, 1902-, English archaeologist. Trained originally as an architect, he gained his first archaeological experience in 1928 as a member of the Egypt Exploration Society's expedition to Tel el Amarna. Acting (1930-37) as field supervisor to the Iraq Expedition of the Univ. of Chicago Oriental Institute, he worked at the sites of Tell Asmar and Khafajah. He was (1949-61) director of the British Institute of Archaeology, Ankara, Turkey. He was (1962-69) professor of archaeology at the Univ. of London. His writings include *Ruined Cities of Iraq* (1945), *Foundations in the Dust* (1947), *The Art of the Ancient Near East* (1961), and *Early Highland Peoples of Anatolia* (1967).

Lloyd George, David, 1st **Earl Lloyd-George of Dwyfor** (dōōē'vôr), 1863-1945, British statesman, of Welsh extraction. Elected (1890) to Parliament as a Liberal, the young Lloyd George soon became known as a radical and an anti-imperialist. He bitterly opposed the South African War. In 1905 he entered Sir Henry Campbell-Bannerman's ministry as president of the board of trade, establishing an outstanding reputation for his welfare reforms. In 1908 he was appointed chancellor of the exchequer by Herbert Asquith, later 1st earl of OXFORD AND ASQUITH. The rejection by the House of Lords of his 1909 budget, which provided for a system of social insurance partly financed by land and income taxes, led to passage of the Parliament Act of 1911, by which the Lords lost its power of veto (see PARLIAMENT). In 1911, Lloyd George made his famous Mansion House speech, in which he warned Germany that Britain would not tolerate interference with its international interests. After the outbreak of World War I, Lloyd George remained chancellor until 1915 when he became minister of munitions. He was then (1916) minister of war before he succeeded (Dec., 1916) in ousting Asquith and formed his own coalition government. Lloyd George immediately reorganized the structure of the government, creating a small war cabinet of five (which when attended also by representatives of the dominions and India became the Imperial war cabinet) and forming for the first time a cabinet secretariat. His war policy was bold and aggressive, and, although he was often at odds with the military leaders, he was largely responsible for the unification of military command under Marshal Ferdinand Foch. At the Paris Peace Conference (1919), Lloyd George exercised a moderating influence on both the harsh demands of Georges CLEMENCEAU and the idealistic proposals of Woodrow WILSON, and to a large extent he shaped the final agreement (see VERSAILLES, TREATY OF). A general election in 1918 had given Lloyd George and his coalition a substantial majority, but he was heavily dependent on Conservative support. This fact accounts at least partially for the repressive policy he adopted in Ireland, although he finally concluded the treaty that set up (1922) the Irish Free State. In 1922 occurred the Chanak crisis, in which Lloyd George delivered an ultimatum to the Turks, who, having seized Smyrna from the Greeks, were poised to strike across the neutralized Straits zone. The Turks agreed to withdraw, but in Britain Lloyd George was accused of recklessness. The Conservatives withdrew from the coalition, and his ministry fell (1922). Lloyd George continued to be active in Parliament and, despite the fact that he was disliked by many Liberals for his treatment of Asquith, served (1926-31) as the leader of the by then shattered Liberal party. In 1936 he visited and was much impressed by Adolf Hitler, but he later attacked the policy of appeasing Nazi Germany. He was raised to the peerage only a few months before his death. Lloyd George was a brilliantly eloquent, forceful, and creative statesman, but he was often unscrupulous and opportunistic in his methods and widely mistrusted. See his *War Memoirs* (6 vol., 1933-36; 2 vol., 1943) and *Memoirs of the Peace Conference* (1939); biographies by Malcolm Thomson (1948), Thomas Jones (1951), William George, his brother (1958), Martin Gilbert (1968), and F. L. Lloyd George, his widow (1971); K. O. Morgan, *The Age of Lloyd George* (1971).

Lloydminster (loid'mĭnstər), city (1971 pop. 8,691), on the Alta.-Sask. boundary, Canada. The city is chartered by both provinces. Farming and ranching are the chief activities of the region, which has oil and natural gas deposits.

Lloyd's, London insurance underwriting corporation of some 300 individual syndicates. Founded in the late 17th cent. by a group of merchants, shipowners, and insurance brokers at the coffeehouse of Edward Lloyd, the association is now international in scope. It is primarily concerned with the underwriting of marine insurance, but issues insurance against many other types of risk, except life insurance. *Lloyd's Register of Shipping,* affiliated with Lloyd's, is an annual publication containing detailed information, such as age, tonnage, class, and construction, of the vessels of all nations, together with supplementary data about docks, harbors, and port facilities. See studies by D. E. W. Gibb (1957, repr. 1972), R. S. Sayers (1957), and Antony Brown (1974).

Llullaillaco (yōōyīyä'kō), extinct volcano, 22,057 ft (6,723 m) high, on the border of Chile and Argentina. One of the highest peaks in the Andes and perpetually snowcapped, it overlooks a pass used for rail and highway traffic between Chile and Argentina.

LNG (liquefied natural gas): see under NATURAL GAS.

Loa (lō'ä), longest river of Chile, 275 mi (443 km) long, flowing S from the Andes, N Chile, then W and N through the Atacama Desert, before turning W to the Pacific Ocean. It is not navigable but affords some water supply and hydroelectric power for nitrate-mining communities in its vicinity.

loadstone: see MAGNETITE.

loam, soil composed of sand, silt, clay, and organic matter in evenly mixed particles of various sizes. More fertile than sandy soils, loam is not stiff and tenacious like clay soils. Its porosity allows high moisture retention and air circulation. The popular confusion of loam with HUMUS is probably due to the superior quality of both soils. According to the preponderance of their ingredients, loams are classified as sandy, clay, or silt loams. Most soils of agricultural importance are some type of loam.

Loammi (lōăm'ī) [Heb.,=not my people], symbolic name of the prophet Hosea's second son and figurative name of Israel before reconciliation with God. Hosea 1.9,10. Cf. AMMI.

loan, in business, sum of money borrowed at a particular interest rate. More generally, it refers to anything given on condition of its return or repayment of its equivalent. A loan may be acknowledged by a bond, a promissory note, or a mere oral promise to repay. Because of biblical injunctions against usury, the early Christian church forbade the taking of interest. In feudal European society, loans were little needed by the great mass of relatively self-sufficient and noncommercial peasants and serfs, but kings, nobles, and ecclesiastics were heavy borrowers for personal expenditures. Merchants and other townsmen, especially the Jews, were the moneylenders, and various devices were found for circumventing the prohibition of usury. With the rise of a commercial society, restrictions on the taking of interest were gradually relaxed. Today, banks and finance companies make most loans, usually on COLLATERAL, such as stocks, personal effects, and mortgages on land and other property, or on assignments of wages. CREDIT UNIONS have attained some importance in making personal loans at relatively low interest rates. A PAWNBROKER lends money on the security of articles left in his shop.

Loanda: see LUANDA, Angola.

Lobachevsky, Nikolai Ivanovich (nyĭkəlī' ēvä'nəvĭch ləbəchĕf'skē), 1793-1856, Russian mathematician. A pioneer in non-Euclidean geometry, he challenged Euclid's fifth postulate that one and only one line parallel to a given line can be drawn through a fixed point external to the line; he developed, independently of János Bolyai, a self-consistent system of geometry (hyperbolic geometry) in which that postulate was replaced by one allowing more than one parallel through the fixed point. Lobachevsky first announced his system in 1826; he subsequently wrote several expositions of it, including *Geometrical Researches on the Theory of Parallels* (originally pub. 1840 in German; tr. 1891, 1914), and a statement of his completed work, *Pangéométrie* (issued 1855 in Russian and French). A graduate of the Univ. of Kazan, he remained there as teacher (1812), professor (1816), and rector (1827). Despite his efficient and devoted service, in 1846 he was relieved by the government of his posts of professor and rector.

lobbying, practice of influencing governmental decisions by agents who serve special interests. The term originated in the 1830s, when representatives of interest groups wanting to influence legislative decisions tended to congregate in the lobbies of Congress and state legislatures. It is now used in a broader sense to include attempts to influence any governmental decision. In the United States lobbying has become an accepted part of the political system, supplementing geographical representation. Many organized groups such as corporations, railroads, labor unions, educational groups, medical interests, and farm groups maintain permanent lobbies both in Washington and in the state capitals in order to protect and further their interests in the consideration of new legislation and the administration of existing legislation. Recently, there has been a growth of self-appointed "public interest" lobbyists for substantially unorganized groups such as consumers. Lobbyists often deal directly with governmental decision makers and exert influence through the supply of technical information, political threats or promises, and personal friendship. Indirect methods employed include the use of the mass media to inspire grass roots support for the aims of particular interests. The potential for corruption, especially bribery, in the seeking of private ends in the public arena has given lobbying an unsavory connotation and has led to many attempts to regulate the practice on both state and national levels. The basic federal law is the Regulation of Lobbying Act of 1946, which requires registration of and regular financial reports from all individuals and agents seeking to influence legislation. There is, in general, less strict regulation at the state level. See L. W. Milbrath, *The Washington Lobbyists* (1963); V. O. Key, *Politics, Parties and Pressure Groups* (5th ed. 1964); James Deakin, *The Lobbyists* (1966); A. M. Scott et al., *Congress and Lobbies: Image and Reality* (1966); Suzanne Farkas, *Urban Lobbying* (1971); Graham Wooton, *Interest Groups* (1971).

lobefin, common name for any of a group of lunged, fleshy-finned, bony FISHES, also called crossopterygians, that were dominant in the Devonian period and gave rise to amphibians. They had heavy, ungainly bodies and stumpy paired fins, the precursors of the limbs of four-footed animals. Known from their fossils, the lobefins were thought to be extinct until 1938, when a live coelacanth was caught in deep water off S Africa. Since then other specimens have been discovered in the Madagascar area. The coelacanths were a marine branch of the lobefins. The living coelacanth, *Latimeria chalumne*, is a brown to steel-blue fish 5 ft (150 cm) long, with circular, overlapping scales, a laterally flattened three-lobed tail, a spiny dorsal fin, and a vestigial lung. It is the nearest living fish relative of the amphibians. Lobefins are classified in the phylum CHORDATA, subphylum Vertebrata, class Osteichthyes, order Crossopterygii. See LUNGFISH.

lobelia (lōbĕl'yə), any plant of the genus *Lobelia*, annual and perennial herbs of tropical and temperate woodlands and moist places. Most lobelias have blue or purple flowers on a long (1-4 ft/30-122 cm), leafy stem. Native North American species, often cultivated as ornamentals, include the only red lobelia, the cardinal flower (*L. cardinalis*), which is becoming rare; the blue lobelia (*L. syphilitica*), used by the Indians for the treatment of syphilis; and the Indian tobacco (*L. inflata*), named for its odor. The dried leaves and stems of Indian tobacco and sometimes of other species furnish medicinal lobelia, which is used as a respiratory stimulant but is poisonous in overdose as are the roots. *L. erinus*, introduced from S Africa, is a common border plant. Some botanists include *Lobelia* and related genera in the family Campanulaceae (bluebell family); others consider them a separate family, the Lobeliaceae. Lobelia is classified in the division MAGNOLIOPHYTA, class Magnoliopsida, order Campanulales, family Lobeliaceae.

Lobengula (lō"bĕng-gōō'lə), c.1833-94, king of Matabeleland (now in Rhodesia). After succeeding his father (1870), he tried to turn aside the approaches of European colonizers. In 1888, however, under pressure from Cecil RHODES, he ceded his mineral rights in exchange for small payment, and Rhodes used those concessions to form the British South Africa Company (1889). When British gold miners began appearing, Lobengula rallied his people and in 1893 attacked the British. The results were disastrous for the MATABELE; Lobengula died while fleeing north.

Lobito (lōbē'tō, lo͝ovē'tō), city (1969 est. pop. 98,000), W central Angola, on the Atlantic Ocean. Angola's chief port, it is also a road hub and the western terminus of the trans-African Benguela railroad. The harbor, protected by a sand bar, is among the best on Africa's west coast. There are bulk loading facilities for ores and grain; other exports include coffee, sisal, sugar, fish, salt, and beans. As an international port, Lobito ships minerals from Zambia and the Shaba (Katanga) region of Zaïre. Among the city's industries are shipbuilding, food processing, and the manufacture of cement and building materials. Lobito was founded in 1843 on orders from Queen Maria II in response to requests by the Portuguese inhabitants of Benguela for a healthier and strategically more favorable living area. The completion of the railroad from Benguela in 1929 made Lobito an important commercial center. It is built mainly on reclaimed land.

loblolly pine, common name for the PINE species *Pinus taeda,* found in the SE United States.

lobotomy (lōbŏt'əmē, lə-), surgical procedure for cutting nerve pathways in the frontal lobes of the BRAIN. The operation has been performed on psychotic patients whose behavioral patterns were not improved by other forms of treatment. The procedure as pioneered by Nobel laureate Egas Moniz in the 1930s consisted of drilling holes through the skull and severing or interfering with nerve fibers to the midbrain, particularly to the thalamus. In a later development, instruments were passed through the eye sockets above the eyeballs in order to sever the connections. Lobotomies were performed on numerous patients between 1936 and 1956. In approximately one half of the cases there was at least temporary relief of symptoms. However, some patients exhibited worse behavior after the operation than before, and others whose tensions were relieved by the surgery degenerated to a vegetablelike state. Since the mid-1950s such psychosurgery has been largely abandoned in favor of less radical means of treatment, e.g., the administration of tranquilizers and other chemical substances. Most psychiatrists today take a very conservative position on lobotomy as an acceptable form of treatment.

lobster, marine CRUSTACEAN with five pairs of jointed legs, the first bearing large pincerlike claws of unequal size adapted to crushing the shells of its prey. The segmented body of the lobster consists of a large cephalothorax (made up of 14 segments) and a moveable, muscular abdomen (composed of 7 segments). It is covered with a chitinous exoskeleton that is dark green in the living animal and bright red when boiled. As the lobster grows, the exoskeleton is periodically molted and a new, larger one is formed in its place. Lobsters have 20 pairs of gills attached to the bases of the legs and to the sides of the body; the gills are protected by the carapace, the large area of the exoskeleton covering the back and sides of the cephalothorax. In addition to the legs, the appendages consist of 2 paired antennae, 6 pairs of mouth parts, and the small swimmerets attached to the abdominal segments. In the female the eggs remain attached to the swimmerets for 10 or 11 months until they hatch into free-swimming larvae. The larvae swim for about a year, molting between 14 and 17 times before they settle to the bottom and begin to take on adult characteristics. Lobsters crawl briskly over the ocean floor and swim backward with great speed by scooping motions of the muscular abdomen and tail, but are clumsy on land. They are scavengers but also prey on shellfish and may even attack live fish and large gastropods. Over a period of five years they grow to an average weight of 3 lb (1.4 kg). The common American lobster, *Homarus americanus,* is found inshore in summer and in deeper waters in winter from Labrador to North Carolina, but especially along the New England coast, where the chief lobster fisheries are located. Lobsters are caught in slatted wooden traps, or "pots," baited with dead fish. In Europe a species of *Homarus* similar to the American is found, but the smaller Norway lobster is the chief seafood variety. The spiny, or rock, lobsters, found in warm seas of both hemispheres, are actually marine crayfish (genus *Panulirus*); they lack claws but have sharp spines on the carapace. The stout-bodied, sometimes brightly colored squat lobsters are close relatives of the hermit crab; their broad abdomens are usually tucked under their bodies, as in crabs, but can be extended and used for backward swimming, as in the true lobsters. Lobsters are protected by law and are raised by several hatcheries on the New England coast; nevertheless, they are still in danger of extinction. Lobsters are classified in the phylum ARTHROPODA, class Crustacea, order Decapoda, family Homaridae.

local government, political administration of the smallest subdivisions of a country's territory and population. Although there are special-purpose local government bodies (e.g., school boards in the United States), much more important are those that carry out a broad range of public activities within a defined area and population. Almost all such local government bodies share certain characteristics: a continuing organization; the authority to undertake public activities; the ability to enter into contracts; the right to sue and be sued; and the ability to collect taxes and determine a budget. An important distinction among types of local government is that between representative bodies, which are elected locally and have decision-making authority, and nonrepresentative bodies, which are either appointed from above or, if elected locally, have no independent governing authority. Most countries have complex systems of local government with varying degrees of local autonomy. Three of these systems, those of France, the Soviet Union, and Great Britain have served as models for much of the rest of the world. The French system is usually considered to be among the most nonrepresentative. Its basic structure, codified by Napoleon I, developed out of the desire of the government of revolutionary France to curtail the influence of the local nobility and hasten governmental reform. It stresses clear lines of authority, reaching from the central government's ministry of the interior through the centrally appointed prefect of the department to the municipality, which has a locally elected mayor and municipal council. The prefect, being both the chief executive of the department and the representative of the central bureaucracy in the department, provides the channel of centralization. He has wide authority to overrule local councils and supervise local expenditures. Variants of this system are found throughout Europe and in former French colonies. The local governments of the Soviet Union, set up following the Russian Revolution of 1917, have much more formal authority than those in France. At each governmental level, down to the city and village, there is a locally elected council with administrative and legislative authority and supposedly close accountability to the local citizens. Most of this local authority, however, is undercut both by the broad powers of more central councils to overrule local ones and by the centralizing influence of the Communist party. The result is a generally nonrepresentative system, which has been largely copied by the East European and other Communist states. The British system of local government, which has been the model for most of that country's former colonies including the United States, is the most representative of the major types. Largely reformed in the 19th cent. and extensively restructured in the 1970s, the system stresses local government autonomy through elected councils on the COUNTY and subcounty levels. This system is marked by less central government interference with local decisions and greater local taxation and budgetary authority than any other system. A special feature of the British system is its use of an extensive committee system, instead of a strong executive, for supervising the administration of public services. Although there are considerable differences among the various states, the local government system of the United States has incorporated the general principles of the British system, except that a strong executive is common in the United States. The county remains the usual political subdivision, although it has retained more authority in rural areas than in the more urban sections, where incorporated municipalities (see CITY GOVERNMENT) have most of the local power. In both rural and urban areas the local government's relationship to the state is a complex one of shared authority and carefully defined areas of legal competence. Areas of local government authority usually include public schools, local highways, municipal services, and some aspects of social welfare and public order. There is inherent tension in the situation whereby local governments are increasingly reliant on state and Federal funding to carry out their traditional duties, while fearful of losing that degree of local control generally associated with the U.S. system of government. See John J. Clarke, *A History of Local Government of the United Kingdom* (1955); H. A. Turner, *American Democracy: State and Local Government* (1968); Duane Lockard, *The Politics of State and Local Government* (2d ed. 1969); Samuel Humes and Eileen Martin, *The Structure of Local Government* (1969).

local group, in astronomy, loose cluster of at least 19 nearby GALAXIES, including our own MILKY WAY galaxy, the ANDROMEDA GALAXY, and the MAGELLANIC CLOUDS. The local group is spread over an ellipsoidal region of space with a major axis of approximately 3 million light-years. The Milky Way galaxy, near one end of the major axis, and the Andromeda Galaxy, near the other end, are the largest members of the group. Two galaxies in the group were detected only recently by their INFRARED RADIATION; a dusty region in space obscures their visible light. There may be other galaxies in the local group that are as yet undetected. As shown by the work of G. de Vaucouleurs, the local group is part of a supercluster containing at least 50 separate clusters, each having from a few dozen to as many as a thousand galaxies. These groups appear to be concentrated in a plane, which indicates that the supercluster is rotating. Its center lies approximately 50 million light-years away in the direction of the constellation Virgo.

local solar time: see SOLAR TIME.

Locarno (lōkär'nō), town (1970 pop. 14,143), Ticino canton, S Switzerland, at the northern end of Lago Maggiore. In a beautiful resort region with a mild climate, Locarno attracts a great number of tourists. It has an annual film festival. Jewelry, motors, soap, and food products are made. In 1512 it was taken from Milan by the Swiss cantons, and in 1803 it was included in Ticino canton. There are many fine churches; among them is the noted pilgrimage church, Madonna del Sasso (first built 1480), which has a painting by Bramantino.

Locarno Pact, 1925, concluded at a conference held at Locarno, Switzerland, by representatives of Great Britain, France, Germany, Italy, Belgium, Czechoslovakia, and Poland. The request of Gustav STRESEMANN for a mutual guarantee of the RHINELAND met with the approval of Aristide BRIAND; under the leadership of Briand, Stresemann, and Austen CHAMBERLAIN, a series of treaties of mutual guarantee and arbitration were signed. In the major treaty the powers individually and collectively guaranteed the common boundaries of Belgium, France, and Germany as specified in the Treaty of Versailles of 1919. Germany signed treaties with Poland and Czechoslovakia, agreeing to change the eastern borders of Germany by arbitration only. Germany also signed arbitration treaties with France and Belgium, and mutual defense pacts against possible German aggression were concluded between France and Poland and France and Czechoslovakia. As an adjunct, Germany was promised entry into the League of Nations. The "spirit of Locarno" symbolized hopes for an era of international peace and good will. In 1936, denouncing the Locarno Pact, Hitler remilitarized the Rhineland.

Locatelli, Pietro (pyĕ'trō lōkätĕl'lē), 1695–1764, Italian violinist and composer. Locatelli was a pupil of Arcangelo Corelli. Much of his life was spent in Amsterdam, where he died. An outstanding virtuoso, he wrote studies and caprices designed to display his great technical skill, as well as concertos and sonatas of solid musical value.

locative (lŏk'ətĭv) [Latin,=placing], in the grammar of certain languages (e.g., Sanskrit), the CASE referring to location. Nouns in this case are often translatable into English phrases beginning with *at, in,* or *on.*

Loch (lŏkh, lŏk). For names of Scottish lakes and inlets beginning thus, see second element; e.g., for Loch Awe, see AWE, LOCH. See also LAKE.

Lochaber (lŏkhăb'ər, -ä'bər), mountainous district, Highland region, W Scotland. It includes Ben Nevis (4,406 ft/1,343 m), Great Britain's highest peak. The Lochaber power scheme provides electricity for Fort William's aluminum works.

Loches (lôsh), town (1968 pop. 6,473), Indre-et-Loire dept., W central France, in Touraine, on the Indre River. It is famous for its medieval buildings, especially the ancient château that dominates the town. Originally established by the counts of Anjou, it later became (mid-13th cent.) a royal residence and a state prison. The royal lodge, built by Charles VII, contains the tomb of Agnès Sorel and the oratory of Anne of Brittany.

Lochiel, Sir Ewen Cameron of: see CAMERON OF LOCHIEL, SIR EWEN.

Lochiel, the Gentle: see CAMERON OF LOCHIEL, DONALD.

Lochner, Stephan (shtĕf'än lōkh'nər), d. 1451, German religious painter of the school of Cologne. He combined the Gothic tradition with a new naturalism and a pure color sense. A *Last Judgment* (panels now in Cologne, Frankfurt, and Munich) is his earliest known work and shows the influence of the van Eycks. In the years c.1440 he painted a *Crucifixion with Saints* (Nuremberg) and the *Virgin with Violets* (Cologne). His best-known work is the Cologne Cathedral altarpiece, called the *Dombild,* which comprises the *Annunciation, St. Ursula, St. Gereon,* and as the central panel the *Adoration of the Magi* (c.1445). A *Presentation of Christ* in Darmstadt (1447) is one of his few dated works. His bright color and tender sentiment have made him one of the best-loved German 15th-century masters.

lock, air: see AIR LOCK.

lock, canal, stretch of water enclosed by gates, one at each end, built into a canal or river for the purpose of raising or lowering a vessel from one water level to another. A lock may also be built into the entrance of a dock for the same purpose. When the ship is to be raised to a higher level, it enters the lock and a gate is closed behind it. Water is let into the lock until its level equals that of the water ahead. The forward gate is then opened, and the ship progresses on the higher level. The procedure is reversed when the vessel is to pass from a higher to a lower level. As many locks as necessary are used in a given waterway. Most modern locks are made of concrete, although some have walls of steel-sheet piles or floors of natural rock or sand. The mitre gate, frequently used in the United States, consists of two swinging sections forming an arc or shallow V, with the apex pointed toward high water so that water pressure keeps both sections tightly sealed when closed. Another type of gate in common use consists of one piece of sheet steel that slides across the entrance to the lock on rollers or is lifted into the air or sunk under water. The gates of most locks are operated by hydraulic or electric power. Water is poured into or out of locks through culverts built into the masonry structure of the lock walls. Among well-known locks are those of the Panama Canal.

lock and key, fastening consisting essentially of a sliding, pivoted, or rotary bolt guarded by an obstacle either fixed (warded) or movable (tumbler) and operated by a key. Usually the key has a shank that is flat or in the form of a pipe or a pin. Known to the Egyptians and other ancient civilizations, locks and keys are mentioned in the Bible; a celebrated passage is Mat. 16.19, the bestowal of the keys of the kingdom of heaven upon Peter. Warded locks were known to the Etruscans, and the combination lock, opened by dialing a sequence of letters or numbers, was used in the 17th cent., but most early locks were of the pin-tumbler type. Until the 19th cent. locks and keys were usually massive and ornate; modern types tend to be utilitarian. The modern door lock is a compact pin-tumbler cylinder lock of the type developed (1860) by the American inventor Linus Yale. The warded lock, the simplest and least secure, is used for cheap padlocks. The lever tumbler is used for safe-deposit boxes. Originally suggested in 1831 and first used successfully c.1875, the time lock has a clock mechanism set to prevent opening until a time previously fixed. Recently a pin-tumbler lock in which the pins are actuated by small magnets on the key has been developed. The key symbolizes authority in religion; the coat of arms of the Holy See bears two keys crossed.

Locke, David Ross: see NASBY, PETROLEUM V.

Locke, John (lŏk), 1632–1704, English philosopher, founder of British empiricism. Educated at Christ Church College, Oxford, he became (1660) a lecturer there in Greek, rhetoric, and philosophy. He studied medicine, and his acquaintance with scientific practice had a strong influence upon his philosophical thought and method. In 1666, Locke met Anthony Ashley Cooper, the future 1st earl of Shaftesbury, and soon became his friend, physician, and adviser. After 1667, Locke had minor diplomatic and civil posts, most of them through Shaftesbury. In 1675, after Shaftesbury had lost his offices, Locke left England for France, where he met French leaders in science and philosophy. Returning to England in 1679, he retired soon to Oxford, where he stayed quietly until, suspected of radicalism by the government, he went to Holland and remained there several years (1683–89). In Holland he completed the famous *Essay Concerning Human Understanding* (1690), which was published in complete form after his return to England at the accession of William and Mary to the English throne. In the same year he published his *Two Treatises on Civil Government;* part of this work justifies the Glorious Revolution of 1688, but much of it was written earlier. His fame increased, and he became known in England and on the Continent as the leading philosopher of freedom. In the *Essay* Locke examines the nature of the human mind and the process by which it knows the world. Repudiating the traditional doctrine of innate ideas, Locke believed that the mind is born blank, a *tabula rasa* upon which the world describes itself through the experience of the five senses. Knowledge arising from sensation is perfected by reflection, thus enabling man to arrive at such ideas as space, time, and infinity. He distinguished the primary qualities of things (e.g., solidity, extension, number) from their secondary qualities (e.g., color, sound). These latter qualities he held to be produced by the impact of the world on the sense organs. Behind this curtain of sensation the world itself is colorless and silent. Science is possible, Locke maintained, because the primary world affects the sense organs mechanically, thus producing ideas that faithfully represent reality. The clear, commonsense style of the *Essay* concealed many unexplored assumptions that the later empiricists George Berkeley and David Hume would contest, but the problems that Locke set forth have occupied philosophy in one way or another ever since. Locke is most renowned for his political theory. Contradicting Thomas Hobbes, Locke believed that the original state of nature was happy and characterized by reason and tolerance. In that state all men were equal and independent, and none had a right to harm another in his "life, health, liberty, or possessions." The state was formed by social contract because in the state of nature each was his own judge, and there was no protection against those who lived outside the law of nature. The state should be guided by natural law. Rights of property are very important, for each man has a right to the product of his labor. Locke forecast the labor theory of value. The policy of checks and balances as followed in the Constitution of the United States was set down by Locke, as was the doctrine that revolution in some circumstances is not only a right but an obligation. At Shaftesbury's behest, he wrote the Fundamental Constitutions for the Carolinas; the colonists, however, never ratified the document. Locke based his ethical theories upon belief in the natural goodness of man. The inevitable pursuit of happiness and pleasure, when conducted rationally, leads to cooperation, and in the long run private happiness and the general welfare coincide. Immediate pleasures must give way to a prudent regard for ultimate good, including reward in the afterlife. He argued for broad religious freedom in three separate essays on toleration. Only atheism and Roman Catholicism should be legislated against as inimical to religion and the state. In his essay *The Reasonableness of Christianity* (1695), he emphasized the ethical aspect of Christianity against dogma. Locke summed up the Enlightenment in his belief in the middle class and its right to freedom of conscience and right to property, in his faith in the new science, and in his confidence in the goodness of man. His influence upon philosophy and political theory has been incalculable. See biographies by M. W. Cranston (1957) and Richard Aaron (3d ed. 1971); John Yolton, ed., *John Locke: Problems and Perspectives* (1969); R. S. Woolhouse, *Locke's Philosophy of Science and Knowledge* (1971); J. W. Gough, ed., *John Locke's Political Philosophy; Eight Essays* (2d ed. 1973); J. D. Mabbott, *John Locke* (1973).

Locker-Lampson, Frederick, 1821–95, English author. He is remembered for his light verse in *London Lyrics* (1857) and other volumes. His memoirs, *My Confidences* (1896), were edited by Augustine Birrell, his son-in-law, who also wrote his biography (1920).

Lockhart, John Gibson, 1794–1854, Scottish editor, lawyer, literary critic, and biographer; son-in-law and biographer of Sir Walter Scott. A major contributor to *Blackwood's Magazine,* he also was editor of and contributor to the *Quarterly Review* (1825–53). He became known as "The Scorpion" because of the fierceness of his criticism. Among his works are a volume of adaptations (1823) from ancient Spanish ballads, several novels, and a biography of Burns (1828). However, his fame rests on his *Memoirs of the Life of Sir Walter Scott* (7 vol., 1837–38). Although eulogistic, the biography is organized in a unique, discursive manner that produces a vivid portrait of Scott. It is generally ranked among English biographies as second only to Boswell's *Johnson.* See Andrew Lang, *The Life and Letters of John Gibson Lockhart* (2 vol., 1897, repr. 1970); biography by F. R. Hart (1971).

Lock Haven, industrial city (1970 pop. 11,427), seat of Clinton co., N central Pa., on the West Branch of the Susquehanna River at the junction of Bald Eagle Creek, in a rich agricultural area; settled 1769, inc. as a city 1870. The city was a lumber center in the 19th cent., and it now has varied industries. Lock Haven State College is there. The surrounding area is mountainous and scenic, and three state parks are in the vicinity.

lockjaw: see TETANUS.

lockout, intentional closing up of a company, factory, or shop by an employer to prevent employees from working during a strike or labor dispute. The term *lockout* is sometimes confused with the term STRIKE, since what employers will frequently designate as a *strike* will in turn be referred to by workers as a *lockout.* Lockouts have generally been regarded as legal by the courts, although in some cases they have been held unlawful if they violate the terms of a joint agreement. See A. W. Kornhauser, ed., *Industrial Conflict* (1954); A. M. Ross, *Changing Patterns of Industrial Conflict* (1960); Leon Wolff, *Lockout* (1965).

Lockport, industrial city (1970 pop. 25,399), seat of Niagara co., W N.Y., on the New York State Barge Canal, in a rich fruit and dairy region; settled 1821, inc. 1865. Automotive radiators, wood, metal, and paper products are among the many manufactures. The city was built around a series of locks on the old Erie Canal.

Lockwood, James Booth, 1852–84, American arctic explorer, b. Annapolis, Md. In 1873 he was commissioned second lieutenant in the U.S. army. In 1881, Lockwood joined the arctic expedition of Adolphus W. Greely, in the course of which he performed two noteworthy feats—he led a sledging party to Mary Murray Island, off N Greenland, thus achieving a record for the northernmost point reached up to that time (lat. 83°24′ N, according to his calculations), and later (1883) he crossed Grant Land on Ellesmere Island to the west shore. He died at Cape Sabine, as did other members of the ill-fated Greely expedition.

Lockyer, Sir Joseph Norman (lŏk'yər), 1836–1920, English astronomer, educated on the Continent. One of the first to make a spectroscopic examination of the sun and stars, he devised (1868), independently of P. J. C. Janssen, a method of observing solar prominences with the spectroscope in daylight. In the same year he identified the element helium in the sun and applied the name chromosphere to the layer, or envelope, of gas around the sun. He was elected to fellowship in the Royal Society (1869) and served as professor of astronomical physics of the newly founded Royal College of Science and director of the Solar Physics Observatory (1890–1913). Between 1870 and 1905 he headed eight government expeditions to observe total eclipses of the sun. He was knighted in 1897. His works include *Studies in Spectrum Analysis* (1872), *Contributions to Solar Physics* (1874), *The Chemistry of the Sun* (1887), and *The Sun's Place in Nature* (1897). See biography by A. J. Meadows (1972).

Locle, Le (lə lôk'lə), town (1970 pop. 14,452), Neuchâtel canton, NW Switzerland, in the Jura mts. near the French border. It has been a watchmaking center since the 17th cent.

Locofocos (lō"kōfō'kōz), name given in derision to the members of a faction that split off from the Democratic party in New York in 1835. Tension had been growing between radical Democrats, who believed that Andrew Jackson's war against the national bank should be extended to state banks and other monopolies, and the regular TAMMANY Democrats in New York City. When the Tammany leaders expelled (Sept., 1835) William Leggett, the radical editor of the New York *Evening Post,* from the party, the radicals decided to act. At a Tammany Hall meeting held in the Wigwam on Oct. 29, 1835, to ratify the Tammany nominations the revolt began. The antibank men voted down the chairman selected by the organization; before the meeting could be reorganized, the gas was turned off and the hall plunged in darkness. The reformers, however, continued their work by the light of candles and of self-igniting "locofoco" matches, from which their nickname derived. In Jan., 1836, this group organized a new party, called the Friends of Equal Rights or the Equal Rights party. They opposed the chartering of state banks and other forms of monopoly and exclusive privilege as antidemocratic and advocated the suspension of paper money and legal protection for labor unions. By nominating fusion candidates with the Whigs, the Locofocos defeated (April, 1836) Tammany men for city office and elected (Nov., 1836) two of their members to the state assembly. However, their intention was not to build a permanent new party, but to convert the regular Democrats to their platform.

After Martin Van Buren and his administration adopted a large part of their program, especially its financial policies, Tammany also accepted much of their platform, and by 1838 most of the Locofocos had been reabsorbed into the Democratic party. See Fitzwilliam Byrdsall, *The History of the Loco-Foco or Equal Rights Party* (1842, repr. 1967).

locomotive, vehicle used to pull a train of unpowered RAILROAD cars. The Englishman Richard TREVITHICK built and operated (1803–4) the first successful STEAM ENGINE locomotive for hauling cars on a track. The English engineer George Stephenson built his first locomotive, the *Blucher,* in 1814, and in 1829 he demonstrated with his famous *Rocket* the practicability of the steam engine for commercial transportation. The locomotive, when running light, attained 29 mi per hr (47 km per hr). The first American-built locomotive was designed and tested on a private track by the American engineer John Stevens in 1826. The English-built *Stourbridge Lion,* imported c.1829, was not a commercial success, being too heavy for the American track. The *Tom Thumb* (1830), built by Peter Cooper, an American manufacturer, for the BALTIMORE & OHIO RAILROAD, was the first practical American-built locomotive. The American manufacturer Matthias Baldwin's first locomotive, *Old Ironsides,* built in 1832, long remained in operation. In 1832, the American engineer John B. Jervis built the first locomotive with a swivel truck, a wheel assembly on which part of the body was mounted. Placed at the forward end of a locomotive, a swivel truck permitted a locomotive to negotiate curves more safely. The reciprocating steam locomotive is a self-contained power unit consisting essentially of a steam engine and a BOILER with fuel and water supplies. Superheated steam, controlled by a throttle, is admitted to the cylinders by a suitable valve arrangement, the pressure on the pistons being transmitted through the main rod to the driving wheels. The driving wheels, which vary in number, are connected by side rods. Steam locomotives are usually classified under the Whyte system, by the number and arrangement of the wheels—an engine classified as 2-6-0 would have one pair of wheels under the front truck, three pairs of coupled or driving wheels, and no wheels under the trailing truck. In some cases the truck wheels of the tender (fuel carrier) are added. Electric locomotives, introduced c.1895, range from the small type used in plants and coal mines for local hauling to the large engines used on railroads. Electric locomotives are generally provided with two or more motors. Power is collected from an electric trolley, or pantograph, running on an overhead wire or from a third rail at one side. Battery locomotives, used only for local haulage, carry electric storage batteries that act as their primary source of power. Electric railroad locomotives are used chiefly on steep grades and on runs of high traffic density, and although highly efficient they are not more widely used because of the cost of electric substations and overhead wires or third rails. Diesel-electric locomotives have almost entirely replaced steam locomotives in the United States, where they were introduced c.1924. In the United States they are the most widely used type of locomotive. In such vehicles electric power is produced by a generator driven by a diesel engine; this power runs electric motors that turn the driving wheels. Gas turbine-electric locomotives, a new type, are similar to the diesel-electric but use a gas turbine to drive the generator. See H. C. Casserley, *The Historic Locomotive Pocketbook* (1960); J. R. Day and B. K. Cooper, *Railway Locomotives* (1961); J. H. White, *American Locomotives: An Engineering History, 1830–1880* (1967); Angus Sinclair, *Development of the Locomotive Engine* (1907; annotated by J. J. White, Jr., 1970); H. B. Comstock, *The Iron Horse* (1971); Don Ball, *Portrait of the Rails: From Steam to Diesel* (1972); see also bibliography under STEAM ENGINE.

locoweed or **crazyweed** [Span. *loco*=crazy], any of several species of the genera *Astragalus* and *Oxytropus,* leguminous plants of the family Leguminosae (PULSE family), that, when eaten by horses, cattle, or sheep, cause a nervous disorder called loco disease. The locoweeds, perennials native to the West and Southwest, have pealike flowers and pinnately compound leaves. Not all species of these genera have been found poisonous. An Old World plant related to the *Astragalus* locoweeds is the source of gum TRAGACANTH. Locoweed is classified in the division MAGNOLIOPHYTA, class Magnoliopsida, order Rosales, family Leguminosae.

Locris (lō'krĭs), region of central Greece. The state was probably in existence before the arrival of the Phocians. The rise of Doris and Phocis split the original region into western and eastern portions. Eastern Locris, along the Malian Gulf (now Maliakós Kolpós) and Gulf of Euboea (now Vórios Evvoïkós Kolpós) between Thermopylae and Larymna, was again split (6th cent. B.C.) by Phocis into Epicnemedian in the west and Opuntian in the east. Western, or Ozolaean, Locris was on the north coast of the Gulf of Corinth and had for its principal towns Amphissa (now Ámfissa) and Naupactus (now Návpaktos). Largely hemmed in by stronger states, the Locrians played a minor role in Greek history. However, they founded (c.700 B.C.) one of the earliest Greek colonies in S Italy, Epizephyrian Locris near the promontory of Zephyrium; it was in the toe of the peninsula. The earliest written legal code in Europe, attributed to Zaleucus (7th cent. B.C.), was used there.

locust, in botany, any species of the genus *Robinia,* deciduous trees or shrubs of the family Leguminosae (PULSE family) native to the United States and Mexico. The locusts have clusters of flowers similar to the sweet pea; these are very fragrant in the black, or yellow, locust (*R. pseudoacacia*), which is the common locust, sometimes also called acacia, or false acacia. This species has been widely planted in the past for ornamental purposes, for erosion control, and for its useful wood, but the locust borer has killed it in many areas. Its heavy, hard, durable wood is used extensively for treenails in shipbuilding, for fence posts, for turning, and for fuel. The shoots and bark of the black locust are poisonous. The HONEY LOCUST belongs to a different genus of this family, as does the CAROB, which is thought to have been the biblical locust. Locust is classified in the division MAGNOLIOPHYTA, class Magnoliopsida, order Rosales, family Leguminosae.

locust, in zoology, name for certain migratory members of the short-horned GRASSHOPPER family (Acrididae). Like other members of this family, locusts have antennae shorter than their bodies, song-producing organs on the forewings and hind legs, and hind legs well developed for jumping. Typical locusts (e.g., species of the Old World genus *Locusta*) have two distinct adult forms, a short-winged migratory form and a long-winged nonmigratory form. Locust migration is an occasional event, which follows an enormous buildup of a locust population. The young locusts, called nymphs, only develop into the migratory form under certain environmental conditions, which also lead to a population increase. Not all of the environmental factors involved are known, but one is hot weather. When migration occurs the locust swarms are so dense as to blacken the sky over an area of many miles. When the insects finally settle, after traveling hundreds or thousands of miles, they begin to feed, consuming enormous quantities of vegetation. Locusts lay their eggs in the ground; when the nymphs hatch they are wingless and move across the land by walking. The first generation produced after a migration is not usually migratory. Locusts are serious agricultural pests. They are most common in Africa and Asia, but also occur in the United States. The Rocky Mountain locust, *Melanopolus spratus,* destroyed millions of dollars worth of crops on the Great Plains between 1874 and 1877. A single swarm contained an estimated 124 billion insects. Spraying with solutions of arsenic and overturning the soil can destroy the eggs. Locusts are classified in the phylum ARTHROPODA, class Insecta, order Orthoptera, suborder Caelifera, family Acrididae.

Locust Grove, uninc. town (1970 pop. 11,626), Nassau co., SE N.Y., on Long Island.

Lod (lōd), city (1972 pop. 30,500), central Israel. It is also known as Lydda. Its manufactures include chemicals, oil products, electronic equipment, and cigarettes. Nearby is Israel's chief international airport, which is also the site of the nation's aircraft industry. The city is a railroad and road junction. Lod was probably of Hebrew foundation and is frequently mentioned in the Bible. It was the scene of Peter's healing of the paralytic. It was destroyed (A.D. 66–70) by the Romans in the Jewish-Roman war and, after the destruction of the Temple in Jerusalem (A.D. 70), became the temporary seat of many famous Jewish teachers. HADRIAN rebuilt the city and named it Diospolis. It is the traditional home and place of burial of St. George (4th cent.?), England's patron saint, and has a church in his honor. In the 5th cent. it was the seat of a bishop; a synod of bishops met there in 415. Lod was occupied by the Crusaders in 1099, destroyed by Saladin in 1191, and rebuilt by King Richard I (Richard Coeur de Lion) of England. After the Arab-Israeli War of 1948 most Arabs left the city, which was then settled by Jewish immigrants.

lode, deposit of ORE.

Lo-debar (lō-dē'bär), unidentified town of Gilead, E of the Jordan River. 2 Sam. 9.4; 17.27.

lodestone: see MAGNETITE.

Lodge, Henry Cabot, 1850–1924, U.S. Senator (1893–1924), b. Boston. He was admitted to the bar in 1876. Before beginning his long career in the U.S. Senate he edited (1873–76) the *North American Review,* was lecturer (1876–79) on American history at Harvard, and edited (1880–81) the *International Review* with John Torrey Morse. He was (1880–81) a member of the Massachusetts house of representatives and was (1887–93) a U.S. Representative. He also wrote some historical works, as well as biographies of his great-grandfather George Cabot (1877), of Alexander Hamilton (1882), of Daniel Webster (1883), and of George Washington (1889); he edited an edition of the works of Hamilton (9 vol., 1885). As a Senator he was a close friend of Theodore Roosevelt, welcomed war with Spain in 1898, and favored the acquisition of the Philippines and the development of a strong army and navy. A conservative party-line Republican, he supported the gold standard and a high protective tariff, was a bitter opponent of President Wilson's peace policy, and, as chairman of the Senate Committee on Foreign Relations, opposed U.S. entry into the League of Nations unless specified and highly limiting reservations were made to protect U.S. interests. He later opposed U.S. entry into the World Court. In 1920 he was one of the group of Senators who brought about Warren G. Harding's nomination. See his *Early Memories* (1913); biographies by William Lawrence (1925), Karl Schriftgiesser (1944), and J. A. Garraty (1953).

Lodge, Henry Cabot, Jr., 1902–, American public official and diplomat, U.S. Senator from Massachusetts (1937–44, 1947–53), b. Nahant, Mass.; grandson of Henry Cabot Lodge. He was a journalist on the Boston *Evening Transcript* and then on the New York *Herald Tribune* until 1931 and a member of the Massachusetts legislature from 1933 to 1936. Elected to the U.S. Senate in 1936 and reelected in 1942, he served until his resignation to enter the army in World War II. Lodge was returned to the Senate in 1946, but in 1952, despite the nationwide Republican landslide, he was defeated by the Democrat John F. Kennedy. An early supporter of Dwight D. Eisenhower (he was his campaign manager in 1952), he was then appointed (1953) U.S. representative at the United Nations, serving until 1960. In 1960, he was the Republican candidate for Vice President on the unsuccessful ticket headed by Richard M. Nixon. He served as U.S. ambassador to South Vietnam in 1963–64 and again from 1965 to 1967, was (1968–69) ambassador to West Germany, and was (1969) chief U.S. representative to the Paris peace talks on Vietnam. He wrote *The Stream Has Many Eyes* (1973), a personal memoir.

Lodge, Sir Oliver Joseph, 1851–1940, English physicist, grad. University College, London (B.S., 1875; D.Sc., 1877). He made valuable contributions to the development of wireless telegraphy and conducted research on electrons, the ether, and lightning. From 1881 to 1900 he was professor of physics at University College, Liverpool, and from 1900 to 1919 principal of the Univ. of Birmingham. In 1902 he was knighted. Lodge was greatly interested in reconciling science and religion and was an ardent believer in spiritualism and in survival after death. His writings on both physical and psychical research are listed in *Bibliography of Sir Oliver Lodge* (1935), compiled by Theodore Besterman. See his autobiography (1932).

Lodge, Thomas, 1558?–1625, English writer, grad. Oxford, 1577. After abandoning the study of law for literature, he published (c.1580) his defense of poetry and other arts, usually called *Honest Excuses,* in reply to the attacks made by Stephen Gosson in *The School of Abuse.* Lodge wrote in nearly every form of literature. His pamphlets include *Alarm against Usurers* (1584) and *Wits Misery and World's Madness* (1596). He wrote several euphuistic romances, the best of which are *Scillaes Metamorphosis* (1589), a source of Shakespeare's *Venus and Adonis; Rosalynde* (1590), Shakespeare's source for *As You Like It;* and *A Margarite of America* (1596). *Phillis* (1593), a collection of amorous sonnets, is his chief volume of verse. He also wrote plays and a book of verse satires, *A Fig for Momus* (1595). Lodge pursued several careers in addition to his literary efforts. He sailed on a few expeditions, the most notable being the Thomas Cavendish expedition to South America in 1591. He received a medical degree from Avignon in 1598 and another from Oxford in 1603. He wrote very little original work during his later life, devoting himself primarily to translating and to the practice of medicine. See his complete works ed. by E. W. Gosse (1883, repr. 1966); biography by P. M. Ryan, Jr. (1958); studies by C. J. Sisson (1933, repr. 1966) and E. A. Tenney (1935, repr. 1969).

lodgepole pine, common name for the PINE species *Pinus contorta,* found in the Rocky Mts. and the northwestern coast of the United States.

Lodi (lô'dē), city (1971 pop. 43,938), Lombardy, N Italy, on the Adda River, near Milan. It is an important dairy center. Machines, electrical goods, and ceramics are also produced. The city is located near the site of ancient Laus Pompeia, which was destroyed by Milan in A.D. 1111. At Lodi on May 10, 1796, Napoleon Bonaparte defeated the Austrians after personally leading his troops across the bitterly contested bridge over the Adda. Of note in the city are the Romanesque cathedral (12th cent.) and the beautiful Renaissance-style Church of the Incoronata.

Lodi (lō'dī). **1** City (1970 pop. 28,691), San Joaquin co., central Calif., on the Mokelumne River, in a rich farm area; inc. 1906. The city has foundries, a cannery, and a meat plant. Wine is made, as well as other diverse manufactures. Lodi was founded in 1869 and settled by wheat farmers from the Dakotas, mostly of German descent. **2** Industrial borough (1970 pop. 25,213), Bergen co., NE N.J.; inc. 1894. It has chemical industries.

Lodomeria, Latinized name of the duchy of Vladimir. See VLADIMIR-VOLYNSKI.

Łódź (lōōj), city (1970 pop. 761,760), central Poland. The second largest city of Poland and an important industrial center, Łódź is the center of the Polish textile industry. Other important manufactures include machinery, electrical equipment, chemicals, and metals. Chartered in 1423, the city passed to Prussia in 1793 and to Russia in 1815. It reverted to Poland in 1919. The first textile mills were established in the city c.1830, but the industry grew only after 1870. The city was also the center of the Polish labor and socialist movements. In World War II it was incorporated into Germany, renamed Litzmannstadt, and subjected to ruthless Germanization. The city has a university (founded in 1945).

Loeb, Jacques (lōb), 1859–1924, American physiologist, b. Germany, M.D. Univ. of Strasbourg, 1884. He came to the United States in 1891 and taught at Bryn Mawr, the Univ. of Chicago, and the Univ. of California. From 1910 he was a member of the Rockefeller Institute (now Rockefeller Univ.). Best known for his tropism theory and for his experiments in inducing parthenogenesis and regeneration by chemical stimulus, he also propounded the mechanistic philosophy that all ethics were the outgrowth of man's inherited tropisms. He was a founder and editor of the *Journal of General Physiology.* His works include *The Mechanistic Conception of Life* (1912), *Artificial Parthenogenesis and Fertilization* (1913), and *The Organism as a Whole* (1916).

Loeb, James, 1867–1933, American banker and philanthropist, b. New York City; son of Solomon Loeb. He entered (1888) Kuhn, Loeb and Company and retired from business at 34. Most of the rest of his life was spent abroad. He founded and endowed the Loeb Classical Library, a series of inexpensive yet attractive books containing on facing pages the original Greek and Latin texts and the English translations. He also founded (1905) in New York City the Institute of Musical Art, now part of the JUILLIARD SCHOOL, and a clinic for psychiatric study in Munich.

Loeb, Solomon, 1828–1903, American banker, b. Germany. After he came (1849) to the United States, he settled in Cincinnati and became wealthy as a dry-goods merchant. He moved (1865) to New York City and with Abraham Kuhn started the banking house of Kuhn, Loeb and Company. After his retirement, most of his financial interests were taken over by his son, James Loeb. His philanthropies included large amounts to Jewish charities. See biography by Cyrus Adler (1928).

Loeffler, Charles Martin (lĕf'lər), 1861–1935, American composer and violinist, b. Alsace, France; he studied in Kiev, Berlin, and Paris. In 1881 he emigrated to the United States, and from 1882 until 1903 he shared with Franz Kneisel the position of first violinist and soloist of the Boston Symphony Orchestra. His *Pagan Poem* (1906) for orchestra shows the influence of French impressionism, but it also reflects an attempt to evoke the style of *ars antiqua.* Other works include *Memories of My Childhood* (1925), for orchestra, inspired by Russian folk music. He also wrote chamber music and choral works.

loess (lō'ĕs, Ger. lös), unstratified soil deposit of varying thickness, usually yellowish and composed of fine-grained angular mineral particles mixed with clay. It is found in many regions of the world and is probably related to the CHERNOZEM of the USSR; extensive deposits occur along the Mississippi River and its tributaries, on the Columbia Plateau in Oregon, Washington, and Idaho, and in China. Although some authorities believe loess was deposited by running water, a more commonly accepted theory is that it originated as dust carried by the wind from adjacent deserts, from frost-pulverized outwash of glaciers (during the Pleistocene epoch), or from the floodplains of glacier-fed streams. Studies of particles transported by wind from plains recently denuded by tillage show that the material is sorted to about the same degree as loess. Much of the loess in the United States is of glacial origin; in China, of desert origin. Loess is usually deep, fertile soil, rich in organic remains (especially the shells of snails) and characterized by slender, vertical tubes that are said to represent stems and roots of plants buried by sediment. When cut by streams or other agencies, loess remains standing in cliffs exhibiting a vertical, columnar structure; this is attributed to the vertical tubes and to the angularity of the grains and their consequent tendency to interlock. The uncompacted character of loess makes it subject to rapid erosion.

Loewi, Otto (lō'ē), 1873–1961, American physiologist and pharmacologist, b. Frankfurt, Germany. He was professor of pharmacology (1909–38) at the Univ. of Graz, Austria, until forced into exile after the Nazi purge of professors; from 1940 he was professor of pharmacology at the college of medicine of New York Univ. For his discovery of the chemical transmission of nerve impulses he shared the 1936 Nobel Prize in Physiology and Medicine with Sir Henry Dale. Loewi investigated the physiology and pharmacology of metabolism, the kidneys, the heart, and the nervous system. In 1954 he was made a member of the Royal Society of London.

Löffler, Friedrich (frē'drĭkh löf'lər), 1852–1915, German bacteriologist. From 1888 he taught hygiene at the Univ. of Greifswald. Among his many contributions to bacteriology are his demonstrations of the relationship of diphtheria to the organism known as the Klebs-Löffler bacillus and of foot and mouth disease to a virus.

Lofoten (lōō'fōōtən) and **Vesterålen** (vĕ'stərôlən), two contiguous island groups (1971 pop. 63,365), Nordland and Troms counties, NW Norway, in the Norwegian Sea. Situated within the Arctic Circle, the islands extend c.150 mi (240 km) from northeast to southwest and are from 1 to 50 mi (1.6–80 km) off the mainland. The North Atlantic Drift gives these northern islands a temperate climate. The chief islands of the Lofoten group are Røstøya, Vaerøya, Moskenesøya, Vestvågøya, and Austvågøya; the celebrated MOSKENSTRAUMEN is S of MOSKENESØYA. The Vesterålen group, separated from the Lofoten by the narrow Raftsundet, includes the islands of Hinnøya (the largest island of Norway), Langøya, and Andøya. Svolvaer, on Austvågøya, and Hårstad, on Hinnøya, are the main trading centers. The chief economic importance of these island groups lies in their cod and herring fisheries, which are among the richest in the world. The codfish shoal on the eastern coast of the islands from February to April, the herrings on the western coast from August to November. During these seasons thousands of fishing craft come to the fish banks, but treacherous tidal currents make operations dangerous and difficult. The local population also engages in cattle and sheep raising. Coal and magnetite are mined on Andøya and Langøya.

Lofting, Hugh, 1886–1947, American writer of juvenile stories, b. Maidenhead, England. He settled in the United States in 1912. His famous "Dr. Dolittle" stories, which concern an extraordinary country doctor with a great love of animals, began as letters to his children during World War I. They include *The Story of Dr. Dolittle* (1920), *The Voyages of Dr. Dolittle* (1922), and *Dr. Dolittle and the Secret Lake* (1948). All were illustrated by Lofting himself.

Logan, Benjamin, c.1743–1802, American frontiersman, b. Augusta co., Va. He built (1775) Fort Logan (now Stanford, Ky.) and led a number of retaliatory expeditions against the Indians in Ohio during the American Revolution. He was a leading figure in Kentucky history both during and after the Revolution, serving in the Virginia assembly (1781–82, 1785–87), in Kentucky's first constitutional convention (1792), and in the Kentucky legislature (1792–95, 1797–98). See biography by C. B. Talbert (1962).

Logan, George, 1753–1821, American political figure and agriculturist, b. near Germantown (now part of Philadelphia), grandson of James Logan. After obtaining a medical degree abroad, he returned to America during the Revolution and turned from medicine to farming; at the same time he served several terms in the Pennsylvania legislature. A friend and supporter of Thomas Jefferson, he went (1798) on his own authority to France to secure its accord with the United States. His mission, in part successful, was resented by Federalists, who secured the passage of the so-called Logan Act, prohibiting civilian participation in diplomatic negotiations except by official authority. He served as U.S. Senator (1801–7) and, despite the Logan Act, went to England to reconcile differences between that country and the United States. Logan was active for many years in the furtherance of agricultural advancement. See biography by F. B. Tolles (1953, repr. 1972).

Logan, James, 1674–1751, American colonial statesman and scholar, b. Ireland. While engaged in the shipping trade, Logan met William PENN and became (1699) his secretary. He emigrated to Philadelphia with Penn and remained his confidential adviser for many years. He served as provincial secretary and clerk of the provincial council, where he was a member from 1702 to 1747. A leader of the aristocratic proprietary party, he often came into bitter conflict with David LLOYD. Logan became mayor of Philadelphia (1722), justice of the court of common pleas (1727), and chief justice of the supreme court (1731). He was acting governor of the province from 1736 to 1738. Logan became very wealthy through land investment and trade with the Indians. He maintained a large estate, where his hospitality to the Indians established their long-lasting friendship with the colony. Logan's wide scholarly interests included botanical research that received recognition from Carolus Linnaeus, who named the genus *Logania* after him. He was also the author of numerous scientific works, and at his death he left his large library of classical and scientific books to Philadelphia. See *Correspondence between William Penn and James Logan,* ed. by Deborah Logan and Edward Armstrong (2 vol., 1870–72, repr. 1972); biography by F. B. Tolles (1957).

Logan, James, c.1725–1780, chief of the Mingo Indians, b. Pennsylvania. He took his name from James Logan (1674–1751) and is frequently called simply Logan. He was a leader of the Indians on the Ohio and Scioto rivers. Logan was long the friend of the whites, but when his family was massacred by white settlers (1774), his attacks against them helped bring on Dunmore's War. Logan refused to participate in making the treaty, and his eloquent speech became famous. He served with the British during the American Revolution. See biography by G. S. Haber (1958).

Logan, John Alexander, 1826–86, American politician, Union general in the Civil War, b. Murphysboro, Ill. He fought in the Mexican War and practiced law in Illinois. A Democrat who supported Stephen A. Douglas, he served several terms in the state legislature and was elected to Congress in 1858 and 1860. At the first battle of Bull Run (July, 1861), Logan fought in the ranks. Afterward he organized the 31st Illinois Infantry, of which he was made colonel. He served at Fort Donelson (1862) and in the Vicksburg campaign (1862–63). Logan led a corps of the Army of the Tennessee in General Sherman's Atlanta campaign (1864) and commanded that army for a short time. However, Oliver O. Howard was given the permanent command, and Logan returned to his corps for the march through the Carolinas. A radical Republican Congressman (1867–71), he was one of the House managers of the impeachment trial of Andrew Johnson. From 1871 to 1877 and from 1880 until his death he was a U.S. Senator from Illinois. He was the Republican candidate for Vice President in 1884. A founder, and three times president, of the Grand Army of the Republic, Logan was a prominent supporter of legislation for veterans. He inaugurated MEMORIAL DAY in 1868. He wrote *The Volunteer Soldier of America* (1887). See studies by J. P. Jones (1967) and by his wife, M. S. Logan (1913, abr. ed. 1970).

Logan, Joshua, 1908–, American theatrical and film director, b. Texarkana, Texas. After 1938 he directed several successes in New York. Later he was director, producer, and coauthor of *Mr. Roberts* (1948), *South Pacific* (1949; film, 1958), and *Fanny* (written with S. N. Behrman, 1954; film, 1961). His other films include *Picnic* (1955), *Sayonara* (1957), and *Camelot* (1967).

Logan, Stephen Trigg, 1800–1880, American lawyer, b. Franklin co., Ky. He moved to Illinois in 1832 and practiced law at Springfield until his death. Regarded in his day as a leader of the Illinois bar, he is chiefly remembered as the senior law partner of Abraham Lincoln from 1841 to 1844. Logan served several terms in the state legislature and was a delegate to the Republican convention at Chicago that nominated Lincoln for President in 1860.

Logan, Sir William Edmond, 1798–1875, Canadian geologist. Educated in England, he managed (1831–38) coal mines and a copper smelter in Wales. In addition to making studies of clays underlying coal seams, he made extensive geological maps and sections. These were used for the first geological map of Britain by H. T. De la Beche. As head of the Canadian Geological Survey (1843–69), Logan became known as the father of Precambrian geology. His pioneering work included the mapping of areas for which no topographical maps existed. His results were summarized in *The Geology of Canada* (1863), written with T. S. Hunt. See biography by B. J. Harrington (1883).

Logan, city (1970 pop. 22,333), seat of Cache co., N Utah, on the Logan River; inc. 1859. It is the center of an irrigated dairy and farm area, with huge cheese plants, other food-processing facilities, and factories making farm machinery, pianos, plastics, and knitted goods. Logan was founded (1859) by Mormons. A Latter-Day Saints tabernacle, Logan Temple (also Mormon), and Utah State Univ. are located there. Cache National Forest is nearby, and Logan Peak is visible from the city.

Logan, Mount [for Sir William Logan, a Canadian geologist], 19,850 ft (6,050 m) high, extreme SW Yukon Territory, Canada, just E of Alaska; highest mountain in Canada and second highest in North America. It caps an immense tableland and is the center of the greatest glacial expanse in North America. The first ascent was made in 1925.

loganberry, blackberrylike plant of the genus *Rubus* of the family Rosaceae (ROSE family). See BRAMBLE.

logania (lōgā′nēə), common name for the Loganiaceae, a family of herbs, shrubs, and trees of warmer climates, including many woody climbing species. Some plants of this family are grown in the United States as ornamentals, and several are sources of medicines and poisons. The former include introduced species of *Logania* (native to New Zealand and Australia) and several species of buddleja, or butterfly bush (genus *Buddleja* or *Buddleia),* introduced from China and naturalized in the South. Two species of buddleja are native to Arizona and California. Carolina yellow jessamine, or jasmine, (*Gelsemium sempervirens*), also called false jasmine, is the state flower of South Carolina. It is often grown as a porch vine in the South, and its dried roots are used medicinally as an antispasmodic and sedative. The strong poisons STRYCHNINE and CURARE, which also affect the central nervous system, come respectively from the seeds of *Strychnos nux-vomica,* of tropical Africa, and from the bark and roots of *S. toxifera* and other related tropical American species. Logania is classified in the division MAGNOLIOPHYTA, class Magnoliopsida, order Gentianales.

Logansport, city (1970 pop. 19,255), seat of Cass co., N central Ind., at the confluence of the Wabash and the Eel rivers; inc. 1838. In a fertile farm area, it has diversified industries. Its products include fabricated metals, transportation equipment, electrical goods, building materials, precision machinery, beverages, and processed meats. Grissom Air Force Base is nearby.

logarithm (lŏg′ərĭthəm) [Gr.,=relation number], number associated with a positive number, being the power to which a third number, called the base, must be raised in order to obtain the given positive number. For example, the logarithm of 100 to the base 10 is 2, written $\log_{10} 100=2$, since $10^2=100$. Logarithms of positive numbers using the number 10 as the base are called common logarithms; those using the number *e* (see separate article) as the base are called natural logarithms or Napierian logarithms (for John Napier). The natural logarithm of a number *x* is denoted by ln *x* or simply log *x*. Since logarithms are EXPONENTS, they satisfy all the usual rules of exponents. Consequently, tedious calculations such as multiplications and divisions can be replaced by the simpler processes of adding or subtracting the corresponding logarithms. Logarithmic tables are generally used for this purpose.

Logau, Friedrich, Freiherr von (frē′drĭkh frī′hĕr fən lō′gou), 1604–55, German poet, b. Silesia. Influenced by Martin Opitz, Logau wrote epigrams in the contemporary fashion, bringing a wide range of literary expression to this succinct poetic form. The chief collection of his epigrams is *Deutscher Sinngetichte drey Tausend* (1654).

log cabin or **log house,** style of home typical of the American pioneer on the Western frontier of the United States in the great westward expansion after 1765. It was constructed with few tools, usually an axe or an adz and an auger. All the fastenings were of wood. The log walls were chinked with mud to make them reasonably impervious to the wind. There was no glass, and greased paper might be used across window openings to let some light through. The shutters and doors were fastened on with wooden pegs. There was usually only one door. When the ridgepole of the roof was put in place, roughly hewn flat slabs were laid for a roof. Frequently there was no floor; if there was, it was usually of puncheons, logs split in half, placed with the flat sides up. The furniture was very often roughly made with the same tools that were used in making the house. All were of crude but efficient workmanship. In settlements where Indian attacks were feared the log houses were sometimes placed to form a protected rectangle. The BLOCKHOUSE on the Western frontier was often made of logs. Log cabins were frequently built by community enterprise, a "house-raising" being an occasion for entertainment as well as work. Log houses were unknown to the American Indian, and the first English settlers did not build them. They are known in some countries of Europe, especially Scandinavia, Germany, and Switzerland, and it is a generally accepted hypothesis that they were introduced in America by Swedish settlers on the Delaware in 1638. The log cabin was later adopted by the other settlers in America, and by the end of the 18th cent. at the latest the log house was the typical backwoods dwelling. It was universally used by settlers in the West until they reached the Great Plains, when the SOD HOUSE appeared as the customary dwelling. Reappearing in the Rockies, the log house became a symbol of the frontier. See H. R. Shurtleff, *The Log Cabin Myth* (1939, repr. 1967); C. A. Weslager, *Log Cabin in America* (1969).

loggerhead: see SEA TURTLE.

logic, systematic study of valid inference. A distinction is drawn between logical validity and truth. Validity merely refers to formal properties of the process of inference. Thus, a conclusion whose value is true may be drawn from an invalid argument, and one whose value is false from a valid sequence. For example, the argument *All professors are brilliant; Smith is a professor, therefore, Smith is brilliant* is a valid inference, even if Smith himself is a dolt, but the argument *All professors are brilliant; Smith is brilliant; therefore, Smith is a professor* is an invalid inference, even if Smith is a professor. In Western thought, systematic logic is considered to have begun with Aristotle's collection of treatises, the *Organon* [tool]. ARISTOTLE introduced the use of variables: While his contemporaries illustrated principles by the use of examples, Aristotle generalized, as in: *All x are y; all y are z; therefore, all x are z.* Aristotle posited three laws as basic to all valid thought: the law of identity, *A is A;* the law of contradiction, *A cannot be both A and not A;* and the law of the excluded middle, *A must be either A or not A.* Aristotle believed that any logical argument could be reduced to a standard form, known as a SYLLOGISM. A syllogism is a sequence of three propositions: two premises and the conclusion. By varying the form of the proposition and the modifiers (such as *all, no,* and *some*), a few specific forms may be delimited. Although Aristotle was concerned with problems in modal logic and other minor branches, it is usually agreed that his major contribution in the field of logic is his elaboration of syllogistic logic; indeed, the Aristotelian statement of logic held sway in the Western world for 2,000 years. Nonetheless, various logicians did, during that time, take issue with parts of Aristotle's thought. One of his tacit assumptions was that there is a correspondence linking the structures of reality, the mind, and language (and hence logic). This position came to be known in the Middle Ages as REALISM. The opposing school of thought, NOMINALISM, is exemplified by William of Occam, a medieval logician, who maintained that the structure of language and logic corresponds only to the structure of the mind, not to that of reality. Since knowledge is a study of generalizations, while nature occurs in myriad single instances, the distinction between the world and our conception of it is stressed by the nominalists. In the 19th cent. John Stuart Mill noticed the same dichotomy between man's generalizations and nature's instances, but moved toward a different conclusion. Mill held that the scientist or experimenter is not interested in moving from the general to the specific case, which characterizes deductive logic, but is concerned with inductive reasoning, moving from the specific to the general (see INDUCTION). For example, the statement *The sun will rise tomorrow* is dependent on no particular deductive process, but is based on a psychological calculation of probability based on past experience. Mill's chief contribution to logic rests on his efforts to formulate rules of inductive logic. Although since the criticisms of David Hume there has been disagreement about the validity of induction, modern logicians have argued that inductive logic does not need justification any more than deductive logic does. The real problem is to establish rules of induction, just as Aristotle established rules of deduction. With the development of SYMBOLIC LOGIC by George Boole and Augustus De Morgan in the 19th cent., logic has been studied in more purely mathematical terms, and mathematical symbols have replaced ordinary language. Reference to external interpretations of the symbols (formulated in ordinary language) was also rejected by the formalist movement of the early 20th cent. Bertrand Russell and Alfred North Whitehead, in *Principia Mathematica,* attempted to develop logical theory as the basis for mathematics. Pure formal logic attempts to prove that a logical system is dependent only on the perceptual recognition and valid manipulation of symbols and requires no interpretive reference to content. Intuitionism, rejecting such formalism, holds that words and formulas have significance only as a reflection of activity in the mind. Thus a theorem has meaning only if it represents a mental construction of a mathematical or logical entity. Kurt Gödel, in the 1930s, brought forth his "incompleteness theorem," which demonstrates that an infinitude of propositions that are underivable from the axioms of a system nevertheless have the value of true within the system. Neither these Gödel Propositions, as they are called, nor their negations are provable. One implication for the modern logician is that Aristotle's law of the excluded middle (*either A or not A)* is neither so simple nor so self-evident as it once seemed.

logical positivism, also known as scientific empiricism, modern school of philosophy that attempted to introduce the methodology and precision of mathematics and the natural sciences into the field of philosophy. The movement, which began in the early 20th cent., was the fountainhead of the modern trend that considers philosophy an analytical, rather than a speculative, inquiry. It began in the group called the Vienna Circle, which formed around Moritz Schlick when he occupied (1920s) a chair of philosophy at the Univ. of Vienna. Among its members were the philosophers Friedrich Waismann, Otto Neurath, Rudolf Carnap, Herbert Feigl, and Victor Kraft, and the mathematicians Hans Hahn, Karl Menger, and Kurt Gödel. The movement soon had a widespread following in Europe and the United States. Among those philosophers whose work was influenced by the Vienna Circle are A. J. AYER and Gilbert Ryle. The position of the original logical positivists was a blend of the positivism of Ernst MACH with the logical concepts of Gottlob FREGE and Bertrand RUSSELL, but their inspiration was derived from the writings of Ludwig WITTGENSTEIN, who lived for a time near Vienna, and G. E. MOORE. The Vienna Circle in general subscribed to Wittgenstein's dictum in *Tractatus Logico-Philosophicus* that the object of philosophy was the logical clarification of thought; philosophy was not a theory but an activity. The logical positivists held that metaphysical speculation was nonsensical, propositions of logic and mathematics tautological, and moral or value statements merely emotive. The meaning of a statement could be determined only by tests that applied empirical observation. However, philosophy still had a useful function to perform in clarifying the concepts of both everyday and scientific language. For the logical positivists, philosophy was to become the logic of science. The Vienna Circle disintegrated after the Nazis took control of Austria in the late 1930s. The influence of the movement, as a movement, ended c.1940. However, the concepts of the movement, particularly in its emphasis on the function of philosophy as the analysis of language, has been carried on throughout the West. Several rudimentary works on ethics, published by followers of the school, may yet be the most important outgrowth of logical positivism. See A. J. Ayer, ed., *Logical Positivism* (1959, repr. 1966); Ernest Gellner, *Words and Things* (rev. ed. 1968, repr. 1972); B. R. Gross, *Analytic Philosophy* (1970).

logic circuit, electric circuit whose output depends upon the input in a way that can be expressed as a function in SYMBOLIC LOGIC; it has one or more binary inputs (capable of assuming either of two states, e.g., "on" or "off") and a single binary output. Logic circuits that perform particular functions are called gates. Basic logic circuits include the AND gate, the OR gate, and the NOT gate, which perform the logical functions AND, OR, and NOT. Logic circuits can be built from any binary electric or electronic devices, including switches, relays, electron tubes, solid-state diodes, and transistors; the choice depends upon the application and design requirements. Modern technology has produced integrated logic circuits, modules that perform complex logical functions. A major use of logic circuits is in electronic digital computers. Fluid logic circuits have been developed whose function depends on the flow of a liquid or gas rather than on an electric current.

Logos (lō'gŏs) [Gr.,=word], in Greek and Hebrew metaphysics, the unifying principle of the world. The central idea of the Logos is that it links God and man, hence any system in which the Logos plays a part is monistic. The Greek HERACLITUS held (c.500 B.C.) that the world is animated and kept in order by fire—this fire is the Logos; it is the power of order in the world and the order itself. It thus became the unifying feature of the Heraclitean system. The Stoics (see STOICISM) were influenced in part by Platonism and Aristotelianism in their conception of the Logos. To them God was immanent in the world, its vitalizing force, and God as the law guiding the universe they called Logos; with the additional idea that all things develop from this force, it is called the Spermaticos Logos. The Logos reappears in Greek philosophy in a much restricted form in the system of emanations of NEOPLATONISM. Certain books of the Old Testament present a principle called the Wisdom of God active in the world. At the same time there was a very ancient Hebrew idea of the Word of God, also active in the world. Thus the Wisdom and the Word of God, sometimes quasi-distinct from Him, coalesced. PHILO, in his synthesis of Judaism and Greek thought, naturally hit upon the Logos as a union between the systems; hence his Logos retains qualities both of the Stoic Logos and the Hebrew Word of God. Philo's God is remote, unaffected by the world, without attributes, unmoving; hence He must have mediation to connect Him with the world. At times Philo's Logos is independent of God (because of God's remoteness); at other times the Logos is simply the Reason of God (because Philo's monism obliges God to act in the world through His mediating forces). St. John in his Gospel adapted the term to his purpose. In the prologue of 14 verses the idea of the Gospel is stated clearly and simply. The Logos, which is the eternal God, took flesh and became man, in time. The Logos is Jesus. The impersonal, remote God of Philo is not there; the intermediate Logos, neither God nor man, has been replaced by a Logos that is both God and man. This explanation of the relation of God and man became an abiding feature of Christian thought. See W. J. Ong, *Presence of the Word* (1967).

Logroño (lōgrō'nyō), city (1970 pop. 84,456), capital of Logroño prov., N Spain, in Old Castile, on the Ebro River. It is a farm-processing center noted for its Rioja wine; wood products and textiles are also made there. The kings of Navarre and Castile fought over Logroño from the 10th cent. until its final annexation (1173) to Castile. The charter granted by Alfonso VI served as a model for those of other cities.

logwood, small, thorny tree (*Haematoxylon campechianum)* of the family Leguminosae (PULSE family) native to tropical America and introduced into other tropical regions. The brown-red heartwood is the source of the dye haematoxylin and was exported to Europe as a major purple textile dye from the 16th cent. until the recent development of synthetic aniline dyes. It is still used more than are most natural dyes—as a histological stain, for ink, and as a special-purpose dye. Local names for the wood include campeachy wood and blackwood. The name logwood is sometimes applied to other similar woods. Logwood is classified in the division MAGNOLIOPHYTA, class Magnoliopsida, order Rosales, family Leguminosae.

Lohengrin (lō'ən-grĭn), in medieval German story, a knight of the Holy GRAIL, son of Parzival. He is sent to rescue Princess Elsa of Brabant from an unwanted suitor. Led to Antwerp by a swan, Lohengrin saves Elsa and marries her. She is forbidden to ask his identity, but, overcome by curiosity, she asks. As a result, Lohengrin must return to the castle of the Grail. The swan reappears and is revealed to be Elsa's brother. In its fullest form the story is treated in a German epic poem composed c.1285-1290 and ascribed to WOLFRAM VON ESCHENBACH by its unknown author. Wagner based his libretto for the opera *Lohengrin* (1850) on this source. The swan's metamorphosis is also a theme in classical, Celtic, and other mythologies.

Lohenstein, Daniel Caspar von (dä'nēĕl käs'pär fən lō'ənshtīn), 1635-83, German dramatist, novelist, and poet. Lohenstein is credited with having created baroque tragedy in Germany. He employed ancient themes of sensuality and inhumanity in *Cleopatra* (1661), *Sophonisbe* (1680), and *Ibrahim Bassa* (1650). His mammoth courtly novel *Grossmütiger Feldherr Arminius* [magnanimous General Arminius] (1689-90) is a roman à clef dedicated to the German nobility. A collection of his poetry, *Gedichte*, was published in 1966.

Loir (lwär), river, 193 mi (310 km) long, rising S of Chartres, N central France, and flowing generally SW through a fertile agricultural region to join the Sarthe River N of Angers.

Loire, department (1968 pop. 722,383), E central France, in part of Beaujolais and Lyonnais. SAINT-ÉTIENNE is the capital.

Loire, longest river of France, c.630 mi (1,010 km) long, rising in the Cévennes mts., SE France, and flowing in an arc through central and W France to the Atlantic Ocean at Saint-Nazaire. The upper Loire swiftly flows northwestward through numerous gorges in the Massif Central. At Orléans it swings southwest and enters a wide fertile valley; Tours and Angers are there. In the Loire basin lie the rich fields, gardens, and vineyards of Orléanais, Touraine, and Anjou. At the head of the Loire estuary, c.35 mi (55 km) from the sea, is the industrial city of Nantes. The Loire's chief tributaries are the Allier, Cher, and Vienne. Silting, shallowness, and seasonal volume fluctuations limit the use of the Loire for navigation. Because the Loire is subject to heavy flooding, its banks are lined with dikes. The Loire Lateral Canal parallels the river from Roanne to Briare. Other canals connect the river with the Seine and Rhône river systems. The Loire valley has fostered traditions of civilized living that have become a heritage of all France. The châteaus of the Loire region are embodiments of French history and civilization.

Loire-Atlantique (lwär-ätläNtēk'), formerly **Loire-Maritime,** department (1968 pop. 861,452), NW France, in S Brittany, on the Atlantic coast. The main cities are NANTES (the capital) and ST. NAZAIRE.

Loiret (lwärā'), department (1968 pop. 430,629), N central France, partly in Orléanais. ORLÉANS is the capital.

Loir-et-Cher (lwär-ā-shĕr), department (1968 pop. 267,896), N central France, in Orléanais. BLOIS is the capital.

Lois (lō'ĭs), grandmother of Timothy. 2 Tim. 1.5.

Loisy, Alfred Firmin (älfrĕd' fērmăN' lwäzē'), 1857-1940, French theologian and biblical critic. He was ordained (1879) a Roman Catholic priest and was (1881-93) professor at the Catholic Institute in Paris. He lost his position because of an article he wrote that was suspected of heresy by the authorities. He taught (1900-1904) at the École des Hautes Études and (1909-26) at the Collège de France. At the beginning of the 20th cent. he became the principal leader of the movement called Catholic MODERNISM, which accepted the theories of the HIGHER CRITICISM and developed a kind of liberal humanitarianism. His books were condemned severally and collectively by the Holy See, and in 1908 he was excommunicated. Thereafter he became increasingly opposed to the teachings of the church. Among his works are *L'Évangile et l'église* [the gospel and the church] (1902), *Le IVe Évangile* [the fourth gospel] (1903), and *Les Évangiles synoptiques* [the synoptic gospels] (1908). His autobiography appeared in 1924. See John Ratté, *Three Modernists* (1968).

Loja (lō'hä), city (1970 est. pop. 38,300), capital of Loja prov., S Ecuador, on the Zamora River, at the terminus of the Ecuadorian section of the Pan American Highway. It is a commercial center for the agricultural and mineral resources (gold, silver, and copper) of the area. Cattle are raised in the surrounding region. Founded in 1546, the city was the site of the Ecuadorian declaration of independence in 1820. Loja has a law school.

Lokayata (lōkä'yətə): see INDIAN PHILOSOPHY.

Loki (lō'kē), Norse giant (or deity) who personified evil. He hated the gods of Asgard and continually sought to overthrow them. His worst exploit was the murder of BALDER, for which he was punished by Thor. It was prophesied that when Ragnarok (the doom of the gods) occurs, Loki, with the aid of his monstrous children—the Fenris wolf, the Midgard serpent, and the goddess Hel—will lead the enemies of heaven.

Lokoja (lōkōjä'), town (1963 pop. 25,000), central Nigeria, at the junction of the Niger and Benue rivers. Lokoja is the trade and distribution center for an agricultural (chiefly cotton) region and has food-processing industries. Undeveloped iron ore deposits are found nearby. In 1859 a British trading and missionary settlement was founded in Lokoja. From 1867 to 1869 a British consulate was maintained there. In 1900, Lokoja served as the staging point for the British conquest of N Nigeria and became the temporary capital of the protectorate of Northern Nigeria.

Løland, Rasmus (räs'mōōs lö'län), 1861-1907, Norwegian novelist. Løland, who suffered from poor health throughout his life, produced numerous works after a late start as a writer. His autobiographical novel *Aasmund Arak* (1902) describes the anguish of an individual at odds with the rural society in which he lives. In *Barnebøker* [children's books] (3 vol., 1923-25), considered his finest work, he shows remarkable insight into the world of children.

Lolland or **Laaland** (both: lô'län), island (1965 pop. 81,760), 479 sq mi (1,241 sq km), SE Denmark, in the Baltic Sea, E of Langeland, S of Sjaelland, and W of Falster. The island is low-lying and agricultural; sugar beets are the main crop. The chief cities are Maribo, Sakskøbing, and Nakskov. There are numerous summer resorts on the island's southwest coast.

Lollardry (lŏl'yōōrdrē) or **Lollardy,** medieval English movement for ecclesiastical reform, led by John WYCLIF, whose "poor priests" spread his ideas about the countryside in the late 14th cent. The church in England was ridden with abuses, especially in the ownership and management of great ecclesiastical properties, and its apparent wealth stood in stark contrast to the miserable poverty of most of the common people. Wyclif's central doctrine of evangelical poverty was close to the actual conditions of the people and gave form to widespread discontent with the church. The Great Schism (1378) had also served to deepen the general disillusionment and to foster the belief, taught by Wyclif, that the church had surrendered its divine calling. The Bible, which a man could interpret for himself, was set up as the only reliable rule of faith and standard of holiness. Wyclif supplied his bands of preachers with portions of his translation of the Bible. The most complete statement of the Lollard creed is in the document commonly known as the *Conclusions,* presented to Parliament in 1395. It denied transubstantiation; it condemned the use of sacramentals, images, prayers for the dead, and auricular confession; it declared against all war; and it attacked clerical celibacy and the chastity vows of nuns as unnatural. At its peak just before the turn of the century, Lollardry appealed to members of the middle and upper classes as well as to those of the lower. Oxford became an intellectual center of Lollardry. Severe repressive measures began with the accession (1399) of Henry IV. The statute *De haeretico comburendo* [on the burning of the heretic] was passed by Parliament in 1401, but burnings at the stake were actually rare. Under persecution the Lollards tended to fanaticism, and a petty rebellion broke out among followers of Sir John OLDCASTLE. The rebellion was easily put down (1414), and Oldcastle was executed (1417). There was another uprising, again easily suppressed, in 1431, but stricter suppression drove the movement underground, where it survived until the 16th cent. The alarm of the clergy in England over the Lutheran doctrines was partly caused by a fear that Lollardry would be revived. It is difficult to state how much Lollardry actually encouraged the English Reformation. Undoubtedly it weakened the hold of the church on the people, and the popular use of the Bible helped to stimulate the later movement. Finally, although Lollardry knew nothing of Martin Luther's doctrine of justification by faith, it did in effect proclaim the direct responsibility of the individual soul to God—the essential idea of the Reformation. See James Gairdner, *Lollardy and the Reformation in England* (1908-13); J. A. F. Thomson, *The Later Lollards, 1414-1520* (1965).

L'Olonnois, François: see NAU, JACQUES JEAN DAVID.

Lomax, John Avery (lō'măks), 1867-1948, American folklorist, b. Goodman, Miss. Lomax's first book, *Cowboy Songs* (1910), contained for the first time in print such songs as "The Old Chisholm Trail," "Git Along Home Little Dogies," and "Home on the Range." Collecting and recording songs in the Southern penitentiaries, he discovered Huddie LEDBETTER, known as Leadbelly, who provided the material for his *Negro Folk Songs as Sung by Lead Belly* (1936), which he compiled with his son, **Alan Lomax,** 1915–, b. Austin, Texas. In addition to the Leadbelly collection, father and son collaborated in compiling *American Ballads and Folk Songs* (1934), *Our Singing Country* (1941), and, with Mr. and Mrs. Charles Seeger, *Folk Song: U.S.A.* (1947). See John Avery Lomax's autobiographical *Adventures of a Ballad Hunter* (1947).

Lombard, Peter: see PETER LOMBARD.

Lombard, village (1970 pop. 35,977), Du Page co., NE Ill., a residential suburb of Chicago; inc. 1869. It is known for its lilacs.

Lombardi, Vince (Vincent Thomas Lombardi), 1913–70, American football coach, b. New York City. He played football in high school and at Fordham Univ. After great success as a high school coach (1939–46) Lombardi coached at Fordham (1947–48) and West Point (1949–53), working with the T formation. Entering professional football, he coached (1954–58) with the New York Giants and became (1958) head coach of the Green Bay Packers. He led the team to six conference titles and five national championships. In 1968 he became general manager of the club, but the following year he returned to coach the Washington Redskins to a second place finish. In 10 seasons his professional teams won more than 160 games. He was elected to the Professional Football Hall of Fame in 1971.

Lombard League, an alliance formed in 1167 among the communes of Lombardy to resist Holy Roman Emperor Frederick I when he attempted to assert his imperial authority in Lombardy. Previously the communes had been divided, some favoring the emperor and others favoring the pope. However, after Frederick proclaimed his sovereignty in Italy at the Diet of Roncaglia (1158), twice invaded Italy (1158, 1166), and appointed German officials in all Lombard towns, even the imperial cities joined the coalition against him. The league was supported by Pope Alexander III, for whom its fortified city of Alessandria was named. In 1176 the league defeated Frederick at Legnano. After the peace of Constance (1183), which confirmed the freedom of the cities, the alliance tended to break again into rival factions. The league was revived in 1226 against Holy Roman Emperor Frederick II, who in 1237 defeated it at Cortenuova. The Lombard communes then ranged themselves on opposing sides in the quarrels between the popes and the Honhenstaufen.

Lombardo (lōmbär'dō), Italian family of sculptors and architects. Emigrants from Lombardy c.1470, they were leaders in the architectural Renaissance in Venice. **Pietro Lombardo,** c.1435–1515, architect of numerous churches and palaces, worked on the court facades of the doge's palace from 1498. As sculptor, he is noted for the mausoleum of Doge Pietro Mocenigo in Santi Giovanni e Paolo and for other tombs, including that of Dante at Ravenna. In most of his undertakings he had as associates his sons, **Antonio Lombardo,** c.1458–1516?, and **Tullio Lombardo,** c.1455–1532. One of their greatest joint productions was the Church of Santa Maria dei Miracoli.

Lombardo Toledano, Vicente (vāsān'tā lōmbär'dō tōlātħä'nō), 1894–1968, Mexican labor leader. A successful lawyer, he became (1920) governor of the state of Puebla. In 1921 he joined the Mexican Regional Confederation of Workers (CROM). After the CROM lost the support of Plutarco Elías CALLES it collapsed (1929), and Lombardo Toledano, a zealous Marxist, later founded (1936) the Confederation of Mexican Workers (CTM) and became its first secretary. With the backing of President Lázaro Cárdenas the CTM soon rose in power and promoted urgent labor and welfare reforms. Under the conservative regime (1940–46) of Manuel Ávila Camacho, Lombardo Toledano was stripped of most of his power in the Mexican labor movement. He left the CTM in 1948 and founded the Popular party (later the Popular Socialist party), which he headed until his death. In 1949 he organized the Latin American Confederation of Labor (CTAL). He ran unsuccessfully for president in 1952. See biography by R. P. Millon (1966).

Lombards (lŏm'bərdz, -bärdz), ancient Germanic people. By the 1st cent. A.D. the Lombards were settled along the lower Elbe. After obscure migrations they were allowed (547) by Byzantine Emperor Justinian I to settle in Pannonia and Noricum (modern Hungary and E Austria). In 568, under the leadership of ALBOIN, they invaded N Italy and established a kingdom with Pavia as its capital. They soon penetrated deep into central and S Italy, but RAVENNA, the Pentapolis, and much of the coast remained under Byzantine rule while Rome and the Patrimony of St. Peter (see PAPAL STATES) were kept by the papacy. After Alboin's death (572?) and the brief reign of Cleph (d. 575), no king was elected and Lombard Italy fell under the disunited rule of 36 dukes. The Lombard duchies of SPOLETO and BENEVENTO in central and S Italy were set up independently. In 584 the Lombard nobles united to elect Cleph's son, AUTHARI, as the new king, in order to strengthen themselves against the enmity of the Franks, the Byzantines, and the popes. The Lombard kingdom reached its height in the 7th and 8th cent. Paganism and Arianism, which were at first prevalent among the Lombards, gradually gave way to Catholicism. Roman culture and Latin speech were accepted, and the Catholic bishops emerged as chief magistrates in the cities. Lombard law combined Germanic and Roman traditions. King LIUTPRAND (712–44) consolidated the kingdom through his legislation and reduced Spoleto and Benevento to vassalage. One of his successors, Aistulf, took Ravenna (751) and threatened Rome. Pope Stephen II appealed to the Frankish King PEPIN THE SHORT, who invaded Italy; the Lombards lost the territories comprised in the Donation of Pepin to the papacy. After Aistulf's death King DESIDERIUS renewed (772) the attack on Rome. CHARLEMAGNE, Pepin's successor, intervened, defeated the Lombards, and was crowned (774) with the Lombard crown at Pavia. Of the Lombard kingdom only the duchy of Benevento remained, and it was conquered in the 11th cent. by the Normans. The iron crown of the Lombard kings (now kept at MONZA, Italy) was also used for the coronation (951) of Otto I (the first Holy Roman emperor) as king of Italy and for the crowning of several succeeding emperors. The Lombards left their name to the Italian region of Lombardy. The chief historian of the Lombards was PAUL THE DEACON. See Thomas Hodgkin, *Italy and Her Invaders,* Vol. V and VI (1895, repr. 1967); Pasquale Villari, *Barbarian Invasions of Italy* (2 vol., tr. 1902).

Lombard Street, in London, England. It is a street of banks and financial houses that takes its name from the Lombard merchants and moneylenders who settled there in the 13th cent.

Lombardy (lŏm'bərdē), Ital. *Lombardia,* region (1971 pop. 8,526,718), c.9,200 sq mi (23,830 sq km), N Italy, bordering on Switzerland in the north. MILAN is the capital of the region, which is divided into the provinces of Bergamo, Brescia, Como, Cremona, Mantua, Milan, Pavia, Sondrio, and Varese (named for their capitals). Lombardy has Alpine peaks and glaciers in the north, several picturesque lakes, and upland pastures that slope to the rich, irrigated Po valley in the south. The VALTELLINA valley is in the northeast. Rice, cereals, forage, flax, and sugar beets are the main crops of Lombardy, and the mulberry is extensively cultivated for use in sericulture. Milan is the chief commercial, industrial, and financial center in Italy, and Lombardy is the country's leading industrial region. Manufactures include textiles, clothing, iron and steel, machinery, motor vehicles, chemicals, and wine. The Lombard plain, located in the central part of Lombardy at the confluence of several Alpine passes, has for centuries been a much coveted and frequently invaded area, and it has been a battlefield in many wars. First inhabited by a Gallic people, the region became (3d cent. B.C.) part of the Roman province of Cisalpine Gaul. It suffered heavily during the barbarian invasions that took place towards the end of the Roman Empire. In A.D. 569 the region was made the center of the kingdom of the LOMBARDS, for whom it was named. Lombardy was united in 774 with the empire of CHARLEMAGNE. After a period of confusion (10th cent.), power gradually passed (11th cent.) from feudal lords to autonomous communes, and a general economic revival occurred. Trade between N Europe and the E Mediterranean was largely carried on via the Po valley, and Lombard merchants and bankers did business throughout Europe. In the 12th cent. several cities united in the LOMBARD LEAGUE in order to defy Emperor Frederick I, who wanted to assert his authority over the communes, and defeated him at Legnano (1176). The 13th cent. was marked by struggles between Guelphs (pro-papal) and Ghibellines (pro-imperial), which resulted in wars among cities and rivalries between families within cities. Except for MANTUA (ruled by the GONZAGA family), Lombardy fell (14th–15th cent.) under the sway of the VISCONTI family and the SFORZA dukes of Milan; however, Bergamo and Brescia (1428) and Cremona (1529) were lost to Venice and the Valtellina valley was taken by the Grisons (1512). After the end (mid-16th cent.) of the ITALIAN WARS, the rest of Lombardy followed the fortunes of Milan. Spanish rule (1535–1713) was followed by that of Austria (1713–96) and of France (1796–1814). The Lombardo-Venetian kingdom was established under Austrian rule in 1815. Lombardy briefly ousted the Austrians in 1848–49; in 1859 they were permanently removed and the kingdom was dissolved. In the 11th–12th cent. there was a characteristic Lombard Romanesque architecture, and during the Renaissance Lombardy had a flourishing school of painting whose leading figures were Bernardino Luini and Gaudenzio Ferrari. There are universities at Milan and Pavia.

Lombok (lŏmbŏk'), island (1961 pop. 1,300,324), c.1,825 sq mi (4,725 sq km), E Indonesia, one of the Lesser Sundas, separated from Bali by the Strait of Lombok. Mataram, with the port of Ampenan nearby, is the chief town. The volcanic and mountainous terrain rises to 12,224 ft (3,726 m) at Mt. Rinjani (Rindjani). Its southern area is a fertile plain producing maize, rice, coffee, cotton, and tobacco. The inhabitants, known as Sassacks, are skilled weavers and metalworkers. The island is dominated by the Balinese, who are Hindu. First visited by the Dutch in 1674, Lombok became part of the Netherlands East Indies in 1894. The English naturalist A. R. Wallace noted that Lombok is on the line where the fauna of Asia and Australia meet. A state university is in Mataram.

Lombroso, Cesare (chĕ'zārā lōmbrô'zō), 1835–1909, Italian criminologist and physician. In 1876 he published a pamphlet setting forth his theory of the origin of criminal traits. In the study, later enlarged into the famous *L'uomo delinquente* (5th ed., 3 vol., 1896–97; partial tr. as *Criminal Man,* 1911), he compared anthropological measurements and developed the concept of the atavistic, or born, criminal. In his later works, less importance was given to that concept. Although the usefulness of the concept has been questioned by other criminologists, Lombroso is still credited with turning attention from the legalistic study of crime to the scientific study of the criminal. Lombroso advocated humane treatment of criminals and limitations on the use of the death penalty. See biography by H. G. Kurella (tr. 1911).

Lomé (lômā'), city (1970 pop. 83,845), capital of Togo, on the Gulf of Guinea. It is the country's administrative, communications, and industrial center, and the chief port, handling such items as coffee, cocoa, copra, and palm nuts. Railroads connect the city with Togo's agricultural interior and with Dahomey. Lomé was a small village until 1897, when it became the capital of the German colony of Togo. The Univ. of Benin (1970; formerly the Institute of Higher Studies of Benin) is there. Togo's main airport is outside Lomé.

Loménie de Brienne, Étienne Charles (ātyĕn' shärl lōmānē' də brēĕn'), 1727–94, French statesman, cardinal of the Roman Catholic Church. He was archbishop of Toulouse (1763–88) and of Sens (1788) and a member of the French Academy. In the Assembly of the Notables (1787) he worked against the minister of finance Charles Alexandre de CALONNE and, though King Louis XVI looked with disfavor on his notorious immorality, he succeeded (1787) Calonne in control of finances. Thereupon he adopted Calonne's plans for a direct land tax, for calling of provincial assemblies to apportion the tax, and for other reforms. The opposition of the Parlement of Paris to the land tax led him to exile the parlement to Troyes for a time and finally resulted in the calling of the fateful STATES GENERAL. Having done nothing to relieve the financial ills of France, Brienne was forced out of office (Aug., 1788). He was made a cardinal. Brienne was one of the few French prelates to take oath to the civil constitution of the clergy, promulgated in 1790; for this he was deprived of the cardinalate. Arrested by the revolutionary government (1793), he died in prison.

Lomita (ləmē'tə), city (1970 pop. 19,784), S Calif., a residential suburb of Los Angeles; inc. 1964.

Lomond, Loch (lŏkh lō'mənd, -mən), largest lake of Scotland, 23 mi (37 km) long and from 1 to 5 mi (1.6–8.1 km) wide, between Strathclyde and Central regions, W Scotland. The Leven River drains it into the Clyde. At the southern end of the lake, near its outlet, there are numerous wooded islands. The northern end is overlooked by Ben Lomond (3,192 ft/973 m high). The hydroelectric power plant at the northwestern end of the lake is fed by water from Loch Sloy. Loch Lomond has numerous associations with Rob Roy, and a cave there was once used as a refuge by Robert I.

Lomonosov, Mikhail Vasilyevich (mēkhəyēl' vəsē'lyəvĭch ləmənô'səf), 1711–65, Russian scientist, scholar, and writer, an outstanding figure in 18th-century Russia. Lomonosov was the son of a prosperous fisherman. Concealing his peasant background, he obtained an extraordinarily broad education. He was chosen by the St. Petersburg Academy to study the sciences and philosophy in Germany. In 1741 he received a lifetime appointment to the Russian Academy of Sciences. In his experiments he anticipated such modern principles as the mechanical nature of heat and the kinetic theory of gases. To promote education, Lomonosov wrote a history of Russia (1766) and a Russian grammar (1755). In his poetry he adopted tonic versification, thus altering the character of Russian prosody. For his reform of the Russian literary language he chose an idiom midway between the Old Church Slavonic and spoken Russian. See biography by Boris Menshutkin (1912, tr. 1952); study by F. R. Silbajoris (1968).

Lomonosov (ləmənô'səf), formerly **Oranienbaum** (orä'nyənboum), city (1967 est. pop. 32,000), NW European USSR, on the Gulf of Finland. It is a rail terminus and summer resort and has foundries and brick factories. In Lomonosov are a palace built (1710–25) by Peter I and the "Chinese Palace," built (1762–68) by Catherine the Great. The city was part of the Soviet bridgehead on the Gulf of Finland during the German siege of Leningrad in World War II. It was renamed in 1948 in memory of M. V. Lomonosov, who founded a glass and mosaic works there in 1752.

Lompoc (lŏm'pōk), city (1970 pop. 25,284), Santa Barbara co., S Calif., in an oil area; inc. 1888. It has a huge flower seed industry and two large diatomaceous earth mines. Petroleum and food are processed, and phonograph records are manufactured. Nearby is La Purisima Mission (1791), a state historic monument. Vandenberg Air Force Base, a large missile testing base with a launch site for military satellites, is to the west.

Łomża (lôm'zhä), town (1970 pop. 25,500), NE Poland, on the Narew River. It is a railway terminus. Manufactures include cotton cloth, agricultural machinery, and bricks. There are clay deposits in the vicinity. Łomża dates from c.1000; it passed to Prussia in 1795 and to Russia in 1815 and reverted to Poland in 1921.

London, Jack (John Griffith London), 1876–1916, American author, b. San Francisco. The illegitimate son of an astrologer and a Welsh farm girl, he had a poverty-stricken childhood, brought up by his mother and her husband, John London. At 17, Jack London shipped as an able seaman to Japan and the Bering Sea. He was an oyster pirate, a gold-seeker in the first Klondike rush, a newspaper correspondent during the Russo-Japanese War, and in 1914 a war correspondent in Mexico. His stories, romantic adventures with realistic setting and character, began to appear first in the *Overland Monthly.* In 1900, *The Son of the Wolf: Tales of the Far North* was published. London's Klondike tales are exciting, vigorous, and brutal, often emphasizing a kind of red-blooded energy and virility. *The Call of the Wild* (1903), about a tame dog who eventually leads a wolf pack, is one of the best dog stories ever written. Among his other works are *The Sea-Wolf* (1904), *White Fang* (1905), and *Smoke Bellew* (1912). *Martin Eden* (1909) and *Burning Daylight* (1910) are partly autobiographical. Although he was a highly paid writer of extremely popular fiction, London, a socialist, considered his social tracts—*The People of the Abyss* (1903) and *The Iron Heel* (1907)—as his most important work. *The Cruise of the Snark* (1911) is a vivid account of his interrupted voyage around the world in a 50-ft (15.2-m) ketch-rigged yacht, and *John Barleycorn; or, Alcoholic Memoirs* (1913) is autobiographical. Beset in his later years by alcoholism and financial difficulties, London committed suicide at the age of 40. See Charmian London (his second wife), *The Log of the Snark* (1915), *Our Hawaii* (1917), and *The Book of Jack London* (2 vol., 1921); biographies by Richard O'Connor (1964) and London's daughter, Joan London (1969); study by Franklin Walker (1966).

London, capital of Great Britain and chief city of the Commonwealth of Nations, SE England, on both sides of the Thames River. Since the 1965 London Government Act, London is officially **Greater London** (1971 pop. 7,379,014), c.620 sq mi (1,610 sq km), consisting of the Corporation of the City of London and the following 32 boroughs: WESTMINSTER, CAMDEN, ISLINGTON, HACKNEY, TOWER HAMLETS, GREENWICH, LEWISHAM, SOUTHWARK, LAMBETH, WANDSWORTH, HAMMERSMITH, KENSINGTON AND CHELSEA (the inner boroughs); WALTHAM FOREST, REDBRIDGE, HAVERING, BARKING, NEWHAM, BEXLEY, BROMLEY, CROYDON, SUTTON, MERTON, KINGSTON UPON THAMES, RICHMOND UPON THAMES, HOUNSLOW, HILLINGDON, EALING, BRENT, HARROW, BARNET, HARINGEY, and ENFIELD (the outer boroughs). Greater London includes the area of the former county of London, most of the former county of Middlesex, and areas that were formerly in Surrey, Kent, Essex, and Hertfordshire. Greater London is governed by the Greater London Council. Each of the boroughs also elects a council. The Corporation of the City (1971 pop. 4,234), 1 sq mi (2.6 sq km), the core of London historically and commercially, elects a lord mayor, aldermen, and councilmen.

Economy. London is one of the world's foremost financial, commercial, industrial, and cultural centers. The BANK OF ENGLAND, LLOYDS, and numerous banks and investment companies have their headquarters there, primarily in the City. London is one of the world's greatest ports. It exports manufactured goods and imports petroleum, tea, wool, raw sugar, timber, butter, metals, and meat. London is also a great manufacturing city. About one fourth of the London area's workers are employed in manufacturing. Clothing, furniture, precision instruments, jewelry, cement, chemicals, and stationery are produced. Engineering and scientific research are also important. London is rich in artistic and cultural activity with numerous theaters, cinemas, museums, galleries, and opera and concert halls.

History. Little is known of London prior to A.D. 61, when, according to the Roman historian Tacitus, the followers of Queen Boadicea rebelled and slaughtered the inhabitants of the Roman fort Londinium. Roman authority was soon restored, and the first city walls were built, remnants of which still exist. After the final withdrawal of the Roman legions in the 5th cent., London was lost in obscurity. Celts, Saxons, and Danes contested the general area, and it was not until 886 that London again emerged as an important town under the firm control of King Alfred, who rebuilt the defenses against the Danes and gave the city a government. London put up some resistance to William I in 1066, but he subsequently treated the city well. During his reign the White Tower, the nucleus of the TOWER OF LONDON, was built just east of the city wall. Under the Normans and Plantagenets (see GREAT BRITAIN), the city grew commercially and politically and during the reign of Richard I (1189–99) obtained a form of municipal government from which the modern City Corporation developed. In 1215, King John granted the city the right to elect a mayor annually. The GUILDS of the Middle Ages gained control of civic affairs and grew sufficiently strong to restrict trade to freemen of the city. The guilds survive today in 80 LIVERY COMPANIES, of which members were once the voters in London's municipal elections. Medieval London saw the foundation of the INNS OF COURT and the construction of WESTMINSTER ABBEY. By the 14th cent. London had become the political capital of England. It played no active role in the Wars of the Roses (15th cent.). In the 16th cent. many monastical buildings were destroyed or converted to other uses by Henry VIII, who founded several grammar schools for the poor. The reign of Elizabeth I brought London to a level of great wealth, power, and influence—the undisputed center of England's Renaissance culture. This was the time of Shakespeare and the beginnings of overseas trading companies such as the MUSCOVY COMPANY. With the advent (1603) of the Stuarts to the throne, the city became involved in struggles with the crown on behalf of its democratic privileges, culminating in the English Civil War. In 1665 the great PLAGUE took some 75,000 lives. A great fire in Sept., 1666, lasted five days and virtually destroyed the city. Sir Christopher Wren played a large role in rebuilding the city. He designed more than 51 churches, notably the rebuilt ST. PAUL'S CATHEDRAL. Much of the business as well as literary and political discussion was transacted in coffeehouses, forerunners of the modern club. Until 1750, when Westminster Bridge was opened, LONDON BRIDGE, first built in the 10th cent., was the only bridge to span the Thames. Since the 18th cent. several other bridges have been constructed. In the 19th cent. London began a period of extraordinary growth. The area of present-day Greater London had about 1.1 million people in 1801; by 1851 the population had increased to 2.7 million, and by 1901 to 6.6 million. During the Victorian era London acquired tremendous prestige as the capital of the British Empire and as a cultural and intellectual center. Britain's free political institutions and intellectual atmosphere continued to make London a haven for persons unsafe in their own countries. The Italian Giuseppe Mazzini, the Russian Alexander Herzen, and the German Karl Marx were among many politically controversial figures who lived for long periods in London. Many buildings of central London were completely destroyed or partially damaged in air raids during World War II. These include the Guildhall (scene of the lord mayor's banquets and other public functions); No. 10 DOWNING STREET, the British Prime Minister's residence; the Inns of Court; Westminster Hall and the Houses of Parliament; St. George's Cathedral; and many of the great halls of the ancient livery companies. Today there are numerous blocks of new office buildings and districts of apartment dwellings constructed by the government authorities. The growth of London in the 20th cent. has been extensively planned. One notable feature has been the concept of a "Green Belt" to save certain areas from intensive urban development. The best-known streets of London are FLEET STREET, the STRAND, PICCADILLY, WHITEHALL, PALL MALL, Downing Street, LOMBARD STREET, and Bond and Regent streets (noted for their shops). Municipal parks include HYDE PARK, Kensington Gardens, and Regent's Park. Besides the BRITISH MUSEUM, the art galleries and museums of London include the VICTORIA AND ALBERT MUSEUM, the NATIONAL GALLERY, and the TATE GALLERY. The Univ. of London is the largest in Great Britain.

London, city (1971 pop. 223,222), SE Ont., Canada, on the Thames River. The site was chosen in 1792 by Governor Simcoe to be the capital of Upper Canada, but York was made capital instead. London was settled in 1826. Its streets and bridges are named for those of old London in England. In a rich agricultural district, it has become a notable industrial, commercial, and financial center. Electrical goods and locomotive and automobile parts are among the products made. The Univ. of Western Ontario (coeducational; 1878) and the affiliated Ursuline and Huron colleges are in the city.

London, Declaration of, international code of maritime law, especially as related to war, proposed in 1909. The declaration grew largely out of the attempt at the second of the HAGUE CONFERENCES to set up an international prize court with compulsory jurisdiction. Great Britain, then the chief naval power, felt that such a court should be governed by defined principles. At British invitation the leading European naval powers and the United States and Japan assembled at London in 1908. The Declaration of London that they issued comprised 71 articles dealing with many controversial points, including BLOCKADE, CONTRABAND, and PRIZE. In general it was a restatement of the existing law, but in its high regard for the rights of neutrals it represented a distinct advance. Although the U.S. Senate ratified the declaration, unanimous ratification by the signatories did not follow, and the code never went into effect officially. In World War I a proposal of the United States that the belligerents voluntarily abide by the code was not adopted. See study by Norman Bentwich (1911).

London, University of, at London, England; founded 1836 as an examining and degree-giving body. Teaching functions were not added until 1898. It comprised at first University College (which had been founded in 1826 as the Univ. of London, a nonsectarian school) and King's College (founded 1829 by adherents of the Church of England). It is now a large aggregation of affiliated schools, colleges, institutes, and hospitals. Besides University and King's, its schools and colleges include Royal Veterinary College (1791), Birkbeck (1823), School of Pharmacy (1842), Bedford (1849; for women), Queen Elizabeth College (1881), Westfield College (1882; for women), Royal Holloway College (1883; for women), Queen Mary College (1887), Wye College (1894), London School of Economics and Political Science (1895), Imperial College of Science and Technology (1907), and the School of Oriental and African Studies (1916); it also has several theological and medical schools. Among its famous institutes are the Warburg Institute and the Institute of Historical Research.

London Bridge, granite, five-arched bridge formerly over the Thames, in London, England. It is 928 ft (283 m) long and was designed by John Rennie and built between 1824 and 1831. The early wooden bridge (963–75) was replaced (1176–1209) by a stone bridge with houses and a chapel. The buildings were removed from 1756 to 1762. The bridge was many times damaged by fire and was finally removed in 1832 after the opening of a new bridge in

1831. In 1968, London Bridge was dismantled and purchased by Lake Havasu City, Ariz., and a new six-lane concrete bridge was begun. London Bridge was the only bridge over the Thames in London until the construction (1739-50) of Westminster Bridge.

London Company, corporation composed of stockholders residing in and about London, which, together with the Plymouth Company (see VIRGINIA COMPANY), was granted (1606) a charter by King James I to found colonies in America. The London Company was granted a tract of land fronting 100 mi (160 km) on the sea and extending 100 mi inland, somewhere between lat. 34°N and lat. 41°N. Government was vested in an English council, appointed by the king, which was to appoint a local council for the colony. The company's expedition, under the command of Capt. Christopher NEWPORT, founded (1607) JAMESTOWN in Virginia, the first permanent English settlement in America. In May, 1609, the company received a new charter, extending its territory and enabling it to replace the local council with an absolute governor. Thomas West, Baron DE LA WARR, was the first to hold that office, with Sir Thomas GATES as his deputy. A third charter, granted in March, 1612, made the London Company a self-governing body. There was, however, dissension within the company over governing policies, and the governing council was soon divided into two parties. The court party, headed by Sir Robert Rich (later the 2d earl of Warwick) and Sir Thomas Smythe, favored prolongation of martial law in the colony. The country, or patriot, party, led by Sir Edwin SANDYS, Sir John Danvers, and John and Nicholas Ferrar, favored discontinuance of the system of servitude. The country party was in the majority, but a liberal form of government was not established until after the appointment of Sir George YEARDLEY as governor of Virginia. Yeardley convened America's first legislative assembly at Jamestown in 1619. Although affairs in Virginia gradually improved, a petition was presented (1623) to the king calling for an investigation of conditions in the colony. Shortly afterward there appeared a paper, *The Unmasked Face of Our Colony in Virginia.* Already offended by the company, the king now took extreme measures. A report was made by an investigating commission, the case was tried before the King's Bench, and the unfavorable decision, rendered in May, 1624, resulted in the dissolution of the company. About £200,000 had been expended by the company and more than 10,000 emigrants sent to Virginia. See S. M. Kingsbury, ed., *The Records of the Virginia Company of London* (4 vol., 1906-35); H. L. Osgood, *The American Colonies in the Seventeenth Century,* Vol. I (1904, repr. 1957); W. F. Craven, *Dissolution of the Virginia Company* (1932, repr. 1964); C. M. Andrews, *The Colonial Period of American History,* Vol. I (1934, repr. 1964); C. W. Sams, *The Conquest of Virginia: The Third Attempt, 1610-1624* (1939).

London Conference, several international conferences held at London, England, in the 19th and 20th cent. The following list includes only the most important of these meetings. At the **London Conference of 1830-31** the chief powers of Europe met to discuss the status of Greece. It was decided that Greece should be a fully independent principality, instead of an autonomous state as had been provided in the London Protocol of 1829. The territory of Greece was, however, considerably reduced from that provided in the London Protocol, and the decision was rejected by the Greeks. A new protocol (1831) that restored the 1829 border but retained the sovereign status of Greece was accepted. While the Greek problem was under discussion, the Belgians revolted against the Dutch king. The matter was taken up at the conference, which ordered (Nov., 1830) an armistice between the Dutch and the Belgians. The first draft for a treaty of separation of Belgium and the Netherlands was rejected by the Belgians. A new draft (June, 1831) was rejected by William I of the Netherlands, who resumed hostilities. Franco-British intervention compelled the Dutch to evacuate their forces from Belgium late in 1831, and in 1833 an armistice of indefinite duration was concluded. William's designs to recover Luxembourg and Limburg led to renewed tension, and the **London Conference of 1838-39** followed. This prepared the final Dutch-Belgian separation treaty of 1839 and divided Luxembourg and Limburg between the Dutch and Belgian crowns. The neutrality of Belgium was guaranteed. For the **London Conference of 1852,** see SCHLESWIG-HOLSTEIN; for the **London Conference of 1867,** see LUXEMBOURG, duchy; for the **London Conference of 1908,** see LONDON, DECLARATION OF. The **London Conference of 1933** was the World Monetary and Economic Conference, which had as its object the checking of the world depression by means of currency stabilization and economic agreements. Unbridgeable disagreements among the participants and the attitude of the United States made the meeting a total failure; customs and currency restrictions instead became increasingly stringent throughout the world. After World War II several meetings of the Council of FOREIGN MINISTERS took place at London. For the **London Conference of 1954,** see PARIS PACTS.

Londonderry, Robert Stewart, 2d **marquess of:** see CASTLEREAGH, ROBERT STEWART, 2D VISCOUNT.

Londonderry (lŭn″dəndĕr′ē, lŭn′dəndĕr″ē) or **Derry,** county (1971 pop. 130,296), 804 sq mi (2,082 sq km), NW Northern Ireland. The county town is LONDONDERRY. Much of the county is mountainous. Along the border with Co. Tyrone to the west are the Sperrin Mts., and there is a low cultivated plain along Lough Foyle and the Bann River. Agriculture is the main occupation; cattle, sheep, and pigs are raised. Distilling and the manufacture of linen are the chief industries of the region, and fishing is important. The district was dominated for many centuries by the O'Neill family, whose confiscated estates were granted, in 1609, to the city companies of London, whence the name of the county.

Londonderry or **Derry,** county borough (1971 pop. 83,287), county town of Co. Londonderry, NW Northern Ireland, on the Foyle River near the head of Lough Foyle. Londonderry is the second most important city in Northern Ireland. It is a naval base and seaport with extensive exporting of livestock. The staple industry is the manufacture of linen shirts and collars, but a program of industrial development and diversification was begun in 1969. Londonderry, originally called Derry, grew up around an abbey founded in 546 by St. Columba. The town was burned by the Danes in 812. In 1311 it was granted to Richard de Burgh, earl of Ulster. When it was turned over (1613) to the corporations of the City of London, the name was changed from Derry to Londonderry. Town walls from this period are well preserved. In the siege of Londonderry by the forces of James II (beginning in April, 1689), the town was held for 105 days under the leadership of George Walker; a triumphal arch, a column, and one of the town gates commemorate the siege. The city contains a Protestant cathedral (built 1628-33; restored 1886-87), a Roman Catholic cathedral, and a monastery church (founded 1164). Magee Univ. College in Londonderry is affiliated with Queens Univ., Belfast.

London School of Economics and Political Science, at London, England; founded 1895, recognized as a school of the Univ. of London (see LONDON, UNIV. OF) in 1900. It publishes many periodicals, including the *British Journal of Sociology,* the *British Journal of Industrial Relations,* and the *Journal of Transport Economics and Policy.* The Higher Education Research Unit and the Centre for Urban Economics are affiliated.

Lone Wolf, d. 1879, Kiowa Indian Chief. He led some KIOWA INDIANS on raids in 1874 after his son had been killed by whites, but he was defeated and with a number of followers was deported to Florida, where he remained in military confinement for three years; he died one year after his release.

Long, Crawford Williamson, 1815-78, American physician, b. Danielsville, Ga., M.D. Univ. of Pennsylvania, 1839. He practiced in Jefferson, Ga. In 1842 he excised a tumor of the neck using ether anesthesia, but this was not made public until after the demonstration by W. T. G. Morton in Boston in 1846.

Long, Earl Kemp, 1895-1960, American political figure, b. Winnfield, La.; brother of Huey Long. A lawyer, he was given a state office when his brother became governor. He ran for lieutenant governor in 1931 without Huey Long's support and lost. Later, the two were reconciled. In 1936, he was elected lieutenant governor and served (1939-40) as governor, after his predecessor resigned. Although defeated for reelection in 1940, he twice again served as governor of Louisiana (1948-52, 1956-60). From 1935 to 1960, he was a leader in the "Long machine" created by his brother, which dominated Louisiana politics after 1928. His last administration was marred by personal troubles, which at one point caused him to be committed to a mental hospital. He was elected to the U.S. House of Representatives in 1960 but died before taking office. See biography by A. J. Liebling (1961).

Long, Huey Pierce, 1893-1935, American political leader, b. Winnfield, La.; brother of Earl Long. Originally a farm [illegible]
traveling sal[illegible]
Univ. He wa[illegible]
ticed in Winn[illegible]
to the state ra[illegible]
became the pu[illegible]
elected to the [illegible]
man, and was a[illegible]
litigation. Narro[illegible]
ana in 1924, Lon[illegible]
later. When the [illegible]
gram of economi[illegible]
control of the stat[illegible]
age. Long was resp[illegible]
needed roads and [illegible]
owned hospitals, and [illegible]ool
system into remote rural re[illegible] also increased the taxes of large businesses in Louisiana, especially the oil companies. The state legislature was bludgeoned or bought into passing his laws. In 1929, Long was impeached on charges of bribery and gross misconduct, but he was not convicted. "The Kingfish," as he was called, was elected to the U.S. Senate in 1930, but he did not take his seat until Jan., 1932, after he had assured the succession as governor of one of his own supporters. From Washington, Long continued to direct the Louisiana government. In 1934 he began a reorganization of the state, which virtually abolished local government and gave Long the power to appoint all state employees. As Senator, Long was at first a supporter of the New Deal, but soon became one of Franklin Delano Roosevelt's most vociferous critics. A presidential aspirant, Long gained a steadily increasing national following. Early in 1934 he introduced his plan for national social and economic reform, the "Share-the-Wealth" program; it proposed a guaranteed family annual income and a homestead allowance for every family. Meanwhile, in Louisiana, Long continued to expand his powers. In Sept., 1935, on a trip to the state, Long was assassinated. The assassin, Dr. Carl A. Weiss, was slain by Long's bodyguards. Long's political machine flourished for several years after his death and the Long family remained important in the state; his son Russell Long entered the U.S. Senate in 1948. See his *My First Days in the White House* (1935, repr. 1972); biography by T. H. Williams (1970); H. T. Kane, *Louisiana Hayride* (1941, repr. 1971); A. P. Sindler, *Huey Long's Louisiana* (1972).

Long, John Luther, 1861-1927, American playwright, b. Hanover, Pa. In 1900, in collaboration with David Belasco, he dramatized his short story "Madame Butterfly" (1897), which Puccini later made (1906) into an opera. Belasco and Long also collaborated successfully on *The Darling of the Gods* (1902) and *Adrea* (1905).

Long, Stephen Harriman, 1784-1864, American explorer, b. Hopkinton, N.H. As an army engineer, Long was sent on several exploring and surveying expeditions. The first in 1817 was to the region of the upper Mississippi and the Fox-Wisconsin portage; it is recorded in his *Voyage in a Six-oared Skiff to the Falls of St. Anthony* (1860). A journey to the Rocky Mts. in 1819-20 provided much new knowledge of the mountains. He climbed several peaks, including Long's Peak, and explored the regions of the Platte and Arkansas rivers. Edwin James's *Account of an Expedition from Pittsburgh to the Rocky Mountains* (2 vol. and an atlas, 1822-23) tells of that journey. In 1823, Long led an expedition to determine the source of the Minnesota River and to study the United States-Canadian boundary W of the Great Lakes. Some of his notes were used in W. H. Keating's *Narrative of an Expedition to the Source of the St. Peter's River* (1824). Chosen to select a route for the Baltimore and Ohio RR, he made a survey that resulted in an authoritative railroad manual, with tables of grades and curves.

Long, Loch (lŏkh), inlet of the Firth of Clyde, extending from northeast to southwest in Strathclyde region, W Scotland. Oil is imported there and piped 57 mi (92 km) to the Grangemouth refinery.

Long Beach. 1 City (1970 pop. 358,633), Los Angeles co., S Calif., on San Pedro Bay; inc. 1888. Having an excellent harbor, it serves as a port and a year-round resort noted for its long, wide beaches and active marina. The city has a large oil industry; oil (discovered in 1921) is found both underground and offshore. Manufactures include aircraft, automobile and missile parts, electronic equipment, building materials, canned seafoods, liquid gas, detergents, valves, thermostats, and metal, rubber, and chemical products. A large shipyard and drydock are there. Points of interest in the city include an adobe ranch useum; four man-made ... nd the ocean liner *Queen* ... nased in 1967 and converted ... el, and tourist center. California ... ong Beach, a junior college, and a ... tal are in the city. **2** City (1970 pop. ... ssau co., SE N.Y., on Long Island; inc. ... s a beach resort on the Atlantic Ocean. La- ... clothing, and umbrellas are manufactured ... ere.

Long Branch, city (1970 pop. 31,774), Monmouth co., E central N.J., on the Atlantic coast; settled 1740, inc. 1904. It has garment and electronics industries. Long Branch has been a popular ocean resort since the early 19th cent. Presidents Grant, Hayes, Garfield, and Arthur summered there, and President Wilson's summer house (now part of Monmouth College) was at West Long Branch. President Garfield died in Long Branch in 1881. A historical museum and an art center are in the city, and the Monmouth Park Racetrack is nearby.

Longchamp, William of (lông'shămp, lôNshäN'), d. 1197, chancellor and justiciar of England, bishop of Ely. After service with Geoffrey, duke of Brittany, he joined Richard (later RICHARD I) and JOHN in their uprising (1189) against their father, Henry II. Upon Richard's accession (1189) to the throne, William was made chancellor and bishop of Ely. When the king went on crusade in 1190, William was appointed joint justiciar, and within the same year he had ousted the other justiciar and been appointed papal legate, thus becoming the acting head in England of both state and church. His strong administration was very unpopular, and in 1191 a series of disputes led to a rebellion by the king's brother John and the barons. A settlement was reached, but shortly thereafter the justiciar's high-handed arrest of Geoffrey, archbishop of York, provoked another uprising, and William was deposed from office. In 1193 he joined the captive Richard in Germany and was active in the negotiations to secure his release. He remained chancellor to the king and visited England with him in 1194.

Long Eaton, urban district (1971 pop. 33,694), Derbyshire, central England. A large number of products are manufactured, including synthetic fabrics and apparel, electrical equipment, and railroad carriages.

longevity (lŏnjĕv'ĭtē), term denoting the length or duration of the life of an animal or plant, often used to indicate an unusually long life. The average human life-span of threescore and ten years cited in the Bible has been attained only in recent years in areas of the world where man has been largely freed from disease and social and economic disadvantages. Only 200 years ago the average life span in the United States was less than 35 years. In the more undeveloped areas of the world the life span is lower, depending on the existing conditions. Many individuals are reported to have lived unusually long lives. Thomas Parr of England is said to have lived 152 years. The whale leads the mammalian group at 500 years. The eagle and the swan have the longest lives (100 years) among birds; of the fishes, the carp and pike are believed to live as long as 150 years. Among plants, the bristlecone pine of California has the greatest longevity, up to 4,600 years.

Longfellow, Henry Wadsworth, 1807-82, American poet, b. Portland, Maine. He wrote some of the most popular poems in American literature, in which he created a new body of romantic American legends. Descended from an established New England family, Longfellow was educated at Bowdoin College, graduating in 1825. He spent the next three years in Europe, preparing himself for a professorship of modern languages at Bowdoin, where he taught from 1829 to 1835. After the death of his young wife in 1835, Longfellow traveled again to Europe, where he met Frances Appleton, who was to become his second wife after a long courtship. She was the model for the heroine of his prose romance, *Hyperion* (1839). From 1836 to 1854, Longfellow was professor of modern languages at Harvard, and during these years he became one of an intellectual triumvirate that included Oliver Wendell Holmes and James Russell Lowell. Although a sympathetic and ethical person, Longfellow was uninvolved in the compelling religious and social issues of his time; he did, however, display interest in the abolitionist cause. He achieved great fame with long narrative poems such as *Evangeline* (1847), *The Song of Hiawatha* (1855), *The Courtship of Miles Standish* (1858), and *Paul Revere's Ride* (1861). In all of these works he used unusual, "antique" rhythms to weave myths of the American past. His best-known shorter poems include "The Village Blacksmith," "Excelsior," "The Wreck of the Hesperus," "A Psalm of Life," and "A Cross of Snow." Although he was highly praised and successful in his lifetime, Longfellow's literary reputation has declined in the 20th cent. His unorthodox meters, while contributing to the unique effects of his poems, have been much parodied, and many critics have viewed harshly his simple, sentimental, often moralizing verse. Longfellow made a poetic translation of Dante's *Divine Comedy* (1867), for which he wrote a sequence of six outstanding sonnets. After his death, he was the first American whose bust was placed in the Poet's Corner in Westminster Abbey. See his letters, ed. by Andrew Hilen (4 vol., 1967-1972); biographies by his brother, Samuel (3 vol., 1891; repr. 1969), Newton Arvin (1963), E. C. Wagenknecht (1966), and T. W. Higginson (1902, repr. 1973).

Longfellow, Samuel, 1819-92, American clergyman and hymn writer, b. Portland, Maine; brother and biographer of Henry Wadsworth Longfellow. He was a Unitarian pastor in Fall River, Mass., Brooklyn, N.Y., and Germantown, Pa. Among the four hymnals he compiled are *Vespers* (1859), containing his own *Now on Land and Sea Descending,* and *Hymns of the Spirit* (1864).

Longfellow National Historic Site: see NATIONAL PARKS AND MONUMENTS, (table).

Longford, Elizabeth (lông'fərd), 1906-, British author. Born Elizabeth Harman, she married (1931) Frank Pakenham, later earl of Longford. Educated at Oxford, she lectured for the Workers Education Association (1929-35) and was an unsuccessful Labour candidate for Parliament (1935 and 1950). Her chief works are *Jameson's Raid* (1960), *Victoria* (1964), and *Wellington* (2 vol., 1969-72). She is the mother of the biographer Antonia Fraser.

Longford, county (1971 pop. 28,227), 403 sq mi (1,044 sq km), N central Republic of Ireland. The county town is LONGFORD. A part of the central plain of Ireland, it has level land with numerous small lakes, bogs, and marshes. The River Shannon and Lough Ree form its western border. Raising beef cattle is the principal occupation; oats and potatoes are the chief crops.

Longford, urban district (1971 pop. 3,875), county town of Co. Longford, N central Republic of Ireland, on the Camlin River. It is a farm market and is the seat of the Roman Catholic bishop of Ardagh and Clonmacnois.

Longhi, Pietro (pyā'trō lông'gē), 1702-85, Venetian genre painter. Longhi studied with Crespi in Bologna. He is best known for his small pictures depicting the life of upper-middle-class Venetians of his day. Pastel-colored, doll-like figures move stiffly but daintily through *The Visit* (Metropolitan Mus.) and *Exhibition of a Rhinoceros* (National Gall., London). Apart from early frescoes done in a more lively and vigorous style (Sagredo Palace, Venice) Longhi's artistic life was devoted primarily to his small-scale genre works. He duplicated several of his own works, many of which were also copied by his followers. Examples are in the Museo Correr, Venice; the National Gallery, Washington, D.C.; and the City Art Museum, St. Louis. His son, **Alessandro Longhi,** 1733-1813, was a portrait painter and author of a work on the lives of 18th-century Venetian painters, for which he engraved the illustrations. A portrait attributed to him is in the Metropolitan Museum.

Longhorn Cavern, limestone cave, central Texas, at Burnet. On the northern edge of the Edwards Plateau, the cave (explored length c.8 mi/13 km) lies beneath a triangular ridge rising above the valley of the Colorado River. Guided trails, 2 mi (3.2 km) long, have electric lighting.

Longinus (lŏnjī'nəs), fl. 1st cent.? A.D., Greek writer of the famous treatise *On the Sublime.* Nothing is known of his life, and for a long time his work was attributed to Cassius Longinus. *On the Sublime* is one of the monuments of literary criticism; it defines the qualities of mind and technique that constitute what would now be called "loftiness of style." The work is the sole source for Sappho's second ode.

Longinus (Cassius Longinus), c.213-273, Greek rhetorician and philosopher of the Neoplatonic school. He taught rhetoric at Athens. He later became counselor to Queen Zenobia of Palmyra; when the anti-Roman policy he had advocated failed, he was delivered to the Romans, who executed him as a traitor. Of his numerous rhetorical, philosophical, and critical works, only fragments remain. *On the Sublime,* a Greek treatise of literary criticism, was long attributed to Longinus, but it is now agreed that the author, often known as Pseudo-Longinus, lived in the 1st cent. A.D. See Demetrio St. Marin, *Bibliography of the Essay on the Sublime* (1967).

Long Island: see BAHAMA ISLANDS.

Long Island (1970 pop. 7,141,515), 1,723 sq mi (4,463 sq km), 118 mi (190 km) long, and from 12 to 20 mi (19-32 km) wide, SE N.Y.; fourth largest island of the United States and the largest outside of Alaska and Hawaii. It is separated from Staten Island by the Narrows, from Manhattan and the Bronx by the East River, and from Connecticut by the Long Island Sound; on the south is the Atlantic Ocean. Long Island comprises four counties—Kings, Queens, Nassau, and Suffolk; Kings (coextensive with Brooklyn) and Queens are part of New York City. Eastern Long Island has two flukelike peninsulas that are separated by Peconic Bay. The northern fluke, terminating in Orient Point, follows part of the Harbor Hill moraine, a hilly ridge that extends west along N Long Island to the Narrows and was deposited by melting ice during the last (Wisconsin) stage of the Ice Age (Pleistocene epoch). The southern fluke, terminating in Montauk Point, follows the Ronkonkoma moraine, a somewhat older (also Wisconsin) morainal ridge that extends west to join the Harbor Hill moraine at Lake Success. Low, wooded hills, capped by glacial deposits lie north of the moraines and contrast with a broad, low-lying outwash plain to the south; the highest point on the island is c.400 ft (120 m) above sea level. Long beaches, backed by dunes and shallow lagoons, fringe the south shore; the north shore has low cliffs and is deeply indented by bays. With no large streams, water supply is limited and is obtained from groundwater or from reservoirs on the mainland; large recharge basins catch surplus rainwater to replenish underground supplies, and strict conservation measures have been imposed to prevent further contamination of groundwater from sewage disposal and detergents and from encroachment by seawater. Both the Dutch and the English established farming, whaling, and fishing settlements on Long Island, but it remained sparsely settled until bridges, highways, and railroads provided easy access to New York City. Industrial and residential growth has been especially rapid since 1945. Farming has declined in importance but continues to be profitable in E Long Island. Sand and gravel are quarried from the island's glacial deposits. Sport and commercial fishing is important on the south and east coasts. The south shore is a popular recreational area and includes Fire Island National Seashore, Robert Moses and Jones Beach state parks, Coney Island, and parts of Gateway National Recreation Area. La Guardia and John F. Kennedy International airports are on W Long Island; the Brookhaven National Laboratory is in the east.

Long Island, battle of, Aug. 27, 1776, American defeat in the American Revolution. To protect New York City and the lower Hudson valley from the British forces massed on Staten Island, George Washington sent part of his small army to defend Brooklyn Heights, on Long Island. After several unsuccessful peace overtures, Sir William HOWE landed at Gravesend while the British fleet under his brother, Richard HOWE, shelled New York. After Sir William's troops defeated an American force under John Sullivan and William ALEXANDER (Lord Stirling), Israel Putnam, the corps commander, prepared for the main attack. Sir William, not wanting another Bunker Hill, decided to lay siege instead of storming Brooklyn Heights. Washington saw the position was hopeless and evacuated (night of Aug. 29-30) his army back to Manhattan. Shortly afterward, the Americans began the retreat northward in which delaying actions were fought at Harlem Heights, White Plains, and Fort Washington. Washington managed to extricate most of his troops, and he regrouped them before striking at Trenton.

Long Island City, area of New York City, in Queens co., SE N.Y., on Long Island. An industrial and residential district, it has a long waterfront on the East River and is connected with Manhattan by the Queensborough Bridge.

Long Island Sound, arm of the Atlantic Ocean, c.90 mi (145 km) long and 3-20 mi (5-32 km) wide, separating Long Island, N.Y., from the SE New York mainland and Connecticut. On the W the East River joins it with New York Bay. The sound is fed from the north by the Housatonic, Connecticut, and Thames rivers. The Long Island Sound is an important shipping route and popular pleasure-boating center. New Haven, New London, and Bridgeport, Conn., are the largest port cities; many residential communities line the sound.

Long Island University, mainly at Brooklyn, N.Y.; coeducational; chartered 1926, opened 1927. It also includes C. W. Post College (est. 1954) at Brookville, Long Island, a College of Pharmacy (chartered 1886) at Brooklyn, and a branch at Southampton, Long Island.

longitude (lŏn'jĭto͞od"), angular distance on the earth's surface measured along the equator east or west of the PRIME MERIDIAN. A meridian of longitude is an imaginary line on the earth's surface from pole to pole; two opposite meridians form a great circle dividing the earth into two hemispheres. By international agreement, the meridian passing through the original site of the ROYAL GREENWICH OBSERVATORY at Greenwich, England, is designated the prime meridian, and all points along it are at 0° longitude. All other points on the earth have longitudes ranging from 0° to 180°E or from 0° to 180°W. Except where it is changed to account for populated areas, the INTERNATIONAL DATE LINE lies along the 180° meridian. Meridians of longitude and parallels of LATITUDE together form a grid by which any position on the earth's surface can be specified. The term *longitude* is also used in various celestial coordinate systems (see ECLIPTIC COORDINATE SYSTEM).

long march [Chin.,= *ch'ang cheng*], the journey of c.6,000 mi (9,660 km) undertaken by the Red Army of China in 1934–35. When their Kiangsi prov. soviet base was encircled by the Nationalist army of Chiang Kai-shek, some 90,000 men and women broke through the siege (Oct., 1934) and marched westward to Kweichow prov. There, at the Tsunyi Conference (Jan., 1935), MAO TSE-TUNG won leadership of the Communist party and decided to join the remote Shensi prov. soviet base. Overcoming numerous natural obstacles (such as towering mountain ranges and turbulent rivers) and despite constant harassment by Nationalist troops and the armies of provincial warlords, the Red Army arrived at its new home in the north in Oct., 1935. However, more than half of the original marchers were lost in this almost incredible trek. Those who survived settled around the city of YEN-AN. See Edgar Snow, *Red Star over China* (rev. ed. 1968) and R. G. Wilson, *The Long March, 1935* (1971).

Longmeadow, town (1970 pop. 15,630), Hampden co., SW Mass., a residential suburb adjoining Springfield, on the Connecticut River; settled 1644, set off and inc. 1783. It has a junior college.

Longmont, city (1970 pop. 23,209), Boulder co., N Colo.; inc. 1885. It is the trading and processing center for a rich farm area irrigated by the Colorado-Big Thompson project. Sugar is produced, turkeys are processed, and campers, trailers, and batteries are made.

Longo, Luigi (lo͞oē'jē lông'gō), 1900–, Italian political leader. He was a founder of the Italian Communist party in 1921. In the Spanish civil war he served as inspector-general of the international brigades and fought personally against Benito Mussolini's troops at Guadalajara. Returning to Italy during World War II, he organized partisan units to fight against the Germans. He was elected to the constituent assembly in 1946 and to parliament in 1948. From 1945 to 1964 he was deputy secretary of the Italian Communist party. He became secretary-general of the party in 1964 and served until 1972, when he was given the largely honorary post of party president.

Long Parliament: see ENGLISH CIVIL WAR.

Long Range, mountain range, extending c.300 mi (480 km) along the west coast of Newfoundland island, Canada; rises to 2,672 ft (814 m) in the Lewis Hills. It forms the Great Northern Peninsula of NW Newfoundland. Part of the Appalachian system, the range consists of parallel ridges that rise steeply from the coast and slope gently eastward. A depression, of which Grand Lake and St. George's Bay are part, divides Long Range into two sections. The densely forested range is economically important for timber. Gros Morne National Park is there.

Long Sault Rapids (sō, so͞o), in the Ottawa River, Canada, midway between Ottawa and Montreal. There in 1660 the Iroquois defeated a party of 18 Frenchmen, led by Dollard des Ormeaux, who were attempting to save Montreal.

Longs Peak [for Stephen H. LONG], 14,255 ft (4,345 m) high, N Colo., in the Front Range of the Rocky Mts. From the east side of its snow-capped peak there is a 2,000 ft (610 m) drop to Chasm Lake. It is in Rocky Mountain National Park.

Longstreet, James, 1821–1904, Confederate general in the American Civil War, b. Edgefield District, S.C. He graduated (1842) from West Point and served in the Mexican War, reaching the rank of major. At the outbreak of the Civil War he resigned from the U.S. army and became a Confederate brigadier general. He took part in the first battle of Bull Run and in the Peninsular campaign. His creditable performance at the second battle of Bull Run (1862), at Antietam, and at the battle of FREDERICKSBURG led to his promotion (Oct., 1862) to lieutenant general. In 1862–63 he held a semi-independent command S of the James River, returning too late to aid General Lee at Chancellorsville. He commanded the right wing at Gettysburg (1863), where his delay in taking the offensive is generally said to have cost Lee the battle (see GETTYSBURG CAMPAIGN). He fought at Chickamauga in the Chattanooga campaign and unsuccessfully besieged Knoxville (1863). Returning to Virginia in 1864, he distinguished himself in the WILDERNESS CAMPAIGN, where he was wounded. Longstreet participated in the last defense of Richmond, surrendering with Lee at Appomattox. After the war he settled in New Orleans, became a Republican, and held a number of Federal posts. He criticized Lee's conduct at Gettysburg harshly and was long unpopular in the South. As a general, he is considered to have been a poor independent commander and strategist but an excellent combat officer. His opinions on the war are expressed in his *From Manassas to Appomattox* (1896, repr. 1960). See biographies by H. J. Eckenrode and Bryan Conrad (1936), and by D. B. Sanger and T. R. Hay (1952); Glenn Tucker, *Lee and Longstreet at Gettysburg* (1968).

Longton: see STOKE-ON-TRENT, England.

Longueuil, Charles le Moyne, sieur de (shärl lə mwän, syör də lôNgö'yə), 1626–85, French colonial leader in Canada, founder of a famous Canadian family, b. Dieppe, France. Emigrating to Canada in 1641, he worked for the Jesuits among the Hurons, was a trader, soldier, and interpreter at Trois Rivières (Three Rivers), and finally settled at Ville Marie (Montreal). For his services to France, especially his dealings, both warlike and peaceful, with the Iroquois, Le Moyne was ennobled (1668) and granted the seigniory he named Longueuil. Of his 11 sons, all of whom distinguished themselves in the French service, the sieur d'IBERVILLE and the sieur de BIENVILLE were most famous.

Longueuil, city (1971 pop. 97,590), S Que., Canada, on the St. Lawrence River opposite Montreal. It is a residential suburb of Montreal.

Longueville, Anne Geneviève de Bourbon-Condé, duchesse de (än zhənəvyĕv' də bo͞orbôN'-kôNdā' düshĕs' də lôNgvēl'), 1619–79, daughter of Henry II de Condé and sister of the Great Condé, Louis II de Bourbon, prince de Condé. A noted beauty, she maintained a long liaison with the duc de La Rochefoucauld and joined him as a leader of the FRONDE. A determined enemy of Cardinal Mazarin, she obtained the assistance of her brother Armand de Bourbon, prince de CONTI, during the first Fronde, and that of the Vicomte de Turenne and her brother, the Great Condé, during the second Fronde. She made her peace with the court in 1653. Much of her remaining life was spent in convents, notably that of Port-Royal, which through her influence was saved from persecution in her lifetime.

Longus (lông'gəs), fl. 3rd cent. A.D., Greek writer. The pastoral romance *Daphnis and Chloë* is attributed to him. Idyllic in nature, the poem tells the improbable but charming story of the love of a goatherd and a shepherdess. *Daphnis and Chloë* was widely popular in France and England in the 17th and 18th cent.

Longview. 1 City (1970 pop. 45,547), seat of Gregg co., E Texas; inc. 1872. It is a manufacturing, business, and distributing center for the rich East Texas oil field. The city has oil and natural gas wells, oil refineries, and plants making a wide variety of products. It is also a livestock center. Decline set in when pine lumbering began to fall off, but the city boomed with the discovery of the oil field in 1930. It is the seat of LeTourneau College. Annual horse and cattle shows are held in Longview. **2** City (1970 pop. 28,373), Cowlitz co., SW Wash., a port of entry at the junction of the Columbia and the Cowlitz rivers; inc. 1924. It is a transportation center, with a bridge across the Columbia to Oregon. Its manufactures include aluminum, metal, paper, pulp, and wood products. The city was founded in 1922 as a lumber town on the site of the historic settlement Monticello, which had been swept away by a flood in 1867. A junior college is there.

long-wall mining: see COAL MINING.

Long Walls, Greece: see PIRAIÉVS.

Longworth, Nicholas, 1869–1931, American legislator, b. Cincinnati. A lawyer, he practiced in Cincinnati, where his family had long been prominent. He served (1899–1903) in the Ohio legislature and, with the support of George B. Cox, was elected (1903) to the U.S. House of Representatives. In 1906 he married Alice Lee Roosevelt, the daughter of President Theodore Roosevelt, in a wedding that took place at the White House. As a Representative (1903–13, 1915–31), Longworth was (1925–31) Speaker of the House and became recognized as a master of congressional procedure. See biography by Clara Chambrun (1933); Alice Roosevelt Longworth, *Crowded Hours* (1933).

Longwy (lôNwē'), town (1968 pop. 21,509), Meurthe-et-Moselle dept., NE France, near the Belgian and Luxembourg borders. It is a center of the Lorraine iron and steel industry, with its furnaces and foundries concentrated in Longwy-Bas, the lower town. Longwy-Haut, c.500 ft (150 m) higher, has kept the fortifications built (17th cent.) by Vauban.

Longyearbyen (lông'yērbü"ən), town and administrative center of Svalbard, on Isfjorden, Spitsbergen island. It is a coal-mining settlement, founded (1905) by an American company and named after the American miner J. M. Longyear. Its coal mines were transferred to a Norwegian company in 1916. It was destroyed (Sept., 1943) by German battleships but was quickly rebuilt.

Lon Nol (lŏn nōl), 1913–, Cambodian general and political leader. He held various army commands and was a provincial governor before he became defense minister and army chief of staff in 1955 in Norodom Sihanouk's government. He held these posts until 1966, when he became premier. He became a first vice president in 1967 and then premier again in 1969. In 1970 he led the coup that deposed Sihanouk, and Lon Nol assumed control of the government. He attempted unsuccessfully to suppress Communist guerrillas, and his efforts plunged the country into civil war. He temporarily relinquished power after suffering a stroke in April, 1971, but in 1972 he seized control, took the title of president, and suspended the constitution.

Lönnrot, Elias (ĕlē'äs lön'ro͞ot), 1802–84, Finnish philologist, compiler of the KALEVALA. Although he was trained as a physician, he spent his life, after 1828, traveling through Finland, Lapland, and NW Russia, collecting fragments of the *Kalevala* from the rune singers. Of these he published in 1835 about 12,000 lines. A second edition of nearly 23,000 lines appeared in 1849. To Lönnrot must go the credit of creating a national epic from the scattered fragments sung or recited.

Lons-le-Saunier (lôN-lə-sōnyā'), town (1968 pop. 21,715), capital of Jura dept., E France, at the foot of the Jura mts. A saltwater spa since Roman times, the town has food and textile industries and varied manufactures. Parts of its Romanesque church date from the 11th cent.

Loo-choo Islands: see RYUKYU ISLANDS.

Lookout, Cape, point of a sandy reef (Core Banks), off E N.C., SW of Cape Hatteras. The reef guards the port entrance to Beaufort and Morehead City. A lighthouse on the point was built in 1859 and is included in Cape Lookout National Seashore (see NATIONAL PARKS AND MONUMENTS, table).

loom, frame or machine used for WEAVING; there is evidence that the loom has been in use since 4400 B.C. Modern looms are of two types, those with a shuttle (the part that carries the weft through the shed) and those without; the latter draw the weft from a stationary supply. There are basically three kinds of shuttleless looms. The dummy shuttle, the most widely used, contains no weft but moves through the shed depositing a trail of yarn. A second type, the newest of looms, makes use of jets of air or water to force the weft through the shed. A third kind, called the rapier type and widely used in carpet weaving, uses steel rods to move the weft into the shed. The fundamental parts of all looms are the warp beam, a cylinder on which the warp threads are wound; heddles (rods or cords), each with an eye through which is drawn a warp thread; the harness, a rectangular frame set with a series of heddles operated to form a shed between the warp threads for the insertion of the weft threads; the reed, a comblike frame that pushes the filling yarn firmly against the finished cloth after each pick, or row; the breastbeam, over which the cloth is wound creating a tension with the warp beam; the cloth beam, on which the cloth is rolled as it is constructed; and the shuttle, if it is not a shuttleless loom. Vertical looms, such as the Navaho and some tapestry looms, developed from the practice of hanging the warp beam from a tree and holding the yarns taut with stones, pegs, or a weighted pole. The horizontal form, at first two poles holding the warp extended on the ground, was widely used for the

Western European handloom and for the foot loom, the forerunner of the modern power loom. In the foot loom the harnesses were operated by treadles, leaving the hands free to pass and catch the shuttle. John Kay invented (1733) the automatic fly shuttle, and in 1760 his son Robert devised a drop box by which trays automatically brought bobbins of colored threads in line as desired. These aids to weaving encouraged inventions to speed up SPINNING, which in turn made faster weaving essential. Edmund Cartwright patented (1785) the first practical power loom, the basis of the modern loom with its multiplicity of automatic devices. By 1804, Joseph Marie JACQUARD had perfected an attachment applicable to the power loom whereby any design might be woven on it. In the modern Jacquard, one repeat of the design is laid out on squared paper, then punched on cards that are laced into a continuous chain rotated on an overhead device. The cards are brought in contact with needles each controlling a wire that lifts a heddle when the needle passes through a hold in the card. In the Lefier robot, a design made on copper with insulating paint is transmitted by electricity to needles which lift the heddles.

looming: see MIRAGE.

loon, common name for migratory aquatic birds found in fresh and salt water in the colder parts of the Northern Hemisphere. Its strange, laughing call carries for great distances. Like the grebes, loons float low in the water and their legs are placed far back. They are expert swimmers and divers, sometimes slipping below the surface to swim underwater, but they cannot walk on land and at nesting time must use bill and wings to inch along. In taking flight they patter across the water with their feet. Their long, sharp, strong beaks are well adapted for catching fish. North American species include the common loon, or great northern diver (*Gavia immer*), a black and white bird about 32 in. (80 cm) long; the red-throated loon (*G. stellata*); and the Arctic loon (*G. arctica*). Loons are classified in the phylum CHORDATA, subphylum Vertebrata, class Aves, order Gaviiformes, family Gaviidae.

looper, name for caterpillars that move with a looping motion, including the INCHWORM and the CABBAGE LOOPER.

Loos, Adolf (ä'dôlf lōs), 1870-1933, Austrian architect. His design theories were strongly influenced by his stay in the United States from 1893 to 1896. He built mainly residences in and around Vienna. Among these the most noted was the Steiner House (1910), composed of austere, prismatic forms. In the same year he designed his best-known work, the office building on Michaelerplatz. Loos's emphasis on pure form and proper material and his polemics against ornament and decoration had a strong influence upon the development of the functional style. Two volumes of his essays were published as *Ins Leere gesprochen* [spoken into a void] (1921) and *Trotzdem* [nevertheless] (1931).

loosestrife, common name for the Lythraceae, a widely distributed family of plants most abundant as woody shrubs in the American tropics but including also herbaceous species (chiefly of temperate zones) and some trees. Several shrubs of this family have been introduced in the United States as ornamentals and are now naturalized, e.g., the crape (or crepe) myrtle (*Lagerstroemia indica*) and the henna shrub, or mignonette tree (*Lawsonia inermis*). The latter, cultivated especially in Muslim countries, is the source of HENNA dye (from the leaves), oil and pomade scents (from the flowers), and a medicament (from the bark). The wild marsh plants called loosestrifes (genus *Lythrum*) include several native American species with pink or lavender flowers, but the tall, showy species that blankets moist meadows and swamps with magenta to purple flowers in late summer and autumn is the spiked loosestrife (*L. salicaria*), introduced from Europe and now so widespread as to be a weed. Several species of the unrelated family Primulaceae (primrose family) are also called loosestrife. True loosestrife is classified in the division MAGNOLIOPHYTA, class Magnoliopsida, order Myrtales.

Lop Buri (lŭp bo͝orē'), town (1960 pop. 21,232), capital of Lop Buri prov., S Thailand. Originally called Lavo, it was ruled by the Mons in the 7th and 8th cent. and by the Khmers from the 10th to the 13th cent. While Ayutthaya was the capital of Thailand, Lop Buri served as an alternate capital.

Lope de Rueda (lō'pā dā ro͞oā'thä), 1510?-1565, Spanish dramatist. A precursor of the Golden Age of Spanish literature, Rueda was an actor and a manager as well as a playwright. He is said to have created the genre known as *pasos* (short farces), noted for their use of rustic language and ordinary subjects. One of these is *Paso de las aceitunas* [incident of the olives]. His work was published posthumously.

Lope de Vega Carpio, Félix (fā'lēks lō'pā dā vā'gä kär'pyō), 1562-1635, Spanish dramatic poet, founder of the Spanish drama, b. Madrid. Lope, born a peasant, was orphaned at an early age. He wrote the first of his nearly 1,800 plays at 12, and by 25 he was an established playwright and a celebrated wit. He was involved in countless amorous adventures and several scandals, one of which caused him to be banished from Madrid for some years. In 1588 he joined the Spanish Armada and, surviving the campaign, took up his theatrical career and acquired a lifelong patron, the duke of Sessa. Lope's first wife, Isabel de Urbino, was immortalized in his poetry and plays as Belisa. Although he wrote lyric verse and several epic poems (e.g., *La hermosura de Angélica,* 1502, a sequel to Ariosto's *Orlando Furioso*), his masterworks were his *comedias.* These graceful and vigorous plays combined the comic, the serious, and the ironic. Major examples are *El mejor alcalde el rey* (tr. *The King, the Greatest Alcade,* 1936), *El rey don Pedro en Madrid, El castigo sin venganza* [punishment without vengeance], and *Peribáñez* (tr. 1937). Lope's themes were the varied aspects of honor, human dignity, justice, and the conflict of peasant and nobleman. He developed many genres, including historical drama, cloak-and-dagger love intrigues, and romantic extravaganzas, in addition to writing tragedies and religious plays. He invented a comic type known as *el gracioso,* which became a stalwart of Spanish theater. In 1609, Lope set down his dramatic precepts in *El arte nuevo de comedias* [the new art of writing plays] (tr. 1914). To hold the attention of his audiences, he kept the length of his plays relatively short, consciously ignored the classical unities, convoluted his plots to produce the unexpected, and wrote so as to be easily understood by the common people. Adhering to these self-imposed rules, Lope gained the adulation of his public and the scorn of his rival, the classicist Góngora. Lope took religious orders in 1614 and achieved important church positions despite his continued love affairs. In his last years he finished *La Dorotea* (1632), an autobiographical novel begun in his youth. Nearly 500 of Lope's works are extant. Famed for vitality, wit, and ingenuity, they assure his position as the foremost and most prolific Spanish literary innovator. See *Four Plays of Lope de Vega* (tr. with an introd. by J. G. Underhill, 1936); biographies by H. A. Rennert (1904, repr. 1968) and Angel Flores (1930, repr. 1969); studies by F. C. Hayes (1967) and A. S. Trueblood (1974).

López, Carlos Antonio (kär'lōs äntô'nyō lō'pās), 1790?-1862, president of Paraguay (1844-62). He rose to power shortly after the death of J. G. Rodríguez Francia and soon became president. An arbitrary but enlightened ruler, he improved the armed forces, encouraged education, and attempted to strengthen the economy by creating government monopolies. He made vigorous attempts to end the isolationism that Francia had imposed on Paraguay, but his foreign policy caused friction with neighboring nations. Many of his reforms came to a halt during the regime of his successor, Francisco Solano LÓPEZ.

López, Francisco Solano (fränthēs'kō sōlä'nō), 1826?-1870, president of Paraguay (1862-70). He was the son of Carlos Antonio LÓPEZ, who made him a brigadier general at 18. Appointed head of a diplomatic mission, he went to Europe in 1853, where he negotiated the building of the first railroad in Paraguay. Upon his return he was made minister of war, and in 1862, on the death of his father, he assumed power as a dictatorial caudillo. A megalomaniac who considered himself the Napoleon of South America, López fanatically sought to increase the prestige of Paraguay and waged (1865) a disastrous war with Brazil, Argentina, and Uruguay (see TRIPLE ALLIANCE, WAR OF THE). He was defeated and killed (1870) after retreating with the remnants of his army. López demanded blind allegiance and even had members of his family killed on suspicion of conspiracy. An incident with the United States arose over his imprisonment of Porter Cornelius Bliss. Many of the cruelties that marked his rule were attributed to Eliza Lynch, his Irish mistress, whom he had met in Paris. Solano López, however, is today regarded by some Latin Americans as the champion of the rights of small countries against the aggression of more powerful neighbors. See biography by R. B. Graham (1933).

López, Narciso (närsē'sō), 1798?-1851, Spanish American soldier, b. Venezuela. After serving in the Spanish army during the Venezuelan revolution against Spain, he left his native country for Cuba (1823). He went to Spain, fought against the Carlists, and became a field marshal and a senator in the Cortes. He obtained an appointment as governor of Trinidad, Cuba, but lost it when the supreme command in Cuba was changed in 1843. A liberal, he began to plan a revolution against Spain, and in 1848 he was forced to flee to the United States when his scheme was discovered. He obtained American aid and planned a filibustering expedition to Cuba (1848). It did not succeed, and, two years later, a new expedition against Cárdenas was scarcely more successful. In 1851 a third expedition did gain a foothold on the island, but ended in complete defeat—López himself was captured and executed. See R. G. Caldwell, *The Lopez Expeditions to Cuba, 1848-51* (1915).

López, Vicente Fidel (vēsān'tā fēthāl'), 1815-1903, Argentine historian, journalist, and politician; son of Vicente LÓPEZ Y PLANES. A member of the liberal group that opposed the dictatorship of Juan Manuel de Rosas, he had to seek refuge in Chile (1840-52), where he founded a political review and aided the educational schemes of Domingo Faustino Sarmiento. He returned to Argentina to aid Justo José de Urquiza and was again an expatriate after Urquiza's fall from power. Later he became rector of the Univ. of Buenos Aires. With Juan Maria Gutierrez he edited (1871-77) the *Revista del Río de la Plata.* Of his historical works the most important is the 10-volume *Historia de la república argentina* (1883-93). He also wrote novels, essays, and political tracts.

López Arellano, Osvaldo (ōsvä'dō lō'pās äräyä'-nō), 1922-, president of Honduras (1963-71, 1972-). An army colonel, he led the violent coup that ousted (Oct., 1963) President Ramón VILLEDA MORALES. In 1965 he was selected as president by a constituent assembly. He reversed most of Villeda's liberal economic policies and temporarily restored financial stability until the serious five-day war with El Salvador in 1969. He engineered the national unity plan under which Ramón Cruz was elected president in 1971. As commander of the armed forces under President Cruz, López Arellano retained enormous power, with the constitutional right to ignore presidential orders. He ousted President Cruz in Dec., 1972, when the political coalition of the national unity plan appeared to be breaking down.

López Bravo, Gregorio (grāgō'rēō lō'pāth brä'vō), 1923-, Spanish politician. Employed first as the managing director of several shipbuilding companies, he entered government service in 1959, serving as director general of foreign trade to Dec., 1960, director general of the Spanish Institute of Foreign Currency (1960-62), and minister of industry (1962-69). A member of OPUS DEI and one of the nonpolitical technocrats who rose to power under Francisco Franco, he became minister of foreign affairs in 1969. López Bravo was relieved of that post in June, 1973, because of right-wing opposition to his quest for closer relations with Communist countries, the United States, and Western Europe. In 1973 he became chairman of the ministerial council of the Organization for Economic Cooperation and Development in Paris.

López de Ayala, Pedro (pā'thrō lō'pāth thā äyä'lä), 1332-1407, Spanish statesman and the first important modern Spanish historian. As a royal official in Castile, he served Peter the Cruel, Henry II, John I, and Henry III, rising to become chancellor of Castile (1398-1407). He is best known for his chronicle of the reigns of the four kings he served; avoiding the fantastic interpretations of earlier historians, he wrote with accuracy and realism. He also wrote a satiric poem, *Rimado de Palacio,* on the social and political problems of his era.

López de Legaspi, Miguel (mēgĕl' lō'pāth dā lägäs'pē), d. 1572, Spanish navigator, conqueror of the Philippines. In 1545 he went to Mexico and was later chosen by the viceroy, the elder Luis de Velasco, to head an expedition for the conquest of the Philippines. He sailed in 1563, occupied the Ladrone Islands (the present-day Marianas), and in 1564 reached the Philippines. With tact and ability he took possession of the islands (Cebu in 1565, Luzon in 1570) almost without fighting. The Austin friars who accompanied him helped in organizing the government. His conquest was nonviolent, and his short rule was beneficial. In 1571 he founded modern Manila. See C. A. Sharp, *Adventurous Armada* (1961).

López de Mendoza, Iñigo, marqués de Santillana: see SANTILLANA.

López de Santa Anna, Antonio: see SANTA ANNA, ANTONIO LÓPEZ DE.

López Mateos, Adolfo (āthôl'fō lō'pās mätā'ōs), 1910-69, president of Mexico (1958-64). A lawyer, he became active in the government party. He served as senator (1946-52) and as minister of labor (1952-58), during which time he settled more than 13,000 disputes. As president, he fostered industrial growth and diversification, attracted large amounts of foreign capital, and presided over an economic boom. He instituted profit sharing for workers and promoted agrarian reform. Maintaining close relations with the United States, he negotiated the return to Mexico of a long-disputed 437-acre (177-hectares) border strip along the Texas boundary. After retiring as president, he headed the committee that arranged for the 1968 Olympic games to be held in Mexico City.

López Velarde, Ramón (rämōn' lō'pās välär'thā), 1888-1921, Mexican poet. One of the major poets of Mexico, he deeply influenced the work of later poets, notably Xavier VILLAURRUTIA. Although his poetry sometimes shows the influence of MODERNISMO, he was one of the first poets to rebel against its labored aestheticism. His excesses are the result of a passionate quest for originality. It was his masterful treatment of the Mexican landscape, the contrast between the traditions of the countryside and the turbulence of the city, and his own anguished struggle between ascetic leanings and pagan sensuality that give his lyrics their peculiar tension, expressiveness, and drama. His first work, *La sangre devota* [the devout blood] (1916), was followed by *Zozobra* (1919). *El son del corazón* [the sound of the heart] and *Poemas escogidos* [selected poems] (1935) were published posthumously.

López y Planes, Vicente (vēsān'tā lō'pās ē plä'nās), 1784-1856, Argentine statesman and poet. He served (1806-7) under Jacques de Liniers against the British invaders. After the resignation of Rivadavia, he became (1827) provisional president of the United Provinces of La Plata. He was a minister under Dorrego and a prominent jurist under Juan Manuel de Rosas. After the fall of Rosas, López y Planes was made (1852) governor of Buenos Aires prov. Outstanding among his poems are *Triunfo argentino,* a ballad celebrating the successful Argentine defense against the British, and a war song commemorating the triumph of the revolution, which was adopted as the national hymn in 1813. He was the father of Vicente Fidel López.

Lop Nor: see LO-PU PO, China.

Lo-pu po (lô-bōō bô) or **Lop Nor** (lôp nôr), salt basin, SE Sinkiang Uigur Autonomous Region, China, in the Tarim River basin. Since 1964, Lo-pu po has been used by the Chinese Communist government for its nuclear test explosions. Once a large salt lake (as mapped by ancient Chinese geographers), it is now largely dried up, with marshes and small, shifting lakes receiving the channels of the Tarim River. The region was explored by N. M. PRZHEVALSKY and Sven Hedin. In 1928, at the time of the last expedition, the lake covered c.1,200 sq mi (3,100 sq km).

loquat (lō'kwŏt), small ornamental evergreen tree (*Eriobotrya japonica*) and its fruit. It belongs to the family Rosaceae (ROSE family) and is probably indigenous to China. It has been grown from antiquity in Japan and N India and is cultivated also in Indochina, the Mediterranean region, and to some extent in the New World subtropics. The yellowish, oval fruits are borne in clusters and taste somewhat like apples or pears but are slightly tart. They are commonly eaten fresh but are used also for making jam, jelly, pie, and sauces. Sometimes the loquat is called Japanese medlar, probably because it somewhat resembles the medlar of Europe and Asia. The loquat is one of the few important fruit trees of the tropics belonging to the rose family. Loquat is classified in the division MAGNOLIOPHYTA, class Magnoliopsida, order Rosales, family Rosaceae.

Lorain (lôrān'), city (1970 pop. 78,185), Lorain co., N Ohio, on Lake Erie at the mouth of the Black River; inc. 1834. It is an important ore-shipping port, with shipyards, steel works, automobile-assembly plants, and commercial fisheries. Power equipment, building materials, navigation equipment, and toys are among the manufactures. Situated in a popular vacation area, Lorain has numerous boating facilities. A cosmetology school and an electronic technological institute are there. An international festival, with 55 nationality groups participating, is held yearly.

loran, long-range, accurate radio navigational system used by a ship or aircraft to confirm or to determine its geographical position. The term *loran* is derived from the words *lo*ng-*ra*nge *n*avigaton. Loran, operating in the 1,700-kHz range, measures the time-of-arrival difference between two signals transmitted from two geographically separated ground stations. The pulse from the first station, called the master, triggers the second station, called the slave, into transmitting a similar pulse after a set time delay. Knowing the elapsed time difference, the navigator refers to a loran chart and selects his line of position. The chart contains groups of hyperbolic curves of constant time differences between particular station pairs. The position of the receiver (ship or airplane) will be somewhere along the curve that corresponds to the measured time difference. By taking a similar time-difference reading from a second pair of stations whose curves intersect those of the first pair, a definite geographic fix may be obtained. Loran stations are located throughout the world so as to cover the more frequently traveled areas of the Atlantic and Pacific oceans.

Lorca, Federico García: see GARCÍA LORCA.

Lorca (lôr'kä), city (1970 pop. 243,759), Murcia prov., SE Spain, in Murcia, on the Guadalentín River. It is a market center for a fertile, irrigated region producing cereals and livestock. Hemp sandals and woolen products are made in Lorca. Nearby are gypsum quarries and sulfur and iron mines. Taken by the Moors in the 8th cent., the city was liberated in 1234. It has a Moorish castle, a 17th-century collegiate church, and several old mansions.

Lord Howe Island, volcanic island (1969 pop. 280), 5 sq mi (12.9 sq km), S Pacific, a dependency of New South Wales, Australia. It is a resort c.300 mi (480 km) E of the Australian coast. The island was discovered in 1788 by the British and was settled in 1834. Palm seeds are the only export.

Lords, House of: see PARLIAMENT.

Lord's Prayer or **Our Father,** the principal Christian prayer, beginning, "Our Father, which art in heaven." Mat. 6.9-13; Luke 11.2-4. As a result of differences in translation, in the manuscripts and in the Gospels themselves, several English versions are current; thus, for example, many say "Forgive us our debts as we forgive our debtors" while others say "Forgive us our trespasses." In the liturgy formulated after the Second Vatican Council, Roman Catholics added the doxology ("For thine is the kingdom,"etc.), which had been adopted earlier by most Protestants from a version of Matthew. The prayer is called, in Latin, paternoster. The first three phrases of the Lord's Prayer parallel the opening words of the kaddish, an ancient Jewish prayer.

Lord's Supper, Protestant sacrament of the EUCHARIST. In the REFORMATION the leaders generally rejected the traditional belief in the sacrament as a sacrifice and as an invisible miracle of the actual changing of the bread and wine into the body and blood of Christ (transubstantiation) but retained the belief in it as mystically uniting the believers with Christ and with one another. The Lutherans held that there is a change by which the body and blood of Christ join with the bread and wine; this principle (consubstantiation) was rejected by Huldreich Zwingli who, in a controversy over the sacrament, held that communion was only symbolic. Calvinists, on the other hand, maintained the spiritual, but not the real presence of Christ in the sacrament. The Church of England affirmed the real presence but denied transubstantiation. However, since the Oxford Movement, Anglicans tend to accept either transubstantiation or the Calvinist interpretation. In another point of departure from the Roman Catholic Church, while the Lutheran and Anglican communion services follow the Roman Catholic MASS in outline, the service books have eliminated references to a sacrifice and have shortened the service. Anglicans hold to Western tradition in using unleavened bread. Most Protestant churches use raised bread; many use unfermented grape juice instead of wine. Communion in which the laity receive only the body (bread) of Christ is rejected by Protestants; this was a crucial point with the Hussites. Lutherans and Anglicans (especially since the Oxford Movement) celebrate communion much more frequently than most other Protestant churches, which often restrict it to a few times a year. The Quakers are one of the few Protestant groups to reject the sacrament entirely.

Lorelei (lôr'əlī, Ger. lō'rəlī), cliff, 433 ft (132 m) high, on the right bank of the Rhine River, near St. Goarshausen, W West Germany, about midway between Koblenz and Bingen. There the Rhine forms a dangerous narrows, and in German legend a fairy similar to the Greek Sirens lived on the rock and by her singing lured the sailors to their death. Heinrich Heine's poem, *Die Lorelei,* is world famous. The rock has sometimes been identified as the place where the hoard of the Nibelungs is hidden under the Rhine.

Loren, Sophia, 1934–, Italian film actress; her original name was Sophia Scicoloni. She grew up in the slums of Naples. With the help of Italian producer Carlo Ponti (later her husband) she gained international fame as a beautiful and accomplished film actress. Her movies include *The Gold of Naples* (1954), *The Pride and the Passion* (1957), *Houseboat* (1958), *Two Women* (1961), *Yesterday, Today and Tomorrow* (1963), *Marriage Italian Style* (1964), and *Man of La Mancha* (1972).

Lorentz, Hendrik Antoon (hĕn'drək än'tōn lō'rĕnts), 1853-1928, Dutch physicist, a pioneer in formulating the relations between electricity, magnetism, and light. He was one of the first to postulate the existence of electrons. On this he based his explanation of the Zeeman effect (a change in spectrum lines in a magnetic field), for which he shared with Pieter Zeeman the 1902 Nobel Prize in Physics. He extended the hypothesis of G. F. Fitzgerald, an Irish physicist, that the length of a body contracts as its speed increases (see LORENTZ CONTRACTION), and he formulated the Lorentz transformation, by which space and time coordinates of one moving system can be correlated with the known space and time coordinates of any other system. This work influenced, and was confirmed by, Einstein's special theory of relativity. Lorentz also discovered (1880), simultaneously with L. V. Lorenz of the Univ. of Copenhagen, the relations (known as Lorentz-Lorenz relations) between the refraction of light and the density of a translucent body. He was professor (1878-1912) at the Univ. of Leiden and director from 1912 of the Teyler laboratory, Haarlem. His works in English include *The Theory of Electrons* (1909) and *Problems of Modern Physics* (1927). See his collected papers (9 vol., 1934-39); study ed. by G. L. de Haas-Lorentz (tr. 1957).

Lorentz contraction (lôr'ĕnts), in physics, contraction or foreshortening of a moving body in the direction of its motion, proposed by H. A. Lorentz on theoretical grounds and based on an earlier suggestion by G. F. Fitzgerald; it is sometimes called the Fitzgerald, or Lorentz-Fitzgerald, contraction. The Lorentz contraction hypothesis was put forward in an attempt to explain the negative result of the Michelson-Morley experiment of 1887 designed to demonstrate the earth's absolute motion through space (see ETHER; RELATIVITY). The hypothesis held that any material body is contracted in the direction of its motion by a factor $\sqrt{1-v^2/c^2}$, where v is the velocity of the body and c is the velocity of light. Although the Lorentz contraction did not succeed entirely in reconciling the results of the Michelson-Morley experiment with classical theory, it did serve as the basis for the mathematics of Einstein's theory of relativity. The equations used in relativity theory to change from a coordinate system, or frame of reference, in which the observer is at rest to a second system that is moving at constant velocity with respect to the first system are known as the Lorentz transformation. The Lorentz transformation will result in a stationary observer recording an effect equivalent to the Lorentz contraction when observing an object in uniform motion relative to his system of coordinates. Einstein showed, however, that this effect is due not to the actual deformation of the body in question, as Lorentz had originally supposed, but to the equivalence of the two systems with respect to the laws of electricity and magnetism.

Lorenz, Konrad (kôn'rät lôr'ĕnts), 1903–, Austrian zoologist and ethologist. He received medical training at the Univ. of Vienna and spent two years at the medical school of Columbia Univ. He received a Ph.D. (1936) in zoology from the Univ. of Munich and subsequently taught at Vienna and Königsberg. For his work in establishing the science of ethology, particularly his studies concerning the organization of individual and group behavior patterns, Lorenz was awarded the Nobel Prize for Physiology and Medicine in 1973. He derived his insights into behavior from studying fish and birds, most extensively the greylag goose. With Oscar Heinroth, he discovered imprinting, an especially rapid and relatively irreversible learning process that occurs early in the individual's life. A central concept complementary to imprinting is the innate release mechanism, whereby organisms are genetically predisposed to be especially responsive to certain stimuli. Some of his views are expressed in the popular book *On Aggression* (tr. 1966). His assertion that aggressive impulses are to a degree innate, and the analogies he draws between human and animal behavior, have engendered considerable controversy. After World War II, a Max Planck Institute was established for Lorenz's group of students and co-workers in ethology. Lorenz is a foreign member of the Royal Society of London.

Lorenzetti (lōrān-tsĕt'tē), two brothers who were major Sienese painters. **Pietro Lorenzetti,** c.1280–c.1348, was first influenced by Duccio di Buoninsegna and Giovanni Pisano. His earliest known work, an altarpiece at Arezzo, already shows the impact of Giotto's style in its concern with profound emotion and simple grandeur of form. In Siena he painted several works together with his brother, which have been lost. Pietro's altarpiece (1329) for the Church of the Carmelites is now in the Pinacoteca. His last works are the magnificent *Birth of the Virgin* (c.1342; Opera del Duomo, Siena) and an altarpiece for the Church of St. Francis at Pistoia (now in the Uffizi). Of uncertain date are the imposing frescoes attributed to Pietro in the Lower Church at Assisi—*Virgin and Child with St. Francis* and scenes from the *Passion*. See study by E. T. De Wald (1930). **Ambrogio Lorenzetti,** d. 1348?, was the more inventive brother. Also influenced by Giotto and Giovanni Pisano, he developed great simplicity of style and a remarkable ability to depict spatial depth. Several times he is recorded as having been in Florence. There he painted an altarpiece for the Church of San Procolo which includes scenes from the life of St. Nicholas. His greatest achievement is the cycle of frescoes (1337–39) in the Palazzo Pubblico, Siena. It consists of allegories of good and bad government and is a revealing portrayal of Italian life in the 14th cent. The paintings are invaluable from the aesthetic as well as the historical viewpoint. Other works by Ambrogio are three frescoes depicting the *Maestà* in Siena, *Presentation in the Temple* (Uffizi), and *Annunciation* (Siena Pinacoteca). See monograph by George Rowley (1958). No records of the brothers appear after 1348; they are believed to have perished in the plague. See study by G. Rowley (2 vol., 1958).

Lorenzini, Carlo: see COLLODI, CARLO.

Lorenzo de' Medici: see MEDICI, LORENZO DE'.

Lorenzo di Credi (lōrĕn'tsō dē krĕ'dē), 1459–1537, Florentine painter. He spent his early years in the workshop of Verrocchio, whom he assisted in the painting of an altarpiece at the Cathedral of Pistoia. He was strongly influenced by his fellow pupil Leonardo da Vinci, whose works he copied with a considerable loss of flavor. Technically accomplished, he lacked imagination. Examples of his art are two of the *Madonna* (Turin); *Annunciation* (Uffizi); *Madonna Adoring the Child* (Metropolitan Mus.); and *Boy's Head* (Mus. of Fine Arts, Boston).

Lorenzo di Pietro (pyā'trō), c.1412–1480, Sienese painter, sculptor, and goldsmith, called Il Vecchietta. He has been linked with Donatello because of his vigorous style. He painted a group of frescoes and a relic press in the hospital at Siena; four ceilings in the Baptistery of San Giovanni at Siena; an altarpiece, *The Assumption of the Virgin,* his masterpiece (cathedral, Pienza); a triptych, *Madonna with Saints* (Uffizi); *St. Catherine* and the *Virgin of Mercy,* fragments of frescoes (Palazzo Pubblico, Siena); and a *Madonna* (Siena). Vecchietta was one of the most important painters of the later Sienese school. He also executed many sculptures, including *The Risen Christ* (Santa Maria della Scala, Siena) and a bronze relief, *The Resurrection* (Frick Coll., N.Y.).

Lorenzo Monaco (mō'näkō), c.1370–1425?, Italian painter, one of the leading artists in Florence at the beginning of the 15th cent. His real name was Piero di Giovanni. Born in Siena, he came to Florence (c.1391) and became a Camaldolite monk. His early works show a Sienese influence, evidenced in his sophisticated use of line and delicate rendering of texture. His only signed work is the *Coronation of the Virgin* (1414; Uffizi). His *Adoration of the Magi* (Uffizi) reflects the international Gothic style, with its elongated figures and rich pageantry. Other works include an altarpiece, *Annunciation,* and frescoes from the *Life of the Virgin* (Bartolini Chapel, Santa Trinita, Florence); a smaller *Coronation of the Virgin* (National Gall., London); a *Madonna and Child* (Metropolitan Mus.); and a *Madonna and Child* (National Gall. of Art, Washington, D.C.). See B. Berenson, *The Drawings of the Florentine Painters* (Vol. II and III, 1938, repr. 1970).

Loreto (lōrĕ'tō), town (1971 pop. 9,530), in the Marche, central Italy, on a hill overlooking the Adriatic Sea. It has silk industries and is a famous place of pilgrimage. According to legend, the Holy House of the Virgin in Nazareth was brought to Loreto through the air by angels in 1294. Around the Holy House (a small brick building) there is a church—the Santuario della Santa Casa—begun in 1468 by Pope Paul II; Bramante contributed to its construction. It has fine bronze doors (16th–17th cent.) and frescoes by Melozzo da Forlì and Luca Signorelli. Our Lady of Loreto is a patron of aviators. The Loretto (or Loreto) order of nuns, named for the town, was founded in Ireland in 1822.

Loria, Isaac ben Solomon: see LURIA, ISAAC BEN SOLOMON.

Loria, Roger of: see ROGER OF LORIA.

Lorient (lôryăN'), town (1968 pop. 68,760), Morbihan dept., NW France, a port and naval station on the Atlantic Ocean. It is a great shipbuilding center. Established (17th cent.) as a port to serve the French East India Company, it was developed as a naval base by Napoleon I and became the country's chief naval yard. In World War II it was the Germans' major submarine base on the Atlantic. Almost totally destroyed by Allied bombs in 1942–43, it has been rebuilt.

Lorimer, George Horace, 1867–1937, American editor, b. Louisville, Ky. After working for the Armour Packing Company (1887–95) and as a wholesale grocer, he went to work as a newspaper reporter in Boston. He became editor in chief of the *Saturday Evening Post* in 1899, and until 1936 his guidance was responsible for its growth. His success was attributed to his ability to ascertain the literary tastes of the middle class. He was president (1932–34) of the Curtis Publishing Company. *Letters from a Self-made Man to His Son* (1902) was reprinted from the *Post.* See John Tebbel, *George Horace Lorimer and the Saturday Evening Post* (1948).

loris, name for slow-moving, nocturnal, arboreal primates of the family Lorisidae, found in India, Sri Lanka, and SE Asia. Lorises have round heads, large round eyes, and furry bodies. They have no tails, and their index fingers are vestigial. Lorises move hand over hand through the trees, gripping the branches firmly with hands and feet; they feed on insects and vegetable matter. Best known are the slender loris (*Loris tardigradus*), with an 8-in.-long (20-cm) body and very thin legs, and the slow loris (*Nycticebus coucang*), with a 16-in.-long (40-cm) body and short, thick legs. The slow loris has pale brownish fur with a darker dorsal stripe. African members of the loris family are the potto (*Perodicticus potto*), which has a stumpy tail, the angwantibo (*Arctocebus calabarensis*), characterized by its pointed face, and the BUSH BABIES, or galagos, a distinctive group of small, swift-moving animals. Lorises are classified in the phylum CHORDATA, subphylum Vertebrata, class Mammalia, order Primates, family Lorisidae.

Loris-Melikov, Mikhail Tarielovich (mĕkhəyĕl' təryĕl'əvĭch lô'rĭs-mĕ'lyĭkəf), 1826–88, Russian general and statesman, of Armenian descent. He was created count for his services in the Russo-Turkish War of 1877–78 and in 1880 was made minister of the interior by Alexander II. He promoted some liberal reforms, specifically in the educational system, and drafted a program to allow members of the zemstvos to play a minor advisory role in legislation. Alexander II approved this reform on the day he was assassinated (1884), but Alexander III voided the reform and dismissed its author. Loris-Melikov in his youth is charmingly portrayed in Leo Tolstoy's *Hadjii Murad.*

Lorme, Marion de: see DELORME, MARION.

Lorrain, Claude: see CLAUDE LORRAIN.

Lorraine (lôrĕn'), Ger. *Lothringen,* region and former province, NE France, bordering in the N on Belgium, Luxembourg, and West Germany, in the E on Alsace, in the S on Franche-Comté, and in the W on Champagne. It is now divided into four departments—Moselle, Meurthe-et-Moselle, Meuse, and Vosges. In Moselle dept., of which METZ is the capital, German is widely spoken along with French. The rest of Lorraine is French-speaking. NANCY is its economic and intellectual center. Except for the Vosges mts. in the southeast and the ridges paralleling the Moselle and Meuse rivers, Lorraine is a slightly rolling plateau with pastures and some agricultural districts. Hops are grown (Lorraine has large breweries), and there are numerous vineyards. In the east salt is mined; some coal is found in the north. The principal wealth of Lorraine lies in its iron deposits, concentrated along the Belgian and Luxembourg borders in the Briey, Longwy, and Thionville basin and near Nancy. Despite the low grade of the ore, these deposits constitute the richest fields of iron in Europe outside the USSR and Sweden. The major obstacle to their full exploitation is the necessity of importing coal and coke from the Ruhr basin in West Germany or from Belgium and N France. Lorraine, as its name indicates, was in the 9th cent. part of the kingdom of LOTHARINGIA; it became a duchy under the Holy Roman Empire. It passed in 1048 to the house of Alsace, which then became the house of Lorraine and controlled the duchy until 1738. Several fiefs emerged in the 12th–13th cent. that escaped the control of the dukes. Chief of these were the county of Barrois, later the duchy of Bar (see BARLE-DUC), and the three bishoprics of Metz, TOUL, and VERDUN. Bar and Lorraine were reunited when Lorraine passed by marriage to RENÉ of Anjou, duke of Bar; the three bishoprics were finally annexed by France in 1552. René II of Lorraine helped (1477) to defeat, at Nancy, CHARLES THE BOLD of Burgundy, who had seized most of the duchy. In the 16th cent. a cadet branch of the house of Lorraine, the GUISE family, gained tremendous influence in France, while Lorraine itself, under Duke Charles II (1559–1608), enjoyed a period of relative order and prosperity amidst a Europe torn by religious and imperialistic strife. Lorraine was occupied by France in the Thirty Years War (1618–48). Duke CHARLES IV spent most of his life trying to recover his lands, and his successor, CHARLES V, although he helped to recover Hungary from Turkey, never managed to recover Lorraine. At last, in the Treaty of Ryswick (1697), Leopold I was recognized in possession of the duchy. His heir, Francis III, married Maria Theresa of Austria, became emperor as FRANCIS I, and founded the house of Hapsburg-Lorraine. By an arrangement (1735) with Louis XV, he exchanged the duchies of Lorraine and Bar for Tuscany; Lorraine and Bar were given to Louis XV's father-in-law, STANISLAUS I, ex-king of Poland, upon whose death (1766) they passed to France. As a French province, Lorraine continued to enjoy certain exemptions and privileges. In 1871, as a result of the Franco-Prussian War, the eastern part of Lorraine was ceded to Germany and united with Alsace as the imperial land (Reichsland) of Alsace-Lorraine. Those parts of Lorraine remaining French were organized into the present department of Meurthe-et-Moselle. After World War I, Alsace-Lorraine was returned to France, but it was again annexed (1940–44) by Germany during World War II. (The unique problems of Alsace-Lorraine are discussed in the article ALSACE.) During both World Wars Lorraine suffered heavily.

Lorraine, Lower and **Upper:** see LOTHARINGIA.

Lorris, Guillaume de: see GUILLAUME DE LORRIS.

Lortzing, Gustav Albert (go͝os'täf äl'bĕrt lôr'tsĭng), 1801–51, German opera composer. Lortzing's first opera was written in 1824. Among his best-known works are the comic operas *Zar und Zimmerman* [the Czar and the carpenter] (1837), about Peter the Great, and *Der Wildschutz* [the poacher] (1842). He also wrote a romantic opera, *Undine* (1845), as well as an oratorio, various songs, and incidental music. His works are rarely heard outside Germany. Lortzing had 11 children and was in financial difficulty for much of his life.

Lo-ruhamah (lō"-ro͞ohä'mə), daughter of Hosea. Hosea 1.6,8.

lory: see PARROT.

Los Alamitos (lŏs ăləmē'təs), city (1970 pop. 11,346), Orange co., S Calif., in a farm area; inc. 1960. It has a race course.

Los Alamos (lŏs ăl'əmōs), uninc. town (1970 pop. 11,310), seat of Los Alamos co., N central N.Mex. It is on a long mesa extending from the Jemez Mts. The U.S. government chose the site in 1942 for atomic research, and the first atomic bombs were produced there. In 1947 the Atomic Energy Commission took over the town. In 1962 government control ended and Los Alamos became a self-governing community. The county was incorporated in 1969. The Los Alamos Scientific Laboratory, operated by the Univ. of California, is a national historic landmark.

Los Altos, residential city (1970 pop. 24,956), Santa Clara co., W Calif.; inc. 1952. A junior college is in nearby Los Altos Hills.

Los Angeles (lŏs ăn'jələs), city (1970 pop. 2,809,596), seat of Los Angeles co., S Calif.; inc. 1850. A port of entry on the Pacific coast, with a fine harbor at San Pedro Bay, it is the third largest U.S. city in population. Two mountain ranges, the Santa Monica and Verdugo, cut across the center of the city. Los Angeles is the shipping, industrial, communication, financial, and distribution hub of an agricultural area that produces citrus fruit, vegetables, grains, nuts, and dairy products. The site of the city was visited by the Spanish explorer Gaspar de PORTOLÁ in 1769, and in 1781 El Pueblo de Nuestra Señora de los Angeles de Porciuncula (The Town of Our Lady the Queen of the Angels of Porciuncula) was founded. The city served several times as the capital of the Spanish colonial province of ALTA CALIFORNIA and was a cattle-ranching center under Spanish and Mexican rule. In 1846, Los Angeles was captured from the Mexicans by U.S. forces. The arrival of the railroads (Southern Pacific in 1876; Santa Fe in 1885) and the discovery of oil in the early 1890s stimulated expansion, as did the development of the motion picture industry in the early 20th cent. More recently, the establishment of radio and television studios and the development of a great variety of industries have contributed to the city's rapid growth. Today, Los Angeles is a leading producer of aircraft, military ordnance, stone and clay, glass, furniture, lumber and wood products, electrical machinery, transportation equipment, and fabricated metal. The Los Angeles metropolitan area covers five counties (Los Angeles, Orange, Riverside, San Bernardino, and Ventura) and encompasses 34,000 sq mi (88,000 sq km) and nearly 10 million people. The region is a great industrial and urban complex in which the problems of urban society are magnified; residues of industry, combined with a high motor-vehicle density, have created a serious problem of smog pollution. Los Angeles is the only major U.S. city without a public transportation system. Water for the city is obtained from the Colorado and Owens rivers and the Mono Basin, at distances of c.240 to c.400 mi (380-640 km). Over the years the city has absorbed numerous communities and enclosed independent municipalities. Among the communities now part of Los Angeles are Central City, Hollywood, San Pedro, Sylmar, Watts, Westwood, Bel-Air, and Boyle Heights. Independent municipalities surrounded by Los Angeles include SANTA MONICA (1970 pop. 88,289), BEVERLY HILLS (1970 pop. 33,416), and SAN FERNANDO (1970 pop. 16,571). Incorporated cities in the broader metropolitan region with populations of 80,000 or more are Anaheim, Burbank, Downey, Fullerton, Garden Grove, Glendale, Huntington Beach, Inglewood, Lakewood, Long Beach, Norwalk, Pasadena, Pomona, Riverside, San Bernardino, Santa Ana, Santa Monica, and Torrance (see separate articles), in addition to Los Angeles itself. In Los Angeles are botanical gardens; art, history, movie, industrial, and science museums; and many parks, including Griffith Park, the largest urban park in the world, with a zoo and a planetarium. The La Brea Tar Pits are one of the world's biggest sources of Ice Age fossils. There are large ethnic communities from Mexico and Latin America, India, Japan, and China, as well as a substantial American Indian population. Los Angeles has a symphony orchestra and professional baseball, football, basketball, and hockey teams. The motion picture and television industries, the proximity of many resorts, the fine beaches, and a climate that encourages year-round outdoor recreation attract thousands of tourists annually to Los Angeles. Other attractions in the region include the Santa Anita and Hollywood racetracks and Disneyland (at Anaheim). Among the city's many educational institutions are the Univ. of Southern California; the Univ. of California, Los Angeles; Occidental College; Loyola Marymount Univ.; and Pepperdine Univ. Los Angeles is governed by a mayor, elected at large, and 15 councilmen, elected by district. See C. Rand, *Los Angeles* (1967); R. M. Fogelson, *The Fragmented Metropolis* (1967).

Los Angeles County Museum, Los Angeles, Calif. The original museum opened in 1913. Among its important patrons was William Randolph HEARST, whose enormous collection brought the museum major status among the country's art houses. The museum's finest collections include furnishings from France and England, paintings by Holbein, Christus, Renoir, Matisse, Rothko, and Pollock, and works by the German expressionists. The new Wilshire Boulevard building was designed by W. L. Pereira and Associates.

Los Angeles Philharmonic Orchestra, founded in 1919 by William Andrews Clark, Jr. After his death the Southern California Symphony Association was formed in 1934 to sponsor the orchestra. The orchestra was housed in Philharmonic Auditorium from 1920 until 1964, when it moved to the newly constructed Los Angeles Music Center. The orchestra holds summer concerts in the Hollywood Bowl, which seats 20,000 people. Zubin MEHTA has been its music director since 1962.

Losey, Joseph (lō'zē), 1909–, American film director, b. La Crosse, Wis. Among his Hollywood works are *The Boy With Green Hair* (1948) and *The Big Night* (1952). Losey was blacklisted in Hollywood because of alleged Communist sympathies and left for England in 1952. Among his numerous films made there are *The Servant* (1963), *Accident* (1967), and *The Go-Between* (1970), all with screenplays by Harold Pinter. Losey set these studies of moral penury—underscored by Pinter's spare, ambiguous dialogue—against opulent physical backgrounds. His other films include *King and Country* (1964) and *A Doll's House* (1973). See study by James Leahy (1967).

Los Gatos (lōs gä'tōs, găt'əs), city (1970 pop. 23,735), Santa Clara co., W Calif.; inc. 1887. It is a residential community in a fruit and poultry area. Wine and electronic equipment are produced. Los Gatos, Spanish for "the cats," got its name from the wildcats that abounded in the Santa Clara valley at the time the city was founded.

Lo-shan or **Loshan** (both: lō-shän), city, central Szechwan prov., China, just S of Ch'eng-tu, on the Min River. Machine tools and textiles are manufactured. Nearby are decorated grottoes, a colossal stone Buddha, and the sacred peak Omei. Lo-shan was formerly called Kiating.

Losonczi, Pál (päl lōshōn'tsē), 1919–, Hungarian Communist politician. He joined the Communist party in 1945 and became a member of parliament in 1953. Active in the cooperative farm program, Losonczi was minister of agriculture (1960-67). In 1967 he was appointed president.

Lost Battalion, in World War I, popular name given to those American units of the 77th Division—six companies of the 1st and 2d battalions of the 308th Infantry, one company of the 307th Infantry, and the platoons of the 306th Machine Gun Battalion—that were cut off by German forces after the launching of an American attack in the Argonne Forest in early Oct., 1918. The Lost Battalion, numbering about 600 men and under the command of Major Charles W. Whittlesey, put up a heroic five-day defense in the Binarville Ravine without food, water, or reserve ammunition. After withstanding several heavy barrages and attacks, the Lost Battalion, which defiantly refused the German demand of surrender, was rescued (Oct. 8, 1918) by American relief troops. Some 400 men of the Lost Battalion perished. See T. M. Johnson and Fletcher Pratt, *The Lost Battalion* (1938).

Lost Dauphin: see LOUIS XVII, titular king of France.

lost property: see FINDER.

lost tribes, 10 Jewish tribes that, according to the Bible, were transported to Assyria by Tiglathpileser III or Shalmaneser after the conquest of Israel. Numerous conjectures have been advanced as to the fate of these tribes: they have been identified with the people of Arabia, India, Ethiopia, and America (North, Central, South) and with other groups, including the Nestorians of Mesopotamia, the Afghans, the high-caste Hindus, and the holy Shindai class of Japan. The Anglo-Israelite theory, still maintained by some, identifies the English people with the lost tribes; it was, in the 17th cent., a factor in helping the Jews to reenter England. The identification of the North American Indians with the 10 lost tribes figured in the writings of the early New England Christian theologians.

lost wax casting: see CIRE PERDUE.

Lot, son of Abraham's brother Haran. Lot settled in Sodom and received a warning of its destruction. As he fled with his family, his wife, disobeying God's orders, looked back at the city and was turned into a pillar of salt. Lot is considered the eponym of the Moabites and Ammonites. Gen. 11–14; 19.

Lot (lôt), department (1968 pop. 151,198), S central France, in Quercy. CAHORS is the capital.

Lot, river, c.300 mi (483 km) long, rising in the Cévennes mts., SE France, and flowing W past Mende and Cahors to join the Garonne River. The limestone plateaus through which the Lot winds are intersected by fertile valleys and vineyards.

Lota (lō'tä), city (1970 pop. 51,548), S central Chile, a port on the Gulf of Arauco, an inlet of the Pacific Ocean. Founded in the 17th cent., the city grew rapidly after coal was discovered in the region (1837). There are also industries producing copper and ceramics. The botanical park on a hill above the city is famous for its landscaping and sea views.

Lotan (lō'tăn), duke of Edom. Gen. 36.20,22,29.

Lot-et-Garonne (lôt-ā-gärôn'), department (1968 pop. 290,592), in Agenais and parts of Bazadais and Bezaume, SW France. AGEN is the capital.

Lothair I (lōthâr'), 795–855, emperor of the West (840–55), son and successor of LOUIS I. In 817 his father crowned him coemperor. He was recrowned (823) at Rome by the pope and issued (824) a constitution, proclaiming his right to confirm papal elections. He twice (830, 833) revolted against his father, who favored Lothair's half brother Charles (Charles the Bald, later CHARLES II) at his elder son's expense, and in 833, with his brothers Pepin and LOUIS THE GERMAN, he succeeded in temporarily deposing Louis I. However, his brothers deserted him and restored Louis. Lothair retained only Italy. He later was reconciled with his father, who in 838 allotted him almost the whole eastern half of the empire, the west (France) going to Charles. After Louis's death Charles and Louis the German made war on their brother Lothair, who tried to reunite the whole empire under his sole rule. The battle of Fontenoy (841), although indecisive, checked Lothair. Renewing their alliance in 842 (see STRASBOURG, OATH OF), Charles and Louis the German forced (843) Lothair to sign the fateful Treaty of Verdun (see VERDUN, TREATY OF), which partitioned the empire of Charlemagne among the three brothers; Lothair retained the imperial title. He subdivided his domains among his sons LOUIS II, who was crowned emperor at Rome in 850, LOTHAIR, king of Lotharingia, and Charles.

Lothair II, also called **Lothair III,** 1075–1137, Holy Roman emperor (1133–37) and German king (1125–37); successor of Holy Roman Emperor Henry V. His predecessor invested him with the duchy of Saxony in 1106, but after 1112 Lothair, in several rebellions, successfully championed local independence against the royal authority. When Henry V died (1125), the ELECTORS chose Lothair over Frederick of HOHENSTAUFEN, Henry V's nephew, to succeed him; this was the first victory of elective over hereditary kingship. Frederick and his brother Conrad (who later became German king as CONRAD III) made war on Lothair, and Conrad was elected (1127) antiking. However, Lothair and his son-in-law, HENRY THE PROUD of Bavaria, defeated the Hohenstaufen and peace was made in 1135. In Italy, Lothair promised his support to Pope INNOCENT II, whose election was disputed. In 1132 he entered Italy and was crowned emperor in Rome (1133). After the defeat of the Hohenstaufen he returned (1136) to Italy and campaigned successfully against Roger II of Sicily, supporter of the antipope Anacletus II. Lothair died on the journey home. As emperor, Lothair adhered loyally to the Concordat of Worms (see WORMS, CONCORDAT OF), and actively supported both political expansion and revival of missionary activity in the East. He forced various heathen princes to pay tribute and established German suzerainty in Denmark, Bohemia, and Poland (see BOLESLAUS III). At his death his rival, Conrad III, was elected king. Lothair is known also as Lothair of Saxony or Lothair of Supplinburg.

Lothair, 941–86, French king (954–86), son and successor of King Louis IV. During the early part of his reign he was dominated by HUGH THE GREAT. Even after Hugh's death he was involved in conflict with the great feudal lords and controlled only a small part of France. He alienated his protector, Holy Roman Emperor Otto II, by his unsuccessful attempt to occupy Lotharingia (Lorraine) in 978. Otto retaliated by invading France. Although Lothair renounced all claims to Lotharingia at a meeting with Otto in 980, he tried to regain it after Otto's death in 983. He died during the campaign and was succeeded by his son Louis V.

Lothair, sometimes called **Lothair II,** d. 869, king of Lotharingia (855–69), second son of Emperor of the West Lothair I. He inherited the region bounded by the Rhine, Scheldt, Alps, and North Sea, which became known as LOTHARINGIA. He was married to Theutberga, the sister of one of his father's vassals, and after the death of Lothair I he repudiated her and married his mistress by whom he had a son. Theutberga appealed to Bishop HINCMAR, a counselor to King Charles the Bold of the West Franks (later Emperor of the West Charles II). Charles, Lothair's uncle, hoped to annex Lotharingia if Lothair should die without an heir, which was likely since Theutberga was barren. Hincmar supported Theutberga and with the aid of Pope NICHOLAS I forced Lothair to reinstate her. When Lothair died suddenly his lands were divided between his uncles, Charles the Bald and LOUIS THE GERMAN, by the Treaty of Mersen (870).

Lotharingia (lōthərĭn'jə), name given to the northern portion of the lands assigned (843) to Emperor of the West LOTHAIR I in the first division of the

Carolingian empire (see VERDUN, TREATY OF). It comprised, roughly, the present Netherlands, Belgium, Luxembourg, Lorraine, Alsace, and NW Germany, including Aachen and Cologne. Lothair also received Italy and Burgundy (including Provence and W Switzerland) in the division of 843. Before his death (855), Lothair subdivided his lands among his three sons. His son, King LOTHAIR (for whom the region is named), was given Lotharingia as a kingdom, while Italy and Burgundy went to LOUIS II and Charles. King Lothair died in 869, and in 870 his lands were fairly evenly divided between the East Frankish and West Frankish kingdoms (i.e., Germany and France) in the Treaty of MERSEN. After a period of confusion and warfare, Holy Roman Emperor Otto I, whose predecessor, the German King Henry I, had gained (925) control over all Lotharingia, gave it in 953 to his brother St. Bruno, archbishop of Cologne. Bruno's difficulties with the Lotharingian nobles caused him to divide (959) the country into the duchies of Lower Lorraine, in the north, and Upper Lorraine, in the south (the name Lorraine being the modern form of Lotharingia). The ducal titles in both duchies subsequently were awarded in confusing succession to various noble houses, but their significance became nothing as the great feudal lords gained in power. In Upper Lorraine, the ducal title continued until 1766 in what became known simply as the duchy of LORRAINE; this was greatly restricted in extent and did not include Alsace, Luxembourg, the bishoprics of Metz, Toul, and Verdun, and the archbishopric of Trier, all of which were originally in Upper Lorraine. In Lower Lorraine, the title soon lapsed completely; chief among the fiefs that emerged here were the duchies of Brabant, Bouillon, Limburg, Jülich, Cleves, and Berg, the county of Hainaut, and the bishopric of Liège. Cologne and Aachen became free imperial cities. Both Upper Lorraine and Lower Lorraine thus ceased in the 11th cent. to have a unified history. From the Treaty of Verdun until the present time the territories comprised in Lotharingia, particularly Upper Lorraine, have been chronically contested between Germany and France.

Lothian, Philip Henry Kerr, 11th **marquess of** (kär, lō'thēən), 1882–1940, British statesman. He served (1905–10) on various government commissions in South Africa and was a member of Milner's "kindergarten" (see MILNER, ALFRED MILNER, 1ST VISCOUNT). After his return to England he edited (1910–16) the *Round Table,* a liberal scholarly journal, which he had helped to found. As David Lloyd George's private secretary (1916–21) he was active at the Paris Peace Conference (1919). He inherited his title in 1930, represented the Liberal party in the National government as chancellor of the duchy of Lancaster (1931–32), and served (1932) as chairman of the India franchise committee. Lothian advocated appeasement of Nazi Germany until 1939 when he came round to a vigorous advocacy of resistance to Adolf Hitler. A proponent of closer Anglo-American cooperation, he was secretary of the Rhodes Trust after 1925, and he was appointed ambassador to Washington in 1939. See biography by J. R. M. Butler (1960).

Loti, Pierre (pyĕr lôtē'), pseud. of **Julien Viaud** (zhülyăN' vyō), 1850–1923, French novelist, an officer in the French navy. He achieved popularity with his impressionistic romances of adventure in exotic lands, such as *Aziyadé* (1879), set in Constantinople, *Rarahu* (1880, later titled *Mariage de Loti*), set in Tahiti, and *Madame Chrysanthème* (1888), set in Japan. His most enduring novels, however, are *Pêcheur d'Islande* (1886; tr. *An Iceland Fisherman*), a tale of Breton fishermen, and *Ramuntcho* (1897; tr. 1897), a story of French Basque peasant life. Of his many travel books, *Vers Ispahan* (1904) is highly esteemed.

Lotophagi: see LOTUS-EATERS.

lots. The casting of lots was an ancient method of making a choice, settling a dispute, or determining a course of action. In biblical times lots were cast to determine the will of God (it is believed that the Urim and Thummim, mysterious sacred objects placed on the breastplate of the high priest, were originally used for casting lots and determining a course of action), to discover the guilty (1 Sam. 14.41, 42), to select officials (1 Sam. 17–27; Acts 1.24–26), and in numerous other instances. The lot, probably a stone, die, or other object, was cast upon the ground, the manner of its fall determining the question in doubt; in other cases, lots were cast into a receptacle and drawn from it. It is possible that dice originated, not as a game, but as a device for casting lots.

Lötschberg Railway (löch'bĕrkh), electrical railroad, crossing the Bernese Alps from Thun, W central Switzerland, to Brig, on the Rhône River, S Switzerland. It passes through the **Lötschberg Tunnel** (9 mi/14 km long; alt. 4,078 ft/1,243 m) under Lötschen Pass and emerges in the Lötschen Valley. Built in 1911, it is one of the world's longest railway tunnels.

lottery, scheme for distributing prizes by lot or other method of chance selection to persons who have paid for the opportunity to win. The term is not applicable when lots are drawn without payment by the interested parties to determine some matter, e.g., the distribution of property among heirs. The lottery is distinguished as a form of gambling by the absence of any element of skill or play. Under common law in England and the United States lotteries were lawful. They paid for many public buildings, and founded and supported educational, charitable, and religious enterprises. Private lotteries, which were particularly susceptible to fraudulent practices, were first generally prohibited in the early 19th cent. Most publicly sponsored lotteries were discontinued not long afterwards. With the adoption in 1890 of a Federal statute prohibiting the transportation of lottery tickets or prizes by mail or in interstate commerce, the largest American state lottery—that of Louisiana—came to an end. It was not until more than 50 years later that state lotteries were again legalized in the United States, when New Hampshire authorized (1963) a sweepstakes lottery, the proceeds of which were to go to education. Other states, including New York and New Jersey, soon followed suit, initiating similar programs. Lotteries are lawful in many countries of Europe (including France, Spain, Italy, and the Republic of Ireland) as well as in Latin America and the USSR.

Lotto, Lorenzo (lōrĕn'tsō lôt'tō), c.1480–1556, Venetian painter. His work reflects the influence of several great contemporaries from Bellini to Titian, but preserves throughout a fine sensibility and intimacy quite his own. Notable among his early works are *St. Jerome* (Louvre); the fresco *Annunciation* (Church of San Domenico, Recanati, Italy); and *Madonna and Saints* (cathedral, Asolo, Italy). Of a later period are *Bridal Couple* (Prado); *Christ and the Adulteress* (Louvre); and portraits in the galleries of London, Milan, Rome, and Vienna. After 1554 Lotto lived with the monks of the sanctuary at Loreto, where his *Presentation in the Temple* remains. He is represented in numerous American collections including the Philadelphia Museum; the National Gallery of Art, Washington, D.C.; and the Metropolitan Museum. See study by Bernard Berenson (1955).

lotus: see WATER LILY.

lotus-eaters or **Lotophagi** (lətŏf'əjī"), a fabulous people who occupied the north coast of Africa and lived on the lotus, which brought forgetfulness and happy indolence. They appear in the *Odyssey.* When Odysseus landed among them, some of his men ate the food. They forgot their friends and home and had to be dragged back to the ships. "The Lotus-Eaters" by Tennyson has become a classic of English poetry.

Lotze, Rudolf Hermann (rōō'dôlf hĕr'män lō'tsə), 1817–81, German philosopher and psychologist. After studying medicine and philosophy at Leipzig, he was lecturer in both departments and professor after 1842. He succeeded Herbart as professor at Göttingen (1844–81) and in 1881 was appointed professor at Berlin. Among his works, which include medical and biological discussions, are *Allgemeine Physiologie des körperlichen Lebens* (1851), *Medizinische Psychologie oder Physiologie der Seele* (1852), and *Mikrokosmus* (1856–64, tr. 1885). The first parts of his projected, though never completed, *System der Philosophie* appeared as *Logik* (1874, tr. 1884) and *Metaphysik* (1879, tr. 1888). Lotze sought to reconcile the views of mechanistic science with the principles of romantic idealism. He started from the idea that all phenomena are determined by the interaction of atoms. Since these exist in extension, there must also be some deeper mode of existence through which they interact and exhibit their quality of extension. He saw the atoms as centers of force operating in a matrix of a more basic substance. By analogy from the immediate knowledge of spiritual existence in the self, he argued that the centers of force are stages of development within the underlying substance of the world mind. Lotze's psychology reflects his metaphysics, though his scientific background brought him to an empirical position that helped insure the advance of scientific psychology. His theory of space perception was an important contribution to philosophy. See studies by E. E. Thomas (1921) and George Santayana (new ed. 1971).

Loubet, Émile François (āmēl' fräNswä' lōōbā'), 1838–1929, president of the French republic (1899–1906). As a member of the chamber of deputies, he advocated secular education. After serving (1887–88) as minister of public works he became premier in 1892. His hesitance to investigate the PANAMA CANAL scandal forced his resignation, but he continued as minister of the interior until 1893 and became president of the senate in 1896. In 1899 he succeeded Félix Faure as president of the republic. Favoring revision in the DREYFUS AFFAIR, Loubet pardoned Alfred Dreyfus in 1899; in foreign affairs his reception of King Edward VII of Great Britain symbolized the growing rapprochement between the two countries. During his presidency premiers René WALDECK-ROUSSEAU and Émile COMBES secured the limiting of Church privilege, culminating (1905) in the separation of Church and state in France. Loubet retired in 1906 and was succeeded by Armand Fallières.

Loucheux Indians: see KUTCHIN INDIANS.

loudspeaker or **speaker,** device used to convert electrical energy into sound. It consists essentially of a thin flexible sheet called a diaphragm that is made to vibrate by an electric signal from an AMPLIFIER. The vibrations create sound waves in the air around the speaker. In a dynamic speaker, which is the most common kind, the diaphragm has the shape of a cone. It is attached to a coil of wire that is suspended in a magnetic field produced by a permanent magnet or an electromagnet. A signal current in the suspended coil creates another magnetic field that interacts with the already existing field, causing

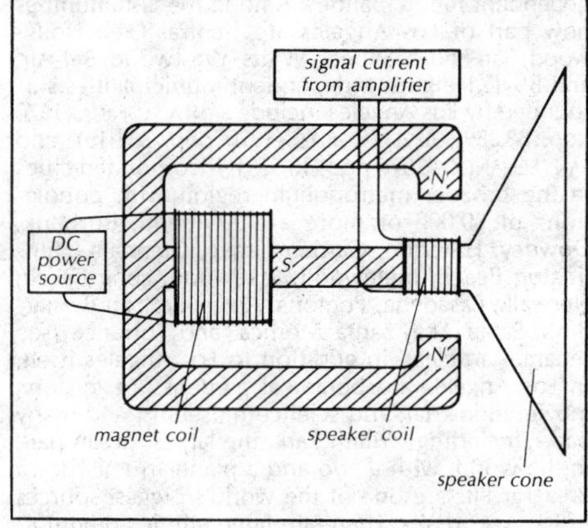

Electrodynamic loudspeaker

the coil and the diaphragm attached to it to vibrate. In an electrostatic speaker a movable electrode made of a metal-covered plastic sheet acts as the diaphragm. It is placed between two fixed screenlike electrodes; a high, constant DC voltage is maintained between the three electrodes. When a signal voltage is added to the high voltage, the electrostatic force on the diaphragm varies, causing it to vibrate. In order to provide a faithful reproduction of music or speech, a loudspeaker must be able to reproduce a wide range of frequencies. Since it is difficult for a single speaker to do this adequately, many quality sound systems employ three different sized speakers. The largest one, called a woofer, is used to reproduce low frequencies. The medium-sized one, called a mid-range speaker, is used to reproduce middle frequencies. The smallest one, called a tweeter, is used to reproduce high frequencies. In a stereophonic radio or phonograph, the three different sized speakers come in pairs; in a quadraphonic system, they come in sets of four each. The quality of a speaker can be enhanced by a well-designed enclosure. Such an enclosure can reduce the tendency of a speaker to resonate.

Louga (lōō'gä), town, W Senegal. Located in a region where peanuts, cassava, and gum arabic are produced, the town manufactures peanut oil and processes hides and skins. Louga is a road junction and has rail connections with Saint-Louis in NW Senegal. An agricultural school and a branch of the Institute for Research in Seed Oils are in Louga.

Lough (lŏkh, lŏk). For names of Irish lakes and inlets beginning thus, see second part of name; e.g., for Lough Erne, see ERNE, LOUGH. See LAKE.

Loughborough (lŭf'bərə), municipal borough (1971 pop. 45,863), Leicestershire, central England, on the

Soar River. It is a market town with engineering works; its products include hosiery, shoes, pharmaceuticals, boilers, and pottery. Bell foundries were built in 1840; the great bell of St. Paul's Cathedral in London was cast there in 1881. Loughborough's war memorial, with a carillon of 47 bells, was built in 1923. Loughborough has a technical university and a grammar school, founded in 1495.

Louis, Saint: see LOUIS IX, king of France.

Louis I or **Louis the Pious,** Fr. *Louis le Pieux* or *Louis le Débonnaire,* 778–840, emperor of the West (814–40), son and successor of Charlemagne. He was crowned king of Aquitaine in 781 and coemperor with his father in 813. In 817 he made his eldest son, LOTHAIR I, coemperor and gave Aquitaine and Bavaria to his sons PEPIN I and LOUIS THE GERMAN. Louis's attempts to create a kingdom for Charles (later Emperor of the West CHARLES II), his son by a second marriage, provoked several revolts by his older sons. In 830, Lothair rebelled and became virtually sole ruler of the empire. However, Pepin and Louis the German, fearing Lothair's supremacy, soon restored their father to power. Another revolt by all three sons occurred in 833. Louis met the rebels near Colmar on a field known since then as the Field of Lies (Ger. *Lügenfeld*) because of the general defection of the imperial troops. Louis, compelled to surrender, was formally deposed, and Lothair became sole emperor. Yet in 834, Louis the German and Pepin once more joined against Lothair and restored Louis. Later he partitioned his empire between Lothair and Charles and died while attempting to uphold the partition against the Aquitanians and Louis the German.

Louis II, d. 875, emperor of the West (855–75), king of Italy (844–75), son of Emperor of the West Lothair I. In 844, Lothair I designated him king of Italy and in 850 he was crowned emperor of the West in Rome. He became sole emperor when his father died; the title had little meaning, however, since he ruled only in Italy. Throughout his reign, his power there was challenged by the independent Lombard dukes and by the Arab invaders of S Italy. In the dispute between his brother LOTHAIR, king of Lotharingia, and Pope Nicholas I, concerning Lothair's divorce, he supported his brother. However, the pope refused to allow Lothair to set aside his wife even after Louis occupied Rome (864). Subsequently, Louis submitted to the pope's decision. At Lothair's death (870) Louis claimed Lotharingia, but the Treaty of Mersen divided it between his two uncles, Charles the Bald (who succeeded Louis as Emperor of the West CHARLES II) and LOUIS THE GERMAN.

Louis IV or **Louis the Bavarian,** 1287?–1347, Holy Roman emperor (1328–47) and German king (1314–47), duke of Upper Bavaria. After the death of Holy Roman Emperor Henry VII the Luxemburg party among the electors set aside Henry's son, John of Luxemburg, because of his youth and chose Louis as rival king to FREDERICK THE FAIR. The popes Clement V and his successor JOHN XXII refused to approve Louis's election and, claiming that the imperial throne was vacant, declared the Holy Roman Empire to be under papal rule. This doctrine fitted in well with the papacy's ambition to restore papal authority in Italy. In 1322, Louis defeated and captured Frederick at Mühldorf. Despite this victory, John XXII refused to ratify Louis's election and in 1324 excommunicated him. In 1327–30 Louis was in Italy, where he was crowned emperor by the representatives of the Roman people, and set up Pietro RAINALDUCCI as Antipope Nicholas V. Rainalducci was soon reconciled with the pope, however, and Louis unsuccessfully attempted to reach a settlement. The failure of protracted negotiations with the papacy led (1338) to the declaration at Rhense by six electors to the effect that election by all or the majority of the electors automatically conferred the royal title and rule over the empire, without papal confirmation. Throughout his reign Louis kept adding to the possessions of his family, the house of WITTELSBACH. He conferred Brandenburg on his son and added Lower Bavaria to Upper Bavaria. In 1342 he acquired Tyrol by voiding the first marriage of MARGARET MAULTASCH and marrying her to his own son, thus alienating the house of Luxemburg. In 1346 he further antagonized the lay princes by conferring Holland, Zeeland, and Friesland upon his wife. Meanwhile, the pope, CLEMENT VI, took advantage of the hostility to Louis and deposed him (1346), securing the election of a new German king, Charles of Luxemburg (later Holy Roman Emperor CHARLES IV). Louis was successfully resisting his rival when he was killed in a hunting accident. The controversy between Louis and the popes caused the publication of many books and pamphlets, notably the *Defensor pacis* by MARSILIUS OF PADUA, which supported Louis's claims. WILLIAM OF OCCAM was another of his supporters.

Louis I, 1786–1868, king of Bavaria (1825–48), son and successor of King Maximilian I. He was chiefly responsible for transforming Munich into one of the handsomest capitals of Europe and for making it a center of the arts. His reign, liberal at first, became reactionary, and his unpopularity was heightened by his liaison with Lola MONTEZ. The Revolution of 1848 forced him to abdicate in favor of his son, Maximilian II.

Louis II, 1845–86, king of Bavaria (1864–86), son and successor of King Maximilian II. Much was hoped from the handsome, talented, and liberal young prince at his accession, but his prodigality and eccentricity soon alienated his subjects. Louis was the patron and friend of Richard WAGNER, who for many years exerted a strong influence over him. Louis aided Austria in the Austro-Prussian War (1866) but sided with Prussia against France in 1870 and in 1871 reluctantly joined the newly created German Empire. In 1886 his insanity necessitated his confinement at his château on Lake Starnberg, Bavaria, where he drowned himself. His brother, Otto I, who was insane, succeeded him under the regency of an uncle, Luitpold. See biographies by Werner Richter (1939, tr. 1954), Desmond Chapman-Huston (1955), and Wilfred Blunt (1970).

Louis III, 1845–1921, last king of Bavaria (1913–18). He succeeded (1912) his father, LUITPOLD, as regent for the insane OTTO I but proclaimed himself king in 1913. He was overthrown in the Bavarian revolution of Nov., 1918.

Louis I, French king: see LOUIS I, emperor of the West.

Louis II or **Louis the Stammerer,** 846–79, French king. He succeeded (877) his father, Emperor of the West Charles II, as king. On Louis's death his kingdom was divided between his sons Carloman and Louis III.

Louis III, c.863–882, French king, son of King Louis II. He became joint ruler with his brother CARLOMAN on the death of Louis II (879), despite the attempts of LOUIS THE YOUNGER to become French king. Louis III and Carloman fought against the secessionists of Burgundy and Provence and resisted an invasion of the Normans, whom Louis routed (881) at Saucourt. His death left Carloman sole ruler.

Louis IV or **Louis d'Outremer** (lwē dōōtramĕr') [Fr.,=Louis from overseas], 921–54, French king (936–54), son of King Charles III (Charles the Simple). He spent his youth as an exile in England, but at the death of King RAOUL he was recalled by the nobles under the leadership of HUGH THE GREAT. However, Louis's energy and independence displeased Hugh, who fought against him with the German king, Otto I, until 942. Captured by the Normans (945), Louis was surrendered to Hugh, by whom he was released only on the cession of Laon (946). Now in alliance with Otto, Louis made war on Hugh and received his submission in 950. Louis was succeeded by his son Lothair.

Louis V (Louis the Sluggard), c.967–987, last French king of the Carolingian dynasty; son of King Lothair. His father had him crowned in 979, but he did not become king until Lothair's death in 986. He was childless and was succeeded by HUGH CAPET.

Louis VI (Louis the Fat), 1081–1137, king of France (1108–37). He succeeded his father, Philip I, with whom he was associated in government from c.1100. He firmly established his authority within the royal domain, suppressing brigandage by robber barons and besieging their castles, and punishing wrongdoers. He continued his father's policy of opposing the English in Normandy and was almost continuously at war with King Henry I (1109–13, 1116–20, 1123–35); he often met with defeat, but his resistance checked a greater English advance. In 1124, strongly supported by the nobles, he resisted the invasion of Holy Roman Emperor Henry V, who had come to the aid of Henry I. As a part of his plan for strengthening royal authority, Louis favored the church, liberally endowing its enterprises and selecting churchmen—notably the Abbé SUGER—as his ministers; he was vigorous, however, in enforcing his privilege of interference in ecclesiastical affairs. To gain support from the towns, he began to grant them royal charters. He obtained a foothold in Guienne (Aquitaine) by marrying his son Louis (his successor as Louis VII) to the heiress of the duchy, ELEANOR OF AQUITAINE. His enforcement of order and justice made Louis popular with the middle classes, the peasantry, and the clergy. See J. W. Thompson, *The Development of the French Monarchy under Louis VI le Gros* (1895).

Louis VII (Louis the Young), c.1120–1180, king of France (1137–80), son and successor of King Louis VI. Before his accession he married ELEANOR OF AQUITAINE. A controversy with Pope Innocent II over Louis's refusal to accept the papal appointee to the archbishopric of Bourges led to a papal interdict on Louis and to warfare between the king and the count of Champagne, who supported the papal candidate. It was settled, after the intervention of St. BERNARD OF CLAIRVAUX, by Louis's capitulation (1144) to Pope Celestine II, Innocent's successor. In the course of that war Geoffrey IV (Geoffrey Plantagenet), count of Anjou, completed his conquest of Normandy; Louis, in return for a small concession, acquiesced in the conquest. In 1147, Louis left on the Second Crusade (see CRUSADES), after appointing Abbé SUGER as regent. The crusade failed, and he returned in 1149. In 1152 Louis, suspecting Eleanor of being unfaithful, had his marriage with her annulled. Her subsequent marriage with Henry Plantagenet (later King HENRY II of England), Geoffrey's son, resulted in Henry's claims to AQUITAINE and precipitated recurrent warfare between Louis and Henry. Louis supported THOMAS À BECKET during his exile from England and joined in the revolt of Henry's sons (1173–74), but won no territory. He completed his father's work of subduing the barons on the royal domain and continued to increase his influence over more distant vassals. His son Philip II succeeded him.

Louis VIII, 1187–1226, king of France (1223–26), son and successor of King PHILIP II. He fought (1215, 1219) against the ALBIGENSES in S France. Invited by English lords in rebellion against their king, JOHN, to become king of England, he invaded (1216) England, although his action caused his excommunication by Pope Innocent III. The death of John and the accession of Henry III as king of England lost Louis much support among the English nobility. After his defeat (1217) at Lincoln, he withdrew. In 1224 he conquered Poitou from the English. To make his peace with the church, he pledged to go on crusade, and in 1226 he resumed the Albigensian Crusade and conquered most of Languedoc. He continued his father's policy of strong central authority.

Louis IX or **Saint Louis,** 1214–70, king of France (1226–70), son and successor of Louis VIII. His mother, BLANCHE OF CASTILE, was regent during his minority (1226–34), and her regency probably lasted even after Louis reached his majority; she was his chief adviser until her death. During the early years of the reign, the queen mother suppressed several revolts of the great nobles, led by Pierre Mauclerc (PETER I), duke of Brittany, and supported by Duke RAYMOND VII of Toulouse and King HENRY III of England. In 1240–43, Louis subdued new revolts in S France, securing the submission of Poitou and of Raymond VII, and repulsing a weak invasion (1242) by Henry III. Louis took the cross in 1244, but did not leave on the crusade to Egypt (the Seventh Crusade; see CRUSADES) until 1248. Defeated and captured (1250) at Al Mansurah, he was ransomed but remained in the Holy Land until 1254, helping to strengthen the fortifications of the Christian colonies. After his return he attempted to bring about a peaceful settlement of territorial claims with Henry III. Agreement was reached in the Treaty of Paris, ratified in 1259. By its terms Louis ceded Limoges, Cahors, and Périgueux to Henry in exchange for Henry's renunciation of Normandy, Anjou, Maine, Touraine, and Poitou and his recognition of the king of France as suzerain for the reduced duchy of Aquitaine. Louis made a favorable treaty with King James I of Aragón by yielding the French claim to Roussillon and Barcelona in return for James's abandonment of his claim to Provence and Languedoc. A respected arbitrator, Louis settled succession disputes in Flanders and Hainaut and in Navarre; he attempted unsuccessfully to settle the bitter controversy between Henry III and the English barons by judging in favor of the king. In 1270, Louis undertook the Eighth Crusade, but he died soon after landing in Tunis. He was succeeded by his son, Philip III. Under Louis IX, France enjoyed unprecedented prosperity and peace. Louis continued the reforms of his grandfather, Philip II. He curbed private feudal warfare, simplified administration, improved the distribution of taxes, encouraged the use of Roman law, and extended the appellate jurisdiction of the crown to all cases. Louis was the ideal medieval Christian monarch, pious and ascetic, yet a good administrator and diplomat. His religious fervor, however, led him to encourage the Inquisition. He was canonized in 1297. Feast: Aug. 25. See memoirs of his contemporary, Jean de JOINVILLE; biography by M. W. Labarge (1968).

Louis X, Fr. **Louis le Hutin** [the quarrelsome], 1289–1316, king of France (1314–16), son and successor of Philip IV. His reign was dominated by his uncle, Charles of Valois, and was distinguished by his concessions to the barons in the form of charters. The death soon after birth of his posthumous son and successor, John I, opened the succession to Philip V.

Louis XI, 1423–83, king of France (1461–83), son and successor of Charles VII. As dauphin he was almost constantly in revolt against his father. He was pardoned after joining (1440) the PRAGUERIE; after conspiring (1446) against Agnès SOREL and Pierre de Brézé, he was exiled to the Dauphiné, which he governed himself. His continued intrigues forced another exile (1456–61), this time to the court of PHILIP THE GOOD of Burgundy. Louis began his reign by dismissing many of his father's best advisers; but he soon deserted his former allies of the Praguerie and began the task of centralizing all authority in the crown. His measures to curb the power of the great nobles aroused (1465) the League of the Public Weal, headed by CHARLES THE BOLD, son of Philip the Good; FRANCIS II, duke of Brittany; Jean, comte du DUNOIS; Antoine de CHABANNES; and the dukes of Alençon and Bourbon, under the nominal leadership of the king's brother Charles. The lesser nobility, the bourgeoisie, and the lower classes supported Louis, who also allied with the citizens of Liège, a Burgundian protectorate, against Charles the Bold. Louis successfully defended Paris, but in Oct., 1465, he granted the demands of the rebels in the treaties of Conflans and Saint-Maur-des-Fossés. He soon violated the treaties, taking Normandy from his brother Charles, to whom it had been granted. In 1467 a new coalition against the king was formed by Charles the Bold, now duke of Burgundy, with Francis II; Charles also obtained the support of King Edward IV of England. When the duke of Brittany invaded Normandy, Louis arranged a truce with him. In 1468, at the expiration of the truce with Brittany, he subdued Normandy and forced Francis II to sign the Peace of Ancenis (1468). Having visited Péronne for an interview with Charles the Bold, Louis was made (1468) prisoner and forced to sign a treaty granting important concessions and compelling him to participate in suppressing the revolt of Liège, which he had helped instigate. After his release, he involved himself in English affairs against Edward IV (see ROSES, WARS OF THE), aiding the restoration of King Henry VI. Conflict with the French nobles continued. The death (1472) of Louis's brother Charles removed one opponent, and after a brief campaign Louis signed truces with Francis II and Charles the Bold. Charles renewed his alliance with Edward IV, who had regained the English throne. Louis, however, succeeded in buying off Edward IV when he invaded (1475) France to aid Charles, and in uniting the enemies of Charles the Bold, among whom the Swiss were the strongest. The Swiss victories over Charles and his death (1477) at Nancy enabled Louis to take Burgundy, Picardy, Boulogne, Artois, and Franche-Comté from Charles's daughter, MARY OF BURGUNDY. Mary's husband, Maximilian of Austria (later Holy Roman Emperor MAXIMILIAN I), defeated (1479) Louis at Guinegate, but was ultimately forced to concede the Burgundian territories to Louis in the Treaty of Arras (see ARRAS, TREATY OF). On the extinction of the house of Anjou, Louis acquired Anjou, Maine, Bar, and Provence. A born diplomat, Louis skillfully checked his foreign and domestic enemies and set up an efficient central administration. He used commissions (and the one States-General he convoked) to give his acts the appearance of popular approval. He diminished the prestige of the courts. Despite his revocation (1461) of his father's PRAGMATIC SANCTION of Bourges, he intervened freely in church affairs. He imposed heavy taxes, using much of the revenue to purchase support. He also encouraged industry and expanded domestic and foreign trade. Louis preferred men of humble origin, and among his advisers were Olivier LE DAIM, Louis Tristan L'Hermite, and Cardinal BALUE, whom he rewarded liberally, though he was niggardly in his own expenses. Fearing assassination, he spent his last years in virtual self-imprisonment near TOURS. He was succeeded by his son, Charles VIII. See writings of a contemporary, COMINES; biographies by P. H. Champion (tr. 1929, repr. 1970), D. B. Wyndham Lewis (1929), James Cleugh (1970), and P. M. Kendall (1971).

Louis XII, 1462–1515, king of France (1498–1515), son of Charles, duc d'ORLÉANS. He succeeded his father as duke. While still duke, he rebelled against the regency of Anne de Beaujeu and was imprisoned (1488), but was released (1491) by his cousin King Charles VIII, whom he succeeded (1498) on the throne. Immediately after his accession he ensured the continuance of the personal union of Brittany and France by having his first marriage annulled and marrying his predecessor's widow, ANNE OF BRITTANY. Thereafter the king and his minister, Georges d'AMBOISE, attempted to assert French claims in Italy (see ITALIAN WARS). Louis conquered Milan and Genoa, but he failed to secure Naples, which he had conquered in alliance with King FERDINAND II of Aragón. By the treaties of Blois (1504), Louis attempted a compromise with Spain and with Holy Roman Emperor Maximilian I, who had so far remained an inactive opponent; the treaties subsequently collapsed, and the king's daughter Claude, whose marriage to Maximilian's grandson Charles of Austria (later Holy Roman Emperor Charles V) was to have been the keystone of the new entente, was betrothed to her cousin, Francis of Angoulême, later King FRANCIS I. In 1507, Louis suppressed the revolt of Genoa (1506–7), and in 1508 he joined the League of Cambrai (see CAMBRAI, LEAGUE OF) against Venice, defeating the Venetians at Agnadello (1509). When his Italian territories were attacked (1511) by Pope Julius II's HOLY LEAGUE, he committed their defense to Gaston de Foix, but after Gaston's death (1512) his troops were forced by the Swiss (then the pope's main allies) to evacuate Milan. In 1513 the Swiss routed his army at Novara while another army was defeated at Guinegate by Maximilian and King Henry VIII of England, also the pope's allies. In 1514 he made a truce with all his enemies save Maximilian. Louis endeavored to rule France with justice and moderation, and was known as the Father of the People. See J. S. C. Bridge, *A History of France from the Death of Louis XI*, Vol. III–IV (1929).

Louis XIII, 1601–43, king of France (1610–43). He succeeded his father, HENRY IV, under the regency of his mother, MARIE DE' MEDICI. He married ANNE OF AUSTRIA in 1615. Even after being declared of age in 1614, he was excluded from affairs of state by his domineering mother. In 1617 he caused the assassination of her minister Concino CONCINI, with the aid of his own favorite, Charles d'Albert, duc de LUYNES, and Marie de' Medici was forced into retirement. He was reconciled to her in 1622 and entrusted (1624) the government to her protégé, Cardinal RICHELIEU. In 1630, urged by his mother to discharge Richelieu, he instead sent his mother again into exile. Melancholy and retiring by nature, Louis thenceforth gave full support to Richelieu and his successor, Cardinal MAZARIN. Richelieu strengthened royal authority and centralized government control. Louis's reign was remarkable for the establishment of the French Academy and for the work of St. FRANCIS OF SALES and St. VINCENT DE PAUL in religion, René DESCARTES in philosophy, and Pierre CORNEILLE in literature. See V. L. Tapié, *La France de Louis XIII et de Richelieu* (1952); H. W. Chapman, *Privileged Persons* (1966).

Louis XIV, 1638–1715, king of France (1643–1715), son and successor of King Louis XIII. After his father's death, his mother, ANNE OF AUSTRIA, was regent for Louis, but the real power was in the hands of Anne's adviser, Cardinal MAZARIN. Although Louis's majority was declared in 1651, he did not take over the government until Mazarin's death (1661). By that time France was economically exhausted by the Thirty Years War, by the outbreaks known as the FRONDE, and by fiscal abuses. But the centralizing policies of RICHELIEU and Mazarin had prepared the ground for Louis, under whom absolute monarchy, based on the theory of divine right, reached its height. Louis's reign can be characterized by the remark attributed to him, "L'état, c'est moi" [I am the state]. Gathering power into his own hands, Louis continued the nobility's exemption from taxes but forced its members into financial dependence on the crown, thus creating a court nobility that spent its energy on ceremonial etiquette and petty intrigues. The provincial nobles lost political power. Louis used the bourgeoisie to build his centralized bureaucracy. He curtailed local authorities and created specialized ministries, filled largely by professionals responsible solely to him. Under his minister Jean Baptiste COLBERT, industry and commerce expanded on mercantilist principles, a navy was developed, and colonial trade was increased. Under the war minister, the marquis de LOUVOIS, the foundations of French military greatness were laid. In foreign policy Louis strove vigorously for supremacy. His marriage (1660) to the Spanish princess Marie Thérèse served as a pretext for the War of DEVOLUTION (1667–68), which netted him part of Flanders, although the Dutch then moved against him with the TRIPLE ALLIANCE of 1668. Bad relations with the Dutch were exacerbated by commercial rivalry and in 1672 Louis, determined to crush Holland, began the third of the DUTCH WARS. It gave him Franche-Comté but depleted his treasury. For the next 10 years the king limited his aggressive policies to diplomacy. He set up "chambers of reunion" to unearth legal grounds for claims on a number of cities, which Louis promptly annexed. Notable among these was Strasbourg, seized in 1681. Fear of Louis's rapacity resulted in a European coalition (see AUGSBURG, LEAGUE OF; GRAND ALLIANCE, WAR OF THE), which confronted him when he attacked the Holy Roman Empire in 1688. This war ended with the Treaty of RYSWICK (1697), through which Louis lost minor territories. Louis's last war, the War of the SPANISH SUCCESSION (1701–14), left France in debt and greatly weakened militarily; nevertheless, Louis's grandson retained the Spanish throne. In religious affairs Louis was at first tolerant of dissent, but later began to impose religious uniformity. In the 1680s he resorted to persecution of the HUGUENOTS, which culminated (1685) in the revocation of the Edict of Nantes (see NANTES, EDICT OF). This measure, which resulted in an exodus of Protestants, many of whom were merchants and skilled artisans, intensified the kingdom's economic decline and further alienated the Protestant powers. Louis also suppressed Jansenism (see under JANSEN, CORNELIS). Despite this concern with religious orthodoxy, he favored GALLICANISM, and controversy with the popes approached schism (1673–93) before Louis abandoned this position. In his personal life Louis had a series of mistresses, among them Mlle de LA VALLIÈRE and Mme de MONTESPAN. He finally came under the influence of Mme de MAINTENON, whom he married morganatically (1684) after the queen's death and who had an important share in bringing him to the religious devotion and quiet domesticity of his later years. A great supporter of the arts, Louis encouraged and patronized the foremost writers and artists of his time, including MOLIÈRE, Jean RACINE, Jean de LA FONTAINE, and Charles LE BRUN. The architect Jules MANSART supervised the building of the lavish palace of VERSAILLES for Louis. Because of the brilliance of his court, Louis was called "Le Roi Soleil" [the Sun King] and "Le Grand Monarque." He was succeeded by his great-grandson, Louis XV. For contemporary sources see the incisive memoirs of the Cardinal de RETZ; the extremely prejudiced but indispensable memoirs of the duc de SAINT-SIMON; the letters of Mme de SÉVIGNÉ, which brilliantly portray the social life of the time. See biographies by Vincent Cronin (1964), David Ogg (2d ed. 1967), J. B. Wolf (1968), and Philippe Erlanger (tr. 1970); study by Pierre Gaxotte (tr. 1970).

Louis XV, 1710–74, king of France (1715–74), great-grandson and successor of King Louis XIV, son of LOUIS, titular duke of Burgundy, and Marie Adelaide of Savoy. He succeeded to the throne with Philippe II, duc d'Orléans (see ORLÉANS, family) as regent. After the regent died (1723), Louis was guided by André Hercule de FLEURY, his main adviser from 1726. When Fleury died in 1743, the king decided not to appoint a chief minister. Louis, however, lacked both the will and interest to govern forcefully, and his reign was influenced by a succession of favorites; of these Mme de POMPADOUR and her adherents were the most important. While Louis was king, France was involved in a series of wars. As a result of the king's marriage (1725) to MARIE LESZCYNSKA, France took part in the War of the Polish Succession (see POLISH SUCCESSION, WAR OF THE), and eventually obtained (1766) the duchy of Lorraine for its efforts. Louis's diplomacy, which was often conducted secretly by the king's personal agents rather than through his official ministers, involved France in the War of the Austrian Succession against Austria (see AUSTRIAN SUCCESSION, WAR OF THE) and, after a switch of alliances that realigned (1756) France with Austria, in the SEVEN YEARS WAR. The Treaty of Paris (see PARIS, TREATY OF, 1763), ending the Seven Years War, marked the loss of most of France's colonial empire and a low point in French prestige on the Continent. In domestic affairs, the abuses of Louis XIV's rule and the disastrous financial policy of the regency were partly liquidated by Fleury, but the extravagances of Louis XV's court, the expense of warfare, and the defeat of attempts at reform left the monarchy weak by the time of Louis XV's death. Efforts to reform the inequitable tax system failed, as did the attempt by René Nicolas de MAUPEOU to suppress opposition to reform from the PARLEMENT. Throughout Louis's reign, the aristocracy asserted more influence, and the upper bourgeoisie gained more financial power. The country knew general prosperity, but the government was near bankruptcy. The apathy of Louis XV in the face of these problems found expression in the saying "Après moi le déluge" [after me, the flood], wrongly attributed to the king himself. The failure of the monarchy to solve its fiscal difficulties led directly to the French Revolution during the reign of Louis's successor, Louis XVI. See Pierre Gaxotte, *Louis the Fifteenth and His Times* (1934); G. P. Gooch, *Louis XV; the Monarchy in Decline* (1956); Alfred Cobban, *A History of Modern France*, Vol. I (1957, repr. 1969).

Louis XVI, 1754-93, king of France (1774-92), third son of the dauphin (Louis) and Marie Josèphe of Saxony, grandson and successor of King Louis XV. His early attempts to enact reforms and to appoint competent and upright ministers met with general approval, but his character was unsuited to provide the leadership needed to control the complex social and political conflict smoldering in France. Shy, dull, and corpulent, he preferred the hunting field and his locksmith's workshop to the council chamber; his indecision made him subject to the poor advice of his intimates. The reforms begun by his able ministers A. R. J. TURGOT and Chrétien de MALESHERBES were opposed by the court faction, with his queen, MARIE ANTOINETTE, among those who persisted in ignoring the threat of bankruptcy and the plight of the lower classes. A more important obstacle to Turgot's plans was the opposition of the parlements, which were revived after the dismissal of René de MAUPEOU. Turgot was dismissed in May, 1776, and Louis appointed (Oct., 1776) Jacques NECKER director of the treasury. The king supported most of Necker's reforms and economies, but the costly French intervention in the American Revolution more than canceled the savings, and Necker's borrowing greatly swelled the debt. The jealousy of the chief minister, the comte de Maurepas, caused the reluctant king to dismiss Necker in May, 1781. Necker's successors, Charles Alexandre de CALONNE (1783-87) and Étienne Charles LOMÉNIE DE BRIENNE (1787-88), were unable to ward off bankruptcy. When the interest-bearing debt had risen to a huge figure, the king convoked (1787) the Assembly of Notables and asked their consent to tax the privileged classes. The notables made a few minor reforms but refused to consent to taxation, referring this to the STATES-GENERAL. Louis finally convoked the States-General in 1789. Necker, restored in 1788, prevailed upon Louis to double the number of deputies from the third, or lowest, estate. This increase, however, would be meaningless if the estates met separately and voted as units rather than as individuals; the privileged classes, the nobles (first estate) and the clergy (second estate), could still outvote the third estate. The king's opposition to the combined meeting of the estates and his procrastination on this issue led the third estate to proclaim itself a National Assembly, thus signaling the end of absolutism in France. Louis ordered the estates to meet and vote separately, but he was forced (June 27, 1789) to yield and allow the estates to sit together and vote by head. Shortly afterward Louis sent troops to Paris, where he suspected the French Guards of being too sympathetic to the assembly. Rumors circulated that the king intended to suppress the assembly, and the dismissal of the popular Necker provoked the storming of the Bastille (July 14, 1789), which set off the FRENCH REVOLUTION. Louis again had to capitulate; he ordered the retirement of the royal troops, reinstated Necker, and accepted the new national red, white, and blue cockade. Despite his outward acceptance of the revolution, Louis allowed the reactionary plotting of the queen and court, and in August refused to approve the abolition of feudal rights. In Oct., 1789, a mob marched on Versailles and forced the royal family to return to Paris, where they were confined in the Tuileries palace. Louis's position, further compromised by the plots of ÉMIGRÉ circles, was definitively ruined when the royal family attempted (June, 1791) to flee France in disguise. They were apprehended at Varennes, and their attempted flight was considered proof of their treasonable dealings with foreign powers. Louis was forced to accept the constitution of 1791, which made him a mere figurehead. After his return he was in communication with Austria and Prussia, urging them to rescue him. In 1792 the early reverses of the French army in the war with Austria and Prussia and the duke of Brunswick's threat to destroy Paris if the royal family were harmed infuriated the revolutionists; the king was "suspended" and the royal family imprisoned (Aug., 1792) in the Temple. When the Prussians were repulsed (September) at Valmy, the monarchy was abolished in France. Incriminating evidence against Louis was discovered, and he was tried (December-January) by the Convention, which had replaced the National Assembly; Louis was condemned to death by an absolute majority of one. He was guillotined on Jan. 21, 1793, facing death with steadfast courage. See biographies by S. K. Padover (new ed. 1963) and Bernard Fay (tr. 1968); S. H. MacLehose, *The Last Days of the French Monarchy* (1901).

Louis XVII (Louis Charles), 1785-1795?, titular king of France (1793-95), known in popular legend as the "lost dauphin." The second son of King Louis XVI and Queen MARIE ANTOINETTE, he became dauphin at the death (1789) of his elder brother. In 1792 the revolutionists imprisoned him with the royal family in the Temple. After the execution (1793) of Louis XVI, the comte de Provence (later King Louis XVIII) proclaimed the dauphin king as Louis XVII, but he remained in prison until his death. Cruel treatment by his jailer, Antoine SIMON, was said to have hastened his end. His death has often been disputed; it was rumored that someone had taken the true dauphin from prison and substituted another boy in his place. The various stories of his escape and speculations on his fate opened the way for a series of impostors claiming to be the lost dauphin. Of these claimants, the most important in the United States was Eleazer WILLIAMS. The most important in Europe was a German watchmaker, Karl Wilhelm Naundorff, who gathered a number of followers. Evidence indicates that the boy really died in prison in 1795, and historians, for the most part, disregard the lost dauphin theory altogether. For the life of Louis XVII and discussion of the claims of various pretenders see study by H. G. Francq (tr. 1971).

Louis XVIII, 1755-1824, king of France (1814-24), brother of King Louis XVI. Known as the comte de Provence, he fled (1791) to Koblenz from the French Revolution and intrigued to bring about foreign intervention against the revolutionaries. He was recognized as king by the émigrés after the death (1795) of Louis XVII. He passed his exile on the Continent and in England. With the assistance of Charles de TALLEYRAND, he was restored (1814) to the French throne by the allies after their entry into Paris. He adopted a conciliatory policy towards the former revolutionists and granted a constitutional charter. Forced to flee once more on the news of the return of Napoleon I, he returned with the allies (1815) after the defeat at Waterloo had ended Napoleon's rule of a HUNDRED DAYS. His chief ministers were at first moderates—Armand Emmanuel, duc de RICHELIEU, and Élie DECAZES—but the ultraroyalists, led by Louis's brother, the comte d'Artois (later CHARLES X), triumphed after the assassination (1820) of the count's son, Charles Ferdinand, duc de Berry. Louis, then old and suffering from gout, allowed the ultraroyalists to take control. The new ministry headed by the comte de VILLÈLE was thoroughly reactionary. Electoral laws were revised to increase the influence of the wealthy classes, and civil liberties were curbed. This trend continued and was intensified during the reign (1824-30) of his successor, Charles X. See RESTORATION, in French history.

Louis I or **Louis the Great,** 1326-82, king of Hungary (1342-82) and of Poland (1370-82). He succeeded his father, Charles I, in Hungary, and his uncle, Casimir III, in Poland. He continued the internal policy of his father, favoring the church and the commerce of the towns. In 1351 he confirmed the Golden Bull of ANDREW II, but to assure the continuance of a strong and wealthy military class he applied the system of ENTAIL to the estates of the nobles and made it mandatory for serfs to pay one ninth of their farm produce to their overlords. He was rarely forced to appeal to the diet for funds; as a result, its meetings became less frequent. The murder (1345) of his brother Andrew at the court of Andrew's wife, JOANNA I of Naples, broke Hungary's alliance with the western branch of the ANGEVIN dynasty and slowed Louis's reconquest of Dalmatia. Two successful wars (1357-58, 1378-81) against Venice, however, gained him Dalmatia and Ragusa. The rulers of Serbia, Walachia, Moldavia, and Bulgaria became his vassals. In Poland, where his campaign (1354) against the Tatars and the Lithuanians had made him popular, he was unable to prevent revolts after his accession. In 1377, Louis campaigned successfully against the Turks. He brought Hungarian power to its peak and also fostered art and learning, which were influenced both by Louis's French background and by his campaigns that brought Hungarians in contact with the Italian Renaissance. Louis had no male heir but provided for his succession by marrying his eldest daughter, Mary, to SIGISMUND (later Holy Roman emperor). After a period of turmoil following Louis's death, Mary and Sigismund ruled Hungary jointly. Poland refused to continue the union of the crowns, so his younger daughter, JADWIGA, succeeded him as queen of Poland.

Louis II, 1506-26, king of Hungary and Bohemia (1516-26), son and successor of Uladislaus II. He was the last of the Jagiello dynasty in the two kingdoms. In the face of intensified attacks by Sultan SULAYMAN I, Louis hastily sought (1526) to unite Hungary and Christendom behind him, but only the pope sent help. With a pitiful army, Louis joined battle with the Turks at MOHÁCS. The Hungarian army was destroyed, and Louis was killed. Through the marriage treaty concluded by his father (see ULADISLAUS II) the crowns of Hungary and Bohemia passed to Louis's brother-in-law, Ferdinand of Hapsburg (later Holy Roman Emperor FERDINAND I), but Hungary fell under Turkish rule.

Louis I, 1339-84, king of Naples (1382-84; rival claimant to CHARLES III), duke of Anjou, count of Provence, second son of John II of France. He founded the second ANGEVIN line in Naples. As a regent for his nephew, CHARLES VI of France, he was noted for his rapacity. In 1380, JOANNA I of Naples adopted Louis as heir to the throne and to Provence, repudiating her first choice, Charles of Durazzo. Charles, supported by his uncle, Pope Urban VI, conquered the kingdom (1381) and was crowned king of Naples as Charles III. Supported by the antipope Clement VII (Robert of Geneva), Louis I invaded the kingdom, but his troops soon deserted, and he died shortly thereafter. His claim then passed to his son, Louis II.

Louis II, 1377-1417, king of Naples (1384-1417), duke of Anjou, count of Provence, son and successor of Louis I of Naples. In 1389 the antipope Clement VII (Robert of Geneva) invested him with the kingdom, LANCELOT, rival claimant of Naples, having been expelled in 1386. Louis took possession of Naples in 1390, but he was ousted in turn by Lancelot in 1399. In 1409, Louis liberated Rome from Lancelot's occupation; in 1410, as an ally of the antipope John XXIII (see COSSA, BALDASSARRE), he attacked Lancelot and defeated him at Roccasecca (1411). Eventually Louis lost his Neapolitan support and had to retire. His claim to Naples passed to his son, Louis III.

Louis III, 1403-34, king of Naples (1417-34; rival claimant to JOANNA II), duke of Anjou, count of Provence, son and successor of Louis II. He invaded Naples in 1420. Queen Joanna called in the aid of ALFONSO V of Aragón and Sicily and adopted him as heir (1421), but Alfonso's domineering attitude caused her (1423) to adopt Louis instead. Louis had gained control of most of the kingdom when he died. Joanna made his brother RENÉ heir.

Louis I, 1838-89, king of Portugal (1861-89), son of Maria II and Ferdinand II. He succeeded to the throne on the death of his brother Peter V. His reign was marked by much political turmoil and by a growth of republicanism, while a succession of alternating liberal and conservative ministries accomplished little. After the overthrow (1868) of Isabella II of Spain, there was talk of Louis's claiming the Spanish throne, but it led to nothing. In 1886, Portugal secured French and German recognition of its claim to the African interior between Angola and Mozambique, but this was challenged by Great Britain. Slavery was abolished in the Portuguese colonies during Louis's reign, and Portugal made considerable progress in transportation, commerce, and industry. Louis was succeeded by his son, CHARLES I.

Louis, 1682-1712, titular duke of Burgundy; grandson of King Louis XIV of France. He became heir to the throne on the death (1711) of his father, Louis the Great Dauphin. François de FÉNELON was his tutor and wrote *Télémaque* for his use. Louis was the rallying point of the opposition to Louis XIV—reactionary nobles and liberals alike—and miracles were expected of him. When he died suddenly during an epidemic (possibly of scarlet fever), rumors of poisoning circulated. His death is described in a famous passage in the memoirs of the duc de Saint-Simon. He was the father of King Louis XV of France and the brother of King Philip V of Spain.

Louis, Joe (Joseph Louis Barrow) (lo͞o'ĭs), 1914-, American boxer, b. Lafayette, Ala. His father, a Negro sharecropper, died when Louis was four years old, and in 1926 his stepfather took the family to Detroit, where Louis became interested in boxing. At 18 he began an amateur career in the ring. After winning (1934) the National Amateur Athletic Union light heavyweight title, Louis immediately turned professional. In an unprecedented meteoric rise in professional boxing, Louis—with magnificent physique, lightning punches, and stolid calmness—

fought his way from the ranks of beginners to become (1937) the world heavyweight champion by knocking out James J. Braddock in the eighth round at Chicago. In 1938 he knocked out Max Schmeling—who had been the only man ever to defeat Louis (by a 12-round knockout in 1936) in professional boxing—in the first round in New York City. By the time he announced his retirement from the ring in 1949, Louis, often called the "Brown Bomber" by his admirers, had defended his title a record 25 times, scoring 21 knockouts. Louis came out of retirement in 1950, lost a decision to Ezzard Charles, and was knocked out (1951) by Rocky Marciano, after which he finally retired. In 71 professional bouts Louis was defeated only three times. See his autobiography (1947).

Louis, Morris, 1912-62, American painter, b. Baltimore. Louis is noted for soaking poured paint through unsized and often unstretched canvas. Prior to 1960 he did a series of veil and floral paintings using overlapping areas of muted, transparent colors in organic patterns. After 1960, Louis worked with more precisely defined poured columns of color in a vertical or diagonal format, e.g., *Lambda* (1960-61; Emmerich Gall., New York City). See study by Michael Fried (1971).

Louis, Séraphine (säräfēn' lwē), 1894-1934, French neoprimitive painter. Louis was a shepherdess and kitchen helper who taught herself to paint. Her powerful floral paintings are fantasies of twining stems and colorful blooms, with bits of human anatomy scattered into flat, frontal designs.

Louisburg (lo͞o'ĭsbərg), town (1971 pop. 1,582), E Cape Breton Island, N.S., Canada. The town, an ice-free port, is near the site of the great fortress of Louisbourg, built (1720-40) by France as its Gibraltar in America. Plans were drawn by the great French engineer Vauban, but the work was poorly done, and the garrison was inadequately supplied and at odds with the civilian population. French privateers, using the harbor as a base, preyed on New England fishermen working the Grand Banks, until 1745, when a small force of New Englanders under William Pepperrell, supported by a fleet of merchantmen commanded by Sir Peter Warren, attacked Louisbourg and forced its surrender. Three years later it was returned to France by the Treaty of Aix-la-Chapelle, in exchange for Madras, India, but it fell (1758) to a British land and sea attack led by Gen. Jeffrey Amherst and Admiral Boscawen, which reduced it to ruins. The site is a national historic park, and reconstruction of the buildings is scheduled to be completed by 1976.

Louisburgh, Scotland: see WICK.

Louis d'Outremer: see LOUIS IV, French king.

Louise, 1776-1810, queen of Prussia, consort of FREDERICK WILLIAM III; a princess of Mecklenburg-Strelitz. During the Napoleonic Wars her patriotism and bravery won her lasting popularity. In 1807 she humiliated herself in vain at Tilsit before the French emperor, Napoleon I, begging him to lighten the peace terms for Prussia. See biography by Constance Wright (1969).

Louise, Lake, 1½ mi (2.4 km) long, alt. 5,680 ft (1,731 m), SW Alta., Canada, in the Rocky Mts., in Banff National Park. Noted for its scenic beauty, it is surrounded by high peaks, glaciers, and snow fields, which are reflected in its waters. The lake was discovered in 1882 and later was named for Princess Louise. It has become a popular year-round tourist and mountain-climbing center. The lake drains to the E into the Bow River.

Louise of Savoy, duchesse d'Angoulême (düshĕs' däNgo͞olĕm'), 1476-1531, regent of France; daughter of Duke Philip II of Savoy and mother of King FRANCIS I of France and Margaret, queen of Navarre. During Francis's absence in the Italian Wars, she acted as regent. She had much influence over Francis, and during his captivity in Spain (1525-26) she made an alliance with King Henry VIII of England, in which Henry deserted his alliance with Holy Roman Emperor Charles V, Francis's opponent in the Italian Wars. She also negotiated (1529) the so-called Ladies' Peace (see CAMBRAI, TREATY OF) with Margaret of Austria, Charles V's aunt. See her journal (in French; ed. by J. F. Michaud and J. J. F. Poujoulat, 1854); D. M. Mayer, *The Great Regent* (1966).

Louisiade Archipelago (lo͞oē"zēäd', -äd'), SW Pacific, part of Papua New Guinea. The archipelago comprises c.10 volcanic islands and numerous coral reefs. The major islands are Tagula (the largest), Rossel, Misima, and Deboyne. The inhabitants are Papuans. Bwagaoia, on Misima island, is the chief village of the group. Most of the islands had gold reserves, but mining largely ceased after World War II. The archipelago was discovered by the French navigator J. A. B. d'Entrecasteaux and was named in honor of the king of France.

Louisiana (ləwē"zēăn'ə, lo͞oē"-), state (1970 pop. 3,643,180), 48,523 sq mi (125,675 sq km), S central United States, admitted to the Union in 1812 as the 18th state. BATON ROUGE is the capital and the third largest city. The largest city is NEW ORLEANS, whose seaport is second only to New York City's as the busiest in the nation. Other major cities are SHREVEPORT, LAKE CHARLES, and LAFAYETTE. Louisiana is bounded on the N by Arkansas, on the E by Mississippi (the line is formed by the Mississippi River in the north, by the Pearl in the extreme south), on the S by the Gulf of Mexico, and on the W by Texas (the Sabine River marks most of the boundary). A low country on the Gulf coastal plain and the Mississippi alluvial plain, Louisiana rises in uplands near Arkansas only to some 535 ft (163 m). The rainy coast country contains marshes and fertile delta lands; inland are rolling pine hills and prairies. The Mississippi dominates the many waterways, but there are other rivers (e.g., the Red River, the Ouachita, the Atchafalaya, and the Calcasieu) and the coast is threaded by many slow bayous (e.g., the

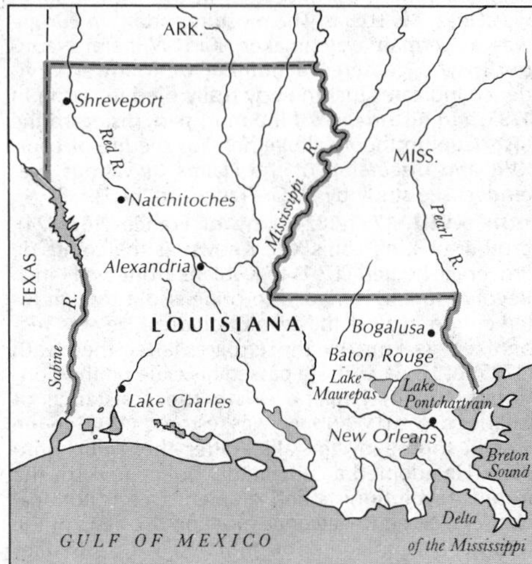

Teche, the Macon, and the Lafourche). There are lagoons such as Lake Ponchartrain; oxbow lakes made by Mississippi River cutoffs, and other lakes where the slow streams are clogged. The climate (subtropical in the south and temperate in the north), together with the rich alluvial soil, makes the state one of the nation's leading producers of sweet potatoes, rice, and sugarcane. Other major commodities are soybeans, cotton, cattle, and dairy products. Almost any North American crop can be grown in Louisiana, and strawberries, corn, hay, pecans, and truck vegetables are also produced in quantity. Fishing is a major industry; shrimp, menhaden, and oysters are principal catches. Louisiana is a leading fur-trapping state; its marshes (7,409 sq mi/19,189 sq km of the state's area is under water) supply most of the country's muskrat furs. Pelts are also obtained from mink, coypus, opossums, otter, and raccoon. The state has great mineral wealth. It leads the nation in the production of salt and sulfur, and it ranks second in the production of crude petroleum (of which many deposits are off shore), natural gas, and natural-gas liquids. Timber is plentiful; forests cover more than 50% of the land area. There is one national forest. The state is rapidly industrializing. It has giant oil refineries, petrochemical plants, metal foundries, and sawmills and paper mills. Other industries produce foods, clay, glass, and transportation equipment. Tourism brings in over $600 million revenue a year, New Orleans being the major attraction with its exciting night life and Old World charm. It is especially noted for its picturesque French quarter, which has many celebrated restaurants, and for the colorful Mardi Gras—perhaps the most famous festival in the United States—held annually since 1838. Another yearly attraction is the Sugar Bowl football game, staged on New Year's Eve. Elsewhere a variety of recreational facilities makes the state an excellent vacationland; some of its lakes (e.g., Pontchartrain) have been highly developed as resort areas, and there is superb hunting and fishing throughout much of the region. Louisiana is rich in tradition and legend. Three different groups have contributed to its unique heritage: the Creoles, descendants of the original Spanish and French colonists; the Cajuns, whose French ancestors were expelled from Nova Scotia by the British in 1755; and the American cotton planters. Today, along the rivers and bayous overhung with Spanish moss, many old mansions remain, recalling the elegance and splendor of Southern antebellum days. Plantation tours from Baton Rouge and Natchitoches are very popular, while the Cajun country in the Mississippi delta land also attracts visitors—most particularly the areas around St. Martinville. Louisiana has a long and colorful history. The region was possibly visited by Cabeza de Vaca and his fellow survivors of a Spanish expedition of 1528, and it was certainly seen by some of De Soto's men (1541-42). In 1682, La Salle reached the mouth of the Mississippi and claimed for France all of the land drained by that river and its tributaries, naming it Louisiana after Louis XIV. Europeans did not permanently settle there until 1699, when Pierre le Moyne, sieur d'Iberville, founded a settlement near Biloxi. This settlement became the seat of government for Louisiana, an enormous territory embracing the entire Mississippi drainage basin. In 1702, Iberville's brother, the sieur de Bienville, was appointed governor and moved the territorial government to Fort Louis on the Mobile River. This colony was later moved (1710) to the present site of Mobile (in what is now the state of Alabama), and Mobile became the capital of Louisiana. French missionaries and fur traders explored some of the vast territory, and Natchitoches (the oldest settlement within the present boundaries of the state of Louisiana) grew from a French military and trading post established (c.1714) to protect the Red River area from the Spanish. In order to increase the value of the colony, France granted (1712) a monopoly of commercial privileges, which in 1717 passed to a company organized by John Law. The promise of riches under Law's MISSISSIPPI SCHEME brought many settlers to Louisiana, and a large number of them remained even after his scheme had collapsed. New Orleans was founded in 1718, and in 1723 the capital was transferred there. Large numbers of Negroes were brought in as slaves, and the *Code Noir*, adopted in 1724, provided for the rigid control of their lives and the protection of the whites. Additional provisions established Catholicism as the official religion. The settlers were menaced by Indians, and in 1729 the garrison at Fort Rosalie (see NATCHEZ, Miss.) was destroyed by the Natchez Indians, who were then wiped out by the French and their Choctaw Indian allies. Indigo plantations and fur trading brought some wealth, but the colony did not prosper. The French and Indian War was ending disastrously for the French, and in order to keep the entire Louisiana territory from falling into the hands of the British, the French secretly ceded (by the Treaty of Fontainebleau in 1762) the area W of the Mississippi and the "Isle of Orleans" to Spain. By the Treaty of Paris (1763; see PARIS, TREATY OF), Great Britain gained control of all Louisiana E of the Mississippi except the "Isle of Orleans"; these changes were announced in 1764. The French colonists resisted the new Spanish rule, and Spanish control was not confirmed until after the arrival (1769) of Count Alexander O'Reilly with a strong Spanish force. Then the insurrectionist leaders were executed or imprisoned, and Spanish mercantilistic monopoly of trade was instituted. During the Spanish years agriculture flourished with the cultivation of rice and sugarcane, and New Orleans grew as a major port and trading center. The Spanish government welcomed thousands of Acadians (see ACADIA) from Nova Scotia, and they settled what came to be known as the Cajun country. During the American Revolution New Orleans was a center for Spanish aid to the colonies. After Spain declared war on Great Britain in 1779, Louisiana's governor, Bernardo de Gálvez, became an active ally of the revolutionists, capturing Baton Rouge and Natchez (1779), Mobile (1780), and Pensacola (1781). After the war Louisiana's control of the great inland trade route, the Mississippi, led to heated controversy with the Americans. Conflicts over shipping rights were partly resolved by the Pinckney Treaty (1795), in which Spain granted Americans free navigation of the river and the right to deposit goods in New Orleans. This policy was briefly reversed (1802) by a Spanish official before it became known that Napoleon I had forced the retrocession of the territory to France, as confirmed in the secret Treaty of SAN ILDEFONSO (1800). Revelation of this treaty caused profound concern in the United States. The threat posed by having Napoleon as a neighbor and the fear that the Mississippi might be closed to Western commerce under French possession led President Jefferson to attempt to purchase the "Isle of Orleans" from France. To the surprise of the American representatives in France, Napoleon decided to sell all of Louisiana to the United States (see LOUISIANA PURCHASE). Americans took possession in 1803, and in 1804 the territory was divided into two parts. That north of lat. 33°N (the present northern boundary of the state of Louisiana) was first called the District of Louisiana (1804–5), then the Territory of Louisiana (1805–12), and finally Missouri Territory. The southern part, which was called the Territory of Orleans, was admitted to the Union in 1812 as the state of Louisiana. Settlement (1819) of the WEST FLORIDA CONTROVERSY gave Louisiana the area between the Mississippi and Pearl rivers, which formerly had been part of Florida. After statehood French and Spanish influence remained, not only in the Creole and Cajun societies but also in the civil law (based on French and Spanish codes) and in the division of the state into parishes rather than counties. In the early years of the 19th cent. the people of Louisiana—the French, the Spanish, the Germans, and Isleños brought by Gálvez from the Canary Islands—resisted the American minority and American ways. However, the whole population, including the pirate and adventurer Jean Laffite, united behind Andrew Jackson to defeat (1815) the British at the Battle of New Orleans during the War of 1812. (Today the battle site is contained in Chalmette National Historical Park; see NATIONAL PARKS AND MONUMENTS, table.) With settlers pouring in from other Southern states, great sugar and cotton plantations developed rapidly in the fertile lowlands, and the less productive uplands were also settled. The state capital was moved several times: from New Orleans (1812–25), to Donaldsonville (1825–31), again to New Orleans (1831–49), and to Baton Rouge in 1849. The advent of steam propulsion on the Mississippi (the first steamboat to navigate the river arrived in New Orleans in 1812) was a boon to the state's economy; by 1840, New Orleans was the nation's second-largest port. Plantation owners, with their large landholdings and many slaves (more than half the population was Negro) dominated politics and largely controlled the state. On Jan. 26, 1861, Louisiana seceded from the Union and six weeks later joined the Confederacy. The fall of New Orleans to David G. Farragut in 1862 prefaced the detested military occupation under Gen. B. F. Butler. Grant's VICKSBURG CAMPAIGN and the fall of Port Hudson left only W Louisiana in the hands of the Confederates. It was successfully defended by Confederate Gen. Richard Taylor at SABINE CROSSROADS and remained unoccupied throughout the war; during those years Shreveport served as the Confederate state capital. Occupied Louisiana was a proving ground for Lincoln's moderate restoration program, but after Lincoln's assassination radical Republicans seized control and Louisiana suffered greatly during RECONSTRUCTION. With Texas it was organized into a military district under the rule of Gen. Philip H. Sheridan. The state was readmitted to the Union in 1868 under a constitution giving the Negro power at the expense of the former governing classes; the result was confusion, corruption, and great economic distress in the bitter years from 1868 to 1877. The KU KLUX KLAN was particularly active from 1866 to 1871. In the election of 1872 the radical Republican candidate for governor lost but was installed with the help of Federal troops. Reconstruction in Louisiana finally ended with the disputed presidential election of 1876, when Louisiana's electoral votes were "traded" to the Republicans (whose candidate was Rutherford B. Hayes) in exchange for the withdrawal of Federal troops from the state. Francis R. T. Nicholls, a Democrat, became governor of Louisiana, and white control of the state was reestablished. Economic recovery was slow. The disrupted plantation system was largely replaced by farm tenancy and sharecropping. The decline of steamboat traffic was offset somewhat by new railroad building and the opening of the Mississippi River for oceangoing vessels from New Orleans to the sea (a feat accomplished by James B. Eads). Mississippi floods constituted a serious problem, and levee building increased after the flood of 1882; it was only after the disastrous flood of 1927, however, that the Federal government undertook a vast control system. The water resources development program today encompasses flood control, navigation, drainage, and irrigation. The pattern of Louisiana economy was changed by the discovery of oil and natural gas in the early 1900s, and industries began to grow on the basis of cheap fuel and cheap labor. Medical advances helped to curb the yellow-fever epidemics that had periodically disrupted the state. Industrial growth and the continuing woes of the tenant farmers did not alter control of the state by "Bourbon" Democrats, but in 1928 a virtual revolution occurred when Huey P. Long was elected governor. His almost dictatorial rule, detested by liberals across the nation, brought material progress at the cost of widespread official corruption. Long withstood all outside pressures, including the opposition of President F. D. Roosevelt's administration. After his assassination in 1935 (he had resigned the governorship in 1931 to become a U.S. Senator but had retained control over the state), his political heirs made their peace with the New Deal, and Federal funds, withheld during Long's last years, were poured into the state. In 1948, Huey's brother, Earl Long, invoking the memory of his dead brother (still regarded by many as a savior and a martyr), gained the governorship, and Huey's son Russell was elected to the U.S. Senate. In 1956, Earl Long was again elected governor, and his second term was marked by scandal and controversy. Louisiana, almost solidly Democratic in its state politics since 1877 and traditionally Democratic nationally, bolted in the presidential elections in 1948 (to the States Rights party candidate, J. Strom Thurmond), 1956 (to the Republican, Dwight D. Eisenhower), 1964 (to the Republican, Barry Goldwater), 1968 (to the independent candidate, George Wallace), and 1972 (to the Republican, Richard M. Nixon). The state has a large black population, and the issue of black rights has long been a bitter one. The process of racial INTEGRATION following the 1954 Supreme Court ruling against racial segregation in the public schools has been difficult. Despite much public furor, integration is continuing, with considerable progress in recent years. In 1965, Louisiana suffered one of the worst natural disasters in its history when it was struck by Hurricane Betsy; many lives were lost and property damage exceeded $1 billion. In April, 1973, the Mississippi River rose to its highest level recorded in Louisiana. Its floodwaters, together with those from its tributaries and distributaries, covered more than 10% of the state and caused millions of dollars of damage to crops and property; New Orleans was saved from inundation by the opening of spillways that diverted much of the river's flow away from the city. The state has had 11 constitutions since it was admitted to the Union in 1812. Its present constitution (effective Jan., 1975) replaced the constitution of 1921, which had been amended more than 500 times. The state's executive branch is headed by a governor elected for a four-year term and permitted one reelection. Louisiana's bicameral legislature has a senate with 39 members and a house of representatives with 105 members, all elected for four-year terms. Louisiana is the only state to call its counties parishes, a holdover from the Spanish religious divisions. The state elects 2 Senators and 8 Representatives to the U.S. Congress and has 10 electoral votes. Edwin W. Edwards was elected governor in 1972 to succeed John J. McKeithen, who had completed two full terms. All of Louisiana's governors have been Democratic since 1877. Among the state's more prominent institutions of higher learning are Tulane Univ., Dillard Univ., and Loyola Univ., all at New Orleans; Louisiana State Univ. and Agricultural and Mechanical College, mainly at Baton Rouge; and Louisiana Tech Univ., at Ruston. Louisiana's distinctive life and customs have been portrayed in the works of George W. Cable, Lafcadio Hearn, C. E. A. Gayarré, and Grace King. See also Federal Writers' Project, *Louisiana: a Guide to the State* (1941); E. A. Davis, *Louisiana* (1959) and *The Story of Louisiana* (1960); J. D. Winters, *The Civil War in Louisiana* (1963); H. Carter, *Doomed Road of the Empire* (1963); F. Gaillardet, *Sketches of Early Texas and Louisiana* (1966); C. L. Dufour, *Ten Flags in the Wind* (1967); S. H. Lockett, *Louisiana As It Is* (1969).

Louisiana Purchase, 1803, acquisition from France of the formerly Spanish region of Louisiana. The revelation in 1801 of the secret agreement of 1800, whereby Spain retroceded Louisiana to France, aroused uneasiness in the United States both because Napoleonic France was an aggressive power and because Western settlers depended on the Mississippi River for commerce. In a letter to the American minister to France, Robert R. Livingston (1746–1813; see LIVINGSTON, family), President Jefferson stated that "The day that France takes possession of New Orleans . . . we must marry ourselves to the British fleet and nation." Late in 1802 the right of deposit at New Orleans, granted to Americans by the Pinckney treaty of 1795, was withdrawn by the Spanish intendant (Louisiana was still under Spanish control). Although Spain soon restored the right of deposit, the acquisition of New Orleans became of paramount national interest. Jefferson instructed Livingston to attempt to purchase the "Isle of Orleans" (i.e., New Orleans) and West Florida from France. He appointed James MONROE minister

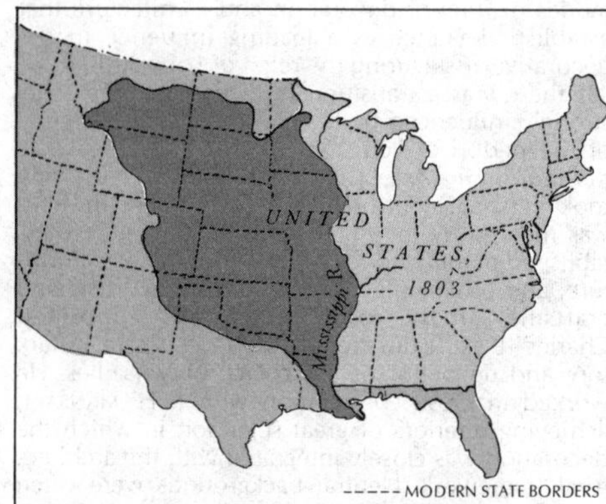

Louisiana Purchase (1803)

extraordinary and plenipotentiary to serve with Livingston. Congress granted the envoys $2 million to secure their object. The international situation favored the American diplomats. Louisiana was of diminishing importance to France. The costly Negro revolt in Haiti forced the French emperor Napoleon I to reconsider his plan to make Hispaniola the keystone of his colonial empire, and impending war with Great Britain made him question the feasibility of holding Louisiana against that great naval power. He decided to sell Louisiana to the United States. On April 11, 1803, the French foreign minister Charles Maurice de Talleyrand opened negotiations by asking the surprised Livingston what the United States would give for all of Louisiana. Bargaining began in earnest the next day, on Monroe's arrival in Paris. On April 29, the U.S. envoys agreed to pay a total of $15 million to France; about $3,750,000 of this sum covered claims of U.S. citizens against France, which the U.S. government agreed to discharge. The treaty, dated April 30, 1803, was signed several days later. Jefferson's scruples about the constitutionality of the purchase were overcome by his fears that Napoleon might change his mind (as intimated in reports from Livingston) and by the overwhelming public approval of the Louisiana Purchase (although there was some objection from Federalists, especially in New England). The treaty was ratified by the U.S. Senate in October, and the U.S. flag was raised over New Orleans on Dec. 20. The Louisiana Purchase, extending from the Mississippi River to the Rocky Mts. and from the Gulf of Mexico to British North America, doubled the national domain, increasing it c.828,000 sq mi (c.2,144,500 sq km). The final boundaries of the territory were not settled for many years (see WEST FLORIDA CONTROVERSY), since the 1803 treaty did not set the limits of the region. See J. K. Hosmer, *The History of the Louisiana Purchase* (1902); J. A. Robertson, *Louisiana under the Rule of Spain, France, and the United States, 1785–1807* (2 vol., 1910–11, repr. 1969); E. S. Brown, *The Constitutional History of the Louisiana Purchase* (1920, repr. 1972), A. P. Whitaker, *The Mississippi Question, 1795–1803* (1934, repr. 1962).

Louisiana State University and Agricultural and Mechanical College, mainly at Baton Rouge; land-grant and state supported; coeducational; chartered 1853, opened as a state seminary 1860 near Alexandria (with W. T. Sherman as president), moved 1869. It became a university in 1870 and merged with the Agricultural and Mechanical College 1877. Its medical and nursing schools and an undergraduate division are at New Orleans. The Audubon Sugar School is at Baton Rouge, and the university also has branches at Alexandria, Eunice, and Shreveport.

Louisiana Tech University, at Ruston; coeducational; state supported; chartered 1894, opened 1895 as an industrial institute. The name was formerly Louisiana Polytechnic Institute.

Louis le Hutin: see LOUIS X, king of France.

Louis Napoleon: see NAPOLEON III.

Louis of Baden (bä'dən), 1655–1707, margrave of Baden (1677–1707), military commander in the service of the Holy Roman Empire. In 1689 he was made chief commander of the imperial army in Hungary, where he scored (1691) a resounding victory against the Turks at Slankamen. Shortly afterward he was sent to head the army of the Rhine in the War of the GRAND ALLIANCE (1688–97). He later fought in the War of the SPANISH SUCCESSION (1701–14), but gave up his commands after being forced to retreat; he died a few months later.

Louis period styles, 1610–1793, succession of modes of interior decoration and architecture that established France as a leading influence in the decorative arts. During the reign of Louis XIII (1610–43) there was a transition from the baroque style, strongly influenced by Italy, to the classical dignity of the period of Louis XIV (1643–1715). The Louis XIV [*Louis Quatorze*] style, established after the king took personal control of the government in 1661, was molded by the chief minister, Colbert. He established manufactories of tapestries, textiles, furniture, and ornaments; assembled leading artists and craftsmen in the royal service; and appointed Charles LE BRUN director of the GOBELINS manufactory and decorator of the palace of Versailles. He worked in close cooperation with J. H. MANSART, achieving interiors of great splendor, in which the decoration was closely integrated with the architectural framework. Neutral backgrounds were often used to emphasize the strong, rich colors of Gobelin, Aubusson, and Beauvais tapestries, Savonnerie and Oriental rugs, velvet or brocade upholstery, hangings, and large paintings on walls and ceilings. Such ornaments as scrolls, acanthus leaves, caryatids, busts, and full figures with festoons of flowers and fruit were employed. Large mirrors decorated the walls. Furniture scaled to the huge proportions of the rooms was made of ebony or covered with silver, gilt, or lacquer and decorated with carving and with marquetry in the manner of A. C. BOULLE. In contrast to the heavy, massive members and curves used in the period of Louis XIV, the RÉGENCE STYLE, established during the regency of Philippe II, duc d'Orléans (1715–23), began to employ delicate lines and intricate curves. Finely sculptured bronze reliefs became the outstanding mode of furniture decoration under the leadership of the cabinetmaker Charles CRESSENT. The Louis XV [*Louis Quinze*] (1723–74) style was characterized by free curves and the use of ROCOCO ornament and CHINOISERIE. Rooms were smaller, specialized, and arranged for convenient use. Colors were delicate. Tinted wood, veneer, lacquer panels, marquetry, mounts by CAFFIERI and Pierre GOUTHIÈRE, and porcelain plaques of SÈVRES WARE distinguish the designs. The style in its later phase was more restrained and presaged the strong reaction of the Louis XVI [*Louis Seize*] (1774–93) period, during which simplicity replaced excess and the CLASSIC REVIVAL influenced decorative motifs and brought a return to straight lines and symmetry. Slenderness of proportion was emphasized in furniture. Colors were light in tone; ornament delicate and in low relief, embossed, or painted. Furniture details included slender fluted legs, convex moldings, and rosette, leaf, and flower motifs in the carved frames often painted white and touched with gilt. Upholstery and hangings used varied fabrics. The Revolution abolished the guilds, which had maintained high standards of craftsmanship, and weakened the practice, instituted under Louis XIV, of cooperation between artists and masters of the various crafts in producing fine furniture and decorative accessories. See Seymour de Ricci, *Louis XIV and Regency Furniture and Decoration* (1929); Geneviève Souchal, *French Eighteenth-Century Furniture* (tr. 1961); Jacqueline Viaux, *French Furniture* (tr. 1964).

Louis Philippe (lwē fēlēp'), 1773–1850, king of the French (1830–48), known before his accession as Louis Philippe, duc d'Orléans. The son of Philippe Égalité (see ORLÉANS, LOUIS PHILIPPE JOSEPH, DUC D'), he joined the army of the French Revolution, but deserted (1793) with Gen. Charles François DUMOURIEZ. Although in exile for the next 20 years, he did not collaborate with France's enemies. Reconciled with the BOURBONS, he returned to France after their restoration and soon recovered his huge fortune. He figured in the liberal opposition to kings LOUIS XVIII and CHARLES X and was supported by the discontented upper bourgeoisie and by the liberal journalists. In the JULY REVOLUTION of 1830, Louis Philippe was made lieutenant general of the realm and, with the support of the marquis de LAFAYETTE, was chosen "king of the French." His reign, known as the July Monarchy, marked the triumph of the wealthy bourgeoisie. Although the constitutional charter of 1814 was revised (1830) in a liberal direction, the new legislature was unresponsive to the economic needs and political desires of the lower classes. In the early years of his reign, Louis Philippe's basically conservative outlook was strengthened by a number of workers' outbreaks and by several attempts on his life, notably that of Giuseppe FIESCHI (1835). Although the king was a constitutional monarch, he gained considerable personal power by splitting the liberal movement and appointing weak ministers, such as Louis MOLÉ. Eventually a conservative ministry, dominated (1840–48) by François GUIZOT, who had the king's confidence, came to power. In foreign policy, Louis Philippe promoted Anglo-French friendship and supported colonial expansion; Algeria was conquered in his reign. He cooperated with England in support (1831) of Belgian independence and in the QUADRUPLE ALLIANCE of 1834. The Franco-British rapprochement was ended (1846), however, by the Spanish marriages (see ISABELLA II), which violated a previous Franco-British agreement. In France, Louis Philippe became increasingly unpopular. On the right he was opposed by the legitimists (who supported the senior Bourbon line) and by the Bonapartists. The leftist elements organized numerous secret revolutionary societies. The opposition to the government undertook (1847–48) a banquet campaign to propagate the demand for electoral reform. The campaign led to the FEBRUARY REVOLUTION of 1848. Louis Philippe abdicated in favor of his grandson (see ORLÉANS, family), but a republic was set up. The king fled to England, where he died. Louis Philippe was known as the "citizen king" because of his bourgeois manner and dress, and he and his regime were satirized by Honoré DAUMIER. See Jean Lucas-Dubreton, *The Restoration and the July Monarchy* (tr. 1929); biographies by J. S. C. Abbott (1902), Catherine Gavin (1933), Agnes de Stoeckl (1958), T. E. Howarth (1961), and P. H. Beik (1965).

Louis the Bavarian: see LOUIS IV, Holy Roman emperor.

Louis the Child, 893–911, German king (900–911), son and successor of King Arnulf. He was the last of the German line of the Carolingians. The archbishop of Mainz was regent for him. During his reign the Magyars began devastating raids into Bavaria, Saxony, and Thuringia; these invasions together with internal weakness brought on a revival of autonomous ducal power. Louis was succeeded by Conrad I.

Louis the German, c.804–876, king of the East Franks (817–76). When his father, Emperor of the West LOUIS I, partitioned the empire in 817, Louis received Bavaria and adjacent territories. In the conflict between his brother LOTHAIR I (who succeeded Louis I as emperor) and their father, Louis the German repeatedly changed sides. In 839 Louis I transferred some of Louis's holdings to Lothair; Louis again rebelled and his father died in the ensuing campaign. Louis now joined with his half brother Charles (Charles the Bald, later Emperor of the West CHARLES II) against Lothair, who sought to gain supremacy in their kingdoms. They checked Lothair at FONTENOY (841), renewed their alliance (842; see STRASBOURG, OATH OF), and forced Lothair to accept the Treaty of Verdun (843; see VERDUN, TREATY OF), which made them independent sovereigns. In 858–59 Louis turned on Charles and unsuccessfully invaded the West Frankish kingdom (France), but both brothers soon directed their attention to the lands of Lothair's heirs, Emperor of the West LOUIS II and King LOTHAIR of Lotharingia. After King Lothair's death LOTHARINGIA was divided between them by the Treaty of MERSEN (870). The death (875) of Louis II renewed the war between Louis the German and Charles; Charles quickly conquered Italy and was crowned emperor of the West. Louis the German, in the course of his reign, defended his frontiers against the Slavs and the Danes and suppressed several revolts of his sons, CARLOMAN of Bavaria, LOUIS THE YOUNGER, and Charles the Fat (later Emperor of the West CHARLES III).

Louis the Great: see LOUIS I, king of Hungary.

Louis the Pious: see LOUIS I, emperor of the West.

Louis the Stammerer: see LOUIS II, French king.

Louis the Younger, c.830–882, German king, ruler (876–82) over Saxony, Franconia, and Thuringia, son of LOUIS THE GERMAN. He shared the succession to his father's lands with his brothers CARLOMAN (d. 880) and Charles the Fat (later Emperor of the West CHARLES III). In 876 at Andernach, Louis the Younger defeated his uncle, Emperor of the West CHARLES II (Charles the Bald), who had claimed a portion of Louis's share of Lotharingia. Louis attempted twice (879, 880) to win France from the grandsons of Charles II, Louis III and Carloman, but instead settled for the cession of the remainder of Lotharingia. At his death Germany was reunited under Charles III.

Louisville (lo͞o'ēvĭl), city (1970 pop. 361,958), seat of Jefferson co., NW Ky., at the Falls of the Ohio; inc. 1780. It is the largest city in Kentucky, a port of entry, and one of the most important industrial, financial, marketing, and shipping centers in the South. The city has some of the nation's largest whiskey distilleries and cigarette factories. There are also railroad shops, sawmills, meat-packing houses, glassworks, chemical plants, and a wide variety of other industries. A settlement grew after George Rogers Clark built (1778) a fort as a base of operations against the British and the Indians. The city was chartered by the Virginia legislature in 1780 and named for Louis XVI of France. Louisville developed as a portage place around the falls (until a canal was built in 1830) and as a river port and major commercial center. After the arrival of the railroads in the mid-19th cent., its shipping became even more important; both the southern and midwestern rail lines terminated there. During the Civil War it was a center of pro-Union activity in the state and a military and supply base for Federal forces. The Univ. of Louisville (est. 1798), Bellarmine College, Spalding College, Louisville Presbyterian Theological Seminary, Southern Baptist Theological Seminary, and a junior college are there. Churchill Downs, a noted racetrack and scene of the famous annual Kentucky Derby (first held in 1875), is in Louisville. The city has a fine park system and is the site of the state fairgrounds. Among the many points of interest are the American Printing House for the Blind; the J. B. Speed Art Museum; a railway museum; "Farmington" (built 1810); the Filson Club, with a historical library and museum; the Jefferson County Courthouse (1850); and old Cave Hill Cemetery, where George Rogers Clark is buried. Nearby is "Locust Grove," the last home (1809–18) of Clark, and the Zachary Taylor National Cemetery, where Taylor is buried. Fort Knox is in the area. See I. M. McMeekin, *Louisville: the Gateway City* (1946); Caroline Williams, *Louisville Scenes* (1970).

Louisville, University of, at Louisville, Ky.; coeducational; founded 1798 as a seminary, became a college and merged in 1837 with the Medical Institute of the City of Louisville (chartered 1833). In 1846 it was reorganized and chartered as the University of Louisville. Of note are its schools of social work and medicine and the Speed Scientific School (of engineering).

Lourdes (lo͝ord), town (1968 pop. 18,310), Hautes-Pyrénées dept., SW France, at the foot of the Pyrenees. It is famous for its Roman Catholic shrine where Our Lady of Lourdes (Feast: Feb. 11) is believed to have repeatedly appeared (1858) to St. BERNADETTE. Millions of people make the pilgrimage to Lourdes each year, drawn by their faith in the miraculous cures attributed to the waters of the shrine.

Lourenço Marques (lôrĕn'sō mär'kĕs, Port. lōrān'tsō mär'kĭsh), city (1972 est. pop. 230,000), capital of Mozambique, a port on the Indian Ocean. It is Mozambique's largest city and its administrative, communications, and commercial center. The economy is dominated by the modern port, on Delagoa Bay; coal, cotton, sugar, chrome, ore, sisal, copra, and hardwood are the chief exports. The city's main manufactures are food products, beverages, cement, pottery, furniture, shoes, and rubber. People of Indo-Pakistani background play an important role in retail trade. Tourists from South Africa and Rhodesia frequent the city and its excellent beaches. Lourenço Marques is linked by rail with South Africa, Swaziland, and Rhodesia and by an all-weather road with Johannesburg, South Africa. Founded in the late 18th cent., the city is named for the Portuguese trader who first explored the area in 1544. Its main growth dates from 1895, when a railroad to Pretoria, South Africa, was completed. In 1907, Lourenço Marques became the capital of Mozambique. The Univ. of Mozambique (1962) is in the city, which also has a museum on Mozambique's history, a military museum, and the Roman Catholic Cathedral of Our Lady of Fatima.

louse, common name for members of either of two distinct orders of wingless, parasitic, disease-carrying INSECTS. Lice of both groups are small and flattened with short legs adapted for clinging to the host. The sucking lice, of the order Anoplura, are external parasites of man and other mammals, feeding on blood by means of their piercing-and-sucking mouthparts. The group includes the body lice and head lice, considered varieties of the same species, *Pediculus humanus*, and the crab, or groin, louse, *Phthirus pubis*, named for its crablike appearance. A female sucking louse lays about 300 eggs in her lifetime, cementing them to body hairs and underclothing. The larva resembles the adult; the life cycle takes about 16 days. Sucking lice infestations are common in crowded living conditions and where clothing is not changed or washed frequently. Body lice may transmit rickettsial diseases (see RICKETTSIA) and bacterial infections such as relapsing fever; infection results from scratching the crushed louse or its feces into the skin. The biting lice, of the order Mallophaga, have chewing mouthparts and feed on hair, skin, or feather fragments of the host. They attack birds, rodents, and domesticated animals. Although they do not actually puncture the skin, and thus are scavengers and not true parasites, they often multiply so rapidly that they irritate, weaken, and may even kill the host. The chicken louse, *Menopon pallidum,* if left uncontrolled, can be a major problem in poultry production. Biting lice may produce 6 to 12 generations annually. The eggs, sometimes called nits, hatch into rapidly developing young in which METAMORPHOSIS is incomplete, as in many parasites. The book louse is a tiny, wingless, cosmopolitan insect which damages books by feeding on glue, paste, and paper. The APHID is sometimes called plant louse. Lice are classified in the phylum ARTHROPODA, class Insecta, orders Anoplura and Mallophaga. See bulletins of the U.S. Dept. of Agriculture.

Louth (louth, louth), county (1971 pop. 74,899), 317 sq mi (821 sq km), NE Republic of Ireland. The county town is DUNDALK. Smallest of the Irish counties, it borders on the Irish Sea from the mouth of the Boyne River to Carlingford Lough. The terrain is an undulating plain except for a hilly district in the north. Principal rivers are the Fane, the Glyde, and the Dee. Nonagricultural enterprises are the chief employers. Among the industries are cotton and linen manufacturing, brewing, and food processing. Dundalk, DROGHEDA, and Greenore are ports. The region is associated with the exploits of the legendary Irish hero Cuchulain.

Louth (louth), municipal borough (1971 pop. 11,746), in the Parts of Lindsey, Lincolnshire, E England, on the Lud River. Although a canal was built to the Humber estuary in the 18th cent., Louth is no longer an important river port. The town's industries include trading and processing of farm produce and the manufacture of agricultural implements, malt, and lime. Tennyson was a pupil at the 13th-century grammar school (rebuilt 1869). There are ruins of a Cistercian abbey founded in 1139; for centuries Louth was an important religious center. The parish church of St. James, noted for its spire, dates from the early 16th cent. The first protests of the PILGRIMAGE OF GRACE took place in Louth in 1536.

Louvain (lo͞ovăN'), Flemish *Leuven,* city (1970 pop. 30,623), Brabant prov., central Belgium, on the Dijle River. It is a commercial, industrial, and cultural center and a rail junction. Mentioned in the 9th cent., Louvain was a center of the wool trade and of the cloth industry in the Middle Ages. It was for a time the capital of the duchy of BRABANT, and in 1356 the *Joyeuse Entrée,* a charter of liberties, was granted there. In the 14th cent. there was also much strife between the nobles and the weavers, and after the nobles gained sway (1383) most of the weavers emigrated to Holland and England, and the city declined. In 1426, Duke John IV of Brabant founded a famous Roman Catholic university there. The excellent university library was destroyed by the Germans in World Wars I and II, but was rebuilt after each. In 1968, as a result of a long-standing dispute between Flemish and French-speaking sectors, the university was divided into two autonomous units. The Flemish-speaking Universitiet de Leuven remained in Louvain, and the French-speaking Université Catholique de Louvain was established at Ottignies. Among the noted buildings of Louvain are the magnificent Gothic city hall (15th cent.; damaged in both world wars); the 14th-century Cloth Workers' Hall, and several medieval churches.

L'Ouverture, Toussaint: see TOUSSAINT L'OUVERTURE, FRANÇOIS DOMINIQUE.

Louvière, La (lă lo͞ovyâr'), town (1970 pop. 23,310), Hainaut prov., S Belgium. It is an industrial center of the Bassin du Centre coal-mining region. Manufactures include steel and machinery.

Louvois, François Michel Le Tellier, marquis de (frăNswä' mēshĕl' lə tĕlyā' märkē' də lo͞ovwä'), 1641–91, French statesman, minister during the reign of King Louis XIV. After 1654 he was associated in office with his father, Michel LE TELLIER, and from 1666 he functioned as war minister, officially replacing his father in 1677. His father shared in the reforms credited to Louvois. Among these reforms were the creation of an efficient provisioning system, the introduction of the bayonet and the flintlock rifle, the close coordination of the artillery and the corps of engineers with the infantry, the creation of grades to which officers might be promoted without purchasing their commissions, and the establishment of a fixed rate of pay. By these measures the French army became the most powerful military force in Europe. After the death of Jean Baptiste COLBERT (1683), Louvois became the most influential of Louis's ministers. He supported the revocation of the Edict of Nantes (see NANTES, EDICT OF) and was largely responsible for the brutal enforcement of that measure. Louvois also was instrumental in the shaping of Louis's aggressive policies. The devastation of the Palatinate (1689) by the French army under his orders during the War of the Grand Alliance earned him condemnation throughout Europe.

Louvre (lo͞o'vrə), foremost French museum of art, located in Paris. The building was a royal fortress and palace built by Philip II in the late 12th cent. In 1546 Pierre Lescot was commissioned by Francis I to erect a new building on the site of the Louvre. During his reign, several paintings by Leonardo, including the *Mona Lisa,* and works of other Italian masters came into the royal collections. In 1564, Catherine de' Medici commissioned Philibert Delorme to build a residence at the Tuileries and to connect it to the Louvre by a long gallery. The Grande Galerie was completed in 1606 under Henri IV. While Cardinal Richelieu collected art with state funds, work was continued on the buildings under Louis XIII. Lescot's architectural designs were expanded by Lemercier in 1624, and under Louis XIV the magnificent colonnade was brought to completion (1670) by Louis Le Vau and Claude Perrault. In 1750 part of the royal collections was put on view in the Luxembourg palace. In 1793 the Musée Central des Arts was created by decree and the Grande Galerie of the Louvre was officially opened. For many years the area beneath the Grande Galerie served as artists' studios and workshops. Napoleon I by his conquests added vastly to its collections and in 1803 the museum was proclaimed the Musée Napoléon, but many famous works were returned after his downfall. The grand architectural scheme of the Louvre was completed by Napoleon III. The museum is famous for its enormous collection of Greek, Roman, and Egyptian antiquities, and for its superb old masters, a collection especially rich in works by Rembrandt, Rubens, Titian, and Leonardo. Its most famous sculptures include the *Nike,* or *Victory, of Samothrace* and the *Venus of Milo.* Outstanding works of the impressionist school are exhibited in a separate building at the other end of the Tuileries garden and park, the Jeu de Paume. Special exhibits are frequently housed in the Orangerie, near the Jeu de Paume. A part of the museum building houses the Museum of Decorative Arts, a private institution. See René Huyghe, ed., *Art Treasures of the Louvre* (1960); G. D. Regoli et al., *Louvre, Paris* (1968); Pierre Schneider, *Louvre Dialogues* (tr. 1971).

Louÿs, Pierre (pyĕr lo͞oē'), 1870–1925, French writer of the Parnassian school, whose real name was Pierre Louis. His early poems, collected as *Astarté* (1891), first appeared in the *Conque,* a review that he helped to found. *Aphrodite* (1896), the novel that made him famous, was made into an opera in 1906. *Chansons de Bilitis* (1894) are lyrics in the manner of Sappho.

lovage, tall perennial herb (*Levisticum officinale*) of the family Umbelliferae (CARROT family), native to the mountains of S Europe and cultivated elsewhere. Its aromatic fruits are used in soups and as a flavoring for confectionery and for some liqueurs. An aromatic oil extracted from the roots is used medicinally and also for flavoring. The edible leaves are usually used like celery. Lovage is classified in the division MAGNOLIOPHYTA, class Magnoliopsida, order Umbellales, family Umbelliferae.

Lovat, Simon Fraser, 11th **Baron** (lŭv'ət), 1675?–1747, Scottish nobleman and Jacobite conspirator. The nephew of the 9th baron, he and his father contested the passing of the title to his cousin Amelia. In an attempt to assert his claim he eloped with Amelia, but she returned to her mother. He then abducted her mother, widow of the 9th baron, and forced her to marry him, for which he was outlawed in 1701. He returned to Scotland in 1703 to join James Douglas, 2d duke of QUEENSBERRY, in plotting against John MURRAY, 2d marquess and later 1st duke of Atholl, brother of the aunt he had abducted. When the plot failed he fled abroad and was imprisoned by the exiled Jacobites for betraying them to the English in an attempt to regain his estates. Returning to Scotland in 1714, he again betrayed the Jacobites in the uprising of 1715 by siding with the Hanoverians at the last minute. He thus won a pardon. In 1730 he successfully contested his cousin's claim to the peerage and was decreed Baron Lovat. In the Jacobite rising of 1745, however, having posed as loyal to the crown, he sent his son and clan to fight for the Pretender. He was captured in hiding, tried by impeachment before the House of Lords, and convicted. He was the last British peer to be executed for high treason. See biography by Moray McLaren (1957); study by G. W. Keeton (1959).

Love, Alfred Henry, 1830–1913, American pacifist, b. Philadelphia. Love, a Quaker, remained firm in his principles at the outbreak of the Civil War, refusing even to hire a substitute when he was drafted; he set forth his position in *An Appeal in Vindication of Peace Principles* (1862). With others he formed the Universal Peace Union and until his death remained the leader of this body and editor of its publications and periodical. He urged outlawing war, the negotiation of treaties of arbitration, the establishment of an international court, and arbitration in industrial disputes.

love-apple: see TOMATO.

love bird: see PARROT.

love-in-a-mist, hardy annual garden plant (*Nigella damascena*) of the family Ranunculaceae (BUTTERCUP family), having finely cut foliage and blue or white flowers surrounded by a cluster of thready bracts. It is also called fennel-flower—as are other plants of the genus—and devil-in-the-bush. The seeds have been used medicinally. Seeds of another species (*N. sativa*) are called black cumin and have been used in the Old World for seasoning; they are thought to be the fitch of the Bible (Isa. 28.25, 27). True cumin and true fennel are unrelated plants of the carrot family. Love-in-a-mist is classified in the division MAGNOLIOPHYTA, class Magnoliopsida, order Ranunculales, family Ranunculaceae.

Lovejoy, Arthur Oncken, 1873–1962, American philosopher and intellectual historian, b. Germany, grad. Univ. of California, 1895, M.A. Harvard, 1897. He also studied at the Sorbonne before he began teaching (1899–1910) at Stanford, Washington Univ., Columbia, and Univ. of Missouri. From 1910 to 1938 he taught at Johns Hopkins. The founder and first editor of the *Journal of the History of Ideas,* Lovejoy was the chief promoter in the United States of the historiography of ideas. He made a distinction between the history of a philosophical system and the history of an idea—which may be shared by different systems and unlike the system may originate in or influence areas far removed from philosophy. His work argued for and encouraged an interdisciplinary approach in the study of philosophy, history, literature, and science. His major philosophical work was *The Revolt Against Dualism* (1930); *The Great Chain of Being* (1936) was his most influential publication on the history of ideas. His other books included *Essays in the History of Ideas* (1948), *Reflections on Human Nature* (1961), and *The Reason, the Understanding, and the Time* (1961).

Lovejoy, Elijah Parish, 1802–37, American abolitionist, b. Albion, Maine, grad. Waterville (now Colby) College, 1826, and later studied theology at Princeton. In 1833 he became editor of the *Observer,* a Presbyterian weekly in St. Louis. His antislavery views (he advocated gradual emancipation) became extremely unpopular, and in 1836 he moved to Alton, Ill. There he advocated immediate abolition in his Alton *Observer.* Mobs destroyed three of his presses, and on Nov. 7, 1837, while guarding another new press, he was killed. Lovejoy's martyrdom helped advance the cause of the ABOLITIONISTS. See biographies by John Gill (1958), M. L. Dillon (1961), and Paul Simon (1964).

Lovejoy, Owen, 1811–64, American abolitionist, b. Albion, Maine, educated at Bowdoin College. He witnessed the killing of his brother Elijah P. Lovejoy, under whom he had studied for the ministry. Taking up Elijah's cause, he became the recognized leader of Illinois abolitionists, persuading them to accept the more conservative leadership of Lincoln and become a part of the Republican strength. For many years pastor of the Congregational Church at Princeton, Ill., he also served in Congress from 1857 until his death. See study by Edward Magdol (1967).

Lovelace, Richard, 1618–1657?, one of the English CAVALIER POETS. He was the son of a Kentish knight and was educated at Oxford. In 1642 he was briefly imprisoned for having presented to Parliament a petition for the restoration of the bishops. An ardent royalist, he served with the French army during the English civil war. On his return to England in 1648, he was imprisoned by the Commonwealth. His royalist sympathies lost him his entire fortune, and he died in extreme poverty. He is remembered almost solely for two extremely graceful, melodic, and much-quoted lyrics, "To Althea, from Prison" and "To Lucasta, Going to the Wars." The first volume of his poems, *Lucasta: Epodes, Odes, Sonnets, Songs, &c.,* appeared in 1649; the companion volume, *Lucasta: Posthume Poems,* in 1660. See edition of his poems ed. by C. H. Wilkinson (1930); biography by Manfred Weidhorn (1970).

Loveland, city (1970 pop. 16,220), Larimer co., N Colo.; inc. 1881. It is a food-processing center in a fertile farm area irrigated by the Colorado-Big Thompson project, as well as a growing industrial hub.

Lover, Samuel, 1797-1868, Irish painter, novelist and song writer. Before turning to literature, Lover was a painter, and in 1828 he became a member of the Royal Hibernian Academy of Art. However, he is best known for his ballad *Rory O'More* (1836), which he expanded into a novel and a play (both appeared in 1837), and for *Handy Andy* (1842), a farcical novel of Irish life. His other works include *Legends and Stories of Ireland* (1831), which he illustrated, and *Songs and Ballads* (1839).

Loves Park (lŭvz), city (1970 pop. 12,390), Winnebago co., N Ill., on the Rock River; inc. 1947. It is chiefly residential.

Lovestone, Jay, 1898-, American labor official, b. Russia, grad. College of the City of New York, 1918. Lovestone joined the left wing of the Socialist party in 1916 and participated in the formation (1919) of the COMMUNIST PARTY of America. He was a member (1919-23) of the central committee of that party and in 1923 became director of research of the Workers (Communist) party. Lovestone was associated with the faction of Nikolai Ivanovich Bukharin in the Communist International, and, when Joseph Stalin consolidated his control of the Communist movement in 1929, Lovestone and his followers were expelled from the party. During the 1930s Lovestone led a small left-wing anti-Stalinist group. Subsequently he became a trade-union official and was an adviser to the AFL-CIO on anti-Communist matters.

Low, Sir David (lō), 1891-1963, British cartoonist, b. New Zealand. In 1919 Low went to England, where he worked on the London *Star* (1919-27). Thereafter he successively joined the staff of the *Evening Standard* (1927-50), the *Daily Herald* (1950-53), and finally the Manchester *Guardian* (from 1953). At the *Standard* he became noted for his sharp and perceptive caricatures and cartoons on national and international affairs. He created "Colonel Blimp," a caricature of the pompous British ultraconservative. Low's cartoons have been collected in *A Cartoon History of Our Times* (1939), *Low on the War* (1941), *Years of Wrath* (1946), which covers the period from 1931 to 1945, and *The Fearful Fifties* (1960). See his autobiography (1956).

Low, Seth, 1850-1916, American political reformer and college president, b. Brooklyn, N.Y., grad. Columbia, 1870. He entered his father's tea and silk importing firm, but became interested in politics and was reform mayor of the city of Brooklyn for two terms (1882-86). His support of Grover Cleveland in 1884 angered his fellow Republicans and cost Low a third term. As president of Columbia (1889-1901) he reorganized the existing schools, added to their number, increased affiliations with other institutions, supervised the removal of the university to Morningside Heights (1897), and gave it a library building in memory of his father. In 1901 he was elected mayor of Greater New York City (including the present five boroughs) as Fusion candidate against Tammany, then under Richard CROKER. He reformed the police and education departments, reorganized the city finances, compelled the electrification of the New York Central RR within the city, and attacked the continued existence of unsanitary tenements. He was not reelected. Low was a delegate to the First Hague Conference. See biographies by his nephew Benjamin R. C. Low (1925, repr. 1971) and Gerald Kurland (1971).

Low Archipelago: see TUAMOTU ISLANDS.

Low Church: see ENGLAND, CHURCH OF.

Low Countries, region of NW Europe comprising the NETHERLANDS, BELGIUM, and the grand duchy of LUXEMBOURG. The northern parts of the Netherlands and Belgium form a low plain bordering on the North Sea, but S Belgium and Luxembourg are part of the Ardennes plateau. The name Low Countries thus is a political and historic rather than a strictly geographic concept. One of the wealthiest areas of medieval and modern Europe, it also has been chronically a theater of war. For the history of the Low Countries, see articles on the individual countries and on their provinces (e.g., FLANDERS; BRABANT, DUCHY OF; HOLLAND). See also NETHERLANDS, AUSTRIAN AND SPANISH.

Lowden, Frank Orren, 1861-1943, American political leader, b. Chisago co., Minn. He practiced law in Chicago after 1887 and gained extensive agricultural holdings in Illinois. A leading member of the Republican party from 1900, Lowden served in the U.S. House of Representatives (1906-11) and as governor of Illinois (1917-21). He gained wide notice as governor by his reorganization of the state government and by his effective handling of the Chicago race riots in 1919. A contender for the Republican presidential nomination in 1920, he was deadlocked with Leonard Wood at 311½ votes on the eighth ballot, which enabled Warren G. Harding to gain the nomination. In 1924 he refused to run as Vice President on the Republican ticket, but he remained an influential party leader and a spokesman of the farmer. See biography by W. T. Hutchinson (1957).

Lowe, Sir Hudson (lō), 1769-1844, British general. He fought with credit throughout the French Revolutionary and Napoleonic Wars, mainly in the Mediterranean region, and served (1815-21) as governor of St. Helena and custodian of Napoleon I. He was criticized severely for his alleged mistreatment of the French exiles on St. Helena. His later years were largely spent in controversy on this score, and he wrote a self-vindication. See William Forsyth, *History of the Captivity of Napoleon at St. Helena* (1853); R. C. Seaton, *Napoleon's Captivity in Relation to Sir Hudson Lowe* (1903).

Lowe, Robert, Viscount Sherbrooke: see SHERBROOKE, ROBERT LOWE, VISCOUNT.

Lowe, Thaddeus Sobieski Coulincourt, 1832-1913, American aeronaut and inventor, b. Coos co., N.H. He flew (1861) a distance of 900 mi (1,448 km) in a balloon he built himself. Later that year President Lincoln appointed him chief of the corps of aeronautics of the U.S. army. During the Civil War he built up a fleet of observation balloons that served in many engagements. Lowe invented (1865) a machine for making ice, equipped (1868) a steamer with refrigeration for haulage of perishable food, and built regenerative metallic furnaces for gas and petroleum and a coke-oven system for simultaneously producing gas and metallic coke.

Lowell, Abbott Lawrence, 1856-1943, American educator, president of Harvard (1909-33), b. Boston, grad. Harvard (B.A., 1877; LL.B., 1880); brother of Percival Lowell and Amy Lowell. He practiced law in Boston for 17 years and joined the Harvard faculty in 1897 as a lecturer in political science, becoming a professor in 1900. In 1909 he succeeded Charles W. Eliot as president. As Eliot had developed the graduate schools of Harvard, Lowell turned his attention to the undergraduate college. To combat specialization, he introduced (1914) a modification of the elective system, established (1917) the requirement of a general examination in their major subject for candidates for the bachelor's degree, and instituted (1917) the tutorial system for upper classmen. He also put into operation (1931), in seven new residence halls along the Charles River, his "house plan," whereby, through residential units like those in English universities, he hoped to secure the advantages of intellectual and social cohesion. Lowell is remembered for his spirited defense of academic freedom and for his advocacy of American participation in the League of Nations. His presidency saw a period of tremendous physical growth at Harvard and the reorganization of the finances of the university. His writings include *Essays on Government* (new ed. 1969), *Public Opinion and Popular Government* (1913, repr. 1969), *Conflicts of Principle* (1932), *Biography of Percival Lowell* (1935), and *What a University President Has Learned* (1938, repr. 1969). See biography by H. A. Yeomans (1948).

Lowell, Amy, 1874-1925, American poet, biographer, and critic, b. Brookline, Mass., privately educated; sister of Percival Lowell and Abbott Lawrence Lowell. In 1912 she published *A Dome of Many-Colored Glass,* a volume of conventional verse. The next year she went to England, where she met Ezra Pound and became identified with the IMAGISTS. After Pound abandoned the group, she became its leader and champion, publishing a three-volume anthology entitled *Some Imagist Poets* (1915, 1916, 1917). Lowell's own poetry is particularly notable for its rendering of sensuous images. Her experiments with polyphonic prose, a free-verse form that combines prose and poetry, are considered unsuccessful. Among her volumes of poetry are *Sword Blades and Poppy Seed* (1914), *Men, Women, and Ghosts* (1916), *Can Grande's Castle* (1918), *What's o'Clock* (1925; Pulitzer Prize), *East Wind* (1926), and *Ballads for Sale* (1927). Her best-known poems are "Patterns" and "Lilacs." Lowell's perceptive and dynamic criticism includes *Six French Poets* (1915) and *Tendencies in Modern American Poetry* (1917). Her most ambitious work is her two-volume biography of Keats (1925). See biographies by Horace Gregory (1958) and S. F. Damon (1935, repr. 1966).

Lowell, Francis Cabot, 1775-1817, pioneer American cotton manufacturer, b. Newburyport, Mass.; son of John LOWELL (1743-1802). A merchant in Boston, he traveled (1810) to England, where he studied closely the new machinery used in the textile industry of Lancashire. Upon his return, with the aid of Paul Moody, he designed and constructed the first power loom in America, which had important improvements over its English prototypes. With Patrick T. Jackson (his brother-in-law), Nathan Appleton, and others, he formed the Boston Manufacturing Company and at Waltham, Mass., built the first factory in America to perform all the operations involved in converting raw cotton into cloth. He succeeded in having a duty on cotton incorporated into the tariff law of 1816. Lowell, Mass., founded after his death, was named for him. John Lowell (1799-1836) was his son. See C. F. Ware, *The Early New England Cotton Manufacture* (1931, repr. 1966).

Lowell, James Russell, 1819-91, American poet, critic, and editor, b. Cambridge, Mass. He was influential in revitalizing the intellectual life of New England in the mid-19th cent. Educated at Harvard (B.A., 1838; LL.B., 1840), he abandoned law for literature. In 1843 he started a literary magazine, the *Pioneer,* which failed after two issues. The next year Lowell married Maria White, an ardent abolitionist and liberal, who encouraged him in his work. Lowell's *Poems* (1844, 1846), *A Fable for Critics* (1848), *The Vision of Sir Launfal* (1848), and *The Bigelow Papers* (1848; 2d series, 1867) brought him considerable notice as a poet and critic. The best remembered of these are *The Bigelow Papers,* political and social lampoons written in Yankee dialect, which established his reputation as a satirist and a wit. The first of these two series of verses expressed opposition to the Mexican War, and the second supported the cause of the North in the Civil War. In 1855, Lowell became professor of modern languages at Harvard, a position he held until 1876. In addition to teaching, he served as first editor (1857-61) of the *Atlantic Monthly* and later (1864-72) of the *North American Review.* In his later writings he turned to scholarship and criticism. Collections of his essays and literary studies appeared as *Fireside Travels* (1864), *Among My Books* (1870; 2d series, 1876), and *My Study Windows* (1871). In 1877 he was appointed minister to London, where he remained until 1885. While abroad Lowell did much to increase the respect of foreigners for American letters and American institutions; his speeches in England, published as *Democracy and Other Addresses* (1887), are among his best work. Lowell's letters (ed. by C. E. Norton, 2 vol., 1893) and *New Letters* (ed. by M. A. De Wolfe Howe, 1932) remain valuable for their shrewd and lively comments on public affairs and the literary activities of his generation. See his collected works (12 vol., 1890-92); biographies by M. B. Duberman (1966) and H. E. Scudder (2 vol., 1901, repr. 1969); study by Leon Howard (1952, repr. 1971).

Lowell, John, 1743-1802, American jurist, b. Newburyport, Mass. He became (1762) a lawyer and later served in the provincial assembly (1776, 1778), in the state constitutional convention (1779-80), and in the Continental Congress (1782-83). Lowell was a member (1784) of the commission that settled the New York-Massachusetts boundary dispute, and after 1789 he held several major judicial posts. He was a founder of the American Academy of Arts and Sciences. He was the father of Francis Cabot Lowell and John Lowell (1769-1840).

Lowell, John, 1769-1840, American political writer, b. Newburyport, Mass.; son of John Lowell (1743-1802). He practiced law, but devoted most of his time to supporting his Federalist views in newspapers and pamphlets. *Mr. Madison's War* (1812) was his most effective piece of writing.

Lowell, Percival, 1855-1916, American astronomer, b. Boston, grad. Harvard, 1876; brother of Abbott Lawrence Lowell and Amy Lowell. He visited Korea and Japan, where he acted as counselor and foreign secretary to the Korean Special Mission to the United States and wrote several books about the Orient. Becoming interested in astronomy, he established (1894) the Lowell Observatory at Flagstaff, Ariz., and devoted himself to making personal observations. It was his belief that Mars was inhabited and that the Martian canals were artificial waterways. He also contended that there was a planet beyond Neptune (confirmed in 1930 by the discovery of Pluto). From 1902 he was nonresident professor of astronomy at the Massachusetts Institute of Technology. Among his many writings on astronomy are *Mars and Its Canals* (1906) and *The Genesis of Planets* (1916). See biography by A. L. Lowell (1935).

Lowell, Robert, 1917–, American poet, b. Boston. A grandnephew of James Russell Lowell, he graduated from Kenyon College in 1940. In that same year he converted to Roman Catholicism and married the writer Jean STAFFORD. During World War II he served a jail sentence as a conscientious objector. He has taught at Boston Univ. and at Harvard. His second wife was the novelist and critic Elizabeth Hardwick. Lowell's poetry is individualistic and intense, rich in symbolism and marked by great technical skill. Although much of his verse treats the meaninglessness and corruption of life in both the past and in the 20th cent., his later work indicates a philosophic acceptance of life and the world. His highly praised *Life Studies* (1959) is a frank and highly personal autobiographical volume in verse and prose. Among his books of poetry are *Lord Weary's Castle* (1946; Pulitzer Prize), *The Mills of the Kavanaughs* (1951), *For the Union Dead* (1964), *Near the Ocean* (1967), *Notebook: Nineteen Sixty-Seven to Nineteen Sixty-Eight* (1969), and *The Dolphin* (1973; Pulitzer Prize). His other works include translations of Racine's *Phèdre* (1969), Aeschylus' *Prometheus Bound* (1969), and of miscellaneous European verse, collected as *Imitations* (1961). His dramatic adaptation of Melville's story "Benito Cereno" was successfully produced off Broadway in 1965; it is part of Lowell's trilogy of plays, *The Old Glory* (1968).

Lowell, city (1970 pop. 94,239), a seat of Middlesex co., NE Mass., at the confluence of the Merrimack and Concord rivers; settled 1653, set off from Chelmsford 1826, inc. as a city 1836. Its manufactures include electronic and electrical equipment, textiles, rubber products, chemicals, machine parts, foodstuffs, shoes, and plastics. The city developed after textile mills were built at Pawtucket Falls, and it became one of the great textile centers of the country. Lowell State College and Lowell Technological Institute are there. The city has several fine parks, and Whistler's birthplace is preserved. Charles Dickens visited Lowell in 1842 and described it in *American Notes.* See J. P. Coolidge, *Mill and Mansion* (1942, repr. 1967); M. T. Parker, *Lowell: A Study of Industrial Development* (1970).

Lowell Observatory, astronomical observatory located in Flagstaff, Ariz.; it was founded in 1894 by Percival Lowell, the American astronomer who popularized the idea that Mars may support intelligent life. Its equipment includes 72-in. (183-cm), 42-in. (107-cm), 31-in. (79-cm), 24-in. (61-cm), and 21-in. (53-cm) reflecting TELESCOPES, plus 24-in., 20-in. (51-cm), and 13-in. (33-cm) refracting telescopes and an 8-in. (20-cm) Schmidt camera. Many discoveries of fundamental importance were made at the observatory, especially by V. M. SLIPHER, its director from 1916 to 1954. By 1917 he had determined through spectroscopic analysis the RADIAL VELOCITIES of most spiral NEBULAS then known. Beginning in 1905 the observatory made a concerted search for a trans-Neptunian planet; this search, under Slipher's supervision, led to the discovery of Pluto in 1930. Principal research programs conducted by Lowell Observatory involve the search for nearby stars and the measurement of light and motion of close double stars, nebulas, and other galactic objects.

Lower Austria, Ger. *Niederösterreich,* province (1971 est. pop. 1,411,000), c.7,400 sq mi (19,170 sq km), NE Austria. Vienna, although outside its boundaries, is the seat of the provincial government. Lower Austria is the largest of the Austrian provinces, and it borders on Czechoslovakia in the north and northeast. It is a picturesque, hilly region, drained by the Danube River and containing peaks of the Eastern Alps and the WIENERWALD (Vienna Woods). The province includes roughly half of the country's arable land and is noted for its grain production and its wines. The valleys and basins around Vienna and Wiener Neustadt contain more than half of all Austrian industry. Much petroleum is produced N of the Danube, especially near Zistersdorf. Baden is a well-known spa, and the Semmering region in the south is a tourist and health center. The province has several medieval castles and abbeys. The history of Lower Austria coincides with that of AUSTRIA.

Lower Avon, river: see AVON **1**, river, England.

Lower Burrell (bərĕl'), city (1970 pop. 13,654), Westmoreland co., SW Pa., 20 mi (32 km) NE of Pittsburgh; inc. 1959. Steel is produced there. A campus of Pennsylvania State Univ. is nearby.

Lower California: see BAJA CALIFORNIA.

Lower Canada: see QUEBEC, province, Canada.

Lower Hutt, city (1971 pop. 58,561), S North Island, New Zealand, at the mouth of the Hutt River, near Wellington. It is a manufacturing city with automobile assembly plants and railroad workshops. Several scientific research institutions are located in Lower Hutt.

Lower Saint Croix National Scenic River: see NATIONAL PARKS AND MONUMENTS (table).

Lower Saxony, Ger. *Niedersachsen* (nē'dərsäk"sən), state (1970 pop. 7,082,000), 18,295 sq mi (47,384 sq km), N West Germany. Hanover is the capital. The state was formed in 1946 by the merger of the former Prussian province of HANOVER and the former states of BRUNSWICK, OLDENBURG, and SCHAUMBURG-LIPPE. Situated on the North German plain, it is bordered by the Netherlands on the west; the states of North Rhine-Westphalia and Hesse on the south; East Germany on the east; and the states of Bremen, Schleswig-Holstein, and Hamburg and the North Sea on the north. The state is mountainous in the south (notably the Harz and Weser mts.); heaths and moors form the central belt. Lower Saxony is drained by the Weser, Ems, Aller, Leine, and Elbe rivers. Farming and cattle raising are important occupations. Industry (including the manufacture of iron and steel, textiles, machinery, food products, and chemicals) is well developed in the cities of Brunswick, Celle, Goslar, Hanover, and Osnabrück. There are oil wells in the Emsland, large iron-ore deposits at Watenstedt-Salzgitter, and lignite mines near Helmstedt. Emden, Wilhelmshaven, and Cuxhaven are the chief North Sea ports. The region of Lower Saxony has had no historic unity since 1180, when Emperor Frederick I broke up the duchy of Henry the Lion of Saxony, of which it was a part. The term "Lower Saxony" continued, however, as a geographic expression. It also designated (16th cent. to 1806) one of the imperial circles of the Holy Roman Empire; the circle included, besides present-day Lower Saxony, Mecklenburg, Holstein, and Bremen.

Lowestoft (lō'stôft, -stəf), municipal borough (1971 pop. 52,182), East Suffolk, the easternmost town in England. It is a popular seaside resort and has fishing, shipbuilding, food processing, and other light industries. The new resort area is separated from Old Lowestoft by Lake Lothing and the harbor. Oliver Cromwell took the town in 1643, and in 1665 the coastal waters were the scene of a naval victory of the English under the duke of York (later James II) over the Dutch. Most of the old houses were destroyed by a fire in the 17th cent., but St. Margaret's Church, from the 15th cent., has an older tower. Fine bone china was produced in Lowestoft from about 1750 to 1800. The town was the birthplace of the satirist Thomas Nashe. In 1974, Lowestoft became part of the new nonmetropolitan county of Suffolk.

Lowie, Robert Harry, or **Robert Heinrich Lowie,** 1883–1957, American anthropologist, b. Vienna, grad. College of the City of New York, 1901, Ph.D. Columbia, 1908. He was on the staff of the American Museum of Natural History from 1908 until 1921. From that year until his death he taught at the Univ. of California. Lowie gained international fame through his studies of the North American Indian, especially the northern Plains tribes, and his contributions to ethnological theory. His book, *Primitive Society* (1920, 2d ed. 1947), and its sequel, *Social Organization* (1948), are regarded as classics in their field. Other writings include *Primitive Religion* (1924, rev. ed. 1948), *An Introduction to Cultural Anthropology* (1934, rev. ed. 1940), *The History of Ethnological Theory* (1938), and *Indians of the Plains* (1954). His autobiography was published in 1959; the *Crow Texts* translated and edited by him and *Selected Papers in Anthropology* appeared in 1960. See biography by R. F. Murphy (1972).

Lowndes, Rawlins (loundz), 1721–1800, president of South Carolina (1778–79), b. St. Kitts, British West Indies. In 1730 his family moved to Charleston, S.C., where Lowndes later became a noted lawyer. In the colonial assembly (where he was speaker several times) and as associate judge of the court of common pleas, he took a leading part in opposing British measures before the American Revolution, but did not favor armed rebellion or independence. Nevertheless he helped draft the state constitution and was chosen president in 1778; he declined reelection. After the war he was the leading opponent in South Carolina of ratification of the Federal Constitution.

Lowry, Malcolm (Clarence Malcolm Lowry), 1909–57, English novelist. After his death Lowry was recognized as an important writer who effectively articulated the spiritual desolation of 20th-century man. While still a student at Cambridge he wrote his first novel, *Ultramarine* (1933), later reworked and published in final form in 1962. His reputation is founded on his second novel, *Under the Volcano* (1947), a subtle and complex study of the dissolution of an Englishman's character. Set in Mexico, the novel is highly autobiographical. Like his hero Geoffrey Firmin, Lowry was an alcoholic whose addiction all but destroyed his family life and caused him to seek peace in such disparate places as British Columbia and Mexico. Lowry's other works, all published posthumously, include *Selected Poems* (1962); two volumes of short stories, *Hear Us O Lord from Heaven Thy Dwelling Place* (1961) and *Dark As The Grave Wherein My Friend Is Laid* (1968); and a novel, *Lunar Caustic* (1968). See biography by Douglas Day (1973).

low-temperature physics, science concerned with the production and maintenance of temperatures much below normal, down to almost absolute zero, and with various phenomena that occur only at such temperatures. The TEMPERATURE scale used in low-temperature physics is the KELVIN TEMPERATURE SCALE, or absolute temperature scale, which is based on the behavior of an idealized gas (see GAS LAWS; KINETIC-MOLECULAR THEORY OF GASES). Low-temperature physics is also known as cryogenics, from the Greek meaning "producing cold." Since HEAT is internal ENERGY, low temperatures are achieved by removing energy from a substance. This may be done in various ways. The simplest way to cool a substance is to bring it into contact with another substance that is already at a low temperature. Ordinary ice, dry ice (solid carbon dioxide), and LIQUID AIR may be used successively to cool a substance down to about 80°K (about −190°C). The heat is removed by CONDUCTION, passing from the substance to be cooled to the colder substance in contact with it. If the colder substance is a liquefied gas (see LIQUEFACTION), considerable heat can be removed as the liquid reverts to its gaseous state, since it will absorb its LATENT HEAT of vaporization during the transition. Various liquefied gases can be used in this manner to cool a substance to as low as 4.2°K, the BOILING POINT of liquid helium. If the vapor over the liquid helium is continually pumped away, even lower temperatures, down to less than 1°K, can be achieved because more helium must evaporate to maintain the proper VAPOR PRESSURE of the liquid helium. Most processes used to reduce the temperature below this level involve the heat energy that is associated with magnetization (see MAGNETISM). Successive magnetization and demagnetization under the proper combination of conditions can lower the temperature to only about a millionth of a degree above absolute zero. Reaching such low temperatures becomes increasingly difficult, as each temperature drop requires finding some kind of energy within the substance and then devising a means of removing this energy. Moreover, according to the third law of THERMODYNAMICS, it is theoretically impossible to reduce a substance to absolute zero by any finite number of processes. Among the phenomena that occur only at temperatures near absolute zero are SUPERCONDUCTIVITY and SUPERFLUIDITY. Superconductivity is the vanishing of all electrical resistance in certain substances when they reach a transition temperature that varies from one substance to another; this effect can be used in superconducting magnets for memory units in computers and other applications. Superfluidity occurs only in liquid helium and is the tendency of liquid helium to flow over the sides of any container it is placed in without being stopped by friction or gravity. See D. K. C. MacDonald, *Near Zero* (1961); Michael McClintock, *Cryogenics* (1964).

Loyalists, in the American Revolution, colonials who adhered to the British cause. The patriots referred to them as Tories. Although Loyalists were found in all social classes and occupations, a disproportionately large number were engaged in commerce and the professions, or were officeholders under the crown. They also tended to be foreign born and of the Anglican religion. Their motives for remaining loyal were complex and embraced both ideological and material reasons. In 1774–75, when most colonials hoped for reconciliation with the British government, the line between Loyalist and non-Loyalist was not very sharp; many Loyalists voiced opposition to the acts of Parliament. But the Declaration of Independence created a sharp dividing line between supporters and opponents of independence.

Figures on public opinion in the Revolution are obviously mere guesswork, but John Adams estimated that one third of the colonials were Loyalists; probably another third were neutral, apathetic, or opportunistic. The Loyalists were strongest in the far southern colonies—Georgia and the Carolinas—and in the Middle Atlantic colonies, especially New York and Pennsylvania. In those places particularly the fighting became bitter civil war with raids and reprisals. The Revolutionaries deeply hated the leaders of the Loyalist armed bands, such as Thomas Browne, Edmund Fanning, and John and Walter Butler. Even before warfare began many Loyalists were seeking refuge in British-held lands. Feeling against them, in addition to natural cupidity, led the patriots to enact harsh penal laws against the Loyalists and to confiscate many of their estates. The matter of restoring these properties to their owners was discussed in negotiations for the Treaty of Paris (1783), and the treaty provided that Congress should urge the states to make restitution, but little was done, and there were stray lawsuits concerning particular properties for many years. A great many of the dispossessed Loyalists settled in the Maritime provs. of Canada, in the Bahamas, in other parts of the West Indies, and in England. See W. H. Nelson, *The American Tory* (1961, repr. 1964); Wallace Brown, *The Good Americans: Loyalists in the American Revolution* (1969); G. N. D. Evans, ed., *Allegiance in America: The Case of the Loyalists* (1969); studies of Loyalism in individual provinces by A. C. Flick (1901, repr. 1970; New York), O. G. Hammond (1917; New Hampshire), I. S. Harrell (1926, repr. 1965; Virginia), E. A. Jones (1927, New Jersey; 1930, Massachusetts), R. O. Demond (1940, repr. 1964; North Carolina), and H. B. Hancock (1940; Delaware).

Loyalty Islands, coral group, S Pacific, a part of the French overseas territory of NEW CALEDONIA. The group comprises three islands (Lifu, Maré, and Uvéa) and many islets, and has a total land area of c.800 sq mi (2,070 sq km). The chief exports are copra, rubber, and sugarcane.

Lo-yang or **Loyang** (both: lō-yäng), city (1970 est. pop. 750,000), NW Honan prov., China, on the Lo River. The city is the hub of several highways and is located on the Lung-hai RR. A new industrial center, it has grown about fourfold since 1949. Manufactures include ball and roller bearings, tractors, heavy machinery, glass, cement, and textiles. Lo-yang, a major Chinese cultural center, was the capital of several ancient dynasties, particularly that of the Eastern Chou kingdom (770-256 B.C.) and the T'ang dynasty (A.D. 618-906). Under the Chou it was the seat of several schools of philosophy. The nearby Lung-men grottoes, embellished in the 6th cent. A.D., contain colossal carvings of Buddha. Lo-yang was formerly called Honanfu.

Loyola, Ignatius of: see IGNATIUS OF LOYOLA, SAINT.

Loyola University, at New Orleans, La.; Jesuit; coeducational. The university was established through a merger in 1911 of the College of the Immaculate Conception (opened 1849) and Loyola College and Academy (opened 1904). The school has a seismographic observatory.

Loyola University of Chicago, at Chicago, Ill.; Jesuit; coeducational; founded (1870) as St. Ignatius College. The present name was adopted in 1909.

Loyson, Charles (shärl lwäzôN'), 1827-1912, French preacher, called Père Hyacinthe. He was successively a Sulpician, a Dominican, and a Carmelite. In 1869, when he was perhaps the best-known preacher in France, he opposed the calling of the Vatican Council. He opposed enunciation of the doctrine of the infallibility of the pope, and in 1871 he left the Church. In 1878 he founded a Gallican church at Paris; this joined later (1893) with the Jansenists of Utrecht.

Lozère (lôzĕr'), department (1968 pop. 77,258), S central France. MENDE is the capital.

LPG: see LIQUEFIED PETROLEUM GAS.

Lr, chemical symbol of the element LAWRENCIUM.

LSD: see LYSERGIC ACID DIETHYLAMIDE.

LSI: see INTEGRATED CIRCUIT.

Lu, chemical symbol of the element LUTETIUM.

Lualaba, river, Zaïre: see CONGO, river.

Luanda (lo͞oăn'də,-än'də), city (1970 pop. 475,328), capital of Angola, a port on the Atlantic Ocean. It is Angola's largest city and its administrative center. Manufactures include processed foods, beverages, textiles, cement and other construction materials, plastic products, metalware, cigarettes, and shoes. Petroleum, found nearby, is refined in the city. Luanda has a natural harbor, with a modern port. The chief exports are coffee, cotton, sugar, palm products, and manganese ore. Founded in 1575 by the Portuguese as São Paulo de Luanda, the city has been the administrative center of Angola since 1627 (except for 1640-48). From c.1550 to c.1850 it was the center of a large slave trade to Brazil. Today Luanda is an attractive, modern city. It is the seat of a Roman Catholic archbishop. The Univ. of Angola, the 17th-century Fort of São Miguel, and the Governor's Palace are in Luanda.

Luang Prabang (lwäng prəbäng'), city (1970 est. pop. 25,000), capital of Luang Prabang prov. and the royal capital of Laos, NW Laos, on the Mekong River. The economic center of N Laos, it is a river port and a market for rubber, rice, teak, and fish. Most shops are Chinese owned. Zinc is mined nearby. According to tradition, Luang Prabang was founded by Indian Buddhist missionaries. For several centuries it was the center of a Laotian-Thai kingdom that controlled most of Laos and parts of Siam. Luang Prabang came under French rule in 1893.

Luanshya (lwänsh'yä), city (1972 est. pop., with suburbs, 110,500), N central Zambia, near Zaïre. It is a copper-mining center, located on the COPPERBELT.

Luapula: see CONGO, river.

Lubbock, Sir John (lŭb'ək), 1834-1913, English banker, statesman, and naturalist. As a member of Parliament from 1870, he introduced many reform bills, especially in banking, including legislation establishing bank holidays. His scientific contributions were in entomology and anthropology and include his *Prehistoric Times* (1865), long used as a textbook in several languages; popular works include *Ants, Bees, and Wasps* (1882) and *The Pleasures of Life* (2 vol., 1887-89). He was created Baron Avebury in 1900. See biographical compilation, ed. by his daughter, U. L. Grant Duff (1924). His father was **Sir John William Lubbock,** 1803-65, an astronomer and mathematician. He made a special study of tides and of the lunar theory and developed a method for calculating the orbits of comets and planets. In mathematics he applied the theory of probability to life insurance problems.

Lubbock, city (1970 pop. 149,101), seat of Lubbock co., NW Texas; inc. 1909. In the Llano Estacado on a branch of the Brazos River, Lubbock was settled in 1879 by Quakers. It is the trade center for the cotton and grain-growing Great Plains region of Texas and E N.Mex. Its manufactures include sprinkler heads, earth-moving equipment, mobile and modular homes, sausage casings, and sheets. In Mackenzie State Park a prairie-dog town has been preserved. Lubbock Lake Site is an important geological formation. Texas Tech Univ. and Lubbock Christian College are in the city. Reese Air Force Base, where jet pilots are trained, is nearby.

Lübeck (lü'bĕk), city (1970 pop. 239,339), Schleswig-Holstein, NE West Germany, on the Trave River near its mouth on the Baltic Sea, and near the border with East Germany. It is a major port and a commercial and industrial center. The city contains foundries, machinery plants, textile mills, and large shipyards; it is also noted for the manufacture of marzipan and other sweets. Known in the 11th cent., Lübeck was destroyed by fire in 1138 but was refounded in 1143. It was acquired and chartered by Henry the Lion c.1158; the charter, which granted far-reaching communal rights, was copied by more than 100 other German cities. In 1226, Frederick II made Lübeck a free imperial city. Ruled by a merchant aristocracy, it soon rose to great commercial prosperity, acquired hegemony over the Baltic trade, and headed the HANSEATIC LEAGUE. However, the rise of the maritime powers of Denmark and Sweden and the revolution in commerce caused by the discovery and development of the Americas resulted in the decline of the League and, with it, of Lübeck. In 1630 the last of the Hanseatic diets was held there. The city escaped the ravages of the Thirty Years War (1618-48); and, in spite of a decline in Lübeck's power, its patrician merchant families continued to prosper. In the French Revolutionary Wars, Lübeck was sacked by French troops in 1803; and, after the Prussian army under Blücher capitulated (1806) to the French at nearby Ratekau, the city was occupied by the French. Lübeck, governed by a senate, joined the North German Confederation and later the German Empire as a free Hanseatic city; it retained that status until 1937, when it was incorporated into Schleswig-Holstein. The opening (1900) of the Elbe-Lübeck Canal (formerly called the Elbe-Trave Canal) helped increase Lübeck's trade. Despite heavy damage by bombing in World War II, the inner city of Lübeck remains one of the finest examples of medieval Gothic architecture in N Europe. Among the buildings that have been restored are the magnificent city hall (13th-15th cent.); the churches of St. Catherine and St. Jacob (both: 14th cent.); the Hospital and Church of the Holy Ghost (13th cent.); the Holstentor (completed 1477), an imposing city gate flanked by two round towers; the cathedral (founded in 1173); the large brick Church of St. Mary (13th-14th cent.); and many of the old patrician residences. There are also several museums in the city. Dietrich Buxtehude, the composer and organist, was active in Lübeck from 1668 to 1707. The life and decline of a Lübeck patrician family is the subject of the novel *Buddenbrooks,* by Thomas Mann, who, with his brother Heinrich Mann, was born in the city. The city of Lübeck should not be confused with the former **bishopric of Lübeck,** whose rulers resided from c.1300 at nearby Eutin. The bishops were territorial princes of the Holy Roman Empire and accepted the Reformation in the 16th cent. The prince-bishopric of Lübeck passed into a branch of the Danish house of Holstein-Gottorp, which in 1773 also acquired the duchy of Oldenburg. Secularized in 1803, the former bishopric (which did not include the city of Lübeck) became a district of Oldenburg until it was transferred to Schleswig-Holstein in 1937.

Lubim (lo͞o'bĭm), in the Bible, the Libyans. 2 Chron. 12.3; 16.8; Nahum 3.9. For other possible occurrences, see CHUB; LEHABIM; LUD.

Lubin, David (lo͞o'bĭn), 1849-1919, American agriculturist, b. Poland. After prospering as a merchant in California, he devoted himself to helping farmers with their problems. Through his efforts the California Fruit Growers Association, a cooperative marketing group, was established. His plan to found a worldwide agricultural institute found favor in Italy, and in 1905 the International Institute of Agriculture was founded in Rome, with 46 nations participating. Lubin was the U.S. representative until his death. In 1945 the institute's activities were absorbed by the United Nations Food and Agriculture Organization.

Lublin (lo͞o'blēn), city (1970 pop. 235,937), SE Poland. It is a railway junction and industrial center. Manufactures include textiles, automobiles, trucks, agricultural machinery, and electrical products. One of the oldest Polish towns, Lublin became the capital of a province in 1474 and the seat of a tribunal in 1578. It was the meeting place of several diets (16th-18th cent.), one of which united (1569) Poland with Lithuania. Lublin passed to Austria in 1795 and to Russia in 1815. It was (1918) the seat of a temporary Polish Socialist government. In 1944 it was the seat of a provisional government rivaling the Polish government-in-exile in London. At the Yalta Conference (Feb., 1945) it was agreed to broaden the Lublin government by including members of the London cabinet; the Lublin government was recognized as the sole Polish authority at the Potsdam Conference (Aug., 1945). The Catholic Univ. at Lublin (founded 1918) was reopened in 1944 and renamed Maria Curie-Sklodowska Univ. Lublin's most notable buildings are a 14th-century city hall (rebuilt 1787), a 14th-century castle (rebuilt 1826), and a 16th-century cathedral.

lubrication, introduction of a substance between the contact surfaces of moving parts to reduce friction and to dissipate heat. A lubricant may be oil, grease, graphite, or any substance—gas, liquid, semiliquid, or solid—that permits free action of mechanical devices and prevents injury by abrasion and "seizing" of metal or other components through unequal expansion caused by heat. In machining processes lubricants also function as coolants to forestall heat-caused deformities. Lubricants can be classified by their origin—animal (e.g., sperm oil, goose grease), vegetable (e.g., soybean oil, linseed oil), or mineral (e.g., petroleum, molybdenum sulfide). But whatever their derivation or properties, their purpose is to replace dry friction with either thin-film or fluid-film friction, depending on the load, speed, or intermittent action of the moving parts. Thin-film lubrication, in which there is some contact between the moving parts, usually is specified where heavy loads are a factor. In fluid, or thick-film, lubrication a pressure film is formed between moving surfaces and keeps them completely apart. This type of lubrication cannot easily be maintained in high-speed machinery and therefore is used where reciprocating or oscillating conditions are moderate. From ancient times until the late 19th cent. lubricants were obtained from vegetable oils or animal fats and oils. Today most are derived from mineral oils, such as petroleum and shale oil, which can be distilled and condensed without decomposition. Differing widely in viscosity, specific gravity, vapor pressure, boiling point, and other properties, lubricants also offer a wide range of selection for the increasingly varied needs of modern industry. Efficient operation of machinery largely depends not only on the lubricant selected but also on its method of application. Lubricants formerly were applied by hand, but modern machinery requires exact methods that can be precisely controlled. Mechanical devices to supply lubricants are called lubricators. A simple form of lubricator is a container mounted over a bearing or other part and provided with a hole or an adjustable valve through which the lubricant is gravity-fed at the desired rate of flow. Wick-feed oilers are placed under moving parts, and by pressing against them they feed oil by capillary action. Horizontal bearings are frequently oiled by a rotating ring or chain that carries oil from a reservoir in the bearing housing and distributes it along the bearing through grooves or channels. Bath oiling is useful where an oil-tight reservoir can be provided in which the bearing journal may be submerged; the pool of oil helps to carry away heat from contact surfaces. Splash-oiling devices are used where gears, bearings, or other parts contained in housings have moving parts that dip into the lubricant and splash it on the bearings or into distribution channels. Centralized oiling systems usually consist of a reservoir, pump, and tubes through which oil is circulated, while heaters or coolers may be introduced to change the viscosity of the lubricant for various parts of the system. Many oiling operations are automatically synchronized to start and stop with the machinery. GREASE lubricants are semisolid and have several important advantages: They resist being squeezed out, they are useful under heavy load conditions and in inaccessible parts where the supply of lubricant cannot easily be renewed, and they tend to form a crust that prevents the entry of dirt or grit between contact surfaces. Grease is a mixture of a lubricant and a thickener; often it is made from a mineral oil and a soap. It may be applied in various ways: by packing enclosed parts with it, by pressing it onto moving parts from an adjacent well, by forcing it through grease cups by a spring device, and by pumping it through pressure guns. Solid lubricants are especially useful at high and low temperatures, in high vacuums, and in other applications where oil is not suitable; common solid lubricants are graphite and molybdenum disulfide. Synthetic lubricants, such as silicones, are of great value in applications involving extreme temperatures. In certain types of high-speed machinery films of gas under pressure have been successfully used as lubricants. For most machinery, different methods of lubrication and types of lubricants must be employed for different parts. In an automobile, for example, the chassis is lubricated with grease, the manual transmission and rear-axle housings are filled with heavy oil, the automatic transmission is lubricated with a special-grade light oil, wheel bearings are packed with a grease that has a thickener composed of long fibers, and the crankcase oil that lubricates engine parts is a lightweight, free-flowing oil.

Lubumbashi (lo͞obo͞obo͞om'bä'shē), formerly **Elisabethville,** city (1970 est. pop. 318,000), capital of Shaba region, SE Zaïre, near the border with Zambia. The second largest city of the country, it is a commercial and industrial center. Copper is smelted there, and textiles, food products and beverages, printed materials, and bricks are manufactured. Founded in 1910, Lubumbashi prospered with the development of the region's copper-mining industry. It was the capital of the secessionist state of Katanga (1960–63), as Shaba was then called, and was the scene of bloody strife between UN troops and Katangan forces. The city is the site of a university (founded 1955), a regional museum, and a modern airport. It is situated on a transcontinental railroad that links Luanda on the west coast of Africa with Beira on the east coast.

Luca Giordano: see GIORDANO, LUCA.

Lucan (Marcus Annaeus Lucanus) (lo͞o'kən), A.D. 39–A.D. 65, Latin poet, b. Corduba (Córdoba, the modern Cordova), Spain, nephew of the philosopher Seneca. At first in Nero's favor, he was later forced to kill himself when his part in a plot against the emperor was discovered. Ten books of his epic *Bellum Civile* (on the civil war between Caesar and Pompey), erroneously called Pharsalia, survive. Though the poem is written in a severe style and is often digressive and extravagant, it has a kind of vigorous beauty and grandeur which gave Lucan a high place in the esteem of later writers. See study by R. J. Getty (1940, repr. 1955).

Lucan, Patrick Sarsfield, earl of: see SARSFIELD, PATRICK, EARL OF LUCAN.

Lucania (lo͞okā'nēə), ancient region of S Italy. It was bounded on the east by the Gulf of Tarentum (now Taranto) and by Apulia, on the north by Samnium and Campania, on the west by the Tyrrhenian Sea, and on the south by Bruttium. Italic tribes and Greek colonists lived there before the Roman conquest in the 3d cent. B.C. (see MAGNA GRAECIA). Their chief cities were Heraclea and Metapontum on the Gulf of Tarentum and Paestum and Buxentum on the Tyrrhenian coast. The non-Greek Lucanians were Samnites. The western portion of ancient Lucania is now in Campania; the larger eastern part is in BASILICATA.

Lucania, Mount, 17,147 ft (5,226 m) high, in the St. Elias Mts., SW Yukon Territory, Canada, near the Alaska line; Canada's third tallest peak.

Lucaris, Cyril (lyo͞okä'rĭs), 1572–1637, Greek churchman, b. Crete (then belonging to Venice). He studied at Venice and Padua and was elected patriarch of Alexandria (1602–20) and of Constantinople (1620–37). In Western Europe he had become imbued with Calvinistic ideas, and he attempted to synthesize them with Orthodoxy. He published a *Confession of Faith* (1629) to this end and sent many young priests to study in the West. He corresponded with leading Anglicans and Lutherans and sent the Codex Alexandrinus of the Bible to Charles I. His Protestant tendencies had no lasting effect in the East, and after his death a synod condemned his teachings. In Constantinople he was deposed several times. The sultan, Murad IV, had him murdered on charges that he was involved in an anti-Turkish plot. He is also called Cyril Lucar. See G. A. Hadjiantoniou, *Protestant Patriarch* (1961).

Lucas (lo͞o'kəs), variant of LUKE.

Lucas, Edward Verrall, 1868–1938, English author and critic. For several years he was assistant editor of *Punch.* He wrote many volumes of gently satirical essays and travel books, including *Old Lamps for New* (1911), *Saunterer's Rewards* (1933), and *Only the Other Day* (1936). He is chiefly remembered, however, for his biography of Charles Lamb (1905) and his collection of the letters of Charles and Mary Lamb (1903–5). Of his several novels, *Over Bemerton* (1908) is considered his best. See biography by his daughter Audrey Lucas (1939, repr. 1969).

Lucas van Leyden (lü'käs vän lī'dən), 1494–1533, Dutch historical and genre painter and engraver. With Lucas, Dutch painting of scenes from daily life may be said to begin. His art is notable for its realistic treatment, dramatic power, and careful execution. He studied with his father, Huig Jacobsz, a Leiden artist, and with Cornelis Engelbrechtsz and soon established himself as an engraver of extraordinary ability, as well as a painter of originality and power. A child prodigy and prolific artist, Lucas executed more than 200 engravings, etchings, and designs for woodcuts, including *Mohammed and the Monk* (1508), *Ecce Homo* (1510), and *Adam and Eve* (1519). From c.1510 his works show the influence of Dürer, whom he met on a visit to Antwerp in 1521. They drew and exchanged portraits of each other. Later Lucas's style reflected his study of the prints of Marcantonio Raimondi. Among his paintings are *Moses Striking Water from the Rock* (Mus. of Fine Arts, Boston); *Chess Game, St. Jerome,* and *Virgin Enthroned* (Berlin); and *Last Judgment* (Leiden). See his complete engravings, etchings, and woodcuts, ed. by Jacques Lavalleye (tr. 1967).

Lucca (lo͝ok'kä), city (1971 pop. 89,944), capital of Lucca prov., Tuscany, N central Italy, near the Ligurian Sea. It is a commercial and industrial center and an agricultural market (olive oil, wine, and tobacco). Manufactures include textiles, paper, and food products. A Ligurian settlement, later a Roman town, Lucca became (6th cent.) the capital of a Lombard duchy and (12th cent.) a free commune, which soon developed into a republic. In spite of ruthless strife between Guelphs and Ghibellines and frequent wars (especially with Pisa and Florence) the city prospered. Its bankers and merchants were noted throughout Europe, as were its velvets and damasks. The arts also flourished after the 12th cent.; Lucchese sculpture reached its zenith in the 15th cent. with Matteo Civitali, whose fine works adorn the cathedral. Numerous churches, showing Pisan influence, were built from the 12th to the 14th cent. Save for short periods of rule by foreign powers and by tyrants (notably, Castruccio Castracani), Lucca remained an independent republic until Napoleon I made it a principality (1805) for his brother-in-law, Felice Baciocchi, and his sister Elisa. In 1817, Lucca became part of the duchy of Parma and in 1847 of the grand duchy of Tuscany; in 1860 it was annexed to the kingdom of Sardinia. The cathedral (11th–15th cent.) and the churches of San Frediano (begun in the 6th cent.) and San Michele (12th cent.) have fine marble facades. The city's ramparts (16th–17th cent.) are also notable.

Luce, Clare Boothe, 1903–, American playwright and diplomat, b. New York City. She was educated in private schools. After her marriage to the wealthy George T. Brokaw ended in divorce (1929), she served on the staffs of *Vogue* and of *Vanity Fair,* of which she was managing editor (1933–34). In 1935 she married magazine publisher Henry R. LUCE. She first achieved theatrical success with her play *The Women* (1936), a witty satire of wealthy New York matrons. *Kiss the Boys Goodbye* (1938) and *Margin for Error* (1939) were also theatrical hits. Her other writings include *Stuffed Shirts* (1933) and *Europe in the Spring* (1940). Long active in politics, she supported Franklin Roosevelt in 1932, but was a Republican afterwards. She supported Wendell Willkie in 1940, and served two terms (1943–47) as a U.S. Representative from Connecticut. From 1953 to 1956 she served as ambassador to Italy. She is generally acknowledged to have been an able diplomat (ill health forced her to resign), and in Feb., 1959, President Eisenhower named her ambassador to Brazil. Although the Senate confirmed her, she submitted her resignation (May 1, 1959) without having served, because of a controversy over her qualifications. See biography by Stephen Shadegg (1971).

Luce, Henry Robinson, 1898–1967, American publisher, b. Tengchow, China, the son of a Presbyterian missionary. After studying at Oxford, he worked (1921–22) as a reporter on the Chicago *Daily News* and the Baltimore *News.* In 1923, with Briton Hadden, he founded *Time,* a weekly news magazine that features capsulated news accounts written in a brisk, adjective-laden style. After Hadden's death, Luce became editor in chief of *Time* and subsequently founded *Fortune* (1930), a business monthly; *Life* (1936), a pictorial news magazine; and *Sports Illustrated* (1954). In 1932 he purchased *Architectural Forum.* Generally considered the most influential magazine publisher in the United States since S. S. McClure, Luce was also one of the most controversial. He believed that objective reporting was impossible and encouraged his editors to express their own views in their articles even though they did not sign them. During the years that Luce headed Time, Inc., his critics maintained that Luce's publications reflected his personal leanings—for example, their tendency to favor the Republican party and big business. Luce and his wife, Claire Boothe Luce, were influential in national politics. See R. T. Elson, *Time, Inc.* (1968); biographies by J. Kobler (1968) and W. A. Swanberg (1972).

Luce, Stephen Bleecker, 1827–1917, American naval officer, b. Albany, N.Y. He entered the navy as a midshipman in 1841. In the Civil War he was head of the department of seamanship at the Naval Academy (then at Newport, R.I.) and served on blockade duty off the South Carolina coast. After the war he was commandant (1865–68) of midshipmen at Annapolis and saw varied service afloat and ashore. It was largely owing to his efforts that the naval war college was established at Newport in 1884. He was its first superintendent (1884–86). Promoted rear admiral in 1886, he was retired in 1889. Luce's *Seamanship* (1863), which went through many editions, was long an authoritative text. See biography by Albert Gleaves (1925).

Lucera (lo͞ochĕ'rä), town (1971 pop. 31,270), Apulia, S Italy. It is an agricultural and industrial center. Already important in the 4th cent. B.C., the town was destroyed by the Byzantines in the 7th cent. A.D. It was revived (13th cent.) by Emperor Frederick II, who built a great castle (now in ruins) that was the most important fortress in Apulia. Lucera also has a 14th-century cathedral.

lucern: see ALFALFA.

Lucerne (lo͞osûrn'), Ger. *Luzern* (lo͞otsĕrn'), canton (1970 pop. 144,129), 576 sq mi (1,492 sq km), central Switzerland. Drained by the Reuss and Kleine Emme rivers, Lucerne is mainly an agricultural and pastoral region, with orchards and large forested areas. It contains the Lake of Sempach and borders on the Lake of Lucerne. There are several resort areas, notably along the northwest shores of the Lake of Lucerne. The population is mainly German-speaking and Roman Catholic. Manufactures of the canton include machinery, textiles, and paper and other wood products. One of the FOUR FOREST CANTONS, its history is that of its capital, **Lucerne** (1970 pop. 69,879), which is on both banks of the Reuss where it flows out of the Lake of Lucerne. One of the largest resorts (mainly summer) in Switzerland, Lucerne has manufactures of textiles, metal goods, and chemicals, and has a printing industry. The city grew around the monastery of St. Leodegar, founded in the 8th cent. An important trade center on the St. Gotthard route, it became a Hapsburg possession in 1291. Lucerne joined the Swiss Confederation in 1332 and gained full freedom after the battle of SEMPACH (1386). It became capital of the HELVETIC REPUBLIC in 1798. Lucerne was one of the chief towns of the SONDERBUND (1845–47). The noted monument, the Lion of Lucerne, designed by A. B. Thorvaldsen, was erected (1820–21) in memory of the SWISS GUARDS killed in Paris in 1792. Other points of interest are a mainly 17th-century church (Hofkirche), the Glacier Garden, the cantonal buildings, and several museums. An international music festival is held in Lucerne every summer.

Lucerne, Lake of, Ger. *Vierwaldstätter See,* irregular-shaped lake, 44 sq mi (114 sq km), central Switzerland. It has a maximum depth of c.700 ft (210 m). The lake is fed and drained by the Reuss River. Surrounded by mountains, the Lake of Lucerne is noted for its scenic beauty; many resort towns are along its shores. Lucerne (Ger. *Luzern*), the principal lakeside city, is located at its northern outlet. The three arms of the Lake of Lucerne are called the Lake of Küssnacht (northern arm), the Lake of Alpnacht (southwestern), and the Lake of Uri (southeastern).

Luchaire, Achille (äshēl' lüshĕr'), 1846–1908, French historian. He edited, in collaboration with Berthold Zeller, *L'Histoire de France racontée par les contemporains* (65 vol., 1880–90), a collection of excerpts from original sources. His *Histoire des institutions monarchiques de la France sous les premiers Capétiens* (2d ed., 2 vol., 1891), *Manuel des institutions françaises: Période des Capétiens directs* (1892), *Les Communes françaises à l'époque des Capétiens directs* (rev. ed. 1890), and *Social France at the Time of Philip Augustus* (1909, tr. 1912, repr. 1970) are authoritative studies of medieval France under the Capetians and are written in a style noted for its lucidity.

Luchon: see BAGNERES-DE-LUCHON, France.

Luchow: see HO-FEI, China.

Lu-chu Islands: see RYUKYU ISLANDS.

Lucia, Santa: see LUCY, SAINT.

Lucian (lo͞o'shən), b. c.125, d. after 180, Greek prose writer, also called Lucianus, b. Samosata, Syria. In late life he held a government position in Egypt. Lucian wrote an easy, masterly Attic prose, which he turned to satirical use. His wit and characterizations give his satires a vigor and an interest that have made him highly admired and often imitated. Some of Lucian's 82 extant works are falsely attributed to him. The most important and characteristic are his dialogues (e.g. *Dialogues of the Gods, Dialogues of the Dead, The Sale of Lives*), which deal with ancient mythology (the Olympian fables, which he satirizes) and with contemporary philosophers (whose ineptitude he exposes). *The True History,* a fantastic tale parodying incredible adventure stories, influenced such later writers as Rabelais and Swift; *Lucius; or, The Ass,* doubtfully by Lucian, seems to have been the model for APULEIUS. Lucian also wrote poems and rhetorical, critical, and biographical works. See studies by F. G. Allinson (1963) and Peter Gay (1970).

Luciani, Sebastiano: see SEBASTIANO DEL PIOMBO.

Lucie-Smith, Edward, 1933–, English poet and art critic, b. Jamaica, grad. Oxford, 1951. He has lived in London since 1951, where he has worked as an advertising copywriter since 1956. Among his works are *A Tropical Childhood* (1961) and *Confessions and Histories* (1964), poems; and *Art in Britain 1969–70* (1970) and *Symbolist Art* (1973). He has also edited *The Penguin Book of Elizabethan Verse* (1968), *British Poetry Since 1945* (1970), and *Primer of Experimental Poetry* (1972).

Lucifer (lū'sĭfər) [Lat.,=light-bearing], a name for SATAN. In Isaiah 14.12 the reference to Lucifer is figurative for the king of Babylon, but it was misunderstood to mean the fallen angel. Hence the name passed into tradition as a name for the devil. In early times Lucifer was the name given Venus as the morning star.

Lucifer of Cagliari (kälyä'rē), d. 370, bishop of Cagliari, Sardinia (353–70), violent opponent of ARIANISM. As legate of Pope Liberius he went to the council at Milan (355) that Constantius disbanded by exiling the Catholic delegates. Lucifer was bitter against those who seemed to submit to Arianism, and on his return to Sardinia (362) he formed a sect of his own, barring all who had strayed into Arianism at all. His peremptory consecration of a bishop for Antioch (outside his jurisdiction) perpetuated the schism of MELETIUS.

Lucilius, Gaius (gā'əs lo͞osĭl'ēəs, gī'əs), c.180–102? B.C., Latin satiric poet, considered the founder of Latin satire, b. Campania, Italy. About 1,300 fragments survive from his 30 books. He influenced Horace, Persius, and Juvenal.

Lucite: see POLYACRYLICS.

Lucius III, d. 1185, pope (1181–85), a native of Lucca named Ubaldo Allucingoli; successor of Alexander III. He was a Cistercian with St. Bernard and was created a cardinal in 1141 by Innocent II. He was a successful diplomat under Alexander, notably in the peace negotiations (1177) with Holy Roman Emperor Frederick I. During his reign his relations with Frederick were cool; Lucius refused to crown Henry VI, Frederick's son, and there was the perennial question of the lands of MATILDA, countess of Tuscany. The pope and the emperor had a long conference at Verona in 1184 that resembled a council from the attendance; there they issued a joint decree (*Ad abolendam*) on the extirpation of heresies. The decree had a new stringency and detail, but death was not yet invoked as a penalty. The Waldensians were condemned at the same meeting. Lucius was succeeded by Urban III.

Lucius. 1 Christian teacher at Antioch, a Cyrenian. Acts 13.1. **2** Christian at Rome. Rom. 16.21.

Luck: see LUTSK, USSR.

Luckner, Felix, Graf von (fā'lĭks gräf fən lo͝ok'nər), 1886–1966, German naval officer. In World War I he commanded (1916–17) the commerce raider *Seeadler.* Luckner slipped through the British blockade and before his capture near the Fiji Islands (Sept., 1917), destroyed Allied shipping worth more than $25 million. His bold operations earned him the nickname "the Sea Devil." See biography by Lowell Thomas (1927).

Lucknow or **Lakhnau** (both: lŭk'nou), city (1971 pop. 750,512), capital of Uttar Pradesh state, N central India. An educational and cultural center, it also has varied manufactures. It was the capital of the kingdom of Oudh (1775–1856) and then of Oudh prov. It became the capital of the United Provinces when Agra and Oudh merged in 1877. Except for the Imambara [mausoleum] of Asuf-ad-daula, Oudh's greatest king, the architectural remains of the royal period are undistinguished. In the INDIAN MUTINY, one of the causes of which was the abolition of the kingdom of Oudh, the British garrison in Lucknow suffered heavy casualties during the five-month siege (June–Nov., 1857). Although the siege was broken, the British evacuated the city (Nov.). Lucknow was a focus of the movement (1942–47) for an independent Pakistan.

Lucrece (lo͞okrēs') or **Lucretia** (lo͞okrē'shə), in Roman legend, Roman matron, illustrious for her virtue. She was the victim of rape by Sextus, son of Tarquinius Superbus. Having enjoined her husband, Lucius Tarquinius Collatinus, and his friends to avenge her, she stabbed herself to death. The ensuing revolt drove the Tarquins from Rome (see TARQUIN). See Shakespeare's *Rape of Lucrece.*

Lucretius (Titus Lucretius Carus) (lo͞okrē'shəs), c.99 B.C.–c.55 B.C., Roman poet and philosopher. Little is known about his life. A chronicle of St. Jerome speaks of the loss of his reason through taking a love potion. It states that in sane intervals he had written books that were later emended by Cicero. The poetry of Lucretius constitutes one great didactic work in six books, *De rerum natura* [on the nature of things]. In dignified and beautiful hexameter verse the poet sets forth arguments founded upon the philosophical ideas of Democritus and Epicurus. He seeks to persuade man that there need be no fear of the gods or of death, since "man is lord of himself." His proof is based upon the so-called atomic theory of the ancients, which held that everything, even the soul, is made up of atoms, and the laws of nature control all. The soul is itself material and so closely associated with the body that whatever affects one affects the other. Consciousness ends with death. There is no immortality of the soul. The universe came into being through the working of natural laws in the combining of atoms, instead of by the creative power of a deity. Although not the same as the modern atomic theory, many of the principles he gives in his scientific discussions have been upheld by later investigations. See the translation by Cyril Bailey (3 vol., 1947); studies by G. D. Hadzsits (1935) and E. E. Sikes (1936, repr. 1971).

Lucullus (Lucius Licinius Lucullus Ponticus) (lo͞okŭl'əs), c.110 B.C.–56 B.C., Roman general. He served in the Social War under Sulla, who made him his favorite. He fought in the East (87 B.C.–85 B.C.), always loyal to Sulla, who made him curule aedile (79 B.C.) and praetor (78 B.C.). Lucullus was made consul (74 B.C.) and obtained for his proconsulship the province of Cilicia. With his colleague, Caius Aurelius Cotta, he went to the East to attack MITHRADATES VI, who was advancing steadily through Asia Minor. Mithradates defeated Cotta, but Lucullus camped behind the Pontic king, drew him out, and annihilated his army. Mithradates withdrew into Pontus but the following year (72 B.C.) was forced by Lucullus into Armenia, where he took refuge with King Tigranes. Lucullus then applied himself to the establishment of order in Asia, provoking great unpopularity in Rome by reforming the provincial finances. Pompey had always been Lucullus' enemy, and now his party joined with the capitalists in urging the recall of Lucullus. They also sent out emissaries to stir up discontent in Lucullus' army, which had never been devoted to him. In 69 B.C., Lucullus invaded Armenia and took the capital, Tigranocerta. This was the climax of his career, for mutiny then became an almost daily occurrence in his army. In 66 B.C. he was recalled, and Pompey replaced him. Lucullus retired to Rome. He kept out of state affairs and spent huge sums sponsoring public shows and improving his estates. The term *Lucullan* derives from his extravagant standard of living.

Lucy, Saint, d. 304?, Sicilian virgin martyr, commemorated daily in the canon of the Mass. According to legend, at an early age she vowed herself to God. She rejected a pagan suitor, who then denounced her during the persecutions under Diocletian. She is popular in Sicily and in S Italy. In Italian her name is Lucia. Her attributes: a lamp, an awl, a sword, or a wound in her throat. Feast: Dec. 13.

Lud, eponym of an Asiatic people, probably the Lydians. Gen. 10.22; 1 Chron. 1.17. There is probably textual confusion at some points with the LUBIM. Isa. 66.19; Ezek. 27.10; 30.5.

Luddites, name given to bands of workingmen in the industrial centers of England who rioted between 1811 and 1816. The uprisings began in Nottinghamshire, where groups of textile workers, in the name of a mythical figure called Ned Ludd, or King Ludd, destroyed knitting machines, to which they attributed the prevailing unemployment and low wages. In 1812 workers in Lancashire, Cheshire, and the West Riding of Yorkshire began to wreck cotton power looms and wool shearing machines. There was no political aim involved and no cohesion in the movement. Outbreaks of Luddism were very harshly suppressed by the government. See study by M. I. Thomis (1972).

Ludendorff, Erich (ā'rĭkh lo͞o'dəndôrf), 1865–1937, German general. A disciple of SCHLIEFFEN, he served in WORLD WAR I as chief of staff to Field Marshal HINDENBURG. As such, he was largely responsible for the military decisions made by the team of Hindenburg and Ludendorff. After Hindenburg became supreme military commander in 1916, Ludendorff intervened also in all aspects of civilian rule. In 1917 he forced Chancellor BETHMANN-HOLLWEG to resign; his successors were subordinate to the military leaders. When the German military offensive collapsed (Aug., 1918), Ludendorff demanded an armistice (Sept. 29, 1918). Several days later he was dismissed by the new government of MAXIMILIAN, PRINCE OF BADEN and fled to Sweden. Returning in 1919, he took part in the ultranationalist Kapp putsch (1920) and in the "beer-hall putsch" (1923) of Adolf HITLER. He was acquitted in the subsequent trial, was a National Socialist member of the Reichstag (1924–28), and ran for president in 1925 but won few votes. Meanwhile he and his second wife, Mathilde, were proponents of a new "Aryan" racist religion. Ludendorff wrote pamphlets accusing the pope, the Jesuits, the Jews, and the Freemasons of a common plot against Aryan man. Later he became alienated from Hitler. His writings include *Ludendorff's Own Story* (tr. 1919) and *The General Staff and Its Problems* (tr. 1920).

Lüdenscheid (lü'dənshīt), city (1970 pop. 78,993), North Rhine-Westphalia, W West Germany. It is an industrial center; manufactures include metal products and household goods. Lüdenscheid was chartered in 1287 and later was a member of the Hanseatic League. Noteworthy buildings include Neuenhof (1694), a moated castle.

Lüderitz, Franz Adolf (lü'dərĭts), 1834–86, German colonialist in South West Africa. A Bremen merchant, he bought (1883) land including the present town of Lüderitz from a Hottentot chief. This purchase was the nucleus from which he helped create Germany's first colony, SOUTH WEST AFRICA. Lüderitz drowned while exploring the coast of the colony.

Lüderitz (lü'dərĭts), town (1970 pop. 6,642), SW South West Africa, on Lüderitz Bay, an arm of the Atlantic Ocean. Fish and lobsters are processed in the city, and diamonds are mined nearby. The town was founded in 1883 by Adolf Lüderitz.

Ludhiana (lo͝odēä'nə), city (1971 pop. 401,124), Punjab state, NW India. It was founded in the late 15th cent.; today it is an industrial center. Hosiery, cotton textiles, bicycle parts, and sewing machines are the important manufactures.

Ludim (lo͞o'dĭm), African people, unknown unless Ludim is a textual error for LUBIM. Gen. 10.13; 1 Chron. 1.11. See LUD.

Ludlow, Edmund, 1617?–1692, English parliamentarian and regicide. He commanded a regiment of cavalry in the English civil war and served on the court that condemned King Charles I, signing his death warrant. In 1651–52 he was assistant and then successor to Henry IRETON in the subjugation of Ireland. He sympathized with the republican Puritans and opposed the Protectorate of Oliver Cromwell and his son Richard and likewise the restoration of Charles II. After the Restoration (1660) he fled to Switzerland. He returned to England briefly in 1689, meeting with survivors of the republican party, but the government issued a warrant for his arrest, and he returned to Switzerland. See his memoirs (ed. by C. H. Firth, 1894).

Ludlow, Roger, b. 1590, d. after 1664, one of the founders of Connecticut, b. England. Educated at Oxford and admitted to the Inner Temple to study law, he was elected (1630) an assistant of the Massachusetts Bay Company and in the same year sailed to America. He was one of the founders of Dorchester, Mass., and served (1634) as deputy governor of Massachusetts. Moving to the new settlements along the Connecticut River, he presided (1636) at Windsor over the first court held in Connecticut and is credited with the final drafting of the FUNDAMENTAL ORDERS, adopted by the colony in 1639. He also completed the first codification of Connecticut laws, known as Ludlow's Code or the Code of 1650. In 1639 he founded the settlement of Fairfield, Conn., and for many years served as a magistrate and deputy governor of Connecticut. He represented (1651–53) the colony in the New England Confederation. Disagreement over his proposed expedition against the Dutch settlers of New Netherland caused him to return (1654) to England, after which he settled in Ireland. See biography by J. M. Taylor (1900).

Ludlow, town (1970 pop. 17,580), Hampden co., SW Mass., on the Chicopee River; settled c.1750, set off from Springfield 1774, inc. 1775. It is a residential suburb of Springfield and Chicopee. Its manufactures include brassieres, shoelaces, and electronics and television components. Ludlow State Park is within the town.

Ludus Coventriae (lo͞o'dəs kəvĕn'trēā), one of four extant cycles of English miracle plays. In the 17th cent. it was mistakenly designated as originating in the town of Coventry. Because of its stylistic distinction from other Coventry plays, the *Ludus Coventriae* is presently believed to have been produced by a traveling troupe. See also MIRACLE PLAY.

Ludwig. For German rulers thus named, see LOUIS.

Ludwig, Emil (ā'mĕl lo͞ot'vĭkh), 1881–1948, German biographer. His vivid and dramatic (although sometimes unreliable) portraits of great men include *Goethe* (1920, tr. 1928), *Napoleon* (1924, tr. 1926), *Bismarck* (1926, tr. 1927), *The Son of Man* (1928, tr. 1928), and *Schliemann of Troy* (1931, tr. 1931). Among his other works are the "biographies" *The Mediterranean* (1927, tr. 1942) and *The Nile* (1935, tr. 1936). Ludwig left Germany for Switzerland in 1907.

Ludwig, Karl Friedrich Wilhelm (kärl frē'drĭkh vĭl'hĕlm), 1816–95, German physiologist. He became world famous as professor (from 1865) and head of the physiological institute at the Univ. of Leipzig. He pioneered in the study of physiology as related to the physical sciences and introduced improved laboratory methods and apparatus, notably the kymograph.

Ludwig, Otto (ô'tō), 1813–65, German writer. He was one of Germany's first modern realists; although his plots were melodramatic, he sketched accurate and detailed backgrounds. After Hebbel, he was the most notable national dramatist of the period. Among his plays is the tragedy *The Forest Warden* (1850, tr. 1912). Ludwig's best-remembered works, however, are two tales, *Die Heiterthei* (1853) and, especially, *Between Heaven and Earth* (1856, tr. 1911).

Ludwigsburg (lo͞ot'vĭkhsbo͝orkh"), city (1970 pop. 78,019), Baden-Württemberg, SW West Germany, near the Neckar River. It is a transportation and industrial center. Manufactures include machine tools, metal goods, chemicals, porcelain, and organs. There are hot mineral springs in the suburb of Hoheneck. Ludwigsburg grew around the large baroque castle built (1704–33) in imitation of Versailles by Duke Eberhard Ludwig of Württemberg. Schiller lived in Ludwigsburg from 1768 to 1773 and from 1793 to 1794 and attended a nearby military school. The city is the birthplace of the poets J. Kerner and E. Mörike, the theologian D. F. Strauss, and the philosopher F. T. Vischer.

Ludwigshafen am Rhein (lo͞ot"vĭkhs-hä'fən äm rīn), or **Ludwigshafen,** city (1970 pop. 176,031), Rhineland Palatinate, W West Germany, a port on the left bank of the Rhine River. It is connected by bridge with Mannheim, on the opposite shore of the Rhine. The city is a major transshipment point and is a leading center of the West German chemical industry. Machinery and motor vehicles are also produced there. Founded as a small fortress in the 17th cent., Ludwigshafen was named and developed by King Louis I of Bavaria in the mid-19th cent. It was badly damaged in World War II and was the scene (1948) of a disastrous explosion of several chemical plants.

Lueger, Karl (kärl lü'gər), 1844–1910, Austrian politician. He was the leader of the Christian Social party. Lueger appealed to the lower middle classes of Vienna through his anti-Semitism, which was partly religious but mostly opportunist. He was elected mayor of Vienna in 1897, despite the initial opposition of Emperor Francis Joseph, and he held that post until his death. During his administration the public utilities and municipal parks of Vienna were expanded and improved. Lueger was primarily concerned with increasing the church's influence and getting votes. His views and tactics may have influenced the young Adolf Hitler, who then lived in Vienna.

Luening, Otto, 1900–, American flutist and composer, b. Milwaukee. Luening studied at conservatories in Munich and Zurich and with Ferruccio Busoni. He has had a long career as a teacher. Having composed electronic music with Vladimir Ussachevsky for several years, in 1959 he became a director of the new Columbia-Princeton Electronic Music Center in New York City. Luening's electronic works include *Sonority Canons for Four Live Flutes and Thirty-three Recorded Flutes* (1960) and *Gargoyles* (1961) for violin and synthesizer.

Lufkin, city (1970 pop. 23,049), seat of Angelina co., E Texas; inc. 1890. Situated in the deep pine woods, it is the core of a region of forest industries with many sawmills and the first plant to make newsprint from native pine. While lumbering is its major industry, there are numerous other manufactures, including oilfield equipment, engines, gears, and iron and steel castings. Fuller's earth is found in the region. A junior college and a state school for the retarded are in Lufkin. Angelina National Forest, David Crockett National Forest, and Sam Rayburn Lake are in the area.

Lugano (lo͞ogä'nō), city (1970 pop. 22,280), Ticino canton, S Switzerland, near the Italian border. A commercial center in the Middle Ages, Lugano today is a popular resort noted for its scenery and climate. Textiles, tobacco products, and chocolate are made. It was taken from Milan by the Swiss cantons in 1512. Lugano is Italian in character. Notable buildings are the Romanesque Cathedral of San Lorenzo and the 15th-century Monastery of Santa Maria degli Angioli, with its frescoes by Bernardino Luini. Its art museum has a fine collection of European masters. The town, the largest in Ticino canton, is situated on the **Lake of Lugano,** Ital. *Lago di Lugano* (lä'gō dē) or *Ceresio* (chārā'zyō), narrow and irregular in shape (c.20 sq mi/50 sq km), which lies between Switzerland and Italy.

Lugansk: see VOROSHILOVGRAD, city, USSR.

Lugard, Frederick John Dealtry Lugard, 1st **Baron** (lo͞ogärd'), 1858–1945, British colonial administrator. After an early military career, he entered (1889) the service of the British East Africa Company and was sent (1890) to Uganda. After securing British predominance in the area he returned (1892) to England and was instrumental in persuading the British government to assume (1894) a protectorate over Uganda. Appointed British commissioner for N Nigeria, he created the West African Frontier Force in 1897 and by 1903 had subdued N Nigeria. Lugard was governor of all Nigeria from 1912 to 1919, welding its diverse territories into a single administrative unit. He developed the doctrine of indirect rule, which Great Britain employed in many of its African colonies. According to his views the colonial administration should exercise its control of the subject population through traditional native institutions. Lugard expounded his theory in *The Dual Mandate in British Tropical Africa* (1922). He was raised to the peerage in 1928. See biography by Margery Perham (2 vol., 1956; repr. 1968).

luge (lo͞ozh): see TOBOGGANING.

Lugo (lo͞o'gō), city (1970 pop. 63,830) and episcopal see, capital of Lugo prov., NW Spain, in Galicia, on the Miño River. The city is the processing and trade center for a fertile farm area. It has well-preserved Roman walls (3d cent. B.C.) and a 12th-century cathedral (restored).

Lugones, Leopoldo (lāōpōl'dō lo͞ogō'nās), 1874–1938, Argentine poet and journalist. Lugones was a friend of Rubén Darío and was the outstanding *modernista* poet of Argentina. His early work *Las montañas de oro* [the golden mountains] (1897) was influenced by Victor Hugo. It was followed by *Los crepúsculos del jardín* [twilights in the garden] (1905) and *El lunario sentimental* [sentimental almanac] (1909). Later he turned to realism and satire, as in *Odas seculares* [centennial odes] (1910), and emphasized native scenes in collections like *Poemas solariegos* [poems of the manor house] (1928). He is also known for works in linguistics and in history (e.g., *El imperio jesuítico,* 1904). Lugones committed suicide at 63.

lugworm: see ANNELIDA.

Luhith (lo͞o'hĭth), unidentified path in Moab, leading to a sanctuary on a hill. Isa. 15.5; Jer. 48.5.

Luini, Bernardino (bārnärdē'nō lo͞oē'nē), c.1480–1532, b. Luino, Italian painter, son of Giovanni Lutero. Among the extant works of his early years (before 1510) are a *Pietà* (Santa Maria della Passione, Milan) and *Madonna and Child with St. John* (National Gall., London), in the manner of the Lombard school. He soon came under the influence of Leonardo da Vinci, whose style he echoed for the rest of his life. Thus his paintings, particularly of the Madonna, are characterized by a serenity and grace distilled from his master. Panels of the *Madonna and Child* are in the Brera, Milan; the Cincinnati Art Museum; and the Louvre. He executed many large works in towns near Milan: the altarpiece for the church at Legnano; frescoes for Santa Maria Miracoli at Saronno; the *Crucifixion* in Santa Maria degli Angioli, Lugano; and works in the cathedral at Como. These paintings are marked by a more inventive quality, with enchanting landscape backgrounds filled with delightful details. Other works include *Modesty and Vanity* (San Diego) and a portrait and several mythological paintings (National Gall. of Art, Washington, D.C.).

Luitpold (lo͞o'ĭtpôlt), 1821–1912, regent of Bavaria (1886–1912); third son of King Louis I of Bavaria. He ruled for his insane nephews LOUIS II and OTTO I. His son succeeded him as regent and became king (1913) as Louis III.

Lukács, György (dyör'dyə lo͞o'käch), 1885–1971, Hungarian writer, one of the foremost modern literary critics. Converted to Communism in 1918, Lukács served (1919) in the cabinet of Béla Kun. On Kun's fall he fled and lived in Berlin until the rise of Hitler, when he went to the Soviet Union. In 1945 he returned to Hungary, became professor of aesthetics at Budapest, and was important in the Communist party and in national intellectual life. He was attacked for his sympathy for Western literature as expressed in *The Destruction of Reason* (1954), and after the Hungarian revolution he was stripped of political importance. Lukács' powerful criticism combines Marxist social theory with aesthetic sensibility, flexibility, and humanism. His central theme, expounded in *History and Class Consciousness* (1923, tr. 1971), is the link between creative works and the social struggle. His works include studies on Goethe (1947, tr. 1969), Hegel (1948), Lenin (1970), and Solzhenitsyn (1970, tr. 1971) as well as on Marxism and literary values. His other writings include *The Historical Novel* (1955, tr. 1962) and his outstanding *Studies in European Realism* (1946, tr. 1950). His *Political Writings, 1919–1929* was translated in 1972. See studies by George Lichtheim (1970) and E. Bahn and R. G. Kunzer (1972).

Luke, Saint [Gr. *Lucas*], early Christian, traditional author of the third Gospel (see LUKE, GOSPEL ACCORDING TO SAINT) and of its sequel, the ACTS OF THE APOSTLES. He was a Gentile and is called by St. Paul "the beloved physician." Luke accompanied Paul on his second missionary journey and went with him to Rome. Acts 20.5–21.18; 27.1–28.16; Col. 4.14; 2 Tim. 4.11; Philemon 24. According to tradition he was a painter and died a martyr. As an evangelist his symbol is an ox. Feast: Oct. 18.

Luke, Gospel according to Saint, third book of the New Testament. It has been ascribed since the 2d cent. to St. Luke and was composed in the latter part of the 1st cent. A prologue addressed to one Theophilus (1.1-4) precedes the biography. The whole is a literary composition, showing thoughtful working over of matter from different sources, which included St. Mark's Gospel among others (see SYNOPTIC GOSPELS). It contains a unique account of the birth and boyhood of Jesus (1-2), and the center of the book (9.51-18.14) is mainly unparalleled in the other Gospels. A fourfold division of St. Luke after the prologue would be the coming of the Savior (1.5-4.13), his first two years of preaching (4.14-9.17), his third year (9.18-21.38), and the passion and resurrection (22-24). The Gospel shows Pauline influences (St. Paul was a friend of St. Luke), especially with regard to the equality of men and the universality of salvation. The Acts of the Apostles is the sequel to St. Luke's Gospel.

Lukeman, Augustus (Henry Augustus Lukeman), 1871-1935, American sculptor, b. Richmond, Va., studied at the National Academy of Design, New York City, and the École des Beaux-Arts, Paris. Among his works are *Manu, the Law Giver of India* (Appellate Court) and the fountain in memory of Isidore and Ida Straus (both: New York City), and equestrian statues of Francis Asbury (Washington, D.C.) and Kit Carson (Trinidad, Colo.). In 1925 he took over the completion of the colossal sculptures on Stone Mt. in Georgia, started by Gutzon Borglum.

Luks, George Benjamin (lo͝oks), 1867-1933, American portrait and genre painter, b. Williamsport, Pa., studied at the Pennsylvania Academy of the Fine Arts and in Düsseldorf. He worked as a newspaper illustrator, for a time drawing the comic strip *The Yellow Kid* for the New York *World.* In 1902 he became a painter and art teacher. A member of the EIGHT, Luks is best known for his spirited portraits, painted with dash and verve and bordering on caricature. *The Spielers* (Addison Gall., Andover, Mass.) is characteristic of his work. Luks is represented in many leading American galleries.

Luleå (lü'ləō"), city (1970 pop. 50,538), capital of Norrbotten co., NE Sweden, a port on the Gulf of Bothnia at the mouth of the Luleälv River. Although its harbor is icebound most of the winter, large quantities of iron ore and timber are exported. The city has a large smelting plant and railroad shops. Luleå was chartered by Gustavus II in 1621. It was destroyed by fire in 1887, and was rebuilt in a modern style.

Luleälv (lü'ləĕlv'), river, c.275 mi (440 km) long, rising near the Norwegian border, Norrbotten prov., N Sweden, and flowing SE to the Gulf of Bothnia at Luleå. It has spectacular falls at Stora Sjöfallet, Porjus, and Harsprånget. Great power plants constructed at Porjus (1910-14) and at Harsprånget (1945-52)—the latter, with a 350,000-kw capacity, is one of Europe's largest—have harnessed much of the river's potential power, and have impounded huge lakes. Power from Porjus operates many industries in N Sweden, especially the iron mines at Kiruna and Gallivare. Power is transported by high tension wires from Harsprånget to Hallsberg in central Sweden.

Luling: see CHI'AN, China.

Lull, Ramón (rämōn' lo͞ol) or **Raymond Lully,** c.1232-1316?, Catalan philosopher, b. Palma, Majorca. Of a wealthy family, he lived in ease until c.1263, when he had a religious experience and was fired with ambition to convert Muslims to Christianity. He studied Arabic language and literature and founded (1276) a college in Majorca for the study of Arabic. In 1292 he went to Tunis and challenged Muslim scholars to public debates. He was forcibly deported but made a second trip to North Africa in 1307 to combat the teachings of Averroës and again was banished. The tradition that he was stoned to death on a third trip that began in 1315 cannot be substantiated. Lull's chief work—*Ars magna* [the great art]—was a defense of Christianity against the teachings of Averroës. Lull maintained that philosophy (including science) was not divorced from theology and that every article of faith could be demonstrated perfectly by logic. See biographies by E. A. Peers (1946, repr. 1969) and Liam Brophy (1960); study by J. N. Hillgarth (1971).

Lully, Jean Baptiste (zhäN bätēst' lülē'), 1632-87, French operatic composer, b. Florence, Italy. His name originally was Giovanni Battista Lulli. A self-taught violinist, he went to France in 1646 and in 1652 entered the service of Louis XIV. He became chamber composer and conductor of one of the king's orchestras. Lully composed numerous ballets, many for plays by Molière, until 1672, when he obtained a patent for the production of opera. He established the Académie royale de Musique, where he held a virtual monopoly on the French operatic stage, amassing a fortune producing his own works. Among his many operas are *Cadmus et Hermione* (1673), *Alceste* (1674), *Amadis* (1684), and *Armide* (1686). His librettist, Philippe Quinault, was a dramatist in his own right, and Lully called their works *tragédies lyriques.* He established the form of the French overture, wrote recitatives well suited to the French language, and set the style for French opera until the advent of Gluck.

Lully, Raymond: see LULL, RAMON.

Luluabourg: see KANANGA, city, Zaïre.

lumbago (ləmbā'gō), pain in the lumbar region of the back, between the chest cavity and the pelvis. It may be caused by a sudden strain, as from lifting or bending, or by a structural weakness of the tendons or muscles. Treatment consists of rest, analgesics, and application of heat. It is important to avoid further strain on the back muscles. Pain in the lower back can also result from disease of the spine.

lumbar puncture: see SPINAL PUNCTURE.

lumber, term for timber that has been cut into boards for use as a building material. The major steps in producing lumber involve logging (the felling and preparation of timber for shipment to sawmills), sawing the logs into boards, grading the boards according to defects and intended use, drying, and finishing the rough boards into smoother products. The leading lumber-producing countries in the world are the Soviet Union and the United States, which together produce over 50% of the world's lumber supply. In the United States, Maine early took the lead in production, but as the industry spread the forests of the West acquired increasing importance and Oregon, Washington, and California became leading producers. More recently, the forests of the S United States have taken over a large share of lumber production. Lumbering was one of the first industries in North America—its first exports were ship timbers. Logging was a frontier industry, the work being rough, dangerous, and difficult. Romantic, exaggerated stories and legends of the feats of the lumberjack are a colorful chapter in U.S. folklore. For lumber cuts and preparations, see WOOD. See N. C. Brown, *Lumber* (2d ed. 1958); R. E. Pike, *Tall Trees, Tough Men* (1967); Louie Blanchard, *The Lumberjack Frontier* (1969).

Lumberton, city (1970 pop. 16,961), seat of Robeson co., S N.C., on the Lumber River; founded 1787, inc. 1852. It is a tobacco market and has textile and lumber mills. Nearby Pembroke is a center for Lumbee Indians and the seat of Pembroke State Univ.

lumen: see PHOTOMETRY.

Lumière, Louis Jean (lwē zhäN lümyĕr'), 1864-1948, and **Auguste Lumière** (ōgüst'), 1862-1954, French inventors, brothers. They invented the Cinématographe, which was patented and demonstrated in 1895. This mechanism was the first to photograph, print, and project moving pictures onto a screen where they could be viewed by an audience. The portable Cinématographe was an important improvement upon the Edison kinetoscope.

luminescence, general term applied to all forms of cool light, i.e., light emitted by sources other than a hot, incandescent body, such as a BLACK BODY radiator. Luminescence is caused by the movement of electrons within a substance from more energetic states to less energetic states. There are many types of luminescence, including chemiluminescence, produced by certain chemical reactions, chiefly oxidations, at low temperatures; electroluminescence, produced by electric discharges, which may appear when silk or fur is stroked or when adhesive surfaces are separated; and triboluminescence, produced by rubbing or crushing crystals. BIOLUMINESCENCE is luminescence produced by living organisms and is thought to be a type of chemiluminescence. The luminescence observed in the sea is produced by living organisms, many of them microscopic, that collect at the surface. Other examples of bioluminescence include glowworms, fireflies, and various fungi and bacteria found on rotting wood or decomposing flesh. If the luminescence is caused by absorption of some form of radiant energy, such as ultraviolet radiation or X rays (or by some other form of energy, such as mechanical pressure), and ceases as soon as (or very shortly after) the radiation causing it ceases, then it is known as FLUORESCENCE. If the luminescence continues after the radiation causing it has stopped, then it is known as PHOSPHORESCENCE. The term *phosphorescence* is often incorrectly considered synonymous with *luminescence.*

luminism (lo͞o'mĭnĭz"əm), American art movement of the 19th cent., related to impressionism. Its practitioners sought to render the effect of diffused light. Painting majestic vistas bathed in the mystical light of a pristine sky, the luminists, including Frederick E. CHURCH, FitzHugh LANE, and John F. KENSETT, portrayed the American landscape.

luminosity, in astronomy, the rate at which energy of all types is radiated by a star in all directions. A star's luminosity depends on its size and its temperature, varying approximately as the square of the radius and the fourth power of the absolute surface temperature. The sun is a medium-sized star with a luminosity of 3.8×10^{33} ergs per sec, so it radiates 70,000 horsepower per sq yd. The luminosities of other stars are commonly expressed in terms of the sun's luminosity. The known luminosities of stable stars range from about 1/1,000,000 that of the sun for a WHITE DWARF to about 1,000,000 times that of the sun for the hottest known supergiant star. See MAGNITUDE; MASS-LUMINOSITY RELATION; STELLAR EVOLUTION.

lumpy jaw, infectious disease of cattle and swine caused by the bacterium *Actinomyces bovis.* It is characterized by an infection of the bone of the head, particularly the mandible and the maxilla, with abscesses forming near the lower jaw bones. Its scientific name is actinomycosis. Treatment consists of the oral or intravenous administration of iodide compounds and surgical drainage of the affected areas.

Lumumba, Patrice Emergy (pətrēs' ĕmârzhē' lo͞omo͞om'bä), 1925-61, prime minister (1960) of the Republic of the Congo (now Zaïre). A member of the Batatele tribe, he was educated in mission schools and later worked as a postal clerk. He became a member of the permanent committee of the All-African Peoples Conference (founded in Accra, 1958) and president of the Congolese National Movement, an influential political party. After the uprising (Jan., 1959) in the Congo, he fled the country to escape arrest but soon returned. Late in 1959, accused of instigating public violence, he was jailed by the Belgians but was released (1960) to participate in the Brussels Congo conference, where he emerged as a leading negotiator. When the Republic of the Congo came into existence (June, 1960) Lumumba was its first premier and minister of defense. Shortly after independence, the army mutinied, the Belgian government flew in troops to protect Belgian citizens, and Katanga province declared its independence. Lumumba appealed for aid to the United Nations, which sent troops to reestablish order. In September, President KASAVUBU, his rival for power, dismissed him as prime minister and he, in turn, dismissed Kasavubu as president. Shortly afterward, Lumumba was put under house arrest by Colonel MOBUTU. Lumumba escaped but was recaptured and then flown (Jan., 1961), on orders from Mobutu and Kasavubu, to Katanga (now Shaba), where in February, it was announced that he had been killed. Riots of protest took place in many parts of the world. See his *Congo: My Country* (1962) and *Lumumba Speaks* (ed. by Jean van Lierde, tr. 1972); study by T. R. Kanza (1972).

Luna, Alvaro de (älvä'rō dā lo͞o'nä), 1391?-1453, constable of Castile, grand master of the Order of Santiago. The favorite of JOHN II of Castile, he virtually ruled the kingdom, winning victories over the Moors (1431) and the rebellious nobles (1445). However he aroused the enmity of John's second wife, Isabel of Portugal, whose schemes led to Luna's trial and execution.

Luna, Pedro de (pā'thrō), 1328?-1423?, Aragonese churchman, antipope (1394-1417) with the name Benedict XIII. He was a doctor of canon law and as cardinal (1375) became an outstanding member of the Curia Romana. He supported the election of URBAN VI, but later switched his allegiance to ROBERT OF GENEVA, who, as Antipope Clement VII, launched the Great Schism (see SCHISM, GREAT). As Robert's legate in Spain, Cardinal de Luna secured the adherence of his country to the Avignon obedience. On Robert's death, the cardinals at Avignon elected Cardinal de Luna, having first elicited his promise to abdicate should that be necessary to bring an end to the schism. As Benedict XIII, the new antipope proved himself the most able of all of the popes and antipopes of the period. He showed himself unwilling, however, to negotiate an end to the schism. His outright refusal to abdicate at the Council of Pisa (see PISA, COUNCIL OF) only made matters worse, and Benedict lost all his obedience but Scotland, Sicily,

Castile, and Aragón. The Council of Constance (see CONSTANCE, COUNCIL OF) moved Benedict to even greater intransigence. The council deposed him in 1417. Benedict, forsaken by all but his household, lived on in his fortress at Peñiscola (near Valencia), claiming to be the rightful pope until his death.

Lunacharsky, Anatoli Vasilyevich (ənətô'lyē vəsē'lyəvĭch lo͝onəchär'skē), 1875–1933, Russian revolutionary, dramatist, and critic. He began his revolutionary career in 1892 and joined the Bolshevik party when it appeared, forming with Gorky and Bogdanov the left wing of the group, which was in opposition to Lenin. Later he was Lenin's ally in overthrowing the Kerensky government. His most important position was as commissar of education (1917–29). He advocated the creation of a new proletarian literature. Of his many plays, three are translated in *Three Plays* (1923).

lunacy: see INSANITY.

lunar caustic: see SILVER NITRATE.

lunar exploration: see SPACE EXPLORATION.

Lund (lŭnd), city (1970 pop. 53,469), Malmöhus co., S Sweden. It is a commercial and industrial center and a rail junction. Manufactures include paper, printed materials, and clothing. Mentioned (c.920) in the sagas as Lunda, it became the Roman Catholic archiepiscopal see for Scandinavia in 1103–4 and subsequently flourished as an ecclesiastical and trade center. The city declined after it became (1536) a Lutheran bishopric, and it was devastated during the Danish-Swedish wars of the 17th cent. It passed definitively to Sweden in 1658 with Skåne prov. In 1668 Charles XI dedicated the Univ. of Lund, where the poet Esaias Tegner (1782–1846) later taught. The theological faculty of the university was well known in the 19th cent. The city is also the site of a technical university. Lund has a fine 11th-century Romanesque cathedral and a museum of folk customs.

Lunda (lo͝on'də), ethnic group of central Africa. The Lunda speak a Bantu language and now live in S Zaïre, E Angola, and N Zambia. In the 16th cent. Lunda living near the upper Lulua and Kasai rivers assimilated political ideas from the Luba (especially regarding divine kingship and bureaucratic administration) and formed a kingdom ruled by the mwata yamvo, or king. The kingdom grew powerful, partly through trade (especially for firearms) with the Portuguese in Angola, and by the 18th cent. had expanded to include most of the area between the Kwango and Luangwa rivers. At the same time, dissident Lunda migrated eastward; some of them founded the kingdom of the Mwata Kazembe, centered near the Luapula River, which was a flourishing trading state in the period from the late 18th to the early 19th cent. Both kingdoms declined with the establishment of European rule in the late 19th cent. See Jan Vansina, *Kingdoms of the Savanna* (1966).

Lundy, Benjamin, 1789–1839, American abolitionist, b. Sussex co., N.J., of Quaker parentage. A pioneer in the antislavery movement, Lundy founded (1815) the Union Humane Society while operating a saddlery in Ohio. He soon began to devote his efforts full time to the abolitionist cause by founding (1819) the antislavery periodical *Philanthropist.* In 1821 he began publishing the better-known *Genius of Universal Emancipation.* William Lloyd GARRISON became associate editor of the *Genius* in 1829, but Lundy's belief in forming colonies abroad for freed slaves led the two to part. The *Genius* ceased publication in 1835, and in 1836, at Philadelphia, Lundy founded the *National Enquirer,* edited after 1838 by John Greenleaf Whittier as the *Pennsylvania Freeman.* See biography by Marshall L. Dillon (1966); Thomas Earle, ed., *The Life, Travels and Opinions of Benjamin Lundy* (1847, repr. 1971).

Lundy Isle, 3 mi (4.8 km) long, off Devonshire, SW England, at the mouth of the Bristol Channel. Granite was quarried there for centuries. Inhabited in prehistoric times, the island was a stronghold of pirates and smugglers from the Middle Ages until the 18th cent. There are ruins of a 13th-century castle.

Lundy's Lane, locality in S Ontario just W of the Niagara Falls, scene of a stubborn engagement of the War of 1812, fought July 25, 1814. The American forces commanded by Gen. Winfield Scott and led by Gen. Jacob J. Brown, pushing into Canada, encountered British troops posted along Lundy's Lane. After prolonged fighting, the Americans fell back to Fort Erie, their former position. They had gained no advantage but had shown themselves able to hold a superior enemy force. There were heavy casualties on both sides.

Lüneburg (lü'nəbo͝orkh), city (1970 pop. 59,516), Lower Saxony, N West Germany, on the Ilmenau River. It is a rail junction and river port. There are large saltworks and chemical and textile industries in the city. Its hot salt springs and mud baths have long been frequented. Dating from the 10th cent., Lüneburg was long the capital of the dukes of Brunswick-Lüneburg (see HANOVER, former independent kingdom). It was an important member of the Hanseatic League. Predominately built in the late-Gothic and Renaissance styles, the city has several fine churches, a large city hall (begun 13th cent., additions as late as the 18th cent.), and many gabled houses in the characteristic north German style. The **Lüneburger Heide** (lü'nəbo͝orgər hī'də), a vast heath, SW of Lüneburg, lies between the Elbe and Aller rivers. It is a sandy region; sheep are raised and petroleum is produced. Parts of the heath are game preserves.

Lünen (lü'nən), city (1970 pop. 71,658), North Rhine-Westphalia, N central West Germany, on the Lippe River. Its manufactures include machinery, metal fittings, textiles, and aluminum. Motor vehicles are assembled there and coal is mined. First mentioned in 1195, Lünen was chartered in 1265 and passed to the counts of Mark in 1302.

Lunenburg (lo͞o'nənbərg), town (1971 pop. 3,215), SW N.S., Canada, on Lunenburg Bay, SW of Halifax. It has a large fishing fleet. The district was chiefly settled c.1750 by Germans from Hanover.

Lunéville (lünāvēl'), town (1968 pop. 25,367), Meurthe-et-Moselle dept., NE France, on the Meurthe River in Lorraine. It is known for its crockery. Railroad equipment, textiles, and wooden toys are also made. The 18th-century palace in Lunéville was the residence of Stanislaus I. The treaty signed there in 1801 between France and Austria confirmed and supplemented the terms of the treaty that had been signed at CAMPO FORMIO.

lungfish, common name for any of a group of fish belonging to the families Ceratodontidae and Lepidosirenidae, found in the rivers of South America, Africa, and Australia. Like the lobefins, the lungfishes are ancestrally related to the four-footed land animals. Fossil lungfish have been found in the United States, Europe, and India. Of the living specimens, the most primitive is an Australian species, a stout-bodied 5-ft (150-cm) fish with paired fins set on short stumps. The function of its lungs is not clearly understood. The fins of other lungfishes have become long, wispy sense organs. They are in general more eellike in appearance. Best-known are the African species, which hibernate in hard clay balls during the dry season. They line their retreat with a waterproof membrane of dried mucus and apply their mouths to tubes of this material that serve as airshafts from the cocoons to the surface of the ground. They can remain dormant in this manner for up to three years. In water, the African lungfishes breathe with gills. The South American loalach is totally dependent on air and will drown if held under water. Its eggs are laid in a long tunnel at the bottom of a swamp and are guarded by the male, which sprouts red filamental gills from his pelvic fins. The young are also equipped with temporary external gills. Lungfish feed on snails and plants, storing quantities of fat for sustenance during hibernation. Lungfish are classified in the phylum CHORDATA, subphylum Vertebrata, class Osteichthyes, order Dipteriformes, families Ceratodontidae and Lepidosirenidae.

Lung-men: see LO-YANG, China.

lungs, pair of elastic organs used for breathing in vertebrate animals. In man they are located on either side of the heart, occupying a large portion of the chest cavity from the collarbone to the diaphragm. Air enters the body through a series of passages, beginning with the nose or mouth. It travels to the chest cavity through the TRACHEA, which divides into two bronchi, each of which enters a lung. The bronchi divide and subdivide into a network of countless tubes. The smallest tubules, or bronchioles, enter cup-shaped air sacs known as alveoli, which number about 700 million in both lungs. Each alveolus is surrounded by a net of capillaries. As blood flows through these vessels, carbon dioxide passes into the alveoli and oxygen diffuses into the bloodstream. The capillaries are part of a vast network of pulmonary blood vessels that connect the lungs directly to the heart via the large pulmonary arteries and veins. The alveoli are clustered in groups, or lobules, and the lobules are clustered into lobes. In man the left lung has two lobes; the right lung three. The lungs are covered by a thin membrane called the PLEURA. They are expanded and contracted (thereby inhaling and exhaling air) by the combined movement of the diaphragm and the rib cage, which is alternately raised (and expanded) and lowered (and contracted) by the chest muscles. See RESPIRATION.

Lunt, Alfred, 1893–, b. Milwaukee, **and Lynn Fontanne** (fŏntăn'), 1887?–, b. England, American acting couple. Lunt made his debut in Boston (1913), toured in vaudeville, and won fame in Tarkington's *Clarence* in 1919. Fontanne made her London debut in 1905 and her first appearance in New York City in 1910. The couple were married in 1922 and appeared together (1924–29) in many Theatre Guild productions, including *The Guardsman* and *Pygmalion.* The Lunts first appeared in London in *Caprice* in 1929. They excelled especially in sophisticated modern comedy, such as Coward's *Design for Living* (1933). The Lunts played in *There Shall Be No Night* (1940) and in *The Visit* (1957–60) and performed together in films and television plays. See Maurice Zolotow, *Stagestruck* (1965).

Lupercalia (lo͞opərkāl'yə), ancient Roman festival held annually on Feb. 15. The ceremony of the festival was intended to secure fertility and keep out evil. Two male youths, clad in animal skin, ran around the city slapping passersby with strips of goat skin. Because the youths impersonated male goats (the embodiment of sexuality), the ceremony was believed to be in honor of FAUNUS. The festival survived into Christian times and was not abolished until the end of the 5th cent.

Lupescu, Magda (mäg'dä lo͞opĕ'sko͞o), 1896?–, wife of CAROL II of Rumania. Her given name was Elena. Carol renounced (1925) his succession to the throne for her, but after becoming king (1930) he installed her as his official mistress. She was accused of exerting a corrupting influence on Rumanian politics; part of her unpopularity was due to her Jewish origin. Lupescu shared Carol's exile from 1940 and was married (1947) to him in Brazil, becoming Princess Elena. After his death (1953) she lived in Portugal and in France. See biography by A. L. Moats (1955).

lupine or **lupin** (lo͞o'pĭn); any species of the genus *Lupinus,* annual or perennial herbs or shrubs of the family Leguminosae (PULSE family). These leguminous plants have been cultivated in the Mediterranean region since ancient times for enriching the soil. The seeds of some species (e.g., *L. albus,* the white lupine) have been boiled and used as food to some extent in that locality, and the leafy parts are used as forage both there and in America. Some of the many species native to the American West are poisonous as forage, causing the disease lupinosis to which sheep are especially susceptible. Poisonous species and their effects have not been fully determined. As a garden flower the lupine is a favorite because of the various colors and the tall spikes of bonnet-shaped blossoms. The leaves are usually composed of leaflets radiating to form a rounded handlike leaf. Certain movements, as from the horizontal to a vertical position, are characteristic of the leaves of some of these plants, e.g., the common wild lupine (*L. perennis*), also called sundial and quaker bonnet. The bluebonnet, or buffalo clover (*L. subcarnosus*), is the state flower of Texas, where it carpets the plains in springtime with its blue blossoms. In Scotland the name bluebonnet is given to the cornflower. The false lupine belongs to the genus *Thermopsis.* Lupine is classified in the division MAGNOLIOPHYTA, class Magnoliopsida, order Rosales, family Leguminosae.

lupus, noninfectious disease in which antibodies in an individual's immune system attack the body's own substances. In lupus, also known as systemic lupus erythematosus, antibodies are produced against the individual's own nucleic acids and cell organelles such as ribosomes and mitochondria, causing tissue inflammation and cell damage. Because the vascular and connective tissue of any body organ may be affected, a multiplicity of symptoms may result. Generalized symptoms include fever, weakness, weight loss, anemia, enlargement of the spleen, and a characteristic butterfly-shaped skin rash on the face. Heart, joint, and kidney disease are common (see NEPHRITIS). It is believed that the disease may be suddenly triggered by certain drugs or foreign proteins, exposure to ultraviolet radiation, or psychic trauma; it has also been suggested that some undetected virus infection may alter cells and thus destroy the normal immunological tolerance of the body to its own substances. The disease, which may range from mild to fatal, most commonly occurs in young women. It is treated with IMMUNOSUPPRESSIVE DRUGS and STEROIDS. See IMMUNITY; AUTOIMMUNE DISEASE.

Luray (lo͞orā'), tourist town (1970 pop. 3,612), seat of Page co., N Va., in the Shenandoah valley, in a farm area; inc. 1812. It is the headquarters of Shenandoah

National Park. George Washington National Forest is north and west of the town. The **Luray Caverns** there, discovered in 1878, are remarkable for the beauty and color of their large stalagmite and stalactite formations and pools. In a park adjoining the caverns there is a 47-bell carillon; recitals are given throughout the year.

Lurçat, Jean (zhäN lürsä'), 1892–1966, French artist and writer. Lurçat worked as a painter and lithographer, illustrating numerous books. He is best known, however, as a tapestry designer. His gay, brightly colored tapestries hang in many European royal and presidential palaces. A major example hangs in the Musée national d'Art moderne, Paris. Lurçat's writings include *Designing Tapestry* (tr. 1950). His brother **André Lurçat,** 1894–1970, architect and city-planner, worked extensively on the rebuilding of French cities after World War II.

Lurgan (lûr'gən), municipal borough (1971 pop. 24,055), Co. Armagh, central Northern Ireland, near Lough Neagh. A textile center since the 17th cent., Lurgan also has factories for the production of machinery. The town was founded in the early 17th cent. by settlers from England; its castle dates from that period. The poet George William Russell was born in Lurgan.

Luria or **Loria, Isaac ben Solomon** (lo͝or'ēə, lôr'-), 1534–72, Jewish cabalist, surnamed Ashkenazi, called Ari [lion] by his followers, b. Jerusalem. At the age of about 22 he became a hermit and a visionary. He settled (c.1570) at Safed, Palestine, where he became the teacher and leader of a large circle of students who formed an important school of mysticism. Combining Messianism with reinterpreted cabalistic doctrines from an earlier period (see CABALA), Luria sought to understand the nature and connection between earthly redemption and cosmic restoration. Man's deeds, linked to the secret processes of creation and thus an integral part of the cosmic drama, work toward man's redemption by aiding in the restoration of the cosmos to its original state. It is the Jewish people, through their adherence to God's HALAKAH, who will effect this restoration and thereby bring forth the Messiah as the consummate act of earthly redemption. Luria's philosophy has come down to us through the numerous works of his chief disciple, Hayim Vital. See Gershom Scholem, *Major Trends in Jewish Mysticism* (3d rev. ed. 1954, repr. 1967); Yehudah Ashlag, *The Kabbalah: A Study of the Ten Luminous Emanations from Rabbi Isaac Luria* (tr. vol. 1, 1969).

Luria, Roger of: see ROGER OF LORIA.

Luristan (lo͝orĭstän'), governorate (1966 pop. 686,307), c.11,700 sq mi (30,300 sq km), W Iran. The chief cities are the capital Khurramabad and Burujird. The region consists mainly of mountain ranges; the highest point is c.14,200 ft (4,330 m). It has large petroleum deposits. Sheep are raised. The inhabitants are mainly Lurs and Bakhtiari. From Luristan came (18th cent. B.C.) the Kassite conquerors of Babylonia. The noted **Luristan bronzes,** found in the governorate beginning around 1930, include cups, horse bits, daggers, and shields, ornamented with animal motifs, checkerboards, wavy lines, and crosses. They were probably made in the 8th and 7th cent. B.C. by local metalworkers for Scythian, Cimmerian, or Median nomads. See Freya Stark, *The Valley of the Assassins* (1934).

Lusaka (lo͞osä'kə), city (1972 est. pop. 188,000), alt. 4,200 ft (1,280 m), capital of Zambia, S central Zambia. A sprawling city located in a productive farm area, Lusaka is an administrative, financial, and commercial center. Manufactures include foodstuffs, beverages, clothing, and cement (made from limestone quarried nearby). The city is at the junction of the Great North Road (to Tanzania) and the Great East Road (to Malawi) and is on Zambia's main railroad. The Great Uhuru (or Tan Zam) Railway (begun in 1970) is scheduled to connect Lusaka and Dar-es-Salaam, Tanzania, by 1975. Lusaka was founded by Europeans in 1905 and was named after the headman of a nearby African village. Its main growth occurred after 1935, when it replaced Livingstone as the capital of the British colony of Northern Rhodesia. The Univ. of Zambia (1965) and Hodgson Technical College are in Lusaka.

Lusatia (lo͞osā'shə), Ger. *Lausitz,* Pol. *Łużyce,* region of E East Germany and SW Poland. It extends N from the Lusatian Mts., at the Czechoslovak border, and W from the Oder River. The hilly and fertile southern section is known as Upper Lusatia, the sandy and forested northern part as Lower Lusatia. The Lusatian Neisse separates E East Germany and SW Poland. Forestry, farming, and stock raising are the chief occupations. There are lignite mines, textile mills, and glass-making factories. Bautzen, Cottbus, Görlitz, Żagań, and Zittau are the main towns. The Lusatians are descended from the Slavic WENDS, and part of the population, particularly in the Spree Forest, still speaks Wendish and has preserved traditional dress and customs. The region was colonized by the Germans beginning in the 10th cent. and was constituted into the margraviates of Upper and Lower Lusatia. Both margraviates changed hands frequently among Saxony, Bohemia, and Brandenburg. In 1346 several towns of the region formed the Lusatian League and preserved considerable independence. Under the Treaty of Prague (1635) all of Lusatia passed to Saxony. The Congress of Vienna awarded (1815) Lower Lusatia and a large part of Upper Lusatia to Prussia. After World War II the Lusatian Wends (or Sorbs, as they are also called) sought unsuccessfully to obtain national recognition.

Lusatian Neisse, river: see under NEISSE.

Lü Shan: see CHIU-CHIANG, China.

Lü-shun (lü-sho͞on), formerly **Port Arthur,** Jap. *Ryojun,* city, SW Liaoning prov., China, at the tip of the Liao-tung peninsula. It has been combined with Ta-lien (Dairen) into the joint municipality of LÜ-TA. Lü-shun is an important naval base dominating the entrance to the Po Hai; it is also a southern terminus of the South Manchurian RR. The city was the administrative center of the Liao-tung (or Kwantung) leasehold from 1898 to 1945 (see LIAONING). As a Russian base (1898–1905), it was the site on Feb. 8, 1904, of the surprise Japanese naval attack that precipitated the Russo-Japanese War. The city passed to Japan by the Treaty of Portsmouth (1905). In 1945 it became the headquarters of the Port Arthur Naval Base District under joint Sino-Soviet administration. China regained exclusive control in 1955.

Lusiads, The: see CAMÕES, LUÍS DE.

Lusignan (lüzēnyäN'), French noble family. The name is derived from a castle in Poitou, built, according to legend, by MÉLUSINE. The family was powerful in the Middle Ages and ruled (13th–14th cent.) the county of Marche. One branch was prominent in the history of the Crusades. GUY OF LUSIGNAN succeeded (1186) Baldwin V as king of Jerusalem; compelled (1192) to resign this title, he received the island of Cyprus from King Richard I of England. His brother, AMALRIC II, succeeded (1194) him as king of Cyprus and was also king of Jerusalem; his descendants continued to claim the kingship of Jerusalem. In 1342 a branch of their line ascended the throne of Lesser Armenia (Cilicia); in 1375 the last Lusignan king of Armenia was overthrown by the Mamelukes, and the Lusignans of Cyprus added the empty title of king of Armenia to the equally empty one of king of Jerusalem. Cyprus flourished under Lusignan rule until about 1370, but then it declined and eventually became dependent on Venice and was obliged to pay tribute to Egypt. The royal capital, Nicosia, was long a center of French medieval culture. Famagusta, however, was ceded in the mid-1370s to Genoa as security for an indemnity in return for the release of the captive King Peter II. In the next century the Lusignan rulers of Cyprus had little power. The situation changed in 1460, however, when Queen Charlotte was expelled by the half-Greek illegitimate son of her late husband. The usurper became king as James II, recovered (1464) Famagusta, and married the Venetian heiress Caterina CORNARO. Their son, James III, died in 1474, and with him the Lusignan dynasty ended; in 1489 Venice took complete control of Cyprus.

Lusin (lo͞o'sĭn'), 1881–1936, Chinese author, whose original name was Chou Shu-jen. He left medical school in Japan to devote himself to literature. Lusin sought to arouse the Chinese people from their cultural lethargy and isolation and to teach them the values of Western science and philosophy. His gift of satire, expressed in terse and mordant style, and his use of the vernacular gained him great popularity during the Chinese literary renaissance. At first attacked as a bourgeois writer by the Chinese Communists, he was later honored as the Gorky of China. He is also known as Lu Hsin and Lu Hsun. See his selected works (tr., 4 vol., 1956–60).

Lusitania (lo͞osĭtān'ēə), Roman province in the Iberian Peninsula. As constituted (A.D. c.5) by Augustus it included all of modern central Portugal as well as much of W Spain. The province took its name from the Lusitani, a group of warlike tribes who, despite defeats, resisted Roman domination until their great leader, Viriatus, was killed (139 B.C.) by treachery. In the 1st cent. B.C. they joined in supporting Sertorius, who set up an independent state in Spain. The old identification of Portugal with Lusitania and of the ancestors of the Portuguese with the Lusitanians (hence Camões's great epic was entitled *Os Lusíadas*) is now largely ignored, but the creation of Lusitania may have had some faint echoing effect in the setting up of the separate kingdom of Portugal many centuries later.

Lusitania, liner under British registration, sunk off the Irish coast by a German submarine on May 7, 1915. In the sinking, 1,195 persons lost their lives, of whom 128 were U.S. citizens. A warning to Americans against taking passage on British vessels, signed by the Imperial German Embassy, appeared in morning papers on the day the vessel was scheduled to sail, but too late to accomplish its purpose. The vessel was unarmed, though the Germans made a point of the fact that it carried munitions for the Allies. The considerable sympathy for Germany that had previously existed in the United States to a large extent disappeared, and there were demands from many for an immediate declaration of war. President Wilson chose the course of diplomacy and sent Germany a strong note asking for "reparation so far as reparation is possible." Germany refused to accept responsibility for the act in an argumentative reply, but issued secret orders to submarine commanders not to attack passenger ships without warning. After prolonged negotiations, Germany finally conceded its liability for the sinking of the *Lusitania* and agreed to make reparations and to discontinue sinking passenger ships without warning. The immediate crisis between the United States and Germany subsided. The incident, however, contributed to the rise of American sentiment for the entry of the United States into World War I. See Adolph and Mary Hoehling, *The Last Voyage of the Lusitania* (1956); C. L. Droste, *The Lusitania Case* (1972); Colin Simpson, *The Lusitania* (1973).

lusterware, kind of pottery with an overglaze finish containing copper and silver or other materials that give the effect of iridescence. The process may have been invented and was certainly first popularized by Islamic potters of the 9th cent. The most beautiful and brilliantly colored ware—pottery that was made between 836 and 883 for the Abbasid caliphs—has been found at Samarra. During the reign (10th–12th cent.) of the Fatimids in Egypt a high standard was maintained. Iranian and Egyptian potters continued to produce lusterware, while in Europe it was manufactured chiefly in Spain and then in Italy, where in the 15th cent. it was sometimes used to enhance majolica. In England the technique came into vogue in the 19th cent. and was utilized by Josiah Wedgwood and Josiah Spode.

Lü-ta (lü-tä), city (1970 est. pop. 4,000,000), S Liaoning prov., China, at the tip of the Liaotung peninsula. It comprises the important and historic municipalities of LÜ-SHUN (Port Arthur) and TA-LIEN (Dairen). In addition to the industrial, commercial, and naval activities carried on in Lü-shun and Ta-lien, Lü-ta has within its municipal boundaries notable vineyards and fields that produce winter wheat and cotton.

lute, musical instrument that has a half-pear-shaped body, a fretted neck, and a variable number of strings, which are plucked with the fingers (see FRETTED INSTRUMENT). The long lute, with its neck much

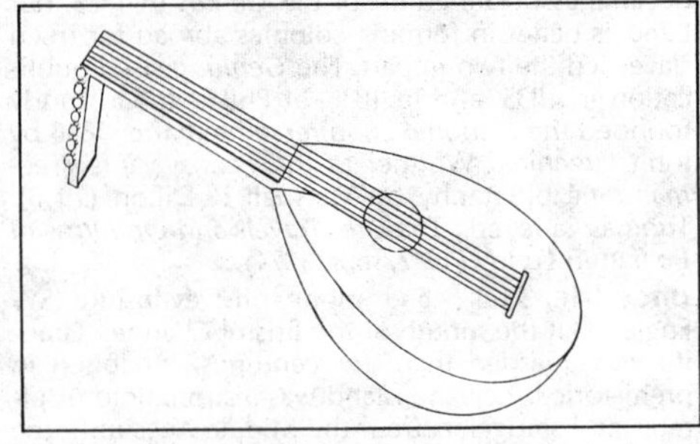

Lute

longer than its body, seems to have been older than the short lute, existing very early in the Egyptian and Middle Eastern cultures, whence the word lute derives. The short lute was known in Spain as early as the 10th cent., having been brought there by the Saracens. Its greatest development came in the 15th cent. The lute was the most popular English and European instrument of the late Middle Ages and the Renaissance. During these periods it amassed a vast literature. In the 17th cent. a larger form (the archlute) was developed; it gave rise to the THEORBO and to the *chitarrone,* which was supplanted by the

Spanish vihuela and the modern GUITAR. Lute music is notated in TABLATURE.

lutenizing hormone (LH): see GONADOTROPIC HORMONE.

Luteri, Giovanni de: see DOSSO DOSSI.

Lutetia: see PARIS, France.

lutetium (lo͞otē'shēəm), formerly **lutecium,** metallic chemical element; symbol Lu; atomic number 71; at. wt. 174.97; m.p. about 1655°C; b.p. about 3315°C; sp. gr. 9.835 at 25°C; valence +3. Lutetium is a silver-white metal that is relatively stable in air. One of the RARE-EARTH METALS, it is the last member of the LANTHANIDE SERIES in group IIIb of the PERIODIC TABLE. The metal may be prepared by reduction of the chloride or fluoride with an alkali or alkaline earth metal. Rare and expensive, it has few commercial uses. The chief commercial source of lutetium is the mineral MONAZITE, which contains lutetium in a concentration of about three parts per hundred thousand. A process for separating lutecia (lutetium oxide, a rare earth) from ytterbia was described in 1907 by Georges Urbain, a French chemist, who is credited with the discovery of the element. It was discovered independently in 1908 by Carl Auer von Welsbach, an Austrian chemist, who called the element *cassiopeium*.

Luther, Hans (häns lo͞o'tər), 1879–1962, German statesman. As minister of finance he aided Hjalmar SCHACHT in stabilizing the German currency. He succeeded Wilhelm Marx as chancellor, heading two successive conservative coalition cabinets (1925–26). He and his foreign minister, Gustav STRESEMANN, negotiated the LOCARNO PACT in 1925. Luther was president (1930–33) of the Reichsbank and German ambassador (1933–37) to the United States. His memoirs appeared in 1960.

Luther, Martin, 1483–1546, German leader of the Protestant Reformation, b. Eisleben, Saxony, of a family of small, but free, landholders. He was educated at the cathedral school at Eisenach and at the Univ. of Erfurt (1501–5). In 1505 he completed his master's examination and began the study of law. Several months later, after what seems to have been a sudden religious experience, he entered a monastery of the Augustinian friars at Erfurt. There, devoutly attentive to the rigid discipline of the order, he began an intensive study of Scripture and was ordained a priest in 1507. In 1508 he was sent to the Univ. of Wittenberg to study and to lecture on Aristotle. In 1510, Luther was sent to Rome on business for his order, and there he was shocked by the spiritual laxity apparent in high ecclesiastical places. Upon his return he completed the work for his theological doctorate and became a professor at Wittenberg. This period was the beginning of the intimacy between Luther and John von Staupitz, whose influence led Luther to say in 1531, "I have received everything from Staupitz." For Luther these years were times of profound spiritual and physical torment. Obsessed with anxieties about his own salvation, he sought relief in frequent confession and extreme asceticism. His search for peace of mind led him, under the guidance of Staupitz, to further study of the Scriptures. In preparation for his university lectures in 1513, especially on the letters of Paul, Luther resolved his turmoil. In the Scriptures Luther found a loving God who bestowed upon sinful humans the free gift of salvation, to be received through faith, against which all good works were as nothing. Luther devoted himself with increasing vigor to the work of the church, and in 1515 he became district vicar. From 1516 on, as a consequence of his new convictions, he felt compelled to protest the dispensation of indulgences (see INDULGENCE). The arrival of Johann TETZEL in Saxony in 1517 to proclaim the indulgence granted by Leo X prompted Luther to post his historic 95 theses on the door of the castle church. The abuse of indulgences had been condemned by many Catholic theologians, but it had had great financial success, and ecclesiastical authorities had not halted it. Luther's theses were widely distributed and read, finding sympathy among the exploited peasantry and among the civil authorities, who deplored the drainage of funds to Rome. The propositions were brought to the attention of the pope, who ordered the head of the Augustinians to keep peace in his order. Meanwhile Tetzel was committed to the struggle against Luther, and he found an able colleague in Johann ECK. Although Luther still considered his activities as directed toward reforms within the church, his opponents found his ideas heretical. In the following years several attempts were made to reconcile Luther to the church, but the basis of compromise was lacking on both sides. At a meeting with the papal legate at Augsburg in 1518, Luther refused to recant, and in 1519 in a public disputation with Eck in Leipzig he was forced to declare his stand as one at variance with some of the doctrines of the church. As the break with Rome became inevitable, Luther broadened his position to include widespread reforms. In his *Address to the Christian Nobility of the German Nation* (1520) he supported the new nationalism by advocating German control of German ecclesiastical matters and appealed to the German princes to help effect the reformation in Germany. He attacked the claim of the papacy of authority over secular rulers and denied that the pope was the final interpreter of Scripture, enunciating the doctrine of the priesthood of all believers. He assailed the corruption of the church and attacked usury and commercialism, recommending a return to a primitive agrarian society. Catholic theologians were further aroused with the publication of *The Babylonian Captivity of the Church,* in which Luther, in an uncompromising attack on the papacy, denied the authority of the priesthood to mediate between the individual and God and rejected the sacraments except as aids to faith. He followed this work with a tract entitled *The Freedom of a Christian Man* in which he reiterated his doctrine of justification by faith alone and presented a new ideal of piety—that of the Christian man, free in conscience by virtue of faith and charged with the duty of conducting himself properly in a Christian brotherhood. By the time the papal bull *Exsurge Domine,* condemning his views and threatening excommunication, reached Germany, Luther's position was well understood and widely supported. In a dramatic renunciation of papal authority, Luther held a public burning of the bull and of the canon law. In 1521 formal excommunication was pronounced. In the same year Luther was given a safe-conduct and was summoned before the Diet of Worms (see WORMS, DIET OF). The opinions at the diet were divided, but when an edict of the diet called for Luther's seizure, his friends placed him for safekeeping in the Wartburg, the castle of Elector FREDERICK III of Saxony. There Luther translated the New Testament into German and began the translation of the entire Bible, a work not completed until 10 years later. Meanwhile at Wittenberg the iconoclasts under CARLSTADT had instituted radical changes that Luther greatly deplored. Fearing that his movement was endangered, Luther disregarded his personal safety and returned to Wittenberg, where he spent most of the remainder of his life organizing and spreading the new gospel. Luther suffered a loss of popular appeal when he stoutly opposed (1524–25) the PEASANTS' WAR, a revolt that his own spirit of independence had helped to foster. His position was further weakened by a break with the humanists brought about by Erasmus's work, *Freedom of the Will* (1524), in which Erasmus attacked Luther's doctrine of the enslaved will. Nevertheless, through his forceful writings and preaching his doctrines spread to many towns and free cities, strengthened by the support of many German nobles. He married (1525) a former nun, Katharina von Bora, and raised six children. His closest friends and associates, Philip MELANCHTHON and Justus JONAS, helped carry forward his endeavors, and after the death of Frederick III he enjoyed the active support of JOHN FREDERICK I, who succeeded to the electorate. Luther worked actively to build a competent educational system; his extensive writing on church matters included the composition of hymns, a liturgy, and two catechisms that are basic statements of the Lutheran faith. His attitude hardened toward various sects, especially the Anabaptists, whose growth presented a serious challenge to his conception of the church. His uncompromising attitude in doctrinal matters helped break up the unity of the Reformation that he was anxious to preserve; the controversy with Huldreich ZWINGLI and later with Calvin over the LORD'S SUPPER divided Protestants into the Lutheran Church and the Reformed Churches. After attempts at union, the Lutherans drew up their own articles of faith in the Augsburg Confession (see CREED **4**), which was written by Melanchthon at the Diet of Augsburg in 1530 with the sanction of Luther, who was not permitted to attend. About this time the control of the Lutheran Church had passed further into the hands of the Protestant princes. During the last years of Luther's life he was troubled with ill health of increasing severity and the plagues of political and religious disunion within the nation. He died in Eisleben and was buried at Wittenberg, leaving behind an evangelical doctrine that spread throughout the Western world and marked the first break in the unity of the Catholic Church. In Germany his socio-religious concepts laid a new basis for German society. His writings, in forceful idiomatic language, helped fix the standards of modern German. Luther's works have been published frequently and in many languages; the first attempt at an edition of them was in 1539–58. See Hartmann Grisar, *Martin Luther, His Life and Work* (tr. 1930, repr. 1971); Heinrich Boehmer, *Luther and the Reformation in the Light of Modern Research* (tr. 1930) and *The Road to Reformation* (tr. 1946, repr. 1957); R. H. Fife, *The Revolt of Martin Luther* (1957); James MacKinnon, *Luther and the Reformation* (4 vol., 1962); V. H. H. Green, *Luther and the Reformation* (1964, repr. 1969); Paul Althaus, *The Theology of Martin Luther* (tr. 1966); James Atkinson, *Martin Luther and the Birth of Protestantism* (1968); E. G. Rupp, comp., *Martin Luther* (1970); H. G. Koenigsberger, comp., *Luther: A Profile* (1973).

Lutheranism, branch of Protestantism that arose as a result of the REFORMATION, whose religious faith is based on the principles of Martin LUTHER, although he opposed such a designation. It became apparent to Luther that the reforms he desired could not be carried out within the Roman Catholic Church. He then devoted himself to questions of faith rather than form in the new Evangelical churches that developed. His was the conservative attitude, as distinguished from the views of the Reformed (Calvinistic) communions. Luther's major departures from Roman Catholic doctrine rest on these beliefs: the Scriptures contain the one necessary guide to truth, and it is the right of the individual to reach God through them with responsibility of his individual conscience to God alone; salvation comes through faith alone, available to man through the redeeming work of Christ; and the sacraments are valid only as aids to faith. The principal statements of faith are found in Luther's two catechisms, the unaltered Augsburg Confession, the Apology of the Augsburg Confession, the Schmalkald Articles, and the Formula of Concord. These are all included in the Book of Concord (1580). Baptism was counted necessary for spiritual regeneration, but no form was specified. The sacrament of the LORD'S SUPPER was retained, but the doctrine of transubstantiation was rejected. As to the manner of worship, Luther chose to retain altars and vestments; he prepared an order of liturgical service, but with the understanding that no church was bound to follow any set order. There is today no uniform liturgy belonging to all branches of the Lutheran body; characteristically, however, an important place is given to preaching and congregational singing. Because of Luther's conservatism and the political conditions of 16th-century Germany, the Lutheran churches originated as territorial churches, subject to the local princes. The history of Lutheranism is generally divided into several distinct periods. The first period, from 1520 to 1580, was one of doctrinal consolidation. Doctrinal disputes, especially that concerning ANTINOMIANISM, began even during Luther's lifetime, but they became more heated in the generation after his death, when the controversy raised by Andreas OSIANDER over the meaning of Christ's death on the cross shook the whole German Evangelical Church. In these disputes the opposing factions were the strict Lutherans, who refused any compromise with Rome or Calvinism, and the moderate wing, headed by Philip MELANCHTHON, who strove for reconciliation. The period from 1580 to 1700 was called "the age of orthodoxy." Almost exclusive emphasis was put on right doctrine, and faith was understood as intellectual assent. During the early years of the 17th cent., Germany was racked by the THIRTY YEARS WAR, and Lutheranism lost much of its territory. Religious boundaries were stabilized by the Peace of Westphalia (1648), which maintained that with slight exceptions the religion of the prince was to be the religion of his subjects. The latter part of the century saw a reaction against the prevailing orthodoxy in the form of PIETISM. In 1817, Frederick William III of Prussia sought to merge forcibly the Lutheran and Reformed churches of Prussia into a single organization called the Prussian Union. Some conservative Lutherans opposed this move and withdrew from the union to found the Evangelical Lutheran Church of Prussia, as a free church. By the end of the 19th cent. there were five or six such independent Lutheran bodies in Germany in addition to the state churches. In 1919, after World War I, the supervision of churches by territorial rulers disappeared completely. The churches were no longer governed by state laws but still received state support. In the unification of German culture under the Nazi regime, the church did not escape. In 1933 a national organization, the German Evangelical Church, was formed. Under the direction of the Nazi party it tried to develop a national racial church, with pure Aryan blood as a prerequisite for membership. A revolt against this movement, led by Martin NIEMOELLER, resulted in the founding of the CONFESSING CHURCH and the formation of the Confessional Synod, which issued (1934) its declaration rejecting the Reich's interference with the church. The end of the war saw the formation of the Evangelical Church in Germany (EKID), which is made up of members of both Lutheran and Reformed churches, and the United Evangelical Lutheran Church of Germany (VELKD), which functions as an expressly Lutheran constituency within the EKID. German churches have also cooperated wholeheartedly in the formation of the Lutheran World Federation (1947) and the World Council of Churches. The Lutheran Church is the established state church of Denmark, Iceland, Norway, Sweden, and Finland. In North America, Lutherans from the Netherlands were among the settlers on Manhattan island in 1625. A congregation was formed there in 1648, but it was antedated by one established (1638) by Swedish settlers at Fort Christina (Wilmington) on the Delaware River. On nearby Tinicum Island the first Lutheran church building in the country was dedicated in 1646. Early in the 18th cent. exiles from the Palatinate established German Lutheran churches in New York, Pennsylvania, Delaware, and Maryland. The Salzburger migration to Georgia (1734) introduced Lutheranism in the South. In the 18th cent., organization of the churches was begun by Heinrich Melchior MÜHLENBERG, who brought about the formation (1748) in Pennsylvania of the first synod in the country. The Synod of New York and adjoining states followed (1786); that of North Carolina was created in 1803. With the settlement of the Midwest, the West, and the Northwest, many small synods were formed by Norwegians, Danes, Finns, and other national groups. Once there were about 150 distinct Lutheran bodies, but in 1918 many of the autonomous Lutheran bodies merged into the United Lutheran Church of America. That marked the beginning of Lutheran unification in the United States. Since then, most American Lutherans have united into three main groups: the American Lutheran Church, formed in 1961; the Lutheran Church in America, formed in 1962; and the Evangelical Lutheran Synodical Conference of North America, formed in 1872 and including the Lutheran Church–Missouri Synod. These groups comprise all but about 50,000 of the 8 million American Lutherans. The local organization still has the most important place in church polity, but there is a growing tendency towards a more organized church. Lutheranism has traditionally stressed education, and there are many Lutheran schools, colleges, and seminaries throughout the world. Since the mid-18th cent., Lutherans have had a program of Christian service for women called the Deaconess movement. The world membership of Lutherans is about 70 million. See A. R. Wentz, *The Lutheran Church in American History* (2d ed. rev. 1933); L. P. Qualben, *The Lutheran Church in Colonial America* (1940); Edmond Vermeil et al., *The Churches in Germany* (1949); Jaroslav Pelikan, *From Luther to Kierkegaard* (1950, repr. 1963); A. K. Swihart, *Luther and the Lutheran Church* (1960); J. H. Bodensieck, ed., *The Encyclopedia of the Lutheran Church* (3 vol., 1965); E. C. Nelson, *Lutheranism in North America* (1971).

Luther College, at Decorah, Iowa; American Lutheran; coeducational; chartered and opened 1861.

Luthuli, Albert John (ləthōō'lē), 1898?–1967, African political leader in the Republic of South Africa. Descended from a line of Christian Zulu chiefs, he was educated at Adams College, a mission school near Durban, and taught there for 15 years. He was appointed chief (1935) and, remaining active in church affairs, preached non-violence in the Africans' campaign against racial discrimination. Although devoutly religious, he grew disillusioned with the church's racial position and became active politically. In 1946 he joined the African National Congress (ANC). When he refused to resign (1952) from the presidency of the ANC, the South African government deposed him as chief and applied severe restrictions on his activities. Nevertheless, he led a campaign of passive resistance against the apartheid laws. In 1956, with some 150 other critics of the government, he was arrested on charges of treason; after a prolonged mass trial he was acquitted. In 1959 the government banished him to his village and outlawed (1960) the ANC, which continued to operate underground. A government law in 1962 banned publication of his statements in the media. A firm believer in the political and spiritual force of passive resistance, he was awarded the 1960 Nobel Peace Prize. Despite some criticism of his passive philosophy, he was highly regarded by most black South Africans. He is the author of an autobiography, *Let My People Go* (1962). See biography by Mary Benson (1963); study by Edward Callan (rev. ed. 1965).

Luton (lōō'tən), county borough (1971 pop. 161,178), Bedfordshire, S central England on the Lea River. Luton is the largest city in Bedfordshire. Automobiles, ball bearings, and aircraft parts are among the products manufactured in Luton. It is also the center of the English millinery industry, established in Luton in the time of James I.

Lutsk (lōōtsk) Pol. *Łuck,* city (1970 pop. 94,000), capital of Volyn oblast (see VOLHYNIA), SW European USSR, in the Ukraine, on the Styr River. A river port, it has industries producing machinery, food products, textiles, and shoes. First mentioned in 1085 as Luchesk, it is one of the oldest cities of Volhynia. It was the main fortress of the Luchan tribe and was called Luchesky Veliki. Lutsk, together with all of Volhynia, was part of Kievan Russia until 1154, when it became the capital of the Lutsk independent principality. It was included in the Galich-Volhynian principality, was taken by Lithuania in the 14th cent., and was an important trade city from the 14th to the 16th cent. Lutsk was part of Poland from the second half of the 16th cent., was taken by Russia in 1791, was Polish again from 1919 to 1939, and was ceded to the Ukrainian SSR in 1939. Architectural monuments include the walls and turrets of a castle (13th–16th cent.), churches (14th–17th cent.), and a synagogue (1626–29).

Lutyens, Sir Edwin Landseer (lŭ'chənz, lŭ'tyənz), 1869–1944, English architect. He began his career designing small houses in Surrey and later executed a long series of large country establishments, many of them complete with their furniture and gardens. In these works he developed a style of domestic architecture that was based upon traditional English design and craftsmanship and yet was highly individual. The noteworthy public achievement of his career was the planning of New Delhi, India, which included the design of the palace for the viceroy. Among his principal works are the Cenotaph in London and other war memorials, including those at Manchester and at Johannesburg, South Africa; domestic and public buildings at Hampstead garden suburb; Hampton Court bridge; and the British embassy at Washington, D.C. He was knighted in 1918. See study by Christopher Hussey (1950).

Lützelburger, Hans (häns lü'tsəlbōōrgər), d. 1526, German wood engraver, assumed to be the same man as Hans Franck, active from c.1516. He worked in Augsburg and Basel and probably in Mainz. His remarkable technical abilities are evident in his wood engravings after Holbein the Younger's *Dance of Death* and in a curious print, *Peasants Fighting with Naked Men.*

Lützen (lüt'sən), town (1965 est. pop. 4,800), Leipzig district, S central East Germany. There, in the Thirty Years War, Gustavus II of Sweden defeated (1632) General Albrecht Wallenstein, but was killed in the battle; Marshal Gottfried zu Poppenheim, on the imperial side, was also mortally wounded. In 1813, Napoleon I defeated the Russian and Prussian forces at nearby Grossgörschen (also spelled Gross Görschen).

Lützow, Adolf, Freiherr von (ä'dôlf frī'hĕr fən lü'tsō), 1782–1834, Prussian officer. He commanded a volunteer corps, the Black Troops (or Black Rifles), in the War of Liberation against Napoleon I in 1813–14. The corps was distinguished for its daring exploits, which were glorified by the poet Karl Theodor Körner, one of its members.

Luxembourg, François Henri de Montmorency-Bouteville, duc de (fräNswä' äNrē' də môNmôräNsē'- bōōtvēl' dük də lüksäNbōōr'), 1628–95, marshal of France. Under his cousin, the Great Condé, he served in the FRONDE, in the conquest of Franche-Comté (1668), and in the Dutch War. Made a marshal in 1675, he was given (1676) command on the Rhine and shared in the victory of Cassel (1677). He was implicated in the POISON AFFAIR and was sent to the Bastille (1679–80). Although still out of favor at the beginning of the War of the Grand Alliance, he was eventually given command in Flanders and won three battles on which his reputation chiefly rests—Fleurus (1690), Steenkerke (1692), and Neerwinden (1693).

Luxembourg (lŭk'səmbûrg, Fr. lüksäNbōōr') or **Luxemburg** (lŭk'səmbûrg, Ger. lōōk'səmbōōrkh), grand duchy (1972 est. pop. 343,000), 998 sq mi (2,586 sq km), W Europe. Roughly triangular, it borders on Belgium in the west and north, West Germany in the east, and France in the south. The city of Luxembourg (1970 est. pop. 77,500) is the capital.

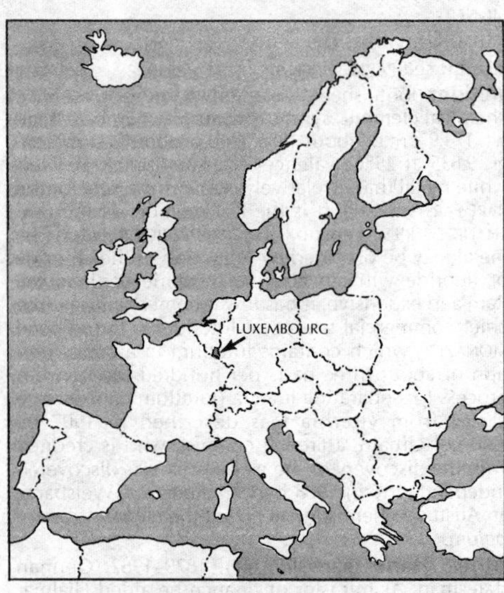

In Letzeburgesch, the prevailing Low German dialect, the name of Luxembourg is Letzeburg. French is the official language and, along with German, is widely spoken. The great majority of the population is Roman Catholic. Luxembourg is drained by the Sauer and Alzette rivers, both tributaries of the Moselle, which forms part of its eastern border. The Ardennes Mts. extend into N Luxembourg. The southwestern section is part of the Luxembourg-Lorraine iron-mining basin and is of international importance; Esch-sur-Alzette is its main center. Despite its smallness, Luxembourg is a major iron and steel producer. Other industries are food processing, tanning, and the production of textiles, chemicals, and cement. Grains and potatoes are grown and livestock are raised. Iron and steel products are the main exports; imports include fuel, food, cloth, and manufactured goods. Luxembourg's neighbors are the main trade partners. The grand duchy is a constitutional monarchy with a bicameral legislature, the upper chamber being appointed by the sovereign, the lower chamber elected by direct universal suffrage. The county of Luxembourg (originally Lützelburg), extending between the Meuse and Moselle rivers and including the present Luxembourg prov. of Belgium, was one of the largest fiefs in the Holy Roman Empire and rose to prominence when its ruler was elected emperor as HENRY VII in 1308. His son was JOHN OF LUXEMBURG, king of Bohemia, father of Emperor CHARLES IV, who made Luxembourg a duchy in 1354. The elder line of the house continued in Bohemia and the empire, with Emperors Wenceslaus and Sigismund, while the younger line, descended from Charles's brother, Duke Wenceslaus, continued in Luxembourg. (The French noble family of Luxembourg was descended in collateral line from an early count of Luxembourg.) In 1443, Philip the Good of Burgundy seized the duchy, and in 1451 he was confirmed in possession by the estates of Luxembourg. Luxembourg passed in 1482 to the house of Hapsburg following the death of Mary of Burgundy. For the following three centuries it shared the history of the S Netherlands (see NETHERLANDS, AUSTRIAN AND SPANISH), passing from Spanish to Austrian rule in 1714. The southern part of the duchy, including Montmédy, Thionville, and Longwy, was ceded to France in the Peace of the Pyrenees (1659); in 1684, Louis XIV of France seized Luxembourg, but he was obliged to restore it to Spain by the Treaty of Ryswick (1697). Occupied by the French during the French Revolutionary Wars, the duchy was formally ceded to France by the Treaty of Campo Formio (1797). The Congress of Vienna (1814–15) made Luxembourg a grand duchy, in personal union through the sovereign with the Netherlands; at the same time, Luxembourg became a member of the German Confederation, and the fortress in the capital was garrisoned by Prussian troops. When in 1830 the Belgians rebelled against William I of the Netherlands, Luxembourg shared in the revolt. Belgium, on gaining its independence, claimed the entire grand duchy; it finally obtained (1839) the major part, i.e., the present Belgian Luxembourg prov. The remainder, continuing in personal union with the Netherlands and as a member of the German Confederation, became autonomous and was granted a constitution in 1848. When the German Confederation was dissolved in

1866, William III of the Netherlands agreed to sell the grand duchy to France, nearly provoking war between France and Prussia. At the London Conference of 1867 the European powers declared Luxembourg a neutral territory; its fortress was dismantled and the Prussian garrison withdrawn. William III died (1890) without male heir; while his daughter Wilhelmina succeeded him in the Netherlands, Duke Adolf of NASSAU, from a collateral line, became grand duke of Luxembourg. He was followed in 1905 by William IV and in 1912 by Marie Adelaide. In 1914, Germany violated the neutrality of the grand duchy and occupied it for the duration of World War I. Grand Duchess Marie Adelaide abdicated in 1919 in favor of her sister, Charlotte, who married Prince Felix of Bourbon-Parma. In 1922, Luxembourg formed an economic union with Belgium. Germany once again invaded (May, 1940) neutral Luxembourg in World War II. The grand duchess and her cabinet fled abroad, and a government in exile was established in London. Allied troops liberated Luxembourg in Sept., 1944. Luxembourg entered the UN (1946) and the North Atlantic Treaty Organization (1949) and received Marshall Plan aid. In 1947, Luxembourg joined with Belgium and the Netherlands in a customs union. A treaty signed in 1958 provided for a full economic union of the three countries, and in 1960 the BENELUX ECONOMIC UNION went into effect. Luxembourg is also a member of the EUROPEAN COMMUNITY. A constitutional revision (1948) abolished the perpetual neutrality of the grand duchy, a status which in practice had ended with the introduction (1944) of compulsory military service (ended 1967). In 1961, Prince Jean (b. 1921), son and heir of Grand Duchess Charlotte, was made the representative of his mother as head of state. Charlotte formally abdicated in 1964. See Arthur Herchen, *History of the Grand Duchy of Luxembourg* (tr. 1950); J. A. Gade, *Luxemburg in the Middle Ages* (1951); K. C. Edwards, *Historical Geography of the Luxembourg Iron and Steel Industry* (1961); Roger Pilkington, *Small Boat to Luxembourg* (1967); F. G. Gunther, *The Benelux Countries* (1959, repr. 1972).

Luxembourg, Flemish *Luxemburg,* province (1970 pop. 217,310), 1,706 sq mi (4,419 sq km), SE Belgium, in the Ardennes, bordering on the Grand Duchy of Luxembourg in the east and on France in the south. The chief towns are Arlon (the capital), Bastogne, and Marche-en-Famenne. The province is drained by the Ourthe, Semois, and Lesse rivers. It is mainly agricultural, producing grain, livestock, and dairy goods. The population is largely French-speaking, although Letzeburgesch, a Low German dialect, is spoken in the east. The province was detached from the Grand Duchy of Luxembourg in 1839. In World War II it was a major battleground in the Battle of the Bulge (Dec., 1944–Jan., 1945).

Luxembourg or **Luxemburg,** city (1970 est. pop. 77,500), capital of the Grand Duchy of Luxembourg, S Luxembourg, at the confluence of the Alzette and Pétrusse rivers. It is a commercial, industrial, administrative, and cultural center and a rail junction. Manufactures include iron and steel, furniture, leather goods, machinery, textiles, beer, and processed food. A picturesque city, Luxembourg developed around a 10th-century castle that was one of Europe's strongest fortresses until its fortifications were dismantled according to the terms of the Treaty of London (1867). Of note are the Cathedral of Notre Dame and the city hall (both 16th cent.). The city is the seat of a university (founded 1958), Radio Luxembourg, and several institutions of the European Communities (including the Court of Justice and the European Investment Bank).

Luxembourg Palace, large Renaissance palace in Paris, on the left bank of the Seine near the Sorbonne. It was built (1615–20) for Marie de' Medici by Salomon de Brosse on the site of a former palace belonging to the duke of Piney-Luxembourg (hence its name), and it was enlarged in the 19th cent. Poussin, Philippe de Champaigne, and Rubens were commissioned to decorate the interior; the 24 panels painted by Rubens are now at the Louvre. The palace was used for the Paris Peace Conference of 1946. It contains valuable paintings, notably those by Delacroix, but the collection of contemporary art, long exhibited at the Luxembourg, has been moved to another building. The beautiful Luxembourg Gardens are a favorite playground for children and, by long tradition, a favorite walk for the students and professors of the Sorbonne.

Luxemburg, Rosa (rō'zä lo͝ok'səmbo͝ork), 1871–1919, German revolutionary, b. Russian Poland. Involved as a student in revolutionary activities, she was forced to flee to Switzerland in 1889. While there she became a Marxist. One of the founders of the Polish Socialist party (1892), she formed (1894) a splinter group (later known as the Social Democratic party of Poland and Lithuania) that favored unity with Russia as the best means of achieving socialist revolution. She acquired German citizenship through marriage and after 1898 was a leader in the German Social Democratic party. A brilliant writer and orator, she participated in the revolution of 1905 in Russian Poland and was active in the Second International. Differences with other socialist leaders in Germany led her to form with Karl LIEBKNECHT the SPARTACUS PARTY in Germany during World War I. In protective custody during much of the war and released in 1918 upon the outbreak of the German revolution, she aided in the tranformation of the Spartacists into the German Communist party and edited its organ, *Rote Fahne.* For their part in the Spartacist uprising in Berlin, she and Liebknecht were arrested (Jan., 1919). While being taken to prison they were killed by soldiers. See her *Rosa Luxemburg Speaks,* ed. with an introd. by M. A. Waters (1970); J. P. Nettl, *Rosa Luxemburg* (2 vol., 1966); Paul Frölich, *Rosa Luxemburg* (tr. 1972).

Luxemburg, grand duchy, province, and city: see LUXEMBOURG.

Luxeuil (lüksö'yə), former abbey, E France, at the present-day town of Luxeuil-les-Bains. It was founded c.590 by St. COLUMBAN on the site of the Roman town Luxovium, destroyed (451) by Attila, later established in Franche-Comté and now in the Haute-Saône dept. The ascetic rule of Columban was soon modified and replaced (8th cent.) by that of St. Benedict. Although constantly troubled by the interference of the Merovingian kings, the monks of Luxeuil were important in upholding Christianity, and enjoyed independence until the abbey's inclusion in Franche-Comté. The abbey, devastated (c.732) by the Saracens, was rebuilt by Charlemagne and soon became one of the early centers of medieval learning; its abbots came to rank as princes of the Holy Roman Empire. The French Revolution secularized the abbey.

Luxor (lŭk'sôr, lo͝ok'-), city (1970 est. pop. 84,600), central Egypt, on the Nile. It is 1 mi (1.6 km) W of KARNAK and occupies part of the site of THEBES. The temple of Luxor, the greatest monument of antiquity in the city, was built in the reign of Amenhotep III as a temple to Amon. The temple, 623 ft (190 m) long, was much altered by succeeding pharaohs, especially by Ramses II, who had many colossal statues of himself erected on the grounds. In early Christian times the temple was made into a church, and later a shrine to a Muslim saint was built in the great hall. The temple was restored, beginning in 1883. Numerous temples and burial grounds, including the Valley of the Tombs of the Kings, are nearby.

luxury tax, levy on articles that are not essential to a normal standard of living. Such taxes may be imposed strictly for revenue purposes or they may be intended to discourage consumption of certain articles, e.g., the tax on French lawns and laces in the 18th cent. in England. In modern times such "conventional necessities" as alcohol, tobacco, jewelry, furs, amusements, private automobiles, and candy have been taxed. In the United States, luxury taxes have been levied frequently, especially in wartime, to raise revenue as well as to discourage the flow of essential resources into the production of items not related to the national effort. See J. F. Due, *Sales Taxation* (1957).

Luynes, Charles d'Albert, duc de (shärl dälbĕr' dük də lüēn'), 1578–1621, constable of France, minister and favorite of King Louis XIII. With the king's collaboration he caused the assassination of Concino CONCINI (1617), took over the government, and forced MARIE DE' MEDICI into exile. His power was twice threatened (1619, 1620) by the activities of Marie and her partisans among the nobles. He became constable in 1621 and shortly afterward died while on a campaign against the Protestants of Béarn.

Luz. 1 Place in Palestine, apparently to be identified with BETHEL **1.** Gen. 28.19; 35.6; 48.3; Joshua 16.2; 18.13; Judges 1.23. **2** City of N Palestine. Judges 1.26.

Luzán, Ignacio de (ēgnä'thyō thā lo͞othän'), 1702–54, Spanish scholar and critic. He studied the classics and the humanities in Italy. From 1747 to 1749 he was secretary at the Spanish embassy in Paris. Luzán's most famous work is *La poética* (1737), in which he voices the need for neoclassical rules and principles in poetry. About a third of the book, which had great influence, is a critical study of the Spanish drama. Luzán was the translator of many Latin, French, English, and Italian works. See study by I. L. McClelland (1973).

Luzern: see LUCERNE, Switzerland.

Luzon (lo͞ozŏn'), island (1970 pop. 16,669,724), 40,420 sq mi (104,688 sq km), largest, most populous, and most important of the Philippine Islands. The irregular coastline provides several fine bays, most notably Manila Bay, which is considered the best natural harbor in the Orient and one of the finest in the world. N Luzon, which is drained by the Cagayan River, is very mountainous; the highest peak, Mt. Pulog, rises to 9,606 ft (2,928 m). In the east, the great Sierra Madre range so closely parallels the shore that almost no coastal plain exists. Mountains extend generally along the entire length of the island, into the irregular Bicol peninsula to the southeast, where Mt. Mayon is the most famous volcano. In the west, the Zambales range runs from Lingayen Gulf S to Bataan peninsula. The island has two large lakes, Laguna de Bay and Taal. Between the rugged coastal mountains, in central Luzon, lies a great fertile plain watered by the Pampanga and Agno rivers. Barely above sea level, c.100 mi (160 km) long and 40 mi (64 km) wide, it is the most important agricultural land in all the Philippines. It supplies food for almost the entire Manila area and is the nation's major rice-producing region and its second (after Negros island) sugarcane-producing area. Elsewhere, the Bicol peninsula is important in the production of hemp, and the Cagayan River valley is known for its tobacco and corn. Other major crops are fruits, vegetables, and cacao. Luzon has important lumbering and mining industries; there are gold, manganese, chromite, nickel, copper, and iron deposits, and the mountain pines and the bamboo on Bataan peninsula have many commercial uses. Manufacturing is centered in the Manila metropolitan area, where the major industries produce textiles, chemicals, metal products, and automobiles. Scattered throughout the island are fertilizer plants, an occasional oil refinery, cement factories, and plywood mills and wood product plants. The inhabitants are almost all Christian and are principally Tagalogs and Ilocanos. Primitive groups include the Negritos and Igorots (the latter's famous rice terraces on steep mountain slopes are considered one of the agricultural wonders of the world). As the major island, Luzon has played the leading role in the nation's history. Manila harbor has been important since the arrival of the Spanish in the late 16th cent. It was on Luzon that the Filipino revolt against Spanish rule began (1896), that U.S. forces wrested control of the islands from Spain (1898), and that the Philippine insurrection against U.S. rule broke out (1899). In World War II, Manila Bay was the prize that most attracted the Japanese and was most stubbornly defended by the U.S.-Filipino army, the bulk of which was concentrated on Luzon. The island was invaded by Japanese forces in several places on Dec. 10, 1941, and in early 1942 the Allied forces made their last stand on BATAAN peninsula and CORREGIDOR. Luzon was recovered (1945) after a major landing from Lingayen Gulf (January), a bloody fight for Manila (February), and protracted mop-up operations, which were not completed until June. After the war, Luzon's central plain (where most of the farms are owned by a few wealthy families and worked by poor tenants) was the focus of a Communist-dominated land reform movement, the Hukbalahap, which resorted to terrorism and caused much civil strife until it was finally brought under control (c.1954). In 1968 the movement became active again; mounting assassinations and violence spurred President Marcos to initiate (Aug., 1969) an intensive military campaign to restore order in central Luzon. In mid-1972, Luzon experienced the worst flooding in the nation's history; more than 400 lives were lost and there was extensive property damage.

Luzzatti, Luigi (lo͞oē'jē lo͞ot-tsät'tē), 1841–1927, Italian political leader and economist. As minister of finance in several cabinets and as premier (1910–11) he promoted liberal legislation and was noted especially for his advocacy of peoples' banks and minority rights. He also secured 24 commercial treaties, one of which (1898) ended the Franco-Italian tariff struggle.

Luzzatto, Moses Hayyim (hä'yēm lo͞ot-tsät'tō), 1707–47, Hebrew playwright, poet, and mystic, a leader of the renaissance of Hebrew literature, b. Padua. At 15 he formed a group to study Cabalistic mysteries and at 17 he wrote *Samson and Delilah,* a drama in verse. He studied the mystic book *Zohar* closely and claimed divine revelation for his own works of mysticism, most of which did not survive rabbinic denunciation. He wrote of love with Biblical lyricism in the *Migdal 'Oz* (1727). His finest work is the allegorical *Glory to the Righteous* (1743). See biographies by Simon Ginzburg (1931) and I. Landman (1908).

Lvov, Prince Georgi Yevgenyevich (gēôr'gē yĭvgā'- nyəvĭch lyəvôf'), 1861–1925, Russian public official, head of the provisional government (March–July, 1917). He played a prominent part in the development of the ZEMSTVO system of local self-government and was chairman of the all-Russian union of zemstvos in World War I. A deputy of the Constitutional Democratic party in the Duma, he became head of the provisional government after the February Revolution of 1917 (see RUSSIAN REVOLUTION). Lvov's idealism and fear of violence made him particularly unfit for coping with the turbulent situation. While he sought to organize a constitutional and democratic government, the Social Democrats gained the actual power by organizing and dominating the workers' and peasants' councils (soviets). Agitation for peace with the Central Powers forced (May, 1917) the resignation of the foreign minister, MILYUKOV, and of the war minister, Guchkov, and Lvov formed a second government. After a popular uprising in Petrograd was suppressed (July, 1917), he resigned and a moderate Socialist government under KERENSKY was organized. Lvov subsequently emigrated to Paris, where he died.

Lvov (lyəvôf'), Ukr. *Lviv,* Ger. *Lemberg,* city (1970 pop. 553,000), capital of Lvov oblast, SW European USSR, in the Ukraine, at the watershed of the Western Bug and Dnestr rivers and in the northern foothills of the Carpathian Mts. The chief city of W Ukraine, Lvov is a major rail and highway junction and an industrial and commercial center. Machine building, food processing, oil refining, and the manufacture of chemicals and pharmaceuticals, motor vehicles, radio and electrical apparatus, and textiles are the leading industries. Lvov is also an educational and cultural center, with a famous university (est. 1661) and several institutes of the Ukrainian Academy of Sciences. Founded c.1256 by Prince Daniel of GALICH, the city was named for his son Lev and developed as a great commercial center on the trade route from Vienna to Kiev. It also served as an outpost against Tatar invasions. Lvov was captured by the Poles in the 1340s, the Turks in 1672, and the Swedes in 1704. During the first partition of Poland (1772) it passed to Austria, and became the capital of GALICIA. Lvov was the chief center of the Ukrainian national movement in Galicia after 1848. The capital of the short-lived West Ukrainian Democratic Republic after World War I, the city was taken by Poland in 1919 and confirmed as Polish by the Soviet-Polish Treaty of Riga (1921). Lvov was annexed to the Ukraine by the USSR in 1939. German forces held the city during much of World War II and exterminated most of the Jewish population. In 1945, Poland formally ceded Lvov to the USSR. Landmarks include a 16th-century palace and two 14th-century cathedrals.

Lw, former symbol of the element LAWRENCIUM, now Lr.

Lwoff, André (äNdrā' ləwôf'), 1902–, French microbiologist, b. Allier dept., central France, of Russian-Polish origin. He was educated in France and in 1925 became associated with the Pasteur Institute in Paris. In 1959 he also became professor at the Sorbonne. In the 1920s his study of the morphogenesis of protozoa led to the discovery of extranuclear inheritance in these organisms. Publication in 1941 of his treatise *L'évolution physiologique* developed the thesis of biochemical evolution by progressive losses of biosynthetic capacity. He shared the 1965 Nobel Prize in Physiology and Medicine with Jacques Monod and François Jacob for discoveries related to genes, the structures within cells that determine hereditary characteristics and control the production of enzymes and other proteins.

Lyakhov Islands (lyä'khəf), c.2,700 sq mi (7,000 sq km), southern group of the NEW SIBERIAN ISLANDS, N Siberian USSR, between the Laptev Sea and the East Siberian Sea, Yakut Autonomous SSR. They include Bolshoy Lyakhov, Maly Lyakhov, and Stolbovoy islands and are separated from the Anjou group of the New Siberian Islands by Sannikov Strait and from the mainland by Dmitri Laptev Strait. They were discovered (1770) by Ivan Lyakhov, a Russian merchant. In 1928 the Soviet government established a geophysical station there.

Lyall, Sir Charles James (lī'əl), 1845–1920, British Orientalist and civil servant in India. He held various offices in India and became chief commissioner of the Central Provs. (1895–98). In London he held (1898–1910) an important post in the India Office. Lyall was a student of Arabian poetry. His works include *Translations of Ancient Arabian Poetry* (1885, 1930), *The Diwan of Abid ibn al-Abras* (1913), *The Poems of Amr Son of Qamiah* (1919), and *The Mufaddaliyat* (1921).

Lyallpur (lī'əlpo͝or), city (1972 metropolitan area est. pop. 1,109,000), NE Pakistan, in a cotton- and wheat-growing area. It is an important commercial center, especially for grains, cloth, and ghee (clarified butter). Manufactures include textiles, pharmaceuticals, bicycles, textile machinery, hosiery, flour, sugar, vegetable oil, and soap. The city was founded by Sir James Lyall c.1895 and named in his honor. Punjab Agricultural Univ., several colleges affiliated with the Univ. of Punjab, and numerous experimental farms and cattle-breeding stations are in Lyallpur.

Lyautey, Louis Hubert Gonzalve (lwē übĕr' gôNzälv' lyōtā'), 1854–1934, colonial administrator and marshal of France. A career soldier, he served in Indochina, Madagascar, and Algeria before being sent (1912) to Morocco as French resident general after the establishment of a French protectorate. With a brief interruption in 1916–17, when he was French war minister, Lyautey devoted the next 13 years to administering the protectorate, developing the economy, extending the borders, and pacifying native resistance. During World War I he maintained French rule over Morocco despite a depleted force, and after the war he saw the campaign against the Berber mountain tribes under Abd el-Krim brought to a successful conclusion. Lyautey supported traditional forces in Morocco and focused his policy on the sultanate rather than on the French settlers. See André Maurois, *Lyautey* (tr. 1931); Alan Scham, *Lyautey in Morocco* (1970).

lycanthropy (lĭkăn'thrəpē), in folklore, assumption by a human of the appearance and characteristics of an animal. Ancient belief in lycanthropy was widespread, and it still exists in parts of the world. Certain African tribes have their "leopardmen" and the like, and literatures all over the world have tales of men changing to animals. One of the most widely held of these superstitions is the belief in the werewolf (a person who either willingly or unwillingly changes into a wolf, eats human flesh or drinks human blood, then returns to his natural form). The lycanthrope, akin to the vampire, is thought to undergo his change by means of witchcraft or magic. In the Middle Ages the church condemned lycanthropy as a form of sorcery and often ruthlessly punished the supposed offenders. The term is also applied to a form of insanity in which a person believes himself to be an animal and behaves accordingly.

Lycaonia (lĭk"āō'nēə), ancient country of S Asia Minor (now in Turkey), between Galatia and Cilicia on the north and south and Phrygia and Cappadocia on the west and east. Passing successively to the Persians, Syrians, and Romans, it was divided by the Romans between Galatia and Cappadocia. It was visited by Paul and Barnabas (Acts 14.6). Its chief city was ICONIUM.

Lyceum (līsē'əm), gymnasium near ancient Athens. There Aristotle taught; hence the extension of the term *lyceum* to Aristotle's school of philosophers, the Peripatetics.

lyceum (līsē'əm, lī'-), 19th-century American association for popular instruction of adults by lectures, concerts, and other methods. Lyceum groups were concerned with the dissemination of information on the arts, sciences, history, and public affairs. The National American Lyceum (1831) developed from the lectures given by Josiah Holbrook at the first lyceum group in Millbury, Mass. (1826). The movement spread through groups formed in other states and was a powerful force in adult education, social reform, and political discussion. Many of the ablest leaders of the time lectured to lyceum audiences, and public interest in general education was greatly stimulated by the movement. The lyceum movement waned after the Civil War, but much of its work was later taken up by the CHAUTAUQUA MOVEMENT. See Carl Bode, *The American Lyceum* (1956, repr. 1968).

Lycia (lĭsh'ə), ancient country, SW Asia Minor. A mountainous promontory, it was never politically important. Egyptian sources ally the Lycians to the Hittites at the time of Ramses II. Lycia was frequently mentioned by Homer in Greek mythology. In historic times it was held by the Persians, the Seleucids, and the Romans (from 189 B.C.). Its chief towns, Patara and Myra, were visited by St. Paul (Acts 27.5). Ruins include rock-cut tombs and Grecian sculptures dating from the 5th cent. B.C.

Lycomedes (lī"kəmē'dēz): see ACHILLES; THESEUS.

Lycophron (lĭk'əfrŏn), fl. early 3d cent. B.C., b. Chalcis, Alexandrian Greek poet, one of the PLEIAD. His only extant poem, *Cassandra* or *Alexandra,* is an occult work. In ancient times his tragedies were highly esteemed.

Lycopodiophyta (lī"kōpō"dēōf'ətə), division of the plant kingdom consisting of the organisms commonly called CLUB MOSSES and quillworts. As in other vascular plants, the sporophyte, or spore-producing phase, is the conspicuous generation, and the GAMETOPHYTE, or gamete-producing phase, is minute. The living representatives are all rather small herbaceous plants, usually with branched stems and small leaves, but their fossil ancestors were trees. The stems and roots grow in length by means of an apical MERISTEM and have epidermis, cortex, and a central cylinder, or stele, of conducting tissue. The spore cases, or sporangia, are borne at the base of leaves, either scattered along the stem or clustered into a terminal cone, or strobilus. At maturity, the sporangia split across the top, releasing great quantities of spores. The spores germinate by successive cell divisions to produce small, green, fleshy gametophytes, which bear both sperm-producing antheridia and egg-producing archegonia. The motile sperms swim to the egg through a film of water. The fertilized egg, or zygote, gives rise to an embryo and eventually to a mature sporophyte. The order Lycopodiales includes the common genus *Lycopodium,* the larger of two genera belonging to this order and containing some 600 species. The order Selaginellales contains only one living genus, *Selaginella,* with perhaps 500 species, although fossil forms resembling *Selaginella* are known from deposits of the Carboniferous period (see RESURRECTION PLANT). The order Isoetales (quillworts) contains the small genus *Isoetes,* which grows in shallow water in lakes, ponds, and marshy places. The plants have a grass-like appearance and are therefore often not readily identified. The order Lepidodendrales contains members known only from fossil specimens dating from the Upper Devonian to Permian times. *Lepidodendron* (see separate article), the most common genus, was of tree size.

Lycopolis: see ASYUT, city, Egypt.

Lycurgus (lĭkûr'gəs), traditional name of the founder of the Spartan constitution. The earliest mention of him is in Herodotus. Nothing is known of his life—when he lived or if he was a real man, a god, or a mythical figure. However, he is generally associated with the 7th cent. B.C. at the time when a revolt of the Messenian subjects nearly ruined Sparta. Lycurgus led a reform in the government and in the city's social system to establish a machine of war that would preclude further trouble from the helots and other subjects. Some features of the unique Spartan system were certainly more recent than 600 B.C. Later classical writers added details to his life as the tradition developed until Plutarch actually wrote a biography.

Lycurgus, c.396–c.325 B.C., one of the Ten Attic Orators of the Alexandrian canon; pupil of Isocrates. A capable and honored public official, he administered the state finances from 338 to 326 B.C. and led (with Demosthenes) the anti-Macedonian party. One of his official acts ordered the editing and preserving of the works of Aeschylus, Sophocles, and Euripides. A single oration (*Against Leocrates*) is extant. See R. C. Jebb, *The Attic Orators* (1893).

Lydd (lĭd), municipal borough (1971 pop. 4,301), Kent, SE England. A military training center, the borough gave its name to lyddite (picric acid), an explosive that was tested at the military camp there in 1888. Lydd was a member of the CINQUE PORTS but is no longer a seaport because of changes in the shore line.

Lydda: see LOD, Israel.

lyddite (lĭd'īt), a high EXPLOSIVE containing PICRIC ACID.

Lydgate, John (lĭd'gāt), c.1370–c.1450, English poet, a monk of Bury St. Edmunds. A professed disciple of Chaucer, he was one of the most influential, voluminous, and versatile writers of the Middle Ages. His works may be divided into three classes: (1) poems written in the Chaucerian manner, such as the *Complaint of the Black Knight,* which resembles Chaucer's *Book of the Duchess,* and the allegory *The Temple of Glass;* (2) lengthy translations, of which the *Troy Book* (from the Latin of Guido della Colonna), *The Fall of Princes* (from the French of Laurent de Premierfait), and *The Siege of Thebes* (also from the French), are the best known; (3) short pieces, including fables, saints' lives, and devotional, philosophic, and occasional poems. After

Lydgate's death his fame diminished rapidly. His poetry has been criticized for its prolixity and prosaic style. See his *Poems,* ed. by John Norton-Smith (1966); study by D. A. Pearsall (1970).

Lydia (lĭd'ēə), Christian convert at whose house in Philippi Paul stayed. She was from Thyatira. Acts 16.14–40.

Lydia, ancient country, W Asia Minor, N of Caria and S of Mysia (now NW Turkey). The tyrant Gyges was the founder of the Mermnadae dynasty, which lasted from c.700 B.C. to 550 B.C. The little kingdom grew to an empire in the chaos that had been left after the fall of the Neo-Hittite kingdom. Lydia was proverbially golden with wealth, and the capital, SARDIS, was magnificent. To Lydian rulers is ascribed the first use of coined money in the 7th cent. B.C. Lydia had close ties with the Greek cities of Asia, which were for a time within the Lydian empire. The last ruler was CROESUS, who was defeated (c.546 B.C.) by Cyrus the Great of Persia. Lydia was then absorbed into the Persian Empire.

Lydia, Mount, Turkey: see MYCALE.

lye, name commonly used for a strongly alkaline solution. It originally meant a solution of POTASSIUM CARBONATE (potash) prepared by leaching wood ashes with water, but now the name also means a solution of SODIUM HYDROXIDE or POTASSIUM HYDROXIDE. *Lye* is also used to refer to the undissolved solute. Common household lye is usually sodium hydroxide. Lye should be used with caution as it is caustic and poisonous.

Lyell, Sir Charles (lī'əl), 1797–1875, English geologist, b. Forfarshire, Scotland. After studying and briefly practicing law, he spent most of his life in travel and in popularizing scientific ideas. He championed and won general acceptance of the theory of UNIFORMITARIANISM of James Hutton (as opposed to the theory of CATASTROPHISM) in his *Principles of Geology* (3 vol., 1830–33), which went into 12 editions in his lifetime. Besides *Elements of Geology* (1838) and *The Geological Evidences of the Antiquity of Man* (1863), he wrote two books on his travels in North America. Lyell's work was greatly influential in shaping 19th-century ideas not only in geology but in scientific fields generally; he thus facilitated later acceptance of Darwin's theory of evolution. Among Lyell's most important contributions was the division of the Tertiary period into the Eocene, Miocene, and Pliocene epochs. See his *Life, Letters, and Journals,* ed. by his sister-in-law, K. M. Lyell (2 vol., 1881); study by L. G. Wilson (3 vol., 1972–).

Lyly or **Lilly, John** (both: lĭl'ē), 1554?–1606, English dramatist and prose writer. An accomplished courtier, he also served as a member of Parliament from 1589 to 1601. His *Euphues,* published in two parts (*The Anatomy of Wit,* 1578, and *Euphues and His England,* 1580), was an early example of the novel of manners and was one of the most influential works of its time. In it Lyly tried to establish an ideal of perfected prose style, which was actually convoluted and artificial (see EUPHUISM). His early plays, the most notable being *Campaspe* (1584) and *Endimion* (1591), followed *Euphues* in their elaborate style, but his later work, specifically *Mother Bombie* (1594), employed the realistic, robust manner of Roman comedy. Shakespeare and other Elizabethan playwrights were indebted to him for his innovation of prose as the vehicle for comic dialogue and for his development of the romantic comedy. See his complete works edited by R. W. Bond (new ed. 1967); studies by G. K. Hunter (1962 and 1968) and Peter Saccio (1970).

Lyman, Theodore, 1833–97, American naturalist, b. Waltham, Mass., grad. Harvard, 1855, and Lawrence Scientific School, Harvard, 1858. He was in the Union army as an aide (1863–65) on the staff of Gen. George Meade. As Massachusetts commissioner of inland fisheries (1866–83) he was a leader in the movement for the conservation of food fish. For the Harvard Museum of Comparative Zoology (with which he was associated, 1859–87) he published many scientific papers on marine forms. He served in Congress (1882–85) as an independent in favor of civil service reform.

Lyman series: see SPECTRUM.

Lyme Regis (līm rē'jĭs), municipal borough (1971 pop. 3,394), Dorset, SW England. It is a tourist resort. Paleontological discoveries have been made in the blue Lias rocks quarried near Lyme Regis.

Lymington (lĭm'ĭngtən), municipal borough (1971 pop. 35,644), Hampshire, S England, on the Solent channel at the mouth of the Lymington River. It is a market town, resort, and port; coast trading and yacht building are pursued and piston rings are produced. A Roman camp was in the vicinity. Henry II landed at Lymington in 1154 on the way to his coronation.

lymphatic system (lĭmfăt'ĭk), network of vessels carrying lymph, or tissue fluid, from the tissues into the veins of the circulatory system. Like the blood circulatory system, the lymphatic system is composed of fine capillaries that lie adjacent to the fine

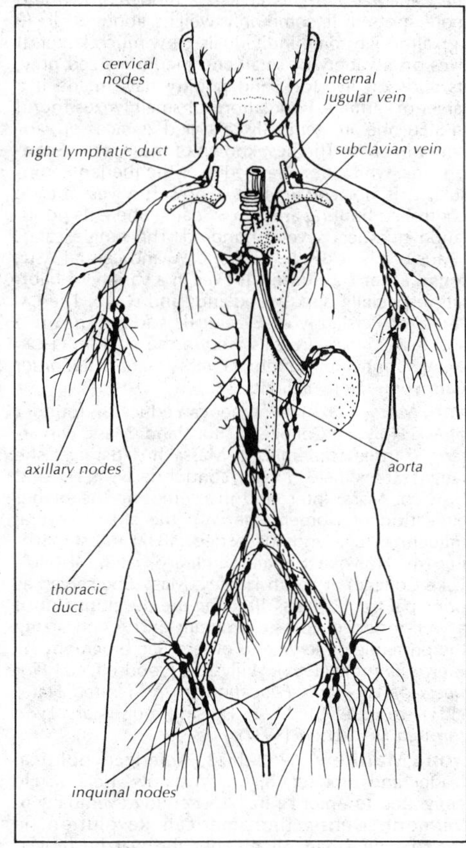

Lymphatic system

blood vessels. These merge into larger tributaries called trunks, the latter merging into two still larger vessels called ducts. The thoracic and right lymphatic ducts empty into the venous system in the region of the collarbones. Lymph, a colorless fluid whose composition is like that of blood except that it does not contain red blood cells or platelets and contains considerably less protein, is continuously passing through the walls of the capillaries. It transports nutrients and oxygen to the cells and collects waste products. Most of the lymph passes back into the venous capillaries; however, a small amount (about 10%) enters the terminal lymphatic capillaries and is returned to the blood via the lymphatic system. The fluid that flows through the lymphatic system is functionally important because it contains substances having large molecules (such as proteins and bacteria) that cannot enter the small pores of the venous capillaries. Along the lymphatic network in certain areas of the body (neck, armpit, groin, abdomen, chest) are small reservoirs, the lymph nodes, which collect bacteria and other deleterious agents and act as a barrier against the entrance of these substances into the bloodstream. In a disease state, therefore, the lymph nodes may become filled with harmful material to the degree where they can be seen or felt; therefore, enlarged lymph nodes are of diagnostic importance. In addition, the lymphatic system functions along with the circulatory system in absorbing nutrients from the small intestines. A large portion of digested fats are absorbed via the lymphatic capillaries.

lymphocyte: see BLOOD.

lymphogranuloma venereum: see VENEREAL DISEASE.

lymphoma: see NEOPLASM.

Lympne, England: see HYTHE.

Lynaker, Thomas: see LINACRE, THOMAS.

Lynbrook, village (1970 pop. 23,776), Nassau co., SE N.Y.; inc. 1911. It is a suburb of New York City on the south shore of Long Island. There is some light manufacturing. Old Church dates from 1800. The area was settled in 1785 and was called Bloomfield. The name *Lynbrook* (formed by reversing the syllables in *Brooklyn*) was adopted in 1895.

Lynch, Charles, 1736–96, American Revolutionary soldier, b. near the site of Lynchburg, Va. A member (1767–76) of the Virginia house of burgesses, he took a prominent part in the preparations for war. When a Tory conspiracy was discovered (1780) in Bedford co., where he had been a justice of the peace from 1774, Lynch, a zealous patriot, presided over an extralegal court that meted out summary punishment to the Loyalists. From this action comes the origin of the term "lynch law." Lynch clearly exceeded his authority, but he was later exonerated by the state legislature. He led a volunteer regiment at the battle of Guilford Courthouse in 1781.

Lynch, John, 1917–, Irish statesman. Before he embarked upon his political career he gained nationwide fame as an athlete, captaining several winning hurling teams in the 1930s and 40s. He studied law at Univ. College in Cork and at the King's Inns in Dublin and was admitted to the bar in 1945. He entered the Dáil (parliament) in 1948 as a member of the Fianna Fáil party. In 1951, Lynch was named parliamentary secretary to the government and to the minister for lands. Thereafter, he rose steadily in office. He was minister for education (1957–59) and minister for industry and commerce (1959–65). During his tenure in the latter office, he demonstrated outstanding ability as a mediator in major labor disputes. He was minister of finance when, in 1966, his party elected him to succeed Sean F. Lemass as prime minister of the Republic of Ireland. Reelected as prime minister in 1969, he soon became involved in a series of tense political disputes over the policy of his government regarding the escalation of violence between Protestants and Roman Catholics in Northern Ireland. When Fianna Fáil was defeated in the 1973 election, Lynch surrendered his office to Liam Cosgrave.

Lynch, Thomas, 1749–79, political figure in the American Revolution, signer of the Declaration of Independence, b. Prince George's Parish, Winyaw, S.C. He was the son of a Carolina statesman, Thomas Lynch, and is known as Thomas Lynch, Jr. He was elected (1776) to the Continental Congress but soon resigned because of ill health. In an attempt to regain his health, Lynch sailed for the West Indies and was lost at sea.

Lynchburg, independent city (1970 pop. 54,083), central Va., on the James River; settled 1757, inc. as a city 1852. It is a trade center and tobacco market in the foothills of the Blue Ridge Mts. Its manufactures include shoes, foundry and fabricated metal products, clothing, electronic equipment, machinery, tools, printed materials, furniture, wood products, and medical supplies. There is a nuclear research facility. Lynchburg was a Confederate supply base in the Civil War; in 1864 a Union attempt to take the city failed. Randolph-Macon Woman's College, Lynchburg College, Virginia Theological Seminary and College, Lynchburg Baptist College, and Central Virginia Community College are there. There is a fine arts center. Several old houses are notable, including Poplar Forest, built by Thomas Jefferson.

lynching, unlawfully hanging or otherwise killing a person by mob action. The origin of the word is unknown; there are various explanations, one being that it is derived from the name of Col. Charles LYNCH. North American pioneers whose settlements had not yet established legal institutions frequently took the law into their own hands. The pioneers so situated sometimes punished lesser crimes by exile, compelling the persons believed guilty to leave their community. Crimes that seemed to them capital, such as rape, were punished by lynching. Horse stealing and cattle rustling were such crimes, since often pioneers who lost their horses and cattle thereby lost their livelihood. Pioneers formed vigilance committees to repress crime (see VIGILANTES). When legal institutions had been duly established, such vigilance committees normally tended to disappear. Measures by such committees were extralegal and had the intrinsic danger of resort to violence and hasty injustice. Lynching in a community adequately supplied with law officers was generally regarded as a threat to their authority and to the basis of the law. In the chaotic social conditions of the S United States during Reconstruction days there was considerable resort to lynching, particularly by the KU KLUX KLAN. The tradition of using violence against blacks accused of crime (especially rape of a white woman or murder of a white man) was maintained in the period after Reconstruction. It should be noted, however, that the practice was exceptional rather than common and that a large body of Southern opinion was steadfastly opposed to the practice. It should also be noted that many lynchings occurred in other sections of the nation. More than 3,000 blacks were lynched in the United States from the 1880s to the early 1960s. Since then there have been no reported lynchings. See J. E. Cutler, *Lynch-law* (1905, repr. 1969); A. F. Raper, *The Tragedy of Lynching* (1933, repr. 1969); J. W. Caughey, *Their Majesties, the Mob* (1960).

Lynd, Robert Staughton, 1892–1970, American sociologist, b. New Albany, Ind.; grad. Princeton (B.A., 1914), Ph.D. Columbia, 1931. He taught at Columbia for 30 years (1931–61). With his wife, Helen Merrell Lynd, he made a noted sociological study of Muncie, Ind., published in 1929 as *Middletown: A Study in Contemporary American Culture,* and wrote *Middletown in Transition* (1937). Lynd also wrote *Knowledge for What?* (1939).

Lyndhurst, John Singleton Copley, Baron, 1772–1863, British jurist, b. Boston, Mass.; son of John Singleton Copley, the American painter. Educated in England, he was called to the bar in 1804. He attained notice by his successful defense of Arthur THISTLEWOOD and James Watson (1817). He entered (1818) Parliament, became solicitor general (1819), attorney general (1824), and master of the rolls (1826). Between 1827 and 1846 he was three times lord chancellor. Although he defended radicals earlier in his career, in political life he was a Tory and a leader of his party in the House of Lords. See biography by Sir Theodore Martin (1883).

Lyndhurst, city (1970 pop. 19,749), Cuyahoga co., NE Ohio; inc. 1917. It is a residential suburb of Cleveland.

Lyndon B. Johnson National Historic Site: see NATIONAL PARKS AND MONUMENTS (table).

Lyndsay, Sir David: see LINDSAY, SIR DAVID.

Lynen, Feodor (fāō'dôr lē'nən), 1911–, German biochemist, grad. Univ. of Munich (Ph.D. 1937). He began teaching at the Max Planck Institute for Cell Chemistry in Munich in 1947. His research on the B vitamin called biotin, the basic function of which is to regulate carbon-dioxide usage by cells, led to work on the mechanism and regulation of cholesterol and fatty-acid metabolism for which he shared the 1964 Nobel Prize in Physiology and Medicine with K. E. Bloch.

Lynn, city (1970 pop. 90,294), Essex co., E Mass.; inc. as a town 1631, as a city 1850. Lynn is an old industrial center. The first ironworks (1643) and the first fire engine (1654) in America were built there. Formerly the shoe industry was important, but today jet engines, marine turbines, and electrical instruments are major products. The home of Mary Baker Eddy, the founder of Christian Science, is in Lynn.

Lynn Canal, natural inlet, c.90 mi (145 km) long, 7–12 mi (11–19 km) wide, SE Alaska. It connects in the S with Chatham Strait and Stephens Passage and thrusts north between mountains to break finally into the inlets of the Chilkoot and Chilkat rivers. Navigable to its head, Lynn Canal connects Skagway with Juneau and is an important shipping lane. During the Alaska gold rush (1896) it was a major route to the gold fields.

Lynnfield, town (1970 pop. 10,826), Essex co., NE Mass.; inc. 1814. It is mostly residential.

Lynnwood, city (1970 pop. 16,919), Snohomish co., W central Wash., a suburb of Seattle; inc. 1959. Lynnwood has a junior college.

Lynwood, city (1970 pop. 43,353), Los Angeles co., S Calif., a suburb of Los Angeles; founded 1896, inc. 1921. It has various light manufacturing industries.

lynx, name given to several related small, ferocious members of the CAT family. All have small heads, tufted ears, and heavy bodies with long legs and short tails. All are primarily terrestrial, although they are able to climb trees. The northern lynx, *Felis lynx,* is found in coniferous forests of N North America and N Eurasia. As a result of the general deforestation of Europe, the northern lynx is now very restricted in its European range and may be extinct in W Europe. The North American variety of the northern lynx, similar in size and appearance to its Old World counterpart, is also known as the Canadian lynx; it ranges from the northern limits of the Canadian forests to the extreme N United States. The Canadian lynx may attain a length of over 3 ft (90 cm), with a 5-in. (13-cm) tail, and may weigh up to 40 lb (18 kg). Its long fur is yellow-brown to grayish, slightly spotted with black. It has long black ear tufts and large feet, adapted to moving on deep snow. A nocturnal hunter, it preys on a variety of game, sometimes as large as deer, but is particularly dependent on the snowshoe rabbit as its staple diet. The Canadian lynx population fluctuates in cycles correlated with the fluctuation of the snowshoe rabbit population. The bobcat, *F. rufa,* also known as bay lynx, red lynx, or wildcat, is a small North American lynx found in thickets, swamps, and rocky areas from the S of Canada to central Mexico. It has a longer tail, shorter ear tufts and smaller feet than the Canadian lynx; its coat is a redder brown and more spotted. It commonly weighs about 20 lb (9 kg), although some individuals grow much larger. It lives on a variety of small and medium-sized prey; its raids on livestock and poultry have made it a target of farmers. Populations of small lynxes found in S Europe are generally regarded as races or varieties of *F. lynx.* The best known of these is the Spanish lynx, which once ranged over the Iberian Peninsula. It is not certain that it now survives outside controlled hunting areas in S Spain, where its population numbers several hundred. The jungle cat *F. chaus* is a lynx of N Africa and W and central Asia, found as far E as Burma. It lives in a variety of habitats, especially open woodlands and scrub. The CARACAL, or Persian lynx, *F. caracal,* is found in Africa and Asia. Lynxes are classified in the phylum CHORDATA, subphylum Vertebrata, class Mammalia, order Carnivora, family Felidae.

Lyon, Mary, 1797–1849, American educator, founder of Mt. Holyoke College, b. Buckland, Mass. She attended three academies in Massachusetts; later she taught at Ashfield, Mass., Londonderry, N.H., and Ipswich, Mass. Interested in promoting the higher education of women, she won the aid of several influential men and succeeded (1837) in establishing Mt. Holyoke Female Seminary (later Mt. Holyoke College) at South Hadley, Mass. She served as principal for 12 years, directing the development of a well-rounded college program and emphasizing the principle of service to others. See biography by Evelyn Banning (1965); Willystine Goodsell, ed., *Pioneers of Women's Education in the United States* (1931, repr. 1970); M. F. Lansing, ed., *Mary Lyon through Her Letters* (1937).

Lyon, Matthew, 1750–1822, American political leader and pioneer, b. Co. Wicklow, Ireland. He emigrated to America in 1765, settling eventually in Vermont. During the American Revolution he served with Ethan Allen. After the war he moved (1783) to the town of Fair Haven, Vt., and, active in various business ventures, became its leading citizen. From 1797 to 1801 he was a vociferous Anti-Federalist member of the U.S. House of Representatives. In 1798 he was convicted under the Sedition Act for the publication in the *Vermont Journal* of a letter criticizing President John Adams. While serving a short jail sentence, he was reelected to Congress. Moving to Eddyville, Ky., in 1801, he represented (1803–11) that state in Congress. Lyon was appointed (1820) U.S. agent to the Cherokee Indians in Arkansas, where he was elected the second delegate of that territory to Congress, but died before taking his seat. He was a hero of three successive frontiers, an able exponent of frontier views in Congress, and a man of shrewd business ability. See biography by R. P. Williams (1972).

Lyon, Nathaniel, 1818–61, Union general in the American Civil War, b. Eastford, Conn. After serving against the Seminole and in the Mexican War, he was stationed in California and Kansas until the outbreak of the Civil War, when he was put in command of the St. Louis arsenal. He immediately broke up Camp Jackson, where the secessionist governor, Claiborne F. JACKSON, had quartered the state militia. By the spring of 1861, Lyon had subdued all the hostile sections of the state. When a Confederate force from Arkansas advanced into Missouri and was joined by Missouri's secessionist militia, Lyon attacked them at WILSON'S CREEK, Aug. 10. He was killed in the battle. See H. C. Adamson, *Rebellion in Missouri, 1861* (1961).

Lyonnais (lyônā'), region and former province, E central France, now divided into the Rhône and Loire depts. It included Lyonnais proper (the region around LYONS, its capital), which Philip IV acquired c.1307; the former counties of Forez and Beaujolais, annexed in 1531; and the tiny dependency of Franc-Lyonnais. It is primarily a grazing region, with great industrial centers (noted especially for their textile production) at Lyons, Saint-Étienne, and Roanne.

Lyonnesse (lī'ənĕs"), region W of Cornwall, now sunk beneath the sea more than 40 fathoms deep. The Lyonnesse of Celtic legend, the home of Tristram and of the Lady of Lyones, has been identified with Lothian in Scotland.

Lyons, Joseph Aloysius, 1879–1939, Australian statesman, b. Tasmania. He left schoolteaching in 1909 to enter political life, was a Labour member of the Tasmanian House of Assembly until 1929, and was premier of Tasmania. He became a member of the commonwealth Parliament in 1929 and held cabinet posts, but in 1931 he repudiated the Labour government's proposals of inflation to solve the depression and helped form a coalition United Australia party. As prime minister of Australia for three terms (1932–39), he reduced the national debt and restored the country to solvency.

Lyons, Fr. *Lyon* (both: lyôN'), city (1968 pop. 535,000), capital of Rhône dept., E central France, at the confluence of the Rhône and Saône rivers. As an economic center and a densely populated metropolis it is second only to Paris. It leads Europe in silk and rayon production; it has important metal, machine, clothing, and chemical industries; a river port; a stock exchange (founded 1506, the oldest in France); a university (founded 1808); and several fine museums. It is, moreover, a gastronomic capital. Founded in 43 B.C. as a Roman colony, ancient Lugdunum soon became the principal city of GAUL. There Christianity was first introduced into Gaul, and the importance of Lyons until c.1300 was chiefly religious. One of the earliest archiepiscopal sees in France, Lyons (which after the breakup of the Carolingian empire passed to the kingdom of Arles) was ruled by its archbishops until c.1307, when Philip IV incorporated the city and LYONNAIS proper into the French crownlands. Of great importance were the emergence (12th cent.) of the WALDENSES and the councils held there in 1245 and 1274. Lyons became a silk center in the 15th cent.; at first the silkworms raised in SE France sufficed the needs of the industry, but in recent times Lyons has become increasingly dependent on Far Eastern imports of raw material. In 1793, Lyons was devastated by French Revolutionary troops after a counterrevolutionary insurrection, but it recovered quickly thanks to the invention of the Jacquard loom. During the German occupation in World War II (1940–44), Lyons was the capital of the French resistance movement. A handsome modern city, Lyons has preserved interesting old sections, notably around the primatial Cathedral of St. John (12th–14th cent.). Annual international trade fairs are held at Lyons.

Lyons (lī'ənz), village (1970 pop. 11,124), Cook co., NE Ill., a residential suburb of Chicago, on the Des Plaines River; inc. 1888. It was settled at the edge of an early travel route, the portage between the Chicago and the Des Plaines rivers.

Lyons, First Council of (lyôN'), 1245, 13th ecumenical council of the Roman Catholic Church, convened at Lyons, France, by Pope INNOCENT IV to deal with his struggle with Holy Roman Emperor FREDERICK II. In spite of the defense of Frederick by his ambassador, he was declared deposed by the council. The action was without effect.

Lyons, Second Council of, 1274, 14th ecumenical council of the Roman Catholic Church. It was summoned by Pope GREGORY X to discuss problems in the Holy Land, to remove the schism of East and West, and to reform the church. The reunion of Constantinople and Rome had been proposed by the Byzantine emperor, Michael VIII, who hoped to avert the imperial designs of Charles of Anjou and other Latin leaders. There were long preliminaries at Constantinople, and at the council the Greek delegates made all the necessary concessions, including the concession on the *Filioque* issue (see CREED), and reunion was proclaimed. The reunion, however, was unpopular in the East and ignored in the West and was officially denounced by Michael's successor Andronicus II. The legislation of the council for church reform was well prepared, supported by statements submitted by the bishops for the pope. Emphasis was laid on abuses at the diocesan level (e.g., plural benefices, absentee clerics, and faulty elections). Perhaps the most important decrees were those that established the system whereby popes are elected by a conclave of cardinals, that set regulations for religious orders, and that granted special protections to the Dominicans and the Franciscans. The double procession of the Holy Spirit from the Father and the Son (*Filioque*) was formally defined. St. Bonaventure died at the council, and St. Thomas Aquinas died on his way there.

Lyra (lī'rə) [Lat.,=the lyre], northern CONSTELLATION lying S of Draco, E of Hercules, and W of Cygnus. Although many civilizations represented it as a bird, it was also depicted as a tortoise. The white star VEGA (Alpha Lyrae), the brightest star in the constellation, is one of the brightest in the entire sky. Just NE of Vega is Epsilon Lyrae, one of the few double stars that can be resolved with the naked eye. Also in Lyra is the Ring Nebula, the most famous of the planetary nebulas, consisting of a shell of gas separated from and expanding from a central star. Lyra reaches its highest point in the evening sky in August.

lyre, generic term for stringed musical instruments having a sound box from which project curved arms, joined by a crossbar. The strings are stretched between the crossbar and the sound box and are plucked with the fingers or with a plectrum. In ancient times Sumer, Babylonia, Israel, and Egypt had various sorts of lyres. Ancient Greece had two lyres—the KITHARA, which was the larger instrument used by the professional musician, and the lyra, the smaller instrument of the amateur. Each had from 3 to 12 strings, made of hemp. After the 10th cent. the lyres of N European countries were bowed instead of being plucked. The bowed lyre that persisted longest was the Welsh crwth, known as early as the 11th cent. and still in use in the early 19th cent. At some time in its history a fingerboard was added, making it an early member of the violin family.

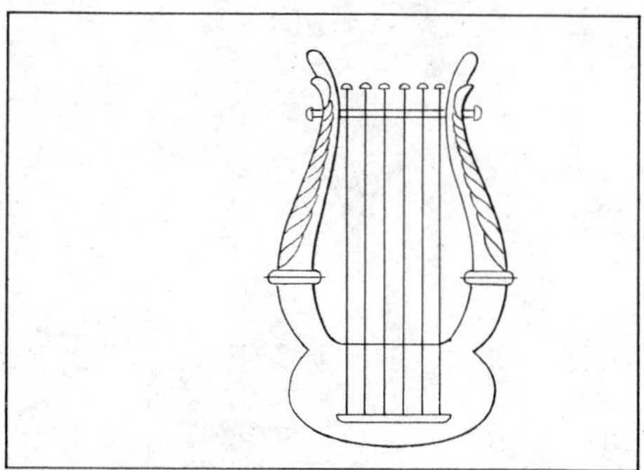

Greek lyre

lyrebird, common name for Australian passerine birds named for the appearance of the tail plumage of the male superb lyrebird, *Menura novaehollandiae,* when displayed during courtship. There are only two species. The superb lyrebird, about the size of a rooster, is brown above and ash below. It has a long, pointed bill, a longish neck, and large, strong legs and feet with which it runs swiftly. The Albert's lyrebird is smaller. Lyrebirds are shy, solitary forest and scrubland dwellers. They seldom fly; at night they roost in trees. Their diet consists of insects, worms, and land crustaceans and mollusks. The frame of the lyre, which develops when the male is three years old, is formed by the two long (2 ft/60 cm), curved outer tail feathers; the "strings" between are lacy white quills. The lyre position of the tail is assumed only fleetingly during the courtship dance, which is performed on a mound of earth scraped together by the male. This dance is accompanied by elaborate vocalizing, the birds being excellent mimics as well as distinctive singers. The female lays her single egg in a bulky domed nest built on or near the ground. The lyrebird appears on the seals and stamps of Australia. Lyrebirds are classified in the phylum CHORDATA, subphylum Vertebrata, class Aves, order Passeriformes, family Menuridae.

lyric, in ancient Greece, a poem accompanied by a musical instrument, usually a lyre. Although the word is still often used to refer to the songlike quality in poetry, it is more generally used to refer to any short poem that expresses a personal emotion, be it a sonnet, ode, song, or elegy. In early Greek poetry a distinction was made between the choral song and the monody sung by an individual. The monody was developed by Sappho and Alcaeus in the 6th cent. B.C., the choral lyric by Pindar later. Latin lyrics were written in the 1st cent. B.C. by Catullus and Horace. In the Middle Ages the lyric form was common in Christian hymns, in folk songs, and in the songs of TROUBADOURS. In the Renaissance and later, lyric poetry achieved its most finished form in the sonnets of Petrarch, Shakespeare, Spencer, and Sidney and in the short poems of Ronsard, Ben Jonson, John Donne, Herrick, and Milton. The romantic poets emphasized the expression of personal emotion and wrote innumerable lyrics. Among the best are those of Robert Burns, Blake, Wordsworth, Shelley, Keats, Lamartine, Hugo, Goethe, Heine, and Leopardi. American lyric poets of the 19th cent. include Emerson, Whitman, Longfellow, Lanier, and Emily Dickinson. Among lyric poets of the 20th cent. are W. B. Yeats, A. E. Housman, Rainer Maria Rilke, Federico García Lorca, W. H. Auden, Stephen Spender, Edna St. Vincent Millay, Wallace Stevens, Elinor Wylie, Dylan Thomas, and Robert Lowell. See J. M. Cohen, *The Baroque Lyric* (1963); Cecil Day Lewis, *The Lyric Impulse* (1965); John Erskine, *The Elizabethan Lyric* (1967); Peter Dronke, *The Medieval Lyric* (1968).

Lyrids: see METEOR SHOWER.

Lys (lēs), Flemish *Leie,* river, c.135 mi (220 km) long, rising in the hills of Artois, N France, and flowing northeast, forming the Franco-Belgian border between Armentières and Menen. It continues into Belgium past Kortrijk to empty into the Scheldt (Schelde) River at Ghent (Gent). The Lys is canalized from Aire to Ghent. The Lys valley is known for flax spinning and weaving. It was the scene of severe fighting in World War I.

Lysander (lĭsăn'dər), d. 395 B.C., Spartan naval commander and statesman. Toward the end of the PELOPONNESIAN WAR he was made admiral and built up the Spartan fleet so that it defeated (407 B.C.) the Athenians off Notium. Later he was responsible for the capture (405 B.C.) of the Athenian fleet at the mouth of the Aegospotamos and for the final submission (404 B.C.) of Athens to Sparta. He set up, in each of Athens' allied states, 10 oligarchs and, in Athens, the Thirty Tyrants. Sparta itself soon changed his severe system by modifying the oligarchies and by restoring Athenian democracy. Ambitious that Sparta should control all Greece and that he should be the leading power in Sparta, Lysander supported the succession of Agesilaus II as king, but the latter proved more able and independent than had been anticipated. When in 395 B.C. the Boeotians, with Thebes and Corinth at their head, made war upon Sparta, Lysander led an army against them, but he fell in battle at Haliartus.

Lysanias (lĭsā'nēəs), tetrarch of Abilene. Luke 3.1. A rock inscription mentioning his name was found on the site of ancient Abila.

Lysenko, Trofim Denisovich (lĭsĕng'kō, Rus. trəfēm' dyĭnyē'səvĭch lĭsyĕn'kə), 1898–, Russian agronomist. As president of the Lenin All-Union Academy of Agricultural Sciences he became the scientific and administrative leader of Soviet agriculture. In 1937 he was made a member of the Supreme Soviet and head of the Institute of Genetics of the Soviet Academy of Sciences. He first became known for his process (vernalization) of moistening and refrigerating the seed of spring wheat, thereby reputedly imparting to it characteristics of winter wheat. He became the leader of the Soviet school of genetics that opposed the theories of heredity accepted by most geneticists and supported the doctrine that characteristics acquired through environmental influences are inherited (see ACQUIRED CHARACTERISTICS). Lysenko rejected neo-Mendelism and was a disciple of the Russian horticulturist I. V. Michurin. Lysenko's theories were offered as Marxist orthodoxy and won the official support (1948) of the Soviet Central Committee. However, they were severely criticized after the death of Stalin in 1953, and in 1956 his resignation as president of the All-Union Academy of Agricultural Sciences was announced. In 1965 he was removed as director of the Institute of Genetics, which resulted in the return of Soviet biological thought to the mainstream of international scientific ideas. Lysenko stated his theories of inheritance of acquired characteristics in *Heredity and Its Variability* (1943, tr. 1946) and in *The Science of Biology Today* (1948, tr. 1948). See Julian Huxley, *Heredity: East and West* (1949, repr. 1969); Z. A. Medvedev, *The Rise and Fall of T. D. Lysenko* (tr. 1969); David Joravsky, *The Lysenko Affair* (1970).

lysergic acid diethylamide (lī"sûr'jĭk, dī"ĕth'ələmĭd, dī"ĕthəlăm'īd) or **LSD,** alkaloid synthesized from lysergic acid, which is found in the fungus ERGOT (*Claviceps purpurea*). It is a PSYCHOTOMIMETIC DRUG that produces intensification of sense perceptions, hallucinations, mood changes, and changes in the sense of time. Although lysergic acid itself is without hallucinogenic effects, lysergic acid diethylamide, one of the most powerful drugs known, is weight for weight 5000 times as potent as the psychotomimetic drug mescaline and 200 times as potent as psilocybin. The effects usually last from 6 to 14 hours. An occasional experience, especially among repeating users, is recurrence, i.e., the triggering of a hallucinogenic experience even though the individual has not recently taken the drug. Side effects include delayed or prolonged reactions, suicidal and homicidal tendencies, and convulsions. Repeated use sometimes precipitates severe psychosis, and there is some evidence linking the use of LSD and chromosome damage. The drug has been proposed as an aid in psychotherapy and chronic alcoholism. Research projects investigating lysergic acid diethylamide pharmacology have been conducted under governmental supervision.

Lysias (lĭs'ēəs), c.459–c.380 B.C., Attic orator; son of Cephalus, a Syracusan. After the capture (404 B.C.) of Athens by the Spartans, the Thirty Tyrants caused the arrest of Lysias and his brother Polemarchus, who was put to death. Lysias escaped to Megara, from which he returned when the tyrants were expelled (403 B.C.). He prosecuted Eratosthenes for his brother's death, and his oration against Eratosthenes is a model of Greek oratory. The tyrants had deprived him of his wealth, and he adopted the profession of writing speeches for litigants. Only 34 of his orations are extant. The clarity and elegance of his style place him among the very finest Greek orators and prose writers.

Lysias, Claudius: see CLAUDIUS LYSIAS.

Lysimachus (lĭsĭm'əkəs), c.355–281 B.C., Thessalian general of Alexander the Great. He was a commander in Alexander's fleet on the Hydaspes as well as his bodyguard. On Alexander's death (323 B.C.) Lysimachus took control of Thrace. He joined (314 B.C.) the other Diadochi—CASSANDER, PTOLEMY I, and SELEUCUS I—in the league against ANTIGONUS I, and after the defeat of Antigonus at Ipsus, Lysimachus took W Asia Minor as his share (301 B.C.). In 286 B.C. he added Macedonia to his kingdom by defeating Pyrrhus. Five years later Lysimachus was defeated in a war with Seleucus and was killed in battle at Corupedium near Magnesia ad Sipylum. A legend says that Lysimachus' wife, Arsinoë (daughter of Ptolemy I), persuaded him to kill his son by a former marriage and that the son's widow took refuge with Seleucus and provoked the final war.

lysine (lī'sēn), organic compound, one of the 22 α-AMINO ACIDS commonly found in animal proteins. Only the L-stereoisomer appears in mammalian protein. It is one of several essential amino acids needed in the diet; the human body cannot synthesize it from simpler metabolites. Young adults need about 23 mg of this amino acid per day per kilogram (10 mg per lb) of body weight. Lysine is found in particularly low concentrations in the proteins of cereals; wheat gluten, for example, is relatively poor in lysine. This deficiency in lysine is probably the reason for the failure of diets that employ cereal protein as a sole source of essential amino acids to support growth in children and general well-being in adults. Once lysine is incorporated into protein, its basic side chain often provides a positive electrical charge to the protein, thereby aiding its solubility in water. Its side chain has also been implicated in the binding of several COENZYMES (pyridoxal phosphate, lipoic acid, and biotin) to ENZYMES. In addition, the basic amino group of the side chain of lysine is said to participate directly in the catalytic function of several enzymes without the aid of a coenzyme. The amino acid was first isolated from casein (milk protein) in 1889, and its structure was elucidated in 1902.

$H_2C—NH_2$
CH_2
CH_2
CH_2
$H_2N—C—C(=O)OH$
H

lysine

Lysippos (lĭsĭp'əs), fl. late 4th cent. B.C., Greek sculptor, head of the Sicyon school. Hellenistic sculpture was based largely on the style he introduced. In treating the human figure, he modified the proportions set by the canon of POLYKLEITOS, making the head smaller, the form slender, the muscles close-lying. There is also a new sense of movement—torso, head, and limbs all face in different directions, indicating a momentary change of action. Of the many bronze statues and groups mentioned by Pliny and other ancient writers as his work, no certain original exists, and the marble statues accepted as copies of his bronzes probably do not follow his modeling exactly. The figure of an athlete, *Apoxyomenus,* in the Vatican and the *Agias* at Delphi are the most famous of these copies or adaptations. The copy by GLYCON of the Farnese Hercules (National Mus., Naples) of Lysippos stood originally in the Baths of Caracalla and later in the Farnese Palace. It is one of more than three dozen copies of this work. Lysippos made numerous statues of Alexander the Great after 340 B.C. According to tradition, he produced 1,500 works. The subjects were gods, heroes, and athletes. The sizes ranged from small bronzes to a statue of Zeus 60 ft (18 m) high.

lysogeny: see BACTERIOPHAGE; RECOMBINATION.

lysozyme: see IMMUNITY.

Lystra (lĭs'trə), ancient city of Lycaonia, S Asia Minor, in present Turkey. It was visited by Paul and Barnabas (Acts 14.6). An ancient altar found there mentioned the city and helped to identify the site.

Lytham Saint Anne's (lĭth'əm), municipal borough (1971 pop. 40,089), Lancashire, NW England, on the north shore of the Ribble estuary. It is a seaside resort. Lytham Saint Anne's was founded in the 12th cent. by Benedictine monks.

Lyttelton, Sir Thomas: see LITTLETON, SIR THOMAS.

Lytton, Edward George Earle Lytton Bulwer-Lytton, 1st Baron: see BULWER-LYTTON.

Lytton, Edward Robert Bulwer-Lytton, earl of, pseud. Owen Meredith: see BULWER-LYTTON.

Lytton, Victor Alexander George Robert Lytton, 2d earl of, 1871–1947, British diplomat, son of Edward Robert Bulwer-Lytton, 1st earl of Lytton. He was undersecretary of state for India (1920–22) and governor of Bengal (1922–27). He achieved prominence as chairman of the League of Nations mission to Manchuria (1932); his report recommended in effect economic sanctions against Japan. Lytton's writings include a biography of his father (1913), *Antony Viscount Knebworth: A Record of Youth* (letters to and from his son, 1935), and *The Web of Life* (1938).

M

M, 13th letter of the ALPHABET, usually representing a bilabial nasal as in the English *much.* It corresponds with the Greek mu. M is the Roman numeral for 1,000.

M'. Gaelic names beginning thus are entered as if spelled Mac-. See MAC.

Maacah (mā'əkə), in names of persons and places in the Bible, variant of MAACHAH.

Maachah (mā'əkə). **1** Absalom's mother. 1 Chron. 3.2. Maacah: 2 Sam. 3.3. **2** See MAOCH. **3** Idolatrous wife of Rehoboam. She was Absalom's daughter and mother of Abijah. 1 Kings 15.2; 2 Chron. 11.20. Michaiah: 2 Chron. 13.2. **4** Caleb's concubine. 1 Chron. 2.48. **5** Wife of Machir the Manassite. 1 Chron. 7.15. **6** Child of Nahor. Gen. 22.24. **7** Wife of Jehiel. 1 Chron. 8.29; 9.35. **8, 9** Fathers of two of David's men. 1 Chron. 11.43; 27.16.

Maachah, ancient city-state of Syria, S of Mt. Hermon. It was held by Arameans in biblical times. The inhabitants are Maachathi or Maachathites. Deut. 3.14; Joshua 12.5; 13.11; 2 Sam. 23.34; 1 Chron. 19. Maacah: 2 Sam. 10. The town of ABEL-BETH-MAACHAH may have been in Maachah.

Maadai (māăd'ī, māədā'ī), one who had a foreign wife. Ezra 10.34.

Maadiah (mā"ədī'ə), family returned from exile. Neh. 12.5. Moadiah: Neh. 12.17.

Maai (mā-ā'ī), one who took part in the dedication of the wall. Neh. 12.36.

Maaleh-acrabbim (mā'əlē-ăkrăb'ĭm), pass, S of the Dead Sea, called also "the ascent of Akrabbim." Num. 34.4; Joshua 15.3.

Maan (məăn'), town (1961 pop. 6,643), S Jordan. It is the terminus of the country's main rail line (which extends to Damascus, Syria) and carries on trade in agricultural produce. Important since biblical times, Maan was a point on an early Middle Eastern caravan route and on the pilgrimage road to Mecca.

Maarath (mā'ərăth), unidentified town in the mountains S of Jerusalem. Joshua 15.59.

Maarianhamina (mä'rēänhä"mīnä), Swed. *Mariehamn,* city (1970 pop. 8,570), capital of Ahvenanmaa prov., SW Finland, on Ahvenanmaa island. It is an active trade center and a popular summer resort. It was founded in 1861 by Czar Alexander II.

Maas, Nicolaes: see MAES, NICOLAES.

Maas, river: see MEUSE.

Maaseiah (mā"əsē'yə). **1** Musician under David. 1 Chron. 15.18,20. **2** Captain who aided the restoration of Joash. 2 Chron. 23.1. **3** Officer of King Uzziah. 2 Chron. 26.11. **4** Son of King Ahaz. 2 Chron. 28.7. **5** Man charged by Josiah with repairing the Temple. 2 Chron. 34.8. **6** The same as ASAIAH **4. 7** Father of ZEDEKIAH **3. 8** Father of ZEPHANIAH **5. 9** Grandfather of SERAIAH **3. 10, 11, 12, 13** Men who had foreign wives. Ezra 10.18,21,22,30. **14** Father of AZARIAH **20. 15** Man with Ezra at the reading of the Law. Neh. 8.4. **16** Levite instructor of the Law. Neh. 8.7. **17** Sealer of the covenant. Neh. 10.25. **18** Ancestor of SALLU **2. 19, 20** Priests at the dedication of the wall. Neh. 12.41,42.

Maasiai (māās'īā"), priest. 1 Chron. 9.12. See AMASHAI.

Maastricht (mäs'trĭkht"), city (1971 pop. 112,465), capital of Limburg prov., SE Netherlands, on the Maas (Meuse) River and on the Albert Canal system. It is an important rail and river transportation point and an industrial center. Its manufactures include textiles, ceramics, glass, paper, printed materials, and chemicals. The Maas was forded there in Roman times, and the city derives its name from the Latin *Mosae Trajectum* [Maas ford]. An episcopal see from 382 to 721, Maastricht has the oldest church in the Netherlands, the Cathedral of St. Servatius, founded in the 6th cent. In 1284 the city came under the dual domination of the dukes of Brabant and the prince-bishop of Liège. It was for many years a strategic fortress and suffered many sieges. The Spanish under Farnese captured it (1579) from the Dutch rebels during the revolt of the Netherlands and massacred a large part of the population. In 1632 the Dutch under Prince Frederick Henry recovered the city, which, however, fell several times into French hands in the wars of the 17th and 18th cent., notably in 1673 and 1794. A historic city, Maastricht has many old structures including the Romanesque Church of Our Lady (11th cent.), a 13th-century bridge across the Maas, and the town hall (17th cent.). The city is a cultural center. The district of Wijk occupies the right bank of the Maas.

Maath (mā'ăth), ancestor of Joseph. Luke 3.26.

Maaz (mā'ăz), descendant of Judah. 1 Chron. 2.27.

Maaziah (mā"āzī'ə), family of chief priests. 1 Chron. 24.18; Neh. 10.8.

Mabillon, Jean (zhäN mäbēyôN'), 1623–1707, French scholar, a Benedictine monk. His *De re diplomatica* (1681; with a supplementary volume, 1704) was the first attempt to develop a critical method of determining the authenticity of documents. Mabillon thus created the science of diplomatics, which made historiography far more scientific. The work remains a classic in its field.

Mabinogion (măbĭnō'gēən), title given to a collection of medieval Welsh stories. Scholars differ as to the meaning of the word *mabinogion:* some think it to be the plural of the Welsh word *mabinogi,* which means "youthful career"; others think it derives from the Welsh word *mabinog,* meaning "aspirant to bardic honor." The stories in the *Mabinogion* are found in two manuscripts, the *White Book of Rhydderch* (c.1300–1325) and the *Red Book of Hergest* (c.1375–1425). The first four tales, which are called collectively *The Four Branches of the Mabinogi,* are divided into *Pwyll, Branwen, Manawydan,* and *Math;* their connecting link, now obscured by many accretions, is the story of Prince Gwri or, as he is later called, Pryderi. In the first tale he is born and fostered, inherits the kingdom and marries; in the second he is barely mentioned; in the third he is imprisoned by enchantment and released; and in the fourth he falls in battle. Another tale, the story of *Kilhwch and Olwen,* which was composed before 1100, is an early example of an Arthurian tale. *The Dream of Rhonabwy,* which was written before 1175, also contains Welsh traditions about King Arthur. A story apparently based on the legend of Emperor Maximus is *The Dream of Maxim Wledig. Llud and Llevelys* is a short folktale full of fairy tale elements. The last group in the *Mabinogion* consists of three Arthurian romances, *Geraint, The Lady of the Fountain,* and *Peredur.* It seems probable that the first two shared with the works of Chrétien de Troyes common sources written in French, and that the last drew on the vast body of Grail tradition. *The Four Branches, Kilhwch,* and the romances are invaluable in the study of the ARTHURIAN LEGEND. Using just the *Red Book of Hergest* as her source, Lady Charlotte Guest (1812–95) published the first English translation of the *Mabinogion* between 1838 and 1849; she also gave the volume its title. Later the *White Book of Rhydderch* was discovered, containing older, finer versions of the tales in Guest's work. In 1929, T. P. Ellis and J. Lloyd published a translation based on a composite of the tales in both the *Red* and *White* books. A later composite translation is *The Mabinogion* (1949) of Gwyn Jones and Thomas Jones.

Mabuse, Jan de (yän də mäbüz'), c.1478–c.1533, Flemish painter, b. Maubeuge. His real name was Jan Gossaert or Gossart. He may have studied in Bruges before joining the Antwerp guild in 1503. In 1508 he went for a year with his patron, Philip of Burgundy, to Italy, where he was strongly influenced by Italian art and ancient sculpture. He was among the first Flemish artists to represent the nude and classical mythology in a manner derived from Italy. His forms are solid and heavy, and their surfaces are rendered with smooth precision. Mabuse also executed some impressive portraits. The imperious attitude he gave to his subjects was highly popular in his time. *A Donor and His Wife* (Brussels), *Neptune and Amphitrite* (Berlin), *Danaë* (Munich), *St. Luke Painting the Virgin* (versions in Vienna and National Gall., Prague), and *Jean Carondelet Adoring the Virgin* (Louvre) are characteristic paintings. See H. B. Wehle and M. Salinger, *Early Flemish, Dutch and German Painters* (1947).

Mac, Mc, or **M'** [Irish, = son], element in names derived from Irish and Scottish Gaelic patronymics. In most of these names the second element was a forename (e.g., *Macdonald,* in various spellings). Other names included titles or epithets (e.g., *McIntosh* [son of the chief]). Notions that some forms of the prefix are more typically Scottish or Irish are fallacious. Some of the names, however, have typical local distribution; thus, McLeod is Hebridean, McSweeney is especially Irish. See O; NAME.

macadamia (măk"ədā'mēə), name for the nut of the *Macadamia ternifolia,* an evergreen tree native to Australia. The nut is eaten roasted or raw. The macadamia tree is classified in the phylum MAGNOLIOPHYTA, class Magnoliopsida, order Proteales, family Proteaceae.

macadam road (məkăd'əm): see PAVEMENT.

McAdoo, William Gibbs (măk'ədōō), 1863–1941, American political leader, U.S. Secretary of the Treasury (1913–18), b. near Marietta, Ga. The son of a prominent Georgia jurist, McAdoo became a lawyer in Chattanooga, Tenn. After 1892 he practiced in New York City and was president of the Hudson and Manhattan RR Company, which built and operated the railroad tunnels known as the Hudson Tubes. He actively promoted Woodrow Wilson for the presidency in 1912 and was given a cabinet post. In 1914, after the death (1912) of his first wife, he married Eleanor Randolph Wilson, daughter of the President. The Federal Reserve System was begun during McAdoo's administration of the Dept. of the Treasury, and he was its first chairman. He also managed the financing of American participation in World War I and served as director general of railroads during the period of government operation (1917–19). After leaving public office, McAdoo returned to law practice in New York City, then moved to Los Angeles. He was prominent as a contender for the Democratic presidential nomination in 1920, and in 1924 the supporters of McAdoo and the adherents of Alfred E. Smith balanced each other and forced the choice of a compromise candidate. In 1928 he was unable to halt Smith's nomination. His California delegation at the convention in 1932 was joined with the Texas delegation in support of John N. Garner. When this bloc of voters was shifted to Franklin Delano Roosevelt, Roosevelt was nominated. McAdoo later served (1933–39) as Senator from California. His autobiography, *Crowded Years* (1931), ends with his resignation from the cabinet. See biography by J. J. Broesamle (Vol. I, 1974).

McAlester (məkăl'ĭstər), city (1970 pop. 18,802), seat of Pittsburg co., SE Okla.; inc. 1899. Once a coal-mining and farming community, it is now a regional distribution center with a busy stockyard. Aircraft and truck parts, boats, and clothing are manufactured. Nearby are a huge U.S. naval ammunition depot and a state penitentiary. The prison is the site of an annual rodeo.

McAllen, city (1970 pop. 37,636), Hidalgo co., extreme S Texas, on the Rio Grande; inc. 1911. It is a port of entry and a packing and processing center for the citrus fruit, truck crops, and other produce of the lower Rio Grande valley. The city has oil refineries, chemical plants, and other manufacturing industries. It is also a winter resort, and is known as the City of Palms, since 40 varieties of that tree flourish there. It is connected by bridge with Reynosa, Mexico.

McAllister, Ward (Samuel Ward McAllister), 1827–95, American society leader, b. Savannah, Ga. He practiced law (1850–52) in San Francisco and became wealthy. He moved (1852) to New York City, married (1853) Sarah T. Gibbons, a millionaire's daughter, and then went to Europe, where he mingled widely with figures of European society. Upon his return to the United States, he established a second residence at Newport, R.I., and soon became the arbiter of the New York and Newport social set. It was McAllister who chose (1872) the "patriarchs," a group of leaders from prominent New York families, and sifted out (1892) the Four Hundred—people whom he deemed members of "true" New York society. It was McAllister who groomed the famous Mrs. William Astor for her role as queen of New York society. He wrote *Society as I Have Found It* (1890). See Cleveland Amory, *Who Killed Society?* (1960).

Macao (məkou'), Port. *Macau,* Mandarin *Ao-men,* Portuguese overseas province (1970 est. pop. 300,000), 6 sq mi (15.5 sq km), adjoining Kwangtung prov., SE China, on the estuary of the Canton (Pearl) River, 40 mi (64 km) W of Hong Kong and 65 mi (105 km) S of Canton. It consists of a rocky, hilly peninsula (c.2 sq mi/5 sq km), connected by a sandy 700-ft-wide (213-m) isthmus to China's Chung-Shan (T'ang-chia-huan) island; and the two small islands of Taipa and Colôane. The city of Macao is approximately coextensive with the peninsula and contains almost the entire population of the province, which is overwhelmingly Chinese. Macao, a free port, is a leading trade, tourist, and fishing center, with gambling casinos and a recently established textile industry. In 1971 textiles accounted for 60% of the exports; other leading products are fresh and salted fish and handicraft items, especially firecrackers and matches. Most of Macao's transit trade with China is by way of its shallow harbor on the west side of the peninsula. The colony's name is derived from the Ma Kwok temple, built there in the 14th cent. Macao is the oldest permanent European settlement in the Far East. First visited by Vasco da Gama in 1497, it was a parched and desolate spot when the Portuguese established a trading post there in 1557. For nearly 300 years the Portuguese paid China an annual tribute for the use of the peninsula, but in 1849 Portugal proclaimed it a free port; this was confirmed by China in the Protocol of Lisbon in 1887. With the gradual silting up of its harbor and the rise (19th cent.) of Hong Kong, Macao lost is preeminent position and became identified to a large extent with smuggling and gambling interests. Since 1949 the population has been greatly swelled by an influx of Chinese refugees from the Communist mainland. In the winter of 1966–67, Communist-organized riots shook the province, resulting in a capitulation by the Portuguese authorities to Chinese demands to bar entry to refugees and prohibit anti-Communist activities. Macao's historic structures include the remaining facade of St. Paul's Basilica (built 1635 by Roman Catholic Japanese artisans; burned 1835), a fascinating example of late Italian Renaissance architecture, with mixed Western and Oriental motifs; St. Domingo's church and convent (founded c.1670); the fort and chapel of Guia (1626); the fort of São Paulo de Monte (16th cent.); and statues to Gama and Luís de Camões, who wrote (1558–59) part of *The Lusiads* there. Macao is separated from China by a barrier gate (built 1849, replacing one erected by the Chinese in 1573). There is daily ferry and bus service to Canton and ferry, hydrofoil, and helicopter service to Hong Kong. Taipa and Colôane islands are connected by a causeway (finished 1967). Construction of a 1-mi-(1.6-km-) long bridge to Taipa island was begun in 1974.

Macapá (məkəpä'), city (1970 pop. 86,307), capital of Amapá federal territory, extreme N Brazil, on the Amazon River. Its economy is based on mining (manganese and iron) and tropical forest products. Macapá's rubber resources have not been fully exploited. Founded (1688) by military men in the vicinity of a fortress, Macapá grew very slowly until it became the capital of the federal territory, which was created in 1944. The old fortress is now a regional museum.

Macapagal, Diosdado (dēōsdä'thō mäkäpägäl'), 1911–, Philippine president (1962–65). A forceful orator, Macapagal practiced law and later served in the Philippine diplomatic service and in the house of representatives (1949–56). In 1951 he led the Philippine delegation to the United Nations. In 1957, Macapagal was elected vice president on a split ticket, serving under Carlos P. Garcia. In 1961 he defeated Garcia for president, although his Liberal party was in the minority. As president, Macapagal fought poverty, unemployment, and corruption. He was defeated (1965) for reelection by Ferdinand Marcos.

macaque (məkăk'), name for Old World MONKEYS of the genus *Macaca,* related to mangabeys, mandrills, and baboons. All but one of the twelve species are found in Asia, from Pakistan to Japan, the Philippines, and Borneo. Macaques are stocky monkeys with short limbs and a short tail or, in a few species, no tail. They are highly intelligent and display a great variety of calls and facial expressions. A typical macaque is the rhesus monkey (*Macaca mulatta*) of S Asia. It is yellowish brown with a pale, naked face and a tail about half as long as the body. A large male may reach a body length of 2 ft (60 cm). Rhesus monkeys live in large colonies in forests and on rocky hillsides, ranging to high altitudes. Omnivorous feeders, they often raid cultivated fields and gardens. The rhesus monkey has been widely used in medical and other scientific experiments; the Rh blood factor, found in humans as well as monkeys, is named for it. The stump-tailed macaque (*M. speciosa*) is a nearly tailless, very hairy macaque with a naked pink face, found at high altitudes in SE Asia. Its close relative the Japanese macaque (*M. fuscata*) is the northernmost primate other than man. Its social organization has been extensively studied, and it has been found that there are culturally transmitted behavioral differences among different troops. The single non-Asian macaque is the so-called Barbary ape (*M. sylvana*), a large, tailless species of NW Africa, with one colony on the Rock of Gibraltar; it is the only nonhuman primate found in Europe. Macaques are classified in the phylum CHORDATA, subphylum Vertebrata, class Mammalia, order Primates, family Cercopithecidae.

macaroni, generic name for shaped and dried doughs prepared from selected wheat flour and water, originally peculiar to Italy. Macaroni noodles are made from dough mixed with eggs or egg solids, rolled thin and sliced. Similar flour and rice pastes have been known in Asia for a long time and are believed to have been introduced into Europe during the Mongol invasions in the 13th cent. The basic ingredient of macaroni is semolina, a durum wheat flour, coarsely ground and free from bran; farina, similarly prepared from other varieties of hard wheat, is also used. The sifted flour is moistened with hot water, kneaded to a stiff dough, forced through holes of the desired size and shape, then slowly dried in a current of warm air. In modern factories open-air drying has been replaced by the use of air-conditioned rooms. Long-cut macaroni is hung to dry on racks or sticks. Short-cut pastes are dried on trays. The dough is made in various shapes, ribbons, tubes, and disks, and may be twisted or ribbed. Thinner forms of the same material are known as spaghetti (cords of medium diameter) and vermicelli (fine strands). The increased use of alimentary pastes in the United States in the 20th cent. has led to widespread cultivation of durum wheat and to the establishment of factories producing quantities sufficient for export as well as for domestic use.

MacArthur, Arthur, 1845–1912, American army officer, b. Springfield, Mass.; father of Douglas MacArthur. Raised in Wisconsin, he served with the 24th Wisconsin Volunteers in the Civil War and fought in many Western campaigns and in the Chattanooga campaign of 1863. He received the Medal of Honor for gallantry. Joining the regular army after the war, he fought in both Cuba and the Philippines in the Spanish-American War and was (1900–1901) military governor of the Philippines. He had risen (1906) to the rank of lieutenant general when he retired in 1909.

MacArthur, Douglas, 1880–1964, American general, b. Little Rock, Ark.; son of Arthur MacArthur. He was reared on army posts and attended military school in Texas. At West Point he achieved an outstanding scholastic record, and after graduation (1903) he served in the Philippines and in Japan. He was (1906–7) aide to his father's friend President Theodore Roosevelt and from 1913 to 1917 was attached to the army general staff. After the United States entered World War I he fought in France, first as chief of staff of the 42d (Rainbow) Division and then, having been promoted (June, 1918) to brigadier general, as commander of the 84th Infantry Brigade. As superintendent of West Point (1919–22) he helped modernize the academy's military training program. After holding various commands (1922–25) in the Philippines, he returned to the United States and served (1925) on the court-martial of Gen. William MITCHELL. He was (1928–30) department commander in the Philippines and then served (1930–35) as chief of the general staff. In 1932 he provoked much criticism by personally commanding the troop action that evicted the BONUS MARCHERS from Washington. In the tense and threatening days of Japanese expansion President Franklin Delano Roosevelt appointed (1935) MacArthur head of the American military mission to the new Philippine Commonwealth. Accepting command of the Philippine military establishment, he retired (1937) from the U.S. army, but later returned to duty (July, 1941) to command U.S. armed forces in the Far East. After the Japanese attack on Pearl Harbor on Dec. 7, 1941, he commanded the defense of the Philippines until March, 1942, when, under the orders of President Roosevelt, he left for Australia to take command of Allied forces in the Southwest Pacific. From Australia he launched the New Guinea campaign and later (Oct., 1944–July, 1945) directed the campaigns that led to the liberation of the Philippines. He was promoted (Dec., 1944) to the new rank of general of the army (five-star general). MacArthur accepted the surrender of Japan on the U.S.S. *Missouri* on Sept. 2, 1945. He was then named commander of the Allied powers in Japan and directed the Allied occupation of Japan. He was seriously considered for the Republican presidential nomination in 1948, but defeat in the Wisconsin state primary discouraged his supporters. At the beginning (1950) of the KOREAN WAR he was appointed commander of UN military forces in South Korea, retaining his command of Allied forces in Japan. After driving the North Korean forces back over the 38th parallel, MacArthur received President Truman's permission to press into North Korea and advance all the way to the Yalu River—the border between North Korea and Communist China—despite warnings that this might provoke Chinese intervention. When China did intervene, causing the UN forces to fall back in disarray, MacArthur began to press for permission to bomb Chinese bases in Manchuria. Truman refused such permission and finally (after MacArthur had made the dispute public) removed him from command in April, 1951. On his return to the United States, MacArthur was given a hero's welcome and invited to address a joint session of Congress. Another attempt to nominate MacArthur for the presidency was unsuccessful in 1952. Retired from active service, he became an officer of a large business corporation. See biography by D. C. James (Vol. I, 1970); studies by John Gunther (1951), Frazier Hunt (1954, repr. 1964), Courtney Whitney (1956), J. W. Spanier (1959, repr. 1965), and G. M. Long (1969).

Macarthur, Mary Reid, 1880–1921, British labor organizer, b. Glasgow. Working in her father's draper's shop, she became prominent in the shop assistants' union. As the representative of the women chain makers of Cradley Heath, she secured a minimum wage for them in 1909 and led a strike to compel employers to pay the increase without delay. She visited the United States in 1920 as a British representative in the first labor conference convened under the League of Nations. In 1911 she married William Crawford Anderson, chairman of the Independent Labour party. See M. A. Hamilton, *Mary Macarthur* (1925).

Macassar: see MAKASAR, Indonesia.

Macau: see MACAO.

Macaulay, Dame Rose (məkôl'ē), 1889?–1958, English author. Remembered primarily for her novels satirizing middle-class life, she first achieved fame with *Potterism* (1920). Her subsequent novels include *Told by an Idiot* (1923), *Staying with Relations* (1930), *The World My Wilderness* (1950), and *The Towers of Trebizond* (1956). She also wrote two volumes of verse, several books on travel, and studies of Milton (1934) and E. M. Forster (1938). She was named a Dame of the British Empire in 1958. See biography by A. R. Benson (1970).

Macaulay, Thomas Babington, 1800–59, English historian and author, b. Leicestershire, educated at Cambridge. After the success of his essay on Milton in the Edinburgh *Review* (Aug., 1825), he contributed regularly to that journal. He was called to the bar in 1826 and, elected to Parliament in 1830, distinguished himself as a Whig orator. In India, 1834–38, as a member of the supreme council of the East India Company he reformed the Indian educational system and composed a legal code for the colony. On his return to England, Macaulay devoted himself to writing history, but returned to public office as secretary of war (1839–41), paymaster of the forces (1846–47), and member of Parliament (1839–47, 1852–56). In 1857 he was raised to the peerage as Baron Macaulay of Rothley. Macaulay's greatest work and one of the great works of the 19th cent. was *The History of England from the Accession of James the Second* (5 vol., 1849–61). Its brilliant narrative style and its vivid recreation of the social world of the 17th cent. made it an unprecedented success. The work has been criticized, however, for its failure to achieve objectivity, primarily because of Macaulay's Whig and Protestant bias. He also wrote several notable short biographical essays on Bacon, Johnson, Warren Hastings, and others. His poetical work, the *Lays of Ancient Rome* (1842), celebrated the great events of Roman history. See his letters, ed. by Thomas Pinney (2 vol., 1974); Sir G. O. Trevelyan (his nephew), *The Life and Letters of Lord Macaulay* (1876; repr., 2 vol., 1961); biographies by R. C. Beatty (1938, repr. 1971) and John Clive (1973).

macaw: see PARROT.

McBain, Howard Lee, 1880-1936, American political scientist, b. Toronto, Ont., grad. Richmond (Va.) College, 1900, Ph.D. Columbia, 1907. After teaching at George Washington and Wisconsin universities, he became, in 1913, associate professor of municipal science and administration and, in 1917, professor of constitutional law at Columbia. In 1929 he was made dean of the graduate faculties at Columbia. An authority on constitutional law, he revised (1933) the Cuban electoral code. His books include *The Law and the Practice of Municipal Home Rule* (1916), *American City Progress and the Law* (1917), *The New Constitutions of Europe* (with Lindsay Rogers, 1922), and *The Living Constitution* (1927).

Macbeth (măkbĕth'), d. 1057, king of Scotland (1040-57). He succeeded his father as governor of the province of Moray c.1031 and was a military commander for Duncan I. In 1040 he killed Duncan in battle and seized the throne. Possibly of royal descent himself, he acquired a direct claim to the throne through his wife, Gruoch; she was a granddaughter of Kenneth III, who had been overthrown by Duncan's ancestor Malcolm II. Macbeth represented northern elements in the population who were opposed to the ties with the Saxons advocated by Duncan. Macbeth was defeated in 1054 by SIWARD, earl of Northumbria, who regained the southern part of Scotland on behalf of Malcolm Canmore, Duncan's son. Malcolm himself regained the rest of the kingdom after defeating and killing Macbeth in the battle of Lumphanan. He then succeeded to the throne as MALCOLM III. William Shakespeare's version of the story comes from the accounts of Raphael Holinshed and Hector Boece.

MacBeth, George, 1932-, Scottish poet, grad. Oxford, 1955. He is a producer for the British Broadcasting Corp. His poetry, often treating violent subjects, combines fantasy and reality. He writes with wit and vitality, blending an enthusiasm for many formal poetic forms and figures of speech with an exciting lack of restraint. His volumes of poetry include *A Form of Words* (1954), *The Colour of Blood* (1967), *Collected Poems* (1972), and *Shrapnel and A Poet's Year* (1974).

MacBride, Sean, 1904-, Irish diplomat, b. South Africa. The son of John MacBride and Maud Gonne, both revolutionary Irish nationalists, he was a leader of the Irish Republican Army and was several times imprisoned. Later he became a lawyer and in 1946 founded a new Irish republican party, the Clann na Poblachta. Elected to the Dáil Eireann in 1947, he became minister of external affairs in the coalition government of 1948-51, under which Ireland became an independent republic. Active in many international organizations, he was a founder of Amnesty International and secretary general (1963-70) of the International Commission of Jurists. In 1974 he was appointed UN Commissioner for Namibia (South West Africa); in the same year he shared the Nobel Peace Prize with Eisaku Sato of Japan.

Maccabees or **Machabees** (both: măk'əbēz), Jewish family of the 2d and 1st cent. B.C. that brought about a restoration of Jewish political and religious life. They are also called Hasmoneans or Asmoneans after their ancestor, Hashmon. They appear in history as the family of a priest, Mattathias, dwelling in Modin, who opposed the Hellenizing tendencies of the Syrian ruler ANTIOCHUS IV. Antiochus had taken advantage of factionalism among the Jews and had stripped and desecrated the Temple and begun a religious persecution. Mattathias, after killing an apostate Jew who took part in a pagan sacrifice, killed the royal enforcing officer. With his five sons he fled to the mountains and was joined by many HASIDIM. Thus began a guerrilla war. On Mattathias' death (166 B.C.) the leadership passed to his son Judas Maccabeus, from whose surname the family name is derived. Judas, an excellent military leader, defeated an expedition sent from Syria to destroy him. Having occupied Jerusalem, he rededicated the Temple; the feast of HANUKKAH celebrates this event (165 B.C.). At that time there was civil strife in Syria. DEMETRIUS I, then in control, sent the general Nicator with an army against Judas; that expedition was routed, but another, led by Bacchides, defeated and killed Judas (161? B.C.). Judas' brother Jonathan, the new leader, was successful for a time; he supported Demetrius' rival, Alexander Balas, and made treaties of friendship with Sparta and Rome. Jonathan was killed by treachery in 143 B.C., and the last brother, Simon, succeeded; he was recognized by the other powers as civil ruler as well as high priest, and Palestine enjoyed some years of peace. Eventually Antiochus VII sent an expedition against the Jews; Simon defeated it, but in the disorder afterward he was murdered (135 B.C.) by an ambitious son-in-law. John Hyrcanus, Simon's son, managed to gain the ascendancy in the subsequent strife. He fought against Antiochus and remained in power until his death (105? B.C.). Under him Judaea enjoyed its greatest political power. He was succeeded by his son Aristobulus I, who died a year later. Another son, Alexander Jannaeus, then took the throne; he governed with great severity and headed the Sadducees in their strife with the Pharisees. Upon his death (78? B.C.) his widow, Salome Alexandra, who had also been married to Aristobulus, became queen. She favored the Pharisees and governed well. After her death, her son John Hyrcanus II, who had been high priest, acquired the temporal rule as well, but his more energetic brother, Aristobulus II, revolted. A civil war followed and resulted in Roman intervention and the taking of Jerusalem by Pompey (63 B.C.). The house of the Maccabees made several efforts to throw off Roman rule. One of its members, Alexander, led an abortive rebellion in Syria, and in 40 B.C. Antigonus, the son of Aristobulus II, invaded Judaea with Parthian aid. Some of the Jews rallied to his standard, but he was defeated and put to death (37 B.C.) at the request of Herod the Great. Hyrcanus II, who had been reinstated as high priest by the Romans, was captured by the Parthians and deprived of his ears in order to render him unfit for priestly service. He returned (33 B.C.) to Judaea but was put to death (30 B.C.) on a charge of treason. The name Maccabees has been extended to include the Jewish martyrs of the persecution, notably those of 2 Mac. 6; 7. The chief sources for the Maccabees are the books of First and Second Maccabees and the *Antiquities* of Josephus. For bibliography, see OLD TESTAMENT and JEWS. See also Elias Bickerman, *The Maccabees* (tr. 1947); Avigdor Tcherikover, *Hellenistic Civilization and the Jews* (1959).

Maccabees, two books of the Old Testament; they are the last two books in the Western canon, but they are not included in the Hebrew Bible and are placed in the Apocrypha in the Authorized Version. First Maccabees is a straight narrative, originally written in Hebrew, concerning the struggles of the house of Maccabees against Antiochus IV of Syria, beginning with the rebellion of Mattathias (c.167 B.C.) and ending with the murder of Simon (135 B.C.). Its order is chronological, as follows: introduction (1); Mattathias as leader (2); Judas Maccabeus' leadership (3.1-9.22), including the restoration of the Temple as the high point (4.36-59); Jonathan's career (9.23-12.53); and Simon's career (13-16). The book is the best source for the period of history that it treats; it is careful in citing and dating. There is an interesting account of the reputation of republican Rome (8.1-16) and of Maccabean relations with that power (8.17-32; 12.1-18; 14.16-24; 15.15-24). First Maccabees is usually dated c.100 B.C. Second Maccabees claims to be a condensation of five books by one Jason of Cyrene about the Maccabees; it was probably composed in Greek late in the 1st cent. B.C. It is a devout history of the persecutions of Antiochus and the career of Judas Maccabeus. The contents are as follows: a seemingly extraneous letter from Palestinian Jews to Jews in E Egypt referring to the feast of the restoration of the Temple in 165 B.C. (1-2.18); literary preface (2.19-32); the intrigues and troubles leading to the persecution (5-6.17); two accounts of martyrdom (6.18-31; 7); Judas' glorious career (8-15), including the horrible death of Antiochus (9) and a vision of Judas (15.12-16). Second Maccabees is composed in a self-deprecatory, witty style; cf. 2.23-32; 4.40; 5.21; 7.42; 15.37-39. It sheds interesting light on Jewish belief of the period, as on creation (7.22-23) and on the resurrection and prayers for the dead (12.43-45). There are other books of Maccabees among the PSEUDEPIGRAPHA. See studies by E. J. Bickerman (tr. 1947) and Moshe Pearlman (1973).

Maccabees, Feast of the: see HANUKKAH.

McCall, Samuel Walker, 1851-1923, American political leader, U.S. Congressman (1893-1913), governor of Massachusetts (1916-18), b. East Providence, Pa. He was a lawyer in Boston when he entered politics. Although a Republican, he spoke out strongly against Theodore Roosevelt's vigorous use of executive power and opposed Federal regulatory legislation. He promoted the building of the Lincoln Memorial in Washington, D.C. He wrote biographies of Thaddeus Stevens (1898) and Thomas B. Reed (1914) and *The Business of Congress* (1911). See biography by L. B. Evans (1916).

McCarthy, Charles, 1873-1921, American political scientist and author, b. Brockton, Mass. He organized and directed (1901-21) at Madison, Wis., the first official legislative reference library in the country. Through published articles, lectures, and contact with legislators he became one of the chief minds behind the progressive legislation enacted in Wisconsin in the gubernatorial administration of Robert M. La Follette. He wrote *The Wisconsin Idea* (1912). McCarthy served (1914-15) as the first director of the U.S. Commission on Industrial Relations. See biography by E. A. Fitzpatrick (1944).

McCarthy, Eugene Joseph, 1916-, U.S. political leader, b. Watkins, Minn. He served (1942-46) as a technical assistant for military intelligence during World War II and then taught (1946-49) at the College of St. Thomas in St. Paul, Minn. As a Democratic member of the U.S. House of Representatives (1949-59) and the Senate (1959-71), McCarthy gained a reputation as an intellectual in politics. In 1967 he announced his candidacy for the Democratic nomination for the presidency as a direct challenge to President Lyndon B. Johnson's Vietnam policies. His antiwar position won the support of many liberals and his strong showing (March, 1968) in the New Hampshire primary brought Sen. Robert F. Kennedy into the race and helped persuade Johnson not to seek reelection. Defeated for the nomination by Hubert H. Humphrey, McCarthy retired from the Senate and resumed (1973) teaching. He is the author of *The Limits of Power* (1967) and *The Year of the People* (1969). See studies on his presidential campaign by Arthur Herzog (1969), Ben Stavis (1969), and Jeremy Larner (1970); A. Q. McCarthy, *Private Faces/Public Places* (1972).

McCarthy, Joseph Raymond, 1908-57, U.S. Senator from Wisconsin (1947-57), b. near Appleton, Wis. He practiced law in Wisconsin and became (1940) a circuit judge. He served with the U.S. marines in the Pacific in World War II, achieving the rank of captain. In 1946, McCarthy defeated Senator Robert M. La Follette, Jr., for the Republican senatorial nomination and then overwhelmed his Democratic opponent in the election. His career in the Senate was undistinguished and obscure until Feb., 1950, when he won national attention with a speech at Wheeling, W.Va., in which he charged that the State Dept. had been infiltrated by Communists. Although a Senate investigating committee under Millard Tydings exonerated the State Department and branded the charges a fraud and a hoax, McCarthy repeated his claims in a series of radio and television appearances. Challenged to produce his evidence, he refused and instead made new accusations. When the Republicans assumed control of Congress in 1953, McCarthy, who had been reelected in 1952, became chairman of the Senate permanent investigations subcommittee (Government Operations Committee), a post in which he wielded great power; he used his position to exploit the public's fear of Communism. Through widely publicized hearings, the use of unidentified informers, and reckless accusation, McCarthy doggedly pursued those whom he classified as Communists and subversives. Careers were ruined on the flimsiest evidence, and his methods came under increasing attack by the press and his colleagues. In April, 1954, McCarthy accused Secretary of the Army Robert T. Stevens and his aides of attempting to conceal evidence of espionage activities that McCarthy and his staff had allegedly uncovered at Fort Monmouth, N.J. The army, in turn, accused McCarthy, his chief counsel, and a staff member of seeking by improper means to obtain preferential treatment for a former consultant to the subcommittee, then a private in the army. After widely publicized hearings McCarthy and his aides were cleared (Aug., 1954) of the army's charges. However, in December the Senate, acting on a motion of censure against him, voted to "condemn" McCarthy for contempt of a Senate elections subcommittee that had investigated his conduct and financial affairs in 1952, abuse of certain Senators, and insults to the Senate itself during the censure proceedings. After this rebuke, and with the Democrats again in control of Congress after the 1954 elections, McCarthy's influence in the Senate and on the national scene steadily diminished until his death. McCarthy's indiscriminate attacks gave rise to the term "McCarthyism," which denotes similar assaults characterized by sensationalist tactics and unsubstantiated accusations. See studies by R. H. Rovere (1960, repr. 1973), M. P. Rogin (1967),

A. J. Matusow (1970), Robert Griffith (1970), F. J. Cook (1971), Roberta Feuerlicht (1972), and Robert Goldston (1973).

McCarthy, Joseph Vincent, 1887–, American baseball manager, b. Philadelphia, Pa. A manager in the American Association and later (1926–30) in the National League, "Marse Joe," as he was known, became manager of the American League's New York Yankees in 1931. During his 16-year tenure with the Yankees his teams won eight league pennants and seven world championships. He later managed (1948–50) Boston in the American League. In 1957 he was elected to the National Baseball Hall of Fame.

M'Carthy, Justin, 1830–1912, Irish historian, politician, and novelist. After a long career in journalism, he entered the British Parliament in 1879, advocating home rule for Ireland. He was at first a supporter of, then head of the opposition to, Charles Parnell. His novels include *Dear Lady Disdain* (1875) and *Miss Misanthrope* (1878). Best known as a historian, he wrote *A History of Our Own Times* (7 vol., 1879–1905) and began *The Four Georges and William IV* (4 vol., 1884–1901). It was completed by his son, **Justin Huntly M'Carthy,** 1860–1936. Also a member of Parliament (1884–92) and a versatile writer, he was best known for his novel *If I Were King* (1901), which he based on the life of François Villon. His later dramatization of the novel became the basis for the operetta *The Vagabond King.*

McCarthy, Mary Therese, 1912–, American writer, b. Seattle, Wash., grad. Vassar, 1933. As drama critic for the *Partisan Review* (1937–45), she gained a reputation for wit, intellect, and acerbity, qualities she brings to her fiction. Her novel *The Oasis* (1949) satirizes left-wing intellectuals whereas *The Group* (1963), while analyzing the lives of eight Vassar graduates, satirizes an entire generation. Her other fictional works include *Cast a Cold Eye* (1950), *The Groves of Academe* (1952), and *Birds of America* (1971). Among her nonfiction works are *Venice Observed* (1956), *The Stones of Florence* (1959), *Vietnam* (1967) and *The Mask of State: Watergate Portraits* (1974). She was married to Edmund WILSON.

Macchiaioli, I (ē mäk-kēīō'lē), a group of Italian artists active primarily in Florence c.1855–65. Influenced by members of the BARBIZON SCHOOL, the Macchiaioli reacted against stilted academic art and worked to emphasize painterly immediacy and freshness. Silvestro Lega, Giovanni Fattori, Vito d'Ancona, Giovanni (Nino) Costa, and Giovanni Boldini were among the artists of this school. They were best known for their landscapes, portraits, and GENRE scenes.

McClellan, George Brinton, 1826–85, Union general in the American Civil War, b. Philadelphia. After graduating (1846) from West Point, he served with distinction in the Mexican War and later worked on various engineering projects, notably on the survey (1853–54) for a Northern Pacific RR route across the Cascade Range. Resigning from the army in 1857, he was a railroad official until the outbreak of the Civil War. In May, 1861, McClellan was made commander of the Dept. of the Ohio and a major general in the regular army. He cleared the western part of Virginia of Confederates (June–July, 1861) and consequently, after the Union defeat in the first battle of Bull Run, was given command of the troops in and around Washington. In November he became general in chief. The administration, reflecting public opinion, pressed for an early offensive, but McClellan insisted on adequate training and equipment for his army. In March, 1862, he was relieved of his supreme command, but he retained command of the Army of the Potomac, with which in April, 1862, he initiated the PENINSULAR CAMPAIGN. The collapse of this campaign after the SEVEN DAYS BATTLES was charged by many to his overcaution. In Aug., 1862, most of McClellan's troops were reassigned to the Army of Virginia under John POPE. After Pope's defeat at the second battle of Bull Run, McClellan again reorganized the Union forces, and in the ANTIETAM CAMPAIGN he checked Robert E. Lee's first invasion of the North. He was slow, however, to follow Lee across the Potomac and in Nov., 1862, was removed from his command. In 1864, McClellan was the Democratic candidate for President, although he rejected the party's peace platform. McClellan's candidacy caused the administration much uneasiness, but President Lincoln was reelected by a substantial majority. McClellan resigned from the army on the day of the election and afterward traveled extensively with his family in Europe. He was later chief engineer of the New York City department of docks and was governor of New Jersey (1878–81). Despite his faults "Little Mack" was an able general and was loved and trusted by his men of the Army of the Potomac. He wrote *McClellan's Own Story* (1887) in defense of his military record. See biographies by W. S. Myers (1934), H. J. Eckenrode and Bryan Conrad (1942), and W. W. Hassler, Jr. (1957); T. H. Williams, *McClellan, Sherman, and Grant* (1962).

McClellan, George Brinton, 1865–1940, American politician and educator, b. Dresden, Saxony, Germany; son of Gen. George B. McClellan. He studied law and joined (1889) Tammany Hall, becoming one of its most prominent orators. He was president of the board of aldermen of New York City (1893–94), served as a Democrat in Congress (1895–1903), and was mayor of New York (1903–9). While serving as mayor, he broke with Tammany boss Charles Murphy over patronage, thereby ending his political career. Afterwards he taught at Princeton, where he was professor of economic history from 1912 to his retirement in 1931. McClellan, an authority on Venetian history, wrote *Venice and Bonaparte* (1931) and *Modern Italy* (1933). See his autobiography, *The Gentleman and the Tiger* (ed. by Harold Syrett, 1956).

McClernand, John Alexander, 1812–1900, Union general in the American Civil War, b. Breckinridge co., Ky. He was admitted (1832) to the Illinois bar and sat as a Democrat in the U.S. House of Representatives (1843–51, 1859–61). At the outbreak of the Civil War he resigned from Congress, raised a brigade of Illinois volunteers, and was made a brigadier general (May, 1861). He fought at Fort Donelson (Feb., 1862) and at Shiloh (April). Through political influence he superseded William T. Sherman (Jan. 2, 1863) in command of the river expedition in the VICKSBURG CAMPAIGN. After McClernand—upon Sherman's suggestion—had successfully assaulted ARKANSAS POST (Jan. 11), Ulysses S. Grant assumed his command. In Grant's successful advance on Vicksburg, McClernand led the 13th Corps, fighting at Port Gibson and Champion's Hill, but he was subsequently relieved (June) for insubordination. Restored to his command in Feb., 1864, he resigned his commission in November and returned to the legal profession.

Macclesfield (măk'əlzfēld), municipal borough (1971 pop. 44,240), Cheshire, W England. Silk manufacture, of which Macclesfield is the principal center in England, was introduced in the town in 1756; other industries manufacture clothing, shoes, electrical appliances, and paper. The Church of St. Michael dates from 1278 and the grammar school from the beginning of the 16th cent. Macclesfield Forest is a moorland east of the town.

McClintock, Sir Francis Leopold, 1819–1907, British Arctic explorer. As a lieutenant in the navy he was assigned to his first Arctic service in 1848, when Sir James Clark Ross went in search of the lost expedition of Sir John Franklin. On this voyage and on the Franklin search expedition (1850–51) under Capt. Horatio Austin, McClintock learned and developed the Eskimo art of sledging. On the Austin expedition he mapped much of the south coast of Melville Island; while on Sir Edward Belcher's expedition (1852–54), he discovered and mapped most of Prince Patrick Island. In 1857, Lady Franklin placed him in command of the *Fox,* in which he set forth in search of more definite knowledge of Franklin's fate. The *Fox* remained in the Arctic until 1859; McClintock discovered the channel that bears his name, explored Prince of Wales Island and the east coast of King William Island, and sledged to Boothia Peninsula. He found records that disclosed that Franklin and his party had left their ships alive and had begun the march toward Hudson Bay. McClintock also proved that Franklin had found the existence of the Northwest Passage before he perished. The account of McClintock's findings was published as *The Voyage of the Fox* (1859), which achieved great popularity. He retired from the navy in 1884 with the rank of admiral. See biography by Sir Clements Markham (1909).

McClintock, John, 1814–70, American Methodist Episcopal clergyman and educator, b. Philadelphia. From 1836 to 1848 he taught at Dickinson College, resigning to edit (1848–56) the *Methodist Quarterly Review.* He preached in New York City (1857–60), and at the American Chapel in Paris (1860–64). He served (1867–70) as first president of Drew Theological Seminary. With James Strong, McClintock began in 1853 the noted *Cyclopaedia of Biblical, Theological, and Ecclesiastical Literature* (10 vol., 1867–81), three volumes of which were published before his death.

McCloy, John Jay, 1895–, U.S. government official, b. Philadelphia. A lawyer, he gained an international reputation when after a long investigation he fixed responsibility on the German government for the Black Tom munitions explosion in Hoboken, N.J., in 1917. He was Assistant Secretary of War in World War II and in 1947 became president of the International Bank for Reconstruction and Development (the World Bank). He resigned in 1949 and was U.S. military governor and high commissioner for Germany (1949–52). He returned (1961–63) to government service to act as President Kennedy's principal disarmament adviser. He is the author of *The Challenge of American Foreign Policy* (1953) and *The Atlantic Alliance* (1969).

McClung, Clarence Erwin, 1870–1946, American zoologist, b. Clayton, Calif., grad. Univ. of Kansas (B.A., 1896; Ph.D., 1902). He made extensive studies of germ plasm and chromosomes and in 1901 stated that sex is determined by the chromosomal constitution of the germ cells. For many years he was managing editor of the *Journal of Morphology* and was editor of the *Handbook of Microscopical Technique* (1929, rev. ed. 1950).

McClure, Alexander Kelly, 1828–1909, American journalist and political leader, b. Perry co., Pa. He edited and published the *Juniata Sentinel* of Mifflintown, Pa., before acquiring and editing (1850–56, 1862–64) the *Franklin Repository* at Chambersburg. He was an early and active Republican, and, at the party's national convention in 1860, he and Andrew G. Curtin swung the pivotal Pennsylvania delegation to Lincoln. As chairman of the state committee, McClure built up the Republican organization that secured the governorship for Curtin and Pennsylvania's electoral votes for Lincoln. He served in both houses of the state legislature and after the Civil War practiced law in Philadelphia. McClure supported Gen. U. S. Grant in 1868, but in 1872 was one of the leaders of the Liberal Republican party, which nominated Horace Greeley for President. In 1874 he was defeated for mayor of Philadelphia. He founded (1875) the Philadelphia *Times* and was its editor until 1901. He wrote *Abraham Lincoln and Men of War Time* (1892), *Old Time Notes of Pennsylvania* (1905), and accounts of his varied travels, and he edited *Famous American Statesmen and Orators* (6 vol., 1902). See his recollections (1902).

McClure, Sir Robert John Le Mesurier, 1807–73, British arctic explorer. He entered the navy and in 1848 accompanied Sir James Clark Ross to the arctic. As a naval captain he was given command (1850) of the *Investigator,* one of the two ships that were to search the western part of the Arctic Archipelago for Sir John Franklin. Passing through the Bering Strait, he coasted along Alaska and Canada, then went by way of Prince of Wales Strait into the western part of Viscount Melville Sound. He wintered (1850–51) in Prince of Wales Strait and by a sledging journey along its shores reached Barrow Strait. He discovered McClure Strait and established the insularity of Banks Island. On the north coast of Banks Island the *Investigator* was frozen in the ice for several winters. Finally he abandoned ship in 1853 and by sledge retreated over Barrow Strait eastward across the ice to Dealy Island, where his party was ultimately rescued by Sir Edward Belcher's expedition. McClure became the first man to prove the existence of the Northwest Passage. Although he was censured for having returned without his ship, he was highly commended for his work and knighted in 1854.

McClure, Samuel Sidney, 1857–1949, American editor and publisher, b. Co. Antrim, Ireland. He emigrated to America as a boy. In 1884 he established the McClure Syndicate, the first newspaper syndicate in the United States. He founded *McClure's Magazine* in 1893 and, as editor, made it a great success, particularly during the era of the MUCKRAKERS, when it published the articles of many of the journalistic leaders of the muckraking movement. McClure's works include *Obstacles to Peace* (1917), *The Achievements of Liberty* (1935), and *What Freedom Means to Man* (1938). See his autobiography (1914); biography by Peter Lyon (1963, repr. 1967).

McClure Strait, arm of the Beaufort Sea, c.170 mi (270 km) long and 60 mi (100 km) wide, W Franklin dist., Northwest Territories, Canada. It extends W from Viscount Melville Sound, between Melville and Eglinton islands on the north and Banks Island on the south. In 1954, U.S. icebreakers cut through the strait for the first time, opening the last obstacle to the shortest water route across the Canadian arctic region.

McComb, John, 1763–1853, American architect, b. New York City. He was chiefly known for the New

York City Hall (1803-12), one of the finest American buildings of the postcolonial period, designed with the collaboration of Joseph Mangin, a French architect; its elegant composition was inspired by the monumental work of the mid-18th cent. in France. His other New York works include St. John's Church, Varick St. (now demolished); the facade of the old government house (built in 1790, demolished in 1815); and the fort at the Battery (begun c.1807). McComb also designed churches and public and private buildings in other places, including Alexander Hall (1815) at Princeton Theological Seminary, Queen's Building (1808-9) at Rutgers College, New Brunswick, N.J., and the Cape Henry lighthouse.

McComb, city (1970 pop. 11,969), Pike co., SW Miss., near the La. line; inc. 1872. It is the trade and rail center of a cattle, soybean, and timber area. It has railroad shops and light manufacturing industries. A state park is nearby, and a junior college is in neighboring Summit.

McCormack, John, 1884-1945, Irish-American tenor, b. Athlone, Ireland. He made his debut in London in 1907. In 1909, Oscar Hammerstein brought him to the United States. After his debut in New York City he sang with the Boston and Chicago opera companies but after 1914 sang principally in concert and for phonograph records. He was widely beloved for the singing of simple sentimental songs. He became a U.S. citizen in 1919. In 1938 he retired. See biography by L. A. G. Strong (1941).

McCormick, Cyrus Hall, 1809-84, inventor of the reaper, b. Rockbridge co., Va. His father, Robert McCormick (1780-1846), had worked intermittently for over 20 years at his blacksmith shop on a reaping machine, but had given it up before Cyrus, his eldest son, began working on different principles. The first public demonstration of the reaper, as constructed by Cyrus, took place in July, 1831, and was a success, although he did not patent it until after Obed Hussey announced his invention in 1834. McCormick's reaper contained the straight reciprocating knife, guards, reel, divider, platform, main-drive wheel, and other innovations that are essential features of every satisfactory harvesting machine. His early machines were made for local use, and not until more than 10 years later did he begin in earnest to expand his market. In 1847 he built his Chicago factory; in 1851 he introduced the reaper into England and, subsequently, into other European countries. He continued to patent improvements and demonstrated his machine in the field, often in competition with Hussey's reaper. After 1850 many strong competitors appeared and Hussey gave up, while only McCormick's unusual business ability kept him in the running. He was quick to purchase promising inventions and added the self-rake, hand binder, and twine binder. See biographies by W. T. Hutchinson (2 vol., 2d ed. 1968) and H. N. Casson, (1909, repr. 1971).

McCormick, Joseph Medill: see under McCormick, Robert Sanderson.

McCormick, Robert Rutherford, 1880-1955, American journalist, b. Chicago. He held local public offices, was admitted (1907) to the bar, and practiced law in Chicago. He worked with his brother, Joseph Medill McCormick, in the management of the Chicago *Tribune,* and, after serving in World War I, he became sole owner of the newspaper. He rapidly extended his journalistic holdings, took control of paper mills, and soon was dominant in the Midwestern newspaper world. The Chicago *Tribune* steadily and vehemently maintained an extreme right wing position on various issues—it condemned labor unions and attacked the participation of the United States in world affairs. McCormick's works include *The American Revolution and Its Influence on World Civilization* (1945) and *The War without Grant* (1950).

McCormick, Robert Sanderson, 1849-1919, American diplomat, b. Rockbridge co., Va.; nephew of Cyrus Hall McCormick. President McKinley appointed (1901) him minister to Austria-Hungary, and the next year the first American ambassador to Austria-Hungary. McCormick then served as ambassador to Russia (1902-5) and to France (1905-7). He married Katherine Von Etta Medill, daughter of Joseph Medill. His son **Joseph Medill McCormick,** 1877-1925, b. Chicago, began his journalistic career as a reporter on the family newspaper, the Chicago *Tribune.* By 1908 the newspaper was under his management. He was a leading figure in Theodore Roosevelt's Progressive party campaign (1912) and later served in the Illinois legislature (1913-17), in the U.S. House of Representatives (1917-19), and in the U.S. Senate (1919-25). He was a strong opponent of the League of Nations. His brother was Robert Rutherford McCormick (see separate article). His wife was **Ruth Hanna McCormick,** 1880-1945, b. Cleveland, daughter of Mark HANNA. She early became interested in Republican party politics. She served (1929-31) in the U.S. House of Representatives but was defeated as a candidate for the U.S. Senate in 1930.

McCosh, James, 1811-94, Scottish-American philosopher and educator, b. Ayrshire, grad. Univ. of Edinburgh, 1833. He was called to the United States in 1868 to become president of the College of New Jersey (now Princeton Univ.), and he retained the position until 1888. His successful career as administrator and teacher laid an enduring foundation for the liberal development of the college. His philosophical position was that of the Scottish school of Thomas Reid and Sir William Hamilton; he is philosophically important as the expounder of the Scottish tradition to America. Chief among his works are *Method of Divine Government* (1850), *The Intuitions of the Mind Inductively Investigated* (1860), *Christianity and Positivism* (1871), *Scottish Philosophy from Hutchinson to Hamilton* (1875), and *Psychology* (1886-87). See W. M. Sloane, ed., *The Life of James McCosh* (1896).

McCoy, Joseph Geating, 1837-1915, American cattle-trade pioneer, b. Sangamon co., Ill. He selected Abilene, Kansas, as the site for a railroad shipping center for the marketing of Western cattle. In 1867 he purchased a tract of land, built stockyards and facilities, and advertised his plan, which resulted in the shipment of 350,000 cattle the first year and of tens of millions of cattle in succeeding years. In 1881 the Cherokee Indians employed him as their agent for the collection of revenue on tribal lands. His *Historic Sketches of the Cattle Trade* (1874, rev. ed. 1940) is an important source book.

MacCracken, Henry Mitchell, 1840-1918, American educator, b. Oxford, Ohio, grad. Miami Univ. (Ohio), 1857. After a brief teaching career MacCracken entered the Presbyterian ministry in 1863. From 1881 to 1884 he was chancellor of Western Univ. (now the Univ. of Pittsburgh). In 1884 he was appointed professor of philosophy and vice chancellor of the Univ. of the City of New York (now New York Univ.), becoming chancellor in 1891. Before his retirement in 1910, the University Heights campus was acquired, a graduate school and schools of commerce and pedagogy were founded, and the university medical school was strengthened by union with Bellevue Hospital medical college. Henry Noble MacCracken and John Henry MacCracken, president (1915-26) of Lafayette College, were his sons. See T. F. Jones, *New York University, 1832-1932* (1933).

McCracken, Paul W., 1915-, American economist, b. Richland, Iowa, educated at William Penn College (B.A., 1937), Harvard (M.A., 1942; Ph.D., 1948). After teaching at Berea College (1937-40) and serving in the Commerce Dept. (1942-43) and the Federal Reserve System (1943-48), he joined the faculty of the Univ. of Michigan school of business administration in 1948. A specialist in the fields of banking and finance, he took a leave of absence in 1956 to serve for three years on President Dwight D. Eisenhower's Council of Economic Advisers. He returned to the university in 1959, but again entered government to serve (1969-72) as chairman of the Council of Economic Advisers under President Nixon. McCracken stressed a balance between fiscal and monetary policy to fight inflation and unemployment. Although wary of governmental regulation of the economy, he supported the imposition of wage and price controls in 1971. McCracken returned to the Univ. of Michigan in 1972.

McCrae, John (məkrā'), 1872-1918, Canadian physician and poet. His famous poem "In Flanders Fields," written under fire during World War I, was published anonymously in *Punch* in 1915 and under his name in a posthumous volume, *In Flanders Fields* (1919). He died of pneumonia during the war.

McCullers, Carson, 1917-67, American novelist, b. Columbus, Ga., studied at Columbia. The central theme of her novels is the spiritual isolation that underlies the human condition. Her characters are usually outcasts and misfits whose longings for love are never fulfilled. In her first novel, *The Heart Is a Lonely Hunter* (1940), a deaf-mute is the focus of a circle of sad and tormented people. *The Member of the Wedding* (1946; dramatization, 1950), her best-known work, is the tender story of a lonely adolescent girl. Her other works include the novels *Reflections in a Golden Eye* (1941) and *Clock Without Hands* (1961); *The Ballad of the Sad Cafe,* a volume of stories (1951; title story dramatized by Edward ALBEE in 1963); and a play, *The Square Root of Wonderful* (1958). While she was in her 20's, McCullers suffered a series of strokes that left her partially paralyzed; during her last years she was confined to a wheelchair. A posthumous collection of her writings, *The Mortgaged Heart,* was published in 1972. See biography by O. W. Evans (1965).

McCulloch, Ben (məkŭl'ə), 1811-62, American scout and soldier, b. Rutherford co., Tenn. He followed David Crockett to Texas (1835), distinguished himself at San Jacinto (1836) in the Texas Revolution, and took part in campaigns against the Indians in Texas. He also served in the Mexican War. In 1849 he went to California but returned in 1852 to Texas, where he was a U.S. marshal. Made a Confederate brigadier general (1861), he commanded in Arkansas and fought at the battle of WILSON'S CREEK and at Pea Ridge, where he was killed.

McCulloch, Hugh, 1808-95, American financier and public official, b. Kennebunk, Maine. Educated at Bowdoin College, he studied law in Boston and practiced two years at Fort Wayne, Ind., before turning to banking and eventually becoming president of the State Bank of Indiana. In 1863 he became U.S. comptroller of the currency and launched the new national banking system. Appointed (1865) Secretary of the Treasury by Abraham Lincoln, he held office through Andrew Johnson's term. While in office, despite congressional opposition, he favored rapid reduction of the huge debt left by the Civil War as well as retirement of the legal tender notes (see GREENBACK) and a return to specie payments in order to prevent overspeculation and a panic. After leaving the Treasury in 1869, McCulloch went into the investment business. From Oct., 1884, to March, 1885, he again served as Secretary of the Treasury. See his *Men and Measures of Half a Century* (1888).

McCulloch vs. Maryland, case decided in 1819 by the U.S. Supreme Court. Congress had established (1816) the Second Bank of the United States to help control the unregulated issuance of currency by state banks. Maryland replied by imposing a tax on all banks not chartered by the state and brought suit for collection against the U.S. branch bank in Baltimore. Chief Justice John Marshall, who wrote the opinion, gave trenchant expression to the doctrine of implied powers: "Let the end be legitimate, let it be within the scope of the constitution, and all means which are appropriate, which are plainly adapted to that end, which are not prohibited, but consist with the letter and spirit of the constitution, are constitutional." The chartering of a bank was a power implied from the power over Federal fiscal operations. Because the state cannot impede constitutional Federal laws, the tax was unconstitutional. Marshall's opinion, based on a loose constructionist interpretation of the constitution, greatly expanded the scope of Federal power.

McCumber, Porter James, 1858-1933, American political leader, b. Crete, Ill. He began law practice in North Dakota and served (1885-89) in the territorial legislature. From 1899 to 1923 he was a Republican U.S. Senator. He actively supported the Pure Food and Drug Act (1906). As chairman of the finance committee he had a leading part in the framing of the Fordney-McCumber Tariff Act of 1922. He was obliged to agree to high tariffs on industrial goods in order to secure protection for many farm products.

McCutcheon, John Tinney, 1870-1949, American cartoonist, b. Tippecanoe co., Ind. He had been associated with the Chicago *Record* and *Record-Herald* when in 1903 he joined the staff of the Chicago *Tribune,* remaining with that paper until he retired (1945). He was war correspondent during the Spanish-American and Boer wars, during the Mexican expedition in 1914, and during World War I. In 1931 he won the Pulitzer Prize for one of his cartoons, *A Wise Economist Asks a Question.* Several collections of his cartoons have been published.

Macdhui, Ben, peak: see BEN MACDHUI, Scotland.

MacDiarmid, Hugh (məkdĭr'mĭd), pseud. of **Christopher Murray Grieve,** 1892-, Scottish poet and critic, b. Langholm, Dumfrieshire, Scotland. Passionately devoted to Communism and to Scottish independence from England, he was a founder of the Scottish Nationalist Party. He is credited with stimulating a Scottish literary revolution, emphasizing indigenous literature. Among his many works are *At the Sign of the Thistle* (1934), essays; *A Drunk Man Looks at the Thistle* (1962, rev. ed. 1971), a long poem castigating his fellow Scots; *Collected Poems* (1962) and *More Collected Poems* (1971). See his autobiography, *Lucky Poet* (1943, rev. ed. 1972); *The Hugh McDiarmid Anthology,* ed. by Michael Grieve and Alexander Scott (1972).

Macdonald, Dwight, 1906–, American author and editor, b. New York City, grad. Yale, 1928. As an associate editor (1928–36) of the business magazine *Fortune,* he acquired a distaste for capitalism, and in 1937 he became editor of the radical *Partisan Review.* In the left-wing factionalism of the 1930s and 40s, Macdonald moved from Stalinism to Trotskyism and then to pacifism and to anarchism. In 1943 he left *Partisan Review,* protesting its support of World War II. As a vehicle for his wry and intensely personal essays he founded *Politics* (monthly 1944–47; quarterly 1947–49). His works include *Henry Wallace: The Man and the Myth* (1948), *The Root Is Man* (1953), and *The Ford Foundation* (1956). His *Memoirs of a Revolutionist* (1957) traces his philosophy through his articles. In the 1950s, Macdonald turned to writing about culture in various magazines and to reviewing motion pictures. *Against the American Grain* (1962) comprises his essays deploring the effects of mass culture on the arts. Other collections of his essays and reviews include *Dwight Macdonald on Movies* (1969), *Politics Past* (1970) and *Discriminations* (1974).

Macdonald, Flora, 1722–90, Scottish Jacobite heroine. She aided Charles Edward STUART, known as Bonnie Prince Charlie, to escape to France after the defeat of the Jacobites at Culloden Moor in 1746. For smuggling the prince, disguised as a woman, to the Isle of Skye, she was imprisoned briefly in the Tower of London. Later she was visited by many celebrities, including Dr. Samuel Johnson (1773). Her romantic aid to the prince is commemorated in Highland ballad and legend.

Macdonald, George, 1824–1905, Scottish author. Ordained a Congregational minister, he eventually abandoned his vocation to become a writer and free-lance preacher. His first published works were several volumes of poetry, including the narrative poem *Within and Without* (1855), *Phantastes* (1858), and *Lilith* (1895), the last two both moral allegories. Macdonald achieved his first real success with his novels of life in rural Scotland, notably *David Elginbrod* (1863), *Alec Forbes* (1865), and *Robert Falconer* (1867). His lasting reputation, however, rests upon his superb allegorical fairy stories for children; they include *At the Back of the North Wind* (1871), *The Princess and the Goblin* (1872), and *The Princess and Curdie* (1882). See biography by his son Greville Macdonald (1924, repr. 1971).

Macdonald, Jacques Étienne Joseph Alexandre (zhäk ātyĕn'zhôzĕf' älĕksäN'drə mäkdônäl'), 1765–1840, marshal of France, of Scottish descent. He distinguished himself in the French Revolutionary Wars, particularly in Italy, but was defeated by Russian forces under Aleksandr SUVOROV at the battle of Trebbia (June, 1799). He aided Napoleon's coup d'etat of 18 Brumaire (1799). Temporarily in disgrace for defending Jean Victor MOREAU, he returned to favor, was created duke of Taranto, and played an important part in the battle of Wagram (1809), the Peninsular War, and the Russian campaign. In the Hundred Days he was loyal to King Louis XVIII.

Macdonald, Sir John Alexander, 1815–91, Canadian statesman, first prime minister of the Dominion of Canada, b. Glasgow. His parents settled in 1820 in Kingston, Ont. Macdonald first practiced law. With his election (1844) as a Conservative to the legislative assembly, he entered upon his long political career. A forceful man and a vigorous fighter, he quickly rose to leadership in the government of Upper Canada (Ontario). He and Georges Étienne CARTIER of Lower Canada headed the Liberal-Conservatives (a coalition largely of Macdonald's creating), and he became prime minister in 1857. This government fell in 1858, but he continued as a cabinet minister until 1862. He briefly returned (1864) as prime minister before he was joined by George BROWN and others in the "great coalition" ministry (1864–67), which paved the way for the union of the British North American provinces. Macdonald was the most potent figure in bringing about confederation (1867) of the provinces as the Dominion of Canada. His policy as prime minister was dominated by the vigorous attempt to build Canada. Believing that the dominion's prosperity required strong bonds with England, he worked throughout his career to that end. The Northwest Territories were taken over from the Hudson's Bay Company in 1869; to facilitate their development, Macdonald's government decided to construct the Canadian Pacific Railway. His personal popularity was not enough when the PACIFIC SCANDAL, which involved the railroad, broke (1873), and the government resigned. Changing industrial conditions made Macdonald the advocate of a protectionist policy (known as the National Policy), and he was returned as prime minister in 1878 and served until his death. The transcontinental railroad was completed (1885), and other public works were accomplished. Macdonald was knighted in 1867. See his correspondence, ed. by Joseph Pope (1921); biographies by his nephew, J. P. Macpherson (2 vol., 1891) and D. G. Creighton (1952 and 1956); study by Donald Swainson (1971).

Macdonald, John Sandfield, 1812–72, Canadian political leader. He was elected (1841) as a Conservative to the Legislative Assembly, but he afterward developed considerable political independence. He was solicitor general for Upper Canada (1849–51), speaker of the Legislative Assembly (1852–54), and attorney general for Upper Canada (1858). He was prime minister from 1862 to 1864. Although he was loyal to confederation after it was effected (1867), he had previously opposed it. He was chosen first prime minister of Ontario in 1867, but in 1871 he resigned when his coalition party was defeated by the Liberals. See biography by B. W. Hodgins (1971).

MacDonald, Ramsay, 1866–1937, British statesman, b. Scotland. The illegitimate son of a servant, he went as a young man to London, where he joined the Social Democratic Federation (1885) and the Fabian Society (1886). He became (1894) a member of the newly formed Independent Labour party and was instrumental in organizing the Labour Representation Committee (later the LABOUR party), in which he served (1900–1912) as first secretary. MacDonald was elected to Parliament in 1906 and was leader of the Labour party in the House of Commons (1911–14) until he was discredited and labeled a traitor for his pacifist stand at the outbreak of World War I. He lost his seat in Parliament in 1918 but was reelected in 1922 and again chosen to lead the Labour party. In Jan., 1924, he became prime minister and foreign secretary of the first Labour government of Great Britain. Although unemployment benefits were extended, his minority government did not enact strong socialist measures. In foreign affairs, however, MacDonald helped secure acceptance of the DAWES PLAN and sponsored the Geneva Protocol (later rejected by the Conservative government), which provided for compulsory arbitration of international disputes. A trade agreement with the Soviet Union and the government's withdrawal of charges against a Communist newspaper editor led to a vote of censure that forced MacDonald to call an election in Oct., 1924. Publication of the Zinoviev Letter (see under ZINOVIEV, GRIGORI EVSEYEVICH) helped secure Labour's defeat. In 1929, MacDonald became prime minister in the second Labour government. Again it was a minority government and could not press a socialist program, and its strictly orthodox economic measures proved ineffective against the serious depression. In 1931, when proposed cuts in unemployment benefits split the Labour cabinet, MacDonald agreed to lead a coalition government (the National government), leaning heavily on Conservative support. This action was regarded as apostasy by most of the Labour party, which however was roundly defeated in the election that followed. Never completely trusted by his new Conservative allies, MacDonald was no more than a figurehead in the National government. In 1935 he resigned the premiership to Stanley BALDWIN and became lord president of the council. He lost his parliamentary seat in the same year but was returned in a by-election and remained in the cabinet until his death. MacDonald's writings include *Parliament and Revolution* (1920) and *Socialism: Critical and Constructive* (1924). See L. M. Weir, *The Tragedy of Ramsay MacDonald* (1938; an unsympathetic account of his political career); biography by Lord Elton (1939; covering his career to 1919); studies by Benjamin Sacks (1953) and David Carlton (1970).

Macdonald, Ross, pseud. of **Kenneth Millar,** 1915–, American novelist, b. Los Gatos, Calif. He was educated in Canada and at the Univ. of Michigan. Macdonald's highly complex mystery novels center on the tough but compassionate private detective Lew Archer. They often deal with the effect of a person's past on his present behavior, with the crimes parents commit against their children, and with the nature of evil in a shallow, transient society. His novels include *The Galton Case* (1959), *The Zebra-Striped Hearse* (1962), *The Chill* (1964), *The Good-bye Look* (1969), *The Underground Man* (1971), and *Sleeping Beauty* (1973). His wife, **Margaret Millar,** 1915–, b. Kitchner, Ont., Canada, is also a mystery writer. Her works include *The Invisible Worm* (1941), *Beast in View* (1956), and *The Fiend* (1964).

McDonald Observatory, astronomical observatory located on Mt. Locke, near Fort Davis, Texas; founded in 1932, sponsored by the Univ. of Texas in cooperation with the Univ. of Chicago. Its equipment includes 107-in. (272-cm), 82-in. (208-cm), 32-in. (81-cm), and 30-in. (76-cm) reflecting TELESCOPES plus a 16-ft (4.9-m) parabolic radio-astronomy dish. The 107-in. reflector, which began operation in 1968 as the third largest telescope in the world, was built under contract with the National Aeronautics and Space Administration. It is primarily used for the study of bodies within the solar system, particularly the planets, satellites, and asteroids, to gather information for possible use in future space exploration. Principal research programs conducted by McDonald Observatory are on lunar occultations, planetary atmospheres, and interstellar molecules as well as the spectroscopic and photometric analysis of stellar, interstellar, and extragalactic matter.

Macdonald-Wright, Stanton, 1890–1973, American artist, b. Charlottsville, Va. Macdonald-Wright was among the first Americans to paint in a totally abstract mode. Together with Morgan RUSSELL, he founded synchromism in 1912. In paintings such as *Oriental Synchromy in Blue-Green* (1918; Whitney Mus., New York City), Macdonald-Wright uses color to build an illusion of space and depth.

Macdonnell, Arthur Anthony (măk''dənĕl'), 1854–1930, British Sanskrit scholar. Macdonnell was one of the greatest figures in his field. Besides many other authoritative works, he wrote the standard grammar of Vedic and a Sanskrit-English dictionary.

Macdonough, Thomas (məkdŏn'ə), 1783–1825, American naval officer, b. New Castle co., Del. In the TRIPOLITAN WAR he took part in the burning of the captured *Philadelphia* and the attack on the Tripolitan gunboats. In the War of 1812, given command of a small fleet on Lake Champlain, Macdonough augmented his strength by building ships from the local forests. On Sept. 11, 1814, in a pitched battle, his makeshift fleet defeated the British and thoroughly disrupted the British plans that required control of the lake. By superior skill and planning Macdonough on his flagship, the *Saratoga* (26 guns), was able to defeat the *Confiance* (37 guns) in one of the most significant naval battles in U.S. history. See C. G. Muller, *The Proudest Day: Macdonough on Lake Champlain* (1960) and *Hero of Two Seas* (1968).

McDougall, Alexander, 1731–86, American Revolutionary political leader and general, b. Islay, Inner Hebrides, Scotland. He was taken (1738) as a child to New York. He became a fiery opponent of British restrictions on trade and helped to form the SONS OF LIBERTY in New York City. In 1770 he was arrested on the charge of having written a seditious broadside. In 1774 he presided over the meeting that decided to send New York delegates to the Continental Congress. He served in the army throughout the Revolution and was notable in the battles of White Plains and Germantown and in the fighting in New Jersey. In 1780, after Benedict Arnold's treason, McDougall succeeded to the charge of West Point. After the war he was (1781–82, 1784–85) a member of Congress from New York.

McDougall, William, 1822–1905, Canadian leader in the movement for Canadian confederation, b. Ontario. He was elected (1858) to the Legislative Assembly, and in 1864 he entered the "great coalition" ministry led by John A. Macdonald and George Brown. He was a delegate to the two Canadian conferences (1864) on confederation and to the Anglo-Canadian conference held in England (1866). In 1868 he again went to England, with Georges Étienne Cartier, to arrange the transfer to Canada of the territories of the Hudson's Bay Company, a project he had long urged. The following year he was appointed lieutenant governor of the newly acquired region, but on his way to assume his post he was turned back near the border by rebels of the Red River Settlement. This setback, for which he was removed from office, as well as the success of his opponents within the Liberal party, led to the decline of McDougall's influence.

McDougall, William, 1871–1938, American psychologist, b. Lancashire, England, educated at Cambridge, Oxford, and Göttingen. He was professor (1920–27) of psychology at Harvard and later at Duke. A pioneer in physiological and social psychology, he was known also for his biological approach to the problems of psychology. He studied eugenics and heredity and for 17 years conducted experiments in the inheritance of acquired characteristics. He was also much interested in psychical research. His works include *An Introduction to Social Psychology* (1908) and *Outline of Psychology* (1923).

MacDowell, Edward Alexander, 1861-1908, American composer, b. New York City. He studied at the conservatories in Paris and Frankfurt and taught (1881-82) at the Darmstadt Conservatory. He held the first chair of music at Columbia Univ. from 1896 until 1904. His outstanding works for four programmatic piano sonatas—*Tragica* (1893), *Eroica* (1895), *Norse* (1900), and *Keltic* (1901)—and his *Indian Suite* (1897) for orchestra, which employs adaptations of native Indian melodies. In addition, he wrote two piano concertos and numerous smaller works, including the popular *Woodland Sketches* (1896) and *Sea Pieces* (1898) for piano. The MacDowell Colony for composers, artists, and writers, founded by his widow, Marian Nevins MacDowell, at their summer home in Peterborough, N.H., is a fulfillment of a plan of MacDowell's. See biographies by Lawrence Gilman (rev. ed. 1909) and J. F. Porte (1922) and biography of Mrs. MacDowell by Nancy McKee (1962).

McDowell, Ephraim, 1771-1830, American pioneer surgeon, b. Virginia. He studied with the Scottish surgeon John Bell in Edinburgh and practiced in Danville, Ky. He was noted especially for his success in lithotomy, and in 1809 he made surgical history by performing the first ovariotomy.

McDowell, Irvin, 1818-85, Union general in the American Civil War, b. Columbus, Ohio. He taught at West Point (1841-45) and was made captain for his service in the Mexican War. In the Civil War, McDowell, promoted to brigadier general in the regular army (May, 1861), commanded the Union troops at the first battle of BULL RUN. After that defeat he commanded a corps under his successor, George B. McClellan. When the PENINSULAR CAMPAIGN began, McDowell's 1st Corps (then called the Army of the Rappahannock) was withdrawn from McClellan's command to defend Washington. In the summer of 1862, McDowell's force fought at the second battle of Bull Run. McDowell shared in the blame for that defeat and was removed from command. He later commanded various territorial departments until his retirement in 1882. He was promoted to major general in 1872. See study by R. S. Harper (1961).

McDuffie, George, 1790-1851, American politician, b. Columbia co., Ga. He was a member of the South Carolina legislature and served (1821-34) in the U.S. House of Representatives, where he quickly became noted as an ebullient debater. He bitterly opposed the administration of John Quincy Adams and as ardently supported Andrew Jackson. McDuffie later broke with Jackson; he supported the Bank of the United States and also was a leader of the South Carolina group that advocated the doctrine of NULLIFICATION. He was (1834-36) governor of South Carolina and served (1842-46) in the U.S. Senate.

mace, in botany: see NUTMEG.

Mace, chemical spray device used by police in riot control. Mace is ordinary TEAR GAS (chloroacetophenone, or CN) in a volatile solvent contained in a spray can. It causes severe lacrimation and temporary blindness. If sprayed directly into the face from a distance of less than 6 ft (1.8 m), it may cause permanent injury.

Macedon (măs'ədŏn), ancient country, N Greece, the modern Macedonia. Macedon proper constituted the coast plain NW, N, and NE of the Chalcidice (now Khalkidhikí) peninsula; Upper Macedon was the highland to the west and the north of the plain. The plain was fertile and productive, and there were important silver mines in the eastern part. The population of the region was complex when first known and included Anatolian peoples as well as several Hellenic groups. The first influence of Greek culture in Macedon came from the colonies along the shore founded in the 8th cent. B.C. and after; they had ties to their mother cities that tended to isolate them politically from Macedon. By the 7th cent. B.C. there was developing in W Macedon a political unit led by a Greek-speaking family, which assumed the title of king and aggrandized itself. Macedon was a Persian tributary in 500 B.C. but took no real part in the Persian Wars. Alexander I (d. 450 B.C.) was the first Macedonian king to enter into Greek politics; he began a policy of imitating features of Greek civilization. For the next century the Hellenic influences grew and the state became stronger. With Philip II (reigned 359-336 B.C.) these processes reached their culmination, for by annexing Upper Macedon, Chalcidice, and Thrace he made himself the strongest power in Greece; then he became its ruler. He created an excellent army with which his son, Alexander the Great, forged his empire. That empire, although it was a Macedonian conquest, was a personal creation. The Macedonian generals carved it up after Alexander's death (323 B.C.); these were the successors (the Diadochi), founders of states and dynasties—notably Antipater, Perdiccas, Ptolemy I, Seleucus I, Antigonus I, and Lysimachus. They had armies largely Macedonian and Greek in personnel, and most of them founded cities with colonies of their soldiers. Thus began the remarkable spread of the Hellenistic (Greek, rather than Macedonian) civilization. All the armies constituted a fatal drain on the population of Macedon. Macedon, with Greece as a dependency, was one of the states cut out of the Alexandrian empire. Almost immediately, however, there was struggle for the hold over Greece and even over Macedon itself. Cassander took (319-316 B.C.) Macedon and held it until his death (297); he refounded Salonica (now Thessaloníki). After a period of short-lived attempts by Demetrius I, Pyrrhus of Epirus, Lysimachus, and others to hold Macedon, Antigonus II established himself as king. He fought off the Galatian invaders and used his long reign (277-239 B.C.) to restore Macedon economically. There was constant trouble with the Greek city-states; many of them regained independence, but Antigonus III (reigned 229-221 B.C.), another strong king, reestablished Macedonian hegemony. Under his successor, Philip V (reigned 221-179 B.C.), Macedon engaged in war against Rome. Although the First Macedonian War (215-205 B.C.) ended favorably for Philip, he was decisively defeated in the Second Macedonian War (200-197 B.C.), was forced to give up most of his fleet and pay a large indemnity, and was confined to Macedonia proper. By collaborating with the Romans, however, he was able to reduce the indemnity. His successor, Perseus (reigned 179-168 B.C.), foolishly aroused Roman fears and lost his kingdom in the Third Macedonian War (171-168 B.C.). Now Rome divided Macedon into four republics. Later (150-148 B.C.) a pretender, Andriscus, tried to revive a Macedonian kingdom. This time Macedonia was annexed to Roman territory and became (146 B.C.) the first Roman province. It never again had political importance in ancient times. In the history of Greek culture Macedon had its single significance in producing the conquerors and armies who created the Hellenistic empires and civilizations. The capital of Macedon from c.400 to 167 B.C. was PELLA. See Stanley Casson, *Macedonia, Thrace, and Illyria* (1926); W. W. Tarn, *Hellenistic Civilization* (3d ed. 1952); F. E. Adcock, *The Greek and Macedonian Art of War* (1957); N. G. C. Hammond, *A History of Macedonia* (Vol. I, 1972).

Macedonia (măsədō'nēə), Macedonian *Makedoniya,* region, SE Europe, on the Balkan Peninsula, divided among Greece, Yugoslavia, and Bulgaria. Corresponding roughly with ancient Macedon, it extends from the Aegean Sea northwards between Epirus in the west and Thrace in the east and includes the Vardar, Struma, and Mesta (in Greece, the Axiós, Strimón, and Néstos) river valleys. The region is predominately mountainous, encompassing parts of the Pindus and Rhodope mts. Tobacco is the main crop; grains and cotton are also grown, and sheep and goats are raised. The mining of iron, copper, lead, and chromite is important. Greek, or Aegean, Macedonia (c.13,000 sq mi/33,670 sq km) includes the KHALKIDHIKÍ (Chalcidice) peninsula, the site of THESSALONÍKI (Salonica), a major industrial and shipping center. As a result of population movements after World War I, Greek Macedonia has a largely homogeneous Greek population. Bulgarian or Pirin Macedonia is largely coextensive with the Blagoyevgrad (formerly Gorna Dzhumaya) province of Bulgaria (c.2,500 sq mi/6,475 sq km). The population consists of Macedonians, Bulgarians, Turks, and others. Yugoslav Macedonia is a constituent republic (c.9,930 sq mi/25,720 sq km) within Yugoslavia; the main cities are Skopje, Bitola (Bitolj), and Prilep. The population is largely Macedonian (see SLAVS), and Macedonian is an official language. Like neighboring Thrace and Epirus, Macedonia has been, since the early Middle Ages, a meeting place of nations, a fact which has contributed in large measure to its complex and turbulent history. With the division (395) of the Roman Empire, Macedonia came under Byzantine rule. Devastated by the Goths and Huns, it was settled (6th cent.) by the Slavs, who quickly made most of Macedonia a Slavic land. However, it continued under intermittent Byzantine domination until the 9th cent., when most of Macedonia was wrested from the Byzantine Empire by Bulgaria. Emperor Basil II recovered it (1014-18) for Byzantium, but after the temporary breakup (1204) of the Byzantine Empire during the Fourth Crusade, Macedonia was bitterly contested among the Latin Empire of Constantinople, the Bulgars under Ivan II, the despots of Epirus, and the emperors of Nicaea. It again became part of the Byzantine Empire, which was restored in 1261, but in the 14th cent. Stephen Dushan of Serbia conquered all Macedonia except for present-day Thessaloníki. The fall of the Serbian empire in the late 14th cent. brought Macedonia under the rule of the Ottoman Turks, which lasted for five centuries. In the 19th cent. the national revival in the Balkans began; national and religious antagonism flared, and conflict was heightened by the Ottoman policy of playing one group against the other. Meanwhile the Ottoman Empire lost control over the major sections of Greece, Serbia, and Bulgaria, each of which claimed Macedonia on historical or ethnical grounds. In the Treaty of SAN STEFANO (1878), which terminated the Russo-Turkish War of 1877-78, Bulgaria was awarded the lion's share of Macedonia. However, the settlement was nullified by the European powers in the same year (see BERLIN, CONGRESS OF), and Macedonia was left under direct Ottoman control. A secret terrorist organization working for Macedonian independence sprang up in the late 19th cent. and soon wielded great power. The *komitadjis,* as the terrorist bands were called, were generally supported by Bulgaria, which gained a major share of Macedonia in the first of the BALKAN WARS (1912-13). Greece and Serbia turned against Bulgaria in the Second Balkan War, and the Treaty of Bucharest (1913) left Bulgaria only a small share of Macedonia, the rest of which was divided roughly along the present lines. Thousands of Macedonians fled to Bulgaria. In World War I the Salonica (present-day Thessaloníki) campaigns took place in Macedonia. After the war Macedonia became a hotbed of agitation and terrorism, directed largely from Bulgaria. The population exchange among Greece, Turkey, and Bulgaria after 1923 resulted in the replacement by Greek refugees from Asia Minor of most of the Slavic and Turkish elements in Greek Macedonia. Charging that the Greek minority in Bulgarian Macedonia was being mistreated, Greece in 1925 invaded Bulgaria. The League of Nations, however, forced a cession of hostilities and awarded (1926) a decision favorable to Bulgaria. Bulgarian relations with Yugoslavia (before 1929 the kingdom of the Serbs, Croats, and Slovenes) remained strained over the Macedonian question. Frontier incidents were frequent, as were Yugoslav charges against Bulgaria for fostering the Internal Macedonian Revolutionary Organization (IMRO), a nationalist group that used violence, in Yugoslavia. Macedonian agitation against Serbian rule culminated (1934) in the assassination of King Alexander of Yugoslavia by a Macedonian nationalist at Marseilles. In World War II all Macedonia was occupied (1941-44) by Bulgaria, which sided with the Axis against Yugoslavia and Greece, but the Bulgarian armistice treaty of 1944 restored the prewar boundaries, which were confirmed in the peace treaty of 1947. The Yugoslav constitution of 1946 made Yugoslav Macedonia an autonomous unit in a federal state, and the Macedonian people were recognized as a separate nationality. Tension over Macedonia continued in the early postwar years. During the Greek civil war there was much conflict between Greece and Yugoslavia over Macedonia, and the breach between Yugoslavia and Bulgaria after 1948 helped to make the Macedonian question explosive. However, with the settlement of the civil war and with the easing of Yugoslav-Bulgarian relations after 1962, tension over Macedonia was reduced. See H. N. Brailsford, *Macedonia: Its Races and Their Future* (1971).

Maceió (məsāô'), city (1970 pop. 263,583), capital of Alagoas state, E Brazil, on a narrow strip of land between a lagoon and the Atlantic Ocean. Its port is at Jaraguá. A commercial and distribution center, Maceió exports sugar and textiles. On the outskirts are coconut plantations. The city grew around a sugar mill following the Dutch occupation during the early 17th cent. The Portuguese gained control of Maceió in 1654. By the early 19th cent. it had developed as an important sugar export center, and in 1839 it became the provincial capital. Maceió is an important cultural center, with a state university, historical institute, and academy of letters. The most outstanding landmark is a lighthouse in the center of the city.

Maček or **Machek, Vladimir** (both: vlădē'mĭr mä'chĕk), 1879-1964, Croatian political leader. He headed the Croatian Peasant party from 1928. A vigorous opponent of the dictatorship of King Alexander of Yugoslavia, he fought for Croatian autonomy and was imprisoned several times. After Alexander's death, Maček was granted amnesty, and largely through his negotiations with Prince Paul, regent for King Peter II, Croatia obtained (1939) substantial autonomy within Yugoslavia. Maček entered (1939) the Yugoslav government as vice premier. After the occupation (1941) of Yugoslavia by the Axis forces, he was under close surveillance. Later, he opposed the Tito regime, which came into power in 1944. He left Yugoslavia in 1945, settling eventually in the United States. See his *In the Struggle for Freedom* (1957).

Macenta (mäsĕn'tä), town (1961 est. pop. 22,500), SE Guinea. It is the market center for a rain forest region where rice, manioc, millet, coffee, tea, and kola nuts are grown. Diamond mines are found nearby.

Macer: see under LICINIUS, Roman gens.

Macerata (mächärä'tä), town (1971 pop. 43,698), capital of Macerata prov., in the Marche, central Italy. It is an agricultural and industrial center. Manufactures include musical instruments, furniture, and construction materials. Macerata was ruled by the papacy from the mid-15th cent. to 1797. It retains its medieval walls and has a university that was founded in 1290.

MacEwen, Sir William (məkyo͞o'ən), 1848-1924, Scottish surgeon. A professor of surgery at the Univ. of Glasgow, he was noted for his work on bone grafting, on the radical cure of hernia, and especially on surgery of the brain and spinal cord.

MacGahan, Januarius Aloysius (məgăn'), 1844-78, American newspaper correspondent. He reported the Franco-Prussian War for the New York *Herald* and in 1873 penetrated central Asia to join the Russian army against Khiva. An account of the venture, *Campaigning on the Oxus* (1874), made him famous. He was sent by the London *Daily News* to investigate the Turkish massacres in Bulgaria, and his dispatches were collected in *The Turkish Atrocities in Bulgaria* (1876) and were an incitement to the Russo-Turkish War of 1877-78.

McGee, Thomas D'Arcy (məgē'), 1825-68, Canadian journalist and statesman, a leader in the movement for confederation, b. Ireland. He emigrated (1842) to Boston, where he became editor of the Boston *Pilot,* but in 1845 he returned to Ireland to join the staff of the Dublin *Freeman's Journal.* Later McGee transferred to the *Nation,* journal of the Young Ireland party. Implicated in the uprising of 1848, he fled to America. He edited Irish papers in New York City and Boston before settling (1857) in Montreal, where he started the *New Era.* Entering (1858) the Canadian legislature, McGee became president of the council (1862) and minister of agriculture (1864). His anti-British position had changed, and he lent his brilliant oratory to the cause of Canadian confederation within the empire. He lived to see it take place (1867), but the following year he was assassinated by a member of the FENIAN MOVEMENT, whose tactics McGee had denounced.

McGill, William James, 1922-, American educator and psychologist, b. New York City, grad. Fordham (A.B., 1943) and Harvard (Ph.D., 1953). A specialist in psychophysics and one of the leading mathematical psychologists in the United States, he was professor of psychology at Columbia (1956-65) and at the Univ. of California at San Diego (1965-68). From 1968 to 1970 he served as chancellor of that university. In 1970 he became president of Columbia Univ.

Macgillicuddy's Reeks (məgĭl'əkŭd'ēz rēks), highest mountain range of Ireland, Co. Kerry, SW Republic of Ireland. It includes Carrantuohill and other peaks more than 3,000 ft (914 m) high.

McGillivray, Alexander (məgĭl'ĭvrā), 1759-93, American Indian chief. He was born in the Creek country now within the borders of the state of Alabama, the son of Lachlan McGillivray, a Scots trader, and Sehoy Marchand, his French-Creek wife. Given a classical education at Charleston, S.C., he returned to his mother's people at the beginning of the American Revolution when Georgia confiscated the property of his Loyalist father, who thereupon returned to Scotland. In the war he was a British agent, influential in maintaining Creek loyalty to the crown. At Pensacola in 1784, McGillivray, now dominant in his nation's councils, concluded with the Spanish a treaty confirming the Creek Indians in their lands, giving the Spanish a trade monopoly, and making him Spanish commissary. With arms provided by the Spanish, his warriors periodically attacked American frontier settlements from Georgia to the Cumberland River. In 1790, President Washington, seeking to end the depredations, invited him to a conference in New York City. McGillivray, an intelligent diplomat, accepted, meanwhile assuring Spanish authorities of his loyalty, and was well received. By the Treaty of New York (1790), the Creek acknowledged U.S. sovereignty over part of their territory, acquired lands claimed by Georgia, and agreed to keep the peace. McGillivray himself accepted a brigadier generalcy and a yearly pension. He continued in the pay of the Spanish, however; in 1792 when they increased his subsidy, he entered upon another treaty with them that practically repudiated his treaty with the Americans, and the Indian attacks were resumed. See J. W. Caughey, *McGillivray of the Creeks* (1938).

McGill University, at Montreal, Que., Canada; coeducational; chartered 1821, opened 1829. It was named for James McGill, who left a bequest to establish it. Its real development dates from 1855 when John W. DAWSON became principal. Besides its faculties of arts, science, dentistry, engineering, agriculture, graduate studies and research, education, management, religious studies, law, medicine, and music, it has schools of architecture, social work, commerce, library science, nursing, food science, and physical and occupational therapy. Anglican, Presbyterian, and United Church theological colleges are affiliated. Royal Victoria College at Montreal is the women's college of the university. Macdonald College at Ste Anne de Bellevue, Que., includes the faculty of agriculture and the school of food science. McGill is noted for its graduate work in chemistry, medicine (especially neurology and psychiatry), and biology. It has a fine medical library and medical museum.

McGilvary, Evander Bradley (məgĭl'vərē"), 1864-1953, American realist philosopher, b. Bangkok, Thailand, grad. Davidson College, 1884, and Univ. of Calif., Ph.D. 1897. He taught at California (1894-99) before going to Cornell Univ. as professor of ethics (1899-1905) and to the Univ. of Wisconsin as chairman of the philosophy department (1905-34). His only book, *Toward A Perspective Realism* (ed. by A. G. Ramsperger, 1956), was taken from lectures given in 1939 and contained his thinking on the nature of consciousness.

McGinley, Phyllis, 1905-, American poet, b. Ontario, Oregon. Her light verse treats aspects of modern life with humor and underlying seriousness. Among her best-known collections of verse are *A Pocketful of Wry* (1940), *The Love Letters of Phyllis McGinley* (1950), and *Times Three* (1960; Pulitzer Prize). She has also written many light essays as well as criticism, children's books, and song lyrics. *Saint-Watching* (1969) recounts the lives of various saints with irreverence and affection.

McGovern, George Stanley, 1922-, U.S. political leader, b. Avon, S.D. He was (1942-45) a pilot during World War II and later taught (1949-53) American history. After serving as a Democrat (1957-61) in the U.S. House of Representatives, he was (1961-62) director of President Kennedy's Food for Peace Program. Elected (1962) to the U.S. Senate, McGovern became an outspoken critic of defense spending and was among the first Senators to oppose the Vietnam War. At the 1968 Democratic convention he tried unsuccessfully to rally the antiwar supporters of the late Robert F. Kennedy. McGovern announced (1971) his candidacy for the presidency on a platform promising to end the war in Vietnam, cut defense spending by $30 billion, and provide a guaranteed annual income for all Americans. His grass-roots campaign won (1972) for him the Democratic nomination, but McGovern's handling of the Thomas EAGLETON affair, in which he first announced complete support for his running mate, only to drop Eagleton from the ticket later, and Republican charges of radicalism, led to his defeat by Richard M. Nixon in the election. He wrote *War Against Want* (1964), *A Time of War, A Time of Peace* (1968), and *The Great Coalfield War* (1972). See biography by R. S. Anson (1972); studies by Richard Dougherty (1973), G. W. Hart (1973), and Eleanor McGovern (1974).

McGraw, John Joseph, 1873-1934, American baseball manager, b. Cortland co., N.Y. He began playing professional baseball in 1890 and was (1891-1900) the star third baseman of the renowned Baltimore Orioles of the National League. McGraw managed the Orioles in 1899, and after the team was dropped (1900) by the National League he helped organize (1900) the American League. As manager (1902-32) of the New York Giants of the National League, the fiery, efficient John J. McGraw became one of the outstanding figures of baseball. He led the Giants to 10 pennants (1904-5, 1911-13, 1917, 1921-24) and three world series victories (1905, 1921-22). In 1914 and again in 1924, McGraw, together with Charles Comiskey, led groups of baseball players on worldwide tours to popularize the sport in Europe and the Orient. He was named to the National Baseball Hall of Fame in 1937. He wrote *How to Play Baseball* (1914). See his autobiography, *My Thirty Years in Baseball* (1923); biography by Frank Graham (1944); Frank Durso, *The Days of Mr. McGraw* (1969).

McGready, James (məgrā'dē), c.1758-1817, American Presbyterian minister and evangelist, b. Pennsylvania. His preaching (1797-99) in Logan co., Ky., began the great religious revival which in 1800 swept over the South and the West. Gatherings encamped for McGready's revivals were the forerunners of later CAMP MEETINGS. Some of his methods were questioned by the Presbyterian Church; in the division that resulted, the Cumberland Presbyterian Church was established. Later McGready was received back into his presbytery and sent (1811) to Indiana to found churches.

MacGregor, Robert: see ROB ROY.

McGuffey, William Holmes (məgŭf'ē), 1800-1873, American educator, b. near Claysville, Pa. He was graduated from Washington and Jefferson College in 1826, having meanwhile taught in rural schools, and became professor of languages at Miami Univ., Ohio. He remained at Miami until he became (1836) president of Cincinnati College. He later served as president of Ohio Univ. at Athens (1839-43), as professor of philosophy at Woodward College, Cincinnati (1843-45), and as professor of moral philosophy at the Univ. of Virginia (1845-73). He helped to organize the public school system of Ohio but is now remembered chiefly as the compiler of the McGuffey Eclectic Readers, the First and Second of which were published in 1836, the Third and Fourth in 1837, the Fifth in 1844, and the Sixth in 1857. These were constantly revised and passed through edition after edition, maintaining their place for nearly two generations; their estimated sales totaled 122 million copies. Concerned with traditional morality as much as with reading, their influence in shaping the American mind of the mid-19th cent. can scarcely be exaggerated. A memorial was erected to McGuffey at his birthplace in West Finley township, Pa., in 1931. See *Old Favorites from the McGuffey Readers, 1836-1936* (1936, repr. 1969); biographies by H. C. Minnich (1936) and A. M. Ruggles (1950); R. D. Mosier, *Making the American Mind* (1947, repr. 1965).

Mach, Ernst (ĕrnst mäkh), 1838-1916, Austrian physicist and philosopher, b. Moravia. He taught (1864-67) mathematics at Graz and later, until his retirement in 1901, was professor of physics at Prague and Vienna. Mach, one of the leaders of modern positivism, did his major work in the philosophy of science. Following strictly empirical principles, he strove to rid science of all metaphysical and religious assumptions. He felt science should confine itself to the description of phenomena that could be perceived by the senses. This view challenged science's traditional claim of yielding absolute knowledge and was greatly influential in the development of LOGICAL POSITIVISM. Mach also did research in the field of ballistics; the Mach number is named for him. His works include *Die Mechanik in ihrer Entwicklung* (1883; tr. *The Science of Mechanics,* 1893); *Die Analyse der Empfindungen* (1886); *Erkenntnis und Irrtum* [perception and error] (1905).

Mácha, Karel Hynek (kä'rel hē'nĕk mä'khä), 1810-36, Czech romantic poet. After studying law at the Univ. of Prague he became a civil servant. He published a number of promising poems and wrote *Pictures from My Life,* introspective autobiographical sketches. This work was followed by *Gypsies* (1835-36), a novel. His long iambic poem *May* (1836, tr. 1932) is considered the finest lyric work in the Czech language; Czech iambic verse dates from this work. Mácha's profoundly melancholy and nostalgic verse reveals his strong response to nature, medievalism, and Czech civilization as well as his fatalistic philosophy. See Milada Souckova, *The Czech Romantics* (1958).

Machabees: see MACCABEES.

Machado, Antonio (äntō'nyō mächä'thō), 1875-1939, Spanish poet of the GENERATION OF '98. He spent most of his life in Castile and wrote his best poetry under the sober and dramatic influence of its landscape. His *Poesías completas* appeared in 1936. Forced to leave Spain because of his important contributions to the Loyalist cause during the Spanish civil war, he crossed the Pyrenees on foot and died in France a month later. With his brother, the poet Manuel Machado (1874–1947), he also wrote plays and translated Rostand's *L'Aiglon* and Hugo's *Hernani.* See studies by A. J. McVan (1959) and H. T. Young (1964).

Machado, Gerardo, 1871–1939, president of Cuba (1925–33). With the support of ZAYAS, Machado defeated MENOCAL in the campaign of 1924. A businessman, he gave considerable attention to economic welfare and reform. His primary concern was to free Cuba from the political bonds of the Platt Amendment and from economic dependence on the United States. He attempted to achieve this by taxing American capital investments, by constructing a 700-mi (1,127-km) central highway, by building up Havana and the tourist trade, and by fostering industrial and mining expansion. Increasingly dictatorial, he succeeded in amending the constitution to permit a six-year term. Secret societies, notably the ABC, banded together and led an abortive revolt in 1931. Liberal student groups subsequently rebelled. A prominent opposition figure was Ramón GRAU SAN MARTÍN. Retaliating by murderous activities of secret police, the president began a terrorism so bloody that the United States intervened. Machado refused to resign, but a general strike and loss of army support forced him to flee. The opposition chose Carlos Manuel de CÉSPEDES as provisional president. Machado died in Miami Beach, Fla.

Machado de Assis, Joaquim Maria (zhwäkēm' mərē'ə məshä'dōō dĭ əsēz'), 1839–1908, Brazilian novelist, b. Rio de Janeiro. Machado de Assis received his education from a priest and became a typesetter, a proofreader, and finally a journalist. His poetry and short stories were well received, but his reputation as the greatest of Brazilian writers rests upon his realistic novels. His major novels are *Memórias póstumas de Braz Cubas* (1881, tr. *Epitaph of a Small Winner,* 1952), *Quincas Borba* (1891, tr. *Philosopher or Dog?,* 1954), and *Dom Casmurro* (1900, tr. 1953). They are distinguished by psychological insight and a profound awareness of social conditions; their objective attitude stands in sharp contrast to the prevalent romantic tendency of the time. His pessimistic view of life is impelled by irony. See studies by José Bettencourt Machado (1953) and Helen Caldwell (1970).

Machar, Josef Svatopluk (yô'zĕf svä'tôplōōk mä'khär), 1854–1942, Czech poet and essayist. A leader of the realist movement in Czech poetry and a master of colloquial Czech, Machar was active in anti-Austrian political circles in Vienna. Many of his poems were satires of political and social conditions. In the poetic cycle *The Conscience of the Ages* (1901–21), of which *Golgotha* was the initial volume, he contrasted antique with Christian civilization, favoring the former. His *Magdalena* (1894, tr. 1916), a satirical play, concerns the oppression of women. Both Machar's use of colloquial diction and his brilliantly expressed skepticism greatly influenced Czech literature and public opinion.

Machault d'Arnouville, Jean Baptiste de (zhäN bätēst' də mäshō' därnōōvēl'), 1701–94, French statesman. He held a succession of government offices and was (1743–45) intendant of Valenciennes. King Louis XV appointed him controller general of finances in 1745. To raise funds for the War of the Austrian Succession and to alleviate the government's chronic deficit he proposed (1749) that a tax of one twentieth (*vingtième*) of all incomes be levied. Opposition and evasion by the nobility, clergy, and certain privileged groups made the tax inequitable and decreased its revenue. Finally in Dec., 1751, he was forced to suspend payment of the *vingtième* by the clergy and to abandon fiscal reform. In 1754, Machault was made naval minister. Having incurred the enmity of Mme de Pompadour, he was dismissed (1757) by Louis XV. He was arrested (1794) during the French Revolution and died in prison.

Machaut, Guillaume de (gēyōm' də mäshō'), c.1300–1377, French poet and composer. Variants of his name include Machault, de Machaudio, and de Mascaudio. He studied theology and took holy orders. In the service of King John of Bohemia he traveled through Europe on chivalric expeditions. Later, while in the service of King Charles of Navarre, he wrote the long narrative poems *Confort d'ami* and *Le Jugement du roi de Navarre.* The recipient of numerous papal benefices, Machaut was canon at Rheims from 1340 until his death. In *Le Livre du voir dit* (1361–65) he wrote a long poem of courtly love with musical interpolations. Considered the greatest French musician of the 14th cent. and the exponent of ars nova in France, he wrote lais, motets, ballads, rondeaux, virelais, and one mass. He contributed to the secularization of the motet by using French texts of courtly love instead of Latin liturgy. Most important perhaps was his skillful use of rhythm with counterpoint, which made his music widely known and admired. His mass, the first complete polyphonic version, was still in use in the 16th cent. and led to the great masses of Josquin Desprez and Palestrina.

Machbanai (măk'bənā, măkbā'nā, măkbānā'ī), Gadite ally of David. 1 Chron. 12.13.

Machbenah (măkbē'nə), son of Sheva. 1 Chron. 2.49.

Machebeuf, Joseph Projectus (zhôzĕf' prôzhĕktüs' mäshbŏf'), 1812–89, French missionary in the American Southwest, a Roman Catholic priest. He was a friend and associate of Jean Baptiste LAMY, coming with him to Ohio in 1839 and accompanying him to New Mexico in 1850. He did much missionary work, establishing churches, schools, and hospitals in New Mexico, Arizona, Utah, and Colorado. He was made bishop of Denver in 1887. Father Machebeuf is the Father Vaillant of Willa Cather's novel *Death Comes for the Archbishop.* See biography by W. J. Howlett (1908).

Machek, Vladimir: see MAČEK, VLADIMIR.

Machen, Arthur (măk'ən), 1863–1947, English author, b. Wales. He wrote a series of semiautobiographical fantasies, notably *The Hill of Dreams* (1907) and *Far Off Things* (1922), and tales of horror and the supernatural. Machen achieved transient fame during World War I with "The Bowman," a tale relating how St. George and his ghostly archers rescue the British army and slaughter the Germans. See his autobiography, ed. by Morchard Bishop (1951); biography by W. D. Sweetser (1964).

Machen, John Gresham (grĕ'səm mā'chən), 1881–1937, American Presbyterian clergyman, b. Baltimore. Ordained a Presbyterian minister in 1914, he became a leader of the fundamentalists in his denomination. He objected to the liberalism of the Presbyterian Board of Foreign Missions and in 1933 set up an independent board. Suspended (1935) from the ministry for this action, Machen, with certain ministers and lay groups, established in 1936 an independent body that later took the name Orthodox Presbyterian Church. See biography by N. B. Stonehouse (1954).

McHenry, James, 1753–1816, American political leader, b. Ireland. He emigrated to Philadelphia in 1771 and, after studying medicine under Benjamin Rush, served as a surgeon in the Continental Army in the American Revolution. Captured by the British at Fort Washington on Harlem Heights, N.Y., he was exchanged in the spring of 1778. He was George Washington's secretary from 1778 to 1780, when he became attached to General Lafayette's staff. McHenry was (1781–86) a member of the Maryland senate, served (1783–86) as a delegate to the Confederation Congress, and attended (1787) the Federal Constitutional Convention, where he maintained a conservative course. Later he advocated adoption of the Constitution. As Secretary of War (1796–1800), he followed the political leadership of Alexander Hamilton rather than that of President John Adams. Adams finally demanded and received his resignation, and thereafter McHenry lived in retirement. Fort McHenry at Baltimore was named for him.

McHenry, Fort: see FORT MCHENRY.

Machi (mā'kī), father of a spy. Num. 13.15.

Machiavelli, Niccolò (nēk-kōlô' mäkyävĕl'lē), 1469–1527, Italian author and statesman, one of the outstanding figures of the Renaissance, b. Florence. A member of the impoverished branch of a distinguished family, he entered (1498) the political service of the Florentine republic and rose rapidly in importance. As defense secretary he substituted (1506) a citizens' militia for the mercenary system then prevailing in Italy. This reform sprang from his conviction, set forth in his major works, that the employment of mercenaries had largely contributed to the political weakness of Italy. Machiavelli became acquainted with power politics through his important diplomatic missions. He met Cesare BORGIA twice and was sent by Florence to Louis XII of France (1504, 1510), to Pope Julius II (1506), and to Holy Roman Emperor Maximilian I (1507). The return (1512) of the Medici to Florence caused his dismissal; in 1513 he was briefly imprisoned and was tortured for his alleged complicity in a plot against the Medici. Machiavelli retired to his country estate, where he wrote his chief works. He humiliated himself before the Medici in a vain attempt to recover office. When, in 1527, the republic was briefly reestablished, Machiavelli was distrusted by many of the republicans, and he died thoroughly disappointed and embittered. Machiavelli's best-known work, *Il Principe* [the prince] (1532), describes the means by which a prince may gain and maintain his power. His "ideal" prince (seemingly modeled on Cesare Borgia) is an amoral and calculating tyrant who would be able to establish a unified Italian state. The last chapter of the work pleads for the eventual liberation of Italy from foreign rule. Interpretations of *The Prince* vary: it has been viewed as sincere advice, as a plea for political office, as a detached analysis of Italian politics, as evidence of early Italian nationalism, and as political satire on Medici rule. However, the adjective *Machiavellian* has come to be a synonym for amoral cunning and for justification by power. Less widely read but more indicative of Machiavelli's politics is his *Discorsi sulla prima deca di Tito Livio* [discourses on the first 10 books of Livy] (1531). In it Machiavelli expounded a general theory of politics and government that stressed the importance of an uncorrupted political culture and a vigorous political morality. Vaster in conception than *The Prince,* the *Discourses* show clearly Machiavelli's republican principles, which are also reflected in his *Istorie Fiorentine* [history of Florence] (1532), a historical and literary masterpiece, entirely modern in concept. Other works include *Dell' arte della guerra* [on the art of war] (1521), which viewed military problems in relation to politics, and numerous reports and brief works. He also wrote many poems and plays, notably the lively and ribald comedy *Mandragola* (1524). His correspondence has been preserved and is of great interest. The chief works of Machiavelli are available in several popular English editions. See Pasquale Villari, *Life and Time of Niccolò Machiavelli* (2 vol., tr. 1878, repr. 1973); Federico Chabod, *Machiavelli and the Renaissance* (1926, tr. 1959, repr. 1965); Dorothy Erskine Muir, *Machiavelli and His Times* (1936); Roberto Ridolfi, *The Life of Niccolò Machiavelli* (1942, tr. 1963); Herbert Butterfield, *The Statecraft of Machiavelli* (1956); Sydney Anglo, *Machiavelli* (1970); two volumes of essays ed. by Anthony Parel (1972) and Martin Fleisher (1972).

Machida (mächē'dä), city (1970 pop. 208,801), Tokyo Metropolis, E central Honshu, Japan, on the Tsurumi River. It is an industrial and residential suburb of Tokyo.

machine, arrangement of moving and stationary mechanical parts used to perform some useful WORK or to provide transportation. By means of a machine an applied force is increased, its direction is changed, or one form of motion or energy is changed into another form. Thus defined, such simple devices as the LEVER, the PULLEY, the INCLINED PLANE, the SCREW, and the WHEEL AND AXLE are machines; they are called simple machines; more complicated machines are merely combinations of them. Of the five, the lever, the pulley, and the inclined plane are primary; the wheel and axle and the screw are secondary. The wheel and axle combination is a rotary lever, while the screw may be considered an inclined plane wound around a core. The WEDGE is a double inclined plane. By means of a machine, a small force, or effort, can be applied to move a much greater resistance, or load. In doing so, however, the applied force must move through a much greater distance than it would if it could move the load directly. The mechanical advantage (MA) of a machine is the factor by which it multiplies any applied force. The MA may be calculated from the ratio of the forces involved or from the ratio of the distances through which they move. Ideally, the two ratios are equal, and it is simpler to calculate the ratio of the distance the effort moves to the distance the resistance moves; this is called the ideal mechanical advantage (IMA). In any real machine some of the effort is used to overcome friction. Thus, the ratio of the resistance force to the effort, called the actual mechanical advantage (AMA), is less than the IMA. The efficiency of any machine measures the degree to which friction and other factors reduce the actual work output of the machine from its theoretical maximum. A frictionless machine would have an efficiency of 100%. A machine with an efficiency of 20% has an output only one fifth of its theoretical output. The efficiency of a machine is equal to the ratio of its output (resistance multiplied by the distance it is moved) to its input (effort multiplied by the distance through which it is exerted); it is also equal to the ratio of the AMA to the IMA. This does not mean that low-efficiency machines are of limited use. An automobile jack, for example, must overcome a great deal of friction and therefore has low efficiency, but it is extremely valuable because small effort can be applied to lift a great weight. Although most machines are used to multiply an effort so that it may move a greater resistance, they may have other purposes. For example, a single, fixed pulley merely changes the direction of the applied force; the pulley may make it easier to lift the load, since one can pull down on a rope, thus adding his own weight to the effort, rather than simply lifting the load. In a catapult an effort greater than the load moves through a short distance, causing the load to be moved through a large distance before being released. As the load is being moved, it picks up speed so that it is traveling at a considerable velocity when it leaves the catapult. Machines are designated, as a rule, by the operations they perform, and the complicated devices used for sawing, planing, and turning, for example, are known as sawing machines, planing machines, and turning machines respectively and as machine tools collectively. Machines used to transform other forms of energy (as heat) into mechanical energy are known as engines, i.e. the STEAM ENGINE or the INTERNAL COMBUSTION ENGINE. The electric motor transforms electrical energy into mechanical energy. Its operation is the reverse of that of the electric generator, which transforms the energy of falling water or steam into electrical energy. From a historical perspective, the first machines were the result of man's efforts to improve his war-making capacity; the term *engineer* at one time had an exclusively military connotation. In America the original colonies were not permitted to make or import machine tools; it was only after the Revolution that the first manufacturing machines were built (c.1790) by Samuel Slater for a textile mill in Pawtucket, R.I.

machine gun: see SMALL ARMS.

machine tool, power-operated tool used for finishing or shaping metal parts, especially parts of other machines. An establishment that is equipped with such tools and specializes in such work is known as a machine shop. Machine tools operate by removing material from the workpiece. In some operations chips, shavings, or large pieces are removed, while in others only very small particles are taken off. Basic machining operations are: (1) turning, the shaping of a piece having a cylindrical or conical external contour; (2) facing, the shaping of a flat circular surface; (3) milling, the shaping of a flat or contoured surface; (4) drilling, the formation of a cylindrical hole in a workpiece; (5) boring, the finishing of an existing cylindrical hole, as one formed by drilling; (6) broaching, the production of a desired contour in a surface; (7) threading, the cutting of an external screw thread; and (8) tapping, the cutting of an internal screw thread. In addition there are operations such as sawing, grinding, gear cutting, polishing, buffing, and honing. The tools themselves vary in size from hand-held devices that can be used for drilling and grinding to large stationary tools that perform a number of operations. Many machine tools have a name that indicates their principal function, e.g., drill press, broach machine, milling machine, and jig borer. The LATHE can perform turning, facing, threading, drilling, and other operations. In all machining operations there must be some relative motion between the tool and the workpiece while they are in contact. In some cases the tool moves and the workpiece is stationary; in other cases this situation is reversed or both are moving. In order to withstand the great heat that this motion generates, the materials used in machine tools must be very hard and very tough. Thus their working surfaces are made of such substances as high-speed steels, sintered carbides, and diamonds. To help dissipate the heat, the area of contact between the working surface and the workpiece is usually lubricated with a fluid that may also improve the finish of the workpiece's surface. See BORING MILL.

Machir (mā'kər). **1** Son of Manasseh. Joshua 17.1; Num. 26.29. **2** One who helped David and Mephibosheth. 2 Sam. 9.4–6; 17.27.

Machnadebai (măknədē'bī, –năd'ə–), one who had a foreign wife. Ezra 10.40.

Mach number (mäk), ratio between the speed of an object and the speed of sound in the medium in which the object is traveling. An airplane that has the velocity of Mach 3.0 is traveling at three times the speed of sound as measured in the prevailing atmospheric conditions.

Machpelah (măkpē'lə), cave, near Hebron. It was bought by Abraham from Ephron, son of Zohar the Hittite, for a family burial place. The Mosque of Hebron, now on the site, may be a successor to a structure built by the Herods. Gen. 23; 25.9,10; 49.29–32; 50.13.

Mach's principle (mäks) [for E. Mach], assertion that the inertial effects of MASS are not innate in a body, but arise from its relation to the totality of all other masses, i.e., to the universe as a whole. Thus, the inertial forces experienced by a body in accelerated motion have the same physical origin as the gravitational forces it experiences near mass concentrations, namely the mass-energy FIELD described by the general theory of RELATIVITY. Inertial forces have a much longer range than gravitational forces, so the role of very distant matter becomes preponderant. According to Mach's principle, a body experiences no inertial forces when it is at rest or in uniform motion with respect to the CENTER OF MASS of the entire universe. When its motion is nonuniform (accelerated) with respect to the total mass of the universe, it experiences forces such as centrifugal force (see CENTRIPETAL FORCE and CENTRIFUGAL FORCE) and the CORIOLIS effect. Hence, the "local" behavior of matter is influenced by the "global" properties of the universe, i.e., those properties that describe the universe as a whole, which are studied in COSMOLOGY.

Machu Picchu (mä'cho͞o pēk'cho͞o), fortress city of the ancient Incas, Peru, about 50 mi (80 km) NW of Cuzco. It is perched high upon a rock in a narrow saddle between two sharp mountain peaks and overlooks the Urubamba River 2,000 ft (600 m) below; it was unknown to Spanish explorers. Discovered in 1911 by the American explorer Hiram Bingham, the imposing city is one of the few urban centers of pre-Columbian America found virtually intact. Perhaps the most extraordinary ruin in the Americas, Machu Picchu contains 5 sq mi (13 sq km) of terrace and construction, with over 3,000 steps linking it to many levels. It shows admirable architectural design and execution, although the stonework is not always as refined as in other Inca sites. The period of occupancy is doubtful, but legend indicates that the city may have been the home of the Incas prior to their migration to Cuzco as well as their last stronghold after the Spanish Conquest. See Hiram Bingham, *Lost City of the Incas* (1948, repr. 1969).

Maciá, Francisco (fränsēs'kō mäsē'ä), 1859–1933, Spanish politician, Catalan nationalist leader. An army officer, he joined the separatist movement in CATALONIA and was elected to the Cortes in 1907. Exiled briefly in 1917 for political activism, he returned to found (by 1922) the Catalan nationalist movement, Estat Catalá. He was exiled again in 1924. From Paris he directed an ineffective movement to establish a Catalan republic, plotting unsuccessfully an invasion of Catalonia (1926). After the fall of Primo de Rivera, he returned (1930) to Barcelona and became (1931) the first president of the Catalan republic. In 1932 he made an agreement with the central government at Madrid by which Catalonia was recognized as an autonomous region.

McIlwain, Charles Howard, 1871–1968, American historian, b. Saltsburg, Pa. He received his Ph.D. from Harvard in 1911 and, after teaching history at Miami Univ. in Ohio (1903–5) and at Princeton (1905–10), he became (1911) a professor of history and government at Harvard, serving as Eaton professor of the science of government (1926–46). He was president (1935–36) of the American Historical Association. Among his books are *The American Revolution: A Constitutional Interpretation* (1923), for which he won the 1924 Pulitzer Prize in history; *The Growth of Political Thought in the West, from the Greeks to the End of the Middle Ages* (1932); *Constitutionalism and the Changing World* (1939); and *Constitutionalism, Ancient and Modern* (1940, rev. ed. 1947)

MacInnes, Colin, 1914–, English novelist, b. London. Son of the novelist Angela Thirkell, MacInnes was educated in Australia and served in the British intelligence corps during World War II. He is best known for his "London novels," which delineate various types of London life. They all reveal MacInnes's talent for acute observation, sympathy for the underdog, and interest in sociology. *City of Spades* (1957), for example, vividly depicts the life of Negro immigrants to England. The other "London novels" are *Absolute Beginners* (1959) and *All Day Saturday* (1966). *Three Years To Play* (1971) is a novel set in Elizabethan London in which Shakespeare is a character.

MacInnes, Helen: see under HIGHET, GILBERT.

McIntire, Samuel, 1757–1811, American architect and woodcarver, b. Salem, Mass. He developed high skill as a joiner and housewright and in wood sculpture. McIntire's opportunities, both as builder and carver, came in designing houses for the shipowning aristocracy of Salem. In the interiors of these houses are beautiful carved cornices and mantelpieces, inspired by the elegant style of Robert Adam. At first McIntire executed most of this work himself, but later he employed his son, his two brothers, and his nephew, all skilled craftsmen. His Salem works include the Pierce-Nichols, the Peabody-Silsbee, the Gardner-White-Pingree, and the Elias Haskett Derby residences. His public buildings are Assembly Hall, Hamilton Hall, Washington Hall, and the courthouse, all in Salem, of which the latter two no longer stand. In 1792, McIntire competed for the design of the capitol at Washington. Among his works in sculpture are portrait busts of Governor Winthrop and Voltaire (both: American Antiquarian Society, Worcester); medallions of President Washington (Essex Inst., Salem); and various ship carvings. See study by Fiske Kimball (1940); *Samuel McIntire, a Bicentennial Symposium* (ed. by B. W. Labaree, 1957).

Macintosh, Charles, 1766–1843, Scottish chemist and inventor. In 1823 he developed a waterproof fabric used to make raincoats that were named for him. His other research included preparing sugar of lead and inventing a commercially successful bleaching powder.

McIntosh, Millicent Carey, 1898–, American educator, b. Baltimore, grad. Bryn Mawr, 1920, Ph.D. Johns Hopkins Univ., 1926. From 1926 to 1930 she taught at Bryn Mawr and was acting dean in 1929–30. She was headmistress of Brearley School, New York City, from 1930 until her appointment in 1947 as dean of Barnard College, Columbia Univ. In 1952 she became president of the college, retiring in 1962.

McIntosh, William, c.1775–1825, American Indian chief, b. in the Creek country now within the limits of Carroll co., Ga.; son of a British army officer and a Creek woman. Friendly to the Americans, McIntosh led the lower Creek Indians against the British in the War of 1812 and was made a brigadier general. He later fought alongside Andrew Jackson against the Seminole Indians. In Feb., 1825, he signed a treaty ceding the Creek lands E of the Chattahoochee River to Georgia and was shortly thereafter slain by the upper Creek Indians, who opposed the cession.

Macip or **Masip, Vicente Juan** (vēthān'tā hwän mäthēp', mäsēp'), c.1523–1579, Spanish religious painter of the Valencian school, known as Juan de Juanes and Vicente Joanes. One of the Spanish mannerists, Macip shows the influence of Italian painters, especially Raphael, in his design. Among his chief works are *Holy Family* (Academy, Madrid); the *Last Supper* (Church of St. Nicholas, Valencia); and scenes from the life of St. Stephen (Prado).

MacIver, Loren (məkī'vər), 1909–, American painter, b. New York City. MacIver's fanciful compositions owe a debt to surrealism. Her imaginative, lyrical paintings are often filled with mist, subdued light, and pale color. Her subjects include fallen leaves and the delicate rainbows formed by oil slicks. *The Street* (1956; Corcoran Gall., Washington, D.C.) is a representative work.

MacIver, Robert Morrison (məkē'vər), 1882–1970, Scottish-American sociologist, b. Scotland, grad. Edinburgh and Oxford. He began teaching at Columbia Univ. in 1927. His books, in which he discusses the complexities of social and political organization, include *Community: A Sociological Study* (1917), *Society: Its Structure and Changes* (1931), *The Web of Government* (1947), *The Pursuit of Happiness* (1955), *Life: Its Dimensions and Its Bounds* (1960), *The Challenge of the Passing Years* (1962), *Social Causation* (1964), *The Prevention and Control of Delinquency* (1966), *Politics & Society* (1969), and *On Community, Society, and Power; Selected Writings*, ed. by L. Bramson (1970).

Mack, Connie (Cornelius McGillicuddy), 1862–1956, American baseball player and manager, b. East Brookfield, Mass. He was a star catcher for the Washington Senators (1886–89) and the Pittsburgh Pirates (1891–94). After gaining managerial experience with the Pittsburgh (1891–96) and the Milwaukee (1897–1900) clubs, Mack became (1901) manager, and ultimately chief owner, of the Philadelphia Athletics of the newly organized American League. Under his guidance the Athletics won nine pennants (1902, 1905, 1910–11, 1913–14, 1929–31) and five world series (1910–11, 1913, 1929–30). In 1937 he was named to the National Baseball Hall of Fame. After 1937 he met with repeated illnesses, and increasing managerial responsibilities were given to his son, Earle Mack. Connie Mack continued as president of the Athletics until 1954, when the team was moved to Kansas City. See his autobiography (1950).

McKay, Claude, 1890–1948, American poet and novelist, b. Jamaica, British West Indies, studied at Tuskegee and the Univ. of Kansas. A major figure of the Harlem Renaissance, McKay is best remembered for his poems treating racial themes. His works include the volumes of poetry *Spring in New Hampshire* (1920) and *Harlem Shadows* (1922); and the novels *Home to Harlem* (1927), *Banjo* (1929), and *Banana Bottom* (1933). For years McKay was involved in radical political activities, but he became increasingly disillusioned, and in 1944 he converted to Roman Catholicism. See his autobiography (1937).

McKay, Donald, 1810–80, American shipbuilder, b. Nova Scotia. He opened his own shipyard in Newburyport, Mass., in 1841, then moved to Boston in 1845. He grew celebrated as designer and builder of the largest ships of his time and sleek, swift clippers, some of the most beautiful ships ever to sail the seas. Some of the vessels he built were the *New World,* a three-decker, the largest ship known in 1845; the *Lightning* and the *James Baines,* clippers which established new speed records for the long England-to-Australia route; and the *Glory of the Seas,* which in 1869 made a record run of 94 days from New York to San Francisco. He built several ships for the Union navy in the Civil War.

Mackay, Hugh (məkī'), 1640?–1692, Scottish soldier. After service with several continental armies, he joined the Dutch forces in 1673, took his regiment to England (1685) to help suppress the uprising in favor of the duke of MONMOUTH, and in 1688 accompanied William of Orange (William III) to England. Commanding English troops in Scotland, he was defeated by the Jacobites under Viscount Dundee at Killiecrankie (1689) but later put down the Jacobite rising. He was killed fighting the French in the battle of Steenkerke.

Mackay, John William (măk'ē), 1831–1902, American financier, b. Dublin, Ireland. He immigrated to the United States in 1840. In 1859 he joined the rush to Nevada, where silver had been discovered. He and J. G. Fair, later joined by William Shoney O'Brien and J. C. Flood, acquired control of valuable silver mines, which yielded them great fortunes. With James Gordon Bennett he founded (1883) the Commercial Cable Company and laid two submarine cables to Europe. Later (1886) he organized the Postal Telegraph Cable Company.

Mackay (məkī'), city (1971 urban agglomeration pop. 28,416), Queensland, NE Australia on the Pioneer River. A port city, Mackay exports sugar.

MacKaye, Benton (məkī'), 1879–, American forester and regional planner, b. Stamford, Conn., grad. Harvard (B.A., 1900; M.A. School of Forestry, 1905); son of Steele MacKaye. He was a research forester of the U.S. Forest Service; he planned and helped in the construction of the Appalachian Trail (1921) and served on the regional planning staff of the Tennessee Valley Authority (1934–36) and on the staff of the Rural Electrification Administration (1942–45). MacKaye's philosophy of regional planning is given in *The New Exploration (1928).*

MacKaye, Steele (James Morrison Steele MacKaye), 1842–94, American dramatist and inventor in theatrical scene design. After studying in Europe he went to the United States (c.1872) and first appeared in New York with a group of students he had trained in the DELSARTE system. He opened the Madison Square Theatre in 1879, where his most successful melodrama, *Hazel Kirke,* was presented (1880). It was in this theater that he invented and installed overhead and indirect stage lighting, movable stages or wagons, and folding seats. He then took over the Lyceum where he established the first school of acting in New York City, later known as the American Academy of Dramatic Art. See *Epoch* (1927) by his son, Percy MacKaye.

Macke, August (ou'go͝ost mä'kə), 1887–1914, German painter. Trained in Germany, he made several trips to Paris, where he came in contact with impressionism and the fauvist and cubist painters. A brilliant colorist, he joined the artists Franz Marc and Kandinsky and exhibited with the BLAUE REITER group. In 1914 he traveled with Paul Klee to Tunisia. There he created watercolors of a fine transparency with subtle prismatic patterns. Macke had barely finished *Farewell* (Cologne) when he was conscripted. He was killed in World War I.

McKean, Thomas (məkēn'), 1734–1817, political leader in the American Revolution, signer of the Declaration of Independence, b. New London, Pa. He settled at New Castle, Del., and became a lawyer and a political figure, one of the strong opponents of the British colonial system. He was (1765) a delegate to the Stamp Act Congress. McKean promoted concerted action by the colonies and was (1774–76, 1778–83) a member of the Continental Congress. Absent when the Declaration of Independence was signed, he affixed his signature later. McKean helped to frame the Delaware constitution, was president (governor) of Delaware for a short time (1777), and then was chief justice of Pennsylvania (1777–99), where he also had a home. He was (1781) briefly president of the Continental Congress and was a supporter of the Articles of Confederation, which he signed. He worked to obtain the ratification of the Constitution by Pennsylvania and was a member of Pennsylvania's state constitutional convention. A supporter of Thomas Jefferson, McKean was (1799–1808) governor of Pennsylvania. With James Wilson he wrote *Commentaries on the Constitution of the United States* (1792). See study by William Cobbett (1798, repr. 1970).

McKeesport, city (1970 pop. 37,977), Allegheny co., SW Pa., in hilly terrain at the confluence of the Monongahela and Youghiogheny rivers; settled 1755, inc. as a city 1890. It is primarily an industrial city, with factories that manufacture steel, machine parts, and automobile bodies. Pennsylvania State Univ. has a campus there.

McKees Rocks, borough (1970 pop. 11,901), Allegheny co., SW Pa., an industrial suburb of Pittsburgh, on the Ohio River, in a coal-mining region; settled c.1764, inc. 1892.

McKenna, Joseph, 1843–1926, American jurist, Associate Justice of the U.S. Supreme Court (1898–1925), b. Philadelphia. Admitted to the bar in 1865, he practiced law in California and served in the state legislature (1875–76) and the U.S. Congress (1885–92). A Federal circuit judge from 1892 to 1897, he was appointed (1897) U.S. Attorney General by President McKinley. He held this office for only a few months before President McKinley appointed him to the Supreme Court. Although he never developed a consistent legal philosophy, McKenna wrote a number of important decisions. Most notable was his opinion in the case of *United States* vs. *U.S. Steel Corporation* (1920) in which the "rule of reason" principle, asserting that only those combinations that are in unreasonable restraint of trade are illegal, finally triumphed in antitrust cases. See biography by Matthew McDevitt (1946, repr. 1974).

McKenna, Reginald, 1863–1943, British politician and banker. Elected to Parliament as a Liberal in 1895, he entered the cabinet as president of the board of education in 1907. As first lord of the admiralty (1908–11), he increased the rate of battleship construction and thus helped to ensure Britain's naval supremacy at the outbreak (1914) of World War I. After serving as home secretary (1911–15), McKenna became chancellor of the exchequer in Herbert Asquith's coalition cabinet (1915–16) and imposed new income taxes and import duties. He resigned when David Lloyd George displaced Asquith as prime minister. Defeated in the 1918 election, he retired from politics. From 1919 until his death he was chairman of the Midland Bank.

McKenna, Siobhan (shəvôn'), 1923–, Irish actress. From 1940 to 1942, McKenna performed with the Gaelic Repertory Theatre. At the ABBEY THEATRE in Dublin (1943–46) she appeared in *The Countess Cathleen, Purple Dust,* and *Saint Joan.* She made her New York debut in *The Chalk Garden* (1955) and appeared on Broadway in a one-woman show, *Here Are Ladies* (1972), portraying several heroines of Irish literature. McKenna's films include *Daughter of Darkness* (1948) and, for television, Shaw's *Misalliance* and *Don Juan in Hell.*

Mackensen, August von (ou'go͝ost fən mä'kənzən), 1849–1945, German field marshal. In World War I he defeated the Russians in the battle of the MASURIAN LAKES (1914–15), conducted successful operations in Galicia, Serbia, and Rumania, and in 1917 occupied Rumania. Held by the French until Dec., 1919, he retired (1920) from service and became a leader of the Stahlhelm, a monarchist veterans' organization. He later supported Adolf Hitler, although he protested against the murder (1934) of Kurt von SCHLEICHER.

Mackenzie, Sir Alexander, 1764?–1820, Canadian fur trader and explorer, b. Scotland. His family took him to the colony of New York in 1774, and later he was sent to Canada. He entered (c.1779) a Montreal fur-trading firm and in a short time became partner of one of the firms that merged (1787) to form the North West Company. Given (1788) supervision of the important Athabasca fur district, Mackenzie set out (1789) from his headquarters at Fort Chipewyan on Lake Athabasca on the first of his two noted trips of exploration. After reaching Great Slave Lake, he followed the then unknown Mackenzie River to the Arctic Ocean. Disappointed because the great river that now bears his name did not prove an avenue to the Pacific and unable to relinquish his hope of discovering a route to the Pacific, Mackenzie made careful preparations for a second expedition and set out again in 1793. He and his party fought their way up the Peace River and its tributary the Parsnip River, crossed the Continental Divide, and discovered the Fraser River, down which they traveled a short distance before they struck overland for the coast. Following the course of the Blackwater River, a western tributary of the Fraser, they reached and crossed the Coast Ranges to the Bella Coola River, which they descended, in a borrowed dugout, to its mouth in a tidal inlet of the Pacific. Thus Mackenzie completed the first overland journey across North America N of Mexico. Shortly after this historic exploit, he left the West, never to return. His *Voyages . . . to the Frozen and Pacific Oceans* (1801) won him wide recognition and a knighthood in 1802. Mackenzie was elected in 1805 to the Legislative Assembly of Lower Canada, but he soon returned (1808) to Scotland, where he lived the rest of his life. See his journals and letters, ed. by W. K. Lamb (1972); biographies by Philip Vail (1964) and Roy Daniells (1969).

Mackenzie, Alexander, 1822–92, Canadian political leader, b. Scotland. Emigrating (1842) to Canada, he worked first as a stonemason in Kingston, Ont., and then as a builder and contractor in Sarnia. In Lambton he became editor (1852) of a Liberal newspaper. Elected (1861) to the Canadian Legislative Assembly, Mackenzie supported the confederation movement and the Liberal leader, George BROWN. A member of the first dominion House of Commons (1867), Mackenzie headed the Liberal opposition to Sir John A. MACDONALD'S government; upon its fall (1873) as a result of the PACIFIC SCANDAL he became the first Liberal prime minister of the dominion. In 1878, Macdonald came back into power, and Mackenzie, who remained in Parliament until his death, led the Liberal opposition until 1880. During his ministry the courts and provincial governments were strengthened, trade expanded, and immigration, especially to the western provinces, encouraged. See his life and times by William Buckingham and G. W. Ross (1892, repr. 1969); biography by D. C. Thomson (1960).

MacKenzie, Sir Compton, 1883–1972, English author, b. West Hartelpool, Durham, educated at Oxford. In April, 1923, he founded the *Gramophone,* a periodical devoted to reviewing recordings. A prolific and versatile writer, MacKenzie was particularly noted for his novels, which were often set in exotic locations. They include *Carnival* (1912), *Sinister Street* (1913), and *On Moral Courage* (1962). Among his nonfiction works is *Mr. Roosevelt* (1944). See his autobiography, *My Life and Times* (10 vol., 1963–71); study by Kenneth Young (1968).

Mackenzie, Henry, 1745–1831, English author, b. Scotland. He had an active political and legal life, serving as comptroller of taxes for Scotland from 1804 until his death. His first and most famous novel, *The Man of Feeling* (1771), is a series of loosely joined episodes describing the adventures of a highly sentimental and good-natured man. His other novels are *The Man of the World* (1773) and *Julia de Roubigne* (1777). Of his four plays the only one to achieve any success was *The Prince of Tunis* (1773). See his letters, ed. by Horst Drescher (1967); biography by H. W. Thompson (1931).

Mackenzie, Sir Morell, 1837–92, English physician and laryngologist. A skillful surgeon, he was called to Germany to treat the crown prince (later Frederick III, emperor of Germany), who eventually died of cancer of the larynx. He was prompted by political and professional criticism to write *The Fatal Illness of Frederick the Noble* (1888). See biography by R. S. Stevenson (1946).

Mackenzie, Sir William, 1849–1923, Canadian railroad builder and financier, b. Ontario. In the early 1870s he became a railroad contractor. He constructed portions of the Canadian National and the Canadian Pacific railroads. Entering (c.1888) into partnership with Sir Donald Mann, another Canadian Pacific contractor, he began the organization and construction of the far-flung network later known as the Canadian Northern Railway, of which Mackenzie became president. Taken over by the Canadian government in 1918, the railroad is now a part of the Canadian National Railways system. Mackenzie was knighted in 1911.

Mackenzie, William Lyon, 1795–1861, Canadian journalist and insurgent leader, b. Scotland; grandfather of William Lyon Mackenzie KING. Emigrating to Upper Canada in 1820, he published (1824–34), first at Queenston, then at York (later Toronto), his noted *Colonial Advocate.* In it he vigorously attacked the governing clique called the FAMILY COMPACT, and in 1826 his printing office was partly demolished. Elected (1828) to the Legislative Assembly of Upper Canada, Mackenzie was five times expelled for "libel" and five times reelected by his constituency. As a leader of the Reform party of Upper Canada he went to London in 1832 to obtain redress of grievances. In 1834 he became the first mayor of Toronto. In 1836 he founded the *Constitution* as a Reform party organ. Enraged by the policies of Sir Francis Bond HEAD and by the defeat of the Reform party, Mackenzie and a group of insurgents attempted (1837) to seize Toronto, but the rebellion was quickly put down. Mackenzie and others escaped to the United States. He set up a provisional government with fortified headquarters on Navy Island in the Niagara River, but he was later imprisoned for 18 months by the U.S. authorities for violating the neutrality laws (see CAROLINE AFFAIR). After his release Mackenzie worked as a journalist and writer until the proclamation of general amnesty allowed his return (1849) to Canada. There he was a member (1851–58) of the Legislative Assembly of United Canada (Upper and Lower Canada). See Stephen Leacock, *Mackenzie, Baldwin, LaFontaine, Hincks* (1926 ed.); E. C. Guillet, *The Lives and Times of the Patriots* (1938).

Mackenzie, river, c.1,120 mi (1,800 km) long, issuing from Great Slave Lake, S Mackenzie dist., Northwest Territories, Canada, and flowing generally NW to the Arctic Ocean through a great delta. Between Great Slave Lake and Lake Athabasca it is known as the Slave River. At Lake Athabasca, the Finlay-Peace river system and the Athabasca River join the Mackenzie. The Finlay-Peace-Mackenzie system (c.2,600 mi/4,180 km long) is the second longest continuous stream in North America. The Liard River is the largest tributary flowing directly into the Mackenzie. The river is navigable from the Arctic Ocean to Great Slave Lake between June and October. Between Great Slave Lake and Lake Athabasca there are rapids (14 mi/23 km) that must be portaged; above the rapids are more than 400 mi (644 km) of navigable waters. The Liard River affords transportation between Fort Nelson, British Columbia, and the Arctic; the Athabasca-Mackenzie system is followed by a major shipping route between Edmonton, Alta., and the Arctic. Numerous lakes in the Mackenzie basin act as reservoirs and natural flood controls. The basin, flanked by the Rocky Mts. and the Canadian Shield, is the northern portion of the Great Plains of North America; arctic air masses follow the valley south into the interior of the continent. Much of the Mackenzie valley is heavily forested and, where climate permits, its deep soil is well suited to agriculture. Numerous trading posts were established along the Mackenzie in the early part of the 19th cent. and fur trapping is still an important activity there; the chief trading posts are Fort Simpson, Fort Providence, and Aklavik. The region was the domain of fur traders until the 1930s when vast oil fields and other mineral resources were discovered; Norman Wells is the chief oil-producing town. In the early 1970s large natural gas fields were discovered in the Mackenzie delta region. Peter Pond was possibly the first white man to enter (1777) the Mackenzie drainage area, but Sir Alexander Mackenzie, the Canadian explorer, was the first to descend (1789) the river to the Arctic Ocean.

Mackenzie District, 527,490 sq mi (1,366,199 sq km), one of the three districts of the NORTHWEST TERRITORIES, Canada. Established in 1920, it lies between Yukon Territory (on the west) and the district of Keewatin (on the east) and includes the lower two thirds of the Mackenzie valley, Great Bear Lake, Great Slave Lake, and many smaller lakes. Yellowknife, the territorial capital, is the largest city of the district. Part of Wood Buffalo National Park (est. 1922) and all of Nahanni National Park (est. 1972) are in the district.

Mackenzie King, William Lyon: see KING, WILLIAM LYON MACKENZIE.

mackerel, common name for members of the family Scombridae, 60 species of open-sea fishes, including the albacore, bonito, and TUNA. They are characterized by deeply forked tails that narrow greatly where they join the body; small finlets behind both the dorsal and the anal fins; and sleek, streamlined bodies with smooth, almost scaleless skins having an iridescent sheen. All members of the mackerel family are superb, swift swimmers. The firm, oily texture of their powerful muscles and their generally large size make them of great commercial importance as food fish. They travel in schools, feeding on other fish (chiefly HERRING) and on squid, and migrate between deep and shallow waters. The smaller species rely on the constant rush of water through their gills for sufficient oxygen and will suffocate if motionless. The largest of the family, the enormous (up to ¾ ton/680 kg) tunas, are among the few warm-blooded fishes, due to the constant operation of their huge banks of muscles. Of the smaller members of the family, the Atlantic, or common, mackerel, *Scomber scombrus,* found in colder waters off North America and Europe, is one of the smallest (1½ lb/0.675 kg average). Despite its size, the annual catch is 50 million lb (22.5 million kg), which is marketed fresh, salted, and canned. Intermediate between the Atlantic mackerel and the bonitos (see TUNA) are the frigate mackerels, found in warm seas. Spotted species found off the Florida and Gulf coasts include the Spanish, painted, and Sierra mackerels, averaging 10 to 15 lb (4.5–6.7 kg). Other species are the king mackerel, also called kingfish and cero (up to 60 lb/27 kg); the chub mackerel, similar to the Atlantic mackerel; and the cosmopolitan and more solitary wahoo, or peto. Related to the mackerels are the escolars and rabbit fishes of Mediterranean and Cuban waters and the cutlass, or scabbard, fish, a degenerate eellike offshoot of the mackerels, found off Florida. Mackerels are classified in the phylum CHORDATA, subphylum Vertebrata, class Osteichthyes, order Perciformes, family Scombridae.

mackerel shark: see MAKO.

McKim, Charles Follen, 1847–1909, American architect, b. Chester co., Pa., studied (1867–70) at the École des Beaux-Arts. He was one of the founders of the firm of McKim, Mead, and Bigelow, which in 1879 became McKim, Mead, and White. A vast number of important commissions came into the firm's offices, in which McKim's spirit and taste were the controlling forces. Following a policy of adhering to classical architecture and its Renaissance derivatives, the partners erected a long series of buildings with a restrained classical sobriety that turned the tide away from the vagaries of the prevailing romanticism. Early examples of the style were the old Madison Square Garden (1891, now demolished), New York City, and the Boston Public Library (1888–95). McKim was influential in the development of the Chicago World's Columbian Exposition, for which he built the Agricultural Palace. He designed a fine series of clubhouses in New York City, of which the Harvard Club and the University Club are two; a number of buildings for Columbia Univ., including the present-day Low Memorial Library; the Pennsylvania RR station (1904–10); the Pierpont Morgan Library; and numerous fine commercial and residential works. His restorations include the work on Thomas Jefferson's buildings at the Univ. of Virginia and on the White House at Washington, D.C. McKim was associated with D. H. Burnham, Augustus Saint-Gaudens, and F. L. Olmsted, Jr., on the Senate Park Commission, which drew up plans for the development of Washington and the District of Columbia. He was first president of the American Academy in Rome, to the founding of which he had devoted many years of zealous effort. See biographies by Charles Moore (1929) and F. P. Hill (1950).

Mackinac (măk'ĭnô"), historic region of the Old Northwest (see NORTHWEST TERRITORY), a shortening of Michilimackinac. The name, in the past, was variously applied to different areas: to Mackinac Island; to the whole fur-trading region supplied from the island; to the northern mainland shore (St. Ignace, Mich., has been sometimes called Ancient Michilimackinac); and to the southern mainland shore, where Mackinaw City, Mich. is today and where a fort called Old Mackinac once stood. The Straits of Mackinac, a passage between the Upper and Lower peninsulas of N Mich., connecting Lake Michigan and Lake Huron, served for many years as an important Indian gathering place. In 1634 the French explorer Jean Nicolet was the first white man to pass through the straits. The French Jesuit Claude Allouez, in 1665, was the first missionary to go there; he was followed by Father Jacques Marquette, who established a mission at St. Ignace in 1671. A fort was later built there, and it became the headquarters of French trade operations in New France and an important military post in the Old Northwest; its importance declined in 1701 when Detroit was founded. The region passed into British hands in 1761 during the FRENCH AND INDIAN WARS. In 1763 the British garrison at Old Mackinac was massacred by Ottawa Indians during PONTIAC'S REBELLION. During the American Revolution, the fort and town at Old Mackinac, threatened by the exploits of the American general George Rogers Clark, was moved to Mackinac Island. The island and the straits were awarded to the United States in 1783 by the Treaty of Paris but remained in British hands until 1794. One of the first events of the War of 1812 was the British capture of Mackinac; it was returned to U.S. control by the Treaty of GHENT in 1814. After the war, Mackinac Island became the center of operations of John Jacob Astor's AMERICAN FUR COMPANY and thrived until the 1830s, when fur trading declined. After the 1840s the straits area changed from an important crossroads to an out-of-the-way shipping point; the U.S. army post on the island was abandoned in 1894. Mackinac Island became a Michigan state park and, along with Bois Blanc Island, a popular summer resort. Iron-ore mining revitalized the area in the early 20th cent., but the ore was depleted after World War II. The Mackinac Straits Bridge, the third longest suspension bridge in the world (3,800 ft/1,158 m long; opened 1957) spans the straits and links St. Ignace with Mackinaw City. It was built to stimulate the economy of the Upper Peninsula by opening it to tourists, vacationers and sportsmen. The straits are an important link in the Great Lakes–St. Lawrence waterway.

Mackinaw City, resort village (1970 pop. 810), Sheboygan and Emmet counties, N Mich., on the south shore of the Straits of Mackinac; settled 1681, inc. 1882. The region was well traveled by traders, missionaries, and explorers during the 17th and 18th cent. French troops, sent to garrison Fort Michilimackinac in 1715, remained for several years until the fort was occupied by British forces. A reconstructed stockade of the fort is in Michilimackinac State Park, and another state park is nearby. Mackinaw City was formerly linked with the Upper Peninsula by car ferry. It is now the southern terminus of the Mackinac Straits Bridge (completed 1957), the world's third longest suspension bridge.

Mackinder, Sir Halford John, 1861–1947, English geopolitician. He was educated at Oxford, where, as reader in geography (1887–1905), he led in the revival of British geographical learning. He established geography as an academic subject, teaching at the universities of Reading and London, and was (1903–8) director of the London School of Economics. He was a member of Parliament (1909–22), and he later held various imperial posts. In *Democratic Ideals and Reality* (1904) Mackinder propounded the view of Eurasia as the geographical pivot and "heartland" of history. The theory received little attention in Great Britain and the United States before World War II, but the idea of the heartland as a natural seat of power was adopted in Germany, notably by Karl Haushofer, and was used to support Nazi GEOPOLITICS.

McKinley, William, 1843–1901, 25th President of the United States (1897–1901), b. Niles, Ohio. He was educated at Poland (Ohio) Seminary and Allegheny College. After service in the Union army in the Civil War, he returned to Ohio and became a lawyer at Canton. He entered politics and was elected as a Republican to Congress in 1876. As a Congressman until 1891 (except for part of one term when his election was declared invalid), he strongly advocated protective tariffs, thus pleasing Ohio industrialists. The highly protective McKinley Tariff Act of 1890 was unpopular and helped to bring about the Republican defeat in 1892. It had already cost McKinley his seat in Congress in the election of 1890, but he had attracted the attention of the powerful capitalist-politician Marcus A. HANNA, who put the force of the efficiently organized Ohio Republican machine behind the ex-Congressman. McKinley was elected governor in 1891 and again in 1893. Hanna in 1895 began a skillful and successful preconvention campaign to have McKinley nominated by the Republicans for President in 1896. The Democrats took a radical position and nominated William Jennings Bryan with a platform favoring free silver. Although McKinley had earlier favored bimetallism and voted for the Bland-Allison Act, he accepted a platform endorsing the gold standard, and the issue was squarely joined. Many conservative Democrats viewed their party's stand as reckless, and Hanna's handling of the campaign was a masterpiece of adroitness. Conservatism and McKinley won. The Republicans also had control of

Congress, and in 1897 a thoroughgoing Republican tariff was adopted. Interest then swung to external affairs. There was much sympathy in the United States for the rebels in Cuba, who were seeking independence from Spain. The destruction of the battleship MAINE gave the advocates of war a rallying cry, and McKinley made the decision to ask Congress for a declaration of war. The SPANISH-AMERICAN WAR was brief, and from it the United States emerged a world power. McKinley directed the peace commissioners to demand the Philippine Islands for the United States. Cuba became a U.S. protectorate. The President also signed the bill to annex Hawaii and supported the Open Door policy in China, thus vigorously advancing the interests of the United States and American commerce. The Currency Act of 1900 consolidated the gold standard policy on which McKinley had been elected in 1896. He was reelected in 1900, but his new administration was short. On Sept. 5, 1901, he addressed the Pan-American Exposition at Buffalo, N.Y., advocating commercial reciprocity among nations. The next day he was shot down by an anarchist, Leon CZOLGOSZ, and on Sept. 14 he died. Theodore Roosevelt succeeded him. See biographies by C. S. Olcott (1916, repr. 1972) and W. C. Spielman (1954); Margaret Leech, *In the Days of McKinley* (1959); H. W. Morgan, *William McKinley and His America* (1963).

McKinley, Mount, peak, 20,320 ft (6,194 m) high, S central Alaska, in the Alaska Range; highest point in North America. Permanent snowfields cover more than half the mountain and feed numerous glaciers. Known locally as Denali, Mt. McKinley was first successfully scaled by the American explorer Hudson Stuck in 1913. It is included in MOUNT MCKINLEY NATIONAL PARK.

McKinney, city (1970 pop. 15,193), seat of Collin co., N Texas; inc. 1849. It is a shipping point for cotton and grains and has small industries. Located on the fertile blackland prairie, it was one of the queen cotton cities before the Civil War. The restored home of Collin McKinney (1836) is there, and a wildlife sanctuary and a museum of natural science are just outside the city.

Mackintosh, Charles Rennie, 1868–1928, Scottish architect, artist, and furniture designer. His decorative and graphic works are some of the finest manifestations of art nouveau. He created the architectural equivalent of this sumptuous decorative mode in the interiors that he designed for Miss Cranston's four tearooms in Glasgow. His few buildings, however, are notable for their absence of external decoration and their subtlety of proportion—both qualities derived from Scottish medieval precedent. Among these buildings are the Glasgow School of Art and two country houses—"Windyhill," Kilmacolm, and "Hill House," Helensburgh—all built around the turn of the century. See study by Thomas Howarth (1952).

Mackintosh, Sir James, 1765–1832, British writer and public servant, b. Scotland. He was trained as a physician, but after settling (1788) in London he became a writer and lawyer. His *Vindiciae Gallicae* (1791), a spirited reply to Edmund Burke's *Reflections on the French Revolution,* was the leading Whig statement in favor of the French Revolution, but from 1796 he grew hostile to French radicalism. Mackintosh served as recorder of Bombay (1804–6) and judge in Bombay vice-admiralty court (1806–12). As a member of Parliament after 1812, he supported penal and parliamentary reform. His writings include several historical works.

Macklin, Charles, 1697?–1797, English actor and dramatist, whose original name was Charles McLaughlin, b. Ireland. He began his career as a strolling player. His style of acting was radically different from the prevailing declamatory style of James Quin and Barton Booth. At first unsuccessful, he won fame with his dignified, tragic portrayal of Shylock in his production (1741) of *The Merchant of Venice.* This performance foreshadowed the naturalistic school of acting which was to be realized with David Garrick. His production (1772) of *Macbeth,* in which he used Scottish dress, was noted as an early attempt to achieve historical accuracy in costuming. Macklin's eccentricities and violent temper were notorious. He wrote and acted in *Love à la Mode* (1759) and *The Man of the World* (1781). See biographies by E. A. Perry (1891) and W. W. Appleton (1960).

Mack von Leiberich, Karl, Freiherr (kärl frī'hĕr mäk fən lī'bərĭkh), 1752–1828, Austrian general. In 1798 he led the Neapolitan army against the French. Through connections at court he gained (1805) command of the Austrian forces. He soon showed his incompetence, however, and had to surrender (1805) his army to Napoleon I at Ulm.

McLane, Louis, 1786–1857, American statesman, b. Smyrna, Del. He served in the U.S. House of Representatives (1817–27) and in the Senate (1827–29), resigning to become minister to England (1829–31). He was Secretary of the Treasury (1831–33) in Andrew Jackson's cabinet, but when he refused Jackson's demand to transfer deposits from the Bank of the United States to state banks, he was made Secretary of State (1833–34). President of the Baltimore and Ohio RR (1837–47), he was again (1845–46) minister to England, where he conducted the negotiations to establish the Oregon boundary.

McLaughlin, Andrew Cunningham, 1861–1947, American educator and historian, b. Beardstown, Ill., grad. Univ. of Michigan (B.A., 1882; LL.B., 1885). He taught history at the Univ. of Michigan (1887–1906), becoming a full professor in 1891, and was professor of history at the Univ. of Chicago (1906–29), serving as head of the department from 1906 to 1927. After 1929 he was professor emeritus. From 1898 to 1914 he was an associate editor of the *American Historical Review,* acting as managing editor (1901–5). His reputation as an authority on constitutional history was acquired by writing such books as *The Confederation and the Constitution, 1783–1789* (1905), *The Courts, the Constitution, and Parties* (1912), *The Foundations of American Constitutionalism* (1932), and *A Constitutional History of the United States* (1935), which won the 1936 Pulitzer Prize in history. He also wrote a biography of Lewis Cass (1891), *A History of the American Nation* (1899; rev. ed., 1913), *America and Britain* (1918), and *Steps in the Development of American Democracy* (1920). He was joint editor with Albert Bushnell Hart of the *Cyclopedia of American Government* (3 vol., 1914).

Maclaurin, Colin, 1698–1746, Scottish mathematician and natural philosopher, one of the greatest mathematicians of his time. He was professor at Aberdeen and from 1725 at the Univ. of Edinburgh. He was an authority on fluxions (as Newton's version of the CALCULUS was called), on Newton's gravitational theory, and on geometry. He also contributed to astronomy, cartography, and did actuarial computation for insurance companies. His writings include *Geometria organica* (1720) and *A Treatise on Fluxions* (1742).

Maclay, William (məklā'), 1734–1804, U.S. Senator from Pennsylvania (1789–91), b. Chester co., Pa. A lawyer and a provincial and state official before serving as Senator, he kept a journal, not published until 1880 (later ed. by Charles A. Beard, 1927), which gives the fullest, firsthand account of the debates in the Senate during the 1st Congress (1789–91). The journal reveals Maclay's opposition to Alexander Hamilton's policies and his defense of the interests of the small farmer.

McLean, John (məklān'), 1785–1861, American political figure and jurist, b. Morris co., N.J. His family moved to Ohio, where he studied law, was admitted (1807) to the bar, and practiced in Lebanon. He served in the House of Representatives (1813–16), was an associate justice of the Ohio supreme court (1816–22), and commissioner of the U.S. General Land Office (1822–23). President Monroe appointed him Postmaster General in 1823, and he was reappointed by John Quincy Adams. McLean resigned in 1829 because of disagreement with Andrew Jackson on the question of patronage. Jackson, however, appointed (1829) him to the U.S. Supreme Court where he served as an Associate Justice until his death; he is perhaps best remembered for his dissenting opinion in the DRED SCOTT CASE. See biography by F. P. Weisenburger (1937, repr. 1971).

McLean, city (1970 pop. 17,698), Fairfax co., N Va., a suburb of Washington, D.C.

McLean Canyon, Labrador: see CHURCHILL FALLS.

MacLeish, Archibald (məklēsh'), 1892–, American poet and public official, b. Glencoe, Ill., grad. Yale, 1915, LL.B Harvard, 1919. He practiced law for only three years and during the 1920s lived mostly in France. There he produced several volumes of verse, including *The Pot of Earth* (1925) and *The Hamlet of A. MacLeish* (1928), expressing his disillusionment with the contemporary postwar scene. *Conquistador* (1932; Pulitzer Prize) is a narrative poem about the conquest of Mexico. MacLeish returned to the United States in the 1930s; the volume of poetry *Frescoes for Mr. Rockefeller's City* (1933), the verse play *Panic* (1935), and the verse play for radio *The Fall of the City* (1937) reveal his deepening concern with the rise of fascism in the world. A strong New Deal advocate, he was librarian of Congress (1939–44) and undersecretary of state (1944–45) during the administrations of Franklin D. Roosevelt. MacLeish spoke for democracy in many vigorous articles. From 1949 to 1962 he was Boylston Professor of Rhetoric at Harvard. Among his later works are the verse drama *J. B.* (1958; Pulitzer Prize), a retelling of the story of Job in modern setting; volumes of poetry including *Collected Poems 1917–1952* (1952; Pulitzer Prize), *The Wild Wicked Old Man* (1968), and *The Human Season* (1972); two collections of essays, *Poetry and Experience* (1961) and *A Continuing Journey* (1968); and *Scratch* (1971), a play based on Stephen Vincent Benét's short story "The Devil and Daniel Webster."

MacLennan, Hugh (məklĕn'ən), 1907–, Canadian writer, b. Cape Breton Island, N.S. Although his works usually treat aspects of Canadian life, they are also paradigms of the human condition. Among his novels are *Barometer Rising* (1941); *Two Solitudes* (1945), a study of the conflicts between English and French Canadians; *Each Man's Son* (1951); *The Watch That Ends the Night* (1959); and *Return of the Sphinx* (1967). He has also published several nonfiction works including *Cross Country* (1949), *Thirty and Three* (1955), *The Scotsman's Return and Other Essays* (1960), and *Colour of Canada* (1967).

McLennan, Sir John Cunningham, 1867–1935, Canadian physicist, grad. Univ. of Toronto (B.A., 1892; Ph.D., 1900). He taught at the Univ. of Toronto from 1892 to 1932, was professor of physics from 1907, and was dean of the school of graduate studies and research from 1930. He is known for his studies in the fields of radioactivity, low-temperature research, the superconductivity of metals, spectroscopy, and the treatment of cancer by radium. He was knighted in 1935.

Macleod, Fiona: see SHARP, WILLIAM.

MacLeod, Sir George, 1895–, Scottish clergyman. He was educated at Oxford and, after serving in World War I, was ordained a Church of Scotland minister in 1924. Disaffected with his church's tenuous relations with its parishoners, MacLeod left his ministry in a Glasgow slum and in 1938 organized a multidenominational religious community with unemployed workers and fellow clerics on the Scottish island of IONA. A pacifist dedicated to political and social involvement, MacLeod served as moderator of the Church of Scotland in 1957–58. In 1967 he was created a life peer as Baron MacLeod of Fuinary.

Macleod, John James Rickard (məkloud'), 1876–1935, Scottish physiologist, educated at Aberdeen and Leipzig. He was a professor at Western Reserve Univ. (1903–18) and at the Univ. of Toronto (1918–28) and later taught at the Univ. of Aberdeen. For the discovery of insulin and the studies of its use in treating diabetes he shared with F. G. Banting the 1923 Nobel Prize in Physiology and Medicine. His works include *Diabetes* (1913), *Physiology and Biochemistry in Modern Medicine* (with others, 1918; 9th ed. *Macleod's Physiology in Modern Medicine,* 1941), and *Carbohydrate Metabolism and Insulin* (1926).

Macleod, Norman, 1812–72, Scottish clergyman. He was one of the foremost preachers of his time and was also noted for his work among the poor of Glasgow. He was editor (1860–72) of *Good Words,* to which he contributed many stories. His works include *Eastward* (1866) and *Reminiscences of a Highland Parish* (1867). See the memoir (1876) by his brother, Donald Macleod.

Maclise, Daniel (məklēs'), 1811–70, British painter and illustrator, b. Ireland. His character sketches contributed (1830–38) to *Fraser's Magazine* under the pseudonym Alfred Croquis were later published as *The Maclise Portrait Gallery* (1871). He was an excellent portraitist and painted his friend Dickens (National Gall., London). Maclise also executed the dramatic narrative scenes, *The Meeting of Wellington and Blücher* and *The Death of Nelson* in Westminster Palace, London. Among the writings he illustrated were Dickens's Christmas books and Moore's *Irish Melodies.* See memoir by W. J. O'Driscoll (1871).

McLoughlin, John (məklŏk'lĭn), 1784–1857, Canadian-American fur trader in Oregon, b. Rivière du Loup, near Quebec. A physician and then a trader, he was (1824–46) chief agent and administrator of the Hudson's Bay Company in the Columbia River country, when it was hotly disputed by British and Americans. McLoughlin used his power to monopolize and expand trade and to maintain peace with the Indians. Recognizing the rich farming potential of the Willamette valley, he helped French Canadians to settle there and urged a land colonization scheme on the Hudson's Bay Company. At Fort Vancouver (now Vancouver, Wash.), his headquarters after 1825, aid and shelter were given to American adventurers, missionaries, and settlers. In 1849 he became a U.S. citizen. See his letters to the Hudson's Bay Company governor and committee (3 vol., 1941–45); biographies by R. C. Johnson (new ed. 1958) and R. G. Montgomery (1934, repr. 1971).

McLoughlin House National Historic Site: see NATIONAL PARKS AND MONUMENTS (table).

McMahon, Brien (James O'Brien McMahon), 1903–52, American statesman, b. Norwalk, Conn. After practicing law, he became a judge in Norwalk, and from 1933 to 1936 he served in the office of the U.S. Attorney General. McMahon, a Democrat, was elected to the U.S. Senate in 1944 and reelected in 1950. He was chairman (1945–47) of the Joint Committee on Atomic Energy and the author of the McMahon Act for the control of atomic energy, which led to the establishment of the Atomic Energy Commission.

MacMahon, Marie Edmé Patrice de (märē' ĕdmā' pätrēs' də mäkmäō'), 1808–93, president of the French republic (1873–79), marshal of France. MacMahon, of Irish descent, fought in the Algerian campaign, in the Crimean War, and in the Italian war of 1859. For his victory at Magenta (1859), Napoleon III created him duke of Magenta. He was governor general (1864–70) of Algeria and a commander in the FRANCO-PRUSSIAN WAR, taking part in the battle resulting in the great defeat of the French at Sedan (1870). He aided (1871) in the bloody suppression of the COMMUNE OF PARIS. A monarchist, he was chosen by the monarchist majority in the national assembly to succeed Adolphe THIERS in 1873 as president of France for a seven-year term. MacMahon inaugurated measures designed to repress the republicans but was unwilling to go to the illegal extremes necessary to reestablish a monarchy. This reluctance, as well as dissension among the monarchists, served to preserve the Third Republic, and France received its new constitution in the organic laws of 1875. On May 16 (*le Seize Mai*), 1877, MacMahon precipitated a crisis by forcing the republican premier, Jules SIMON, to resign, although Simon had the support of the newly elected (1876) chamber of deputies, which had a republican majority. MacMahon appointed a royalist cabinet, dissolved the chamber of deputies, and ordered new elections; this was the only time during the Third Republic that the chamber was dissolved. Despite a Republican victory in the elections in Oct., 1877, MacMahon again named a royalist ministry. He was finally forced (December) to accept a ministry that had the approval of the chamber of deputies. This incident established the principle of ministerial responsibility to the chamber rather than to the president, thus limiting presidential power in the Third Republic. Involved in continuing conflict with the chamber of deputies, MacMahon resigned in Jan., 1879, before the end of his seven-year term. Jules Grévy succeeded him.

McMaster, John Bach, 1852–1932, American historian, b. Brooklyn, N.Y. Having practiced engineering in New York City and written two books, *Bridge and Tunnel Centres* (1875) and *High Masonry Dams* (1876), McMaster was appointed (1877) an instructor in civil engineering at the College of New Jersey (now Princeton). On a trip to Wyoming (1878) to collect fossils and study geology, he was struck with the drama of the frontier, and his determination to write a history of the United States was renewed. After the successful appearance of his first volume in 1883, he was offered a newly created professorship of American history at the Univ. of Pennsylvania, where he remained until he retired in 1920 as professor emeritus. His *History of the People of the United States* (8 vol., 1883–1913), covering the period from the American Revolution to the Civil War, is marked by an emphasis on social and economic affairs, by the use of newspapers and other contemporary sources previously neglected by historians, and by a simple and straightforward narrative. He wrote a ninth volume, *A History of the People of the United States during Lincoln's Administration* (1927), a number of highly successful school textbooks, *Benjamin Franklin as a Man of Letters* (1887), *Daniel Webster* (1902), *The Life and Times of Stephen Girard* (2 vol., 1918), and *The United States in the World War* (2 vol., 1918–20). See biography by E. F. Goldman (1943).

McMaster University, at Hamilton, Ont., Canada; nondenominational; founded 1887. It has faculties of humanities, science, social sciences, business, engineering, theology, and medicine as well as schools of graduate studies, nursing, and social work.

MacMillan, Donald Baxter, 1874–1970, American arctic explorer, b. Provincetown, Mass., grad. Bowdoin College, 1898, and studied at Harvard. After a decade of teaching, he went on the expedition (1908–9) of Robert E. Peary to the North Pole. Later (1911, 1912) he made ethnological studies among the Labrador Eskimos. Leader of the Crocker Land expedition (1913–17), MacMillan established a base at Etah, Greenland, from which he explored the Greenland coast and Ellesmere and Axel Heiberg islands. By a notable march over the frozen ocean NW of Ellesmere Island he proved the nonexistence of Peary's supposed Crocker Land. His experiences are told in *Four Years in the White North* (1918, new ed. 1933). He subsequently commanded a number of arctic expeditions and brought back much valuable scientific information. In his polar expedition of 1925 he was accompanied by Richard E. Byrd, who commanded a naval air unit of exploration. For the Field Museum (now the Chicago Natural History Museum) he led expeditions to Greenland, Baffin Island, and Labrador in 1926 and 1927–28. In 1938 he brought back over 40,000 plants from the Arctic. As a member of the U.S. naval reserve, he was recalled to the navy in 1941, made a commander in 1942, and assigned to the hydrographic office in Washington. Later he was placed in command of arctic expeditions in 1944, 1946, and 1947. In the 1944 voyage to Greenland, Baffin Island, and Labrador he made extensive air surveys and brought back some 10,000 photographs. He received the Congressional Medal of Honor that year. Sponsored by Bowdoin College (after which he named his noted exploration ship, the *Bowdoin*), MacMillan conducted expeditions to Ellesmere Island in 1948 and to Baffin Island in 1949, returning with rare bird specimens and other material. The expedition of 1949 was his 28th voyage of arctic exploration. On a polar trip in 1954, MacMillan and his party barely escaped having their ship destroyed. His other writings include *Etah and Beyond* (1927) and *How Peary Reached the Pole* (1934). See E. S. Allen, *Arctic Odyssey* (1962).

McMillan, Edwin Mattison, 1907–, American physicist, b. Redondo Beach, Calif., grad. California Institute of Technology, 1928, Ph.D. Princeton, 1932. On the faculty of the Univ. of California since 1932, he was appointed professor of physics in 1946 and director of the Lawrence Radiation Laboratory (now the Lawrence Berkeley Laboratory) in 1958. With P. H. Abelson he discovered neptunium (element 93) and with Glenn Seaborg and others, plutonium (element 94). For his work on the chemistry of the transuranium elements he shared the 1951 Nobel Prize in Chemistry with Seaborg. He also contributed to microwave radar and sonar, and to the design of particle accelerators. He worked (1942–45) on the atomic bomb at Los Alamos.

Macmillan, Harold (Maurice Harold Macmillan), 1894–, British statesman. He was educated at Eton and at Oxford and served in World War I. He entered Parliament in 1924 as a Conservative. Throughout the 1930s he was an advocate of social and economic reforms and an outspoken critic of the government's policy of appeasement. When sanctions against Italy were abandoned in 1936, he voted against his party leaders and sat for a year as an independent. He held several government posts during World War II. He was minister of housing and local government (1951–54), minister of defense (1954–55), and chancellor of the exchequer (1955–57). In 1957 he succeeded Sir Anthony Eden as prime minister. He restored close Anglo-American relations, damaged by the Suez Canal crisis, and attempted to establish a firmer basis for East-West negotiations by making personal appeals to Moscow and Washington. He also strove for the admission of Great Britain to the European Common Market but met with the opposition of French President De Gaulle. In the 1959 election, Macmillan told the country, "You've never had it so good," pointing to the full employment and substantial rise in real earnings of the 1950s, and he and his party won a landslide victory. However, by 1961 balance of payments difficulties had forced the government to introduce an austerity program. In 1963 the revelation that John Profumo, secretary for war, had been involved with a call girl who had also had dealings with a Russian official caused a scandal that seriously damaged the government's prestige. Macmillan resigned from office in Oct., 1963, after major surgery and retired from Parliament in 1964. See his memoirs, *Winds of Change, 1914–1939* (1966), *The Blast of War, 1939–1945* (1967), *Tides of Fortune, 1945–1955* (1969), *Riding the Storm, 1956–1959* (1971), *Pointing the Way, 1959–1961* (1972), and *At the End of the Day, 1961–1963* (1973). See also biography by Anthony Sampson (1967).

Macmillan, river, c.200 mi (320 km) long, rising in two main forks in the Selwyn Mts., E Yukon Territory, Canada, and flowing generally W to the Pelly River. It was an important route to the gold fields from c.1890 to 1900.

McMinnville. 1 City (1970 pop. 10,125), seat of Yamhill co., NW Oregon; inc. 1876. It is a trade and processing center in the fertile Willamette valley, and it also has a large lumber industry. Linfield College is there. **2** Town (1970 pop. 10,662), seat of Warren co., central Tenn.; inc. 1809. It has various manufacturing industries.

MacMonnies, Frederick William (məkmŏn'ēz), 1863–1937, American sculptor and painter, b. Brooklyn, N.Y., studied with Augustus Saint-Gaudens and with Falguière in Paris. His fountain for the Court of Honor at the World's Columbian Exposition, Chicago, 1893, brought him fame. Among his numerous other works are a statue of Nathan Hale (City Hall Park, New York City); reliefs on the central bronze doors and the Shakespeare statue (Library of Congress); the army and navy groups for the Brooklyn Arch (Prospect Park, Brooklyn, N.Y.); and the *Pioneer Monument* (Denver).

McMurdo Sound, Antarctica: see ROSS SEA.

McMurray, town, (1971 pop. 6,750), NE Alta., Canada, on the Athabasca River. It is an important river port and transshipment point for the Northwest Territories. It is also known as Fort McMurray.

McMurrough, Dermot: see DERMOT MCMURROUGH.

MacNab, Sir Allan Napier, 1798–1862, Canadian political leader, b. Ontario. He fought in the War of 1812 and later became a lawyer. A staunch supporter of English policies, he commanded "the men of Gore" against the rebels in the uprising of 1837 and later took charge of the forces opposing the insurgents under William Lyon Mackenzie. MacNab was knighted (1838) for these actions. He served in the Legislative Assembly of Canada from 1841 to 1857; he became prime minister in 1854 but was forced to resign in 1856.

MacNally, Leonard, 1752–1820, Irish political informer. A lawyer, he joined the United Irishmen and defended many of their members in court. His clients, however, were invariably convicted, and after his death it was discovered that MacNally had been in the pay of the British government. It was he who betrayed Lord Edward Fitzgerald (1798) and Robert Emmet (1803). MacNally wrote many plays and the song "The Lass of Richmond Hill."

McNamara, Robert Strange, 1916–, U.S. Secretary of Defense (1961–68), b. San Francisco. He taught (1940–43) business administration at Harvard, served in World War II, and was (1946–60) an executive of the Ford Motor Company, where he was responsible for many of the managerial and product changes that enabled the company to regain its high rank among the nation's corporations. In Nov., 1960, he became the first president of the corporation who was not a member of the Ford family, but he resigned shortly afterward to become (Jan., 1961) President Kennedy's Secretary of Defense. McNamara introduced modern management techniques in the Defense Dept. and asserted civilian control over the defense establishment. He also shifted U.S. military strategy away from heavy reliance on nuclear weaponry and strengthened conventional fighting capacity. Although he at first supported escalation of the VIETNAM WAR, growing doubts about the war led McNamara to resign from the cabinet. In 1968 he became president of the World Bank. McNamara wrote *The Essence of Security* (1968) and *One Hundred Countries, Two Billion People* (1973). See biography by H. L. Trewhitt (1971); study by J. M. Roherty (1970).

McNary, Charles Linza, 1874–1944, U.S. Senator (1917–44), b. near Salem, Oregon. Admitted (1898) to the bar in Oregon, he became prominent in the Republican party. In the Senate he sponsored farm aid measures and, as minority leader after 1932, supported much New Deal legislation, although he opposed the reciprocal trade agreements and President Franklin Delano Roosevelt's proposals for Supreme Court reform. He ran for Vice President on the unsuccessful Republican ticket along with Wendell Willkie in the campaign of 1940.

McNary Dam, 7,265 ft (2,214 m) long and 183 ft (56 m) high, on the Columbia River between Oregon and Washington, near Umatilla, Oregon; built 1947–56 by the U.S. Corps of Engineers. Located at the head of the slack water pool created by John Day Dam, it provides slack-water navigation 61 mi (98 km) upstream to the mouth of the Snake River; locks permit vessels to pass around the dam. McNary Dam is one of the largest (986,000-kw capacity) hydroelectric power facilities in the United States.

McNaughton, Andrew George Latta (məknôt'ən), 1887-1966, Canadian general, b. Saskatchewan. An artillery officer in World War I, he was later (1929-35) Canadian chief of staff. In World War II he commanded the Canadian forces in Great Britain and staunchly supported the policy of keeping the Canadian army a complete and separate force. He became a general in 1944, returned to Canada that year, and was appointed minister of national defense. He served (1946-48) as president of the Canadian Atomic Energy Control Board, was (1948) Canada's representative on the UN Security Council, and represented (1946-66) Canada on the UN Atomic Energy Commission. He was also Canadian chairman (1950-62) of the International Joint Commission with the United States.

MacNeice, Louis (məknēs'), 1907-63, Irish poet. Educated in England, he became a classical scholar and teacher and later was a producer for the British Broadcasting Corporation. In the 1930s MacNeice allied himself with a group of poets of social protest led by W. H. AUDEN. His later poetry, expressing the futility of modern life, retains the sparkling wit, ironical flatness of statement, and colloquial tone of his earlier verse. His volumes of poetry include *Poems, 1925-1940* (1940), *Springboard* (1945), *Holes in the Sky* (1948), *Ten Burnt Offerings* (1952), and *Solstices* (1961). He also rendered poetic translations of Aeschylus' *Agamemnon* (1936) and Goethe's *Faust* (1951). See his *Strings Are False: An Unfinished Autobiography* (1966); *Collected Poems,* ed. by E. R. Dodds (1967); studies by W. T. McKinnon (1971) and D. B. Moore (1972).

MacNeil, Hermon Atkins, 1866-1947, American sculptor, b. Chelsea, Mass., studied in Paris and in Rome. His first work of importance was for the World's Columbian Exposition, Chicago, 1893, but he is perhaps best known for his Indians and Western pioneers. Among his monuments are *The Coming of the White Man* (Portland, Oregon); the McKinley Memorial (Columbus, Ohio); the Soldiers and Sailors Monument (Albany, N.Y.); and the Marquette Memorial (Chicago). Among smaller sculptures is *The Sun Vow* (Metropolitan Mus.). MacNeil designed the 25¢ piece (Liberty quarter) that was accepted for minting in 1916.

Macomb, Alexander (məkōm'), 1782-1841, American army officer, b. Detroit, Mich. He entered the army in 1799. In the War of 1812, as brigadier general in command at Plattsburg, N.Y., in the absence of Gen. Ralph Izard, he repulsed (Sept. 11, 1814) the assault of a greatly superior force under Sir George Prevost; this action, accompanied by the complete defeat of a squadron on Lake Champlain by Thomas Macdonough, caused the British to retreat to Canada. From 1828 until his death he was commanding general of the U.S. army.

Macomb, city (1970 pop. 19,643), seat of McDonough co., W Ill.; inc. as a city 1856. A trade and manufacturing center in a rich farm, clay, and coal region, the city is known for its artistic clay products. Among its other manufactures are insulated containers and roller bearings. Western Illinois Univ. is there, and a state park is nearby.

Macon, Nathaniel (mā'kən), 1758-1837, American political leader, b. near the present Warrenton, N.C. He served in the American Revolution and later became a political figure in North Carolina and an ardent champion of states' rights. He opposed the U.S. Constitution because he thought it gave too much power to the Federal government. In the early years of the republic he was a national figure, serving as U.S. Representative (1791-1815; speaker of the House, 1801-7) and U.S. Senator (1815-28; president pro tempore of the Senate, 1826-28). He was a stout Jeffersonian, although briefly in Jefferson's second administration he sided with a small faction called the QUIDS, who favored James Monroe rather than James Madison as the presidential candidate to succeed Jefferson. From the time that he opposed the Alien and Sedition Acts to the end of his career he stood for Jeffersonian ideas of personal liberty and states' rights. He opposed protective tariffs, the reestablishment of the Bank of the United States, most of the plans for internal improvement, and (ironically enough) Macon's Bill No. 2, which bears his name (see EMBARGO ACT OF 1807). Some of his correspondence was edited by Kemp P. Battle (1902). See biography by W. E. Dodd (1908, repr. 1970).

Mâcon (mäkôN'), town (1968 pop. 35,264), capital of Saône-et-Loire dept., E central France, in Burgundy, on the Saône River. It is famous for its quality wines. The town also has foundries and plants that manufacture motorcycles, electrical equipment, and clothing. Mâcon was acquired by the French crown in 1238, passed to Burgundy by the Treaty of Arras (1435), and was recovered by France in 1477. In the 16th cent. it was a Huguenot stronghold. Lamartine was born there.

Macon (mā'kən, mā'kŏn), city (1970 pop. 122,423), seat of Bibb co., central Ga., at the head of navigation on the Ocmulgee River; inc. 1823. The third-largest city in the state, it is the industrial, processing, and shipping center for an extensive farm area. Textiles, clay products, insulation board, tile brick, rockets, explosives, and fabricated steel are among its manufactures. Fort Hawkins was established on the east side of the river in 1806 and renamed Newtown in 1821. Macon (for Nathaniel Macon) was laid out on the west side in 1823, and Newtown was annexed in 1829. Wesleyan College, Mercer Univ., a state school for the blind, and a junior college are there. Also in Macon are the birthplace of Sidney Lanier, a restored grand-opera house (1884), Fort Hawkins (1806; partially restored), a museum of arts and sciences, and a planetarium. Nearby are Robins Air Force Base, and the Ocmulgee National Monument, which contains prehistoric Indian mounds.

Macon, Bayou (bī'ō), c.145 mi (230 km) long, rising in SE Ark. and flowing S into NE La. to the Tensas River. It was used as a rendezvous by the bandits Frank and Jesse James.

Macphail, Agnes Campbell (məkfāl'), 1890-1954, Canadian legislator, b. Ontario. She was elected (1921) to the Canadian House of Commons as a representative of the United Farmers of Ontario and Labor, the first woman in Canada to enter Parliament; she served until her defeat in 1940. She later became a member of the Ontario legislature (1943-45; 1948-51). On the formation (1933) of the Cooperative Commonwealth Federation, she became a leading member of this party. See biography by M. Stewart and D. French (1959).

McPherson, Aimee Semple, 1890-1944, U.S. evangelist, founder of the International Church of the Foursquare Gospel, b. near Ingersoll, Ont. Born Aimee Elizabeth Kennedy, she was converted to Pentecostalism as a young girl and married a preacher, Robert Semple. The couple went as missionaries to China, but when he died a year later, she returned to the United States. Not long afterward she married Harold McPherson, but she left him to take up a life of itinerant preaching, holding revival meetings along the Atlantic coast. With her mother, Minnie Kennedy, as business manager, she went to Los Angeles in 1918. There she became phenomenally successful and was noted for her healing sessions. In 1923, she opened Angelus Temple in Los Angeles and began to preach the religion of the foursquare gospel (see FOURSQUARE GOSPEL, INTERNATIONAL CHURCH OF THE). Her disappearance in May, 1926, while swimming in the Pacific, and then reappearance in June with a bizarre tale of kidnapping caused a huge uproar that resulted in a trial for fraud. Although she was acquitted, her business activities as head of Angelus Temple resulted in numerous other legal actions. She died as a result of an accidental overdose of sleeping pills.

Macpherson, James, 1736-96, Scottish author. Educated at Aberdeen and Edinburgh, he spent his early years as a schoolmaster. In later life he held a colonial secretaryship in West Florida (1764-66), and he was a member of Parliament from 1780 until his death. In 1760, at the insistence of John Home and others, he published *Fragments of Ancient Poetry Collected in the Highlands of Scotland,* supposedly his own translations of ancient Gaelic poems. Later he published translations of two epic poems, *Fingal* (1761) and *Temora* (1763), which were represented as the work of a 3d-century Irish bard named Ossian. A collection, *The Works of Ossian,* appeared in 1765. Samuel Johnson and others heatedly challenged the authenticity of the poems. After Macpherson's death an investigating committee of scholars agreed that he had used some ancient Gaelic poems and traditions, but composed most of the supposedly ancient poetry himself. His prose poems, written in a loose, rhythmical style, filled with supernaturalism and melancholy, influenced powerfully the rising romantic movement in literature, especially German literature. Macpherson also wrote several histories. See T. B. Saunders, *Life and Letters of James Macpherson* (1894, repr. 1969); study by D. S. Thomson (1951).

McPherson, James Birdseye, 1828-64, Union general in the American Civil War, b. Sandusky co., Ohio. After teaching (1853-54) at West Point, he worked on various engineering projects. In the Civil War, he became aide-de-camp to General Halleck in Missouri and then chief engineer to Ulysses S. Grant in the Union advance through Tennessee. McPherson, promoted to brigadier general of volunteers in May, 1862, and major general in October, commanded the 17th Corps in the VICKSBURG CAMPAIGN, distinguishing himself at Port Gibson and Raymond. He commanded the Dist. of Vicksburg (July, 1863-March, 1864) and upon Grant's recommendation was made a brigadier general in the regular army (Aug., 1863). In the ATLANTA CAMPAIGN he ably commanded the Army of the Tennessee until he was killed in the battle of Atlanta (July 22). See biography by E. J. Whaley (1955).

McPherson, city (1970 pop. 10,851), seat of McPherson co., central Kansas, in a farm area on the old Santa Fe Trail; inc. 1874. The city has an oil refinery, a flour mill, and factories that make a variety of products. The city is named for Gen. James B. McPherson, the highest ranking Union general to die in the Civil War. McPherson College and a junior college are there.

Macquarie, Lachlan (məkwä'rē), 1761-1824, governor (1809-21) of the British colonies in Australia. Sent to replace the corrupt rule of the officers of the original convict guard, he established a sensible and humane administration, stressing public building, land reform, and fair treatment of convicts and freedmen.

Macquarie, river, 590 mi (950 km) long, rising in the Blue Mts., E New South Wales, Australia, and flowing NW to the Darling River. It flows through an important sheep-and wheat-raising area.

macramé (măk'rəmā''), a technique of decorative knotting employing simple basic knots to create a multitude of patterns. The term derives from an Arabic word for braided fringe. Its first known use was recorded by Arabs in the 13th cent. During the next hundred years it spread to S Europe. Macramé has been used extensively by sailors as a pastime. The craft revival of the 1960s brought the technique to life after decades of obscurity. It remains popular for the making of handbags, wall hangings, plant hangers, and jewelry. See Eugene Andes, *Practical Macramé* (1971).

Macready, William Charles (məkrē'dē), 1793-1873, English actor and manager. The son of a provincial manager, he first appeared as Romeo in his father's company in 1810. His London debut (1816) was as Orestes in *The Distressed Mother.* With his portrayal of Richard III at Covent Garden in 1819, Macready established himself as a tragedian of the first rank and the only rival to Edmund Kean. Although he was at his best in the plays of his own day, his Lear, Hamlet, and Macbeth were noteworthy. He was manager of Covent Garden (1837-39) and of Drury Lane (1841-43). In 1849, on his last visit to the United States, the Astor Place riot occurred, in which several people were killed, brought on by his fierce rivalry with Edwin FORREST. He retired in 1851. Macready sought to uphold the standards of fine drama in a period of decline, and he pointed the way toward the drawing-room realism of the 19th cent. See his *Reminiscences,* ed. by Sir Frederick Pollock (2 vol., 1875); his journal, from 1832 to 1851, ed. by J. C. Trewin (1967); biographies by A. S. Downer (1966) and William Archer (1890, repr. 1971).

McReynolds, James Clark (məkrĕn'əldz), 1862-1946, U.S. Attorney General (1913-14) and Associate Justice of the U.S. Supreme Court (1914-41), b. Elkton, Ky. He received his law degree from the Univ. of Virginia in 1884. He was a professor of law at Vanderbilt when, although a Democrat, he was appointed Assistant Attorney General by Theodore Roosevelt. He served from 1903 to 1907, and later, while practicing law, he was a special assistant to the Attorney General in several antitrust cases. He continued his active antitrust work as Attorney General. As a member of the Supreme Court, to which he was appointed by President Wilson, he had a name as a strict constructionist; he wrote more opinions finding acts of Congress unconstitutional than any other Supreme Court Justice before him. He particularly opposed the New Deal legislation, which he believed violated the Constitution. As a result, he was a key target in President Franklin Delano Roosevelt's unsuccessful attempt to reconstitute the Supreme Court.

Macrinus (Marcus Opellius Severus Macrinus) (məkrī'nəs), 164-218, Roman emperor (217-18). A Moorish officer, prefect of the Praetorian Guard under CARACALLA, he was threatened by the emperor's murderous plans. Macrinus therefore had the emperor killed and became the first emperor who was not a senator. He himself lost the favor of the soldiers, who revolted. He was killed, and HELIOGABALUS succeeded.

Macrobius (məkrō'bēəs), fl. c.400, Latin writer and philosopher. His *Saturnalia,* a dialogue in seven books chiefly concerned with a literary evaluation of Vergil, incorporates valuable quotations from other writers. He also wrote a commentary on Cicero's *Dream of Scipio,* which was popular in the Middle Ages and influenced Chaucer.

macromolecule, term that may refer either to a CRYSTAL such as a diamond, in which the atoms are identical and held by covalent bonds (see CHEMICAL BOND) of equal strength, or to one of the units that compose a POLYMER. Macromolecules such as proteins and nucleic acids are vital to the functions of living cells.

McTaggart, John McTaggart Ellis, 1866–1925, British philosopher. A student of G. W. Hegel, by whom he was strongly influenced, he taught at Trinity College, Cambridge (1897–1923). Believing that the ultimate reality was spiritual, he denied the real existence of the material, of space, and of time. He was also a determinist but held that determinism was not incompatible with moral obligation. His writings included *Some Dogmas of Religion* (1906), *A Commentary On Hegel's Logic* (1910), and his great work *The Nature of Existence* (2 vol., 1921–27). See biography by G. L. Dickinson (1931); C. D. Broad, *Examination of McTaggart's Philosophy* (2 vol., 1933, 1938); R. M. Gale, *The Language of Time* (1968).

Mactan (mäktän'), coral island (1960 pop. 57,844), 24 sq mi (62 sq km), Cebu prov., the Philippines, just off the coast of Cebu island. Magellan was killed by natives there in 1521. The spot is marked by a monument.

MacVeagh, Isaac Wayne (məkvā'), 1833–1917, American political figure, U.S. Attorney General (1881), b. Chester co., Pa. A lawyer, he was the son-in-law of Simon Cameron, Republican boss of Pennsylvania. He became prominent in the Republican party and was (1870–71) minister to Turkey. After 1871 he began to oppose Cameron and his political machine. In 1877 he was appointed by President Hayes to lead a commission (the MacVeagh Commission) to adjust political difficulties in Louisiana following the disputed presidential election; this resulted in the withdrawal of Federal troops from the state. MacVeagh was appointed to the cabinet by President Garfield but resigned after Garfield's death. Because of his support of civil service and other reforms he left the Republican party and supported (1892) Grover Cleveland for the presidency. He served (1893–97) as ambassador to Italy and was (1903) chief counsel of the United States in the VENEZUELA CLAIMS question.

Macy, Anne Sullivan, 1866–1936, American educator, friend and teacher of Helen KELLER, b. Feeding Hills, Mass. Placed in Tewksbury almshouse (1876), she was later admitted (1880) to Perkins Institution for the Blind, since her eyes had been seriously weakened by a childhood infection. Although a series of operations partially restored her sight, she learned the manual alphabet in order to talk with Laura BRIDGMAN, a fellow resident at Perkins. She was graduated in 1886 and one year later was chosen to teach Helen Keller. The two remained constant companions until Anne Sullivan's death. As Helen Keller's teacher, Anne Sullivan pioneered in techniques of education for the handicapped. She based her instruction on a system of touch teaching; rather than attempt to explain the properties of an object, she would allow her student to experience it directly. In 1905 she married John Macy, who later became a noted writer and literary critic. During the early 1920s, Anne Macy and her former student helped to publicize the new American Foundation for the Blind (founded 1921) and lobbied for its program of increased opportunities for the sightless. See biographies by Nella Braddy (1933) and L. A. Hickock (1961); H. A. Keller, *Teacher* (1955, rev. ed. 1966).

Madách, Imré (ĭm'rĕ mŏ'däch), 1823–64, Hungarian poet and dramatist. Madách is best known for his dramatic epic, *The Tragedy of Man* (1861, tr. 1908), which relates the history of mankind in somber, philosophical terms. Influenced by Goethe's *Faust,* it reveals Madách's profound pessimism. An adapted version is frequently performed in Hungarian theaters.

Madagascar: see MALAGASY REPUBLIC.

Madai (măd'āī, mā'dī), biblical form of the name of the Medes. Gen. 10.2; 1 Chron. 1.5.

Madang (mä'däng), town (1970 est. pop. 11,100), Papua New Guinea, on NE New Guinea island. A seaport on Astrolabe Bay, Madang exports copra and gold. It was an important Japanese air base during World War II. Madang was formerly known as Friedrich-Wilhelmshafen.

Madariaga, Salvador de (Salvador de Madariaga y Rojo) (sälvä*th*ōr' dā mä*th*äryä'gä ē rō'hō), 1886–, Spanish author and diplomat. In 1922 Madariaga became head of the disarmament section of the League of Nations. After teaching at Oxford (1928–31), he served as Spanish ambassador to the United States and France. His resignation (1936) followed his disaffection with the republic; he took no part in the civil war. Living in England, Madariaga became prominent in the 1950s and 60s as spokesman for the anti-Franco Spaniards in exile. His literary work, written in Spanish, French, and English, is voluminous; it includes history, international relations, literary criticism, and social psychology. Madariaga's point of view is liberal and humanist, his style classical. His historical works include *Spain* (1930), *The Rise of the Spanish American Empire* and *The Fall of the Spanish American Empire* (both: 1947), and essays on Christopher Columbus (1940) and Hernán Cortés (1941). Madariaga's other works include *The Genius of Spain* (1923), essays on contemporary literature; *Don Quixote* (tr. 1934) and *Englishmen, Frenchmen, and Spaniards* (1928), psychological studies; *Victors, Beware* (1946), and *Democracy versus Liberty?* (1958), defenses of liberal philosophy; and *Portrait of Europe* (1952), on the effects of European militarism. See his memoirs (1974).

madder, common name for the Rubiaceae, a family of chiefly tropical and subtropical trees, shrubs, and herbs, especially abundant in N South America. The family is important economically for several tropical crops, e.g., coffee, quinine, and ipecac, and for many ornamentals, e.g., the gardenia, bluet, madder, bedstraw, and partridgeberry. COFFEE beans come from species of the genus *Coffea,* bushes and trees of the Old World tropics; many are African. The medicine QUININE comes from the bark of evergreen trees (CINCHONA) native to the Andes. The drug IPECAC, or ipecacuanha, is obtained from the dried rhizomes and roots of *Cephaëlis ipecacuanha* and related species, shrubby herbaceous perennials of tropical forests in Central and South America. Madder (*Rubia tinctorum*), also called turkey red, is an Old World dye plant native to S Europe. The herb's long fleshy root was the principal source of various fast, brilliant red dye pigments until artificial production of ALIZARIN, the color principle of madder. The plant was known to ancient peoples—madder-dyed cloth has been found in Egyptian mummy cases—and was cultivated in the East for centuries and in Europe from the late Middle Ages. Madder and the two major sources of blue pigment, indigo and woad, were the most important dye plants until the development of synthetic aniline dyes in the 19th cent. Gardenias [for naturalist Alexander Garden] are evergreen shrubs and trees (genus *Gardenia*) of the Old World subtropics. Most of the cultivated types are varieties of *G. jasminoides,* called also Cape jasmine but unrelated to the true jasmine. The heavily fragrant and showy blossoms make gardenias popular corsage and greenhouse plants. Several native North American wild flowers belong to the madder family. The bedstraws (species of *Galium,* an almost cosmopolitan weed) were formerly used for mattress filling because of their pleasing odor. The partridgeberry, or squawberry (*Mitchella repens*), is a small, trailing evergreen plant with scarlet berrylike fruits sometimes used medicinally or for winter decorations. The bluet (*Houstonia caerulea*) is a favorite spring flower of open woods and grassy meadows in the Northeast. Called also innocence and quaker-ladies, it has a distinctive tiny four-petaled blue flower. Other species of *Houstonia,* as well as the unrelated cornflower, are also called bluets. Phylogenetically, the madder family is closely related to the honeysuckle family. The madder family is classified in the division MAGNOLIOPHYTA, class Magnoliopsida, order Campanulales.

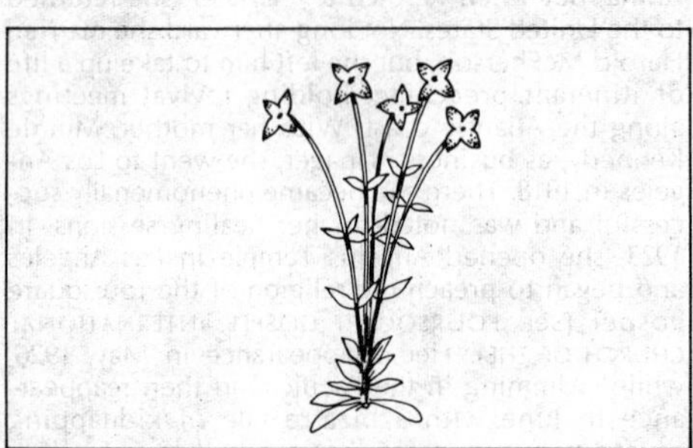

Bluet, Houstonia caerulea,
a member of the madder family

Maddox, Lester G., 1915–, U.S. public official, governor of Georgia (1967–71), b. Atlanta. He achieved national notoriety in 1964 when he drove Negroes from his restaurant in defiance of Federal civil rights legislation and then closed the establishment rather than desegregate it. Elected (1966) governor as an avowed segregationist with the support of the Ku Klux Klan, he was unable to stem the tide of integration. Although prevented by the state constitution from succeeding himself as governor, he was elected (1970) lieutenant governor. He lost the 1974 primary election for the Democratic gubernatorial nomination. See biography by Bruce Galphin (1968).

Madeira, island: see MADEIRA ISLANDS, Portugal.

Madeira (mədā'rə), river, c.900 mi (1,450 km) long, formed by the junction of the Beni and Mamoré rivers on the Bolivia-Brazil border. It flows north along the border for c.60 mi (100 km), then northeast in a winding course through the Rondônia and Amazonas sections of NW Brazil into the Amazon River. At its mouth is Ilha Tupinambaranas, an extensive marshy region formed by the Madeira's distributaries. The river receives numerous tributaries from the southeast and is navigable by ocean vessels to the falls and rapids near Pôrto Velho, Brazil. There the Madeira-Mamoré RR begins a 227 mi (365 km) run around the unnavigable section to Guajará-Mirim on the Mamoré River.

Madeira Islands (mədēr'ə, -dâr'ə), archipelago (1970 pop. 268,700), 308 sq mi (798 sq km), coextensive with Funchal dist., Portugal, in the Atlantic Ocean c.350 mi (560 km) off Morocco. Madeira, the largest island (35 mi/56 km long and 13 mi/21 km wide), and Porto Santo are inhabited. Two island groups, the Desertas and the Selvagens, are uninhabited. The chief town is FUNCHAL on Madeira. Sugarcane and Madeira wine are produced on the islands, and there are light industries such as embroidering and the manufacture of reed furniture and baskets. Madeira is a year-round resort. Mountain peaks, which descend steeply into deep, green valleys and advance to the sea as precipitous basalt cliffs, give the island unusual scenic beauty. The delightful climate is marred only by the occasional *leste,* a hot Saharan wind. The islands were known to the Romans as the Purple Islands and were rediscovered (1418–20) by João Gonçalves Zarco and Tristão Vas Teixeira. Settlement took place rapidly under the orders of Prince Henry the Navigator. Madeira was temporarily occupied by the British in the early 19th cent.

Madeira wine, red or amber fortified wine produced on the island of Madeira; it is matured about six years in the cask and improved by heat and motion. The chief types are sercial, a dry wine; bual, rich, with a fine bouquet; malmsey, a sweet dessert wine; and verdeilho, dark and full-bodied.

Madeleine (măd'əlĭn, Fr. mädlĕn') [Fr.,=Magdalen, i.e., Mary Magdalen], large church of Paris, in the Place de la Madeleine. It was originally planned by J. A. Gabriel as a part of his layout for the Place de la CONCORDE, the location being selected so as to close the vista of the Rue Royale. The building was begun in 1764, but construction was halted by the French Revolution. Napoleon I selected Barthélemy Vignon to convert the structure into a Temple of Glory. Vignon worked on the Madeleine from 1807 until his death in 1828, and his successor, J. J. M. Huvé, completed it in 1842. After the Bourbon restoration the building became a church again. Externally it is a peripteral temple (surrounded by one row of columns) of the Roman Corinthian order, with its columns (63 ft/19 m high) surpassing the height of all those of the ancient Greek or Roman temples. The interior contains a vestibule, a nave of three bays covered by domes on pendentives, and a semicircular apse. The building is without windows, and light is furnished by an oculus, or round opening, in the crown of each dome.

Madera (mədâr'ə), city (1970 pop. 16,044), seat of Madera co., central Calif., in the San Joaquin valley; inc. 1907. It is known for its wines; other products include olives, packed meats, lumber, paper, glass, and air-cooling and farm equipment. A U.S. vocational training center for Indians is there. Part of the Central Valley project is nearby. To the northeast is Yosemite National Park, and Kings Canyon National Park and Sequoia National Park are to the east.

Maderna, Bruno (bro͞o'nō mäděr'nä), 1920–73, Italian composer and conductor, b. Venice. Maderna studied composing with Gian Francesco Malipiero and conducting with Hermann Scherchen. As a conductor he introduced many avant-garde works to Italy. Maderna's music is based on mathematical structures. He collaborated with Luciano Berio in electronic music at the Milan Radio. Among his works are two serenades (1946, 1954), an oboe concerto (1962), the electronic ballet *Oedipus the King*, and the *Juilliard Serenade* for chamber orchestra and tape.

Madero, Francisco Indalecio (fränsē'skō ēndälā'syō mät͟hä'rō), 1873–1913, Mexican statesman and president (1911–13). A champion of democracy and social reform, he established various humanitarian institutions for the peons on his family's vast estates in Coahuila. In 1908, after Porfirio DÍAZ announced that Mexico was ready for democracy, Madero published *La sucesión presidencial en 1910*, a mild protest against the Díaz regime; the book made Madero a national figure. In 1910 he was the Anti-Reelectionist party's presidential candidate, with a program emphasizing effective suffrage and non-reelection. Díaz, at first contemptuous of his opponent, finally imprisoned Madero and won the election, as usual, without difficulty. Madero, released, fled to Texas and there proclaimed a revolution. Returning to Mexico, he found several groups in Chihuahua already in arms. These rebels, some led by Francisco VILLA, rallied to Madero's standard. On May 9, 1911, they captured Juárez; the prestige of the government was destroyed. At almost the same time an independent band rose under ZAPATA in the south. Throughout the republic the movement quickly gathered strength. The revolution triumphed. Díaz resigned on May 25, 1911. Madero, elected president, took office in Nov., 1911. His administration was anything but successful, and he was unable to accomplish any notable reforms because of division among his followers and his own administrative inability. Numerous revolts ensued. In Feb., 1913, an insurrection broke out in the capital. Victoriano HUERTA, appointed commander of the government forces, plotted with the rebels for Madero's fall. Pretending to punish the insurgents, Huerta staged a bloody show of force. Finally, after striking a clandestine bargain, he treacherously assassinated Madero's brother, assumed power, and caused Madero's arrest and imprisonment. Madero was shot, supposedly in an attempt to escape. See biography by S. R. Ross (1955, repr. 1970); C. C. Cumberland, *Mexican Revolution: Genesis under Madero* (1952, repr. 1969).

Madhva: see VEDANTA.

Madhya Bharat or **Madhyabharat** (mədyəbŭ'rət), former state, 46,400 sq mi (120,176 sq km), W central India. It comprised 25 former princely states. In 1956 it was incorporated into Madhya Pradesh state. Gwalior was the winter capital; Indore was the summer capital.

Madhyamika (mädyŭ'mĭkə) [Skt.,=of the middle], philosophical school of Mahayana BUDDHISM, based on the teaching of "emptiness" (see SUNYATA) and named for its adherence to the "middle path" between the views of existence or eternalism and nonexistence or nihilism. The school was founded by Nagarjuna (2d cent. A.D.) who came from S India to the Buddhist university of Nalanda and entered into debate with other schools including the Hindu logic school, or Nyaya, and the Buddhist ABHIDHARMA. About 25 works are attributed to Nagarjuna, the most important being the *Middle Stanzas* (*Madhyamika Karika*). Nagarjuna took key ideas from early Mahayana scriptures and expounded them using a rigorous dialectic. He attacked the concept of essence or "self-nature" (*svabhava*) as self-contradictory, holding that nothing self-existent can be subject to change. He then refuted all possible answers to philosophical problems such as causality, identity, and change by showing their logical inconsistency, with the aim of freeing the mind from all speculative views, which are the source of attachment that prevents enlightenment. He claimed to have no view of his own and to be attempting only to refute the views of his opponents. Nagarjuna's ultimate principle of emptiness was equated by him with "dependent co-arising," the causally conditioned, relative nature of all phenomena. He declared that there is no distinction between NIRVANA and *samsara* (bondage in birth-and-death) when the latter is seen without delusory concepts. He recognized two levels of truth, the absolute and the conventional. Thus his system does not deny the validity of empirical experience in its own sphere, although it does not accept the possibility of statements about absolute reality, which is beyond conceptualization. Nagarjuna's immediate disciple Aryadeva carried on his teaching. About A.D. 500 Bhavaviveka, heading the Svatantrika school of the Madhyamika, held that the Buddhist position can be put forward by positive argument. The Prasanga school, championed by Candrakirti, opposed him and reaffirmed the simple refutation of opponents by *reductio ad absurdum* as the true Madhyamika position. Santideva (691–743) wrote the philosophical and inspirational classic *Bodhicaryavatara* (tr. by M. L. Matics, *Entering the Path of Enlightenment*, 1970). Santaraksita and Kamalasila were the chief representatives of the Madhyamika's last phase, a syncretism with the YOGACARA school that was transmitted to Tibet. Madhyamika was also transmitted to China as the San-lun, or Three Treatises, school, introduced by KUMARAJIVA. See T. R. V. Murti, *The Central Philosophy of Buddhism* (2d ed. 1960, repr. 1970); D. T. Suzuki, *Outlines of Mahayana Buddhism* (1963); R. H. Robinson, *Early Madhyamika in India and China* (1967); Frederick Streng, *Emptiness: A Study in Religious Meaning* (1967).

Madhya Pradesh (mäd'yə prä'dĭsh), state (1971 pop. 41,650,684), 171,210 sq mi (443,434 sq km), central India, between the Deccan and the Ganges plain. The capital is BHOPAL. The second largest state of India, Madhya Pradesh consists, from north to south, of upland zones separated by plains. Adequate rainfall and plentiful good soil permit a prosperous, predominantly agricultural economy. Grains, especially wheat, are the main crops of the north. In the southeast, rice is the largest crop. The abundant cotton of the southwest (especially Berar) makes this state second only to Gujarat in cotton production. Spinning and weaving are the chief industries; there is a huge steel mill at Bhilainagar, built with Soviet aid. The state is rich in minerals; manganese, bauxite, iron ore, and coal are exploited. Nominally within the Mogul empire, the area was ruled during the 16th and 17th cent. by the GONDS and in the 18th cent. by the MAHRATTAS. The British occupied it in 1820. Berar, originally belonging to the domain of the Nizam of Hyderabad, was incorporated in 1903; from then until 1950 the state was called Central Provinces and Berar. In 1956 it greatly increased its area with the addition of Madhya Bharat, Vindhya Pradesh, and Bhopal, and part of Rajasthan. The majority of the inhabitants are Hindi-speaking Hindus, but Urdu and other languages are spoken. A large aboriginal population (c.5 million), principally Gonds, inhabits the forested regions. There are four major universities and numerous colleges in the state. Madhya Pradesh is governed by a chief minister and cabinet responsible to a bicameral legislature with one elected house and by a governor appointed by the president of India.

Madian (măd'ēən), variant of MIDIAN.

Madinat ash Shab (mədē'nət ăsh shăb), town (1967 est. pop. 20,000), SW Southern Yemen, just N of Aden. Formerly called al-Ittihad, it was built in the 1960s as the federal capital of the Federation of South Arabia. From 1967 to 70 it was the capital of Southern Yemen along with Aden.

Madison, Dolley, 1768–1849, wife of President James Madison, b. Guilford co., N.C. Born Dolley Payne of Quaker parents, she was brought up in simplicity and was married (1790) to a Quaker, John Todd, who died in the yellow fever epidemic of 1793. She left the Friends to marry Madison in 1794. In later years as official White House hostess for President Jefferson (who was a widower) and for her husband, both in the White House and at MONTPELIER, she was noted for the magnificence of her entertaining as well as for charm, tact, and grace. See her memoirs and letters (1886, repr. 1971); biography by E. S. Arnett (1972).

Madison, James, 1751–1836, 4th President of the United States (1809–17), b. Port Conway, Va. A member of the Virginia planter class, he attended the College of New Jersey (now Princeton Univ.), graduating in 1771. Like George Washington and others, he opposed the colonial measures of the British. His distinctive contribution to the colonial cause was a deep knowledge and understanding of government and political philosophy—resources that first proved their value in 1776 when Madison helped to draft a constitution for the new state of Virginia. He served in the Continental Congress (1780–83, 1787) and represented his county in the Virginia legislature (1784–86), where he played a prominent part in disestablishing the Anglican Church. During this time he watched the ineffectual floundering of Congress under the Articles of Confederation with apprehension and became convinced of the necessity for a strong national authority. Madison was an important figure in bringing about the conference between Maryland and Virginia concerning navigation of the Potomac. The meetings at Alexandria and Mt. Vernon in 1785 led to the Annapolis Convention in 1786, and at that conference he endorsed New Jersey's motion to call a FEDERAL CONSTITUTIONAL CONVENTION for May, 1787. With Alexander Hamilton he became the leading spokesman for a thorough reorganization of the existing government, and his influence on the Virginia plan, which advocated a strong central government, is evident. At the convention his skills in political science and his persuasive logic made him the chief architect of the new governmental structure and earned him the title "master builder of the Constitution." His journals are the principal source of later knowledge of the convention. He fought to get the Constitution adopted. He contributed with Alexander HAMILTON and John JAY to the brilliantly polemical papers of The FEDERALIST, and in Virginia he led the forces for the Constitution against the opposition of Patrick HENRY and George MASON. As a Congressman from Virginia (1789–97) he had a hand in getting the new government established, and he was a strong advocate of the first 10 amendments to the Constitution, the Bill of Rights. Yet, although modern historians have demonstrated the conservative nature of the Constitution and its founders, Madison was an opponent of the policies of the conservative wing in the Washington administration, a steadfast enemy of Alexander Hamilton and his financial measures, and a supporter of Thomas JEFFERSON. He especially deplored Hamilton's frank Anglophilia. After the passage of the Alien and Sedition Acts, Madison attacked these measures and prepared the protesting Virginia resolutions (see KENTUCKY AND VIRGINIA RESOLUTIONS). When Jefferson triumphed in the election of 1800, Madison became (1801) his Secretary of State. He served through both of Jefferson's terms, and he was Jefferson's choice as presidential candidate. As President, Madison had to deal with the results of the foreign policy that, as Secretary of State, he had helped to shape. The EMBARGO ACT OF 1807 was in effect dissolved by Macon's Bill No. 2. The bill provided, however, that if either Great Britain or France should remove restrictions on American trade, the President was empowered to reimpose the trade embargo on the other. Madison, accepting an ambiguous French statement as a bona fide revocation of the Napoleonic decrees on trade, reinstated the trade embargo with Great Britain, an act that helped bring on the WAR OF 1812. This move alone, however, did not bring about the war with Great Britain; equally significant were the activities of the "war hawks," led by Henry Clay and John C. Calhoun, who, hungry for the conquest of Canada and for free expansion, clamored for action. They helped to bring about the declaration of war against Great Britain on June 18, 1812. The War of 1812 was the chief event of Madison's administration. New England merchants and industrialists were already disaffected by the various embargoes, and their malcontent grew until at the HARTFORD CONVENTION they talked of sedition rather than continuing "Mr. Madison's War." Even the friends of the President and the promoters of the war grew discouraged as the fighting went badly. Victories in late 1813 and in the autumn of 1814 lifted the gloom somewhat, but disaster came in Sept., 1814, when the British took Washington and burned the White House. Nevertheless the war ended in stalemate with the Treaty of Ghent. Madison's remaining years in office witnessed the beginning of postwar national expansion. He encouraged the new nationalism, which hastened the split in the Democratic party, evident in the rise of Jacksonian democracy. Through these later upheavals Madison lived quietly with his wife, Dolley Madison, after his retirement in 1817 to MONTPELIER. His writings were edited by Gaillard Hunt (9 vol., 1900–1910). See biography in his own words, ed. by M. D. Peterson (1974); other biographies by Irving Brant (6 vol., 1941–61; abr. ed. 1970), Neal Riemer (1968), and Ralph Ketcham (1971).

Madison. **1** City (1970 pop. 13,081), seat of Jefferson co., SE Ind., on the Ohio River; settled c.1806, inc. 1838. It is a port of entry and a major tobacco marketing center. Among its manufactures are machinery, electric motors, organs, and metal products. The city has fine examples of Federal, Regency, Gothic, Georgian, Classic Revival, and Italianate architecture. An annual regatta is held on the river there. Hanover College, a state park, and a state mental hospital are nearby. **2** Borough (1970 pop. 16,710), Morris co., NE N.J., a residential suburb of the New York–New Jersey area; settled 1685, inc. 1889. Drew Univ. and part of Fairleigh Dickinson Univ. are there. Originally called Bottle Hill, it was renamed in 1834. Sayre House (1745) in Madison was Anthony Wayne's headquarters. The borough is noted for its roses. **3** City (1970 pop. 172,007), state capital, and seat of Dane co., S central Wis., on an isthmus between lakes Monona and Mendota, in the Four Lakes group; inc. 1856. It is a trading and manufacturing center in a fertile agricultural region. Meat products, dairy machinery, batteries, and medical equipment are made. Madison was founded in 1836, and was chosen (through the efforts of James Duane Doty) territorial capital before it was settled. It is the seat of the Univ. of Wisconsin, Edgewood College and a junior college. Many parks dotting the wooded lake shores make it an attractive residential city. Among its points of interest are the elaborate capitol, which houses the legislative library organized by Charles McCarthy; a Unitarian church designed by Frank Lloyd Wright; a large arboretum; and Vilas Park, which contains a zoo. A U.S. forest-products laboratory and a state mental hospital are there.

Madison, river, 183 mi (295 km) long, rising in Yellowstone National Park, NW Wyo., and flowing W then N through SW Montana to join the Jefferson and Gallatin rivers at the Three Forks of the Missouri. It is impounded by Hebgen Dam in its upper course and by Madison Dam, a power facility, at mid-course. The river is used for irrigation. Earthquake Lake was formed in 1959.

Madison Avenue, celebrated street of Manhattan, borough of New York City. It runs from Madison Square (23d St.) to the Madison Bridge over the Harlem River (138th St.). Its midtown section is known for towering office buildings and exclusive shops. Some of the major U.S. advertising agencies have headquarters in this section, and the name of the avenue has become synonymous with the advertising industry.

Madison Heights, city (1970 pop. 38,599), Oakland co., SE Mich., a suburb of Detroit; inc. 1955. Steel is processed, and automobile and aircraft parts, tools and dies, filters, and electrical equipment are manufactured there.

Madisonville, city (1970 pop. 15,332), seat of Hopkins co., W Ky., in a coal and farm area; inc. 1807. Coal is mined there, both underground and by stripping. Food is processed and canned, and there is some light manufacturing. The city has a junior college.

Madmannah (mădmăn'ə), place, SW Palestine, perhaps the same as BETH-MARCABOTH. Joshua 15.31; 1 Chron. 2.49.

Madmen, unidentified town in the plains E of the Red Sea. Jer. 48.2.

Madmenah (mădmē'nə), unidentified village N of Jerusalem. Isa. 10.31.

Madoc or **Madog** (Madoc ap Owain Gwynedd) (măd'ək, mä'-), fl. 1170?, quasi-historical Welsh prince. According to Welsh legend, Madoc, said to be a son of Owain Gwynedd, discovered America 300 years before Columbus. Witnesses' accounts of finding supposedly Welsh-speaking Indians have served to keep alive the story, which is otherwise unsupported by evidence. He is the subject of Robert Southey's *Madoc.*

Madoera: see MADURA, island, Indonesia.

Madon (mā'dŏn), unidentified royal Canaanite city, N Palestine. Joshua 11.1; 12.19.

Madonna lily: see LILY.

Madras (mədrăs', mədräs'), city (1971 pop. 2,470,-288), capital of Tamil Nadu state, SE India, on the Bay of Bengal. A commercial and manufacturing center, it has large textile mills, chemical plants, and tanneries. Leather, peanuts, and cotton are exported. Largely built around Fort St. George, a British outpost completed in 1640, the city soon became an important British trading center. The French under Dupleix captured it in 1746, but the British recovered it two years later. A cultural center, the city houses the Univ. of Madras (1857), one of the finest in India. There are many large public buildings and a famous shore drive, the Marina. Near the city is Mt. St. Thomas, the traditional site of the martyrdom (A.D. 68) of Thomas the apostle. He is supposedly buried in Madras at the Cathedral of St. Thomé.

Madre de Dios (măd'rā thā dyōs), river, c.700 mi (1,130 km) long, rising in the Andes of SE Peru and flowing NE through NW Bolivia to the Beni River. It is a major artery of NW Bolivia, but frequent rapids make its lower course only partly navigable. It drains a rubber-producing region.

Madrid (mədrĭd', Span. mäthrēth'), city (1970 pop. 3,146,071), capital of Spain and of Madrid prov., central Spain, in New Castile, on the Manzanares River. The newest of the great Spanish cities, it lacks the traditions of the ancient Castilian and Andalusian towns. Lying on a vast open plateau, it is subject to extremes of temperature; the daily variation is sometimes 40°F (22°C). Madrid is almost in the exact geographic center of Spain and is Spain's chief transportation and administrative center. Its commercial and industrial life developed very rapidly after the 1890s and is rivaled in Spain only by that of Barcelona. Besides its many manufacturing industries, Madrid is foremost as a banking, education, printing, publishing, and motion-picture center. An archiepiscopal see, Madrid also has a university, transferred from ALCALÁ DE HENARES in 1836. Madrid was first mentioned in the 10th cent. as a Moorish fortress. Alfonso VI of Castile drove out the Moors in 1083. The Cortes of Castile met in Madrid several times, and Ferdinand and Isabella as well as Emperor Charles V often resided there, but Madrid became the capital of Spain only in 1561, in the reign of Philip II. The city developed slowly at first but it expanded rapidly in the 18th cent. under the Bourbon kings (especially Charles III). From that period date the royal palace and the Prado, which houses one of the finest art collections in the world. At the beginning of the PENINSULAR WAR a popular uprising against the French took place at Madrid on May 2, 1808, and a fierce battle was fought in the Puerta del Sol, the city's central square. In reprisal, hundreds of citizens were shot at night along the Prado promenade. The events of that day were immortalized by two of Goya's most celebrated paintings, both in the Prado gallery. Madrid again played a heroic role in the Spanish civil war (1936–39), when, under the command of Gen. José Miaja, it resisted 29 months of siege by the Insurgents, suffering several bombardments and air attacks and surrendering, thus ending the war, only late in March, 1939. The general aspect of Madrid is modern, with tree-lined boulevards and fashionable shopping areas, but the old quarters have picturesque winding streets. Among the many landmarks are the huge royal palace; the Buen Retiro park, opened in 1631; and the imposing 19th-century building containing the national library (founded 1712), the national archives, a museum of Spanish modern art, and an archaeological museum. Also noteworthy is the modern Ciudad Universitaria [university city].

Madrid, Treaty of, 1526: see ITALIAN WARS.

madrigal, name for two different forms of Italian music, one related to the poetic madrigal in the 14th cent., the other the most common form of secular vocal music in the 16th cent. The poetic madrigal is a lyric consisting of one to four strophes of three lines followed by a two-line strophe called a ritornello. The most important 14th-century madrigal composers were Giovanni da Cascia (also known as Giovanni da Florentia) and Jacopo da Bologna (both fl. c.1350). Their madrigals are usually for two voices in long and florid melodic lines. The 16th-century madrigal is poetically a free imitation of its earlier counterpart; musically it is unrelated. The earliest of these madrigals were usually homophonic in four and sometimes three parts, emotionally restrained, and lyric in spirit. The classic madrigals of Cipriano da Rore (1516–65), Andrea Gabrieli, Orlando di Lasso, and Filippo da Monte (1550–80) were usually for five voices in a polyphonic and imitative style, the expression closely allied to the text. In the last part of the 16th cent. composers such as Luca Marenzio, Carlo Gesualdo (c.1560–1614), and Monteverdi intensified the expression of the text by the use of chromaticism, word painting, and declamatory effects. In the 17th cent. *madrigal* was used to designate certain expressive solo songs. In England the polyphonic madrigal had a late flowering in the Elizabethan era. Celebrated English madrigal composers included Byrd, Morley, Dowland, Campion, and Orlando Gibbons. See E. H. Fellowes, *English Madrigal Composers* (2d ed. 1948); Alfred Einstein, *The Italian Madrigal* (3 vol., 1949); Denis Stevens, ed., *Second Penguin Book of English Madrigals* (1970).

madroño (mədrōn'yə), tree or shrub (*Arbutus menziesii*) of the family Ericaceae (HEATH family), native to the Pacific coast of North America and Mexico. It has glossy evergreen leaves, white flowers, and red berries and is cultivated in warm regions for ornament. The bark, which peels off naturally from the trunk to give the tree a naked appearance, is a source of a brown dye and of tannin, and the hardwood is sometimes used for furniture. A related Mediterranean species, the strawberry tree (*A. unedo*), also supplies tannin and has edible berries used in preserves, wines, and liqueurs. This genus should not be confused with the plant of the same family whose common name is TRAILING ARBUTUS. Madroño is classified in the division MAGNOLIOPHYTA, class Magnoliopsida, order Ericales, family Ericaceae.

madtom: see CATFISH.

Madura or **Madoera** (both: mädōō'rä), island (1961 est. pop. 2,000,000), c.1,760 sq mi (4,560 sq km), Indonesia, near the northeast coast of Java, from which it is separated by Madura Strait. The island and its offshore islets are part of the province of East Java. Pamekasan is the capital, and Sumenep is the largest town. Principal products are salt, obtained from pans along the coast, and fish. Cattle are extensively raised, and bull races are held annually. The island is densely populated. The generally chalky soil limits agriculture, and much food has to be imported. From the 11th to the 18th cent., Madura was dominated by the rulers of Java.

Madurai (mədōōrī), city (1971 pop. 548,298), Tamil Nadu state, S India, on the Vaigai River. It is known as the "city of festivals and temples." The Meenakshi temple, which has 1,000 carved pillars, is especially famous. Madurai is also an educational and cultural center and a market for tea, coffee, and cardamom. Important industries are the weaving and dyeing of silk and muslin cloth, the making of brassware, and wood carving. As Mathurai, the city was the capital of the Pandya kingdom from the 5th cent. B.C. until the 11th cent. A.D. In the 14th cent. it was captured by Muslim invaders, who held it until 1378, when it became part of the Hindu Vijayanagar kingdom. From c.1550 until 1736 the city was the capital of the Nayak kingdom. The Carnatic Nawabs then gained control and in 1801 ceded it to the British. (See INDIA.) The Nayak palace (17th cent.) is a notable building in Madurai.

Madvig, Johan Nikolai (yōhän' nĭkōlī' mäthvĭg), 1804–86, Danish classical scholar. Educated at the Univ. of Copenhagen, he served (1829–79) as professor of Latin there. As minister of education (1848–51), he worked for the improvement of classical schools. He was interested in the careful editing of classics as the basis of philology and in history as the primary background of philology. His edition of Cicero's *De finibus* (1839, 3d ed. 1876) is particularly fine.

Maeander (mēăn'dər), ancient name of the Büyük Menderes River, c.250 mi (400 km) long, W Turkey. It rises in three branches W of Afyonkarahisar and flows generally W into the Aegean Sea. Its valley is extremely fertile. Its winding and wandering course gave rise to the word *meander.*

Maebashi (mää'bäshē), city (1970 pop. 233,631), capital of Gumma prefecture, central Honshu, Japan, on the Tone River. Now a silk textile center, it was formerly the castle town of the Matsudaira clan.

Maecenas (Caius Maecenas) (mĭsē'nəs, mē-), d. 8 B.C., Roman statesman and patron of letters. He was born (between 74 B.C. and 64 B.C.) into a wealthy family and was a trusted adviser of Octavian (AUGUSTUS), who employed Maecenas as his personal representative for various political missions. Later he retired and devoted all his time to his famous literary circle, which included Horace, Vergil, and Propertius. Although his friendship with Octavian became strained in later years, he bequeathed all his property to the emperor. To the great poets of his day he proved a friend and a munificent patron. His name is the symbol of the wealthy, generous patron of the arts.

Maelstrom, whirlpool, Norway: see MOSKENSTRAUMEN.

maenads (mē'nădz), in Greek and Roman mythology, female devotees of Dionysus. They roamed mountains and forests, adorned with ivy and skins of animals, waving the thyrsus. When they danced, they often worked themselves into an ecstatic frenzy, during which they were capable of tearing wild animals to pieces with their bare hands. The maenads were also called (for Bacchus) bacchantes or bacchae.

Mae Nam Chao Phraya, river, Thailand: see CHAO PHRAYA.

Maeotis, Palus: see AZOV, SEA OF, USSR.

Maerlant, Jacob van (yä'kōp vän mär'länt), c.1235–c.1300, Flemish poet, earliest important figure of Dutch literature. He wrote lyric poems and chivalric verse romances after the French as well as long didactic poems, chief of which is *Spiegel historiael,* an adaptation of the *Speculum* of VINCENT OF BEAUVAIS.

Jacob van Maerlant is an early literary representative of the bourgeois spirit.

Maes or **Maas, Nicolaes** (both: nē'kōläs mäs), 1632–93, Dutch genre and portrait painter. His earlier genre pictures bear, in their manner and coloring, a certain resemblance to those of his master, Rembrandt. In Dordrecht (1653–73) he painted chiefly domestic genre on a smaller scale. His later works, mostly portraits, show the influence of Flemish art in their smooth elegance. Among his paintings are *Old Woman Praying* (Rijks Mus.); and *Woman Dozing over a Book* and *Portrait of a Lady* (National Gall. of Art, Washington, D.C.).

Maeshowe (mās'hou), prehistoric chambered mound, on Pomona in the Orkney Islands, off N Scotland, near Stenness. It is a tomb with chambers inside a hollow mound about 300 ft (90 m) in circumference. There are runic inscriptions on the walls.

Maesteg (mīstāg'), urban district (1971 pop. 20,970), Mid Glamorgan, S Wales. It is a coal-mining town.

Maestra, mts., Cuba: see SIERRA MAESTRA.

Maeterlinck, Maurice (môrēs' mätĕrlăNk'), 1862–1949, Belgian author who wrote in French. After practicing law unsuccessfully for several years, he went to Paris in 1897. He had already been touched by the influence of the SYMBOLISTS and the mystical thought of Novalis and Emerson; his eventual 60-odd volumes can be read as a symbolist manifesto. Their suggestion of universal mystery, their insistence on ennui and impending doom affected the mood of a whole generation before World War I. Maeterlinck was awarded the 1911 Nobel Prize in Literature, but after 1920 his creative powers declined. His works include the short story "Le Massacre des innocents" (1886); the plays *Les Aveugles* (1891, tr. *The Blind*), *Pelléas et Mélisande* (1892), which inspired Debussy's opera (1902), *Monna Vanna* (1902), and *L'Oiseau bleu* (1909, tr. *The Blue Bird*), an allegorical fantasy for children that denies the reality of death; the essays *La Vie des abeilles* (1901, tr. *The Life of the Bee*) and *L'Intelligence des fleurs* (1907, tr. *Life and Flowers*); and poems. See critical study by Auguste Bailly (tr. 1974).

Maetzu, Ramiro de (rämē'rō thä mäĕt'thōō), 1875–1936, Spanish essayist and journalist, b. Vitoria. A member of the GENERATION OF '98, he believed in exposing Spain to European influence. Although considered radical in his youth, he later turned conservative and became a spokesman for the Spanish Catholic tradition. Among his works are *Hacia otra España* [toward another Spain] (1899), *La revolución y los intelectuales* [the revolution and the intellectuals] (1911), and *Defensa de la Hispanidad* [in defense of the Spanish essence] (1934).

Mafeking (măf'əkĭng), town (1970 pop. 6,900), Cape Prov., N central South Africa. It is the market for the surrounding cattle-raising and dairy-farming area and is an important railroad depot. Mafeking was founded in 1885 on the site of a black African settlement. In the SOUTH AFRICAN WAR (1899–1902) the British garrison there, under Lord BADEN-POWELL, withstood a BOER siege for 217 days; the fort is now a national monument. Mafeking was the extraterritorial capital of the Bechuanaland protectorate until it became independent as BOTSWANA in 1965.

Mafia (mä'fēä), name given to a number of organized groups of Sicilian brigands in the 19th and 20th cent. Unlike the CAMORRA in Naples, the Mafia had no hierarchic organization; each group operated on its own. The Mafia originated in feudal times, when lords hired brigands to guard their estates in exchange for protection from the royal authority. The underlying assumption of the Mafia was that legal authorities were useless and that justice must be obtained directly, as in the VENDETTA. Political corruption gave the Mafia tremendous influence. Benito Mussolini in a vigorous campaign attempted to suppress the Mafia, which revived after World War II. Through emigration the organization spread to the United States (where it was sometimes called the Black Hand), and it created particular trouble in Louisiana in the late 19th cent. It is reputed to control many illegal operations—trade in narcotics, gambling, prostitution, labor union racketeering—and certain legal enterprises in the United States. In Nov., 1957, more than 60 of its alleged leaders were surprised conferring at Apalachin (near Endicott), N.Y. About one third of them were convicted of obstructing justice, but the convictions were reversed on appeal. See ORGANIZED CRIME. See Michele Pantaleone, *The Mafia and Politics* (tr. 1966); Donald Cressey, *Theft of the Nation* (1969); Peter Maas, *The Valachi Papers* (1969); Joseph Albini, *The American Mafia* (1971); Nicholas Gage, *Mafia U.S.A.* (1972); Francis Ianni, *A Family Business* (1972).

Mafra (mä'frə), town (1970 pop. 7,149), Lisboa dist., W central Portugal, in Estremadura. It is noted for its huge 18th-century palace and monastery, built by John V in imitation of Spain's Escorial. Rectangular in shape, the edifice is surmounted by two towers and by a central dome. It contains a church, a fine library, and extensive royal quarters.

Maga, Hubert (übâr' mä'gä), 1916–, political leader in Dahomey. A teacher, he became active in politics and was (1951–58) a representative in the French national assembly. When Dahomey achieved independence (1960), he became its first president. The country's deteriorating economy led (1963) to his removal in a coup, and he later went into exile. He subsequently returned and served (1970–72) as head of a rotating three-man presidential commission designed to reduce domestic turmoil.

Magadan (măg'ədăn), in the Bible: see MAGDALA.

Magadan (məgədăn'), city (1970 pop. 92,000), capital of Magadan oblast, Far Eastern USSR, a port on the Sea of Okhotsk. It has shipyards, canning factories, and a major airport. A highway leads from Magadan to the gold-mining region on the upper Kolyma River.

Magadha (mŭ'gädə), ancient Indian kingdom, situated within the area of the modern state of Bihar. Its capital was Pataliputra (now Patna). The kingdom rose to prominence in the mid-7th cent. B.C. and rapidly extended its frontiers, especially under the rule of Bimbisara (c.540–c.490). Magadha fell (c.325) to CHANDRAGUPTA, who made the kingdom the nucleus of the Mauryan empire. After a period of obscurity, it recovered importance in the 4th cent. A.D. as the power-base of the GUPTA dynasty. Buddhism and Jainism first developed in Magadha, and the Buddha used the Magadhi dialect of Sanskrit.

Magadi, Lake (məgä'dē), c.20 mi (30 km) long and 2 mi (3.2 km) wide, S Kenya, in the Great Rift Valley. Formed and constantly resupplied by volcanic springs, the lake has a thick crust of carbonate of soda. The crust is removed by a floating dredge and then pumped to refineries, where it is processed into soda ash (used in glassmaking).

Magallanes, Chile: see PUNTA ARENAS.

magazine: see PERIODICAL.

Magbish (măg'bĭsh), family in the return. Ezra 2.30.

Magdala (măg'dələ), home of St. Mary Magdalen. It is probably to be identified with Majdol (Israel), a hamlet on the west shore of the Sea of Galilee. In some Bible sources Magdala is read in Mat. 15.39; others give Magadan, a place not otherwise known. The comparable passage (Mark 8.10) reads DALMANUTHA.

Magdala (mäg'dälä, măg'dələ), village, Wallo prov., central Ethiopa. Emperor Theodore II (Tewodros II) in the mid-19th cent. used Magdala as the base of operations for his conquest of the surrounding GALLA territory. In 1867 he made it his capital and imprisoned several British diplomats there. In 1868 a British military expedition under Sir Robert Napier rescued the prisoners, destroyed Magdala, and prompted Theodore's suicide. For his exploits Napier was later named Baron Napier of Magdala.

Magdalen: see MARY MAGDALEN.

Magdalena, (mägthälä'nä), river, c.1,000 mi (1,600 km) long, rising in the Cordillera Central, SW Colombia and flowing N to the Caribbean Sea near Barranquilla. It flows in a fault-block valley (c.50 mi/80 km wide) through the Andes to a broad, swampy, alluvial plain where the Cauca River, the chief tributary, joins its lower course. The Magdalena is a natural and important avenue of communication, linking the interior highlands with the coastal lowlands. Its navigability is hampered by sandbars, rapids, and fluctuating water levels. La Dorada, c.600 mi (970 km) upstream, is the head of navigation. Railways connect navigable sections. The tropical valley of the Magdalena is thinly populated. Economic development has been retarded except for the oil industry. Coffee is the chief crop along the river's upper course. Rodrigode Bastidas, the Spanish explorer, discovered (1501) the Magdalena, and since the time of exploration (1536) by Gonzalo Jiménez de Quesada, the Spanish conquistador, the river has profoundly influenced the economic and political life of Colombia.

Magdalenian: see PALEOLITHIC PERIOD.

Magdalen Islands (măg'dələn) or **Îles-de-la-Madeleine** (ēl-də-lä-mädlĕn'), group of nine main islands and numerous islets (1971 pop. 13,303), Que., Canada, in the Gulf of St. Lawrence N of Prince Edward Island. They were discovered (1534) by Jacques Cartier. The main islands are Alright, Amherst, Brion, Coffin, East, Entry, Grindstone, Grosse, and Wolf Fishing and sealing are the chief occupations of the islanders, most of whom are of French descent.

Magdeburg (mäk'dəbōōrkh), city (1970 pop. 270,692), capital of Magdeburg district, W East Germany, on the Elbe River. It is a large inland port, an industrial center, and a rail and road junction. Manufactures include steel, paper, textiles, machines, and chemicals. There are lignite and potash mines nearby. Known in 805, Magdeburg became, under Emperor Otto I, an outpost for the colonization of the Wendish territories. In 968 it was made an archiepiscopal see. The archbishops of Magdeburg ruled a large territory as princes of the Holy Roman Empire. The city of Magdeburg obtained from them (13th cent.) a charter that was the model of hundreds of medieval town charters in Germany, Austria, Bohemia, and Poland. Under this Magdeburg Law a town governed itself through an elected council, had its own courts of justice, and was exempt from all duties except the payment of rent to the prince of the land. Magdeburg prospered and became one of the chief members of the Hanseatic League. It accepted (1524) the Reformation, joined (1531) the SCHMALKALDIC LEAGUE, and continued its resistance against Emperor Charles V until its fall (1551) to Maurice of Saxony. The archbishops were converted to Protestantism, and the family, members of the house of Brandenburg, ruled the archbishopric as administrators. The *Magdeburg Centuries,* the first comprehensive history of Protestantism, was edited there in the late 16th cent. During the Thirty Years War the imperial forces laid siege to Magdeburg in 1630. On May 20, 1631, the imperial troops under Tilly and Pappenheim stormed the city and put the garrison to the sword. Fires mysteriously broke out in various quarters, and by the following day virtually the entire city had burned down. Roughly 25,000 persons (about 85% of the city's population) perished in the conflagration and the sacking. The sack of Magdeburg produced an immense impression and caused the Protestant princes to conclude a closer alliance. The Protestant charge that Tilly had ordered the fire is unfounded. The theory that the defenders themselves put fire to the city is equally doubtful. The city was rebuilt and its trade revived after the Peace of Westphalia (1648), which transferred both the city and the archbishopric (which was secularized and made a duchy) to the electorate of Brandenburg. From the late 17th cent. Magdeburg was an important Prussian fortress. The city was severely damaged in World War II. Historic landmarks of Magdeburg include an 11th-century Romanesque church and the 13th-century cathedral. The city is the birthplace of Otto von Guericke (1602–86), the physicist and inventor of the Magdeburg hemispheres (which demonstrate air pressure); the composer G. P. Telemann (1681–1767); and Baron von Steuben (1730–94), the Prussian general who fought in the American Revolutionary War.

Magdiel (măg'dēēl), duke or chief of Edom. Gen. 36.43; 1 Chron. 1.54.

Magellan, Ferdinand (məjel'ən), Port. *Fernão de Magalhães,* Span. *Fernando de Magallanes,* c.1480–1521, Portuguese navigator. Born of a noble family, he was reared as a page in the royal household. He served (1505–12) in Portuguese India under Francisco de ALMEIDA and later under Alfonso de ALBUQUERQUE. While in service (1513–14) in Morocco, he was accused of financial irregularities; he lost the favor of Manuel I, who rejected his proposal to reach the MOLUCCAS by a western route. In 1517 he went to Spain, where his plan was approved (1518) by Charles I (later Holy Roman Emperor Charles V). Portuguese efforts failed to prevent the voyage. With five vessels and about 265 men, Magellan sailed from Sanlúcar de Barrameda on Sept. 20, 1519. Sighting the South American coast near Pernambuco, he searched for the suspected passage to the South Sea. In Jan., 1520, the Río de la Plata was explored. While wintering in Patagonia (March–Aug., 1520), he summarily put down a mutiny of some of his officers. On Oct. 21, Magellan discovered and entered the strait which bears his name, and on Nov. 28 he reached the Pacific. His fleet, by then consisting of three vessels, the *Concepción,* the *Trinidad,* and the *Victoria,* sailed NW across the Pacific. No land was sighted for nearly two months, no provisions obtained for three; the men suffered intensely. On March 6, 1521, Magellan reached the Marianas and 10 days later the Philippines, where he was killed (April 27) while supporting one group of natives against another. Soon after, the *Concepción* was burned as unseaworthy, but the remaining two vessels visited Borneo and then the Moluccas, where they loaded spices. The *Trinidad* sailed for Panama but was wrecked; only four of her crew eventually reached Spain. The *Victoria,* commanded by Juan Sebastián del CANO, sailed across the Indian Ocean and rounded the Cape of Good Hope. The Portuguese detained 13 of her crew at the Cape Verde Islands, but finally, with only 18 men, she reached Sanlúcar on Sept. 6, 1522, thus completing the first voyage around the world. Although he did not live to complete the journey, Magellan provided the skill and determination that took the vessels over the great unknown portion of the globe, one of the greatest achievements of navigation. The voyage proved definitely the roundness of the earth, it revolutionized ideas of the relative proportions of land and water, and it revealed the Americas as a new world, separate from Asia. See the firsthand account of Antonio Pigafetta, *Magellan's Voyage around the World,* tr. by R. A. Skelton (1969); biographies by F. H. H. Guillemard (1890, repr. 1971), E. F. Benson (1929), and C. M. Parr (2d ed. 1964).

Magellan, Strait of, c.330 mi (530 km) long and 2½ to 15 mi (4–24 km) wide, separating South America from Tierra del Fuego and other islands south of the continent. Except for a few miles at its eastern end in Argentina, it passes through Chile. The strait, discovered by Ferdinand Magellan in 1520, was important in the days of sailing ships, especially before the building of the Panama Canal, and is still used by ships rounding South America. One of the most scenic waterways in the world, it affords an inland passage protected from almost continuous ocean storms. However, the strait is often foggy. The only city on the strait is Punta Arenas on Tierra del Fuego.

Magellanic Clouds (măj″əlăn′ĭk), two galaxies located in the far southern sky and visible to the unaided eye; they are classified as irregular because they show no definite symmetry or nucleus. The larger of the two, known as the Large Cloud or Nubecula Major, is located mostly in the constellation Dorado, with its center at R.A. 5^h21^m, Dec. −69°25′; its angular diameter measures approximately 7°. The Small Cloud, or Nubecula Minor, is almost completely in the constellation Tucana, with its center at R.A. 0^h53^m, Dec. −72°32′, and measures approx. 4° in diameter. Both are nearly 200,000 light-years from the earth and appear to be rotating about a common center of mass. They are part of the LOCAL GROUP of galaxies, which includes our own galaxy, the Milky Way, and are the nearest extragalactic objects. The Magellanic Clouds, named for the Portuguese navigator Magellan, were known to the Arabs in the 11th cent.; they were first studied in detail by Sir John Herschel in the 19th cent. While studying CEPHEID VARIABLE stars in the Small Cloud, Henrietta Leavitt of Harvard discovered (1910) the period-luminosity relation. This relation offered a technique for measuring the distances of stars and galaxies.

Magendie, François (fräNswä′ mäzhäNdē′), 1783–1855, French physician. He taught at the Collège de France and is considered a founder of experimental physiology. He distinguished the motor and sensory portions of peripheral nerves and studied the function of veins, the effect of air in arteries, and the uses and effects of various drugs.

Magenta (mäjān′tä), town (1971 pop. 23,690), Lombardy, N Italy, near Milan. Manufactures include matches, textiles, and plastics. At the Ticino River nearby, the French and the Sardinians won a decisive victory (1859) over the Austrians, which opened the way to Milan. General MacMahon was made duke of Magenta by Napoleon III for his leading role in the battle.

magenta: see FUCHSIN.

Maggiore, Lago (lä′gō mäd-jô′rā), or **Verbano** (vārbä′nō), second largest lake in Italy, 82 sq mi (212 sq km), in the Alpine foothills of Piedmont and Lombardy. The lake is c.40 mi (65 km) long and has a maximum depth of c.1,220 ft (370 m). It is formed by the Ticino River and lies partly in Switzerland. Along part of its western shore run the Simplon Road (built by Napoleon) and railroad. The lake is dotted with villas and resorts, notably at Stresa, Baveno, Pallanza, Intra, and (on the Swiss side) Locarno. On Isola Bella, one of the four Borromean Islands near Stresa, is the Borromeo palace (17th cent.; now a museum) with beautiful gardens.

maggot: see BLOWFLY; FLY; LARVA.

Maghreb or **Magrib** (both: mä′grĭb) [Arabic,=the West], Arabic term for NW Africa. It is generally applied to all of MOROCCO, ALGERIA, and TUNISIA but actually pertains only to the area of the three countries between the high ranges of the Atlas Mts. and the Mediterranean Sea. Some writers also included Spain—especially during its period of Muslim domination—in the definition. Isolated from the rest of the continent by the Atlas Mts. and the Sahara, the Maghreb is more closely related in terms of climate, landforms, population, economy, and history to N Mediterranean areas than to the rest of Africa. The region was united politically only during the first years of Arab rule (early 8th cent.), and again under the Almohads (1159–1229).

Magi (mā′jī), priestly caste of ancient Persia. Probably Median in origin, they were, according to Herodotus, a tribe rather than a priestly family. ZOROASTER is thought to have been a Magus. Study of the Magi is hampered by the lack of original source material. They are thought to have molded a pre-Zoroastrian religion, but nothing is known of it except by inference. After Zoroaster, Magian priests headed Zoroastrianism; the greatest was Saena. The Magi were revered by classic authors as wise men, and their reputed power over demons gave rise to the word *magic.* For the Magi of Mat. 2, see WISE MEN OF THE EAST.

magic, practice of manipulating and controlling the course of nature by preternatural means. Magic is based upon the belief that the universe is populated by unseen forces or spirits that permeate all things. Since human beings seek to control nature and since these supernatural forces are thought to govern the course of natural events, the control of these forces gives humans control over nature. The practice of magic is held to depend on the proper use of both the ritual and the spell. The spell, or incantation, is the core of the magical ceremony; it unlocks the full power of the ritual. The practice of magic, in seeking its desired end, also frequently combines within its scope elements of religion and science. In the art of ALCHEMY the process of transmuting a base metal into gold would require precise weights and volumes of acids, bases, and catalysts as well as the reciting of holy passages and prayers. Anthropologists often distinguish between two forms of magic, the sympathetic and the contiguous. Sympathetic magic works on the principle that like produces like. The Ojibwa Indian of North America makes a wooden image of his enemy and then sticks pins into it. Since the doll represents the enemy, harm done to the doll will harm the enemy. Contiguous magic operates on the belief that things that have been in contact will continue to act on each other after the physical contact has ceased. The aborigines of Australia believe that they can lame a man by placing sharp pieces of quartz, glass, bone, or charcoal in his footprints. Sometimes both sympathetic and contiguous magic are used in conjunction; certain African tribesmen will build a clay effigy around nail clippings, hairs, or bits of cloth belonging to the enemy and roast the completed image slowly in a fire. Not all magic is performed in order to harm or destroy, and for this reason a distinction is made between black magic and white magic. White magic is characterized by those rites and spells designed to produce beneficial effects for the community (see FERTILITY RITES) or for the individual, particularly in those cases where an illness is considered to be the result of evil demons or of black magic (see VOODOO; WITCHCRAFT). See James Frazer, *The Golden Bough* (12 vol., 1907–15); Lynn Thorndike, *History of Magic and Experimental Science* (8 vol. 1923–58); Bronislaw Malinowski, *Magic, Science, and Religion* (1948); Maurice Bouisson, *Magic: Its History and Principal Rites* (tr. 1961); John Middleton, comp., *Magic, Witchcraft, and Curing* (1967); Max Marwick, *Witchcraft and Sorcery* (1970); Milbourne Christopher, *The Illustrated History of Magic* (1973).

magic lantern: see STEREOPTICON.

magic square, a square divided into parts with letters or numbers inscribed therein that, whether combined vertically, horizontally, or diagonally, form the same sum or the same word. In ancient times such squares were thought to have magic properties, perhaps connected with the stars. Magic squares have been found in such widely divergent cultures as ancient China, Egypt, and India, as well as W Europe. Example:

4	9	2
3	5	7
8	1	6

See W. S. Andrews, *Magic Squares and Cubes* (2d ed. 1917, repr. 1960).

Maginn, William (məgĭn′), 1793–1842, Irish writer. Some of his best stories and essays appeared in *Blackwood's Magazine.* His short story "Bob Burke's Duel with Ensign Brady" is considered one of the most humorous Irish tales ever written. In 1830 he established the highly successful *Fraser's Magazine,* for which he wrote satires and parodies in both verse and prose.

Maginot Line (măzh′ĭnō, Fr. mäzhēnō′), system of fortifications along the eastern frontier of France, extending from the Swiss border to the Belgian. It was named for André Maginot, who was French minister of war (1929–32) and who directed its construction. Although considered impregnable, the line was still not complete at the outbreak (1939) of World War II. Its actual strength was never tested, for the line was flanked by the Germans in their French campaign of 1940. Like fortified lines since the Great Wall of China, the chief effect it had was to create a false sense of security; it could not eliminate the necessity for mobile warfare, and that particular lesson was thoroughly learned after the French collapse of 1940. See Vivian Rowe, *The Great Wall of France* (1959); J. M. Hughes, *To the Maginot Line* (1971).

Maglemosian: see MESOLITHIC PERIOD.

Magliabechi, Antonio (äntō′nyō mälyäbĕ′kē), 1633–1714, Italian librarian, b. Florence. Magliabechi was a trained goldsmith who devoted his life to learning, and mastered Greek, Latin, and Hebrew. He became known throughout Europe for his prodigious memory. In 1673 he was appointed court librarian by Cosimo III de' Medici, grand duke of Tuscany. At his death Magliabechi bequeathed his library of 30,000 volumes to the grand duke, who gave it to the city of Florence, where it now forms part of the National Library.

magma (măg′mə): see LAVA.

Magna Carta or **Magna Charta** [Lat.,=great charter], the most famous document of British constitutional history, issued by King JOHN at Runnymede under compulsion from the barons and the church in June, 1215. Charters of liberties had previously been granted by Henry I, Stephen, and Henry II, in attempts to placate opposition to a broad use of the king's power as feudal lord. John had incurred general hostility. His expensive wars abroad were unsuccessful, and to finance them he had charged excessively for royal justice, sold church offices, levied heavy aids, and abused the feudal incidents of wardship, marriage, and escheat. He had also appointed advisers from outside the baronial ranks. Finally in 1215 the barons rose in rebellion. Faced by superior force, the king entered into parleys with the barons at Runnymede. On June 15, after some attempts at evasion, John set his seal to the preliminary draft of demands presented by the barons, and after several days of debate a compromise was reached (June 19). The resulting document was put forth in the form of a charter freely granted by the king—although in actuality its guarantees were extorted by the barons from John. The original charter, in Latin, is a relatively brief, and somewhat vague, document of some 63 clauses, many of which were of only transient significance. The charter was in most respects a reactionary document; its purpose was to insure feudal rights and dues and to guarantee that the king would not encroach upon baronial privileges. There were provisions guaranteeing the freedom of the church and the customs of the towns, special privileges being conferred upon London. The charter definitely implies that there are laws protecting the rights of subjects and communities that the king is bound to observe or, if he fails to do so, will be compelled to observe. Historically most important were the vaguely worded statements against oppression of all subjects, which later generations interpreted as guarantees of trial by jury and of habeas corpus. Such interpretations, however, were the work of later scholars and are not explicit in the charter itself. However, the fact that many of the early interpretations of its provisions were based upon bad historical scholarship or false reasoning does not vitiate the importance of the Magna Carta in the development of the British constitution. As an actual instrument of government the charter was, at first, a failure. The clumsy machinery set up to prevent the king's violation of the charter never had an opportunity to function, and civil war broke out the same year. On John's death in 1216, the charter was reissued in the name of young King Henry III, but with a number of significant omissions relative to safeguards of national liberties and restrictions on taxation. It was reissued with further changes in 1217 and again in 1225, the latter reissue being the one that was incorporated into British statute law. In later centuries it became a symbol of the supremacy of the constitution over the king, as opponents of arbitrary royal power extracted from it various "democratic" interpretations. This movement reached its height in the 17th cent. in the work of such apologists for Parliament as Sir Edward COKE. It came to be thought that the charter forbade taxation without representation, that it guaranteed trial by jury, even that it invested the House of Commons (nonexistent in 1215) with great powers. These ideas persisted until the 19th cent., when certain scholars came to maintain that the Magna Carta was a completely reactionary, not a progressive, document—that it was merely a guarantee of feudal rights. It is generally recognized now, however, that the charter definitely did show the viability of opposition to excessive use of royal power and that this constitutes its chief significance. There are four extant copies of the original charter. See W. S. McKechnie, *Magna Carta: A Commentary* (2d ed. 1914, repr. 1960); H. E. Malden, ed., *Magna Carta Commemoration Essays* (1917); Faith Thompson, *The First Century of Magna Carta* (1925; repr. 1967); Maurice Ashley, *Magna Carta in the Seventeenth Century* (1965); J. C. Holt, *Magna Carta* (1965, repr. 1969); Anne Pallister, *Magna Carta* (1971); J. C. Holt, *Magna Carta and the Idea of Liberty* (1972).

Magna Graecia (măg'nə grē'shə)[Lat.,=great Greece], Greek colonies of S Italy. The Greek overseas expansion of the 8th cent. B.C. founded a number of towns that became the centers of a new, thriving Greek territory. They were on both coasts from the Bay of Naples and the Gulf of Taranto southward. Unlike Greek Sicily, Magna Graecia began to decline by 500 B.C., probably because of malaria and endless warfare among the colonies. Only Tarentum (now Taranto) and Cumae remained individually very significant. Magna Graecia was the center of two philosophical groups in the 6th cent. B.C., that of Parmenides at Elea and that of Pythagoras at Crotona. Through Cumae especially, the Etruscans of Capua and the Romans came into early contact with Greek civilization. The following are the chief cities of Magna Graecia (those colonized from Greece, except Thurii and Elea, go back to the 8th or early 7th cent. B.C.; those colonized locally are perhaps a century younger)—on the east coast from north to south, Tarentum (colonized from Sparta), Metapontum (from Achaea), Heraclea (from Tarentum), Siris (from Colophon), Sybaris (from Achaea), Thurii (from Athens, replacing Sybaris), Crotona (from Achaea), Caulonia (from Crotona), Epizephyrian Locris (from Locris); on the west coast from north to south, Cumae (from Chalcis), Neapolis (now Naples; from Cumae), Paestum, or Posidonia (from Sybaris), Elea (from Phocaea in Ionia), Laos (from Sybaris), Hipponium (from Epizephyrian Locris), and Rhegium (now Reggio de Calabria; from Chalcis). See David Randall-MacIver, *Greek Cities of Italy and Sicily* (1931); T. J. Dunbabin, *The Western Greeks* (1948); A. G. Woodhead, *The Greeks in the West* (1962).

magnalium (măgnā'lēəm), alloy of aluminum and about 5% magnesium. Although weak and soft in the elemental state, magnesium alloys with aluminum, manganese, zinc, tin, zirconium, and cerium to produce alloys useful in engineering materials. The strength and hardness of aluminum increases when it is alloyed with such substances as magnesium, manganese, nickel, chromium, zinc, iron, copper, and silicon. Magnalium—lighter and more workable than aluminum—is used in making metal mirrors and scientific instruments.

Magnasco, Allessandro (ālĕs-sän'drō mägnäs'kō), 1667–1749, Italian painter. Magnasco's style developed from an early apprenticeship to a Venetian painter and from his exposure to Lombard MANNERISM during his years as a Tuscan court painter. His works are characteristically gloomy, storm-torn landscapes and ruins, peopled with small, attenuated figures, and illuminated by flickering light. Magnasco's themes are primarily religious, and his paintings have a mystical, fantastic quality often compared to that of El Greco. Among his works are *The Baptism of Christ* (National Gall., Washington, D.C.) and the late work *Synagogue* (Cleveland Mus. of Art). The influence of his style was felt after his death in the works of Guardi, Goya, and Daumier.

Magnesia, two ancient cities of Lydia, W Asia Minor (now W Turkey). They were colonies of the Magnetes, a tribe of E Thessaly. One city (Magnesia ad Maeandrum), SE of Smyrna (İzmir), was later colonized by Ionians and given by Artaxerxes I to Themistocles, who died there. There are important ruins on the site, including the celebrated temple of Artemis Leucophryene, built in the 2d cent. B.C. Magnesia ad Sipylum, on the Hermus River at the foot of Mt. Sipylus, NE of Smyrna, was (190 B.C.) the scene of the defeat of Antiochus III (Antiochus the Great) by the Romans. The modern MANISA is nearby.

magnesia, common name for the chemical compound magnesium oxide, MgO. It occurs as colorless, cubic crystals. It is refractory, melting at about 2800°C. It is very slightly soluble in pure water but is soluble in acids and solutions of ammonium salts. The magnesia of commerce is a fine white powder used in soaps, cosmetics, pharmaceuticals, and as a filler in rubber goods. Magnesia is used to make crucibles and other ceramic goods. Crude magnesia is prepared by roasting dolomite (calcium magnesium double carbonate) or magnesite (magnesium carbonate). Pure magnesia is prepared by refining the crude product. Magnesia is also extracted from sea water. It occurs in nature as the mineral periclase.

magnesite (măg'nəsīt), mineral, magnesium carbonate, $MgCO_3$, white, yellow, or gray in color. It originates through the alteration of olivine or of serpentine by waters carrying carbon dioxide; through the replacement of calcium by magnesium in calcareous rocks, sometimes limestone but more often dolomite; and through precipitation from waters rich in magnesium that have undergone reaction with sodium carbonate. Caustic magnesite is not thoroughly calcined, 3% to 4% of carbon dioxide being left; mixed with magnesium chloride it makes oxychloride cement, which is extensively used for floorings and as a stucco. Dead-burned magnesite is calcined in kilns until it contains less than 1% of carbon dioxide; it is made into an excellent FIREBRICK. Magnesite is also used in the manufacture of Epsom salts, face powder, boiler wrappings, and disinfectants.

magnesium (măgnē'zēəm, -zhəm), metallic chemical element; symbol Mg; at. no. 12; at. wt. 24.312; m.p. about 651°C; b.p. about 1110°C; sp. gr. 1.738 at 20°C; valence +2. Magnesium is a ductile, silver-white, chemically active metal with a hexagonal close-packed crystalline structure. It is malleable when heated. Magnesium is one of the ALKALINE-EARTH METALS in group IIa of the PERIODIC TABLE. It reacts very slowly with cold water. It is not affected by dry air but tarnishes in moist air, forming a thin protective coating of basic magnesium carbonate, $MgCO_3 \cdot Mg(OH)_2$. When heated, magnesium powder or ribbon ignites and burns with an intense white light and releases large amounts of heat, forming the oxide, magnesia, MgO. A magnesium fire cannot be extinguished by water, since water reacts with hot magnesium and releases hydrogen. Magnesium reacts with the halogens and with almost all acids. It is a powerful reducing agent and is used to free other metals from their anhydrous halides. Magnesium is the eighth most abundant element in the earth's crust but does not occur uncombined in nature. It is found in abundance in the minerals brucite, MAGNESITE, DOLOMITE, and carnallite. It is also found (as the silicate) in asbestos, meerschaum, serpentine, and talc. Magnesium chloride is found in seawater, brines, and salt wells. Mineral waters often contain salts of magnesium; the magnesium ion imparts a bitter flavor. Magnesium is a constituent of the chlorophyll in green plants and is necessary in the diet of animals and man. Two methods of producing magnesium commercially are used. The principal method is the electrolysis of fused magnesium chloride, which is used in the extraction of magnesium from seawater (the principal source) and from dolomite. In recovery from seawater, the magnesium is precipitated as magnesium hydroxide by treatment with lime (calcium oxide) obtained from oyster shells. The hydroxide is collected and treated with hydrochloric acid to form the chloride. The chloride is fused and electrolyzed, forming magnesium metal and chlorine gas. The molten metal is cast into ingots for further processing; the chlorine gas is made into hydrochloric acid and is reused to form magnesium chloride. About 1 lb of magnesium is recovered from each 100 gal of seawater; the oceans are a virtually inexhaustible source of this metal. A second method of magnesium production, called the ferrosilicon process, involves the reduction of magnesium oxide (prepared by calcining dolomite) with an iron-silicon alloy. Magnesium is a commercially important metal with many uses. It is only two thirds as dense as aluminum. It is easily machined, cast, forged, and welded. It is used extensively in alloys, chiefly with aluminum and zinc, and with manganese. Magnesium alloys were used as early as 1910 in Germany. Early structural uses of magnesium alloys were in aircraft fuselages, engine parts, and wheels. They are now also used in jet-engine parts, rockets and missiles, luggage frames, portable power tools, and cameras and optical instruments. DURALUMIN and MAGNALIUM are alloys of magnesium. The metal is also used in pyrotechnics, especially in incendiary bombs, signals, and flares, and as a fuse for THERMITE. It is used in photographic flashbulbs and is added to some rocket and missile fuels. It is used in the preparation of malleable cast iron. An important use is in preventing the corrosion of iron and steel, as in pipelines and ship bottoms. For this purpose a magnesium plate is connected electrically to the iron. The rapid oxidation of the magnesium prevents the slower oxidation and corrosion of the iron. Magnesium forms many compounds. The oxide, hydroxide, chloride, carbonate, and sulfate are commercially important. They are used in ceramics, cosmetics, fertilizers, insulation, leather tanning, and textile processing. EPSOM SALTS (magnesium sulfate heptahydrate, $MgSO_4 \cdot 7H_2O$), milk of magnesia (magnesium hydroxide, $Mg(OH)_2$), and citrate of magnesia are used in medicine. Magnesium reacts with organic halides to form the GRIGNARD REAGENTS of organic chemistry. In 1808, Sir Humphry Davy discovered magnesium in its oxide, although it is not certain that he isolated the metal. Pure magnesium was isolated substantially by A. A. B. Bussy in 1828 by chemical reduction of the chloride. Magnesium was first isolated electrolytically by Michael Faraday in 1833.

magnet: see ELECTROMAGNET; MAGNETISM.

magnetic core: see COMPUTER.

magnetic pole, either of two regions on the surface of the earth, one in the Northern Hemisphere and one in the Southern, that attracts one end of a compass needle and repels the opposite end. It is to this magnetic pole rather than to the geographical pole that the needle of a compass points. Near either magnetic pole the magnetic force is vertical, rendering the magnetic compass useless. In these regions a gyrocompass must be used. The study of magnetism in rocks (PALEOMAGNETISM) indicates that throughout geological time the locality of either magnetic pole has varied considerably. The north magnetic pole, first located (1831) by English explorer Sir James C. Ross at lat. 70° 51'N and long. 96° 46'W, was placed in 1970 at about 76°N and 101°W. The south magnetic pole, reached (1909) by English geologists Sir T. W. E. David and Sir Douglas Mawson, was tentatively located by them at lat. 72°25'S and long. 155°16'E on Antarctica. In 1970, it was estimated to be at about 66°S and 139°E. The magnetic poles follow circular paths with the circles having diameters of about 100 miles (160 km). Recent studies of paleomagnetism indicate that the earth's magnetic field has reversed its polarity many times in the geologic past. The origin of terrestrial magnetism is imperfectly known. The best hypothesis to date is the self-exciting dynamo theory. It holds that the earth's magnetic field, and hence the magnetic poles, are generated and maintained by the interaction of motion and electrical currents in the earth's liquid outer core.

magnetic pyrite: see PYRRHOTITE.

magnetic resonance, in physics and chemistry, phenomenon produced by simultaneously applying a steady magnetic field and ELECTROMAGNETIC RADIATION (usually radio waves) to a sample of atoms and then adjusting the frequency of the radiation and the strength of the magnetic field to produce absorption of the radiation. The resonance refers to the enhancement of the absorption that occurs when the correct combination of field and frequency is reached. The procedure is analogous to tuning a radio dial exactly to a desired station. Several distinct kinds of magnetic resonance exist. In cyclotron resonance the magnetic field is adjusted so that the frequency of revolution of a charged particle around the field lines is exactly equal to the frequency of the radiation. This principle is used to produce beams of energetic particles in PARTICLE ACCELERATORS. Other magnetic resonance phenomena depend on the fact that both the proton and the electron exhibit intrinsic spin about their own axes and thus act like microscopic magnets. Electron paramagnetic resonance (EPR) arises from unpaired electron spins in liquids or solid crystals. Because of their own magnetism, the spins line up with the external magnetic field. For a given magnetic field the spins can be made to "flip" to the opposite direction when they absorb radiation at a corresponding "resonant" frequency. From the point of view of quantum mechanics, the spin flips can be considered as transitions between states that become separated in energy when the magnetic field is applied. The effect is related to the splitting of spectral lines when an atom is subjected to a magnetic field (see

SPECTRUM; ZEEMAN EFFECT). Nuclear magnetic resonance (NMR) is analogous to EPR; however NMR is produced by the much smaller magnetism associated with unpaired nuclear spins. The NMR resonant frequency (usually that of protons in complex molecules) is slightly shifted by interactions with nearby atoms in the sample, thus providing information about the chemical structure of organic molecules and other materials. Magnetic resonance can also occur in the absence of an external magnetic field as a result of the interactions of the electron and nuclear spins; such resonance produces the fine and hyperfine structure of atomic spectra.

magnetic tape: see COMPUTER; TAPE RECORDER.

magnetism, FORCE of attraction or repulsion between various substances, especially those made of iron and certain other metals; ultimately it is due to the motion of electric charges. The term *magnetism* is derived from *Magnesia,* the name of a region in Asia Minor where lodestone, a naturally magnetic iron ore, was found in ancient times. Any object that exhibits magnetic properties is called a magnet. Every magnet has two points, or poles, where most of its strength is concentrated; these are designated as a north-seeking pole, or north pole, and a south-seeking pole, or south pole, because a suspended magnet tends to orient itself along a north-south line. Since a magnet has two poles, it is sometimes called a magnetic dipole, being analogous to an electric dipole, composed of two opposite charges. The like poles of different magnets repel each other, and the unlike poles attract each other. From his study of magnetism, C. A. Coulomb in the 18th cent. found that the magnetic forces between two poles followed an inverse-square law of the same form as that describing the forces between electric charges. The law states that the force of attraction or repulsion between two magnetic poles is directly proportional to the product of the strengths of the poles and inversely proportional to the square of the distance between them. As with electric charges, the effect of this magnetic force acting at a distance is expressed in terms of a FIELD of force. A magnetic pole sets up a field in the space around it that exerts a force on magnetic materials. The field can be visualized in terms of lines of induction (similar to the lines of force of an electric field). These imaginary lines indicate the direction of the field in a given region. By convention they originate at the north pole of a magnet and form loops that end at the south pole either of the same magnet or of some other nearby magnet (see also FLUX, MAGNETIC). The lines are spaced so that the number per unit area is proportional to the field strength in a given area. Thus, the lines converge near the poles, where the field is strong, and spread out as their distance from the poles increases. A picture of these lines of induction can be made by placing a piece of paper over a magnet and sprinkling iron filings on it. The individual pieces of iron become magnetized by entering a magnetic field, i.e., they act like tiny magnets, lining themselves up along the lines of induction. By using variously shaped magnets and various combinations of more than one magnet, representations of the field in these different situations can be obtained. Iron is not the only material that is easily magnetized when placed in a magnetic field; others include nickel and cobalt. Materials that respond strongly to a magnetic field are called ferromagnetic [Lat. *ferrum*=iron]. The ability of a material to be magnetized or to strengthen the magnetic field in its vicinity is expressed by its magnetic permeability. Ferromagnetic materials have permeabilities of as much as 1,000 or more times that of free space (a vacuum). A number of materials are very weakly attracted by a magnetic field, having permeabilities slightly greater than that of free space; these materials are called paramagnetic. A few materials, such as bismuth and antimony, are repelled by a magnetic field, having permeabilities less than that of free space; these materials are called diamagnetic. One remarkable property of magnets is that whenever a magnet is broken, a north pole will appear at one of the broken faces and a south pole at the other, such that each piece has its own north and south poles. It is impossible to isolate a single magnetic pole, regardless of how many times a magnet is broken or how small the fragments become. (The theoretical question as to the possible existence in any state of a single magnetic pole, called a monopole, is still considered open by physicists; experiments to date have failed to detect one.) The connections between magnetism and electricity were discovered in the early part of the 19th cent. In 1820, H. C. Oersted found that a wire carrying an electrical current deflects the needle of a magnetic compass because a magnetic field is created by the moving electric charges constituting the current. It was found that the lines of induction of the magnetic field surrounding the wire (or any other conductor) are circular. If the wire is bent into a coil, called a solenoid, the magnetic fields of the individual loops combine to produce a strong field through the core of the coil. This field can be increased many fold by inserting a piece of soft iron or other ferromagnetic material into the core; the resulting arrangement constitutes an ELECTROMAGNET. Following Oersted's discovery the various magnetic effects of an electric current were extensively investigated by J. B. Biot, Félix Savart, and A. M. Ampère. Ampère showed in 1825 that not only does a current-carrying conductor exert a force on a magnet, but magnets also exert forces on current-carrying conductors. In 1831, Michael Faraday and Joseph Henry independently discovered that it is possible to produce a current in a conductor by changing the magnetic field about it. The discovery of this effect, called electromagnetic induction, together with the discovery that an electric current produces a magnetic field, laid the foundation for the modern age of electricity. Both the electric GENERATOR, which makes electricity widely available, and the electric MOTOR, which converts electricity to useful mechanical work, are based on these effects. Another relationship between electricity and magnetism is that a regularly changing electric current in a conductor will create a changing magnetic field in the space about the conductor, which in turn gives rise to a changing electrical field. In this way regularly oscillating electric and magnetic fields can generate each other. These fields can be visualized as a single wave that is propagating through space. The formal theory underlying this ELECTROMAGNETIC RADIATION was developed by James Clerk Maxwell in the middle of the 19th cent. Maxwell showed that the speed of propagation of electromagnetic radiation is identical with that of LIGHT, thus revealing that light is intimately connected with electricity and magnetism. The electric basis for the magnetic properties of matter has been verified down to the atomic level. Because the ELECTRON has both an electric charge and a spin, it can be called a charge in motion. This charge in motion gives rise to a tiny magnetic field. In the case of many atoms, all the electrons are paired within energy levels, according to the EXCLUSION PRINCIPLE, so that the electrons in each pair have opposite (antiparallel) spins and their magnetic fields cancel. In some atoms, however, there are more electrons with spins in one direction than in the other, resulting in a net magnetic field for the atom as a whole; this situation exists in a paramagnetic substance. If such a material is placed in an external field, e.g., the field created by an electromagnet, the individual atoms will tend to align their fields with the external one. The alignment will not be complete, due to the disruptive effect of thermal vibrations. Because of this, a paramagnetic substance is only weakly attracted by a magnet. In a ferromagnetic substance, there are also more electrons with spins in one direction than in the other. The individual magnetic fields of the atoms in a given region tend to line up in the same direction, so that they reinforce one another. Such a region is called a domain. In an unmagnetized sample, the domains are of different sizes and have different orientations. When an external magnetic field is applied, domains whose orientations are in the same general direction as the external field will grow at the expense of domains with other orientations. When the domains in all other directions have vanished, the remaining domains are rotated so that their direction is exactly the same as that of the external field. After this rotation is complete, no further magnetization can take place, no matter how strong the external field; a saturation point is said to have been reached. If the external field is then reduced to zero, it is found that the sample still retains some of its magnetism; this is known as hysteresis. If the external field is applied again in the opposite direction (increasing negative values), the magnetism of the ferromagnetic sample decreases to zero, then increases in the opposite direction to a second saturation point. Reversing the external field again will return the sample to its first saturation point. A graph of this cyclic process with the magnetism of the sample (more properly, magnetic induction or magnetic flux density) plotted as a function of external field strength is known as a hysteresis loop. The area enclosed within the hysteresis loop, which has the shape of an elongated S, reveals the relative ease or difficulty with which the sample may be magnetized and demagnetized. Soft iron and the iron-silicon alloys used for electromagnets and transformers have narrow hysteresis loops, so that the energy loss during changes in the magnetic field is minimized. The materials used for permanent magnets, on the other hand, have large hysteresis loops, reflecting their resistance to demagnetization. Carbon steel was long the material commonly used for permanent magnets, but more recently other materials have been developed that are much more efficient as permanent magnets, including certain ferroceramics and Alnico, an alloy containing iron, aluminum, nickel, cobalt, and copper. *Geomagnetism,* or *terrestrial magnetism,* as it was formerly called, refers to the magnetic properties of the earth. William Gilbert in his *De Magnete* (1600), the first scientific work on magnetism, showed that the earth behaves like a gigantic magnet. Freely suspended magnets, e.g., compass needles, line themselves up in a north-south direction along the lines of induction of the earth's magnetic field. The earth's magnetic poles are near, but not coincident with, the geographic poles. The angle between the direction of a compass needle at a given location and true north is the angle of declination for that location. Lines on a map connecting points with equal angles of declination are called isogonic lines; they correspond roughly to lines of magnetic longitude. If a compass needle is suspended so that it can move in a vertical direction as well, it is found that its position differs from the horizontal in most locations, the angle between the needle and the horizontal being known as the angle of dip, or angle of inclination; lines of equal dip are called isoclinic lines and correspond to lines of magnetic latitude. At the magnetic north pole a suspended compass needle, or dipping needle, will point straight down, and at the magnetic south pole it will point straight up. Along the magnetic equator the angle of dip is 0°. Because of various factors, such as deposits of ferromagnetic minerals, isogonic and isoclinic lines are not straight, as are lines of geographic longitude and latitude, but vary in an irregular manner. The earth's magnetic field is thought to be due to motions of charges within the dense, liquid core of the earth. It is affected by various factors, such as sunspots and the solar wind, and undergoes a regular daily variation. A number of scientists have made studies of geomagnetism, including Alexander von Humboldt, C. F. Gauss, and Johann von Lamont. An important discovery related to geomagnetism was that of the Van Allen radiation belts, bands of charged particles in the upper atmosphere trapped by the earth's magnetic field. See Francis Bitter, *Magnets* (1959); Dieter Wagner, *Introduction to the Theory of Magnetism* (1972).

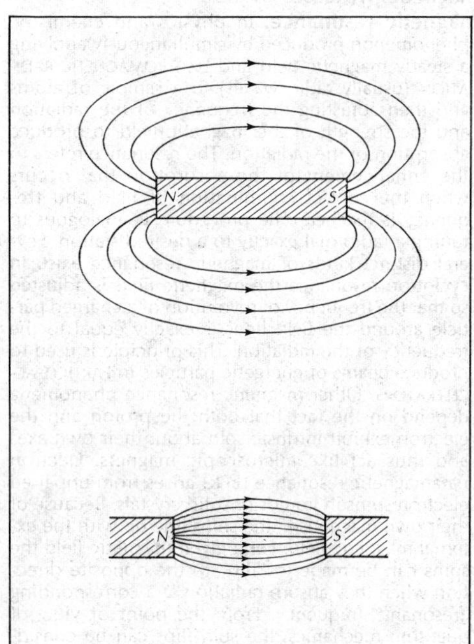

Lines of induction around a single bar magnet and between opposite poles of different magnets

magnetite (măg'nətīt), lustrous black, magnetic mineral, Fe_3O_4. It occurs in crystals of the cubic system, in masses, and as a loose sand. It is one of the important ores of iron (magnetic iron ore) and is a common constituent of igneous and metamorphic rocks. It is found in Norway, Sweden, the Urals, and various parts of the United States. A variety of magnetite, lodestone (or loadstone) exhibits polarity and is especially interesting for its natural magnetism; Magnet Cove, Ark., became famous as a source.

magneto: see GENERATOR.

magnetohydrodynamics (măgnē″tōhī″drōdĭnăm′ĭks) or **MHD,** study of the motions of electrically conducting fluids and their interactions with magnetic fields. The principles of magnetohydrodynamics are of particular importance in PLASMA physics. See NUCLEAR ENERGY.

magnetosphere: see VAN ALLEN RADIATION BELTS.

magnetron (măg′nĭtrŏn″), vacuum tube oscillator (see ELECTRON TUBE) that generates high-power electromagnetic signals in the MICROWAVE frequency range. Its operation is based on the combined action of a magnetic field applied externally and the electric field between its electrodes. The tube is a diode having a cathode and an anode and is surrounded by an external magnet. Without this external magnetic field, the tube would work much like a simple diode, with the electrons flowing directly from the cathode to the anode. The magnetic field forces the cathode-emitted electrons to assume a curved path and thus creates a rotating electron cloud about the tube axis. The magnetron is noted for its high efficiency (ability to convert electrical power input to microwave power output). Magnetrons are available for generating microwave energies ranging from a few kilowatts to a few megawatts.

Magnificat (măgnĭf′ĭkăt) [Lat.,=magnifies], song of the Virgin Mary, beginning "Magnificat anima mea Dominum" [my soul doth magnify the Lord], from Luke 1.46–55. It is the daily vesper hymn of the Roman Catholic Church and is usually sung at evening prayer in the Church of England.

magnifying glass: see MICROSCOPE.

Magnitogorsk (məgnyē″təgôrsk′), city (1970 pop. 364,000), SW Siberian USSR, on the slopes of Mt. Magnitnaya in the S Urals, on the Ural River. Built (1929–31) under the first Five-Year Plan on the site of iron and magnetite deposits, the city became an important symbol of Soviet industrial growth. Coking coal for steel production comes from the Kuznetsk and Karaganda basins; there are also coke and chemical plants. Magnitogorsk was a leading steel manufacturer during World War II and is still a major Soviet metallurgical center.

magnitude, in astronomy, measure of the brightness of a star or other celestial object. The stars cataloged by Ptolemy (2d cent. A.D.), all visible with the unaided eye, were ranked on a brightness scale such that the brightest stars were of 1st magnitude and the dimmest stars were of 6th magnitude. The modern magnitude scale was placed on a precise basis by N. R. Pogson (1856). It was found by photometric measurements that stars of the 1st magnitude were about 100 times as bright as stars of the 6th magnitude, i.e., 5 magnitudes lower. Pogson defined a difference of 5 magnitudes to be exactly equal to a hundredfold change in brightness, so that stars differing by 1 magnitude differ in brightness by a factor of 2.512 (the 5th root of 100). The modern magnitude scale permits a precise expression of a star's relative brightness and extends to both extremely bright and very dim objects. Thus, an object 2.512 times as bright as a 1st-magnitude star is of 0 magnitude; brighter objects have negative magnitudes. The sun's magnitude, for example, is −26.8. On the other hand, a faint star of 16th magnitude is only 1/10,000 as bright as a 6th-magnitude star, the dimmest that can be seen with the naked eye. Magnitudes determined on the basis of an object's relative brightness as seen from the earth are known as apparent magnitudes. Astronomers also assign a star an absolute magnitude, which is the magnitude that a star would have if it were located at a standard distance of 10 PARSECS (32.6 light-years). Absolute magnitude is a measure of the intrinsic LUMINOSITY of the star, i.e., its true brightness. Since in modern times magnitudes are measured with photometers and photographic plates, which may be more sensitive to light at one wavelength than at another wavelength, it is necessary to specify the method used when comparing two or more magnitudes. The magnitude usually referred to is the visual, or photovisual, magnitude, measured with a photometer. Magnitudes determined with standardized photographic plates, which are more sensitive to blue light, are called photographic magnitudes. A star's COLOR INDEX is the difference between its photographic magnitude and its visual magnitude.

Magnolia, city (1970 pop. 11,303), seat of Columbia co., SW Ark.; inc. 1855. Its oil industry has been important since 1938. Textiles, chemicals, lumber, and metal and plastic products are also produced. Southern State College is there.

magnolia, common name for plants of the genus *Magnolia,* and for the Magnoliaceae, a family of deciduous or evergreen trees and shrubs, often with showy flowers. They are principally of north temperate regions with centers of distribution in Asia and E North America. Among the few native American species of the chiefly Asian genus *Magnolia* are the deciduous umbrella tree (*M. tripetala*); the cucumber tree (*M. acuminata*), named for the appearance of its unripe fruits; the evergreen sweet, or swamp, bay (*M. virginiana*); and the bull bay, or Southern magnolia (*M. grandiflora*), with enormous blossoms resembling water lilies. Many imported magnolias are also cultivated in the South, as are several species of the Asiatic genus *Michelia.* The only other member of the family native to America is the tulip tree (*Liriodendron tulipfera*), named for the tulip-like shape of its greenish-yellow, orange-centered blossoms. The tulip tree, relic of a past geological era when it was widespread throughout North America and Europe, now grows only in the E United States and in China. Its yellowish softwood, prized for cabinetwork and furniture, is commonly called yellow poplar, canary wood, or whitewood. The magnolia family is possibly the most primitive group of angiosperms. The magnolia family is classified in the division MAGNOLIOPHYTA, class Magnoliopsida, order Magnoliales.

Magnoliophyta (măg″nōlēŏf′ətə), division of the plant kingdom consisting of those organisms commonly called the flowering plants, or ANGIOSPERMS. The angiosperms have leaves, stems, and roots, and vascular, or conducting, tissue (xylem and phloem). The ovules, which develop into seeds, are enclosed within an ovary, hence the term angiosperm, meaning "enclosed seed." The flowering plants are the source of all agricultural crops, cereal grains and grasses, ornamentals, garden and roadside weeds, and familiar broad-leaved shrubs and trees.

Class Magnoliopsida (dicotyledons). Plants of this class have two seed leaves, or cotyledons, and cambium tissue in the stems (see MERISTEM). Much the larger of the two classes of flowering plants, dicots are divided into many families, among which several of the more conspicuous and easily recognized are the WILLOW, BUTTERCUP, PINK, MUSTARD, SAXIFRAGE, ROSE, PEA, heather (see HEATH), GENTIAN, BLUEBELL, and ASTER families.

Class Liliatae (monocotyledons). Plants of this class have only one seed leaf, or cotyledon, and generally lack cambium tissue. The most common families are the GRASS, PALM, ARUM, SEDGE, LILY, AMARYLLIS, and ORCHID families.

Magnus I (Magnus the Good), 1024–47, king of Norway (1035–47) and Denmark (1042–47), son of OLAF II. He was recalled from exile in 1035 by the former opponents of Olaf when they rebelled against Sweyn, son of CANUTE. In 1038 he made a treaty with another son of Canute, Harthacanute of Denmark, by which either king, if he died without an heir, was to be succeeded by the other. Magnus at first dealt harshly with his father's enemies and kept the oppressive laws of Sweyn in force, but later he granted an amnesty and revoked Sweyn's laws. He succeeded (1042) Harthacanute in Denmark and claimed the throne of England, but he was prevented from pressing his claim by the necessity of crushing a Danish revolt and of fighting against the WENDS. In 1046 he consented to dividing the Norwegian realm with his uncle HAROLD III, who became sole king at Magnus's death.

Magnus VI (Magnus the Law Mender), 1238–80, king of Norway (1263–80), son of Haakon IV. A man of peace, he brought an end to the Scottish war by ceding (1266) the Hebrides and the Isle of Man to Alexander III of Scotland for a large sum. He immediately undertook a general revision of the laws, introducing (1274) a new code for the kingdom and subsequently new municipal laws. His code introduced the concept that crime is an offense against the state rather than against the individual and thus narrowed the possibilities of personal vengeance. It greatly increased the power of the king, making the throne the source of justice. The municipal law gave the cities increased freedom from rural control. One of his enactments fixed the law of succession to the throne; another, by its creation of a new royal council and of new ranks of nobility, laid the foundation of a new governing class. In 1277, Magnus and the church reached an agreement on the limits of church and state power. He was succeeded by his sons, Eric II (reigned 1280–99), who was the father of Margaret Maid of Norway, and Haakon V (reigned 1299–1319). See L. M. Larson, *The Earliest Norwegian Laws* (1934).

Magnus VII (Magnus Ericsson), b.1316, d.1373 or 1374, king of Norway (1319–43) and Sweden (1319–63). He succeeded his grandfather, Haakon V, in Norway; at the same time he was elected king by the Swedish nobles to succeed his exiled uncle, King Birger of Sweden. He was declared of age in 1332. Educated in Sweden, he neglected Norway and soon became unpopular there. Norwegian opposition to union with Sweden forced him to recognize (1343) his son Haakon (later Haakon VI) as his successor in Norway, over which he exercised a nominal regency until Haakon came of age (1355). Early in his reign Magnus had acquired the Danish provinces of Skåne and Blekinge in S Sweden, but in 1343 Waldemar IV of Denmark forced him to sell these acquisitions back to Denmark. Magnus's son Eric revolted in 1356 and gained part of Sweden, but Magnus regained control after Eric's death (1359). The threat of the Hanseatic League, which established its colony at Bergen during Magnus's reign, induced Magnus and Haakon VI to enter (1363) an alliance with Denmark. Haakon married Waldemar's daughter MARGARET I, thus preparing the union of Sweden, Norway, and Denmark. The Danish alliance was unpopular with the Swedish nobles, who deposed both Magnus and Haakon and offered the Swedish crown to the duke of Mecklenburg. The duke's son, Albert, thus became (1363) king of Sweden. Magnus was imprisoned until 1371 and spent his last years in Norway. The codification of Swedish law was completed in Magnus's reign.

Magnus, Heinrich Gustav (hīn′rĭkh gōōs′täf mäg′nōōs), 1802–70, German chemist, physicist, and educator. In 1831 he became lecturer and in 1834 professor of physics and technology at the Univ. of Berlin. A brilliant and highly popular teacher, Magnus introduced the seminar and the teaching laboratory and was influential in the science of his time. The scope of his interests was broad; he was the first to prepare a platino-ammonium compound (Magnus's green salt) and several acids and their salts. From his study of projectiles was developed the theory of the "Magnus effect," the lateral force on rotating cylinders in air currents. His other investigations included studies in thermoelectricity, electrolysis, and vapor pressure.

Magnus Colorado: see MANGAS COLORADAS.

Magnusson, Árni or **Árne** (our′nĭ mäg′nōōsôn), 1663–1730, Icelandic historian and antiquarian. He taught at the Univ. of Copenhagen, and his important collection of ancient Icelandic manuscripts is housed there.

Magnusson, Finnur (fĭn′nər), 1781–1847, Icelandic archaeologist and scholar. Educated at the Univ. of Copenhagen, he was appointed (1815) professor of Northern literature and mythology there. He compiled, edited, and translated the *Elder Edda* and published a lexicon of Norse mythology (1828) and works on the origin of the *Edda* sayings.

Magog (mā′gŏg), in the Bible. **1** Son of Japheth. Gen. 10.2. **2** See GOG.

Magog, city (1971 pop. 13,281), S Que., Canada, on Lake Memphremagog, SW of Sherbrooke. Founded by Loyalist emigrants from the United States after 1776, Magog is a resort and trade center, with textile mills and dairying.

Magoon, Charles Edward (məgōōn′), 1861–1920, American administrator, b. Steele co., Minn. As an attorney (1899–1904) for the Bureau of Insular Affairs in the War Dept., he dealt with the legal problems of American expansion. In 1904 he was made counsel for the Panama Canal Commission and prepared laws for the Canal Zone, and in 1905 he became governor of the Canal Zone and minister to Panama. He was provisional governor of Cuba during the U.S. military occupation of 1906 to 1909. He wrote *The Law of Civil Government under Military Occupation* (1902).

Magor-missabib (mā′gôr-mĭs′əbĭb), name given by Jeremiah to the man who put him in the stocks. Jer. 20.3.

Magpiash (măgpī′ăsh), signer of the Covenant. Neh. 10.20.

magpie, common name for certain birds of the family Corvidae (crows and jays). The black-billed magpie, *Pica pica,* of W North America has iridescent black plumage, white wing patches and abdomen, and a long wedge-shaped tail. It is altogether about 20 in. (50 cm) long. Magpies build large, domed nests in trees. Nest-building is part of courtship. The female alone incubates the eggs. Magpies destroy other birds' eggs and young and kill sickly, wounded, or newborn sheep and cows by pecking. They are scavengers (often collecting small bright objects), but they also eat harmful insects as well as fruits, berries, and leaves. Noisy, chattering birds, in captivity they can be taught to imitate some words. The yellow-billed magpie is found in the valleys of California. The European magpie is closely related to the American; other species are found in Asia and Africa. The magpie-lark belongs to a different family, Grallinidae. Magpies are classified in the phylum CHORDATA, subphylum Vertebrata, class Aves, order Passeriformes, family Corvidae.

Magritte, René (rənä' mägrĕt'), 1898–1967, Belgian surrealist painter. Strongly influenced by CHIRICO, Magritte developed a style in which a misleading sort of realism is combined with mocking irony. His paintings are dominated by an intense quietude and restraint, despite a startling juxtaposition of images. Characteristic works, such as *The Red Model* (1935; Modern Mus., Stockholm), contain elaborate fantasies constructed around commonplace situations. See studies by Suzi Gablik (1970) and A. M. Hammacher (tr. 1974).

Magruder, John Bankhead (məgro͞o'dər), 1810–71, Confederate general in the American Civil War, b. Winchester, Va. His reckless daring in the Mexican War won him quick promotion in the army. At the outbreak of the Civil War he resigned and was made colonel in the Confederate army. In June, 1861, he defeated Benjamin F. Butler at Big Bethel. Promoted to major general (Oct., 1861), Magruder distinguished himself in the Peninsular campaign (1862). As commander of the Dept. of Texas (1862–64), he recaptured Galveston on Jan. 1, 1863. After the war he served (1866–67) as a major general in the army of Emperor Maximilian of Mexico.

Magsaysay, Ramón (rämōn' mägsī'sī), 1907–57, president of the Philippines (1953–57), b. Iba, Zambales prov., Luzon. When the Japanese invaded the Philippines (1941), he joined the army and was commissioned a captain. He was a guerrilla leader throughout the Japanese occupation and was named (1945) military governor of Zambales prov. by Gen. Douglas MacArthur. While serving in the Philippine Congress (1946–50) Magsaysay presented a plan for subduing the Hukbalahap (Huk) guerrillas, who were then at the height of their power. The plan was approved, and Magsaysay was appointed secretary of national defense by President Elpidio QUIRINO. With often unorthodox but direct methods, he reformed the army, captured the top members of the Communist party, and fought the Huks under a strategy that combined strong military action with a land resettlement program. After a dispute with President Quirino, however, Magsaysay resigned his post (1953). He left the ruling Liberal party and ran for president on the Nationalist ticket, defeating Quirino by a large majority. As president he cooperated closely with the United States and pursued a program of land and governmental reform. He was favored to win reelection to a second term but died in an airplane crash (1957) before the voting began. See biographies by Carlos Quirino (2d. ed. 1964) and M. M. Gray (1965).

maguey: see AMARYLLIS.

Magyars (mŏd'yärz, măg'yärz), the dominant people of HUNGARY, but also living in Rumania, the Soviet Union, Czechoslovakia, and Yugoslavia. Although in the past it was thought that some common origin existed among the Magyars, the Huns, the Mongols, and the Turks, modern research has disproved this claim. The only similarity between the Magyars and the peoples named above was their mode of life when they first appeared in Europe in the 9th cent. The Magyar or Hungarian language belongs to the Finno-Ugric family. A nomadic nation, the Magyars migrated (c.460) from the Urals to the Northern Caucasus region. They remained there for about 400 years; during a portion of that time they were allied with the Khazars. Contact with Turkic peoples seems to have been close, for many Magyar words of Turkish origin, relating to animal husbandry and political and military organization, were in use before the 9th cent. Late in the 9th cent. the advance of the PECHENEGS forced the Magyars westward across S Russia and into present Rumania. Under their leader Arpad they defeated the Bulgar czar Simeon I, but Simeon, with the help of the Pechenegs, forced them northward into Hungary, which they permanently settled c.895. They were described as ferocious warriors. They conquered Moravia and penetrated deep into Germany until they were checked (955) by Holy Roman Emperor Otto I at the Lechfeld. Under St. STEPHEN, Christianity was introduced early in the 11th cent., and the Magyars consolidated their state. They absorbed the other ethnic groups of Hungary proper. The SZÉKELY are presumably closely related to them. The terms *Magyar* and *Hungarian* are identical, but in non-Hungarian languages the word *Magyar* is frequently used to distinguish the Hungarian-speaking population of Hungary from the German, Slavic, and Rumanian minorities, which were considerable until the end of World War I, when Hungary lost its border provinces. For Magyar literature, see HUNGARIAN LITERATURE. See C. A. Macartney, *The Magyars in the Ninth Century* (1930, repr. 1968); I. M. Bobula, *Origin of the Hungarian Nation* (1966).

Mahabalipuram (məhä'bəlĭpo͝orəm), village, Tamil Nadu state, SE India, on the Coromandel Coast. Archaeological remains there represent some of the earliest-known examples of Dravidian architecture (c.7th cent. A.D.) in India. Under the patronage of the Pallava dynasty, numerous temples, hewn from granite hillocks, were carved. The site is often called the Seven Pagodas because of the high pinnacles of seven of its temples. It is also called Mamallapuram.

Mahabharata (məhä'bär'ətə), classical Sanskrit epic of India, probably composed between 200 B.C. and A.D. 200. The *Mahabharata,* comprising more than 90,000 couplets, usually of 32 syllables, is the longest single poem in world literature. The 18-book work is traditionally ascribed to the ancient sage, Vyasa, but it was undoubtedly composed by a number of bardic poets and later revised by priests, who interpolated many long passages on theology, morals, and statecraft. It is the foremost source concerning classical Indian civilization and Hindu ideals. While there are many subplots and irrelevant tales, the *Mahabharata* is primarily the fabulous account of a dynastic struggle and great civil war in the kingdom of Kurukshetra, which in the 9th cent. B.C. encompassed the region around modern Delhi. The throne of Kurukshetra fell to the prince Dhritarashtra, but he was blind and therefore, according to custom, not eligible to rule. Pandu, his younger brother, became king instead, but he renounced the throne and retired as a hermit to the Himalayas; Dhritarashtra then became king. When the five sons of Pandu, the Pandavas, came of age, the eldest, Yuddhisthira, demanded the throne from his uncle, Dhritarashtra. However, the hundred sons of Dhritarashtra, the Kauravas, treacherously plotted against the Pandavas, the rightful heirs. The five brothers were eventually driven from the kingdom by the Kauravas, and in exile as soldiers of fortune they married in common the Princess Draupadi. Dhritarashtra renounced the throne and divided the kingdom between them and his own sons. The Kauravas, not content with the territorial settlement, challenged the Pandavas to a great dice match, at which they won the entire kingdom by devious means. After many years of wandering the Pandavas returned with their friend KRISHNA to reclaim the kingdom, but the Kauravas refused to abdicate and a great battle ensued. Before the battle began, Krishna preached the exalted BHAGAVAD-GITA. The forces engaged, and after three weeks of fighting, the Pandavas won. Yuddhisthira, the eldest, ascended the throne. After a long and peaceful reign he and his brothers abdicated and with their wife Draupadi set out for the Himalayas, where they entered the blissful City of the Gods. The philosophy set forth throughout the work emphasizes social duty and ascetic principles. Its theology is enormously complex. The other great Sanskrit epic is the RAMAYANA. See translations of the *Mahabharata* by M. N. Dutt (8 vol., 1895–1905, repr. 1960), C. V. Narasimhan (1965), J. A. B. van Buitenen (Vol. I, 1974; 6 vol. projected); study by R. K. Sharma (1964).

Mahalah (mähä'lə), child of the sister of Gilead. 1 Chron. 7.18.

Mahalaleel (mä"həlā'lēĕl). **1** Descendant of Adam. Gen. 5.12; 1 Chron. 1.2. Maleleel: Luke 3.37. **2** Judahite. Neh. 11.4.

Mahalath and **Mahalath Leannoth:** see AIJELETH SHAHAR.

Mahali (mähä'lī), variant of MAHLI.

Mahan, Alfred Thayer (məhăn'), 1840–1914, U.S. naval officer and historian, b. West Point, N.Y. A Union naval officer in the Civil War, he later lectured on naval history and strategy at the Naval War College, Newport, R.I., of which he was president (1886–89, 1892–93). Out of his lectures grew his two major works on the historical significance of sea power—*The Influence of Sea Power upon History, 1660–1783* (1890) and *The Influence of Sea Power upon the French Revolution and Empire, 1793–1812* (2 vol., 1892). In these he argued that naval power was the key to success in international politics; the nation that controlled the seas held the decisive factor in modern warfare. Mahan's work appeared at a time when the nations of Europe and Japan were engaged in a fiercely competitive arms race. His books were quickly translated into several languages and were widely read by political leaders, especially in Germany, where they were used as a justification for a naval buildup. In the United States, Theodore Roosevelt and other proponents of a big navy and overseas expansion were much influenced by Mahan's writings. Among his many works are biographies of David Farragut and Horatio Nelson and the autobiographical *From Sail to Steam* (1907, repr. 1968). See biography by W. D. Puleston (1939).

Mahan, Dennis Hart, 1802–71, American soldier and educator, b. New York City; father of Alfred Thayer Mahan. He graduated (1824) from West Point, and from that year until 1871, except for four years (1826–30) spent in France studying public works and institutions, Mahan taught civil and military engineering at the Military Academy. A recognized authority on military engineering, Mahan wrote texts long considered as standard. As a member of the academic board he also contributed greatly to the development of education at West Point. His works include *Complete Treatise on Field Fortifications* (1836), *Summary on the Cause of Permanent Fortifications and of the Attack and Defense of Permanent Works* (1850), and *An Elementary Course of Military Engineering* (2 vol., 1866–67).

Mahanadi (məhä'nədē), river, c.550 mi (885 km) long, rising in SE Madhya Pradesh state, central India, and flowing north then east through a gorge in the Eastern Ghats, across Orissa state, forming a delta before entering the Bay of Bengal near Cuttack. The Tel and Hasdo rivers are its main tributaries. During the rainy season, the river causes severe floods. The Mahanadi irrigates a fertile valley whose chief crops are rice, oilseed, and sugarcane.

Mahanaim (mā"hənā'ĭm), unidentified city E of the Jordan River near the Jabbok. There Jacob met angels; there, also, David took refuge from Absalom. Gen. 32.2,22; Joshua 21.38; 2 Sam. 2.8; 17.24–27; 19.32; 1 Kings 4.14.

Mahaneh-dan (mähä'nĕ-dăn"), unidentified place near Jerusalem. Judges 13.25; 18.12.

Maharai (mā'hərī), one of David's men. 2 Sam. 23.28; 1 Chron. 11.30; 27.13.

Maharashtra (məhä'rəshtrə), state (1971 pop. 50,335,492), 118,530 sq mi (306,993 sq km), W India, on the Arabian Sea. The city of BOMBAY is the capital. The state was formed in 1960, when the old state of Bombay was split along linguistic lines into two new states, Maharashtra and Gujarat. Marathi is the official language of the state, and Hinduism is the predominant religion. The mountains of the Western Ghats run parallel to the coast of the state, leaving a narrow strip known as the Konkan between the Arabian Sea and the lofty mountain barrier. There is a series of small ports along the coast in addition to Bombay. Beyond the Western Ghats is a vast plateau drained by the Tapti, Godavari, Bhima, Krishna, Wardha, and Valnganga rivers. The great Tapti trough, a fertile belt where cotton is cultivated, is there. The heaviest rainfall is along the coastal area, where it averages 80 to 120 in. (203–305 cm) a year. In the plateau areas, 25 to 80 in. (64–203 cm) of rain fall annually. The climate in general is tropical. Rice, grown in the coastal area, is the principal food crop. The state is rich in minerals; manganese, iron ore, bauxite, coal, and salt are mined. Industry, including the manufacture of textiles, electrical products, and chemicals, is mainly concentrated in Bombay, Poona, Aurangabad, and Nagpur. The Muslim rulers of India controlled the area of Maharashtra from the early 14th cent. to the mid-17th cent., when the great Mahratta leader SIVAJI formed a Maharashtran confederacy. In the 16th cent., Portugal was the leading foreign power in the region, but Great Britain gradually gained influence and by the early 19th cent. had incorporated the Maharashtran area into the Bombay presidency, which later became a province of British India. Maharashtra is governed by a chief minister and cabinet responsible to a bicameral legislature with one elected house and by a governor appointed by the president of India. See Ravindar Kumar, *Western India in the Nineteenth Century* (1968) and C. D. Deshpande, *Geography of Maharashtra* (1971).

Mahath (mā'hăth). **1** Ancestor of the singer Heman. 1 Chron. 6.35. **2** Levite serving under Hezekiah. 2 Chron. 31.13.

mahatma (məhăt'mə, -hät'-) [Sanskrit,=great-souled], title used in India among Hindus for a person of superior holiness. It is without theological significance. Mohandas Gandhi is the best-known figure to whom the title was applied.

Mahavira: see JAINISM.

Mahavite (mā'hăvīt, măhā'vīt), obscure family name of one of David's guard. 1 Chron. 11.46.

Mahayana Buddhism: see BUDDHISM.

Mahazioth (məhā'zēōth), leader of temple musicians. 1 Chron. 25.4,30.

Mahdi (mä'dē) [Arab.,=he who is divinely guided], in Sunni ISLAM, the restorer of the faith. He will appear at the end of time to restore justice on earth and establish universal Islam. The Mahdi will be preceded by al-Dajjal, a Muslim antichrist, who will be slain by Jesus. This belief is not rooted in the Koran but has its origins in Jewish ideas about the Messiah and in the Christian belief of the second coming of Christ. Among the SHIITES the concept of the Mahdi takes a different form (see IMAM). In the history of Islam, many men have arisen who claimed to be the Mahdi. They usually appeared as reformers antagonistic to established authority. One such man, who became famous in Western history, was **Muhammad Ahmad,** 1844–85, a Muslim religious leader in the Anglo-Egyptian Sudan. He declared himself in 1881 to be the Mahdi and led a war of liberation from the oppressive Egyptian military occupation. He died soon after capturing Khartoum. In his reform of Islam the Mahdi forbade the pilgrimage to Mecca and substituted the obligation to serve in the holy war against unbelievers. His followers, known as Mahdists, for a time made pilgrimages to his tomb at Omdurman. The final defeat of the Mahdists in 1898 at Omdurman by an Anglo-Egyptian army under Lord Kitchener gave Great Britain control of the Sudan. See P. M. Holt, *The Mahdist State in the Sudan* (2d ed. 1970).

Mahdia: see AL MAHDIYAH, Tunisia.

Mahé: see SEYCHELLES.

Maher-shalal-hash-baz (mā'ər-shăl'əl-hăsh-băz), symbolic name of a son of Isaiah. Isa. 8.1,3.

Mahgoub, Muhammad Ahmad (mōōhăm'mäd äkhmäd' mä'gōō), 1908–, Sudanese political leader. After twice serving as Sudan's minister of foreign affairs (1956–58, 1964–65), he was elected prime minister (1965) but was forced by the constituent assembly to resign in the following year. He was again elected prime minister in 1967, and in August of that year he hosted an Arab summit conference designed to coordinate strategy against Israel. Mahgoub's government was deposed (1969) in a coup led by Muhammad Gaafur al-Nimeiry and other left-wing officers. A writer, Mahgoub has published several volumes of poetry in Arabic.

Mahican Indians (məhē'kən), confederacy of North American Indians of the Algonquian branch of the Algonquian-Wakashan linguistic stock (see AMERICAN INDIAN LANGUAGES). The Mahican were of the Eastern Woodlands culture area. In the early 17th cent. they occupied both banks of the upper Hudson River extending north almost to Lake Champlain. Living to the northeast were the Pennacook Indians, and to the southwest the Wappinger Indians; both were closely related to the Mahican. The MOHEGAN INDIANS were a tribe of the Mahican Confederacy and are to be distinguished from the larger group. However, both groups have on occasion been referred to as Mohicans. When the Dutch arrived in what is now New York the Mohawk had been at war with the Mahican for some time and had steadily driven the Mahican east of the Hudson River. The Mahican council fire, or capital, had been moved (1664) from Schodac, near Albany, eastward to what is now Stockbridge, Mass. The complete subjection and dispersal of the Mahican were hastened by the firearms provided to their enemies by the Dutch. Some of the Mahican moved west to join the Delaware Indians, with whom they afterwards moved to the Ohio region (where the Mahican refugees lost their identity). Others placed themselves under the protection of the Iroquois Confederacy in S central New York. Those remaining in Massachusetts joined the Massachusetts STOCKBRIDGE INDIANS; other Mahican descendants live in Connecticut and Wisconsin. See Alanson Skinner, *Notes on Mahikan Ethnology* (1925).

mahimahi: see DOLPHIN (fish).

mah jongg (mä jông), four-handed game, probably of Chinese origin, popular in the United States. It is played in many variations throughout China. In 1920, Joseph P. Babcock, an American traveler in China, devised a set of rules for Western play and invented a complete terminology. He patented the game under the trade mark Mah Jongg. The game enjoyed a remarkable popularity. The goal of the game, which is similar in principle to rummy, is to accumulate sets. The equipment for the currently popular mah jongg set consists of 152 tiles—small rectangular blocks of wood with ivory or bone faces. There are 108 suit tiles, 16 wind tiles, 12 dragon tiles, 8 flower tiles, and 8 jokers. The three suits are bamboo, or sticks; circles, or dots; and characters, or cracks. Both the distribution of tiles and succeeding play are complicated.

Mahlah (mā'lə), daughter and coheiress of Zelophehad. Num. 27.1–11.

Mahler, Gustav (gōōs'täf mä'lər), 1860–1911, composer and conductor, born in Austrian Bohemia of Jewish parentage. Mahler studied at the Univ. of Vienna and the Vienna Conservatory. He was conductor of the Budapest Imperial Opera (1888–90), the Hamburg Municipal Theater (1891–97), the Vienna State Opera (1897–1907), and the New York Philharmonic (1909–11). He also conducted the Metropolitan Opera (1908–10). As a conductor Mahler achieved high standards of performance that have become legendary. His refusal to compromise artistic integrity aroused intense personal opposition in Vienna and New York. Composing mainly during summers, he completed nine symphonies (the unfinished tenth has been completed by Deryck Cooke) and several songs and song cycles, mostly with orchestral accompaniment. Of the cycles, *Lieder eines fahrenden Gesellen* [songs of a wayfarer] (1883–85), *Kindertotenlieder* [songs on the death of children] (1901–4), and *Das Lied von der Erde* [song of the earth] (1907–10) are most notable. Mahler followed Bruckner in the Viennese symphonic tradition. He added folk elements to the symphony and expanded it in terms of length, emotional contrast, and orchestral size. He used choral or solo voices in four symphonies: the Second, Third, Fourth, and Eighth; the Eighth is known as the Symphony of a Thousand because of the enormous performing forces required. The thinner texture, wide-ranging melodies, and taut, intense emotionalism of Mahler's late works strongly influenced the next generation of Austrian composers, especially Arnold Schoenberg and Alban Berg. See his letters ed. by Alma Mahler and Donald Mitchell (3d ed., tr. 1973); biographies by Bruno Walter (tr. 1941, repr. 1970), Kurt Blaukopf (tr. 1972), and H. L. de LaGrange (vol. I, 1973).

Mahli (mā'lī, mä'-). **1** Son of Merari. 1 Chron. 6.19,29; 23.21; 24.26. Mahali: Ex. 6.19. **2** Grandson of Merari. 1 Chron. 6.47; 23.23; 24.30.

Mahlon (mā'lən), Ruth's husband. Ruth 1.2,5; 4.9,10.

Mahmud I (mämōōd', mä'mōōd), 1696–1754, Ottoman sultan (1730–54), son of Mustafa II, nephew and successor of AHMED III. A revolt of the JANISSARIES put him on the throne of the Ottoman Empire (Turkey). Affairs of state were largely in the capable hands of the Nubian agha [officer], Beshir (1653–1746), who was the power behind a number of successive grand viziers (chief executive officers). During Mahmud's reign the Ottoman Empire was involved in wars with Persia. War with Russia broke out in 1736. Holy Roman Emperor CHARLES VI entered the war in 1737 on the Russian side, but by the separate peace of Belgrade (1739) he restored N Serbia to Turkey. Russia made peace soon afterward and was forced to raze Azov. Mahmud built many splendid buildings in Constantinople. He was succeeded by his brother, Osman III, who was in turn succeeded (1757) by Mustafa III, son of Ahmed III.

Mahmud II, 1784–1839, Ottoman sultan (1808–39), younger son of Abd al-Hamid I. He was raised to the throne of the Ottoman Empire (Turkey) upon the deposition of his brother, MUSTAFA IV, and continued the reforms of his cousin, SELIM III. During his reign the EASTERN QUESTION assumed increasing importance. Mahmud inherited the Russo-Turkish War of 1806–12, which ended with Turkey's loss of Bessarabia. However, Russia was obliged to end its support of the Serbian rebels under KARAGEORGE, and Serbia returned (1813) to Turkish control. In 1817, Mahmud recognized MILOŠ as prince of Serbia, a Turkish vassal. He suppres[illegible]
and defeated th[illegible]
Greek War of Ind[illegible]
power he ruthlessly [illegible]
ished project—the de[illegible]
whose political power [illegible]
Turkish successes in Gree[illegible]
troops sent by the viceroy [illegible]
under the command of IBRAH[illegible]
sian, and French intervention l[illegible]
(1827) of the Egyptian fleet at Na[illegible]
Turkish War of 1828–29, a humili[illegible]
ADRIANOPLE, TREATY OF), and the in[illegible] of
GREECE. The sequel of the Greek war [illegible] inva-
sion of Turkey by Ibrahim Pasha after M[illegible]hmud had refused to give Syria to Muhammad Ali as reward for his aid against the Greeks. At Konya the Turkish army was completely routed (1832), and Constantinople was saved only by the intervention of a Russian fleet. Mahmud was obliged to accede (1833) to Muhammad Ali's demands and, by a secret agreement with Russia, promised to close the Dardanelles to all warships hostile to Russia. In 1839 war with Egypt was resumed, and on the day of Mahmud's death news came of the ignominious surrender of the Turkish fleet in the harbor of Alexandria. Mahmud's son and successor, Abd al-Majid, granted Egypt virtual independence. Thus, despite the efforts of one of its most forceful and able rulers, the decay of the Ottoman Empire had still advanced. However, Mahmud laid the basis for a modern Turkey. He not only initiated the reform of the Turkish army, begun in 1835 by H. K. B. von MOLTKE, but he sought to Westernize the whole structure of the state and he destroyed the old feudal pattern of his empire.

Mahmud of Ghazni (mämōōd', gŭz'nē), 971?–1030, Afghan emperor and conqueror. He defeated (c.999) his elder brother to gain control of Khurasan (in Iran) and of Afghanistan. Mahmud, a staunch Muslim, was the scourge of the heterodox and the infidel. In his raids against the states of N India he destroyed Hindu temples, forced conversions to Islam, and carried off booty and slaves. Hindus especially abhorred his destruction of the temple to Siva at Somnath in Gujarat. Mahmud's territorial gains lay mainly W and N of Afghanistan and in the Punjab. He was a patron of literature and art. At Ghazni, his capital, he built a magnificent mosque. His successors in the Ghaznavid dynasty, which he founded, ruled over a reduced domain with the capital at Lahore until 1186. See biographies by Muhammed Nazim (1931) and M. Habib (2d ed. 1967).

mahogany, common name for the Meliaceae, a widely distributed family of chiefly tropical shrubs and trees, often having scented wood. The valuable hardwood called mahogany is obtained from many members of the family; in America and Europe it is imported for cabinetmaking and similar uses. According to tradition it was first introduced to England from the West Indies when Sir Walter Raleigh had a mahogany table made for Queen Elizabeth I; the popularity of the wood increased steadily in the 18th cent. The different mahoganies vary in color from golden to deep red brown; most are close-grained and resistant to termites. The principal sources are the tropical American genus *Swietenia* (especially *S. mahogani,* found as far north as Florida) and the W African genus *Khaya* (especially *K. ivorensis*). Another member of the family is the West Indian cedar, or cigar-box tree (*Cedrela odorata*), whose scented, insect-repellent wood is commonly used for cigar boxes. The wood of the chinaberry tree (*Melia azedarach*) of Asia, introduced to the United States as an ornamental and now naturalized in the South, is also used for lumber. The name mahogany is also given to numerous unrelated tropical trees that provide similar lumber. The mahogany family is classified in the division MAGNOLIOPHYTA, class Magnoliopsida, order Lapindales.

Mahol (mā'hŏl), father of wise men. 1 Kings 4.31.

Mahomet: see MUHAMMAD.

Mahón (mäōn'), town (1970 pop. 19,279), capital and chief town of Minorca island, Baleares prov., Spain, in the W Mediterranean Sea. A port with an excellent natural harbor defended by two fortresses, it is also an important air and naval base. Mahón was named for the Carthaginian general Mago. It shared the history of MINORCA.

Mahone, William (məhōn'), 1826–95, Confederate general in the American Civil War and Virginia politician, b. Southampton co., Va. He was president, chief engineer, and superintendent of the Norfolk-Petersburg RR when the Civil War broke out. Ma-

[illegible] the Confederate army and [illegible] the campaigns of the Army of [illegible]inia. He distinguished himself particu[illegible] [illegible]ETERSBURG, where on June 30, 1864, he re[illegible]ed the Union assault at "the Crater." For this he was immediately promoted to major general. After the war he resumed his railroad activities and entered politics. Mahone became the leader of the Readjusters, Virginia Democrats who advocated the partial repudiation of the state debt and popular social and economic reforms. He led them to victory in the state elections of 1879 and 1881, and was himself elected (1880) to the U.S. Senate. By allying himself with the Republicans there, Mahone was able to build a powerful machine that controlled Virginia Republican politics for several years. See biography by N. M. Blake (1935).

Mahoning (məhōn'ĭng), river, c.90 mi (140 km) long, rising in NE Ohio, E of Canton. It flows NW to Alliance, then NE past Warren, where it turns southeast to flow past Youngstown into NW Pennsylvania and joins the Shenango River to form the Beaver River. It drains an exceptionally fertile valley. Berlin Dam (completed 1943), on the upper Mahoning, provides flood control and water supply.

Mahony, Francis Sylvester, pseud. **Father Prout,** 1804–66, Irish humorist. He was dismissed from the Jesuit order in 1830 for a minor offense. In 1832 he became a parish priest but lived most of his life as a man of letters. His witty essays and poems—all purported to be the work of a priest named Father Prout—contributed to *Fraser's Magazine* and other periodicals, were collected as *The Reliques of Father Prout* (1836) and *The Final Reliques of Father Prout* (1875). His best-known work is the poem "The Bells of Shandon."

Mahrattas or **Marathas** (both: mərăt'əz, mərä'təz), Marathi-speaking people of W central India, known for their ability as warriors and their devotion to Hinduism. From their homeland in MAHARASHTRA these Hindu warriors rose to power in the 17th cent. The Mahrattas helped bring about the fall of the Mogul empire and were the most determined rivals to British supremacy in India. Under the leadership of SIVAJI, who successfully resisted the Mogul emperor, AURANGZEB, Mahratta power was extended throughout the Deccan and much of S India. By the mid-18th cent. the Mahrattas, with their capital at Poona, were the leading power in India, but their domain soon split into several territories that warred among themselves. In the 18th cent. power passed to a succession of Brahmans who had been serving as peshwas (prime ministers) to the weaker descendants of Sivaji. Great Britain, determined to end the threat to its control over India, waged several wars with the Mahrattas, finally subduing them in 1818. The major states of the Mahratta confederation included Baroda, Gwalior, and Indore. See J. G. Duff, *History of the Mahrattas* (rev. ed. 1921, repr. 1971); Rao Bahadur G. S. Sardesai, *New History of the Marathas* (3 vol., 1957); M. G. Ranade, *Rise of the Maratha Power* (1962); Ravinder Kumar, *Western India in the Nineteenth Century* (1968).

Mährisch Ostrau: see OSTRAVA, Czechoslovakia.

Mai, Angelo (än'jālō mī), 1782–1854, Italian philologist and, from 1838, cardinal of the Roman Catholic Church. As an official at the Ambrosian Library in Milan and the Vatican Library, he discovered and published many manuscripts, some of them highly valuable. His most famous discovery was Cicero's *De republica.*

Maia (mā'ə, mī'ə). **1** In Greek mythology, oldest of the PLEIADES. She was the mother of Hermes by Zeus. **2** In Roman mythology, goddess of fertility; also called Maiesta. She was often identified with BONA DEA. The month of May was probably named for her.

Maiden Castle, prehistoric fortress, Dorset, S England, near Dorchester. The finest earthwork in the British Isles, c.115 acres (50 hectares) in area, is there. Excavations in 1934–37 revealed evidences of a Neolithic village, with a two-ditch irrigation system, indicating occupation c.2000 B.C. On the same site are remains of an Iron Age fortified village (300 B.C.), which was eventually taken by the Romans. The inhabitants ceased to occupy Maiden Castle about A.D. 70 when they moved to a town in the nearby valley.

maidenhair tree: see GINKGO.

Maidenhead, municipal borough (1971 pop. 45,306), Berkshire, S central England, on the Thames River. It is a residential town and a resort. There are also brewing and milling industries. The 13th-century stone bridge was rebuilt in the 1770's.

Maidstone (mād'stən), municipal borough (1971 pop. 70,918), county town of Kent, SE England, on the Medway River. It is a market town. There are paper, printing, quarrying, brewing, engineering, and agricultural industries. There is evidence of a Roman station. Chillington Manor (Elizabethan) contains the Maidstone Museum, the public library, and the headquarters of the Kent Archaeological Society. The grammar school dates from 1549. Noteworthy are the Church of All Saints, founded in the 14th cent.; the palace of the archbishops; and Penenden Heath, a recreation ground. There are technical, art, and adult-education schools. William Hazlitt was born in Maidstone, and Cobtree Manor, nearby, is the "Dingley Dell" of Dickens's *Pickwick Papers.*

Maiduguri (mīdo͞o'gərē), town (1969 est. pop. 162,000), NE Nigeria. Leather goods made from the hides of crocodiles caught in Lake Chad are a leading product of the town. Groundnuts, cotton, and hides and skins produced in the area are exported. The city is a rail, road, and air transportation center serving NE Nigeria and parts of Niger and Chad. Maiduguri was founded near Yerwa in 1907 as a British military post.

Maidu Indians (mī'do͞o), North American Indians belonging to the Penutian linguistic stock (see AMERICAN INDIAN LANGUAGES). In the early 19th cent. they were located on the eastern tributaries of the Sacramento River. Maidu culture was typical of the California area; the people lived in brush shelters, gathered acorns, and practiced the spirit-impersonating Kuksu religion. Of the three divisions of the Maidu—valley, foothill, and mountain groups—the valley Indians, or Nisenan, were the most prosperous and culturally developed. The Maidu numbered about 9,000 in the late 18th cent., but now only a few survive, sharing the Round Valley Reservation, Calif., with other Indians. See A. L. Kroeber, *Valley Nisenan* (1929); R. L. Beals, *Ethnology of the Nisenan* (1933).

Maikop (mīkôp'), city (1970 pop. 110,000), capital of Adyge Autonomous Oblast, Krasnodar Kray, S European USSR, at the foot of the Greater Caucasus and on the Belaya River. It has machinery, lumber, and food-processing industries. Nearby are the important Maikop oil fields, discovered in 1900–1901 and linked by pipeline with the refineries at Krasnodar and the Black Sea port of Tuapse. Maikop was founded in 1857 as a Russian fortress. It was captured by German troops in 1942 and retaken by Soviet forces in 1943.

Mailer, Norman, 1923–, American writer, b. Long Branch, N.J., grad. Harvard, 1943. An uninhibited and irreverent critic of American life, Mailer has become almost as famous for his unconventional opinions and activities as for his writing. He served in the army during World War II and at the age of 25 published *The Naked and the Dead* (1948), one of the most significant novels to emerge from the war. His next two novels, *Barbary Shore* (1951) and *The Deer Park* (1955), were generally considered failures. More successful was *An American Dream* (1966) in which he explored sex, violence, and death in America through the experiences of his semiautobiographical protagonist. Mailer introduced a new kind of journalism with *The Armies of the Night* (1968; Pulitzer Prize), an account of the 1967 peace march on Washington, D.C. Poetic and witty in style, the book combines factual analysis with the intimacy of a memoir and the perceptive density of a novel. Among his other journalistic works are *Miami and the Siege of Chicago* (1969), a report on the 1968 Republican and Democratic conventions; and *A Fire on the Moon* (1971), an account of the Apollo 11 moon shot. *The Prisoner of Sex* (1971) is Mailer's response to the women's liberation movement. Mailer has made several experimental films, and in 1969 he ran unsuccessfully for mayor of New York City. Among his other works are *The White Negro* (1958), *Advertisements for Myself* (1959), *Why Are We in Vietnam?* (1967), *St. George and the Godfather* (1972), and *Marilyn* (1973), a controversial biography of Marilyn Monroe.

Maillart, Robert (mīyär'), 1872–1940, Swiss engineer, renowned for his inventive and beautiful reinforced-concrete bridges. Maillart's basic structural principles—integration of the supporting arch, the stiffening wall, and the traffic platform into one cohesive unit—were applied as early as 1901 in a bridge at Zuoz, Switzerland. These ideas were further refined in Maillart's later works. The Schwandbach Bridge (1933) is constructed on a curving plan to facilitate traffic movement over a mountain gorge. Maillart was also an innovator in the development of reinforced-concrete beamless floor slab (mushroom-column) construction, which has been used in warehouses, factories, and other multistoried buildings. See study by Max Bill (3d ed. 1969).

Maillol, Aristide (ärēstēd' mäyôl'), 1861–1944, French sculptor, woodcut artist, and painter. At first a painter, Maillol studied at the École des Beaux-Arts, Paris, and then allied himself with the NABIS. In his forties he turned to sculpture and quickly developed his characteristic style, creating strong, energetic nude figures of women. His affinity to classical sculpture was strengthened by a trip to Greece in 1908. Maillol's massive nudes were idealized, yet endowed with robustness and an impressive controlled tension. *The River* and several other works are in the Museum of Modern Art, New York City. Maillol also made woodcuts illustrating *Daphnis and Chloë* and the works of Ovid and Vergil. See his catalogue raisonné (in French) by Marcel Guérin (2 vol., 1965–67); his woodcuts, ed. by John Rewald (1943); study by John Rewald (1939).

Maimana (mī'mənə), city (1967 pop. 48,750), N Afghanistan, near the USSR border. A walled city inhabited mainly by Uzbeks, Maimana is a district administrative center and a market for leather goods, silk, wheat, and barley.

Maimon, Salomon (mī'môn), c.1754–1800, German philosopher, b. Polish Lithuania. He received a Jewish religious education and was influenced by the Talmudic tradition and particularly by Maimonides. Wandering through Germany, he reached Berlin c.1779 and later went to school in Hamburg. An important critic of Immanuel KANT, Maimon argued that the "thing in itself" was to be understood not as an external entity underlying phenomena but as something residing in consciousness, a limit of the possible cognition of an object. Maimon posited the idea of an infinite reason, which he sometimes understood as a limit of understanding but tended to regard as an ontological entity. See his autobiography (tr. by J. C. Murray, 1946); studies by Samuel Atlas (1964) and S. H. Bergman (tr. 1967).

Maimonides (mīmŏn'ĭdēz) or **Moses ben Maimon** (mī'mən), 1135–1204, Jewish rabbi, physician, and philosopher, one of the greatest Hebrew scholars, b. Cordoba, Spain, d. Cairo. He is sometimes called Rambam, from the initials of the words Rabbi Moses ben Maimon. His greatest scholastic work was his attempt to organize the vast mass of Jewish oral law, or Mishna, in what was to be a reference book for laymen as well as for rabbis and judges; the work is called the *Mishneh Torah,* generally known in English as the *Strong Hand.* He also produced a great commentary on the six orders of the Mishna; a collection of discourses; a work on logic; a treatise on the calendar; several medical books, including an important work on hygiene; and the great philosophical work *Moreh Nevukhim* (tr., *Guide for the Perplexed,* 1919), in which he explained the esoteric ideas in the Bible, formulated a proof of the existence of God, expounded the principle of creation, and elucidated baffling metaphysical and religious problems. The *Moreh Nevukhim,* which reflects Maimonides's great knowledge of Aristotelian philosophy, has dominated Jewish thought and exerted a profound influence upon Christian thinkers. See biographies by Izak Münz (1912, tr. 1935), Solomon Zeitlin (2d ed. 1955), and J. S. Minkin (1957); studies by F. G. Bratton (1967) and Jehuda Melber (1968).

Main (mīn), river, c.310 mi (500 km) long, formed near Kulmbach, E West Germany, by the confluence of the Roter Main and the Weisser Main, both of which rise in the Fichtelgebirge. It then winds generally west through the rich farmland of central West Germany and past the industrial areas of Schweinfurt, Würzburg, Aschaffenburg, and Frankfurt to the Rhine River at Mainz. Navigable from its junction with the Regnitz River, its chief tributary, the Main is an important east-west route. The Ludwig Canal connects it with the Danube River. There are about 40 hydroelectric power plants on the Main, of which Griesheim (62,000-kw capacity) is the largest.

Mainbocher (Main Rousseau Bocher): see under FASHION.

Maine, Sir Henry James Sumner, 1822–88, English jurist and historian, educated at Cambridge. A pioneer in the historical and comparative study of institutions, he viewed the history of laws as the most certain way of studying the history of civilization. He drew analogies between 19th-century institutions in India and those of Anglo-Saxon society and believed that society progressed from custom to law, with Roman law demonstrating the intermediate stage between ancient usage and modern British law. Parts of his theories have been discredited, but his influence on the study of the history of jurisprudence is incalculable. His first work, *Ancient Law* (1861; new ed., with introd. by C. K. Allen, 1931, repr. 1970), was his most famous. He was (1862–69) legal member of the viceroy's council in India, where he planned the codification of Indian law. He embodied his lectures on legal history, given at Oxford and Cambridge, in several books, including *Village Communities in the East and the West* (1871) and *The Early History of Institutions* (7th ed. 1966). In *Popular Government* (1885) he challenged the thought of his day by warning that democracy and progress were not necessarily equated. See biography by George Feaver (1969).

Maine (mĕn), region and former province, NW France, S of Normandy and E of Brittany. It now comprises the departments of Mayenne and Sarthe and parts of Loire-et-Cher, Eure-et-Loir, and Orne. LE MANS, the historic capital, is an important industrial and commercial center. Other towns in the region are Laval, Mayenne, and Vendôme. Maine is primarily agricultural, with important stock raising in the hilly Perche; it is well irrigated by the Mayenne, Loire, and Sarthe rivers. Important during Roman times, Maine was Christianized between the 4th and 6th cent. Made a county in the 10th cent., it passed (1126) to Anjou and was held for long periods by England. It frequently reverted to the French crown, or to members of the royal family, until it was finally united with the crown in 1584 upon the death of the Duke of Alençon.

Maine, state (1970 pop. 993,663), 33,215 sq mi (86,027 sq km), in the extreme northeast corner of the United States, largest of the New England states; admitted as the 23d state of the Union in 1820. AUGUSTA is the capital; PORTLAND, LEWISTON, and BANGOR are the largest cities. The Canadian provinces of Quebec and New Brunswick border Maine from the northwest around to the southeast coast, with the St. John and the St. Croix rivers forming part of the international boundary with New Brunswick. To the south is the Atlantic Ocean (the Bay of Fundy lies off to the east). New Hampshire (to the west) is the only state bordering Maine. Geologic action laid down a bedrock of sandstoné, shale, and limestone. Much of the soft rock eroded into tableland valleys, while the more resistant rock remained, forming the generally mountainous west, the mountains of Mt. Desert Island in the east, and isolated peaks including Katahdin (5,268 ft/1,606 m), the highest point in the state. Receding glaciers deposited long drift ridges across the countryside and dammed the valleys to form more than 2,200 lakes (Moosehead Lake is the largest) and to establish new, rugged watercourses for more than 5,000 streams and rivers. The major rivers are the St. John, the Penobscot, the Kennebec, the Androscoggin, and the Saco. The sea has encroached on the low coastal valleys, leaving a jigsawed coastline of 2,500 mi (3,219 km) and numerous irregular and rocky islands offshore. East of the Kennebec the coast of Maine is rugged and wild, but west of the river the shoreline has sandy beaches and marshy lowlands. The great stands of white pine (for which Maine is known as the Pine Tree State) are now virtually extinct, but four fifths of the state (17.4 million acres/7 million hectares) is still forested with hemlock, spruce, fir, and hardwoods. In the shelter of lakes and woods, particularly in the north counties, wildlife has found refuge. Moose, deer, black bears, and smaller game are still found; fish and fowl are plentiful. Much of Maine's abundant natural and industrial resources remain undeveloped. The mineral wealth of the state is considerable. Many varieties of granite, including some superior ornamental types, have been used for construction throughout the nation. Sand and gravel, zinc, and peat are found in addition to stone. Gold was discovered at Pembroke in 1965. Maine is the third largest producer of beryllium concentrate in the United States. The population of Maine is centered on the cleared land along the coast and major rivers. With many factors operating against the establishment of a stable and prosperous economy—a generally poor soil and a short growing season, geographical remoteness from production centers, an inadequate distribution system, lack of coal and steel, and a reluctance to adopt modern methods of production and merchandising—Maine has had a very low population increase in the last century. The economic revival experienced in port and factory towns during World War II did not continue after the war, and in 1949–50 the textile industry, after enjoying a brief expansion, suffered severely

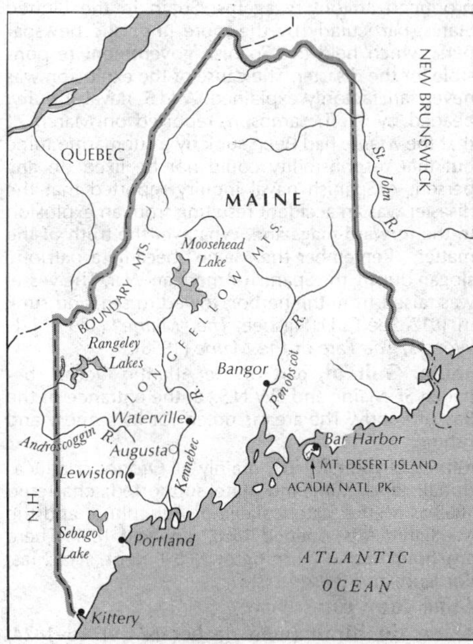

from competitive markets, and many of the old mills and plants were closed. However, the picturesque coastal and island resorts of Maine hold a strong appeal for visitors and tourists and, combined with abundant wildlife to attract sportsmen, make the tourist trade a most important feature of Maine's economy. Maine's other economic assets are its protected harbors, which serve as fishing ports; rapid rivers, which provide power for mills and factories; extensive lumber and fishing resources; and farming regions. Fishing, one of the state's earliest industries, remains important (Rockport and ROCKLAND have important fisheries), and Maine lobsters are nationally famous. Lumbering—the first sawmill in America was built in 1623 on the Piscataqua River—dominated industry and the export trade from the days when the straight white pines provided masts for the British navy. However, since the virgin timber has been largely cut off and forest fires have been costly, the timber trade has declined. But conservation and reforestation programs are in progress, and pulpwood products and paper are still manufactured at mill and factory towns along the rivers. Maine is a leading producer of paper and paper products, which account for about one third of the value of all manufactures in the state. The proximity of harbors and forests early encouraged extensive shipbuilding, which reached its peak in the 19th cent. Although the days are past when clipper ships and freighters slipped down the tidal rivers to carry the skill of Maine artisans and seamen around the world, the construction of fishing and pleasure craft remains a skilled and valuable industry. After the decline of shipbuilding and timber trading, commercial activity slackened, and today Portland, the largest port, operates far below its capacity. However, Portland, Bangor, and Rockland are still important cities and during the summer months serve a vast resort region. Manufacturing is the largest economic sector, accounting for one third of all production. Leather goods, food products, textiles, and transportation equipment are produced in addition to paper and wood products. Printing and publishing are also important. Agriculture, which occupies approximately one third of the population, has been developed despite adverse soil and climatic conditions. Since the opening of the prairie and grasslands of the West, Maine has tended to concentrate on dairying, poultry raising, and market gardening to serve local and New England markets. The state is a leading producer of broiler chickens. The growing of potatoes, particularly in Aroostook co., was stimulated by the completion of the Aroostook RR in 1894; only Idaho produces more potatoes than Maine. Hay, apples, and oats are the other chief crops. The earliest human habitation in what is now Maine extends back to prehistoric times, as evidenced by the burial mounds of the Red Paint people found in the south central part of the state. The Indians who came later left enormous shell heaps, variously estimated to be from 1,000 to 5,000 years old. At the time of settlement by white men the friendly ABNAKI INDIANS were scattered along the coast and in some inland areas. The coast of Maine may have been visited by the Norsemen and was known to British, French, and Spanish mariners before the sieur de Monts and Samuel de Champlain established a short-lived French colony in 1604 at the mouth of the St. Croix River. The region was included in the grant that James I of England awarded to the Plymouth Company, and colonists set out under George POPHAM in 1607. This settlement, Fort St. George, on the present site of Phippsburg, at the mouth of the Kennebec (then called the Sagadahoc) River, did not prosper, and the colonists returned to England in 1608. The French returned to the area in 1613 and established a new colony and a Jesuit mission on Mt. Desert Island; however, the English under Sir Samuel ARGALL expelled them. In 1620 the Council for New England (successor to the Plymouth Company) granted Ferdinando Gorges and Captain John Mason the territory between the Kennebec and Merrimack rivers extending 60 mi (97 km) inland. At this time, the region became known as Maine, either to honor Henrietta Maria, queen of Charles I, who was feudal proprietor of the province in France called Maine, or to distinguish the mainland from the offshore islands. Gorges and Mason divided (1629) their grant, with Gorges taking the area E of the Piscataqua, in which he was confirmed by Charles I, who issued him a royal charter in 1639 for "the Province and Countie of Maine." Meanwhile, permanent settlements had been established at Monhegan, Saco, and York (originally known as Gorgeana, York was the first city in America chartered by England and became the capital of Gorges's province in 1642). Neglected after Gorges's death in 1647, Maine settlers came under the jurisdiction of the Massachusetts Bay Colony in 1652. With the restoration of Charles II in 1660, however, the Massachusetts title to Maine was disputed until, in 1677, Massachusetts purchased the proprietary rights of Gorges's heirs. KING PHILIP'S WAR (1675–76) was the first of many struggles between the British on one side and the French and Indians on the other that slowed down the further settlement of Maine. French influence, which had been reasserted E of the Penobscot, declined rapidly after 1688, when Sir Edmund Andros, royal governor of all New England, seized French fortifications there. After the colonists overthrew Andros, Massachusetts received a new charter (1691) that confirmed its hold on Maine, and with Sir William PHIPS, a Maine native, as governor and the territorial question settled, local government and institutions in the Massachusetts tradition really took root in Maine. Because it was on the frontier, the province was repeatedly ravaged by Indians, but their strength was broken during Queen Anne's War (1702–3), at the end of which Kittery, Wells, and York were the only remaining settlements. Maine nevertheless recovered quickly and soon had prosperous fishing, lumbering, and shipbuilding industries. In one of the last French and Indian Wars its militia won distinction serving under Sir William Pepperrell, a Maine man, in the capture (1745) of Louisburg, a French stronghold on Cape Breton Island. Dissatisfaction with British rule was first expressed openly after Parliament passed the STAMP ACT in 1765; in protest, a mob at Falmouth (Portland) seized a quantity of the hated stamps. As conflict increased between the colonies and England, nonimportation societies to boycott English goods were formed in Maine. During the AMERICAN REVOLUTION, Falmouth paid dearly for its defiance; it was devastated by a British fleet in 1775. A regiment from Maine fought at BUNKER HILL. In that same year, 1775, Benedict Arnold led his grueling, unsuccessful expedition against Quebec N through Maine. During the war supplies were cut off and Indian attacks were frequent, but with American independence won, economic development was rapid in what was then called the Dist. of Maine, one of the three admiralty districts of Massachusetts set up by the Continental Congress in 1775. However, the EMBARGO ACT OF 1807 and the WAR OF 1812 interrupted the thriving commerce and turned the district to industrial development. Agitation for statehood, which had been growing since the Revolution, now became widespread. Dissatisfaction with Massachusetts was aroused by the inadequate military protection provided during the War of 1812; by the land policy, which encouraged absentee ownership; and by the political differences between conservative Massachusetts and democratic Maine. The imminent admission of Missouri into the Union as a slave state hastened the separation of Maine from Massachusetts, and equality of power between North and South was preserved by admitting Maine as a free state in 1820, as part of the MISSOURI COMPROMISE. With Portland as its capital (moved to Augusta in 1832) the new state entered a prosperous period. During the first half of the 19th cent. Maine enjoyed its greatest population increase. A highly profitable timber trade was carried on with the West Indies, Europe, and Asia, and towns such as BATH became America's leaders in shipbuilding. The long-standing NORTHEAST BOUNDARY DISPUTE almost precipitated border warfare between Maine and New Brunswick in the so-called AROOSTOOK WAR of 1839; the controversy was settled by the WEBSTER-ASHBURTON TREATY with Great Britain in 1842. Political life was vigorous, particularly in the 1850s, when the reluctance of the Democrats, who had been dominant since 1820, to take a firm antislavery stand swept the new Republican party into power. Hannibal HAMLIN was a leading Republican politician and was Vice President during Abraham Lincoln's first administration. Antislavery sentiment was strong, and Maine made sizable contributions of men and money to the Union in the Civil War. Generals Oliver O. HOWARD and Joshua L. CHAMBERLAIN were from Maine. For decades regulation of the liquor traffic was the chief political issue in Maine, and the state was the first to adopt (1851) a prohibition law. It was incorporated into the constitution in 1884 and was not repealed until 1934. State politics entered a hectic stage in 1878 when the newly organized Greenback party combined with the Democrats to carry the election, ending more than 20 years of Republican rule. The following year the coalition was accused of manipulating election returns, a charge sustained by the state supreme court, which seated a rival legislature elected by the Republicans. In 1880 the fusionists were again successful, but from that time until the 1950s the state was generally Republican, providing that party with such national leaders as James G. Blaine, Thomas B. Reed, and Margaret Chase Smith, who in 1948 became the first Republican woman U.S. Senator. A Democratic resurgence began in 1954 with the election of Edmund S. Muskie as governor. In 1964 and 1968 (when Muskie, then a U.S. Senator, ran unsuccessfully for Vice President) the state voted Democratic in the presidential election for the first times since 1912. Prior to 1960, Maine was unique in holding elections in September, giving rise to the slogan coined by the usually successful Republican party, "as Maine goes, so goes the nation." In the 20th cent. the nationwide interest in progressive legislation led to the adoption of the direct primary, the initiative and referendum, and a corrupt practices act. The state's economy was aided by the construction of the Ripogenus Dam (1917), the Wyman Dam (1930), and the Maine Turnpike from Kittery to Augusta (completed 1955). The principal ground station for the first communications satellite was built at Andover in 1962. In 1969 personal and corporate income taxes were added to the sales tax within the state. Maine is governed under the 1820 constitution as amended. There is a two-house legislature of 33 senators and 151 representatives, all elected for two-year terms; the governor is elected for a four-year term and may succeed himself once. In 1971, Kenneth M. Curtis, a Democrat, became governor. In 1974, James B. Longley, an Independent, was elected governor. Maine elects two Representatives and two Senators to the U.S. Congress and has four electoral votes. Places of interest in Maine include Acadia National Park on Mt. Desert Island; Baxter State Park, which includes the beginning of the APPALACHIAN TRAIL at Mt. Katahdin in the N Maine wilderness; and the Old York Gaol (1653), one of the oldest public buildings in New England. Among the state's leading educational institutions are Bowdoin College, at Brunswick; Colby College, at Waterville; Bates College, at Lewiston; and the Univ. of Maine, at Orono. See W. B. Smith, *The Lost Red Paint People of Maine* (1930); G. W. Starkey, *Maine: Its History, Resources and Government* (4th ed. 1947); H. P. Beck, *The Folklore of Maine* (1957); Berenice Abbott, *A Portrait of Maine* (1968); R. F. Banks, comp., *A History of Maine* (1969); Federal Writers' Project, *Maine, a Guide to the Vacation State* (2d ed. 1969) and *Maine, a Guide Down East* (2d ed. 1970); L. D. Rich, *The Coast of Maine* (3d ed. 1970); Martin Dibner, *Seacoast Maine, People and Places* (1973).

Maine, U.S. battleship destroyed (Feb. 15, 1898) in Havana harbor by an explosion that killed 260 men. The incident helped precipitate the SPANISH-AMERICAN WAR (April, 1898). Commanded by Capt. Charles Sigsbee, the ship had been sent (Jan., 1898) to Cuba to protect American life and property from the revolutionary turmoil there. The sinking of the *Maine* produced an outcry against Spain in the United States, particularly by the more jingoistic newspapers, which held the Spanish government responsible for the disaster. The cause of the explosion was never satisfactorily explained. A U.S. naval inquiry, headed by W. T. Sampson, reported on March 21 that the *Maine* had been sunk by a submarine mine but that responsibility could not be fixed on any person. A Spanish naval inquiry reported that the disaster was an accident resulting from an explosion in the forward magazine. Whatever the truth of the matter, "Remember the Maine" became a patriotic slogan during the Spanish-American War. The vessel was raised from the harbor, towed to sea, and sunk in 1912. See C. D. Sigsbee, *The "Maine"* (1899); J. E. Weems, *The Fate of the Maine* (1958).

Maine, Gulf of, part of the Atlantic Ocean, between SE Maine and SW N.S., at the entrance of the Bay of Fundy. The area is noted for its scenery and fishing.

Maine, University of, mainly at Orono; coeducational; land-grant and state supported; chartered 1865 as Maine State College of Agriculture and the Mechanic Arts, opened 1868, renamed 1897. There are branches at Farmington, Fort Kent, Machias, Portland, and Presque Isle.

Maine coon cat: see CAT.

Maine de Biran (mĕn də bĕräN'), 1766–1824, French philosopher, member of the Council of Five Hundred (1797), and councilor of state (1816). His real name was Marie François Pierre Gonthier de Biran. Although interested in the theories of Condillac and the ideologues, he was unable to accept Condillac's view of knowledge as derived solely from sensation. Maine de Biran emphasized the importance of inner consciousness of the self, finding the basis of morality in the consciousness of volitional activity. He later inclined toward mysticism. His writings were collected as *Œuvres inédites de Maine de Biran* (1859). See studies by P. P. Hallie (1959) and F. C. T. Moore (1970).

Maine-et-Loire (mĕn-ā-lwär), department (1968 pop. 584,709), NW France, roughly coextensive with ANJOU. ANGERS is the capital.

Mainland. 1 Island (1971 pop. 6,502), 178 sq mi (461 sq km), N Scotland. The largest of the Orkney Islands (see under ORKNEY), it is also called Pomona. KIRKWALL, the county town of Orkney, is on the island. Kirkwall Bay and Scapa Flow deeply indent its shores. The interior has hills, moors, several lakes, and fertile valleys. Cattle and sheep are raised; eggs are a leading product. There is also a distilling industry. Local customs in some districts reveal the Norse ancestry of many of the inhabitants. There are numerous Pictish remains—mounds, underground dwellings, circles, and standing stones. Most famous of these are MAESHOWE and the Standing Stones of STENNESS. SKARA BRAE is an excavated prehistoric village. **2** Island, 375 sq mi (971 sq km), extreme N Scotland. It is the largest of the SHETLAND ISLANDS (see under SHETLAND). LERWICK, the county town of Shetland, is in the southeastern part of the island. There are remains of a prehistoric village at Jarlshof.

Maino, Juan Bautista: see MAYNO, JUAN BAUTISTA.

main-sequence star: see HERTZSPRUNG-RUSSELL DIAGRAM.

Maintenon, Françoise d'Aubigné, marquise de (fräNswäz' dōbĕnyä' märkēz' də măNtənôN'), 1635–1719, second wife of the French king Louis XIV. Her grandfather was Agrippa d'Aubigné, the Huguenot hero. The family spent some years in Martinique, but upon her father's death she and her mother returned to France. Although baptized a Roman Catholic, the child was educated by a Protestant aunt. Later cared for by Catholic relatives, she became a very devout Catholic. At 16 she married the poet Paul SCARRON and became a figure in the literary and intellectual world of Paris. After his death in 1660 the queen mother continued the poet's pension to his widow, and later Mme de MONTESPAN obtained a pension for her. She became (1669) the governess for the children of Mme de Montespan and the king and gradually supplanted Mme de Montespan in the esteem and affections of Louis XIV, who made her a marquise. Mme de Maintenon exercised considerable influence over Louis and greatly lifted the moral tone of the court, although the ascription to her of Louis's mistakes (particularly the revocation of the Edict of Nantes) is an exaggeration. The queen, Marie Thérèse, was devoted to her and died in her arms. In 1684 she was morganatically married to the king. In her later years Mme de Maintenon gave much of her attention to the famous school of Saint-Cyr, which she had founded for the daughters of poor but noble families. She also wrote remarkable essays and letters dealing with education. See biographies by C. C. Dyson (1910) and Charlotte Haldane (1970).

Mainz (mīnts), city (1970 pop. 172,195), capital of Rhineland-Palatinate, W central West Germany, a port on the left bank of the Rhine River opposite the mouth of the Main River. Its French name, also sometimes used in English, is Mayence. The city is an industrial, commercial, and transportation center. Chemicals, motor vehicles, machinery, cement, champagne, and printed materials are produced; the city is also a trade center for Rhine wines. Mainz is one of the great historical cities of Germany. It grew on the site of the Roman camp of Maguntiacum, or Mogontiacum (founded 1st cent. B.C.). The city was made (746–47) the seat of the first German archbishop, who was St. Boniface (c.675–754). The later archbishops acquired considerable territory around Mainz and in Franconia, on both sides of the Main, which they ruled as princes of the Holy Roman Empire. They very early received a vote in the imperial elections and had precedence over the other ELECTORS; they crowned the German kings. From the 16th cent., with the emperors-elect, the archbishops-electors were, ex officio, archchancellors of the Holy Roman Empire. Under the rule of the archbishops-electors Mainz flourished as a commercial and cultural center. Jews, who had one of their oldest settlements in Germany at Mainz, played an important part in the prosperity of the city. Johann Gutenberg (c.1397–1468) lived in Mainz, which he made the first printing center of Europe. Occupied in 1792 by the French, the city was ceded to France by the treaties of Campo Formio (1797) and Lunéville (1801), and the archbishopric was secularized and reduced to a diocese in 1803. The last archbishop, K. T. von Dalberg, became (1806) prince-primate of the Confederation of the Rhine. The Congress of Vienna made (1815) Mainz a federal fortress of the German Confederation and awarded it, with Rhenish Hesse, to the grand duchy of Hesse-Darmstadt. The city was made (1816) the provincial capital of Rhenish Hesse. It was (1873–1918) a fortress of the German Empire. Mainz was severely damaged during World War II, but was largely restored and rebuilt after 1945. Noteworthy structures in the old inner city include the six-towered Romanesque cathedral (consecrated 1009; restored 19th cent.); the Renaissance-style electoral (archiepiscopal) palace (17th–18th cent.), which houses an art gallery and a museum of Roman and Germanic antiquities; and the Church of St. Peter (18th cent.). The Univ. of Mainz was founded in 1477, was discontinued in 1816, and was reestablished in 1946 as the Johannes Gutenberg Univ. Mainz is a television broadcasting center. In 1945 the city's suburbs on the right bank of the Rhine were transferred to the state of Hesse.

maiolica: see MAJOLICA.

Maipú (mīpōō'), battlefield, central Chile, a few miles S of Santiago. On April 5, 1818, SAN MARTÍN routed the Spanish royalist army at Maipú and assured Chilean independence. The victory made possible his liberating expedition to Peru.

Maisonneuve, Paul de Chomedey, sieur de (pōl də shômdā' syör də măzôNnöv'), 1612–76, founder and first governor of Montreal, b. France. A soldier, he fought in European wars before being sent by the Société de Notre Dame de Montréal to take possession of their grant in the new world. He landed (1642) on Montreal island, where he established the city of Ville Marie, later Montreal, and administered the colony for 22 years (1642–63). He returned (1665) to France and died in obscurity in Paris.

Maisons-Alfort (măzôNz-älfôr'), suburb SE of Paris (1968 pop. 53,671), Val-de-Marne dept., N central France. There is some agriculture, but it is mainly an industrial town producing chemicals and metals. A 13th-century church and a veterinary school are in Maisons-Alfort.

Maistre, Joseph de (zhôzĕf' də mĕs'trə), 1754?–1821, French writer and diplomat. Born in Savoy, he was Sardinian ambassador at St. Petersburg from 1803 to 1817. A passionate Roman Catholic and royalist, he was master of a rigidly logical doctrine and the possessor of a great store of knowledge. These qualities, combined with a fine ability in writing French prose, made him perhaps the most powerful literary enemy of 18th-century rationalism, in which he delighted to detect logical weakness and shallowness. His principal works were *Du pape* [on the pope] (1819) and *Les Soirées de Saint-Pétersbourg* [discussions in St. Petersburg] (1821). They develop his idea that the world should be one, ruled absolutely by the pope as the spiritual ruler, with no temporal ruler having an independent authority.

Maistre, Xavier de (zävyā'), 1763-1852, French writer, b. Savoy; brother of Joseph de Maistre. He served in the Russian army and lived most of his life in St. Petersburg. His works are distinguished for their polished wit. *Voyage autour de ma chambre* [trip around my room] (1794), written when he was in prison for dueling, is a simple peregrination from object to object allowing each to call up recollections. *Le Lépreux de la cité d'Aoste* [the leper of Aosta] (1811) is a dialogue between a soldier and a leper, notable for its portrayal of Christian resignation. *La Jeune Sibérienne* [the Siberian girl] is the story of a plea of a Russian girl to the czar for mercy for her father in Siberia.

Maitland, Frederic William, 1850-1906, English legal historian, educated at Cambridge. A thorough scholar, he founded the Selden Society for the publication of early English documents and edited many texts himself, such as Henry de Bracton's notebook and the *Year Books of Edward II* (completed by G. J. Turner, 4 vol., 1903-7). *The History of English Law before the Time of Edward I* (1895), which he wrote with Sir Frederick Pollock, is a brilliant work, still standard. Other studies by him, notable for their prose style as well as sound elucidation of the ideas and attitudes embodied in legal institutions, are *Domesday Book and Beyond* (1897, repr. 1966), a model for the use of a source; *English Law and the Renaissance* (1901); *Equity* (ed. by A. H. Chaytor and W. J. Whittaker, 1909; rev. ed. by John Brunyate, 1937); and *The Forms of Action at Common Law* (ed. by A. H. Chaytor and W. J. Whittaker, 1909 and 1937). His *Constitutional History of England* (ed. by H. A. L. Fisher, 1908) is a valuable series of lectures. See his collected papers (ed. by H. A. L. Fisher, 3 vol., 1911) and *Selected Essays* (ed. by H. D. Hazeltine, G. T. Lapsley, and P. H. Winfield, 1936, repr. 1968); biography by C. H. S. Fifoot (1971); studies by J. R. Cameron (1961) and H. E. Bell (1965).

Maitland, John: see LAUDERDALE, JOHN MAITLAND, DUKE OF.

Maitland, William (Maitland of Lethington), 1528?-1573, Scottish statesman. He began his career in the service of the regent MARY OF GUISE but deserted her in 1559, joining the revolt of the Protestant nobles, the lords of the congregation. When MARY QUEEN OF SCOTS returned to Scotland two years later, he became her secretary and close adviser. A skilled diplomat, Maitland was unique in an age of religious wars for his refusal to be swayed by religious passions, and he resisted attempts of the Church to dominate government. This led to suspicion from both Catholics and Protestants, although his abilities were recognized by all. His chief desire was to effect a union of Scotland and England based on Mary's right of succession to the English throne after the death of Elizabeth I. He was implicated in the murders of both Rizzio and Darnley. After Mary's marriage to Bothwell, Maitland joined the opposition, but he later worked for her restoration. In the civil war following the murder (1570) of the earl of MURRAY, Maitland led the queen's party and held out in Edinburgh Castle from 1571 to 1573. His death shortly afterward saved him from execution. It has been suggested that if portions of the so-called Casket Letters were forged, Maitland was the probable forger. See Ernest Russell, *Maitland of Lethington, the Minister of Mary Stuart* (1912).

Maitland, city (1971 pop. 30,963), New South Wales, SE Australia, on the Hunter River. It is a railroad junction and agricultural center with light manufacturing. Maitland began as a convict settlement in 1824. The river has flooded in 1893, 1949, and 1955. There is a Roman Catholic cathedral in the city.

maize: see CORN.

Maizuru (mī'zo͞oro͞o), city (1970 pop. 95,895), Kyoto prefecture, SW Honshu, Japan, on Maizuru Bay. It is an important port and naval base with the best natural harbor on the Japan Sea coast. The city has spinning mills and chemical, rolling stock, and glass industries.

Majano, Benedetto da: see BENEDETTO DA MAJANO.

Majdanek (mīdä'nĕk), village, SE Poland, a suburb of Lublin. The Germans established and operated a concentration camp there in World War II. About 1,500,000 persons of 22 nationalities (chiefly Jews, Russians, and Poles) were annihilated there in gas chambers.

majolica (məjŏl'ĭkə, məyŏl'-) or **maiolica** (məyŏl'ĭkə) [from Majorca], type of FAÏENCE usually associated with wares produced in Spain, Italy, and Mexico. The process of making majolica consists of first firing a piece of earthenware, then applying a tin enamel that upon drying forms a white opaque porous surface. A design is then painted on and a transparent glaze applied. Finally the piece is fired again. This type of ware was produced in the ancient Middle East by the Babylonians, and the method remained continuously in use. It was extensively employed by the Hispano-Moresque potters of the 14th cent. By the mid-15th cent. majolica was popular in Italy, where it became justly famous through the decorations of the DELLA ROBBIA family. The method is still extensively employed in folk art. See Bernard Rackham, *Italian Majolica* (1952); Giuseppe Liverani, *Five Centuries of Italian Majolica* (tr. 1960).

Major, John, 1469-1550, Scottish theologian and historian. He studied and taught at the Univ. of Paris. His works, all in Latin, were published there. He was one of the most famous teachers of scholastic philosophy of his day, at Paris and later at the Univ. of Glasgow and at St. Salvator's College, St. Andrews. The best known of his works is *Historia Majoris Britanniae, tam Angliae quam Scotiae* (Paris, 1521; Edinburgh, 1740). This *History of Greater Britain, both England and Scotland* was the first critical history of Scotland. An English translation by Archibald Constable was published (1892) with a biography by Aeneas J. G. Mackay. Major's name was also spelled Mair.

Majorca (məjôr'kə), Span. *Mallorca* (mälyôr'kä), island (1970 pop. 460,030), 1,405 sq mi (3,639 sq km), Spain, largest of the Balearic Islands, in the W Mediterranean. Palma is the chief city. Majorca is mountainous in the northwest, rising to 4,739 ft (1,444 m) in the Puig Major; the south and east form a gently rolling, fertile region. Its mild climate and beautiful scenery have long made Majorca a popular resort; tourism is its major industry. Cereals, flax, grapes, and olives are grown, a light wine is produced, hogs and sheep are raised, and lead, marble, and copper are mined. For the history of Majorca before 1276, see BALEARIC ISLANDS. In 1276 the kingdom of Majorca was formed from the inheritance of James I of Majorca. It comprised the Balearic Islands, Roussillon and Cerdagne (between France and Spain), and several fiefs in S France. Perpignan, in Roussillon, was the capital. In 1343, Peter IV of Aragón took the kingdom from James II and reunited it with the crown of Aragón. The island's flourishing commerce declined, partly because of the warfare between the native peasantry and the Aragonese nobels and Catalan traders, but mainly because of the change in trade routes after the discovery of America. Majorca is known for its stalagmite caves and for its architectural treasures and prehistoric monuments. The abandoned old monastery where Chopin and George Sand lived is an island landmark. The inhabitants speak their own dialect.

Majorian (Julius Maiorianus) (məjôr'ēən), d.461, Roman emperor of the West (457-61). He became emperor after he and RICIMER had deposed Avitus. An able and honest ruler, Majorian enacted laws to protect the people from unfair taxation and to preserve the ancient monuments of Rome. He attempted to recover the provinces but was defeated (460) in his expedition against GAISERIC. Ricimer, jealous of Majorian's strength, deposed him and had him murdered. Majorian's death was the beginning of the disintegration of the West Roman Empire.

Majuba Hill (məjo͞o'bə), E Natal, South Africa, in the Drakensberg Range. On Feb. 27, 1881, a British force of 500 was routed there by Boer troops under the command of P. J. Joubert.

Majunga (məjŭng'gə), city (1970 est. pop. 54,000), NW Malagasy Republic, on Madagascar, on the Mozambique Channel. Despite its shallow harbor, Majunga is one of the nation's chief ports. The Betsiboka River valley provides access to the interior. Majunga has food processing, cement, and sisal processing industries. The city was the capital of the Sakalava kingdom, which flourished in the 18th cent. France occupied Majunga from 1883 to 1885 and retook it in 1894.

Majuro: see MARSHALL ISLANDS.

Makah Indians (mäkô'), North American Indians who in the early 19th cent. inhabited Cape Flattery, NW Wash. According to Lewis and Clark they then numbered some 2,000. The Makah are the southernmost of the Wakashan branch of the Algonquian-Wakashan linguistic stock, being the only member of the Wakashan group within the United States (see AMERICAN INDIAN LANGUAGES). Makah culture was fundamentally that of the Pacific Northwest Coast area. In 1855 they ceded all their lands to the United States except a small area on Cape Flattery that was set aside as a reservation. Today they live on Makah Reservation, where they number some 500; their main tribal income is from forestry. See Elizabeth Colson, *The Makah Indians* (1953, repr. 1974).

Makarios III (mäkä'rēôs), 1913-, Orthodox Eastern archbishop and Cypriot statesman, first president of Cyprus (1960-). Born Michael Mouskos, Makarios was elected bishop of Kition in 1948 and archbishop of Cyprus in 1950. Leader of the Greek Cypriots in the movement for enosis (union with Greece), he was exiled by the British in 1956 on charges of encouraging terrorism. He was released in 1957. In 1958 he began to press for Cypriot independence from Great Britain rather than union with Greece. When agreement was reached on the independence of Cyprus, he was elected president. Makarios pursued a neutralist policy, favoring a peaceful solution between the island's Greek and Turkish communities. After his term of office had expired in 1965 and had been extended to 1968, Makarios was reelected in 1968 and 1973. In 1972 he came under increasing pressure from the Greek government to allow for greater Greek influence in Cypriot affairs; the Cypriot Orthodox Church pressured him to resign if he failed to do so. Gen. George Grivas, leader of the enosis movement, launched a terrorist campaign aimed at overthrowing Makarios. This effort finally succeeded (July 1974), when a Greek-sponsored coup deposed Makarios. After several months of exile he returned to Cyprus in Dec., 1974, and resumed the presidency. See biography by P. N. Vanezis (1971); study by Stanley Mayes (1960).

Makart, Hans (häns mä'kärt), 1840-84, Austrian history painter, studied with Karl von PILOTY. His early success was phenomenal. The emperor of Austria provided him with a studio, and his short life was crowded with official honors and triumphs. In his large history paintings he strove to emulate Titian and Veronese in the use of lush color. Characteristic of his glittering costume pieces is *Entry of Charles V into Antwerp* (1878, Hamburg).

Makasar (məkăs'ər), city (1961 pop. 384,159), SW Celebes, capital of South Sulawesi prov., Indonesia. The largest city in Celebes, it is one of Indonesia's important seaports, a distribution and transshipment point for goods from Europe and Asia. Exports include coffee, teak, spices, copra, rubber, rattan, and gums and resins. The city is also a commercial center, with a large central market. Industries include the manufacture of cement and paper, and automobile assembly. Once a center of spice smuggling, Makasar was a thriving port when the Portuguese arrived (16th cent.). The Dutch supplanted the Portuguese, triumphing over the indigenous sultan in 1667. Makasar became a free port in 1848. It is the seat of a superior court, a state university, and two private universities. In World War II, Makasar Strait (between Borneo and Celebes) was the scene of a Japanese naval defeat.

Makatea (mäkätā'ä), formerly **Aurora,** island, South Pacific, one of the most northwesterly of the TUAMOTU ISLANDS, FRENCH POLYNESIA. The center of the island was once a solid mass of phosphate that was mined jointly by the British and the French until 1966, when the phosphate reserves were depleted. Makatea is administered as part of the Windward group of the SOCIETY ISLANDS and is no longer inhabited.

Makaz (mā'kăz), unidentified town, W central Palestine. 1 Kings 4.9.

Makemie, Francis (məkĕ'mē), c.1658-1708, American clergyman, considered the founder of Presbyterianism in America. Born in Ireland, he studied in Scotland and c.1682 was ordained a missionary to America. In 1683 he arrived in Maryland. He traveled and preached from the Carolinas to New York. Makemie organized Presbyterian churches at Snow Hill and Rehobeth, Md. In 1704 he went to England for funds and men to strengthen Presbyterianism in America; in 1706, through his efforts, the first presbytery in the country was organized in Philadelphia. Makemie was arrested and imprisoned (1707) by Governor Cornbury of New York on the charge of preaching there without a license. Though acquitted, he had to pay heavy costs. He died in Virginia. See biography by I. M. Page (1938); biographical study ed. by B. S. Schlenther (1971); C. A. Briggs, *American Presbyterianism* (1885).

Makeyevka (məkyä'yəfkə), city (1970 pop. 392,000), S European USSR, in the Ukraine, in the Donets Basin. It is a leading metallurgical and coal-mining center and has machinery and coking plants. Makeyevka was founded in 1899 as a metallurgical settlement then called Dmitriyevsk.

Makhachkala (məkhäch"kəlä'), city (1970 pop. 186,000), capital of Dagestan Autonomous Republic, SE European USSR, a port on the Caspian Sea. It is an important commercial and industrial center with oil refineries that are linked by pipeline with the Grozny fields. Aircraft and textiles are manufactured. Founded in 1844 as a Russian stronghold, the city, called Petrovsk, was renamed Makhachkala in 1921.

Makheloth (măkhē'lŏth), unidentified desert encampment. Num. 33.25.

Makin: see BUTARITARI.

Makkedah (măkē'də), unidentified Canaanite royal city, SW Palestine, taken by Joshua. Joshua 10.

Makó (mŏ'kō), town (1970 pop. 30,097), S Hungary, on the Mureşul River near the Rumanian border. It is an administrative and trade center and a road hub in a fertile agricultural region. The center of the Hungarian onion industry, Makó also has textile mills. There is a large Slovak population. The journalist Joseph Pulitzer was born in Makó.

mako (mä'kō), heavy-bodied, fast-swimming SHARK, genus *Isurus,* highly prized as a game fish. Also known as the sharp-nosed mackerel shark, it is a member of the mackerel shark family, which also includes the great WHITE SHARK and the porbeagle. The mako is deep blue above and white below, with a conical head and sharply pointed snout. It may reach a length of 12 ft (3.7 m) and weigh 1,000 lb (450 kg). Extremely active, makos have been known to attack boats and are probably dangerous to swimmers, although they have no particular reputation as maneaters; they put up a ferocious fight when hooked, leaping out of the water. The mako feeds on large fishes, including swordfishes, and usually swallows its prey whole. There are two species, *Isurus oxyrinchus,* of the Atlantic, and *I. paucus,* of the Pacific and Indian oceans. The porbeagles, or common mackerel sharks, genus *Lamna,* are similar to the makos, but smaller. One species, *Lamna nasus,* is found in the Atlantic and in the Mediterranean; another, *L. ditropus* occurs along the eastern coast of the Pacific. They are regarded as pests by fishermen, because they tear fishnets to feed on the catch. Makos and other mackerel sharks are classified in the phylum CHORDATA, subphylum Vertebrata, class Chondrichthyes, order Selachii, family Isuridae.

Maksutov telescope: see TELESCOPE.

Maktesh (măk'tĕsh), unidentified district of Jerusalem. Zeph. 1.11.

Makurdi (mäko͝or'dē), town (1969 est. pop. 63,000), central Nigeria, a port on the Benue River. Sesame seeds and cotton grown in the region are collected at Makurdi for transshipment. There is a small boatbuilding industry. The town has an airport and is a rail and road center and the terminus of a bridge across the Benue. Makurdi was developed by the British in the early 20th cent. as a transportation and local administration center.

Malabar Coast (măl'əbär), SW coast of India stretching c.525 mi (845 km) from Goa to the southern tip of the peninsula at Cape Comorin. It is a narrow coastal plain bounded by the Western Ghats. There is extensive fishing from the ports of Cochin and Calicut. Monsoon rains make the coast a fertile rice-growing region. It was the scene of trade struggles in the 16th and early 17th cent. between the Portuguese and their European and Indian rivals.

Malabo, formerly **Santa Isabel** (săn'tä ēsäbāl'), city (1970 est. pop. 20,000), capital of Equatorial Guinea, on Fernando Po island, in the Gulf of Guinea. It is the chief port and commercial center of Fernando Po island. Fish processing is the city's main industry, and cacao and coffee are the leading exports. The city was founded in 1827 by the British as a base for the suppression of the slave trade and was called Port Clarence, or Clarencetown. An international airport is on the city's outskirts.

Malacca: see MELAKA, Malaysia.

Malacca, Strait of, c.500 mi (800 km) long and from c.30 to 200 mi (50–320 km) wide, between Sumatra and the Malay Peninsula. Linking the Indian Ocean with the South China Sea, it is one of the world's most important sea passages. Pinang and Melaka (Malaysia) and Belawan (Indonesia) are chief ports; Singapore is at the southern end of the strait.

Malachi (mă'ləkī, -kē), **Malachias** (măl"əkī'əs), or **Malachy** (măl'əkē), book of the Old Testament, the 39th and last book in the order of the Authorized Version, 12th of the books of the Minor Prophets. Its author is anonymous (the title *Malachi,* meaning "my messenger," is taken from the opening verse of chapter 3), but on internal evidence the book is usually dated shortly before the reforms of Nehemiah and Ezra, probably c.460. After a protestation of God's love for Israel (1.1–2), the prophet rebukes the priests (1.6–2.9) for their negligence and the people (2.10–16) for their foreign marriages. Finally, there is a prophecy of the coming Day of Judgment (2.17–4.6). For bibliography, see OLD TESTAMENT.

malachite (măl'əkīt), a mineral, the green basic carbonate of copper occurring in crystals of the monoclinic system or (more usually) in masses. It is translucent or opaque; the luster is silky, vitreous, adamantine, or dull. It takes a good polish. An important ore of copper, it also serves as a gem and for various ornamental purposes and, when finely ground, as a pigment. It is found associated with other ores of copper (especially AZURITE) in various parts of the United States and in Chile, the USSR, Rhodesia, Zaïre, and Australia.

Malachy, Saint (măl'əkē), 1095–1148, Irish churchman, reformer of the church in Ireland. His Irish name was Máel Máedoc ua Morgair. He was assistant to Cellach (Celsus), bishop of Armagh, who was attempting to reduce the disorderly ecclesiastical system to a state of discipline. Malachy was ordained, studied at Lismore, and became abbot of Bangor (1123?), bishop of Connor (1124), and archbishop of Armagh (1134–37). He resigned to be bishop of Down in 1137. The church in Ireland was still organized with the tribal hierarchy set up by St. Patrick, a situation that did not at that time encourage reform. Paganism was rife in Ireland following the invasions of the Danes. To deal with the problem, St. Malachy reorganized the Irish church into a territorial hierarchy, following the example of the church in England and on the Continent. He disciplined the clergy and generally ushered in a religious revival. He went to Rome to seek confirmation of his deeds and to request the pallium for newly created Irish archbishops. On the way he visited Clairvaux (1140), where he became the friend of St. Bernard. They planned a Cistercian house for Ireland; this resulted (1142) in the abbey of Mellifont (near Brobheda). On a later trip to the Continent, he died at Clairvaux, where he was buried. Feast: Nov. 3. The primary source is the biography by St. Bernard of Clairvaux (Eng. tr. by H. J. Lawlor, 1920).

Maladetta Mountains (mälädĕt'ä), Span. *Montes Malditos* [Span., =cursed mountains], massif of the central Pyrenees, NE Spain, near the French border. Its highest point, Pico de Aneto (11,168 ft/3,404 m), is also the highest in the Pyrenees. The Garonne River rises in this group.

Málaga (mä'lägä), city (1970 pop. 374,452), capital of Málaga prov., S Spain, in Andalusia, on the Guadalmedina River and the Costa del Sol. Picturesquely situated on the Bay of Málaga, it is one of the best Spanish Mediterranean ports. Olives, almonds, and dried fruits are exported. Málaga's mild climate and luxurious flora, as well as the beautiful beaches nearby, make it also a popular resort. The sweet Malaga wine is celebrated throughout the world. Founded (12th cent. B.C.) by the Phoenicians, the city passed to the Carthaginians, the Romans, the Visigoths, and finally (711) the Moors. It flourished from the 13th cent. as a seaport of the Moorish kingdom of Granada, until it fell to Ferdinand and Isabella in 1487. Although largely modern in aspect, the city has several historic buildings, including a cathedral begun in the 16th cent., the ruins of a Moorish alcazar, and an imposing citadel called the Gibralfaro. Picasso was born in Málaga.

Malagasy Republic (măl"əgăs'ē), Malagasy *Repoblika Malagasy,* Fr. *République Malgache,* republic (1971 pop. 7,655,134), 226,658 sq mi (587,045 sq km), in the Indian Ocean, separated from E Africa by the Mozambique Channel. The nation is made up of Madagascar, the world's fourth largest island, and several small islands including Sainte-Marie, Nossi-Bé (Nosy-Bé), Juan de Nova, Europa, and Bassas da India. The capital of the country, which is divided into six provinces, is TANANARIVE; other cities include Antsirabe, Diégo-Suarez (Antsirane), Fianarantsoa, Majunga, Tamatave, and Tuléar. Madagascar is made up of a highland plateau fringed by a lowland coastal strip, narrow (c.30 mi/50 km) in the east and considerably wider (c.60–125 mi/100–200 km) in the west. The plateau attains greater heights in the north, where Mount Maromokotro (9,450 ft/2,880 m), the loftiest point in the country, is located, and in the center, where the Ankaratra Mts. reach c.8,670 ft (2,640 m). Once heavily wooded, the plateau is now largely deforested. A series of lagoons along much of the east coast is connected in part by the

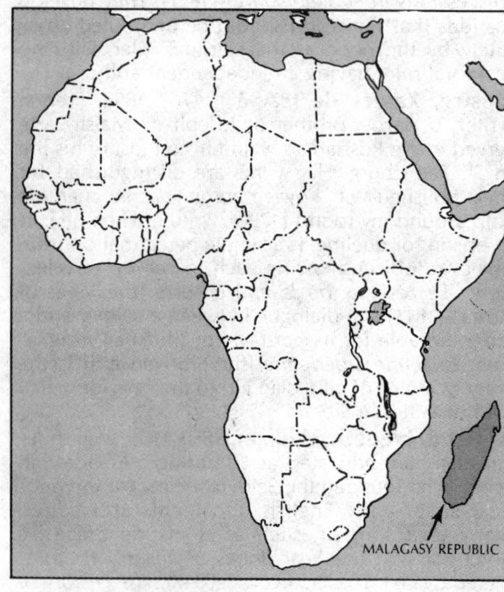

Pangalanes Canal, which runs (c.400 mi/640 km) between Farafangana and Foulpointe and can accommodate small boats. The island has several rivers, including the Sofia, Betsiboka, Manambao, Mangoro, Tsiribihina, Mangoky, Mananara, and Omilahy, all of which flow to the sea. The inhabitants of the Malagasy Republic fall into two main groups—those largely of Indonesian descent and those principally of black African descent. The groups are divided into a total of 18 ethnic groups. The main Indonesian ethnic groups are the Merina (with some 1,744,000 members in 1968), who live near Tananarive, and the Bétsiléo (about 806,000), who live around Fianarantsoa. The principal black African groups are the Betsimisáraka (numbering approximately 998,000), who live near Tamatave; the Tsimihety (477,000), who live near Majunga; the Sakalawa (382,000) and the Antandroy (about 370,000), who live in the west; and the Antaisaka (about 356,000), who live in the southeast. All the people speak Malagasy, a language of Indonesian origin; it and French are official languages. About 40% of the people are Christian (equally divided between Roman Catholics and Protestants), 5% are Muslim, and the rest follow traditional beliefs. The economy of the Malagasy Republic is overwhelmingly agricultural, largely of a subsistence type; the best farmland is in the east and northwest. The principal crops are rice, manioc, millet, pulses, sugarcane, groundnuts, coffee, raffia, tobacco, cloves, and vanilla. In addition, large numbers of poultry, cattle, goats, sheep, and hogs are raised. Manufactures are mostly confined to agricultural products, beverages, and basic consumer goods like clothing. Refined petroleum, cement, paper, and radio and television receivers are also produced, and motor vehicles are assembled. The country has a small but growing mining industry; the chief minerals extracted are chromite, graphite, phosphates, ilmenite, mica, zircon, and industrial beryl and garnets. There is an extensive road system but only a very limited rail network. Tamatave and Majunga are the chief ports. The Malagasy Republic carries on a relatively small foreign trade, and the annual value of imports is usually considerably higher than the value of exports. The main imports are metals, machinery, transport equipment, textiles, and food products; the leading exports are coffee, vanilla, rice, sugar, cloves, raffia, and tobacco. The principal trade partners are France, the United States, and West Germany.

History. The earliest history of Madagascar is unclear. Black Africans and Indonesians reached the island about 2,000 years ago, the Indonesian immigration continuing until the 15th cent. From the 9th cent., Muslim traders (including some Arabs) from E Africa and the Comoro Islands settled in NW and SE Madagascar. Probably the first European to see Madagascar was Diogo Dias, a Portuguese navigator, in 1500. Between 1600 and 1619, Portuguese Roman Catholic missionaries tried unsuccessfully to convert the Malagasy. From 1642 until the late 18th cent. the French maintained footholds, first at Fort-Dauphin in the southeast and finally on Sainte Marie Island off the east coast. By the beginning of the 17th cent. there were a number of small Malagasy kingdoms, including those of the Antemoro,

Antaisaka, Bétsiléo, and Merina. Later in the century the Sakalawa under Andriandahifotsi conquered W and N Madagascar, but the kingdom disintegrated in the 18th cent. At the end of the 18th cent. the Merina people of the interior were united under King Andrianampoinimerina (reigned 1787–1810), who also subjected the Bétsiléo. RADAMA I (reigned 1810–28), in return for agreeing to end the slave trade, received British aid in modernizing and equipping his army, which helped him to conquer the Betsimisáraka kingdom. The Protestant London Missionary Society was welcomed, and it gained many converts, opened schools, and helped to transcribe the Merina language. Merina culture began to spread over Madagascar. Radama was succeeded by his wife Ranavalona I (reigned 1828–1861), who, suspicious of foreigners, declared (1835) Christianity illegal and halted most foreign trade. During her rule the Merina kingdom was wracked by intermittent civil war. Under Radama II (reigned 1861–63) and his widow and successor Rasoherina (reigned 1863–68) the anti-European policy was reversed and missionaries (including Roman Catholics) and traders were welcomed again. Rainilaiarivony, the prime minister, controlled the government during the reigns of Ranavalona II (1868–83) and Ranavalona III (1883–96); by then the Merina kingdom included all Madagascar except the south and part of the west. Ranavalona II publicly recognized Christianity, and she and her husband were baptized. In 1883 the French bombarded and occupied Tamatave, and in 1885 they established a protectorate over Madagascar, which was recognized by Great Britain in 1890. Rainilaiarivony organized resistance to the French, and there was heavy fighting from 1894 to 1896. In 1896, French troops under J. S. Gallieni defeated the Merina and abolished the monarchy. By 1904 the French fully controlled the island. Under the French, who governed the Malagasy through a divide-and-rule policy, development was concentrated in the Tananarive region, and thus the Merina benefited most from colonial rule. Merina nationalism developed early in the 20th cent., and in 1916 (during World War I) a Merina secret society was suppressed by the French after a plot against the colonialists was discovered. During World War II, Madagascar was aligned with Vichy France until 1942, when it was conquered by the British; in 1943 the Free French regime assumed control. From 1947 to 1948 there was a major uprising against the French, who crushed the rebellion, killing between 11,000 and 80,000 (estimates vary) Malagasy in the process. As in other French colonies, indigenous political activity increased in 1956, and the Social Democratic Party (PSD), led by Philibert Tsiranana (a Tsimihety), gained predominance in Madagascar. On Oct. 14, 1958, the country—renamed the Malagasy Republic—became autonomous within the French Community and Tsiranana was elected president. On June 26, 1960, it became fully independent. Under Tsiranana (reelected in 1965 and 1972), an autocratic ruler whose PSD controlled parliament, government was centralized, the coastal peoples (*côtiers*) were favored over those of the interior (especially the Merina), and French economic and cultural influence remained strong. In a controversial move beginning in 1967, Tsiranana cultivated economic relations with white-ruled South Africa. After Tsiranana was reelected in Jan., 1972, students and workers, discontented with the president's policies and with the deteriorating economic situation, staged a wave of protest demonstrations. At the height of the crisis Tsiranana handed over (May 18) power to General Gabriel Ramanantsoa, who became prime minister. In Oct., 1972, a national referendum overwhelmingly approved Ramanantsoa's plan to rule without parliament for 5 years; Tsiranana, who opposed the plan, resigned the presidency shortly after the vote. Ramanantsoa freed political prisoners jailed by Tsiranana, began to reduce French influence in the country, broke off relations with South Africa, and generally followed a moderately leftist course. See D. O. Mannoni, *Prospero and Caliban: the Psychology of Colonization* (tr., 2d ed. 1964); Virginia Thompson and Richard Adloff, *The Malagasy Republic* (1965); Raymond Kent, *From Madagascar to the Malagasy Republic* (1962) and *Early Kingdoms in Madagascar, 1500–1700* (1970); Hubert Deschamps, *Histoire de Madagascar* (4th ed. 1972).

Malakhov (məlă'khəf), hill overlooking Sevastopol, SW European USSR, in the Ukraine, in the Crimea, just east of the city. A major fortified point in the Crimean War, it was stormed (1855) by the French after an 11-month siege. The name is often spelled Malakoff.

Malamud, Bernard (măl'əməd), 1914–, American author, b. Brooklyn, N.Y., grad. College of the City of New York (B.A., 1936) and Columbia (M.A., 1942). His works often reflect a concern with Jewish tradition and the nobility of the humble man. *The Fixer* (1966; Pulitzer Prize), set in the Soviet Union, reveals the courage of a handyman falsely accused by the government of ritual murder. *The Tenants* (1971) describes the confrontation of two writers, one Jewish, one black, and probes the nature of the art of writing. Malamud's other works include the novels *The Natural* (1952), *The Assistant* (1957), and *A New Life* (1961); and the short-story collections *The Magic Barrel* (1958), *Idiots First* (1963), and *Rembrandt's Hat* (1973).

malamute: see ALASKAN MALAMUTE.

Malan, Daniel François (dänyĕl' fräNswä' məlän'), 1874–1959, South African political leader. A minister of the Dutch Reformed Church, he left the pulpit after the outbreak of World War I to become editor of an Afrikaner nationalist paper. Rising to prominence in the National party in Cape Province, he was elected to Parliament in 1918. He served (1924–33) as minister of the interior, public health, and education in the cabinet of J. B. M. Hertzog. After World War II, Malan's National party and the small Afrikaner party, campaigning on the issue of white supremacy, came (1948) to power with Malan as prime minister. His government initiated the racial separation laws known as apartheid. He retired as prime minister in 1954.

Malaparte (mäläpär'tā), pseud. of **Curzio Suckert,** 1898–1957, Italian journalist and short-story writer. After action in World War I and two years in the diplomatic service, he became a free-lance writer. The *enfant terrible* of Italian letters, he first defended and later criticized Fascism. He suffered a five-year exile to Lipari, which he described in *Fughe in prigione* (1936). His other works—erratic, eclectic, and often obscene—include the short-story collections *Donna come me* [woman like me] (1940) and *Kaputt* (1944, tr. 1946) and *Das Kapital,* a play produced in 1949.

Mälaren (mĕ'lärən), lake, c.440 sq mi (1,140 sq km), E central Sweden. Third largest of the Swedish lakes, it extends c.70 mi (110 km) W from Stockholm, which is situated on the strait connecting the lake with the Baltic Sea. The lake's scenic shores and more than 1,000 islands have many villas and historic castles and ruins, notably Skokloster and Gripsholm. There are many important small industrial towns on the lake.

malaria, infectious parasitic disease that can be either acute or chronic and is frequently recurrent. It has been and still is a widespread disease; its victims at any given time are counted in the millions. Malaria is common in Central and South America, the Mediterranean countries, Asia, and many of the Pacific islands. In the United States it is found in the South and less frequently in the northern and western parts of the country. Malaria is usually transmitted by an *Anopheles* mosquito that has picked up the causative organism, *Plasmodium,* from the blood of an infected person and transferred it to that of a healthy person in the course of its feeding. At the onset of malaria, bouts of chills (ague) and fever lasting several hours and occurring every three or four days are the usual symptoms. If the disease is not treated, the spleen and the liver become enlarged, anemia develops, and jaundice appears. Death may occur from general debility, anemia, or invasion of the cerebral tissues. Quinine and cinchona, the specific drugs in the treatment of malaria for centuries, have been largely replaced since World War II by several superior synthetic antimalarials, among them chloroquine. Drainage of swamps and other breeding places of mosquitoes and education of the populace in the use of screens, netting, insecticides, and repellents have greatly diminished incidence of the disease; however, much preventive work remains to be done.

Malaspina (mäləspē'nə), glacier, c.1,500 sq mi (3,890 sq km), SE Alaska, between Yakutat Bay and Icy Bay and flowing into the Gulf of Alaska. The glacier was named for an Italian navigator who explored this region for Spain in 1791.

Malatesta (mälätĕ'stä), Italian family, ruling RIMINI and nearby cities for almost 300 years from the 13th to 16th cent. Malatesta da Verucchio (d. 1312), a powerful Guelph leader, became (1239) podesta, or chief magistrate, of Rimini and used this position to entrench his family's position in the area. His hunchback son Gianciotto was married to FRANCESCA DA RIMINI. With the expulsion of the family's Ghibelline rivals in 1295 the Malatesta rule in Rimini became well established, but papal investiture was made only in the following century. Branches of the family came to rule also Pesaro, Cesena, and Fano. In the 14th and 15th cent. several members of the family were noted CONDOTTIERI in the service of various Italian states. The most famous was Sigismondo Pandolfo Malatesta (1417–68), a typical lord of the Italian Renaissance. A patron of arts and letters, he had the church of San Francesco in Rimini transformed into the Tempio Malatestiano [the temple of the Malatesta]. A despot excommunicated for numerous crimes, he engaged in a bitter conflict with the papacy over territorial claims, but he finally lost (1463) all his possessions except Rimini. His brother Novello, lord of Cesena, built there the fine Malatesta library. Sigismondo's son and grandson held the little state with difficulty, eventually losing it in 1500 to Cesare Borgia. Although the Malatesta family returned for brief intervals in the early 16th cent., Rimini passed definitively to the Holy See in 1528.

Malathion (măl"əthī'ŏn): see INSECTICIDE.

Malatya (mälät'yä), city (1970 pop. 130,340), capital of Malatya prov., E central Turkey, in the E Taurus mts. It is the commercial center for a rich farm region that produces apricots, grapes, and grains. Manufactures of the city include cement, cotton textiles, and sugar. Situated at a strategic crossroads in ancient times, the city was the capital of a small Hittite kingdom c.1100 B.C.; it was then known as Milidia. In Roman times it was called Melitene and was a military headquarters. An important city of Cappadocia, it became a metropolitan see in early Christian times. The city frequently suffered from attack and changed hands many times. In 1516 it was annexed by the Ottoman Empire. In 1895, Christians were massacred in Malatya.

Malawi (məlä'wē), formerly **Nyasaland** (nīăs'əlănd"), republic (1973 est. pop. 4,700,000), 45,200 sq mi (117,068 sq km), E central Africa, bordering on Zambia in the west, on Tanzania in the north, and on Mozambique in the east, south, and southwest. The capital is LILONGWE; other cities include BLANTYRE, Mzuzu, and ZOMBA. Malawi is long and narrow, and about 20% of its total area is made up of Lake Nyasa (Lake Malawi). Several rivers flow into Lake Nyasa from the west, and the Shire River (a tributary of the Zambezi) drains the lake in the

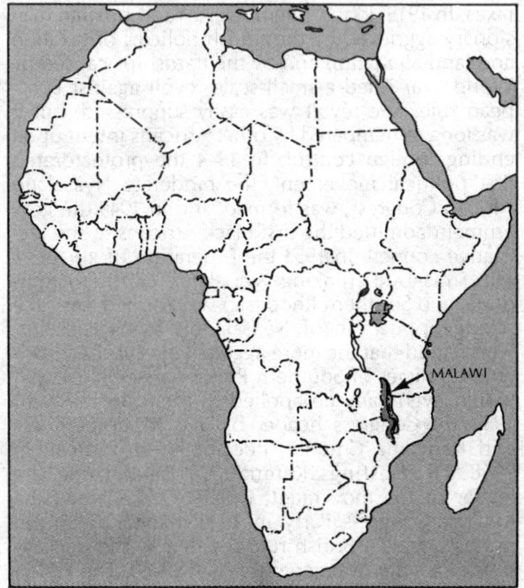

south. Both the lake and the Shire lie within the Great Rift Valley. Much of the rest of the country is made up of a plateau that averages 2,500 to 4,500 ft (762–1,372 m) in height, but reaches elevations of c.8,000 ft (2,440 m) in the north and almost 10,000 ft (3,050 m) in the south. Almost all of the country's inhabitants are Bantu-speaking black Africans, of which the Tumbuka, Ngoni, and Tonga (in the north) and the Cewa, Yao, Nguru, and Nyanja (in the center and south) are the main subgroups. About 1.7 million Malawians are Christian (mostly Roman Catholic and Presbyterian), and more than 500,000 are Muslim; the rest follow traditional beliefs. English, Cinyanja, and Citumbuku are official languages. Malawi is an overwhelmingly agricultural country, with a very low per capita income. About 85% of the cultivated land is made up of small farms held under traditional terms of tenure; the principal crops raised are maize, pulses, millet, sorghum, groundnuts, cassava, and potatoes. The rest of the farmland is included in large estates, where tea, tobacco, sugarcane, and tung oil are produced. Large numbers of poultry, goats, cattle, and pigs are raised in the country. There are also small fishing and forest products industries. Practically no minerals are extracted, but there are substantial deposits of bauxite. Malawi's few manufactures are limited to basic goods, such as processed food, beverages, clothing, footwear, construction materials, and radios. In the early 1970s about 250,000 Malawians worked as migratory laborers in Rhodesia, South Africa, and Zambia. The annual value of Malawi's imports is usually considerably higher than the value of its exports, the leading imports being manufactured consumer goods, machinery, transport equipment, chemicals, and foodstuffs; the principal exports are tobacco, tea, groundnuts, and maize. The chief trade partners are Great Britain, Rhodesia, and South Africa. Most of the country's foreign trade is conducted via Salima, a port on Lake Nyasa, which is connected by rail with the seaports of Beira and Nacala in Mozambique.

History. The first inhabitants of present-day Malawi were probably Pygmy-like hunter-gatherers. In the 15th cent., Bantu-speaking persons migrated from the west and north, and they soon coalesced into the Malawi kingdom (late 15th–late 18th cent.), centered in the Shire River valley. In the 18th cent. the kingdom conquered much of modern Rhodesia and Mozambique. However, shortly thereafter it declined as a result of internal rivalries and incursions by the Yao, who sold their Malawi captives as slaves to Arab and Swahili merchants living on the Indian Ocean coast. In the 1840s the region was thrown into further turmoil by the arrival from S Africa of the predatory Ngoni. In 1859, David Livingstone, the Scots explorer, visited Lake Nyasa and drew European attention to the effects of the slave trade there; in 1873 two Presbyterian missionary societies established bases in the region. Missionary activity, the threat of Portuguese annexation, and the influence of Cecil Rhodes led Great Britain to send a consul to the area in 1883 and to proclaim the Shire Highlands Protectorate in 1889. In 1891 the British Central African Protectorate (known from 1907 until 1964 as Nyasaland), which included most of present-day Malawi, was established. During the 1890s British forces ended the slave trade in the protectorate. At the same time, Europeans established coffee-growing estates in the Shire region; they were worked by Africans who thereby earned the cash necessary to pay taxes. In 1915, John Chilembwe, a Yao Christian missionary aggrieved by the British policies of taxation and land alienation and by the hardships caused by World War I, led a small-scale revolt against European rule. The revolt was easily suppressed, but it was long remembered by other Africans intent upon ending foreign control. In 1944 the protectorate's first political movement, the moderate Nyasaland African Congress, was formed, and in 1949 the government admitted the first black Africans to the legislative council. In 1953 the Federation of RHODESIA AND NYASALAND (linking Nyasaland, Northern Rhodesia, and Southern Rhodesia) was formed, over the strong opposition of Nyasaland's black Africans, who feared that the more aggressively European-oriented policies of Southern Rhodesia (see RHODESIA) would eventually be applied to them. In the mid-1950s the Congress, headed by H. B. M. Chipembere and Kanyama Chiume, became more radical. In 1958, Dr. Hastings Kamuzu BANDA became the leader of the movement, which was renamed the Malawi Congress Party in 1959. Banda organized protests against British rule that led to the declaration of a state of emergency in 1959–60. The Federation of Rhodesia and Nyasaland was ended in 1963, and on July 6, 1964, Nyasaland became independent as Malawi. Banda led the country in the era of independence, first as prime minister and, after Malawi became a republic in 1966, as president; he was made president for life in 1971. He quickly alienated other leaders by governing autocratically, by allowing Europeans to retain considerable influence within the country, and by refusing to oppose white-minority rule in South Africa. Banda crushed a revolt led by Chipembere in 1965 and one led by Yatuta Chisiza in 1967. Arguing that the country's economic well-being depended on friendly relations with the white-run governments in S Africa, Banda established diplomatic ties between Malawi and South Africa in 1967. In 1970, Prime Minister Balthazar J. Vorster of South Africa visited Malawi, and in 1971 Banda became the first head of an independent black African nation to visit South Africa. See M. J. Morris, *A Brief History of Nyasaland* (1952); Colin Black, *The Lands and Peoples of Rhodesia and Nyasaland* (1961); Robert I. Rotberg, *The Rise of Nationalism in Central Africa* (1966); J. G. Pike, *Malawi: A Political and Economic History* (1968); B. Pachai, *The Early History of Malawi* (1972).

Malawi, Lake, E central Africa: see NYASA, LAKE.

Malay: see MALAYAN.

Malaya: see MALAYSIA, FEDERATION OF.

Malayalam (mä″ləyä′ləm), Dravidian language of India. See DRAVIDIAN LANGUAGES.

Malayan (məlā′ən) or **Malay** (mā′lā), general term for one of a population of persons inhabiting SE Asia and the adjacent islands. The Malays vary greatly in physical appearance. The term *Indonesian,* used as an alternative for *Malayan,* is sometimes applied to the people of interior districts, who are thought to be related to the Pygmies or Negritos (probably the earlier inhabitants of the region). In the coastal districts there has been intermixture with the Arabs, the Chinese, the Indians, and the Siamese. Scores of languages or dialects are spoken; they form a group of the Malayo-Polynesian languages. Among anthropologists the term *Malayan* is used exclusively to describe an inhabitant of the Malayan Peninsula.

Malay Archipelago, great island group of SE Asia formerly called the East Indies. It lies between the Asian mainland and Australia, separating the Pacific Ocean from the Indian Ocean.

Malay language: see MALAYO-POLYNESIAN LANGUAGES.

Malayo-Polynesian languages (məlā′ō-pŏlĭnē′-zhən), sometimes also called Austronesian languages, family of languages estimated at from 300 to 500 tongues and spoken by more than 130 million people in the Malay Peninsula, Madagascar, Taiwan, Indonesia, New Guinea, the Melanesian, Micronesian, and Polynesian islands, the Philippine Islands, and New Zealand. It is thought that the original Malayo-Polynesian speakers came from a part of Asia near the Malay Peninsula and later migrated west as far as Madagascar and east to the Pacific. This migration probably began well over two thousand years ago. Because Malayo-Polynesian speakers lived on thousands of islands that were often widely separated, and because in earlier times communication among them was difficult, if not impossible, many dialects and, in time, languages evolved from the ancestor language, Proto-Malayo-Polynesian. Although it has been suggested that the Malayo-Polynesian and Southeast Asian (or Austroasiatic) languages form a single Austric family, this has not been proved. In fact, the Malayo-Polynesian tongues do not seem to be related to any other linguistic family. Today four Malayo-Polynesian languages have official status in four important states: Malay, in Malaysia; Indonesian (also called Bahasa Indonesia), in the Republic of Indonesia; Malagasy, in the Malagasy Republic of the island of Madagascar; and Tagalog, in the Republic of the Philippines, where it has been called Filipino since 1959. The Malayo-Polynesian family has two subfamilies, Western Malayo-Polynesian and Eastern Malayo-Polynesian. The Western subfamily has the greater significance from both a cultural and a commercial viewpoint. Western Malayo-Polynesian languages are spoken by about 130 million people and include Malagasy, the language of 5 million people on the island of Madagascar; Malay, native to 17 million in Malaya, Borneo, and Sumatra; Indonesian or Bahasa Indonesian [Indonesian language], which is based on Malay and spoken by about 12 million people in Indonesia; Javanese, the mother tongue of 45 million people on Java; Sundanese, the language of 14 million, also on Java; Madurese, with 7 million speakers on Madura; Balinese, spoken by 2 million on Bali; Batak, native to 2 million on Sumatra; Bugi, with 2 million speakers on Celebes; Dayak, the language of more than 1 million on Borneo and Sumatra; Visayan, spoken by 11 million in the Philippines; Tagalog, the tongue of 6 million, also in the Philippines; Ilocano, with 3 million speakers in the Philippines; Bikol, native to another 2 million in the Philippines; and some Western Malayo-Polynesian dialects spoken by several thousand people on Taiwan. The Eastern branch consists of the Melanesian, Micronesian, and Polynesian groups of languages. Although there is a very large number of these languages, all together they are spoken by only one million people. Melanesian languages are found on the Fiji Islands, the Solomon Islands, New Hebrides, New Caledonia, the Bismarck Archipelago, and New Guinea. Among the leading Polynesian languages are Samoan, the tongue of 100 thousand people of Western Samoa and American Samoa; Maori, native to 75 thousand people in New Zealand; Tongan, spoken by 70 thousand people of Tonga; Tahitian, the language of 30 thousand on Tahiti; and Hawaiian, spoken by 25 thousand people of Hawaii. Chomorro of Guam, a Micronesian language, has 30 thousand speakers. The Malayo-Polynesian languages exhibit an abundance of vowels and a comparative paucity of consonants. They also tend to have disyllabic roots, form derivatives by means of affixes, and use reduplication to indicate the plural and other grammatical concepts. Writing varies, some forms being based on the Roman alphabet and others on alphabets derived from Indian or Arabic scripts. See R. C. Green and Andrew Pawley, *The Linguistic Subgroup of Polynesia* (1966).

Malay Peninsula (məlā′, mā′lā), southern extremity (c.70,000 sq mi/181,300 sq km) of the continent of Asia, lying between the Andaman Sea of the Indian Ocean and the Strait of Malacca on the west and the Gulf of Siam and the South China Sea on the east. It stretches south for c.700 mi (1,100 km) from the Isthmus of Kra, where it is narrowest, to Singapore. The northern part of the peninsula forms a part of Thailand; the southern part constitutes West Malaysia, the Malayan part of the Federation of Malaysia. A mountain range (the highest point of which is Gunong Tahan, 7,186 ft/2,190 m, in Malaysia) forms the backbone of the peninsula; from it numerous short, swift rivers flow east and west. More than half of the land surface is covered with tropical rain forest; the only open areas, aside from man-made clearings, are the alluvial plains of the west-central portion of the peninsula and stretches along the rivers. The region is one of the richest of the world in the production of tin and rubber; other products include timber, copra and coconut oil, palm oil, tapioca, peanuts, pineapples, and bananas. Rice is the chief foodstuff. The peninsula forms a physical and cultural link between the mainland of Asia and the islands of Indonesia (often included in the Malay Archipelago). The Malays, historically the dominant cultural group, probably came originally from S China (c.2,000 B.C.), but marriages with other peoples have modified their ethnic characteristics. The Chinese are now nearly as numerous as the Malays; Indians and Thais form important minority groups. Small tribes of aborigines, descendants of pre-Malay immigrants, are found in the hills and jungles. The Malay Peninsula was visited near the beginning of the Christian era by traders from India and in the succeeding centuries received, like Indonesia and Indochina, Buddhist and Brahman missionaries and Hindu colonists. Small Hinduized states sprang up, like Langkasuka in the area of modern Kedah. In the second half of the 8th cent. the peninsula fell under the domination of the Sailendra rulers of Sri Vijaya (from Sumatra), who adopted Mahayana Buddhism. Their cities in Kedah and Pattani rivaled the importance of their capital at Palembang. The peninsula was overrun in the 11th cent. by the Cholas from the Coromandel Coast of India; after about 50 years, the Sailendras, somewhat weakened, resumed their sway. It ended in the late 13th cent., when Sumatra and some southern areas of the Malay Peninsula fell to a Javan invasion and when the Thai king of Sukhothai swept over the peninsula from the north. The Sumatran kingdom of Melayu next ruled over the south of the peninsula, to be followed in turn (late 14th cent.) by Madjapahit, which was the last Hindu empire of Java, and by the Thai king of Ayutthaya. The fall of Madjapahit opened the way for the primacy of a Malay state, Malacca (see MELAKA). In the 15th cent., the Malays, beginning with the Malaccans, were converted to Islam (which remains the religion of most Malays). The 16th cent. brought the first Europeans. The Portuguese seized Malacca (1511), and soon afterward Dutch traders appeared in Malayan waters. Malacca fell to the Dutch in 1641. The important British role on the peninsula began with the founding of settlements at PINANG (1786) and SINGAPORE (1819). The coming of the Portuguese had plunged the peninsula into anarchy. The last sultan of Malacca, in flight from the Portuguese, founded a kingdom based on the Riau Archipelago and JOHOR, but the rulers of the petty states in the south gradually achieved independence, while the rising power of Siam and an increasingly imperial Britain became rivals. The British established protectorates over several Malay states, and in 1909 the boundary between Siam and Malaya was fixed by Siam's transfer to Great Britain of suzerainty over Kedah, Perlis, Kelantan, and Terengganu. See MALAYSIA, FEDERATION OF.

Malaysia, Federation of, country (1971 pop. 10,424,325), 128,430 sq mi (332,633 sq km), Southeast Asia. Malaysia consists of two parts: **West Malaysia** (1971 pop. 8,791,690), 50,700 sq mi (131,313 sq km), on the MALAY PENINSULA, comprising the states of PERLIS, KEDAH, PINANG, PERAK, KELANTAN, TERENGGANU, PO-

HANG, SELANGOR, NEGERI SEMBILAN, MELAKA (Malacca), and JOHOR, and coextensive with the former Federation of Malaya; and **East Malaysia** (1971 pop. 1,632,635), 77,730 sq mi (201,320 sq km), comprising the

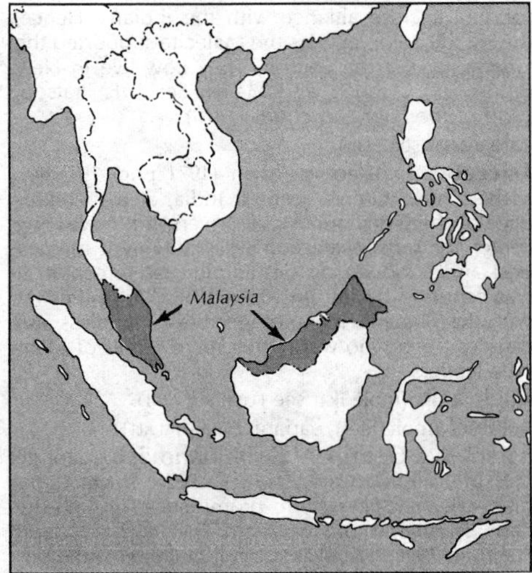

states of SABAH and SARAWAK (the former British colonies of North Borneo and Northwest Borneo) on the island of Borneo. The two parts are separated by c.400 mi (640 km) of the South China Sea. West Malaysia is bordered on the north by Thailand, on the east by the South China Sea, on the south by Singapore (separated by the narrow Johore Strait), and on the west by the Strait of Malacca and the Andaman Sea. East Malaysia is bordered on the north by the South China Sea and the Sulu Sea, on the east by the Celebes Sea, and on the south and west by Kalimantan (Indonesian Borneo). Along the coast within Sarawak are the two small portions of the British protectorate of Brunei. The capital of Malaysia is KUALA LUMPUR. Both East and West Malaysia have mountainous interiors and coastal plains. The highest point is Mt. Kinabalu (13,455 ft/4,101 m) in Sabah. The longest of the country's many rivers are the Rajang (c.350 mi/560 km) in Sarawak, the Kinabatangan in Sabah, and the Pahang in West Malaysia. Lying close to the equator, Malaysia has a tropical rainy climate. Nearly three fourths of the land area is forested, and many parts of the country have not yet been explored. The federation is largely a producer of raw materials, and it is one of the world's leading suppliers of tin and rubber. Other large exports are timber and forest products, palm oil, and iron ore. Pinang city is the chief port. Other minerals found in Malaysia are petroleum, bauxite, ilmenite, copper, and gold. Subsistence agriculture, however, remains the basis of livelihood for most Malaysians; rice is the staple food, while fish supply most of the protein. Industry, mainly processing and light manufacturing, is largely concentrated in West Malaysia. The major cities on the Malay Peninsula are connected by state-owned railroads with Singapore, and an extensive road net covers the west coast, where most of the population is concentrated. Malaysia is a country of vast ethnic diversity. Of the total population a little more than two fifths are Malays, a little less than two fifths are Chinese, about one tenth are Indians and Pakistanis, and the remainder belong to sixteen indigenous ethnic groups. In West Malaysia, Malays comprise about one half of the population, Chinese one third, and Indians and Pakistanis one tenth. In East Malaysia, the two largest groups are the Chinese and the Ibans (Sea Dayaks), an indigenous people, who together make up about three fifths of the total. Malays account for a little less than one fifth. Conflict between the ethnic groups, particularly between Malays and Chinese, has played a large role in Malaysian history. The official language is Bahasa Malaysia (Malay), although English is used in the legal system. Chinese, Tamil, and tribal languages and dialects are also widely spoken. There are three universities: Kebangsaan Univ. and the Univ. of Malaya in Kuala Lumpur and the Univ. of Penang in Gelugor, Pinang.

History. (For early history of West Malaysia, see MALAY PENINSULA; for history of East Malaysia, see SABAH and SARAWAK.) When the Portuguese captured Malacca (1511), its sultan fled first to Pahang and then to Johor and the Riau Archipelago. One of his sons became the first sultan of Perak. From both Johor and ACHEH in Sumatra unsuccessful attacks were made on Malacca. Acheh and Johor also fought each other. The main issue in these struggles was control of trade through the Strait of Malacca. Kedah, Kelantan, and Terengganu, north of Malacca, became nominal subjects of Siam. In the early 17th cent. the Dutch established trading bases in Southeast Asia. By 1619 they had established themselves in Batavia (Djakarta), and in 1641, allied with Johor, they captured Malacca after a six-month siege. Another power entered the complicated Malayan picture in the late 17th cent. when the Bugis from Celebes, a Malay people economically pressured by the Dutch, began settling in the area of Selangor on the west coast of the peninsula, where they traded in tin. The Bugis captured Johor and Riau in 1721 and, with a few interruptions, maintained control there for about a century, although the Johor sultanate was permitted to remain. The Bugis were also active in Perak and Kedah. Earlier, in the 15th and 16th cent., another Malay people, the Minangkabaus from Sumatra, had peacefully settled inland from Malacca. Their settlements eventually became the state of Negeri Sembilan. The British role on the peninsula began in 1786, when Francis Light of the British East India Company, searching for a site for trade and a naval base, obtained the cession of the island of Pinang from the sultan of Kedah. In 1791 the British agreed to make annual payments to the sultan, and in 1800 the latter ceded Province Wellesley on the mainland. In 1819 the British founded SINGAPORE, and in 1824 they formally (actual control had been exercised since 1795) acquired Malacca from the Dutch. A joint administration was formed for Pinang, Malacca, and Singapore, which became known as the STRAITS SETTLEMENTS. During this period Siam was asserting its influence southward on the peninsula. In 1816, Siam forced Kedah to invade Perak and made Perak acknowledge Siamese suzerainty. In 1821, Siam invaded Kedah and exiled the sultan. The Anglo-Siamese treaty of 1821 recognized Siamese control of Kedah but left the status of Perak, Kelantan, and Terengganu ambiguous. In 1841 the sultan of Kedah was restored, but Perlis was carved out of the territory of Kedah and put under Siamese protection. Later in the century a number of events led Great Britain to play a more direct part in the affairs of the peninsula. There was conflict between Chinese settlers, who worked in the tin mines, and Malays; there were civil wars among the Malays; and there was an increase in piracy in the western part of the peninsula. Merchants asked the British to restore order. The British were also concerned that Dutch, French, and German interest in the area was increasing. As a result, treaties were made with Perak, Selangor, Pahang, and the components of what became (1895) Negeri Sembilan. In each state a British "resident" was installed to advise the sultan (who received a stipend) and to supervise administration. The Pangkor Treaty of 1874 with Perak served as a model for subsequent treaties. In 1896 the four states were grouped together as the Federated Malay States with a British resident general. Johor, which had signed a treaty of alliance with Britain in 1885, accepted a British adviser in 1914. British control of the four remaining Malayan states was acquired in 1909, when, by treaty, Siam relinquished its claims to sovereignty over Kedah, Kelantan, Perlis, and Terengganu. These four, along with Johor, became known as the Unfederated Malay States. In the latter half of the 19th century Malaya's economy assumed essentially its present character. The output of tin, which had been mined for centuries, increased greatly with the utilization of modern methods. Rubber trees were introduced (Indian laborers were imported to work the rubber plantations), and Malaya became a leading rubber producer. Malaya's economic character, as well as its geographic position, gave it great strategic importance, and the peninsula was quickly overrun by the Japanese at the start of World War II and held by them for the duration of the war. Malaya's Chinese population received particularly harsh treatment during the Japanese occupation. When the British returned they arranged (1946) a centralized colony, called the Malayan Union, comprising all their peninsula possessions. Influential Malays vehemently opposed the new organization; they feared that the admission of the large Chinese and Indian populations of Pinang and Malacca to Malayan citizenship would end the special position Malays had always enjoyed, and they were unwilling to surrender the political power they enjoyed within the individual sultanates. The British backed down and established in place of the Union the Federation of Malaya (1948) headed by a British high commissioner. The Federation was an expansion of the former Federated Malay States. Pinang and Malacca became members in addition to the nine Malay states, but there was no common citizenship. In that same year a Communist insurrection began that was to last more than a decade. The Communist guerrillas, largely recruited from among the Chinese population, employed terrorist tactics. In combatting the uprising the British resettled nearly 500,000 Chinese. "The Emergency," as it was called, was declared ended in 1960, although outbreaks of terrorism have continued sporadically. The insurrection had the positive effect of spurring the movement for Malayan independence: In 1957 the Federation became an independent state within the Commonwealth of Nations and was admitted to the United Nations. The first prime minister was Tengku (Prince) Abdul Rahman, the leader of the Alliance Party, a loose coalition of Malay, Chinese, and Indian parties. The constitution guaranteed special privileges for Malays. In 1963 Singapore, Sabah, and Sarawak were added to the federation, creating the Federation of Malaysia. Since Singapore has a large Chinese population, the latter two states were included to maintain a non-Chinese majority. Brunei was also included in the plan but declined to join. Malaysia retained Malaya's place in the United Nations and the Commonwealth. The new state was immediately confronted with the hostility of Indonesia, which described the federation as a British imperialist subterfuge and waged an undeclared war against it. In the struggle Malaysia received military aid from Great Britain and other Commonwealth nations. Hostilities continued until President Sukarno's fall from power in Indonesia (1965). Nonviolent opposition came from the Philippines, which still claims Sabah, but the claim has not been pressed. The merger with Singapore did not work out satisfactorily. Friction developed between Malay leaders and Singapore's prime minister, Lee Kuan Yew, who worked to improve the position of Chinese in the Federation. In 1965, Singapore peacefully seceded from Malaysia. Inter-communal tension continued, however, and serious violence broke out in 1969 following general elections in West Malaysia in which the Chinese made gains at the expense of the Malays. Parliament was suspended for 22 months. General elections in Aug., 1974, resulted in an overwhelming victory for the National Front coalition government of Prime Minister Abdul Razak.

Government. Malaysia is a constitutional monarchy with parliamentary democracy. The sovereign (the Yang di-Pertuan Agong) is elected by and from the nine hereditary rulers of Perlis, Kedah, Perak, Kelantan, Terengganu, Pahang, Selangor, Negeri Sembilan, and Johor. The sovereign appoints the cabinet, headed by the prime minister, who must be a member and have the confidence of the house of representatives (Dewan Ra'ayat). The parliament has two chambers. The house consists of 154 members, all elected by popular vote in single-member districts. The house sits for a maximum of five years but may be dissolved by the sovereign. The senate (Dewan Negara) consists of 58 members chosen for six-year terms; each state legislature elects two and the sovereign appoints the remaining 32. There is a high court for each half of Malaysia and a federal court. West Malaysia has five main political parties: the leading Alliance Party, a coalition of the United Malays National Organization, the Malayan Chinese Association, and the Malaysian Indian Congress; the Pan-Malayan Islamic Party, representing extreme Malay nationalist views; the Democratic Action Party, which is Chinese-oriented; the socialist Gerakan Ra'ayat Malaysia (Malaysian People's Movement); and the People's Progressive Party, a moderately socialist party appealing largely to Chinese. There are also separate parties in Sabah and Sarawak. See N. J. Ryan, *The Making of Modern Malaysia and Singapore* (4th ed. 1969); R. O. Winstedt, *Malaya and its History* (7th ed. 1966, repr. 1969); J. W. Henderson, and others, *Area Handbook for Malaysia* (1970); Joseph Kennedy, *A History of Malaya* (2d ed. 1970); M. J. Esman, *Administration and Development in Malaysia* (1972); R. C. McKie, *The Emergence of Malaysia* (1963, repr. 1973).

Malay States: see MALAYSIA.

Malazgirt: see MANZIKERT.

Malbone, Edward Greene (mălbōn′), 1777-1807, American portrait painter and miniaturist, b. Newport, R.I. After painting portraits in Providence and Boston, he accompanied Washington Allston to Charleston, S.C., and then to Europe. He was urged by Benjamin West to settle in London, but he returned to America, where he met with great success. His miniatures are noted for their grace and delicacy of tone. See monograph by R. P. Tolman (1958).

Malbork (mäl'bôrk), Ger. *Marienburg,* town (1970 pop. 30,900), N Poland, on the Nogat River. It is a rail junction with sugar refineries and manufactures of rubber and pharmaceuticals. Originally a castle founded (1274) by the TEUTONIC KNIGHTS, Malbork became the seat of their grand master in 1309. It successfully withstood sieges by the Poles in 1410 and 1454, but in 1457 Malbork was sold to Poland by mercenaries whose pay was in arrears. The town passed to Prussia in 1772. The castle (rebuilt in the 14th and 19th cent.) is one of the finest examples of German secular medieval architecture.

Malcham (măl'kəm). **1** One of the Benjamite chiefs. 1 Chron. 8.9. **2** Heathen god, perhaps to be identified with MOLECH. Zeph. 1.5.

Malchiah (mălkī'ə). **1** Priest. 1 Chron. 6.40. **2, 3, 4, 5** Israelites in the return to Palestine. Ezra 10.25; Neh. 3.14,31; 8.4. **6** Israelite in the return. Ezra 10.31. Malchijah: Neh. 3.11. **7** Owner of Jeremiah's prison. Jer. 38.6 **8** See MALCHIJAH **1.**

Malchiel (măl'kēĕl, mălkī'əl), founder of an Asherite family. Gen. 46.17; Num. 26.45. 1 Chron. 7.31.

Malchijah (mălkī'jə). **1** Priest. 1 Chron. 9.12. Jer. 38.1. Malchiah: Neh. 11.12. Melchiah: Jer. 21.1. **2** Priest, perhaps the same as **1.** 1 Chron. 24.9. **3** Sealer of the covenant, perhaps the same as **1.** Neh. 10.3. **4** Israelite in the return. Ezra 10.25. **5** Priest in the return. Neh. 12.42. **6** See MALCHIAH **6.**

Malchiram (mălkī'rəm), son of King Jeconiah. 1 Chron. 3.18.

Malchi-shua (măl'kī-shōō'ə), son of Saul. 1 Chron. 8.33; 9.39. Melchishua: 1 Sam. 14.49; 31.2.

Malchus (măl'kəs), servant of the high priest whose ear Peter cut off and Jesus healed. John 18.10,11.

Malcolm III (Malcolm Canmore), d. 1093, king of Scotland (1057-93), son of Duncan I; successor to MACBETH (d. 1057). It took him some years after Macbeth's death to regain the boundaries of his father's kingdom. About 1068, EDGAR ATHELING, pretender to the English throne, took refuge with Malcolm, who soon married Edgar's sister Margaret (see MARGARET OF SCOTLAND, SAINT). On behalf of Edgar, Malcolm invaded N England, but in 1072 WILLIAM I of England invaded Scotland, and Malcolm made peace with him. In the reign of WILLIAM II, Edgar joined Malcolm in his raid into England in 1091, but William forced both men to submit and to do homage. Malcolm was killed at Alnwick on still another raid into England. His frequent wars insured the independence of his kingdom, which made possible the great ecclesiastical reorganization initiated by his wife, Margaret. Malcolm was succeeded by his brother Donald Bane, but later three of Malcolm's sons were kings of Scotland—Edgar (reigned 1097-1107), Alexander I, and David I. Malcolm's daughter Edith (renamed Matilda) married Henry I of England, and another daughter was mother to the wife of King Stephen of England.

Malcolm IV, 1141-65, king of Scotland (1153-65), grandson and successor of DAVID I. On his accession the young king was at once faced with a rebellion of the western Gaels, supported by the Norse, which he put down. Henry II of England insisted he give up his claim to Northumbria in 1157 in return for a re-grant of the earldom of Huntingdon, which was largely useless to the Scottish kings because of its distance from Scotland. Malcolm fought on Henry's behalf in France (1159) and, on his return, completed the subjection of Galloway. He was succeeded by his brother William the Lion.

Malcolm X, 1925-65, militant black leader in the United States, also known as El-Hajj Malik El-Shabazz, b. Malcolm Little in Omaha, Neb. He was introduced to the BLACK MUSLIMS while serving a prison term and became a Muslim minister upon his release in 1952. He quickly became very prominent in the movement with a following perhaps equalling that of its leader, Elijah Muhammad. In 1963, Malcolm was suspended by Elijah after a speech in which Malcolm suggested that President Kennedy's assassination was a matter of the "chickens coming home to roost." He then formed a rival organization of his own, the Muslim Mosque, Inc. In 1964, after a pilgrimage to Mecca, he announced his conversion to orthodox Islam and his new belief that there could be brotherhood between black and white. In his Organization of Afro-American Unity, formed after his return, the tone was still that of militant black nationalism but no longer of separation. In Feb., 1965, he was shot and killed in a public auditorium in New York City. His assassins were vaguely identified as Black Muslims, but this is a matter of controversy. See his autobiography (as told to Alex Haley, 1964) and selected speeches, *Malcolm X Speaks* (1965); biography by Peter Goldman (1973); J. H. Clarke, ed., *Malcolm X* (1969).

Malden (môl'dən), city (1970 pop. 56,127), Middlesex co., E Mass., a suburb of Boston, in the Mystic valley; settled 1640, inc. 1882. Among its varied manufactures are processed foods, cans, aluminum products, and tools. A number of old historic churches are there. Michael Wigglesworth was minister in Malden for many years, and Adoniram Judson was born there.

Malditos, Montes: see MALADETTA MOUNTAINS.

Maldives (măl'dīvz), formerly **Maldive Islands,** republic (1970 pop. 114, 469), 115 sq mi (298 sq km), S Asia, stretching c.500 mi (800 km) from north to south in the N Indian Ocean, SW of Sri Lanka. Male Island (1970 est. pop. 13,000) is the capital and the largest island. The Maldives consist of 19 atolls made up of nearly 2,000 coral islands that are the exposed tops of a submarine ridge. They have a tropical monsoon climate modified by their marine location. The islands are covered with tropical vegetation, particularly coconut palms. About 200 of the islands are inhabited, and some have freshwater lagoons. Maldivians are of mixed Indian, Sinhalese, and Arab stock. Islam is the offical religion. Tropical fruit and corn are raised; fish, coconuts, and coconut products (especially copra) are the nation's chief sources of income. Sri Lanka is the Maldives' principal trading partner. The Maldives are governed under the constitution of 1968. The president, who is both the head of state and of government, is elected by popular vote for a four-year term. The *Majlis,* the legislative body, consists of 54 members who serve five-year terms. The Maldives were orginally settled by peoples who came from S Asia. In the 12th cent. Islam was brought to the islands. Starting in the 16th cent., with the coming of the Portuguese, the Maldives were intermittently under European influence. In 1887 they became a British protectorate and military base but retained internal self-government. The Maldives obtained complete independence as a sultanate in 1965, but in 1968 the ad-Din dynasty, which had ruled the islands since the 14th cent., was ended and a republic was declared. The Maldives are a member of the Commonwealth of Nations and the United Nations.

Maldon (môl'dən), municipal borough (1971 pop. 13,840), Essex, E England, on the Blackwater estuary. It is a market town with iron foundries and other small industries. The 13th-century Church of All Saints has a unique triangular tower with a hexagonal spire, and the town hall dates from the 15th cent. Prehistoric traces have been found in the vicinity and there may have been a Saxon settlement. A battle against Danish raiders was fought near Maldon in 991; the leader of the East Saxons, Byrhtnoth (or Brihtnoth), was killed. The battle was celebrated in one of the last Anglo-Saxon heroic poems, "The Battle of Maldon," of unknown authorship but probably written by a contemporary.

Mâle, Émile (āmēl' mäl), 1862-1954, French art historian. Mâle pioneered the study of French art of the Middle Ages, its forms, and especially the Eastern sources of sculptural iconography of the cathedrals of France. He was a director of the Académie de France à Rome and a member of the Académie Française. Among Mâle's major works are *L'Art religieux du XIIIe siècle en France* (1913, tr. *The Gothic Image,* 1958) and *L'Art religieux du XIIe au XVIIIe siècle* (1945, tr. 1949).

Malebo Pool, Zaïre: see STANLEY POOL.

Malebranche, Nicolas (nēkôlä' mälbräNsh'), 1638-1715, French philosopher. Malebranche's philosophy is a highly original synthesis of Cartesian and Augustinian thought. Its purpose was to reconcile the new science with Christian theology. Beginning with Descartes's dualism between mind and body, Malebranche developed a theory called OCCASIONALISM, which denied any interaction of the two realms. To Malebranche, the eternal truths are contained in the divine intellect, and scientific knowledge is possible only because the soul is part of the divine intellect. He summarized his beliefs in his famous assertion that we see all things in God, a statement that led to an extended controversy with the theologian Antoine Arnauld. The philosophy of Malebranche influenced such diverse minds as Leibniz, Berkeley, and John NORRIS. His chief works are *De la recherche de la vérité* (1674; tr. *The Search for Truth,* 1694) and *Traité de la nature et de la grâce* (1680). See studies by R. C. Church (1931, repr. 1970), A. A. Luce (1934, repr. 1967), B. K. Rome (1963), and Desmond Connell (1967).

Malecite Indians (măl'əsīt), North American Indians whose language belongs to the Algonquian branch of the Algonquian-Wakashan linguistic stock (see AMERICAN INDIAN LANGUAGES). In the early 17th cent. they occupied the valley of the St. John River in New Brunswick, Canada. The French settlers in this area intermarried with the Malecite, thus forming a close alliance with the Indians. Hence, during the colonial wars the Malecite supported the French against the English. They now live in New Brunswick, Quebec, and Maine. See J. F. Pratson, *Land of the Four Directions* (1970).

male fern: see FERN.

Malegaon (mälä'goun), town (1971 pop. 197,784), Maharashtra state, W central India, at the confluence of the Girna and Masam rivers. It is a weaving center for saris. Malegaon was formerly a military post and is now a district administrative center. It was captured by the British in 1818 during the war with the Pindaris, marauding tribes of landless and casteless men who were often mercenaries of Mahratta leaders.

maleic acid (məlē'ĭk): see FUMARIC ACID.

Maleleel (məlē'lēĕl), variant of MAHALALEEL.

Malenkov, Georgi Maksimilianovich (gāôr'gē mäksĭmĭlyä'nəvĭch məlyĭnkôf'), 1902–, Soviet Communist leader. He rose to prominence through the party secretariat and was a trusted aide of Joseph Stalin. In 1946, he became a full member of the politburo and a deputy premier. He succeeded Stalin as premier in March, 1953, and was also very briefly first secretary of the Communist party. However, Nikita Khrushchev replaced him as party head. Malenkov's premiership was marked by a conciliatory foreign policy and by the curtailment of the power of the secret police. In Feb., 1955, he was forced to resign, assuming blame for the failure of the government's agricultural policy; he was succeeded by Nikolai Bulganin, whom Khrushchev supported for the post. In 1957, Malenkov was removed from all important posts for his role in the "antiparty faction" opposing Khrushchev. He was expelled from the party in 1961.

Malesherbes, Chrétien Guillaume de Lamoignon de (krātyăN' gēyōm' də lämwänyôN' də mälzĕrb'), 1721-94, French minister of state. After serving as counselor to the Parlement of Paris, he succeeded (1750) his father as president of the Court of Aids at Paris. His father, then chancellor, entrusted him with the censorship of the press; the publication of the ENCYCLOPÉDIE was largely due to his liberal policy. He protested against the dissolution of the PARLEMENT in 1771 and was exiled to his country estate, but upon the accession of Louis XVI (1774), Malesherbes was appointed secretary of state for the royal household. His responsibilities included ecclesiastical affairs, the administration of Paris and some provinces, and appointments at court. He attempted to improve prison conditions and limit the use of LETTRES DE CACHET. Malesherbes resigned (1776) after the failure of the reform program of his friend A. R. J. TURGOT. Recalled in 1787, he was made minister without portfolio but resigned the next year and retired from political life. In 1792, at his own request, he was appointed a defender of Louis XVI in the king's trial. Malesherbes was soon afterwards arrested as a royalist and guillotined. See biography by J. M. S. Allison (1938); study by E. P. Shaw (1966).

Malevich, Casimir or **Kasimir** (both: kā'sĭmēr mälyä'vĭch), 1878-1935, Russian painter. Malevich worked first in a style related to FAUVISM, then as a cubist, before he founded SUPREMATISM in 1913. He created nonobjective paintings composed of bare geometric forms—often just a single square on the flatly painted surface. Characteristic is his famous *White on White* (Mus. of Modern Art, New York City). His written theories were published in Germany in 1928 as *The Non-Objective World* (tr. 1959). His controversial work was influential in the development of abstract art.

Malherbe, François de (fräNswä' də mälĕrb'), 1555-1628, French poet and critic, official poet of Henry IV and Louis XIII. His own poems approach technical perfection but lack verve and fire; the best-known is *Consolation à Monsieur du Périer* (c.1590). As a critic Malherbe had considerable influence on French literature. He consistently advocated objectivity, precision of language, and seriousness of purpose, ideals which were soon to be associated with classicism. See study by C. K. Abraham (1971).

Malheur (məlōōr'), river, c.165 mi (270 km) long, rising in several branches in the Strawberry Mts., E Oregon. The united stream flows generally NE to the Snake River at Ontario. There are flood-control projects on the river, and the Vale project uses the Malheur for irrigation.

Malheur Lake, c.15 mi (25 km) long and up to 5 mi (8 km) wide, in Harney Basin, SE Oregon. It receives the basin's interior drainage. A national wildlife refuge is there.

Mali (mä'lē), independent republic (1973 est. pop. 5,300,000), 478,764 sq mi (1,240,000 sq km), the largest country in W Africa. BAMAKO is the capital. Mali is bordered on the N by Algeria, on the E and SE by Niger, on the S by Upper Volta and Ivory Coast, and on the W by Guinea, Senegal, and Mauritania. In the south, traversed by the Niger and Senegal rivers, are fertile areas where peanuts, rice, and cotton are grown. Elsewhere the country is arid desert or semidesert and barely supports grazing (mainly cattle, sheep, and goats). The Niger serves as an important transportation artery and a source of fish. Peanuts and cotton are the country's only significant cash crops, but subsistence agriculture (the growing of rice, maize, sorghum, millet, and cassava) is also practiced. Live animals and preserved fish are the most important exports. Mali has varied light industries, including canning and preserving, cotton ginning, peanut-oil extraction, brickmaking, and the production of textiles, cigarettes, matches, and hardware. Some salt and gold are mined for local

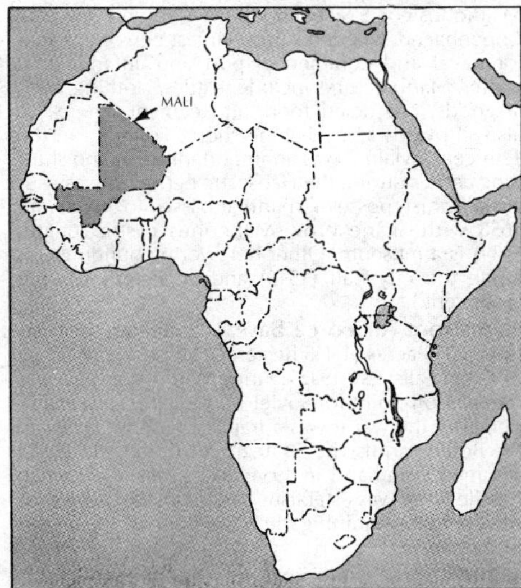

trade, but the country's extensive mineral resources (bauxite, manganese, iron ore, phosphates, lithium, diamonds) remain largely unexploited. There is hope of finding oil in the desert regions. Mali's main ethnic groups are the Bambara, Marka, Songhai, and Malinké, who are chiefly farmers and fishermen, and the Fulani and the Tuareg, who are pastoralists. About 65% of the population is Muslim, while most of the remainder are animists. The Mali region has been the seat of extensive empires and kingdoms, notably those of GHANA (4th–11th cent.), Mali, and Gao. The medieval empire of Mali was a powerful state and one of the world's chief gold suppliers; it attained its peak in the early 14th cent. under Emperor Mansu Musa (reigned c.1312–1337), who made a famous pilgrimage to Mecca in 1324 laden with gold and slaves. During his rule Muslim scholarship reached new heights in Mali, and such cities as TIMBUKTU and Djenné became important centers of trade, learning, and culture. The Mali empire was followed by the Songhai empire of Gao, which rose to great power in the late 15th cent. Its most notable ruler, Askiya Muhammad I, also made a pilgrimage to Mecca. In 1590 the empire, already weakened by internal divisions, was shattered by a Moroccan army. The Moroccans, however, could not effectively dominate the vast region, which broke up into petty states. By the late 18th cent., the area was in a semianarchic condition and was subject to incursions by the Tuareg and Fulani. The 19th cent. witnessed a great resurgence of Islam. The Tukolor empire of Al Hajj Umar (1794–1864) and the empire of Samory (1870–98) emerged as Muslim states opposing French invasion of the region. By 1898 the French conquest was virtually complete; Mali, called French Sudan, became part of the Federation of French West Africa. A nationalist movement, spearheaded by trade unions, student groups, and other associations, blossomed during the period between the two World Wars. The Sudanese Union, a militantly anticolonial party, became the leading political force. Its leader, Modibo KEITA, was a descendant of the Mali emperors. In the French constitutional referendum of 1958, French Sudan voted to join the French Community as the autonomous Sudanese Republic. In 1959 the republic joined Senegal to form the Mali Federation, but political differences shattered the union in 1960. That same year, the Sudanese Republic, renamed the Republic of Mali, obtained full independence from France and severed ties with the French Community. Seeking to promote African unity, Mali joined in a largely symbolic union with Guinea and Ghana, and in 1963 it joined the newborn Organization of African Unity. Under Keita's presidency Mali became a one-party state committed to socialist policies. In 1962 the country withdrew from the franc zone and adopted a nonconvertible national currency. The resulting economic and financial difficulties forced an accommodation with France in 1967; Mali devalued its currency, returned to the franc zone, and permitted French technicians and administrators to assume a supervisory role in the economy. Militant elements in the Sudanese Union opposed this rapprochement, however, and Keita formed a people's militia to destroy opposition. The arrest of several dissenting army officers by the militia in 1968 provoked a bloodless military coup that overthrew the Keita regime. Under Keita, who served both as president of the republic and as chief of the Sudanese Union, the party exercised dominant authority. The new rulers, however, governed through the Military Committee of National Liberation, with Lt. Moussa Traoré as president. Mali's constitution provides for a unicameral national assembly elected every five years by universal adult suffrage. The country has continued to pursue a course of nonalignment in international affairs but is also an associate member of the European Common Market. In 1968, Mali joined with Senegal, Guinea, and Mauritania in founding the Organization of Senegal River States to develop the Senegal valley. In the early 1970s, Mali suffered from the effects of a prolonged drought that desiccated the Sahel region of Africa. The drought, which parched the semiarid grasslands and further reduced the country's already meager water supplies, shattered Mali's agriculture economy by killing thousands of head of livestock and hindering crop production. The resulting famine, disease, and poverty contributed to the deaths of untold thousands and forced the southward migration of many tribes. Mali received emergency aid from UN-supervised international relief programs. The drought may have permanently extended desert conditions into central and S Mali. See W. J. Foltz, *From French West Africa to Mali Federation* (1965); F. G. Snyder, *One-Party Government in Mali* (1965); Anton Bebler, ed., *Military Rule in Africa: Dahomey, Ghana, Sierra Leone, and Mali* (1973); Nehemia Levtzion, *Ancient Ghana and Mali* (1973).

Malibran, Maria Felicità (märē'ä fālēsētä' mälēbräN'), 1808–36, French-Spanish contralto. Malibran was the daughter of the tenor Manuel García and the sister of the mezzo Pauline Viardot. She made her opera debut in 1825 as Rosina in the *The Barber of Seville* in London. Her unhappy marriage to an elderly, bankrupt French merchant, Malibran, lasted less than a year. In 1836 she married the violinist Charles de Bériot shortly before a fall from a horse led to her death. Malibran's voice was of unusual color and great range, extending into the soprano register. She acquired enormous popularity in London, Paris, and Italy for the passionate character of her interpretations.

Malibu Beach (măl'ĭbo͞o), resort and residential area, S Calif., W of Los Angeles and near Santa Monica.

malic acid: see CITRIC ACID CYCLE.

malice, in law, an intentional violation of the law of crimes or torts that injures another person. Malice need not involve a malignant spirit or the definite intent to do harm. To prove malice, it is sufficient to show the willful doing of an injurious act without lawful excuse. A malicious state of mind may be inferred from reckless and wanton acts that a normal person should know might produce or threaten injury to others. Malice aforethought is a technical element of MURDER.

Mali Federation: see MALI.

malignancy: see CANCER.

Malik, Adam, 1917–, Indonesian government official. A militant nationalist as a youth, he helped to found a news bureau that eventually became the official Indonesian news agency, and after World War II he fought for Indonesian independence. He entered the house of representatives in 1956 and later served as ambassador to the USSR (1959–63) and minister of commerce (1963–65) under President Sukarno. He was (1966) a key figure in Sukarno's removal from power and became foreign minister in the new government. In this post he negotiated Indonesia's readmittance to the United Nations and a peace treaty with Malaysia, while reversing Sukarno's pro-Chinese policies.

Malik, Charles Habib, 1906–, Lebanese statesman and educator, grad. American Univ. of Beirut, 1927, Ph.D. Harvard, 1937. After teaching philosophy at the American Univ. of Beirut (1937–45), Malik served as minister (1945–53) and ambassador (1953–55) to the United States. As foreign minister (1956–58), he supported President Eisenhower's decision to send troops to Lebanon in 1958. Malik was a signer of the UN Charter (1945) and served as delegate to the UN from 1945 to 1955 and from 1957 to 1959. He was elected (1958) president of the 13th UN General Assembly. In 1962 he returned to the American Univ. of Beirut as distinguished professor of philosophy. His publications include *The Problem of Asia* (1951) and *Man in the Struggle for Peace* (1963). He is the editor of *God and Man in Contemporary Christian Thought* (1970) and *God and Man in Contemporary Islamic Thought* (1972).

Malina, Judith: see BECK, JULIAN.

Malindi (mälĭn'dē), town (1962 pop. 5,818), SE Kenya, on the Indian Ocean. It is a beach resort and a commercial center. Probably founded in the 10th cent. by Arab traders, Malindi became an important city-state and a major port. The Portuguese navigator Vasco da Gama landed there in 1498 and erected a monument that still stands. Nearby are the ruins of Gedi, an ancient walled city.

Malines: see MECHELEN, Belgium.

Malinovsky, Rodion Yakovlevich (rō'dyōn yä'kəvlyĭvĭch mälyĭnŏf'skē), 1898–1967, Soviet marshal, b. the Ukraine. He joined the Communist party in 1926. In World War II Malinovsky commanded an army in the Stalingrad (later Volgograd) offensive and later in the Ukraine. He became (1956) a member of the central committee of the Communist party and commander in chief of Soviet land forces. In 1957, upon the demotion of Marshal Zhukov, Malinovsky was made minister of defense of the USSR. He held that post until his death.

Malinowski, Bronislaw (brōnē'slŏf mälĭnŏf'skē), 1884–1942, English anthropologist, b. Poland, Ph.D. Univ. of Kraków, 1908. Working in the field of cultural anthropology, he gained renown through his studies (1914–18) of the indigenous peoples of the Trobriand Islands off New Guinea. He began teaching at the Univ. of London in 1924, becoming a professor in 1927. Malinowski traveled and did research in Africa, Latin America, and the United States. His research techniques and insistence on the study of different cultures in terms of their particular internal dynamics caused him to be regarded as the founder of "functionalism" in social anthropology. In 1939, Malinowski became a visiting professor at Yale. Among his writings are *Argonauts of the Western Pacific* (1922), *Crime and Custom in Savage Society* (1926, 4th ed. 1947), and *The Sexual Life of Savages in North-Western Melanesia* (1929, 3d ed. 1948). Posthumous works include the volumes of essays *The Dynamics of Culture Change* (1945; ed. by P. M. Kaberry) and *Magic, Science and Religion* (1948; introd. by Robert Redfield). See studies by Max Gluckman (1949 and 1963), Raymond Firth (1957, repr. 1964), and J. P. S. Uberoi (1971).

Malipiero, Gian Francesco (jän fränchä'skō mälēpyä'rō), 1882–1973, Italian composer. Malipiero studied in Venice and Bologna with Enrico Bossi and taught at the Conservatory of Parma, at the Univ. of Padua, and in Venice. He did important research in early Italian music, edited the works of Monteverdi (16 vol., 1926–42), Vivaldi, and others, and published studies of the music. *Rispetti e strambotti* (1920) is among his best-known chamber works. His compositions include songs, concertos, choral works, orchestral music, and numerous operas. His work is strongly influenced by older Italian music and French innovations of the early 20th cent.

mallard: see DUCK.

Mallarmé, Stéphane (stāfän' mälärmā'), 1842–98, French poet. Mallarmé's great importance is as the chief forebear of the SYMBOLISTS; many poets and other writers of the mid-1880s drew inspiration at the Tuesday evening gatherings where Mallarmé expounded his theories. He held that the poet should express the ideas of a transcendental world, that poetry should evoke thoughts through suggestion rather than description, and that it should approach the abstraction of music. Mallarmé's language defies traditional syntax and is frequently so obscure that it must be read with commentary. His best-known poems are *Hérodiade* (1869), *L'Après-Midi d'un faune* (1876; *The Afternoon of a Faun*), which inspired a composition by Debussy, and *Un Coup de dés jamais n'abolira le hasard* (1897; *A Throw of the Dice Will Never Eliminate Chance*). Editions of Mallarmé's poetry were published in 1887 and 1899, and a selection of prose, *Divagations*, in 1897. Mallarmé earned his living by teaching English. The influence of his poetry was particularly felt by Valéry. See biography by Anatole France (1967); studies by F. C. St. Aubyn (1969) and T. A. Williams (1970).

Mallawi (mäl'läwē), town (1970 est. pop. 65,000), E central Egypt, on the Nile. Situated in a farm area, the town produces textiles and handicrafts.

Mallea, Eduardo (ā"thwär'thō mäyä'ä), 1903–, Argentine novelist and essayist. Mallea is considered one of the outstanding literary figures of Spanish America. His stories in *Cuentos para una inglesa desesperada* (1926) are written in a lighthearted vein. With *Nocturno Europeo* (1934) and *Ciudad junto al rio immóvil* (1936) he reveals a profound concern with philosophical questions. Existentialist thought, particularly in the writings of Kierkegaard and Kafka, influenced his intense and sometimes anguished analysis of modern urban society. In *Historia de una pasión Argentina* (1935) he excoriates the Argentine political oligarchy. *El sayal y la púrpura* (1941) is a collection of essays. Some of his other works are *The Bay of Silence* (1940, tr. 1944), *Las Águilas* (1943), *La Torre* (1951), *Simbad* (1957), *Posesión* (1958), *Las Travesías* (2 vol., 1961–62), *La barea de hielo* (1967), and *Gabriel Andaral* (1971). Some of Mallea's stories and novellas were translated in *All Green Shall Perish* (1966). See study by John Herman Polt (1959).

malleability, property of a metal describing the ease with which it can be hammered, forged, pressed, or rolled into thin sheets. Metals vary in this respect; pure gold is the most malleable. Silver, copper, aluminum, lead, tin, zinc, and iron are also very malleable. Some heating usually increases malleability. Zinc, for example, at ordinary temperatures is very brittle, but is malleable in the temperature range from about 120°C. to 150°C. Impurities adversely affect the malleability of metals.

Mallet or **Malloch, David** (măl'ĭt, -əkh), c.1705–1765, English poet and dramatist, b. Scotland. His best-known work is the ballad *William and Margaret* (1720). Although he wrote several tragedies, he is usually remembered as the author (with James Thomson) of the masque *Alfred* (1740), which contained the song *Rule Britannia.*

Mallet-Joris, Françoise (fräNswäz' mälā'-zhôrē'), 1930–, French novelist, b. Belgium. Her works often portray social convention as an instrument of human self-destruction. They are sharply analytical and descriptive, particularly of Flemish settings. Among her novels are *Into the Labyrinth* (tr. 1951), *The Red Room* (tr. 1955), *House of Lies* (tr. 1957), and *The Witches* (tr. 1969). See her autobiographical *Paper House* (tr. 1971).

Mallorca: see MAJORCA.

Mallory, George Herbert Leigh (măl'ərē), 1886–1924, English mountain climber. After some spectacular ascents in the Alps, he participated in the Everest expeditions of 1921, 1922, and 1924. The 1924 expedition culminated in a bold and possibly successful drive toward the summit made by Mallory and Andrew Irvine, from which they did not return. Mallory's intelligence, resolution, and superb leadership, together with the mystery surrounding his final effort, have made his name legendary among mountaineers. His name also appears as George Herbert Leigh-Mallory. See biographies by Showell Styles (1967) and D. A. Robertson (1969).

Mallory, Stephen Russell, c.1813–73, U.S. Senator, secretary of the navy in the Confederacy, b. Trinidad, West Indies. He was raised in Key West, Fla., where he practiced law and was a customs official. Elected to the U.S. Senate in 1851 and reelected in 1857, Mallory served until Florida seceded. Long chairman of the Senate committee on naval affairs, he became (Feb., 1861) secretary of the navy in the Confederacy. Mallory ardently advocated ironclad warships for the navy. However, efforts to secure ironclads from England and France proved futile, and of the few constructed in the Confederacy the most outstanding, the *Virginia* (see MONITOR AND MERRIMACK) and the *Mississippi,* had to be destroyed to prevent their falling into Union hands. Mallory was captured in flight with Jefferson Davis in 1865 and was imprisoned. On his release in 1866, he resumed the practice of law in Florida. See biography by J. T. Durkin (1954).

Mallothi (măl'əthī, məlō'thī), leader of temple singers. 1 Chron. 25.4,26.

mallow, common name for members of the Malvaceae, a family of herbs and shrubs distributed over most of the world and especially abundant in the American tropics. Tropical species sometimes grow as small trees. The family is characterized by often mucilaginous sap and by showy, five-part flowers with a prominent column of fused stamens. The true mallows (genus *Malva*) are native to north temperate regions of the Old World, although many species have escaped from cultivation and become naturalized in the United States. North American species, sometimes cultivated and most common in the South and West, include the false mallows (genus *Malvastrum*) and the rose, or swamp, mallows (genus *Hibiscus*) found in marshy areas across the

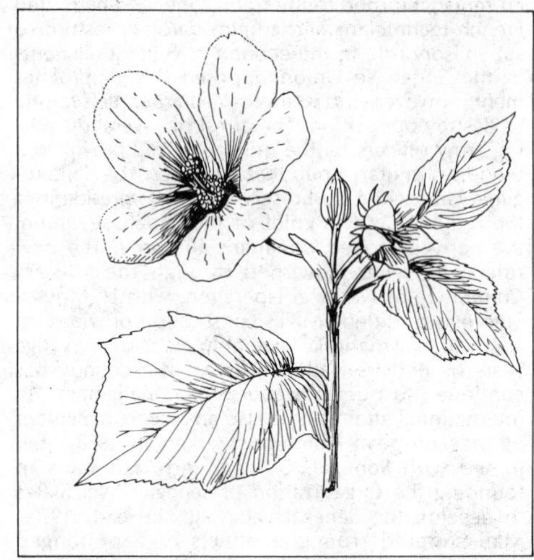

Rose mallow, Hibiscus moscheutos

country. Introduced species of hibiscus include the rose of Sharon, or shrubby althea *(H. syriacus),* a popular ornamental bush or small tree native to Asia, and okra, or GUMBO *(H. esculentus),* native to Africa, whose mucilaginous pods are used as a vegetable and in soups and stews. *Althea* is an Old World genus. The hollyhock *(A. rosea),* the most popular ornamental of the family, is a Chinese perennial now widely naturalized and cultivated as a biennial or annual in many varieties of diverse colors. *A. officinalis* is the marsh mallow, a name sometimes used also for the larger-blossomed rose mallows. The root of the true marsh mallow, a native of Europe, is used medicinally. It was formerly used for the confection marshmallow, which is now usually made from syrup, gelatin, and other ingredients. The tropical and subtropical flowering maple genus *Abutilon,* named for the maplelike foliage of some species, includes several house and bedding ornamentals. Some Asiatic species yield a fiber known as China jute—e.g., the velvetweed *(A. theophrasti),* called also Indian mallow and velvetleaf for the texture of its foliage. This plant, introduced to the United States as an ornamental, has become a noxious weed. Economically, the most important plant in the family is COTTON (genus *Gossypium*), with species native to both the Old and New World and cultivated independently in both areas from early times. The mallow family is classified in the division MAGNOLIOPHYTA, class Magnoliopsida, order Malvales.

Mallowan, Max Edgar Lucien, 1904–, British archaeologist, educated at Oxford. He participated in the British Museum–Univ. of Pennsylvania excavations at Ur (1925–1930) and Nineveh (1931–32), both in present-day Iraq. From 1947 to 1961 he served as director of the British School of Archaeology in Iraq, supervising the Nimrud excavations of 1949–1958 and those at numerous other sites. He taught at the Univ. of London from 1947 until 1962 and was knighted in 1968. He is married to the popular mystery novelist Agatha Christie. His writings include *Twenty-five Years of Mesopotamian Discovery* (1956).

Malluch (măl'ək). **1** Merarite. 1 Chron. 6.44. **2, 3** Two who gave up foreign wives. Ezra 10.29,32. **4, 5** Two signers of the covenant. Neh. 10.4,27. **6** Priestly family returned with Zerubbabel. Neh. 12.2. Melicu: Neh. 12.14. Some of these may be the same.

Malmberg, Aino (ī'nō mälm'bĕr"yə), 1866–1933, Finnish patriot and feminist, grad. Univ. of Helsinki, 1887, in the first class to include women students. She was active in the nationalist movement that sought independence from Russia, and in the nationwide strike of 1905, which resulted in universal suffrage. Exiled by Russia in 1910, she went to England. Her home in London was long a center for exiles from Finland and other oppressed nations. She was a pacifist during World War I. She returned to Finland after it became independent in 1917, and her later years were devoted to bettering the position of the peasantry.

Malmédy (mälmādē'), town (1970 pop. 6,464), Liège prov., E Belgium, near the West German border. It is a manufacturing and tourist center. The town and the surrounding district belonged to the abbey of nearby Stavelot until they passed (1815) to Prussia. Malmédy and EUPEN were transferred to Belgium by the Treaty of Versailles after World War I. In World War II there was heavy fighting at Malmédy during the Battle of the Bulge (Dec., 1944).

Malmesbury (mämz'bərē), municipal borough (1971 pop. 2,526), Wiltshire, S England. It is famous for its magnificent Benedictine abbey, founded in the 12th cent., of which only the nave remains. King Athelstan of Wessex was buried in Malmesbury. Thomas Hobbes was born in the present borough, and at nearby Garsdon are tombs of George Washington's ancestors.

Malmö (mäl'mö), city (1970 pop. 262,260), capital of Malmöhus co., S Sweden, on the Øresund opposite Copenhagen. Sweden's third largest city, it is a major naval and commercial port and an industrial center. Manufactures include textiles, clothing, metal goods, processed food, and cement. There are also shipyards and machine shops. Founded in the 12th cent., Malmö was an important trade and shipping center during the Hanseatic period. It was usually a Danish possession until it passed to Sweden in 1658 with Skåne prov. Malmöhus castle (begun 1434) is a museum. Other noteworthy buildings include the city hall (1546) and St. Peter's Church (14th cent.).

Malmstrom Air Force Base, U.S. military installation, 3,573 acres (1,446 hectares), W central Mont., E of Great Falls; est. 1942. During World War II, it was the take-off point for Soviet-bound LEND-LEASE materiel; after the war it was a training base for crews in the Berlin Airlift. The Strategic Air Command (SAC) assumed command in 1954; SAC's first Minuteman missile wing was established there in 1961. The missile complex adjoining the base is one of the largest in the world.

malnutrition, insufficiency of one or more nutritional elements necessary for health and well-being. Primary malnutrition is caused by the lack of essential foodstuffs—usually vitamins, minerals, or proteins—in the diet. In some areas of the world a poor economy or such regional conditions as drought or overpopulation cause a scarcity of certain foodstuffs, and a certain portion of the population is malnourished because essential nutrients are not available. However, even when food is plentiful, malnutrition can result from poor eating habits. Secondary malnutrition is caused by failure of absorption or utilization of nutrients (as in disease of the gastrointestinal tract, thyroid, kidney, liver, or pancreas), by increased nutritional requirements (growth, injuries, burns, surgical procedures, pregnancy, lactation, fever), or by excessive excretion (diarrhea). Anemia may follow lack of iron; rickets, scurvy, beriberi, and pellagra result from lack of vitamins.

Maloja (mälō'yä), pass, 5,960 ft (1,817 m) high, Grisons canton, SE Switzerland, leading from the Engadine valley to Italy. The lowest of passes to Italy, it crosses the Rhaetian Alps.

Malolos (mälō'lōs), town (1969 est. pop. 67,100), capital of Bulacan prov., SW Luzon, the Philippines, N of Manila. It is an old marketing center for surrounding farms. The Spanish settled there in 1580. Malolos was the capital of the Philippine republic proclaimed (June, 1898) by the insurrectionary leader Emilio Aguinaldo; U.S. forces captured the town in March, 1899. It is the seat of the Bulacan College of Arts and Trades.

Malone, Dumas (dōōmä' məlōn'), 1892–, American historian and editor, b. Coldwater, Miss. He received his Ph.D. from Yale in 1923 and was an instructor of history at Yale (1919–23) and associate professor (1923–26) and professor (1926–29) at the Univ. of Virginia. He was an editor of the *Dictionary of American Biography* from 1929 to 1931 and editor in chief from 1931 to 1936. After serving as director of the Harvard Univ. Press (1936–43), Malone was (1945–59) professor of history at Columbia and managing editor (1953–58) of the *Political Science Quar-*

terly. Among his books are *The Public Life of Thomas Cooper* (1926), *Saints in Action* (1939), *Edwin A. Alderman* (1940), *The Story of the Declaration of Independence* (1954), and *Jefferson and His Time* (5 vol., 1948–74), a multivolume biography of Thomas Jefferson.

Malone, Edmond, 1741–1812, English literary critic and Shakespearean scholar, b. Ireland. His studies (1778) in the chronology of Shakespeare's plays are still considered highly valuable. He was among the first to see through the supposed antiquity of the poems of Thomas CHATTERTON, and in 1796 he exposed the Shakespearean forgeries of William Ireland. His monumental edition of Shakespeare was left unfinished at his death and was completed (21 vol., 1821) by Boswell's son James. The Malone Society, founded in 1907 for the purpose of furthering the study of early English drama by printing dramatic texts and documents, was named after him.

Malory, Sir Thomas (măl'ərē), d. 1471, English author of *Morte d'Arthur.* It is almost certain that he was Sir Thomas Malory of Newbold Revell, Warwickshire. Knighted in 1442, he served in the Parliament of 1445. He was evidently a violent, lawless individual who committed a series of crimes, including poaching, extortion, robbery, and murder. Most of his life from 1451 was spent in prison, and he probably did most of his writing there. Malory's original book was called *The Book of King Arthur and His Noble Knights of the Round Table* and was made up of eight romances that were more or less separate. William Caxton printed the work in 1485 and gave it the misleading title of *Morte d'Arthur.* The last medieval English work of the ARTHURIAN LEGEND, Malory's tales are supposedly based on an assortment of French prose romances. The *Morte d'Arthur* is noted for its excellent dramatic narrative and the beauty of its rhythmic and simple language. It is the standard source for later versions of the legend. See *The Works of Sir Thomas Malory,* ed. by Eugene Vinaver (3 vol., 2d ed., 1967); study by P. J. C. Field (1971).

Maloyaroslavets (mä"ləyärəslä'vyĭts), city (1967 est. pop. 20,000), E central European USSR, on the Luzh River. Founded in the 14th cent., it was a fort in the 15th and 16th cent. In October, 1812, Russian forces in the city barred the road to Kaluga against Napoleon's retreating army, forcing it to retreat by way of Mozhaysk through devastated territory.

Malpighi, Marcello (märchĕl'lō mälpē'gē), 1628–94, Italian anatomist. A pioneer in the use of the microscope, he made many valuable observations on the structure of plants and animals. He completed Harvey's theory of circulation by his observation of the movement of blood through capillaries and recorded this, as well as his work on the structure of the lung, in *De pulmonibus* (1661). He is noted also for his studies of the structure of glands and of the brain, spleen, liver, and kidneys; of the anatomy of the silkworm; of the embryology of the chick; and of plant tissues. Several anatomical parts bear his name, including a layer in the human skin and the excretory tubules in insects. He was professor at the Univ. of Bologna (1666–91).

Malplaquet, battle of (mälpläkā'), a major engagement in the War of the Spanish Succession (see SPANISH SUCCESSION, WAR OF THE). On Sept. 11, 1709, the combined forces of England and the Holy Roman emperor, led by the Duke of MARLBOROUGH and Prince EUGENE OF SAVOY met the French army under Marshal VILLARS. Although the French were forced to retreat, the Anglo-imperial army, attacking strongly fortified positions, suffered more than 20,000 casualties, twice the number of French casualties. The battle was a strategic victory for France as it prevented an allied advance to Paris.

Malraux, André (äNdrā' mälrō'), 1901–, French man of letters and political figure. An intellectual with a broad knowledge of archaeology, art history, and anthropology, Malraux led from early manhood a remarkably adventurous life. He participated with the Communists in the uprisings in Shanghai (1925–27), helped to organize the Loyalist air force in the Spanish civil war, and was a founder of the World League against Anti-Semitism. A French tank commander during World War II, he was captured by the Germans but escaped and became a resistance leader and hero. Malraux served (1945, 1958) as minister of information under Charles de Gaulle; an enthusiastic adherent of De Gaulle, he became minister of cultural affairs in 1959. His writings on De Gaulle include *Fallen Oaks* (1971, tr. 1972). His outstanding novels, reflecting the tumult of his time, include *La Condition humaine* (1933; tr. *Man's Fate,* 1934), concerning the Shanghai uprisings, and *L'Espoir* (1938; tr. *Man's Hope,* 1938), set in Spain during the civil war. Amid violence and political chaos, Malraux's heroes struggle to maintain their dignity and humanity. Among his writings on art and civilization are *Les Voix du silence* (1951; tr. *The Voices of Silence,* 1953); *The Metamorphosis of the Gods* (tr. 1960), drawn from several of his works, including *Le Musée imaginaire de la sculpture mondiale* (3 vol., 1953–54); and *Le Triangle noir* (1970), studies of Goya, Laclos, and Saint-Just. In these works Malraux portrays art as an outgrowth of past art rather than a reaction to contemporary stimuli. See his *Antimemoirs* (1967, tr. 1968); memoir by Clara Malraux (tr. 1967); biographies by Robert Payne (1970) and Pierre Galante (tr. 1971); studies by V. M. Horvath (1969), T. J. Kline (1973), and W. M. Frohock (1974).

malt, a grain (usually barley) steeped in water, partially germinated, then dried and cured. Enzymes, chiefly diastase, are produced by germination. Malt is used in brewing for the conversion of cereal starches to sugars by means of the enzymes. Its high carbohydrate and protein content makes it a valuable nutrient.

Malta (môl'tə), independent state (1967 pop. 315,765), 122 sq mi (316 sq km), in the Mediterranean Sea S of Sicily. It comprises the islands of Malta (95 sq mi/246 sq km), Gozo (26 sq mi/67 sq km), and Comino (1 sq mi/2.6 sq km), as well as two uninhabited rocks. The group is sometimes called the Maltese Islands. VALLETTA is the capital. Malta has no rivers or lakes, no natural resources, and very few trees. Nevertheless it is of great strategic value and has long been an important British military base. The decline in activity at the base, beginning in the late 1960s, created serious economic problems for the country. Although the soil is poor, agriculture is the principal occupation in Malta. The chief crops are wheat, barley, potatoes, and other vegetables and fruits. Tourism is of increasing importance, and efforts have been made to stimulate food processing and other light industries; manufactured goods such as textile threads and rubber products are the lead-

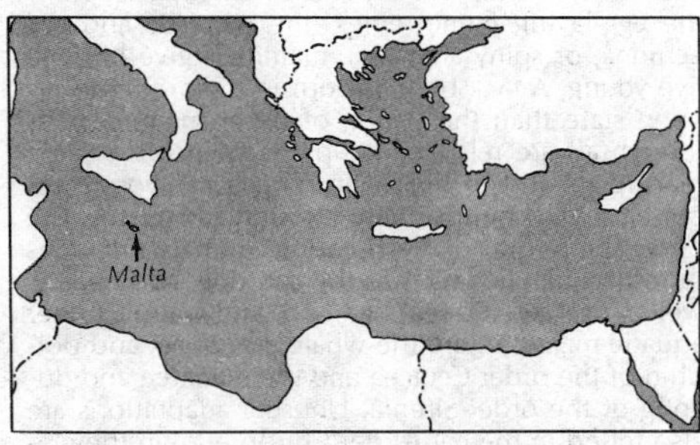

ing exports. Machinery, textiles, foods, motor vehicles, and fuels are the largest imports. Most trade is with Great Britain. English and Maltese, a Semitic dialect, are the official languages, although Italian is also widely spoken. Roman Catholicism is the state religion. Malta has a very high population density. The country is governed under a 1964 constitution. The prime minister and cabinet are responsible to the 50-member house of representatives. The Labour and Nationalist parties dominate politics. It is a member of the Commonwealth of Nations. The island of Malta (ancient Melita) belonged successively to the Phoenicians, Greeks, Carthaginians, Romans, and Saracens. St. Paul was shipwrecked there (A.D. 60). The Normans of Sicily occupied it c.1090. In 1530 the Hapsburg Charles V granted Malta to the Knights Hospitalers (therefore sometimes known as the Knights of Malta). Notwithstanding a determined siege by the Turks in 1565, the knights held it until 1798, when it was surrendered to Napoleon. The British ousted the French in 1800, and for most of the 19th cent. Malta was ruled by a military governor. The opening of the Suez Canal (1869) increased its strategic value. During World War II Malta was subjected to extremely heavy bombing by Italian and German planes, and in 1942 King George VI awarded the entire population the George Cross for bravery. Almost from the start of the period of British rule the Maltese agitated for increased political freedom. A constitution promulgated in 1921 granted considerable self-government but was revoked in 1936. Malta reverted to the status of crown colony. A similar constitution was granted in 1947 but was revoked after civil disturbances in 1959. Malta became fully independent in 1964 and chose to remain in the Commonwealth of Nations. In 1965 it joined the United Nations. When the Labour party came to power in 1971 Prime Minister Dom Mintoff threatened to break ties with the West if the British did not increase rental payments for the naval base. A compromise agreement (effective through 1979) was reached by which the rent would be paid by the British while Malta would also receive a sum from the North Atlantic Treaty Organization and aid from Italy. In Aug., 1973, Malta initiated a seven-year economic development plan intended to free the country, after 1979, from its dependence on the rental payments, and in Sept., 1973, Malta pledged at a conference of nonaligned nations to eliminate the military bases by 1979. See Dennis Austin, *Malta and the End of the Empire* (1971); Brian Blouet, *The Story of Malta* (rev. ed. 1972); D. H. Trump, *Malta, an Archaeological Guide* (1972).

Malta, Knights of: see KNIGHTS HOSPITALERS.

Malta fever: see BRUCELLOSIS.

Malte-Brun, Conrad (kôn'răth măl'tə-brōōn", Fr. mältə-brôN'), 1775–1826, Danish geographer, b. Jutland but later settled in Paris; originally named Malthe Konrad Bruun. He is responsible for the descriptive, readable style that became characteristic of the French school of geography. He wrote an encyclopedic geography of the world, a geography of Poland, and a dictionary of geography. He was secretary of the French Society of Geography, as was his son, **Victor Adolphe Malte-Brun,** 1816–89, who also wrote extensively on geographical subjects.

Maltese (môltēz'), breed of very small TOY DOG of obscure origin that was widely popular in Europe by the beginning of the 19th cent. It stands about 5 in. (12.7 cm) high at the shoulder and weighs from 2 to 7 lb (0.9–1.4 kg). Its long, flat-lying, silky coat is pure white and hangs down on either side of the body almost to the ground. The Maltese is probably an ancient breed; dogs closely resembling the modern type were kept as lap dogs in Rome and Greece before the Christian era. Today it is a popular house pet. See DOG.

Maltese cat: see CAT.

Maltese Islands: see MALTA.

Malthus, Thomas Robert (măl'thəs), 1766–1834, English economist, sociologist, and pioneer in modern POPULATION study. In *An Essay on the Principle of Population* (1798, rev. ed. 1803), he contended that poverty and distress are unavoidable, since population increases by geometrical ratio and the means of subsistence by arithmetical ratio. As checks on population growth, Malthus first accepted only war, famine, and disease, but in his revised work he admitted also the preventive check of "moral restraint." Although his theory caused general controversy, it was later adapted by neo-Malthusians, and its implications influenced classical economists, especially David Ricardo. With the help of BIRTH CONTROL and technological advances, particularly in food production, subsequent trends have shown some of his predictions to be false. However, much of his analysis remains valid even today, especially in underdeveloped areas of Asia and Africa. He wrote *Principles of Political Economy* (1820) and other books. See biography by James Bonar (2d ed. 1924, repr. 1966); study by D. V. Glass (1953); Morton Paglin, *Malthus and Lauderdale; the Anti-Ricardian Tradition* (1956, repr. 1973).

maltose (môl'tōs) or **malt sugar,** crystalline disaccharide (see CARBOHYDRATE). It has the same empirical formula ($C_{12}H_{22}O_{11}$) as sucrose and lactose but differs from both in structure (see ISOMER). Maltose is produced from starch by hydrolysis in the presence of diastase, an ENZYME present in malt. Maltose is hydrolyzed to GLUCOSE by maltase, an enzyme present in yeast; the glucose thus formed may be fermented by another enzyme in yeast to produce ETHANOL. Maltose is important in the brewing of beer. It is an easily digested food.

Maluku: see MOLUCCAS, Indonesia.

Malus, Étienne Louis (ätyĕn' lwē mälüs'), 1775–1812, French artillery officer and physicist. In 1810 he stated his discovery of the polarization of light by reflection and published a memoir of his theory of double refraction.

Malvasia (mălvəsē'ə) or **Monemvasía** (mô"nĕmväsē'ä), village, S Greece, in the Peloponnesus, on a rocky island joined to the mainland by a mole. In the Middle Ages it was a fortress and an important commercial port, exporting Malvasian or malmsey wine, a type now made in many places. It was (1821) the seat of the first Greek national assembly.

Malvern (môl'vərn, mô'-), urban district (1971 pop. 29,004), Worcestershire, W central England, on the eastern slopes of the scenic Malvern Hills. Occupying the site of the medieval Chase of Malvern (a royal forest of 7,000 acres/2,833 hectares), Malvern today is primarily a health (mineral springs) and holiday resort. Malvern College, a public school for boys, was founded in 1862. The priory church of Great Malvern dates from 1085; the Norman arches of the interior remain intact. The annual Malvern festival of dramatics, associated with the plays of G. B. Shaw, was instituted in 1928. In 1974, Malvern became part of the new nonmetropolitan county of Hereford and Worcester.

Malverne, residential village (1970 pop. 10,036), Nassau co., SE N.Y., on Long Island; settled in the early 1800s, inc. 1921.

Malvern Hill: see SEVEN DAYS BATTLES.

Malvern Hills, range of hills, c.9 mi (14.5 km) long, W central England, in Hereford and Worcester. The highest points are the Worcester Beacon (1,395 ft/425 m) and the Hereford Beacon (1,114 ft/340 m); on the latter was an ancient British camp.

Mamallapuram: see MAHABALIPURAM.

Mamaroneck (mənăr'ənĕk), village (1970 pop. 18,909), Westchester co., SE N.Y., a suburb of New York City, on Long Island Sound; settled 1661, inc. 1895. It is a boating center, with a fine marina. Although it is primarily residential, there is considerable industry.

mamba, name for African snakes of the genus *Dendroaspis,* in the COBRA family. Widely distributed throughout Africa except in the deserts, mambas have extremely toxic venom. When attacking they raise the front of the body high off the ground and aim at the head or trunk of the victim. They do not have hoods (as do the Asian cobras), but some can inflate their necks in a threatening gesture. Members of some species are very aggressive, displaying a greater tendency to attack than do most snakes; nevertheless, their reaction to danger is often flight. The so-called black mamba (*Dendroaspis polylepis*), actually dark brown to gray, may grow up to 14 ft (4.3 m) long and is the most feared of the mambas. It lives mostly in open country and preys on small mammals and birds. The green mamba (*D. angusticeps*) is a more arboreal snake, found in forest and bush country. Both are distributed throughout most of sub-Saharan Africa. Mambas are classified in the phylum CHORDATA, subphylum Vertebrata, class Reptilia, order Squamata, family Elapidae.

Mamelukes (măm'əlo͞oks) [Arabic, = slaves], a warrior caste for over 700 years dominant in Egypt and influential in the Middle East. Originally slaves of non-Arab extraction, they were used as soldiers by the Fatimid caliphs and Ayyubite sultans from the 10th cent. onward. Although at first slaves, the Mameluke soldiers grew powerful enough to challenge the existence of the rulers who were theoretically their masters. Aybak, the first Mameluke to actually become a ruler, was able (1250) to force the mother of the last Ayyubite sultan to marry him after she had murdered her son. For more than 250 years thereafter, Egypt was ruled by Mameluke sultans supported by a caste of warrior-slaves, from which the sultans were chosen. This Mameluke ruling class of soldiers took advantage of their power to become the principal landholders in Egypt. The Mameluke sultans are usually divided into two dynasties, the Bahrites (1250–1382), chiefly Turks and Mongols, and the Burjites (1382–1517), chiefly Circassians who were chosen from the garrison of Cairo. The Bahrite sultans were usually selected from a few chief families, but during Burjite times there was scant respect for the hereditary principle in the selection of rulers. Neither dynasty was able to exercise more than a limited power over the turbulent Mameluke soldiers. The sultans reigned, on the average, less than seven years and usually met violent ends. In spite of the dangers that threatened the sultans at home, they usually conducted a vigorous foreign policy. They defeated the last of the Crusaders and repulsed the Mongol invasions of Syria. At times they held all Palestine and Syria and the holy places of Arabia. One of the strongest Mameluke rulers, Baybars, owed his elevation to the sultanate to the victory he won (1260) over the Mongols at Ain Jalut in Syria. This defeat was the first serious check that the expansion of the Mongols had received. Baybars, who reigned from 1260 to 1277, also put an end to the power of the Assassins. The most spectacular event of his reign was the inauguration of a new line of caliphs. A relative of the last Abbasid caliph of Baghdad was installed as a Mameluke puppet at Cairo. The long reign of al-Nair from 1293 to 1340, although interrupted three times, was one of ostentation and luxury that helped to undermine the Bahrite dynasty. The Burjite period that followed was one of bloodshed and treachery. It was marked by war against Tamerlane and by the conquest (1424–26) of the Christian-held island of Cyprus. Toward the end of the 15th cent. the Mamelukes became involved in a series of disputes with the Ottoman Turks. These difficulties finally led to an invasion by the Turks who captured Cairo in 1517. The Ottoman ruler, Selim, put an end to the Mameluke sultanate, carried away the last of the puppet line of caliphs to Constantinople, and established a small Turkish garrison in Egypt. He did not, however, destroy the Mamelukes as a class. They kept their lands. Mameluke governors remained in control of the provinces and were even allowed to keep private armies. In the 18th cent., when Turkish power began to decline, the Mamelukes were able to win back an increasing amount of self-rule. In 1769 one of their number, Ali Bey, even proclaimed himself sultan and independent of Constantinople. Although he fell in 1772, the Turks still felt compelled to concede an ever greater measure of autonomy to the Mamelukes and appointed a series of them as governors of Egypt. The Mamelukes were defeated by Napoleon during his invasion of Egypt in 1798, but their power as a class was ended only in 1811 by MUHAMMAD ALI. See studies by Sir William Muir (1896, repr. 1973), N. A. Ziadeh (1953), David Ayalon (1956), and Sir John Glubb (1974).

Mamison or **Mamisson** (both: məmĕsôn'), pass, 9,550 ft (2,911 m) high, S European USSR, in the central Greater Caucasus, on the border between the Georgian and Russian republics. Crossed by the Ossetian Military Road, it links the cities of Kutaisi and Alagir, and the Ardon and Rioni river valleys.

mammal, an animal of the highest class of vertebrates, the Mammalia. The female has mammary glands, which secrete milk for the nourishment of the young after birth. In the majority of mammals the body is partially or wholly covered with hair; the heart has four chambers, and only the left aortic arch is present; and a muscular diaphragm separates the chest from the abdominal cavity. Mammals are warm-blooded; that is, they have a relatively constant body temperature independent of the temperature of the surroundings. The mature red blood cells (erythrocytes) usually lack a nucleus. Except for the egg-laying monotremes (the PLATYPUS and the echidna, or spiny anteater), mammals give birth to live young. A MARSUPIAL is born in a more undeveloped state than the young of other mammals, although all are relatively helpless at birth. In some marsupials and in higher mammals the young receive prenatal nourishment through a PLACENTA. The order Carnivora, or flesh-eating animals, includes terrestrial families such as the cat, dog, and bear as well as the aquatic seal, sea lion, and walrus. Other aquatic mammals are the whale, porpoise, and dolphin of the order Cetacea and the manatee and dugong of the order Sirenia. Unusual adaptations are also found in the bat (order Chiroptera); in the elephant (order Proboscidea); in the sloth, armadillo, and anteater (order Edentata); and in the beaver, woodchuck, porcupine, and squirrel (order Rodentia). The order Insectivora includes the shrew and the mole. There are two groups of ungulates, or hoofed mammals: Most members of the order Perissodactyla, including the horse and the rhinoceros, are odd-toed, with the third digit the largest; those of the order Artiodactyla, including the deer, antelope, camel, pig, and cow, are even-toed, with the third and fourth digits symmetrical and functional. Man, the monkey, the ape, and the lemur belong to the order of Primates. Some remains of mammals are identified as from the Jurassic period of the Mesozoic era; the group became diversified in the Tertiary period of the Cenozoic era. See E. P. Walker, et al., *Mammals of the World* (2 vol., rev. ed. 1968); Björn Kurtén, *The Age of Mammals* (1972); T. A. Vaughan, *Mammalogy* (1972); A. F. DeBlase and R. E. Martin, *A Manual of Mammalogy* (1974).

mammary gland, organ of the female mammal that produces and secretes milk for the nourishment of the young. A mammal may have from 1 to 11 pairs of mammary glands, depending on the species. Generally those with larger litters have more glands. In humans there is one pair of mammary glands, also known as mammae, or breasts. They are rudimentary in both sexes until the age of puberty when, in response to ovarian hormones, they begin to develop in the female. During pregnancy they distend still further in preparation for nursing the infant. Pregnant women are prevented from lactating (producing milk) by the presence in the blood of high levels of estrogen and progesterone secreted by the placenta until birth occurs. Then response to prolactin, the milk-stimulating hormone, is no longer inhibited by placental hormones and lactation begins. Mammary tissue is composed of from 12 to 20 compartments or lobules, like a cluster of grapes, each containing a network of tubes whose cells manufacture the liquid and fatty substances that form milk. The tubes of each lobe connect with a duct, and all ducts lead to the nipple, where the milk is secreted when the nipple is sucked by the young. The mammary gland of the cow and of some other mammals is known as the udder.

mammon (măm'ən), Aramaic term, meaning worldly riches, retained in the New Testament Greek. "Ye cannot serve God and mammon" is one of the most noted biblical strictures. Mat. 6.24; Luke 16.9,11,13.

mammoth, name for several large prehistoric elephants of the extinct genus *Mammuthus,* which ranged over Eurasia and North America in the Pleistocene epoch. The shoulder height of the Siberian, or woolly, mammoth, which roamed throughout the Northern Hemisphere, was about 9 ft (2.7 m), and that of the imperial mammoth of the North American Great Plains was about 13½ ft (4.1 m). Mammoths were covered by a long, shaggy, black outer coat and a dense, woolly undercoat. They had complex, many-ridged molar teeth; long, slender upward-curved tusks; and a long trunk. Ivory hunters have collected their tusks for centuries in Siberia, where some 50,000 have been discovered; it is from these and from the drawings left by the Cro-Magnon people in the caves of S France that the mammoth's appearance is known. Paleolithic (Old Stone Age) people hunted mammoths, as is evidenced by remains of the animals found together with tools, and may have contributed to their extinction. Mammoths are classified in the phylum CHORDATA, subphylum Vertebrata, class Mammalia, order Proboscidea, family Elephantidae.

Mammoth Cave National Park, 51,354 acres (20,783 hectares), S Ky.; est. 1936. Located in a hilly and forested region, the park offers numerous outdoor activities. It is the site of **Mammoth Cave,** one of the largest known caves in the world. Composed of a series of subterranean chambers and narrow passages formed by the dissolution of limestone, the cave has five separate levels. Its full extent is still unexplored, but the known passages extend c.150 mi (240 km), disclosing limestone formations (stalactites, stalagmites, and columns), lakes, and rivers. Echo River, c.360 ft (110 m) below the surface, flows through the cave's lowest level and drains into the Green River. Hanson's Lost River, an underground stream, joins Mammoth Cave with the extensive Flint Ridge cave system; this long-sought link was discovered in 1972. The temperature (54°F/12°C) and relative humidity (87%) remain constant during the year throughout the cave. The cave contains the mummified body of a man believed to date from the pre-Columbian period. Eyeless fish, bats, and insects are also found. Mammoth Cave was discovered by white men in 1799 but was an Indian habitation long before it was visited by Kentucky pioneers. During the War of 1812, saltpeter was mined in the cave for gunpowder.

Mamoré (məmo͞orĕ'), river, c.600 mi (965 km) long, formed by tributaries rising in the Andes and plains of central Bolivia. It flows north, past Trinidad, to the Brazilian border. After forming part of the Bolivia-Brazil border, the Mamoré joins with the Beni River to form the Madeira River. With the Río Grande, its chief tributary, the Mamoré flows c.1,100 (1,770 km) through the Bolivian lowlands (where it is navigable) and the Cordillera Oriental.

Mamre (măm'rē), ally of Abraham and owner of part of HEBRON. Gen. 14.24.

Mamun, al- (Abu al-Abbas Abd-Allah al-Mamun) (mämo͞on'), 786–833, 7th ABBASID caliph (813–33); son of HARUN AR-RASHID. He succeeded his brother al-Amin but was unable to enter Baghdad until 819. His reign was troubled, particularly because of al-Mamun's preference for Persians and rationalists. He was himself one of the Mutazilites, the greatest rationalistic sect of Islam, holding that the Koran was created in time, i.e., that it was not an uncreated eternal existent, as orthodox Muslims maintain. He persecuted the orthodox bitterly. Al-Mamun's reign was one of great cultural achievement, and he was especially interested in scientists, particularly when they knew Greek. He established (830) in Baghdad the *House of Wisdom,* an institution that translated Greek works into Arabic. The poet Abu Tammam, the scholar Bukhari, and the jurist Ahmad ibn Hanbal all flourished under al-Mamun.

Man, town (1967 est. pop. 30,000), W central Ivory Coast, at the foot of the Toura Mts. It is an administrative and commercial center for a region producing coffee, cacao, kola nuts, rice, and cassava. Iron ore, bauxite, copper, and gold are mined nearby.

man: see ANTHROPOLOGY; MAN, PREHISTORIC; RACE.

Man, Isle of, island (1971 pop. 49,743), 227 sq mi (588 sq km), off Great Britain, in the Irish Sea. The coast is rocky with precipitous cliffs; the Calf of Man is a detached rocky islet off the southwest coast. The rounded hills in the center of the island rise to 2,034 ft (620 m) at Snaefell. The scenery is varied and beautiful, the climate very mild (subtropical plants are grown without protection), and the island is a popular resort. Oats, barley, turnips, and potatoes are grown, and sheep are raised. Dairying and fishing are carried on, and Manx tweeds are made from locally produced wool. There is some light industry. Traces of occupants of the isle from Neolithic times exist; there are ancient crosses and other stone monuments, a round tower, an old fort, and castles. Occupied in the 9th cent. by Vikings, the island was a dependency of Norway until 1266, when it passed to Scotland, but from the 14th to the 18th cent. (except for brief periods when it reverted to the English crown) it belonged to the earls of Salisbury and of Derby. Since 1765, when Parliament purchased it from the Duke of Atholl, the Isle has been a dependency of the crown, but it is not subject to acts of the British Parliament. The traditional open-air assembly of the Tynwald (one of the world's oldest legislative bodies) on July 5th was attended for the first time by the British king in 1945. The isle is rich in folklore and legend. Its towns include DOUGLAS (the capital), Peel, Ramsey, and Castletown. The Manx language (Celtic) is now known by very few of the inhabitants—English is generally spoken. Thomas Edward Brown, a native Manxman, used the dialect in his poetry. Sir Hall Caine lived on the island and wrote about Manx life.

man, prehistoric, or **early man.** For centuries, but especially since the late 19th cent. with the development of the theory of biological evolution, or DARWINISM, scientists have been interested in discovering man's origins. Modern knowledge of man's evolutionary development is largely derived from the findings of PALEONTOLOGY, ANTHROPOLOGY, and GENETICS. In these fields scientific knowledge is incomplete, but a clear anatomical relationship has been established between man and the apes, and there is much evidence to support the thesis that man evolved from apelike ancestors. While there are many gaps and uncertainties in the line of descent, there is definitely a continuous, gradual evolution from simple PRIMATES to man, involving a change from an arboreal to a terrestrial environment; the achievement of erect, bipedal locomotion; and increase of body size, life span, period of dependency of young, brain size, and intelligence. The physical evolution of man was accompanied by the development of CULTURE, including tools, language, and social activity. The earliest remains of human culture are the stone tools of the PALEOLITHIC PERIOD (2,000,000–40,000 years ago), which manifest a cultural evolution somewhat parallel to the physical evolution shown by fossil skeletal remains.

The Evolutionary Tree. Man is a mammal of the order Primates. The earliest primates evolved about 70 million years ago in the geological time period known as the Paleocene epoch. They were small, arboreal fruit eaters, like modern tree shrews. Primates of the Eocene epoch, 50 million years ago, were similar to contemporary tarsiers, LEMURS and tree shrews. In the late Eocene and early Oligocene periods, about 35 million years ago, the higher primates developed along three lines: New World (or platyrrhine) monkeys, Old World (or catarrhine) monkeys, and apes. The ancestors of modern apes and of man were among the fossil genus DRYOPITHECUS, an extinct group of apes of the Miocene and early Pliocene epochs, 25 million to 14 million years ago. About 14 million to 12 million years ago man and apes began to develop along separate lines. The fossil group RAMAPITHECUS is the earliest known representative of the hominid family to which modern man belongs. Early hominids were most likely arboreal animals that adapted increasingly to existence on the ground, an adaptation possibly necessitated by deforestation of their environment.

The Dawn of Man. The appearance of early man occurs in the Pleistocene period, the most recent geological era. This period was marked by four advances and recessions of a north polar ice cap, and the vast climatic changes that ensued may have influenced the anatomical and social transition from apelike to manlike species. AUSTRALOPITHECUS, which preceded man, was in many ways transitional between apes and man. The Australopithecines lived in Africa 5 million to one million years ago. They were short, generally less than 5 ft (152 cm) tall, walked nearly erect, and had an average brain size of 500 cc (compared to an average 1,350 cc in modern man). They may have used stone tools. The species of man called HOMO ERECTUS seems to have evolved from *Australopithecus* more than a million years ago. They walked fully erect, were over 5 ft tall, and had projecting jaws and brow ridges. They used stone tools, in some areas fire, and probably had a spoken language. They were food gatherers and hunters of small animals. Fossils of *Homo erectus* have been found in Africa, Asia, and Europe, and indicate regional variations, perhaps local adaptations. From *Homo erectus* there evolved, about 300,000 years ago, early *Homo sapiens* such as Swanscombe man (England) and Steinham man (Germany). *Homo sapiens* is distinguished from *Homo erectus* by changes in skull shape, development of the forehead, reduction of the jaws, and increase in brain size. While the average brain size of *Homo erectus* was about 1,000 cc, differences in intelligence of the two species are related to other factors besides brain size and not easily measured. About 75,000 years ago there evolved a type of *Homo sapiens* called NEANDERTHAL MAN. Neanderthal man was slightly more than 5 ft tall, had a long and full face, brow ridges, deep-set eyes, and a robust body. He had an average brain size of 1,450 cc, somewhat larger than the modern average. Neanderthal populations predominated in Europe, Africa, and Asia in late Pleistocene times until about 40,000 years ago. The relationship of the Neanderthals to later types is unclear. The classic, European Neanderthal, with such extreme specialized features as the outstanding brow ridges, may have become extinct. There is no definite continuity between Neanderthal man and the later CRO-MAGNON MAN in Europe. In the Middle East, however, fossils found at Mt. Carmel indicate an evolution or an intermixing between Neanderthal and more modern forms of man. The first types physically indistinguishable from modern man appeared about 35,000 years ago. Early fossils of modern *Homo sapiens* include Cro-Magnon man, Grimaldi man (Italy), Boskop man (South Africa), and Wadjak man (Java). PILTDOWN MAN (England), which long troubled scientists as to its place in the evolution of prehistoric man, proved a forgery. There have been many scientific attempts to discern the genetic characteristics of modern man in these early populations of *Homo sapiens;* as yet, their relationship is undetermined. No remains of man of great antiquity have been discovered in the New World. The view generally held is that the prehistoric populations of America were predominantly Mongoloid, possibly with some admixture of AINU and perhaps Caucasoid elements, descendants of Asiatic immigrants who entered the continent about 25,000 years ago by way of Bering Strait and Alaska. See Marcellin Boule and H. V. Valois, *Fossil Men* (tr. 1957); C. S. Coon, *The Origin of Races* (1962); T. G. Dobzhansky, *Mankind Evolving* (1962, repr. 1967); C. Loring Brace and M. F. Ashley Montagu, *Man's Evolution* (1965); W. W. Howells, *Mankind in the Making* (rev. ed. 1967); W. E. LeGros Clark, *The Fossil Evidence for Human Evolution* (2d ed. 1964), *History of the Primates* (10th ed. 1970), and *The Antecedents of Man* (rev. ed. 1971).

mana: see ANIMISM; TABOO.

Manado (mänä'dō) or **Menado** (mānä'dō), town (1961 pop. 129,912), capital of North Sulawesi prov., on the northeast coast of Celebes, Indonesia. It is a trade center and seaport on an inlet of the Celebes Sea; exports include copra, coffee, spices, sugarcane, and lumber. In Manado is the Univ. of North and Central Sulawesi, as well as an extension facility of the Islamic Univ. of Indonesia.

Manaen (măn'āĕn), Antiochene Christian, foster brother of Herod the tetrarch. Acts 13.1.

management: see INDUSTRIAL MANAGEMENT.

Managua (mänä'gwä), city (1970 est. pop. 374,178), W Nicaragua, capital and largest city of Nicaragua, on the southern shore of Lake Managua. It is the commercial and industrial center of the country. Situated on the Inter-American Highway, the city is the hub of Nicaragua's railroads. Managua was made permanent capital in 1855 to end the bitter feud between GRANADA and LEÓN. During periods of disorder (1912–25 and 1926–33) it was occupied by U.S. marines. Managua is generally hot and sultry. A fairly constant wind blows from nearby Lake Managua, notable for the same marine phenomena as Lake Nicaragua and flanked by the smoking volcano Momotombo. Many residences and farms have been established on the cooler heights rising in the southern outskirts of the city. Managua was damaged by earthquake and fire in 1931 and by fire in 1936. On Dec. 23, 1972, it was almost completely destroyed in an earthquake that took more than 10,000 lives. Plans were made to reconstruct a new city on the ruins of the old.

Manahath (măn'əhăth, mănā'hăth). **1** Unidentified place. 1 Chron. 8.6. **2** Descendant of Seir. 1 Chron. 1.40.

manakin (măn'əkən), common name for stocky, tiny birds, most measuring less than 5 in. (12.5 cm) long, comprising 59 species in the family Pipridae. Manakins are found throughout the forested areas of Central and South America, where they feed on a diet of small fruits picked on the wing, and occasional insects. They are noted for their curiously modified wing feathers, with which the birds produce a series of whirring and snapping sounds during flight. The sexes differ markedly. The females of most of the species are inconspicuous olive green birds. Males are strikingly arrayed. Primarily greenish brown to black, they have brilliant patches of red, blue, and yellow, often with further ornamental modifications, such as the long central tail feathers of the Fandango birds, genus *Chiroxiphia.* In manakins, as in their relatives, the cotingas, male ornamentation is often coupled with elaborate mating displays. Among the Fandango birds, e.g., *C. pareola,* two or more males cooperate to perform a complex series of acrobatics in order to attract female onlookers. Gould's manakin, *Manacus vitellinus,* clears an area of the forest floor of litter between two saplings and performs a leaping dance, snapping his wings noisily and flitting from branch to branch. When he is joined by a female, mating occurs and the female flies off to lay her 2 pale brown, mottled eggs. The male is polygamous and mates with as many females as he attracts. The female weaves delicate hammock nests of grass, slung in ferns or saplings and typically overlying water. She is entirely responsible for incubation and care of the young. Manakins are classified in the phylum CHORDATA, subphylum Vertebrata, class Aves, order Passeriformes, family Pipridae.

Manamah: see AL MANAMAH, Bahrain.

Manas: see MA-NA-SSU, China.

Manassas (mənăs'əs), town (1970 pop. 9,164), seat of Prince William co., N Va., in a farm area; inc. 1873, rechartered 1938. It was a key railroad junction during the Civil War, and the battles of BULL RUN were fought nearby. Today its population is growing rapidly as the Washington, D.C., suburbs expand further into N Virginia. The town of Manassas Park (1970 pop. 6,844) is adjoining, and near both is the Manassas National Battlefield Park.

Manassas National Battlefield Park: see BULL RUN; NATIONAL PARKS AND MONUMENTS (table).

Manasseh (mənăs'ē) [Heb.,=forgetfulness] or **Manasses** (-əs). **1** First son of Joseph by his Egyptian wife, Asenath, and eponymous ancestor of one of the 12 tribes of Israel. Manasseh was divided into two halves: in Palestine it occupied the land just S of the Vale of Jezreel. In the land beyond the Jordan, Manasseh received land E of Gad. Gen. 41.51; Num. 26.28–34; Deut. 3.13; Joshua 17; 2 Kings 10.33; 1 Chron. 2.21–23; 5.23–26; 7.14–19; Rev. 7.6. **2** King of Judah (c.696–c.642 B.C.), son and successor of Hezekiah. Under him Judah reached a low point of degradation. 2 Kings 21; 2 Chron. 33; Mat. 1.10. The **Prayer of Manasses,** one of the PSEUDEPIGRAPHA, placed in the Apocrypha in the Authorized Version, is a penitential psalm. It is given as the king's prayer in captivity, alluding to 2 Chron. 33.13. **3, 4** Men who had foreign wives. Ezra 10.30,33 **5** Textual error for Moses. Judges 18.30. **6** Husband of Judith. Judith 8.2.

Manasseh ben Israel, 1604–57, Jewish scholar and communal leader, b. Portugal. Early in his life he settled in Amsterdam, where he became a rabbi and started (1627) the first Hebrew press there. He is best known for his efforts to obtain the readmission of Jews into England, where they had been forbidden to live since 1290; he managed to obtain Oliver Cromwell's unofficial assent for Jews to settle in London. His *Conciliador,* an elaborate discussion of hundreds of conflicting passages in the Old Testament, was intended to make Judaism more understandable and acceptable to the Christian world. He wrote in five languages. See biography by Cecil Roth (1934); Lucien Wolf, *Menasseh Ben Israel's Mission to Oliver Cromwell* (1910).

Manasses (mənăs'əs), variant of MANASSEH.

Ma-na-ssu (mä-nä-sōō) or **Manas** (mänäs'), town and oasis, central Sinkiang Uigur Autonomous Region, China, on the Ma-na-ssu River, in the Dzungarian basin. It is the center of a large mechanized-farm area. Wheat, millet, sugar beets, melons, and cotton are grown. Since 1952 an extensive irrigation project, directed by the Chinese army, has reclaimed much acreage for cultivation. Oil deposits are in the area.

manatee: see SIRENIAN.

Manaus (mänous'), city (1970 pop. 312,160), capital of Amazonas state, NW Brazil, on the Rio Negro. It is the chief commercial and cultural center of the upper Amazon region and an important river port, with floating docks that can accommodate ocean-going vessels. Surrounded by jungle, Manaus is the only major city in a c.600-mi (1000-km) radius. Founded in 1669, Manaus grew slowly until the late 19th cent., when the wild-rubber boom brought prosperity and short-lived splendor. In recent years, renewed interest in the Amazon basin and the discovery of oil nearby brought new importance to Manaus. The city is now the seat of several organizations dealing with Amazonian problems, is a free port, and has an international airport and several industries (including an oil refinery). Manaus exports Brazil nuts, rubber, hardwoods, and animal skins. It has a cathedral, zoological and botanical gardens, and a regional museum.

Mancha, La (lä män'chä), region of central Spain, in New Castile, comprising Ciudad Real prov. and part of the provinces of Toledo, Albacete, and Cuenca. This high, barren plateau, dotted with windmills, was made famous as the scene of most of the adventures of Don Quixote de la Mancha in the novel by Cervantes.

Manche (mäNsh), department (1968 pop. 451,939), NW France, in NORMANDY, on the English Channel. Manche is coextensive with the COTENTIN peninsula and extends S into the Norman woods. SAINT-LÔ (the capital), CHERBOURG, and AVRANCHES are the chief towns, and MONT-SAINT-MICHEL is off the coast. Manche is largely agricultural, with extensive animal breeding and raising. Although industry is secondary, there are textile, copper, tile, and food industries, and, at Cherbourg, shipbuilding. The name Manche derives from the French name for the English Channel.

Manchester, county borough (1971 pop. 541,468), Lancashire, NW England, on the Irwell, Medlock, Irk, and Tib rivers. Manchester is the center of the most densely populated area of England. It has long been the leading textile city (its textile industry dates back to the 14th cent.) of England and among the world's foremost cotton cities, serving as a distribution point for the mills of surrounding towns and a center of industries closely allied to the textile trade. It is also the center of printing and publishing in N England. The first application of steam to machinery for spinning cotton was made in Manchester in 1789, and a terminus of the first English passenger railroad (to Liverpool) was constructed here by George Stephenson in 1830. The Manchester Ship Canal, opened in 1894, gave the city access to the sea. After World War I the artificial-silk industry tended to balance losses in the cotton market. A Celtic settlement is believed to have existed on the site of Manchester. The Romans called the town Mancunium, and there are remains of their occupation. Manchester's first charter was granted in 1301. Representation in Parliament was achieved in 1832, and in 1838, thanks to the efforts of Richard Cobden, Manchester was incorporated as a borough. The PETERLOO MASSACRE occurred there in 1819. Manchester has played a prominent role in liberal reform movements. It was the center of the MANCHESTER SCHOOL of economics and the ANTI-CORN LAW LEAGUE, led by Cobden and John Bright. The influential liberal daily the Manchester *Guardian* was founded in 1821. During World War II, Manchester suffered extensively from air raids. The borough has several libraries, including the John Rylands Library (founded 1899) and the Chetham Library (founded 1653), one of Europe's first free public libraries. The Victoria Univ. of Manchester, formerly Owens College, opened in 1851. Manchester has been an important center for scientific research. John Dalton, Lord Rutherford, and Niels Bohr, among others, did significant work in nuclear physics there. At Jodrell Bank, nearby, is the world's largest radio telescope. Manchester has several art galleries and a symphony orchestra of international repute, the Hallé Orchestra, founded in 1857 by Sir Charles Hallé. The first municipal airport in Britain was established at Manchester in 1929. Robert Peel, the statesman, and Thomas de Quincy, the author, were born in Manchester. In 1974, Manchester became part of the new metropolitan county of Greater Manchester.

Manchester. 1 Town (1970 pop. 47,994), Hartford co., central Conn.; settled c.1672, inc. 1823. Among its many manufactures are fiberboard, electrical goods, and textiles. A junior college is there, and Hartford's Bradley International Airport is nearby. **2** City (1970 pop. 87,754), seat of Hillsboro co., S N.H., on both sides of the Merrimack River; settled 1722, inc. as a city 1846. It is the largest city in New Hampshire. Among its various manufactures are textiles, shoes, machinery, and electrical and electronic products. The Amoskeag Falls on the Merrimack provided power for the first textile mills. In 1838 textile interests founded the city and established a giant textile-manufacturing company. Until the depression of the 1930s and the moving of much of the textile industry to the south, Manchester was heavily dependent on this industry. Manchester is the seat of St. Anselm's College and the Currier Gallery of Art. John Stark lived in the city and is buried there. A state park and a number of ski areas are in the vicinity.

Manchester, Victoria University of, at Manchester, England; founded 1880 as Victoria University, an outgrowth of Owens College (est. 1851). In 1903 the university was reconstituted and its present name was adopted. It has faculties of arts, business administration, economic and social studies, education, law, medicine, music, science, technology, and theology. The Univ. of Manchester Institute of Science and Technology is affiliated.

Manchester school, group of English political economists of the 19th cent., so called because they met at Manchester. Their most outstanding leaders were Richard COBDEN and John BRIGHT. Their chief tenet was that the state should interfere as little as possible in economic matters (see LAISSEZ FAIRE), and they advocated FREE TRADE. See F. W. Hirst, ed., *Free Trade and other Fundamental Doctrines of the Manchester School* (1903, repr. 1968); W. D. Grampp, *The Manchester School of Economics* (1960).

Manchester Ship Canal, 35.5 mi (57 km) long with a minimum depth of 28 ft (8.5 m), connecting Manchester, W England, with the Mersey estuary at Eastham, above Birkenhead. Begun in 1887, it was opened in 1894 and changed Manchester from a river port to a seaport. There are large oil refineries along the canal.

Manchester terrier, breed of sleek, alert TERRIER developed in England in the 19th cent. There are two varieties, the standard and the toy (see TOY DOG). The standard variety stands from 14 to 16 in. (35.6–40.6 cm) high at the shoulder and weighs about 16 lb (7.3 kg). The toy Manchester, bred down from the standard, weighs from 5 to 12 lb (2.3–5.5 kg) and stands about 7 in. (17.8 cm) high at the shoulder. The only distinction other than size between the two varieties is in ear carriage; when not cropped, the ears of the standard are semierect, while the toy's natural ear carriage is erect. The dense, short, smooth coat is glossy and is a combination of jet black and mahogany tan in color. Believed to have been the product of breeding a whippet to a famous brown crossbred terrier, the Manchester was originally used in destroying rats and in the widely popular sport of rabbit coursing. Today it is raised chiefly as a house pet. See DOG.

Man-chou-li or **Manchouli** (both: män-jō-lē), city, NW Heilungkiang prov., China, on the Soviet-Chinese border. Coal is mined there, and the city has some light industry. Man-chou-li developed after the construction (1903) of the Chinese Eastern RR and was important as a customs station; until recent times virtually all trade between China and the USSR passed through there. Many Russian émigrés settled in the city after the Bolshevik revolution. It was known as Lupin from 1913 until 1949. Before boundary changes in 1969–70, Man-chou-li was in the Inner Mongolian Autonomous Region.

Manchu (măn'cho͞o), people who lived in Manchuria for many centuries and who ruled China from 1644 until 1912. These people, related to the Tungus, were descended from the Jurchen, a tribe known in Asia since the 7th cent. They were first called Manchu in the early 17th cent. Originally pastoral nomads in Manchuria, the Manchu (or Jurchen) swept into N China in the early 12th cent. but were forced by the Mongols to withdraw in the mid-13th cent. The Manchu settled in the Sungari River valley and developed an agrarian civilization. Under the emperor Nurhachu (1559–1626) they secured the allegiance of many tribes and increased their territory. The Manchu claim of relation to the Ch'in dynasty of China was the justification for conquering China in the 17th cent. and establishing the CH'ING dynasty. The Manchu tried to keep themselves from being absorbed by the Chinese, but when the dynasty was overthrown in the 20th cent. these efforts failed; gradually, they became part of the general Chinese population.

Manchukuo (mănchō͞o'kwō), former country, comprising MANCHURIA and Jehol prov., China. The Japanese invaded Manchuria in 1931 and founded Manchukuo in 1932. Changchun, the capital, was renamed Hsinking [Chinese, = new capital]. Henry Pu Yi, last of the Manchu (CH'ING) dynasty of China, ruled as regent and emperor. Manchukuo, ostensibly an independent Manchu state, was actually a Japanese puppet-state. Of the major countries only Japan, Italy, and Germany extended diplomatic recognition; few foreigners were allowed into Manchukuo. The Japanese military kept strict control of the administration and fought a continuing guerrilla war with native resistance groups. To develop Manchukuo as a war base, the Japanese greatly expanded industry and railroads. After World War II, Chinese sovereignty was reasserted over the area.

Manchuria (mănchŏŏr'ēə), Mandarin *Tung-pei-chiu-sheng* [northeastern provinces], region, c.600,000 sq mi (1,554,000 sq km), NE China. It is separated from the USSR largely by the Amur, Argun, and Ussuri rivers, from North Korea by the Yalu and Tumen rivers, and from Mongolia by the Khingan mts. It includes the Liao-tung peninsula. Until 1860 it included territory now in Siberia and until 1955 territory now in the Inner Mongolian Autonomous Region. Provincial divisions have changed frequently, but since 1956 Manchuria has comprised Kirin, Heilungkiang, and Liaoning provs. Much of the region is hilly to mountainous. The Great and Lesser Khingan in the north and the Ch'ang-pai in the east are the greatest ranges. Manchuria has vast timber reserves; the country's finest timber is found in the E Manchurian highlands. Mineral resources, chiefly coal and iron, are concentrated in the southwest; the largest colliery is at Fu-shun and the largest steel mill at An-shan. Magnesite and gold are also important, and there is a large oilfield at Tach'ing, NW of Harbin. Uranium deposits have also been found. The great Manchurian plain (average elevation c.1,000 ft/300 m), crossed by the Liao and Sungari rivers, is the only extensively level area. Fertile and densely populated, it is a major manufacturing and agricultural center of China. One of the few areas in the country suitable for large-scale mechanized agriculture, it has numerous state and collective farms. Long, severe winters limit harvests to one a year, but considerable quantities of soybeans are produced. Sweet potatoes, beans, and cereals (including rice, wheat, millet, and kaoling) are also grown, and cotton, flax, and sugar beets are raised as industrial crops. The processing of soybeans into oil, animal feed, and fertilizer is centered in cities in or near the plain, notably Ch'ang-ch'un, Harbin, and Shen-yang (formerly Mukden). Livestock are raised in the north and the west, and fishing is important off the Yellow Sea coast. The chief commercial port is Ta-lien, and Lü-ta is a leading naval base. All rivers are navigable but only the Sungari is significant for heavy traffic. When the rivers freeze, they are used as roadways. An extensive rail system connects the hinterland with the coastal ports; major lines are the South Manchurian RR and the Chinese Eastern RR. The building of the railroads (after 1896) spurred industrial development. Today Manchuria is a great industrial hub, with huge coal mines, iron and steel works, aluminum reduction plants, paper mills, and factories making heavy machinery, tractors, locomotives, aircraft, and chemicals. Manchuria is traditionally the homeland of peoples that have invaded and sometimes ruled N China. Among the most important of these tribes were the Tungus, Eastern Turks, Khitan, and Jurchen. It was the home of the MANCHU conquerors of China. The Manchus tried to keep Manchuria an imperial preserve by limiting Chinese immigration. In this century, however, emigration to Manchuria from the adjacent provinces has been heavy, and the population is now predominantly Chinese. Japan and Russia long struggled for control of this rich, strategically important region. Japan tried to seize the Liao-tung peninsula in 1895, but was forestalled by the Triple Intervention. From 1898 to 1904, Russia was dominant. As a result of a Russo-Chinese alliance against Japan, the Russians built Harbin, the naval base at Port Arthur, and the Chinese Eastern RR. Japan, after victory in the Russo-Japanese War (1904–5), took control of Port Arthur and the southern half of Manchuria (see LIAONING), limiting Russian influence to the north. Chiefly through the South Manchurian RR, Japan developed the region's economy. From 1918 to 1931 the warlords Chang Tso-lin and Chang Hsueh-liang controlled Chinese military power in Manchuria. Japan occupied Manchuria in 1931–32, when Chinese military resistance, sapped by civil war, was weak. The seizure of Manchuria was, in effect, an unofficial declaration of war on China. Manchuria was a base for Japanese aggression in N China and a buffer region for Japanese-controlled Korea. In 1932, under the aegis of Japan, Manchuria with Jehol prov. was constituted Manchukuo, a nominally independent state. During World War II the Japanese developed the Ta-lien, An-shan, Fu-shun, Mukden, and Harbin areas into a huge industrial complex of metallurgical, coal, petroleum, and chemical industries. Soviet forces, which occupied Manchuria from July, 1945, to May, 1946, dismantled and removed over half of the Manchurian industrial plant. At the end of the war the Chinese Communists were strongly established in Manchuria and by 1948 had captured the major cities and inflicted devastating losses on the Nationalist army. From 1949 to 1954, Manchuria, ruled by Kao Kang, was the most staunch of the Communist areas in China. With the help of Soviet technicians the Communists rapidly restored Manchuria's large industrial capacity. Since the Sino-Soviet rift in the 1960s there has been a massive Soviet military buildup along the border and several border incidents have occurred.

Manchurian Incident or **Mukden Incident,** 1931, confrontation that gave Japan the impetus to set up a puppet government in Manchuria. After the Russo-Japanese War (1904–5), Japan replaced Russia as the dominant foreign power in S Manchuria. By the late 1920s the Japanese feared that unification of China under the Kuomintang party would imperil Japanese interests in Manchuria. This view was confirmed when the Manchurian general CHANG HSUEH-LIANG, a recent convert to the Kuomintang, refused to halt construction of railway and harbor facilities in competition with the SOUTH MANCHURIAN RAILWAY, referring Japan to the Nationalist central government. When a bomb of unknown origin ripped the Japanese railway near Mukden, the Japanese Kwantung army guarding the railway used the incident as a pretext to occupy S Manchuria (Sept., 1931). Despite Japanese cabinet opposition and a pledge before the League of Nations to withdraw to the railway zone, the army completed the occupation of Manchuria and proclaimed the puppet state of MANCHUKUO (Feb., 1932). See SINO-JAPANESE WAR, SECOND. See Takehiko Yoshihashi, *Conspiracy at Mukden* (1963); S. N. Ogata, *Defiance in Manchuria* (1964).

Mancini, Pasquale Stanislao (päskwä'lā stänēzlä'ō mänchē'nē), 1817–88, Italian jurist and public official. After taking part in the Revolution of 1848 in Naples he fled to Turin, where he later became (1860) a deputy in the parliament. He was minister of justice (1876–78) and of foreign affairs (1881–85), and negotiated the Triple Alliance (see TRIPLE ALLIANCE AND TRIPLE ENTENTE). In internal politics Mancini represented the liberal left and was an anticlerical. He taught at the universities of Turin and Rome.

Manco Capac (mäng'kō käpäk'), legendary founder of the Inca dynasty of Peru. According to the most frequently told story, four brothers, Manco Capac, Ayar Anca, Ayar Cachi, and Ayar Uchu, and their four sisters, Mama Ocllo, Mama Huaco, Mama Cura (or Ipacura), and Mama Raua, lived at Paccari-Tampu [tavern of the dawn], several miles distant from Cuzco. They gathered together the tribes of their locality, marched on the Cuzco Valley, and conquered the tribes living there. Manco Capac had by his sister-wife, Mama Ocllo, a son called Sinchi Roca (or Cinchi Roca). Authorities concede that the first Inca chief to be a historical figure was called Sinchi Roca (c.1105–c.1140). Thus the foundation for an empire was laid. Another legend relates that the Sun created a man and a woman on an island in Lake Titicaca. They were given a golden staff by the Sun, their father, who bade them settle permanently at whatever place the staff should sink into the earth. At a hill overlooking the present city of Cuzco the staff of gold disappeared into the earth. They gathered around them a great many people and founded the city of Cuzco and the Inca state.

Manco Capac, d. 1544, last of the Inca rulers, son of HUAYNA CAPAC. After the deaths of HUÁSCAR and ATAHUALPA, Manco Capac was crowned (1534) emperor by the Spanish conquistador Francisco Pizarro but was tolerated only as a puppet. He escaped, levied a huge army, and in 1536 laid siege to Cuzco, the Inca capital; the defense was commanded by Hernando Pizarro. Although the Indians had by now learned some European tactics of war they were outclassed by technical advantages. Also, Manco Capac could not prevent dismemberment of his army at harvest time. The heroic siege, which virtually destroyed the city, was abandoned after ten months, but during the ensuing eight years the Inca's name became a terror throughout Peru. Manco Capac fought a bloody guerrilla war against soldiers and settlers. He was treacherously murdered after giving refuge to the defeated supporters of Diego de Almagro, who had rebelled against Pizarro.

Mandaeans (măn'dēənz), a small religious sect in Iran and S Iraq, who maintain an ancient belief resembling that of GNOSTICISM and that of the PARSIS. They are also known as Christians of St. John, Nasoraeans, Sabians, and Subbi. A few Mandaeans survive, some near the Tigris and Euphrates rivers, others in the area of Shushtar, Iran, and in cities of Asia Minor. Their customs and writings indicate early Christian, perhaps pre-Christian, origin. Their system of astrology resembles those of ancient Babylonia and the cults of the MAGI in the last centuries B.C. Their emanation system and their dualism suggest a Gnostic origin, but unlike the Gnostics, they abhor asceticism and emphasize fertility. Although some of their practices were influenced by Christianity, Judaism, and Islam, they reject all three. The Mandaeans respect St. John the Baptist because of his baptizing, since their principal concern is ritual cleanliness and their chief rite is frequent baptism. The custom, which antedated the baptisms of St. John, stems from the belief that living water is the principle of life. They have a communion sacrament, which is offered for the remembrance of the dead and resembles Parsi ritual meals. The origin of the Mandaeans is not known; it is conjectured that they came from a mountainous region N of Babylonia and Persia, where they settled in ancient times; however, more recent scholarship places their origin in Palestine or Syria. Their chief holy book, the *Ginza Rba,* like their other books, is a compendium of cosmology, cosmogony, prayers, legends, and rituals, written at various times and often contradictory. The sect is diminishing because younger members tend to apostatize. See S. A. F. D. Pallis, *Mandaean Studies* (rev. ed. 1926); Lady Drower, *The Mandaeans of Iraq and Iran* (1937, repr. 1962) and *Secret Adam: A study of Nasorean Gnosis* (1960); E. M. Yamauchi, *Gnostic Ethics and Mandaean Origins* (1970).

Mandal (män'däl), town (1970 pop. 11,143), Vest-Agder co., extreme S Norway, on the Skagerrak. A renowned seaport in the 17th cent., it is now a small trading and shipping center, known for its remarkable beach and for its 18th-century patrician houses.

mandala (mŭn'dələ), a concentric diagram, having spiritual or occult significance, in the form of a square, a circle, or combination, usually quartered. The mandala occurs as a basic pattern in religious art and ritual throughout the world. The psychologist Carl Jung interpreted it as an archetype, the appearance of which in dreams signals the emergence of a period of fulfillment and inner balance. The four corners of a mandala represent the four corners of the world, and thus the diagram may be taken to symbolize the totality of existence, inner or outer. Mandalas are used as subjects for meditation particularly in TIBETAN BUDDHISM, where numbers of deities have specific positions in the diagram, and the symbolism and structure of the mandala are highly elaborated.

Mandalay (măn"dəlā', măn'dəlā"), city (1970 est. pop. 300,000), Mandalay division, central Burma, on the Irrawaddy River. The second largest city in Burma, it is the terminus of the main rail line from Rangoon and the starting point of branch lines to Lashio and Myitkyina. As a city it dates from c.1850. It was the capital of the Burman kingdom, replacing Amarapura, from 1860 to 1885, when it was annexed to British Burma. A center of Burmese Buddhism, the city is noted for the Arakan pagoda, which is built around an ancient shrine. The group of sacred buildings known as the Seven Hundred and Thirty Pagodas was erected in the reign (1853–78) of King Mindon. Mandalay was heavily damaged in World War II.

mandamus (măndā'məs) [Lat.,=we order], in law, WRIT directing the performance of ministerial acts. A ministerial act is one that a person or body is obliged by law to perform under given circumstances; e.g., on receipt of the fee, a license clerk must grant a marriage license to persons legally qualified to marry. If the law allows discretion in performance, the act is not ministerial; thus mandamus will not be issued if, pursuant to statute, a license to sell liquor is refused because of the applicant's immoral character. Mandamus may be used to compel the directors of a corporation to produce the books for inspection in the manner provided by law or to compel a lower court to accept a suit it has illegally refused. Mandamus is an extraordinary remedy; i.e., it will not be issued if the usual remedies, e.g., DAMAGES for the breach of duty, are adequate. Mandamus, originally granted at the will of the English king, is now available from ordinary courts in Great Britain and the United States. In the famous case of MARBURY VS. MADISON the Supreme Court was asked to issue a writ of mandamus against Secretary of State James Madison. See INJUNCTION.

Mandan (măn'dăn), city (1970 pop. 11,093), seat of Morton co., S N.Dak., on the Missouri River opposite Bismarck; inc. 1881. A railroad division point, it is the distributing center for a grain, livestock, and dairy region. It has a large cattle market, food-processing plants, and an oil refinery. Lewis and Clark wintered there (1804–5) in the Mandan Indian villages. A state industrial school is in the city, and a U.S. agricultural experiment station and a state park are nearby.

Mandan Indians, North American Indians whose language belongs to the Siouan branch of the Hokan-Siouan linguistic stock (see AMERICAN INDIAN LANGUAGES). The Mandan Indians were a sedentary tribe of the Plains area and were culturally connected with their neighbors on the Missouri River, the ARIKARA and the HIDATSA Indians. The Mandan had certain distinctive cultural traits, which included a myth of origin in which their ancestors climbed from beneath the earth on the roots of a grapevine. According to tradition, at one time the Mandan lived to the east, but their movements in historic times were westward up the Missouri River. By the mid-18th cent., they lived in nine villages near the mouth of the Heart River in S central North Dakota. After having suffered severely from smallpox and the attacks of the Assiniboin and the Sioux, the Mandan moved farther up the Missouri River to a point opposite the Arikara villages. Here the Mandan survivors merged into two villages on opposite sides of the Knife River. They were visited (1804) by Lewis and Clark, who said that they numbered some 1,250. In 1837, after an epidemic of smallpox and cholera, the Mandan were reduced to some 150, all dwelling in a single village. When the Hidatsa moved (1845) from the Knife River region N to the Fort Berthold trading post, the few Mandan joined them. A large reservation was set aside (1870) for the Mandan, the Hidatsa, and the Arikara in North Dakota (Fort Berthold Reservation), where together they number some 2,700. See George Catlin, *O-Kee-Pa, a Religious Ceremony, and Other Customs of the Mandans* (1867, centennial ed. by J. C. Ewers, 1967).

Mandarin (măn'dərĭn) [from Port. *mandar*=to govern, or from Malay *mantri*=counselor of state], a high official of imperial China. For each of the nine grades there was a different colored button worn on the dress cap. Mandarin Chinese was the language spoken by the official class and was based on the Peking dialect. Mandarin Chinese is now taught throughout the country, and it is the official national language. It is spoken everywhere except along the southeastern coast, where the Cantonese, Fukienese, and Shanghai languages—usually miscalled dialects—are dominant.

mandates, system of trusteeships established by Article 22 of the Covenant of the LEAGUE OF NATIONS for the administration of former Turkish territories and of former German colonies. As finally adopted, the mandates system was principally the work of the South African statesman Gen. Jan Christiaan Smuts. It marked an important innovation in international law with respect to the treatment of dependent territories. A mandated territory differed from a protectorate in that obligations were assumed by the mandate power to the inhabitants of the territory and to the League, which supervised mandates; it differed from a sphere of influence in that the guardians had an acknowledged right to raise and expend revenues, to appoint officials, and to make and enforce laws. The mandated territories were divided into three classes, according to their economic and political development and their location, and were then assigned to individual powers. Class A consisted of Iraq (British), Syria and Lebanon (French), and Palestine (British). The provisional independence of these former Turkish provinces was recognized, subject to administrative control until they could stand alone. By 1949 all former Class A mandates had reached full independence. Class B was composed of the former German African colonies, South West Africa excepted—Tanganyika and parts of Togoland and the Cameroons (British), Ruanda-Urundi (Belgian), and the greater part of Togoland

and the Cameroons (French). The establishment of military or naval bases in these regions by the mandatories was forbidden; commercial equality with other nations and native rights were guaranteed. In Class C were placed South West Africa (South Africa), former German Samoa (New Zealand), New Guinea (Australia), Nauru (Australia), and former German islands in the Pacific, north of the equator (Japan). While fortification of these mandates was forbidden and native rights were guaranteed, these areas were to be administered by the mandatories as integral parts of their empires. The mandates system was administered by the League of Nations through a Permanent Mandates Commission of 11 members. With the creation of the UNITED NATIONS, the mandates system was superseded by the trusteeship system (see TRUSTEESHIP, TERRITORIAL). All remaining mandated territories became trust territories except South West Africa, the status of which remains a point of contention between South Africa and the United Nations. See Quincy Wright, *Mandates under the League of Nations* (1930, repr. 1968); R. N. Chowdhuri, *International Mandates and Trusteeship Systems* (1955).

mandats: see ASSIGNATS.

Mande (män'dā), language group, W Africa, including the Malinke, Dyula, Marka, Mende, Bambara, and Soninke subgroups. The Mande-speakers today number about 3 million and live mainly in Senegal, Mali, Guinea, Sierra Leone, and Liberia. Their societies are patrilineal, and most practice sedentary agriculture and profess Islam. The Mande probably originated in the region of the upper Niger River, and they formed numerous states based on trade. The Soninke founded the ancient empire of GHANA (7th–13th cent.), and the Malinke established the empire of Mali (13th–16th cent.). Mande traders were important in spreading Islam in W Africa.

Mandelstam, Osip Emilyevich (ô'sĭp ĕmyēl'yəvĭch män'dĭlstəm), 1892–1940?, Russian poet. Mandelstam was a leader of the ACMEIST school. He wrote impersonal, fatalistic, meticulously constructed poems, the best of which are collected in *Kamen* [stone] (1913) and *Tristia* (1922). Although he opposed the Bolsheviks, he remained in Russia after the revolution but wrote no poetry after 1925. He was arrested in 1933 or 1934 and died in a concentration camp. See his complete works, tr. by Burton Raffel and Alla Burago (1973); memoirs by Nadezhda Mandelstam (2 vol., 1970 and 1974); study by Clarence Brown (1973).

Mander, Karel van (kä'rəl vän män'dər), 1548–1606, Flemish painter and humanist. He wrote plays on biblical themes and translated from the classics. He is known primarily for his biography of painters, *Het Schilder-Boeck* (1604; tr. *Dutch and Flemish Painters,* 1936), which, despite its inaccuracies, is probably the best early source on Northern painters.

Mandeville, Bernard (măn'dəvĭl), 1670–1733, English author, b. Dordrecht, Holland. A physician, he went to London in 1692 ostensibly to learn the language, but eventually settled there permanently, practicing medicine and writing on ethical subjects. His most important work, *The Fable of the Bees* (1714, enl. ed. 1723, 1728), was an expansion of his poem *The Grumbling Hive* (1705). Mandeville declared that the mainspring of a commercial and industrial society is the self-seeking effort of individuals. Religious or legal restraints are mere fictions invented by rulers and clergymen to put men under domination. Mandeville's attitude was attacked by his contemporaries George Berkeley and William Law. However, his work had a strong influence on the doctrine of utilitarianism of the 19th cent.

Mandeville, Sir John, 14th-century English author of *The Travels of Sir John Mandeville.* Originally written in Norman French, the work became enormously popular and was translated into English, Latin, and most European languages. It purports to recount the author's travels through Jerusalem, Egypt, Turkistan, India, China, and other places. Actually it is a skillful compilation from the recorded travels of other people—e.g., Marco Polo, Ordoric of Pordenone, and William of Boldensele—into which Mandeville interpolated extravagant details of medieval lore. Many scholars believe that Mandeville was a pseudonym and that the work was written by Jean de Bourgogne (or Jean à la Barbe), physician of Liège, or by Jean d'Outremeuse (1338–1400), citizen of Liège and composer of fabulous history. A growing number of scholars, however, contest that the book was composed, as reported in the text, by John Mandeville. Biographical details are not wholly clear, but he seems to have been born at St. Albans in the late 13th cent., to have spent the prime of his life on the Continent, and to have completed the book by 1356 as a travel romance, rather than as an authentic account. For a lucid discussion of the whole scholarly problem and of Mandeville's artistry, see J. W. Bennett, *The Rediscovery of Sir John Mandeville* (1954).

mandolin (măn"dəlĭn', măn'dəlĭn"), musical instrument of the lute family, with a half-pear-shaped body, a fretted neck, and a variable number of strings, plucked with the fingers or with a plectrum.

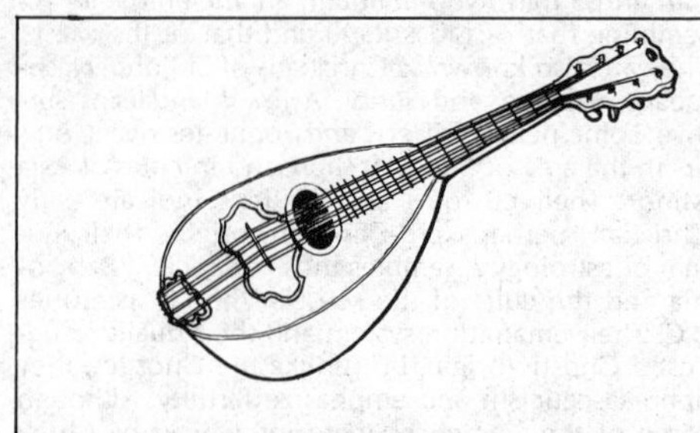

Mandolin

The earlier mandolin, with five double strings, was developed from the mandola, a 17th-century lute. The Neapolitan mandolin, a smaller type having four pairs of strings, became popular in the 18th cent. and is the usual present-day mandolin. In popular music it is generally played with a tremolo motion. Notable uses of the mandolin in serious music are in Mozart's *Don Giovanni* and in pieces by Beethoven.

Mandor, India: see JODHPUR.

mandorla (män'dôrlä), [Ital.=almond], a medieval Christian artistic convention by which an oval or almond-shaped area or series of lines surrounds a deity, most commonly Christ. The mandorla is thought to have derived from either Greek or Roman prototypes. Figures of deities were sometimes placed within semicircular outlines on Greek vases. The Romans surrounded portrait busts with medallions and shields. One of the earliest known uses of the mandorla in Christian ICONOGRAPHY occurs in the 5th-century mosaics in the church of Santa Maria Maggiore, Rome. The principal applications of the mandorla, also sometimes termed aureole or *vesica pisces,* were in paintings depicting the Transfiguration, the Ascension, the Last Judgment, the Harrowing of Hell, and in symbolic portrayals of the evangelists and Christ in Majesty. The Virgin Mary and the major angels were also shown enclosed in a mandorla. The convention, like that of the halo, was discontinued during the Renaissance. See NIMBUS.

mandrake, plant of the family Solanaceae (NIGHTSHADE family), the source of a narcotic much used during the Middle Ages as a pain-killer and perhaps the subject of more superstition than any other plant. The true mandrakes are of the genus *Mandragora* (especially *M. officinalis*), herbaceous perennials native to the Mediterranean and to Himalayan areas. The long root (sometimes called a mandrake), which crudely resembles the human form, has been credited since ancient times with such attributes as the power to magically arouse ardor, increase wealth, and overcome barrenness (e.g., Gen. 30.14–16). It was said that the root gave forth such screams when pulled from the ground that death or madness resulted for any who heard; it was uprooted, therefore, by a dog who was tied to it and then called from a distance. The potency of the mandrake, which contains several alkaloids of medicinal value, has made it one of the most frequently mentioned plants in literature. Also sometimes called mandrake is the May apple (genus *Podophyllum*) of the Berberidaceae (BARBERRY family), which has milder medicinal properties. Mandrake is classified in the division MAGNOLIOPHYTA, class Magnoliopsida, order Polemoniales, family Solanaceae. The May apple is classified in the order Ranunculales, family Berberidaceae.

mandrill, large monkey, *Mandrillus sphinx,* of central W Africa, related to the BABOONS. Mandrills are found in forests, while baboons live in open country. The fur of the mandrill is mostly dark brown, but the bare areas—face and buttocks—are patterned in bright colors that are especially spectacular in the adult male, the most colorful of all mammals. The long, heavy doglike muzzle has bright red skin covering the chin, mouth, and nose and extending upward in a narrow strip to the striking, close-set, yellow-brown eyes. The cheeks are bright blue and are folded into an elaborate pattern of ridges. The fur around the eyes is black, and the beard and the edges of the mane are pale yellow. The buttock pads are bright blue, red, and purple. The tail is a short stump. Male mandrills, about 3 ft (90 cm) long, are considerably larger than females and have enormous canine teeth that they display in yawnlike threatening gestures. Mandrills travel on the ground in small family groups, feeding chiefly on insects and vegetation. Powerful animals, and formidable when provoked, they are retiring in habits and avoid contact with humans. They are extremely difficult to observe in the wild. The closely related drill, *M. leucophaeus,* is also a forest dweller. It is brown with a black face partially outlined in red; the buttock pads are pink. The mandrill and the drill are classified in the phylum CHORDATA, subphylum Vertebrata, class Mammalia, order Primates, family Cercopithecidae.

Mánes, Josef (yô'zĕf mä'nĕs), 1820–71, Czech painter and illustrator, who worked chiefly in Prague. He painted portraits and genre scenes with detailed representations of Czech costumes. Mánes also illustrated the story of Dr. Faust (1858) and Czech folksongs (1856–62).

manes (mā'nēz), in Roman religion, spirits of the dead. They were also called *di manes,* a euphemism meaning the good gods. The Romans placated the manes with offerings at the graves of the dead. In later times, when the family tomb was introduced into burial custom, the *di manes* were identified with the *di parentes,* the ancestors of the family, and as such watched over the welfare of the family along with the lares and penates.

Manet, Édouard (ādwär' mänā'), 1832–83, French painter, b. Paris. Rather than study law Manet went to sea. On his return to Paris in 1850 he studied art with COUTURE. He was influenced by Velázquez and Goya and later by Japanese printmakers. In 1861 the Salon accepted his *Chanteur espagnol.* Two years later his *Déjeuner sur l'herbe* (Louvre) was shown in the Salon des Refusés and was violently attacked; it is a remarkably forthright portrait of a woman, which has not lost its power to shock. Manet's masterpiece, *Olympia* (1863; Louvre), an equally arresting portrait of a well-known courtesan, was shown in 1865. It was met by outrage and abuse from critics and public alike. Apart from their extraordinary psychological insight, these paintings incorporated a number of technical innovations, which were themselves attacked by the academicians as heresy. This hostility of the critics attended Manet throughout his life, yet he never ceased to hope for acceptance from the art establishment. Fortunately he had some independent means, a strong following among his fellow painters, and a companion in Zola, who lost his position on a newspaper because he defended the painter. Manet profoundly influenced the impressionist painters and, indeed, the whole course of French painting. He is often called an impressionist himself, although he declined to exhibit his work with the group, and except for a short time he did not employ broken color or sketchy brush strokes. The whole of his work was a successful attempt to describe the natural immediacy of the eye's perception in terms of paint. He worked in broad, flat areas, using almost no transitional tones, to show what the eye takes in at a glance. By 1900 his techniques and their results were understood and appreciated, and his works were hung in the Louvre. Today examples are to be seen in the most important European and American galleries. Among his many celebrated paintings are *The Balcony* (1869), a portrait of Zola (1868), and *The Fife Player* (1866), all of which are in the Louvre; part of the *Execution of Maximilian* (1867; Tate Gall., London); and *Les Courses à Longchamps* (Art Inst., Chicago). Manet also made many delightful pastels, watercolors, and etchings, including graphic portraits of Baudelaire, and a series of illustrations based on Poe's *Raven.* See catalogs of his pastels by J. Rewald (1947), graphic works by J. C. Harris (1970), and drawings by A. DeLeiris (1971); studies by G. Bataille (tr. 1955), P. Courthion (1962), and G. H. Hamilton (1954, repr. 1969).

Manetho (măn'ĭthō), fl. 300 B.C., Egyptian historian, a priest at Heliopolis, under Ptolemy I and Ptolemy II. His work, covering the history of Egypt from legendary times to 323 B.C., is written in Greek and is known to us only through the later works of Josephus, Sextus Julius Africanus, and Eusebius. Manetho's arrangement of 30 dynasties, in spite of limitations—some dynastic changes are not recorded; some dynasties continued through two or three of Manetho's—has proved to be a convenient device and is still in use.

Manfred, c.1232–1266, king of Sicily (1258–66), the last HOHENSTAUFEN on that throne. An illegitimate son of Holy Roman Emperor Frederick II, Manfred was regent in Sicily for his brother CONRAD IV. Conrad died in 1254, and Manfred seized the regency for Conrad's young son, CONRADIN. However, Pope INNOCENT IV and his successors, Alexander IV and URBAN IV, were determined to stamp out the Hohenstaufen. Papal forces invaded Sicily, and Manfred was forced to restore (1254) the kingdom to the papacy, retaining only the duchy of Taranto in fief from the pope. Soon Manfred rebelled, reconquered S Italy and Sicily, assumed leadership of the antipapal forces throughout Italy, and had himself crowned (1258) at Palermo. Urban IV reacted by investing Charles of Anjou with Sicily as CHARLES I. Invading Italy, Charles defeated Manfred at Benevento (1266). Manfred died in the battle, and Conradin was later captured and executed. After the SICILIAN VESPERS (1282), Manfred's son-in-law, Peter III of Aragón, was chosen king of Sicily and began a new dynasty.

mangabey: see MONKEY.

Mangalore (măng-gəlôr'), city (1971 metropolitan area pop. 214,093), Karnataka state, SW India, on the Arabian Sea. A port, it trades in spices, rice, coffee, nuts, and timber. It was the capital (13th cent.) of the Alupa kingdom. In the late 18th cent., Mangalore was an important shipbuilding center. The British occupied the city in 1799.

Mangan, James Clarence, 1803–49, Irish poet. He spent most of his life as a clerk, eventually slipping into alcoholism and opium addiction. His reputation rests on his English renderings of Gaelic poems, such as the excellent "Dark Rosaleen." See study by James Joyce (1930).

manganese (măng'gənēs, măn'-) [Lat.,=magnet], metallic chemical element; symbol Mn; at. no. 25; at. wt. 54.938; m.p. about 1245°C; b.p. about 2100°C; sp. gr. 7.2 to 7.45, depending on form; valence principally +2, +4, or +7. Manganese is a pinkish-gray, chemically active metal. It is the first element in group VIIb of the PERIODIC TABLE. It resembles iron but is harder and more brittle. The metal exhibits ALLOTROPY; it has four different forms with varying physical properties. It can be highly polished. Manganese tarnishes in moist air and oxidizes when heated to form an oxide, Mn_3O_4. It slowly displaces hydrogen from water. It reacts readily with hydrochloric and sulfuric acids and with the halogens. In compounds, manganese assumes a number of different oxidation states. It is easily raised to the +2 state, for example, by reaction with hydrochloric acid to form manganous chloride, $MnCl_2$. Manganese is also found in the +3 (manganic) state, but this state is unstable and usually reverts to the +2 state. Both manganous and manganic ions form acidic solutions. Manganese is found in the +4 state largely in manganese dioxide, MnO_2; the +4 oxidation state is amphoteric, i.e., in the +4 state manganese can either donate or accept electrons in chemical reactions. Manganese also exists in +6 and +7 states; the +6 state is found in the manganate ion (MnO_4^{--}) and the +7 state in the permanganate ion (MnO_4^{-}). These ions are stable in basic solutions. There is also evidence for a +1 state (in a complex cyanide) and for an unstable +5 state (in basic solutions). Manganese is found in abundance in nature. Pyrolusite (MnO_2) is the major ore. Manganese ores are produced principally in the Soviet Union, India, the Union of South Africa, Ghana, and Morocco, and to a lesser extent in the United States. The metal is prepared commercially by reduction of its ores with aluminum or, with high purity, by electrolysis of a manganese sulfate solution. Manganese is very important in the steel industry, where it is used as a deoxidizing and desulfurizing agent; no substitute has been found. It is also used in large amounts to toughen and harden steel without making it brittle; it is usually added as ferromanganese. Any steel having between 10% and 15% manganese is known as manganese steel, although almost all steel contains some manganese. Manganese is widely used in making alloys. Manganese bronze and manganese brass are alloys containing manganese, copper, tin, zinc, and small amounts of other metals in varying proportions. Certain alloys containing manganese, aluminum, antimony, and small amounts of copper are highly magnetic. Compounds of manganese are widely used in industry. Manganese dioxide is used as a drying agent; it catalyzes the oxidation of oils in paints and varnishes. It is also used in the dry cell and to remove the green color caused by iron impurities in glass. Potassium permanganate ($KMnO_4$) is a powerful oxidizing agent used industrially for bleaching and in chemistry as an analytical reagent. Other compounds find use in glassmaking, as pigments, and as fertilizers. Manganese is needed as a nutrient in small amounts by many plants and animals and by man. The purple color of amethyst is due to manganese. The element was first isolated in 1774 by J. G. Gahn, although its existence was previously recognized by T. O. Bergman and by K. W. SCHEELE.

Mangareva: see GAMBIER ISLANDS.

Mangas Coloradas (mäng'gäs kōlōrä'thäs) [Span.,=red sleeves], c.1797–1863, chief of the Mimbrenos group of Apache Indians of SW New Mexico. Many of the Mimbrenos were massacred by trappers in 1837 as a result of the bounty for Apache scalps offered by the Mexican authorities. Mangas Coloradas, a natural leader because of his intelligence and size (unusually tall for an Apache, he was over 6 ft/180 cm), united the tribes, led them in a successful war of revenge, and cleared the area of settlers. When the Americans took possession of New Mexico in 1846, he pledged friendship to these conquerors of his Mexican enemies, but peace ended as the gold rush began. In 1851 a series of incidents culminated in hostilities when Mangas Coloradas suffered a humiliating flogging at the hands of some miners. Leading his warriors, he waged continuous warfare until he was finally captured and killed by Union soldiers in 1863. The name sometimes appears erroneously as Magnus Colorado.

mange (mānj), contagious skin disease of domestic and wild animals caused by minute parasitic mites. It is known also as follicular mange, red mange, scab, scabies, or barn itch. Several types of mite cause the disease by burrowing into the skin, hair follicles, or sweat glands. This leads to chronic inflammation, loss of hair, itching, and secondary bacterial infection. Treatment of infected animals consists of dipping (see DIP) or spraying with chlorinated hydrocarbons or organophosphate insecticides at regular intervals.

mangel-wurzel: see GOOSEFOOT.

Mangin, Charles Marie Emmanuel (shärl märē' ĕmänüĕl' mäNzhăN'), 1866–1925, French general. A graduate of Saint-Cyr, he served in the Sudan under Jean MARCHAND and in French North Africa. His works on French colonial activities show concern with colonial development and supply a useful exposition of French colonial policy. Mangin, who commanded in World War I and was prominent in the defense of Verdun, supported a policy of offensive warfare as opposed to trench warfare. In 1921 he became a member of the supreme war council and inspector general of colonial troops.

mango (măng'gō), evergreen tree of the Anacardiaceae (SUMAC family), native to tropical E Asia and now grown in both hemispheres. The chief species, *Mangifera indica,* is believed to have been cultivated for about 6,000 years. It was introduced into Brazil by the Portuguese colonists. Many horticultural varieties have been developed. The mango tree grows rapidly and may attain a height of 90 ft (27 m) and a spread of 120 ft (37 m). It is densely covered with glossy leaves and bears small, fragrant yellowish or reddish flowers. The fruit, a fleshy drupe, is about 6 in. (15.2 cm) long and has thick greenish to yellowish-red mottled skin, pale yellow to orange-red flesh, and a large seed, the kernel of which is edible when cooked. Mango fruits are luscious, aromatic, and slightly acid. Equivalent in importance to the apple of Europe and N America, they are a vital food source for millions of inhabitants of the tropics. Mangoes are eaten fresh, often as a dessert fruit, and are also cooked, dried, and canned. They are used in chutneys, jellies, and jams. The tree is propagated by grafting and budding and to a lesser extent by seed. Mangoes are classified in the division MAGNOLIOPHYTA, class Magnoliopsida, order Sapindales, family Anacardiaceae.

Mangravite, Peppino (pĕp-pē'nō mängrävē'tā), 1896–, American painter, b. Italy. Mangravite studied in New York, under Robert Henri. He served on the faculty of art departments in many American schools and as professor of painting at Columbia. Examples of his murals are in the Dept. of Labor, Washington, D.C., and St. Anthony's Shrine, Boston. Mangravite is the author of many articles on art and art education.

mangrove, large tropical evergreen tree, genus *Rhizophora,* that grows on muddy tidal flats and along shore lines. Mangroves are most abundant in tropical Asia, Africa, and the islands of the SW Pacific. The American, or red, mangrove (*Rhizophora mangle*) is found along the muddy shores and in the everglades of the Florida peninsula and on other tropical American coast lines. Mangroves produce from their trunks aerial roots that become embedded in the mud and form a tangled network; this serves both as a prop for the tree and as a means of aerating the root system. Such roots also form a base for the deposit of silt and other material carried by the tides, and thus land is built up which is gradually invaded by other vegetation. Some mangrove species lack prop roots but have special pores on their branching root system for obtaining air. The mangrove fruit is a conical reddish-brown berry. Its single seed germinates inside the fruit while it is still on the tree, forming a large primary root that quickly anchors the seedling in the mud when the fruit is dropped. Mangrove bark is used to a limited extent as a source of tannins and dyes; the wood is used for wharf pilings. The name mangrove is also applied to other unrelated constituents of mangrove vegetation, such as *Avicennia nitida,* a bush of the vervain family, called black mangrove. True mangroves are classified in the division MAGNOLIOPHYTA, class Magnoliopsida, order Cornales, family Rhizophoraceae.

Mangyshlak Peninsula (mən-gĭshläk'), E Central Asian USSR, extending into the NE Caspian Sea. Except for the Kara-Tau range, the peninsula is below sea level; Batyr Sink is c.430 ft (130 m) below sea level. Oil, manganese, and coal are found on the peninsula. Fort Shevchenko is a fishing center.

Manhattan. 1 City (1970 pop. 27,575), seat of Riley co., NE Kansas, at the confluence of the Big Blue and Kansas rivers; inc. 1857. It is the trade and processing center of a farm area. Dress patterns are manufactured. Much of the economy is dependent upon Kansas State Univ. and nearby Fort Riley. The Tuttle Creek Dam and reservoir, with numerous recreational areas, is to the north. Damon Runyon was born in Manhattan. **2** Borough (1970 pop. 1,524,541), 22 sq mi (57 sq km), New York City, SE N.Y., coextensive with New York co. It is composed chiefly of Manhattan Island, and is bounded by the Hudson River on the west, New York Bay on the south, the East River on the east, and the Harlem River and Spuyten Duyvil Creek on the northeast and north. Many bridges, tunnels, and ferries link it to the other boroughs and to New Jersey. A large portion of Manhattan's workers commute to the borough every day. Manhattan is the cultural and commercial heart of the city, and its dramatic skyline symbolizes New York City around the world. The MANHATTAN INDIANS sold the island to Peter Minuit of the Dutch West India Company, supposedly for some $24 worth of merchandise (sale completed 1626). A town built at the tip of the island was called New Amsterdam and served as the capital of the colony of NEW NETHERLAND during the Dutch domination. In 1664 the English captured New Netherland and renamed it New York. The boundary of New York City first extended beyond Manhattan island when some Westchester co. towns were annexed in 1874. In 1898, Manhattan became one of the five boroughs established by the Greater New York Charter. For cultural, educational, and religious institutions and other points of interest, see NEW YORK, city. See I. N. Phelps Stokes, *The Iconography of Manhattan Island* (6 vol., 1915–28). See also bibliography under NEW YORK, city.

Manhattan Beach, city (1970 pop. 35,352), Los Angeles co., S Calif., on Santa Monica Bay; inc. 1912. It is a residential and beach community with an oil refinery and factories that produce aircraft and missile parts, electrical equipment, and pottery. A state park is nearby.

Manhattan College, at Riverdale, Bronx, N.Y.; Roman Catholic; primarily for men; founded 1853 as the Academy of the Holy Infancy. Its present name was adopted in 1863.

Manhattan Indians, North American Indians of the Algonquian-Wakashan linguistic stock (see AMERICAN INDIAN LANGUAGES). They were a small tribe of the Wappinger Confederacy. The Manhattan Indians in the early 17th cent. inhabited N Manhattan Island and the east bank of the Hudson River; their principal village was on the site of present-day Yonkers, N.Y. The Dutch bought Manhattan Island from them (the sale was made final in 1626) and then practically destroyed them in the wars waged between 1640 and 1645.

Manhattan Project, the wartime effort to design and build the first nuclear weapons (ATOMIC BOMBS). With the discovery of fission in 1939, it became clear to scientists that certain radioactive materials could be used to make a bomb of unprecented power. U.S. President Franklin Delano Roosevelt responded by creating the Uranium Committee to investigate this possibility. Progress was slow until Aug., 1942, when the project was placed under U.S. Army control and totally reorganized. The Manhattan Engineer District (MED) was the official name of the project. The MED's commanding officer, Gen. Leslie R. Groves, was given almost unlimited powers to call upon the military, industrial, and scientific resources of the nation. A $2-billion effort was required to obtain sufficient amounts of the two necessary isotopes, uranium-235 and plutonium-239. At Oak Ridge, Tenn., the desired uranium-235 was separated from the much more abundant uranium-238 by a laborious process called gaseous diffusion. At the Hanford installation (Wash.), huge nuclear reactors were built to transmute nonfissionable uranium-238 into plutonium-239. This method was based on the principle of the self-sustaining nuclear reaction (nuclear pile) that had first been achieved under the leadership of Enrico Fermi at the metallurgical laboratory of the Univ. of Chicago. At the radiation laboratory of the Univ. of California at Berkeley costly efforts were made to separate the two uranium isotopes using cyclotrons, but only minute amounts of pure uranium-235 were obtained. The actual design and building of the plutonium and uranium bombs took place at Los Alamos, N.Mex., under the leadership of J. Robert Oppenheimer. Gathered at this desert laboratory were an extraordinary group of American and European-refugee scientists. The only nuclear test explosion, code-named Trinity, was of a plutonium device; it took place on July 16, 1945, near Alamogordo, N.Mex. The first uranium bomb ("Little Boy") was delivered untested to the army and was dropped on Hiroshima on Aug. 6, 1945, killing at least 70,000 inhabitants. On Aug. 9, 1945, a plutonium bomb virtually identical to the Trinity device was dropped on Nagasaki, killing at least 35,000 inhabitants. See Leslie R. Groves, *Now It Can Be Told* (1962); Lansing Lamont, *Day of Trinity* (1965); Herbert Feis, *The Atomic Bomb and the End of World War II* (rev. ed., 1966); Stephane Groueff, *The Manhattan Project* (1967).

Mani (mä'nē): see MANICHAEISM.

manic-depressive psychosis, severe functional mental disorder involving mania or depression or a fluctuation of the two. The term was introduced by the German psychiatrist Emil KRAEPELIN in 1896. In the manic phase the mood of the patient is exalted and is characterized by excitement, activity, extravagance, and a tendency toward lack of rational judgment; in extreme manic states antisocial behavior often occurs as well. During the depressive phase, in which the sufferer may be lethargic and withdrawn, ideas of unworthiness, self-blame, guilt, fear of punishment, and suicide may occur. Attacks occur periodically or they may be chronic, and only a minority of cases show an alternation between the two phases. There may be a hereditary predisposition. SHOCK THERAPY has had some success in shortening the depressive phase of the psychosis; lithium carbonate is used to calm the manic patient. Antidepressant drugs and psychotherapy are also used in treatment. See PSYCHOPHARMACOLOGY.

Manich: see MANYCH, rivers, USSR.

Manichaeism (măn'ĭkēĭzəm) or **Manichaeanism** (mănĭkē'ənĭzəm), religion founded by Mani (c.216–c.276). Much of the evidence for the life of Mani (called Manes by the Greeks and Romans) is contradictory, but the outlines seem clear. He was born near Baghdad, probably of Persian parents; his father may have been a member of the Mandaeans. In his early youth Mani had a vision of an angel, his double. After wandering for several years as a meditative ascetic he had the vision again, then came forward (c.240) as the inspired prophet of a new religion. He was soon expelled by the Zoroastrians as a heretic and went to Bactria in NW India, where he came in contact with Buddhism. He returned to Persia after the coronation (241) of SHAPUR I, who was tolerant of new religious movements; at the Sassanid capital of Ctesiphon he began preaching (c.242) the doctrine that was to become Manichaeism, a great synthesis of elements from GNOSTICISM, from ZOROASTRIANISM, from other Persian religions, and from Christianity, as well as from the teachings of MARCION. However, he rejected all of the Old Testament and parts of the New Testament and claimed Buddha, Zoroaster, Hermes, and Plato as his predecessors. He also called himself "Mani, Apostle of Jesus Christ," and held that he was the Paraclete promised by Christ. During the long reign of Shapur I (d.272), Mani was free to travel about the realm making converts. However, the accession of Bahram I brought a reaction against the Manichaeans (or Manichees) from orthodox Zoroastrian religious circles, and, after 272, Mani and his followers met with increasing persecution. He was martyred c.276, according to most accounts, in SW Persia. Within a century after Mani's death his religion spread rapidly, and it was soon disseminated throughout the Roman Empire and Asia. Basic to the doctrine of Manichaeism was the conflicting dualism between the realm of God, represented by light and by spiritual enlightenment, and the realm of Satan, symbolized by darkness and by the world of material things. To account for the existence of evil in a world created by God, Mani posited a primal struggle in which the forces of Satan separated from God; man, composed of matter, that which belongs to Satan, but infused with a modicum of godly light, was considered a product of this struggle, and was looked upon as a paradigm of the eternal war between the forces of light and those of darkness. Christ, regarded as the ideal, light-clad soul, could redeem for each man the portion of light God had given him. Light and dark were seen to be commingled in our present age as good and evil, but in the last days each would return to its proper, separate realm, as they were in the beginning. Women were considered part of the forces of Satan, seducing man so that the day of emancipation from matter and darkness would never come. Out of the basic opposition of God and Satan, the Manichees developed an elaborate cosmogony, which made much use of the sacred number five. The Christian notion of the Fall and of personal sin was repugnant to the Manichees; they felt that the soul of man suffered not from a weak and corrupt will but from contact with matter. Evil was a physical, not a moral, thing; the misfortunes of man were miseries, not sins. Mani's followers were divided into two classes: the elect, or perfect, who were assured of immediate felicity after death because of the resource of light they had acquired, and the auditors, or hearers, who were laymen with little spiritual attainment. The elect repudiated darkness by leading a life of strict celibacy and austerity, and by teaching and preaching. They were administered to by the auditors, who might marry, but for whom sensual pleasures were discouraged and the begetting of children forbidden. Believing in metempsychosis (see TRANSMIGRATION OF SOULS), the auditors hoped to be reborn as elect. All other were sinners, doomed to hell. Several Christian emperors, including Justinian, published edicts against the Manichees. St. Augustine, in his youth a Manichee, describes in his *Confessions* his conversion from the sect to Christianity. Little is heard of the Manichees in the West after the 6th cent., but their doctrines reappear in the medieval heresies of the CATHARI, ALBIGENSES, and BOGOMILS. It was the practice in the Middle Ages to call by the name of Manichaeism any dualist Christian heresy. The sect survived in the East, notably in Chinese Turkistan, until about the 13th cent. The prime sources for the study of Manichaeism are the so-called Turfan texts, named after the region in Chinese Turkistan where they were found in 1904–5. These include fragments of Mani's long-lost bible and portions of Manichaean literature written in Pahlavi, Saghdian, Old Turkish, and Chinese. Other sources are a collection of documents found in Egypt in 1933 and refutations of Manichaeism by Christian, Muslim, and Zoroastrian polemicists. See F. C. Burkitt, *The Religion of the Manichees* (1925); A. V. W. Jackson, *Researches in Manichaeism* (1932, repr. 1965); Steven Runciman, *The Medieval Manichees* (1947, repr. 1961); Hans Jonas, *Gnostic Religion* (2d ed. 1963).

Manicouagan (mănĭkwäg'ən), river, 310 mi (499 km) long, rising in E central Que., Canada, and flowing S to the St. Lawrence River near Baie Comeau. The river is an important source of hydroelectricity; it has five hydroelectric power plants with a combined capacity of c.5.5 million kilowatts.

Manihiki (mänĭhē'kē), atoll (1966 pop. 584), c.2 sq mi (5.2 sq km), South Pacific, in the COOK ISLANDS. It comprises 12 islets; the whole group that includes Manihiki and Penrhyn is also often designated Manihiki. Manihiki was discovered in 1822 by Americans and became a British protectorate in 1889. In 1901 it became part of the New Zealand Cook Islands administration. Copra and pearl shell are the main exports. Manihiki is also known as Humphrey Island.

Manila (mənĭl'ə), city (1970 pop. 1,330,788), former capital of the Philippines, SW Luzon, on Manila Bay. Although adjacent Quezon City was designated the official capital of the republic in 1948, Manila is still the unique metropolitan center of the country, its largest city, chief port, and focus of all governmental, commercial, industrial, and cultural activities. In addition to its extensive and superb port facilities, Manila has a major international airport and is the terminus of the island's railroads and highways. It is the manufacturing center of the Philippines, with large metal fabrication, automobile assembly, and textile and garment industries. It also has food- and hemp-processing plants, cigarette factories, and establishments making toilet articles, pharmaceuticals, and other chemical products. The navigable Pasig River flows through the city, dividing it into two sections, with Intramuros (the old Spanish walled city) and Ermita (the site of most government buildings and tourist hotels) on the south bank, and the "newer" section (which includes the commercial district, many congested slum areas, and the Chinese quarter in Binondo) on the northern bank. Malacañan Palace, the presidential mansion, is on the Pasig. The fortified walled colony was established there in 1571 by López de Legaspi and developed mainly by Spanish missionaries. Except for two years (1762–64) when the city was in British hands, it remained under Spanish control until the Spanish-American War (1898), when it was seized by U.S. forces three months after the battle of Manila Bay. Filipino uprisings occurred for several years, and not until 1901 was a civil government definitely established. In World War II the city was occupied by the Japanese (Jan. 2, 1942). Its recovery (Feb., 1945) involved fierce house-to-house fighting, which reduced the old walled city to rubble, destroying many fine examples of 17th-century Spanish architecture. Only the Church of San Agustin (1606) survived. Reconstruction of the Manila Cathedral began in 1958. Today Manila, often called the "Pearl of the Orient," is a modern city, one of the most cosmopolitan in Asia. It has many daily newspapers and periodicals, radio and television stations, a symphony orchestra, and more than 20 universities and colleges. These include the Univ. of Santo Tomás (1611), which during World War II served as an internment camp for thousands of American, British, and Dutch civilian prisoners; the Ateneo de Manila (1859); the Univ. of Manila; the Univ. of the East; Centro Escolar Univ.; and Manila Central Univ. The oval-shaped Luneta, the country's national park on Manila Bay, contains a monument to José Rizal, who was executed by a Spanish firing squad there. In 1968, Manila was shaken by a severe earthquake, which killed over 300 people and caused extensive property damage. In 1972 the city was damaged by floodwaters resulting from more than three weeks of torrential rains.

Manila Bay, nearly landlocked inlet of the South China Sea, SW Luzon, the Philippines. About 35 mi (56 km) wide at its broadest point and 30 mi (48 km) long, it is the best natural harbor in the Orient and one of the finest in the world. The city of Manila is on the eastern shore of the bay, and on the southeast is the city of Cavite, a historic naval base and today the site (on Sangley Point) of a large U.S. naval installation. The entrance to Manila Bay (c.11 mi/18 km wide) is divided by the island of Corregidor into two channels; the northern channel, between Corregidor and Bataan peninsula, is only c.2 mi (3.2 km) wide. During the Spanish-American War, in the battle of Manila Bay (May 1, 1898), an American squadron under Commodore George Dewey destroyed the Spanish fleet off Cavite within a few hours. The Manila Bay area was the focus, during the early phase of World War II, of a desperate attempt to save the Philippines from Japanese conquest (see BATAAN; CORREGIDOR). In the Allied recovery of the Philippines (1944–45), many Japanese ships were sunk in the bay.

Manila hemp, the most important of the cordage fibers. It is obtained chiefly from the Manila hemp plant *(Musa textilis)* of the family Musaceae (BANANA family). It is grown mainly in its native Philippine Islands, where it has been cultivated since the 16th cent. and is known as abacá. The abacá is in no way related to the true hemp; it is of the same genus as the common banana, which it closely resembles except for the inedible fruit. At maturity the plants are cut down, and the long fibers are taken from overlapping leaves that converge at the base to form a false stem. The fibers are exceptionally strong and durable. The coarser ones are used for binder twine, matting, and rope, particularly marine cordage because of their resistance to the action of salt water; the finer grades are woven into beautiful native fabrics and hemp hats. Manila paper is made chiefly from old Manila hemp ropes and is valuable as a strong wrapping paper. Manila hemp is classified in the division MAGNOLIOPHYTA, class Liliatae, order Zingiberales, family Musaceae.

Manilius, Marcus, fl. A.D. 20, Roman poet. Of his didactic poem on astrology, the *Astronomica,* five books remain. These may or may not have constituted the whole work.

Manin, Daniele (dänyĕ'lā mänĕn') 1804–57, Venetian leader of the movement to free N Italy from Austrian rule. His father, a Jew, was converted to Christianity and took the name of his patrons, the illustrious Venetian family of Manin. A successful lawyer, Manin was active in revolutionary agitation against Austrian rule in Venice and was imprisoned in Jan., 1848, with the poet Niccolò Tommaseo. Released two months later after the outbreak of the Revolution of 1848, he became head of the Venetian republic. Despite his opposition, Venice voted (July, 1848) its union with the kingdom of Sardinia, and Manin, an ardent republican, resigned. However, he soon returned to power as head of a triumvirate, and in March, 1849, he became president of a provisional government. After the Sardinian rout at Novara in March, 1849, he was given dictatorial powers; he organized the heroic resistance of Venice to its Austrian besiegers. After famine and disease forced Venice to surrender (Aug., 1849), Manin went into exile in Paris. He subsequently supported the leadership of Sardinia in the movement for Italian unification. See G. M. Trevelyan, *Manin and the Venetian Revolution of 1848* (1923).

manioc: see CASSAVA.

Manipur (mənĭpŏŏr'), state (1971 pop. 1,069,555), 8,628 sq mi (22,347 sq km), NE India, bordered by Burma on the south and east. IMPHAL is the capital. The terrain, mostly jungle, is on a high plateau, about 2,600 ft (790 m) above sea level. The Manipur Hills have peaks rising to 8,500 ft (2,590 m). The inhabitants are mainly of Mongoloid stock and speak Tibeto-Burmese languages. The majority are Hindus, with groups of Naga and Kuki tribesmen. The raja of Manipur signed (1762) a treaty of protection with the British, who provided forces against invading Burmese. The area was administered from Assam state until 1947, when it became a union territory under the direct control of the central government of India. Manipur became a state in 1972. It is governed by a chief minister and cabinet responsible to an elected unicameral legislature. The states of Assam, Nagaland, Meghalaya, Manipur, and Tripura and the union territories of Mizoram and Arunachal Pradesh have a common governor appointed by the president of India.

Manisa (mänĕsä'), city (1970 pop. 70,022), capital of Manisa prov., W Turkey. It is a rail junction and the market center of a rich agricultural region. Mineral deposits are nearby. The city has many fine buildings, among them the notable Muradye mosque, and was the residence of Ottoman sultans Murad II and Murad III. The ruins of ancient MAGNESIA ad Sipylum are nearby.

manito (măn'ĭtō), name used among Indians of the Algonquian-Wakashan linguistic stock to describe the supernatural power that permeates all things (see ANIMISM). The idea of a supreme and personified manito, Kitchi Manito, may have been learned from missionaries. Manito is also spelled manitoa, manitua, manitou, and manetto.

Manitoba (mănĭtō'bə), province (1971 pop. 988,247), 246,512 sq mi (638,466 sq km), including 27,239 sq mi (70,549 sq km) of water surface, W central Canada. WINNIPEG is the capital and the largest city; other important cities are SAINT BONIFACE, SAINT JAMES, BRANDON, and SAINT VITAL. Easternmost of the Prairie Provinces, Manitoba is bounded on the N by Keewatin dist. of the Northwest Territories (with a northeast shore line on Hudson Bay), on the E by Ontario, on the S by Minnesota and North Dakota, and on the W by Saskatchewan. The south and central part of Manitoba was once covered by Lake AGASSIZ. As its waters receded into Hudson Bay, it left behind numerous lakes (Winnipeg, Manitoba, and Winnipegosis) and rivers (Nelson, Churchill, and Hayes), which flow northeast into the bay. In some places rock formations were swept bare, and in others they were covered with rich deposits of black loam. Miles of almost uninhabited treeless tundra surround the port of Churchill. Extending S from Churchill and E from Lake Winnipeg, the topography is that of the Canadian Shield; limited areas have been cleared for general farming and dairying, and the mineral and timber resources have been partly developed. The southern part of Manitoba is dominated by lakes, with the Winnipeg paralleled in the W by Winnipegosis and Manitoba. To the W and N of the Red River valley, the land rises in an escarpment extending into the plateaus of the Pembina, Turtle, Riding, Duck, and Porcupine mountains. Much of this heavily forested area has been set off as reserves, and the Riding Mt. area is a national park. To the south, where most of the popula-

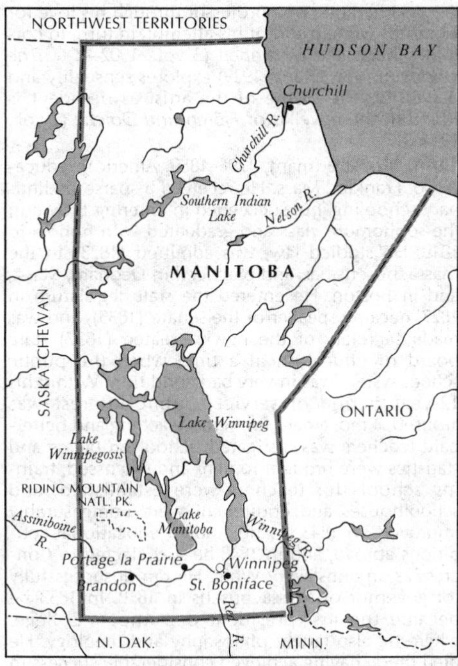

tion is concentrated, are fields of wheat, barley, oats, and flax. The well-settled Souris plains in the southwest are especially famous for their wheat fields. Canada's wheat industry originated in Manitoba, and Manitoba's bread wheat has set the standards for the world. Grain is shipped in quantity from Churchill (the only port in the Prairie Provinces) during the three ice-free months of the year. Although agriculture has been continually extended—especially in mixed farming, dairying, and poultry and stock raising—manufacturing has nevertheless displaced it as the leading industry in the province. Foods, minerals, clothing, electrical items, chemicals, furniture, leather, fabricated metals, and transportation equipment are major products. Continuing developments in mining, pulp and paper manufacturing, and extensive hydroelectric production promise to preserve Manitoba's status as the most industrialized of the Prairie Provinces. In the southwest, near Brandon, are large oil reserves, and the municipal districts of Flin Flon and The Pas, on the Saskatchewan River, are gateways to the rich mineral deposits (chiefly nickel, copper, and zinc) and timberlands of the central west. Manitoba ranks second only to Ontario in the production of nickel; the new town of Thompson was born on a nickel mine and has boomed with the industry. Beluga whales are still caught by native fishermen at Churchill, and fur farming in the north places Manitoba second of all the provinces in the production of fur; there are about 500 licensed fur farms. The history of Manitoba began along Hudson Bay. The search for the elusive Northwest Passage to the Pacific drew such explorers as Henry Hudson, Thomas Button, Pierre Radisson, and Médart Chouard, some of whom returned to England laden with beaver furs. To exploit this fur wealth, King Charles II granted (1670) the HUDSON'S BAY COMPANY propriety over all the lands draining into Hudson Bay. This vast area included the present-day province of Manitoba, then occupied by the Assiniboin, Ojibwa, and Cree Indians. The company established a trading post at Port Nelson and soon extended its operations south to the strategic Red River valley. In 1717, Fort Prince of Wales was built at the mouth of the Churchill River (rebuilt in stone 1732–71, it is now in Fort Prince of Wales National Historic Park). Manitoba was explored and posts were established by the French as well as by the British; their rival claims were resolved when England's conquest of Canada in the French and Indian Wars was confirmed by the Treaty of Paris in 1763. Scotsmen took over much of the French fur trade, organized the NORTH WEST COMPANY, and challenged the monopoly of the Hudson's Bay Company. A crisis came when the earl of Selkirk established the RED RIVER SETTLEMENT in North West Company territory. The resulting violence deterred colonization until the merger of the two companies in 1821. From then until 1870, when the Hudson's Bay Company sold its vast domain to the newly created confederation of Canada, that company was in sole control, and settlement of the area increased. Prearrangements for the transfer of the land to the new dominion government led to conflict between government representatives and the Indians and half-breeds (métis), who had long enjoyed almost total freedom under the Hudson's Bay Company's rule. Fearing political persecution and the loss of their land, they staged (1869) the Red River Rebellion under the leadership of Louis RIEL. Despite this trouble, Manitoba was organized as a province in 1870. Agricultural settlement proceeded slowly, but when the railroads came (1870 and 1881), they provided access to and from the grain markets on the Great Lakes, and, during the 1880s, the population doubled. Manitoba's area was enlarged in 1881, and in 1912 it was given its present extension to Hudson Bay. With the completion of the Hudson Bay Railway to Churchill in 1929, the province was in a position to use the shorter sea route eastward. During the last part of the 19th cent. and the first part of the 20th, the Canadian government advertised for immigrants to settle the prairies, and huge numbers of Russians, Poles, Estonians, Scandinavians, and Hungarians came from Europe. The largest single group was from the Ukraine. Today the Ukrainians are an important part of Manitoban culture. A national Ukrainian festival is held each year, and there is a Ukrainian culture museum in Winnipeg. The province provided a multilingual school system from 1897 to 1916, but abolished it when the number of ethnic groups requesting such facilities grew too large. Further immigration came with World War I when American pacifist sects (e.g., the Mennonites and Hutterites), seeking to avoid military service, set up colonies of their own in the province. Today Manitoba still has problems amalgamating its many ethnic groups; they include the métis, who have settlements (such as St. Boniface) in the province. Politically, Manitoba turned to a socialist government in 1958 when the Progressive Conservative party came into power. That party was displaced (1969) by the New Democrats under the leadership of Edward R. Schreyer. The New Democrats remained in power following the 1972 and 1974 general elections. Manitoba sends 6 senators (appointed) and 13 representatives (elected) to the national Parliament. The Univ. of Manitoba is at Winnipeg. See M. S. McWilliams, *Manitoba Milestones* (1928); W. L. Morton, *Manitoba: A History* (2d ed. 1967); J. A. Jackson, *The Centennial History of Manitoba* (1970); *Manitoba: Past and Present,* ed. by Denise Dawes (tr. 1971).

Manitoba, Lake, 1,817 sq mi (4,706 sq km), SW Man., Canada; one of the largest lakes of North America. A remnant of glacial Lake Agassiz, it is fed by Lake Winnipegosis and drains into Lake Winnipeg. Its shores are marshy. The lake has commercial fisheries.

Manitoba, University of, at Winnipeg, Man., Canada; provincially supported, coeducational; chartered 1877. It has faculties of agriculture, home economics, commerce, graduate studies, law, pharmacy, arts and science, education, engineering, architecture, medicine, and dentistry as well as schools of agriculture, music, art, nursing, physical education, medical rehabilitation, dental hygiene, and social work.

Manitoulin Islands (mănətōō'lĭn), archipelago consisting of three large islands and several smaller ones, in N Lake Huron, NW of Georgian Bay. The islands, in a noted fishing region, are popular resorts. The permanent population is mainly Indian. Dairying, lumbering, mixed farming, and tourism are the major activities. **Manitoulin,** c.80 mi (130 km) long and from 2 to 30 mi (3.2–48 km) wide, is the world's largest lake island. It encloses more than 100 lakes and has a much-indented, rugged coast. Cockburn Island and Drummond Island are also rocky and forested. Drummond Island belongs to Michigan, and the others of the group to Ont., Canada.

Manitowoc (măn"ĭtəwŏk'), industrial city (1970 pop. 33,430), seat of Manitowoc co., E Wis., a port of entry on Lake Michigan at the mouth of the Manitowoc River; inc. 1870. Its shipbuilding industry dates from 1847; submarines were made there in World War II. Among the city's many other products are aluminum ware and soap. The North West Company established a trading post on the site in 1795. Manitowoc and its twin city, Two Rivers, were founded in 1836. Silver Lake College of the Holy Family and a maritime museum are located in the city; to the north are a nuclear power plant and a petrified forest.

Maniu, Iuliu (yo͞o'lyo͞o mänyo͞o'), 1873–1955?, Rumanian politician, head of the Rumanian National Peasants' party. Born in Transylvania, he helped to organize the Rumanian national movement there before and during World War I. In 1918 he headed the Rumanian provisional government. As premier (with one slight interruption) from 1928 to 1930, he enacted liberal reforms, which were soon abrogated by King Carol II. He was briefly premier again in 1932–33. Maniu opposed Carol and the dictatorship of Ion Antonescu. Denounced as a reactionary by the Communists, in 1947 he was convicted of treason and given a life sentence. He was unofficially reported to have died in prison.

Manizales (mänēsä'läs), city (1968 est. pop. 219,500), alt. 7,063 ft (2,153 m), capital of Caldas dept., W central Colombia, on the slopes of the Cordillera Central. It is a commercial and agricultural center in a region that produces a large share of Colombia's coffee. There are minor industries in the city and some gold and silver mines nearby. Manizales was founded in 1847 by gold prospectors. It was destroyed by an earthquake in 1878 and by fire in 1925.

Mankato (mănkā'tō), city (1970 pop. 30,895), seat of Blue Earth co., S Minn., at the confluence of the Blue Earth and Minnesota rivers; inc. 1865. It is a trade and processing center for a farm and dairy region. Mankato stone has been quarried there for over 100 years. It is the home of the huge Mankato State College. Sibley Park in Mankato was the site of Camp Lincoln, where more than 300 Sioux were held and 38 of them hanged, after their revolt in 1862. A state park, with waterfalls, adjoins the city.

Mankato State College, at Mankato, Minn.; coeducational; est. 1866 as a normal school, became Mankato State Teachers College in 1921. Its present name was adopted in 1957. The school focuses on training in various fields of education.

Manley, Mary de la Rivière, 1663–1724, English author, one of the first women to earn a living by writing. Notorious because of her marriage to her cousin, who was already married and who later deserted her, she turned to literature and avenged herself on society by writing several scandalous memoirs disguised as prose romances. *The New Atalantis* (1709), her most notable book, abused every prominent member of the Whig party then in power and involved her in a court suit. She collaborated with Swift on various Tory pamphlets and in 1711 succeeded him as editor of the *Examiner.*

Manley, Norman, 1893–1969, prime minister of Jamaica (1959–62). Of Irish and Negro descent, he was educated at Oxford and became an internationally known lawyer. He founded the moderately socialist People's National party in 1938, and, with his cousin, Alexander Bustamante, dominated Jamaican politics for several decades. He served as chief minister of Jamaica (1955–59) before being designated prime minister. He pushed land reform and encouraged economic growth, especially in the bauxite and tourist industries. He was the architect of the short-lived West Indies Federation (1958–62).

Manlius (măn'lēəs), ancient Roman gens, chiefly patrician but later containing plebeian families. **Marcus Manlius Capitolinus,** d. 384? B.C., consul (392 B.C.), took refuge in the Capitol when Rome was taken (c.389) by the Gauls. Aroused by the cackling of the sacred geese at night, he repulsed the Gauls from the hill. According to legend, he defended plebeian debtors from harsh patrician creditors, and the following year he was impeached for high treason and thrown from the Tarpeian Rock by the tribunes. **Titus Manlius Imperiosus Torquatus,** fl. 4th cent. B.C., served against the Gauls (361 B.C.), one of whom he slew in single combat. He took the Gaul's torque, or collar, hence his name Torquatus. He was dictator twice more, and three times consul. In 340, with his colleague, Publius Decius Mus, he defeated the Latins near Vesuvius and at Trifanum. He killed his own son for disobeying express orders not to engage in single combat with the enemy. Some of his story is legendary. **Titus Manlius Torquatus,** fl. 3d cent. B.C., conquered the Sardinians while consul (235 B.C.), subsequently becoming censor (231), consul (224), and dictator (210). He opposed the ransoming of Roman prisoners taken at the battle of Cannae (216), and he defeated (215) a large Carthaginian force in Sardinia.

Manly, municipality (1971 pop. 39,250), New South Wales, SE Australia, a suburb of Sydney, on Port Jackson, an inlet of the Pacific Ocean. It is a resort.

man-made elements: see SYNTHETIC ELEMENTS.

Mann, Heinrich (hīn'rĭkh män), 1871–1950, German novelist; older brother of Thomas Mann. He was a prolific author; themes of social criticism dominate his works. *The Poor* (1917, tr. 1917) and *The Chief* (1925, tr. 1925) deal with regeneration through democracy. The famous *Professor Unrat* (1905; tr. *The Blue Angel,* 1932, *Small Town Tyrant,* 1944) tells of the degeneration of a professor through his love for a corrupt woman and of his attempt, in turn, to corrupt others. *Die Göttinnen* (3 vol., 1902–4; tr. *The Goddess,* 1918, *Diana,* 1929) explores sensuality and perversity. The theme of the artist as decadent is found in the novellas of *Flöten und Dolche* (2 vol., 1904–5).

Mann, Horace (măn), 1796–1859, American educator, b. Franklin, Mass. He received a sparse preliminary schooling, but succeeded in entering Brown in the sophomore class and graduated with honors in 1819. He studied law, was admitted (1823) to the Massachusetts bar, and practiced in Dedham, Mass., and in Boston. He entered the state legislature in 1827, became speaker of the senate (1835), and was made secretary of the newly created (1837) state board of education at a time when the public school system was in very bad condition. Within his 12-year period of service, public interest was aroused, a movement for better teaching and better-paid teachers was instigated, school problems and statistics were brought to light and discussed, training schools for teachers were established, and schoolhouses and equipment were immeasurably improved. In 1843, Mann studied educational conditions abroad, and in 1848 he was elected to Congress as an antislavery Whig. He ran unsuccessfully for governor of Massachusetts in 1852. In 1853 he became the first president of Antioch College, where he also taught philosophy and theology. He died there, having achieved considerable success in demonstrating the practicality of coeducation and in raising the academic standards of the college. His second wife was Mary T. Peabody, sister of Elizabeth Peabody. See Mary T. P. Mann and others, ed., *The Life and Works of Horace Mann* (5 vol., 1891); biographies by Jonathan Messerli (1972) and R. B. Downs (1974); B. A. Hinsdale, *Horace Mann and the Common School Revival in the United States* (1937); *Selective and Critical Bibliography of Horace Mann* (comp. by the Federal Writers' Project of Massachusetts, 1937).

Mann, James Robert, 1856–1922, American legislator, b. McLean co., Ill. A Chicago lawyer, he held many local offices before serving (1897–1922) as a Republican member of the U.S. House of Representatives. He was (1910) one of the sponsors of the Mann-Elkins Act, which strengthened railroad-rate regulation by the INTERSTATE COMMERCE COMMISSION, and he was author (1910), of the Mann Act, which forbade, under heavy penalties, the transportation of women from one state to another for immoral purposes. In the House, Mann introduced the Pure Food and Drugs Act of 1906 and led the fight for an amendment to the Constitution granting suffrage to women.

Mann, Thomas (tō'mäs män), 1875–1955, German novelist and essayist, outstanding German literary figure of the 20th cent., b. Lübeck; brother of Heinrich Mann. A writer of great intellectual breadth, Mann developed literary themes that not only delved into the inner self but also related inner problems to changing European cultural values. To coordinate this dual focus Mann often wrote in a symbolic vein, although in general he was less experimental than many of his contemporaries. He became famous with the publication of his first novel, *Buddenbrooks* (1901, tr. 1924), which depicts the rise and disintegration of a merchant family. Shorter works of fiction followed, among them *Tonio Kröger* (1903, tr. 1913–15); the verse drama *Fiorenza* (1905); and the classic *Der Tod in Venedig* (1912, tr. *Death in Venice,* 1925), a novella in which the hero, a great writer, falls prey to an uncontrolled passion, weakens, and eventually dies. These works show Mann's preoccupation with the interaction of cultural and psychological problems. The proximity of creative art to neurosis and the affinity of genius and disease are the larger themes; homosexuality and infantile sexuality appear secondarily. The problem of artistic values in a bourgeois society is a constant concern, present also in his rather comic second novel, *Königliche Hoheit* (1909, tr. *Royal Highness,* 1916). Among Mann's other important shorter works of fiction are *Unordnung und frühes Leid* (1925, tr. *Early Sorrow,* 1929), a story; and the short novel *Mario und der Zauberer* (1930, tr. *Mario and the Magician,* 1930), an allegorical attack on fascism. Translations of his shorter fiction are collected in *Stories of Three Decades* (1936). Mann's third novel, *Der Zauberberg* (1924, tr. *The Magic Mountain,* 1927), occupied him for 12 years. Here the protagonist is a young man from a bourgeois background who, after spending seven years in the midst of disease and death in a tuberculosis sanatorium, finds fulfillment in leaving there to fight and die in World War I. Mann then began his tetralogy *Joseph und seine Brüder* (1933–43, tr. *Joseph and His Brothers,* 1934–44), on which he worked intermittently for 16 years. This erudite and detailed recreation of the biblical story of Joseph is a brilliant study of the psychological and the mythological. In *Doctor Faustus* (1947, tr. 1948), Mann used the Faust motif to delve into the conflict between spirituality and sensuality. His last works include the novels *Der Erwählte* (1951, tr. *The Holy Sinner,* 1951) and *Bekenntnisse des Hochstaplers Felix Krull* (1954, tr. *Confessions of Felix Krull, Confidence Man,* 1955), a picaresque comedy adapted from an earlier fragment. Mann's essays fall into two general categories—political and literary. His autobiographical essay *Betrachtungen eines Unpolitischen* [reflections of a nonpolitical man] (1918) marks his decision that the artist must participate in politics in order to preserve a creative society; Mann became an outspoken opponent of fascism. Translations of his major political speeches and essays are published in *Order of the Day* (1942). His own selection of his literary essays appeared in English as *Essays of Three Decades* (1947). These elaborate the recurrent themes of his fiction through studies of thinkers who influenced him. Despite his romanticism, Mann opposed the anti-intellectualism of German 20th-century theorists. He left (1933) Hitler's Germany for Switzerland in self-imposed exile, was deprived (1936) of his citizenship by the Nazis, and after 1938 lived in the United States until he returned to Switzerland in 1953. Mann was awarded the 1929 Nobel Prize in Literature. See his letters (tr. 1971); his *A Sketch of My Life* (1960); Golo Mann, *Thomas Mann: Memories of my Father* (1965); Erika Mann, *The Last Year of Thomas Mann* (tr. 1958, repr. 1970); studies by J. P. Stern (1967), Erich Heller (1958, repr. 1973), and W. E. Berendsohn (1973). Mann's daughter, **Erika Mann,** 1905–69, was an actress and author and was married to the poet W. H. Auden. Mann's son, **Klaus Mann,** 1906–49, was a novelist, essayist, and playwright. He left Germany in 1933 and edited the anti-Nazi journal *Sammlung* in Amsterdam. A resident of the United States from 1935, he became a citizen in 1943 when he entered the U.S. army. His writings include *Alexander: A Novel of Utopia* (1929, tr. 1930); *Pathetic Symphony* (1936, tr. 1948), a novel about Tchaikovsky; the autobiographical *Turning Point* (1942); and *André Gide and the Crisis in Modern Thought* (1943). With his sister he wrote *Escape to Life* (1939) and *The Other Germany* (tr. 1940).

Mann, Tom, 1856–1941, British labor leader and socialist. He was an organizer of the 1889 London dock strike, which was an important step in the unionization of unskilled English laborers. Secretary (1894–97) of the Independent Labour party, he helped to organize (1902) the Labour party in Australia. Mann returned from Australia a proponent of syndicalism, and he was one of the founders (1920) of the British Communist party. He was jailed several times for his radical activities. See his memoirs (1923, repr. 1967).

manna (măn'ə), in the Bible, edible substance provided by God for the people of Israel in the wilderness. It is described as white, small, and flaky and was found on the ground in the morning six days a week. (Ex. 16; Num. 11.7–9; Joshua 5.12; John 6.49–58.) Several species of manna have been identified botanically. These include an exudate of the European flowering ash *(Fraxinus ornus)* and a species of lichen of the genus *Lecanora,* still found on barren plains and mountains in many sections of W Asia and N Africa. According to another theory, the manna of Sinai is the sweet secretion of various plant insects feeding on tamarisk trees.

Mann Act: see MANN, JAMES ROBERT.

Mannaeans (mănē'ənz), ancient people of Asia Minor, occupying the region E of Assyria and SE of Urartu, in present-day NW Iran. Their kingdom, which flourished in the 9th and 8th cent. B.C., seems to have acted as a buffer state between the Urartians and the Assyrians until it was conquered (7th cent.) by Media. Excavations have been conducted since 1956 at the fortified city of Hasanlu.

Mannerheim, Baron Carl Gustav Emil (kärl gŭ'stäv ā'mĭl mä'nərhām), 1867–1951, Finnish field marshal and president of Finland (1944–46). Of a distinguished Swedish-Finnish family in Russian-controlled Finland, Mannerheim rose to the rank of general in the czarist army. In 1918 he led victorious

Finnish antisocialist forces against the Finnish Bolsheviks and their Soviet supporters, and in the following year he headed the new regime in Finland as regent. Defeated in the presidential elections of 1919, he went into retirement and engaged in philanthropic activity. He was appointed head of the Finnish defense council in 1931 and commanded the Finnish forces against the Soviet Union in the FINNISH-RUSSIAN WAR of 1939–40 and again in 1941–44. In Aug., 1944, he succeeded Risto Ryti as president of Finland, and in September he terminated hostilities with the Soviet Union. He resigned the presidency in 1946 because of ill health and was succeeded by Juho Paasikivi. The **Mannerheim Line,** a fortified line of defense across the Karelian Isthmus, was planned by him. The Soviet army broke through the line in 1940, and it was subsequently dismantled.

mannerism, a style in art and architecture (c.1520–1600), originating in Italy as a reaction against the equilibrium of form and proportions characteristic of the High Renaissance. In Florence, Pontormo and Bronzino, and in Rome, Il Rosso, Parmigianino, and Beccafumi created elegant figures elongated and contorted into uncomfortable postures. Mannerists devised compositions in which they deliberately confused scale and spatial relationships between figures, crowding them into the picture plane. Often strange tunnel-like spaces were created, as in the works of Tintoretto and El Greco. Lighting became harsh, and coloring tended to be acrimonious. The mannerists devised sophisticated and obscure allegories. Among the prominent sculptors who created sinuous and sometimes bizarre forms were Giovanni Bologna, Ammanati, and to a certain extent Cellini. The style was carried into France by Primaticcio, Il Rosso, Niccolò dell' Abbate, and Cellini. It flourished particularly at Fontainebleau and was adapted by the sculptor Goujon and the engraver Callot. In architecture the style was manifested in the use of unbalanced proportions and arbitrary arrangements of decorative features. Elements of mannerism can be found in the elegant Laurentian Library in Florence, designed (c.1525) by Michelangelo; the Massimi Palace, Rome, planned by Peruzzi; the Palazzo del Te, Mantua, built and decorated by Giulio Romano; and the Uffizi, planned by Vasari. In Spain, Berruguette was a leading exponent of mannerism. Toward the end of the 16th cent., mannerism assumed an academic formalism in the works of the Zuccaro brothers. By the end of the century it had given way to the BAROQUE. See studies by W. Friedlaender (1957), S. J. Freedburg (2 vol., 1961), F. Würtenberger (1963), and M. Haraszti-Takas (1970).

Mannes, David (măn'ĭs), 1866–1959, American violinist, conductor, and educator, b. New York City. Mannes was violinist in the New York Symphony Orchestra from 1891 and its concertmaster from 1898 to 1912. In 1912 he founded the Music School Settlement for Colored People and in 1916, with his wife, the Mannes Music School, both in New York City. He inaugurated free concerts in the Metropolitan Museum of Art in 1918. *Music Is My Faith* (1938) is his autobiography. His wife, **Clara Damrosch Mannes,** 1870–1948, b. Breslau, the daughter of Leopold Damrosch, was a pianist. A pupil of Busoni, she and her husband toured extensively in joint recitals. She was codirector with him of the Mannes Music School. Their son, **Leopold Damrosch Mannes,** 1899–1964, b. New York City, studied piano and composition in New York and Paris. He taught composition (1924–31) at the Mannes school and theory (1927–31) at the Institute of Musical Art (now Juilliard School of Music). In 1931 he became a research chemist with the Eastman Kodak Company and made significant contributions to the development of color photography. In 1939 he returned to the Mannes school (after 1953 known as the Mannes College of Music), subsequently becoming its president.

Mannheim, Karl, 1893–1947, Austro-Hungarian sociologist and historian, born and educated in Hungary. He taught at Heidelberg and Frankfurt and, from 1933 to his death, at the Univ. of London. In his historical writings he emphasized the role of social values. Mannheim was influenced by—but critical of—Karl Marx, whose approach he adapted for his *Ideology and Utopia* (1929, tr. 1936). See studies by J. J. P. Maquet (1951, repr. 1973) and F. W. Rempel (1965).

Mannheim (män'hīm), city (1970 pop. 332,163), Baden-Württemberg, central West Germany, on the right bank of the Rhine River and at the mouth of the Neckar River. A bridge connects it with Ludwigshafen, on the opposite bank of the Rhine. It is a major inland port and an industrial center. Manufactures include precision instruments, chemicals, building materials, textiles, agricultural machinery, and motor vehicles. Mannheim was mentioned in the 8th cent. as a small fishing village. It was fortified and chartered in 1606–7. In 1720 the city became the residence of the electors palatine (see PALATINATE), who built (1720–60) a large palace and held a brilliant court there. Elector Charles Theodore made (late 18th cent.) Mannheim one of the great musical and theatrical centers of Europe. The famous Mannheim orchestra ranked first among 18th-century orchestras and became the model of many later symphonic groups. Mozart lived (1777–78) there and Schiller began (1782–83) his career at the Mannheim theater. Mannheim was awarded to Baden in 1802. Although many of the historic buildings were heavily damaged in World War II, the city has, since 1945, restored the château and the regularly laid-out 18th-century baroque buildings of the inner city, including the Jesuit church (1733–60) and the city hall (1700–23). Carl Benz is credited with building (1885) the first motor-driven vehicle at Mannheim. There is a university in the city.

Manning, Daniel, 1831–87, American journalist and political leader, b. Albany, N.Y. At the age of 11 he went to work for the Albany *Atlas,* which in 1856 was consolidated with the *Argus;* he became editor in 1865 and owner in 1873. As legislative reporter he had become well known in political circles, and in 1874 he became a member of the New York Democratic committee, serving as chairman from 1881 to 1884. Manning played an important part in electing Grover Cleveland governor in 1882 and in nominating him for President in 1884. He served (1885–87) as Secretary of the Treasury under Cleveland.

Manning, Henry Edward, 1808–92, English churchman, cardinal of the Roman Catholic Church. He was born of a Low Church family and was educated at Harrow and at Balliol College, Oxford (B.A., 1830), gaining some reputation as a debater. He lacked the financial backing to enter politics like his friend William Ewart Gladstone, but worked for a year in a minor post of the colonial office and returned to Oxford as fellow of Merton College. He was ordained (1832) in the Anglican Church and was given a living in Sussex. By 1835 he had become an adherent of the OXFORD MOVEMENT. In 1841 he became archdeacon of Chichester. By 1845 when William George WARD was degraded, Manning had become prominent in the Oxford movement, and his letters of succeeding years, as well as his visit to Rome (1847), foretold his following of John Henry NEWMAN and Ward into the Roman Catholic Church. When the bishop of Exeter was compelled by the privy council (1850) to institute G. C. Gorham to a benefice despite Gorham's open disbelief in the doctrine of baptismal regeneration, Manning left the Church of England and entered (1851) the Roman communion. He was later ordained. He was a celebrated confessor, an ardent advocate of prison reform, and a constant promoter of schemes for alleviating the condition of the poor. His society of Oblates of St. Charles (1857) carried on much of this work. One of the most trusted advisers of Cardinal WISEMAN, Manning was made (1857) provost of the Westminster chapter, and on Wiseman's death, he was appointed archbishop (1865). He greatly expanded Catholic education in England and furthered the education of the poor. He strongly opposed Catholic participation in Anglican universities, thereby bringing himself into conflict with Newman. His advocacy of the rights of workingmen brought much abuse upon him from conservatives, but he fearlessly forwarded the movement within his church that culminated in the encyclical of LEO XIII on the rights of labor. In his later years he was constantly called on to speak at labor-union conventions and to serve on strike arbitration boards. He was an advocate of slum clearance and teetotalism. In 1869 and 1870, Manning was a leader in the movement that favored the dogma of papal infallibility, and he inclined to view Newman and others who thought it an untimely move as decidedly lukewarm Catholics. This intensified the dislike between Newman and Manning. In 1875, Manning was created cardinal. Many regard as the greatest single achievement of Manning's career the strong support he gave the strikers in the great London dock strike (1889) and his single-handed settlement of it. His *Rule of Faith* (1839) and *Unity of the Church* (1842) were important in the history of the Oxford movement. Among his Catholic works, *The Eternal Priesthood* (1883) is best known. See biographies by E. S. Purcell (2 vol., 1895–96, repr. 1973); Shane Leslie (rev. ed. 1954) and V. A. McClelland (1962); G. Donald, *Men Who Left the Movement* (1967); Lytton Strachey, *Eminent Victorians* (1918, repr. 1969).

Manning, Olivia, English novelist, b. Portsmouth, Hampshire. During World War II she served as a journalist in the Middle East. She is best known for her "Balkan trilogy": *The Great Fortune* (1960), *The Spoilt City* (1962), and *Friends and Heroes* (1966). These novels concern a British diplomat and his wife in Eastern Europe during World War II, and they brilliantly juxtapose historical and personal events.

Manning, Robert: see MANNYNG, ROBERT.

Manning, William Thomas, 1866–1949, American Episcopal bishop of New York, b. England, received his collegiate and theological training at the Univ. of the South, Sewanee, Tenn. Ordained a priest (1891), he served parishes in California, Pennsylvania, and Tennessee and taught dogmatic theology at the Univ. of the South before becoming rector of Trinity parish, New York City, in 1908. Manning was bishop of New York from 1921 until his retirement in 1946.

Mannyng or **Manning, Robert,** fl. 1298–1338, English poet, b. Brunne (modern Bourne), Lincolnshire; also called Robert of Brunne. He was a monk in the Gilbertine order. Mannyng is known chiefly for his *Handling Sin,* a lively religious manual adapted from William of Wadington's *Manuel des péchés.* Illustrating the vices and weaknesses of man, this work is an excellent reflection of the manners of the time. Mannyng is also the author of a chronicle of England based on Wace and de Langtoft.

Manoah (mənō'ə), father of Samson. Judges 13.

Manoel. For Portuguese rulers thus named, see MANUEL.

Manolete (mänōlā'tā), 1917–47, Spanish matador, b. Córdoba. Christened Manuel Rodríguez y Sánchez, he was the son and grandson of matadors, who both also had the nickname Manolete. In 1939 at Seville he received his *alternativa* (i.e., became a full-fledged matador), which was confirmed at Madrid the same year. For eight years (1940–47) he was the top matador in the world, rivaled only by Pepe Luis Vásquez and Domingo Ortega at the beginning and by Carlos ARRUZA and Dominguín at the end. Manolete was fatally gored in a *corrida* at Linares, Spain, on August 28, 1947. See his autobiography, *My Life as a Matador* (tr. by Barnaby Conrad, 1956); Barnaby Conrad, *The Death of Manolete* (1958).

manometer (mənŏm'ĭtər): see PRESSURE.

manor house, dwelling house of the feudal lord of a manor, occupied by him only on occasional visits if he held many manors. Although not built specifically for fortification as castles were, many manor houses were partly fortified; they were enclosed within walls or moats that sometimes included the farm buildings as well. The primary feature of the manor house was its great hall, to which subsidiary apartments were added as the lessening of feudal warfare permitted peaceful domestic life. By the beginning of the 16th cent., manor houses as well as smaller castles began to acquire the character and amenities of the residences of country gentlemen. This transformation produced the smaller Renaissance châteaux of France and the numerous country mansions of the Elizabethan and Jacobean styles in England. See J. A. Gotch, *Growth of the English House* (2d ed., 1928); W. H. Ward, *Architecture of the Renaissance in France* (1926); Ralph Dutton, *The English Country House* (1935).

manorial system (mənôr'ēəl, măn-) or **seignorial system** (sēnyôr'ēəl), economic and social system of medieval Europe under which peasant land TENURE and production were regulated and local justice and taxation were administered. The system was intimately related to FEUDALISM but was not itself feudal, since it had no connection with the military and political conception of the fief. The fundamental characteristic of the manorial system was economic—the peasants held land from the lord (Fr. *seigneur*) of an estate in return for fixed dues in kind, money, and services. A similar method of landholding by the peasants has existed in countries outside Europe, notably Japan and India. The manorial system prevailed in France, England, Germany, Spain, and Italy and far into Eastern Europe. Local manorial institutions developed with the decline of central Roman power. Like feudalism, the system received great stimulus from the collapse of Carolingian rule and from the invasions by Norsemen, Arabs, and Magyars. It reached its final form at different times in various countries, but in general it flourished from the 11th to the 15th cent.

Structure and Functions. Essentially the system was a local institution, and general statements concerning it are subject to exceptions. In its simple form it consisted of the division of the land into self-sufficient estates, each presided over by the lord of the manor and tilled by residents of the local village that usually accompanied each manorial estate. The lord, who might be the king, an ecclesiastical lord, a baron, or any lesser noble, owed military protection to his peasants. The land remained in his holding and was loaned to the man who cultivated it in return for services and dues. The lord, however, did not have the right to withdraw the property or to increase the dues; and the rights of cultivation were in general heritable among the peasants. The peasants generally fell into two classes, the free and the unfree, but there was wide diversity in the status of VILLEIN and SERF, and the distinction became confused. The terms *free* and *servile* came to be attached to the land rather than to the man, and a holding was servile or free regardless of the status of the holder. On the typical domain was the manor house of the lord. Some of the land he retained for his own use (the demesne). The domain was divided into arable, meadow (the commons), woodland, and waste. The arable was held by the peasants, and each holding was under its own fixed conditions; usually the holdings were by strips, and a single man might hold widely separated lands. The three-field system of agriculture generally prevailed, with one field devoted to winter crops, one to summer crops, and one lying fallow each year. The meadow was generally held in common. The woodlands and fishponds usually belonged to the lord, and he had to be recompensed for the right to hunt animals, catch fish, and cut wood. In times of poor harvest the lord was to use his coin and credit to prevent starvation. Small local industry was also a function of the manorial system, and dues owed the estate included such items as cloth, building materials, and ironware. The payments made by serf and villein varied with the locality. There were usually fixed dues paid at certain times of the year. In addition to dues for the use of the lands and the use of the lord's mill and oven, there were personal work dues. There were also obligations to supply the lord with services—food, lodging, and the like—when he came to the manor. In addition there were dues for the rights of justice. The manor was an administrative and political unit. There were manorial courts, and the lord or his agent presided over the administration of justice. The manor was also the unit for the raising of taxes and for public improvements. Thus the tenants were obliged to repair roads and bridges, maintain the castles, and take care of the military contributions. The manor was almost always under the charge of an agent of the lord. He might be assisted by provosts or bailiffs. The manor was looked upon as a permanent organization, and even when part of it was transferred to others by the lord it remained a single manor. Thus one manor might have several direct lords. It did not necessarily coincide with a single estate; it might be larger or it might be only part of an estate.

Decline. Many economic and political factors contributed to the extinction of the manorial system. The spread of trade and a money economy promised greater profit to capitalist production than to the subsistence manor; the growth of new centralized monarchies competed with the local administration of the lord. Gradual decline took place with the wide development of towns and capitalistic commerce that tended to break down the small local economic unit, the manor, and to build up larger units. Decline was early in Italy, where Roman city institutions persisted to some extent through the Middle Ages (see COMMUNE). In Spain it was soon modified, especially by Moorish conquest, but still existed in modified form in the 20th cent. In England the dissipation of the system had been long in process before it was hastened by the INCLOSURE of estates. In France its disappearance was consummated by the French Revolution. In Austria and Prussia it was virtually ended by the reforms of Emperor JOSEPH II, Karl vom und zum STEIN, and HARDENBERG, but in Hungary it left traces until the 20th cent. In Russia it was profoundly altered by the abolition of serfdom (1861; see EMANCIPATION, EDICT OF). Everywhere it left its mark upon succeeding institutions.

The Dispute over Origins. The most perplexing problem concerning the manor is the question of the origin of manorial organization. A quarrel between the so-called Romanists and the so-called Germanists as to the sources of the organization has never been settled; there is not sufficient evidence. Romanists point to the process that was, in the days of the later Roman Empire, producing independent estates. Germanists point out the likenesses of the manor to what was supposedly the ancient German system of landholding (see MARK). It is now rather generally agreed that both German and Roman influences contributed to the development of the manorial system. See P. G. Vinogradoff, *Villainage in England* (1892, repr. 1968) and *The Growth of the Manor* (3d. ed. 1920, repr. 1968); N. S. B. Gras and E. C. Gras, *The Economic and Social History of an English Village* (1930, repr. 1969); H. S. Bennett, *Life on the English Manor* (1937, repr. 1960); Marc Bloch, *French Rural History* (tr. 1966); J. W. Thompson, *Economic and Social History of the Middle Ages* (2 vol., new ed. 1959) and *Economic and Social History of Europe in The Later Middle Ages* (new ed. 1960).

Man o' War, 1917–47, American race horse, by Fair Play out of Mahubah, bred by August Belmont near Lexington, Ky., and owned by Samuel D. Riddle after 1918. A large reddish-colored colt capable of tremendously long strides, he raced only as a two-year-old and three-year-old, but in this short time (1919–20) he won 20 out of 21 races and set five world records. His one loss was to a horse named Upset at Saratoga in 1919; he ran second. The most renowned stallion in the history of thoroughbred racing, "Big Red," as Man o' War was often called, became the leading sire of all time.

man-o'-war bird or **frigate-bird,** most aerial of the water birds, found in the tropic seas. The man-o'-war bird's wingspread (7½ ft/228.5 cm) is the largest in proportion to its body (3–4 lb/1.4–1.8 kg) of any bird; it can soar motionless by the hour. It is awkward on land and in the sea, where the feathers quickly become water-logged. The name derives from its grace and swiftness in the air and from its piratical tendencies; it harasses boobies, pelicans, cormorants, and gulls until they drop their catch. Man-o'-war birds feed chiefly on fish but also prey on the young of sea birds and on jellyfish, squid, and young turtles. They have long hooked beaks and forked tails; the male has an inflatable orange throat pouch that becomes red at courtship time. The purplish black magnificent frigate-bird, *Fregata magnificens,* 40 in. (100 cm) long, is found from the Bahamas and Baja California S to Brazil and Ecuador; the great frigate-bird, *F. minor,* is found in the Indian Ocean. Other species, e.g., the Ascension and Christmas Island frigate-birds, are named for their habitats. The lesser frigate-bird, the smallest (32 in./80 cm) of the family, is found in the South Pacific and on the islands off Brazil and Madagascar. Frigate-birds are classified in the phylum CHORDATA, subphylum Vertebrata, class Aves, order Pelecaniformes, family Fregatidae.

Manpower Administration (MA), agency of the U.S. Dept. of Labor; it comprises a number of offices and services that were established to carry out work-experience and manpower-training programs and to administer the Federal-State Employment Security System. MA includes the Office of National Projects Administration, which is responsible for the National On-the-Job Training program; the U.S. Employment Service, which provides assistance to the states in establishing and maintaining a system of over 2,400 local public employment offices, and is responsible for the Veterans Employment Service, the Rural Manpower Service, and the Summer Youth Opportunity Campaign; the Employment Development Program, which provides leadership in the development and improvement of nationwide manpower programs, and is responsible for the Neighborhood Youth Corps program, Operation Mainstream, the Public Service Careers Program, the Private Sector On-the-Job Training program, and the Work Incentive Program; the Unemployment Insurance Service, which is concerned with the development, improvement, and operation of Federal and State employment insurance; Job Corps; and the Public Employment Program.

Manresa (mänrā'sä), city (1970 pop. 57,846), Barcelona prov., NE Spain, in Catalonia, on the Cardoner River. It is an industrial center with textile, metallurgical, and glass industries. Of ancient origin. Manresa has a Roman bridge and a Gothic collegiate church. Below the Jesuit convent is the grotto where St. Ignatius of Loyola retired in prayer during his sojourn (1522–23) at Manresa on his way back from Montserrat. It is now a place of pilgrimage. There is a conservatory of music in Manresa.

Manrique, Jorge (hôr'hā mänrē'kā), c.1440–1479, Spanish poet and soldier. Most of his verse is undistinguished, but his *Coplas* [couplets], on his father's death, are among the treasures of world poetry. Incomparably elegant, they describe an exemplar of medieval knighthood and his stoic acceptance of death. Longfellow's notable English translation appeared in 1833.

Mans, Le (lə mäN), city (1968 pop. 147,651), capital of Sarthe dept., NW France, on the Sarthe River. The historical capital of Maine, it is also an important manufacturing, commercial, educational, and communications center. Le Mans, which dates from pre-Roman times and before Charlemagne was a Merovingian capital, has witnessed frequent sieges and battles throughout its history. The Cathedral of St. Julien du Mans (11th–13th cent.), which contains the tomb of Berengaria, queen of Richard Cœur de Lion (Richard I of England), is partly Romanesque; its Gothic part has perhaps the most daring system of flying buttresses of any Gothic cathedral. Le Mans was the birthplace of Henry II of England and John II of France. Today, Le Mans is famous for its annual international auto race.

Mansa Musa (män'sä mo͞o'sä), died 1337, ruler of the Mali empire (1312–37). A Muslim, he brought the Mali empire to its greatest height. During his reign Timbuktu became a center of Muslim culture and scholarship. His pilgrimage to Mecca in 1324–25 brought Mali fame throughout the world; the emperor traveled with an immense entourage, preceded by 500 slaves carrying staffs of gold. His gifts of gold in Cairo were so lavish that the metal was devalued in Egypt.

Mansard: see MANSART.

mansard roof (măn'särd), type of roof, so named because it was frequently used by the French architect François Mansart. It was not devised by him but was used early in the 16th cent., as in portions of the palace of the Louvre designed by Pierre Lescot. It became particularly characteristic of French Renaissance architecture and later was much used in Victorian buildings in Europe and America. The slope of a mansard roof from eaves to ridge is broken into two portions. The lower portion is built with a steep pitch, sometimes almost vertical; the upper portion has a low pitch or is nearly flat. This results in a higher and more useful interior space than can be obtained with other roof types.

Mansard roof

Mansart or **Mansard, François** (both: fräNswä' mäNsär'), 1598–1666, French architect. His work is noted as being an outstanding expression of French classical design. In 1635 he was commissioned by the duc d'Orléans to make additions to the château of Blois. That same year he designed the Hôtel de la Vrillière, which for a long time served as a classic model for the elegant Paris house. Mansart began construction of the Church of Val-de-Grâce and finished the lower part before the commission was transferred to Lemercier. The best surviving examples of Mansart's work are the château of Maisons and, in Paris, the alterations of the Hôtel Carnavalet, now a museum. See Sir Anthony Blunt, *François Mansart and the Origins of French Classical Architecture* (1941).

Mansart or **Mansard, Jules Hardouin** (zhül ärdwăN'), 1646–1708, French architect. He studied under his great-uncle François Mansart and under Libéral Bruant. Favored by Louis XIV, he was ennobled and in 1699 made chief architect for the royal buildings. After enlarging the royal château of Saint-Germain-en-Laye, he undertook work at the palace of Versailles, where among his accomplishments are the impressive Galérie des Glaces (decorated by Le Brun), the Grand Trianon, the palace chapel, and the vast orangery. As town planner he designed in Paris the Place des Victoires (1684–86) and the superb Place Vendôme (1699). The impressive Dôme des Invalides (1706) in Paris is considered his most splendid achievement; it was added as a second church to the one constructed by Bruant and brought the scheme of the Hôtel des INVALIDES to completion. Much of Mansart's work was executed in the massive Roman baroque style, but some of his designs at Versailles point toward the lightness and elegance of the rococo.

Mansel, Henry Longueville (măn'səl), 1820–71, English philosopher and theologian. A disciple of Sir William Hamilton, he systematized his teacher's conception of the relativity of knowledge, and in his famous Bampton Lectures, *The Limits of Religious Thought Examined* (1858), he applied the conception to religion, denying the possibility of any knowledge of the absolute and asserting the necessity of faith. Other works include *Prolegomena Logica* (1851), *Metaphysics* (1860), and *Philosophy of the Conditioned* (1866). See study by K. D. Freeman (1969).

Mansfeld, Peter Ernst von (pā'tər ĕrnst fən mäns'fĕlt), 1580?–1626, military commander in the THIRTY YEARS WAR. Illegitimate son of a governor for the Hapsburgs in Luxembourg, he rendered distinguished service in the imperial forces in the Netherlands and was legitimized; by 1607 he was styling himself count. At the beginning of the Thirty Years War, Mansfeld and his army were loaned by his employer, the duke of Savoy, to FREDERICK THE WINTER KING, in Bohemia. Frederick's funds ran low, however, and shortly before the battle of the White Mt., Mansfeld refused further service. A promise of Dutch funds later induced him to defend Frederick's possessions in the Palatinate. He was at first successful and proved himself skillful in command. He won an engagement with TILLY in 1622, but he was unable to oust the imperial forces, and his unruly men ravaged and terrorized the country. Frederick dismissed him. He became (1623) a mercenary leader for Holland and in 1625, with a subsidy from England, recruited a force to fight on the Protestant side. He was severely defeated (1626) by Wallenstein near Dessau. Mansfeld attempted then to cooperate with Gabriel Bethlen but without success.

Mansfield, Edward, d. 1667, West Indian buccaneer. Possibly born in Curaçao of Dutch parentage, he is also called Edward Mansveld. He was engaged (1665) by the British governor of Jamaica, Sir Thomas Modyford, to take Curaçao from the Dutch. He set sail with a fleet of 15 vessels, with Henry Morgan as his lieutenant, and made, instead, for Cuba where he sacked Sancti Spiritus. He took the island of Old Providence, ascended the San Juan River to take Granada, Nicaragua, and plundered and burned Spanish possessions along the Central and South American coasts before he returned to Jamaica, where he was mildly reproved by Governor Modyford for his activities. He died shortly afterward and his reputation as chief of the buccaneers passed to Henry (later Sir Henry) Morgan.

Mansfield, Katherine, 1888–1923, British author, b. New Zealand, regarded as one of the masters of the short story. Her original name was Kathleen Beauchamp. A talented violincellist, she did not turn to literature until 1908. Her first volume of short stories, *In a German Pension* (1911), was not remarkable and achieved little notice, but the stories in *Bliss* (1920) and *The Garden Party* (1922) established her as a major writer. Later volumes of stories include *The Dove's Nest* (1923) and *Something Childish* (1924; Am. ed. *The Little Girl,* 1924). Her collected stories appeared in 1937. *Novels and Novelists* (1930) is a compilation of critical essays. After an unhappy first marriage, she married John Middleton MURRY, an editor and critic, in 1918. During the last five years of her life she suffered from tuberculosis and succumbed to the disease at the age of 35. Mansfield's stories, which reveal the influence of Chekhov, are simple in form, luminous and evocative in substance. With delicate plainness they present elusive moments of decision, defeat, and small triumph. John Middleton Murry edited her poems (1923, new ed. 1930); her letters (1928); and a collection of her unfinished pieces (1940). See John Middleton Murry, *Between Two Worlds* (1935); biographies by Antony Alpers (1953) and M. Joseph (1971); studies by S. R. Daly (1965) and M. Magalaner (1971).

Mansfield, Michael Joseph, 1903–, U.S. Senator (1953–), b. New York City. After working (1922–31) as a mining engineer, he taught (1933–42) history at Montana State Univ. before serving (1943–53) as a Democrat in the U.S. House of Representatives. Elected (1952) to the Senate, Mansfield succeeded (1961) Lyndon B. Johnson as Senate majority leader. In this key position he wielded much power and helped win passage of major civil rights legislation and liberal reform programs during the 1960s. He has had the longest tenure of any Senator as majority leader.

Mansfield, Richard, 1854–1907, American actor, b. Germany. Mansfield made his New York debut in 1882. He became a leading romantic actor; among his chief successes were *Beau Brummel* (1890), a play written for him by Clyde Fitch, and *Cyrano de Bergerac* (1898). He introduced the works of Shaw to the United States with his production (1894) of *Arms and the Man* and gave (1906) the first production in English of Ibsen's *Peer Gynt.* See biographies by Paul Wilstach (1909) and William Winter (1910).

Mansfield, William Murray, 1st earl of, 1705–93, English jurist. As solicitor general (1742–54) he prosecuted the Scottish rebel lords, Balmerino (Arthur Elphinstone), Kilmarnock, and Lovat. In 1756 he was raised to the peerage and made lord chief justice, a post he held until 1788. He rationalized many of the rules of procedure, reduced expense and delay, and tried to fuse the principles of law and equity. Though not fully successful in renovating the medieval law of property, he did establish a theory of contract that laid the foundation for modern commercial law. He attempted to apply continental analogies in order to bring English law closer to international practice. Mansfield was unpopular for his opinions on seditious libel and for his judgments in the case of John WILKES, and his house was burned (1780) in the Gordon riots. His wide learning and forceful thinking greatly influenced Sir William Blackstone. See biography by C. H. S. Fifoot (1936).

Mansfield, municipal borough (1971 pop. 57,598), Nottinghamshire, central England, on the western border of Sherwood Forest. It is in a coal district, with manufactures of hosiery, shoes, and metal products. Limestone and sandstone are quarried nearby. Prehistoric cave dwellings are in the vicinity, and there is a medieval church; the grammar school was founded in 1561. Hardwick Hall and NEWSTEAD ABBEY are nearby. Mansfield Woodhouse (1971 pop. 24,787), a nearby mining and quarrying town, was once a forest post for guarding against wolves.

Mansfield. 1 Town (1970 pop. 19,994), Tolland co., NE Conn.; settled c.1692, inc. 1702. The Univ. of Connecticut is in Storrs, which is included within Mansfield. The town also includes Mansfield Hollow, the site of a large flood-control project. **2** Industrial city (1970 pop. 55,047), seat of Richland co., N central Ohio, in a hilly region surrounded by fertile farmlands; inc. 1828. It is a manufacturing, commercial, and insurance center. Among its many diverse products are tires, automobile bodies, electrical appliances, sports vehicles, and brass goods. A branch of Ohio State Univ. is there. The home of Louis Bromfield is now used as an ecological center and experiment farm. Also of interest are South Park, with a reconstructed blockhouse of the War of 1812, and Kingwood Center and Gardens, with landscaped floral displays and a pre-Civil War French-provincial mansion.

Mansfield, Mount, peak, 4,393 ft (1,339 m) high, N central Vt.; highest peak in the Green Mts. and in Vermont. Most of the mountain is in Mt. Mansfield State Forest. At the foot of the mountain is a deep gorge called Smugglers Notch. The Mt. Mansfield area is a winter-sports center offering some of the finest skiing in New England.

Manship, Paul, 1885–1966, American sculptor, b. St. Paul, Minn., studied at St. Paul Institute of Arts, Pennsylvania Academy of the Fine Arts, and the American Academy at Rome. He often went to classical mythology for his subjects. His art is notable for its emphatic musculature and polished contours. Among his works are *Prometheus* (Rockefeller Center, New York City); *Centaur and Dryad, Little Brother,* and *Pauline* (Metropolitan Mus.); and *Indian and Pronghorn Antelope* and *Dancer and Gazelles* (Art Inst., Chicago). He received many awards and was a member of the Legion of Honor. See study by Edwin Murtha (1957).

manslaughter, HOMICIDE committed without justification or excuse but distinguished from MURDER by the absence of the element of MALICE aforethought. Modern criminal statutes usually divide it into degrees, the most common distinction being between voluntary and involuntary manslaughter. Voluntary manslaughter is a killing done in the heat of passion provoked by acts of the victim such as to cause a reasonable man to act rashly and without reflection. Such provocation may include violent assault and an unlawful attempt to arrest him, but not mere insulting words or gestures. Involuntary manslaughter is a killing in which there is no intention to kill at all. It occurs when the killing is the result of the commission of a crime that is neither a FELONY nor an act likely to cause great bodily harm or when it is the result of a lawful act done in a criminal manner, e.g., a case of NEGLIGENCE. The advent of the automobile caused many manslaughter cases that arise from reckless and careless driving; in the statutes of some states of the United States such killing is a separate crime.

Manson, Patrick, 1844–1922, English parasitologist. After receiving his medical degree (1866) from the university at Aberdeen, Scotland, Manson left for China where he was to spend 24 years, studying such diseases as tinea, Calabar swelling, and blackwater fever. In 1878 he observed that filariae, the worms that cause elephantiasis in man, pass part of their life cycle in the *Culex* mosquito; he thus led the way in the study of the transmission of diseases caused by parasites. In 1894 he made the deduction that the parasite of malaria passes part of its life cycle in the mosquito, a theory that Ronald ROSS was to verify three years later. A founder of two schools devoted to the study of tropical diseases, one at Hong Kong (1886) and the other at London (1898), Manson is often described as the father of tropical medicine.

Mansur, al- (äl-mänsŏŏr') [Arab.,=the victorious], d. 775, 2d ABBASID caliph (754–75) and founder of the city of Baghdad. His name was in full Abu Jafar abd-Allah al-Mansur. He was brother and successor of ABU AL-ABBAS. A vigorous and dominating caliph, he successfully consolidated his empire even though it was threatened by internal strife and foreign wars. He could not prevent the secession of Muslim Spain, however, under the Umayyad prince Abd ar-Rahman I. Mansur lived at first, as his brother had, near Kufa, but in 762 he began to build a new city, Baghdad. He was favorable to the Persians, and the Barmecides were his ministers.

Mansur, al- (Muhammad ibn Abi-Amir al-Mansur billah), 914–1002, Moorish regent of Córdoba, known in Spanish as Almanzor. He became steward to Princess Subh, wife of the caliph Hakim II, and under her patronage and by clever manipulation he rose to become (978) royal chamberlain for Hakim's successor, the young Hisham II. Al-Mansur kept Hisham in seclusion at his court and assumed complete control over the caliphate. A great warrior, he reorganized the army and undertook many campaigns against the Christian states of N Spain; he sacked Barcelona (985), razed the city of León (988), and destroyed the church and shrine of St. James at Santiago de Compostela (998). Before he died he appointed one of his sons as his successor.

Mansurah, Al (äl mänsŏŏr'ä), city (1970 est. pop. 212,000), N Egypt, a port in the Nile River delta. It is an agricultural market and industrial center. Manufactures include ginned cotton, cottonseed oil, and textiles. Al Mansurah was founded in 1221 to replace DUMYAT (Damietta), then occupied by Crusaders. In 1250, Crusaders under LOUIS IX of France suffered a crushing defeat there at the hands of the Mamelukes. The city is the seat of a branch of the Univ. of Cairo, the Institute of Al Mansurah (affiliated with Al Azhar Univ. in Cairo), and Al Mansurah Polytechnic Institute.

manta: see RAY.

Manteca (măntē'kə), city (1970 pop. 13,845), San Joaquin co., central Calif.; founded 1870, inc. 1918. Sugar beets are processed, and glass, fertilizer, wine, and chemicals are made. A large army depot and a state park are nearby.

Mantegna, Andrea (ändrĕ'ä mäntē'nyä), 1431–1506, Italian painter of the Paduan school. He was adopted by Squarcione, whose apprentice he remained until 1456, when he procured his release. In 1454 he had married the daughter of Jacopo Bellini and by 1460 he had entered the service of the Gonzagas in Mantua, in which he continued all his life. Outside of Venice Mantegna was the greatest and most celebrated artist of N Italy. His passion for the antique is evidenced in all his work, and he was one of the first artists to make an extensive collection of Greek and Roman works. A rigorous draftsman and anatomist and a perfectionist in perspective, he nevertheless gave to his statuesque forms an intense and dramatic life. Among his early works the most celebrated are his frescoes of the lives of St. James and St. Christopher (Church of the Eremitani, Padua, destroyed in World War II); St. Luke altarpiece (Milan); and San Zeno altarpiece (Verona; parts are at the Louvre and Tours). In Mantua he decorated the bridal chamber of the Gonzaga palace with frescoes portraying many members of the family and other notables (completed 1474). On the ceiling he created the illusion of sky, a form of decoration which became very popular in the baroque period. Mantegna also painted nine cartoons depicting the *Triumph of Caesar* (Hampton Court Palace) and a *Pietà*

(Milan). About 1497 he executed for Isabella d'Este *Parnassus* and *Triumph of Virtue* (Louvre). The Metropolitan Museum has his *Adoration of the Shepherds.* Mantegna is also noted for his drawings and copper-plate engravings. Early in his career he illustrated two manuscripts intended for René, duke of Anjou. In his initial letters for Strabo's *Geography,* he recaptured the art of Roman inscriptions. His lettering had a great influence on the development of printing. Among his engravings are *Virgin and Child, Battle of the Sea Gods,* and the *Entombment.* See *Complete Paintings of Mantegna,* ed. by Luigi Coletti (1970).

Manteuffel, Edwin, Freiherr von (ĕt'vēn frī'hĕr fən män'toifəl), 1809–85, Prussian field marshal. He served in the Danish War (1864) and was appointed Prussian governor in conquered Schleswig. In the AUSTRO-PRUSSIAN WAR of 1866 he commanded brilliantly, and in the Franco-Prussian War (1870–71) he distinguished himself. Manteuffel commanded (1871–73) the German army of occupation in France and from 1879 until his death was governor of Alsace-Lorraine.

mantid or **mantis,** name applied to the large, slender, slow-moving, winged INSECTS of the family Mantidae in the order Orthoptera. The only predatory members of their order, mantids have strong, elongate, spiny front legs, used for grasping prey. While lying in wait for its prey, a mantid holds its front legs in an upraised position suggestive of prayer; hence the Greek name mantis, or prophet, and the common name, "praying mantis." The prothorax, or front portion of the body, is very long in proportion to its width, and the head, with its two large, protruding, compound eyes, can turn in any direction. Members of the 1,800 mantid species range in length from 1 to 5 in. (2.5–12.5 cm). Their typically green or brown color, in some cases with irregular patterns, camouflages them among the leaves and twigs in which they are found. Mantids are voracious eaters, feeding on insects and other invertebrates, including other mantids. They may even catch small vertebrates, such as frogs. Often the female eats the male after mating. The female lays 200 or more eggs contained in a papery case, usually attached to leaves or twigs. The young hatch as bright yellow nymphs (see METAMORPHOSIS), resembling the adults except for their smaller size and lack of wings. Mantids are sometimes used by gardeners, in place of chemical pesticides, to combat insect pests. They are found in all warm regions of the world, and are especially numerous in the tropics. There are about 20 native species in the S and W United States, known regionally as devil's coach horses or mule killers. The commonest of the southern species is the Carolina mantid, *Stagmomantis carolina,* about 2 in. (5 cm) long. Two introduced species, the European mantid, *Mantis religiosa* (about 2 in./5.1 cm long), and the Chinese mantid, *Tenodera sinensis* (up to 4 in./10.2 cm long), are now common in the N and E United States. Mantids are classified in the phylum ARTHROPODA, class Insecta, order Orthoptera, suborder Mantodea, family Mantidae.

Mantinea (măn"tĭnē'ə), city of ancient Greece, in E central Arcadia (now Arkadhía). In the Peloponnesian War a coalition led by Mantinea and Argos and urged on by Athens was defeated (418 B.C.) by Sparta at Mantinea. It was also the scene of the victory of Thebes over Sparta in which EPAMINONDAS was killed (362 B.C.).

mantis: see MANTID.

mantis shrimp, marine crustacean characterized by a pair of enlarged appendages, called maxillipeds, that form powerful claws for seizing prey. The last two segments of each of these legs are strong and sharp, and the end segment is folded back over the next segment to make a scissorslike cut. Mantis shrimps have stalked eyes and flattened abdomens with appendages bearing gills. They prefer warm shallow seas. A number of species are quite large, reaching 1 ft (30 cm) or more in size. Mantis shrimps are an important sea food outside the Western Hemisphere. They are classified separately from either true shrimps or praying mantises, whose forelimbs the maxillipeds superficially resemble. Mantis shrimps are grouped in the phylum ARTHROPODA, class Crustacea, order Stomatopoda.

Mantle, Mickey Charles, 1931–, American baseball player, b. Spavinaw, Okla. In 1951, Mantle joined the New York Yankees of the American League and eventually replaced Joe Di Maggio in center field. An outstanding switch hitter and one of the great sluggers in the history of the game, Mantle hit a total of 536 home runs and had a lifetime batting average of .298. Mantle was voted the league's most valuable player in 1956, 1957 (when he batted a high of .365), and 1962. In 1956 he was named the outstanding professional athlete of the year. Mantle's career was hampered by injuries and by osteomyelitis of his left leg. He retired in 1968 and was elected to the Baseball Hall of Fame in 1974.

mantle, portion of the EARTH's interior lying beneath the crust and above the core. Its upper and lower boundaries have been determined solely by abrupt changes in the velocities and character of seismic waves passing through the earth's interior. No direct observation of the mantle, or even its upper boundary, have been made, although the ill-fated Mohole project was designed for that purpose. It has been suggested that samples of the upper mantle are provided by some volcanic eruptions in ocean areas, e.g., the Hawaiian Islands, and by some rare igneous intrusions. The upper surface of the mantle, called the Mohorovičić discontinuity, or Moho, lies at depths ranging from 12 to 70 km (7.5–43 mi) below the earth's surface. Analysis of seismic waves indicates that rocks below the Moho are less rigid and slightly more dense than rocks making up the crust. A zone of low seismic velocity and low rigidity, called the ASTHENOSPHERE, is present in the upper part of the mantle, and its presence is of critical importance to the PLATE TECTONICS theory of crustal evolution. The base of the mantle is located c.2,900 km (1,800 mi) below the earth's surface.

mantra (măn'trə, mŭn-), in Hinduism and Buddhism, mystic words used in ritual and meditation. A mantra is believed to be the sound form of reality, having the power to bring into being the reality it represents. There are several types of mantras. Sanskrit verses used in the Vedic sacrifice are known as mantras. *Bija-mantra* or "seed-sounds," used mainly in TANTRA, are syllables without semantic value having an occult affinity for particular deities or forces; use of such mantras usually requires initiation by a guru. Extremely common is the repetition (*japa*) of the name of a deity and the singing of devotional phrases (*mahamantra*); for those mantras initiation is not required.

Mantua (măn'cho͞oə, -to͞oə), Ital. *Mantova,* city (1971 pop. 65,926), capital of Mantova prov., Lombardy, N Italy, bordered on three sides by lakes formed by the Mincio River. It is an agricultural, industrial, and tourist center. Manufactures include machinery, furniture, and petroleum. Originally an Etruscan settlement, Mantua was later a Roman town and afterwards a free commune (12th–13th cent.). It flourished under the GONZAGA family (1328–1708), who were magnificent patrons of the arts. Mantua passed to Austria in 1708, was taken by Napoleon I in 1797, was retaken by Austria in 1815, and was returned to Italy in 1866. The Gonzaga palace (13th–18th cent.), among the largest and finest in Europe, has frescoes by Mantegna and Giulio Romano and numerous other works of art. Other landmarks include the Palazzo del Te (1525–35); the Church of Sant' Andrea (15th–18th cent.), designed by Alberti, where Mantegna is buried; and the law courts (13th cent.).

Manu (mŭ'no͞o), semilegendary Hindu lawgiver. Traditionally ascribed to him are the *Laws of Manu,* best known of the Sanskrit *smriti* texts (see SANSKRIT LITERATURE). They were compiled, probably between 200 B.C. and A.D. 200, from diverse ancient sources and provide detailed rules, presumably directed to Brahman priests, governing ritual and daily life. In particular they seek to validate and preserve the high caste position of the Brahmans. See *The Laws of Manu,* tr. by Georg Bühler (1886, repr. 1967).

Manu'a (mäno͞o'ä), island group and district (1970 pop. 2,112) of AMERICAN SAMOA comprising Ta'u, Ofu, and Olosega islands, with a total area of 22 sq mi (57 sq km). According to Samoan tradition, the Manu'a group is the cradle of the race. The main settlement is Luma (1970 pop. 260), on Ta'u Island.

manual language: see SIGN LANGUAGE.

manual training: see VOCATIONAL EDUCATION.

Manuel I (Manuel Comnenus) (kŏmnē'nəs), c.1120–1180, Byzantine emperor (1143–80), son and successor of John II. He began his reign with a war against the Seljuk Turks, the subjugation of Raymond of Antioch, and an alliance with the German king, CONRAD III against Roger of Sicily. In 1147 the Second Crusade (see CRUSADES) was preached and although Manuel aided the Crusaders, he made a truce with the Turks in order to protect his western provinces, which had been invaded by Roger. At first Manuel relied on mercenaries and the help of Venice, but in 1155 he invaded S Italy. Defeated at Brindisi in 1156 by William I of Sicily, in 1158 he made peace with him (which lasted for 30 years) and withdrew his forces. Manuel subsequently directed his diplomacy against Holy Roman Emperor FREDERICK I, supporting Pope ALEXANDER III, and uniting both the Western Empire and Church with his Eastern Empire and Church. With all of his energies directed to the West, Manuel neglected Asia Minor, which led to his crushing defeat (1176) by the Turks at Myriocephalon. Manuel liked Westerners and gave them high positions in the empire. During his reign Genoese, Pisan, and Venetian merchant colonies grew at Constantinople and began to be influential. His son Alexius II, succeeded him.

Manuel II (Manuel Palaeologus), 1350–1425, Byzantine emperor (1391–1425), son and successor of JOHN V. In his youth he was taken captive by the Turks, and during his reign the Turks reduced the empire to Constantinople and its dependencies in the Peloponnesus. After the failure of the crusade of Sigismund of Hungary (later Holy Roman Emperor Sigismund) at NIKOPOL (1396), Manuel appealed to the West for aid and made a futile European journey (1399–1402) for that purpose. His nephew, JOHN VII, was coemperor from 1399 and he and BOUCICAUT defended Constantinople against the siege by Sultan Bayazid I. The victory of Tamerlane over Bayazid at Ankara, in the same year, temporarily saved Constantinople. By 1422 the Turks were again strong enough to attack Constantinople, and in 1425 Manuel was forced to pay tribute to the sultan. Afflicted with partial paralysis in his last years, Manuel devoted himself to religious writing, entrusting the government to his son and successor, John VIII.

Manuel I, 1469–1521, king of Portugal (1495–1521), successor of John II. Cousin and brother-in-law of John, he became heir to the throne on the death (1491) of John's only son, Alfonso. Manuel's reign was most notable for the successful continuation of Portugal's overseas enterprises. John had planned the expedition in search of a sea route to India and had appointed Vasco da Gama to head it, but it was under Manuel that the epochal voyage was made (1497–99) and that the wealth of the Indies began to pour into Portugal. Cabral announced the discovery of the coast of Brazil (1500), and such commanders as Francisco de Almeida and Afonso de Albuquerque built up the Portuguese commercial empire. Portugal became the leading commercial nation of the West. This sudden wealth, however, soon had corrupting effects on officials and started the process of turning interest away from the agricultural and industrial development of Portugal itself. In order to marry Isabel, eldest daughter of Ferdinand and Isabella of Spain, Manuel accepted (1496) the Spanish condition that he expel the Jews and Moors from Portugal. However, because he did not wish to lose a community that had contributed much to learning and science in Portugal and had provided many able artisans, he first attempted a policy of forcible conversion of the Jews. Though Manuel promised that no investigation would be made into the faith of the "new Christians," he could not prevent the departure of some Jews. Nor could he prevent a great massacre of the Jews in Lisbon in 1506, though he punished the perpetrators. Manuel used his new wealth to erect some beautiful buildings, including the Hieronymite monastery at Belém (now in Lisbon), near the spot where Vasco da Gama embarked for India. He also revised the laws and strengthened the power of the king. He was succeeded by his son, John III. Manuel I is sometimes called in English Emmanuel I.

Manuel II, 1889–1932, king of Portugal (1908–10), second son of CHARLES I. He succeeded to the throne after the assassination of his father and elder brother. The tide of republican sentiment continued to rise; economic troubles increased discontent. In Oct., 1910, a revolution dethroned Manuel and established a republic, of which Teófilo Braga became president. The royal family escaped, and Manuel spent most of his remaining years in England enjoying his large fortune.

manueline, sumptuous, composite style of architectural ornamentation of the early 16th cent. It combined contemporary Portuguese, Spanish, Italian, and Flemish elements and was named for King Manuel I of Portugal (reigned 1495–1521). The Chapter House of the Convent of Christ at Tomar, Portugal (early 16th cent.), with its large-scale windows surrounded with sculptured organic and twisted rope forms, is the major monument of the manueline style. The few known architects who originated the style include Mateus Fernandes, Diogo Boytac, the brothers Arruda, and Juão de Castilho. The style was extended to the decorative arts and spread to Spain, Mexico, and India.

manure, term used in the United States to refer to excreta of animals, with or without added bedding; also called barnyard manure. In other countries the term often refers to any material used to fertilize the soil. Properly managed, barnyard manure is a valuable FERTILIZER because of its nitrogen and phosphate content; its composition varies greatly depending upon the animals that produce it. Often it is reinforced with additions of SUPERPHOSPHATE to make it a better balanced fertilizer and to reduce the loss of nitrogen as ammonia. Other organic manures are fish scrap, guano, seaweed, and COMPOST. The claim by so-called organic farmers that crops fertilized by organic manures are more nutritious than those grown with artificial manures (i.e., chemical fertilizers) has not been substantiated. The term *green manure* is applied to crops grown for plowing under (see COVER CROP) and to manure that has not undergone decay.

manure salts: see POTASSIUM CHLORIDE.

manuscript, a handwritten work as distinguished from printing or typescript. The oldest manuscripts, those found in Egyptian tombs, were written on PAPYRUS; the earliest dates from c.3500 B.C. PARCHMENT, which succeeded papyrus as a writing material, was much more durable; most extant ancient manuscripts are of parchment. Both sides were used and palimpsests, which were erased and reused pages, were common. The discovery of the DEAD SEA SCROLLS in the mid-20th cent. added immeasurably to the world's treasury of ancient manuscripts. The manuscripts of the Middle Ages were often beautifully illuminated in colors (see ILLUMINATION, in art) on vellum, a fine variety of parchment. Initial letters of first lines and titles were often highly decorated. Although PAPER was invented in China in the 2d cent. A.D., it was not known in Europe until the 11th cent. Paper bases included silk, cotton, and linen, all used before the advent of printing. Medieval pens were made of quills and INK, most commonly black, of various carbon-containing substances. The study of ancient and medieval manuscripts and handwriting is a highly developed and complex discipline (see PALEOGRAPHY). After the European invention of printing in the 15th cent., the need for hand-copied manuscripts rapidly vanished. They soon came to be valued by collectors of fine books. Among the important manuscript collections in the United States are those in the Library of Congress in Washington, D.C.; and in the New York Public Library and Morgan Library in New York City. There are numerous superb European collections, notably those at the Vatican in Rome and the British Museum in London. Also known as manuscripts are modern authors' typescripts made for publishers and printers. The term includes as well the private and public papers, typed or handwritten, left by public figures for the use of historians and scholars. The Library of Congress holds a very large deposit of manuscripts of this type, including the papers of most U.S. Presidents. Other important collections of this sort are in the New York Public Library and the Massachusetts Historical Society. See BOOK. See Leo Deuel, *Testaments of Time* (1965).

manuscript illumination: see ILLUMINATION, in art.

Manutius, Aldus: see ALDUS MANUTIUS.

Manville, borough (1970 pop. 13,029), Somerset co., central N.J.; laid out 1906, inc. 1929. Clothing and plastics are produced there.

Manx (măngks), virtually extinct language belonging to the Goidelic or Gaelic group of the Celtic subfamily of the Indo-European family of languages. See CELTIC LANGUAGES.

Manx cat: see CAT.

Manych (mä'nĭch), two rivers, SE European USSR. The Western Manych, c.200 mi (320 km) long, rises near Stavropol in the N Caucasus and flows NW through Lake Manych-Gudilo into the lower Don River. The Eastern Manych rises in a marshy area and flows c.100 mi (160 km) east to a system of salt lakes and marshes c.75 mi (120 km) W of the Caspian Sea, but it reaches the sea only in rare spring floods. In spring the Western and Eastern Manych join in the center of the **Manych Depression,** a broad, valley-like lowland extending c.350 mi (560 km) southeast from the lower Don to the Caspian Sea. A variant spelling is Manich.

Manzala, Lake (mänză'lə), or **Lake Menzaleh** (mĕn-), salt water lagoon, c.660 sq mi (1,710 sq km), NE Egypt, near Port Said, partly separated from the Mediterranean Sea by a narrow peninsula. The Suez Canal cuts through the eastern part of the lake's basin.

Manzanares (mänthänä'räs), river, c.55 mi (90 km) long; rising in the Sierra de Guadarrama, central Spain, and flowing S past Madrid (where it is canalized) into the Jarama River. The Manzanares is used for irrigation and hydroelectric-power generation.

Manzanillo (mänsänē'yō), city (1970 pop. 77,880), Oriente prov., SE Cuba, a port on the Guacanayabo Gulf of the Caribbean Sea. A leading city on Cuba's southern coast, Manzanillo is a commercial center and the exportation point for the agricultural produce (sugarcane, rice, tobacco) of the Cauto plain. The city was founded in 1784 and was long a smuggling center involving British merchants from Jamaica. An attack by Great Britain on Manzanillo in 1792 destroyed numerous Spanish ships in the harbor and led to the fortification of the city.

Manzanillo, city (1970 pop. 36,982), Colima state, SW Mexico. The nation's chief Pacific port, Manzanillo has a fine harbor and modern rail and highway connections with Mexico City. It handles many imports and ships out minerals, coffee, and lumber. Excellent beaches, a tropical climate, and resources for hunting and fishing have made Manzanillo a lively resort.

manzanita: see BEARBERRY.

Manzikert (măn'zĭkərt), Turk. *Malazgirt,* village, E Turkey, SE of Erzurum. It was an important town of ancient Armenia. A council held there in A.D. 726 reasserted the independence of the Armenian Church from the Orthodox Eastern Church. There, in 1071, the Seljuk Turks under ALP ARSLAN routed the troops of Byzantine Emperor ROMANUS IV in a decisive battle that resulted in the fall of Asia Minor to the Seljuks.

Manzini (mänzē'nē), formerly **Bremersdorp** (brē'-mərzdôrp), town (1972 est. pop. 20,000), central Swaziland. It is the trade center of a farming region. Founded in 1890, the town was the capital of Swaziland protectorate from 1894 to 1902.

Manzoni, Alessandro (äläs-sän'drō mändzô'nē), 1785–1873, Italian novelist and poet. Taken in his youth to Paris by his mother, he there embraced the deism that he was later to discard for an ardent Roman Catholicism. He returned to Italy in 1807. In his last years he became a senator. He wrote tragedies, e.g., *Il Conte di Carmagnola* (1816–20) and *Adelchi* (1822), and poetry, including the *Inni sacri* and the celebrated *Cinque maggio* (1821), an ode on the death of Napoleon. It was in 1825–26, under the influence of Sir Walter Scott, that he produced his most famous work, *I promessi sposi* (tr. *The Betrothed,* 1828), a novel of 16th-century Milan that reveals a detailed and vast understanding of Italian life and remains one of Italy's most popular novels. By 1875, 118 editions had appeared, and the work was widely translated. As a result Manzoni's influence on the development of a consistent Italian prose style was immense. Goethe admired the work of Manzoni, and Verdi wrote his *Requiem* on the poet's death. See tr. of *The Betrothed* by Archibald Colquhoun (1951); biographies by Bernard Wall (1954) and Archibald Colquhoun (1954).

Manzù, Giacomo (jä'kōmō mänzōō'), 1908–, Italian sculptor. Influenced by the sculpture of antiquity and by Donatello, Rodin, and Maillol, Manzù's representational sculptures, such as *The Cardinal,* are distinguished by their quiet dignity and sensitive craftsmanship. His major works include a door for St. Peter's in Rome and one for Salzburg Cathedral. See study by John Rewald (1967).

Maoch (mā'ŏk), father of Achish. 1 Sam. 27.2. Maachah: 1 Kings 2.39.

Maon (mā'ŏn), town in the hills of Judah, c.10 mi (16 km) S of Hebron. It was Nabal's home. Joshua 15.55; 1 Sam. 23.24–25; 25.2. The Maonites were apparently a Canaanite tribe of S Palestine. Judges 10.12.

Maori (mä'ōrē), people of New Zealand, believed to have migrated in early times from Polynesia. Their tradition asserts that seven canoes brought their ancestors to New Zealand. The Maori language is closely related to Rarotongan, Tahitian, Hawaiian, and other languages spoken on the islands lying E of Samoa in the South Pacific. In the early 19th cent., at the end of their war against European encroachment, they numbered about 100,000. The number later dwindled to 40,000. Largely through the efforts of their own chiefs, however, they have reemerged as an economically self-sufficient minority in New Zealand, and their population today is about 225,000. Few people would claim that the Maoris are fully included in the New Zealand societal community, however. They have their own members of parliament, but tend to be little concerned with general political issues and to limit their interests almost entirely to Maori affairs. See A. J. Metge, *Maoris of New Zealand* (1967); J. A. Williams, *Politics of the New Zealand Maori: Protest and Cooperation, 1891–1909* (1970).

Maori language: see MALAYO-POLYNESIAN LANGUAGES.

Mao Tse-tung (mou dzŭ-dōōng), 1893–, founder of the People's Republic of China. Mao, of Hunanese peasant stock, was trained in the Chinese classics and later received a modern education. As a young man he traveled widely, particularly in central China, where he observed oppressive social conditions. One of the original members of the Chinese Communist party, he organized (1920s) Kuomintang-sponsored peasant and industrial unions and directed (1926) the Kuomintang's Peasant Movement Training Institute. After the Kuomintang-Communist split (1927), Mao led the disastrous "Autumn Harvest Uprising" in Hunan prov. and subsequently was forced out of the central committee of the party. From 1928 until 1931, Mao, with CHU TEH and others, worked in the Chinese hinterlands, establishing rural soviets and building the Red Army. In 1931 he was elected chairman of the newly established Soviet Republic of China, based in Kiangsi prov. After withstanding several military campaigns launched by Chiang Kai-shek, Mao led (1934–35) the Red Army on the LONG MARCH (6,000 mi/9,656 km) from Kiangsi north to Yenan in Shensi prov. During the Second Sino-Japanese War (1937–45) the Communists and the Kuomintang continued their civil war, even while both groups were battling the Japanese invaders. The civil war continued after the conflict with Japan had ended, and in 1949, after the Communists had taken almost all of mainland China, Mao became chairman of the central government council of the newly established People's Republic of China; he was reelected to the post, the most powerful in China, in 1954. In an attempt to break with the Russian model of Communism and to imbue the Chinese people with renewed revolutionary vigor, Mao launched (1958) the Great Leap Forward. Small, labor-intensive industries, controlled by local peasant groups, were set up throughout China. The program was a failure economically, causing Mao to withdraw temporarily from public view. In 1959, Liu Shao-ch'i, an opponent of the Great Leap Forward, replaced Mao as chairman of the central government council, but Mao retained his chairmanship of the Communist party and thus remained the nation's chief policymaker. A power struggle between Mao and Liu developed, culminating in the Cultural Revolution (1966–69), a period of widespread agitation begun and directed by Mao. Liu was removed from power in 1968, and in the following year Mao reasserted his leadership of Communist China by serving as chairman of the Ninth Communist Party Congress. In 1970 he was named supreme commander of the whole nation and the whole army, further consolidating his position as China's most powerful figure. One of the Communist world's most prominent theoreticians, Mao's ideas on active revolutionary struggle and guerrilla warfare have been extremely influential, especially among Third World revolutionaries. His policies have often brought him into conflict with the Soviet Union's leaders, whom Mao accuses of betraying Marxism by taking overly conciliatory attitudes toward the West. His name is also spelled Mao Tze-tung. See his *Selected Works* (4 vol., 1954–56, repr. 1961–65), *Quotations from Chairman Mao Tse-tung* (ed. by S. R. Schram, 1967) and *Poems* (tr. 1972). See also Jerome Ch'en, *Mao and the Chinese Revolution* (1967, repr. 1970); R. J. Lifton, *Revolutionary Immortality* (1968); Edgar Snow, *Red Star over China* (rev. ed. 1968); Jerome Ch'en, ed. *Mao* (1969); Philippe Devillers, *Mao* (tr. 1969); Robert Payne, *Mao Tse-tung* (rev. ed. 1969); S. R. Schram, *Mao Tse-tung* (1967) and *The Political Thought of Mao Tse-tung* (rev. ed. 1969).

Map or **Mapes, Walter,** c.1140–c.1210, English author, b. Wales. A favorite of Henry II, he traveled with the king and became archdeacon of Oxford. The one work indubitably his, *De nugis curialium* [courtiers' trifles], is a Latin prose collection of legends, tales, gossip, and anecdotes. Shrewd, witty, and satirical, the work shows Map as a wit and a man of the world, familiar with court life and public affairs. That he was the author of one or more extant Arthurian romances and of some surviving Goliardic songs is no longer accepted by scholars.

map, conventionalized representation of spatial phenomena on a plane surface. Unlike photographs, maps are selective and may be prepared to show various quantitative and qualitative facts, including boundaries, physical features, patterns, and distribution. Each point on a map corresponds to a geographical position in accordance with a definite SCALE and projection (see MAP PROJECTION). Cartography, or mapmaking, antedates even the art of writing. Diagrams of areas familiar to them were made by Marshall Islanders, Eskimo, American Indians, and many other preliterate peoples. Maps drawn by ancient Babylonians, Egyptians, and Chinese have been found. The oldest known map, now on exhibition in the Semitic Museum of Harvard, is a Babylonian clay tablet dating from c.2500 B.C. Our present system of cartography was established by the Greeks, who remained unexcelled until the 16th cent. Scientific measurements of earth distances by means of meridians and parallels were first made by Eratosthenes (3d cent. B.C.). Of the ancient scholars, the mathematician and geographer Ptolemy (A.D. 2d cent.), expounded on the principles of cartography; his system was followed for many centuries, although his basic error in underestimating the earth's size was not corrected until the age of Mercator. Only the Mediterranean world was represented with any accuracy in early maps. During the Middle Ages, while European cartographers produced artistic, idealized maps, Arabic mapmakers, notably Idrisi (12th cent.), carried on the work of Ptolemy, and the Chinese produced the first printed maps. Three major events contributed to the spectacular renaissance of cartography in Europe around 1500—the rediscovery and translation into Latin of Ptolemy's *Geographia,* the invention of printing and engraving, and the great voyages of discovery. This renaissance was manifested by the work of Gerardus Mercator in the first modern world atlas, published in 1570 by Abraham Ortelius, and by the decorative, paintinglike maps of the French Sanson family (17th cent.). Improvements in the methods of surveying and increased emphasis on accuracy led to the noted work in the 18th cent. of the Frenchmen Guillaume Delisle and J. B. B. d'Anville, the founders of modern cartography. After 1750 many European governments undertook the systematic mapping of their countries. The first important national survey was made in France (published 1756), followed by the Ordnance Survey of Great Britain (published 1801) and the topographic survey of Switzerland (organized 1832). In the United States the Geological Survey (established 1878) has mapped much of the country on varying scales. During the 19th cent. the demand for national maps was fulfilled, and famous world atlases were published. But with the advent of the 20th cent. the need arose for an international map of the world on a uniform scale. Accordingly, at several meetings of the International Geographical Congress (1891, 1909, 1913), the German Albrecht Penck presented and perfected plans for a world map on a scale of 1:1,000,000, to consist of about 1,500 sheets, each covering four degrees of latitude and six degrees of longitude in a modified conic projection. Uniformity of lettering and the use of layer tints to indicate relief were agreed upon. However, only part of the work has been completed. The greatest single contribution to the map of the world was made by the American Geographical Society of New York, which completed (1945) its 107-sheet *Map of Hispanic America.* During World Wars I and II the science and art of mapping was greatly advanced. Aerial and satellite photography, radar, and sonar as the basis for mapmaking have made great technical advances since the end of World War II. Computer mapping was developed in the 1960s. The earliest European printed maps (2d half of the 15th cent.) were made from woodcuts; maps are now reproduced by several processes, including photoengraving, wax engraving, and lithography. See also CHART. See Leo Bagrow, *History of Cartography* (1964); T. W. Birch, *Maps: Topographical and Statistical* (2d ed. 1964); David Greenhood, *Mapping* (rev. ed. 1964); G. R. Crone, *Maps and Their Makers* (3d ed. 1966); A. H. Robinson and R. D. Sale, *Elements of Cartography* (3d ed. 1969); F. J. Monkhouse and H. R. Wilkinson, *Maps and Diagrams* (1971); N. J. W. Thrower, *Maps and Man* (1972).

Mapes, Walter: see MAP, WALTER.

maple, common name for the genus *Acer* of the Aceraceae, a family of deciduous trees and shrubs of the Northern Hemisphere, found mainly in temperate regions and on tropical mountain slopes. *Acer,* the principal genus, includes the many maples and the box elder. Maples are popular as shade trees and often have brilliantly colored foliage in the fall. Several E North American species provide valuable timber, notably the sugar, hard, or rock, maple (*A. saccharum*), and the more brittle-timbered black maple (*A. nigrum*). Their strong, close-grained, easily worked hardwood is used in shipbuilding and aircraft construction, for floors, fuel, and wood pulp, and in many other industries. Bird's-eye and curly maple are decorative cuts used for cabinetmaking. The ashes are rich in potash. In addition, these two maples are the main sources of maple sugar. A prevalent and widely distributed North American species is the swamp, or red, maple (*A. rubrum*). The box elder, or ash-leaved maple (*A. negundo*), is a smaller North American species also planted as a shade tree; its softer wood is used for woodenware, cheap furniture, and paper pulp. Several European and Japanese maples have been introduced to the United States as ornamentals. The only other genus of the family is *Dipteronia,* consisting of two species indigenous to China. All members of the family have characteristic winged seeds. **Maple syrup** is the concentrated sap obtained for commercial purposes from the sugar maple and the black maple. Sap flows intermittently for periods of up to six weeks in the spring, is caught in buckets, strained, and concentrated by boiling to a density of 11 lb (4.9 kg) per gal for syrup or evaporated further for sugar. The syrup and sugar, first prepared by the Indians (by dropping hot rocks into the sap or by freezing out the water) became the staple sweetening used by the colonists and remained important until c.1875. As cane sugar—with a higher saccharine content and a lower manufacturing cost—gained precedence and as the maple forest stands, or "sugar bush," were depleted, maple sugar and syrup became scarcer and are now used mainly for confectionery and for flavoring, especially of tobacco. Vermont is the chief producing state. Maples are classified in the division MAGNOLIOPHYTA, class Magnoliopsida, order Sapindales, family Aceraceae. See Helen and Scott Nearing, *The Maple Sugar Book* (1950, repr. 1970).

Maple Heights, city (1970 pop. 34,093), Cuyahoga co., NE Ohio; inc. 1932. It is chiefly residential, with huge shopping centers and an industrial park.

maple syrup: see MAPLE.

Maplewood. 1 Village (1970 pop. 25,222), Ramsey co., SE Minn., a residential suburb of St. Paul; inc. 1957. **2** City (1970 pop. 12,785), St. Louis co., E Mo., a suburb of St. Louis; settled 1825, inc. 1908. Manufactures include structural steel products, honing tools, and aluminum storm sashes.

map projection, transfer of the features of the surface of the earth or another spherical body onto a flat sheet of paper. Only a globe can represent accurately the shape, orientation, and relative area of the earth's surface features; any projection produces distortion with regard to some of these characteristics. The particular projection chosen for a given map will depend on the use for which the map is intended. Some projections preserve correct relative distances in all directions from the center of the map (equidistant projection); some show areas equal to (equal-area projection) or shapes similar to (conformal projection) those on a globe of the same scale; some are useful in determining direction. Many map projections can be constructed by the use of a light source to project the features of the globe onto a piece of paper (although in practice one performs the operation mathematically rather than with a light); other projections can be constructed only mathematically. Projections are classified as cylindrical, conic, or azimuthal according to the method of projection with a light source; many projections that can be constructed only mathematically are also classified according to this system. In a typical cylindrical projection, one imagines the paper to be wrapped as a cylinder around the globe, tangent to it along the equator. Light comes from a point source at the center of the globe or, in some cases, from a filament running from pole to pole along the globe's axis. In the former case the poles clearly cannot be shown on the map, as they would be projected along the axis of the cylinder out to infinity. In the latter case the poles become lines forming the top and bottom edges of the map. The Mercator projection, long popular but now less so, is a cylindrical projection of the latter type that can be constructed only mathematically. In all cylindrical projections the meridians of longitude, which on the globe converge at the poles, are parallel to one another; in the Mercator projection the parallels of latitude, which on the globe are equal distances apart, are drawn with increasing separation as their distance from the equator increases in order to preserve shapes. However, the price paid for preserving shapes is that areas are exaggerated with increasing distance from the equator. The effect is most pronounced near the poles; e.g., Greenland is shown with enormously exaggerated size, although its shape is preserved. The poles themselves cannot be shown on the Mercator projection. Students using the Mercator projection obtain an incorrect impression of the relative sizes of the countries of the world. In a conic projection a paper cone is placed on a globe like a hat, tangent to it at some parallel, and a point source of light at the center of the globe projects the surface features onto the cone. The cone is then cut along a convenient meridian and unfolded into a flat surface in the shape of a circle with a sector missing. All parallels are arcs of circles with a pole (the apex of the original cone) as their common center, and meridians appear as straight lines converging toward this same point. Some conic projections are conformal (shape preserving); some are equal-area (size preserving). A polyconic projection uses various cones tangent to the globe at different parallels. Parallels on the map are arcs of circles but are not concentric. In an azimuthal projection a flat sheet of paper is tangent to the globe at one point. The point light source may be located at the globe's center (gnomonic projection), on the globe's surface directly opposite the tangent point (stereographic projection), or at some other point along the line defined by the tangent point and the center of the globe, e.g., at a point infinitely distant (orthographic projection). In all azimuthal projections, the tangent point is the central point of a circular map; all great circles passing through the central point are straight lines, and all directions from the central point are accurate. If the central point is a pole, then the meridians (great circles) radiate from that point and parallels are shown as concentric circles. The gnomonic projection has the useful property that all great circles (not just those that pass through the central point) appear as straight lines; conversely, all straight lines drawn on it are great circles. A navigator taking the shortest route between two points (always part of a great circle) can plot his course on a gnomonic projection by simply drawing a straight line between the two points. Among the other commonly used map projections are the Mollweide homolographic and the sinusoidal, both of which are equal-area projections with horizontal parallels; they are especially useful for world maps. Goode's homolosine projection is a composite using the sinusoidal projection between latitudes 40°N and 40°S and the homolographic projection for the remaining parts. Interruptions, or splits, are often made in the ocean areas in order to show land areas with truer shapes. See G. P. Kellaway, *Map Projections* (2d ed. 1970).

Mapp vs. Ohio, case decided in 1961 by the U.S. Supreme Court. Dollree Mapp was convicted in a state court of possessing pornographic material in violation of Ohio law. Her conviction was obtained on the basis of evidence taken by the police when they entered (1957) her boardinghouse without a search warrant while looking for gambling materials. The Supreme Court, in overturning her conviction, declared that the exclusionary rule (based on the Fourth Amendment to the Constitution), which prohibits the use in Federal court of evidence obtained through an illegal search and seizure, extended also to state courts. The ruling provoked a good deal of controversy; while proponents of the exclusionary rule claim that it is the only means of assuring freedom from illegal searches, opponents argue that a criminal should not go free because of a policeman's mistake.

Mapu, Abraham (mä'po͞o), 1808–67, Lithuanian novelist who wrote in Hebrew. For many years an impoverished, itinerant schoolmaster, Mapu gained financial security when he was appointed teacher in a government school for Jewish children. Mapu is considered the creator of the Hebrew novel. Influenced by French romantic literature, he wrote heavily plotted novels about life in ancient Palestine, which he contrasted favorably with 19th-century Jewish life. His style is fresh and poetic, almost biblical in its simple grandeur. Among his novels are *Ayit Zanua* [the hypocrite] (1858) and *Ahavat Zion* (1853; tr. *Amonon, Prince and Peasant,* 1887).

maquis (mäkē'): see GUERRILLA WARFARE.

Mar, John Erskine, 1st (or 6th) **earl of,** d. 1572, regent of Scotland. As Lord Erskine he was keeper of Edinburgh and Stirling castles, a source of much political strength. In the struggle between the regent Mary of Guise and the Protestant nobles, Erskine intervened to a limited degree on both sides, and on the approach of the English (1559) he received the regent into Edinburgh Castle. When Mary Queen of Scots returned from France in 1561 he was made a member of her privy council, and in 1565 he was created earl of Mar. (There is still dispute as to whether this constituted a restoration of the earldom of Mar, as Erskine claimed, or a new creation; hence the alternative numbering.) In 1567, Mar was given custody of Mary's young son, later James VI. The earl of Bothwell tried to gain control of the prince, but Mar evaded him and joined the revolt of the nobles. He was one of the council to whom Mary signed (1567) over the government. Although Mar was chosen regent after the earl of Lennox's death in 1571, James Douglas, the earl of MORTON, held the real power. Mar's death forestalled a proposal by Elizabeth I of England that Mary, a prisoner in England, be turned over to the Scots for execution. His wife continued as a guardian of James.

Mar, John Erskine, 2d (or 7th) **earl of,** 1558–1634, Scottish nobleman; son of the 1st (or 6th) earl. In 1578 he was persuaded by James Douglas, 4th earl of MORTON, to assert his claims to Stirling Castle and the guardianship of the young James VI (later JAMES I of England). Mar emerged in control of the king's person, while Morton attempted to recover his authority. After the rise of Esmé STUART, duke of Lennox, and James STUART, earl of Arran, Mar fell out of favor with the king. He participated in the capture of James in the raid of Ruthven (1582). After James's escape, Mar was received at court, but he was banished in 1584 and fled to England. In 1585 he joined the other banished Scottish nobles who invaded Scotland and overthrew Arran. Mar was made a member of the privy council. In 1601 he was sent as ambassador to England to offer secret assistance to the 2d earl of Essex in his rebellion. This was crushed before his arrival, and Mar spent his time negotiating the question of James's succession to the English throne. In 1603 he accompanied James to England and was made a member of the English privy council. From 1616 to 1630 he was lord high treasurer of Scotland.

Mar, John Erskine, 6th (or 11th) **earl of,** 1675–1732, Scottish nobleman, leader of the JACOBITES. He was nicknamed "Bobbing John," probably because of his political vacillation. He succeeded his father as earl in 1689 and in the following years was generally a member of the court party. He was twice secretary of state for Scotland under Queen Anne and played a leading part in promoting the union (1707) with England. After the accession (1714) of George I, he made an effusive offer of his services but was dismissed. He then withdrew secretly to Scotland, where he raised (1715) the standard for James Francis Edward STUART, the Old Pretender, without orders from him to do so. The rebellion failed, largely through Mar's incompetence. He was defeated at Sheriffmuir and fled (1716) to France with the Pretender. He was attainted of treason in England, but his active dissatisfaction with the Jacobite court and his suspected treachery caused the Pretender also to break with him in 1724. Mar remained in exile until his death. See Alistair Tayler and Henrietta Tayler, *1715: The Story of the Rising* (1936).

Mara (mâr'ə) [Heb.,=bitter], punning name taken by Naomi out of sorrow. Ruth 1.20.

marabou: see STORK.

Marabouts (mâr'əbo͞ots) [Arabic,=devotee hermit], members of a Muslim religious and military community, precursors of the ALMORAVIDS. They spread from NW Africa into Spain in the 11th and 12th cent. The Marabouts later became known as holy men and were greatly venerated as saints. They now live in monasteries or are attached to mosques. Their tombs, also called Marabouts, are often places of pilgrimage.

Maracaibo (märäkī'bō), city (1970 est. pop. 666,000), capital of Zulia state, NW Venezuela, at the outlet of Lake Maracaibo. It is Venezuela's second largest city, a commercial and industrial center, and the oil capital of South America. Besides oil, exports include coffee, cacao, sugar, hardwoods, and some minerals found in the surrounding region. Maracaibo was founded in 1571. In the 17th cent. it was sacked five times, notably by Sir Henry MORGAN in 1669. Until the establishment of the oil industry after 1918, Maracaibo was extremely underdeveloped; but exploitation by foreign interests of the vast petroleum resources of the Maracaibo basin resulted in a rapid expansion and modernization of the city. The dredging of the lake also increased Maracaibo's importance as a shipping point for inland products. The c.5-mi-long (8-km) Lake Maracaibo Bridge is S of the city.

Maracaibo, Lake, largest lake of South America, c.5,100 sq mi (13,210 sq km), NW Venezuela, extending c.110 mi (180 km) inland. A strait, 34 mi (55 km) long, connects it with the Gulf of Venezuela. Discovered in 1499 by Alonso de Ojeda, the Spanish explorer, the lake lies in the extremely hot, humid, and disease-ridden lowlands of the Maracaibo basin, a region which, almost enclosed by mountains, is semiarid in the north but has an average annual rainfall of 50 in. (127 cm) in the south. Much of the indigenous population lives in thatched huts built on stilts over the brackish water. Some areas are still inhabited by hostile Indians, notably the Motilones. Although the fertile soil produces sugarcane, cacao, and a wealth of tropical hardwoods, absentee exploitation, unhealthful living, and scarcity of labor have left the area undeveloped agriculturally. Some livestock is raised. By far the most vital activity is production of petroleum. Developed since 1918 by foreign concerns, the region is one of the greatest oil-producing areas in the world. Lake Maracaibo, with the Catatumbo River, its chief tributary, is a major artery of communication for products of the adjacent region and those of the Colombian-Venezuelan highlands. A dredged channel gives ocean-going vessels access to the lake. Cabimas and the port of Maracaibo are the principal cities on the lake. Lake Maracaibo Bridge (c.5 mi/8 km long; completed 1962), spanning the lake's outlet, is one of the longest bridges in the world.

Maracay (märäkī'), city (1970 est. pop. 193,000), capital of Aragua state, N Venezuela, at the eastern end of Lake Valencia. It is a commercial, agricultural, and industrial city, supplying much of the meat, dairy products, and raw materials for Caracas. Maracay was modernized in the early 20th cent. by the dictator Juan Vicente GÓMEZ, who built an opera house, a bull ring, gardens, and a triumphal arch.

Maradi (märädē'), town (1970 est. pop. 26,000), S Niger, near the border with Nigeria. It is the administrative and commerical center for an agricultural region that specializes in peanut growing and goat raising. A major road connects Maradi with KANO, Nigeria. The town has a technical college and a center for research on poultry and goat breeding.

Maragall i Gorina, Joan (hō'än märägäl'yə ē gōrē'nä), 1860–1911, Catalonian poet and essayist. For many years he wrote articles and essays for the influential newspaper *Diario de Barcelona* [Barcelona daily]. Maragall i Gorina is noted for the serenity and spontaneity of his poetry. Because of his emphasis on external reality, he is regarded by many critics as the first Catalonian modernist. His volumes of poetry include *Visions i Cants* [visions and songs] (1900), which makes much use of Catalonian legend; and *Següencies* (1911), which contains "Cant espíritual," his most famous poem.

Maragha, Iran: see MARAGHEH.

Maragheh (märägā'), city (1966 pop. 54,106), East Azerbaijan prov., NW Iran, on the southern slopes of Mt. Sahand. It is the trade and transportation center of a fertile fruit-growing region; dried fruits are shipped from there. After the Arab conquest in the 7th cent. Maragheh developed rapidly as a provincial capital. In 1029 it was seized by the Oghuz Turks, but they were driven out by a Kurdish chief who established a local dynasty. The city was destroyed by the Mongols in 1221, but Hulagu Khan held court there until the establishment of a fixed capital at Tabriz. The city was temporarily occupied by Russia in 1828. Maragheh's celebrated observatory (13th cent.) is now in ruins. The city is also known as Maragha.

Marah (mâr'ə) [Heb.,=bitter], bitter spring that Moses sweetened. Ex. 15.23.

Marais (märā') [Fr.,=swamp], old quarter of Paris, on the right bank of the Seine. Until the 18th cent. it was the most aristocratic section of Paris. The Hôtel des Tournelles, long the residence of the kings of France (Henry II was killed in its court during a joust), was replaced with the Place des Vosges. The Marais park, surrounded by uniform houses in pink brick and gray slate, remains a perfect ensemble of 17th-century architecture. Nearby is the Carnavalet, once the home of Mme de Sévigné, which now houses the municipal museum of Paris. Although the quarter is now very populous, it still has fine mansions dating from its most prosperous period. Among its many renovated and restored buildings is the sumptuous Hotel Sully (17th cent.).

Marais des Cygnes (mĕr'ē də sēn), river, c.140 mi (230 km) long, rising in E central Kansas, SW of Topeka, and flowing SE into W Mo. to join the Little Osage River and form the Osage River. Subject to heavy floods, the river has many flood control projects.

Marajó (mərəzhô'), island, c.150 mi (240 km) long and c.100 mi (160 km) wide, N Brazil, at the mouth of the Amazon River. It divides the river into the Amazon proper and the Pará. Cattle are raised on the extensive eastern grasslands, and water buffaloes are bred in the low, swampy west. The island is famous for its prehistoric mounds, which yield handsome pottery.

Maralah (mâr'əlä), unidentified boundary mark in N Palestine. Joshua 19.11.

Maranatha (mär"ənä'thə): see ANATHEMA.

Maranhão (mərənyouN'), state (1970 pop. 2,947,576), 126,897 sq mi (328,663 sq km), NE Brazil, on the Atlantic Ocean. The capital is SÃO LUÍS (also known as Maranhão).

Marañón, Gregorio (grāgō'rēō märänyōn'), 1887–1960, Spanish essayist, b. Madrid. A physician and professor of endocrinology, he used his scientific knowledge and approach to analyze literary characters, historical figures, writers, and artists. His works include *Ensayo biológico sobre Enrique IV y su tiempo* [biological essay about Henry IV and his time] (1930), *Las ideas biológicas del Padre Feijo* [the biological ideas of Father Feijo] (1934), and *El Greco y Toledo* [El Greco and Toledo] (1956).

Marañón, river, c.1,000 mi (1,600 km) long, rising in Lake Lauricaucha in the Cordillera Occidental, W central Peru. It flows generally NW, then E across the Andes to join the Ucayali River in NE Peru where it forms the Amazon River; some consider the Marañón to be the authentic headwater of the Amazon. It is navigable to the Pongo de Manseriche, the gorge in NW Peru through which it flows before reaching the Amazon basin. The Huallaga River is its chief tributary. Pedro de Ursúa, the Spanish explorer, descended the Marañón in 1560.

Maraş (märäsh'), city (1970 pop. 105,206), capital of Maraş prov., S central Turkey, in the Taurus mts. It is an agricultural trade center and a transportation hub. Ancient inscriptions found there indicate that Maraş was a Hittite city-state c.1000 B.C. The city was called Germanikeia in Roman times. It was captured by the Arabs in A.D. 638 and was annexed by the Ottoman Empire in the early 16th cent.

maraschino (mâr'əskē'nō), LIQUEUR prepared by distilling the fermented juice of the marasca, a sour cherry originally of Dalmatia (part of present-day Yugoslavia). Maraschino is now produced in Italy and Yugoslavia. The **maraschino cherry** is preserved in maraschino or in imitation syrup.

Marat, Jean Paul (zhäN pōl märä'), 1743–93, French revolutionary, b. Switzerland. He studied medicine in England, acquired some repute as a doctor in London and in Paris, and wrote valuable scientific and medical works (some in English). His *Philosophical Essay on Man* (1773) was attacked by Voltaire for its extreme materialism. When the Revolution began (1789), he abandoned science for politics, founding the propagandist journal *L'Ami du peuple*, in which he vented his bitter hatred and suspicion of all who were in power. Outlawed, he twice fled to England (in 1790 and the summer of 1791) and during the interval between these two flights he hid in the sewers of Paris, thereby exacerbating a skin disease that he had previously contracted; it required treatments in a warm bath. He continued to publish his paper in secret and successively attacked Jacques Necker, the marquis de Lafayette, the commune, the comte de Mirabeau, the émigres, and, finally, the king. Marat's inflammatory articles helped foment the Aug. 10, 1792, uprising and the September massacres (see FRENCH REVOLUTION). Entering public life again in Aug., 1792, he was elected (1792) to the Convention. There he supported the JACOBINS in their fierce power struggle with the GIRONDISTS. He was stabbed to death in his bath by Charlotte CORDAY, an admirer of the Girondists. Selections from his writings have been published as *Textes choisis* (1945). See studies by L. R. Gottschalk (1967) and Marie Scherr (1929, repr. 1970).

Marathas: see MAHRATTAS.

Marathi (mərä'tē), language belonging to the Indic group of the Indo-Iranian subfamily of the Indo-European family of languages. See INDO-IRANIAN LANGUAGES.

Marathon (mâr'əthŏn), village and plain, ancient Greece, 20 mi (32 km) NE of Athens. Here the Athenians and Plataeans under MILTIADES defeated a Persian army in 490 B.C. (see PERSIAN WARS). In legend the plain was the scene of the victory of THESEUS over a great bull.

marathon group therapy: see GROUP PSYCHOTHERAPY.

marathon race, long-distance endurance race deriving its name from Marathon, Greece; in 490 B.C., Pheidippides, a runner from Marathon, carried news of victory over the Persians to Athens. A long-distance foot race called a marathon was first included in the Olympic games at Athens in 1896. The distance was c.25 mi (c.4,000 m) but in 1908 it was standardized at 26 mi, 385 yd (4,537 m). This race has become one of the principal events of the Olympic games. The American Marathon Race, held annually (except for 1918) since 1897 under the auspices of the Boston Athletic Association, is the most famous of such races in the United States. It originates in Hopkinton, Mass., and ends in downtown Boston.

Maratti, or **Maratta, Carlo** (kär'lō märät'tē, -tä), 1625-1713, Italian high baroque painter and engraver of the Roman school. He restored Raphael's frescoes in the Vatican and was appointed curator of the Vatican paintings. Maratti created a number of allegorical pictures in which he attempted to reconcile the baroque and classical trends. An example is the ceiling fresco *The Triumph of Clemency* (Altieri Palace, Rome).

Marbella (märbā'lyä), city (1970 pop. 33,203), Málaga prov., S Spain, in Andalusia, on the Mediterranean Sea. The city is a noted tourist resort.

Marble, Alice, 1913-, American tennis player, b. Plumas co., Calif. She began playing tennis at the age of 15, and after 1931 she rose rapidly in national tennis rankings. She four times took the U.S. singles championship (1936, 1938-40) and, with Sarah Palfrey Cooke, took the U.S. doubles crown (1937-40). She also won the British singles (1939) and doubles (1938-39) championships before entering (1941) the professional tennis ranks. See her autobiography, *The Road to Wimbledon* (1946).

marble, metamorphic ROCK composed wholly or in large part of CALCITE or DOLOMITE crystals, the crystalline texture being the result of METAMORPHISM of LIMESTONE by heat and pressure. The term *marble* is loosely applied to any limestone or dolomite that takes a good polish and is otherwise suitable as a building stone or ornamental stone. Marbles range in color from snow-white to gray and black, many varieties being some shade of red, yellow, pink, green, or buff; the colors, which are caused by the presence of impurities, are frequently arranged in bands or patches and add to the beauty of the stone when it is cut and polished. Marble is used as a material in statuary and monuments, as a facing stone in buildings and residences, and for pillars, colonnades, paneling, wainscoting, and floor tiles. Like all limestones, it is corroded by water and acid fumes and is thus ultimately an uneconomical material for use in exposed places and in large cities. The presence of certain impurities decreases its durability. Marble was extensively used by the ancient Greeks; the Parthenon and other famous buildings were constructed of white Pentelic marble from Mt. Pentelicus in Attica, and the finest statues, e.g., the Venus de' Medici, from the remarkably lustrous Parian marble from Paros in the Cyclades. These same quarries were later used by the Romans. Among the famous marbles of Italy are the Carrara and Siena marbles of Tuscany, which were used by the Romans and the Italian sculptors of the Renaissance. Marbles are quarried in all parts of the world. The finest marbles in the United States come from Vermont, which produces large quantities. Other states important as marble producers are Massachusetts, Maryland, Tennessee, Alabama, Georgia, Missouri, California, Colorado, and Arizona. See ALABASTER.

Marble Canyon National Monument: see NATIONAL PARKS AND MONUMENTS (table).

Marblehead, town (1970 pop. 21,295), Essex co., NE Mass., on the Atlantic coast; inc. 1649. A fishing village for many years, Marblehead became a resort in the 19th cent.; it is famous especially for yachting. There are 18th-century buildings in the picturesque village, including Elbridge Gerry's birthplace. Abbot Hall contains Archibald Willard's *Spirit of '76.* In Burial Hill cemetery are the graves of hundreds of Revolutionary soldiers and a monument to the 65 Marblehead residents who died in a gale in 1846. The Revolutionary Fort Sewall is in a seaside park.

marbling, in bookbinding, a process of coloring the sides, edges, or end papers of a book in a design that suggests the veins and mottles of marble. In tree marbling, as of tree calf bindings, the design suggests also the trunk and branches of a tree. In tree marbling, liquid colors are run over a surface bent to form a trough; the trunk of the tree is produced in the bottom of the trough. In other marbling, the colors are arranged on the surface of a liquid, and to this the surface to be colored is applied. The process of marbling was known in Japan as early as the 9th cent. A.D.; it reached Europe in the 17th cent.

Marburg: see MARIBOR, Yugoslavia.

Marburg an der Lahn (mär'bo͝ork än dĕr län) or **Marburg,** city (1970 pop. 46,968), Hesse, central West Germany, on the Lahn River. It is chiefly known for its Protestant university, founded in 1527 by Philip of Hesse. Manufactures include chemicals, pharmaceuticals, machinery, and surgical and optical instruments. Marburg grew in the 12th cent. around a castle; it was chartered in 1227 and, at intervals during the 13th to 17th cent., served as the residence of the landgraves of Hesse. Marburg became part of the Prussian province of Hesse-Nassau in 1866. The castle, which still dominates the picturesque city, was the scene of the famous Marburg Colloquy, held (1529) under the auspices of Philip of Hesse; it failed to bring about agreement between Luther and Melanchthon on the one side and Zwingli on the other. St. Elizabeth of Hungary is buried in the fine Gothic church (13th-14th cent.) dedicated to her; the remains of Field Marshal Hindenburg and of Frederick William I and Frederick II of Prussia were transferred to the church in 1946.

Marbury vs. Madison, case decided in 1803 by the U.S. Supreme Court. William Marbury had been commissioned justice of the peace in the District of Columbia by President John Adams in the "midnight appointments" at the very end of his administration. When the new administration did not deliver the commission, Marbury sued James Madison, Jefferson's Secretary of State. (At that time the Secretary of State was charged with certain domestic duties as well as with conducting foreign affairs.) Chief Justice John Marshall held that, although Marbury was entitled to the commission, the statute that was the basis of the particular remedy sought was unconstitutional because it gave the Supreme Court authority that was implicitly denied it by Article 3 of the U.S. Constitution. The decision was the first by the Supreme Court to declare unconstitutional and void an act passed by Congress that the Court considered in violation of the Constitution. The decision established the doctrine of judicial review, which vastly expanded the power of the judiciary.

Marbut, Curtis Fletcher, 1863-1935, American geologist, b. Verona, Mo., grad. Univ. of Missouri (B.S., 1889) and Harvard (M.A., 1844). As professor of geology at the Univ. of Missouri, he became interested in soil morphology and classification and developed soil survey maps of southern Missouri. Later working for the U.S. Dept. of Agriculture, he completed a similar survey of the entire Ozark region. In 1913 he devoted himself to the establishment of a permanent system of soil classification for the entire United States. He thus became known as the father of modern soil classification, including soil genesis, morphology, and mapping. Marbut organized and led numerous geological excursions throughout the world and also worked on setting up an international system of soil classification. His most important publication was *Soils of the United States* (1935).

Marc, Franz (fränts märk), 1880-1916, German painter. Influenced by August Macke, he developed a rich, chromatic symbolism. He depicted a mystical world of animals, especially horses, employing devices of distortion to express the animals' own awareness of their lives. Marc's pictorial conception of nature became increasingly abstract, resulting in the formation of colorful, crystalline patterns. Together with Kandinsky and Klee, Marc was a leader of the BLAUE REITER group. He was killed in World War I. Characteristic examples of his art are the *Gazelle* (Mus. of Art, Rhode Island School of Design, Providence, R.I.) and *Blue Horses* (Walker Art Center, Minneapolis, Minn.). See study by Georg Schmidt (tr. 1960).

marc: see BRANDY.

Marcantonio, Vito (vē'tō märkäntō'nēō), 1902-54, American politician, b. New York City. After the age of 18 he was active in community affairs in the Harlem section of New York City. He became a political protégé of Fiorello H. LaGuardia and later managed his political campaigns. Marcantonio served (1930-31) as assistant U.S. district attorney, and in 1934 he ran successfully for Congress on the Republican and Fusion tickets. He was defeated for reelection in 1936. In 1938 he was read out of the Republican party. Nonetheless he won the nomination of that party and of the American Labor party and was reelected to Congress. Thereafter he was repeatedly reelected, several times receiving the Democratic nomination as well as those of the other two parties. In 1948, after a New York state law was passed prohibiting a candidate from entering the primary of a party without its consent, Marcantonio ran only on the ballot of the American Labor party—of which he was (1947-53) state chairman and through which he gave staunch support to the Progressive party's presidential candidate, Henry A. Wallace in 1948. Marcantonio backed much of the New Deal legislation in Congress but aligned himself with President Franklin Delano Roosevelt's foreign policy only after June, 1941, when Germany invaded the USSR. A supporter of close relations between the United States and the USSR, Marcantonio was frequently criticized for allegedly changing his position in accordance with the Communist party line. He was defeated for reelection in 1950 by a coalition candidate. See biographies by A. L. Schaffer (1966) and S. J. LaGumina (1969).

Marc Antony: see ANTONY.

marcasite (mär'kəsīt) or **white iron pyrites,** a mineral closely resembling and having the same chemical composition (FeS_2) as PYRITE. It differs from pyrite in that it is paler in color, becomes darker upon oxidation, and crystallizes in the orthorhombic system. Twinned crystals resembling cockscombs (cockscomb pyrites) or spearheads (spear pyrites) are of common occurrence. The mineral occurs in marls, clays, and limestones in many parts of the world.

Marceau, Marcel (märsĕl' märsō'), 1923-, French mime. Marceau studied under Charles Dullin and Étienne Decroux in Paris. He gained renown in 1947 with the creation of Bip, a sad white-faced clown with a tall, battered hat. Marceau and his Compagnie de Mime have performed frequently in the United States since 1955. He has made several films, including *Un jardin public* (1955). See George Mendoza, *The Marcel Marceau Alphabet Book* (1970).

Marcel, Étienne (ātyĕn' märsĕl'), d. 1358, French bourgeois leader, provost of the merchants of Paris. In the States-General of 1355 he and Robert Le Coq bargained for governmental reforms with the French king, John II, who needed funds for the English war. After John's capture (1356) by the English, Marcel dealt with the dauphin (later CHARLES V). In 1357, the dauphin was forced to agree to the *Grande Ordonnance,* which granted the States-General far-reaching powers. Shortly afterward, Charles managed to escape from Paris and raise an army. Marcel's popularity waned, partly because of his alliance with CHARLES II of Navarre, who coveted the throne, and partly because of his intrigues with the English. The dauphin's troops besieged Paris, and on July 31, 1358, a royalist faction assassinated Marcel as a traitor; the dauphin then entered Paris.

Marcel, Gabriel (gäbrēĕl') 1889-1973, French philosopher, dramatist, and critic, b. Paris. A leading Christian existentialist, he became a Roman Catholic in 1929. He called himself a "concrete philosopher," indicating a reaction to his early idealism. He saw philosophy not as formulation of a system but rather as a personal reflection on the human situation. He held that the philosopher must be *engagé,* or personally involved, because existence and the human person are more significant than any abstraction. Involvement must be with other persons. To counter the impersonality of the mechanistic modern world and to recall man to an awareness of the mystery of being, Marcel spoke of the development of the individual in person-to-person dialogue. Human existence finds its earthly satisfaction in a God-centered communion of persons that is characterized by mutual fidelity and hope. His chief works include *Metaphysical Journal* (1927), *Being and Having* (1935), *The Mystery of Being* (1950), *Presence and Immortality* (1959), and a collection of essays, *Philosophy of Existentialism* (1961). His best-known plays are *Un Homme de Dieu* (1925) and *Le Chemin de Crete* (1936). See his *Tragic Wisdom and Beyond* (tr. 1973); studies by Seymour Cain (1963), T. J. van Ewijk (tr. 1965), and J. B. O'Malley (1967).

Marcellinus Ammianus: see AMMIANUS MARCELLINUS.

Marcellus (märsĕl'əs), principal plebeian family of the ancient Roman gens Claudia. **Marcus Claudius Marcellus,** c.268-208 B.C., was consul five times. In his first consulship he fought (222) against the Insubrian Gauls and killed their king in single combat. In his third consulship he was a colleague of Fabius Maximus, and he went (214) into S Italy and Sicily to prosecute the Second Punic War. He besieged Syracuse and took (212) the city, in spite of the ingenious defenses made by Archimedes. In his fifth consulship he fell in a skirmish with Hannibal's men near Venusia. Plutarch wrote a biography of him. **Marcus Claudius Marcellus,** d. 45 B.C., was a friend of Cicero and subject of the Ciceronian oration, *Pro Marcello.* He held the posts of curule aedile (56 B.C.) and consul (51 B.C.). As a senatorial partisan Marcellus defended Milo against Clodius and joined the opponents of Julius Caesar in the civil war. Caesar pardoned him after Pharsala. **Marcus Claudius Marcellus,** 43? B.C.-23 B.C., was son of Octavia, sister of AUGUSTUS, who greatly favored him.

Marcellus was considered to be Augustus' intended heir; he was adopted as son of the emperor, married to Julia, the emperor's daughter, and made pontifex. He died at Baiae, and Augustus named a theater for him.

Marcellus of Ancyra (ăn'sī'rə), fl. 350, Galatian churchman, the most violent opponent of ARIANISM in Asia Minor. He developed the theory that the Trinity was the result of emanations from God that would ultimately revert to God in the final judgment. Marcellus practically denied all distinction between Father and Son, thus teaching a virtual Sabellianism (see SABELLIUS) that proved embarrassing to his orthodox defenders. His views were eventually condemned.

March, earls of: see MORTIMER, EDMUND DE, EARL OF MARCH, and MORTIMER, ROGER DE, EARL OF MARCH.

March, Fredric, 1897–, American actor, b. Racine, Wis., as Frederick McIntyre Bickel. March made his stage debut (1920) in *Deburau.* Equally distinguished on stage and screen, he won Academy Awards for his performances in *Dr. Jekyll and Mr. Hyde* (1932) and in *The Best Years of Our Lives* (1947). Among his other outstanding films are *Anna Karenina* (1935), *Death of a Salesman* (1952), and *Inherit the Wind* (1960). He appeared on Broadway in 1956 in O'Neill's *Long Day's Journey into Night,* co-starring with his wife, Florence Eldridge, and in 1961 in *Gideon.* See L. J. Quirk, *The Films of Fredric March* (1971).

March: see MORAVA, river, Czechoslovakia.

March: see MONTH.

march, in music, composition intended to accompany marching. The only constant characteristics of a march are duple meter and a fairly simple rhythmic design. In mood, marches range from the moving death march in Wagner's *Götterdämmerung* to the brisk military marches of John Philip Sousa and the martial hymns of the late 19th cent. Examples of the varied use of the march can be found in Beethoven's *Eroica* Symphony, in the *marches militaires* of Schubert, in the *marche funèbre* in Chopin's Sonata in B flat minor, and in the *Dead March* in Handel's *Saul.*

Marchand, Jean Baptiste (zhäN bätēst' märshäN'), 1863–1934, French explorer and general. Sent to Africa (1897) to establish French control of the headwaters of the White Nile, Marchand led a heroic trek through uncharted terrain. In 1898 he established a post at Fashoda (now Kodok) and resisted dervish attacks. When Lord Kitchener arrived with a large British force, France and England stood at the brink of war; the FASHODA INCIDENT ended with Marchand's withdrawal. Marchand fought in China in the Boxer Rebellion (1900) and held a command in France in World War I.

Marche (märsh), region and former province, central France, on the NW margin of the MASSIF CENTRAL. It is coextensive with Creuse dept., much of the Haute-Vienne dept., and parts of Vienne, Indre, and Charente depts. GUÉRET is the chief town. Marche is primarily an agricultural region that also specializes in sheep raising. The wool is manufactured into carpets and tapestries at Felletin and Aubusson. The name of the region derived from its location as a northern border fief (march) of the duchy of AQUITAINE. Marche passed (13th cent.) to the house of Lusignan but was seized (early 14th cent.) by Philip IV of France. Briefly united with the crown lands, it ultimately became an appanage of the house of Bourbon. It came definitively to France in 1531, following the confiscation (1527) of the lands of Constable Charles de Bourbon by Francis I.

Marche (mär'kā) or **the Marches,** region (1971 pop. 1,359,063), 3,742 sq mi (9,692 sq km), E central Italy, extending from the eastern slopes of the Apennines to the Adriatic Sea. ANCONA is the capital of the region, which is divided into the provinces of Ancona, Ascoli Piceno, Macerata, and Pesaro e Urbino (named after their chief cities). The Marche is mostly hilly or mountainous, except for a narrow coastal strip, and is drained by the Metauro, Potenza, Tronto, and Nera rivers. Farming is the chief occupation; cereals, grapes, vegetables, and tobacco are the main products, and livestock is raised. Industry has expanded in the 20th cent. with the construction of hydroelectric facilities. Manufactures include textiles, chemicals, fertilizer, and refined petroleum. Commercial and fishing ports are located at Ancona, Pesaro, Fano, and Senigallia. The Umbri and the Picentes (Greek colonists for whom part of the region was called Picenum) lived in the region when it was colonized (3d cent. B.C.) by Rome. After the fall of Rome the area was invaded by the Goths. In the 6th cent. the northern section, including four of the cities of the Pentapolis and adjoining territories, came under Byzantine rule; the southern section became a part of the Lombard duchy of SPOLETO. In the 8th cent. the region passed, as part of the donations of Pepin the Short (754) and Charlemagne (774), under the nominal rule of the papacy, but later emperors granted fiefs in the area until the 13th cent. The name *Marche* [boundaries] originated around the 10th cent., because the fiefs of Ancona, Fermo, and Camerino were established at the border of the Holy Roman Empire. Despite the strength of the popes and the emperors, who contested for control of the region, some cities established free communes or were governed by noble families (including the Malatesta, the Varano, and the Montefeltro). From the 13th to the 16th cent. the popes gradually established their rule in the Marche and ended local autonomy. The region was occupied by the French from 1797 to 1815, when it was restored to the papacy. The Marche was united with the kingdom of Sardinia in 1860. There are universities at Macerata and Urbino.

Marchesi, Mathilde (mätēl'də märkā'zē), 1821–1913, German mezzo-soprano whose maiden name was Graumann; pupil of Manuel García. She was known especially as the teacher of such singers as Melba, Eames, and Calvé. Marchesi taught at the conservatories of Cologne and Vienna and in Paris.

Marchfeld (märkh'fĕlt"), plain, NE Austria, NE of Vienna, between the Danube and the Morava (Ger. *March*) rivers, on the border of Czechoslovakia. A strategic approach to Vienna, it was the site of several important battles. In 1260, Ottocar II of Bohemia defeated Bela IV of Hungary on the Marchfeld, and in 1278, Ottocar was defeated and slain by the forces of Rudolf I of the house of Hapsburg. In 1809, Napoleon I was defeated on the Marchfeld at Aspern by Archduke Charles, but was victorious at Wagram.

Marchmont, Patrick Home of Polwarth, 1st **earl of:** see HOME OF POLWARTH, SIR PATRICK.

Marcian (mär'shən), 396–457, Roman emperor of the East (450–57); successor of Theodosius II, whose sister PULCHERIA he married in 450. Orthodox in religious affairs, he convoked (451) the Council of Chalcedon (see CHALCEDON, COUNCIL OF). He curtailed court expenses and endeavored to lighten taxation. His refusal to pay tribute to ATTILA precipitated the Hunnic invasion of the Roman Empire. With him the Theodosian dynasty came to an end in the East. Leo I succeeded him.

Marciano, Rocky (märsēä'nō), 1924–69, American boxer, b. Brockton, Mass. His real name was Rocco Francis Marchegiano. Failing to become a professional baseball player, Marciano turned to boxing and won 27 of 30 amateur bouts before he turned professional in 1947. On his climb to the heavyweight title, Marciano became the second boxer ever to knock out (1951) Joe LOUIS. On Sept. 23, 1952, Marciano won the title by knocking out Joe Walcott in 13 rounds at Philadelphia. Undefeated in 49 professional fights, Marciano successfully defended his title six times before retiring in April, 1956. Noted for his powerful punching ability, he won 43 of his professional bouts by knockouts.

Marcion (mär'shən, mär'sēən), fl. 144, early Christian bishop, founder of the Marcionites, the first great Christian heresy to rival Catholic Christianity. He was born in Sinope (A.D. c.85). He taught in Asia Minor, then went (c.135) to Rome, where he perfected his theory. In 144 he presented his ideas to the Romans, who excommunicated him. He then formed a church of his own, which became widespread and powerful. Marcion taught that there were two gods, proclaiming that the stern, lawgiving, creator God of the Old Testament rivaled the good, merciful God of the New Testament. He considered the creator god the inferior of the two. Marcion also rejected the real incarnation of Christ, claiming that he was a manifestation of the Father. He believed in salvation by faith rather than by gnosis; he rejected the Gnostic emanation theory; and he sought truth in his own truncated version of the New Testament, which included only 10 of the Pauline Epistles and an edited version of St Luke. He completely rejected the Old Testament. He explained in his *Antitheses* that since Jewish law was often opposed to St. Paul, all passages in the Bible that suggested the Jewish foundation of Christianity should be suppressed, even including such statements by St. Paul (see ANTINOMIANISM). Marcionism emphasized asceticism and influenced the developments of MANICHAEISM, by which it was later absorbed. Its effect on orthodox Christianity was to cause a canonical New Testament to be assembled and promulgated and the fulfillment of the Old Law in the New Law to be clearly enounced.

Marcomanni: see GERMANS.

Marconi, Guglielmo, Marchese (gōōlyĕl'mō märkā'zā märkô'nē), 1874–1937, Italian physicist, celebrated for his development of wireless telegraphy (see RADIO). In the field of electromagnetic waves he correlated and improved inventions of H. R. Hertz, Édouard Branly, and other scientists and invented a practical antenna. Experimenting with homemade apparatus, in 1895 he sent long-wave signals over a distance of more than a mile. He patented his system in England (1896) and organized a wireless telegraph company (1897) to develop its commercial applications. In 1899 he transmitted signals across the English Channel and in 1901 received in St. John's, N.F., the first transatlantic wireless signals, sent from his station at Poldhu, Cornwall. After World War I he concentrated on short waves, and c.1930 turned his attention to microwaves. He received, jointly with C. F. Braun, the 1909 Nobel Prize in Physics for work in wireless telegraphy. See biographies by his daughter, D. P. Marconi (1962), David Gunston (1965), and W. P. Jolly (1972).

Marco Polo: see POLO, MARCO.

Marcos, Ferdinand Edralin (fĕrdēnänd' ĕd'rälēn" mär'kōs), 1917–, Philippine political leader. A lawyer, he was elected to congress in 1949. He was (1954, 1960–62) also a member of the Philippine delegation to the UN General Assembly. Formerly a Liberal, he bolted the party in 1964, won the Nationalist party nomination for president, and defeated (1965) Diosdado Macapagal for reelection. As president, Marcos maintained close ties with the United States, pushed land reform, and fought government waste and corruption. Faced with increasing Communist terrorist activities, he launched (Aug., 1969) a major military campaign against Communist groups (see HUKBALAHAP). He also sent national troops to Mindanao, where bands of Moros (Muslims) were attacking Christian settlers. Marcos was reelected in 1969. His second term was marked by increasing civil strife. In Sept., 1972, following a series of bombing incidents in Manila, Marcos charged that a Communist takeover was impending and declared martial law. He imposed strict press and radio censorship and directed the arrest of several thousand persons. Early in 1973 he assumed virtual dictatorial control over the country. See biography by Hartzell Spence (1969).

Marcos de Niza (mär'kōs dā nē'sä), c.1495–1558, missionary explorer in Spanish North America. A Franciscan friar, he served in Peru and Guatemala before going to Mexico. There he headed an expedition (1539) planned by Antonio de MENDOZA, who had been excited by Cabeza de Vaca's stories of rich Indian pueblos. Fray Marcos traveled north at least into SE Arizona and perhaps into New Mexico. Probably duped by ZUNI legends, the friar described with enthusiasm and great inaccuracy the fabulous riches of the Seven Cities of Cibola. They proved to be only fables when Francisco Vásquez de CORONADO led (1540) his soldiers there. Fray Marcos was dismissed as guide and sent back in disgrace.

Marculf (mär'kŭlf"), fl. 7th cent., Frankish monk. He compiled the *Marculfi monachi formulae* [formularies of Marculf], usually dated c.650. Formularies were model forms of official documents for the use of the Church, of the state, and of private individuals, and they were used as manuals in chanceries. Marculf's is one of the best collections and is invaluable to scholars.

Marcus, in the Bible: see MARK, ST.

Marcus Aurelius (Marcus Aelius Aurelius Antoninus) (mär'kəs ôrē'lēəs), 121–180, Roman emperor, named originally Marcus Annius Verus. He was a nephew of Faustina, the wife of ANTONINUS PIUS, who adopted him. Marcus married Antoninus' daughter, another Faustina. From youth he was a diligent student and a zealous Stoic. With his adoptive brother, Lucius Verus, as colleague, Marcus succeeded Antoninus in 161. Verus allowed him to dominate, and from 169 Marcus was sole emperor. His reign was spent repressing rebellions and attacks of Parthians, Germans, and Britons. He won a victory over the Marcomanni (167–168), which was commemorated by the Antonine column (Piazza Colonna, Rome), erected by his son and successor, COMMODUS. Devoted to his duty and humanitarian in his conception of it, Marcus Aurelius was notably good to the poor, lowering their taxes. He was always lenient with political criminals and tried to decrease the brutality at gladiatorial shows. He did, however, persecute the Christians, whom he regarded as natural enemies of the empire. His *Medi-*

tations, available in several translations, expresses with great beauty and humanity a philosophy with a Stoic basis. The virtuous character of Marcus Aurelius is revealed in his letters to his tutor FRONTO. See biography by A. R. Birley (1966); study by J. H. Oliver (1970).

Marcuse, Herbert, 1898–, U.S. political philosopher, b. Berlin. He was educated at the Univ. of Freiburg and with Theodore Adorno and Max Horkheimer founded the Frankfurt Institute of Social Research. A special target of the Nazis because of his Jewish origins and Marxist politics, he emigrated (1934) to the United States and became a naturalized citizen in 1940. Marcuse served with the Office of Strategic Services during World War II and later taught at Harvard, Columbia, and Brandeis before becoming (1965) professor of philosophy at the Univ. of California at San Diego. He is best known for his attempt to synthesize Marxian and Freudian theories into a comprehensive critique of modern industrial society. In *One Dimensional Man* (1964), his most popular book, he argued for a sexual basis to the social and political repression in contemporary America; the book made him a hero of the student New Left radicals and provided a rationale for the student revolts of the 1960s in the United States and Europe. His other works include *Reason and Revolution* (1941), *Eros and Civilization* (1955), *An Essay on Liberation* (1969), and *Counterrevolution and Revolt* (1972). See studies by Alasdair MacIntyre (1970), Paul Mattick (1972), and Jack Woddis (1972).

Marcy, William Learned, 1786–1857, American politician, b. Southbridge, Mass. He settled in Troy, N.Y., where he practiced law and, after serving in the War of 1812, held local offices. A Democrat and a partisan of Martin VAN BUREN, Marcy entered the political group known as the ALBANY REGENCY, of which he soon became a dominant figure. He served as state comptroller (1823–29) and as justice of the state supreme court (1829–31) before he entered (1831) the U.S. Senate. There he made a famous speech supporting the nomination of Van Buren as minister to England: his defense of Van Buren's methods of patronage with the claim that "to the victor belong the spoils of the enemy" supposedly gave rise to the term "spoils system." Marcy served (1833–39) as governor of New York for three terms and was a member (1840–42) of the Mexican Claims Commission. He was Secretary of War (1845–49) under President Polk and conducted that office efficiently during the Mexican War. He had drifted into opposition to Van Buren and headed the HUNKERS, a faction of the New York Democratic party. The peak of Marcy's career was reached when he served as Secretary of State (1853–57) under President Pierce. He handled many delicate problems, including the GADSDEN PURCHASE, negotiations concerning the BLACK WARRIOR affair with Spain, and the trouble arising from the filibustering expedition of William WALKER in Nicaragua. He condemned the OSTEND MANIFESTO, but he managed to maintain a neutral attitude in the rising dispute over slavery. See biography by I. D. Spencer (1959).

Marcy, Mount, 5,344 ft (1,629 m) high, NE N.Y., in the Adirondack Mts.; highest peak in the state. Lake Tear of the Clouds, on its southern slope, is the source of the main headstream of the Hudson River.

Mardan (mərdän'), city (1972 metropolitan area est. pop. 131,000), N Pakistan, on the Kalpani River. It is the site of a military cantonment and of a fort built by the British in 1854.

Mar del Plata (mär thĕl plä'tä), city (1970 pop. 317,444), E central Argentina, on the Atlantic Ocean. It is one of the most popular seaside resorts in South America. Fishing and fish processing are also important industries. The city was founded in the 1850s.

Mardi Gras (mär'dē grä), last day before the fasting season of Lent. It is the French name for SHROVE TUESDAY. Literally translated, the term means "fat Tuesday" and was so called because it represented the last opportunity for merrymaking and excessive indulgence in food and drink before the solemn season of fasting. In the cities of some Roman Catholic countries the custom of holding carnivals for Mardi Gras has continued since the Middle Ages. The carnivals, with spectacular parades, masked balls, mock ceremonials, and street dancing, usually last for a week or more before Mardi Gras itself. Some of the most celebrated are held in New Orleans, Rio de Janeiro, Nice, and Cologne. For a full discussion of this subject, see CARNIVAL.

Mardonius (märdō'nēəs), d. 479 B.C., Persian general; son-in-law of Darius I. Darius sent him (492 B.C.) to retaliate against Eretria and Athens for aiding the Ionians in the PERSIAN WARS, but his fleet was lost in a storm off Mt. Athos, and a Thracian tribe destroyed a large part of his army. He helped XERXES I plan his invasion of Greece. Xerxes returned (480 B.C.) to Persia after his defeat at Salamis and left Mardonius in command in Greece. Mardonius was defeated and killed at Plataea.

Marduk (mär'do͝ok), ancient god of Babylonia and chief god of the city of Babylon. His cult rose to prominence in the reign of Hammurabi, and Marduk became the omniscient king of the pantheon—the creator of mankind and the god of light and life. In his various aspects he was the successor of the Sumerian earth god Enlil.

Maree, Loch (lŏkh mərē'), lake, 13 mi (21 km) long and 1 to 3 mi (1.6–4.8 km) wide, Highland region, NW Scotland. It drains into the Minch through the Ewe River and Loch Ewe. Set in the Highlands, Loch Maree is known for its scenery. Isle Maree, near the north shore, has a primitive burial ground and the ruins of a 7th-century chapel.

Maremma (märām'mä), coastal area in Tuscany, central Italy, along the Tyrrhenian Sea and extending E to the Apennines. A flourishing region in Etruscan and early Roman times, it became marshy and was largely abandoned in the Middle Ages because of malaria. Reclamation was begun (19th cent.) by the grand dukes of Tuscany and was continued in the 20th cent. by the Italian government. There are now wide fertile areas, rich borax mines, and good hunting grounds; cattle and a noted breed of horses are raised. Cities include Piombino (a port) and Grosetto (an inland agricultural center).

Marengo (mărĕng'gō), village, Piedmont, NW Italy, near Alessandria. It was the site of a famous battle (June 14, 1800) between the French under Napoleon Bonaparte and the Austrians under Melas. Melas had almost won when Desaix arrived with fresh troops to bolster the French; Desaix lost his life, but the Austrians were completely defeated and retired to the Mincio.

Marengo, battle of, a major engagement of the FRENCH REVOLUTIONARY WARS, fought on June 14, 1800, at the village of Marengo in Piedmont, N Italy. Determined to throw the Austrians back from positions they had recently regained in Lombardy and Piedmont, Napoleon Bonaparte gathered an army at Dijon and crossed into Italy by way of the Great St. Bernard Pass. A surprise attack by the Austrians under Baron Melas at Marengo caught Bonaparte with his forces scattered. A French defeat seemed imminent until a division that Bonaparte had sent off under General Desaix de Veygoux returned in time to lead a successful counterattack. The French lost about 5,800 men, the Austrians 9,400.

Marenzio, Luca (lo͞o'kä mărĕn'tsēō), 1553–1599, Italian composer, in whose works the Renaissance madrigal reached its peak of development. He served in the households of several cardinals and toward the end of his life attended the court of Sigismund III of Poland. See study by Denis Arnold (1966).

Mareotis (mârēō'tĭs) or **Maryut** (mär'yo͞ot), salt lake, c.95 sq mi (250 sq km) excluding marshes, N Egypt, in the Nile delta. It is separated from the Mediterranean Sea by the narrow isthmus on which Alexandria is situated. There are fisheries and saltworks on the lakeshore.

Mareshah (mârē'shə). **1** Descendant of Caleb. 1 Chron. 2.42. **2** Son of Laadan. 1 Chron. 4.21. These passages may refer to places, not persons. **3** Town, Palestine, c.20 mi (32 km) WSW of Bethlehem. In the Hellenistic period it was called Marissa (the present-day Tel Maresha, Israel), and is the best-known preserved town in Hellenistic Palestine. Excavations have revealed Hellenistic inscriptions, painted tombs in caves, and the finest Mosaic pavement yet found in Palestine. Joshua 15.44; 2 Chron. 11.8; 14.9; 20.37; Micah 1.15. Marisa: 2 Mac. 12.35.

mare's-tail, any plant of the genus *Hippuris,* perennial, submerged aquatic herbs of temperate and frigid regions. Mare's-tails have an erect stem bearing whorls of small leaves, in which they resemble some of the horsetails (which are also sometimes called mare's-tails); however, unlike horsetails, they are flowering plants, with the inconspicuous flowers borne in the leaf axils. Mare's-tails are cultivated in bog gardens. They are classified in the division MAGNOLIOPHYTA, class Magnoliopsida, order Haloragales, family Hippuridaceae.

Margai, Sir Milton (mär'gī), 1895–1964, prime minister of Sierra Leone (1961–64). A prominent doctor, he turned to politics in 1949 and led his country to independence (1961) while serving as chief minister (1954–61). He was knighted in 1959. Milton was followed as prime minister by his brother Sir **Albert Margai,** 1910–, who had held important cabinet posts. A lawyer, Albert had frequently disagreed with his brother. As prime minister he initiated radical policies that finally led to his overthrow in a coup in 1967. He was knighted in 1965.

Margaret I, 1353–1412, queen of Denmark, Norway, and Sweden, daughter of Waldemar IV of Denmark. She was married (1363) to King Haakon VI of Norway, son of MAGNUS VII of Norway and Sweden. At the death (1375) of her father, her son Olaf became king of Denmark under the regency of his parents. As Haakon was occupied in Norway, Margaret actually wielded the power in Denmark. The death (1380) of Haakon made Olaf king of Norway as Olaf V, and Margaret became regent. She continued to press her late husband's claim to Sweden, and she styled her son king of that country. When Olaf died (1387), Margaret continued to rule Denmark and Norway. In 1389, near Falkoping, Sweden, she defeated and captured the Swedish king, Albert of Mecklenburg. Sweden and Norway were prey to disorder. However, Margaret succeeded in persuading the Danish, Norwegian, and Swedish diets to accept her grandnephew, Eric of Pomerania, as king. He was crowned (1397) at Kalmar, and at the same time a tentative act of union of the three realms was drawn up (see KALMAR UNION). Stockholm had held out against Margaret, but surrendered in 1398. In spite of Eric's nominal kingship, Margaret remained the actual ruler of all three kingdoms until her death. She ruled autocratically and energetically, leaving many offices unfilled and reducing others to complete dependence on her authority. Norway and Sweden resented her appointment of Danes to office. The empire built by her was one of the largest of Europe, but it was not lasting.

Margaret II (Margrethe), 1940–, queen of Denmark (1972–). The oldest daughter of King Frederick IX and Queen Ingrid (the daughter of King Gustavus VI of Sweden), Princess Margrethe's right to the throne was established (1953) through a new constitution that allowed female succession. She became a member of the Council of State in 1958. In 1967 she married a Frenchman, Comte Henri de Laborde de Monpezat, and she has borne two sons. Upon the death of her father in 1972, Margrethe became Denmark's first ruling queen since Margaret I, who had reigned in the late 14th and early 15th cent.

Margaret, 1930–, British princess, daughter of King George VI and sister of Queen Elizabeth II. In 1960 she married a commoner, Antony Armstrong-Jones, who was created earl of Snowdon. They have two children: David, Viscount Linley (b. 1961), and Sarah (b. 1964).

Margaret Island: see BUDAPEST, Hungary.

Margaret Maid of Norway, 1283–90, queen of Scotland (1286–90), daughter of Eric II of Norway and granddaughter of ALEXANDER III of Scotland. In 1284 the nobles of Scotland recognized the infant Norwegian princess as heiress presumptive to the Scottish throne, and on Alexander III's death Margaret became queen under a regency. Edward I of England arranged a marriage for her with his eldest son, Edward, and this union was agreed to by the Scots in the Treaty of Birgham (1290), which stipulated that Scotland would remain independent. Margaret, however, died on the voyage from Norway to Scotland. The resultant dispute over the succession gave Edward I an opportunity to try to subjugate Scotland.

Margaret Mary, Saint, 1647–90, French nun of the Visitation Convent of Paray-le-Monial, Saône-et-Loire dept., France. Her family name was Alacoque. Jesus appeared to her in a number of visions, in one of which he bade her to inaugurate devotion to his Sacred Heart. Devotion to the Sacred Heart has become one of the principal cultuses of the Roman Catholic Church, largely as a result of St. Margaret Mary's visions. She was canonized in 1920. Feast: Oct. 17. See biography by Henri Ghéon (1937).

Margaret Maultasch (moul'täsh) [Ger.,=pocket mouth], 1318–69, countess of Tyrol, called the Ugly Duchess, probably because of her unattractive appearance, especially her mouth. When Margaret's father, Henry, count of Tyrol and duke of Carinthia, died in 1335, Holy Roman Emperor Louis IV gave Carinthia to the Hapsburgs and tried to take Tyrol from Margaret and her husband, John Henry, son of John of Luxemburg, king of Bohemia. Her Tyrolean subjects remained loyal, and John of Luxemburg forced the emperor to restore Tyrol to his son. However, the nobles found Luxemburg rule oppressive, and Margaret after 12 years of marriage found John Henry both stupid and impotent. Margaret expelled her husband from her country; her marriage was voided by Louis IV, and in 1342 she married his son Louis, margrave of Brandenburg. The secular annulment offended the Tyrolean nobles, who supported Pope Benedict XII's condemnation of the countess's second marriage and rebelled against Margaret's authority. But Margaret stood firmly by her husband. After his death (1361) and that of their son Meinhard, she abdicated (1363), leaving Tyrol to the Hapsburgs. Legend has painted her as a woman of great power and evil. Her portrait was Sir John Tenniel's model for the "duchess" in his illustrations of *Alice in Wonderland,* and Lion Feuchtwanger utilized her story in his novel *The Ugly Duchess* (tr. 1928).

Margaret of Angoulême: see MARGARET OF NAVARRE.

Margaret of Anjou (ăn'jo͞o, Fr. äNzho͞o'), 1430?–1482, queen consort of King HENRY VI of England, daughter of René of Anjou. Her marriage, which took place in 1445, was negotiated by William de la Pole, 4th earl (later 1st duke) of Suffolk (see under POLE, family). Margaret soon asserted influence at the English court, allying herself with Suffolk and Edmund Beaufort, 2d duke of SOMERSET, in their rivalry with Richard, duke of YORK, heir presumptive to the throne. When the king became insane in 1453, York was made protector, but the birth (1453) of Margaret's son, Edward (which destroyed Richard's chances of succession), and Henry's recovery of his faculties (1454), allowed Margaret to regain the ascendancy. With the clash between the followers of York (the Yorkists) and the supporters of the king (the Lancastrians) at St. Albans (1455), the Wars of the Roses began (see ROSES, WARS OF THE). Margaret was very active in the warfare; for 16 years she fought in defense of her son's claim to the throne. Richard of York was killed (1460), but Richard Neville, earl of WARWICK, and Edward, the new duke of York (later EDWARD IV), took up the Yorkist cause. After the Lancastrian defeat at Towton (1461), Margaret went to Scotland with her son and husband and thence to France, where she secured aid for an abortive invasion (1463) of England. Thereafter she was forced to bide her time until, following the quarrel between Warwick and Edward IV, she made common cause with Warwick to invade England and restore Henry VI to the throne (1470). The next year Edward IV triumphed at Tewkesbury, where Margaret was captured and her son killed. The payment of ransom by Louis XI enabled her to return to France (1476), where she spent her last years in poverty. See biographies by J. J. Bagley (1948) and Philippe Erlanger (tr. 1970); E. F. Jacob, *The Fifteenth Century* (1961); J. H. Dahmus, *Seven Medieval Queens* (1972).

Margaret of Austria, 1480–1530, Hapsburg princess, regent of the Netherlands; daughter of Emperor MAXIMILIAN I. She was betrothed (1483) to the dauphin of France, later King CHARLES VIII, and was transferred to the guardianship of Louis XI of France (see ARRAS, TREATY OF, **2**). After Charles renounced the treaty and married ANNE OF BRITTANY, Margaret was returned (1493) to her father. She was married in 1497 to John of Spain (d. 1497), son of Ferdinand and Isabella, and in 1501 to Philibert of Savoy (d. 1504). Made (1507) regent of the Netherlands and guardian of her nephew Charles (later Holy Roman Emperor CHARLES V), Margaret acted as intermediary between her father and his subjects in the Netherlands, negotiated a treaty of commerce with England favorable to the Flemish cloth interests, and played a role in the formation of the League of Cambrai (1508; see CAMBRAI, LEAGUE OF). After his majority (1515), Charles rebelled against her influence, but soon recognized her as one of his wisest advisers. After 1517 she was again regent intermittently until her death. She negotiated the Ladies' Peace with Louise of Savoy (1529; see CAMBRAI, TREATY OF). See biography by Jane de Iongh (tr. 1953).

Margaret of Navarre (nəvär') or **Margaret of Angoulême** (äNgo͞olām'), 1492–1549, queen consort of Navarre; sister of King Francis I of France. After the death of her first husband she married (1527) Henri d'Albret, king of Navarre; their daughter was JEANNE D'ALBRET. Margaret was an ardent supporter of religious liberty and mild church reform. Her brilliant court at Navarre was frequented by literary men, among them Étienne Dolet, Clément Marot, and François Rabelais. A writer herself, she is best known for the *Heptaméron* (1558), an original collection of 72 stories in the manner of Boccaccio. She also wrote plays and poems. See studies of the *Heptameron* by Jules Gelernt (1966) and Marcel Tetel (1973); biography by E. R. Chamberlin (1974).

Margaret of Parma, 1522–86, Spanish regent of the Netherlands; illegitimate daughter of Holy Roman Emperor Charles V. She was married (1536) to Alessandro de' Medici (d. 1537) and (1538) to Ottavio Farnese, duke of Parma. Appointed Spanish governor of the Netherlands (1559), she was restricted in her authority by a council of state headed by Cardinal GRANVELLE. Charged with the difficult task of carrying out the religious policy of her half brother PHILIP II of Spain, she urged and finally secured the recall of the unpopular prelate. She subsequently showed favor to the national party, but after the outbreak of violence she turned against the popular leaders (Egmont, Hoorn, and William the Silent). In 1567 the duke of ALBA arrived at Brussels to suppress the opposition by force. Margaret warned Philip II against harsh measures and resigned as regent, being unable to agree with Alba. She was a woman of great ability and firmness, and her resignation was generally regretted. Margaret's son was the noted general Alessandro Farnese, duke of Parma and Piacenza.

Margaret of Scotland, Saint, d. 1093, queen consort of MALCOLM III and sister of Edgar Atheling. She was married to Malcolm c.1070. A deeply religious woman, she worked to replace the Celtic practices of the Scottish church with those of Rome. She did this partly by bringing many English priests into Scotland and founding new monasteries. She was generous to the poor and led a life of extraordinary piety. She was canonized in 1250. Feast: June 10 or, in Scotland, Nov. 16.

Margaret of Valois (välwä'), 1553–1615, queen of France and Navarre, daughter of King Henry II of France and of Catherine de' Medici. She was known as Queen Margot. Her wedding (1572) with Henry, Protestant king of Navarre (later Henry IV of France), which was intended to mark the peace between Roman Catholics and Protestants, instead was a prelude to the massacre of Protestants on SAINT BARTHOLOMEW'S DAY. The marriage was one of mutual toleration. Margaret took part in the intrigues of her husband and her brother FRANCIS, duke of Alençon and Anjou. In 1583 her brother King Henry III exiled her from Paris because of her promiscuous conduct. Estranged from both her husband and her brother, she took up arms against them and seized Agen. She was taken prisoner by royal troops (1586) and confined at the castle of Usson, but she soon became mistress of the castle. Although sympathetic with the Catholic LEAGUE, she took little part in the succeeding troubles. She refused to agree to Henry IV's demand for the annulment of their marriage so he could marry his mistress, Gabrielle d'ESTRÉES, although she finally consented (1599) to the annulment after Gabrielle's death. In her retirement at Usson (1587–1605), she maintained a small court, in which men of letters were prominent. Her own memoirs (tr. 1892), correspondence, and other writings show considerable literary ability. She spent her last years in Paris. Margaret plays a conspicuous role in literature and legend. See biographies by H. N. Williams (1907), J. H. Mariéjol (1928, tr. 1929), and Charlotte Haldane (1968).

Margaret Tudor, 1489–1541, queen consort of JAMES IV of Scotland; daughter of Henry VII of England and sister of Henry VIII. Her marriage (1503) to James was accompanied by a treaty of "perpetual peace" between Scotland and England, a peace that was ended when James invaded England in 1513 and was killed at Flodden. Margaret then became regent for her infant son, JAMES V, but her marriage (1514) to Archibald DOUGLAS, 6th earl of Angus, led to the loss of the regency to John STUART, duke of Albany. Albany soon obtained custody of the king, and Margaret fled to England. She returned in 1517, during Albany's absence, and shortly thereafter she became estranged from Angus. From this time she played a considerable part in the shifting Scottish political scene. Her political affiliations varied with her personal interest of the moment and her desire for money and power. Her favor alternated between the French party of the Hamiltons (Arran) and the English party of the Douglas's (Angus). James was proclaimed king in 1524 but was for several years virtually a prisoner of Angus. In 1527, Margaret obtained a divorce from Angus and soon married Henry Stuart, later Lord Methven. James, upon his escape from Angus (1528), joined his mother and Methven, and they were for a time his chief advisers. A plan of Margaret's for a meeting between Henry VIII and her son led James to accuse her of betrayal (1534). They were further estranged by James's refusal to allow her to divorce Methven. Margaret's descendants by James IV and by Angus were united by the marriage of Lord Darnley and Mary Queen of Scots, whose son became James I of England (James VI of Scotland). See Michael Glenne, *King Harry's Sister, Margaret Tudor* (1953).

margarine, manufactured substitute for butter. It consists of a blend of vegetable oils or meat fats (or a combination of both) mixed with milk and salt. It was developed in the late 1860s by the French chemist Hippolyte Mège-Mouries in a contest sponsored by Napoleon III for a butter substitute. Beef fat, known as oleo oil, was chiefly used at first, but later was supplemented by pork and other animal fats and by vegetable oils such as coconut oil, olive oil, and cottonseed oil. At present, most margarines contain only vegetable oils; the margarine produced in the United States is usually made from corn, cottonseed, or soybean oil. The oils, refined, deodorized, and hydrogenated to the desired consistency, are churned or homogenized, usually with cultured skim milk, then chilled and reworked to incorporate salt and remove excess water. Margarine is similar in composition to butter, yields practically the same number of calories, and is easily digestible. It is commonly fortified with vitamin A and vitamin D. In the 1960s a new type of margarine was developed made of polyunsaturated fats (see CHOLESTEROL). Margarine is sometimes called oleomargarine.

Margarita (märgärē'tä), island (1961 est. pop. 75,000), 444 sq mi (1,150 sq km), in the Caribbean Sea off the coast of Venezuela. With several smaller islands it constitutes the Venezuelan state of Nueva Esparta. La Asunción is the capital. Island industries produce canned fish, salt, fishing boats, ceramics, tiles, shoes, and sisal hats. Margarita is also a popular tourist resort. The island was discovered by Columbus in 1498. During colonial times it was an important pearl-fishing center and was used (1561) as a base of operations by the Spanish adventurer Lope de AGUIRRE. Because the people supported Simón BOLÍVAR, Margarita and its neighboring islands were made a state after independence was won from Spain.

Margate (mär'gĭt), municipal borough (1971 pop. 50,145), in the Isle of Thanet, Kent, SE England. It is a seaport with light industries and, since the late 18th cent., a popular resort, especially for Londoners. Of interest is the Church of St. John the Baptist (partly Norman). There is regular steamer service from London in the summer.

Margate City (mär'gāt, -gĭt), resort city (1970 pop. 10,576), Atlantic co., SE N.J., on the Atlantic Ocean; inc. 1897.

Margelan (mərgyĭlän'), city (1970 pop. 95,000), Central Asian USSR, in E Uzbekistan, in the Fergana Valley. It is a center for textile and silk industries.

Marggraf, Andreas Sigismund (ändrā'äs zē'gĭsmo͞ont märk'gräf"), 1709–82, German chemist, a pioneer in analytical chemistry. He proved that alumina, magnesia, and lime are distinct earths, found (1743) an improved method for the commercial preparation of phosphorus, and isolated (1746) zinc. In 1747 he announced his discovery of sugar in the beet. Marggraf directed, from 1754, the chemical laboratory of the Berlin Academy of Sciences.

Margherita: see RUWENZORI, mts.

Margiana: see MERV.

margin requirement, that part of a security's price that a buyer must pay for in cash. The balance of the price is met by the broker, who, in effect, is supplying his client with a loan. Thus, if the margin requirement is set at 70%, $100 worth of securities may be bought with only $70 in cash; the remaining $30 is lent to the purchaser by his broker. The smaller the margin, the greater the inducement to speculation. Thus low margin requirements were considered an important cause of the collapse of the American stock market in 1929. Since then, margin requirements have been regulated; the Securities Exchange Act (1934) gave the Federal Reserve Board that power. The amount, set at 50% in 1937, has been reset at various times according to market conditions; it was put at 100% in 1946, but usually varies between 50% and 90%.

Margrethe. For Danish queens thus named, see MARGARET.

Marguerite. For French women so named, see MARGARET.

marguerite: see DAISY.

Mari (mä'rē), ancient city of Mesopotamia (modern Syria). It is on the middle Euphrates, south of its junction with the Habor (Khabur). The site was discovered by chance in the early 1930s by Arabs digging graves and has subsequently been excavated by the French. The earliest evidence of habitation goes back to the Jemdet Nasr period in the 3d millennium B.C., and Mari remained prosperous throughout the early dynastic period. The temple of Ishtar and other works of art show that Mari was at this time an artistic center with a highly developed style of its own. As the commercial and political focus of W Asia c.1800 B.C., its power extended over 300 mi (480 km) from the frontier of Babylon proper, up the Euphrates, to the border of Syria. The inhabitants were referred to as Amorites in the Old Testament and spoke a language related to the Hebrew of the patriarchs. The archives of the great King Zimri-lim, a contemporary of Hammurabi in the 18th cent. B.C., were discovered in 1937. They contain over 20,000 clay documents, which have made it possible to fix the dates of events in Mesopotamia in the 2d millennium B.C. Also found at Mari is the great palace complex of Zimri-lim consisting of more than 200 rooms and covering 5 acres (2 hectares). Hammurabi conquered Mari c.1700 B.C.; and Babylon then became the center of W Asia. Mari never regained its former status.

Maria I, 1734–1816, queen of Portugal (1777–1816), daughter of Joseph I. She was married (1760) to her uncle, who assumed joint rule with her as Peter III. Neither of them was much interested in affairs of state, but they did immediately bring about the fall of Joseph's powerful minister, Pombal. Many of the intellectuals and personal enemies of Pombal who had been imprisoned or exiled returned, and Portugal experienced a mild intellectual revival. The deaths of her husband (1786) and eldest son, Joseph (1788), and, reputedly at least, fears over the revolution in France helped to unhinge Maria's mind. Her second son (later JOHN VI) assumed power in 1792 (though he did not formally become regent until 1799). In 1807, Maria fled with the rest of the court to Brazil, where she died.

Maria II (Maria da Glória), 1819–53, queen of Portugal (1834–53), daughter of Peter IV (PEDRO I of Brazil). Pedro, having succeeded to the Portuguese throne on the death (1826) of his father, John VI, granted a constitutional charter to the Portuguese and then abdicated in favor of Maria. In order to quiet the claims of her uncle, Dom MIGUEL, it was arranged that Maria be betrothed to him and placed under his regency. Miguel promised to abide by Pedro's charter, but in 1828, before Maria had arrived in Europe from Brazil, he convened a Cortes, procured an offer of the throne, and set out to rule in absolutist fashion. Maria's father, having abdicated the Brazilian throne, recruited an army from the liberal opponents of Miguel; he also had the assistance of the English. The armed forces gathered and sailed from the Azores to Oporto in 1832. The subsequent fighting in the so-called Miguelist Wars was severe. Miguel capitulated in 1834 after the English had defeated his fleet. Maria's reign was torn by dissension, revolutions, and counterrevolutions. Some progress was made, however, in the building of roads, the first railroad, and schools. Maria married (1836) Ferdinand of Saxe-Coburg-Gotha (FERDINAND II of Portugal). She was succeeded by her son Peter V.

maria: see MOON.

Maria Christina, (märē'ä krēstē'nä), 1806–78, queen of Spain, daughter of Francis I of the Two Sicilies. The fourth wife of FERDINAND VII, she persuaded him to confirm (1833) the original revocation (1789) of the SALIC LAW to allow their daughter Isabella to succeed him. At the king's death (1833) Maria Christina became regent for ISABELLA II. In the Carlist Wars (see CARLISTS) that this succession provoked, she was aided by the liberals, but the frequent changes in the constitution alienated their support. The opposition of ESPARTERO forced her to resign the regency, and she went to France (1840). She returned after Espartero's overthrow (1843) and regained influence. She had to yield to Espartero again in 1854 but remained a powerful figure to the end of Isabella's turbulent reign in 1868.

Maria Christina, 1858–1929, queen of Spain, consort of Alfonso XII. An Austrian archduchess, she was married to Alfonso in 1879. After his death, she was regent (1886–1902) for his posthumous son, Alfonso XIII. During her regency little was done to remedy the social ills of Spain, and the last Spanish possessions in America were lost in the SPANISH-AMERICAN WAR.

María de Molina (dā mōlē'nä), d. 1321, queen of Castile, consort of Sancho IV. As regent (1295–1301) for her son, Ferdinand IV, she defended his throne against several pretenders, who were at various times supported by France, Aragón, Portugal, Navarre, and Granada. After Ferdinand's death (1312), she acted as a guardian to her grandson Alfonso XI, while the regency was contested among his other relatives.

Maria Feodorovna (märē'ä fyô'dərəvnə), 1847–1928, czarina of Russia, consort of Alexander III and mother of Nicholas II. Originally named Dagmar, she was the daughter of Christian IX of Denmark and the sister of Queen Alexandra of Great Britain. She devoted herself to philanthropic and educational activities, especially the Red Cross. Detained (1917) in the Crimea by the revolutionaries, she was freed by German forces and immigrated to England and then to Denmark, where she spent her last years. Her letters to Nicholas II are published in *The Secret Letters of the Last Tsar* (tr. 1938). See biography by E. E. P. Tisdall (1958).

María Luisa (lo͞oē'sä), 1751–1819, queen of Spain, daughter of Duke Philip of Parma, consort of King CHARLES IV. Dissolute and domineering, she exerted, with her lover GODOY, the real power in the government, thus contributing to the downfall of Spain at the hands of Napoleon I. She was present at the meeting in Bayonne at which Napoleon forced her husband and her son, FERDINAND VII, to abdicate. She shared her husband's confinement and exile. Goya, her favorite, painted several portraits of her.

Mariamne (mārēăm'nē). **1** Second of Herod the Great's 10 wives. She was a descendant of the Maccabees. Herod loved her greatly, but he had her murdered after she was falsely accused by her sister Salome. **2** Another wife of Herod. She was renowned for her beauty. Herod divorced her because she took part in a plot against him.

Mariana, Juan de (hwän dā märyä'nä), 1536?–1623?, Spanish historian and political philosopher, a Jesuit. He taught in Rome and in Paris before going to Toledo, where he wrote his two great works. His *Historiae de rebus Hispaniae* [history of Spain], a notable achievement in history, presented a unified and coordinated history rather than a simple chronicle. Although sometimes credulous, he was to some extent critical of sources; his ability to create a smooth-flowing narrative was remarkable. His *De rege et regis institutione* [on the king and the institution of kingship] achieved particular note because it condoned tyrannicide. Mariana argued that when the state violated the welfare of the people, a desperate remedy was justifiable. He extolled the natural simplicity of the communal life of a lost golden age. His humanitarian ideals were widely influential; he is supposed to have had a great effect on Rousseau. His violent attack on debasement of the coinage, in which he expressed arguments later universally accepted, caused him to be imprisoned for a time. See study by Guenter Lewy (1960).

Marianao (märyänä'ō), city (1970 pop. 368,747), La Habana prov., W Cuba, a suburb of Havana. Marianao encloses the military base of Ciudad Columbia. Chemicals, beer, and textiles are produced in the city, which also has a fine beach. Founded in 1719 by Dominican and Augustinian monks, the city was destroyed by fire in 1726. It was rebuilt in 1765 as Quemados de Marianao and grew with the sugar boom in the 19th cent.

Marianas Islands (mārēă'nās), island group (1970 pop. 9,640), W Pacific, comprising one of the six districts of the U.S. Trust Territory of the PACIFIC ISLANDS and the island of GUAM (1970 pop. 84,996). The Marianas lie E of the Philippines and S of Japan and extend 350 mi (563 km) from north to south. The most important islands are Guam, SAIPAN, and TINIAN. The northern islands are composed of volcanic rock, the southern islands of madrepore limestone covering a volcanic base. All the islands are mountainous, with the highest peak (3,166 ft/965 m) on Agrihan. Sugarcane, coffee, and coconuts are the chief products. There are deposits of phosphate, sulfur, and manganese ore. Most of the inhabitants are Japanese, but there are some Micronesians and Chamorros (mixed Spanish, Filipino, and Micronesian descent). The islands were discovered in 1521 by Ferdinand MAGELLAN, who named them the Ladrones Islands (Thieves Islands). They were renamed the Marianas by Spanish Jesuits who arrived in 1668. Nominally a possession of Spain until 1898, the islands were sold to Germany in 1899, except for Guam, which was ceded to the United States. The islands belonging to Germany were seized by Japan in 1914 and were mandated to Japan by the League of Nations in 1920. U.S. forces occupied the Marianas (1944) during World War II, and in 1947 the group (exclusive of Guam) was included in the U.S. Trust Territory of the Pacific Islands. The Marianas (sometimes called the Marianne Islands) form an important strategic link in the U.S. defense network in the Pacific.

Marianas trench, Marianas trough, or **Marianas deep,** elongated depression on the floor of the Pacific Ocean, 210 mi (338 km) SW of Guam. It is the deepest (36,198 ft/11,033 m) known depression on the earth's surface. The trench was first sounded (1959) by Soviet scientists; its bottom was reached (1960) by two men in a U.S. navy bathyscaphe.

Marianne Islands: see MARIANAS ISLANDS.

Mariánské Lázně (mär'yänskä läz'nyĕ), Ger. *Marienbad,* town (1970 pop. 13,402), W Czechoslovakia, in Bohemia. It is a world-famous spa, with many curative mineral springs and baths, situated on the grounds of a 12th-century abbey. Mariánské Lázně has been the site of numerous international congresses.

Marianus Scotus (mărēā'nəs skō'təs), 1028–c.1082, Irish monk and chronicler, whose Gaelic name was Mael-brigte. He left Ireland in 1056 and lived on the Continent until his death. His chronicle of the world from the creation until 1082 was much used in the Middle Ages, notably by Florence of Worcester and Sigebert of Gembloux.

Marianus Scotus, d. 1088, Irish churchman, whose Gaelic name was Muiredach. He left Ireland in 1067 on a pilgrimage to Rome but settled permanently at Regensburg (Ratisbon), Germany, where he became abbot. He was famous for his calligraphic copies of parts of the Bible, which were usually accompanied by his commentaries.

Marías, Julián (ho͞olyän' märē'äs), 1914–, Spanish philosopher and essayist, b. Valladolid. He was a disciple of José ORTEGA Y GASSET, with whom he founded the Institute of Humanities. His best-known works include *Historia de la filosofía* (1941; tr. *History of Philosophy,* 1967), *Miguel de Unamuno* (1943, tr. 1966), *El método histórico de las generaciones* (1949; tr. *Generations: An Historical Method,* 1970), *Introducción a la filosofía* (1956; tr. *Reason and Life: The Introduction to Philosophy,* 1956), and *Ortega, circunstancia y vocación* (1960; tr. *José Ortega y Gasset, Circumstance and Vocation,* 1970), and *Philosophy as Dramatic Theory* (tr. 1970).

Marias (mərī'əz), river, c.210 mi (340 km) long, rising in several branches in NW Montana near the Continental Divide and flowing SE to the Missouri River near Fort Benton. It receives the Teton River. The Marias is used for irrigation. Tiber Dam (completed 1956), located in the lower course, is part of the Missouri River basin project.

Mariátegui, José Carlos (hōsā' kär'lōs märēä'tāgē), 1895–1930, Peruvian writer and political leader. Of a poor family, he was a tubercular from childhood but rose to prominence as a self-taught journalist. He studied in Europe and became a confirmed Marxist. Returning to Peru he joined other radicals, such as Víctor Raúl HAYA DE LA TORRE, in political agitation during the 1920s, and when Haya de la Torre founded the APRA party (see APRA) in exile, Mariátegui became its leading spokesman in Peru. He broke with the Apristas, as the members of the APRA party were known, in 1928. His *Siete ensayos de interpretación de la realidad Peruana* [seven essays in interpretation of Peruvian reality], published in 1928, is a masterpiece of social analysis. See J. M. Baines, *Revolution in Peru* (1972).

Maria Theresa, (mərē'ə tərā'zə), 1717–80, Austrian archduchess, queen of Bohemia and Hungary (1740–80), consort of Holy Roman Emperor FRANCIS I and dowager empress after the accession (1765) of her son, Joseph II. Her father, Holy Roman Emperor CHARLES VI, altered the Hapsburg family law by the PRAGMATIC SANCTION of 1713 so that she might succeed to the Hapsburg lands. She was recognized by her subjects in the Austrian duchies and the Austrian Netherlands, in Bohemia, and in Hungary. The chief European powers had subscribed to the Pragmatic Sanction in Charles's lifetime, but when Maria Theresa acceded she was immediately confronted with a European coalition against her, and FREDERICK II of Prussia brazenly seized SILESIA. In the War of the AUSTRIAN SUCCESSION (1740–48), Maria Theresa lost most of Silesia to Prussia but secured (1745) in exchange the imperial election for her husband. Her warm personality and strength of will won her the loyalty of her subjects and troops, to whom she appealed directly in moments of crisis. Her husband was given a share in governing her hereditary lands, but the actual government was in the hands of Maria Theresa, assisted by her able chancellor, KAUNITZ. After the Treaty of AIX-LA-CHAPELLE (1748), Kaunitz accomplished a diplomatic revolution in concluding an alliance with France, the traditional enemy. The SEVEN YEARS WAR (1756–63) exhausted the strength of Austria. Maria Theresa lost no territory, but leadership among German states had definitely passed to

Prussia. In 1772, Maria Theresa shared with Prussia and Russia in the first partition of Poland (see POLAND, PARTITIONS OF). Partly under the influence of her son, Joseph II (with whom she jointly ruled her dominions after 1765), Maria Theresa carried out a series of agrarian reforms and centralized the administration of her lands. Unlike her son she followed no particular plan and was, on the whole, conservative. A devout Roman Catholic, her court was the most moral in Europe. During her reign Vienna increased its reputation as a center of the arts and of music. Among her 16 children were emperors Joseph II and Leopold II, Marie Caroline of Naples, and Marie Antoinette of France. Her authoritative biographer is Alfred von Arneth. See biographies by R. Pick (1966) and E. Crankshaw (1970); studies by G. P. Gooch (1965) and C. A. Macartney (1969).

Mari Autonomous Soviet Socialist Republic (mä'rē), autonomous republic (1970 pop. 685,000), c.8,900 sq mi (23,100 sq km), E central European USSR, in the middle Volga valley. Yoshkar-Ola is the capital. The region is a rolling plain, heavily forested with fir and pine. There is an extensive lumbering industry, and the republic produces paper and pulp and varied wood products. In the nonforested agricultural areas, grain and flax are grown, and there is dairy farming and livestock raising. The population is mainly Mari and Russian, with Chuvash, Tatar, and Udmurt minorities. In the 18th cent. the Mari were under Khazar rule. Ruled by the Eastern Bulgars from the 9th to the 12th cent., the Mari were then conquered (1236) by the Golden Horde. The Russians under Ivan IV assumed control in 1552. The autonomous republic was organized in 1936. Previously called Cheremiss, the Mari speak a Finno-Ugric language and are known for their wood and stone carving and embroidery.

Maria Wörth (märē'ä vört), village, Carinthia prov., S Austria. It is a popular resort on the south shore of the Wörther See, a small lake. It is also a place of pilgrimage with two 12th-century churches.

Mariazell (märē''ätsĕl'), town, Styria prov., E central Austria. It is a winter and summer resort. Chiefly noted as a place of pilgrimage, it is famous for its 12th-century wood carving of the Virgin and Child.

Marib (mä'rĭb), ancient city, Yemen, SW Arabia, 140 mi (225 km) inland at an altitude of 3,900 ft (1,190 m). It was one of the chief cities, perhaps the capital, of SHEBA. The site was visited by Joseph Halévy, who found numerous inscriptions and ruins, including the famous dam that was built in the 6th cent. B.C. and was one of the great engineering feats of antiquity. The dam collapsed in the 6th cent. A.D., flooding the countryside.

Maribo (mä'rēbō), city (1970 com. pop. 12,294), Storstrøm co., SE Denmark, on Lake Søndersø. It is a commercial and industrial center with sugar refineries. The playwright Kaj Munk (1898–1944) was born there.

Maribor (mä'rĭbôr), Ger. *Marburg,* city (1971 pop. 172,155), NW Yugoslavia, in Slovenia, on the Drava River. One of Yugoslavia's leading manufacturing cities, it has industries that produce machinery, armaments, automobiles, airplanes, chemicals, and textiles. Known as early as the 12th cent., it was an important city of Styria until its transfer (1919) to Yugoslavia. The city has a 12th-century Gothic cathedral, a 15th-century castle, and a fine Renaissance town hall.

Maricopa Indians (mărĭkō'pə, mâr-), North American Indians whose language belongs to the Yuman branch of the Hokan-Siouan linguistic stock (see AMERICAN INDIAN LANGUAGES). At some time in the past the Maricopa, under pressure from the Yuma, moved up the Gila River in Arizona from the Colorado River. In 1775 they lived near the mouth of the Hassayampa River in S Arizona. They then numbered some 3,000. The Maricopa were sedentary farmers who lived in somewhat permanent villages. In alliance with the Pima, they severely defeated the Yuma in 1857. Now numbering less than 200, the Maricopa live with the Pima on the Gila River and the Salt River reservations in Arizona. See Leslie Spier, *Yuman Tribes of the Gila River* (1933, repr. 1970); P. H. Ezell, *The Maricopas* (1963).

Marie (mərē'), 1875–1938, queen of Rumania, consort of FERDINAND I. The daughter of Alfred, duke of Edinburgh and of Saxe-Coburg-Gotha, she was the granddaughter of Czar Alexander II of Russia and of Queen Victoria of England. Marie was instrumental in bringing Rumania into the Allied camp in World War I, and she followed the Rumanian armies as a Red Cross nurse. Her writings, in English, include novels and collections of fairy tales, as well as her autobiographies, *The Story of My Life* (1934) and *Ordeal* (1935).

Marie, Alexandre Thomas (älĕksäN'drə tômä' märē'), 1795–1870, French minister of public works. He served in the revolutionary provisional government of 1848 and in the executive committee that replaced it (April, 1848). Supposedly to fulfill the plan of Louis BLANC for social workshops, Marie opened national workshops, but they proved impracticable and costly. It is thought that he deliberately discredited the plan. The abandonment of the program led to the workers' rebellion of the JUNE DAYS of 1848. After 1848, Marie actively opposed Louis Napoleon (later Napoleon III).

Marie Antoinette (ăntwənĕt', äNtwänĕt'), 1755–93, queen of France, wife of King LOUIS XVI and daughter of Austrian Archduchess Maria Theresa and Holy Roman Emperor Francis I. She was married in 1770 to the dauphin, who became king in 1774. Her marriage had been made to strengthen France's alliance with its longtime enemy, Austria. The union, however, was not altogether popular, and Marie Antoinette's actions only increased hostility toward her. She constantly sought the advice of the Austrian ambassador and attempted to influence French foreign policy in favor of Austria. Unhappy in her marriage, which remained unconsummated for seven years, she surrounded herself with a dissolute clique, led by Yolande de POLIGNAC and Marie Thérèse de LAMBALLE, and threw herself into a life of pleasure and careless extravagance. Her notorious reputation led to scandals such as the Affair of the DIAMOND NECKLACE and to rumors concerning her relations with officers of the guard and with Hans Axel FERSEN. The famous solution to the bread famine, "Let them eat cake," is unjustly attributed to the queen, but it is certain that Marie Antoinette lacked understanding of economic problems. With the birth of her first son, her life became more sedate. Although she had contributed to the downfall of A. R. J. Turgot in 1776 and was hostile to Jacques Necker, her influence on the king's decisions during the first two years of the French Revolution (1789–91) has been exaggerated. She was brought with the king from Versailles to Paris (Oct., 1789) and was seized at Varennes when the royal family attempted to escape (1791). Despite her hatred of the Revolution, the apathy of the king forced her to conduct negotiations first with the comte de MIRABEAU, then with Antoine BARNAVE. Simultaneously, however, she secretly urged Austrian intervention; after war was declared, she fully identified the cause of the Bourbon dynasty with that of France. After the storming of the Tuileries palace (Aug., 1792), she and her husband were removed to the Temple and accused of treason. The king was executed in Jan., 1793. Marie Antoinette's son was taken from her (see LOUIS XVII), and she was transferred to the Conciergerie. Known derisively as the "Widow Capet," she was tried before the Revolutionary Tribunal (Oct. 14–15, 1793), found guilty, and guillotined (Oct. 16). In her last misfortunes she displayed steadfastness, courage, and dignity. Her portraits, notably by Élisabeth VIGÉE-LEBRUN, are well known. Among Marie Antoinette's published correspondence see *Lettres de Marie Antoinette* (2 vol., 1895–96) and O. G. von Heidenstam, ed., *The Letters of Marie Antoinette, Fersen, and Barnave* (1913, tr. 1926). See also biographies by Stefan Zweig (tr. 1933), André Castelot (tr., 1957), D. M. Mayer (1969), and Philippe Huisman (tr. 1971).

Marie Byrd Land, area of W ANTARCTICA, E of the Ross Shelf Ice and the Ross Sea and S of the Amundsen Sea; the Ford Ranges lie in the northwest part. The region was discovered and claimed for the United States by Richard E. Byrd in 1929. Much of this region was explored during the second Byrd expedition (1933–35) and the U.S. Antarctic Service Expedition (1939–41).

Marie Caroline, 1752–1814, queen of Naples, consort of Ferdinand IV (later FERDINAND I of the Two Sicilies), daughter of Holy Roman Emperor Francis I and Maria Theresa, and sister of Queen Marie Antoinette of France. She was married to Ferdinand, son of Charles III of Spain, in 1768. Strongly influenced by her favorites, Sir John ACTON and Emma, Lady HAMILTON, she sought to eliminate Spanish influence in the kingdom and to establish close ties with Austria and England. Her court was a center of scandal and intrigue. Late in 1798 she and Ferdinand were forced to flee Naples with the advent of the short-lived Parthenopean Republic set up by the French Revolutionary army. The couple was again expelled from Naples in 1806 by Napoleon; they took up residence in Sicily. Marie was subsequently banished because of her intrigues, and she died at Vienna.

Marie de France (də fräNs), fl. 1155–90, poet. Born in France, she spent her adult life in England in aristocratic circles and wrote in Anglo-Norman. She is best known for some dozen lais; several are of Celtic origin, and some are Arthurian. See *Lais,* ed. by Alfred Ewert (1944). See translations by J. L. Weston (1900), Edith Rickert (1901), and Eugene Mason (1911); study by E. J. Mickel, Jr. (1974).

Marie de l'Incarnation (də lăNkärnäsyôN'), 1599–1672, French missionary. Her name was originally Marie Guyard. She was married in her youth and bore a son; when her son was 12 years old, her husband being dead, she entered the Ursuline order. At her entreaty, the authorities gave her and another nun permission to go to New France to work among the Indians. In 1639 she arrived in Quebec, where she was soon head of an Ursuline convent. She administered her house with great success and worked among the Indians with notable results. Her letters are valuable sources of French Canadian history. She wrote devotional works and catechisms, not only in French but in Indian languages. See Agnes Repplier, *Mère Marie of the Ursulines* (1931).

Marie de' Medici (mĕd'ĭchē), 1573–1642, queen of France, second wife of King Henry IV and daughter of Francesco de' Medici, grand duke of Tuscany. She was married to Henry in 1600. After his assassination (1610) she became regent for her son Louis XIII. She reversed the policies set by her husband; the duc de SULLY was replaced by her favorite, Concini, and the carefully hoarded treasury surplus was dissipated in court extravagance and in pensions to the discontented nobles. In foreign affairs she abandoned the traditional anti-Hapsburg policy. A new Franco-Spanish alliance was formed by the marriage of Louis to Anne of Austria, daughter of King Philip III of Spain, and was further cemented by the marriage of the French princess Elizabeth to the future Philip IV of Spain. Having remained in power for three years beyond the king's majority, Marie was forced into exile after the murder of Concini (1617). In 1619 her partisans rose in revolt, but she was reconciled to her son in 1622. After the rise to power of her former favorite, Cardinal RICHELIEU, she attempted (1630) to regain influence by urging the king to dismiss his minister of state; instead Louis forced his mother into a new exile at Compiègne, whence she fled to the Netherlands (1631), never to return to France. She was the mother of Henrietta Maria, queen of Charles I of England. The marriage of Marie and Henry IV was the subject of a celebrated series of paintings by Peter Paul Rubens. See biographies by Julia Pardoe (3 vol., 1852), A. P. Lord (1903), and Louis Batiffol (1906; tr. 1908, repr. 1970).

Marie Galante: see GUADELOUPE.

Mariehamn: see MAARIANHAMINA, Finland.

Marie Leszczynska (lĕshchĭn'skə), 1703–68, queen of France, wife of Louis XV, and daughter of STANISLAUS I of Poland. Married in 1725, she bore 10 children and was the grandmother of Louis XVI. Of retiring disposition, she made no attempt to rival the king's mistresses. Her marriage facilitated French involvement in the War of the Polish Succession.

Marie Louise, 1791–1847, empress of the French (1810–15) as consort of NAPOLEON I and duchess of Parma, Piacenza, and Guastalla (1816–47), daughter of Holy Roman Emperor Francis II (later Emperor of Austria as Francis I.) She was married (1810) to Napoleon I and was the mother of NAPOLEON II. When Napoleon I was defeated (1814), she fled to Vienna. Her duchies were awarded to her at the Congress of Vienna; she ruled them ineptly from Parma, with the assistance of her lover, Count Adam Adalbert von Neipperg, whom she married morganatically in 1821. After his death (1829) she married the comte de Bombelles. See biographies by J. A. Mahan (1931) and Patrick Turnbull (1971).

Marienbad: see MARIANSKÉ LÁZNĚ.

Marienburg: see MALBORK, Poland.

Mariestad (märē''əstäd'), town (1970 pop. 9,801), capital of Skaraborg co., S Sweden, on Lake Vänern. It is a commercial and industrial center. Manufactures include paper, textiles, and furniture. Chartered in 1583, Mariestad was rebuilt (1895) after a destructive fire.

Marietta (mârēĕt'ə). **1** City (1970 pop. 27,216), seat of Cobb co., NW Ga.; inc. 1834. Aircraft are manufactured there. A summer resort area, Marietta is at the foot of Kennesaw Mt. and was the scene of a Union defeat in the Civil War (see ATLANTA CAMPAIGN). Kennesaw Mountain National Battlefield Park (see NATIONAL PARKS AND MONUMENTS, table) marks the site. Many Civil War dead are buried in the city. A junior college and a division of the Georgia Institute of Technology are there, and Dobbins Air Force Base is nearby. **2** City (1970 pop. 16,861), seat of Washington co., SE Ohio, at the confluence of the Muskingum and Ohio rivers; inc. 1801. It is a trading center for an agricultural and dairying area. Among the city's varied manufactures are office equipment, alloys, plastics, ventilators, and paints. It was the first planned, permanent settlement in Ohio and the Northwest Territory. Founded in 1788 by the Ohio Company of Associates under Manasseh Cutler and Rufus Putnam, among mound builders' earthworks, it was named for Marie Antoinette and grew as a shipbuilding and shipping center for a farm area. The first houses were in a stockaded enclosure called Campus Martius. The city is the seat of Marietta College. General Putnam's house is preserved in the Campus Martius Memorial State Museum. Other points of interest are the Ohio River Museum (est. 1972); and Mound Cemetery, named for a large Indian mound within its enclosure, where numerous Revolutionary officers are buried.

Mariette, Auguste Édouard (ōgüst' ādwär' märyĕt'), 1821–81, French Egyptologist. On a visit (1850–54) to Egypt to collect Coptic manuscripts for the Louvre, he excavated (1851) the ruins of the Serapeum at Memphis. He was (1854–58) curator of the Egyptian department at the Louvre and in 1858 returned to Egypt as director of excavations, receiving the title of bey and later of pasha. Mariette founded (1863) at Bulak (now part of Cairo) the Egyptian national museum. He suggested the story for the libretto of the opera *Aïda*.

Marignano, battle of (märēnyä'nō), 1515, in the Italian Wars, fought by Francis I of France and his Venetian allies against the Swiss Confederates, who then controlled the duchy of Milan. It was fought (Sept. 13–14) near the town of Marignano (now Melegnano), 10 mi (16.1 km) SE of Milan. One of the bloodiest engagements in the ITALIAN WARS, its outcome was decided by the timely arrival of Venetian cavalry. The Swiss retreated in good order but evacuated Milan, which was thus surrendered by their protégé, Massimiliano SFORZA. Their military ambitions broken, the Swiss made peace with Francis and negotiated (1516) the "perpetual alliance" (see SWITZERLAND). Described as a "battle of giants," Marignano established the superiority of artillery and cavalry over the reputedly invincible Swiss infantry tactics.

marigold, any plant of the genus *Tagetes* of the family Compositae (COMPOSITE family), mostly Central and South American herbs cultivated elsewhere as garden flowers. The two common species of marigold, both annuals, are distinguished as African, or Aztec (*T. erecta*), and French (*T. patula*) although both are native to Mexico and Guatemala. The African commonly has large yellow or orange flower heads and the strong-scented foliage typical of the genus, but an odorless kind has been developed; the French has smaller flower heads, single or double, usually two tones of yellow or orange and red. Other plants sharing the name marigold include MARSH MARIGOLD, BUR MARIGOLD, and pot marigold (see CALENDULA). Marigolds are classified in the division MAGNOLIOPHYTA, class Magnoliopsida, order Asterales, family Compositae.

marihuana: see MARIJUANA.

Mariinsk System: see VOLGA-BALTIC WATERWAY.

marijuana or **marihuana,** drug obtained from the flowering tops, stems, and leaves of the hemp plant, *Cannabis sativa* (see HEMP). It has been used as an agent for achieving euphoria since ancient times; it was described in a Chinese medical compendium alleged to date from 2737 B.C. Its use spread from China to India and then to N Africa and reached Europe at least as early as A.D. 500. A major crop in colonial North America, marijuana was grown as a source of fiber. It was extensively cultivated during World War II, when Asian sources of hemp were cut off. It was probably introduced as an intoxicant into the United States in the early 20th cent. by Mexican laborers and Latin American seamen. In the United States, where it is usually smoked, it is also called weed, grass, stuff, pot, or tea. The plant grows as a common weed in many parts of the world, and drug preparations vary widely in potency according to climate, cultivation, and method of preparation. The resin found on flower clusters and top leaves of the female plant is the most potent drug source and is used to prepare HASHISH, the highest grade of marijuana. The primary active component is tetrahydrocannabinol, although other cannabinol derivatives are also thought to be intoxicating. Marijuana is chemically and pharmacologically unlike other hallucinogens, or PSYCHOTOMIMETIC DRUGS, such as LYSERGIC ACID DIETHYLAMIDE, mescaline, and psilocybin. Although it produces some of the same effects, such as heightened sensitivity to colors, shapes, music, and other stimuli and distortion of the sense of time, it is much less potent, does not alter perception as drastically, and does not lead to increasing tolerance of drug dosage. A campaign conducted in the 1930s by the U.S. Federal Bureau of Narcotics (now the Bureau of Narcotics and Dangerous Drugs) sought to portray marijuana as a powerful, addicting substance that would lead users into narcotics addiction, but current evidence indicates that these assertions are untrue. Much of the prevailing public apprehension about marijuana may stem from the drug's effect of inducing introspection and bodily passivity, which are antipathetic to a culture that values aggressiveness, achievement, and activity. Although the possibility that marijuana, like other perception-altering drugs, produces psychosis has not been entirely disproved, the drug is probably most dangerous to persons with already existing psychotic tendencies; most evidence indicates that marijuana does not induce mental or physical deterioration. The drug has been used experimentally to help withdraw addicts from NARCOTICS. With the increase in the number of middle class users, there has been a growing acceptance of the view that marijuana should not be considered in the same class as narcotics and that U.S. marijuana laws should be relaxed. Opponents arguing against easing marijuana laws assert that it is an intoxicant less controllable than alcohol, that our drug-using society does not need another widely used intoxicant, and that the United States should not act to weaken United Nations policies, which are opposed to the use of marijuana. See John Kaplan, *Marijuana—the New Prohibition* (1970); Lester Grinspoon, *Marihuana Reconsidered* (1971); J. S. Hochman, *Marijuana and Social Evolution* (1972).

marimba: see XYLOPHONE.

Marin, John (măr'ĭn), 1870–1953, American landscape painter, b. Rutherford, N.J. After a year at Stevens Institute of Technology, he worked for four years as an architectural draftsman. At 28 he entered the Pennsylvania Academy of the Fine Arts and in 1905 went abroad, where he painted and etched and lived precariously for several years. In 1909 his work was exhibited at Stieglitz's gallery in New York City. He was quickly recognized as a leading American watercolorist. Marin painted scenes of New York, Taos, and particularly Maine seascapes, which he rendered with a few powerful zigzag strokes, often employing angular abstract forms to enclose the composition. His color ranged from subtle, delicate tones to bold, eerie effects. Marin's work in oil and watercolor is in more than 40 public collections in the United States. See his letters edited by H. J. Seligman (1931, repr. 1970); study by Helm MacKinley (1948, repr. 1970).

Marinduque (märēndōō'kä), island, 346 sq mi (896 sq km), the Philippines, between Mindoro and S Luzon. The island is a major iron-producing area. There is also a lumbering industry, and resins are produced. Subsistence farming is carried on.

marine biology, study of ocean plants and animals and their ecological relationships. Marine organisms may be classified (according to their mode of life) as nektonic, planktonic, or benthic. Nektonic animals are those that can swim and migrate freely, e.g., adult fishes, whales, and squid. Planktonic organisms, usually very small or microscopic, have little or no power of locomotion and merely drift or float in the water. Benthic plants or animals live on the sea bottom and include sessile forms (e.g., sponges, oysters, and corals), creeping organisms (e.g., crabs and snails), and burrowing animals (e.g., many clams and worms). The distribution of organisms depends on the chemical and physical properties of seawater (temperature, salinity, and dissolved nutrients), on ocean currents (which carry oxygen to subsurface waters and serve to disperse nutrients, wastes, spores, eggs, larvae, and plankton), and on penetration of light. Plants, the ultimate source of food, exist only in the photic zone (to a depth of about 300 ft/90 m), where there is sufficient light for photosynthesis. Since only about 2% of the ocean floor lies in the photic zone, benthic plants are far less abundant than plant plankton, which is distributed in a shallow oceanwide area. Among the most numerous plant forms (phytoplankton) are the diatoms and dinoflagellates. Planktonic animals (zooplankton) include such protozoans as the Foraminifera and Radiolaria; they are found at all depths but are more numerous near the surface, especially at night. Bacteria are abundant in upper waters and in bottom deposits. The scientific study of marine biology dates from the early 19th cent.; important marine biological laboratories include those at Naples; at Plymouth and Millport in England; and at Woods Hole, Mass., La Jolla, Calif., and Coral Gables, Fla., in the United States. The science has contributed to the efficient exploitation of fisheries and to the understanding of problems in the evolution and growth of organisms. See also OCEANOGRAPHY. See Rachel Carson, *The Sea Around Us* (rev. ed. 1961); A. C. Hardy, *The Open Sea* (2 vol., 1956, repr. 1970); Otto Kinne, *Marine Ecology* (1970); W. D. Russell-Hunter, *Aquatic Productivity* (1970).

Marine Corps, United States: see MARINES.

marine engine, machine for the propulsion of watercraft. The earliest marine power plants, reciprocating steam engines, were used almost exclusively until the early 1900s. In later ship construction these were largely replaced by the steam turbine and the INTERNAL-COMBUSTION ENGINE (see also DIESEL ENGINE). For some applications, notably ferries, electric motors are used to allow greater maneuverability. Steam turbines having 1,000 shaft horsepower and more are used for the most powerful ships. Diesel engines may supply power for vessels ranging in size from small boats to medium-size ships requiring as much as 40,000 total horsepower. Gas turbines and fast diesels usually have a reduction-gear drive making it possible to run them at high speeds (for maximum economy) while the propeller turns at low speeds (for maximum efficiency). Gas turbines have been used experimentally in merchant ships and naval patrol boats. Some submarines, merchant ships, and icebreakers have nuclear power plants in which a nuclear reactor replaces the boiler of a stream turbine plant. Conventional submarines have a diesel-electric drive and run on batteries when submerged. Small boats usually have gasoline outboard engines that clamp on the stern or inboard engines to drive propeller shafts. Shallow-draft boats for use in swamps have aircraft engines and air propellers. A few small boats are propelled by a pumped jet of water. The inboard-outboard motor for small vessels incorporates features of both types: the engine, the reduction gearing, and the vertical propeller shaft compose a self-contained unit that is mounted with the engine inboard, usually just forward of the transom; the gear housing projects through an opening in the transom and the propeller shaft extends down from it. This arrangement makes possible the combination of a relatively large power plant with the convenience and maneuverability of an outboard installation; e.g., the propeller may be tilted up in order to beach the boat. See Conrad Miller, *Small Boat Engines* (1961); J. E. Flack, et al., *Marine Combustion Practice* (1969); K. T. Rowland, *Steam at Sea* (1971).

marine insurance: see INSURANCE.

marine pollution: see WATER POLLUTION.

Mariner space program: see SPACE EXPLORATION.

marines, troops that serve on board ships of war or in conjunction with naval operation. A British marine corps was established in 1664, and the need for skilled riflemen aboard military vessels brought about intermittent renewal of this organization. In 1775 the Continental Congress established the Continental Marines in the American Revolution, and after this organization had disappeared with the end of the war, the U.S. Congress created (1798) its successor, the present U.S. marine corps. The corps played a distinguished role on the Barbary coast and has been prominent in all major wars in which the United States has participated. In the early 20th cent. U.S. marines were sent to quell disturbances in several Central American and Caribbean countries—Panama, Honduras, Nicaragua, Haiti, and the Dominican Republic. In a controversial move, the United States also sent some 22,000 marines and paratroopers into the Dominican Republic during the revolution of April, 1965. In World War II the marines played a key role in the invasion of several Pacific islands held by the Japanese, and they also served with distinction in Korea and Vietnam. Under the organization (1947) of the National Military Establishment, the U.S. marine corps functions as a branch of the U.S. navy but is a complete operating unit within itself and has all military arms except cavalry. See C. L. Lewis, *Famous American Marines* (1950); R. D. Heinl, *Soldiers of the Sea* (1962); J. B. Moran, *Creating a Legend* (1973).

Marinette (mârĭnĕt'), city (1970 pop. 12,696), seat of Marinette co., NE Wis., on Green Bay at the mouth of the Menominee River; inc. 1887. A port of entry, it is the center of a tri-city area embracing Peshtigo, Wis., and Menominee, Mich. Among the city's manufactures are pulp and paper, machinery, and aluminum castings. Fur trading began there c.1795 and gave way to lumbering, which flourished until the 1930s. The city was named for a Menominee Indian queen, who established a trading post on the river and built the first frame house there.

Marinetti, Filippo Tommaso (fēlēp'pō tōm-mä'zō märēnĕt'tē), 1876–1944, Italian poet, novelist, and critic. He is best known as the founder of FUTURISM (1909), on which he wrote and lectured, and as an advocate of Fascism; he was one of the first members of the Fascist party. He wrote in both French and Italian; among his works are *Le Roi Bombance* (1905) and *Mafarka il futurista*, published (1910) simultaneously in French and Italian. See his writings ed. by R. W. Flint (tr. 1972).

Maringá (mərēng-gä'), city (1970 pop. 121,461), Paraná state, SE Brazil. It is an agricultural center whose chief products are coffee, maize, beans, rice, wheat, and sugarcane. Coffee processing is the main industry.

Marini, Marino (märē'nō märē'nē), 1901–, Italian sculptor. Marini is best known for his many vigorous sculptures of horses and horsemen, (e.g., *Horse and Rider*, 1949–50), although he has created notable portrait busts, group statues, and paintings and drawings. After 1955 he tended toward a more dramatic expression of form. His works are in many European and American museums. See study by Edward Trier (1961).

Marino, Giambattista (jäm"bät-tē'stä märē'nō), 1569–1625, Italian poet. His florid, highly elaborated style, called *Marinismo*, which was akin to euphuism, was much admired and imitated in his time. He had a strong influence on writing in all European literature. Among his principal works is *Adone* (1623), a long narrative poem. His name sometimes appears as Marini. See study by J. V. Mirollo (1963).

Mario (mär'yō), 1810–83, stage name of Giovanni Matteo, Cavaliere di Candia, Italian tenor. An officer of the Piedmontese guard, he went to Paris in 1836 and studied at the Paris Conservatory, making his debut (1838) at the Paris Opera in *Robert le Diable*. He sang with great success in Paris, London, and St. Petersburg, appearing often with his wife, Giulia Grisi. Mario had a very beautiful voice, which, united with personal grace and charm, made him the idol of his public. He retired in 1867.

Mariology: see MARY.

Marion, Francis, c.1732–1795, American Revolutionary soldier, known as the Swamp Fox, b. near Georgetown, S.C. He was a planter and Indian fighter before joining (1775) William Moultrie's regiment at the start of the American Revolution. In 1779 he fought under Benjamin Lincoln at Savannah and escaped (1780) capture at Charleston by being on sick leave. Marion organized a troop (1780), which, after the American defeat at Camden in the Carolina campaign, constituted the chief colonial force in South Carolina. Engaging in guerilla warfare, he disrupted the British lines of communication, captured scouting and foraging parties, and intimidated Loyalists. His habit of disappearing into the swamps to elude the British earned him his nickname. When Nathanael Greene had succeeded in ousting the British from North Carolina (see CAROLINA CAMPAIGN), his lieutenant, Light-Horse Harry Lee, brought reinforcements to Marion, and they took part together in several battles, notably that at Eutaw Springs (Sept. 8, 1781). After the war, Marion served in the South Carolina senate, where he advocated a lenient policy toward the Loyalists. See biographies by W. G. Simms (1844, repr. 1971) and H. F. Rankin (1973).

Marion. **1** City (1970 pop. 11,724), seat of Williamson co., S Ill.; inc. 1841. It is the commercial and retail center of a farm and coal area and has a large soft drink bottling plant. A veterans' hospital and home and a Federal prison are there. Robert Ingersoll and John A. Logan lived in Marion. Nearby is a U.S. wildlife refuge. **2** City (1970 pop. 39,607), seat of Grant co., E central Ind., on the Mississinewa River; settled 1826, inc. 1889. It is a trade, processing, and industrial center in a farm area. Its diversified manufactures include auto parts and television and radio tubes. The city developed with the discovery of gas and oil in the late 1880s. It is the seat of Marion College and a U.S. veterans' hospital. Taylor Univ. is in nearby Upland. **3** City (1970 pop. 18,028), Linn co., E central Iowa, adjoining Cedar Rapids; inc. 1865. It is chiefly residential. Home construction and mobile home manufacturing are its main industries. An airport for small craft is there. **4** City (1970 pop. 38,646), seat of Marion co., central Ohio; inc. 1830. A rail, industrial, and agricultural center, it is noted for its production of power shovels, cranes, and road-building equipment. Limestone quarries are in the area. Marion was the home of President Harding; his house is preserved as a museum, and his burial place is marked by a circular marble monument. A branch of Ohio State Univ. is in the city.

Marion, Fort: see SAINT AUGUSTINE, Fla.

marionette: see PUPPET.

Mariotte, Edme (ĕd'mə märyôt'), 1620?–1684, French physicist. His *De la nature de l'air* (1676) includes a statement of Boyle's law (see GAS LAWS), which he discovered independently and which is sometimes called Mariotte's law in France. One of the founders of experimental physics, Mariotte investigated a wide range of phenomena, including the motion of bodies, sound, hydrodynamics, barometry, color, and vision.

mariposa lily: see LILY.

Maris (mä'rĭs), three Dutch painters, who were brothers. **Jacob** or **Jakob Maris**, 1837–99, the most celebrated, painted domestic interiors but is particularly famous for his vigorous landscapes in oil and watercolor. Rich in color and large and simple in composition and handling, these paintings are among the finest of the Hague school. They usually depict the rich countryside under luminous gray skies. The Rijks Museum has a notable collection, including *Arrival of the Boats*. Other works are *The Bridge* (Frick Coll., New York City) and *Canal in Holland* (Metropolitan Mus.). **Matthew** or **Matthijs Maris**, 1839–1917, genre and landscape painter and etcher, worked with his brother Jacob and in 1877 settled in London. He developed a vein of mysticism in his later work, shown in such paintings as *Reverie* (Metropolitan Mus.) and *Memory of Amsterdam* (Rijks Mus.). **William** or **Willem Maris**, 1844–1910, achieved an early reputation for his bright landscapes, usually with cattle. The Rijks Museum has several, including *Cows beside a Ditch*.

Maris, Roger Eugene (măr'ĭs), 1934–, American baseball player, b. Hibbing, Minn. He played (1957–59) for the Cleveland Indians and the Kansas City Athletics before joining (1960) the New York Yankees. In 1961, Maris hit 61 home runs, thus establishing a new record for the most home runs hit in a single major-league season. The spectacular feat surpassed by one the 60 home runs that Babe Ruth hit in 1927. However, Ford C. Frick, commissioner of baseball, ruled that since Maris played in a 162-game schedule and Ruth in only a 154-game schedule, Ruth's record would stand unless bettered within 154 games; Maris had 59 home runs in 154 games. Maris won the league's most valuable player award in 1960 and again in 1961. He hit 275 home runs in his 12-year major league career (1957–68). The amount of publicity Maris received for his feat in 1961 and the debate surrounding the validity of his accomplishment led him into an early retirement from the sport.

Marisa: see MARESHAH.

Marisco, Adam de: see MARSH, ADAM.

Marisol (Escobar) (măr'ĭsōl," āskō'bär), 1930–, Venezuelan-American sculptor, b. Paris. Marisol was first influenced by pre-Columbian sculpture and South American folk art. She is noted for her large, satirical, wooden figure groups; these place her within the POP ART movement. Many of her works, such as *The Family* (1962; Mus. of Modern Art, New York City), contain found objects and plaster or painted replicas of parts of her own body.

Maritain, Jacques (zhäk märĕtăN'), 1882–1973, French Neo-Thomist philosopher. He was educated at the Sorbonne and the Univ. of Heidelberg and was much influenced by the philosophy of Henri Bergson. He was originally Protestant, but became a Roman Catholic through association with Léon BLOY and devoted himself to the study of Thomism and its application to all aspects of modern life. Maritain opposed what he regarded as the modern tendency to disown the proper function of reason; he valued philosophy highly and posed the "metaphysics of existence," the study of being, as the highest type of human intellectual activity. He urged Christian involvement in secular affairs, a view that greatly influenced the Second Vatican Council. Maritain was French ambassador to the Vatican (1945–48) and taught in France and the United States. His works include *The Degrees of Knowledge* (1932, tr. 1937); *True Humanism* (1936, tr. 1938); *Art and Scholasticism* (1920, tr. 1929); *Man and the State* (1951); *On the Use of Philosophy* (1961); and *The Peasant of the Garonne* (1966, tr. 1968). See studies by J. W. Evans, ed. (1963) and J. W. Hanke (1973).

maritime law, system of law concerning navigation and overseas commerce. Because ships sail from nation to nation over seas no nation owns, nations need to seek agreement over customs related to shipping. From such agreements between nations has grown a body of customs and usages that is the basis for maritime law. It was, in origin, based on customs only, but it felt the influence of the Roman civil law. In the later Middle Ages, when traders were more and more venturous in crossing the waters, the rules of the sea were compiled into widely recognized collections such as the *Consolato del mare* [consulate of the sea], *The Rolls of Oléron* or *The Laws of Oléron*, and the English *Black Book of the Admiralty*. In England, special courts were set up to administer the law under the high court of admiralty. The Judicature Act of 1873 abolished these courts and assigned their functions to the high court of justice. In the United States the Constitution gives the Federal courts authority in "all cases of admiralty and maritime jurisdiction." This jurisdiction covers all maritime contracts, torts, injuries or offenses, and questions of PRIZE. In cases of collision at sea, the parties may under the Judiciary Act of 1789 bring suits at common law; otherwise all maritime cases come to the Federal courts. The jurisdiction extends to all navigable waters of the United States, and much of the law is now governed by Federal statutes. Though maritime law is general in character, only those parts that determine the relations among nations—particularly those that deal with problems arising on the seas in wartime, such as questions of BELLIGERENCY and NEUTRALITY—are part of the international law proper. See ADMIRALTY; BLOCKADE; PIRACY; PRIVATEERING; SEAS, FREEDOM OF THE; LONDON, DECLARATION OF; PARIS, DECLARATION OF. See Henry Reiff, *The United States and the Treaty Law of the Sea* (1959); D. W. Bowett, *The Law of the Sea* (1967); C. J. Colombos, *The International Law of the Sea* (6th ed. 1967).

Maritime Provinces, Canada, term applied to NOVA SCOTIA, NEW BRUNSWICK, and PRINCE EDWARD ISLAND, which before the formation of the Canadian confederation (1867) were politically distinct from Canada proper.

Maritime Territory: see PRIMORSKY KRAY, USSR.

Maritsa (märē'tsä), river, c.300 mi (480 km) long, rising in the Rila Mts., W Bulgaria, and flowing SE between the Balkans and Rhodope Mts., past Plovdiv, to Edirne, Turkey, where it turns south to enter the Aegean Sea near Enez. The Tundzha is its chief tributary. The Maritsa's lower course forms part of the Bulgarian-Greek border and the Greek-Turkish line. The upper Maritsa valley is a principal east-west route in Bulgaria. The unnavigable river is used for power production and irrigation. It is known as the Évros by the Greeks and the Meriç by the Turks.

Maritzburg: see PIETERMARITZBURG.

Mariupol: see ZHDANOV, USSR.

Marius, Caius, c.157 B.C.–86 B.C., Roman general. A plebeian, he became tribune (119 B.C.) and praetor (115 B.C.) and was seven times consul. He served under Scipio Africanus Minor at Numantia and under Quintus Metellus against Jugurtha. Later, when he was commander of Roman forces against Jugurtha, he hastened the end of the war by a bold attack against the Numidians. In 102 B.C. he defeated the Teutones at Aix, and the next year he bested the Cimbri at Vercelli. Rivalry with Sulla over the command against Mithridates VI of Pontus turned into civil war; Sulla won, and Marius fled Rome. When Sulla went off to fight, Marius, now allied with the consul Cinna, returned and slaughtered (88 B.C.) his opponents. Marius had no political program, but the enmity of the senate and of Sulla gained him recognition as a friend of the people. This reputation had an important influence on the early career of Julius Caesar, who was the nephew of Julia, Marius' wife. See biographies by P. A. Kildahl (1968) and T. F. Canney (2d. ed. 1970).

Marivaux, Pierre Carlet de Chamblain de (pyĕr' kärlā' də shāblē' də märēvō'), 1688–1763, French dramatist and novelist. He enjoyed popularity for a time with his numerous comedies, including *Le Jeu de l'amour et du hasard* (1730, tr. *Love in Livery*) and *Le Legs* (1736, tr. *The Legacy*, 1915), which analyze the sentiments and complications of love in a graceful, though often precious, style. The term *marivaudage* was thenceforth applied to his brand of artificiality. He also wrote two unfinished novels of middle-class life, *La Vie de Marianne* (1731–41) and *Le Paysan Parvenu* (1735–36), which are important early examples of the genre. See K. N. McKee, *The Theater of Marivaux* (1958); R. C. Rosbottom, *Marivaux's Novels* (1975).

marjoram or **sweet marjoram** (mär'jərəm), Old World perennial aromatic herb *(Marjorana hortensis)* of the family Labiatae (MINT family), cultivated in gardens for flavoring. The tops yield origanum oil, once used medicinally but more recently for perfuming soaps. The closely related European pot, or wild, marjoram (*Origanum vulgare*) has similar uses and is the spice usually sold as OREGANO, although other species may be called oregano. The generic names *Marjorana* and *Origanum* are frequently interchanged. Marjoram is classified in the division MAGNOLIOPHYTA, class Magnoliopsida, order Lamiales, family Labiatae.

Mark, Saint [Lat. *Marcus*], Christian apostle, traditional author of the 2d Gospel (see MARK, GOSPEL ACCORDING TO ST.). His full name was John Mark. His mother, named Mary, had a house in Jerusalem, which the Christians used as a meeting place. Mark accompanied St. Paul and St. Barnabas, who was his cousin or uncle, on their mission to Cyprus, but he left them at Perga and returned to Jerusalem. Paul refused to take Mark on his second trip, thus creating a breach with Barnabas. Acts 12.12,25; 13.5,13; 15,37-39; Col. 4.10; 2 Tim. 4.11; Philemon 24; 1 Peter 5.13. Tradition identifies Mark with the young man who "fled from them naked" at Gethsemane (Mark 14.51-52). Tradition also makes him an associate of St. Peter, who is thought to have furnished many of the evangelist's facts. The Alexandrian church claims Mark as its founder—the liturgy of that church is called the Liturgy of St. Mark. St. Mark is the patron of Venice and of its famous cathedral, where his relics are shown. His symbol as an evangelist is a lion. Feast: April 25.

Mark, Gospel according to Saint, 2d book of the New Testament. This is the simplest and earliest of the four Gospels (composed probably A.D.c.70), and it was used as a source by the authors of the Gospels of St. Matthew and St. Luke (see SYNOPTIC GOSPELS). The Gospel may be divided into four parts: beginning of the ministry of Jesus (1.1-13); his first two years of preaching (1.14-6.56); his third year (7-13); the passion and resurrection (14-16). Because of manuscript discrepancies, there is uncertainty about the conclusion (16.9-20); some versions conclude with 16.8. The Gospel has traditionally been ascribed to St. Mark, who is supposed to have obtained his material from St. Peter; some modern scholars have questioned the attribution.

mark, designation for the free village community that was supposed to have been the unit of primitive German social life. According to a theory formulated in the 19th cent. by G. L. von MAURER and others, the mark was composed of free men in voluntary association, holding lands communally, and governed by a chief elected for a short term. The theory was expanded by other scholars, among them E. A. FREEMAN, but it later was bitterly attacked by the historians N. D. FUSTEL DE COULANGES and Frederic SEEBOHM. It has become generally accepted that Roman as well as Germanic institutions influenced the formation of the medieval MANORIAL SYSTEM and that the idyllic democratic society depicted by Maurer never existed. See VILLAGE.

market gardening, cultivation, on suburban land of high value, of vegetables and flowers for the supply of nearby cities. Heavy fertilizing and the planting of successive crops are employed to obtain continuous returns from the acreage. Sales are to greengrocers and florists, principally through commission agents. With modern transportation, market gardens can be located at greater distances from market cities. See TRUCK FARMING. See Ronald Webber, *Market Gardening* (1972).

marketing, in economics, that part of the process of production and exchange that is concerned with the flow of goods and services from producer to consumer. In popular usage it is defined as the distribution and sale of goods, the word *distribution* being understood in a broader sense than the technical economic one. Marketing includes the activities of all those who are engaged in the transfer of goods from producer to consumer—not only those who buy and sell directly, wholesale and retail, but also those who warehouse, grade, transport, insure, finance, or otherwise have a hand in the process of transfer. In a modern capitalist economy, where all production is for a market, such activities are of first importance; it is estimated that more than 50% of the price paid by the final consumer is made up of the cost of marketing. Where production is for direct use, as in the subsistence farm, the feudal manor, or the communal group, there is little need for exchange of goods because the division of labor is poorly developed and most people produce the same or similar goods. Interregional exchange between disparate geographic areas depends on adequate means of transportation. Thus, before the development of caravan travel and navigation, there was little exchange of the products of one region for those of another. Where systems of transportation are well developed, as in the Mediterranean in ancient times and throughout most of the world in modern times, interregional trade has been substantial. The village market or fair, the itinerant merchant or peddler, and the shop where customers could have such goods as shoes and furniture made to order were features of marketing in rural Europe. The general store superseded the public market in England, and it was an institution of the American country town until recent times. In the United States in the 19th cent. the typical marketing setup was one in which wholesalers assembled the products of various manufacturers or producers and sold them to jobbers and retailers. A picturesque figure in this setup was the "drummer," or traveling salesman, who, after the advent of a network of railroads, was able to penetrate to every town and hamlet in the country, calling on retailers and receiving their orders for goods. The independent STORE, operated by its owner, was the chief retail marketing agency; however, in the 20th cent. it met stiff competition from chain stores, which were organized for the mass distribution of goods and enjoyed the advantages of large-scale operation. Today chain stores dominate the field of retail trade; the 50 largest retail businesses, comprising less than 3% of the total, now account for more than 40% of the nation's annual retail sales. The advent of the motor truck and paved highways, making possible the prompt delivery of lots of goods in any quantity, have still further modified the marketing setup, and the proliferation of the automobile has continuously widened the area in which consumers could make retail purchases. People at all points of the marketing system have grouped together or eliminated various middlemen, in order to form more efficient marketing units. Manufacturers maintain their own wholesale departments and deal directly with retailers. Independent stores operate their own wholesale agencies to supply them with goods. Wholesale houses operate voluntary chains as outlets for their wares, and farmers sell their products through wholesale cooperatives of their own. Commodity exchanges, such as those of grain and cotton, enable businessmen to buy and sell commodities for both immediate and future delivery. Methods of merchandising have also been changed to attract customers. The one-price system, said to have been introduced (1841) by A. T. Stewart in New York, saves the time of salesmen, previously wasted in haggling, and promotes faith in the integrity of the merchant. Advertising has created a nationwide market for many goods, especially trademarked and labeled goods. The number of customers, especially for durable goods, has been greatly increased by the practice of INSTALLMENT BUYING AND SELLING. It is possible to speak of the marketing of services as well as of goods or commodities. Sometimes a service, like that of a barber, repairman, or physician, is marketed through the same act that produces it. Personal services may, however, also be disposed of by intermediaries, such as employment agencies, booking agents for concert or theatrical performers, and the like. Methods of marketing now include market research, motivational research, and other means of determining consumer acceptability of a product before the producer decides to manufacture and market it. See G. B. Hotchkiss, *Milestones of Marketing* (1939); R. D. Crisp, *Marketing Research* (1957); C. F. Phillips and D. J. Duncan, *Marketing: Principles and Methods* (6th ed. 1968); D. J. Luck and others, *Marketing Research* (3d ed. 1970).

Markham, Sir Clements Robert, 1830-1916, English geographer and writer. While in the navy he served on a British expedition (1850-51) to the Arctic to search for the explorer Sir John Franklin. From 1867 to 1877 he supervised the geographical work of the India Office, and he is credited with the introduction of cinchona cultivation into India from Peru. He was president (1893-1905) of the Royal Geographical Society. Secretary (1858-86) and president (1889-1909) of the Hakluyt Society, he edited and translated for it accounts of early travels. His own 50 works include accounts of his many travels and a number of biographies, chiefly of explorers and travelers. He was an authority on Inca civilization and wrote *The Incas of Peru* (1910) and edited early accounts of the Inca. Markham was an important promoter of antarctic exploration and helped to raise funds for Robert Scott's 1901 expedition.

Markham, Edwin, 1852-1940, American poet, b. Oregon City, Oregon. He grew up in California and later taught school there. In 1899 he achieved widespread popularity for the poem "The Man with the Hoe." Inspired by Millet's famous painting, the poem was a protest against the degradation and exploitation of labor. His other famous poem, "Lincoln, the Man of the People," appeared in *Lincoln and Other Poems* (1901). See biography by Louis Filler (1966).

Markham, Gervase, 1568-1637, English writer on horses and English country life. His chief work is *Cavelarice; or the English Horseman* (1607). Included among his other works are *Country Contentments* (1615) and several plays. He is said to have imported the first Arabian horse into England.

Markham, village (1970 pop. 15,987), Cook co., NE Ill., a residential suburb of Chicago; inc. 1925.

markhor (mär'kôr), wild goat, *Capra falconeri,* found in the rugged mountains of central Asia, from S Russia to the W Himalayas. Largest of the goats, the male may stand over 40 in. (100 cm) at the shoulder and weigh over 200 lb (90 kg). The coat is short and reddish brown in summer; in winter it is long, silky, and gray. Males have long, thick beards. The distinctive corkscrew-shaped horns are extremely thick and heavy. Markhors live in small herds of between 4 and 30 individuals, grazing up to the snow line. The isolated populations of the different mountain ranges constitute distinct races; most are near extinction because of extensive hunting. In the USSR, where the markhor has been protected since the 1930s, its numbers have increased to about 1,000. The markhor is classified in the phylum CHORDATA, subphylum Vertebrata, class Mammalia, order Artiodactyla, family Bovidae.

Markiewicz, Constance Georgine, Countess (märkyā'vĭts), 1868?-1927, Irish politician and patriot. A member of SINN FEIN, she was sentenced to death for her militant part in the Easter Rebellion of 1916 but was released in 1917. The daughter of an Irish baronet, she was married (1900) to a Polish count. In 1918 she was the first woman to be elected to the British House of Commons, but she never took her seat. Instead she sat in the DÁIL ÉIREANN until her death. See her *Prison Letters* (1934, repr. 1970); biography by Sean O'Faoláin (rev. ed. 1968).

Markova, Dame Alicia (märkō'vä), 1910-, English ballerina. Her original name was Lilian Alicia Marks. Markova joined Diaghilev's Ballet Russe in 1925 and, in 1932, the Vic-Wells Ballet as prima ballerina. In 1935 she formed a company with Anton DOLIN. After appearing (1938-41) with the Ballet Russe de Monte Carlo she danced with a number of American ballet companies. She worked again with Dolin from 1945 to 1952 in their Festival Ballet company. She was named Dame of the British Empire in 1963. Markova was noted for her precise style and ethereal grace. She excelled in all the classic roles. Her interpretations of *Giselle, Pas de Quatre, Petrouchka, Swan Lake,* and *Romeo and Juliet* were exceptionally celebrated. She wrote *Giselle and I* (1960).

Marl (märl), city (1970 pop. 76,697), North Rhine-Westphalia, W West Germany. It is an industrial and mining (coal, lead, and zinc) center. Now a modern city, Marl was first mentioned in the 9th cent. and was chartered in 1936.

marl or **bog lime,** soil, essentially clay mixed with carbonate of lime, highly valued as a dressing or fertilizer. It crumbles rapidly and easily. Marl in which the lime is in the form of invertebrate shells is called shell marl. The term is loosely used for a variety of soils, some of which are low in lime content, e.g., the greensand marl of New Jersey. Marling of soil tends to lighten it, to correct acidity, and to promote nitrification.

Marlboro or **Marlborough** (märl'bərō), city (1970 pop. 27,936), Middlesex co., E Mass.; settled on the site of an Indian village 1657, inc. as a city 1890. It has been a shoe-manufacturing center for many years. The community was almost destroyed (1676) in King Philip's War.

Marlborough, John Churchill, 1st **duke of** (märl'bərə, môl'-), 1650-1722, English general and statesman, one of the greatest military commanders of history. The son of an impoverished squire, he became (1665) a page of the duke of York (later JAMES II) and entered (1667) the army. He rose rapidly under York's patronage and c.1678 married Sarah Jennings (see MARLBOROUGH, SARAH CHURCHILL, DUCHESS OF), attendant and friend of Princess (later Queen) ANNE. Under James II he was active in crushing the rebellion (1685) of the duke of MONMOUTH and was raised to the peerage and made a major general. Nevertheless, fearing the religious policies of the

Roman Catholic king, and concerned about his own career, he corresponded with William of Orange (later WILLIAM III) and supported him against James in the Glorious Revolution of 1688. He was created earl of Marlborough at William's coronation (1689). Marlborough was successful as a military commander in 1689 and 1690, but William's poor treatment of Anne offended him, and William began to resent Marlborough's ambition and ability. When Marlborough began secret communication with the exiled James II, he was discovered and lost royal favor (1692-98). In 1702, when Anne ascended the throne, he reached the fullness of his power. His military genius and remarkable gift for foreign diplomacy were given wide scope in the War of the SPANISH SUCCESSION. His personal efforts long held together the anti-French alliance. He and Prince EUGENE OF SAVOY together won such victories as Blenheim (1704), Oudenarde (1708), and Malplaquet (1709), and he alone is credited with Ramillies (1706) and countless other triumphs. Marlborough, made a duke in 1702, also enjoyed political ascendancy, largely as a result of his wife's influence over the queen. Marlborough and his friend Sidney GODOLPHIN, as well as the queen, although earlier bound by personal and religious ties to the Tories, now turned to the Whigs, who favored the war while the Tories opposed it. They secured the dismissal of Robert HARLEY in 1708 and were momentarily paramount in politics. The duchess, however, quarreled with Anne, who came under the influence of Abigail MASHAM, Harley's cousin; the war was costly, and Marlborough was accused of prolonging it for his personal glory; the prosecution of Henry SACHEVERELL was unpopular; and in 1710 the Whigs fell, yielding power to Harley and Henry St. John (later Viscount Bolingbroke). The duke was falsely charged with misappropriating public funds and was dismissed (1711) from office. He returned to England from self-imposed exile upon the accession of George I in 1714 and was given chief command of the army again, but he took little further part in public affairs. A great strategist and a shrewd diplomat, he has been criticized for inordinate love of wealth and power and for unstable loyalties in politics. See the duke's letters and dispatches (ed. by Sir George Murray, 1845); the exhaustive biography of him by his descendant Winston S. Churchill (1933-38, repr. 1972) and a short one by M. P. Ashley (1939, repr. 1957); studies of his military career by C. T. Atkinson (1921), Frank Taylor (1921), I. F. Burton (1968), and D. G. Chandler (1973).

Marlborough, Sarah Churchill, duchess of, 1660-1744, confidante of Queen Anne of England. Born Sarah Jennings, she was a childhood friend of Princess Anne. In 1677 she married John Churchill, later 1st duke of Marlborough. On Anne's marriage (1683) she was appointed lady of the bedchamber and became a close confidante. Although temporarily out of favor (1692-94) owing to the political disgrace of her husband, Sarah maintained a close relationship with Anne (who succeeded to the throne in 1702) until 1705, when they began to quarrel over Whig cabinet appointments. Until then Sarah had wielded considerable influence at court, but gradually Abigail MASHAM, a kinswoman both of Sarah herself and of the Tory leader Robert HARLEY, replaced her in Anne's affections. Finally dismissed in 1711, she and her husband went abroad in 1713. After the death (1722) of the duke of Marlborough, the duchess supervised completion of the building of Blenheim Palace, quarreling bitterly with its architect, Sir John Vanbrugh, and with most of her relatives.

marlin, common name for open-sea fish related to the SAILFISH and SWORDFISH (family Istiophoridae) and prized by sportsmen. The best known is the blue marlin of the genus *Makaira,* found in the Gulf Stream as far north as Long Island. It may reach 1,000 lb (454 kg) in weight. The upper jaw of the marlin extends into a long spike with which it clubs the small fish on which it feeds. The striped marlin of the Pacific reaches a weight of 300 to 400 lb (135-180 kg); the paler white marlin of the Atlantic rarely exceeds 100 lb (45 kg). Marlins are classified in the phylum CHORDATA, subphylum Vertebrata, class Osteichthyes, order Perciformes, family Istiophoridae.

Marlinsky, Cossack: see BESTUZHEV, ALEKSANDR ALEKSANDROVICH.

Marlowe, Christopher, 1564-93, English dramatist and poet, b. Canterbury. Probably the greatest English dramatist before Shakespeare, Marlowe broke with the tradition that tragedies should be patterned after those of Seneca. Educated at Cambridge, he went to London in 1587, where he became an actor and dramatist for the Lord Admiral's Company. In 1593 the playwright Thomas Kyd, with whom Marlowe had at one time lived, supported charges that Marlowe held and disseminated heretical and lewd religious and moral principles. Before Marlowe could appear for questioning, he was stabbed in a barroom brawl by a drinking companion. Although a coroner's jury certified that the assailant acted in self-defense, the murder may have resulted from a definite plot, due, as some scholars believe, to Marlowe's activities as a government agent. Marlowe's dramas have heroic themes, usually centering on a great personality who is destroyed by his own passion and ambition. Although filled with violence, brutality, passion, and bloodshed, Marlowe's plays are never merely sensational. The poetic beauty and dignity of his language raise them to the level of high art. Indeed, Marlowe is considered more a poet of the theater than a dramatist. His innovation of blank verse as the appropriate medium for the drama prepared the way for the great plays of Shakespeare. Marlowe's most important plays are the two parts of *Tamburlaine the Great* (c.1587), *Dr. Faustus* (c.1588), *The Jew of Malta* (c.1589), and *Edward II* (c.1592). Some authorities detect traces of his work in the Shakespeare canon, notably in *Titus Andronicus* and *King Henry VI.* Of his nondramatic pieces, the best-known are the long poem *Hero and Leander* (1598), which was finished by George Chapman, and the beautiful lyric that begins "Come live with me and be my love." See his *Works and Life* (6 vol., 1949-55); biographies by F. S. Boas (1940) and Charles Norman (rev. ed. 1971); studies by J. E. Bakeless (1942), P. H. Kocher (1946), H. Levin (1952, repr. 1964), W. Sanders (1969), B. Morris (1970), J. B. Steane (1964, repr. 1970), and J. P. Cutts (1973).

Marlowe, Julia, 1865?-1950, American actress, b. England, originally named Sarah Frances Frost. She moved to the United States with her parents in 1871 and in 1887 made her New York debut. As a leading actress, she was known for her success in acting various roles of the entire Shakespearean repertory with her second husband, E. H. Sothern. See biographies by C. E. Russell (1926) and E. H. Sothern (1954).

Marly-le-Roi (märlē'-lə-rwä), town (1968 pop. 12,016), Yvelines dept., N France, on the Seine River near Versailles. Nearby is the hamlet of Marly-la-Machine, where in 1682 a huge hydraulic engine, the *machine de Marly,* was built to supply the fountains of Versailles. Considered one of the wonders of the world, the engine was in use until 1804. In the town is a church (1689) built by J. H. Mansart.

Marmaduke, John Sappington, 1833-87, Confederate general in the American Civil War, b. Arrow Rock, Mo. He served in the expedition against the Mormons and in Western army posts. At the outbreak of the Civil War he resigned from the U.S. army. He served for a time with the Missouri militia and then accepted a commission in the Confederate army. Marmaduke distinguished himself at Shiloh (1862) and was sent to Arkansas and Missouri as brigadier general. Commanding the cavalry on Sterling Price's raid into Missouri (1864), he was captured at Marais des Cygnes River and was held prisoner until the end of the war. Marmaduke was elected governor of Missouri in 1884. He died in office.

marmalade [Port.,=quince preparation], thick preserve of fruit pulp, originally made from quinces (*marmelos*) and known in England from the 15th cent. Marmalade has a jellylike consistency and a slightly bitter flavor, caused by including the rind of some tart fruit such as the Seville orange or the grapefruit. The name is also applied to various jams made tart by the addition of lemon juice or other acid ingredients.

Marmara, Sea of, or **Sea of Marmora,** c.4,430 sq mi (11,474 sq km), NW Turkey, between Europe in the north and Asia in the south. The Sea of Marmara, c.175 mi (280 km) long and 50 mi (80 km) wide, is connected on the east with the Black Sea through the Bosporus and on the west with the Aegean Sea (part of the Mediterranean Sea) through the Dardanelles. İstanbul (Constantinople) is located at the entrance of the Bosporus into the Sea of Marmara. The sea has no strong currents and the tidal range is minimal. In ancient times the sea was known as Propontis [Gr.,=fore-sea] from its position relative to the Black Sea. Its modern name is derived from the small island of Marmara or Marmora (ancient *Proconnesus*), famous for its extensive marble quarries.

Mármol, José (hōsā' mär'môl), 1817-71, Argentine writer of the romantic school. His invectives against Juan Manuel de Rosas earned him the nickname "the poetic hangman of Rosas." He was imprisoned by Rosas in 1839 and later fled to Montevideo, where he lived until the overthrow of the dictator. Mármol's fame rests primarily upon his novel *La Amalia* (1851-55, tr. 1919), which, despite its stilted style, presents a powerful description of the tyranny of Rosas. He also wrote *El peregrino* (1847) [the pilgrim], a long poem in imitation of Byron's *Childe Harold's Pilgrimage.*

Marmolada, peak, Italy: see DOLOMITES.

Marmont, Auguste Frédéric Louis Viesse de (ōgüst' frādārĕk' lwē vyĕs də märmôN'), 1774-1852, marshal of France. He fought with Napoleon in Italy and Egypt and took part in his coup d'etat of 18 Brumaire (1799). In 1808 he was made duke of Ragusa and later governor of Illyria. He succeeded André Masséna as commander in the PENINSULAR WAR, but was defeated (1812) at Salamanca. In command of the defense of Paris in 1814, he was forced to surrender and later signed a convention with the allies that prevented Napoleon from retaking Paris. During the Restoration he supported King Charles X, and he left France when Charles was overthrown in 1830. He wrote memoirs.

Marmontel, Jean François (zhäN fräNswä' märmôNtĕl'), 1723-99, French critic, dramatist, and story writer, contributor to Diderot's *Encyclopédie.* Educated by the Jesuits, he taught in Jesuit schools until 1745, when, encouraged by Voltaire, he went to Paris. His works, popular in his day, include *Denys le tyran* (1748), a tragedy; *Contes moraux,* which appeared in the *Mercure* between 1761 and 1786; *Bélisaire* (1767), a plea for tolerance; and his *Mémoires* (4 vol., 1804), written for his children. He was a member of the French Academy.

Marmora: see MARMARA.

marmoset (mär'məzĕt''), name for many of the small, squirrellike New World MONKEYS of the family Callithricidae. Members of this family are all found in tropical South America, with one species found also in Central America. They range in size from the pygmy marmoset, which is 8 in. (20 cm) long including the tail and weighs 3 oz (85 g), to species about the size of house rats. Many of the larger species are called tamarins. Most marmosets and tamarins are brightly colored, and many are ornamented with manes, ear tufts, or mustaches. Their tails are long and furry. Day active, gregarious animals, they scurry through trees and chatter in shrill voices. They feed on plant matter as well as on insects and other small animals. Females usually bear twins, and it is claimed that in some species the male takes a large part in the care of the young. Most spectacular is the golden lion marmoset, with flaming, golden fur and a luxuriant mane. Marmosets have long been valued as pets. They are classified in the phylum CHORDATA, subphylum Vertebrata, class Mammalia, order Primates, family Callithricidae.

marmot, ground-living RODENT of the genus *Marmota,* of the SQUIRREL family, closely related to the ground squirrel, prairie dog, and chipmunk. Marmots are found in Eurasia and North America; the best-known North American marmot is the WOODCHUCK, *M. monax,* of Canada and the E United States. Marmots inhabit plains or open country in mountainous regions. They live in burrows (some species in large colonies) and hibernate during the winter. Active during the day, they feed chiefly on grasses and other green plants. Marmots have stout bodies, rounded ears, and powerful digging claws. They vary in length from 15 to 25 in. (38-64 cm), excluding 5- to 12-in. (16- to 30-cm) bushy tails. The coarse fur, which is usually brown on the upper parts, is often tipped with white. The yellow-bellied marmot, *M. flaviventris,* is found in W North America from S Canada to New Mexico. The hoary marmot, *M. caligata,* also called whistler from its shrill warning call, is found in Siberia and from Alaska S to Idaho. A colonial animal, it lives in mountains above the timberline. Largest of the marmots, it is also distinguished by its pale yellow-gray fur and black and white head. The Alpine marmot, *M. marmota,* lives below the snow level in the Alps. The bobac, *M. bobak,* is a marmot found in mountains from E Europe through central Asia. It is hunted for its flesh by the Mongols, and its fur is used as imitation marten. Marmots are classified in the phylum CHORDATA, subphylum Vertebrata, class Mammalia, order Rodentia, family Sciuridae.

Marmousets (märmo͞ozā'), [Fr.,=little fellows], ministers of King CHARLES V of France, so called by the great nobles, who were contemptuous of their humble origins. Olivier de CLISSON was the most prominent Marmouset. They were recalled by King

CHARLES VI when he reached his majority, but they fell from power after he became mad (1392). Their administration attempted to restore sound and conservative government.

Marne (märn), department (1968 pop. 485,388), NE France, in CHAMPAGNE. CHÂLONS-SUR-MARNE is the capital.

Marne, river, c.325 mi (520 km) long, rising in the Langres plateau, NE France, and flowing in an arc generally NW to the Seine River near Paris. It passes through Chaumont and Châlons-sur-Marne. The Marne-Rhine Canal and the Marne-Saône Canal also connect with the Aisne, Meuse, Moselle, and Saar rivers. During World War I and World War II, the Marne region was the scene of much fighting.

Marne, battle of the, two important battles of World War I that are named for the Marne River. In the first battle (Sept. 6-9, 1914) the German advance on Paris was halted at the Marne by the Allies under JOFFRE, GALLIENI, and Sir John French. The German retreat that followed signified the abandonment of the Schlieffen plan (see under SCHLIEFFEN, ALFRED, GRAF VON). In the second battle (July, 1918) the last great German offensive was decisively repulsed by the Allies. See studies by R. H. Asprey (1962), Georges Blond (tr. 1965), and Henri Isselin (tr. 1965).

Marnix, Philip van (fē'lĭp vän mär'nĭks), 1540-98, Flemish patriot, lord of Sainte-Aldegonde. He became a Calvinist in his youth and was the chief author of the Compromise of Breda (1566; see GUEUX). A leader in the Dutch and Flemish struggle for independence from Spain, he actively supported William the Silent. He wrote (c.1570) the hymn *Wilhelmus van Nassauwe*, which was used as the rallying song of the insurgents and which remains the national anthem of the Netherlands. In 1572 he represented William at the estates of Holland, held at Dordrecht, and secured the recognition of William as lawful stadholder of Holland. Among his writings are the vehement anti-Catholic pamphlet, *De Biënkorf der H. Roomsche Kercke* (1569; tr. *The Bee Hive of the Romish Church*, 1578?) and a versification of the Psalms (1580).

Maronites (mâr'ənīts), Christian community of Arabs in Lebanon, in communion with the pope. By emigration they have spread to Cyprus, Palestine, Egypt, South America, and the United States and now number about one million. Their liturgy (said mainly in liturgical Syriac) is of the Antiochene type, with innovations taken from the Latin rite. Their ecclesiastical head, under the pope, is called patriarch of Antioch; he lives in Lebanon. As in other Eastern rites, the parish priests are usually married. The Maronites have been a distinct community since the 7th cent., when they separated in the doctrinal dispute over MONOTHELETISM; they returned to communion with the pope in the 12th cent. In the 19th cent., massacres of Maronites by the Druses brought French intervention; this gave France its modern hold in Lebanon and Syria. Besides the Maronites there are two other groups in Syria in communion with the pope—the MELCHITES and the Syrian Catholics. See Donald Attwater, *The Christian Churches of the East*, Vol. I (1947).

maroon, term for a fugitive slave in the 17th and 18th cent. in the West Indies and Guiana, or for a descendant of such slaves. They were called *marron* by the French and *cimarrón* by the Spanish. Formerly much used in the West Indies and South America, the term later came to be used with particular reference to certain Negroes living in W Jamaica. The maroons fled when the British began their conquest of the island from the Spanish in 1655 and maintained a hostile independence until 1739, when a treaty granting them lands of their own and virtual independence was concluded. See R. C. Dallas, *The History of the Maroons* (1803); Carey Robinson, *The Fighting Maroons of Jamaica* (1969).

Marot, Clément (klāmäN' märō'), 1496?-1544, French court poet. Accused of heresy, he spent years in exile, writing in prison at Chartres his allegory *Enfer*. His light, graceful rondeaux, ballades, and epigrams won him the patronage of Francis I and Margaret of Navarre. He also translated the Psalms into French verse for the Genevan Psalter (see HYMN).

Maroth (mā'rŏth), unidentified town, SW Palestine. Micah 1.12.

Marozia (mərō'zhēə, Ital. märô'tsyä), c.892-c.937, Italian noblewoman. Daughter of the Roman consul Theophylact and his wife Theodora, Marozia was strongly influenced by her mother who controlled Roman politics and the papacy in what has been called the "pornocracy." The mistress of Pope Sergius III (904-11), Marozia married, in succession, Albert I of Spoleto (d. 926), Guido of Tuscany (d. 929), and Hugh of Provence, to help maintain her political control. Marozia received the titles "senatrix" and "patricia" from Pope John X (914-28); she nevertheless had him put to death in 928 in order to install her favorite candidates in papal office (including one of her sons as Pope John XI; 931-35). In 932, Marozia was overthrown by Albert II of Spoleto, a son of her first marriage, who had her imprisoned until her death.

Marprelate controversy (mär'prĕl''ĭt), a 16th-century English religious argument. Martin Marprelate was the pseudonym under which appeared several Puritan pamphlets (1588-89) satirizing the authoritarianism of the Church of England under Archbishop John Whitgift. The church replied in kind, but silenced the pamphleteer only after a reaction against him by the more conservative Puritans and after the use of police powers by Whitgift. A flood of both Martinist and anti-Martinist literature followed, to which Thomas Nashe, John Lyly, and Richard Harvey are supposed to have contributed. The true identity of Martin Marprelate has never been determined, but John PENRY may have been the chief author. See *The Marprelate Tracts* (ed. by William Pierce, 1911, repr. 1967); Edward Arber, *An Introductory Sketch to the Martin Marprelate Controversy, 1558-1590* (1895, repr. 1967); D. J. McGinn, *John Penry and the Marprelate Controversy* (1966).

Marquand, John Phillips (mär'kwŏnd), 1893-1960, American novelist, b. Wilmington, Del., grad. Harvard, 1915. Most of Marquand's gently satirical novels examine life among the rich and socially prominent of New England. Often they concern people too hidebound by money or tradition to change their lives for the better. He first won popularity with a series about a Japanese detective, "Mr. Moto," which ran in the *Saturday Evening Post*. His reputation as a novelist was established with *The Late George Apley* (1937, Pulitzer Prize) about a conservative Bostonian. Among his other novels are *Wickford Point* (1939), *H. M. Pulham, Esquire* (1941), *So Little Time* (1943), *Point of No Return* (1949), *Melville Goodwin, U S A* (1951), and *Life at Happy Knoll* (1957).

marque and reprisal: see PRIVATEERING.

Marquesas Islands (märkā'säs), volcanic group (1966 est. pop. 5,000), South Pacific, a part of FRENCH POLYNESIA. There are 12 islands in the group, which lies c.740 mi (1,190 km) NE of Tahiti. The largest island is NUKU HIVA; the second largest, HIVA OA, is the seat of the capital, ATUONA. The Marquesas, famous for their rugged beauty, are fertile and mountainous, rising to c.4,130 ft (1,260 m) on Hiva Oa. There are breadfruit, pandanus, and coconut trees; the limited fauna includes wild cattle and hogs. The chief exports are copra, tobacco, cotton, and vanilla. Taiohae Bay, on Nuka Hiva, and the Bay of Traitors, on Hiva Oa, are the major harbors. The islands are divided into two groups. The southern cluster (sometimes called the Mendaña Islands), including Fatu Huku, Hiva Oa, Tahuata, Motane, and Fatu Hiva, was discovered in 1595 by the Spanish navigator Alvaro de Mendaña de Neira; the northern group (sometimes called the Washington Islands), including Hatutu, Eiao, Motu Iti, Nuku Hiva, Ua Huku, Ua Pou, and Motu Oa, was discovered in 1791 by the American navigator Captain Joseph Ingraham. In 1813, Commodore David Porter claimed Nuku Hiva for the United States, naming it Madison Island, but the U.S. Congress never ratified the claim. France took possession of the islands in 1842 and established a settlement on Nuku Hiva, which was abandoned in 1859. In 1870 the French administration over the Marquesas was reinstated. Of all the Polynesian peoples, the Marquesans suffered the greatest decline from the spread of European diseases; in the 1850s they numbered some 20,000, about four times the present population. The islands are the setting for Herman Melville's novel *Typee*.

Marquet, Albert (älbĕr' märkā'), 1875-1947, French painter. In 1894 he met Matisse and later became associated with FAUVISM. His exuberantly colored figure studies are clearly fauvist. Marquet was a gifted draftsman. Many of his later landscapes and port scenes, painted with great clarity, are in American museums.

marquetry (mär'kətrē), branch of cabinetwork in which a decorative surface of wood or other substance is glued to an object on a single plane. Unlike inlaying, in which the secondary material is sunk into portions of a solid ground cut out to receive it, the technique of marquetry applies both field and pattern material as a veneer of equal thickness. Wood is most often used for the ground, or field, and to a considerable extent also—when of differing color, grain or kind—for the decorative sections. Tortoise shell, metal, ivory, and bone are also used. The process was derived from the true wood inlay known as INTARSIA and reached a high point of development in its use by the Dutch in the 17th cent.; subsequently the French were its chief exponents, with the Boulle family (see BOULLE, ANDRÉ CHARLES) creating a distinctive style through the use of copper and tortoiseshell. Marquetry in England was never carried to the heights of elaboration or technical brilliance reached on the Continent, but in the latter part of the 18th cent. work of considerable distinction and refinement was produced. See W. A. Lincoln, *The Art and Practice of Marquetry* (1974).

Marquette, Jacques (zhäk märkĕt'), 1637-75, French missionary and explorer in North America, a Jesuit priest. He was sent to New France in 1666 and studied Indian languages under a missionary at TROIS RIVIÈRES. In 1668 he was sent as a missionary to the Ottawa Indians, spent a winter at Sault Ste Marie, and in 1669 reached La Pointe mission on Chequamegon Bay. When fear of the Sioux drove the Ottawa and Huron Indians away from La Pointe, Marquette accompanied them to Mackinac, where he founded a new mission on Point St. Ignace. Contact with the Indians of Illinois had led Marquette to plan a mission among them, and he was also interested in the reports of a great south-running river. Therefore he welcomed his appointment by Frontenac, governor of New France, to accompany Louis JOLLIET on an expedition to find the river. They were the first to establish the existence of a water highway from the St. Lawrence to the Gulf of Mexico. On his return from the Mississippi voyage, Marquette stayed at Mackinac for a time, recovering his health and writing a journal of the voyage, which was first published (1681) in Thévenot's *Recueil de voyages*. In 1674 he set out to establish a mission in present-day Illinois, but his health broke. He was hastening back to Mackinac when he died near present-day Ludington, Mich. In 1677 his body was removed to St. Ignace. See edition (1900) of his journal in the *Jesuit Relations;* biographies by J. P. Donnelly (1968) and R. N. Hamilton (1970).

Marquette, city (1970 pop. 21,967), seat of Marquette co., N Mich., Upper Peninsula, on Lake Superior; settled 1849, inc. as a city 1871. It is a center of iron-ore shipping and of industry and trade for a mining, lumbering, farming, and resort region. Chemicals, wood products, and machinery are manufactured. Marquette is the seat of Northern Michigan Univ., and it also has a branch of the state prison. Nearby are a U.S. air force base, two state parks, and a fish hatchery.

Marquette University at Milwaukee, Wis.; Jesuit; coeducational; chartered 1864, opened 1881. The school achieved university status in 1907.

Marquis, Don (Donald Robert Perry Marquis) (mär'kwĭs), 1878-1937, American author, b. Walnut, Ill. In 1912 he began the humorous column "The Sun Dial" in the New York *Sun* and later conducted "The Lantern" in the *Herald Tribune*. He invented various characters of gay satire, notably "archy the cockroach" and "mehitabel the cat." Their saga is told in *Lives and times of archy and mehitabel* (3 vol. in 1, 1943). Marquis published innumerable stories, poems, and plays. He was most successful when writing satire.

Marrakesh (märä'kĕsh, mə-), Fr. *Marrakech*, city (1970 est. pop. 305,000), W central Morocco. The city, renowned for leather goods, is one of the principal commercial centers of Morocco. It was founded (1062) by the Almoravid leader Yusuf ibn Tashfin and was the capital of Morocco from then until 1147 and again from 1550 to 1660. It was captured by the French in 1912. Beautifully situated near the Atlas Mts., Marrakesh has extensive gardens, a 14th-century palace, and a former palace of the sultan that is now a museum of Moroccan art. The 220-ft (67-m) minaret (completed 1195) of the Koutoubya mosque dominates the city. The Université Ben Youssef, a center of Islamic studies, is in Marrakesh.

marram grass: see BEACH GRASS.

Marranos (mərä'nōs): see SEPHARDIM.

marriage, socially sanctioned union of one or more men with one or more women. In all societies limitations are placed on the choice of mates according to the rules of exogamy (the obligation to marry outside the group) and endogamy (the obligation to marry within the group). Exogamy usually applies to close relatives (see INCEST) and broad kinship groups such as the CLAN; endogamy applies chiefly to social groups such as the CASTE or to social classes. Rules of endogamy and exogamy frequently coexist. For example, marrying a cousin may be disapproved under the rules of exogamy, while marrying someone of a different race may be disapproved under the rules of endogamy. Until recent times, the selection of mates was guided primarily by social, economic, and political considerations aimed at the establishment of new ties or the consolidation of existing ones. Marriages were often arranged by the families through the services of a matchmaker or go-between (e.g., among the Australian aborigines, the Dayaks of Borneo, the Basutos and the Bambara of Africa, and the Arabs, as well as among many South American Indian tribes and the Slavic peoples of Europe). It was not unusual for the prospective husband and wife to be pledged in childhood, sometimes in infancy or even before birth. In such cases, the young female would often go to live with her future husband's family several years before the marriage was consummated. The exchange of property has often been a concomitant of marriage. When the property passes from the family of the wife to that of the husband, it is called a DOWRY. In the opposite case, it is called a bride price. The practice of exacting a bride price was prevalent in those societies where the woman was an important economic asset whose loss needed to be compensated. Sometimes, as among certain Siberian tribes, the bride price was paid in months or even years of labor by the husband to his father-in-law. In most societies the wedding celebration is ritualistic, often elaborately so. After the marriage the couple have three choices of residence. Depending upon the custom, they may establish patrilocal residence (with or near the husband's family), matrilocal residence (with or near the wife's family), or neolocal residence (independent of either). Another consideration is the number of husbands or wives permitted each spouse. Monogamy (the union of one wife to one husband) is the prevalent form almost everywhere, although polygyny (having several wives at one time) has been a prerogative in many societies (see HAREM). Polyandry (having several husbands at one time) is rare, occurring only in Tibet and a few other localities. Polygynous households are usually ruled by the first wife. The practice of wedding sisters to one husband is known as sororate marriage. The custom of marrying a widow to her late husband's brother is known as levirate marriage; it was common among the ancient Hebrews. Although marriage tends to be regarded in most places as a permanent tie, unsuccessful unions may be terminated in most societies. The causes of termination vary, but adultery, sterility, failure to provide the necessities of life, and mistreatment are the most common. The bride price, or dowry, if one has been given, usually has to be returned upon separation. In societies (usually preindustrial) where marriage is associated with extensive economic, political, religious, or social ties beyond the couple, divorce is relatively rare. It is most frequent in societies that approve marriage by free choice, a comparatively recent cultural phenomenon associated with the widespread social and economic changes of modern times (see FAMILY). Civil unions are now permitted in Western countries, but for nearly a thousand years marriage in the Western world was a religious contract. The Christian church undertook its supervision in the 9th cent., when newly wed couples instituted the practice of coming to the church door to have their union blessed by the priest. Eventually the church regulated marriage through canon law. The Roman Catholic and Orthodox churches consider matrimony a sacrament and an indissoluble contract. For the legal aspects of marriage, see HUSBAND AND WIFE; CONSANGUINITY; DIVORCE. See E. A. Westermark, *The History of Human Marriage* (5th ed., 3 vol., 1921; repr. 1971); M. B. Sussman, *Sourcebook in Marriage and the Family* (3d ed. 1968); M. W. Weil, ed., *Sociological Perspectives in Marriage and the Family* (1972).

marrow, soft tissue filling the spongy interiors of animal bones. Red marrow is the principal organ that forms blood cells in mammals, including man (see BLOOD). In children the bones contain only red marrow. As the skeleton matures, fat-storing yellow marrow displaces red marrow in the shafts of the long bones of the limbs. In adults red marrow remains chiefly in the ribs, the vertebrae, the pelvic bones, and the skull. Erythrocytes (red blood cells), platelets, and all but one kind of leucocyte (white blood cell) are manufactured in human red marrow. The marrow releases about 10 million to 15 million new erythrocytes every second, while an equivalent number are destroyed by the spleen. Disease of the marrow, such as leukemia, or injury to it from metallic poisons can interfere with the production of erythrocytes, causing ANEMIA.

Marryat, Frederick (mâr'ēăt), 1792–1848, English novelist. He is famous for his thrilling tales of sea adventure. His 24 years of service in the British navy in various parts of the world provided background for his stories. Noted for their humor and robust vigor, his novels include *Frank Mildmay* (1829), *Peter Simple* (1834), *Mr. Midshipman Easy* (1836), and *Snarleyyow; or, The Dog Fiend* (1837). In his later years he devoted himself to writing adventure books for children, notably *Masterman Ready* (1841) and *The Children of the New Forest* (1847). A trip (1837–39) to North America resulted in his unfavorable account of American manners, *A Diary in America* (1839). See *The Life and Letters of Captain Marryat* (1872) by his daughter Florence Marryat; biography by David Hannay (1889, repr. 1973).

Mars, in astronomy, 4th planet from the sun, with an orbit next in order beyond that of the earth. Mars has a striking red appearance, and when most favorably seen, it is twice as bright as Sirius, the brightest star. The mean distance of Mars from the sun is about 141 million mi (228 million km); its period of revolution is about 687 days, almost twice that of the earth. At those times when the sun, earth, and Mars are aligned (i.e., in opposition) and Mars is at its closest point to the sun (perihelion), its distance from the earth is about 35 million mi (56 million km); this occurs every 15 to 17 years. At oppositions when Mars is at its greatest distance from the sun (aphelion) it is about 63 million mi (101 million km) from the earth. Mars has a diameter of 4,200 mi (6,800 km), just over half the diameter of the earth, and its mass is only 11% of the earth's mass. It rotates on its axis with a period of about 24 hr 37 min, a little more than one earth day. The planet has a very thin atmosphere composed mainly of carbon dioxide. Scientists have also detected a slight amount of water vapor and traces of ammonia and methane, two vital substances in the early atmosphere of the earth. From these, together with other substances known to be in the Martian atmosphere, basic forms of life may have evolved. The greater part of its surface area appears to be a vast desert, dull red or orange in color. This color may be due to various oxides in the surface composition, particularly those of iron. About one fourth to one third of the surface is composed of darker areas whose nature is still uncertain. Because the plane of rotation is tilted about 25° to the plane of revolution, Mars experiences seasons somewhat similar to those of the earth. One of the most apparent seasonal changes is the growing or shrinking of white areas near the poles known as polar caps. These polar caps may be composed of ordinary ice or of dry ice (frozen carbon dioxide) and are thought to be only a few inches thick. During the Martian summer the polar cap in that hemisphere shrinks and the dark regions grow darker; in winter the polar cap grows again and the dark regions become paler. Studies of these changes (1969) indicate a migration of water vapor between the polar caps and the dark areas suggesting that the dark areas are a simple type of vegetation; however, no direct evidence confirms this, and other nonorganic explanations are possible. Photographs sent back by space probes show the surface of Mars to be pitted with a number of large craters, much like the surface of the moon. One interesting surface feature is a network of linelike markings first studied in detail (1877) by G. V. Schiaparelli and referred to by him as *canali*, the Italian word meaning "channels" or "grooves." Percival Lowell, then a leading authority on Mars, created a long-lasting controversy by accepting these "canals" to be the work of intelligent beings. It now appears clear that they are some sort of natural feature, perhaps rock faults similar to those on the earth. In addition to its barren surface, Mars has an extreme day-to-night temperature range, from about 80°F (27°C) at noon to about -100°F (-73°C) at midnight, resulting from its thin atmosphere. Mars has two natural satellites, discovered by Asaph Hall in 1877. The innermost of these, Phobos, is about 7 mi (11 km) in diameter and orbits the planet with a period far less than Mars's period of rotation (7 hr 39 min), causing it to rise in the west and set in the east. The outer satellite, Deimos, is about 4 mi (6 km) in diameter and is the smallest known satellite of the planets. See Patrick Moore and C. A. Cross, *Mars* (1973).

Mars, in Roman religion, god of war. In early Roman times he was a god of agriculture, but in later religion (when he was identified with the Greek Ares) he was primarily associated with war. Mars was the father of Romulus, the founder of the Roman nation, and, next to Jupiter, he enjoyed the highest position in Roman religion. The Salii, his priests, honored him by dancing in full armor in the Campus Martius, the site of his altar. Chariot races and the sacrifice of animals were primary features of the festivals held in his honor in March (named for him) and October. Mars was represented as an armed warrior. His attributes include the spear and shield, and the wolf and woodpecker were sacred to him. He was frequently associated with Bellona, the Roman goddess of war.

Marsala (märsä'lä), city (1971 pop. 79,568), W Sicily, Italy, a port on the Mediterranean Sea, located on Cape Boeo. It is noted for its sweet wine. The ancient LILYBAEUM, it was later renamed Marsah al Allah [port of God] by the Arabs. In 1860, Garibaldi landed there at the start of his successful campaign to conquer the kingdom of the Two Sicilies.

Marschner, Heinrich August (hīn'rĭkh ou'go͝ost märsh'nər), 1795–1861, German opera composer. Marschner's first opera was produced by Carl Maria von Weber in Dresden in 1820. He worked with Weber at the Dresden Opera from 1823 to 1826. His most famous works are *Der Vampyr* (1828); *Der Templer und die Jüdin* (1829), based on Scott's *Ivanhoe;* and *Hans Heiling* (1833). Marschner's operas continued Weber's romantic style; his use of full orchestration influenced Wagner.

Marsden, Samuel, 1764–1838, Anglican clergyman and chaplain of a convict colony in New Zealand. He introduced domestic animals (especially sheep) into New Zealand. As director of the first missionary settlement there in 1814, Marsden began a tradition of missionary protection of the Maori natives against the incursion of European settlers.

Marseilles (märsā'), Fr. *Marseille,* city (1968 pop. 893,771), capital of Bouches-du-Rhône dept., SE France, on the Gulf of Lions, an arm of the Mediterranean Sea. It is the second largest city of France and one of its most important seaports; an underground canal (see ROVE TUNNEL) links it with the Rhône River. Marseilles is a major industrial city where flour, vegetable oil, soap, cement, sugar, sulfur, chemicals, and processed foods are produced. The oldest town of France, it was settled by Phocaean Greeks from Asia Minor c.600 B.C. Known as Massilia, it became an ally of Rome, which annexed it (49 B.C.) after it supported Pompey against Caesar in the Roman civil war. Although the city retained its internal autonomy, it was of secondary importance during the Middle Ages. The upper city was ruled by its bishops from A.D. 539 until 1288, when it was reunited with the lower city, which had been governed independently by a city council since 1214. During the CRUSADES (11th–14th cent.) Marseilles was a commercial center and a transit port for the Holy Land. The city declined commercially in the first half of the 14th cent. Marseilles was taken by Charles I of Anjou (13th cent.) and then absorbed by Provence and bequeathed (with Provence) to the French crown in 1481. In the 1700s commerce revived, mainly with the LEVANT and the BARBARY STATES; although the plague wiped out almost half its population in 1720, Marseilles continued to enjoy prosperity until the French Revolution, during which it was torn by civil strife. In the 19th cent. the French conquest of Algeria and the opening of the Suez Canal led to a tremendous expansion of the port of Marseilles and to the city's industrialization. The sight of Marseilles from the sea, a gleaming white city rising on a semicircle of bare hills, is famous. Despite its long history, Marseilles has few buildings dating back further than the 18th cent. The Canebière, the principal thoroughfare, is one of the great avenues of the world. The science and medical schools of the university of Aix-en-Provence are in Marseilles. There are also industrial and engineering schools, the National School of Marine Commerce, and an observatory. A landmark of Marseilles harbor is the CHATEAU D'IF, a castle built on a small, rocky isle. Excavations in 1966–67 uncovered what are believed to be vestiges of the ramparts of old Massilia.

Marsena (mär'sēnə), counselor of King Ahasuerus. Esther 1.14.

Marsh, Adam, or **Adam de Marisco** (mâr'ĭskō), d. 1259?, English Franciscan scholar. He was a student of Robert GROSSETESTE. When Grosseteste became bishop, Marsh took his place in the Franciscan school at Oxford. Marsh's advice and his services as a peacemaker were constantly sought, and Grosseteste relied heavily on him. Actively supporting the reform party of Simon de MONTFORT (1208?–1265),

Marsh was able nevertheless to retain the confidence of Henry III. Of his writings only his letters survive.

Marsh, Dame Ngaio (nī'ō), 1899- detective story writer, b. New Zealand. She was an art student, actress, and theatrical producer before her first novel, *A Man Lay Dead,* was published in 1934. Her many mystery novels, acute in characterization and literate in style, reflect her knowledge of the art studio and the theater. They include *Artists in Crime* (1938), *Died in the Wool* (1945), *False Scent* (1959), *Killer Dolphin* (1966) and *Black As He's Painted* (1974). She was made a Dame of the British Empire in 1966. See her autobiography (1966).

Marsh, Reginald, 1898-1954, American painter and illustrator, b. Paris. Both his parents were artists. After their return to the United States, he studied at Yale (B.A., 1920). He worked as an illustrator for *Vanity Fair, Harper's Bazaar,* and the New York *Daily News,* and later he was a scene designer. He then studied under John Sloan and K. H. Miller at the Art Students League. From 1925 to 1939 he made two trips to Europe and sketched for the *New Yorker.* His lively recordings of Manhattan street life in many media were popular. *"Why Not Use the 'L'?"* (1930; Whitney Mus., New York City) is typical. Marsh painted two celebrated murals in the Post Office Building, Washington, D.C. See study by Lloyd Goodrich (1972).

marsh: see SWAMP.

Marshal, William: see PEMBROKE, WILLIAM MARSHAL, 1ST EARL OF.

Marshall, Alfred, 1842-1924, English economist. At Cambridge, where he taught from 1885 to 1908, he exerted great influence on the development of economic thought of the time. He systematized the classical economic theories and made new analyses in the same manner, thus laying the foundation of the neoclassical school of economics. He was concerned with theories of costs, value, and distribution and developed a concept of marginal utility. His *Principles of Economics* (1890) was for years the standard work and is still accepted by some. Among his other works is *Industry and Trade* (1919). See A. C. Pigou, ed., *Memorials of Alfred Marshall* (1925, repr. 1966). *What I Remember* (1947), by M. P. Marshall, his wife, has some biographical material on him. See studies by H. J. Davenport (1935, repr. 1965) and Clark Kerr (1969).

Marshall, George Catlett, 1880-1959, American army officer and cabinet member, b. Uniontown, Pa. A career army officer, Marshall distinguished himself as a staff officer in World War I and later (1919-24) was aide to General Pershing. After varied tasks, including service in China (1924-27), he headed (1939-45) the army as Chief of Staff, becoming General of the Army (five-star general) in Dec., 1944. Helping to direct Allied strategy in World War II, Marshall advocated the conquest of Germany through France, and his plan was finally adopted. Many of his wartime tasks were diplomatic. When he resigned as Chief of Staff, he was promptly appointed (Nov., 1945) special ambassador to China by President Truman and was later recalled (Jan., 1947) to be made Secretary of State. After engineering (Feb., 1947) immediate aid to Greece and Turkey, he fostered the European Recovery Program (called the MARSHALL PLAN) to promote postwar economic recovery in Europe. He resigned because of ill health in Jan., 1949. In Sept., 1950, he was called out of retirement to become Secretary of Defense, but he resigned from this post in Sept., 1951. For the Marshall Plan he received the 1953 Nobel Peace Prize. See biography by F. C. Pogue (3 vol., 1963-73).

Marshall, James Wilson, 1810-85, American pioneer, discoverer of gold in California, b. Hunterdon co., N.J. Migrating to California for his health, he arrived at Sutter's Fort (site of present Sacramento) in 1845 and soon acquired land and livestock. After fighting in the Mexican War, he returned in 1847 to find his livestock gone. Having sold his land, he undertook to build a sawmill for John A. SUTTER. In Jan., 1848, while supervising the digging of the mill race, Marshall discovered gold. This discovery launched the famous gold rush of 1849. The claims of Marshall and Sutter were ignored, the sawmill failed, and Marshall ended his days, embittered and misanthropic, working as a gardener. See biography by Theressa Gay (1967).

Marshall, John, 1755-1835, American jurist, 4th Chief Justice of the United States (1801-35), b. Virginia. The eldest of 15 children, John Marshall was born in a log cabin on the Virginia frontier (today in Fauquier co., Va.) and spent his childhood and youth in primitive surroundings. His father rose to prominence in local and state politics. Through his mother he was related to the Lees and the Randolphs and to Thomas Jefferson, later his great antagonist. Marshall first left home for any length of time to serve as an officer in the American Revolution. He returned in 1779 after attending for a few months lectures on law given by George Wythe at the College of William and Mary (his only formal education). Admitted to the bar in 1780, he practiced law in the West and was elected (1782) a delegate to the Virginia assembly. He married and settled in Richmond, his home until his death. His brilliant skill in argument made him one of the most esteemed of the many great lawyers of Virginia. A defender of the new U.S. Constitution at the Virginia ratifying convention, Marshall later staunchly supported the Federalist administration, and after refusing Washington's offer to make him U.S. Attorney General or minister to France, he finally accepted appointment as one of the commissioners to France in the diplomatic dispute that ended in the XYZ AFFAIR. Marshall's effectiveness there made him a popular figure, and he was elected to Congress as a Federalist in 1799. One of the tiny group that continued to support President John Adams, he was prevailed upon to become Secretary of State (1800-1801). Before he left the cabinet he was appointed Chief Justice and confirmed by the Senate despite some opposition. In his long service on the bench, Marshall raised the Supreme Court from an anomalous position in the Federal scheme to power and majesty, and he molded the Constitution by the breadth and wisdom of his interpretation; he eminently deserves the appellation the Great Chief Justice. He dominated the court equally by his personality and his ability, and his achievements were made in spite of virulent quarrels with Jefferson and later Presidents. A loyal Federalist, Marshall saw in the Constitution the instrument of national unity and Federal power and the guarantee of the security of private property. He made incontrovertible the previously uncertain right of the Supreme Court to review Federal and state laws and to pronounce final judgment on their constitutionality. He viewed the Constitution on the one hand as a precise document setting forth specific powers and on the other hand as a living instrument that should be broadly interpreted so as to give the Federal government the means to act effectively within its limited sphere (see MCCULLOCH VS. MARYLAND). His opinion in the DARTMOUTH COLLEGE CASE was the most famous of those that dealt with the constitutional requirement of the inviolability of contract, another favorite theme with Marshall. His interpretation of the interstate commerce clause of the Constitution, most notably in GIBBONS VS. OGDEN, made it a powerful extension of Federal power at the expense of the states. In general Marshall opposed STATES' RIGHTS doctrines, and there were many criticisms advanced against him and against the increasing prestige of the Supreme Court. The sometimes undignified quarrel with Jefferson (which had one of its earliest expressions in MARBURY VS. MADISON) reached a high point in the trial (1807) of Aaron BURR for treason. Marshall presided as circuit judge and interpreted the clause in the Constitution requiring proof of an "overt act" for conviction of treason so that Burr escaped conviction because he had only engaged in a conspiracy. Marshall's difficulties with President Jackson reached their peak when Marshall declared against Georgia in the matter of expelling the Cherokee Indians, a decision that the state flouted. Marshall in his arguments drew much from his colleagues, especially his devoted adherent, Justice Joseph Story, and he was stimulated and inspired by the lawyers pleading before the court, among them some of the most brilliant legal minds America has seen, including Daniel Webster, Luther Martin, William Pinkney, William Wirt, and Jeremiah Mason. Marshall in his manners combined the unceremonious heartiness of the frontier with the leisurely grace of the Virginia aristocracy. So great was his winning charm and so absolute his integrity that he gained the admiration of his enemies and the unbounded affection of his friends. His style combined conciseness and precision. He wrote each opinion as a series of logical deductions from self-evident propositions, and it was almost never his practice to cite legal authority. It is in these opinions that his literary skill is shown rather than in his major nonlegal work, *The Life of George Washington* (5 vol., 1804-7). Marshall's constitutional opinions are collected in editions by J. M. Dillon (1903) and J. P. Cotton (1905). An autobiographic sketch was published in 1937. See biography by Leonard Baker (1974); John E. Oster, *The Political and Economic Doctrines of John Marshall* (1914, repr. 1967); R. K. Faulkner, *Jurisprudence of John Marshall* (1968); William M. Jones, ed., *Chief Justice John Marshall: A Reappraisal* (1956, repr. 1971).

Marshall, Samuel Lyman Atwood (S. L. A. Marshall), 1900-, American author and military analyst, b. Catskill, N.Y. After serving in World War I, he embarked upon a career in journalism, working as an editorial writer and military critic for the *Detroit News.* In World War II he was chief combat historian in the Central Pacific (1943) and chief historian for the European Theater of Operations (1945) and during the Korean War was an infantry operations analyst for the U.S. army, with the rank of brigadier general. Marshall developed several systems to analyze infantry performance in battle. Among his many works are *Blitzkrieg* (1940); *Armies on Wheels* (1941); *Men against Fire* (1947); *The River and the Gauntlet* (1953); *Pork Chop Hill* (1956); *Sinai Victory* (1958); *Night Drop* (1962); and *Crimsoned Prairie* (1972).

Marshall, Thomas Riley, 1854-1925, U.S. Vice President (1913-21), b. North Manchester, Ind. A lawyer in Columbia City, Ind., he was Democratic governor of the state (1909-13) and sponsored much labor and social legislation before being elected Vice President on the ticket with Woodrow Wilson. His was the expression "What this country needs is a really good five-cent cigar." See his recollections (1925).

Marshall, Thurgood, 1908-, U.S. lawyer and Associate Justice of the U.S. Supreme Court (1967-), b. Baltimore, Md. He received his law degree from Howard Univ. in 1933. After private practice in Baltimore he joined (1936) the legal staff of the National Association for the Advancement of Colored People. Becoming head of the legal staff in 1938, he was extremely active and successful in civil-rights litigation; he argued the landmark 1954 desegregation in education case before the U.S. Supreme Court. Appointed a judge of the U.S. Court of Appeals in 1961, he became U.S. Solicitor General in 1965. President Lyndon B. Johnson appointed him to the Supreme Court two years later; he was the first black to sit on the high court. There he became aligned with the other liberal activist justices. See study by R. W. Bland (1973).

Marshall. **1** City (1970 pop. 12,051), seat of Saline co., N central Mo.; inc. 1839. It is the processing center of a farm area, with meat-packing houses, grain and seed mills, and cold storage facilities. Shoes are also manufactured. It is the seat of Missouri Valley College. George Caleb Bingham lived there. **2** City (1970 pop. 22,937), seat of Harrison co., E Texas, in a pine-covered hill and lake area; inc. 1844. Live-oak-shaded streets and mansions recall the plantation past of the city, which now has railroad shops and chemical and aluminum industries. It is the seat of East Texas Baptist College and Wiley College.

Marshall Islands, archipelago (1970 pop. 22,888), central Pacific, an administrative district of the U.S. Trust Territory of the PACIFIC ISLANDS. The Marshalls extend over a 700-mi (1,130-km) area and comprise two major groups: the Ratak Chain in the east, and the Ralik Chain in the west, with a total of 34 atolls, c.900 reefs, and a land area of 70 sq mi (181 sq km). KWAJALEIN, the largest atoll, is the district headquarters of the Ralik Chain; Majuro, the chief island of the Ratak Chain, is also the administrative center of all the Marshalls; JALUIT, with a fine natural harbor, is the archipelago's chief trade center. The population of the Marshalls is largely Micronesian. The chief industry is coconut planting; copra, sugar, and coffee are the major exports. Some of the islands were discovered by Spanish explorers in the early 16th cent. and were named after a British captain who visited them in 1788. Much mapping was done on Russian expeditions under Adam Johann von KRUSENSTERN (1803) and Otto von KOTZEBUE (1815 and 1823). Germany annexed the group in 1885 and tried with little success to establish a colony. The administrative affairs of the islands continued to be managed largely by private German and Australian interests. In 1914, Japan seized the Marshalls and in 1920 received a League of Nations mandate over them. In World War II the islands were taken by U.S. forces (1943-44); they were included in the Trust Territory of the Pacific Islands in 1947. See E. H. Bryan, *Life in the Marshall Islands* (1972).

Marshall Plan or **European Recovery Program,** project instituted at the Paris Economic Conference (July, 1947) to foster economic recovery in certain European countries after World War II. The Marshall Plan took form when U.S. Secretary of State George

C. Marshall urged (June 5, 1947) that European countries decide on their economic needs so that material and financial aid from the United States could be integrated on a broad scale. In April, 1948, President Truman signed the act establishing the Economic Cooperation Administration (ECA) to administer the program. The ECA was created to promote European production, to bolster European currency, and to facilitate international trade. Another object was the containment of growing Soviet influence (through national Communist parties), especially in Czechoslovakia, France, and Italy. Paul G. Hoffman was named (April, 1948) economic cooperation administrator, and in the same year the participating countries (Austria, Belgium, Denmark, France, West Germany, Great Britain, Greece, Iceland, Italy, Luxembourg, the Netherlands, Norway, Sweden, Switzerland, Turkey, and the United States) signed an accord establishing the Organization for European Economic Cooperation (later called the Organization for Economic Cooperation and Development) as the master coordinating agency. The ECA functioned until 1951, when its activities were transferred to the Mutual Security Agency. Over $12 billion was dispersed (1948–51) under the program. From the start the Soviet Union strongly opposed the Marshall Plan while the various countries in Eastern Europe denounced or ignored it. The Marshall Plan, completed in 1952, was one aspect of the FOREIGN AID program of the United States and greatly contributed to the economic recovery of Europe. See S. E. Harris, ed., *Foreign Economic Policy for the United States* (1948, repr. 1968); H. B. Price, *The Marshall Plan and Its Meaning* (1955).

Marshalltown, city (1970 pop. 26,219), seat of Marshall co., central Iowa, on the Iowa River; inc. 1863. It is the rail and trade center of a rich grain and livestock area and a busy manufacturing city with the nickname of "Little Pittsburgh." The state soldiers' home and a junior college are there.

Marshall University, at Huntington, W.Va.; state supported; coeducational. It achieved university status in 1961.

marsh antelope, name for members of a group of deerlike African ANTELOPES, usually found in reeds or tall grasses near water. The males of this group have horns that curve back, up, and forward; females are hornless. Most marsh antelopes travel in small herds. The waterbucks are large marsh antelopes with long, coarse, brown hair. The males stand up to 50 in. (125 cm) at the shoulder and weigh up to 500 lb (225 kg). They are found in reedy or grassy country but may wander several miles from water. Strong swimmers, they often take to water when pursued. The common waterbuck (*Kobus ellipsiprymnus*) is found in S and E Africa, the Defassa waterbuck, (*K. defassa*) in central Africa. The kob (*K. kob*) and the puku (*K. vardoni*), of equatorial Africa, are smaller, reddish antelopes, always found close to water or swamps. The lechwes are the most aquatic of the marsh antelopes; they often spend the day submerged up to the neck. The red lechwe (*K. leche*) is found in S Africa, and the Nile lechwe (*K. megaceros*) in the Sudan. The reedbucks (genus *Redunca*), whose different species are distributed over most of Africa, are small, generally solitary antelopes about 30 in. (76 cm) high; the smallest, the mountain reedbuck (*Redunca fulvorufula*), is found in the hills and mountains of E Africa. The rhebok *(Pelea capreolus)* resembles the reedbuck but has a woolly coat; it is found in hilly country in S Africa. Marsh antelopes are classified in the phylum CHORDATA, subphylum Vertebrata, class Mammalia, order Artiodactyla, family Bovidae.

marsh buck: see BUSHBUCK.

Marshfield. 1 Resort town (1970 pop. 15,223), Plymouth co., SE Mass., on the Atlantic coast; settled 1632, inc. 1640. Sand and gravel are the major industrial products. Points of interest include Winslow House, home of Edward Winslow, and several other colonial buildings. Daniel Webster lived in Marshfield and is buried there. **2** City (1970 pop. 15,619), Marathon and Wood co., central Wis., in a dairy area; inc. 1883. Cheese, lumber, fabricated metal, concrete, and mobile homes are among the city's products. A branch of the Univ. of Wisconsin Center System is there.

marsh gas: see METHANE.

Mars' Hill, name given in the Bible for the AREOPAGUS at Athens. Acts 17.22.

marsh mallow and **marshmallow:** see MALLOW.

marsh marigold, perennial spring-blooming Old World and North American plant (*Caltha palustris*) of the family Ranunculaceae (BUTTERCUP family), found in wet places. It has rounded glossy leaves and large buttercuplike flowers of bright and shining yellow. The tops are reputed to be toxic but with boiling become edible and are often eaten as greens while young; the flower buds are pickled and used as capers, and the flowers have been used for beverages. In the United States it is sometimes called cowslip. Other species of *Caltha* are also called marsh marigold. Marsh marigolds are classified in the division MAGNOLIOPHYTA, class Magnoliopsida, order Ranunculales, family Ranunculaceae.

Marsh test, method for the detection of ARSENIC, so sensitive that it can be used to detect minute amounts of arsenic in foods (the residue of fruit spray) or in stomach contents. The sample is placed in a flask with arsenic-free zinc and sulfuric acid. Arsine gas (also hydrogen) forms and is led through a drying tube to a hard glass tube in which it is heated. The arsenic is deposited as a "mirror" just beyond the heated area and on any cold surface held in the burning gas emanating from the jet. Antimony gives a similar test, but the deposit is insoluble in sodium hypochlorite, whereas arsenic will dissolve. The test was named for its inventor, the English chemist James Marsh.

Marsic War: see SOCIAL WAR.

Marsilius of Padua (märsĭl'ēəs, pă'dyo͞oə), d. c.1342, Italian political philosopher. He is satirically called Marsiglio. Little is known with certainty of his life except that he was rector of the Univ. of Paris c.1312. When Holy Roman Emperor LOUIS IV was seeking a theorist to assist him in his struggle with Pope JOHN XXII, Marsilius composed a tract, *Defensor pacis* [the defender of peace], probably in collaboration with the Averroist John of Jandun. It was published in 1324 and proved to be one of the most revolutionary of medieval documents. The work held that all power is derived from the people and their ruler is only their delegate; there is no law but the popular will, as expressed in the ruler. The church too has no authority apart from the people, and the actual power of the Holy See is self-arrogated; the church should be under the ruler, its province should be purely that of worship, and it should be governed by periodic councils. The notion that princes derive their power from the people was current in scholasticism, but the antiecclesiastical argument of the work aroused great scandal. It was repeatedly condemned by the Holy See. Marsilius, however, continued under the emperor's protection and went in Louis's train to Rome for his coronation and attended him afterwards. His lesser works include an argument that the emperor had final jurisdiction in matrimonial cases (1342). The *Defensor pacis* had a long life; John GERSON recommended it, and in England, during Henry VIII's fight with the church, Thomas Cromwell patronized its translation into English (1535). See the modern edition of Alan Gewirth (1967); also Alan Gewirth, *Marsilius of Padua and Medieval Political Philosophy* (1951).

Marston, John, 1576–1634, English satirist and dramatist, b. Oxfordshire, grad. Oxford, 1594. In accordance with his father's wishes he studied law at Middle Temple, but his interests soon turned to literature. His first published works, a licentious, satiric love poem entitled *The Metamorphosis of Pigmalion's Image* and *The Scourge of Villanie*, a volume of coarse verse satires, appeared in 1598. After both these works were burned in 1599 by order of the archbishop of Canterbury, Marston began writing for the stage. His most notable plays are the love story *Antonio and Mellida* (1599); its sequel, the revenge tragedy *Antonio's Revenge* (1599); his masterpiece, *The Malcontent* (1604), a tragicomedy that examines moral deformity; and *The Dutch Courtezan* (1605), a bitterly anti-female comedy. Marston was involved in the war of the theaters against Ben Jonson from 1599 to 1601, while both playwrights were writing for rival companies of child actors. Later, the two men became friends and collaborated with George Chapman in writing *Eastward Ho!* (1605). Marston ended his literary career c.1607, and two years later he took holy orders. See his plays ed. by H. H. Wood (3 vol., 1934–39); his poems ed. by A. Davenport (1961); study by P. J. Finckelpearl (1969).

Marston, John Westland, 1819–90, English author. Although his poetic dramas, including *The Patrician's Daughter* (1842) and *The Favourite of Fortune* (1866), were popular, he is more noteworthy for his literary criticism, most particularly his review of Swinburne's *Atalanta in Calydon.* His son **Philip Bourke Marston** (1850–87), blind from the age of three, wrote four volumes of verse in the manner of the PRE-RAPHAELITES; they include *Songtide* (1871) and *Wind Voices* (1883).

Marston Moor, battlefield, West Riding of Yorkshire, N England, near York. The battle fought there on July 2, 1644, between the royalists, under Prince Rupert and the duke of Newcastle, and the parliamentarians, under Lord Fairfax of Cameron, Oliver Cromwell, and the earl of Leven, resulted in the first major victory for the parliamentarians in the ENGLISH CIVIL WAR.

marsupial (märso͞o'pēəl), member of the order Marsupialia, or pouched mammals. With the exception of the New World OPOSSUMS and an obscure S American family (Caenolestidae), marsupials are now found only in Australia, Tasmania, New Guinea, and a few adjacent islands. They are generally distinguished from the higher, or placental, mammals by the absence of a placenta connecting the embryo with its mother, although in a few forms the female has a rudimentary placenta that functions for a short time. The embryo is nourished during its brief gestation by a fluid secreted by the mother's uterus. The young are born in a very undeveloped state; at birth the great gray KANGAROO is about 1 in. (2.5 cm) long and the opossum about 1½ in. (3.8 cm) long. Immediately after birth the young crawl to the mother's nipples and remain attached to them while continuing their development. As they are still too helpless to suckle, milk is squirted into them by the periodic contraction of muscles over the mother's mammary glands. In nearly all marsupials the female's nipples are covered by a pouch, or marsupium, formed by a fold of abdominal skin. Even after the suckling stage the young return at times to the pouch for shelter and transportation. In many species the young are carried on the mother's back after the suckling stage. In addition to having a less efficient reproductive system than the placental mammals, marsupials are of generally lower intelligence. They were once widespread over the earth, but were displaced in most regions as the more successful placental mammals evolved. The Australian region, which has been isolated from contact with other regions since the Cretaceous period, had almost no native placental mammals, and the marsupials were able to continue their evolution there without competition. They underwent an ADAPTIVE RADIATION in Australia comparable to that of placental mammals in the rest of the world, evolving many forms that superficially resemble various placental mammals and fill the same ecological niches. Thus, there are animals known as Tasmanian wolves (see THYLACINE), marsupial moles, marsupial mice, and native cats (see DASYURE), which live very much like the correspondingly named placental mammals and, in many cases, are strikingly similar in appearance. See BANDICOOT, NUMBAT, PHALANGER, TASMANIAN DEVIL, WOMBAT. See Hugh Tyndale-Biscoe, *Life of Marsupials* (1973).

marsupial anteater: see NUMBAT.

Marsyas (mär'sēəs), in Greek mythology, Phrygian satyr. He found the flute that Athena had invented but had thrown away. He became so skillful with the instrument that he challenged the lyre-playing Apollo to a contest. Apollo accepted on the condition that the victor might do as he would with the vanquished. The Muses, acting as judges, awarded the contest to Apollo. Apollo promptly flayed Marsyas for his presumption. The river Marsyas sprang from his blood or from the tears of his mourners. Among the many statues depicting this event is the *Flaying of Marsyas,* in the Villa Albani, Rome.

Martaban, Gulf of (märtəbăn', -băn'), arm of the Andaman Sea, indenting S Burma and receiving the waters of the Rangoon, Sittang, and Salween rivers. The small port of Martaban, located at the mouth of the Salween across the river from Moulmein, is famous for its glazed pottery.

marten, name for carnivorous, largely arboreal mammals (genus *Martes*) of the WEASEL family, widely distributed in North America, Europe, and central Asia. Martens are larger, heavier-bodied animals than weasels, with thick fur and bushy tails. Members of most species are brown above and light-colored below. The American marten, *Martes americana,* also called American pine marten and American, or Hudson Bay, sable, is from 20 to 25 in. (51–64 cm) long, including the 7- to 8-in. (18- to 20-cm) tail, and has yellow-brown fur. It lives in coniferous forests from Alaska to the extreme N United States, extending south in western mountain ranges. It is mostly nocturnal and spends much of the time in trees, where it leaps from branch to branch, although it also forages on the ground; it makes its den in a hollow tree or log. Its diet consists chiefly of small animals, especially red squirrels (*Tamiasciurus*), but it also eats berries and nuts. The other

North American species, *M. pennanti,* is called FISHER; both are valued for their fur. Similar to the American marten are the European pine marten, *M. martes,* and the stone, or beech, marten, *M. foina,* of Europe and central Asia. The stone marten is grayish. The Siberian SABLE, *M. zibellina,* is a marten species that produces extremely valuable fur. The yellow-throated martens, *M. flavigula* of E Asia and *M. gwatkinsi* of S Asia, are patterned in shades of brown, yellow, and orange. Martens are classified in the phylum CHORDATA, subphylum Vertebrata, class Mammalia, order Carnivora, family Mustelidae.

Martens, Feodor (fyô'dər mär'tĕns), 1845-1909, Russian diplomat and authority on international law. He became an official in the foreign ministry in 1868 and was professor of international law at the Univ. of St. Petersburg from 1873 to 1907. He was a representative at many international conferences, including the Hague Conferences of 1899 and 1907, for which he helped lay the foundation. His decisions as arbitrator and his many books contributed much to international law, and his efforts toward international understanding earned him the Nobel Peace Prize in 1902.

Martens, Georg Friedrich von, 1756-1821, German writer on international law, b. Hamburg. He was professor of international law at Göttingen (1783-89), a state councilor of Westphalia (1808-13), and the representative of the king of Hanover in the diet of Frankfurt (1816-21). His two great works (written in French) were a comparative study of European law, *Précis du droit des gens modernes de l'Europe* (2 vol., 1789; tr. *Summary of the Law of Nations,* 1795; a revision of an earlier work in Latin), and an enormous collection of treaties signed after 1761, *Recueil des principaux traités . . .* [collection of treaties] (7 vol., 1791-1801), which was continually brought up to date until the end of World War II (3d series, 41 vol., 1908-44).

Martha, friend of Jesus, sister of Mary and Lazarus of Bethany. Luke 10.38-42; John 11.1-46; 12.1-9. In medieval Christian literature, Martha was a symbol of the active, as opposed to the contemplative, life. Feast: July 29.

Martha's Vineyard (vĭn'yərd), island (1970 est. pop. 6,000), c.100 sq mi (260 sq km), SE Mass., separated from the Elizabeth Islands and Cape Cod by Vineyard and Nantucket sounds. As a result of glaciation, the island has morainal hills composed of boulders and clay deposits in the north, and low, sandy plains in the south. The English were the first to settle the island (1642); they engaged in farming, brickmaking, salt production, and fishing. Martha's Vineyard became an important commercial center, with whaling and fishing as the main occupations, in the 18th and early 19th cent. In the late 1800s the island, with its harbors, beaches, and scenic attractions, developed into a summer resort. It is divided into the towns of Chilmark, Edgartown, Gay Head, Oak Bluffs, Tisbury, and West Tisbury. Much of the island's interior is set aside as a state forest.

Martí, José (hōsā' märtē'), 1853-95, Cuban essayist, poet, and patriot, leader of the Cuban struggle for independence. One of the greatest prose writers of Spanish America, he is noted for his fluent style and vivid imagery. In *Nuestra América* (1891) and other essays he brilliantly analyzed the sociopolitical problems of Latin America. As a poet he wrote the famous *Ismaelillo* (1882), *Versos libres* (c.1882, pub. 1913), and a collection of exquisite lyrics, *Versos sencillos* (1891). His disregard for the stilted rhetoric of most 19th-century Spanish literature made him a precursor of the MODERNISMO movement. Simultaneously a poet and a man of action, Martí led a life of heroic dedication to the cause of Cuban independence. At the age of 16 he was arrested and exiled. A long and arduous pilgrimage ensued during which he lived and worked in Mexico, Spain, Guatemala, Venezuela, and the United States, chiefly in New York City. He earned his living mostly by contributing articles (including some perceptive appraisals of literary, artistic, and political life in the United States) to South American newspapers and to the New York *Sun.* A great admirer of the United States, he nevertheless feared the effect of U.S. power and influence on the South American republics. During his last stay in the United States (1881-95) he founded the Cuban Revolutionary party and became the leading figure of the liberation movement. A major tragedy at the commencement of the final insurrection against Spain was his untimely death at the battle of Dos Ríos in May, 1895. See biographies by Felix Lizoso (1953, repr. 1974) and R. B. Gray (1962).

Martial (Marcus Valerius Martialis) (mär'shəl), A.D. c.40-A.D. c.104, Roman epigrammatic poet, b. Bilbilis, Spain. After 64 A.D. he lived in Rome for many years, winning fame by his wit and poetic gifts. He enjoyed the patronage of Domitian, Titus, and Pliny the Younger and the friendship of Juvenal and Quintilian. His verses are characterized by a twist of wit at the end of each and by original meter and form. They have become models for the modern epigram. See *The Epigrams of Martial,* tr. by James Michie (1973).

martial law, temporary government and control by military authorities of a territory or state when war or overwhelming public disturbance makes the civil authorities of the territory or state unable to enforce its law. The body of principles and doctrines under which the military authorities act is also called martial law. Martial law refers to rule by the domestic army only; the rule of occupied territory by an invading army is termed MILITARY GOVERNMENT. During a war a nation may invoke martial law in some or all of its territory as part of the war effort. Martial law is also applied in serious cases of internal dissension; the army authorities may take over the administrative and judicial functions, and civil safeguards (e.g., HABEAS CORPUS and freedom of speech) are suspended. Where the civil courts remain open, even if their orders are executed by the military, martial law is not applicable. In the United States the Federal government is limited in applying martial law by the provision of Article 1, Section 9, Subsection 2, of the Constitution, which concerns the suspension of habeas corpus. In most U.S. states, martial law may be proclaimed when rendered necessary for public safety. Martial law, which applies to all persons, civil and military, in the area is to be distinguished from MILITARY LAW, the system of rules of government applying only to those in military service.

Martianus Capella: see CAPELLA, MARTIANUS.

Martignac, Jean Baptiste Sylvère Gay, vicomte de (zhäN bätēst' sēlvĕr' gā vēkôNt' də märtēnyäk'), 1778-1832, French statesman. He was elected (1821) to the chamber of deputies and was named a member of the council of state in 1822. In 1828 he was made minister of the interior and virtual head of the new cabinet by King Charles X after the fall of the ministry of the comte de VILLÈLE. Martignac's cabinet, composed of both liberals and reactionaries, was ineffective; his liberal reforms were killed by the ultraroyalists. The king had never liked Martignac's moderate concessions to the liberals and in 1829 dismissed him and appointed the reactionary prince de Polignac to succeed him.

Martin, Saint, c.316-397, bishop of Tours. Born a heathen in Pannonia (in modern Hungary), the son of a soldier, he became a convert and refused to fight Christians. He went (c.360) to St. Hilary of Poitiers and built himself a hermitage. In 371 he was acclaimed bishop, against his will. He continued to live as a monk in the monastery of Marmoutiers, near Tours, which became the training ground for Celtic missions. He was a staunch Catholic, but his zeal for orthodoxy did not prevent his withholding communion from those bishops who connived at the ruthless slaughter of the Priscillianist heretics. St. Martin was universally loved, and his cloak is a symbol of heroic charity (see CHAPEL). His principal shrine was at Tours. Feast: Nov. 11 (known in England as Martinmas). St. Martin's summer is an English counterpart of the American Indian summer; it occurs in mid-November around the time of Martinmas.

Martin I, Saint, d. 655?, pope (649-55?), an Italian, b. Todi; successor of Theodore I. On his accession he summoned a great council at the Lateran, as St. MAXIMUS had urged, to deal with MONOTHELETISM, discussion of which had been forbidden by Byzantine Emperor CONSTANS II. The council condemned all Monothelete utterances, including the imperial edicts of Heraclius (*Ecthesis*) and Constans (*Typus*) and the private letter of Pope HONORIUS I. It also enunciated the Catholic dogma of two natures, two wills, and two energies in one Person in Jesus Christ. Martin issued an encyclical confirming the council's acts. To punish his defiance Constans ordered Martin taken to Naxos and imprisoned with great privations. Later, he was publicly humiliated in Constantinople and finally exiled in the Crimea. He soon died there and was immediately acclaimed a martyr (the last pope to be martyred) by Catholics of East and West. He was succeeded by St. Eugene I. Feast: Nov. 12.

Martin IV, d. 1285, pope (1281-85), a Frenchman named Simon de Brie; successor of Nicholas III. He was chancellor under Louis IX of France and was created cardinal by Urban IV. He was thus a supporter of the ANGEVIN dynasty in S Italy and Sicily. In supporting the design of Charles of Anjou (see CHARLES I) to restore the Latin Empire of Constantinople, and in his excommunication of Byzantine Emperor MICHAEL VIII, Martin sacrificed (1281) the recent union of East and West made at Lyons (1274). After the revolt known as the SICILIAN VESPERS he turned all his powers against PETER III of Aragón. Martin adopted the title Martin IV because it was believed then that the two popes named Marinus were named Martin. He is actually only the second pope named Martin. He was succeeded by Honorius IV.

Martin V, 1368-1431, pope (1417-31), a Roman named Oddone Colonna; successor of Gregory XII. He was created cardinal by Innocent VII, and in the schism (see SCHISM, GREAT) he attended and supported the decisions of the Council of Pisa (see PISA, COUNCIL OF). His election (Nov. 11, 1417) by the conclave at the Council of Constance (see CONSTANCE, COUNCIL OF) as pope ended the schism. The election was greeted with almost universal joy and relief. Declining invitations to settle elsewhere, Martin made his way slowly to Rome (1420) and set about rehabilitating the city and the Papal States. His chief concern was the consolidation of the restored Church unity and the papal prestige, and to this end he made concordats with various rulers. More significant was his denunciation of the conciliar theory (i.e., that councils are supreme in the Church) that had gained wide following at Pisa and Constance. Nevertheless he followed the wishes of the last council and summoned a new one; this met at Pavia (1423), moved to Siena, and accomplished nothing; Martin dissolved it (1424) and summoned a council for 1431 to meet at Basel. In Martin's reign an attempt to prolong the schism was made in Spain by the followers of Antipope Benedict XIII (see LUNA, PEDRO DE), who chose (1425) a successor to him called Clement VIII (otherwise Gil Sánchez Múñoz). Alfonso V of Aragón patronized this antipope out of political motives, but, gaining nothing, he made Clement resign (1429) and recognized Martin. Eugene IV succeeded Martin.

Martin, 1356-1410, king of Aragón and count of Barcelona (c.1395-1410) and, as Martin II, king of Sicily (1409-10). He succeeded his brother, John I, in Aragón and became king of Sicily on the death of his son, Martin I of Sicily, who had married Maria, last of the Sicilian branch of the house of Aragón. Martin of Aragón and Sicily died without a male heir and thus was the last ruler from the Catalan dynasty of Aragón. After a two-year interregnum, his nephew, Prince Ferdinand of Castile, was chosen (1412) king of Aragón and Sicily as FERDINAND I.

Martin, Agnes, 1912–, American painter, b. Maklin, Canada. Martin's paintings are allover grids penciled on monochrome or muted canvases. Her use of line expresses strength and delicacy within a restrained form. Her *Tree* (1964) is in the Museum of Modern Art and *Mill River* (1963) is in the Whitney Museum, both in New York City.

Martin, Archer John Porter, 1910–, English biochemist, educated at Cambridge Univ. From 1938 to 1946 he carried on chemical research in the laboratories of the Wool Industries Association at Leeds, Yorkshire. In 1948 he joined the staff of the National Institute for Medical Research, London, where from 1953 to 1956 he was head of the physical chemistry division. After 1956 he was chemical consultant to the institute. A specialist in the development of chromatographic and other methods of chemical analysis, he was awarded jointly with R. L. M. Synge the 1952 Nobel Prize in Chemistry for his contributions to paper partition chromatography, a method for separating and identifying chemical substances in a mixture.

Martín, Esteban (ĕstā'bän märtēn'), fl. 1539, printer in Mexico. Martín is reputed to have preceded Juan PABLOS. There is evidence that he printed *Escala espiritual para llegar al cielo,* a translation of a work by St. John Climax, in 1535, and *Catechismo mexicano* in 1537.

Martin, François Xavier (fräNswä' zävyā' märtăN'), 1762-1846, American jurist, b. Marseilles, France. He emigrated to the United States (c.1786) and was admitted to the North Carolina bar in 1789. He held Federal positions as judge for Mississippi Territory (1809) and for Louisiana Territory (1810). In the government of the state of Louisiana he was attorney general (1813), justice of the state supreme court (1815), and chief justice (1836). His wide learning did much to harmonize the strands of English, Spanish, and French law in the legal system of Louisiana. Besides digests of Louisiana cases, Martin wrote *A History of Louisiana* (1827) and *A History of North Carolina* (1829).

Martin, Homer Dodge, 1836-97, American landscape painter, b. Albany, N.Y. His earlier works are in the style of the Hudson River school, but after his stay in France (1881-86) his work showed the influence of the Barbizon school, notably Corot; his style, however, retained its individuality. Martin's landscapes are melancholy, poetical interpretations of nature, subtle in coloring and in the treatment of light and atmosphere. Among his best-known works are *Harp of the Winds* (1895), *Sand Dunes at Lake Ontario, White Mountains* (all: Metropolitan Mus.), and *Sea at Villerville* (Kansas City Art Inst.). His last years were spent in St. Paul, Minn., where, nearly blind, he painted *Adirondack Scenery* from memory. See study by F. J. Mather (1912).

Martin, John, 1789-1854, English painter and engraver. Martin's visionary and grandiose landscapes, the pictorial counterparts of English romantic poetry, won him international popularity. He is also known for his illustrations for the Bible and Milton's *Paradise Lost* (1827).

Martin, Joseph William, 1884-1968, American politician, Speaker of the House of Representatives (1947-49, 1953-55), b. North Attleboro, Mass. He was a reporter (1902-8) for several newspapers until he formed a combine to purchase the North Attleboro *Evening Chronicle*. His newspaper work led to an interest in politics, and he served (1912-17) in the state legislature before entering the U.S. House of Representatives in 1925, where he served continuously until 1967. A staunch conservative, Martin became minority leader of the House in 1939, a position he held until 1959, except for those periods when he was Speaker. He served as permanent chairman of every Republican National convention from 1940 to 1956. After the Republican congressional defeat in the 1958 elections, Martin was ousted as Republican leader on the grounds that his leadership was not vigorous enough. See his autobiography (1960).

Martin, Josiah, 1737-86, British colonial governor, b. West Indies. An army officer, he had attained the rank of lieutenant colonel when he was appointed governor of North Carolina in 1771. He established cordial relations with the leaders of the REGULATOR MOVEMENT on the frontier but clashed with the assembly over the collection of taxes and court regulations. He unsuccessfully attempted to organize the Loyalists of the colony to resist the American Revolution. When his Loyalist Highlanders were defeated (1776) and the Revolution became general, he left the colony. Later he took part in the attack on Charleston and was an advisor to generals Clinton and Cornwallis. He returned to England in 1781.

Martin, Luther, c.1748-1826, American lawyer and political leader, b. New Brunswick, N.J. He practiced law in Maryland and became the first attorney general of the state, holding office from 1778 to 1805 and again from 1818 to 1822 (although he was inactive in his last two years of office). He was a delegate to the Federal Constitutional Convention but refused to sign the Constitution because he felt it violated states' rights. Martin, considered one of the nation's leading lawyers, was one of the defense counsel in the trials of Justice Samuel Chase (1805) and of Aaron Burr (1807). He was a bitter opponent of Thomas Jefferson. See biography by P. S. Clarkson and S. R. Jett (1970).

Martin, Mary, 1913-, American musical comedy star, b. Weatherford, Texas. Since Martin's first stage appearance in *Leave It to Me* (1938), she has starred in several enormously successful musicals, including *One Touch of Venus* (1943), *South Pacific* (1949); *Peter Pan* (1954), and *The Sound of Music* (1959). Her films include *The Great Victor Herbert* (1939) and, for television, *Peter Pan* and *Annie Get Your Gun*.

Martin, William McChesney, Jr., 1906-, U.S. banker, chairman of the Board of Governors of the Federal Reserve System (1951-70), b. St. Louis. After an early career as a stockbroker, Martin became (1938) the first salaried president of the New York Stock Exchange. He served in World War II and then held high-level positions in the Export-Import Bank, the U.S. Treasury Dept., and the International Bank for Reconstruction and Development. President Harry Truman appointed him chairman of the Federal Reserve Board in 1951, and he continued to hold the position under six successive administrations until his retirement in 1970. Favoring a "hard money" policy, Martin continually fought to keep the Federal Reserve System independent of political control, and he frequently expressed opposition to an excessive expansion of the monetary supply, which he considered a major cause of inflation. He reentered private business after his retirement from the Federal Reserve Board.

martin: see SWALLOW.

Martin de Porres: see PORRES, MARTIN DE.

Martin du Gard, Roger (rôzhā' märtăN' də gär), 1881-1958, French novelist. Long associated with the *Nouvelle Revue française*, he first gained recognition with *Jean Barois* (1913), a novel of France during the Dreyfus Affair. His fame, however, rests chiefly on his eight-part novel cycle *The World of the Thibaults* (1922-40, tr. 1939-41). A story of two families, one Roman Catholic and the other Protestant, it explores the conflicts of French society in the early 20th cent. He also wrote *Confidence africaine* (1931) and *Vieille France* (1933, tr. *The Postman*, 1954). Martin du Gard was awarded the 1937 Nobel Prize in Literature. See studies by Denis Boak (1963), D. I. Schalk (1967), and C. H. Sarage (1968).

Martineau, Harriet (mär'tĭnō), 1802-76, English author. A journalist rather than a writer of literature, she was an enormously popular author. Her success is the more remarkable since she was deaf from childhood and the victim of various other illnesses throughout her life. The sister of the Unitarian minister James Martineau, she began her career writing articles on religious subjects. Her fame spread with *Illustrations of Political Economy* (9 vol., 1832-34) and *Illustrations of Taxation* (1834), two series of stories interpreting classical economics to the layman. After a visit to the United States in 1834, she became an advocate for the abolition of slavery and wrote several unflattering works on the American way of life, including *Society in America* (1837) and *Retrospect of Western Travel* (1838). Her later writings include *Deerbrook* (1839), a novel; *The Playfellow* (4 vol., 1841), tales for children; *Letters on Mesmerism* (1845); *The Positive Philosophy of Auguste Comte* (1853); and a very candid autobiography (1877), containing commentaries on the literary figures of her day. See biography by Vera Wheatley (1957); study by R. K. Webb (1960).

Martineau, James, 1805-1900, English philosopher and Unitarian clergyman; brother of Harriet Martineau. He strongly upheld the theist position against the negations of physical science. A renowned teacher and minister, he achieved international distinction in academic and religious circles. Besides numerous essays contributed to periodicals, he was the author of *A Study of Spinoza* (1882), *Types of Ethical Theory* (1885), and *A Study of Religion* (1888). See study by Henry Sidgwick (1902, repr. 1968).

Martinelli, Giovanni (jōvän'nē märtĕnĕl'lē), 1885-1969, Italian-American operatic tenor. He made his debut in Milan in 1910 and sang (1913-46) at the Metropolitan Opera. His repertoire of about 50 roles included the leading tenor roles in nearly all the principal Italian operas.

Martinez (märtē'nəs), city (1970 pop. 16,506), seat of Contra Costa co., W Calif., on Carquinez Strait between San Pablo and Suisun bays, in a farm area; inc. 1884. Its major industries are petroleum refining and food canning. John F. Kennedy Univ. and the John Muir National Historic Site are there. A naval weapons station adjoins the city, and part of the Central Valley project is nearby.

Martínez de Campos, Arsenio (ärsā'nyō märtē'nĕth dā käm'pōs), 1831-1900, Spanish general. He served in Morocco (1859-60), in Mexico (1861-63), and in Cuba (1869-72). He played a leading role in the proclamation (1874) of Alfonso XII as king and helped bring the Carlist Wars to an end (1876). In 1877 he was sent to Cuba, where he ended the TEN YEARS WAR. In 1879 he was briefly premier of Spain and later war minister. In 1895 he was sent to put down the insurgents in the Cuban revolution, but his lenient attitude caused his replacement by Weyler. He later was president of the Spanish senate.

Martínez de la Rosa, Francisco (fränthēs'kō märtē'nĕth dā lä rō'sä), 1787-1862, Spanish dramatic poet, statesman, and historian. He was an outspoken liberal professor of philosophy, a deputy, and an ambassador. His major plays include *La conjuración de Venecia* [the conspiracy of Venice] (1834), a landmark of the romantic theater in Spain; *Abén Humeya* (in French, 1830, Span. tr. 1836); and the neoclassic *Edipo* [Oedipus] (1829). Among his poems the best known are the elegy entitled *Epístola al duque de Frias* and *El recuerdo de la patria* [memory of our country]. Martínez de la Rosa also wrote historical novels and political histories.

Martínez de Rozas, Juan (hwän märtē'nās dā rō'säs), 1759-1813, Chilean revolutionist, b. Mendoza, Argentina. A lawyer and scholar, he was a leading instigator of revolutionary ideas. In 1810 he headed the junta that deposed the Spanish governor, but the next year he was forced out because his ideas were too radical for the more conservative element of the revolution. Subsequently opposing the military dictatorship of José Miguel CARRERA, he was exiled and died at his birthplace.

Martínez Ruiz, José (hōsā' märtē'nĕth rōōēth'), 1873?-1967, Spanish writer. He often used the pseudonym Azorín. A political radical in the 1890s, he moved steadily to the right. In literature Martínez exemplified the GENERATION OF '98 (a term he coined), especially in his attempt to define the eternal qualities of Spanish life. Collections of his essays and criticism, written in a simple, compact style, include *Castilla* (1912), *Lecturas españolas* (1912), *Clásicos y modernos* (1913), and *An Hour of Spain* (1924, tr. 1933). Particularly notable are his impressionistic descriptions of Castilian towns and landscape. Among his many other works are the autobiographical novels *La Voluntad* (1902) and *Antonio Azorín* (1903); the novel *Don Juan* (1922, tr. 1923); the dramatic trilogy *Lo invisible* (1928); and a collection of short stories (1929, tr. 1931). See studies by Anne Krause (1948) and L. A. LaJohn (1961).

Martínez Sierra, Gregorio (grāgō'rēō märtē'nĕth syā'rä), 1881-1947, Spanish dramatist, novelist, and poet. His masterpiece is *Canción de cuna* (1911, tr. *The Cradle Song*, 1917), but he is also known for his tale *El Amor Brujo*, which is the subject of a ballet set to music by Manuel de Falla. In addition to many plays, he wrote novels, the most popular of which is *Tu eres la paz* (1907, tr. *Ana María*, 1921). *Flores de escarcha* [flowers of frost] (1900) is a collection of verse. He also translated Shakespeare and Maeterlinck, founded several literary magazines, and was active in the theater. In much of his work he collaborated with his wife, the poet María Lejárraga.

Martini, Giovanni Battista (jōvän'nē bät-tēs'tä märtē'nē), 1706-84, Italian composer and teacher, also known as Padre Martini. Martini became a priest in 1722. He acquired great prestige as a teacher, particularly of counterpoint. His students included J. C. Bach, Gluck, Grétry, and Mozart. Martini built up a vast library devoted to the historical, scientific, and mathematical aspects of music.

Martini, Simone (sēmô'nā) or **Simone di Martino** (dē märtē'nō), c.1283-1344, major Sienese painter. His art is admired for its Gothic spirituality combined with a vibrancy and a great elegance of line. A follower of Duccio di Buoninsegna, his earliest known work (1315) was a fresco depicting the *Maestà* (*Madonna and Child Enthroned with Saints and Angels*) in the Palazzo Pubblico, Siena. In 1317, King Robert of Anjou invited him to Naples to paint *St. Louis Enthroned* (Naples Mus.). He created altarpieces for the Dominicans of Pisa and Orvieto. One of these is now in the Gardner Museum, Boston. In 1328 he painted one of the first commemorative portraits, an impressive almost heraldic image of the soldier Guidoriccio da Fogliano, with a starkly landscaped background (Palazzo Pubblico, Siena). His painting of the *Annunciation* (1333; Uffizi) is famous for its exquisitely refined use of outline. In this work, as in others, he was assisted by his brother-in-law Lippo Memmi. At the invitation of Pope Benedict XII, he went to Avignon in 1339 and decorated the portal of Notre Dame des Dons (almost obliterated). He became friends with Petrarch and designed a frontispiece for him for a Vergil codex (Ambrosian Library, Milan). His frescoes (of uncertain date) at Assisi include lively scenes from the life of St. Martin. Other works by Simone are in Siena, Berlin, Liverpool, and in the Louvre. See study by Giovanni Paccagnini (tr. 1957).

Martinique (märtĭnēk'), overseas department of France (1973 est. pop. 343,100), 425 sq mi (1,101 sq km), in the Windward Islands, West Indies. FORT-DE-FRANCE is the capital. The department and the island

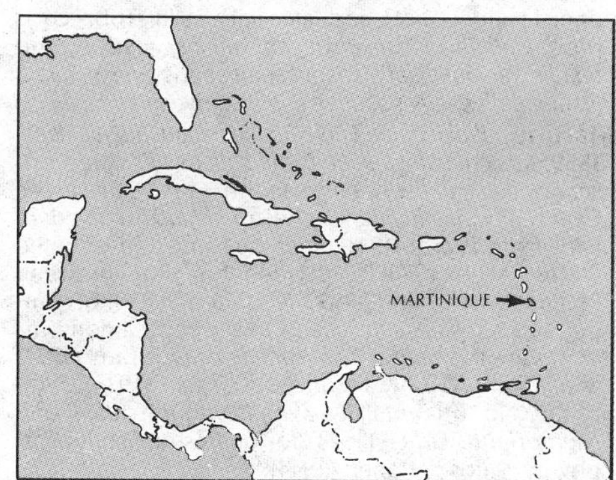

of Martinique are coterminous. Of volcanic origin, the island is rugged and mountainous and reaches its greatest height in Pelée volcano. Most agriculture is carried on in the hot valleys and along the coastal strips; about 80% of this area is devoted to sugarcane, which was introduced from Brazil in 1654 and which provides Martinique's two major exports, sugar and rum. The island's industries consist mainly of sugar and rum production and pineapple canning. Tourism is a growing source of revenue. The population is mostly Negro or mulatto. French is the official language, but most of the people speak a creole patois. Discovered by Columbus, probably in 1502, the island was ignored by the Spanish; colonization began in 1635, when the French, who had promised the native Carib Indians the western half of the island, established a settlement. The French proceeded to eliminate the Caribs and later imported African slaves as sugar plantation workers. In the 18th cent. Martinique's sugar exports made it one of France's most valuable colonies; although slavery was abolished in 1848, sugar continued to hold a dominant position in the economy. A target of dispute during the Anglo-French worldwide colonial struggles, Martinique was finally confirmed as a French possession after the Napoleonic wars. Martinique supported the Vichy regime after France's collapse in World War II, but in 1943 a U.S. naval blockade forced the island to transfer its allegiance to the Free French. It became a department of France in 1946.

Martinsburg, industrial city (1970 pop. 14,626), seat of Berkeley co., NE W.Va., in the Eastern Panhandle; settled 1732, inc. as a city 1859. It is a railroad center in a region that grows apples and peaches. Manufactures include textiles, hosiery, glassware, and cement. Limestone is quarried nearby. In the Civil War the city's strategic location on the railroad made it a frequent military objective. Belle Boyd, the Confederate spy, lived there and was imprisoned in the old courthouse. Nearby Bunker Hill, settled c.1729, is the oldest recorded settlement in the state. Sleepy Creek State Park is also near the city.

Martins Ferry, industrial city (1970 pop. 10,757), Belmont co., E Ohio, on the Ohio River opposite Wheeling, W.Va.; settled 1780, inc. as a city 1885. It is a coal-mining and steel-manufacturing city. The novelist William Dean Howells was born in Martins Ferry. In Walnut Grove Cemetery are the graves of Elizabeth (Betty) and Ebenezer Zane.

Martinson, Harry, 1904–, Swedish writer. Orphaned early, Martinson was self-educated. His works reveal his appreciation of nature and his distrust of modern technological society. He is best known for his long narrative poem *Aniara* (1956), about the journey of a spaceship. It was set to music in 1959 by K. B. Blomdahl. Noted for their novel, expressive style, his major works include *Kap Farväl!* [Cape Farewell] (1933), based on his travels; a volume of poetry, *Nässlorna blomma* (flowering nettle] (1936); and *Vägen till Klockricke* (1948, tr. *The Road,* 1956), a sympathetic portrayal of society's outcasts. Martinson was the first writer of the working classes to be admitted to the Swedish Academy. He shared the 1974 Nobel Prize in Literature with the Swedish writer Eyvind Johnson.

Martinson, Moa (mo͞o'ə märtĭnso͞on'), 1890–1964, Swedish novelist and poet. The mother of five children before she was 25, Martinson began writing late; her first novel was *Kvinnor och äppelträd* [women and apple trees] (1933). *Mor gifter sig* [Mother marries] (1936), considered her best work, depicted the miseries of working-class women, as did most of her novels. Her works are often autobiographical as well as historical in content. Martinson is ranked among the foremost of Swedish literary realists.

Martinsville, city (1970 pop. 19,653), seat of Henry co., S Va., in the Blue Ridge foothills near the N.C. line; founded 1793, inc. as a city 1928. Tobacco is processed, and furniture, chemicals, textiles, and textile products are manufactured. The city has a junior college. A state park is nearby.

Martinů, Bohuslav (bô'ho͝osläf mär'tĭno͞o), 1890–1959, Czech composer; studied at the Prague Conservatory. He played the violin (1913–23) in the Czech Philharmonic Orchestra. Martinů lived in Paris from 1923 to 1941, when he came to the United States. After 1946 he divided his time between Prague, Switzerland, and the United States, becoming a U.S. citizen in 1952. Outstanding among his works are the operas *The Miracle of Our Lady* (1934) and *Juliette* (1938), a *Concerto Grosso* (1938), Symphony No. 6 (*Fantaisies Symphoniques*, 1955), and *Memorial to Lidice* (1943) for orchestra. See biography by Milos Safranek (1944).

Martin vs. Hunter's Lessee, case decided in 1816 by the U.S. Supreme Court. From 1779 to 1785, Virginia passed a series of laws by which the state confiscated all lands owned by foreigners. David Hunter was granted 800 acres of confiscated lands that had been willed to Denny Martin Fairfax, a British subject. Fairfax brought suit against Hunter for return of the land. On Fairfax's death the suit was taken over by his heir, Philip Martin. Martin argued that Fairfax's ownership had been protected by treaties between the United States and Great Britain guaranteeing British subjects the right to hold land in America. The Virginia court of appeals upheld the grant to Hunter, but on appeal the U.S. Supreme Court voided the grant (1813). The Virginia court refused to obey the Supreme Court ruling, declaring that it had no right to review the decisions of state courts under the U.S. Constitution. When the case again came before the Supreme Court, Justice STORY ruled that section 25 of the Judiciary Act of 1789, which granted the U.S. Supreme Court appellate jurisdiction over state courts in certain situations (as in this case, where a state court denied the validity of a federal statute), was constitutional. His decision affirmed the Supreme Court's right to review state court decisions.

Marugame (märo͞o'gämē), city (1970 pop. 59,214), Kagawa prefecture, N Shikoku, Japan, on the Inland Sea. It is an important port with extensive food-processing industries.

Marvell, Andrew, 1621–78, one of the English METAPHYSICAL POETS. Educated at Cambridge, he worked as a clerk, traveled abroad, and returned to serve as tutor to Lord Fairfax's daughter in Yorkshire. In 1657 he was appointed John Milton's assistant in the Latin secretaryship, and in 1659 he was elected to Parliament, where he served until his death. He was one of the chief wits and satirists of his time as well as being a Puritan and a public defender of individual liberty. Today, however, he is known chiefly for his brilliant lyric poetry, which includes "The Garden," "The Definition of Love," "Bermudas," and "To His Coy Mistress," and for his "Horatian Ode" to Cromwell. See his poems and letters edited by H. M. Margoliouth (2d ed. 1952); biographies by M. C. Bradbrook and M. G. L. Thomas (1940) and V. Sackville-West (1929, repr. 1971); studies by H. E. Toliver (1965), P. Legouis (rev. ed. 1966), J. M. Wallace (1969), D. M. Friedman (1970), and R. L. Colie (1971).

Marvin, Charles Frederick, 1858–1943, American meteorologist, b. Putnam (now part of Zanesville), Ohio, grad. Ohio State Univ., 1883. He entered (1884) the U.S. Signal Service, predecessor of the Weather Bureau, which he helped to develop and later directed (1913–34). He is especially noted for his work on humidity tables and on the measurement of wind velocity, for the invention and improvement of meteorological instruments, and for his advocacy of calendar reform.

Marwar, India: see JODHPUR.

Marx, Karl, 1818–83, German social philosopher, the chief theorist of modern SOCIALISM and COMMUNISM. His father, a lawyer, converted from Judaism to Lutheranism in 1824. Marx studied law at Bonn and Berlin, but became interested in philosophy and took a Ph.D. degree at Jena (1841). He early rejected the idealism of Georg Wilhelm Friedrich HEGEL and turned toward materialism, partly through the influence of Ludwig FEUERBACH and Moses HESS. In 1842 he became editor of the *Rheinische Zeitung,* but his demands for radical reforms led to its suppression in 1843. He then went to Paris, where he began his lifelong association with Friedrich ENGELS. At this time Marx became a socialist. He devoured the works of Adam Smith, David Ricardo, the comte de Saint-Simon, and many others. Antagonized by the individualistic radicalism of Pierre Joseph Proudhon, Marx attacked him in *The Poverty of Philosophy* (1847, tr. 1910), an early attempt to systematize his own thought. In this period also he wrote, with Engels, *The German Ideology* (tr. 1933), which provided an exposition of his DIALECTICAL MATERIALISM. Breaking with the tradition of justifying social reform by appeal to natural rights, he invoked "inevitable" laws of history to predict the eventual triumph of the working class. He joined (1847) the Communist League and with Engels wrote for it the famous *Communist Manifesto* (1848), which strikingly expressed his general view of the class struggle. The failure of the revolutions of 1848 convinced Marx of the need to stimulate the consciousness and solidarity of the working class through the founding of open revolutionary parties. Exiled from most continental centers, he settled permanently in London in 1849. He lived in poverty, made more bitter by his own chronic illness and the death of several of his children. At times he was able to earn funds as a correspondent for the New York *Tribune,* but he was continually dependent on Engels for financial aid. Nonetheless, he pursued research in the British Museum and continued to write steadily. In 1864 he helped to found the International Workingmen's Association. Through this First INTERNATIONAL and through the work of Ferdinand LASSALLE and others, Marx's ideas began to gain primacy in European socialist and radical thought. This primacy was greatly furthered with the publication of the first volume of *Das Kapital* (Vol. I, 1867, tr. 1886; Vol. II–III, ed. by Engels, 1885–94; tr. 1907–9). The manuscript for the fourth volume was edited by Karl Kautsky and published as *Theorien über den Mehrwert* (3 parts, 1905–10; tr. of 1st part, *A History of Economic Theories,* 1952). A monumental work, *Das Kapital* provided a thorough exposition of MARXISM and became the foundation of international socialism. As Marx's reputation spread, so too did public fear of him. He insisted on authoritarian sway within the International, and finally, after controversy with Mikhail BAKUNIN, virtually destroyed the International for fear of losing control over its direction. He remained the prophet of socialism and was often consulted by the various socialist party leaders. His role was frequently that of urging more hard-minded policies, further removed from bourgeois embellishments; *The Gotha Program* (1891, tr. 1922), a critique, illustrates this position. The complexity and vituperation of this polemic characterizes much of Marx's prose. In his last years Marx's great intellectual vigor continued unabated. The importance of his dialectical method and of his theories goes far beyond their immense political influence; many scholars consider him a great economic theoretician and the founder of economic history and sociology. There are many translations and editions of Marx's best-known works and of his and Engels's selected correspondence. The standard biography of Marx is that by Franz Mehring (tr. 1935); other notable works include those by Otto Rühle (tr. 1929), E. H. Carr (1938), C. J. S. Sprigge (1938), Karl Korsch (1939), and Isaiah Berlin (3d ed. 1963). Recent biographies are by Robert Payne (1968), Werner Blumenberg (tr. 1972), and David McLellan (1973). See also bibliography under MARXISM.

Marx, Wilhelm (vĭl'hĕlm), 1863–1946, German statesman. A Reichstag member, he was a leading figure of the Catholic Center party and was elected its president in 1921. As chancellor (1923–24) he secured the passage of the Dawes Plan. He was succeeded by Hans Luther, whom he followed again as chancellor (1926–28). In the presidential elections of 1925, Marx was the unsuccessful candidate of the Center and the Social Democratic parties against Paul von HINDENBURG.

Marx Brothers, team of American movie comedians. The members were Julius (1895–), known as Groucho; Arthur (1893–1964), called Harpo; Leonard (1891–1961), known as Chico; and two other brothers, Gummo and Zeppo, who withdrew from the team by 1935; all were born in New York City. After appearing in vaudeville they began their film work in 1929. Their outstanding films include *Animal Crackers* (1930), *Monkey Business* (1931), *Horse Feathers* (1932), *Duck Soup* (1933), *A Night at the Opera* (1935), and *A Day at the Races* (1937). Their zany and anarchic brand of humor depended on slapstick, sight gags, and outrageous puns and wisecracks. Groucho conducted a popular television quiz show in the 1950s. See autobiographies by Groucho (1959) and Harpo (1961); Arthur Marx, *Life with Groucho* (1954) and *Son of Groucho* (1972); Groucho Marx and R. J. Anobile, *The Marx Bros. Scrapbook* (1973).

Marxism, economic and political philosophy named for Karl MARX. It is also known as scientific (as opposed to utopian) socialism. Marxism has had a profound impact on contemporary culture; modern COMMUNISM is based on it, and most modern socialist theories derive from it (see SOCIALISM). Although no one treatise by Marx and his co-worker Friedrich ENGELS covers all aspects of Marxism, the *Communist Manifesto* suggests many of its premises, and the monumental *Das Kapital* develops many of them most rigorously. Many elements of the Marxist system were drawn from earlier economic and historical thought, notably that of Georg Wilhelm Friedrich HEGEL, the comte de Saint-Simon, J. C. L. de Sismondi, David Ricardo, Charles Fourier, and Louis Blanc; but Marxist analysis as fully developed by Marx and Engels was unquestionably original. The Marxist philosophical method is DIALECTICAL MATERI-

ALISM, a reversal of the dialectical idealism of Hegel. Dialectical materialism presumes the primacy of economic determinants in history. Through dialectical materialism was developed the fundamental Marxist premise that the history of society is the inexorable "history of class struggle." According to this premise, a specific class could rule only so long as it best represented the economically productive forces of society; when it became outmoded it would be destroyed and replaced. From this continuing dynamic process a classless society would eventually emerge. In modern capitalist society, the bourgeois (capitalist) class had destroyed and replaced the unproductive feudal nobility and had performed the economically creative task of establishing the new industrial order. The stage was thus set for the final struggle between the bourgeoisie, which had completed its historic role, and the proletariat, composed of the industrial workers, or makers of goods, which had become the true productive class. Supporting Marxism's historical premises are its economic theories. Of central importance are the labor theory of value and the idea of surplus value. Marxism supposes that the value of a commodity is determined by the amount of labor required for its manufacture. The value of the commodities purchasable by the worker's wages is less than the value of the commodities he produces; the difference, called surplus value, represents the profit of the capitalist. Thus the bourgeois class has flourished through exploitation of the proletariat. The capitalist system and the bourgeoisie were seen as riven with weaknesses and contradictions, which would become increasingly severe as industrialization progressed and would manifest themselves in increasingly severe economic crises. According to the *Communist Manifesto,* it would be in a highly industrialized nation, where the crises of capitalism and the consciousness of the workers were far advanced, that the proletarian overthrow of bourgeois society would first succeed. Although this process was inevitable, Marxists were to speed it by bringing about the international union of workers, by supporting (for expediency) whatever political party favored "the momentary interests of the working class," and by helping to prepare workers for their revolutionary role. The proletariat, after becoming the ruling class, was "to centralize all instruments of production in the hands of the state" and to increase productive forces at a rapid rate. Once the bourgeoisie had been defeated, there would be no more class divisions, since the means of production would not be owned by any group. The coercive state, formerly a weapon of class oppression, would be replaced by a rational structure of economic and social cooperation and integration. Such bourgeois institutions as the family and religion, which had served to perpetuate bourgeois dominance, would vanish, and each individual would find true fulfillment. Thus social and economic utopia would be achieved, although its exact form could not be predicted. The first impact of Marxism was felt in continental Europe. By the late 19th cent., through the influence of the INTERNATIONALS, it had permeated the European trade union movement, and the major socialist parties (see SOCIALIST PARTIES, in European history) were committed to it in theory if not in practice. A major division soon appeared, however, between those socialists who believed that violent revolution was inevitable and those, most notably Eduard BERNSTEIN, who argued that socialism could be achieved by evolution; both groups could cite Marx as their authority because he was inconsistent in his writings on this question. The success of the revolutionary socialists (hereafter called Communists) in the Russian Revolution and the establishment of an authoritarian Communist state in Russia split the movement irrevocably. In disassociating themselves from Russian Communism, many of the democratic socialist parties also moved slowly away from Marxist theory. Communists, on the other hand, regard Marxism as their official dogma, and it is chiefly under their aegis that it has spread through the world, although its concepts of class struggle and exploitation have helped to determine policies of welfare and development in many nations besides those adhering to Communism. However, although useful as a revolutionary ethic and also as a frame of reference and a cue to policy, Marxism has found far less practical application than is often presumed. The Soviet and Chinese and other Communist states are at most only partly structured along Marxist "classless" lines, and while such Communist leaders as Vladimir Ilyich LENIN, Joseph STALIN, and MAO TSE-TUNG have staunchly claimed Marxist orthodoxy for their pronouncements, they have, in fact, greatly stretched the doctrine in attempting to mold it to their own uses. Furthermore, the evolution of laissez-faire capitalism to the present mixed world economy and to varied forms of welfare capitalism, as well as the improved condition of workers in modern industrial societies, has tended to discredit Marx's dire and deterministic economic predictions. The history of Communist nations has also belied Marx's predictions; the Russian Revolution occurred in an industrially retarded country, and the Soviet and Chinese regimes have resulted not in the disappearance of the state but in the erection of huge, monolithic state structures. Many Western intellectuals see Marxism as a valid response to the conditions of the 19th cent. but reject the application of Marxist methods to the economic problems of the 20th cent. Instead, a number have turned to Marx's more psychologically oriented writings and explored the present-day value of such Marxist concepts as alienation. In less stable societies Marxism's combination of materialistic analysis with a militant sense of justice remains a powerful attraction. See M. M. Bober, *Karl Marx's Interpretation of History* (2d ed. 1948); J. P. Plamenatz, *German Marxism and Russian Communism* (1954); Sidney Hook, *From Hegel to Marx* (1962); Shlomo Avineri, *The Social and Political Thought of Karl Marx* (1968); George Lukács, *History and Class Consciousness* (tr. 1971); Wolfgang Leonhard, *Three Faces of Marxism* (1974); collections of essays by George Novack (1972), Herbert Marcuse (tr. 1972), and Isaac Deutscher (1972); see also bibliographies under MARX, KARL; COMMUNISM; SOCIALISM.

Mary, the Virgin, mother of Jesus, the principal saint, called Our Lady. Her name is the Hebrew *Miriam.* The events of her life mentioned in the New Testament include the archangel Gabriel's annunciation to her of Jesus' birth, her visitation to Elizabeth, Jesus' nativity, her purification at the Temple, and her station at the Cross. According to Scripture she was first betrothed, then married, to Joseph and was the cousin of Elizabeth, mother of John the Baptist. (Mat. 1. 18-25; 2; Luke 1. 26-56; 2; John 2; Mark 3.31-35; 6.3; Luke 11.27,28; Mat. 12.46-50; John 19.25-27; Acts 1.14.) From ancient times Mary has been highly honored by Christians. Details of the Virgin's life are not mentioned in Scripture, but tradition has it that she was the daughter of St. JOACHIM and St. ANNE, announced miraculously to them, that she was presented and dedicated at the Temple as a virgin, that she was later betrothed to Joseph to be protected by him, that after the Ascension she was cared for by St. John the Divine, and that she was "assumed" directly into heaven. The Orthodox, Roman Catholic, and Anglican churches all teach the perpetual virginity of Mary, placing a nonliteral interpretation on New Testament references to Jesus' "brothers." The Roman Catholic Church additionally has proclaimed the dogma of the Immaculate Conception (declared in a bull of Pius IX, 1854), according to which Mary is said to have been conceived and born without original sin. The Roman Catholic Church further teaches that Mary was freed from actual sin by a special grace of God. In 1950, Pope Pius XII's bull *Munificentissimus Deus* made Mary's bodily assumption into heaven an article of faith. From earliest times Mary's intercession was believed to be especially efficacious on behalf of men and the church, and she is called upon to meet every kind of need. The Roman Catholic Church teaches that Mary is the mediatrix of all graces. As the Second Eve, she also cooperates in the redemption of mankind and is spoken of as co-Redemptress with Jesus Christ. The body of teachings about Mary is called Mariology. (Mariolatry is an opprobrious term used since the Reformation to mean the worship of Mary—a criticism leveled by many Protestant bodies at the cult of Mary within the Roman Catholic Church.) Catholics assert that the veneration (hyperdulia) accorded Mary, while higher than that accorded any other creature, is infinitely lower than the worship (latria) due to her Son. The principal feasts honoring Mary are those of the Assumption (Aug. 15), the Birthday of Our Lady (Sept. 8), the Immaculate Conception (Dec. 8), the Purification (Feb. 2: see CANDLEMAS), and the Annunciation or Lady Day (March 25). Apparitions of the Virgin have been reported since ancient times, and some have led to new cultuses and shrines, typically associated with cures. Some of these cultuses have been approved by the Roman Catholic Church, without vouching for the authenticity of the apparition or the cures. These apparitions include those at GUADALUPE HIDALGO, Mexico, in 1531, associated with a miraculous painting (Our Lady of Guadalupe); at Paris (Our Lady of the Miraculous Medal) in 1830; at Lourdes, France, in 1858; and at Fatima, Portugal, in 1917. Two great pilgrim shrines of medieval England were Our Lady of Glastonbury and Our Lady of Walsingham (Norfolk). Our Lady of CZESTOCHOWA is a rallying point of Polish nationalism. Artistic representations of Mary are innumerable; for differing aspects, see Christian iconography under ICONOGRAPHY. She has been the subject of countless works from the time of the pseudepigrapha. Mary in her aspect of the Immaculate Conception is the patroness of the United States. Our Lady of Guadalupe was declared Empress of all the Americas by Pope St. Pius X. See M. J. Scheeben, *Mariology,* Vol. 1 (1946); R. M. Rilke, *The Life of Mary* (tr. 1947, repr. 1972); Adrienne von Speyr, *Handmaid of the Lord* (1956); Donald Attwater, *A Dictionary of Mary* (1957); for the Protestant view, see Giovanni Miegge, *Virgin Mary* (1956); in art, Henri Ghéon, *Mary, Mother of God* (1956); H. C. Graef, *Mary: A History of Doctrine and Devotion* (2 vol., 1963-65).

Mary I (Mary Tudor), 1516-58, queen of England (1553-58), daughter of HENRY VIII and KATHARINE OF ARAGÓN. While she was a child, various husbands were proposed for her—the eldest son of Francis I of France (1518), Holy Roman Emperor Charles V (1522), Francis I himself (1527), and several others. She was a pawn in her father's diplomatic intrigues. In 1525 she was given a separate household as the Princess of Wales; but in 1527, Henry began negotiations for a divorce from Katharine, and Mary, remaining loyal to her mother and to the Roman Catholic Church, spent the next nine years in misery. She was separated from Katharine, denied presence at court, treated as illegitimate, and forced to serve her half sister Elizabeth as lady in waiting. Plans to escape to the Continent failed, and in 1536 Mary was finally forced to acknowledge herself as illegitimate and to repudiate her church, statements from which she was later absolved by the pope. During the spread of Protestantism in the reign of her half brother, EDWARD VI, Mary was steadfastly loyal to her faith, observing Mass in her private chapel in defiance of the Act of Uniformity and appealing to Emperor Charles V for protection. On Edward's death John Dudley, duke of NORTHUMBERLAND, arranged the short-lived usurpation of the throne by Lady Jane GREY; Mary, however, supported by an overwhelming number of loyal subjects, soon ascended the throne. In the early part of her reign Mary showed considerable clemency toward her political opponents, but she and her advisers were set upon two policies—her marriage to Philip (later PHILIP II of Spain), son of Emperor Charles, with the consequent Spanish alliance, and the restoration of papal supremacy in England. The former aroused violent opposition, which was focused in the unsuccessful rebellion of Sir Thomas WYATT, but both the marriage and alliance were carried out in 1554. Late in the same year papal authority was reestablished in England. Early in 1555, Parliament repealed the antipapal laws of Henry VIII and restored the ecclesiastical courts and the laws against heresy. However, they refused to restore church property that had been seized. There then began the religious persecutions that lasted for the rest of the reign; the number burned at the stake amounted almost to 300 and included such men as Nicholas RIDLEY, John ROGERS, Hugh LATIMER, and Thomas CRANMER. The queen's title of "Bloody Mary" is something of a misnomer, for Mary was by temperament a gentle and merciful person; however, though the persecutions of her reign were no more severe than many on the Continent, they were unprecedented in England. In 1555, Philip, frustrated by Parliament in his attempt to win coronation, left his wife and went to his dominions in the Netherlands. He returned briefly in 1557, mainly for the purpose of drawing England into the existing war between Spain and France, the chief results of which were the loss (1558) of Calais and the increasing hostility of the English people toward their queen. Mary, whose general ill health may have been aggravated by her grief over Philip's absence, died childless. She was succeeded by her half sister, Elizabeth I. See biographies by H. F. M. Prescott (rev. ed. 1953) and Milton Waldman (1972).

Mary II, 1662-94, queen of England, wife of WILLIAM III. The daughter of James II by his first wife, Anne Hyde, she was brought up a Protestant despite her father's adoption of Roman Catholicism. In 1677 she married her cousin William of Orange and went with him to Holland. She returned to England after the GLORIOUS REVOLUTION of 1688 and was proclaimed joint sovereign with her husband in 1689, though she actually ruled only during his absences. Although she was relatively popular with the Dutch and English peoples, she led an unhappy life because of the political conflicts between her husband, her father, and her sister Anne. She sided faithfully with her husband. See biographies by H. W. Chapman (1953, repr. 1972) and Elizabeth Hamilton (1972).

Mary, 1867–1953, queen consort of George V of England. Daughter of the duke of Teck and great-granddaughter of George III, she was engaged first to George's elder brother, the duke of Clarence, who died in 1891. She married George, then duke of York, in 1893. Among her sons were Edward VIII and George VI.

Mary, in the Bible. **1** MARY, the Virgin. **2** MARY MAGDALEN. **3** Wife of CLEOPHAS. **4** Mary of Bethany, sister of Lazarus and Martha. She sat at Jesus' feet while Martha served. She has come to symbolize the life of contemplative love of God. Luke 10.38–42; John 11.1–46; 12.1–9. Some identify her with St. Mary Magdalen. **5** Roman lady saluted by Paul. Rom. 16.6. **6** Mother of St. Mark. Acts 12:12. **7** Mother of Saint James the Less. Mark 15.40, 16.1; Mat. 27.56.

Mary (mä'rē), city (1969 est. pop. 61,000), capital of Mary oblast, Central Asian USSR, in Turkmenistan. Lying in a large oasis of the Kara-Kum desert, on the Murgab River delta, Mary is the center of a rich cotton-growing area. It is a rail junction and carries on extensive trade in cotton, wool, grain, and hides. Mary is also a major textile center. Mary arose in 1884 as a Russian military-administrative center c.20 mi (30 km) from the site of ancient MERV and was itself called Merv until 1937.

Maryborough, city (1971 pop. 19,304), Queensland, E Australia, on the Mary River. Sugar, fruit, coal, and timber are exported, and there are shipyards and locomotive works in the city. The Maryborough School of Arts was established there in 1861.

Maryknoll, headquarters of the Catholic Foreign Mission Society of America, near Ossining, N.Y. A Roman Catholic community of priests (the "Maryknoll Fathers") are there especially trained for foreign missionary work. The community was established in 1911 and sent out its first missionaries in 1918. At first the territory assigned was the Far East, especially China and Korea. During World War II, Maryknoll priests began to be sent to Ecuador, Peru, Bolivia, and Chile, to supplement the shortage of native clergy. There is an affiliated community of nuns (the "Maryknoll Sisters"). See Robert Considine, *The Maryknoll Story* (1950); G. D. Kittler, *The Maryknoll Fathers* (1961).

Maryland, state (1970 pop. 3,922,399), 10,577 sq mi (27,394 sq km), E United States, in the Middle Atlantic region, one of the original Thirteen Colonies. ANNAPOLIS is the capital; BALTIMORE, with a large percentage of the state's population, is the metropolis. A seaboard state, Maryland is divided by Chesapeake Bay, which runs almost to the northern border; thus the section of Maryland called the Eastern

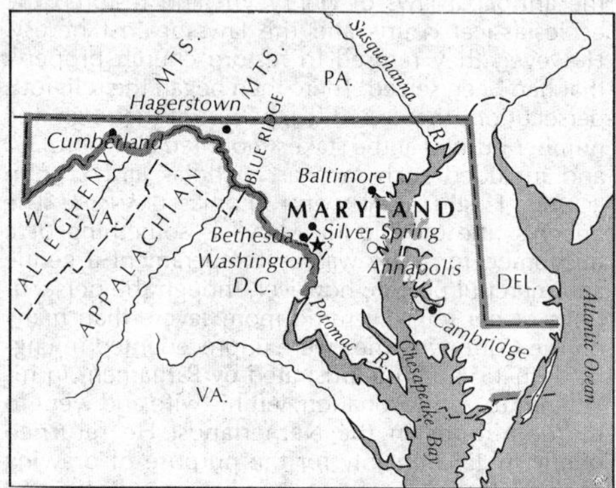

Shore is separated from the main part of the state. Maryland is bounded on the N by Pennsylvania (see MASON-DIXON LINE) and on the E by Delaware and the Atlantic Ocean. For the most part, the erratic course of the Potomac River separates the main part of Maryland from Virginia (to the south) and the long, narrow western handle from West Virginia (to the south and west). The District of Columbia cuts a rectangular identation into the state at the estuary of the Potomac. The main part of the state is divided by the fall line, which runs between Baltimore and Washington, D.C.; to the north and west is the rolling Piedmont, rising to the Blue Ridge and to the Pennsylvania hills. The heavily indented shores of Chesapeake Bay fringe the land with bays and estuaries, which helped in the development of a farm economy relying on water transport. In the mild winters and hot summers of the coastal plains typically southern trees, such as the loblolly pine and the magnolia, flourish, while the cooler uplands have woods of black and white oak and beech. Maryland has nearly 3 million acres (1.2 million hectares) of forest land. Chesapeake Bay dominates the eastern section of the state, where the countryside is sharp with the smell of salt water. Although the fishing industry is declining, the catch of fish and shellfish from Chesapeake Bay yields an annual income in the millions of dollars. The coastal marshes abound in wild fowl. In the western part of Maryland are the mineral resources of building stone and coal. The iron mines, active in the 19th cent., have declined along with other mining activity. The making of iron and steel products is, however, still a major industry, and Maryland, although not a leading mineral producer, is an important mineral processor. Along with Baltimore, CUMBERLAND and HAGERSTOWN are the chief industrial centers. Shipbuilding flourished early and reached an artistic high point in the days when the Baltimore clipper was queen of the seas; in later years shipbuilding continued, but on more massive lines. Other important industries include the manufacture of primary metals, food products, transportation equipment, electrical machinery, chemicals, and apparel. Shipping (Baltimore is a major port), tourism (especially in the Chesapeake Bay cities), and printing and publishing are also big industries. Manufacturing is the largest sector of the economy except for government work. Although manufacturing well exceeds agriculture as a source of income, Maryland's farms yield corn, hay, tobacco, soybeans, and other crops. Income from livestock, especially cattle and chickens, and livestock products is almost twice that from crops; dairy and poultry farms thrive, and Maryland is famous for breeding horses. Farm productivity has remained constant in recent years, despite the growth in manufacturing. John Cabot was probably the first white man to see what is today Maryland when he sailed along the eastern coast in 1498. Giovanni da Verrazano, an Italian navigator in the service of France, probably visited (1524) the Chesapeake region, which was certainly later explored (1574) by Pedro Menéndez Marqués, governor of Spanish Florida. In 1603 the region was visited by an Englishman, Bartholomew Gilbert, and it was charted (1608) by Capt. John Smith. William Claiborne of Virginia, under license from Charles I of England, set up a fur-trading post on Kent Island in 1631. The next year Charles granted a charter to George Calvert, 1st Baron Baltimore, yielding him feudal rights to the region between lat. 40°N and the Potomac River. Disagreement over the boundaries of the grant led to a long series of border disputes with Virginia that were not resolved until 1930. The states still dispute the use of the Potomac River. The territory was named Maryland in honor of Henrietta Maria, queen consort of Charles I. Before the great seal was affixed to the charter, George Calvert died, but his son Cecilius Calvert, 2d Baron Baltimore, undertook development of the colony as a haven for his persecuted fellow Catholics and also as a source of income. In 1634 the ships *Ark* and *Dove* brought settlers (both Catholic and Protestant) to the Western Shore, and a settlement called St. Mary's (see SAINT MARYS CITY) was set up with Leonard Calvert, brother of the proprietor, as governor. The land was largely parceled out in the quasi-feudal holdings and turned over to the colonizers. The Algonquian-speaking Indian tribes withdrew gradually and for the most part peacefully from the area during the colonial period, sparing Maryland the conflicts other colonies experienced. The royal charter gave the assembly of freemen, which first met in 1635, no power to initiate laws. However, in 1638 Lord Baltimore granted that power. Shortly afterwards freemen began electing delegates rather than meeting themselves. The council of advisors to the governor began to sit as the upper house of the legislature, so that by 1650 a bicameral legislature existed. Religious conflict was strong in ensuing years as the Puritans, growing more numerous in the colony and supported by Puritans in England, set out to destroy the religious freedom guaranteed with the founding of the colony. A toleration act (1649) was passed in an attempt to save the Catholic settlers from persecution, but it was repealed (1654) after the Puritans seized control. A brief civil war ensued (1655), from which the Puritans emerged triumphant. By a compromise in 1657 the proprietorship was briefly restored to Lord Baltimore; but after England's Glorious Revolution of 1688, the government of the colony passed to the Crown; the Church of England was made the established Church, and Maryland became (1691) a royal province. Although the proprietorship was again restored in 1715, Maryland remained indistinguishable in government from other royal provinces. Anti-Catholic activity persisted until the 19th cent., when by a curious reversal many Catholic immigrants came to Baltimore. In 1694, when the capital was moved from St. Mary's to Annapolis, those were the only towns in the province, but the next century saw the emergence of commercially oriented Baltimore, which by 1800 had a population of more than 30,000 and a flourishing coastal trade. Public education began in 1723 when the general assembly authorized a free school in each county. Tobacco became the basis of the economy by 1730. In 1767 the demarcation of the Mason-Dixon line ended a long-standing boundary dispute with Pennsylvania. Economic and religious grievances led Maryland to support the growing colonial agitation against England. At the time of the American Revolution most Marylanders were stalwart patriots and vigorous opponents of the British colonial policy. In 1776, Maryland adopted a declaration of rights and a state constitution and sent soldiers and supplies to aid the war for independence; supposedly the high quality of its regular "troops of the line" earned Maryland its nickname, the Old Line State. Although reluctant to sign the Articles of Confederation until the states yielded their claims to Western lands to the national government, Maryland finally signed in 1781. At Annapolis Congress ratified the Treaty of Paris ending the Revolutionary War in 1783. A party advocating states' rights, in which Luther Martin was prominent, was unsuccessful in opposing ratification of the Constitution, and in 1791 Maryland and Virginia contributed land and money for the new national capital in the District of Columbia. Industry, already growing in conjunction with renewed commerce, was furthered by the skills of German immigrants. The War of 1812 was marked for Maryland by the British attack of 1814 on Baltimore and the defense of Fort McHenry, immortalized in Francis Scott Key's "Star-Spangled Banner." After the war the state entered a period of great commercial and industrial expansion. This was accelerated by the building of the National Road, which tapped the rich resources of the West; the opening of the Chesapeake and Delaware Canal (1829); and the opening (1830) of the Baltimore & Ohio RR, first railroad in the United States open for public traffic. Southern ways and sympathies persisted, however, among the plantation owners, and as the rift between North and South widened, Maryland was torn by conflicting interests and the intense internal struggle of the true border state. In 1860 there were 87,000 slaves in Maryland, but industrialists and businessmen had special interests in adhering to the Union; and despite the urgings of Southern sympathizers, made famous in J. R. Randall's song, "Maryland, My Maryland," the state remained in the Union. At the beginning of the Civil War a pro-Southern mob in Baltimore attacked units of the Massachusetts militia that were passing through the city en route to Washington. Gov. Thomas H. Hicks, a Unionist, opposed the pro-Southern legislature in its desire for secession, and President Lincoln suspended habeas corpus and sent troops to Maryland who imprisoned large numbers of secessionists. Nevertheless, Marylanders fought on both sides, and families were often split. General Lee's Army of Northern Virginia invaded Maryland in 1862 and was repulsed by Union forces at Antietam (see ANTIETAM CAMPAIGN). In 1863, Lee again invaded the North and marched across Maryland on the way to and from Gettysburg. Throughout the war Maryland was the scene of many minor battles and skirmishes. With the end of the Civil War, industry was quickly revived and became a dominant force, economically and politically. Senator Arthur P. Gorman, a Democrat, president of the Baltimore & Ohio RR, ran the controlling political machine from 1869 to 1895, when two-party government was restored. New railroad lines traversed the state, making it more than ever a crossing point between North and South. Labor troubles hit Maryland with the Panic of 1873, and four years later railroad wage disputes resulted in large-scale rioting in Cumberland and Baltimore. During the 20th cent., however, Maryland became a leader in labor and other reform legislation. The administrations of governors Austin L. Crowthers (1908–12) and Albert C. Ritchie (1920–35) were noted for reform. Ritchie, a Democrat, became nationally known for his efforts to improve the efficiency and economy of state government. The great influx of population into the state during World War I was repeated and accelerated in World War II—war workers poured into Baltimore, where vital shipbuilding and aircraft plants were in operation, and military and other government employees moved into the area around Washington, D.C. Since World War II, public-works legislation, particularly that concerning roads and other traffic arteries, has brought major changes. The opening of the Chesapeake Bay Bridge in 1952 spurred significant industrial expansion on the Eastern Shore; a parallel bridge was opened in 1973. The Patapsco River tunnel under Baltimore harbor, completed in 1957, represents the state's largest single engineering project. Other projects include the Baltimore-Washington International Airport, formerly called Friendship International Airport (1950), SW of Baltimore, and the Baltimore-Washington Expressway (1954). In 1968, Maryland Gov. Spiro T. Agnew was elected Vice President. Maryland is governed under a constitution adopted in 1867. The general assembly consists of 43 senators and 123 delegates, all elected for four-year terms. The governor, also elected for a four-year term, may succeed himself once. The state elects two U.S. Senators and eight Representatives. It has 10 electoral votes. Marvin Mandel, a Democrat, was appointed governor in 1969 to complete Agnew's term, was elected to a full term in 1970, and was reelected in 1974. Maryland has become increasingly popular as a vacation area—Ocean City is a popular seashore resort, and both sides of Chesapeake Bay are lined with beaches and small fishing towns. The new Chesapeake Bay Bridge has brought the culture of the Eastern Shore, formerly quite distinctive, into a more homogenous unity with that of the rest of the state; the area, however, is still noted for its unique rural beauty and architecture, strongly reminiscent of the English countryside left behind by early settlers. Annapolis, with its well-preserved Colonial architecture and 18th-century waterfront, is the site of the U.S. Naval Academy. Tourists are also attracted to the Antietam National Battlefield Site and the national cemetery at Sharpsburg (see NATIONAL PARKS AND MONUMENTS, table); the Fort McHenry National Monument, at Baltimore harbor; and the historic towns of Frederick and St. Marys City. Racing enthusiasts attend the annual Preakness and Pimlico Cup horse races at Baltimore. There are several military establishments, including Fort George G. Meade and Andrews Air Force Base. The National Institutes of Health in Bethesda is a civilian government establishment. A 12,000-acre (4,856-hectare) National Agricultural Research Center is located at Beltsville. Maryland's medical, educational, and cultural institutions greatly benefited from philanthropic gifts in the late 19th cent. from Johns Hopkins, George Peabody, and Enoch Pratt. Institutions of higher learning in the state include Johns Hopkins Univ., at Baltimore; St. John's College, at Annapolis; Towson State College, at Towson; and the Univ. of Maryland, at College Park. See Federal Writers' Project, *Maryland: A Guide to the Old Line State* (1940); H. Footner, *Rivers of the Eastern Shore* (1944) and *Maryland Main and the Eastern Shore* (1942, repr. 1967); J. T. Scharf, *History of Maryland from the Earliest Period to the Present Day* (1967) and *History of Western Maryland* (1968); F. Van Wyck Mason, *The Maryland Colony* (1969); W. Eddis, *Letters from America*, ed. by A. C. Land (1792, repr. 1970).

Maryland, University of, mainly at College Park; coeducational; land-grant and state supported; chartered and opened 1807 as the College of Medicine of Maryland, became a university in 1812. It has absorbed Maryland Agricultural College (chartered 1856), Baltimore College of Dental Surgery (1840; the first U.S. dental school), and several other colleges and professional schools. The university hospital and the professional schools are at Baltimore. In 1966 a new campus was opened at Catonsville. An autonomous division of the university, now called Maryland State College, is located at Princess Anne. The university operates extension centers throughout the state.

Mary Magdalene (măg'dələn; formerly, and still in Magdalen College, Oxford, and Magdalene College, Cambridge, môd'lən, hence *maudlin,* i.e., tearful) [traditionally Greek=of MAGDALA], Christian saint, a woman widely venerated in Christendom. The name Madeleine is a French form of Magdalene. She appears in the New Testament as a woman whose evil spirits are cast out by Jesus, as a watcher at the Cross, as an attendant at Jesus' burial, and as one of those who found the tomb empty (Mat. 27.56,61; 28; Mark 15.47; 16; Luke 8.2; 24; John 19.25; 20). A universal tradition identifies her with the repentant prostitute who anointed Jesus' feet (Luke 7.36–50). Some also identify her with the sister of Martha (Luke 10.38). Because of the legend (held completely improbable by the Roman Catholic Church) that St. Mary Magdalene lived in penitence at Sainte-Baume, W Var dept., France, the grotto there became a place of pilgrimage. The principal aspect of her cult is as the penitent, hence the word *Magdalen.* Artistic representations deal particularly with her repentance, with her bathing of the feet of Jesus, and with her meeting with Jesus after the resurrection. She appears in representations of Jesus' crucifixion and burial. Frequently she is shown with red hair. Feast: July 22.

Mary of Burgundy, 1457–82, wife of Maximilian of Austria (later Holy Roman Emperor MAXIMILIAN I), daughter and heiress of CHARLES THE BOLD of Burgundy. The marriage of Mary was a major event in European history, for it established the Hapsburgs in the Low Countries and initiated the long rivalry between France and Austria. At her father's death (Jan., 1477) Louis XI of France seized Burgundy and Picardy and prepared to annex the Low Countries, Artois, Luxembourg, and Franche-Comté—Mary's entire inheritance. To gain the assistance of Flanders, Brabant, Hainaut, and Holland, whose representatives met at Ghent in Feb., 1477, Mary granted the Great Privilege, which restored the liberties of the provincial estates that her father and grandfather had abrogated. She then rejected Louis XI's proposal that she marry the dauphin Charles, and in May she married Maximilian, who had hastened to her assistance with an army. However, the Low Countries remained in turmoil; despite his victory at Guinegate (1479), Maximilian was forced (1483) to agree to the Treaty of Arras (see ARRAS, TREATY OF), by which Franche-Comté and Artois passed to France. Mary's premature death, caused by a fall from horseback, left her young son Philip (later PHILIP I of Castile) her heir, but only in 1493 was Maximilian able to regain control over the Low Countries, where Philip had been a virtual prisoner until 1485. The Treaty of Senlis (1493) with France restored Artois and Franche-Comté to Philip, but Burgundy and Picardy remained French.

Mary of England (Mary Tudor), 1496–1533, queen consort of Louis XII of France, daughter of Henry VII of England and sister of Henry VIII. She was betrothed in 1507 to the future Holy Roman Emperor Charles V, but the contract was broken, and in Oct., 1514, she was married to Louis XII of France, then a man of 52 and in poor health. Soon after Louis's death (Jan. 1, 1515), Mary secretly married the man of her choice, Charles Brandon, duke of SUFFOLK. With great reluctance Henry VIII pardoned the marriage. Mary was the grandmother of Lady Jane GREY.

Mary of Guise (gēz), 1515–60, queen consort of James V of Scotland and regent for her daughter, MARY QUEEN OF SCOTS. The daughter of Claude de Lorraine, duc de GUISE, she was also known as Mary of Lorraine. Before her marriage (1538) to James V she had been married (1534) to Louis d'Orléans, 2d duc de Longueville, who died in 1537. When James died (1542), shortly after his daughter's birth, James HAMILTON, 2d earl of Arran, became regent. He negotiated (1543) the betrothal of the infant Queen Mary to Prince Edward (later Edward VI) of England, but the queen mother persuaded the Scottish Parliament to repudiate the agreement. After the outbreak of war with England, Mary of Guise arranged the betrothal of her daughter to the French dauphin, and the young queen was sent to France. By 1554, with French aid, Mary of Guise had replaced the ineffectual Arran as regent, and she made no secret of her desire to bring France and Scotland together. Meanwhile, Protestantism was spreading rapidly in Scotland, and Mary, though at first conciliatory toward the reformers, began a campaign of suppression. In 1559 the Protestants, exhorted by John KNOX, rose against the regent and declared her deposed. Mary received French aid, but the Protestants, allied with the English, proved the stronger force. The civil war was concluded shortly after Mary's death by the Treaty of Edinburgh (1560), which ended the French domination of Scotland and opened the way for the establishment of the Protestant church.

Mary of Modena (mŏd'ĭnə), 1658–1718, queen consort of JAMES II of England; daughter of Alfonso IV, duke of Modena. Her marriage (1673) to James, then duke of York, was brought about through the influence of Louis XIV of France. Mary was a devout Roman Catholic and therefore unpopular in Protestant England. When she bore a son in 1688, it was widely rumored that this Catholic heir to the throne was a changeling, and fear of a Catholic succession precipitated the GLORIOUS REVOLUTION that overthrew James II. Mary fled to France with her son, James Francis Edward STUART, and worked tirelessly to advance his claims to the English throne (see JACOBITES).

Mary Queen of Scots (Mary Stuart), 1542–87, only child of James V of Scotland and MARY OF GUISE. Through her grandmother MARGARET TUDOR, Mary had the strongest claim to the throne of England after the children of Henry VIII. This claim (and her Roman Catholicism) made Mary a threat to ELIZABETH I of England, who finally had her executed. However, Mary's son, James VI of Scotland, succeeded Elizabeth to the English throne as JAMES I.

Early Life. Born at Linlithgow in Dec., 1542, Mary became queen of Scotland on the death of her father only 6 days later. Mary of Guise betrothed her daughter to the French dauphin (later Francis II) and sent the girl to France in 1548 to be brought up by her powerful relatives the GUISE family. In 1558, Mary and Francis were married under an agreement that would unite the crowns of Scotland and France if the union produced male issue. At the same time Mary signed a secret contract that bequeathed Scotland to France should she die without issue. The young couple was crowned in 1559, but Francis died the following year. The accession of Charles IX in France led to the fall of Mary's Guise uncles. This situation, together with the recent death of her own mother, prompted Mary to return to Scotland in 1561. As a Frenchwoman and a Catholic, Mary faced a nation of hostile subjects, but her great personal charm quickly won over many lords and commoners. She took as her principal counselors her illegitimate half brother James Stuart (later earl of MURRAY) and William MAITLAND, both friends of England, thus dispelling fears of a return of French interference in Scottish affairs. She also accepted the establishment of the Presbyterian Church and, under pressure from John KNOX and his associates, consented to certain laws against Catholics. She refused, however, to abandon the Mass in her own chapel, or to approve a law for compulsory attendance at Protestant services.

Darnley and Bothwell. Mary's chief diplomatic project was to secure recognition as successor to the English throne, and she sought a marriage that would reinforce her claim. In 1565 she married her English Catholic cousin, Henry Stuart, Lord DARNLEY, whose descent from Margaret Tudor gave him a claim to the English throne almost as close as Mary's. Murray and some other Protestant nobles opposed the marriage and tried to raise a revolt, but they were defeated and fled to England. Though infatuated with him at first, Mary soon came to dislike her husband and consistently refused his demands for the crown matrimonial (i.e., parliamentary assurance of power during her lifetime and after). Chagrined at his own lack of power and jealous of David RIZZIO, an Italian musician who had become Mary's most trusted friend, Darnley joined a plot against Rizzio. In March, 1566, a band of nobles led by Darnley and the earl of MORTON broke into Mary's apartment and murdered Rizzio, perhaps hoping that the shock would prove fatal to the pregnant queen. Mary, with great courage, talked Darnley over to her side, escaped to Dunbar to be joined by the earl of BOTHWELL and other loyal nobles, and so defeated the coup. In June, 1566, Mary bore her son, James. According to tradition, about this time she fell in love with Bothwell, who had been consistently loyal to her. Darnley, meanwhile, had succeeded in making himself ever more unpopular, and all the royal counselors urged Mary to get rid of him. On the night of Feb. 9, 1567, the house in which Darnley was staying was blown up, and Darnley was found strangled outside. Bothwell was universally suspected of the murder, but was acquitted by a packed court. On April 24, Mary was intercepted by Bothwell on her way to Edinburgh and carried off to Dunbar Castle. In the ensuing two weeks Bothwell secured a divorce from his wife, and on May 15 he and Mary were married by Protestant rites. Aroused by outraged Protestant preachers, the Scots rebelled. Mary had lost the support of the people and the lords, first by her failure to punish the man believed to be her husband's murderer and then by the flagrant act of marrying him. She was forced to surrender to the rebels at Carberry Hill on June 15. Bothwell escaped, only to die insane in a Danish prison. Imprisoned at the castle of Lochleven, Mary abdicated in favor of her son and named Murray regent. In May, 1568, she escaped and soon accumulated a considerable force of men. However, she was defeated by Murray at Langside, near Glasgow, and she immediately fled to N England.

Elizabeth's Prisoner. Elizabeth welcomed Mary to England and refused to turn her over to the Scottish government. She then persuaded both parties to present their cases before an English tribunal, first at York and then at Westminster (1568–69). At the inquiry Murray presented the famous Casket Letters, poems and letters allegedly written by Mary to Bothwell that supposedly proved her share in the plot against Darnley. Mary insisted that parts of the letters were forgeries, and the available evidence suggests that this was the case. In any event, the judgment was that the abdication and Murray's regency were legal, but that Mary's complicity in Darnley's murder was unproven (as it remains). Mary became a prisoner of the English government, living for the next 16 years in the lenient custody of the earl of Shrewsbury and then under the stricter surveillance of Sir Amias Paulet. She schemed ceaselessly to regain her liberty and was party to a succession of plots that would have raised her to the English throne with the help of a Catholic uprising and a Spanish invasion. The uncovering of such plots, real and alleged, some involving important English nobles in schemes to murder Elizabeth, led Parliament to clamor for Mary's execution. Elizabeth refused to take action until the discovery by Sir Francis Walsingham of a plot led by Anthony BABINGTON. The evidence implicated Mary, and she was arrested and taken to Fotheringay Castle. At her trial she defended herself with eloquence and dignity, but there was no doubt of her complicity. Elizabeth hesitated to sign the death warrant, but after assurance from James in Scotland that he would not interfere, and under great pressure from her counselors, she reluctantly consented. Mary was beheaded at Fotheringay on Feb. 8, 1587. Mary's reported beauty and charm and her undoubted courage have made her a particularly romantic figure in history. She is the subject of Schiller's great drama *Maria Stuart* and of plays by Vittorio Alfieri, A. C. Swinburne, and Maxwell Anderson. See biographies by T. F. Henderson (1905, repr. 1969) and Antonia Fraser (1969); studies by G. M. Thomson (1967) and I. B. Cowan, comp. (1971).

Mary Tudor, queen of England: see MARY I.

Maryut, salt lake, Egypt: see MAREOTIS.

Maryville, city (pop. 13,808), seat of Blount co., E Tenn.; settled around Fort Craig (built 1785), inc. as a town 1830, as a city 1927. With its twin city, Alcoa, it is an important center for the production of aluminum and aluminum products. Textile, rubber, and plastic products are also manufactured. Sam Houston went there in 1807; nearby is the log schoolhouse where he taught. Maryville College is in the city and the Great Smoky Mountains National Park and the Tuckaleechee Caverns are in the area.

Mary Washington College: see VIRGINIA, UNIVERSITY OF.

Marzuq (mär'zo͝ok) or **Murzuk** (mo͝or'–), town, SW Libya. With Sabhah, it is one of the chief settlements of Fazzan. Marzuq developed around a fort built c.1310 (now in ruins).

Masaccio (mäzät'chō), 1401–1428?, Italian painter. Masaccio is considered one of the foremost figures of the Florentine Renaissance. His original name was Tommaso Guidi. He was enrolled in the guild of St. Luke in 1424. Most of the creations of his brief lifetime have perished. Only four remain that are attributed to him without question: a polyptych (1426) painted for the Church of the Carmine, Pisa, many of its panels dispersed (now in London, Pisa, Naples, and Vienna) and some lost; the great *Trinity* fresco in Santa Maria Novella, Florence, which revolutionalized the understanding of perspective in painting; the *Virgin with St. Anne* (Uffizi), an early work in collaboration with the lesser painter MASOLINO DA PANICALE; and his masterpiece—a major monument in the history of art—the frescoes in the Brancacci Chapel of Santa Maria del Carmine, Florence, begun by Masolino and completed many years later by Filippino LIPPI. Leaving the chapel unfinished, Masaccio went to Rome, where he died. Masaccio's independent works in the chapel include *Expulsion from Eden, Peter and John Healing the Sick, Peter and John Distributing Alms, Peter Baptizing, The Raising of the King's Son,* and *The Tribute Money.* These frescoes had a great impact on Florentine painting and were for generations the training school and inspiration of painters, among them Michelangelo and Raphael. Masaccio imparted a new sense of grandeur and austerity to the human figure. He used light to give dimension to the contour and achieved a classic sense of proportion. At the same time he created a diversity of character within a unified group and emphasized the range of emotional expression in heroic individuals. His achievement was described by Vasari, who noted Masaccio's debt to Brunelleschi for his system of central perspective and to Donatello for sculptural modeling of forms. His naturalistic approach places his work in the tradition of Giotto and Michelangelo. See studies by Ugo Procacci (tr. 1962) and Luciano Berti (1967).

Masada (məsä'də), ancient mountaintop fortress in Israel, the final outpost of the Zealot Jews in their rebellion against Roman authority (A.D. 66–73). Located in the Judaean Desert, the fortress sits atop a mesa-shaped rock that towers some 1,300 ft (400 m) above the western shore of the Dead Sea. According to the ancient historian Josephus, Masada was first fortified sometime during the 1st or 2d cent. B.C. Between 37 and 31 B.C. Herod the Great, king of Judaea, further strengthened Masada, building two ornate palaces, a bathhouse, aqueducts, and surrounding siege walls. In A.D. 66, with the outbreak of the Jewish war against Rome, the ZEALOTS, an extremist Jewish sect, seized the fortress in a surprise attack and massacred its Roman garrison. Masada remained under Zealot control until A.D. 73, when, after a siege of almost two years, the 15,000 soldiers of Rome's tenth legion finally subdued the 1,000 men, women, and children holding the fortress. In a final act of defiance, however, almost all of the Jewish defenders had killed themselves rather than be captured and enslaved by the Romans. Only two women and five children survived to tell of the Zealots' last action. Excavated (1963–65) by Yigael Yadin and an international team of volunteer archaeologists, Masada is now a major tourist site and an Israeli historical shrine. See Yigael Yadin, *Masada* (tr. 1966).

Masai (mäsī'), a people of E Africa, mainly in Kenya and Tanzania. They are mostly nomadic pastoralists, living off the milk, blood, and meat of their livestock. Men are initiated into the warrior age group, which is responsible for herding cattle and killing lions and other predators. The Masai have been particularly resistant to many of the cultural changes occurring in Africa. See A. C. Hollis, *The Masai: Their Language and Folklore* (1905, repr. 1971); Gerald Hanley, *Warriors and Strangers* (1971).

Masaniello (mäzänyĕl'lō), 1620?–1647, Neapolitan revolutionist, whose original name was Tommaso Aniello. A fisherman, he led a revolt of the lower classes, burdened by high taxes, against the Spanish rulers of Naples. Tumults broke out in 1647 and soon became so serious that the Spanish viceroy came to terms with Masaniello, promised the reforms demanded, and recognized him as captain general. Demented by his sudden success, Masaniello was killed shortly afterward either by agents of the Spanish viceroy or by his own disillusioned supporters. The revolution was soon repressed.

Masaryk, Jan (yän mä'särĭk), 1886–1948, Czechoslovak diplomat, son of Thomas G. Masaryk. He was (1925–38) Czechoslovak minister to Great Britain, and in London he became (1940) foreign minister in the Czechoslovak government in exile headed by Eduard Beneš after the German occupation of Czechoslovakia. During World War II, Masaryk supported a policy of cooperation with the Soviet Union as well as with the Western powers. He continued to hold his post after his government returned (1945) to Prague, and he remained in office after the Communist coup d'etat of Feb., 1948. A few days later it was officially announced that he had committed suicide by throwing himself from a window. The announcement aroused world consternation. No real evidence was ever adduced to prove whether his death was or was not voluntary. See Claire Sterling, *The Masaryk Case* (1969).

Masaryk, Thomas Garrigue (gərēg'), 1850–1937, Czechoslovak political leader and philosopher, first president and chief founder of CZECHOSLOVAKIA. Born in Moravia, he received (1876) his doctorate from the Univ. of Vienna and married an American, Charlotte Garrigue. Masaryk's first important work, *Der Selbstmord als sociale Massenerscheinung der modernen Civilisation* [suicide as a mass phenomenon of modern civilization], was published in 1881, and in 1882 he became professor of philosophy at the new Czech Univ. of Prague. He launched (1883) a monthly review, *The Atheneum;* became associated temporarily with the liberal nationalist Young Czech party; assumed the editorship (1889) of *Čas* [time], a political journal; and was elected (1891) to the Austrian parliament and the Bohemian diet. In 1893, he turned away from parliamentary activity to devote himself to the political education of his people. Disciples had gathered around him, and they launched (1900) the Czech Peoples party (later the Progressive party), based on Masaryk's ideas. Known as the Realist party, it emphasized the economic and social foundations of political power and strove for Czech equality, suffrage, and autonomy; the protection of minorities; and the unity of Czechs and Slovaks. In 1907, Masaryk was reelected to parliament as a member of this party. He did not openly advocate independence at this point, but favored the transformation of the Austro-Hungarian Empire into a federation of self-governing nationalities. He also called for an end to anti-Semitism and opposed (1908) Austria-Hungary's annexation of Bosnia-Hercegovina. At the outbreak of World War I, Masaryk fled abroad and with Eduard BENEŠ formed the Czechoslovak national council, which in 1918 was recognized by the Allies as the de facto government of Czechoslovakia. Traveling widely during the war years, Masaryk raised funds in the United States for the Czech cause, and in Russia he organized (1917–18) the CZECH LEGION, an independent Czech army composed largely of former prisoners of war. The national council, of which Masaryk was president, maintained close secret contact with Czech nationalist leaders (notably Charles KRAMAŘ) at home. Upon the collapse of Austria-Hungary at the end of World War I, Masaryk became (1918) the first president of the Czechoslovak republic. He was reelected in 1920, 1927, and 1934. An extensive land reform was one of the first acts of his government. He steered a moderate course on such sensitive issues as the status of minorities (particularly the Slovaks and Germans) and the relations between Church and state. In foreign policy, he fully backed his foreign minister, Beneš. Masaryk resigned in 1935 because of advanced age, and Beneš succeeded him. He was revered by the majority of the Czech people and was internationally recognized as a great democratic leader. His extensive writings on philosophical, social, and political subjects include *The Making of a State* (tr. 1927, repr. 1969), *Ideals of Humanity* (tr. 1938, repr. 1969), *Modern Man and Religion* (tr. 1938), and *The Spirit of Russia* (tr., 2d ed., 1955). See biographies and studies by Karel Čapek (1935, repr. 1971), Emil Ludwig (1936, repr. 1971), D. A. Lowrie (new and enl. ed. 1937), Paul Selver (1940), Victor Cohen (1941), W. P. Warren (1941), and R. W. Seton-Watson (1943).

Masaya (mäsä'yä), city (1970 est. pop. 50,000), W Nicaragua, capital of Masaya dept. Connected by rail and highway to Granada and Managua, Masaya is a commercial and light manufacturing center in a rich agricultural district. It is noted for Indian crafts and flower gardens.

Masbate (mäsbä'tā), island (1970 pop. 492,868), 1,262 sq mi (3,269 sq km), the Philippines, one of the Visayan Islands, S of SE Luzon. Gold, which has been mined there for centuries, is still produced in quantity; copper is also mined. Lumbering is important, resins are manufactured, and there is general farming. The densely populated coastal plains are intensively cultivated.

Mascagni, Pietro (pyā'trō mäskä'nyē), 1863–1945, Italian operatic composer. He is known for his opera *Cavalleria rusticana* (1890), based on the tale by Giovanni Verga; it is a classic example of the style of realism known as *verismo.* His other operas were less successful.

mascagnite: see AMMONIUM SULFATE.

Mascara (măs'kərə, mäs'kärä), town (1966 pop. 36,930), NW Algeria. It is an administrative center, a garrison town, and a marketplace, noted for its white wine and for its trade in cereals and tobacco. Mascara occupies the site of a Roman settlement. During the 18th cent. it served as capital of the Turkish province in W Algeria. It later became a headquarters of the Algerian emir Abd al-Kadir, from whom the French captured it in 1835; they lost it briefly and then reoccupied it in 1841.

Mascarene Islands (măskərēn'), in the Indian Ocean, E of Madagascar. They include MAURITIUS, RÉUNION, and RODRIGUEZ. Apparently known to the Arabs, they were rediscovered by the Portuguese at the beginning of the 16th cent. The islands are named for Pedro Mascarenhas, who visited them c.1512.

Maschil (măs'kĭl), in the titles of Pss. 32, 42, 44, 45, 52, 53, 54, 55, 74, 78, 88, 89, and 142, a term of unknown significance, probably an indication of the character of the Psalm.

mascon: see MOON.

Masefield, John (māS–), 1878–1967, English poet. He went to sea as a youth and later spent several years in the United States. In 1897 he returned to England and was on the staff of the Manchester *Guardian.* His first volumes of poetry, *Salt-Water Ballads* (1902), containing "Sea Fever" and "Cargoes," and *Ballads* (1903), earned him the title "Poet of the Sea." It was, however, for his realistic, long narrative poems—*The Everlasting Mercy* (1911), *The Widow in the Bye Street* (1912), *Dauber* (1913), and *Reynard the Fox* (1919)—that he won his greatest fame. He was also a playwright and novelist of some note. His plays, written in both verse and prose, include *The*

Tragedy of Nan (1909), *The Tragedy of Pompey the Great* (1910), and *The Coming of Christ* (1928). Among his novels are *Multitude and Solitude* (1909), *Sard Harker* (1924), and *The Bird of Dawning* (1933). Masefield is the author of several literary studies, of which his *William Shakespeare* (1911) is the most notable. Other works include adventure stories for boys and two war sketches, *Gallipoli* (1916) and *The Nine Days Wonder* (1941), and the posthumous volume of poetry *In Glad Thanksgiving* (1968). He was poet laureate from 1930 until his death and was awarded the Order of Merit in 1935. See his autobiographical works *In the Mill* (1941), *So Long to Learn* (1952), and *Grace Before Ploughing* (1966); biography by G. O. Thomas (1933); study by William Hamilton (1922, repr. 1969); bibliography by Geoffrey Handley-Taylor (1960).

maser (mā'zər), device for creation, amplification, and transmission of an intense, highly focused beam of high-frequency radio waves. The name *maser* is an acronym for microwave amplification by stimulated emission of radiation, microwaves being radio waves of short wavelength, or high frequency. The maser is an OSCILLATOR in which the basic frequency control arises from an atomic resonance rather than a resonant electronic circuit. The waves produced by the maser are coherent, that is, all of the same frequency, direction, and phase relationship, while the waves produced by most sources of ELECTROMAGNETIC RADIATION are emitted in all directions over a wide range of frequencies and have all possible phase relationships. Maser radiowaves are much closer to an ideal single-frequency source than those of ordinary radio transmitters. As a result, the maser output can be transmitted over fairly large distances with relatively little loss. The principle of the maser was conceived of in the early 1950s, based on the developments of the QUANTUM THEORY, and the first maser was operated in 1954 by C. H. Townes, J. P. Gordon, and H. J. Zeiger. In 1960 the first optical maser was developed by T. H. Maiman (the optical maser is now called a LASER). Masers have been developed to operate at many different wavelengths, so that the original designation "microwave" is no longer strictly accurate. In the maser, electromagnetic radiation is produced by stimulated emission; an atom or molecule in an excited state (i.e., a state of increased energy) emits a PHOTON of a specific frequency when struck by a second photon of the same frequency. The emitted photon and the bombarding photon emerge in phase and in the same direction. For such emissions to take place in sufficient numbers to produce a steady source of radiation, many atoms or molecules must first be "pumped" to the higher energy state. The first maser used molecules of ammonia gas, which oscillate at a characteristic natural frequency between two energy states. Paramagnetic ions in crystals have also been used as the source of coherent radiation for a maser. A maser may be used as an amplifier or as an oscillator, the latter application requiring a higher power level. One of the most useful types of maser is based on transitions in atomic hydrogen occurring at a frequency of 1,421 megahertz. The hydrogen maser provides a very sharp, constant oscillating signal, and thus serves as a time standard for an ATOMIC CLOCK. See Manfred Brotherton, *Masers and Lasers* (1964).

Masereel, Frans (fräns mäsərāl'), 1889–1972, Belgian painter and illustrator. Essentially self-taught, Masereel is famous for his many series of satiric, expressionist woodcuts. He illustrated many books, including Rolland's *Jean-Christophe*.

Maseru (măz'əro͞o), city (1972 est. pop. 20,000), capital of the Kingdom of Lesotho, on the Caledon River, near the border with the Republic of South Africa. It is Lesotho's only sizable city and its administrative center. A trade and transportation hub, it lies on Lesotho's main road and is linked with South Africa's rail network. An international airport is nearby. The city's few manufactures include candles, carpets, and retreaded tires. Maseru was a small trading town when it was made the capital of the Basuto people by Moshesh I, their paramount chief, in 1869 (see LESOTHO). It was the capital of the British Basutoland protectorate from 1869 to 1871 and from 1884 to 1966, when Lesotho achieved independence. The Univ. of Botswana, Lesotho, and Swaziland is nearby.

Mash, son of Aram. Gen. 10.23.

Mashal (mā'shăl), variant of MISHAL.

Masham, Abigail, Lady (măsh'əm), d. 1734, favorite of Queen ANNE of England. Her maiden name was Abigail Hill. A plain, intelligent person, she became (1704) bedchamber woman to the queen through the influence of her cousin Sarah Churchill, duchess of MARLBOROUGH. In 1707 she married Samuel Masham (later a baron), a groom to Anne's husband, Prince George of Denmark. Mrs. Masham gradually supplanted the duchess of Marlborough in the queen's affection and became the instrument through which Robert HARLEY, her kinsman, exerted his influence on Anne. In 1714, however, Mrs. Masham quarreled with Harley, secured his dismissal as lord treasurer, and assured Viscount Bolingbroke (Henry St. John) of supreme political power. After Anne's death (1714), she lived in retirement.

Mashhad (măsh-häd'), city (1966 pop. 409,616), capital of Khorasan prov., NE Iran. It is an industrial and trade center and a transportation hub. Manufactures include carpets, textiles, pharmaceuticals, and processed foods. Formerly known as Sanabadh, it is the site of the beautiful shrine of the Imam Ali Riza, a Shiite holy person. Imam Riza died (819) in the city after visiting the grave of Caliph Harun ar-Rashid, who had died there 10 years before; he was buried next to Harun, and the shrine was built over both graves. The city was attacked by the Oghuz Turks (12th cent.) and by the Mongols (13th cent.), but recovered by the 14th cent., when it came to be known as Mashhad [Arab.,="place of martyrdom" or "shrine"]. It prospered under the Safavids, who were devout Shiite Muslims; Shah Abbas I embellished Mashhad with many fine buildings. It reached its greatest glory in the 18th cent., when Nadir Shah made Mashhad the capital of Persia. The city took on strategic importance in the late 19th cent. because of its proximity to the Russian and Afghan borders. The bombing of the sanctuary of the Imam Riza by the Russians in 1912 caused widespread resentment in the Shiite Muslim world. Near Mashhad are the remains of the former city of Tus, birthplace of the poet Firdausi and the philosopher al-Ghazali. Mashhad itself is the seat of a university (founded 1947). The city is also known as Meshed.

Mashin, Draga: see DRAGA.

Mashona: see BANTU.

Mašin, Draga: see DRAGA.

Masinissa or **Massinissa** (both: măsĭnĭs'ə), c.238–148 B.C., king of Numidia. He succeeded (c.207 B.C.) his father as king of E Numidia. Brought up in Carthage, he fought in a Carthaginian campaign in Spain in the Second Punic War (see PUNIC WARS) but eventually went over (c.206) to the Roman side. After defeating his old rival Syphax, king of W Numidia, he joined Scipio Africanus Major and led his cavalry in a decisive charge at the battle of Zama (202), which ended the war. Rome awarded him the Punic territory E of Carthage. His tragic relationship with SOPHONISBA at the end of the Second Punic War has been the subject of numerous literary interpretations. During his long reign he extended his power and converted his land of turbulent tribesmen into a formidable and prosperous kingdom. He goaded Carthage into resisting Numidian encroachments; the resistance furnished Rome with a pretext for beginning the Third Punic War.

Masip, Vicente Juan: see MACIP, VICENTE JUAN.

Masjed Soleyman (mäsjĕd' sōlāmän'), city (1966 pop. 64,488), Khuzistan prov., SW Iran, on the Karun River. The site of the first discovery of petroleum in Iran (1908), it is now an oil-refining center.

mask, cover or partial cover for the face or head used as a disguise or protection. Masks have been worn from time immemorial throughout the world. They are used by primitive peoples chiefly to impersonate supernatural beings or animals in religious and magical ceremonies. Particularly notable are the masks of W and central Africa; the wooden masks of the Indians of NW North America, which sometimes represented totemic animals; the False Face Society of the Iroquois Indians, whose masked dancers were thought to ward off evil spirits; and the gold and turquoise-mosaic masks of Aztec warriors and priests. Masks have always been especially important in drama, and their use has been continued into modern times. They are an integral part of Japanese drama, especially of the No plays, and of Chinese temple dramas (see ORIENTAL DRAMA). The many masks used in ancient Greek drama represented the character being portrayed by the actor and were constructed to portray a fixed emotion such as grief or rage. Greek masks had metallic mouthpieces that enhanced the resonance of an actor's voice. The use of masks was preserved in the Roman theater, passed into the early Italian theater, and was a characteristic device of the COMMEDIA DELL' ARTE. The mask was used in the miracle dramas of the Middle Ages and appeared in the 20th cent. in the works of the German expressionist playwrights and in Eugene O'Neill's plays *The Great God Brown* and *Lazarus Laughed.* The making of death masks (reproduction of the face of a dead person) is an ancient practice. Roman death masks were made of wax, and Egyptian death masks of thin gold plate. The modern method first applies oil or grease to the face and next a coat of plaster of paris, which is permitted to harden and is then removed. This procedure results in a mold that is used to cast the mask. A similar process has been used for life masks but is often dangerous to the sitter and unsatisfactory in results. Protective masks include those used by medieval horsemen, gas masks, surgeon's masks, and masks used in certain athletic events. See AFRICAN ART; NORTH AMERICAN INDIAN ART; MASQUE. See Roy Sieber, *Masks as Agents of Social Control* (1962); Josef Gregor, *Masks of the World* (1937, repr. 1968); Andreas Lommel, *Masks* (tr. 1972).

Maskat: see MUSCAT, Oman.

Maskelyne, Nevil (măs'kəlĭn), 1732–1811, English astronomer. Maskelyne received his education at Westminster School and Trinity College. Appointed director of the Greenwich Observatory in 1765, he held this post for 46 years. He introduced the determination of longitude by lunar distances into English navigation, calculated these distances annually, and had them and other pertinent observations published in the *Nautical Almanac,* the first of which was available in 1766. At Schieballion, a mountain in England, he devised a method of measuring the mean density of the earth by using a pendulum.

masochism (măs'əkĭzəm), sexual abnormality in which pleasure is derived from subjection to physical maltreatment. More broadly it refers to a tendency to suffer humiliation, domination, or defeat by which unconscious needs are satisfied. In psychoanalysis the term describes a destructive attitude which the individual turns inward upon himself rather than outward upon others. The word *masochism* was suggested by Leopold von Sacher-Masoch, an Austrian novelist, whose books depicted this abnormality. See Gilles Deleuze, *Masochism* (tr. 1971); Gerald Green and Caroline Green, *S-M: The Last Taboo* (1973); Shirley Panken, *The Joy of Suffering* (1973).

Masolino da Panicale (mäzōlē'nō dä pänēkä'lā), 1383–c.1447, Florentine painter of the early Renaissance, whose real name was Tommaso di Cristoforo Fini. His versatile painting incorporated his feeling for decorative color with strong modeling and spatial organization. He was admitted (1423) to the apothecaries' guild in Florence, in which painters were enrolled, and was soon commissioned to paint the frescoes in the Brancacci Chapel in Florence. These were continued by his pupil Masaccio upon Masolino's departure (1427) for Hungary and were completed by Filippino Lippi, thus greatly complicating the question of authorship; currently scholars attribute to Masolino *St. Peter Preaching, St. Peter Healing the Cripple, The Raising of Tabitha,* and *The Fall of Adam and Eve.* Upon his return to Florence, Masolino found painters occupied with problems of perspective, light and shade, and classical architecture and decoration, ideas which he utilized while retaining much of the old Giottesque tradition. He went to Rome where he painted frescoes in the Church of San Clemente for the Cardinal Branda Castiglione. For the same patron he decorated the church of Castiglione di Olona in the province of Como, Italy. There he represented scenes from the life of the Virgin and of St. John the Baptist. Attributed to Masolino are *The Foundation of Santa Maria Maggiore* and a *Madonna and Christ in Glory* (Naples); *Madonna with Angels* (Church of San Fortunato, Todi); two *Annunciations* (National Gall. of Art, Washington, D.C.); and *Saints* (Philadelphia Museum). See B. Berenson, *The Italian Painters of the Renaissance* (3 vol., 1930, repr. 1968); study by Henrik Lindberg (1931); monograph by Emma Micheletti (1959).

Mason, Daniel Gregory: see MASON, LOWELL.

Mason, George, 1725–92, American political leader, b. Fairfax co., Va. He was one of the most affluent of the colonial Virginia planters. In his triple capacity as trustee of Alexandria (1754–79), justice of the Fairfax county court, and vestryman of Truro parish, Mason exercised great influence in local politics. In 1752 he became a member of the Ohio Company (serving as treasurer until 1773), and in 1759 he was elected to the Virginia house of burgesses. An early opponent of British colonial policy, he drafted the nonimportation resolutions adopted (1769) by the burgesses against the British and also wrote (1774) the Fairfax Resolves, which restated the constitutional position of the colonies in relation to the crown. Mason served on the Virginia committee of safety, and as a member of the Virginia constitutional convention of 1776 he drafted the well-known declaration of rights, which was extensively copied by other American states, and which was drawn on by Thomas Jefferson in the first part of the Declaration of Independence. He was a member of the Federal Constitutional Convention at Philadelphia (1787) and took an active part in drafting the Constitution; however, he objected to provisions for the centralization of power, the compromise between the New England and the Southern states on the tariff and slave trade issues, and the failure to include a bill of rights. Mason refused to sign the Constitution, and with Patrick Henry he led the fight in Virginia against its ratification; the bill of rights he advocated was the basis for some of the first 10 amendments (the Bill of Rights) to the Constitution. See his papers, ed. by R. A. Rutland (3 vol., 1970); biographies by K. M. Rowland (1892, repr. 1964), Helen Hill (1938, repr. 1966), R. A. Rutland (1961, repr. 1963), and Florette Henri (1971).

Mason, James, 1909–, British stage and film actor. Mason, trained at Cambridge as an architect, made his stage debut in 1931. He became a leading man in British films in the 1940s and thereafter an international star. Since the 1950s he has often played deeply introspective or menacing character parts. Among his best-known films are *Odd Man Out* (1946), *Rommel, Desert Fox* (1951), *Julius Caesar* (1953), *A Star is Born* (1954), *Lolita* (1962), *Georgy Girl* (1966), and *The Seagull* (1968).

Mason, James Murray, 1798–1871, U.S. Senator and Confederate diplomat, b. Georgetown, D.C.; grandson of George Mason. He began to practice law in Winchester, Va., in 1820. Mason served in the Virginia legislature (1826–27, 1828–31), in the House of Representatives (1837–39), and in the U.S. Senate (1847–61). A staunch supporter of Southern rights, he drafted the Fugitive Slave Act of 1850 and advocated secession. Jefferson Davis appointed him Confederate commissioner to England in Aug., 1861. Along with John Slidell, Mason was seized aboard the British ship *Trent* by Capt. Charles Wilkes, commanding the U.S. warship *San Jacinto,* and was held prisoner at Fort Warren, Boston, until Jan., 1862 (see TRENT AFFAIR). After his release he went on to England, but he was never officially recognized by the British government. See biography by his daughter, Virginia Mason (1903).

Mason, John, 1586–1635, founder of NEW HAMPSHIRE, b. England. After serving (1615–21) as governor of Newfoundland, he and Sir Ferdinando GORGES received (1622) a patent from the Council for New England for all the territory lying between the Merrimack and Kennebec rivers. In 1629 they divided the grant, Mason taking as his share an area 60 mi (95 km) deep between the Merrimack and Piscataqua rivers, which he named New Hampshire. This grant was confirmed to him when the Council for New England surrendered its charter in 1635. Attempts by his heirs to make good their claims to this land led to long litigation. The inhabitants were finally compelled to recognize the Mason rights, which were sold (1746) by one of Mason's descendants to a group of 12 Portsmouth men, who became known as the **Masonian Proprietors.** They issued settlement permits and land titles in the undeveloped parts of Mason's grant. The grant was redefined by the state in 1788. See J. W. Dean, ed., *Captain John Mason* (1887, repr. 1972).

Mason, John, c.1600–1672, American colonial military commander, b. England. He was an army officer before emigrating (c.1630) to Massachusetts and then (1635) to Windsor, Conn. When the PEQUOT INDIANS threatened to wipe out the new colonies on the Connecticut River, he and John UNDERHILL led an expedition (1637) against them with the aid of other Indians under UNCAS and MIANTONOMO and virtually destroyed the tribe. After this campaign—generally called the Pequot War—Major Mason was a distinguished political leader in Connecticut until his death. See his narrative of the Pequot War in *A Brief History of the Pequot War* (1736, repr. 1971); biography by L. B. Mason (1935).

Mason, John Young, 1799–1859, American statesman, b. Greensville co., Va. He studied law under Tapping Reeve at Litchfield, Conn., and was admitted to the Virginia bar in 1819. Mason served in the state legislature (1823–31), in Congress (1831–37), and as a Federal judge (1837–44). He was Secretary of the Navy (1844) under President Tyler, and in President Polk's cabinet he was Attorney General (1845–46) and again Secretary of the Navy (1846–49). From 1853 until his death he was minister to France, where with James BUCHANAN and Pierre SOULÉ he drew up (1854) the OSTEND MANIFESTO.

Mason, Lowell, 1792–1872, American composer and music educator, b. Medfield, Mass. While working as a bank clerk in Savannah, Ga., he helped compile an anthology that was published as *The Boston Handel and Haydn Society's Collection of Church Music* (1822). He went to Boston to direct the music in three churches, added music to the curriculum of Boston public schools, and, with George J. Webb, founded (1832) the Boston Academy of Music, where he introduced the principles of Pestalozzi in the teaching of music. He arranged many hymns and composed 1,210 of his own, including *Nearer, My God, to Thee, My Faith Looks Up to Thee,* and *From Greenland's Icy Mountains.* Lowell Mason had four sons, all active musically. The two eldest, Daniel Gregory and Lowell, formed a publishing company in New York City. Lowell, the third son, Henry, and Emmons Hamlin founded Mason & Hamlin, a firm that first made organs and later made pianos. The youngest son, **William Mason,** 1829–1908, b. Boston, was a distinguished concert pianist and teacher. He studied in Europe with Liszt and others. With Theodore Thomas he organized a chamber-music ensemble that did much to interest Americans in chamber music. See his *Memories of a Musical Life* (1901). The son of Henry Mason, **Daniel Gregory Mason,** 1873–1953, b. Brookline, Mass., was important as a composer, writer, and lecturer. He studied with John K. Paine at Harvard and with D'Indy in Paris. In 1909 he joined the faculty of Columbia, where he was professor of music from 1929 to 1940. His writings include *Music in My Time* (1938) and *The Quartets of Beethoven* (1947). Among his compositions are the *Chanticleer Overture* (1928); three symphonies, of which the third, known as *Lincoln Symphony* (1936), is outstanding; and chamber music.

Mason, William, 1724–97, English poet, editor, and cleric. His works include two plays, *Elfrida* (1752) and *Caractacus* (1759), based on classical dramas. He was a friend of Thomas GRAY, whose *Life and Letters* he published in 1775. Although he confused the texts of the letters, Mason is noted for developing the method of combining a life with letters.

Mason and Slidell Affair: see TRENT AFFAIR.

Mason City, city (1970 pop. 30,379), seat of Cerro Gordo co., N central Iowa; inc. 1874. It is the rail, trade, and industrial center of a large agricultural area. The major industries are food processing and the manufacture of cement, brick, tile, doors and windows, fertilizers, feeds, apparel, and mobile homes. Its public junior college (1918) is the oldest in the state. A large band festival is held annually in Mason City. A state park is nearby.

Mason-Dixon Line, boundary between Pennsylvania and Maryland (running between lat. 39°43'26.3"N and lat. 39°43'17.6"N), surveyed by the English astronomers Charles Mason and Jeremiah Dixon between 1763 and 1767. The ambiguous description of the boundaries in the Maryland and Pennsylvania charters led to a protracted disagreement between the proprietors of the two colonies; the dispute was submitted to the English court of chancery in 1735. A compromise between the Penn and Calvert families in 1760 resulted in the appointment of Mason and Dixon. By 1767 the surveyors had run their line 244 mi (393 km) W from the Delaware border, every fifth milestone bearing the Penn and Calvert arms. The survey was completed to the western limit of Maryland in 1773; in 1779 the line was extended to mark the southern boundary of Pennsylvania with Virginia (the present-day West Virginia). Before the Civil War the term "Mason-Dixon Line" popularly designated the boundary dividing the slave states from the free states, and it is still used to distinguish the South from the North.

Masonic orders: see FREEMASONRY.

masonry: see BRICK; CONCRETE; STONEWORK; TILE.

Masora or **Massorah** (məsō'rə) [Heb.,=tradition], collection of critical annotations made by Hebrew scholars, called the Masoretes, to establish the text of the Old Testament. A principal problem was to fix the vowels, as the Hebrew alphabet has only consonants. Through assiduous study the Masoretes formulated rules for an accurate reading of each verse, evolving a system of vowels and punctuation for the purpose of pronunciation and intonation. Two systems of vowels were evolved: the Tiberian (now in use), consisting of curves, dots, and dashes, which can be traced to the 7th cent.; and the Babylonian, of earlier origin, a more complicated superlinear system. The language of the Masora is mostly Aramaic, although some of the notes are written in Hebrew. The Masoretic compilation that consists of notes in the margins is called the Small, or Marginal, Masora; the one that consists of notes written at the top or the bottom of the text is known as the Great, or Final, Masora. Masoretic work was begun at an unknown time; the first traces of it appear in some halakic works on the Pentateuch. Innumerable scholars contributed to this work, which ceased c.1425. See Robert Gordis, *Biblical Text in the Making* (1937, repr. 1971); C. D. Ginsburg, *Introduction to the Masoretico-Critical Edition of the Hebrew Bible* (rev. ed. 1966).

Masovia (məsō'vēə), Pol. *Mazowsze,* historic region, almost coextensive with Warsaw province, central Poland. At the death (1138) of Boleslaus III, Masovia became an independent duchy under the PIAST dynasty. It became a suzerainty of Great Poland in 1351 and was finally united with it in 1526. Masovia passed to Prussia during the 18th-century partitions of Poland and was later a part of the Russian Empire. It reverted to Poland in 1918.

Maspero, Gaston Camille Charles (gästôN' kämē'yə shärl mäspərō'), 1846–1916, French Egyptologist. He taught at the Collège de France and was director of excavations in Egypt, where he established the French School of Oriental Archaeology at Cairo and accomplished valuable work, especially in Luxor and Karnak. Maspero returned to France in 1914 as permanent secretary of the Académie des Inscriptions et Belles Lettres. Among his chief works is *L'Histoire ancienne des peuples de l'Orient Classique,* of which three volumes were translated as *The Dawn of Civilization* (1884), *The Struggle of Nations* (1897), and *The Passing of the Empires* (1900). An excellent brief version is his *Histoire ancienne des peuples de l'Orient* (1875).

Masqat: see MUSCAT, Oman.

masque, courtly form of dramatic spectacle, popular in England in the first half of the 17th cent. The masque developed from the early 16th-century disguising, or mummery, in which disguised guests bearing presents would break into a festival and then join with their hosts in a ceremonial dance. As the form evolved, the important elements retained were the use of the mask and the mingling of actors and spectators. Reaching its height in the early 17th cent., the masque became a magnificent and colorful spectacle, presented in the open air on huge wooden platforms. The actors personified pastoral and mythological figures, with great emphasis placed on music and dance. The foremost writer of the masque was Ben JONSON. However, it was Inigo JONES, the theatrical architect, famous for his elaborate costume designs, settings, and scenic effects, who gave the masque its greatest popularity. The popular masquerade or costume ball originated in France. See Allardyce Nicoll, *Stuart Masques and the Renaissance Stage* (1937); Enid Welsford, *The Court Masque* (1927, repr. 1962); S. K. Orgel, *The Jonsonian Masque* (1965).

Masrekah (măsrē'kə), unidentified birthplace of an Edomite king. Gen. 36.36; 1 Chron. 1.47.

Mass, religious service of the Roman Catholic Church, a performance of the sacrament of the EUCHARIST. It is based on the ancient Latin liturgy of the city of Rome, now used in most, but not all, Roman Catholic churches. For non-Roman liturgies, see LITURGY. The term Mass [from Latin *missa,*=dismissed] probably derives from the practice of dismissing the catechumens—those not yet initiated into the mystery of the Eucharist—before the offertory and from the words *Ite, missa est* [Go, you are dismissed] spoken to the faithful at the end of the Mass. The term is also used among Anglo-Catholics; in the Eastern churches the Mass is generally called the Holy Liturgy or the Offering. In the Roman Catholic Church, except for the altogether distinct Ambrosian rite (see AMBROSE, SAINT) and for some variant forms among religious orders, especially that of the Dominicans, the service is the same everywhere, under regulation of the Holy See. The language of the liturgy is typically terse. The celebrant, who must be a priest or a bishop, follows a prescribed missal and wears certain vestments. Mass is said at an altar containing relics; two candles must be burning. A congregation is not essential, but solitary Mass is discouraged. In full form there are priest, deacon, and choir; this is High (solemn) Mass. Low Mass, much commoner, is the same service said by one priest. Most of the text is invariable, or "ordinary," but certain parts, called "proper," change with the occasion or day. Of the sung portions, some are chanted solo at the altar with choral response; there are also nine hymns for the choir. Four of these are proper and related in theme, with texts usually from the Psalms: introit, anthem after the epistle (alleluia, gradual, tract, or sequence), offertory, and communion. The five ordinary choral pieces are KYRIE ELEISON, GLORIA IN EXCELSIS, Credo (see CREED), SANCTUS, and AGNUS DEI. PLAINSONG is prescribed for all texts, but latitude is permitted the choir. A musical setting for the five ordinary hymns, called a Mass, has been a major musical form. The principal period of Mass composition lasted from 1400 to 1700. It came to an end with shift of interest to instrumental music, although later composers did use the form. Among the many composers who produced Masses are Josquin des Prés, Palestrina, Monteverdi, Bach, Haydn, Mozart, Beethoven, Verdi, and Stravinsky. The Mass begins with an entrance hymn, a greeting, and a brief penetential rite that includes the *Kyrie eleison*, the *Gloria in excelsis* (not always), a COLLECT or collects, the proper EPISTLE, an anthem and the proper GOSPEL (chanted with all standing), and a homily on the texts. This ends the part of the Mass known in primitive times as the Mass of the Catechumens. Mass continues with the creed (sometimes), the OFFERTORY (anthem with offering of bread and wine), offering of incense (sometimes), washing of the celebrant's hands, and proper prayers called "secrets." Then there is a chanted dialogue and proper preface of thanksgiving, ending in the *Sanctus*. That opens the long eucharistic prayer, or canon. It begins with prayers for the living. The consecration follows; then the celebrant raises Host and chalice above his head for all to see and adore. The canon ends with prayers for the dead and a doxology, which is the solemn climax of the eucharistic prayer. After the canon the Mass consists of the Lord's Prayer, a prayer amplifying the supplication "Deliver us from evil," the symbolic breaking of the Host and putting a piece into the cup, the kiss of peace (shared by the members of the congregation), the *Agnus Dei*, the communion, the ablution of vessels, the communion anthem, postcommunion prayers, the dismissal, and the blessing. There are ceremonial adjuncts such as processions, blessings, censings, and in some places, the ringing of a handbell at the consecration. Normally at Low Mass a server (altar boy) or acolyte, often a boy, helps the celebrant. Mass may be offered with a special intention, as in thanksgiving or for peace. A REQUIEM is a proper Mass for the dead. Most priests say Mass daily. Sunday Mass is an important sociocultural factor in Roman Catholic life. All members are required to attend Mass on Sunday as a minimum participation in public worship. The basic structure of the Mass is largely unchanged since the 6th cent. In the Catholic Reformation the forms were restricted and local variants eliminated. As a result of the Constitution on the Sacred Liturgy of the Second Vatican Council, the Roman Mass liturgy has undergone extensive reformation. The revisions include the use of the vernacular languages in the place of Latin, an emphasis on congregational singing, latitude for modifications that may be introduced by local bishops, additional eucharistic prayers, and communion in both bread and wine. See J. A. Jungmann, *The Mass of the Roman Rite* (rev. ed. 1959); François Amiot, *History of the Mass* (tr. 1959); Henry Daniel-Rops, *This Is the Mass* (rev. ed. 1965).

mass, in physics, the quantity of matter in a body regardless of its volume or of any forces acting on it. The term should not be confused with *weight*, which is the measure of the force of gravity (see GRAVITATION) acting on a body. Under ordinary conditions the mass of a body can be considered to be constant; its weight, however, is not constant, since the force of gravity varies from place to place. There are two ways of referring to mass, depending on the law of physics defining it: *gravitational* mass and *inertial* mass. The gravitational mass of a body may be determined by comparing the body on a beam balance with a set of standard masses; in this way the gravitational factor is eliminated. The inertial mass of a body is a measure of the body's resistance to acceleration by some external force. One body has twice as much inertial mass as another body if it offers twice as much force in opposition to the same acceleration. All evidence seems to indicate that the gravitational and inertial masses of a body are equal, as demanded by Einstein's equivalence principle of RELATIVITY; so that at the same location equal (inertial) masses have equal weights. Because the numerical value for the mass of a body is the same anywhere in the world, it is used as a basis of reference for many physical measurements, such as density and heat capacity. According to the special theory of relativity, mass is not strictly constant but increases with the speed according to the formula $m=m_0/\sqrt{1-v^2/c^2}$, where m_0 is the rest mass of the body, v is its speed, and c is the speed of light in vacuum. This increase in mass, however, does not become appreciable until very great speeds are reached. The rest mass of a body is its mass at zero velocity. The special theory of relativity also leads to the Einstein mass-energy relation, $E=mc^2$, where E is the energy, and m and c are the (relativistic) mass and the speed of light, respectively. Because of this equivalence of mass and ENERGY, the law of conservation of energy was extended to include mass as a form of energy.

Massa (măs'ə), seventh son of Ishmael. Gen. 25.14; 1 Chron. 1.30.

Massa (mäs'ä), city (1971 pop. 62,797), capital of Massa-Carrara prov., Tuscany, N central Italy, near the Ligurian Sea. Marble is quarried, and chemicals are produced there. From the 15th to the 19th cent. Massa was the capital of the independent principality, later duchy, of Massa and Carrara, which was ruled by the Malaspina and the Cybo-Malaspina families. In 1829 the city passed through marriage to the house of Austria-Este, dukes of Modena. It united with the kingdom of Sardinia in 1859. The old town centers around the 15th-century Malaspina castle; in the new section are the Cybo-Malaspina Palace, a 15th-century cathedral, and a fine marble fountain.

Massachuset Indians (măsəchōō'sĭt), confederation of North American Indians whose language belongs to the Algonquian branch of the Algonquian-Wakashan linguistic stock (see AMERICAN INDIAN LANGUAGES). In the early 17th cent. they occupied the territory around Massachusetts Bay and ranged northward. They then numbered some 3,000, but by 1631, after wars and pestilence, they were reduced to some 500. Soon thereafter they adopted Christianity and moved, with other converts, into the villages of the PRAYING INDIANS. Here they ceased to have a separate tribal existence. The Massachuset owned and occupied the site of Boston.

Massachusetts (măsəchōō'sĭts), state (1970 pop. 5,689,170), 8,257 sq mi (21,386 sq km), NE United States, in NEW ENGLAND, one of the Thirteen Colonies. BOSTON is the capital and largest city. Other important cities include WORCESTER, SPRINGFIELD, CAMBRIDGE, NEW BEDFORD, FALL RIVER, SOMERVILLE, LYNN, and LOWELL. Massachusetts is bounded on the N by Vermont and New Hampshire, on the E and S by the Atlantic Ocean, further on the S by Rhode Island (which also borders SE Massachusetts on the W) and Connecticut, and on the W by New York. The eastern part of the commonwealth (its official designation), including the CAPE COD peninsula and the islands lying off it to the south— the ELIZABETH ISLANDS, MARTHA'S VINEYARD, and NANTUCKET—is a low coastal plain. In this area short, swift rivers such as the Merrimack have long supplied industry with power, and an indented coastline provides many good natural harbors, with Boston a major port. In the interior rise uplands separated by the rich Connecticut River valley, and farther west lies the Berkshire valley, surrounded by the Berkshire Hills, part of the Taconic Mts. The western streams feed both the Hudson and the Housatonic rivers. The state has a mean altitude of c.500 ft (150 m), and Mt. Greylock in the Berkshires is the highest point (3,491 ft/1,064 m). The climate, of the northeast temperate zone variety, is variable. Massachusetts is an overwhelmingly industrial state, and, with its predominantly urban population, one of the most densely settled in the nation. It has many diverse manufactures; chief among them are electrical and electronic equipment, plastic products, shoes and leather goods, clothing and textiles, firearms, paper and paper products, machinery, tools, and metal and rubber products. Shipping, printing, and publishing are important, and the jewelry industry dates from before the American Revolution. Leading agricultural products include cranberries, tobacco, hay, apples, vegetables, greenhouse and nursery items, and milk and other dairy goods; poultry is also raised. The fishing fleets of Gloucester and New Bedford still bring in a large and varied catch, and the coastal waters abound in shellfish. Lime, clay, sand, gravel, and stone are the chief mineral resources. The coast of what is now Massachusetts was probably skirted by Norsemen in the 11th cent., and Europeans of various nationalities (but mostly English) sailed offshore in the late 16th and early 17th cent. Settlement began when the PILGRIMS arrived on the Mayflower and landed (1620) at a point which they named PLYMOUTH (for their port of embarkation in England). Their first governor, John Carver, died the next year, but under his wise successor, William Bradford, the PLYMOUTH COLONY took firm hold. Weathering early difficulties, the colony eventually prospered. Other Englishmen soon established fishing and trading posts nearby—Andrew Weston (1622) at Wessagusset (now Weymouth) and Thomas Wollaston (1625) at Mt. Wollaston, which was renamed Merry Mount (now QUINCY) when Thomas Morton took charge. The fishing post established (1623) on Cape Ann by Roger Conant failed, but in 1626 he founded Naumkeag (SALEM), which in 1628 became the nucleus of a Puritan colony led by John Endecott of the New England Company and chartered by the private Council for New England. In 1629 the New England Company was reorganized as the MASSACHUSETTS BAY COMPANY after receiving a more secure patent from the crown. In 1630, John Winthrop led the first large Puritan migration from England (900 settlers on 11 ships). Boston supplanted Salem as capital of the colony, and Winthrop replaced Endecott as governor. After some initial adjustments to allow greater popular participation and the representation of outlying settlements in the General Court (consisting of a governor, deputy governor, assistants, and deputies), the "Bay Colony" continued to be governed as a private company for the next 50 years. It was also a thoroughgoing Puritan theocracy (see PURITANISM), in which clergymen such as John Cotton enjoyed great political influence. The status of freeman was restricted (until 1664) to church members, and the state was regarded as an agency of God's will on earth. Since their chief aim was to prove the feasibility of such a theocracy to less "pure" Protestants

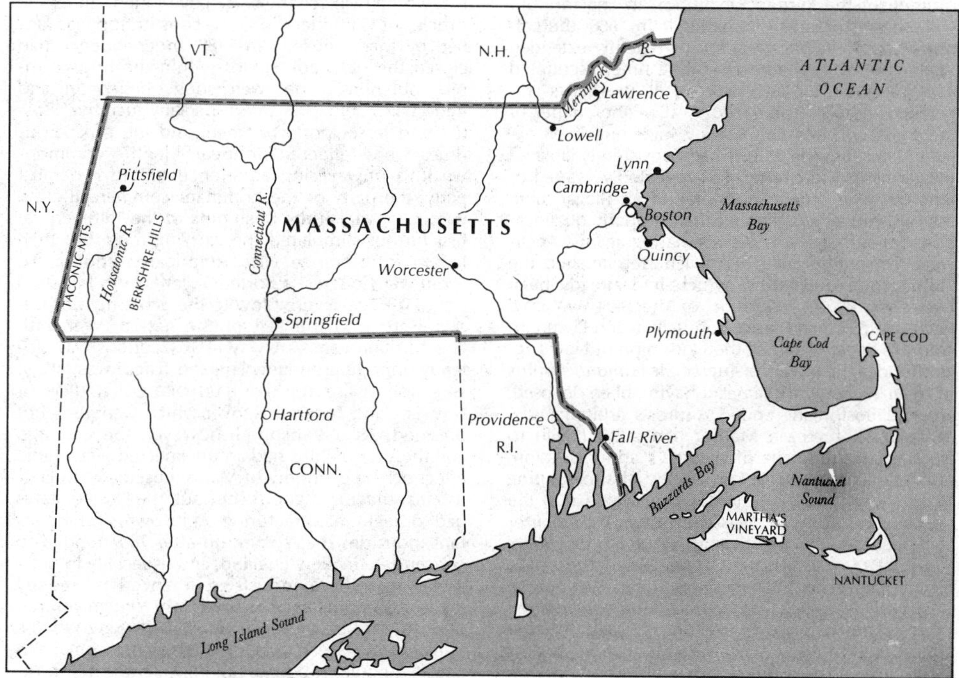

in England, the authorities of the Bay Colony made every effort to suppress dissent. When Roger Williams spoke out in favor of religious toleration he was expelled (1635). In 1636 he founded Rhode Island as a haven for religious dissenters and was soon joined by Anne Hutchinson, a principal figure in the controversy over ANTINOMIANISM. Her brother-in-law, John Wheelwright, was also banished (1638) and founded Exeter in New Hampshire. Connecticut, on the other hand, was established by prominent orthodox Puritans such as John Haynes and Thomas Hooker. The steady stream of newcomers from England more than offset these departures, and soon the South Shore (i.e., S of Boston), the North Shore, and the interior were dotted with firmly rooted communities. The early Puritans were primarily agricultural people, although a merchant class soon formed. Most of the inhabitants lived in villages, beyond which lay their privately owned fields. The typical village was composed of houses (also individually owned) grouped around the common—a plot of land held in common by the community. The dominant structure on the common was the meetinghouse, where the pastor, the most important figure in the community, held long Sabbath services. In the meetinghouse of the chief village of a town (in New England a town corresponds to what is usually called a township elsewhere in the United States) was also held the town meeting, traditionally regarded as a foundation of American democracy. In practice the town meeting served less to advance democracy than to enforce unanimity and conformity, and participation was as a rule restricted to male property holders and church members. The Puritans, however, were not invariably grim and dictatorial. Life in the New World was hard, and they took it seriously; but, like 17th-century Englishmen in general, the Puritans also had a gregarious and bawdy side. Because they valued the ability of everyone to study scripture and always insisted on a learned ministry, the Puritans also zealously promoted the development of educational facilities. The BOSTON LATIN SCHOOL was founded in 1635, one year before HARVARD UNIVERSITY was established, and in 1647 a law was passed requiring elementary schools in towns of 50 families. These were not free schools, but they were open to all and are considered the beginning of popular education in the United States. This vigorous missionary activity, largely carried on by John Eliot, even included attempts to educate the Indians. While the Indians probably did not mind learning the English alphabet, they did become increasingly resentful of English land grabbing. After the Pequot War (see PEQUOT INDIANS) of 1637, the four Puritan colonies (Massachusetts Bay, Plymouth, Connecticut, and New Haven) formed the NEW ENGLAND CONFEDERATION, the first voluntary union of American colonies, which in 1675–76 broke the power of the Indians of southern New England in King Philip's War. In the course of the drawn-out FRENCH AND INDIAN WARS, however, frontier settlements such as DEERFIELD were subjected to devastating Indian attacks. Massachusetts Bay Colony naturally rejoiced at the triumph of the Puritan Revolution in England, but with the restoration of Charles II in 1660, the colony's happy prospects faded. Its recently extended jurisdiction over Maine was for a time discounted by royal authority, and, worse still, its charter was revoked in 1684. The withdrawal of the charter of the Massachusetts Bay Colony had long been expected because the colony had consistently violated the terms of the charter and repeatedly evaded or ignored royal orders by operating an illegal mint, establishing religious rather than property qualifications for suffrage, and discriminating against Anglicans. The withdrawal of the charter finished the "Bible commonwealth," which had already been weakened by the adoption of the HALF-WAY COVENANT in 1657. The Massachusetts Bay and Plymouth colonies became part of the Dominion of New England under the governorship of Sir Edmund Andros in 1686. In 1689, with James II having been deposed, aroused Bostonians ended Andros's arbitrary rule. Meanwhile, Increase Mather had gone (1688) to England to complain of Andros's administration. Mather managed to obtain a new charter uniting Massachusetts Bay, Plymouth, and Maine into the one royal colony of Massachusetts. This charter abolished church membership as a test for voting, although CONGREGATIONALISM remained the established religion. Sir William Phips, a native of Maine, was the first royal governor under the new charter. Widespread anxiety over loss of the original charter contributed to the witchcraft panic that reached its climax in Salem in the summer of 1692. Nineteen persons were hanged and one crushed to death for refusing to confess to the practice of witchcraft. The Salem trials ended abruptly when colonial authorities, led by Cotton Mather, became alarmed at their excesses. By the mid-18th cent. the Massachusetts colony had come a long way from its humble agricultural beginnings. Fish and lumber were exported along with farm products in a lively trade carried by ships built in Massachusetts and manned by local seamen. That the menace of French Canada was removed by 1763 was due in no small measure to the unstinting efforts of the mother country, but the increasing British tendency to regulate colonial affairs, especially trade (see NAVIGATION ACTS), without colonial advice, was most unwelcome. Because of the colony's extensive shipping interests, e.g., the traffic in molasses, rum, and Negro slaves (the "triangular trade"), it sorely felt these restrictions. In 1761, James Otis opposed a Massachusetts superior court's issue of the writs of assistance (general search warrants to aid customs officers in enforcing collection of duties on imported sugar), arguing that this act violated the natural rights of Englishmen and was therefore void. He thus helped set the stage for the political controversy which, coupled with economic grievances, culminated in the AMERICAN REVOLUTION. In Massachusetts a bitter struggle developed between the governor, Thomas Hutchinson, and the anti-British party in the legislature led by Samuel Adams, John Adams, James Otis, and John Hancock. The STAMP ACT (1765) and the TOWNSHEND ACTS (1767) preceded the BOSTON MASSACRE (1770), and the Tea Act (1773) brought on the BOSTON TEA PARTY. The rebellious colonials were punished for this with the INTOLERABLE ACTS (1774), which troops under Gen. Thomas Gage were sent to enforce. Through Committees of Correspondence, Massachusetts and the other colonies had been sharing their grievances, and in 1774 they called the First CONTINENTAL CONGRESS at Philadelphia for united action. The mounting tension in Massachusetts exploded in April, 1775, when General Gage decided to make a show of force. Warned by Paul Revere and William Dawes, the Massachusetts militia engaged the British force at Lexington and Concord (see LEXINGTON AND CONCORD, BATTLES OF). Patriot militia from other colonies hurried to Massachusetts, where, after the battle of BUNKER HILL (June 17, 1775), George Washington took command of the patriot forces. The British remained in Boston until March 17, 1776, when Gen. William Howe evacuated the town, taking with him a considerable number of Tories. British troops never returned, but Massachusetts soldiers were busy fighting elsewhere for the independence of the colonies. In 1780 a new constitution, drafted by a constitutional convention under the leadership of John Adams, was ratified by direct vote of the citizenry. Victorious in the Revolution, the colonies faced depressing economic conditions. Nowhere were those conditions worse than in W Massachusetts, where discontented Berkshire farmers erupted in SHAYS'S REBELLION in 1786. The uprising was promptly quelled, but it frightened conservatives into support of a new national constitution that would displace the weak government under the Articles of Confederation; this constitution was ratified by Massachusetts in 1788. Independence had closed the old trade routes within the British Empire, but newer ones were soon opened up, and trade with China became especially lucrative. Boston and lesser ports boomed, and the prosperous times were reflected politically in the commonwealth's unwavering adherence to the Federalist party, the party of the dominant commercial class. European wars at the beginning of the 19th cent. at first further stimulated the carrying trade but then led to interference with American shipping. To avoid war Congress resorted to Jefferson's EMBARGO ACT OF 1807, a severe blow to the economy of Massachusetts and the rest of the nation. War with Great Britain came anyway in 1812, and it was violently unpopular in New England. There was talk of secession at the abortive HARTFORD CONVENTION of New England Federalists, over which George Cabot presided. As it transpired, however, the embargo and the War of 1812 had an unexpectedly favorable effect on the economy of Massachusetts. With English manufactured goods shut out, the United States had to begin manufacturing on its own, and the infant industries that sprang up after 1807 tended to concentrate in New England, and especially in Massachusetts. These industries, financed by money made in shipping and shielded from foreign competition by protective tariffs after 1816, grew rapidly, transforming the character of the commonwealth and its people. Labor was plentiful and often ruthlessly exploited. The power loom, perfected by Francis Cabot Lowell, as well as English techniques for textile manufacturing (based on plans smuggled out of England) made Massachusetts an early center of the American textile industry. Agriculture, on the other hand, went into a sharp decline because Massachusetts could not compete with the new agricultural states of the West, a region more readily accessible after the opening of the ERIE CANAL (1825). Farms were abandoned by the score; some farmers turned to work in the new factories, others moved to the West. In 1820, Maine was separated from Massachusetts and admitted to the Union as a separate state under the terms of the MISSOURI COMPROMISE. In the same year the Massachusetts constitution was considerably liberalized by the adoption of amendments which abolished all property qualifications for voting, provided for the incorporation of cities, and removed religious tests for officeholders. (Massachusetts is the only one of the original 13 states that is still governed under its original constitution, the one of 1780, although this was extensively amended by the constitutional convention of 1917–19.) In the 1830s and 40s the state became the center of religious and social reform movements. UNITARIANISM, a more charitable creed than the stern old-time Congregationalism (finally disestablished in 1833), swept through the commonwealth under the guidance of William Ellery Channing and, later, Theodore Parker. Horace Mann set about establishing an enduring system of public education in the 1830s, and Dorothea Lynde Dix began her crusade to help the mentally ill in the 1840s. Of the transcendentalists (see TRANSCENDENTALISM), Ralph Waldo Emerson and Henry Thoreau were quick to perceive and decry the evils of industrialization, while Bronson Alcott, Margaret Fuller, Nathaniel Hawthorne, and Emerson had some association with BROOK FARM, an outgrowth of Utopian ideals. The intellectual and cultural center of the nation, Massachusetts gave to the nation the architect Charles Bulfinch; such writers and poets as Richard Henry Dana, Emily Dickinson, Oliver Wendell Holmes, Henry Wadsworth Longfellow, James Russell Lowell, and John Greenleaf Whittier; the historians George Bancroft, John Lothrop Motley, Francis Parkman, and William Hickling Prescott; and the scientist Louis Agassiz. In the 1830s reformers began to devote energy to the antislavery crusade. This was regarded with great displeasure by the mill tycoons, who feared that an offended South would cut off their cotton supply. William Lloyd Garrison was the boldest, though not the most effective, of the ABOLITIONISTS. Equally sincere were Wendell Phillips and the poet Whittier, who attacked the great Whig leader Daniel Webster for his part in effecting the Compromise of 1850. Charles Sumner, who soon took Webster's seat in the U.S. Senate, satisfied even the most fiery abolitionist. While he eloquently denounced the Kansas-Nebraska Act (1854), other Massachusetts men organized the EMIGRANT AID COMPANY to save "bleeding" Kansas from slavery. With the Whig party broken on the slavery issue, Massachusetts turned to the new Republican party and voted for John C. Frémont in 1856 and Abraham Lincoln in 1860. Largely because of its efficient governor John Andrew, Massachusetts was the first state to answer Lincoln's call for troops after the firing on Fort Sumter. Massachusetts men were the first to die for the Union cause when the 6th Massachusetts Regiment was fired on by a secessionist mob in Baltimore. In the course of the war over 130,000 men from the state served in the Union forces. After the war Massachusetts, with other northern states, experienced rapid industrial expansion. Massachusetts capital financed many of the nation's new railroads, especially in the West. Although people continued to leave the state for the West, labor remained cheap and plentiful as European immigrants streamed into the state. The Irish, oppressed by both nature and the British, began arriving in droves even before the Civil War (beginning in the 1840s), and they continued to land in Boston for years to come. After them came French Canadians, arriving later in the 19th cent., and, in the early 20th cent., Portuguese, Italians, Poles and other Slavs, and Scandinavians. Also from the British Isles came Englishmen, Scots, and Welshmen. Of all the immigrant groups, English-speaking and non-English-speaking, the Irish came to be the most influential, especially in politics. Their religion (Roman Catholic) and their political faith (Democratic) definitely set them apart from the old native Yankee stock. Practically all of the immigrants went to work in the factories. The halcyon days of shipping were over. The carrying trade had bounded back triumphantly after the War of 1812, but the supplanting of sail by steam, the growth of railroads, and the destruction caused by Confederate cruisers in the Civil War helped reduce shipping to its present negligible state—a far cry from the colorful era of the clipper ships, which were perfected by Donald McKay of Boston. Whaling, once the glory of New Bedford and Nantucket, faded quickly with the introduction of petroleum. The rise of industrialism was accompanied by a growth of cities, although the small mill town, where the factory hands lived in company houses and traded in the company store, remained important. Labor unions struggled for recognition in a long, weary battle marked by strikes, sometimes violent, as was the Lawrence textile strike of 1912. World War I, which caused a vast increase in industrial production, improved the lot of workingmen, but not of Boston policemen, who staged and lost their famous strike in 1919. For his part in breaking the strike, Gov. Calvin Coolidge won national fame and went on to become Vice President and then President, the third Massachusetts citizen (after John Adams and John Quincy Adams) to hold the highest office in the land. The SACCO-VANZETTI CASE, following the police strike, attracted international attention, as liberals raged over the seeming lack of regard for the spirit of the law in a state which had given the nation such an eminent jurist as Oliver Wendell Holmes (1841-1935). Labor unions finally came into their own in the 1930s under the New Deal. Industry spurted forward again during World War II, and in the postwar era the state has continued to develop. The decline of the textile industry has been offset by the growth of the electronics industry, attracted by the skilled labor in the Boston area. In 1973 the state's economy was dealt a severe blow when several U.S. military installations, including the 172-year-old Boston Naval Shipyard and Westover Air Force Base, were closed by the Federal government in an economy move. On the political scene, Massachusetts gave the nation its 35th President, John F. Kennedy. The governor of Massachusetts is elected for a four-year term. The legislature (the General Court) has a senate of 40 members and a house of representatives with 240 members, all of whom serve two-year terms. Massachusetts sends 12 Representatives and 2 Senators to the U.S. Congress, and has 14 electoral votes. In 1974, Michael S. Dukakis, a Democrat, was elected governor. As a recreation and vacation land, Massachusetts has great stretches of seashore in the east and many lakes and streams in the wooded Berkshire Hills in the west. There are numerous state parks, forests, and beaches, and Cape Cod is the site of a national seashore. Provincetown, on Cape Cod, and Rockport, on Cape Ann, are artist colonies; Marblehead is a noted yachting center. The state is also famed for its historic points of interest, among them being those at Sturbridge, Concord, and Lexington; at Minute Man Historical Park; and at six historic sites—Adams, Salem Maritime, Longfellow, John Fitzgerald Kennedy, Saugus Iron Works, and Dorchester Heights (see NATIONAL PARKS AND MONUMENTS, table). Cultural attractions include the noted Tanglewood music festival (see BERKSHIRE FESTIVAL) and the many educational facilities of the state. In the field of higher learning Massachusetts continues strong. Besides Harvard Univ. and the Massachusetts Institute of Technology, at Cambridge, educational institutions include Radcliffe College, also at Cambridge; Amherst College and the Univ. of Massachusetts, at Amherst; Boston College, at Chestnut Hill; Boston Univ., Simmons College, and Northeastern Univ., at Boston; Brandeis Univ., at Waltham; Clark Univ., College of the Holy Cross, and Worcester Polytechnic Institute, at Worcester; Lowell Technological Institute, at Lowell; Mount Holyoke College, at South Hadley; Smith College, at Northampton; Tufts Univ., at Medford; Wellesley College, at Wellesley; Wheaton College, at Norton; Williams College, at Williamstown; and several state teachers colleges. The state is also renowned for its excellent private secondary schools, such as Phillips Academy. See J. T. Adams, *The Founding of New England* (new ed. 1962), *Revolutionary New England* (1923), and *New England in the Republic* (1926); A. B. Hart, ed., *Commonwealth History of Massachusetts* (5 vol., 1927–30, repr. 1966); Van Wyck Brooks, *The Flowering of New England* (1936) and *New England: Indian Summer* (1940); Federal Writers' Project, *Massachusetts: a Guide to Its Places and People* (1937); Perry Miller, *The New England Mind: the Seventeenth Century* (1939) and *The New England Mind from Colony to Province* (1953); Edmund S. Morgan, *The Puritan Dilemma: the Story of John Winthrop* (1958); H. F. Howe, *Massachusetts: There She Is, Behold Her* (1960); S. E. Morison, *Builders of Bay Colony* (1930) and *Maritime History of Massachusetts, 1783–1860* (new ed. 1961); Chadwick Hansen, *Witchcraft at Salem* (1969); Michael Zuckerman, *Peaceable Kingdoms: New England Towns in the Eighteenth Century* (1970).

Massachusetts, University of, at Amherst; land-grant and state supported; coeducational; chartered 1863, opened 1867 as Massachusetts Agricultural College. It was called Massachusetts State College from 1931 to 1947. Agricultural facilities include an experiment station and a statewide extension service. The university's library houses a noted collection of rare books and periodicals relating to agriculture.

Massachusetts Bay, inlet of the Atlantic Ocean. The bay, with its arms (Boston, Cape Cod, and Plymouth bays), extends 65 mi (105 km) from Cape Ann on the north to Cape Cod on the south. Its coastline varies from the irregular, rocky shore of the north to the sandy beaches of the south. In the War of 1812, the battle between the *Chesapeake* and the *Shannon* took place there off Boston Harbor.

Massachusetts Bay Company, English chartered company that established the Massachusetts Bay colony in New England. Organized (1628) as the New England Company, it took over the Dorchester Company, which had established a short-lived fishing colony on Cape Ann in 1623. The group obtained (1628) from the Council for New England a grant of land between the Charles and Merrimack rivers, extending westward to "the South Sea." One of the men who negotiated for this patent, John ENDECOTT, became leader of the colony at Naumkeag (later Salem), founded (1626) by Roger CONANT and others from the Cape Ann settlement. In 1629 the New England Company obtained a royal charter as the "Governor and Company of the Massachusetts Bay in New England." Almost immediately the emphasis changed from trade to religion, as the Puritan stockholders conceived of the colony as a religious and political refuge for their sect. A group led by John WINTHROP (1588-1649) signed the so-called Cambridge Agreement (1629), by which they engaged to emigrate to New England provided that they could buy out the stock of the company and thus gain complete control of the company's government and charter. Since the royal charter did not specify where the stockholders should meet, this arrangement was made, and the Massachusetts Bay Company became the only one of the English chartered colonization companies not subject to the control of a board of governors in England. The colonists sailed for New England in 1630. They reached Salem, soon moved to Charlestown, but decided to make their chief settlement at the mouth of the Charles River, a commanding position on Massachusetts Bay. There Boston was established. Attempts were made by the Council for New England, under the leadership of Sir Ferdinando GORGES, to annul the colony's land claims, but the efforts were unsuccessful. The company and the colony were synonymous until 1684, when the charter was withdrawn, and the company ceased to exist. In 1691 a new charter made Massachusetts a royal colony and extended its jurisdiction over Plymouth and Maine. See N. B. Shurtleff, ed., *Records of the Governor and Company of the Massachusetts Bay in New England* (5 vol., 1853–54, repr. 1968), G. L. Beer, *The Origins of the British Colonial System, 1578–1660* (1908, repr. 1959); J. T. Adams, *The Founding of New England* (1921, repr. 1963), C. M. Andrews, *The Colonial Period of American History,* Vol. I (1934, repr. 1964); Thomas Hutchinson, *The History of the Colony and Province of Massachusetts Bay* (ed. by L. S. Mayo, 3 vol., 1936, repr. 1970); T. J. Wertenbaker, *The Puritan Oligarchy* (1947, repr. 1970); R. E. Wall, *Massachusetts Bay: The Crucial Decade, 1640–1650* (1972).

Massachusetts Institute of Technology, at Cambridge; coeducational; chartered 1861, opened 1865 in Boston, moved 1916. It has long been recognized as an outstanding technical college. Among its facilities are five high-energy accelerators, a large nuclear reactor, and a noted nuclear engineering laboratory. The institute also operates a research center (Round Hill) near South Dartmouth, Mass., the Lincoln Laboratory at Lexington, Mass., and an engineering practice school at Oak Ridge, Tenn. Significant among its more than 70 special laboratories are an instrumentation laboratory, a computation center, and a spectroscopy laboratory. The institute also has cooperative arrangements with the Woods Hole Oceanographic Institution as well as the Brookhaven National Laboratory. Primarily a technological institute, it maintains a center for international studies and, with Harvard, a center for urban studies. The institute's Boston Stein Club Map Room in the Hayden Library and Hart Nautical Museum are noteworthy. See S. C. Prescott, *When M.I.T. Was Boston Tech, 1861–1916* (1954).

Massachusetts State Teachers College: see FRAMINGHAM STATE COLLEGE.

massage (məsäzh'), treatment of superficial parts of the body by systematic rubbing, stroking, kneading, or slapping. Massages can be administered manually or with mechanical devices. They are sought most often to relieve muscle stiffness, spasms, or cramps and to relieve anxiety and tension. Gentle massage has a soothing action on the sensory nerves. More vigorous massage quickens the circulation and aids the muscles in disposing of accumulated waste products. Some methods of massage cause the muscles to contract and thus exercise them when movement of the entire body is not possible or desirable, as in illness or paralysis. However, there is no evidence that massage can reduce or alter fat or adipose tissue. Men and women who are trained in the art of massage are known as masseurs and masseuses, respectively.

Massah (măs'ə) or **Meribah** (mĕr'ĭbə) or **Massah and Meribah,** symbolic name of place, near Horeb, where Moses brought forth water from the rock. Ex. 17.7. A similar event and an equally symbolic name concern the spring at Kadesh. Num. 20.13,24. Allusions to the event are found in Deut. 6.16; 9.22; 32.51; 33.8; Ps. 81.7.

Massamba-Debat, Alphonse (älfôNs' mäsĕm'bä-däbä'), 1921–, president (1963–68) of the Republic of the Congo (now People's Republic of the Congo.) He headed a provisional government that replaced Fulbert YOULOU and late in 1963 was elected to a five-year term under a new constitution. His anti-West, pro-Communist policies contributed to the domestic unrest that marked his regime; he was removed from office in 1968.

Massapequa (măsəpēk'wə), uninc. city (1970 pop. 26,951), Nassau co., SE N.Y., on the south shore of Long Island. It is chiefly residential.

Massapequa Park, residential village (1970 pop. 22,112), Nassau co., SE N.Y., on Long Island; inc. 1931. A state park is nearby.

Massasoit (măsəsoit'), c.1580–1661, chief of the Wampanoag Indians. He was also known as Ousamequin (spelled in various ways). One of the most powerful native rulers of New England, he went to Plymouth in 1621 and signed a treaty with the Pilgrims, which he faithfully observed until his death. He befriended Roger Williams and was a friend of Edward Winslow. In 1632 he fought his enemy, Canonicus, ruler of the Narragansett. Massasoit's son, Metacomet, became famous as King Philip (see KING PHILIP'S WAR). See biography by A. G. Weeks (1919).

Massawa (məsä'wə), city (1965 est. pop. 25,000), Eritrea prov., N Ethiopia, a port on the Red Sea. It is the main port for N Ethiopia and is linked by rail with Asmara. Major industries include meat processing and the production of cement and salt. Fishing is also important to the city's economy. Long a commercial port, Massawa was part of the kingdom of Aksum (c.1st–8th cent. A.D.). In 1577 it was captured by the Ottoman Turks, who in 1868 transferred it to Egyptian control. In 1885, Massawa was taken by Italy, and from 1889 to 1900 it was the capital of the Italian colony of Eritrea. It is the main base of the Ethiopian navy and has a naval training school. The city is also known as Massaua and Mitsiwa.

Masséna, André (äNdrä' mäsānä'), 1758–1817, marshal of France, b. Nice. Of humble origin, he entered (1791) the French army and rose rapidly because of his brilliant tactical abilities. He served under Napoleon Bonaparte in the Italian campaign, won the battle of Rivoli (1797), where he earned a reputation for rapaciousness, and distinguished himself in Napoleon's campaigns of 1800 and 1809 against Austria. In 1799, Masséna's victory over the Russians at Zürich saved France from invasion by the Second Coalition (see FRENCH REVOLUTIONARY WARS). Masséna's subsequent failure in the PENINSULAR WAR is often attributed to the lack of cooperation of the other French commanders. Masséna's relations with Napoleon were somewhat strained because of Masséna's republican convictions, but he lacked political ambition, and Napoleon honored his military achievements by making him duke of Rivoli (1808) and prince of Essling (1810). After Napoleon's fall in 1814, Masséna supported Louis XVIII, who raised him to the peerage (1815). His neutral attitude during the Hundred Days was attacked by the royalists after the Restoration. See his *Mémoires* (7 vol., 1848–50, repr. 1966–67); biography by J. H. Marshall-Cornwall (1965).

Massena (məsē'nə), village (1970 pop. 14,042), St. Lawrence co., extreme N N.Y., on the St. Lawrence River; settled 1792, inc. 1886. Aluminum and aluminum products are the chief manufactures. Two locks and two dams of the St. Lawrence Seaway are nearby. Massena is the center of a vast summer resort area and has a state park. An international bridge connects the village with Cornwall, Ontario.

Massenet, Jules (zhül mäsənā'), 1842-1912, French composer. He studied at the Paris Conservatory, where he taught from 1878 to 1896. In addition to many songs, several oratorios, and a number of orchestral suites, he composed more than 20 operas. His most famous work is *Manon* (1884), which exemplifies his sensuous style and contains accompanied spoken dialogue instead of traditional recitative. His other operas are *Werther* (1892), *Thaïs* (1894), and *Le Jongleur de Notre Dame* (1902). See his memoirs (tr. 1919); study by James Harding (1970).

Massey, Vincent, 1887-1967, Canadian statesman, b. Toronto; brother of actor Raymond Massey. After a brief career as a professor he served (1918-19) as a government official before joining his family's farm machinery company, of which he was (1921-25) president. A Liberal party supporter, he served as Canada's first minister to the United States (1926-30) and as high commissioner in England (1936-46). He was (1947-52) chancellor of the Univ. of Toronto and then served (1952-59) as governor-general of Canada; he was the first native-born Canadian to hold the post. See his memoirs (1963).

massicot: see LITHARGE.

Massif Central (mäsēf' säNträl') [Fr.,=central highlands], great mountainous plateau, c.33,000 sq mi (85,470 sq km), S central France, covering almost a sixth of the surface of the country. The chief water divide of France, it borders on the Paris basin in the north, the Rhône valley and basin in the east and south, and the Aquitanian basin in the west. The core of the Massif is the volcanic mass of the Auvergne mts. that rises to the Massif's highest point, Puy de Sancy (6,187 ft/1,886 m). The Cévennes limit the Massif Central on the southeast and the Causses form its southwest border. The Massif Central is the most rugged and geologically diverse region within France. It is also France's most varied region climatically. All four chief rivers of France (the Seine, Loire, Rhône, and Garonne) receive tributaries from the Massif Central; the Loire, Dordogne, and Charente originate there. Sheep and goat grazing, dairying, cattle raising, and, in the fertile valleys, agriculture are the chief occupations of the region. Coal and kaolin are mined extensively. Hydroelectricity is produced along the western edge of the Massif Central. Clermont-Ferrand, Le Creusot, Limoges, Saint-Étienne, and Roanne are important industrial centers.

Massillon, Jean Baptiste (zhäN bätēst' mäsēyôN'), 1663-1742, French clergyman, bishop of Clermont from 1717. He was celebrated for his preaching, especially at the courts of Louis XIV and Louis XV. Collections of sermons include a series for Advent and a series for Lent.

Massillon (măs'ĭlŏn), city (1970 pop. 32,539), Stark co., NE Ohio, on the Tuscarawas River; inc. 1853. It is an industrial city; among its manufactures are surgical gloves, food products, aluminum cans, and plastics. Jacob S. Coxey, the social reformer, lived in Massillon and was mayor of the city in the early 1930s. A state mental hospital is there and a state park is nearby.

Massine, Léonide (lāônēd' mäsēn'), 1896-, American choreographer and ballet dancer, b. Russia. Massine attended the Imperial Ballet School, St. Petersburg, and became principal dancer and choreographer for Diaghilev's Ballet Russe (1914-20) and for the Ballet Russe de Monte Carlo (1932-42). He was noted especially as a character dancer. Massine's choreographical works include *Parade* (1917), *La Boutique fantasque* (1919), *The Three-cornered Hat* (1919), *Gaité parisienne* (1938), *Commedia umana* (1960), and the films *The Red Shoes* (1948) and *Tales of Hoffman* (1951). He worked in the 1940s in the United States with the Ballet Theatre.

Massinger, Philip, 1583-1640, English dramatist, b. Salisbury. He studied at Oxford (1602-6) but left without a degree, apparently to go to London to write plays. Massinger wrote more than 40 plays (often in collaboration), but many of them are now lost. He is best known for his realistic comedies of domestic life—*A New Way to Pay Old Debts* (1625) and *The City Madam* (1632). His other extant works, most of which were produced between 1620 and 1630, include the romantic dramas *The Duke of Milan* and *The Great Duke of Florence* and the tragicomedies *The Fatal Dowry* (with Nathaniel Field), *The Virgin Martyr* (with Thomas Dekker), and *The Bondman*. A sober, meticulous writer, Massinger was a harsh moralist and frequently employed HUMOR characters to illustrate the evils of a frivolous and avaricious society. See studies by A. H. Cruickshank (1920, repr. 1971) and T. A. Dunn (1957).

Massinissa: see MASINISSA.

Massive, Mount, peak, 14,421 ft (4,396 m) high, W central Colo., in the Sawatch Mts.; second-highest peak in the U.S. Rocky Mts.

mass-luminosity relation, in astronomy, law stating that the LUMINOSITY of a star is proportional to some power of the mass of the star. More massive stars are in general more luminous. For stars on the main sequence of the HERTZSPRUNG-RUSSELL DIAGRAM, it is found empirically that the luminosity varies as the 3.5 power of the mass. This means that if the mass is doubled, the luminosity increases more than tenfold. The law can be derived theoretically and was confirmed by independently measuring the masses of many visual binary stars, all at approximately the same distance. A more exact formulation of the law takes into account the chemical composition of the star. One important use of the mass-luminosity relation is in estimating the mass of a star of known luminosity that is not in a binary system.

mass number, often represented by the symbol *A*, the total number of nucleons (neutrons and protons) in the nucleus of an ATOM. All atoms of a chemical ELEMENT have the same atomic number (number of protons in the nucleus) but may have different mass numbers (from having different numbers of neutrons in the nucleus). Atoms of an element with the same mass number make up an ISOTOPE of the element. Different isotopes of the same element cannot have the same mass number, but isotopes of different elements often do have the same mass number, e.g., carbon-14 (6 protons and 8 neutrons) and nitrogen-14 (7 protons and 7 neutrons).

Masson, André (äNdrā' mäsôN'), 1896-, French painter and graphic artist. An exponent of SURREALISM until 1928, Masson developed "automatic writing"—spontaneous linear expressions of his personal mythology. After World War II he painted superb landscapes in Aix-en-Provence. His *Meditation on an Oak Leaf* and other works are in the Museum of Modern Art, New York City.

Masson, Frédéric, 1847-1923, French historian, an authority on Napoleon I and his family. His work is uncritically laudatory with regard to Napoleon himself; his admiration, however, did not deter his severe indictment of Napoleon's relatives in *Napoléon et sa famille* (13 vol., 1897-1919). Among his books translated into English are *Napoleon at Home* (1894), *Napoleon, Lover and Husband* (1894), and *Napoleon and His Coronation* (1911). Other writings include, in collaboration with Guido Biagi, *Napoléon inconnu* (1895), containing unpublished manuscripts of Napoleon and valuable notes on his early life.

Massorah: see MASORA.

mass production: see PRODUCTION.

mass spectrograph, device used to separate electrically charged particles according to their masses; a form of the instrument known as a mass spectrometer is often used to measure the masses of ISOTOPES of elements. J. J. Thomson and F. W. Aston showed (c.1900) that magnetic and electric fields can be used to deflect streams of charged particles traveling in a vacuum, and that the degree of bending depends on the masses and electric charges of the particles. In the mass spectrograph the particles, in the form of ions, pass through deflecting fields (produced by carefully designed magnetic pole pieces and electrodes) and are detected by photographic plates. The beam of ions first passes through a velocity selector, consisting of a combination of electric and magnetic fields that eliminates all particles except those of a given velocity. The remaining ion beam then enters an evacuated chamber where a magnetic field bends it into a semicircular path ending at the photographic plate. The radius of this path depends upon the mass of the particles (all other factors, such as velocity, being equal). Thus, if in the original stream isotopes of various masses are present, the position of the blackened spots on the plate makes possible a calculation of the isotope masses. The mass spectrograph is widely used in chemical analysis and in the detection of impurities.

mass transit, passenger transportation system in which large numbers of individuals share the same vehicle. Railroads, bus systems, airlines, shipping lines, and ferries are commonly considered to be mass transit systems. Moving sidewalks and building elevators may also be included. Mass transit systems offer considerable savings in manpower, materials, and energy over private transit systems. Since far fewer operators are required per passenger transported, they can be better trained and more strictly licensed and supervised. When utilized to any reasonable fraction of their capacity, mass transit vehicles carry a far higher passenger load per unit of weight and volume than do private vehicles. They thus require less raw materials to build than an equivalent number of private vehicles. They also offer fuel savings, not only because of the relative reduction in weight transported, but also because they are large enough to carry more efficient engines. Furthermore, if emphasis is given to mass transit in the planning of future ground transportation systems, smaller rights of way will be possible, lessening the amount of landscape that must be paved over for highways and roads. Although mass transit offers many savings, it does require some sacrifices in personal convenience. These are the necessity to travel on a fixed rather than an individually selected schedule and to enter and disembark from the system only at certain designated locations. The successful operation of a mass transit system depends upon careful studies of traffic flows throughout the region that the system is intended to serve. Such studies should be used early in the planning stage to ensure an optimal choice of route and of the location of stations along the route, and later, especially in large systems, as a basis for determining which stations will have express service and which stations only local service. These studies, as well as subsequent monitoring of the system's operation, provide a basis for the scheduling of services. The obvious goal for a mass transit operation is to have as few unused passenger accommodations as possible. In most mass transit systems presently operational, this goal has not been achieved sufficiently well to allow of their survival independent of public subsidy. See BUS; RAPID TRANSIT; STREETCAR; AIR POLLUTION.

Massys, Matsys, Messys, or **Metsys, Quentin** (kvĕn'tĭn măsĭs', mätsĭs', mĕ-, mĕt-), c.1466-1530, Flemish painter. After studying in Louvain, he moved to Antwerp by 1491, remaining in that city throughout his life. Influences of Italian art, especially of Leonardo da Vinci, may be seen in his work, particularly in the delicate modeling, the subtle nuances of tone, and in the adoption of Leonardo's grotesque head studies for such pictures as *The Old Man* (Jacquemart-André Mus., Paris) and *Ugly Duchess* (National Gall., London). Massys sought inspiration also in works of earlier Flemish artists, especially of Jan van Eyck. The combined Flemish and Italian influences aided Massys in evolving a calm and measured style, with solid figures and soft textures. He developed a type of portraiture, in which the sitter was placed against an appropriate background, as in his painting of St. Erasmus surrounded by books and papers (National Gall., Rome). There are religious subjects and portraits by Massys in the museums of Munich, Brussels, Antwerp, Chicago, and Philadelphia. Quentin's son, **Jan Massys,** c.1509-1575, painted satirical and later more elegant works under French influence. *Judith* (Mus. of Fine Arts, Boston) is characteristic. Another son, **Cornelis Massys,** d. after 1560, was a landscape painter and engraver. His *Arrival in Bethlehem* is in the Metropolitan Museum. See Max J. Friedländer, *From Van Eyck to Bruegel* (2 vol., 3rd ed. 1969).

mast, large metal or timber pole secured vertically or nearly vertically in a ship, used primarily for supporting sails and rigging. The mast is as old as sailing vessels, and the oldest sailboats depicted (those of ancient Egypt) had a small mast placed forward and carrying a single sail. The Phoenician bireme had one mast, the Greek trireme had two. Viking ships had one central mast. In the Middle Ages, a topmast was added, fixed to the single mast, to carry more sail; after the 16th cent., topmasts were generally demountable. By that time the building of larger vessels and the desire for greater speed on longer journeys had already brought increase in sails and in the masts—a process that continued until the clipper ships of the middle of the 19th cent. were rushed forward by clouds of sails. Above the topmast was added the topgallant mast and above that the topgallant mast royal. In vessels having more than one mast, a small forward mast is called the foremast and a small mast abaft the mainmast is called the mizzenmast. A platform for lookout on a mast is called a crow's nest. The modern merchant ship often has a mast made of hollow steel tubes which is used mainly for signaling and for supporting radio antennas and lifts or derricks for cargo. In some modern warships the mast has a steel platform on which are mounted instruments for controlling gunfire.

mastaba (măs'təbə), in Egyptian architecture, a sepulchral structure built aboveground. The mastabas of the early dynastic period (3200-2680 B.C.), such as those of the I dynasty at Sakkara, were elaborate, having many storage or offering compartments, and were quite evidently close copies of contemporary houses. Better known are the mastabas of the Old Kingdom (2680-2181 B.C.), which were an elaboration of the predynastic burial-pit and mound form. The typical mastaba was generally rectangular in plan with a flat roof and inward-sloping walls, built of brick and faced with limestone slabs. The sarcophagus was placed in a small chamber at the bottom of a deep shaft below the structure and sealed off. The superstructure was filled in solidly except for the offering chamber—a decorated chapel where offerings were placed for the spirit of the deceased—and the serdab—a small chamber containing a portrait statue of the deceased. The offering chamber opened to a street or courtyard, but the serdab connected with the chapel by a false door. The decorated offering chambers became increasingly elaborate until by the end of the VI dynasty the inside of the superstructure was filled with a complex arrangement of chambers and halls.

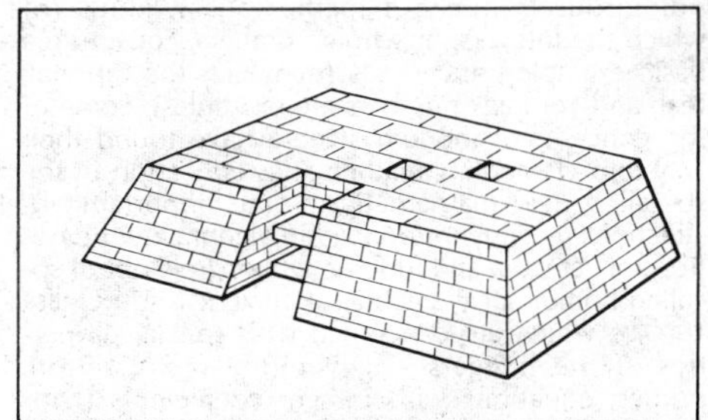

Mastaba

mastectomy (măstĕk'təmē), surgical removal of all or part of the breast. In a simple mastectomy for nonmalignant growths, only breast tissue is removed. When cancer is present, a radical mastectomy may be performed: The breast, underlying chest muscles, and lymph nodes of the adjacent armpit are excised. Early detection and surgery increase the chances for arresting breast cancer, but there is some controversy as to the efficacy of radical mastectomy.

Master Honoré (ōnôrā'), French manuscript illuminator, active c. 1288-1318. Honoré worked in Paris for the court of Philip the Fair (1285-1314). A breviary (Bibliothèque nationale) made in 1296 for the king is typical of his work: the lively figures are drawn with a remarkable sense of volume, achieved by a delicate modeling of the garments that fall in weighty, elegantly curved folds. An influential element of Honoré's style are the long ivy tendrils terminating in pointed leaves that frame entire pages. Imitated throughout Europe, Honoré's works influenced stained-glass-window design, particularly the modeling of figures, as well as painting. See study by E. G. Millar (1959).

Master of the Housebook (Meister des Hausbuchs), fl. 1475-1500, German graphic artist. The master is named for a series of vigorous and sophisticated drawings of everyday life found in the *Hausbuch* at Castle Wolfegg. Many of his engravings are in the Rijksmuseum, Amsterdam. His work is thought to have influenced Bosch, Bruegel, and Dürer.

Masters, Edgar Lee, 1869-1950, American poet and biographer, b. Garnett, Kansas. He maintained a successful law practice in Chicago from 1892 to 1920. Masters' *Spoon River Anthology* (1915), a collection of epitaphs in free verse revealing the secret lives of dead citizens, was acclaimed for its treatment of small-town American life. Less successful volumes that followed include *Starved Rock* (1919), *Domesday Book* (1920), *Poems of People* (1936), and *Illinois Poems* (1941). His *Lincoln the Man* (1931) is a bitter and prejudiced attack. Other biographies are *Vachel Lindsay* (1935), *Whitman* (1937), and *Mark Twain* (1938). See his autobiography *Across Spoon River* (1936).

mastic, RESIN obtained from the small mastic tree *Pistacia lentiscus* (of the SUMAC family), found chiefly in Mediterranean countries. When the bark of the tree is injured, the resin exudes in drops. It is transparent and pale yellow to green in color. Mastic is used chiefly in making varnish but is also used medicinally as an astringent and, with aniseed, to flavor a distilled liquor called mastic. The term *mastic* is also applied to certain caulking and adhesive compounds, especially those consisting of a mineral filler, a resinous binder (e.g., ASPHALT), and a volatile solvent.

mastiff (măs'tĭf), breed of very large, powerful WORKING DOG developed in England more than 2,000 years ago. It stands from 27 to 33 in. (68.6-83.8 cm) high at the shoulder and weighs from 165 to 185 lb (74.9-83.9 kg). Its coarse, short, close-lying coat may be silver fawn, apricot, or dark fawn brindle in color, with a black muzzle, nose, and ears and black around the eyes. The mastiff was first bred as a fighting dog and guardian. As a fighter it was cited for its physical prowess and courage by Caesar in his account of the Roman invasion of Britain in 55 B.C. Indeed, it was later imported to Rome to fight in the arena. In its native country the mastiff was a popular antagonist in bullbaiting and bearbaiting contests and in organized dogfights until these blood sports were outlawed in 1835. However, throughout the entire history of the breed in England its greatest popularity has derived from its widespread use as a guardian of home and family. This centuries-old association with man is undoubtedly responsible for the mastiff's unexcelled suitability for the role of family companion and its particular devotion to and gentleness with children. The term *mastiff* is also applied to a general type of giant dog whose origin has been traced to Asia and of which the modern Tibetan mastiff, infrequently seen in the United States, is representative. See DOG.

mastitis (măstī'tĭs), inflammation of the breast. Mastitis most commonly occurs in nursing mothers between the first and third weeks after childbirth, usually of the first child. It is an infection that results when bacteria enter through cracked nipples; the organisms may already be in the body and attack breast tissue weakened by injury. The breast becomes swollen and painful and a high fever may be present. Mastitis is usually easily treated with ANTIBIOTICS. In severe cases, when an ABSCESS forms within the breast, the suckling baby must be weaned completely. Chronic cystic mastitis is a common, noninfectious but often painful condition in women between 30 and 50 years old, in which cystic nodules develop in the breasts, giving them a lumpy appearance. It sometimes results from a hormonal imbalance. Biopsy may be necessary to distinguish the condition from breast cancer. Another type of mastitis may occur during puberty, and another is associated with other infectious diseases, e.g., mumps and tuberculosis.

mastodon, name for a number of prehistoric mammals of the extinct genus *Mammut,* from which modern elephants are believed to have developed. The earliest known forms lived in the Oligocene epoch in Africa. These were long-jawed mastodons about 4½ ft (137 cm) high, with four tusks and a greatly elongated face. Their descendants in the Miocene epoch were the size of large elephants, the latest forms having long, flexible trunks, like those of elephants, and only two tusks. During Miocene times they spread over Europe, Asia, and North America. The mastodons were forest dwellers; they obtained their food by browsing and their teeth were more numerous and of a simpler form than those of the elephant. They were apparently extinct in the Old World by the early Pleistocene epoch but survived in North America until late Pleistocene times. They are classified in the phylum CHORDATA, subphylum Vertebrata, class Mammalia, order Proboscidae, family Mammutidae.

Mastroianni, Marcello (märchĕl'lō mästrōyän'nē), 1923–, Italian movie actor, b. Fontana Liri, Italy. He became internationally famous for his role as the world-weary hero of *La Dolce Vita* (1959). His many other films include *La Notte* (1961), *Divorce Italian Style* (1962), *8½ (1963), Yesterday, Today and Tomorrow* (1964), *The Organizer* (1965), *The Stranger* (1967), and *Melampo* (1972).

Masuda (mäsōō'dä), city (1970 pop. 50,071), Shimane prefecture, SW Honshu, Japan, on the Sea of Japan at the mouth of the Takutsu River. It is an agricultural and communications center.

Masudi (mäsōō'dē), d. 956, Arab historian, geographer, and philosopher, b. Baghdad. He traveled in Spain, Russia, India, Ceylon, and China and spent his last years in Syria and Egypt. His *Muruj adh-Dhahab* [meadows of gold], an epitome of a longer history of the world from creation to A.D. 947, is a compilation of his observations and studies in all these lands and embraces social and literary history and discussions of religions, as well as geographic descriptions. A French version of this work was published between 1861 and 1878. The first volume has been translated into English. See R. A. Nicholson, *A Literary History of the Arabs* (2d ed. 1930).

Masulipatam (məsōō''ləpŭ'təm) or **Bandar** (bŭn'dər), town (1971 pop. 112,636), Andhra Pradesh state, E central India, a port on the Bay of Bengal. In the 17th cent. it was a center of French, British, and Dutch trade. It has a cotton industry; other products include chemicals and scientific instruments. The town is a district administrative headquarters and educational center.

Masuria (məzōō'rēə), Ger. *Masurenland,* Pol. *Mazury,* region, N Poland. It is a low-lying area covered by large lakes and forests and drained by many small rivers. The original population of the region was expelled by the Teutonic Knights and replaced (14th cent). with Polish settlers. Masuria later became part of East Prussia and was largely Germanized by the early 20th cent. After Masuria passed to Poland in 1945, most of the German-speaking population was expelled and replaced by Poles. The **Masurian Lakes** region, where more than 2,700 lakes are located, was the scene of heavy fighting early in World War I. Two Russian armies, commanded by generals Samsonov and Rennenkampf, were defeated in the region—Samsonov by Hindenburg at Tannenburg (Aug., 1914) and Rennenkampf by Mackensen in the lake country (Sept., 1914). The Russians were also repulsed (Feb., 1915) in Masuria in the so-called Winter Battle.

masurium: see TECHNETIUM.

Matabei, Iwasa (ēwä'sä mätäbā'), 1578-1650, Japanese genre and portrait painter. His works had a strong influence on later genre painters. He is often confused with a legendary painter, Otsu no Matabei, and falsely claimed as the founder of the ukiyo-e school of painting.

Matabele (mătəbē'lē) or **Ndebele** (ĕndəbē'lē), Bantu-speaking people inhabiting Matabeleland, W Rhodesia. The Matabele, now numbering about 300,000, originated as a tribal following in 1823, when Mzilikazi, a general under the Zulu king Chaka, fled with a number of warriors across the Drakensberg into present-day Transvaal. Reinforced by other Zulu deserters, the Matabele raided as far south as the Orange River, destroying or absorbing the surrounding tribes except for the Bamangwato of Bechuanaland, who paid tribute. Driven north (1837) by the Boers and by the Zulus, Mzilikazi crossed the Limpopo River and established his people in Matabeleland, their present homeland. From his successor, Lobengula (1870-94), the British South Africa Company secured (1888) the mineral concession for all of Matabeleland. Restive under the restrictions placed on them by European settlers, the Matabele attacked the settlers. Lobengula was soon defeated by the British and died in hiding. With the suppression of a revolt in 1896 the Matabele abandoned war and became herdsmen and farmers. See David Carnegie, *Among the Matabele* (1894, repr. 1970); J. M. Selby, *Shaka's Heirs* (1971).

Matadi (mətä'dē), city (1970 pop. 110,000), Bas-Zaïre region, W Zaïre, on the Congo River. Matadi is the main port of the country. Situated c.80 mi (130 km) from the mouth of the Congo, at the farthest point navigable by oceangoing vessels, the city is linked by rail with Kinshasa. Chief exports are palm products, coffee, cotton, rubber, and bananas.

Matagorda Bay (mătəgôr'də), inlet of the Gulf of Mexico, c.50 mi (80 km) long and from 3 to 12 mi (4.8-19 km) wide, SE Texas, protected by a long sandspit, Matagorda Peninsula. It receives the Colorado River and is crossed by the Intracoastal Waterway. The bay, with its arm, Lavaca Bay, was probably visited (1685) by the French explorer Robert La Salle on his last expedition. Matagorda Island is a sandbar farther south at the entrance of San Antonio Bay. On the shore of Matagorda Bay is the site of the former town of **Matagorda,** which was settled in 1825 and served as a port for Stephen F. Austin's colony. Today Matagorda is known principally for fishing and oyster gathering. The area is often struck by hurricanes.

Mata Hari (mä'tə hä'rē), 1876-1917, Dutch dancer and spy in German service during World War I. Her real name was Margaretha Geertruida Zelle. A dancer in Paris, she joined the German secret service in 1907, and during the war she betrayed important military secrets confided to her by the many high Allied officers who were on intimate terms with her. In 1917 she was arrested, convicted, and executed by the French. See biography by Sam Waagenaar (1965).

matamata: see SIDE-NECKED TURTLE.

Matamoros, Mariano (märyä'nō mätämō'rōs), d. 1814, Mexican revolutionist in the war against Spain. He was, like Miguel Hidalgo y Costilla and José María Morelos y Pavón, a priest with liberal political opinions. Much harassed by the Spanish authorities after the outbreak of the revolution of 1810, he joined Morelos (1811) and became a prominent military leader. After the defeat of Morelos's army by Agustín de Iturbide, Matamoros was captured, degraded from priestly office, and shot.

Matamoros, city (1970 pop. 182,881), Tamaulipas state, NE Mexico, near the mouth of the Rio Grande, opposite Brownsville, Texas. Matamoros, linked by rail and highway with the United States, is an international trading center and a point of entry. Fishing is an important industry, and maize, cotton, and cattle are raised in the surrounding area. Founded in 1700 as San Juan de los Esteros, the city was renamed in 1851 in honor of the leader for Mexican independence Mariano Matamoros. Noted for its heroic defense against numerous U.S. adventurers during the 19th cent., the city fell to the forces of Zachary Taylor in the Mexican War in 1846.

Matane (mətăn'), town (1971 pop. 11,841), SE Que., Canada, on the St. Lawrence River at the mouth of the Matane River at the beginning of the Gaspé Peninsula. Matane is a fishing, lumbering, and pulpwood-shipping center, and a summer resort.

Matanzas (mätän'säs), province (1970 pop. 501,273), W central Cuba. MATANZAS is the capital. The northern coast is lined with ports and bays and contains one of the world's finest beaches, at Varadero ("Playa Azul"). The northern half of the province is mountainous; in the south and west are plains. The Yomuri and the San Juan are the chief rivers of Matanzas. Sugarcane and henequen are the major crops; subsistence agriculture is also practiced, and there is some cattle raising. Despite its many mineral springs, Matanzas lacks mineral resources.

Matanzas, city (1970 pop. 85,376), capital of Matanzas prov., W central Cuba. A port with a large, deep harbor, it exports sugar, fruits, and sisal. Industries in the city include sugar refineries and textile mills. Matanzas is located on the turnpike between Havana and Varadero Beach, and is a popular stopover for vacationers, who explore the picturesque Yumurí River valley and the caves of Bellamar, famous for their calcite crystal formations. Founded in 1693, it was once a pirate haven but by the early 19th cent. had become Cuba's second city, mainly because of the growth of the sugar industry. As the industry moved eastward, the city's importance declined. Matanzas remains an important cultural center.

Matapan, Cape (măt'əpăn") or **Cape Taínaron** (tâ'närôn), S Greece, southern extremity of the Greek mainland, of the Peloponnesus, and of the Taygetus mts., projecting into the Ionian Sea. It was known to the ancients as Taenarum. In World War II the British won an important naval battle (1941) over the Italians off Cape Matapan.

Matapedia, Lake (mătəpē'dēə), 14 mi (23 km) long and 2 mi (3.2 km) wide, E Que., Canada, at the base of the Gaspé Peninsula and S of Matane. It is drained southward by the Matapedia River, famous for salmon fishing. The lake is a well-known tourist center.

Mataró (mätärō'), city (1970 pop. 73,129), Barcelona prov., NE Spain, in Catalonia. It is a Mediterranean port and a manufacturing center, especially of knitted goods. The first railroad in Spain was built (1848) from Barcelona to Mataró. The city's baroque church of Santa María is notable.

match, small stick whose chemically coated tip bursts into flame when struck on a rough surface. Before the introduction of the match, fire was made by friction methods using the stick and the groove, the fire drill, or flint, tinder, and steel, or by employing a magnifying glass. Attempts in the 18th cent. to cause ignition by the use of chemicals resulted in a friction match devised in 1827 by an Englishman, the apothecary John Walker, and in a phosphorus match invented in France in 1831 by the French student Charles Sauria. In the United States a practical phosphorus match was patented in 1836. The safe, cheap modern match was made possible by mechanized large-scale manufacture and by the use of nontoxic chemicals, notably the sesquisulfide of phosphorus. In the safety match, invented in Sweden in 1855, an oxidizing agent on the match tip is ignited only when struck on a combustible material affixed to the matchbox.

maté (mätā', mătā'), **yerba maté** (yĕr'bä, -bə), or **Paraguay tea,** evergreen tree of the family Aquifoliaceae (HOLLY family). From ancient times South American Indians have made a tea (also called maté) from the young leaves and tender shoots of *Ilex paraguensis,* the source of the best brew, and from closely related species. Maté is the most popular beverage in much of South America, and its culture is an important industry in Brazil and Paraguay. The tea is a stimulant and restorative, less astringent than genuine tea, and contains considerable caffeine. The word *maté* refers also to the cups in which the tea is infused, which are made from curiously shaped gourds or calabashes, with small openings cut in the top and sometimes decorated with silver mountings. The dried leaves are put in a container and covered with boiling water, and the tea is drunk through a *bombilla,* a tube provided at the lower end with a strainer of fine basketwork, metal, or perforated wood. The word *maté* frequently appears as *mate.* Maté is classified in the division MAGNOLIOPHYTA, class Magnoliopsida, order Celastrales.

Matera (mätĕ'rä), city (1971 pop. 44,750), capital of Matera prov., in Basilicata, S Italy, in the Apennines. It is an agricultural and industrial center with woolen textile mills and food-processing factories. A Romanesque cathedral and a castle (both 13th cent.) are in the city.

materialism, in philosophy, a widely held system of thought that explains the nature of the world as entirely dependent on matter, the fundamental and final reality beyond which nothing need be sought. Certain periods in history, usually those associated with scientific advance, are marked by strong materialistic tendencies. The doctrine was formulated as early as the 4th cent. B.C. by DEMOCRITUS, in whose system of atomism all phenomena are explained by atoms and their motions in space. Other early Greek teaching, such as that of EPICURUS and STOICISM, also conceived of reality as material in its nature. The theory was later renewed in the 17th cent. by Pierre GASSENDI and by his associate, Thomas Hobbes, who believed that the sphere of consciousness essentially belongs to the corporeal world, or the senses. The investigations of John Locke were adapted to materialist positions by David Hartley and Joseph Priestley. They were a part of the materialist development of the 18th cent., strongly manifested in France, where the most extreme thought was that of Julien de LA METTRIE. The culminating expression of materialist thought in this period was the *Système de la nature* (1770), for which Baron d'HOLBACH is considered chiefly responsible. A reaction against materialism was felt in the later years of the 18th cent., but the middle of the 19th cent. brought a new movement, largely psychological in interpretation. Two of the modern developments of materialism are DIALECTICAL MATERIALISM and physicalism, a position formulated by some members of the Logical Positivist movement. Closely related to materialism in origin are naturalism and sensualism. See D. M. Armstrong, *Materialist Theory of the Mind* (1968).

materials, strength of: see STRENGTH OF MATERIALS.

materia medica: see PHARMACOLOGY.

Mater Matuta: see MATUTA.

mathematical logic: see SYMBOLIC LOGIC.

mathematics, deductive study of numbers, geometry, and various abstract constructs, or structures. The latter often arise from analytical models in the empirical sciences, but many emerge from purely mathematical considerations.

Branches. Mathematics is very broadly divided into foundations, algebra, analysis, geometry, and applied mathematics. The term *foundations* is used to refer to the formulation and analysis of the language, axioms, and logical methods on which all of mathematics rests (see LOGIC; SYMBOLIC LOGIC). The scope and complexity of modern mathematics requires a very fine analysis of the formal language in which meaningful mathematical statements may be formulated and perhaps be proved true or false. Most apparent mathematical contradictions have been shown to derive from an imprecise and inconsistent use of language. A basic task is to furnish a set of AXIOMS effectively free of contradictions and at the same time rich enough to constitute a deductive source for all of modern mathematics. The modern axiom schemes proposed for this purpose are all couched within the theory of SETS, originated by Georg Cantor, which now constitutes a universal mathematical language. Historically, ALGEBRA is the study of solutions of one or several algebraic equations, involving the POLYNOMIAL functions of one or several variables. The case where all the polynomials have degree one (systems of linear equations) leads to linear algebra. The case of a single equation, in which one studies the roots of one polynomial, leads to field theory and to the so-called Galois theory. The general case of several equations of high degree leads to algebraic geometry, so named because the sets of solutions of such systems are often studied by geometric methods. Modern algebraists have increasingly abstracted and axiomatized the structures and patterns of argument encountered not only in the theory of equations, but in mathematics generally. Examples of these structures include GROUPS (first witnessed in relation to symmetry properties of the roots of a polynomial and now ubiquitous throughout mathematics), RINGS (of which the integers, or whole numbers, constitute a basic example), and FIELDS (of which the rational, real, and complex numbers are examples). Some of the concepts of modern algebra have found their way into elementary mathematics education in the so-called new mathematics. Some important abstractions recently introduced in algebra are the notions of category and functor, which grew out of so-called homological algebra. ARITHMETIC and NUMBER THEORY, which are concerned with special properties of the integers—e.g., unique factorization, primes, equations with integer coefficients (Diophantine equations), and congruences—are also a part of algebra. Analytic number theory, however, also applies the nonalgebraic methods of analysis to such problems. The essential ingredient of ANALYSIS is the use of infinite processes, involving passage to a LIMIT. For example, the area of a circle may be computed as the limiting value of the areas of inscribed regular polygons as the number of sides of the polygons increases indefinitely. The basic branch of analysis is the CALCULUS. The general problem of measuring lengths, areas, volumes, and other quantities as limits by means of approximating polygonal figures leads to the integral calculus. The differential calculus arises similarly from the problem of finding the tangent line to a curve at a point. Other branches of analysis result from the application of the concepts and methods of the calculus to various mathematical entities. For example, VECTOR analysis is the calculus of functions whose variables are vectors. Here various types of derivatives and integrals may be introduced. They lead, among other things, to the theory of differential and integral equations, in which the unknowns are functions rather than numbers, as in algebraic equations. Differential equations are often the most natural way in which to express the laws governing the behavior of various physical systems. Calculus is one of the most powerful and supple tools of mathematics. Its applications both in pure mathematics and in virtually every scientific domain are manifold. Euclidean GEOMETRY is concerned with the axiomatic study of polygons, conic sections, spheres, polyhedra, and related geometric objects in two and three dimensions, in particular, with the relations of congruence and of similarity between such objects. The unsuccessful attempt to prove the "parallel postulate" from the other axioms of Euclid led, in the 19th cent., to the discovery of two different types of NON-EUCLIDEAN GEOMETRY. The 20th cent. has seen an enormous development of TOPOLOGY, which is the study of very general geometric objects, called topological spaces, with respect to relations that are much weaker than congruence and similarity. Other branches of geometry include algebraic geometry, which is now in a vigorous state of development, and DIFFERENTIAL GEOMETRY, in which the methods of analysis are brought to bear on geometric problems. *Applied mathematics* is a term loosely designating a wide range of studies with significant current use in the empirical sciences. It includes numerical methods and COMPUTER science, which seeks concrete solutions, sometimes approximate, to explicit mathematical problems (e.g., differential equations, large systems of linear equations). It also includes mathematical physics, which involves in some instances rather sophisticated branches of group theory. In addition, PROBABILITY theory and mathematical STATISTICS are often considered parts of applied mathematics. The strong distinction between pure and applied mathematics is of relatively recent origin.

History. The earliest records of mathematics show it arising in response to practical needs in agriculture, business, and industry. In Egypt and Mesopotamia, where evidence dates from the 2d and 3d millennia B.C., it was used for surveying and mensuration; estimates of the value of π are found in both locations. There is some evidence of similar developments in India and China during this same period, but few records have survived. This early mathematics is generally empirical, arrived at by trial and error as the best available means for obtaining results, with no proofs given. However, it is now known that the Babylonians were aware of the necessity of proofs prior to the Greeks, who had been presumed the originators of this important step. A profound change occurred in the nature and approach to mathematics with the contributions of the Greeks. The earlier (Hellenic) period is represented by THALES (6th cent. B.C.), PYTHAGORAS, PLATO, and ARISTOTLE, and the schools associated with them. The Pythagorean theorem, known earlier in Mesopotamia, was discovered by the Greeks during this period. During the Golden Age (5th cent. B.C.), Hippocrates of Chios made the beginnings of an axiomatic approach to geometry and ZENO OF ELEA proposed his famous paradoxes concerning the infinite and the infinitesimal, raising questions about the nature of and relationships among points, lines, and numbers. The discovery through geometry of irrational numbers, such as $\sqrt{2}$, also dates from this period. EUDOXUS OF CNIDOS (4th cent. B.C.) resolved certain of the problems by proposing alternative methods to those involving infinitesimals; he is known for his work on geometric proportions and for his exhaustion theory for determining areas and volumes. The later (Hellenistic) period of Greek science is associated with the school of Alexandria. The greatest work of Greek mathematics, EUCLID'S *Elements* (c.300 B.C.), appeared at the beginning of this period. Elementary geometry as taught in high school is still largely based on Euclid's presentation, which has served as a model for deductive systems in other parts of mathematics and in other sciences. In this method primitive terms, such as *point* and *line*, are first defined, then certain axioms and postulates relating to them and seeming to follow directly from them are stated without proof; a number of statements are then derived by deduction from the definitions, axioms, and postulates. Euclid also contributed to the development of arithmetic and presented a geometric theory of quadratic equations. In the 3d cent. B.C., ARCHIMEDES, in addition to his work in mechanics, made an estimate of π and used the exhaustion theory of Eudoxus to obtain results that foreshadowed those much later of the integral calculus, and APOLLONIUS OF PERGA named the conic sections and gave the first theory for them. A second Alexandrian school during the Roman period included contributions by Menelaus (A.D. c.100, spherical triangles), HERON OF ALEXANDRIA (geometry), PTOLEMY (150, astronomy, geometry, cartography), PAPPUS (3d cent., geometry), and DIOPHANTUS (3d cent., arithmetic). Following the decline of learning in the West, the development of mathematics continued in the East. In China, Tsu Ch'ung-Chih estimated π by inscribed and circumscribed polygons, as Archimedes had done, and in India the numerals now used throughout the civilized world were invented and contributions to geometry were made by ARYABHATA and BRAHMAGUPTA (5th and 6th cent. A.D.). The Arabs were responsible for preserving the work of the Greeks, which they translated, commented upon, and added to. In Baghdad, AL-KHOWARIZMI (9th cent.) wrote an important work on algebra and introduced the Hindu numerals for the first time to the West, and AL-BATTANI worked on trigonometry. In Egypt, IBN AL-HAYTHAM was concerned with the solids of revolution and geometrical optics. The Persian poet Omar Khayyam wrote on algebra. These works began to reach the West in the 12th and 13th cent. One of the first important European mathematicians was Leonardo da Pisa (Leonardo FIBONACCI), who wrote on arithmetic and algebra (*Liber abaci*, 1202) and on geometry (*Practica geometriae*, 1220). With the Renaissance came a great revival of interest in learning, and the invention of printing made many of the earlier books widely available. By the end of the 16th cent. advances had been made in algebra by Niccolò TARTAGLIA and Geronimo CARDANO, in trigonometry by François VIÈTE, and in such areas of applied mathematics as mapmaking by Mercator and others. The 17th cent., however, saw the greatest revolution in mathematics, as the scientific revolution spread to all fields. Decimal fractions were invented by Simon STEVIN, logarithms by John NAPIER and Henry BRIGGS, the beginnings of projective geometry were made by Gérard DESARGUES and Blaise PASCAL, number theory was greatly extended by Pierre de FERMAT, and the theory of probability was founded by Pascal, Fermat, and others. In the application of mathematics to mechanics and astronomy, GALILEO and Johannes KEPLER made fundamental contributions. The greatest mathematical advances of the century, however, were the invention of analytic geometry by René DESCARTES and that of the calculus by Isaac NEWTON and, independently, by G. W. LEIBNIZ. Descartes's invention (anticipated by Fermat, whose work was not published until later) made possible the expression of geometric problems in algebraic form and vice versa. It was indispensable in creating the calculus, which built upon and superseded earlier special methods for finding areas, volumes, and tangents to curves, developed by F. B. CAVALIERI, Fermat, and others. The calculus is probably the greatest tool ever invented for the mathematical formulation and solution of physical problems. The history of mathematics in the 18th cent. is dominated by the development of the methods of the calculus and their application to such problems, both terrestrial and celestial, with leading roles being played by the BERNOULLI family (especially Jakob, Johann, and Daniel), Leonhard EULER, Guillaume de L'Hopital, and J. L. LAGRANGE. Important advances in geometry began toward the end of the century with the work of Gaspard MONGE in descriptive geometry and in differential geometry and continued through his influence on others, e.g., his pupil J. V. PONCELET, who founded projective geometry (1822). The modern period of mathematics dates from the beginning of the 19th cent., and its dominant figure is C. F. GAUSS. In the area of geometry Gauss made fundamental contributions to differential geometry, did much to found what was first called analysis situs but is now called topology, and anticipated (although he did not publish his results) the great breakthrough of non-Euclidean geometry. This breakthrough was made by N. I. LOBATCHEVSKY (1826) and independently by János BOLYAI (1832), the son of a close friend of Gauss, who each proceeded by establishing the independence of Euclid's fifth (parallel) postulate and showing that a different, self-consistent geometry could be derived by substituting another postulate in its place. Still another non-Euclidean geometry was invented by G. F. B. RIEMANN (1854), whose work also laid the foundations for the modern tensor calculus description of space, so important in the general theory of relativity. In the area of arithmetic, number theory, and algebra, Gauss again led the way. He established the modern theory of numbers, gave the first clear exposition of complex numbers, and investigated the functions of complex variables. The concept of number was further extended by W. R. HAMILTON, whose theory of quaternions (1843) provided the first example of a noncommutative algebra (i.e., one in which $ab \neq ba$). This work was generalized the following year by H. G. GRASSMANN, who showed that several different consistent algebras may be derived by choosing different sets of axioms governing the operations on the elements of the algebra. These developments continued with the group theory of M. S. LIE in the late 19th cent. and reached full expression in the wide scope of modern abstract algebra. Number theory received significant contributions in the latter half of the 19th cent. through the work of Georg CANTOR, J. W. R. DEDEKIND, and K. W. WEIERSTRASS. Still another influence of Gauss was his insistence on rigorous proof in all areas of mathematics. In analysis this close examination of the foundations of the calculus resulted in A. L. CAUCHY'S theory of limits (1821), which in turn yielded new and clearer definitions of continuity, the derivative, and the definite integral. A further important step toward rigor was taken by Weierstrass, who raised new questions about these concepts and showed that ultimately the foundations of analysis rest on the properties of the real number system. In the 20th cent. the trend has been toward increasing generalization and abstraction, with the elements and operations of systems being defined so broadly that their interpretations connect such areas as algebra, geometry, and topology. The key to this approach has been the use of formal axiomatics, in which the notion of axioms as "self-evident truths" has been discarded. Instead, the emphasis is on such logical concepts as consistency and completeness. The roots of formal axiomatics lie in the discoveries of alternative systems of geometry and algebra in the 19th cent.; the approach was first systematically undertaken by David Hilbert in his work on the foundations of geometry (1899). The emphasis on deductive logic inherent in this view of mathematics and the discovery of the interconnections between the various branches of mathematics and their ultimate basis in number theory led to intense activity in the field of mathematical logic after the turn of the century. Rival schools of thought grew up under the leadership of Hilbert, Bertrand RUSSELL and A. N. WHITEHEAD, and L. E. J. Brouwer. Important contributions in the investigation of the logical foundations of mathematics were made by Kurt GÖDEL and A. Church. See Richard Courant and Herbert Robbins, *What Is Mathematics?* (1941); E. T. Bell, *The Development of Mathematics* (2d ed. 1945) and *Men of Mathematics* (1937, repr. 1961); J. R. Newman, ed., *The World of Mathematics* (4 vol., 1956); D. J. Struik, *A Concise History of Mathematics* (3d ed. 1967); Morris Kline, *Mathematical Thought from Ancient to Modern Times* (1973).

Mather, Cotton, 1663-1728, American Puritan clergyman and writer, b. Boston, grad. Harvard (B.A., 1678; M.A., 1681); son of Increase Mather and grandson of Richard Mather and of John Cotton. He was ordained (1685) and became a colleague of his father at North Church, Boston, serving as pastor in his father's absences and after his father's death (1723). It was principally by his indefatigable writing that he became one of the most celebrated of all New England Puritan ministers. He was a scholar of parts, working industriously to gather a library and volubly setting forth what he learned. Thus his *Magnalia Christi Americana* (1702) is a miscellany of materials on the ecclesiastical history of New England, vaguely intended to show how the history of Massachusetts demonstrated the working of God's will. His theological writings, now largely forgotten, had great influence in his time. He was a power in the state as well as in the church, was a leader in the revolt against the rule of Sir Edmund ANDROS and an adviser in Sir William Phips's government. Today he is generally pictured unsympathetically as the archetype of the narrow, intolerant, severe Puritan, and his part in the Salem witch trials in 1692 is often recalled. Although he did not approve of all the trials, he had helped to stir up the wave of hysterical fear by his *Memorable Providences relating to Witchcraft and Possessions* (1689). Later he further pursued his inquiries into satanic possession with *Wonders of the Invisible World* (1693, new ed. 1956), which was sharply answered by Robert CALEF. Even Mather's benevolence—expressed in his actions and reflected in his writings, as in *Essays to Do Good* (1710)—had a core of smugness. Yet he helped to forward learning and education and to make New England a cultural center. He was disappointed in his hopes of being president of Harvard but was one of the moving spirits in the founding of Yale. He was deeply interested in science and was the first native-born American to be a fellow of the Royal Society. He persuaded Zabdiel Boylston to inoculate against smallpox and supported the unpopular inoculation even when his life was threatened. See biographies by Barrett Wendell (1891, repr. 1963) and R. P. Boas and Louise Boas (1928, repr. 1964); studies by Robert Middlekauff (1971) and J. P. Wood (1971); bibliography by T. J. Holmes (3 vol., 1940).

Mather, Frank Jewett, Jr., 1868-1953, American art critic and teacher, b. Deep River, Conn., grad. Williams, 1889, Ph.D. Johns Hopkins, 1892. He taught (1893-1900) at Williams and was professor (1910-33) of art and archaeology at Princeton. Art critic of the New York *Evening Post* and other papers, he also wrote many books.

Mather, Increase, 1639-1723, American Puritan clergyman, b. Dorchester, Mass.; son of Richard Mather. After graduation (1656) from Harvard, he studied at Trinity College, Dublin (M.A., 1658), and preached in England and Guernsey until the Restoration. After returning to Massachusetts (1661), he became (1664) pastor of North Church, Boston, and retained that position through his life. Cotton Mather, his son and colleague, cooperated with him in many of the affairs that occupied their busy lives. They were outstanding upholders of the old Puritan theocracy and of the established order in church and state. This conservatism led to trouble with the government during the Restoration period, and Increase Mather was a particularly bitter opponent of Edward RANDOLPH and Sir Edmund ANDROS over the withdrawal of the Massachusetts charter and the conduct of the royal government. In 1688 he went to England to present the grievances of Massachusetts, and, after the Glorious Revolution of 1688 and the subsequent revolt in Massachusetts against Andros, he obtained a new charter that united Plymouth Colony with Massachusetts Bay Colony. Increase Mather looked with favor on the government of Sir William PHIPS. After 1692 his influence declined somewhat, but he remained powerful to the end. He was president of Harvard College (1685-1701), but he was inactive and spent little time in Cambridge. His writing reflected the concerns of his career. *Cases of Conscience Concerning Evil Spirits*

(1693), appearing soon after the Salem witch furor, denounced "spectral evidence" in witch trials. He also wrote a biography of his father (1670); *A History of the War with the Indians* (1676), written just after King Philip's War; and *Remarkable Providences* (1684), based on an earlier work by other writers. See biography by K. B. Murdock (1953, repr. 1966); study by Robert Middlekauff (1971); bibliography by T. J. Holmes (1931).

Mather, Richard, 1596–1669, British Puritan clergyman in North America, b. Lancashire, England. He studied at Oxford, began preaching, and was ordained in 1620. His Puritan beliefs led him into difficulties, and he fled to Massachusetts (1635), where he was pastor of Dorchester until his death. He helped to draw up the CAMBRIDGE PLATFORM and, with John Eliot and Thomas Welde, prepared the *Bay Psalm Book.* See T. J. Holmes, *The Minor Mathers* (1940); Robert Middlekauff, *The Mathers* (1971).

Mathew, Theobald, 1790–1856, Irish social worker and temperance leader, a Capuchin priest. Father Mathew spent many years working for the welfare and education of the poor. In 1838 he took a pledge of total abstinence and thereafter devoted himself to the cause of temperance, campaigning in Ireland, England, and North America. See biography by Patrick Rogers (1943).

Mathews, Shailer, 1863–1941, American theologian, educator, and author, b. Portland, Maine, studied at Colby College, at Newton Theological Institution, and at the Univ. of Berlin. After seven years of teaching at Colby College (then called Colby Univ.) he entered (1894) upon his long association with the Univ. of Chicago. There he was associate professor and professor of New Testament history and interpretation (until 1905), professor of systematic theology (1905–6), and professor of history and comparative theology (1906–33); he was dean of the divinity school from 1908 to 1933 and dean emeritus thereafter. He was editor (1903–11) of the *World Today,* editor (1913–20) of the *Biblical World,* and president (1912–16) of the Federal Council of Churches of Christ in America. His writings include an autobiography, *New Faith for Old* (1936); *The French Revolution* (1901), *The Church and the Changing Order* (1907), *The Faith of Modernism* (1924), *The Church and the Christian* (1938).

Mathewson, Christy (Christopher Mathewson), 1880–1925, American baseball player, b. Factoryville, Pa., grad. Bucknell Univ., 1902. A righthander, he showed great promise while pitching with the Norfolk, Va., team in 1900. He was purchased by the New York Giants in midseason, but was returned to the Norfolk club in 1901; the same year he joined the Cincinnati Reds and was traded back to the Giants. Under John J. McGRAW, Mathewson rose to greatness as a pitcher and won 373 games and struck out 2,499 batters before he retired from active play in 1918. In three consecutive seasons (1903–5) Mathewson won 30 games or more each season, and in 1905 he led the Giants in their world-series victory over the Philadelphia Athletics by pitching three shutouts in six days. He pitched two no-hit games and in 1908 recorded 37 victories. Mathewson was traded (1916) to the Cincinnati Reds and successfully managed the team until 1918, when he joined the army in World War I. He became a victim of poison gas in France. He returned to baseball in 1923 as president of the Boston Braves, but he died of tuberculosis shortly after. In 1936 he was elected to the National Baseball Hall of Fame.

Mathieu, Georges (zhôrzh mätyö'), 1921–, French painter. Mathieu's works are executed with spontaneous splashes and smears against a brightly colored ground. Improvised with lightning speed, they are calligraphic in style. Some of them were created as performances before an audience.

Mathiez, Albert (älbĕr' mätyā'), 1874–1932, French historian, an authority on the French Revolution. He studied under AULARD, whose scientific method he adopted, though it led him to different conclusions. Although not a member of the Socialist party, Mathiez was a follower of Jean JAURÈS. Mathiez's chief work, *La Révolution française* (3 vol., 1922–27; tr. 1928, repr. 1962), was essentially a socialist interpretation; he viewed the Revolution as the product of the class struggle and of economic necessity. His factual presentation was so unbiased that the royalist historian Pierre Gaxotte used much of Mathiez's work to support entirely opposite conclusions. Mathiez extolled Robespierre, damned Danton, and interpreted the Thermidorian reaction after Robespierre's fall in 1794 as the triumph of the bourgeoisie over the working class. Among Mathiez's other works are *Autour de Robespierre* (1925, tr. *The Fall of Robespierre,* 1927, repr. 1970), *La Réaction thermidorienne* (1929), and other more specialized studies of the Revolutionary period.

Mathura (mŭ'thŏŏrä, mŭ'trə) or **Muttra** (mŭ'trə), city (1971 pop. 131,813), Uttar Pradesh state, N central India, on the Jumna River. An agricultural market town and district administrative center, it is best known as a Hindu pilgrimage site, the reputed birthplace of the god Krishna. The region, which may have been inhabited since the 7th cent. B.C., is rich in archaeological remains. Muslim rulers (16th–18th cent.) destroyed all Hindu temples in the city and erected many mosques.

Mathurai, India: see MADURAI.

Mathusala (məthōō'sələ): see METHUSELAH.

Matilda, Saint: see HENRY I (Henry the Fowler).

Matilda or **Maud,** 1102–67, queen of England, daughter of HENRY I of England. Henry arranged for her a marriage with Holy Roman Emperor Henry V, and she was sent to Germany, betrothed, and five years later (1114) married to him. Empress Matilda was popular in Germany and seemed more German than English, but after her husband's death (1125) she returned to England. Since her only legitimate brother had died (1120), her father devoted himself to securing for her the succession to the English throne, and the barons did in fact recognize her as Henry's heir in 1127. In 1128 she married GEOFFREY IV of Anjou, to whom she bore three sons, the eldest being the future HENRY II. Her life with Geoffrey was stormy, but they managed to compose their differences. Both she and her marriage were unpopular in England, however, and on Henry I's death in 1135 the barons gave their support to Matilda's cousin STEPHEN, who seized the throne. In 1139, Matilda, aided by her half brother Robert, earl of GLOUCESTER, undertook to recover the throne. After the defeat and capture of Stephen in 1141, she was elected "Lady of the English"; but her arrogance alienated supporters, and the captive Stephen had to be freed in a prisoner exchange for Gloucester. Before the end of the year her forces were routed at Winchester, and the same powerful clergy who had enthroned her then deposed her and declared for Stephen. The struggle continued, but never greatly in her favor. In 1148 she withdrew; her son Henry inherited her claim to the throne and was in 1153 recognized as heir. Matilda spent her remaining years in Normandy and became noted for her charity.

Matilda, 1046–1115, countess of Tuscany, called the Great Countess; supporter of Pope Gregory VII in the papal conflict with the Holy Roman emperors. Ruling over Tuscany and parts of Emilia-Romagna and Umbria, she controlled the most powerful feudal state in central Italy. It was at her castle at Canossa that Holy Roman Emperor Henry IV humiliated himself before Pope Gregory VII in 1077. Soon afterward Matilda made a donation (renewed in 1102) of her lands to the Holy See; she retained them as fiefs from the papacy. Her first husband having died in 1076, she married (1089) Duke Welf V of Bavaria. After the expedition (1110–11) of Holy Roman Emperor HENRY V to Italy, Matilda willed her lands to him on her death. He seized them in 1116. The dispute over the ownership of Matilda's lands played a large part in the conflicts between the popes and the emperors, particularly the Hohenstaufen. The cities of Tuscany emerged as independent communes from the struggle; the other lands left by Matilda eventually fell under papal rule.

Matisse, Henri (äNrē' mätēs'), 1869–1954, French painter, sculptor, and lithographer. Matisse is considered, with Picasso, one of the two foremost artists of the modern period. His contribution to 20th-century art is inestimably great. He began to study law and, during an illness in 1890, took up painting, thereafter forsaking law entirely. He studied first with the academician Bouguereau and then with Gustave MOREAU, in whose studio he met many painters who would soon attain prominence with him in the fauvist movement. Matisse's earliest work was exceptionally mature. He explored impressionism (e.g., *La Desserte,* 1897; Niarchos Coll., Athens) and, coming into contact with the theories of Paul SIGNAC, drew upon neo-impressionist styles as in *Luxe, calme et volupté* (c.1905; private coll.). To learn aspects of composition he made variations on the works of the old masters in the Louvre, a practice he continued for many years (e.g., *Variation on a Still-life by de Heem,* c.1915; S. A. Marx Coll., Chicago). Matisse began exhibiting in 1896 and at first was unsuccessful. In 1905 at Collioure, a Mediterranean village, he began using pure primary color as a significant structural element. His portrait of Mme Matisse, known as *The Green Line* (1905; State Mus., Copenhagen), exemplifies this abstract, intellectual use of color. In 1905 he exhibited at the Salon d'automne with the group of artists called fauves [Fr.,= wild beasts], so-named for their remarkable, exuberant use of color. Matisse became a leader of FAUVISM, delighting in vivid color for its sensual and decorative value. After the demise of fauvism, he continued to use color to communicate his joy in bold pattern and striking ornament, e.g., in *The Moorish Screen* (1921; Phila. Mus. of Art) and *Lady in Blue* (1937; private coll.). He experimented frequently with different sorts of expressive abstraction, as in *The Blue Nude* (1907; Baltimore Mus. of Art), *Mlle Landsberg* (1914; Phila. Mus. of Art), and *The Piano Lesson* (1916; Mus. of Modern Art, New York City), but he rejected cubism in order to develop his own ideas. In 1908, Matisse wrote out his theories for *La Grande Revue,* emphasizing his preeminent desire to render the emotion evoked in him by a subject rather than its literal appearance. By 1909 the artist's fame was worldwide. His early sculptured works reveal an interest in African sculpture and in Rodin's treatment of forms. Matisse designed for the ballet (1920, 1938) and illustrated works by Mallarmé (1932) and Baudelaire (1944) among many others. His superbly simple line drawings rank among the greatest works of graphic art of the 20th cent. When he was nearly 80, Matisse volunteered to decorate the Dominican nuns' chapel at Vence, France. The fresh, joyous windows, murals, altar, and myriad details attest to his indomitable spirit and sense of adventure. In his last years he made brilliant paper cutouts and stencils (e.g., *Jazz,* 1947; Phila. Mus. of Art), as gay and as strong in design as his earliest work. The largest collections of his works may be found in the Baltimore Museum of Art; the Art Institute of Chicago; the Museum of Modern Art, New York City; and the Hermitage, Leningrad. See studies by A. H. Barr, Jr. (1951, repr. 1966), Jean Guichard-Meili (tr. 1967), and Louis Aragon (2 vol., tr. 1972).

Mato Grosso (mä'tōō grô'sōō) [Port.,= thick forest], state (1970 pop. 1,600,494), 475,501 sq mi (1,231,548 sq km), central and W Brazil. The capital is CUIABÁ.

Matred (mā'trĕd), mother of Mehetabel, the wife of Hadar, king of Edom. Gen. 36.39.

Matri ((mā'trī), Saul's family. 1 Sam. 10.21.

matrix, in mathematics, a rectangular array of elements (e.g., numbers) considered as a single entity. A matrix is distinguished by the number of rows and columns it contains. The matrix

$$\begin{matrix} 2 & 4 & -6 \\ 5 & 3 & 2 \end{matrix}$$

is a 2×3 (read "2 by 3") matrix, because it contains 2 rows and 3 columns. A matrix having the same number of rows as columns is called a square matrix. The matrix

$$\begin{matrix} 3 & 5 \\ 2 & 7 \end{matrix}$$

is a 2×2 matrix, or square matrix of order 2; a square matrix of order n contains n rows and n columns. Definitions are made for certain operations with matrices; for example, a matrix may be multiplied by a number, and two matrices of the same order may be added or multiplied using an algebra of matrices that has been developed. Matrices find application in such fields as vector analysis and the solution of systems of linear equations by means of electronic computers. See R. C. Dorfi, *Matrix Algebra* (1969).

matrix mechanics: see QUANTUM THEORY.

Matruh (mätrōō'), town (1970 est. pop. 11,800), NW Egypt, near the Mediterranean Sea. Built at the site of the Roman town of Paraetonium, it is located on the coast road and is linked to the coast railroad. During World War II several battles between German and British forces were fought nearby.

Ma-tsu (mä'-dzōō'), island, in the East China Sea, off Fukien prov., China, E of Fu-chou, and c.100 mi (160 km) from Taiwan. It remained a Chinese Nationalist-held outpost after the Communist takeover of the mainland in 1949. Periodically since 1958 the heavily defended island has suffered bombardment from artillery as well as propaganda leaflets from the mainland.

Matsubara (mätsōō'bärä), city (1970 pop. 111,562), Osaka prefecture, SW Honshu, Japan. It is an industrial and residential suburb of Osaka.

Matsudaira, Tsuneo (tsōōnā'ō mätsōōdī'rä), 1877–1949, Japanese diplomat. He was much involved in negotiations with the United States and Great Britain and as a delegate to the post-World War I naval conferences. He served as ambassador in Washington from 1924 to 1928 and later as ambassador to Britain. In 1929 he headed the Japanese delegation to the London Disarmament Conference. From 1936 to 1945 he was imperial household minister. After Japan surrendered to end World War II, he was elected (1947) first head of the new house of councilors.

Matsudo (mätsō͞o'dō), city (1970 pop. 253,591), Chiba prefecture, E central Honshu, Japan. It is a suburb of Tokyo.

Matsue (mätsō͞o'ā), city (1970 pop. 118,005), capital of Shimane prefecture, SW Honshu, Japan, a port on the Sea of Japan. It is an important distribution center and a popular tourist spot. Landmarks include an old castle and a museum containing a collection of the manuscripts and letters of Lafcadio Hearn, who lived in Matsue in 1890–91.

Matsukata, Masayoshi (mäsī'ōshē mätsō͞o'kä''tä), 1835–1924, Japanese statesman. A Satsuma clansman and a GENRO, he was a leading figure in the modernization of Japan. As finance minister (1881–91) his programs stimulated economic activity, increased exports, and laid the basis for armament expansion. As prime minister (1891–92) he dissolved the diet and used the police in the subsequent election, which he nonetheless lost. He became prime minister again (1896–97) and was keeper of the privy seal (1917–22).

Matsumoto (mätsō͞omō'tō), city (1970 pop. 162,924), Nagano prefecture, central Honshu, Japan. It is a market for silkworms and raw silk. Industries include food processing, machine-building, and textile manufacturing. Shiroyama Park has remains of a 16th-century castle.

Matsuoka, Yosuke (yōsō͞o'kē mätsō͞o'ōkä), 1880–1946, Japanese statesman and diplomat. After graduating from the Univ. of Oregon, he served briefly in the foreign ministry and then entered the SOUTH MANCHURIAN RAILROAD Company (1921). He became a spokesman for the expansionist Japanese policy and led the Japanese delegation out of the League of Nations in 1933. He was appointed president of the South Manchurian RR in 1935. Matsuoka was the principal promoter of the Japanese alliance with the fascist powers, and as foreign minister (1940–41) in the second Konoye cabinet he followed a policy of strengthening ties with the Axis, neutralizing the USSR, and making a settlement with the United States. He helped forge the Pact of Berlin (Sept. 27, 1940), which bound Japan to the Axis, and early in 1941 he signed a five-year peace pact with the USSR. After the German attack on Russia (June, 1941) he left the cabinet. Matsuoka was indicted as a war criminal after World War II but died before his trial ended.

Matsushima (mätsō͞o'shĭmä), town (1970 pop. 16,004), Miyagi prefecture, N Honshu, Japan, on Ishinomaki Bay. It is a tourist center for the hundreds of scenic pine-covered islets in the bay. One island is the site of the noted Buddhist temple of Zuiganji (founded 828).

Matsuyama (mätsō͞oyä'mä), city (1970 pop. 322,881), capital of Ehime prefecture, NW Shikoku, Japan, a port on the Inland Sea. It is an important agricultural distribution point and fishing port. Cotton textiles and paper products are manufactured. Matsuyama has two universities. Its feudal castle (built 1603), one of the best preserved in Japan, stands in a magnificent park.

Matsys, Quentin: see MASSYS, QUENTIN.

Matta Echaurren, Roberto (māt'tä ĕkhär'rĕn), 1912–, Chilean painter working in Europe and the United States, b. Santiago. Matta was an exponent of SURREALISM in the group around André BRETON in the late 1930s. His pictures present volatile forms engulfed in cosmic holocaust; their weird effects have been compared to science fiction. Matta cultivated the "accident" of spilled pigment in his canvases. His ideas on abstraction influenced his friend Arshile GORKY. His *Let's Phosphoresce by Intellection, II* is in the Nelson Gallery-Atkins Museum, Kansas City, Mo. See studies by William Rubin (1957) and Irene Clurman (1970).

Mattagami (mətăg'əmē), river, 275 mi (443 km) long, rising in the lake district, E Ont., Canada, SW of Timmins, flowing N to join the Missinaibi River, with which it forms the Moose River.

Mattan (măt'ən). **1** Priest of Baal. 2 Kings 11.18. **2** Father of Shephatiah. Jer. 38.1.

Mattanah (măt'ənä), unidentified resting place, SE of the Dead Sea. Num. 21.18,19.

Mattancheri, India: see COCHIN.

Mattaniah (măt''ənī'ə). **1** Early name of King ZEDEKIAH. **2** Asaphite Levite. 1 Chron. 9.15; Neh. 11.17; 12.8,25,35. **3** Temple musician. 1 Chron. 25.4,16. **4** Levite contemporary with Hezekiah. 2 Chron. 29.13. **5, 6, 7, 8** Men who had foreign wives. Ezra 10.26,27,30,37. **9** Levite. Neh. 13.13.

Mattatha (măt'əthə), ancestor of Joseph. Luke 3.31.

Mattathah (măt'əthə), Jew who had a foreign wife. Ezra 10.33.

Mattathias (măt''əthī'əs) [Gr. variant of MATTITHIAH]. **I, 2** Two in Luke's genealogy. Luke 3.25,26. **3** Father of the MACCABEES. 1 Mac. 2. **4** Captain under Jonathan, the Maccabee. 1 Mac. 11.70. **5** Son of Simon, the Maccabee, murdered with his father. 1 Mac. 16. **6** Envoy from Nicanor to Judas Maccabeus. 2 Mac. 14.19.

Mattei, Enrico (ānrē'kō mät-tā'), 1906–62, Italian public administrator. After World War II he was given the task of dismantling the Italian Petroleum Agency, a Fascist state enterprise. Instead Mattei enlarged and reorganized it into the Ente Nazionale Idrocarburi (ENI), or National Fuel Trust. Under his direction ENI developed large deposits of natural gas in Italy and negotiated important oil concessions in the Middle East as well as a large-scale trade agreement with the USSR. Mattei, who became a powerful figure in Italy, introduced the principle whereby the country that owned exploited oil reserves received 75% of the profits. A left-wing Christian Democrat, Mattei was a member of parliament from 1948 to 1953. He died in a plane crash in 1962.

Mattenai (mătēnā'ī) **I, 2** Two who had taken foreign wives. Ezra 10.33,37. **3** Priest. Neh. 12.19.

Matteotti, Giacomo (jä'kōmō mät-tāôt'tē), 1885–1924, Italian Socialist leader; the outstanding opponent of the Fascist regime during its early days. He was a member of parliament, and his murder by Fascist hirelings precipitated a parliamentary crisis that Mussolini overcame by disavowing the murder and by tightening police control. With Matteotti's removal Mussolini's dictatorship may be said to have begun. The murderers and their accomplices received only nominal sentences.

matter, anything that has MASS and occupies space. The general properties of matter are due to these two criteria. Because of its mass, all matter has INERTIA (the mass being the measure of its inertia) and WEIGHT, if it is in a gravitational field (see GRAVITATION). Because it occupies space, all matter has volume and impenetrability, since two objects cannot occupy the same space simultaneously. The special properties of matter, on the other hand, depend on internal structure and thus differ from one form of matter, i.e., one substance, to another. Such properties include DUCTILITY, ELASTICITY, HARDNESS, MALLEABILITY, porosity (ability to permit another substance to flow through it), and tenacity (resistance to being pulled apart). Matter is ordinarily observed in three different states, or phases (see STATES OF MATTER), and scientists distinguish still a fourth state. Matter in the solid state has both a definite volume and a definite shape; matter in the liquid state has a definite volume but no definite shape, assuming the shape of whatever container it is placed in; matter in the gaseous state has neither a definite volume nor a definite shape and expands to fill any container. The properties of a PLASMA, or hot, ionized gas, are sufficiently different from those of a gas at ordinary temperatures for scientists to consider plasma a fourth state of matter. In ancient times various theories were suggested about the nature of matter. Empedocles held that all matter is made up of four "elements"—earth, air, fire, and water. Leucippus and his pupil Democritus proposed an atomic basis of matter, believing that all matter is built up from tiny particles differing in size and shape. Anaxagoras, however, rejected any theory in which matter is viewed as composed of smaller constituents, whether atoms or elements, and held instead that matter is continuous throughout, being entirely of a single substance. The modern theory of matter dates from the work of John Dalton at the beginning of the 19th cent. The ATOM is considered the basic unit of any element, and atoms may combine chemically to form molecules, the MOLECULE being the smallest unit of any substance that possesses the properties of that substance. An ELEMENT in modern theory is any substance all of whose atoms are the same (i.e., have the same ATOMIC NUMBER), while a compound is composed of different types of atoms together in molecules. Different atoms may also be present together in a mixture, but in a mixture they are not bound together chemically as they are in a compound. The difference between a mixture and a compound helps to illustrate the difference between a physical change and a chemical change. In a physical change, such as a change of state (e.g., from solid to liquid), the substance as a whole changes, but its underlying structure remains the same; water is still composed of molecules containing two hydrogen atoms and one oxygen atom whether it is in the form of ice, liquid water, or steam. In a chemical change, however, the substance participates in a CHEMICAL REACTION, with a consequent reordering of its atoms. As a result, it becomes a different substance with a different set of properties. Many of the physical properties and much of the behavior of matter can be understood without detailed assumptions about the structure of atoms and molecules. For example, the KINETIC-MOLECULAR THEORY OF MATTER provides a good explanation of the nature of TEMPERATURE and the basis of the various GAS LAWS and also gives insight into the different states of matter. Substances in different states vary in the strength of the forces between their molecules, with intermolecular forces being strongest in solids and weakest in gases. The force holding like molecules together is called cohesion, while that between unlike molecules is called adhesion (see ADHESION AND COHESION). Among the phenomena resulting from intermolecular forces are SURFACE TENSION and CAPILLARITY. An even larger number of aspects of matter can be understood when the nature and structure of the atom are taken into account. The QUANTUM THEORY has provided the key to understanding the atom, and most basic problems relating to the atom have been solved. The development of the atomic theory of matter has not, however, settled the question of the basic nature of matter. It is now known that matter and energy are intimately related. According to the law of mass-energy equivalence, developed by Albert Einstein as part of his theory of RELATIVITY, a quantity of matter of mass m possesses an intrinsic rest mass energy E given by $E = mc^2$, where c is the speed of light. This equivalence is dramatically demonstrated in the phenomena of nuclear fission and fusion (see NUCLEAR ENERGY; NUCLEUS), in which a small amount of matter is converted to a rather large amount of energy. The conversion of energy to matter has been observed frequently in the creation of many new ELEMENTARY PARTICLES. The study of elementary particles has not solved the question of the nature of matter but only shifted it to a smaller scale. Matter is sometimes called koinomatter (Gr. *koinos*=common) to distinguish it from antimatter, or matter composed of ANTIPARTICLES. See Ginestra Amaldi, *The Nature of Matter* (1966); V. H. Booth, *Elements of Physical Science: The Nature of Matter and Energy* (1970).

Matterhorn (mä'tərhôrn), Fr. *Mont Cervin,* Ital. *Monte Cervino,* peak, c.14,700 ft (4,480 m) high, in the Pennine Alps, on the Swiss-Italian border, near Zermatt. Its distinctive pyramidal peak was formed by the enlargement of several cirques. It was first scaled in 1865 by Edward Whymper, the English mountaineer. The nearby **Matterjoch** (mä'təryôkh) or **Théodule** (tāôdül'), a pass (alt. 10,800 ft/3,292 m), links Italy with Switzerland.

Matteson, Tompkins Harrison (măt'əsən), 1813–84, American genre and portrait painter, b. Peterboro, N.Y. His subjects were taken from American history and rural life, and he is famous chiefly for his painting of *The Spirit of '76.*

Matthan (măth'ăn), name appearing in the Gospel genealogy. Mat. 1.15.

Matthat (măth'ăt), name appearing twice in the Gospel genealogy. Luke 3.24,29.

Matthew, Saint, one of the Twelve Disciples. Also called Levi, he was a publican (tax collector) from Capernaum (Mat. 9.9–13; 10.3; Mark 2.14; 3.18; Luke 5.27,29; Acts 1.13). Since the 2d cent. the first Gospel (see MATTHEW, GOSPEL ACCORDING TO SAINT) has been attributed to him, but the attribution is almost certainly incorrect. Matthew is said to have died a martyr. His symbol as an evangelist is a winged young man or an angel. Feast: Sept. 21.

Matthew, Thomas: see ROGERS, JOHN (1500?–1555).

Matthew, Gospel according to Saint, 1st book of the New Testament. Although traditionally regarded as the earliest Gospel, it is now generally accepted as postdating the Gospel of St. Mark, from which the author drew considerable material (see SYNOPTIC GOSPELS). It differs from the other Gospels, however, in its unique material on the birth of Jesus (1–2), in the arrangement of the Sermon on the Mount (5–7), and in the length of the discourse on the end of the world (24–25). There are more allusions to the Old Testament in this Gospel than in the others; it was clearly written for Jewish Christians, the purpose being to prove that Jesus was the Messiah foretold in the Old Testament. A fourfold division of the book would be: the coming of the Messiah (1–4.11); his first two years of preaching (4.12–14.36); his third year (15–25); the passion and resurrection (26–28). The Gospel was composed in the last quarter of the 1st cent. The traditional ascription to St. Matthew, which dates from the 2d cent., is questioned by most scholars. See studies by J. C. Fenton (1964) and H. A. Guy (1971).

Matthew of Paris or **Matthew Paris,** d. 1259, English historian, a monk of St. Albans. He became the historiographer of the convent after the death (c.1236) of ROGER OF WENDOVER. The first part of his *Chronica majora* [great chronicle], a history of the world, is largely a reworked version of Wendover's chronicle. However, the second part, from 1235 to 1259, is original and extremely valuable because its material was carefully collected from eyewitnesses or written from personal knowledge. Paris was an excellent stylist and narrator, and in his rewriting of Wendover's chronicle he formulated the hostile image of King John that has been copied by historians until very recent times. The standard edition of this work is by H. R. Luard (7 vol., 1872–83); a translation by J. A. Giles (1852–54) begins with 1235. Paris wrote a history of England, the *Chronica minora* [little chronicle], also called the *Historia Anglorum,* largely taken from the great chronicle but with some added material. See biography by Richard Vaughan (1958).

Matthew of Westminster, name for many years given to the imaginary author of an English chronicle in Latin, the *Flores historiarum.* The chronicle was actually written by various monks. The portion covering the period from the creation to 1265, written at St. Albans, derived largely from the *Chronica majora* of MATTHEW OF PARIS. The portion covering 1265–1326 was written at Westminster, the entries for the period from 1307 to 1325 being written by Robert of Reading (d. 1325). A translation to 1307 was made by C. D. Yonge (1853).

Matthew Paris: see MATTHEW OF PARIS.

Matthews, Brander (James Brander Matthews), 1852–1929, American author and teacher, b. New Orleans. Matthews was a well-known figure in theatrical and literary circles in Paris and London as well as in New York City. He began to teach at Columbia in 1891 and in 1900 was appointed the first professor of dramatic literature in any American university. A founding member of several writers' clubs, he had considerable influence on the playwrights of the period from 1890 to 1915. His works include *The Development of the Drama* (1903), *Principles of Playmaking* (1919), and *Playwrights on Playmaking* (1923). His gift of model stage sets, costumes, and books is now the Brander Matthews Dramatic Museum at Columbia. See his autobiography, *These Many Years* (1917).

Matthews, Stanley, 1915–, British soccer player. Matthews' career began in 1931, and he continued to play through 1965. From 1934 on he played wing for England in international matches 56 times. Considered one of the finest athletes ever to play professional soccer, he was knighted in 1965. See his autobiography, *The Stanley Matthews Story* (1960).

Matthias, Saint (məthīʹəs), apostle chosen by lot to fill the place of Judas Iscariot. Acts 1.23–26. He is said in ancient tradition to have died a martyr at Colchis. Feast: Feb. 24.

Matthias, 1557–1619, Holy Roman emperor (1612–19), king of Bohemia (1611–17) and of Hungary (1608–18), son of Holy Roman Emperor Maximilian II. He was appointed governor of Austria (1593) by his brother, Holy Roman Emperor RUDOLF II. He formed a close association there with the bishop of Vienna, Melchior KLESL, who later became his chief adviser. In 1605, Matthias forced the ailing emperor to allow him to deal with the Hungarian Protestant rebels. The result was the Peace of Vienna (1606), which guaranteed religious freedom in Hungary. In the same year Matthias was recognized as head of the house of Hapsburg and as future Holy Roman emperor, as a result of Rudolf's illness. Allying himself with the estates of Hungary, Austria, and Moravia, Matthias forced (1608) his brother to yield rule of these lands to him; Rudolf later ceded (1611) Bohemia. After Matthias's accession as Holy Roman emperor, his policy was dominated by Klesl, who hoped to bring about a compromise between Catholic and Protestant states within the empire in order to strengthen it. Matthias had already been forced to grant religious concessions to Protestants in Austria and Moravia, as well as in Hungary, when he had allied with them against Rudolf. His conciliatory policies were opposed by the more intransigent Catholic Hapsburgs, particularly Matthias's brother Archduke Maximilian, who hoped to secure the succession for the inflexible Catholic archduke Ferdinand (later Holy Roman Emperor FERDINAND II). The start of the Bohemian Protestant revolt in 1618 provoked Maximilian to imprison Klesl and revise his policies. Matthias, old and ailing, was unable to prevent Maximilian's takeover. Ferdinand, who had already been crowned king of Hungary (1617) and of Bohemia (1618), succeeded Matthias as Holy Roman emperor.

Matthias Corvinus (kôrvīʹnəs), 1443?–1490, king of Hungary (1458–90) and Bohemia (1478–90), second son of John HUNYADI. He was elected king of Hungary on the death of LADISLAUS V. Holy Roman Emperor FREDERICK III sought to contest the election, but recognized him in 1462. Matthias won a reputation as a crusader against the Turks. He was persuaded by Pope PIUS II to take up arms against GEORGE OF PODEBRAD, king of Bohemia. Having conquered Moravia, Silesia, and Lusatia, Matthias had himself crowned (1469) king of Bohemia, but was not recognized by the Bohemian diet. The war continued after the accession of Ladislaus II as king of Bohemia. In 1478 peace was made: both Ladislaus and Matthias were to keep the title king of Bohemia; Matthias was to retain his conquests, which were, however, to revert to Bohemia after his death. After fighting two wars (1477, 1479) against Frederick III, Matthias began (1482) a third campaign. He took Vienna (1485) and conquered Styria, Carinthia, and Carniola, but his conquests were lost again after his death. His military success was largely due to the establishment of a standing army. During his rule Hungary reached its last flowering before its fall to Turkey. He respected the national institutions but was harsh in his fiscal policy and in his administration of justice. A true Renaissance ruler, he protected learning and science. His library at Buda, the Corvina, was one of the finest in Europe. He was succeeded in Hungary by Ladislaus II of Bohemia, who ruled as ULADISLAUS II of Hungary.

Matthiessen, F. O. (Francis Otto Matthiessen) (măthʹĭsĕn), 1902–50, American critic, b. Pasadena, Calif., grad. Yale, 1923, Rhodes Scholar at Oxford (B.Litt., 1925), Ph.D. Harvard, 1927. He was professor of history and literature at Harvard (1929–50). As a critic Matthiessen was interested in the history of American literature and the relationship of literature to society. He was a devout Christian and a committed socialist. His works include *Sarah Orne Jewett* (1929), *American Renaissance* (1941), *Henry James: The Major Phase* (1944), and *Theodore Dreiser* (1951). Matthiessen committed suicide at the age of 48.

Mattithiah (măt″ĭthīʹə). **1** Overseer in the temple. 1 Chron. 9.31. **2** Musician of David. 1 Chron. 15.18; 16.5. **3** Man who had a foreign wife. Ezra 10.43. **4** Assistant of Ezra. Neh. 8.4.

Mattoon (măt″o͞onʹ), city (1970 pop. 19,681), Coles co., E central Ill.; inc. 1859. It is a processing, rail, and industrial center for a rich farm and dairy region. Among its manufactures are road-building equipment, paper and brass products, and springs. Nearby are many oil wells, a fish hatchery, and Paradise Lake. The farm and grave of Abraham Lincoln's father and stepmother are southeast of the city. Gen. Ulysses S. Grant took command of his first Civil War troops in Mattoon. A junior college is there.

Maturin, Charles Robert (mătʹyo͝orĭn), 1782–1824, Irish author. A minister by vocation, he wrote novels in the manner of the Gothic horror tale of Ann Ward RADCLIFFE. They include *The Fatal Revenge* (1807), *The Milesian Chief* (1812), and his masterpiece *Melmoth the Wanderer* (1820). He wrote several tragedies, but only *Bertram* (1816) was a success. See study by Dale Kramer (1973).

Matuta or **Mater Matuta** (māʹtər məto͞oʹtə), Roman goddess. Sometimes called the goddess of dawn, she was more properly the goddess of childbirth. Her festival, the Matralia (June 11), was attended only by matrons. She was also identified with the Greek goddess LEUCOTHEA and as such was worshiped as a sea deity.

Matute, Ana María (äʹnä märēʹä mäto͞oʹtā), 1926–, Spanish novelist and short-story writer, b. Barcelona. In simple, delicate prose she writes of isolation, suffering, and anguish. As characters in her novels she favors children, adolescents, and the humble and rejected. Her works include *Los Abel* (1948), *Fiesta al noroeste* [fiesta to the northeast] (1952), *Los hijos muertos* (1958; tr. *The Lost Children,* 1965), and *Historias de la Artámila* [stories of Artámila] (1961). See studies by M. E. W. Jones (1970) and J. W. Díaz (1971).

Maubeuge (mōbözhʹ), city (1968 pop. 32,172), Nord dept., N France, on the Sambre River near the Belgian border. Iron and steel products, glass, and china are major manufactures. An abbey was founded on the site of Maubeuge by St. Aldegone in the 7th cent. During World War I the city was held by the Germans. Its position on an extension of the MAGINOT LINE resulted in heavy destruction during World War II. Still standing are remains of fortifications built in 1685 by the famous military engineer Sébastien Vauban.

Mauclerc, Pierre: see PETER I, duke of Brittany.

Maud: see MATILDA, queen of England.

Maudling, Reginald, 1917–, British politician. A lawyer, he entered Parliament in 1950 as a Conservative and rapidly rose to prominence, serving as minister of supply (1955–57), paymaster-general (1957–59), president of the board of trade (1959–61), colonial secretary (1961–62), and chancellor of the exchequer (1962–64). He was narrowly defeated by Edward Heath in a contest for the Conservative party leadership in 1965. When the Conservatives returned to power in 1970, he became home secretary, assuming responsibility for two explosive matters—race relations and Northern Ireland. However, he resigned in 1972 because of his past connection with a bankrupt company that was under police investigation for corruption.

Maugham, William Somerset (môm), 1874–1965, English author, b. Paris. He was noted as an expert storyteller and a master of fictional technique. An introverted child afflicted with a stammer, Maugham was orphaned at 10 and sent to live with his uncle, a vicar. Although he later studied medicine and completed his internship, he never practiced, having decided at an early age to devote himself to literature. Maugham wrote with wit and irony, frequently expressing a cynical attitude toward life. Famous as a dramatist before he became known for his novels and short stories, he achieved his first success with the sardonically humorous play *Lady Frederick* (1907). This was followed by a series of commercial successes, the best being *The Circle* (1921), *Our Betters* (1923), and *The Constant Wife* (1927). He had written eight novels before his masterpiece, the partly autobiographical *Of Human Bondage* (1915), appeared. It is the story of the painful growth to self-realization of a lonely, sensitive young physician with a clubfoot. Maugham's other famous novels include *The Moon and Sixpence* (1919), based on the life of the French painter Paul Gauguin; *Cakes and Ale* (1930), satirizing Thomas Hardy and Hugh Walpole; and *The Razor's Edge* (1944), dealing with a young American's search for spiritual fulfillment. Frequently his writings, notably the short stories "Miss Thompson" and "The Letter," use as background the exotic places he had visited. In his later work Maugham limited himself primarily to essays; *The Art of Fiction: an Introduction to Ten Novels and Their Authors* (1955) is representative. See biographies by J. Weidman (1959) and R. Maugham (1966); study by R. A. Cordell (2d ed. 1969).

Maui (mouʹē), island (1970 pop. 38,691), 728 sq mi (1,886 sq km), second largest island in the state of Hawaii, separated from the island of Hawaii by the Alenuihaha Channel and from Molokai by the Pailolo Channel. Maui is made up of two mountain masses, which constitute the east and west peninsulas, connected by an isthmus. The highest point on the island is the Haleakala volcano (10,023 ft/3,055 m) in HALEAKALA NATIONAL PARK. In the west Puu Kukui rises to 5,788 ft (1,764 m). The island's chief industries are the cultivation of sugarcane and pineapples. The principal ports are Kahului and Lahaina. Wailuku is the largest town and the county seat of Maui co., which includes the islands of Maui, Kahoolawe, and Molokai.

Mauldin, Bill (William Henry Mauldin), 1921–, American cartoonist, b. Mountain Park, N. Mex. During World War II he achieved fame with his sardonic cartoons depicting the squalid reality of the enlisted man's life. These appeared in *Stars and Stripes* and elsewhere. Mauldin's cartoons won him two Pulitzer Prizes (1944 and 1958). He is political cartoonist for the Chicago *Sun-Times.* Among his principal books of cartoons are *Up Front* (1945), *A Sort of a Saga* (1949), *Bill Mauldin in Korea* (1952), and *The Brass Ring* (1971). Mauldin appeared in the movie *The Red Badge of Courage* (1951).

Mau Mau, secret terrorist organization in KENYA, comprising mainly Kikuyu tribesmen. They were bound by oath to force the expulsion of white settlers from Kenya. In 1952 the Mau Mau began bloody reprisals against the Europeans, especially in the "white highlands," which had long been claimed by the Kikuyu as tribal lands. The settlers retaliated, and casualties grew. Kikuyu who refused to join the Mau Mau were slain by the terrorists. By 1956, however, British troops had driven the Mau Mau into the mountain forests, where they were killed or eventually captured. Later the entire Kikuyu tribe was resettled within a guarded area, and Jomo KENYATTA was imprisoned. The state of emergency decreed (1952) in Kenya was ended in 1960; Kenyatta was released. See Fred Majdalany, *State of Emergency* (1962); C. J. Rosberg, Jr., *The Myth of Mau Mau* (1966).

Maumbury Rings: see DORCHESTER, England.

Maumee (mômē'), village (1970 pop. 15,937), Lucas co., NW Ohio, on the Maumee River; inc. 1838. It is largely residential. Maumee was the site of Fort Miami, a British post surrendered to the Americans during the War of 1812. Nearby is Fallen Timbers, the historical monument commemorating the battle fought in 1794.

Mauna Kea (mou'nə kā'ə), dormant volcano, 13,796 ft (4,205 m) high, in the south central part of the island of Hawaii. It is the loftiest peak in the Hawaiian Islands and the highest island mountain in the world, rising c.32,000 ft (9,750 m) from the Pacific Ocean floor. It has many cinder cones on its flanks and a great crater at the summit. Its fertile lower slopes are used for agriculture, especially the growing of coffee beans. The upper slopes are snow-covered in winter.

Mauna Kea Observatory, astronomical OBSERVATORY located on Mauna Kea peak, Hawaii, at an altitude of more than 13,600 ft (4,145 m). It is operated by the Institute for Astronomy of the Univ. of Hawaii. Instruments include an 88-in. (224-cm) reflecting telescope and twin 24-in. (61-cm) reflectors, and a 3.6-m (142-in.) reflector is to be erected at Mauna Kea by 1977-78 by France and Canada.

Mauna Loa (mou'nə lō'ə), mountain, 13,680 ft (4,170 m) high, in the south central part of the island of Hawaii, in Hawaii Volcanoes National Park. Its many craters include Kilauea and Mokuaweoweo, two of the world's largest active craters. Mauna Loa has erupted twice (1942, 1949) since its period of greatest activity in 1881. Its lava flows have reached the sea.

Maundy Thursday (môn'dē) [Latin *mandatum,* word in the ceremony], traditional English name for Thursday of HOLY WEEK, anniversary of the institution of the Eucharist by Jesus at the Last Supper. In some churches, Jesus' washing of the disciples' feet is symbolically reenacted. In Great Britain there is a survival in the distribution by the sovereign of special "maundy money" to certain of the poor at Westminster Abbey. In the Roman Catholic Church, Maundy Thursday is a general communion day; a single Mass is sung, in the evening, and a Host, consecrated for the morrow, is placed in a specially adorned chapel of repose. The altars are stripped bare until the Easter vigil mass.

Maupassant, Guy de (gē də mōpäsäN'), 1850-93, French novelist and short-story writer, of an ancient Norman family. He worked in a government office at Paris and became known c.1880 as the most brilliant of the circle of Zola. He poured out a prodigious number of short stories, novels, plays, and travel sketches until 1891, when he went mad. He died in a sanitarium. Maupassant's style and treatment of subject resemble those of Flaubert in classic simplicity, clarity, and objective calm. Maupassant is a modern exemplar of traditional French psychological realism; he portrays his characters as unhappy victims of their greed, desire, or vanity, but presents even the most sordid details of their lives without sermonizing. His best novels are considered to be *Une Vie* (1883, tr. *A Life*), about the disillusioning life of a lonely woman; *Bel-Ami* (1885), describing the career of a selfish journalist; *Pierre et Jean* (1888), a study of the hatred of two brothers; and *Notre Cœur* (1890, tr. *Our Hearts*), showing the emotional life of an unhappily married man. His short stories, 300 in all, are superior to the rest of his work, and many of them are said to be unsurpassed in their genre. A list of his masterpieces would include "Boule de suif" ("Tallow Ball"), "L'Héritage" ("The Heritage"), "La Parure" ("The Necklace"), "La Maison Tellier" ("The House of Mme Tellier"), "Clair de lune" ("Moonlight"), "La Ficelle" ("The Piece of String"), "Mlle Fifi," and "Miss Harriet." Maupassant had tremendous influence on all European literature, and his works are often translated. See studies by Edward D. Sullivan (1954, repr. 1971); A. H. Wallace (1973), and Stanley Jackson (1938, repr. 1974).

Maupeou, René Nicolas de (rənā' nēkôlā' də mōpo͞o'), 1714-92, chancellor of France (1768-74). He was president of the Parlement of Paris before he succeeded his father as chancellor. He was the chief mover in the attempt of King Louis XV to master the PARLEMENT and end its opposition to the fiscal measures needed to replenish the treasury. Maupeou dissolved (1771) the parlement, exiled its members from Paris, and abolished the sale of judicial offices. He then substituted a new parlement (nominating all the members) and a system of superior courts. Some of the provincial parlements suffered similar treatment. Although he strove for judicial reform he became highly unpopular. King Louis XVI on his accession dismissed Maupeou and restored the old parlements.

Maupertuis, Pierre Louis Moreau de (pyĕr lwē môrō' də mōpĕrtüē'), 1698-1759, French mathematician and astronomer. For his skillful support of Newton's theory he was admitted to the Royal Society of London in 1728. He headed (1736-37) an expedition of academicians to Lapland, where he confirmed Newton's theory of the flattening of the earth at the poles. In 1740 he went to Berlin upon the invitation of Frederick II of Prussia, who later placed him in charge of the new academy. Besides his numerous astronomical writings, including *Discours sur la figure des astres* (1732) and *Discours sur la parallaxe de la lune* (1741), he wrote a work setting forth a mechanistic view of the universe, *Essai de cosmologie* (1750), and several biological studies. Quarrels, particularly with Samuel Koenig and Voltaire (who satirized him in several writings, especially *Diatribe du Docteur Akakia*), and illness complicated his later years.

Maura y Montaner, Antonio (äntō'nyō môr'ä ē mōn'tänär), 1853-1925, Spanish politican. He entered the Cortes in 1881 as a liberal but later joined the Conservative party. As premier (1903-4, 1907-9), he attempted to carry through a program for reform (a "revolution from above"), but he was fiercely opposed by the liberals. He fell from power after the brutal suppression of an uprising in Barcelona in 1909 (caused by the call-up of Catalan troops to fight in Morocco), but later (1918, 1919, 1921-22) headed coalition cabinets.

Maurepas, Jean Frédéric Phélippeaux, comte de (zhäN frādārĕk' fālēpō' kôNt də môrəpä'), 1701-81, French statesman. He succeeded his father as minister of state at 14, the post being administered for him in his minority. He was later made minister of marine and attempted to apply scientific methods to naval affairs. A satirical epigram against the king's mistress, Mme de Pompadour, caused his dismissal and exile (1749). After King Louis XVI's accession (1774) Maurepas returned, became minister of state, and covered his mediocre abilities by a judicious selection of his council, which included the comte de Vergennes, A. R. J. Turgot, and Lamoignon de Malesherbes. He supported the alliance with the American colonies and the war against Great Britain. His failure to give full support to the ministers helped to bring about the downfall of both Turgot (1776) and his successor, Jacques Necker (1781).

Maurer, Alfred Henry, 1868-1932, American painter, b. New York City; son of Louis Maurer. He was apprenticed as a lithographer, taught himself painting, and went to Europe in 1897, studying briefly at the Académie Julian, Paris. While in Paris he was the first American painter to take a significant interest in fauvist and cubist painting. Most of his later work retains this influence; his paintings vary from elongated female heads to subtly restrained and balanced still lifes. Among his works in museums are *Two Heads* (Berkshire Mus., Pittsfield, Mass.); *Still Life with Pears* (Addison Gall., Andover, Mass.); and *Self-Portrait with a Hat* (Walker Art Center, Milwaukee). See biography by Elizabeth McCausland (1951).

Maurer, Georg Ludwig von (gā'ôrkh lo͞ot'vĭkh fən mou'rər), 1790-1872, German jurist and historian. He taught at the Univ. of Munich, helped to introduce legal reforms, and held various public offices. Deeply interested in early Germanic institutions, particularly the MARK, or village, he believed that he could distinguish in them the roots of the principles of liberty and democracy. His theory of the mark found enthusiastic adherents but has been generally abandoned, at least in its extreme form.

Maurer, Ion Gheorghe (yôn gāôr'gā), 1902-, Rumanian statesman. A lawyer, he defended Rumanian Communists in the 1930s and later became (1945) a member of the central committee of the Communist party. In the postwar decades he was minister of economic affairs (1946-47), minister of industry and trade (1947-48), foreign minister (1957-58), and chairman of the presidium of the national assembly (1958-61). In 1961 he became chairman of the council of ministers, or premier. An intimate of Nicolae Ceauşescu, Maurer supported Rumania's nationalist and independent policy. He curtailed his activities after a serious car accident in 1970 and resigned as premier in 1974.

Mauretania, ancient district of Africa in Roman times. In a vague sense it meant only "the land of the Moors" and lay W of Numidia, but more specifically it usually included most of present-day N Morocco and W Algeria. The district was not the same as modern Mauritania. It was a complex of native tribal units, but by the 2d cent. B.C. when Jugurtha of Numidia was rebelling against Rome, Jugurtha's father-in-law, Bocchus, had most of Mauretania under his control. The Roman influence became paramount, and Augustus, having met opposition in restoring JUBA II to the throne of Numidia, placed him instead (25 B.C.) as ruler of Mauretania. Revolts later occurred, and Mauretania was subdued (A.D. 41-A.D. 42); Emperor Claudius I made it into two provinces—Mauretania Caesariensis, with Caesarea (modern Cherchel) as capital, and Mauretania Tingitana, with Tingis (modern Tangier) as capital. Roman influence was never complete, and native chieftains remained powerful. With the onset of the barbarian invasions, Roman control weakened, and by the end of the 5th cent. A.D. it had disappeared.

Mauriac, François (fräNswä' mōryäk'), 1885-1970, French writer. Mauriac achieved success in 1922 and 1923 with *Le Baiser au lépreux* and *Genitrix* (tr. of both in *The Family,* 1930). Generally set in or near his native Bordeaux, his novels are imbued with his profound, though nonconformist, Roman Catholicism. His characters exist in a tortured universe; nature is evil and man eternally prone to sin. His major novels are *The Desert of Love* (1925, tr. 1929), *Thérèse* (1927, tr. 1928), and *Vipers' Tangle* (1932, tr. 1933). Other works include *The Frontenacs* (1933, tr. 1961) and *Woman of the Pharisees* (1941, tr. 1946); a life of Racine (1928) and of Jesus (1936, tr. 1937); and plays, notably *Asmodée* (1938, tr. 1939). Also a distinguished essayist, Mauriac became a columnist for *Figaro* after World War II. Collections of his articles and essays include *Journal, 1932-39* (1947, partial tr. *Second Thoughts* 1961), *Proust's Way* (1949, tr. 1950), and *Cain, Where Is Your Brother?* (tr. 1962). Mauriac received the 1952 Nobel Prize in Literature. See his memoirs (1959, tr. 1960); study by Cecil Jenkins (1965).

Maurice (môr'ĭs), c.539-602, Byzantine emperor (582-602). He was a successful general when, on his deathbed, Tiberius II, his father-in-law and the successor of Justin II, proclaimed him emperor. He failed to halt the Lombards in Italy but ended (591) the war with Persia, restored Khosru II to the throne, and defeated the Avars. His strict discipline caused mutiny in the Danubian army, and he was obliged to flee. He was killed by order of the usurper Phocas, who was deposed (610), in turn, by Heraclius I.

Maurice, 1521-53, duke (1541-47) and elector (1547-53) of Saxony. A member of the Albertine branch of the ruling house of Saxony, he became duke of Albertine Saxony during the Protestant Reformation. Although a Protestant, he was more swayed by political than by religious motives. In 1546 he made an agreement with Holy Roman Emperor CHARLES V by which he was to receive, in return for deserting the Protestants of the SCHMALKALDIC LEAGUE, the lands and title of his cousin, Elector JOHN FREDERICK I of Saxony, ruler of the Ernestine portion of Saxony. He fought for Charles in the Schmalkaldic War and after the battle of Mühlberg (1547) received the electorate and a portion of his cousin's lands. However, Maurice's disgust with the emperor's ill-treatment of the Protestant leader PHILIP OF HESSE, and his still unsatisfied ambition, led him to turn against Charles. After raising an army for the execution of the ban against Magdeburg, with which he had been entrusted, he formed an alliance with HENRY II of France (1551). In the war that followed Maurice nearly captured Charles at Innsbruck. He forced Charles to free Philip and to conclude (1552) the Treaty of PASSAU. In 1553, Maurice was killed in a battle against Albert Alcibiades of Brandenburg-Kulmbach.

Maurice, Frederick Denison, 1805-72, English clergyman and social reformer. He was brought up a Unitarian but became an Anglican. He studied law at Cambridge and was a founder of the Apostles' Club. Entering Oxford in 1830, he took holy orders in 1831, but in 1853 he lost the post of professor of divinity at King's College, London, because of the views contained in his *Theological Essays* (1853). He held the chair of moral philosophy at Cambridge from 1866 until his death. Besides one novel, *Eustace Conway* (1834), he wrote many religious works, including *Lectures on Ecclesiastical History* (1854) and *The Doctrine of Sacrifice* (1854). Maurice was a leader of the CHRISTIAN SOCIALISM movement and also a leader in education, being a founder of Queen's College for women (1848) and the Working Men's College (1854), both in London. See biographies by his son, Sir J. F. Maurice (1884), and C. F. G. Masterman (1907); studies by F. M. McClain (1972) and O. J. Brose (1972).

Maurice of Nassau (năs'ô), 1567–1625, prince of Orange (1618–25); son of WILLIAM THE SILENT by Anne of Saxony. He became stadtholder of Holland and Zeeland after the assassination (1584) of his father. He was later appointed (1588) captain general and admiral of the United Netherlands and became (1589) stadtholder of Utrecht, Gelderland, and Overijssel. In 1618 he succeeded his elder brother, Philip William, as prince of Orange. Throughout his career the NETHERLANDS continued to struggle for independence from Spain. In 1590 he took the offensive against the Spanish under Alessandro Farnese. His campaigns were primarily distinguished by his skill in siegecraft. His successes on land and on sea enabled the Netherlands to conclude (1609) a 12-year truce with the Spanish (then commanded by Spinola). The truce virtually established the independence of the seven United Provinces. During the first part of Maurice's career his principal adviser was OLDENBARNEVELDT, chief author of the truce of 1609. Relations between the two men were, however, strained after 1600 and flared into open conflict when the struggle between REMONSTRANTS and strict Calvinists broke out. Maurice took the part of the Calvinists and in 1618 compelled the summoning of the Synod of Dort, which suppressed the Remonstrants. Oldenbarneveldt, as a leader of the Remonstrants, was arrested, tried, and executed. Thus the house of Orange became supreme in the Netherlands. Maurice's campaigns after the resumption (1621) of hostilities with Spain met with little success. He was succeeded by his brother Frederick Henry.

Maurice of Saxony: see MAURICE (1521–53); SAXE, MAURICE, COMTE DE (1696–1750).

Mauritania, Islamic Republic of (môrĭtā'nēə), republic (1973 est. pop. 1,250,000), 397,953 sq mi (1,030,700 sq km), NW Africa, bordering on the Atlantic Ocean in the west, on Spanish Sahara in the northwest and north, on Algeria in the northeast, on Mali in the east and southeast, and on Senegal in the southwest. NOUAKCHOTT is the capital and largest town; other towns include Atar and Kaédi. Most of Mauritania is made up of low-lying desert, which forms part of the Sahara. Along the Senegal River (which forms the border with Senegal) in the southwest is the semiarid Sahel with some fertile alluvial soil. A wide sandstone plateau (rising to c.1,500 ft/460 m) runs through the center of the country from north to south. In the southeast is the Hodh, a large basin in the desert. About 80% of the population is made up of nomadic and seminomadic persons of Berber, Arab, Tuareg, and Fulani descent. Those of Berber, Arab, and mixed Berber-Arab background are sometimes called MOORS or Maures. The remaining 20% of the population are mostly black Africans who belong to the Tukolor, Soninke, Bambara, and Wolof ethnic groups and live as sedentary agriculturalists near the Senegal River. About 90% of Mauritania's population lives in rural areas. Virtually all the inhabitants of the country are Muslim, and many belong to the Qadirriya brotherhood. The great majority of Mauritanians speak Arabic, which, along with French, is an official language. Mauritania's economy is sharply divided between a traditional agricultural sector and a modern mining industry that was developed in the 1960s. The great majority of the country's workers are engaged either in raising crops or pasturing livestock and are largely unaffected by the mining industry. The principal agricultural products, produced chiefly near the Senegal and in scattered oases, are millet, pulses, dates, maize, groundnuts, gum arabic, rice, and wheat. Large numbers of sheep, goats, cattle, and camels are raised. There is a small but growing fishing industry based in the Atlantic and on the Senegal River. A large deposit of high-grade iron ore was discovered in N Mauritania in the late 1950s and production for export began in 1963. Mining is controlled by the Iron Mining Co. of Mauritania (MIFERMA), which is jointly owned by French (56%), British (19%), Italian (15%), and West German (5%) concerns; Mauritania holds a 5% interest. Foreign sales of iron ore account for about 80% of the country's export earnings, which are derived from a percentage of MIFERMA's foreign sales paid to the government of Mauritania. Copper ore is found in W Mauritania, and its exploitation is controlled by a firm owned principally by U.S. and British interests. Although little copper was mined in the early 1970s, output was expected to rise by the end of the decade. Salt is also produced, and there are untapped deposits of gypsum and titanium. The country's few manufactured goods are made up principally of basic consumer items such as processed food (especially fish), clothing, and matches. Mauritania has one railroad and a very small network of all-weather roads that serves mainly the south. The chief exports, in addition to iron ore, are copper ore, cattle, processed fish, and gum arabic; the leading imports are machinery, transportation equipment, chemicals, foodstuffs, and refined petroleum. The principal trade partners are France, Great Britain, the United States, and West Germany. In 1974, Mauritania became a charter member of the West African Economic Community.

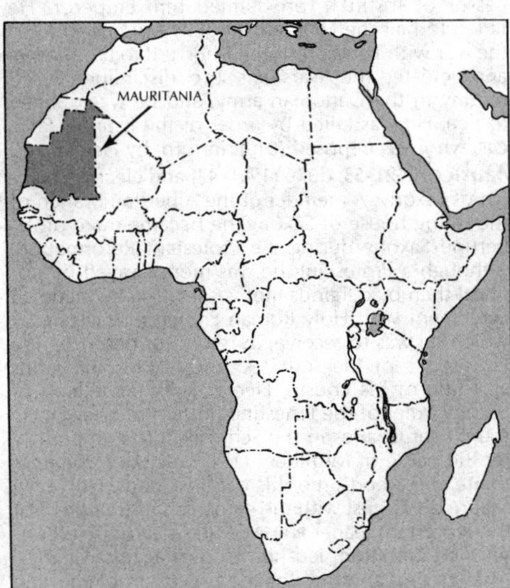

History. The remains of paleolithic and neolithic cultures have been discovered in N Mauritania. By the beginning of the 1st millennium A.D. Sanhaja Berbers had migrated into Mauritania, pushing the black African inhabitants (especially the Soninké) southward toward the Senegal River. The Hodh region, which became desert only in the 11th cent., was the center of the ancient empire of Ghana (700–1200), whose capital, Kumbi-Saleh, located near the present-day border with Mali, has been unearthed by archaeologists. Until the 13th cent., Oualata, Awdaghost, and Kumbi-Saleh, all in SE Mauritania, were major centers along the trans-Saharan caravan routes linking Morocco with the region along the upper Niger River. In the 11th cent. the ALMORAVID movement was founded among the Muslim Berbers of Mauritania. In the 14th and 15th cent., SE Mauritania was part of the empire of Mali, centered along the upper Niger. By this time the Sahara had encroached on much of Mauritania, consequently limiting agriculture and reducing the population. In the 1440s, Portuguese navigators explored the Mauritanian coast and established a fishing base on Arguin Island, located near the present-day boundary with Spanish Sahara. From the 17th cent., Dutch, British, and French traders were active along the S Mauritanian coast; they were primarily interested in the gum arabic gathered near the Senegal. Under Louis Faidherbe, governor of Senegal (1854–61; 1863–65), France gained control of S Mauritania. The region was declared a protectorate in 1903, but parts of the north were not pacified until the 1930s. Until 1920, when it became a separate colony in FRENCH WEST AFRICA, Mauritania was administered as part of Senegal. Saint-Louis, in Senegal, continued to be Mauritania's administrative center until 1957, when it was replaced by Nouakchott. The French ruled through existing political authorities and did little to develop the country's economy or to increase educational opportunities for the population. National political activity began only after World War II. In 1958, Mauritania became an autonomous republic within the FRENCH COMMUNITY, and on Nov. 28, 1960, it became fully independent. Its leader at independence was Makhtar Ould Daddah, who in 1961 formed the Party of the Mauritanian People (which in 1965 became the country's only legal party) and was the leading force in establishing a new constitution. Under the 1961 constitution, Mauritania's chief executive is the president, who is popularly elected to a five-year term and who must be a Muslim. Legislative power is vested in the national assembly, whose 50 members are also popularly elected to five-year terms. Ould Daddah was elected president in 1961 and reelected in 1966 and 1971. The 1960s were marked by tensions between the black Africans of the south and the Arabs and Berbers of central and N Mauritania, some of whom sought to join Mauritania with Morocco. By the early 1970s the main conflicts in the country were over economic and ideological rather than ethnic matters, as dissident workers and students protested what they considered an unfair wage structure and an undue concentration of power in Ould Daddah's hands. Ould Daddah attempted to act as a bridge between N Africa and black Africa and in the early 1970s was on good terms with Libya, Algeria, Tunisia, and Morocco as well as with black African nations like Senegal and Liberia. In 1973, Mauritania became a member of the Arab League. In the same year the country began to loosen its ties with France by withdrawing from the franc zone and establishing its own currency. Ould Daddah was a strong advocate of independence for Spanish Sahara. The long-term drought in the semiarid Sahel region in the south, which began in the late 1960s, was estimated in mid-1974 to have caused the death of about 80% of the country's livestock; in addition, the drought caused extremely poor harvests in the region bordering on the Senegal River, thus necessitating sharply increased imports of foodstuffs. See Alfred Gerteiny, *Mauritania: A Survey of a New African Nation* (1967); R. N. Westebbe, *The Economy of Mauritania* (1971).

Mauritius (môrĭsh'ēəs, –əs), island country (1970 est. pop. 811,000), 790 sq mi (2,046 sq km), in the SW Indian Ocean, part of the Mascarene Island group, c.500 mi (800 km) E of the Malagasy Republic. The island of RODRIGUEZ and two groups of small islands, Agalega and Cargados Carajos, are dependencies of Mauritius. The capital is PORT LOUIS (1969 est. pop. 138,150). Mauritius is surrounded by coral reefs. A central plateau is ringed by mountains of volcanic origin which rise to c.2,700 ft (820 m) in the southwest. The island has a tropical rainy climate. Mauritius was originally uninhabited; today three fifths of the population are of Indian descent and two fifths are either Creole (mixed French and African) or of French descent. There is a Chinese community of about 25,000. More than half the population is Hindu, about 30% are Christian, and about 14% are Muslim. Overpopulation—a result of the eradication of malaria in the 1960s—is a serious problem. French and English are the official languages. Sugarcane is the chief crop raised and sugar and molasses are the major exports; tea and food crop production have been encouraged to diversify the economy and reduce the need to import food. The fishing industry is of some importance. Mauritius was probably visited by Arabs and Malays in the Middle Ages. Portuguese sailors visited it in the 16th cent. The island was occupied by the Dutch from 1598 to 1710 and named after Prince Maurice of Nassau. The French settled the island in 1722 and called it Île de France. It became an important way station on the route to India. The French introduced the cultivation of sugarcane and imported large numbers of African slaves to work the plantations. The British captured the island in 1810 and restored the Dutch name. After the abolition of slavery in the British Empire in 1833, indentured laborers were brought from India; their descendents constitute a majority of the population today. Politics on Mauritius was long the preserve of the French and the Creoles, but the extension of the franchise under the 1947 constitution gave the Indians political power. Indian leaders in the 1950s and 1960s favored independence, while the French and Creoles wanted continuing association with Britain, fearing domination by the Hindu Indian majority. The 1967 election gave a majority in the assembly to Sir Seewoosagur Ramgoolam's Independence party. Independence was granted in 1968, and Ramgoolam became the first prime minister. Mauritius joined the Commonwealth of Nations and the United Nations. Clashes among the island's ethnic groups have frequently resulted in bloodshed. High unemployment has been a serious problem. In the 1960s a multiracial militant left-wing party became active. See Burton Benedict, *Mauritius: Problems of a Plural Society* (1965); J. E. Meade, *The Economic and Social Structure of Mauritius* (1968).

Maurocordatos, Alexander: see MAVROKORDATOS.

Maurois, André (äNdrā′ mōrwä′), 1885–1967, French biographer, novelist, and essayist. His name was originally Émile Herzog. His first work, *The Silence of Colonel Bramble* (1918, tr. 1920), describing British military life, was highly successful. *Ariel* (1923, tr. 1924), a life of Shelley, was followed by lives of Byron, Disraeli, Chateaubriand, Washington, George Sand, Victor Hugo, and others. Other works include *A History of England* (1937, tr. rev. ed., 1958), *Tragedy in France* (1940, tr. 1940), *From My Journal* (1946, tr. 1948), and *Proust* (1949, tr. 1950). Maurois wrote discerningly on the art of biography as well as on writing and on living. See his memoirs (2 vol., tr. 1942 and 1970).

Maury, Jean Siffrein (zhäN sēfrăN′ môrē′), 1746–1817, French churchman, cardinal of the Roman Catholic Church. A court preacher and writer before the French Revolution, he was known in the Constituent Assembly as a defender of the nobility and clergy. He fled (1791) France, passed some years (1792–98) in Rome, and was made cardinal in 1794. Leaving (1799) Italy after the French occupation, he spent some time in Russia. After his return (1804) to France, he was made archbishop of Paris in 1810 and refused to surrender this office when commanded to do so by the pope. After the fall of Napoleon he again fled (1814) to Rome, where he was imprisoned for a time.

Maury, Matthew Fontaine (fŏntān′ môr′ē), 1806–73, American hydrographer and naval officer, b. near Fredericksburg, Va. Appointed a midshipman in 1825, he saw varied sea duty until a stagecoach accident (1839) made him permanently lame. In 1842 he was placed in charge of the Depot of Charts and Instruments (later the U.S. Naval Observatory and Hydrographical Office). Soon his wind and current charts of the Atlantic began to appear, and they eventually cut sailing time on many routes. He wrote widely on navigation and naval reform, and his *Physical Geography of the Sea* (1855) was the first classic work of modern oceanography. With the outbreak of the Civil War, he resigned and served the Confederacy, first in harbor defense and then as an agent in England. After the war he served (1865–66) under Maximilian in Mexico, where he attempted to establish colonies of ex-Confederates. He returned to the United States in 1868 and was professor of meteorology at the Virginia Military Institute until his death. See biographies by F. L. Williams (1966), C. L. Lewis (1927, repr. 1969), and V. P. Parriott (1973).

Maurya (mou′ərya), ancient Indian dynasty, c.325–c.183 B.C., founded by CHANDRAGUPTA (Chandragupta Maurya). He conquered the Magadha kingdom and established his capital at Pataliputra (now Patna). After defeating (c.305) Seleucus Nicator, he extended his empire west into Afghanistan; on the east it was bounded by the Bay of Bengal and on the south by the Narbada River. His son, Bindusara (d. c.273), probably conquered the Deccan, and his grandson, ASOKA, the most notable ruler of ancient India, for the first time in history brought nearly all India, together with Afghanistan, under one rule. Asoka made Buddhism the state religion of India. The culture of the Mauryan empire, although it shows the influences of Persia and Greece, represents the first great flowering of native Indian civilization, not to be equalled until the coming of the Gupta dynasty. See D. R. Bhandarkar, *Asoka* (4th ed. 1969); Lallanji Gopal, *Chandragupta Maurya* (tr. 1969).

mausoleum (môsəlē′əm), a sepulchral structure or TOMB, especially one of some size and architectural pretension, so called from the sepulcher of that name at Halicarnassus, Asia Minor, erected (c.352 B.C.) in memory of MAUSOLUS of Caria. It was a magnificent white marble structure, one of the seven wonders of the ancient world. Presumably in the form of an Ionic peristyle set on a lofty and massive base that contained the sarcophagus, it was surmounted by a stepped pyramid, on whose truncated apex was a marble quadriga, or four-horse chariot. It was richly decorated with sculpture, including works of Scopas and, quite probably, of Praxiteles. The building itself was demolished for the purpose of reusing the material, but some of the sculpture was recovered (1846) for the British Museum. A notable Roman mausoleum (135–39) is that of Hadrian in Rome. It was originally a great circular drum sheathed in marble and perhaps covered by a conical stepped roof of masonry; its form, however, has been changed beyond recognition. It is now called CASTEL SANT' ANGELO. Under the Mogul emperors of India was built a remarkable series of domed mausoleums, many of them used as pleasure pavilions during the owner's lifetime. The most celebrated mausoleum, built by Shah Jehan at Agra, is known as the TAJ MAHAL. Notable mausoleums of modern times are those of Napoleon under the Dôme des Invalides, Paris; of Gen. U. S. Grant on Riverside Drive, New York City; and of Lenin in Red Square, Moscow. In the United States the term *mausoleum* is used loosely to describe any sepulchral building above the surface of the ground.

Mausolus (môsō′ləs), d. 353 B.C., Persian satrap, ruler over Caria (c.376–353 B.C.). He was always more or less independent. One of the satraps who revolted against ARTAXERXES II, he later allied himself with the Persian kings. He extended his power greatly, even to hegemony over Rhodes. After his death his wife, Artemisia, erected at Halicarnassus a tomb that he had planned, called the MAUSOLEUM.

Mavrokordatos or **Mavrocordatos, Alexander** (both: mäv″rôkôr-thä″tôs), 1791–1865, Greek statesman. A leading patriot of modern Greece, he took an active part in the Greek revolt (1821) against Turkey and wrote the Greek declaration of independence. He was (1822) president of the first national assembly and commander of the army. Mavrokordatos was appointed (1832) minister of finance by King Otto I, held numerous ambassadorial posts, and served several times as premier (1833–34, 1841, 1843–44, and 1854–55). Associated with the pro-English party, he opposed Russian influence in Greece.

Mawenzi, peak, Africa: see KILIMANJARO.

Mawson, Sir Douglas, 1882–1958, Australian antarctic explorer and geologist, b. England. His first geographical expedition was to the New Hebrides Islands as a geologist in 1903. As a member of the scientific staff of Sir Ernest Shackleton's south polar expedition (1907–9), Mawson took part in the famous ascent of Mt. Erebus and the journey to the south magnetic pole. From 1911 to 1914 he commanded the Australian antarctic expedition; he studied the antarctic coast W of Cape Adare, spent two winters in Adélie Land (now Adélie Coast), and discovered King George V Land (now George V Coast), while a subordinate party discovered and explored Queen Mary Land (now Queen Mary Coast). On this trip Mawson's two companions died, and he was barely able to save himself. His *Home of the Blizzard* (1915) describes these explorations. In 1920 he became professor of geology and mineralogy at the Univ. of Adelaide. As commander of the British, Australian, and New Zealand antarctic expedition (1929–30), he revisited Enderby Land, not seen since its reported discovery a century earlier, and discovered MacRobertson Coast. Using a seaplane in conjunction with his ship, he made many short flights; in the course of this expedition, Mawson charted over 1,000 mi (1,600 km) of previously unknown antarctic coast and recharted c.1,500 mi (2,400 km) of vaguely known coasts. In his three trips between 1907 and 1931, Mawson claimed 2,225,000 sq mi (5,762,750 sq km) of antarctic territory for Australia. In recognition of his accomplishments he received the King's Polar Medal. He wrote many scientific papers.

Max, Gabriel (gä′brēēl mäks), 1840–1915, German painter and illustrator, b. Prague; son and pupil of the sculptor Josef Max (1803–54). A student of psychology and anthropology, Gabriel Max is best known as a painter of mystical subjects. Characteristic of his ethereal style is *The Last Token* (Metropolitan Mus.).

Max, Peter, 1937–, American artist, b. Berlin. Max is noted for his undulating graphic designs in bright, vibrating colors. His style has influenced much commercial art. It is reminiscent of ART NOUVEAU and comic strip art, incorporating psychedelic colors in floral and celestial motifs.

Maxentius (Marcus Aurelius Valerius Maxentius) (măksĕn′shəs), d. 312, Roman emperor (306–12), son of MAXIMIAN. After Diocletian and Maximian had retired, the successor to Maximian, Constantius, died. The Romans, discontented with the shift of power away from Rome, supported Maxentius, who claimed the throne. His father came out of retirement to help him when SEVERUS (d. 307) and GALERIUS came to force him to submission. Severus was compelled to surrender, and Galerius had to withdraw from Italy, while a fourth seeker for power, Constantine (CONSTANTINE I) was persuaded to recognize Maxentius. Maxentius and his father fell out, however, and Constantine turned against Maxentius, whom he defeated (312) in the battle of Milvian Bridge.

Maxim, name of a family of inventors and munition makers. **Sir Hiram Stevens Maxim,** 1840–1916, was born near Sangerville, Maine. After launching on a career of inventing, he moved to England and there invented (1884) the Maxim machine gun. Among his numerous other inventions were a smokeless powder, a delayed-action fuse, and an airplane. His arms company was consolidated (1896) with the Vickers firm. He became a British subject in 1900 and was knighted in 1901. His brother, **Hudson Maxim,** 1853–1927, was born in Orneville, Maine, and remained in the United States. A chemist, he developed numerous inventions, including a high explosive (maximite), smokeless powders (one of them stabilite), and a self-combustive compound to propel torpedoes (motorite). **Hiram Percy Maxim,** 1869–1936, son of Sir Hiram, was born in Brooklyn, N.Y., and remained in the United States. After graduation from the Massachusetts Institute of Technology, he held many positions as a mechanical engineer and created several inventions, among them an automobile. The most spectacular was the Maxim silencer for explosive weapons (1908), but perhaps more useful were silencers for gasoline engines and the like.

Maximian (Marcus Aurelius Valerius Maximianus) (măksĭm′ēən), d. 310, Roman emperor, with DIOCLETIAN (286–305). An able commander, he was made Caesar (subemperor) by Diocletian in 285 and Augustus in 286. He was in general charge of the empire in the West but failed to put down the revolt of Carausius. Two new Caesars, GALERIUS and CONSTANTIUS I, were created in 293, and Constantius was successful against Carausius. Maximian abdicated with Diocletian in 305, but the death of Constantius in 306 brought confusion to the political scene—there was a struggle for power among SEVERUS (d.307), Galerius, Constantine (CONSTANTINE I, son of Constantius), and MAXENTIUS (son of Maximian). Maximian plunged into the conflict, at first to aid his son in Italy; he captured Severus, repulsed Galerius, and won over Constantine, to whom he gave his daughter Fausta in marriage. Then Maximian and Maxentius became enemies, and, having failed to depose his son, Maximian fled to Constantine and abdicated again (308). He could not, however, rest content but revolted against Constantine. In 310 he was forced to commit suicide.

Maximilian I, 1459–1519, Holy Roman emperor and German king (1493–1519), son and successor of Holy Roman Emperor Frederick III. In 1486 he was elected king of the Romans (i.e., emperor-elect) and assumed an increasing share of the imperial duties until his father's death. As emperor, he aspired to restore forceful imperial leadership and inaugurate much-needed administrative reforms in the increasingly decentralized empire. In both domestic and foreign policy, however, he sacrificed the interests of Germany as a whole to the aggrandizement of Hapsburg possessions. Maximilian's marriage (1477) to MARY OF BURGUNDY involved him in defense of her inheritance—including Burgundy, the Netherland provinces, and Luxembourg—against the designs of King Louis XI of France. By Mary's death (1482), Maximilian had secured Franche-Comté, the county of Artois, and the Low Countries, but he yielded a sizable part of French-speaking Burgundy in the Treaty of Arras of 1483 (see ARRAS, TREATY OF). Louis XI's successor, CHARLES VIII, repudiated the treaty; moreover, instead of marrying Maximilian's daughter MARGARET OF AUSTRIA, he forced ANNE OF BRITTANY into marrying him (1491), disregarding her marriage by proxy to the widowed Maximilian the preceding year. Renewed warfare with France was settled temporarily by the Treaty of Senlis (1493), which basically retained the status quo; but the Burgundian question remained a key issue in Hapsburg relations with the French crown. Maximilian became embroiled in the ITALIAN WARS in order to regain the rest of the Burgundian inheritance and also to expand Hapsburg dominions and check any extension of French power. His Italian campaigns also afforded him an opportunity to aid Ludovico Sforza, whose niece he had married (1493) and whom, in exchange for a dowry, he had invested with the duchy of Milan (also claimed by Louis XII of France). His involvement in Italy led him to join the League of Cambrai (see CAMBRAI, LEAGUE OF) and later the HOLY LEAGUE. Both alliances cost him money, of which he was chronically short, and forced him to borrow heavily from the FUGGER family. Moreover, his interference in Italy encouraged the French to exert pressure on the Swiss to turn a jurisdictional dispute with imperial authorities into an open war (1499), which resulted in an imperial defeat. Despite these difficulties, Maximilian made the Hapsburgs into a powerful dynasty through his astute marriage diplomacy. The marriage of his son Philip (see PHILIP I of Castile) to Joanna, the heiress of Ferdinand

and Isabella, eventually gave his grandson, the future Holy Roman Emperor Charles V, one of the largest territorial inheritances in history. The double marriage of Maximilian's grandson and granddaughter to the daughter and son of King ULADISLAUS II of Hungary (1516) ultimately assured Hapsburg succession to the Hungarian and Bohemian thrones and ascendancy in central Europe. The very extent and diversity of the Hapsburg territories were a detriment as well as an asset, making the imperial title the essential bond of unity. At the beginning of his reign Maximilian attempted to modernize the cumbersome imperial administration, but his reform program fell victim not only to his dynastic aspirations but also to the competition between the princes and the emperor for ultimate power. Maximilian was forced in 1500 to adhere temporarily to a council of regency (see REICHSREGIMENT), although he eventually dispensed with this restriction. Nevertheless the Diet of Worms (1495) established a supreme court of justice to adjudicate disputes among princes and to apply Roman law throughout the empire; levied a general property tax to defray military costs; and issued a ban on private warfare. The limited constitutional reforms proved inadequate, however, to cope with future problems, least of all with the political, social, and religious upheaval of the REFORMATION. See biography by R. W. Seton-Watson (1902); G. E. Waas, *The Legendary Character of Kaiser Maximilian* (1941, repr. 1966).

Maximilian II, 1527-76, Holy Roman emperor (1564-76), king of Bohemia (1562-76) and of Hungary (1563-76), son and successor of Holy Roman Emperor Ferdinand I. Before acceding he evidenced a sympathy for Lutheranism that caused grave concern in imperial and papal circles and led Holy Roman Emperor Charles V to urge that his son King Philip II of Spain succeed Ferdinand. However, Maximilian yielded and in 1562 swore to remain a Catholic and to allow his immediate heirs to be educated in Spain. He thereupon was elected king of the Romans, or Holy Roman emperor-elect (1562), and king of Hungary (1563). On Ferdinand's death (1564) he took full direction of imperial affairs. He obtained funds from the diet for the defense of Austria against the Turks but did not press his advantage, and by the truce of 1568 with Selim II he agreed to continue paying tribute to the sultan for his part of Hungary. Maximilian granted a large degree of religious toleration in his Bohemian and Austrian possessions. His policy of neutrality, however, also allowed the Catholic Reformation to make considerable gains in some parts of the empire. A candidate for the throne of Poland to succeed Henry of Anjou (HENRY III of France), he was elected (1575) by the Polish diet as rival king to STEPHEN BÁTHORY. Maximilian died, refusing the sacraments, while preparing to invade Poland. His son Rudolf II succeeded him.

Maximilian, 1832-67, emperor of Mexico (1864-67). As the Austrian archduke Ferdinand Maximilian, he was denied a share in the imperial government by his reactionary brother, Emperor Francis Joseph. Maximilian served as commander in chief of the Austrian fleet and was governor general of Lombardo-Venetia (1857-59), but he found no outlet for his dreams of liberal reform. When Mexican conservatives negotiated with Napoleon III to found a Mexican empire, Maximilian was persuaded to accept the crown. He and his wife, CARLOTTA, left their palace near Trieste and sailed (1864) to Mexico. The empire was a failure from the start. Maximilian, who had no real understanding of Mexico, found most of the country hostile to him and loyal to Benito JUÁREZ. He alienated the conservatives by his liberal tendencies and others of his supporters by his decree (1865) ordering the summary execution of all followers of Juárez. Indeed, Maximilian's tenure rested solely on French soldiers, who drove Juárez and his liberal army to the north. The European monarchs, except Napoleon III, were lukewarm. The United States, irked by this violation of the MONROE DOCTRINE, was frankly hostile and was prevented from interfering only by the American Civil War. When affairs in France and the cessation of the Civil War impelled Napoleon III to withdraw (1866-67) the French troops from Mexico, the flimsy fabric of the empire dissolved. For a time Maximilian considered abdication, but he was irresolute. In 1866, Empress Carlotta went to Europe and vainly sought aid from Napoleon III and the pope. Maximilian, in desperation, assumed personal command of his forces, then mostly concentrated at Querétaro. There, after a siege (March-May, 1867), he was captured and shot. He wrote *Aus meinem Leben* (1865, tr. *Recollections of My Life,* 1868). See John Musser, *The Establishment of Maximilian's Empire in Mexico* (1918); Egon Corti, *Maximilian and Charlotte of Mexico* (1928, repr. 1968); *Maximilian, Emperor of Mexico: Memoirs of His Private Secretary, José Luis Blasio* (tr. and ed. by R. H. Murray, 1934).

Maximilian I, 1756-1825, king (1806-25) and elector (1799-1806) of Bavaria as Maximilian IV Joseph. His alliance with French Emperor Napoleon I earned him the royal title and vast territorial increases at the Treaty of PRESSBURG (1805) and made him one of the chief members of the CONFEDERATION OF THE RHINE. His daughter was married to Napoleon's stepson, Eugène de Beauharnais. In 1813, after Napoleon's retreat from Russia, he joined the coalition against Napoleon a few days before the battle of Leipzig. At the Congress of Vienna (1814-15) Maximilian lost some of his territorial gains. Devoted to Bavarian independence, he opposed all moves to unite Germany. With his minister, Maximilian von Montgelas, he carried out important social reforms and abolished most of the relics of feudalism in Bavaria. In 1818 he granted a liberal constitution and, unlike the neighboring reactionary rulers, he continued to rule as an "enlightened monarch." He was succeeded by his son, Louis I.

Maximilian II, 1811-64, king of Bavaria (1848-64), son and successor of LOUIS I. He had strong liberal tendencies and was a patron of art and learning. He hoped to create a union of small German states under Bavarian leadership as a counterweight to Austrian and Prussian influence in German affairs, but he was unable to do so. His son, Louis II, succeeded him.

Maximilian I, 1573-1651, elector (1623-51) and duke (1597-1651) of Bavaria, one of the outstanding figures of the THIRTY YEARS WAR and an ardent supporter of the Catholic Reformation. His occupation (1607) of Donauwörth, a Protestant stronghold then under the imperial ban, aroused Protestant indignation and spurred the formation (1608) of the Protestant Union. To oppose this, Maximilian founded (1609) the Catholic League. Until 1619 he tried to maintain a moderate course in the great quarrel within the empire. Then, in return for concessions, he brought the army of the League to the support of Holy Roman Emperor FERDINAND II against FREDERICK THE WINTER KING. Frederick, who was elector of the Palatinate, headed the Protestant Union; he had been elected king of Bohemia to replace Ferdinand. In 1620, Maximilian entered Upper Austria and, after the victory of the commander of the Catholic League, TILLY, at the White Mt., entered Prague. Maximilian then conquered the Palatinate, and in 1623 the emperor transferred Frederick's electoral vote and the Upper Palatinate to Maximilian. In 1628, Maximilian was given the Rhenish Palatinate in return for Upper Austria, which he had been holding. Maximilian protested against the ascendancy of the imperial commander Albrecht von WALLENSTEIN and secured his dismissal (1630). Later in the war, Bavaria was ravaged by Swedish and French forces, and Maximilian was forced to conclude the truce of Ulm and to renounce his alliance with the emperor; however, he soon broke the truce. By the Peace of Westphalia (1648), Maximilian retained the electorate and the Upper Palatinate.

Maximilian, prince of Baden (Max of Baden), 1867-1929, German statesman, last chancellor of imperial Germany. A liberal, he was made imperial chancellor at the end of World War I as Germany neared defeat. He formed a coalition cabinet that included members of the Center, Progressive, and Socialist parties, the three major parties in the Reichstag. At the recommendation of the supreme command, he began to negotiate for an armistice with the Allies. In late Oct., 1918, mutiny broke out among the sailors at Kiel. It spread and soon erupted into revolution. Prince Max hoped to save the monarchy by forcing Emperor William II to abdicate. William refused, but Max nevertheless announced his abdication (Nov. 9). Several hours later he surrendered the government to the Socialist leader Friedrich EBERT.

Maximin (Caius Julius Verus Maximinus) (măk'sĭmĭn), d. 238, Roman emperor (235-38). A rough Thracian soldier of great physical strength, he rose in the army, and when the soldiers revolted against ALEXANDER SEVERUS, they proclaimed Maximin emperor at Mainz. He established order among the troops and conducted (235-38) highly successful campaigns against the Germans. In 238 there was a rebellion in Africa, and Gordian (Gordian I) was named emperor by the landowners. Maximin marched on Italy and advanced on Aquileia. In the siege he was assassinated by the soldiers.

Maximin (Galerius Valerius Maximinus), d. 313, Roman emperor (308-13); kinsman of Galerius. He is called Maximin Daia. He was made Caesar in 305 and in 308 proclaimed himself Augustus in opposition to Emperor LICINIUS. After the death of Galerius (310), Maximin exercised considerable power. He persecuted the Christians and tried to revive paganism. He later allied himself with MAXENTIUS against Licinius and Constantine (CONSTANTINE I); Maxentius was crushed by Constantine, and Maximin was defeated by Licinius. A last-minute effort to win the Christians by an edict of toleration did not help him. He died a fugitive.

Maximus, Saint, c.580-662, Greek theologian. He was secretary to Emperor HERACLIUS and subsequently abbot at the monastery of Chrysopolis. To curb MONOTHELETISM he went to Rome and persuaded Pope St. MARTIN I to convene the synod of 649, which denounced as heretical the *Typus* of Emperor Constans. Back at Constantinople, Maximus demanded that the decrees of the synod be accepted. He was imprisoned (653-62) by imperial order, mutilated, then exiled. He is important in the history of Byzantine mysticism. St. Maximus leaned much upon the Pseudo-Dionysius (see DIONYSIUS THE AREOPAGITE, SAINT). St. Maximus' works influenced Erigena, who translated them into Latin. Feast: Aug. 13.

Maximus, Magnus Clemens, d. 388, Roman emperor of the West (383-88). After his followers murdered GRATIAN, he was recognized as ruler of Britain, Gaul, and Spain by THEODOSIUS I. He invaded Italy in 387, expelling VALENTINIAN II, but the following year he was defeated and put to death by Theodosius. In the reign of Maximus the heresy of PRISCILLIAN was suppressed.

Max of Baden: see MAXIMILLIAN, PRINCE OF BADEN.

Maxwell, James Clerk (klärk), 1831-79, great Scottish physicist. After a brilliant career at Edinburgh and Cambridge, where he won early recognition with mathematical papers, he was professor at Marischal College, Aberdeen (1856-60), and at King's College, London (1860-65). In 1871 he was appointed first professor of experimental physics at Cambridge, where he directed the organization of the Cavendish Laboratory. He is known especially for his work in electricity and magnetism, summarized in *A Treatise on Electricity and Magnetism* (1873). Basing his own study and research on that of Faraday, he developed the theory of the electromagnetic field on a mathematical basis and made possible a much greater understanding of the phenomena in this field. He was led to the conclusion that electric and magnetic energy travel in transverse waves that propagate at a speed equal to that of light; light is thus only one type of ELECTROMAGNETIC RADIATION. Maxwell's electromagnetic theory occupies a position in classical physics comparable to Newton's work on mechanics. One of his early papers, "On the Stability of Motion of Saturn's Rings" (1859), was especially important and foreshadowed his later investigations of heat and the kinetic theory of gases. He is also known for his studies of color (which led to his invention of the color disk named for him), and color blindness. In addition to his papers in these fields, he wrote a classic elementary text in dynamics, *Matter and Motion* (1876).

May, Philip William (Phil May), 1864-1903, English pen-and-ink caricaturist, b. Leeds. After living in poverty for many years, he made numerous drawings for the *St. Stephen's Review. Phil May's Winter Annual,* which began in 1892, was followed by collections of his sketches in albums such as *Phil May's Gutter-Snipes* (1896). During his last years he worked exclusively for *Punch* and the *Graphic.* May's work is distinguished for its economy of line, its brilliant characterization and gentle, kindly humor. Most of his types are taken from the stage, sporting events, and London street life. See biography by James Thorpe (1949).

May, Thomas, 1595-1650, English author, b. Sussex, grad. Cambridge, 1612. Besides writing several tragedies on classical subjects, he wrote two comedies, *The Heir* (1620) and *The Old Couple* (c.1620). He made translations of Lucan's *Pharsalia* (1626-27) and Vergil's *Georgics* (1628) and wrote two historical poems on the reigns of Henry II (1633) and Edward III (1635). An ardent Puritan, he was secretary to the Long Parliament and wrote an objective *History of the Parliament of England* (1650).

May, Thomas Erskine, 1st **Baron Farnborough,** 1815-86, English constitutional jurist and historian. A period of long service to Parliament, including his tenure (1871-86) as clerk of the House of Commons, led to his great *Treatise upon the Law, Privileges, Proceedings, and Usage of Parliament* (1844).

May: see MONTH.

may, name for several plants; in England, particularly the HAWTHORN. See also MAYFLOWER.

May, Cape: see CAPE MAY.

Maya (mī'ə, Span. mä'yä), Central American Indians ethnically and linguistically related, occupying an area comprising the Yucatán peninsula and the highland crescent of E Chiapas in Mexico, much of Guatemala, and extreme W Honduras. The Mayan languages are spoken in this area and in the PÁNUCO basin. The contemporary Maya population is about 2 million. They have maintained many aspects of their ancient culture while changing under the influence of Spanish-American cultures. Many inscriptions written in a hieroglyphic exist in Maya ruins. The system, which contains about 850 characters, is almost entirely undeciphered. Attempts to understand the script have been made through the study of the standard Maya language written in documents under Spanish influence and of modern Maya (see AMERICAN INDIAN LANGUAGES). Archaeologists have assembled masses of evidence about the Maya, but their early history is still obscure. One theory holds that they were an offshoot of the OLMEC culture, another that the civilization originated c.1000 B.C. among nomadic tribes in N central PETÉN. Located there are the ruins of TIKAL and Uaxactún, early examples of the flourishing culture of a sedentary, agricultural people well advanced in art and science. Generally, scholars agree on three major epochs of Maya history—Pre-Classic (1500 B.C.?–A.D. 300), Classic (300–900), and Post-Classic (900–1697). Pre-Classic is divided into I, II, and III. Material remains from I and II are rare, but during this time the cultivation of maize was practiced. In Pre-Classic III came the invention of the Maya calendar, the development of chronology and hieroglyphic writing, and the first major works of stone architecture. Both the Classic and Post-Classic eras likewise are broken into periods. In the Early Classic (300–600) archaism vanished from sculpture and epigraphy, and Maya culture spread over the entire area. Territorial and cultural consolidation took place, leading to the greatest developments in arts and sciences of the Maya in the Late Classic (600–900) at COPÁN, Quiriguá, PALENQUE, PIEDRAS NEGRAS, UXMAL, and Tikal. These centers of culture were all abandoned within a century; the reasons are uncertain, although several hypotheses have been suggested, ranging from soil exhaustion to peasant revolts against the rulers. Two migrations probably occurred; they have been named the Lesser Descent and the Great Descent (ended 889). The latter migration took the Maya N through E Yucatán. The Lesser Descent resulted in the founding of several cities, one of them CHICHÉN ITZÁ. The Great Descent took them farther west. The Post-Classic period, thus begun, falls into two periods—Early (900–1200) and Late (1200–1697). A Mexican migration or invasion begun under Kukulcán (see QUETZALCOATL) strongly influenced the culture of the Maya by introducing TOLTEC elements. Kukulcán, probably in league with the reigning Itzá, gained control of Chichén Itzá. Toltec influence, dominant for a time, disappeared from the area c.1200, the Mexicans probably being absorbed by the more numerous Maya. Chichén Itzá, still in the hands of the Itzá, remained a prominent center. Around 1200 a group of Itzá migrated westward from Chichén Itzá and founded Mayapán, which developed rapidly, becoming the civil capital under the Cocom lineage of Itzá by 1283. A new group, the Xiu, appeared and, after reoccupation of Uxmal, centered themselves at Mayapán in alliance with the Cocoms. Probably to secure the new rulers' control, a loose confederation of the three cities, called the league of Mayapán, was formed, and a long period of stability ensued. Civil war finally broke out, and Chichén Itzá was destroyed by Mayapán. The federation was ended, and the ITZÁ had to abandon their city. The victorious Cocom maintained a tyrannical ascendancy until the Xiu revolted (1441), destroying Mayapán and the last vestige of central authority. The cities were abandoned. The Xiu founded a new center, Mani. Subsequent Maya history was dominated by civil wars, a series of calamities, and the Spanish Conquest under the elder and younger Francisco de MONTEJO. The governmental and probably the ecclesiastical organization of the Maya was headed by a hereditary chieftain, who appointed lesser chieftains to govern dependent villages. All ranking officials probably constituted, with the priesthood, a hereditary nobility. The leading priest was second only to the chieftain. He and his hierarchy were not only able administrators but also outstanding scholars, astronomers, and mathematicians. Below them came the vast majority of common people (laborers and artisans) and then the slaves (war prisoners and criminals). Religious practices in the Classic epoch were stately and well organized, and they probably involved little human sacrifice, but with the Post-Classic and Mexican influence human sacrifice and complex idol worship were introduced. The chief gods were Hunab Ku and his son, ITZAMNA. Since the religion of the Maya was dualistic, there was also a chief malevolent deity, Ah Puch, god of death, presiding over hell. Other important deities were the god of corn and Chac, god of rain. The number of gods later grew considerably. The Spanish destroyed the worship of all except the lesser gods of nature and fertility; the rites for these idols were to a large extent incorporated by the common people into Christian practices. The Maya, recording not deeds of human glorification but chronology, astronomy, and religion, were the only people in the Americas to develop an original system of writing (ideographic), which was probably borrowed by other Mexican Indians. The most important of the Spanish documents giving information on the language is Bishop Diego de Landa's *Relación de las cosas de Yucatán* (1566; tr. by A. M. Tozzer, 1941). He had destroyed all but three perishable records, the Dresden Codex, the Tro-Cortesianus Codex, and the Peresianus Codex. The paperlike codices were made from the pounded bark of the wild fig tree (*copó*), folded in strips and fastened with natural gum. Shortly after the Spanish conquest some of the natives, educated to write their language in Spanish script, recorded much of their history and life in the *Books of Chilam Balam* (tr. 1945) and the POPOL VUH (tr. 1950). There were two Mayan calendars—a 365-day year (*haab*), recurring in 52-year cycles, and a sacred or ceremonial year (*tzolkin*) of 260 days grouped into 13 months of 20 days each. The corrected calendar year of 18 months of 20 days and one month of 5 days approximated the astronomically determined year with even more accuracy than the Gregorian calendar. The mathematics of the Maya, developed for accurate time computation, was a magnificent abstract intellectual achievement, based on the vigesimal (base 20) rather than the decimal system but having no fractions. It was an advance in knowledge that was not equaled for many centuries in Western Europe. To record numbers the Maya used bars and dots (a bar equal to five, a dot equal to one) and had variant pictures, or glyphs, for names. Mayan architecture was displayed in ceremonial buildings grouped around plazas. The majority of the population, estimated to have been about 14,000,000 in the 8th cent., lived in suburban agricultural communities in wattle, or sometimes adobe, houses with thatched roofs. Temples (usually marked by a molding on all four sides and often by a flying facade or roof comb of stone rising from the flat roof as high again as the temple itself) were built on pyramidal substructures. The pyramid usually had a core of rubble faced with limestone and was ascended by steep stairways. Interiors, universally without windows, were small chambers roofed by a corbeled vault (the Maya had no arch), by flat slabs of lime concrete, or by wooden beams. Walls were covered with limestone plaster, and some buildings were decorated by elaborate stucco or sculpturing on wall panels, stairway ramps, and doorjambs. Post-Classic architecture, showing Toltec influence, was characterized by ornate moldings, the feathered serpent, and great open colonnades. In general, Post-Classic buildings were less massive and more graceful than those of other periods. Sculpture as an independent art reached its highest expression in the Classic epoch, when magnificent carved stone steles marking the calendric periods were erected. Usually they were painted dark red, less often blue and other colors. Sculpture, at its height between 731 and 889, declined as an independent art in the Post-Classic period but as an adjunct of architecture reached a dignity and beauty equaled nowhere else in aboriginal America. Comparing accomplishments of the Maya with those of other American Indian civilizations, the Maya emerge as undisputed masters of abstract knowledge—writing, astronomy, calendric development, chronology, the recording of history, and mathematics. Their architecture, though not as massive as that of the Inca, the Toltec, or the Aztec nor as advanced as that of the Inca in technical achievement, was outstanding in harmony of line and decorative motifs; the Maya excelled in sculpture in relief and in round. Their painting, as in codices and in wall frescoes, was superb. Their ceramics were beautiful in polychromatic design. In metalwork and in lesser arts the Maya were inferior to other great pre-Columbian civilizations. Neither in governmental nor in social organization did they quite equal the Aztec or the Inca. For an outstanding account of the first thorough exploration of Maya ruins, see J. L. Stephens, *Incidents of Travel in Central America, Chiapas, and Yucatan* (1841, repr. 1949) and *Incidents of Travel in Yucatan* (1843, repr. 1963). For the Spanish Conquest, see P. A. Means, *History of the Spanish Conquest of Yucatan* (1917); R. S. Chamberlain, *The Conquest and Colonization of Yucatan* (1949, repr. 1966). For art and architecture, see E. O. Winzerling, *Aspects of Maya Culture* (1956); Paul Rivet, *Maya Cities* (tr. 1960); Ferdinand Anton, *Art of the Maya* (1970). For the culture as a whole, see S. G. Morley, *Ancient Maya* (rev. ed. 1957); J. E. S. Thompson, *The Rise and Fall of the Maya Civilization* (rev. ed. 1966) and *Maya History and Religion* (1970); M. D. Coe, *The Maya* (1966); E. P. Benson, *The Maya World* (1967); Pierre Ivanoff, *Mayan Enigma* (1971); R. L. Brunhouse, *In Search of the Maya* (1973); T. P. Culbert, ed., *The Classic Maya Collapse* (1973).

maya (mä'yä), in Hinduism, term used in the VEDA to mean magic or supernatural power. In Mahayana Buddhism it acquires the meaning of illusion or unreality. The term is pivotal in the VEDANTA system of Shankara, where it signifies the world as a cosmic illusion and also the power that creates the world.

Mayaguana: see BAHAMA ISLANDS.

Mayagüez (mīägwās', mīäwās'), city (1970 pop. 68,872), W Puerto Rico, on Mona Passage. It is a port of entry as well as a shipping and manufacturing center in an area where sugarcane, coffee, tobacco, and livestock are raised. Sugar, tropical fruits, coffee, and needlework are exported. Mayagüez has long been known for embroidery. The city, founded c.1760, is also a communications and cultural center. It has colleges of liberal arts, agriculture, and mechanics, a center for nuclear studies, and a U.S. government agricultural research station.

Mayakovsky, Vladimir Vladimirovich (vlədyē'mĭr vlədyē'mĭrəvĭch mī''əkôf'skē), 1893–1930, Russian poet and dramatist. Mayakovsky was a leader of the futurist school in 1912, and he was chief poet of the revolution. His lyrics are highly original in rhythm, rhyme, and imagery. *The Cloud in Trousers* (1915), a poem written almost entirely in metaphors, describes the agony of unrequited love. After the revolution he devoted almost all his energies to propaganda verse. His early play, *Mystery Bouffe* (1918, tr. 1933), is an allegory prophesying the victory of the revolution. His later plays, such as the satires *The Bedbug* (1928, tr. 1960) and *The Bathhouse* (1929), were more critical of the new order. Mayakovsky grew increasingly disillusioned with Soviet life and committed suicide in 1930. His *Complete Plays* were published in English in 1971. See biography by Wiktor Woroszylski (tr. 1971); study by E. J. Brown (1973); Viktor Shklovsky, *Mayakovsky and his Circle* (tr. 1972).

May apple: see BARBERRY.

Maybeck, Bernard, 1862–1957, American architect, b. New York City. After studying at the École des Beaux-Arts, Paris, he became one of the leading architects in California. From the 1890s to the 1920s, Maybeck created warm and intimate houses of redwood and shingles. His mastery of larger spaces was apparent in Hearst Hall (1899; destroyed by fire 1922) at the Univ. of California, Berkeley, a building in which he introduced the laminated wooden arch. In his masterpiece, the Christian Science church in Berkeley (1910), he unified elements from many styles, using a wide range of materials—industrial steel sash, cement asbestos panels, and exposed concrete. For the San Francisco Exposition of 1915 he designed the Palace of Fine Arts. See Esther McCoy, *Five California Architects* (1960).

May beetle: see JUNE BEETLE.

May Day, first day of May. Its celebration probably originated in the spring fertility festivals of India and Egypt. The festival of the Roman goddess of spring, Flora, was celebrated from April 28 to May 3. In medieval England the chief feature of the celebration of May Day was the Maypole; this was decorated with flowers and streamers, the loose ends of which were held by dancers, who encircled the pole, weaving intricate patterns as they passed each other in the dance. These dances are still performed for exhibition purposes in England and the United States. The Second Socialist International in 1889 designated May Day as the holiday for radical labor, and since that time it has been the occasion for demonstrations, parades, and speeches among

Socialists and Communists. It is a very important holiday in the USSR.

Mayence: see MAINZ, West Germany.

Mayenne, Charles de Lorraine, duc de (shärl də lôrĕn' dük də mäyĕn'), 1554–1611, French Catholic general in the Wars of Religion (see RELIGION, WARS OF); brother of Henri, 3d duc de GUISE, and Louis de Lorraine, Cardinal de Guise. After the murder of his brothers (1588), he became the head of the Catholic LEAGUE. Defeated by King Henry IV of France at Arques (1589) and Ivry (1590), he nevertheless raised Henry's siege of Paris (1590). For a time he wielded almost royal power over the parts of France that supported the League. He became estranged from the pro-Spanish faction, which supported the claim to the French crown of the Spanish infanta Isabella, a granddaughter of King Henry II of France. In 1596, Mayenne made his final peace with Henry IV, who had previously abjured Protestantism.

Mayenne, department (1968 pop. 252,762), NW France, in parts of MAINE and ANJOU. It is an agricultural region. LAVAL is the capital.

Mayer, Johan Tobias (yō'hän tōbē'äs mī'ər), 1723–62, German mathematician and astronomer. In 1751 he became professor of economics and mathematics at the Univ. of Göttingen, and in 1754 director of the observatory there. He is especially noted for his lunar tables (1752), which were important in precisely determining longitude at sea. Mayer is remembered also for his improvements in mapmaking and for the invention of the repeating circle, later used in measuring the arc of the meridian. A collection of his memoirs was published in 1775; a revision of his catalog of 998 zodiacal stars, newly computed, appeared in 1894.

Mayer, Julius Robert von, 1814–78, German physician and physicist, studied medicine at Tübingen, Munich, and Paris. From a consideration of the generation of animal heat, he was led to determine the general relationship between heat and work. This resulted in his announcement in 1842, independently of J. P. Joule, of the mechanical equivalence of heat, a consequence of the law of conservation of energy. In 1845 he gave a still more general statement of this law. Controversy arose, however, as to the priority of the discovery, and it was only years later that he received due credit for his contribution. See study by R. B. Lindsay (1973).

Mayer, Louis Burt, 1885–1957, American movie producer, b. Russia. Mayer began his career (1907) as the operator of a theater in Haverhill, Mass., and gradually gained control of all the theaters in the city. In 1924 he merged his Louis B. Mayer Corp. with Metro Pictures Corp., which he had organized, and eventually with Goldwyn Pictures Corp.; the company was called Metro-Goldwyn-Mayer. Mayer was one of the most powerful film tycoons of early Hollywood. He was known for his strict paternalistic management of his studio and stars. See biography by Bosley Crowther (1960); Bosley Crowther, *The Lion's Share* (1957).

Mayerling (mī'ərlĭng), village, Lower Austria prov., E Austria, on the Schwechat River, in the Wienerwald (Vienna Woods). It is the site of the hunting lodge (now a convent) where Crown Prince Rudolf and Baroness Maria Vetsera died mysteriously in Jan., 1889.

Mayfield, city (1970 pop. 10,724), seat of Graves co., SW Ky., in an area of farms and clay deposits; founded 1823. It is an agricultural trade center with a large tobacco market. In a plot at the local cemetery are the curious Wooldridge monuments—stone figures of an eccentric aristocrat (buried there in 1899), his family, friends, and animal pets.

Mayfield Heights, city (1970 pop. 22,139), Cuyahoga co., NE Ohio, a residential suburb of Cleveland; inc. 1925.

Mayflower, ship that in 1620 brought the PILGRIMS from England to New England. She set out from Southampton in company with the *Speedwell,* the vessel that had borne some of the English separatists from the Netherlands back to England for the momentous voyage. However, the *Speedwell* proved unseaworthy, and the ships put back to Plymouth, where the *Mayflower* took on some of the smaller ship's passengers and supplies. The *Mayflower,* under the captaincy of Christopher Jones, then set sail alone on Sept. 16. After a two-month voyage the ship sighted land (Cape Cod) on Nov. 19. Some time was spent in selecting a suitable place for the colony, and on Dec. 26 the Pilgrims landed at Plymouth. Before landing, an agreement for the temporary government of the colony by the will of the majority was drawn up in the famous MAYFLOWER COMPACT. Much effort has been spent on the identification of the *Mayflower.* It is known that she was a wineship, of 180 tons burden, and presumed that she was of a type commonly used in that period. In 1957 a British group sponsored the voyage of a replica of the original *Mayflower* from Plymouth, England, to Plymouth, Mass. The vessel was given to the United States as an expression of international goodwill and remains on exhibit at Plymouth, Mass. See studies by Warwick Charlton (1957) and Crispin Gill (1970).

mayflower, in botany, name for several spring-blooming plants. In England the HAWTHORN is called mayflower, or may; in North America the name is used for the TRAILING ARBUTUS, the HEPATICA, and an herb (*Maianthemum canadense*) of the family Liliaceae (LILY family). The latter, a common wild flower of northern forests, bears a cluster of small white blossoms and has many local names, e.g., Canada mayflower and false lily-of-the-valley. It is classified in the division MAGNOLIOPHYTA, class Liliatae, order Liliales, family Liliaceae.

Mayflower Compact, in U.S. colonial history, an agreement providing for the temporary government of Plymouth colony. The compact was signed (1620) on board the *Mayflower;* it created the first American settlement based upon a social contract. In it, the colonists combined together in a "civil Body Politick" whose purpose was to frame just and equal laws for the general good of the colony. The compact remained the basis of government in Plymouth for ten years, and all later governments in the colony developed out of the compact.

mayfly, any INSECT of the order Ephemeroptera, so named because the adults live for a short time, often only a single day, during which they molt twice, mate, and lay their eggs in fresh water. The adults are medium to large, shiny, slender insects with two pairs of fragile, transparent, many-veined wings, and two or three long threadlike tails. The long forelegs of the male are used to clasp the female during the mating flight. Mayflies, also called June bugs, shad flies, and salmon flies, emerge by the thousands from streams, ponds, and lakes at twilight in the early spring; the males form large mating swarms and when a female flies into the swarm she is seized by a male and the two depart to mate. Mayflies lack fully developed mouthparts and do not feed. The insect undergoes incomplete METAMORPHOSIS, the egg hatching directly into an aquatic naiad, or nymph, with chewing mouthparts, which passes through some 20 nymphal stages over a period of two years or more, feeding on algae and diatoms and breathing oxygen taken directly from water by gills. It emerges from the water to transform into a subadult phase known as the subimago, unique among insects, in which it has wings and can fly but has immature legs, tail, and reproductive system. Adult mayflies are an important food source for many animals; several fishing flies are modeled after them. Mayflies are classified in the phylum ARTHROPODA, class Insecta, order Ephemeroptera.

May Fourth Movement (1919), first mass movement in modern Chinese history. The Versailles Conference (April 28, 1919) ruled against China, awarding the former German leasehold of Kiaochow, Shantung prov., to Japan. On May 4, about 5,000 university students in Peking marched protesting the Versailles decision and secret government agreements with Japan that had prejudiced China's case. Demonstrations and strikes spread to students and workers in Shanghai, and a nationwide boycott of Japanese goods followed. Under pressure, the Chinese delegation refused to sign the Treaty of Paris. The May Fourth Movement spurred continuing intellectual ferment. Biting attacks on Confucian ethics, traditional customs, and warlord politics were published in hundreds of new periodicals. Intellectuals turned to foreign ideas and ideologies. HU SHIH expounded the pragmatic, democratic method of John Dewey, while Ch'en TZ'U HSI and LI TA-CHAO introduced Marxism. Other consequences of the movement were popularization of vernacular literature, increased labor organization, political participation by women, and educational reforms. See Hu Shih, *The Chinese Renaissance* (2d ed. 1964); Chow Tse-tsung, *The May Fourth Movement* (1960).

mayhem (mā'hĕm, mā'əm), in law, originally the crime of willfully and violently injuring a person so as to diminish his capacity for self-defense. Cutting off an arm or leg would constitute the offense, while such a BATTERY as cutting off an ear would not. In the United States, however, statutes treat all mutilations (including those which are self-inflicted to escape some duty, such as military service) as the same offense. The victim may sue for damages.

Maynard, George Willoughby, 1843–1923, American figure, marine, and mural painter, b. Washington, D.C., studied at the National Academy of Design and in Florence and Antwerp. Maynard created decorations for the Library of Congress and the old Metropolitan Opera House, New York City. His *In Strange Seas* is in the Metropolitan Museum.

Mayno or **Maino, Juan Bautista** (hwän boutēs'tä mī'nō), 1578–1649, Spanish painter. He entered the Dominican order in Toledo, where he is thought to have studied with El Greco. He was drawing teacher to the young Philip (later Philip IV). *The Reconquest of the Bay of San Salvador* and *Adoration of the Kings* (both: Prado) and *Adoration of the Shepherds* (Leningrad) are examples of his high baroque work.

Maynooth (mā'nōōth, mānōōth'), town, Co. Kildare, E Republic of Ireland. It is the seat of St. Patrick's College (1795), the principal institution in Ireland for training Roman Catholic clergy, now a constituent college of the National Univ. of Ireland. Some of the buildings were designed by A. W. Pugin. Near the college are the ruins of Maynooth Castle, also called Geraldine Castle, founded c.1176. It was besieged in the reign of Henry VIII and dismantled in the 17th cent.

Mayo, Charles Horace (mā'ō), 1865–1939, American surgeon, b. Rochester, Minn., M.D. Northwestern Univ., 1888. He specialized in goiter and cataract operations. His brother, **William James Mayo,** 1861–1939, b. Le Sueur, Minn., M.D. Univ. of Michigan, 1883, was also a surgeon; he specialized in abdominal surgery. From a small clinic opened by their father, William Worrall Mayo, in Rochester, Minn., in 1889, the brothers developed the great **Mayo Clinic** of international reputation. In 1915 they established the Mayo Foundation for Medical Education and Research as a branch of the graduate school of the Univ. of Minnesota. See G. W. Nagel, *The Mayo Legacy* (1966); H. Clapesattle, *The Doctors Mayo* (2d ed. 1968); C. W. Mayo, *The Story of My Family and My Career* (1968).

Mayo, Henry Thomas, 1856–1937, American naval officer, b. Burlington, Vt. In 1913 he became commander of the Atlantic Fleet. At Tampico in 1914 he precipitated an international incident by demanding an apology and salute to the American flag after Mexican officials had arrested U.S. sailors. President Wilson supported Mayo's demands, and he was made (1915) vice admiral. He was commander of the Atlantic Fleet in World War I and for a time in 1919 commanded the entire U. S. fleet. He was given the permanent rank of rear admiral and in 1920 was retired.

Mayo, county (1971 pop. 109,497), 2,084 sq mi (5,398 sq km), W Republic of Ireland. The county town is CASTLEBAR. The western portion, including large Achill island, is mountainous; the eastern part is more level. There are numerous lakes (Mask, Carrowmore, Cullen, Conn, and Carra), and the irregular coast line is deeply indented by bays (Killala, Broadhaven, Blacksod, and Clew). Oats and potatoes are grown and cattle, sheep, pigs, and poultry are raised. Bacon curing, woolens manufacturing, and flour milling are carried on. The region was granted to the De Burghs after the Anglo-Norman invasion of Ireland, but the county was not brought fully under English control until the late 16th cent.

Mayo Clinic: see MAYO, CHARLES HORACE.

Mayon, Mount (mäyōn'), active volcano, c.8,000 ft (2,440 m) high, SE Luzon, the Philippines. It is considered one of the world's most perfect cones. The last major eruption took place in 1947.

Mayo-Smith, Richmond, 1854–1901, American statistician, b. Troy, Ohio, grad. Amherst, 1875. After graduation he studied for two years in Germany. From 1877 to 1901 he taught at Columbia. He is best known as a pioneer in the teaching of statistics and the application of statistics to social science. He also worked directly in economics. After 1886 he was an editor of the *Political Science Quarterly,* and he was one of the founders (1885) of the American Economic Association. His principal works are *Science of Statistics* (2 vol., 1895–99; issued also as *Statistics and Sociology* and *Statistics and Economics*) and *Emigration and Immigration* (1890).

Mayow, John (mā'ō), 1643?–1679, English chemist and physiologist. In his studies on air he recognized the presence in it of a substance (oxygen) that supports burning and respiration; he called the substance the "nitro-aerial" spirit. His writings include *Medico-physical Works* (tr. from the Lat., 1907).

maypop: see PASSIONFLOWER.

Mays, Willie Howard, Jr. ("Say Hey" Willie Mays), 1931–, American baseball player, b. Fairfield, Ala. He began his professional career at 17 with the Black

Barons of the Negro National League. He signed (1950) with the New York Giants of the National League and joined them in 1951. Mays was a superb outfielder, an agile base stealer, and a devastating hitter. In 1954 he led the Giants to their first world championship in 21 years; in 1954 and 1965 Mays won the most valuable player award. He won the league's home-run title four times (1955, 1962, 1964, 1965). Mays played his final two seasons with the New York Mets and despite numerous injuries sparked the team to the National League championship in 1973. At his retirement in 1973, Mays was third in career home runs with 660 and batted .302.

Ma Yüan (mä yüän), fl. c.1190–1225, Chinese painter of the Sung dynasty and foremost of the Ma family of painters. He became one of the most important landscape painters of the 12th and 13th cent., the other being HSIA KUEI. He was known for his "one-cornered" compositions, in which dramatic effect was achieved by crisp, forceful brush strokes, asymmetrical arrangement of elements, and drastic elimination of all but essentials. Attribution of his works is difficult because many later painters followed his style and because toward the end of his life he collaborated with his son Ma Lin, often signing his own name to his son's works. *Four Old Recluses in the Shang Mountains* (Cincinnati Art Mus.) and *Landscape with Willows* (Mus. of Fine Arts, Boston) are generally attributed to Ma Yüan.

Maywood. **1** City (1970 pop. 16,996), Los Angeles co., S Calif., a suburb of Los Angeles, in a highly industrialized area; inc. 1924. Although chiefly residential, it has plants that make a variety of products. **2** Village (1970 pop. 30,036), Cook co., NE Ill., a suburb of Chicago, on the Des Plaines River; inc. 1881. A farm marketing and processing point, it is also a manufacturing center. In the village are a veterans' hospital and the Loyola Univ. hospital and dental school. **3** Borough (1970 pop. 11,087), Bergen co., NE N.J., a residential suburb between Hackensack and Paterson; inc. 1894.

Mazaca: see CAESAREA MAZACA.

Mazagan: see AL-JADIDA, Morocco.

Mazanderan (mäzän"dĕrän'), province (1966 pop. 1,841,637), c.20,400 sq mi (52,840 sq km), N Iran, bordering on the Caspian Sea in the north. Sari is the capital; other cities include Babol, Amul, and Gorgan. It is traversed by the Elburz mts., which run parallel to the Caspian Sea and divide the province into many isolated valleys. Rice, grain, fruits, cotton, sugarcane, and silk are produced in the lowland strip along the Caspian shore. Mazanderan changed hands often early in its history and was incorporated into the Persian Empire by Shah Abbas I in 1596. It was formerly known as Tabaristan.

Mazarin, Jules (zhül mäzäräN'), 1602–61, French statesman, cardinal of the Roman Catholic Church, b. Italy. His original name was Giulio Mazarini. After serving in the papal army and diplomatic service and as nuncio at the French court (1634–36), he entered the service of France and made himself valuable to King Louis XIII's chief minister, Cardinal Richelieu, who brought him into the council of state. Although he had received only minor orders and had never been ordained a priest, he was raised to cardinal upon the recommendation of Louis XIII (1641). After the deaths of Richelieu (1642) and Louis XIII (1643), Mazarin was the principal minister of the regent ANNE OF AUSTRIA. The theory that Mazarin was secretly married to the widowed queen has been widely credited. He won favorable terms for France in the Peace of Westphalia (1648), but his attempts to raise money through taxation and his centralizing policy provoked the troubles of the FRONDE (1648–53), during which he was several times forced to leave France. After the defeat of the Fronde, Mazarin was securely in control of France. By clever diplomacy he strengthened the crown and negotiated the favorable Peace of the PYRENEES at the end of the war with Spain (1659). See J. B. Perkins, *France under Mazarin* (1886); Arthur Hassall, *Mazarin* (1903, repr. 1970); W. F. Church, *The Impact of Absolutism in France* (1969).

Mazarin Bible (măz'ərĭn), considered to be the first important work printed by GUTENBERG and the earliest book printed from movable types. The Bible, printed at Mainz, probably required several years of work; it was completed not later than 1455. The text of the Bible is Latin. The type is a Gothic style related to Old English and similar to the best handwriting of the time. Colored initials and other illuminations were hand drawn. The pages of the book are folio, each page is in two columns, and, with few exceptions, each column has 42 lines. The edition includes both vellum and paper copies. In design and workmanship, the Mazarin Bible holds its place as one of the finest of all printed books. It is called the Mazarin Bible because the first copy to recapture attention was in the library of Cardinal Mazarin, in Paris. It is called also the Gutenberg Bible and the 42-line Bible.

Mazar-i-Sharif (mäzär'-ē-shärēf'), city (1967 pop. 43,197), capital of Mazar-i-Sharif prov., N Afghanistan, near the USSR border. It is held sacred as the alleged burial place of Ali, son-in-law and cousin of Muhammad; a noted mosque of Ali is in the city. Mazar-i-Sharif, the center of Afghanistan's rug and carpet industry, also has cotton and silk industries. Most of the inhabitants are Uzbeks. An active trade is carried on with the Soviet republic of Uzbekistan, across the Amu Darya River. The surrounding agricultural area is especially known for its horses and karakul lambs; Mazar-i-Sharif is a center of the karakul fur trade.

Mazaruni (mäzəro͞o'nē), river, c.350 mi (560 km) long, rising in the Guiana Highlands, NW Guyana, and flowing generally E to the Essequibo River at Bartica. The river is the center of Guyana's diamond industry.

Mazatlán (mäsätlän'), city (1970 pop. 171,835), Sinaloa state, W Mexico, on the Pacific coast. One of the largest commercial and industrial centers of W Mexico, Mazatlán is a major seaport and is also on a railroad between the United States and Mexico City. Although the climate is hot, Mazatlán is a popular resort with a beautiful setting. Spanish colonial trade with the Philippines stimulated the development of the port. Present exports include metals, woods, hides, fish products, and oregano.

Mazdaism: see ZOROASTRIANISM.

maze, detail of landscape gardening based on the Greek LABYRINTH, consisting of intricate paths or alleys lined with high hedges and having a center and exit difficult to find. It was a prominent feature in the formal English gardens of the 17th and 18th cent., the most notable being that Hampton Court Palace, London. Some medieval cathedrals, e.g., Amiens, had a pattern of contrasting stones on the floor of the nave that was also called a maze.

Mazepa, Ivan (ēvän' məzyä'pə), c.1640–1709, Cossack hetman [leader] in the Russian Ukraine. He was made hetman (1687) on the insistence of Prince Gallitzin, adviser to the Russian regent, Sophia Alekseyevna, and he aided Gallitzin in his campaign against the Tatars (1689). Mazepa was able for some years to maintain Ukrainian autonomy while keeping good relations with Czar Peter I. Under Mazepa's direction, churches were built and libraries and educational institutions were established. He did not, however, attain his goal of uniting all Ukrainian lands (see UKRAINE) with his territory, which lay on the left bank of the Dnepr River. Eventually, Peter's harsh demands on the Ukraine threatened Cossack autonomy. When the Northern War between Russia and Sweden began (1700), the hetman established secret contact with pro-Swedish elements in Poland. Peter, who trusted Mazepa, refused to believe reports of his treason. In 1708, however, Mazepa openly joined Charles XII of Sweden when the latter's army advanced into the Ukraine. The hetman found himself with few enthusiastic followers in this venture; most Ukrainian Cossacks remained loyal to the czar. After the Swedish defeat at Poltava (1709), Mazepa and Charles fled to Bender, where Mazepa died. According to a legend, Mazepa, in his youth, was tied to the back of a wild horse and sent into the steppes by a jealous husband. This legend was described in Lord Byron's poem, *Mazeppa.* See biography by C. A. Manning (1957); studies by Theodore Mackiw (1967); H. F. Babinsky, *The Mazeppa Legend in European Romanticism* (1974).

Mazo, Juan Bautista Martínez del (hwän boutēs'tä märtē'nĕth dĕl mä'thō), c.1612–1667, Spanish portrait and landscape painter. He was the pupil and son-in-law of Velázquez, with whom he lived and collaborated and whom he succeeded in 1661 as first court painter to Philip IV. There are few extant paintings that scholars agree are his. These include *View of Saragossa* (1647, Prado); *Portrait of Queen Mariana* (1666, National Gall., London); and *Mazo's Family* (Vienna). Although he adopted the externals of Velázquez's style, his painting lacks vigor and originality.

mazurka (məzûr'kə, -zo͝or'-), Polish national dance that spread to England and the United States at the beginning of the 19th cent. Danced by four or eight couples and characterized by stamping of the feet and clicking of the heels, it is in moderate triple meter and permits improvisation. Chopin composed more than 50 mazurkas for piano.

Mazurov, Kiril (kĭrēl' mäzo͞o'rôf), 1914–, Soviet political leader. A construction technician, he joined the Communist party in 1940, and was active in the Communist youth organization. Rising in the party hierarchy in Byelorussia, Mazurov served as chairman of the Byelorussian council of ministers (1953–56) and first secretary of the Byelorussian Communist party (1956–65) before becoming (1965) first deputy premier of the USSR. The same year, he was promoted to membership in the presidium (later renamed the politburo) of the Communist party central committee.

Mazzaroth (măz'ərŏth), name probably signifying the signs of the Zodiac. Job 38.32.

Mazzini, Giuseppe (jo͞ozĕp'pā mät-sē'nē), 1805–72, Italian patriot and revolutionist, an outstanding figure of the RISORGIMENTO. His youth was spent in literary and philosophical studies. He early joined the CARBONARI, was imprisoned briefly, and went into exile. In Marseilles he founded the secret society Giovine Italia [young Italy], which led a vigorous campaign for Italian unity under a republican government. Mazzini went to Switzerland, then to London (1837), working untiringly at revolutionary propaganda. His influence on Italian liberals was tremendous. During the REVOLUTIONS OF 1848, when uprisings occurred in Milan, the Papal States, and the Two Sicilies, Mazzini returned to Italy; in 1849 he was one of the leaders of the Roman republic. After its fall he resumed his propaganda from abroad. He organized unsuccessful uprisings in Milan (1853) and an ill-fated expedition in S Italy (1857). He often came secretly to Italy, although he had been condemned to death in absentia. Back in London in 1858 he founded the newspaper *Pensiero ed azione* [thought and action]. He supported Giuseppe Garibaldi's expedition to Sicily, but unlike Garibaldi, he remained a confirmed republican. His relations with Camillo Benso di Cavour, the Sardinian premier, were strained; although both strove for Italian unification, their ideas were opposite, Cavour relying for help on a foreign power (France), Mazzini believing in revolution and war based on direct popular action. He was briefly imprisoned (1870) in Italy for revolutionary activities. Mazzini's work was inspired by his great moral strength. His program was not only political, but deeply social, aiming at human redemption on a religious and moral basis, at liberty, and at justice. His literary style is remarkably fine. He wrote on politics, social science, philosophy, and literature. A selection of his works has appeared in English (6 vol., 1890–91). See biographies by G. O. Griffith (1932, repr. 1970), Stringfellow Barr (1935), and Edgar Holt (1967); study by Gaetano Salvemini (tr. 1957).

Mazzola, Francesco: see PARMIGIANO.

Mazzuchelli, Samuel Charles (mä'zho͝okĕlē), 1806–64, Italian missionary in America. He was a Dominican. He was ordered (1830) to the island of Mackinac to be the only permanent priest in the upper Great Lakes region. He founded the first Catholic school in Wisconsin at Green Bay and visited various Indian tribes as a missionary. About 1835 he moved to Galena, Ill.; he established churches in Galena, Dubuque, Davenport, Potosi, Burlington, Iowa City, Bloomington, Bellevue, Shullsburg, Sinsinawa, and other places. He founded a college for men at Sinsinawa and for three years was its first president. He excelled in music, painting, and architecture and designed all his churches and several lay buildings. He probably drew plans for the first statehouse of Iowa, now the administration building of the state university. See his memoirs (tr. 1915); biography by M. E. Evans (1950).

M'Ba, Léon (lāōN' əmbä'), 1902–67, Gabonese political leader. He was a member of the dominant Fang tribe. When Gabon became a self-governing republic in the French Community (1958), he became (1959) its first prime minister. In 1961 he was elected as the country's first president, was briefly removed by a coup (1964), and then served until his death. Albert-Bernard Bongo was his handpicked successor.

Mbabane (əmbäbä'nā), town, (1966 pop. 13,803), capital of Swaziland, NW Swaziland, in the Mdimba mts. It is primarily an administrative center but serves as a commercial hub for the surrounding agricultural region. Tin and iron are mined nearby.

Mbandaka (əmbändä'kä), formerly **Coquilhatville** (kôkēyävēl'), city (1970 pop. 107,910), capital of Equateur region, W Zaïre, a port on the Congo River. It is a commercial and transportation center and has tanning and fishing industries. The city was founded in 1883 by the explorer Henry M. Stanley, who called it Equator.

M'Bour (əmbo͞or'), town, W Senegal, on the Atlantic Ocean. Ilmenite, rutile, and yirconium are extracted from the titanium ore mined nearby. M'Bour also processes and trades peanuts grown in the area and has a fishing industry. There is a geophysics research institute in the city.

Mboya, Thomas Joseph (mboi'ə), 1930–1969, Kenyan political leader. The son of a Luo farmer, he was born in the "white highlands" of Kenya and educated at Roman Catholic mission schools. Early involved in trade union activities, he joined Jomo Kenyatta's Kenya African Union and soon became one of its leaders. In 1953 he was elected general secretary of the Kenya Federation of Labor. After studying in India and England, Mboya returned (1956) to Kenya and, under the first elections held (1957) for African members of the Kenya Legislative Council, was one of eight elected. Heading a delegation to the All-African People's Conference (1958) in Accra, Ghana, he was elected its president. As leader of the Kenya Independence Movement, he was instrumental in securing a constitution assuring African political supremacy. Merging his group with the newly formed Kenya African National Union in 1960, he became general secretary of the organization. After Kenya gained (1963) its independence, Mboya served as minister of labor (1962–63), minister of justice and constitutional affairs (1963–64), and minister of economic planning and development (1964–69). His popularity established him as a likely successor to Kenyatta, and his assassination in 1969 set off widespread rioting. He wrote *Kenya Faces the Future: A Statement of the African Case in Kenya* (1959). See a collection of his speeches and writings in *The Challenge of Nationhood* (1970); biography by Alan Rake (1962).

Mbuji-Mayi (əmbo͞o'jē-mī'yē), formerly **Bakwanga** (bäkwäng'gä), city (1970 pop. 256,154), capital of Kasai-Oriental region, S central Zaïre, on the Sankuru River. A commercial center in Luba country, it handles most of the industrial diamonds produced in Zaïre. After Zaïre attained independence (1960) the city's population grew rapidly with the immigration of Luba people from other parts of the country. From 1960 to 1962 it was the capital of the secessionist Mining State of South KASAI.

Mbundu (əmbo͞on'do͞o), black African ethnic group, W Angola. The Mbundu speak a Bantu language and number about 1.1 million. By the late 15th cent. they had formed the Ndongo kingdom, ruled by the *ngola* (from which the Portuguese derived the name *Angola*). Beginning in the early 16th cent. Ndongo was raided for slaves by its northern neighbor, the kingdom of the Kongo, which sold them to the Portuguese. In 1579 the Portuguese first attempted to conquer Ndongo; however, the Mbundu resisted fiercely and it was not until 1683 that the kingdom was definitively defeated.

Mc-. Names beginning thus are entered as if spelled Mac-. See MAC.

Md, chemical symbol of the element MENDELEVIUM.

Mdina: see CITTÀ VECCHIA, Malta.

Mead, George Herbert (mēd), 1863–1931, American philosopher and psychologist, b. South Hadley, Mass., grad. Oberlin, 1883, and Harvard, 1888, and studied in Leipzig and Berlin. He taught at the Univ. of Chicago from 1894 until his death. The work of John Dewey and of Mead may be regarded as complementary. Mead, studying the development of the mind and the self, regarded mind as the natural emergent from the interaction of the human organism and its social environment. Within this biosocial structure the gap between impulse and reason is bridged by the use of language. Mastering language, man sets up assumptions as to his role in life, and self and consciousness-of-self emerge, giving intelligence a historical development that is both natural and moral. Mead called his position social behaviorism, using conduct—both social and biological—as an approach to all experience. Mead's work, collected posthumously, includes *The Philosophy of the Present* (1932), *Mind, Self, and Society* (1934), and *The Philosophy of the Act* (1938). See Paul Pfuetze, *The Social Self* (1954, repr. 1973 under the title *Self, Society, Existence*); study by D. L. Miller (1973).

Mead, Margaret, 1901–, American anthropologist, b. Philadelphia, grad. Barnard, 1923, Ph.D. Columbia, 1929. In 1926 she became assistant curator, in 1942 associate curator, and from 1964 to 1969 she was curator of ethnology of the American Museum of Natural History, New York City. After 1954 she served as adjunct professor of anthropology at Columbia. A student and collaborator of Ruth BENEDICT, she focused her interests on problems of child rearing, personality, and culture. Her field work was carried out primarily among the peoples of Oceania. She was also active with the World Federation for Mental Health. Her works include *Coming of Age in Samoa* (1928), *Growing Up in New Guinea* (1930), *The Changing Culture of an Indian Tribe* (1932), *Sex and Temperament in Three Primitive Societies* (1935), *Male and Female* (1949), *New Lives for Old: Cultural Transformation in Manus, 1928–1953* (1956), *People and Places* (1959), *Continuities in Cultural Evolution* (1964), *Culture and Commitment* (1970), and a biographical account of her early years, *Blackberry Winter* (1972). She is also the author of a book for young people, *People and Places* (1959). She edited *Cultural Patterns and Technical Change* (1953) and a volume of Ruth Benedict's writings, *An Anthropologist at Work* (1959, repr. 1966). See study by Allyn Moss (1963).

Mead, William Rutherford, 1846–1928, American architect, b. Brattleboro, Vt. He entered the office of Russell Sturgis in New York City. In 1872 he began to practice architecture with C. F. MCKIM, and their partnership was joined by Stanford White in 1879 to make the famous firm of McKim, Mead, and White.

mead (mēd), wine made of fermented honey and water, sometimes flavored with spices. It is highly intoxicating. Mead was known in classical Greece and Rome and was the favorite drink of the tribes of N and W Europe.

Mead, Lake, 247 sq mi (640 sq km), on the Nev.-Ariz. border, formed by Hoover Dam across the Colorado River. The lake is 115 mi (185 km) long, from 1 to 8 mi (1.6–12.9 km) wide, and 589 ft (180 m) at its maximum depth; it has the greatest capacity of any reservoir in the United States and is one of the largest in the world. Lake Mead, with its 550 mi (885 km) shoreline, is the focal point of Lake Mead National Recreation Area. See NATIONAL PARKS AND MONUMENTS (table).

Meade, George Gordon, 1815–72, Union general in the American Civil War, b. Cádiz, Spain. Graduated from West Point in 1835, he resigned from the army the next year and became a civil engineer. In 1842, Meade reentered the army in the corps of topographical engineers. He served in the Mexican War and on various engineering projects. In the Civil War he was made a brigadier general of volunteers (Aug., 1861). In the Seven Days battles (1862), he was severely wounded at Frayser's Farm (or Glendale), but he recovered in time to lead his brigade ably at the second battle of Bull Run. In the Antietam campaign, in the battle of Fredericksburg (1862), and in the battle of Chancellorsville (1863) he distinguished himself further. Meade took command of the Army of the Potomac on June 28, 1863. Several days later he won the important battle of Gettysburg (see GETTYSBURG CAMPAIGN). This brought him a brigadier generalcy in the regular army. He was criticized, however, for not following up his victory. Mead commanded the Army of the Potomac until the end of the war, but Ulysses S. Grant really directed his army in the WILDERNESS CAMPAIGN and subsequent operations. He was promoted to major general in the regular army on Grant's recommendation in Aug., 1864. After the war Meade commanded various military departments. See George Meade, *The Life and Letters of General George Gordon Meade* (2 vol., 1913); biography by Freeman Cleaves (1960).

meadow beauty, any plant of the genus *Rhexia,* herbaceous perennials of wet places E of the Rockies, particularly damp pine barrens and sands along the southeast coast. A widespread species, *R. virginica,* is a common component of cranberry-bog vegetation. Meadow beauties (also called deer grass) are sometimes cultivated, often in bog gardens. They are classified in the division MAGNOLIOPHYTA, class Magnoliopsida, order Myrtales, family Melastomataceae.

meadowlark, common North American meadow bird of the family Icteridae, also called meadow starling. Unlike other members of the family, which comprises blackbirds, GRACKLES, orioles, and others, the meadowlark does not travel in large flocks, and it eats harmful insects rather than grain. The eastern meadowlark, *Sturnella magna,* known for its clear, whistling song, is about 10 in. (25 cm) long. In color, it is brown streaked with black above and yellow below with a broad black crescent across the chest. The Western species, *Sturnella neglecta,* is slightly smaller, and its call is lower. Recent experiments have shown that the two species do not interbreed in the wild, although they are nearly indistinguishable. Meadowlarks are classified in the phylum CHORDATA, subphylum Vertebrata, class Aves, order Passeriformes, family Icteridae.

meadow mouse: see VOLE.

meadow rue, any plant of the genus *Thalictrum* of the family Ranunculaceae (BUTTERCUP family). Most are tall perennials (up to 7 ft/2.1 m high) bearing summer flowers with showy, pendant tassels of long stamens, greenish sepals, and no petals. Meadow rues are found in moist, open places throughout northern temperate regions; in the United States they are especially abundant in the Northeast. A few species are cultivated for ornament. The European herb called RUE is an unrelated plant. Meadow rue is classified in the division MAGNOLIOPHYTA, class Magnoliopsida, order Ranunculales, family Ranunculaceae.

meadow saffron or **autumn crocus,** perennial garden ornamental (*Colchicum autumnale*) of the family Liliaceae (LILY family). Native to Europe and N Africa, it has escaped from gardens to meadows and fields in some parts of the United States. Its poisonous corms and seeds yield the drug COLCHICINE. The purplish flowers, which bloom in the fall when the leaves are gone, resemble those of the true crocus and true saffron (of the IRIS family) but have six stamens instead of three. Other species of *Colchicum* are also popular garden plants. Meadow saffron is classified in the division MAGNOLIOPHYTA, class Liliatae, order Liliales, family Liliaceae.

meadowsweet: see SPIRAEA.

Meadville, city (1970 pop. 16,573), seat of Crawford co., NW Pa.; settled 1788, inc. 1866. It is an industrial city in a rich agricultural region. There is a railroad shop and factories that manufacture zippers, acetate yarn, flat glass, furnaces, and machines and machine parts. Allegheny College is there.

Meagher, Thomas Francis (mär), 1823–67, Irish revolutionary and Union general in the American Civil War, b. Waterford, Ireland. A leader of the Young Ireland movement, he was arrested and condemned to death for his part in the abortive rebellion of 1848, but the sentence was commuted to penal servitude in Van Diemen's Land (now Tasmania). Escaping, he went to New York City in 1852, practiced law, and edited the *Irish News.* In the Civil War, Meagher fought at the first battle of Bull Run with the famous 69th Regiment and organized (1861–62) the Irish Brigade of New York. His brigade was eventually decimated in fighting with the Army of the Potomac from the Peninsular campaign through Chancellorsville, and Meagher resigned (1863) as brigadier general of volunteers. His resignation was soon canceled, and at the end of the war he was serving under General Sherman. He was appointed secretary of Montana Territory in 1865 and served as temporary governor, but his rule was unpopular. He drowned in the Missouri River near Fort Benton while awaiting a shipment of weapons for the Montana militia. His *Speeches on the Legislative Independence of Ireland* was published in 1853. See biography by R. G. Athearn (1949); P. J. Jones, *The Irish Brigade* (1969).

Meah (mē'ə), tower of the wall of Jerusalem. Neh. 3.1; 12.39.

mealybug, common name for certain unarmored SCALE INSECTS that exude a granular white secretion, giving them a mealy appearance. Many are common greenhouse and crop pests. Adult females are wingless, with oval, segmented bodies and well-developed legs. The females and young feed on various parts of plants with their sucking mouthparts. Adult males have no mouthparts and do not feed. In egg-laying species the female produces several hundred eggs in a mass covered with waxy threads. In other species the young are born alive. The most serious pests are mealybugs that feed on citrus; other species damage sugarcane, grapes, pineapple, coffee trees, ferns, and orchids. Mealybugs are classified in the phylum ARTHROPODA, class Insecta, order Homoptera, family Pseudococcidae.

mean, in statistics, a type of AVERAGE. The arithmetic mean of a group of numbers is found by dividing their sum by the number of members in the group; e.g., the sum of the seven numbers 4, 5, 6, 9, 13, 14, and 19 is 70 so their mean is 70 divided by 7, or 10. Less often used is the geometric mean (for two quantities, the square root of their product; for *n* quantities, the *n*th root of their product).

Means, Philip Ainsworth, 1892–1944, American historian and archaeologist, b. Boston. An assistant on a Yale expedition to Peru (1914–15), he was later (1920–21) director of the National Museum of Archaeology at Lima, Peru. He traveled widely in Latin American countries, and between 1921 and 1932 he was several times an associate in anthropology at the Peabody Museum, Harvard. He wrote many books and articles, in both English and Spanish; these are admired for their scholarship and literary style. Among his works are *History of the Spanish Conquest of Yucatan and of the Itzas* (1917), *Ancient Civilizations of the Andes* (1931), *Fall of the Inca Empire and the Spanish Rule in Peru, 1530-1780* (1932), *The Spanish Main: Focus of Envy, 1492-1700* (1935), and *Newport Tower* (1942).

mean solar time: see SOLAR TIME.

Meany, George, 1894–, American labor leader, president of the American Federation of Labor and Congress of Industrial Organizations (AFL-CIO; 1955–), b. New York City. A plumber, he was elected business agent of his local union in 1922 and rose in 1934 to the presidency of the New York State Federation of Labor. He proved an able lobbyist before the Albany legislature, where he successfully helped promote the passage of 72 prolabor bills. Elected secretary-treasurer of the AFL in 1939, he held that post until his elevation to the presidency upon the death of William Green (1952). When the AFL and the CIO merged in 1955, Meany was elected head of the new federation and was reelected after that without opposition. Angered by reforms in the Democratic party in 1972, Meany was influential in leading the traditionally Democratic AFL-CIO into a neutral stance, supporting neither one of the major candidates in the presidential election. Many observers agreed that this was a significant element in President Nixon's landslide victory. Meany later broke with Nixon, however, and became an early advocate of his resignation or impeachment. See Joseph C. Goulden, *Meany* (1972).

Mearah (mē'ərə) [Heb.,=cave], unknown cave region, NW Palestine. Joshua 13.4.

Meares, John (mērz), 1756?–1809, British naval officer, explorer, and trader. He served in the navy, in which he attained the rank of lieutenant, until after the Peace of Paris (1783), when he entered the merchant service. In Macao he formed a commercial company for trade with the northwest coast of America, to which he paid his first visit in 1786. He explored along the coast of Alaska, wintered in Prince William Sound, and then returned to the Orient. Two years later he went to NOOTKA SOUND, erected a trading post on its shores, and built the *Northwest America*, first ship launched in British Columbia. In 1789 his establishment at Nootka Sound was seized by the Spanish; war between England and Spain was narrowly averted. Meares later returned to the British navy and became (1795) a commander. He wrote *Voyages Made in the Years 1788 and 1789 to the North West Coast of America* (1790).

Mearns, the, Scotland: see KINCARDINESHIRE.

measles or **rubeola** (ro͝obē'ələ), highly contagious disease of young children caused by a filtrable virus and spread by droplet spray from the nose, mouth, and throat of individuals in the infective stage. This period begins 2 to 4 days before the appearance of the rash and lasts from 2 to 5 days thereafter. The first symptoms of measles, after an incubation period of 7 to 14 days, are fever, nasal discharge, and redness of the eyes. Characteristic white spots appear in the mouth, followed by a rash on the face that soon spreads to the rest of the body. The symptoms disappear in 4 to 7 days. Measles, if uncomplicated by secondary infections, is not dangerous, and one attack confers lifelong immunity. However, it renders the patient highly susceptible to other more serious infections such as bronchial pneumonia and encephalitis, either of which can be fatal or lead to permanent aftereffects. For this reason measles is now considered a disease against which children should be guarded and immunized. Immunization by injection of live measles-virus vaccine, first marketed in 1963, was proved effective. Given at first with gamma globulin, the vaccine was further developed by 1965 so that one shot alone is generally safe and gives long-term, probably lifetime, immunity; a nationwide program was then established in the United States for the vaccination of all children over nine months old to avoid the dangerous and sometimes fatal complications of the disease.

measure, in music, a metrical unit having a given number of beats, the first of which normally is accented, although the accent may be displaced by syncopation. Measures are separated on the staff by vertical lines called bars. The term *bar* has become synonymous with measure. The consistent division of music into measures with regularly recurring accent did not become prevalent until the 17th cent. See also METER and RHYTHM.

measurement, determination of the magnitude of a quantity by comparison with a standard for that quantity. Quantities frequently measured include time, length, area, volume, pressure, mass, force, and energy. To express a measurement, there must be a basic unit of the quantity involved, e.g., the inch or second, and a standard of measurement (instrument) calibrated in such units, e.g., a ruler or clock. For convenience, such a standard is usually marked off both in multiples and in fractions of the basic unit. Although various systems of units exist for measuring different quantities (see WEIGHTS AND MEASURES), the most important and widely used are the METRIC SYSTEM and the ENGLISH UNITS OF MEASUREMENT. Certain units have been defined for special applications, e.g., the LIGHT-YEAR and PARSEC in astronomy and the ANGSTROM in physics. Measurement is one of the fundamental processes of SCIENCE. It provides the data on which new theories are based and by which older theories are tested and retested. A good measurement should be both accurate and precise. Accuracy is determined by the care taken by the person making the measurement and the condition of the instrument; a worn or broken instrument or one carelessly used may give an inaccurate result. Precision, on the other hand, is determined by the design of the instrument; the finer the graduations on the instrument's scale and the greater the ease with which they can be read, the more precise the measurement. The choice of the instrument used should be appropriate to the desired precision of the results. The human foot may be a suitable instrument for pacing off short distances if precision is not important; at the other extreme, the interferometer (see INTERFERENCE) is used for extremely precise measurements of distance in science. There is a basic distinction between measurement and counting. The result of counting is exact because it involves discrete entities that are not subdivided into fractions. Measurement, on the other hand, involves entities that may be subdivided into smaller and smaller fractions and is thus always an estimate. This distinction between measurement and counting seems, on the surface, to break down at the atomic level, where the QUANTUM THEORY reveals that not only mass (in the form of elementary particles and atoms) but also many other quantities occur only in discrete units, or quanta. It would seem, therefore, that one could, in theory, reduce measurement to counting at this level. However, the quantum theory also places limitations on the possibility of such counting, stressing such concepts as the wavelike nature and indistinguishability of particles and proposing the UNCERTAINTY PRINCIPLE as an absolute limitation on certain pairs of related measurements.

measures: see WEIGHTS AND MEASURES.

measuring worm: see INCHWORM.

meat, term for the flesh of animals used for food, especially that of cattle, sheep, lambs, and swine, as distinct from game, poultry, and fish; sometimes it is inclusive of all animal flesh. The chief constituents of meat are water, protein, and fat. Phosphorus, iron, and vitamins are also contained in meat, especially in some of the edible organs (e.g., liver). Although meat is digested more slowly than starches or sugars, it has a high food value, with more than 95% of the protein and fat being digested; the fattier meats (e.g., pork) take somewhat longer to digest than the leaner ones. The edible parts of a carcass include lean flesh, fat flesh, and edible glands or organs, such as the heart, liver, kidneys, tongue, tripe, brains, and SWEETBREAD. The comparative toughness of meat depends on the character of the muscle walls and connective tissue, the part of the animal from which the meat is taken, and the age and condition of the animal. Ripening meat, i.e., hanging it for a time at a temperature just above freezing (or, in a more recently developed technique, at a high temperature) permits enzyme action and the formation of lactic acid, which tenderizes it. Good meat may be recognized by a uniform color; a firm, elastic texture; being barely moist to the touch; and having a scarcely perceptible, clean odor. The choicer cuts should be of fine texture and well marbled with fat. Cooking meat not only softens tissues, kills parasites and microorganisms, and coagulates blood and albumen, but makes the meat more palatable by developing its flavors or introducing new ones by means of seasonings and sauces. Meat, where available, has been a staple food since prehistoric times. The meat supply, obtained at first by using the raw flesh of animals found dead, was augmented by trapping; then, as humans developed their tools and a community life, by hunting; and finally, by the domestication of animals. Meat has been subject to prohibitions (see VEGETARIANISM), as well as to butchering regulations on religious and hygienic grounds. Meat consumption has been commonly based on the supply, lamb and mutton being preferred in the Middle East, veal in Italy, and pork and beef in most of Europe and the Americas. The leading producers of meat for export are Argentina, Australia, and New Zealand.

Meath (mēth, mēth), county (1971 pop. 71,616), 903 sq mi (2,339 sq km), E Republic of Ireland. The county town is NAVAN. The land is mostly level, being a part of the central plain of Ireland, with extensive fertile areas near the Boyne and the Blackwater, the principal rivers. There is a sandy coastline of some 10 mi (16 km) along the Irish Sea. Grain and potato cultivation and cattle raising support the bulk of the population, and there is some manufacturing in the larger towns. The region is important in Irish history. TARA was long the seat of the ancient high kings of Ireland. Meath was considered a fifth province of Ireland for many centuries and was not finally organized as a county until the 17th cent. Remains of archaeological interest have been found in the Newgrange mounds.

meat-packing, industry involved with the buying, inspection, and slaughter of food-producing animals; the preparation of their carcasses for food and various other purposes; and the conduct of departments for advertising, distribution, and sales. It is one of the largest industries in the modern world. In the United States, the practice of assembling livestock at a central plant where they can be slaughtered and all parts utilized is a natural outgrowth of American conditions. The plains of the Midwest and the Southwest support cheap stock raising, but the livestock must be marketed in the densely populated Eastern states. Losses entailed in driving animals, especially swine, to distant markets led, as early as 1820, to the shipment of brine-packed meat from central points. Cincinnati was a leading center from 1840, and in the 1850s Chicago attained prominence in the industry. Its Union Stock Yards (1864) was the nation's major livestock and packing center until the mid-20th cent. It was closed in 1971, largely because it was unable to compete with newer, more modern plants. Modern meat-packing dates from the introduction of refrigeration. In 1870 fresh beef was shipped from Hammond, Ind., to Boston in an iced car. The Union Stock Yards began (c.1877) the use of refrigerated cars. Distribution extended even to export trade, and the handling of fresh meat assumed predominant importance. Storage and distribution warehouses, coordinated with the extensive operation of refrigerated cars and steamships, make possible the rapid and efficient marketing of even the most perishable products. Research has found profitable uses for even those by-products formerly considered waste, e.g., hoofs, hair, horns, bones, fats, intestines, blood, and viscera. Federal laws of 1906 and subsequent years require humane slaughtering methods and the examination of all animals killed for export or interstate trade. The Wholesome Meat Act of 1967 extended such inspection to intrastate trade. The laws are administered through the Animal and Plant Health Inspection Service of the U.S. Dept. of Agriculture, and all plants are open to inspection day and night. Kansas City, South Omaha, St. Louis, South St. Joseph, Indianapolis, Fort Worth, Ottumwa, and Sioux City are distribution centers of packinghouse products in the United States. Packers may avail themselves of a grading service, offered at cost by the Dept. of Agriculture, which classes beef as prime, choice, good, medium, common cutter, and low cutter steer or heifer. See BEEF; MUTTON; SAUSAGE.

Meaux (mō), city (1968 pop. 31,420), Seine-et-Marne dept., N France, in BRIE, on the Marne River. It is an industrial center where metals, flour, chemicals, carbon paper, candy, and cheeses are manufactured. An episcopal see since the 4th cent., Meaux has a cathedral (13th–14th cent.) that contains the tomb of Bossuet, the city's most famous bishop. In the massacre of Meaux (1358), thousands of peasants who had participated in the JACQUERIE were slain.

Mebunnai (mēbŭn'ī), the same as SIBBECAI.

Mecca (mĕk'ə), city (1965 est. pop. 185,000), capital of the Hejaz, W Saudi Arabia. The birthplace A.D. c.570 of MUHAMMAD the Prophet, it is the holiest city of ISLAM. It is c.45 mi (70 km) from its port, JIDDA, and is in a narrow valley overlooked by hills crowned with castles. Unlike those of most Middle Eastern cities, many of the buildings, constructed of stone, are more than three stories high. The city, called Macoraba by Ptolemy, was an ancient center of commerce and a place of great sanctity for idolatrous Arab sects before the rise of Muhammad. Muhammad's flight (the hegira) from Mecca in 622 is the beginning of the Muslim era. He captured the city shortly after. Although Mecca never lost its sanctity, it declined rapidly in commercial importance after its capture by the UMAYYADS in 692. It was sacked in 930 by the KARMATHIANS and taken by the Ottoman Turks in 1517. The WAHABIS held it from 1803 to 1813. In Mecca, in 1916, Husayn ibn Ali proclaimed his independence from Turkey and maintained himself as king of the HEJAZ until Mecca fell to Ibn Saud in 1924. At the center of Mecca is the Great Mosque, the Haram, which encloses the KAABA, the chief goal of Muslim pilgrimage. Next to the Kaaba is the Zamzam, a holy well used solely for religious and medicinal purposes. The bazaar outside the mosque is noted for its silks, beadwork, and perfumes. The commerce of the city depends almost wholly on the pilgrims, as little else is manufactured save articles of devotion. Despite the ban against unbelievers, the holy city was visited and described in the 19th cent. by Richard Burton and others. In some years more than 400,000 Muslims from outside Saudi Arabia make the pilgrimage to Mecca, MEDINA, and ARAFAT. See C. S. Hurgronje, *Mekka in the Latter Part of the 19th Century* (1931, repr. 1970); H. Y. Hirashima, *The Road to Holy Mecca* (1972).

mechanical advantage: see MACHINE.

mechanical engineering: see ENGINEERING.

mechanics, branch of PHYSICS concerned with MOTION and the FORCES that tend to cause it; it includes study of the mechanical properties of MATTER, such as DENSITY, ELASTICITY, and VISCOSITY. Mechanics may be roughly divided into STATICS and DYNAMICS; statics deals with bodies at rest and is concerned with such topics as BUOYANCY, EQUILIBRIUM, and the principles of simple MACHINES, while dynamics deals with bodies in motion and is sometimes further divided into kinematics (description of motion without regard to its cause) and kinetics (explanation of changes in motion as a result of forces). The science of mechanics may also be broken down, according to the state of matter being studied, into solid mechanics and fluid mechanics. The latter, the mechanics of liquids and gases, includes hydrostatics, hydrodynamics, pneumatics, aerodynamics, and other fields. Mechanics was studied by a number of ancient Greek scientists, most notably Aristotle, whose ideas dominated the subject until the late Middle Ages, and Archimedes, who made several contributions and whose approach was quite modern compared to other ancient scientists. In the Aristotelian view, ordinary motion required a material medium; a body was kept in motion by the medium rushing in behind it in order to prevent a vacuum, which, according to this philosophy, could not occur in nature. Celestial bodies, on the other hand, were kept in motion through the vacuum of space by various agents that, in the Christianized version of Aquinas and others, acquired an angelic character. This explanation was rejected in the 14th cent. by several philosophers, who revived the impetus theory proposed by John Philoponos in the 6th cent. A.D.; according to this theory a body acquired a quantity called impetus when it was set in motion, and it eventually came to rest as the impetus died out. The impetus school flourished in Paris and elsewhere during the 14th and 15th cent. and included William of Occam (Ockham), Jean Buridan, Albert of Saxony, Nicolas Oresme, and Nicolas of Cusa, although it was never successful in replacing the dominant Aristotelian mechanics. Modern mechanics dates from the work of Galileo, Simon Stevin, and others in the late 16th and early 17th cent. By means of experiment and mathematical analysis, Galileo made a number of important studies, particularly of falling bodies and projectiles. He enunciated the principle of INERTIA and used it to explain not only the mechanics of bodies on the earth but also that of celestial bodies (which, however, he believed moved in uniform circular orbits). The philosopher René Descartes advocated the application of the mathematical-mechanical approach to all fields and founded the mechanistic philosophy that was so important in science for the next two centuries or more. The first system of modern mechanics to explain successfully all mechanical phenomena, both terrestrial and celestial, was that of Isaac Newton, who in his *Principia (Mathematical Principles of Natural Philosophy,* 1687) derived three laws of motion and showed how the principle of universal GRAVITATION can be used to explain both the behavior of falling bodies on the earth and the orbits of the planets in the heavens. Newton's system of mechanics was developed extensively over the next two centuries by many scientists, including Johann and Daniel Bernoulli, Leonhard Euler, J. le Rond d'Alembert, J. L. Lagrange, P. S. Laplace, S. D. Poisson, and W. R. Hamilton. It found application to the explanation of the behavior of gases and thermodynamics in the statistical mechanics of J. C. Maxwell, Ludwig Boltzmann, and J. W. Gibbs. In 1905, Albert Einstein showed that Newton's mechanics was an approximation, valid for cases involving speeds much less than the speed of light; for very great speeds the relativistic mechanics of his theory of RELATIVITY was required. Einstein showed further in his general theory of relativity (1916) that gravitation could be explained in terms of the effect of a massive body on the framework of space and time around it, this effect applying not only to the motions of other bodies possessing mass but also to light. In the quantum mechanics developed during the 1920s as part of the QUANTUM THEORY, the motions of very tiny particles, such as the electrons in an atom, were explained using the fact that both matter and energy have a dual nature—sometimes behaving like particles and other times behaving like waves. Two different but mathematically equivalent forms of quantum mechanics were presented, the wave mechanics of Erwin Schrödinger and the matrix mechanics of Werner Heisenberg. See J. L. Synge and B. A. Griffith, *Principles of Mechanics* (3d ed. 1959); K. R. Symon, *Mechanics* (3d ed. 1971); I. B. Cohen, *Introduction to Newton's Principia* (1971); Ernst Mach, *Science of Mechanics* (6th ed. 1973); T. W. Kibble, *Classical Mechanics* (2d ed. 1973); N. C. Barford, *Mechanics* (1973).

mechanism, philosophical theory about the nature of organic systems, holding that organisms are machines in the sense that they are material systems. Mechanism seeks to explain biological processes, including behavior, within the framework of classical physics and chemistry. The mechanistic approach has caused great controversy and is considered by its opponents, including vitalists (who contend that living organisms must be explained in terms of a mysterious self-determining principle rather than in physical or chemical terms) as inadequate and oversimplified. See A. R. Anderson, *Minds and Machines* (1964); R. E. Schofield, *Mechanism and Materialism* (1969).

mechanized warfare, employment of modern mobile attack and defense tactics that depend upon machines, more particularly upon vehicles powered by gasoline and diesel engines. Central to the waging of mechanized warfare are the tank and armored vehicle, with support and supply from motorized columns and aircraft. Automobiles were of great use in World War I. The TANK was introduced at Cambrai in 1917, and its use was enthusiastically endorsed by the British general J. F. C. FULLER. The need for air protection and support was emphasized by the American general William MITCHELL. Although the basic essentials of mechanized warfare were thus established early, it was not until Germany attacked Poland at the start of World War II that its full potentials were revealed. German armored (Panzer) divisions, supported by aircraft, proved their worth in Poland and France and later won spectacular successes in the Balkans, the Soviet Union, and Africa. Outstanding among the German proponents of this type of warfare were Heinz Guderian and Erwin Rommel. The German triumphs brought recognition to other advocates of mechanized warfare, e.g., Liddell Hart and Charles de Gaulle. The British and American armies also created armored divisions, and they developed weapons for defense against mechanized attack, e.g., the antitank gun and the tank destroyer. The Germans used their mechanized forces for deep penetrations into enemy territory but were ultimately beaten by superior use of artillery and aircraft as shown by the Allies in the battle of Alamein and other engagements. The Allies themselves developed the use of mechanized warfare with brilliant success, as in the overrunning of Western Europe (1944–45) by Allied forces under such leaders as Gen. George S. Patton. The Israeli desert offensives of 1956 and 1967 involved close coordination of motorized infantry units with air and parachute forces; in the Vietnam War helicopters helped to increase the mobility of troops and equipment.

Mechelen (mĕkh'ələn), Fr. *Malines,* city (1970 pop. 65,466), Antwerp prov., N central Belgium, on the Dijle River. In English it is also known as Mechlin. It is a commercial, industrial, and transportation center and was formerly a famous lace-making center. Manufactures include textiles, steel, motor vehicles, and processed food. Founded in the early Middle Ages, Mechelen was until 1356 a fief of the prince-bishops of Liège. It then passed to Louis de Mâle and the dukes of Burgundy. It was made an archiepiscopal see in 1559. The city was damaged often in the many wars that were fought in the Low Countries. However, Mechelen retains many noteworthy buildings, including the Gothic Cathedral of St. Rombaut (13th cent.), which has a 319-ft (97-m) tower and a famous carillon and which contains Anthony Van Dyck's great painting, the *Crucifixion;* the churches of Notre Dame and of St. John, both of which have paintings by Rubens; the archiepiscopal palace (16th cent.); and the city hall (14th cent.; rebuilt 18th cent.).

Mecherathite (mĕk'ərāthīt), obscure designation of one of David's guards. 1 Chron. 11.36.

Mechitar (mĕk'ĭtär''): see ARMENIAN LITERATURE.

Mechlin: see MECHELEN, Belgium.

Mecklenburg (mĕk'lənbo͝orkh), former state, c.8,850 sq mi (22,920 sq km), N East Germany, bordering on the Baltic Sea. Schwerin was the capital. As constituted in 1947 under Soviet military occupation, Mecklenburg consisted of the former states of Mecklenburg-Schwerin (5,068 sq mi/13,126 sq km) and Mecklenburg-Strelitz (1,131 sq mi/2,929 sq km), and of that part of the former Prussian province of POMERANIA situated W of the Oder River (but not including Stettin). In 1952 it was abolished as an administrative unit, and its territory was included in the districts of Schwerin, Rostock, and Neubrandenburg. The region embraced by the former state of Mecklenburg is a low-lying, fertile agricultural area, with many lakes and forests. Until the end of World War II it was characterized by great estates and farms, but after 1945 the region was divided into innumerable small farms. On the Baltic coast are the cities of Rostock, Wismar, and Stralsund, long important as Hanseatic ports, and the island of Rügen. (Rügen and Stralsund were formerly in Pomerania.) The region of Mecklenburg was occupied (6th cent. A.D.) by the WENDS. Later awarded as a march to the dukes of Saxony, it was subdued (12th cent.) by Henry the Lion, and the Wendish prince Pribislaw became a vassal of the Holy Roman Empire. In 1348 the princes were raised to ducal rank. In 1621 the duchy divided into Mecklenburg-Schwerin and Mecklenburg-Güstrow, but during the Thirty Years War both dukes were deposed (1628) and the entire duchy was given to WALLENSTEIN, the imperial general, who had conquered it. However, it was retaken by Gustavus II of Sweden and restored (1631) to its former rulers. The line of Mecklenburg-Güstrow died out in 1701, and the line of Mecklenburg-Strelitz took its place. At the Congress of Vienna both divisions of Mecklenburg were raised (1815) to grand duchies. They both joined the German Confederation, sided with Prussia in the Austro-Prussian War of 1866, and joined the German Empire at its founding in 1871. The grand dukes were deposed in 1918. In 1934 the separate states of Mecklenburg-Schwerin and Mecklenburg-Strelitz were united.

Mecklenburg Declaration of Independence, resolution alleged to have been proclaimed at Charlotte, N.C., by the citizens of Mecklenburg co. on May 20, 1775. Although North Carolina's seal and flag bear that date, the declaration is widely regarded as a spurious document. It is known, however, that the Mecklenburg citizens adopted (May 31, 1775) strong anti-British resolutions that declared all crown officials, civil and military, suspended from their offices, thus implying independence without actually declaring it. An account of the Mecklenburg Resolves, as they are called, was published in 1819, with embellishments from the national Declaration of Independence. From this grew the tale of the declaration of May 20, which still persists in North Carolina but which has not been supported by documentary evidence. See studies by W. M. Hoyt (1907, repr. 1972), J. H. Moore (1908), and V. V. McNitt (1960).

Medad (mē'dăd), one who, with Eldad, received the prophetic power of Moses. Num. 11.26, 27.

medal, a piece of metal, cast or struck, often coin-shaped. The obverse and reverse bear bas-relief and inscription. Commemorative medals are issued in memory of a notable person or event. Civil and military DECORATIONS are those medals (disk, cross, or star) conferred by state, order, or organization for signal bravery or service or for distinction in science or the arts. Religious medals, often worn by Roman Catholics, are believed to be efficacious if blessed by the Church; an INDULGENCE may be attached to a blessed medal. Medals have ranked as works of art since Greek times; Roman medals are notable for their realistic portraiture. Medals returned to fashion during the Renaissance, especially through the fine work of PISANELLO. Many sculptors and painters were famous also as medalists, notably Leone Leoni, Benvenuto Cellini, and Albrecht Dürer. France in the 19th cent. became the leader in producing medals of artistic merit. Cast medals were predominant in the 15th cent., but by the 16th had been largely superseded by die-struck medals. Dies may be cut direct, or a wax or plaster model about four times the intended size of the medal may be reproduced as a metal electrotype from which a die is made in the desired size by a reducing machine operating on the principle of the pantograph. See also NUMISMATICS. See Jean Babelon, *Great Coins and Medals* (tr. 1959).

Medan (mē'dăn), son of Abraham and Keturah. Gen. 25.2; 1 Chron. 1.32.

Medan (mädän'), city (1961 pop. 479,098), capital of North Sumatra prov., NE Sumatra, Indonesia, on the Deli River, c.15 mi (25 km) from its mouth, where the city's port (Belawan) is situated. The largest city in Sumatra, Medan is the marketing, commercial, and transportation center of a rich agricultural area containing great tobacco, rubber, and palm oil estates. Coffee and tea are also grown in the vicinity. Industries include the production of machinery and tile, and automobile assembly. Medan, gateway to the beautiful Lake Toba region, is a tourist center, with an international airport. The city is the seat of a superior court and of the Univ. of North Sumatra and the Islamic Univ. of North Sumatra.

Medary, Samuel (mĕd'ərē), 1801–64, American journalist, b. Montgomery co., Pa. In Ohio after 1825, he edited the *Ohio Sun* at Bethel and later the *Ohio Statesman* at Columbus and was superintendent of public printing (1837–47). Medary, a leading Western Democrat, championed the annexation of Texas and Oregon. He was territorial governor of Minnesota (1857–58) and of Kansas (1858–60). He founded the *Crisis* (1860) in Columbus, Ohio. In the Civil War, as a Peace Democrat who opposed Lincoln's policies because they were destructive to the Union, he was bitterly hated by Union patriots, who wrecked his press in 1863.

Medawar, Peter Brian (mĕd'əwär), 1915–, British zoologist, b. Brazil. After graduate work at Oxford he held research and teaching posts there. He was professor of zoology (1947–51) at the Univ. of Birmingham and in 1951 became professor of zoology and comparative anatomy at University College, London. During World War II he discovered a method for joining ends of severed nerves and later became noted for his experimental work in transplanting living tissue from one body to another. Working on a theory proposed by Sir Macfarlane Burnet, he proved it was possible under certain circumstances for an organism to be made to overcome its normal tendency to reject foreign tissue or organs. He was awarded the 1960 Nobel Prize for Physiology and Medicine jointly with Sir Macfarlane Burnet for this discovery of acquired immunological tolerance.

Medea (mīdē'ə), in Greek mythology, princess of Colchis, skilled in magic and sorcery. She fell in love with JASON and helped him, against the will of her father, Aeëtes, to obtain the Golden Fleece. When Jason left Colchis, she fled with him and lived as his wife for many years, bearing him two children. Jason later wished to marry Creusa, daughter of King Creon of Corinth, but Medea sent her an enchanted wedding gown that burned her to death. Medea then completed her revenge by killing her own two children; in another version of the legend the angered citizens of Corinth stoned them to death. Afterward, Medea fled to Athens, where she married King Aegeus.

Medeba (mĕd'ĭbə, mē'–), town, Jordan, the modern Madaba, E of the Dead Sea. An ancient Moabite town, it changed hands between Moab and Israel several times. In early Christian times it was a bishop's see. One of the oldest maps of Palestine (probably 6th cent.) was found there in a mosaic in a Byzantine church. Num. 21.30; Joshua 13.9–16; 1 Chron. 19.7; Isa. 15.2.

Medellín (māthäyēn'), city (1971 est. pop. 1,039,800), capital of Antioquia dept., W central Colombia. It is the country's second largest city and its chief manufacturing center. Textiles, steel, sugar, and coffee are the principal products. Coal, gold, and silver are mined in the surrounding region. The city, which was founded in 1675, is located in a small intermontane valley at an altitude of c.5,000 ft (1,520 m). Until the development of transportation in the 19th cent., it was practically isolated. Medellín, rich in cultural institutions, has three universities, several 17th-century churches, and a national mint.

Medes: see MEDIA, ancient country of W Asia.

Medford. 1 City (1970 pop. 64,397), Middlesex co., E Mass., a residential and industrial suburb of Boston, on the Mystic River; settled 1630, inc. as a city 1892. Truck bodies, valves, wax, paper, and furniture are among its products. A shipping and shipbuilding center from the 17th to the 19th cent., Medford was also known for its rum. It is the seat of Tufts Univ. Several 18th-century buildings are in the city. **2** City (1970 pop. 28,454), seat of Jackson co., SW Oregon, on Bear Creek; inc. 1884. It is a trade, shipping, and medical center in an agricultural area. There are fruit-packing plants and lumber mills in the city. Between 1836 and 1856 the area was the scene of a number of bloody conflicts between white settlers and the Rogue River Indians. Gold was discovered nearby in 1851. The gold-mining town of Jacksonville has been restored. Medford is the headquarters for Crater Lake National Park (see NATIONAL PARKS AND MONUMENTS, table) and Rogue River National Forest.

Media (mē'dēə), ancient country of W Asia whose actual boundaries cannot be defined, occupying generally what is now W Iran and S Azerbaijan. It extended from the Caspian Sea to the Zagros Mts. The Medes were an Indo-European people who spoke an Iranian language closely akin to old Persian. Some scholars claim they were an Aryanized people from Turan. Since there are no Median records, Assyrian and Greek sources must be relied upon for Median history. The Medes extended their rule over PERSIA during the reign of Sargon (d. 705 B.C.) and under Cyaxares captured Nineveh in 612 B.C.; they were the first people subject to Assyria to secure their freedom. The dynasty continued until the rule of ASTYAGES, when it was overthrown (c.550 B.C.) by Cyrus the Great and united with the Persian Empire. In the 2d cent. B.C. Media became part of the Parthian kingdom. It was divided by the Romans into Media Atropatene in the north and Media Magna in the south.

median. 1 In statistics, a type of AVERAGE. In a group of numbers as many numbers of the group are larger than the median as are smaller. In the group 4, 5, 6, 9, 13, 14, 19, the median is 9, three numbers being larger and three smaller. When there is an even number of numerals in the group, the median is usually defined as the number halfway between the middle pair. **2** In geometry, the line segment connecting any vertex of a triangle to the midpoint of the opposite side; the three medians of a triangle intersect in a single point, called the median point, or centroid. The median of a trapezoid is the line segment connecting the midpoints of the nonparallel opposite sides.

mediation, in international law, type of intervention in which the disputing states accept the offer of a third state to recommend a solution for their controversy. Mediation by an international commission is usually termed conciliation. Mediation differs from arbitration in being a diplomatic rather than a judicial procedure; thus, the parties to the dispute are not bound to accept the mediator's recommendation. Certain formal procedures appear in mediation that are absent from diplomatic good offices (i.e., informal consideration of a dispute by a third country friendly with both disputants); in effect, however, the two methods are identical. Resort to mediation has become increasingly frequent. The Declaration of Paris (1856) expressed the hope that the signatories would ask for mediation in their disputes. At the Second Hague Conference (1907) the right of friendly powers to offer mediation was recognized. The Covenant of the League of Nations provided that the whole League, acting through the League Council, should offer conciliation, and the Charter of the United Nations requires all members to submit disputes to mediation on recommendation of the Security Council. Mediation has been successful in many cases of international conflict. The United States served as mediator between Bolivia and Chile (1882) and between Russia and Japan (1905). The United Nations served as a mediator in the conflict in ISRAEL in 1948. In 1966 the Soviet Union mediated the border clashes between India and China. The Secretary General of the United Nations mediated successfully in several international disputes, particularly that over IRIAN BARAT.

medic: see ALFALFA.

Medicaid, national health insurance program in the United States for low-income persons; established 1965 with passage of the Social Security Amendments. The Federal role is limited to setting standards, issuing regulations and guidelines, and overseeing the state operation of the program. Of the various services covered under Medicaid, almost 40% of the funds are used to purchase in-patient hospital services; 30%, nursing home services; 12%, physician services; and the remaining 18% for drugs, laboratory services, X rays, and other covered services.

medical jurisprudence or **forensic medicine,** the application of medical science to legal problems. It is typically involved in cases concerning paternity, insanity, injury, or death resulting from violence. It also defines the relation of physician and patient. See studies by W. J. Curran (2d ed. 1970) and C. K. Simpson (6th ed. 1969).

Medicare, national health insurance program in the United States for persons aged 65 and over. It was established in 1965 with passage of the Social Security Amendments and is run by the Social Security Administration. It provides for a basic program of hospital insurance, under which most persons aged 65 and over are protected against major costs of hospital and related care; and a supplementary medical insurance program, through which persons aged 65 and over are aided in paying doctor bills and other health care bills. In the early 1970s Medicare paid for about 40% of the aged's total health bill.

Medici (mĕ'dĭchē, Ital. mā'dēchē), Italian family that directed the destinies of FLORENCE from the 15th cent. until 1737. Of obscure origin, they rose to immense wealth as merchants and bankers, became affiliated through marriage with the major houses of Europe, and, besides acquiring (1569) the title grand duke of Tuscany, produced three popes (LEO X, CLEMENT VII, and Leo XI), two queens of France (CATHERINE DE' MEDICI and MARIE DE' MEDICI), and several cardinals of the Roman Catholic Church. They also ruled for a brief period (1516–21) the duchy of Urbino. The rise of the Medici in Florence coincided with the triumph of the capitalist class over the guild merchants and artisans. Until 1532 the democratic constitution of Florence was outwardly upheld, but the Medici exerted actual control over the government without holding any permanent official position. They were driven from power and expelled from Florence in 1433–34, from 1494 to 1512, and from 1527 to 1530. However, the attempts (such as the PAZZI CONSPIRACY, 1478) of the Florentine republicans to restore the former liberties failed ultimately because of the Medici's wealth and powerful connections. When their influence began, in the early 15th cent., much of the glorious period of the RENAISSANCE in Florence lay already in the past; however, the magnificence and liberality of many of the members of the house, who were passionate patrons of the arts, literature, and learning, allowed Florence to become the richest repository of European culture since the Athens of Pericles. Florence as it is today is largely the accomplishment of the Medici. This cultural flowering was accompanied by tremendous economic prosperity and expansion and also by territorial aggrandizement (see TUSCANY) that reached its climax in the 16th cent. The rule of the Medici, though denounced by their enemies as tyrannical, was at first generally tolerant and wise, but became stultifying and bigoted in the 17th and 18th cent. The genealogy of the family is complicated by numerous illegitimate offspring and by the tendency of some of the members to dispose of each other by assassination. The first important member was Giovanni di Bicci de' Medici (1360–1429). His elder son, Cosimo de' Medici, founded the senior line, which included Piero de' Medici (1416–69); Lorenzo de' Medici (Lorenzo il Magnifico); Piero de' Medici (1471–1503); Pope Leo X; Giuliano de' Medici, duke of Nemours; Lorenzo de' Medici, duke of Urbino; Catherine de' Medici; Ippolito de' Medici; Alessandro de' Medici; and Pope Clement VII. Giovanni di Bicci's younger son, Lorenzo (d.1440), founded the younger line, which included Lorenzino de' Medici; Giovanni de' Medici (Giovanni delle Bande Nere); and the grand dukes of Tuscany—Cosimo I, Francesco (whose daughter was Marie de' Medici), Ferdinand I, Cosimo II, Ferdinand II, Cosimo III, and Gian Gastone, last of the line. See separate articles on the most important members of the family. See Lacy Collison-Morley, *The Early Medici* (1936); Ferdinand Schevill, *The Medici* (1949, repr. 1970); H. M. M. Acton, *The Last Medici* (rev. ed. 1958, repr. 1973); Marcel Brion, *The Medici* (tr. 1969). See also bibliographies under FLORENCE and RENAISSANCE.

Medici, Alessandro de' (älĕs-sän'drō dā), 1510?–37, duke of Florence (1532–37); probably an illegitimate son of Lorenzo de' Medici, duke of Urbino. After his father's death (1519), young Alessandro lived in Florence with his cousin Ippolito de' Medici (see separate article) and with Cardinal Silvio Passerini, who administered the city under the orders of Pope CLEMENT VII, then head of the Medici family. In 1527 the Medici were banished from Florence as a result of the invasion of Italy by the army of Holy Roman Emperor Charles V. After peace was reestablished between the pope and the emperor, Clement succeeded (1530) in restoring the Medici to power in Florence. With Clement's support Alessandro was made head of the republic (1531) and hereditary duke (1532) by Charles V, whose illegitimate daughter Margaret of Austria (later known as Margaret of Parma) he married. His arbitrary rule brought him general hatred. The Florentines sent (1535) Ippolito to appeal to Charles V against the duke, but Ippolito died en route, apparently of malaria, although he may have been poisoned at Alessandro's orders. Alessandro, who continued to enjoy imperial favor, was murdered in turn two years later by a relative, Lorenzino de' Medici (see separate article). The elder Medici line was then extinct, and the headship of the family passed to Cosimo I de' Medici.

Medici, Catherine de': see CATHERINE DE' MEDICI.

Medici, Cosimo de' (kô'zēmō), 1389–1464, Italian merchant prince, first of the MEDICI family to rule Florence. He is often called Cosimo the Elder. After the death of his father, Giovanni di Bicci de' Medici, Cosimo and his family were banished (1433) from Florence by a faction headed by the powerful Albizzi family. He returned a year later and, supported by the people, soon became the acknowledged leading citizen of the republic. An able financier, he vastly expanded the family's banking business. In spite of his lavish expenses for the state, for charities, and for the arts and learning, he doubled his fortune. He respected the republican institutions of the city, always sought popular support, and made his power as little felt as possible. Guiding Florentine foreign policy, he sought a balance of power among the Italian states. From the traditional alliance with Venice against Milan, he shifted to an alliance with the SFORZA family, helping the Sforzas to gain control over Milan. Cosimo's claim to greatness, however, rests chiefly on his generosity toward artists and scholars. He founded the famous Medici Library and an academy for Greek studies (headed by Marsilio FICINO), built extensively in Florence, and protected such artists as Brunelleschi, Donatello, Ghiberti, and Luca della Robbia. After his death Florence voted him the official title Pater Patriae. His son, Piero de' Medici, known as Il Gottoso [the gouty], succeeded as head of the family. See biographies by K. D. Vernon (1899, repr. 1970) and K. S. Gutkind (1939).

Medici, Cosimo I de', 1519–74, duke of Florence (1537–69), grand duke of Tuscany (1569–74); son of Giovanni de' Medici (Giovanni delle Bande Nere). In 1537, Lorenzino de' Medici (see separate article) murdered Cosimo's predecessor, Alessandro de' Medici, and fled from Florence, leaving the succession to Cosimo. Cosimo, despite promises to the contrary, assumed absolute authority as soon as he was installed. A group of exiles who tried to restore the republic were defeated and were either imprisoned or beheaded. In 1539, Cosimo married a Spanish noblewoman, Eleonora de Toledo, whose enormous dowry replenished his empty coffers. Under Cosimo's able, though ruthless, rule Florence reached its highest political importance and material prosperity and almost doubled its territories—notably by the acquisition (1555) of the republic of SIENA. In 1569, Pope Pius V made Cosimo grand duke of Tuscany. Cosimo centralized his state. His son, Francesco de' Medici, succeeded him.

Medici, Cosimo II de', 1590–1621, grand duke of Tuscany (1609–21); son and successor of Ferdinand I de' Medici. Although Cosimo played a role in the War of the Mantuan Succession, he generally avoided intervention in foreign affairs; in domestic policy he was less energetic than his father, particularly in economic matters, but he maintained a large fleet. He was a patron of Galileo, whom he appointed court philosopher and mathematician. His son, Ferdinand II de' Medici, succeeded him.

Medici, Cosimo III de', 1642–1723, grand duke of Tuscany (1670–1723); son and successor of Ferdinand II de' Medici. During his reign the government of Tuscany degenerated into bigoted and corrupt despotism. His son and successor, Gian Gastone de' Medici, was the last of the family to rule Tuscany.

Médici, Emílio Garrastazú (əmē'lyo͞o gərăsh'təzo͞o mĕd'ĭsē), 1905–, president of Brazil (1969–74). An army general, he served as head of the national intelligence service. He was selected president (Oct., 1969) by a military junta to succeed the ailing Artur da Costa e Silva. Sharply suppressing all dissent, he imposed a military dictatorship. Under his leadership the country experienced a major economic boom. He was succeeded (March, 1974) by his hand-picked successor, Ernesto Geisel.

Medici, Ferdinand I de', 1549–1609, grand duke of Tuscany (1587–1609); brother and successor of Francesco de' Medici. He was made a cardinal in his youth, and he built the famous Villa Medici at Rome. To become grand duke at his brother's death he resigned his cardinalate (he had never been ordained). Ferdinand improved the administration, strengthened the fleet, and created the port of Leghorn. His son, Cosimo II de' Medici, succeeded him.

Medici, Francesco de' (frănchās'kō), 1541–87, grand duke of Tuscany (1574–87); son and successor of Cosimo I de' Medici. In his reign the decline of the Medici family began. He allowed the Austrian and Spanish branches of the house of Hapsburg to establish a virtual protectorate over his dominion, devoting himself to alchemy and other nonpolitical pursuits. He first married Joanna, daughter of Holy Roman Emperor Ferdinand I, and then, after Joanna's death, Bianca CAPELLO. His daughter by the first marriage was Marie de' Medici, queen of Henry IV of France. Francesco was succeeded by his brother, Ferdinand I de' Medici.

Medici, Gian Gastone de' (jän gästô'nā), 1671–1737, grand duke of Tuscany (1723–37); son and successor of Cosimo III de' Medici. Gian Gastone was the last male member of his family, and the question of succession caused agitation even before his father's death. In 1735 it was settled, in connection with the general territorial exchanges caused by the War of the POLISH SUCCESSION, that on Gian Gastone's death Tuscany should fall to Francis of Lorraine (later Holy Roman Emperor FRANCIS I), husband of Maria Theresa, in exchange for Lorraine, which went to Stanislaus I of Poland. When Francis became grand duke, Tuscany had fallen from its former glory to decadence and impoverishment.

Medici, Giovanni de' (1475–1521): see LEO X.

Medici, Giovanni de', or **Giovanni delle Bande Nere** (jōvän'nē dĕl'lā bän'dā nā'rā) [Ital.,=of the black bands], 1498–1526, Italian condottiere; great-grandson of Lorenzo de' Medici (d. 1440, brother of Cosimo de' Medici, 1389–1464). The son of Caterina Sforza (see under SFORZA, family), he was trained from childhood for the military life, and in 1516 his relative Pope Leo X gave him command of a troop. He soon won great reputation as a military leader. His nickname was probably acquired because of the black stripes of mourning on his banners after the death (1521) of Leo X. In the Italian Wars, Giovanni fought (1521–22) in N Italy for the pope, on the side of Holy Roman Emperor Charles V, against Francis I of France. He later changed sides, however, and fought with Francis in the battle of Pavia (1525), where he was severely wounded. In 1526 he again sided with Francis, fighting for the League of Cognac. He died of a wound received in battle. Giovanni delle Bande Nere possessed great courage and tactical ability. His hold over his men was remarkable, and his corps remained together long after his death. His wife, Maria Salviati, was a granddaughter of Lorenzo de' Medici (Lorenzo il Magnifico), and his son became grand duke of Tuscany as Cosimo I.

Medici, Giuliano de' (jo͞olyä'nō), 1479–1516, duke of Nemours (1515–16); younger son of Lorenzo de' Medici (Lorenzo il Magnifico) and brother of Pope Leo X. He entered Florence in 1512 when the Holy League restored his family to rule the city. Having married a princess of the Nemours branch of the house of Savoy, he was invested with the duchy by Francis I of France, who also intended to place him on the throne of Naples. Giuliano was a patron of the arts and letters. His statue, by Michelangelo, together with the statues of Day and Night, adorn his tomb in the Church of San Lorenzo, Florence. Ippolito de' Medici was his illegitimate son.

Medici, Giulio de': see CLEMENT VII.

Medici, Ippolito de' (ēp-pô'lētō), 1511–35, cardinal of the Roman Catholic Church; an illegitimate son of Giuliano de' Medici, duke of Nemours. Pope CLEMENT VII, head of the Medici family, after his election to the papacy in 1523, continued to rule Florence through Ippolito and Ippolito's cousin, Alessandro de' Medici (see separate article), entrusting to Cardinal Silvio Passerini the actual conduct of Florentine affairs. Clement favored Alessandro more and more, and in 1531 he made him head of the republic. At the same time he made Ippolito a cardinal and sent him on a temporary mission to Hungary to remove him from the scene. In 1535, Ippolito was deputed by the Florentines to bring their grievances against Alessandro before Holy Roman Emperor Charles V. He died on his way, probably of malaria, although he may have been poisoned at Alessandro's command.

Medici, Lorenzino de' (lōräntsē'nō), 1515–47, member of the cadet branch of the Medici family. A boon companion of Alessandro de' Medici (see under MEDICI, family), he secretly plotted the duke's murder—possibly out of republican convictions. With a hired assassin, he stabbed Alessandro to death (1537) and fled to Venice. Alessandro had named Cosimo I de' Medici, Lorenzino's distant cousin, heir to the duchy, and Cosimo succeeded upon Alessandro's death. Lorenzino was eventually assassinated in Venice on Cosimo's orders. He is the hero of Alfred de Musset's drama, *Lorenzaccio* (1833).

Medici, Lorenzo de' (lōrĕn'tsō), 1449–92, Italian merchant prince, called Lorenzo il Magnifico [the magnificent]. He succeeded (1469) his father, Piero de' Medici, as head of the Medici family and as virtual ruler of Florence. One of the towering figures of the Italian Renaissance, he was an astute politician, firm in purpose, yet pliant and tolerant; a patron of the arts, literature, and learning; and a reputable scholar and poet. Without adopting any official title, he subtly managed to conduct the affairs of the Florentine state. His lavish public entertainments contributed to his popularity, but, in combination with his mediocre success as a businessman, they helped to drain his funds. His growing control of the government alarmed Pope SIXTUS IV, who helped to foment the PAZZI CONSPIRACY (1478) against Lorenzo and his brother, Giuliano de' Medici. Giuliano was stabbed to death during Mass at the cathedral, but Lorenzo escaped with a wound, and the plot collapsed. Lorenzo retaliated against the Pazzi, and Sixtus excommunicated him and laid an interdict on Florence. An honorable peace was made not long afterward. In 1480, in order to retrieve his huge financial losses, Lorenzo used his political power to gain control over the public funds of Florence. The city, however, flourished, and Lorenzo, who played an important role on the international scene, constantly worked to preserve general peace by establishing a balance of power among the Italian states. Through his credit with Pope Innocent VIII he obtained a cardinal's hat for his son Giovanni (later Pope Leo X). In spite of the attacks of Girolamo SAVONAROLA, Lorenzo allowed him to continue his preaching. Lorenzo spent huge sums to purchase Greek and Latin manuscripts and to have them copied, and he urged the use of Italian in literature. His brilliant literary circle included Politian, Ficino, Luigi Pulci, and Giovanni Pico della Mirandola. He was a patron of Sandro Botticelli, Ghirlandaio, Filippino Lippi, Andrea del Verrocchio, Michelangelo, and other famed artists. His own poetry—love lyrics, rustic poems, carnival songs, sonnets, and odes—shows a delicate feeling for nature. His son Piero de' Medici succeeded him as head of the family but was expelled from Florence two years later. See C. M. Ady, *Lorenzo de' Medici and Renaissance Italy* (1955, repr. 1964); C. L. Mee, *Lorenzo de Medici and the Renaissance* (1969).

Medici, Lorenzo de', 1492–1519, duke of Urbino (1516–19); son of Piero de' Medici. His uncle, Pope LEO X, who controlled Florence through him, made Lorenzo duke of Urbino. After Lorenzo's death, however, Urbino reverted (1521) to the Della Rovere family. A patron of the arts and humanities, Lorenzo has been immortalized by MICHELANGELO, who designed and made his tomb in the Church of San Lorenzo, Florence. Of the three statues adorning his tomb, one represents Lorenzo in a pensive attitude (hence it is known as the *Pensieroso*) and the other two represent Dawn and Dusk. Lorenzo was the father of Catherine de' Medici, queen of France, and, probably, of Alessandro de' Medici.

Medici, Marie de': see MARIE DE' MEDICI.

Medici, Piero de' (pyĕ'rō), 1416–69, Italian merchant prince. He succeeded his father, Cosimo de' Medici, as head of the Medici family and as leader of the Florentine state. His ill health earned him the nickname Il Gottoso [the gouty]. In 1466, Piero put down a conspiracy of nobles headed by the Pitti family, and although it was directed at his life, he allowed the conspirators to go free. His son, Lorenzo de' Medici (Lorenzo il Magnifico), succeeded him as head of the family.

Medici, Piero de', 1471–1503, Italian merchant prince. He succeeded his father, Lorenzo de' Medici

(Lorenzo il Magnifico), as head of the Medici family and as leader of the Florentine state. In 1494 he surrendered the chief fortresses of Tuscany to the invading army of Charles VIII of France. The democratic party in Florence, led by SAVONAROLA, took advantage of Charles's approach and of Piero's weakness to expel the Medici, who had virtually ruled Florence for half a century. After Piero's death the Medici regained (1512) control over Florence with the help of the HOLY LEAGUE. Giuliano de' Medici and Pope Leo X were brothers of Piero. Piero's son, Lorenzo de' Medici, became (1516) duke of Urbino.

medicine, science and art of treating and preventing disease. The art, if not the science, undoubtedly began with man's first appearance on earth, for since man became capable of thought he has been seeking cures for illness. Of prehistoric medicine there is evidence only of those diseases that affected the bony structure. Prehistoric skulls found in Europe and South America indicate that Neolithic man was already able to trephine, or remove disks of bone from, the skull successfully, but whether this delicate operation was performed to release evil spirits or as a surgical procedure is not known. Nevertheless, those records available that concern early medicine reveal that many civilizations, amidst all the magic and incantation, had discovered scientific principles held valid today. Although earliest Egyptian medical papyri are replete with ritual prayers and spells against demons, a more rational, empirical practice also developed, involving the use of many potent drugs still in use today, such as castor oil, senna, opium, colchicine, and mercury. In spite of their skill in embalming, however, the Egyptians had little knowledge of anatomy. In Sumerian medicine the Laws of Hammurabi established the first known code of medical ethics and laid down a fee schedule for specific surgical procedures. In the absence of a strong lay professional caste, every Babylonian considered himself a physician and, according to Herodotus, gave advice freely to the sick man who was willing to exhibit himself to passersby in the public square. The Mosaic Code of the Hebrews indicated concerns with social hygiene and prevention of disease by dietary restrictions and sanitary measures. Although ancient Chinese medicine was also influenced adversely by the awe felt for the sanctity of the human body, the *Nei Ching,* attributed to the emperor Huang-Ti (2698–2598 B.C.), contains a reference to a theory of the circulation of the blood and the vital function of the heart that presupposes some familiarity with anatomy. In addition, accurate location of the proper points for ACUPUNCTURE implies some familiarity with the nervous and vascular systems. The Chinese pharmacopeia was the most extensive of all the older civilizations. The Hindus seem to have been familiar with every surgical procedure except the use of ligature; they were skilled in such techniques as reconstructing the nose (rhinoplasty) and cutting for removal of bladder stones. In Greek medicine, the impetus for the rational approach came largely from the speculations of the pre-Socratic philosophers and such philosopher-scientists as Pythagoras, Democritus, and Empedocles. Hippocrates taught the prevention of disease through a regimen of diet and exercise; he emphasized careful observation of the patient, the recuperative powers of nature, and a high standard of ethical conduct, as incorporated in the Hippocratic Oath. By the 4th cent. B.C., Aristotle had already stimulated interest in anatomy by his dissections of animals, and work in the 3d cent. B.C. on human anatomy and physiology was of such high quality that it was not equalled for fifteen hundred years. The Roman conquest was accompanied by a gradual decline in medical originality. However, through the construction of aqueducts, baths, sewers, and hospitals, the conquerors did much to improve sanitation and public health, and by dredging marshy areas they learned to control malaria. The encyclopedic writings of GALEN constitute a final synthesis of the medicine of the ancient world. Revered by Arabic and Western physicians alike, his concepts were to stand virtually unchallenged until the 16th cent. Unfortunately his prolific researches on anatomy and physiology were not invariably accurate, and reliance on them later impeded progress in anatomy. The gradual spread of Christianity, followed by the barbarian invasions and the Arab conquests, brought on a period of stagnation in European medicine and a resurgence of priestly medicine. With the destruction or neglect of the Roman sanitary facilities, there followed a series of local epidemics that culminated many centuries later in the great PLAGUE of the 14th cent. known as the Black Death. During the Middle Ages certain monastic libraries, notably those at Monte Cassino, Bobbio, and St. Gall, preserved a few ancient medical manuscripts, and Arab and Jewish physicians such as Avicenna and Maimonides continued medical investigation. The first real breakthrough in the medical isolation of Europe came with the translation of many writings from the Arabic at Salerno, Italy, and through continuing trade and cultural exchange with Byzantium. By the 13th cent. there were flourishing medical schools at Montpellier, Paris, Bologna, and Padua. At Bologna a renewal of interest in surgery led to the first public dissection of the human body. The center of anatomical studies was Padua, where VESALIUS proved that Galen had made anatomical mistakes. Prominent among those who pursued the new interest in experimental medicine were Paracelsus, Ambroise Paré, and Fabricius (who discovered the valves of the veins); others experimented with new drugs derived from plants. In the 17th cent. William HARVEY, using careful experimental methods, demonstrated the circulation of the blood, a concept that met with considerable early resistance. The introduction of quinine marked a triumph over malaria, one of the oldest plagues of mankind. The introduction of the compound microscope led to the discovery of minute forms of life, and the discovery of the capillary system of the blood filled the final gap in Harvey's explanation of blood circulation. In the 18th cent. the heart drug digitalis was introduced, scurvy was controlled, SURGERY was transformed into an experimental science, and reforms were instituted in mental institutions. Edward Jenner introduced VACCINATION to prevent smallpox, laying the groundwork for the science of immunization. The 19th cent. saw the beginnings of modern medicine, with demonstration of the germ theory of DISEASE; the use of disinfection and the consequent improvement in medical, particularly obstetrical, care; the use of inoculation; the introduction of anesthetics in surgery (see ANESTHESIA); and a revival of better PUBLIC HEALTH and sanitary measures. A decline in maternal and infant mortality followed. Medicine in the 20th cent. has been characterized by the rise of CHEMOTHERAPY, especially the use of ANTIBIOTICS and SULFA DRUGS; increased understanding of the mechanisms of IMMUNITY and the increased prophylactic use of vaccination; utilization of knowledge of the endocrine system to treat diseases resulting from hormone imbalance, such as the use of insulin to treat diabetes; and increased understanding of nutrition and the role of VITAMINS in health. Much medical research is now directed toward such problems as CANCER, HEART DISEASE, and organ TRANSPLANTATION. With the growth of general and specialized medical knowledge, the educational requirements of the medical profession have increased. In addition to the four-year medical course and the general hospital internship required almost everywhere, additional years of study in a specialized field are usually required. Similar progress and increased requirements in education are reflected in ancillary professions such as nursing. Modern medicine, characterized by growing specialization and a complex diagnostic and therapeutic technology, faces problems in the allocation of capital and personnel resources. Some authorities advocate an increase in the use of paramedical personnel to supervise the care of individuals with common, chronic, or terminal illnesses, leaving the physician in charge of treating curable disease. Others emphasize the physician's responsibility to help patients and families in the overall management of their health problems, many of which are thought to reflect the social ills and concomitant emotional problems of urban, industrialized society. In some countries, e.g., Great Britain, medical care is under government control and is available virtually without charge to all. In the United States, medical practice is characterized by a patchwork mixture of government and private control. The Kefauver-Harris amendments to the Federal Food, Drug, and Cosmetic Act of 1962 empower the Food and Drug Administration to require stricter testing and licensing of new drugs. There have also been federal, state, and local programs for mass vaccination and other public health programs, e.g., for the control of venereal disease. The Medicare program, enacted in 1965, provides subsidized hospital and nursing home care for persons over 65 and, with the Hill-Burton Act, provides funds for state aid to the medically indigent (Medicaid). A wide variety of private medical insurance plans are also available, and health maintenance organizations, or group practice plans, such as the Kaiser-Permanente plan, provide comprehensive care to keep people healthy rather than merely to treat them after they have become ill. However, the great rise in the cost of health care in recent years has led to a growing belief that the United States should adopt some form of nationwide health insurance plan. See the histories of medicine by H. E. Sigerist (2 vol., 1951–61), C. J. Singer (2d ed. 1962), and E. H. Ackerknecht (rev. ed. 1968); C.E.A. Winslow, *The Conquest of Epidemic Disease* (1943, repr. 1967); Edwin Clarke, ed., *Modern Methods in the History of Medicine* (1971); Noel Poynter, *Medicine and Man* (1971); William Osler, *The Evolution of Modern Medicine* (1922, repr. 1972).

Medicine Bow Mountains, outlying eastern range of the Rocky Mts., SE Wyo. and N Colo. It extends from Medicine Bow town, Wyo., NW of Laramie, southward c.100 mi (160 km) to Cameron Pass, Colo. Peaks include Medicine Bow Peak (12,013 ft/3,662 m) and Elk Mt. (11,156 ft/3,400 m). Much of the area is in Medicine Bow National Forest.

Medicine Hat, city (1971 pop. 26,518), SE Alta., Canada, on the South Saskatchewan River. It is the center of a farming and ranching area. Natural-gas deposits are exploited. There are light industries and glassblowing and rubber plants.

medicine man, among American Indian tribes and other primitive peoples as far back as Paleolithic times, a sorcerer supposed to possess mysterious healing powers. Like the SHAMAN and the African witch doctor, the medicine man was a specialist in the use of supernatural healing agencies. Usually the medicine man's functions were quite extensive, and he served not only as healer of bodily diseases but as tribal priest, with powers to inflict pain, promote fertility, and secure good hunting and fishing. Most Indian tribes regarded illness as the visitation of some malignancy that had gained access to the body by either natural or supernatural means—through violation of a taboo or through the activities of a sorcerer from an enemy tribe. The function of the medicine man was to remove or cast out the illness from the patient by means of spells, charms, and sympathetic magic. Sometimes scientific or pseudoscientific methods were used, such as bloodletting, physical manipulation, application of herbs, or sucking out the malignancy from the patient's body.

Medieval Latin literature. With the slow dissolution over centuries of the Roman Empire in the West, Latin writing dwindled and changed like the rest of Roman culture. It was formerly conventional to say that in the 6th cent. the *De consolatione philosophiae* of Boethius was the last great work of classical Latin and that Boethius' younger contemporary Cassiodorus was the first notable figure of medieval literature (though he wrote in classical form). However, the transition was, in fact, so gradual as to be imperceptible. One of the main characteristics of the emerging literature was the fundamentally Christian tone; the other was the use of a simpler and more flexible Latin, which drew from the common speech of Rome and the provinces. The Christian tradition had already been firmly established by early Christian writers—St. Jerome, St. Ambrose, St. Augustine, and others—using exact classical language. Notable poets wrote Christian hymns, Prudentius as early as the 4th cent., Fortunatus of Gaul in the 6th cent. Hymns, which were joined to music and shaped to new poetry with accentual rhythm and rhyme unknown to the classics, were to be one of the glories of medieval literature. From the 6th cent. on learning was preserved mostly in the monasteries (see MONASTICISM), and almost all writers were clergymen. The Latin used in the Church services, based on the simplified language, was therefore preserved long after all Latin was replaced in common speech by the vernacular tongues. Medieval literature, secular as well as religious, was permeated with quotations from, and allusions to, the Vulgate version of the Bible. The bulk of prose writing was given over to theological treatises, homilies, sermons, pastoral instructions, and devotional works. Some of it is of great force and beauty, as in writings of St. Gregory the Great (Pope Gregory I). Sporadic efforts were made to revive classical learning, but these were successful only in promoting learning in general and establishing educational standards. By far the most important was the Carolingian revival in the late 8th and early 9th cent. Charlemagne persuaded an Englishman, Alcuin, to establish a court school. The writers, such as Einhard, were medieval rather than classical in spirit, but the effects of the revival were lasting. The great Church schools at Chartres, Rheims, Paris, and Bologna and the many other schools preserved academic standards, and many writers, such as Paul the Dea-

con, Rabanus Maurus Magnentius, and John Scotus Erigena, show the vigorous effect of the school movement. The poetry of Walafrid Strabo and Gottschalk seems to be related to academic exercises, and *Waltharius,* a Latin rendition of a Germanic epic, bears marks of the schoolroom. The dramas of Hrotswith von Bandersheim were a deliberate attempt to imitate Terence in Christian terms. Abelard, outstanding theologian and competent poet, was primarily a schoolman, although he is best known today for his letters and the pathetic account of his misfortunes. His school was the precursor of the Univ. of Paris, one of the great medieval universities (see UNIVERSITY). St. Bernard of Clairvaux, vigorous opponent of Abelard, is usually considered one of the greatest of medieval writers; some of his contemplative works and hymns are widely known today. Perhaps more renowned as a theologian than Bernard was the learned St. Anselm, and certainly more vociferous in polemics was Hugh of St. Victor. Among the mystical writers Richard of St. Victor is ranked by many as a peer of St. Bernard. The volume of writing was steadily growing and was of truly universal Western authorship. Secular poetry and prose were being composed for sheer enjoyment. Chroniclers and historians were found in all lands—Bede, Geoffrey of Monmouth, Matthew Paris, Walter Map, Suger, and William of Tyre are examples—and many monasteries had completely anonymous chronicles such as those of St. Gall. Letters, tracts, and scientific works all added to the bulk of written matter. The quality of writing and of scholarship was steadily rising, and the way was being prepared for the great flowering of medieval culture in the 13th cent. Most notable was the full development of SCHOLASTICISM by St. Bonaventure, St. Albertus Magnus, and St. Thomas Aquinas, together with Duns Scotus, William of Occam, and others. The simple Latin dialogues on the mysteries of Christ's life had become the MIRACLE PLAY. Secular poetry had since the 11th cent. given rise to well-wrought and exquisitely rhymed lyrics and satires commonly called the GOLIARDIC SONGS. The type of encyclopedic compendium popular since St. Isidore of Seville's 7th-century *Etynologiae* was represented by the work of Vincent of Beauvais. The lives of saints were collected in *The Golden Legend* by Jacobus de Voragine. Other genres were also represented in Latin: the mock epic, the fabliau, the romance, the beast tale, the folk story. But these forms were already being taken over by writing in the vernacular, which had begun in the 10th cent. and was to replace Latin entirely by the 14th. This advance of the dialects, which were already being formed into the modern European languages, doomed the older "learned" literature. Meanwhile the revival of classical learning and the scholarship of the Renaissance moved to undermine Medieval Latin literature. Dante's precise Latin writing could scarcely be called medieval in its form, and the humanists with their Ciceronian prose and Vergilian eclogues were setting out to destroy, not to reform, Medieval Latin. Except for the persistence of Church Latin, they succeeded. See H. O. Taylor, *The Medieval Mind* (1925); Maurice Hélin, *A History of Medieval Latin Literature* (tr. 1949); E. R. Curtius, *European Literature and the Latin Middle Ages* (tr. 1953); F. J. E. Raby, *A History of Christian Latin Poetry* (2d ed. 1953) and *A History of Secular Latin Poetry* (2d ed. 1957); W. T. H. Jackson, *The Literature of the Middle Ages* (1960).

medieval philosophy: see SCHOLASTICISM.

Medill, Joseph (mədĭl'), 1823–99, American journalist, b. near St. John, N.B., Canada. His family moved to a farm near Massillon, Ohio, in 1832. He was admitted to the bar in 1846, but in 1849 abandoned law and with his three brothers bought the Coshocton *Whig,* which he renamed the *Republican.* In 1851 he founded the *Daily Forest City* in Cleveland and later merged it with a Free-Soil paper to form the Cleveland *Leader.* Medill bought an interest in the Chicago *Tribune* in 1855, became its managing editor and business manager, and from 1874 until his death had absolute control of the paper. He was important in the formation of the Republican party (he is credited with having suggested its name) and was a warm supporter and friend of Lincoln. In the Civil War he advocated the emancipation and arming of the slaves and in Reconstruction days backed the radical Republicans in Congress. He was a member of the Illinois constitutional convention of 1869, was one of the first U.S. civil service commissioners (1871), and was elected (1871) mayor of Chicago. See Philip Kinsley, *The Chicago Tribune* (3 vol., 1943–46); John Tebbel, *An American Dynasty* (1947).

Medina, José Toribio (hōsā' tōrē'byō māthē'nä), 1852–1930, Chilean scholar. He traveled widely in Latin America, Europe, and the United States, collecting documents relevant to Latin American history. His numerous works cover a vast range of learning—history, biography, bibliography, archaeology, and journalism. Among them are a history of colonial literature in Chile; *Los aborígenes de Chile* (1882); biographical works on Juan Díaz de Solis and others; several volumes on the Inquisition; numerous books on the history of printing in Spanish America; and the monumental *Biblioteca hispanoamericana* (7 vol., 1898–1907). See biography by S. E. Roberts (1941).

Medina (mĭdē'nə), Arabic *Medinat an-Nabi* [city of the Prophet] or *Madinat Rasul Allah* [city of the apostle of Allah], city (1965 est. pop. 100,000), Hejaz, W Saudi Arabia. It is situated c.110 mi (180 km) inland from the Red Sea in a well-watered oasis where much fruit is raised. Before the flight (hegira) of MUHAMMAD from MECCA to the city in 622, Medina was called Yathrib. Muhammad quickly gained control of Medina, successfully defended it against attacks from Mecca, and used it as the base for converting and conquering Arabia. Medina grew rapidly until 661, when the UMAYYAD dynasty transferred the capital of the caliphate to Damascus. Thereafter Medina was reduced to the rank of a provincial town, ruled by governors appointed by the distant caliphs. Local warfare drained the city's prosperity. It came under the sway of the Ottoman Turks in 1517. The WAHABIS captured it in 1804, but it was retaken for the Turks by Muhammad Ali in 1812. In World War I the forces of Husayn ibn Ali, who revolted against Turkey, captured Medina. In 1924 it fell to Ibn Saud, Husayn's rival, after a 15-month siege. The city is surrounded by double walls flanked by bastions and pierced by nine gates. The chief building is the large mosque, which contains the tombs of Muhammad, his daughter Fatima, and the caliph Omar. A pilgrimage to Mecca usually includes a side trip to Medina. Medina is the seat of Islamic Univ. (1962). See Eldon Rutter, *The Holy Cities of Arabia* (2 vol., 1928); Emel Esin, *Mecca, The Blessed; Madinah, the Radiant* (1963).

Medina (mədī'nə), city (1970 pop. 10,913), seat of Medina co., N Ohio; laid out 1818, inc. as a city 1950. It is a processing point in a farm area, with a bee industry.

Medina del Campo (māthē'nä thĕl käm'pō), town (1970 pop. 14,327), Valladolid prov., central Spain, in León. It is a communications center and agricultural market with food-processing industries. The town was almost completely destroyed by fire in the 16th cent. Medina del Campo was the favorite residence of Queen Isabella I.

Medina Sidonia, Alonso Pérez de Guzmán, duque de (älōn'sō pā'rĕth thā gōōthmän' dōō'kā thā māthē'nä sēthō'nyä), 1550–1615, Spanish nobleman and commander in chief of the Spanish ARMADA. The 7th duke of one of Spain's most ancient, illustrious, and wealthy houses, Medina Sidonia was appointed captain general of Andalusia early in 1588. Following the death of the marqués de Santa Cruz shortly afterward, Philip II of Spain made him leader of the Armada, a command that he accepted with reluctance because he had no previous naval experience. Aware of the fleet's deficiencies in supplies, arms, and crew, he nevertheless set out in May, 1588, to fulfill almost impossible instructions: he was to skirt the French coast through the English Channel while avoiding a naval engagement and to effect a rendezvous in the Netherlands with the land army of Alessandro FARNESE, duke of Parma, and cover its attack on England. Weather conditions and a running battle with the English fleet prevented this liaison, and Medina Sidonia took the remnants of his defeated and scattered Armada around Scotland and Ireland, reaching Spain by late September. He retained royal favor and continued to serve in high offices until his death. Although defamed by contemporaries and subsequent historians, Medina Sidonia has been rehabilitated by recent scholars who have recognized his courage, loyalty to the crown, leadership, and administrative ability.

Mediolanum: see MILAN, Italy.

Mediterranean fever: see BRUCELLOSIS.

Mediterranean fruit fly: see FRUIT FLY.

Mediterranean race: see RACE.

Mediterranean Sea [Latin,=in the midst of lands], the world's largest inland sea, c.965,000 sq mi (2,499,350 sq km), surrounded by Europe, Asia, and Africa. It is c.2,400 mi (3,900 km) long with a maximum width of c.1,000 mi (1,600 km); its greatest depth is c.14,450 ft (4,400 m), off Cape Matapan, Greece. It connects with the Atlantic Ocean through the Strait of Gibraltar; with the Black Sea through the Dardanelles, the Sea of Marmara, and the Bosporus; and with the Red Sea through the Suez Canal. Its chief divisions are the Tyrrhenian, Adriatic, Ionian, and Aegean seas; its chief islands are Sicily, Sardinia, Corsica, Crete, Cyprus, Malta, Rhodes, the Dodecanese, the Cyclades, the Sporades, the Balearic Islands, and the Ionian Islands. Shallows (Adventure Bank) between Sicily and Cape Bon, Tunisia, divide the Mediterranean into two main basins. It is of higher salinity than the Atlantic and has little variation in tides. The largest rivers that flow into it are the Po, Rhône, Ebro, and Nile. The shores are chiefly mountainous. Earthquakes and volcanic disturbances are frequent. The region around the sea has a warm, dry climate characterized by abundant sunshine. Strong local winds, such as the hot, dry sirocco from the south and the cold, dry mistral and bora from the north, blow across the sea. Fish (about 400 species), sponges, and corals are plentiful. Some of the most ancient civilizations (see AEGEAN CIVILIZATION) flourished around the Mediterranean. It was opened as a highway for commerce by merchants trading from PHOENICIA. Carthage, Greece, Sicily, and Rome were rivals for dominance of its shores and trade; under the Roman Empire it became virtually a Roman lake and was called *Mare Nostrum* [our sea]. Later, the Byzantine Empire and the Arabs dominated the Mediterranean. Products of the Orient passed to Europe over Mediterranean trade routes until the establishment of a route around the Cape of Good Hope (late 15th cent.). With the opening of the Suez Canal (1869) the Mediterranean resumed its importance as a link on the route to the East. The development of the northern regions of Africa and of oil fields in the Middle East has increased its trade. Its importance as a trade link and as a route for attacks on Europe resulted in European rivalry for control of its coasts and islands and led to campaigns in the region during both world wars. Since World War II the Mediterranean region has been of strategic importance to both the United States and the USSR. See William Reitzel, *The Mediterranean: Its Role in America's Foreign Policy* (1948, repr. 1969); E. D. Bradford, *Mediterranean, Portrait of a Sea* (1971); J. E. Swain, *The Struggle for the Control of the Mediterranean Prior to 1848* (1973); L. G. Pine, *The Middle Sea* (1973).

medium: see SPIRITISM.

medlar (mĕd'lər), small deciduous tree (*Mespilus germanica*) of the family Rosaceae (ROSE family), native to Europe and Asia. It has luxuriant foliage and large white or pinkish flowers; in the wild state it is sometimes thorny. The medlar has long been cultivated in parts of Europe for its acid, apple-shaped fruit. It is usually not picked until after it has been touched by frost, which causes the hard fruit to begin to mellow; then the fruit is stored until the ripening process is completed. It is commonly eaten fresh but is sometimes used for preserves. Medlar is classified in the division MAGNOLIOPHYTA, class Magnoliopsida, order Rosales, family Rosaceae.

Médoc (mādôk'), region, SW France, a peninsula extending NW of Bordeaux between the Bay of Biscay and the Gironde River estuary. The region is covered with some of France's most famous vineyards; Château Lafite, Château Latour, and Château Margaux are the most renowned of the many wines produced in Médoc.

medulla: see BRAINSTEM.

Medusa (mədo͞o'sə), in Greek mythology, most famous of the three monstrous GORGON sisters. She was once a beautiful woman, but she offended Athena, who changed her hair into snakes and made her face so hideous that all who looked at her were turned to stone. When Medusa was with child by Poseidon, Perseus killed her and presented her head to Athena. Chrysaor and Pegasus sprang from her blood when she died. Medusa's head retained its petrifying power even after her death. Because of this power, her image frequently appeared on Greek armor. In some myths Athena used the Medusa head on her aegis.

medusa, in zoology, scientific name for the JELLYFISH, i.e., the free-swimming stage of various animals in the phylum CNIDARIA. See POLYP AND MEDUSA.

Medveditsa (mĭdvĕ'dyĭtsə), river, c.430 mi (690 km) long, SE European USSR. It rises NW of Volsk, flows roughly parallel to the Volga past Petrovsk, and empties into the Don River near Serafimovich.

Medwall, Henry, fl. 1486, first known English dramatist. He was chaplain to Cardinal Morton. His *Fulgens and Lucrece* (1497), a love story, is the earliest known secular English play. Medwall also wrote *Nature*, a morality play.

Meer, Jan or **Johannes van der:** see VERMEER, JAN.

meerkat: see MONGOOSE.

meerschaum (mēr'shəm), a mineral that looks like white clay and is used chiefly for making tobacco pipes and cigar and cigarette holders (all have mouthpieces of amber). It is about as dense as water. Lighter pieces sometimes float to shore, and the mineral has been erroneously thought to be petrified sea foam. It is relatively soft before drying, and meerschaum pipes are often carved into ornate forms. Vienna is the chief center of meerschaum carving. Meerschaum is absorbent, and pipes that are made of it and waxed become a rich brown with use. The mineral is found in many parts of the world, the chief source being Asia Minor. Chips from the carving of meerschaum are pulverized and pressed into inferior pipes. Chemically, meerschaum is a hydrous magnesium silicate; in mineralogy it is named sepiolite.

Meerut (mē'rət), city (1971 pop. 271,325), Uttar Pradesh state, N central India. An agricultural market, it processes flour and vegetable oil. Meerut was conquered by Muslims in 1192, ravaged by TAMERLANE in 1399, and became part of the Mogul empire. An important town of the Jat Bharatpur kingdom (mid 18th cent.), it subsequently fell to the British. The first outbreak of the INDIAN MUTINY occurred in Meerut in May, 1857, but the British held the city. See study by Julian Palmer (1966).

Megaera: see FURIES.

megalithic monuments (mĕgəlĭth'ĭk) [Gr.,=large stone], in archaeology, a construction involving one or several roughly hewn stone slabs of great size; it is usually of prehistoric antiquity. These monuments are found in various parts of the world, but the best-known and most numerous are concentrated in Western Europe, especially in Brittany and the British Isles. Aside from the standing stones and stone heaps that are still raised occasionally as boundary marks or memorials of personal and public events, most megalithic monuments seem to have been erected for funerary and religious purposes. Most of those in Western Europe were constructed between 2,000 and 1,500 B.C. and may be divided into four categories: the chamber tomb, or DOLMEN; the single standing stone, or MENHIR; the stone row; and the stone circle. Chamber tombs were usually covered with earth mounds, forming a BARROW. Menhirs sometimes stood alone near the entrance of a tomb or on top of the mound. Sometimes they were set in long rows called alignments, as at CARNAC in Brittany; in other places they were arranged in a circle, usually a CROMLECH, the most elaborate of which is STONEHENGE in England. The individual stone slabs may reach 65 ft (20 m) in length and 100 tons in weight. Such massive structures testify to the engineering feats possible to the concerted efforts of relatively ill-equipped peoples. See Glyn Daniel, *The Megalith Builders of Western Europe* (1958).

Megalopolis (mĕgəlŏp'əlĭs) [Gr.,=great city], ancient city of Greece, S central Arcadia (now Arkadhía). It was founded (c.370 B.C.), on Epaminondas' advice, as headquarters for the new, anti-Spartan Arcadian League. Inhabitants of many villages moved to the city, and it was the home of PHILOPOEMEN and of POLYBIUS. There has been much excavation.

Meganthropus: see HOMO ERECTUS; AUSTRALOPITHECUS.

megapode (mĕg'əpōd"), common name for large, stout-bodied, long-tailed, terrestrial, nonmigratory birds comprising six genera in the family Megapodiidae. Members of the family have large, strong feet, hence the name megapode (from the Greek meaning "large foot"). Also called mound birds and incubator birds, they are remarkable in that they do not brood their eggs, but rather deposit them in mounds of earth and leaves and allow them to be incubated by the heat from the sun and from rotting vegetable material. The territory of each male contains a single mound, often the work of generations, reaching up to 15 ft (4.5 m) in height and 50 ft (15.2 m) in diameter. The male remains in the vicinity of the mound throughout the brood season, constantly checking and regulating the temperature by adding or removing material. The megapodes are commonly divided into three groups: the generally dullish-colored jungle fowl of the New Guinea rain forest, the blackish brush turkeys (e.g. *Allectura lathami*) of coastal Australia, and the reddish-brown, white-spotted Mallee fowl (*Leipoa ocellata*) of Australia's semiarid scrub region. Many megapode species were early carried by canoe to the South Pacific. Omnivorous, their diet includes insects, small animals, fruit, and seeds. Egg-laying details are well known for the Mallee fowl, which over a period of time in the early spring, deposits from 5 to 35 eggs. The eggs begin to incubate immediately, the heat inside the mound being carefully watched and regulated by the parents. This is accomplished by adding sand to cover the eggs if there is too much heat from the sun, or scratching it away, thereby increasing the amount of heat reaching the eggs. The Mallee fowl usually builds a new mound every year, unlike other members of the family. Megapodes are classified in the phylum CHORDATA, subphylum Vertebrata, class Aves, order Galliformes, family Megapodiidae.

Mégara (mĕ'gərə, -gärä), town (1971 pop. 17,294), E central Greece, on the Saronic Gulf. Wine, olive oil, and flour are produced. It is the site of the ancient town of Mégara, the capital of Mégaris, a small district between the Gulf of Corinth and the Saronic Gulf. The DORIANS who succeeded the earliest known inhabitants made Mégara a wealthy city by means of maritime trade, and they founded many colonies, including, in the 7th cent. B.C., Chalcedon and Byzantium. After the Persian Wars the citizens of Mégara summoned the aid of Athens against Corinth (459 B.C.), but soon thereafter expelled the Athenians. The mathematician Euclid was probably born in Mégara.

Megarian school, Greek school of philosophy at Mégara from late 5th cent. to early 3rd cent. B.C. Influenced by the ELEATIC SCHOOL and by Socrates, it was known for its interest in logic and for argumentation. Its founder was EUCLID OF MEGARA, who maintained that good was an unchanging absolute under various names, such as wisdom, God, and mind. His successor Eubulides was famed for his paradoxes, such as "If I say that I am lying, am I telling the truth?" Other members included Stilpo, Diodorus Cronus, Cleinomachus, and Panthoides. No Megarian writings survive.

megatherium (mĕgəthēr'ēəm) [Gr.=large beast], extinct ground sloth, of the genus *Megatherium*, that was widely distributed in North and South America in the Pleistocene epoch. Fossil evidence shows that these mammals became extinct comparatively recently, about the time that the first explorers reached the New World. A huge beast, the megatherium attained a length of 18 ft (5.5 m) and probably weighed several tons. The hind legs and tail were massive, the forelegs slender and supple; the animal probably supported itself much of the time in a semierect position on its hind legs and tail and used its forelegs to pull from trees the foliage on which it fed. The megatherium is classified in the phylum CHORDATA, subphylum Vertebrata, class Mammalia, order Edentata, family Megatheriidae.

Meghalaya (mā"gəlā'yə), state (1971 pop. 983,336), c.8,700 sq mi (22,530 sq km), NE India, bordered on the S by Bangladesh. The capital is SHILLONG. Meghalaya is in the Garo, Khasi, and Jaintia hills, at an elevation of 4,000–6,000 ft (1,220–1,830 m). The inhabitants are Khasi, Synteng, and Pner tribesmen, who speak a Mon-Khmer language. Christian missionaries have had considerable influence among them. Meghalaya was formerly part of Assam state; it became a separate state in 1972. It is governed by a chief minister and cabinet responsible to an elected unicameral legislature. The states of Assam, Nagaland, Meghalaya, Manipur, and Tripura and the union territories of Mizoram and Arunachal Pradesh have a common governor appointed by the president of India.

Meghna (mĕg'nə), river, c.130 mi (210 km) long, formed at the western end of the Surma valley, NE Bangladesh, by the branches of the Surma River. It flows south, receiving arms of the Ganges and Brahmaputra rivers, to the Bay of Bengal. The Meghna is an important inland waterway, navigable throughout its length by river steamers. In the springtime, at high tide, tidal bores, c.20 ft (6.1 m) high, rush upstream with great destructive force.

Megiddo (məgĭd'ō), ancient city, Palestine, by the Kishon River on the southern edge of the plain of Esdraelon, N of Samaria. It was inhabited from the 4th millennium B.C. to c.450 B.C. Situated in a strategic position, controlling the route that connected Egypt with Mesopotamia, it has been the scene of many battles throughout history, from Thutmose III (c.1468 B.C.) to Gen. Edmund Allenby (later Viscount Allenby of Megiddo) in World War I. Excavations have unearthed 20 strata of settlements. Found in the latest 6 strata, from the Canaanite period to c.500 B.C., were the Megiddo Ivories, one of the most important examples of Canaanite art, and Solomon's chariot stables. Judges 5.19; 2 Kings 23.29,30. The plain is called the valley of **Megiddon** in Zech. 12.11. See also ARMAGEDDON. See *Megiddo* (Univ. of Chicago, Parts I-II, 1939-48); Gordon Loud, *The Megiddo Ivories* (1939).

Meharry Medical College (məhâr'ē), at Nashville, Tenn.; coeducational; organized 1876 as the medical department of Central Tennessee College, granted an independent charter 1915.

Mehemet. For persons thus named, see MUHAMMAD.

Mehetabeel (mēhĕt'əbēl), ancestor of Shemaiah the prophet. Neh. 6.10.

Mehetabel (mēhĕt'əbĕl), wife of Hadad, king of Edom. Gen. 36.39.

Mehida (mēhī'də), family returned from Babylon. Ezra 2.52; Neh. 7.54.

Mehir (mē'hĭr), descendant of Judah. 1 Chron. 4.11.

Mehmed: see MUHAMMAD.

Meholathite (mēhō'ləthīt), biblical epithet, perhaps referring to ABEL-MEHOLAH. 1 Sam. 18.19.

Mehta, Zubin (zo͞o'bĭn mä'tə), 1936–, Indian conductor. Son of the violinist Mehli Mehta, founder and conductor of the Bombay Symphony, Mehta studied medicine for two years before continuing the family's musical tradition. After two years of study at the Vienna Music Academy, he won first prize at the International Conducting Competition in Liverpool, England, in 1958. Master of a flamboyant style, Mehta specializes in late romantic and early modern symphonic repertoire and in opera. He served as director of the Montreal Symphony (1961–67) and in 1962 was named permanent director of the Los Angeles Philharmonic Orchestra. Since 1965 he has regularly conducted at the Metropolitan Opera in New York City.

Mehujael (mēhyo͞o'jāĕl), descendant of Cain. Gen. 4.18.

Méhul, Étienne Nicolas (ātyĕN' nēkôlä' māül'), 1763–1817, French operatic composer. Encouraged by Gluck, he became one of France's outstanding composers in the Revolutionary period. Méhul's masterpiece was the biblical opera *Joseph* (1807). His *Euphrosine et Coradin* (1790) and *Stratonice* (1792) were the first operas to be called opéras comiques—signifying at that time not that they contained humorous elements but that they employed spoken dialogue.

Mehuman (mēhyo͞o'mən), chamberlain of King Ahasuerus. Esther 1.10.

Mehunim (mĕhyo͞o'nĭm) or **Meunim** (mēyo͞o'-), Canaanite tribe, located SE of Petra, near the modern Maan (Jordan). 1 Chron. 4.41; 2 Chron. 20.1; Ezra 2.50; Neh. 7.52.

Meighen, Arthur (mē'ən), 1874–1960, Canadian political leader, b. Ontario. A lawyer, he began his career in Manitoba. Entering (1908) the Canadian House of Commons as a Liberal-Conservative, he became solicitor general (1913), secretary of state and minister of mines (1917), and minister of the interior (1917). He was chosen prime minister in 1920 but resigned in 1921 after his defeat in the general election. As leader of the Conservative party, Meighen was again prime minister in 1926 but resigned within the year. In 1932, Richard B. Bennett appointed him to the Senate, from which he resigned in 1941 to contest a seat for the House of Commons. Defeated, he retired to private life. See biography by W. R. Graham (1960).

Meigs, Return Jonathan (mĕgz), 1740–1823, American Revolutionary army officer, b. Middletown, Conn. He accompanied Benedict Arnold on the Quebec expedition, where he was taken prisoner and later exchanged (1776). Meigs is best remembered for the expedition he led against the British at Sag Harbor, Long Island, in 1777. After the Revolution he became interested in the OHIO COMPANY OF ASSOCIATES. He later became (1801) Indian agent to the Cherokees. His son, **Return Jonathan Meigs,** 1764–1825?, American cabinet member, b. Middletown, Conn., also went to Ohio and became prominent in politics there. Meigs served consecutively as Senator from Ohio (1808–10), governor of Ohio (1810–14), and as U.S. Postmaster General (1814–23).

Meigs, Fort: see FORT MEIGS.

Meiji (mā'jē), 1852–1912, reign name of emperor of Japan (1867–1912). His given name was Mutsuhito. He ascended the throne when he was 15. A year later the SHOGUN fell, and the power that had been held by the TOKUGAWA military house was returned to the emperor. This was the MEIJI RESTORATION, the chief event in the modern history of Japan, for it meant the downfall of Japanese feudalism and the forging of a new and modern state. Emperor Meiji himself had little political power, but he was a paramount symbol of the unity of Japan. A constitution adopted in 1889 provided for a diet with an upper house selected mainly from the peerage, and an elected lower house to advise the government. The cabinet was not directly responsible to the diet but was regarded as above politics and responsible only to the emperor. In practice, the emperor delegated selection of premiers to a group of close advisers known as the GENRO, or elder statesmen. Under the direction of these oligarchs (among them Hirobumi ITO, Aritomo YAMAGATA, and Kaoru INOUYE), Japan was transformed into a modern industrial state, and its military power was demonstrated in the first Sino-Japanese War (1894–95) and the Russo-Japanese War (1904–5). When the Meiji period ended in 1912, Japan was a world power. See D. B. Sladen, *Queer Things About Japan* (4th ed. 1913, repr. 1968); W. G. Beasley, *The Meiji Restoration* (1972); Paul Akamatsu, *Meiji, 1868* (tr. 1972).

Meiji restoration, 1868. Just after the accession of Emperor MEIJI (1867) occurred the revolution in Japanese life and government known as the Meiji restoration. The power of the TOKUGAWA military dictatorship, weakened by debt and internal division, had declined, and much opposition had built up in the early 19th cent. The intrusion of foreigners, particularly the Americans under Admiral Matthew C. PERRY, precipitated further discontent. Under pressure, the Tokugawa shogunate submitted (1854) to foreign demands and ended Japan's isolation. The powerful Choshu and Satsuma domains of W Japan attempted resistance to the foreigners on their own and were defeated (1863). These domains, excluded from the Tokugawa governing councils because of their status as *tozama,* or outside DAIMYO, then demanded creation of a new government loyal to the emperor to expel the foreigners. Samurai from these domains recognized that this could only be accomplished by adopting Western armaments, and some even advocated institutional reform on the Western model. The shogun was finally forced to relinquish power to the emperor (1867), and remnants of the shogunal army were defeated (1868). The court was moved from Kyoto to Tokyo, and the emperor placed (1868) the power of government in the hands of the Westernizers (among them Toshimichi OKUBO, Shigenobu OKUMA, Tomomi IWAKURA, and Koin KIDO), who worked assiduously to modernize Japan. The feudal domains were abolished (1871) and a centralized administration was created. The effectiveness of the new conscript army of commoners was proved and the possibility of a return to feudalism was definitely ended when the rebellion of the great Satsuma clan (see Takamori SAIGO) was crushed in 1877. See Sir Ernest Mason Satow, *A Diplomat in Japan* (1921, repr. 1968); studies by Ken Yamaguchi (1873, repr. 1972), Paul Akamatsu (tr. 1972), and W. G. Beasley (1972).

Meiklejohn, Alexander (mĭk'əljŏn), 1872–1964, American educator, b. Rochdale, England, grad. Brown Univ., 1893, Ph.D. Cornell Univ., 1897. He taught philosophy at Brown (1897–1912), serving as dean after 1901 and, after 1906, as professor of logic. From 1912 to 1924 he was president of Amherst College. Meikeljohn was professor of philosophy at the Univ. of Wisconsin from 1926 to 1938 and was chairman of the Experimental College for the five years of its existence (1927–32). This experiment, in which a period of Greek civilization was studied intensively, inspired similar programs in other colleges, e.g., St. John's College. From 1933 to 1936 he taught at the Social Studies Center in San Francisco. Meiklejohn's educational theories are set forth in *The Liberal College* (1920), *Freedom and the College* (1923), and *The Experimental College* (1932). He also wrote *What Does America Mean?* (1935), *Education between Two Worlds* (1942), *Free Speech and Its Relation to Self-Government* (1948), and *Political Freedom* (1960, repr. 1965).

Meinecke, Friedrich (frē'drĭkh mī'nĕkə), 1862–1954, German historian and intellectual figure. Educated at the Univ. of Berlin, he became a professor there in 1914 and directed (1893–1935) the *Historische Zeitschrift.* In 1948 he was made rector of the Free Univ. of Berlin. During the Nazi era his liberal views led to official disfavor and his withdrawal from active teaching. Meinecke was both a nationalist and a classic liberal; his early historical works, many of them on Prussia, reveal his belief that the state, besides functioning as the repository of power, must serve cultural values and promote individualism. In *Weltbürgertum und Nationalstaat* (1919, 7th ed. 1928) he wrote with approval of German unification through power at the necessary expense of cultural cosmopolitanism. However, shocked by World War I, Meinecke sought in his masterful *Idee der Staatsraïson in der neueren Geschichte* (1924; tr. *Machiavellism,* 1957) to expose irresponsible power in the frame of intellectual history. *Die deutsche Katastrophe* (1946; tr. *The German Catastrophe,* 1950) reflected on the rise of National Socialism and the extent of German guilt. See R. W. Sterling, *Ethics in a World of Power* (1958) and R. A. Pois, *Friedrich Meinecke and German Politics in the Twentieth Century* (1972).

Meiningen (mīn'ĭng-ən), city (1970 pop. 25,357), Suhl district, SW East Germany, on the Werra River. Manufactures include machinery, textiles, lumber, and metal products. Meiningen was first mentioned in the 10th cent. and passed to the dukes of Saxony in 1583. It was the capital of the duchy of SAXE-MEININGEN from 1680 to 1918. In the second half of the 19th cent. the ducal theater of Meiningen acquired an international reputation and long set the style for German dramatic performances. The ducal orchestra, conducted (1880–85) by Hans von Bülow, was also famous. The ducal palace in Meiningen dates from the 16th and 17th cent.

Meiningen Players, German theatrical company that toured Europe from 1874 to 1890. The group, inspiring theatrical reforms wherever it performed, was a major influence in the movement toward modern theater. George II, duke of Saxe-Meiningen, who had organized the company, strove to perfect ensemble acting and as a designer used historically accurate costumes and settings. He was the first to recognize the importance of central artistic control, which anticipated the function of the director in the production of plays.

Meinong, Alexius (älĕk'syo͞os mīn'ông), 1853–1920, Austrian philosopher and psychologist; pupil of Franz Brentano. He was professor at the Univ. of Graz from 1889, founding (1894) the first psychological laboratory in Austria. Opposed to the school of content, which regarded perception as a composite of elementary sensations, Meinong's school of the act believed its necessary constituent to be a definite mental act. Establishing a general theory of values based on psychological grounds, Meinong distinguished between perception as the recognition of relationships inherent in the perceived object and conception as dependent on the mental act itself. See J. N. Findlay, *Meinong's Theory of Objects* (2d ed. 1963); Gustav Bergmann, *Realism: A Critique of Brentano and Meinong* (1967).

meiosis (mīō'sĭs), process of nuclear division in a living cell by which the number of chromosomes is reduced to half the original number. Meiosis occurs only in the process of gametogenesis, i.e., when the gametes, or sex cells (OVUM and SPERM), are being formed. Because FERTILIZATION consists of the fusion of two separate nuclei, one from each of the sex cells, meiosis is necessary to prevent the doubling of the chromosome number in each successive generation. An ordinary body cell is diploid; i.e., it contains two of each type of chromosome. An ovum or sperm is haploid; i.e., it contains only a single chromosome of each type and, therefore, half the number of chromosomes of the diploid cell. When the two haploid cells fuse, the diploid number is restored, and the plant or animal growing from the fertilized egg (zygote) has the usual diploid number of chromosomes in its body cells. In the first stage of meiosis, called reduction division, the members of each pair of homologous chromosomes, which are double-stranded, lie side by side. Each member of the pair then moves away from the other toward opposite ends of the dividing nucleus, and two nuclei, each with the haploid number of double-stranded chromosomes, are formed. In the second meiotic sequence, called equational division, each haploid cell nucleus contains double-stranded chromosomes, the halves of the original homologous pairs. The chromosomes in the nucleus sepa-

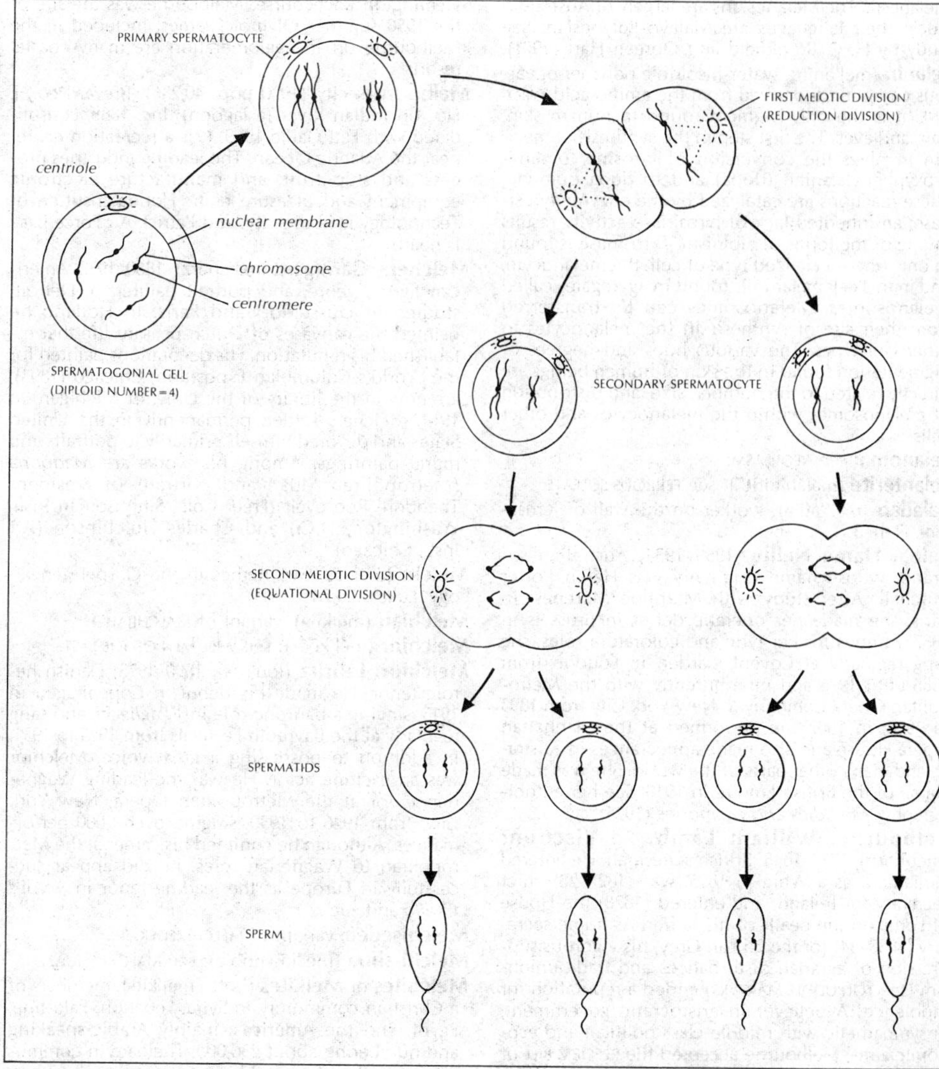

Formation of sperm cells through meiosis

rate into their single strands and the strands move toward opposite ends of the dividing nucleus. The result of meiotic division is four cells, each haploid, with one chromosome of each pair.

Meir, Golda (māĕr'), 1898–, Israeli political leader, b. Kiev, Russia, originally named Golda Mabovitch. Her family emigrated to the United States in 1906, settling in Milwaukee. She became a school teacher and early involved herself in the Zionist labor movement. In 1921 she and her husband, Morris Meyerson (the name was hebraized to Meir in 1956), emigrated to Palestine. She joined the Palestine labor movement and became (1936) head of the political department of the Histadrut (General Federation of Jewish Labor). After Israeli independence was achieved (1948), she served as minister to Moscow, minister of labor (1949–56), and foreign minister (1956–66). She became secretary general of the Mapai party (later the Labor party) in 1966. On the death (1969) of Levi Eshkol, Meir became interim prime minister pending elections, but she retained her post after the elections were held (Oct., 1969). As prime minister she maintained a difficult coalition at home, while negotiating abroad with the hostile Arab nations and with the United States. In 1971 she managed to defeat a "no-confidence" vote in parliament engineered by opposition members on the grounds that she had made excessive concessions to Egypt in peace negotiations. Despite criticism, however, she retained tremendous personal popularity. In Oct., 1973, she rallied Israeli forces following a surprise combined Egyptian-Syrian offensive (see ARAB-ISRAELI WARS). After the hostilities ceased, her government, particularly defense minister Moshe DAYAN, was criticized for its unpreparedness. After two unsuccessful attempts to form a new coalition government, she resigned in April, 1974, and left office in May. See her *This Is Our Strength: Selected Papers,* ed. by H. M. Christman (1962), and *A Land of Our Own: An Oral Autobiography,* ed. by Marie Syrkin (1973); biographies by Eliyahu Agres (1969) and Peggy Mann (1971).

Meiss, Millard (mēs), 1904–, American art historian, b. Cincinnati. Meiss taught art history at Columbia from 1934 to 1953 and thereafter was professor at Harvard until 1958, when he joined the Institute for Advanced Study, Princeton, N.J. He has edited several leading art journals and has written articles and books on medieval and Renaissance painting. His books include *Painting in Florence and Siena after the Black Death* (1951), *Andrea Mantegna as Illuminator* (1957), *Giotto and Assisi* (1960), *The Painting of the Life of St. Francis in Assisi* (with Leonetto Tintori, 1962), *French Painting in the Time of Jean de Berry* (2 vol., 1967–68), and *The Great Age of Fresco* (1970).

Meissen (mī'sən), city (1970 pop. 45,571), Dresden district, SE East Germany, on the Elbe River. A porcelain manufacturing center since 1710, Meissen is famous for its figurines (often called "Dresden" china). Other manufactures include metal products and leather goods. Nearby are large kaolin deposits. Meissen was founded (929) by Henry of Saxony (later German king as Henry I), and it became (965) the seat of the margraviate of Meissen, where the WETTIN dynasty of Saxony originated. The diocese of Meissen was founded in 968, was suppressed in 1581, and was restored in 1921 with its see at Bautzen. The Albrechtsburg (15th cent.), a large castle, dominates the city; it housed (1710–1864) the royal porcelain manufacture, begun by J. F. Böttger under the patronage of Elector Frederick Augustus I (Augustus II of Poland). Among the other noteworthy buildings of Meissen are the cathedral and the Church of St. Afra (both 13th–15th cent.).

Meissonier, Jean Louis Ernest (zhäN lwē ĕrnĕst' māsônyā'), 1815–91, French genre and military painter. His study of the Dutch masters was evident in his first Salon-exhibited painting, *A Visit to the Burgomaster* (1834). His small genre paintings are meticulous as to furnishings and costumes. Among Meissonier's battle scenes, chiefly of the Napoleonic Wars, are *Napoleon I with His Staff* (Louvre) and *Friedland, 1807* (Metropolitan Mus.). His genre pictures include *The Voyagers* (Louvre) and *The Lute Player* (Metropolitan Mus.). See study by V. C. O. Gréard (tr. 1897).

Meissonier, Juste Aurèle (zhüst ōrĕl'), 1695–1750, French designer, b. Turin. At first a goldsmith, in 1724 he was appointed designer to the king under Louis XV, a position he held until his death. Meissonier designed mainly interiors, usually in a novel, capricious, and asymmetrical manner. His only complete architectural venture was the house of Léon de Brethous, Paris (1733; now the Chamber of Commerce). Several volumes of his engravings were of great importance in spreading the ROCOCO style throughout Europe.

meistersinger (mī'stərsĭng"ər, Ger. mī'shtərzĭng"ər) [Ger., = mastersinger], a member of one of the musical and poetic guilds that flourished in German cities during the 15th and 16th cent. The guilds or schools comprised chiefly artisans who claimed artistic descent from the courtly MINNESINGERS. Each member was required to compose and sing according to rigid technical formulas laid down in the *Tabulatur.* Candidates for the coveted rank of *Meister* were judged in public contest. Some of the song texts of Hans Sachs and others became famous, but it was Richard Wagner's opera *Die Meistersinger von Nürnberg* (1862–67) that popularized knowledge of the movement. Wagner's libretto faithfully represents guild practices.

Meister Stephan: see LOCHNER, STEPHAN.

Meitner, Lise (lē'zə mīt'nər), 1878–1968, Austrian-Swedish physicist and mathematician. She was professor at the Univ. of Berlin (1926–33). A refugee from Germany after 1938, she became associated with the Univ. of Stockholm and with the Nobel Institute at Stockholm and was visiting professor (1946) at the Catholic Univ. of America. In 1917, working with Otto Hahn, she discovered the element protoactinium and is noted for her work on the disintegration products of radium, thorium, and actinium and on the behavior of beta rays. In 1938 she participated in experimental research in bombarding the uranium nucleus with slow-speed neutrons. Meitner interpreted the results as a fission of the nucleus and calculated that vast amounts of energy were liberated. Her conclusion contributed to the development of the atomic bomb. In 1949 she became a Swedish citizen.

Me-jarkon (mē-jär'kŏn), unidentified town, W Palestine. Joshua 19.46.

Meknès (mĕknĕs'), city (1966 est. pop. 195,000), N central Morocco. It has a noted carpet-weaving industry. There are also woolen mills, cement and metal works, oil distilleries, and food-processing plants. Meknès was founded (c.1672) by Sultan ISMAIL, who undertook such palatial building operations that the city was called the Versailles of Morocco. Little of his construction has survived. A European town is laid out beside the old one.

Mekonah (mēkō'nə), unlocated town, apparently in S Palestine. Neh. 11.28.

Mekong (mā'kŏng, mē'–), Chinese *Lan-ts'ang Chiang,* one of the great rivers of SE Asia, c.2,600 mi (4,180 km) long. It rises in the Tibetan highlands of China as the Dza Chu and flows generally S through Yünnan prov. in deep gorges and over rapids. Leaving Yünnan, the Mekong forms the Burma-Laos border, then curves E and S through NW Laos before marking part of the Laos-Thailand border. From SW Laos the river descends onto the Cambodian plain, where it receives water from Tônlé Sap during the dry season by way of the Tônlé Sap River; during the rainy season, however, the floodwaters of the Mekong reverse the direction of the Tônlé Sap River and flow into Tônlé Sap, a lake that is a natural reservoir. The Mekong River finally flows into the South China Sea through many distributaries in the vast Mekong delta (c.75,000 sq mi/194,250 sq km), which occupies SE Cambodia and S South Vietnam. The delta, crisscrossed by many channels and canals, is one of the greatest rice-growing areas of Asia. It is a densely populated region; Vinh Long, Can Tho, and Long Xuyen are the chief towns there. Saigon is located just east of the delta. The Mekong River is navigable for large vessels c.340 mi (550 km) upstream; Phnom Penh is a major port. North of the Cambodian border, the Mekong is navigable in short sections. At Khone Falls, a series of rapids (6 mi/9.7 km long) in S Laos, the Mekong drops 72 ft (22 m). The falls are the site of a hydroelectric power station, part of the Mekong Scheme, a project undertaken by the United Nations in the early 1960s to develop the potentials of the lower Mekong basin. The project seeks to improve navigation, provide irrigation facilities, and produce hydroelectricity. The

Mekong delta was the scene of heavy fighting in the Vietnam War.

Mela, Pomponius: see POMPONIUS MELA.

Melaka or **Malacca** (both: məlăk'ə), state (1971 pop. 403,722), 640 sq mi (1,658 sq km), Malaysia, S Malay Peninsula, on the Strait of Malacca. Formerly one of the STRAITS SETTLEMENTS, it was constituted a state of Malaya in 1957 (see MALAYSIA, FEDERATION OF). Nearly half the population are Malay; about two fifths are Chinese. The capital, on the strait, is the historic city of **Melaka** or **Malacca** (1971 pop. 86,357). Until the 17th cent., Malacca was one of the leading commercial centers of the Far East. It was founded c.1400 by a Malay prince who had been driven from Singapore after a brief reign there. The city quickly gained wealth as a center of trade with China, Indonesia, India, and the Middle East. Its sultans, aided by the decline of the Madjapahit empire of Java and by the friendship of China, extended their power over the nearby coast of Sumatra and over the Malay Peninsula as far north as Kedah and Pattani. More importantly, Gujarati traders introduced Islam to the Malay world through Malacca. In 1511, Malacca was captured by the Portuguese under Alfonso de Albuquerque. The sultan fled first to Pahang and then to JOHOR. In the mid-16th cent. St. Francis Xavier preached in Malacca. Portugal's control was frequently contested by ACHEH and Johor. In the early 17th cent. the Dutch entered the region, allied themselves with Johor, and captured Malacca in 1641 after a long siege. They utilized the city more as a fortress guarding the strait than as a trading port. The Dutch retained nominal control until 1824, although during the wars of the French Revolution and the Napoleonic period (1795–1818) the British occupied Malacca at the request of the Dutch government-in-exile. In 1824 the Dutch formally transferred Malacca to Great Britain. The modern city, of slight economic importance, retains traces of its past in its Portuguese and Dutch buildings and Portuguese-Eurasian community. The majority of the city's inhabitants are Chinese, who are unusual in that they have acquired many Malay customs.

melamine (mĕl'əmēn''), common name for 2,4,6-triamino-1,3,5-triazine. Melamine is a trimer (see POLYMER) of cyanamide, $H_2NC{\equiv}N$, and is synthesized from calcium carbide. It condenses with formaldehyde to give a thermosetting RESIN. Melamine resins have many uses, including the manufacture of plastic dishes under the trade name Melmac.

Melampus (mĭlăm'pəs), in Greek mythology, seer who understood the speech of all creatures. It was said that he introduced the worship of Dionysus into Greece.

melancholia (mĕlənkō'lēə) [Gr.,=black bile], state of general DEPRESSION associated with certain neuroses and PSYCHOSES. See INVOLUTIONAL PSYCHOTIC REACTIONS; MANIC-DEPRESSIVE PSYCHOSIS; PSYCHONEUROSIS.

Melanchthon, Philip (məlăngk'thən), 1497–1560, German scholar and humanist. He was second only to Martin Luther as a figure in the Lutheran Reformation. His original name was Schwarzerd [Ger.,= black earth; "melanchthon" is the Greek rendering of "black earth"]. A man of great intellect and wide learning, he was professor of Greek at the Univ. of Wittenberg when he met Luther, and they soon became intimate friends and associates. Melanchthon's influence on the Lutheran movement had many sides. In *Loci communes* (1521) he made the first systematic presentation of the principles of the Reformation and so clarified the new gospel to those outside the movement. He served as mediator between Luther and the humanists, tempering the Protestant disapproval of worldly culture. He represented Luther at many conferences. At the Marburg Conference he opposed Huldreich ZWINGLI, and at the Diet of Augsburg (1530) he wrote and presented the Augsburg Confession (see CREED). Melanchthon was more conciliatory than Luther, as evidenced by his friendship with John Calvin after Luther's death and by his willingness to compromise on doctrinal issues. Luther had great confidence in Melanchthon as his successor, but Melanchthon was ill-suited for leadership. For his powerful role in creating the German schools, Melanchthon is known as preceptor of Germany. His *Loci communes* appeared in a modern critical edition and translation by Charles Leander Hall (1944). See biography by Robert Stupperich (tr. 1965); study by Clyde Manschreck (1958).

Melanesia (mĕlənē'zhə, -shə), one of the three main divisions of OCEANIA, in the SW Pacific Ocean, NE of Australia and S of the equator. Melanesia includes the SOLOMON ISLANDS, NEW HEBRIDES, NEW CALEDONIA, the BISMARCK ARCHIPELAGO, and the Admiralty and FIJI islands. NEW GUINEA is sometimes included in Melanesia. The Melanesians are largely of Australoid stock; their languages are Malayo-Polynesian. See study by H. C. Brookfield and Doreen Hart (1971).

melanin (mĕl'ənĭn), water-insoluble polymer of various compounds derived from the amino acid TYROSINE; it is the only pigment found in human skin, hair, and eyes. The first step in the synthesis of melanin involves the conversion of tyrosine to dihydroxyphenylalanine (dopa) and to dopa quinone. These reactions are catalyzed by the enzyme tyrosinase; an inherited lack of tyrosinase activity results in one of the forms of albinism. Tyrosinase is found in only one specialized type of cell, the melanocyte, and in this cell melanin is found in aggregates called melanosomes. Melanosomes can be transferred from their site of synthesis in the melanocytes to other cell types. The various hues and degrees of pigmentation found in the skin of human beings are directly related to the number, size, and distribution of melanosomes within the melanocytes and other cells.

melanoma: see NEOPLASM.

melanterite (məlăn'tərīt''): see FERROUS SULFATE.

Melatiah (mĕl''ətī'ə), worker on the wall of Jerusalem. Neh. 3.7.

Melba, Dame Nellie, 1859–1931, Australian soprano, whose name originally was Helen Porter Mitchell. After study with Mathilde Marchesi in Paris, she made her operatic debut in Brussels in 1887. Famous for her lyric and coloratura roles, she sang regularly at Covent Garden in London from 1888 until 1926 and intermittently with the Metropolitan Opera Company in New York City from 1893 to 1910; in 1907 she performed at the Manhattan Opera House and also made appearances in Australia and many other parts of the world. She was made Dame of the British Empire in 1918. See her autobiography, *Melodies and Memories* (1925).

Melbourne, William Lamb, 2d Viscount (mĕl'bərn), 1779–1848, British statesman. He entered Parliament as a Whig in 1805, was (1827–28) chief secretary for Ireland, and entered (1828) the House of Lords on the death of his father. As home secretary (1830–34) for the 2d Earl Grey, his vigorous suppression of agrarian disturbances and trade unionism (see TOLPUDDLE MARTYRS) ended a reputation for indolence. A believer in aristocratic government, unsympathetic with middle-class political and economic aims, Melbourne accepted the REFORM BILL of 1832 as a political necessity. As prime minister (1834, 1835–39, 1839–41) his views brought him support from Whigs and moderate Tories, and he excluded radicals from his ministries. He conceded such reforms as amendment of the POOR LAW (1834), the Municipal Corporations Act (1835), and liberalization of the Canadian government. He was also conciliatory in his policy toward Ireland. However, he resisted further parliamentary reform and repeal of the corn laws. Melbourne viewed the prime ministership as a supervisory position; cabinet members, such as Lord PALMERSTON, played a vital role in developing policy. Handsome and urbane, Melbourne was a favorite of the young Queen VICTORIA and taught her important lessons in statecraft. It was at her request that he returned to office (1839) after the queen's quarrel with Sir Robert Peel over her Whig bedchamber ladies. See Lord Melbourne's papers (ed. by L. C. Sanders, 1889, repr. 1971); biography by Lord David Cecil (1954, repr. 1965). Melbourne's wife, **Lady Caroline Lamb,** 1785–1828, was clever and beautiful, but also eccentric, impulsive, and indiscreet. She is remembered less for the minor novels that she wrote than for her love affair with Lord Byron. Lady Caroline and her husband separated in 1825. See biography by Henry Blyth (1972).

Melbourne, city (1971 pop. 74,877; urban agglomeration pop. 2,388,941), capital of Victoria, SE Australia, on Port Phillip Bay at the mouth of the Yarra River. Melbourne, Australia's second largest city, is a rail hub and financial and commercial center. Wool and raw and processed agricultural goods are exported. The city is heavily industrialized; industries include shipbuilding and the manufacture of automobiles, farm machinery, textiles, and electrical goods. Settled in 1835, it was named (1837) for Lord Melbourne, the British prime minister. From 1901 to 1927 the city was the seat of the Australian federal government. Melbourne has three universities: the Univ. of Melbourne (1853), Monash Univ. (1958), and La Trobe Univ. (1964). Melbourne Technical College, the Australian Ballet School, and the National Art Gallery are also in the city. Melbourne is the seat of Roman Catholic and Anglican archbishops. The botanical gardens are a notable attraction. The Melbourne Cup Race is run annually at the Flemington Racecourse. Melbourne was the site of the 1956 summer Olympic games. Included in the Melbourne urban agglomeration are many coastal resorts.

Melbourne, city (1970 pop. 40,236), Brevard co., E Fla., on Indian River (a lagoon); inc. 1888, consolidated with Eau Gallie 1969. It is a recreation center near the Atlantic Ocean. The leading industries process and ship fruit, and manufacture electronic equipment and pleasure craft. Florida Institute of Technology is in the city, and Patrick Air Force Base is nearby.

Melchers, Gari (gâr'ē mĕl'chərz), 1860–1932, American figure, genre, and portrait painter, b. Detroit, studied in Düsseldorf and Paris. In Holland he painted the canvases of Dutch peasant life that established his reputation. His decorations painted for the World's Columbian Exposition, Chicago (1893), are now in the library of the Univ. of Michigan. In 1914, Melchers settled permanently in the United States and devoted himself primarily to portraits and mural paintings. Among his works are *Madonna* (Metropolitan Mus.) and portraits of President Theodore Roosevelt (Freer Coll., Smithsonian Inst., Washington, D.C.) and Charles Hutchinson (Art Inst., Chicago).

Melchi (mĕl'kī), two names in the Gospel genealogy. Luke 3.24,28.

Melchiah (mĕlkī'ə), variant of MALCHIJAH **1.**

Melchior (mĕl'kēôr): see WISE MEN OF THE EAST.

Melchior, Lauritz (lou'rĭts), 1890–1973, Danish heroic tenor. He made his debut in Copenhagen in 1913, singing a baritone role in *I Pagliacci,* and sang regularly at the Bayreuth Festivals from 1925 to 1931. In addition to possessing a great voice, Melchior was an exciting actor. He was the leading Wagnerian tenor at the Metropolitan Opera, New York City, from 1926 to 1950, singing over 1,000 performances. Although he confined his career at the Metropolitan to Wagnerian roles, he did appear successfully in Europe as the leading tenor in Verdi's *Otello* and *Aïda.*

Melchisedec, variant of MELCHIZEDEK.

Melchi-shua (mĕl'kī-shōō'ə): see MALCHI-SHUA.

Melchites or **Melkites** (both: mĕl'kīts), members of a Christian community in Syria, Lebanon, Palestine, Egypt, and the Americas, mainly Arabic-speaking and numbering about 250,000. They are in communion with the pope and have a Byzantine rite much like that of Constantinople but in the Arabic language. Their head, under the pope, is called patriarch of Antioch; he lives in Damascus or Egypt. The name Melchites (which derives from the syriac word for "king") was first applied to all who followed the emperor Marcian in accepting the Council of Chalcedon (451) and came back into use in the 18th cent. to designate that segment of the Orthodox Eastern Church that reunited with Rome; it is now, however, also sometimes applied to the Orthodox of Syria and Egypt. Like the Maronites and the Syrian Catholics, the Melchite community has its own hierarchy under the pope and its own rite. See Donald Attwater, *The Christian Churches of the East,* Vol. I (1947).

Melchizedek or **Melchisedec** (both: mĕlkĭz'ədĕk), king of Salem and "priest of the most high God." He blessed Abraham after the defeat of Chedorlaomer, and Abraham gave him tithes from the spoils of the enemy. Gen. 14.18–20. Later Melchizedek is regarded as typifying the priesthood of the future Messiah. Ps. 110.4; Heb. 5–7.

Melcombe Regis, England: see WEYMOUTH AND MELCOMBE REGIS.

Melea (mē'lēə), ancestor of Joseph. Luke 3.31.

Meleager (mĕlēā'jər), hero in Greek mythology. He was the son of Oeneus, king of Calydon, and Althaea. When Meleager was born, a prophecy said that he would die when a certain log in the fire was burned. His mother snatched the log from the fire and hid it. Meleager grew to be a famous warrior. When Oeneus failed to sacrifice to Artemis, the goddess sent a huge wild boar to ravage his land. To kill the boar Greece's bravest heroes were summoned. Those who came included Castor and Pollux, Theseus, Jason, Nestor, and Atalanta. Meleager led the hunt, known as the Calydonian hunt, and killed the boar. He gave its pelt to Atalanta, with whom he had fallen in love. When his mother's brothers tried to take the pelt, Meleager killed them. In revenge his mother angrily burned the hidden log, and Meleager died as prophesied. In Homer, the Atalanta account is absent, and Meleager is killed in a battle for possession of the pelt.

Melech (mē'lĕk), great-grandson of Jonathan. 1 Chron. 8.35; 9.41.

Melegnano: see MARIGNANO, BATTLE OF.

Meléndez Valdés, Juan (hwän mälān'dāth väldās'), 1754–1817, Spanish neoclassic poet. He studied classics and law and later taught humanities at Salamanca. After much political vacillation during the rise and fall of the Bonapartes, he was forced to flee to France. As poet he was outstanding in an otherwise undistinguished age of Spanish poetry. Although often sentimental and obvious, his work is musical, rich in language and imagery, and distinguished by a fine sensibility. His themes range from the sensual and joyous, celebrating love and nature (e.g., *Los Besos de Amor*), to the philosophical, deploring Spanish poverty and backwardness and pleading for liberal reforms. See study by R. M. Cox (1974).

Meletius, Saint (mĭlē'shəs), d. 381, Catholic bishop, leader of the Meletian faction in the Antiochene schism. The Arians had deposed the Catholic Patriarch EUSTATHIUS and in 361 appointed Meletius. He proved to be orthodox in his views, but the Eustathians opposed him for his Arian sponsorship. The Arians, unhappy with him, secured his exile. A party of Meletians arose to defend him. Athanasius sought to conciliate the Eustathians, but LUCIFER OF CAGLIARI deepened the schism by uncanonically consecrating Paulinus from the Eustathian ranks. Antioch then had two Catholic bishops. Meletius returned in 378, but Rome favored Paulinus, and the parties would not unite. Meletius died while presiding at the First Council of Constantinople, which sought to end the schism by electing FLAVIAN OF ANTIOCH successor to his see. He was the teacher of St. John Chrysostom. Feast: Feb. 12. He is sometimes confused with his contemporary, Meletius of Lycopolis, who organized the widespread Meletian Schism in Egypt, which was aligned with the Arians.

Melfi (mĕl'fē), town (1971 pop. 15,194), in Basilicata, S Italy. It is an agricultural and manufacturing center noted for its wine. In 1041 it was made the first capital of the Norman county of Apulia. At Melfi Emperor Frederick II promulgated (c.1231) his important code, the Constitutions of Melfi, or *Liber Augustalis*. In 1528 the town was sacked by the French under Lautrec, and it never recovered its position as a flourishing commercial center. Earthquakes have damaged the Norman castle (11th–13th cent.) and the cathedral (reconstructed 18th cent.), but the campanile (1153) still stands.

Melicertes (mĕl"ĭsûr'tēz): see ATHAMAS; INO.

Melicu (mĕl'ĭkyōō), same as MALLUCH **6.**

Melilla (mālē'lyä), city (1970 pop. 60,843), Spanish possession, on the Mediterranean coast of Morocco, NW Africa. It is a fishing port and an export point for iron ore. Spain has held the city since 1496 despite many attacks by Moroccans. The revolt that began (1936) the Spanish Civil War broke out in Melilla.

melilot: see SWEET CLOVER.

melinite (mĕl'ənīt"), a high EXPLOSIVE containing PICRIC ACID.

melissa: see BEE BALM.

Melita: see MALTA.

Melitene: see MALATYA.

Melitopol (mălyĕtō'pəl), city (1970 pop. 137,000), S European USSR, in the Ukraine, on the Molochnoy River. A manufacturing center, it produces heavy machinery and has flour mills and food-processing plants. It was founded in the early 19th cent. as the settlement Novo-Aleksandrovka but was renamed in 1841.

Melk (mĕlk), town (1971 pop. 5,100), Lower Austria province, N central Austria, on the Danube River. A noted tourist spot, it was one of the earliest residences of the Austrian rulers. The large Benedictine abbey there, founded in 1089, has a library whose holdings include about 2,000 old manuscripts and 80,000 volumes. The abbey was completely rebuilt by the architect J. Prandtauer in the 18th cent. and is a splendid example of the baroque style.

Melkites: see MELCHITES.

Mellon, Andrew William, 1855–1937, American financier, industrialist, and public official, b. Pittsburgh. He studied at the Western Univ. of Pennsylvania (now the Univ. of Pittsburgh), but he left college to organize a lumber business with his brother, Richard B. Mellon. Soon they joined interests with their father, Thomas Mellon, a successful Pittsburgh banker and lawyer, who had helped Henry C. Frick to expand his holdings in the coke industry. When Thomas Mellon retired (1886), his two sons took over the banking firm of Thomas Mellon and Sons. In 1889, Andrew Mellon led in establishing the Union Trust Company of Pittsburgh—later to become one of the larger financial institutions in the United States—and then the Union Savings Bank was created as a subsidiary firm. Meanwhile Andrew Mellon expanded his holdings in key American industries and held large interests in the Gulf Oil Company, the American Locomotive Company, the Pittsburgh Coal Company, and in hydroelectric, bridge-building, public-utility, steel, insurance, and traction companies. Mellon also played an important role in originating the huge Aluminum Company of America. He resigned (1921) as president of the Mellon National Bank to become U.S. Secretary of the Treasury and held that cabinet post until 1931 under Presidents Harding, Coolidge, and Hoover. As secretary, Mellon worked for a downward revision of income taxes and surtaxes, and in spite of drastic tax curtailments, he reduced the national debt from $24,298,000,000 in 1920 to $16,185,000,000 in 1930. He later served (1931–32) as U.S. ambassador to Great Britain. His income-tax return for the year of 1931 was the subject of a Federal investigation in 1935, but he was exonerated in Dec., 1937, four months after he died. He gave $10 million for the founding (1913) of the Mellon Institute of Industrial Research in Pittsburgh; in 1937 he donated his art collection to the public, with funds for the erection of a building in Washington in which to house it (see NATIONAL GALLERY OF ART). He wrote *Taxation: The People's Business* (1924). See F. D. Denton, *The Mellons of Pittsburgh* (1948).

Mellon Foundation, officially known as the Andrew W. Mellon Foundation, philanthropic trust formed (1969) through the merger of the Avalon Foundation (est. 1940 by Ailsa Mellon Bruce) and the Old Dominion Foundation (est. 1941 by Paul Mellon). Prior to the merger, the Avalon Foundation distributed funds to hospitals and health agencies, educational institutions, and cultural programs including the Metropolitan Opera and the New York Philharmonic. The Old Dominion Fund concentrated on the humanities and liberal education, giving support to such schools as St. John's College, Yale and Harvard universities, and Hampton and Tuskegee institutes. The merged foundation continued to support the areas of health, education, and the humanities, and also added programs in conservation and community services. In 1972 it had assets of approximately $703 million. Other philanthropic foundations endowed by members of the Mellon family include the A. W. Mellon Educational and Charitable Trust (est. 1930), and the Richard King Mellon Foundation (est. 1947).

Melloni, Macedonio (mächādô'nyō mäl-lō'nē), 1798–1854, Italian physicist. Known especially for his investigations of heat, he pointed out the similarity of heat to light, showing that it also is refracted, reflected, and polarized.

Mellon Institute of Industrial Research: see CARNEGIE-MELLON UNIV.

melodeon or **melodium:** see REED ORGAN.

melodrama [Gr.,=song-drama], originally a spoken text with musical background, as in Greek drama. The form was popular in the 18th cent., when its composers included Georg Benda, J. J. Rousseau, and Pietro Metastasio, among many others. The variation of the form to include drama interspersed with song is seen in John Gay's *Beggar's Opera.* Modern examples of the true music melodrama are found in Richard Strauss's setting of Tennyson's *Enoch Arden*, and in Arnold Schönberg's *Pierrot Lunaire.* In 18th-century melodramas the action was generally romantic, full of violent action, and often characterized by the final triumph of virtue. The term was used extensively in England in the 19th cent. as a device to circumvent the law that limited legitimate plays to certain theaters. The term is now applied to all plays with overdrawn characterizations, smashing climaxes, and appeal to sentiment, whether or not the climaxes are heightened by the use of music. *East Lynne* by Mrs. Henry Wood and *Ten Nights in a Barroom* by W. W. Pratt are among the most famous melodramatic "tearjerkers." See study by J. L. Smith (1973).

melody, succession of single tones of varying pitch. Melody is the linear aspect of music, in contrast to harmony, the chordal aspect, which results from the simultaneous sounding of tones. It is impossible to consider melody without RHYTHM. These two are the necessary elements to music. Melody by itself, i.e., monophonic music, was the principal form of composition in Western cultures before the year 1000. It remains in FOLK SONG and ORIENTAL MUSIC and in the music of many primitive cultures. From 1000 melody was combined with one or more different melodies. The polyphonic music thus created dominated composition until about 1750 when homophonic music, melody supported by harmonies, was developed. See POLYPHONY and HARMONY.

melon, fruit of *Cucumis melo,* a plant of the family Curcurbitaceae (GOURD family) native to Asia and now cultivated extensively in warm regions. There are many varieties, differing in taste, color, and skin texture—e.g., Persian, honeydew, casaba, muskmelon, and cantaloupe. The true cantaloupe (var. *cantalupensis*), introduced in Cantalupo, Italy, from Armenia, is a hard-shelled or rock melon. It is little grown outside of the Mediterranean countries; the cantaloupes of the United States are varieties of the muskmelon. Melon is classified in the division MAGNOLIOPHYTA, class Magnoliopsida, order Violales, family Curcurbitaceae.

Melos, Greece: see MÍLOS.

Melozzo da Forlì (mālôt'tsō dä fōrlē'), 1438–94, Umbrian painter. His extant works, though few, reveal him as a painter of power and individuality. He is especially notable for his bold foreshortening, in the use of which, particularly in vaultings, he was a pioneer. His known works include the great fresco of the *Ascension*, in the cupola of the Church of the Santi Apostoli, Rome (Quirinal Palace, Rome); a fresco, *Pope Sixtus IV Giving Custody of the Vatican Library to Platina*, painted for the Vatican Library, and *Angels Making Music*, a fragment (Vatican).

Melpomene (mĕlpŏm'ənē"): see MUSES.

Melrose, burgh (1971 pop. 2,188), Roxburghshire, S Scotland, on the Tweed River. It is the site of one of the finest ruins in Scotland—Melrose Abbey, founded for Cistercians by David I in 1136 and now owned by the nation. Scott's *Lay of the Last Minstrel* has descriptions of its beauty. Several times partly destroyed and rebuilt, the abbey contains the heart of Robert I (Robert Bruce). In 1975, Melrose became part of the Borders region.

Melrose, city (1970 pop. 33,180), Middlesex co., E Mass., a suburb of Boston; settled c.1629, set off from Malden and inc. 1850. It is chiefly residential. The opera star Geraldine Farrar was born in Melrose.

Melrose Park, village (1970 pop. 22,716), Cook co., NE Ill., an industrial suburb of Chicago; inc. 1893. It has large railroad yards and shops, steel mills, and factories that make a wide variety of products.

melting point, TEMPERATURE at which a substance changes its state from solid to liquid. Under standard atmospheric pressure different pure crystalline solids will each melt at a different specific temperature; thus melting point is a characteristic of a substance and can be used to identify it. When heat is applied continuously and in sufficient quantity to such solids, the temperature rises steadily until it reaches the point at which liquefaction occurs. Here the rise ceases and no further change in temperature is observed until all of the substance has been converted to liquid. The heat being applied to the substance at that temperature is consumed in bringing about the change of state, and none is available to raise the temperature of that part of the substance already liquefied until all of it has changed to the liquid. If heat is still applied when liquefaction is complete, the temperature will begin to rise again. The quantity of heat necessary to change one gram of any substance from solid to liquid at its melting point is known as its LATENT HEAT of fusion and differs for different substances. Ice, for example, requires approximately 80 calories of heat to change each gram to water at its melting point. Because its heat of fusion is relatively high, ice is used in refrigeration. In freezing (the reverse process, i.e., the change from liquid to solid), heat is given off by the substance undergoing the change, and the amount given off is the same as that absorbed in melting.

Melun (məlŏN'), town (1968 pop. 36,269), capital of Seine-et-Marne dept., N central France, SE of Paris. It is an important industrial center where automobile bodies, airplane engines, leather products, pharmaceuticals, and elastics are produced. An ancient town of ÎLE-DE-FRANCE, Melun was founded on an island in the Seine and during Gallo-Roman times expanded to both banks of the river. It was ravaged often by the Normans. Melun became an early residence of the CAPETIAN kings. The town has a Romanesque church (12th cent.) and vestiges of a Roman fortress and a Capetian castle. Nearby is the famous Château of Vaux-le-Vicomte, built for Nicholas Fouquet.

Mélusine (mālüzēn') or **Melusina** (mĕlyōōsē'nä), in French legend, a fairy who changed into a serpent from the waist down every Saturday. She married a mortal, Count Raymond, said to be the ancestor of the house of Lusignan, and made him promise never to visit her on that day. When he broke his agreement and discovered her secret, she fled. The Mélusine story has many parallels in Europe and Asia.

Melville, Andrew, 1545–1622, Scottish religious reformer and scholar. He studied abroad, came under the influence of Theodore BEZA, and was a professor at Geneva. He was principal (1574–80) of the Univ. of Glasgow; in 1580 he became principal of St. Mary's College, St. Andrews, and in 1590 he was made rector of St. Andrews. He reorganized the Scottish universities and greatly broadened their educational scope. However, Melville's greater task was the molding of the Scottish church; upon him fell the mantle of John Knox. He was entrusted (1575) with drawing up *The Second Book of Discipline* and was largely responsible for the introduction of a presbyterian system into the somewhat tentative church organization developed by Knox. A foe of prelacy and of royal supremacy, Melville asserted the independence of the church, which brought him into conflict with the court party of James VI (later James I of England). He was called before the privy council on a charge of treason in 1584 and fled to England, but shortly returned to Scotland. He was several times moderator of the general assembly. Melville's struggle to protect the independence of the Scottish church continued. In 1606 he and other clergymen were summoned to confer with James I, but no settlement was reached. Melville offended the court by his harsh criticism of the king and particularly by a Latin epigram directed against Anglican practices. In 1607 he was committed to the Tower of London, where he remained for four years. On his release he was allowed to teach at Sedan, France, a leading Calvinist center. Melville wrote a number of Latin poems of some merit. The standard biography is that of Thomas McCrie (1819).

Melville, Henry Dundas, 1st Viscount, 1742–1811, British lawyer and politician. He was solicitor general for Scotland (1766–75), entered Parliament in 1774, and became lord advocate in 1775. During the American Revolution he favored harsh punishment of the colonists and considered Lord North much too conciliatory. A close friend and lieutenant of William Pitt the younger, he displayed remarkable administrative talents as treasurer of the navy (1783–1800), member of the board of control for India (1784–1801), home secretary (1791–94), secretary for war during the early Napoleonic Wars (1794–1801), and first lord of the admiralty (1804–5). He was impeached (1806), charged with mismanagement of navy funds, and despite acquittal he never returned to office. See his correspondence with Lord Wellesley, ed. by Edward Ingram (1970); biographies by H. E. Furber (1931) and C. E. Matheson (1933).

Melville, Herman, 1819–91, American author, b. New York City, considered one of the great American writers and a major figure in world literature. Born into an impoverished family of distinguished Dutch and English colonial descent, Melville was 12 when his father died. He left school at 15, worked at a variety of jobs, and in 1839 signed on as a cabin boy on a ship bound for Liverpool, an experience reflected in his romance *Redburn.* In 1841–42 he spent 18 months on a whaler, but intolerable hardships on board caused him and a companion to escape from the ship at the Marquesas Islands. The two were captured by a tribe of cannibals, by whom they were well-treated. After being rescued by an Australian whaler, Melville spent some time in Tahiti and other Pacific islands before shipping home in 1844. The immediate results of his experiences were *Typee: A Peep at Polynesian Life* (1846), *Omoo: A Narrative of Adventures in the South Seas* (1847), and *Redburn* (1849), all fresh, exuberant, and immensely popular romances. In 1847, Melville married Elizabeth Shaw, the daughter of Lemuel Shaw, Chief Justice of Massachusetts. The popularity of his books brought him prosperity, business trips to Europe, and admission to literary circles in New York City. In 1850 he bought a farm near Pittsfield, Mass., and became friends with his neighbor Nathaniel Hawthorne. The allegorical implications evident in his romances *Mardi: and a Voyage Thither* (1849) and *White-Jacket; or, The World in a Man-of-War* (1850) reached full development in Melville's masterpiece, *Moby-Dick; or, The Whale* (1851). The story of a deranged whaling captain's obsessive voyage to find and destroy the great white whale that had ripped off his leg, the novel is at once an exciting sea story, a sociological critique of various American class and racial prejudices, a repository of information about whales and whaling, and a philosophical inquiry into the nature of good and evil, of man and his fate. The novel is heavily symbolic, and many critical formulations have been made as to the meaning of its central symbol, the great white whale Moby-Dick himself. *Moby-Dick* is greatly enhanced by Melville's rhythmic, rhetorical prose style. Although it is now considered one of the greatest of all novels, *Moby-Dick* was misunderstood and ill-received in its time. Readers were confused by the book's symbolism, and they failed to grasp Melville's complex view of the world. Similarly, *Pierre; or, The Ambiguities* (1852), a psychological study of guilt and frustrated good, was disregarded by the public. Disheartened by debts, ill health, and the failure to win an audience, Melville became absorbed in mysticism. He was unable to accept the optimism of TRANSCENDENTALISM, for he was always able to see the cruel as well as the beautiful in nature; although he searched for a faith that would satisfy his yearning for the Absolute, he never found one. He continued to produce important works in *The Piazza Tales* (1856), a collection which includes "Benito Cereno" and "Bartleby the Scrivener," and *The Confidence Man: His Masquerade* (1857), a pessimistic satire on materialism. He was forced to sell his farm, and in 1866 he secured a poorly paying position in New York City as a district inspector of customs, a job which he held for 19 years. Melville's later works include the volumes of poetry *Battle-Pieces and Aspects of the War* (1866) and *John Marr and Other Sailors* (1888); the long poem *Clarel* (1876); and the novella *Billy Budd, Foretopman* (1924), the tragedy of an innocent. Melville died in poverty and obscurity. Although neglected for many years, he was rediscovered around 1920 and has been enthusiastically studied by critics and scholars ever since. Many of his unpublished works were issued posthumously, notably *The Apple Tree Table* (1922), a collection of magazine sketches; *Journal of a Visit to London and the Continent* (1948); and *Journal of a Visit to Europe and the Levant* (1955). See his letters ed. by M. R. Davis and W. H. Gilman (1960); biographies by Leon Howard (1951) and Newton Arvin (1950, repr. 1972); studies by John Seelye (1970), Richard Chase (1949, repr. 1971), and G. W. Allen (1971).

Melville, Sir James, 1535–1617, Scottish diplomat. He was a page to Mary Queen of Scots in France and, after her return to Scotland, was employed as Mary's representative at the court of Elizabeth I of England. He later performed important diplomatic missions for James VI. His memoirs, written after James's accession (1603) to the English throne (as James I) and first published in 1683, are one of the principal sources for the history of the period. See edition by A. F. Steuart (1929).

Melville, Lake, salt water lake, 1,133 sq mi (2,934 sq km), SE Labrador, Canada, extending c.120 mi (190 km) inland from Hamilton Inlet, an arm of the Atlantic Ocean. It receives the Churchill River in Goose Bay, its southwest arm, and the Naskaupi River. Rigolet, a Hudson's Bay Company post, is on the lake.

Melville Bay, broad indentation of the western coast of Greenland, opening to the SW into Baffin Bay. The inland ice cap comes down to the coast, and glaciers discharge much ice into its waters.

Melville Island, 2,240 sq mi (5,802 sq km), Northern Territory, N Australia, in the Timor Sea 16 mi (26 km) off the coast. It is 65 mi (105 km) long and 45 mi (72 km) wide and is separated from Bathurst Island by Apsley Strait. It consists largely of mangrove jungle with sandy soil. An aboriginal reservation is on the island.

Melville Island, c.16,400 sq mi (42,500 sq km), W Franklin dist., Northwest Territories, Canada, N of Victoria Island; largest of the Parry Islands. Generally hilly (rising to c.1,500 ft/460 m), it has several ice-covered areas in the interior. There are musk oxen on the island. Sir William Parry, the British explorer, discovered Melville Island in 1819, and its south coast was explored (1851) by Sir Francis McClintock.

Melville Peninsula, 24,156 sq mi (62,564 sq km), c.250 mi (400 km) long and from 70 to 135 mi (113–217 km) wide, S Franklin dist., Northwest Territories, Canada, between the Gulf of Bothnia and Foxe Basin, and separated from Baffin Island to the N by the Fury and Hecla Strait; it is joined to the mainland by the Rae Isthmus. Numerous streams radiate from the peninsula's central hilly section, which rises to 1,850 ft (564 m). Hall Lake (c.200 sq mi/520 sq km) lies near the northeast coast, and in the southern portion of the peninsula are many connected lakes. The tundra-covered region is virtually uninhabited and is of little importance economically. There is a trading post at Repulse Bay on the south coast and an air station near Hall Lake.

Melville Sound, Canada: see VISCOUNT MELVILLE SOUND.

Melvindale, city (1970 pop. 13,862), Wayne co., SE Mich., a residential suburb of Detroit; settled 1870, inc. as a city 1932.

Melzar (mĕl'zär), title of the guardian of King Jehoiakim's wards. Dan. 1.11,16.

membrane, structure composed primarily of fat and protein that forms the outer boundary of a cell, of organelles within cells, or of tissues or organs. The external membrane of cells is a three-layered sheet up to 150 ANGSTROMS thick, in which two protein layers enclose a layer of PHOSPHOLIPID. It is selectively permeable, i.e., some ions and molecules, but not others, diffuse freely across it. Other substances are actively transported by enzyme processes that take place within the membrane structure and involve the expenditure of chemical energy. In the processes of pinocytosis, the bulk transport of fluid across the cell boundary, and phagocytosis, the movement of solids, the membrane moves substances into the cell by the mechanical process of infolding and enveloping the substances, or ejects them by a reverse sequence. Cell membranes also carry receptors that can bind specific substances. Sudden variations in membrane permeability, with the consequent passage of certain charged particles (ions), is responsible for the transmission of nerve impulses and muscle contraction in specialized cells. Within the cell a system of membranes, the endoplasmic reticulum, structurally similar to the external membrane, is the site of protein synthesis. The term *membrane* also describes any layer of pliable tissue that encloses an organ or that lines a body cavity, such as the PLEURA.

Memel: see KLAYPEDA, USSR.

Memel: see NEMAN, river, USSR.

Memel Territory, Ger. *Memelland,* name applied to the district (1,092 sq mi/2,828 sq km) of former East Prussia situated on the east coast of the Baltic Sea and the right (northern) bank of the Neman River. In 1919 the Treaty of Versailles placed the district, containing the city and port of Memel (see KLAYPEDA) under League of Nations–sponsored French administration. Lithuanian troops occupied the area in 1923, forcing the French garrison to withdraw. The Allied council of ambassadors then drew up a new status for the territory, which in 1924 became an autonomous region within Lithuania with its own legislature. The 1938 electoral victory of the National Socialists in the Memel Territory was followed in March, 1939, by a German ultimatum demanding the district's return. Lithuania complied. In 1945 the area was taken by Soviet forces and was restored to Lithuania, by then a part of the USSR.

Memling or **Memlinc, Hans** (häns mĕm'lĭng, -lĭngk), c.1430–1494, Flemish religious and portrait painter, b. Germany. He may have studied with Roger van der Weyden in Brussels, but after 1466 he was in Bruges, working for Flemish patrons and for the many Italian businessmen there. His religious works reflect van der Weyden's figure types, but without their religious intensity; Memling's religious art is pleasing, but somewhat bland. His portraits are more original, combining accuracy of representation with imaginative and varied treatment of the backgrounds. In general, his compositions are symmetrical, with figures often placed frontally. Details, such as flowers, animals, or architecture, are often sensitively observed. An example is his accurate view of Cologne Cathedral as it was in 1489 in the background of the *St. Ursula Shrine* panels (Bruges). His earliest known work is a triptych of *The Madonna Enthroned with Saints and Donors* (1468; Duke of Devonshire Coll., Chatsworth). Other important works are *The Adoration of the Magi Triptych* and the *Diptych of Martin van Nieuwenhoven* (both Bruges) and pictures in the Metropolitan Museum and the Pierpont Morgan Library, New York City; the National Gallery of Art, Washington, D.C.; and the museums of San Diego, Houston, and Montreal. See study by K. B. McFarlane (1972).

Memmingen (mĕm'ĭng-ən), city (1970 pop. 32,917), Bavaria, S West Germany. Manufactures include metal products, textiles, machinery, beer, and chemicals. It is also a rail junction. Historically a Swabian town, Memmingen was first mentioned in the early 12th cent. and became a free imperial city in 1286. The Twelve Articles of the Peasantry (1525) were drawn up there during the PEASANTS WAR. Memmingen passed to Bavaria in 1803. Parts of the city's 15th-century walls and gates remain. There are also two 15th-century Gothic churches, a 16th-century city hall, and the 16th-century Fugger House.

Memminger, Christopher Gustavus (mĕm'ĭnjər), 1803–88, American politician, Confederate secretary of the treasury; b. Württemberg, Germany. He was brought to Charleston, S.C., as a child and became a successful lawyer. As a state legislator and Charleston school commissioner he did much to effect financial and educational reform. He took a prominent part in the proceedings of the South Carolina secession convention of 1860 and was chairman of the committee that drafted the provisional constitution of the Confederacy. Appointed (1861) Confederate secretary of the treasury, Memminger, although a believer in hard currency, was forced by circumstances to direct an inflationary financial program. He was blamed for the collapse of Confederate credit and compelled to resign in 1864. After the war he practiced law again in Charleston. See biography by H. D. Capers (1893).

Memnon (mĕm'nŏn), in Greek mythology, king of Ethiopia, son of Tithonus and Eos. In the Trojan War he fought against the Greeks, and after he had killed Antilochus, he himself was killed by Achilles. Eos obtained immortality from Zeus for her son. Memnon was supposed to have lived in Egypt, and the Greeks gave his name to the great statue of Amenhotep III at Thebes. This statue was said to make a musical sound at daybreak, at which time Memnon greeted his mother, goddess of dawn.

Memorial Day, holiday in the United States observed in late May. Previously designated Decoration Day, it was inaugurated in 1868 by Gen. John A. Logan for the purpose of decorating the graves of Civil War veterans and has since become a day on which all war dead are commemorated.

Memorial University of Newfoundland, at St. John's, N.F., Canada; provincially supported; coeducational; founded 1925 as Memorial University College. It achieved university status in 1949. The school has faculties of arts, science, education, engineering, medicine, junior studies, and graduate studies.

memory, in electronics: see COMPUTER.

memory, in psychology, the storing of learned information, and in certain situations, the ability to recall that which has been stored. It has been hypothesized that three processes occur in remembering: perception and registering of a stimulus; temporary maintenance of the perception, or short-term memory; and lasting storage of the perception, or long-term memory. For long-term memory to occur, there must be a period of maturation, or information consolidation. Retrograde AMNESIA, i.e., the failure to remember an event just preceding a head injury, is evidence of interrupted consolidation; SHOCK THERAPY has the same amnesic effect. Experiments have suggested that many factors enhance retention of information, including high motivation and presentation of material that is interesting and that allows one to recognize past experience or relearn. Forgetting was first studied scientifically by Hermann Ebbinghaus, the German experimental psychologist, using nonsense syllables (groups of disconnected syllables without associative connection); he showed that the rate of forgetting is greatest at first, gradually diminishing until a relatively constant level of retained information is reached. Theories to explain forgetting include the theory of disuse, that is, that forgetting occurs because stored information is not used; and the psychoanalytic theory that forgetting is purposeful and that some memories are rarely recalled except through hypnosis or PSYCHOANALYSIS. According to the theory of interference, memory is impeded when irrelevant material interferes with the material to be learned; proactive inhibition is the inability to remember one thing because of having learned another thing first; retroactive inhibition is interference with remembering one thing because of having learned another thing afterward. In a physiological sense, learning is believed to be a modification of the transmission pathways of the nervous system. Some authorities have hypothesized that synthesis of ribonucleic acid (RNA) or related substances is involved in memory. See B. B. Murdock, Jr., *Human Memory: Theory and Data* (1974).

Memphis (mĕm'fĭs), ancient city of Egypt, capital of the Old Kingdom (c.3100–c.2258 B.C.), at the apex of the Nile delta and 12 mi (18 km) from Cairo. It was reputedly founded by Menes, the first king of united Egypt. Its god was Ptah. The temple of Ptah, the palace of Apries, and two huge statues of Ramses II are among the most important monuments found at the site. The necropolis of SAKKARA, near Memphis, was a favorite burial place for pharaohs of the Old Kingdom. Across the Nile are the great pyramids, extending for 20 mi (32 km) to Al Jizah (Gizeh). Memphis remained important during the long dominance by Thebes and became the seat of the Persian satraps (525 B.C.). Second only to Alexandria under the Ptolemies and under Rome, it finally declined with the founding of nearby Fustat by the Arabs, and its ruins were largely removed for building in the new city and, later, in Cairo.

Memphis, city (1970 pop. 623,530), seat of Shelby co., SW Tenn., on the Fourth, or Lower, Chickasaw Bluff above the Mississippi, at the mouth of the Wolf River; inc. 1826. An important river port with excellent anchorages on the Wolf, Memphis is the largest city in the state, a port of entry, a great rail center, and a leading hardwood lumber, cotton, poultry, and livestock market. Its wide variety of manufactures includes textiles, heating equipment, pianos, and automobile and truck parts. A number of corporations have their national headquarters there, and the city is one of the four regional headquarters for the U.S. Postal Service. De Soto possibly crossed the Mississippi near the site of Memphis, and La Salle's Fort Prudhomme may have been built there. The area was strategically important during the time of the British, French, and Spanish rivalries in the 18th cent. A U.S. fort was erected there in 1797. The city was established (1819) by Andrew Jackson (who named it), Marcus Winchester, and John Overton. In the Civil War it fell, on June 6, 1862, to a Union force led by the elder Charles Henry Davis and was an important Federal base for the rest of the war. Severe yellow-fever epidemics occurred in the 1870s; thousands died, and so many people fled the city that its charter had to be surrendered (1879); the charter was not restored until 1891. E. H. "Boss" Crump ruled Memphis from 1909 until his political hold was broken after 1948. The city is the seat of Memphis State Univ., the Univ. of Tennessee Medical Units, Southwestern at Memphis, Christian Brothers College, Le Moyne-Owen College, the Memphis Academy of Arts, Southern College of Optometry, and a technical institute. It has a museum of natural history, a planetarium, an art gallery, a notable park system, botanical gardens, a zoo, an aquarium, a coliseum, a speedway, and a greyhound park. It is the seat of a large medical center, St. Jude Children's Research Hospital, a veterans hospital, and a state mental hospital. The Mid-South Fairgrounds are there, and a new convention hall has been built. An annual week-long cotton carnival is held, and the Liberty Bowl postseason college football game is played there each year. A number of antebellum homes in the city have been restored. A leading tourist attraction of Memphis is Beale St., made famous by W. C. Handy, the black composer and compiler of the blues. There are a number of military installations in and near the city. A trans-Mississippi bridge connects Memphis with Arkansas, and the city has an international airport. See Shields McIlwaine, *Memphis Down in Dixie* (1948); G. W. Lee, *Beale Street: Where the Blues Began* (1934, repr. 1969).

Memphis State University, at Memphis, Tenn.; coeducational; opened 1912 as a normal school, became West Tennessee State Teachers College in 1925. The school was renamed Memphis State College in 1941 and in 1957 received university status.

Memucan (mēmyōō'kən), counselor of King Ahasuerus. Esther 1.14.

Mena, Juan de (hwän dā mā'nä), 1411–56, Spanish poet and scholar. Influenced by the Italian school, he modeled his chief work *Laberinto de Fortuna* (1444) upon Dante. This 300-stanza allegorical poem was the major Spanish harbinger of the Renaissance. His *Coronación*, a didactic allegory, is more conventionally medieval.

Menado: see MANADO, Indonesia.

Menahem (mĕn'əhĕm), d. c.737 B.C., king of Israel (c.749–c.737 B.C.). He was governor of Tirzah and murdered Shallum for the throne of Samaria. Menahem was made a tributary by Tiglath-pileser III of Assyria, who helped him to gain his throne. The book of Kings represents him unfavorably. His son, Pekahiah, succeeded him.

Menai Strait (mĕn'ī), channel of the Irish Sea, 14 mi (23 km) long and from 200 yd (183 m) to 2 mi (3.2 km) wide, between the island of Anglesey and mainland Gwynedd, NW Wales. Thomas Telford's suspension bridge (1826; rebuilt 1938–41) carries the road from Bangor on the mainland to Anglesey, over the strait, and Robert Stephenson's tubular bridge (1850) carries a railroad. Caernarvon is on the strait; Llanfairpwllgwyngyll is nearby.

Menam or **Menam Chao Phraya,** river, Thailand: see CHAO PHRAYA.

Menan (mē'nən), ancestor of Joseph. Luke 3.31.

Menander (mĭnăn'dər), 342?–291? B.C., Greek poet, the most famous writer of New Comedy. He wrote ingenious plays using the love plot as his theme; his style is elegant and elaborate and his characters are highly developed. Many fragments of his plays survive; *The Curmudgeon*, discovered in Cairo in 1957, is Menander's only complete play now extant (tr. by Gilbert Highet, 1959). Through the imitations of PLAUTUS and TERENCE he influenced late-17th-century comedy. See studies by T. B. L. Webster (1950, repr. 1960), D. B. Durham (1969), and A. W. Gomme and F. H. Sandbach (1973).

Menasha (mənăsh'ə), city (1970 pop. 14,905), Winnebago co., E Wis., on Lake Winnebago and the Fox River, adjacent to its twin city of Neenah; settled 1840s, inc. 1874. Menasha is a great paper-making center. The industry, which is served by water power, dates from the late 19th cent. The region at the lake outlet was visited by Jean Nicolet (c.1634; the site is marked) and other French explorers and was described by Jonathan Carver in his *Travels* (1778).

Mencius (mĕn'shəs), Mandarin *Meng-tse*, 371?–288? B.C., Chinese Confucian philosopher. The principal source for Mencius' life is his own writings. He was born in the ancient state of Ch'ao, in modern Shantung prov. He lost his father as a child and was reared by his mother, who, in Chinese folklore, is synonymous with maternal devotion. Appalled at the anarchic condition of society, he traveled through several petty states urging the rulers to practice the doctrines of CONFUCIUS. Central to the philosophy of Mencius was the belief that man is by nature good. His innate moral sense can be developed by cultivation or perverted by an unfavorable environment. The duty of the ruler is to ensure the prosperous livelihood of his subjects. He should particularly eschew warfare except for defense. If the ruler's conduct reduces his subjects to penury and self-seeking, he must be deposed. Many of the specific reforms in landholding and other economic relations that Mencius proposed are difficult to understand from the sole text of his works, *The Book of Mencius,* which is one of the *Shih Shu* [four books] (see CHINESE LITERATURE). Not until the late 11th cent. A.D. was Mencius regarded with veneration. Since then his image has been placed in temples dedicated to Confucius, and his work is considered second only to that of Confucius. The complete text of Mencius was translated by James Legge (1861; 2d ed. 1895, repr. 1970), L. A. Lyall (1935), Lionel Giles (1942), and D. C. Lau (1970). Excerpts were translated by Arthur Waley in *Three Ways of Thought in Ancient China* (1939). See I. A. Richards, *Mencius on the Mind* (1932); A. F. Verwilghen, *Mencius: The Man and His Ideas* (1967).

Mencken, Henry Louis, 1880–1956, American editor, author, and critic, b. Baltimore, grad. Baltimore Polytechnic. He began his journalistic career on the Baltimore *Morning Herald,* became editor of the Baltimore *Evening Herald,* and from 1906 until his death was on the staff of the Baltimore *Sun* or *Evening Sun.* From 1914 to 1923 he was coeditor of the *Smart Set* with George Jean Nathan; together they started the *American Mercury* in 1924, and Mencken was the sole editor from 1925 to 1933. His pungent and iconoclastic criticism, although aimed at all complacent attitudes, was chiefly directed at the middle class. These essays have been collected in a series of six volumes, *Prejudices* (1919–27). In the field of philology he compiled a monumental and lively study, *The American Language* (1st ed. 1919; 4th ed. 1936; with supplements, 1946, 1948). Among his other works are *George Bernard Shaw: His Plays* (1905), *In Defense of Women* (1917), *Treatise of the Gods* (1930), and the autobiographical *Happy Days, 1880–1892* (1940), *Newspaper Days, 1899–1906* (1941), and *Heathen Days, 1890–1936* (1943), collected in one volume in 1947. Mencken was also important as the literary champion of Theodore Dreiser, Sherwood Anderson, Sinclair Lewis, and Eugene O'Neill. See his letters (ed. by G. L. Forgue, 1961); biographies by Sara Mayfield (1968) and Carl Bode (1969); studies by D. C. Stenerson (1971) and F. C. Hobson, Jr. (1974).

Mende (mäNd), city (1968 pop. 11,472), capital of Lozère dept., S France, on the Lot River. Mende is a tourist resort. It was originally a small Gallo-Roman city that became an episcopal see in the 5th cent. Bishops ruled the town until 1306, when they were forced to cede a portion of it to Philip the Handsome. During the Wars of Religion (1562–98) the city was often sacked. Points of interest include a 14th-century bridge over the Lot River, a 14th-century Gothic cathedral, and an 18th-century town hall.

Mendel, David: see NEANDER, JOHANN AUGUST WILHELM.

Mendel, Gregor Johann (grā'gôr yō'hän mĕn'dəl), 1822–84, Austrian monk noted for his experimental work on heredity. He entered the Augustinian monastery in Brno in 1843, taught at a local secondary school, and carried out independent scientific investigations on garden peas and other plants until his election as prelate in 1868. Failing eyesight and his duties as prelate somewhat curtailed his researches; although he anticipated Oscar Hertwig's discovery that fertilization of an egg involved only one male sex cell, these findings went unpublished. At a time of avid interest in Darwinism and of many speculative theories about speciation, Mendel was the first to fashion, by means of a controlled pollination technique and careful statistical analysis of his results, an accurate and scientific explanation for hybridization. His account of the experiments and his conclusions, published in 1866, were ignored during his lifetime. Rediscovered by three separate investigators (Correns, De Vries, and Tschermak) in 1900, Mendel's conclusions have become the basic tenets of genetics and a notable influence in plant and animal breeding. Mendel's classic article on his experiments with peas has been published as a pamphlet (tr. *Experiments in Plant Hybridization,* 1926) and in Curt Stern and E. R. Sherwood, ed., *The Origin of Genetics* (1966). See biography by Hugo Iltis (tr. 1932, repr. 1966). **Mendelism** is the system of heredity formulated from Mendel's conclusions. Briefly summarized, the Mendelian system states that an inherited characteristic is determined by the combination of two hereditary units (now called genes), one from each of the parental reproductive cells, or gametes. In the body cells the genes are found in pairs representing alternative or contrasting factors (e.g., in the pea plant, the pair determining tallness or dwarfness). The law of segregation (Mendel's first law) states that in the process of the formation of the gametes (see MEIOSIS) the pairs separate, one going to each gamete, and that each gene remains completely uninfluenced by the other. Mendel found that when a pure strain of one factor, inbred for many generations, was crossed with a pure strain of its alternative, one of these factors consistently prevailed over the other; he therefore termed the two factors *dominant* and *recessive,* and called the phenomenon itself the law of dominance. Given A as the dominant factor and a as the recessive, the offspring of the purebred strains AA and aa are hybrids, individuals each having one A factor and one a. When the hybrids are crossed, the offspring exhibit the characteristic in question in a ratio of three dominant to one recessive; i.e., the four possible combinations of Aa and Aa are AA, aA, Aa, and aa. By the same rule, when a hybrid is crossed with a purebred recessive (Aa with aa) the ratio is one to one. Breeders often use these ratios to trace the hybrid or purebred nature of the parent stock. The law of independent assortment (Mendel's second law) states that characteristics are inherited independently of each other; e.g., the dominant trait of yellow seed color in pea plants can appear in combination with either the dominant trait of plant tallness or the recessive trait of dwarfness. This law has been modified by the discovery of linkage (see GENETICS). See also HEREDITY. See K. R. Lewis, *The Matter of Mendelian Heredity* (1964); R. C. Olby, *Origins of Mendelism* (1966); T. H. Morgan et al., *The Mechanism of Mendelian Heredity* (1915, repr. 1972).

Mendeleev, Dmitri Ivanovich (mĕndəlā'əf, Rus. dəmē'trē ēvä'nəvĭch myĭndyĭlyā'əf), 1834–1907, Russian chemist. He is famous for his formulation (1869) of the PERIODIC LAW and the invention of the PERIODIC TABLE, a classification of the elements; with Lothar Meyer, who had independently reached similar conclusions, he was awarded the Davy medal in 1882. From his remarkable table Mendeleev predicted the properties of elements then unknown; three of these (gallium, scandium, and germanium) were later discovered. He studied also the nature of solutions and the expansion of liquids. An outstanding teacher, he was professor at the Univ. of St. Petersburg (1868–90). He directed the bureau of weights and measures from 1893 and served as government adviser on the development of the petroleum industry. His *Principles of Chemistry* (2 vol., 1868–71; tr. 1905) was long a standard text. Various spellings of his surname are common, among them Mendeleyev and Mendelejeff. See biographies by D. Q. Posin (1948) and Peter Kelman and A. H. Stone (1970).

Mendele mocher sforim (mĕn'dələ môkh'ər sfô'rĭm), pseud. of **Sholem** (or **Solomon**) **Yakob Abramovich** (shō'ləm yä'kôp əbrä'məvĭch), 1836–1917, Yiddish novelist. Born in Minsk, Russia, and orphaned at 14, he traveled with beggars through the Ukraine. His early writings were in Hebrew, but his later novels and short stories were written in Yiddish. He perfected a Yiddish prose style that greatly influenced later writers. Mendele translated many of his later works into Hebrew and is considered the father of modern prose literature in Hebrew. Among his best-known writings, dealing with Jewish life in Russia, are *Di kliatche* [the mare] (1873) and *The Travels of Benjamin the Third* (1878). He attempted to influence the people to free themselves from the ghetto. See Leo Wiener's *The History of Yiddish Literature in the Nineteenth Century* (1899).

mendelevium (mĕndəlāv'ēəm), artificially produced radioactive chemical element; symbol Md; at. no. 101; mass no. of most stable isotope 258; m.p., b.p., and sp. gr. unknown; valence +2 or +3. Mendelevium is a synthetic radioactive metal of the ACTINIDE SERIES in group IIIb of the PERIODIC TABLE. It is named for the Russian chemist Dmitri Ivanovich Mendelejeff. Five isotopes of mendelevium are known. Mendelevium-256 (half-life about 90 min) was the first isotope produced; it was detected in 1955 by A. Ghiorso, B. G. Harvey, G. R. Choppin, S. G. Thompson, and G. T. SEABORG, who produced it one atom at a time by bombarding einsteinium-253 with alpha particles in a cyclotron at the Univ. of California at Berkeley. Studies of mendelevium-256 suggest +2 and +3 valence in aqueous solutions. However, little is known of the properties of this element, since its isotopes are unstable and difficult to produce. Mendelevium-258 (the most stable isotope) has a half-life of about 2 months; its synthesis (by bombarding einsteinium-255 with alpha particles) may make possible studies of the physical and chemical properties of the element.

Mendelism: see MENDEL, GREGOR JOHANN.

Mendelsohn, Erich (ā'rĭkh mĕn'dəlzōn), 1887–1953, German architect, an exponent of expressionism. His designs included that of the Steinberg hat factory (1919–20) at Luckenwalde near Berlin and several department stores in Germany (1926–29). The Potsdam observatory, also known as the Einstein tower (1919–21), was a highly original structure conceived as a concrete tower and suggestive of sculpture in its plastic conformation of volumes and surfaces. In his later works Mendelsohn turned to more simplified forms. He emigrated to England in 1933 and after 1934 designed medical centers and other buildings in Haifa and Jerusalem. In 1941, Mendelsohn became a resident of the United States, where he built some works in San Francisco and several impressive synagogues in the Midwest. See study by Wolf von Eckardt (1960).

Mendelssohn, Felix (Jacob Ludwig Felix Mendelssohn) (mĕn'dəlsən, Ger. yä'kôp lo͝ot'vĭkh fā'lĭks mĕn'dəlszōn"), 1809–47, German composer; grandson of the Jewish philosopher Moses Mendelssohn. Mendelssohn was one of the major figures in 19th-century music. His father, Abraham, upon conversion to Christianity, changed his surname to Mendelssohn-Bartholdy, a form which is seldom used. A prodigy, reared in a highly cultured atmosphere, Felix as a child presented his orchestral compositions to illustrious audiences at the family estate. His first mature work, the Overture to *A Midsummer Night's Dream,* was composed at 17, and he showed similar precocity at the piano. In 1829 he conducted a performance of the St. Matthew Passion which stimulated a revival of interest in the music of J. S. Bach. He was musical director (1833–35) at Düsseldorf and in 1835 became conductor of the Gewandhaus concerts, Leipzig. There he helped found (1842–43) the Leipzig Conservatory. He was director of the music section of the Academy of Arts, Berlin, in 1841. On many occasions he conducted the London Philharmonic Orchestra. His music is characterized by emotional restraint, refinement, and sensitivity, and a fastidious adherence to classical forms. Of his five symphonies, the *Scottish* (1830–42), *Italian* (1833), and *Reformation* (1830–32) are best known. Frequently performed are his Violin Concerto in E Minor (1844); *The Hebrides Overture* or *Fingal's Cave* (1830–32); and two oratorios, *St. Paul* (1836) and *Elijah* (1846). Outstanding piano works include the *Variations sérieuses* (1841) and eight sets of *Songs without Words* (1832–45). He also composed chamber music, songs, choral music, and six organ sonatas. See his letters (ed. by Gisela Selden-Goth, 1945); biographies by G. R. Marek (1972) and Wilfred Blunt (1974); Herbert Kupferberg, *The Mendelssohns* (1972).

Mendelssohn, Moses, 1729–86, German-Jewish philosopher; grandfather of Jakob Ludwig Felix Mendelssohn. He was a leader in the movement for cultural assimilation. In 1743 he went to Berlin, where he studied and worked, becoming (1750) a partner in a silk merchant's firm. In 1754 he met Lessing, and a life-long friendship began, out of which grew Lessing's play *Nathan the Wise* (1779). Mendelssohn's philosophy anticipated the aesthetics of Kant and Friedrich Schiller. His writings include *Philosophische Gespräche* (1755), *Philosophische Schriften* (1761), *Phädon* (1767), and *Jerusalem; oder, Über religiöse Macht und Judentum* (1783). He also translated the Psalms and the Pentateuch into German. See biography by Alexander Altman (1973).

Menderes, Adnan (ädnän'mĕndĕrĕs'), 1889–1961, Turkish premier (1950–60). In Jan., 1946, he formed the Democratic party, the first legal opposition party in Turkey. When the party came to power (1950), Menderes became premier, and in 1955 he also assumed the duties of foreign minister. In May, 1960, an army coup under General Cemal GÜRSEL toppled the government, and Menderes was arrested, charged with violating the constitution, and executed.

Menderes (mĕndĕrĕs'), name of several rivers in Turkey. The Büyük Menderes is the ancient MAEANDER; the Küçük Menderes is the ancient SCAMANDER.

Mendès, Catulle (kätül' mäNdĕs'), 1841–1909, French poet, critic, and novelist of the Parnassian school. He founded (1861) the *Revue fantaisiste,* contributed to the *Parnasse contemporain,* and wrote volumes of verse, including *Philoméla* (1863) and *La Grive des vignes* (1895).

Mendès-France, Pierre (pyĕr mäNdĕs'-fräNs), 1907–, French statesman. A lawyer and economist, he entered (1932) the chamber of deputies as a Radical Socialist. In World War II he was a pilot in the Free French forces. Popular as a democratic leader, he became premier in 1954. At the Geneva Conference (1954), he arranged the armistice that halted the fighting in Indochina. He also helped to bring about the formation of the Western European Union, and he proposed far-reaching economic reform. His cabinet fell (1955) on the issue of his liberal North African policy. His conflict with the doctrinaire conservative Radical Socialists led to a party split; in 1957 he resigned as party head. He failed to gain reelection to the national assembly in 1958, and in 1959 he was expelled from the party. Mendès-France opposed the return to power (1958) of Charles de Gaulle, and he led the Union of Democratic Forces, an anti-Gaullist group. See his *Economics and Action* (tr. 1955), *The Pursuit of Freedom* (tr. 1956), and *A Modern French Republic* (tr. 1963); biography by Alexander Werth (1958).

Méndez Montenegro, Julio César (ho͞o'lyō sä'sär män'dās mōntänā'grō), 1915–, president of Guatemala (1966–70). A law professor and author of a number of books on law, he was elected president after three years of military rule. He attempted to curb inflation, promote new industry, and institute social reform, and succeeded in bringing a degree of economic prosperity to the country. However, his attention was chiefly absorbed by the increasing violence and terrorism that gripped the country.

Mendieta y Montefur, Carlos (kär'lōs mändyā'tä ē mōntäfo͞or'), 1873–1960, Cuban political leader. He was one of the chief opponents of Gerardo MACHADO. Mendieta, installed as provisional president (1934) by a coup led by Fulgencio Batista, was unable to establish political stability and resigned (1935).

Mendip Hills, range of hills, c.25 mi (40 km) long, across N Somerset, SW England, extending SE from the vicinity of Hutton to the Frome valley. Composed primarily of limestone, the hills have numerous caves (Wookey Hole, Cheddar Caves), some of which show signs of prehistoric occupation. In the hills are ruins of Roman lead mines, an amphitheater, and a Roman road. The gorges near Cheddar are particularly notable. Livestock raising and quarrying are important there.

Mendoza, Antonio de (äntō'nyō dā mändō'thä), 1490?–1552, Spanish administrator, first viceroy of New Spain (1535–50) and viceroy of Peru (1551–52). Of noble family, Mendoza held high offices before going to Mexico, where his wise rule earned him the appellation "the good viceroy." He alleviated the condition of the Indians (though opposing enforcement of the New Laws of Bartolomé de Las Casas), fostered religion, and encouraged education.

He brought the first printing press to America at the request of Bishop ZUMÁRRAGA. He quelled numerous revolts, notably the Indian insurrection in Nueva Galicia (called the MIXTÓN WAR) in which Pedro de ALVARADO was killed. By fostering expeditions, especially those under MARCOS DE NIZA and CORONADO, he pushed exploration far northward. Industry and agriculture were also developed, bringing prosperity. In brief, he extended and consolidated the conquest begun by Hernán CORTÉS, and established the sure basis for Spain's long rule in Mexico. Efforts to discredit and oust him, originating with Cortés, ended in failure. In 1551 he took office as viceroy of Peru and again opposed enforcement of the New Laws. The audiencia, however, overruled him. See biography by A. S. Aiton (1927).

Mendoza, Diego Hurtado de: see HURTADO DE MENDOZA, DIEGO.

Mendoza, Iñigo López de: see SANTILLANA, IÑIGO LÓPEZ DE MENDOZA, MARQUÉS DE.

Mendoza, Pedro de (pā'thrō), b. 1501 or 1502, d. 1537, Spanish conquistador, first adelantado [civil and military governor] of Río de la Plata (present-day Argentina). After a military career in Europe, he received (1534) from Emperor Charles V a commission to conquer and colonize the Río de la Plata region. With 11 vessels and 1,200 men, he sailed from Sanlúcar de Barrameda on Aug. 24, 1535. He reached the estuary of the Río de la Plata in January and founded Buenos Aires early in Feb., 1536. Attacks by the Indians, scarcity of food, and disaster of every sort made the site untenable. Leaving Juan de AYOLAS in charge, Mendoza sailed for Spain in April, 1537, and died at sea. Buenos Aires was abandoned in 1541, by order of Domingo Martínez de Irala, and the colonists moved to Asunción.

Mendoza, Pedro González de (pā'thrō gōnthä'lĕth dā), 1428–95, Spanish cardinal and archbishop of Toledo. He was the son of the poet Iñigo López de Mendoza, marqués de Santillana. He supported Henry IV of Castile in his struggles against the nobles and later sided with Isabella I against Juana la Beltraneja. More a soldier than a prelate, he fought in the battle of Toro (1476) against the Portuguese and later took part in the conquest of Granada. He also cultivated literature and wrote religious and political works.

Mendoza, city (1970 pop. 118,568), capital of Mendoza prov., W Argentina. With a backdrop of snow-capped mountains, Mendoza is surrounded by a fertile oasis, known as the "Garden of the Andes," irrigated by the Mendoza River. It is a major metropolis and the center of a rich wine-producing region, largely settled by Italian immigrants. Mendoza was founded in 1561 and belonged to Chile until the creation of the viceroyalty of Río de la Plata (1776). Destroyed by earthquake in 1861, the town was rebuilt and expanded rapidly after the completion of the railroad to Buenos Aires late in the 19th cent. It is also the eastern terminus of the TRANSANDINE RAILWAY. It was in Mendoza that SAN MARTÍN began (1817) the final liberation of Chile from Spain. The city's landmarks include a Franciscan monastery where several Argentine national heroes are buried.

Mene, Mene, Tekel, Upharsin (mē'nē, mē'nē, tē'kəl, yōōfär'sĭn), in the Bible, the mysterious riddle written by a hand on the wall at Belshazzar's feast. These Aramaic words may be translated literally as, "It has been counted and counted, weighed and divided." Daniel interpreted this to mean that the king's deeds had been weighed and found deficient and that his kingdom would therefore be divided. Dan. 5.5–29.

Menelaus (mĕnəlā'əs), in Greek mythology, king of Sparta, son of Atreus. He was the husband of Helen, the father of Hermione, and the younger brother of Agamemnon. When Paris, prince of Troy, abducted Helen, Menelaus asked the other Greek kings to join him in an expedition against Troy. Thus the Trojan War began. Menelaus, although subordinate to Agamemnon, took a prominent part in the war. After the fall of Troy, he became reconciled with Helen, but before they finally reached Sparta they experienced a long series of adventures. Menelaus appears in the *Iliad* and in the *Odyssey*.

Menelik II (mĕn'əlĭk), 1844–1913, emperor of Ethiopia after 1889. He was originally ras (ruler) of Shoa (central Ethiopia). After the death (1868) of Emperor Theodore II, Menelik, with Italian support, gained strength steadily. He seized the throne after Emperor Johannes IV died. In 1889, Menelik concluded the Treaty of Uccialli with Italy. When he learned, however, that the Italian version of the treaty made Ethiopia a protectorate of Italy, he denounced the agreement. The Italian invasion that followed (1895–96) was crushed by Menelik's great victory near ADUWA. Italy was forced to renounce all claim to Ethiopia and to pay an indemnity. Menelik took important steps to strengthen and modernize his domain. He made Addis Ababa his capital, constructed a railroad, attempted to end the slave trade, and curbed the feudal nobility. His conquests doubled the size of the country and brought the present S Ethiopia (largely Muslim in population) into the realm. Gradually his health failed, and the end of his reign was marked by intrigue and maneuvering for the succession. He was succeeded as emperor by Lij Yasu.

Menen, Aubrey Clarence, 1912–, English novelist, b. London. The son of an Indian father and an Irish mother, he has been a drama critic, theater director, and advertising agency executive. Menen is primarily a satirist, and his novels are aimed more at amusing than reforming. For example, *The Abode of Love* (1956), which is about a harem in Victorian London, satirizes Victorianism. His other works include *A Prevalence of Witches* (1948), *Dead Man in the Silver Market* (1953), *Upon This Rock* (1972), and *The Mystics* (1974).

Menen (mā'nən), Fr. *Menin*, city (1970 pop. 22,037), West Flanders prov., SW Belgium, on the Leie River, near the French border. Manufactures include machinery, textiles, and tobacco products. Founded in 1578, Menen was strongly fortified in the 17th cent. In World War I it changed hands several times during the bitter fighting between German and English forces in the Ypres sector.

Menéndez de Avilés, Pedro (pā'thrō mānān'dĕth dā ävēlās'), 1519–74, Spanish naval officer and colonizer, founder of SAINT AUGUSTINE, Fla., b. Avilés, Asturias. He went to sea as a youth and so distinguished himself that by the time he was 35 he held the captain generalcy of the Indies fleet, which convoyed treasure ships from the New World to Spain. In 1565, Philip II of Spain charged him with driving the French Huguenots from Fort Caroline and establishing a Spanish colony in Florida. Menéndez's expedition of 11 ships and 500 colonists sailed from Spain on June 29 and on Aug. 28 entered the harbor he named for St. Augustine. At the mouth of the St. Johns River on Sept. 4 he encountered a French fleet under Jean RIBAUT, which he was unable to bring to combat. Menéndez then returned to St. Augustine, where he began to build a fort. Ribaut, hoping to take the Spanish by surprise, sailed to attack them, but his fleet was wrecked in a storm. With Fort Caroline, under the command of René de LAUDONNIÈRE, virtually defenseless, Menéndez marched overland and on Sept. 21 killed most of the French there. Ribaut and his men, driven ashore S of St. Augustine, were captured as they tried to reach Fort Caroline by land, and all but a few were slain. The massacres, which aroused France, were later (1568) avenged by Dominique de GOURGUES. Part of his mission accomplished, Menéndez went to Cuba for supplies and then explored the Gulf Coast, where he made friendly contacts with the Indians. Before he returned to Spain in 1567 there were Spanish posts on St. Helena Island (S.C.) and on Chesapeake Bay in addition to St. Augustine and San Mateo (Fort Caroline). Although he remained governor of Florida until his death, Menéndez returned only for a brief stay in 1571. The establishment of the Florida colony was due almost wholly to his energy and ability. An early account is Gonzalo Solís de Merás, *Pedro Menéndez de Avilés* (tr. and ed. by J. T. Connor, 1923, repr. 1964). See Woodbury Lowery, *The Spanish Settlements* (1905, repr. 1959); study by A. C. Manucy (1965).

Menéndez Pidal, Ramón (rämōn' mānān'dĕth pēthäl'), 1869–1968, Spanish scholar and philologist. Menéndez was a noted authority on Spanish epic literature and the Spanish language, and was also a major modern historian. He directed the *Revista de filología española* and wrote *Orígenes del español* (1926). Among his studies in medieval literature are *El romancero español* (1910) and *Poesía juglaresca y juglares* (1924), as well as several works on the Cid. *Spaniards in Their History* (tr. 1950) is one of his best-known works.

Menéndez y Pelayo, Marcelino (märthālē'nō mānān'dĕth ē pälä'yō), 1856–1912, Spanish literary historian and critic. His vast contribution to Spanish scholarship includes *Historia de los heterodoxos españoles* (1880–82), a panoramic history of Spain; *Historia de las ideas estéticas en España* (1883–91), an equally panoramic cultural history of Spain; an anthology of Castillan poetry (13 vol., 1890–1908); and the important anthology of Latin American poetry (1893–95). His masterpiece was the *Orígenes de la novela española* (1905–15). See study by Manuel Olguín (1950).

Menes (mē'nēz), fl. 3200 B.C., king of ancient Egypt, of the first dynasty, the first Egyptian ruler for whom there are historical records. According to tradition, he seems to have united the southern and northern kingdoms and to have settled on a new capital, the later Memphis. A recent theory identifies Menes with King Narmer, whose famous slate palette is in the Cairo museum.

Menevia, Wales: see SAINT DAVID'S.

Mengelberg, Josef Willem (yō'zəf vĭl'əm mĕng'əlbĕrk), 1871–1951, Dutch conductor. He was conductor of the Amsterdam Concertgebouw Orchestra from 1895 to 1945. Mengelberg was noted for interpretations of Mahler and of Richard Strauss, whose *Ein Heldenleben* is dedicated to him. From 1921 to 1929 he conducted the New York Philharmonic Orchestra. His health failed in 1941, and in 1945 he retired to Switzerland.

Menger, Karl (kärl mĕng'ər), 1840–1921, Austrian economist, a founder of the Austrian school of economics. He was professor of economics at the Univ. of Vienna from 1873 until 1903, when he retired to devote himself to research. Following an empirical approach rather than the historical method, he formulated a theory of marginal utility. The basic principle is that consumer goods have value of two orders, as they serve human needs directly or indirectly; thus he explained the economic phenomena of price and distribution in terms of social value. His theories are well known to the English-speaking world through the works of some of his associates, especially Friedrich von Wieser and Eugen von Böhm-Bawerk. His chief work is *Principles of Economics* (1871; tr. 1950).

Mengs, Anton Raphael (än'tôn rä'fäĕl mĕngs), 1728–79, German historical and portrait painter, b. Bohemia. He was the pupil of his father, Ismael Mengs (c.1688–1764), a Dresden miniaturist who took him to Italy in 1741. Anton was appointed Dresden court painter in 1749. Influenced by the theories of WINCKELMANN, he became the leading light of the neoclassical movement. His major works include *Parnassus* (1761; Villa Albani, Rome) and *Apotheosis of Trajan* (Madrid), which he created as court painter to Charles III of Spain. His portrait of Queen María Luisa is in the Metropolitan Museum. Mengs was also an important theoretician. His most famous work was *Considerations on Beauty and Taste in Painting* (1762).

Meng-tse: see MENCIUS.

Mengtsz: see MENG-TZU, China.

Meng-tzu or **Mengtsz** (both: mŭng-dzŭ), city, SE Yünnan prov., China, c.12 mi (20 km) E of Ko-chiu. It is the commercial hub of a district where tin and antimony are mined.

menhaden: see HERRING.

menhir (mĕn'hēr") [Breton, = long stone], in archaeology, name given to the single standing stones of Western Europe, and by extension to those of other lands. Their size varies and their shape is rough and squared, tapering toward the top. See MEGALITHIC MONUMENTS.

Ménière's syndrome (mən-yĕrz'), disorder of the inner ear characterized by recurrent episodes of loss of balance combined with deafness and a ringing sensation. It was first described by the French otologist Prosper Ménière, in 1861. The sufferer of Ménière's syndrome experiences severe dizziness, in which objects may seem to spin around, and often nausea, vomiting, and sweating. Attacks may last for several hours. In the disorder, which occurs most often in men between the ages of 40 and 60, the cochlear duct of the inner ear is found to be enlarged; the causes are not known. The disease is treated by administration of antihistamines, atropine, or diuretics. In severe cases, surgery to destroy part of the acoustic nerve is necessary.

Menin: see MENEN, Belgium.

meninges (mĭnĭn'jēz), three membranous layers of CONNECTIVE TISSUE that envelop the brain and spinal cord (see NERVOUS SYSTEM). The outermost layer, or dura mater, is extremely tough and is fused with the membranous lining of the skull. In the brain it forms a vertical sheet that separates the cerebral hemispheres and a horizontal sheet that lies between the cerebrum and the cerebellum. The thin arachnoid membrane lies below and in close contact with the dura mater. The innermost layer, or pia mater, is in direct contact with the brain and spinal cord and contains the blood vessels that supply them. The pia mater and arachnoid membrane are separated by the subarachnoid space containing the cerebrospinal fluid, which carries nutrients, absorbs the impact of shocks, and acts as a barrier to disease organisms.

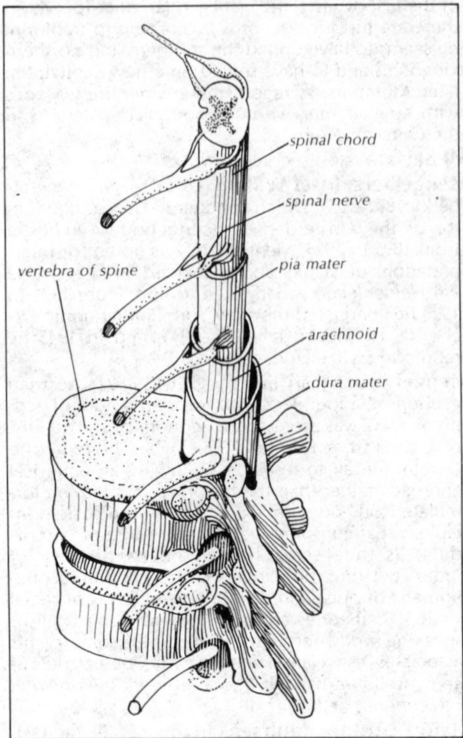

Meninges: Section of spine showing meningeal layers

Thus, the meninges provide a fluid-filled jacket for the protection of neural tissues and allow for the flexing and twisting of the vertebral column about the spinal cord.

meningitis (mĕnĭnjī'tĭs) or **cerebrospinal meningitis** (sĕr″əbrōspī'nəl), acute inflammation of the membranes of the brain or spinal cord, or both. It can be caused by bacteria, viruses, protozoa, yeasts, or fungi, usually introduced from elsewhere in the body. The most common form is meningococcal meningitis; it is attributed to an infection with *Neisseria meningitidis* and has occurred in epidemic form. The use of sulfa and antibiotic drugs has greatly reduced mortality and has lessened the incidence of aftereffects (hydrocephalus, deafness, paralysis, infection of the iris, arthritis). Symptoms are high fever, severe headache, projectile vomiting (sudden ejection of vomit to some distance, frequently without nausea), delirium, coma, pronounced neck and back rigidity, and twitchings or obvious convulsions. In especially severe cases, extensive spotting of the skin occurs; the disease is therefore sometimes called "spotted fever." A spinal tap permits a specific diagnosis as well as a therapeutic route directly into the spinal column.

Ménippée, Satyre: see SATYRE MÉNIPPÉE.

Menkaure (mĕnkoo͞'rā) or **Mycerinus** (mĭsərī'nəs), fl. 2525? B.C., king of ancient Egypt, of the IV dynasty; successor of Khafre. He built the third pyramid at Gizeh.

Menlo Park, residential city (1970 pop. 26,906), San Mateo co., W Calif.; inc. 1874. Space products are manufactured in the city. Menlo College and a Stanford Univ. research institute are there.

Menninger, Karl Augustus (mĕn'ĭnjər), 1893–, and **William Claire Menninger,** 1899–1966, American psychiatrists, brothers, b. Topeka, Kansas. Karl was graduated from Harvard (M.D., 1917), and William from Cornell (M.D., 1924). The Menninger Clinic, conceived with the idea of collecting many specialists in one center, was founded in Topeka in 1920 by Karl and his father, Charles Frederick (1862–1953), and in 1926 they were joined by William. The Menninger Foundation, for the purposes of research, training, and public education in psychiatry, came into existence in 1941 and soon became a psychiatric center of the United States. Karl Menninger, whose writings include *The Human Mind* (1930), *Man Against Himself* (1938), and *Theory of Psychoanalytic Technique* (1959), was instrumental in founding the Winter Veterans' Administration Hospital at Topeka at the close of World War II. This institution functioned not only as a mental hospital but as the center of the largest psychiatric training program in the world. See Karl Menninger's *Psychiatrist's World: The Selected Papers of Karl Menninger* (1959) and *The Crime of Punishment* (1968); William Menninger's *Psychiatry in a Troubled World* (1948), *You and Psychiatry* (1948), and *A Psychiatrist for a Troubled World* (1967); and Walker Winslow, *The Menninger Story* (1956).

Mennonites (mĕn'ənīts), sect of Protestant Christians, originating among the ANABAPTISTS in Switzerland and for a time called Swiss Brethren. They derive their name from MENNO SIMONS, a Dutch reformer. In Zürich a congregation formed by Conrad Grebel and others separated (1523–25) from the state church because they believed the concept of a state church to be unauthorized by Scripture and because they rejected the practice of baptizing infants. They believed in nonresistance and refused to take oaths. With the Bible as their sole rule of faith, they proposed to restore the Christianity of apostolic times. Two sacraments were recognized—baptism (for adult believers only) and the Lord's Supper. Persecution drove many of the Brethren to Germany, where new congregations were formed. The movement spread also to France, Russia, and the Netherlands, where it became influential. The Dordrecht Confession of Faith, embodying the distinctive features of Mennonite belief, was issued (1632) in Holland. Mennonites are numerous in the United States, where they have settled mainly in Pennsylvania, Ohio, and the Middle West. The first permanent Mennonite settlement in America was made (1683) at Germantown, Pa., by a group from Krefeld, Germany. Mennonites from Switzerland, Russia, and other parts of Europe increased the numbers in America. While each congregation is at liberty to decide independently on its form of worship and other matters, all Mennonites agree on certain points—baptism of believers only, the necessity of regeneration, refusal to bear arms and to take oaths, and the importance of rejecting worldly concerns. They preserve simplicity of dress and habits and disapprove of marriage with one outside their faith. In celebrating the Lord's Supper, some branches include the rite of foot washing and the kiss of charity. Differences of opinion on matters of discipline and performance of church services have resulted in a division of the church into a number of branches. The Mennonite Church, whose members are sometimes known as Old Mennonites, is the original body in the United States and has the largest membership. It carries on missionary and other kinds of organized Christian work and publishes denominational literature in both English and German. The General Conference of the Mennonite Church of North America (1860), the next largest body, may be listed among the liberal branches of the sect. One of the most conservative divisions is the Amish Church, which, under the leadership of Jacob Amman, broke away from the main body in Europe. The principal Amish groups in the United States are the Old Order Amish, who do not use churches but worship in homes and conduct their services in German, and the Conservative Amish, who abide by the Dordrecht Confession of Faith but hold services in English as well as German and accept such innovations as the Sunday school. The terms "House Amish" and "Church Amish" are sometimes used to distinguish the branches. Another conservative body is the Reformed or Herrite branch, established (1812) under the leadership of John Herr. The Church of God in Christ (1859) and the Old Order Mennonites, formed in 1870 under Jacob Wisler, are among the other branches. Large numbers of Mennonites are to be found in Canada, and a number of American, Canadian, and European Mennonites have moved to colonies in Mexico and South America. Although attempts at unification have not been particularly successful, the Mennonite Central Committee, which represents almost all the Mennonite groups in North America, has enabled the branches to cooperate in many activities. See Robert Friedmann, *Mennonite Piety through the Centuries* (1949); Kiehl Newswanger and Christian Newswanger, *Amishland* (1954); E. L. Smith, *The Amish People* (1958); C. H. Smith, *Mennonites and Their Heritage* (1964); J. C. Wenger, *The Mennonite Church in America* (1966).

Menno Simons (mĕn'ō sē'mōns), 1496?–1561, Dutch religious reformer. The name of the MENNONITES was derived from his name, although he was not the actual founder of the sect. In 1524 he became a Roman Catholic priest but in 1536 he left the church when he announced that he no longer believed in infant baptism and other Catholic teachings. His test of the true Christian was regeneration. He was active in Holland and Germany as an organizer and leader of the less aggressive division of Anabaptists. His writings and sermons were published as *Opera omnia theologica* (1681). See his *complete writings* ed by J. C. Wenger (tr 1956); C. J. Dyck, ed., *A Legacy of Faith* (1962); W. E. Keeney; *The Development of Dutch Anabaptist Thought and Practice from 1539-1564* (1968).

Menocal, Mario García (mä'ryō gärsē'ä mānokäl'), 1866–1941, president of Cuba (1913–21). A leader in the fight for liberation from Spain, he later became a Conservative politician. As president he initiated a "businessman" government that was widely criticized as corrupt and arbitrary. His victory in the 1916 election was challenged by the Liberals, and José Miguel Gómez subsequently led an unsuccessful revolt against his regime. Menocal secured U.S. support by taking Cuba into World War I on the side of the Allies. The Cuban sugar boom known as the "dance of the millions" occurred in his time. In 1920, Menocal backed Alfredo ZAYAS and in 1924 he lost to Gerardo MACHADO. After leading (1931) an abortive revolt, he sought exile in the United States; when the Machado government fell, he returned to Cuba. He ran unsuccessfully for president in 1936.

Menominee (mənŏm'ənē), city (1970 pop. 10,748), seat of Menominee co., N Mich., W Upper Peninsula, on Green Bay at the mouth of the Menominee River; inc. 1883. It is a car-ferry port, a distribution center for upper Michigan and N Wisconsin, and the marketplace for a cheese-producing area. A fur-trading post was established near there in 1796, and several sawmills were operating along the river by 1832. Menominee became a great shipping point for lumber; at one time it was known as the white-pine capital of the world. Today its diversified manufacturing is augmented by a growing tourist industry; the harbor has excellent small-craft anchorages, and the city is the gateway to a vast resort and sports region. Of interest is the "mystery ship," raised (1969) from the bottom of Green Bay, where it sank in 1864. A bridge connects Menominee with its sister city of Marinette, Wis.

Menominee, river, 118 mi (190 km) long, formed by the union of the Brule and the Michigamme rivers above Iron Mountain, W Upper Peninsula, N Mich., and flowing SE into Green Bay at Menominee. It passes through an iron-ore region and forms part of the Wisconsin-Michigan line. Once used for lumbering, it now furnishes water power.

Menominee Indians, North American Indians whose language belongs to the Algonquian branch of the Algonquian-Wakashan linguistic stock (see AMERICAN INDIAN LANGUAGES). Also called the Menomini, they were a sedentary people who chiefly subsisted on the gathering of wild rice; the Algonquian name for wild rice is *manomin*. In c.1634, when they were visited by the missionary Jean Nicolet, the Menominee were living at the mouth of the Menominee River in Wisconsin and Michigan. From 1671 until 1854 they inhabited settlements that extended from the Menominee River S to the Fox River and bordered the western shore of Green Bay. Although some of the Menominee supported the British in the American Revolution and the War of 1812, they were generally peaceful toward the American settlers. The Menominee were, however, bitter enemies of the neighboring Algonquian tribes, who waged constant warfare to drive the Menominee out of the rich wild-rice area. In 1854 the Menominee were settled on a reservation (Menominee Reservation) on the Wolf River, in N central Wisconsin. The reservation became a county of Wisconsin in 1961 when the Menominee became independent of Federal control. By the 1970s the Menominee numbered some 4,000. See Felix Keesing, *The Menomini Indians of Wisconsin* (1939, repr. 1971); Louise Spindler, *Menomini Women and Culture Change* (1962).

Menomonee Falls (mənŏm'ənē), village (1970 pop. 31,697), Waukesha co., SE Wis., on the Menomonee River; inc. 1892. The village's economy is based on small businesses and light industry.

Menomonie (mənŏm'ənē), city (1970 pop. 11,275), seat of Dunn co., W Wis., on the Red Cedar River; platted 1859, inc. 1882. Once a lumber town, it is now a trade center in an area of poultry and dairy farms. The Univ. of Wisconsin at Stout is there. The ornate civic center building was erected (1890s) by a lumber baron.

menopause (mĕn'əpôz) or **climacteric** (klīmăk'tərĭk, klī″măktĕr'ĭk), transitional phase in a woman's life when menstruation ceases, also known as change of life. It is the result of declining ovarian function due to aging of the ovaries and the process is usually a gradual one. Natural menopause usually occurs between 40 and 50 years of age. Premature menopause (due to premature aging of the ovaries, debilitating disease, or infection) and artificial menopause (due to destruction of the ovaries by surgery or irradiation) may occur much earlier. The menopause is sometimes accompanied by deficient or excessive functioning of the glandular and autonomic nervous systems, giving rise to nervousness, flushes, excitability or depression, dizziness, headaches, sweating, and other disorders. Such disturbances are usually severe when cessation of ovarian function is relatively rapid. When menstruation ceases gradually, menopausal symptoms are mild or nonexistent. If symptoms are severe, they may be eased by hormone therapy.

Menorca, Spain: see MINORCA.

Menotti, Gian-Carlo (jän'-kär'lō mänôt'tē), 1911–, Italian composer. Menotti was taught music by his mother and composed his first opera at 10. He studied at the Milan Conservatory and at the Curtis Institute of Music, Philadelphia, where he later taught. Enormously successful in the United States as a composer of operas, he wrote his own librettos—all in English except *Amelia al Ballo* (1937; tr. *Amelia Goes to the Ball*). In 1946 his melodrama *The Medium* had unprecedented success with New York audiences. Menotti's major works include *The Old Maid and the Thief* (1939) and *Amahl and the Night Visitors* (1951), both written for radio broadcast; *The Telephone* (1947); *The Consul* (1950); *The Saint of Bleecker Street* (1954; Pulitzer Prize); *Maria Golovin* (1958); *Labyrinth* (1963), a short opera; *Martin's Lie* (1964); and *Tamu-Tamu* (1973). His operas are celebrated for their powerful dramatic impact and superb use of language and polytonality. Menotti instituted the Festival of Two Worlds at Spoleto, Italy, in 1958. See study by M. I. Casmus (1962).

Menshevism: see BOLSHEVISM AND MENSHEVISM.

Menshikov, Aleksandr Danilovich, Prince (əlyĭksän'dər dənyē'ləvĭch mĕn'shĭkəf), 1672?–1729, Russian field marshal and statesman. Of lowly origin, he became an intimate companion of PETER I (Peter the Great), and after the death of François Lefort (1699) he was the czar's chief adviser. Despite his vices, Menshikov proved an able military commander and was created prince and later field marshal. Menshikov was successively governor of Schlüsselburg, St. Petersburg, and Estonia. He energetically carried out Peter's reforms, but he was notorious for his financial misdeeds. Peter's second wife, Catherine (see CATHERINE I), had previously been Menshikov's mistress, and she continued to look out for his interests. Upon Peter's death (1725), Menshikov helped her to accede to the throne, and he was the real ruler during her reign. Although his administration was efficient, it was also high-handed, and his enemies were legion. Shortly after the accession (1727) of the child czar, Peter II, Menshikov was removed from office through the intrigues of Count Osterman and others. He died in exile in Siberia. Several of his descendants held high posts in the empire.

menstruation, periodic flow of bloody fluid from the UTERUS, occurring about every 28 days in women. Menstruation commences at puberty (about age 12) and continues until MENOPAUSE (about age 45). It is associated with the release of an ovum from the OVARY and is controlled by hormonal activity of the pituitary gland and the ovary. During the childbearing years the lining, or endometrium, of the uterus undergoes rapid proliferation of cells and venous channels in preparation for pregnancy. When the ovum is not fertilized this tissue and blood is shed. The proliferation of the uterine wall then begins once more in expectation of the next release of an ovum, and if conception does not take place, it sloughs off again. The process continues monthly until pregnancy occurs or until ovulation ceases at menopause. The natural rhythm of the menstrual cycle may be broken or temporarily halted by hormonal imbalance, illness, or emotional disturbance.

mental age: see INTELLIGENCE.

mental disorders: see MANIC-DEPRESSIVE PSYCHOSIS; PSYCHONEUROSIS; PARANOIA; PSYCHIATRY; PSYCHOSIS; SCHIZOPHRENIA.

mental hygiene, the science of promoting mental health and preventing mental illness through the application of psychiatry and psychology. Throughout the 19th cent. there were periodic waves of interest in the problems of persons then called insane, generally stimulated by the crusading zeal of such reformers as Dorothea L. DIX. In reaction to public ignorance of the facts of insanity, as well as to callousness in official quarters, the National Association for the Protection of the Insane and the Prevention of Insanity was formed in 1880. While this organization performed great service in the area of public enlightenment, it could not survive the internal dissensions that caused its dissolution in 1886; in 1908 the mental hygiene movement took root as a direct result of public reaction to Clifford W. Beers's autobiography, *A Mind That Found Itself,* which described his experiences in institutions for the insane. That year the Connecticut Society for Mental Hygiene was organized, to be followed in 1909 by the National Committee for Mental Hygiene and in 1950, the National Association for Mental Health. In the United States the major Federal mental health agency is the National Institute for Mental Health. The mental hygiene movement has accomplished, among many other advances, wide reforms in institutional care, the establishment of child-guidance clinics, and public education concerning mental hygiene. See also PSYCHIATRY; PSYCHOTHERAPY; PSYCHOSIS. See William Glasser, *Mental Health or Mental Illness* (1961, repr. 1970); Nina Ridenour, *Mental Health in the United States: A Fifty-Year Survey* (1961); H. A. Carroll, *Mental Hygiene* (5th ed. 1969); L. E. Martin, *Mental Health/Mental Illness: Revolution in Progress* (1970); M. H. Brenner, *Mental Illness and the Economy* (1973).

mental illness, any of a variety of disorders in which an individual, as a result of inappropriate behavior and outlook, is unable to function adequately. Mental illness varies from mild forms, the PSYCHONEUROSES, to more severe forms, the PSYCHOSES. See also PSYCHOANALYSIS.

mental illness, legal: see INSANITY.

mental retardation, subnormal mental development, manifested from birth or early childhood, that may be caused by a variety of conditions. In the United States the term refers to the mental deficiency, or feeble-mindedness, of those at the lower end of the intelligence spectrum. INTELLIGENCE is classified largely on the basis of tests of intelligence quotient (IQ). An IQ between 65 and 85 is borderline; subjects with IQs below this level have traditionally been classified as morons (51–70), imbeciles (26–50), and idiots (0–25). However, these categories do not now serve any useful function, and other characteristics besides IQ are used to evaluate mental incompetence, e.g., social maturity and the ability to sustain personal and social independence. Many mental deficients, especially in the higher IQ levels, can achieve some language development and can be taught to perform manual labor of moderate complexity. Observable physical defects, found in less than 10% of the mentally retarded, include CRETINISM, caused by an underactive thyroid gland; mongolism, or Down's syndrome, most often caused by chromosomal disorders in offspring of older mothers; microcephalia, characterized by a small skull resulting from injury to the fetus; hydrocephalia, an accumulation of cerebrospinal fluid in the brain; and various metabolic disorders, such as PHENYLKETONURIA. See L. S. Penrose, *The Biology of Mental Defect* (3d ed. 1963); Margaret Adams, *Mental Retardation and Its Social Dimensions* (1971).

mental tests: see INTELLIGENCE; PSYCHOLOGICAL TESTS.

Mentana (māntä'nä), town (1971 pop. 16,543), in Latium, central Italy. On Nov. 3, 1867, Garibaldi was defeated there by French and papal troops during his unsuccessful campaign to capture nearby Rome.

Menteith (mĕntēth'), lake, up to 1.5 mi (2.4 km) across, SW Perthshire, central Scotland, near Stirling. Mary Queen of Scots, as a child of five, was hidden at Inchmahome priory on the largest of the lake's three islands.

menthol, white crystalline substance with a characteristic pungent odor. It is derived from the oil of the peppermint herb *Mentha piperita* (see MINT) or prepared synthetically from coal tar. An alcohol, menthol is freely soluble in ethyl alcohol, ether, and chloroform. It is an ANTISEPTIC, and because it imparts a tingling sensation to the skin, it is used in after shave lotions and skin fresheners. As an irritant it brings blood to the skin surface and is helpful in relieving minor aches and pains.

Menton (mäNtôN'), town (1968 pop. 25,271), Alpes-Maritime dept., SE France, near the Italian border and on the Mediterranean Sea. A popular resort of the RIVIERA, it was a part of MONACO until 1848 when it declared itself a free city under the protection of Sardinia. It passed to France after a plebiscite in 1860. Menton has a 16th-century fort overlooking its harbor and a 17th-century Baroque church. The town is noted for its music and art festival.

Mentor, residential village (1970 pop. 36,912), Lake co., NE Ohio, on Lake Erie; founded 1799, inc. 1855. James Garfield was living there when he was elected President, and his home, "Lawnfield," is preserved.

Mentor (mĕn'tər, -tôr''), in Greek mythology, friend of Odysseus and tutor of Telemachus. On several occasions in the *Odyssey*, Athena assumes Mentor's form to give advice to Telemachus or Odysseus. His name is proverbial for a faithful and wise adviser.

Menuhin, Yehudi (yəho͞o'dē mĕn'yo͞oĭn), 1916–, American violinist, b. New York City. Menuhin, an extraordinary prodigy, began playing the violin at the age of four. He made his debut with the San Francisco Symphony Orchestra at the age of seven and afterward studied in Europe with Adolph Busch and Georges Enesco. After a world tour (1934–35) of unprecedented success, he retired to study for two years. His triumphant career has included many hundreds of concerts for the Allied forces and relief efforts of World War II. Menuhin has introduced little-known works and promoted Eastern music in lectures and performances. Bartók's Sonata for Solo Violin was written for Menuhin. See his *Theme and Variations* (1972); biographies by Robert Magidoff (1955) and Norman Wymer (1961). His sister, the pianist **Hepzibah Menuhin,** 1920–, b. San Francisco, also a prodigy, has often appeared in recital with him.

Menzaleh, Lake, Egypt: see MANZALA.

Menzel, Adolph Friedrich Erdmann von (ä'dôlf frē'drĭkh ĕrt'män fən mĕn'tsəl), 1815–1905, German painter and illustrator. Self-taught, Menzel made lithographic illustrations for Goethe's *Künstlers Erdenwallen,* which attracted attention. His 400 designs for woodblocks illustrating Kugler's *History of Frederick the Great* (1840–42) established his reputation and gave a stimulus to German wood engraving. While best known for historical paintings, he sketched scenes from nature related to IMPRESSIONISM in style. His work is best represented in Berlin.

Menzel, Donald Howard, 1901–, American astrophysicist, b. Florence, Colo., grad. Univ. of Denver, 1920, Ph.D. Princeton, 1924. From 1926 to 1932 he was with the Lick Observatory, Mt. Wilson, Calif. In 1932 he joined the faculty at Harvard, where he became professor (1938) of astrophysics and director (1954) of the observatory. An authority on the sun's chromosphere, he discovered (1933) with J. C. Boyce that the sun's corona consists, in part, of oxygen. With W. W. Salisbury he made (1941) the first of the calculations that led to radio contact with the moon in 1946. In his *Flying Saucers* (1953), Menzel advanced the theory that the so-called flying saucers were merely natural optical phenomena. Other writings include *Stars and Planets* (1931), and *Our Sun* (1949, rev. ed. 1959), and *Stellar Interiors* (with others, 1971).

Menzel Bourguiba (mĕnzĕl' bərgē'bə), formerly Ferryville, town (1966 pop. 33,800), N Tunisia, on Lake Bizerte. It was founded as a naval installation during the period of French rule. After Tunisia became independent (1956), it was renamed in honor of Habib Bourguiba, Tunisia's leader.

Menzies, Sir Robert Gordon (mĕn'zēz), 1894–, Australian statesman. A barrister, Menzies was elected to the Australian House of Representatives in 1934 and was attorney general (1935–39) in Joseph A. Lyons's government. Upon Lyons's death (1939) Menzies succeeded as leader of the United Australia party (later the Liberal party) and as prime minister. In 1941 he lost the premiership, and he led the opposition in the House from 1943 until late in 1949, when the Liberal-Country party coalition defeated the Labour government at the polls. Menzies, as leader of the Liberal party, again became prime minister. He retired in 1966, making him the longest continuously serving prime minister in Australian history. During his term in office, Menzies pursued a conservative, anti-Communist policy. He unsuccessfully tried (1951) to ban Australia's Communist party, and he dispatched Australian troops to support the U.S. war effort in South Vietnam.

Meonenim (mēŏn'ĕnĭm), unidentified location adjacent to Shechem. Judges 9.37.

Meonothai (mēŏn'ōthā), son of Caleb's brother Othniel. 1 Chron. 4.14.

meperidine (məpĕr'ədēn), name for an ANALGESIC marketed under the trade name Demerol.

Mephaath (mĕf'āăth, mēfā'ăth), Levitical city, later Moabite, E of the Dead Sea. Joshua 13.18; 21.37; 1 Chron. 6.79; Jer. 48.21.

Mephibosheth (mĭfĭb'əshĕth). **1** Jonathan's lame son to whom David restored Saul's lands. 2 Sam. 4.4; 9; 16.1,4; 19.24. Merib-baal: 1 Chron. 8.34; 9.40. For the relation between the names of this man, see BAAL. **2** Son of Saul. 2 Sam. 21.8.

Mephistopheles: see FAUST.

meprobamate (məprō'bəmāt"), tranquilizing drug that acts as a DEPRESSANT of the central NERVOUS SYSTEM and is commonly used in the treatment of ANXIETY and sometimes SCHIZOPHRENIA. Although meprobamate is chemically unlike BARBITURATES and has lower toxicity, it has similar pharmacological effects, especially the ability to induce sleep and alleviate anxiety. The drug possesses some anticonvulsant properties and is used to suppress some forms of EPILEPSY. A muscle relaxant, meprobamate is also used to treat abnormal motor activity. It is marketed under the trade names Equanil and Miltown.

Mequon (mĕk'wŏn), city (1970 pop. 12,150), Ozaukee co., SE Wis., a suburb of Milwaukee, on Lake Michigan and the Milwaukee River; est. 1846, inc. 1957. It has varied industries. A Catholic training center for teaching sisters, a Lutheran seminary, and an automotive museum are there.

Merab (mĭr'ăb), daughter of Saul. 1 Sam. 18.17–19. She is referred to (by a textual error, no doubt) as Michal at 2 Sam. 21.8.

Meraiah (mĕr"ā'ə), one of the priestly family of Seraiah. Neh. 12.12.

Meraioth (mĕrā'yŏth). **1** Descendant of Aaron. 1 Chron. 6.7,52; Ezra 7.3. **2** Priest. 1 Chron. 9.11; Neh. 11.11. **3** See MEREMOTH **3.**

Merari (mĕr'ārī, mĕrā'rī), ancestor of a division of the Levites. Gen. 46.11; Num. 26.57.

Mercalli scale: see RICHTER SCALE.

mercantilism (mûr'kəntĭlĭzəm), economic system of the major trading nations during the 16th, 17th, and 18th cent., based on the premise that national wealth and power were best served by increasing exports and collecting precious metals in return. It superseded the medieval feudal organization in Western Europe, especially in Holland, France, and England. The period 1500–1800 was one of religious and commercial wars, and large revenues were needed to maintain armies and pay the growing costs of civil government. Mercantilist nations were impressed by the fact that the precious metals, especially gold, were in universal demand as the ready means of obtaining other commodities; hence they tended to identify money with wealth. As the best means of acquiring bullion, foreign trade was favored above domestic trade, and manufacturing or processing, which provided the goods for foreign trade, was favored at the expense of the extractive industries (e.g., agriculture). State action, an essential feature of the mercantile system, was used to accomplish its purposes. Under a mercantilist policy a nation sought to sell more than it bought so as to accumulate bullion. Besides bullion, raw materials for domestic manufacturers were also sought, and duties were levied on the importation of such goods in order to provide revenue for the government. The state exercised much control over economic life, chiefly through corporations and trading companies. Production was carefully regulated with the object of securing goods of high quality and low cost, thus enabling the nation to hold its place in foreign markets. Treaties were made to obtain exclusive trading privileges, and the commerce of colonies was exploited for the benefit of the mother country. In England mercantilist policies were effective in creating a skilled industrial population and a large shipping industry. Through a series of NAVIGATION ACTS England finally destroyed the commerce of Holland, its chief rival. As the classical economists were later to point out, however, even a successful mercantilist policy was not likely to be beneficial, because it produced an oversupply of money and, with it, serious inflation. Mercantilist ideas did not decline until the coming of the INDUSTRIAL REVOLUTION and of LAISSEZ FAIRE. Henry VIII, Elizabeth I, and Oliver Cromwell conformed their policies to mercantilism. In France its chief exponent was Jean Baptiste COLBERT. See J. W. Horrocks, *A Short History of Mercantilism* (1925); P. W. Buck, *The Politics of Mercantilism* (1942, repr. 1964); E. F. Heckscher, *Mercantilism* (2 vol. rev. ed. 1955, repr. 1962); D. C. Coleman, ed., *Revisions in Mercantilism* (1969).

mercaptan (mərkăp'tăn) or **thiol** (thī'ōl), any of a class of organic compounds containing the group —SH bonded to a carbon atom. Many of the volatile low-molecular-weight mercaptans have disagreeable odors resembling that of hydrogen sulfide, H_2S (which smells like rotten eggs). Mercaptans are often produced as a decay product of animal and vegetable matter and are found in crude petroleum. They are produced by certain plants and animals; e.g., propanethiol (propyl mercaptan) is released when onions are cut, and butanethiol (butyl mercaptan) is present in skunk secretion. Ethanethiol (ethyl mercaptan) is often added to the odorless natural gas used for cooking and serves to warn of gas leaks. Mercaptans take part in a wide variety of chemical reactions.

mercaptopurine: see METABOLITE.

Mercator, Gerardus (jərär'dəs mûrkā'tər), Latin form of his real name, **Gerhard Kremer** (gār'härt krā'mər), 1512–94, Flemish geographer, mathematician, and cartographer. He studied in Louvain, where he had a geographical establishment (1534). From 1537 to 1540 he surveyed and mapped Flanders; in 1538 he produced his first map of the world (based on Ptolemy's map); in 1541 he made a terrestrial, and in 1551 a celestial, globe. He was appointed (1552) to the chair of cosmography in Duisburg, where he subsequently lived and worked. In 1554 he made a six-sheet map of Europe. In 1568 appeared his first map using the projection that has since borne his name and that has been more generally used than any other projection for navigators' maps of the world. In 1585, Mercator began a great atlas, including many of his earlier maps; this atlas was completed by his son and published in 1594. Mercator did cartographical work for Charles V and was cosmographer to the duke of Jülich and Cleves. He wrote several books, mainly on the science and mathematics of geography and cartography and on ancient geography.

Mercator map projection: see MAP PROJECTION.

Merced (mərsĕd'), city (1970 pop. 22,670), seat of Merced co., central Calif.; inc. 1889. It is a center for tourism and farm trade in a cotton, fruit, and dairy region. Castle Air Force Base and Yosemite National Park are nearby.

Mercedes (mĕrsā'thĕs), city (1963 pop. 31,352), capital of Soriano dept., SW Uruguay, a port on the Río Negro. An agricultural and livestock center, the city has a shipyard and several fine beaches and resorts. Mercedes was founded in 1781. It has a famous cathedral.

Mercer, Hugh, c.1725–1777, American Revolutionary general, b. Aberdeen, Scotland. A physician, he was a surgeon in the forces of Charles Edward Stuart (the Young Pretender) and after the defeat at Culloden (1746) emigrated to America. In the French and Indian Wars, Mercer served with Edward Braddock (1755) and John Forbes (1758) in their expeditions against Fort Duquesne. Mercer moved to Virginia, and, at the start of the American Revolution, helped organize the Virginia militia. He fought at Trenton (1776) and was mortally wounded at Princeton (Jan. 3, 1777). See J. M. Waterman, *With Sword and Lancet* (1941).

Mercer University, at Macon, Ga.; Southern Baptist; coeducational; opened 1833 as Mercer Institute. The name was changed to its present form in 1837.

Merchant Adventurers, name given originally to all merchants in England who engaged in export trade, but later applied to loosely organized groups of merchants in the major ports concerned with exporting cloth to the Netherlands. They were incorporated as a trading company in 1407. Originally the company's activities centered in Bruges, but in 1446 it obtained trading privileges from the duke of Burgundy and established its staple (i.e., trading center) at Antwerp. Despite strong competition from the HANSEATIC LEAGUE, whose dominance in the Baltic caused the exclusion of the Merchant Adventurers from that area, the company flourished, established depots in several cities, and in 1560 was given the monopoly on exporting cloth to W Germany and the Netherlands. It continued to prosper throughout the 16th and 17th cent., although political rivalries forced it to move its staple to Hamburg (1567) and Dordrecht (1655). The company was dissolved in 1808. See E. M. Carus-Wilson, *Medieval Merchant Venturers* (2d ed. 1967).

merchant marine: see SHIPPING.

Merchants of the Staple or **Merchant Staplers,** English trading company that controlled the export of English raw wool. The first wool staple (i.e., a place designated by royal ordinance as special center of commerce) was established in 1294, and the first compulsory staple, where all wool exporters were required to trade, was set up in 1314. The staple was moved from place to place according to political needs, but in 1363 a group of 26 English merchants was incorporated as the Company of the Staple at Calais with a complete monopoly of wool exports. The staple thereafter remained almost continuously at Calais until 1558, and the company's resources contributed heavily to the defense of that city against the French. The company's wealth and importance diminished with the rise of the English cloth trade and the loss of Calais to the French in 1558. The staple was moved to Bruges, and the staplers retained their monopoly until 1617, when the export of raw wool was prohibited and home staples established. They then became domestic wool brokers. The staplers were the only trading company to be organized on a commodity rather than a regional basis. See E. E. Power, *The Wool Trade in English Medieval History* (1941); E. M. Carus-Wilson, *Medieval Merchant Venturers* (2d ed. 1967).

Mercia (mûr'shə), one of the kingdoms of Anglo-Saxon England, consisting generally of the region of the Midlands. It was settled by Angles c.500, probably first along the Trent valley. Its history emerges from obscurity with the reign of PENDA, who extended his power over Wessex (645) and East Anglia (650) to gain overlordship of England S of the Humber River. After his death Mercia suffered a three-year loss of ascendancy during which it was converted to Christianity by a Northumbrian mission. Penda's son, Wulfhere, then reestablished a Greater Mercia that finally under ÆTHELBALD in the 8th cent. extended over all S England. This hegemony was strengthened by OFFA (reigned 757–96), who controlled East Anglia, Kent, and Sussex and maintained superiority of a sort over Wessex and Northumbria. He had the great Offa's Dyke built to protect W Mercia from the Welsh. After his death, Mercian power gradually gave way before that of Wessex. The victories of EGBERT of Wessex in Mercia established him briefly as overlord. In 874, Mercia weakly succumbed to the invading Danish army, and ultimately the eastern part became (886) a portion of the DANELAW, while the western part was controlled by ALFRED of Wessex. Thereafter Mercia had no independent history, although it had one more distinguished ruler in ÆTHELFLÆD, Lady of the Mercians. See F. M. Stenton, *Anglo-Saxon England* (2d ed. 1947).

Mercier, Désiré Joseph (dāzērā' zhôzĕf' mârsēā'), 1851–1926, Belgian churchman, cardinal of the Roman Catholic Church. He was ordained in 1874 and eight years later became professor of philosophy at the Univ. of Louvain, where, under the auspices of Pope Leo XIII, he organized an institute for the study of the teachings of St. Thomas Aquinas. He became a foremost leader in the 20th-century revival of interest in Thomistic scholasticism and in its integration with modern developments. He was made archbishop of Malines (1906) and cardinal (1907). Cardinal Mercier worked to secure greater cooperation between the Catholic clergy and the laity and to promote social well-being. In World War I, Cardinal Mercier became the spokesman of Belgian opposition to the German occupation, for which the Germans placed him under house arrest. See his autobiography, *Cardinal Mercier's Own Story* (1920); biographies by H. L. Dubly (1928) and J. A. Gade (1934).

Mercier, Honoré (ōnôrā' mĕrsyā'), 1840–94, Canadian political leader, b. Quebec prov. Opposing confederation (1867) on the ground that unification of the Canadian provinces would imperil the influence of the French element, Mercier was (1871) a founder of the Parti national. He sat (1872–74) in the Canadian House of Commons, entered (1879) Quebec's legislative assembly, and became (1883) leader of the Liberal party of Quebec. Strong feeling stirred by the execution of the rebel Louis RIEL enabled Mercier to form a coalition of the disaffected and to become premier of Quebec in 1887. His laws indemnifying the Jesuits for lands earlier confiscated by the government aroused much opposition (see JESUIT ESTATES ACT). After four years as prime minister, he was dismissed by the lieutenant governor for alleged misuse of public funds and was defeated in the elections that followed. His son, **Honoré Mercier,** 1875–1937, was also a lawyer and a politician in Quebec. He served from 1907 to 1936 in the provincial legislative assembly. He was minister of colonization, mines, and fisheries (1914–19) and minister of lands and forests (1919–36).

Merck, Johann Heinrich (yō'hän hīn'rĭkh mĕrk), 1741–91, German critic. He was the counselor of many young writers, including Goethe, whose genius he was first to recognize.

Merckx, Eddy, 1945–, Belgian bicycle racer. He won the world amateur cycling championship in 1964 and became world professional champion in 1967. He won the 2,237-mi (3,600-km) Tour de France bicycle race five times (1969–72, 1974), a record equaled only by Jacques Anquetil (1957, 1961–64). It has been estimated that Merckx rode up to 30,000 mi

(48,300 km) a year in practice and competition together.

mercuric chloride or **mercury (II) chloride,** chemical compound, $HgCl_2$, a white powder of colorless rhombohedral crystals, somewhat soluble in water. It is also called bichloride of mercury or corrosive sublimate. It is extremely poisonous. Raw egg white may be given as an antidote, since mercuric chloride reacts with egg albumin to form a nearly insoluble precipitate; medical treatment should be sought immediately. Mercuric chloride is sometimes used in dilute solution as an antiseptic for inanimate objects and as a fungicide. It is also used in preparing other mercury compounds; it reacts with mercury metal to form MERCUROUS CHLORIDE. Mercuric chloride is prepared by reacting mercury with chlorine gas or by subliming a mixture of mercuric sulfate and sodium chloride (common salt).

mercurous chloride, mercury (I) chloride, or **calomel,** chemical compound, Hg_2Cl_2, a white crystalline powder, very slightly soluble in water. It was once used medicinally as a purgative, cathartic, liver stimulant, and to eliminate parasitic worms, but is rarely so used today because it is readily decomposed into metallic mercury and the very poisonous MERCURIC CHLORIDE on exposure to sunlight or if heated in the presence of moisture. Mercurous chloride is a less dangerous poison than mercuric chloride chiefly because it is much less soluble; it is highly toxic if retained in the body. Mercurous chloride is prepared by sublimation from a mixture of mercury and mercuric chloride or by precipitation from a mercurous chloride solution on adding chloride ion. It is also found in nature as horn quicksilver. The calomel electrode, often used as a reference in determining electric potentials and for measuring the pH of solutions, contains mercurous chloride, mercury metal, and potassium chloride solution.

mercury or **quicksilver** [from the Roman god Mercury], metallic chemical element; symbol Hg [Lat. *hydrargyrum*=liquid silver]; at. no. 80; at. wt. 200.59; m.p. −38.87°C; b.p. 356.58°C; sp. gr. 13.55 at 20°C; valence +1 or +2. Mercury is the only common metal existing as a liquid at ordinary temperatures. The pure metal has a silver-white mirrorlike appearance. Mercury is below cadmium in group IIb of the PERIODIC TABLE. It is relatively stable in dry air, but in moist air slowly forms a gray oxide coating. Mercury forms numerous compounds, assuming +1 valence in mercurous compounds and +2 valence in mercuric compounds. Mercury is not attacked by dilute hydrochloric or sulfuric acid. It reacts with hot nitric acid to form mercuric nitrate, $Hg(No_3)_2$. An excess of mercury reacts with nitric acid to form mercurous nitrate, $HgNO_3$. Mercury reacts with hot concentrated sulfuric acid to form mercuric sulfate, $HgSO_4$; with excess mercury, mercurous sulfate, Hg_2SO_4, is formed. Mercury reacts directly with the halogens to form mercuric salts. At elevated temperatures mercury reacts slowly with oxygen to form mercuric oxide, HgO. A mercurous oxide may be formed chemically but is unstable, decomposing to a mixture of mercury and mercuric oxide. Mercury occurs uncombined in nature to a limited extent. The metal is obtained commercially from CINNABAR, a mercuric sulfide ore; it is easily separated by roasting the ore in air. The metal is usually purified by repeated vacuum distillation. Mercury metal has many uses. Because of its high density, it is used in BAROMETERS and manometers. Because it has a high rate of thermal expansion that is fairly constant over a wide temperature range, it is used extensively in THERMOMETERS. Mercury is important as a liquid contact material for electric switches. It is used in mercury-vapor lamps, which emit light rich in ultraviolet radiation; various kinds of such lamps are used for street lighting, as sun lamps, and in "black lights" (see LIGHTING). Mercury is used as an electrode in the production of chlorine and sodium hydroxide. It is also used in certain electric batteries. With some other metals mercury forms a special type of alloy called an AMALGAM; a special amalgam (mostly mercury, silver, and tin) is used in dentistry for filling teeth. Mercury compounds have many uses. Calomel (mercurous chloride, Hg_2Cl_2) is used as a standard in electrochemical measurements and in medicine as a purgative. MERCURIC CHLORIDE (corrosive sublimate, $HgCl_2$) is used as an insecticide, in rat poison, and as a disinfectant. Mercuric oxide is used in skin ointments. Mercuric sulfate is used as a catalyst in organic chemistry. Vermilion, a red pigment, is mercuric sulfide; another crystalline form of the sulfide (also used as a pigment) is black. Mercury FULMINATE, $Hg(CNO)_2$, is used as a detonator. Mercury forms many organic compounds. Mercurochrome (in 2% aqueous solution) is used in medicine as a topical antiseptic. Mercury compounds were formerly used in the treatment of syphilis. Mercury and most of its compounds are poisonous. Some symptoms of chronic mercury poisoning (mercurialism) are red, bleeding gums, tremors of the hands, digestive disturbances, and deafness. Mercury should be handled with extreme caution, especially to prevent spills, since it is volatile and hard to clean up. At room temperature the concentration of vapor in air from spilled mercury may be as much as 100 times the safe concentration. Mercury has high surface tension; when spilled, it breaks up into tiny beads which often become lodged in cracks. Mercury is a cumulative poison; it is not easily discharged from the body. Mercury pollution in rivers, lakes, and oceans is a serious problem, since mercury (especially in its organic compounds) becomes increasingly concentrated in the food cycle of aquatic life and may reach dangerous levels in fish used for food. Mercury was discovered in antiquity, and was known to the ancient Chinese, Hindus, and Egyptians, but was not recognized as an element. It was used as a medicine by Paracelsus. It was first recognized as a chemical element (in the modern sense) by A. L. Lavoisier about the end of the 18th cent.

Mercury, in astronomy, nearest planet to the sun, at a mean distance of 36 million mi (58 million km); its period of revolution is 88 days. Mercury passes through phases similar to those of the moon as it completes each revolution about the sun, although the visible disk varies in size with respect to its distance from the earth. Because its greatest ELONGATION is 28°, it is seen only for a short time after sunset or before sunrise. Since observation of Mercury is particularly unfavorable when it is near the horizon, the planet has often been studied in full daylight, with the sun's light blocked off. Mercury has the second most elliptic orbit in the solar system, only Pluto's being greater among the planets. Its great eccentricity of orbit and its great orbital speed provided one of the important tests of Einstein's general theory of RELATIVITY. Mercury's perihelion (its closest point to the sun) is observed to advance by 43" each century, more than can be explained from planetary perturbations using Newton's theory of GRAVITATION, yet in nearly exact agreement with the prediction of the general theory. Mercury is the smallest planet in the solar system, having a diameter of about 3,000 mi (4,800 km). Its mean density is comparable to that of the earth. Its small mass and proximity to the sun prevent it from having an appreciable atmosphere, although a slight amount of carbon dioxide, with some hydrogen and argon, has been detected. The surface of Mercury is probably much like that of the moon, as indicated by its ALBEDO, the light-reflecting power of its surface. It was long thought that Mercury's period of rotation on its axis was identical to its period of revolution, so that the same side of the planet always faced the sun. However, radar studies in 1965 showed a period of rotation of about 59 days. This results in periods of daylight and night of 90 earth days each, with the daylight temperatures reaching as high as 800°F (430°C). Night temperatures are believed to drop as low as 32°F (0°C).

Mercury, in Roman religion, god of commerce and messenger of the gods; identified with the Greek HERMES. He was honored at the Mercuralia, a festival held in May and attended primarily by traders and merchants.

mercury dry cell: see CELL, in electricity.

mercury poisoning, tissue damage resulting from the ingestion of more than trace amounts of the element mercury or its compounds. Mercury and its salts, absorbed by the skin and mucous membranes or ingested by eating contaminated food, can cause skin disorders, hemorrhage, destruction of kidney tubules, liver disease, and gastrointestinal disturbances. Organic mercury compounds, especially methylmercury, are the most toxic; such compounds can cross the blood-brain barrier and cause irreversible nervous system and brain damage, e.g., loss of motor control, numbness in limbs, blindness, and inability to speak. Women who have eaten methylmercury-contaminated food while pregnant have given birth to children who are blind, retarded, and subject to convulsive seizures. Mercury has long been known to be toxic; the phrase "mad as a hatter" refers to the 19th-century occupational disease that resulted from prolonged contact with the mercury used in the manufacture of felt hats. Workers in many industries in which mercury is used, such as mercury mining, chemicals, and dentistry, have also been affected. Mercury has become an environmental pollutant in areas where agricultural and industrial wastes containing the metal escape or are discharged into waterways. It is believed that elemental mercury and inorganic mercury salts, although fairly inert when deposited on the bottom of waterways, are converted into methylmercury by microorganisms, and that this compound then enters the food chain and will contaminate fish used as food by man. Recent research suggests that mercury is a naturally occurring environmental contaminant in some areas. Minamata disease was named after the occurrence, in the 1950s and 1960s in Minamata, Japan, of many cases of severe mercury poisoning. It was found that a chemicals factory was discharging its mercury-containing wastes into the local waters, contaminating fish that residents caught for food. Mercury poisoning in the United States came to public attention in 1969, when it was learned that the children in a New Mexico family were afflicted by mercury poisoning after eating hog meat from animals fed with mercury-treated seed. In 1970, swordfish, tuna, and other large fish at the top of the food chain were found to contain significant levels of the metal. Most mercury pesticides have been withdrawn from the U.S. market, and in 1972, 91 countries approved a ban on ocean dumping of mercury and other pollutants. See WATER POLLUTION. See L. J. Goldwater, *Mercury* (1972).

Mercury space program: see SPACE EXPLORATION.

mercy killing: see EUTHANASIA.

Mer de Glace (mĕr də gläs) [Fr.,=sea of ice], glacier (3.5 mi/5.6 km long; 16 sq mi/41 sq km), Haute-Savoie dept., E France, on the northern slope of Mont Blanc. It is formed by the junction of three smaller glaciers and extends a few miles NE of Chamonix. There are deep crevasses and high seracs (ice needles). The glacier is renowned for its majestic beauty and is a tourist attraction.

Mered (mē'rĕd), husband of Pharaoh's daughter Bithiah. 1 Chron. 4.17,18.

Meredith, Edwin Thomas, 1876–1928, American publisher and U.S. Secretary of Agriculture (1920–21), b. Avoca, Iowa. After 1896 he owned and edited the *Farmers' Tribune,* founded (1902) *Successful Farming,* and started (1922) the magazine that became *Better Homes and Gardens.* An unsuccessful Democratic candidate for public office, Meredith was appointed to several government posts before he entered President Wilson's cabinet.

Meredith, George, 1828–1909, English novelist and poet. One of the great English novelists, Meredith wrote complex, often comic yet highly cerebral works that contain striking psychological character studies. As a youth he attended a Moravian school in Germany and eventually became apprenticed to a London lawyer. He began his career as a free-lance journalist, contributing to newspapers and magazines in London. His first volume of poems appeared in 1851 and received the praises of Tennyson. In 1849 he married Mary Ellen Nicoll, the widowed daughter of Thomas Love Peacock; she left him in 1858. *Modern Love* (1862), a series of 50 connected poems, reflects his own experience in relating the tragic dissolution of a marriage. He married Marie Vulliamy, happily, in 1864 and settled in Surrey, the location that inspired many of his later nature poems. Although Meredith began and ended his literary career as a poet, he is best remembered as a novelist. His first distinguished work, *The Ordeal of Richard Feverel,* appeared in 1859. His other notable books include *Evan Harrington* (1860), *The Adventures of Harry Richmond* (1871), *The Egoist* (1879), and *Diana of the Crossways* (1885). His famous critical essay, *On the Idea of Comedy and the Uses of the Comic Spirit* (1897), was first delivered as a lecture in 1877. Meredith's novels and poems are written in a brilliant but oblique style that has prevented him from becoming a popular author. Highly intellectual, his novels often treat social problems. Prominent in all his works is his joyful belief in evolution—in life as a process of becoming. See various volumes of his letters; biography by Lionel Stevenson (1953, repr. 1967); studies by G. M. Trevelyan (1906, repr. 1966), Siegfried Sassoon (1948, repr. 1969), J. B. Priestley (1926, repr. 1970), and Gillian Beer (1970).

Meredith, Owen: see BULWER-LYTTON, EDWARD ROBERT.

Meremoth (mĕr'ĭmōth). **1** Priest under Nehemiah. Ezra 8.33; Neh. 3.4. **2** Israelite who married a foreigner. Ezra 10.36. **3** Sealer of the Covenant. Neh. 10.5; 12.3. He is probably the Meraioth of Neh. 12.15.

Meres (mē'rēz), counselor of King Ahasuerus. Esther 1.14.

Merezhkovsky, Dmitri Sergeyevich (dəmē'trē syĭrgā'yəvĭch mârĭshkôf'skē), 1865–1941, Russian critic and novelist. His principal critical study is *Tolstoi as Man and Artist; with an Essay on Dostoievsky* (1901–2, tr. 1902), in which he represented the authors as seers of, respectively, the flesh and the spirit. This type of antithetical thought is developed in his trilogy of historical novels entitled *Christ and Antichrist,* which concerns Julian the Apostate (1896, tr. 1899), Leonardo da Vinci (1902, tr. 1902), and Peter the Great (1905, tr. 1905). With his wife, Zinaida GIPPIUS, he actively promoted the theories embodied in his novels through the Religious-Philosophic Society, which he founded in 1903. Merezhkovsky and Gippius were twice forced into exile—in 1905 temporarily, because of their support of the revolution, and after 1918 permanently, because they opposed the Bolsheviks. From his exile in Paris he attacked Bolshevism in *The Kingdom of Antichrist* (1922, tr. 1922) and other works.

merganser: see DUCK.

Mergenthaler, Ottmar (ôt'mär mĕr'gən-tä"lər), 1854–99, American inventor of the LINOTYPE. Mergenthaler was born in Germany, learned the watchmaker's trade, emigrated to America in 1872, and was employed to inspect and repair clocks in the government buildings in Washington. After 1876 he made his home in Baltimore, where he perfected his linotype, first patented in 1884 and put into operation in 1886.

merger, in corporate business, fusion of two or more corporations by the transfer of all property to a single corporation. The remaining corporation continues in existence, having absorbed the others. A merger differs from a consolidation (called amalgamation in Great Britain), wherein all the corporations terminate their existence and become parties to a new one. Mergers may be effected to increase profits and reduce losses through the reduction of competition, to diversify production, to protect against the liabilities of concentration in a single area, or to revive or rejuvenate failing businesses by the infusion of new management and personnel. The methods of effecting mergers vary. Often the corporation that continues to function makes an outright purchase of the property and stock of the others; exchange of bonds, options, and other agreements are also employed by the corporations involved. Mergers for monopolistic purposes were among the unfair practices that the Sherman Antitrust Act (1890) and, more especially, the Clayton Antitrust Act (1914) attempted to correct. Frequent mergers have taken place in the railroad industry, and important mergers have taken place in banking, the textile industry, and among international telegraph carriers. See CONGLOMERATE.

Merian, Maria Sibylla (märē'ä zĭbü'lä mä'rēän), 1647–1717, Swiss naturalist and painter of insects and flowers; daughter of Matthäus MERIAN, the elder. Her first book on insects, with plates she engraved and colored, was published in 1699. The same year she went to Dutch Guiana to study tropical insects, and her work on that subject appeared in 1705. Her remarkable painting of a Guianan bird-eating spider was ridiculed as a flight of female fancy until 1863 when an English naturalist observed a similar spider in the Amazon forest. Merian's careful research in natural history, combined with her exquisite pictorial studies, mostly in watercolor, earned her considerable esteem. The British Museum has two volumes of her drawings.

Merian, Matthäus (mätĕ'o͞os), the elder, 1593–1650, Swiss engraver and draftsman. In Frankfurt am Main from c.1623, he produced, with help from assistants, numerous engravings of battles and hunts, and topographic prints of European towns. His notable prints include *Dance of Death,* illustrations for Gottfried's *Chronik,* and the series *Theatrum Europaeum.* His son, **Matthäus Merian,** the younger, 1621–87, portrait and historical painter, worked throughout Europe. He is best represented by *Martyrdom of St. Lawrence* (cathedral, Bamberg) and a portrait of his sister, the artist Maria Sibylla MERIAN (Basel).

Meribah (mĕr'ĭbə): see MASSAH.

Merib-baal (mērĭb'-bāäl): see MEPHIBOSHETH **1.**

Meriç: see MARITSA, river.

Mérida (mä'rētħä), city (1970 pop. 253,856), capital of Yucatán state, SE Mexico. It is the chief commercial, communications, and cultural center of the Yucatán peninsula. Founded (1542) by Francisco de MONTEJO, the younger, on the site of a ruined Mayan city, Mérida has many fine examples of Spanish colonial architecture, notably the 16th-century cathedral. Rooftop windmills, curious landmarks, are used to pump water from underground wells and streams. The limited nature of the soil has made Mérida dependent commercially on the large crops of henequen (see SISAL HEMP) from the surrounding region and on tourists visiting nearby Mayan ruins, notably CHICHÉN ITZÁ and UXMAL.

Mérida, city (1970 pop. 40,059), Badajoz prov., SW Spain, in Estremadura, on the Guadiana River. It is a rail hub and agricultural center. The colony Emerita Augusta, founded by the Romans in the 1st cent. B.C., it became the capital of LUSITANIA. Its Roman remains, among the most important in Spain, include a magnificent bridge, a triumphal arch, a theater with marble columns, an aqueduct, a temple, an imposing circus, and an amphitheater. Mérida was later the chief city of Visigothic Lusitania. It fell (713) to the Moors, under whom it prospered. Conquered (1228) by Alfonso IX of León, it was given to the Knights of Santiago but quickly declined.

Meriden (mĕr'ĭdən), city (1970 pop. 55,959), New Haven co., S central Conn.; settled 1661, inc. as a town 1806, as a city 1867, town and city consolidated 1922. Meriden is known for its large silver industry. Silverware and pewter were made there in the 18th cent. by Samuel Yale and later by the Rogers Brothers and a forerunner of the International Silver Company. Jewelry and bathroom and lighting fixtures are also manufactured. Hubbard Park is in the city.

Meridian, city (1970 pop. 45,083), seat of Lauderdale co., E Miss., near the Ala. line; settled 1831, inc. 1860. The third largest city in the state, it is an important rail and highway focus and the trade, shipping, and industrial center for a farm, livestock, and timber area. In the Civil War the city was the temporary capital of Mississippi (1863); it was destroyed by General Sherman in Feb., 1864. Two junior colleges and a state mental hospital are there. A huge naval jet training base is to the north. Nearby Okatibbee Reservoir offers recreational activities.

meridian circle: see TRANSIT INSTRUMENT.

meridian of longitude: see LONGITUDE.

Mérimée, Prosper (prôspĕr' mārēmā'), 1803–70, French author. He first wrote a collection of plays in imitation of Spanish drama, *The Plays of Clara Gazul* (1825, tr. 1825), and a collection of so-called Illyrian ballads, *La Guzla* (1827). His important historical novel, *The Chronicle of the Reign of Charles IX* (1829; tr. 1830, 1890), is marked by an objectivity and psychological penetration rare among the romanticists. He was master of a concise and understated style, most fully realized in his *nouvelles,* or long stories, for which he is best known. Outstanding examples include *Colomba* (1852, tr. 1853); *Carmen* (in *Revue des Deux Mondes,* 1845; as a book, 1846, tr. 1881), which was the basis of Bizet's opera; *La Vénus d'Ille* (1837); and *Letters to an Unknown* (in *Revue des Deux Mondes,* 1873; as a book, 1874, tr. 1874). His short story, "Mateo Falcone" (1876), is a masterpiece of the genre. A cultivated man of the world, Mérimée was a painstaking student of archaeology, a linguist who translated Russian authors into French, and a senator under the Empire. He also wrote literary and art criticism and historical studies. See biography by A. W. Raitt (1970); study by M. A. Smith (1973).

Merino sheep, breed intermediate in body size having fine wool, developed in Spain. These sheep are noted for their hardiness and their herding instincts and have been used as parents of several other breeds, notably the Rambouillet of France. Three strains have been developed. Types A and B are strongly and moderately wrinkled, respectively; the C, or Delaine, type is much smoother, and has better combinations of wool and meat qualities. Merinos are white-faced with the rams horned and the ewes hornless.

Merionethshire (mĕrēŏn'əthshĭr), county (1971 pop. 35,277), 660 sq mi (1,709 sq km), NW Wales, on Cardigan Bay. The county town is DOLGELLAU. The region is mountainous, some peaks (Aran Mawddwy, Cader Idris) rising to nearly 3,000 ft (914 m). The chief rivers are the Dysynni, the Dovey, the Dee, and the Mawddach. The soil is generally poor, but provides good sheep pasturage. The main wealth of the county lies in its deposits of manganese and slate. The beautiful scenery makes it a popular tourist district. Merionethshire was organized as a shire by the English in the 13th cent., but the remoteness of the region made it one of the last districts in Wales to submit to English influence. Many of the inhabitants speak Welsh. In 1974, Merionethshire became part of the new nonmetropolitan county of Gwynedd.

meristem (mĕr'ĭstĕm"), any plant tissue characterized by cell division and differentiation into specialized tissues. Stems and roots and their branches increase in length through the activity of rapidly dividing groups of cells at their tips, called apical meristems, which produce the primary tissues. Stems and roots may grow in thickness or in diameter through cell divisions in lateral, or secondary, meristems, found just under the surface of the stem or root. Tissues derived from differentiated lateral meristem are known as secondary tissues. In one type of lateral meristem, called cambium, or vascular cambium, the cells divide and differentiate to form the conducting tissues of the plant, i.e., the WOOD, or xylem, and the phloem (see BARK; STEM). The growth in diameter of tree trunks is wholly dependent on the division of cambium cells. Other meristematic tissues include CORK cambium, which divides to produce waterproofing and protective cork tissue at the surface of the stem and root; and intercalary meristems, modified apical meristems found in different positions than either apical or lateral meristems, e.g., in the stem nodes of grasses. See also DIFFERENTIATION, in biology.

Merleau-Ponty, Maurice (mōrēs' mĕrlō'-pôNtē'), 1908–61, French philosopher. He graduated (1931) from the École normale supérieure, Paris, and after World War II taught at the Univ. of Lyon, the Sorbonne, and the Collège de France. Merleau-Ponty stressed the primacy of perception as a mode of access to the real, but, unlike many phenomenologists, he affirmed the reality of a world that transcends our consciousness of it. In his studies of perception he laid emphasis on the physical and the biological (or vital) as levels of conceptualization that preconditioned all mental concepts. This emphasis led him to a sympathy for Karl Marx's historical materialism, although he differed from most Marxians in regarding history as irreducibly plural and contingent: No single movement could claim to be the unique agency of the historical process. His study of perception also laid stress on the stratum of socially founded meanings that to him was intermediary between pure individual subjectivity and the objective existence of things. Since language was the chief repository of these meanings, he became interested, particularly in his later work, in the role of language in perception. Merleau-Ponty's works include *The Structure of Behavior* (1942, tr. 1963), *Phenomenology of Perception* (1945, tr. 1962), *Humanism and Terror* (1947, tr. 1969), *Sense and Nonsense* (1948, tr. 1964), *Adventures of the Dialectic* (1955, tr. 1973), and *Signs* (1960, tr. 1964). See studies by Thomas Langan (1966), J. F. Bannan (1967), Albert Rabil (1967), and John O'Neill (1970).

Merle d'Aubigné, Jean Henri (zhäN äNrē' mĕrl dōbēnyā'), 1794–1872, Swiss ecclesiastical historian and Protestant preacher. After studying theology at Geneva and in Berlin, he was pastor of the French Protestant church in Hamburg for five years, then court preacher to King William at Brussels until the Revolution of 1830 separated Holland from Belgium. Returning to Geneva, he helped establish the new Evangelical Church there and became distinguished as professor of Church history in its theological seminary. His history of the Reformation (1835–53) was translated into most of the languages of Europe and was widely read.

Merlin, in ARTHURIAN LEGEND, magician, seer, and teacher at the court of King Vortigern and later at the court of King Arthur. He was a bard and culture hero in early Celtic folklore. In Arthurian legend he is famous as a magician and as the counselor of King Arthur. In Tennyson's *Idylls of the King* Merlin is imprisoned eternally in an old oak tree by the treacherous Vivien (or Nimue), when he reveals the secrets of his knowledge to her.

Merlo (mĕr'lō), city (1970 pop. 188,868), Buenos Aires prov., E Argentina. An administrative and agricultural center of the Greater Buenos Aires area, it was founded in 1730 by Francisco de Merlo y Barbossa.

mermaid, in folklore, sea-dwelling creature commonly represented as having the head and body of a woman and fishtails instead of legs. Belief in mermaids, and in their counterpart, mermen, has existed since earliest times. They are often described as having great beauty and charm, which they use to lure sailors to their deaths (see SIREN). In some legends they assumed human shape and married mortals (see MÉLUSINE). The original of the mermaid is thought by some to be the DUGONG.

mermaid's purse: see RAY.

Merman, Ethel, 1909–, American musical comedy star, b. Astoria, N.Y., originally named Ethel Zimmerman. Merman's theater debut was in *Girl Crazy* (1930). Noted for her booming voice, she has appeared on Broadway in *Annie Get Your Gun, Call Me Madam* (also the film version, 1953), and *Gypsy.* Among her films are *Alexander's Ragtime Band* (1938) and *There's No Business Like Show Business* (1954).

mermen: see MERMAID.

Merneptah (mĕrnĕp'tä), d. c.1215 B.C., king of ancient Egypt, of the XIX dynasty; son and successor of Ramses II. He succeeded (1224 B.C.) to the throne when he was already advanced in years. He quelled a revolt in Syria and repulsed a Libyan invasion of the western delta of the Nile. The first recorded mention of the name of Israel was found in an inscription on a stele of Merneptah exulting in a victory. His reign was apparently the beginning of the decline of Egypt. After his death a period of palace intrigues began. Seti II was one of the kings who reigned briefly after Merneptah.

Merodach (mĕr'ōdăk, mērō'dăk), biblical form of the name of the god Marduk of Babylon. Jer. 50.2.

Merodach-baladan (mĕr'ōdăk-băl'ədăn), fl. 722–702 B.C., Chaldaean prince, who usurped (721) the Babylonian throne. Sargon of Assyria put down the allies of Merodach-baladan in Syria and Palestine and eventually drove (c.710) the usurper from Babylon. After Sargon's death, Merodach-baladan reoccupied (703–702) the throne. During his rule of Babylonia, he strengthened the Chaldaean Empire. He is also called Baladan and Berodach-baladan and is mentioned in the Bible (Isa. 39; 2 Kings 20).

Meroë (mĕr'ōē), ancient city in the northern province of the Republic of the Sudan, on the east bank of the Nile, N of Khartoum. In the mid-6th cent. B.C., Meroë replaced Napata as the central city of the Cushite dynasty and from 530 B.C. until A.D. 350 served as the capital of the dynasty. By the 1st cent. B.C., Meroë was a major center for iron smelting. It is believed that knowledge of iron casting was carried (7th–10th cent.) from the middle Nile to the middle Niger by a great African overland route. Among Meroë's extensive ruins are royal palaces (6th cent. B.C.) and a temple of Amon. Nearby are cemeteries and three groups of pyramids.

Merom, Waters of: see HULA, LAKE.

Meronothite (mērŏn'ōthīt), obscure designation used of two men. 1 Chron. 27.30; Neh. 3.7.

Merope (mĕr'əpē), in Greek mythology. **1** One of the Pleiades. She was the wife of Sisyphus, king of Corinth, and the mother of Glaucus. According to one legend she became the lost Pleiad because of the shame she felt for having married a mortal. **2** Daughter of Oenopion. Orion loved her, but when he failed to gain her father's approval, he raped her. In revenge, Oenopion blinded him.

Merovingian art and architecture (mĕr"əvĭn'-jēən). This period is named for Merovech, the founder of the first Germanic-Frankish dynasty (A.D. c.500–751). The Merovingian period was marked by the gradual decline of the classical tradition and by the absorption of a radically new element into the artistic mainstream—the abstract and brilliantly ornamental style of the barbarian tribes. The art of these tribes was confined to small and portable objects because of their nomadic way of life. The migratory waves of settlers from Central Europe and the East have been credited with the introduction into Western art of the CLOISONNÉ technique. They also excelled in several other types of enamelwork and metalwork. Merovingian architecture, monumental sculpture, and painting were dependent upon the legacy of the classical and Early Christian traditions. Little remains of the architecture of the Merovingian period, although contemporary sources, such as the writings of Gregory of Tours, indicate that building activity was substantial. Larger churches were timber roofed and adhered to the basilican plan. The most original aspect of Gallic churches was their use of a bell tower. Constructions of Merovingian date have been found in Auxerre, Jouarre, Lyons, and Poitiers. Merovingian stone sculpture was characterized by a simplification of antique forms, sometimes culminating in a rather crude graphic shorthand. Animal motifs, especially birds and lambs disposed in rows or within geometric patterns, were tirelessly repeated on sarcophagi. The human figure became an abstract sign. Illumination of manuscripts was almost entirely restricted to the elaboration of colorful initial letters based on animal forms, notably bird and fish motifs.

Merovingians, dynasty of Frankish kings, descended, according to tradition, from Merovech, chief of the Salian FRANKS, whose son was CHILDERIC I and whose grandson was CLOVIS I, the founder of the Frankish monarchy. After the death (511) of Clovis I, the kingdom was divided among his descendants into various kingdoms, which later became known as AUSTRASIA, NEUSTRIA, and BURGUNDY. These kingdoms, whose borders were constantly shifting, were often combined; for brief periods, they were all united in a single realm under CLOTAIRE I (558–61), CLOTAIRE II (613–23), and DAGOBERT I (629–39). The rule of the Merovingians before Dagobert I was disturbed by chronic warfare among aristocrats and rivals for power, notably between Queen BRUNHILDA of Austrasia and Queen FREDEGUNDE of Neustria. Dagobert I was the last active ruler; his descendants were called the *rois fainéants,* or idle kings. They were entirely subject to their mayors of the palace, the CAROLINGIANS, who became the nominal as well as the actual rulers of the Franks when PEPIN THE SHORT deposed (751) the last Merovingian king, Childeric III. See CHILDEBERT I; THEODORIC I; GUNTRAM; CHILPERIC I; SIGEBERT I; CHILDEBERT II. See Samuel Dill, *Roman Society in Gaul in the Merovingian Age* (1926, repr. 1966); Peter Lasko, *The Kingdom of the Franks: Northwest Europe before Charlemagne* (1971).

Meroz (mē'rŏz), unidentified place, denounced in the Song of Deborah. Judges 5.23.

Merriam, city (1970 pop. 10,851), Johnson co., NE Kansas, a suburb of Kansas City; inc. 1950. It has various light industries.

Merrick, David, 1912?–, American theatrical producer, b. St. Louis, Mo. With a short, prosperous legal career as prelude to his theatrical experience, Merrick began his remarkably successful series of productions in 1954 with *Fanny,* his first Broadway musical. Between 1955 and 1974 he presented more than 70 plays and musicals, notably *Gypsy* (1958), *Becket* (1960), *Carnival* (1961), *Oliver!* (1962), *Luther* (1963), *Hello, Dolly!* (1964), *Marat/Sade* (1965), *Child's Play* (1970), and *Dreyfus in Rehearsal* (1974).

Merrick, uninc. city (1970 pop. 25,904), Nassau co., SE N.Y., on Long Island. Although chiefly residential, it has some light manufacturing.

Merrill, Robert, 1919–, American baritone, b. Brooklyn, N.Y. He studied with his mother, Lillian Miller Merrill, and in 1943 began singing at Radio City Music Hall. In 1945 he won the Metropolitan Opera's Auditions of the Air and in the same year made his debut as Germont in Verdi's *La Traviata.* He subsequently became one of the most popular baritones in the company, singing the French and Italian repertoires. Among his important roles have been Renato in Verdi's *Un Ballo in maschera,* Amonasro in *Aïda,* and Escamillo in Bizet's *Carmen.* In 1970 he celebrated his 25th anniversary at the Metropolitan.

Merrimack, river, c.110 mi (180 km) long, formed at Franklin, S central N.H., by the junction of the Pemigewasset (rising in the White Mts.) and Winnipesaukee rivers. It flows S past Concord and Manchester into NE Mass., where it flows NE past Lowell and Lawrence to the Atlantic Ocean at Newburyport. With its numerous tributaries, the river drains most of S New Hampshire. It has long been used as a source of power for textile and other mills.

Merrimack: see MONITOR AND MERRIMACK.

Merritt Island, c.40 mi (60 km) long and c.6 mi (10 km) wide, E Fla., separated from the mainland by Indian River (a lagoon) and from the Canaveral peninsula on the east by Banana River (a lagoon). It produces citrus fruits and is noted for its birds and other wildlife. The village of Merritt Island is there.

Merry del Val, Rafael (räfäĕl' mä'rē dĕl väl), 1865–1930, Spanish prelate, cardinal of the Roman Catholic Church, b. London. He was educated for the priesthood and ordained at Rome (1888). He was secretary of the pontifical commission that studied the validity of Anglican orders (1897). He went as apostolic delegate to Canada (1897) on the occasion of the closing of Catholic and private schools in Manitoba. In 1903, Pius X created him cardinal and made him papal secretary of state; in that office he was said to have increased the bitterness between France and the Holy See. Benedict XV made him archpriest of St. Peter's and secretary of the Congregation of the Holy Office. He was a co-worker with Cardinal Gasparri in the negotiations leading to the Lateran Treaty. See his diary ed. by F. J. Weber (1964); biography by M. B. Quinn (1958).

Merryman, ex parte, case decided in 1861 by Chief Justice Roger B. Taney sitting as a Federal circuit judge in Baltimore, Md. John Merryman, a citizen of Maryland, was imprisoned by the U.S. army on suspicion of favoring the Confederacy. He obtained a writ of HABEAS CORPUS. The commanding general refused to respect this action, alleging that President Lincoln had authorized him to suspend the writ. Taney held that Article 1, Section 9, of the U.S. Constitution gave to Congress alone the power to suspend the writ in case of rebellion or invasion and that consequently the President's action had been without warrant and represented a threat to the liberties of all Americans. Lincoln, however, continued to adhere to the same practice throughout the Civil War. Congress ratified the suspension in 1863. See H. S. Commager, ed., *Documents of American History* (8th ed. 1968).

Merry Mount: see MORTON, THOMAS.

Merseburg (mĕr'zəbo͝ork), city (1970 pop. 55,986), Halle district, S central East Germany, on the Saale River. It is an industrial city and a lignite-mining center. Manufactures include chemicals, paper, steel, bricks, and beer. A fortress in the 9th cent., Merseburg was a favorite residence of Henry I (Henry the Fowler) and of Emperor Otto I. It served as a German outpost for subduing the Slavs and Poles. Merseburg was an episcopal see from 968 until its suppression (1561) during the Reformation, when the bishopric passed to Saxony. From 1656 to 1738 the city was the seat of the dukes of Saxe-Merseburg. In 1815 it passed to Prussia. Merseburg was badly damaged in World War II. Among its noted buildings are the cathedral (founded 1015, rebuilt in the 13th and 16th cent.) and the episcopal palace (15th cent.).

Mers-el-Kebir (mĕrs-ĕl-kəbĭr'), town, NW Algeria, on the Gulf of Oran. Originally a Roman port, it has a long history of maritime importance. During the 15th cent. it was a center of activity for corsairs and was twice occupied by the Portuguese. The Spanish held the town from 1505 to 1792; the French arrived in the 19th cent. After France's defeat by Germany in June, 1940, the French fleet sought refuge at Mers-el-Kebir, but the British navy sank or damaged most of the ships. The great French naval base at Mers-el-Kebir came to include subterranean installations where atomic tests were held. In 1962 the Evian Agreement, by which Algerian independence was acknowledged, allowed France to maintain the Mers-el-Kebir base for 15 years; however, the French evacuated the base in 1967.

Mersen, Treaty of, 870, redivision of the Carolingian empire by the sons of LOUIS I, Charles the Bald (later CHARLES II) of the West Franks (France) and LOUIS THE GERMAN of the East Franks (Germany), signed at Mersen (Dutch *Meersen*), now in the Netherlands. The treaty superseded the tripartite division of the empire in 843 (see VERDUN, TREATY OF). It divided the kingdom of LOTHARINGIA between Charles and Louis, following the death (869) of their nephew, Lothair, king of Lotharingia. France obtained the territories roughly corresponding to the modern Netherlands, Belgium, and Lorraine and Germany received Alsace and the left bank of the Lower Rhine. The borders established did not last long, but the treaty had the permanent effect of establishing a common frontier between Germany and France.

Mersey (mûr'zē), river, c.70 mi (110 km) long, formed at Stockport, W England, by the confluence of the Etherow and Goyt rivers. It flows east to the Irish Sea near Liverpool. The estuary of the Mersey, which is 16 mi (26 km) long and c.2 mi (3.2 km) wide, is navigable for oceangoing vessels. Its chief tributaries are the Irwell and Bollin rivers. The Manchester Ship Canal uses the waters of the Mersey. Mersey Tunnel or Queensway, a vehicular tunnel (opened 1934) with a length of 2.3 mi (3.7 km), is the longest subaqueous tunnel in the world; it connects Liverpool and Birkenhead. Kingsway Tunnel (1.5 mi/2.4 km long; opened 1971) connects Liverpool and Wallasey. The Mersey River is of great commercial importance to the cities served by it, especially Liverpool and Manchester. Shipbuilding, milling, and oil refining are important industries along the river.

Merseyside, metropolitan county (1972 est. pop. 1,659,000), NW England, created under the Local Government Act of 1972 (effective 1974). It is subdivided into five metropolitan districts. Merseyside is composed of the county boroughs of BIRKENHEAD, BOOTLE, LIVERPOOL, SAINT HELENS, SOUTHPORT, and WALLASEY, and parts of the former counties of CHESHIRE and LANCASHIRE.

Mersin (mĕrsĭn'), formerly **İçel** (ēchĕl'), city (1970 pop. 114,302), capital of İçel prov., S Turkey, on the Mediterranean Sea. A rail terminus and modern seaport, it exports cotton, chrome, copper, and agricultural produce. Excavations at Mersin in the 1930s showed that the site was occupied in early Neolithic times (c.3600 B.C.).

Merthyr Tydfil (mûr'thər tĭd'vĭl), county borough (1971 pop. 55,215), Glamorganshire, S Wales, on the Taff River. It is connected to Cardiff by canal. In the center of the great coal field of Glamorganshire, it has ironworks and steelworks. After World War II, light industries were stressed to revive the economy. Textiles, clothing, and leather goods are also made. The name comes from the story of the martyrdom of St. Tydfil, a Welsh princess killed in the 5th cent. In 1974, Merthyr Tydfil became part of the new non-metropolitan county of Mid Glamorgan.

Merton, Robert King, 1910–, American sociologist, b. Philadelphia, grad. Temple Univ. (A.B., 1931) and Harvard Univ. (M.A., 1932; Ph.D., 1936). He has been a professor of sociology at Columbia Univ. since 1941. He was Giddings Professor of Sociology from 1963 until 1974, when he was named university professor, Columbia's highest academic rank. He is especially known for his contributions to the fields of social structure, sociology of science, bureaucracy, and mass communications. Among his writings are *Mass Persuasion* (1946), *Social Theory and Social Structure* (1957), and *The Sociology of Science* (1973).

Merton, Thomas, 1915–68, American religious writer and poet, b. France. He grew up in France, England, and the United States and studied at Cambridge Univ. and at Columbia (B.A., 1938; M.A., 1939). Converted to the Roman Catholic Church during his college career, he became in 1941 a Trappist monk. He was later ordained a priest and is known in religion as Father M. Louis. Merton died as a result of an accident in Thailand while attending an ecumenical council of Catholic and Buddhist monks. Among his volumes of poems are *Figures for an Apocalypse* (1947), *The Tears of the Blind Lions* (1949), and *The Strange Islands* (1957). Best known of his books are his autobiography, *The Seven Storey Mountain* (1948, repr. 1970), two volumes on Trappist life, *The Waters of Siloe* (1949) and *The Sign of Jonas* (1953, repr. 1973), and *Mystics and Zen Masters* (1967). His *Seeds of Contemplation* (1949), *The Silent Life* (1957), and *New Seeds of Contemplation* (1962, rev. ed. 1972) are volumes of meditations. See also his *Disputed Questions* (1960), *Conjectures of a Guilty Bystander* (1966), *Faith and Violence* (1968), *Contemplation in a World of Action* (1971), and his Asian journal, ed. by Naomi Burton et al. (1973); *A Thomas Merton Reader*, ed. by T. P. McDonnell (1962); study by J. T. Baker (1971).

Merton, Walter de, d. 1277, English bishop, founder of Merton College, Oxford. He was lord chancellor from 1261 to 1263, was reappointed after the death of Henry III (1272), and was made bishop of Rochester in 1274. In 1261 he obtained a charter from the earl of Gloucester for the assignation of lands for the support of scholars, and in 1264 a regular charter of incorporation established a "House of Scholars" at Malden, Surrey; this was later transferred to Oxford. The establishment of a corporate body to rule and control the scholars marks the beginning of the collegiate system of education, and Merton College became the model for other colleges at Oxford and Cambridge.

Merton, borough (1971 pop. 176,524) of Greater London, SE England. Merton was created in 1965 by the merger of the metropolitan London boroughs of Mitcham and Wimbledon and the urban districts of Merton and Morden. The area is largely residential with some industry, including tanning and the manufacture of silk and calico prints, varnish and paint, and toys. An annual fair dating from Elizabethan times is held in Mitcham, and cricket is played on the town common. Wimbledon is England's tennis headquarters; the first Wimbledon Championship match took place in 1877. Cricket and golf matches are also played. George Eliot lived in Wimbledon. Merton has remains of a priory that was founded in 1115 and destroyed by Oliver Cromwell. Walter de Merton, Lord High Chancellor to Henry III and founder of Merton College, Oxford, and Thomas à Becket were educated at Merton Priory. Admiral Horatio Nelson and Lady Emma Hamilton lived together in Merton Park.

Merton and Morden: see MERTON.

Meru, Mount (mä'ro͞o), extinct volcano, 14,979 ft (4,566 m) high, NE Tanzania, near Mt. Kilimanjaro. Coffee is grown on its lower slopes.

Merv (myĕrf), ancient city, Central Asian USSR, in Turkmenistan, in a large oasis of the Kara-Kum desert, on the Murgab River. The city, known in antiquity as Margiana, or Antiochia Margiana, was founded in the 3d cent. B.C. on the site of an earlier settlement. Its periods of greatness were from A.D. 651 to 821, when it was the seat of the Arab rulers of Khorasan and Transoxania and one of the main centers of Islamic learning, and from 1118 to 1157, when it was the capital of the Seljuk Empire under the last sultan, Sandzhar. The Mongols destroyed the city early in the 13th cent., but it was slowly rebuilt, to be destroyed again by the Bukharans in 1790. The Russians conquered the area in 1884. Several mausoleums, mosques, and castles of the 11th and 12th cent. are preserved and are among the best monuments of Muslim art in Central Asia. Present-day Merv, c.20 mi (30 km) from the old city, was renamed Mary in 1937. It is the capital of Mary oblast and an important textile center.

Merwin, W. S. (William Stanley Merwin), 1927–, American poet and translator, b. New York City. After graduating from Princeton in 1948, he traveled in Europe, studying romance languages. His volumes of poetry include *A Mask for Janus* (1952), *Drunk in the Furnace* (1960), and *Lice* (1967). Merwin is also well known for his translations, among them *The Cid* (1959) and *The Life of Lazarillo de Tormes* (1962).

Meryon, Charles (shärl mĕryôN'), 1821–68, French etcher. His short life was saddened by poverty and neglect and complicated by recurring forms of mental aberration. Prevented by color blindness from painting, he became an etcher and evolved an incomparable technique. Reflecting the romanticism of the period, he depicted architectural settings with great structural clarity, often inserting grotesque or enigmatic figures. His fame rests largely on his poetic series of 22 etchings of old sections of Paris, *Eaux-Fortes sur Paris* (1850–54). Meryon died insane at 47. See studies by Loÿs Delteil (1928) and Campbell Dodgson (1931).

Mesa (mā'sə), city (1970 pop. 62,583), Maricopa co., S central Ariz., in the lush Salt River valley; inc. 1883. Electronic components, fabricated metals, aircraft, and machine tools are among the manufactures of this city, which almost doubled in population between 1960 and 1970. Tourism is also important, and the citrus and farm products of the area are packed and processed in Mesa. The Mormons who founded the city in 1878 used old Indian irrigation canals. A Mormon temple, a junior college, and the chief agricultural experimental farm of the Univ. of Arizona are there. In the city are training sites for major-league baseball teams.

mesa (mā'sə) [Span.,=table], name given in the SW United States to a small, isolated tableland or a flat-topped hill. Two or more of the sides are steep and usually perpendicular. Some have all four sides practically perpendicular and are very difficult of access. Their bold lines make them a picturesque part of the landscape, and they are frequently deep red or yellow in color. The usual explanation of their origin is that a hard stratum acted as a cap to protect the layers beneath it from the erosion that wore down the surrounding softer rock, once level with the summit of the mesa in a plateau. The strata, or layers of rock, in a mesa are horizontal, or nearly so. The many "table mountains" are mesas. Two celebrated mesas are the Mesa Verde in Colorado and the Enchanted Mesa (Mesa Encantada) in New Mexico. A butte is a small mesa that usually has less precipitous sides.

Mesabi, range of low hills, NE Minn., famous for its extensive iron ore deposits. The ores are found in a belt c.110 mi (180 km) long and from 1 to 3 mi (1.6–4.8 km) wide between Babbitt and Grand Rapids; they occur in horizontal layers (up to 500 ft/152 m thick) near the surface and are mined by the open pit method. Reserves of high-grade hematite iron are nearly exhausted, and lower-grade taconite deposits are now being worked. The taconite contains mostly chert and magnetite (an iron-bearing mineral) and must undergo a costly and complex beneficiation process before being shipped in the form of pellets containing c.60% iron. Most of the ore is shipped by rail to Duluth, Minn., and other ports on Lake Superior and then by lake vessels to iron and steel plants on the lower lakes. The Mesabi iron ore deposits were first discovered in 1887 by Leonidas Merritt and his brothers, who organized the Mountain Iron Company in 1890 to mine the ore; John D. Rockefeller gained control of the company in the Panic of 1893.

Mesa Verde National Park, 52,074 acres (21,074 hectares), SW Colo.; est. 1906. It includes the most notable and best-preserved cliff dwellings (see CLIFF DWELLERS) and relics in the United States, covering four archaeological periods. There are museums and a library.

mescal (mĕskăl'), Mexican spirituous liquor, obtained by distilling a liquid made from the leaves, juicy stalk, and roots of certain species of maguey (see AMARYLLIS). The name is sometimes given to liquor distilled from agave sap, which, fermented, is PULQUE. Tequila and sotol are similar to mescal. Presumably because of a slight similarity of effect, the name mescaline is commonly applied to a powerful alkaloid drug obtained from PEYOTE.

mescaline (mĕs'kəlēn"), perception-altering substance found in PEYOTE. See PSYCHOTOMIMETIC DRUG.

Mesdag, Hendrik Willem (hĕn'drĭk vĭl'əm mĕs'-däkh), 1831–1915, Dutch marine painter. He gave up banking at 35 to study painting. He later lived at The Hague and was known as a painter and wealthy patron of the arts. He presented to the nation his fine collection, containing many paintings of the Barbizon school, together with a building to house it—Mesdag Museum, The Hague. His simple and realistic marine paintings are found in many Dutch galleries. *The Return of the Fishing Boats* (The Hague) is characteristic.

Mesech (mē'sĕk), variant of MESHECH.

mesentery: see PERITONEUM.

Meseta: see IBERIAN PENINSULA.

Mesha (mē'shə). **1** King of Moab contemporary with Ahab. Ahab was his overlord, after whose death Mesha attempted a revolt against Israel. The account of this is inscribed on the MOABITE STONE. 2 Kings 3. **2** Son of Caleb. 1 Chron. 2.42. **3** Benjamite. 1 Chron. 8.9. **4** Unidentified region of Arabia. Gen. 10.30.

Meshach (mē'shăk), one of the THREE HOLY CHILDREN.

Meshech (mē'shĕk). **1** Son of Japheth. Gen. 10.2; Ezek. 32.26; 38.2; 39.1. Mesech: Ps. 120.5. **2** Son of Shem. 1 Chron. 1.17.

Meshed: see MASHHAD, Iran.

Meshelemiah (mĕshĕl"ĕmī'ə), gatekeeper. 1 Chron. 9.21; 26.1,2,9. Shallum: 1 Chron. 9.19,31; Ezra 2.42; Neh. 7.45. Shelemiah: 1 Chron. 26.14. Meshullam: Neh. 12.25.

Meshezabeel (mēshĕz'əbēl"). **1** Worker on the wall. Neh. 3.4. **2** Signer of the covenant. Neh. 10.21. **3** Descendant of Judah. Neh. 11.24.

Meshillemith (mēshĭl'ēmĭth) or **Meshillemoth** (-mōth). **1** Ephraimite chief. 2 Chron. 28.12. **2** Priest. 1 Chron. 9.12; Neh. 11.13.

Meshobab (mēshō'băb), descendant of Simeon. 1 Chron. 4.34.

Meshullam (mĕshŭl'əm). **1** Ancestor of Shaphan. 2 Kings 22.3. **2** Son of Zerubbabel. 1 Chron. 3.19. **3** See MESHELEMIAH. **4** See SHALLUM **7.** **5** Father-in-law of JOHANAN **10.** Neh. 3.4,30; 6.18. **6** Repairer of the wall. Neh. 3.6. **7** Assistant of Ezra. Ezra 10.15. **8** Man who had a foreign wife. Ezra 10.29. **9** Father of SALLU **2.** **10** Ancestor of ADAIAH **4.** **11** Gadite chief. 1 Chron. 5.13. **12** Chief man of the Exile. Ezra 8.16. **13, 14** Sealers of the covenant. Neh. 10.7,20. **15** Grandfather of AZARIAH **24.** **16, 17** Priests in the time of Jehoiakim. Neh. 12.13,16. **18** Benjamite. 1 Chron. 8.17. **19** Kohathite Levite. 2 Chron. 34.12. **20** Prince of Judah. Neh. 12.33. **21** One present at the reading of the Law. Neh. 8.4. **22** A porter. Neh. 12.25.

Meshullemeth (mĭsho͝ol'əmĕth) [Heb.,=fem. of MESHULLAM], wife of King Manasseh. 2 Kings 21.19.

Mesilla (māsē'yä), town (1970 pop. 1,713), SW N.Mex., on the Rio Grande and near Las Cruces; settled c.1850. The whole Mesilla Valley became part of the United States under the Gadsden Purchase (1853). Mesilla was a central station on the overland mail route. During the Civil War it changed hands several times. From July, 1861, to Aug., 1862, it was headquarters for Col. John R. Baylor of the Confederate army, who proclaimed Mesilla the capital of the new Confederate territory. A museum commemorates Billy the Kid, who once stood trial there.

Mesmer, Friedrich Anton (frē'drĭkh än'tôn mĕs'-mər), or **Franz Anton Mesmer** (fränts), 1734–1815, German physician. He studied in Vienna. His interest in "animal magnetism" developed into a system of treatment through hypnotism that was called mesmerism. It seems now that Mesmer was actually treating psychosomatic illness, but an unsympathetic medical and scientific community caused him to be expelled first from Vienna, and in 1778 from Paris. He retired to his native Austria and to obscurity. See his memoir (1799, tr. 1957); biography by D. M. Walmsley (1967).

mesmerism: see HYPNOTISM.

Mesobaite (mēsō'bāīt, mĕs"ōbā'īt), obscure term applied to one of David's guards. 1 Chron. 11.47.

mesoderm, in biology, middle layer of tissue formed in the gastrula stage of the developing embryo. At the end of the blastula stage, cells of the embryo are arranged in the form of a hollow ball.

Continued cell movement results in an invagination of the bottom region of the embryo, producing a form that resembles a double-layered cup. A third layer, the mesoderm, is formed between the other two by growth of cells derived from a marginal zone. The mesoderm is the germ layer that forms many muscles, the circulatory and excretory systems, and the dermis, skeleton, and other supportive and connective tissue. It also gives rise to the NOTOCHORD, a supporting structure between the neural canal and the primitive gut. In many animals, including vertebrates, the mesoderm surrounds a cavity known as the COELOM, the space that contains the viscera. See EMBRYO.

Mesolithic period (mĕz"əlĭth'ĭk) or **Middle Stone Age,** period in human development between the end of the PALEOLITHIC PERIOD and the beginning of the NEOLITHIC PERIOD. It began with the end of the last glacial period over 10,000 years ago and evolved into the Neolithic period; this change involved the gradual domestication of plants and animals and the formation of settled communities at various times and places. While Mesolithic cultures lasted in Europe until almost 3000 B.C., Neolithic communities developed in the Middle East between 9000 and 6000 B.C. Mesolithic cultures represent a wide variety of hunting, fishing, and food gathering techniques. This variety may be the result of adaptations to changed ecological conditions associated with the retreat of glaciers, the growth of forests in Europe and deserts in N Africa, and the disappearance of the large game of the Ice Age. Characteristic of the period were hunting and fishing settlements along rivers and on lake shores, where fish and mollusks were abundant. Microliths, the typical stone implements of the Mesolithic period, are smaller and more delicate than those of the late Paleolithic period. Pottery and the use of the bow developed, although their presence in Mesolithic cultures may only indicate contact with early Neolithic peoples. The Azilian culture, which was centered in the Pyrenees region but spread to Switzerland, Belgium, and Scotland, was one of the earliest representatives of Mesolithic culture in Europe. The Azilian was followed by the Tardenoisian culture, which covered much of Europe; most of these settlements are found on dunes or sandy areas. The Maglemosian, named for a site in Denmark, is found in the Baltic region and N England. It occurs in the middle of the Mesolithic period. It is there that hafted axes, an improvement over the Paleolithic hand axe, and bone tools are found. The Ertebolle culture, also named for a site in Denmark, spans most of the late Mesolithic. It is also known as the kitchen-midden culture for the large deposits of mollusk shells found around the settlements. Other late Mesolithic cultures are the Campignian and Asturian, both of which may have had Neolithic contacts. The Mesolithic period in other areas is represented by the Natufian in the Middle East, the Badarian and Gerzean in Egypt, and the Capsian in N Africa. The Natufian culture provides the earliest evidence of an evolution from a Mesolithic to a Neolithic way of life. See study by J. G. D. Clark (1953, repr. 1970).

Mesolóngion (mĕsôlông'gēôn) or **Missolonghi** (mĭsəlông'gē), town (1971 pop. 11,614), capital of Aetolia and Acarnania prefecture, W central Greece, a port on the Gulf of Pátrai. It trades in fish, wine, and tobacco. Mesolóngion was a major stronghold of the Greek insurgents in the Greek War of Independence. Its inhabitants successfully resisted a siege by forces of the Ottoman Empire in 1822–23 and held out heroically against a second siege from 1825 to 1826, when the Ottoman forces captured the town. Lord Byron, the English poet who supported the Greek insurgents, died there in 1824.

meson (mē'zŏn) [Gr.,=middle (i.e., middleweight)], class of ELEMENTARY PARTICLES whose masses are generally between those of the LEPTON class of lighter particles and those of the BARYON class of heavier particles. From a technical point of view mesons are strongly interacting bosons; i.e., they participate in the strong nuclear FORCE and are described by the Bose-Einstein statistics, which apply to all particles not covered by the Pauli EXCLUSION PRINCIPLE. The lightest meson is the PION, whose mass is about 270 times that of the ELECTRON. Heavier mesons include the kaon (K meson), eta meson, and a number of higher-mass recurrences of the lighter mesons. The heaviest mesons are heavier than some baryons, such as the proton and neutron, but their classification as mesons is based on their behavior rather than on their mass. The existence of mesons was first predicted in 1935 by Hideki Yukawa, who theorized that they could be responsible for the force holding the NUCLEUS of an atom together. In 1936 a particle was discovered by Carl D. Anderson and Seth Neddermeyer that had a mass close to that predicted for the Yukawa particle. However, the behavior of this particle, the MUON, did not correspond to that of the theory at all. The muon was subsequently reclassified as a lepton rather than a meson. The particle predicted by Yukawa was the pion, which was not discovered until 1947 by C. F. Powell and coworkers. Both the muon and the pion were first observed in secondary COSMIC RAYS, being produced in the upper atmosphere by collisions between primary cosmic rays and the atoms of the atmosphere. Since then mesons have been produced and observed in large numbers in laboratories where high-energy particle collisions can be achieved with the aid of a PARTICLE ACCELERATOR.

mesopeak: see ATMOSPHERE.

Mesopotamia (mĕs"əpətā'mēə) [Gr.,=between rivers], ancient country of Asia, the region about the Tigris and Euphrates rivers, included in modern Iraq. The region extends from the Persian Gulf north to the mountains of Armenia and from the Zagros and Kurdish mts. on the east to the Syrian Desert. From the mountainous north, Mesopotamia slopes down through grassy steppes to a central alluvial plain, which was once rendered exceedingly fertile by a network of canals. The south was long thought to be the cradle of civilization until earlier settlements (which probably date from about 5000 B.C.) were found in N Mesopotamia; Jarmo, the earliest of these, was superseded by a succession of cultures: Tell Hassuna, Samarra, and Tell Halaf. Tell Halaf, the most advanced of these early cultures, is famous for Halaf ware, the finest prehistoric pottery in Mesopotamia. It is found at such sites as Nineveh and Tepe Gawra. While these advances were being made in the north, civilization was just beginning in the south, particularly at Eridu. The Al Ubaid culture that followed flourished in both N and S Mesopotamia. During the next period (called the proto literate phase) the south was the important region, and the transformation of the village culture into an urban civilization took place. Erech (modern Warka), the foremost site at the beginning of this period, has yielded such monumental architecture as the temple of Inanna and the ziggurat of Anu. Also found at Erech were tablets including the earliest pictographic writing. The early dynastic phase that followed saw the development of city-states all over the Middle East as far as N Syria, N Mesopotamia, and probably Elam. The famous sites of this period are Tell Asmar, Kafaje, Ur, Kish, Mari, Farah, and Telloh (Lagash). The Sumerians, the inhabitants of these city-states of S Mesopotamia, were unified at Nippur, where they gathered together to worship Enlil, the wind god. The famous first dynasty of Ur came at the end of the early dynastic period. Sargon founded (c.2340) the Akkadian dynasty, the first empire in Mesopotamia, whose example of empire building was later followed by the old Babylonian dynasty and late Assyrian Empire (see BABYLONIA; ASSYRIA). There was also a great cultural exchange between the Mesopotamians and the Elamites (and other Iranians), who for centuries had threatened each other. Mesopotamia still had prestige at the time of Alexander the Great, but later it was generally a part of the Roman Empire. The Arabs took it from the Byzantine Empire, and it rose to great prominence after Baghdad was made (A.D. 762) the capital of the Abbasid caliphate. This glory was destroyed when the Mongols under Hulagu Khan devastated the area in 1258, destroying the ancient irrigation system. In the centuries following, Mesopotamia never regained its former prominence. In World War I, however, it was an important battlefield. The kingdom of IRAQ was formed in 1921 (Iraq became a republic in 1958) and is of international importance because of its rich oil fields, but its status in the world is enhanced by the rich archaeological finds of the incredibly distant past. See Henri Frankfort, *The Birth of Civilization in the Near East* (1951, repr. 1968); Georges Roux, *Ancient Iraq* (1966); S. N. Kramer, *Cradle of Civilization* (1967); David Oakes, *Studies in the Ancient History of Northern Iraq* (1968); Leo Oppenheim, *Ancient Mesopotamia* (1968).

Mesopotamian art: see ASSYRIAN ART; HITTITE ART; PHOENICIAN ART; SUMERIAN AND BABYLONIAN ART.

mesosphere: see ATMOSPHERE.

Mesozoic era (mĕz"əzō'ĭk), (Gr.,=middle life), major division of geologic time (see GEOLOGIC ERAS, table). Great crustal disturbances that marked the close of the Paleozoic and the beginning of the Mesozoic eras brought about drastic changes in the topography of North America. The Appalachian geosyncline, or downward thrust of the earth's crust, was replaced by the Appalachian Mts., and the eastern part of the continent was elevated and exempt from submergence during most of the era. The Appalachians were subjected to erosion, the products of which were deposited along the Atlantic coast, which had become a lowland region, or in the ocean beyond. Aside from the Appalachians, the other positive (consistently dry) areas of the continent were the Canadian Shield, the Antilles areas, and a mountain range elevated in part of the Cordilleran geosyncline. The negative (always or often submerged) areas were the Pacific geosyncline of the west coast; the Colorado geosyncline, successor to the Cordilleran geosyncline and occupying much of the western interior of the continent; and the Mexican geosyncline, which formed at the beginning of the Mesozoic. The Atlantic Ocean began to open along an extensive rift zone that became an underwater mountain range called the Mid-Atlantic Ridge, separating the Americas from Europe and Africa (see SEA FLOOR SPREADING). The life of the Mesozoic was dominated by the reptiles that evolved into the large land-dwelling dinosaurs of the Jurassic and Cretaceous periods. Flying reptiles and birds first appeared during the Mesozoic. Mammals probably evolved from some common ancestor of the reptiles early in the Triassic Period, but were subordinate to the reptiles until the end of the era, when the dominance of reptiles was ended by the extinction of the dinosaurs. Conifers dominated the plant life, with modern pines and sequoias first appearing. Flowering plants, deciduous trees, and grasses also appeared during this era. With an estimated duration of 160 million years, the Mesozoic was less than half as long as the Paleozoic.

Mesquite (məskēt'), city (1970 pop. 55,131), Dallas co., N Texas, a suburb of Dallas; inc. 1887. The leading manufacture is telephone equipment. A junior college is there.

mesquite (mĭskēt', mĕs'kēt), any plant of the genus *Prosopis,* leguminous spiny trees or shrubs of the family Leguminosae (PULSE family), native to tropical and subtropical regions. The seed pods of *P. juliflora,* a common mesquite, contain a sweet pulp eaten by numerous mammals, including domestic livestock. The mesquite still provides a staple food for many Indians and Mexicans, who grind the bean pod into meal for bread and also use it to make a fermented beverage. The flowers are an excellent honey source. The stems yield a gum somewhat like gum arabic; the very durable wood is valued for fence posts and fuel. Mesquites, which grow in barren sites unsuited to most crops, are good water indicators; their roots may penetrate 50 to 60 ft (15–18 m) into the earth to find moisture. Mesquites are a characteristic part of the vegetation in arid western regions of the Americas (e.g., the CHAPARRAL of the SW United States). Mesquite is classified in the division MAGNOLIOPHYTA, class Magnoliopsida, order Rosales, family Leguminosae.

Messalina (Valeria Messalina)(mĕsəlī'nə), d. A.D. 48, Roman empress, wife of CLAUDIUS I. She was the mother of his children, BRITANNICUS and Octavia. Her reputation for greed and lust was supposedly unknown to her husband until, in Claudius' absence, she publicly married her lover Caius Silius. A political plot was apparently involved, and Claudius' secretary Narcissus informed the emperor. Messalina was killed.

Messana: see MESSINA, Italy.

Messene (mĕsē'nē), ancient city, central Messenia (now Messinías prov.), Greece. It was founded (c.369 B.C.) under Theban auspices to be a capital and fort for the Messenians, whom the battle of Leuctra had just freed from the Spartans. The ruins, notably of the city walls dating from the 4th cent. B.C., are well preserved. Modern Messíni is at some distance.

Messenia (mĕsē'nēə), ancient region of SW Greece, in the Peloponnesus and corresponding to the modern nome of Messinías. Excavation has revealed an important center of Mycenaean culture at PYLOS dating from the 13th cent. B.C. From the 8th cent. B.C. the Messenians were engaged in a series of revolts against expanding Sparta. After the First Messenian War the Spartans annexed (c.700 B.C.) the eastern part of Messenia. With the Second Messenian War the remaining inhabitants were reduced (7th cent. B.C.) to helots. The Third Messenian War (464–459 B.C.) was a failure for Messenia, but very costly to Sparta. The battle of LEUCTRA (371 B.C.) freed Messenia, and Messene was founded (c.369 B.C.) as the capital. The region gave its name to Messina, Sicily, because of an influx of Messenian colonists (c.490 B.C.). See C. A. Roebuck, *A History of Messenia from 369 to 146 B.C.* (1941); *The Minnesota Messenia Expedition*, ed. by W. A. McDonald and G. R. Rapp (1972).

Messiaen, Olivier (ôlēvyā' mĕsyäN'), 1908–, French composer and organist. Messiaen was a pupil of Paul Dukas at the Paris Conservatory. He became organist of La Trinité, Paris, in 1931 and taught at the Schola Cantorum and the École normale de Musique. He was appointed professor of harmony at the Paris Conservatory in 1941. Messiaen's music is remarkably original and personal, often based on scale formulas of his own invention or on his studies of Oriental music and birdsong. His works reflect his religious mysticism, which is also expounded in his didactic prose works. Messiaen's major works include *L'Ascension* (1935), for orchestra; *La Nativité du Seigneur* (1936), *Le Banquet céleste* (1936), and *Les Corps glorieux* (1939), for organ; *Quartet for the End of Time* (1941); *Visions de l'amen* (1943), for two pianos; *Oiseaux exotiques* (1956); *Chronochromie* (1960); *The Transfiguration* (1969), an oratorio; and *Et exspecto resurrectionem mortuorum*. He has written masses, songs, and much chamber music. His symphony in 10 movements, *Turangalila* (1949) is considered the most grandiose expression of his theories. See his *Technique of my Mystical Language* (tr. 1957).

Messiah (məsī'ə) or **Messias** (məsī'əs) [Heb.,=anointed], in Judaism, a man who would be sent by God to restore Israel and reign righteously for all mankind. The idea developed among the Jews especially in their adversity, and such a conception is clearly indicated in Isaiah 9. Messianic expectations generally focused on a kingly figure of the house of David, who would be born in Bethlehem (Micah 5.2). However, a second Messianic figure, the Messiah son of Joseph, was said to precede the Messiah son of David, preparing the way for him by combating the enemies of Israel and reuniting the twelve tribes for the return to Jerusalem where he would die in combat with the enemies of God before the final redemption under the Davidic Messiah. Jesus Christ considered himself, and is considered by Christians, to be the promised Messiah to whom the whole Old Testament pointed; the name Christ is Greek for Messiah (Mat. 16.16). The Christian ideal of the Messiah is fundamentally different from the early Jewish conception in the aspect of suffering; the common idea of Jesus' time was that the Messiah should reign in glory as an earthly king, a political figure sent by God, not a savior in the Christian sense. The expectation of the second coming of Jesus is similar to the Jewish belief in the Messianic advent. The idea of a messiah, a redeemer sent by God, is common among many different peoples throughout history and may reflect a universal psychological pattern. Ancient Middle Eastern texts foretell the coming of savior-kings. Buddhists, Zoroastrians, and Confucians believe in the redemption of mankind, or the advent of a golden age, through the arrival of a Holy One. In Islam, the coming of the MAHDI is closely related to the messiah concept. Other peoples also believe in messiah figures; among the North American Indians, WOVOKA is the most famous. See W. D. Wallis, *Messiahs, Their Role in Civilization* (1943); Joseph Klausner, *The Messianic Idea in Israel* (1955); A. H. Silver, *A History of Messianic Speculation in Israel* (1955); Vittorio Lanternari, *The Religions of the Oppressed: A Study of Modern Messianic Cults* (1963); and Gershom Scholem, *The Messianic Idea in Judaism* (1971).

Messier catalog (mĕsyā'), systematic list of nebulas and star clusters. A first list, compiled and published in 1771 by Charles Messier, contained 45 objects. The final list, published in 1784, contained 103 objects; some of these were later removed from the list. Of the remaining objects, about 50 are extragalactic nebulas, i.e., galaxies. Designations from Messier's catalog are frequently used to refer to the brighter nebulas and star clusters; for example, M31 is the Andromeda Galaxy, M1 the Crab Nebula, M42 the Great Nebula in Orion, and M45 the Pleiades.

Messina (mās-sē'nä), city (1971 pop. 275,623), capital of Messina prov., NE Sicily, Italy, on the Strait of Messina, opposite the Italian mainland. It is a busy seaport and a commercial and industrial center. Manufactures include processed food, chemicals, and pharmaceuticals. Founded (late 8th cent. B.C.) by Greek colonists and named Zancle, the city was captured (5th cent. B.C.) by Anaxilas of Rhegium and renamed Messana. It became involved in several wars, particularly against Syracuse and Carthage, and was taken in 282 B.C. by mercenaries called Mamertines. The Romans answered an appeal for help from the Mamertines and intervened in Sicily, thus precipitating the first of the PUNIC WARS. Messina was subsequently allied with Rome, and it shared the history of the rest of SICILY. The city was conquered by the Arabs in the late 9th cent. A.D. but was liberated by the Normans in 1061. It developed a thriving silk industry (which declined in the 18th cent.). Messina later came under the rule of the Angevins, the Aragonese, and the Spanish Bourbons. A heroic insurrection against the Bourbons took place from 1774 to 1778. Garibaldi took Messina in July, 1860, but the Bourbon garrison resisted in the citadel until March, 1861. The city suffered a severe plague in 1743 and major earthquakes in 1783 and 1908. The earthquake of Dec. 28, 1908, destroyed 90% of Messina's buildings, including fine churches and palaces, and cost about 80,000 lives; afterward the city was completely rebuilt in conformity with standards for quake-resistant construction. In World War II, the Sicilian campaign ended with the fall of Messina to the Allies on Aug. 17, 1943. Of interest in the city are the Norman-Romanesque cathedral (rebuilt after 1908) and the National Museum. Messina has a university, founded in 1548.

Messina, Strait of, channel, c.20 mi (32 km) long and from 2 to 10 mi (3.2–16 km) wide, separating the Italian peninsula from Sicily and connecting the Ionian and Tyrrhenian seas. Reggio di Calabria, SW Italy, and Messina, NE Sicily, are the main ports. A ferry crosses the strait from Messina to Villa San Giovanni. There is much spearfishing. The currents, whirlpools, and winds of the strait, which still hamper navigation, gave rise in ancient times to many legends about its dangers to navigators (see SCYLLA).

Messmer, Pierre (pyĕr mĕsmā'), 1916–, French political leader. In World War II he fought with the Free French forces before joining General De Gaulle's staff. After the war he held several overseas administrative posts. A devoted supporter of De Gaulle, he served (1960–69) as minister of defense until De Gaulle's resignation as French president. In 1971 he became minister of overseas departments and territories. Considered a hard-line Gaullist, he was appointed by French President Pompidou to replace Jacques Chaban-Delmas as premier in 1972. He was succeeded in 1974 by Jacques Chirac.

Messys, Quentin: see MASSYS, QUENTIN.

mesta (mā'stä), association of Spanish sheep farmers, formed to regulate sheep raising and to prevent cultivation of pastureland. Its date of origin is uncertain, but by 1273 Alfonso X of Castile formally recognized its long-established privileges, which were confirmed and extended by his successors. The mesta gradually escaped local jurisdiction and came under direct supervision of the crown. It prospered, especially in the 15th and 16th cent., by exporting wool from its highly prized MERINO SHEEP. The mesta yielded large revenues to the crown, but its monopoly of large areas of land exhausted the soil and contributed to the economic decline of Spain by preventing intensive agriculture. Attacked by reforming ministers in the 18th cent., it was not abolished until 1837. See studies by Julius Klein (1920) and W. H. Dusenberry (1963).

mestizo (māstē'sō) [Span.,=mixture], person of mixed race, particularly in Latin American countries a person of European (Spanish or Portuguese) and American Indian descent. The mestizos constitute a large part of the population in those countries; they are in various places also called by other names, e.g., ladinos in Guatemala, caboclos in Brazil. The word is primarily applied to a mixture of racial strains (including at times Negro elements), but it has acquired social and cultural connotations; it may be applied to pure-blooded Indians who adopt European dress and customs. All persons of mixed race are called mestizos in the Philippines. See MISCEGENATION.

Meštrović, Ivan (ē'vän mĕsh'trōvyĭch), 1883–1962, Yugoslav sculptor. He was a shepherd and then an apprentice to a marble cutter. At 17 he went to the Vienna Academy, and then to Rome. His figures and reliefs were strongly influenced by Rodin and classical Greek sculpture. Many of Meštrović's sculptures are of biblical scenes, often in wood. He traveled to the United States in 1946 and taught at Syracuse and Notre Dame universities. See study by Laurence Schmeckebier (1959).

metabolism, sum of all biochemical processes involved in life. Two subcategories of metabolism are anabolism, the building up of complex organic molecules from simpler precursors, and catabolism, the breakdown of complex substances into simpler molecules, often accompanied by the release of energy. Organic molecules involved in these processes are called METABOLITES, and their interconversions are catalyzed by ENZYMES. The transformation of one molecule into another, and then into another and another in sequence, is termed a metabolic pathway; the intermediates in these pathways are often identified with the aid of a chemical TRACER. Exercise, food, and environmental temperature influence metabolism. Basal metabolism is the heat produced by an organism at rest; it represents the minimum amount of energy required to maintain life at normal body temperature. The measurement of basal metabolism (the basal metabolic rate) can be made by noting the amounts of oxygen and carbon dioxide exchanged during breathing under certain standard conditions, i.e., complete rest in a room temperature of 68°F (20°C), 12 to 14 hours after ingestion of food. A less cumbersome method of estimating basal metabolic rate involves the quantitative assay of the hormone THYROXINE, known to regulate the body's rate of metabolism. Often the word metabolism is associated with a particular organic compound or class of compounds, as in phenylalanine metabolism or amino acid metabolism. In this usage the word refers to the sum of all interconversions, both anabolic and catabolic, in which the particular compound or class of compounds is involved.

metabolite, organic compound which is a starting material in, an intermediate in, or an end product of METABOLISM. Starting materials are substances, usually small and of simple structure, absorbed by the organism as food. These include the vitamins and essential amino acids. They can be used to construct more complex molecules, or they can be broken down into simpler ones. Intermediary metabolites are by far the most common; they may be synthesized from other metabolites, perhaps used to make more complex substances, or broken down into simpler compounds, often with the release of chemical energy. For example, glucose, perhaps the single most important metabolite, can be synthesized in a process called gluconeogenesis, can be polymerized to form starch or glycogen, and can be broken down during glycolysis in order to obtain chemical energy. End products of metabolism are the final result of the breakdown of other metabolites and are excreted from the organism without further change; they usually cannot be used to synthesize other metabolites. Urea, for example, is an end product of protein degradation in man, the other primates, and the Dalmatian dog. Carbon dioxide is usually thought of as an end product of carbohydrate, protein, and fat degradation in aerobic organisms, although technically, carbon dioxide, as carbonic acid, can participate in the biosynthesis of some substances, particularly in plants. Complex substances such as proteins, although end products of a synthetic process, can almost always be broken down again and are usually not considered to be true end products of metabolism. A compound that closely resembles a metabolite in molecular structure but is metabolically inactive is called an antimetabolite; such a substance is often used as a drug in the treatment of malignant disease. When introduced into the body, it is mistaken by the cell for the metabolite it simulates, thus preventing the cell from using the genuine substance necessary to its life and growth. It is difficult to design molecules so that they will be metabolic poisons for malignant cells and not for normal cells as well. Folic acid (see COENZYME) antagonists such as Aminopterin and amethopterin (Methotrexate) are used in the treatment of acute leukemias in children. The purine antagonist mercaptopurine is also used for the treatment of acute leukemia, while azathioprine (Imuran) is used to prevent the rejection of transplanted organs. Pyrimidine antagonists used in cancer chemotherapy include fluorouracil and fluorodeoxyuridine. Most of the agents are designed to halt cell division in rapidly dividing malignant cells by the disruption of the metabolism of purines and pyrimidines, two classes of compounds necessary for NUCLEIC ACID synthesis and hence necessary for cell division.

metal, chemical ELEMENT displaying certain properties by which it is normally distinguished from a nonmetal, notably its metallic luster, the capacity to lose electrons and form a positive ION, and the ability to conduct heat and electricity. The metals comprise about two thirds of the known elements (see PERIODIC TABLE). Some elements, e.g., arsenic and antimony, exhibit both metallic and nonmetallic properties and are called metalloids. The metals differ so widely in hardness, ductility (the potentiality of being drawn into wire), malleability, tensile strength, density, and melting point that a definite line of distinction between them and the NONMETALS cannot be drawn. Furthermore, although all metals form crystals, this is also characteristic of certain nonmetals, e.g., carbon and sulfur. The hardest elemental metal is chromium; the softest, cesium. Copper, gold, platinum, and silver are especially ductile. Most metals are malleable; gold, silver, copper, tin, and aluminum are extremely so. Some metals exhibiting great tensile strength are copper, iron, and platinum. Three metals (lithium, potassium, and sodium) have densities of less than one gram per cubic centimeter at ordinary temperatures and are therefore lighter than water. Some heavy metals, beginning with the most dense, are osmium, iridium, platinum, gold, tungsten, uranium, tantalum, mercury, hafnium, lead, and silver. For many industrial uses, the melting points of the metals are important. Tungsten fuses, or melts, only at extremely high temperatures (3370°C.), while cesium has a melting point of 28.5°C. The best metallic conductor of electricity is silver. Copper, gold, and aluminum follow in the order named. All metals are relatively good conductors of heat; silver, copper, and aluminum are especially conductive. The metal uranium is used in reactor piles to generate steam and electric power. Some of the radioactive metals not found in nature are produced by nuclear bombardment. On the basis of their ability to be oxidized, i.e., lose electrons, metals can be arranged in a list called the ELECTROMOTIVE SERIES, or replacement series. Metals toward the beginning of the series, like cesium and lithium, are more readily oxidized than those toward the end, like silver and gold. In general, a metal will replace any other metal, or hydrogen, in a compound that it precedes in the series, and under ordinary circumstances it will be replaced by any metal, or hydrogen, that it follows. Metals fall into groups in the PERIODIC TABLE determined by similar arrangements of their orbital ELECTRONS and a consequent similarity in chemical properties. Groups of similar metals include the ALKALI METALS (Group Ia in the periodic table), the ALKALINE EARTH METALS (Group IIa in the periodic table), and the RARE-EARTH METALS (LANTHANIDE and ACTINIDE series). Most metals other than the alkali metals and the alkaline earth metals are called transition metals (see TRANSITION ELEMENTS). The oxidation states, or VALENCE, of the metal ions vary from +1 for the alkali metals to as much as +7 for some transition metals. Chemically, the metals differ from the nonmetals in that they form positive ions and basic oxides and hydroxides. Upon exposure to moist air, a great many undergo corrosion, i.e., enter into a chemical reaction; e.g., iron rusts when exposed to moist air, the oxygen of the atmosphere uniting with the metal to form the oxide of the metal. Aluminum and zinc do not appear to be affected, but in fact a thin coating of the oxide is formed almost at once, stopping further action and appearing unnoticeable because of its close resemblance to the metal. Tin, lead, and copper react slowly under ordinary conditions. Silver is affected by compounds such as sulfur dioxide and becomes tarnished when exposed to air containing them. The metals are combined with nonmetals in their salts, as in carbides, carbonates, chlorides, nitrates, phosphates, silicates, sulfides, and sulfates. They are also mixed with each other in definite amounts to form ALLOYS. A mixture of mercury and another metal is called an AMALGAM. BRONZE is an alloy of copper and tin, and BRASS contains copper and zinc. STEEL is an alloy of iron and other metals with carbon added for hardness. Some metals, including copper, tin, iron, lead, gold, silver, and mercury, were known to the ancients; copper is probably the oldest known metal. Although a few metals occur uncombined in nature, the great majority are found combined in their ORES. The extraction of metals from their ores is called METALLURGY. Since metals form positive ions readily, i.e., they donate their orbital electrons, they are used in chemistry as reducing agents (see OXIDATION AND REDUCTION). Finely divided metals or their oxides are often used as surface CATALYSTS. Iron and iron oxides catalyze the conversion of hydrogen and nitrogen to ammonia in the HABER PROCESS. Finely divided catalytic platinum or nickel is used in the HYDROGENATION of unsaturated oils. Metal ions orient electron-rich groups called LIGANDS around themselves, forming COMPLEX IONS. Metal ions are important in many biological functions, including ENZYME and COENZYME action, NUCLEIC ACID synthesis, and transport across membranes. For the uses of specific metals, see separate articles.

metallic bond: see CHEMICAL BOND; METAL.

metallurgy (mĕt'əlûr"jē), science of extracting metals from their ores. The processes employed depend upon the chemical nature of the ORE to be treated and upon the properties of the METAL to be extracted. When an ore has a low percentage of the desired metal, a method of physical concentration must be used before the extraction process begins. In one such method, the ore is crushed and placed in a machine where, by shaking, the heavier particles containing the metal are separated from the lighter rock particles by gravity. Another method is the FLOTATION PROCESS, used commonly for copper sulfide ores. In certain cases (as when gold, silver, or occasionally copper occur "free," i.e., uncombined chemically in sand or rock), mechanical or ore dressing methods alone are sufficient to obtain relatively pure metal. Waste material is washed away or separated by screening and gravity; the concentrated ore is then treated by various chemical processes. Gold and silver are often removed from the impurities associated with them by treatment with mercury, in which they are soluble. Another method for the separation of gold and silver is the so-called CYANIDE PROCESS. The Parkes process is used to free silver from lead ores. Since almost all the metals are found combined with other elements in nature, chemical reactions are required to set them free. These chemical processes are classified as pyrometallurgy, electrometallurgy, and hydrometallurgy. Pyrometallurgy, or the use of heat for the treatment of an ore, includes SMELTING and roasting. If the ore is an oxide, it is heated with a reducing agent, such as carbon in the form of coke or coal; the oxygen of the ore combines with the carbon and is removed in carbon dioxide, a gas (see OXIDATION AND REDUCTION). The waste material in the ore is called gangue; it is removed by means of a substance called a flux which, when heated, combines with it to form a molten mass called slag. Being lighter than the metal, the slag floats on it and can be skimmed or drawn off. The flux used depends upon the chemical nature of the ore; limestone is usually employed with a siliceous gangue. A sulfide ore is commonly roasted, i.e., heated in air. The metal of the ore combines with oxygen of the air to form an oxide, and the sulfur of the ore also combines with oxygen to form sulfur dioxide, which, being a gas, passes off. The metallic oxide is then treated with a reducing agent. When a carbonate ore is heated, the oxide of the metal is formed, and carbon dioxide is given off; the oxide is then reduced. Electrometallurgy includes the preparation of certain active metals, such as aluminum, calcium, barium, magnesium, potassium, and sodium, by ELECTROLYSIS: a fused compound, commonly the chloride, is treated, the metal collecting at the cathode. Hydrometallurgy, sometimes called leaching, involves the selective dissolution of metals from their ores. For example, certain copper oxide and carbonate ores are treated with dilute sulfuric acid, forming water-soluble copper sulfate. The metal is recovered by electrolysis of the solution. If the metal obtained from the ore still contains impurities, special REFINING processes are required. Modern metallurgical research is concerned with the preparation of radioactive metals, with obtaining metals economically from low-grade ores, with obtaining and refining rare metals hitherto not used, and with the formulation of alloys. The methods for the treatment of ores are quite diverse; see ALUMINUM, COPPER, GOLD, IRON, LEAD, NICKEL, SILVER, TIN, and ZINC for the special procedures followed. See Edward Slade, *Metals in the Modern World* (1968); P. S. Hurd, *Metallic Materials* (1968); D. K. Allen, *Metallurgy Theory and Practice* (1969); E. N. Simons, *Outline of Metallurgy* (1969).

metalwork. Copper, gold, and silver were probably fashioned into ornaments and amulets as early as the Neolithic period. GOLDWORK and SILVERWORK have since employed the talents of leading craftsmen and artists in making JEWELRY, plate, inlays, and sculpture. The first great advance in metalworking occurred when techniques for making BRONZE SCULPTURE were developed during the Bronze Age. Brass, an alloy of copper with zinc, came into use later (see BRASSES, MONUMENTAL; BRASSES, ORNAMENTAL). The Iron Age provided a cheaper medium used chiefly for tools and ornamental IRONWORK until modern times, when improved methods, alloys, and machinery made iron available and essential to the industrial and structural trades. PEWTER, tin, and lead have been used in industrial and art metalwork. Methods of shaping metals include drawing, spinning, hammering, and casting; various decorative processes include chasing, DAMASCENING, EMBOSSING, ENAMEL work, FILIGREE, GILDING, INLAYING, NIELLO, and REPOUSSÉ.

metamorphic rocks: see ROCK.

metamorphism, in geology, process of change in the structure, texture, or composition of ROCKS caused by agents of heat, deforming pressure, hot, chemically active fluids, or a combination of these, acting while the rock being changed remains essentially in the solid state. Theoretically, rocks are formed when their constituents are in equilibrium with ambient physical conditions. If the conditions are changed by movements in the earth's crust or by igneous activity, metamorphism occurs to reestablish equilibrium. Metamorphism results in obvious changes in the physical character of the rock mass. In general, a metamorphic rock is coarser and has a higher density and lower porosity than the rock from which it was formed. High pressure and temperature can result in recrystallization of the minerals forming the rock with little or no chemical change, causing mineral grains to interpenetrate and pore spaces between grains to be filled with mineral matter. For example, a limestone will recrystallize to marble consisting of tightly interlocking crystals of calcite. Alteration of texture commonly results in a rearrangement of mineral particles into a parallel alignment, called foliation, as a result of directed pressure stress. Foliation is probably the single most characteristic property of metamorphic rocks. Thus, slate is a rock in which there has been barely enough recrystallization of fine-grained sedimentary rocks such as shale to give the rock a tendency to break along smooth planes. Slate breakage along planes of foliation is termed slaty cleavage. Schist is formed when tabular minerals, such as hornblende, graphite, mica, or talc dominate. These are aligned and tightly packed in a parallel fashion, not separated by bands of alternating minerals. Other minerals in schists are enclosed by tiny pods of the platy minerals. Gneiss is a metamorphic rock with coarse parallel bands of alternating light- and dark-colored minerals. Chemical changes occurring during metamorphism tend to rearrange the chemical constituents into assemblages stable in their new environment, thus often forming new minerals of essentially the same chemical composition as those occurring in the rock prior to metamorphism. For example, hornblende can be changed into garnet or pyroxene. The mineral composition of rocks may also be altered by the addition of new elements or by the removal of elements formerly present through the action of circulating liquids or gases or by recrystallization under pressure. Local metamorphism of significant extent occurs when a large igneous mass is intruded into older rock. Some of the changes that occur in the older rock are due simply to the heat radiated from the igneous mass and to the pressures it creates. More extensive alterations are produced by the fluids and gases given off by the igneous mass. Metamorphic rocks of this type rarely show foliation. Metamorphism on a grander scale, called regional, or dynamic, metamorphism, accompanies mountain-building activity. Metamorphic rocks pervade regions that have been subjected to intense pressures and temperatures during the development of mountain chains along boundaries between crustal plates. Large scale, intense regional metamorphism is particularly great in the "roots" of these mountains, which were at considerable depths when the pressures forming the mountains were active. These kinds of metamorphic rocks are most commonly exposed in old mountain chains, like the Blue Ridge Mts., that have largely eroded away with time, leaving only disturbed structure and regional metamorphic rocks. A broad-scale, relatively gentle regional metamorphism is represented by gneisses, schists, and marbles exposed in Manhattan, the Bronx, and Westchester co. in New York and in NW New Jersey. These represent early Paleozoic or older rocks metamorphosed several times in the past.

metamorphosis (mĕt"əmôr'fəsĭs) [Gr.,=transformation], in zoology, term used to describe a form of development from egg to adult in which there is a series of distinct stages. Many INSECTS, amphibians, mollusks, crustaceans, and fishes undergo metamorphosis, which may involve a change in habitat, e.g., from water to land. Metamorphosis is called complete when there is no suggestion of the adult form in the larval stage, e.g., in the transformation from TADPOLE to FROG or from LARVA to PUPA to adult in bees and butterflies. When the successive larval stages resemble the adult (as in the grasshopper and the lobster), metamorphosis is called incomplete.

metaphor [Gr.,=transfer], in rhetoric, a figure of speech in which one class of things is referred to as if it belonged to another class. Whereas a simile states that *A* is like *B*, a metaphor states that *A* is *B* or substitutes *B* for *A*. Some metaphors are explicit, like Shakespeare's line from *As You Like It*: "All the world's a stage." A metaphor can also be implicit, as in Shakespeare's Sonnet X, where old age is indicated by a description of autumn:

That time of year thou mayst in me behold
Where yellow leaves, or none, or few, do hang
Upon those boughs which shake against the cold,
Bare ruined choirs, where once the sweet birds sang.

A dead metaphor, such as "the arm of a chair," is one that has become so common that it is no longer considered a metaphor.

metaphysical poets, name given to a group of English lyric poets of the 17th cent. The term was first used by Samuel Johnson (1744). The hallmark of their poetry is the metaphysical conceit (a figure of speech that employs unusual and paradoxical images), a reliance on intellectual wit, learned imagery, and subtle argument. Although this method was by no means new, these men infused new life into English poetry by the freshness and originality of their approach. The most important metaphysical poets are John Donne, George Herbert, Henry Vaughan, Thomas Traherne, Abraham Cowley, Richard Crashaw, and Andrew Marvell. Their work has considerably influenced the poetry of the 20th cent. See studies by H. J. C. Grierson (1934), T. Spencer and M. Van Doren (1939), H. C. White (1936, repr. 1962), J. F. Bennett (3d ed. 1964), H. Gardner, ed. (1967), G. Williamson (1967), and Patricia Beer (1972).

metaphysics (mĕtəfĭz'ĭks), branch of philosophy concerned with the ultimate nature of existence. It perpetuates the *Metaphysics* of Aristotle, a collection of treatises placed after the *Physics* [Gr. *metaphysics*=after *physics*] and treating what Aristotle called the First Philosophy. The principal area of metaphysical speculation is generally called ontology and is the study of the ultimate nature of being. However, philosophical theology and cosmology are also usually considered branches of metaphysics. In the history of philosophy there have been many great metaphysical systems. One of the most carefully constructed systems is that of the scholastic philosophy (see SCHOLASTICISM), which essentially is based on Aristotle's metaphysical system. In the 17th cent. the great rationalistic systems of René Descartes, Baruch Spinoza, Nicolas Malebranche, and G. W. von Leibniz were developed. They were followed in the 18th cent. by Immanuel Kant's critical philosophy, which demonstrated the impossibility of a scientific metaphysics. This was in turn succeeded by the metaphysics of German idealism (of J. G. Fichte, Friedrich von Schelling, and G. W. F. Hegel). Since the middle of the 19th cent. the dominant philosophical trend has been in the direction of positivism, which denies the validity of any metaphysical assertion. This is clearly reflected in the contemporary movement called LOGICAL POSITIVISM. See R. T. De George, *Classical and Contemporary Metaphysics* (1962); A. E. Taylor, *Elements of Metaphysics* (1956, repr. 1961); Bruce Wilshire, *Metaphysics: An Introduction to Philosophy* (1969).

Metapontum (mĕtəpŏn'təm), ancient city of MAGNA GRAECIA, on the Gulf of Taranto, SE Italy. Settled by Greeks, c.7th cent. B.C., it flourished and gave refuge to Pythagoreans expelled from Crotona. Pythagoras taught and died there. There are remains of a Doric temple, called Tavole Paladine, and other ruins.

Metasequoia: see SEQUOIA.

Metastasio, Pietro (pyĕ'trō mātästä'zēō), 1698–1782, Italian poet and librettist, whose original name was Pietro Bonaventura Trapassi. A prodigy at poetic improvisation, he was adopted, educated, and renamed by the jurist and critic Gravini, who left him a fortune that he quickly wasted. Befriended by the singer La Romanina (Marianna Bulgarelli), his fame and fortune increased. He became court poet at Vienna in 1729. He wrote melodious lyric verse; a masque, *The Gardens of the Hesperides* (1721–22); and librettos of many operas, including *Didone abbandonata* (1723), *Artaxerxes* (1730, tr. 1761), *La clemenza di Tito* (1734, tr. 1811), and *The Shepherd King* (1751, tr. 1765). These librettos were set to music by many composers, including Gluck, Handel, Mozart, Pergolesi, and Rossini. Metastasio, with Apostolo Zeno, whom he succeeded as imperial poet laureate at Vienna, created the rigid *opera seria* (see OPERA). His melodrama *Attilio Regolo* (1750) is generally considered his masterpiece. See his *Dramas and Other Poems* (3 vol., tr. 1800).

Metauro (mätou'rō), river of the Marches, c.68 mi (110 km) long, rising in the Etruscan Apennines, central Italy, from a double source (the Meta and the Auro) and flowing NE into the Adriatic Sea near Fano. On its banks the Romans defeated (207 B.C.) the Carthaginians under Hasdrubal in the Second Punic War.

Metaxas, John (mĭtăk'səs, Gr. mä'täksäs''), 1871–1941, Greek general and statesman. A career soldier, he served in the Greco-Turkish War of 1897 and in the Balkan Wars of 1912–13, in which he was assistant chief of staff. He was later chief of staff, but was exiled (1917) as pro-German when Greece joined the Allies in World War I. He returned in 1920, led a coup d'etat, and was exiled again (1923–24). He was prominent as a royalist politician and held several ministerial posts from 1928 to 1936. After the monarchy had been reestablished (1935) in Greece, Metaxas became premier on April 13, 1936. His administration became a reactionary dictatorship after he dissolved parliament in Aug., 1936. In 1938 he was named premier for life. After the Italian attack on Greece (Oct., 1940) he successfully directed Greek resistance. His death was considered even by his opponents to be a blow to the Greek cause.

Metazoa (mĕt''əzō'ə), subkingdom of the animal kingdom, comprising the many phyla of multicellular animals; it is distinguished from the subkingdom Protozoa, which contains a single phylum, PROTOZOA, of unicellular animals. In some schemes of classification there are three subkingdoms: the metazoan animals are divided into the Parazoa, which includes only the phylum PORIFERA, or sponges, and the Eumetazoa, the more complex multicellular animals.

Metcalfe, Charles Theophilus Metcalfe, 1st **Baron,** 1785–1846, British colonial administrator, b. India. He entered the Indian civil service as a young man, rose quickly, and was provisional governor-general in 1835. He later served (1839–42) as governor of Jamaica. He was appointed governor-general of Canada in 1843. His experience in India and Jamaica had little prepared Metcalfe for service in a colony in which the movement for self-government was strongly under way. In 1843 his ministers, headed by Robert Baldwin and Louis Hippolyte LaFontaine of the Reform parties, resigned. He formed a Conservative administration, and a general election resulted in his favor. Impaired in health, he retired in 1845, the same year in which he was created a baron. See biography by E. J. Thompson (1937); D. N. Panigrahi, *Charles Metcalfe in India* (1968).

Metchnikoff, Élie (ālē' mĕch'nĭkôf), 1845–1916, Russian biologist. He studied in Russia and Germany, lectured at the Univ. of Odessa, and, after working with Pasteur in Paris, became (1904) deputy director of the Pasteur Institute there. He introduced the theory of phagocytosis, i.e., that certain white blood cells are able to engulf and destroy harmful substances such as bacteria. For his work on immunity he shared with Paul Ehrlich the 1908 Nobel Prize in Physiology and Medicine. He developed a theory that lactic-acid bacteria (*B. acidophilus*) in the digestive tract could, by preventing putrefaction, prolong life; and with P. P. É. Roux he experimented with calomel ointment as a treatment for syphilis. His writings include *Immunity in Infectious Diseases* (1905) and *The Nature of Man* (1938). See biography by Olga Metchnikova (1921).

Metellus (mĕtĕl'əs), ancient Roman family of the plebeian gens Caecilia. It was one of the families that controlled the senate. **Lucius Caecilius Metellus,** d. c.221 B.C., consul (251 B.C.), fought in the First Punic War. He was pontifex maximus (from 243) and was said to have been blinded (241) in rescuing the Palladium from the burning temple of Vesta. His grandson, **Quintus Caecilius Metellus Macedonicus,** d. 115 B.C., was an important general in the final pacification of Greece (146). He was consul in 143 and defeated the Celtiberians in N Spain. As censor (131) he proposed that marriage be made compulsory for Roman men, to increase the birthrate. **Quintus Caecilius Metellus Numidicus,** d. 91? B.C., nephew of Macedonicus, was a leader of the senatorial party. As consul (109 B.C.) he conducted the Numidian War against Jugurtha. He antagonized his legate, MARIUS, who later received his command. While serving as censor (102), Numidicus tried to remove Lucius Appuleius Saturninus, of the popular party, from the senate. In 100 B.C., Saturninus and Marius took revenge by passing a law requiring senators to swear acceptance of an agrarian law; they tricked Numidicus into refusing to swear and succeeded in having him exiled for it. His son, **Quintus Caecilius Metellus Pius,** d. c.63 B.C., named Pius because of his filial devotion during his father's exile, continued his father's opposition to Marius. As praetor (89 B.C.) he fought in the Social War; in the civil war that followed he was called to Rome by the senate to defend the city against Marius and Lucius Cornelius CINNA. Foreseeing its capitulation, he fled to Africa, but he returned (83 B.C.) to join SULLA. He defeated the Marians in Umbria and Cisalpine Gaul and became (80 B.C.) consul with Sulla. In his proconsulship in Spain (79 B.C.) he began an eight-year war with SERTORIUS, in which he was continually unsuccessful, in spite of the aid brought by Pompey. After the murder of Sertorius (72 B.C.), Metellus won at Italica and Segovia. For his adopted son, **Quintus Caecilius Metellus Pius Scipio,** see under SCIPIO. A great-grandson of Metellus Macedonicus was **Quintus Caecilius Metellus Celer,** d. 59 B.C. He fought in Asia under Pompey and was praetor (63 B.C.) in Cicero's consulship. He was consul in 60 B.C. Celer was a leader in the stubborn defense of every senatorial prerogative. This policy led him to oppose Pompey in every detail, thus driving Pompey into the fateful alliance with Julius Caesar. Celer's wife, CLODIA, was said to have poisoned him. **Quintus Caecilius Metellus Nepos,** d. c.55 B.C., brother of Celer, served with Pompey (67–64 B.C.). He supported Pompey against the senatorial party and was (63 B.C.) his candidate for the tribunate. He was elected with Cato but had to flee Rome temporarily to escape senatorial hatred. In his consulship (57 B.C.) he allowed his sworn enemy, Cicero, to return from exile, chiefly to curry favor with Julius Caesar. His proconsulship (56 B.C.) was in Hither Spain. **Quintus Caecilius Metellus Creticus,** d. c.55 B.C., grandson of Macedonicus, was consul with Quintus Hortensius (69 B.C.). Crete was his proconsular assignment, and he set out to subjugate the pirate-infested island. When he had conquered most of the island, the pirates sent a message to Pompey (Creticus' superior officer) offering to surrender to him, hoping for easy terms. Creticus disregarded the surrender and captured the rest of Crete.

metempsychosis: see TRANSMIGRATION OF SOULS.

meteor, small piece of matter flying through space that becomes visible when it enters the earth's atmosphere. While still outside the atmosphere, it is known as a meteoroid. Countless meteoroids of varying sizes are moving about the solar system at any time. Perhaps a billion meteoroids a day enter the atmosphere, their speeds ranging from 10 to 45 mi (16–72 km) per sec. As meteors they experience friction due to collisions with air molecules. By the time they reach 50 to 75 mi (80–120 km) from the earth's surface, they have been heated to incandescence through friction and are visible as "shooting stars," or "falling stars." Most disintegrate completely before they reach the earth; those large enough to reach the ground are called METEORITES. A meteor of considerable duration and brightness is known as a FIREBALL; a fireball that breaks apart with an explosion is a bolide. Meteors are composed of stone, iron, or a mixture of stone and iron, with other metals present in very small proportions. Although most meteors are quite small, and even though only a very small fraction of them reach the earth's surface, their large quantity accounts for several tons of matter falling on the earth each day. A single observer without the aid of a telescope can see an average of 5 to 10 meteors per hour. More meteors are visible after midnight because the earth's rotation has then positioned the observer's part of the earth in the direction of the earth's motion about the sun. The frequency of meteors also increases when the earth passes through certain swarms of particles that intersect the earth's orbit. Such METEOR SHOWERS are named for the constellation from which they appear to originate.

meteorite, METEOR that survives the intense heat of atmospheric friction and reaches the earth's surface. Because of the destructive effects of this friction, only the very largest meteors become meteorites. Three general categories are used to classify meteorites. The siderites, or irons, are composed entirely of metal (chiefly nickel and iron). The aerolites, or stony meteorites, show a diversity of mineral elements including large percentages of silicon and magnesium oxides; the most abundant type of aerolite is the chondrite, so called because the metal embedded in it is in the form of grainlike lumps, or chondrules. The siderolites, which are rarer than the other types, are of both metal and stone in varying proportions. A particular characteristic of meteorites are the Widmanstätten figures, caused by the conditions of pressure and temperature encountered in their passage through the atmosphere. These figures, found only in siderites, appear after the meteorite is cut, polished, and treated with nitric acid; they are patterns surrounded by dark bands and are formed as the acid reacts with iron salts. As a meteor speeds through the atmosphere, its outer surface becomes liquefied; the friction of the atmosphere finally reduces its velocity, and the surface cools and solidifies into a dark, smooth crust. Lines of flow in the hardened surface can indicate its motions in flight. Cone-shaped meteorites show that one end was directed forward. Others, which are unevenly shaped, probably spun while falling. Friction with the atmosphere has little effect in slowing down a very large meteorite because it is offset by gravity. When it reaches the earth, it strikes with tremendous force and becomes buried beneath the surface. This sudden impact causes great compression, heating, and partial vaporization of the outer part of the meteorite and of the materials in the ground; expansion of the gases thus formed and of steam produced from groundwater causes an explosion that shatters the meteorite and carves out a crater in the ground. Such a crater is the huge Meteor Crater near Winslow, Ariz. Other craters believed to have been produced by meteorites have been discovered in N Quebec, Canada; near Odessa, Texas; in the Chaco, Argentina; in the great desert of Arabia; and in N Siberia. A meteorite estimated to weigh 60 tons rests where it was discovered, near Grootfontein, South West Africa. Among the exhibits at the Hayden Planetarium in New York City are three large meteorites brought from Greenland by R. E. Peary (one weighing 36½ tons) and the conical Willamette meteorite, weighing about 14 tons, found (1902) near Portland, Oregon. In N Mexico a number of meteorites have been found weighing a ton or more each. Siderites weighing more than a ton have been discovered in Brazil, Argentina, and Australia. Not until the early 19th cent. did scientists fully accept the fact that meteorites came to the earth from outer space. Since then many studies have been made of their composition and crystalline structure; the use of microchemical analysis, X rays, and the mass spectrograph has facilitated such work. The age of meteorites can be determined by measuring their radium and helium contents. The origin of meteorites is as yet undetermined. Among prevalent theories is the belief that they are fragments of COMETS that are left in their orbital paths or of some large body from which asteroids also originated. In examining sections of certain meteorites, Harold Urey and other scientists have found what they believe to be chemical evidence of organic life. The dispute that has arisen in this connection is whether the organic material in the meteorite comes from outer space or represents contamination from life on our own planet. Recent studies by C. Ponnamperuma of a meteorite that fell on Australia in 1969, together with the detection of organic molecules in space by the techniques of RADIO ASTRONOMY, suggest that the organic substances in meteorites may in fact originate in outer space. See H. H. Nininger, *Our Stone-Pelted Planet* (1933); F. G. Watson, *Between the Planets* (rev. ed. 1955); B. H. Mason, *Meteorites* (1962); G. J. H. McCall, *Meteorites and Their Origins* (1973); publications of the American Museum of Natural History, New York.

meteorological satellite: see SATELLITE, ARTIFICIAL.

meteorology, branch of science that deals with the ATMOSPHERE of a planet, particularly that of the earth, the most important application of which is the analysis and prediction of WEATHER. Aristotle's *Meteorologica* (c.340 B.C.) is the oldest comprehensive treatise on meteorological subjects. Although most of the discussion is inaccurate in the light of modern understanding, Aristotle's work was respected as the authority in meteorology for some 2,000 years. In addition to further commentary on the *Meteorologica,* this period also saw attempts to forecast the weather according to astrological events, using techniques introduced by Ptolemy. As speculation gave way to experimentation following the scientific revolution, advances in the physical sciences made contributions to meteorology, most notably through the invention of instruments for measuring atmospheric conditions, e.g., Leonardo da Vinci's wind vane (1500), Galileo's THERMOMETER (c.1593), and Torricelli's mercury BAROMETER (1643). Further developments included Halley's account of the TRADE WINDS and MONSOONS (1686) and Ferrel's theory of the general circulation of the atmosphere (1856). The invention of the telegraph made possible the rapid collection of nearly simultaneous weather observations for large continental and marine regions, thus providing a view of the large-scale pressure and circulation patterns that determine the weather. In 1917 the Norwegian physicist Vilhelm Bjerknes introduced his theory describing the formation of wave CYCLONES on the POLAR FRONT and laid the foundation for modern methods of weather forecasting. In 1922, L. F. Richardson perceived the basis for the mathematical prediction of the atmospheric circulation and in 1938 C. G. Rossby made additional mathematical contributions. Application of this treatment by Richardson and Rossby awaited the introduction of high-speed electronic computers, which were first used for weather forecasting in the late 1940s by J. G. Charney and John Von Neumann. By 1955 computer forecasts were being made operationally and computer forecasting models have been improved steadily since then. Since 1959 meteorological SATELLITES have provided an overview of the atmosphere's cloud patterns, serving among other things as an early warning and detection system for HURRICANES, typhoons, and tropical cyclones. Infrared sensors mounted on meteorological satellites now provide observations of the vertical temperature structure of the atmosphere, and research efforts continue the development of computer forecasting models capable of utilizing these and other satellite data to improve current weather-predicting skills. The National Oceanic and Atmospheric Administration (NOAA) has the major governmental responsibility in the United States for monitoring and forecasting the weather and conducting meteorological research. The Air Weather Service and the Fleet Numerical Weather Control have similar responsibilities within the U.S. air force and U.S. navy, respectively; space applications to meteorology are researched by the National Aeronautics and Space Administration (NASA) as well as by the National Environmental Satellite Service, which is under the auspices of NOAA. In addition to a host of universities conducting meteorological research, there is the National Center for Atmospheric Research, which is operated by an affiliation of universities and sponsored by the U.S. National Science Foundation. A number of private companies also engage in operational and research meteorological activities. See T. F. Malone, ed., *Compendium of Meteorology* (1953); R. E. Huschler, ed., *Glossary of Meteorology* (1960); W. L. Donn, *Meteorology* (3d ed 1965); R. G. Barry and R. J. Chorley, *Atmosphere, Weather, and Climate* (1970).

meteor shower, increase in the number of METEORS observed in a particular part of the sky. Meteor showers usually occur annually and with varying intensity. The meteors of a meteor shower all appear to originate at a single point in the sky known as the radiant point, or radiant. A shower is named for the constellation in which its radiant is located, e.g., the Lyrids appear to come from a point in Lyra, the Perseids from Perseus, and the Orionids from Orion. While the average counting rate of meteors for the entire sky is between 5 and 10 per hr, an observer may see twice this number in one part of the sky during a shower, and in the case of the Perseids, possibly more than 100 in an hour. Meteor showers are closely associated with COMETS. When a comet breaks up, a swarm of particles eventually becomes scattered out over its entire orbit. If this orbit intersects that of the earth, a meteor shower will be observed. The shower will be particularly intense in those years when the original comet would have been observed. The Andromedids are associated with Biela's comet, and the Aquarids and Orionids are thought to be associated with Halley's comet. Some of the better-known meteor showers and their approximate dates are: Lyrids, Apr. 21; Perseids, Aug. 12; Orionids, Oct. 20; Taurids, Nov. 4; Leonids, Nov. 16; Geminids, Dec. 13.

meter, abbr. m, fundamental unit of length in the METRIC SYSTEM. The meter was originally defined as 1/10,000,000 of the distance between the equator and either pole; however, the original survey was inaccurate and the meter was later defined simply as the distance between two scratches on a bar made of a platinum-iridium alloy and kept at Sevres, France, near Paris. More recently it has been defined in terms of a reproducible, universally available atomic standard, being equal to 1,650,763.73 wavelengths of the red-orange LIGHT given off by krypton-86 under certain conditions. The meter is now the legal standard of length for most of the world, other standards, such as the yard, being defined in terms of the meter.

meter, in music, the division of a composition into units of equal time value called measures. In general, the first beat of a MEASURE receives an accent. Meter is usually indicated by a time signature, a fraction whose numerator indicates the number of beats in a measure and whose denominator indicates the note value that is the unit of beating. The time signature may be changed at any point in the composition, and frequent changes of meter occur in much 20th-century music. In music of the 18th and 19th cent., however, the same meter is usually adhered to throughout a section or movement in a composition. See RHYTHM. For meter in poetry, see VERSIFICATION; for meter as a unit of measure, see METRIC SYSTEM.

methadone (mĕth'ədōn", -dŏn"), synthetic narcotic similar in effect to MORPHINE. Synthesized in Germany, it came into clinical use after World War II. Given to addicts, it blocks the euphoric action of HEROIN without itself causing euphoria, dulling of the senses, or other narcotic effects; i.e., if an addict maintained on methadone takes heroin, he will not experience the heroin euphoria. In the 1960s the doctors Marie Nyswander and Vincent Dole promoted methadone as a therapeutic tool to rehabilitate narcotics addicts. The drug is currently in use in maintenance programs throughout the United States. It is used to wean the patient from heroin and to help him break out of the addictive life style. Critics of methadone point out that methadone patients are still addicts and that methadone therapy does not help addicts with their personality problems. In most maintenance programs methadone is dispensed under supervision, but some addicts manage to resell the methadone they receive in order to buy heroin, and methadone has joined the group of addictive drugs sold on the street. Methadone is slightly more potent than morphine and as an ANALGESIC, or pain killer, has a more lasting effect. Withdrawal symptoms are less severe than with morphine. When methadone is given to a heroin addict and the addict is later withdrawn from methadone, he will undergo methadone withdrawal instead of the more severe heroin withdrawal. Methadone is also sometimes used as an analgesic and to suppress the cough reflex. See DRUG ADDICTION AND DRUG ABUSE.

methamphetamine (mĕth"ămfĕt'əmēn): see AMPHETAMINE; METHEDRINE.

methanal, IUPAC name for FORMALDEHYDE.

methane (mĕth'ān), CH_4, colorless, odorless, gaseous saturated hydrocarbon; the simplest ALKANE. It is less dense than air, melts at −184°C, and boils at −161.4°C. It is combustible and can form explosive mixtures with air. Methane occurs naturally as the principal component of NATURAL GAS; it is formed by the decomposition of plant and animal matter. When this decomposition occurs underwater in swamps and marshes, marsh gas is released. The firedamp of coal mines is chiefly methane. Methane can be prepared in the laboratory by heating sodium acetate with sodium hydroxide, by the reaction of aluminum carbide with water, by the direct combination of carbon and hydrogen, or by the destructive distillation of coal or wood. It is unaffected by many common chemical reagents but reacts violently with chlorine or fluorine in the presence of light. As natural gas, methane is widely used for fuel. It is also used for carbonizing steel and is important as a starting material for the synthesis of solvents, e.g., methylene chloride, chloroform, and carbon tetrachloride, and of some of the Freon refrigerants.

methane series: see ALKANE.

methanoic acid, IUPAC name for FORMIC ACID.

methanol, methyl alcohol, or **wood alcohol,** CH_3OH, a colorless, flammable liquid that is miscible with water in all proportions. Methanol is a monohydric ALCOHOL. It melts at −97.8°C and boils at 67°C. It reacts with certain acids to form methyl esters. Methanol is a fatal poison. Small internal doses, continued inhalation of the vapor, or prolonged exposure of the skin to the liquid may cause blindness. As a result, commercial use of methanol has sometimes been prohibited. Methanol is used as a solvent for varnishes and lacquers and as an antifreeze. Large amounts of it are used in the synthesis of FORMALDEHYDE. Because of its poisonous properties, methanol is also used as a denaturant for ethanol. Methanol is often called wood alcohol because it was once produced chiefly as a by-product of the destructive distillation of wood. It is now produced synthetically by the direct combination of hydrogen and carbon monoxide gases, heated under pressure in the presence of a catalyst.

methanometer, in mining, portable instrument used to measure the concentration of methane (firedamp; see DAMP) in the air of coal mines.

methedrine (mĕth'ədrēn), drug of the AMPHETAMINE group. Also known as methamphetamine, it is used as a STIMULANT.

Metheg-ammah (mē'thĕg-ăm'ə), place, conquered by David from the Philistines. It is identified by some with Gath. There is some doubt whether it was an actual place; the spelling may be a textual corruption. 2 Sam. 8.1.

methionine (mĕthī'ənēn), organic compound, one of the 22 α-AMINO ACIDS commonly found in animal proteins. Only the L-stereoisomer appears in mammalian protein. It is one of several essential amino acids needed in the diet; the human body cannot synthesize it from simpler metabolites. Young adults need about 31 mg of this amino acid per day per kilogram (14 mg per lb) of body weight. Methionine reacts with ADENOSINE TRIPHOSPHATE to form S-adenosyl methionine, a potent donor of methyl groups (composed of one carbon and three hydrogen atoms); S-adenosyl methionine is the principal methyl donor in the body and contributes to the synthesis of many important substances, including EPINEPHRINE and choline (see ACETYLCHOLINE; VITAMIN). However, once methionine is incorporated into protein, it appears to be relatively unreactive and is said to participate directly in the catalytic function of only one enzyme, horseradish peroxidase. Methionine was isolated from casein (milk protein) in 1922, and its structure was proved by laboratory synthesis in 1928.

SCH_3 | CH_2 | CH_2 | $H_2N—C(H)—C(=O)OH$

methionine

Methodism, the doctrines, polity, and worship of those Protestant Christian denominations that have developed from the movement started in England by the teaching of John WESLEY. He, his brother Charles, George WHITEFIELD, and others belonged to a group at Oxford that in 1729 began meeting for religious exercises. From their resolution to conduct their lives and religious study by "rule and method," they were given the name Methodists. The beginning of Methodism as a popular movement dates from 1738, when both of the Wesley brothers, influenced by contact with the Moravians, undertook evangelistic preaching. From the Moravians, too, they took the emphasis on conversion and holiness that are still central to Methodism. The leaders of the movement were ordained ministers of the Church of England; neither of the two Wesleys ever disclaimed the holy orders of that church, but they were barred from speaking in most of its pulpits, in disapproval of their evangelistic methods. They preached in barns, houses, open fields, wherever an audience could be induced to assemble. Societies were formed, class meetings of converts were held, and lay preachers were trained and given charge of several congregations. The moving of preachers from one appointment to another was the beginning of the system of itinerancy. Theologically, John Wesley was essentially a follower of Jacobus ARMINIUS. Whitefield, unable to accept the Arminian doctrines of Wesley, broke with him in 1741 and became the leader of the Calvinistic Methodists. In 1744 the first annual conference was held and the Articles of Religion were drawn up. They were based to a considerable extent upon the Thirty-nine Articles of the Church of England, but great emphasis was laid upon repentance, faith, sanctification, and the privilege of full, free salvation for everyone. By 1784 the spread of the movement, especially in America, made an organization separate from the Church of England necessary. In 1784, Wesley issued a Deed of Declaration giving legal status to the yearly Methodist conference. That same year he ordained Thomas Coke superintendent of the societies in America. In 1791, after Wesley's death, the English Methodists were formally separated from the Church of England and established the Wesleyan Methodist Church. In both England and America various groups seceded from the main branch to form independent Methodist churches. Some of them later reunited. In Great Britain the Methodist New Connection was the first group to form a separate branch. Then followed the Primitive Methodists, the Bible Christians, the Protestant Methodists, the Wesleyan Methodist Association, and the Wesleyan Reformers. In 1857 the last three formed a union as the United Methodist Free Churches; in 1907 these were incorporated with the Methodist New Connection and the Bible Christians as the United Methodist Church. Finally, in 1932, the Wesleyan Methodists, the Primitive Methodists, and the United Methodists gathered together as the Methodist Church. In the early 1970s there were about 650,000 Methodists in Great Britain.

Methodism in America. John Wesley (with his brother) visited America in 1735 as spiritual adviser to James Oglethorpe's colony in Georgia, but the actual beginnings of Methodism in America were in New York, after 1766, when Philip Embury, a Wesleyan convert who had earlier come from Ireland, began to preach. In Maryland, Robert Strawbridge started a congregation. In 1769, Wesley sent several itinerant preachers into the new field; Francis ASBURY arrived in 1771. The first annual conference in America was held in 1773. In 1784, Coke, acting on authority from Wesley, proceeded with the organization of the Methodist Episcopal Church in America. At a Christmas conference in Baltimore, Asbury and Coke were elected superintendents (and shortly thereafter styled bishops), and the order of worship and articles of religion prepared by Wesley were adopted. The first General Conference of the new church was held in 1792. In 1830, after controversy over lay representation in conferences and other questions, the Methodist Protestant Church was formed, without bishops or presiding elders. The Wesleyan Methodist Connection was organized (1843) at Utica, N.Y., in a strong antislavery protest. The independent career of the Methodist Episcopal Church, South, began in 1845 over the issue of slavery. In 1939 a great reunion was realized—the Methodist Episcopal Church (North), the Methodist Episcopal Church, South, and the Methodist Protestant Church united as the Methodist Church. In 1968 the Methodist Church joined with the Evangelical United Brethren Church to form the United Methodist Church, now the largest body of Methodists in the world. The many activities of this vast body are administered by boards, among which are the council of bishops; boards of education, missions and church extension, publication, hospitals and homes, and evangelism; and the commission on world peace. Among other branches of Methodism in the United States are the Primitive Methodist Church (introduced c.1830 by emigrants from England), the Congregational Methodist Church (1852), and the Free Methodist Church of North America (1860). Black Methodists formed denominations of their own, under the leadership of such men as Richard ALLEN. These include the African Methodist Episcopal Church, the African Methodist Episcopal Zion Church, and the Christian Methodist Episcopal Church (formerly the Colored Methodist Episcopal Church), which became in 1870 a separate body approved in the General Conference of the Methodist Episcopal Church, South. In the early 1970s there were about 13 million Methodists in the United States. See R. M. Cameron, *The Rise of Methodism* (1954); Umphrey Lee, *Our Fathers and Us: The Heritage of the Methodists* (1959); N. B. Harmon, *The Organization of the Methodist Church* (2d rev. ed. 1962); E. S. Bucke et al., ed., *The History of American Methodism* (3 vol. 1964); A. D. Ward, *The Social Creed of the Methodist Church* (rev. ed. 1965); C. W. Ferguson, *Organizing to Beat the Devil* (1971); Bernard Semmel, *The Methodist Revolution* (1973).

Methodius, Saint: see CYRIL AND METHODIUS, SAINTS.

Methuen (mĭthōō'ən), town (1970 pop. 35,456), Essex co., NE Mass., a suburb of Boston; settled c.1642, set off from Haverhill 1725. The town's industries produce boxes and food products. The Memorial Music Hall in Methuen contains a large organ. The Tenney Estate is now St. Basil's Seminary and Presentation of Mary Academy.

Methusael (mēthyōō'sāĕl), father of Lamech. Gen. 4.18.

Methuselah (mēthyōō'zələ), descendant of Seth; son of Enoch. The Bible says he lived 969 years. Gen. 5.21–27. Mathusala: Luke 3.37.

methyl (mĕth'əl), CH_3, organic FREE RADICAL or ALKYL GROUP derived from METHANE by the removal of one hydrogen atom.

methyl alcohol: see METHANOL.

methylbenzene, IUPAC name for TOLUENE.

methylphenol: see CRESOL.

methyl salicylate (səlĭs'əlāt"), methyl ester of SALICYLIC ACID.

Metonic cycle: see SYNODIC PERIOD.

metonymy (mĭtŏn'əmē), figure of speech in which an attribute of a thing or something closely related to it is substituted for the thing itself. Thus, "sweat" can mean "hard labor," "Joyce" indicates the works of James Joyce, "Capitol Hill" represents the U.S. Congress.

metric system, system of WEIGHTS AND MEASURES planned in France and adopted there in 1799; it has since been adopted by most of the technologically developed countries of the world. It is based on a unit of length, called the METER (m), and a unit of mass, called the KILOGRAM (kg). The system has changed somewhat since it was first developed; e.g., the definition of the meter has changed, and the unit for mass is different. The meter was originally intended to be 1/10,000,000 of the distance on the earth's surface between the equator and either pole; however, because of errors in the original survey for determining the meter and because of the impracticality of referring to such a standard, the meter was later redefined in terms of the standard prepared and kept at Sèvres, France, near Paris. Long defined as the distance between two scratches on a bar of platinum-iridium alloy, the meter in 1960 was redefined in terms of an atomic standard. The original unit of mass, the GRAM, was first defined as the mass of pure water at maximum density that would fill a cube whose edges are each 0.01 m. The unit of mass is now the kilogram, defined as the mass of a platinum-iridium cylinder kept at Sèvres. (A gram is now defined as a mass 1/1,000 kg.) Other metric units can be defined in terms of the meter and the kilogram. For example the are, the unit of area, is equal to the area of a square whose edges are each 10 m long. The liter, the metric unit of volume, is equal to the volume of a cube whose edges are each 1/10 m long. Fractions and multiples of the metric units are related to each other by powers of 10, allowing conversion from one unit to a multiple of it simply by shifting a decimal point, and avoiding the lengthy arithmetical operations required by the English units of measurement. The prefixes in the accompanying table have been accepted for designating multiples and fractions of the meter, gram, are, and other units. Thus, 1,000 grams are a kilogram, 100 ares are a HECTARE, and 1/100 of a meter is a centimeter. Several other systems of units based on the metric system have been in wide use. The CGS SYSTEM is based on the centimeter of length, the gram of mass, and the SECOND of time; the MKS SYSTEM is based on the meter of length, the kilogram of mass, and the second of time. Units in the mks system are larger than the corresponding cgs units. ELECTRIC AND MAGNETIC UNITS have been defined for both of these systems; in fact, two different sets of electric units are defined in the cgs system. The mks system serves as the basis for the INTERNATIONAL SYSTEM OF UNITS, a com-

PREFIXES FOR BASIC METRIC UNITS

Multiples				*Fractions*			
PREFIX	ABBREVIATION	POWER OF 10	EQUIVALENT	PREFIX	ABBREVIATION	POWER OF 10	EQUIVALENT
tera-	T	10^{12}	trillion	deci-	d	10^{-1}	tenth part
giga-	G	10^{9}	billion	centi-	c	10^{-2}	hundredth part
mega-	M	10^{6}	million	milli-	m	10^{-3}	thousandth part
kilo-	k	10^{3}	thousand	micro-	μ	10^{-6}	millionth part
hecto-	h	10^{2}	hundred	nano-	n	10^{-9}	billionth part
deka-	da	10^{1}	ten	pico-	p	10^{-12}	trillionth part

prehensive system of units for all physical quantities adopted in 1960 by the 11th General Conference on Weights and Measures. See DECIMAL SYSTEM. See Lewis Van Hagen Judson, *Units of Weight and Measure (U.S. Customary and Metric)—Definitions and Tables of Equivalents* (1961; U.S. National Bureau of Standards, Miscellaneous Publication 233) and *Weights and Measures Standards of the United States: A Brief History* (1963; U.S. National Bureau of Standards, Miscellaneous Publication 247).

metronome, in music, pyramid-shaped clockwork mechanism to indicate the exact tempo in which a work is to be performed. It has a double pendulum whose pace can be altered by sliding the upper weight up or down. The sliding bob indicates the rate of oscillation by means of calibrations on the pendulum. A number to indicate the rate at which the metronome is to be set and a note whose value is to equal one beat of the metronome are often given on a piece of music, preceded by the initials MM, for Mälzel's Metronome—Johann Mälzel (1772–1838) having made in 1816 the type of metronome in general use today. Beethoven and Schumann left such tempo indications for many of their compositions, but for earlier music and often for later music such indications are those of the editor. A pocket-watch type of metronome was developed in the 1940s; a boxlike electric metronome has also become popular.

Metropolitan Museum of Art, New York City, founded in 1870. The Metropolitan Museum is the foremost repository of art in the United States. It opened in 1880 on its present site on Central Park facing Fifth Ave. The building was designed by Calvert Vaux and J. W. Mould. It is owned by the city, which contributes a certain sum yearly for upkeep, but otherwise the museum is supported by private endowment and income from memberships and admission fees that are requested as voluntary contributions. The museum's most outstanding collections include European paintings and sculpture of the Renaissance, baroque, and modern periods; pastels; watercolors; miniatures; and a vast number of drawings and graphic art works. The Egyptian wing has the mastaba of Perneb (erected c.2460 B.C.), rebuilt here in its original form. Much of the extensive and remarkable medieval art collection is housed in the CLOISTERS, a separate building erected from various medieval components in 1938. The collection of armor is outstanding. The museum houses a great number of works of art from the Orient in many media. The American collection shows the development of furniture and decorative arts from the colonial period to the mid-19th cent. and paintings and sculpture up to the present day. A new museum to house American works of all sorts is scheduled to open in the U.S. bicentennial year, 1976. The print collection includes woodcuts and engravings, dating from the 15th cent., and etchings and lithographs. The Costume Institute provides a practical source of inspiration and reference for designers through its collection of thousands of authentic costumes and accessories, international in scope and covering four centuries. The museum houses an important exhibition of antique and primitive musical instruments. Its hundreds of examples of Greek pottery and its Greek and Roman sculptures are among the finest such collections in the world. The museum's need for greatly increased space in which to house its fast-growing collections led to the plan to expand into Central Park, a decision of grave concern to Park conservationists. In the early 1970s the museum acquired the Egyptian Temple of Dendur, the Michael C. Rockefeller collection of primitive art, and the extensive Robert Lehman collection of European art, housed in a new wing constructed especially for it. See Leo Lerman, *The Museum* (1969); Calvin Tomkins, *Merchants and Masterpieces* (1970); two guidebooks (*The Cloisters,* 3d ed. 1963; *Guide to the Metropolitan Museum of Art,* ed. by Nora B. Beeson, 1972).

Metropolitan Opera Company, term used in referring collectively to the organizations that have produced opera at the Metropolitan Opera House, New York City. The original house was built by members of New York society who could not be accommodated with boxes at the Academy of Music. The first presentation, on Oct. 22, 1883, was Gounod's *Faust.* Among the early managers were Henry E. Abbey, Leopold Damrosch, Edmond Stanton, and Maurice Grau. A devastating fire prevented production of any opera during the season 1892–93, and rebuilding was undertaken by a new company, the Metropolitan Opera and Real Estate Company. The first of the galaxy of great stars to make the house famous had already appeared. There was no resident company in the season 1897–98, but the Maurice Grau Opera Company was active from 1898 to 1903, and the period was brilliant with virtuoso singers. The Conried Metropolitan Opera Company was formed with Heinrich Conried as manager in 1903. In Nov., 1903, Enrico Caruso made his debut and by the following season had assumed his place as the dominant figure of the company. Conried retired in 1908, and the following season saw the coming of Giulio Gatti-Casazza as director and Alfred Hertz, Gustav Mahler, and Arturo Toscanini as conductors; the name was now Metropolitan Opera Company. Toscanini's departure in 1915 was a serious artistic loss for the company. In Feb., 1935, during Gatti-Casazza's final season, Kirsten Flagstad made her debut. Herbert Witherspoon was appointed in May, 1935, to succeed Gatti-Casazza but died only a few weeks later. Edward Johnson was appointed in his place. In 1932 the Metropolitan Opera Association, Inc., was formed, and performances were thenceforth underwritten by public subscription. In 1940 the association bought the house from the Metropolitan Opera and Real Estate Company, marking the final step in transference from private to public sponsorship. In June, 1949, Rudolf Bing was appointed to succeed Johnson. A controversial figure, he brought many noted singers to the company, including Marian Anderson, Renata Tebaldi, Franco Corelli, Joan Sutherland, Maria Callas, Birgit Nilsson, Tito Gobbi, and Leontyne Price. The new Metropolitan Opera House in Lincoln Center for the Performing Arts opened in 1966 with a premier performance of Samuel Barber's *Antony and Cleopatra,* written especially for the occasion; the new building featured acoustics superior to those in the old building and a lobby decorated with murals by Marc Chagall. Bing retired in 1972. He was replaced by Goeran Gentele, who was killed in an automobile accident in July, 1972, a few weeks after he had succeeded Bing. The opera's assistant manager, Schuyler Chapin, was named interim manager and in 1973 was appointed manager. See W. H. Seltsam, *Metropolitan Opera Annals* (1947, with two supplements, 1957 and 1968); Irving Kolodin, *The Metropolitan Opera* (4th ed. 1966); the official guidebook to the opera house, by H. E. Krawitz (1967).

Metsu or **Metzu, Gabriel** (both: gä'brēĕl mĕt'sü), 1630?–1667, Dutch genre painter, b. Leiden. In 1657 he moved to Amsterdam, where he remained for the rest of his life. In his youth he painted biblical subjects, such as *Woman Taken in Adultery* (Louvre), which show Rembrandt's influence. His true gift was for genre, and he is best known for his quiet, charming interiors that reveal the influence of DOU, his teacher. His work is distinguished by fine draftsmanship and exquisite handling of light and texture. Among his well-known works are *Music Lesson* (The Hague); *Duet* (National Gall., London); *Mother with a Sick Child* (c.1660, Amsterdam); *Music Lesson, Visit to the Nursery,* and *Tavern Scene* (all: Metropolitan Mus.).

Metsys, Quentin: see MASSYS, QUENTIN.

Metternich, Clemens Wenzel Nepomuk Lothar, Fürst von (klā'mĕns vĕn'tsəl nä'pōmo͝ok lō'tär fürst fən mĕt'ərnĭkh), 1773–1859, Austrian statesman and arbiter of post-Napoleonic Europe, b. Koblenz, of a noble Rhenish family. While a student in Strasbourg he witnessed revolutionary excesses, to which he later credited his extreme conservatism and hatred of political unrest. In 1795 he married Eleonora von Kaunitz, granddaughter of the Austrian statesman Wenzel von Kaunitz. She brought Metternich great estates and admission to the highest court circles. He began his state career in 1797 as representative of the Westphalian college of counts at the Congress of Rastatt, and he became Austrian ambassador to Saxony (1801) and to Prussia (1803). The favorable impression he made upon the French envoy while in Berlin led Napoleon I to request that he be sent as Austrian representative to France (1806). His influence greatly increased when he succeeded Johann Philipp von Stadion as foreign minister (1809). Until 1813 he pursued a policy of acquiescence to French supremacy, but he constantly sought to strengthen the diplomatic and military position of Austria in order to make future resistance possible and to disrupt the alliance between Napoleon and Czar Alexander I. He was successful in securing the marriage of Archduchess MARIE LOUISE to Napoleon (1810) and a temporary alliance with France (1812). The middle course that he pursued between France and Russia developed into a policy of armed mediation, and was supplanted by one of substituting Austrian for French supremacy in 1813. The Quadruple Alliance was formed, and war of the coalition against France resulted in the allied victory at Leipzig (1813). Although Metternich wished French domination checked, he had no desire to see the country crushed, for he did not want Prussia and Russia too greatly strengthened and the balance of power upset. He hoped to make Austrian influence supreme in Italy and, while vigorously opposing German unity, sought Austrian ascendancy in the newly formed GERMAN CONFEDERATION. Although his role in Austrian affairs was weakened by rivalry with the liberal minister Franz Kolowrat, the period 1815–48 has been called the Age of Metternich, for during this time he was the chief arbiter of Europe. Metternich, using skillful diplomacy as the leader of conservatism in Europe, was the guiding spirit of the international congresses at Vienna (1814–15; see VIENNA, CONGRESS OF), Aachen (1818), Carlsbad (1819; see CARLSBAD DECREES), Troppau (1820; see TROPPAU, CONGRESS OF), Laibach (1821; see LAIBACH, CONGRESS OF), and Verona (1822; see VERONA, CONGRESS OF) and was the chief statesman of the so-called HOLY ALLIANCE. In 1813 he was created prince. His brilliant assistant was Friedrich von GENTZ. The Metternich system depended upon political and religious censorship, espionage, and the suppression of revolutionary and nationalist movements. His name became anathema to liberals, and the REVOLUTIONS OF 1848 (which forced him to seek refuge in England) were in part directed at his repressive system. He returned to Austria in 1851. His memoirs were published posthumously (1880–84), as was his correspondence (1899). The authoritative work on Metternich is Heinrich, Ritter von Srbik's *Metternich, der Staatsmann und der Mensch* (1925). See also biographies by Helène du Coudray (1935), Algernon Cecil (3d ed. 1947), Constantin de Grunwald (tr. 1953), and Alan Palmer (1972); studies by E. E. Kraehe (1963) and A. G. Haas (1963); A. J. May, *The Age of Metternich* (rev. ed. 1963).

Metuchen (mətŭch'ən), borough (1970 pop. 16,031), Middlesex co., NE N.J.; settled before 1700, inc. 1900. Although chiefly residential, it has manufactures of electronic and electrical equipment and cleaning compounds. In June, 1777, a brief but bloody skirmish occurred there between British troops under Gen. William Howe and a small American force led by William Alexander.

Metz, Christian: see AMANA CHURCH SOCIETY.

Metz (Eng. and Ger. mĕts, Fr. mĕs), city (1968 pop. 113,586), capital of Moselle dept., NE France, on the Moselle River. It is a cultural and commercial center of LORRAINE and an industrial city producing metals, machinery, tobacco, clothing, and food products. Of pre-Roman origin, the city was the capital of the Mediomatrici, a Gallic people. One of the most important cities of Roman Gaul, it was invaded and destroyed by the Vandals (406) and the Huns (451). Metz was an early episcopal see and became the capital of AUSTRASIA (the eastern portion of the MEROVINGIAN Frankish empire) in the 6th cent. After the division of the Frankish empire (8th cent.) the bishops of Metz greatly increased their power, ruling a relatively vast area as a fief of the Holy Roman Empire. Metz was a major cultural center of the Carolingian Renaissance (8th cent.) and was later (10th cent.) a prosperous commercial city with an important Jewish community. Metz became a free imperial city in the 12th cent. and was then one of the richest and most populous cities of the empire. During the REFORMATION the bourgeoisie of Metz welcomed Protestantism, but the city never became a bastion of Calvinism, and the uneasy bourgeoisie accepted the protection of the French crown. In 1552, Henry II annexed the three bishoprics of Lorraine (Metz, Toul, and VERDUN), and soon after, Metz, under the command of François de Guise, resisted a long siege (1552–53) by Emperor Charles V. The Peace of Westphalia (1648), ending the THIRTY YEARS WAR, confirmed the three bishoprics in French possession. An important fortress and garrison town, Metz was besieged (1870) by the Germans in the FRANCO-PRUSSIAN WAR, and after a two-month siege, 179,000 French soldiers under Marshall Achille Bazaine capitulated. During the German annexation of E Lorraine (1871–1918), Metz, largely French-speaking, was a center of pro-French sentiment. During World War II the city suffered greatly under German occupation. There are many Gallo-Roman ruins in Metz, including an aqueduct, thermal baths, and part of an amphitheater. Much has also been preserved from the medieval period. The celebrated Cathedral of St. Étienne was built from c.1221 to 1516. The Place Sainte-Croix is a square surrounded by medieval houses (13th–15th cent.). Metz has several other churches, including St. Pierre-de-la-Citadelle Basilica, mansions from the Middle Ages, and many beautiful promenades. Paul Verlaine was born in Metz.

Metzinger, Jean (zhäN mĕtsăNzhär'), 1883–1956, French painter and writer. With Gleizes he wrote *Du cubisme* (1912, tr. 1913), which presented the philosophical basis of the cubist aesthetic. In his paintings he employed cubist faceting and a stylized, richly detailed manner that was never wholly abstract. The *Dancer* (Albright-Knox Art Gall., Buffalo, N.Y.) is characteristic.

Metzu, Gabriel: see METSU, GABRIEL.

Meudon (mödôN'), town (1968 pop. 51,481), Hauts-de-Seine dept., N central France, a suburb SW of Paris. Metal products, automobile bodies, and explosives are the chief manufactures. The astrophysics department of the Paris Observatory is located in the pavilion of an 18th-century château, which commands a magnificent view of Paris. François Rabelais, Richard Wagner, and Auguste Rodin lived in Meudon. Rodin is buried in the garden of his villa.

Meulen, Adam Frans van der (ä'däm fräns vän dĕr möl'ən), c.1632–1690, Flemish painter of battle scenes and portraits. He was invited to Paris c.1665 and accompanied Louis XIV on military campaigns, carefully recording battles in drawings that he used as preparation for his detailed paintings and tapestry designs. All of these are now of considerable historical interest. The Metropolitan Museum has Meulen's *Combat of Cavalry* and *Encounter of Cavalry.*

Meun, Jean de: see JEAN DE MEUN.

Meunier, Constantin (kôNstäNtăN' mönyā'), 1831–1905, Belgian sculptor and painter. In paintings of monastic life and of factory workers and miners, his work expressed the dignity of labor, in a style marked by romantic idealism. Turning to sculpture exclusively at the age of 50, he produced the bronze reliefs and monuments for which he is known. His masterpiece, the unfinished *Monument to Labor* (Brussels), comprises four stone reliefs, *Industry, The Mine, Harvest,* and *Harbor;* four bronze statues, *The Sower, The Smith, The Miner,* and *The Ancestor;* and a bronze group, *Maternity.* Many of his works are housed in the Constantin Meunier Museum in Brussels.

Meurthe (mört), river, c.105 mi (169 km) long, rising in the Vosges, NE France, and flowing NW past Lunéville to join the Moselle River just N of Nancy. Its very irregular level has necessitated an intricate system of controls.

Meurthe-et-Moselle (mör"tāmôzĕl'), department (1968 pop. 705,413), NE France, in Lorraine, bordering on Belgium and Luxembourg. NANCY is the capital.

Meuse (möz), department (1968 pop. 209,513), NE France, in LORRAINE, bordering on Belgium. BAR-LE-DUC, the capital, and VERDUN are the chief towns. Its industries include the manufacture of metals, foundry products, wood products, ceramics, and glass. Agriculture is concentrated in the Meuse River valley, where most of the department's people live. Part of the Argonne forest is in the north, and in the forested west and central regions there is extensive animal breeding.

Meuse (myo͞oz, Fr. möz), Dutch and Flemish *Maas,* river, c.560 mi (900 km) long, rising in the Langres Plateau, NE France and flowing N past Sedan (the head of navigation) and Charleville-Mézières into S Belgium. It is joined by the Sambre River at Namur. From Namur the Meuse winds eastward skirting the Ardennes, passes Liège, and turns north, where it forms part of the Belgian-Dutch border before swinging westward through SE Netherlands (where it is called the Maas). Near 'sHertogenbosch it branches out to form a common delta with the Rhine River. One branch joins with the Waal River near Gorinchem to form the Merwede River, which flows into the North Sea. The other branch, called the Bergsche Maas, flows into an inlet of the North Sea S of Dordrecht. The Oude Maas (Old Meuse), which is a branch of the Waal, and the Nieuwe Maas (New Meuse), which is a continuation of the Lek River, actually belong to the Rhine estuary. The Meuse is linked with the Belgian port of Antwerp by the Albert Canal and with Rotterdam and other Dutch ports by the intricate system of Dutch waterways; it is thus one of the chief thoroughfares of Europe. The Belgian section of the Meuse valley, especially around Namur and Liège, is an important industrial and mining region. A strategic line of defense, particularly in Belgium and France, the valley has been a battleground in many wars, and most of the cities along its course have been strongly fortified since the Middle Ages.

Mewar, India: see UDAIPUR.

Mexía, Pedro (pä'thrō māksē'ä), 1499–1551?, Spanish humanist, b. Sevilla. A man of broad knowledge and erudition, he was influenced by ERASMUS. His works include *Silva de varia lección* [literary miscellany] (1540), a collection of observations and notes on customs, travels, superstitions, etc.; *Historia imperial y Cesárea* [history of the emperors and caesars] (1545), and the unfinished *Historia del Emperador Carlos V* [history of the emperor Charles V].

Mexicali (māhēkä'lē), city (1970 pop. 390,411), capital of Baja California state, NW Mexico, across the border from Calexico, Calif. Once noted chiefly as the center of a cotton- and cereal-raising area, it has more recently acquired both wealth and notoriety as a gaudy border resort. Mexicali is also a commercial center and the seat of an episcopal see.

Mexican art and architecture were already highly developed in the ancient civilizations flourishing before the conquest of Cortés. For the artistic achievements of the AZTEC, the MAYA, and other native cultures, see PRE-COLUMBIAN ART AND ARCHITECTURE. With the coming of the Spanish to Mexico, the native peoples were introduced to European art, especially painting, and building techniques. A good many Spanish paintings were brought there, and during the 17th cent. gifted native artists became adept at religious oil painting, modeling religious figures in wax, and the art of polychrome wood sculpture (see SPANISH COLONIAL ART AND ARCHITECTURE). The serenity and sensitivity of the early native art combined with the Spanish influence to give to Mexican painting a mellowness and richness of color not yet achieved in Spain at that time. Fifty years or so before Murillo made his mark as a colorist, Mexican artists were already giving their works rich red and blue tones. This type of work is sometimes referred to as Mexican baroque to distinguish it from the more rigid European BAROQUE. Baltásar de Echave, the elder (c.1548–1620), is considered to be the first great Mexican artist; he founded the first native school in 1609. His *Agony in the Garden* (begun 1582) is an example of a Renaissance work with a Spanish character. More important, however, was the work of Alonso Vázquez (c.1565–1608). Painting declined toward the middle of the 17th cent., and sculpture and architecture gained ascendancy; the dominant style in both was the Churrigueresque (named after José CHURRIGUERA), a fanciful form of the baroque, but Mexican PLATERESQUE art and architecture also appeared. The 18th cent. produced a large number of artists; outstanding among them were José Ibarra and Miguel Cabrera. A period of academic art followed, producing no very distinctive works; this period of imitation was broken at the close of the 19th cent. by the painter José María VELASCO, whose landscapes again reaffirmed a national style. The political broadside became a popular and pungent native art. José Guadalupe POSADA was famous for his satirical prints. With the coming of independence, architecture went into a general decline, but wealthy creoles were responsible for the erection of a profusion of luxurious mansions, some of them of great beauty. In the latter half of the 19th cent., during the ill-starred regime (1864–67) of Emperor Maximilian, the heavy splendor of French Second Empire architecture was imported into Mexico. The famous gardens and castle at CHAPULTEPEC were beautified by the emperor and made even more lavish by the dictator Porfirio Díaz, under whose administration (1876–1911) the French accent became stronger, especially in the mansions along the famous Paseo de la Reforma in Mexico City. The influence of ART NOUVEAU is evident in the portentous and elaborately decorated Palacio de Bellas Artes, also commissioned by Díaz but not completed until 1930. Since the revolution of 1910 Mexican artists have enjoyed unusually strong government patronage and have been, as a result, committed principally to the expression of revolutionary ideals. The foremost have been muralists employing broad techniques in the service of their political and social themes. The three internationally acclaimed painters Diego RIVERA, José Clemente OROZCO, and David Alfaro SIQUEIROS produced masterpieces of mural art and initiated a revival of fresco painting. Miguel COVARRUBIAS attained international fame as a caricaturist and illustrator, and Dr. Atl (pseud. of Gerardo Murillo) was influential as a teacher and art critic as well as a painter. Francisco Goita was noted for his paintings stressing the hardships of Indian peasant existence. Of the abstract easel painters, Rufino TAMAYO is the outstanding 20th-century figure. Contemporary Mexican painters and sculptors have continued to produce an extraordinary variety of works in many styles and techniques; major figures include José Luis Cuevas, Jorge G. Camarena, Martínez de Hoyos, Frida Kahlo (Diego Rivera's wife), Enrique Echeverría, and Leonora Carrington. Modern architecture has also flourished. Functionalism, expressionism, and other schools have left their imprint on a large number of works in which Mexican stylistic elements have been combined with European and North American techniques. In the great manufacturing center of Monterrey there are fine examples of industrial architecture. Perhaps the most outstanding achievement of contemporary Mexican architecture is the Ciudad Universitaria outside Mexico City, a complex of buildings and grounds housing the National Univ. of Mexico. A cooperative venture, the project was directed by Carlos Lazo. A major structure is the central library, with a brilliant mosaic facade by the architect and painter Juan O'GORMAN. Another architect of note is Felix CANDELA, who designed the expressionistic church Nuestra Señora de los Milagros. Folk arts, including the weaving of magnificent textiles, pottery making, and silver work have flourished in Mexico throughout its history. See also NATIONAL MUSEUM OF ANTHROPOLOGY. See Bernard Myers, *Mexican Painting in Our Time* (1956); Max Cetto, *Modern Architecture in Mexico* (tr. 1961); Gerd Dörner, *Folk Art of Mexico* (tr. 1963); Justino Fernandez, *A Guide to Mexican Art* (tr. 1969).

Mexican jumping bean: see SPURGE.

Mexican literature: see SPANISH AMERICAN LITERATURE.

Mexican War, 1846–48, armed conflict between the United States and Mexico. While the immediate cause of the war was the U.S. annexation of Texas (Dec., 1845), other factors had disturbed peaceful relations between the two republics. In the United States there was agitation for the settlement of long-standing claims arising from injuries and property losses sustained by U.S. citizens in the various Mexican revolutions. Another major factor was the American ambition, publicly stated by President POLK, of acquiring California, upon which it was believed France and Great Britain were casting covetous eyes. Despite the rupture of diplomatic relations between Mexico and the United States that followed congressional consent to the admission of Texas into the Union, President Polk sent John SLIDELL to Mexico to negotiate a settlement. Slidell was authorized to purchase California and New Mexico, part of which was claimed by Texas, and to offer the U.S. government's assumption of liability for the claims of U.S. citizens in return for boundary adjustments. When Mexico declined to negotiate, the United States prepared to take by force what it could not achieve by diplomacy. The war was heartily supported by the outright imperialists and by those who wished slave-holding territory extended. The settlement of the Oregon boundary dispute (June, 1846), which took place shortly after the official outbreak of hostilities, seemed to indicate British acquiescence, for it granted the United States a free hand.

The Course of Hostilities. Early in May, 1845, American troops under Gen. Zachary TAYLOR had been stationed at the Sabine River preliminary to an advance to the Rio Grande, the southern boundary claimed by Texas. They advanced to Corpus Christi in July. In March, 1846, after the failure of Slidell's mission, Taylor occupied Point Isabel, a town at the mouth of the Rio Grande. To the Mexicans, who claimed the Nueces River as the boundary, this was an act of aggression, and after some negotiations Gen. Mariano Arista ordered his troops to cross the Rio Grande. On April 25 a clash between the two armies occurred, and Taylor reported to Washington that hostilities had begun. On May 3 the guns of Matamoros began to shell Fort Brown (then Fort Taylor), an advanced American position near the present Brownsville, Texas. President Polk called these Mexican actions an invasion of American soil, and on May 13, 1846, the United States declared war. Meanwhile, Taylor had defeated the Mexicans at PALO ALTO (May 8) and RESACA DE LA PALMA (May 9). The Mexicans retreated across the Rio Grande. Taylor followed them and on May 18 took Matamoros. After a delay he then advanced on Monterrey, which he occupied after a five-day battle (Sept. 20–24, 1846). In June, 1846, Gen. Stephen W. KEARNY left Fort Leavenworth for New Mexico with some 1,600 men, including a force of Missouri volunteers under Alexander DONIPHAN. Santa Fe was taken (August), a provisional government was set up, and Doniphan was placed in command of the area. Kearny pushed on to California to find that this province, through the agency of Commodore John D. SLOAT (later relieved by Robert F. STOCKTON) and John C. FRÉMONT, was already under American rule. After reinforcements reached Santa Fe, Doniphan invaded (Dec., 1846) N Mexico, taking El Paso and Chihuahua before he joined forces with Gen. John E. WOOL (who had advanced southwest from San Antonio) and with Taylor at Saltillo. Gen. Antonio López de SANTA ANNA, who had been in exile in Cuba and had been allowed passage through the U.S. blockade at Veracruz, had now assumed the presidency of Mexico; he gathered a large force to stop Taylor's advance. Taylor, whose army had been greatly reduced in size, was in an extremely vulnerable position when hit by Santa Anna in the battle of BUENA VISTA (Feb., 1847). The fighting was hard and appeared indecisive for a time, but in the end the Mexicans withdrew in confusion. The final campaign of the war began with the landing of U.S. forces under Gen. Winfield SCOTT at Veracruz in March, 1847. Scott was supported by a naval task force under David Conner (who was relieved by Matthew C. PERRY); they landed some 12,000 men and after a three-day bombardment took the city. Scott then began his drive on Mexico City. Santa Anna was defeated at the mountain stronghold of CERRO GORDO (April). After hard fighting Mexican forces were also routed at CONTRERAS and Churubusco (August). On Aug. 24 the Mexicans accepted an armistice, but after two weeks of futile peace negotiations, fighting was resumed. The Mexican capital was heavily defended by garrisons at Casa Mata and Molino del Rey and by the great fortress of CHAPULTEPEC. William J. WORTH carried Casa Mata and Molino del Rey, and the supposedly impregnable Chapultepec was stormed in a savage American assault led by Gen. John A. QUITMAN. On Sept. 14, 1847, American troops entered Mexico City, where they remained until peace was restored.

The Settlement. The United States had won an easy victory, partly because Mexico, torn by civil strife, could not present a united front to face the invader. The Mexican presidency had changed hands a number of times during the war, and some of the states had refused to cooperate with the central government. Peace negotiations were conducted on behalf of the United States by Nicholas P. TRIST, a secret envoy, whose relations with General Scott were at first strained. Although recalled by President Polk, Trist decided to ignore the order and continue his negotiations, which resulted in the Treaty of GUADALUPE HIDALGO (Feb. 2, 1848). By the terms of the treaty, Mexico ceded to the United States two fifths of its territory and received an indemnity of $15 million and the assumption of American claims against Mexico by the U.S. government. The boundary between the two countries, as outlined, was to follow the Rio Grande from its mouth to the New Mexico line, then run west to the Gila River, follow the Gila to the Colorado River and then follow the boundary between Upper California and Lower California to the Pacific. See G. L. Rives, *The United States and Mexico, 1821–1848* (1913, repr. 1969); J. H. Smith, *The War with Mexico* (1919, repr. 1963); Bernard De Voto, *The Year of Decision* (1943, repr. 1961); A. H. Bill, *Rehearsal for Conflict* (1947, repr. 1969); R. S. Henry, *The Story of the Mexican War* (1950, repr. 1961); O. A. Singletary, *The Mexican War* (1960); R. E. Ruiz, *The Mexican War: Was It Manifest Destiny?* (1963); K. J. Bauer, *The Mexican War* (1974); J. H. Schroeder, *Mr. Polk's War* (1974).

Mexico (mĕk'sĭkō), Span. *México* or *Méjico* (both: mä'hēkō), officially United States of Mexico, republic (1970 pop. 48,377,363), 761,600 sq mi (1,972,544 sq km), S North America, bordering on the United States in the north, on the Gulf of Mexico (including its arm, the Bay of Campeche) and the Caribbean Sea in the east, on British Honduras (Belize) and Guatemala in the southeast, and on the Pacific Ocean in the south and west. Mexico is divided into 31 states and the Federal District, which includes the country's capital and largest city, MEXICO City. The states are AGUASCALIENTES, BAJA CALIFORNIA, Baja California Sur, CAMPECHE, CHIAPAS, CHIHUAHUA, COAHUILA, COLIMA, DURANGO, GUANAJUATO, GUERRERO, HIDALGO, JALISCO, MEXICO, MICHOACÁN, MORELOS, NAYARIT, NUEVO LEÓN, OAXACA, PUEBLA, QUERÉTARO, QUINTANA ROO, SAN LUIS POTOSÍ, SINALOA, SONORA, TABASCO, TAMAULIPAS, TLAXCALA, VERACRUZ, YUCATÁN, and ZACATECAS. Most of Mexico is highland or mountainous and only about 15% of the land is arable; about 20% of the country is forested. Most of the Yucatán peninsula and the Isthmus of Tehuantepec in the southeast is lowland, and there are lowlying strips of land along the Gulf of Mexico, the Pacific Ocean, and the Gulf of California (which separates the Baja, or Lower, California peninsula from the rest of the country). The heart of Mexico is made up of the Mexican Plateau (c.700 mi/1,130 km long and c.4,000–8,000 ft/1,220–2,440 m high), which is broken by mountain ranges and segmented by deep rifts. The plateau is fringed by two mountain ranges, the Sierra Madre Oriental (in the east) and the Sierra Madre Occidental (in the west), which converge just south of the plateau. Within the plateau are drainage basins, which have no outlet to the sea and which contain some of the country's major cities. The LAGUNA DISTRICT, one of the drainage basins, was (1936) the scene of a major experiment in land reapportionment. In the north the plateau is arid except for irrigated areas and is used principally for raising livestock. In the south the deserts yield to the broad, shallow lakes of a region, comprising the Valley of Mexico, known as the ANÁHUAC and famous for its rich cultural heritage. South of the Anáhuac, which includes Mexico City, is a chain of extinct volcanoes, including ORIZABA, or Citlaltepétl (18,700 ft/5,700 m, the highest point in Mexico), POPOCATÉPETL, and IXTACIHUATL. To the south are jumbled masses of mountains and the Sierra Madre del Sur. Among Mexico's few large rivers are the Rio Grande (in Mexico, Río Bravo), which forms the boundary with Texas, and its tributaries the Río Conchos and the Río Sabinas; the Río Yaqui, Río Fuerte, Río Mezquital, Río Grande de Santiago, and Río Balsas, which flow into the Pacific; and the Río Grijalva and Río Usumacinta, which flow into the Bay of Campeche. The climate of the country varies with the altitude, so that there are hot, temperate, and cool regions—*tierra caliente* (up to c.2,000 ft/610 m), *tierra templada* (c.2,000–c.6,000 ft/610–1,830 m), and *tierra friá* (above c.6,000 ft/1,830 m). The great majority of the population are of mixed Spanish and Indian descent and speak Spanish, the official language, as their first language. Of the 3 million Indians in 1970, 1.1 million spoke only an Indian language, and the rest had but a poor command of Spanish. Since 1920 the population of Mexico has had a very high rate of growth, almost entirely the result of natural increase; from 1940 to 1970 the population grew from 19.6 million to 48.4 million. About 96% of the people are Roman Catholic and only 2% are Protestant. Since 1945, Mexico has enjoyed considerable economic growth, especially of its industrial plant. By 1970 manufacturing and commerce each contributed about 26% of the annual national product and agriculture (including forestry and fishing) about 16%. The Mexican government plays a major role in planning the economy and owns and operates basic industries and means of transport. About half of the country's workers (including those largely outside the money economy) are engaged in farming, which is still run in large measure according to inefficient, outmoded methods. Because rainfall is not adequate outside the coastal regions, agriculture depends largely on irrigation, the development of which began on a large scale only in the 1940s. The leading crops raised are maize, wheat, sugarcane, beans, citrus fruits, tomatoes, plantains, cotton, rice, coffee, sisal, and chili peppers. Maguey (see AMARYLLIS) is widely grown and is processed into the alcoholic beverages PULQUE and MESCAL. Mexico has considerable mineral resources. The great majority of operating mines are foreign-owned, but laws passed in the early 1960s provide for a gradual transition to Mexican control. The chief minerals produced are antimony, barite, copper, graphite, gypsum, lead, manganese, mercury, petroleum (large deposits were discovered in Chiapas and Tabasco states in Oct., 1974), salt, silver, sulfur, and zinc. The principal industrial centers in Mexico are Mexico City, MONTERREY, VERACRUZ, DURANGO, TAMPICO, MÉRIDA, GUADALAJARA, and PUEBLA. The leading manufactures include iron and steel, motor vehicles, processed food, cement, refined petroleum and petrochemicals, chemical fertilizers, rubber products, forest products, textiles, and aluminum. Mexico is also known for its handicrafts, especially pottery, woven goods, and silverwork. There is a large tourist industry; favorite tourist centers include ACAPULCO, CUERNAVACA, and TIJUANA. The country's chief ports are Veracruz, Tampico, COATZACOALCOS, and MAZATLÁN. The annual value of Mexico's imports is usually considerably higher than the value of its exports. The leading imports are machinery, motor vehicles, iron and steel, chemicals, and manufactured consumer goods; the main exports are cotton, sugar, coffee, tomatoes, shrimp, sulfur, and zinc. The principal trade partners are the United States, Japan, and West Germany. Mexico is a charter member of the Latin American Free Trade Association (founded 1961). The country has numerous universities, notably in Mexico City, Saltillo, Guadalajara, Monterrey, and Puebla.

History to the early 19th cent. Before the arrival of the Spanish conquistadores in the early 16th cent., great Indian civilizations developed and flourished in Mexico. The MAYA, the AZTEC, the TOLTEC, the MIXTEC, the ZAPOTEC, and the OLMEC all left behind impressive remains of great interest. The first Europeans to visit Mexico were Francisco Fernández de Córdoba in 1517 and Juan de GRIJALVA in 1518. The conquest was begun from Cuba in 1519 by Hernán CORTÉS, who with able lieutenants like Pedro de ALVARADO managed to conquer the Aztec capital, TENOCHTITLÁN; to capture MONTEZUMA, the Aztec ruler, and to bring down his empire; and to ward off Spanish rivals like Pánfilo de Narváez. In 1528 the first AUDIENCIA (royal court) was set up under Nuño de GUZMÁN, who later carried the conquest N to NUEVA GALICIA. The territory was constituted the viceroyalty of New Spain under Antonio de MENDOZA in 1535, and the process of Christianizing and Europeanizing the Indians went forward under such men as Juan de ZUMÁRRAGA. Nevertheless, the Spanish remained a small minority among the vast Indian population, and establishing control over the Indians remained an arduous task, interrupted by serious revolts like the MIXTÓN WAR (1541). The population developed slowly into three groups—whites, Indians, and mestizos (mixed white and Indian). The groups did not coalesce easily, despite the efforts of able viceroys like Luis de VELASCO (both father and son) and the younger conde de REVILLA GIGEDO. The efforts of the church resulted in at least nominal conversion of the Indians to Roman Catholicism. However, the church failed to mend the tissue of society, and the concentration of land and political power in its hands did nothing to close the gap in status between the wealthy, almost exclusively Spanish landowning class and the depressed laboring class on the land, in the mines, and in the small factories (chiefly the textile mills, called *obrajes*). The growth of an underprivileged mestizo class and the antagonism between those whites born in Spain (*gachupines*) and those born in America (*criollos,* or creoles) added to the stress. The mercantilist system, under which manufacturing was largely forbidden in New Spain, drained the wealth of the country to Spain. Lesser officials often were corrupt and ignored the country's problems. At the same time, new territory was conquered. Most of present-day Mexico and the former Spanish holdings in the present-day United States were occupied early. In the 16th cent. California was explored, but it was not until the middle and late 18th cent. that NE Mexico and Texas were occupied in any large degree. Many of the administrative evils were ended by the reforms (especially that of 1786) of José de GÁLVEZ, but discontent with Spanish rule continued to grow among the creoles.

Independence. The establishment of the United States and the ideas of the French Revolution had considerable influence on Mexicans. The occupation (1808) of Spain by Napoleon I, who placed his brother Joseph Bonaparte on the Spanish throne, opened the way for a revolt in Mexico. The priest HIDALGO Y COSTILLA began the rebellion by issuing (Sept. 16, 1810) the *Grito de Dolores* [cry of Dolores], a revolutionary tract calling for racial equality and the redistribution of land. Armies, made up mostly of lower-class mestizos and Indians and shunned by the creoles, sprang up under the command of Ignacio ALLENDE, José María MORELOS Y PAVÓN, Vicente GUERRERO, and Mariano MATAMOROS. Hidalgo was at first successful, but lost (1811) the decisive battle of Calderón Bridge. By 1815, Morelos and Matamoros had been defeated, and Guerrero had been driven into the wilds. When the liberals came to power in Spain in 1820, the more conservative elements in Mexico (primarily the higher clergy and the creoles) sought independence as a means of maintaining the status quo. The royalist general Augustín de ITURBIDE negotiated with Guerrero, and they arrived (Feb., 1821) at the Plan of Iguala (see under IGUALA), which called for an independent monarchy, equality for gachupines and creoles, and the maintenance of the privileged position of the church. Spain accepted Mexican independence in Sept., 1821, and a short-lived empire with Iturbide at its head was established (1822). In 1823, the republican leaders SANTA ANNA and GUADALUPE VICTORIA drove out Iturbide and a republic was set up with Guadalupe Victoria as its first president. Politics was dominated by groups formed around individuals (mostly army officers), each seeking his personal ends. There was a frequent turnover of governments, and the national budget usually ran a deficit. Guerrero, with the support of Santa Anna, became president in 1829, but was ousted in 1830 by Anastasio BUSTAMANTE. In 1832, the ambitious Santa Anna, who had a great influence over Mexican politics until 1855, toppled Bustamante and became president. Santa Anna fell from power after being captured during the Texas revolution (1836), but he served again as president from 1841 to 1844. Waste, corruption, and inefficiency were rampant at the time, and all the inequities of the social order went unchallenged. The war with Texas led to an all-out war with the United States, the MEXICAN WAR (1846–48), which was ended by the Treaty of GUADALUPE HIDALGO, by which Mexico lost a large block of territory. After the war, Santa Anna returned to power as "perpetual dictator," but he was overthrown (1855) by a revolution started (1854) at AYUTLA. A group of reform-minded men came to the fore—Juan ÁLVAREZ, Ignacio COMONFORT, Miguel and Sebastián LERDO DE TEJADA, and, especially, Benito JUÁREZ—and drafted the liberal constitution of 1857, which secularized church property and reduced the privileges of the army. Conservative opposition was bitter, and civil war ensued; Juárez led the liberals to victory in the War of Reform (1858–61). The conservatives then sought foreign aid and received it from Napoleon III of France, who had colonial ambitions. French intervention followed and led to a brief and ill-starred interlude of empire (1864–67) under MAXIMILIAN, a Hapsburg prince. With the end of French aid the empire collapsed and Juárez again ruled Mexico, but political disturbances prevented the accomplishment of his reform program. Porfirio DÍAZ led a successful armed revolt in 1876 and, except for the period from 1880 to 1884, firmly held the reins of power as president until 1911. It was a period of considerable economic growth, but social inequality was increased by the favoritism shown the great landowners and foreign investors; the Indians sank deeper into peonage. The democratic institutions remained only as a veneer for oligarchic rule.

The Revolution. In Nov., 1910, an idealistic liberal leader, Francisco I. MADERO, began an armed revolt against Díaz, who had gone back on his word not to seek reelection in 1910. Madero was quickly successful, and in May, 1911, Díaz resigned and went into exile. Madero was elected president in Nov., 1911. Well-meaning but ineffectual, he was attacked by conservatives and revolutionaries alike and was harassed by U.S. ambassador Henry Lane Wilson. In Feb., 1913, Madero was overthrown by his general, Victoriano HUERTA, and was murdered. President Huerta's regime was dictatorial and repressive, and revolts soon broke out under the leadership of Venustiano CARRANZA, Francisco "Pancho" VILLA, and Emiliano ZAPATA. In 1914, Huerta resigned, partly because of U.S. military intervention ordered by President Woodrow Wilson, and Carranza became president. Civil war broke out again in late 1914, but by the end of 1915 Carranza had established control over the country, although Villa and Zapata maintained opposition bands for a number of years. In 1916, Villa led a raid into the United States, which resulted in an unsuccessful U.S. expedition into Mexico. Carranza sponsored the constitution of 1917, which was similar to the 1857 constitution, but which in addition provided for the nationalization of mineral resources, for the restoration of communal lands to the Indians, for the separation of church and state, and for educational, agrarian, and labor reforms. However, most provisions of the constitution were not implemented, and in 1920 Carranza was deposed by General Álvaro OBREGÓN, his former military chief, who was subsequently elected president. Under the Obregón regime (1920–24) some land was redistributed and, under the leadership of José VASCONCELOS, numerous schools were built. Obregón was succeeded by Plutarco Elías CALLES, who continued the agrarian and educational programs, but who became embroiled in serious controversies with the United States over rights to petroleum and with the church over the separation of church and state. In some regions Catholic militants, called *Cristeros* because of their rallying cry—*Viva Cristo Rey!* [long live Christ the King]—were in open revolt, and in the country as a whole from 1926 to 1929 church schools were closed and no church services were held. Both controversies subsided, partly because of the intervention of the U.S. ambassador, Dwight MORROW. Reelected in 1928, Obregón was assassinated before taking office. Calles remained the most powerful person in Mexico during the administrations of Portes Gil (1928–30), Ortiz Rubio (1930–32), and Abelardo Rodríguez (1932–34). In 1929 he organized the National Revolutionary party (in 1946 renamed the Institutional Revolutionary party), the chief political party in Mexico. Calles's hegemony ended, however, with the inauguration (1934) of Lázaro CÁRDENAS. Vigorous and idealistic, Cárdenas instituted reforms to improve the lot of the underprivileged and to make the Indian an organic part of the state. He redistributed much land under the EJIDO system and supported the Mexican labor movement, which had suffered a setback under Calles (see Vicente LOMBARDO TOLEDANO). Railroads were nationalized, and foreign holdings, particularly in petroleum fields, were expropriated with compensation. Educational opportunities were increased and illiteracy reduced, medical facilities were extended, transport and communications were improved, and plans were drawn up for land reclamation and for hydroelectric and industrial projects. A settlement with the church was reached. The pace of reform slowed under Manuel ÁVILA CAMACHO, who became president in 1940. Relations with the United States improved. In World War II, Mexico declared war (1942) on the Axis powers; it made substantial contributions to the Allied cause and also received considerable U.S. economic aid.

Post-1945 Developments. Since World War II, Mexico has enjoyed considerable economic development, but most of the benefits have accrued to the middle and upper classes and the relative welfare of poorer persons (small farmers and laborers) has remained the same or deteriorated. Under President Miguel ALEMÁN (1946–52) vast irrigation projects and hydroelectric plants were constructed, and industrialization advanced rapidly. The improvements made in Mexico's rail network during World War II and the opening of the INTER-AMERICAN HIGHWAY after the war encouraged more U.S. tourists to visit Mexico and thus increased the commercial value of one of the country's greatest assets, the beauty of its land. Under the moderate presidents Adolfo Ruiz Cortines (1952–58), Adolfo López Mateos (1958–64), and Gustavo Díaz Ordaz (1964–70), the government continued to play a dominant role in national affairs, and attempts were made to improve the conditions of the lower classes. The tax structure was reformed somewhat, some large estates were confiscated and the land redistributed, and educational opportunities in rural areas were increased. In foreign affairs, Mexico maintained friendly relations with the United States, ratifying treaties settling long-standing border disputes in the El Paso, Texas, region (1964, 1967) and calling (1965) for the United States to maintain the freshwater content of the Colorado River, whose waters are used for irrigation in Mexico. Unlike most other American nations, Mexico maintained diplomatic relations with revolutionary Cuba, but it supported the United States during the Cuban missile crisis (1962). In 1970, Luis Echevarría Álvarez became president. He took significant steps toward reforming the government and opening it to persons with new ideas and toward reviving the spirit of the Mexican revolution. However, the first years of his administration were plagued by clashes between rightist and leftist students and by the activities of guerrilla groups. Also, within the Catholic Church there was a serious rift between politically active leftist clerics and conservatives who eschewed politics.

Government. Under the constitution of 1917 as amended, Mexico is a federal republic whose chief executive and head of state is the president, directly elected to a nonrenewable six-year term and assisted by a cabinet. The bicameral legislature is made up of the Senate, comprising 64 members directly elected to six-year terms, and the Chamber of Deputies, consisting of 219 members serving three-year terms (194 of the deputies are directly elected, and 25 are chosen by a system of proportional representation). Since precolonial times Mexican architects, painters, writers, and musicians have produced a rich cultural heritage. See articles on SPANISH COLONIAL ART AND ARCHITECTURE, MEXICAN ART AND ARCHITECTURE, and SPANISH AMERICAN LITERATURE. A number of historical sources have been translated into English, notably the letters of Cortés and the account of the conquest by Bernal DÍAZ DEL CASTILLO. See W. H. Prescott, *The Conquest of Mexico* (3 vol., 1843; many subsequent editions); Octavio Paz, *The Labyrinth of Solitude* (tr. 1962) and *The Other Mexico* (tr. 1972); François Chevalier, *Land and Society in Colonial Mexico* (tr. 1963); L. B. Simpson, *Many Mexicos* (4th ed. 1966); C. C. Cumberland, *Mexico, the Struggle for Modernity* (1968) and *Mexican Revolution: The Constitutionalist Years* (1972); Frank Tannenbaum, *The Mexican Agrarian Revolution* (1929, repr. 1968); J. W. Wilkie, *The Mexican Revolution* (2d ed. 1970); A. J. Hanna and K. A. Hanna, *Napoleon III and Mexico* (1971); R. D. Hansen, *The Politics of Mexican Development* (1971); R. H. Marett, *Mexico* (1971); Nicolas Cheetham, *A History of Mexico* (1972); Peter Calvert, *Mexico* (1973); T. R. Fehrenbach, *Fire and Blood: A History of Mexico* (1973).

Mexico, Span. *México* or *Méjico*, state (1970 pop. 3,797,861), 8,286 sq mi (21,461 sq km), S central Mexico. TOLUCA is the capital. The northern section of the state, containing most of the Valley of Mexico (part of the Anáhuac plateau), has broad, shallow lakes and is broken by low mountains. There are steeper mountains and valleys in the east, and the southern and western areas are dominated by the rugged volcanic belt extending across the center of the country. On the state's southeastern border are the Popocatépetl and Ixtacihuatl volcanoes. The principal river is the Lerma. Except on the south, the state encircles the Federal District, with the nation's capital, Mexico City. Mining (gold, silver, copper, iron), agriculture (maguey, coffee, tobacco, beans, cereals), and dairy farming are the state's chief economic activities. It is a leading national producer of iron and steel, chemicals, and textiles. Other industrial products include glassware and pottery. Mexico is one of the country's most densely populated states.

Mexico, Span. *México* or *Méjico,* city (1970 pop. 3,025,564), central Mexico, capital and largest city of

Mexico, near the southern end of the plateau of Anáhuac, at an altitude of c.7,800 ft (2,380 m). The horizons of the city are almost obscured by mountain barriers, and the peaks of Popocatépetl and Ixtacihuatl are not far off. The climate is cool, dry, and healthful. Much of the surrounding valley is a lake basin with no outlet, and in the past during the rainy seasons mountain floods swelled the lakes. From the time when the Aztec capital of Tenochtitlán stood on an island in Lake Texcoco—now the heart of the metropolis—measures have been taken to protect the city and provide for expansion by draining Texcoco and the other lakes, Chalco and Xochimilco. In the 17th cent. the Spanish viceroys, notably Louis de Velasco, the younger, initiated important works. In 1900 a central canal was completed that reached to the headwaters of the Pánuco River. The Caracol [Span.,=snail], a 12-mi (19-km) spiral canal fed in turn by longitudinal canals begun in 1936, acts as an evaporating basin, from which valuable minerals are taken. Drainage and artesian wells have lowered the water table so that the surface crust, formerly supported by subsoil water, can no longer sustain the heavier buildings of the city, which are sinking some 4 to 12 in. (10.2-30 cm) a year. Some of Mexico's finest buildings have been damaged, among them the old cathedral (begun in 1553 on the site of an Aztec temple) and the Palace of Fine Arts (which has sunk 10 ft/3.1 m). Modern office buildings have been shored up with pilings. Nevertheless, many monuments of Spanish colonial architecture remain. The cathedral and the National Palace are on the great central square, or Plaza de la Constitución, where the streets of the old town crisscross in a rough gridiron. From the Plaza the great avenues span out to the far sections of the capital. Many colonial churches are to be found, notably on the Paseo de la Reforma, which cuts across the city to CHAPULTEPEC. Public buildings of the 19th cent. have a ponderous grandeur that shows French influence, but the recent edifices are starkly modern. Some old buildings as well as the newer (e.g., the Palace of Fine Arts, the National Palace, and the National Preparatory School) have murals by the modern artists Diego Rivera, José Clemente Orozco, and David Alfaro Siqueiros. The National Univ. of Mexico, founded in the 16th cent., is now housed in University City (opened 1952), built on a lava outcrop in the outskirts. The city has been the metropolis of Mexico since New Spain was created. It was taken in 1847 by Winfield Scott's American army, after an inland march from Veracruz in the MEXICAN WAR. The French army captured Mexico City in 1863, and Emperor Maximilian, crowned in 1864, did much to beautify it before it was recaptured by Mexicans under Benito JUÁREZ. In the years of revolution after 1910 it was a magnet for divergent insurrectionary forces. Perhaps the most spectacular incidents were the occupations (1914-15) by Francisco VILLA and Emiliano ZAPATA. Today Mexico City forms the core of the Federal Dist. and is the commercial, industrial, financial, political, and cultural center of the nation. Among its important manufactures are iron and steel, petroleum, food products, textiles, glassware, machinery, chemicals, and consumer items. Population has increased rapidly in a city that had already spread out in many residential sections called *colonias.* Beyond these lie the cities of the Federal Dist.; Atzcapotzalco and Gustavo A. Madero are the largest. Of the many suburbs of Mexico City, Coyoacán is the oldest, with a palace built by Cortés. Among noted religious and recreational centers are Guadalupe Hidalgo and Xochimilco. The city, with its rich local color and extraordinary cultural attractions, has become a focal point for tourists, especially from the United States. In 1957 an earthquake caused extensive damage. The Olympics were held in Mexico City in 1968.

Mexico, city (1970 pop. 11,807), seat of Audrain co., central Mo., in a farm area; inc. 1857. Firebrick and shoes are manufactured, and there are livestock markets and horse stables in the city. A saddle horse museum, the county historical society museum, and Missouri Military Academy are in the city.

Mexico, Gulf of, arm of the Atlantic Ocean, c.700,000 sq mi (1,813,000 sq km), SE North America. The Gulf stretches more than 1,100 mi (1,770 km) from west to east and c.800 mi (1,290 km) from north to south. It is bordered by the southeast coast of the United States from Florida to Texas, and the east coast of Mexico from Tamaulipas to Yucatán. At the entrance of the Gulf is the island of Cuba. On the northern side of Cuba the Gulf is connected with the Atlantic Ocean by the Straits of Florida (through which the Gulf Stream passes); on the southern side of Cuba it is connected with the Caribbean Sea by the Yucatán Channel. The Bay of Campeche (Bahía de Campeche), Mexico, and Apalachee Bay, Florida, are the Gulf's largest arms. Sigsbee Deep (12,714 ft/3,875 m), the deepest part of the Gulf, lies off the Mexican coast. The shoreline is generally low, sandy, and marshy, with many lagoons and deltas. Chief of the many rivers entering the Gulf are the Alabama, Mississippi, Brazos, and Rio Grande. The U.S. Intracoastal Waterway follows the Gulf's northern coast. Oil deposits from the continental shelf are tapped by offshore wells, especially along the coast of Texas and Louisiana. Most of the U.S. shrimp catch comes from the Gulf Coast; menhaden is another important catch. The chief ports along the Gulf of Mexico are at Tampa and Pensacola, Fla.; Mobile, Ala.; Galveston and Corpus Christi, Texas; Tampico and Veracruz, Mexico; and Havana, Cuba.

Mexico, National University of, at Mexico City, Mexico; founded 1551 by the Spanish king Charles I (Holy Roman Emperor Charles V). It has faculties of accounting and business administration, chemistry, engineering, law, medicine, philosophy and letters, political and social sciences, psychology, science, and veterinary medicine and zoology as well as schools of architecture, dentistry, economics, music, nursing and obstetrics, and plastic arts.

Meyer, Adolf (ä'dôlf mī'ər) 1866-1950, American neurologist and psychiatrist, b. Switzerland, M.D. Zürich, 1892. He emigrated to the United States in 1892 and was professor of psychiatry at Cornell Univ. (1904-9) and at Johns Hopkins (1910-41), where he was also director of the Henry Phipps Psychiatric Clinic. He was active in the mental hygiene movement from its inception (1908) and suggested the term "mental hygiene." His system of treating mental illness, called psychobiology, demanded that each problem be considered in the light of the patient's total personality. His selected papers, *Commonsense Psychiatry,* were edited by Alfred Lief (1948). See his collected papers, ed. by E. E. Winters (4 vol., 1950-52).

Meyer, Conrad Ferdinand (kôn'rät fĕr'dēnänt mī'ər), 1825-98, Swiss poet and novelist. He studied history and art and later turned to literature. He is best known for his historical novellas, which are marked by a feeling for the spirit of past ages, keen psychological insight, and deep concern for ethical problems. Among these works are *Das Amulett* (1873), *Jürg Jenatsch* (1876), *Der Heilige* (1880; tr. *Thomas à Becket the Saint,* 1885), and *Die Hochzeit des Mönchs* (1884; tr. *The Monk's Wedding,* 1887). Meyer's verse, like his prose, dealt mainly with Renaissance themes, but its underlying symbolism made it a link between classical and impressionistic poetry. See study by Heinrich Henel (1954).

Meyer, Eugene, 1875-1959, American financier and newspaper publisher, b. Los Angeles. He was a successful broker and a director of many corporations. In 1917 he was appointed to guide American war production and finance, serving in many government agencies. He was director of the War Finance Corp. from 1918 to 1920 and from 1921 to 1925. After organizing the Reconstruction Finance Corp. (1931), he became its first chairman. In 1946 he was appointed first president of the International Bank for Reconstruction and Development (World Bank). Meyer bought the Washington *Post* in 1933 and made it one of the country's most influential newspapers. In 1954 it absorbed the *Times-Herald.* Succeeded as publisher in 1946 by his son-in-law, Philip L. Graham, Meyer remained board chairman until his death.

Meyer, Gustav: see MEYRINK, GUSTAV.

Meyer, Hannes (hän'əs mī'ər), 1889-1954, Swiss architect. Meyer was a lecturer and studio master at the BAUHAUS in Dessau. He succeeded Gropius as its director (1928-30). Meyer is noted for his rejection of the concept of individual design in favor of designs produced by the collaboration of architects. He worked in Germany, Switzerland, Mexico, and the USSR. One of his best-known designs is the German Trades Union School at Bernau (1928-30).

Meyer, Julius Lothar, 1830-95, German chemist. He taught at Breslau, Karlsruhe, and Tübingen (from 1876) and is known especially for his work in the development of the PERIODIC LAW, for which, with Mendeleev, he received the Davy medal in 1882. He evolved the atomic volume curve (1869), which represented graphically the relation between the atomic weights and the atomic volumes of the elements.

Meyerbeer, Giacomo (jä'kōmō mī'yərbĕr), 1791-1864, German operatic composer. He traveled in Italy and experimented in various styles of composition, but his real success came only with his spectacular French grand operas—*Robert le Diable* (1831) and his masterpiece, *Les Huguenots* (1836). For these and two other grand operas, *Le Prophète* (1849) and *L'Africaine* (1865), Scribe was the librettist. Two opéras comiques are noteworthy, *L'Étoile du nord* (1854) and *Dinorah* (1859). He calculated the taste of his public with tremendous success and was much imitated, notably by Wagner in *Rienzi.*

Meyerhof, Otto (ô'tō mī'ərhōf), 1884-1951, American physiologist, b. Germany, M.D. Heidelberg, 1909. He was professor at the Univ. of Kiel (1912-24) and at the Univ. of Berlin and director of the Kaiser Wilhelm Institute of Medical Research at Heidelberg (1929-38). Forced to leave Germany, he became professor of biochemistry at the Univ. of Pennsylvania in 1940. He studied cellular oxidation and discovered the transformation of lactic acid in muscles. For this he shared with A. V. Hill the 1922 Nobel Prize in Physiology and Medicine. His works include *The Chemical Dynamics of Life Phaenomena* (1924).

Meyerhold, Vsevolod (fəsyĕ'vəlŭt mē'ûrhōlt), 1874-1940?, Russian theatrical director and producer. Meyerhold led the revolt against naturalism in the Russian theater. Working with the Moscow Art Theatre, he experimented with his own directing ideas until the outbreak of the Revolution. Meyerhold was a member of the Bolshevik party, and as head of theatrical activities for the state he directed the first theater to specialize in Soviet plays. He was among the earliest advocates of the theater of the absurd. In his avant-garde productions he employed various grotesque elements, pantomimes, and acrobatics, emphasizing the plays' visual, nonverbal aspects. He produced Bolshevik propaganda dramas, using bare constructivist settings and formalized scenery, and eliminating the curtain. Meyerhold directed his actors according to his principle of "biomechanics," reducing the actors' individual contributions to a minimum, in the interests of the play as a whole. His work eventually became unprofitable, and the state discontinued his subsidy. He was an outspoken opponent of SOCIALIST REALISM. A victim of the Soviet purges, Meyerhold died under circumstances that remain unclear; the date of his death is open to question. See *Meyerhold on Theater,* ed. by Edward Braun (1969); biography by M. L. Hoover (1974); J. M. Symons, *Meyerhold's Theatre of the Grotesque* (1971).

Meyer-Lübke, Wilhelm (vĭl'hĕlm mī'ər-lüp'kə), 1861-1936, Swiss philologist. Meyer-Lübke taught at the universities of Jena, Vienna, and Bonn. He was the author of many works on Romance languages, chief among them being a four-volume grammar of Romance languages (1890-1902) and an etymological dictionary (in 13 parts, 1911-20).

Meynell, Alice (Thompson) (mĕn'əl), 1847-1922, English poet and essayist. She spent most of her youth in Italy. Converted to Roman Catholicism in 1872, she wrote much on religious subjects. In 1877 she married Wilfrid Meynell (1852-1948), the founder and editor of *Merry England,* a Catholic paper, to which she was a frequent contributor. The Meynells befriended and encouraged Francis THOMPSON, whose work also appeared in their magazine. A complete edition of Meynell's poetry was published in 1923. Her verse, characterized by control and religious emotion, includes "The Shepherdess," "A Letter from a Girl to Her Own Old Age," and the sonnet "Renouncement." *The Rhythm of Life* (1893) and *The Second Person Singular* (1921) are among her many books of essays. See biography by her daughter Viola Meynell (1929).

Meyrink, Gustav (go͝os'täf mī'rĭngk), 1868-1932, German author, b. Vienna. His original name was Gustav Meyer. A staff member of *Simplicissimus* from 1902, he became famous for his sketches, parodies, and comedies. His novels, including *The Golem* (1916, tr. 1928), about an artificial man who runs amok, and *Walpurgisnacht* (1917), have a surrealistic blend of comedy, grotesquerie, and symbolism.

Mezahab (mĕz'āhăb), grandfather of Mehetabel. Gen. 36.39; 1 Chron. 1.50.

Mezen (myĕ'zĭnyə), river, c.565 mi (910 km) long, rising in the Timan Hills, Komi Autonomous Republic, NE European USSR, and flowing NW into the Mezen Bay of the White Sea. Its lower course is navigable from May to November. Near its mouth is the city of Mezen, a river port exporting lumber.

Mézières, France: see CHARLEVILLE-MÉZIÈRES.

mezzo-soprano: see SOPRANO.

mezzotint (mĕt'sətĭnt, mĕd'zə-, mĕz'ə-) [Ital.,=halftint], method of copper or steel engraving in tone. A Dutch officer, Ludwig von Siegen, is given credit for the invention of mezzotint c.1640. The process then came into prominence in England early in the 18th cent. Mezzotint involves uniform burring with a curved, sawtoothed tool by cradling it back and forth until the surface of the plate presents an all-over, even grain. This yields a soft effect in the print. The picture is developed in chiaroscuro with a scraper and a burnisher, every degree of light and shade from black to white being attainable. In pure mezzotint, no line drawing is employed, the result being soft without the sharp lines of an etching. Mezzotint was often used for the reproduction of paintings, particularly, in England, for landscapes and portraits. The process is essentially extinct today.

Mfumbiro, mountains, Africa: see VIRUNGA.

Mg, chemical symbol of the element MAGNESIUM.

MHD: see MAGNETOHYDRODYNAMICS.

Miami (mīăm'ē, -ə). **1** City (1970 pop. 334,859), seat of Dade co., SE Fla., on Biscayne Bay at the mouth of the Miami River; inc. 1896. The second largest city in the state and a port of entry, it is also one of the most popular and famous resorts of the E United States. Tourism is its major industry, and there are extensive recreational facilities for fishing, swimming, golf, yachting, and horse and dog racing, with many related businesses and enterprises. The city has an international airport and is a major port for cruise ships to the Caribbean. It is also the processing and shipping hub of a large agricultural region and a center for rebuilding and repairing aircraft. Its manufactures include aluminum products, clothing, furniture, transportation equipment, machinery, stone, clay, glass, lumber, and wood products. Other industries are printing and publishing, fishing, and shellfishing. The first settlement was made there in the 1870s near the site of Fort Dallas, built in 1836 during the Seminole War. In 1895, Henry M. Flagler became interested in the area. He made Miami a railroad terminus in 1896, dredged the harbor, and began the development of a recreation center. The city received its greatest impetus during the Florida land boom of the mid-1920s. Biscayne Boulevard, with its park and causeways spanning Biscayne Bay and leading to Miami Beach, is well known, as is the Dade County Art Museum. The Orange Bowl is the home of the city's major league football team, the Miami Dolphins, and site of a traditional New Year's festival and college bowl game. Marine Stadium is known for its water sports. Miami is the seat of Barry College, Biscayne College, Florida Memorial College, and the largest junior college in the country (Miami-Dade Junior College). The Univ. of Miami is in nearby Coral Gables. A veterans hospital is in the city, and a number of state parks, gardens, and major tourist attractions are in the area. The region of Greater Miami encompasses all of Dade co., and includes Miami, Miami Beach, Coral Gables, Hialeah, and many smaller communities. See S. D. Dietriech, *Miami* (1964); W. W. Jenna, *Metropolitan Miami* (1972). **2** City (1970 pop. 13,880), seat of Ottawa co., extreme NE Okla., in the foothills of the Ozarks and on the headwaters of Grand Lake, which provides both electric power and recreation. It is a trade, shipping, and marketing center for a tri-state region where lead and zinc are mined. A two-year state agricultural and mechanical college is there.

Miami (mīăm'ə, -ē) or **Great Miami,** river, c.160 mi (260 km) long, formed in W Ohio near Indian Lake and flowing generally SW past Dayton to the Ohio River at the Ind. line. The Miami River system has large-scale flood-control projects. The Miami and Erie Canal (c.240 mi/390 km long; opened in the 1830s) linked the upper Miami River with Lake Erie and was the principal transportation route of W Ohio until the 1850s. The Little Miami River (95 mi/152 km long) to the east and generally parallel, rises SE of Springfield and enters the Ohio River at Cincinnati.

Miami, University of, mainly at Coral Gables, Fla.; partly supported by city, county, and state; coeducational; chartered 1925, opened 1926. Besides the main campus there are the north and south campuses nearby and a marine laboratory on Virginia Key. The university also maintains extension centers at Fort Lauderdale and at Patrick Air Force Base.

Miami Beach, city (1970 pop. 87,072), Dade co., SE Fla., on an island between Biscayne Bay and the Atlantic Ocean; inc. 1915. It is connected to Miami by four causeways. Miami Beach is a popular year-round resort, world famous for its "gold coast" hotel strip (with over 350 hotels and motels), palatial estates, and recreational facilities; the city's chief source of income is from tourism. It has approximately 3 million visitors each year. The 34,000-seat Convention Hall complex has hosted several national political conventions, including the Democratic and Republican conventions in 1972. The area was originally a jungle wilderness; a wooden bridge was built from the mainland in 1913, but development was slow until the Florida land boom in the 1920s. The U.S. coast guard and the U.S. army Corps of Engineers have bases there. See Harold Mehling, *The Most of Everything; the Story of Miami Beach* (1960); P. Redford, *Billion Dollar Sandbar* (1970).

Miami Indians, group of North American Indians of the Algonquian branch of the Algonquian-Wakashan linguistic stock (see AMERICAN INDIAN LANGUAGES). They shared the cultural traits of the Eastern Woodlands area and the Plains area, hunting the buffalo that ranged through much of their territory. In the mid-17th cent. the Miami held land in W Wisconsin, NE Illinois, and N Indiana. In the mid-18th cent., however, the invading northern tribes drove the Miami to NW Ohio. The Miami occupied this territory until the treaty of 1763, when they retired to Indiana. They then numbered some 1,700. The Miami had aided the French in the French and Indian Wars, and they helped the British in the American Revolution. With their chief LITTLE TURTLE, the Miami were prominent in the Indian wars of the Old Northwest. By 1827 they had ceded most of their lands in Indiana and had agreed to move to Kansas. Most of them went (1840) to Kansas and then moved (1867) to Oklahoma, where they were placed on a reservation. Since then the land has been divided among them. There is also a group of Miami in Indiana. See Bert Anson, *The Miami Indians* (1970).

Miamin (mī'əmĭn). **1** One separated from a foreign wife. Ezra 10.25. **2** Family of priests. Neh. 12.5. Mijamin: 1 Chron. 24.9; Neh. 10.7. Miniamin: Neh. 12.17.

Miamisburg (mīăm'ēzbərg), city (1970 pop. 14,797), Montgomery co., SW Ohio, on the Miami River; laid out 1818, inc. 1932. Metal and paper products are the leading manufactures. The Atomic Energy Commission operates a research corporation there. A large Indian mound is nearby.

Miami Springs, city (1970 pop. 13,279), Dade co., SE Fla., a residential suburb of Miami; inc. 1926. The wells in the city supply water to much of Dade co. Miami International Airport is adjacent to the city.

Miami University, mainly at Oxford, Ohio; coeducational; state supported; chartered 1809, opened 1824. The library has extensive collections in literature and American history including the William Holmes MCGUFFEY Library and Museum and the Edgar W. King collection of children's literature. The Scripps Foundation for Research in Population Problems library is there. Branch campuses are located at Hamilton and Middletown.

Miantonomo (mēăn"tənō'mō, mīăn"-), d. 1643, chief of the Narragansett Indians; nephew of another chief, Canonicus. In 1637 he aided the English colonists in the Pequot War. The following year he was induced to make a treaty of peace with the English and with his ancient enemy, UNCAS. Miantonomo was friendly with the settlers of Rhode Island, particularly with Roger Williams, but was viewed with suspicion in Massachusetts and accused of instigating plots against the English. He defended himself (1640) in Boston, where he was ill-treated. In 1643 he was captured by Uncas and delivered to the English at Hartford, but was returned by them to Uncas, who killed him. See H. M. Chapin, *Sachems of the Narragansetts* (1931).

Mianwali (myän'välē), town (1961 pop. 31,398), N Pakistan, on the Indus River. It is the administrative center and market for a district that produces food grains, oilseed, hides, and wool.

Miaskovsky, Nikolai Yakovlevich (nyĭkəlī' yä'kəvlyĭvĭch myəskôf'skē), 1881–1950, Russian composer, b. near Warsaw, grad. St. Petersburg Conservatory, 1911. Professor of composition at the Moscow Conservatory from 1921 to 1950, he is perhaps the most prolific composer of symphonies in the 20th cent., having completed 27. He also wrote much chamber and piano music, choruses, operas, and scores for films. See A. A. Ikonnikov, *Myaskowsky: His Life and Work* (tr. 1946).

Miass (mēäs'), river (c.390 mi/630 km long), W Siberian USSR. It rises in the eastern slopes of the S Urals and flows N and NE past Chelyabinsk into the Iset, a tributary of the Ob River. The city of **Miass** (1970 pop. 130,000) is the center of a major gold-mining area and has instrument and metallurgical plants.

Mibhar (mĭb'här), one of David's men. 1 Chron. 11.38.

Mibsam (mĭb'săm). **1** Son of Ishmael. Gen. 25.13; 1 Chron. 1.29. **2** Son of Simeon. 1 Chron. 4.25.

Mibzar (mĭb'zär), duke of Edom. Gen. 36.42.

mica (mī'kə), general term for a large group of minerals, hydrous silicates of aluminum and potassium, often containing magnesium, ferrous iron, ferric iron, sodium, and lithium and more rarely containing barium, chromium, and fluorine. All crystallize in the monoclinic system, but mica is most commonly found in the form of scales and sheets. All the micas have an excellent basal cleavage, splitting into very thin, elastic laminae. Some varieties are transparent; resistance to heat is high. Commercially, the most important micas are muscovite (potassium mica) and phlogopite (magnesium mica). Muscovite, the commoner variety, is usually colorless, but it may be red, yellow, green, brown, or gray, with a vitreous to pearly luster. It occurs in granites, syenites, mica schists, and gneisses, but is commonest in pegmatite dikes. It is widely distributed. Phlogopite varies in color from yellow to brown, some specimens having a coppery tint and others being greenish. It occurs in crystalline limestones, dolomites, and serpentines in Canada, New York, New Jersey, and Finland. Mica mining, because of the necessity of keeping the crystals intact, is a delicate operation; drills and blasting powder must be used carefully, if at all. The mined crystals are first "cobbed," i.e., roughly trimmed of rock and cut, then split with a hammer into plates, and further split into sheets with a knife. Sheet mica is used as an insulating material and as a resonant diaphragm in certain acoustical devices. Scrap and ground mica is used in wallpaper, fancy paint, ornamental tile, roofing, lubricating oil, and Christmas-tree snow. Ground mica is sometimes pressed into sheets (micanite) that can be used as sheet mica. Most of the sheet mica used in the United States is imported, chiefly from India and also from Brazil. Synthetic mica was produced in the United States after intensive government-sponsored research began in 1946.

Micaëlis de Vasconcelos, Carolina (kärōlē'nä mēkää'lĭs dĭ väsh"kōnsĕl'ōōsh), 1851–1925, Portuguese scholar, b. Berlin. As a youth she gained a considerable reputation as a Romance philologist. After her marriage in 1876 to Joaquim de Vasconcelos, a Portuguese art critic, she moved to Portugal. Her careful and brilliant work, especially her edition of the *Cancioneiro de Ajuda* (1904), masterfully reconstructed the history of early Portuguese literature and language. She was a professor at the Univ. of Coimbra. Her name is sometimes written as Michaëlis de Vasconcellos.

Micah (mī'kə). **1** Prophet, author of the book of MICAH. **2** Levite. 1 Chron. 23.20. Michah: 1 Chron. 24.24. **3** Ephraimite whose sacred belongings were taken from him. Judges 17–18. **4** Son of Mephibosheth. 1 Chron. 8.34; 9.40. Micha: 2 Sam. 9.12. **5** Same as MICHAIAH **1.** **6** Same as MICHAIAH **2.** **7** Reubenite. 1 Chron. 5.5.

Micah (mī'kə) or **Micheas** (mīkē'əs), book of the Old Testament, 33d in the order of the Authorized Version, 6th of the books of the Minor Prophets. The book contains the prophecy of Micah, a contemporary of Isaiah and Hezekiah (second half of the 8th cent. B.C.). The main divisions of the prophecy are as follows: the doom of Israel and Judah, which are to be punished for hypocritical worship, social injustice, and personal immorality (1–3); ultimate redemption (4–5); a recapitulation in different form of the same themes (6–7). The book includes a famous Messianic passage (5.2–6), alluded to in Mat. 2.6 and John 7.42. Some scholars attribute chapters 4 through 7 to later authorship. See study by T. M. Bennett (1968); see also bibliography under OLD TESTAMENT.

Micaiah (mīkā'yə, mī"kā'ə), Samaritan prophet who foretold the death of Ahab. 1 Kings 22.

Micha (mī'kə). **1** Same as MICAH **4.** **2** Sealer of the covenant. Neh. 10.11. **3** Same as MICHAIAH **2.**

Michael (mī'kəl) [Heb.,=Who is like God?], archangel prominent in Jewish, Christian, and Muslim traditions. In the Bible he is mentioned as a prince or a warrior and as the guardian angel of Israel (Dan. 10.13,21; 12.1; Jude 1.9; Rev. 12.7). In Christian tradition he is the angel with the sword, the conqueror of Satan. In the Roman Catholic Church and in the Eastern Church he has had widespread veneration. His feast (jointly with the other archangels) is Michaelmas, Sept. 29; it is the anniversary of the dedication of a Roman basilica to him. On May 8 he is honored for his apparition (492?) on Monte Gargano, Italy. He is supposed to have appeared to Joan of Arc and on the site of Mont-Saint-Michel.

Michael I (Michael Rangabe), d. c.845, Byzantine emperor (811–13), son-in-law of Nicephorus I. He supported orthodoxy against iconoclasm and recalled THEODORE OF STUDIUM from exile. He recognized (812) Charlemagne's claim as emperor. Defeated by the Bulgars, he was deposed and exiled. Leo V succeeded him.

Michael II (Michael the Stammerer), d. 829, Byzantine emperor (820-29). A native of Phrygia, he fought with Emperor Leo V, whom he had helped gain the throne. Leo had him arrested for heading a conspiracy, but the plotters murdered Leo and raised Michael to the throne. In the religious controversy, Michael tolerated both orthodoxy and iconoclasm but personally favored iconoclasm. He lost (825) Crete to the Arabs, who began (827) the invasion of Sicily. He was succeeded by his son Theophilus and by (842) his grandson Michael III.

Michael III (Michael the Amorian or Phrygian), 836-67, Byzantine emperor (842-67), son and successor of Theophilus and grandson of Michael II. His minority saw the final overthrow of ICONOCLASM and a severe persecution of the PAULICIANS. Upon coming of age he entrusted the government to his capable uncle, Bardas, whose administration (856-66) was marked by the missions of saints CYRIL AND METHODIUS to the Slavs and by the conversion of Czar Boris I of Bulgaria. The Arabs continued their raids into the empire and extended their conquests in Sicily, although their eastward expansion was temporarily stopped (863). In the north, he defeated (860-61) the Russians. Michael made Basil of Macedonia (later Basil I) one of his favorites and together they had Bardas assassinated in 866. Basil was made coemperor. He then murdered Michael and became sole emperor. The schism precipitated by the patriarch PHOTIUS began in the last year of Michael's reign.

Michael VIII (Michael Palaeologus), c.1225-1282, Byzantine emperor (1261-82), first of the PALAEOLOGUS dynasty. Following the murder of the regent for Emperor JOHN IV of Nicaea, he was appointed (1258) regent and, soon afterward (1259), coemperor. He successfully defended (1259) Nicaea against the coalition of the despotat of Epirus, Sicily, and Achaea. Michael then led his army against the crumbling Latin Empire of Constantinople and recovered (1261) its capital from Emperor BALDWIN II. With the Byzantine Empire thus restored, Michael was crowned by the patriarch. He later had John IV blinded and imprisoned. The remainder of Michael's reign was taken up by his fight against CHARLES I of Naples and Sicily, and against the despotat of Epirus. He concluded peace with the Tartars and Mamelukes in 1272. For support against Charles he vacillated between Venice and Genoa as allies. He negotiated with Pope Gregory X for a union of the Eastern and Western Churches, and in 1274 his emissaries at the Second Council of Lyons (see LYONS, SECOND COUNCIL OF) agreed to recognize the spiritual supremacy of the pope. However, in 1281 Pope MARTIN IV, a supporter of Charles, broke the union by excommunicating Michael, while Charles's troops with those of Venice invaded Epirus. Michael saved his throne by financing a rebellion in Sicily, which broke Charles's power in the SICILIAN VESPERS. Michael was distinguished for his learning and left an autobiography. His son Andronicus II succeeded him. See study by Deno Geanakoplos (1959).

Michael (Michael Romanov), 1596-1645, czar of Russia (1613-45), founder of the ROMANOV dynasty; grandnephew of Anastasia, first wife of Ivan IV. His election as czar, following successive appearances of false pretenders (see DMITRI), ended the so-called Time of Troubles, a period of social and political chaos in Russia that had begun in the late 16th cent. The real power in the government was Michael's father, the patriarch Philaret (d. 1633). During Michael's reign the peasantry was further reduced to serfdom; peace was temporarily obtained with Poland and Sweden; and some Western industrial and military techniques were introduced by foreign manufacturers and other experts. Michael was succeeded by his son Alexis.

Michael, 1921-, king of Rumania (1927-30, 1940-47). His father, Prince Carol (later CAROL II), renounced his right of succession in 1925, and young Michael ascended the throne under a regency on the death of Ferdinand. However, in 1930 his father returned to be recognized as king. When Carol II abdicated in 1940, Michael once more became king. In 1944 he overthrew the dictatorship of Ion ANTONESCU and concluded an armistice with the Allies (see RUMANIA). Increasing difficulties with the Communist-dominated coalition government after World War II led to his abdication (Dec., 1947) and exile. He married (1948) Princess Anne of Bourbon-Parma.

Michael (Michael Obrenović) (ōbrĕ'nəvĭch), 1823-68, prince of Serbia (1839-42, 1860-68); younger son of Prince MILOŠ. He succeeded his brother, Milan, but was deposed (1842) several years later by supporters of ALEXANDER (Alexander Karadjordjević). In 1858, Miloš was restored to the throne and Michael returned with his father, on whose death (1860) he once more became prince. Michael modernized his country and prepared its complete liberation from Turkish vassalage. At the end of his reign, the last Turkish garrisons withdrew from the Serbian fortresses, including Belgrade. Michael was assassinated and was succeeded by his cousin Milan.

Michael. **1** Father of Sethur the spy. Num. 13.13. **2** Chief of Issachar. 1 Chron. 7.3; 27.18. **3** One of David's captains at Ziklag. 1 Chron. 12.20. **4** Jehoshaphat's murdered son. 2 Chron. 21.2. **5, 6** Gadites. 1 Chron. 5.13,14. **7** Kohathite. 1 Chron. 6.40. **8** Benjamite. 1 Chron. 8.16. **9** Ancestor of a companion of Ezra. Ezra 8.8.

Michaelis, Georg (gā'ôrkh mĭkh"āā'lĭs), 1857-1936, German chancellor (July-Oct., 1917). A Prussian bureaucrat, he succeeded Theobald von BETHMANN-HOLLWEG as imperial chancellor and was dominated by the military leaders, particularly Erich LUDENDORFF. When asked to endorse the resolution passed by the Reichstag favoring peace without annexation or indemnities, he tried to avoid committing himself by stating that he would support the resolution "as I understand it."

Michaëlis, Karin (kä'rĕn mĭkāā'lĭs), 1872-1950, Danish novelist, sociologist, and lecturer. Her chief interest, the psychological study of women and their problems, was the theme of her controversial novel *The Dangerous Age* (1910, tr. 1911). Her memoirs include *Wonderful World* (1948-49) and *Little Troll* (1946, in English).

Michaëlis de Vasconcellos, Carolina: see MICAËLIS DE VASCONCELOS, CAROLINA.

Michaelmas: see MICHAEL, archangel.

Michaelmas daisy: see ASTER.

Michael the Brave, d. 1601, prince of Walachia (1593-1601), of Transylvania (1599-1600), and of Moldavia (1600). Michael was one of Rumania's greatest medieval rulers, as well as a celebrated military commander. Having been obliged to pay a large sum to the Ottoman emperor for his appointment as prince of Walachia, he did away with his Turkish creditors, who had advanced him the money, by summoning them to his palace and then having them massacred. This act was imitated throughout Walachia and became known as the Walachian Vespers. Michael repeatedly routed a Turkish retaliatory army with the help of Sigismund Báthory, prince of Transylvania, and mercenaries; Michael's subjects were oppressively taxed to pay for the victory. In 1596 the sultan made peace, leaving Walachia virtually independent. Michael now turned to the conquest of Transylvania, which he accomplished after defeating (1599) Andrew Cardinal Báthory, to whom Sigismund had given up his throne. Initially, Michael had the support of Holy Roman Emperor Rudolf II and he was able to unite all Rumanians under his sole rule. However, Rudolf II soon came to suspect Michael's increased power, and when Transylvanian nobles provoked a rebellion against Michael, the imperial army in Hungary under Gen. George Basta came to their aid. Defeated, Michael fled and presented himself at the imperial court in Vienna, where he was pardoned and reinstated as governor of Transylvania. Returning, he defeated Sigismund Báthory, who had renewed his claim to the principality, but Michael was shortly afterward assassinated on the order of General Basta. After his death Walachia and Moldavia reverted to Turkish control, while Transylvania came under Austrian domination; the union of the three areas became a national ideal in succeeding generations, and Michael himself a national hero.

Michah, the same as MICAH 2.

Michaiah (mĭkā'yə, mī"kā'yə). **1** Father of ABDON **2.** 2 Kings 22.12. Micah: 2 Chron. 34.20. **2** Asaphite. Neh. 12.35. Micah: 1 Chron. 9.15. Micha: Neh. 11.17. **3** Priest. Neh. 12.41. **4** Same as MAACHAH **3. 5** Prince sent by Jehoshaphat to teach in Judah. 2 Chron. 17.7. **6** Son of Gemariah who read Jeremiah's prophecies to the princes. Jer. 36.11-13.

Michal (mī'kəl), wife of David and daughter of Saul. 1 Sam. 18.20; 19.12; 2 Sam. 6.16. See MERAB.

Michaud, Joseph François (zhôzĕf' fräNswä' mēshō'), 1767-1839, French journalist and historian. Under the Directory he was deported for advocating the restoration of the Bourbons. On his return (1799) to France he wrote a *History of the Crusades* (tr., 3 vol., 1852; repr. 1972), still widely read. He was chief editor of the *Biographie universelle* (52 vol., 1811-28; rev. ed., 45 vol., 1853-66), a biographical reference work.

Michaux, André (äNdrā' mēshō'), 1746-1802, French botanist. He collected botanical specimens in Europe and Asia. In 1785 he was sent by the French government to establish nurseries in the United States to cultivate plants for naturalization in France. Until 1796 he made botanical journeys over the United States and recorded his studies in a book on the oaks of North America (1801) and in a work on North American botany, *Flora Boreali-Americana* (1803). His son, **François André Michaux,** 1770-1855, is known chiefly for his work on the forest trees of North America (1810-13, tr. *The North American Sylva*, 1817).

Micheas (mīkē'əs), variant of MICAH.

Michel, Claude: see CLODION.

Michelangelo Buonarroti (mīkəlăn'jəlō, Ital. mēkālän'jālō bwōnär-rô'tē), 1475-1564, Italian sculptor, painter, architect, and poet, b. Caprese, Tuscany. Michelangelo was a towering figure of Renaissance, mannerist, and baroque art. After serving a year of apprenticeship to the painters Domenico Ghirlandaio and his brother David at Florence, Michelangelo entered (1489) the art school held in the Medici gardens under the directorship of Bertoldo (a pupil of Donatello). His early essays in sculpture attracted the attention of Lorenzo de' Medici, who took him to live in his household between 1490 and 1492. There he was influenced by the neoplatonic ideas of Poliziano, Pico della Mirandola, and Marsilio Ficino. Drawings of this youthful period (now in the Louvre) attest to Michelangelo's study of works by Giotto and Masaccio, while the marble reliefs of the *Madonna of the Stairs* and *Battle of Centaurs* (Casa Buonarroti, Florence) show the influence of Donatello and of ancient Roman sarcophagi. He had occasion to study the reliefs of Jacopo della Quercia on the portal of San Petronio, Bologna, when he executed statuettes for the shrine of San Domenico in the same church in 1494. At this time the apocalyptic vision of the fanatic monk Savonarola impressed the artist and was to fuse with his own tragic sense of human destiny later in his work. Between 1496 and 1501, Michelangelo worked in Rome where he executed the marble *Bacchus* (Bargello, Florence) and the exquisitely balanced *Pietà* (St. Peter's, Rome), which was badly damaged by a madman wielding a hammer in 1972 and thereafter expertly restored. After returning to Florence in 1501, he was commissioned by the city to execute the magnificent giant *David* for the Piazza della Signoria, later moved into the Academy to protect it. The city asked him to paint, with Leonardo da Vinci, one of two frescoes for the council hall of the Palazzo Vecchio. The cartoons (now lost) for these projected frescoes exerted enormous influence in their period. From these years date the marble *Bruges Madonna* (Notre Dame, Bruges) and the painted tondo of the *Holy Family* (Uffizi). In 1505 he was called to Rome to execute a sepulchral monument for Pope Julius II. This was to become the most frustrating project of his life. As penance for a quarrel with the pope, Michelangelo spent more than a year creating a gigantic bronze portrait of Julius; it was shortly thereafter melted down for cannon. Soon after the contract for the tomb was awarded, Julius changed his mind in favor of the decoration of the ceiling of the SISTINE CHAPEL. The Sistine ceiling was executed between 1508 and 1512. In its profundity of spiritual content and sublimity of style it stands as one of the world's greatest masterpieces. A vast architectonic framework divides the ceiling into three superimposed zones. In the highest zone are nine panels with scenes from Genesis. Below are prophets and sibyls. In the lunettes and spandrels of the lowest zone are enigmatic scenes with groups of figures which have been variously identified as the ancestors of Christ or of the Virgin and which seem to suggest a vision of primordial humanity. After the death of Julius II, the heirs again contracted for the execution of his monument, and litigations dragged on some 30 years. It was a major tragedy for Michelangelo that his plan for a vast temple-mausoleum within St. Peter's had to be abandoned, and that the monument finally erected in San Pietro in Vincoli, Rome, was a mere travesty of his heroic conception. Works that were to have been included in the scheme were the colossal *Moses* (San Pietro in Vincoli) and statues known as *Slaves* (Academy, Florence; Louvre). He worked (1520-34) on the sepulchral chapel of the Medici in the second sacristy of San Lorenzo, Florence, and designed the elegant, mannerist Laurentian Library which forms a part of the church. In the sacristy he combined sculpture and architecture into a powerful expressive unity. A forceful contrast between contemplation and action is embodied in his statues of Giuliano and Lorenzo de' Medici and the allegorical figures of *Dawn, Evening, Night,* and *Day.* Michelangelo assisted (1529) as engineer in the defense of Florence and then established himself in Rome where he became deeply attached to a young nobleman, Tommaso Cavalieri, to whom he dedicated many sonnets and several drawings of an allegorical nature. From 1534 to 1541 he worked on the *Last Judgment* of the Sistine Chapel. From this period dates his friendship with Vittoria Colonna, to whom he dedicated many religious sonnets. After executing (1541-50) the Pauline Chapel (Vatican) frescoes of the *Conversion of Paul* and *Martyrdom of Peter,* he devoted himself principally to architecture. In 1547 he succeeded Antonio da Sangallo, the younger, as chief architect of St. Peter's. Michelangelo was responsible for the dominant features of the main body of the church, its centralized Greek-cross plan and the great dome which was completed, after his death, by Domenico Fontana and Giacomo della Porta, who only slightly modified Michelangelo's plan. Other architectural works included remodeling the tepidarium of the baths of Diocletian into the Church of Santa Maria degli Angeli and designing the facades and court of the palace group on the Capitoline Hill. Two unfinished sculptured *Pietà* groups testify to the tendency toward increasingly spiritualized and abstract form in Michelangelo's last years. The one now in the Cathedral of Florence was intended by Michelangelo for his own tomb; it was smashed and survives as reassembled by another sculptor, who may have added or entirely reworked the figure of the Magdalen. The Rondanini *Pietà* (now Castello Sforzesco, Milan) was begun c.1555 and was left unfinished at Michelangelo's death. Michelangelo thought of himself primarily as a sculptor, and a feeling for the expressive potentialities of sculptural form manifests itself in all phases of his work. As a 16th-century artist, he was forced to depend on the favor of great patrons who had the means and power to award commissions worthy of his genius. Throughout his career his artistic ambitions were thwarted by the caprices of these patrons, by the social instability of the times, by jealousy of other artists, and by the deep moral conflicts that arose within his own spirit. This struggle is expressed in an art whose universality transcends definition in terms of one style and which scholars have variously categorized as best associated with the High Renaissance, mannerist or baroque periods. Many of Michelangelo's designs have survived only through his drawings. Using a technique of vigorous cross-hatching, he did many anatomical studies and created numerous forceful compositions. His compositions were adapted by his followers and imitated for generations. There are great collections of his drawings in the Louvre; Uffizi and Casa Buonarroti, Florence; British Museum; Windsor Castle; and Ashmolean Museum, Oxford. See Michelangelo's poems (tr. by C. Gilbert 1963, repr. 1970); letters (tr. by E. H. Ramsden, 1963); autobiographical selections by I. and J. Stone (1962); biographies by J. A. Symonds (1936, repr. 1961) and C. I. De Tolnay (5 vol., 1943-60; repr. 1969-70); his paintings, sculptures, and architecture (ed. by L. Goldscheider, 4th ed. 1964); J. S. Ackerman, ed., *Architecture* (rev. ed. 1967); F. Hartt, *Michelangelo: Paintings* (1965), *Sculpture* (1969), and *Drawings* (1970); Herbert von Einem, *Michelangelo* (tr. 1974).

Michelet, Jules (zhül mĕshəlā'), 1798-1874, French writer, the greatest historian of the romantic school. Born in Paris of poor parents, he visualized himself throughout his life as a champion of the people. He headed the historical section of the national archives and was professor of history at the Collège de France, but he lost his positions when he refused (1851) the oath of allegiance to Louis Napoleon (later Napoleon III). His major work is his *Histoire de France* (many volumes, 1833-67; several partial translations into English); its style, its emotional strength, and its powerful evocation make it a masterpiece of French literature. Michelet traced the biography of the nation as a whole, instead of concentrating on persons or groups of persons. His most convincing pages deal with the Middle Ages. Michelet had vast knowledge of factual detail and original documents, but his history, especially the latter part, is marred by emotional bias against the clergy, the nobility, and the monarchic institutions. Many of Michelet's other political and historical works are outgrowths of his history of France; especially notable are *Le Peuple* (1846) and the biography of Joan of Arc (1853). He also wrote romantic impressions of nature and life.

Michelozzo Michelozzi (mĕkālôt'tsō mĕkālôt'tsē), 1396-1472, Italian sculptor, architect, goldsmith, and founder. He was long associated with Donatello and Ghiberti. His first independent sculpture was the Aragazzi Tomb for the cathedral at Montepulciano; some of the statues and reliefs for that work remain in the cathedral, and two angels are in the Victoria and Albert Museum, London. His fame rests chiefly on the architectural and decorative works to which he devoted himself after 1435; he shared leadership with Brunelleschi and Alberti in establishing the Renaissance style. Michelozzo's best work was at Florence. The Medici-Riccardi Palace, which he built as architect and art adviser to Cosimo de' Medici, is one of the finest city houses ever built. He also enlarged and rebuilt the Monastery of San Marco and worked on the restoration of the Palazzo Vecchio. In 1446-51 he was director of works, succeeding Brunelleschi, of Santa Maria del Fiore. Michelozzo planned or remodeled several VILLAS for the Medici. The one at Fiesole (1458-61), with its terraced gardens, had an important influence upon the design of later villas.

Michelson, Albert Abraham, 1852-1931, American physicist, b. Strelno, Prussia, grad. Annapolis, 1873, and studied at Berlin, Heidelberg, and Paris. He was professor of physics at Clark Univ. (1889-92) and later was head of the department of physics at the Univ. of Chicago (1892-1931). He is known especially for his determinations of the speed of light; in some of his earliest work he tested the data of Foucault's experiments and, then and later, with apparatus (including the interferometer) that he designed and built himself, measured the speed of light to an unequaled degree of accuracy. He measured (1892-93) the length of the standard meter in Paris in terms of the wave length of the red line of the cadmium spectrum, using his interferometer method. The wave length thus provided an absolute and exactly reproducible standard of length. With E. W. Morley he conducted the Michelson-Morley experiment, which led to the refutation of the ether hypothesis and contributed to the development of Einstein's theory of relativity. Michelson was the first to measure the diameter of a star. He also demonstrated that the earth as a whole is rigid, not molten. Awarded the 1907 Nobel Prize in Physics, he was the first American scientist to receive the honor. Michelson's major writings include *Velocity of Light* (1902) and *Studies in Optics* (1927). See biography by his daughter, Dorothy Michelson Livingston (1973).

Michener, James Albert, 1907-, American author, b. New York City, grad. Swarthmore, 1929. Most of his popular novels are set in the Far East. His short-story collection *Tales of the South Pacific* (1947; Pulitzer Prize) was adapted by Rodgers and Hammerstein into a successful musical. His novels include *Return to Paradise* (1951), *The Bridges at Toko-ri* (1953), *Sayonara* (1954), *Hawaii* (1959), *The Source* (1965), and *Centennial* (1974). His nonfiction works include *The Modern Japanese Print* (1969) and *Kent State: What Happened and Why* (1971).

Michigan (mĭsh'ĭgən), state (1970 pop. 8,875,083), 58,216 sq mi (150,779 sq km), not including c.38,575 sq mi (99,909 sq km) of the Great Lakes; N United States, in the Great Lakes region, admitted to the Union 1837 as the 26th state. LANSING is the capital,

and DETROIT is the largest city. The Lower Peninsula, shaped like a mitten, thrusts northward from Indiana and Ohio. On the east it is separated from Ontario, Canada, by Lake Erie and Lake Huron, and by the Detroit River and the St. Clair River, which together link the two Great Lakes; on the west it is separated from Wisconsin by Lake Michigan. Across Lake Michigan, NE of Wisconsin, the Upper Peninsula stretches eastward, separating Lake Michigan from Lake Superior, and itself separated from Ontario only by the narrow St. Marys River. The Upper Peninsula is separated from the Lower Peninsula by the Straits of Mackinac; a bridge connecting the two peninsulas was opened in 1957 and has spurred the development of the Upper Peninsula. Meanwhile, an extensive ferry system across Lake Michigan facilitates travel between the Lower Peninsula and Wisconsin. The eastern portion of the Upper Peninsula has swampy flats and limestone hills on the Lake Michigan shore, while sandstone ridges rise abruptly from the rough waters on Lake Superior; in the west the land rises to forested mountains, still rich in copper and iron. The whole of the Upper Peninsula is northern woods country, with what has been described as "ten months of winter and two months of poor sledding." The abundance of furred animals and the trees early attracted fur traders and lumbermen. The animals were trapped out, many of the virgin forests were ruthlessly stripped, and even the pure copper and the high-grade iron ore were rapidly wrested from the earth. Today, mines, though reduced in significance, are still active, and lower-grade ores are being exploited. Deer, bears, and other big and small game in the forests, as well as abundant fish in streams and the lakes, make the area a sportsman's delight. The scarred timberlands are being reforested with second growth, and selective cutting and replanting of trees have replaced the rapacious methods of the old-time lumber barons. The Lower Peninsula is a different sort of country, less wild but in parts no less beautiful. Its forests were also cut over in the lumber boom of the late 19th cent., when busy sawmills made Michigan the temporary leader in lumber production. Tne soil of these cut-over lands, unlike the productive earth in other areas of the Lower Peninsula, proved generally unsuitable for agriculture, and reforestation has been undertaken. The Lower Peninsula also has its mineral riches, including gypsum, sandstone, limestone, salt, cement, petroleum, and sand and gravel, but its great wealth lies in the many farms and factories. The surrounding waters temper the climate, allowing a long growing season. Fields of grain and corn cover much of the southern counties, and Michigan's noted fruit belt lines the shore of Lake Michigan. Livestock raising and dairying are of great importance, but crops account for almost half of farm income. Corn is the chief crop, followed by hay, dry beans, wheat, oats, and soybeans. The manufacture of transportation equipment is by far the state's chief industry, and Detroit, Dearborn, Flint, Pontiac, and Lansing are centers for automobile manufacturing. Michigan's automobile factories are known the world over, and their mass-production methods were the core of a 20th-century industrial revolution. Michigan's other leading industries produce nonelectrical machinery, fabricated metal products, primary metals, chemicals, and food products. Industrial centers include Saginaw, Bay City, Muskegon, and Jackson. The chemical industry in Midland is one of the nation's largest; Kalamazoo is an important paper-manufacturing center; Grand Rapids is noted for its furniture, and Battle Creek for its breakfast foods. Although mining contributes less to income in the state than either agriculture or manufacturing, Michigan in 1972 was the nation's 13th leading state in mineral production. The chief minerals produced are iron ore, cement, copper, and sand and gravel. In 1972, Michigan ranked first among the states in production of peat, bromine, calcium-magnesium chloride, gypsum, and magnesium compounds, and ranked second to Minnesota in iron-ore production and second to California in sand and gravel. Fishing is also important to Michigan's economy, both commercially and as a resource attracting visitors to the state. The OJIBWA, the OTTAWA, the POTAWATOMI, and other Algonquian-speaking Indian tribes were living in what is now Michigan when the French explorer Étienne Brulé landed at the narrows of Sault Ste Marie in 1618, probably the first white man to have reached present Michigan. Later French explorers, traders, and missionaries came, including Jean Nicolet, who was searching for the Northwest Passage; Jacques Marquette, who founded a mission in the Mackinac region; and the empire builder, Robert

Cavelier, sieur de La Salle, who came on the *Griffon*, the first ship to sail the Great Lakes. French posts were scattered along the lakes and the rivers, and Mackinac Island (in the Straits of Mackinac) became a center of the fur trade. Fort Pontchartrain, later Detroit, was founded in 1701 by Antoine de la Mothe Cadillac. All this vast region was weakly held by France until lost to Great Britain in the French and Indian War (1754–63). In 1760, Detroit was surrendered to the American frontiersman Robert Rogers and his Rangers. The Indians of Michigan, who had lived in peace with the French, resented the coming of the British, who were the allies of the much-hated Iroquois. Under Pontiac the Indians rose in bloody revolt (see PONTIAC'S REBELLION) and terrorized the British in their newly acquired territory. The rebellion, which began in 1763, was short-lived, ending in 1766, and the Indians subsequently supported the British during the American Revolution. Despite provisions of the Treaty of Paris, which ended the American Revolution (1783; see PARIS, TREATY OF), the British held stubbornly to Detroit and Mackinac until 1796, when they evacuated the area under the terms of Jay's Treaty. After passage of the Northwest Ordinance in 1787, Michigan became part of the NORTHWEST TERRITORY. However, even after the Northwest Territory was broken up and Detroit was made (1805) capital of Michigan Territory, British agents still maintained great influence over the Indians, who fought on the British side in the War of 1812. In that war Mackinac and Detroit fell almost immediately to the British as a result of the ineffective control of U.S. Gen. William Hull and his troops. Michigan remained in British hands through most of the war until William Henry Harrison in the battle of Thames and Oliver Hazard Perry in the battle of Lake Erie restored U.S. control. After peace came, pioneers moved into Michigan, slowly at first and then more rapidly. Much of the credit for the policy of pushing the Indians westward and opening the lands for settlement is given to Gen. Lewis Cass, who was governor of Michigan Territory (1813–31) and later a U.S. Senator. He negotiated treaties with the Indians, in which the latter ceded their lands to the whites, and he encouraged the Federal government to build five military highways in the area. Steamboat navigation on the Great Lakes and sale of public lands in Detroit both began in 1818, and the Erie Canal was opened in 1825. Farmers came to the Michigan fields, and the first sawmills were built along the rivers. The move toward statehood was retarded by the desire of Ohio and Indiana to absorb parts of present S Michigan, and by the opposition of southern states to the admission of another free state. The Michigan electorate organized a government without U.S. sanction and in 1836 operated as a state, although outside the Union. To resolve the boundary dispute Congress proposed that the Toledo strip be ceded to Ohio and Indiana with compensation to Michigan of land in the Upper Peninsula. Though the Michigan electorate rejected the offer, a group of Democratic leaders accepted it, and by their acceptance Michigan became a state in 1837. (The admission of Arkansas as a slaveholding state offset that of Michigan as a free state.) Detroit served as the capital until 1847, when it was replaced by Lansing. After statehood Michigan promptly adopted a program of internal improvement through the building of railroads, roads, and canals, including the Soo Ship Canal at Sault Ste Marie. A survey of mineral resources made in 1837 by Douglas Houghton, the state geologist, and William A. Burt, U.S. deputy surveyor, prefaced the development of the copper and iron mines in the state. At the same time lumbering was expanding, and the population grew as German, Irish, and Dutch immigrants arrived. In 1854 the Republican party was organized at Jackson, Mich. During the Civil War, Michigan fought on the side of the Union. After the war the state remained firmly Republican until 1882. Then Michigan farmers, moved by the same financial difficulties and outrage at high transportation and storage rates that aroused other Western farmers, supported movements advocating agrarian interests, such as the GRANGER MOVEMENT and the GREENBACK PARTY. The farmers joined with the growing numbers of workers in the mines and lumber camps to elect a Greenback-Democratic governor in 1882 and succeeded in getting legislation passed for agrarian improvement and public welfare. Reforms influenced by the labor movement were the creation of a state board of labor (1883), a law enforcing a 10-hr day (1885), and a moderate child-labor law (1887). The lumbering business, with its yield of wealth to the timber barons, declined to virtually nothing. Some of the loggers joined the ranks of industrial workers, which were further swelled by many Polish and Norwegian immigrants. With the invention of the automobile and the construction of automotive plants, industry in Michigan was altered radically. Henry Ford established the Ford Motor Company in 1903 and introduced conveyor-belt assembly lines in 1918. General Motors and the Chrysler Corp. were established shortly after Ford. Along with the development of mass-production methods came the growth of the labor movement. In the 1930s, when the automobile industry was well established in the state, labor unions struggled for recognition. The conflict between labor and the automotive industry, which continued into the 1940s, included sit-down strikes and was sometimes violent. In World War II, Michigan produced large numbers of tanks, airplanes, and other war matériel. Industrial production again expanded after the Korean War broke out in 1950. In the early 1960s, however, economic growth lagged and unemployment became a problem in the state. The Saint Lawrence Seaway opened in 1959 and increased export trade by bringing many oceangoing vessels to the port of Detroit. In 1963, Michigan adopted a new constitution which reapportioned the upper house of the state legislature. Detroit was shaken by severe race riots in 1967 that left 43 persons dead and many injured. In the wake of the rioting, programs were undertaken to improve housing facilities and job opportunities in the city, deficiencies thought to have fueled racial tensions. Violence erupted again in the state in 1971 when opponents of a busing program to achieve integration in Pontiac schools destroyed 10 empty schoolbuses with explosives. Resistance to busing was a major political issue in the state in the early 1970s. The northern Michigan wilds, numerous inland lakes, and some 3,000 mi (4,800 km) of shoreline, combined with a pleasantly cool summer climate, have long attracted thousands of vacationers. In the winter Michigan's snow-covered hills bring skiers from all over the Midwest. Places of interest in the state include Greenfield Village, a re-creation of a 19th-century American village, and the Henry Ford Museum, both at Dearborn; Pictured Rocks and Sleeping Bear Dunes national lake shores; and Isle Royal National Park. Michigan's constitution, adopted in 1963, provides for an elected governor as the state's chief executive. The governor serves for a term of four years and may succeed himself in the office. The state legislature is made up of a senate and house of representatives. The senate has 38 members elected for terms of four years and the house of representatives has 110 members elected for two-year terms. Michigan sends 19 Representatives and 2 Senators to the U.S. Congress and has 21 electoral votes in presidential elections. William G. Milliken, a Republican, became governor in 1969, succeeding George Romney, who resigned to accept a Cabinet appointment; Milliken was elected to a full term in 1970 and was reelected in 1974. Higher education is well represented by such institutions as the Univ. of Michigan, at Ann Arbor; Michigan State Univ., at East Lansing; the Univ. of Detroit and Wayne State Univ., at Detroit; and many other private and state colleges. See George Fuller, ed., *Michigan: A Centennial History* (5 vol., 1939); K. I. Gillard, *Our Michigan Heritage* (1956); F. C. Bald, *Michigan in Four Centuries* (1960); W. F. Dunbar, *Michigan: A History of the Wolverine State* (1965); J. A. Door, Jr., and D. F. Eschman, *Geology of Michigan* (1970); Alec R. Gilpin, *Territory of Michigan, 1805–1887* (1971); Federal Writers' Project, *Michigan: A Guide to the Wolverine State* (1941, repr. 1972).

Michigan, Lake, 22,178 sq mi (57,441 sq km), 307 mi (494 km) long and 30 to 120 mi (48–193 km) wide, bordered by Mich., Ind., Ill., and Wis.; third largest of the Great Lakes and the largest freshwater lake entirely within the United States. Its surface is 581 ft (177 m) above sea level, and the lake is 923 ft (281 m) deep. The Straits of Mackinac, its only natural outlet, connect the lake with Lake Huron to the northeast; the Illinois Waterway links Lake Michigan with the Mississippi River and Gulf of Mexico. Many islands are found in the northern part of the lake; the northern shoreline is indented, with Green Bay and Grand Traverse Bay the largest bays. The southern part of Lake Michigan has a regular shoreline necessitating the building of man-made harbors such as the Calumet Harbor, NE Ill. The Muskegon, Grand, Kalamazoo, Fox, and Menominee are the chief rivers flowing into Lake Michigan; the lake's current tends to clog the mouths of the rivers with sand. The Chicago River formerly flowed into the lake, but its course was reversed in 1900. Sand dunes border the eastern and southern shores of the lake; Indiana Dunes National Lakeshore (see NATIONAL PARKS AND MONUMENTS, table) is there. The forested northern region of Lake Michigan is generally sparsely populated. The southern portion, located near the heart of the Midwest, is one of the most important urban industrial areas in the United States; the Gary-Chicago-Milwaukee urbanized area extends along the southwestern shore. Michigan City, Gary, Chicago, Evanston, Waukegan, Kenosha, Racine, Milwaukee, Sheboygan, Manitowoc, and Escanaba are the major lakeside cities. This concentration has led to a growing pollution problem that can affect the availability of potable water to the area. Prevailing westerly winds tempered by the lake give the eastern shore a moderate climate, making it a rich fruit belt and popular resort area. Lake Michigan was discovered in 1634 by the French explorer Jean Nicolet and was later explored by the French traders Marquette and Jolliet. French missionary and trade centers thrived there by the late 1600s. As part of the bitterly contested NORTHWEST TERRITORY, the area passed to England in 1763 and then, in 1796, to the United States. The area was isolated until the 1830s, when improvements in transportation brought settlers there. Ore, coal, and grain are the main items moved on the lake. The Saint Lawrence Seaway has opened Lake Michigan to international trade. The southern part of the lake does not freeze over in the winter, but storms and ice halt interlake movement from December to April.

Michigan, University of, mainly at Ann Arbor; state supported; coeducational; chartered 1817 at Detroit as the Catholepistemiad, or University, of Michigania, rechartered 1821 (as Univ. of Mich.) and 1837 when it was relocated at Ann Arbor. Two senior colleges, Dearborn Center at Dearborn, and Flint College at Flint, are operated by the university in addition to centers at Battle Creek, Detroit, Escanaba, Grand Rapids, Port Huron, Saginaw, and Traverse City. Michigan has an outstanding school in astronomy and maintains two observatories at Ann Arbor and others at Portage Lake, Lake Angelus (where important solar physics research is done), and Bloemfontein, South Africa. At Ann Arbor are the Phoenix Memorial Laboratory, which carries on instruction and research in the peaceful uses of atomic energy, and the Aeronautical Engineering Laboratory. Michigan has a noted law school, an extensive system of hospitals, clinics, and medical institutes, and several museums. The university library houses many notable collections including the Hubbard Collection on Imaginary Voyages, an outstanding papyrus collection, the Worcester collection on the Philippines, a collection on American colonial and Revolutionary history, and the Stellfeld music collection. See W. B. Shaw, ed., *The University of Michigan* (4 vol., 1942–58); H. H. Peckham, *The Making of the University of Michigan, 1817–1967* (1967).

Michigan City, city (1970 pop. 36,369), La Porte co., NW Ind., on Lake Michigan; inc. 1836. A resort area with sand dune beaches and a state park, it also has industries that produce air compressors, plumbing products, metal furniture, and truck trailers. A state prison is there.

Michigan State University, at East Lansing; land-grant and state supported; coeducational; chartered 1855. It opened in 1857 as Michigan Agricultural College, the first state agricultural college. From 1925 to 1959 it was known as Michigan State College of Agriculture and Applied Science, and in 1964 its present name was adopted. The state agricultural experiment station is there. The university operates the Kellogg Biological Station at Gull Lake. Its library contains an outstanding collection of books relating to veterinary medicine.

Michmas (mĭk'măs) or **Michmash** (–măsh), town, c.8 mi (12.9 km) NE of Jerusalem. It is identified with modern Mukhmas (Jordan). It was a bivouac of Jonathan in his Philistine wars. 1 Sam. 13; 14; Ezra 2.27; Neh. 7.31.

Michmethah (mĭk'mĕthä), unidentified place, central Palestine. Joshua 17.7.

Michoacán (mĕchōäkän'), state (1970 pop. 2,341,556), 23,202 sq mi (60,093 sq km), S Mexico. MORELIA is the capital. Dominated by the mountains of the Sierra Madre Occidental and the volcanic chain of central Mexico, Michoacán extends from the Pacific Ocean northeastward into the central plateau. The Lerma River and Lake Chapala form part of its northern boundary with the state of Jalisco; the Río de las Balsas constitutes the southern border with Guerrero. The climate and soil variations caused by topography and differences in elevation make Michoacán predominantly an agricultural state. Sugarcane, coffee, vanilla, tobacco, cereals, and subsistence crops are grown, and cattle and sheep are raised. Michoacán's forests yield fine cabinet woods and dyewoods. Mining is a leading industry; gold and silver are most important, but lead, cinnabar, iron, copper, sulfur, coal, and oil are also exploited. Michoacán, having no important Pacific port, ships its products from the cities of Morelia and Uruapan. Federally sponsored irrigation and hydroelectric power projects have aimed at developing Michoacán's Pacific coastal region. Lake Pátzcuaro (where UNESCO and the Organization of American States have a training center for Latin American rural teachers) and the Paricutín volcano attract many tourists. Most of the state's inhabitants are TARASCAN Indians. Michoacán played a leading role in Mexico's revolution against Spain and in subsequent struggles.

Michri (mĭk'rī), ancestor of Elah. 1 Chron. 9.8.

Michtam (mĭk'tăm), in the titles of Pss. 16, 56, 57, 58, 59, 60, a word of uncertain meaning, perhaps indicating the type of psalm.

Michurinsk (mēcho͞o'rĭnsk), city (1970 pop. 94,000), central European USSR. It is a railway junction and has an iron and steel plant, locomotive and automobile repair works, and varied manufactures. Founded in 1636, it was known as Kozlov until 1932, when it was renamed in honor of the 19th-century Russian scientist Michurin, who founded a horticultural experimental institute in the city.

Mickiewicz, Adam (ä'däm mētskyĕ'vĭch), 1798–1855, Polish romantic poet and playwright, b. Belorussia. He studied at the Univ. of Vilna, where he was arrested (1823) for pan-Polish activities and deported to Russia. He was permitted (1829) to travel through Europe and served as professor of literature in Lausanne (1839) and in Paris (1840–44). In the revolutionary upheavals of 1848 and again in the Crimean War he organized legions for Polish emancipation. He died in Constantinople during a cholera epidemic. Mickiewicz's poetry gave international stature to Polish literature. His powerful verse expressed a romantic view of the soul and the mysteries of life, often employing Polish folk themes. His major works include the epic *Grazyna* (1823, tr. 1940), concerning female heroism; the fantastic drama *The Forefathers* (1823); *Sonnets from the Crimea* (1825); the philosophical poem *Konrad Wallenrod* (1828); *The Books of the Polish Nation and of Polish Pilgrimage* (1832); and the great epic *Pan Tadeusz* (1834, tr. 1917). This poem, Mickiewicz's masterpiece, is a comprehensive and Homeric treatment of the life of the Polish gentry. See biographies by Marion Coleman (1956) and M. M. Gardner (1911, repr. 1971); studies by Wiktor Weintraub (1954 and 1959) and Manfred Kridl, ed. (1951, repr. 1969).

Micmac Indians, North American Indians whose language belongs to the Algonquian branch of the Algonquian-Wakashan linguistic stock (see AMERICAN INDIAN LANGUAGES). They are found in Nova Scotia, Cape Breton Island, Prince Edward Island, Newfoundland, and New Brunswick. French missionaries came into contact with them in the early 17th cent., and the Micmacs were allies of the French throughout the history of New France. Contact with the whites has not had the usual effect of tribal disintegration, and the Micmacs still thrive, though their culture has changed radically. Many are Roman Catholics. The Micmacs are expert canoeists, and, although their economy once centered on fishing and hunting, they now derive their income from agriculture. See W. D. and R. S. Wallis, *The Micmac Indians of Eastern Canada* (1955); J. F. Pratson, *Land of the Four Directions* (1970).

Micon: see MIKON.

microbiology: see BIOLOGY.

microcephalia: see MENTAL RETARDATION.

microcline: see FELDSPAR.

microelectronics, branch of electronic technology devoted to the design and development of extremely small electronic devices that consume very little electric power. The simplest, but least effective, approach used in microelectronics is to make circuit elements, such as resistors, capacitors, and semiconductor devices, extremely small but discrete. In another approach, circuit elements are thin films of conductive, semiconductive, and insulating materials deposited in sandwich form on an insulating substrate. This method is costly and allows but a limited size reduction. The most advanced method is to form circuits, called INTEGRATED CIRCUITS, within and upon single semiconductor crystals.

micrometer (**1** mīkrŏm'ətər, **2** mī'krōmē"tər). **1** Instrument used for measuring extremely small distances. Typical examples are devices used in astronomical telescopes to measure the apparent diameter of celestial objects and similar devices used in microscopes. In both of these devices a fine hair or filament is moved from one extremity to the other of the image of an object and the distance read on a calibrated scale. Another typical micrometer is the micrometer caliper, a device in which an object to be measured is enclosed between two jaws, one fixed and the other movable by means of a fine screw. When the jaws are just touching the object, the distance between the jaws can be read on an associated scale, often to an accuracy of 10^{-4} (one ten-thousandth) in., or 10^{-6} (one millionth) m. **2** Unit of linear distance equal to 10^{-6} (one millionth) m. It was formerly known as a micron.

micron: see MICROMETER.

Micronesia (mīkrōnē'zhə, -shə), one of the three main divisions of Oceania, in W Pacific Ocean, north of the equator. Micronesia includes the CAROLINE ISLANDS, MARSHALL ISLANDS, MARIANAS ISLANDS, GILBERT ISLANDS, and NAURU. The inhabitants are of Australoid and Polynesian stock. They speak Malayo-Polynesian languages.

microphone, device for converting sound into electrical energy, used in radio broadcasting, recording, and sound amplifying systems. Its basic component is a diaphragm that responds to the pressure or particle velocity of sound waves. The microphone, various forms of which were developed independently c.1877 by inventors Emile Berliner, David E. Hughes, and Thomas A. Edison, was first used as a telephone transmitter. The modern telephone transmitter, which is essentially a carbon microphone, contains loosely packed carbon grains. When someone speaks into the transmitter, the diaphragm vibrates, causing the grains to be compressed and released. The motion of the grains varies the flow of current in the associated electric circuit. All other microphones in common use generate minute voltages of their own in response to the vibrations of the diaphragm. Crystal microphones generate voltages by the PIEZOELECTRIC EFFECT. They are often found in inexpensive tape recorders and public address systems. Both the ribbon microphone and the dynamic microphone generate voltages by electromagnetic INDUCTION. For example, in the dynamic microphone, the diaphragm is attached to a light movable coil that generates a voltage as it moves back and forth between the poles of a magnet. In the CAPACITOR, or condenser, microphone two parallel metal plates are given opposite electrical charges. One of the plates is attached to the diaphragm and moves in response to its vibrations, generating a varying voltage. The ribbon, dynamic, and capacitor microphones are all used in high-quality sound systems. See M. L. Gayford, *Electroacoustics* (1971).

microscope, optical instrument used to increase the apparent size of an object. A magnifying glass, an ordinary double convex LENS having a short focal length, is a simple microscope. The reading lens and hand lens are instruments of this type. When an object is placed nearer such a lens than its principal focus, i.e., within its focal length, an IMAGE is produced that is erect and larger than the original object. The image is also virtual; i.e., it cannot be projected on a screen as can a real image. The magnification is commonly expressed in diameters. For example, if a lens magnifies an object 5 times, the magnification is said to be 5 diameters, commonly written simply "5x." The compound microscope consists essentially of two or more such lenses fixed in the two extremities of a hollow metal cylinder. This cylinder is mounted upright on a screw device, which permits it to be raised or lowered above the object until a clear image is formed. The lower lens (nearest to the object) is called the objective; the upper lens (nearest to the eye of the observer), the eyepiece. The total magnification of the compound microscope is computed by multiplying the magnifying power of the objective by the magnifying power of the eyepiece. When an object is in focus, a real, inverted image is formed by the lower lens at a point inside the principal focus of the upper lens. This image serves as an "object" for the upper lens which produces another image larger still (but virtual) and visible to the eye of the observer. The compound microscope is widely used in bacteriology, biology, and medicine in the examination of such extremely minute objects as bacteria, other unicellular organisms, and plant and animal cells and tissue. It has been extremely important in the development of the biological sciences and of medicine. Its invention is variously accredited to Zacharias Janssen, a Dutch spectaclemaker, c.1590, and to Galileo, who announced his invention in 1610. Other men are known for their discoveries made by the use of the instrument and for their new designs and improvements, among them G. B. Amici, Nehemiah Grew, Robert Hooke, Antony van Leeuwenhoek, Marcello Malpighi, and Jan Swammerdam. The ultramicroscope is an apparatus consisting essentially of a compound microscope with an arrangement by which the material to be viewed is illuminated by a point of light placed at right angles to the plane of the objective and brought to a focus directly beneath it. This instrument is used especially in the study of Brownian movement in colloidal solutions (see COLLOID). The phase-contrast microscope, a modification of the compound microscope, makes transparent objects visible; it is used to study living cells. The television microscope uses ultraviolet light. Since this light is not visible, the apparatus is used with a special camera and may be connected with a television receiver on which the objects (e.g., living microorganisms) may be observed in color. The electron microscope, which is not limited by the powers of optical lenses and light, permits greater magnification and greater depth of focus than the optical microscope and reveals more details of structure. Instead of light rays it employs a stream of electrons controlled by electric or magnetic fields. The image may be thrown on a fluorescent screen or may be photographed. It was first developed in Germany c.1932; James Hillier and Albert Prebus, of Canada, and V. K. Zworykin, of the United States, contributed notably to its development in this hemisphere. The field-ion microscope, invented by the German-American E. W. Müller, is a modification of his own, less powerful, field-emission microscope. In the former a high positive voltage is applied to a metal needle enclosed in a gas-filled tube; ionization of the gas occurs, and the positive ions, repelled by the needle, impinge on a fluorescent screen, forming a pattern corresponding to the atomic structure of the metal used. In the field-emission microscope the needle is used as an electron gun, the expelled electrons being directed against the screen.

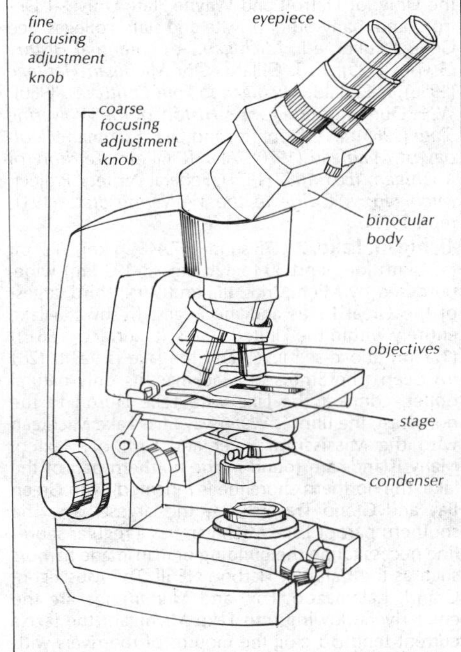

Compound microscope

microwave, electromagnetic wave having a frequency range from 1,000 megahertz (MHz) to 300,000 MHz, corresponding to a wavelength range from 300 mm (about 12 in.) to 1 mm (about 0.04 in.). Like light waves, microwaves travel essentially in straight lines. They are used in radar, in communications links spanning moderate distances, and in other applications, such as microwave ovens. The equipment used to generate, process, and transmit microwaves is in many respects different from that used with ordinary radio waves. See WAVEGUIDE; MAGNETRON.

microwave oven: see STOVE.

Midas (mī'dəs), in Greek mythology, king of Phrygia. Because he befriended Silenus, the oldest of the satyrs, Dionysus granted him the power to turn everything into gold by touch. But when even the food that he touched turned to gold, Midas begged to be relieved of his gift. Dionysus allowed him to wash away his power in the Pactolus River, which afterwards had gold-bearing sands. In another legend Midas was given ass's ears by Apollo for preferring, in a contest, the music of Pan (in another account Marsyas) to that of Apollo. Midas preserved his shame from all but his barber, who, wishing to tell it, whispered it into a hole in the ground. The reeds that grew out of that hole, however, murmured the secret whenever the wind blew through them. There was also a historical king of Phrygia named Midas in the 8th cent. B.C.

Mid-Atlantic Ridge: see ATLANTIC OCEAN.

midbrain: see BRAIN.

Middelburg (mĭd'əlbûrgh"), city (1971 pop. 30,873), capital of Zeeland prov., SW Netherlands, on the former island of WALCHEREN. It is a trade, manufacturing, and tourist center. Chartered in 1217, Middelburg developed into an important medieval trade center. The last Spanish fortress in Zeeland, it was captured (1574) by the Beggars of the Sea (see GUEUX). Although heavily damaged in World War II, Middelburg retains many beautiful old buildings, including a 12th-century abbey and the 16th-century town hall.

Middelfart (mĭ'thəlfärt), city (1970 com. pop. 16,184), Fyn co., central Denmark, on the Lille Baelt, which is spanned there by a road and rail bridge. Middelfart has long been a port and fishing base.

Middin, unidentified town, S Palestine. Joshua 15.61.

Middle Ages, period in Western European history that followed the disintegration of the West Roman Empire in the 4th and 5th cent. and lasted into the 15th cent., i.e., into the period of the Renaissance. The transitions were gradual, and exact dates for the demarcation of the Middle Ages are misleading. Although the entire Middle Ages period was once called the Dark Ages, medieval civilization is no longer thought to have been so dim, and the term "Dark Ages," if used at all, usually refers to the period before c.1000. The unifying force of the Middle Ages was Christendom. With the collapse of the Roman Empire, Christianity became the standard-bearer of Western civilization. The PAPACY gained secular authority; monastic communities, generally adhering to the Rule of St. BENEDICT, did yeoman service in preserving civilized life; and missionaries, sent to convert the GERMANS and other tribes, spread Latin civilization. By the 8th cent. a cultural milieu centered on Christianity had been established; it incorporated both Latin traditions and German institutions, such as GERMANIC LAWS. The far-flung empire created by CHARLEMAGNE illustrated this fusion. However, the empire's fragile central authority was shattered by a new wave of invasions, notably those of the VIKINGS and MAGYARS. FEUDALISM, with the MANORIAL SYSTEM (see also TENURE) as its agricultural base, became the typical social and political organization of Europe. The new framework gained stability from the 11th cent., as the invaders became Christian and settled and as prosperity was created by agricultural innovations, increasing productivity, and population expansion. As Europe entered the period known as the High Middle Ages, the church remained the universal and unifying institution. Conceptually, feudalism, the HOLY ROMAN EMPIRE, and CHIVALRY fused Christian ideals with military and political institutions. Medieval asceticism was an outgrowth of a more singularly religious ethic. While some independence from feudal rule was gained by the rising towns (see COMMUNE, in medieval history), their system of GUILDS perpetuated the Christian and medieval spirit of economic life, which stressed the collective entity, disapproved of unregulated competition, and minimized the profit motive. In the church itself the CLUNIAC ORDER brought new life to moribund ideals, and strong popes, notably GREGORY VII, worked for a reinvigorated Europe guided by a centralized church, a goal virtually realized under INNOCENT III. Militant religious zeal was expressed in the CRUSADES, which also stemmed from the growing strength of Europe. Security and prosperity stimulated intellectual life, newly centered in burgeoning UNIVERSITIES, which developed under the auspices of the church. From the Crusades and other sources came contact with Arab culture, and new learning was acquired. This was assimilated into the tenets of the Christian faith and the prevailing philosophy of SCHOLASTICISM, synthesized by St. THOMAS AQUINAS. Christian values dominated scholarship and literature, especially MEDIEVAL LATIN LITERATURE, but PROVENÇAL LITERATURE also reflected Arab influence, and other flourishing medieval literatures, including GERMAN LITERATURE, OLD NORSE LITERATURE, and MIDDLE ENGLISH LITERATURE, incorporated the materials of pre-Christian tradition. The complex currents, vitality, and religious fervor of medieval culture are evident in GOTHIC ARCHITECTURE; the inner spirit of the age is penetrated in the classics of DANTE and CHAUCER. However, the splendors of such cities as Florence and Paris were in cruel contrast to the primitive medical knowledge and sanitation that brought such horrors as the Black Death (see PLAGUE). The transition from the medieval to the modern world was foreshadowed by economic expansion, political centralization, and secularization. A money economy weakened serfdom, and an inquiring spirit stimulated the age of exploration that preceded the COMMERCIAL REVOLUTION. In growing towns there flourished banking, the bourgeois class, and secular ideals; all lent support to the expanding monarchies. The church was weakened by internal conflicts as well as by quarrels between CHURCH AND STATE. As feudal strength was sapped, notably by the the HUNDRED YEARS WAR and the Wars of the ROSES, there emerged in France and England the modern nation state. A forerunner of intellectual modernity was the new humanism of the RENAISSANCE. Finally, the great medieval unity of Christianity was shattered by the religious theories that culminated in the Protestant REFORMATION. There is a vast body of scholarship dealing with the Middle Ages. A general bibliography to provide a helpful introduction to aspects of the period should include the works by Henry ADAMS, Marc BLOCH, J. B. BURY, C. H. HASKINS, Johan HUIZINGA, Henri PIRENNE, H. O. TAYLOR, Lynn THORNDIKE, Geoffrey Barraclough, G. G. Coulton, E. S. Duckett, Ferdinand Lot, C. W. C. Oman, Sidney Painter, Eileen Power, F. M. Powicke, R. W. Southern, F. M. Stenton, and J. R. Strayer. See also bibliographies under such related articles as countries, e.g., FRANCE, GERMANY, and peoples, e.g., ANGLO-SAXONS, MOORS.

Middleboro, town (1970 pop. 13,607), Plymouth co., SE Mass.; inc. 1669. Cranberry-processing is a major industry in the town. Fire apparatus, brass products, and shoes are also made. The town was destroyed by Indians in King Philip's War and later rebuilt. Points of interest include an Indian site believed to date from 2500 B.C.; restored Revolutionary industries, such as a slitting mill and an iron foundry; and the Tom Thumb historical museum. The name is also spelled Middleborough.

Middleburg Heights, city (1970 pop. 12,367), Cuyahoga co., NE Ohio, a residential suburb of Cleveland; inc. as a village 1928, as a city 1960.

Middlebury College, at Middlebury, Vt.; coeducational; chartered and opened 1800. It is a small liberal arts college noted for its summer language schools, which pioneered in the development of segregated, specialized language study. It also operates graduate language schools in France, Italy, Germany, and Spain. The Bread Loaf School of English and the Bread Loaf Writers' Conference are also conducted by Middlebury College. See W. Storrs Lee, *Father Went to College* (1936) and *Stagecoach North* (1941).

middlebuster: see PLOW.

middle class: see BOURGEOISIE.

Middle Congo: see CONGO, PEOPLE'S REPUBLIC OF THE.

Middle Country: see MIDDLE KINGDOM.

Middle East, term applied to the countries of SW Asia and NE Africa lying W of Afghanistan, Pakistan, and India. Thus defined it includes the Asian part of Turkey, Syria, Israel, Jordan, Iraq, Iran, Lebanon, the countries of the Arabian peninsula (Saudi Arabia, Yemen, Southern Yemen, Oman, United Arab Emirates, Qatar, Bahrain, Kuwait), and Egypt and Libya. The term is sometimes used in a cultural sense to mean the group of lands in that part of the world predominantly Islamic in culture, thus including the remaining states of N Africa as well as Afghanistan and Pakistan.

Middle Eastern religions, in ancient times. Little was known about the religions of the city-states of W Asia until stores of religious literature were uncovered by excavations in the 19th and 20th cent. The picture is still incomplete, although from the available information it appears that the various religions shared many beliefs and concepts. It was from these roots that three of the world's major religions—Judaism, Christianity, and Islam—developed. Probably the most important of the Middle Eastern religions was that which was developed by the peoples of Mesopotamia (i.e., the Sumerians, the Babylonians, and the Assyrians). These peoples, besides spreading their influence, absorbed contributions of the Hittites, the Phrygians, the Ugarites, and the Phoenicians. It was in Mesopotamia that the Sumerians implanted reverence for the sky and for high places. Later, when they came into contact with the Semites, new gods were absorbed into the pantheon. The result was a blend of religious thought, Sumerian and Semitic, in which everything—a tree, a stone, a fish, a bird, a man, or even an abstract idea—had a particular significance in the universe. The highest authority was the triad of gods: the sky god ANU, the storm god ENLIL, and the water god EA, or Enki. Later a second triad arose: the moon god SIN, the sun god SHAMASH, and the goddess ISHTAR (sometimes replaced by the weather god HADAD). As Babylon rose to supremacy in the 2d millennium B.C. the local god MARDUK became important; a thousand years later ASHUR of Assyria took his place. Thus many deities were determined by political conquest as well as by interchange. There was a gradual development among the Middle Eastern cultures toward belief in a supreme god. One of the most widespread cults was that of the mother goddess (Inanna, Ishtar, Astarte, Cybele; see GREAT MOTHER OF THE GODS). She was considered as more kindly disposed toward man than the other deities, but was also capable of cruelty and vengefulness. Man was, according to Middle Eastern beliefs, created for the benefit of the gods: he was to serve and obey, provide the gods with food, clothing, and shelter, and offer them reverence. There were personal gods who were protective of the individual and linked man with the great deities, but essentially the ancient Mesopotamian peoples were at the mercy of gods whose behavior was arbitrary and often abusive. In response to this belief in negligence on the part of the gods, various city-states enacted public laws or codes of ethics (in addition to promulgating a large body of wisdom literature) that sought to promote justice and truth and to destroy wickedness. Of these law collections the most famous was probably the code of HAMMURABI. While originally the functions of priesthood were borne by the city rulers, in later times priests became a separate group and were assigned special and significant duties: some pacified the gods with hymns and liturgy; others were trained in divination and astrology (special functions in Middle Eastern religion that indirectly contributed to the growth of science); others—perhaps the most important—were concerned with protecting men from demons, who were considered actual creatures with distinct shapes and names and were to be repelled by magic, daily recitations, and exorcism. Some beliefs—the story of creation, the perpetuation of life, the inevitable fate of man—have come down to us in Sumerian and Babylonian mythology, which was preserved in cuneiform writing on clay tablets. The epic of creation, the *Enuma elish* (2d millennium B.C.), describes the battle between the young gods (forces of order), led by Marduk, and the old gods (forces of chaos), led by Tiamat and her consort Kingu. Another well-known myth, symbolizing the death and rebirth of vegetation, is that of Ishtar's descent to the underworld in search of her lover TAMMUZ and her triumphant return to earth. Here is the resurrection theme common to later religions. Perhaps the most famous of all Babylonian myths is the story of GILGAMESH. Although the people of the ancient Middle East conceived of a sort of after-existence, they generally believed that man's fate was decay and dust. Their beliefs did foreshadow, at least, the change from polytheism to monotheism, faith in some sort of divine benevolence, even the idea of salvation so important in the religious MYSTERIES and later in Christianity. See S. N. Kramer, *Sumerian Mythology* (rev. ed. 1961); Thorkild Jacobsen's essay in *The Intellectual Adventure of Ancient Man* (ed. by Henri Frankfort, 1946, repr. 1957); S. H. Hooke, *Babylonian and Assyrian Religion* (1953, repr. 1963); Isaac Mendelsohn, ed., *Religions of the Ancient Near East* (1955; tr. of texts).

Middle East Treaty Organization: see CENTRAL TREATY ORGANIZATION.

Middle English literature, English literature of the medieval period, c.1100 to c.1500. The Norman conquest of England in 1066 traditionally signifies the beginning of 200 years of the domination of French in English letters. French cultural dominance, moreover, was general in Europe at this time. French language and culture replaced English in polite, court society and had lasting effects upon English culture. But the native tradition survived, although little 13th-century, and even less 12th-century, vernacular literature is extant, since most of it was transmitted orally. Anglo-Saxon fragmented into several dialects and gradually evolved into Middle English, which, despite an admixture of French, is unquestionably English. By the mid-14th cent., Middle English had become the literary as well as the spoken language of England. There are several poems in early Middle English extant. The ORRMULUM (c.1200) is a verse translation of parts of the Gospels that is of linguistic and prosodic rather than literary interest. Of approximately the same date, *The Owl and the Nightingale* (see separate article) is the first example in English of the *débat,* a popular continental form; in the poem, the owl, strictly monastic and didactic, and the nightingale, a free and amorous secular spirit, charmingly debate the virtues of their respective ways of life. Middle English prose of the 13th cent. continued in the tradition of Anglo-Saxon prose—homiletic, didactic, and directed toward ordinary people rather than polite society. The "Katherine Group" (c.1200), comprising three saints' lives, is typical. The ANCREN RIWLE (c.1200) is a manual for prospective anchoresses; it was very popular, and it greatly influenced the prose of the 13th and 14th cent. The fact that there was no French prose tradition was very important to the preservation of the English prose tradition. In the 13th cent., the ROMANCE, an important continental narrative verse form, was introduced in England. It drew from three rich sources of character and adventure: the legends of Charlemagne, the legends of ancient Greece and Rome, and the British legends of King Arthur and the Knights of the Round Table. Layamon's BRUT, a late 13th-century metrical romance (a translation from the French), marks the first appearance of Arthurian matter in English (see ARTHURIAN LEGEND). Original English romances based upon indigenous material include KING HORN and HAVELOCK THE DANE, both 13th-century works that retain elements of the Anglo-Saxon heroic tradition. However, French romances, notably the Arthurian romances of CHRÉTIEN DE TROYES, were far more influential. They popularized in England ideas of adventure and heroism quite contrary to those of Anglo-Saxon heroic literature and were representative of wholly different values and tastes. Ideals of courtly love, together with its elaborate manners and rituals, replaced those of the heroic code; adventure and feats of courage were pursued for the sake of the knight's lady rather than for the sake of the hero's honor or the glory of his tribal king. Continental verse forms based on metrics and rhyme replaced the Anglo-Saxon alliterative line in Middle English poetry, with the important exception of the 14th-century alliterative revival. Many French literary forms also became popular, among them the FABLIAU; the exemplum, or moral tale; the animal fable; and the dream vision. The continental allegorical tradition, which derived from classical literature, is exemplified by the ROMAN DE LA ROSE, which had a strong impact on English literature. Medieval works of literature often center upon a popular rhetorical figure, such as the *ubi sunt,* which remarks on the inevitability—and sadness—of change, loss, and death; and the *cursor mundi,* which harps on the vanity of human grandeur. A 15,000-line, 13th-century English poem, the *Cursor Mundi,* retells human history (i.e., the medieval version—biblical plus classical story) from the point of view its title implies. There are a number of secular and religious Middle English lyrics of the 13th cent. extant, including the exuberant SUMER IS ICUMIN IN, but like Middle English literature in general, the LYRIC reached its fullest flower during the second half of the 14th cent. Lyrics continued popular in the 15th cent., from which time the BALLAD also dates. The poetry of the alliterative revival (see ALLITERATION), the unexplained reemergence of the Anglo-Saxon verse form in the 14th cent., includes some of the best poetry in Middle English. The Christian allegory *The Pearl* (see separate article) is a poem of great intricacy and sensibility that is meaningful on several symbolic levels. *Sir Gawain and the Green Knight,* by the same anonymous author, is also of high literary sophistication, and its intelligence, vividness, and symbolic interest render it possibly the finest Arthurian poem in English. Other important alliterative poems are the moral allegory *Piers Plowman,* attributed to William LANGLAND, and the alliterative *Morte Arthur,* which, like nearly all English poetry until the mid-14th cent., was anonymous. The works of Geoffrey Chaucer are the brilliant culmination of Middle English literature. *The Canterbury Tales* are stories told each other by pilgrims—who comprise a very colorful cross section of 14th-century English society—on their way to the shrine at Canterbury. The tales are cast into many different verse forms and genres, and collectively explore virtually every significant medieval theme. Chaucer's wise and humane work also illuminates the full scope of medieval thought. Overshadowed by Chaucer but of some note are the works of John Gower. The 15th cent. is not distinguished in English letters, due in part to the social dislocation caused by the prolonged Wars of the Roses. Of the many 15th-cent. imitators of Chaucer the best-known are John Lydgate and Thomas Hoccleve. Other poets of the time include Stephen Hawes and Alexander Barclay, and the Scots poets William Dunbar, Robert Henryson, and Gavin Douglas. The poetry of John Skelton, which is mostly satiric, combines medieval and Renaissance elements. William Caxton introduced printing to England in 1475 and in 1485 printed Sir Thomas Malory's *Morte d'Arthur.* This prose work, written in the twilight of chivalry, casts the Arthurian tales into coherent form and views them with an awareness that they represent a vanishing way of life. The MIRACLE PLAY, a long cycle of short plays based upon biblical episodes, was popular throughout the Middle Ages in England. The MORALITY PLAY, an allegorical drama centering on the struggle for man's soul, originated in the 15th cent. The finest of the genre is EVERYMAN. For further information see ENGLISH LITERATURE, ANGLO-SAXON LITERATURE, and separate articles on individual authors mentioned in this entry, e.g., Geoffrey CHAUCER. See E. K. Chambers, *English Literature at the Close of the Middle Ages* (1945); J. W. Wells, *Manual of the Writings in Middle English* (1916–51); R. M. Wilson, *Early Middle English Literature* (3d ed. 1968); Margaret Schlauch, *English Medieval Literature and Its Social Foundation* (1956, repr. 1971).

Middle Kingdom or **Middle Country,** Mandarin *Chung Kuo,* Chinese name for China. It dates from c.1000 B.C., when it designated the Chou empire situated on the North China Plain. The Chou people, unaware of high civilizations in the West, believed their empire occupied the middle of the earth, surrounded by barbarians. Since 1949, when the Communists took power, the official name for China has been *Chung Hua Jen Min Kung Ho Kuo* [middle glorious people's republican country] or, in English, the People's Republic of China.

Middle River, uninc. town (1970 pop. 19,935), Baltimore co., N Md., an industrial suburb of Baltimore.

Middlesborough, city (1970 pop. 11,878), Bell co., S Ky., in the Cumberland Mts. near the point where Kentucky, Tennessee, and Virginia meet; inc. 1890. It is a coal-mining center, with diversified manufacturing, and a railroad division point. Cumberland Gap National Historical Park (see NATIONAL PARKS AND MONUMENTS, table), Pinnacle Mt., and a resort lake are nearby.

Middlesex, former county adjoining London, SE England. In 1965 most of the county was reorganized into the Greater London boroughs of Barnet, Brent, Ealing, Enfield, Haringey, Harrow, Hillingdon, Hounslow, and Richmond-upon-Thames. The remainder became part of the counties of Hertfordshire and Surrey. Middlesex has been important from Roman times, when the Roman road known as Watling Street traversed the district. The name means middle Saxons.

Middlesex, borough (1970 pop. 15,038), Middlesex co., N central N.J.; inc. 1913. The borough has diversified manufacturing industries.

Middle Temple: see INNS OF COURT; TEMPLE, THE.

Middleton, Arthur, 1742–87, political leader in the American Revolution, signer of the Declaration of Independence, b. near Charleston, S.C.; son of Henry Middleton. He was educated in England, returning to America in 1763. Middleton was elected (1776) to succeed his father as a delegate to the Continental Congress. He also fought at Charleston (1780), where he was captured by the British. After being exchanged, he again served (1781–83) in the Congress.

Middleton, Conyers, 1683–1750, English clergyman, one of the earliest English rationalistic theologians. A fellow of Trinity College, Cambridge, he became known through his disputes with Richard Bentley, master of Trinity. Middleton was made principal librarian of Cambridge in 1721. A storm of protest followed his *Letter from Rome, Showing an Exact Conformity between Popery and Paganism* (1729). It was in his controversy with Daniel Waterland over the historical accuracy of the Bible that doubts about his orthodoxy were raised. The *Life of Cicero* (1741) brought the author wide recognition, but later critics charged that it owed much to a work by William Bellenden. He was regarded as a latitudinarian (i.e., one who advocates opening the church to a broad spectrum of beliefs), an attitude plainly shown in his *Free Inquiry into the Miraculous Powers* (1749), concerning the claims to miraculous powers in the church; his view was severely criticized. His *Miscellaneous Works* (4 vol., 1752) include many of his writings.

Middleton, Henry, 1717–84, American Revolutionary leader, b. near Charleston, S.C. A wealthy, influential planter, he held many official positions before resigning (1770) in protest against the British trade policies. He was a member (1774–76) and president (1774–75) of the Continental Congress, but he opposed independence and resigned. His son Arthur Middleton took his place. The elder Middleton returned to South Carolina and continued to hold public offices. Although he resumed allegiance to the crown after the fall of Charleston (1780), his estates were not confiscated.

Middleton, Thomas, 1580–1627, English dramatist, b. London, grad. Queen's College, Oxford, 1598. His early plays were chiefly written in collaboration with Dekker, Drayton, and others. Between 1604 and 1611 he wrote realistic, satiric comedies of London life, including *Michaelmas Term, A Trick to Catch the Old One, A Mad World, My Masters, The Roaring Girl* (with Dekker), and *A Chaste Maid in Cheapside.* His comedies, like his early pamphlets, aimed to expose contemporary vice and give graphic pictures of the more scabrous side of Jacobean life. During the years 1613 to 1618 he devoted himself to writing tragicomedies. From 1621 to the end of his career he wrote his most notable plays, two powerful tragedies about the corruption of character, *The Changeling* (with William Rowley) and *Women Beware Women.* He was severely reproved by the Privy Council for his anti-Spanish political satire, *A Game of Chess* (1624). In addition to his plays, he wrote civic pageants and masques. See his works (ed. by A. H. Bullen, 8 vol., 1885–86); studies by R. H. Barker (1958) and N. A. Brittin (1972).

Middleton, municipal borough (1971 pop. 53,419), Lancashire, NW England, on the Irk River. Manufactures include cotton and silk textiles, soap, plastics, and chemicals. In 1974, Middleton became part of the new metropolitan county of Greater Manchester.

Middletown. 1 Industrial city (1970 pop. 36,924), Middlesex co., central Conn., on the west bank of the Connecticut River; settled 1650, inc. 1784, town and city consolidated 1923. Its manufactures include brake linings, marine hardware, rubber footwear, clothing, and textiles. Shipping brought early prosperity to Middletown, and during colonial days it was the state's leading shipping, commercial, and cultural center. It is the seat of Wesleyan Univ. and a junior college. Also in the city are a state mental hospital, a state girls' correctional school, and a state park. A bridge (1938) spans the Connecticut River to Portland. **2** Industrial city (1970 pop. 22,607), Orange co., SE N.Y., on the Walkill River; settled 1756, inc. as a city 1888. It is a farm trade center with railroad shops and foundries. Among its products are clothing and leather goods. A state mental hospital and a junior college are in Middletown. **3** Industrial city (1970 pop. 48,767), Butler co., SW Ohio, on the Great Miami River, in a farm area; inc. 1866. Its major industry is steel production. Miami Univ. has a branch there. **4** Rural and resort town (1970 pop. 29,290), Newport co., SE R.I., on Rhode Island and Narragansett Bay; set off from Newport and inc. 1743. Its name is derived from its location between Newport and Portsmouth. "Whitehall," where Bishop Berkeley lived (1729–31), has been preserved. During the Revolution the town was pillaged (1776) by the British.

Middletown: see LYND, ROBERT STAUGHTON.

middle voice, in grammar: see VOICE.

Middle West or **Midwest,** section of the United States about the Great Lakes and the upper Mississippi valley. It is a vague regional term and has been by some applied to all the northern section of the land between the Allegheny and the Rockies. More usually it is restricted to the Old Northwest and the neighboring states to the southern border of Missouri, E of the Great Plains. It thus includes Ohio, Indiana, Illinois, Michigan, Wisconsin, Minnesota, Iowa, Missouri, Kansas, and Nebraska. The term may be extended internationally to include the Ontario Peninsula of Canada. The area has some of the richest farming land in the world and is known for its corn and hogs. The extended area also includes great wheat fields. Parts of the Middle West also have an enormous amount of industry (e.g., the automobile factories of Michigan and the rubber factories of Ohio). The chief cities are Chicago, Detroit, St. Louis, and Minneapolis-St. Paul. In popular tradition the Middle West is conservative, isolationist, Protestant, and "American." Actually it has all sorts and shades of political, economic, and religious opinion and a great mixture of peoples. It does, however, constitute a dialect area of American speech. See Walter Havighurst, *The Heartland* (1962); D. E. Clark, *The Middle West in American History* (1966); K. R. Walker, *A History of the Middle West* (1972).

Midgard: see GERMANIC RELIGION.

midge, name for any of numerous minute, fragile FLIES in several families. The family Chironomidae consists of about 2,000 species, most of which are widely distributed. The herbivorous larvae are found in all fresh waters; the larvae of some species live in salt water. Midge larvae are an important source of food for larger aquatic insects and fish. The larvae of some species of the genus *Chironomus*, which are called freshwater bloodworms, are unusual in that they contain the protein hemoglobin. The pupae are active and aquatic. The adults, which look like slender mosquitoes, are often seen swarming over or near water, and large courting and mating swarms may contain millions of insects. The larvae and pupae of the net-wing midges, family Blepharoceridae, live in fast-flowing fresh water; they attach to rocks by suction disks and feed mainly on algae. The biting midges belong to the genus *Culicoides* of the family Ceratopogonidae; they are the smallest of the bloodsucking insects and are common pests in the NE United States, where they are called punkies, sand flies, and no-see-ums. The adults have mouthparts that pierce and suck and inflict irritating bites on humans; some species ride the wings of dragonflies and lacewings, sucking the blood of their hosts. Gall midges, family Cecidomyiidae, damage many plants by causing formation of plant galls in which the larvae live (see GNAT). Midges are classified in the phylum ARTHROPODA, class Insecta, order Diptera.

midget: see DWARFISM.

Mid Glamorgan (glәmôr'gәn), nonmetropolitan county, S Wales, created under the Local Government Act of 1972 (effective 1974). It comprises the county borough of MERTHYR TYDFIL, and portions of the former counties of GLAMORGANSHIRE, BRECONSHIRE, and MONMOUTHSHIRE.

Midhat Pasha (mĭdhät' päshä'), 1822–83, Turkish politician. As governor of Bulgaria he succeeded within the few years of his tenure (1864–69) in raising the country from misery to relative prosperity. Schools, roads, and granaries were built from funds obtained by local taxation. His hostility to Pan-Slavism caused the Russian ambassador at Constantinople to secure his transfer to Baghdad. He was briefly grand vizier (chief executive officer) in 1872. In 1876, at the head of the reforming party, he led the revolution that deposed Sultan Abd al-Aziz. The new sultan, Murad V, was in turn shortly deposed because of his insanity, and ABD AL-HAMID II succeeded. Late in 1876, as grand vizier, Midhat secured the promulgation of the first Turkish constitution, but as soon as Abd al-Hamid regained control over the situation he sent Midhat into exile. After being recalled as governor of Syria, Midhat was charged with the murder of Abd al-Aziz, imprisoned, and strangled.

Midi, Pic du: see PIC DU MIDI D'OSSAU.

Midian (mĭd'ēәn) or **Midianites** (-īts), in the Bible, a nomadic Bedouin people of N Arabia and of the lands E of Palestine. They were closely associated with the Israelites. Moses took refuge with them and married the daughter of their priest Jethro. At the time of the Judges, they invaded and oppressed Israel and were defeated by Gideon. Their eponym was a son of Abraham. They were among the first to use the camel. Gen. 25.2; 37.28,36; Ex. 3.1; Num. 31.1–9; Judges 6–8. Madian: Acts 7.29.

Midland, town (1971 pop. 10,992), S Ont., Canada, on Georgian Bay, NW of Toronto. Midland is a port, and has grain elevators and plants that manufacture textiles, cameras, optical goods, and other products. The Martyrs' Shrine, commemorating the deaths of five Jesuit priests who were among the eight North American martyrs canonized in 1930, and other remembrances of the early colonial period are nearby.

Midland. 1 City (1970 pop. 35,176), seat of Midland co., central Mich., in the Saginaw valley at the confluence of the Tittabawassee and Chippewa rivers; inc. 1887. Midland owes its development after 1890 to the Dow Chemical Company, whose corporate headquarters are there. Silicone products, chemicals, cans, magnesium, and plastics are among the manufactures. Oil, coal, and salt are found in the area. The Dow Gardens Library and Center for Arts are in Midland, and Saginaw Valley College and a junior college are in nearby University Center. **2** City (1970 pop. 59,463), seat of Midland co., W Texas, on the southern border of the Llano Estacado; inc. 1906. Midland has prospered partly because of its cattle ranches, but the city's reputation for spectacular wealth and its great spurt in population after 1940 resulted from the location of many oil-company offices there. Clothing, mobile homes, aircraft, fabricated steel, plastic products, and tools for mining and drilling are manufactured. The prosperous, bustling city attracts travelers, and the airport between Midland and Odessa is important in transcontinental traffic. The city has a junior college, a symphony orchestra, a planetarium, and a petroleum museum and hall of fame.

Midland Canal, Ger. *Mittelland Kanal,* artificial waterway system of West Germany and East Germany, extending c.200 mi (320 km) along the North German plain from the Dortmund-Ems Canal, West Germany, to Magdeburg, East Germany, on the Elbe River. An eastward extension of the Midland Canal passes through Berlin and connects with the Oder River. The system is made up of a series of canals that join parallel north-flowing rivers. The canal facilitates east-west transportation of raw materials and manufactured goods.

Midlands, region of central England. It is usually considered to include the present counties of Derbyshire, Leicestershire, Northamptonshire, Nottinghamshire, Staffordshire, Warwickshire, West Midlands, and E Hereford and Worcester. The region is highly industrialized. See BLACK COUNTRY; POTTERIES, THE.

Midlothian (mĭdlō'thēәn), formerly **Edinburghshire,** county (1972 pop. 598,500), 366 sq mi (948 sq km), SE Scotland, on the south shore of the Firth of Forth. The county town is EDINBURGH, capital of Scotland. More than four fifths of the county's population lives in Edinburgh. In the south are the Pentland and Moorfoot hills, which rise to c.2,000 ft (610 m). The main rivers are the Gala Water, Water of Leith, the Esk, the Almond, and the Tyne. The coal fields of the Esk valley and the Calders are extensively mined and are the largest employers. Oil is refined near Edinburgh. Other industries are engineering, brewing, and the manufacture of paper, textiles, and carpets. Grains, potatoes, and fruit are grown. LEITH is one of Scotland's greatest ports. There are numerous vestiges of Roman occupation and medieval secular and ecclesiastical remains. In the country were fought the battles of PINKIE and of Carberry Hill (see MARY QUEEN OF SCOTS). The Heart of Midlothian was a popular name for the former Tolbooth prison at Edinburgh and became the title of a novel by Sir Walter Scott. Under the Local Government Act of 1973, Midlothian was divided between the Lothian and Borders regions.

Midlothian (mĭdlō'thēәn), village (1970 pop. 15,939), Cook co., NE Ill., a residential suburb of Chicago; inc. 1927.

Midnapore (mĭd'nәpûr''), town (1971 pop. 71,521), West Bengal state, E India, on the Kasai River. It is a district administrative center and a market for agricultural products and timber. A canal links Midnapore with Calcutta.

midnight sun, phenomenon in which the sun remains visible in the sky continuously for 24 hr or longer, occurring only in the polar regions. The midnight sun is due to the fact that the plane of the earth's equator is tilted about 23½° to the plane of the ECLIPTIC (the apparent path of the sun through the sky). Thus, at the summer SOLSTICE (about June 22), the sun is still visible on the horizon at midnight at all points along the ARCTIC CIRCLE, 23½° of latitude from the North Pole. At points north of the Arctic Circle, the midnight sun is visible for longer than one day, the North Pole having a full six months of continuous sun from the vernal EQUINOX (about March 21) to the autumnal equinox (about Sept. 23). In the south polar regions the midnight sun is visible along the ANTARCTIC CIRCLE at the winter solstice (about Dec. 22) and south of the Antarctic Circle for longer periods.

Midrash (mĭd'räsh) [Heb.,=to examine, to investigate], verse by verse interpretation of Hebrew Scriptures, consisting of homily and exegesis, by Jewish teachers since about 400 B.C. Distinction is made between Midrash HALAKAH, dealing with the legal portions of Scripture, and Midrash haggada, dealing with biblical lore. Midrashic exposition of both kinds appears throughout the Talmud. Individual midrashic commentaries were composed by rabbis after the 2d cent. A.D. up to the Middle Ages, and they were mostly of an aggadic nature, following the order of the scriptural text. Important among them are the *Midrash Rabbah,* a collection of commentaries on the Pentateuch and the Five Scrolls, and the *Pesikta Midrashim,* concerning the festivals. This body of rabbinic literature contains the earliest speculative thought (including what might be termed Jewish theology) in the Jewish tradition. See H. L. Strack, *Introduction to the Talmud and Midrash* (1931, repr. 1969); Louis Ginzberg, *Legends of the Bible* (1956); N. N. Glatzer, *Hammer on the Rock: A Short Midrash Reader* (1962).

midshipman: see TOADFISH.

midsummer day and midsummer night, names given to the feast of the nativity of St. John the Baptist (June 24) and the preceding night (St. John's Eve, June 23). Because midsummer is about the time of the solstice, it has been associated with solar ceremonies since long before Christianity. Relics of such ceremonies are the bright bonfires and the merrymaking of midsummer night. Formerly it was considered the one night of the year when supernatural beings were about. The importance of this night to love and lovers is undoubtedly a survival of fertility rites. Shakespeare and Mendelssohn are among the masters who have used the festival as a subject for a major work.

Midway, island group (2 sq mi/5.2 sq km), central Pacific, c.1,150 mi (1,850 km) NW of Honolulu, comprising Sand and Eastern islands with the surrounding atoll. It is a U.S. military base, with no indigenous population. Discovered by Americans in 1859, Midway was annexed in 1867. A cable station was opened in 1903. In 1935 Midway became a commercial air station of Pan American Airways, and in 1941 a U.S. naval base was opened. The **battle of Midway** (June 3–6, 1942), one of the decisive Allied victories of World War II, occurred nearby. The battle, fought mostly with aircraft, resulted in the destruction of three Japanese aircraft carriers, crippling the Japanese navy. The islands are now administered by the U.S. Dept. of the Interior.

Midwest: see MIDDLE WEST.

Midwest City, city (1970 pop. 48,212), Oklahoma co., central Okla., a residential suburb of Oklahoma City; founded 1942 with the activation of adjoining Tinker Air Force Base, a logistics center.

midwifery (mĭd'wī''fәrē), art of assisting at childbirth. The term *midwife* for centuries referred to a woman who was an overseer during the process of delivery. In ancient Greece and Rome these women had some formal training, but as the medical arts declined during medieval times whatever skills the midwives possessed were gained from experience, and the lore was passed on from mother to daughter or to apprentices. With the upsurge of medical science about the 16th cent. the delivery of babies was accepted into the province of physicians, and as formal training and licensing of medical practitioners became more prevalent these requirements extended also to the women still engaged in that important skill. At this time professional schools of midwifery were established in Europe. When midwifery finally became recognized as an important branch of medicine and worthy of the interest and attention of physicians, the practice of obstetrics was established. Professional midwives are still used widely in Europe, but in the United States, midwifery is practiced mostly in areas where there are few doctors and nurses, principally in the Southern states. Recently there has been renewed interest in the United States in training women who are not physicians to deliver infants.

Mie (mē'ä), prefecture (1970 pop. 1,543,083), S Honshu, Japan, on Ise Bay. TSU (the capital), ISE (a major Shintoist center), YOKKAICHI, Matsusaka, and Kuwana are the chief cities. Mie has textile, ceramic, woodworking, and fishing industries. Ise-shima National Park is there.

Mieczyslaw: see MIESZKO.

Mielziner, Jo (mēlzē'nәr), 1901–, American theatrical scene designer, b. Paris. Mielziner made his Broadway design debut in 1924 with *The Guardsman.* Among the more than 200 productions for which he has designed sets are *Strange Interlude, Hamlet, Carousel, Annie Get Your Gun, A Streetcar Named Desire, Death of a Salesman, The Prime of Miss Jean Brodie,* the film *Picnic,* and the ballet *Who Cares?* During World War II he was a camouflage specialist with the U.S. air force. Mielziner was, with Eero SAARINEN, codesigner of the Vivian Beaumont Theater in New York City's Lincoln Center. See his memoirs, *Designing for the Theatre* (1965), and his *The Shapes of Our Theatre,* ed. by C. R. Smith (1970).

Mieres (mēā'rĕs), city (1971 pop. 64,552), Oviedo prov., N Spain, in Asturias, on the Lena River. It is an important mining center for coal, sulfur, and cinnabar and has iron and steel plants.

Mierevelt, Miereveld, or **Miereveldt, Michiel Janszen van** (all: mēkhēl' yän'sən vän mē'rəvĕlt), 1567-1641, Dutch portrait painter. He was court painter to the house of Orange, working chiefly in Delft and at The Hague. Mierevelt had many pupils and assistants, whose numerous, and usually inferior, works bear his name. His thousands of portraits included those of nearly all the major court figures. The Rijks Museum and the Metropolitan Museum have examples of his works. His son and pupil, **Pieter van Mierevelt,** 1595-1623, painted portraits in the manner of his father. His *Anatomy Lesson* is in the hospital at Delft.

Mieris (mē'rĭs), family of Dutch genre and portrait painters of Leiden. **Frans van Mieris,** 1635-81, the most important, was the son of a goldsmith and pupil of Gerard Dou. His tiny, meticulous paintings won him distinguished patrons and a lucrative practice. Mieris excelled in the rendering of texture and was an admirable portraitist. Among his numerous well-known works in major museums are *Oyster Breakfast* (Hermitage, Leningrad); *Sleeping Girl* (Uffizi); and *Lady in a Crimson Jacket* (National Gall., London). His sons and pupils, **Jan van Mieris,** 1660-90, and **Willem van Mieris,** 1662-1747, continued his tradition, but failed to equal him. None of Jan's work is extant. A grandson, **Frans van Mieris,** 1689-1763, also followed in his steps with only slight success, being better known as an antiquarian and writer.

Miës van der Rohe, Ludwig (lo͝ot'vĭkh mē'ĕs vän dĕr rō'ə), 1886-1969, German-American architect. He is one of the founders of modern architecture. He was an assistant to Peter Behrens, in whose office Gropius and Le Corbusier had also been trained. In 1921 Miës produced a design for an all-glass skyscraper that attracted international attention. In 1927 he was placed in charge of the Werkbund Housing Exposition at Stuttgart, for which he built a modern apartment house, and in 1929 had charge of the German section of the Barcelona International Exposition. He was appointed (1930) director of the BAUHAUS at Dessau. In 1937 he left Germany. At the Armour Institute (now the Illinois Institute of Technology), Chicago, he headed the department of architecture until his retirement in 1958. He planned the new campus and designed several of its buildings. The 860 Lake Shore apartments (Chicago; 1949-51) incorporate the principles of the glass skyscraper with a surface expression of steel-frame construction. He and Philip Johnson elaborated on this concept in the Seagram Building, New York City (1956-58). Miës also experimented with buildings of a single great space. In his last years his most notable works were the School of Social Service Administration of the University of Chicago (1963-65) and the impressive Chicago Federal Center (1963-68), which consists of three skyscraper slabs. See his works ed. by M. Pawley (1970); studies by P. Johnson (1953), A. Drexler (1960), P. Blake (1964), and W. Blaser (rev. ed. 1972).

Mieszko I (myĕsh'kô) or **Mieczyslaw I** (—chĭsläf), c.922-992, duke of Poland (962-92), the first important member of the PIAST dynasty. The first German invasions of Poland began in 963. To avert this threat, Mieszko obtained (c.963) a friendly treaty with Holy Roman Emperor Otto I, to whom he agreed to pay tribute. Mieszko later conquered Pomerania. In 966 he accepted Christianity and immediately began the conversion of Poland. Late in his reign he placed Poland under the protection of the pope, thus gaining papal support of Polish integrity. His son BOLESLAUS I succeeded him.

Mieszko II or **Mieczyslaw II,** 990-1034, king of Poland (1025-34), son and successor of Boleslaus I. His reign was marked by internal and external strife. Moravia was lost to Bohemia, Lusatia to Germany, and sections of Ruthenia to Kiev. The kingdom was in chaos when it passed to his son, CASIMIR I.

Mifflin, Thomas, 1744-1800, American Revolutionary general and political leader, b. Philadelphia. Turning from business to public affairs, he was a member of the Pennsylvania provincial assembly and of the First Continental Congress. He joined the army early in the American Revolution and rose to the rank of quartermaster general. He held that post, except for a brief interruption, until 1778, when he resigned after being accused of misuse of funds. The charges were never substantiated. Dissatisfied with George Washington's conduct of the war, he became involved in the CONWAY CABAL and tried to undermine Washington, but later he renewed his friendship with the commander in chief. Mifflin again served in the Continental Congress (1782-84) and was its president (1783-84). He was later a delegate to the Federal Constitutional Convention (1787), and was governor of Pennsylvania (1790-99) during the WHISKEY REBELLION and the revolt of the Pennsylvania Germans under John FRIES. Although he initially refused to commit the Pennsylvania militia to suppressing the Whiskey Rebellion, he eventually cooperated with President Washington against the insurgents. See study by K. R. Rossman (1952).

Migdal-el (mĭg'dəl-ĕl), fortified town, N Palestine. It is believed to be identical with the biblical MAGDALA. Joshua 19.38.

Migdal-gad (mĭg'dəl-găd), town, SW Palestine. Joshua 15.37.

Migdol (mĭg'dŏl). **1** Place near which the Israelites crossed the Red Sea. Ex. 14.2; Num. 33.7. **2** City, Egypt, where Jews lived. It is the modern Tall al Hayr, S of Pelusium. Jer. 44.1; 46.14.

Mignard, Pierre (pyĕr mēnyär'), 1612-95, French painter. In 1657 he was summoned by Louis XIV to portray the king and celebrities of the court. In 1664 he decorated, in fresco, the cupola of the Church of Val-de-Grâce, Paris. In his theories, rather than in his painting, he led the opposition against Le Brun and the Académie royale, but after the death of Le Brun, Mignard succeeded to the directorship of the Académie and of the Gobelin tapestry works. Among his best-known works are *St. Luke Painting the Virgin,* and *Mme de Maintenon* (Louvre).

Migne, Jacques Paul (zhäk pôl mē'nyə), 1800-1875, French publisher of theological works, a Roman Catholic priest (ordained 1824). He set up a printing press in Paris and printed many religious and theological works. His principal publication was *Patrologia,* an ambitious project the aim of which was to publish the writings of all Christian writers into the Middle Ages. Its principal value lies in the fact that the volumes were not expensive and that in Migne's edition countless works had been published for the first time. There were three series: Latin Fathers to Innocent III (217 vol. and an index in 4 vol.); Greek Fathers (to 1438) in Latin translation (81 vol.); and Greek Fathers in Greek and Latin (166 vol.).

Mignet, François Auguste Marie (fräNswä' ôgüst' märē' mēnyā'), 1796-1884, French historian and journalist. With his lifelong friend, Adolphe THIERS, Mignet edited the *National,* a powerful liberal daily, and helped to overthrow Charles X in the July Revolution of 1830. As a historian, Mignet is best known for *L'Histoire de la Révolution française* (1824; many later editions and translations). A moderate, Mignet deplored the violence of the Terror but defended the French Revolution as the necessary product of economic and social conditions. He also made significant contributions to the history of the 16th cent., including works on Spanish history.

mignonette (mĭn''yənĕt'), common name for some members of the Resedaceae, a small family of herbs and a few shrubs inhabiting arid regions. The main genus, the mignonettes (genus *Reseda*), chiefly of the Mediterranean area, has several species naturalized to waste places of the United States, e.g., the dyer's-weed (*R. luteola*), which has been a source of a yellow dye since Neolithic times. A few species are cultivated for their fragrant flowers, e.g., the common mignonette (*R. odorata*), formerly highly valued in perfumery for its essential oils. The mignonette family is classified in the division MAGNOLIOPHYTA, class Magnoliopsida, order Capparales.

migraine (mī'grān), headache characterized by recurrent attacks of severe pain, usually on one side of the head. It may be preceded by flashes or spots before the eyes or a ringing in the ears, and accompanied by double vision, nausea, vomiting, or dizziness. The attacks vary in frequency from daily occurrences to one every few years. Migraine affects women twice as often as men and is often inherited. Many disturbances, such as allergy, temporary swelling of the brain, and endocrine disturbances, have been suspected of causing the disorder. Although the exact cause is unknown, the pain is believed to be associated with constriction followed by dilation of blood vessels leading to and within the brain. Untreated attacks may last for many hours. Mild attacks are often relieved by common sedatives such as aspirin. Severe attacks are treated with ergotamine, a drug derived from a fungus, which will often stop the headache if given at the early stage.

migrant labor, term applied in the United States to laborers who travel from place to place harvesting crops that must be picked as soon as they ripen. Although migrant labor patterns exist in other parts of the world (e.g., Africa, Australia, Canada, Europe, and South America), none compares with the extent and magnitude of the system in the United States. Migrant laborers may travel on their own or they may be transported by a contractor who has agreed to supply the farmer with the needed workers. They may be urban dwellers who go on the land only for the season or migrants whose only means of living is to follow the crops from one place to another. Efforts to enforce sanitary conditions, prevent child labor, and protect the workers from exploitation met with only slight success until the 1960s. In the 1930s, a combination of droughts, the depression, and the increased mechanization of farming prompted a migration of small farmers and laborers from Arkansas, Kansas, Oklahoma, and Texas to the W United States. It was estimated that this type of permanent migrant worker, without home, voting privileges, or union representation, numbered more than 3 million. John Steinbeck's *Grapes of Wrath* is a dramatic representation of the life of those migrants. In World War II another type of migrant worker sprang into being with the need for labor in the defense industries. These uprooted workers experienced housing problems, but they were protected by wage and hour laws that did not apply to agricultural labor. Since the 1940s, thousands of workers each year have been brought into the United States from foreign countries, principally from Mexico. Migrant labor, which remains almost exclusively agricultural, continues to receive little legal protection. However, in the mid-1960s, under the leadership of Cesar CHAVEZ, organization of migrant workers began in the West, mainly in California. In 1970, after years of strikes, marches, and a nationwide boycott, more than 65% of California's grape growers signed contracts with the AFL-CIO's United Farm Workers Organizing Committee headed by Chavez. That organization, which became a full-fledged union as the United Farm Workers (UFW) in 1972, had some success in negotiating contracts in other states as well. However, it found itself locked in a fierce struggle with the Teamsters Union, which also claimed to represent migrant laborers and succeeded in renegotiating many of the UFW's contracts in California. The Teamsters' attempt to break up the UFW led to many strikes and some violence. See Carey McWilliams, *Factories in the Field* (1939, repr. 1971); Dorothy Nelkin, *On the Season* (1970).

migration, of people, geographical movements of individuals or groups for the purpose of permanently resettling. Migrations have occurred throughout human history and have played an important part in the peopling of all the areas of the world. Primitive migrations were usually made in search of food. Physical changes, such as the advance of the glacial mass, and invasion by other peoples also accounted for prehistoric mass migration. The most important migrations in European history were the Gothic invasions from the 3d through the 6th cent. (see GERMANS), the Arab invasions of the 7th and 8th cent. (see ARABS), the westward migration of the Golden Horde of JENGHIZ KHAN in the 13th cent., and the invasions of the Ottoman Turks in the 14th to 16th cent. (see OTTOMAN EMPIRE; TURKS). From the 17th to the 20th cent. migration became a matter for individuals and families rather than nations or mass groups. The basic motive for migration in this period was economic pressure, as areas of low population density attracted people from areas where density was high and economic opportunity consequently low. The desire for religious and political freedom has also been important, and national policies have played a part in the movement of peoples. In the largest international migration in history, c.65 million people migrated from Europe to North America and South America between the 17th cent. and World War II, while another 17 million to Africa and Oceania. Regulation of migration by governments became significant in the 20th cent. (see IMMIGRATION). The development of totalitarianism and World War II resulted in a new pattern of forced mass migration within Europe. Over 30 million people were forcibly moved or scattered by the Nazis during the war. In the postwar period c.10 million Germans and persons of German descent were forcibly expelled from Eastern Europe. Other forced migrations since World War II have included the partitioning of India and Pakistan, which uprooted 18 million, and the establishment of the state of Israel, which created about one million refugees (see REFUGEE). Normal internal migration has been characterized in modern times by a population shift from rural to urban areas. In some countries, especially the United States, MIGRANT LABOR has become an important problem. See J. A. Jackson, ed., *Migration* (1969); C. J. Jansen, *Readings in the Sociology* *of Migration* (1970); J. M. Simmie, *The Sociology of Internal Migration* (1972).

migration of animals, movements of animals in large numbers from one place to another. In modern usage the term is usually restricted to regular, periodic movements of populations away from and back to their place of origin. A single round trip may take the entire lifetime of an individual, as with the Pacific SALMON; or an individual may make the same trip repeatedly, as with many of the migratory birds and mammals. The animals may travel in groups along well-defined routes; or individuals may travel separately, congregating for breeding and then spreading out over a wide feeding area, as do some of the SEALS. The term *emigration* refers to irregular movements out of an area, with no return. When such emigration is the result of sudden, explosive population increase, it is called an irruption. Irruptions are common among small rodents, notably LEMMINGS, and various species of birds and insects. The mass movements of the so-called migratory locusts of N Africa (*Locusta*) and North America (*Melanoplus*) are actually irruptions; however, the N African desert locust (*Schistocerca*) makes true migrations between its winter and summer breeding grounds. Another type of one-way travel is the regular dispersal of the young of most species. The simplest type of regular migration is the diurnal movement of some marine microorganisms from one depth to another in response to light changes. Certain marine invertebrates, such as the palolo worm (see ANNELIDA) have a monthly migration pattern influenced by the phase of the moon. Seasonal migrations occur in many species of insects, birds, marine mammals, and large herbivorous mammals. These migrations often provide the animals with more favorable conditions of temperature, food, or water. Many birds and a few BATS of cold and temperate regions migrate to warmer areas during the winter. Herbivores of cold regions, such as WAPITI (elk), CARIBOU, and MOOSE, have summer and winter ranges; many herbivores of warm regions, such as the African ANTELOPES, migrate seasonally to avoid drought. These migrations may involve a change of latitude, of altitude, or both. In many cases the chief function of seasonal migration is to provide a suitable place for reproduction, which may not be the place most suitable for the feeding and other daily activities of adults. Many fishes migrate to spawning grounds, and in some cases this involves a change from salt water to fresh water (e.g., salmon) or vice versa (e.g., fresh water EELS). SEA TURTLES, seals, and many sea birds come ashore to breed, and most AMPHIBIANS gather near water at the breeding season. FUR SEALS and many WHALES make ocean voyages of thousands of miles to their breeding grounds, the former coming ashore on islands. Various factors are involved in the initiation of migration. In some cases external pressures—temperature, drought, food shortage—alone may cause the animals to seek better conditions. For example, most of the mule deer of Yellowstone Park, Wyo., migrate between summer and winter pastures, but those living near hot springs, where grazing is available all year, do not. In many species migration is initiated by a combination of physiological and external stimuli. In birds the migratory instinct is related to the cycle of enlargement of the reproductive organs in spring and their reduction in fall. Experiments have shown that variation in day length is the chief external stimulus for this cycle: Light received by the eye affects production of a hormone by the anterior pituitary gland, which stimulates growth of the reproductive organs. Much work has been done in recent decades on the problems of orientation and navigation in migrating animals, although the subject is still not well understood. Studies of salmon indicate that they depend on the olfactory sense to locate and return to their stream of origin. Herbivorous mammals often follow well-established trails, and probably also make use of the sense of smell. Bats, whales, and seals use echolocation to navigate in the dark or under water; in addition, some whales appear to take visual bearings on objects on the shore in their migrations. Many migratory birds travel by night, and experiments in planetariums indicate that they navigate at least in part by the stars. Night-migrating birds are sometimes disoriented in prolonged heavy fog. Day-flying birds navigate by the sun, and also make some use of geographical features, particularly of shorelines. It has long been proposed that birds perceive the direction of the earth's magnetic field and use it for navigation, but experimental evidence for that hypothesis is inconclusive. Most migratory birds travel within broad north-south air routes known as flyways. There are four major flyways in North America, called the Pacific, central, Mississippi, and Atlantic flyways. The space within the flyway used by a particular group of birds is called a corridor. Bird migration is not always in a north and south direction. Many European birds migrate in an east-west direction, wintering in the more temperate British Isles, and many mountain-dwelling birds descend to lower altitudes in winter. The breeding grounds of a bird species are regarded as its home territory. Some migratory birds winter only a few hundred miles from their breeding grounds, while others migrate between the cold or temperate zones of the two hemispheres. The longest journey is made by the arctic TERN, which alternates between the Arctic and the Antarctic. The movements of migrating animals are often studied by tagging individuals. Bird banding has been carried on extensively since the 1920s; more recently there has been tagging of fishes, butterflies, and marine mammals. Use is now made of radar, sonar, and radio for following migrations, particularly those of marine animals. Radio transmitters attached to whales or seals emit signals that can be picked up by weather satellites at regular intervals. See Otto von Frisch, *Animal Migration* (1969); R. T. Orr, *Animals in Migration* (1970).

Migron (mĭg'rŏn). **1** Unidentified place or places N of Jerusalem. 1 Sam. 14.2; Isa. 10.28. **2** Place, mentioned on the route of the Assyrian army, possibly the same as Migron **1.** Isa. 10.28.

Miguel (mēgĕl'), 1802–66, Portuguese prince; son of JOHN IV of Portugal and younger brother of PEDRO I of Brazil. He led an unsuccessful revolt against his father in 1824. On John's death (1826) the Portuguese succession was in dispute. The liberals supported Pedro, who was in fact recognized as King Peter IV, but the reactionary absolutists favored Miguel for the throne. Pedro abdicated in favor of his daughter, MARIA II, on condition that Miguel act as guardian for and marry the young queen and that he accept a constitutional charter issued by Pedro. Migeul accepted this arrangement, but immediately upon taking power he convened (1828) a nonconstitutional Cortes and took the crown it offered him. The liberal leaders gathered forces and established themselves in the Azores. Pedro joined them in 1832, and they sailed to Oporto. There Miguel besieged them until an English sea force in the employ of the liberals destroyed (1833) his fleet. By 1834 his cause was lost, and he agreed to leave Portugal. He later denounced his capitulation, and although he himself took no part, there were several attempted Miguelist risings during Maria's reign.

Mihailović, Draža: see MIHAJLOVIĆ, DRAŽA.

Mihajlović or **Mikhailovich, Draža** or **Dragoljub** (drä'zhä mēhī'lôvĭch, drä'gôlyo͞ob"), 1893?–1946, Yugoslav soldier. He fought with the *chetniks,* a Serbian guerrilla force, in the Balkan Wars (1912–13) and in World War I, and after the conquest (1941) of Yugoslavia in World War II he headed the revived *chetnik* forces. His successful operations earned him promotion to general and appointment (1942) as minister of war by the Yugoslav government-in-exile. An ardent royalist and Serbian nationalist, he soon clashed with the partisans of Marshal TITO. Mihajlović's forces gradually dwindled while Tito's increased, and by 1944 he had lost Allied support and was reluctantly dismissed by King Peter II. Mihajlović continued antipartisan warfare with the remnants of his forces, but he was captured by the Tito authorities and tried on charges of collaboration and treason. Evidence indicates that Mihajlović, who considered the Communists a greater threat than the Axis Powers, did at times act against the Tito forces in an understanding with the enemy, but his death sentence was based on internal political considerations rather than on his actual guilt. The name also appears as Mihailović.

Mihara (mēhä'rä), city (1970 pop. 82,621), Hiroshima prefecture, W Honshu, Japan, on the Inland Sea. It is a production center for sake, rayon, rolling stock, and cement. It was a castle town during the Edo era.

Mijamin (mĭj'əmĭn), variant of MIAMIN.

mikado (mĭkä'dō), a former title of the emperor of JAPAN used chiefly in the English language.

Mikan, George Lawrence (mī'kən), 1924–, American basketball player, b. Joliet, Ill. A star basketball player at DePaul Univ., he was three times chosen All-American; he scored a total of 1,870 points in collegiate games. Mikan, 6 ft 10 in. tall, played center and in 1946 turned professional, joining the Minneapolis Lakers of the National Basketball Association. In his nine years as a professional he won three scoring championships (1948–49, 1949–50, and 1950–51) and scored a total of 11,764 points in 520 games, for a career average of 22.6 points a game. His high for a single game was 61 points. Mikan retired in 1955.

Mikhailovich, Draja: see MIHAJLOVIĆ, DRAŽA.

Mikkeli (mĭk'kĕlē), Swed. *Sankt Michel,* city (1970 pop. 25,218), capital of Mikkeli prov., S central Finland. It is in the Saimaa lake region and is an important lake port, commercial center, and transportation hub. It was chartered in 1838.

Mikloth (mĭk'lŏth). **1** Son of Jehiel and Maachah. 1 Chron. 8.32; 9.37,38. **2** Captain of a division of David's army. 1 Chron. 27.4.

Mikneiah (mĭknē'yə), temple doorkeeper. 1 Chron. 15.18,21.

Mikołajczyk, Stanislaus (stänēs'läs mēkôlī'chĭk), 1901–66, Polish politician and leader of the Polish Peasant party. After the German conquest of Poland, he became vice premier (1941) and premier (1943) in the Polish government in exile at London. He sought to reach agreement with the USSR concerning the Polish-Russian border and with the Polish Committee of National Liberation (see LUBLIN) concerning the future Polish government. After the YALTA CONFERENCE he joined the new Polish government as vice premier and minister of agriculture. He soon was the only center of opposition to the Communist and left-wing Socialist leaders of the state, and the procedure adopted in the elections of 1947 resulted in his defeat. Midołajczyk fled and settled in the United States. He remained active in the politics of Polish exiles.

Mikon (mī'kŏn), fl. c.460 B.C., Greek painter and sculptor. In collaboration with Polygnotus he painted *The Greeks and the Amazons* and the celebrated *Battle of Marathon* in the Stoa Poecile (Gr. *Poikile*) at Athens. He is supposed to have contributed paintings for the decoration of the temple of the Dioscuri at Athens and the Theseum.

Míkonos or **Mykonos** (both: mē'kônôs), mountainous island (1971 pop. 3,823), c.35 sq mi (90 sq km), SE Greece, in the Aegean Sea; one of the Cyclades. It is a tourist resort and has fisheries. There are many churches.

Mikoyan, Anastas Ivanovich (ənəstäs' ēvä'nəvĭch myĭkəyän'), 1895–, Soviet Communist leader. He joined the Communist party in 1915, became a member of the party's central committee in 1923, and subsequently held cabinet posts concerned with trade and the food industry. In 1935 he was elected to the politburo, the ruling body of the central committee of the Communist party. He held other high government posts before serving (1955–57, 1958–64) as first deputy premier. In 1964–65, Mikoyan was chairman of the presidium of the Supreme Soviet, or titular head of state. Although not reelected to the politburo in 1966, he continued to serve on the central committee. In 1974 he was dropped from the Supreme Soviet, thereby completing his retirement from public office.

Mikszáth, Kálmán (käl'män mĭk'sät), 1849–1910, Hungarian writer. He wrote witty novels and tales satirizing the decaying gentry and petty civil servants of Hungary before 1914. These include the novel *St. Peter's Umbrella* (1895, tr. 1900).

Mikulov (mĭ'ko͝olôf), Ger. *Nikolsburg,* town (1970 pop. 6,267), S central Czechoslovakia, in Moravia, near the Austrian border. It is an agricultural market and has textile and food-processing industries. Mikulov was the site in 1621 of the signing of a treaty between Emperor Ferdinand II and Gabriel Bethlen, who renounced his kingship of Hungary. Armistice agreements ending the Franco-Austrian War (1805) and the Austro-Prussian War (1866) were also signed at Mikulov.

Milalai (mĭl"əlā'ī, mĭlā'lāī), musician in the dedication of the wall. Neh. 12.36.

Milan (Milan Obrenović) (mĭl'än ōbrĕ'nəvĭch), 1854–1901, prince (1868–82) and king (1882–89) of Serbia; grandnephew of Miloš Obrenović. He succeeded his cousin Michael Obrenović as prince. He was educated in Paris, and a regency, which undertook constitutional reform in 1869, ruled for him until 1872. Under Russian influence he declared war (1876) on Turkey in support of the rebellion in Bosnia and Hercegovina (see RUSSO-TURKISH WARS). At the Congress of Berlin (1878) he secured Austrian support and obtained European recognition of the full independence of Serbia from the Ottoman Empire. In 1882 he took the title king of Serbia after signing a secret treaty granting Austria considerable influence. Heavy taxation, his pro-Austrian policy, his scandalous private life, and his unsuccessful campaign (1885) against Bulgaria aroused bitter opposition. After proclaiming (1889) a liberal constitution, he abdicated in favor of his son, ALEXANDER

(Alexander Obrenović), and went abroad. He returned in 1897 and became commander in chief of the army but resigned upon his son's marriage to Draga Mašin.

Milan (mĭlăn', –än'), Ital. *Milano*, Lat. *Mediolanum*, city (1971 pop. 1,724,173), capital of Lombardy and of Milano prov., N Italy, at the heart of the Po basin. Because of its strategic position in the Lombard plain, at the intersection of several major transportation routes, it has been since the Middle Ages an international commercial, financial, and industrial center. Today Milan is Italy's second largest city and its economic heart. Manufactures include textiles, clothing, machinery, chemicals, printed materials, motor vehicles, airplanes, and rubber goods. The city has a large construction industry, and it is one of the most important silk markets in Europe. Probably of Celtic origin, Milan was conquered by Rome in 222 B.C. In later Roman times it was the capital (A.D. 305–402) of the Western Empire and the religious center of N Italy. In 313, Constantine I issued the Edict of Milan, which granted religious toleration. From 374 to 379 the city's bishop was St. Ambrose, known for the liturgy he wrote and for his eloquence. Milan was severely damaged by the Huns (c.450) and again by the Goths (539) and was conquered by the LOMBARDS in 569. In the 12th cent. it became a free commune and gradually gained supremacy over the cities of Lombardy. From the 11th to the 13th cent. Milan suffered from internal warfare between rich and poor, from the Guelph and Ghibelline strife, and from the enmity of rival cities, which assisted Emperor Frederick I in destroying it (1163). As a member of the Lombard League, Milan later contributed to the defeat of Frederick I at Legnano (1176). The city's independence was recognized in the Peace of Constance (1183). In the 13th cent. Milan lost its republican liberties; first the Torriani, then the VISCONTI (1277) became its lords. Galeazzo Visconti received (1395) the title of duke of Milan from the emperor, and under him the duchy became one of the most important states in Italy. After the death of the last Visconti (1447) the SFORZA became dukes of Milan. The city flourished until it became involved in the ITALIAN WARS and passed under Spanish domination (1535). At the end of the War of the Spanish Succession, Austrian rule of Milan was established (1713–96). Napoleon I made the city the capital of the Cisalpine Republic (1797) and of the kingdom of Italy (1805–14). In 1815, Milan again came under Austria. It was a leading center throughout the RISORGIMENTO; after five days of heroic fighting in 1848 the citizens of Milan succeeded in expelling the Austrians, who returned, however, a few months later. In 1859 the city was united with the kingdom of Sardinia. Its industrial importance grew after it was incorporated (1861) into Italy. In World War II, Milan suffered widespread damage from Allied air raids; many significant buildings were damaged beyond repair. The most striking feature of the city is the large, white-marble cathedral (1386–1813), which shows traces of many styles (especially Gothic). It is elaborately ornamented with 135 pinnacles and more than 200 marble statues. A statue of the Madonna is on the highest pinnacle (354 ft/108 m). Other points of interest in Milan include Brera Palace and Picture Gallery (17th cent.), which includes major works by Mantegna and Bellini; the Castello Sforzesco (15th cent., with 19th-century additions), which houses a museum of art; the Church of Santa Maria delle Grazie (1465–90), containing the famous fresco, the *Last Supper*, by Leonardo da Vinci; the Basilica of Sant' Ambrogio (founded in the 4th cent., rebuilt in the 11th–12th cent.); the Ambrosian Library, which houses a rich collection of paintings; the Church of Sant' Eustorgio (9th cent.); the Leonardo da Vinci Museum of Science and Technology; and the gallery of modern art. Long a center of music, Milan has a conservatory and an opera house, Teatro alla Scala (opened in 1778). The city also has three universities and a polytechnic institute.

Milan Decree, issued Dec., 1807, by Napoleon I of France in an attempt to enforce the CONTINENTAL SYSTEM. Designed to strengthen the BERLIN DECREE, it authorized French warships and privateers to capture neutral vessels sailing from any British port or from countries occupied by British armies. It also declared that neutral ships that submitted to search by British authorities on the high seas were to be considered lawful prizes if captured by the French or their allies. The British government issued replies by ORDERS IN COUNCIL.

Milarepa, 1040–1143, saint and poet of TIBETAN BUDDHISM. He was the second patriarch of the Kargyupa sect, the first being Milarepa's guru Marpa (1012–97), who studied under Naropa, the Bengali master of Tantra, at Nalanda. Milarepa's autobiography recounts how in his youth he practiced black magic in order to take revenge on relatives who deprived his mother of the family inheritance. He later repented and sought Buddhist teaching. After undergoing many tests and ordeals under Marpa, he received initiation from him. He spent the rest of his life meditating in mountain caves and teaching his disciples. See W. Y. Evans-Wentz, ed., *Tibet's Great Yogi, Milarepa* (1928; 2d ed. 1951, repr. 1969).

Milazzo (mēlät'tsō), town (1971 pop. 26,623), NE Sicily, Italy, on a peninsula in the Tyrrhenian Sea. It is the ancient MYLAE. The town is a wine-trade and tuna-fishing center and is the gateway to the nearby Lipari Islands. Garibaldi completed his conquest of Sicily by defeating (June, 1860) the Bourbon troops there. Milazzo has an imposing 13th-century castle (now a prison) and a 16th-century cathedral.

Milcah (mĭl'kə). **1** Wife of Abraham's brother Nahor. Gen. 22.20. **2** Daughter and coheiress of Zelophehad. Num. 27.1–12.

Milcom (mĭl'kəm) [Heb.,=their king], god of the Ammonites. 1 Kings 11.5,33; 2 Kings 23.13. In Judges 11.24 the name is replaced (probably by mistake) by Chemosh. Milcom may be identifiable with MOLECH.

mildew, name for certain fungi and the diseases they cause in various crops and for the discoloration (and sometimes the weakening and disintegration) of materials, such as leather, fabrics, and paper, caused by other, related fungi. The powdery mildews usually grow on the surface of plant tissues, forming a gray or white coating and absorbing nourishment from the host. The downy mildews are more properly called molds. Methods of making fabrics and leather resistant to mildew have been devised. For the occurrence and control of mildews in agriculture, see DISEASES OF PLANTS. Mildews are classified in the division FUNGI; powdery mildews belong to the class Ascomycetes, downy mildews to the class Phycomycetes.

Milé, Jean François: see MILLET, JEAN FRANÇOIS (c.1642–1679).

mile: see ENGLISH UNITS OF MEASUREMENT.

Miles, Nelson Appleton, 1839–1925, American army officer, b. near Westminster, Mass. In 1861, at the outbreak of the Civil War, he left his job in a Boston store and organized a company of volunteers. He served throughout the war, distinguishing himself at Antietam, Fredericksburg, Chancellorsville, and in other important battles, and was made brigadier general (1864) and major general (1865) of volunteers. Remaining in the army as a colonel, he led many campaigns against the Indians of the West. He helped subjugate the Sioux in Montana and in 1877 destroyed the village of Chief CRAZY HORSE. In the same year he defeated and captured Chief JOSEPH of the Nez Percé. In 1886, as commander of the Dept. of Arizona, he accepted the surrender of the Apache under Geronimo, and in 1890–91, in Dakota, he suppressed another Sioux outbreak. He commanded (1894) the troops that were called out during the PULLMAN STRIKE. In 1895 he became commander in chief of the army, rising to the rank of lieutenant general in 1901. During the Spanish-American War (1898), he led the troops that occupied Puerto Rico. He visited the Philippines in 1902, made an official inspection, and reported on the mistreatment of insurgents by Americans. In 1903 he was retired. He wrote *Personal Recollections and Observations* (1896, repr. 1969), *Military Europe* (1898), and *Serving the Republic* (1911). See biography by V. W. Johnson (1962); study by N. F. Tolman (1968).

Milesians (mīlē'zhənz), in Irish mythology, the ancestors of the present inhabitants of Ireland. The last invaders of ancient Ireland, they were said to have dwelt in Spain before attacking Ireland, where they defeated the TUATHA DE DANANN.

Milesian school: see IONIAN SCHOOL.

Miletus (mīlē'təs), ancient seaport of W Asia Minor, in Caria, on the mainland not far from Sámos. It was occupied by Greeks in the settlement of the E Aegean (c.1000 B.C.) and became one of the principal cities of Ionia. From the 8th cent. B.C. it led in colonization, especially on the Black Sea. The Milesians were strong enough to resist the Lydian kings and were not molested by the Persians. In 499 B.C., however, they stirred up the revolt of Ionian Greeks against Persia; the Persians sacked the city (494 B.C.). Although less flourishing, Miletus remained an important seaport until the harbor silted up early in the Christian era. Miletus produced some of the earliest Greek philosophers, including Thales and Anaximander. St. Paul visited Miletus twice. (Acts 20.15; 2 Tim. 4.20.) The biblical name appears as Miletum. The site was excavated by German archaeologists.

milfoil: see YARROW.

Milford. **1** City (1970 pop. 50,858), New Haven co., SW Conn., on Long Island Sound; settled 1639, inc. as a city 1959. Writing pens, electrical products, thermostats, and rivets are produced. Milford Academy, a preparatory school, is there. **2** Industrial town (1970 pop. 19,352), Worcester co., S Mass., on the Charles River, in a farm area; settled 1662, set off from Mendon and inc. 1780. Pink granite has been quarried there since the mid-1800s.

Milford Haven, urban district (1971 pop. 13,745), Pembrokeshire, SW Wales. It is a seaport on the northern side of the estuary called Milford Haven. The bay forms a splendid natural harbor that can handle large oil tankers, making the town a key oil port and refining center. Other imports are cattle, food, and fertilizer. From early times the town was a port for trade with Ireland. Henry II invaded Ireland from Milford Haven in 1172; Henry Tudor (who became Henry VII) landed there from France in 1485. In 1974, Milford Haven became part of the new metropolitan county of Dyfed.

Milford Sound, fjord, arm of the Tasman Sea, indenting SW South Island, New Zealand. Part of Fjordland National Park, it is a well-known resort area. Mountains rise steeply from the shore to a height of more than 5,000 ft (1,524 m).

Milhaud, Darius (däryüs' mēyō'), 1892–1974, French composer. Milhaud studied at the Paris Conservatory. In Brazil (1917–19) as an aide to Paul Claudel, poet and French minister to Brazil, he became acquainted with Brazilian folk music. Upon his return to France, he became known as one of Les Six. Milhaud became professor of composition at Mills College, Oakland, Calif., in 1940. He is especially celebrated as a composer for the stage; his operas include *Le Pauvre Matelot* (1927; libretto by Jean Cocteau) and *Christophe Colombe* (1930; libretto by Claudel). Milhaud's outstanding ballets are *La Création du Monde* (1923) and *Le Boeuf sur le toit; or, The Nothing Doing Bar* (1920). A prolific composer, Milhaud also wrote symphonies, concertos, orchestral music, chamber music, and songs. He was among the first to exploit polytonality and developed new rhythmic structures influenced by Brazilian and jazz elements. See his autobiography, *Notes without Music* (tr. 1953, repr. 1970).

Milic of Kremsier (mē'lēch, krām'zēr), d. 1374, Bohemian reformer. He was a Roman Catholic priest In 1363 he began a career of preaching in Moravia as well as in Prague. Believing that the end of the world was near, he went to Rome in 1367 to urge the remedying of abuses in the church. He was imprisoned by the Inquisition and there wrote *Libellus de Antichristo*. Released by Pope Urban V, Milic continued (1369–72) his preaching in Prague. He later acquitted himself of heresy charges before the pope at Avignon. He was the author of devotional writings in both Latin and Czech. As one of the most influential preachers in Bohemia, he has been called a precursor of John Huss, but there is no question of Milic's doctrinal orthodoxy.

military engineering: see ENGINEERING.

military government, rule of enemy territory under military occupation. It is distinguished from MARTIAL LAW, which is the temporary rule by domestic armed forces over disturbed areas. The practices of military government were standardized before World War I, notably at the Hague Conferences (1899, 1907) and form a part of the laws of war (see WAR, LAWS OF). During and after World War II, vast territories came under military government. During the war, Germany administered occupied countries through a hierarchy of *Kommandaturen* [military government headquarters], but this normal army administration was often duplicated by civilian economic agencies and Gestapo personnel. In France, Norway, Greece, and Serbia, local puppet governments were authorized to operate under German control; Belgium and NE France were under purely military government; in Eastern Europe, authority was concentrated in 1941 in the ministry for eastern occupied territories. German military government often violated the rules laid down by the Hague Conventions. The Germans held and executed hostages for acts committed by unknown individuals and deprived the conquered nations of their basic resources; they rounded up slave labor for German industries and committed wholesale executions and massacres. Allied Military Government (AMG) began to function in Sicily and in Italy in 1943; it sought to utilize local civilian authorities to the widest possible extent. When operating in Allied territory, such as France, AMG became Civil Affairs and was limited to combat areas. After the termination of military operations, Germany and Austria were divided (1945) into four occupation zones and military government was reorganized. At first it was subject in general policy to the authority of the U.S.-Russian-British-French Allied Control Councils in Berlin and Vienna. In time, the growing dissension between the Western powers and the USSR led to the breakdown of the quadripartite system in Germany and in BERLIN. The British, French, and American zones were soon amalgamated for most purposes and ultimately became the state of West Germany; in opposition to them stood the Russian zone, which later became the East German State. In Austria and Vienna disharmony was less evident, and military control ended in 1955 with the signing of a peace treaty between Austria and the four Allied occupying powers. In Japan, military government became a solely American responsibility, though subject to suggestions of an 11-power Allied council. It was ended by the signing of the peace treaty with Japan (1951). In response to the experiences of World War II, a new convention covering military occupation was signed in Geneva in 1949. See Ernst Fraenkel, *Military Occupation and the Rule of Law* (1944); Raphaël Lemkin, *Axis Rule in Occupied Europe* (1944); C. J. Friedrich, ed., *American Experiences in Military Government in World War II* (1948); D. A. Graber, *Development of the Law of Military Occupation, 1863–1914* (1948, repr. 1969); Gerhard von Glahn, *The Occupation of Enemy Territory* (1957); A. D. McNair and A. D. Watts, *The Legal Effects of War* (4th ed. 1967); J. J. McGinnis, *Military Government Journal* (1971).

military law, system of rules established for the government of persons in the armed forces. In most countries the legislature establishes the code of military law. It is distinguished from both MARTIAL LAW (rule by domestic military forces over an area) and MILITARY GOVERNMENT (rule by the military over occupied foreign territory). Regular systems of military law existed in ancient Rome, with severe penalties for such offenses as desertion. In the Middle Ages procedures were less regularized, but written codes began to appear . The origin of much military law is found in the codes and statutes enacted in England in the 17th cent. These were substantially adopted in the United States. The scope of military law differs somewhat in peace and in war. In time of peace it is generally limited to military offenses—e.g., absence without leave, desertion, breach of orders; during war it usually extends to crimes of a civil nature as well, and the penalties may be more severe. It was widely felt after World War II that many abuses had occurred in the administration of American military justice and that excessively severe sentences had been imposed, especially on enlisted men. The armed forces responded by establishing civilian review boards, which recommended reduction of the punishment inflicted on a large percentage of those convicted (some 100,000) by general courts-martial during the war. In 1951, Congress extensively revised the codes of military law enacting a uniform code of military justice for all branches of the armed services. This code placed operations more in the hands of professional lawyers and ensured fairer review procedures. An important change permitted an enlisted man tried by a general court-martial to demand that one third of the court be composed of enlisted personnel. This uniform code defines the offenses for which a person under the jurisdiction of the armed forces may be subjected to court-martial. In addition to allowing punishments by the commanding officer, including confinement not to exceed one week, the code establishes three levels of courts-martial. The summary court-martial consists of a single officer, and may impose a maximum penalty of imprisonment for one month. The special court-martial consists of at least three officers and may impose a prison sentence of up to six months. The general court-martial is composed of five members and one law officer who must be a trained lawyer admitted to practice before a state's highest court. The general court-martial may impose any authorized sentence including dishonorable discharge or death. One of the principal differences between the procedure in courts-martial and in criminal cases in civil courts is the absence of a jury. Cases are decided by a vote of two thirds or three fourths of the court, depending on the severity of the offense. For the death penalty, the vote must be unanimous. The accused is permitted to have counsel, to compel the attendance of witnesses, and to enjoy the usual protections of the law of evidence. See W. B. Aycock and S. W. Wurfel, *Military Law under the Uniform Code of Military Justice* (1955, repr. 1973); R. O. Everett, *Military Justice in the Armed Forces of the United States* (1956); R. S. Rivkin, *G.I. Rights and Army Justice* (1970); W. E. Schug, *United States Law and the Armed Forces* (1972); J. W. Bishop, Jr., *Justice under Fire* (1974).

military pension: see PENSION.

military science: see STRATEGY AND TACTICS.

militia (məlĭsh'ə), military organization composed of citizens enrolled and trained for service in times of national emergency. Its ranks may be filled either by enlistment or conscription. An early prototype was the national militia developed by Philip of Macedon. However, the modern concept of the militia as a defensive organization against invaders grew out of the Anglo-Saxon *fyrd.* The militiaman, in times of crisis, left his civilian duties and became a soldier until the emergency was over, when he returned to his civilian status. Militia persisted through the Middle Ages, especially in England, Italy, and Germany; after the rise of large standing armies it declined. In America, however, it continued. The Military Company of Massachusetts was the first militia organization in America and was followed by similar groups in the other colonies. Local control and voluntary service prevailed. Although the militia was valuable throughout the American Revolution, it proved undependable in the War of 1812. Therefore, no militia was used in the MEXICAN WAR. However, during the Civil War, when manpower needs were greater, both sides resorted to the use of militia. During the 19th cent. various states of the United States had their own militia, which served in all of America's wars. After World War I, state military units were established under the term NATIONAL GUARD. In other countries the militia is known generally as the special reserve or the territorial reserve. See J. D. Hill, *The Minute Man in Peace and War* (1964).

Miliukov, Pavel Nikolayevich: see MILYUKOV.

Milk, river, 729 mi (1,173 km) long, rising in the Rocky Mts., NW Mont. It flows N into Alberta, Canada, then in long curves eastward, S into Montana again, and generally SE to the Missouri River, entering just below Fort Peck Dam. The Milk River reclamation project (est. 1911) irrigates c.134,000 acres (54,230 hectares). The largest of several dams is the Fresno Dam (completed 1939). Malta, Chinook, Glasgow, and Harlem, Mont., are in the project area.

milk, liquid secreted by the mammary glands of female mammals as food for their young. The milk of the cow is most widely used by humans, but the milk of the mare, goat, ewe, buffalo, camel, ass, zebra, reindeer, llama, and yak is also used. Milk, an almost complete food, consists of fats, proteins (mainly casein), salts, and sugar (lactose), as well as vitamins A, C, and D, certain B vitamins, and lesser amounts of others. Commercial dairies sometimes supplement the natural vitamin D with a vitamin D concentrate. The mineral content of milk is chiefly calcium and phosphorus. The composition of milk varies with the species, breed, feed, and condition of the animal. Jersey and Guernsey cows produce milk of high butterfat content; Holsteins produce larger quantities of milk but with a lower butterfat content. Milk prepared for sale is often homogenized; in this process it is pumped under pressure through small openings to break up the milk fat globules, thus ensuring an equal distribution of fat throughout the milk rather than permitting it to rise to the top as cream. In most countries where milk is a commercial product it is subject to regulations concerning its composition, i.e., the proportion of butterfat and other solids; its nonadulteration; and its purity, with sanitary measures in force that cover milk handlers, herds, plant, and equipment; dairy herds are also commonly disease tested. PASTEURIZATION (partial sterilization by heating) checks bacterial growth, thereby making milk safer to drink and increasing its keeping qualities and range of transportation. The consumption of concentrated milk, both whole and skim, has steadily increased since its commercial production was inaugurated. A patent was issued for the production of dried milk in Great Britain in 1855, and for concentrated milk in the United States to Gail Borden in 1856. The two types of concentrated milk are condensed and evaporated; condensed milk is a sweetened product (over 40% sugar); while evaporated is unsweetened. The latter is preserved by sterilization, the former by the high sugar content. Dried, or powdered, milk is made by passing a film of partially evaporated milk over a heated drum or by spraying it into a heated chamber in which the particles dry as they fall to the floor. Malted milk is a dried mixture made of milk and the liquid from a mash of barley malt and wheat flour. Skim milk is valuable in fat-free diets; although much of the nutritive value of milk remains, most of the vitamin A is removed in the cream. See BUTTER; CHEESE; DAIRYING; FERMENTED MILK. See L. M. Lampert, *Milk and Dairy Products* (1947); C. L. Roadhouse and J. L. Henderson, *The Market-Milk Industry* (2d ed. 1950); J. H. Frandsen, *Dairy Handbook and Dictionary* (1958).

Milking Shorthorn cattle: see SHORTHORN CATTLE.

milk of magnesia, common name for the chemical compound magnesium hydroxide, $Mg(OH)_2$. The viscous, white, mildly alkaline mixture used medicinally as an antacid and laxative is a suspension of approximately 8% magnesium hydroxide in water.

milk snake: see KING SNAKE.

milk sugar: see LACTOSE.

milkweed, common name for members of the Asclepiadaceae, a family of mostly perennial herbs and shrubs characterized by milky sap, a tuft of silky hairs attached to the seed (for wind distribution), and (usually) a climbing habit. Forms of this primarily pantropical family are especially abundant in South America and in Africa, where many are succulents. Only a few genera are temperate; those species native to the United States are mostly of the genus *Asclepias,* the milkweeds, or silkweeds. The common milkweed, a plentiful roadside and field plant of the eastern and central states, is *A. syriaca.* A number of western species are poisonous to livestock, especially sheep. The milkweeds have been utilized as food (particularly the young shoots and buds), masticatory, medicament, and fiber by the Indian and to some extent by the white man. Some species yield an excellent bast fiber, like flax, but are difficult to cultivate and refine. The readily obtainable seed hairs from wild plants are sometimes used as a rather inferior substitute for kapok. Several temperate species are a source of natural rubber; Palay rubber comes from a species of *Crypostegia* native to Madagascar. Among the milkweeds grown as ornamentals, the showy-blossomed butterfly weed or pleurisy root (*A. tuberosa*), native to the United States, was eaten by the Indians for lung and throat ailments. *Hoya* is an Old World genus that includes the wax plant (*H. carnosa*), a tropical climbing shrub cultivated as a pot plant for its fleshy leaves and fragrant waxy flowers. The milkweed family is classified in the division MAGNOLIOPHYTA, class Magnoliopsida, order Gentianales.

milkwort, common name for the Polygalaceae, a family including herbs, shrubs, and trees found in all parts of the world except New Zealand and the arctic regions. Several milkworts (genus *Polygala*), perennial herbs, are native to moist habitats of the United States and are sometimes cultivated as ornamentals. The Seneca snakeroot (*P. senega*), used by the Seneca Indians for snakebite, yields the medicinal substance senegin. The milkwort family is classified in the division MAGNOLIOPHYTA, class Magnoliopsida, order Polygalales.

Milky Way, broad band of light arching across the night sky from horizon to horizon; if not blocked by the horizon, it would be seen as a circle around the entire sky. The Milky Way passes through the constellations Sagittarius (where it is brightest), Aquila, Cygnus, Perseus, Auriga, Orion, and Crux (the Southern Cross). In the direction of Cygnus is the Great Rift, a dark band that lies along the Milky Way, dividing it into two forks. Another dark region is the Coalsack, in Crux. Once believed to be vast empty regions in space, these dark areas are now known to be clouds of dust blotting out the light behind them. The Milky Way is actually a collection of about a hundred billion stars, sometimes referred to as the Milky Way GALAXY, of which the sun is a member. Rather than being randomly distributed, the stars are arrayed in the form of a disk, which we see edgewise. The glow is due to the combined light of the stars in the region of the plane of the disk. The Milky Way is a typical large spiral galaxy, characterized by a central nucleus of closely-packed stars lying in the direction of Sagittarius and a flat disk marked by spiral arms, which wind out from the nucleus like a giant pinwheel. The diameter of the disk is c.100,000 light-years; its average thickness is 10,000 light-years, increasing to 30,000 light-years at the nucleus. The position of the sun was at first thought to be very near the central nucleus; later studies showed it to be c.30,000 light-years distant and lying in the galactic plane. Although its motion is not readily apparent, the entire galaxy is rotating about its center with the spiral arms trailing. The sun, traveling at a speed of c.155 mi per sec (c.250

km per sec) in a nearly circular orbit, takes 200 million years to complete one revolution. Surrounding the galaxy is a thin halo of STAR CLUSTERS. Studies of their distribution provided the first realistic estimate of the size of the galaxy and of the sun's location in the plane of the disk. Nonluminous clouds of dust and gas, called dark NEBULAS, obscure many parts of the sky from sight; in the direction of the galactic center, the view is almost entirely obscured. Certain features of the region near the sun have suggested that our galaxy is very similar to the ANDROMEDA GALAXY. Using this galaxy as a guide, astronomers were able to map short sections of three spiral arms of the Milky Way located within 15,000 light-years of the sun. With the recent development of radio astronomy, scientists have produced a nearly complete map of the spiral structure of the galaxy. See B. J. and P. F. Bok, *The Milky Way* (3d ed. 1957); Thornton and L. W. Page, ed., *Stars and Clouds of the Milky Way* (1968); Howard Shapley, *Galaxies* (3d ed. 1972); S. L. Jaki, *The Milky Way* (1973).

Mill, James, 1773-1836, British philosopher, economist, and historian, b. Scotland; father of John Stuart Mill. Educated as a clergyman at Edinburgh through the patronage of Sir John Stuart, Mill gave up the ministry and went to London in 1802 to pursue a career writing for and editing periodicals. He met Jeremy Bentham c.1808 and became an ardent advocate of utilitarianism. On the strength of his *History of British India* (3 vol., 1817), on which he had worked for over 10 years, he secured a permanent position with the East India Company. Others of his works were *Elements of Political Economy* (1821), *Analysis of the Phenomena of the Human Mind* (2 vol., 1829), and *A Fragment on Mackintosh* (1835), which contains the best exposition of his psychological and ethical theories. Mill furnished a psychological basis for utilitarian ethics by expanding the associationism of David Hume. Association by contiguity, where ideas that occur frequently together form combinations, may be such a subtle process that the merging of ideas may occur without leaving any trace of the elements that went into their formulation. Derived conceptions may thus achieve autonomy of value quite apart from their obvious utilitarian effect. This is the origin of altruistic motives, which are otherwise difficult to explain on utilitarian grounds. It is also the origin of conscience. See W. H. Burston, *James Mill on Philosophy and Education* (1973).

Mill, John, 1645-1707, English clergyman and biblical scholar. The masterpiece of scholarly critical work to which 30 years of his life were devoted is an edition (1707) of the Greek New Testament. Dr. John Fell, bishop of Oxford, encouraged Mill to undertake the task, giving over his own notes and assuming the expense of printing.

Mill, John Stuart, 1806-73, British philosopher and economist. A precocious child, he was educated privately by his father, James Mill. In 1823, abandoning the study of law, he became a clerk in the East India company, where he rose to become head of the examiner's office by the time of the company's dissolution (1858). During this period he contributed to various periodicals and met with discussion groups, one of which included Thomas Macaulay, to explore the problems of political theory. His *A System of Logic* (1843) was followed in 1848 by the *Principles of Political Economy.* In 1851, following the death of her husband, he married Harriet Taylor, whom he had loved for 20 years. She died in 1858, and Mill, profoundly affected, dedicated to her the famous *On Liberty* (1859), on which they had worked together. In 1863, *Utilitarianism* was published, and his *Auguste Comte and Positivism* appeared in 1865. From 1865 to 1868 he served as a member of Parliament, after which he retired, spending much of his time at Avignon, France, where his wife was buried and where he died. In the year of his death appeared his celebrated *Autobiography*. John Stuart Mill's philosophy followed the doctrines of his father and Jeremy Bentham, but he sought to temper them with humanitarianism. At times Mill came close to socialism, a theory repugnant to his predecessors. His urge for reform and increased democracy was in part due to the influence of his wife. In logic he formulated rules for the inductive process and stressed the method of empiricism as the source of all knowledge. In his ethics he pointed out the possibility of a sentiment of unity and solidarity that may even develop a religious character, as in Comte's religion of humanity. In addition he introduced into the utilitarian calculus of pleasure a qualitative principle that goes far beyond the simpler conception of quantity (see UTILITARIANISM). He constantly advocated political and social reforms, such as proportional representation, emancipation of women, and the development of labor organizations and farm cooperatives. He strongly supported the Union cause in the American Civil War. Mill's influence has been strong in economics, politics, and philosophy. See Maurice Cowling, *Mill and Liberalism* (1963); Edward Alexander, *Matthew Arnold and John Stuart Mill* (1966); J. M. Robson, *The Improvement of Mankind: The Social and Political Thought of John Stuart Mill* (1968); H. J. McCloskey, *John Stuart Mill: A Critical Study* (1971).

mill: see MILLING.

Millais, Sir John Everett (mĭlā'), 1829-96, English painter. A prodigy, he began studying at the Royal Academy at the age of 11. In 1848, together with William Holman Hunt and Dante Gabriel Rossetti, he initiated the PRE-RAPHAELITE movement. His early work shows a painstaking rendering of minute detail and great clarity. His *Christ in the Carpenter's Shop* (1850; Tate Gall., London) was attacked because of its realism, but his reputation was soon established. He was created a baronet in 1885, and in 1896 he became president of the Royal Academy. John Ruskin was a close friend and champion of his work until 1855 when Millais married Mrs. Ruskin, after the nullification of her marriage. His work, well represented in many British galleries, is generally considered overly sentimental by modern critics. His *Portia* is in the Metropolitan Museum. See biographies by J. G. Millais (1899), M. H. Spielmann (1899), A. L. Baldry (1902), and Arthur Fisk (1923).

Millar, John, 1735-1801, Scottish philosopher and historian. Millar studied at Glasgow, where he became the chief disciple of Adam Smith. In 1761 Millar became professor of civil law at Glasgow, and his lectures there made him a national figure. He was one of the earliest advocates of the view that later became known as economic determinism, and in his *Origin of the Distinction of Ranks* (1778) he advanced the view that all social relations, even relations between the sexes, are determined by the economic organization of society. His *Historical View of the English Government* (1787) was one of the first constitutional histories of England. Drawing upon the histories of other peoples for comparative purposes, and emphasizing the social and economic bases of political institutions and developments, it represented a marked advance in historical scholarship. See biography by W. C. Lehmann (1960).

Millar, Kenneth: see MACDONALD, ROSS.

Millau (mēyō'), town (1968 pop. 23,442), Aveyron dept., S France, on the Tarn River. The center of the French glove industry, the town also has tanning and dyeing industries. At the nearby village of Roquefort, the famous cheese is manufactured from sheep's milk. Millau was a HUGUENOT stronghold in the 16th cent. Points of interest include Gallo-Roman ruins, a 16th-century church, and a belfry (partly from the 11th cent.).

Millay, Edna St. Vincent (mĭlā'), 1892-1950, American poet, b. Rockland, Maine, grad. Vassar, 1917. One of the most popular poets of her era, Millay was admired as much for the bohemian freedom of her youthful life style as for her verse. During the early 1920s she lived in Greenwich Village, New York City, and wrote satiric sketches for *Vanity Fair* under the pseudonym Nancy Boyd. Among her friends were Edmund Wilson and John Peale Bishop. *Renascence,* Millay's first volume of poetry, appeared in 1917 and was praised for its freshness and vitality. It was followed by *A Few Figs from Thistles* (1920), *Second April* (1921), and *The Ballad of the Harp Weaver* (1922; Pulitzer Prize). She was a member of the PROVINCETOWN PLAYERS, a group that produced several of her verse dramas, including *Aria da Capo* (1920) and *Two Slatterns and a King* (1921). In 1923 she married Eugen Jan Boissevain, a Dutch coffee importer, and moved to "Steepletop," a farm near Austerlitz, N.Y. Although her socially conscious later poetry is generally considered inferior to her early work, it exhibits her absolute mastery of the sonnet form. Among her later volumes are *Fatal Interview* (1931), a superb sonnet cycle; *Conversation at Midnight* (1937); and *Make Bright the Arrows* (1940). She also wrote the libretto for Deems Taylor's opera *The King's Henchman* (1927) and, with George Dillon, she translated Baudelaire's *Flowers of Evil* (1936). Eugen Boissevain died in the autumn of 1949, and Millay died of a heart attack less than a year later. In Feb., 1974, her sister, Norma Millay, announced that "Steepletop" would become an arts colony, opening in 1976. See Millay's collected poems, ed. by Norma Millay (1956); her letters, ed. by A. R. Macdougal (1952); biography by Jean Gould (1969).

Millbrae (mĭlbrā'), city (1970 pop. 20,920), San Mateo co., W Calif., on San Francisco Bay; inc. 1948. It is mainly a residential area. San Francisco International Airport adjoins the city.

Millbury, town (1970 pop. 11,987), Worcester co., S Mass., on the Blackstone River; settled 1716, inc. 1813. Felt and felt products and valve spring wire are manufactured there.

Milledge, John (mĭl'ĭj), 1757-1818, American political leader, b. Savannah, Ga. In the American Revolution he was a prominent figure in the group that seized (1775) the colonial government at Savannah. A lawyer, he was a U.S. Representative (1792-93, 1795-99, 1801-2), governor of Georgia (1802-6), and a Senator (1806-9). The Univ. of Georgia campus is situated on land that he donated, and the city of Milledgeville was named in his honor.

Milledgeville, city (1970 pop. 11,601), seat of Baldwin co., central Ga., on the Oconee River, in a fertile farm area; inc. 1836. Among the industries are the manufacture of textiles, pharmaceuticals, prefabricated homes, and food products. Laid out in 1803 as the site of the state capital, Milledgeville was the seat of government from 1807 to 1868. Many antebellum homes survive; among them are the old executive mansion (1838) and the old state capitol (1807), now part of Georgia Military College. The city is also the site of Georgia College and contains a large state hospital.

Mille Lacs Lake (mĭl lăks), 207 sq mi (536 sq km), E central Minn., N of Minneapolis. It drains into the Rum River. Sieur Duluth, a French explorer, visited Ojibwa Indians living on its shore in 1679. In 1680, Louis Hennepin, a French friar and explorer of North America, and his companions were held captive near the lake by the Indians for several weeks. The region is a center for tourists and sportsmen. There is an Indian reservation on the southwest shore.

millennium [Lat.,=1,000 years], the period of 1,000 years in which, according to some schools of Christian eschatology, Christ will reign again gloriously on earth. Belief in the millennium, based on Rev. 20, has recurred in Christianity since the earliest times. Today it is held and taught by the ADVENTISTS and some other conservative evangelical bodies. Belief in the millennium is called chiliasm by historians of the ancient church. See JUDGMENT DAY.

Miller, Alfred Jacob, 1810-74, American artist, b. Baltimore, studied under Thomas Sully and in Europe. In 1837 he joined an expedition to the American West and was probably the first artist to depict the Rocky Mts. On that trip he produced his most important works, chiefly studies of Indian and frontier life, valuable for their documentary detail. These sketches and watercolors were entirely forgotten for nearly a century until they were rediscovered in a storeroom of the Peale Museum, Baltimore. See study by Marvin Ross (1951).

Miller, Arthur, 1915-, American dramatist, b. New York City, grad. Univ. of Michigan, 1938. Miller is a serious playwright, profoundly concerned with morality and the pressures exerted on people by family and society. His masterpiece, *Death of a Salesman* (1949; Pulitzer Prize), is the story of an ordinary man betrayed by his own hollow values and those of American society. *The Crucible* (1953) is both a dynamic dramatization of the 17th-century Salem witch trials and a parable about the United States in the McCarthy era (see MCCARTHY, JOSEPH RAYMOND). In *A View From the Bridge* (1955; Pulitzer Prize) Miller studies a Sicilian-American longshoreman whose unacknowledged lust for his niece destroys him and his family. Miller's life with his second wife, Marilyn MONROE, is depicted in *After the Fall* (1964). His other plays include *All My Sons* (1947), *Incident at Vichy* (1965), *The Price* (1968), and *The Creation of the World and Other Business* (1972). He has written a novel, *Focus* (1945), and a study of the contemporary Soviet Union, *In Russia* (1969), with photographs by his third wife, Inge Morath. See studies by Benjamin Nelson (1970) and Ronald Hayman (1972).

Miller, Cincinnatus Heine (or **Hiner**): see MILLER, JOAQUIN.

Miller, George Abram, 1863-1951, American mathematician, b. Lehigh co., Pa., grad. Muhlenberg College (B.A., 1887), Ph.D. Cumberland Univ., 1893. He was professor at the Univ. of Illinois (1907-31). His chief work was in the theory of groups of finite order, in the development and use of determinants, and in the history of mathematics.

Miller, Henry, 1860–1926, American actor, director, and manager, b. England. After his New York debut in *Cymbeline* (1880), Miller became the leading man of the Empire Theatre stock company. In 1918 he bought his own theater, which became known for sophisticated drama. His major performances included roles in *The Only Way, Shenandoah, Heartease,* and *The Servant in the House.* His son Gilbert Heron Miller was also an actor, producer, and director.

Miller, Henry, 1891–, American author, b. New York City. A vigorous and highly controversial writer, Miller sought to reestablish the liberty and freedom of the natural man. His books are mainly potpourris of sexual description, quasi-philosophical speculation, reflection on literature and society, surrealistic imaginings, and autobiographical incident. After living in Paris in the 1930s, he returned to the United States and settled in Big Sur, Calif. Miller's first publications, *Tropic of Cancer* (Paris, 1934) and *Tropic of Capricorn* (Paris, 1939), were, because of alleged obscenity, denied publication or entry in the United States until the early 1960s. *The Colossus of Maroussi* (1941), a travel book of modern Greece, is considered by some critics his best work. His other writings include *The Cosmological Eye* (1939), *The Air-Conditioned Nightmare* (2 vol., 1945–47), *Big Sur and the Oranges of Hieronymus Bosch* (1957), a trilogy, *The Rosy Crucifixion,* composed of *Sexus* (1949), *Plexus* (1953) and *Nexus* (1960), and the autobiographical *My Life and Times* (1972). See *The Henry Miller Reader* (ed. by Lawrence Durrell, 1959); letters to Durrell (1962) and Anaïs Nin (1965); E. B. Mitchell, ed., *Henry Miller: Three Decades of Criticism* (1971).

Miller, Joaquin (wäkēn'), pseud. of **Cincinnatus Heine** (or **Hiner**) **Miller,** 1839?–1913, American poet, b. Liberty, Ind. In 1852 his family moved to frontier Oregon. He lived in gold-mining camps, later with Indians, and was in turn an express rider, an editor, and an Oregon judge. His first two volumes of poems, *Specimens* (1868) and *Joaquin et al* (1869), contained energetic, rhetorical celebrations of frontier life. They brought him only local acclaim, but in England, where he went next, his colorful personality, his dramatic Western costume, and his *Songs of the Sierras* (1871) made him famous as a frontier poet. See his autobiography (1898; ed. by S. G. Firman, 1930).

Miller, Jonathan, 1934–, English director, actor, writer, and physician. Forsaking medicine, Miller made his first London (1961) and New York (1962) stage appearances as coauthor and actor in the zany satirical revue *Beyond the Fringe.* Miller directed *The Old Glory* in New York and *Danton's Death, The School for Scandal,* and *The Merchant of Venice* for the National Theatre. He has written and directed television and radio shows, written theater criticism, and in 1969 toured the United States as director of the Oxford and Cambridge Shakespeare Company.

Miller, Perry, 1905–63, U.S. historian, b. Chicago. He received his Ph.D. from the Univ. of Chicago in 1931 and taught at Harvard from 1931 until his death. A towering figure in the field of American intellectual history, Miller wrote extensively, especially about colonial New England. In *The New England Mind* (1939) he argued that the Puritans had a coherent world view firmly rooted in theology and that religion rather than economics was the prime motive behind the settling of New England. Miller's work stimulated a renewed interest in American Puritanism. His other books include *Orthodoxy in Massachusetts* (1933), *From Colony to Province* (1953), *Errand into the Wilderness* (1956), and intellectual biographies of Jonathan Edwards (1949) and Roger Williams (1953).

Miller, William, 1782–1849, American sectarian leader, b. Pittsfield, Mass. He was the founder of the sect of Second ADVENTISTS, sometimes called Millerites. In 1831, convinced from study of the Bible that the prophecies pointed to the second coming of Christ in 1843, he went about spreading his belief among large audiences. Many prepared for the Day of Judgment, and when the year passed without a fulfillment of Miller's prophecy, a date in 1844 was set. In 1845 Miller and his followers founded the Adventist Church.

Miller, William, 1795–1861, British soldier in South America. After service with the British army he went (1817) to South America, where he distinguished himself fighting under José de SAN MARTÍN. He played an important and heroic part in the liberation of Peru and Chile from Spain and became commander in chief and grand marshal of Peru. However, he was exiled (1839) from that politically tumultuous country for his support of Andrés SANTA CRUZ. In 1843 he became British consul general in the Pacific. See his memoirs (2d ed. 1829; repr., 2 vol., 1973).

Millerand, Alexandre (älěksäN'drə mēlräN'), 1859–1943, French politician, president of France (1920–24). A Socialist member of the chamber of deputies, he was the first Socialist to serve in a bourgeois cabinet; he was (1899–1902) minister of commerce in the ministry of Rene Waldeck-Rousseau. Millerand was sharply criticized by his party for accepting the post and was also censured for supporting antilabor decisions. He was eventually expelled from the Socialist party. Moving further to the right on the political spectrum, he became an ardent nationalist and, as minister of war (1912–13), he attempted to restore the morale and prestige of the army. He was again minister of war in 1914–15, and after World War I he became commissioner general in recovered Alsace and Lorraine (1919) and premier (1920). In 1920 he succeeded Paul Deschanel as president. Opposed by the newly elected (1924) chamber of deputies, which had a socialist and radical majority, and accused of favoring the right, Millerand was forced to resign. Gaston Doumergue succeeded him. Elected (1925) to the senate, Millerand continued to exert influence as a rightist and nationalist.

Milles, Carl (mĭl'əs), 1875–1955, Swedish-American sculptor, whose name originally was Carl Emil Wilhelm Anderson. Influenced by Rodin, he studied in Paris from 1897 until 1904, when he returned to Stockholm. In 1929 he visited the United States for the first time and in 1931 began to teach sculpture at Cranbrook Academy, Cranbrook, Mich. His work, at first inspired by Rodin, later became more angular and abstract. Millesgården near Stockholm contains many of his works. He is represented in the United States by the *Peace Monument* at St. Paul, Minn.; the *Fountain of the Meeting of the Waters* at St. Louis; a fountain in the Metropolitan Museum; and statues in Rockefeller Center, New York City. See study by M. R. Rogers (1940, repr. 1948).

Millet, Francis Davis, 1846–1912, American illustrator, painter, and journalist, b. Mattapoisett, Mass. He had been a drummer boy in the Civil War before going to college. As a correspondent, Millet covered the Russo-Turkish War of 1877–78 for the New York *Herald* and the London *Daily News* and *Graphic.* He was war correspondent in the Philippines in 1898 for the London *Times* and for *Harper's Weekly.* His mural paintings, for which he was later well known, include *Evolution of Navigation* (Customhouse, Baltimore). Of his genre pictures, *A Cozy Corner* and *An Old-Time Melody* are in the Metropolitan Museum, and *Between Two Fires* is in the Tate Gallery, London. He became a member of the National Academy in 1885 and was first secretary of the American Academy at Rome. Millet lived in England much of his later life; he died in the sinking of the *Titanic.*

Millet or **Milé, Jean François** (both: zhäN fräNswä' mēlā'), c.1642–1679, French landscape painter, known as Francisque, b. Antwerp. The Arcadian and imaginary Italian landscapes that are attributed to him (e.g., *The Storm;* National Gall., London) are painted in the manner of Gaspar Poussin and may be seen in numerous European galleries. His son, Jean François Millet (1666–1732), was also a landscape painter.

Millet, Jean François, 1814–75, French painter. He was born into a poor farming family. In 1837 an award enabled him to go to Paris, where he studied with Delaroche. In 1849 he settled in Barbizon, where he executed such celebrated works as the *Gleaners* (1857) and the *Angelus* (1859), both now in the Louvre. He was associated with members of the Barbizon school by proximity and friendship rather than by stylistic approach or treatment of subject. As a painter of melancholy scenes of peasant labor, he has been considered a social realist. Millet's paintings are noted for their power and simplicity of drawing. His work is well represented in American museums, notably in the Museum of Fine Arts, Boston. His drawings are executed with more spontaneity than his more sentimental paintings. See study by J. M. C. Ady (1896, repr. 1971).

millet, common name for several species of grasses cultivated mainly for cereals in the Eastern Hemisphere and for forage and hay in North America. The principal varieties are the foxtail, pearl, and barnyard millets and the proso millet, called also broomcorn millet and hog millet. Much millet is grown in China, India, Manchuria, the USSR, and Africa. Of the millets grown in the United States, 90% are of the foxtail variety. Proso millet is the chief cereal in parts of India, Africa, and the USSR; in the United States it is used for feeding poultry and cage birds. Millet seeds or grain have served man and domestic animals as food (e.g., groats) since ancient times. The plant is known to have been grown by the lake dwellers of Switzerland in the Stone Age, and it was sown by the Chinese in religious ceremonies as early as 2700 B.C. Millets are classified in the division MAGNOLIOPHYTA, class Liliatae, order Cyperales, family Gramineae.

Milligan, ex parte, case decided by the U.S. Supreme Court in 1866. By authorization of Congress, President Lincoln in 1863 suspended the writ of HABEAS CORPUS in cases where military officers held persons for offenses against the armed services. Army authorities had arrested Lambdin Milligan, a civilian who was involved in Copperhead, or pro-Confederate, activities in Indiana, and in 1864 he was tried by a military commission, convicted of fomenting rebellion, and condemned to death. The Supreme Court did not deal directly with the question of habeas corpus but with the limitation of martial law. It held that civilians might be tried by a military tribunal only where civil courts could not function because of invasion or disorder. It decided that even though the United States was at war, the Federal courts of Indiana were operating, and they alone might try the case. See Samuel Klaus, ed., *The Milligan Case* (1929, repr. 1970); Darwin Kelley, *Milligan's Fight Against Lincoln* (1973).

Millikan, Robert Andrews (mĭl'ĭkən), 1868–1953, American physicist and educator, b. Morrison, Ill., grad. Oberlin College, 1891, Ph.D. Columbia, 1895, and studied in Germany. He taught (1896–1921) physics at the Univ. of Chicago and from 1921 to 1945 was chairman of the executive council of the California Institute of Technology and director of the Norman Bridge Laboratory there. The 1923 Nobel Prize in Physics was awarded him for his measurement of the charge on the electron and for his work on the PHOTOELECTRIC EFFECT. He also made important studies of cosmic rays (which he named), X rays, and physical and electric constants and wrote and lectured on the reconciliation of science and religion. His books include *Science and Life* (1924), *Evolution in Science and Religion* (1927; 7th printing with addition, 1949), *Science and the New Civilization* (1930), *Time, Matter, and Values* (1932), and *Electrons (+ and −), Protons, Photons, Neutrons, Mesotrons, and Cosmic Rays* (rev. ed. 1947; 1st ed. with title *The Electron,* 1917; enl. ed. 1935). See his autobiography (1950).

Millin, Sarah Gertrude (Liebson), 1889–1968, South African writer. The first of her novels about colonial and racial problems in South Africa is *Dark River* (1920). Later novels include *God's Stepchildren* (1924), *What Hath a Man?* (1938), *The King of the Bastards* (1949), and *Two Bucks without Hair* (1958). She has also written a study, *The South Africans* (1926), and biographies of Cecil Rhodes (1933) and General Smuts (1936). See her autobiography, *The Measure of My Days* (1955).

milling, mechanical grinding of wheat or other grains to produce flour. Milling separates the fine, mealy parts of grain from the fibrous bran covering. In prehistoric times grain was crushed between two flat stones. Later a stone with a rounded end was used to grind grain in a cup-shaped stone; this led to the development of the mortar and pestle. The more advanced peoples began to use the quern, a primitive mill in which the grain is placed on a flat, circular lower millstone and ground by revolving a similar upper millstone to which a handle is attached. Such a device, operated at first by hand, was adapted to the use of animal, water, or wind power. The Greeks probably used water power c.450 B.C.; the Romans used gears to connect several sets of millstones with one waterwheel. Windmills are said to have become widespread in Europe following the Crusades and were probably introduced from Asia Minor. The Industrial Revolution initiated the use of steam power and of transportation facilities that resulted in the rise of large-scale milling centers. Machinery was improved, with metal replacing wood and steel rollers replacing millstones. The invention of the middlings purifier, by which, after preliminary grinding, the flour is separated from bran particles by strong air currents, improved the quality of flour prepared from hard spring wheat and, in the United States, led to the development of great milling centers in the spring-wheat areas of Minnesota (notably Minneapolis), the Dakotas, and Montana. In Europe modern rolling methods were developed during the 19th cent. in Hungary, and Budapest became one of the chief milling centers. In modern processing, grain is usually blended, cleaned, scrubbed to remove wheat hairs, tempered by heat and moisture (to prevent brittleness in the bran and consequent pulverization resulting in speckled flour), passed through sets of steel rolls with successively finer corrugations, and sifted after each grinding. It is then blown in a middlings purifier, ground between sets of smooth rolls, and bolted through a very fine mesh sieve. The entire, highly automated process takes about an hour and comprises some 180 operations. The term *milling* is applied also to the processing of other materials, e.g., soap, textiles, and metals; processing establishments are often called mills, e.g., lumber mill or sawmill, cotton mill, and sugar mill. See Martha and Murray Zimilies, *Early American Mills* (1973).

Millington, city (1970 pop. 21,177), Shelby co., SW Tenn., a suburb of Memphis, in a livestock, poultry, and cotton region; inc. 1903. A huge U.S. naval air station provides a major source of employment. Nearby is a state forest.

millipede (mĭl'əpēd"), elongated arthropod having many body segments and pairs of legs. Millipedes, sometimes termed thousand-legged worms, have two pairs of legs on each body segment except the first few and the last. They do not have a poisonous bite, but many protect themselves by offensive odors produced by stink glands; some produce highly irritating compounds that can injure the skin or eyes of attackers; and some can roll up into a ball

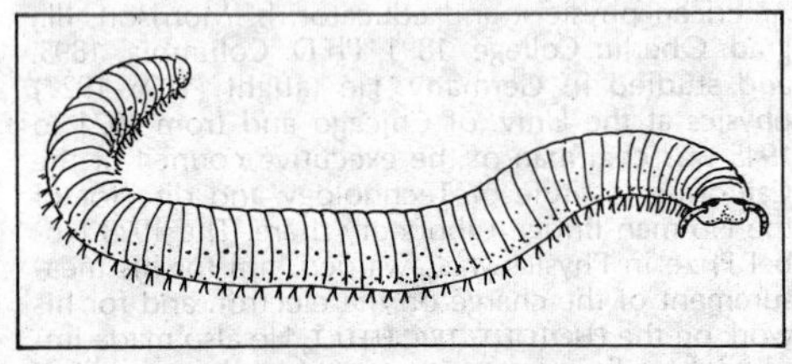

Millipede, representative of the class Diplopoda

or spiral for protection. They are widely distributed in temperate and warmer regions, living in surface litter, under stones or logs, and in relatively humid surroundings. They feed mostly on decaying vegetation, although some will consume decaying animal food. Some species attack plant roots and cause crop damage. Most temperate region millipedes are rather small and dull in appearance, but a few tropical species are brightly colored, and some reach 1 ft (30 cm) in length. The millipede body is nearly circular in cross section, with two pairs of legs on most segments. In contrast, CENTIPEDES, with which millipedes are often confused, are carnivorous, have a single pair of legs on each segment, and a body that is flat in cross section. Millipedes belong to the phylum ARTHROPODA, class Diplopoda.

Millo (mĭl'ō), fortification, N Jerusalem, built in the time of David. At Shechem there was a similar fortification called Beth-millo. Judges 9.6,20; 2 Sam. 5.9; 1 Kings 9.15,24; 11.27; 2 Kings 12.20; 1 Chron. 11.8; 2 Chron. 32.5.

Mills, Clark, 1810–83, American sculptor, b. Onondaga co., N.Y. Self-taught in art, he designed and in 1852 cast in an experimental foundry the statue of General Jackson for Lafayette Square, Washington, D.C. Mills had never seen his subject nor an equestrian statue. The daring pose of the horse was a mechanical triumph. Later Mills made a colossal statue of Washington on horseback, and he cast in his foundry Thomas Crawford's *Armed Freedom* for the Capitol dome.

Mills, Ogden Livingston, 1884–1937, American political leader, b. Newport, R.I. He practiced law in New York City and became an active Republican party leader. He served (1914–17) in the New York state legislature and then (1921–27) in the U.S. Congress, where he was noted as a fiscal expert. He was appointed (1927) Under Secretary of the Treasury, succeeded Andrew Mellon as Secretary of the Treasury (Feb., 1932–March, 1933), and afterward severely criticized the New Deal. His works include *Liberalism Fights On* (1936) and *The Seventeen Million* (1937).

Mills, Robert, 1781–1855, American architect of the CLASSIC REVIVAL period, b. Charleston, S.C. From 1800 to 1820 he worked as an architect in Washington, Philadelphia, and Baltimore, being associated at different times with Thomas Jefferson, James Hoban, and B. H. Latrobe. He then returned to Charleston as state engineer and architect. In 1836, President Jackson appointed Mills architect of public buildings in Washington. In this post he was responsible for designing and supervising the construction of the Treasury Building in 1836 and the Patent Office and the old Post Office, both begun in 1839. His design (1833) for the Washington Monument was executed (1848–84) without the base originally intended for it. Mills had planned to have the great obelisk superimposed upon a large Greek Doric Pantheon. He also designed the Washington Monument in Baltimore, the Bunker Hill Monument, and the Monumental Church in Richmond, Va. Seeking to create a truly American architecture, Mills devised plans for public buildings that were highly practical. His buildings give the effect of great dignity and massiveness, corresponding to their solidity of construction. See biography by H. M. Pierce Gallagher (1935).

Mills College, at Oakland, Calif.; mainly for women; est. 1852 as the Young Ladies' Seminary at Benicia, Calif., moved 1871, chartered as Mills College 1885. The first women's college in the Far West, it has schools of home and community services, fine arts, humanities, and natural sciences. It is noted for its fine arts department.

Mill Springs, village, on the Cumberland River, S of Frankfort, SE Ky.; site of the opening battle of the Kentucky-Tennessee campaign of the Civil War and the first important Union victory in the West. On Jan. 19, 1862, the Union forces of Gen. George Thomas repulsed a Confederate attack led by Gen. George Crittenden at Logan's Crossroads, 10 mi (16 km) north of the river; E Tennessee was thus left open to a Union advance.

Mill Valley, city (1970 pop. 12,942), Marin co., W Calif., a suburb on Richardson Bay, an inlet of San Francisco Bay; inc. 1900. It is a residential community set in heavily timbered hills and valleys; redwood trees predominate. Golden Gate Baptist Theological Seminary and an artists' colony are there. Mt. Tamalpais State Park is adjacent to the city, and Muir Woods National Monument (see NATIONAL PARKS AND MONUMENTS, table) is nearby.

Millville, city (1970 pop. 21,366), Cumberland co., S N.J., on the Maurice River, in a poultry, fruit, and truck-farm area; settled 1756, inc. 1866. The principal industries produce glass and clothing and repair aircraft engines. Nearby Union Lake attracts summer tourists.

Milman, Henry Hart, 1791–1868, English clergyman, poet, and historian, dean of St. Paul's Cathedral, London, from 1849. He was the author of several dramatic poems as well as some important historical works. His *History of the Jews* (1830) was the first work of English theology to subject the Bible to historical criticism. Other works include *History of Christianity under the Empire* (1840) and his chief work, *History of Latin Christianity* (6 vol., 1854–55). See biographies by A. Milman (1900) and C. H. E. Smyth (1949).

Milne, Alan Alexander (mĭln), 1882–1956, English author. A. A. Milne began his literary career as a journalist and later became a regular contributor to *Punch.* He is best known for his collections of verses for children, including *When We Were Very Young* (1924) and *Now We Are Six* (1927), and for the books *Winnie-the-Pooh* (1926) and *The House at Pooh Corner* (1928), which established the characters Christopher Robin and his toy animal friends Pooh Bear, Piglet, and Eeyore. These stories have become classics, beloved by adults as well as children. Milne's detective novel, *The Red House Mystery* (1921), is one of the best in its genre. Also a successful dramatist, he wrote several comedies, including *Mr. Pim Passes By* (1920) and *The Dover Road* (1921). See his autobiography (1939).

Milne, David, 1882–1953, Canadian painter, b. Ontario. He grew up in the country and returned to Canada after studying at the Art Students League in New York City. Milne chose simple, ordinary subjects which he imbued with dignity and significance. His landscapes and still lifes reveal a decorative sense and fluidity of touch.

Milne, John, 1850–1913, British seismologist, b. Liverpool, educated at King's College and the Royal School of Mines. He worked as a mining engineer in Newfoundland and Labrador and served (1874) as a geologist on a mining expedition to NW Arabia. From 1875 to 1894 he was professor of geology at the Imperial Univ. in Tokyo, where he helped to organize the seismic survey of Japan. After his return to England he was influential in promoting the establishment of seismological stations throughout the world; he designed several seismographs. His writings include two standard works, *Earthquakes* (1883), and *Seismology* (1898).

Milne-Edwards, Henri (äNrē' mĕl"nădwärs'), 1800–85, French naturalist. He became professor at the Sorbonne (1843) and served at the Museum of Natural History, Paris, as professor (from 1841) and director (from 1864). He wrote important works on the crustaceans, mollusks, and corals and a noted textbook on zoology (1834). His principal work was a series on comparative anatomy and physiology (14 vol., 1857–81).

Milner, Alfred Milner, 1st **Viscount,** 1854–1925, British statesman and colonial administrator. He distinguished himself as a student at Oxford and was briefly a journalist in London. He became (1887) private secretary to George Goschen, chancellor of the exchequer, and served (1890–92) as undersecretary of finance in Egypt. His *England in Egypt* (1892) effectively argued for greater British involvement there. In 1897, Milner was appointed high commissioner for South Africa and governor general of Cape Colony. His efforts to gain political rights for English settlers in Boer territories heightened growing tension between the rival groups and helped precipitate (1899) the SOUTH AFRICAN WAR. After the war, Milner's financial policies aided economic recovery, but his importation of indentured Chinese laborers raised strong opposition. He remained in South Africa until 1905, working for the assimilation of the Boer territories into a South African federation firmly linked to Britain. During this period he gathered around him a group of able young administrators, including Philip Kerr, later marquess of LOTHIAN, who became known as "Milner's kindergarten." Milner was one of the Conservative lords who opposed the revolutionary budget of 1909 introduced by David LLOYD GEORGE, but in 1916 Lloyd George appointed him to his war cabinet. After serving (1918) as secretary of war, he was (1919–21) colonial secretary and in 1920 led a commission to Egypt that recommended Egyptian independence. He was created viscount in 1902. See Cecil Headlam, ed., *The Milner Papers, 1897–1905* (1931–33); study by Edward Crankshaw (1952, repr. 1974).

Milner, Moses Embree: see CALIFORNIA JOE.

Milnes, Richard Monckton: see HOUGHTON, RICHARD MONCKTON MILNES, 1ST BARON.

Milo (mī'lō) or **Milon** (mī'lŏn), fl. 500 B.C., athlete of ancient Greece, b. Crotona. He won numerous victories in wrestling at the Olympic and Pythian games. He is said to have carried a heifer on his shoulders through the Olympic stadium, killed her with a blow of his fist, and devoured her in the course of a day. Finding a tree partially split, he attempted, according to legend, to tear it apart but caught his hand and was eaten alive by wolves.

Milo (Titus Annius Papianus Milo), 95 B.C.–47 B.C., Roman partisan leader. As tribune of the people (57 B.C.) he obtained the recall from exile of Cicero. At the instance of POMPEY, Milo hired a gang to fight the gang of CLODIUS. The rivals kept Rome in an uproar until it ended (52 B.C.) in the death of Clodius in an affray at Bovillae, on the Appian Way. Pompey was appointed sole consul to restore order in the city, and Milo was brought to trial. Cicero, his advocate, was so intimidated that he did not deliver his oration, which he later published (*Pro Milone*). Milo was exiled to Massilia, joined the insurrection of Marcus Caelius in Italy, and was defeated, captured, and killed. Milo's wife was Sulla's daughter.

milo or **milo maize:** see SORGHUM.

Milon, Greek athlete: see MILO.

Miloš or **Milosh** (Miloš Obrenović) (both: mĭ'lôsh ōbrĕ'nəvĭch), 1780–1860, prince of Serbia (1817–39, 1858–60), founder of the OBRENOVIĆ dynasty and of modern SERBIA. An illiterate swineherd, he was a revolutionary chieftain fighting the Turks under KARAGEORGE. After Karageorge's defeat he temporarily submitted to the Turks, but in 1815 he began a new and successful rebellion. In 1817, having probably killed his rival, Karageorge, he was named prince of Serbia, a title confirmed by the national assembly (1827) and by the sultan (1830), who remained his suzerain. In 1838 the sultan, backed by Russia, forced the appointment of a council of senators hostile to Miloš, who abdicated in favor of his son Milan in 1839. When Milan died in the same year, Miloš's younger son, Michael (Michael Obrenović), became prince. He was deposed in turn in 1842 and was succeeded by Alexander Karadjordjević. In 1858 the Serbian parliament recalled Miloš, but he died two years later.

Milos (mē'lôs) or **Milo** (mē'lō, mī'-), mountainous island (1971 pop. 4,499), 58 sq mi (150 sq km), SE Greece, in the Aegean Sea; one of the CYCLADES. The main town is Mílos (1971 pop. 952), formerly known as Plaka. The island's products include grain, cotton, fruits, and olive oil. Mílos flourished as a center of early Aegean civilization because of its deposits of obsidian and its strategic location between the Greek mainland and Crete. It lost importance when bronze replaced obsidian as a material for tools and weapons. Despite its neutrality in the Peloponnesian War, Mílos fell victim to Athens, which conquered the island in 416 B.C. and then massacred the men, enslaved the remaining persons, and founded an Athenian colony. Much excavation has been done on Mílos. The most famous find is the Venus of Milo (now in the Louvre, Paris), discovered in 1820.

Milosh: see MILOŠ.

Milpitas (mĭl″pē'təs), city (1970 pop. 27,149), Santa Clara co., W Calif., a suburb of San Jose, in a truck-farm and citrus-fruit area; inc. 1954. Industries are automobile assembling, food distributing, and the installation and maintenance of irrigation systems.

Milstein, Nathan, 1904–, Russian violinist, b. Odessa. Milstein attended the music school in Odessa before entering the St. Petersburg conservatory, where he studied under Leopold Auer. He toured Russia from 1920 to 1926. Milstein left Russia (1926) for Paris, where his reputation brought him engagements throughout Europe. Moving to the United States in 1928, he made his debut (1929) with the St. Louis Symphony Orchestra. Since then he has made numerous world tours. Milstein is known for the precision of his technique and the discriminating taste of his interpretation.

Miltiades (mĭltī'ədēz), d. 489 B.C., Athenian general who commanded at Marathon. He succeeded his uncle as ruler (c.524 B.C.) of an Athenian dependency in the Gallipoli Peninsula. He accompanied (c.513) Darius in the Persian expedition into Scythia. Later he took part in the revolt of Ionian Greece against the Persians (499–493) and afterward fled to Athens. His experience and ability made him a powerful figure and he was elected to the board of generals to oppose the impending Persian invasion (see PERSIAN WARS). When the enemy arrived at Marathon (490), Miltiades went there to protect Athens from the land side. After a few days' delay the Persians began the march toward Athens, and Miltiades attacked. He had an infantry that was greatly outnumbered, but the Greek spears and armor outweighed Persian arms. The Athenian center gave way and the wings enveloped the Persians, vanquishing them. The Persians retreated to their ships and set out at once by sea to attack Athens, the army being absent. Perhaps the chief glory of Miltiades was that he brought his army, which had been fighting all day, in a 20-mi (32-km) race back to Athens; in the morning when the Persian fleet arrived off Athens, Miltiades and his army were ready. After the battle Miltiades was given a fleet. In 489, he made an unsuccessful attack on Paros. His enemies took advantage of the failure and had him fined. He died of a wound soon after.

Milton, John, 1608–74, English poet, b. London. The son of a wealthy scrivener, he was educated at St. Paul's School and Christ's College, Cambridge. While Milton was at Cambridge he wrote poetry in both Latin and English, including the ode "On the Morning of Christ's Nativity" (1629). Although the exact dates are unknown, "L'Allegro" and "Il Penseroso" were probably written not long after this. His dislike of the increasing ritualism in the Church of England was the reason he later gave for not becoming a minister as he had earlier planned to do. Resolved to be a poet, Milton retired to his father's estate at Horton after leaving Cambridge and devoted himself to his studies. There he wrote the masque *Comus* (1634) and "Lycidas" (1638), one of his greatest poems, an elegy on the death of his friend Edward King. In 1638, Milton went to Italy, where he traveled, studied, and met many notable figures, including Galileo. Returning to England in 1639, he supported the Presbyterians in their attempt to reform the Church of England. His pamphlets, which attacked the episcopal form of church government, include *Of Reformation in England* (1641) and *The Reason of Church Government Urged against Prelaty* (1642). In 1643 he married Mary Powell, a young woman half his age, who left him the same year. Disillusioned by the failure of his marriage, he started work on four controversial pamphlets (1643–45) upholding the morality of divorce for incompatibility. *Areopagitica* (1644), one of the great arguments in favor of the freedom of the press, grew out of his dissatisfaction with the strict censorship of the press exercised by Parliament. Milton gradually broke away from the Presbyterians, and in 1649 he wrote *The Tenure of Kings and Magistrates,* which supported the Independents who had imprisoned King Charles in the Puritan Revolution. In it he declared that subjects may depose and put to death an unworthy king. This pamphlet secured Milton a position in Oliver Cromwell's government as Latin secretary for foreign affairs, and he continued to defend Cromwell and the Commonwealth government in his *Eikonoklastes* [the image breaker] (1649)—an answer to *Eikon Basilike*—and in the Latin pamphlets *First Defense of the English People* (1651), *Second Defense of the English People* (1654) and *Defense of Himself* (1655). In the midst of his heavy official business and pamphleteering, Milton, whose sight had been weak from childhood, became totally blind, and he had to carry on his work through secretaries, one of whom was Andrew Marvell. Mary Powell returned to Milton in 1645 but died in 1652 after she had borne him three daughters. He married Catharine Woodcock in 1656, and she died two years later. She is the subject of one of his most famous sonnets, beginning "Methought I saw my late espoused saint." In 1663 he married Elizabeth Minshull, who survived him. Milton supported the Commonwealth to the very end, and after the Restoration (1660) he was forced into hiding for a time, and some of his books were burned. He was included in the general amnesty, however, and lived quietly thereafter. For many years Milton had planned to write an epic poem, and he probably started his work on *Paradise Lost* before the Restoration. The blank-verse poem in 10 books appeared in 1667; a second edition, in which Milton reorganized the original 10 books into 12, appeared in 1674. It was greatly admired by Milton's contemporaries, and has since then been considered the greatest epic poem in the English language. In telling the story of Satan's rebellion against God and the story of Adam and Eve in the Garden of Eden, Milton attempted to account for the evil in this world and, in his own words, to "justify the ways of God to man." *Paradise Regained,* a second blank-verse poem in four books, describes how Christ, a greater individual than Adam, overcame the temptations of Satan. In both works, Milton's characterizations of Satan, Adam, Eve, and Christ are penetrating and moving. Indeed, his portrayal of Satan is so compelling that many 19th-century critics maintained that he rather than Adam was the hero of *Paradise Lost.* Milton's language is dignified and ornate, replete with biblical and classical allusions, allegorical representations, metaphors, puns, and rhetorical flourishes. *Samson Agonistes,* a poetic drama modeled on classical Greek tragedy but with biblical subject matter, appeared together with *Paradise Regained* in 1671. Milton's theology, which, although in the Protestant tradition, is extremely unorthodox and individual on many points, is set forth in the Latin pamphlet *De doctrina Christiana* [on Christian doctrine], unpublished during Milton's lifetime and discovered and published in 1825. Milton wrote 18 sonnets in English and 5 in Italian, which generally follow the Petrarchan style and are accepted as among the greatest ever written. See his complete works (ed. by F. A. Patterson, 20 vol., 1931–40); 1-vol. collections by F. A. Patterson (rev. ed. 1933), D. Bush (1965), and J. T. Shawcross (1971); variorum commentary on the poems (M. Y. Hughes, general editor; Vol. I, 1970; Vol. II, in 3 parts, 1972); Yale edition of his complete prose works (Vol. I-VI, 1953–1973; two more volumes are projected); biographies by W. A. Raleigh (1900, repr. 1967), J. H. Hanford (1949), W. R. Parker (2 vol., 1968), and E. Wagenknecht (1971); studies by M. Nicolson (1963), D. Bush (1964), E. M. W. Tillyard (3 studies: 1938, repr. 1963; 1951, repr. 1960; and rev. ed. 1965), D. Daiches (1957, repr. 1966), J. M. Steadman (1967 and 1968), A. D. Ferry (1963 and 1969), J. T. Shawcross (1966, 1967, and 1970), F. Kermode (1960, repr. 1971), C. A. Patrides (1971), and J. D. Simmonds, ed. (1969 and 1971). See also J. H. Hanford and V. G. Taffe, *A Milton Handbook* (1970); Lois Potter, *A Preface to Milton* (1972); John Broadbent, ed., *John Milton: Introductions* (1973); Michael Lieb and J. T. Shawcross, eds., *Achievements of the Left Hand* (1974).

Milton, town (1970 pop. 27,190), Norfolk co., E Mass., a residential suburb of Boston, on the Neponset River; settled 1636, set off from Dorchester and inc. 1662. Granite quarries are nearby. Milton is the seat of Curry College and several preparatory schools, including Milton Academy (1798). Harvard's meteorological observatory is on Blue Hill.

Milton Keyes, new town (1971 pop. 46,473), Buckinghamshire, S central England. Milton Keyes was designated one of the NEW TOWNS in 1967 to alleviate overpopulation in London. The town's population is planned to increase to 250,000 by the end of the century.

Miltown: see MEPROBAMATE.

Milvian Bridge or **Mulvian Bridge,** Latin *Pons Milvius* or *Pons Mulvius.* It was built by Marcus Aemilius Scaurus in 109 B.C. over the Tiber near Rome as part of the FLAMINIAN WAY. By defeating Maxentius here in A.D. 312, Constantine I became the unchallenged ruler of the West. It was here that Constantine saw the cross in the sky.

Milwaukee (mĭlwô̆k'ē), city (1970 pop. 717,372), seat of Milwaukee co., SE Wis., at the point where the Milwaukee, Menomonee, and Kinnickinnic rivers enter Lake Michigan; inc. 1846. The largest city in the state, it is a port of entry, shipping heavy cargo from the entire Midwest to world ports via the St. Lawrence Seaway. It is a major producer of heavy machinery and electrical equipment and one of the world's leading manufacturers of diesel and gasoline engines, tractors, and beer. Motorcycles, refrigeration equipment, chocolate, and electronic products are also produced. In 1673, Father Jacques Marquette visited the site, which was then an Indian gathering and trading center. In 1795 the North West Company established a fur-trading post. Solomon Juneau, the fur trader, arrived in 1818, and in 1838 several settlements merged to form Milwaukee village. It grew as a shipping center and became famous for its numerous industries, notably brewing and meat packing. German refugees arrived in large numbers after 1848, stimulating the city's political, economic, and social growth. The Knights of Saint Crispin foreshadowed the city's growing labor movement after the Civil War. Victor L. Berger, the Socialist leader, exerted a dominant influence there, and Daniel W. Hoan made Milwaukee known for efficient administration. Among the city's educational institutions are Marquette Univ., the Univ. of Wisconsin at Milwaukee, Alverno College, Layton School of Art, Cardinal Stritch College, and three junior colleges. Local attractions include the breweries, with their guided tours; a public library and museum; an art center; a church built by Frank Lloyd Wright; a performing arts center; and the water tower. Among the numerous parks are Washington Park; Mitchell Park, with enclosed botanical gardens; Juneau Park; and Estabrook Park, containing one of the city's oldest houses. A large U.S. veterans hospital is in the city. Milwaukee has professional basketball and baseball teams as well as the Green Bay Packers professional football team. In the 1960s, Milwaukee was the scene of much racial disorder. A Catholic priest, Father James Groppi, won national attention, mobilizing the city's blacks and leading them in demonstrations.

Milwaukie, city (1970 pop. 16,379), Clackamas and Multnomah counties, NW Oregon, on the Willamette River; inc. 1903. The city is a distribution center for farms and orchards of the Willamette valley and has numerous warehouse facilities. Chief among its varied manufactures are tools and textiles. Fruit trees brought there from Iowa by covered wagon in 1848 inaugurated the state's important cherry-growing industry.

Milyukov or **Miliukov, Pavel Nikolayevich** (both: pä'vĭl nyĭkəlī'əvĭch mēlyōōkôf'), 1859–1943, Russian political leader and historian. An advocate of parliamentary democracy, he was a founder and leader of the Constitutional Democratic party, organized in 1905, and a member of the Duma. After the overthrow of the czarist government in March, 1917 (Feb., 1917, O.S.), he became foreign minister in the provisional government of Prince Lvov. His insistence on carrying out Russia's military obligations toward the Allies in World War I made him highly unpopular with the war-weary masses, and in May, 1917, he was forced to resign. An uncompromising opponent of Bolshevism, he settled in Paris after the failure of the counterrevolution against Lenin. Among his historical works is *Outlines of Russian Culture* (tr., 3 vol., 1942).

Mimas (mī'măs), in astronomy, one of the 10 known moons, or natural satellites, of SATURN.

mime: see PANTOMIME.

mimeograph, process used for producing copies of printed or drawn material. The material to be copied is typed, written, or drawn on a stencil, or master, which is a sheet with a wax coating. As the material is being transcribed, the instrument used, such as a typewriter key or a stylus, cuts through the wax in the areas that it strikes or moves over. After the transcription, the stencil is placed top side down over an ink pad on the drum of a mimeograph machine. As the drum rotates, sheets of paper are drawn past it. Since ink from the pad can only pass through the stencil in the areas from which the wax has been removed, an image of the material on the stencil is formed on each sheet of paper. Up to 10,000 copies can be made from a single stencil. If a stencil is not worn out on a single run, it can be stored and reused later.

Mimico (mĭm'ĭkō) (1966 pop. 19,341), part of metropolitan TORONTO, S Ont., Canada, on Lake Ontario.

mimicry, in biology, the advantageous resemblance of one species to another, often unrelated, species or to a feature of its own environment. (When the latter results from pigmentation it is classed as PROTECTIVE COLORATION.) Mimicry serves either to protect the mimic from its predators, as when the model is inedible or dangerous, or to deceive its prey (e.g., certain ant-eating spiders that themselves resemble ants). Mimicry occurs in both plants and

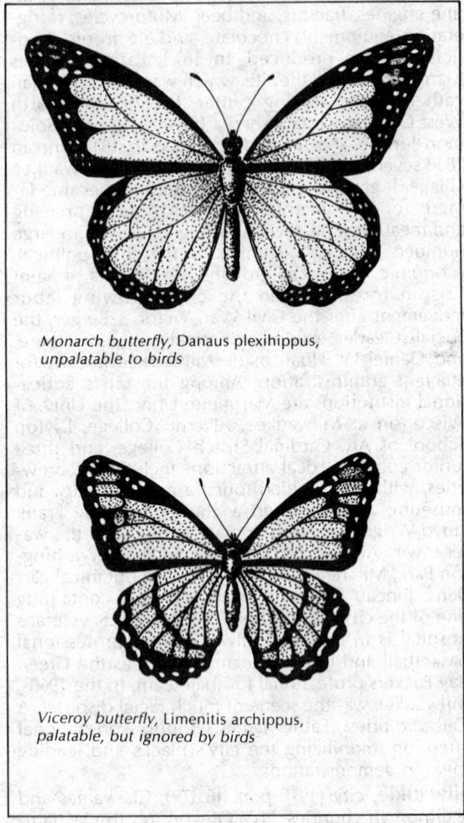
Monarch butterfly, Danaus plexihippus, unpalatable to birds
Viceroy butterfly, Limenitis archippus, palatable, but ignored by birds
Mimicry in butterflies

animals, but is most prevalent among insects, particularly butterflies and moths. The first scientific studies on the subject were published by English naturalists H. W. Bates (1862) and A. R. Wallace (1865). The Batesian theory is based on the operation of natural SELECTION: if, say, a harmless snake acquires a deceptive resemblance to a poisonous variety it is then more likely to escape its predators and thus to survive and propagate, producing offspring with the same appearance. Examples of mimicry are the resemblance of the viceroy butterfly to the monarch butterfly, which is repugnant to birds; harmless nettles that resemble stinging nettles; and the many fishes, crabs, and slugs of the Sargasso Sea that resemble the floating seaweed masses they inhabit. See Wolfgang Wickler, *Mimicry in Plants and Animals* (tr. 1968).

mimic thrush, common name for members of the Mimidae, a family of exclusively American birds, allied to the wrens and thrushes, that includes the mockingbird, the catbird, and the thrashers. Mimic thrushes are most numerous in Mexico. They are about the size of a robin or slightly larger but are proportionately slimmer and have slender, downcurved bills, long tails which they twitch vigorously when excited, and strong legs suited to scratching through dead leaves and underbrush for insects; they also eat berries and fruit. All these birds are famous for their vocal powers. The preeminent songster of all North American birds is the common mockingbird, *Mimus polyglottos,* found in the E United States S of Maryland—the northernmost of nine similar species. It is gray above, with white wing patches and whitish underparts. Its song, usually delivered from a high, exposed perch, is unrestricted as to season or time of day and includes phrases from other birds' songs (of which it will repeat as many as 30 in succession), imitations of familiar sounds, and a melodious song of its own. Two species of blue mockingbirds, genus *Melanotis,* are found in Mexico. Another member of the family, the catbird, *Dumatella carolinensis,* slate gray with a black cap and a chestnut patch under the tail, is also an expert singer, with a plaintive mewing call that gives it its name. Of the 17 species of thrashers, the brown thrasher, *Toxostoma rufum,* of the E United States is typical. It is a rich chestnut above, with whitish underparts streaked with brown; it is sometimes erroneously called the brown thrush. Thrashers also are tuneful singers and are valuable destroyers of harmful insects. Mimic thrushes are classified in the phylum CHORDATA, subphylum Vertebrata, class Aves, order Passeriformes, family Mimidae.

Mimir (mē'mĭr), in Norse mythology, giant who guarded the well of wisdom. According to one legend Mimir was beheaded by the enemies of the gods of Asgard; his head was then preserved by Odin, who consulted it for information and advice.

Mimnermus (mĭmnûr'məs), fl. late 7th cent. B.C., Greek elegiac poet of Colophon in Ionia. Only fragments of his poetry survive. Although he mainly wrote love poetry, he did write some martial and historical verse as well. His work is marked by tenderness and melancholy sentiment. One collection was called *Nanno,* for a girl he loved.

mimosa (mĭmō'sə), any tree, shrub, or herb of the genus *Mimosa* of the family Leguminosae (PULSE family), chiefly tropical plants. They usually have feathery foliage and rounded clusters of fragrant pinkish flowers atop the branches. Mimosas are used for ornamental purposes in warm regions. The yellow-flowered plants sold as mimosa by florists are usually of the similar and related genus *Acacia* (see ACACIA). Most widely known of the mimosas is the sensitive plant (*M. pudica*), considered a weed in the American tropics but cultivated as a greenhouse annual elsewhere because of its interesting movements. Its leaves fold up and collapse under stimulus (e.g., touch, darkness, or drought) until the whole plant may assume temporarily a thoroughly wilted appearance. When stimulated at frequent intervals, the plant soon fails to respond. It is now naturalized in many warm regions and grows wild in the Gulf states. The name sensitive plant is also applied to other plants of this family that show similar movements. Mimosa is classified in the division MAGNOLIOPHYTA, class Magnoliopsida, order Rosales, family Leguminosae.

Mimosa or **Beta Crucis,** bright star in the constellation CRUX (Southern Cross); 1970 position R.A. $12^h46.0^m$, Dec. −59°32′. It is sometimes called Becrux, from its Bayer name, analogous to Acrux (Alpha Crucis) and Gacrux (Gamma Crucis). A bluish-white giant of SPECTRAL CLASS B0 III, its apparent MAGNITUDE of 1.28 makes it one of the 20 brightest stars in the sky. Mimosa's distance is more than 400 light-years.

Mims, Fort: see FORT MIMS.

Min (mĭn). **1** Chief river of Fukien prov., SE China, c.350 mi (560 km) long, rising in Wu-i Shan and flowing SE to the South China Sea near Fu-chou; it receives several tributaries near Nan-p'ing. Fu-chou, a transshipment point, has a deep-water anchorage for oceangoing vessels. **2** River, W Szechwan prov., central China, c.500 mi (800 km) long, rising in the Min Shan and flowing S through the Ch'eng-tu Plain to the Yangtze River at I-pin. The Ta-tu River, c.400 mi (640 km) long, is its chief tributary. In the 2d cent. B.C., the Min's water was diverted by Li Ping, governor of Ch'eng-tu, into numerous channels that reunite downstream near P'eng-shan. The irrigation system is still used today to water the fertile Ch'eng-tu Plain.

minaret (mĭnərĕt'), tower, used in Islamic architecture, from which the faithful are called to prayer by a muezzin. Most MOSQUES have one or more small towers, which are usually placed at the corners. The first constructions used as minarets were the four watchtowers built during Hellenic times at the corners of the ancient temple enclosure later converted into the Great Mosque at Damascus. The earliest structures specifically built as minarets were the four low square towers at the four corners of the Mosque of Amr in Egypt (A.D. 673), modeled after those of Damascus. The square form remained in use in Syria until the 13th cent. and in the Maghreb until modern times; the minaret of Giralda in Seville (A.D. 1195) is famous. The free-standing conical minaret surrounded by a spiral staircase, probably deriving from the ancient Babylonian ziggurat, was built at Samarra, Iraq, and in Cairo in the second half of the 9th cent. The most typical Egyptian development is

Minaret

seen in the octagonal minarets of the two 15th-century Cairo mosques of El-Azhar and Kait-bey; both have two balconies, the upper smaller than the lower, over projecting friezes of stalactite vaulting and are surmounted by an elongated and bulbous finial. The most distinctly Persian development (see PERSIAN ART AND ARCHITECTURE) are the two pairs of slim, towering minarets flanking the huge entrance arches of the Isfahan Masjid-i Shah (c.1612); the conical shafts terminate in covered balconies and are entirely encased in brilliant blue tiles. See ISLAMIC ART AND ARCHITECTURE.

Minas de Ríotinto, Spain: see RÍO TINTO.

Minas Gerais (mē'nəs zhərīs') [Port.,=various mines], state (1970 pop. 11,497,574), 226,707 sq mi (587,171 sq km), E Brazil. The capital is BELO HORIZONTE.

mincemeat: see PIE.

Minch (mĭnch) or **North Minch,** strait, 20 to 45 mi (32–72 km) wide, separating the N Outer Hebrides from the mainland of Scotland. Little Minch, to the southwest, 14 to 20 mi (23–32 km) wide, separates Skye island from the middle Outer Hebrides islands.

Mincio (mēn'chō), river, c.47 mi (76 km) long, in Lombardy, N Italy. It flows generally south from the southern end of Lake Garda through Mantua (where it forms three lakes) to the Po River. Above Lake Garda it is called the Sarca. The Sarca-Garda-Mincio line, which is 120 mi (193 km) long, marks the natural border between Lombardy and Venetia and has been of strategic importance, especially in the wars of the Risorgimento (1848–49).

Mindanao (mĭndənä'ō, -nou'), island (1970 pop. 7,292,691), 36,537 sq mi (94,631 sq km), 2d largest of the Philippines, NE of Borneo. The terrain is generally mountainous and heavily forested, rising to 9,690 ft (2,954 m) at Mt. Apo, an active volcano and the highest point in the Philippines. The island is indented by several deep bays and has a large western peninsula, the Zamboanga or Sibuguey Peninsula. Its main rivers are the Pulangi (known as the Mindanao in its lower course), c.200 mi (320 km) long and navigable by small steamers for c.40 mi (60 km); and the Agusan, c.240 mi (390 km) long. The largest lake is Lake Lanao, for centuries the habitat of Muslim Moros. Off the northeast coast in the Philippine Sea is the Mindanao Trench (c.35,000 ft/10,670 m deep), one of the greatest known ocean depths. Mindanao lies below the typhoon belt, and its climate is more favorable than that of Luzon to the north. Most of the fertile arable land is now intensively cultivated. Mindanao is the country's major pineapple-and hemp-producing island. Coffee and rice are also grown in abundance. There are commercial coconut and rubber plantations, fish culture areas, and crocodile grounds. The many natural resources are being rapidly exploited. Lumbering and mining are major industries. Mindanao is a prime source of Philippine mahogany, and iron, gold, and coal are produced in quantity. Zamboanga and Davao are the principal cities; Davao is the most important port. There was considerable industrial growth during the 1960s. The extensive development of the water resources of the Lake Lanao-Agus River basin, including the harnessing of Maria Christina Falls, has resulted in the establishment of heavy industrial plants, especially in the Iligan area. About one third of the island's population is Muslim (see MOROS). In the middle of the 14th cent. Islam spread from Malaya and Borneo to the Sulu Archipelago, and from there to Mindanao. The arrival of the Spanish in the late 16th cent. united the various Muslim groups in a holy war against the conquerors that lasted some 300 years. The Moros likewise resisted American domination; fighting between U.S. garrisons and Muslim groups occurred early in the 20th cent. Although many of the Philippine Islands suffered extensive damage in World War II, Mindanao emerged relatively unscathed. As the chief frontier left in the difficult reconstruction years, it was the object of government colonization projects. During the 1960s it experienced a phenomenal population increase and very rapid development. These changes brought serious problems. The native Moros, finding themselves outnumbered and in many cases pushed off their lands, retaliated with terrorist activities. When the Philippine army attempted to restore order, fierce fighting often resulted. In 1969 and the early 1970s several thousand people were killed and hundreds of villages were burned. Many pagan tribes formerly isolated in the wilds of Mindanao are also being threatened by the advancing civilization. The amazing discovery in 1971 of a gentle Stone Age people, the Tasaday, living in an area now under rapid exploitation, strengthened the government's desire to protect such peoples against encroaching (and often ruthless) lumbering, mining, and ranching interests.

Minden (mĭn'dən), city (1970 pop. 48,912), North Rhine-Westphalia, N West Germany, a port on the Weser River and the Midland Canal. It is an industrial center and rail junction. Manufactures include ships, machinery, textiles, clothing, coffee filters, chemicals, beer, and foundry products. Minden was the see of a bishopric founded c.800 by Charlemagne. The city struggled throughout the Middle Ages against the temporal rule of its bishops. In the 13th cent. it joined the Hanseatic League, and in 1530 it accepted the Reformation. Minden and the secularized bishopric passed to Brandenburg in the Peace of Westphalia (1648). In the Seven Years War the English and the Hanoverians defeated (1759) the French at Minden. The city passed to Prussia in 1814. Noteworthy buildings include the cathedral (11th-13th cent.) and the city hall (13th-17th cent.).

Minden, city (1970 pop. 13,996), seat of Webster parish, NW La.; inc. 1850. It is the shipping center of an area rich in timber, oil, and natural gas. Industries include lumbering, gas and oil production, steel fabrication, and the manufacture of plywood and of sand and gravel. An army ammunition production center is there.

Mindoro (mĭndô'rō), island (1970 pop. 473,940), 3,759 sq mi (9,736 sq km), 7th largest of the Philippines, SW of Luzon. Its mountainous interior rises to c.8,500 ft (2,590 m), at Mt. Halcon. Although there is relatively little arable land, subsistence farming is carried on. Coal is mined, lumbering is an important industry, and there are major crocodile grounds.

mind reading: see PARAPSYCHOLOGY; TELEPATHY.

Mindszenty, Jozsef (mĭnd'sĕntē), 1892–, Hungarian prelate, cardinal of the Roman Catholic Church. He was bishop of Veszprém during the German occupation of Hungary in World War II. His anti-German attitude led to his imprisonment for several months by the Hungarian puppet government. After the war he was made archbishop of Esztergom and Catholic primate of Hungary, and in 1946 he was raised to the cardinalate. A strong opponent of Communism, Mindszenty was arrested by the Hungarian government late in 1948 on the charges of treason and illegal monetary transactions. At a sensational public trial Mindszenty pleaded guilty to most charges. It was widely held that his confession had been obtained by drugging him, because he had disclaimed in advance any confession he might make in case of arrest. The court sentenced him to life imprisonment. Released from prison because of ill-health in 1955, Mindszenty was kept under close watch. During the Hungarian revolution he was freed by rebel forces. When the revolt was crushed, he took refuge in the U.S. legation and thereafter refused to leave Hungary unless the Hungarian government rescinded his conviction and sentence. In 1971, after an agreement between the Vatican and the Hungarian government, Mindszenty left Hungary for the Vatican. Shortly afterwards, he settled in Vienna. In 1974, in an effort to improve church relations with Hungary, Pope Paul VI removed him as primate of Hungary. A selection of his writings was published as *Cardinal Mindszenty Speaks* (1949). See biographies by S. K. Swift (1950) and Josef Vecsey (1972).

mine, in industry: see MINING.

mine, in warfare, term formerly applied to a system of tunnels dug under an army fortification and ending in a chamber where explosives were placed to be detonated at the chosen moment. Modern mines are encased explosives detonated by contact, magnetic proximity, or electrical impulse. Land mines, equipped with pressure sensors slightly above or below ground, came into wide use in World War II. They are of two general types—antipersonnel and antitank; the latter are designed so that lighter objects will not cause them to explode. No completely safe way of removing land mines is known. In World War II the United States and Great Britain developed several types of mine-detecting and mine-exploding equipment, but they proved inadequate. Naval mines of various types have been used periodically since the 16th cent., but it was not until World War I that they entered into wide use. Modern naval mines, equipped with sonar or magnetic sensors, are laid on the surface of the sea or sometimes anchored below. They fall within two broad classifications—automatic and controlled. The automatic mine, once planted and armed, is activated by the presence of a ship; it is incapable of discriminating between friendly and enemy ships. The controlled mine, in contrast, is connected by electric cable to a shore station and can be disarmed to allow the passage of friendly vessels. In waters not under enemy control, mines are laid by specially equipped vessels, called minelayers; in enemy waters aircraft and submarines are used for mine laying. Minesweepers are employed as a countermeasure. Since naval mines can only be laid in shallow water (less than 100 fathoms deep), avoidance of shallow water is the best protection against them.

Mineola (mĭnēō'lə), village (1970 pop. 21,744), seat of Nassau co., SE N.Y., on Long Island, a suburb of New York City; inc. 1906. Chiefly residential, it is a commercial center, with some light industry.

mineral, inorganic substance occurring in nature, having a characteristic and homogeneous chemical composition, definite physical properties, and, usually, a definite crystalline form. A few of the minerals (e.g., carbon, arsenic, bismuth, antimony, gold, silver, copper, lead, mercury, platinum, and iron) are elements, but the vast majority are chemical compounds. A generalized formula can usually be assigned to each mineral that is a chemical compound, although sometimes one element in a mineral may be replaced by another without changing the species of the mineral (ISOMORPHISM). Minerals combine with each other to make up rocks, which, as distinguished from minerals, are of heterogeneous composition. Minerals may occur in the massive state when conditions for the formation of crystals are unfavorable. Among the important physical properties of minerals are specific gravity, hardness, cleavage, fracture, luster, color, transparency, streak, striations, tenacity, fusibility, heat conductivity, taste, odor, feel, magnetism, and electrical properties. Minerals originate by precipitation from solution, by the cooling and hardening of magmas, by the condensation of gases or gaseous action on country rock, and by METAMORPHISM. Minerals in rocks are frequently replaced by other minerals through the action of water or gases (metasomatism). Minerals, especially the metals, are of great economic importance to a highly industrialized civilization, entering into the composition of many manufactured articles. Many minerals which would otherwise be of no economic significance are highly valued as gems (see GEM). Mineralogy, a branch of geology, is the science of minerals. See J. L. Gillson, *Industrial Minerals and Rocks* (1960); C. S. Hurlbut, Jr., *Minerals and Man* (1968); Brian Mason and L. G. Berry, *Elements of Mineralogy* (1968); C. J. Morrissey, ed., *Mineral Specimens* (1968); J. D. Dana, *Manual of Mineralogy* (18th ed., rev. by C. S. Hurlbut, Jr., 1971).

mineral oil: see PETROLATUM.

mineral water, spring water containing various mineral salts, especially the carbonates, chlorides, phosphates, silicates, sulfides, and sulfates of calcium, iron, lithium, magnesium, potassium, sodium, and other metals. Various gases may also be present, e.g., carbon dioxide, hydrogen sulfide, nitrogen, and inert gases. Ordinary well or spring water, in contrast, contains far fewer substances, mostly dissolved sulfates and carbonates, and calcium and other alkali and alkaline earth metals. Many mineral waters also contain trace elements that are thought to have therapeutic value. Spa therapy, widely practiced in Europe, advocates bathing in and drinking mineral waters as a cure for a variety of diseases. Many authorities believe that the success of such therapy really results from the beneficial effects of rest and relaxation. Famous European resorts include Bath, Spa, Aix-les-Bains, Aachen, Baden-Baden, and Karlovy Vary (Carlsbad). Prominent among resorts in the United States are Poland, Maine; Saratoga Springs, N.Y.; Berkeley Springs and White Sulphur Springs, W.Va.; Hot Springs, Ark.; French Lick, Ind.; Waukesha, Wis.; and Las Vegas Hot Springs, N.Mex. Many mineral waters are now prepared synthetically, the various mineral ingredients being added to ordinary water in proportions determined by careful chemical analysis of the original ingredients. See SPRING.

Mineral Wells, city (1970 pop. 18,411), Palo Pinto and Parker counties, N Texas; inc. 1882. Among its industrial products are clay pipe, electronic equipment, and craft instruments. The mineral water there made this hill city a popular health resort in the late 19th and early 20th cent., and oil activity in the area also spurred the city's growth. Tourists and sportsmen are attracted by Possum Kingdom Lake and State Park to the northwest. To the east is Lake Mineral Wells, a reservoir in the Trinity River system. Nearby is Fort Wolters, a helicopter training school.

miner's lung: see PNEUMOCONIOSIS.

Minerva (mĭnûr'və), in Roman religion, goddess of handicrafts and the arts. Probably of Etruscan origin, she was worshiped in various parts of ancient Rome, most notably with Jupiter and Juno in the great Capitoline temple. Her temple on the Aventine Hill was a meeting place for skilled craftsmen, actors, and writers. She was identified with the Olympian Athena.

Ming (mĭng), dynasty of China that ruled from 1368 to 1644. The first Ming emperor, Chu Yüan-chang (ruled 1368–98), a former Buddhist monk, expelled the Mongol YÜAN dynasty (1371) and unified all of China proper (1382). Succeeding emperors from their capitals at Nanking and Peking consolidated an empire that at its height extended from Burma to Korea. Seven great naval expeditions were sent at considerable cost to SE Asia, India, and Arabia for tribute and trade (1405–33), but ceased when the dynasty resumed the traditional Chinese preoccupation with Central Asian relations. Despite a strong effort to exclude foreign maritime trade, European settlements were made at Macao and Canton. Christian missionaries penetrated the Chinese hinterlands, and Europeans, such as Matteo RICCI, brought Western ideas to the Ming court. In government and in cultural life the Ming attempted to eradicate all Mongol influences. Civil service examinations were reinstituted and strict Confucianism was enforced. An encyclopedia, a dictionary, and many scholarly works were produced, and the novel and drama reached great heights. Painting generally reflected the Sung style, but architecture soared to a new magnificence. The delicate monochromatic porcelain of the Ming period is often considered the finest achievement of Chinese ceramics. Oppressive taxation and factionalism in government in the later years of the dynasty incited revolts among peasants in the border regions and prepared the way for the Manchu conquest of China (see CH'ING). See L. C. Goodrich, *Dictionary of Ming Biography, 1368–1644* (1975).

Mingan Islands (mĭng'gən), group of 15 small islands and many islets, E Que., Canada, in the St. Lawrence River, N of Anticosti island. They were discovered (1535) by Jacques Cartier, the French explorer. In 1836 the islands were acquired by the Hudson's Bay Company.

Minghetti, Marco (mär'kō mĕngĕt'tē), 1818–86, Italian political leader. A former papal minister, Minghetti—a liberal conservative—became a supporter of Italian unification as a result of his association with Count Cavour, under whom he served in the foreign office of the kingdom of Sardinia and as minister of the interior. He became premier in 1863 but was forced to resign the following year over questions of regional loyalties and the location of the Italian capital. After unification Minghetti headed a conservative cabinet (1873–76), until the leftists under Agostino Depretis gained power in March, 1876. He then led the opposition in the parliament, although toward the end of his life he advocated closer cooperation between conservatives and liberals.

Mingrelia (mĭn-grē'lēə), lowland region, SE European USSR, in Georgia, bordering the Black Sea. Tea and grapes are the chief products. Poti is the main port. The COLCHIS of the ancients, Mingrelia was a vassal principality (with Zugdidi as capital) under the Ottoman Empire. It was annexed to Russia in 1803. The Mingrelians (also called Megrelians) are closely related in culture and language to the Georgians.

Minh, Duong Van (dōōng vän mĕn), 1916–, Vietnamese army officer and political leader. He served (1940–52) in France's colonial army and later fought (1955–62) against the Viet Cong guerrillas. He was a military advisor (1962–63) to President Diem, whom he helped to overthrow (1963), and he was head of government in 1963–64. Minh subsequently went into exile in Thailand, but he returned in 1968 and became a rallying point for opponents of President THIEU. Originally a presidential candidate in 1971, Minh withdrew, charging Thieu with rigging the elections.

Minho, Span. *Miño* (both: mē'nyō), river, c.210 mi (340 km) long, rising in Galicia, NW Spain, and flowing generally SW to the Atlantic Ocean. The Sil is its chief tributary. The lower part of the Minho forms a section of the border between Spain and Portugal. Hydroelectricity is produced near Orense, Spain.

Miniamin (mĭnĭ'əmĭn). **1** See MIAMIN **2.** **2** Officer under Hezekiah. 2 Chron. 31.15. **3** Trumpeter at the dedication of the wall. Neh. 12.41.

miniature bull terrier, breed of small, muscular dog developed in England in the early 19th cent. It stands up to 14 in. (35.6 cm) high at the shoulder and weighs about 17 lb (7.7 kg). Its short, flat, harsh coat is glossy white or white with brindle patches. As the bull terrier was being created from the bulldog and the white English terrier, dogs were produced in a wide variety of sizes. The toys, weighing from 4 to 7 lb (1.8–3.2 kg), were selectively bred and exhibited until about 1914, when interest in them waned. The medium-sized or miniature bull terriers have retained their popularity to this day and have continued to be bred to resemble in every detail the standard-sized bull terriers. The miniature is shown in the miscellaneous class at dog shows sanctioned by the American Kennel Club. See DOG.

miniature painting [Ital.,=artwork, especially manuscript initial letters, done with the red lead pigment *minium;* the word originally had no implication as to size]. In a general sense the term denotes any small, detailed kind of painting, including medieval ILLUMINATION and much of the finest painting of India and Persia. It is also used to refer to diminutive portraits. Among the earliest European masters of this latter art were Holbein the Younger, Jean Clouet, and Jean Fouquet. English masters famous for their miniatures in the 16th and 17th cent. were Nicholas Hilliard, Isaac Oliver, Samuel Cooper, and Richard Cosway. The early portrait miniatures were executed in a precise, sometimes precious style. Two artists of the 18th cent., the Swede Peter Adolphe Hall and the Venetian Rosalba Carriera, introduced a new freedom of brushstroke, even within the small format. Among those who executed elegant and intimate miniatures in France during the 18th and 19th cent. were Nattier, Fragonard, Boucher, and Isabey. In colonial America, C. W. Peale, Benbridge, Copley, Peter Pelham, and E. G. Malbone were notable exponents of the art. Watercolor on parchment, paper, porcelain, or ivory was the most frequently employed medium for miniatures. The art virtually died with the advent of photography. The Metropolitan Museum, the Louvre, and the Wallace Collection in London have notable collections of miniatures. See articles on individuals, e.g., Nicholas HILLIARD and articles on INDIAN ART AND ARCHITECTURE and on PERSIAN ART AND ARCHITECTURE. See T. H. Colding, *Aspects of Miniature Painting* (1953); Elvehjem Art Center, *Indian Miniature Painting* (1971); S. C. Welch, *A King's Book of Kings* (1972).

miniature pinscher, breed of lively TOY DOG originating in Germany in the late 19th cent. It stands from 10 to 12 in. (25.4–30.5 cm) high at the shoulder and weighs from 8 to 10 lb (3.6–4.5 kg). Its short, smooth, flat-lying coat may be red, black with tan markings, or brown marked with rust or yellow. The miniature pinscher was produced by breeding down the Doberman pinscher. It makes an excellent house pet and watchdog. See DOG.

miniature schnauzer: see SCHNAUZER.

minibike: see MOTORCYCLE.

Minidoka project, S Idaho, in the Snake River valley. Developed by the U.S. Bureau of Reclamation, it irrigates more than one million acres (404,700 hectares) of land, extending c.300 mi (480 km) from Ashton, discontinuously along the Snake River, to Gooding. The Snake is impounded by Minidoka Dam (completed 1906), forming Lake Walcott, and by American Falls Dam (1927), which forms American Falls Reservoir. Some of the Snake's tributaries are also impounded for use by the project. Jackson Lake, in Wyoming, stores water for the project, and additional water is furnished by Palisades Reservoir (part of the Palisades project), just W of the Idaho-Wyoming line. Minidoka also provides flood control on the river.

minimum wage, lowest wage legally permitted in an industry or in a government or other organization. The goal in establishing minimum wages has been to assure wage earners a standard of living above the lowest permitted by health and decency. The minimum has been set by labor unions through collective bargaining, by arbitration, by board action, and, finally, by legislation. Introduced (1894) in New Zealand through compulsory arbitration, it rapidly became part of the social legislation of almost all countries. Although Federal minimum wage laws were at first held unconstitutional in the United States, a strong fight by organized labor for enactment culminated in the passage (1938) of the Fair Labor Standards Act, which set minimum wages for workers engaged in interstate commerce (with some exceptions); the act also set up industry committees to recommend rates for every industry. In 1949 the minimum wage was set at $.75 per hour. Thereafter, it was raised several times (in 1955 to $1.00, in 1961 to $1.25, in 1966 to $1.60, and in 1974 to $2.30 per hour). The 1974 law covered between 7 and 8 million workers not previously covered, including, among others, state and local government employees, most domestic workers, and some employees of chain stores. See WAGES and PRICE. See Seth Richardson, *The Minimum Wage* (1927); W. G. Bowen, *Wage Behavior in the Postwar Period* (1961); E. N. Votaw, *Cases and Materials on Government Regulation of Wages* (1966).

mining, extraction of solid mineral resources from the earth. These resources include ores, which contain commercially valuable amounts of metals, such as iron and aluminum; precious stones, such as diamonds; building stones, such as granite; and solid fuels, such as coal and oil shale. The search for and discovery of mineral deposits is called PROSPECTING, or exploration. When a mineral deposit is found, it is studied to determine if it can be mined profitably. If so, the deposit can be worked or extracted by a variety of mining methods. Surface mining, open-pit, or open-cut, mining, strip mining (see COAL MINING), and QUARRYING are the most common mining methods that start from the earth's surface and maintain exposure to the surface throughout the extraction period. The excavation usually has stepped, or benched, side slopes and can reach depths as low as 1,500 ft (460 m). In strip mining the soft overburden, or waste soil, overlying the ore or coal is easily removed. In open-pit mining the barren rock material over the ore body normally requires drilling and blasting to break it up for removal. A typical mining cycle consists of drilling holes into the rock in a pattern, loading the holes with explosives, or blasting agents, and blasting the rock in order to break it into a size suitable for loading and hauling to the mill, concentrator, or treatment plant. There the metals or other desired substances are extracted from the rocks (see METALLURGY). Under certain circumstances surface mining can become prohibitively expensive and underground mining may be considered. A major factor in the decision to operate by underground mining rather than surface mining is the strip ratio, or the number of units of waste material in a surface mine that must be removed in order to extract one unit of ore. Once this ratio becomes large, surface mining is no longer attractive. The objective of underground mining is to extract the ore below the surface of the earth safely, economically, and with as little waste as possible. The entry from the surface to an underground mine may be through an adit, or horizontal tunnel, a shaft (see SHAFT SINKING), or vertical tunnel, or a declined shaft. A typical underground mine has a number of roughly horizontal levels at various depths below the surface, and these spread out from the access to the surface. Ore is mined in stopes, or rooms. Material left in place to support the ceiling is called a pillar and can sometimes be recovered afterward. A vertical internal connection between two levels of a mine is called a winze if it was made by driving downward and a raise if it was made by driving upward. A modern underground mine is a highly mechanized operation requiring little work with pick and shovel. Rubber-tired vehicles, rail haulage, and multiple drill units are commonplace. In order to protect miners and their equipment much attention is paid to mine safety. Mine ventilation provides fresh air underground and at the same time removes noxious gases as well as dangerous dusts that might cause lung disease, e.g., silicosis. Roof support is accomplished with timber, concrete, or steel supports or, most commonly, with roof bolts, which are long steel rods used to bind the exposed roof surface to the rock behind it. There are a number of other mining methods. In solution mining the valuable mineral is brought into a liquid solution by some chemical or bacteria. The resultant liquid is pumped to the surface, where the mineral or metal is taken out of solution by PRECIPITATION or by ion exchange (e.g., the FRASCH PROCESS). In glory-hole mining a steep-sided, funnel-shaped surface excavation is connected to tunnels below it. Rocks blasted off the sides of the excavation fall into the tunnels, from which they are then removed. Gopher mining is an old-fashioned method still used in very small mines. Narrow, small holes are driven in order to extract the ore (e.g., gold) as cheaply as possible. In placer mining no excavation is involved; instead, gravel, sand, or talus is removed from deposits by hand, hydraulic nozzles, or dredging. The ore is separated from the waste by panning or sluicing. See Robert Peele and J. A. Church, ed., *Mining Engineer's Handbook* (3d ed.; 2 vol., 1941); R. S. Lewis and G. B. Clark, *Elements of Mining* (3d ed. 1964); Eugene Pfleider, ed., *Surface Mining* (1968); G. C. Amstutz, *Glossary of Mining Geology* (1971).

mining engineering: see ENGINEERING.

minister, in diplomacy: see DIPLOMATIC SERVICE; EXTRATERRITORIALITY.

minister, in government: see CABINET.

ministry, in religion, term used to designate the clergy of Protestant churches, particularly those who repudiate the claims of APOSTOLIC SUCCESSION. The ceremony by which the candidate receives the office of a minister is called ordination. Protestant ordination, unlike holy orders in the Roman Catholic Church, is not a sacrament. The Reformation doctrine of the "priesthood of all believers" underlies the inclination of many Protestant bodies to reduce the distinction between ministry and laity. In certain Protestant groups, e.g., the Plymouth Brethren, the ordination of ministers is dispensed with altogether. The Society of Friends (Quakers) ordains but makes little practical distinction between ministers and laity. Lutheranism and Presbyterianism invest the office with great dignity. Methodism (in the United States but not in Great Britain) has an episcopal form of church organization but one quite unlike the episcopacy of the Church of England. Fundamental to most Protestant groups is the belief that the soul can go to God without the need of priestly mediation. Hence the function of the ministry is interpreted strictly as one of assistance to the religious life through preaching, the administration of sacraments, and counseling. See H. R. Niebuhr and D. D. Williams, ed., *The Ministry in Historical Perspective* (1956); R. S. Paul, *Ministry* (1965); D. D. Hall, *The Faithful Shepherd* (1972).

Minitari Indians: see HIDATSA INDIANS.

minium: see RED LEAD.

mink, semiaquatic carnivorous mammal of the genus *Mustela,* closely related to the WEASEL and highly prized for its fur. One species, *Mustela vison,* is found over most of North America and another, *M. lutreola,* inhabits Europe—where it is now rare except in Russia—and central Asia. The mink has a slender, arched body, with a long neck, short legs, and a bushy tail. The fur is thick and shiny; in wild strains it is rich brown all over the body, except for a white throat patch. Like other members of the weasel family, minks have musk glands that produce an acrid secretion. Excellent swimmers, they usually live near water, where they catch much of their food. The American mink feeds on aquatic mammals, such as muskrat, as well as fish, frogs, crustaceans, and birds. It is about 20 to 28 in. (51–71 cm) long, including the 7 to 9 in. (18–23 cm) tail. Much of the mink used in the fur trade is bred and raised on farms, where many color varieties have been produced. Descendants of escaped farm animals have established mink populations where none previously existed, e.g., in Great Britain and Iceland. Minks are classified in the phylum CHORDATA, subphylum Vertebrata, class Mammalia, order Carnivora, family Mustelidae.

Minkowski, Hermann (hĕr'män mĭnkôf'skē), 1864–1909, Russian mathematician. He was educated in Germany and was professor at the Univ. of Königsberg (1894–96), the Federal Institute of Technology, Zürich (1896–1902), and the Univ. of Göttingen (1902–9). He is well known for his contribution to the development of the theory of numbers and for having evolved a four-dimensional geometry of space and time that influenced the formulation of the general theory of relativity. He also contributed to the theory of quadratic forms.

Minneapolis (mĭn″ēăp′əlĭs), city (1970 pop. 434,400), seat of Hennepin co., E Minn., at the head of navigation on the Mississippi River, at St. Anthony Falls; inc. 1856. The largest city in the state and a port of entry, it is also a major industrial and rail hub. With adjacent St. Paul (the two are known as the Twin Cities), it is the processing, distributing, and trade center for a vast grain and cattle area. Four of the world's five largest milling companies have their headquarters there. Chief among the many manufactures are computers and electronic equipment, instruments, graphic art products, machinery, fabricated metals, and textiles and garments. The falls were visited by Louis Hennepin in 1683; Fort Snelling was established in 1819; and a sawmill was built at the falls in 1821. The village of St. Anthony was settled c.1839 on the east side of the river near the falls. Minneapolis originated on the west side of the river c.1847 and included much of the reservation of Fort Snelling. It annexed St. Anthony in 1872. The city became the country's foremost lumber center, and after the plains were planted with wheat and the railroads were built, flour milling developed, with the 50-ft (15-m) falls supplying power. The city was laid out with wide streets and has 22 lakes and 153 parks. In Minnehaha Park is the Stevens House (1849), the first frame house in Minneapolis. Also of interest are Fort Snelling State Park, several art galleries and museums (including the American Swedish Institute), The Guthrie Theater, and the Minneapolis Grain Exchange. The Minnesota Symphony was founded there in 1903. The city is the seat of the Univ. of Minnesota, Augsburg College, and the Minnesota College of Art and Design. In extensive redevelopment programs begun in the early 1960s, the main shopping avenue was converted into a 10-block mall lined with trees and flowers; a skyway system of sidewalks was provided for pedestrians; and a 51-story skyscraper and other noteworthy buildings were erected. See Stanley Baldinger, *Planning and Governing the Metropolis: The Twin Cities Experience* (1971); C. R. Walker, *American City*, (1937, repr. 1971).

Minnehaha Falls (mĭn″ēhä′hä) [laughing water], 53 ft (16.1 m) high, SE Minn., in Minnehaha Creek, which flows from Lake Minnetonka (23 sq mi/60 sq km) SE to the Mississippi River. The surrounding area, including the gorge cut by the receding falls, is a state park. Most of the year only a thin trickle of water passes over the falls. The name Minnehaha is immortalized in Longfellow's *Hiawatha*.

minnesinger (mĭn′ĭsĭng″ər), a medieval German knight, poet, and singer of *Minne*, or courtly love. Originally imitators of Provençal TROUBADOURS, minnesingers developed their own style in the 13th and 14th cent. Some of their poems are among the best of Middle High German lyric verse. Important exponents of *Minnesang* included Heinrich von Morungen, Walther von der Vogelweide, and Oswald von Wolkenstein, as well as Gottfried von Strassburg, Wolfram von Eschenbach, and other authors of epics. Wagner's opera *Tannhäuser* is based on minnesinger art and tradition.

Minnesota (mĭn″ĭsō′tə), state (1970 pop. 3,805,069), 84,068 sq mi (217,736 sq km), N central United States, in the Great Lakes region, admitted as the 32d state of the Union in 1858. SAINT PAUL, the capital, and its twin city MINNEAPOLIS, together have almost a third of the state's population. DULUTH is the third-largest city. Except for Alaska, Minnesota is the most northerly of all the states (reaching lat. 49°23′55″N). Minnesota is bounded on the north by the Canadian provinces of Manitoba and Ontario, on the east by Lake Superior and Wisconsin (the St. Croix and Mississippi rivers forming much of the border with that state), on the south by Iowa, and on the west by South Dakota and North Dakota. The climate is humid continental. Winter locks the land in snow, and spring is brief; summers are hot. Prehistoric glaciers left marshes, boulder-strewn hills, and rich, gray drift soil stretching from the northern pine wilderness to the broad southern prairies. In the eastern part of the state are mountains from which iron ore is extracted. In the Vermilion and Cuyuna ranges the iron (discovered in 1884 and 1911) is mined underground, but in the rich MESABI iron range (1890) open-pit methods are used. As richer ores diminish, new methods are being developed to use lower-grade ores such as taconite. Plants set up to concentrate taconite into pellets for easy shipment have given rise to new communities like Silver Bay. Minnesota ranks first in the nation in the production of iron and manganiferous ore. Granite (from St. Cloud) and sand and gravel production are

also among the largest in the country. South of the iron country, famous for its still remembered raw boom towns, lie rolling hills. In the south and the west are prairies, the fine farming country of Minnesota. Wheat, once paramount in the fields, has yielded its preeminence to corn and livestock. The state is a leader in the production of creamery butter, dry milk, cheese, sweet corn, and soybeans. In the early 1950s manufacturing displaced agriculture as the major source of income in Minnesota. Major industries in the state include the manufacture of processed foods, electronic equipment, machinery, paper products, chemicals, and stone, clay, and glass products. St. Paul is one of the nation's largest meat-packing centers. Printing and publishing are also important. Reforestation and the use of smaller trees for pulpwood have helped to keep timber as one of Minnesota's assets, even though the "big woods" of the early 19th cent. have been to a large extent recklessly felled. Today the state has more than 19 million acres (7.7 million hectares) of woodland and two national forests. The days of logging in Minnesota, immortalized in the stories of the legendary Paul Bunyan and his prized possession, Babe the Blue Ox, were brief, but they helped build a number of large fortunes, such as that of Frederick Weyerhaeuser. Another great resource of Minnesota is its water, which has been extensively developed near industrial centers. The state has more than 11,000 lakes and numerous streams and rivers. The rivers feed three great river systems: the Red River of the north and its tributaries in the west run N to Hudson Bay; the streams that run E into Lake Superior eventually help to supply the St. Lawrence; and the Mississippi flows south from its sluggish beginning in Minnesota in Lake Itasca, gathering volume from the waters of the St. Croix and Minnesota rivers before leaving the state. Locks and other improvements enable barge traffic to pass over the Falls of St. Anthony into Minneapolis. Duluth, at the western tip of Lake Superior, has the largest inland harbor in the United States. With the completion of the SAINT LAWRENCE SEAWAY (1959) and a marine terminal, the city became a key port for overseas trade. Archaeological evidence indicates that Minnesota was inhabited long before the time of the Mound Builders. A skeleton ("Minnesota Man"), found in 1931 near Pelican Falls, is believed to date from the Pleistocene epoch, c.20,000 years ago. Much important archaeological information concerning the early inhabitants of North America has been found in Minnesota. There are some experts who argue on the basis of the KENSINGTON RUNE STONE and other evidence that the first white men to reach Minnesota were the Norsemen, but others refute this. That French fur traders came in the mid-17th cent. is undeniable. Other traders, explorers, and missionaries of New France also penetrated the country. Among these were Radisson and Groseilliers, Verendrye, the sieur Duluth, and Father Hennepin and Michel Aco, who discovered the Falls of St. Anthony (the site of Minneapolis). At the time the French arrived, the dominant groups of Indians were the Ojibwa Indians in the east and the Sioux Indians in the west. Both were friendly to the French and contributed to the fur-trading empire of New France. Minnesota remained excellent country for fur trade throughout the British regime that followed the French and Indian Wars and continued so after the War of 1812, when the AMERICAN FUR COMPANY became dominant and the company's men helped to develop the area. The eastern part of Minnesota had been included in the NORTHWEST TERRITORY and was governed under the Ordinance of 1787; the western part was joined to the United States by the LOUISIANA PURCHASE. Further exploration was pursued by Jonathan Carver (1766-67), Zebulon M. Pike (1805-6), Henry Schoolcraft (1820, 1829), and Stephen H. Long (1823). The fisheries of Lake Superior were tapped by the American Fur Company, and they later became important economically. Only after the War of 1812, however, did settlement begin in earnest. In 1820, Fort St. Anthony (later Fort Snelling) was founded as a guardian of the frontier. There, a gristmill established in 1823 initiated the industrial development of Minneapolis. Treaties (1837, 1845, 1851, and 1855) with the Ojibwa and the Sioux, by which the U.S. government acquired Indian lands, and the opening of a land office at St. Croix Falls in 1848 initiated a period of real expansion. By 1848 the settlers were already clamoring to organize the area as a territory. They held a convention at Stillwater in that year and elected Henry H. Sibley, an American fur trader, to petition Congress for territorial status, which was granted in 1849. The Missouri and White Earth rivers were the western boundary. A land boom grew as towns were platted, railroads chartered, and roads built. Attention was turned to education, and the Univ. of Minnesota was started in 1851. At present the school, with its many associated campuses, exerts a great influence on the cultural life of the state. The building (1851-53) of the Soo Ship Canal at Sault Ste Marie, Mich., opened a water route for lake shipping eastward. The Panic of 1857 hit Minnesota particularly hard because of land speculation, but difficult times did not prevent the achievement of statehood in 1858, with St. Paul as the capital and Sibley as the state's first governor. The population had swelled from 6,000 in 1850 to more than 150,000 in 1857. By 1870 there were nearly 440,000 people. Chiefly a land of small farmers (mainly of British, German, and Irish extraction), Minnesota supported the Union in the Civil War and supplied much wheat to the Northern armies. During the war years and afterward the Sioux reacted to broken promises, fraudulent dealings, and the encroachment of the white men on their lands with massacres and raids. A band of Sioux under Little Crow was defeated by H. H. Sibley, at that time a colonel, and Minnesota was consequently freed of Indian wars. Meanwhile, settlement boomed, aided by the Homestead Act of 1862. Later in the century came immigrants from Scandinavia—Swedes, Norwegians, and Finns. Lumbering, which had begun in 1839 with a sawmill on the St. Croix, became paramount, and logging camps were established. Fortunes were made quickly in the '70s and '80s, as the railroads pushed west, aided by the efforts of James J. Hill. A boom in wheat made the Minnesota flour mills famous across the world and brought wealth to flour manufacturers such as John S. Pillsbury. Farmers, however, suffered from such natural disasters as the blizzard of 1873 and insect plagues from 1874 to 1876. To these were added the miseries that accompanied the downward trend of the national economy, and Minnesota became a center of farmers' discontent, expressed in the GRANGER MOVEMENT. The opening of the iron mines gave new impetus to Minnesota's economy but also created discontent among the laborers. They joined forces with the farmers in the 1890s in the POPULIST PARTY, one of several third-party movements that challenged the Republican party's traditional leadership in Minnesota. Ignatius Donnelly was one of the Populists' most powerful figures. Renewed agrarian discontent led to the founding of the NONPARTISAN LEAGUE in 1915 by Arthur C. Townley. Farmers and laborers joined forces again in 1920 in the FARMER-LABOR PARTY, which was dominant in the 1930s; Knute Nelson, Floyd B. Olson, and Henrik Shipstead were among its leading figures. The Republicans returned to power in 1939 with the election of Harold Stassen as governor. In 1944 the Farmer-Labor party and the Democrats merged. The most successful leader of the new party, the Democratic Farmer Labor party (DFL), has been Hubert H. Humphrey, who has been elected to the U.S. Senate four times and was Vice President from 1965 to 1969. Orville Freeman, DFL governor from 1955 to 1961, was Secretary of Agriculture from 1961 to 1969. Since the 1950s the DFL and the Republicans have vied sharply in contests for state offices. With the exception of 1952, 1956, and 1972, Minnesota has voted Democratic in every presidential election since 1932. The state is governed under the 1858 constitution. The legislature has 67 senators elected for four-year terms and 134 representatives elected for two-year terms. The governor is elected for a four-year term and may succeed himself. Wendell R. Anderson, a member of the DFL, was elected governor in 1970 and was reelected in 1974. Minnesota sends 2 Senators and 8 Representatives to Congress; it has 10 electoral votes. The state has been notable for experimentation in novel features of local government and has also been a leader in the use of cooperatives. This phenomenon is perhaps explained by the cooperative heritage present among its many people of Scandinavian descent. Credit unions, cooperative creameries, grain elevators, and purchasing associations were supported by legislation in 1919 that protected the institutions and instructed the state department of agriculture to encourage them. Today there are several thousand cooperative associations in Minnesota serving diversified needs. A nuclear power plant built by the Atomic Energy Commission is located at Elk River. Since the mid-19th cent. the state has become progressively more urban. In 1970 the urban population was two thirds of the total. Many people come to Minnesota for treatment at the famous Mayo Clinic in Rochester, and surgeons at the Univ. of Minnesota have won recognition for their development of new heart-surgery techniques. The beauty of Minnesota's lakes and dense green forests, as seen in Voyageurs National Park, has long attracted vacationers, and the abundant fish in the state's many rivers, lakes, and streams provide excellent fishing. Also of interest to tourists are the Grand Portage and Pipestone national monuments (see NATIONAL PARKS AND MONUMENTS, table), Itasca State Park (site of the headwaters of the Mississippi River), the Minnesota Museum of Mining (near Chisholm), and the world's largest open-pit iron mine at HIBBING. The Minnesota Symphony Orchestra is nationally known, and a theater in Minneapolis houses the professional company of Tyrone Guthrie. Minnesota has contributed important literary figures to the nation, including Sinclair Lewis, F. Scott Fitzgerald, and O. E. Rølvaag. The economist Thorstein Veblen and Charles A. Lindbergh were also born in the state. See William Watts Folwell, *A History of Minnesota* (4 vol., 1921–30); Theodore Christianson, *Minnesota: The Land of the Sky-tinted Water* (5 vol., 1935); James Gray, *Pine, Stream, and Prairie* (1945); T. C. Blegen and T. L. Nydahl, *Minnesota History* (1960); Lowry Nelson, *The Minnesota Community: County and Town in Transition* (1960); Theodore C. Blegen, *Minnesota: A History of the State* (1963); Elden Johnson, *Prehistoric Peoples of Minnesota* (1969).

Minnesota, river, 332 mi (534 km) long, rising in Big Stone Lake at the W boundary of Minnesota and flowing SE to Mankato, then NE to the Mississippi S of Minneapolis. Early called the St. Peter or St. Pierre, it was an important route of explorers and fur traders. The river follows the valley of the prehistoric River Warren, the outlet of Lake Agassiz. See Evan Jones, *The Minnesota: Forgotten River* (1962).

Minnesota, University of, mainly at Minneapolis; land-grant and state supported; coeducational; chartered 1851 and 1868, opened as a university 1869. The schools of agriculture, forestry, home economics and veterinary medicine are at St. Paul. Other branches are at Duluth, Morris, and Crookston. The university is affiliated with the Mayo Foundation for medical research and education at Rochester as well as with the Institute of Technology, the Heart Hospital (heart treatment and research), and the Mayo Memorial Medical Center (see MAYO, Charles H.), at Minneapolis. The Northrop Memorial Auditorium is on the Minneapolis campus. The university's library houses extensive research materials in American and European history, and the Museum of Natural History has a noted collection of animal life displays. See histories by James Gray (1951, 1958).

Minnetonka (mĭnĭtŏng'kə), village (1970 pop. 35,737), Hennepin co., SE Minn., a residential suburb of Minneapolis, near Lake Minnetonka; inc. 1956.

Minnetonka, Lake: see MINNEHAHA FALLS.

Minni, biblical name of part of Armenia. Jer. 51.27.

Minnith, unidentified place, E Palestine, E of the Jordan. It was associated with Jephthah. Judges 11.33; Ezek. 27.17.

minnow, common name for the Cyprinidae, a large family of freshwater fish which includes the CARP (*Cyprinus carpio*), and of which there are some 300 American species. The European minnow is *Phoxinus phoxinus.* Minnows have soft-rayed fins and teeth in the throat only. Together with the closely allied sucker and catfish families they form the "hearing-aid" group of freshwater fishes, so-called for the complex set of bones extending from the airfloat to the inner ear, which gives them a superior sense of hearing and accounts for their characteristic wariness. The carp is generally considered the largest of the minnow family, although the squawfishes of the Columbia and Colorado rivers average 30 lb (13.5 kg) and the mahseer, a game fish of India, is also large. However, most minnows are small. They have great importance in the cycle of freshwater aquatic life, since they consume aquatic insects, larvae, and crustaceans and in turn serve as food for many larger fish. Most species are dully colored, though a few are brilliantly hued in greens, reds, and yellows. Various members of the family are called shiners, chubs, daces, roaches, breams, and bleaks. The Sacramento chub of California rivers, the creek chub, and the golden shiner, a greenish fish that turns golden during the breeding season, attain a length of 12 in. (2.5 cm). The red-sided and red-bellied daces are also named for the seasonal color changes in the male. The GOLDFISH, genus *Carassius,* is also a member of the minnow family. Certain varieties of KILLIFISH of the family Cyprinodontidae are called topminnows and toothed minnows. The carnivorous mudminnows of the family Umbridae, found in the sluggish waters in the Great Lakes region and the Atlantic coastal lowlands, superficially resemble toothed minnows but are more closely related to the pike; they are also called dogfishes. Minnows are classified in the phylum CHORDATA, subphylum Vertebrata, class Osteichthyes, order Cypriniformes, family Cyprinidae.

Miño, river: see MINHO.

Minoan civilization (mĭnō'ən), ancient Cretan culture representing a stage in the development of the AEGEAN CIVILIZATION. It is named for the legendary King Minos of Crete. The culture was divided by Sir Arthur EVANS into three periods that include the whole of the Bronze Age: Early Minoan (c.3000 B.C.–2200 B.C.), Middle Minoan (c.2200 B.C.–1500 B.C.), and Late Minoan (c.1500 B.C.–1000 B.C.). Early Minoan saw the slow rise of the culture from a neolithic state with the importation of metals, the tentative use of bronze, and the appearance of a hieroglyphic writing. In the Middle Minoan period the great palaces appeared at Cnossus and Phaestus; a pictographic script (known as Linear A) was used; ceramics, ivory carving, and metalworking reached their peak; and Minoan maritime power extended across the Mediterranean. Toward the end of the period an earthquake, and possibly an invasion, destroyed Cnossus, but the palace was rebuilt. During this period there is evidence of a new script (Linear B) at Cnossus, which argues the presence of Mycenaean Greeks. Other luxurious palaces existed at this time at Gournia, Cydonia (now Khánia), and elsewhere. Cnossus was again destroyed c.1500 B.C., probably as a result of an earthquake and subsequent invasion from the Mycenaean mainland. The palace at Cnossus was finally destroyed c.1400 B.C., and the Late Minoan period faded out in poverty and obscurity. After the final destruction of Cnossus, the cultural center of the Aegean passed to the Greek mainland (see MYCENAEAN CIVILIZATION). See Sir Arthur J. Evans, *Palace of Minos* (4 vol., 1921–25, repr. 1964); J. D. S. Pendlebury, *Archaeology of Crete* (1939, repr. 1963); Keith Branigan, *Foundations of Palatial Crete* (1970); Sinclair Hood, *The Minoans* (1971); Nicholas Platon, *Zakros* (1971).

Minobe, Tatsukichi (tä'tso͞okē'chē mēnō'bā), 1873–1948, Japanese professor of law at Tokyo Imperial Univ. After serving in the ministry of home affairs and studying in Europe, he became dean of the faculty of law at Tokyo Univ. and a member of the Imperial Academy (1911). Because in an early book he stated that power rested with the people and described the emperor as an "organ of the state," he was accused (1935) of lese majesty and was forced to resign from the house of peers. After World War II, he was appointed to the privy council. See study by F. O. Miller (1965).

Mino da Fiesole (mē'nō dä fyā'zōlā) or **Mino di Giovanni** (dē jōvän'nē), 1429–84, Florentine sculptor of the early Renaissance. He produced many tombs and sculptures for churches. Among the best are the altar in the cathedral at Fiesole, the monument to Count Hugo in the Badia of Florence, and the tombs of Bishop Salutati at Fiesole and of Francesco Tornabuoni in Rome. From 1474 to 1477 he worked on the monument to Pope Paul II in St. Peter's. His religious works vary in execution from a delicate to an overly sweet style. His conception of portrait busts is more vigorous and includes those of Niccolò Strozzi (Berlin) and Astorgio Manfredi (National Gall. of Art, Washington, D.C.). See W. R. Valentiner, *Studies of Renaissance Sculpture* (1950).

Minorca (mĭnôr'kə), Span. *Menorca,* Spanish island (1970 pop. 50,217), 271 sq mi (702 km), in the W Mediterranean Sea, the second largest of the BALEARIC ISLANDS. Port MAHÓN is the chief city and port. The terrain is mostly low but has a hilly center. Cereals, wine, olive oil, and flax are the chief products. Much of the agriculture is irrigated. Lobster fishing, the export of livestock, and shoe making add to the economy. Tourism is also important. A great number of megalithic monuments have been found. Minorca shared the history of the other Balearic Islands until 1708, when it was occupied by the English during the War of the Spanish Succession. England retained it until the Seven Years War, when it was seized by the French. The Treaty of Paris (1763) restored Minorca to Britain, but the French and Spanish again seized it (1782) in the American Revolution. In 1798, in the French Revolutionary Wars, England regained control; the Peace of Amiens (1802) awarded Minorca to Spain. In the Spanish civil war of 1936–39 Minorca remained in Loyalist hands until Feb., 1939, while Majorca, the largest of the Balearic Islands, early passed to the Nationalists.

minority, in international law, population group with a characteristic culture and sense of identity occupying a subordinate political status. Religious minorities were known from ancient times, but ethnic minorities did not become an issue in European politics until the rise of NATIONALISM in the 19th cent. The potential conflict arose from nationalism's equation of the nation with the identity of the dominant cultural group. The dominant group often tried to compel the minority to conform with the so-called national identity and to eradicate the minority's separate identity. The minority group, in turn, sought to establish its own culture as a national identity by either incorporating with a nearby country that shared its identity or, if none existed, by seceding and forming its own nation. Before World War I the minority problem was especially acute in the AUSTRO-HUNGARIAN MONARCHY, the Ottoman Empire (Turkey), and Russia. During the war each side promised autonomy or independence to minorities in enemy states, and revolts (e.g., of Arabs and Czechs) were encouraged. One of President Woodrow Wilson's FOURTEEN POINTS was the freeing of minorities. The treaties of peace attempted to accomplish this in various ways: they established new nations of one predominant stock (e.g., Hungary, Poland, and Austria) or combined several former minorities (e.g., in Czechoslovakia and Yugoslavia), and they made transfers of territory (e.g., Alsace-Lorraine was returned to France from Germany). Hitler made adroit use of the minority issue to annex the Sudetenland in Czechoslovakia and to attack Poland, thus launching World War II. After the war Czechoslovakia and Poland took the extreme step of deporting all Germans. Communist countries, especially the USSR, have asserted that they do not have minority problems because all ethnic groups are allowed full expression; it has been charged, however, that the USSR represses any overt assertion of an ethnic consciousness as anti-internationalist and therefore counterrevolutionary. Newly emerging African nations often include disparate, sometimes even traditionally inimical tribes, because the national boundaries were artificially set by European colonialists. The resulting conflicts are a major problem for the new nations, e.g., in NIGERIA tension between Hausas and Ibos eventually resulted in the unsuccessful Ibo attempt to form the nation of Biafra. Pakistan was formed in 1947 for the Muslim minority of Hindu India. But the nation combined different peoples who shared only a religion, and in 1971 the Bengalis of East Pakistan, themselves a minority in Pakistan, seceded to form the nation of Bangladesh. Since 1945 the United Nations has been active with respect to minority problems, especially through the Commission on Human Rights. In 1948 the United Nations approved two important documents concerning minorities, the Genocide Convention (see GENOCIDE) and the Universal Declaration of Human Rights. The United States, however, is not a party to either. See. L. P. Mair, *The Protection of Minorities* (1928); O. I. Janowsky, *Nationalities and National Minorities* (1945); I. L. Claude, Jr., *National Minorities* (1955, repr. 1969); Charles Wagley and Marvin Harris, *Mi-*

norities in the New World (1958); J. A. Laponce, *The Protection of Minorities* (1960).

minor planet: see ASTEROID.

Minos (mī'nŏs, -nəs), in Greek mythology, king of Crete, son of Zeus and Europa. He was the husband of Pasiphaë, who bore him Androgeus, Glaucus, Ariadne, and Phaedra. Because Minos failed to sacrifice a beautiful white bull to Poseidon, the god caused Pasiphaë to conceive a lustful passion for the animal, by whom she bore the Minotaur, a monster with the head of a bull and the body of a man. The craftsman Daedalus constructed the labyrinth into which the monster was confined. When King Aegeus of Athens killed Androgeus, Minos vengefully forced Athens to pay him an annual tribute of seven youths and seven maidens. These he shut up inside the labyrinth, where they either starved or were devoured by the Minotaur. Finally THESEUS joined a group of the victims and killed the Minotaur. Minos became the most prosperous king of the Mediterranean area, renowned as much for his justness as his power. Along with Aeacus and Rhadamanthus, he became one of the three judges of Hades. Minos was presumably the name or title of an ancient Cretan king. The MINOAN CIVILIZATION is named for him.

Minot, George Richards (mī'nət), 1885–1950, American physician and pathologist, b. Boston, M.D. Harvard, 1912. From 1928 to 1948 he was professor of medicine at Harvard and director of the Thorndike Memorial Laboratory, Boston City Hospital. He specialized in diseases of the blood, and for his research on the value of liver in treating pernicious anemia he shared with W. P. Murphy and G. H. Whipple the 1934 Nobel Prize in Physiology and Medicine. See biography by F. M. Rackemann (1956).

Minot, Laurence, fl. 1333–52, English poet. He was the author of fervently patriotic war poems on Halidon Hill, the siege of Calais, and other battles. Probably a Yorkshireman, he may have been a soldier or a professional minstrel.

Minot, city (1970 pop. 32,290), seat of Ward co., NW N.Dak., on the Souris River; inc. 1887. It is a commercial and transportation center for an extensive agricultural area. There are lignite mines and oil basins in the region. Industries in the city manufacture concrete, construction blocks, dentures, insulation, farm tools, and carbonated beverages. Minot State College and a state agricultural experiment station are there. Nearby is Minot Air Force Base and a U.S. army missile center. Points of interest include the Theodore Roosevelt Park and Zoo and a nearby wildlife refuge.

Minotaur: see MINOS.

Minquiers, Great Britain: see CHANNEL ISLANDS.

Minseito (mēn"sā'tō), Japanese political party. It is usually called the Liberal party in English. Founded by Shigenobu OKUMA in 1882 as the Kaishinto, or Progressive party, it was dissolved in 1884, reformed into the Shimpoto, and merged with the Jiyuto (see SEIYUKAI) in 1898 to form the Kenseito. Okuma later took his group out of the Kenseito and set up the Kenseihonto, which became the Kokuminto in 1910. A faction of the Kokuminto joined Taro Katsura's Doshikai in 1913 and became the nucleus of the Kenseikai. In 1927 the Kenseikai was reorganized as the Minseito. The cabinets of Takaaki Kato (1924–26), Reijiro Wakatsuki (1926–27, 1931), and Osachi Hamaguchi (1929–31) were Kenseikai or Minseito governments. All parties were dissolved in 1940. After World War II, the Minseito reemerged under the leadership of Shigeru Yoshida and Ichiro Hatoyama as the Liberal party, one of the two strong conservative groups in postwar Japan. It merged with the Democrats in 1955 to form the Liberal-Democratic party. The Minseito was traditionally identified with the Mitsubishi financial interests. See Peter Duus, *Party Rivalry and Political Change in Taishō Japan* (1968).

Minsk (mĭnsk, Rus. mēnsk), city (1970 pop. 916,000), capital of the Belorussian Soviet Socialist Republic and of Minsk oblast, W European USSR, on a tributary of the Berezina. It is one of the largest cultural and industrial centers of the USSR and a large railroad junction with machine, machine-tool, tractor, automobile, textile, and food-processing factories. First mentioned in 1067, it was an outpost on the road from Kiev to Polotsk and was part of the Polotsk principality. It became the capital of the Minsk principality in 1101 and part of Lithuania in 1326. At the end of the 15th cent. it became a great craft and trade center. Magdeburg Law was introduced into the local government of the city in 1499. Joined to Poland in 1569, it passed to Russia in the second partition of Poland (1793). The city's industrial development began in the 1870s. It was one of the largest Jewish centers of Eastern Europe in the Middle Ages, and before World War II some 40% of the population was Jewish. From 1941 to 1943, Minsk was a concentration center for Jews prior to their extermination by the Nazis. Although the city was heavily damaged in the war, several monuments remain. These include a former 17th-century Bernardine convent and the 17th-century Ekaterin Cathedral (formerly called the Petropavlovsk church). Minsk is the site of the Academy of Sciences of the Belorussian SSR (founded 1928), the Belorussian Lenin State Univ. (opened 1919), and the Lenin State Library (founded 1921).

minstrel, professional secular musician of the Middle Ages. The modern application of the term is general and includes the JONGLEURS. Certain very able jongleurs ceased their wanderings and were attached to a court to play or sing the songs of the TROUBADOURS or TROUVÈRES who employed them. To these and to some itinerant musicians was applied in the 14th cent. the term *ménétrier* and later *ménestrel,* from which the word *minstrel* is derived, to indicate a higher social class than jongleur. Increasing in number and influence, these minstrels were organized and given protection of the law. Their function was at times similar to that of the Welsh BARD. See Edmondstoune Duncan, *The Story of Minstrelsy* (1907, repr. 1969).

minstrel show, stage entertainment by white performers made up as Negroes. Thomas Dartmouth Rice, who gave (c.1828) the first solo performance in blackface and introduced the song-and-dance act *Jim Crow,* is called the "father of American minstrelsy." The first public performance of a minstrel show was given in 1843 by the Virginia Minstrels, headed by Daniel Decatur Emmett. Christy's Minstrels (for whom Stephen FOSTER wrote some of his most popular songs) appeared in 1846, headed by Edwin P. CHRISTY. In the first part of the minstrel show the company, in blackface and gaudy costumes, paraded to chairs placed in a semicircle on the stage. The interlocutor then cracked jokes with the end men, and, for a finale, the company passed in review in the "walk around." This part of the minstrel show caricatured the black man, misrepresenting him by grotesque stereotypes that were retained in the minds of white American audiences for many decades. In the second part of the show vaudeville or olio (medley) acts were presented. The third or afterpart was a burlesque on a play or an opera. The minstrel show was at its peak from 1850 to 1870, but passed with the coming of vaudeville, motion pictures, and radio. See Carl Wittke, *Tambo and Bones: A History of the American Minstrel Stage* (1930, repr. 1968).

mint, place where legal coinage is manufactured. The name is derived from the temple of Juno Moneta, Rome, where silver coins were made as early as 269 B.C. Mints existed earlier elsewhere, as in Lydia and in Greece; from there coinage was introduced into Italy. The first U.S. mint was established in Philadelphia in 1792. In 1974, U.S. mints were operated in Philadelphia and Denver. See also NUMISMATICS; COIN; MEDAL.

mint, in botany, common name for members of the Labiatae, a large family of chiefly annual or perennial herbs. Several species are shrubby or climbing forms or, rarely, small trees. Members of the family are found throughout the world, but the chief center of distribution is the Mediterranean region, where these plants form a dominant part of the vegetation. The Labiatae typically have square stems, paired opposite leaves, and white flowers with two lips, the upper divided into two lobes and the lower into three. The leaves sometimes grow in whorls; the flowers may also be shades of red, blue, or purple. The family is well known for the aromatic volatile or essential oils in the foliage, which are used in perfumes, flavorings, and medicines. Among the more important essential oils are those derived from SAGE, LAVENDER, ROSEMARY, PATCHOULI, and the true mints. Many of the commonly used potherbs are from the mint family, e.g., BASIL, THYME, SAVORY, MARJORAM, OREGANO, and the plants mentioned above. As is true of most potherbs and spices, these have a history of medicinal use in domestic remedies. CATNIP, PENNYROYAL, HYSSOP, SELF-HEAL, the HOREHOUND of confectionery, and curative teas from such plants as BEE BALM and YERBA BUENA have been similarly used. Species of the Labiatae are often grown as ornamentals as well as in herb gardens, and in the United States several have escaped cultivation and become naturalized as wild flowers. Types of hyssop, sage, pennyroyal, mint, and lavender are among the prevalent native species. The true

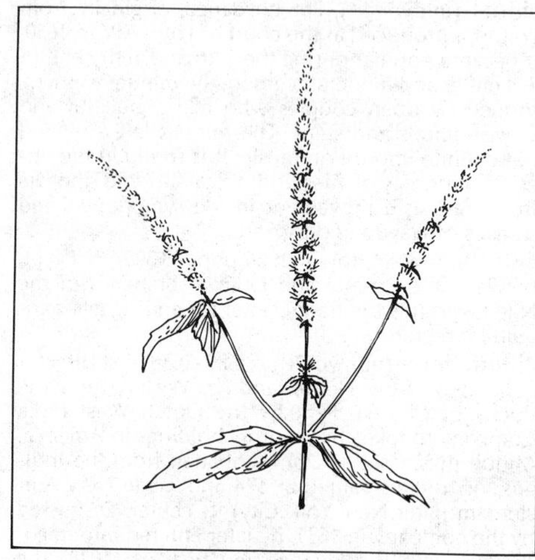

Spearmint, Mentha spicata

mints belong to the genus *Mentha.* Commercially the most important species is peppermint (*M. piperita*). The leaves and tops are sometimes dried and utilized for flavoring and in medicine but are chiefly in demand for the oil, distilled out for use as a carminative and stimulant, for its derivative MENTHOL (obtained also from other mints), and for flavoring purposes, especially in chewing gum and candy and as a disguise for disagreeable tastes of drugs. Spearmint (*M. spicata*) is distinguishable from peppermint by the absence of a leafstalk. Its flavor is milder (the aromatic principle is carvone), and it too is used in chewing gum and medicines and is often cultivated in gardens as a flavoring. Both plants are European perennials now naturalized in the United States. Also useful medicinally and as a source of an essential oil is the pennyroyal. True, or European, pennyroyal (*M. pulegium*) is a prostrate perennial. The species name [Lat.,=fleabane] is a herbalist's name given for the plant's supposed property of driving away fleas. The related American pennyroyal (*Hedeoma pulegioides*) is a branching annual; pennyroyal tea was a traditional domestic remedy. Other American species of *Hedeoma* and similar genera are also called pennyroyal. The mint family is classified in the division MAGNOLIOPHYTA, class Magnoliopsida, order Lamiales.

mint julep: see JULEP.

Minto, Gilbert John Elliot-Murray-Kynynmound, 4th earl of (kĭnĭn'mənd), 1845–1914, British colonial administrator. He entered the army in 1867 and served in several countries before becoming (1884) military secretary to Lord Lansdowne, governor general of Canada. As governor general himself (1898–1904) Minto maintained cordial relations with the Canadian prime minister, Sir Wilfred LAURIER, and became very popular. He then served (1905–10) as viceroy of India, where his personal diplomacy improved relations with Afghanistan. He also worked with John MORLEY to produce the Morley-Minto reforms (1909), which increased native membership on the advisory legislative councils of the viceroy and began India's advance to self-rule. See biography by John Buchan (1924); study by S. R. Wasti (1964).

Minton, English family of potters. The first important member of the family was **Thomas Minton,** 1765–1836, who founded a small pottery at Stoke-on-Trent. He first engraved the famous WILLOW-PATTERN WARE. **Herbert Minton,** 1793–1858, succeeded his father as head of the firm, and to him was due its development and reputation. He enlisted the services of artists and skilled artisans. A memorial museum and library building was erected to him at Stoke-on-Trent.

Minturnae (mĭntûr'nē), ancient town of Latium, Italy, 7 mi (11.3 km) E of Formia. It was important because it controlled the bridge on the Appian Way over the Liris River. Founded by a people called the Aurunci or Ausones, it became a Roman colony (295 B.C.) and a flourishing commercial center. There are important ruins (including an aqueduct), two theaters, forums, and other buildings N of modern Minturno.

Minucius Felix, Marcus (mär'kəs mĭnyōō'shəs fē'lĭks), fl. 2d cent., Christian apologist, author of a dialogue, *Octavius,* one of the earliest Latin apologies. In it a pagan and a Christian discuss the merits of Christian life. See J. H. Freese, *The Octavius of Minucius Felix* (1919).

minuet (mĭnyōōĕt'), French dance, originally from Poitou, introduced at the court of Louis XIV in 1650. It became popular during the 17th and 18th cent. In 3-4 meter and moderate tempo, the minuet was performed by open couples who made graceful and precise glides and steps. The minuet left a refined but definite imprint on music; it is found in the operatic sinfonias of Alessandro Scarlatti and appears frequently as a movement in the symphonies and sonatas of Haydn and Mozart.

Minuf (mĭnōōf'), town (1966 pop. 48,300), N Egypt, between the Rosetta and Dumyat branches of the Nile River. It is the trade center for an irrigated agricultural region.

Minuit, Peter (mĭn'yōōĭt), c.1580–1638, first director general of New Netherland, b. Wesel (then the duchy of Cleves). Sent by the Dutch West India Company to take charge of its holdings in America, Minuit purchased (1626) Manhattan from the Indians for trinkets valued at $24 and made New Amsterdam (later New York City) its center. Dismissed by the company in 1631, he later entered into negotiations with the Swedes and headed (1638) the group sent out to found NEW SWEDEN. He was lost in a hurricane in the West Indies.

Minusinsk (mēnōōsēnsk'), city (1970 pop. 41,000), S central Siberian USSR, in Krasnoyarsk Kray, in the Minusinsk basin and on the Yenisei River. It is a river port and the center of the Minusinsk agricultural and gold- and coal-mining basin. There is a food-processing industry. Minusinsk, founded in 1822, has a natural history museum.

Minute Man National Historical Park: see NATIONAL PARKS AND MONUMENTS (table).

minutemen, in the American Revolution, colonial militiamen or armed citizens who agreed to turn out for service at a minute's notice. The term *minutemen* is used especially for the men who were enrolled (1774) for such service by the Massachusetts provincial congress. These were "the embattled farmers" who fought against the British at Lexington and Concord.

Minya, Al (äl mē'nyə), city (1970 est. pop. 122,000), capital of Al Minya governorate, N central Egypt, on the Nile River. It is an agricultural trade center. Products include ginned cotton, flour, and rugs.

Minya Konka (mĭn'yə kŏng'kə), Chinese *Kung-ka Shan,* peak, 24,900 ft (7,590 m) high, SW Szechwan prov., central China, in the Himalayas; one of the highest points in China. It was climbed (1932) by an American expedition.

Miocene epoch (mī'əsēn), fourth epoch of the TERTIARY PERIOD in the Cenozoic era of geologic time (see GEOLOGIC ERAS, table). North America was more extensively submerged in the Miocene than in the preceding OLIGOCENE EPOCH and underwent considerable crustal disturbances. The Atlantic and Gulf coasts were flooded about as extensively as in the EOCENE EPOCH. Miocene rocks are found along the Atlantic as far N as Martha's Vineyard, but the series, everywhere thin, is thickest and least interrupted from New Jersey to Maryland. On the Gulf coast it extends from Florida westward to Texas. The Atlantic series is chiefly marls, clays, and sands, with diatomaceous earth; the Florida series, chiefly limestone (Florida having risen as an island in the late Oligocene); the Gulf series, limestone and clastic sediments. On the Pacific coast, the Great Valley of California was submerged at the beginning of the Miocene. The deposition of the Vaqueros sandstone, clay, and conglomerate was followed by the formation of the Monterey series, partly sandstone and shale but largely diatomaceous tufa; the Monterey is an important source of oil. In mid-Miocene time there was extensive mountain building in this region, the Cascades and Coast Ranges being elevated, although the Rocky Mts. had by now been eroded to low relief. This disturbance was accompanied by volcanic activity—the Columbia and Snake river plateaus consist of over 200,000 sq mi (520,000 sq km) of basaltic lava flows up to 10,000 ft (3,000 m) thick—and by the first known movement along the San Andreas fault zone, engendered by the collision of the North American continental plate with the Pacific Ocean plate (see PLATE TECTONICS). Late in the Miocene a new, extensive submergence resulted in the deposition of the San Pablo shale and sandstone. The sediments of the California Miocene came chiefly from the Sierra Nevada and the Klamaths, which, through erosion, were peneplained by the close of the epoch. In the western interior of North America the Columbia River basalt plateau of Idaho, Washington, Oregon, N California, and N Nevada was formed by a great ourpouring of lava, which continued in the succeeding Pliocene epoch. During the Miocene most of N Europe was elevated, but marine waters covered E Spain, S France, Italy, and a depressed area extending through Hungary to a basin around Vienna. In addition to considerable mountain making, lagoons were formed at the base of the Carpathians and N of the Caucasus, in the regions now occupied by the Rumanian and Baku oil fields. The mammalian life of the Miocene was marked by further stages in the development of the horse, by the multiplication and final extinction of the giant hogs, and by the appearance of the mastodons, raccoons, and weasels. Cats, camels, doglike carnivores, and rhinoceroses were common, and species of a great ape (*Dryopithecus*) inhabited S Europe, Asia, and Africa. In the Miocene a distinct cooling of the climate resulted in the reduction of the area occupied by forests and an increase in that occupied by grassy plains.

Miphkad (mĭf'kăd), [Heb.,=muster gate], gate in the postexilic wall of Jerusalem. It was east of the Temple. Neh. 3.31.

Miquelon, French island: see SAINT PIERRE AND MIQUELON.

mir (mēr), Russian peasant community. The mir, which antedated serfdom (16th cent.) in Russia, persisted in its primitive form until after the Russian Revolution of 1917. In a community of free peasants the land was owned jointly by the mir; in a community of serfs, lands reserved for serf use were assigned to the mir for allocation. The mir, like a corporate body, had an assembly, obligations, and rights; it was responsible for allocating the arable land to its members and for reallocating such lands periodically. Woodlands, pastures, and waters were used jointly. With the abolition of serfdom in 1861 (see EMANCIPATION, EDICT OF) land was allotted, not to individual peasants, but to the mir. The amount of land allotted, however, was insufficient to support the number of people on the land. Also, retention of the mir perpetuated archaic agricultural methods. After the Revolution of 1905, STOLYPIN introduced reforms that he hoped would lead to the breakup of the mir. The reforms (1908) were not wholly effective, but many mirs were broken into individual holdings. With the success of the Bolshevik Revolution in 1917, the mir was abolished and the COLLECTIVE FARM was introduced. See I. A. Hourwich, *Economics of the Russian Village* (1892, repr. 1970); D. J. Male, *Russian Peasant Organisation Before Collectivisation* (1971).

Mira (mī'rə), [Lat.,=marvelous], VARIABLE STAR in the constellation CETUS; Bayer designation Omicron Ceti; 1970 position R.A. $2^h17.8^m$, Dec. $-3°07'$. The most famous long-period variable, Mira ranges in apparent MAGNITUDE from a maximum of about 2.0 to a minimum of about 10.1 with a period of a little less than a year (332 days). Thus, it is visible to the naked eye for about half a year and can be seen only through a telescope for the remainder of its period. Mira is of SPECTRAL CLASS M6e III, the spectrum showing some emission lines. There is some variation in maximum brightness that is thought to be due to clouds of hydrogen gas surrounding the star. Mira's distance from the earth is about 100 light-years.

Mirabeau, Honoré Gabriel Riquetti or **Riqueti, comte de** (ōnôrā' găbrēĕl' rēkĕtē' kôNt də mĕrăbō'), 1749–91, French revolutionary and political leader; son of Victor de Mirabeau. His life before 1789 was characterized by wild excesses, which ruined his health and caused him to be repeatedly jailed—several times on the request of his father, with whom he carried on a public quarrel. For a while he supported himself by writing. The year 1785 found him an exile in England, where he moved in Whig circles, but in 1786 he was sent on a secret mission to Prussia. He betrayed his government's trust by publishing his unedited reports to Paris, containing accounts of scandal and intrigue in the Prussian court. The author of numerous pamphlets in which he violently denounced various abuses of the *ancien régime,* he was elected (1789) a delegate of the third estate for Aix-en-Provence in the States-General. His clear and practical ideas, his fiery eloquence, and his terrifying yet imposing appearance exerted a fascination over the delegates and the populace. Despite his unsavory personal reputation, he found himself the spokesman of the third estate, particularly when, on June 23, the king ordered the States-General to leave the hall after the day's session had been declared closed. To the marquis de Dreux-Brézé, who announced the king's order, Mirabeau replied (his words have been variously reported): "We shall not leave our places save by the force of bayonets." The assembly remained in session and adopted Mirabeau's motion that its members were inviolable. However, despite his sonorous phrases, Mirabeau from the very beginning of the French Revolution sought to create a strong constitutional monarchy on the British model, which would permit him to play a decisive role as prime minister. In the Constituent Assembly he endeavored to strengthen the king's constitutional powers. However, members of the Assembly were barred from cabinet posts by a decree (Nov., 1789) specifically directed against him. Shortly afterward Mirabeau began secret dealings with the court. He entered the pay of the king and queen and, beginning in May, 1790, dispatched a series of advisory notes to them. The royal couple did not heed his counsel, for he never entirely gained the confidence of the court, particularly of the queen. Meanwhile, he was increasingly criticized in the assembly, particularly by the JACOBINS, who opposed his moderation; his political position was becoming untenable. He died in April, 1791, amid impressive manifestations of public sorrow and respect, for he had never lost his popularity with the masses. He was buried in the Panthéon, but his body was later removed when his dealings with the court were discovered. See Louis de Loménie and Charles de Loménie, *Les Mirabeau* (5 vol., 1879–81); F. M. Fling, *Mirabeau and the French Revolution* (1908); biographies by P. F. Willert (1898, repr. 1970), Henry de Jouvenel (tr. 1929), Pierre Nezelov (tr. 1937), Antonina Vallentin (1948), and O. J. G. Welch (1951).

miracle, preternatural occurrence that is viewed as the expression of a divine will. Its awe and wonder lie in the fact that the cause is hidden. The idea of the miracle occurs especially with the evolution of those highly developed religions that distinguish between natural law and divine will. Many supernatural or inexplicable events have been called miracles, but in the strict religious sense a miracle refers only to the direct intervention of divine will in the affairs of men. The adherents of Judaism, Christianity, and Islam attribute miracles to the omnipotence of God, the Creator, who alone can change the natural events of the world or can delegate that power to a disciple, such as Moses, Jesus, or Muhammad. In the history of Christianity miracles have played a major role, two of the most important examples of divine intervention being the Resurrection (Mat. 28; Mark 16; Luke 24; John 20; 21) and the Virgin Birth. Miracles in Christianity are also associated with saints' bodies and relics and with shrines. Some saints had in their lifetime great repute for curing the sick by supposed miracles. The Roman Catholic Church requires rigid attestation of miracles before CANONIZATION, but does not officially require belief in other than biblical miracles. The miracles of Jesus recorded in the Gospels are as follows. *Raising the dead:* Jairus' daughter (Mat. 9.18–26, Mark 5.22–43, Luke 8.41–56); the widow's son at Nain (Luke 7.11–18); Lazarus (John 11). *Casting out demons:* Gadarene swine (Mat. 8.28–34; Mark 5.1–20; Luke 8.26–40); dumb demoniac (Mat. 9.32–35); deaf-mute (Mat. 12.22; Luke 11.14); Syrophoenician woman's daughter (Mat. 15.21–28; Mark 7.24–30); child (Mat. 17.14–21; Mark 9.17–29; Luke 9.37–42); in the synagogue (Mark 1.23–28; Luke 4.33–37). *Healing:* leper (Mat. 8.2–4; Mark 1.40–45; Luke 5.12–15); centurion's palsied servant (Mat. 8.5–13; Luke 7.1–10); Peter's mother-in-law, sick of a fever (Mat. 8.14,15; Mark 1.30,31; Luke 4.38,39); palsied man (Mat. 9.1–8; Mark 2.1–12; Luke 5.18–26); two blind men (Mat. 9.27–31); withered hand (Mat. 12.10–13; Mark 3.1–6; Luke 6.6–11); two blind men (Mat. 20.30–34); deaf-mute (Mark 7.31–37); blind man (Mark 8.22–26); blind Bartimaeus (Mark 10.46–52; Luke 18.35–43); crippled woman (Luke 13.11–17); dropsical man (Luke 14.1–6); 10 lepers (Luke 17.11–19); Malchus' ear (Luke 22.50,51); nobleman's sick son (John 4.46–54); feeble man at the pool of Bethesda (John 5.1–16); man born blind (John 9). *General:* still the storm (Mat. 8.23–27; Mark 4.37–41; Luke 8.22–25); feeding 5,000 (Mat. 14.15–21; Mark 6.35–44; Luke 9.12–17; John 6.5–14); walking on the water (Mat. 14.22–33; Mark 6.45–52; John 6.15–21); feeding 4,000 (Mat. 15.32–38; Mark 8.1–9); withering the fig tree (Mat. 21.18–22; Mark 11.12–14,20–26); the draught of fish (Luke 5.1–9); turning water into wine at Cana (John 2.1–11); the draught of fish after the Resurrection (John 21.1–14). See also Mat. 4.24,25; 8.16,17; 9.20–22; 15.30,31; Mark 1.32–34; 3.10–12; 5.25–34; Luke 4.40,41; 8.43–48; John 11.47,48.

miracle play or **mystery play,** form of medieval drama that came from dramatization of the liturgy of the Roman Catholic Church. It developed from the 10th to the 16th cent., reaching its height in the 15th cent. The simple lyric character of the early texts, as shown in the *Quem Quœritis,* was enlarged by the addition of dialogue and dramatic action. Eventually the performance was moved to the churchyard and the marketplace. Rendered in Latin, the play was preceded by a prologue or by a herald who gave a synopsis and was closed by a herald's salute. When a papal edict in 1210 forbade the clergy to act on a public stage, supervision and control of presenting the plays passed into the hands of the town guilds, and various changes ensued. The vernacular language replaced Latin, and scenes were inserted that were not from the Bible. The acting became more dramatic as characterization and detail became more important. Based on the Scriptures from the creation to the Second Coming and on the lives of the saints, the plays were arranged into cycles and were given on church festival days, particularly the feast of Corpus Christi, lasting from sunrise to sunset. Each guild was responsible for the production of a different episode. With simple costumes and props, guild members, who were paid actors, performed on stages equipped with wheels (see PAGEANT); each scene was given at one public square and drawn on to its next performance at another, while a different stage succeeded it. Named after the towns in which they were performed, the principal English cycles are the York Plays (1430–40), the longest, containing 48 plays; the Towneley or Wakefield Plays (c.1450, in Yorkshire); the Coventry Plays (1468); and the Chester Plays (1475–1500). The PASSION PLAY is the chief modern example of the miracle play. The French *mystère* distinguished those plays containing biblical stories from those about the lives of the saints. The *auto,* the medieval religious drama in Spain, was acted concurrently with the secular drama throughout the Golden Age and into the 18th cent. CALDERÓN was the greatest composer of the *auto sacramental,* which dealt with the mystery of the Mass in allegory. In Italy the *laudi* were basically choral in form and so distinguished from the later *sacre rappresentazioni,* which became lavish artistic productions comparable to the French *mystère.* See Karl Young, *The Drama of the Medieval Church* (2 vol., 1933); and anthologies ed. by A. W. Pollard (8th ed. 1927) and V. F. Hopper and G. B. Lahey (1962).

mirage (mĭräzh'), atmospheric optical illusion in which an observer sees in the distance a nonexistent body of water or an image, sometimes distorted, of some object or of a complete scene. Examples of mirages are pools of water seen over hot desert sand or over hot pavement; at sea, an inverted image of a ship seen in the heavens or, also at sea, some object that is actually over the horizon but seems to loom up a relatively short distance away. These phenomena can be explained by the facts (1) that light rays undergo refraction, i.e., are bent, in passing from a medium of one density into another of different density and (2) that the boundary between two such media acts as a mirror for rays of light coming in at certain angles (see REFLECTION). Ordinarily the density of the atmosphere gradually decreases with altitude. Variations in temperature disturb the normal state (the density of warm air is less than that of cold air), producing unusual variations in the density of the atmosphere. The "lake" mirage in the desert is essentially a reflection of the sky. Light rays coming at a grazing angle from the sky just above the horizon are thrown upward by the surface of the area of extremely hot air just above the sand, and the effect to an observer is a shimmering reflecting expanse resembling the surface of a body of water. The inverted image of a ship seen in the heavens at sea is caused by a layer of dense cool air over the water; this layer bends the rays of light from the ship (below the horizon) in a curved path that arches over the horizon and back to earth. The image formed appears to be that produced by an object somewhere distant in a straight line from the observer and, therefore, at a position in the sky. It is sometimes inverted because in the bending process the light rays coming from the object are changed in relative position. The type of mirage described as looming, in which distant objects appear much nearer than they actually are, is explained in the same way as the image of the ship, except that the image is not inverted; the density variations may also act as a magnifying glass. Mirages can be photographed. The strange phenomenon known as the fata morgana [Ital., = Morgan le Fay, of the Arthurian legend, the supposed author of the mirage] is a complex mirage especially in evidence at the Strait of Messina; in this mirage images of objects such as ships, houses, or men, often two of the same object with one inverted, are seen suspended in the air over the object itself or on the water.

Miramar (mĭr'əmär"), city (1970 pop. 23,973), Broward co., SE Fla.; inc. 1955. It is a residential community in the rapidly growing area between Miami and Fort Lauderdale.

Miramichi (mĭrəmĭshē'), river, c.135 mi (220 km) long, rising in several forks and tributaries in central N.B. and flowing E past Newcastle into the Gulf of St. Lawrence at Miramichi Bay. The bay was visited (1534) by Jacques Cartier, the French explorer. Several Acadian fishing villages are on its shores.

Miranda, Francisco de (fränsē'skō thā mērän'dä), 1750–1816, Venezuelan revolutionist and adventurer. A hero of the struggle for independence from Spain, he is sometimes called the Precursor to distinguish him from Simón BOLÍVAR, who completed the task of liberation. Before he championed the independence of the Spanish colonies, Miranda involved himself in a number of adventures. As an officer in the Spanish army he served under Bernardo de Gálvez in the Spanish attack on Pensacola (1781), when Spain was an ally of the rebels in the American Revolution. He later visited Philadelphia and Boston and met George Washington, Alexander Hamilton, and other notables. He traveled widely in Europe, particularly in Russia, where he became a favorite of Catherine the Great. In France he fought in the French Revolutionary Wars; running afoul of the Jacobins he fled to England, where he was helped by William Pitt. Imbued with revolutionary ideas, Miranda sought foreign aid and led (1806) an unsuccessful expedition to the Venezuelan coast. After the start of the revolution in 1810, he returned to Venezuela and soon took a commanding position in the patriot forces. He was dictator for a short time, but after increasing misfortunes, including the loss of Puerto Cabello by Bolívar and a destructive earthquake in Caracas, he surrendered (1812) to the Spanish. Bolívar and other patriots, angered by his capitulation, seized him and turned him over to the Spanish who failed to honor the terms of surrender, deported him to Cádiz, and kept him in a dungeon the rest of his life. See *History of Don Francisco de Miranda's Attempt to Effect a Revolution in South America* by James Biggs (1808); biographies by W. S. Robertson (1929, repr. 1969) and J. F. Thorning (1952).

Miranda, in astronomy, one of the five known moons, or natural satellites, of URANUS.

Miranda vs. Arizona, case decided in 1966 by the U.S. Supreme Court. The decision reversed an Arizona court's conviction of Ernesto Miranda on charges of kidnapping and rape. After being identified in a police lineup, Miranda had been questioned by police; he confessed and signed a written statement without being told that he had a right to a lawyer. Miranda's confession was later used at his trial to obtain his conviction. In overturning the conviction Chief Justice Earl Warren ruled that the prosecution may not use statements made by a person in police custody unless certain minimum procedural safeguards were followed. Known as the Miranda warnings, these include informing arrested persons prior to questioning that they have a right to remain silent, that anything they say may be used as evidence against them, and that they have a right to the presence of an attorney, either retained or appointed. Once a person in police custody answers some questions, he or she still retains the right to stop or to request an attorney. The Miranda decision was one of the most controversial of the Warren Court; some thought it unduly hampered the police.

Mirandola, Giovanni Pico della: see PICO DELLA MIRANDOLA, GIOVANNI, CONTE.

Miriam (mĭr'ēəm). **1** Sister of Moses and Aaron. After the crossing of the Sea of Reeds, she led the women in the song of Miriam. Later she sided with Aaron against Moses and was stricken with leprosy, but was cured when Moses interceded for her. Ex. 15.20,21; Num. 12. **2** Descendant of Judah. 1 Chron. 4.17. Miriam and Mary are diverse forms of the same original name.

Mirma (mûr'mə), chief Benjamite. 1 Chron. 8.10.

Mirny (mēr'nē), town (1970 pop. 24,000), NE Siberian USSR, in Yakut Autonomous Republic. Founded in 1956, when diamonds were discovered, Mirny grew rapidly and is now the center of the Soviet diamond-mining industry.

Miró, Joan (hōän' mērō'), 1893–, Spanish surrealist painter. After studying in Barcelona, Miró went to Paris in 1919. In the 1920s he came into contact with CUBISM and SURREALISM. His work has been characterized as psychic automatism, an expression of the subconscious in free form. By 1930 Miró had developed a lyrical style that remained fairly consistent. It is distinguished by the use of brilliant pure color and the playful juxtaposition of delicate lines with abstract, often amoebic shapes (e.g., *Dog Barking at the Moon,* 1926; Philadelphia Mus. of Art). In many of his works there is a distinct undertone of nightmare and horror. After 1941, Miró lived mainly in Majorca. He painted murals for hotels in New York City and Cincinnati and for the Graduate Center at Harvard. In 1958 he completed ceramic decorations for the UNESCO buildings in Paris. Many of his canvases are in the Museum of Modern Art and the Solomon R. Guggenheim Museum, both in New York City. See studies by J. T. Soby (1959), Umbro Apolonio (tr. 1969), and Roland Penrose (1971).

Miró Ferrer, Gabriel (gäbrēēl', fĕrĕr'), 1879–1930, Spanish novelist and short-story writer. One of the GENERATION OF '98, he achieved his powerful individual style through unusual combinations of words and cadences. His novels are sensuous in tone, haunting, and evocative. Their themes are the beauty and cruelty of nature and of man. Among them are *Figuras de la pasión del Señor* (1916, tr. *Figures of the Passion of Our Lord,* 1924), his masterpiece *Libro de Siguënza* (1917), and *Nuestro Padre San Daniel* (1921, tr. *Our Father, San Daniel,* 1930).

Mirpur Khas (mēr'po͝or khäs), town (1961 pop. 60,861), S Pakistan, on the Let War canal. Founded in 1806, the town is a market for cotton and food grains.

mirror, in optics, a reflecting surface that forms an IMAGE of an object when light rays coming from that object fall upon it (see REFLECTION). Usually mirrors are made of plate glass, one side of which is coated with metal or some special preparation to serve as a reflecting surface. The junction of this reflecting surface and the plate glass is called the mirror line. Highly polished metal and other materials serve also as mirrors. Three common types of mirror are the plane mirror, which has a flat, or plane, surface; the convex mirror; and the concave mirror. In a plane mirror the rays of light falling on it are reflected with little change in their original character and their relationship to one another in space. The apparent position of the image is the same distance behind the mirror as the actual object is in front of the mirror; the image is the same size as the object and is called a virtual image (i.e., the rays of light from the object do not actually go to the image, but extensions of the reflected light rays appear to intersect behind the mirror). Convex and concave mirrors are known collectively as spherical mirrors, since their curved reflecting surfaces are usually part of the surface of a sphere. The concave type is one in which the midpoint or vertex of the reflecting surface is farther away from the object than are the edges. The center of the imaginary sphere of which it is a part is called the center of curvature and each point of the mirror surface is, therefore, equidistant from this point. A line extending through the center of curvature and the vertex of the mirror is the principal axis, and rays parallel to it are all reflected in such a way that they meet at a point on it lying halfway between the center of curvature and the vertex. This point is called the principal focus. The size, nature, and position of an image formed by a concave spherical mirror depend on the position of the object in relation to the principal focus and the center of curvature. If the object is at a point farther from the mirror than the center of curvature, the image is real (i.e., it is formed directly by the reflected rays), inverted, and smaller than the object. If the object is at the center of curvature, the image is the same size as the object and is real and inverted. If the object is between the center of curvature and the principal focus, the image is larger, real, and inverted. If the object is inside the principal focus, the image is virtual, erect (right side up), and larger than the object. The position of the object can be found from the equation relating the focal length f of the mirror (the distance from the mirror to the principal focus), the distance d_o of the object from the mirror, and the distance d_i of the image from the mirror: $1/f = 1/d_o + 1/d_i$. In the case of the virtual image, this equation yields a negative image distance, indicating that the image is behind the mirror. In the case of both the real and the virtual image, the size of the image is to the size of the object as the distance of the image from the mirror is to the distance of the object from the mirror. In a convex spherical mirror the vertex of the mirror is nearer to the object than the edges—the mirror bulges toward the object. The image formed by it is always smaller than the object and always erect. It is never real because the reflected rays diverge outward from the face of the mirror and are not brought to a focus, and the image, therefore, is determined by their prolongation behind the mirror as in the case of the plane mirror. The mirror of the ancient Greeks and Romans was a disk of metal with a highly polished face, sometimes with a design on the back, and usually with a handle. Glass mirrors date from the Middle Ages. They were made in large quantities in Venice from the 16th cent., the back being covered with a thin coating of tin mixed with mercury; after 1840 a thin coating of silver was generally substituted. The introduction of plate glass for mirrors (17th cent.) stimulated the use of large stationary mirrors as part of household furniture. Small bits of silvered glass were much used in the East to adorn articles of dress and of decoration. The metal trench hand mirror of World War I revived the manufacture of mirrors of this type. Mirrors also play an important part in the modern astronomical TELESCOPE. See I. G. Gluch, *It's All Done with Mirrors* (1968).

Mirs Bay: see HONG KONG.

MIRV: see GUIDED MISSILE.

Mirzapur (mēr'zäpo͝or''), town (1971 pop. 105,920), Uttar Pradesh state, N central India. It is a district administrative center. Shellac and cement are manufactured. Many Hindu pilgrims visit the shrine of the goddess Vindhyeshwari.

Misael (mĭs'āəl), one of the THREE HOLY CHILDREN.

miscarriage: see ABORTION.

miscegenation (mĭs''ĭjĭnā'shən), interbreeding, or hybridization of persons of different racial types. Before the development of modern anthropology and genetics, opinions differed sharply as to the effects of racial interbreeding. Some held that it produced anatomical disharmony, others that it produced hybrid vigor, sometimes also sought by interbreeding domestic animals. It is now known that racial interbreeding has been continuous from prehistoric times and that modern populations are products of this process on a grand scale. It is generally believed today that the only ill effect seems to be on the personality of the offspring when there is social disapproval of mixed unions. Interracial marriages between blacks and whites were prohibited by statute in some states of the United States until 1967, when the U.S. Supreme Court, in *Loving* vs. *Commonwealth of Virginia,* ruled such laws illegal. See APARTHEID. See J. R. Washington, *Marriage in Black and White* (1971); M. L. Barron, comp., *The Blending American* (1972).

misdemeanor, in law, a minor crime, in contrast to a FELONY. At COMMON LAW a misdemeanor was a crime other than treason or a felony. Although it might be a grave offense, it did not affect the feudal bond or take away the offender's property. By the 19th cent. serious crimes were labeled felonies, and minor crimes misdemeanors. In the United States a misdemeanor usually is an offense that may be punished summarily by fine and by imprisonment for less than a year. Commission of a misdemeanor does not cancel citizenship or subject an ALIEN to deportation. In some states of the United States certain minor law violations are not even classified as misdemeanors, e.g., traffic offenses and breach of municipal regulations.

Miseno, Cape (mēzĕ'nō), S Italy, at the northwest end of the Bay of Naples. Augustus founded (1st cent. B.C.) a naval station (*Misenum*) there, which was destroyed by the Arabs (9th cent. A.D.). Remaining are ruins of the imperial villa, baths, a theater, and a reservoir.

Miserere (mĭzərâr'ē), the 51st (or 50th) Psalm, beginning "Miserere mei, Deus (Have mercy upon me, O God)." It is one of the penitential PSALMS. Noteworthy musical settings are those of Josquin des Prés and Palestrina.

misericords (mĭz''ərəkôrdz'), carvings in Gothic churches that adorn choir stalls provided for the use of the clergy during services. The stalls were carved with biblical scenes that demonstrated the artist's skill and wit. Superb examples of misericords are at Ely, Wells, and Lincoln cathedrals in England.

Misgab (mĭs'găb), unlocated place, SE of the Dead Sea, which was denounced by Jeremiah. Jer. 48.1.

Mishael (mĭsh'āəl). **1** Kohathite Levite. Ex. 6.22; Lev. 10.4. **2** Companion of Ezra. Neh. 8.4. **3** One of the THREE HOLY CHILDREN.

Mishal (mī'shəl), unidentified town, N Palestine. Joshua 21.30. Misheal: Joshua 19.26. Mashal: 1 Chron. 6.74.

Misham (mī'shăm), descendant of Shaharaim. 1 Chron. 8.12.

Mishawaka (mĭshəwôk'ə), city (1970 pop. 35,517), St. Joseph co., N Ind., on both banks of the St. Joseph River and adjacent to South Bend; settled c.1830, inc. 1899. Primarily an industrial city, Mishawaka's industries are closely associated with those of South Bend. Bethel College is there.

Misheal (mī'shēəl), variant of MISHAL.

Mishima, Yukio (yo͞o'kēō mĭsh'ēmä), 1925–70, Japanese author, b. Tokyo. His original name was Kimitake Hiraoka and he was born into a samurai family. Mishima wrote novels, short stories, essays, and plays. He appeared on stage in some of his plays as well as directing and starring in films. During World War II he worked in an aircraft factory. Upon graduation (1947) from the Univ. of Tokyo, he served a brief time in the finance ministry before devoting himself entirely to writing. Mishima and the youthful members of his Tatenokai [Shield Society] practised physical fitness and the ancient arts of the samaurai, e.g., karate, swordsmanship, attempting to return to the ideals of Japan under Imperial rule. His tetralogy *The Sea of Fertility* traces the fading of the old Japan in the first decade of the 20th cent. and continues through the aftermath of World War II. The individual novels of this group are: *Spring Snow* (tr. 1972), *Runaway Horses* (tr. 1973), *The Temple of Dawn* (tr. 1973), and *The Decay of the Angel* (tr. 1974). Other important novels include the semiautobiographical *Confessions of a Mask* (1949; tr. 1958); *The Sound of Waves* (1954; tr. 1956), a simple love story of a boy and girl in a Japanese fishing village; *The Temple of the Golden Pavilion* (1956; tr. 1963), a brilliant depiction of a psychopathic monk who destroys the temple he loves; *After the Banquet* (1960; tr. 1963), the story of a successful businesswoman who marries an aging politician and attempts to restore his former glory; and the horror tale *The Sailor Who Fell from Grace with the Sea* (1963; tr. 1965). All contain paradoxes: beauty equated with violence and death; the yearning for love and its rejection when offered; plus an exquisite attention to detail in the delineation of character. After an unsuccessful demonstration in which he harangued the Japanese self-defense "army" for its lack of power under the Japanese constitution, Mishima committed ritual suicide (seppuku). See biography by John Nathan (1974).

Mishima (mē'shēmä), city (1970 pop. 78,141), Shizuoka prefecture, central Honshu, Japan. It is a hot-spring resort, an agricultural market, and a center for mechanical and textile industries. It is noted for its Mishima (Shinto) shrine and Rakujuen Park.

Mishma (mĭsh'mə). **1** Son of Ishmael. Gen. 25.14; 1 Chron. 1.30. **2** Son of Simeon. 1 Chron. 4.25.

Mishmannah (mĭshmăn'ə), Gadite ally of David. 1 Chron. 12.10.

Mishna (mĭsh'nə), codified collection of legal interpretations of the legal portions of the Biblical books of Exodus, Leviticus, Numbers, and Deuteronomy. Together with the Gemara, or Amoraic commentary on the Mishna, it comprises the TALMUD. Next to the Scriptures the Mishna is the basic textbook of Jewish life and thought. It was the work of the TANNAIM, the final compilation being made under the direction of JUDAH I (ha-Nasi). The Mishna is divided into six Orders (Sedarim)—Zeraim [seeds], laws pertaining to agriculture; Moed [seasons], laws concerning observation of the Sabbath and festivals; Nashim [women], laws regarding vows, marriage, and divorce; Nezikim [damages], laws concerning civil and criminal matters; Kodashim [holy things], laws regulating ritual slaughter, sacrifice, and holy objects; and Tohorot [purities], laws regarding ceremonial purity. Each Order is divided into tractates, which in turn are divided into chapters. These contain paragraphs called mishnayyot. The last tractate of the fourth Order is called *Avot* or *Pirke Avot* [chapters of the fathers] and contains the sayings and teachings of the sages from the 3d cent. B.C. to the 3d cent. A.D. It has been translated into many languages and has had a considerable influence beyond the confines of Judaism. See translation by Herbert Danby (1958); Louis Ginzberg, *Studies in the Origin of the Mishnah* (1920); H. L. Strack, *Introduction to the Talmud and Midrash* (1931, repr. 1969); J. H. Hertz, *Sayings of the Fathers* (1945); Judah Goldin, *The Living Talmud; the Wisdom of the Fathers and Its Classical Commentaries* (1959, repr. 1964); R. Travers Herford, ed., *Pirke Aboth: the Ethics of the Talmud* (tr. 1962).

Mishraites (mĭsh'rāīts, mĭshrā'īts), one of the four families of Kirjath-jearim. 1 Chron. 2.53.

Miskolc (mĭsh'kôlts), city (1970 pop. 172,952), NE Hungary, on the Sajó River. Hungary's second largest city and a major industrial center, Miskolc has large iron and steel mills, lime and cement works, and machinery and motor vehicle factories. Iron ore and lignite are mined nearby, and the region's numerous limestone caves are used as cellars by local winemakers. Miskolc also has an important trade in metal products and agricultural goods. The city is the seat of a Protestant bishopric. An old settlement, Miskolc was granted the status of a free city in the 15th cent. Frequent invasions (by Mongols in the 13th cent., Turks in the 16th and 17th cent., and German imperial forces in the 17th and 18th cent.) marked the city's history. Industrialization began in the second half of the 19th cent. Present-day landmarks include the Avas Reformed Church (15th cent.), the remains of a 13th-century castle, and a museum containing Scythian art. The city also has a law school and a technical university.

Mispereth (mĭs'pērĕth), exile who returned from Babylon. Neh. 7.7. Mizpar: Ezra 2.2.

mispickel: see ARSENOPYRITE.

Misr: see EGYPT.

Misratah (mĭsrä'tä) or **Misurata** (mēzo͞orä'tä), city (1964 pop. 37,000), NW Libya, located in an oasis. A seaport on the Mediterranean Sea, the city exports dates and grain and is noted for its handwoven carpets. Misratah was known to the Romans as Tubartis. The Italians built its port in the 20th cent.

Misrephoth-maim (mĭs'rĕfŏth-mā'ĭm), place, NW Palestine, to which Joshua drove the defeated Canaanites. Joshua 11.8.

missal [Lat.,=of the mass], in the Roman Catholic Church, liturgical book containing all directions and texts necessary for the performance of MASS throughout the year. The Roman Missal (*Missale Romanum*) published by Pope Pius V in 1570 over the years replaced the widespread use of separate missals by each diocese. A number of religious orders (e.g., the Dominicans) and certain privileged dioceses (e.g., Milan) still use missals containing elements proper to themselves. The missal is in Latin and vernacular forms. The Constitution on the Sacred Liturgy, issued by the Second Vatican Council in 1963, initiated a full-scale reform of the text of the Roman Missal.

missile, guided: see GUIDED MISSILE.

Missinaibi (mĭsĭnä'bē), river, c.265 mi (430 km) long, rising in Missinaibi Lake, central Ont., Canada, and flowing N and NE to the Mattagami River, SW of Moosonee, to form the Moose River.

Mission, city (1970 pop. 13,043), Hidalgo co., extreme S Texas; inc. 1910. It is a processing and canning center for citrus fruits (especially grapefruit) and vegetables grown in the irrigated lower Rio Grande valley. It was founded on property that had belonged to the Oblate Fathers; their chapel still stands on the Rio Grande.

Missionary Ridge: see CHATTANOOGA CAMPAIGN.

Mission Indians, Indians of S and central California; so called because they were placed under the jurisdiction of some 21 Spanish missions that were established between 1769 and 1823. The major groups were the Chumash, Costanoan, Diegueño, Gabrielino, Juaneño, and Luiseño. The first mission was established at San Diego. The Mission Indians were taught and forced to work at agriculture. The land and the herds of sheep were theoretically owned by the Indians themselves, but were held in trust by the Franciscan fathers. In the early 1970s there were some 2,000 Mission Indians on reservations in California.

missions, term generally applied to organizations formed for the purpose of extending religious teaching, whether at home or abroad. It also indicates the stations or the fields where such teaching is given. In a more particular sense it designates the efforts to disseminate the Christian religion. From the first steps taken by the disciples of Jesus to carry out his direction to preach his gospel throughout "all the world," the history of the Christian church has been in great part a history of missions. Christianity rapidly gained converts, spreading through Asia Minor to Alexandria and into Europe by way of Greece and Rome. A missionary college was founded in Alexandria in the 2d cent., one at Constantinople in 404. The following centuries were marked by notable missionary labors in Scotland, Ireland, Central Europe, and among the Northmen, reaching even to Iceland and Greenland. St. PATRICK, St. AUGUSTINE OF CANTERBURY, and St. BONIFACE are great names of that era. After the Christianization of Europe there was little missionary effort until the 16th cent. Roman Catholic missions were then, as now, almost entirely in the hands of the religious orders. The great missionary orders are the Benedictines (which virtually civilized medieval Germany), Franciscans (especially the Capuchins), Dominicans (founded for missions among the Albigenses), Carmelites, and Jesuits (founded for the education of boys). The Jesuits were the great missionaries of the Catholic Reformation (see JESUS, SOCIETY OF). They went to the Far East (see FRANCIS XAVIER, SAINT), to America, and to Protestant N Europe. It was the Jesuits who kept up the English missions in the 16th and 17th cent. The first Catholic missionaries in Canada were Recollects, who worked in the first part of the 17th cent.; they were soon followed by Jesuits. Notable of these Jesuits were Jerome Lalemant, Jean de Brébeuf, and Isaac Jogues; they may be regarded as a principal factor in the growth of the Canadian frontier and in the exploration of Canada and the upper Mississippi. The *Jesuit Relations,* the individual journals of these Jesuits, are exceedingly important sources of early American history. In the period of the conquest of Central and South America by Spain the church sent its missionaries with the conquerors. The Franciscans and Jesuits were the most important orders in Mexico. In the late 18th and early 19th cent. there was an extensive Catholic missionary interest in the Mississippi valley, and many Italians and French came to America to teach in the newly opened country. Bardstown, Ky., was the chief center. Since the 17th cent. practically all Roman Catholic missions have been administered by one of the Roman congregations, Congregatio de Propaganda Fide (Congregation for the Propagation of the Faith), usually called the Propaganda. This is made up of cardinals, whose office is in Rome. The foreign missions are administered by the religious orders, the missionaries being responsible to the Propaganda. In Propaganda countries where there is a strong hierarchy, the missionaries are responsible to the hierarchy. In order to prevent overlapping, the Propaganda divides up among the various orders the territory in which there are few Catholics. A new missionary policy was adopted in the middle of the 19th cent., which emphasizes the training of native clergy and the ordination of native bishops. Roman Catholic missions are supported by the Propaganda, by the religious orders, and by lay missionary societies. Two unsuccessful attempts were made to establish Protestant missions in the middle of the 16th cent., one by French Protestants for a colony in Brazil and the other a plan of King Gustavus I of Sweden for work among the Laplanders. The Dutch East India Company sent missionaries to the Malaysians early in the 17th cent., and a seminary for the training of missionaries for work among the American Indians was carried on in New England in the 17th cent. by John ELIOT and Roger WILLIAMS (see also STOCKBRIDGE INDIANS). The Society of Friends also made converts among the Indians. In Great Britain associations were formed to encourage the extension of the faith among the American colonists—the Society for the Propagation of the Gospel in New England (1649), the Society for Promoting Christian Knowledge (c.1698), and the Society for the Propagation of the Gospel in Foreign Parts (1701). The Scottish Society for the Promotion of Christian Knowledge appointed (1742) David BRAINERD as a missionary to the American Indians. Denmark sent into its colonial fields of the East and West Indies the first Lutheran missionaries—mainly German Pietists—in 1705. Members of the MORAVIAN CHURCH went as missionaries to all continents except Australia before 1760. A new missionary spirit was aroused in Great Britain at the end of the 18th cent. by the evangelistic fervor of John Wesley and George Whitefield. The Baptist Missionary Society was formed (1792), and William CAREY went to India. Then followed the founding of the London Missionary Society (1795), which in 1797 laid the foundations of missionary work in the South Sea Islands, and, among the Anglicans, the Church Missionary Society for Africa and the East (1799). In 1813 the Wesleyan Methodist Missionary Society was added. In Holland, Germany, Switzerland, and France missionary societies were organized. In the United States they sprang up all through the early part of the 19th cent.—the American Board of Commissioners for Foreign Missions (1810), the American Baptist Missionary Union (1814), which supported the mission in Burma of Adoniram JUDSON, the Missionary Society of the Methodist Episcopal Church (1819), and the Domestic and Foreign Missionary Society of the Protestant Episcopal Church (1820). Although its work had started much earlier, the Presbyterian Board of Foreign Missions was not actually constituted until 1837. American home mission societies began addressing their efforts to Indians, Eskimo, Negroes, and settlers on the expanding Western frontier, and, later, to immigrants from Europe and Asia and to persons in isolated mountain regions of the South. Many missionaries have specialized in providing medical and educational services as an effective means of opening the way for spiritual ministry. Two of the most famous missionaries to Africa, David LIVINGSTONE and Albert SCHWEITZER, were medical missionaries. Organized medical work in India started in the middle of the 19th cent. under doctors sent by the London Missionary Society and the American Board. With the work of Alexander DUFF in India in 1830, a new enterprise in missionary effort on educational lines was launched. In China a number of Christian colleges and universities were established. Work there was started (1807) by Robert Morrison, representing the London Missionary Society. The China Inland Mission, with funds and personnel drawn from several denominations and countries, was founded (1865) by J. H. Taylor. The opening of Japan by treaties in 1858 offered an opportunity to introduce foreign missionaries. Educational work has been an important part of missionary activity there. A marked trend in missionary work in recent years has been the training of indigenous leadership for church offices and administrative positions in mission enterprises. In 1921 the International Missionary Council, composed of some 26 national and regional missionary organizations and Christian councils in various parts of the world, was formed. During and after World War II missionary accomplishments in many lands were severely curtailed or destroyed, but as quickly as possible new mission schools, hospitals, orphanages, and churches were built to replace those destroyed (except in China, which was closed to missionaries after 1949). In 1961 the International Missionary Council became part of the World Council of Churches, and there has been a high level of cooperation among Protestant churches in mission work. To disprove the widespread belief in Asia and Africa that Christianity is only for Westerners, non-Western missionaries have been encouraged to go to these regions. There continues to be a strong emphasis on medical care and education in mission work throughout the world. See K. S. Latourette, *A History of the Expansion of Christianity* (7 vol., 1937–45; repr. 1971); H. P. Van Dusen, *World Christianity, Yesterday, Today, and Tomorrow* (1947); W. C. Lamott, *Revolution in Missions* (1954); R. H. Glover, *The Progress of World-wide Missions* (rev. ed. 1960); Bernard de Vaulx, *History of the Missions* (1961); S. C. Neill, *Christian Missions* (1964) and *Colonialism and Christian Missions* (1966); publications of the International Missionary Council. For Roman Catholic missions, see works on the religious orders and the publications (in America) of the Society for the Propagation of the Faith and the Society of the Divine Word.

Mississippi (mĭs″əs-sĭp′ē), state (1970 pop. 2,216,912), 47,716 sq mi (123,584 sq km), S United States, admitted as the 20th state of the Union in 1817. JACKSON is the capital and largest city. Other important cities are MERIDIAN, BILOXI, GREENVILLE, HATTIESBURG, GULFPORT, VICKSBURG, and LAUREL. The Mississippi River, which gives the state its name, forms most of the state's western boundary. Across the Mississippi River lie Arkansas and Louisiana. The latter, also bordering a stretch of Mississippi on the south, cuts eastward like the toe of a boot until it reaches the Pearl River, which forms the lower part of Mississippi's southern line; Alabama is on the east, Tennessee on the north. The generally hilly land reaches its highest point (806 ft/246 m) in the northeastern corner along the Tennessee River. The most distinctive region in the state's varied topography is the Delta, a flat alluvial plain between the Mississippi and the Yazoo rivers. The Delta is a highly productive cotton area. A wide belt of longleaf yellow pine (the piny woods) covers most of S Mississippi to within a few miles of the coastal-plain meadows. Important there are lumbering and allied industries. Most of the state's rivers belong to either the Mississippi or the Alabama river systems, with the Pontotoc Ridge the divide. The climate of Mississippi is subtropical in the southern part of the state and temperate in the northern part; the average annual rainfall is more than 50 in. (127 cm). One of the more predominantly rural states in the Union, it is a leader in the production of cotton. Soil erosion, resulting from overcultivation of the crop, and the destruction caused by the boll weevil have led to the increased adoption of scientific farming techniques and to agricultural diversification. The most important crops are cotton lint, soybeans, cotton-

seed, and hay. There has been a great rise in livestock raising and, especially, dairying. The state's most important and valuable mineral resources, petroleum and natural gas, have been developed only since the 1930s. More than one third of the state's land is subject to oil and gas development. Sand and gravel and clays are also produced. Industry has grown rapidly since oil development began and has been helped by the TENNESSEE VALLEY AUTHORITY and the state's program to balance agriculture with industry. Under this program many communities have subsidized and attracted new industries; and industrial products, including clothing, wood products, foods, and chemicals, have exceeded in value those of agriculture in recent years. On the Gulf coast there is a profitable fishing and seafood processing industry. Despite modernization efforts, however, the state's per capita income is one of the lowest in the nation. Hernando De Soto's expedition undoubtedly passed (1540–42) through the region, then inhabited by the Choctaw, Chickasaw, and Natchez Indians, but the first permanent white settlement was not made until 1699, when Pierre le Moyne, sieur d'Iberville, established a French colony on Biloxi Bay. Settlement accelerated in 1718, when the colony came under the French Mississippi Company, headed by the speculator John Law. The region was part of Louisiana until 1763, when, by the Treaty of Paris (see PARIS, TREATY OF) England received practically all the French territory E of the Mississippi River and also East Florida and West Florida, which had belonged to Spain. English colonists, many of them retired soldiers, had made the Natchez district a thriving agricultural community, producing tobacco and indigo, by the time Bernardo de Gálvez captured it for Spain in 1779. By the Treaty of Paris of 1783 at the end of the American Revolution, the United States, with English approval, claimed as its southern boundary in the West lat. 31°N (most of the present-day state of Mississippi was included in the area). Spain denied this claim, and the long, involved WEST FLORIDA CONTROVERSY ensued. In the Pinckney Treaty (1795), Spain accepted lat. 31°N as the northern boundary of its territory but did not evacuate Natchez until the arrival of American troops in 1798. Congress immediately created the Mississippi Territory, with Natchez as the capital and William C. C. Claiborne as the governor. After Georgia's cession (1802) of its Western lands to the United States (see YAZOO LAND FRAUD) and the Louisiana Purchase (1803), a land boom swept Mississippi. The high price of cotton and the cheap, fertile land brought settlers thronging in, most of them via the NATCHEZ TRACE, from the Southern Piedmont region and even from New England. A few attained great wealth, but most simply managed a living. In 1817, Mississippi became a state, with substantially its present-day boundaries; the eastern section of the Mississippi Territory was organized as Alabama Territory. David Holmes was elected governor of Mississippi. The aristocratic planter element of the Natchez region initially dominated Mississippi's government, as the state's first constitution (1817) showed. With the spread of Jacksonian democracy, however, the small farmer came into his own, and the new constitution adopted in 1832 was quite liberal for its time. Land hunger increased as more new settlers arrived, lured by the continuing cotton boom. By a series of Indian treaties (1820, 1830, 1832), all the Indians in the state were pushed westward across the Mississippi. Mississippians were among the leading Southern expansionists seeking new land for cotton and slavery, and Robert J. Walker, Henry S. Foote, John A. Quitman, and Jefferson Davis agitated for or fought in the MEXICAN WAR. After 1840 slaves in the state outnumbered whites. On Jan. 9, 1861, Mississippi became the second state to secede from the Union. State pride was highly gratified by the choice of Jefferson Davis as president of the CONFEDERACY. Civil War fighting did not reach Mississippi until April, 1862, when Union forces were victorious at CORINTH and Iuka. Grant's brilliant VICKSBURG CAMPAIGN ended large-scale fighting in the state, but further destruction was caused by Gen. W. T. Sherman in his march from Vicksburg to Meridian. Moreover, cavalry of both the North and South, particularly the Confederate forces of Gen. N. B. Forrest, continued active. After the war Mississippi abolished slavery but refused to ratify the Thirteenth and Fourteenth Amendments, and in March, 1867, under the Congressional plan of Reconstruction, it was organized with Arkansas into a military district commanded by Gen. E. O. C. Ord. After much agitation, a Republican-sponsored constitution guaranteeing basic rights to Negroes was adopted in 1869. Mississippi was readmitted to the Union early in 1870 after ratifying the Fourteenth and Fifteenth Amendments and meeting other Congressional requirements. While Republicans were in power, the state government was composed of new immigrants from the North, blacks, and cooperative white Southerners. A Negro, A. K. Davis, became lieutenant governor in 1874. The establishment of free public schools was a noteworthy aspect of Republican rule. As former Confederates were permitted to return to politics and blacks were increasingly intimidated (see KU KLUX KLAN), the Democrats regained strength. The Republicans were defeated in the bitter election of 1875. Lucius Q. C. Lamar figured largely in the Democratic triumph and was the state's most prominent national figure for many years. In Reconstruction days the Republicans could win only with solid black support. After Reconstruction the Negroes were virtually disenfranchised. White supremacy was bolstered by the Constitution of 1890, later used as a model by other Southern states; under its terms a prospective voter could be required to read and interpret any of the constitution's provisions. Because at the turn of the century most Mississippi blacks could not read (neither could many whites, but the test was rarely applied to them) and because the county registrar could disqualify a prospective voter if he disagreed with the interpretation of the constitution, the Negroes were legally disenfranchised. On the ruins of the shattered plantation economy rose the sharecropping system, and the merchant and the banker replaced the planter in having the largest financial interest in farming. Too often the system made the sharecroppers, white as well as black, little more than economic slaves. The landowners, however, maintained their hold on politics until 1904, when the small farmers, still the dominant voting group, elected James K. Vardaman governor. Nevertheless this agrarian revolt did not alter a deep-seated obscurantism that was reflected in the JIM CROW LAWS (1904) and the ban on the teaching of evolution in the public schools (1926). Another reflection of the social structure of the state was prohibition, put into effect in 1908 and not repealed until 1959. Since the disastrous flood of 1927 the Federal government has taken over flood-control work—constructing levees, floodwalls, floodways, and reservoirs; stabilizing river banks; and improving channels. Navigation, too, has not been neglected; the Intracoastal Waterway provides a protected channel along the entire Mississippi coastline and links the state's ports with all others along the Gulf coast and with all inland waterway systems emptying into the Gulf of Mexico. The state has made attempts to wipe out illiteracy (for a long time it had the highest illiteracy rate in the country), but its per capita expenditure on education was among the lowest of any state in 1972. Mississippi is still plagued by racial problems, which have changed the state's alignment in national politics. In 1948, Mississippi abandoned the Democratic party because of the national Democratic party's stand on civil rights, and the state supported J. Strom Thurmond, the States' Rights party candidate, for President. The 1954 Supreme Court ruling against racial segregation in public schools (see INTEGRATION) occasioned massive resistance. Citizens Councils, composed of white men and dedicated to maintaining segregation, began to spring up throughout the state. In the 1960 presidential election Mississippians again rebelled against the Democratic national platform by giving victory at the polls to unpledged electors, who cast their electoral college votes not for John F. Kennedy but for Harry F. Byrd, the conservative Senator from Virginia. In 1964 the conservative Republican Barry Goldwater carried the state; in 1968 Gov. George Wallace of Alabama, who had become famous for opposing integration, won the state. In 1961 mass arrests and violence were touched off when "freedom riders," actively seeking to spur integration, made Mississippi a major target. However, there was not even token integration of public schools in Mississippi until 1962, when the state government under the leadership of Gov. Ross R. Barnett tried unsuccessfully to block the admission of James H. Meredith, a Negro, to the Univ. of Mississippi law school at Oxford. In the conflict the Federal and state governments clashed, and the U.S. Dept. of Justice took legal action against state officials, including Barnett. Two persons were killed in riots, and Federal troops had to restore order. Racial antagonisms resulted in many more acts of violence. Churches and black homes were bombed. Medgar Evers, an official of the National Association for the Advancement of Colored People, was killed in 1963. Three civil rights workers (two white, one black) were murdered the next year. James Meredith was wounded during a civil rights march in 1965. In 1970 two students were killed by state police at Jackson State College, a predominantly black school. Despite the violence, some progress has been made. After the Federal Voting Rights Act of 1965, many blacks succeeded in registering and voting. In 1967, for the first time since 1890, a Negro was elected to the legislature, and other black local officials have since been elected. Mississippi is governed under the 1890 constitution. The bicameral legislature consists of 52 senators and 122 representatives, all elected for four-year terms. The governor is also elected for a four-year term. The state has two U.S. Senators, five Representatives, and seven electoral votes. William L. Walker, a Democrat, became governor in 1972. In August, 1969, Mississippi and Louisiana were devastated by a hurricane. In April, 1973, the Mississippi River rose to record levels in the state. The floodwaters from the river and its tributaries covered about 9% of the state, including parts of Vicksburg and Natchez, causing millions of dollars of damage to property and delaying the planting of spring crops. Especially hard hit was the Delta region, where the Yazoo River and its tributaries flooded some 3,100 sq mi (8,030 sq km) of fertile lowlands. Besides the Univ. of Mississippi the institutions of higher education in the state include Mississippi State Univ., at State College, and Mississippi State College for Women, at Columbus. Historical sites in the state include Old Spanish Fort, the oldest house on the Mississippi River, near Pascagoula, and Vicksburg National Military Park, Brices Cross Roads National Battlefield Site, and Tupelo National Battlefield Site (see NATIONAL PARKS AND MONUMENTS, table). Mississippi, in the path of waterfowl migrations down the Mississippi valley, is noted for its duck and quail hunting. Along the Gulf Coast, a favorite fishing area, are several resort cities and part of Gulf Islands National Seashore. In Natchez and Biloxi are many fine antebellum mansions. In the recent literature of Mississippi the most important figures have been William Faulkner and Eudora Welty. See J. R. Bettersworth, *Confederate Mississippi* (1943); E. A. Miles, *Jacksonian Democracy in Mississippi* (1960); J. W. Silver, *Mississippi: The Closed Society* (1966); W. C. Harris, *Presidential Reconstruction in Mississippi* (1967); J. W. Garner, *Reconstruction in Mississippi* (1968); R. A. McLemore, *A History of Mississippi* (2 vol., 1973); Federal Writers' Project, *Mississippi: A Guide to the Magnolia State* (1938, repr. 1973).

Mississippi, river, c.100 mi (160 km) long, rising E of the Kawartha Lakes, S Ont., Canada, and flowing NE through Mississippi Lake, then N to the Ottawa River near Arnprior. It is navigable for small steamers.

Mississippi, river, principal river of the United States, c.2,350 mi (3,780 km) long, exceeded in length only by the Missouri River, the chief of its numerous tributaries. The combined Missouri-Mississippi system (from the Missouri's headwaters in the Rocky Mts. to the mouth of the Mississippi River) is c.3,740 mi (6,020 km) long and ranks as the world's third longest river system after the Nile and the Amazon. With its tributaries, the Mississippi drains c.1,231,000 sq mi (3,188,290 sq km) of the central United States, including all or part of 31 states and c.13,000 sq mi (33,670 sq km) of Alberta and Saskatchewan in Canada. The Mississippi River rises in small streams that feed Lake Itasca (alt. 1,463 ft/446 m) in N Minnesota and flows generally south to enter the Gulf of Mexico through a huge delta in SE Louisiana. A major economic waterway, the river is navigable from the sediment-free channel maintained through South Pass in the delta to the Falls of St. Anthony in Minneapolis, with canals circumventing the rapids near Rock Island, Ill., and Keokuk, Iowa. There is a 40-ft (12.2-m) channel navigable by ocean-going vessels from Head of the Passes to Baton Rouge, La.; a 12-ft (3.7-m) channel from Baton Rouge to Vicksburg, Miss.; and a 9-ft (2.7-m) channel, deep enough for barges and towboats, from Vicksburg to Minneapolis. The Mississippi connects with the Intracoastal Waterway in the south and with the Great Lakes–St. Lawrence Seaway system in the north by way of the ILLINOIS WATERWAY. Along the river's upper course shipping is interrupted by ice from December to March; thick, hazardous fogs frequently settle on the cold waters of the unfrozen sections during warm spells from December to May. In its upper course the river is controlled by 41 dams and falls c.700 ft (210 m) in the 513-mi (826-km) stretch from Lake Itasca to Minneapolis and then falls c.490 ft (150 m) in 856 mi (1,378 km) from Minneapolis to Cairo, Ill. The Mississippi River receives the Missouri River 17 mi (27 km) N of St. Louis and expands to a width of c.3,500 ft (1,070 m); it swells to c.4,500 ft (1,370 m) at Cairo, where it receives the Ohio River. The lower Mississippi meanders in great loops across a broad alluvial plain (25–125 mi/40–201 km wide) that stretches from Cape Girardeau, Mo., to the delta section S of Natchez, Miss. The plain is marked with oxbow lakes and marshes that are remnants of the river's former channels. Natural levees, built up from sediment carried and deposited in times of flood, border the river for much of its length; sediment has also been deposited on the river bed, so that in places the surface of the Mississippi is above that of the surrounding plain, as evidenced by the St. Francis, Black, Yazoo, and Tensas river basins. Breaks in the levees frequently flood the fertile bottomlands of these and other low-lying areas of the plain. After receiving the Arkansas and Red rivers, the Mississippi enters a birdsfoot-type delta, where it discharges into the Gulf of Mexico through a number of distributaries, the most important being the Atchafalaya River and Bayou Lafourche. The main stream continues southeast through the delta to enter the gulf through several mouths, including Southeast Pass, South Pass, and Pass à Loutre. In addition to the present delta, which was built outward by sediment carried by the main stream since c.1500 A.D., geologists recognize three earlier deltas. There are also indications that the river is preparing to abandon its present course and divert through the Atchafalaya River unless man intervenes. Sluggish bayous and freshwater lakes (such as Pontchartrain, Grand, and Salvador) dot the delta region. The flow of the river is greatest in the spring, when heavy rainfall and melting snow on the tributaries (especially the Missouri and the Ohio) cause the main stream to rise and frequently overflow its banks and levees, inundating vast areas of the plain. In the disastrous flood of 1927 the river was 80 mi (129 km) wide in places, and flood waters covered c.18 million acres (7.3 million hectares) of land. Since then the U.S. Congress has authorized the construction of dams on the upper Mississippi and its tributaries to regulate the flow; the building of c.1,600 mi (2,580 km) of levees below Cape Girardeau to contain the swollen river; and the establishment of floodways to divert water at critical points, such as the Cairo–New Madrid, Atchafalaya, and Morganza floodways and the Bonnet Carre Spillway at New Orleans, which diverts water into Lake Pontchartrain. Cutoffs have eliminated the dangerous winding channels, and an improved main channel has increased the river's flood-carrying capacity. Nonetheless, serious, record-breaking floods again occurred in the rainy spring of 1973, when the river crested at St. Louis at 43.3 ft (13.2 m), remained at flood stage for 77 days, flooded c.14 million acres (5.7 million hectares), and drove about 50,000 persons from their homes. The Spanish explorer Hernando De Soto is credited with the European discovery of the Mississippi River in 1541. The French explorers Jacques Marquette and Louis Jolliet reached it through the Wisconsin River in 1673, and in 1682 La Salle traveled down the river to the Gulf of Mexico and claimed the entire territory for France. The French founded New Orleans in 1718 and effectively extended control over the upper river basin with settlements at Cahokia, Kaskaskia, Prairie du Chien, and St. Louis. France ceded the river to Spain in 1763 but regained it in 1800; the United States acquired the Mississippi River as part of the Louisiana Purchase in 1803. A major artery for the Indians and the fur-trading French, the river became in the 19th cent. the principal outlet for the newly settled areas of mid-America; exports were floated downstream with the current, and imports were poled or dragged upstream on rafts and keelboats. The first steamboat plied the river in 1811, and successors became increasingly luxurious as river trade increased in profitability and importance. Traffic from the north ceased after the outbreak of the Civil War. During the Civil War the Mississippi was an invasion route for Union armies and the scene of many important battles. Especially decisive were the capture of New Orleans (1862) by Adm. David Farragut, the Union naval commander, and the victory of Union forces under General Grant at Vicksburg in 1863. River traffic resumed after the end of the war; it is colorfully described in Mark Twain's *Life on the Mississippi* (1883). However, much of the trade was lost to the railroads in the mid-1800s, and the river ports declined in importance. With modern improvements in the channels of the river there has been a great increase in traffic, especially since the mid-1950s, with bulky items such as petroleum products, chemicals, sand, gravel, and limestone being the principal items of freight. River regulation projects in the entire Mississippi basin have made it one of the world's greatest inland waterway systems. Cotton and rice are important crops in the lower Mississippi valley; sugarcane is raised in the delta. The Mississippi is rich in freshwater fish; shrimp are taken from the briny delta waters. The delta also yields sulfur, oil, and gas. There is a 220-acre (89-hectare) model of the Mississippi River basin at Clinton, Miss., which has been used by the U.S. Corps of Engineers to simulate various conditions in the basin. See B. A. Botkin, ed., *A Treasury of Mississippi River Folklore* (1955); Willard Price, *The Amazing Mississippi* (1962); Wright Morris, ed., *The Mississippi River Reader* (1962); Walter Havighurst, *The Upper Mississippi Valley* (1966); Hodding Carter, *Man and the River: The Mississippi* (1970); Bern Keating, *The Mighty Mississippi* (1971); B. L. Burman, *Look Down that Winding River: An Informal Profile of the Mississippi* (1973).

Mississippi, University of, mainly at Oxford; state supported; coeducational; chartered 1844, opened 1848. The university medical center, which includes the schools of medicine and nursing, is in Jackson. The university's additional facilities include an engineering experiment station, a seismological observatory, and an urban research institute. The school also maintains a cooperative program with the national laboratories at Oak Ridge, Tenn.

Mississippian period: see CARBONIFEROUS PERIOD.

Mississippi Scheme, plan formulated by John LAW for the colonization and commercial exploitation of the Mississippi valley and other French colonial areas. In 1717 the French merchant Antoine Crozat transferred his monopoly of commercial privileges in LOUISIANA to Law, who, with the sanction of the French regent, Philippe II, duc d'Orléans, organized the Compagnie d'Occident. Its shares first depreciated in value but rose rapidly when Law, director of the new royal bank, promised to take over the stock at par at an early date. In 1719 the company absorbed several other organizations for the development of the Indies, China, and Africa, and Law thus controlled French colonial trade. The consolidated company, renamed the Compagnie des Indes (but commonly known as the Mississippi Company), was given, among other privileges, the right of farming the taxes. It then assumed the state debt and finally was officially amalgamated (1720) with the royal bank. Public confidence was such that a wild orgy of speculation in its shares had set in. The speculation received a strong impetus from Law's advertising, which described Louisiana as a land full of mountains of gold and silver. One story told of a fabulous emerald rock on the Arkansas River, and an expedition promptly set out to find it. Overexpansion of the company's activities, the almost complete lack of any real assets in the colonial areas, and the haste with which Law proceeded soon brought an end to his scheme. A few speculators sold their shares in time to make huge profits, but most were ruined when the "Mississippi Bubble" burst in Oct., 1720. In the governmental crisis that followed, Law's financial system was abolished, and he fled the country (Dec., 1720). Although a failure in its financial aspects, the Mississippi Scheme was responsible for the largest influx of settlers into Louisiana up to that time.

Mississippi Sound, arm of the Gulf of Mexico, c.100 mi (160 km) long and from 7 to 15 mi (11–24 km) wide, extending from Lake Borgne in Louisiana on the west to Mobile Bay in Alabama on the east. It is part of the Intracoastal Waterway and is separated from the Gulf by a series of narrow islands and sand bars. Cat, Horn, Petit Bois, and Dauphin are the main islands. Gulfport, Biloxi, and Pascagoula, Miss., are on the Mississippi Sound.

Mississippi State College for Women, at Columbus; the first state-supported women's college; chartered 1884, opened 1885 as Mississippi Industrial Institute and College, renamed 1920.

Mississippi State University, at State College, near Starkville; land-grant and state supported; coeducational; chartered 1878 as an agricultural and mechanical college, opened 1880. From 1932 to 1958 it was known as Mississippi State College.

Missolonghi, Greece: see MESOLÓNGION.

Missoula (mĭzo͞o'lə), city (1970 pop. 29,497), seat of Missoula co., W Mont., on the Clark Fork of the Columbia River; inc. 1889. In the midst of five watered valleys, large forests, and an extensive dairy and cattle area, Missoula is a commercial and medical center with a busy lumber industry. The Treaty of Hell Gate in 1855 between the warring Salish (Flathead) and Blackfoot Indian nations brought peace to the area and opened it to settlement. Hell Gate town was founded nearby in 1860 and moved to the present Missoula site six years later. The coming (1883, 1908) of the railroads stimulated Missoula's growth. The Univ. of Montana and a regional headquarters of the U.S. Forest Service are there. Abundant game and fish in the area attract sportsmen.

Missouri (mĭzo͞o'rē, —rə), state (1970 pop. 4,677,399), 69,686 sq mi (180,487 sq km), central United States, admitted as the 24th state of the Union in 1821. The capital is JEFFERSON CITY, and the largest cities are SAINT LOUIS, KANSAS CITY, SPRINGFIELD, and INDEPENDENCE. Missouri is bounded on the N by Iowa; on the W by Nebraska, Kansas, and Oklahoma; on the S by Arkansas; and on the E, where the Mississippi River forms the border, by Illinois, Kentucky, and Tennessee. The state lies north of lat. 36°-30'N except for a small area in the extreme southeast that protrudes into Arkansas. Two great rivers, the Mississippi and the Missouri, have had a great influence on the development of Missouri. The Mississippi tied the region to the South, particularly to New Orleans, and the Missouri, which crosses the state from west to east and enters the Mississippi near St. Louis, was the greatest avenue of pioneer advance westward across the continent. Even today, Missouri represents a merging of the divergent cultures of the South and West—St. Louis and the area to the south still evidence the lower Mississippi influence, but Kansas City and St. Joseph are markedly western cities. The region N of the Missouri River is largely prairie land, where, not unlike the Iowa plains to the north, corn and livestock are raised. Most of the region S of the Missouri is covered by foothills and by the plateau of the Ozark Mts., a unique region of soft hill scenery populated by a relatively isolated, self-reliant people. The rough, heavily forested eastern section of the Ozarks extends into the less hilly farming plateau in the west and encompasses the irregular, twisting Lake of the Ozarks to the northwest. In SW Missouri there is a long, narrow area of flat land, part of the Great Plains, where livestock and forage crops are raised. In the southeast below Cape Girardeau are the cotton fields of the Mississippi flood plain, an area that was once swampy but was improved after the establishment of a drainage system in 1805. The state's rivers have periodically flooded and eroded Missouri's fertile farmlands. Metropolitan areas, too, have occasionally suffered extensive damage, as in the disastrous 1951 flood at the confluence of the Missouri and the Kansas rivers at Kansas City and the record-breaking 1973 flood in the St. Louis area, at the junction of the Mississippi and Missouri rivers. The Missouri River basin project represents a major flood control effort. Early in the area's geologic development swampy prehistoric jungles formed the basis of coal deposits and fire clays in parts of the state. Retreating glaciers of the Ice Age formed the fertile plains in the north, and inland seas laid down deposits of limestone and sandstone. Coal was formed in the west and north central sections, lead in the southeast, and zinc in the southwest. These and other mineral resources are exploited by Missouri's mining concerns. Lead, cement, stone, and iron ore are the chief minerals produced, and in 1972 Missouri was the leading state in the production of lead.

Missouri's economy rests chiefly on industry, however. The manufacture of transportation equipment is the major industry in the state; food products and chemicals are next in commercial importance, followed by printing and publishing. Nonelectrical machinery, fabricated metals, and electrical equipment are also produced. St. Louis is an important center for the manufacture of metals and chemicals. In Kansas City, long a leading market for livestock and wheat, the manufacture of vending machines and of cars and trucks are leading industries. Outside of its major cities, Missouri remains predominantly agricultural, and farming contributes substantially to the state's income. The most valuable farm products are cattle, hogs, soybeans, and dairy items. Missouri ranked fourth in the production of hogs in 1972 and eighth in the production of cattle. After soybeans, the chief crops are corn, hay, and wheat. Springfield is a major agricultural center; Sedalia is the site of the annual state fair; and every fall Kansas City is host to the Midwest's largest horse and cattle show, the American Royal. The development of resorts in the Ozarks has encouraged tourism and added to the state's income. Missouri's recorded history begins in the latter half of the 17th cent. when the French explorers Jacques Marquette and Louis Jolliet descended the Mississippi River, followed by Robert Cavelier, sieur de La Salle, who claimed the whole area drained by the Mississippi River for France and called the territory Louisiana. When the French explorers came the area was inhabited by the Osage and the Missouri Indians, and by the end of the 17th cent. French trade with the Indians flourished. In the early 18th cent. the French worked the area's lead mines and made numerous trips through Missouri in search of furs. Trade down the Mississippi prompted the settlement of Ste Geneviève about 1735 and the founding of St. Louis in 1764 by Pierre Laclede and René Auguste Chouteau, who were both in the fur-trading business. Although not involved in any fighting in the French and Indian War (1754–63), Missouri was affected by the French defeat when in 1762 France secretly ceded the territory W of the Mississippi to Spain. In 1800 the Louisiana Territory (including the Missouri area) was retroceded to France, but in 1803 it passed to the United States as part of the LOUISIANA PURCHASE. French influence remained dominant, even though by this time Americans had filtered into the territory, particularly to the lead mines at Ste Geneviève and Potosi. By the time of the LEWIS AND CLARK EXPEDITION (1803–6), St. Louis was already known as the gateway to the Far West. The U.S. Territory of Missouri was set up in 1812, but settlement was slow even after the War of 1812, and Indian hostilities were not brought under control until 1816. The coming of the steamboat increased traffic and trade on the Mississippi, and settlement progressed. Planters from the South had introduced slavery into the territory, but their plantations were restricted to a small area. However, the question of admitting the Missouri Territory as a state became a burning national issue because it involved the question of extending slavery into the territories. The dispute was resolved by the MISSOURI COMPROMISE, which admitted (1821) Missouri to the Union as a slave state, but excluded slavery from lands of the Louisiana Purchase north of lat. 36°30'. Slaveholding interests became politically powerful, but the state remained principally a fur-trading center. The prominent

Chouteau family and Manuel Lisa of the Missouri Fur Company had set up fur trading on a large scale in the first decade of the century, and by 1821 the AMERICAN FUR COMPANY was allied with the Chouteau interests in St. Louis. In 1822, W. H. Ashley (who later made a fortune in fur trading) led an expedition of the adventurous trappers who became known as MOUNTAIN MEN up the Missouri River to explore the West for furs. The fur trade in St. Louis later came under the dominance of Pierre Chouteau. From Missouri traders established a thriving commerce over the SANTA FE TRAIL with the inhabitants of New Mexico, and pioneers followed the OREGON TRAIL to settle the Northwest. Franklin, Westport, Independence, and St. Joseph became famous as the points of origin of these expeditions. Settlement of Missouri itself quickened, spreading in the 1820s over the river valleys into central Missouri and by 1830s into W Missouri. The present boundaries of the state were formed after the Indians gave up their claim to Platte co. in 1836, and this strip of land in the northwest corner of present-day Missouri was added to the state. Mormon immigrants came to settle Missouri in the 1830s, but their opposition to slavery and their growing numbers made them unwelcome and they were driven from the state in 1839. German immigrants, however, were cordially received during the 1840s and 50s. They settled principally about St. Louis and were to contribute outstanding leaders to the state and nation, notably the political leader, Carl Schurz. In 1846, Missourians took part in the Mexican War, fighting under, among others, the Missouri legislator and soldier, Alexander W. Doniphan. In 1854 the problem of slavery was made acute with the passage of the KANSAS-NEBRASKA ACT, leaving the question of slavery in the Kansas and Nebraska territories to the settlers themselves. The proslavery forces in Missouri became very active in trying to win Kansas for the slave cause and contributed to the violence and disorder that tore the territory apart in the years just prior to the Civil War. Nevertheless Missouri also had leaders opposed to slavery, including one of its Senators, Thomas Hart Benton. During the Civil War most Missourians remained loyal to the Federal government, largely through the activity of Unionists like Francis P. Blair (1821–75), legislator and later Union general. A state convention, which met in March, 1861, voted against secession, and in 1862, after deposing the pro-Southern administration of Gov. Claiborne F. Jackson, the convention set up a provisional government headed by Hamilton R. Gamble. In Aug., 1861, the Union general John C. Frémont issued without authorization a proclamation instituting martial law in Missouri and freeing all slaves; Lincoln promptly countermanded with an order to modify the decree to conform with existing Federal law. Meanwhile, Camp Jackson at St. Louis, which was considered pro-Confederate, was overwhelmed (May, 1861) by a pro-Union force under Gen. Nathaniel Lyon. Union forces under Lyon were defeated at Wilson's Creek (Aug. 10, 1861), but the Confederates were routed (March, 1862) at Pea Ridge (NW Arkansas) and did not again reappear in force until 1864 when Sterling Price led a brief invasion against his native state. However, guerrilla activities persisted during this period, including those of William C. Quantrill. The lawlessness bred by civil warfare persisted in Missouri after the war in the activities of outlaws such as Jesse James. A new Missouri rose out of the war—the semi-Southern atmosphere, along with the river life and steamboating, began to decline, but the flavor of the period was preserved in the works of one of Missouri's most celebrated sons, Mark Twain. The coming of the railroads brought the eventual decay of many of Missouri's river towns and tied the state more closely to the East and North. Urbanization and industrialization progressed, and the Louisiana Purchase Exposition, held at St. Louis in 1904, dramatically revealed Missouri's economic growth. Although during World War I general prosperity prevailed in the state, the depression years of the 1930s sent farm values crashing down, and many banks, especially in rural areas, failed. Prosperity returned, however, during World War II, when both St. Louis and Kansas City served as vital mid-continental transportation centers. After the war Missouri's industrialization increased enormously. In 1945, Missouri adopted a new state constitution that is still in effect today. The governor of the state is elected for a term of four years. The general assembly, or legislature, has a senate with 34 members elected for four years and a house of representatives with 163 members elected for two years. The state also elects 10 Representatives and 2 Senators to the U.S. Congress and has 12 electoral votes in presidential elections. Christopher S. Bond, a Republican, became governor in 1973. Since the brief period of radical Republican rule from 1864 to 1870, Missouri has been permanently wedded to neither major party. While tending toward the Republicans in the days of Theodore Roosevelt, it turned solidly Democratic for Franklin D. Roosevelt and helped to elect Missourian Harry S. Truman to the presidency in 1948. Political machines in the large cities have attracted national attention, notably the machine of Thomas J. Pendergast (1872–1945) in Kansas City. Missouri has contributed to the United States such outstanding statesmen as Champ Clark, James Reed, and W. Stuart Symington. Thomas Hart Benton, a descendant of the Missouri Senator of the same name, was one of the country's important artists. Places of cultural and historic interest in Missouri include the Jefferson National Expansion Memorial, a national historic site, in St. Louis; George Washington Carver National Monument, in Diamond; Wilson's Creek National Battlefield, near Springfield; the William Rockhill Nelson Gallery of Art, in Kansas City; the Harry S. Truman Memorial Library, in Independence; and the Museum of the American Indian, in St. Joseph. Missouri's schools were desegregated following the Supreme Court decision in 1954, and integration has progressed without major incident. Institutes of higher learning include the Univ. of Missouri, at Columbia; Saint Louis Univ., Washington Univ., and Webster College, at St. Louis; Rockhurst College, at Kansas City; and Westminster College, at Fulton. See State Historical Society, *Historic Missouri* (1959); E. C. McReynolds, *Missouri: A History of the Crossroads State* (1962); Federal Writers' Project, *Missouri: A Guide to the "Show Me" State* (1941, repr. 1973). A 5-vol. history of the state is in preparation under the general editorship of W. E. Parrish: Vol. I, W. E. Foley (1971); Vol. II, P. A. McCandless (1972); and Vol. III, W. E. Parrish (1973).

Missouri, river, c.2,565 mi (4,130 km) long (including its Jefferson-Beaverhead-Red Rock headstream), the longest river of the United States and the principal tributary of the Mississippi River. The length of the combined Missouri-Mississippi system from the headwaters of the Missouri to the mouth of the Mississippi is c.3,740 mi (6,020 km), making it the world's third longest river after the Nile and the Amazon. The Missouri River drains an area of c.580,000 sq mi (1,502,200 sq km), including 2,550 sq mi (6,600 sq km) in Canada. The principal headwaters of the Missouri are the Jefferson, Madison, and Gallatin rivers, which rise high in the Rocky Mts., SW Mont., and join to form the Missouri near Three Forks, Mont. The Missouri's upper course flows north through scenic mountain terrain including Gate of the Mountains, a deep gorge. At Great Falls, Mont., the river enters a 10-mi (16-km) stretch of cataracts that prevented navigation to the upper river and effectively established Fort Benton, Mont., as the head of navigation for 19th-century riverboats. Below Fort Benton, the Missouri follows a meandering course east then southeast across the Great Plains of central United States, crossing Montana, North Dakota, and South Dakota, and forming part of the boundaries of Nebraska, Kansas, and Iowa before crossing Missouri and entering the Mississippi River 17 mi (27 km) N of St. Louis. Nicknamed "Big Muddy" for its heavy load of silt, the brown waters of the Missouri do not readily mix with the gray waters of the Mississippi until c.100 mi (160 km) downstream. The Yellowstone and Platte rivers are the Missouri's chief tributaries. Above Sioux City, Iowa, the Missouri's fluctuating flow is regulated by seven major dams (Gavins Point, Fort Randall, Big Bend, OAHE, GARRISON, FORT PECK, and Canyon Ferry) and more than 80 other dams on tributary streams. These dams, with their reservoirs, are part of the coordinated, basin-wide MISSOURI RIVER BASIN PROJECT (authorized by the U.S. Congress in 1944), which provides for flood control, hydroelectric power, irrigation water, and recreational facilities. The dams serve to impound for later use the spring rains and snow melt that swell the volume of the river in March and April and also the second flood stage that frequently occurs in June as the snow melts in the remoter mountain regions. Since the dams have no locks, Sioux City is the head of navigation for the 9-ft (2.7-m) channel maintained over the 760-mi (1,223-km) stretch downstream to the Mississippi. Tugboats pushing strings of barges move freight along this route. From December to March, navigation is interrupted by ice and low water levels (resulting from upstream freezing); summer water levels, which frequently fall so low as to cause river boats to go aground, are now maintained at safe levels by the release of water from Gavin Point Dam. Silt, fertilizers, and pesticides, which are contained in the runoff from agricultural lands, pollute the water above Sioux City, but wastes from industrial plants and from inadequately treated municipal sewage create a more serious level of pollution downstream. The Missouri River was an important artery of commerce for the village Indians of the Plains culture long before the French explorers Jacques Marquette and Louis Jolliet passed the mouth of the river in 1683 and the Canadian explorer Vérendrye visited the upper reaches of the river in 1738. David Thompson, a Canadian fur trader, explored part of the river in 1797. Meriwether Lewis and William Clark followed the Missouri on their journey (1803–6) to the Pacific Ocean and described it at length (see LEWIS AND CLARK EXPEDITION). The first steamboat ascended the river in 1819 and hundreds more later navigated the uncertain waters to Fort Benton. Mormons bound for Utah and pioneers bound for Oregon and California followed the Missouri valley and that of the Platte overland to the West. River traffic declined with the loss of freight to the railroads after the Civil War, but it has been revitalized in the 20th cent., in the section below Sioux City, through the navigational improvements and flood control efforts of the Missouri River basin project. See P. E. Chappell, *A History of the Missouri River* (1911); Stanley Vestal, *The Missouri* (1964); Rufus Terral, *The Missouri Valley: Land of Drouth, Flood, and Promise* (1947; repr. 1970); Bernard De Voto, *Across the Wide Missouri* (1947; repr. 1972); H. M. Chittenden, *Early Steamboat Navigation on the Missouri River* (1972).

Missouri, University of, at Columbia, Rollo, Kansas City, and St. Louis; land-grant and state supported; coeducational; chartered 1839, opened 1841. It is the oldest state university W of the Mississippi; its journalism school was the first (1908) in the world. The school of mines and metallurgy and the mining experiment station are at Rolla. A forestry camp is near Poplar Bluff, a geology camp at Lander, Wyo., and an experimental farm in St. Charles county.

Missouri Compromise, 1820–21, measures passed by the U.S. Congress to end the first of a series of crises concerning the extension of slavery. By 1818, Missouri Territory had gained sufficient population to warrant its admission into the Union as a state. Settlers came largely from the South, and it was expected that Missouri would be a slave state. To a statehood bill brought before the House of Representatives, James Tallmadge of New York proposed an amendment that would forbid importation of slaves and would bring about the ultimate emancipation of all slaves born in Missouri. This amendment passed the House (Feb., 1819), but not the Senate. The bitterness of the debates sharply emphasized the sectional division of the United States. In Jan., 1820, a bill to admit Maine as a state passed the House. The admission of Alabama as a slave state in 1819 had brought the slave states and free states to equal representation in the Senate, and it was seen that by pairing Maine (certain to be a free state) and Missouri, this equality would be maintained. The two bills were joined as one in the Senate, with the clause forbidding slavery in Missouri replaced by a measure prohibiting slavery in the remainder of the Louisiana Purchase north of 36°30′ (the southern boundary of Missouri). The House rejected this compromise bill, but after a conference committee of members of both houses was appointed, the bills were treated separately, and in March, 1820, Maine was made a state and Missouri was authorized to adopt a constitution having no restrictions on slavery. However, the provision in the Missouri constitution barring the immigration of free Negroes to the state was objectionable to many Northern Congressmen, and necessitated another congressional compromise. Not until the Missouri legislature pledged that nothing in its constitution would be interpreted to abridge the rights of citizens of the United States was the charter approved and Missouri admitted to the Union (Aug., 1821). Henry CLAY, as speaker of the House, did much to secure passage of the compromise—so much, in fact, that he is generally regarded as its author, even though Senator Jesse B. Thomas of Illinois was far more responsible for the first bill. The 36°30′ proviso held until 1854, when the KANSAS-NEBRASKA ACT repealed the Missouri Compromise. See studies by Glover Moore (1953, repr. 1967) and R. H. Brown (1964).

Missouri River basin project, comprehensive plan for the coordinated development of water resources of the MISSOURI River and its tributaries, draining an area of c.513,300 sq mi (1,329,400 sq km) in Nebraska, Montana, South Dakota, North Dakota, Wyoming, Kansas, Missouri, Colorado, Iowa, and Minnesota. The program provides for the construction of 112 dams with a storage capacity of almost 35 million gal/132 million liters; 4,300,000 acres (1,740,000 hectares) of irrigated land; 2.6 million kilowatts of hydroelectric generating capacity; a 9-ft (2.7-m) navigable channel on the Missouri River from Sioux City to its mouth; control of floods and sedimentation; protection of fish and wildlife; and development of recreational facilities and industrial and municipal water supplies. Seven main-stem dams on the Missouri are complete (FORT PECK, GARRISON, OAHE, Big Bend, Fort Randall, Gavins Point, and Canyon Ferry), and 80 other dams have been built on tributaries; 370,000 acres (149,700 hectares) have been irrigated. Small-scale improvements made in the basin in the 1930s led to the development of two separate plans for the region advanced by the U.S. Corps of Engineers in 1943 and by the Bureau of Reclamation (see RECLAMATION, UNITED STATES BUREAU OF) in 1944 that were consolidated into a single plan—commonly called the Pick-Sloan Plan—authorized by Congress in the 1944 Flood Control Act. In 1945 the Missouri Basin Interagency Committee was formed to coordinate the gigantic scheme; on the committee are the governors of the ten states involved and representatives of seven Federal agencies. The program has been modified and expanded over the years and is now integrated with other projects for the region, including the COLORADO-BIG THOMPSON PROJECT, the SHOSHONE PROJECT, and the NORTH PLATTE PROJECT.

mist: see FOG.

Mistassini, Lake, c.840 sq mi (2,180 sq km), S Que., Canada, NW of Lake St. John, in sparsely settled country. It drains W to James Bay by way of the Rupert River (380 mi/612 km long).

Misti, El (ĕl mē'stē), dormant volcano, c.19,150 ft (5,840 m) high, in the Cordillera Occidental, S Peru, rising over the city of Arequipa. El Misti is flanked by two other volcanos—on the NW by Chachani, 19,960 ft (6,083 m) high, and on the SE by Pichu Pichu, 18,400 ft (5,608 m) high. El Misti, with its perfect snow-capped cone, apparently achieved significance in the Inca religion, and has often figured in Peruvian legends and poetry.

mistletoe, common name for the Loranthaceae, a family of chiefly tropical parasitic herbs and shrubs with leathery evergreen leaves and waxy white berries. Mistletoes are aerial parasites, attaching themselves to their hosts by modified roots called haustoria, with which they absorb water and food from the host. The list of hosts is varied and numerous. Mistletoes are widely used for Christmas decoration. The custom of kissing under a branch of mistletoe apparently originated among the Druids and other early Europeans, to whom mistletoe was sacred. From early times it has been associated with folklore and superstition; it was thought to cure many ills. The mistletoe most widely sold in America is *Phoradendron flavescens;* most popular in Europe is the "true" mistletoe, *Viscum album,* which is parasitic especially on apple trees. An American genus (*Arceuthobium*) with several species found along the Pacific coast is parasitic on conifers. The largest genus of the family, *Loranthus,* is predominantly African. The mistletoe family is classified in the division MAGNOLIOPHYTA, class Magnoliopsida, order Sontales.

Mistral, Frédéric (frādārĕk' mĕsträl'), 1830–1914, French Provençal poet. With Théodore Aubanel he was one of the seven founders (1854) of the Félibrige, an organization to promote Provençal as a literary language (see PROVENÇAL LITERATURE). He was the leader of the movement and was recognized as its greatest poet. Besides many short poems he wrote four verse romances, notably *Mirèio* (1859, tr. 1867). He published a Provençal dictionary (1878–86) and wrote memoirs (tr. 1907). His verse is characterized rather by ease and beauty of language than by power of thought. He shared with Echegaray the 1904 Nobel Prize in Literature. See studies by C. A. Downer (1901), Richard Aldington (1960), and Tudor Edwards (1965).

Mistral, Gabriela (gäbrēä'lä), 1889–1957, Chilean poet whose original name was Lucila Godoy Alcayaga. She was a teacher in and director of rural schools in Chile before she attained wider acclaim as an educator. Mistral was noted for her revision of the Mexican school system under José VASCONCELOS. Subsequently, she served as Chilean consul in various European and Latin American cities and represented her country at the League of Nations and the United Nations. The mystery of childbearing, the sorrow of a tragic love, and a burning desire for justice are recurrent themes of her fluent and lyric verse. The early *Sonetos de la muerte* [*sonnets of death*] (1915) is considered one of her finest achievements. *Desolación* (1922), *Tala* (1938), and *Lagar* (1954) are three of her major volumes. *Selected Poems,* translated by Langston Hughes, was published in 1957. In 1945, Mistral received the Nobel Prize in Literature, the first Latin American to be so honored. See studies by M. C. Preston (1964) and M. C. Taylor (1968).

Misurata: see MISRATAH, Libya.

mita: see PEONAGE.

Mitanni, ancient kingdom established in the 2d millennium B.C. in NW Mesopotamia. It was founded by Aryans but was later made up predominantly of Hurrians. Washshukanni was its capital. Mitanni controlled Assyria for a period and was engaged in military efforts to hold back Egyptian forces intent on conquering Syria. In c.1450 B.C. the army of Thutmose III of Egypt successfully advanced as far as the Euphrates; the king of Mitanni surrendered, sending tribute to Egypt, which halted its invasion. Friendly relations later developed between the two powers as evidenced by correspondence between King Tushratta of Mitanni and Amenhotep III of Egypt. In the 14th cent. B.C., Mitanni became involved in struggles with the Hittites and c.1335 fell to the Hittites as well as to resurgent Assyrian forces.

Mitau: see YELGAVA, USSR.

Mitava: see YELGAVA, USSR.

Mitcham: see MERTON.

Mitchel, John, 1815–75, Irish revolutionist and journalist. A practicing lawyer, Mitchel contributed articles to the *Nation* (Dublin) and the *United Irishman,* which he founded in 1848, calling for rebellion against Britain. He was transported to Australia for sedition before the abortive Young Ireland revolt of 1848, which he had helped prepare, was carried out. He escaped to the United States in 1853, where he led a turbulent and contentious career as a journalist, editing the proslavery journal *Citizen* (1854–55) in New York City, and during the Civil War, the Richmond *Enquirer.* After a short imprisonment (1865) for his Confederate activities, he became acknowledged leader of the Irish-American nationalists, and as such edited the *Irish Citizen.* He returned to Ireland and was elected (1875) to Parliament shortly before his death. His *Jail Journal* (1854; new ed., with intro. by Arthur Griffith, 1945) is an Irish revolutionary classic. See biographies by P. S. O'Hegarty (1917) and Seamus MacCall (1938).

Mitchell, Arthur, 1934–, American dancer, b. New York City. Mitchell studied in New York City and appeared on Broadway and with various companies at home and abroad. He joined the New York City Ballet in 1956, becoming a soloist in 1959. The first black premier danseur in history, he remained with the company for 20 years. His performance as Puck in *A Midsummer Night's Dream* (1964) was especially acclaimed. He also performed with distinction in *Western Symphony, Agon, Afternoon of a Faun,* and *Ebony Concerto.* In 1968, Mitchell founded a ballet school in Harlem, New York City, in order to provide classical academic training to black students. By 1970 under his direction the school developed into the DANCE THEATRE OF HARLEM, the first black classical ballet company.

Mitchell, John, 1870–1919, American labor leader, b. Braidwood, Ill. He became a miner at the age of 12 and in 1885 joined the Knights of Labor. When the United Mine Workers of America was formed (1890), he became a member; after his successful leadership of the S Illinois soft-coal miners in the strike of 1897, he was national vice president, then president from 1898 to 1908, when he resigned. His leadership of the anthracite miners' strike in 1902 secured better wages and working conditions in the industry, substantially increased membership in the union, and brought him recognition from members and the public as an outstandingly able leader. As a vice president (1899–1914) of the American Federation of Labor, he was a strong advocate of the "sacredness of contract," in which he was opposed by the more radical factions in the federation. In 1914 he was appointed commissioner of labor for New York state and was from 1915 to 1919 chairman of the state industrial commission. He wrote *Organized Labor* (1903) and *The Wage Earner and His Problems* (1913). See biography by Elsie Glück (1929, repr. 1971).

Mitchell, John Newton, 1913–, U.S. Attorney-General (1969–72), b. Detroit. A law partner of Richard M. NIXON, he managed Nixon's 1968 presidential campaign and was made (1969) Attorney-General. In March, 1972, he became head of the Nixon reelection committee, but he resigned in June, following the break-in at the Watergate offices of the Democratic National Committee by employees of the reelection committee. Subsequent investigations of the WATERGATE AFFAIR led to Mitchell's indictment, trial, and conviction (Jan. 1, 1975) on charges of conspiracy, obstruction of justice, and perjury. He was also tried, but acquitted (April, 1974), on charges related to the secret contributions to Nixon's campaign funds made by financier Robert Vesco.

Mitchell, Margaret, 1900–49, American novelist, b. Atlanta, Ga. Her one novel, *Gone with the Wind* (1936; Pulitzer Prize), a romantic, panoramic portrait of the Civil War and Reconstruction periods in Georgia, is one of the most popular novels in the history of American publishing. The film adaptation (1939) has also been extraordinarily successful.

Mitchell, Maria, 1818–89, American astronomer, b. Nantucket, Mass. She taught school in Nantucket and later became a librarian there. She made a special study of sunspots, nebulas, and satellites and discovered a comet in 1847. After 1865 she was professor of astronomy at Vassar College. She was the first woman to be elected to the American Academy of Arts and Sciences. See biographies by P. M. Kendall (1896), M. K. Babbitt (1912), and Helen Wright (1949).

Mitchell, Silas Weir, 1829–1914, American physician and author, b. Philadelphia, M.D. Jefferson Medical College, 1850, studied in Paris. A pioneer in the application of psychology to medicine, he won special fame for his treatment of nervous disorders and for his study of the nervous system. His medical works include treatises on snake venom and neurology, as well as *Injuries of Nerves and Their Consequences* (1872) and *Fat and Blood* (1877), which summarizes his well-known rest cure. Among his novels are historical romances (*Hugh Wynne, Free Quaker,* 1896) and psychological studies (*Constance Trescot,* 1905). He wrote several volumes of poetry and interspersed lyrics in his novels. See biographies by E. P. Earnest (1950), D. S. Rein (1952), and J. P. Lovering (1971).

Mitchell, Wesley Clair, 1874–1948, American economist, b. Rushville, Ill. He received his Ph.D. (1899) from the Univ. of Chicago, where he studied under Thorstein Veblen and John Dewey, and he taught at several institutions, including the Univ. of California, Columbia, and the New School for Social Research. He also served on many government committees, was chairman of the President's Committee on Social Trends (1929–33), and helped found the National Bureau of Economic Research. One of the most eminent American economists, Mitchell refuted many of the tenets of orthodox economics and turned toward an institutional analysis based on behaviorist psychology. His chief researches were centered on investigation, often statistical, of the business cycle; his *Business Cycles* (1913, 2d ed. 1927) is his most important work. His other books include *A History of the Greenbacks* (1903), *The Backward Art of Spending Money* (1937), and *Measuring Business Cycles* (with A. F. Burns, 1946). See biography (ed. by A. F. Burns, 1952).

Mitchell, William (Billy Mitchell), 1879–1936, American army officer and pilot, b. Nice, France. He enlisted (1898) in the U.S. army in the Spanish-American War and received a commission in the regular army in 1901, serving with the signal corps. Rising during World War I to the rank of brigadier general, he organized and ably commanded the American expeditionary air force. After the war, he became assistant chief of air service in the U.S. army, and, as an advocate of air power, argued vehemently for a large independent air force. He urged the military potential of strategic bombing, airborne forces, and polar air routes, and created a national issue when, to demonstrate the superiority of air power, he directed the sensational sinking (1921–23) of several warships in prearranged tests. However, his sharp public criticisms of military leaders for neglect of air power led to his court martial (1925); he was sentenced to a five-year suspension from duty and forfeiture of pay, but resigned (1926) from the army. He continued to promote air power as a civilian, but not until World War II were his main ideas adopted. Mitchell's writings include *Winged Defense* (1925) and *Skyways* (1930). See biographies by I. D. Levine (1943, repr. 1972), Roger Burlingame (1952), and A. F. Hurley (1964); Burke Davis, *The Billy Mitchell Affair* (1967).

Mitchell, city (1970 pop. 13,425), seat of Davison co., SE S.Dak.; inc. 1881. Mitchell is a trade, distribution, and shipping center for a grain, dairy, and livestock area. It has meat-packing and food-processing plants. Its huge Corn Palace, which has murals of colored corn along its entire exterior, is redecorated annually. Harvest festivals are held every September. The city is the seat of Dakota Wesleyan Univ. Lake Mitchell is close by.

Mitchell, Mount, peak, 6,684 ft (2,037 m) high, W N.C., in the Black Mts. of the Appalachian system; highest peak E of the Mississippi River.

Mitchison, Naomi, 1897–, British writer, b. Scotland, educated at Oxford; daughter of the biologist J. S. Haldane. She has written many types of novels on a variety of subjects. They include historical novels set in ancient Greece and Rome, such as *The Bull Calves* (1945); fantasies, such as *Graeme and the Dragon* (1954); and documentary novels set in Scotland or Africa, such as *Swan's Road* (1954). She is active in local government in Scotland and since 1963 has been tribal advisor to the Bakgatla of Botswana.

mite, small, often microscopic arthropod that, along with the tick, makes up the order Acarina; it is also related to spiders. The unsegmented mite body is typically oval and compact, although a few, mostly parasites, are elongate and wormlike. There are four pairs of legs. The movable head is attached to the body by a hinge. There are four stages in the life cycle: egg, larva, nymph, and adult. The thousands of different species are worldwide in distribution and occupy diverse habitats, including plant galls, mosses, other animals, and surface litter or upper layers of the soil. One group, the water mites, has returned to an aquatic environment, both fresh and salt water. Mites eat plant or animal substances, decaying organisms, and humus, and also infest stored food products such as cheese, meat, grains, and flour. The red spider, a mite and not a spider, feeds on plants and is destructive to crops. Many mites are parasitic on other arthropods, on mollusks, or on vertebrates. Mange and scabies mites lay their eggs in the skin and cause irritation in man and fur-bearing animals. Other species are parasitic on the skin of birds and reptiles, and some live in the respiratory channels of birds and mammals. Chiggers, the larvae of harvest mites, transmit the organism that causes scrub typhus. Fowl mites feed on the blood of poultry. The larger members of the order Acarina, the ticks, are all parasitic in at least one developmental stage; most parasitize mammals and birds although some have reptilian and amphibian hosts. An anchoring structure in the tick's mouth enables it to embed its entire head under the skin of the host, where it sucks the host's blood. If a tick is pulled off the host the head usually remains embedded in the skin. Members of the family of soft ticks, with a membranous outer covering, hide in crevices and come out at night to suck blood. Hard ticks, with thickened outer plates made of CHITIN, remain attached to the host for long periods. Ticks transmit diseases such as ROCKY MOUNTAIN SPOTTED FEVER, TULAREMIA, and EQUINE ENCEPHALITIS. Mites and ticks belong in the phylum ARTHROPODA, class Arachnida, order Acarina.

miterwort: see SAXIFRAGE.

Mitford, Mary Russell, 1787–1855, English author. Her first volume of poetry (1810) sold well despite adverse criticism. Later she turned to playwriting, writing one notable success, *Rienzi* (1828). *Our Village* (5 vol., 1824–32), a series of gently humorous rural sketches, established her reputation and gained for her a wide following. Her later works include a novel, *Belford Regis* (1835); other series of tales, such as *Atherton* (1854); and *Recollections of a Literary Life* (1852). See her letters (ed. by A. G. K. L'Estrange, 2 vol., 1870).

Mitford, Nancy, 1904–73, English novelist and biographer, b. London. She managed a London bookshop during World War II and moved to Paris in 1945. Mitford was born into the British aristocracy, which she satirizes in her novels, notably *In Pursuit of Love* (1945) and *Love in a Cold Climate* (1949). Her writing is sophisticated, malicious, and captivating. Indeed her boring, bigoted, illiterate lords and amoral, irresponsible ladies have taken on the qualities of myth. She also wrote biographies of Madame de Pompadour (1954) and Frederick the Great (1970). Mitford's sister **Jessica Mitford,** 1917–, is also a writer, b. London. Her works include *The American Way of Death* (1963), an exposé of American funeral homes, and *Kind and Usual Punishment* (1973), a critical study of American prisons. See her autobiography, *Daughters and Rebels* (1960).

Mithat Pasha: see MIDHAT PASHA.

Mithcah (mĭth'kə), unlocated desert encampment. Num. 33.28,29.

Mithnite (mĭth'nīt), obscure designation used of one of David's guards. 1 Chron. 11.43.

Mithra (mĭth'rə), ancient god of Persia and India (where he was called Mitra). Until the 6th cent. B.C., Mithra was apparently a minor figure in the Zoroastrian system. Under the Achaemenids, Mithra became increasingly important, until he appeared in the 5th cent. B.C. as the principal Persian deity, the god of light and wisdom, closely associated with the sun. His cult expanded through the Middle East into Europe and became a worldwide religion, called **Mithraism.** This was one of the great religions of the Roman Empire, and in the 2d cent. A.D. it was more general than Christianity. Mithraism found widest favor among the Roman legions, for whom Mithra (or Mithras in Latin and Greek) was the ideal divine comrade and fighter. The fundamental aspect of the Mithraic system was the dualistic struggle between the forces of good and evil. Mithra, who gave to his devotees hope of blessed immortality, represented the fearless antagonist of the powers of darkness. The story of Mithra's capture and sacrifice of a sacred bull, from whose body sprang all the beneficent things of the earth, was a central cultic myth. The ethics of Mithraism were rigorous; fasting and continence were strongly prescribed. The rituals, highly secret and restricted to men only, included many of the sacramental forms common to the mystery religions (e.g., baptism and the sacred banquet). Mithraism, which bore many similarities to Christianity, declined rapidly in the late 3d cent. A.D. See Franz Cumont, *The Mysteries of Mithra* (reissued, 1956) and Esmé Wynne-Tyson, *Mithras* (1958, repr. 1972).

Mithradates VI (Mithradates Eupator) (mĭthrədā'tēz), c.131 B.C.–63 B.C., king of Pontus, sometimes called Mithradates the Great. He extended his empire until, in addition to Pontus, he held Cappadocia, Paphlagonia, and the Black Sea coast beyond the Caucasus. The increasing importance of Rome in Asia Minor brought Mithradates and the republic into open conflict. The First Mithradatic War (88 B.C.–84 B.C.) was the result. Mithradates conquered the whole of Asia Minor (except for a few cities) in 88 B.C. In 85 B.C. the Roman general Fimbria attacked him in Asia Minor, and he was defeated simultaneously with the destruction of his army in Greece. In the resultant treaty Mithradates paid an indemnity and gave up all but Pontus and a few colonies. The Second Mithradatic War (83 B.C.–81 B.C.) was begun by Sulla's lieutenant Lucius Murena, who desired glory. Murena was repelled by Mithradates and was superseded by Aulus Gabinius, who made peace with the king of Pontus. The Third Mithradatic War (74 B.C.–63 B.C.) began when Mithradates resolved to prevent Rome from annexing Bithynia, which had been left to Rome by a royal will. LUCULLUS was sent against Mithradates, who was finally forced to flee to Armenia. In 68 B.C. the Romans invaded Armenia, but were forced to retreat. Mithradates returned to Pontus, and Lucullus was replaced (66 B.C.) by POMPEY. Pompey soon drove Mithradates eastward, and the king fled to the Crimea, the last of his provinces. He had a slave kill him. His fall is the subject of Racine's *Mithridate.* Pharnaces II was his son and Tigranes, his son-in-law. The name is also spelled Mithridates.

Mithredath (mĭth'rēdăth). **1** Cyrus's treasurer. Ezra 1.8. **2** Persian officer who hindered the rebuilding of the Temple. Ezra 4.7.

Mithridates VI: see MITHRADATES VI.

Mitilíni (mētēlyē'nyē) or **Mytilene** (mĭtĭlē'nē), city (1971 pop. 23,426), capital of Lesbos prefecture, E Greece, a port on the island of LESBOS in the Aegean Sea. Roman remains are there.

Mitla (mēt'lä) [Nahuatl,=abode of the dead], religious center of the ZAPOTEC, near Oaxaca, SW Mexico. Probably built in the 13th cent., the buildings, unlike the pyramidal structures of most Middle American architecture, are low, horizontal masses enclosing the plazas. Wall panels, decorated with hard stucco and intricate mosaics, show more than 20 different patterns of a single motif—the stepped spiral representing the plumed serpent QUETZALCOATL. With its subterranean chambers and passages decorated by fine frescoes, Mitla is thought to represent the highest expression of Zapotec architectural talent, although the mosaics have been attributed to the MIXTEC, who conquered Mitla as well as MONTE ALBÁN. See PRE-COLUMBIAN ART AND ARCHITECTURE. See E. W. Parsons, *Mitla: Town of the Souls* (1936, repr. 1966).

Mito (mē'tō), city (1970 pop. 173,789), capital of Ibaraki prefecture, central Honshu, Japan, on the Naka River. It is chiefly a communications center. From 1606 Mito was the seat of a branch of the Tokugawa family. The city's Tokiwa Park is one of the greatest landscape gardens of Japan.

mitochondria: see CELL.

mitosis (mītō'sĭs, mĭ-), process of nuclear division in a living cell by which the hereditary carrier, or CHROMOSOME, is exactly replicated and the two parts distributed to identical daughter nuclei. Mitosis is almost always accompanied by cell division (cytokinesis), and the latter is sometimes considered a part of the mitotic process. The pattern of mitosis is fundamentally the same in all cells. However, while animal cells apparently divide by pinching into two separate cells, plant cells develop a cell plate, which becomes a cellulose cell wall between the two daughter nuclei. In addition, plant cells lack the pairs of centrioles found in the CYTOPLASM of animal cells. Mitosis is simply described as having four stages—prophase, metaphase, anaphase, and

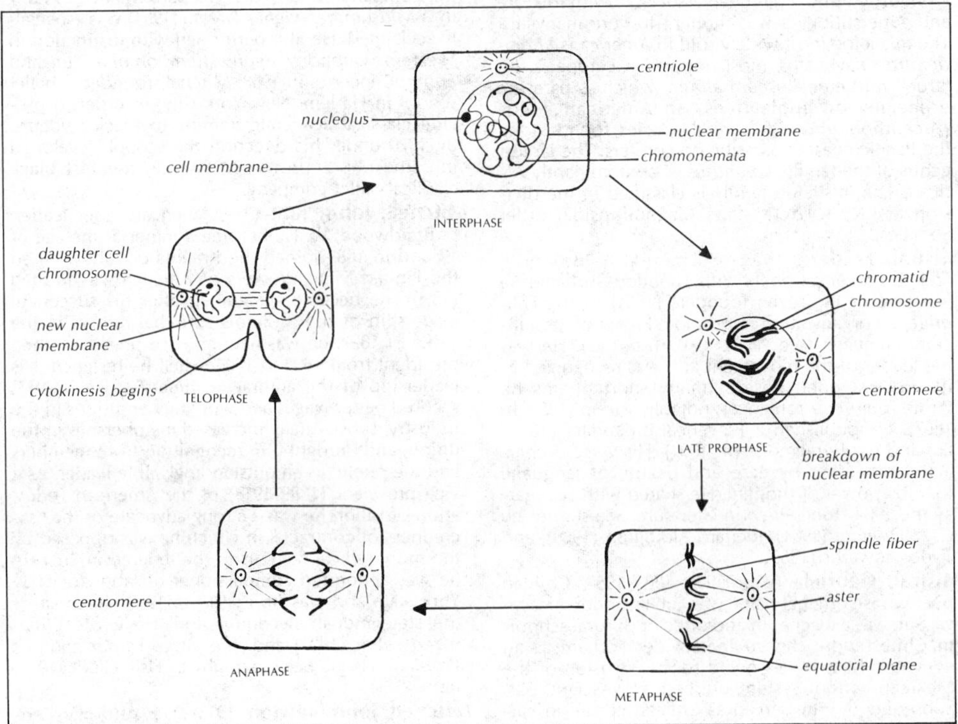

Mitosis in a body cell of an animal

telophase; the steps follow one another without interruption. The entire four-stage division process averages about one hour in duration, and the period between cell divisions, called interphase or interkinesis, varies from 10 to 20 hours. During interphase, the cell's resting stage, the chromosomes are dispersed in the nucleus and appear as an intertwined network of long, thin threads or filaments, called the chromonemata. At some point before prophase begins, the chromosomes replicate themselves to form pairs of identical sister chromosomes, or chromatids. The evidence for this assumption is that deoxyribose NUCLEIC ACID (DNA) is synthesized only during interphase, not while mitosis is in process. During prophase the chromatids contract into compact, tightly coiled pairs, and the nucleolus and, in most cases, the nuclear membrane break down and disappear. Also during prophase the spindle begins to form. In animal cells the centrioles separate and move apart, and radiating fibers, called asters, appear around them. Some of these fibers run from one centriole to the other; these are the spindle fibers. In plant cells the procedure is the same except that there are no visible centrioles. During metaphase the rodlike chromatid pairs assemble at a plane midway between the two narrower ends of the spindle. This is called the equatorial plane and marks the point where the whole cell will divide when nuclear division is completed; the ends of the spindle are the poles to which the chromatids will migrate. The chromatids are attached to the spindle fibers at specific points called spindle attachments, or centromeres. During anaphase the chromatids separate and move to opposite poles, apparently pulled along the spindle fibers by the centromeres. During telophase the spindle fibers first elongate, while new nucleoli appear and nuclear membranes form around the two groups of daughter chromosomes (as they are now called), and then, as the formation of the two daughter nuclei is completed, disappear. The chromosome fibers again disperse into a filamentous network, in which no individual chromosome can be identified. Cytokinesis, which may begin before or after mitosis is completed, finally separates the daughter nuclei into two new individual daughter cells. Despite the relative ease of observation of the physical stages of mitosis under the microscope (primarily because the chromosomes stain readily when in their coiled state), the exact chemical and kinetic nature of mitosis is not yet fully understood. For instance, the spindle has been variously described as a series of solid fibers, of contractile fibers, of hollow tubules, or of longitudinally arranged protein molecules, possibly linked by sulfur bonds. In any case, the explanation of how and why it forms and of how it influences the movement of the chromosomes is still conjecture. The importance of mitosis is that by this mechanism each cell thus formed receives chromosomes that are alike in composition and equal in number to the chromosomes of the parent cell, that composition and number being characteristic of the species. Mitotic division is the method of nuclear division of the somatic (body) cells, as distinguished from the gametes or sex cells (eggs and sperm). In plants and animals that reproduce sexually, i.e., by the union of two gametes, the complex process of MEIOSIS takes place, which produces cells that each contain only half the normal number of chromosomes. Direct cell division, in which the nucleus simply cleaves in two (sometimes but not always followed by division of the cytoplasm), is called amitosis and is very rare.

Mitre, Bartolomé (bär″tōlōmā′ mē′trā), 1821–1906, Argentine statesman, general, and author, president of the republic (1862–68). An opponent of Juan Manuel de ROSAS, he was forced into exile and had a colorful career as a soldier and journalist in Uruguay, Bolivia, Peru, and Chile. He returned to aid URQUIZA in defeating Rosas (1852). A leader of the revolt of Buenos Aires against Urquiza's federal system, Mitre held important posts in the provincial government after Buenos Aires seceded from the confederation. He was defeated by Urquiza in the civil war of 1859, and Buenos Aires reentered the confederation. As governor after 1860, he again assumed leadership when fresh difficulties led to open war in 1861. At Pavón he won a victory for Buenos Aires; he then assumed national authority. In Oct., 1862, Mitre was elected president, and national political unity was finally achieved; a period of internal progress and reform began. He served for a time as commander of the allied forces of Argentina, Brazil, and Uruguay in the war against Paraguay. His political views led to attacks by ALBERDI. In 1868, Mitre was succeeded as president by SARMIENTO, and although still a force in politics, he devoted himself chiefly to literary work. He founded *La Nación* (Buenos Aires), which became one of South America's leading newspapers. Mitre was known in his youth as a poet and in later years as a historian. His important historical works are *Historia de Belgrano* (1858–59, 4th ed. 1887) and *Historia de San Martín y de la emancipación sudamericana* (1877–88, tr. *The Emancipation of South America,* 1893). See W. H. Jeffrey, *Mitre and Argentina* (1952).

Mitropoulos, Dimitri (dēmē′trē mētrô′pōōlôs), 1896–1960, Greek-American conductor. A piano pupil of Busoni, in 1930 he substituted for an indisposed piano soloist and simultaneously conducted the Berlin Philharmonic Orchestra. He made guest appearances in the United States and became conductor of the Minneapolis Symphony Orchestra in 1937. He resigned from that position in 1949 to share with Stokowski the conductorship of the New York Philharmonic. From 1950 to 1958 he was its music director. Mitropoulos wrote an opera and transcribed for orchestra many of J. S. Bach's organ works. He became a U.S. citizen in 1946.

Mitscherlich, Eilhard (īl′härt mĭch′ərlĭkh), 1794–1863, German chemist. He was professor at Berlin from 1822. Noted for his discovery of the principle of ISOMORPHISM, he did important work also on the compounds of phosphorus and arsenic and on benzene derivatives, and he discovered permanganic and silenic acids and nitrobenzene.

Mitsubishi: see ZAIBATSU.

Mitsui: see ZAIBATSU.

Mittag-Leffler, Magnus Gösta (mäng′nōōs yö′stä mĭt′äg-lĕf′lər), 1846–1927, Swedish mathematician. He was (1877–81) professor at Helsingfors (Helsinki) and at the Univ. of Stockholm from 1881. In 1882 he founded *Acta Mathematica,* which he edited until his death. He made important contributions to analysis (including the Mittag-Leffler theorem on single-valued functions) and to linear differential equations and greatly stimulated mathematical research.

Mittelland Kanal: see MIDLAND CANAL.

Mitterrand, François Maurice (fräNswä′ mōrēs′ mĕtəräN′), 1916–, French political leader. He entered parliament in 1946. As head of a small left-of-center party he held ministerial posts in many cabinets from 1947 until 1958, when Charles De Gaulle became president. Mitterrand later merged his party with several other leftist groups, leading them into a unified Socialist party, of which he became head, in 1971. An outspoken opponent of De Gaulle, Mitterrand ran for president against him in 1965, winning 45% of the vote in a runoff election. In 1974 he again ran for president as the Socialist party candidate with the support of the Communists but lost by a small margin in a runoff to Valéry Giscard d'Estaing.

Mivart, St. George Jackson (mī′vərt), 1827–1900, English anatomist and biologist. He contributed important anatomical studies of the insectivores and carnivores. He was converted to Roman Catholicism in 1844, and his attempts to reconcile religion with his evolutionary views led to his excommunication in 1900. See his *On the Genesis of Species* (1871). See also J. W. Gruber, *A Conscience in Conflict* (1960).

mixer, either of two electronic devices in which two or more signals are combined. In the type of mixer used in radio receivers, radar receivers, and similar systems, a signal is translated upward or downward in frequency. The basic property of such a device is that its output is not directly proportional to its input; when signals of different frequencies are applied to such a device, the output contains not only the original frequencies but also frequencies equal to the sum and difference of the original frequencies. Any desired component of the output can be separated from the others by a suitable filter, and any MODULATION present on one of the input signals is preserved on all of the output signals. In the type of mixer used, for example, to combine the outputs of several microphones into a single channel, several signals are combined to produce an output proportional to their sum. In such a device precautions are taken lest the input devices, e.g., the microphones, cause mutual interference. Also, each of the input signals usually passes through a POTENTIOMETER or similar control that fixes its relative level in the output.

Mixtec (mĭs′tĕk), Indian people of Oaxaca, Puebla, and part of Guerrero, SW Mexico, one of the most important groups in Mexico. Although the Mixtec codices constitute the largest collection of pre-Columbian manuscripts in existence, their origin is obscure. Before the arrival (700?) of the TOLTEC on the central plateau, the Mixtec, possibly influenced by the OLMEC, seem to have been the carriers of the advanced highland culture. Probably c.900 they began spreading southward, overrunning the valley of Oaxaca. By the 14th cent. they had overshadowed their rivals, the ZAPOTEC. The Mixtec produced some of the finest stone and metal work of ancient Mexico and also left elaborately carved wood and bone objects and painted polychrome pottery. Their influence on other cultures was strong and is especially noticeable in MITLA and MONTE ALBÁN, Zapotec cities taken by the Mixtec during the long and bitter warfare between the two tribes. This struggle halted momentarily at the end of the 15th cent. in an alliance to defeat the AZTEC, but the Zapotec soon teamed up with the Aztec and eventually made an alliance with the Spanish conquerors. The Mixtec carried on a bloody resistance until they were subjugated by the Spanish conquistador Pedro de ALVARADO. There are about 300,000 Mixtec-speaking people in Mexico today. See A. K. Romney, *The Mixtecans of Juxtlahuaca, Mexico* (1966); Robert Wauchope, ed., *Handbook of Middle American Indians,* Vol. VII: *Ethnology* (ed. by E. Z. Vogt, 1969).

Mixtón War (mēstōn′), 1541, revolt of the Indians against Spanish rule in Nueva Galicia, W Mexico. The conquest under Nuño de Guzmán had been particularly harsh and the ENCOMIENDA system established obvious injustice. Consequently the Indians were thoroughly discontented. When Coronado's expedition to the north in 1540 drained away many of the Spanish, the Indians rose under Tenamaxtli. They fortified Mixtón, Nochistlán, and other mountain towns and besieged Guadalajara. Unable to cope with the uprising, Cristóbal de Oñate, the acting governor, asked for aid from the viceroy, Antonio de Mendoza. The Spanish, reinforced by a large body of Tlaxcaltec and Aztec, succeeded in recapturing the towns by hard fighting. Pedro de ALVARADO was killed in a rash assault on Nochistlán, and the reconquest was slow, but Spanish authority was reestablished in New Spain.

mixture, in chemistry, a physical combination of two or more pure substances (i.e., elements or compounds). A mixture is distinguished from a compound, which is formed by the chemical combination of two or more pure substances in a fixed, definite proportion. The components of a mixture retain their own chemical properties and may be present in any proportions. For example, iron filings may be mixed with powdered sulfur in any proportions, and even if very fine iron powder is carefully mixed with powdered sulfur, the two components are easily separated by means of a magnet; the magnet will draw out the iron from the mixture. However, if seven parts by weight of iron filings or powder are mixed with four parts by weight of powdered sulfur and the mixture is heated to a red glow (e.g., in a test tube, using a Bunsen burner), the iron and sulfur react to form the compound iron sulfide; they are chemically combined and are not readily separated. The iron sulfide is not attracted by a magnet. Mixtures are often classified as homogeneous or heterogeneous. SOLUTIONS and COLLOIDS are homogeneous mixtures. The components of a homogeneous mixture are too intimately combined to be distinguished from one another by visual observation. A SUSPENSION is a heterogeneous mixture. The particles in a heterogeneous mixture are coarse enough to be distinguished by visual observation. Alloys are mixtures of metals and may be either homogeneous or heterogeneous. The components of a mixture usually can be separated by physical means such as distillation, evaporation, precipitation, filtration, solvent extraction, or chromatography.

Miyagi (mēyä′gē), prefecture (1970 pop. 1,819,223), 2,808 sq mi (7,273 sq km), N Honshu, Japan. SENDAI is the capital. The prefecture yields farm products, lumber, raw silk, and minerals.

Miya-jima: see ITSUKU-SHIMA, Japan.

Miyako (mēyä′kō), city (1970 pop. 59,063), Iwate prefecture, NE Honshu, Japan, on the Hei River and Miyako Bay. It is an important fishing port with a large chemical industry.

Miyakonojo (mē″yäkənō′jō), city (1970 pop. 114,802), Miyazaki prefecture, S Kyushu, Japan. It is an important railway junction and commercial center with textile industries.

Miyazaki (mēyä′zä″kē), city (1970 pop. 202,859), capital of Miyazaki prefecture, SE Kyushu, Japan, on the Hyuga Sea. It is a popular tourist and resort center and the seat of the great Shinto shrine, Miyazaki-jingu (with an archaeological museum), dedicated to Jimmu, first emperor of Japan. The Oyodo River traverses the city. Miyazaki prefecture (1970 pop. 1,051,097), 2,998 sq mi (7,765 sq km), produces rice, lumber, raw silk, and charcoal.

Miyazu (mēyä'zōō), town (1970 pop. 31,602), Kyoto prefecture, S Honshu, Japan, on Miyazu Bay. It is a fishing port and processes marine products. Nearby is Ama-no-hashidate, or "heaven's bridge," a long promontory covered with pine trees whose fantastic shapes are reflected in the waters of the bay. This was the site, according to legend, where Izanagi and Izanami stood while they created the islands of Japan (see SHINTO).

Mizar (mī'zər), unidentified hill, near Mt. Hermon. Ps. 42.6.

Mizoram (mĭzôr'əm), union territory (1971 pop. 321,686), c.8,000 sq mi (20,720 sq km), NE India, in the Mizo Hills, bordered on the E by Burma. The capital is Aijal. Mizoram became a union territory in 1972. Formerly, its area was part of Assam state. The tribal population is closely related to the Chins of Burma. Secessionist factions are active in Mizoram; before the creation of BANGLADESH, India accused Pakistan of encouraging and aiding secessionist movements in the area. Mizoram is administered by the home minister in the central Indian government but has an elected advisory council. The states of Assam, Nagaland, Meghalaya, Manipur, and Tripura and the union territories of Mizoram and Arunachal Pradesh have a common governor appointed by the president of India.

Mizpah or **Mizpeh** (both: mĭz'pə). **1** See GALEED. **2** See RAMATH-MIZPEH. **3** Place, on the boundary between Israel and Judah, a religious center with a sanctuary in the time of Judges. Judges 20.1; 21.1,5,8; 1 Sam. 7.5. **4** Town at the foot of Mt. Hermon. Joshua 11.3. **5** Town in the lowland of Judah. Joshua 15.38. **6** Home of Jephthah. Judges 10.17; 11.11,34. **7** David's refuge in Moab. 1 Sam. 22.3.

Mizpar (mĭz'pär), variant of MISPERETH.

Mizraim (mĭzrā'ĭm), son of Ham and eponym of Egypt. Gen. 10.6,13.

Mizzah (mĭz'ə), duke of Edom. Gen. 36.13,17; 1 Chron. 1.37.

Mjøsa (myö'sä), largest lake of Norway, 141 sq mi (365 sq km), and 1,453 ft (443 m) deep, on the Oppland-Hedmark border, SE Norway. It is fed by the Lågen River and is drained by the Vorma River into the Glåma River. The lake is the center of a fertile agricultural region; grains are the chief crops. The region is also one of the most populated areas of Norway; Hamar, Gjøvik, and Lillehammer are the principal cities on the lake.

mks system, system of units of measurement based on the METRIC SYSTEM and having the METER of length, the KILOGRAM of mass, and the SECOND of time as its fundamental units. Other mks units include the NEWTON of force, the JOULE of work or energy, and the WATT of power. The units of the mks system are generally much larger and of a more practical size than the comparable units of the CGS SYSTEM. This fact, coupled with the greater simplicity of the electrical engineering units, e.g., volts and amperes, used with the mks system, has led most scientists to favor the mks system over the cgs system. The mks system provides the basis for the INTERNATIONAL SYSTEM OF UNITS (SI).

Mladá Boleslav (məlä'dä bô'lĕsläf), Ger. *Jungbunzlau*, city (1970 pop. 31,086), NW Czechoslovakia, in Bohemia. The city is an industrial center that manufactures automobiles, tractors, transportation equipment, agricultural machinery, and textiles. Founded in the 10th cent., it became a center of the Bohemian Brethren (see MORAVIAN CHURCH) in the 15th to 16th cent.

Mn, chemical symbol of the element MANGANESE.

Mnason (mənā'sən), Cyprian, an early convert. Acts 21.16.

Mnemosyne (nēmŏs'ĭnē, nēmŏz'-), in Greek mythology, the personification of memory. She was a Titan, daughter of Uranus and Gaea. The Muses were her daughters by Zeus.

Mnesicles (nĕs'ĭklēz), Greek architect, 5th cent. B.C. He designed the PROPYLAEA, and the ERECHTHEUM is also sometimes ascribed to him. Both are on the ACROPOLIS at Athens.

Mo (mō), town, Nordland co., central Norway, just S of the Arctic Circle, at the head of the Rana channel. It is the center of a region where iron, copper, lead, and zinc are mined. The town has large government-owned steelworks.

Mo, chemical symbol of the element MOLYBDENUM.

moa (mō'ə) [Maori], common name for an extinct flightless bird of New Zealand related to the KIWI, the emu, the cassowary, and the OSTRICH. The various species ranged in size from that of a turkey to the 13-ft (396-cm) *Dinornis maximus.* The bird had a short stout bill and was wingless—even the shoulder girdle was lacking in most species. Remains preserved in caves and bogs include bones, pieces of skin, feathers, and egg shells. Although the birds were hunted largely by the Maoris, the reason for the moas' extinction is not precisely known. Moas, along with several other orders of extinct and extant birds, belong to a group called RATITES, all of which are flightless and share other common anatomical features. It is estimated that there were 22 species of moas, in the family Dinornithidae. Moas are classified in the phylum CHORDATA, subphylum Vertebrata, class Aves, order Dinornithiformes, family Dinornithidae.

Moab (mō'ăb), ancient nation located in the uplands E of the Dead Sea, now part of Jordan. The area is unprotected from the east, hence its history is a chain of raids by the Bedouin. The Moabites were close kin to the Hebrews, and the language of the MOABITE STONE is practically the same as biblical Hebrew. The relations of Moab with Judah and Israel are continually mentioned in the Bible. As a political entity, Moab came to an end after the invasion (c.733 B.C.) of Tiglath-pileser III. Its people were later absorbed by the Nabataeans. The Moabite religion was much like that of Canaan. Archaeological exploration in Moab has shown that settlements first occurred in the 13th cent. B.C. See Gen. 19.37; Num. 22–24; Judges 3; 2 Kings 3; Isa. 15–16; Jer. 48; Ezek. 25; Amos 2; Zeph. 2.

Moabite stone, ancient slab of stone erected 850 B.C. by MESHA of Moab; it contains a long inscription commemorating a victory in his revolt against Israel. It was discovered at Dibon, Jordan (1868) by F. A. Klein, a German clergyman. Although it was later broken when Klein tried to purchase it from the Arabs, most of the fragments were recovered. They are in the Louvre. The language of the Moabite is very similar to biblical Hebrew.

Moadiah (mō"ədī'ə), variant of MAADIAH.

Moallakat: see MUALLAQAT.

Moawiyah: see MUAWIYA.

mob, in psychology, a group of people in direct contact who strongly interact upon each other and act under the influence of suggestion and emotion rather than of reason. A crowd may be said to be more stable than a mob and also to lack its intense common emotional element. However, under conditions of stress or danger, a crowd may quickly turn into a mob. Throughout history, fervent and often hysterical leaders have succeeded in driving crowds to acts of moblike heroism as well as to extreme brutality. In a mob the individual is in a state of heightened suggestibility not unlike that prevailing in hypnosis. Differing from the isolated individual, the member of the mob, by reason of his loss of controlling inhibitions, is capable of behaving in a manner foreign to his everyday manner. Mobs and group dynamics are studied in SOCIAL PSYCHOLOGY.

Moberg, Vilhelm (vĭl'hĕlm mōō'bĕryə), 1898–1973, Swedish novelist and dramatist. Moberg's stories, often dealing with farm life, are characterized by brooding, somber beauty and concern with human destiny. Substantial recognition came with his partly autobiographical *Knut Toring* trilogy (1935–39; tr. *The Earth is Ours,* 1940). The historical novel *Ride This Night!* (1941, tr. 1943) was Moberg's impassioned argument against totalitarianism. His epic of Swedish emigration to the United States includes *The Emigrants* (1949, tr. 1951), *Unto a Good Land* (1952, tr. 1954), *The Settlers* (1956), and *The Last Letter to Sweden* (1959, tr. 1961). Two films, *The Emigrants* and *The New Land,* based on these novels and directed by Jan Troell, appeared in 1973. Among his plays are *Our Unborn Son* (1945) and *Fulfillment* (tr. 1953). Moberg also wrote *A History of the Swedish People* (tr. 1972).

Moberly (mō'bərlē), city (1970 pop. 12,988), Randolph co., N central Mo.; inc. 1868. Its manufactures include brake parts, fans, and paints. A state prison is there.

Mobile (mōbēl'), city (1970 pop. 190,026), seat of Mobile co., SW Ala., at the head of Mobile Bay and at the mouth of the Mobile River; inc. 1814. One of the country's major ports, the only seaport in Alabama, and the second-largest city in the state, Mobile is an important shipping and shipbuilding center. There are oil refineries and industries that produce paper, textiles, aluminum, and chemicals. Mobile was founded at its present site in 1710 by the sieur de Bienville. It was the capital of French Louisiana from 1710 to 1719. The British held it from 1763 to 1780, when Bernardo de Gálvez took it for Spain. Mobile was seized for the Americans by Gen. James Wilkinson in 1813. During the Civil War, ships from Mobile evaded the Federal blockade until Admiral Farragut's victory at Mobile Bay (1864). Gen. E. R. S. Canby captured the city in April, 1865. Mobile has many beautiful antebellum homes and magnificent gardens. Also noteworthy are a Roman Catholic cathedral, the city hall (1858), and Marine Hospital (1842), which was designed by Robert Mills. Of historical interest are the homes of Admiral Raphael Semmes and Gen. Braxton Bragg, the headquarters of Gen. E. R. S. Canby, and forts Morgan and Gaines at the entrance to Mobile Bay. Mobile is the seat of Spring Hill College (the oldest in the state), Mobile College, the Univ. of South Alabama, and a junior college. Brookley Air Force Base, a coast guard station, and a coast guard aviation training center are there. The colorful annual Mardi Gras was begun in the early 1700s; the Azalea Trail Festival dates from 1929. The Bankhead Tunnel is under the Mobile River there. See C. G. Summersell, *Mobile, History of a Seaport Town* (1949).

mobile (mō'bēl), a type of moving sculptural artwork developed by Alexander CALDER in 1932 and named by Marcel DUCHAMP. Often constructed of colored metal pieces connected by wires or rods, the mobile has moving parts that are sensitive to a breeze or light touch; it can be designed to hang from the ceiling or stand free on the floor. Mobiles became popular in the 1950s for interior decoration.

Mobile Bay, arm of the Gulf of Mexico, SW Ala., from 8 to 18 mi (12.9–29 km) wide, extending c.35 mi (56 km) from the Gulf to the mouth of the Mobile River. A ship channel connects Mobile Bay with the Gulf. The Intracoastal Waterway passes through the southern part of the bay. Mobile, Ala., is on the northwest shore. Admiral David Farragut, a Civil War naval hero, won the celebrated battle of Mobile Bay on Aug. 5, 1864.

mobile home, larger modification of the trailer house on wheels that can be transported by coupling it to an automobile. Mobile homes, built by many different corporations, are semipermanent dwellings, unlike most trailers, campers, and other recreational vehicles designed to be used for short periods at frequent intervals. Efficiently designed to utilize every available inch, mobile homes are remarkably spacious; many have two or three bedrooms, a complete kitchen, large living and dining areas, and considerable storage space. Most mobile homes remain in trailer parks that tend to have the look of suburban housing developments. While there is a growing demand for mobile homes among retired people, the majority of mobile-home owners appear to be young married couples whose livelihood causes them to move frequently from one part of the country to another; their sense of continuity and permanence is thought to be maintained by not having to change houses. Trailers have been in wide use in the United States since the 1930s, and the mobile-home industry has grown rapidly since the 1940s.

Mobutu, Joseph Désiré: see MOBUTU SESE SEKO.

Mobutu Sese Seko (mōbōō'tō sā'sā sā'kō), 1930–, president of Zaïre. Born Joseph Désiré Mobutu, he studied in Brussels and then returned to the Belgian Congo (later Democratic Republic of the Congo). In 1956 he joined the nationalist movement of Patrice Lumumba. However, in 1960 he led an army coup against the central government, deposing Lumumba; Mobutu soon became the army chief of staff. He staged another coup in 1965, assumed the office of prime minister in 1966, and established a presidential form of government, headed by himself, in 1967. As part of his program of "national authenticity," Mobutu changed the Congo's name to Zaïre (1971) and his own name to Mobutu Sese Seko (1972). Citizens were required to drop their Christian names, and the names of geographical features were Africanized.

Moçambique (mōōsəmbē'kə) or **Mozambique** (mō"zəmbēk'), city (1960 pop. 12,166), NE Mozambique, a seaport on a small coral island in the Mozambique Channel (an arm of the Indian Ocean). It is c.3 mi (5 km) from the mainland town of Lumbo, a terminus of a railroad into the interior. The city is a trade center; exports include cashew nuts and timber. Moçambique was occupied by the Portuguese in 1505 and was the capital of the Portuguese holdings in Mozambique until 1907. Still standing are three old forts and the governor's palace, which attract numerous tourists.

moccasin, snake: see WATER MOCCASIN.

moccasin, skin shoe worn by North American Indians, excepting the sandal wearers of the Southwest area. There were two general types of moccasins, the hard-soled, which was used in the Eastern woodlands and the Southeast cultural areas, and the soft-soled, used in the Plains area. The hard-soled moccasin was made by sewing, with sinew thread, a rawhide sole to a leather upper piece; the soft-soled moccasin was one piece of soft leather with a seam at the instep and the heel. Boot or legging moccasins (sometimes reaching the hip) were worn from Alaska to Arizona and New Mexico, but they were generally part of the woman's costume. The moccasins of certain tribes were distinctive, and sometimes a moccasin track could indicate the tribe of the wearer. Moccasins were usually symbolically decorated with porcupine quills and, after the coming of the Europeans, with glass beads. Special moccasins were used for ceremonies such as the Iroquois adoption service, which required that a recruit put on Iroquois moccasins to indicate that he would follow Iroquois ways.

moccasin flower: see ORCHID.

Mocha (mō'kə), town, S Yemen, a port on the Red Sea. It was noted for the export of the coffee to which it gave its name but declined as a trading port in the late 19th cent. with the rise of Hodeida and Aden.

mocha stone: see AGATE.

Mochi, Francesco (fränchĕs'kō mô'kē), 1580–1654, Italian sculptor. Mochi's attraction to the baroque aesthetic led him to create dramatic sculptures notable for swirling drapery (e.g., *Archangel of the Annunciation*, Mus. dell'Opera del Duomo, Orvieto). His later work exhibited an elegant, artificial, mannerist style.

Mochica (mōchē'kə), ancient Indian civilization on the coast of N Peru. Previously called Early Chimu (see CHIMU), the Mochica were warriors with a highly developed social and political organization. They built temples, pyramids, and aqueducts of adobe brick, were skilled in irrigation, and produced remarkable ceramics. In their stirrup jars, painted with scenes of everyday life, and their figure-modeled portrait jars they revealed fantasy and humor and achieved an astonishing fidelity to human forms. The civilization, which began c.100 B.C., is believed to have lasted 1,000 years.

mockernut hickory: see HICKORY.

mockingbird: see MIMIC THRUSH.

mock orange: see SAXIFRAGE.

Moctezuma: see MONTEZUMA.

modacrylic, man-made copolymer fiber. Modacrylics are soft, strong, resilient, and dimensionally stable. They can be easily dyed, show good press and shape retention, and are quick to dry. They have outstanding resistance to chemicals and solvents, are not attacked by moths or mildew, and are nonallergenic. Among their uses are in apparel linings, furlike outerwear, paint-roller covers, scatter rugs, carpets, work clothing, and as hair in wigs.

mode, in grammar: see MOOD.

mode, in music. **1** Any pattern or arrangement of the intervals of a SCALE. In the Middle Ages eight modes were developed as the basis of plainsong composition. These modes, obscurely derived from ancient Greek theory, were grouped in pairs, each pair containing an authentic mode and a plagal mode. They are distinguished by the difference in the position of their octave ranges, the plagal being at the INTERVAL of a fourth below the corresponding authentic mode. Each pair shared the same lowest (final) note, or *finalis.* The range of each mode was an octave. Although Greek names came to be used for these modes—Dorian, Phrygian, Lydian, mixolydian, hypophrygian, etc.—there is no proof of direct relation to Greek theory. These eight modes were the basis for 11 centuries of musical composition. Freely treated, they have reappeared in the works of some 20th-century composers such as Vaughan Williams. In the late Middle Ages and during the Renaissance certain other modes were adopted, and in 1547 the Swiss theorist Glareanus described 12 as useful for composition. In the late 16th cent. and early 17th cent. the series was limited to the major and minor modes in use today. The use of medieval modes by later composers is called modality in contrast to TONALITY. An extension of the term *mode* allows its application to the tonal systems of HINDU MUSIC, ARABIAN MUSIC, and BYZANTINE MUSIC. See G. Reese, *Music in the Middle Ages* (1940); E. A. Wienandt, *Choral Music of the Church* (1965). **2** In the 13th cent., six rhythmical patterns in ternary meter. Greek names—e.g., trochaic and iambic—were applied to these rhythmic patterns at a fairly late date, but there is no evidence of derivation from the meters of Greek poetry. These rhythmic modes governed composition until they were finally dissolved in the 14th cent. by Philippe de Vitry in his treatise *Ars nova* (see MUSICAL NOTATION). **3** In 20th-century music, the various forms of the tone row in 12-tone composition (see SERIAL MUSIC). The row, an arbitrary arrangement of the 12 chromatic tones of Western music, can be used in four different forms: the original row, the original row reversed (from the last note back to the first note), the original row inverted (upside down), and the inversion reversed. Each of these is a mode.

mode, in statistics, an infrequently used type of AVERAGE. In a group of numbers governed composition until they were ber occurring most frequently. In the group 1, 4, 5, 5, 6, 6, 6, 6, 9, 9, the mode is 6 because it occurs four times and the others only once or twice.

model and modeling, in painting, the use of light and shade to simulate volume in the representation of solids. In sculpture the terms denote a technique involving the use of a pliable material such as clay or wax. As opposed to CARVING, modeling permits addition as well as subtraction of material and lends itself to freer handling and change of intention. The technique is exemplified also by those works in cast metal and plaster that are made from the mold of a clay original. The mold is made by the process of CIRE PERDUE. The noun *model* is used to describe such an original and also any three-dimensional scale model for a larger or more elaborate project in architecture, landscaping, or industry. It also denotes a person or object used as an aid to representation in painting.

modello (mōdĕl'lō), small plan of a major work presented by Renaissance and baroque artists to the patron who commissioned the work. The *modello* was intended to show the patron how the finished project would look. Many *modelli* exist as works of art in their own right, e.g., El Greco's *Worship in the Name of Jesus* (National Gall., London).

Model Parliament: see PARLIAMENT.

Modena (mô'dänä), city (1971 pop. 171,063), capital of Modena prov., Emilia-Romagna, N central Italy, on the Panaro River. It is an agricultural, commercial, and industrial center. Manufactures include motor vehicles, shoes, and machine tools. An Etruscan settlement, the city was the site of a Roman colony called Mutina, founded in the early 2d cent. B.C. and located on the Aemilian Way. Modena became a free commune in the 12th cent. and in 1288 permanently passed to the ESTE family of Ferrara. The duchy of Modena, established in 1452, became the seat of the Este family after it lost (1598) Ferrara. From the fall of Napoleon I in 1814 until 1859 the house of Austria-Este ruled harshly. Among the city's notable structures are the cathedral (12th cent.), which has a massive white marble campanile (289 ft/88 m high) called the Ghirlandina; the Palazzo dei Musei (1753–67), which contains several art collections and the Este library; and the ducal palace (17th cent.). The nearby Nonantola abbey (founded 752) was a center of learning in the Middle Ages. Modena has a university.

modern architecture. In the decade after World War I there emerged in most Western countries a new architectural style displaying an essential homogeneity despite many individual and national variations. By mid-century this style, no longer new, had undergone three decades of experimentation and growth. It possesses no appellation more precise than modern, although the labels INTERNATIONAL STYLE and FUNCTIONALISM have also been used. Since the mid-19th cent., a conscious attempt to assimilate modern technology, first in architectural practice and later also in formulated theory, has been continuously in progress. The totally new technical requirements of the modern era forced the evolution of new styles of building and eventually replaced the eclectic approach to design. Even earlier, at the beginning of the 19th cent., Sir John Soane's work in England had turned away from heavy masonry to a use of light, widely-spaced supports. Technical progress in the development of materials made possible the construction in 1851 of Sir Joseph Paxton's celebrated Crystal Palace in London, in which a remarkable airiness and delicacy was achieved with iron and glass. In the ensuing years iron, steel, and glass determined the architectural form of many train sheds, department stores, and market halls; but the structural forms were cluttered by irrelevant ornament, and as late as 1889 the newly erected Eiffel Tower found the public not yet ready to conceive of pure structure as beautiful in itself. The pioneering use of a complete steel skeleton for tall buildings appeared in the first SKYSCRAPER, built in Chicago in 1883 by William Le Baron Jenney. The English architects R. N. Shaw, Baillie Scott, and C. F. A. Voysey were largely responsible for renewed interest in natural building materials for houses. The pioneers of industrial architecture in Europe included Peter Behrens, Josef Hoffmann, Otto Wagner, Adolf Loos, H. P. Berlage, and Auguste Perret. At the end of the 19th cent. an enormously significant architectural revolution occurred in the works and writings of Louis H. Sullivan and Frank Lloyd Wright (see AMERICAN ARCHITECTURE). Wright in the United States and the exponents of ART NOUVEAU in Europe introduced the concept of a rhythmic flow of space in an attempt to eliminate the angular boundaries between rooms. Conversely, the architects of de STIJL returned to a more disciplined structural form in which they sought to organize building elements into new combinations of rectangular planes. By 1920 there was an increasingly wide understanding that building types must come to terms with their functions and materials if they were to achieve intrinsic significance or beauty. Instead of viewing a building as heavy volumes supported and enclosed by ponderous materials, the leading innovators considered it as areas of space, resting upon slender piers and slabs and enclosed by light, thin curtain walls. The very element of enclosure was given minimum emphasis in order that the basic structural skeleton might be all the more in evidence. In giving form and coherence to this new rationale of an organic modern architecture, Le Corbusier's book *Vers une architecture* (1923, tr. 1927) played an eminent role, and the writings of the Dutch J. J. P. Oud and the German Walter Gropius (head of the BAUHAUS) were also of major importance. In these early consolidations of the modern style, abstract painting and sculpture offered new ideas to the architects; they also conditioned the public to accept a form of beauty based solely upon spatial relationships and pure geometrical shapes, free from past associations. By the mid-20th cent. modern architecture had become an instrument for dealing with the multiple building needs of a complex society in which such problems as housing for population masses, structures for intricate industrial uses, and highly integrated community planning could scarcely be handled except in terms of completely contemporaneous architectural concepts adjusted to the vast resources of current technology and the mass production of modern materials. Large areas of glass, sometimes forming the entire exterior of a building, constitute one important identification of modern works. Reinforced concrete is also intimately involved with the style's development, as are the advances in elevator transportation, air conditioning, and electric illumination. The use of an unvarying module or basic dimensional unit throughout a design, used in contemporary works by R. Buckminster Fuller and Moshe Safdie among many others, makes evident the structural regularity and machine-tool precision of the buildings in which it is employed. Noted pioneers of the 1920s who later practiced in the United States included Miës van der Rohe and Walter Gropius. Important contributions to the evolution of modern design were made by Raymond Hood, Albert Kahn, Marcel Breuer, Richard J. Neutra, William E. Lescaze, the firms of Harrison & Abramovitz and Skidmore, Owings & Merrill, and later by I. M. Pei in skyscraper and industrial architecture. In the 1950s the International style was criticized for its sterility and "institutional" anonymity. More varied and individual modes of expression were sought, while emphasis on basic structure and materials continued. This tendency is evidenced in the works of Louis Kahn, E. D. Stone, Philip Johnson, and the architects of the so-called new brutalism movement in England and in the United States. A dynamic sculptural unity distinguishes the buildings of Le Corbusier and Eero Saarinen. Among the other leading contemporary architects are Alvar Aalto of Finland and the Italians Pier Luigi Nervi and Paolo Soleri. In Central and South America Lúcio Costa, Oscar Niemeyer, Juan O'Gorman, and Felix Candela have evolved distinctive, original, and intensely personal building styles. See articles on individual architects, e.g., Walter GROPIUS. See Walter Gropius, *The New Architecture and the Bauhaus* (1937); Vincent Scully, Jr., *Modern Architecture: The Architecture of Democracy* (1961); Sigfried Giedion, *Space, Time, and Architecture* (5th ed. 1967); Leonardo Benevolo, *History of Modern Architecture* (2 vol., 1966; tr. 1972); J. W. Cook and Heinrich Klotz, *Conversations with Architects* (1973); Dennis Sharp, *A Visual History of Twentieth-Century Architecture* (1973); C. E. Jeanneret-Gris, *The Athens Charter by Le Corbusier* (tr. 1973);

Charles Jencks, *Modern Movements in Architecture* (1974).

modern art. From the 19th cent. to the present day artists have veered away from the traditional concepts and techniques of painting that had been practiced since the Renaissance. In the second half of the 19th cent. painters began to revolt against the classic codes of composition, careful execution, harmonious coloring, and heroic subject matter. Patronage by the church and state sharply declined at the same time that artists' views became more independent and subjective. Courbet, Corot, and others of the BARBIZON SCHOOL, Manet, Degas, and Toulouse-Lautrec chose to paint scenes of ordinary daily and nocturnal life that often offended the sense of decorum of their contemporaries. Monet, Renoir, and Pissarro, the great masters of IMPRESSIONISM, painted café and city life, as well as landscapes, working most often directly from nature and using new modes of representation. While art had always been to a certain extent abstract, painters, beginning with the impressionists in the 1870s, took new delight in freedom of brushwork. They made random spots of color and encrusted the canvas with strokes that did not always correspond to the object that they were depicting but that formed coherent relationships. Thus began a definite separation of the image and the subject. The impressionists exploited the range of the color spectrum, directly applying strokes of pure pigment to the canvas rather than mixing colors on the palette. In the 1880s, Seurat and Signac developed the more detailed and systematic approach of neo-impressionism, while Van Gogh and Gauguin, using bold masses, gave to color an unprecedented excitement and emotional intensity (see POSTIMPRESSIONISM). At the same time, Cézanne painted subtler nuances of tone and sought to achieve greater structural clarity. Flouting the laws of perspective, he extracted geometrical forms from nature and created radically new spatial patterns in his landscapes and still lifes. In sculpture, dynamic forms and variations of impressionism were created by Rodin, Renoir, Degas, and the Italian Medardo Rosso. Other important innovations of the late 19th cent. can be seen in the paintings of the Norwegian Edvard Munch and the vivid fantasies of the Belgian James Ensor. In the 1890s the NABIS developed pictorial ideas from Gauguin, while sinuous linear decorations were produced throughout Europe by the designers of ART NOUVEAU. From the early 20th cent. color reigned supreme and invaded the contours of recognizable objects with the gay, brilliant patterns of FAUVISM (1905-8), dominated by Matisse and Rouault in France, the ORPHISM of Robert Delaunay and František Kupka, and the explosive hues of the German group, the Brücke (see BRÜCKE, DIE), which included Kirchner and Nolde (see EXPRESSIONISM). Kandinsky transformed (c.1910) color into a completely abstract art absolutely divorced from subject matter. The fauvists and expressionists shared an appreciation of the pure and simplified shapes of various examples of primitive art, an enthusiasm that was generated by Gauguin and extended to Picasso, Brancusi, Modigliani, Derain, and others. Meanwhile, the implications of Cézanne's highly organized yet revolutionary spatial structures were being carried through by Picasso and Braque. About 1909 they invented an abstract art of still lifes converted into shifting volumes and planes. CUBISM, developed by the artists of the SCHOOL OF PARIS, went through several stages and had an enormous influence on European and American painting and sculpture. In sculpture it was adopted by Picasso, Duchamp-Villon, Lipchitz, González, and Archipenko, who began to realize the possibilities of convex and concave volumes. Cubism was absorbed in Italy by the exponents of FUTURISM (c.1909–c.1915) and in Germany by the BLAUE REITER group (1911–14); both these movements were cut short by the advent of World War I. Fauvism and cubism were introduced by members of the EIGHT to shocked Americans in the ARMORY SHOW of 1913, and from then on Americans began to participate significantly in the development of modern art (see AMERICAN ART). At that time Russia made extraordinary contributions to the current of nonfigurative art. The sculptors Naum Gabo and Antoine Pevsner joined the movement known as CONSTRUCTIVISM (c.1913–c.1921), and the painter Malevich founded SUPREMATISM (1913). In Holland members of the STIJL group (1917–31), including Mondrian and Theo van Doesburg, created a disciplined, nonobjective art. These Russian and Dutch developments in the second decade of the 20th cent. were applicable to many varieties of art and industrial design, and their principles converged in the teachings of the BAUHAUS in the 1920s. Kandinsky, the highly imaginative Paul Klee, and the American Lyonel Feininger were among the celebrated exponents of the Bauhaus. A more fanciful art was created by Jean Arp, Marcel Duchamp, and Kurt Schwitters in the irreverent manifestations of the DADA movement. Dada artists devised "readymades" and COLLAGE objects from diverse bits of material. The movement was linked with Freudianism in the 1920s, producing the wild imagery of SURREALISM and VERISM, as seen in the paintings of Salvador Dali, Yves Tanguy, Max Ernst, and Joan Miró. The 1920s also saw the beginning of an art of social protest by exponents of NEW OBJECTIVITY, among them George Grosz, Otto Dix, and Max Beckmann. With the rise of fascism and the Great Depression of the 1930s, the protest increased in intensity. The Mexicans Orozco, Rivera, and Siqueiros painted murals in which the human figure was restored to its fullest dignity (see MEXICAN ART AND ARCHITECTURE). The development of a new art movement was held in abeyance until after World War II—when the United States took the lead in the formation of an art known as ABSTRACT EXPRESSIONISM, with the impetus of such artists as Arshile Gorky, Jackson Pollock, and Willem de Kooning. Action painting made its impact felt throughout the world in the 1950s. A number of notable developments have been led by artists associated with the New York school, a loosely defined group working in many styles during the 1960s and early 70s whose works have had international influence. The various styles and movements reflected in their works include POP ART, OP ART, POST-PAINTERLY ABSTRACTION, conceptual art (see Sol LEWITT), HAPPENINGS, EARTHWORKS, and the new realism (see REALISM, in art). One abstract development known as minimalism emphasizes the least discernible variation of technique in painting, sculpture, and other media. In sculpture the explorations of Julio González led to abstract configurations of welded metal that can be seen in the works of Americans such as David Smith, Theodore Roszack, Seymour Lipton, and Herbert Ferber. Alexander Calder stands apart with his brightly colored MOBILES and STABILES, which have been widely imitated. The tradition of Brancusi's organic abstract forms has been inventively exploited by Henry Moore and Barbara Hepworth in England and by Jean Arp in France, while the Swiss Alberto Giacometti and the Italians Giacomo Manzù and Marino Marini have each achieved a distinctive style of sculpture. Nearly every phase of modern art has been greeted by the public with ridicule, but as the shock has worn off, the movement, settling into history, has influenced and inspired new generations of artists. See articles on individual artists and movements, e.g., PICASSO and ABSTRACT EXPRESSIONISM. See also PHOTOGRAPHY, STILL. See Robert Goldwater, *Primitivism in Modern Painting* (1938); Fritz Novotny, *Painting and Sculpture in Europe, 1780–1880* (1960); G. H. Hamilton, *Painting and Sculpture in Europe, 1880–1940* (1967); A. C. Ritchie, *Sculpture of the Twentieth Century* (1952); Alfred H. Barr, Jr., ed., *Masters of Modern Art* (1954); Robert Rosenblum, *Cubism and Twentieth-Century Art* (1966); Irving Sandler, *A History of Abstract Expressionism* (1970); Clement Greenberg, *Art and Culture* (1961); H. H. Arnason, *History of Modern Art* (1968); Werner Haftmann et al., *Art Since Mid-Century* (2 vol., tr. 1972).

modern dance, serious theatrical dance forms that are distinct from both BALLET and the show dancing of the musical comedy or variety stage. Developed in the 20th cent., primarily in the United States, modern dance resembles modern art and music in being experimental and iconoclastic. Modern dance began at the turn of the century when its three pioneers, Isadora DUNCAN, Loie Fuller, and Ruth ST. DENIS, began separate rebellions against the rigid formalism, artifice, and superficiality of classical academic ballet and against the banality of show dancing. Each sought to inspire audiences to a new awareness of inner or outer realities, a goal shared by all subsequent modern dancers. Duncan shocked or delighted audiences by baring her body and soul in what she called "free dance." Wearing only a simple tunic like the Greek vase figures that inspired many of her dances, she weaved and whirled in flowing natural movements that emanated, she said, from the solar plexus. She aimed to idealize abstractly the emotions induced by the music that was her motivating force, daringly chosen from the works of serious composers including Beethoven, Wagner, and Gluck. Although Duncan established schools and had many imitators, her improvisational technique was too personalized to be carried on by direct successors. The work of the two other pioneers was far less abstract although no less free. Fuller used dance to imitate and illustrate natural phenomena: the flame, the flower, the butterfly. Experimenting with stage lighting and costume, she created illusionistic effects that remained unique in the history of dance theater until the works of Alwin NIKOLAIS in the 1960s. The pictorial effects achieved by St. Denis had a different source: the ritualistic dance of Oriental religion. She relied on elaborate costumes and sinuous improvised movements to suggest the dances of India and Egypt and to evoke mystical feelings. With Ted Shawn, who became her partner and husband in 1914 and who advocated and embodied the vigor of the virile male on the dance stage, St. Denis enlarged her repertoire to include dances of the American Indian and other ethnic groups. In 1915 St. Denis and Shawn formed the Denishawn company, which increased the popularity of modern dance throughout the United States and abroad and nurtured the leaders of the second generation of modern dance: Martha GRAHAM, Doris HUMPHREY, and Charles WEIDMAN. At the end of the 1920s these rebels against the art nouveau exoticism and commercialism of Denishawn devised their own choreography and launched their own companies. Their dances were based on new techniques developed as vehicles for the expression of human passions and universal social themes. Graham found the breath pulse the primary source of dance; exaggerating the contractions and expansions of the torso and flexing of the spine caused by breathing, she devised a basis for movement that for her represented man's inner conflicts. To Humphrey, gravity was the source of the dynamic instability of movement; the arc between balance and imbalance of the moving human body, fall and recovery, represented man's conflicts with the world around him. Forsaking lyrical and imitative movement and all but the most austere costumes and simplest stage effects, Graham and Humphrey composed dances so stark, intellectual, and harshly dramatic as to shock and anger audiences accustomed to being pleased by graceful dancers. Graham explored themes from Americana, Greek mythology, and the Old Testament; she viewed music merely as a frame for the dance. Humphrey experimented more with sound; in a 1924 work she discarded music altogether and performed in silence, and later she used nonmusical sound effects, including spoken texts and bursts of hysterical laughter. Her themes were social and often heroic in scale, e.g., the trilogy *New Dance* (1935), which treats man's relation to man. Charles Weidman's gestural mime of movements abstracted from everyday situations provided a different kind of social commentary—comic satire. Winning ardent devotees, the Graham and Humphrey-Weidman companies dominated modern dance for 20 years; the former continues as a major company today. Nonetheless, by the end of World War II, young choreographers had begun breaking the rules of the modern dance establishment—creating dances that had no theme, expressed no emotion, dispensed with the dance vocabulary of fall and recovery, contraction and release. Sybil Shearer's random fantasies, Katherine Litz's surrealistic vignettes, and Erick Hawkins's impressionistic soft rhythms changed the emphasis of choreography. They had no desire to uplift or inform. Foremost of this third generation of modern dancers is Merce CUNNINGHAM, whose company bred avant-garde choreographers for more than 25 years. Cunningham freed dance from spatial restraints, eliminating strong central focus from choreographic patterns, devising dances that can be viewed from any angle. He also released dance from traditional musical constraints by using electronic music and other compositions of his musical director, John CAGE. In addition, he liberated his own choreography from structural limitations by using techniques of chance, such as throws of the dice, to determine the order in which sections of a work should occur. In 1957 Paul TAYLOR, a Cunningham and Graham veteran, presented an evening of minimal dance, which consisted of Taylor standing on the stage alone in street clothes and making only tiny posture changes to the accompaniment of the recorded voice of a telephone operator announcing the time at 10-second intervals; outraged dance critics deliberately ignored the performance. The social and artistic ferment of the 1960s provided a fertile ground for even more radical departures. Twyla Tharp did away with any sound accompaniment that might distract the viewer's attention from the dance itself. She also took dance outside the theater, staging it in such spaces as the staircase of the Metropolitan Museum of New York City and New York's Central Park. Yvonne Rainer pioneered in the use of improvisations based on ordinary, nondance movements ranging from acrobatics, to military marching, to sports and games. Steve Paxton incorporated even more mundane actions into his dances (e.g., dressing and undressing) and went so far as to perform a duet with a chicken. Paxton, like other dancers and pop artists of the 1960s and 70s, was largely concerned with breaking down the barriers between dancers and audience, between art and life. He staged dance events for large numbers of laymen. In *Satisfyin' Lover*, 42 nonprofessional performers were asked to walk across, stand, and sit on a stage; the dance derived its character and tone from the variations in their individual styles of movement. By the 1970s distinctions between modern dance, ballet, and show dancing were not as rigid as they once had been. Ballet technique and choreography remain more formal than those of modern dance, but its themes and stage effects are often similar. Important modern dancers have been invited to perform with and create dances for ballet companies. Paul Taylor has performed with the New York City Ballet in a work created for him by George Balanchine and Twyla Tharp. Taylor has himself created dances for Rudolf Nureyev and Tharp's dancers joined the Joffrey Ballet to perform her *Deuce Coupe*. Since Agnes DE MILLE first introduced a dance sequence as an integral part of the plot development of *Oklahoma!* in 1942, dance has become more than just light entertainment during interludes in the action of Broadway musicals. Anna Sokolow, of the Graham company, brought her modern dance technique to the Broadway stage, as did Hanya Holm, choreographer of *Kiss Me, Kate* (1948) and *My Fair Lady* (1956). The dance style that has evolved in musical comedy usually combines elements of modern dance, modern ballet, and the jazz dance that is based on Afro-Caribbean ethnic dances. See autobiographies by Isadora Duncan (1927, repr. 1972) and Ruth St. Denis (1939); biographies of individual dancers; John Martin, *The Book of the Dance* (1963); Selma Jeanne Cohen, ed., *The Modern Dance* (1965); Don McDonagh, *The Rise & Fall & Rise of Modern Dance* (1970); Margaret Lloyd, *The Borzoi Book of Modern Dance* (1970).

modernism, in religion, a general movement in the late 19th and 20th cent. that tried to reconcile historical Christianity with the findings of modern science and philosophy. Modernism arose mainly from the application of modern critical methods to the study of the Bible and the history of dogma and resulted in less emphasis on historic dogma and creeds and in greater stress on the humanistic aspects of religion. Importance was placed upon the immanent rather than the transcendent nature of God. The movement as a whole was profoundly influenced by the pragmatism of William James, the intuitionism of Henri Bergson, and the philosophy of action of Maurice Blondel. Modernist ideas were accepted in all or in part by many of the Protestant denominations, but there was also a reaction against them in the movement called FUNDAMENTALISM. In reformed Judaism, especially among Americans, there developed a modernist movement resembling Protestant modernism. Within the Roman Catholic Church there was a movement specifically referred to as Modernism; it was condemned as the "synthesis of all heresies" by Pius X in his encyclical *Pascendi* (1907). Among the leaders of Catholic Modernism were A. F. LOISY in France and George Tyrrell in England. Vital to the Catholic movement were the adoption of the critical approach to the Bible, which was by that time accepted by most Protestant churches, and the rejection of the intellectualism of scholastic theology, with the corresponding subordination of doctrine to practice. Many modernists applied the pragmatic method to the sacraments, to dogma, and to prayer. They considered the sacraments to have no reality as a divinely ordained means of grace, but valuable only for their psychological effect. These tendencies led them naturally to deny the authority of the church and the traditional Christian conception of God; a decree declared the beliefs heretical, ending Roman Catholic Modernism. See A. L. Lilley, *Modernism: A Record and a Review* (1908, repr. 1970); Michele Rancheti, *The Catholic Modernists* (tr. 1969); B. M. Reardon, comp., *Roman Catholic Modernism* (1970); A. R. Vidler, *A Variety of Catholic Modernists* (1970); L. F. Barmann, *Baron Friedrich von Hügel and the Modernist Crisis in England* (1972).

modernismo (mōthārnē'smō), movement in Spanish literature that had its beginning in Latin America. It was paramount in the last decade of the 19th cent. and the first decade of the 20th cent. *Modernismo* derived from French symbolism and the Parnassian school, but too much stress can be laid on the French influence, for *modernismo* was spontaneous, and it borrowed from many sources, including the Spanish classics, Edgar Allan Poe, and Walt Whitman. Modernist poetry often created an exotic tapestry of distant landscapes dotted with symbolic swans, peacocks, lilies, and princesses. In some of its aspects it represented, like contemporary movements in other literatures, a rejection of the materialist world of the day. *Modernismo* is now usually said to have first appeared in the poetry of the Cuban leader, José Martí. Julian del Casal, Salvador Díaz Mirón, José Asunción Silva, and Manuel Gutiérrez Nájera were also writing fin dè siècle verse in the modernist vein before *modernismo* became an acknowledged world event with the publication, in Chile, of *Azul* [blue], a volume of poetry by Rubén DARÍO in 1888. The Nicaraguan Darío was the great genius of the movement. His exotic, highly colored, and finely wrought verse made a sensation, and soon a host of little magazines and literary groups were forwarding his ideas of elegant form, carefully chosen images, and subtle word music. The modernists were supremely conscious of their art, and there was more than a hint of artificiality in their works. Among the leading figures of the movement were Leopoldo LUGONES, Julio HERRERA Y REISSIG, Ricardo Jaimes Freyre, Guillermo VALENCIA, José Santos CHOCANO, and Amado NERVO. *Modernismo* had an extraordinary prose writer in José Enrique RODÓ. The movement constituted a sudden and vigorous intellectual awakening in Latin America and had profound repercussions even in politics and economics. Manuel Ugarte, Francisco and Ventura García Calderón, and Rufino Blanco-Fombona all had their roots in *modernismo*. It had a powerful effect in remolding Spanish literary ideas and language and was the first Spanish American movement to affect peninsular Spain deeply. The Spanish writers of the GENERATION OF '98, notably Miguel de Unamuno, Ramón del Valle Inclán, and Juan Ramón Jiménez were influenced by *modernismo*. The force of the movement began to wane after 1914 as many writers became increasingly concerned with the consideration of the social and economic problems of a changing world. Other more extreme aesthetic movements arose, such as *ultraísmo* (see BORGES, JORGE LUIS), but in general the social and political strains grew stronger. After World War I the writers of the new generation revolted against the mannerisms and hollow elegance of early *modernismo*, and in the words of Enrique GONZÁLEZ MARTÍNEZ they "wrung the neck of the deceitful swan." The Brazilian artistic renaissance, which began in 1922, was regional in nature and is also termed *modernismo*. See G. M. Craig, *The Modernist Trend in Spanish-American Poetry* (1934, repr. 1971), an anthology.

Modestinus, Herennius (hərĕn'ēəs mōdəstī'nəs), fl. A.D. c.250, Roman jurist; student of Ulpian. Under the Roman Empire he was one of the five jurists, including PAPINIAN, whose views were considered decisive in resolving legal controversies. Extensive sections of his work are preserved in the Corpus Juris Civilis.

Modesto (mōdĕs'tō), city (1970 pop. 61,712), seat of Stanislaus co., central Calif., on the Tuolumne River, near the northern end of the San Joaquin valley; inc. 1884. The center of a farming and fruit-growing area, it has food-processing plants and companies that manufacture paper cartons and cans. A winery and a cannery there are said to be among the world's largest. A junior college is in the city.

Modica (mô'dĕkä), city (1971 pop. 43,590), SE Sicily, Italy. It is the center of an agricultural region where livestock is raised. Known in ancient times as Motyca, it was a feudal county in the 12th cent. and enjoyed a high degree of independence from the 14th to 18th cent. Nearby are the Cava d'Ispica (a series of limestone grottoes containing cave dwellings) and prehistoric and early Christian tombs.

Modigliani, Amedeo (ämādĕ'ō mōdēlyä'nē), 1884–1920, Italian painter, b. Livorno. In Paris after 1906, Modigliani's first work as a sculptor was influenced by cubism and African art. Soon, however, he developed a unique style in painting characterized by an elongation of form, a purity of line, and a languorous atmosphere reminiscent of Florentine MANNERISM. Although known to other artists, he remained unknown to the public during his short life, which was one of poverty, dissipation, and disease. Shortly after his death from tuberculosis, his magnificent portraits and figure studies became highly prized by collectors. Modigliani is well represented in the Art Institute of Chicago and in the Museum of Modern Art, New York City. See biography by Pierre Sichel (1967); studies by Jeanne Modigliani (1958), J. T. Soby (1963), and Alfred Werner (1967).

Modjeska, Helena (məjĕ'skə), 1844–1909, Polish actress who achieved fame in the United States primarily for her Shakespearean interpretations. After initial acclaim in Warsaw, she emigrated in 1876 to the United States with her second husband. Despite her faulty English, she was an immediate success in *Adrienne Lecouvreur* in San Francisco a year later. Her portrayal (1883) of Nora in *A Doll's House* at Louisville, Ky., marked the first production of Ibsen in the United States. After playing opposite Edwin Booth (1889–90) she toured the United States with Otis Skinner and Maurice Barrymore. Her charm, intelligence, and dignity contributed to her reputation as one of the great tragic actresses of her time. Her admirers were so numerous that the Metropolitan Opera House, New York City, was used (1905) for her farewell testimonial. See her *Memories and Impressions* (1910, repr. 1969); biographies by Antoni Gronowicz (1956) and Marion Coleman (1969).

Modoc Indians (mō'dŏk), North American Indians whose language belongs to the Sahaptin-Chinook branch of the Penutian linguistic stock (see AMERICAN INDIAN LANGUAGES). They lived in SW Oregon and N California, particularly around Modoc Lake (also known as Lower Klamath Lake) and Tule Lake. Modoc culture was similar to the culture of the KLAMATH INDIANS, but the Modoc did not rely as heavily on the wokas, or water-lily seeds, for food. There was considerable trouble between the Modoc and the early white settlers, with atrocities being committed on both sides. The Modoc were finally constrained to go (1864) on the Klamath Reservation in Oregon, but most of the tribe was dissatisfied. In 1870, Chief Kintpuash, or CAPTAIN JACK, led a group back to California and refused to return to the reservation. The attempt to bring them back brought on the MODOC WAR (1872–73). After the Modoc War, the Modoc people were divided; some were sent to Oklahoma (where a few remain), and some to the Klamath Reservation in Oregon. The Modoc in Oregon share lands with the Klamath and Snake Indians; together they number some 1,100. See V. F. Ray, *Primitive Pragmatists: The Modoc Indians of Northern California* (1963), R. H. Dillea, *Burnt-Out-Fires* (1973).

Modoc War, 1872–73, series of battles between the Modoc Indians and the U.S. army fought as a result of the attempt to force a group of the Modoc to return to the Klamath Reservation in S Oregon. Beginning in Nov., 1872, U.S. soldiers were engaged in sieges against the Modoc who were encamped in the lava beds near Tule Lake, Calif. The soldiers, after losing battle after battle, increased their forces to 1,000 by March, 1873. During peace negotiations Gen E. R. S. Canby and Eleazer Thomas were killed; the soldiers intensified their efforts to subdue the Modoc and finally in late May, 1873, CAPTAIN JACK and his much reduced force of 30 warriors were captured. Captain Jack and five other leaders were hanged in October. The Modoc War proved costly to both sides: 87 soldiers were killed and 83 were wounded. Although the Modoc lost only 8 warriors and an unlisted number of women and children in the fighting, they were thereafter divided as a people.

Modred, Sir: see ARTHURIAN LEGEND.

modulation, in communications, process in which some characteristic of a WAVE (the carrier wave) is made to vary in accordance with an information-bearing signal wave (the modulating wave); demodulation is the process by which the original signal is recovered from the wave produced by modulation. The original, unmodulated wave may be of any kind, such as sound or, most often, ELECTROMAGNETIC RADIATION. In modulation the carrier is generated or processed in such a way that its amplitude, frequency, or some other property varies. Amplitude modulation (AM) is widely used in RADIO. In this system the intensity, or amplitude, of the carrier wave varies in accordance with the modulating signal. When the carrier is thus modulated, 50% of its energy is converted to SIDEBANDS extending above and below the carrier frequency by an amount equal to the highest modulating frequency. If the modulated carrier is rectified (see RECTIFIER) and the carrier frequency filtered out, the modulating signal can be recovered. In a variant of amplitude modulation, the carrier and the modulating signal are in effect multiplied together. The resultant signal contains all sidebands and no carrier; it can be demodulated only with the carrier as a reference. This is normally accomplished by generating a wave in the receiver at or very near the carrier frequency. In another variant of amplitude modulation, called single sideband modulation (SSB), only one sideband is sent; demodulation is essentially the same as when two sidebands are sent. Frequency modulation (FM) is variation of the frequency of the carrier wave in such a way that the change in frequency at any instant is proportional to another signal that varies with time. Its principal application is also in radio, where it offers increased noise immunity (see NOISE, ELECTRICAL) and decreased distortion at the expense of greatly increased bandwidth. For example, in the system of FM broadcasting used in the United States, the maximum variation in frequency is 75 kilohertz (kHz) above or below the nominal carrier frequency. However, since sidebands exist at far greater separations than this, FM stations in the same area are at least 400 kHz apart and rarely interfere with each other. By contrast, AM broadcast channels need only be 10 kHz apart. Phase modulation, because of the intimate relation between the frequency and phase of a wave, differs from frequency modulation in only minor ways. In pulse modulation the carrier may be a series of pulses that are all of the same amplitude and width and are all equally spaced. By controlling one of these three variables, a modulating wave may impress its information on the pulses. In pulse code modulation (PCM) the pulses are not varied in any of the above ways, but instead are arranged in groups with some pulses "missing" to form a binary code that contains the information from a modulating wave. When the code pulses are detected by a receiver, the modulating wave can be reconstructed. Developed in 1939 by the English inventor Alec H. Reeves, pulse code modulation is the most important form of pulse modulation because it can be used to transmit information over long distances with hardly any interference or distortion.

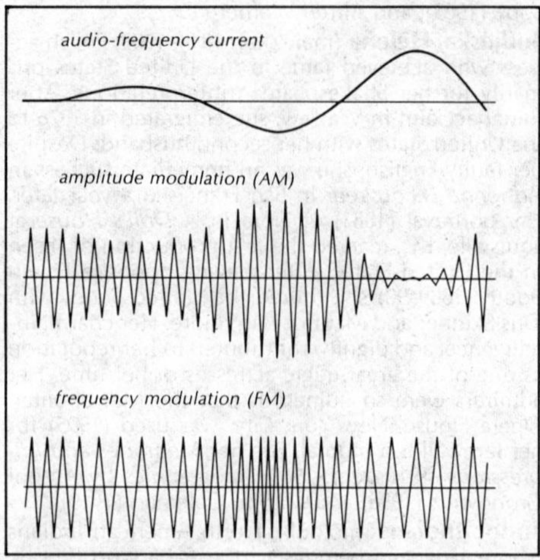

Modulation

modulation, in music, shift in the KEY center of a composition. For its accomplishment use is made of the fact that each chord figures in the harmonic relationships of several keys. In modulating from one key to another, a chord that is common to both keys is used as a pivot chord. If there is no chord common to the two keys, a passage may move through several keys before the desired modulation has been effected. Modulation is commonly employed as a means of achieving variety in a composition and has been in use since the late 15th cent. See Carli Zöller, *The Art of Modulation* (1930); Max Reger, *On the Theory of Modulation* (tr. 1948).

module. 1 Term derived from the Latin *modulus,* a unit of measure in classical architecture equal to half the diameter of a column at its base. This unit was used in proportioning the classical ORDERS OF ARCHITECTURE. **2** The modern module is an interchangeable building unit used in construction; these units are mass-produced and therefore easily replaced and economical. Moshe Safdie's "Habitat," built for Expo 67 in Montreal, is a well-known example of residential modular construction.

Moe, Jørgen Engebretsen, (yör'gən ĕng'əbrĕtsən mō'ə), 1813–82, Norwegian folklorist and poet, bishop of Kristiansand. He collected and revised sagas and folk songs, and he collaborated with P. C. ASBJØRNSEN on the collection *Norwegian Folk Stories* (1841–44, tr. 1859). *Fairy Tales from the Far North* (tr. 1881), and *East o' the Sun and West o' the Moon* (tr. 1917) are selections from *Norwegian Folk Stories.* Moe's son Moltke became Norway's greatest scholar of folklore.

Möen: see MØN, Denmark.

Moerae: see FATES.

Moeris (mēr'ĭs), ancient name of Lake Karun (Arab. *Birkat Qarun*), c.90 sq mi (230 sq km), NE Egypt, in Al Fayyum. The size of the lake is much reduced from that described by ancient travelers, such as Herodotus. Crocodilopolis (later Arsinoë) was the chief town on the lake and a residence of the Ptolemies. Ancient irrigation works were excavated in the late 1920s.

Moesia (mē'shə), ancient region of SE Europe, south of the lower Danube River. Inhabited by Thracians, it was captured by the Romans in 29 B.C. It was later organized as a Roman province, comprising roughly what is now Serbia (Upper Moesia) and Bulgaria (Lower Moesia). Under the empire Roman colonies flourished in the Danube valley.

mofaddaliyat: see MUFADDALIYAT.

Moffat Tunnel (mŏf'ət), railroad tube, 24 ft (7.3 m) high, 18 ft (5.5 m) wide, and 6.4 mi (10.3 km) long, N central Colo., in the Continental Divide, NW of Denver. One of the longest railroad tunnels in the world, it was built between 1922 and 1928. At an elevation of 9,094 ft (2,772 m), it pierces James Peak. An adjacent bore carries water to Denver.

Mogadisho (mŏgədĭsh'ōō), Ital. *Mogadiscio,* city (1969 est. pop. 200,000), capital of the Somali Republic, on the Indian Ocean. It is the country's largest city, a port, and a commercial and financial center. Mogadisho has little industry except for food and beverage processing. Uranium ore has been discovered nearby. The city is linked by road with Kenya and Ethiopia and has an international airport. Mogadisho was settled by Arab colonists c.900, and by the early 12th cent. it had become an important trade center for the east coast of Africa. During the 16th cent. it was controlled by Portugal. In 1871 the city was occupied by the sultan of Zanzibar, who leased it to the Italians in 1892. In 1905, Italy purchased the city and made it the capital of its colony of Italian Somaliland. Mogadisho was captured and occupied during World War II by British forces operating from Kenya. Among the city's historic buildings are the Mosque of Fakr ad-Din (1269) and Garesa Palace, built in the late 19th cent. for the local administrator of the sultan of Zanzibar and now housing a museum and library. Mogadisho is the seat of the University Institute of Somalia.

Mogador: see ESSAOUIRA, Morocco.

Mogi das Cruzes (mōōzhē' däs krōō'zəs), city (1970 pop. 110,156), São Paulo state, SE Brazil, on the Tietê River. It is an industrial center and an agricultural distribution point for São Paulo and Guanabara states. Among its manufactures are paper, pasteboards, textiles, towels, and chemical products. The city was founded in the early 17th cent.

Mogilev (məgĕlyôf'), city (1970 pop. 202,000), capital of Mogilev oblast, W European USSR, on the Dnepr River. It is an important rail and highway junction, a river port, and an industrial center where metal products, machinery, chemicals, and artificial fibers are produced. Arising in the 13th cent. on the territory of Smolensk principality, the city grew around a castle dating from 1267 and became a noted commercial center from the 14th cent. Mogilev was part of the grand duchy of Lithuania (united with Poland in 1569), was later held by Sweden, and passed to Russia during the first partition of Poland (1772). It was occupied and heavily damaged by the Germans during World War II. A tower built by the Tatars and several old churches survive.

Mogilev-Podolski (məgĕlyôf'-pŭdôl'skē), city (1967 est. pop. 24,000), SW European USSR, in the Ukraine, at the confluence of the Dnestr and Derlo rivers. A river port, it has machine and food-processing plants. There are limestone quarries in the area. It was founded at the end of the 16th cent. and grew around a fortress. In the 17th cent. it became an important commercial point on the road from the Ukraine to Turkey and was periodically ruled by the Ukrainian Cossacks, Poles, and Turks. It passed to Russia in 1795. Around the city there are archaeological remains dating from the 3d cent. B.C.

Mogok (mō'gôk"), village, N central Burma, on the Shan Plateau. It is the centuries-old center of the Burmese ruby trade.

Mogollon Plateau or **Mogollon Mesa** (mōgōyōn'), tableland, part of the Colorado Plateau, from 7,000 to 8,000 ft (2,134–2,438 m) high, E central Ariz. It is covered by pine forests, parts of which are included in Coconino, Tonto, and Sitgreaves national forests. Its southern edge is a rugged escarpment called the Mogollon Rim. The plateau is not directly connected with the Mogollon Mts. in W New Mexico.

Mogul (mō'gəl, mōgŭl') or **Mughal** (mōōgŭl'), Muslim empire of India, 1526–1857. The name *Mogul,* a variant of *Mongol,* is incorrectly derived since the founders of the empire were mainly Turks and not descendants of Jenghiz Khan. Turks and Afghans, sweeping from central Asia, had long overrun N India, and in 1206 the DELHI SULTANATE, the first Muslim kingdom of India, was established there. After the fall of the sultanate, a period of turbulence engulfed N India. It was then that BABUR launched his invasion of India; it culminated in the battle of Panipat (1526) and the occupation of Delhi and Agra, thereby marking the beginning of the Mogul empire. Babur was succeeded by his son, HUMAYUN, who soon lost the empire to the Afghan Sher Khan. AKBAR, the son of Humayun and the greatest of the Mogul emperors, reestablished Mogul power in India. At the time of Akbar's death (1605), the empire occupied a vast territory from Afghanistan E to Orissa and S to the Deccan Plateau; Persian culture was implanted in India and the country was free from divisive wars. Mogul expansion continued under Akbar's son JAHANGIR and under his grandson SHAH JAHAN, who built many architectural marvels at Delhi and at Agra (including the Taj Mahal). AURANGZEB, a fanatic Muslim, expanded Mogul territory to its greatest extent, but at the same time the empire suffered the blows of major Hindu revolts. The most serious of these was the Mahratta rising, which brought the empire near ruin. Weakened by the Mahratta wars and by dynastic struggles, the empire came to an effective end as the British established control of India in the late 18th and early 19th cent. However, the British maintained puppet emperors until 1857. Many features of the Mogul administrative system were adopted by Great Britain in ruling India, but the most lasting achievements of the Moguls were in art and architecture (see MOGUL ART AND ARCHITECTURE). See S. M. Edwards and H. L. O. Garrett, *Mughal Rule in India* (1930); Jadunath Sarkar, *Fall of the Mughal Empire* (2d ed., 4 vol., 1949–52, repr. 1972); A. L. Srivastava, *The Mughal Empire, 1526–1803* (6th rev. ed. 1971); Bamber Gascoigne, *The Great Moghuls* (1971); Waldemar Hansen, *The Peacock Throne* (1972).

Mogul art and architecture. ISLAMIC ART AND ARCHITECTURE were introduced into India during the DELHI SULTANATE (1192–1398) and great monuments such as the QUTB MINAR were erected. However, it was under the Mogul emperors that a characteristic Indo-Islamic style, evolved from PERSIAN ART AND ARCHITECTURE, developed on the Indian subcontinent. Mogul monuments are found chiefly in N India, but there are also many remains in Pakistan. The school of Mogul painting began in 1549 when HUMAYUN (1530–56) invited two Persian painters to his court, then at Kabul. They came to direct the illustration of the *Amir Hamza,* a fantastic narrative of which some 1,400 large paintings were executed on cloth. In architecture the first great Mogul monument was the mausoleum to Humayun, erected during the reign of AKBAR (1556–1605). Set in a garden at Delhi, it is a well-composed Persian type of building with two wide octagonal towers, joined by an archway with an elegant facade and surmounted by cupolas, kiosks, and pinnacles. At the same time Akbar was building his fortress-palace in his capital, Agra. Native red sandstone was inlaid with white marble, and all the surfaces were ornately carved on the outside and sumptuously painted inside. Akbar went on to build the entire city of FATEHPUR SIKRI, in which extensive use was made of the low arches and bulbous domes that characterize the Mogul style. Under Akbar, Persian artists directed an academy of local painters. Although at first strong Iranian influence was apparent in the drawing, costumes, and ornamentation of their illuminated manuscripts, by the end of the 16th cent. there was an injection of Indian tastes and manners in the bright coloring and detailed landscape backgrounds. Modeling and perspective also began to be adapted from Western pictures. Basawan, Lal, and Daswanth were Akbar's most famous painters. JAHANGIR (1605–27) favored paintings of events from his own life rather than illustrated fiction. He encouraged portraiture and scientific studies of birds, flowers, and animals, which were collected in albums. Mansur and Manohar were among his famous painters. Jahangir, who resided at Lahore, built less than his predecessors but effected the significant change from sandstone to marble. It was SHAH JAHAN (1628–58) who perfected Mogul architecture and erected at Agra its most noble and famous building, the tomb of his favorite wife, which is known as the TAJ MAHAL. A huge white marble building of simple, symmetrical Persian plan, it is inlaid with colorful semiprecious materials and is set in an equally beautiful and symmetrical garden. Shah Jahan established (1638) Delhi as his capital and built there the famous Red Fort and imperial Mogul palace. This period saw the amalgamation of influences into a truly Mogul style. Portraiture was most highly developed at the sophisticated court of Shah Jahan, and ink drawings were of high quality. Under the puritanical AURANGZEB (1659–1707) the decline of the arts began, although the ornate Pearl Mosque (1662) at Delhi is worthy of mention. During his reign the Mogul academy was dispersed. Artists joined Rajput courts, where their influence upon Hindu painting is clearly evident. See INDIAN ART AND ARCHITECTURE. See also J. V. S. Wilkinson, *Mughal Painting* (1948); Percy Brown, *Indian Architecture: The Islamic Period* (3d ed. 1960); S. C. Welsh, *The Art of Mughal India: Painting and Precious Objects* (1964).

Mohács (mô'häch), town (1970 pop. 19,583), S Hungary, on the Danube and near the Yugoslav border. It is an important river port and railroad terminus and has a modern metallurgical industry. Leather and silk goods, foodstuffs, textiles, and hemp are also produced in the city. Mohács is best known for the crushing defeat (Aug. 29, 1526) there of Louis II of Hungary and Bohemia by Sulayman I of Turkey. Hungary was ill-prepared for the attack, and when Louis hastily tried to unite Hungary and Christendom behind him, only the pope sent help. With a poorly equipped and badly organized army of 28,000, Louis joined battle with a Turkish army of 200,000. The king and almost 25,000 of his army were killed in the battle; the rest were taken captive and massacred. The defeat brought with it more than 150 years of Ottoman domination in Hungary. At Mohács are monuments to the slain, regarded ever since as martyrs to Christianity and to Hungarian independence. Mohács was also the scene (1687) of a Turkish defeat by Charles V of Lorraine, which hastened the end of Turkish rule in Hungary.

mohair, hair of the Angora goat or a large group of fabrics made from it, either wholly or in combination with wool, silk, or cotton. The Angora goat, native of Asia Minor for 2,000 years, is bred in other lands, e.g., the SW United States and South Africa. Mohair is cool, firm, and resistant to dust and moisture. The fiber is especially valuable in the manufacture of sweaters, upholstery plushes, heavy cloaking, and "fur" cloths such as astrakhan.

Mohammed: see MUHAMMAD.

Mohammedan and **Mohammedanism:** see MUSLIM and ISLAM respectively.

Mohave, river and desert: see MOJAVE.

Mohave Indians (mōhä'vē), North American Indians whose language belongs to the Yuman branch of the Hokan-Siouan linguistic stock (see AMERICAN INDIAN LANGUAGES). In the mid-18th cent. they lived on both banks of the Colorado River, in Arizona and California. They then numbered some 3,000. The Mohave were semisedentary farmers who generally cultivated bottomland along the river. They lived in low brush dwellings. Most of the Mohaves are now settled on the Colorado River Reservation, which was established in 1865. By the early 1970s the Mohave numbered about 1,000. See Herman Grey, *Tales from the Mohaves* (1970); study by A. L. Kroeber (1974).

Mohawk, river, c.140 mi (230 km) long, rising in central New York and flowing S then SE past Utica and Schenectady to enter the Hudson River at Cohoes. The Mohawk is canalized from Rome to its mouth (completed 1918) as part of the New York State Barge Canal, which links the Hudson River with the Great Lakes; it is now mainly used by pleasure craft. Rapids and small waterfalls are found at Little Falls and Oriskany, near Cohoes, and on many tributaries. Pollution from industries and from municipal raw sewage is a special target of cleanup efforts under the Clean Waters Program of 1965. The beautiful and fertile Mohawk valley, named for its original Indian inhabitants, was the scene of many battles and raids in the French and Indian War and in the American Revolution. The valley was long an important route to the West. The Erie Canal followed the river.

Mohawk Indians: see IROQUOIS CONFEDERACY.

Mohawk Trail. 1 Old road (c.100 mi/160 km long) in central New York state following the Mohawk River. It was an easy route through the Appalachians by which thousands of settlers emigrated from the Eastern seaboard to the Midwest. It traverses territory once occupied by the Iroquois Confederacy. In the Colonial period it was a series of turnpikes beginning at Schenectady and extending to Rome, with lesser trails stretching westward. The Erie Canal rendered the road less important, and when the railroads were built its value was further diminished. **2** Motor highway extending c.30 mi (50 km) across N Massachusetts from Greenfield to North Adams. It follows a trail blazed originally by the Mohawk Indians. Traversing the scenic Hoosac Range and Berkshire Hills, this route is popular with tourists.

Mohegan Indians, North American Indians, whose language belongs to the Algonquian branch of the Algonquian-Wakashan linguistic stock (see AMERICAN INDIAN LANGUAGES). Also called the Mohican, they were the eastern branch of the MAHICAN INDIANS. In the early 17th cent. the Mohegan occupied most of SW Connecticut, their chief village being on the site of the present village of Mohegan on the Thames River. When the white settlers arrived in this region, the Mohegan and the Pequot were one tribe, living under the rule of Sassacus. Later UNCAS, a subordinate chief, rebelled against Sassacus and assumed the leadership of a small group of Indians on the Thames River near Norwich. This group was known as the Mohegan Indians. After the fall of Sassacus the greater part of the Pequot joined the Mohegan, who in 1643 numbered some 2,300. Uncas thereby obtained control of the territory of the two tribes. The Mohegan, supported by the British, became one of the most powerful tribes in S New England. As white settlements were extended, the Mohegan sold most of their land and accepted a reservation on the Thames. They declined quickly and were practically extinct by the early 19th cent. The Mohegans became known to the world in the early part of the 19th cent. with the publication of James Fenimore Cooper's novel, *The Last of the Mohicans.* In the early 1970s the Mohegan and the Pequot shared a small reservation in Connecticut; together they number about 35. See A. L. Peale, *Uncas and the Mohegan-Pequot* (1939).

Mohenjo-Daro: see INDUS VALLEY CIVILIZATION.

Mohican Indians: see MAHICAN INDIANS; MOHEGAN INDIANS.

Mohl, Hugo von (hōō'gō fən mōl), 1805–72, German botanist. He is noted for his research on the nature of PROTOPLASM and chlorophyll and on the physiology of higher plant forms. Mohl was professor of botany at the Univ. of Tübingen from 1835. He was an expert on microscopy and laid the foundation for later work on the structure of palms and cycads. His works include *Principles of the Anatomy and Physiology of the Vegetable Cell* (1851, tr. 1852) and a collection of important papers *Vermischte Schriften botanischen Inhalts* [miscellaneous botanical writings] (1845).

Moho (mō'hō) or **Mohorovičić discontinuity** (mō"hōrō'vəchĭch): see EARTH.

Mohole Project, program proposed in 1957 to drill a hole down through the earth's crust to the denser material below it, called the mantle, from which the crust is separated by a boundary known as the Mohorovičić discontinuity (see EARTH). The main purposes of the project were to determine the nature of this boundary, to attempt to fill gaps in the evolutionary record from samples of the rocks encountered, and to obtain from the samples further information about the origin of the earth and the solar system. Although several test borings were made in the E Pacific Ocean, the project was abandoned, as funding to support the ever-increasing costs of the project failed to gain congressional approval. Nevertheless, ship positioning and deepwater drilling technology developed for the project have been employed in the recent DEEP SEA DRILLING PROJECT and may facilitate future drilling to tap reserves of oil and gas that lie below the ocean floor.

Moholy-Nagy, László (lä'slō mō'hôlē-nŏ'dyə), 1895–1946, Hungarian painter, designer, and experimental photographer. He turned to art after studying law. While living in Berlin he was one of the founders of CONSTRUCTIVISM, experimenting with photograms and translucent materials. As a professor in the newly opened BAUHAUS from 1923 to 1928, Moholy-Nagy was coeditor with Walter Gropius of the school's regular publications. He worked in Berlin until 1934 as a typographer and designer of stage sets. In 1937 he directed the Bauhaus School of Design in Chicago until it failed (1938). Thereafter he opened the Chicago Institute of Design, which he headed until his death. His greatest contribution to modern art lay in his teaching, which deeply influenced American commercial and industrial design. He was the author of *The New Vision* (tr. 1928) and *Vision in Motion* (1947). See study by his wife Sibyl Moholy-Nagy (1950).

moiety: see CLAN.

Moirai: see FATES.

Moiseyev, Igor Alexsandrovich (ē'gər əlyĭksän'-drəvĭch moisä'yĕv), 1906–, Soviet dancer and choreographer. He was a soloist with the Bolshoi Theatre from 1924 to 1929 and ballet master from 1929 to 1939. In 1936 he organized the Moiseyev Dance Company, a folk dance group, which has since toured Europe and the United States.

Moisie (mwäzē'), river, 210 mi (338 km) long, rising in E Que., Canada, near the Labrador border, and flowing S to the St. Lawrence. The Hudson's Bay Company has an important trading post at the village of Moisie near the river's mouth.

Moivre, Abraham de (äbrä-äm'də mwä'vrə), 1667–1754, French-English mathematician. He fled to England after the revocation of the Edict of Nantes. He was called upon by the Royal Society to help decide the issue between Newton and Leibniz on the priority of the invention of the differential calculus. De Moivre made important contributions to trigonometry and to the theory of probabilities, on which he published *Doctrine of Chances* (1718). There are three mathematical theorems which bear his name.

mojarra (mōhär'ə), common name for a member of the family Gerridae, small tropical food fishes. The many American species are found chiefly off the S Atlantic coast but also along the Pacific coast. Mojarras are rarely over a foot (30 cm) in length and are silvery in color. The fins can be retracted into specialized grooves located under the anal and dorsal fins. They feed on plant life, extending their jaws in order to engulf their food. The thick-lipped mojarra belongs to the genus *Cichlasoma.* Mojarras are classified in the phylum CHORDATA, subphylum Vertebrata, class Osteichthyes, order Perciformes, family Gerridae.

Mojave (mōhä'vē), river, c.100 mi (160 km) long, rising in the San Bernardino Mts., S Calif., and flowing generally north to disappear in the Mojave Desert. Due to the porous soil and rapid evaporation, much of its course is underground except during the short wet season.

Mojave or **Mohave Desert,** c.15,000 sq mi (38,850 sq km), region of low, barren mountains and flat valleys, 2,000 to 5,000 ft (610–1,524 m) high, S Calif.; part of the Great Basin of the United States. It is bordered on the N and W by the Sierra Nevada and the Tehachapi, San Gabriel, and San Bernardino mts. and merges with the Colorado Desert in the southeast. Once a part of an ancient interior sea, the desert was formed by volcanic action (lava surfaces with cinder cones are present) and by material deposited by the Colorado River. The temperature is uniformly warm throughout the year, although there is a wide variation from day to night. Strong, dry winds blow in the afternoon and evening. Located in the rain shadow of the Coast Ranges, the Mojave receives an average annual rainfall of 5 in. (12.7 cm), mostly in winter. Juniper and Joshua trees are found on the higher, outer mountain slopes; desert-type vegetation and numerous intermittent lakes and streams are present in the valleys. The Mojave River is the largest stream. Minerals found in the desert include borax and other salines, gold, silver, and iron. The desert is crossed by two rail lines and two highways. Military installations were established in the Mojave during World War II. Death Valley National Monument and Joshua Tree National Monument are located in the region. See E. C. Jaeger, *The California Deserts* (4th ed. 1965).

Moji: see KITAKYUSHU, Japan.

Moki Indians: see HOPI INDIANS.

Moksha (môk'shə), river, c.375 mi (600 km) long, rising NW of Penza, central European USSR, and flowing generally NW into the Oka River. Its lower course is navigable.

Mokuaweoweo (mōkōō'əwä'ōwä'ō), volcanic crater at the summit of Mauna Loa, south-central part of the island of Hawaii. The second largest active crater in the world, it has a depth of c.800 ft (240 m) and is 3.7 mi (6 km) in circumference and 1.7 mi (2.7 km) wide. During active periods, lava streams flow from Mokuaweoweo down the slopes of Mauna Loa. The lava flow of 1880–81 was c.50 mi (80 km) long.

Mol (môl), city (1970 pop. 28,823), Antwerp prov., N Belgium, near the Dutch border; founded in the 9th cent. It is a manufacturing city and the center of nuclear research in Belgium.

Mola, Emilio (āmē'lyō mō'lä), 1887–1937, Spanish nationalist general. Entering the army in 1904, he rose to the rank of general by 1927, when he commanded a military district in Morocco. He was made director general of the Spanish police in 1930, but lost favor the following year under the new republican government. He regained his Moroccan command in 1935, only to be relieved of it by the leftist government a year later. In July, 1936, he was among the first officers to adhere to Francisco Franco's nationalist cause. A superb strategist, he recruited the antirepublican army in Navarre. As commander of this Army of the North, he was in charge of the operations against Irún, San Sebastian, and Bilbao, but he was killed in a plane crash in 1937. His memoirs (3 vol.) were published in 1934.

Moladah (mŏl'ədə, mōlā'də), unidentified city, S Palestine. Joshua 15.26; 19.2; 1 Chron. 4.28; Neh. 11.26.

molality: see CONCENTRATION.

molarity: see CONCENTRATION.

molar volume, the volume occupied by a MOLE of a substance at STP (see separate article). According to Avogadro's law, at a given temperature and pressure a given volume of any gas contains the same number of molecules. At STP 1 mole of gas occupies 22.414 liters. This volume is what is usually meant by the molar volume, although one can also speak of molar volumes of substances that are not gaseous at STP. Since at STP water occupies very nearly 1 cc per gram, and since 1 mole of water molecules weighs very nearly 18 grams, the molar volume of water is about 18 cc. The molar volume of osmium, one of the densest metals, is only about 8.4 cc; that of beryllium is only about 4.86 cc.

molasses, sugar by-product, the brownish liquid residue left after heat crystallization of sucrose (commercial sugar) in the process of refining. Molasses contains chiefly the uncrystallizable sugars as well as some remnant sucrose. Centrifuges are used to drain the molasses off from the sucrose crystals. Molasses is often reprocessed to retrieve more of this remnant sucrose. The better grades, such as New Orleans drip molasses and Barbados molasses—unreprocessed and therefore lighter in color and containing more sucrose—are used in cooking and confectionery and in the production of rum. The lowest grade, called blackstrap, is mainly used in mixed cattle feed and in the manufacture of industrial alcohol. SUGARCANE is the major source of molasses; other sugar plants, e.g., the sugar beet, yield inferior types. The name molasses is sometimes applied to syrups obtained from sorghum and the sugar maple. In Great Britain, molasses is called treacle.

Molay, Jacques de (zhäk də môlā'), 1243?–1314, last grand master of the KNIGHTS TEMPLARS. He distinguished himself in defending Palestine against the Saracens. After the Templars were driven from the Holy Land, he moved to Cyprus, where he began to organize a new force to recapture the lost territory. He was summoned (1306) to Avignon by Pope CLEMENT V to discuss a new crusading effort. PHILIP IV, king of France, was jealous of the Templars' riches and fearful of their power. In 1307 all of the Templars in France were arrested, and their property was confiscated. De Molay and his knights were brought before an inquisitorial court, charged with heresy and other accusations, and tortured. The grand master, thus subjected, admitted certain charges (later recanted) and was burned at the stake in Paris.

mold, name for certain multicellular organisms of the various classes of the division FUNGI, characteristically having plant bodies composed of a cottony mycelium. The colors of molds are caused by the spores, which are borne on the mycelium. Most molds are saprophytic and can obtain moisture and nutriment from fruits, vegetables, jelly, cheese, butter, bread, silage, and almost any dead organic matter. Among the commonest forms is the black bread mold (*Rhizopus nigricans*), which grows on decaying vegetables and fruits as well as on bread. Some molds, e.g., species of *Penicillium*, are useful in the preparation of Camembert, Roquefort, and other cheeses. PENICILLIN and other antibiotic substances are obtained from molds. A few molds are pathogenic, e.g., those which cause ringworm and other skin diseases and several which cause DISEASES OF PLANTS. See also SLIME MOLD.

Moldau: see VLTAVA, river, Czechoslovakia.

Moldavia (mŏldā'vēə), historic province (c.14,700 sq mi/38,100 sq km), E Rumania, separated in the E from the Moldavian SSR by the Prut River and the W from Transylvania by the Carpathians. Moldavia borders on the Ukraine in the north and on Walachia in the south. It comprises roughly the modern administrative divisions of Bacău, Galaţi, and Iaşi. SUCEAVA and Iaşi, its historic capitals, and GALAŢI, its port on the Danube, are the chief cities. Moldavia, a fertile plain drained by the Siretul, is the granary of Rumania. Besides farming there is livestock raising, and orchards and vineyards dot the countryside. Lumbering and petroleum extraction are the main industries. The region was part of the Roman province of DACIA and has retained its Latin speech despite the centuries of invasion and foreign rule. Greek, Slavic, Turkish, Jewish, and other elements have influenced its culture. Moldavia was part of the Kievan state from the 9th to the 11th cent. In the 13th cent. the Cumans, who then held Moldavia, were expelled by the Mongols. When the Mongols withdrew, Moldavia became (early 14th cent.) a principality under native rulers. It then included BUKOVINA and BESSARABIA. Like its sister principality, Walachia, it was torn by strife among the boyars—the great landowners and officeholders—and among rival claimants to the throne. The rural population was reduced to misery and virtual slavery (which lasted well into the 19th cent.) by the princes, who ruled with Oriental absolutism and cruelty. Moldavia reached its height under Stephen the Great (1457–1504), who in 1475 routed the Turks, but in 1504 it became tributary to the sultans. Although it was frequently occupied by foreign powers in the continuous wars among Turkey, Austria, Transylvania, Poland, and Russia, Moldavia remained under the Ottoman Empire. S Bessarabia early passed under the rule of the khans of Crimea. Early in the 18th cent. the Turks ended the rule by native princes—who had sided with the enemy as often as with Turkey—and appointed governors (hospodars), mostly Greek Phanariots (see under PHANAR). The Greeks surpassed their predecessors in avarice, while the nobility fell into total decay and corruption. Their rule was ended (1822) after the Greek insurrection instigated by Alexander Ypsilanti, and native hospodars were appointed. Meanwhile, Bukovina was taken (1775) by Austria and Bessarabia by Russia (1812). After the Russo-Turkish War of 1828–29, Moldavia and Walachia were made virtual protectorates of Russia (see ADRIANOPLE, TREATY OF), although they continued to pay tribute to the sultan. A Rumanian national uprising (1848–49) was suppressed by Russian intervention. In the Crimean War, Moldavia was again occupied by Russia, but in 1856 the two Danubian principalities, Walachia and Moldavia, were guaranteed independence under the nominal suzerainty of Turkey (see PARIS, CONGRESS OF). With the accession (1859) of Alexander John Cuza as prince of both Moldavia and Walachia the history of modern Rumania began.

Moldavian Soviet Socialist Republic, constituent republic (1970 pop. 3,572,000), c.13,000 sq mi (33,670 sq km), SW European USSR. KISHINEV is the capital. Moldavia, second smallest of the USSR's 15 republics, is landlocked. The Prut River separates it from Rumania in the west. In the north and east, the Dnestr River forms its approximate boundary with the Ukraine, on which it also borders in the south. Mostly a hilly plain, Moldavia occupies all but the southernmost and northernmost sections of former BESSARABIA. Its proximity to the Black Sea gives it one of the mildest climates in the USSR. The fertile soil supports wheat, corn, barley, tobacco, sugar beets, soybeans, and sunflowers, as well as extensive fruit orchards, vineyards, and walnut groves. Horticulture is important for the production of such essences as rose oil and lavender. Beef and dairy cattle are raised, and beekeeping and silk breeding are widespread. Food processing is the main industry; others include metalworking, engineering, and the manufacture of electrical equipment. The majority of the population is Moldavian, but there are large Ukrainian, Russian, Jewish, and Bulgarian minorities. A historic passageway between Asia and S Europe, Moldavia was often subject to invasion and warfare. The main part of Moldavia was an independent principality in the 14th cent. and came under Ottoman Turkish rule in the 16th cent. It became a highly fortified Turkish border region and was a frequent target in Russo-Turkish wars. E Moldavia passed to Russia in 1791. Russia acquired further Moldavian territory in 1793 and especially in 1812, when the Russians received all of Bessarabia (the name for the area of Moldavia between the Prut and Dnestr rivers). The rest of Moldavia remained with the Turks and later passed to Rumania, which seized Bessarabia in 1918. In 1924, the USSR, refusing to sanction the seizure, established the Moldavian ASSR in the Ukraine, with Tiraspol as the capital. Rumania was forced to cede Bessarabia to the USSR in 1940. The predominantly Ukrainian districts in the south and around Khotin in the north were incorporated into the Ukraine, as were parts of the Moldavian ASSR; the rest was merged with what remained of the Moldavian ASSR and made a constituent republic. Taken by Rumania in 1941, the republic was reconquered by the USSR in 1944.

moldboard: see PLOW.

Molde (môl'də), town (1970 pop. 19,186), capital of Møre og Romsdal co., W Norway, on the Moldefjord (an arm of the Romsdalfjord). Commanding a panoramic view of the snow-capped Romsdal Mts., it is a favorite tourist center. Textiles and furniture are manufactured.

molding, in architecture, furniture, and decorative objects, a surface or group of surfaces of projecting or receding contours. A molding may serve as a defining element, terminating a unit or an entire composition (e.g., in the cap of a column or the crowning cornice of a building) or establishing a boundary or transition between portions of a design. One of the primary considerations in the design of a molding is the type of shadow it will cast. It may also serve to break the monotony of a plain surface. The shape of a molding is termed its profile or section. The various architectural styles have developed such specialized character in their moldings that, generally, these accurately reveal the period of a work. Moldings formed an important part of most past styles; in Babylonia, Assyria, and Persia, however, their place was taken by flat ceramic enrichments in color. In Egypt, moldings were limited to the cove, or cavetto, and the half round, or torus, which, used together, formed the cornices for the walls of temple or pylon. Moldings were an essential feature of Greek orders and buildings. The Greek profiles form the basic molding vocabulary for classic types such as the fillet and the fascia, flat vertical surfaces; the ovolo, of an egglike convex outline; the bead and the torus, both convex, three fourths of a circle and one half, respectively; the cavetto, a quarter circle, and the scotia, of elliptical curvature, both concave; and the *cyma recta* and the *cyma reversa*, both of compound curvature, being half concave and half convex. The ovolo was carved with the alternating egg and dart; the acanthus leaf and the anthemion were used for the *cyma recta*, or ogee, and the water leaf for the *cyma reversa*. Roman designers, substituting simple segments of circles for the elliptical and parabolic curvatures, never attained the beauty of Greek forms, although in ornament they added numberless innovations. In Byzantine architecture the tendency was to flatten the classic outlines, transforming them into bands of pierced enrichment. Romanesque moldings were chiefly simple segments of a circle, as in the especially characteristic boltel, or three-quarter round. Moldings changed with the development of Gothic architecture. Cornices, jambs, archivolts, and capitals show a richly varied interplay between projecting rounds and deep concavities. In England, as the style advanced, the boltel became pear-shaped with its tip brought to a point. This, the keel molding, is distinctively Gothic. In the late Gothic (15th cent.) of France and Germany there were ingenious combinations of differing elements to produce broken, merging, and interpenetrating moldings. In developed Gothic a rich assortment of naturalistic forms appeared, e.g., flowers and intertwining vines. The Renaissance return to purely Roman forms was followed in the baroque by heavier, projecting moldings, which cast dramatic shadows. Later a wide variety of styles was employed, but since the 19th cent., decorative molding has been little used in modern architecture.

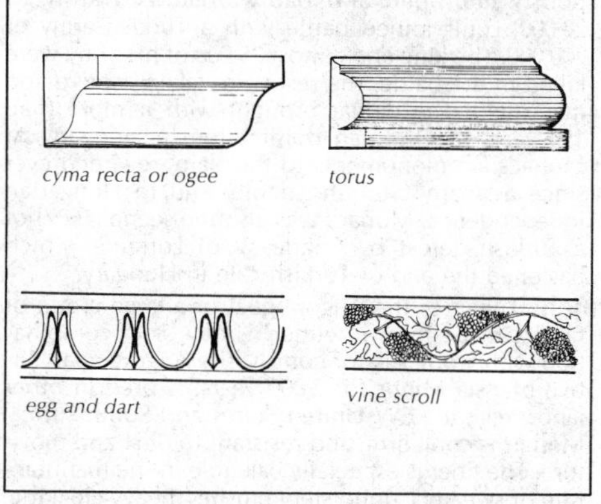

Moldings

Moldoveanu (môldôvyä'no͞o), peak, 8,343 ft (2,543 m) high, central Rumania, NW of Cîmpulung in the Transylvanian Alps; highest point in Rumania.

Molé, Louis Mathieu, Comte (lwē mätyö' kôNt môlā'), 1781–1855, French politician. He was made a count and minister of justice by Emperor Napoleon I and later served in several cabinets under King Louis XVIII. King Louis Philippe appointed him foreign minister (1830) and premier (1836–39). Molé was Louis Philippe's personal favorite for the post of premier, since he was willing to follow the king's lead, a policy that earned him criticism from both the right and left in the chamber of deputies. Because of this opposition Molé persuaded the king to dissolve the chamber and to order new elections. A large majority voted in favor of the parliamentary opposition, and Molé resigned. He was active in the Second Republic (1848–52) but retired after the coup d'etat of Louis Napoleon (later Napoleon III) in 1851.

mole: see BIRTHMARK.

mole, in chemistry, a quantity of particles of any type equal to Avogadro's number, or 6.02×10^{23} particles. One GRAM-MOLECULAR WEIGHT of any molecular substance contains exactly one mole of molecules. The term *mole* is often used in place of *gram-molecular weight;* e.g., one speaks of 18 grams of water as one mole of water rather than as one gram-molecular weight of water. The mole is a unit in the INTERNATIONAL SYSTEM OF UNITS (SI).

mole, in zoology, common name for the small, burrowing, insectivorous mammals of the family Talpidae, found throughout the temperate Northern Hemisphere. Moles are trapped as pests, although they probably do less damage than the animals they destroy, and for their fur, which is highly valued. Typical moles have rounded bodies about 6 in. (15.2 cm) long covered with soft black or gray fur; they have pointed muzzles and lack external ears. They have acute hearing and a highly developed sense of touch at the ends of their noses and tails; their tiny eyes are covered with skin or buried in fur and are capable only of distinguishing light from dark. Moles have short, powerful legs and extremely broad front feet, which are used as shovels and are equipped with enormous digging claws. They can move backwards almost as rapidly as forwards, and most are good swimmers. Moles tunnel just below the surface of the ground, where they hunt for food. Their tunnels make ridges and mounds in fields, gardens, and lawns; quarters for living, nesting, and wintering are in deeper burrows. A single mole can dig about 20 yd (18 m) of tunnel in a day. Moles are voracious eaters, consuming about half their own weight daily. Their diet consists mainly of earthworms and insects, but also includes small mammals such as mice; one mole may even kill and eat another when they happen to meet. They are solitary most of the year, but during the breeding season they travel in pairs. The litter, born in the spring after four weeks of gestation, consists of two to seven young. Typical species include the common European mole, *Talpia europaea,* and the eastern, or garden, mole of North America, *Scalopus aquaticus,* both about 6 in. (15.2 cm) long with a 1-in. (2.54-cm) tail. The largest moles are the western moles of North America, genus *Scapanus,* which may reach a length of 9 in. (22.9 cm). The smallest New World mole is the 3-in. (7.6-cm) shrew mole, *Neurotrichus gibsii,* of the Pacific Northwest, which resembles a shrew and prefers a forest habitat, spending much time above ground. The strangest-looking of the family is the star-nosed mole, *Condylure christata,* of northeastern North America, which has a ring of mobile fleshy protuberances around its snout. This mole is a good diver and leads a semi-aquatic life; apparently it uses the protuberances to pick up sounds in the water. There are no true moles in the Southern Hemisphere. The golden moles of S Africa are members of the insectivorous family Chrysochloridae; they are burrowing animals with bright golden fur. There are burrowing rodents in Africa called strand moles and burrowing marsupials in Australia called marsupial moles. True moles are classified in the phylum CHORDATA, subphylum Vertebrata, class Mammalia, order Insectivora, family Talpidae. See study by Kenneth Mellanby (1973).

Molech (mō'lĕk) or **Moloch** (mō'lŏk), Canaanite god of fire to whom children were offered in sacrifice. He is also known as an Assyrian god. He had a sanctuary at Tophet, in the valley of Hinnom near Jerusalem. Both Solomon and Ahaz were said to have introduced this worship. The practice was contrary to Hebrew law, and the prophets strongly condemned it. Lev. 18.21; 20.2; 1 Kings 11.7; 2 Kings 23.10; Jer. 32.35; Amos 5.26. MALCHAM and MILCOM may be identifiable with Molech.

molecular formula: see FORMULA.

molecular orbital theory, detailed explanation of how electrons are distributed in stable MOLECULES. In the simpler valence theory of the CHEMICAL BOND, each ATOM in a molecule is assumed to retain its own electrons. Even when electrons are shared, as in the covalent bond, it is possible to identify which electron came from which atom. The molecular orbital theory, however, treats each electron as associated with the molecule as a whole. Just as a free atom has certain allowed electron orbits and energies, each molecule has its own allowed molecular orbitals. The orbitals give the probability of finding the electron at any point in space. Each orbital can hold a maximum of two valence electrons and the structure of the molecule is built up by filling the lowest energy orbitals first. The calculations involved are extremely complex, and only the simplest molecules can be treated exactly.

molecular weight, weight of a MOLECULE of a substance expressed in ATOMIC MASS UNITS (amu). The molecular weight may be calculated from the molecular FORMULA of the substance; it is the sum of the ATOMIC WEIGHTS of the atoms making up the molecule. For example, water has the molecular formula H_2O, indicating that there are two atoms of hydrogen and one atom of oxygen in a molecule of water. Rounded to three decimal places, the atomic weight of hydrogen is 1.008 amu and that of oxygen is 15.999 amu. The molecular weight of water is thus $(2 \times 1.008) + (1 \times 15.999) = 2.016 + 15.999 = 18.015$ amu. Since atomic weights are average values, molecular weights are also average values. On the average, a molecule of ordinary water weighs 18.015 amu. Both hydrogen and oxygen are made up of several isotopes. One isotope of hydrogen is deuterium, or heavy hydrogen. Atoms of deuterium are about twice as massive as the average for all hydrogen atoms in ordinary water. Therefore water that contains only atoms of deuterium, called heavy water, has a higher molecular weight than ordinary water. Some substances, especially ionic compounds such as common salt, are not made up of molecules and thus have neither a molecular formula nor a molecular weight. Molecular weights of substances may be determined experimentally in various ways, the method employed usually depending on the state (solid, liquid, or gas) of the substance. Methods for determining the molecular weights of gaseous substances are based on Avogadro's law, which states that under given conditions of temperature and pressure a given volume of any gas contains a specific number of molecules of the gas; thus a comparison of the weights of equal volumes of different gases under the same conditions of temperature and pressure is equivalent to a direct comparison of the weights of molecules of the gases. The molecular weights of substances that are not normally gaseous and do not evaporate without decomposition are sometimes determined from their effects on the melting point, boiling point, vapor pressure, or osmotic pressure of some solvent (see COLLIGATIVE PROPERTIES). However, if the substance ionizes or does not completely separate into molecules, the molecular weight so determined will be erroneous. Highly accurate molecular weights are sometimes determined by using the MASS SPECTROGRAPH. Some substances, e.g., proteins, viruses, and certain synthetic polymers, have very high molecular weights. These molecular weights may be determined by measurement of sedimentation rate in an ultracentrifuge, by light-scattering photometry, or by other methods. The methods may give different results, since usually the molecules of a substance such as a polymer do not all have exactly the same molecular weight. These methods determine an average molecular weight for the molecules in the sample. The number-average molecular weight determined by the ultracentrifuge method gives a value that is equal to the weight of the sample divided by the number of molecules in the sample. This number-average molecular weight can also be determined by other methods based on measurement of colligative properties. The light-scattering method determines what is called the weight-average molecular weight. Although this may be the same value as the number-average molecular weight if all the molecules have nearly the same weight, it will be higher if some of the molecules are heavier than others.

molecule (mŏl'əkyo͞ol) [New Lat.,=little mass], smallest particle of a COMPOUND that has all the chemical properties of that compound. Molecules are made up of two or more ATOMS, either of the same ELEMENT or of two or more different elements, joined by one or more covalent CHEMICAL BONDS. A single atom is usually not referred to as a molecule, and ionic compounds such as common salt are not made up of molecules. Unlike IONS, molecules carry no electrical charge. According to the kinetic molecular theory, the molecules of a substance are in constant motion. The state (solid, liquid, or gaseous) in which matter appears depends on the speed and separation of the molecules in the matter. Substances differ according to the structure and composition of their molecules. A molecular compound is represented by its molecular FORMULA; for example, water is represented by the formula H_2O. A more complex structural formula is sometimes used to show the arrangement of atoms in the molecule. Molecules differ in size and MOLECULAR WEIGHT as well as in structure. In a chemical reaction between molecular substances, the molecules are often broken apart into atoms or radicals that recombine to form other molecules, i.e., other substances. In other cases two or more molecules will combine to form a single larger molecule, or a large molecule will be broken up into several smaller molecules. Molecules can assume many shapes and sizes. Molecules of hydrogen gas, H_2, are very small; each consists of two atoms of hydrogen. Water molecules, H_2O, are much larger, containing an atom of oxygen as well as two of hydrogen. The atoms in a water molecule are arranged at the corners of an isosceles triangle; the oxygen atom is located where the two equal sides meet and the angle between these sides is about 105°. A carbon dioxide molecule, CO_2, is linear, with the two oxygen atoms an equal distance on either side of the carbon atom. In methane, CH_4, the hydrogen atoms are arranged at the corners of a tetrahedron with the carbon atom in the center. In benzene, C_6H_6, the carbon atoms form a hexagonal ring with a hydrogen atom joined to each carbon atom. More complex molecules resemble rings, chains, helices, or other forms. Many molecules occurring in living organisms are very complex. RNA and DNA molecules resemble giant helices. Viruses are single large molecules that can be crystallized and their molecular weight determined. By polymerization a large number of small molecules may be joined to form a single large polymer molecule. Typical polymers include synthetic resins, rubbers, and plastics.

History. The terms *atom* and *molecule* were used interchangeably until the early 19th cent. Initial experimental work with gases led to what is essentially the modern distinction. J. A. C. Charles and R. Boyle had shown that all gases exhibit the same relationship between a change in temperature or pressure and the corresponding change in volume. J. L. Gay-Lussac had shown that gases always combine in simple whole-number volume proportions and had rediscovered the earlier findings of Charles, which had not been published. One early theorist was John Dalton, best known for his atomic theory. Dalton believed that gases were made up of tiny particles, which he thought were atoms. He thought that these atoms were stationary and in contact with one another and that heat was a material substance, called caloric, that was contained in shells around the atom (these shells of caloric were actually what was in contact). When a gas was heated, the amount of caloric was increased, the shells became larger, and the gas expanded. Dalton did not accept Gay-Lussac's findings about combining volumes of gases, perhaps because it could not be explained by his theory. A different theory that could explain the combining volumes was proposed by the Italian physicist Amadeo Avogadro in 1811. According to his theory, under given conditions of temperature and pressure, a given volume of any gas contains a definite number of particles. From the earlier observation that one volume of hydrogen gas and one volume of chlorine gas react to form two volumes of hydrogen chloride gas he deduced that the particles in gaseous hydrogen or chlorine could not be single atoms, but must be some combination of atoms. He called this combination a molecule. He reasoned that the two volumes of hydrogen chloride that are formed must contain twice as many particles as either single volume of hydrogen or chlorine. Thus, if there were 100 particles each of hydrogen and chlorine, there would be 200 particles of hydrogen chloride produced; but there could be only 100 particles produced if the original particles of hydrogen and chlorine were indivisible atoms, since each particle of hydrogen chloride contains both hydrogen and chlorine. An assumption that there are two atoms in a molecule of gaseous hydrogen or chlorine and one atom each of hydrogen and chlorine in a molecule of hydrogen chloride preserves both the hypothesis of indivisible atoms and the hypothesis of equal numbers of particles in equal volumes of gases. Similar reasoning would allow a larger even number of atoms in the molecules of hydrogen or chlorine, but Avogadro favored a rule of simplicity, using the smallest possible number. In the model of gases proposed by Avogadro, the particles were not in contact and much of the volume of the gas was empty space. Avogadro's theory was not well accepted; most responses were very critical. Meanwhile, Dalton's theory prompted extensive experimentation and especially the determination of combining weights of the elements. Many shortcomings of Dalton's theory were uncovered, and although a number of modifications were suggested, none were very successful. It was not until 1858 that the Italian chemist Stanislao Cannizaro suggested a merging of Avogadro's and Dalton's theories. The acceptance of this revised theory was assisted by the acceptance by physicists at about the same time of the KINETIC-MOLECULAR THEORY OF GASES, first proposed in 1738 by Daniel Bernoulli.

Moley, Raymond Charles (mō'lē), 1886–, American political economist, b. Berea, Ohio, grad. Baldwin-Wallace College, 1906, Ph.D. Columbia, 1918. He taught at Western Reserve Univ. (1916–19) and at Columbia after 1923, becoming professor of public law (1928) and an expert on the treatment of criminals. He was an economic adviser to Gov. Alfred E. Smith and became a central figure in the BRAIN TRUST, a group of advisers to Franklin Delano Roosevelt. After Roosevelt was elected President, Moley served (1933) as Assistant Secretary of State and delegate to the World Economic Conference at London, resigning because he felt that Roosevelt did not support him. As editor of *Today* (1933–37) and later associate editor of *Newsweek,* he energetically criticized Roosevelt's administration. He wrote much on government, the treatment of criminals, and politics. His writings include *After Seven Years* (1939), which deals with the Roosevelt administration, *27 Masters of Politics* (1949), *The Republican Opportunity* (1962), and *The First New Deal,* with E. A. Rosen (1966).

Molfetta (mōlfĕt'tä), city (1971 pop. 63,422), in Apulia, S Italy, on the Adriatic Sea. It is a fishing port and industrial center. Manufactures include furniture, boats, and food products. There is an Apulian-Romanesque cathedral (12th–13th cent.).

Molid (mō'lĭd), descendant of Jerahmeel. 1 Chron. 2.29.

Molière, Jean Baptiste Poquelin (zhäN bätēst' pôklăN' môlyĕr'), 1622–73, French playwright and actor, b. Paris; son of a merchant who was upholsterer to the king. His name was originally Jean Baptiste Poquelin. Molière was the creator of French high comedy; his genius lay in exposing the hypocrisies and follies of his society through brilliant humor. In his youth he joined the Béjart troupe of professional actors. Madeleine Béjart was for years his mistress; her younger sister, Armande, became his wife in 1662. The little company, headed by Molière and called the Illustre Théâtre, settled (1643) in Paris, but their venture failed (1645), and they spent the next 13 years touring the provinces, returning in triumph with a performance of Molière's *Le Docteur amoureux* for Louis XIV. Under royal patronage this troupe, performing at the Palais Royal, enjoyed continuous success; it is known as the ancestor of the Comédie Française. Molière had, nevertheless, to contend with attacks on technical matters from the rival theater of the HÔTEL DE BOURGOGNE and with cries of impiety and slander from critics and rival authors. The great variety in Molière's work stems from his being at once actor, director, stage manager, and writer. Influenced by the COMMEDIA DELL' ARTE, he wrote farces, comedies, masks, and ballets on short notice for the entertainment of the court. He is best known for the great comedies of character in which he ridicules a vice or a type of excess by caricaturing a person who is its incarnation: *Le Tartuffe* (1664), on the religious hypocrite; *Le Misanthrope* (1666), on the antisocial man; *L'Avare* (1668, tr. *The Miser*); *Le Bourgeois Gentilhomme* (1670, tr. *The Would-Be Gentleman*), on the parvenu; *Les Femmes savantes* (1672, tr. *The Learned Women*), on the fashionable, affected intellectuals whom he had already lampooned in *Les Précieuses ridicules* (1659), often called the first comedy of manners; and *Le Malade imaginaire* (1673), on the hypochondriac. Molière was acting the title role of the latter when he was fatally stricken. Also comedies of character, but depending more on absurdities, are *L'École des maris* (1661, tr. *The School for Husbands*) and *L'École des femmes* (1662, tr. *The School for Wives*), which was followed by a skit against the critics, *La Critique de l'École des femmes* (1663); and *Don Juan* (1665), an adaptation of the old story of the libertine. Molière's farces are uproarious—*Sganarelle* (1660), *Le Médecin malgré lui* (1666, tr. *The Doctor in Spite of Himself*), *George Dandin* (1668), *Monsieur de Pourceaugnac* (1669), *Les Fourberies de Scapin* (1671, tr. *Scapin, the Trickster*), and *La Comtesse d'Escarbagnas* (1671). Among Molière's other works are the poetic *Amphitryon* (1668), after Plautus; *L'Étourdi* (1653?, tr. *The Blunderer*); *Le Dépit amoureux* (1656, tr. *The Amorous Quarrel*); and *Le Mariage forcé* (1664, tr. *The Forced Marriage*). A primary source on Molière's career is the careful *Registre* or daybook of programs, expenditures, and receipts of the Paris company from 1658. It was kept by the actor Charles Varlet de la Grange (1639?–1692). Molière's comedies have been much translated. See biographies by H. M. Trollope (1905), D. B. Wyndham Lewis (1959), and John Palmer (1930, 2d ed. 1965); studies by Will G. Moore (1949), Ramon Fernandez (1929, tr. 1958), L. Gossman (1963), and Percy A. Chapman (1941, repr. 1965).

Molina, Luis (lwēs mōlē'nä), 1535–1600, Spanish Jesuit theologian. He taught at Coimbra and Évora. In 1589 he published *Concordia,* a work in which he expounded the doctrine known as Molinism. Molinism tries to reconcile the dogma of the efficacy of God's grace with the dogma of the freedom of man's will. Discarding St. Thomas's reconciliation of the two dogmas (see GRACE), Molina made the condition of grace dependent upon the free consent of the will. The Dominicans attacked Molinism and Molina; the Jesuits defended him in a dispute that grew extremely bitter. The theology of Francisco SUÁREZ attempted to bridge the differences.

Molina, Maria de: see MARÍA DE MOLINA.

Molina, Tirso de: see TIRSO DE MOLINA.

Moline (mōlēn'), city (1970 pop. 46,237), Rock Island co., NW Ill., on the Mississippi River, in a coal area; inc. 1848. It is a transportation and industrial center with railroad repair shops, and has been a major producer of farm machinery since John Deere moved there in 1847. Other manufactures are elevators and industrial equipment. A military arsenal is nearby. Moline, with East Moline, Rock Island, and Davenport, Iowa, is part of an economic unit called the Quad Cities. Moline has a junior college.

Molinos, Miguel de (mēgĕl' dā mōlē'nōs), 1640–1697?, Spanish priest and mystic. He was the founder of QUIETISM, which he adhered to in its most extreme form. From 1669 he lived principally at Rome. His *Guida spirituale* (1675) set forth his quietistic principles—the complete contemplative passivity of the soul before God. In 1685 he was tried by the Holy Office, imprisoned, and condemned (1687) by the Inquisition. He died in prison, but received the rites of the Church before dying. See biography by John Bigelow (1882).

Molise (mōlē'zā), region (1971 pop. 319,629), 1,714 sq mi (4,439 sq km), S central Italy, bordering on the Adriatic Sea in the east. CAMPOBASSO is the capital of the region, which is divided into the provinces of Campobasso and Isérnia. Mostly mountainous, Molise is crossed by the Apennines; there is a narrow coastal strip. The main occupation in the generally poor region is farming; cereals, pigs, and sheep are raised. Molise's few industries include the processing of food and the manufacture of clothing. Molise was conquered by the Romans in the 4th cent. B.C. After the fall of Rome it came under the Lombard duchy of Benevento (6th–11th cent.). From the 12th cent., it shared the history of ABRUZZI. From 1948 to 1965, Molise was included in the region of Abruzzi e Molise.

Mollendo (mōyĕn'dō), town (1961 pop. 12,500), S Peru, a port on the Pacific Ocean. Mollendo exports wool and has industries producing textiles, shoes, canned fish, and furniture. It is also a popular beach resort.

Mollet, Guy (gē môlĕ'), 1905–, French politician. A former schoolteacher and a wartime resistance fighter, he rose to prominence in the Socialist party after World War II. He served as minister of state in the Léon Blum government (1946–47) and as vice premier (1951). As premier of a left-of-center anti-Communist cabinet of socialists and radicals, Mollet pursued a foreign policy of unification in Western Europe. He served as minister of state under President De Gaulle (1958–59). Mollet was secretary-general of the Socialist party from 1946 to 1969.

mollie or **molly,** New World fish of the genus *Mollienesia,* in the same family as the guppy (see KILLIFISH). Mollies are found from the E and central United States to Argentina. Top-living fish, they are found in fresh or brackish water, where they feed on algae. Fertilizing internally and giving birth to live young, mollies are of great interest to geneticists because of the reproductive peculiarities of one species, the Amazon mollie (*M. formosa*). This species, which ranges as far N as Texas, consists only of females, which copulate with males of other mollie species; the male does not contribute to the heredity of the all-female offspring. The sailfin mollie, or sailfin (*M. latipinna*), is found in fresh and salt water from South Carolina to Mexico. Sailfins are olive-green with black markings and brightly colored fins. The saillike dorsal fins of the male make it an especially popular aquarium fish. Solid black mollies are artificially bred from any of several mollie species, although mottled black sailfin mollies sometimes occur in nature. Mollies are classified in the phylum CHORDATA, subphylum Vertebrata, class Osteichthyes, order Cyprinodontiformes, family Poeciliidae.

Mollusca (məlŭs'kə), taxonomic name for the second largest phylum of invertebrate animals (Arthropoda is the largest) comprising more than 150,000 living mollusk species and about 35,000 fossil species dating back to the Cambrian period. Mollusks are soft-bodied and most have a prominent shell. The members of this highly successful and diverse phylum are mostly aquatic and include the familiar SCALLOP, CLAM, OYSTER, MUSSEL, SNAIL, SLUG, SQUID, CUTTLEFISH, OCTOPUS, CHITON, and a variety of others. Mollusks occupy habitats ranging from the deep ocean to shallow waters to moist terrestrial niches. Certain mollusks, such as clams, squids, and scallops, constitute important food staples, and molluskan shells are highly valued by collectors. In times past these shells were used as money and today are used ornamentally for such items as buttons and jewelry. Although highly diverse, all members of the phylum share certain general features. Most have a well-developed head, which may bear sensory tentacles; in some, like the clam, the head is very reduced. All possess a flexible body wall, which surrounds a body cavity containing the internal organs. The wall, which varies greatly in shape in different species, is usually folded to form a structure called the mantle, which is attached at the top of the body and surrounds it like a tent; the shell is formed on the outside of the mantle. On the underside of the body the wall is usually stretched out to form a thickened mass called the foot. The wall is covered by an outer epidermis and an underlying dermis. The epidermis usually contains gland cells that secrete mucus, which in mollusks has a variety of important uses, such as locomotion, food-trapping, and prevention of water loss. Muscle tissue is found in the body wall, and is particularly plentiful in the foot, which is used for locomotion in most mollusks (although some swim and some are sedentary), and in the mantle in species with reduced shells. The shell is formed by secretions of glandular cells in the mantle. Except in the chitons, the shells of all mollusks are basically similar, differing only in certain mineralogical details. The shell is composed of an outer, prismatic layer containing densely packed cells of calcareous material, secreted by the edge of the mantle; and an inner, nacreous layer of thin, laminated plates of calcareous material laid down by the entire mantle surface. When very thin, the nacreous lining of the shell is pearly and iridescent. Layers of this material may form around a grain of sand or other irritant that lodges between the mantle and the shell; this process eventually forms a pearl. Pearl oysters of the genus *Pinctada* are the most commercially important pearl formers. The digestive tract of the Mollusca is complex. The foregut region consists of an esophagus and a mouth cavity, which contains a toothed belt called the radula, found in almost all mollusks and peculiar to the phylum. The radula is usually used for scraping food, such as algae, from surfaces. The number and form of radula teeth is highly variable; some species have a single radula tooth while others may have several hundred thousand. In some the teeth are hollow and poison-containing and are used as weapons; other radula modifications exist. The stomachs of mollusks are generally complex, and these, too, differ with the species and according to the feeding habits of the animal. Respiration is through gills called ctenidia (sing. ctenidium), located in the mantle cavity (the space between the mantle and the body wall proper) and varies with the species and with the type of habitat. For example, intertidal marine mollusks are exposed to air and water alternately and must be able to respire in both conditions; terrestrial species have lost their ctenidia, replacing them with lungs that can function both in water and air. Excretion of wastes is through structures called metanephridia and through the body and gill surfaces. The blood circulates through the gill filaments, where exchange of carbon dioxide and oxygen occurs between the blood and the water flowing over the gill surface. Most molluskan blood contains a respiratory pigment called hemocyanin, a copper compound. When oxygenated, such blood is bluish in color; when deoxygenated, the blood is colorless. Only a few mollusks have hemoglobin in their blood. Blood circulation is variable within the phylum, but is generally mediated by a muscular heart, which distributes the blood to the tissues. Most mollusks possess well-developed sensory organs. The highest degree of development of the nervous system is found in the class Cephalopoda (octopuses, squids, and nautiluses). Reproduction is sexual and may be simple or highly complex. The fertilized egg develops into a swimming form called a trochophore larva, and is seen also in the development of annelids; this then elongates to become a veliger larva, characteristic of mollusks, and differing in form in the different classes. There are six classes of mollusks.

Class Amphineura. This class contains two very different kinds of mollusk. The subclass Polyplacophora contains about 600 species of sedentary animals commonly known as chitons, marine forms found from shallow waters to depths of about 1,300 ft (400 m). A chiton has a broad foot and a shell consisting of eight overlapping plates. The subclass Aplacophora contains about 100 species of wormlike, deep-water marine mollusks.

Class Monoplacophora. This class was created for the genus *Neopilina,* a mollusk discovered in 1952, when specimens were dredged from a deep trench off the Pacific coast of Central America. *Neopilina* displays primitive molluskan characteristics; it is the only mollusk with a segmented internal structure, and is thought to show a relationship between mollusks and annelids. The animal is about 1 in. (2.5 cm) long and has characteristics of both chitons and gastropods, but does not quite fit into either class.

Class Gastropoda. This class, containing over 35,000 living and 15,000 fossil gastropod species, comprises the largest class of Mollusca, and includes the LIMPETS, top shells, PERIWINKLES, slipper shells, snails, slugs, sea-hares, ABALONES, nudibranches, or SEA SLUGS, and sea butterflies. Gastropods are primarily marine, but freshwater and terrestrial forms occur. When present, the typical gastropod shell is a three-layered, spiral whorl of calcium carbonate, which varies in color, shape, ornamentation, and size according to the species. Within this shell is the tall, coiled body mass. Some forms, such as slugs, are shell-less and do not have a tall body mass. Gastropod larvae undergo a twisting, or torsion, that brings the rear of the body (mantle cavity, gills, and anus) to a position near the head and results in the twisting of internal organ systems. In many this twisted form is retained by the adult; in others it is partially lost. There are three subclasses, the Prosobranchia, which contains the majority of gastropods; the Pulmonata, which contains the land snails; and the Opisthobranchia, which includes the sea hares and sea slugs. The latter subclass consists of animals with reduced shells or none at all. Most gastropods are motile, but some, e.g., the slipper shell (*Crepidula*), are sedentary. Some, such as the sea butterflies, swim, and others, including the terrestrial snails, move by means of a well-developed foot. Many gastropods are herbivores, or plant-eaters, with multitoothed radulas for scraping algae from various substrata. Among the carnivorous, or animal-eating, species is the CONCH, which feeds on smaller mollusks, and the cone shells (*Conus*), which feed on fish and annelid worms that they first paralyze with poison contained in their hollow radula teeth. The poison is also toxic to humans, causing paralysis and sometimes death. Gastropods have a complex nervous system with ganglia. Reproduction is variable, but most gastropods have separate sexes. Fertilization of the egg occurs in sea water. Some gastropods are hermaphrodites (having both sexes in the same individual) and some are protandric hermaphrodites, i.e., they are male first and become female as they age. Gastropods are economically valuable as food for many animals, including man. Some gastropods are serious pests, for example, the common slug, which causes much garden damage.

Class Pelecypoda. This class (also called Lamellibranchia) contains the mollusks known as bivalves, including the mussels, oysters, scallops, and clams. All have shells composed of two pieces known as valves. In most, the valves are of similar size, but in some sedentary species, such as the oysters, the upper valve, which covers the left side of the body, is larger than the lower valve, which covers the right side and is attached to the substratum. Two large muscles, called adductors, hold the valves together at the top of the body. Pelecypod shells vary greatly in size, color, and ornamentation. The fresh water seed shells are among the smallest known, being less than .1 in. (c.2 mm) in length, while the shell of the GIANT CLAM may exceed 4 ft (120.4 cm) in length. The foot of pelecypods is adapted for burrowing in all species except the sedentary ones, where it is reduced in size. Some species, e.g., the COCKLES, use the foot to hop about from place to place. Pelecypods have a greatly reduced head and no radula. Most have a single pair of large gills used for respiration and for trapping minute food particles. Members of the order Protobranchia use another structure, the proboscis, to feed on bottom detritus. The order Septibranchia contains animals that have lost their gills; they are carnivores or scavengers. Pelecypods have a relatively simple nervous system with three pairs of ganglia and two pairs of long nerve cords. An organ of equilibrium, called a statocyst, is present in most. Fertilization normally occurs in surrounding sea water, and most pelecypods have separate sexes. All are aquatic, and they constitute an important food source for many animals, including man.

Class Scaphopoda. This small class of marine mollusks includes 200 species of burrowing animals commonly known as the tusk, or tooth, shells. The shell is long, cylindrical and tooth- or tusk-shaped, and open at both ends. The foot and the small head project from the larger end. Threadlike tentacles hang from the head and are used for gathering the microscopic organisms on which tusk shells feed. Most scaphopods are tiny, usually only several inches (about 6 cm) long. They are found in both shallow and deep waters; they burrow into the bottom, with only the upper opening protruding.

Class Cephalopoda. This class contains the CEPHALOPODS, animals commonly known as squid, cuttlefish, octopus, and NAUTILUS. The giant squid is the largest of all mollusks. Most cephalopods are highly adapted for swimming. The body mass is very tall. There is no foot; the lower part of the body wall is drawn out to form a ring of arms, or tentacles, around the head. Among living cephalopods, only the nautilus (subclass Nautiloidea) has a complete external shell; extinct members of the subclass and the extinct AMMONITES (subclass Ammonoidea) had similar spiral shells. Members of the subclass Coleoidea (the squid, cuttlefish, and octopus), have an internal shell or no shell at all. All cephalopods are carnivorous and possess a radula and powerful beaks. The nervous system and the sense of vision are highly developed. In most cephalopods the sexes are separate and reproduction requires copulation. Fertilization may occur inside or outside the mantle cavity. Cephalopods are worldwide in distribution and are found in all depths of the ocean. They are an important food staple for many animals, including man.

Mollweide map projection (môl'vīdə): see MAP PROJECTION.

Molly Maguires (məgwī'ərz), secret organization of Irish-Americans in the Scranton anthracite mining districts of Pennsylvania. Its name came from an extralegal, antilandlord organization in Ireland, and its membership was drawn from the Ancient Order of Hibernians, an Irish-American fraternal society. For several years, especially from c.1865 to 1875, the Molly Maguires dominated the mining industry of E Pennsylvania. The movement arose to combat the oppressive industrial and living conditions. Since the police and the forces for law and order were entirely controlled by the mine owners, the Molly Maguires often resorted to murdering or intimidating the police. Agents and superintendents were continually molested. The Mollies reached the height of their power c.1875, when they managed to organize a union in a region otherwise virtually unorganized and to call a strike. Franklin Gowen, president of the Reading RR, which had extensive mining interests, hired the Pinkerton agency to infiltrate the union, and the power of the Molly Maguires was finally broken by the spying activities of James McParlan, a Pinkerton detective. Twenty of the Molly Maguires were hanged. McParlan's secret reports were released for study in 1947. See study by Wayne Broehl (1964, repr. 1968).

Molnár, Ferenc (fĕ'rĕnts môl'när), 1878–1952, Hungarian dramatist and novelist. He studied law in Budapest and Geneva and was for some time a journalist in Budapest. He was a prolific author of plays, novels, stories, sketches, dialogues, and war reports. His best-known works are the plays *Liliom* (1909, tr. 1921), which was made into the musical comedy *Carousel*; *The Guardsman* (1910, tr. 1924); and *The Swan* (1920, tr. 1922). Although technically of high caliber, his plays rely upon superficial theatrical effects. Molnár emigrated to the United States during the Nazi regime; he wrote film scripts and was famed as a wit. See his autobiography (1950).

Mölndal (möln'däl''), city (1970 pop. 33,107), Göteborg och Bohus co., SW Sweden, an industrial suburb of Göteborg.

Moloch (mō'lŏk), in the Bible: see MOLECH.

Molokai (mō'lōkī'), island (1970 pop. 5,261), 261 sq mi (676 sq km), Maui co., Hawaii, between Oahu and Maui islands. Molokai is generally mountainous, with Mt. Kamakou (4,970 ft/1,515 m) the highest peak. On the north coast, separated by a rocky mountain wall from the rest of the island and accessible only over a 2,000-ft (610-m) pass, is the Kalaupapa peninsula, the site of a government leper colony (est. 1860); Father Damien, the Belgian missionary, worked there until his death. Molokai has many cattle ranches and pineapple plantations; the poor soil is unfit for the cultivation of sugarcane. The chief port is Kaunakakai (1970 pop. 1,070), from which the island's products are shipped to Honolulu for export.

Molotov, Vyacheslav Mikhailovich (vyĕ''chĭsläf' mĕkhī'ləvĭch mô'lətəf), 1890–, Soviet political leader. A Communist from 1906, he changed his name from Skriabin to Molotov [the hammer] to escape the imperial police. He was, however, arrested and exiled in 1909. He returned (1911) to St. Petersburg, and when the Bolshevik daily *Pravda* was founded in 1912, he became acting editor. On the eve of the February Revolution of 1917, Molotov was one of the few leading Bolsheviks actually in Russia, and after the October Revolution he rose rapidly in the party and was a strong supporter of Stalin. He was chairman of the council of people's commissars (i.e., premier of the USSR) from 1930 to 1941, when that post was assumed by Joseph Stalin and Molotov became vice chairman. In 1939 he succeeded Maxim Maximovich LITVINOV as commissar of foreign affairs (a title later changed to foreign minister), and in this capacity he negotiated with Joachim von Ribbentrop the Russo-German nonaggression pact, signed at Moscow in Aug., 1939. After the German invasion (1941) of Russia Molotov helped to strengthen the Soviet alliance with the West, shared in the founding of the United Nations, and took part in all major international conferences until 1949, when Andrei Vishinsky succeeded him as foreign minister. As a diplomat Molotov gained a reputation for personal inflexibility and unswerving adherence to Soviet policies. After Stalin's death (1953) he was again foreign minister until 1956. An opponent of Nikita KHRUSHCHEV, he was expelled from the central committee of the Communist party in 1957 after having unsuccessfully tried to oust Khrushchev. He subsequently held minor posts. From 1957 to 1960 he served as ambassador to the Mongolian People's Republic; he was then transferred to Vienna, where he represented (1960–61) the USSR in the International Atomic Energy Agency. In 1964, the USSR revealed that Molotov had been expelled from the Communist party. See biography by Bernard Bromage (1956).

Molotov: see PERM, USSR.

molting, periodical shedding and renewal of the outer skin, exoskeleton, fur, or feathers of an animal. In most animals the process is triggered by secretions of the thyroid and pituitary glands. Nearly all birds molt annually in the late summer, losing and replacing their feathers gradually over a period of several weeks. Except among ducks, rails, and diving birds the ability to fly is not lost. Some birds undergo a second or prenuptial molt in the spring, changing from dull to bright plumage. The development of the young bird is marked by successive molts: first, from the down of the very young to the juvenal plumage, which resembles that of the female in species showing color differences between the sexes; then to the first winter plumage, when the bird is called an immature; and finally to the first nuptial plumage, the adult stage. Arthropods (e.g., insects and crustaceans) must molt their exoskeletons periodically in order to grow; in this process the inner layers of the old cuticle are digested by a molting fluid secreted by the epidermal cells, the animal emerges from the old covering, and the new cuticle hardens. In insects the stages between molts are called instars. Amphibians and snakes usually shed their skins several times a year. Mammals change from heavy winter to light summer pelage.

Protective coloration is exhibited in the color changes of such mammals as the ermine and the varying hare and, more dramatically, among such birds as the ptarmigan.

Moltke, Helmuth Johannes Ludwig, Graf von (hĕl'-mo͞ot yōhä'nəs lo͞ot'vĭkh gräf fən môlt'kə), 1848-1916, German army officer. He fought in the Franco-Prussian War (1870-71) and became adjutant to his uncle, Field Marshal H. K. B. von Moltke, in 1882. A favorite of Emperor William II, he succeeded Alfred von SCHLIEFFEN as chief of general staff in 1906. Shortly before the outbreak of World War I, Moltke modified his predecessor's famous plan by withdrawing several divisions from the right wing of the potential Western front, in order to reinforce the left. This revision weakened the initial attack on France when war broke out. On Sept. 14, 1914, Moltke was succeeded as chief of staff by General Erich von FALKENHAYN.

Moltke, Helmuth Karl Bernhard, Graf von, 1800-1891, Prussian field marshal. Following his graduation from the Royal Military Academy of Denmark, he entered the Danish service, but resigned his commission in 1822 to join the Prussian army. He became (1833) a member of the general staff, and three years later with official sanction he entered the service of the Turkish sultan as military adviser. His advice was not followed in the campaign against Muhammad Ali of Egypt, and he returned (1839) to Prussia, where he advanced rapidly and was made chief of the general staff in 1858. He worked tirelessly to mold the Prussian army into a formidable war machine. The successful completion of the Danish War (1864) and of the Austro-Prussian War (1866) was due to his tactics, and in the FRANCO-PRUSSIAN WAR (1870-71) Moltke's genius, evinced especially in his plan of mobilization, led to complete Prussian victory. On receiving news of the fall of Metz, William I made him a count. Moltke owed many of his military successes to the elasticity of his strategy. Unlike Napoleon, he gave his subleaders liberty in making decisions. When he resigned as chief of staff in 1888, he was made chairman of the committee for national defense. Moltke was a member of the diet of the North German Confederation (1867-71) and of the Reichstag (1871-91). He wrote noteworthy books on tactics, including *The Franco-German War of 1870-71* (tr. 1892). See his *Essays, Speeches, and Memoirs* (tr., 2 vol., 1893).

Moluccas (məlŭk'əz, mō-) or **Spice Islands,** Bahasa Indonesian *Maluku,* Du. *Molukken,* island group and prov. (1970 est. pop. 995,000), c.32,300 sq mi (83,660 sq km), E Indonesia, between Celebes and New Guinea. The capital of the province is Ambon, on Ambon island. The group's many islands include HALMAHERA (the largest), CERAM, BURU, AMBON, TERNATE, and Tidore and the Aru and Kai island groups. Of volcanic origin, the Moluccas are mountainous, fertile, and humid. They are the original home of nutmeg and cloves. Other spices, copra, and forest products are also produced. Sago is the staple food The islands were explored by Magellan in 1511-12 and thereafter settled by the Portuguese, who established a trading center at Ternate. In the 17th cent. they were taken by the Dutch, who secured a monopoly in the clove trade. Twice the British gained a foothold in the islands, which passed definitively to the Dutch in the first quarter of the 19th cent.

molybdenite (məlĭb'dənīt, mō-), a mineral, molybdenum disulfide, MoS_2, blue-gray in color, with a metallic luster and greasy feel. It occurs in crystals of the hexagonal system but more commonly in scales, grains, or foliated or massive form. It has an excellent basal cleavage and the laminae are flexible. It is found in granites, syenites, gneisses, and crystalline limestones. Molybdenite is an important ore of molybdenum. The major sources are quartz veinlets in granite at Climax, Colo., and copper mines in Utah, New Mexico, and Arizona. Minor amounts are recovered in Mexico, Chile, Canada, and Norway.

molybdenum (məlĭb'dənəm) [Gr.,=leadlike], metallic chemical element; symbol Mo; at. no. 42; at. wt. 95.94; m.p. about 2610°C; b.p. about 5560°C; sp. gr. 10.22 at 20°C; valence +2, +3, +4, +5, or +6. Molybdenum is a hard, malleable, ductile, high-melting, silver-white metal with a body-centered cubic crystalline structure. It is below chromium in group VIb of the PERIODIC TABLE. Molybdenum resists corrosion at ordinary temperatures. In forming compounds, as in oxides, sulfides, and halides, it exhibits its variable valence. In its most important compounds, however, it has an oxidation state of +6, as in the trioxide, which forms a series of compounds known as the molybdates. Molybdenum does not occur uncombined in nature. Its chief ore is MOLYBDENITE (molybdenum disulfide, MoS_2). It also occurs in wulfenite (a lead molybdate) and powellite (a calcium molybdate-tungstate). It is widely but sparingly distributed throughout the world; it is found in the United States, Canada, Europe, Australia, Chile, the Soviet Union, and China. Large amounts of molybdenite are mined at Climax, Colo. Molybdenum ore is also obtained as a by-product of copper mining. The ores are usually concentrated by the FLOTATION PROCESS before being refined. The actual refining process depends on the ultimate use. The molybdenite may be purified for use in lubricants. Almost all molybdenum ore is converted by roasting to molybdic oxide, MoO_3. The oxide may be added directly to steel or may be converted to ferromolybdenum by a thermal process; this alloy is used to add molybdenum to other iron and steel alloys. The oxide may be further purified by sublimation, or converting directly from the solid to vapor state, and then reduced to molybdenum powder by reaction with carbon, aluminum, or hydrogen. The oxide may be dissolved in ammonium hydroxide; the solution is filtered and evaporated to yield ammonium molybdate, $(NH_4)_2Mo_2O_7$. In alloy, STEEL molybdenum acts as a hardening agent and also improves the properties of the alloy at high temperatures; such alloys are used in making high-speed cutting tools, aircraft parts, and forged automobile parts. The pure metal in the form of thin sheets or wire is used in X-ray tubes, electronic tubes, and electric furnaces because it can withstand high temperatures. It was used in early incandescent light bulbs. Because it retains its strength and structure at very high temperatures, it has found use in certain critical rocket and missile parts. Useful compounds of molybdenum include molybdenum disulfide, used as a lubricant; ammonium molybdate, used in chemical analysis for phosphates; and lead molybdate, used as a pigment in ceramic glazes. Molybdenum was recognized as a distinct element in 1778 by K. W. Scheele; its ore had earlier been confused with lead ore, hence its name. The element was isolated by P. J. Hjelm in 1782.

Moma (mō'mä), town, E central Mozambique. It is important mainly as a harbor for the export of tropical produce.

Mombasa (mōmbă'sə, -bä'sə), city (1969 pop. 246,000), capital of Coast prov., SE Kenya, mostly on Mombasa island in the Indian Ocean and partly on the mainland (with which it is connected by a causeway). It is Kenya's chief port and an important commercial and industrial center. Manufactures include processed food, cement, and glass. From the 8th to the 16th cent. Mombasa was a center of the Arab trade in ivory and slaves. The city was visited (1498) by Vasco da Gama on his first voyage to India. Mombasa was burned three times by the Portuguese, notably by Francisco de Almeida in 1505. The Portuguese controlled the city until 1698, when it was regained by the Arabs; the Portuguese briefly held the city again in 1729. It came under Zanzibar in the mid-19th cent. and passed to Great Britain in 1887. Mombasa was the capital of the British East Africa Protectorate from 1887 to 1907. Of note are the remains of Fort Jesus, built by the Portuguese in 1593-94.

Mombert, Alfred (äl'frĕt môm'bĕrt), 1872-1942, German poet. He was briefly a lawyer and public official. His works, characterized by mysticism, fantasy, and simplicity of style, include *Die Glühende* [aglow] (1896), *Die Schöpfung* [the creation] (1897), *Die Blüte des Chaos* [the blossoming of chaos] (1905), the trilogy *Aeon* (1907-11), *Der Held der Erde* [the hero of the earth] (1919), and *Atair* (1925). A Jew, Mombert was arrested by the Nazis in 1940. He fell ill in a concentration camp, was released (1941), and died in Switzerland.

mombin (mōm'bēn), any tree of the tropical genus *Spondias* of the family Anacardiaceae (SUMAC family). The plum-shaped fruits, 1 to 2 in. (2.54-5.1 cm) long, are much eaten in the tropics. They are spicy and slightly acid in taste and are eaten fresh, boiled, dried, or in preserves. Best known are the red mombin, or Spanish plum (*S. purpurea*), marketed chiefly in Mexico and Guatemala, the yellow mombin (*S. mombin,* called also hog plum or jobo), and the otaheite apple or ambarella (*S. cytherea*), found in both the Old and New World tropics. The local common names vary widely. Mombin is classified in the division MAGNOLIOPHYTA, class Magnoliopsida, order Sapindales, family Anacardiaceae.

moment, in physics and engineering, term designating the product of a quantity and a distance to some point associated with that quantity. The most theoretically useful moments are moments of masses, areas, lines, and forces, including magnetic force. The concept of torque (propensity to turn about a point) is the moment of force. If a force tends to rotate a body about some point, then the moment, or turning effect, is the product of the force and the distance from the point to the direction of the force. The application of this concept is illustrated by pushing open a door: the farther from the hinge the push is applied, the less force is required. The principle of the moment of a force is perhaps best seen in the use of a LEVER. Extensions of this concept are important in mechanics, in topics such as inertia, center of gravity, equilibrium, and stability of structures and in architectural problems. The moment of inertia of a body about a point is the sum, for each particle in the body, of the mass of the particle and the square of its distance from the point. The angular momentum of a body about a fixed axis is equal to the product of the moment of inertia about that axis and the angular velocity. A torque acting on a rigid body acts to change its angular momentum by producing an angular acceleration.

momentum (mōmĕn'təm), in mechanics, the quantity of motion of a body, specifically the product of the mass of the body and its VELOCITY. Momentum is a vector quantity; i.e., it has both a magnitude and a direction, the direction being the same as that of the velocity vector. When an external force acts upon a body or a system of bodies in motion, it causes a change in the momentum of the body. The impulse of a force acting on a body is the product of the force and the duration of time in which it acts and is equal to the change in momentum of the body. When no external force acts upon a body in motion or a system of bodies there is no change in the total momentum even though, as in the case of a system of bodies, there may be an internal disturbance of the system resulting in changes in the momenta of individual bodies. This conclusion is commonly known as the principle of the conservation of momentum (see CONSERVATION LAWS, in physics). The momentum of a body should not be confused with its kinetic ENERGY. The distinction between them can be seen in the action of a pile driver. The distance to which the pile is driven depends upon its kinetic energy; the length of time required for the action to cease, upon its momentum. In addition to the momentum a body has because of its linear motion, the body may also have angular momentum because of rotation. The angular momentum of a particle rotating about a point is equal to the product of the mass of the particle, its angular velocity, and the square of its distance from the axis of rotation. More simply, the angular momentum is the product of the instantaneous linear momentum and the distance. Angular momentum is a vector quantity directed perpendicular to the plane of motion.

Mommsen, Theodor (tā'ōdōr môm'sən), 1817-1903, German historian. Appointed (1848) professor of civil law at the Univ. of Leipzig, he supported the Revolution of 1848 and lost his chair because of his political opinions. He subsequently taught Roman law at Zurich and Breslau and, from 1858, ancient history at the Univ. of Berlin. After the unification (1870) of Germany he came to publicly oppose the policies of Bismarck. His greatest work is his *History of Rome* (3 vol., 1854-56; several English translations), a classic of historical writing. The fourth volume was never completed, but the fifth appeared in 1885. Mommsen's work, an unmatched re-creation of Roman society and culture, is based largely on his study of ancient coins, inscriptions, and literature. His liberal politics prejudiced his view of ancient history; his German contemporaries are clearly visible on his Roman scene. Although a great admirer of Caesar, he vigorously denounced Caesarism. Mommsen also wrote authoritatively on Roman law, notably in *Römisches Staatsrecht* (3 vol., 1871-76) and *Römisches Strafrecht* (1899), and on archaeology. He edited several volumes of the *Monumenta Germaniae historica.* Mommsen received the 1902 Nobel Prize in Literature. A selection of his articles has been published as *Medieval and Renaissance Studies* (1959).

Momus (mō'məs), figure in Greek mythology. He was the personification of censure and mockery.

Møn or **Möen** (both: mō'ən), island (1970 pop. 12,338), 84 sq mi (218 sq km), SE Denmark, in the Baltic Sea, south of Sjaelland and northeast of Falster. Stege (1970 pop. 3,869) is the main town. Møn is largely agricultural; sugar beets are the main crop, and cattle are also raised. At the island's eastern point are the Møns Klint, scenic white chalk cliffs that rise to 420 ft (128 m).

Mona, Roman name for Anglesey island, Wales. It was also sometimes used to designate the Isle of Man.

Monaco, Lorenzo: see LORENZO MONACO.

Monaco (mŏn'əkō, mōnä'kō, Fr. mônäkō'), independent principality (1968 pop. 23,035), c.370 acres (150 hectares), on the Mediterranean Sea, an enclave within Alpes-Maritimes dept., SE France, near the Italian border. It consists of three adjoining sections—La Condamine, the business district; MONTE CARLO, the site of the famous casino; and Monaco-Ville, the capital, atop a rocky promontory. Its beautiful location, natural harbor, exceptionally mild climate, and the gambling tables of Monte Carlo make Monaco one of the best known resorts of the RIVIERA. The ruling prince, Rainier III, succeeded his grandfather, Louis II, in 1949. In accordance with

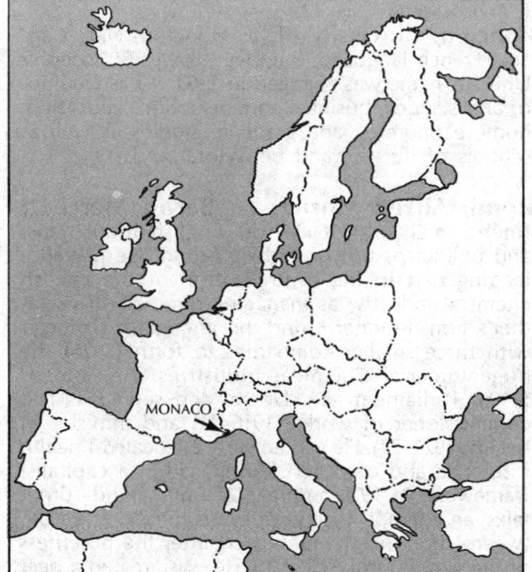

the 1962 constitution, Monaco is governed by the prince, who is assisted by a minister of state (traditionally a Frenchman), a cabinet (the Council of the Crown), and the National Council, which is elected by universal suffrage every five years. The prince may initiate legislation, but all laws must be approved by the National Council. Monaco has a police force and a Royal Guard that has some 65 members. By a treaty of 1918, the succession to the throne must be approved by the French government. Should the throne become vacant for any reason, Monaco would become an autonomous state under French protection. In 1956, Prince Rainier III married Grace Kelly, an American motion-picture actress, and a male heir was born in 1958. Monaco has a customs union with France, and its currency is interchangeable with the French. There are neither income nor corporation taxes; the chief sources of state revenue are excise, stamp, transfer, and estate taxes. Contrary to popular belief, the gambling casino (which is managed as a concession by a private corporation), accounts for only a small portion of government revenue, although it contributes greatly to the economy by attracting tourists. In addition to tourism and the foreign businesses attracted to Monaco by freedom from taxation, shipping and the manufacture of perfumes are also important. Only about 2,500 of the total population are citizens of Monaco (Monegasques), and they are not admitted to the gambling tables. Probably settled by Phoenicians in ancient times, Monaco was annexed by Marseilles and Christianized in the 1st cent. A.D. In the 7th cent. it was part of the kingdom of the LOMBARDS, and in the 8th cent. of the kingdom of ARLES. It was under Muslim domination (8th cent.) after the SARACENS invaded France. Monaco was ruled by the Genovese Grimaldi family from the 13th cent. In 1731 the male line died out, but the French Goyon-Matignon family, which succeeded by marriage, assumed the name Grimaldi. Monaco was under Spanish protection from 1542 to 1641, under French protection from 1641 to 1793, annexed to France in 1793, and under Sardinian protection from 1815 to 1861. The districts of MENTON and Roquebrune (long part of Monaco) were incorporated (1848) into Sardinia, which in turn ceded them to France in 1860. Monaco came under French protection in 1861. Until 1911, when the first constitution was promulgated, the prince was an absolute ruler. In 1962 serious economic disagreements arose between France and Monaco, and new fiscal agreements (1963) severely curtailed the right of French citizens to use Monaco as a tax haven. The Monaco government also came into conflict with the Greek shipping magnate Aristotle Onassis, who owned a majority interest in most businesses in the principality. The issue was settled (1967) when the government purchased these interests. Monaco has a 16th-century palace, a 19th-century cathedral in the Byzantine style, and a noted oceanographic museum, founded in 1910 by Prince Albert I.

monad: see BRUNO, GIORDANO; LEIBNIZ, GOTTFRIED WILHELM, BARON VON.

Monadhliath Mountains (mō'nəlē'ə), Inverness-shire, N central Scotland, between the Spey River and Loch Ness. Carn Ban (3,087 ft/941 m) is the highest point.

Monadnock (mənăd'nŏk), isolated peak, 3,165 ft (965 m) high, SW N.H. It is much visited for its fine view. The peak lends its name to the geomorphic term *monadnock*, an isolated mountain remnant standing above the general level of the land because of its greater resistance to erosion.

Monagas, José Tadeo (hōsā' täthā'ō mōnä'gäs), 1784–1868, Venezuelan political leader. He fought under Bolívar in the revolt against Spain. Chosen by José Antonio PÁEZ as president in 1847, he set up a compromise administration. Páez subsequently revolted, but Monagas crushed the insurrection. In 1851, José Gregorio Monagas, a brother, was inaugurated, and in 1855 José Tadeo again took office. Reforms, including the emancipation of slaves, were introduced, but adoption of a new constitution led to a successful revolution (1858) against him. Ten years later he headed a counterrevolution with forces called the Azules [blues], but he died just after returning to power. His son, José Ruperto Monagas, continuing the dynasty, was overthrown by a new revolution that brought GUZMÁN BLANCO to power.

Monaghan (mŏn'əgən), county (1971 pop. 46,231), 498 sq mi (1,290 sq km), N Republic of Ireland, bordered on the N by Northern Ireland. The county town is MONAGHAN. The northwest portion of the county is a part of the fertile central plain of Ireland; to the south and east are hilly sections. It is primarily an agricultural county. The main enterprise is the raising of beef and dairy cattle. Potatoes, oats, and turnips are the chief crops, and pigs, sheep, and poultry, as well as cattle, are raised in large numbers. Other industries are bacon curing and the manufacture of furniture and footwear.

Monaghan, urban district (1971 pop. 5,255), county town of Co. Monaghan, N Republic of Ireland. It is a farm market with some manufacturing and houses the cathedral of the Roman Catholic diocese of Clogher.

Mona Passage (mō'nə), strait, c.80 mi (130 km) wide, between Puerto Rico and the Dominican Republic. Connecting the N Atlantic Ocean with the Caribbean Sea, it is a favored shipping lane. In it is **Mona Island** (1970 pop. 6), c.20 sq mi (50 sq km), part of the Commonwealth of Puerto Rico. It was discovered by Columbus in 1493, and in 1508 Ponce de León stopped there. In 1511 the island was ceded to Columbus's younger brother Bartolomew, but it soon became a haven for pirates and corsairs.

monarchianism (mōnär'kēənĭzəm) [Gr.,=belief in the rule of one], the concept of God that maintains his sole authority even over Christ and the Holy Spirit. Its characteristic tenet, that God the Father and Jesus Christ are one person, was developed in two forms in early Christianity. Dynamistic monarchians, such as the THEODOTIANS and PAUL OF SAMOSATA, held that Jesus was born a man and received the Christ as a power from God at a later time (see ADOPTIONISM). Modalistic monarchians taught that God is unknowable, except for his manifestations, or modes; Christ is one of these. Because of the consequent implication that God the Father must have died on the cross, they were called Patripassians [from Lat.,= the Father suffering]. SABELLIUS fully developed modalism.

monarchy, form of government in which sovereignty is vested in a single person whose right to rule is generally hereditary and who is empowered to remain in office for life. The power of this sovereign may vary from the absolute (see DESPOTISM) to that strongly limited by custom or constitution. Monarchy has existed since the earliest history of mankind and was often established during periods of external threat or internal crisis because it provided a more efficient focus of power than ARISTOCRACY or DEMOCRACY, which tended to diffuse power. Most monarchies appear to have been elective originally, but dynasties early became customary. In primitive times, divine descent of the monarch was often claimed. Deification was general in ancient Egypt and the Orient, and it was also practiced during certain periods in ancient Greece and Rome. A more moderate belief arose in Christian Europe in the Middle Ages; it stated that the monarch was the appointed agent of divine will. This was symbolized by the CORONATION of the king by a bishop or the pope, as in the Holy Roman Empire. Although theoretically at the apex of feudal power, the medieval monarchs were in fact weak and dependent upon the nobility for much of their power. During the Renaissance and after, there emerged "new monarchs" who broke the power of the nobility and centralized the state under their own rigid rule. Notable examples are Henry VII and Henry VIII of England and Louis XIV of France. The 16th and 17th cent. mark the height of absolute monarchy, which found its theoretical justification in the doctrine of DIVINE RIGHT. However, even the powerful monarchs of the 17th cent. were somewhat limited by custom and constitution as well as by the delegation of powers to strong bureaucracies. Such limitations were also felt by the "benevolent despots" of the 18th cent. Changes in intellectual climate, in the demands made upon government in a secular and commercially expanding society, and in the social structure, as the BOURGEOISIE became increasingly powerful, eventually weakened the institution of monarchy in Europe. The Glorious Revolution in England (1688) and the French Revolution (1789) were important landmarks in the decline and limitation of monarchical power. Throughout the 19th cent. royal power was increasingly reduced by constitutional provisions and parliamentary incursions. In the 20th cent., monarchs have generally become symbols of national unity, while real power has been transferred to constitutional assemblies. Over the past 200 years democratic self-government has been established and extended to such an extent that a true functioning monarchy is a rare occurrence in both East and West. Among the few remaining are Iran, Morocco, and Saudi Arabia. Notable constitutional monarchies include Belgium, Denmark, Great Britain, Japan, the Netherlands, Norway, Sweden, and Thailand.

Monasterboice (mŏn''əstərbois'), village, Co. Louth, E Republic of Ireland. It is one of the oldest monastic sites in Ireland, established near the end of the 5th cent. There are ruins of a round tower, two churches, and crosses.

monasticism (mənăs'tĭsĭzəm, mō–), form of religious life, usually conducted in a community under a common rule. Monastic life is bound by ascetical practices expressed typically in the vows of CELIBACY, poverty, and obedience, called the evangelical counsels. Monasticism is traditionally of two kinds: the more usual form is known as the cenobitic, and is characterized by a completely communal style of life; the second kind, the eremitic, entails a hermit's life of almost unbroken solitude, and is now rare (see HERMIT). Monasticism in general has played an important role in BUDDHISM (including TIBETAN BUDDHISM), JAINISM, ISLAM, and Christianity. Practitioners of monasticism in ancient times included the VESTAL virgins of Rome, the Jewish ESSENES, the THERAPEUTAE of Egypt, and the Peruvian virgins of the sun. The life of the SHAKERS had many analogies with monasticism. The Reformation saw the sudden end of monasticism in the Protestant countries of Europe. The Oxford movement, however, reintroduced religious orders into the Church of England in the 19th cent.; and since World War II renewed interest in monasticism has led to the establishment of a Protestant monastery at Taizé, France.

Monasticism in the Eastern Church. Christian monasticism had its origin in the Egyptian deserts in the 3d–4th cent. with the anchorites, who sought perfection in the most extreme ASCETICISM. Most famous of these hermits was St. ANTHONY, who is called the father of monasticism. From among loose associations of these hermits, the monk St. Pachomius organized (c.320) the first cenobitic community. Somewhat similar was the laura—cells arranged into a monastic village, sometimes of very great size. Uniformity was gradually wrought in Eastern monasticism by the rules of St. BASIL THE GREAT. He favored the cenobitic style and stressed manual labor and obedience in opposition to the extravagances of much of early monasticism (see, e.g., SIMEON STYLITES, SAINT). Monasticism in the East has changed little since the 4th cent.; the monks devote their day to lengthy liturgies and simple work. They do not usually become priests and do not value learning. In contrast to the development in the West, Eastern monks do not belong to different orders with specialized functions; the monasteries or lauras are basically alike in nature and autonomous in organization (see BASILIAN MONKS). Mount Athos is the great center of monasticism in the Eastern Church.

Monasticism in the Western Church. The earliest Western forms of monasticism imitated those of the East and spread with Christianity to Ireland, where the church was organized (6th cent.) around the monasteries, which served as centers. Meanwhile, in Italy, St. BENEDICT (5th cent.) began the work from which sprang the BENEDICTINES and the more moderate monastic rule that, from the time of Pope Gregory I, gradually became universal in the West—even the Celtic foundations assimilating to the Benedictine practice. The role of the monks in the rise of the new civilization of the West is incalculable (see BONIFACE, SAINT, d.754). Their abbeys were a focus of stability, and they, almost alone, preserved learning. In the 10th cent. there began at Cluny a reform that affected all Europe (see CLUNIAC ORDER). Out of another reform arose the CISTERCIANS (12th cent.). The DOMINICANS and FRANCISCANS (early 13th cent.) abandoned enclosure as a principle and with the other friars (see FRIAR) became a feature in the town life of Europe until the Reformation. Their energy gave the universities and schools definitive form, and they dominate the whole history of scholasticism. At this time such semimonastic groups as the BEGHARDS and BEGUINES also began to appear all over Europe. After two centuries of decline, the 16th cent. saw a monastic revival with the founding of the Jesuits (see JESUS, SOCIETY OF). In the 18th cent. anticlericalism among European governments succeeded in suppressing the Jesuits and in causing another general subsidence of monasticism. Since the 19th cent., the number of religious orders has been steadily increasing. The Paulists and the Sisters of Charity of Mother Seton are examples of new American communities.

Monasticism in Modern Times. Roman Catholic religious orders of men fall into seven classes: monks, canons regular (see CANON), friars, clerks regular, ecclesiastical congregations, religious institutes, and secular institutes. Monks are attached to their monastery, subordinate chiefly to their abbot, and are typically Benedictine; the Cistercians are a class of Benedictines, and the TRAPPISTS are a division of the Cistercians. The CARTHUSIANS, of a quasi-hermit type, are the only non-Benedictine monks of the West. Canons regular are priests living in a community usually attached to a church; such have been the Lateran canons, the religious of the Alpine pass of St. Bernard, the Premonstratensians, and the old Austin canons (see AUGUSTINIANS). The rest of the religious orders are highly centralized systems and usually have their work outside their house. The friars are the oldest of this type, chiefly Dominicans, Franciscans, Augustinians, and CARMELITES. Clerks regular are represented principally by the Jesuits, the largest single order in the church today. The communities of priests called loosely ecclesiastical congregations number more than 50; they include the Oratory of St. Philip Neri, the Redemptorists, the Vincentians, and Maryknoll. Religious institutes are separate organizations of unordained persons who have taken vows and who are engaged mostly in teaching, as, notably, the Christian Brothers, founded by St. John Baptist de la Salle. Secular institutes (officially recognized since 1947) are organizations of laymen bound by religious promises; they wear no special garb and, except for special purposes, live separately and hold conventional jobs in the world. Roman Catholic communities of women are generally smaller and more numerous—there are more than 1,000. There are enclosed nuns following the rule of most orders of monks and friars; they are called second orders. Most Roman Catholic sisterhoods are devoted to teaching or charitable work; many of them are tertiaries (see TERTIARY). The term *contemplative* is ordinarily applied to the life of monks and nuns who are enclosed, i.e., who rarely leave the monastery or convent in which they live and work; but many unenclosed religious also lead contemplative lives. See the classic of the comte de Montalembert, *The Monks of the West* (tr., 6 vol., 1896; repr. 1966); Louis Bouyer, *The Meaning of the Monastic Life* (1955); Thomas Merton, *The Silent Life* (1957); Jean Canu, *Religious Orders of Men* (tr., 1960); David Knowles, *The Monastic Order in England* (2d ed. 1963) and *Christian Monasticism* (1969).

Monastir: see BITOLA, Yugoslavia.

monazite (mŏn'əzīt), yellow to reddish-brown natural phosphate of the RARE EARTHS, mainly the CERIUM and LANTHANUM metals, usually with some THORIUM. Yttrium, calcium, iron, and silica are frequently present. Monazite sand is the crude natural material and is usually purified from other minerals before entering commerce. Monazite occurs in North Carolina, South Carolina, Idaho, Colorado, Montana, and Florida in the United States, and in Brazil, India, Australia, and South Africa. It is an important source of cerium, thorium, and other rare-earth metals and compounds.

Monboddo, James Burnett, Lord, 1714–99, English writer, b. Scotland. A pioneer in anthropology, he wrote *Of the Origin and Progress of Language* (6 vol., 1774–92), in which he anticipated Darwin and much of modern evolutionary theory. His *Antient Metaphysics* (6 vol., 1779–99) is a defense of Greek philosophy.

Moncenisio: see CENIS, MONT.

Mönchengladbach (mön'khən-gläd'bäkh), formerly **München-Gladbach** (mün'-), city (1970 pop. 151,090), North Rhine-Westphalia, W West Germany. It is the twin city of adjacent RHEYDT and is a major center of the West German cotton textile industry. Machinery is also manufactured. Mönchengladbach developed around a Benedictine abbey (founded c.972), which was rebuilt several times between the 14th and the 18th cent. and which now serves as the city hall.

Monck, Charles Stanley, 4th **Viscount,** 1819–94, governor general of Canada, b. Ireland. An Irish peer, he was elected (1852) to the British House of Commons as a Liberal and was (1855–58) a lord of the treasury in Lord Palmerston's government. As governor general (1861–67) of British North America (Canada), he worked to prevent a rupture between the United States and Great Britain during the American Civil War and to bring about confederation of the Canadian provinces. Created (1866) a baron in the peerage of the United Kingdom, he was appointed (1867) the first governor general of the Dominion of Canada. He resigned in 1868 and returned to Ireland, where he served (1874–92) as lord lieutenant of Dublin county.

Monck or **Monk, George,** 1st **duke of Albemarle,** 1608–70, English soldier and politician. He took part (1625) in the disastrous expedition against Cádiz and fought against the Spanish in the Netherlands. After service in the BISHOPS' WARS, he was given a command in Ireland and was there when the ENGLISH CIVIL WAR began (1642). He returned to England to fight for Charles I, was captured (1644) at Nantwich, and was not released until 1646. He gained the confidence of Parliament and was commissioned to help subdue the Irish rebellion. In 1650 he accompanied Oliver CROMWELL to Scotland and in 1651 was left to complete the subjugation of the Scots. In 1652 he became a general of the fleet in the first of the DUTCH WARS, and in 1654 he resumed his command in Scotland, which he held until 1660. Monck believed in the supremacy of civil authority over the military, and when the Protectorate of Richard CROMWELL collapsed (1659), he supported the reassembled Rump Parliament (what remained of the Long Parliament after Pride's Purge of 1648) against the army under Gen. John LAMBERT. Having marched (1660) on London and seized control, however, he ordered the Rump to fill its vacant seats and then dissolve itself prior to the election of a "free" Parliament. Monck was an effective diplomat as well as an able soldier. In the next months he applied himself to the delicate task of reconciling the army (largely republican) to growing public sympathy for a restoration of the Stuart monarchy. Following the election of the strongly royalist Convention Parliament, he finally declared openly for the RESTORATION of Charles II, convinced that it was the only alternative to anarchy. Acting on Monck's advice, Charles issued the Delcaration of Breda, and Monck secured an invitation for Charles to return. After the Restoration, honors were heaped upon Monck: he was appointed gentleman of the bedchamber, privy councillor, master of the horse, and commander of all military forces; created duke of Albemarle; and granted estates and a pension. In 1666 he shared with Prince Rupert command of the fleet in the second Dutch War. He was left in charge of London at the time of the great plague (1665) and the great fire (1666). See biographies by Julian Corbett (1889) and Oliver Warner (1936).

Monckton, Robert (mŭngk'tən), 1726–82, British general. After service in Flanders and Germany during the War of the Austrian Succession (1740–48), he was sent (1752) to Nova Scotia, where he suppressed (1753) an insurrection of German settlers at Lunenburg. In 1755 he led a large force that took Fort Beauséjour and other forts from the French, establishing British control of Nova Scotia. He was made lieutenant governor of the colony and carried out the governor's orders in deporting the Acadians (see ACADIA). He was second in command to James WOLFE in the campaign against Quebec (1759). In 1761 he was made governor of New York. He was commander of the land forces in Admiral George Rodney's expedition against Martinique (1761–62). He returned to England in 1763 and was succeeded as governor in 1765.

Monckton Milnes, Richard: see HOUGHTON, RICHARD MONCKTON MILNES, 1ST BARON.

Moncton (mŭngk'tən), city (1971 pop. 47,891), SE N.B., Canada, on the Petitcodiac River. It is an air and rail transportation center. Textiles as well as wood, metal, meat, and petroleum products are manufactured, and wood and meat are processed. It was called The Bend until 1833, when it was renamed in honor of the British general Robert Monckton. Magnetic Hill, an optical illusion, and the Tidal Bore, a high tide occurring twice daily, are features of the city. The Université de Moncton (1963) is there.

Moncton, University of, at Moncton, N.B., Canada; French language; founded 1864 as St. Joseph's Univ. Its name was changed in 1963. It has faculties of arts, science, business administration, education, home economics, and graduate studies as well as schools of nursing and behavioral and social sciences.

Mond, Alfred Moritz, 1st **Baron Melchett** (mŏnd, mĕl'chĭt), 1868–1930, English industrialist and politician; son of Ludwig Mond. He played a leading part in the centralization of the English chemical industry; as managing director of his father's firm, Brunner-Mond, he arranged its merger with three smaller companies to form (1926) the huge Imperial Chemical Industries. He entered (1906) Parliament as a Liberal and served as first commissioner of works (1916–21) and minister of health (1921–22). He was an early advocate of health insurance and of profit sharing within a capitalist framework. In 1928 he organized the Mond-Turner talks, an attempt to achieve some collaboration between labor and the employers after the bitterness of the general strike of 1926. He was created a peer in 1928. See biography by Hector Bolitho (1933).

Mond, Ludwig, 1839–1909, chemist; father of Alfred Moritz Mond. He was born in Germany and became a naturalized British subject. Mond experimented with alkalies and also developed a producer gas known by his name. He was cofounder and director of Brunner-Mond (1872), which became the world's largest producer of alkalies. Another outstanding discovery of his was nickel carbonyl, a gas formed from carbon monoxide and metallic nickel. Mond developed a valuable method known as the **Mond process** for extracting nickel from its ores by use of this carbonyl. In the process, carbon monoxide passing over the crushed and smelted ore containing nickel produces the volatile nickel carbonyl; this is decomposed to yield metallic nickel.

Monday: see WEEK.

Mond process: see under MOND, LUDWIG.

Mondrian, Piet (pēt môn'drēän), 1872–1944, Dutch painter. He studied at the academy in Amsterdam and passed through an early naturalistic phase. In 1910 he went to Paris, where the influence of cubism stimulated the development of his geometric, nonobjective style, which he called neoplasticism. He and Theo van Doesburg—leaders of the so-called STIJL group of artists—founded (1917) a magazine *De Stijl,* in which Mondrian published articles until 1925. In 1920 he published a book on his theory that appeared as *Le Neo-Plasticisme* in French and as *Neue Gestaltung* in German. His art and theory influenced the BAUHAUS movement and the development of the international style in architecture. In 1940 he settled in New York City. Typical of his art are compositions employing only vertical and horizontal lines at 90° angles and using only the primary colors and sometimes grays or black against a white background. Sensuality, three-dimensionality, and representation are utterly eliminated from his works, as is the curved line. Within these restrictions, his paintings are executed with consummate perfection of design and craftsmanship. Much of Mondrian's work is in American and European private collections. He is represented in the Museum of Modern Art, New York City, and in the Art Institute of Chicago. See his essays (1945); studies by Michel Seuphor (tr. 1957), Frank Elgar (tr. 1968), and H. L. C. Jaffé (1970).

Mondsee: see SALZKAMMERGUT, Austria.

Monel metal (mōnĕl'), trademark for a silver-white alloy of nickel and copper comprising about 66% nickel, 30% copper, and a small percentage of other metals, notably iron. It is produced directly by smelting a Bessemerized (see BESSEMER PROCESS) ore containing nickel, copper, iron, and sulfur. The alloy is strong, resists corrosion well, and holds a bright finish. It is used for making scientific instruments, chemical processing equipment, machinery parts, corrosion-resistant containers, condenser tubes for steamships and much other marine equipment, and domestic appliances, and for various other purposes.

Monemvasía, Greece: see MALVASIA.

Monera, in some systems of biological CLASSIFICATION, a kingdom comprising the BACTERIA and the blue-green algae. This group of organisms may also be classified with other simple organisms in the kingdom PROTISTA, or as the division SCHIZOPHYTA of the plant kingdom. Moneran cells lack a well-defined nucleus bound by a membrane, such as is found in all other cells.

Monessen (mənĕs'ən), city (1970 pop. 15,216), Westmoreland co., SW Pa., in a hilly region, on the Monongahela River; founded 1898, inc. 1921. It has a steel mill.

Monet, Claude (klōd mônā'), 1840–1926, French landscape painter, b. Paris. Monet was a founder of IMPRESSIONISM. He adhered to its principles throughout his long career and is considered the most consistently representative painter of the school as well as one of the foremost painters of landscape in the history of art. As a youth in Le Havre, Monet was encouraged by the marine painter BOUDIN to paint in the open air, a practice he never forsook. After two years (1860–62) with the army in Algeria, he went to Paris, over parental objections, to study painting. There he lived in grim poverty, and his young wife's death was partially caused by malnutrition. In Paris, Monet formed lasting friendships with the artists who would become the major impressionists, including Pissarro, Cézanne, Renoir, Sisley, and Bazille. He and several of his friends painted for a time out-of-doors in the Barbizon district. Typical of his work of this period is *Terrace at Le Havre,* a sunny, exhilarating seaside scene (1866; Metropolitan Mus.) that retains considerable clarity of form compared to later works. Monet soon began to concern himself with his lifelong objective: portraying the variations of light and atmosphere brought on by changes of hour and season. Rather than copy in the Louvre, Monet learned from his friends, from the landscape itself, and from the works of his older contemporaries Manet, Corot, and Courbet. He was restless by temperament, living in several countryside villages, moving in and out of Paris, and frequently traveling and painting around France and abroad. Monet deduced much of his knowledge of light from the scientific laws of optics, complementing the information he received from his own nearly infallible eye. In hundreds of paintings he caught the flickering, fleeting effects of light by breaking it down into its color components as a prism does. Eliminating black and grey from his palette, Monet rejected entirely the academic approach to landscape. In his later works he allowed his vision of light to dissolve the real structures of his subjects so that he might describe freely and in a luminous, abstract way what he felt about them. To do this he chose simple matter, making several series of studies of the same object at different times of day or year: haystacks, morning views of the Seine, the Gare Saint-Lazare (1876–78), poplars (begun 1890), the Thames, the celebrated group of Rouen Cathedral (1892–94), and the last great lyrical series of water lilies (1899, and 1904–25), painted in his own garden at Giverny (one version, a vast triptych c.1920; Mus. of Modern Art, New York City). In 1874, Sisley, Morisot, and Monet organized the first impressionist group show, which was ferociously maligned by the critics, who coined the term *impressionism* after Monet's *Impression: Sunrise, 1872* (Mus. Marmottan, Paris). The show failed financially and for some years Monet continued to suffer desperate poverty. However, by 1883 he had prospered, and he retired from Paris to Giverny. In the last decade of his life Monet, nearly blind, painted a group of large water lily murals (*Nymphéas*) for the Musée de l'Orangerie in Paris. His work is well represented in the Louvre, the Marmottan (Paris), the National Gallery (London), the Metropolitan Museum of Art, and the Art Institute of Chicago, as well as in many famous private collections. See biographies by W. C. Seitz (1960) and C. M. Mount (1967); studies by C. P. Weekes (1960) and Raymond Cogniat (1966).

Moneta, Ernesto Teodoro (ārnĕs'tō tāōthô'rō mōnĕ'-tä), 1833–1918, Italian editor and pacifist; winner of the 1907 Nobel Peace Prize. He joined the movement for Italian unification, serving (1859–66) with Garibaldi. From 1867 he devoted himself to the cause of peace, editing the daily *Secolo.* He was president (1906) of the International Peace Congress in Milan.

monetary agreement, attempt by two (bilateral) or more (multilateral) nations to regulate and coordinate their financial relations by treaty. The objectives are usually to promote trade by facilitating payment of international debts and to maintain in each nation a stable exchange rate by making available credits to meet temporary difficulties with BALANCE OF PAYMENTS. After World War II there was a significant movement towards multilateral monetary agreements, of which the most important were the INTERNATIONAL MONETARY FUND and the European Payments Union (1950). Customs unions such as the European Common Market and the European Free Trade Association often require a large degree of monetary cooperation. See W. M. Scammell, *International Monetary Policy* (2d ed. 1961).

money, term that actually refers to two concepts, the abstract unit of account in terms of which the value of goods, services, and obligations can be measured, and anything that is generally acceptable as a means of payment. Frequently the standard of value also serves as a medium of exchange, but that is not always the case. While the Code of Hammurabi contains evidence that a single commodity—silver—was used for both purposes, many ancient communities took cattle as their standard of value but used more manageable objects as means of payment. Thus the Homeric talent of gold was equivalent to an ox in value; both in Latin and in Anglo-Saxon the word for cattle also denotes money. Exchange involving the use of money is a great improvement over barter, since it permits elaborate specialization and provides generalized purchasing power that the participants to the exchange may use in the future. The growth of monetary institutions has largely paralleled that of trade and industry; while some societies, such as the Inca, were able to benefit from extensive division of labor without making significant use of a monetary medium, such a situation was possible only through rigid reliance on custom and status and a system of extreme regimentation. Today almost all economic activity is concerned with the making and spending of money incomes. A great variety of objects have served as money, e.g., stones, shells, ivory, wampum beads, tobacco, furs, dried fish, and cigarettes. From the earliest times precious metals have had particularly wide monetary use, owing to convenience of handling, durability, divisibility, and the high intrinsic value commonly attached to them. Whether an article is to be regarded as money does not, however, depend on its value as a commodity, except where intrinsic worth is necessary to make it generally acceptable in exchange; the relation between the face value of an object used as money and its commodity value has, in fact, tended to become increasingly remote. State coinage, which is said to have originated in Lydia during the 7th cent. B.C., often enabled governments to issue coins with nominal values in excess of their value as metals—i.e., they were not "full-bodied." Paper currency first appeared about 300 years ago; it was usually backed by some "standard" commodity of intrinsic value into which it could be freely converted on demand, but even during the early development of currency, issuance of inconvertible paper money, also called FIAT MONEY, was not infrequent (see, for example, LAW, JOHN). The monetary system of the United States was based on BIMETALLISM during most of the 19th cent. A full gold standard was in effect from 1900 to 1933, providing for free coinage of gold and full convertibility of currency into gold coin; the volume of money in circulation was closely related to the gold supply. The passage of the Gold Reserve Act of 1934, which put the country on a modified gold standard, presaged the end of the gold-based monetary system in domestic exchange. With the dollar legally defined as 15$\frac{5}{21}$ grains of gold $\frac{9}{10}$ fine (i.e., $35 for an ounce of gold), gold still served as the standard of value. Federal Reserve notes, moreover, had to have a gold reserve backing of at least 25%. In spite of those requirements, however, there were indications that, while gold was still thought to be important for maintenance of confidence in the dollar, its connection with the actual use of money was at best vague. The 1934 act stipulated that gold could not be used as a medium of domestic exchange and made it illegal for private persons or firms to own gold bullion; it also restricted private ownership to those who must use gold for industrial or export purposes (a stipulation rescinded as of Dec. 31, 1974). In the years since the passage of the Gold Reserve Act a number of other measures have been taken to emphasize the dollar's dependence on gold; by now practically all U.S. currency, paper or coin, is essentially fiat money with neither gold backing nor gold convertibility. For all practical purposes, the dollar was completely removed from gold in 1970 when the requirement that the Treasury maintain a 25% gold backing for all Federal Reserve notes was dropped. International payments are still settled by central bank gold movements, but DEVALUATION of the dollar and the establishment of SPECIAL DRAWING RIGHTS have created changes in even that system. About seven eighths of the currency circulating in the United States consists of Federal Reserve notes, which are issued in denominations ranging from $1 to $10,000 by the Federal Reserve System, are guaranteed by the U.S. government, and are secured by government securities and eligible commercial paper. Approximately one eighth of the currency supply is made up of the various types of COIN, none of which has a commodity value equal to its face value. Finally, a very small part of the circulating currency is composed of bills that are no longer issued. Such bills include silver certificates, which were redeemable in silver until 1967; U.S. notes, remnants of the greenbacks used to finance the Civil War; and Federal Reserve bank notes and national bank notes. All are in the process of being removed from circulation. Under the Legal Tender Act of 1933, all American coin and paper money in circulation is now legal tender, i.e., under the law it must be accepted at face value by creditors in payment of any debt, public or private. Today currency and coin are less widely used as a means of payment than checks, which probably account for about 90% of payments made in the United States; commercial bank demand deposits (checking accounts) are, therefore, generally considered part of the money supply (see BANKING; on the regulation of the supply, availability, and cost of money, see FEDERAL RESERVE SYSTEM and INTEREST). Certain assets, sometimes called near-monies, come close to possessing the characteristics of money in that they can usually be readily converted into cash without loss; they include, for example, time deposits and very short-term obligations of the Federal government. The importance of money has been variously interpreted. While the advocates of MERCANTILISM tended to identify money with wealth, the classical economists, e.g., John Stuart MILL, usually considered money as a veil obscuring real economic phenomena. Since the mid-20th cent., a group known as the monetarists has given increasing attention to the role of money in determining national income and economic fluctuations. Monetarist theory, now accepted by only a small minority of American economists, maintains that control over the money supply alone will lead to control over virtually all aspects of macroeconomic activity. For a complete statement of monetarist theory see M. Friedman and A. Schwartz, *A Monetary History of the United States* (1963). See J. M. Keynes, *General Theory of Employment, Interest, and Money* (1936, repr. 1964); J. A. Todd, *The Mechanism of Exchange* (5th ed. 1939, repr. 1946); Karl Olivecrona, *The Problem of the Monetary Unit* (1957); E. V. Morgan, *A History of Money* (1965); Antoine Ascain, *History of Money and Finance* (tr. 1968); S. E. Rolfe and James Burtle, *The Great Wheel* (1974).

Monfalcone (mōnfälkô'nā), city (1971 pop. 29,687), in Friuli-Venezia Giulia, extreme NE Italy, near the Adriatic Sea. Manufactures of this modern industrial center include ships, airplanes, textiles, and chemicals.

Monferrato: see MONTFERRAT, Italy.

Monge, Gaspard, comte de Péluse (gäspär' mōNzh kôNt də pälüz'), 1746–1818, French mathematician, physicist, and public official. He was distinguished for his geometrical research, which laid the foundations of modern descriptive geometry, a field essential to mechanical drawing and architectural drawing. He also made important contributions to differential geometry and inspired his pupils, who included J. B. Biot, J. V. Poncelet, and C. Dupin, to new advances in several branches of geometry. He was professor of mathematics (1768) and of physics (1771) at Mézières. One of the founders of the École polytechnique, he served there as professor of descriptive geometry. From 1792 to 1793 he was minister of marine. He was a close and loyal friend of Napoleon and was stripped of all his honors and positions following the restoration of the monarchy in 1815. He wrote *Feuilles d'analyse appliquée à la géometrie* (1795) and *Géometrie descriptive* (1799).

Monghyr (mŭng'gēr), city (1971 pop. 102,462), Bihar state, NE India, on the Ganges River. It is a district administrative center. The city has one of India's largest railroad workshops and a firearms industry that dates back to the 18th cent. Monghyr is famous for its goldsmiths and silversmiths. Cigarettes, chemicals, and steel trunks are also manufactured, and sugar is refined. According to tradition the city was founded during the Gupta dynasty (c.320–545 B.C.). The Muslim leader Mir Kasim Ali used Monghyr as a base during his war against the British in 1764.

Mongkut (mông'ko͞ot) or **Rama IV,** 1804–68, king of Siam, now Thailand (1851–68). A devout Buddhist monk, he was displaced in succession to the throne by his brother, who ascended as Rama III. Mongkut became king as Rama IV in 1851, and then used his knowledge, especially of the West, accumulated during his long years of study, to further his country's interests. He established diplomatic relations with several European countries and the United States, opened Siam to Western trade, and undertook extensive internal reform in all fields. Because of these measures, Siam was the only country in Southeast Asia not to fall under Western control in the 19th cent. He was succeeded by his son CHULALONGKORN. Mongkut was made famous throughout the Western world by Margaret Landon's book *Anna and the King of Siam* (1944), which was based on the reminiscences of Anna Leonowens, a British governess at the court of Siam.

Mongolia (mŏng-gō'lēə, mŏn-), Asian region (c.906,000 sq mi/2,346,540 sq km), bordered roughly by Sinkiang Uigur Autonomous Region, China, on the west; the Manchurian provinces of China on the east; Siberia on the north; and the Great Wall of China on the south. It now comprises the MONGOLIAN PEOPLE'S REPUBLIC (Outer Mongolia) and the INNER MONGOLIAN AUTONOMOUS REGION of China. Mongolia is chiefly a region of desert and of steppe plateau from c.3,000 to 5,000 ft (910–1,520 m) high. The climate is cold and dry and the population sparse. The Gobi desert, which is entirely wasteland, is in the central section. To the west are the Altai mts., which rise to 15,266 ft (4,653 m). Rivers include a section of the Huang Ho (Yellow River) in the south and the Selenga, Orkhon, and Kerulen in the north. Rainfall averages less than 15 in. (38.1 cm) a year, but irrigation has made some cultivation possible; wheat and oats are the chief crops. Mongolia has traditionally been a land of pastoral nomadism; livestock raising and the processing of animal products are the main industries. Wool, hides, meat, cloth, and leather goods are exported. Coal, iron ore, gold, and oil are important mineral resources. Mongolia is crossed north to south by a railroad linking Peking with the USSR. Camels and horses are the chief means of transportation, although the use of jeeps and trucks is increasing. Trade traditionally has been greater with Russia than with China, but this has been changing in recent years. Great hordes of horsemen have repeatedly swept down from Mongolia into N China, establishing vast, though generally short-lived, empires. In the 1st cent. A.D., Mongolia was inhabited by various Turkic tribes who dwelt mainly along the upper course of the Orkhon River. It was also the home of the Hsiung-nu (the Huns) who ravaged (1st–5th cent.) N China. The Uigur Turks founded their first empire (744–856) with its capital near Karakorum in W Mongolia. The Khitan, who founded the Liao dynasty (947–1125) in N China, were from Mongolia. Many smaller territorial states followed until (c.1205) Jenghiz Khan conquered all Mongolia, united its tribes, and from his capital at Karakorum led the Mongols in creating one of the greatest empires of all time. His successors established the Golden Horde in SE Russia and founded the Hulagid dynasty of Persia and the Yüan dynasty (1260–1368) of China. After the decline of the Mongol empire, Mongolia intruded less in world affairs. China, which earlier had gained control of Inner Mongolia, subjugated Outer Mongolia in the late 17th cent., but in the succeeding years struggled with Russia for control. Outer Mongolia finally broke away in 1921 to form the Mongolian People's Republic. Inner Mongolia remained under Chinese control, although the Japanese conquered Jehol (1933), which they included in Manchukuo, and Chahar and Suiyuan (1937), which they formed into Menchiang (Mongol Border Land). These areas were returned to China after World War II. In 1949 the Chinese Communists joined most of Inner Mongolia to N Jehol prov. and W Heilungkiang prov. to form the Inner Mongolian Autonomous Region. In 1945 Tannu Tuva, long recognized as part of Mongolia, was incorporated within the USSR.

Mongolian languages, group of languages forming a subdivision of the ALTAIC subfamily of the Ural-Altaic family of languages (see URALIC AND ALTAIC LANGUAGES). The Mongolian languages are spoken by about 2 million people, mainly in the Mongolian People's Republic, in China's Inner Mongolia, and in the Soviet Union in the region of Lake Baykal. There are also some speakers of Mongolian tongues in the Sinkiang Uigur Autonomous Region and in Manchuria, both in China. The Mongolian languages fall into two principal divisions: Western Mongolian, to which Kalmuck belongs, and Eastern Mongolian, which consists of Buryat, Khalkha, and others. Khalkha, or Mongol proper, is the most important Mongolian language. The official tongue of the Mongolian People's Republic, it is native to more than one million people. Like the other Uralic and Altaic languages, the Mongolian tongues exhibit vowel harmony and are agglutinative. They lack grammatical gender and use postpositions instead of prepositions. For many centuries the Mongols had their own system of writing, which was ultimately derived from the Aramaic script, a Semitic alphabet. After 1941 the traditional Mongol script yielded to a modified Cyrillic alphabet in the Mongolian People's Republic. In Inner Mongolia, owing to the policy of the People's Republic of China, the traditional Mongol script is being replaced by a writing based on the Roman alphabet. See N. N. Poppe, *Introduction to Mongolian Comparative Studies* (1955) and *Mongolian Language Handbook* (1970); J. E. Bosson, *Modern Mongolian* (1964).

Mongolian People's Republic, country (1970 est. pop. 1,290,000), 604,247 sq mi (1,565,000 sq km), N central Asia. It is unofficially called Outer Mongolia, or often simply Mongolia. The capital is ULAN BATOR (formerly Urga). Bordered on the west, south, and east by China, and on the north by the USSR, it comprises more than half the region historically known as MONGOLIA. A high country, its average elevation exceeds 5,100 ft (1,554 m); the central, northern, western, and southwestern areas are covered with hills, high plateaus, and mountain ranges, reaching 15,266 ft (4,653 m) at Tavan Bogd Uul (Tabun Bogdo) in the Altai mts. Much of the Gobi desert lies to the south and east; at no point is the elevation less than c.1,800 (550 m). Numerous beautiful

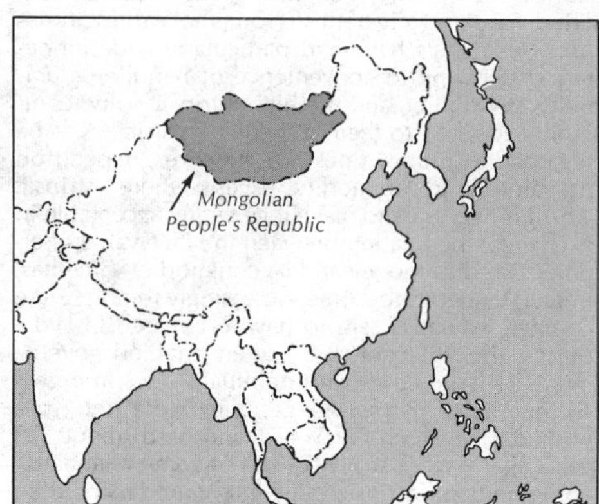

lakes fill the depressions between the mountains; the largest, Uvs Nuur, or Ubsu Nur (c.1,300 sq mi/3,370 sq km) is saltwater. The main rivers are in the north and include the Selenga (Selenge Mörön), with its long tributary the Orkhon (Orhon), which flows into Lake Baykal in the USSR; and the Kerulen. Navigability is limited—the rivers are swift and rough; they freeze in the winter, and many dry up during droughts. The country's climate is dry continental, with little rain or snow and great extremes in temperature. Winters are severe, with low temperatures and high winds that blow away the light snow cover, causing the ground to freeze to unusual depths; summers can be very hot. The paucity of snow permits year-round grazing, and nomadic herding has been the major occupation for centuries. Animal husbandry, now generally organized under state cooperatives, is still the mainstay of the Mongolian economy. Sheep and goats constitute most of the livestock, followed by cattle and horses; yaks are raised in the higher altitudes, and camels are extremely important in the desert and semidesert areas. Agriculture is limited. Wheat is the chief crop, followed by oats. Barley, corn, millet, rye, legumes, and potatoes are also grown. Hunting is a source of revenue; the country abounds in wildlife, and sable, ermine, fox, lynx, woodchuck, marmot, snow leopard, squirrel, and wolf are all trapped for their furs. Mongolia has valuable timberlands, especially in the northern mountainous area; logs are shipped down the Selenga, Orkhon, and Kerulen rivers. Mineral resources are abundant. The extensive coal deposits have been exploited since 1913. Gold, fluorspar, wolframite, iron ore, tungsten, molybdenum, lead, silver, and salt are also mined, and oil was pumped from fields in the E Gobi region from 1951 to 1971. Industry, developed with Soviet aid, is centered chiefly in Ulan Bator. It is based largely on the country's livestock resources, with dairy products, packed meats, leather and leather goods, and woolen textiles and related items (clothing, blankets, carpets) the chief manufactures. The building-material and lumber industries are also important, and cement, glassware, woodwork, furniture, paper, and matches are manufactured. Choybalsan and the new city of Darhan near the Soviet border are budding industrial centers. Mongolia's main exports are livestock, wool, hides, meat, butter, and furs; more than 90% of the trade is with the USSR and countries of eastern Europe. The country has c.1,000 mi (1,610 km) of railroads, consisting of one line running north and south from the Soviet border through Ulan Bator (that section opened in 1950) to the Chinese frontier (opened 1955), with a few spur lines to mining or industrial points. There are c.5,000 mi (8,000 km) of paved roads (the first was built in 1940) and c.50,000 mi (80,500 km) of unimproved dirt roads. The number of motor vehicles (especially Soviet-made trucks and jeeps) is greatly increasing, but beasts of burden are still used, notably in the south, where camel caravans are common. The population is predominantly Khalkha Mongol. Minorities include Oirat Mongols, Kazakhs, Tuvinians, Chinese, and Russians. Khalkha Mongolian, the official language, was until 1946 written in the old Uigur Turkic script; it now uses the Cyrillic alphabet. The dominant religion was long Lamaist Buddhism, but the government undermined its influence, and religion is now openly practiced by very few, mostly the old. For the early history of Mongolia, see MONGOLS. The area was under Chinese control from 1691 until the collapse of the Manchu dynasty in China in 1911, when a group of Mongol princes ousted the Manchu governor and proclaimed an autonomous Mongolia with Jebtsun Damba Khutukhtu (the Living Buddha of Urga) as ruler. The new state was reoccupied by the Chinese in 1919. The Chinese were driven out by White Russian forces under Baron von Ungern-Sternberg in early 1921, and the Whites in turn were ousted by Red Army troops and Mongolian units under the Mongolian Communist leaders Sukhe-Bator and Khorloin Choibalsan. Mongolia was proclaimed an independent state in July, 1921, and remained a monarchy until the Living Buddha died in 1924. The establishment (Nov., 1924) of the Communist-led Mongolian People's Republic was followed by a struggle to divest the old privileged classes of their capital (largely in the form of land and livestock) and persecution of the Lama priests; this in turn led to the Lama Rebellion of 1932, when priests led thousands of people, with some 7 million head of livestock, across the border to Inner Mongolia. In 1936 the USSR signed a mutual aid pact with the republic, thus formalizing the existing close relations between the two countries. A new constitution, adopted in 1940, consolidated the power of the Communist regime. During World War II the Mongolian army joined the USSR in Manchuria in the last, brief stage of the war against Japan. In 1945 a plebiscite was held under a Sino-Soviet agreement, and the republic overwhelmingly voted for continued independence. Khorloin Choibalsan, the prime minister from 1938 until his death in 1952, was succeeded by Yumzhaggiin Tsedenbal. A Soviet-sponsored application for Outer Mongolia's admission to the United Nations was rejected in 1947, but approved in 1961. The border between Mongolia and Communist China was fixed by treaty in Dec., 1962. In the ideological dispute between the Soviet Union and Communist China, Mongolia has maintained its traditional alliance with the Soviet Union. A 20-year treaty of friendship and cooperation was signed with the USSR in 1966. The country's major institute of higher learning is the Mongolian State Univ., at Ulan Bator. See Owen Lattimore, *Nomads and Commissars: Mongolia Revisited* (1962); G. G. Murphy, *Soviet Mongolia* (1966); R. A. Rupen, *The Mongolian People's Republic* (1966); C. R. Bawden, *The Modern History of Mongolia* (1968); A. J. Sanders, *The People's Republic of Mongolia* (1968); T. N. Dupuy et al., *Area Handbook for Mongolia* (1970); V. P. Petrov, *Mongolia* (1970); A. M. Pozdneev, *Mongolia and the Mongols* (Vol. I tr. 1971).

mongolism: see MENTAL RETARDATION.

Mongoloid: see RACE.

Mongols (mŏng'gəlz, -gōlz), Asiatic people, numbering between 2.5 and 3 million and distributed mainly in the Mongolian People's Republic (formerly Outer Mongolia), the Inner Mongolian Autonomous Region of the People's Republic of China, the Buryat Autonomous Soviet Socialist Republic, and the Kalmyk Autonomous Soviet Socialist Republic of the Soviet Union. Mongolian traits include short limbs, skin color ranging from yellow to dark brown, dark hair, and deep-set eyes (so-called slanted eyes). Traditionally the Mongols were a predominantly pastoral people, following their herds of horses, cattle, camels, and sheep on a seasonal round of pasturage, and, when encamped, living in felt-covered yurts. Shamanism was the traditional religion of the Mongols, but Buddhism was introduced in the 16th cent.; competition between the two produced Lamaism, a combination of both. The Mongols have a written language; the earliest extant work written in Mongolian dates from 1240. The origin of the Mongols is obscure, but it is believed that many of the so-called Huns, who invaded Europe, as well as the Khitan, who founded a dynasty (916–1125) in N China, may have been Mongols. However, it was not until the early 13th cent. and the creation of the Mongol empire by JENGHIZ KHAN that the numerous Mongol tribes, hitherto loosely confederated and constantly feuding, emerged in world history as a powerful and unified nation. The Yasa (Jasagh), or imperial code, was promulgated. It laid down the organizational lines of the Mongol nation, the administration of the army, and criminal, commercial, and civil codes of law. As administrators the Mongols employed many UIGURS, whose script they adopted. From their capital at KARAKORUM the Mongol hordes swept W into Europe and E into China, and by c.1260 the sons of Jenghiz Khan ruled a far-flung Eurasian empire that was divided into four khanates. They were the Great Khanate, which comprised all of China and most of E Asia (including Korea) and which under KUBLAI KHAN came to be known as the Yüan dynasty; the Jagatai khanate in TURKISTAN; the Kipchack khanate, or the Empire of the GOLDEN HORDE, founded by BATU KHAN in Russia; and a khanate in Persia. Actually, the Mongol hordes (particularly those who conquered Russia and penetrated as far as Hungary and Germany) included large elements of Turkic peoples; they came to be known collectively as TATARS. TAMERLANE, who conquered most of the Jagatai khanate in the 14th cent. and founded a new empire, claimed descent from Jenghiz Khan, as did BABUR, who in the 16th cent. founded the MOGUL (i.e., Mongol) empire in India. The Mongols were completely expelled from China by 1382 and soon thereafter lapsed into relative obscurity. See H. H. Vreeland, *Mongol Community and Kinship Structure* (2d ed. 1957); Walter Heissig, *A Lost Civilization* (tr. 1966); E. D. Philips, *The Mongols* (1969).

mongoose, name for a large number of small, carnivorous, terrestrial mammals of the CIVET family. They are found in S Asia and in Africa, with one species extending into S Spain. Mongooses are fierce, active hunters, feeding on a variety of ground-living animals, as well as eggs, and in some species, fruits. They live in a variety of habitats and occupy rock crevices or holes, or dig burrows. Unlike civets, they lack scent glands. Typical mongooses, species of the genus *Herpestes,* are weasel-like in appearance, with long, slender bodies, pointed faces, and bushy tails. Their hair is coarse and shaggy. They range in length from 1½ to 3½ ft (45–106 cm) including the tail, which is about as long as the head and body. The Indian gray mongoose, *H. edwardsi,* is known for its ability to kill snakes, including cobras. A medium-sized mongoose, it lives in arid rocky or brushy areas, or cultivated pastures. When attacking a snake, the mongoose provokes it to strike repeatedly, avoiding it by agile dodging; when the snake is exhausted the mongoose seizes its head in its jaws and crushes the skull. Skill in evading the snake is learned, and young mongooses often die of snakebite. However, ingested snake venom is harmless to the mongoose, which eats the snake's head and venom glands. The Indian mongoose is easily tamed and is often kept as a pet and a destroyer of household vermin. Imported into the West Indies to kill rats, it destroyed most of the small, ground-living native fauna. Because of their destructiveness, it is illegal to import mongooses into the United States, even for zoos. The Egyptian gray mongoose, or ichneumon, *H. ichneumon,* is a large species common in most of Africa and in S Spain. It lives in damp, forested regions and preys on small terrestrial and freshwater animals. The ancient Egyptians domesticated this mongoose, which they considered sacred. The marsh mongoose, *Atilax paludinosus,* lives near bodies of water in Africa and dives for food. The meerkat (*Suricata suricatta*), or suricate, is a social mongoose of S African grasslands; meerkats live in large communal burrows and prey chiefly on insects and other small invertebrates. Mongooses are classified in approximately 12 genera of the phylum CHORDATA, subphylum Vertebrata, class Mammalia, order Carnivora, family Viverridae.

Monhegan (mŏnhē'gĭn), island, 2.5 sq mi (6.4 sq km), c.10 mi (16 km) off the coast of S Maine, SE of Boothbay Harbor. It is a summer resort favored by artists for its scenery. In the War of 1812 the U.S.S. *Enterprise* defeated the H.M.S. *Boxer* southeast of the island.

moniliasis: see FUNGUS INFECTION; THRUSH.

monism (mō'nĭzəm) [Gr.,=belief in one], in metaphysics, term introduced in the 18th cent. by Christian von Wolff for any theory that explains all phenomena by one unifying principle or as manifestations of a single substance. Monistic theorists differ considerably in their choice of a basis of unification. It may be material, as with Ernst Haeckel, who took the substance, or energy, as the only reality. It may be spiritual, as with G. W. Hegel, to whom mind, or spirit, is the reality by which all is to be explained. Or, as in Spinoza, it may be a substance, or Deity, of which body and mind are attributes that are held in equipoise. The opposites of monism are dualism and pluralism.

monitor, any of various dragonlike, mostly tropical lizards. A monitor lizard has a heavy body, long head and neck, long tail that comes to a whiplike end, and strong legs with sharp claws. Its slender, forked tongue is protrusible. Monitors range in size from the 8-in. (20-cm) short-tailed species of W Australia to the 10-ft, 300-lb (3-m, 136-kg) Komodo dragon, the giant among living lizards, that lives only on the small Indonesian island of Komodo. Some monitor species spend their lives in trees, and others inhabit lakes and rivers; they can be found on the oceanic islands and continents of the Eastern Hemisphere in all types of warm habitats, from tropical forest to desert. They feed on various kinds of animal matter, including eggs, rats, frogs, and decaying meat. The larger species will attack small deer and pigs. They often tear the prey with claws and teeth, but generally swallow it whole or in large chunks. Monitors lay from 7 to 35 leathery eggs, usually in holes in the ground or in trees. They are classified in the phylum CHORDATA, subphylum Vertebrata, class Reptilia, order Squamata, family Varanidae, genus *Varanus.*

monitor, type of turreted warship (no longer used) carrying heavy guns, having little draft, and lying low in the water. Monitors were so called from the first of the class, the *Monitor,* built for the Union navy in the U.S. Civil War by John ERICSSON. Launched in Jan., 1862, the *Monitor* was 179 ft (55 m) long, of 41.5-ft (13-m) beam, and weighed 1,200 tons. A revolving turret, protected by 8 in. (20.3 cm) of iron armor and containing two 11-in. (27.9-cm) smooth-bore guns, was her main feature. Her sides were covered by iron plates from 3 to 5 in. (7.6–12.7 cm) thick, with about 27 in. (69 cm) of wood backing, and the deck, only 18 in. (46 cm) above water, was shielded with 1-in. (2.54-cm) armor. She was moved by steam power, with a screw propeller. Monitors were used extensively in the Civil War, but the type had limitations and was eventually abandoned. However, they were used by the British navy in World War I.

Monitor and Merrimack, two American warships that fought the first engagement between ironclad ships. When, at the beginning of the Civil War, the Union forces abandoned the Norfolk Navy Yard at Portsmouth, Va., they scuttled the powerful stream frigate *Merrimack.* She was subsequently raised by the Confederates, converted into an ironclad, and renamed the *Virginia.* On March 8, 1862, the *Virginia,* commanded by Capt. Franklin BUCHANAN, sallied forth into Hampton Roads against the wooden ships of the Union blockading squadron. She rammed and sank the *Cumberland,* destroyed the *Congress* after running her aground, and scattered the remaining ships, all the while sustaining practically no damage to herself. But on the next day the *Virginia,* now under command of Lt. Catesby Jones, was challenged by the strange-looking Union ironclad *Monitor,* built by John ERICSSON and commanded by Lt. John L. WORDEN. The *Monitor* had just reached Hampton Roads after a precarious voyage from New York City. The ships engaged in a four-hour close-range duel, which resulted in a draw. In April the *Virginia,* under Capt. Josiah Tattnall, again challenged the *Monitor,* but the Union ship declined combat. When General McClellan's advance in the Peninsular campaign forced the Confederates to abandon Norfolk, Tattnall, unable to lighten the *Virginia* sufficiently for passage up the James River, destroyed her (May, 1862). The *Monitor* foundered and sank in heavy seas off Cape Hatteras in Dec., 1862. The combat between the two ships marked a revolution in naval warfare. See R. M. McCordock, *The Yankee Cheese Box* (1938); H. A. Trexler, *The Confederate Ironclad "Virginia"* (1938); W. C. and Ruth White, *Tin Can on a Shingle* (1957); R. W. Daly, *How the Merrimac Won* (1957).

monitorial system, method of elementary education devised by British educators Joseph LANCASTER and Andrew BELL during the 19th cent. to furnish schooling to the underprivileged even under conditions of severely limited facilities. It was sometimes called the mutual or Lancasterian system. All students met in one room, with about 10 students and one monitor to each bench. The monitors, older and better students, were instructed directly by the teacher and in turn instructed the other pupils. It was often assumed that the monitors would eventually become teachers. This system, which might involve several levels of monitors, used elaborate programs of reward for good deportment and scholarship, supplemented by punishment based on "shame rather than pain." The success of the monitorial system stimulated interest in education for the poor. See Joseph Lancaster, *The Lancasterian System of Education* (1821) and *The Practical Parts of Lancaster's Improvements and Bell's Experiments* (ed. by David Solmon, 1932).

Moniz, Egas (ĕ'gəsh mô'nĕsh), 1874–1955, Portuguese neurologist and diplomat. From 1903 he served in the Cortes several times and was Portuguese minister (1917) in Madrid and secretary for foreign affairs (1918–19). He was professor of neurology at the Univ. of Lisbon from 1911 until 1944. He shared the 1949 Nobel Prize in Physiology and Medicine with W. R. Hess for his work on methods for diagnosing diseases of the brain and for the development of an operation known as prefrontal lobotomy or prefrontal leucotomy, a severing of the nerve fibers connecting the frontal lobes with the lower brain centers. That operation has been used to alleviate uncontrollable pain and to calm victims of severe mental disorders. Moniz was author and coauthor of more than 300 medical works.

Monk, George: see MONCK, GEORGE, 1ST DUKE OF ALBEMARLE.

Monk, Theolonius (Theolonius Sphere Monk), 1920–, American jazz pianist, composer, and arranger, b. Rocky Mount, N.C. Monk is considered one of the most important, and eccentric, figures in modern jazz. His style is astringent, marked by dissonance, alternating rhythms, and melodic interpretations. There is a subtle mixture of cynicism, humor, and warmth in his interpretations. Among the many jazz pieces Monk has composed, the best known is probably "'Round Midnight." Others include "Monk's Mood," "Straight No Chaser," and "Crepuscule with Nellie."

monk: see MONASTICISM.

monkey, any of a large and varied group of mammals of the PRIMATE order. The term *monkey* includes all primates that do not belong to the categories man, ape, or prosimian; however, monkeys do have certain common features. All are excellent climbers, and most are primarily arboreal in their way of life. Nearly all live in tropical or subtropical climates. Unlike most of the prosimians, or lower primates, they are almost all day-active animals. Their faces are usually flat and rather human in appearance, their eyes point forward, and they have stereoscopic color vision. Their hands and feet are highly developed for grasping; the big toes and, where present, the thumbs are opposable. Nearly all have flat nails. Monkeys habitually sit in an erect posture. Unlike the apes, they cannot swing arm-over-arm but move about in trees by running along the branches on all fours. Their skeletal structure is similar to that of other four-footed animals. Monkeys live in troops of up to several hundred individuals and travel about in search of food, having no permanent shelter. As in apes and humans, the female has a monthly reproductive cycle, and mating may occur at any time. Usually only one infant is born at a time; it is cared for by the mother for a long period. There are two large groups, or superfamilies, of monkeys: Old World monkeys (Cercopithecoidea) and New World monkeys (Ceboidea). The Old World monkeys are found in S Asia, with a few species as far N as Japan and N China, and in all of Africa except the deserts. Most are arboreal, but a few, such as BABOONS and some MACAQUE species, are ground dwellers. Some Old World monkeys lack tails; when a tail is present it may be long or short but is never prehensile (grasping). The nostrils are close together and tend to point downward. Many species have cheek pouches for holding food, and many have thick pads (called ischial callosities), on the buttocks. Their gestation period is five to nine months. Adult Old World monkeys have 32 teeth. The Old World monkeys, sometimes called true monkeys, are more closely related to the apes and man than they are to the New World monkeys; the two monkey groups probably evolved separately from ancestral primates. The New World monkeys are found from S Mexico to central South America, except in the high mountains. They are all thoroughly arboreal and most have long, prehensile tails with which they can manipulate objects and hang from branches. In most the thumb is lacking. They have widely separated nostrils that tend to point outward; they lack cheek pouches and ischial callosities. Their gestation period is four to five months. Adults of most New World species have 36 teeth. The Old World monkeys include the many species of macaque, widely distributed throughout Africa and Asia. The rhesus monkey, commonly used in laboratory experiments, is an Asian macaque. Related to the macaques are the baboons of Africa and SW Asia, as well as the MANDRILL and mangabey of Africa. The guerezas, or colobus monkeys (genus *Colobus*), are very large, long-tailed, leaf-eating African monkeys. Their Asian relatives, the langurs and leaf monkeys, include the sacred monkeys of India. The snub-nosed monkey of China and Tibet and the proboscis monkey of Borneo are langurlike monkeys with peculiar snouts. The guenons (*Cercopithecus*) are a large group of long-legged, long-tailed, omnivorous monkeys found throughout sub-Saharan Africa. One very widespread guenon species is the green monkey, or vervet, with olive-brown fur. The New World monkeys include the MARMOSETS and tamarins, small monkeys with claws that are classified in a family of their own, the Callithricidae. The rest of the New World monkeys are classified in the family Cebidae. They include the CAPUCHIN (genus *Cebus*), commonly seen in captivity, which has a partially prehensile tail. Prehensile tails are found in the spider monkey and woolly monkey as well as in the howler monkey, the largest member of the family, which has a voice that carries several miles. Smaller forms with nonprehensile tails are the squirrel monkey and titi, the nocturnal douroucouli, or owl monkey, the saki, and the ouakari. Monkeys are classified in the phylum CHORDATA, subphylum Vertebrata, class Mammalia, order Primates, superfamilies Cercopithecoidea and Ceboidea.

monkeypod: see RAIN TREE.

monkey-puzzle tree, evergreen tree (*Araucaria araucana*) native to Chile and widely cultivated elsewhere as an ornamental. The symmetrical branches have an unusual angularity and are completely covered by the stiff overlapping leaves. The monkey-puzzle tree and related species—e.g., the Norfolk Island pine (*A. excelsa*) and the bunya-bunya (*A. bidwillii*)—are all good timber trees. The edible seeds of the bunya-bunya are highly popular in its native Australia. Species of *Araucaria* form the dominant vegetation of the coniferous forests of Chile and S Brazil. The related kauri pine (*Agathis australis*) of New Zealand is one of the largest commercial trees in the world, sometimes reaching 200 ft (61 m) in height. It yields good timber and the valuable kauri COPAL, collected in fossil or semifossil form. Other species of *Agathis* produce similar copals. The genera *Agathis* and *Araucaria* together comprise the araucaria family. Although now restricted to the temperate regions of South America and of Australia and the neighboring Pacific islands, fossils—e.g., in the Petrified Forest of Arizona—indicate that the group was once abundant in the Northern Hemisphere. The monkey-puzzle tree is classified in the division PINOPHYTA, class Pinopsida, order Coniferales, family Araucariaceae.

Monkey trial: see SCOPES TRIAL.

Mon-Khmer languages (mōn-kəmâr'), group of languages frequently considered as a subfamily of the Southeast Asian family of languages. See SOUTHEAST ASIAN LANGUAGES.

monkshood: see ACONITE.

Monkwearmouth, England: see SUNDERLAND.

Monluc, Blaise de: see MONTLUC, BLAISE DE.

Monmouth, James Scott, duke of (mŏn'məth), 1649–85, pretender to the English throne; illegitimate son of Charles II of England by Lucy WALTER. After his mother's death, he was cared for by Lord Crofts, by whose name the boy was known. In 1662, James went to live at Charles's court. Charles acknowledged him as his son, created him (1663) duke of Monmouth, and married him to Anne Scott, countess of Buccleuch, whose name James now adopted. He held military commands on the Continent (1672–74), became captain general in 1678, and defeated the Scottish Covenanters at Bothwell Bridge in 1679. Politically he became very important after feeling against the succession of the Roman Catholic duke of York (later JAMES II) was heightened by the Popish Plot agitation in 1678. The 1st earl of SHAFTESBURY and other supporters of a Protestant succession championed Monmouth as heir to Charles and tried in vain to get Charles to prove his son legitimate. In 1679, Charles sent both Monmouth and the duke of York into exile. When Monmouth returned without the king's permission, he was forbidden to come to court but was received enthusiastically in London and the western counties. Monmouth worked with Shaftesbury and the Whig party for the exclusion of James from the succession, and after the arrest of Shaftesbury for treason in 1681 he was heard to speak openly of rebellion. When the RYE HOUSE PLOT was discovered (1683) and some of the Whig leaders were arrested, Monmouth fled to Holland. James II succeeded Charles in Feb., 1685. In June, Monmouth landed at Lyme Regis, Dorset, and raised a small force. At Taunton he was proclaimed king, and for a short time his chances for success looked very promising. But the gentry failed to come to his support, and his army was routed at Sedgemoor by James's troops, led by John Churchill (later duke of Marlborough). Monmouth was captured and beheaded in London on July 15.

Monmouth, municipal borough (1971 pop. 6,545), former county town of Monmouthshire, SE Wales, at the junction of the Monnow and Wye rivers. It is a popular tourist attraction and agricultural center with flourishing cattle and produce markets. There are food-processing and paper industries. Remains of a 12th-century castle (in which Henry V was born), a Norman church, and an old bridge (1272) over the Monnow are there. Monmouth School for boys was founded in 1614. In 1974, Monmouth became part of the new nonmetropolitan county of Gwent.

Monmouth, city (1970 pop. 11,022), seat of Warren co., W Ill.; inc. 1852. It is a trade center in a farm area. The city has a packing plant and companies that manufacture pottery, hobby kits, and dog food. Monmouth College is there. Wyatt Earp was born in Monmouth.

Monmouth, battle of, in the American Revolution, fought June 28, 1778, near the village of Monmouth Courthouse (now Freehold, N.J.). Gen. George Washington chose this location to attack the British troops, who were retreating from Philadelphia to New York City. Gen. Charles LEE launched the assault but without warning ordered a retreat. The British, under Sir Henry Clinton, immediately counterattacked, and only the arrival of Washington and Baron von Steuben prevented an American rout. Steuben re-formed Lee's disordered troops and led them back to battle, but the British forces escaped during the night. Lee was later court-martialed and suspended from command for disobeying orders. The legend of Molly PITCHER grew from this battle. See W. S. Stryker, *The Battle of Monmouth* (1927, repr. 1970).

Monmouthshire (mŏn'məth-shĭr), county (1971 pop. 461,459), 542 sq mi (1,404 sq km), SE Wales. The administrative center is NEWPORT. The chief rivers are the Wye and the Usk; the Severn estuary forms the southern border. The lands are low and fertile along the Wye and the seaboard, rising to hills in the west and northwest (Sugar Loaf; 1,955 ft/596 m). Much of the area is devoted to pasturage; wheat and fruitgrowing are important on the lower lands. The region is chiefly important, however, for its extensive coal deposits. Iron ore is now imported. Newport is an important port and steel-producing center. Legally, Monmouth was an English county from 1536 to 1830. Welsh is still spoken by many of its inhabitants. CAERLEON has interesting antiquities. Among the notable architectural remains of the county is TINTERN ABBEY, made famous by Wordsworth. In 1974 most of Monmouthshire was reorganized as the nonmetropolitan county of Gwent; small areas in W Monmouthshire became part of the new nonmetropolitan counties of Mid Glamorgan and South Glamorgan, and a small area of SE Breconshire became part of Gwent.

Monn, Georg Matthias (gä'ôrk mätē'äs môn), 1717–50, Austrian composer. Monn was organist at the Karlskirche in Vienna. His instrumental works exemplify the transition from the baroque to the rococo. In 1932, Arnold Schoenberg transcribed a harp concerto by Monn for cello and orchestra.

Monnet, Jean (zhäN' mônā'), 1888–, French economist and public official, proponent of European unity. In World War I, Monnet served on the Inter-Allied Maritime Commission, an international committee designed to secure war materials, foodstuffs, and shipping facilities for the Allies. He was later (1919–23) deputy general of the League of Nations. During World War II, as a member of the Washington-based British Supply Council (1940–43), he was instrumental in coordinating the Allied war effort. In 1945, Monnet was appointed to draft a plan for French economic revival; the Monnet Plan (1947) called for the modernization of French industry and agriculture with government help and supervision, and provided for a 48-hr work week to achieve economic goals. The resultant redevelopment encouraged French participation in the Marshall Plan and also in the Schuman Plan, drafted by Monnet himself. The Schuman Plan established the European Coal and Steel Community (ECSC), of which Monnet was first president (1952–55); he conceived the ECSC as the initial step towards European economic and political integration (see EUROPEAN COMMUNITY). In 1955, Monnet organized the Action Committee for a United States of Europe, and became its first chairman a year later. The group supported establishment of the COMMON MARKET, which developed from many of Monnet's ideas. See M. and S. Bromberger, *Jean Monnet and the United States of Europe* (tr. 1969).

Monnier, Henri (äNrē' mônyā'), 1799–1877, French lithographer and writer. His work became popular (c.1825) when he illustrated La Fontaine's *Fables* with pen drawings. He wrote and illustrated three series of *Scènes populaires* (1830, 1835, 1862), books of satiric sketches about the people of his day, in which he introduced the imaginary characters Mme Gibou and M. Joseph Prudhomme. Their history was continued in his best-known work, *Mémoires de Monsieur Joseph Prudhomme* (1857), a collection of cartoons, with some text. Some of his numerous plays also concerned themselves with these characters.

Monocacy (mənŏk'əsē), river, c.60 mi (100 km) long, rising in S Pa., and flowing S across Md. to join the Potomac River near Frederick, Md. On its banks, just E of Frederick, was fought the Civil War battle of Monocacy, July 9, 1864. Although the Union forces under Gen. Lew Wallace were defeated, they delayed the Confederate forces under Gen. J. A. Early long enough to give Grant time to dispatch troops to defend Washington and drive Early back into Virginia.

Monod, Jacques (zhäk mônō'), 1910–, French biologist, educated at the Univ. of Paris (D.Sc., 1941). He was a leader of the French resistance in World War II. He shared the 1965 Nobel Prize in Physiology and Medicine with André Lwoff and François Jacob for discoveries concerning molecular genetic mechanisms inside body cells. His publications include *Chance and Necessity* (1971) and *Of Microbes and Life* (ed. with Ernest Borek, 1971).

monoecious plant: see HERMAPHRODITE.

monogamy: see MARRIAGE.

monogram [Gr.,=single letter], symbol of a name or names, consisting typically of a letter or several letters worked together. A famous monogram is that of Christ, consisting of X (chi) and P (rho), the first two letters of *Christ* in Greek. The monogram has been commonly used by artists (e.g., Dürer), monarchs (e.g., E.R. for Elizabeth II), companies, societies, and others. Bridal monograms and monograms on clothing, silverware, jewelry, seals, and letterheads are common.

monologue, an extended speech by one person only. Strindberg's one-act play *The Stronger*, spoken entirely by one person, is an extreme example of monologue. Soliloquy is synonymous, but usually refers to a character in a play talking or thinking aloud to himself, giving the audience information essential to the plot. The most obvious example is Hamlet's "To be or not to be . . ." soliloquy. The dramatic monologue is a lyric poem in which one person speaks, reporting to a silent listener what other characters say and do, while providing insight into his own character, e.g., Browning's "My Last Duchess" and T. S. Eliot's "Love Song of J. Alfred Prufrock." Interior monologue is a narrative technique meant to reproduce a character's thoughts, feelings, and associations in the untidy fashion in which they flow through the mind. The Molly Bloom section at the end of James Joyce's novel *Ulysses* is the most frequently cited example of perfect use of the device.

monomer (mŏn'əmər): see POLYMER.

Monona (mənō'nə), city (1970 pop. 10,420), Dane co., S Wis.; inc. 1938.

Monongahela, river, 128 mi (206 km) long, formed at Fairmont, N W.Va., by the junction of the West Fork and Tygart rivers. It flows north, through a highly industrialized valley in a rich coal mining region, into SW Pennsylvania to join the Allegheny River and form the Ohio River at Pittsburgh. The canalized river is navigable for most of its length. Coal is the chief product moved on the river. The Monongahela River was the first river in the United States to be improved for navigation.

mononucleosis, infectious (mŏn"ənōō"klēō'sĭs), acute infectious disease of older children and young adults, occurring sporadically or in epidemic form. The causative organism is thought to be a herpes virus. The disease occurs most often in patients between the ages of 10 and 35. Its mode of transmission is unknown, but the agent is presumed to be airborne. Diagnosis of mononucleosis follows the exhibition of a large number of abnormal white blood cells (lymphocytes) on microscopic blood examination. Symptoms are varied but include enlarged lymph nodes, fever, enlarged spleen in about half the cases, sore throat, and excessive fatigue. Occasional rashes and throat and mouth infections occur. Hepatitis is common, and the disease occasionally affects the nervous system, lungs, and heart. Fatalities are rare and, when they do occur, usually result from splenic rupture. General therapeutic measures include bed rest and treatment of symptoms.

Monophysitism (mənŏf'ĭsĭt"ĭzəm) [Gr.,=belief in one nature], a heresy of the 5th and 6th cent., which grew out of a reaction against NESTORIANISM. It was anticipated by APOLLINARIANISM and was continuous with the principles of EUTYCHES, whose doctrine had been rejected in 451 at Chalcedon (see CHALCEDON, COUNCIL OF). Monophysitism challenged the orthodox creed of Chalcedon and taught that in Jesus Christ there were not two natures (divine and human) but one (divine). Discussion of this belief was badly confused by misunderstandings of terms and by the lack of knowledge of Greek in the West. In the East the Council of Chalcedon was declared (c.476) invalid by Basiliscus, the imperial usurper. Later, Emperor Zeno, restored to his throne, issued the *Henoticon* (482), based on the doctrines of St. Cyril of Alexandria, in an attempt to settle the dispute. It recommended a formula that, ostensibly orthodox, left a loophole for the Monophysites. Neither side was satisfied; the extreme Monophysites refused to accept the intended compromise, and the pope excommunicated the East for abrogating the Council of Chalcedon. The schism ended in 519 when Emperor Justin I enforced the creed of Chalcedon. Later, Justinian, although strongly Catholic, was tolerant toward the Monophysites, who were becoming more intransigent. The quarrel was further embittered when Justinian in 544 pronounced anathema upon the Three Chapters. These were the person and writings of THEODORE OF MOPSUESTIA, the writings of THEODORET against St. Cyril of Alexandria, and the letters of Ibas of Edessa to Maris the Persian. The anathema was based on the grounds that they were all tainted with Nestorianism. Since many of these writings were considered orthodox by the majority of Catholics, the edict was confusing. The vacillating attitude of Pope VIGILIUS and Justinian's control of the empire procured the convocation of the Second Council of Constantinople (553; see CONSTANTINOPLE, SECOND COUNCIL OF), which condemned the Three Chapters without prejudice to the canons of Chalcedon. The Monophysites remained aloof, and the West was virtually alienated. Justinian's successors alternately favored and suppressed Monophysitism, but by 600 the lines of schism had hardened; the Coptic Church (see under COPT), the JACOBITE CHURCH of Syria, and the ARMENIAN CHURCH, all Monophysite, were established. MONOTHELETISM was a 7th-century attempt to reconcile orthodoxy with Monophysitism. See A. A. Luce, *Monophysitism, Past and Present* (1920); W. H. Frend, *The Rise of the Monophysite Movement* (1972).

monoplane: see AIRPLANE.

monopoly (mənŏp'əlē), market condition in which there is only one seller of a commodity; by virtue of his control over supply, he is able to exert nearly total control over prices. In a pure monopoly the single seller will usually restrict supply to that point on the supply-demand schedule that will maximize both his profit and the market price. Governments have often created public service monopolies by laws excluding competition from an industry. The result is either a public monopoly, such as the U.S. Postal Service, or a publicly regulated private monopoly, such as most power and lighting companies in the United States (see UTILITY, PUBLIC). Such enterprises usually exist in areas of "natural monopoly," where the conditions of the market make unified control necessary or desirable to the public interest. SOCIALISM advocates the extension of the principle of public monopoly to all vital industries, such as coal and steel, that have an immediate effect on the general welfare of the economy. Aside from utility companies, privately controlled monopolies are rare. However, the control of supply by a few producers, which is known as oligopoly, is quite common. In Europe, oligopoly has traditionally taken the form of a CARTEL which often controls the entire production and marketing of a commodity; but in the United States, oligopoly has more often been achieved by the merger of several corporations, by INTERLOCKING DIRECTORATES, or by agreements among members of an industry that restrain price competition. In history, monopoly has often been the source of oppression. In ancient Egypt the pharaohs controlled food, and in England exclusive grants (known as royal charters or patents) were made to court favorites until Parliament limited (1624) the practice during the reign of James I. In modern times, the tremendously increased production and fierce competition brought about by the Industrial Revolution convinced many producers that it would be in their better interest to form monopoly and oligopoly agreements. The U.S. government has made most forms of monopoly, and to a lesser extent oligopoly, illegal under antitrust laws. The objective of such measures is to guarantee that price will be determined by market value rather than by arbitrary contracts among corporations. The government still grants monopolies in the form of patents and copyrights to encourage the arts and sciences. See Joan Robinson, *The Economics of Imperfect Competition* (2d ed. 1969); Edward Chamberlin, *Theory of Monopolistic Competition* (8th ed. 1962); Victor Perlo, *The Empire of High Finance* (1957); Alex Hunter, ed., *Monopoly and Competition* (1969).

monorail, railway system that uses cars that run on a single rail. Typically the rail is run overhead and the cars are either suspended from it or run above it. Driving power is transmitted from the cars to the track by means of wheels that rotate horizontally, making contact with the rail between its upper and lower flanges. One of the principal advantages of a monorail is the relative simplicity of its trackage in comparison with that of a standard railway. Monorails originated and still function as materials-handling systems, similar to traveling cranes, for use in large factories. In the United States short urban transportation monorails have been built in Houston and Seattle.

monosaccharide: see CARBOHYDRATE.

monosodium glutamate: see GLUTAMIC ACID.

monotheism (mŏn'əthēĭzəm) [Gr.,=belief in one God], in religion, a belief in one god. The term is applied particularly to three religions, JUDAISM, CHRISTIANITY, and ISLAM. In general the term is nonphilosophical, the word THEISM being used in metaphysics for the idea of one god. ZOROASTRIANISM in its early stages was monotheistic, and Greek religion in its later stages became monotheistic. Monotheism is opposed to POLYTHEISM, the belief in many gods. The rationalism of the deists is not considered monotheism on the basis that it is not religious. See also GOD.

Monotheletism or **Monothelitism** (both: mənŏth'əlĭtĭz"əm) [Gr.,=one will], 7th-century opinion condemned as heretical by the Third Council of Constantinople in 680 (see CONSTANTINOPLE, THIRD COUNCIL OF). This doctrine, by declaring that Christ operated with but one will, although he had two natures, opposed the intent of the Council of Chalcedon. Monotheletism was first proposed in 622 and was immediately adopted by Byzantine Emperor HERACLIUS I, for political reasons, as a compromise between MONOPHYSITISM and orthodoxy. The Eastern hierarchy, while doubtful of the dogma, tended to support Heraclius. In 631, Cyrus of Phasis, patriarch of Alexandria, promulgated a Monothelite thesis, which was opposed by Sophronius, a Palestinian monk (later patriarch of Jerusalem). At Sophronius' behest, Sergius, patriarch of Constantinople, wrote to Pope HONORIUS I for advice. The pope replied with a letter that apparently supported the doctrine of one will but forbade further discussion of the question. Soon afterwards (638) Heraclius published the *Ecthesis,* which defined Monotheletism as the official imperial form of Christianity. When the *Ecthesis* arrived in Rome, Pope Severinus, Honorius' successor, immediately condemned it, ex cathedra. Heraclius, before he died, disclaimed the *Ecthesis* and attributed it to Sergius. Heraclius' successors, Constantine III and Constans II, however, continued to enforce the heresy. Popes John IV and Theodore I anathematized Monotheletism, but they could do little in face of imperial support of it. Constans II withdrew the *Ecthesis* and promulgated instead the *Typus,* a decree flatly forbidding the mention of one will or two wills or one energy or two energies in the Second Person. The *Typus* was favorable to the Monophysitism established in the empire but would have silenced the orthodox. Intended to make peace, it brought the controversy to a crisis. In 649, Pope St. MARTIN I convened a Lateran Council to condemn Monotheletism and was subsequently seized by the emperor, imprisoned, and exiled. St. MAXIMUS was the most vigorous opponent of Monotheletism. The accession of Constantine IV to the imperial throne brought toleration for the Catholics. After the Council at Constantinople in 680, Monotheletism died out except among the Maronites in Syria. There was a brief revival of imperial Monotheletism from 711 to 713. The last of the Christological controversies, the Monotheletism question enhanced the prestige of the papacy, which took the lead in opposing official imperial heresy.

monotreme (mŏn'ətrēm"), name for members of the primitive mammalian order Monotremata, found in Australia, Tasmania, and New Guinea. The only members of this order are the PLATYPUS, or duckbill, and the several species of ECHIDNA, or spiny anteater. Although monotremes possess the distinguishing mammalian features of hair and mammary glands, they are unique among mammals in laying eggs rather than giving birth to live young. The eggs are like those of reptiles, with large yolks and leathery shells. Like birds and reptiles, monotremes have a single opening, the CLOACA, for the passage of liquid and solid wastes, the transfer of sperm, and, in the female, the laying of eggs. In addition, certain features of the skeletal structure are like those of reptiles, and the regulation of body temperature is less effective than in other mammals. Adult monotremes are toothless. The males possess spurs on their hind feet; these are connected to poison glands and are presumably used as weapons. Mammals are known to have evolved from reptiles; the monotremes probably branched off at an early stage of mammalian evolution and have retained many reptilian features. They are classified in the phylum CHORDATA, subphylum Vertebrata, class Mammalia, order Monotremata.

monotype, TYPE set by the Monotype machine. See PRINTING.

Monreale (mōnrăā'lā), town (1971 pop. 22,980), NW Sicily, Italy, near Palermo. An agricultural market and tourist center, it commands a magnificent view of the fertile Conca d'Oro plain. A famous cathedral, one of the masterpieces of Norman-Sicilian architecture, was begun there (1174) by William II of Sicily. The cathedral has fine copper doors by Bonanno Pisano; its interior is decorated with exceptional Byzantine mosaics. Nearby is a lovely cloister with about 200 twin columns and an Arabian fountain formerly used as a lavabo.

Monro, Harold, 1879-1932, English poet, b. Belgium. In 1911 he founded the *Poetry Review* and the following year established the Poetry Bookshop, which became a refuge and intellectual center for poets. His *Poetry and Drama* (1913), a successor to the *Poetry Review,* was discontinued during World War I, but Monro reestablished it as *Chapbook* (1919-25). Both periodicals had great influence on the poetical work of the time. His own work, first published in 1906, includes *Children of Love* (1914) and *Elm Angel* (1930). See his *Collected Poems* (introd. by T. S. Eliot, 1933); Joy Grant, *Harold Monro and the Poetry Bookshop* (1967).

Monroe, Harriet, 1860-1936, American editor, critic, and poet, b. Chicago. In 1912 she founded *Poetry: a Magazine of Verse,* which paid and encouraged both established and new poets. Monroe's literary reputation is based upon her editorship of this important magazine. She introduced to readers such writers as Carl Sandburg, Rabindranath Tagore, Vachel Lindsay, Rupert Brooke, and Robert Frost. Her own works include several volumes of poetry; her essays *Poets and Their Art* (1933); the anthology she compiled with Alice Corbin Henderson, *The New Poetry* (1917); and her autobiography, *A Poet's Life* (1938). See study by D. J. Cahill (1974).

Monroe, James, 1758-1831, 5th President of the United States (1817-25), b. Westmoreland co., Va. Leaving the College of William and Mary in 1776 to fight in the American Revolution, he served in several campaigns and was wounded (Dec., 1776) at the battle of Trenton. He later studied law (1780-83) under Thomas Jefferson, and the friendship that sprang up was the foundation for Monroe's political career. He was elected to the Virginia legislature in 1782 and served (1783-86) in the Continental Congress under the Articles of Confederation. He was not a delegate to the Federal Constitutional Convention, and in his own state he supported Patrick Henry in opposing the Constitution, which seemed to him to create a government so centralized that it encroached on states' rights. Under the new government, he served (1790-94) in the U.S. Senate, where he proved himself an outstanding lieutenant of Jefferson and a violent assailant of George Washington, Alexander Hamilton, and the Federalists. Appointed (1794) minister to France in the hope that his Francophile sympathies would smooth the ruffled relations between the two nations, he did nothing to lessen French resentment over JAY'S TREATY, and he was recalled in 1796. Governor of Virginia from 1799 to 1802, he was sent (1802) by President Jefferson to France as a special envoy. There he assisted Robert R. Livingston (1746-1813; see LIVINGSTON, family) during negotiations (1803) for the LOUISIANA PURCHASE. The next year, in Spain, he aided Charles Pinckney in the unsuccessful negotiations with the Spanish government. A later mission, to England, was even more disastrous. Monroe and William PINKNEY struggled to arrive at a commercial treaty to end the disputes between Great Britain and the United States over shipping, but they could get no concessions, and Jefferson did not even submit the treaty they drafted (1806) to the Senate for approval. In 1808, Monroe made a bid for the presidential nomination; he thus alienated James Madison, but the estrangement did not last long, and Monroe, after serving again as governor of Virginia, was Madison's Secretary of State (1811-17). For a time he was also Secretary of War (1814-15), after the dismissal of John Armstrong. In 1816 he obtained the presidential nomination and was easily elected. In the 1820 election, despite economic depression, Monroe lost only one vote in the electoral college that reelected him. During Monroe's first administration, serious differences over the question of slavery in the territories were accommodated by the MISSOURI COMPROMISE, which Monroe signed despite his sympathy for the South in this matter. In foreign affairs a number of settlements were reached. The Rush-Bagot agreement with Great Britain (1817) provided for mutual limitation of armaments on the Great Lakes, and the U.S-Canadian boundary question was also settled. U.S. possession of the Floridas was confirmed by Andrew Jackson's campaigns and a treaty with Spain (1819). Late in 1823, Monroe issued what came to be known as the MONROE DOCTRINE, one of the most important principles of U.S. foreign policy. Although this declaration was as much the work of Monroe's Secretary of State, John Quincy Adams, as of the President himself, the initiative for presenting it in the annual message to Congress was Monroe's. The experiment of the American Colonization Society in settling Liberia was undertaken with Monroe's blessing, and Monrovia was named for him. At the end of his term Monroe retired to his estate, Oak Hill, near Leesburg, Va. In 1829 he presided over the Virginia constitutional convention and supported the conservatives on suffrage and slavery. He died on a visit to New York City. His writings were edited by S. M. Hamilton (7 vol., 1898-1903, repr. 1969). See his autobiography (ed. with introd. by S. G. Brown, 1959); biographies by George Morgan (1921, repr. 1969), Arthur Styron (1945), and W. P. Cresson (1946, repr. 1971); study by Lucius Wilmerding (1960).

Monroe, Marilyn, 1926-62, American movie actress, b. Los Angeles; her original name was Norma Jean Baker. Raised in orphanages and married at 14, Monroe became a world-famous sex symbol and, after her death, a Hollywood legend. Her movies, many of which reveal genuine acting talent, include *The Asphalt Jungle* (1950), *All About Eve* (1950), *Niagara* (1952), *The Seven-Year Itch* (1955), *Bus Stop* (1956), *The Prince and the Showgirl* (1957), *Some Like It Hot* (1959), and *The Misfits* (1960). Monroe's second husband was Joe DiMaggio and her third was Arthur Miller. She committed suicide at 36. See controversial study by Norman Mailer (1973).

Monroe, Paul, 1869-1947, American educator, b. North Madison, Ind., grad. Franklin College, 1890, Ph.D. Univ. of Chicago, 1897. At Teachers College, Columbia, he was professor of education from 1902 until his retirement in 1938; he also served as director of the School of Education (1915-23) and of the International Institute after 1923. In 1932 he became president of Robert College and of the American College for Girls, both in Istanbul. Monroe made school surveys in the Philippine Islands, Puerto Rico, and Iraq. He edited the *Cyclopedia of Education* and *Principles of Secondary Education* (1914) and wrote *China, a Nation in Evolution* (1928) and several works on education, including *Founding of the American Public School System* (1940).

Monroe. **1** Residential town (1970 pop. 12,047), Fairfield co., SW Conn.; settled c.1755, inc. 1823. Electronic components are among the town's manufactures. **2** Industrial city (1970 pop. 56,374), seat of Ouachita parish, SE La., on the Ouachita River; founded c.1785, inc. as a city 1900. The center of the great Monroe Natural Gas Field (discovered 1916), it has important chemical and carbon-black plants, as well as pulp, paper, and lumber mills. The first settlers founded (c.1785) Fort Miró. The community was renamed in 1819 after the *James Monroe*, the first steamship to come up the Ouachita. Northeast Louisiana Univ. is in the city. Antebellum houses remain. **3** City (1970 pop. 23,894), seat of Monroe co., SE Mich., on Lake Erie; settled 1778, inc. 1837. Paper products, fuel-burning equipment, chairs, and auto parts are made. The city has large nurseries and is the shipping point for a farm region. Limestone quarries and an atomic breeder reactor plant are nearby. Monroe was the scene of the River RAISIN massacre during the War of 1812 and the center of the "Toledo War" (see TOLEDO, Ohio). George A. Custer lived there, and the local museum has a large collection of Custer memorabilia. A junior college is in the city, and a state park is nearby. **4** City (1970 pop. 11,282), seat of Union co., S N.C., in the Piedmont; settled 1751, inc. 1844. Poultry is processed, and textiles, metal alloys, surgical equipment, and aircraft parts are made. A junior college is just east of the city.

Monroe, Fort: see FORT MONROE.

Monroe Doctrine, principle of American foreign policy enunciated in President James Monroe's message to Congress, Dec. 2, 1823. The doctrine grew out of two diplomatic problems. The first was the minor clash with Russia concerning the northwest coast of North America. In this quarrel, Secretary of State John Quincy Adams expressed the principle that the American continents were no longer to be considered as a field for colonization by European powers. That principle was incorporated verbatim in the presidential message. The other and more important part of the doctrine grew out of the fear that the group of reactionary European governments commonly called the HOLY ALLIANCE would seek to reduce again to colonial status the Latin American states that had recently gained independence from Spain. Great Britain, which wished to maintain open commerce with the newly formed states, supported Latin American independence. The United States had just recognized the independence of these states, and in Aug., 1823, the British foreign minister, George Canning, proposed to the United States that a joint note be sent by the two governments protesting intervention in the New World by the Holy Alliance. President Monroe consulted with two of his predecessors, Thomas Jefferson and James Madison, who recommended that Canning's proposal be accepted. Secretary of State Adams dissented. He feared, with some justification, that the British would try to exact a pledge from the United States not to attempt to acquire any territory in Spanish America. Meanwhile, Canning had secured an agreement with France (which had earlier made the proposal that the Holy Alliance intervene in Latin America), by which France renounced any intention of intervention, thus obviating the need for a joint U.S.-British protest. However, Adams had by then proposed a unilateral action to President Monroe, who finally agreed to this course. The presidential message, therefore, announced that the United States would not interfere in European affairs but would view with displeasure any attempt by the European powers to subject the nations of the New World to their political systems. Thus in a sense the Monroe Doctrine as a dual principle of foreign policy (no colonization and no intervention by European states in the Americas) complemented the policy expressed by George Washington of noninterference in European affairs. The doctrine was not ratified by any congressional legislation; it did not obtain a place in international law, and the term Monroe Doctrine did not come into general circulation until the 1850s. Yet the doctrine became important in American policy, particularly when President Polk reasserted its ideas in 1845 and 1848 with respect to British claims in Oregon, British and French intrigues to prevent the U.S. annexation of Texas, and the aspirations of European nations in Yucatán. The strained relations with Great Britain concerning its sovereignty over several areas in Central America in the 1850s renewed U.S. interest in the doctrine; Great Britain specifically denied its validity. During the Civil War, the doctrine was invoked unsuccessfully after Spain's reacquisition of the Dominican Republic (formerly Santo Domingo). It was also used, somewhat more effectively, to bring pressure on the French government to withdraw support from MAXIMILIAN, who had established an empire in Mexico under French auspices. Under President Grant and his successors the doctrine was expanded. The principle that no territory in the Western Hemisphere could be transferred from one European power to another became part of the Monroe Doctrine. As U.S. imperialistic tendencies grew, the Monroe Doctrine came to be associated not only with the exclusion of European (now extended to mean all non-American) powers from the Americas, but also with the possible extension of U.S. hegemony in the area. This condition explains why the Monroe Doctrine, although it was not formally used to justify American intervention, was viewed with suspicion and dislike by Latin American nations. In 1895, President Cleveland, in a new extension of the Monroe Doctrine, demanded that Great Britain submit to arbitration a boundary dispute between British Guiana and Venezuela (see VENEZUELA BOUNDARY DISPUTE). Following the VENEZUELA CLAIMS question, Theodore Roosevelt expounded (1904) what came to be known as the Roosevelt corollary to the Monroe Doctrine; he stated that continued misconduct or disturbance in a Latin American country might force the United States to intervene in order to prevent European intervention. This frankly imperialistic interpretation met much resistance in Latin America but was used extensively during the administrations of Presidents Taft and Wilson to justify intervention in the Caribbean area. The Monroe Doctrine was so deeply embedded in U.S. foreign policy by the end of World War I that Woodrow Wilson asked for a special exception for it in the Covenant of the League of Nations in 1919. By the end of the next decade the doctrine had become much less important, and its imperialistic aspects were being played down in an effort to foster better relations with Latin America. In the Clark memorandum of Dec., 1928, the U.S. State Department repudiated the Roosevelt corollary. Subsequently, under President Franklin Delano Roosevelt, the doctrine was redefined as a multilateral undertaking to be applied by all the nations of the hemisphere acting together, and emphasis was placed on PAN-AMERICANISM. Nevertheless, in the 1950s and 60s the specter of unilateral intervention in Latin America was again raised, especially by the involvement of the United States with developments in Guatemala, Cuba, and the Dominican Republic. For the most part, however, the United States has continued to support hemispheric cooperation within the framework of the ORGANIZATION OF AMERICAN STATES. See Alejandro Alvarez, *The Monroe Doctrine* (1924); Phillips Bradley, *A Bibliography of the Monroe Doctrine* (1929); Dexter Perkins, *A History of the Monroe Doctrine* (rev. ed. 1963); Frederick Merk, *The Monroe Doctrine and American Expansionism* (1966); C. M. Wilson, *The Monroe Doctrine; an American Frame of Mind* (1971).

Monroeville, borough (1970 pop. 29,011), Allegheny co., SW Pa., a suburb of Pittsburgh; settled 1810, inc. 1952. It has steel, coal, and nuclear industrial research centers. A junior college is there.

Monrovia (mənrō'vēə), city (1970 est. pop. 96,200), capital of the Republic of Liberia, NW Liberia, a port on the Atlantic Ocean at the mouth of the St. Paul River. Monrovia is Liberia's largest city and its administrative, commercial, communications, and financial center. The city's economy revolves around its harbor, which was substantially improved by U.S. forces under LEND-LEASE during World War II. In 1948 the first port capable of handling oceangoing vessels was opened; there are now several ports, including a free port. The main exports are latex and iron ore. The city also has extensive storage and ship repair facilities. Manufactures include cement, refined petroleum, food products, bricks and tiles, furniture, and pharmaceuticals. Roads and railroads connect Monrovia with Liberia's interior. Monrovia was founded in 1822 by the AMERICAN COLONIZATION SOCIETY as a haven for freed slaves from the United States and the British West Indies and was named for James Monroe, then President of the United States. Descendants of those early settlers still control the city. The Univ. of Liberia (1862) and Cuttington College and Divinity School (1889; Episcopal) are in Monrovia.

Monrovia, city (1970 pop. 30,015), Los Angeles co., S Calif., in the foothills of the San Gabriel Mts.; inc. 1886. The city has industries that manufacture electronic equipment, plastics, chemicals, machinery, and printed materials.

Mons (môNs), Flemish *Bergen*, city (1970 pop. 28,324), capital of Hainaut prov., SW Belgium, near the French border. Located at the junction of the Canal du Centre and the Condé-Mons Canal, it is the processing and shipping center of the Borinage coal-mining district and is also a manufacturing center. Known since the 7th cent., Mons became (1295) the seat of the counts of Hainaut. In the wars of the 16th to 18th cent. it was often attacked and occupied by Dutch, Spanish, and French forces. In World Wars I and II the city was the site of several battles. Of note in Mons are the Gothic Church of St. Waltrude (15th–16th cent.), the city hall (15th cent.), and many beautiful houses of the 16th to 18th cent. The city is the scene of an annual pageant and festival of St. George.

Monsalvat: see MONTSERRAT, Spain.

Monserrat: see MONTSERRAT, Spain.

monsignor: see ORDERS, HOLY.

monsoon (mŏnso͞on), wind that changes direction with change of season, notably in India and SE Asia. To a lesser degree, monsoonal winds also develop in portions of all other continents except Antarctica. The change of wind direction is a result of the differences in the heating or cooling of landmasses in contrast to that of oceans. For example, the dry, or winter, monsoon of Asia is largely the result of an area of high pressure that develops over S Siberia. From this area dry winds blow outward, crossing India from northeast to southwest and SE Asia from north to south. The wet, or summer, monsoon is caused by the area of low pressure that develops over S Asia as the landmass warms. Moisture-laden air over the oceans is drawn toward this center of low pressure. The air cools as it ascends the slopes of mountain barriers; it loses its ability to retain moisture, which results in heavy rainfall.

Monstera: see ARUM.

monsters and imaginary beasts in folklore. The mythologies and legends of ancient and modern cultures teem with an enormous variety of monsters and imaginary beasts. A great number of these are composites of different existing animals and of human beings and animals. Among the animal composites are the Babylonian winged bulls and leopards; the Hindu winged elephants; the Greek three-headed dog CERBERUS; the Western European GRIFFIN, with a lion's body and eagle's wings; the DRAGON, with a winged reptilian body and fiery breath; and the Chimera, with a goat's body, lion's head, and lizard's tail. Examples of human-animal composites abound in Greek mythology; the TRITON, with a man's head and torso and a sea-serpent's tail; the SIREN, with a woman's head and a bird's body or a woman's head and torso and a fish's tail; the SATYR, with a man's head and torso, a ram's horns, legs, and hooves, and a horse's ears and tail; the SPHINX, with the body of a lion and a woman's head and bust; and the CENTAUR, with a man's head and torso and a horse's body. Most such creatures represent evil or at least mischievous forces. The restless souls of the living dead are embodied, in ubiquitous legends, by VAMPIRES. Equally grisly and widespread is the werewolf legend (see LYCANTHROPY), in which a man is transformed by night into a wolf that devours human beings. A few imaginary creatures are benign, e.g., the gentle UNICORN, a medieval European symbol of chastity and the power of love. The North American Indians, particularly the Eskimo, who have no epic hero, have created a vast panorama of monsters, ogres, bodiless heads, cannibal mothers, and semihuman beasts. The Zuñi and Pueblo peoples respect many beasts that are considered curers of illness, guardians, and intercessors. Most of these spirits are associated with actual animals. In the folklore of the United States a host of fantastic, impossible "fearsome critters" have been developed. There are the prock, also called the sidehill dodger or the gwinter, an animal with shorter legs on one side that enable him to keep his balance while feeding on steep mountains; the augerino, an underground creature in Colorado that lets the water out of irrigation ditches; and the glitch of the Pentagon in Washington, D.C., that is responsible for general chaos. Legendary monsters and beasts, which appear to be a feature common to all cultures, are the subject of considerable scholarly study. See Stith Thompson, *Tales of the North American Indians* (1929); J. L. Borges, *The Book of Imaginary Beings* (tr. of rev. ed. 1969); Richard Barber and Anne Riches, *A Dictionary of Fabulous Beasts* (1972).

montage (mŏntäzh', Fr. môNtäzh'), the art and technique of motion-picture editing in which contrasting shots or sequences are used to effect emotional or intellectual responses. It was developed creatively after 1925 by the Russian Sergei EISENSTEIN; since that time montage has become an increasingly complex and inventive way of extending the imaginative possibilities of film art. In still photography a composite picture, made by combining several prints, or parts of prints, and then rephotographing them as a whole, is often called a montage or a photomontage.

Montagna, Bartolomeo (bärtōlōmĕ'ō mōntä'nyä), c.1450–1523, Italian painter. He was the founder and most important representative of the school of Vicenza, where he settled in 1480. His works, always religious in subject, are dignified and severe in design and finely colored. The most important are a series of frescoes (damaged) illustrating the life of St. Blaise (Church of San Nazaro, Verona); an altarpiece, *Madonna and Child*, painted for the Church of San Sebastiano, Verona (Academy, Venice); *Madonna Enthroned*, an altarpiece painted for San Michele at Vicenza (Milan); *Ecce Homo* (Louvre); *Madonna and Saints* (Johnson Coll., Philadelphia); *Madonna and Child* and *A Lady of Rank as St. Justina of Padua* (Metropolitan Mus.); and *Madonna and Child* (National Gall. of Art, Washington, D.C.). See Tancred Borenius, *The Painters of Vicenza* (1909); Joseph A. Crowe, *History of Painting in North Italy* (3 vol., 1912, repr. 1972).

Montagnais (mŏntənyā') and **Naskapi** (năs'kəpē) **Indians,** people of Labrador. Their dialects were almost identical, and their customs so clearly alike that the two peoples were hardly distinguishable. The Montagnais covered their conical wigwams with birch bark and hunted principally moose during the winter months, moving down the rivers in the spring to spear salmon and eels, and to harpoon seals along the shores of the St. Lawrence. The Naskapi covered their wigwams with caribou skin and hunted caribou from midsummer until early spring, when some of them moved down the coast, like the Montagnais, while others remained inland to fish in various lakes and rivers, and to hunt hares, porcupines, and other small game. Contact with Europeans was disastrous to both peoples. Both the Montagnais and the Naskapi declined rapidly. Today their combined number is less than 4,000, most of them still hunters and trappers.

Montagnards: see MOUNTAIN, THE.

Montagu, Charles: see HALIFAX, CHARLES MONTAGU, EARL OF.

Montagu, Edward: see SANDWICH, EDWARD MONTAGU, 1ST EARL OF.

Montagu, Elizabeth (Robinson), 1720–1800, English author, one of the BLUESTOCKINGS. She was noted for her wit and beauty, and her London literary salon was frequented by Johnson, Walpole, Burke, and other eminent men. She wrote *An Essay on the Writings and Genius of Shakespeare* (1769), defending the poet against Voltaire's condemnation. She also conducted a voluminous correspondence, edited in part by E. J. Climenson (1906) and in part by Reginald Blunt (1923).

Montagu, John: see SANDWICH, JOHN MONTAGU, 4TH EARL OF.

Montagu, Lady Mary Wortley, 1689–1762, English author, noted primarily for her highly descriptive letters. She was the daughter of the first duke of Kingston. In 1712 she married Edward Wortley Montagu, who became ambassador to Turkey in 1716. On her return to England in 1718 she worked to educate the public in the use of inoculation against smallpox. In 1739 she left her husband and went to live on the Continent. Her *Town Eclogues* (1747), which gives an entertaining picture of contemporary manners, was first published by Edmund Curll in a pirated edition in 1716. She is remembered for her quarrel with Pope, who had once been her ardent admirer and who attacked her viciously in his poetry. Horace Walpole disliked her also and depicted her as a greedy, heartless eccentric. However, recent studies have defended her as a brilliant woman struggling for emancipation. Her letters were first published in 1763. See the complete letters (1965–67) and selections (1970), both ed. by Robert Halsband, also biography by Robert Halsband (1956).

Montague, Charles Edward, 1867–1928, English journalist and author, b. London. He joined the staff of the Manchester *Guardian* in 1890, remaining until his retirement in 1925 except for service (1914–19) in World War I, as a private and later as an intelligence officer. His war experience is reflected in his antiwar essays and novels. Among his best-known novels are *Disenchantment* (1922), *Rough Justice* (1926), and *Right off the Map* (1927). His literary criticism, especially *A Writer's Notes on His Trade* (1930, repr. 1969), is also valuable. See the biography by Oliver Elton (1929).

Montaigne, Michel Eyquem, seigneur de (mŏntān', Fr. mēshĕl' ākĕm' sānyör' də môNtĕn'yə), 1533–92, French essayist. Montaigne was one of the greatest masters of the ESSAY as a literary form. Born at the Château of Montaigne in Périgord, he was the son of a rich Catholic landowner and a mother of Spanish Jewish descent. Montaigne's father, ambitious for his son's education, permitted him to hear and speak only Latin until he was six. After seven years at the Collège de Guyenne in Bordeaux, he studied for the law, held a magistracy until 1570, and was (1581–85) mayor of Bordeaux. From 1571 to 1580, in retirement and ostensibly aloof from the political and religious quarrels of France, he wrote the first two books of his *Esssais* (1st ed. 1580). The third book of *Essais* and extensive revisions and additions to the first two were written in the years between 1586 and his death, and the first complete edition was published in 1595. The essays, which were trials or tests of his own judgment on a diversity of subjects, show the change in Montaigne's thinking as his examination of himself developed into a study of man and nature. The early essays reflect Montaigne's concern with pain and death. To this group belongs the essay "On Friendship," which commemorates Montaigne's association with Étienne de La Boétie. A middle period, characterized by Montaigne's motto "Que sais-je?" [what do I know?], which sums up his skeptical attitude toward all knowledge, is represented by the "Apologie de Raimond Sebond." This essay purportedly defends a Catalan theologian whose work Montaigne had translated (1569), but it is actually an exposition on human fallibility. Montaigne's last essays reflect his acceptance of life as good and his conviction that man must discover his own nature in order to live with others in peace and dignity. The style of his essays is usually formal and familiar, full of concrete images and lively or humorous digressions. Montaigne's works have been widely read abroad and have greatly influenced English literature. The old standard translation of his *Essais* was that of John Florio (1603); other translations include those of Jacob Zeitlin (1934–36) and Donald Frame (1957). See his *Autobiography* (tr. by M. Lowenthal, 1956); biography by Donald Frame (1965); studies by André Gide (tr. 1933, repr. 1939), P. P. Hallie (1967), and Donald Frame (1940, 1955, and 1969).

Montale, Eugenio (āo͞ojĕ'nyō mōntä'lā), 1896–, Italian poet and critic. After working as an editor Montale became chief librarian of the Gabinetto Vieusseux in Florence. His complex poetry expresses external and internal experience. The collection *Poesie* (1958, tr. 1964) includes *Ossi di seppia* (1925), *Le occasioni* (1940), and *La bufera e altro* (1957). Montale's other works include *The Butterfly of Dinard* (1960, tr. 1970) and the volume of essays *La poesia non esiste* (1971). See his *Selected Poems*, ed. by George Kay (tr. 1969), and *Xenia Poems* (tr. 1970); studies by Glauco Cambon (1972) and G. S. Singh (1973).

Montalembert, Charles Forbes, comte de (shärl fôrbz kôNt də môNtäläNbĕr'), 1810–70, French political leader and writer, b. London. He went to Paris (1830), where he became associated with Jean LACORDAIRE and Félicité de LAMENNAIS in the Catholic liberal movement and served as editor of the *Avenir* until 1831; the journal was condemned in 1832 by the pope. He hoped to weld French Catholicism into a united political force, and in the legislature he associated Roman Catholicism with liberalism and worked for civil liberty and for education under churchly auspices. An enthusiastic republican, he was the chief figure in the early liberal opposition to Emperor Napoleon III. For a time he opposed the dogma of papal infallibility. His chief work is *Les Moines de l'occident* (7 vol., 1860–77; tr. *Monks of the West*, 7 vol., 1861–79). See J. C. Finlay, *The Liberal Who Failed* (1968).

Montalván, Juan Pérez de: see PÉREZ DE MONTALVÁN, JUAN.

Montalvo, Juan (hwän mōntäl'vō), 1832–89, Ecuadorean essayist and political writer. A champion of liberalism and a master of political invective, he showered fiery anathemas on the tyrant Gabriel García Moreno and later on the dictator Ignacio Veintimilla. Montalvo's first polemics appeared in his own journal, *El cosmopolita* (1866–69). Exiled in 1879, he went to France. The publication of his *Catilinarias* in 1880 made him famous. Endowed with a lucid and inquisitive intellect and a strong, quasi-romantic temperament, Montalvo turned his vivid style to a variety of historical, philosophical, and cultural themes. The essays in *Siete Tratados* (1882) and in *Geometría moral* (1902) are often speculative and introspective. Montalvo also wrote a witty sequel to *Don Quixote*, entitled *Capítulos que se le olvidaron a Cervantes* [chapters Cervantes forgot] (1921). Montalvo was a dedicated champion of democracy. Many consider him unrivaled as a stylist in 19th-century Spanish letters.

Montana (mŏntăn'ə), state (1970 pop. 694,409), 147,138 sq mi (381,087 sq km), NW United States, in the Rocky Mt. region, admitted as the 41st state of the Union in 1889. HELENA is the capital, BILLINGS and GREAT FALLS are the largest cities; other places of importance include MISSOULA and BUTTE. The state lies on the northwest border of the United States, south of the Canadian provinces of British Columbia, Alberta, and Saskatchewan. It is bounded by North Dakota and South Dakota on the east, by Wyoming and Idaho on the south, and by Idaho on the west. Montana is thinly populated and has many remote areas. Life in the state's western mountain area differs greatly from that on its eastern plains. In the eastern half of the state are broad plains, drained by the Missouri River, which originates in SW Montana, and by its tributaries, the Milk, the Marias, the Sun, and especially the Yellowstone. Much of Montana's western boundary is marked by the crest of the lofty Bitterroot Range, part of the Rocky Mts., which dominate the western section of the state and through which runs the CONTINENTAL DIVIDE. Montana's very name is derived from the Spanish word *montaña*, meaning mountain country. High granite peaks, green forests, blue lakes, and such natural wonders as those of Glacier National Park have helped make tourism a growing industry and a major source of income. The mountains, moreover, offer more than massive beauty, for in and around the mountainous western region are the large mineral deposits for which Montana is famous—copper, silver, gold, zinc, lead, and manganese. The eastern part of the state is noted for its petroleum and natural gas, and there are also vast coal deposits. In addition, Montana also mines vermiculite, chromite, fluorspar, tungsten, uranium, and phosphate rock. In 1972 the most valuable minerals produced were petroleum, copper, sand and gravel, and gold and silver. Leading industries manufacture forest products, processed food, refined petroleum, and coal products. In E Montana the high grass of the Great Plains once nourished herds of buffalo and later sustained the cattle and sheep of huge ranches; now much of the high grass is gone, but the cattle and sheep remain, grazing mainly on short grass. Despite the dangers of drought and the severe years that drove many farmers out of the state, turning farming communities into ghost towns, agriculture today, with the aid of irrigation, provides a major share of Montana's income. Cattle are the most valuable farm item, and dairy products are also important. The principal crops raised are wheat, hay, barley, and sugar beets. Important today for hydroelectric development and for irrigation, Montana's rivers were once avenues of travel for the Indians known to have inhabited the region at the time white men first explored it. These Indians included the Blackfoot, the Sioux, the Shoshone, the Arapaho, the Kootenai, the Cheyenne, the Flathead, and others. Early explorers of the country also traveled along the rivers. The first white men to cross the northern plains were French traders from Canada (possibly the brothers François and Louis Joseph Vérendrye were the earliest in 1742), but the region was not really known to white men until after most of Montana had passed to the United States under the LOUISIANA PURCHASE (1803). The LEWIS AND CLARK EXPEDITION traveled westward across Montana in 1805, and François Antoine Laroque, along with his North West Fur Company of Canada, explored the Yellowstone River after 1805. The first trading post in Montana was established at the mouth of the Bighorn in 1807 by a trading expedition under Manuel Lisa that came up the Missouri from St. Louis. For some years both Canadian and American fur traders continued to open the territory. David Thompson of the North West Company built several trading posts in NW Montana between 1807 and 1812, and beaver in the mountain streams and lakes attracted adventurous trappers, the so-called MOUNTAIN MEN. The American Fur Company, with its posts on the Missouri and the Yellowstone, dominated the later years of the region's fur trade, which diminished in the 1840s. The U.S. claim to present-day NW Montana, the area between the Rockies and the N Idaho border, was legalized in the Oregon Treaty of 1846 with the British. Montana was then still a wilderness of forest and grass, with a few trading posts and some missions established by such stalwart men as Father P. J. De Smet. Settlers were then swarming to the Oregon country and later to the California gold fields, but Montana saw few of these transients. Nevertheless, Fort Benton, at the head of navigation on the Missouri, rose to prominence, and between 1859 and 1863 Capt. John Mullan built a wagon road from Fort Benton across the Rockies to Walla Walla, Wash. However, Indians blocked the travel of white men across the land. Montana's first period of growth was the rapid, boisterous, and unstable expansion brought on by a gold rush. The discovery of gold, made initially in 1852, brought many people to mushrooming mining camps such as those at Bannack (1862) and Virginia City (1864). Crude shanty towns were built, complete with saloons and dance halls—ephemeral settlements as colorful as the earlier gold-rush camps in California and perhaps even more lawless. Previously part of, successively, the territories of Oregon, Washington, Nebraska, Dakota, and Idaho, Montana itself became a territory in 1864. The territory was still a rough frontier, however, and the first governor, Sidney Edgerton, was driven out of the region, and later Thomas Francis Meagher, appointed temporary governor, died mysteriously. After the Civil War the grasslands attracted ranchers, and the first cattle were brought in from Texas in 1866 over the Bozeman Trail, to the area east of the Bighorn Mts. Yet it was not until after wars with the Sioux Indians that ranching was safe. The Sioux did not tamely submit to having their lands taken from them, and in 1876 at the battle of the Little Bighorn they won against Gen. George A. Custer and his force one of the greatest of all Indian victories. The Sioux were, however, subdued, and the gallant attempt of Chief Joseph of the Nez Percé Indians to lead his people into Canada to escape pursuing U.S. troops had its pitiful end in Montana. Great ranches spread out across the plains, and cow towns that were to grow into cities such as Billings and Missoula sprang up as the railroads were built in the West (c.1880–c.1910). Achievement of statehood in 1889 and the building of the railroads put an end to the era of the open range. Mining continued to dominate Montana. The discovery of silver at Butte (1875) had been followed (c.1880) by discovery of copper at that same "richest hill on earth." Montana's fate was subsequently linked to copper, and the Amalgamated Copper Company (later renamed Anaconda Copper Mining Company) came to play a major role in Montana life. The titans of the mines, Marcus Daly and William A. Clark, fought bitterly not only for ownership of the mineral deposits but for political control, and their rivalry was physically fought out by the miners. F. Augustus Heinze also entered the scramble for copper claims, challenging the claims of the Amalgamated Copper Company. Amalgamated ruled triumphant, however, exercising control over state affairs. There were struggles between the company and the workingmen that led to strikes, disorder, and bloodshed, but they led also to enactment of some early measures for social security. This was an important achievement because over the years the livelihood of the residents of the mining towns has been dependent on the market price of copper. Despite fluctuating metals prices, the mines have contributed a large percentage of the state's wealth. After the coming of the railroads James J. Hill and other railroad men brought out farmers by the trainload to develop the lands of E Montana. The farmers planted their fields in the second decade of the 20th cent. The initial yield of wheat was great, and the golden promises seemed fulfilled—but not for long. The calamitous drought of 1919 and the consequent dust storms seared the fields, and in the 1920s the farms began to disappear as rapidly as they had been established. When the great national depression began in 1929 Montana was already accustomed to depression. In subsequent years vigorous measures were taken to aid agriculture in the state and by the late 1940s Federal dam and irrigation projects—on the Missouri, the Yellowstone, the Marias, the Sun, and elsewhere—had opened many acres to cultivation. Some of the vast grazing lands were brought under planned use, and the development of hydroelectric power continues. Major multipurpose dams in Montana producing power include Fort Peck Dam, Hungry Horse Dam, and Canyon Ferry. In addition, there are many reclamation projects. The demand for copper in World War II and the E Montana oil boom of the early 1950s stimulated Montana's economy. On the debit side, Montana must still cope with high transportation costs, lack of manpower, and the necessary regulation of resources. Nevertheless, there has been a beneficial if slow trend toward a more diversified economy, with manufacturing growing in importance in relation to farming and mining. The latter sector of the economy has declined in importance, while tourism has been growing. Development of vast recreational facilities along the Gallatin River stirred protests from conservationists in the early 1970s. Much of Montana is still untamed country where the forces of nature are dominant—Earthquake Lake was formed in 1959 when the top of a mountain tumbled into the Madison River. Places of interest, besides Glacier National Park, include Custer Battlefield National Monument, Big Hole National Battlefield, and Grant-Kohrs Ranch National Historic Site (see NATIONAL PARKS AND MONUMENTS, table) and the National Bison Range, near Ravalli, where herds of buffalo may still be seen. Strips of Yellowstone National Park, including the north and west entrances, are also in Montana, as are such Indian reservations as the Blackfoot, the Fort Belknap, the Fort Peck, and the Crow. The many kinds of fish found in the rushing mountain streams and innumerable lakes bring fishermen to the state, and the abundant wildlife—elk, deer, bear, moose, and waterfowl—attract hunters. The state's outstanding recreational areas also include facilities for skiing, hiking, boating, and swimming. In 1973, Montana implemented a new constitution, which replaced the one adopted in 1889. The governor of the state is elected for a term of four years and may be reelected. The Legislative Assembly is made up of a senate with 50 members and a house of representatives with 100 members. State senators are elected for terms of four years and representatives for terms of two years. Montana is represented in the U.S. Congress by two Representatives and two Senators, and the state has four electoral votes in presidential campaigns. Thomas L. Judge, a Democrat, became governor of the state in 1973. The state's major institutions of higher learning are included in the Univ. of Montana and Montana State Univ. systems. See N. C. Abbott, *Montana in the Making* (rev. ed. 1951); J. M. Hamilton, *From Wilderness to Statehood: A History of Montana (1805–1900)* (1957); R. R. Renne, *The Government and Administration of Montana* (1958); J. K. Howard, *Montana, High, Wide, and Handsome* (rev. ed. 1959); J. H. Bradley, *The March of the Montana Column: A Prelude to the Custer Disaster* (ed. by E. I. Stewart, 1961); Federal Writers' Project, *Montana* (1939, rev. ed. 1962); M. P. Malone, *The Montana Past* (1969); M. S. Mockle, *Montana, An Illustrated History* (1969); K. R. Toole, *Montana, an Uncommon Land* (1959), and *Twentieth-century Montana* (1972).

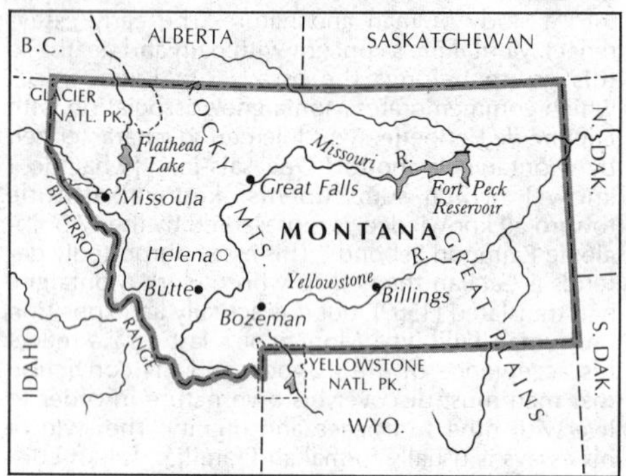

Montana, University of, at Missoula; state supported; coeducational; chartered 1893 as the University of Montana. In 1913 when the Montana University System was established, the school's name was changed to State University of Montana, and in 1935 the name Montana State University was adopted. The name was changed back to its original form in 1965. The school has a noted forestry program. The university system also includes a school of mines at Butte, three teachers colleges, and Montana State Univ.

Montana State University, at Bozeman; land-grant; coeducational; chartered 1893. It is primarily a technical institution specializing in agriculture and engineering.

Montañes, Juan Martínez (hwän märtē'nĕth mōntä'nyās), c.1568–1649, Spanish sculptor. He was known for his polychrome figures in wood. Most of his work was done for the churches and convents of Seville, where it still remains. Among his finest works are his highly spiritual and dignified interpretations of the Crucifixion and of the Immaculate Conception (cathedral, Seville). His work influenced the art of Velázquez and of Zurbarán.

Montanism (mŏn'tənĭzəm), enthusiastic Christian schism of the 2d cent. It arose in Phrygia (c.172) under the leadership of a certain Montanus and two prophets, whose entranced utterances were deemed oracles of the Holy Ghost. They had an immediate expectation of Judgment Day, and they encouraged ecstatic prophesying and strict asceticism. They believed that a Christian fallen from grace could never be redeemed, in opposition to the Catholic view that, since the sinner's contrition restored him to grace, the church must receive him again. Montanism antagonized the church because the sect claimed a superior authority arising from divine inspiration. Catholics were told that they should flee persecution, Montanists were told to seek it. When the Montanists began to set up a hierarchy of their own, the Catholic leaders, fearing to lose the cohesion essential to the survivial of persecuted Christianity, denounced the movement. Even the great TERTULLIAN could not save Montanism, and it died (c.220) as a sect, except in isolated areas of Phrygia, where it continued to the 7th cent. But the puristic anti-intellectual movement had many descendants—NOVATIAN, the Donatists (see DONATISM), the CATHARI, and even Emanuel SWEDENBORG and Edward IRVING.

Montargis (môNtärzhē'), town (1968 pop. 19,891), Loiret dept., N central France, in Orléanais, near the Montargis Forest. Its manufactures include raincoats, machinery, electrical equipment, shoes, and furniture. Ceded (1188) by the house of Courtenay to the crown, it was (14th and 15th cent.) a royal residence. The town retains a medieval aspect. The younger Mirabeau was born at the nearby castle of Bignon. For the story of the Dog of Montargis, see AUBRY DE MONTDIDIER.

Montauban (môNtōbäN'), city (1968 pop. 48,555), capital of Tarn-et-Garonne dept., S France, on the Tarn River. It is a commercial and industrial center where aeronautic and electrical equipment, food products, textiles, shoes, and tiles are produced. Founded in 1144, Montauban was a stronghold of the ALBIGENSES in the 13th cent. and of the HUGUENOTS in the 16th cent. It enjoyed prosperity until the time of Louis XIV's religious persecutions (17th cent.). Points of interest include a 14th-century brick bridge over the Tarn and a cathedral (17th–18th cent.), which contains a celebrated painting by Jean Ingres, who was born in Montauban. The city has several army instruction centers.

Montauk Point (mŏn'tôk"), eastern extremity of the south peninsula of Long Island, SE N.Y. Approximately 115 mi (190 km) E of Manhattan, it is the easternmost point of the state. It has been the site of a lighthouse since 1795. The area is included in Montauk Point State Park.

Montbéliard (môNbālyär'), industrial town (1968 pop. 25,240), Doubs dept., E France, on the Rhône-Rhine Canal. Among its manufactures are clocks, textiles, and wood and metal products. With its surrounding countryside it constituted a county (after the 12th cent.) of the Holy Roman Empire. The county passed (1397) to the counts (later dukes) of Württemberg, who held it, with interruptions, until its capture by French Revolutionary troops in 1793. The town was a Huguenot refuge during the Reformation. It was formally ceded to France by the Treaty of Lunéville (1801). The castle of the Montbéliard counts was rebuilt in the 18th cent.

Mont Blanc (môN bläN), Alpine massif, on the French-Italian border, SE of Geneva. One of its several peaks, also called Mont Blanc (15,771 ft/4,807 m), is the highest peak in France and the second highest in Europe. The southeastern (Italian) face is a massive wall; on the northwestern slopes are numerous glaciers, the largest of which (the Mer de Glace) flows into the valley of Chamonix, a famous French resort region and starting point for mountain climbers. There are many hotels and hostels along the base of Mont Blanc. The first successful ascent of Mont Blanc was made in 1786. In 1965 a highway tunnel (7 mi/11.3 km long) under Mont Blanc, linking Chamonix with Courmayeur, Italy, was opened to traffic. It provides a short, year-round route between Paris and Rome.

Montcalm, Louis Joseph de (mŏntkäm', Fr. lwē zhôzĕf' də môNkälm'), 1712–59, French general. His name in fuller form was Louis Joseph de Montcalm-Gozon, marquis de Saint-Véran. A veteran of the War of the Polish Succession and the War of the Austrian Succession, he was sent (1756) to defend Canada in the French and Indian War. His position was subordinate to that of the marquis de Vaudreuil de Cavagnal, governor of New France, and protests to the home authorities against the dishonesty of the provincial administration and the evil consequences of divided command were without avail. Montcalm's capture of Fort Ontario at Oswego (1756) restored control of Lake Ontario to France, and he besieged and captured (1757) Fort William Henry on Lake George. This victory was marred by the massacre of English prisoners by his Indian allies, although Montcalm finally restored order at the risk of his life. In 1758 he concentrated a force of 3,800 at Ticonderoga and successfully withstood an attack by a large British force under Gen. James Abercromby. In 1759, still handicapped by Vaudreuil's interference, Montcalm successfully defended Quebec against the siege of Gen. James WOLFE until the strategy of the English effected an open engagement (see ABRAHAM, PLAINS OF). The British were victorious (Sept. 13, 1759), but both Wolfe and Montcalm were killed. A classic account is that of Francis Parkman, *Montcalm and Wolfe* (1884, repr. 1965). See bibliography under FRENCH AND INDIAN WARS. See also biography by M. L. Lewis (1961); William Wood, *The Passing of New France* (1914).

Montclair. 1 Residential city (1970 pop. 22,546), San Bernardino co., SE Calif., in a citrus fruit area; inc. 1956. It has some light manufacturing. **2** Town (1970 pop. 44,043), Essex co., NE N.J., a suburb of Newark and New York City, on a slope of the Watchung Mts.; settled c.1666 as part of Newark, set off from Newark 1812, set off from Bloomfield and inc. 1868. Although chiefly residential, it has plants that make chemicals, paint, and metalware. The art museum contains several paintings by George Inness, who lived there. Montclair State College is in Upper Montclair.

Mont-de-Marsan (môN-də-märsäN'), town (1968 pop. 27,749), capital of Landes dept., SW France. It is a commercial center where important fairs are held. The town's products include lumber, goose-liver pâté, and machinery.

Monte Albán (mōn'tā älbän'), ancient city, c.7 mi (11.3 km) from Oaxaca, SW Mexico, capital of the ZAPOTEC. Monte Albán was built on an artificially leveled, rocky promontory above the Valley of Oaxaca. Located around an enormous plaza about 1,000 ft (300 m) long and 650 ft (198 m) wide are long, low buildings set off by sunken courts and stairways. The tombs, particularly Tomb 7, have yielded great archaeological treasure—jewelry of gold, copper, jade, rock crystal, obsidian, and turquoise mosaic and bone and wood carving showing elaborate religious symbolism. Excavation was begun (1931) by the Mexican archaeologist Alfonso CASO. The Zapotec apparently had an advanced culture here c.200 B.C. and already were using the bar and dot system of numerals used by the Maya. The final epoch (c.1300–1521), terminated by the Spanish Conquest, covers the ascendancy of the MIXTEC, when the Zapotec were driven from Monte Albán and MITLA. Tomb 7 belongs to the final period. Cultural links with the OLMEC and the TOLTEC have been found.

Montebello (mŏntĭbĕl'ō), village, SW Que., Canada, on the Ottawa River NE of Ottawa. It is a summer resort in a lumbering and farming area. The political leader Louis Joseph Papineau made his home there after 1854.

Montebello, city (1970 pop. 42,807), Los Angeles co., S Calif., a residential and industrial suburb of Los Angeles; inc. 1920.

Monte Carlo (môNtā' kärlō'), town (1968 pop. 9,948), principality of MONACO, on the Mediterranean Sea and the French RIVIERA. It is a tourist center noted for its world-famous gambling casino (built 1858) and for its scenery, fine villas, and luxurious hotels. In 1954 the concession came under the control of the Greek shipping magnate Aristotle Onassis but has since been returned to the Monaco government. Among the sporting events of the town are the famous Monte Carlo car rally and the Monaco Grand Prix.

Monte Cassino (môn'tā käs-sē'nō), monastery, in Latium, central Italy, E of the Rapido River. Situated on a hill (1,674 ft/510 m) overlooking Cassino, it was founded c.529 by St. BENEDICT of Nursia, whose rule became that of all Benedictine houses in the world. Monte Cassino was throughout the centuries one of the great centers of Christian learning and piety; its influence on European civilization is immeasurable (see BENEDICTINES). Its greatest abbot after St. Benedict was Desiderius (later Pope Victor III) in the 11th cent. The buildings of the abbey were destroyed four times: by the Lombards (c.581); by the Arabs (883); by an earthquake (1349); and, after their restoration in the 17th cent., by a concentrated Allied aerial bombardment in 1944 (see CASSINO). The German garrison, who had used the abbey as a fortress, survived the bombing in previously dug caves, but the buildings were flattened and most of their art treasures destroyed. A considerable part of the library's collection of invaluable manuscripts was saved by the monks. The monastery was rebuilt again after World War II. The tomb of St. Benedict (built before the Lombard invasion) and the tower are the only original parts of the abbey.

Monte Cristo (mŏn"tē krĭs'tō, Ital. môn'tā krē'stō), unpopulated, rocky island, 6 sq mi (15.5 sq km), belonging to Italy, in the Tyrrhenian Sea between Corsica and the Italian coast. It owes its fame to the novel by Alexandre Dumas père, *The Count of Monte Cristo.*

Montecucculi or **Montecuccoli, Raimondo, conte di** (rīmōn'dō kōn'tā dē mōn"tākŏŏk'kŏŏlē, -kōlē), 1609–80, Italian military commander in the service of the Holy Roman Empire. He distinguished himself in the Thirty Years War and was later sent to Hungary to take the field against the Turks. His victory (1664) at Szentgotthárd was the first serious blow to Turkish power in Hungary. In the Dutch War of 1672–78, Montecucculi commanded imperial forces with mixed success against the French generals Turenne and Condé. He was made (1679) a prince of the Holy Roman Empire and duke of Melfi. After retirement he wrote on military subjects.

Montefeltro (mōntāfĕl'trō), Italian noble family. Its members were noted patrons of art and traditionally opposed the papacy in the struggle between GUELPHS AND GHIBELLINES. The county of Montefeltro (created c.1154) included parts of Romagna, the Marches, and San Marino. Oddantonio Montefeltro (d. 1444) was the first Montefeltro duke of Urbino. His successor, **Federico da Montefeltro,** 1422–82, was prominent in Italian politics and gathered an outstanding art collection. His portrait (Uffizi Gall.) was painted by Piero della Francesca. Federico's son, **Guidobaldo da Montefeltro,** 1472–1508, lost and regained (1502–3) the duchy from Cesare Borgia. Guidobaldo's court was a center of Renaissance culture, and he provided the model for *The Courtier* of Baldassare CASTIGLIONE.

Montefiore, Sir Moses Haim (mŏn"tĭfēō'rē), 1784–1885, British-Jewish philanthropist, b. Italy. He married a Rothschild and became affiliated with the family's banking business. He accumulated a fortune on the London stock exchange and retired (1826) from business to devote himself to philanthropy and to the securing of political and civil emancipation for Jews in England. He was knighted (1837) while serving as sheriff of London. In 1846, he was made a baronet. As president (1835–74) of the Board of Deputies of British Jews he worked to alleviate discriminatory practices against Jews in Europe and the Middle East. He founded a hospital and girls' school in Jerusalem in 1855 and was influential in stimulating the rise of Jewish nationalism, the forerunner of modern political Zionism. The *Diaries of Sir Moses and Lady Montefiore* appeared in 1890. See biographies by Lucien Wolf (1884), Eugen Wolbe (1909), and Paul Goodman (1925).

Montego Bay (mŏntē'gō), city (1970 est. pop. 43,000), NW Jamaica. A port, railroad terminus, and commercial center, it is also one of the most popular resorts in the Caribbean. There is an active trade in sugar, bananas, coffee, and rum. The city has various light manufacturing industries.

Montejo, Francisco de (fränthēs'kō dā mōntā'hō), c.1479–c.1548, Spanish conquistador. Coming to the New World with Pedro Arias de Ávila, he served in Cuba under Diego Velásquez. He later commanded a vessel in the expedition of Juan de Grijalva before joining Hernán Cortés in the conquest of Mexico.

Montejo was commissioned to conquer the Maya of Yucatán, but failed in his attempt (1527–28) to take the peninsula from the east. He proceeded to Mexico, subdued (1530) Tabasco, and then conducted (1531–35) a campaign from the west. At first partially successful, he encountered increasingly fierce Maya resistance, and his men, exhausted and finding no booty, deserted. Forced to withdraw from the peninsula, he retired again to Mexico, a disillusioned and impoverished man. In 1540 he entrusted the conquest to his son, Francisco de Montejo, who by 1542 effectively subdued the western part of the peninsula, founding Campeche, Mérida, and other settlements. After a general Indian uprising had been quelled, he finally conquered the eastern portion in 1546.

Monteleone di Calabria: see VIBO VALENTIA, Italy.

Montemezzi, Italo (ē'tälo mōntämĕt'tsē), 1875–1952, Italian composer, studied at the Milan Conservatory. His *Giovanni Gallurese* (1905) had some success, but he is remembered for the opera *L'amore dei tre re* [the love of the three kings] (1913). *La Nave* (1918) is based on a play by D'Annunzio. *L'incantesimo* (1943) was written and broadcast in the United States.

Montenegro (mŏn"tənē'grō), Serbo-Croatian *Crna Gora*, constituent republic of Yugoslavia (1971 pop. 530,361), 5,332 sq mi (13,810 sq km), SW Yugoslavia. Its name means "black mountain." TITOGRAD is the capital. Other principal cities are CETINJE, NIKŠIĆ, and KOTOR (the main port). Situated at the southern end of the Dinaric Alps, Montenegro is almost entirely mountainous and is difficult of access. It consists of two regions: The barren karst of Montenegro proper, on the west, is separated by the Zeta River and its plain from the higher Brda region, on the east, which has forests and pastures. Sheep and goat raising are important occupations. Only about 6% of the area is cultivated, and agriculture, mainly in the Zeta valley and near Lake Scutari (which forms part of the Albanian border), is poorly developed. Although less developed than other regions of Yugoslavia, Montenegro has important mineral resources. The Montenegrin people are Serbs, but they are recognized as a separate ethnic nationality. They belong mostly to the Orthodox faith. From the 14th to the 19th cent. their principal activity was fighting the Turks, who never entirely conquered their mountain stronghold. The region constituting present Montenegro was in the 14th cent. the virtually independent principality of Zeta in the Serbian empire. After Serbia was defeated by the Turks in the battle of Kossovo (1389), Montenegro continued to resist and became a refuge for Serbian nobles who fled Turkish rule. The sultans did not recognize Montenegrin independence, but, although they thrice destroyed Cetinje, they never succeeded in making Montenegro tributary. However, the princes of Montenegro ruled only a small part of the present republic, the rest being governed by Turkey after 1499 and by Venice, which held Kotor. From 1515 until 1851 the rule of Montenegro was vested in the prince-bishops (*vladikas*) of Cetinje; these were assisted by civil governors. Social organization, geared almost exclusively to the needs of war, was largely military and patriarchal. With DANILO I, who ruled from 1696 to 1735, the episcopal succession was made hereditary in the Niegosh family, the office passing ordinarily from uncle to nephew, because the bishops could not marry. Danilo I also inaugurated (1715) the traditional alliance of Montenegro with Russia; the emperors of Russia were henceforth considered as at least the spiritual suzerains of the *vladikas*. Peter I, who reigned from 1782 to 1830, defied both France and Austria when the Treaty of Campo Formio (1797) transferred the Venetian possession of Kotor to Austria, but he failed to obtain the coveted port. However, in 1799, Sultan Selim III recognized the independence of Montenegro. Peter I instituted internal reforms and sought to end the blood feuds and lawlessness that had become a traditional way of life. He was canonized as a saint after his death. Peter II (reigned 1830–51), a gifted poet, continued his predecessor's work of reform and fostered a revival of learning and culture; aside from occasional border warfare, he lived in relative peace with his neighbors, Turkey and Austria. DANILO II, who succeeded him, secularized his principality in 1852 and transferred his ecclesiastic functions to an archbishop. Under NICHOLAS I (reigned 1860–1918) Montenegro was formally recognized as an independent state at the Congress of Berlin (1878), which increased its territory and gave it a narrow outlet on the Adriatic. In 1910, Nicholas proclaimed himself king. He fought Turkey in the BALKAN WARS and took Shkodër in 1913, but was forced by the pressure of the European powers to evacuate the city. Montenegro did, however, receive part of the territory claimed by newly independent Albania, and when World War I broke out (1914), the Montenegrins invaded Albania. Montenegro declared war on Austria in Aug., 1914, but late in 1915 it was overrun by Austro-German forces. In Nov., 1918, a national assembly declared Nicholas deposed and effected the union of Montenegro with Serbia. In 1946, Montenegro became one of the six republics of Yugoslavia, and its territory was enlarged with the addition of part of the Dalmatian coast.

Monterey (mŏntərā'), city (1970 pop. 26,302), Monterey co., W Calif., a port on Monterey Bay; founded 1770, inc. 1850. It is a popular resort and the home of many artists and writers. One of the oldest cities in California, it is rich in historic tradition. The bay was discovered by Juan Cabrillo in 1542 and entered and named by Sebastián Vizcaíno in 1602. In 1770 an expedition under Gaspar de Portolá arrived and established a presidio. Junípero Serra remained to found a Franciscan mission (which a year later was moved near what is now Carmel). Monterey was the capital of Alta California during many of the years between 1775 and 1846. In 1846 the city was taken by a U.S. naval force under Commodore John D. Sloat, and in 1849 the state constitutional convention met there. Monterey became a whaling and fishing center. California's first theater (1844) and first brick building (1847) are still standing, and it was in Monterey that California's first newspaper was established in 1846. The many old structures include the customs house (1827) and the jail (1854). There are numerous museums. The Presidio of Monterey (1770) is the home of a branch of the U.S. army language school. Nearby Fort Ord is an important infantry training and replacement center.

Monterey Park, city (1970 pop. 49,166), Los Angeles co., S Calif., a residential suburb of Los Angeles; inc. 1916. There are two industrial parks in the city.

Montero Ríos, Eugenio (āōōhā'nyō mōntā'rō rē'ōs), 1832–1914, Spanish statesman and jurist. He was professor of canon law at the universities of Oviedo, Santiago, and Madrid. He entered the Cortes (1869), was several times in the cabinet, and helped effect several reforms. Montero Ríos was active in securing the accession of AMADEUS and was one of his most faithful supporters. A liberal, he was chief delegate to the Paris conference that concluded the Spanish-American War (1898) and was premier in 1905.

Monterrey (mōntārā'), city (1970 pop. 830,336), capital of Nuevo León state, NE Mexico, the third largest city of Mexico. Located c.150 mi (240 km) S of Laredo, Texas, in a valley surrounded by mountains, Monterrey is the rail and highway hub of NE Mexico. It is also Mexico's second most important industrial center and the site of the nation's largest iron and steel foundries. Monterrey's numerous industries also include breweries, glass factories, metalworks, paper plants, cotton and flour mills, and factories manufacturing construction materials, electrical equipment, furniture, and textiles. Mexico's chief lead smelting center, Monterrey also produces silver, gold, copper, antimony, and bismuth. Natural gas piped in from Texas has spurred Monterrey's industrialization; coal and petroleum come from the neighboring states of Coahuila and Tamaulipas. Its moderate, dry climate, cool mountains, and hot springs make Monterrey a popular resort. The city was founded in 1579. During the Mexican War, it was captured by Zachary Taylor after a courageous defense (Sept. 19–24, 1846) by the besieged Mexicans. Monterrey is the home of a national university and a technological institute. The Obispado chapel and its cathedral (18th cent.) are good examples of colonial architecture. The city's wealthier suburbs have houses built of stucco in a style derived from Spanish colonial and called Monterrey.

Montes, Ismael (ēsmäēl' mōn'tās), 1861–1933, Bolivian statesman, president of Bolivia (1904–9, 1913–17). He interrupted the study of law in 1879 to fight against Chile in the War of the Pacific. After 1886 he practiced law and journalism, but in the liberal revolution of 1898 he again took up a military career, becoming minister of war in 1900 and serving in the Acre campaign against Brazil. He was chosen president in 1904, and in that year a peace treaty with Chile, officially ending the War of the Pacific, was signed. Montes then launched a program of wide administrative reforms. After diplomatic service in France and England he was elected (1913) for a second term and furthered the construction of railroads and the development of mining. From 1920 to 1928 he lived in France as a political exile.

Montes Claros (môN'təsh klä'rōōsh), city (1970 pop. 116,464), Minas Gerais state, E central Brazil. Cattle breeding is the chief economic activity, and agriculture is important. Montes Claros also has a large cloth industry dating from before World War I. The city has a commercial airport and good road and rail facilities.

Montespan, Françoise Athénaïs, marquise de (fräNswäz' ätänäēs' märkēz' də môNtəspäN'), 1641–1707, mistress of King Louis XIV of France. She was maid of honor to Queen Marie Thérèse and replaced (c.1667) Mlle de LA VALLIÈRE as the king's mistress. She bore the king several children. Their education was entrusted to Mme de MAINTENON, who succeeded her in the king's favor. She later retired to a convent. See H. N. Williams, *Madame de Montespan* (1903); Frances Mossiker, *The Affair of the Poisons* (1970).

Montesquieu, Charles Louis de Secondat, baron de la Brède et de (shärl lwē də səkôNdä' bärôN' də lä brĕd ā də môNtĕskyü'), 1689–1755, French jurist and political philosopher. He was councillor (1714) of the parlement of Bordeaux and its president (1716–28) after the death of an uncle, whom he succeeded in both title and office. He gained a seat in the French Academy in 1728. His *Persian Letters* (1721) brought him immediate fame. In these letters, supposedly written by Persian travelers in Europe and by their friends, he satirized and criticized French insititutions. In 1734 he produced a scientific historical study of the rise and fall of Rome, *Considérations sur les causes de la grandeur des Romains et de leur décadence*. His greatest work, *The Spirit of Laws* (1748), is a comparative study of three types of government—republic, monarchy, and despotism and shows John Locke's influence on Montesquieu. Its main theories are that climate and circumstances determine the form of governments and that the powers of government should be separated and balanced in order to guarantee the freedom of the individual. Written with brilliance of style, it had great historical importance and influenced the formation of the American Constitution. See biography by Robert Shackleton (1961); study by J. R. Loy (1968).

Montessori, Maria (märē'ä mōntās-sô'rē), 1870–1952, Italian educator and physician. She was the originator of the Montessori method of education for the preschool child and was the first woman to receive (1894) a medical degree in Italy. After working with subnormal children as a psychiatrist at the Univ. of Rome, she was appointed (1898) director of the Orthophrenic School. There she pioneered in the instruction of retarded children, especially through the use of an environment rich in manipulative materials. In 1901 she left the school to embark on further study and to serve (1901–7) as lecturer in pedagogical anthropology at the Univ. of Rome. The success of her program at the Orthophrenic School, however, led her to believe that similar improvements could be made in the education of normal preschool children, and in 1907 she opened the first *case dei bambini* [children's house] as a day-care center in the San Lorenzo district of Rome. The success of this venture led Montessori and her followers to establish similar institutions in other parts of Europe and in the United States, where the first Montessori school was established (1912) in Tarrytown, N.Y. In 1929 the Association Montessori Internationale was established to further the Montessori method by sponsoring conventions and training courses for teachers. By this time, however, interest in Montessori education had declined in a number of countries, especially the United States, mainly because of opposition from those who felt that the method was destructive of school discipline. The Montessori method experienced a renaissance in many American schools during the late 1950s, and in 1960 the American Montessori Society was formed. The chief components of the Montessori method are self-motivation and autoeducation. Followers of the Montessori method believe that a child will learn naturally if put in an environment containing the proper materials. These materials, consisting of "learning games" suited to a child's abilities and interests, are set up by a teacher-observer who only intervenes when individual help is needed. In this way, Montessori educators try to reverse the traditional system of an active teacher instructing a passive class. The typical classroom in a Montessori school consists of readily available games and toys, household utensils, plants and animals that are cared for by the children, and child-sized furniture—the invention of which is generally attributed to Dr. Montessori. Montessori educators also stress physical exercise, in accordance with their belief that motor abilities should be developed along with sensory and intellectual capacities. The major outlines of the Montessori system are based on Dr. Montessori's writings, which include *The Montessori Method* (1912), *Pedagogical Anthropology* (1913), *The Advanced Montessori Method* (2 vol., 1917), and *The Secret of Childhood* (1936). See W. H. Kilpatrick, *The Montessori System Examined* (1914, repr. 1971); E. Mortimer Standing, *Maria Montessori* (1958, repr. 1962) and *The Montessori Revolution* (1966).

Monteux, Pierre (pyĕr môNtö'), 1875-1964, French-American conductor, studied at the Paris Conservatory. As conductor (1911-14) of Diaghilev's Ballet Russe, he directed the premieres of ballets by Stravinsky, Ravel, and Debussy. He came to the United States in 1916 to conduct the Ballet Russe on its American tour, and he remained for two seasons at the Metropolitan Opera, New York City, and with the Boston Symphony Orchestra from 1919 to 1924. For the next 10 years he appeared as guest conductor of the Amsterdam Concertgebouw Orchestra. He became conductor of the Paris Symphony Orchestra in 1930 and of the San Francisco Symphony Orchestra in 1936. In 1942 he became a U.S. citizen. From 1960 until his death Monteux led the London Symphony Orchestra. He was known for the purity and self-restraint of his interpretations.

Monteverdi, Claudio (klou'dyō mōntāvĕr'dē), 1567-1643, Italian composer; first great figure in the history of opera. His earliest published works, three sets of madrigals, appeared when he was only 15. In 1590 he entered the service of the duke of Mantua, becoming choir master in the ducal court in 1602. Monteverdi's first opera, *Orfeo*, performed at Mantua in 1607, was revolutionary in its combination of dramatic power and expressive orchestral accompaniment. Of his next opera, *Arianna* (1608), only the celebrated lament, which Monteverdi himself arranged as a five-part madrigal, is extant. In 1613, Monteverdi was appointed choirmaster of St. Mark's, Venice, where he remained until his death. He took holy orders in 1632. Although he wrote mostly church music after settling in Venice, he continued to develop his dramatic gifts in many secular madrigals and dramatic cantatas such as *Il combattimento di Tancredi e di Clorinda* (1624). After the first public opera house opened in Venice in 1637, the aged Monteverdi produced his last operas, including *Il ritorno di Ulisse in Patria* (1641) and *L'incoronazione di Poppea* (1642), which show marked development in characterization and emotional power. They set the style of later Venetian opera. Of his 21 dramatic works, only six, including three operas, are extant. He was among the first composers to use the tremolo and pizzicato effects with strings, and his music shows a strong sense of modern tonality. In his operas he used large orchestras, whose members he grouped into specific combinations to portray characters on stage. See studies by D. Arnold (1963 and 1968) and L. Schrade (1950, repr. 1969). His brother **Giulio Cesare Monteverdi** (1573-?), was a composer, organist, and critic, and Claudio's assistant at the court of Mantua.

Montevideo (mŏntāvēthā'ō), city (1967 est. pop. 1,280,000), S Uruguay, capital and largest city of Uruguay, on the Río de La Plata. It is one of the major ports of South America and the governmental, financial, and commercial center of Uruguay. Much of the S Atlantic fishing fleet is based in Montevideo, and Uruguay's exports—frozen and canned meats and fish, wool, and grains—pass through the port. The city has industries producing textiles, dairy items, wines, and packaged meats. Tourism is also important. Montevideo's origins lay in the colonial rivalry of the Spanish and Portuguese. The Portuguese constructed (1717) a fort on top of the hill that overlooks the harbor. Captured by the Spanish in 1724, the fort became the nucleus of the settlement founded in 1724 by the governor of Buenos Aires. Montevideo became the capital of Uruguay in 1828. It suffered during Uruguay's 19th-century civil wars and was besieged from 1843 to 1851. Today Montevideo is spacious, modern, and attractive, with broad, tree-lined boulevards, numerous beautiful parks, and fine buildings and residences. Notable among the parks is the Prado, which, with its lovely botanical gardens containing many thousands of plant species, is a popular promenade; among the impressive buildings are the cabildo, the legislative palace, the government palace, and the cathedral. Montevideo is the seat of the Univ. of Uruguay. There are fine beaches and luxurious hotels along the Plata estuary east to Punta del Este on the Atlantic Ocean.

Montez, Lola, 1818?-1861, Irish adventuress, whose original name was Marie Dolores Eliza Rosanna Gilbert. Her early marriage to an army officer soon ended in divorce. She adopted the name Lola Montez, claimed Spanish descent, and became a dancer. Her dancing was mediocre, but her beauty, extravagant charm, and adventures (in particular her affairs with Franz Liszt and Dumas père) were legendary. She gained sensational success and by 1846 became the mistress of King LOUIS I of Bavaria, who made her countess of Lansfeld. Her intervention in politics aroused antagonism and helped provoke the Revolution of 1848, when she was banished. She returned (1849) to England and remarried. In 1851 she toured the United States and after the death of her husband married P. P. Hull, a San Francisco newspaperman. After an Australian tour (1855-56), she returned to the United States. She died in New York City. See biographies by Ishbel Ross (1972) and Amanda Darling (1972).

Montezuma (mŏntĕso͞o'mä) or **Moctezuma** (mŏk-), 1480?-1520, Aztec emperor (c.1502-1520). He is sometimes called Montezuma II to distinguish him from Montezuma I (ruled 1440-69), who carried on conquests around TENOCHTITLÁN. His reign was marked by incessant warfare, and his despotic rule caused grave unrest. When Hernán CORTÉS arrived in Mexico he was thus able to gain native allies, notably in the province of the Tlaxcala. Montezuma, believing the Spanish to be descendants of the god QUETZALCOATL, tried to persuade them to leave by offering rich gifts. That failing, he received them in his splendid court at Tenochtitlán in Nov., 1519. Cortès later seized him as a hostage and attempted to govern through him. In June, 1520, the Aztec rose against the Spanish. Montezuma was killed, although whether by the Spanish or the Aztec is not certain. His successor died a few months later and was replaced by CUAUHTÉMOC. Montezuma's name is linked by a legend to fabulous treasures that the Spanish appropriated and presumably lost at sea.

Montezuma Castle National Monument, 842 acres (341 hectares), central Ariz.; est. 1906. Montezuma Castle, built c.1250, is a 5-story, 20-room apartment house perched high in the cavity of a cliff. It was named by early settlers who believed it had been built by the Aztecs. In the region are well-preserved cliff dwellings of prehistoric Indians (see CLIFF DWELLERS).

Montferrat (mŏntfərăt', -răt'), Ital. *Monferrato,* historic region of Piedmont, NW Italy, south of the Po River, now mostly in Alessandria prov. It is largely hilly, and wine, fruit, and cereals are produced. In the late 10th cent. Montferrat was created a marquisate held by the Aleramo family, and its rulers played an important role in the Crusades. In 1310 it passed to the Paleologo family. Casale became the capital of the marquisate in 1435. With the extinction of the Paleologo line, Emperor Charles V gave (1536) Montferrat to the GONZAGA family of Mantua, despite the claims of the house of Savoy. After Francesco Gonzaga's death in 1612, Savoy renewed its claims on Montferrat and invaded (1613) the region. Spain and France intervened. The Treaty of Cherasco (1631) assigned parts of Montferrat to the house of SAVOY, and the rest (including Casale) followed the fortunes of the duchy of Mantua and passed to the Nevers (French) branch of the Gonzaga family. All of Montferrat was recognized by the Peace of Utrecht (1713) as belonging to the house of Savoy.

Montfort, Simon de (mŏnt'fərt, Fr. môNfôr'), c.1160-1218, count of Montfort and earl of Leicester. A participant in the Fourth Crusade (1202-4), he did not join in the sack of Constantinople, but instead proceeded to Syria. He later led the crusade against the ALBIGENESES. Capable, ambitious, and fanatically religious, he commanded the Crusaders who remained in S France after the taking (1209) of Carcassone and, with papal approval, was elected viscount of Béziers and of Carcassone by the armies. In 1211 he attacked the remaining territories of RAYMOND VI of Toulouse and overran all but Toulouse and Montauban. Pope Innocent III attempted to make him recognize PETER II of Aragón as overlord, but in 1213 Simon defeated Peter and Raymond at Muret. He was proclaimed lord of Toulouse and Montauban by the Crusaders (1215), and his title was confirmed by the pope at the Lateran Council. Raymond recaptured (1217) some of his territories, and Simon renewed the warfare; he was killed while besieging Toulouse. Through his mother he claimed the English earldom of Leicester, to which his right was intermittently recognized by King John. His son was Simon de Montfort, the leader of the English barons.

Montfort, Simon de, earl of Leicester, 1208?-1265, leader of the baronial revolt against HENRY III of England. He was born in France, the son of Simon de Montfort, leader of the Albigensian Crusade. After his father's death, he received the claim to the earldom of Leicester, inherited from his grandmother. He went to England in 1229, and two years later his earldom was recognized by Henry III. He became one of the king's advisers and in 1238 married Eleanor, Henry's sister. In 1240, Simon distinguished himself on crusade in Palestine under RICHARD, EARL OF CORNWALL. Returning to France in 1242, he joined Henry III in the Gascon campaigns of 1242-43. Simon was preparing to go on a new crusade when in 1248 Henry sent him to Gascony with unlimited powers to bring order out of the anarchy of petty feudal wars and rebellions against English authority. Simon was skillful and ruthless in using military force to crush the turbulent Gascon barons and achieved a somewhat unstable order. But loud Gascon protests provoked Henry in 1252 to call Simon to an inquiry in England. After a bitter quarrel with the king was temporarily ended, Simon returned to Gascony, only to be interrupted a second time by a royal order to desist in the middle of his campaign so that young Prince Edward (later EDWARD I) might take Gascony in charge. Stung by these insults, Simon was by 1258 an active member of the baronial opposition that forced the king to turn over the power of government to a committee of 15 (of whom Simon was one), which ruled under the PROVISIONS OF OXFORD, supplemented by the Provisions of Westminster of 1259. Divisions soon appeared in the baronial party, and in 1261, when a majority of the barons consented to an unfavorable compromise with the king, Simon left England. There was, however, renewed discontent in England following Henry's annulment (1262) of the provisions, and in 1263 Simon returned to assume leadership in the BARONS' WAR. Simon won a great victory at Lewes in 1264 and became master of England, which he intended to place under a form of government similar to that prescribed in the Provisions of Oxford. However, he could achieve no legal settlement with the king and so ruled as virtual military dictator. His famous PARLIAMENT of 1265, to which he summoned not only knights from each shire but also, for the first time, representatives from boroughs, was an attempt to rally national support, but at the same time he was alienating many of his baronial supporters. In 1265 his most powerful ally, Gilbert de Clare, 8th earl of GLOUCESTER, deserted and with Prince Edward joined the nobles of the Welsh Marches to start the wars again. Simon de Montfort was defeated and killed at Evesham. See Charles Bémont, *Simon de Montfort* (tr. by E. F. Jacob, 1930); R. F. Treharne, *The Baronial Plan of Reform* (1932); F. M. Powicke, *King Henry III and the Lord Edward* (1947) and *The Thirteenth Century* (1953).

Montgolfier, Joseph Michel (zhôzĕf' mĕshĕl' môNgôlfyā'), 1740-1810, and **Jacques Étienne Montgolfier** (zhäk ātyĕn'), 1745-99, French inventors, brothers. Together they invented the first practical BALLOON. On June 5, 1783, they sent up at Annonay, near Lyons, a large linen bag inflated with hot air; its flight covered more than a mile and lasted 10 min. In the same year a Montgolfier balloon sailed over Paris in the first manned free balloon flight.

Montgomerie, Alexander, c.1556-c.1610, Scottish poet. His principal poem, *The Cherry and the Sloe* (1597), is a pedestrian and ambiguous allegory that enjoyed considerable popularity in its time. Montgomerie's other work includes a verse polemic against Home of Polwarth, 70 sonnets, and miscellaneous poems.

Montgomery, Bernard Law, 1st **Viscount Montgomery of Alamein** (məntgŭm'ərē, ăləmān'), 1887-, British field marshal. Educated at Sandhurst, he entered the army in 1908 and served in World War I. In World War II he commanded (1939-40) the 3d Division in France until the evacuation of Dunkirk. In 1942 he was sent to Egypt to command the British 8th Army in Africa under the Middle Eastern Command headed by Gen. Sir Harold Alexander. Winning the battle of ALAMEIN and driving the Germans 2,000 mi (3,200 km) across Africa into Tunisia (see NORTH AFRICA, CAMPAIGNS IN) made Montgomery an idol of the British public. He led the 8th Army in Sicily and Italy until Dec., 1943. He helped formulate the invasion plan for France, and in the Normandy campaign he was field commander of all ground forces until Aug., 1944, then led the 21st Army Group. When the Germans advanced in the Battle of the Bulge, he was given temporary command of two American armies. Afterward his troops thrust across N Germany to the Baltic, and he headed (1945–46) the British occupation forces in Germany. He was made field marshal in 1944 and viscount in 1946. He was chief of the imperial general staff from 1946 to 1948, when he became chairman of the commanders in chief in committee under the permanent defense organization of Britain, France, Belgium, the Netherlands, and Luxembourg. From 1951 to 1958 he was deputy supreme commander of the Allied forces in Europe. His writings include *Forward to Victory* (1946), *Normandy to the Baltic* (1947), *Forward From Victory* (1948), *El Alamein to the River Sangro* (1948), *An Approach to Sanity* (1959), *The Path to Leadership* (1961), and *A History of Warfare* (1968). See his memoirs (1958); biography by Alan Moorehead (1967) and by his brother, Brian Montgomery (1974); R. W. Thompson, *The Montgomery Legend* (1967) and *Montgomery: The Field Marshall* (1969); Ronald Lewin, *Montgomery as Military Commander* (1972).

Montgomery, Gabriel, seigneur de Lorges, comte de (gäbrēĕl' sänyör' də lôrzh kôNt də môNgômərē'), c.1530–1574, French soldier. Captain of the Scottish guards of King Henry II of France, he accidentally killed the king in a tournament in 1559. Disgraced at court, he retired first to Normandy, then to England, where he was converted to Protestantism. He returned to France and there fought (1562–70) with distinction on the Protestant side in the Wars of Religion. He returned again in 1574, but was captured and put to death. The name is also spelled Montgommery.

Montgomery, L. M. (Lucy Maud Montgomery), 1874–1942, Canadian novelist, b. Prince Edward Island. Her first novel, *Anne of Green Gables* (1908), met with immediate success and has been widely translated. Anne Shirley, the novel's heroine, is a spirited, witty young girl with red hair and a wild imagination. The novel's sequels include *Anne of Avonlea* (1909), *Chronicles of Avonlea* (1912), *Anne of the Island* (1915), and *Anne's House of Dreams* (1917).

Montgomery, Richard, 1738?–1775, American Revolutionary general, b. Swords, Co. Dublin, Ireland. After entering the British army, he was sent (1757) to Canada in the French and Indian Wars and saw action at Louisburg, Ticonderoga, and Montreal before participating in operations against Martinique and Havana (1762). In 1772, he sold his army commission and returned from Great Britain to America. He settled near New York City, and married (1773) a daughter of Robert R. Livingston (1718–75). An opponent of British colonial policy, he was (1775) a member of the New York provincial congress. In the same year he became brigadier general in the Continental army and replaced Philip J. Schuyler as commander of the Montreal expedition in the ill-fated QUEBEC CAMPAIGN. After taking Montreal, he joined Benedict Arnold and was killed (Dec. 31, 1775) in the assault on Quebec.

Montgomery, city (1970 pop. 133,386), state capital and seat of Montgomery co., E central Ala., near the head of navigation on the Alabama River just below the confluence of the Coosa and Tallapoosa rivers, and in the rich Black Belt; inc. 1819. It is an industrial city and an important market center for agricultural goods, especially cotton, livestock, and dairy products. Manufactures include machinery, glass products, textiles, refrigeration equipment, axles, furniture, food items, and paper. Montgomery became the state capital in 1847 and boomed as a river port and cotton market. The city has been called the "Cradle of the Confederacy." In the capitol building there (erected 1857) the convention met (Feb., 1861) that formed the Confederate States of America. Jefferson Davis was inaugurated president on the capitol steps, and the city served as the Confederate capital until the seat was moved to Richmond in May, 1861. The city was occupied by Federal troops in the spring of 1865. It is the seat of Alabama State Univ., Auburn Univ. at Montgomery, Huntingdon College, and a junior college. Maxwell Air Force Base adjoins the city on the northwest. Gunter Air Force Base, which adjoins the city on the northeast, has an air force extension institute and a branch of the aviation medical school. A U.S. veterans hospital and a tuberculosis sanitorium are in Montgomery. In addition to the historic state capitol, points of interest include the "first White House of the Confederacy" (built c.1825), preserved as a Confederate museum; a planetarium; a museum of fine arts; the state archives and history museum; and many antebellum homes and buildings. The Cramton Bowl there is the site of the annual Blue and Gray college football classic.

Montgomery, municipal borough (1971 pop. 968), county town of Montgomeryshire, E Wales. OFFA'S DYKE is particularly well preserved there. In 1974, Montgomery became part of the new nonmetropolitan county of Powys.

Montgomeryshire, county (1971 pop. 42,761), 797 sq mi (2,064 sq km), central Wales. The county town is MONTGOMERY; administrative offices are in Welshpool. The region is largely hilly and is drained by the Dovey, the upper Severn, the Tanat, and the Vyrnwy rivers. At one time lead was mined and flannel manufactured, but the region is now devoted mostly to pasturage and, in the valleys on the English border, to farming. In medieval times Montgomeryshire was important as the heavily fortified border district of the Norman lords of the WELSH MARCHES. In 1974; Montgomeryshire became part of the new nonmetropolitan county of Powys.

month, in chronology, the conventional period of a lunation, i.e., passage of the moon through all its phases. It is usually computed at approximately 29 or 30 days. For the computation of the month and its harmony with the solar calendar and for the months in others than the Gregorian calendar, see CALENDAR. For the difference between the sidereal month and the synodic month, see MOON. Certain stones have in ancient and modern times been connected with the months; these lucky stones, or birthstones, are often given as follows: *January* [from the god JANUS]: garnet; *February* [from Lat.,= expiatory, because of ancient rites]: amethyst; *March* [from the god MARS]: bloodstone or aquamarine; *April:* diamond; *May:* agate or emerald; *June* [from the gens *Junius*]: pearl or moonstone; *July* [from Julius CAESAR]: ruby or onyx; *August* [from AUGUSTUS]: carnelian or peridot; *September* [from Lat.,= seven; formerly the 7th month]: chrysolite or sapphire; *October* [eight]: beryl, tourmaline or opal; *November* [nine]: topaz; *December* [ten]: turquoise or ziron.

Montherlant, Henri de (äNrē' də môNtĕrläN'), 1896–1972, French writer. His novels are decadent and egotistical and glorify force and masculine virility. Montherlant fought in World War I and was later an athlete and a bullfighter. Among his novels are *Les Bestiaires* (1926, tr. *The Bullfighters,* 1927), *Les Célibataires* (1934, tr. *The Bachelors,* 1960), the series of four novels *Les Jeunes Filles* (1936–40; tr. *Pity for Women,* 1937, *Costals & the Hippogriff,* 1940), and *Les Garçons* (1969). Montherlant's plays, all very successful, include *Le Maître de Santiago* (1947, tr. 1951), *Port-Royal* (1954), *Don Juan* (1958), *Le Cardinal d'Espagne* (1960), and *La Guerre civile* (1965, tr. 1967 in *Theatre of War*). See biography by Lucille Becker (1970); study by J. W. Batchelor (1967).

Montholon, Charles Tristan, marquis de (shärl trĕstäN' märkē' də môNtôlôN'), 1783–1853, French general in the Napoleonic Wars. He accompanied the former emperor, Napoleon I, to St. Helena. Returning to Europe after the emperor's death, he acted as one of the executors of Napoleon's will. Involved (1840) in Louis Napoleon's unsuccessful coup at Boulogne (see NAPOLEON III), he was imprisoned from 1840 to 1847. After the Revolution of 1848 he was elected to the legislative assembly. He was the author of *Histoire de la Captivité de Ste Hélène* (1846).

month's mind, in the Roman Catholic Church, a solemn commemoration of the death of a person one month (or 30 days) after decease or burial. It is normally a Mass of requiem. It was formerly customary to have a feast also.

Monti, Vincenzo (vēnchān'tsō mōn'tē), 1754–1828, Italian poet and dramatist. Under French rule he became official historiographer of the Italian kingdom and later accommodated himself to Austrian rule as well. Among his many works the best known is the epic *Bassvilliana* (1793), on the assassination of the French envoy Hugo Basseville at Naples. He is also remembered for his tragedies, among them *Aristodemo* (1787; tr. by Fanny Burney, 1818), and for the epic *Il bardo della Selva Nera* (1806), dedicated to Napoleon. His translation of the *Iliad* (1810) was greatly admired in his day. It is the more remarkable because Monti knew hardly any Greek. He was called the "great translator of the translator of Homer."

Monticelli, Adolphe (ädôlf' môNtēsĕlē'), 1824–86, French painter. He worked in Paris and, after 1870, in his native Marseilles. Influenced by Watteau and Delacroix, he portrayed subjects usually of a festive or exotic nature. He has been regarded as a prophet of abstract expressionism because of his free use of dazzling colors applied with a heavy impasto. His work is best represented in Lille and Marseilles. The museums of Boston, Chicago, New York City, St. Louis, and Washington, D.C., have examples of his painting. The *Fête Châmpetre* (Brooklyn Mus.) is characteristic.

Monticello [Ital.,= little mountain], estate, 640 acres (259 hectares), central Va., near Charlottesville; home of Thomas Jefferson for 56 years. The mansion, which he designed, was begun in 1770 on property inherited from his father. The building materials—stone, brick, lumber, and nails—were prepared on the estate, and most of the construction work was carried out by Jefferson's artisan slaves. By 1772, when Jefferson took his bride there to live, part of the house was ready for occupancy; for many years afterward, he added to the building. The house is one of the earliest examples of the American classic revival. Not long after Jefferson's death, his daughter, unable to maintain the property, sold it, retaining only the family burial plot in which Jefferson is interred. Monticello was later bought by Uriah P. Levy, a naval officer, who bequeathed it to "the people of the United States"; but his heirs successfully contested the will. By 1879, Jefferson P. Levy was in full ownership, but he sold Monticello in 1923 to the Thomas Jefferson Memorial Foundation. Dedicated as a national shrine in 1926, and extensively renovated during the next 30 years, the estate was opened to the public in 1954.

Montilla (mōntē'lyä), town (1970 pop. 22,059), Córdoba prov., S Spain, in Andalusia. It is the center of an agricultural district famous for wines. Deriving from Montilla wines, the term *amontillado* now designates a type of sherry wine.

Mont Laurier (môN lō'rēā"), town (1971 pop. 8,240), SW Que., Canada, on the Lièvre River, N of Ottawa. Located in the Laurentian Mts., it is a winter resort in a lumbering and potato-growing region and has a hydroelectric-power station. It is the seat of a Roman Catholic seminary.

Montluc or **Monluc, Blaise de Lasseran-Massencôme, seigneur de** (blĕz də läsräN'-mäsäNkôm', sänyör' də môNlük'), c.1502–1577, marshal of France. A Gascon soldier of fortune, he fought in the Italian Wars and the Wars of Religion. His famous *Commentaires* (1592), which King Henry IV called "the soldier's bible," are admirable military history.

Montluçon (môNlüsôN'), town (1968 pop. 59,983), Allier dept., central France, on the Cher River. Industry developed in the 19th cent. because of nearby coal fields in Commentry and iron-ore deposits around Berry. Today there are metallurgy, rubber, chemical, clothing, synthetic-textile, and wax industries. The southern terminal of the Berry Canal, which links the Commentry coal fields with the Loire River, is at Montluçon. Points of interest include the Romanesque St. Pierre Church, the flamboyant Gothic church of Notre Dame, and many houses dating from the 15th and 16th cent.; the castle (15th–16th cent.) of the dukes of Bourbon now houses a crockery museum.

Montmagny, Charles Jacques Huault de (shärl zhäk üō' də môNmänyē'), fl.1622–54, governor of New France (1636–48). He was an administrator in New France from 1632 and succeeded Samuel de Champlain as governor. The colony prospered under his leadership, the power of the Iroquois was weakened, and a treaty of peace was concluded with them at Trois Rivières (1645). He worked closely with the missionaries, especially the Jesuits.

Montmagny, town (1971 pop. 12,432), SE Que., Canada, on the St. Lawrence River. Manufactures include textiles, furniture, and household appliances.

Montmartre (môNmär'trə) [Fr.,= hill of the martyrs], hill in Paris, on the right bank of the Seine River. The highest point of Paris, it is topped by the famous Church of SACRÉ-COEUR. Parts of the ancient quarter on its slopes were long a favorite residence of the bohemian world. Until the 20th cent. Montmartre retained a rural look and provided material for Van Gogh, Pissarro, Utrillo, and other artists. Montmartre is also famed for its night life; among its many nightclubs is the Moulin Rouge. The cemetery of Montmartre contains the tombs of Stendhal, Renan, Heine, Berlioz, and Alfred de Vigny. The town of Montmartre was annexed to Paris in 1860. The hill, a natural fortress, played a military role during the Paris Commune (1871) and other periods.

Montmorency, Anne, duc de (mŏnt"mərĕn'sē, Fr. än dük də·môNmôräNsē'), 1493?–1567, constable of France. He was made a marshal (1522) by Francis I, was captured with Francis at Pavia (1525), helped negotiate (1526) Francis's release, and soon after the king's return received the governorship of Languedoc, which remained in his family until 1632. He was made constable in 1538. Montmorency's enemies at court and his policy of peace with Holy Roman Emperor Charles V finally led to his disgrace (1541), which lasted until Francis's death (1547). King Henry II restored him to a degree of favor limited by the countervailing influence of François and Charles de GUISE. He took Metz from the Spanish (1552) and was captured (1557) by Emmanuel Philibert of Savoy at Saint-Quentin, but was soon released. Dismissed by Francis II, he was restored to office by Catherine de' Medici. He joined the Guises in the Wars of Religion, was captured at Dreux (1562), and was killed in the siege of St. Denis, near Paris.

Montmorency, Henri, duc de (äNrē'), the elder, 1534–1614, constable of France; younger son of Anne de Montmorency. He was known as Henri, comte de Damville, before 1579. He took Louis I de CONDÉ prisoner at Dreux (1562). In 1563 he succeeded his father as governor of Languedoc and in 1567 was made a marshal. A zealous Roman Catholic and adherent of the GUISE family until his father's death, he was led by the subsequent decline of his family's fortunes and by the murder of his relative Gaspard de COLIGNY to associate himself with the moderates who favored a rapprochement with the Huguenots. He resisted royal efforts to remove him from Languedoc, where he was practically an independent sovereign; he was in alliance with the Huguenots from 1575 to 1577, but thereafter remained aloof from both parties, while attempting to bring about their conciliation. He adhered to King HENRY IV in 1593 and became constable. After Henry's death (1610) he retired to his province.

Montmorency, Henri, duc de, the younger, 1595–1632, admiral and marshal of France; son of the elder Henri de Montmorency. He became governor of Languedoc in 1613 and fought in the religious and foreign wars of Louis XIII's reign. In 1632 he joined in a conspiracy of Gaston d'ORLÉANS against Cardinal Richelieu and was captured and executed.

Montmorency, Mathieu II, baron de (mätyö' bärôN' də), d. 1230, constable of France (1218–30), called the Great Constable. He fought under PHILIP II at Château Gaillard (1203–4) and Bouvines (1214) and under Louis VIII against the English (1224) and the Albigenses (1226). In Louis XI's minority he supported BLANCHE OF CASTILE.

Montmorency (mŏnt"mərĕn'sē), town (1971 pop. 4,949), S Que., Canada, at the confluence of the St. Lawrence and Montmorency rivers. It is a suburb of Quebec city and the site of the scenic Montmorency Falls.

Montmorency, town (1968 pop. 18,948), Val d'Oise dept., N France, a suburb N of Paris. J. J. ROUSSEAU lived there (1756–62), first at the nearby "Hermitage," a cottage on the estate of his friend, Mme d'Épinay, and after his quarrel with her, in Montmorency itself.

Montmorency, river, c.60 mi (100 km) long, rising in the Laurentian Mts., S Que., Canada, and flowing generally S to the St. Lawrence River. Near its mouth are **Montmorency Falls** (275 ft/84 m high), providing hydroelectric power.

Montparnasse (môNpärnäs'), quarter of Paris, on the left bank of the Seine River, centering on the intersection of the Boulevard de Montparnasse and the Boulevard Raspail. Its famous cafés (the Dôme, the Rotonde, the Coupole, and others) were long centers of the Parisian artistic and intellectual world. The quarter contains the Pasteur Institute, the ancient catacombs, and the Montparnasse cemetery, with the tombs of Saint-Saëns, Houdon, Baudelaire, Poincaré, César Franck, Maupassant, and Leconte de Lisle.

Mont Pelée, volcano: see PELÉE.

Montpelier (mŏntpēl'yər), city (1970 pop. 8,609), state capital (since 1805) and seat of Washington co., central Vt., at the junction of the Winooski and North Branch rivers; inc. 1855. Its economy is dominated by state government and insurance industries. It is also a trading center in a lumber, granite, and winter resort area. There are six granite plants in the city. Other manufactures include bakery products, clothespins, plastic products, and sawmill machinery. A junior college, the state historical society, and a state school for retarded children are there. Of interest are the state capitol and an art gallery for wood sculpture. The city, which is surrounded by mountains, has an excellent view of Mt. Mansfield, the highest point in the state. Admiral George Dewey was born in Montpelier.

Montpelier, estate, central Va., near Charlottesville; formerly the home of President James Madison. The brick mansion was built c.1760 by Madison's father. Madison and his wife are buried nearby. The estate is privately owned.

Montpellier (môNpĕlyā'), city (1968 pop. 167,211), capital of Hérault dept., S France, near the Mediterranean coast. It is a great commercial center. Its industries, many of them recently developed, include food processing, salt working, textile milling, printing, and the manufacture of metal items and chemicals. Montpellier's spectacular population increase (c.70% from 1960–70) was due in part to an influx of refugees from Algeria. Dating from the 8th cent., Montpellier was the center of a fief under the counts of Toulouse; it passed (13th cent.) to the kings of Majorca, from whom it was purchased (1349) by Philip VI of France. A Huguenot center, it was besieged and taken by Louis XIII in 1622. It was the seat of the provincial estates of LANGUEDOC. Montpellier's fame rests principally on its university, founded in 1289. Its noted medical faculty is traced to the 10th cent.; Rabelais was its most famous student. The city is also the seat of agricultural and military schools and of an international wine festival. The botanical garden there was founded in 1593.

Montpellier, University of, at Montpellier, France; founded 1220 by Cardinal Conrad and confirmed by papal bull. The university was suppressed during the French Revolution and replaced by faculties of medicine, pharmacy, science, and letters of the Univ. of France. It was reestablished as a university in 1896. In 1970 it was divided into three units: Univ. of Montpellier I, Univ. of Montpellier II (also known as Univ. of Technical Sciences), and Univ. of Montpellier III (Paul Valéry Univ.).

Montpensier, Anne Marie Louise d'Orléans, duchesse de (än märē' lwēz dôrlāäN' düshĕs' də mōpäsyā'), 1627–93, French princess, called Mademoiselle and La Grande Mademoiselle; daughter of Gaston d'Orléans, the brother of Louis XIII. She took an active part on the rebel side in the FRONDE of the Princes; in 1652 she relieved the city of Orléans at the head of her troops and opened the gates of Paris to Louis II de Bourbon, prince de Condé, and his army. Exiled with her father (1652), she returned to court in 1657. She fell in love with the duc de LAUZUN; the king's permission for their marriage was granted only to be revoked (1670). Shortly thereafter, Lauzun was imprisoned (1671). Mademoiselle bought his release in 1681 and apparently married him, but they soon separated. Mademoiselle spent the rest of her life in pious works and the composition of her memoirs. See biographies by Francis Steegmuller (1955) and V. Sackville-West (1959, repr. 1969).

Montreal (mŏntrēôl'), city (1971 pop. 1,214,352; metropolitan pop. 2,743,208), S Que., Canada, on Montreal island in the St. Lawrence River. Montreal is the largest city in Canada (the second largest French-speaking city in the world; most of its inhabitants also speak English) and a cultural, commercial, financial, and industrial center. It lies at the foot of Mt. Royal—the source of its name—and has an excellent harbor on the St. Lawrence Seaway, which connects the city to the great industrial centers of the Great Lakes. Canada's most important port, Montreal is a transshipment point for oil, grain, sugar, machinery, and manufactured goods. Its manufactures include steel, electronic equipment, aircraft, ships, raw textiles, clothing, and tobacco. There are publishing and printing industries and the main offices of many large Canadian transportation firms in the city. A stockaded Indian village, Hochelaga, was found on the site (1535) by Cartier, and the island was visited in 1603 by Champlain, but it was not settled by the French until 1642, when a band of priests, nuns, and settlers under Paul de Chomedey, Sieur de Maisonneuve, founded the Ville Marie de Montréal. The settlement grew to become an important center of the fur trade and the starting point for the western expeditions of Jolliet, Marquette, La Salle, Vérendrye, and Duluth. It was fortified in 1725 and remained in French possession until 1760, when Vaudreuil de Cavagnal surrendered it to British forces under Amherst. Americans under Richard Montgomery occupied it briefly (1775–76) during the American Revolution. The city's growth was aided by the opening in 1825 of the Lachine Canal, making possible water communications with the Great Lakes. From 1844 to 1849, Montreal was the capital of United Canada. The area of Old Montreal has undergone extensive restoration. Among the city's notable buildings are the Gothic Church of Notre Dame (c.1820), St. Sulpice Seminary (1685), and the Château de Ramezay (1705). Montreal is the seat of McGill Univ., the Univ. of Montreal, Sir George Williams Univ., and Loyola College. Expo '67, the international exposition of 1967, was held in the city. See Stephen Leacock, *Montreal, Seaport and City* (1942); E. A. Collard, *Montreal Yesterdays* (1962); Kathleen Jenkins, *Montreal, Island City of the St. Lawrence* (1966); J. I. Cooper, *Montreal, A Brief History* (1969); Leslie Roberts, *Montreal: From Mission Colony to World City* (1969).

Montreal, University of, at Montreal, Que., Canada; French language; established 1876 as a branch of Laval Univ. It became an autonomous university in 1919. It has faculties of graduate studies; theology; law; medicine; arts and sciences; dental surgery; pharmacy; social, economic, and political sciences; environment design; music; nursing; and education sciences, as well as schools of public health; veterinary medicine; and optometry.

Montreuil (môNtrö'yə), town (1968 pop. 95,859), Seine-Saint-Denis dept., N central France, a suburb of Paris. Long famous for its peaches and pears, Montreuil is now an important industrial center. Among its products are metals, furniture, porcelain and glassware, electrical equipment, dresses, and toys. Montreuil was founded before A.D. 1000. In the center of the town is the Church of SS. Peter and Paul (12th cent.), where Charles V was baptized. A nearby public park has a museum dedicated to the Socialist and workers' movements.

Montreux (môNtrö'), resort area (1970 pop. 20,421), on the northeast shore of the Lake of Geneva, Vaud canton, W Switzerland. It is composed of the communes of Le Châtelard and Les Planches, which were merged in 1962. Montreux is a leading resort on the Lake of Geneva.

Montreux Convention, 1936, international agreement regarding the DARDANELLES. The Turkish request for permission to refortify the Straits zone was favorably received by nations anxious to return to international legality as well as to gain an ally against German and Italian expansion. The former signatories to the Treaty of Lausanne (1923; see LAUSANNE, TREATY OF) together with Yugoslavia and Australia met at Montreux, Switzerland, in 1936 and abolished the International Straits Commission, returning the Straits zone to Turkish military control. Turkey was authorized to close the Straits to warships of all countries when it was at war or threatened by aggression. Merchant ships were to be allowed free passage during peacetime and, except for countries at war with Turkey, during wartime. The Black Sea powers (principally the USSR) were authorized to send their fleets through the Straits into the Mediterranean in peacetime. The convention was ratified by Turkey, Great Britain, France, the USSR, Bulgaria, Greece, Germany, and Yugoslavia, and—with reservations—by Japan. It has remained in effect despite Soviet efforts to obtain its revision.

Montrose, James Graham, 5th **earl and** 1st **marquess of** (mŏntrōz'), 1612–50, Scottish nobleman and soldier. He succeeded to the earldom in 1626 and, feeling slighted by CHARLES I, joined the COVENANTERS in 1638. At first he was active in enforcing the Covenant and served in the Covenanters' army in the BISHOPS' WARS. However, he came to fear a Presbyterian oligarchy controlled by Archibald Campbell, 8th earl of ARGYLL, and was imprisoned (1640–41) by Argyll. After the Scottish intervention in the English civil war, Montrose was created marquess and lieutenant general of Scotland by the king. He made an unsuccessful attempt to invade Scotland, then visited the Highlands in disguise and organized a royalist force there. He then defeated the Lowland Presbyterian army of Argyll in six engagements, of which Tippermuir, Inverlochy, and Kilsyth were the greatest (1644–45). Never in command of a very large army, Montrose was successful because of his brilliant strategy and his spirited leadership of the fierce Highland clansmen, whose numbers were augmented by a small Irish force. He was in control of Scotland for a short time, but the defeat of Charles at Naseby (1645) left him without support, and he was finally defeated by David Leslie at Philiphaugh (1645). He fled (1646) to the Continent. In 1650, Montrose returned to Scotland to try to make the nominal rule of Charles II a reality there. However, his expedition was disavowed by Charles himself, and he was captured and hanged. Although the excesses of his wild troops have been sharply criticized, his reckless daring and his successes in battle have made Montrose a romantic figure in Scottish history. He was the author of poetry (ed. by G. L. Weir, 1938). See biography by C. V. Wedgwood (2d ed. 1966).

Montrose, burgh (1971 pop. 9,963), Angus, NE Scotland, on the North Sea at the mouth of the South Esk River. Open to water on three sides, it is a spacious resort town, with flax and jute mills, boat yards, fruit canneries, and a fishing industry. Montrose was the scene of John de Baliol's surrender of the Scottish throne to Edward I of England in 1296.

Montrouge (môNrōozh'), industrial suburb S of Paris (1968 pop. 44,943), Hauts-de-Seine dept., N central France. Papermaking, publishing, construction, aeronautics, and the manufacture of fire-fighting equipment are the chief industries.

Monts, Pierre du Gua, sieur de (pyĕr dü gwä syör də môN), c.1560–c.1630, French colonizer in North America. A wealthy Huguenot and a favorite of Henry IV, he was the holder of a trade monopoly in New France and the patron of Samuel de CHAMPLAIN. Monts had visited the St. Lawrence by 1603. In 1604–5 he and Champlain explored the coast of New Brunswick and New England as far south as Cape Cod. He planted the first French colony in Canada at Port Royal (the modern ANNAPOLIS ROYAL, N. S.) in 1605. Leaving it in Champlain's care, he returned to France but sent ships in 1607 and 1608 to aid the colonists. Monts's monopoly of the fur trade was revoked in 1608, and his influence declined after Henry IV's death (1610), but Monts was involved in Canadian trade into the 1620s. See William Inglis Morse, ed., *Pierre du Gua, sieur de Monts: Records* (1939).

Mont-Saint-Jean (môN-săN-zhäN), village, Brabant prov., central Belgium, on a height S of Waterloo. The British resisted the French onslaught there at the end of the WATERLOO CAMPAIGN (1815).

Mont-Saint-Michel (môN-săN-mēshĕl'), rocky isle (1968 pop. 105) in the Gulf of Saint-Malo, an arm of the English Channel, Manche dept., NW France, 1 mi (1.6 km) off the coast, near AVRANCHES. The isle, accessible by land at low tide, is also linked with the mainland by a causeway (built 1875). The celebrated Benedictine abbey of Mont-Saint-Michel was founded in 708 by Saint Aubert, bishop of Avranches. A gigantic group of buildings, rising three stories high, serves, with the summit of the cone-shaped rock, as a base for the great abbey church. Six of these structures on the side facing the sea form the unit called La Merveille [the marvel], constructed from 1203 to 1228. Mont-Saint-Michel is one of the most imposing achievements of Gothic architecture. Strongly fortified, the abbey was frequently assaulted by the English in the HUNDRED YEARS WAR but was never captured. It remains one of the major tourist attractions of Europe. Henry Adams wrote of it with feeling in *Mont-Saint-Michel and Chartres.*

Montserrat (mŏntsərăt'), island (1970 pop. 12,302), 38 sq mi (98 sq km), British West Indies, one of the Leeward Islands. It is a rugged, scenic island of volcanic origin. Plymouth is the capital and only outlet for the cotton and other agricultural products of the island. Montserrat was discovered in 1493 by Columbus and colonized by the English in 1632. After changing hands several times between France and Britain, it was definitively awarded to Great Britain in 1783. The island was a member of the former Leeward Islands colony and of the Federation of the West Indies. In 1966 it rejected self-government.

Montserrat or **Monserrat** (both: mŏn"sərăt', mŏnt"–, Span. mōnsärät'), mountain, 4,054 ft (1,236 m) high , NE Spain, rising abruptly from a plain in Catalonia, NW of Barcelona. On a narrow terrace, more than halfway up its precipitous cliffs, is a celebrated Benedictine monastery, one of the greatest religious shrines of Spain. Only ruins are left of the old monastery (11th cent.). The present monastery was built in the 18th cent. and restored after being destroyed by French troops in 1812. It has a valuable painting collection, library, and museum. The Renaissance church (16th cent.; largely restored in the 19th and 20th cent.) contains the black wooden image of the Virgin which, according to tradition, was carved by St. Luke, brought to Spain by St. Peter, and hidden in a cave near Montserrat during the Moorish occupation. In the Middle Ages the mountain, also called Monsalvat, was thought to have been the site of the castle of the Holy GRAIL. At Montserrat, St. Ignatius of Loyola devoted himself to his religious vocation just before the founding of the Society of Jesus.

Montt, Jorge (hôr'hā mōnt), 1846–1922, Chilean vice admiral, president of Chile (1891–96). He was a distant relative of Manuel and Pedro Montt. A leader in the ruinous civil war against BALMACEDA, he commanded both the sea and land forces of the insurrectionists and, after the cessation of hostilities, he headed a provisional junta and then became president. An honest but undistinguished administrator, he was only superficially involved with the program of fiscal and political reforms instituted during his presidency.

Montt, Manuel (mänwĕl'), 1809–80, president of Chile (1851–61). From a poverty-stricken childhood he rose to become one of Chile's most notable jurists. He held many prominent academic and governmental posts, distinguishing himself as minister of education. A conservative president, Montt consolidated the great task of progressive reform pioneered by Diego Portales. He especially emphasized educational and scientific advancement, improved relations with Chile's neighbors, and brought prosperity. Although his stern and sometimes illegal methods of suppressing opposition earned him the hatred of liberals, his administration is remembered as a kind of golden age.

Montt, Pedro (pā'thrō), 1848–1910, president of Chile (1906–10). Son of Manuel Montt, he held with distinction several government posts. He was a minister under José Balmaceda but later joined Jorge Montt, a distant relative, in the overthrow of Balmaceda. Elected president in the hope that his energy and prestige would bring moral regeneration to Chile, he was hampered by disruptive social forces and political corruption. He died in office.

Montville, town (1970 pop. 15,662), New London co., SE Conn.; founded 1670, inc. 1786. Textiles, paper products, and boxes are made. Nearby are a Mohegan Indian museum and a state park.

Monumenta Germaniae historica (mŏnyōōmĕn'tə jərmā'nē-ē hĭstôr'ĭkə), comprehensive critical editions of the sources of medieval German history. The first society created to publish them was founded by Karl vom und zum STEIN in 1819, and the first volume appeared in 1826. G. H. Pertz, general editor until 1874, was succeeded by Georg WAITZ. Many eminent scholars took part in the project, and additions and revisions continued into the 20th cent. The *Monumenta* ranks among the great collections of source materials and was instrumental in stimulating research on medieval Germany.

monumental brasses: see BRASSES, MONUMENTAL.

Monvel, Louis Maurice Boutet de: see BOUTET DE MONVEL, LOUIS MAURICE.

Monviso: see VISO, MONTE.

Monza (mōn'tsä), city (1971 pop. 114,421), Lombardy, N Italy. Manufactures of this industrial center include felt hats, carpets, textiles, and machinery. The history of Monza is closely related to that of Milan. The cathedral, founded (6th cent.) by the Lombard queen Theodolinda, contains the iron crown of Lombardy, which was made, according to tradition, from a nail of Christ's cross, and which was used to crown Charlemagne, Charles V, Napoleon I, and other emperors as kings of Lombardy or of Italy. An expiatory chapel was built (1910) at the place where King Humbert I was assassinated in 1900. Monza has a major automobile racetrack (rebuilt 1955).

mood or **mode,** in verb INFLECTION, the forms of a verb that indicate its manner of doing or being. In English the forms are called indicative (for direct statement or question or to express an uncertain condition, e.g., *If they do not send it, we cannot go*), imperative (for commands), and subjunctive (for sentences suggesting doubt, condition, or a situation contrary to fact, e.g., *If I were king . . .* , or *He asked that it be done*). The infinitive (nonpersonal, generalizing), is sometimes considered an example of mood, as are phrases formed with the auxiliaries *may, might, can,* and *could* (termed the potential mood); *should* and *would* (conditional); and *must* and *ought* (obligative). These names of moods are often used for similar categories in other languages, and many languages are far richer in analogous patterns than Romance languages; moods commonly found in other languages are narrative, quotative, mythical, desiderative, optative, and negative. In standard English the verb *to be* has special modal inflections

Moody, Deborah, d. 1659, American colonial religious leader and colonizer, b. England. She emigrated (1639) to Massachusetts Bay and settled in Saugus (now Lynn, Mass.) After being admonished (1643) by the Puritan church for her Anabaptist religious beliefs, Moody led a group of followers to the Dutch colony of New Netherland. She founded the settlement of Gravesend in Brooklyn and was granted (1645) a town charter by the Dutch guaranteeing freedom of worship and self-government; it was the first charter issued to a woman in the New World. Moody became influential in the affairs of New Netherland and was frequently consulted by Governor Peter Stuyvesant on political matters.

Moody, Dwight Lyman, 1837–99, American evangelist, b. Northfield, Mass. He became successful in business in Chicago, where he settled in 1856. His activities there as a Sunday-school teacher and superintendent were so successful that in 1861 he withdrew from business to devote himself to city missionary work. In 1870 he met Ira Sankey, who for a number of years thereafter was associated with him in evangelistic campaigns. They made two extended evangelical tours of Great Britain. Large crowds were also attracted to their meetings in the United States, and their collections of gospel hymns were received with great enthusiasm. Moody's preaching was simple, colorful, and direct; he stressed God's love and mercy rather than retribution and hellfire. His interest in religious education led him to found the Northfield Seminary for girls (1879) and the Mt. Hermon School for boys (1881), both in Northfield, Mass; in 1971 the two schools merged and became the Northfield Mt. Hermon School. In 1889 his Bible Institute for Home and Foreign Missions (now the Moody Bible Institute) opened in Chicago. The conferences for Christian workers that Moody inaugurated at Northfield, Mass., were annual gatherings. See biographies by his sons, W. R. Moody (1900) and P. D. Moody (1938); Gamaliel Bradford, *D. L. Moody, a Worker in Souls* (1927, repr. 1972); J. C. Pollock, *Moody: a Biographical Portrait* (1963, repr. 1967); J. J. Findlay, *Dwight L. Moody* (1969).

Moody, Helen Wills: see WILLS, HELEN NEWINGTON.

Moody, John, 1868–1958, American financial writer, b. Jersey City, N.J. He was working in a Wall Street brokerage house in 1900 when he founded *Moody's Manual of Railroads and Corporation Securities.* It was followed in 1905 by *Moody's Magazine,* a monthly, and in 1909 by *Moody's Analyses of Investments,* an annual. See his two-part autobiography, *The Long Road Home* (1933) and *Fast by the Road* (1942).

Moody, William Vaughn, 1869–1910, American poet and dramatist, b. Spencer, Ind., grad. Harvard, 1893. After writing several verse dramas, Moody achieved wide success with the prose play *The Great Divide* (produced as *A Sabine Woman,* 1906). *The Faith Healer* (1909), however, also written in prose, was less popular. Both his poetry and plays are noted for their lyricism and philosophical idealism. He also wrote *A History of English Literature* (1902) with Robert Morss Lovett. See his poems and plays (2 vol., 1912); studies by Martin Halpern (1964) and M. F. Brown (1973).

Moon, Mountains of the, Africa: see RUWENZORI.

moon, natural satellite of a planet (see SATELLITE, NATURAL), in particular, the single natural satellite of the earth. The moon is the earth's nearest neighbor in space, the only celestial body besides the sun close enough to the earth to be seen as a disk with the naked eye rather than as a point of light. Man has studied the moon since the beginning of time and recorded its apparent motions through the sky. The study of the moon in earnest began with the invention of the telescope by Galileo in 1610 and culminated in 1969 when man first actually set foot on the moon's surface. In addition to its proximity, the moon is also exceptional in that it is quite massive compared to the earth itself, the ratio of their masses being far larger than the similar ratios of other natural satellites to the planets they orbit. For this reason, the earth-moon system is sometimes considered a double planet.

Motions. It is the center of the earth-moon system, rather than the center of the earth itself, that describes an elliptical orbit around the sun in accordance with KEPLER'S LAWS. It is also more accurate to say that the earth and moon together revolve about their common center of mass, rather than saying that the moon revolves about the earth. This common center of mass lies beneath the earth's surface, about 3,000 mi (4800 km) from the earth's center. Looking down on the earth's north pole, the moon moves in a counterclockwise direction with an average orbital speed of about 1 km/sec, which is about 0.6 mi/sec. Because the lunar orbit is elliptical, the distance between the earth and the moon varies periodically as the moon revolves in its orbit. At perigee, when the moon is nearest the earth, the distance is about 227,000 mi (365,000 km); at apogee, when the moon is farthest from the earth, the distance is about 254,000 mi (409,000 km). The average distance is about 240,000 mi (385,000 km), or about 60 times the radius of the earth itself. The plane of the moon's orbit is tilted, or inclined, at an angle of about 5° with respect to the ECLIPTIC. The line dividing the bright and dark portions of the moon is

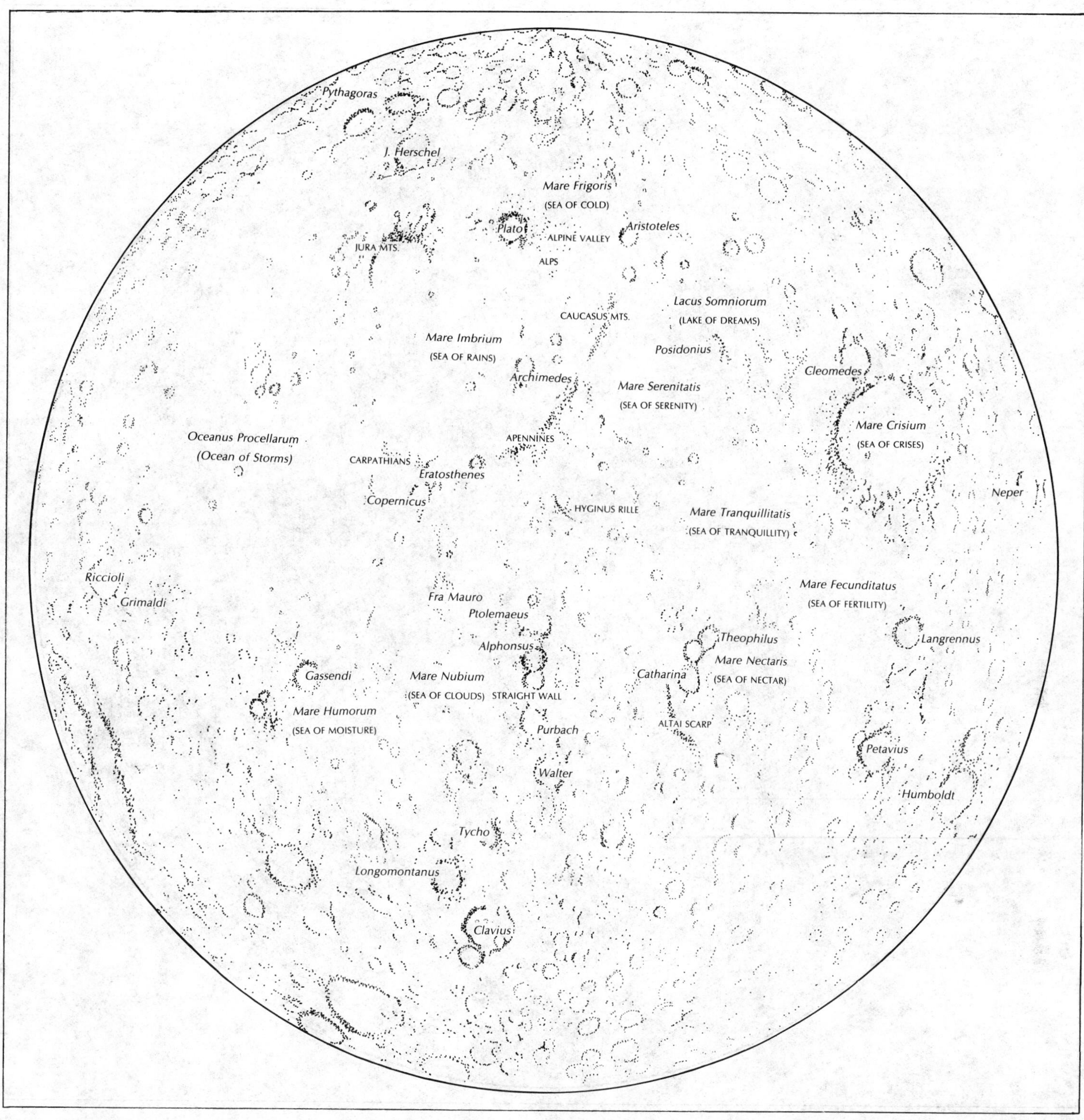

The moon: Near side

called the terminator. Due to the earth's rotation, the moon appears to rise in the east and set in the west, like all other heavenly bodies; however, the moon's own orbital motion carries it eastward against the stars. This motion is much more rapid than the similar motion of the sun. Hence the moon appears to overtake the sun and rises on an average of 50½ minutes later each night. There are many variations in this retardation according to latitude and time of year. In the Northern Temperate Zone, at the autumnal equinox, the harvest moon occurs; moonrise and sunset coincide for several days around full moon. The next succeeding full moon, called the hunter's moon, also shows this coincidence. An optical illusion causes the moon to appear larger when it is near the horizon than when it is near the zenith. The true angular size of the moon's diameter is about ½°, which also happens to be the sun's apparent diameter. This coincidence makes possible total ECLIPSES of the sun in which the solar disk is exactly covered by the disk of the moon. During a solar eclipse, the shadow of the moon strikes part of the earth's surface, making part or all of the sun invisible from that region. An eclipse of the moon occurs when the earth's shadow falls onto the moon, temporarily blocking the sunlight that causes the moon to shine. Eclipses can occur only when the moon, sun, and earth are arranged along a straight line—lunar eclipses at full moon and solar eclipses at new moon. The gravitational influence of the moon is chiefly responsible for the TIDES of the earth's oceans, the twice-daily rise and fall of sea level. The ocean tides are caused by the flow of water toward the two points on the earth's surface that are instantaneously directly beneath the moon and directly opposite the moon. Because of frictional drag, the earth's rotation carries the two tidal bulges slightly forward of the line connecting earth and moon. The resulting torque slows the earth's rotation while increasing the moon's orbital velocity. As a result, the day is getting longer and the moon is moving farther away from the earth. The moon also raises much smaller tides in the solid crust of the earth, deforming its shape. The tidal influence of the earth on the moon was responsible for making the moon's periods of rotation and revolution equal.

Physical Characteristics. The physical characteristics and surface of the moon have been studied telescopically, photographically, and more recently by instruments carried by manned and unmanned spacecraft (see SPACE EXPLORATION). The moon's diameter is about 2,160 mi (3,476 km), somewhat more than ¼ the earth's diameter. The moon has about 1/81 the mass of the earth and is ⅗ as dense. On the moon's surface the force of gravitation is about ⅙ that on earth. It has been established that the moon completely lacks both water and atmosphere. The surface temperature rises above 100°C (212°F) at lunar noon and sinks below −155°C (−247°F) at night. The gross surface features of the moon are visible to the unaided eye and were first studied telescopically in 1610 by Galileo. The lunar surface is divided into the mountainous highlands and the large, roughly circular plains called maria (sing. mare; from Lat., = sea) by early astronomers, who erroneously believed them to be bodies of water. The smooth floors of the maria, varying from flat to gently undulating, are covered by a thin layer of powdered rock that darkens them and accounts for the moon's low ALBEDO (only 7 percent of the incident sunlight is reflected back, the rest being absorbed). The brighter regions on the moon are the mountainous highlands, where the terrain is rough and strewn with rocky rubble. The lunar mountain

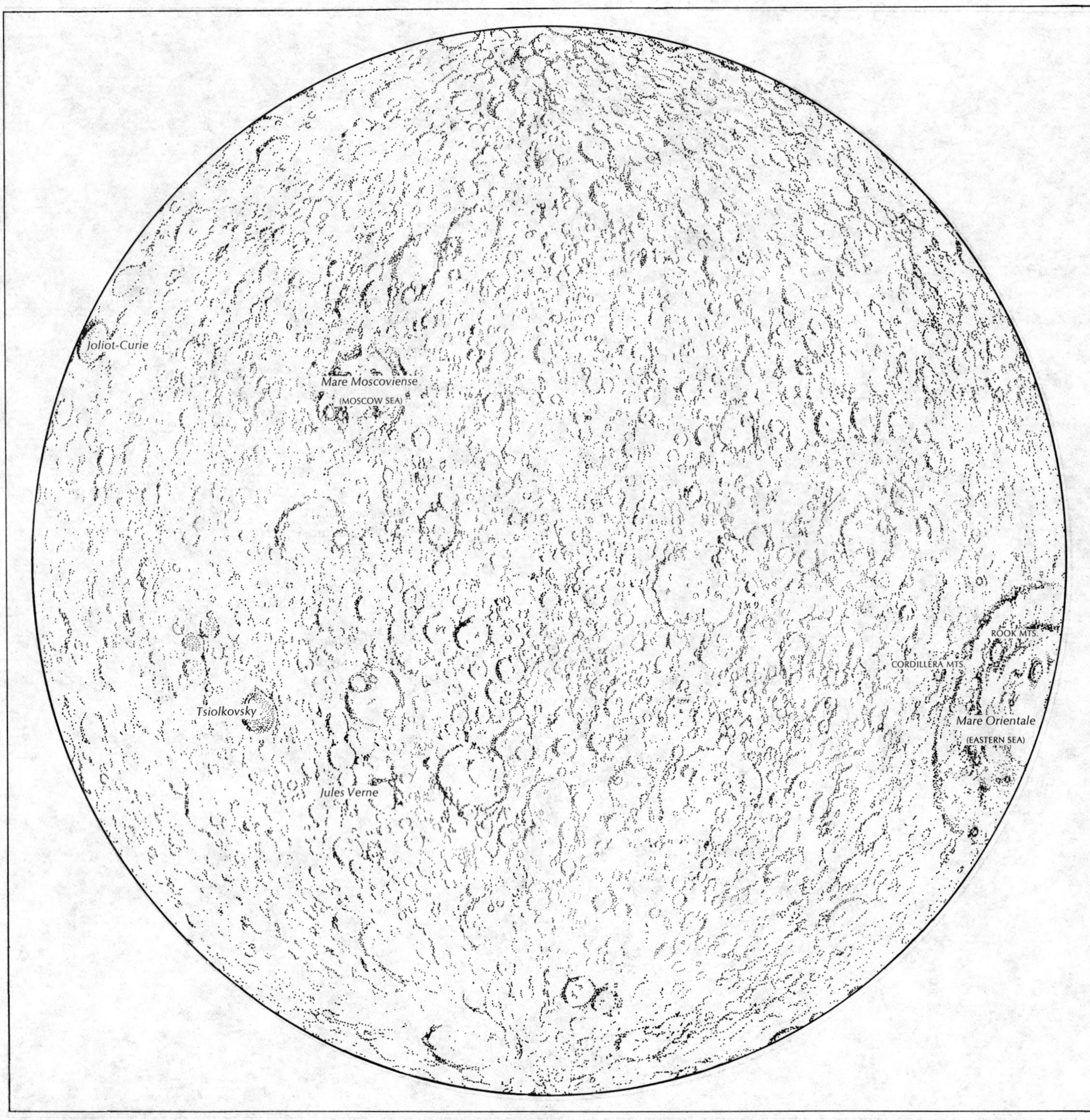

The moon: Far side

ranges, with heights up to 25,000 ft (7,800 m), are comparable to the highest mountains on earth but in general are not very steep. The highlands are densely scarred by thousands of craters—shallow circular depressions, usually ringed by well-defined walls and often possessing a central peak. Craters range in diameter from a few feet to many miles, and in some regions there are so many that they overlap or several smaller craters lie within a large crater. Craters are also found on the maria, although there are nowhere near as many as in the lunar highlands. Other prominent surface features include the rilles and rays. Rilles are sinuous, canyon-like clefts found near the edges of mountain ranges. Rays are bright streaks radiating outward from certain craters, such as Tycho. The origins of the moon and its principal features have become less speculative since the manned exploration of the moon. The moon probably formed by the cold accretion of small particles about 4.5 billion years ago at the same time that the rest of the SOLAR SYSTEM formed; thus, it is now believed that the moon was never in an entirely molten state. The crust, showing pronounced chemical differentiation, formed early. Subsequent impact of very large meteorites depressed the mare basins, at the same time thrusting up the surrounding crust to form the highlands. The mare basins later filled with lava flow, which in turn was covered by a thin layer of lunar "soil"—fine rock dust pulverized by the very slow mechanisms of lunar erosion (thermal cycling, solar wind, and micrometeorites). The craters were probably also formed by meteorite bombardment rather than by internal volcanic action as once believed. The rays are material ejected during the impacts that formed the craters. The moon's rock types are correlated with its major geological periods. The mare and highland rocks differ in both appearance and chemical content. For example, mare rocks are richer in iron and poorer in aluminum than highland rocks. The maria consist largely of basalt, i.e., igneous rock formed from magma. In the highlands the majority of the rocks are breccias—clasts conglomerated from basaltic rock and often studded with small, green, glassy spheres. These spheres probably were formed as the spray of molten rock, originally melted by the heat of meteorite impact, recongealed in midflight. The exposure ages of some rocks (the time their surfaces have been exposed to the action of cosmic rays that produce radioactive isotopes) are as short as 50 million years, much shorter than their crystallization ages. These rocks may have been shifted in position by meteorite impact or seismic activity (moonquakes). However, the present lunar seismic activity is very low, corroborating the image of the moon as an essentially static, nonevolving world. Diffraction of seismic waves provided the first clear-cut evidence for a lunar crust, mantle, and core in analogy to the earth's structure. The lunar crust is about 45 mi (70 km) thick, making the moon a rigid solid to a greater depth than the earth. The inner core has a radius of about 600 mi (1,000 km), about ⅔ of the radius of the moon itself. The internal temperature decreases from 830°C (1530°F) at the center to 170°C (340°F) near the surface. The heat traveling outward near the lunar surface is about half that of the earth but still twice that predicted by current theory. This heat flow is directly related to the rate of internal energy production, so that the internal temperature profile provides information about long-lived radio isotopes and the moon's thermal evolution. The heat-flow measurements indicate that the moon's radioactive content is higher than previously assumed, in particular higher than that of the earth. The moon's magnetic field is a million times weaker than that of the earth, but it varies by a factor of 20 from point to point on the surface. Certain rocks retain a high magnetization, indicating that they crystallized in the presence of magnetic fields much higher than those presently existing on the moon. Mascons are large mass concentrations of unusually high density that are located below certain of the circular maria. Their existence was deduced from short-term deviations of lunar satellites from their predicted orbits. The mascons may have been created by the implantation of very dense, iron-rich meteorites, whose impact formed the mare basins themselves. See Patrick Moore and P. J. Cattermole, *The Craters of the Moon* (1967); David Thomas, ed., *Moon: Man's Greatest Adventure* (1970); George Gamow, *The Moon* (rev. ed. 1971); A. A. Levinson and S. R. Taylor, *Moon Rocks and Minerals* (1971); T. A. Mutch, *Geology of the Moon* (rev. ed. 1973).

Mooney, Thomas J., 1883–1942, American labor agitator, b. Chicago. He was an active leader in several violent labor struggles in California before 1916 and was convicted as a participant in the bomb killings at the San Francisco Preparedness Day parade in 1916 and sentenced to death. His case aroused international interest because of the widely held belief in his innocence and the confessions of perjured testimony at his trial, and in 1918 his sentence was commuted to life imprisonment. Many organizations and individuals sought unsuccessfully to obtain a new trial until Jan., 1939, when Gov. Culbert L. Olson of California pardoned him unconditionally. See the *Mooney-Billings Report* (1932, repr. 1968); E. J. Hopkins, *What Happened in the Mooney Case* (1932, repr. 1970); R. H. Frost, *The Mooney Case* (1968).

moonfish: see POMPANO.

moonflower: see MORNING GLORY.

moon rat: see HEDGEHOG.

moonstone, an orthoclase FELDSPAR found in Sri Lanka (Ceylon) and Burma and on Madagascar, and formerly in the St. Gotthard district of Switzerland. In spite of its pronounced cleavage, it is widely used as a gem; the refraction of light by the thin, paired internal layers causes its milky bluish sheen.

moon worship. Although the moon has not had great prominence in the history of religion, the worship of it has been known since earliest recorded time—in the oldest literatures of Egypt, Babylonia, India, and China—and still exists today in various parts of the world, particularly among certain African and American Indian tribes. Moon worship is founded on the belief that the phases of the moon and the growth and decline of plant, animal, and human life are related. In some societies food was laid out at night to absorb the rays of the moon, which were thought to have power to cure disease and prolong life. Among the Baganda of central Africa it was customary for a mother to bathe her newborn child by the light of the first full moon. The moon was frequently equated with wisdom and justice, as in the worship of the Egyptian god Thoth and the Mesopotamian god Sin. In general, however, the moon has been the basis for many amorous legends and some superstitions (madmen were once considered to be moonstruck, hence the term *lunatic*) and is particularly important in the practice of ASTROLOGY.

Moor, Antonis: see MORO, ANTONIO.

Moorabbin, city (1971 pop. 109,548), Victoria, SE Australia. It is a suburb of Melbourne.

Moore, Archibald Lee (Archie Moore), 1915?–, American prizefighter, b. Collinsville, Ill., or Benoit, Miss. His age and place of birth are uncertain. Moore started his professional boxing career as a middleweight in 1936, winning his first 13 matches by knockouts. In his long and colorful career Moore, a clever boxer and dangerous puncher, engaged in 220 recorded professional bouts and scored 136 knockouts, a record in the history of pugilism. In 1952 he won the light heavyweight championship from Joey Maxim; the National Boxing Association stripped Moore of the title in 1961, but other boxing bodies recognized him as champion. Moore twice fought for the heavyweight championship—in 1955 he was beaten by Rocky Marciano and in 1956 by Floyd Patterson. See his autobiography (1960).

Moore, Brian, 1921–, Anglo-American novelist, b. Belfast, Northern Ireland. He emigrated to Canada in 1948, where he worked as a reporter for the Montreal *Gazette*; he moved to the United States in 1959. His novels usually concern pathetic, failed people who are still capable of hypocrisy and shabby self-delusion. There is a comic vein in all his works. His novels include *The Lonely Passion of Judith Hearne* (1956), *The Luck of Ginger Coffey* (1958), and *Catholics* (1972).

Moore, Clement Clarke, 1779–1863, American educator and poet, b. New York City, grad. Columbia, 1798. A biblical scholar, he was professor of Oriental and Greek literature at the Episcopal General Theological Seminary, erected in New York City on land that he had donated. He is remembered for the well-known poem "Visit from St. Nicholas," which begins "'Twas the night before Christmas"; it was first published in the Troy *Sentinel* in 1823. See biography by S. W. Patterson (1956).

Moore, Douglas Stuart, 1893–1969, American composer and teacher, b. Cutchogue, N.Y. Moore studied with Horatio Parker, Vincent d'Indy, Nadia Boulanger, and Ernst Bloch. In 1926 he joined the music faculty of Columbia Univ. and was its chairman from 1940 to 1962. His major works include *Pageant of P. T. Barnum* (1924) and *Moby Dick* (1928) for orchestra; the operas for children *The Headless Horseman* (1937; libretto by Stephen Vincent Benét) and *The Emperor's New Clothes* (1949); the operas *The Devil and Daniel Webster* (1939), *Giants in the Earth* (1951; awarded a Pulitzer Prize), *The Ballad of Baby Doe* (1956); *The Wings of the Dove* (1961), and *Carrie Nation* (1968); two symphonies (1945, 1948); chamber music; and settings of poetry by Donne, MacLeish, Benét, and Vachel Lindsay. Moore's music is outstanding for its theatricality and use of the American vernacular. His prose works include *Listening to Music* (1932) and *From Madrigal to Modern Music* (1942).

Moore, Edward, 1712–57, English dramatist. He wrote two comedies in the sentimental tradition, *The Foundling* (1748) and *Gil Blas* (1751), but his reputation as a dramatist rests primarily on his prose tragedy *The Gamester* (1753).

Moore, George, 1852–1933, English author, b. Ireland. As a young man he lived in Paris, studying at various art schools. Inspired by Zola, Flaubert, Turgenev, and the 19th-century French realists, Moore turned to writing, publishing his first novel, *A Modern Lover,* in 1883. *A Mummer's Wife* (1885), in portraying the degradation of a woman through alcohol, introduced NATURALISM into the Victorian novel. Moore's most famous novel, *Esther Waters* (1894), poignantly relates the poverty and hardships valiantly endured by a religious girl. Included among his other works are the novels *Confessions of a Young Man* (1888), *Evelyn Innes* (1898), *Sister Teresa* (1901), *The Brook Kerith* (1916), and *Héloise and Abelard* (1921); and the volumes of short stories *Celibates* (1895) and *The Untilled Field* (1903), the latter reminiscent of Dostoevsky. About 1900, Moore returned to Ireland and became associated with William Butler Yeats, George Russell, and others in the IRISH LITERARY RENAISSANCE. His famous three-volume autobiographical work, *Hail and Farewell* (1911–14), is a highly entertaining, and often fictitious, account of his experiences in Ireland. See his letters, ed. by H. E. Gerber (1968); biography by M. J. Brown (1955); study by D. A. Hughes (1971).

Moore, George Edward, 1873–1958, English philosopher, b. Upper Norwood. He was educated at Cambridge, where he was a fellow (1898–1904) and then (1911–25) a lecturer in the department of moral sciences. He was professor of philosophy from 1925 until his retirement in 1939 as professor emeritus. He edited (1921–47) the journal *Mind* and was also visiting professor at various universities in the United States from 1940 to 1944. Moore's earliest writings were strongly influenced by the idealism of F. H. Bradley and the transcendental epistemology of Immanuel Kant, and ranged from idealism to realism. After 1903, however, with the publication of *Principia Ethica* and "The Refutation of Idealism," he became more interested in critical epistemology, i.e., in distinguishing between acts of consciousness and their possible objects, and between the ways in which we can be said to know and the things we can know. Along with Bertrand Russell and Ludwig Wittgenstein he was concerned with the philosophical problems caused by the imprecisions of ordinary language, but he did not consider linguistic analysis the main interest of philosophy. He was also concerned with the distinction between a "sense datum" and a material thing, although he never defined the distinction to his own satisfaction. Similarly, he concerned himself with the definition of "reality" but never arrived at a consistent position on the matter. He defended common sense as a limited but not inadmissible criterion for certainty. Although Moore's philosophy provides no systematic doctrine, and indeed progresses toward fragmented and inconclusive investigations (he himself admitted he had not been "a good answerer of philosophical questions"), he provided closely reasoned investigations of questions important to modern philosophy, and added to an atmosphere of inquiry by his capacity to deal freshly with problems, always placing truth before consistency or the desire for an answer. His other writings include *Ethics* (1912), *Philosophical Studies* (1922), *Some Main Problems of Philosophy* (1953), and *Commonplace Book, 1919–1953* (ed. by Casimir Lewey, 1962). Moore's autobiography and "A Reply to My Critics" appear in *The Philosophy of G. E. Moore* (ed. by P. A. Schilpp, 3d ed. 1968). See E. D. Klemke, *Epistemology of G. E. Moore* (1969) and *Studies in the Philosophy of G. E. Moore* (1969); Alice Ambrose, ed., *G. E. Moore: Essays in Retrospect* (1970); A. J. Ayer, *Russell and Moore: The Analytical Heritage* (1971).

Moore, George Foot, 1851–1931, American biblical scholar, b. West Chester, Pa. In 1878 he was ordained in the Presbyterian ministry. He was professor of Hebrew (1883–1902) at Andover Theological Seminary and professor of theology (1902–4) and of religious history (1904–28) at Harvard. An eminent Oriental scholar and a noted teacher, he wrote a number of books, including *The Literature of the Old Testament* (1913), *History of Religions* (Vol. I, 1913; Vol. II, 1919), *Metempsychosis* (1914), and *Judaism in the First Centuries of the Christian Era* (1927).

Moore, Henry, 1898–, English sculptor. Moore's early sculpture was angular and rough, strongly influenced by pre-Columbian art. About 1928 he evolved a more personal style which has gained him an international reputation. His works, in wood, stone, and cement (done without clay models), are characterized by their smooth, organic shape and often include empty hollows, which he showed to have as meaningful a shape as solid mass. During World War II, when materials for carving were scarce, he was commissioned by the government to do a series of drawings of the London underground bomb shelters (1940). His favorite sculptural subjects have been the mother and child and the reclining figure. Moore executed an abstract screen and a reclining figure for the Time-Life Building in London (1952–53), a bronze group for Lincoln Center of the Performing Arts in New York City (1962–65), and a monument for the Univ. of Chicago (1964–66). See his autobiography, ed. by John Hedgecoe (1968); a collection of his writings, ed. by Philip James (1967); biographies by Ionel Jianou (tr. 1968) and John Russell (rev. ed. 1973); studies by Herbert Read (1967), David Sylvester (1968), and Robert Melville (1970).

Moore, Sir John, 1761–1809, British general. He served with the British army in the American Revolutionary War and between 1793 and 1808 fought successively in the Mediterranean, the West Indies, Ireland, Holland, Egypt, Sicily, and Sweden. He proved himself a master of strategy and a great trainer of men. In 1808, Moore was sent to Portugal with reinforcements for the British army fighting the French there (see PENINSULAR WAR). Made commander in chief after the French evacuation of Portugal, he attempted to go to the aid of the Spanish in defending Madrid. The Spanish defeat, however, forced him to conduct a 250-mi (400-km) retreat over mountainous terrain to La Coruña. There he was victorious over the French but was fatally wounded. His death is commemorated in Charles Wolfe's poem, *The Burial of Sir John Moore* (1817). See his diary, ed. by J. F. Maurice (1904); biographies by Beatrice Brownrigg (with his letters, 1923) and C. M. A. Oman (1953).

Moore, John Bassett, 1860–1947, American authority on international law, b. Smyrna, Del. He was admitted to the Delaware bar in 1883. He was (1885–86) a law clerk in the Dept. of State and was (1886–91) an Assistant Secretary of State before becoming (1891–1924) a professor at Columbia. He represented the United States on several important international commissions. He was (1912–38) on the panel of the Hague Tribunal and was (1921–28) the first American judge on the World Court (the Permanent Court of International Justice). Moore believed that the system of alliances that grew up after World War I threatened to make every conflict worldwide and that maintaining neutrality would tend to localize wars. His *History and Digest of International Arbitrations* (6 vol., 1898), *Digest of International Law* (8 vol., 1906), and *International Adjudications, Ancient and Modern* (8 vol., 1937) are standard compilations. His other books include *American Diplomacy* (1905), *Four Phases of American Development* (1912), *International Law and Some Current Illusions* (1924), *The Permanent Court of International Justice*

(1924), and *Collected Papers* (7 vol., 1945). He also edited the works of James Buchanan (12 vol., 1909–11).

Moore, Marianne, 1887-1972, American poet, b. St. Louis, grad. Bryn Mawr, 1909. She lived mostly in New York City, working first as a librarian and later as acting editor of the *Dial* (1925-29). Her poetry, constructed like a precise mosaic, is witty, intellectual, and often satirical. Volumes of her verse include *Poems* (1921), *Observations* (1924), *What Are Years?* (1941), *Collected Poems* (1951; Pulitzer Prize), *O to Be a Dragon* (1959), and *Complete Poems* (1967). Among her other works are the translation *The Fables of La Fontaine* (1954) and the essays *Predilections* (1955). See *A Marianne Moore Reader* (1961); studies by G. W. Nitchie (1969) and Charles Tomlinson, comp. (1970).

Moore, Thomas, 1779-1852, Irish poet, b. Dublin. He achieved prominence in his day not only for his poetry but also for his love of Ireland and personal charm. A lawyer, he was for a time registrar of the admiralty court in Bermuda. He is remembered today for *Irish Melodies,* a group of lyrics published between 1808 and 1834 and set to music by Sir John Stevenson and others; the songs include several of lasting fame, such as "Believe Me If All Those Endearing Young Charms," "Oft in the Stilly Night," and "The Harp That Once through Tara's Halls." His amusing satires, *Intercepted Letters; or, The Two-Penny Post Bag* (1813) and *The Fudge Family in Paris* (1818), were widely read, and the long poem *Lalla Rookh* (1817), a lush romance of the Orient, was one of the most popular poems of his day. Byron, who was his friend, left him his memoirs, which Moore later—on the advice of Byron's executor and friends—destroyed. His biography of Byron appeared in 1830 and is among his best prose works. See biography by H. M. Jones (1937, repr. 1970).

Moore, Thomas Sturge, 1870-1944, English author. Although his themes were classical and conservative, his poetic technique was innovative. His first volume of poetry, *The Vinedresser,* appeared in 1899. Later works in verse include *Absalam* (1903) and *Mystery and Tragedy* (1930). He wrote several books on art, such as *Albrecht Dürer* (1905) and *Art and Life* (1910), and was a wood engraver, especially noted for his bookplate designs. See his poetical works (4 vol., 1931-33); his correspondence with W. B. Yeats, ed. by Ursula Bridge (1953); biography by F. L. Gwynn (1951).

Moore, city (1970 pop. 18,761), Cleveland co., central Okla., a suburb of Oklahoma City; inc. 1887. It has food industries and a facility that repairs aircraft engines.

Moorea (môrā'ä), volcanic island (1970 pop. 4,842), c.50 sq mi (130 sq km), South Pacific, second largest of the Windward group of the SOCIETY ISLANDS, FRENCH POLYNESIA. The island is mountainous, with Mt. Tohivea (3,975 ft/1,212 m) the highest peak. On the northern coast are Cook Bay and Papetoai Bay. Afareaitu, the chief town, is on the east coast. Copra and coffee are the main products.

Moores Creek National Military Park, 50 acres (20 hectares), SE N.C.; est. 1926. The patriot victory over the Loyalists at Moores Creek Bridge on Feb. 27, 1776, prevented the intended British invasion of North Carolina and spurred revolutionary sentiment in the South; the battle is often called the Lexington and Concord of the South.

Moorestown, township (1970 pop. 15,577), Burlington co., SW N.J., an industrial suburb of the Camden, N.J.-Philadelphia area; settled 1682 by Quakers, inc. 1922. Electronic equipment, metal products, and chemicals are the principal manufactures. A U.S. air force space tracking installation is there. Of interest are several 18th-century houses.

Moorhead, city (1970 pop. 29,687), seat of Clay co., NW Minn., on the Red River; inc. 1881. A sister city of Fargo, N.Dak., it is a shipping and processing center for a dairy and farm (chiefly sugar beets and potatoes) area. Its economy and cultural activities center largely around Moorhead State College and Concordia College. Farm and oil equipment and furniture are manufactured. Moorhead's population is predominantly of Scandinavian origin.

moorhen: see RAIL.

Moorish art and architecture, branch of ISLAMIC ART AND ARCHITECTURE developed in the westernmost lands of the Muslims, known as the Maghreb: N Africa and Spain. The Great mosque at Al Qayrawan in Tunisia is the prototype of western Islamic religious edifices. Reconstructed c.695, it was almost finished in the 9th cent. and comprised a large court surrounded by galleries and opening into a prayer room in the form of a hypostyle hall; the 9th-century mihrab is famed for its luster tile decorations. Another early monument is the Great mosque at Córdoba (785-c.1000), begun by the Umayyad emir Abd ar-RAHMAN I, who had escaped from Damascus. The building is noted for its complex interior consisting of a multitude of low, rounded arches made of alternating black and white stones. In the 12th cent. a closer contact between the art of Spain and that of N Africa was brought about by the ALMOHADS. Under them the mosque of Tin-Mal, in the Atlas Mts., and that of Tlemcen in Algeria were completed. The Almohads also erected the mosque of Seville, known for its minaret, the GIRALDA. The apogee of Moorish architecture was reached in the 13th and 14th cent. with the luxurious palace-fortress, the ALHAMBRA, the only large-scale domestic complex preserved from the first thousand years of Islam, and the madrasahs (schools) of Fez, celebrated for their delicately worked lacy wooden carvings. In these centuries when Spain wrested itself from Moorish domination, the Christians nevertheless showed their admiration of the great Islamic edifices and decoration in their development of MUDÉJAR art, work made by and for Christians in the Moorish style. An example is the 14-century alcazar of Seville, whose flat, intricately carved surfaces are typical of Moorish façades. In Moorish sculpture, stone and wood carving were used mainly as architectural ornament. Many charming ivory boxes remain, which are adorned with scenes of court life or floral and animal motives; boxes were also made of precious metals. Filigreed, inlaid, and enameled jewelry, as well as textiles and rugs, were produced in Moorish Spain. The steel of Toledo was famed throughout the Middle Ages. Although few traces of Moorish painting have survived, an important 13th-century manuscript from Spain is preserved in the Vatican. Moorish pottery was of high quality. Lusterware fragments found near Córdoba dating from the 10th cent. are related to those from Samarra. Lusterware continued to be manufactured. The "Alhambra jars," distinguished by their wing handles, are decorated with golden-brownish designs on a white background with touches of blue. By the 15th cent. Málaga was noted throughout the Christian world for its gold lusterwares. See K. A. C. Creswell, *A Bibliography of the Architecture, Arts and Crafts of Islam* (1961); bibliography under ISLAMIC ART AND ARCHITECTURE.

Moors, nomadic people of the northern shores of Africa, originally the inhabitants of Mauretania. They were chiefly of Berber and Arab stock. In the 8th cent. the Moors were converted to Islam and became fanatic Muslims. They spread SW into Africa (see MAURITANIA, ISLAMIC REPUBLIC OF) and NW into Spain. Under TARIQ IBN ZIYAD they crossed to Gibraltar in 711 and easily overran the crumbling Visigothic kingdom of RODERICK. They spread beyond the Pyrenees into France, where they were turned back at Tours by CHARLES MARTEL (732). In 756, ABD AR-RAHMAN I established the Umayyad dynasty at Córdoba. This emirate became under Abd ar-Rahman III the caliphate of Córdoba. The court there grew in wealth, splendor, and culture. The regent al-Mansur (see under MANSUR, AL-) in the late 10th cent. waged bitter warfare with the Christians of N Spain, where, from the beginning, the Moorish conquest had met with its only opposition. The cities of the south, Toledo, Córdoba, and Seville, speedily became centers of the new culture and were famed for their universities and architectural treasures (see MOORISH ART AND ARCHITECTURE). With the exception of brief periods, there was, however, no strong central government; the power was split up among dissenting local leaders and factions. The caliphate fell in 1031, and the ALMORAVIDS in 1086 took over Moorish Spain, which was throughout the whole period closely connected in rule with Morocco. Almoravid control slowly declined and by 1174 was supplanted by the ALMOHADS. These successive waves of invasion had brought into Spain thousands of skilled Moorish artisans and industrious farmers who contributed largely to the intermittent prosperity of the country. They were killed or expelled in large numbers (to the great loss of Spain) in the Christian reconquest, which began with the recovery of Toledo (1085) by ALFONSO VI, king of León and Castile. The great Christian victory (1212) of Navas de Tolosa prepared the way for the downfall of the Muslims. Córdoba fell to FERDINAND III of Castile in 1236. The wars went on, and one by one the Moorish strongholds fell, until only Granada remained in their hands. Málaga was taken (1487) after a long siege by the forces of Ferdinand and Isabella, and in 1492 Granada was recovered. Many of the Moors remained in Spain; those who remained faithful to Islam were called Mudejares, while those who accepted Christianity were called MORISCOS. They were allowed to stay in Spain but were kept under close surveillance. They were persecuted by Philip II, revolted in 1568, and in the Inquisition were virtually exterminated. In 1609 the remaining Moriscos were expelled. Thus the glory of the Moorish civilization in Spain was gradually extinguished. Its contributions to Western Europe and especially to Spain were almost incalculable—in art and architecture, medicine and science, and learning (especially ancient Greek learning). See Stanley Lane-Poole, *The Moors in Spain* (1886, repr. 1967); Bernard Whishaw and Ellen M. Whishaw, *Arabic Spain* (1912); R. P. A. Dozy, *Spanish Islam* (tr. 1913).

Moos, Ludwig von (lo͝ot'vĭkh fən mo͞os), 1910–, Swiss political leader. Entering politics in his native town of Sachseln, he served (1941-46) as its president. He was later a government (cantonal) councilor (1946-59) before becoming a federal councilor, head of the federal department of justice, and chief of police. A member of the Swiss Conservative party, he served two one-year terms as vice president of the Swiss Confederation (1963, 1968) and two one-year terms as its president (1964, 1969).

Moose, river, c.50 mi (80 km) long, formed in central Ont., Canada, by the Mattagami and Missinaibi rivers. It flows NE to its confluence with the Abitibi River and into SW James Bay near Moosonee.

moose, largest member of the deer family, genus *Alces,* found in the northern parts of Eurasia and North America. The Eurasian species, *A. alces,* is known in Europe as the ELK, a name which in North America is applied to another large deer, the WAPITI. The Eurasian and the American moose are quite similar, but the American moose is somewhat larger and is considered by some to be a separate species, *A. americana.* It inhabits the coniferous forests of Alaska, Canada, and the northern conterminous United States. The moose has a heavy brown body with humped shoulders, and long, lighter-colored legs, the front pair longer than the hind ones. It has a thick, overhanging, almost trunklike muzzle and a short neck; a flap of skin covered with long hair and called the bell hangs from the throat. The male has broad, extremely flattened antlers, with a spread of up to 6 ft (180 cm). The largest variety is the Alaska moose; the adult male weighs from 1,000 to 1,800 lb (450-820 kg) and stands as much as 7½ ft (2.3 m) high at the shoulder. Browsers rather than grazers, moose eat leaves, twigs, buds, and the bark of some woody plants, as well as lichens, aquatic plants, and some of the taller herbaceous land plants. Moose live in small groups during the summer, sometimes forming large herds in the winter. They are polygamous, the males becoming very aggressive during the mating season. They are strong swimmers, reportedly crossing lakes many miles wide. Protection in national parks and reserves in Canada and the United States has saved the moose from extermination. Hunting of moose is strictly regulated. The Eurasian moose, or elk, is found from Scandinavia to E Siberia. Moose are classified in the phylum CHORDATA, subphylum Vertebrata, Class Mammalia, order Artiodactyla, family Cervidae.

Moose Factory, trading post, NE Ont., Canada, near the mouth of the Moose River on James Bay. A fort was built there by Charles Bayly, governor of the Hudson's Bay Company, in the early 1670s. In the struggle between the English and French in Canada, the fort changed hands several times and shortly after 1696 was destroyed. In 1730 the company built a post close to the ruins of the original fort. This post has been in continuous operation to the present day.

Moosehead Lake, 35 mi (56 km) long, from 2 to 10 mi (3.2-16.1 km) wide, with an area of 120 sq mi (311 sq km), W Maine, N of Augusta. It is the largest lake in Maine and has an irregular shoreline and numerous islands. The region around the lake is a picturesque resort area, and there is a state park on the southeast shore. **Mt. Kineo** (1,789 ft/545 m high) is located on a peninsula that extends into the lake.

Moose Jaw, city (1971 pop. 31,854), S central Sask., Canada. It is a railroad and distribution center, with oil refineries, meat-packing and dairy-processing plants, flour, lumber, and woolen mills, and dominion grain elevators and stockyards. There is also an airport.

Moosonee (mo͞o'sənē), village, NE Ont., Canada, on the Moose River near James Bay. It is the northern terminus of the Ontario Northland RR and Ontario's only saltwater port. There is a meteorological station. The area is popular with goose hunters.

moped: see MOTORCYCLE.

Mopti (môp'tē), city (1970 est. pop. 14,000), central Mali, a port at the confluence of the Niger and Bani rivers. The city is built on three islets linked by dikes; one dike, 8 mi (12.9 km) long, connects the islets with the river bank. Mopti is the market center for a region where rice, cotton, peanuts, and manioc are produced and cattle are raised.

Moqui Indians: see HOPI INDIANS.

Mor, Antonis: see MORO, ANTONIO.

Moradabad (môrədəbăd', mōrädäbäd'), city (1971 pop. 258,251), Uttar Pradesh state, N central India. It is an important rail junction and an agricultural market center. The Jama Masjid [great mosque], built in 1631, is in the city.

moraine (mərān'), rock and soil debris carried and finally deposited by a GLACIER. Material that falls on the sides of a valley glacier from the bounding cliffs makes up lateral moraines, running parallel to the valley sides. When two or more valley glaciers unite, the lateral moraines unite to form a medial moraine, running down the center of the glacier. When two or more lobes of a continental ice sheet unite, the debris carried by each lobe intermingles, forming an interlobate moraine. When the climate of a region becomes warmer, glaciers will start receding to their point of origin. The debris deposited by a melting glacier is called a ground moraine. The debris left at the edge of the glacier's extreme forward movement is a terminal moraine. Similar moraines deposited during stillstands or minor readvances of glacial ice are recessional moraines. After the retreat of a glacier the moraines remain as prominent features of the topography of the region that the glacier covered. The margins of the great ice sheets of the PLEISTOCENE EPOCH are marked by terminal moraines stretching across North America and Europe. See DRIFT.

Morais or **Moraes, Francisco de** (both: fränsēsh'kō dĭ môrīsh'), c.1500–c.1572, Portuguese courtier and writer. He was treasurer at the court of John III and was secretary to the Portuguese ambassador to Paris, where he was involved in an unhappy love affair. Morais's fame rests on his *Cronica de Palmeirim de Inglaterra* (1567), a long, fanciful episodic romance of chivalry, very popular in its day. His only other known work was *Dialogos* (1624). Morais's life of adventure ended by assassination.

Morales, Luis de (lwēs dā mōrä'lās), c.1520–1586, Spanish mannerist painter. He lived and worked in Badajoz. Morales executed vivid portrayals of saints suffering and refined devotional images of the Virgin and Child. Influences of Leonardo da Vinci and of Netherlandish art may be seen in his delicate and precisely executed paintings. *The Virgin with the Distaff, Holy Family,* and *Ecce Homo* are at the Hispanic Society, New York City. Other examples of his work are in the Prado and in churches in Badajoz.

morality play, form of medieval drama that developed in the late 14th cent. and flourished through the 16th cent. The characters in the morality were personifications of good and evil usually involved in a struggle for a man's soul. The form was generally static, but it contributed significantly to the secularization of European drama. The first known moralities were called the *Paternoster* plays. The greatest English morality is EVERYMAN. See MIRACLE PLAY.

Moral Re-Armament: see BUCHMAN, FRANK N. D.

morals: see ETHICS.

Moran, Edward (mərăn'), 1829–1901, American painter of marine and historical subjects, b. England. He came to the United States with his family in 1844. In 1899 he completed a series of 13 paintings illustrating epochs in the maritime history of America from the landing of Leif Ericsson to the return of Admiral Dewey's fleet from the Philippines in 1899 (Pennsylvania Mus. of the Fine Arts, Philadelphia). His brother **Thomas Moran,** 1837–1926, was an American landscape painter, illustrator, and etcher. He accompanied the exploring expeditions of Professor F. V. Hayden to the Yellowstone River (1871) and of Major J. W. Powell down the Colorado River (1873). Subsequently, he made the illustrations on wood for both expeditions' reports and the sketches from which he painted the two large canvases now in the Capitol at Washington, D.C., *The Grand Canyon of the Yellowstone* and *Chasm of the Colorado.* In 1884 he became a member of the National Academy of Design. As a painter Moran was strongly influenced by the art of Turner. Other examples of his painting are *Bringing Home the Cattle* (Buffalo, N.Y., Mus.); *The Grand Canal, Venice; The Dream of the Orient;* and *Tower of Cortez, in Mexico,* a watercolor. He also produced many etchings and magazine illustrations on wood. Another brother was **Peter Moran,** 1841–1914, American landscape and animal painter and etcher. Good examples of his painting are *Pasture Land; Santa Barbara Mission; Pueblo of Zia, New Mexico; The Stable Door;* and *Return of the Herd,* awarded a medal at the Centennial Exposition (1876), where his etchings of animals were similarly honored.

Morandi, Giorgio (jôr'jō môrän'dē), 1890–1964, Italian painter and etcher, b. Bologna. After his association with the *pittura metafisica* (1918–20) of CHIRICO, he developed an independent style. In his still lifes of exactingly arranged bottles and jars painted with a limited tonal range, Morandi created an art of quiet eloquence. His work was much respected in Italy for its poetic qualities.

Morat: see MURTEN, Switzerland.

Moratín, Leandro Fernández de: see FERNÁNDEZ DE MORATÍN, LEANDRO.

Morava (môr'ävä), Ger. *March,* river, c.240 mi (390 km) long, rising in the Sudetes, N Czechoslovakia, and flowing generally S past Olomouc into the Danube River, W of Bratislava. It is navigable in its lower course, which also forms part of the Austria-Czechoslovakia border. The Morava Valley is very fertile; sugar beets, grains, and tobacco are raised there. The valley is an important north-south thoroughfare.

Morava or **Velika Morava** (vĕl'ĭkä), river, 134 mi (216 km) long, formed at Stalać, E Yugoslavia, by the junction of the Zapadna Morava and the Južna Morava. It flows N to the Danube River. The Morava's wide valley is fertile and densely populated. Along with the Vardar River it is a major transportation corridor of the Balkan Peninsula.

Moravia, Alberto (älbĕr'tō mōrä'vyä), 1907–, Italian novelist. Moravia's original name was Alberto Pincherle. He is considered one of the foremost contemporary Italian novelists. His first novel, *The Indifferent Ones* (1929, tr. 1932), is a powerful study of spiritual ennui. A flamboyant work is *The Woman of Rome* (1947, tr. 1949). In such novels as *The Empty Canvas* (1960, tr. 1961), the surface tales grimly depict the conflict and interaction between the creative and the sensual, while the underlying theme is the apathy and despair of modern man. *Two Women* (1957, tr. 1958) a compelling story of wartime flight, was superbly filmed in 1961. His other works include *The Conformist* (1951), *Two: A Phallic Novel* (tr. 1972), the drama *Beatrice Cenci* (tr. 1965), the short-story collection *Bought and Sold* (1970, tr. 1973), and the essay collection *Which Tribe Do You Belong To?* (tr. 1974). See studies by Luciano Rebay (1970) and Joan Ross and Donald Freed (1972).

Moravia (mərā'vēə, mō–), Czech *Morava,* Ger. *Mähren,* region, central Czechoslovakia. The region is bordered on the W by Bohemia, on the E by the Little and White Carpathian Mts., which divide it from Slovakia, and on the N by the Sudetes Mts., which separate it from Silesia and which include the Moravian Gate, a historically strategic north-south route. Central Moravia is a valley, opening in the S on Austria and drained by the Morava River and its tributaries. A fertile agricultural area that encompasses the Haná region (noted both for farming and horse-breeding), Moravia is also highly industrialized. Diverse mineral resources, such as lignite, coal, oil, iron, copper, silver, and lead, spurred industrialization in the 20th cent. Among the region's other products are machinery, machine tools, armaments, automobiles, beer, liquor, clothing, furniture, and lumber. Major cities include BRNO, the former Moravian capital and one of Europe's leading textile centers; GOTTWALDOV, famous for its shoe industry; OSTRAVA, a coal-mining center with a large iron and steel industry; and OLOMOUC. With Bohemia and Czech Silesia, Moravia makes up the portion of Czechoslovakia traditionally occupied by the Czechs, a branch of the Western Slavs, who displaced Germanic tribes that occupied the region from the 1st to the 5th cent. A.D.; before then, Moravia had been inhabited by the Celtic Boii and Cotini. Subjugated by the Avars, the Czechs freed themselves under the leadership of Samo (627–c.660), who established the first state of the Western Slavs. The state disintegrated after his death, but by the 9th cent. the Moravians, again united, formed a great empire, including Bohemia, Silesia, Slovakia, S Poland, and N Hungary. In 863 the missionaries CYRIL AND METHODIUS were sent to Moravia on the appeal of Duke Rotislav, and the Moravians accepted Christianity, placing themselves under the Roman Catholic Church. The Moravian empire reached its height under Svatopluk (d. 894), but after his death it broke apart and (early 10th cent.) fell to the Magyars. When Emperor Otto I defeated (955) the Magyars, Moravia became a march of the Holy Roman Empire. From the early 11th cent. it was in effect a crownland of the kingdom of BOHEMIA, with which it passed (1526) under Austrian rule. However, Moravia retained its separate diet and was at times separated from the Bohemian crown (e.g., at periods during the Hussite Wars of the 15th cent. and from 1608 to 1611, when Bohemia was ruled by Emperor Rudolf II and Moravia by his brother Matthias). Moravia, generally more tolerant of Hapsburg authority than Bohemia, suffered less in the religious and civil strife of the 16th cent. and even experienced a flowering of Protestantism during a period of religious toleration. In 1618, however, the Czechs of Bohemia revolted and were crushed at the battle of the WHITE MOUNTAIN by the Hapsburgs, who thereafter took reprisals against the Moravian Czechs as well. Moravia's diet was reduced to total ineffectiveness. The Moravian towns underwent thorough Germanization from the 13th cent. Under Hapsburg rule nearly the entire upper and middle classes were German; cities such as Brno, predominantly German-speaking, were surrounded by a countryside of Czech-speaking people. In 1849, following an abortive revolution during which the Czechs of Bohemia and Moravia demanded unification of their historic lands and creation of a common diet, Moravia was made an Austrian crownland. Hapsburg rule was finally overthrown in 1918, and Moravia was incorporated into Czechoslovakia. In 1927, Moravia, with Czechoslovak SILESIA, was constituted into the province of Moravia and Silesia. The German element, however, continued to play an important part in Moravian life. The MUNICH PACT of 1938 resulted in the annexation by Germany of Czechoslovak Silesia and of NW and S Moravia; in 1939 Moravia and Bohemia became a German "protectorate." After World War II the pre-1938 boundaries were restored, and the larger part of the German-speaking population was expelled. In 1949 the province of Moravia and Silesia was replaced by four administrative regions, and in 1960, in a new administrative reorganization, Moravia was included in the South Moravian region (5,795 sq mi/15,009 sq km) and the North Moravian region (4,271 sq mi/11,062 sq km).

Moravian Church, Renewed Church of the Brethren, or **Unitas Fratrum,** an evangelical Christian communion whose adherents are sometimes called United Brethren or Herrnhuters. It originated (1457) near Kunwald, Bohemia, among some of the followers of John Huss who, after Huss's martyrdom, wished to preserve the spirit of his teaching. The name of this first association was Church of the Brotherhood. In 1467 one of the Brethren was consecrated bishop by Stephen, a bishop of the Waldenses. This brought about a break between the new brotherhood and the church of Rome. Persecution drove many of the Brethren out of Bohemia and Moravia into Poland, Austria, and elsewhere in Eastern Europe. The Moravians established schools and printing presses that were among the finest in Europe. The last of the bishops of the United Church was John Amos Comenius, appointed in 1632. He published a history of the church and an account of its doctrines and order. By the end of the Thirty Years War (1648), only a remnant of the movement remained. In 1722 a company of those still faithful to the teachings of the Brethren took refuge in Saxony on the estates of Graf von ZINZENDORF, where they built a town, Herrnhut. There the elements of the original church were revived and 1727, the year of the rediscovery of Comenius' works, is generally considered the founding date of the Renewed Moravian Church. The sect was immediately active in evangelizing and, after 1732, in missionary work. Its endeavors extended to the West Indies, to North and South America, to Africa, and to Asia, chiefly under the direction of August Gottlieb SPANGENBERG, who later became (1735) the founder of the Moravian Church in America. In 1735, David Nitschmann and a company of fellow workers bound for Georgia met and influenced John Wesley. Bethlehem, Nazareth, and Lititz, Pa., were founded (c.1740); from these Moravian settlements and from that in Salem, N.C., missionary work among Indians and white settlers was actively carried on. Interest in education led to the founding of the Moravian College for Women in 1742 and Moravian College (for men) in 1807 (both now at Bethlehem, Pa.). The Moravians take Scripture as the rule of faith and morals. Their simple liturgy, emotional hymns, and love feasts all tend to stress the subjective aspect of religion. The music in the Moravian churches is famous, especially the part-singing of the congregations. Conceiving of themselves as a "congregation of saints," the Moravians emphasize conduct rather than doctrine. The doctrinal system, which conforms to the major Protestant confessions, is expounded in the *Easter Morning Litany* (1749). The church is governed by provincial synods, the bishops having only spiritual and administrative authority. More than half, or about 50,000, of the Moravians in the world live in North America. The church belongs to the National Council of Churches and the World Council of Churches. See Edward Langton, *History of the Moravian Church* (1956).

Moravian College, at Bethlehem, Pa.; Moravian; coeducational; inc. 1954 with the merger of Moravian Seminary and College for Women (1742) and Moravian College and Theological Seminary (1807).

Moravská Ostrava, Czechoslovakia: see OSTRAVA.

Moray. For Scottish names spelled thus, see MURRAY.

moray: see EEL.

Morayshire (mŭ'rēshĭr) or **Elginshire** (ĕl'gĭnshĭr), county (1971 pop. 51,485), 476 sq mi (1,233 sq km), NE Scotland, on the Moray Firth. ELGIN is the county town. The inland hills reach 2,000 ft (610 m) and slope to a fertile farm belt near the coast. The chief rivers are the Findhorn, the Lossie, and the Spey. Forestry projects have reclaimed many thousands of acres in the northwest of the county, including the sandy wastes of the Culbin sands along the coast. Oats, barley, and livestock are raised; the uplands are used for rough grazing. Whiskey and woolens are the chief manufactures. Fishing is important. Morayshire was colonized by Northern Picts. Forming the eastern part of the province of Moray, it came under crown dominion in the time of Malcolm III of Scotland (late 11th cent.). The region is associated with legends about Macbeth. In 1975, Morayshire was divided between the Highland and Grampian regions.

Morazán, Francisco (fränsēs'kō mōräsän'), 1799–1842, Central American statesman, b. Tegucigalpa, Honduras. He led the revolutionary army that overthrew (1829) the regime of Manuel José Arce and was proclaimed president of the CENTRAL AMERICAN FEDERATION in 1830. The opponents of Guatemalan domination caused Morazán to move the capital from Guatemala to San Salvador. As a liberal he promoted education and abolished most monastic orders. The spiritual father of federalism in Central America, he fought vigorously for his ideals, but when elected for a second term he was unable to combat widespread apathy and the increasing opposition of the conservatives; his congress dissolved the federation in 1838. Nevertheless, in 1839 he attempted to recapture Guatemala from Rafael CARRERA, but was defeated. In the following year he went into voluntary exile until recalled in 1842 by Costa Rica and proclaimed president there. Again he attempted to restore Central American unity but was betrayed and shot Sept. 15, 1842, by his own partisans. See biography by R. S. Chamberlain (1950).

Morbihan (môrbēäN'), department (1968 pop. 540,474), NW France, in Brittany, on the Atlantic coast. VANNES is the capital.

mordant (môr'dənt) [Fr.,=biting], substance used in dyeing to fix certain dyes (mordant dyes) in cloth. Either the mordant (if it is colloidal) or a colloid produced by the mordant adheres to the fiber, attracting and fixing the colloidal mordant dye (see COLLOID); the insoluble, colored precipitate that is formed is called a LAKE. The chemical compounds used as mordants are either acidic or basic. Acid mordants (e.g., tannic acid) are employed with basic dyes; basic mordants (e.g., alum, chrome alum, and certain salts of aluminum, chromium, copper, iron, potassium, and tin) are employed with acid dyes. Cloth to be dyed may be treated first with the mordant and then with the dye, or the mordant and dye may be applied together. The vividness of certain dyes that ordinarily do not require the use of a mordant may be markedly increased when one is employed.

Mordaunt, Charles: see PETERBOROUGH, CHARLES MORDAUNT, 3D EARL OF.

Mordecai (môr'dĕkī, môr''dĕkā'ī), cousin and guardian of ESTHER.

Morden, town (1971 pop. 3,266), S Man., Canada, SW of Winnipeg. Located in an agricultural region, it has farm machinery and food- and fiber-processing plants. There is a government experimental farm in the town.

Mordovian Autonomous Soviet Socialist Republic: see MORDVINIAN AUTONOMOUS SOVIET SOCIALIST REPUBLIC.

Mordred, Sir: see ARTHURIAN LEGEND.

Mordva: see MORDVINIAN AUTONOMOUS SOVIET SOCIALIST REPUBLIC.

Mordvinian Autonomous Soviet Socialist Republic (môrdvĭn'ēən), autonomous republic (1970 pop. 1,030,000), c.10,000 sq mi (25,900 sq km), E European USSR. A densely forested steppe, it consists of the Volga upland in the east and the Oka-Don lowland in the west. Lumbering, agricultural processing, and the manufacture of automobiles, machinery, furniture, paper, and wood chemicals are the major industries. Beekeeping is a long-established economic activity. Cattle and sheep are raised, and grain, hemp, potatoes, and flax are grown. SARANSK, the capital, and Ardatov are the major cities. The population is composed of Russians (more than 50%), Mordvinians, and Tatars. The Mordvinians, an ancient Finno-Ugric ethnic group, were first mentioned by the Gothic historian, Jordanes, in the 6th cent. A.D. They were land tillers and herdsmen, with close ties to the Slavs. In the mid-13th cent. they fell under the Golden Horde and, when it disintegrated, passed to the Kazan khanate. Russia annexed the territory of the Mordvinians in 1552. The Mordvinian Autonomous SSR, also known as the Mordovian Autonomous SSR, was formed in 1934. The Mordvinians (Rus. *Mordva*) speak a Finno-Ugric language and are Orthodox Christians.

More, Sir Anthony: see MORO, ANTONIO.

More, Hannah, 1745–1833, English author and social reformer. She was educated, and later taught, at her sisters' school for girls in Bristol. At the age of 22 she became engaged to William Turner, a wealthy squire 20 years older than she; he never married her, but settled an annuity on her that made her financially independent. She became a friend of many of the notable figures of her time and was one of the BLUESTOCKINGS. Her two ethical tragedies, *Percy* and *Fatal Falsehood,* were produced by Garrick in 1777 and 1779, respectively. Turning to religious and philanthropic works, she wrote *Thoughts on the Importance of the Manners of the Great to General Society* (1788) and was instrumental in founding (1799) the Religious Tract Society. In the area of Wrington she established Sunday schools in which the poor were taught reading, personal hygiene, and religion. In 1808 her pious but popular novel *Coelebs in Search of a Wife* appeared. Her writing is of little interest today, with the exception of her vivacious and highly informative letters, which were published in 1834. See studies by M. A. Hopkins (1947) and M. G. Jones (1952).

More, Henry, 1614–87, English philosopher, one of the foremost representatives of the school of CAMBRIDGE PLATONISTS. His writings emphasized the mystical and theosophic phases of that philosophy, and as he grew older mysticism dominated his writings. Newton studied under him, and his concept of space and time as "the sense organs of God" greatly influenced Newton's theory of absolute space and time. His chief works are *Philosophical Poems* (1647) and *Divine Dialogues* (1668). See P. R. Anderson, *Science in Defence of Liberal Religion* (1933); Ernst Cassirer, *The Platonic Renaissance in England* (tr. 1953); Ahron Lichtenstein, *Henry More: The Rational Theology of a Cambridge Platonist* (1962).

More, Paul Elmer, 1864–1937, American critic, educator, and philosopher, b. St. Louis. More taught Sanskrit and classical literature and then was a newspaper editor until 1914, after which he wrote and lectured. Associated with Irving BABBITT in the movement called the New Humanism, More became an authority on Greek philosophy. His major works are the *Shelburne Essays* (11 vol., 1904–21), *The Greek Tradition* (5 vol., 1921–31), and the *New Shelburne Essays* (3 vol., 1928–36). See biography by A. H. Dakin (1960); study by F. X. Duggan (1967).

More, Sir Thomas (Saint Thomas More), 1478–1535, English statesman and author of *Utopia,* celebrated as a martyr in the Roman Catholic Church. He received a Latin education in the household of Cardinal Morton and at Oxford. Through his contact with the new learning and his friendships with Colet, Lily, and Erasmus, More became an ardent humanist. As a successful London lawyer, he attracted the attention of Henry VIII, served him on diplomatic missions, entered the king's service in 1518, and was knighted in 1521. More held important government offices and, despite his disapproval of Henry's divorce from Katharine of Aragón, he was made lord chancellor at the fall of Wolsey (1529). He resigned in 1532 because of ill health and probably because of increasing disagreement with Henry's policies. Because of his refusal to subscribe to the Act of Supremacy, which impugned the pope's authority and made Henry the head of the English Church, he was imprisoned (1534) in the Tower and finally beheaded on a charge of treason. A man of noble character and deep, resolute religious conviction, More had great personal charm, unfailing good humor, piercing wit, and a fearlessness that enabled him to jest even on the scaffold. His UTOPIA (published in Latin, 1516; tr. 1551) is a picture of an ideal state founded entirely on reason. Among his other works in Latin and English are a translation of *The Life of John Picus, Earl of Mirandula* (1510); a *History of Richard III,* upon which Shakespeare based his play; a number of polemical tracts against the Lutherans (1528–33); devotional works including *A Dialogue of Comfort against Tribulation* (1534) and a *Treatise on the Passion* (1534); poems; meditations; and prayers. More was beatified (1886) by a decree of Pope Leo XIII and canonized (1935) by Pius XI. His English works were published in 1557 (see edition by W. E. Campbell and A. W. Reed, 1931); his correspondence (ed. by E. F. Rogers, 1947) contains all his letters except those to Erasmus. The biography of More by his son-in-law William Roper (ed. by E. V. Hitchcock, 1935) has been the principal source of later biographies (see the standard modern biography by R. W. Chambers, 1935). See studies by E. L. Suntz (1957), R. Pineas (1968), R. Johnson (1969), and E. E. Reynolds (1965 and 1969).

Morea, Greece: see PELOPONNESUS.

Moréas, Jean (zhäN môrāäs'), 1856–1910, French poet, b. Athens. His name was originally Papadiamantopoulos. He went to Paris in 1872. He wrote two volumes of symbolist verse, *Les Syrtes* (1884) and *Le Pèlerin passionné* (1891). With the publication of *Enone au clair visage* (1894) and *Eriphyle* (1894), Moréas returned to classical style, and in *Stances* (1899–1901) and his play *Iphigénie* (1903) he clearly reacted against the new movements in poetry.

Moreau, Gustave (güstäv' môrō'), 1826–98, French painter. He was known for his pictures of the weird and mystical. The recipient of many honors, he refused to sell his paintings except to friends. Moreau was professor at the École des Beaux-Arts, where his pupils included Matisse and Rouault. After his death, his house in Paris (now the Musée Moreau), with his fine art collection, was bequeathed to the nation. *Orpheus* (Louvre) and *Oedipus and the Sphinx* (Metropolitan Mus.) are characteristic works. See study by Jean and J. P. Paladilhe (1972).

Moreau, Jean-Michel (zhäN-mēshĕl'), 1741–1814, French draftsman and engraver, called Moreau le jeune. He is noted for his charming illustrations of the work of Voltaire, Molière, and Rousseau and for his admirable engravings of court masques and fetes. His brother, **Louis Gabriel Moreau,** 1740–1806, called Moreau l'aîné, was a notable landscape painter, watercolorist, and etcher. His *Coteaux de Mendon* is in the Louvre.

Moreau, Jeanne (zhän), 1928–, French movie actress, b. Paris. She studied at the Comédie Française. Moreau is internationally known for her sophisticated portrayals of amoral romantic heroines. Her films include *The Lovers* (1959), *Les Liaisons Dangereuses* (1960), *La Notte* (1961), *Jules et Jim* (1961), *Diary of a Chambermaid* (1964), *Viva Maria* (1965), *The Bride Wore Black* (1967), and *Going Places* (1974).

Moreau, Jean Victor (zhäN vĕktôr'), 1763–1813, French general in the FRENCH REVOLUTIONARY WARS. Despite his successes on the Rhine and in Germany (1796–97), he was dismissed for withholding compromising information about General PICHEGRU after the coup d'etat of 18 FRUCTIDOR (1797); he was later reinstated (April, 1799) at the head of the French army in Italy. After helping Napoleon Bonaparte in the coup d'etat of 18 Brumaire he was given command (1800) in Germany and routed the Austrians at Hohenlinden. At the conclusion of the war Moreau began to oppose Bonaparte, and his name rallied republican sentiment. Informed of the royalist CADOUDAL plot, he neither joined nor revealed it; after its discovery he was arrested and sentenced to imprisonment for two years. The sentence was commuted to exile, which he spent in Spain and America. Returning to Europe in 1813, he assisted the allies as an adviser in their war against Napoleon, but was killed in battle.

Moreau, Louis Gabriel: see MOREAU, JEAN-MICHEL.

Morecambe and Heysham (môr'kəm, hē'shəm, hē'səm), municipal borough (1971 pop. 41,863), Lancashire, NW England, on Morecambe Bay. Morecambe, a seaside resort, and Heysham, a port with service to Belfast, were joined in 1928. Morecambe shrimp are famous. Nearby is an unusual single-celled chapel dating from before the Norman conquest.

Morecambe Bay, shallow inlet of the Irish Sea, 16 mi (26 km) long and 10 mi (16.1 km) wide, separating Furness peninsula from the mainland, NW England. It receives the Kent and Lune rivers. Shrimp are caught there.

Moreh (mō'rē). **1** Place, Palestine, known by its holy tree, near Shechem. It was Abraham's first resting place after entering the land of Canaan. Gen 12.6; Deut. 11.30. **2** Hill of N Palestine by which Gideon camped before he attacked the Midianites. It is identified with modern Nebi Dahi (Israel), S of Mt. Tabor. Judges 7.1.

Morehouse College: see ATLANTA UNIV. CENTER.

Morelia (mōrā'lyä), city (1970 pop. 209,507), capital of Michoacán state, W Mexico. It is the commercial and processing center of an irrigated agricultural and cattle-raising area. Founded as Valladolid in 1541 by Antonio de Mendoza, Morelia is built on a rocky hill and is surrounded by a fertile valley at the western edge of the central plateau. High peaks border the valley on three sides. The climate is warm and healthful. The city is supplied with water by an aqueduct dating from the colonial period. The most imposing Spanish structure is the cathedral, begun in 1640; colonial architecture, some modern buildings, and shaded plazas give the city a pleasant atmosphere. The Colegio de San Nicolás, founded (1540) in Pátzcuaro and transferred in 1580 to Morelia, is the oldest institution of higher learning in Mexico. Morelia was the birthplace of Agustín de ITURBIDE and of the patriot MORELOS Y PAVÓN, for whom it was renamed in 1828.

Morelos (mōrā'lōs), state (1970 pop. 620,392), 1,917 sq mi (4,965 sq km), S Mexico. CUERNAVACA is the capital. Morelos is separated from the Federal District and from Mexico state by the east-west volcanic chain crossing central Mexico. Morelos itself is mountainous, with many broad, semiarid valleys in the south. The climate is cold in the mountains and hot in the valleys. Chiefly agricultural, the state grows sugarcane, rice, coffee, cereals, tropical fruits, and vegetables. Sugar and rum are manufactured. The principal towns are Cuernavaca and Cuautla Morelos, which is famous for its defense (1812) by Morelos y Pavón in the war against Spain. The state, created in 1869, was named in his honor. It is one of Mexico's most densely populated states.

Morelos y Pavón, José María (hōsā' märē'ä mōrā'lōs ē pävōn'), 1765–1815, Mexican leader in the revolution against Spain, a national hero. He was, like HIDALGO Y COSTILLA, a liberal priest. Joining the revolution (1810), he conducted a brilliant campaign in the south and after the execution of Hidalgo he became insurrectionary chief. He defended CUAUTLA against CALLEJA DEL REY for several months, and then cut through the siege. After taking Orizaba and Oaxaca (1812) in a brilliant engagement, Morelos captured Acapulco (1813). The Congress of Chilpancingo, convened in 1813 under his protection, elected him generalissimo with the powers of chief executive. Late in 1813 his forces were routed at Valladolid (later named Morelia in his honor) by ITURBIDE and were later again defeated. In 1815, Morelos was captured, degraded by the Inquisition, and shot. Only a few leaders, notably GUERRERO and GUADALUPE VICTORIA, were left to continue the revolution. See biography by W. H. Timmons (2d ed. 1970).

Moreno, Mariano (märyä'nō mōrā'nō), 1778–1811, Argentine revolutionist and publicist. He became prominent as legal counselor to the royal audiencia and to the cabildo of Buenos Aires. His condemnation of the Spanish colonial system and his advocacy of liberal economic principles attracted attention. A leader in the revolution of May, 1810, which deposed the Spanish viceroy, he was secretary of the first revolutionary governing junta and exerted a significant influence. He founded (June 7, 1810) the *Gazeta de Buenos Aires* and, as editor, championed in its columns his democratic, reform ideas. In 1810 he founded the national library. His liberal policy provoked a conflict with the conservatives, who, in spite of Moreno's opposition, admitted provincial deputies to the junta; Moreno resigned (Dec., 1810). His resignation checked the democratic movement in the Río de la Plata and initiated a protracted struggle between Buenos Aires and the country provinces. Appointed to a diplomatic mission abroad, he sailed for Europe (Jan., 1811) and died at sea.

Moreno, city (1970 pop. 114,041), Buenos Aires prov., E Argentina. It is a residential and district administrative center in the Greater Buenos Aires area. The district was the scene of several major battles during the Argentine War of Independence and the mid-19th century unitarian-federalist conflict.

Møre og Romsdal (mö'rə ô ro͞oms'däl), county (1972 est. pop. 226,000), 5,820 sq mi (15,074 sq km) W Norway, bordering on the Atlantic Ocean in the west. Molde is the capital. It is a scenic mountainous region, with deep valleys, including the Romsdalen valley, numerous fjords, and many islands. Fishing and farming are important, and there are aluminum, textile, shoe, and furniture industries.

mores (môr'āz), concept developed by William Graham SUMNER to designate those FOLKWAYS that if violated, result in extreme punishment. The term comes from the Latin *mos* (customs), and although mores are fewer in number than folkways, they are more coercive. Negative mores are taboos, usually supported by religious or philosophical sanctions. Whereas folkways guide human conduct in the more mundane areas of life, mores tend to control those aspects connected with sex, the family, or with religion.

Moresheth-gath (môr'ĕshĕth-găth), town, SW Palestine. It was the home of the prophet Micah. Micah 1.14.

Moresnet (môrănā'), district, 1.5 sq mi (3.9 sq km), Liège prov., E Belgium, near the West German border. It was formerly a lead- and zinc-mining center. Under joint Prussian and Dutch (after 1830, Belgian) suzerainty from 1816, it was awarded (1919) to Belgium under the Treaty of Versailles.

Moreton Bay (môr'tən), inlet of the Pacific Ocean, 65 mi (105 km) long and 20 mi (32 km) wide, Queensland, E Australia, nearly enclosed by Moreton and Stradbroke islands. Receiving the Brisbane River, the bay is the entrance to the port of Brisbane. There are many resort towns on its western shore.

Moreto y Cabaña, Agustín (ägo͞ostēn' mōrā'tō ē käbä'nyä), 1618–69, dramatic poet of the Spanish Golden Age, b. Madrid. Moreto borrowed and often improved upon the plots of others, chiefly those of Lope de Vega and Calderón. The author of more than 100 plays, he contributed great artistic polish and strong characterization to the Spanish theater. His best-known plays are *El lindo don Diego* [the handsome Don Diego] and his masterpiece, *El desdén con el desdén* [meeting contempt with contempt]. He entered a monastery in 1659. See study by J. A. Augustin (1974).

Moretto, Il (ēl mōrĕt'tō), c.1498–1554, Italian painter, whose real name was Alessandro Bonvicino. He was a leading representative of the Brescian school. While following the art of the Venetian masters, he developed a rather saccharine style. Many of his altarpieces are still in the churches of Brescia. There are portraits by him in the Metropolitan Museum; National Gallery of Art, Washington, D.C.; and National Gallery, London. His most famous pupil was Giovanni Battista Moroni. See B. Berenson, *Italian Pictures of the Renaissance* (1932, repr. 1968).

Moret y Prendergast, Segismundo (sāhēsmo͞on'dō mōrā' ē prāndārgäst'), 1838–1913, Spanish statesman. In 1863 he was elected to the Cortes, and as colonial minister in the cabinet of Juan Prim he advocated the abolition of slavery. After the restoration of Alfonso XII (1875), he reentered the Cortes and held several cabinet posts. Moret was colonial minister, 1897–98, and advocated a policy of conciliation toward Cuba and Puerto Rico. He opposed the Spanish-American War (1898). After the death of Sagasta (1903), he became a Liberal party leader and was twice premier (1905–6, 1909).

Morey, Charles Rufus, 1877–1955, American art historian, b. Hastings, Mich. Morey was considered one of the foremost medievalists of his time. His principal works include *Early Christian Art* (2d ed. 1953) and *Mediaeval Art* (1942). He was instrumental in returning to Italy works of art plundered by the Nazis.

Morgagni, Giovanni Battista (jōvän'nē bät-tēs'tä mōrgä'nyē), 1682–1771, Italian anatomist, called the founder of pathologic anatomy. He was professor of anatomy at Padua for 56 years. A meticulous observer and recorder, he contributed classical descriptions of anatomical parts (many of which are named for him), collected case histories, and carried out exhaustive postmortem examinations, as a result of which he discovered many relationships between diseases and physiological changes.

Morgan, American family of financiers and philanthropists. **Junius Spencer Morgan,** 1813–90, b. West Springfield, Mass., prospered at investment banking. As a boy he became a dry-goods clerk in Boston; later he entered a brokerage house in New York City. He became a partner in mercantile firms in Hartford, Conn., and in Boston and then (1854) went to London to become a partner of George PEABODY. Ten years later he assumed entire control of the firm, which became J. S. Morgan & Company. He expanded this international banking enterprise, handling most of the British funds invested in the United States. His syndicate's loan of $50 million to the French government at the time of the Franco-Prussian War was one of the most spectacular transactions of the time. His son, **John Pierpont Morgan,** 1837–1913, b. Hartford, Conn., built the family fortunes into a colossal financial and industrial empire. He studied abroad and in 1857 entered the New York City banking house of Duncan, Sherman & Company. Three years later he became the New York agent for his father's firm in London. After he became (1864) junior partner in the new firm, Dabney, Morgan & Company, he helped form (1871) the New York firm of Drexel, Morgan & Company—which in 1895 became J. P. Morgan & Company. On the death of his father (1890) he became sole manager of J. S. Morgan & Company—later (1910) Morgan, Grenfell & Company—of London. J. P. Morgan's ascent to power, however, was accompanied by dramatic financial battles. He wrested control (1869) of the Albany and Susquehanna RR from Jay GOULD and Jim FISK, he led the syndicate that broke the government-financing privileges of Jay COOKE, and he developed a railroad empire by reorganizations and consolidations in all parts of the United States. He backed James J. HILL in preventing (1901) the interests of Edward H. Harriman from controlling the Northern Pacific RR and, with it, the Chicago, Burlington & Quincy RR. Agreement between the factions resulted in formation of the Northern Securities Company, which was dissolved (1904) by court action, with Morgan and President Theodore Roosevelt arrayed as antagonists. In the industrial field, Morgan formed (1901) the U.S. Steel Corp., the first billion-dollar corporation in the world. He financed manufacturing and mining and controlled banks, insurance companies, shipping lines, and communications systems. Through his firm came enormous funds from abroad to develop American resources. He was widely criticized on many occasions for backing the sale of obsolete carbines to the Union and for his gold speculations in the Civil War, for the harsh terms of his loan of gold to the Federal government in the 1895 crisis, for his financial dominance in the Panic of 1907, and for bringing on the financial ills of the New York, New Haven & Hartford RR. He was largely deaf to popular criticism. In 1912 he appeared and publicly defended himself before a congressional committee headed by Arsène PUJO, which was investigating the "money trust" and which was aimed particularly at him. He was an ardent sportsman, and his yacht entered many international races. He was a prominent lay leader in the Protestant Episcopal Church. He personally dispensed numerous philanthropies, and he was a renowned art collector. After his death the Metropolitan Museum of Art, of which he had been president, received a valuable portion of his collection, which is housed in the Pierpont Morgan wing. See biographies by J. K. Winkler (1930), Lewis Corey (1930), and F. L. Allen (1949). **John Pierpont Morgan,** 1867–1943, b. Irvington, N.Y., grad. Harvard, 1889, became active head of the house of Morgan when his father died in 1913. The firm was called upon to help finance World War I. As American agent for Allied countries, the banking house raised huge funds—one issue valued at $500 million—and systematized the purchases of military supplies. The Morgan firm was not important in war financing after America's entry, but in the postwar period it floated securities of foreign governments and corporations reaching $2 billion, at the same time sponsoring over $4 billion of domestic securities. Morgan and his partners actively promoted great mergers after 1922 and controlled numerous nonbanking corporations. The younger J. P. Morgan resembled his father in his dislike for publicity and in continuing his father's philanthropic policy. In 1920 he gave his London residence to the U.S. government for use as its embassy and later endowed the Pierpont Morgan Library in New York City as a research institute in memory of his father. A sister of the younger J. Pierpont Morgan, **Anne Morgan,** 1873–1952, was devoted to numerous philanthropic and civic organizations and constantly voiced the rights of the American woman. See L. Corey, *House of Morgan: a Social Biography of the Masters of Money* (1930, repr. 1969); E. P. Hoyt, Jr., *House of*

Morgan (1966); George Wheeler, *Pierpont Morgan and Friends* (1973).

Morgan, Conwy Lloyd, 1852–1936, English psychologist. Professor of zoology at University College, Bristol (1887–1909), he served as first vice chancellor of the Univ. of Bristol (1909–10) and was professor of psychology and ethics until his retirement in 1919. He was one of the founders of animal psychology and a leading advocate of evolution. His works include *Animal Life and Intelligence* (1890), *Habit and Instinct* (1896), *Instinct and Experience* (1912), *Emergent Evolution* (1923), and *The Animal Mind* (1930).

Morgan, Daniel, 1736–1802, American Revolutionary general, b. probably in Hunterdon co., N.J. He moved (c.1753) to Virginia and later served in the French and Indian Wars and several Indian campaigns. In the Revolution, Morgan assumed command of the attack on Quebec (see QUEBEC CAMPAIGN) after Benedict Arnold was wounded, but Morgan himself was captured. He was exchanged (1776) and took part in the Saratoga campaign, but dissatisfied with the congressional policy of promotions, he retired in 1779. He reentered the army in 1780 and joined the Carolina campaign. Serving under Nathanael Greene, he defeated the British at Cowpens (1781). After the war he helped to suppress the Whiskey Rebellion and served (1797–99) as a U.S. Congressman. See biographies by North Callahan (1961) and Don Higginbotham (1961).

Morgan, Edmund Sears, 1916–, U.S. historian, b. Minneapolis. After receiving his Ph.D. from Harvard in 1942, he taught at the Univ. of Chicago (1945–46) and at Brown (1946–55) before becoming (1955) professor of history at Yale. An expert on American colonial history, Morgan writes in a way that appeals to the general reading public while maintaining high scholarly standards. His many books include *The Puritan Family* (1944, rev. and enl. ed. 1966), *The Stamp Act Crisis,* with his wife Helen M. Morgan (1953, rev. ed. 1963), *The Puritan Dilemma* (1958) and biographies of Ezra Stiles (1962) and Roger Williams (1967).

Morgan, George, 1743–1810, American merchant, Indian agent, and land speculator, b. Philadelphia. In 1765 he went as his firm's representative to engage in the fur trade in Illinois, but the venture failed. Morgan, interested in a tract of land (2,862 sq mi/6,565 sq km in what is now West Virginia) that had been ceded by the Indians in repayment for property destroyed in Pontiac's War (1763), helped to form (1776) the Indiana Company, with a land office at Fort Pitt. The state of Virginia successfully contested the company's claim after several years of litigation. In the American Revolution, Morgan served as an Indian agent and as a colonel in the commissary until 1779, when he retired to his estate near Princeton, N.J. In 1789 he entered into a scheme with the Spanish minister to the United States for colonizing Spanish territory and established (1789) the colony of New Madrid in what is now Missouri. The project was opposed by the Spanish governor of Louisiana, and Morgan abandoned it. In 1796 he took up scientific agriculture on a large tract of land he inherited in W Pennsylvania. See biography by Max Savelle (1932).

Morgan, Sir Henry, 1635?–1688, Welsh buccaneer. In his youth he went to the West Indies, eventually joining the buccaneers there. On the death (1667) of Edward MANSFIELD, Morgan took his place as commander of the buccaneers. He operated as a privateer, being commissioned in his activities by the British authorities. His exploits included the capture of Puerto Príncipe (Camagüey, Cuba) and the sack of Puerto Bello (1668), the capture of Maracaibo (1669), the ravaging of the Cuban and American coasts (1670), and the daring capture of Panama (1671). His operations were always marked by indescribable brutality and debauchery, but they were executed with skill and bravery, sometimes against great odds. Sent (1672) as a prisoner to England on complaints of piracy, he soon became a hero, was knighted (1673), and was made lieutenant governor of Jamaica, where he spent the rest of his life and was acting governor (1680–82). See biography by W. A. Roberts (1933).

Morgan, John, 1735–89, American physician, b. Philadelphia, grad. College of Philadelphia (now Univ. of Pennsylvania), 1751. He founded, in Philadelphia (1765), the first medical school in the United States. In 1775 he became director general and physician in chief to the general hospital of the Continental Army. Blamed for a high mortality rate in the hospital, he was removed (1777) by Congress, which later exonerated him. His writings include *A Discourse on the Introduction of Medical Schools in America* (1765).

Morgan, John Hunt, 1825–64, Confederate general in the American Civil War, b. Huntsville, Ala. He spent most of his early life in Kentucky. At the outbreak of the Civil War, Morgan joined the Confederates as a cavalry scout, and in 1862 he began the daring raids behind Union lines that were to make him and his men famous. For his success at Hartsville, Tenn., where he captured a garrison of Federal troops in Dec., 1862, he was made a brigadier general. The raid through Kentucky, Indiana, and Ohio in the summer of 1863 was Morgan's outstanding feat, even though it ended in his capture (July, 1863). He escaped from prison in November and in April, 1864, was assigned to command in SW Virginia. Federals who had penetrated the Confederate lines killed him at Greeneville, Tenn., in Sept., 1864. See studies by B. W. Duke (1867; repr. 1960), C. F. Holland (1942), and D. A. Brown (1959).

Morgan, John Pierpont: see MORGAN, family.

Morgan, Junius Spencer: see MORGAN, family.

Morgan, Lewis Henry, 1818–81, American anthropologist, b. Aurora, N.Y., grad. Union College, Schenectady, 1840. Practicing as a lawyer, he became interested in the Indians of his locality, and in 1847 he was made an adopted member of the Seneca tribe. His *League of the Ho-de-no-sau-nee or Iroquois* (1851, repr. 1954) is unexcelled among early descriptive reports. Morgan was interested in social organization to the almost complete exclusion of other cultural factors, and he devised a theory correlating kinship terminologies with forms of marriage and rules of descent. His *Systems of Consanguinity and Affinity of the Human Family* (1870) presented this principle. *Ancient Society* (1877, repr. 1959), which classified the cultures of the world into progressive stages—savagery, barbarism, and civilization—attracted the attention of Marx and Engels, who interpreted its evolutionary doctrine as support to their materialistic theory of history. Morgan's *Indian Journals* were edited by Leslie A. White and published in 1959. See biographies by B. J. Stern (1931, repr. 1967) and Carl Resek (1960).

Morgan, Thomas Hunt, 1866–1945, American zoologist, b. Lexington, Ky., Ph.D. Johns Hopkins, 1890. He was professor of experimental zoology at Columbia (1904–28) and from 1928 was director of the laboratory of biological sciences at the California Institute of Technology. He is noted for his ingenious demonstration of the physical basis of heredity and the importance of the gene, using in his research the fruit fly, *Drosophila.* He described the phenomena of linkage and CROSSING OVER, which he and his students utilized to map the linear arrangement of genes along the chromosome. Morgan received the 1933 Nobel Prize in Physiology and Medicine. His books, classics in the literature of genetics, include *The Physical Basis of Heredity* (1919), *Mechanism of Mendelian Heredity* (rev. ed. 1923), *Evolution and Genetics* (1925), *The Theory of the Gene* (rev. ed. 1928), and *Embryology and Genetics* (1934).

Morgan, William: see ANTI-MASONIC PARTY.

Morgan City, city (1970 pop. 16,586), St. Mary parish, S La., a fishing port on the Atchafalaya River (connected to the Intracoastal Waterway); inc. 1860. The city is headquarters for offshore petroleum drilling and a trade center for a bayou area where rice and sugarcane are grown. It has shipyards, a large shrimp fleet, and an oyster industry.

Morgan horse, breed of American LIGHT HORSE descended from a single progenitor—the famous JUSTIN MORGAN. Morgans are used as all-purpose light horses and are very popular on cattle ranches. Their average height is just under 15 hands (60 in./150 cm), and their average weight is about 1,000 lb (450 kg). Bay, chestnut, and black are common colors.

morganite: see BERYL.

Morgan Library: see PIERPONT MORGAN LIBRARY.

Morganton, town (1970 pop. 13,625), seat of Burke co., W N.C., on the Catawba River in the foothills of the Blue Ridge Mts.; founded 1784, inc. 1885. A lake resort town, it also has industries that manufacture furniture, textiles, apparel, and electrical parts. A junior college and a state school for the deaf are there.

Morgantown, city (1970 pop. 29,431), seat of Monongalia co., N W.Va., near the Pa. line, on the Monongahela River; inc. 1785. A shipping point for a coal-mining region, it also has glass, textile, and chemical industries. Fort Morgan was built there in 1772, and the first settlers arrived the same year. Iron, discovered in 1789, was the principal industry until the Civil War. The city is the seat of West Virginia Univ., which has two main campuses in town.

Morgarten (môr'gärtən), mountain, 4,084 ft (1,245 m) high, N central Switzerland, on the border of Schwyz and Zug cantons. There, on Nov. 15, 1315, a small Swiss force decisively defeated the Austrians, thus paving the way for Swiss independence. A monument commemorates the battle.

Morgenthau, Henry (môr'gənthô), 1856–1946, American banker, diplomat, and philanthropist, b. Germany; father of Henry Morgenthau, Jr. He emigrated to the United States as a boy. Later, he practiced law in New York City and built up a large fortune in real estate speculation and banking. An ardent supporter of Woodrow Wilson, he became finance chairman of the Democratic National Committee in 1912 and held the same position in 1916. He was (1913–16) ambassador to Turkey, and after the outbreak of World War I he was entrusted with the duty of acting there for Great Britain, France, Italy, Russia, and other nations. He attended the Paris Peace Conference as an adviser on Middle Eastern and East European problems, and later he led (1919–21) in the raising of funds for relief in the Middle East. Morgenthau was made chairman of the Greek Refugee Settlement Commission, created by the League of Nations in 1923, was an incorporator of the Red Cross in the United States, and was prominent in the activities of the Federation of Jewish Charities. See his *All in a Lifetime* (1922; an autobiographical account), *Ambassador Morgenthau's Story* (1918), and *I Was Sent to Athens* (1929).

Morgenthau, Henry, Jr., 1891–1967, American cabinet officer, b. New York City; son of Henry Morgenthau. He became interested in agriculture and bought a farm in Dutchess co., N.Y., where he became an intimate of Franklin Delano Roosevelt. In 1922, Morgenthau purchased the *American Agriculturalist,* a leading Eastern farm journal. After Roosevelt's election (1928) as governor of New York, he appointed Morgenthau chairman of the state agricultural advisory committee and later made him state conservation commissioner. When Roosevelt became President in 1933, he appointed Morgenthau chairman of the Federal Farm Board and governor of the Farm Credit Administration. Upon the illness of William H. WOODIN, Morgenthau was named (Nov., 1933) Undersecretary of the Treasury. As Secretary of the Treasury (1934–45), he administered Federal tax programs that raised unprecedented revenues, supervised the sale of over $200 billion worth of government bonds to finance America's defense and war activities, and advocated international monetary stabilization. Toward the end of World War II, Morgenthau outlined his plan for controlling Germany by converting it from an industrial to an agricultural economy. The plan was briefly considered but never put into operation. Morgenthau was influential in formulating postwar economic policy at the BRETTON WOODS CONFERENCE, which set up the International Monetary Fund and the International Bank for Reconstruction and Development (the World Bank). After resigning as Secretary of the Treasury, Morgenthau became involved in philanthropic activities. See J. M. Blum, *From the Morgenthau Diaries* (2 vol., 1959–65).

Morghab, river, Afghanistan: see MURGAB.

Moriah (mōrī'ə), land in which the mountain where Abraham was to sacrifice Isaac was located. It has been identified by some with Mt. Moriah. Gen. 22.2.

Moriah, Mount, biblical name of the hill of E JERUSALEM. It was the site of Solomon's temple. 2 Chron. 3.1.

Morier, James Justinian, 1780?–1849, English author, b. Smyrna. While with the diplomatic service he traveled through the Middle East and later wrote *A Journey through Persia . . . 1808 and 1809* (1812) and *A Second Journey through Persia* (1818). He is best known, however, for his picaresque romance of Persian life, *The Adventures of Hajji Baba of Ispahan* (1824), and its sequel, *The Adventures of Hajji Baba of Ispahan in England* (1828).

Mörike, Eduard (ā'do͞oärt mö'rĭkə), 1804–75, German poet and clergyman, a leader of the Swabian school. Over 50 of his rich and varied lyrics, among them "Schlafendes Jesuskind" [the sleeping Christ Child] and "Auf ein altes Bild" [to an old painting], were set to music by Hugo Wolf. He also wrote a novel, *Maler Nolten* (1832), and a distinguished novella, *Mozart's Journey from Vienna to Prague* (1856; tr. 1913–15).

Morillo, Pablo (pä'blō mōrē'lyō), 1778–1837, Spanish general. Sent in 1815 to put down the revolution in New Granada, he captured CARTAGENA, quelled (1816) the insurrection in Bogotá, and then marched into present-day Venezuela. His military occupations were ruthless and bloody. Under orders from

Spain he negotiated (1820) an armistice with Simón BOLÍVAR. Soon recalled at his own request, he continued to serve the crown in the wars in Spain.

Morin, Paul (pôl môrăN'), 1889–, French Canadian poet, b. Montreal. After taking degrees in the arts, science, and law at Laval Univ., he studied in Paris. His two books of poems, *Le Paon d'émail* [the enamel peacock] (1911) and *Poèmes de cendre et d'or* [poems in ashes and gold] (1922), are noted for technical brilliance and exotic language.

Morínigo, Higinio (ēhē'nyō mōrē'nēgō), 1897–, president of Paraguay (1940–48). An officer in the Chaco War, he became minister of war in 1940. After President Estigarribia was killed in an airplane crash, Morínigo was named president. He suspended the constitution and established a military dictatorship; public health and housing were bettered, but a disproportionate amount of the national budget went to the army. Several prominent political exiles were brought into a more democratic cabinet in 1946. When they were ousted (March 7, 1947) on suspicions of treason, civil war broke out. In 1948 Morínigo was ousted by a coup. He later lived in exile in Argentina.

Morioka (mōrē'ōkä), city (1970 pop. 196,000), capital of Iwate prefecture, N Honshu, Japan, on the Kitakami River. An industrial and commercial center, it is noted for the production of ironware. Iwate Univ. and a 12th-century castle are in Morioka.

Moriscos (môrĭs'kōz) [from Span.,=Moorish], Moors converted to Christianity after the Christian reconquest (11th–15th cent.) of Spain. The Moors who had become subjects of Christian kings as the reconquest progressed to the 15th cent. were called Mudéjares. They remained Muslim, and their religion and customs were generally respected. After the fall of Granada (1492), Cardinal Jiménez converted many Moors by peaceful means. However, the rigorous treatment of those who refused conversion or apostatized from the new faith led to an uprising (1500–1502) in Granada. This was soon suppressed. Faced with choosing between conversion or banishment, the majority accepted conversion, but many continued secretly to practice Islam. The Moriscos at times provided the Ottoman Turks with information facilitating Turkish raids on the Spanish coast. Persecuted by the Spanish Inquisition and subjected to restrictive legislation (1526, 1527), the Moriscos rose in a bloody rebellion (1568–71), which Philip II put down with the help of John of Austria. The Moriscos prospered in spite of persecutions and furthered Spanish agriculture, trade, and industries. However, in 1609 Philip III, influenced by Lerma, decreed their expulsion for both religious and political reasons. See H. C. Lea, *The Moriscos of Spain* (1901, repr. 1969).

Morison, Samuel Eliot, 1887–, American historian, b. Boston. He received his Ph.D. from Harvard in 1912 and began teaching history there in 1915, becoming full professor in 1925 and Jonathan Trumbull professor of American history in 1941. Between 1922 and 1925 he was Harmsworth professor of American history at Oxford. He was in the U.S. army in World War I and after the war served in the American delegation at the Paris Peace Conference. Among his earlier books are *The Life and Letters of Harrison Gray Otis, Federalist, 1765–1848* (1913), *The Maritime History of Massachusetts, 1783–1860* (1921, new ed. 1941), *Builders of the Bay Colony* (1930, rev. and enl. ed. 1958), and *The Growth of the American Republic* (1930, 6th rev. and enl. ed. 1969), written in collaboration with Henry Steele Commager. In 1926, Morison was appointed the official historian of Harvard and commenced to write the *Tercentennial History of Harvard College and University,* which was completed in 1936 in three volumes. Two of Morison's books won Pulitzer Prizes: *Admiral of the Ocean Sea* (1942), a biography of Christopher Columbus, and *John Paul Jones* (1959). In 1942, Morison was commissioned by President Franklin Delano Roosevelt to write a history of U.S. naval operations in World War II and given the rank of lieutenant commander (he retired from the navy in 1951 as a rear admiral). The 15 volumes of his *History of United States Naval Operations in World War II* appeared between 1947 and 1962. A selection of Morison's essays, *By Land and by Sea,* was published in 1953. His autobiographical *One Boy's Boston: 1887–1901* appeared in 1962. Although he retired from Harvard in 1955, Morison continued his research and writing. Recent works include *The Oxford History of the American People* (1965), *The European Discovery of America* (2 vol., 1971–74) and a biography of Samuel de Champlain (1972). Morison's literary style is much admired for its clarity and classical simplicity.

Morison, Stanley, 1889–1967, English typographer and journalist. Morison was typographical consultant to Cambridge Univ. Press and to the English Monotype Corp. and editor of the *Fleuron* from 1926 to 1930. He was typographical adviser (1929–44) to the London *Times* and designer of a new format and a new type face called Times Roman. In 1945, Morison became editor of *The Times Literary Supplement.* Among his works on type are *Four Centuries of Fine Printing* (1924) and *First Principles of Typography* (1936). His writings cover a wide range and include a multivolume history of *The Times.* See biography by Nicolas Barker (1972); study by James Moran (1971).

Morisot, Berthe (bĕrt môrēzō'), 1841–95, French impressionist painter. She studied with many gifted painters, including Corot. She formed a close friendship with Manet, who became her brother-in-law, and she served as model for several of his best-known paintings. The two greatly influenced each other's artistic development. Morisot is thought to have convinced Manet to work with the impressionist rainbow palette. Her own later work inclined toward pure impressionism in its rendering of light, while retaining an unusual smoothness of brushwork. Her paintings formed an important addition to all but one impressionist exhibit from 1874 through 1885. Her most notable works, including *Young Woman at the Dance* (1880; Paris) and *La Toilette* (Art Inst., Chicago), are painted in clear, luminous colors. See catalog (ed. by D. Rouart, 1960); her correspondence (ed. by D. Rouart; tr., 2d ed. 1959).

Morland, George, 1763–1804, English genre, animal, and landscape painter. A pupil of his father, Henry Morland (1716–97), a London portrait painter, he left his father's studio when he was 21 and began a lifelong career of dissipation. He painted prolifically, producing more than 4,000 pictures in his short life, and although his work was popular and made him a fortune, he squandered his money and was often imprisoned for debt. In 1791 he painted his masterpiece, *Interior of a Stable* (National Gall., London). He painted genre scenes and the English countryside, rendering them in rich colors and with a gusto that modifies their sentimentality. *Dogs Fighting* and *Old English Sportsman* (N.Y. Historical Society) and *Pigs in a Fodder Yard* (N.Y. Public Lib.) are representative. Despite his earlier fame, Morland died in a detention house for debtors. See catalog by Lowndes Lodge Gall. (1966); study by W. Gilbey and E. D. Cuming (1907).

Morley, Christopher, 1890–1957, American editor and author, b. Haverford, Pa., grad. Haverford College, 1910. He was a Rhodes scholar. Morley was one of the founders of the *Saturday Review of Literature,* of which he was an editor from 1924 to 1940. A prolific author, he wrote more than 50 books. His novels, generally in a light vein, include *Parnassus on Wheels* (1917), *The Haunted Bookshop* (1919), *Thunder on the Left* (1925), and *Kitty Foyle* (1939; filmed 1940). He also revised and enlarged Bartlett's *Familiar Quotations* (1937, 1948).

Morley, Edward Williams, 1838–1923, American scientist, b. Newark, N.J., grad. Williams College, 1860. From 1869 to 1906 he was professor of chemistry at Western Reserve College (now Case Western Reserve Univ.). He is known especially for his work with A. A. Michelson and D. C. Miller in investigating the relative motion of the earth and ETHER and in developing the interferometer as a means of measuring length and distance, and particularly for the Michelson-Morley experiment, which led to the refutation of the ether hypothesis and the development of Einstein's theory of relativity. His other important experiments include research on the oxygen content of the atmosphere; determinations of the density of oxygen and hydrogen and their combining ratio in water; determination of the velocity of light in a magnetic field; and work on thermal expansion.

Morley, Felix, 1894–, American journalist, b. Haverford, Pa., grad. Haverford College, 1915, and Oxford, 1921. He worked (1922–29) on the Baltimore *Sun* and was (1933–40) editor of the Washington *Post.* Morley was (1940–45) president of Haverford College and during the same period served as a government adviser. From 1945 to 1950 he was editor of *Human Events.* His championship of internationalism and democracy is seen in *The Society of Nations* (1932), *The Power in the People* (1949), and *Freedom and Federalism* (1959).

Morley, Henry, 1822–94, English man of letters. In 1850 he closed his successful school to assist Dickens in editing *Household Words.* After that he combined an editorial with an academic career, teaching English literature at several universities. Author of several biographies and critical studies, he wrote *English Writers* (1887–95), an unfinished 11-volume history of English literature. As editor of Morley's University Library, Cassell's National Library, and other series, he produced low-priced editions of literary classics.

Morley, John, Viscount Morley of Blackburn, 1838–1923, English statesman and man of letters. Educated at Oxford, he made his reputation as a journalist in London and served (1867–82) as editor of the liberal *Fortnightly Review.* He was elected to Parliament in 1883 as a strong supporter of William Gladstone. As chief secretary for Ireland (1886, 1892–95), Morley helped prepare the first and second Home Rule bills and cautiously modified the coercive laws for the preservation of peace. He lost his seat in Parliament in 1895 but regained it the following year. He was a vigorous opponent of the South African War, leading the "pro-Boer" wing of the Liberal party. As secretary of state for India (1905–10), he worked with the earl of MINTO to produce the Morley-Minto reforms (1909). Raised to the peerage in 1908, Morley helped steer the Parliament Act of 1911 through the House of Lords. He was lord president of the council from 1910 until 1914, when he retired because of Great Britain's entry into World War I. One of the best biographers of his time, Morley wrote lives of Voltaire (1872), Rousseau (1873), Richard Cobden (1881), Robert Walpole (1889), Oliver Cromwell (1900), and Gladstone (1903; perhaps his best work). He was general editor of the "English Men of Letters" series, for which he wrote a life of Edmund Burke (1879). His political and critical writings include *Critical Miscellanies* (1871–77), *On Compromise* (1874), *Diderot and the Encyclopedists* (1878), *Studies in Literature* (1890), and *On Politics* (1914). His *Recollections* provide an explanation of his Victorian liberalism. See F. W. Hirst, *Early Life and Letters of John Morley* (1927); biography by D. A. Hamer (1968); study by Edward Alexander (1972).

Morley, Sylvanus Griswold, 1883–1948, American archaeologist, b. Chester, Pa., grad. Harvard, 1908. He was a specialist in Middle American archaeology and in Mayan hieroglyphics. Morley did fieldwork (1909–14) in Central America and Mexico for the School of American Archaeology. In 1915 he became research associate and in 1918 associate of the Carnegie Institution of Washington, D.C., a post he retained until 1940. He was in charge of its Central American expeditions and directed (1924–40) research at Chichén Itzá. His writings include *An Introduction to the Study of Maya Hieroglyphs* (1915), *The Inscriptions at Copan* (1920), *The Inscriptions of Petén* (5 vol., 1938), and *The Ancient Maya* (1946; 3d ed. 1956, rev. by G. W. Brainerd). See *Morleyana* (ed. by A. J. O. Anderson, 1950); study by R. L. Brunhouse (1971).

Morley, Thomas, c.1557–1603, English composer; pupil of William Byrd. He was gentleman of the Chapel Royal to Queen Elizabeth I and organist of St. Paul's Cathedral. He set to music some of Shakespeare's songs. Morley's works include motets, music for the several Anglican types of services, and madrigals that are among the most charming examples of this form. He wrote a unique guide to 16th-century English musical practice, *A Plaine and Easie Introduction to Practicall Musicke* (1597, new ed. 1952).

Morley, municipal borough (1971 pop. 44,340), West Riding of Yorkshire, N England. Woolen textiles and many other products are made. Coal is mined in the borough. It was besieged by royalists in the English civil war. Henry Asquith was born in Morley. In 1974, Morley became part of the new metropolitan county of West Yorkshire.

Mormon campaign: see UTAH WAR.

Mormons, name commonly used for the members of the Church of Jesus Christ of LATTER-DAY SAINTS (a description of the church and its doctrines is given under that heading). The religion was founded by Joseph SMITH, who claimed that the golden tablets containing the Book of Mormon had been revealed to him at Palmyra, N.Y. He rapidly gathered followers and in 1831 established his headquarters at Kirtland, Ohio. Intensive missionary activity gained many converts both in the United States and (especially later) abroad. Stakes of Zion, as the Mormons called their settlements, were started in W Missouri. Smith prepared (1831) to make W Missouri the permanent home of his people, but the Mormons came into conflict with their gentile Missouri neighbors. The Mormons were a close-knit body with a communal economy, and other settlers feared their aloofness and strange ways. Intolerance and fear grew into violence and persecution; Mormon leaders were jailed and their followers mistreated. Finally, in 1838–39, Gov. Lillburn W. Boggs ordered their expulsion (see also DONIPHAN, ALEXANDER W.). The Mormons sought a new Zion in the Illinois town of Nauvoo. They received a charter giving them virtual autonomy, with the right to maintain their own militia and their own court and the power to pass any laws not in conflict with the state or Federal constitutions. The town expanded as converts poured in from abroad, and by 1842 it was the largest and most powerful town in Illinois. The growing wealth and strength of the Mormon community caused envy and fear among their neighbors. At about that time, Joseph Smith, as mayor of Nauvoo, ordered the suppression of church dissidents. Violence resulted, and Smith called out the Nauvoo militia to protect the city. For this, he and his brother, Hyrum, were arrested by Illinois authorities (June 24, 1844), and charged with treason. They were jailed in Carthage, Ill., where three days later they were murdered by an angry mob. After that many Mormons fled, dissension and suspicion were rife, and there was debate over the succession to Smith's leadership. Possible choices included another brother, William Smith, and several prominent leaders, notably Sidney Rigdon, James Jesse STRANG, Lyman Wight, and Brigham YOUNG. The church leaders chose Young. He proved a forceful and able leader who dominated and worked for the good of his people. Again it was necessary for the Mormons to find a home. Under Young's guidance a remote spot was chosen, the valley of the Great Salt Lake in what is now Utah. Those who rejected Young's leadership and claimed the succession for a son of Joseph Smith declined to accompany the main body to Utah; they ultimately constituted themselves into a separate church (see LATTER DAY SAINTS, REORGANIZED CHURCH OF JESUS CHRIST OF). In July, 1847, the first settlers reached what is now SALT LAKE CITY and began an agricultural community. The first few years were extremely difficult, but the organization of the Mormons for community welfare, their great industry (the beehive is one of their symbols), and the determined leadership of Young made for their success. Through extensive irrigation, farming prospered. In 1849 the Mormons wished to have their communities admitted to the Union as the State of Deseret, but they were disappointed and in 1850 the area was made Utah Territory. Brigham Young was appointed territorial governor and superintendent of Indian affairs, but Mormon isolation was destroyed. Non-Mormons filtered in. They were resented by the Mormons, and in turn the newcomers were resentful of Mormon exclusiveness and church control. Clashes with overland travelers were frequent. Young's formal announcement in 1852 of the doctrine of plural marriage, based on a vision of Joseph Smith in 1843, set the Mormons further apart from non-Mormon Americans. Thereafter polygamy was luridly discussed in newspapers across the country. There were also stories of dark and violent acts by a secret Mormon police force, the Danites, who forced the will of the church on Mormon and non-Mormon alike. The antagonism was very strong in the 1850s, and when Col. Albert S. Johnston was sent out with an army force in 1857, Brigham Young prepared to defend the Mormon state. Fortunately this Mormon campaign, or the UTAH WAR, did not rise to serious proportions, but the bitterness of feeling was shown after the massacre of the innocent members of a wagon train at MOUNTAIN MEADOWS in 1857, for which the Mormons were blamed. The question of plural marriage was the important point in Utah's demand for statehood. Congress passed laws against polygamy aimed solely at Utah. By the time of Brigham Young's death in 1877 the Mormon community was a thoroughly established commonwealth with a large and prosperous population. Statehood finally came after Morman president Wilford Woodruff made (1890) a statement withdrawing church sanction of polygamy; Utah entered the Union as the 45th state in 1896. The history of Utah has been the history of the church, but Mormonism has spread much beyond that state. It has great strength in Idaho and Arizona, and there are Mormon temples and tabernacles in most of the states, particularly in the West. In 1967 the church's traditional rule barring blacks from the ministry turned into a national issue when George Romney, himself a Mormon minister, became a candidate for the Republican presidential nomination. Among the organizations within the church are Deseret Industries, the Welfare Program, and the Mormon Tabernacle Choir. As a result of extensive proselytizing and missionary activity, the church has spread all over the world and has a membership of about 3 million. See Thomas O'Dea, *The Mormons* (1957); R. B. West, Jr., *Kingdom of the Saints: The Story of Brigham Young and the Mormons* (1957). W. A. Linn, *The Story of the Mormons* (1963); W. J. Whalen, *The Latter-Day Saints in the Modern World* (1966); P. D. Bailey, *The Armies of God* (1968).

Mornay, Philippe de, seigneur du Plessis-Marly (fĕlēp' də môrnā' sānyör' dü plĕsē'-märlē'), 1549–1623, French Protestant leader, also known as Du Plessis-Mornay. Until 1572 he spent much time in the Netherlands and Germany. After the massacre of St. Bartholomew's Day he remained a year in England. He became one of the chief agents for Henry of Navarre (later King Henry IV of France), for whom he arranged a reconciliation with King Henry III of France (1589). In reward he was made governor of SAUMUR. After Henry of Navarre's conversion to Roman Catholicism, Mornay became the leader of the Huguenots. Louis XIII ousted him from Saumur, and he died in retirement. Mornay was an excellent organizer and a spirited writer. Among his works are *De l'institution, usage et doctrine du saint sacrement de l'eucharistie en l'église ancienne* (1598, tr. 1600), the subject of a public disputation on the ancient Eucharist with the bishop of Évreux, who was the victor; *Le Mystère d'iniquité, c'est à dire, l'histoire de la papauté* (1611, tr. 1612); and *Mémoires et correspondance* (12 vol., 1824–25).

morning glory, common name for members of the Convolvulaceae, a family of herbs, shrubs, and small trees (many of them climbing forms) inhabiting warm regions, especially the tropics of America and Asia. The family is characterized by milky sap. The largest groups are the predominantly tropical morning-glory genus (*Ipomoea*), with species most abundant in Mexico, and the bindweed genus (*Convolvulus*) of more temperate regions. Many bindweeds are also called morning glory. Species of both are chiefly herbaceous vines of prolific growth and with

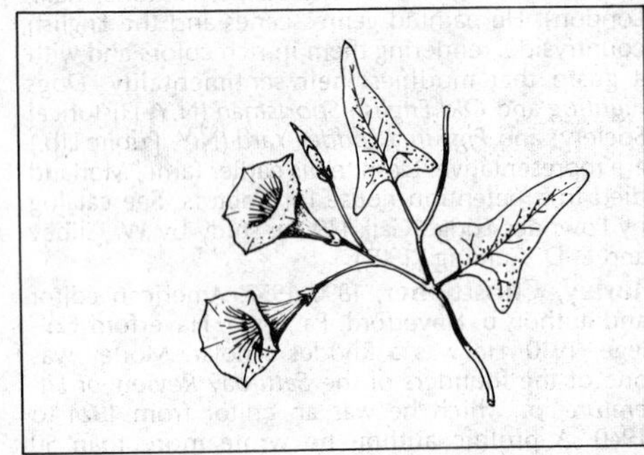

Morning glory, Convolvulus arvensis

colorful funnel-shaped blossoms that often open only in the morning. *I. purpurea* is the morning glory cultivated as an ornamental in North America. The moonflowers (genus *Calonyction*), tropical American night-blooming vines, have similarly shaped but much larger blossoms, often heavily fragrant. *Convolvulus scammonia* is the scammony of Asia Minor; a resin exuded from its roots is exported from Aleppo and Smyrna as a medicine. The most important commercial plant of the family, the SWEET POTATO, belongs to the morning-glory genus. The wild sweet potato or potato vine (*I. pandurata*), a common weed of North America, is not eaten. The dodders (genus *Cuscuta*, sometimes classified as a separate family) are common leafless, parasitic vines that often resemble bright orange threads. Each of the widely distributed species parasitizes a specific host; *C. epilinum*, for example, lives on flax. The morning-glory family is classified in the division MAGNOLIOPHYTA, class Magnoliopsida, order Polemoniales.

morning star: see EVENING STAR.

Morny, Charles Auguste Louis Joseph, duc de (shärl ōgüst' lwē zhōzĕf' dük də môrnē'), 1811–65, French statesman; illegitimate son of Hortense de BEAUHARNAIS and the comte de FLAHAUT DE LA BILLARDERIE. After an army career (1830–38) during which he fought in North Africa, Morny entered politics and was elected a deputy in 1842. In 1851 he was the leading organizer of the coup d'etat that gave his half brother, Louis Napoleon Bonaparte, dictatorial powers. As minister of the interior, Morny used intimidation to assure the outcome of the plebiscite (1852) that made Bonaparte Emperor NAPOLEON III. Morny was created duke in 1862 and subsequently was president of the legislative assembly. As adviser to the emperor, he had a major influence in promoting the liberal, or parliamentary, empire.

Moro, Aldo (äl'dō mô'rō), 1916–, Italian political leader. A lawyer, he entered national politics in 1946, when he was elected to the constituent assembly as a member of the Christian Democratic party. As minister of justice from 1955 to 1957, he worked to reform the prison system, strengthening regulations forbidding corporal punishment and improving food, hygiene, and sanitary conditions. He was political secretary of the Christian Democratic party from 1959 to 1963. In Dec., 1963, he became prime minister, a post he held until 1968. He later served as minister of foreign affairs.

Moro, Antonio (äntō'nyō), c.1519–c.1575, Flemish portrait painter, known as Antonis Mor or Moor and as Sir Anthony More. He studied with Jan van Scorel. In 1547 he was a free master at Antwerp and by 1549 was employed as a court painter to the house of Hapsburg. In the early 1550s he visited Italy, Spain, Portugal, and London, painting state portraits, including a famous one of Mary Tudor (1554; Prado). In his later years, while maintaining a house at Utrecht, Moro traveled widely and made further trips to Italy and Spain. Influenced by Titian, he in turn had a strong effect upon the development of international court portraiture. His figures show his ability for incisive characterization, strong modeling and sharp lighting, and a careful attention to details, textures, and finished surfaces. His portrait subjects include William of Orange (1556; Cassel), Alessandro Farnese (1557; Parma), the artist Hubert Goltzius (1576; Brussels), and a self-portrait (1559; Uffizi).

Morocco (mərŏk'ō), kingdom (1973 est. pop. 15,600,000), 171,834 sq mi (445,050 sq km), NW Africa, on the Mediterranean Sea and the Atlantic Ocean. RABAT is the capital. Morocco is bordered by Spanish Sahara on the south and by Algeria on the south and east. IFNI, formerly a Spanish-held enclave on the Atlantic coast, was ceded to Morocco in 1969. Two cities, Ceuta and Melilla, and several small islands off the Mediterranean coast remain part of metropolitan Spain. The population of Morocco is concentrated in the coastal regions, where rainfall is most plentiful. In parts of the Rif Mts. in the northeast some 40 in. (102 cm) of rain fall each year, and wheat and other cereals can be raised without irrigation. On the Atlantic coast, where there are extensive plains, olives, citrus fruits, and grapes are grown, largely with water supplied by artesian wells. Part of the maritime population fishes for its livelihood. AGADIR, ESSAOUIRA, AL-JADIDA, and LARACHE are among the important fishing harbors. CASABLANCA is by far the largest port for the extensive overseas trade. The main exports are citrus fruits and minerals, while consumer goods and industrial products are the chief imports. France is the leading trade partner. Central Morocco is largely occupied by the Atlas Mts. In the northern foothills, especially, there are large mineral deposits; phosphates are the most important, but there are also iron, zinc, copper, lead, molybdenum, cobalt, and the only sizable coal deposits in all North Africa. Petroleum is also found in Morocco. MARRAKESH, MEKNÈS, and FEZ are the most important centers in the mineral trade. Southern Morocco lies in the Sahara Desert. A few areas of oasis, notably Tafilalt, are all that relieve the desert wastes. The coastal areas and the mineral-producing interior are linked by a barely adequate road and rail network; there are no important rivers. Morocco is governed under a 1972 constitution. The king holds effective power and appoints the ministers, and there is a unicameral parliament. Morocco is a member of the United Nations, the League of Arab States, and the Organization of African Unity. Islam is the state religion and Arabic is the official language, but French and Spanish are also spoken. There are universities at Rabat, Fez, and Marrakesh. BERBERS inhabited Morocco at the beginning of the historic era. In Roman times Morocco was roughly coextensive with the province of Mauretania Tingitania. In the 3d cent. A.D. four bishoprics were created in the province. Jewish colonies were also established during Roman rule. The Vandals were the earliest (5th cent.) of barbarian peoples to take the area as the Roman Empire declined. The Arabs first swept into Morocco c.685, bringing with them Islam. Christianity was all but extirpated, but the Jewish colonies by and large retained their religion. Many Moroccans served in the Arab forces that invaded Spain in the early 8th cent. Later, Berber-Arab conflict fragmented the region. Morocco became an independent state in 788 under the royal line founded by Idris I. After 900 the country again broke into small tribal states. Warfare between the Fatimids of Tunisia and the Umayyads of Spain for control of the region intensified the already-existing political anarchy, which ended only when the ALMORAVIDS overran (c.1062) Morocco and established a kingdom stretching from Spain to Senegal. The ALMOHADS, who succeeded (c.1174) the Almoravids, at first ruled both Morocco and Spain, but the Merinid dynasty (1259–1550), after some triumphs, was limited to Morocco. Rarely, however, was the country completely unified, and conflict between Arabs and Berbers was incessant. Spain and Portugal, after expelling the Moors (i.e., persons from Morocco) from the Iberian Peninsula, attacked the Moroccan coast. Beginning with the capture of Ceuta in 1415, Portugal took all the chief ports except Melilla and Larache, both of which fell to Spain. The Christian threat stimulated the growth of resistance under religious leaders, one of whom established (1554) the Saadian, or first Sherifian, dynasty. At the battle of ALCAZARQUIVIR (1578) the Saadian king decisively defeated Portugal. The present ruling dynasty, the Alawite, or second Sherifian, dynasty, came to power in 1660 and recaptured many European-held strongholds. Morocco, like the other BARBARY STATES, was, from the 17th to the 19th cent., a base for pirates preying upon the Mediterranean trade. In the 19th cent. the strategic importance and economic potential of Morocco excited the interest of the European powers. France, after beginning war with Algeria, defeated (1844) Sultan ABD AR-RAHMAN, who had aided the Algerians. Spain invaded in 1860. In 1880 the major European nations and the United States decided at the Madrid Conference to preserve the territorial integrity of Morocco and to maintain equal trade opportunities for all. Political and commercial rivalries soon disrupted this cordial arrangement and brought on several international crises. France sought to gain Spanish and British support against the opposition of Germany. Thus, in 1904, France concluded a secret treaty with Spain to partition Morocco and secretly agreed with Great Britain (the Entente Cordiale) not to oppose British aims in Egypt in exchange for a free hand in Morocco. In 1905, after France had asked the sultan of Morocco for a protectorate, Germany moved dramatically: Emperor William II visited Tangier and declared support for Morocco's integrity. At German insistence the Algeciras Conference (Jan.–March, 1906) was called to consider the Moroccan question. The principles of the Madrid Conference were readopted and German investments were assured protection, but French and Spanish interests were given marked recognition by the decision to allow France to patrol the border with Algeria and to allow France and Spain to police Morocco. Under the claim of effecting pacification, the French steadily annexed territory. In 1908 friction arose at Casablanca, under French occupation, when the German consul gave refuge to deserters from the French Foreign Legion. This dispute was settled by the Hague Tribunal. Shortly afterward in a coup d'état ABD AL-AZIZ IV was unseated and his brother, Abd al-Hafid, installed on the throne. He had difficulty maintaining order and received help from France and Spain, especially in a revolt that broke out in 1911. In this situation the appearance of the German warship *Panther* at Agadir on July 1, 1911, was interpreted by the French as a threat of war and speeded a final adjustment of imperial rivalries. On Nov. 4, 1911, Germany agreed to a French protectorate in Morocco in exchange for the cession of French territory in equatorial Africa. Finally, at Fez (March 30, 1912), the sultan agreed to a French protectorate, and on Nov. 27 a Franco-Spanish agreement divided Morocco into four administrative zones—French Morocco, nine-tenths of the country, a protectorate with Rabat as capital; a Spanish protectorate, which included Spanish Morocco, with its capital at Tetuán; a Southern Protectorate of Morocco, administered as part of the Spanish Sahara; and the international zone of TANGIER. The French protectorate was placed under the rule of General LYAUTEY, who remained in office until 1925. A strong threat to European rule was posed (1921–26) by the revolt (the Rif War) of ADB-EL-KRIM. In 1934 a group of young Moroccans presented a plan for reform, marking the beginning of the nationalist movement. In 1937 the French crushed a nationalist revolt. Francisco Franco's successful revolt against the republican government of Spain began in Spanish Morocco in 1936. During World War II, French Morocco remained officially loyal to the Vichy government after the fall of France in 1940. On Nov. 8, 1942, Allied forces landed at all the major cities of Morocco and Algeria; on Nov. 11, all resistance ended (see NORTH AFRICA, CAMPAIGNS IN). In Jan., 1943, Allied leaders met at Casablanca. During the war an independence party, the Istiglal, was formed. After the war the nationalist movement gained strength and received the active support of the sultan, Sidi Muhammad, who demanded a unitary state and the departure of the French and Spanish. Faced with growing nationalist agitation, the French outlawed (1952) the Istiglal and in Aug., 1953, deposed and exiled Sidi Muhammad. These measures proved ineffective, and under the pressure of rebellion in Algeria and disorders in Morocco, the French were compelled (1955) to restore Sidi Muhammad. In March, 1956, France relinquished its rights in Morocco; in April the Spanish surrendered their protectorate; in October Tangier was given to Morocco by international agreement. Spain ceded the Southern Protectorate in 1958. The sultan became (1957) King Muhammad V (Sidi Muhammad) and soon embarked on a foreign policy of "positive neutrality," which included support for the Muslim rebels in Algeria. After the king's death (Feb., 1961), his son HASSAN II ascended the throne. In Dec., 1962, a constitution was promulgated that provided Morocco with a bicameral parliament. Border hostilities with Algeria in 1963 cost both sides many lives; Emperor Haile Selassie of Ethiopia aided the cease-fire negotiations. Final agreement on the border was reached in 1970. In June, 1965, following a political crisis that threatened to undermine the monarchy, King Hassan declared a state of emergency and took over both executive and legislative powers. The country returned to a modified form of parliamentary democracy in 1970, with a revised constitution that strengthened the king's authority. Opposition groups, later called the National Front, rejected the constitution and boycotted elections for the national legislature held in August. An abortive coup by military leaders took place on July 10, 1971. Hassan announced another constitution in Feb., 1972. The new constitution, which lessened the king's powers, was approved by referendum despite a boycott by the National Front. In August another assassination attempt took place, when the airplane carrying King Hassan was strafed on its way back from France. Unrest continued in Morocco in 1973. Demonstrations against the government came from the armed forces, students, and opposition parties. King Hassan continued to rule in isolation and maintained relative order through a policy of suppression. In 1974, Morocco pressed its claim to sovereignty over Spanish Morocco. See Budgett Meakin, *Moorish Empire: A Historical Epitome* (1899); Rom Landau, *Moroccan Drama* (1956); Nevill Barbour, *Morocco* (1965); Stéphane Bernard, *The Franco-Moroccan Conflict, 1953–1956* (1968); Louis de Chénier, *The Present State of the Empire of Morocco* (1788, repr. 1972); R. F. Nyrop et al., *Area Handbook for Morocco* (1972); Roger Le Tourneau, *The Modern History of Morocco* (1973).

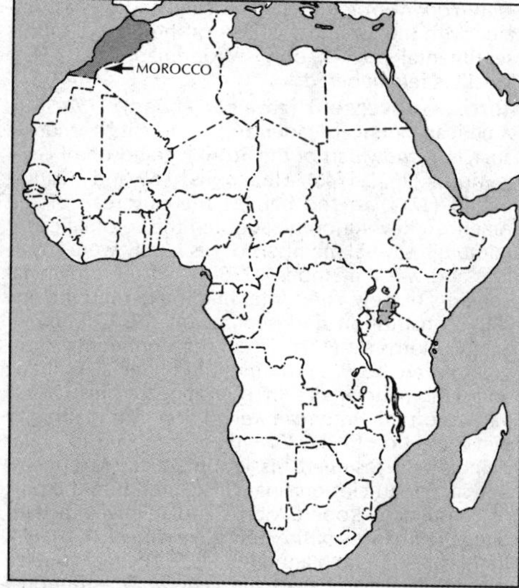

morocco, goatskin leather, dyed on the grain side and boarded by hand or machine to bring up the grain in a bird's-eye effect. It probably originated with the Arabs in North Africa as an alum-tanned product typically dyed red. The process later spread to the Levant, to Turkey, and along the Mediterranean, where sumac was used for tanning. Today the term is also applied to chrome-tanned goat leather whether boarded or embossed to show the characteristic grain; it is often crushed and glazed. Hard, but pliable, it is valued especially for bookbindings and purses. Levant morocco is larger grained; French morocco is a sheepskin imitation.

Morogoro (mō″rōgō′rō), city (1967 pop. 25,262), capital of Morogoro prov., E Tanzania. It is the commercial and transportation center for a region producing sisal, coffee, and livestock. Tobacco is processed there.

Morón (mōrōn′), city (1970 pop. 485,983), Buenos Aires prov., E Argentina. It is a district administrative center in the Greater Buenos Aires area. Settled in the early 16th cent., Morón became an outpost on the route between Buenos Aires and Chile and Peru.

Moroni, Giovanni Battista (jōvän′nē bät-tē′stä mōrô′nē), c.1525–1578, Italian portrait painter of the Brescian school; pupil of Il Moretto. Surpassing his teacher in the ability to capture the expression of the model, Moroni excelled in portraying with tasteful intimacy the aristocratic men and women of his day. He depicted them realistically but with a Venetian flair for style. There are notable examples of his art in the National Gallery, London; the Metropolitan Museum; the Philadelphia Museum; and the Uffizi.

Moroni (mōrō′nē), town (1966 pop. 11,515), capital of the French overseas territory of the Comoro Islands, on Grand Comoro island, at the northern end of the Mozambique Channel, an arm of the Indian Ocean. Moroni is the largest city, main port, and administrative center of the islands. It has an international airport.

moronity: see MENTAL RETARDATION.

Moronobu, Hishikawa (hēshēkä′wä mōrō′nōbo͞o), c.1618–c.1694, Japanese painter and color-print designer of the ukiyoe school. He began his career as an embroiderer. His first of more than 130 illustrated books (1658) is usually regarded as beginning the history of Japanese ukiyoe prints. He produced his first single-sheet prints in about 1673. His prints are mostly in black and white, although occasionally hand colored. For subject matter he drew from classical literature or depicted the daily life of the common people, the celebrated courtesans, and favorite actors. A screen painting of a genre scene at the Museum of Fine Arts, Boston, is one of the few remaining paintings by Moronobu.

Moros (mōr′ōz) [Span., = Moors], a group of Muslim natives, numbering about one million, of Mindanao and the Sulu Archipelago in the Philippines and of Borneo, who were converted in the great missionary extension of Islam from India in the 15th and 16th cent. They are largely of Malayan stock and are neither ethnic nor linguistic units. The Moros are conspicuous as a fierce, proud people, and they long maintained enmity toward the Christian Filipinos. After the Spanish conquered (1564) the Philippines, the Moros waged constant war, which continued even after the United States took over (1898) the islands. Within the Republic of the Philippines they have continued to press for autonomy. Armed conflict with Christians and demands for the secession of Mindanao have continued into the 1970s. See Melvin Mednick, *Encampment of the Lake* (1965); A. C. Glang, *Muslim Secession or Integration?* (1969).

Morosini, Francesco (fränchĕs′kō mōrōzē′nē), 1618–94, Italian soldier, doge of Venice (1688–94), of a family distinguished in Venice for five centuries. Made (1657) captain general of the fleet in a war with the Turks (1651–61), he conducted a brilliant campaign. He again fought against the Turks (1664–69) and was tried and acquitted for being defeated by them in Crete. In a subsequent war with the Turks (1684–88) he conquered the Peloponnesus (1687); under his leadership the Venetian empire had a brief revival.

Morotai (môrōtī′), island (c.695 sq mi/1,800 sq km), E Indonesia, one of the Moluccas. Heavily wooded, it produces timber and resin.

morpheme: see GRAMMAR.

Morpheus (môr′fēəs), in Greek and Roman mythology, god of dreams. The son of Hypnos (or Somnus), the god of sleep, he brought dreams of human forms. His brothers Phobetor and Phantasos induced dreams of animals and inanimate objects, respectively.

morphine, principal derivative of OPIUM, which is the juice in the unripe seed pods of the POPPY (*Papaver somniferum*). It was first isolated from opium in 1803 by the German pharmacist F. W. A. Sertürner. Given intravenously, it is still considered one of the most useful NARCOTICS for the relief of pain. The drug also impairs mental and physical performance, reduces sex and hunger drives, and causes mood changes, inability to concentrate, and apathy. By relieving pain and anxiety, it produces euphoria. It also inhibits the cough reflex and, acting directly on the bowel muscles, produces constipation. Morphine is highly addictive, and for that reason even small quantities must be used with caution. See DRUG ADDICTION AND DRUG ABUSE.

Morphy, Paul Charles (môr'fē), 1837-84, American chess player, b. New Orleans. At 10 he learned the game and at 21 was acknowledged as the greatest player in the world. Not only was Morphy possessed of a phenomenal memory, which he demonstrated in astounding feats of simultaneous blindfold play, but his style of play was in direct contrast to that of his time. He was a master of the open game, in which center pawns are exchanged, open files are utilized, and rapid development of the pieces is demanded. D. Harrwitz, J. Löwenthal, and Adolph Anderssen were among the many who succumbed to his crushing combinations. After 1859, when he had returned to New Orleans from world triumphs, mental instability ended his chessplay. See biography by Regina Morphy-Voitier (1926); studies by J. J. Löwenthal (1860) and W. E. Napier (1957).

Morrice, James Wilson, 1865-1924, Canadian painter, b. Montreal. Abandoning law, he went to Paris, where he studied painting. He visited Venice, Trinidad, Tunis, and periodically returned to Canada. Admired for his subtle coloring and delicate rendering of landscapes, Morrice greatly influenced younger Canadian artists. The National Gallery, Ottawa, has several of his paintings, including *Venice: Night* and *Dieppe: the Beach.* See study by D. W. Buchanan (1936).

morrice dance: see MORRIS DANCE.

Morrill, Justin Smith, 1810-98, American politician, b. Strafford, Vt. A prosperous merchant, he helped organize (1855) the Republican party in Vermont. First elected to Congress in 1854, he served in the House of Representatives until 1867 and then in the Senate until 1898. He is best known for the Morrill Act, a bill first introduced in 1857 and finally passed in 1862, which provided for the granting of public lands for the establishment of educational institutions; these came to be known as land-grant colleges (see LAND-GRANT COLLEGES AND UNIVERSITIES). See biography by W. B. Parker (1924, repr. 1971).

Morris, family of prominent American landowners and statesmen. **Richard Morris,** d. 1672, left England after serving in Oliver Cromwell's army, became a merchant in Barbados, and emigrated to New York City when it was known, under the Dutch, as New Amsterdam. He purchased a tract of land in what is now the Bronx, which, along with other real estate, descended to his son, Lewis Morris (1671-1746; see separate article). The New York estate was erected into a manor, called Morrisania, in 1697. Lewis's eldest son, **Lewis Morris,** 1698-1762, b. Morrisania, was the second lord of the manor and became judge of the high court of admiralty. His brother, **Robert Hunter Morris,** c.1700-1764, b. Morrisania, was appointed (1738) chief justice of New Jersey by his father and later became (1754) governor of Pennsylvania; protests from the western counties over his administration of frontier defenses resulted in his resignation in 1756. The third and last lord of the manor was Lewis Morris (1726-98; see separate article). His brothers included Gouverneur Morris (see separate article) and **Richard Morris,** 1730-1810, b. Morrisania, who was a judge of the admiralty court, like his father, and was appointed (1779) chief justice of the New York state supreme court despite his lack of ardor for the Revolutionary cause. Morrisania was annexed to the city of New York in 1774. Richard Morris's son, **Lewis Richard Morris,** 1760-1825, b. Scarsdale, N.Y., saw active service during the early part of the Revolution and was (1781-83) assistant to the secretary of foreign affairs. He established a manor at Springfield, Vt., was active in Vermont politics, and served (1797-1803) as Representative in the U.S. Congress. Another member of the family was Richard Valentine Morris (see separate article). See L. D. Akerly, *The Morris Manor* (1916).

Morris, Edward Patrick Morris, 1st **Baron,** 1859-1935, Newfoundland political leader, b. St. John's. He became a lawyer and sat (1885-1918) in the Newfoundland parliament. He was a delegate to the conference called (1895) at Ottawa to discuss terms for the possible entry of Newfoundland into the dominion of Canada. Later he represented Newfoundland at many imperial conferences and was (1910) counsel for the British government in the N Atlantic fisheries dispute. From 1909 to 1918 he was prime minister of Newfoundland. After World War I he went to England to live. He was created a baron in 1918.

Morris, George Pope, 1802-64, American poet and journalist, b. Philadelphia. He founded (1823) the *New York Mirror,* a literary weekly, and was associated with the foremost writers of the period. Of his sentimental poems, only "Woodman, Spare That Tree!" is remembered.

Morris, Gouverneur (gəvərnēr',-no͝or'), 1752-1816, American political leader and diplomat, b. Morrisania, N.Y. (now part of the Bronx), grandson of Lewis Morris (1671-1746). He studied law and was admitted (1771) to the bar. At the outbreak of the American Revolution he adopted the colonial cause (although several members of his family were Loyalists) and was a member (1775-77) of the provincial congress of New York. After helping to draft the first state constitution and serving on the Council of Safety, Morris sat (1778-79) in the Continental Congress, where he was prominent in financial, military, and diplomatic affairs. In 1779 appeared his *Observations on the American Revolution.* After failing to win reelection to the Congress he moved to Philadelphia and resumed his law practice. A series of newspaper articles on finance secured him the post of assistant to Robert Morris (no relative) in handling the finances of the new government (1781-85). In this position he planned the U.S. decimal coinage system. As a member of the Federal Constitutional Convention of 1787 he played an active role, defending a strong centralized government and a strong executive, opposing concessions to slavery, and putting the Constitution into its final literary form. He remained, however, a champion of aristocracy who distrusted democratic rule. In 1789 he went to France as a private business agent, remained in Europe, and was appointed (1792) U.S. minister to France. During the French Revolution his sympathies lay with the royalists; he even helped plan a scheme to rescue Louis XVI. His recall was requested in 1794, but he traveled for several years before returning to America in 1798. From 1800 to 1803, Morris, a Federalist, was a U.S. Senator from New York. He then retired to his estate. He condemned the War of 1812, going so far as to recommend the severance of the Federal Union. He was a strong advocate of the Erie Canal, serving as chairman (1810-13) of the canal commission. See his *Diary of the French Revolution* (1939), edited by his great-grand-daughter, Beatrix Cary Davenport; biographies by Theodore Roosevelt (1888, repr. 1972) and Daniel Walther (tr. 1934); M. M. Mintz, *Gouverneur Morris and the American Revolution* (1970).

Morris, Lewis, 1671-1746, American colonial official, first lord of the manor of Morrisania in New York. The son of Richard Morris (d. 1672; see MORRIS, family), he was born in that part of Westchester co. that is now part of the Bronx, New York City. He inherited large properties in New York and New Jersey, and in 1697 his New York estate was patented as the manor of Morrisania. In 1702, Morris traveled to England to help bring about the fall of proprietary government in New Jersey. He became a bitter opponent of the arbitrary rule of Lord Cornbury, who was governor of both New York and New Jersey, and aided in securing his removal (1708). In 1715 he was made chief justice of New York, but a subsequent struggle with Gov. William Cosby resulted in his removal (1733). Upon the separation (1738) of New Jersey from New York, Morris became the first governor of New Jersey, serving until his death. His stern administration was marked by much opposition and quarreling.

Morris, Lewis, 1698-1762: see under MORRIS, family.

Morris, Lewis, 1726-98, American political leader, signer of the Declaration of Independence, b. Morrisania, N.Y. (now part of the Bronx); elder half brother of Gouverneur Morris. A wealthy landowner and third lord of the manor of Morrisania after 1762, he was prominent among the opponents of British policies and was influential in promoting the provincial convention of New York (1775) and in the Continental Congress (1775-77). After the war he restored his estate at Morrisania, which had been burned and plundered by the British. He continued to be prominent in New York affairs.

Morris, Lewis Richard, 1760-1825: see under MORRIS, family.

Morris, Mary Philipse: see under MORRIS, ROGER.

Morris, Richard, d. 1672: see under MORRIS, family.

Morris, Richard, 1730-1810: see under MORRIS, family.

Morris, Richard Brandon, 1904-, American historian, b. New York City. He received his Ph.D. from Columbia in 1930, taught (1927-49) at the College of the City of New York, became a professor at Columbia in 1949, and was made Gouverneur Morris professor of history in 1959. His works in colonial history include *Government and Labor in Early America* (1946), a pioneering study, and *Guide to Sources for Early American History (1600-1800) in New York City* (written with Evarts B. Greene, rev. ed. 1953), an invaluable aid to scholars. Also a student of legal history, Morris wrote *Studies in the History of American Law* (1930) and *Fair Trial* (1952). Morris is also considered an expert on the American Revolution and wrote *The Peacemakers* (1965), *The American Revolution Reconsidered* (1967), and *Seven Who Shaped Our Destiny* (1973). He edited the *Encyclopedia of American History* (enl. and updated, 1970) and, with H. S. Commager, was general editor of the "New American Nation" series (1954-).

Morris, Richard Valentine, 1768-1815, American naval officer, b. Morrisania, N.Y. (now part of the Bronx); son of Lewis Morris (1726-98). After the American Revolution he entered the navy and was commissioned captain in 1798. As commander of a squadron in 1802, he was sent to the Mediterranean to undertake negotiations with Tripoli and the other Barbary States to end the TRIPOLITAN WAR. Unsuccessful in concluding peace with Tripoli and unfortunate in dealing with the other powers, Morris was relieved of his command (1803), and his commission was revoked. His pamphlet, *A Defense of the Conduct of Commodore Morris during His Command in the Mediterranean* (1804), is valuable for its official documents on the negotiations.

Morris, Robert, 1734-1806, American merchant, known as the "financier of the American Revolution," and signer of the Declaration of Independence, b. Liverpool, England. Morris emigrated to America in 1747 and was soon apprenticed to the merchant Charles Willing in Philadelphia. He showed an unusual aptitude for business and by 1754 became a partner in the firm with the son, Thomas Willing, after the elder Willing's death. He opposed British restrictions prior to the Revolution and served (1775-78) as a member of the Continental Congress. Morris voted against the original motion for independence in July, 1776, as premature, but signed the declaration in August. A member of various committees in Congress, Morris was particularly important in obtaining munitions and other supplies and in borrowing money to finance George Washington's army. Although Morris's vast mercantile interests profited greatly from his congressional activities, both he and his firm were acquitted by Congress of charges of fraud. After leaving Congress, Morris expanded his mercantile and investment operations independently of Willing and by 1781 was almost universally acknowledged as the most prominent merchant in America. The collapse of public credit led to his being appointed superintendent of finance (1781-84) by Congress. Morris labored hard and well in this office; he pressed the states for contributions, retrenched expenditures, took steps toward the establishment of a national mint, guided the organization of a national bank, and extensively used his personal credit to raise funds for the government. He framed, but failed to get Congress to approve, a fiscal program including funding at par of the national debt and the assumption of state debts; it paralleled Alexander Hamilton's program of 1790. Morris was later a member of the Federal Constitutional Convention (1787) and served (1789-95) as U.S. Senator from Pennsylvania. His private business, continued in his terms of office, ultimately ended in bankruptcy as a result of the collapse of extensive land speculation. Morris was in debtors' prison from 1798 to 1801 and never recovered his fortune. See biographies by E. P. Oberholtzer (1903, repr. 1968) and Eleanor Young (1950); W. G. Sumner, *The Financier and the Finances of the American Revolution* (1891, repr. 1968); C. L. Ver Steeg, *Robert Morris, Revolutionary Financier* (1954, repr. 1972).

Morris, Robert, 1931-, American artist, b. Kansas City, Mo. Morris was allied in his early work with the minimalists (see MODERN ART), artists who create simple, neutral, impersonal works in reaction against ABSTRACT EXPRESSIONISM. An untitled work (1965) consisting of four blocks of grey fiber glass is in the Dwan Gallery, New York City. His use of nonrigid materials such as felt precluded preconceived or reproducible forms and emphasized the process of art. Morris later experimented in several areas of dance, theater, and the plastic arts, often attempting complex combinations. He is noted also as a theorist and teacher.

Morris, Robert Hunter: see under MORRIS, family.

Morris, Roger, 1727–94, Loyalist in the American Revolution, b. Yorkshire, England. He came (1755) to America as aide-de-camp to Gen. Edward Braddock and fought under James Wolfe at Quebec. After his service in the British army he settled (1764) in New York City with his wife, Mary Philipse. They lived in the famous Morris Mansion (later the JUMEL MANSION). At the outbreak of the American Revolution, Morris was sympathetic to the British but refused to fight against the patriots. His wife, **Mary Philipse Morris,** 1730–1825, inherited her wealth from her father, Frederick Philipse. Handsome and imperious, she is said to have attracted numerous suitors, among them George Washington. After her marriage (1758) her property holdings—including a large estate in Putnam co., N.Y.—were passed on to Roger Morris. Soon after the outbreak of the American Revolution the family's property was confiscated by an act of attainder of the New York state legislature. Subsequently, she left (1783) for England with her husband and four children. Her heirs (who by Mary Philipse's marriage settlement had a right to those estates and had not themselves been attainted) sold their reversionary interests to John Jacob Astor for £20,000. To this the British government added £17,000 in compensation for Morris's losses incurred by New York state's confiscation.

Morris, William, 1834–96, English poet, artist, craftsman, designer, social reformer, and printer. He has long been considered one of the great Victorians. While at Oxford, Morris, along with his lifelong friend BURNE-JONES, became deeply interested in the ritual and architecture of the Middle Ages. However, Morris's great awakening came through his readings of Ruskin, whose ideas on aestheticism and social progress he gradually adopted. In 1856, after being apprenticed to an architect, Morris attached himself to the brotherhood of PRE-RAPHAELITES and through the encouragement of Dante Gabriel Rossetti began to paint and write. In 1858 he published his first volume of poems, *The Defence of Guenevere and Other Poems.* This was followed by *The Life and Death of Jason* (1867) and *The Earthly Paradise* (3 vol., 1868–70), in which a group of medieval Norse wanderers seek a land where there is no death or misery. Although popular in its time, his poetry is not widely read today. With friends in 1861 he started the firm of decorators later famous as Morris and Company, which, in reaction to the growing industrialism, sought a return to the working operations of the Middle Ages and a revitalization of the splendor of the medieval decorative arts (see ARTS AND CRAFTS). He made carvings, stained glass, tapestries, carpets, wallpaper, chintzes, and furniture. In the 1870s he founded the Society for the Preservation of Ancient Buildings. He became interested in politics and reform, joining (1883) the socialist Democratic Federation and forming (1884) the Socialist League. Two notable prose works came out of this political phase, *The Dream of John Ball* (1888) and *News from Nowhere* (1891). In these works Morris contrasts the ugliness of the machine world with the poetry and beauty of the Middle Ages, setting forth the doctrine that art is the expression of joy in labor rather than an exclusive luxury. He made no distinction between art and craft and saw fine design and workmanship as the salvation of the industrial society. His last artistic venture, and one of his most important, was the KELMSCOTT PRESS in Hammersmith (est. 1890), where he designed the type, page borders, and bindings of fine books. Morris had a profound influence on the printing industry with his brilliant graphic contrast of ink with page and his elegantly designed type. See his collected works (24 vol., 1910–15; repr. 1966); his lectures, ed. by E. D. Le Mire (1969); selections, ed. by his daughter, May Morris (1936, repr. 1962); biographies by J. W. Mackail (1912, repr. 1970) and Philip Henderson (1967); studies by P. R. Thompson (1967) and Ray Watkinson (1967).

Morris, Wright, 1910–, American writer, b. Central City, Nev. Since 1962 he has been professor of English at San Francisco State College. A perennially unfashionable writer with an underground reputation, Morris writes numerous types of novels. However, all his fiction treats the American experience, e.g., the relationship of its history to its present, the evolution and continuity of the American character. His novels include *The World in the Attic* (1949), *Love Among the Cannibals* (1957), *Fire Sermon* (1971), and *A Life* (1973). *The Territory Ahead* (1958) is a study of American literary tradition, and *About Fiction* (1975) is a critical work. See studies by David Madden (1964) and Leon Howard (1968).

Morris Brown College: see ATLANTA UNIV. CENTER.

Morrisburg, village, SE Ont., Canada, on the St. Lawrence River. Just east of the village is the Upper Canada Village, a model of a typical 19th-century community.

morris dance or **morrice dance,** rustic dance of the north of England that had its origin in country festivals, such as those of May Day and Whitsunday. Reference to it in English literature is made as early as the 15th cent. The main dancers were called Robin Hood, Maid Marian, the hobbyhorse, and the bavian, or fool. They were accompanied by a piper or taborer. An ambulatory dance, it was often performed from one village to another by the main dancers and six other dancers, three in a row. The morris dance was a sword dance in many vicinities. See C. J. Sharp and H. C. Macilwaine, *The Morris Book* (5 vol., 1909–13).

Morris Jesup, Cape (jĕs'əp), northernmost land point in the world, N Greenland. At lat. 83° 39′ N, it is 440 mi (708 km) from the North Pole. U.S. explorer Robert Peary reached the cape in 1892.

Morrison, Arthur, 1863–1945, English novelist. A journalist, he worked on the *National Observer* for William Ernest Henley. His stories of life in the London slums include *Tales of Mean Street* (1894), *A Child of the Jago* (1896), and *A Hole in the Wall* (1902). He was also the author of a series of detective stories.

Morrison, Mount, Taiwan: see HSIN-KAO SHAN.

Morrison Cave State Park, SW Mont., on the Jefferson River and SE of Butte. The large limestone cavern was in the former Lewis and Clark Cavern National Monument.

Morrison of Lambeth, Herbert Stanley Morrison, Baron, 1888–1965, British statesman. Born in London of poor parents, he went to work at the age of 14. He entered the labor movement as a young man and became secretary of the London Labour party in 1915, a position he held until 1947. He was mayor of Hackney (1920–21), served in Parliament (1923, 1929–31), and was minister of transport in the second Labour government (1929–31). He was a member of the London County Council from 1922 to 1945 and during his leadership in the council (1934–40) brought the transit system of London under a unified system of public ownership and embarked on an ambitious program of slum clearance. Reelected to Parliament in 1935, he was home secretary and minister of home security (1940–45) and served as a member (1942–45) of Winston Churchill's war cabinet. With the Labour victory in 1945, Morrison became lord president of the council, leader in the House of Commons, and deputy prime minister. He favored a moderate policy of socialization designed to keep the support of the middle classes. In 1951, Morrison became foreign secretary, and from 1951 to 1955 he served as deputy leader of the opposition. He became a life peer in 1959. Among his writings are works on government and socialism and his autobiography (1960).

Morristown. 1 Town (1970 pop. 17,662), seat of Morris co., N N.J., on the Whippany River; settled c.1710, inc. 1865. Although chiefly residential, it has stone quarries and plants that make a wide variety of products. This quiet village was a center of Revolutionary activity, particularly in the winters of 1777 and 1779–80, when the Continental army encamped there. Benedict Arnold was court-martialed in the town. Alfred Vail and S. F. B. Morse perfected (c.1837) the telegraph there. Morristown grew with the area's iron industry. It is the seat of Walsh College. The Seeing Eye School (est. 1929) for training dogs to aid the blind is nearby. Of interest are the Schuyler-Hamilton House (1760), where Alexander Hamilton courted (1779–80) Elizabeth Schuyler (it is now headquarters for the Daughters of the American Revolution); the courthouse (1826); and the municipal building, which was built in 1918 as the home and museum of Theodore N. Vail. Other notable residents of Morristown were the cartoonist Thomas Nast, the writer Bret Harte, and the humorist Frank R. Stockton. **Morristown National Historical Park** (see NATIONAL PARKS AND MONUMENTS, table) includes the Ford Mansion, which was Washington's headquarters in 1779–80; a historical museum at the rear of the Ford Mansion; and the reconstructed sites of encampment of the Continental Army at Fort Nonsense and at Jockey Hollow. **2** City (1970 pop. 20,318), seat of Hamblen co., NE Tenn., in a fertile valley of a mountainous region; settled 1783, inc. 1867. Furniture is made there. Two junior colleges are in the city, and nearby Cherokee Lake provides recreation.

Morrisville, borough (1970 pop. 11,309), Bucks co., SE Pa., on the Delaware River opposite Trenton, N.J.; settled c.1624 by the Dutch West India Company, inc. 1804. Golf bags, tiles, and rubber and plastic products are the principal manufactures. Washington had his headquarters there Dec. 8–14, 1776. Nearby is William Penn's manor, Pennsbury, which has been reconstructed.

Morro Castle (môr'ō), fort at the entrance to the harbor of Havana, Cuba. It was erected by the Spanish in 1589 to protect the city from buccaneers. The fort was also used as a prison. Morro Castle was captured by the British under Sir George Pocock in 1762. The fort at the entrance to the harbor of Santiago de Cuba is also called Morro Castle and was built shortly after the Morro Castle of Havana. It was taken by the American forces in the Spanish-American War (1898). Morro Castle on the harbor of San Juan, Puerto Rico, is also a picturesque old Spanish fort.

Morrow, Dwight Whitney, 1873–1931, American banker and diplomat, b. Huntington, W.Va. He practiced law in New York City and entered (1914) the banking house of J. P. Morgan & Company. After the United States entered World War I, he became a member of the allied transport council and chief civilian aide to Gen. John J. Pershing. In the midst of the ill feeling aroused by the Mexican laws expropriating U.S. holdings in Mexico, President Coolidge appointed (1927) Morrow ambassador to Mexico. His service was notable because it marked a new spirit of cooperation in U.S. relations with Latin America. He was afterward (1930) a delegate to the London Naval Conference and served (1930–31) in the U.S. Senate as a Republican from New Jersey. His daughter, Anne Spencer Morrow, married Charles A. LINDBERGH. See biography by Harold Nicolson (1935).

Mors (môrs), island (1965 pop. 25,739), 140 sq mi (363 sq km), NW Denmark, in the Limfjord. Nykøbing is the chief city. The island has considerable fertile soil, and offshore there are oyster fisheries.

Morse, Jedidiah, 1761–1826, American Congregational clergyman, b. Woodstock, Conn., grad. Yale, 1783. Licensed to preach in 1785, he taught and preached in various places before becoming (1789) minister in Charlestown, Mass., where he stayed for 30 years. A staunch conservative, he opposed Unitarianism. He was interested in improving the lot of the Indians and was appointed (1820) to visit various tribes; the result was the well-known *Report to the Secretary of War* (1822, repr. 1972). He produced a series of textbooks in geography that were widely used and caused him to be called the "father of American geography." Sidney Edwards Morse and Samuel F. B. Morse were his sons. See biography by J. K. Morse (1939, repr. 1967).

Morse, John Torrey, 1840–1937, American lawyer and biographer, b. Boston. Admitted to the bar in 1862, he practiced law in Boston until 1880, when he turned all his attention to writing. With Henry Cabot Lodge he was for a time editor of the *International Review.* He wrote legal works and biographies, including those of Alexander Hamilton (1876) and O. W. Holmes (1896), in addition to his biographies of Abraham Lincoln, John Quincy Adams, Thomas Jefferson, and Benjamin Franklin for the "American Statesmen" series, of which he was editor.

Morse, Samuel Finley Breese, 1791–1872, American inventor and artist, b. Charlestown, Mass., grad. Yale, 1810. He studied painting in England under Washington Allston and achieved some success. He returned to the United States in 1815, took up portrait painting, and gained a considerable reputation in this field. He was a founder (1825) of the National Academy of Design. He spent the years from 1829 to 1832 in further European study. His interest in electricity, aroused in his college days, was further stimulated by the lectures of James F. Dana in 1827 and later by contacts with members of the faculty of New York Univ. Learning in 1832 of Ampère's idea for the electric telegraph, Morse worked for the next 12 years, with the aid of Leonard Gale, Joseph Henry, and Alfred Vail, to perfect his own version of the instrument. So many phases of the telegraph, however, had already been anticipated by other inventors, especially in Great Britain, Germany, and France, that Morse's originality as the inventor of telegraphy has been questioned; even the MORSE CODE did not differ greatly from earlier codes, including the semaphore. In any case, Morse in 1844 demonstrated to Congress the practicability of his instrument by transmitting the famous message "What hath God wrought" over a wire from Washington to Baltimore. Morse subsequently was compelled to defend his invention in court, although by then he commanded the acclaim of the world. He later experimented with submarine cable telegraphy. Both Morse and John Draper were instrumental in introducing the daguerreotype in the United States. See his letters and journals, ed. by E. L. Morse (1914, repr. 1973); biography by Carleton Mabee (1943, repr. 1969).

Morse, Wayne Lyman, 1900–1974, U.S. Senator (1945–69), b. Madison, Wis. He was a professor of law and later dean at the Univ. of Oregon law school (1931–44) and gained a nationwide reputation as a labor arbitrator. He served as a member of the National War Labor Board from 1942 to 1944. Elected in 1944 to the U.S. Senate as a Republican (and reelected in 1950), Morse was consistently critical of what he termed reactionary elements in the party. In 1952 he refused to support the Republican presidential nominee, Dwight D. Eisenhower, and declared himself an independent. In 1955 he formally announced himself a Democrat and as such twice won reelection (1956, 1962) to the Senate. As a Senator he strongly supported public-power measures and was a severe critic of the filibuster. Yet Morse in 1953 delivered the longest personal filibuster then on record (22 hr 6 min) in opposing the bill giving offshore oil rights to the states. A long-time opponent of the Vietnam War (he voted against the Gulf of Tonkin resolution in 1964), he was defeated for reelection in 1968. He ran for the Senate in 1972 against Senator Mark Hatfield, also a critic of the war, but failed to unseat him. In 1974 he won the Democratic primary for the Senate but died before the election. See biography by A. R. Smith (1962).

Morse code [for S. F. B. Morse], the arbitrary set of signals used on the TELEGRAPH (see CODE). It may also be used with a flash lamp for visible SIGNALING. The international (or continental) Morse code is a simplified form generally used in radio telegraphy. The American Morse differs from the international Morse in 11 letters, in all the numerals except the numeral 4, and in the punctuation code. The unit of the code is the *dot*, representing a very brief depression of the telegraph key. The *dash* represents a depression lasting three times as long as a dot. Between the depressions there is a pause equal in time to one dot, except in a few letters and signs, when there is a wait of two dots. The pause between letters in a word lasts as long as one dash, between words it lasts as long as two dashes. The international Morse is as follows:

A	.–	J	.–––	S	...
B	–...	K	–.–	T	–
C	–.–.	L	.–..	U	..–
D	–..	M	––	V	...–
E	.	N	–.	W	.––
F	..–.	O	–––	X	–..–
G	––.	P	.––.	Y	–.––
H	....	Q	––.–	Z	––..
I	..	R	.–.		
1	.––––	5	.....	9	––––.
2	..–––	6	–....	0	–––––
3	...––	7	––...	Period	.–.–.–
4	....–	8	–––..	Comma	––..––

The American Morse differs in the following symbols:

C	.. .	O	. .	X	.–..
F	.–.	P	.....	Y	.. ..
J	–.–.	Q	..–.	Z	... .
L	——	R	. ..		
1	.––.	5	–––	9	–..–
2	..–..	6	......	0	———
3	...–.	7	––..	Period	..––..
4	....–	8	–....	Comma	.–.–

mortality: see VITAL STATISTICS.

mortar, in building, mixture of lime or CEMENT with sand and water, used as a bedding and adhesive between adjacent pieces of stone, brick, or other material in masonry construction. Lime mortar, a common variety, consists usually of one volume of well-slaked lime to three or four volumes of sand, thoroughly mixed with sufficient water to make a uniform paste easily handled on a trowel. Lime mortar hardens by absorption of carbon dioxide from the air. Once universally used, lime mortar is now less important because it does not have the property of setting under water and because of its comparatively low strength. It has largely been supplanted by cement mortar, commonly made of one volume of Portland cement to two or three volumes of sand, usually with a quantity of lime paste added to give a more workable mix. Cement mortar, besides having a high strength, generally equal to that of brick itself, has the very great advantage of setting or hardening under water. Other varieties include gauge mortar, for rapid setting, composed of plaster of Paris used either pure or combined with lime or with lime and sand, and grout, a thin liquid mixture of lime or cement, poured into masonry to fill up small interstices. Primitive mortars took various forms: in early Egypt, Nile mud was used as an adhesive; the Mesopotamians used bitumen (the slime mentioned in Genesis) or sometimes a mixture of clay, water, and chopped straw, to cement together their unbaked bricks; Greeks of the Mycenaean era probably employed a soft bituminous clay. The advanced Greek buildings are notable for their construction without mortar, the huge blocks of stone being consummately fitted with dry beds. The Romans likewise used little mortar in cut stonework or vaulting but in later periods bedded the rough stone of their mass masonry in strong cement mortar. In medieval times and in all periods since, mortar of some sort has been almost universally used in masonry construction.

mortar, in warfare, term originally applied to certain types of ARTILLERY with high trajectories, but later applied to an infantry weapon that consists of a tube supported by a bipod that fires a projectile at a very high trajectory. The mortar is not usually classified as artillery. Unlike standard types of artillery, mortars need no complex recoil equipment and are usually smoothbore and muzzle-loaded. Their weight is light in relation to the weight of shell delivered, but at the expense of range and accuracy. First developed by Sir Frederick Stokes during World War I, the mortar was used by infantry in trench warfare and is standard equipment in modern armies.

Morteratsch (môr'tərăch), glacier, SE Switzerland, one of the largest in the country. It lies at the foot of Piz Morteratsch, an Alpine peak, 12,317 ft (3,754 m) high, in the Bernina mts.

mortgage, in law, device for protecting a creditor by giving him an interest in PROPERTY of his debtor. At COMMON LAW a mortgage was a conditional sale; i.e., the mortgagor (debtor) sold realty (real property mortgage) or personal property (chattel mortgage), but if he paid the debt by a certain time the sale was voided. The mortgagee (creditor) held legal title, the mortgagor equitable title; both estates were salable. Today Great Britain and a majority of states in the United States view mortgages as LIENS on property. The practical result under the two systems is the same. If the mortgagor does not pay the debt, the creditor seeks a court-ordered sale of the property (foreclosure), and the debt is paid out of the proceeds. During economic depressions many jurisdictions enact temporary mortgage moratorium statutes that give courts the discretionary power to refuse to foreclose mortgages.

Mortimer, Edmund de, 3d **earl of March** and 1st **earl of Ulster,** 1351–81, English nobleman. He succeeded (1360) his father, Roger, 2d earl of March, married (1368) Philippa, daughter of Edward III's son Lionel, duke of Clarence, and on Lionel's death (1368) inherited his estates and the title of earl of Ulster. Later the house of York (see YORK, HOUSE OF) traced part of its claim to the throne to this union. Mortimer held the office of marshal of England from 1369 to 1377 and supported the party that opposed JOHN OF GAUNT. After the accession of Richard II (1377) he was elected to the boy king's first council. In 1379 he was sent as lieutenant of Ireland to subdue Irish unrest. His daughter Elizabeth married Sir Henry Percy, known as Hotspur.

Mortimer, Edmund de, 5th **earl of March** and 3d **earl of Ulster,** 1391–1425, English nobleman, son of Roger de Mortimer, 4th earl of March. He succeeded (1398) his father not only as earl of March and Ulster but as heir presumptive to the childless Richard II. However, after the usurpation (1399) of the throne by the Lancastrian Henry IV, Mortimer was imprisoned, although allowed to inherit his estates. On the accession of Henry V (1413), he was released and served Henry in the French wars. He refused to countenance plots of partisans to raise him to the throne and even denounced a body of these conspirators to the king. After Henry V's death, Mortimer became (1422) a member of the regency council for the young Henry VI. In 1424 he took the post of lieutenant of Ireland, where his death by plague ended the male line of the Mortimers. His heiress was his sister Anne, whose son by Richard, earl of Cambridge, was Richard, duke of YORK, father of Edward IV and Richard III.

Mortimer, Sir Edmund de, 1376–1409, English nobleman; youngest son of Edmund de Mortimer, 3d earl of March. In 1398 when young Edmund, the 5th earl, nephew of Sir Edmund, succeeded to the title while still a minor, Sir Edmund became the most powerful representative of his family. He supported the usurpation of the throne by the Lancastrian HENRY IV in 1399. In 1402, however, Mortimer was captured by the rebellious Welshman OWEN GLENDOWER, and when the suspicious king forbade his ransom, Edmund entered an alliance with Glendower and married his daughter. Supporting the claim of his young nephew to the throne, he and Glendower continued to fight even after the defeat of their allies, the Percy family (see PERCY, SIR HENRY and NORTHUMBERLAND, HENRY PERCY, 1ST EARL OF). However, Glendower began to suffer defeats, Mortimer's own effectiveness declined, and he died when besieged by royal forces at Harlech.

Mortimer, Roger de, 1st **earl of March,** 1287?–1330, English nobleman. He inherited (c.1304) the vast estates and the title of his father, Edmund, 7th baron of Wigmore. Appointed lieutenant of Ireland in 1316, he was instrumental in securing the defeat of Edward BRUCE and thus was able to consolidate his own holdings in Ireland. His principal estates, however, were in the Welsh Marches, and he joined (1321) the other Marcher lords in opposition to Edward II and the Despensers (see DESPENSER, HUGH LE). He submitted to the king in 1322 and was imprisoned, but in 1323 he escaped to France. When Edward II's queen, ISABELLA, came to France in 1325, Mortimer became her lover. Together they invaded England in 1326 and routed Edward, whom they forced to abdicate (1327) and later had murdered. Having secured the crown for young EDWARD III, Mortimer, with Isabella, virtually ruled England and acquired great wealth. He became earl of March in 1328. Finally in 1330 he was seized by Edward III, tried and convicted by Parliament, and executed as a traitor.

Mortimer, Roger de, 4th **earl of March** and 2d **earl of Ulster,** 1374–98, English nobleman. He succeeded (1381) his father, Edmund de Mortimer, 3d earl of March, and was brought up as a royal ward. In 1385 the childless Richard II proclaimed him heir presumptive to the throne. He came into possession of his estates in 1393, and in 1394 he went to Ireland with Richard to subdue the rebel Irish chiefs. Remaining there as lieutenant of Ireland he won some popularity with the people because of his bravery and liberality. His death in a battle with the clans of Leinster precipitated Richard II's fateful expedition to Ireland in 1399.

Mortimer's Cross, battlefield, Herefordshire, W England, near Leominster. It was the scene of a battle (Feb. 2, 1461) in the Wars of the Roses (see ROSES, WARS OF THE), which ended with a decisive victory for the Yorkist forces under Edward, duke of York, over the Lancastrians. Edward then marched to London, where he proclaimed himself King Edward IV.

mortmain (môrt'mān″) [Fr., = dead hand], ownership of land by a perpetual CORPORATION. The term originally denoted tenure (see TENURE, in law) by a religious corporation, but today it includes ownership by charitable and business corporations. In the Middle Ages the church acquired, by purchase and gift, an enormous amount of land and other property. The struggle over this accumulation of material wealth was an important aspect of the conflict between church and state. Moreover, lands held by monasteries and other religious corporations were generally exempt from taxation and payment of feudal dues, greatly increasing the burden on secular property. Attempts to limit ecclesiastic mortmain began as early as Carolingian times, and by the late 19th cent. the right of religious bodies to own land was in general highly restricted. In many countries the prevailing principle limited such ownership to absolutely necessary holdings. In the United States ecclesiastic mortmain was never a serious problem, and remaining statutes on the subject are essentially inoperative vestiges of former law. See H. C. Lea, *The Dead Hand* (1900); Carl Zollman, *American Civil Church Law* (1917).

Morton, James Douglas, 4th **earl of,** d. 1581, Scottish nobleman. A nephew of Archibald Douglas, 6th earl of Angus, he married Elizabeth Douglas, from whose father he inherited (1553) the earldom of Morton. A member of the Protestant party, he became lord high chancellor to MARY QUEEN OF SCOTS in 1563. He was a principal in the murder of David RIZZIO (1566) and fled thereafter to England. Pardoned, he returned to Scotland the following year and became involved in the plot to murder Lord

DARNLEY. After Mary's marriage to Lord Bothwell, Morton turned against the queen, whose forces he defeated at Langside (1568). He was chief counselor to the regent James Stuart, 1st earl of MURRAY, and became regent himself on the death of the 1st earl of Mar. His rule was devoted to the pacification of a religiously divided and wartorn Scotland. In 1578 he was forced out by a junta of nobles, led by the 6th earl of Argyll and John STUART, 4th earl of Atholl, who persuaded the boy king, James VI (later James I of England), to assert his power. Morton regained control of the king, with the aid of John Erskine, 2d earl of MAR; but in 1581 a plot against him, engineered by Esmé STUART, 1st duke of Lennox, and James STUART, later earl of Arran, resulted in his being tried, convicted, and beheaded for taking part in the murder of Darnley. Morton possessed for some time the Casket Letters, which allegedly implicated Mary in Darnley's death.

Morton, Jelly Roll, 1885-1941, American JAZZ musician, composer, and band leader, originally named Ferdinand Joseph La Menthe, b. Gulfport, La. He began studying piano as a child and in his youth was a pianist in the colorful Storyville district of New Orleans. Later he played with Johnny Dodds, Baby Dodds, Kid Ory, Barney Bigard, and other noted jazz musicians, but his popularity severely declined in the 1930s. Although Morton is regarded by many as the greatest New Orleans pianist, his egocentricity, moodiness, and quarrelsome disposition led many musicians and critics to disparage him. His compositions and arrangements, many of which reflect his Creole background, include *Dead Man Blues, Jelly Roll Blues, King Porter Stomp, Mama Nita, Mamie's Blues* (or *219 Blues*), *Moi pas l'aimez ça, The Pearls, Sidewalk Blues,* and *Wolverine Blues.* See biography by Alan Lomax (1950).

Morton, John, 1420?-1500, English prelate and statesman, archbishop of Canterbury (1486-1500). He studied law at Oxford and practiced in the London ecclesiastical courts. A supporter of the Lancastrian party in the Wars of the Roses, he received a number of church livings, but after the Yorkist victory at Towton (1461) he was attainted and lived in exile at the court of Margaret of Anjou. He returned to England in 1470, taking an active part in the coalition against EDWARD IV, but after Edward's victory at Tewkesbury (1471), his attainder was reversed. He was made a master of the rolls in 1473, was sent (1474) on a mission to Hungary, and became bishop of Ely in 1479. Arrested in the reign of Richard III, he escaped to Flanders and was recalled by Henry VII on his accession (1485) to the throne. Morton became the king's principal counselor, was made archbishop of Canterbury (1486) and lord chancellor (1487), and was created a cardinal in 1493. He was probably the author of the original Latin version of the *History of Richard III,* which is usually ascribed to Sir Thomas More. See biography by R. I. Woodhouse (1895).

Morton, John, c.1724-1777, political leader in the American Revolution, signer of the Declaration of Independence, b. Chester co., Pa. He was a member of the Pennsylvania assembly (1756-66, 1769-75), the Stamp Act Congress (1765), and the Continental Congress (1774-77).

Morton, Julius Sterling, 1832-1902, American cabinet officer, b. Adams, N.Y. He settled (1854) in Nebraska, founded the Nebraska City *News,* and served (1858-61) as territorial secretary. In 1872 he originated ARBOR DAY, which since 1885 has been a legal holiday in Nebraska on April 22, Morton's birthday. He was Secretary of Agriculture (1893-97) under Grover Cleveland. His landed estate at Nebraska City became a memorial park.

Morton, Levi Parsons, 1824-1920, American banker, Vice President of the United States (1889-93), b. Shoreham, Vt. He engaged in business in Hanover, N.Y., and in Boston before organizing (1863) the New York City banking firm of Levi P. Morton and Company—which became one of the more important financial organizations in the country. He became interested in politics and served as a U.S. Representative (1879-81) and as minister to France (1881-85) before he was elected (1888) Vice President on the Republican party ticket along with President Benjamin Harrison. He was later (1895-97) governor of New York. See biography by R. M. McElroy (1930).

Morton, Oliver Perry, 1823-77, American political leader, b. Salisbury, Ind. He was admitted (1847) to the bar and began practice in Centerville, Ind. Morton helped organize the Republican party in Indiana and was its unsuccessful candidate for governor in 1856. When Gov. Henry S. Lane went to the Senate in 1861, Morton, as lieutenant governor, succeeded him; he was elected to the office in his own right in 1864. Despite having to contend with a hostile Democratic legislature for part of his tenure, he was one of the ablest of the Civil War governors and a strong supporter of President Lincoln. In 1867 he resigned to enter the Senate, where he served till his death. There, as one of the leading radical Republicans, he fostered uncompromising Reconstruction legislation and was prominent in the impeachment of President Andrew Johnson. He was a member of the electoral commission in the disputed presidential contest of 1876. See biography by W. D. Foulke (1899, repr. 1974); W. B. Hesseltine, *Lincoln and the War Governors* (1948).

Morton, Rosalie Slaughter, 1876-, American surgeon, b. Lynchburg, Va., M.D. Woman's Medical College of Pennsylvania, 1897. She was the first woman faculty member of both the New York Polyclinic Medical School and Hospital (1912-18) and the College of Physicians and Surgeons (1916-18). During World War I she was active in hospital work, especially during the Salonica campaigns and in Yugoslavia, Serbia, and France. For this work and for her efforts that made possible the education in the United States of 60 Serbian students, she was decorated by foreign governments and by the state of New York. After 1930 she engaged in private practice in Florida. She took part in public health and welfare activities, invented a number of surgical instruments and appliances, and wrote many articles, especially on gynecology and arthritis. See her autobiography (1937).

Morton, Sarah Wentworth, 1759-1846, American author, b. Boston. Under her pseudonym, Philenia, she wrote such works as *Ouâbi: Or the Virtues of Nature* (1790), a sentimental Indian romance. Morton was long thought to be the author of the first American novel, *The Power of Sympathy* (1789), a book that is now attributed to William Hill Brown.

Morton, Thomas, fl. 1622-47, English trader and adventurer in New England. He visited New England in 1622 and returned in 1625 with Captain Wollaston, who founded a settlement at Mt. Wollaston (now Quincy, Mass.). When Wollaston moved on to Virginia, Morton took charge of the settlement, which was renamed Mare Mount, whence it was called Merry Mount. The Plymouth settlers objected to Morton and his companions, who were of the Anglican faith and who started a rival fur trade with the Indians. The Maypole festivities at Merry Mount especially scandalized the Pilgrims. A force under Miles STANDISH seized Morton, who was sent (1628) to England on charges of trading arms to the Indians and harboring runaway servants. He returned in 1629 and resumed his fur trading but was again brought to court in 1630 and sent to England. There he was employed by Sir Ferdinando GORGES as legal counsel in the attempt to void the charter of the Massachusetts Bay Company. Going once more to New England, he was imprisoned (1644-45) in Boston. Later he moved to Maine, where he died. His book, *New English Canaan* (1637, repr. 1883 with notes by Charles Francis Adams, 1835-1915), gives a bitter, satiric view of New England.

Morton, William Thomas Green, 1819-68, American dentist and physician, b. Charlton, Mass., studied at Baltimore College of Dental Surgery. He practiced dentistry in Boston, for a time with Horace Wells, whose unsuccessful demonstration of nitrous oxide, or laughing gas, he sponsored in 1845. C. T. Jackson interested him in ether anesthesia, and in 1846 Morton demonstrated its use during an operation at Massachusetts General Hospital. The prior work of C. W. Long in ether anesthesia had not then been made public. Morton's subsequent claim to the discovery of the anesthetic effects of ether was bitterly disputed. See G. S. Woodward, *The Man Who Conquered Pain* (1962); Betty MacQuitty, *Victory over Pain* (1971).

Morton, village (1970 pop. 10,419), Tazewell co., central Ill., in a grain-farming and livestock area; inc. 1877. Food is canned, and tractor parts and pottery are manufactured.

Morton Grove, village (1970 pop. 26,369), Cook co., NE Ill.; inc. 1895. It has research laboratories and plants that make pumps, electrical equipment, and cosmetics.

Morvan (môrväN'), mountainous region, E central France, in Nivernais and Burgundy. The northernmost part of the Massif Central, this heavily forested region rises to 2,959 ft (902 m) at Bois-du-Roi. Cattle raising and the production of charcoal are the chief industries. The Yonne River rises in the Morvan.

mosaic (mōzā'ĭk), art of arranging colored pieces of marble, glass, tile, wood, or other material to produce a surface ornament. In Egypt and Mesopotamia, furniture, small architectural features, and jewelry were occasionally adorned with inset bits of enamel, glass, and colored stone. Early Greek mosaics (5th-4th cent. B.C.) uncovered at Olynthus were worked in small natural pebbles. The use of cut cubes or tesserae was introduced from the East after the Alexandrian conquest. Roman floor mosaics were probably based upon Greek examples, and glass mosaics applied to columns, niches, and fountains can be seen at Pompeii. In Italy and the Roman colonies the floor patterns were produced both by large slabs of marble in contrasting colors (*opus sectile*) and by small marble tesserae (*opus tessellatum*). The tessera designs varied from simple geometrical patterns in black and white to huge pictorial arrangements of figures and animals; examples were found in Rome, Pompeii, and N Africa. In the early centuries A.D. glass mosaics brought color and decoration to the broad walls of the basilicas. By the 4th cent. the triumphal arch between nave and apse and the walls above the nave arcades received mosaic adornment, while the entire domed apse was lined with a mosaic picture, generally of Christ surrounded by saints and apostles. In this period Byzantium (later Constantinople) became the center of the craft, which reached perfection in the 6th cent. HAGIA SOPHIA exhibits glittering gold backgrounds—a special feature of Eastern mosaic art, which later spread to the West. A gold tessera was produced by applying gold leaf to a glass cube and covering it with a thin glass film to protect against tarnishing; for the other tesserae the colors were produced by metallic oxides. The tesserae were set by hand in the damp cement mortar, and the resulting irregularities, causing the facets to reflect at different angles, were an essential factor of effect. In the 5th and 6th cent. RAVENNA became the Western center of mosaic art, and the Ravenna masterworks (e.g., the decoration of San Vitale), as well as those in Rome, show the Byzantine characteristics of stylized rigidity in the figures. Through the importation of Greek workmen, a revival took place in Italy in the 11th cent. which lasted into the 13th cent., producing the beautiful mural works of Rome, of SAINT MARK'S CHURCH and Torcello at Venice, and of Palermo, Monreale, and Cefalù in Sicily. Rich medieval marble and mosaic floors with geometric patterns appeared in Italy, Sicily, and the East. In Russia, especially in Kiev, remarkable figural mosaics were set into the walls. From the 13th cent., mosaic in Italy and Sicily extended to many architectural elements, such as pulpits, bishops' thrones, paschal candlesticks, and the twisted columns of cloisters. These adornments are commonly termed Cosmati work, after the family of Roman craftsmen especially gifted in their execution. The rise of fresco decoration in the early 14th cent. in Italy superseded mosaic, which then began to deteriorate into mere simulation of painting, although it lingered in Venice, Greece, and Constantinople. The Gothic revival of the 19th cent. produced some modern attempts, as in Westminster Abbey and the houses of Parliament. In the 20th cent. the medium has been used with truer understanding of techniques, as in the modernist mosaics for the Stockholm town hall. In modern work the ancient system shares favor with a new method of fastening the tesserae with glue upon a paper cartoon drawn in reverse, applying fairly large sections of this into proper position upon the damp mortar, and then washing away the paper after the mortar has hardened and the tesserae have set. See E. W. Anthony, *A History of Mosaics* (1935, repr. 1968); Ferdinando Rossi, *Mosaics: A Survey of Their History and Techniques* (1970).

Mosby, John Singleton (môz'bē), 1833-1916, Confederate partisan leader in the American Civil War, b. Edgemont, Va. He was practicing law in Bristol, Va., when the Civil War broke out. Mosby served brilliantly in the cavalry under J. E. B. Stuart until Jan., 1863, when he began his partisan operations in N Virginia—soon called "Mosby's Confederacy." Moving swiftly and secretly, Mosby's men (who never numbered more than 200) continually routed Federal cavalry, destroyed communications, appropriated supplies, and were, in general, a great nuisance to the Army of the Potomac. Perhaps Mosby's most famous exploit was the capture of a Union general, caught asleep in his bed, at Fairfax Courthouse in March, 1863. Protected by the people of the region, Mosby's Partisan Rangers eluded the strong forces sent to capture them and were active until Robert E. Lee surrendered. Mosby secured his parole only through the intercession of Ulysses S.

Grant, of whom he became a great admirer. He joined the Republican party and later held various minor government positions. He wrote *Mosby's War Reminiscences* and *Stuart's Cavalry Campaigns* (1887) and *Stuart's Cavalry in the Gettysburg Campaign* (1908). See C. W. Russell, ed., *The Memoirs of Colonel John S. Mosby* (1917, repr. 1969); biographies by V. C. Jones (1944) and Jonathan Daniels (1959).

Moscheles, Ignaz (ĭg'näts mŏsh'əlĕs), 1794–1870, Bohemian-German musician. Born in Prague, Moscheles was a child prodigy. He studied in Vienna with Johann Albrechtsberger and Antonio Salieri and prepared a piano score of Beethoven's *Fidelio* under the composer's direction. Moscheles toured Europe as a pianist and in 1832 gave the British premier of Beethoven's *Missa Solemnis.* One of his pupils was Mendelssohn, at whose invitation he joined the Leipzig Conservatory faculty in 1846. There he became renowned for his teaching and his piano improvisation. In composition and performance he was unsympathetic to the romanticism of Chopin and Liszt. His works (142 opus numbers) include eight piano concertos. Moscheles translated A. F. Schindler's biography of Beethoven into English.

Moschus (mŏs'kəs), fl. c.150 B.C., Greek bucolic poet of the school of Theocritus. He is called a Syracusan and lived in Alexandria. Among his few extant pieces is an idyl on Europa. Although *Lament for Bion,* a beautiful dirge has traditionally been ascribed to Moschus, it is probably of later date.

Mosconi, Willie (William Joseph Mosconi), 1913–, U.S. professional billiard player, b. Philadelphia. After a brief period as a child prodigy he did not take up the game again until 1931. He won his first world championship in 1941, and defended it successfully through 1955 in all years except 1943 and 1949. Beginning in the mid-1950s, Mosconi gave numerous exhibitions and helped to popularize the game. He wrote *Willie Mosconi on Pocket Billiards* (1954).

Moscow (mŏs'kou, –kō), Rus. *Moskva,* city (1970 pop. 7,061,000), capital of the USSR, of the Russian Soviet Federated Socialist Republic (RSFSR), and of Moscow oblast, W central European USSR, on the Moskva River near its junction with the Moscow Canal. Moscow is the USSR's largest city and leading economic and cultural center. The hub of the Soviet railroad network, it is also an inland port and has several civilian and military airports. Moscow's major industries include machine building, metalworking, oil refining, publishing, brewing, filmmaking, and the manufacture of machine tools, precision instruments, building materials, automobiles, trucks, aircraft, chemicals, wood and paper products, textiles, clothing, and footwear. Although archaeological evidence indicates that the site has been occupied since Neolithic times, the village of Moscow was first mentioned in the Russian chronicles in 1147. Moscow became (c.1271) the seat of the grand dukes of Suzdal-Vladimir, who later assumed the title of grand dukes of Moscow (see MOSCOW, GRAND DUCHY OF). During the rule of DMITRI DONSKOI, the first stone walls of the Kremlin were built (1367). Moscow, or Muscovy, achieved dominance over the Russian lands by virtue of its strategic location at the crossroads of medieval trade routes, its leadership in the struggle against and final defeat of the Tatars, and its gathering of neighboring principalities under Muscovite suzerainty. By the 15th cent. Moscow had become the capital of the Russian national state, and in 1547 Grand Duke Ivan IV became the first to assume the title of czar. Moscow was also the seat of the Metropolitan (later Patriarch) of the Russian Orthodox Church from the early 14th cent. It has been an important commercial center since the Middle Ages and the center of many crafts. Burned by the Tatars in 1381 and again in 1572, the city was taken by the Poles during the Time of Troubles (see RUSSIA). In 1611 the Muscovites, under the leadership of Kuzma Minin (a butcher) and Prince Dmitri Pozharski, attacked the Polish garrison and forced the remaining Polish troops into the Kremlin, where they surrendered in 1612. The large-scale growth of manufacturing in 17th-century Moscow generated a great market and necessitated an outlet to the sea. This commercial consideration was instrumental in Peter I's decision to build St. Petersburg on the Baltic. The Russian capital was transferred from Moscow to St. Petersburg (now Leningrad) in 1712; but Moscow's cultural and social life continued uninterrupted, and the city never ceased to be the religious center of Russia. Built largely of wood until the 19th cent., Moscow suffered from numerous fires, the most notable of which occurred in the wake of Napoleon I's occupation in 1812. Nearly the entire city, except for the great stone churches and palaces, burned down. ROSTOPCHIN denied accusations that he had ordered the blaze ignited in order to drive out the French. It is likely that the fire was accidentally begun by French looters and was intentionally fanned by fanatic patriots among the handful of Russians who had remained behind when Napoleon entered the city. Whatever the cause of the fire, it served as the signal for an anti-French uprising among the peasants, whose raids, along with the cruel winter, helped to force Napoleon's retreat. Rebuilt, Moscow developed from the 1830s as a major textile and metallurgical center. During the 19th and early 20th cent. it was the focus of the Zemstvo cooperative and Slavophile movements and became a principal center of the labor movement and of social democracy. In 1918 the Soviet government transferred the capital back to Moscow and fostered spectacular economic growth in the city, whose population doubled between 1926 and 1939. During World War II, Moscow was the goal of a two-pronged German offensive. Although the spearheads of the German columns were stopped only 20 to 25 mi (32–40 km) from the city's center, Moscow suffered virtually no war damage. (Kuybyshev served as the temporary wartime capital during the German siege of Moscow.) Administratively, Moscow is directly subordinated to the government of the RSFSR. It is governed by a city council and is divided into boroughs. The five major sections of Moscow form concentric circles, of which the innermost is the Kremlin (see under KREMLIN), a walled city in itself. Its walls represent the city limits as of the late 15th cent. Adjoining the Kremlin in the east is the huge Red Square, originally a market-place and a meeting spot for popular assemblies; it is still used as a parade ground and for demonstrations. On the west side of Red Square and along the Kremlin wall are the Lenin Mausoleum and the tombs of other Soviet political figures; on the north side is the historical museum; and at the southern end stands the imposing cathedral of Basil the Beatified, now an antireligious museum. It was built in the 16th cent. to commemorate the conquest of Kazan. One of the most exuberant examples of Russian architecture, the cathedral has numerous cupolas, each a different color, grouped around a central dome. In front of the cathedral stands a monument to the liberators Menin and Pozharski. To the E of Red Square extends the old district of Kitaigorod [Chinatown], once the merchant's quarter, later the banking section, and now an administrative hub with various government offices and ministries. Gorky Street, a main thoroughfare, extends N from the Kremlin and is lined with modern buildings, including the headquarters of the council of ministers; it is connected with the Leningrad highway, which passes the huge Dynamo stadium and the central airport. Near the beginning of Gorky Street is Sverdlov Square, containing the Bolshoi and Maly theaters. Encircling the Kremlin and Kitaigorod are the Bely Gorod [white city], traditionally the most elegant part of Moscow and now a commercial and cultural area; the Zemlyanoy Gorod [earth city], named for the earthen and wooden ramparts that once surrounded it; and the inner suburbs. A notable feature of Moscow are the rings of wide boulevards on the sites where old walls and ramparts once stood. Except for its historical core, Moscow has been transformed into a great modern city under the Soviet government. Among its many cultural and scientific institutions are the Univ. of Moscow (founded 1755), the Academy of Sciences of the USSR (founded 1725 in St. Petersburg and transferred to Moscow in 1934), a conservatory (1866), the Tretyakov art gallery (opened in the 1880s), the Museum of Oriental Cultures, the State Historical Museum, the Lenin Museum and Lenin Library, the Agricultural Exhibition, and the People's Friendship Univ. (1960) for foreign students. Theaters include the Moscow Art Theater, the Bolshoi (opera and ballet), and the Maly Theater (drama). Moscow is also the see of a patriarch, head of the Russian Orthodox Church, and the headquarters of the Communist party of the USSR. A new Palace of Congresses was built (1961) inside the Kremlin walls for meetings of the Supreme Soviet. Moscow's numerous large parks and recreation areas include Gorky Central Park, the forested Izmailovo and Sokolniki parks, and Ostankino Park, with its botanical gardens. The Moscow subway system opened in 1935.

Moscow (mŏs'kō), city (1970 pop. 14,146), seat of Latah co., NW Idaho, at the Wash. line; inc. 1887. It is a trade center for a lumber and farm area that grows wheat and peas. There are saw mills, food-processing plants, and factories that manufacture a variety of products. Originally part of the Nez Percé Indian Reservation, it was first settled by whites in 1871. The Univ. of Idaho is there, as well as a historical museum and a U.S. government forest sciences laboratory.

Moscow or **Muscovy, grand duchy of,** state existing in W central Russia from the late 14th to mid-16th cent., with the city of Moscow as its nucleus. Its formation and eventual ascendancy over other Russian principalities and over the Tatars of the Golden Horde (see GOLDEN HORDE, EMPIRE OF THE) came about gradually and resulted particularly from its central location, its importance as a trade artery, its dynastic continuity, its circumspect loyalty to Tatar overlords, and its prestige as a religious center. After the decline of Kiev in the mid-12th cent., Russian territory broke up into a number of separate political units, among which the principality of Vladimir-Suzdal (see VLADIMIR) was the most important. The rulers of Vladimir were the only Russian princes who bore the title grand duke, and they were regarded as suzerains of the other princes. According to tradition, Moscow was founded on a strategic site on the Moskva River as a military outpost of Vladimir-Suzdal; by the mid-12th cent., when its existence is first mentioned in Russian chronicles, it had become a walled town. The first known prince of Moscow was Daniel (d.1303), son of Grand Duke Alexander Nevsky. Daniel received Moscow as a separate appanage. His son, Yuri (1303–25), launched the struggle for Moscow's predominance in Russia, competing for leadership with the prince of Tver for both the title of grand duke and the allegiance of the less powerful Russian princes. Yuri was temporarily appointed grand duke of Vladimir by the khan of the Empire of the Golden Horde. His younger brother, Ivan I (Ivan Kalita; 1328–41), was not only granted the title of grand duke (1328) but was given the right to collect Tatar tributes from neighboring principalities. Moreover, during Ivan's reign Moscow became the seat of the Russian Orthodox Church. The adjacent areas were subdued or acquired, and Moscow's importance continued to increase, particularly under Ivan I's grandson, DMITRI DONSKOI (1359–89), who was probably the first to bear the title grand duke of Moscow. Dmitri's successors, above all IVAN III (1462–1505) and VASILY III (1505–33), laid the basis of Muscovite absolutism, built the Great Russian state, and threw off the Tatar yoke. By the mid-16th cent., therefore, the unification of the Great Russian lands had been completed under the princely dynasty. The Muscovite rulers now bore the title grand duke of Moscow and of all Russia, and the history of the grand duchy of Moscow became that of Russia. See R. C. Howes, ed., *The Testaments of the Grand Princes of Moscow* (1967); J. L. I. Fennell, *The Emergence of Moscow, 1304–1359* (1968).

Moscow Art Theatre, Russian repertory company founded in 1897 by Constantin STANISLAVSKY and Vladimir NEMIROVICH-DANCHENKO. Its work created new concepts of theatrical production and marked the beginning of modern theater. As director, Stanislavsky worked for an illusion of reality not only in the acting but also in the complete stage picture. Plays were chosen for their literary merit. The plays of CHEKHOV were especially suitable to the intense working atmosphere of the group; their production brought fame to both Chekhov and the theatre. Other memorable productions were Tolstoy's *Czar Fyodor Ivanovitch,* Dostoyevsky's *Brothers Karamazov,* and Gorky's *Lower Depths.* The company made several successful tours of the United States. It has continued its classic repertoire while reflecting in new productions the political changes within Russia over the years. See N. M. Gorchakov, *Stanislavksy Directs* (1954) and *The Theatre in Soviet Russia* (1957); Norris Houghton, *Moscow Rehearsals* (1962) and *Return Engagement* (1962); O. M. Sayler, *Inside the Moscow Art Theatre* (1925, repr. 1970).

Moscow Basin, lignite basin, c.200 mi (320 km) long and 50 mi (80 km) wide, central European USSR, S of Moscow. Tula is the chief city of the region. Low-grade bituminous coal, suitable for the power plants of the Moscow industrial region, is mined there.

Moscow Conferences, meetings held between 1941 and 1947 at Moscow, USSR. At a conference in Sept.–Oct., 1941, American and British representatives laid the basis for LEND-LEASE aid to the USSR in World War II. In Aug., 1942, British Prime Minister Winston Churchill and W. Averell Harriman, representing U.S. President Franklin Delano Roosevelt, met with Soviet Premier Joseph Stalin to discuss the opening of a second front in Europe. The third conference (Oct., 1943), attended by the American, British, and Russian foreign ministers, resulted in the pledge to establish a United Nations organization for the maintenance of peace. At the fourth Moscow Conference (Oct., 1944) Prime Minister Winston Churchill and Joseph Stalin discussed the political difficulties of Poland and agreed on armistice terms for Bulgaria and a joint policy with respect to Yugoslavia. For the foreign ministers' conferences held at Moscow in 1945 and 1947, see FOREIGN MINISTERS, COUNCIL OF.

Moscow University, at Moscow, USSR; founded 1755 by the Russian scientist M. V. Lomonosov. It has faculties of physics, computing mathematics and cybernetics, chemistry, mechanics and mathematics, biology and soil science, geography, geology, history, philology, law, philosophy, economics, journalism, and psychology as well as a faculty for teachers in higher-education institutions, and institutes of Oriental languages, mechanics, nuclear studies, astronomy, and anthropological studies.

Moseley, Henry Gwyn Jeffreys (mōz'lē) 1887–1915, English physicist, grad. Trinity College, Oxford, 1910. He began his research under Ernest Rutherford while serving as lecturer at the Univ. of Manchester and soon devoted himself entirely to research. Extending the work of Max von Laue and of W. H. Bragg and W. L. Bragg on the X-ray spectra of elements, Moseley made systematic studies of the relation between the bright-line spectra of different elements. He found that the frequency of vibration of the X rays emitted by each element when bombarded with cathode rays bore a simple relationship to whole ordinal numbers. These ordinal numbers are the atomic numbers; Moseley concluded that the atomic number is equal to the charge on the nucleus. When the elements are arranged according to their atomic numbers the sequence, although almost the same as Mendeleev's arrangement in order of increasing atomic weight, differs slightly; these differences account for the few discrepancies inherent in the Mendeleev system (see PERIODIC LAW). The genius of Moseley's work was widely recognized. He was killed at Gallipoli in World War I. See biography by J. L. Heilbron (1974).

Moselle (mōzĕl'), department (1968 pop. 971,314), NE France, bordering on Luxembourg and Germany. METZ is the capital.

Moselle, Ger. *Mosel,* river, 320 mi (515 km) long, rising in the Vosges mts., NE France, and winding generally N past Épinal and Metz. Leaving France, it forms part of the border between Luxembourg and West Germany, then enters West Germany, passes Trier, and cuts between the Eifel and the Hunsrück ranges to reach the Rhine River at Koblenz. The Moselle receives the Saar River near Trier. The West German section of the Moselle valley is dotted with numerous old castles and is covered with celebrated vineyards. The Moselle is canalized and is able to accommodate large vessels.

Mosera (mō'sērə), unidentified place, S Palestine, where Aaron died. It is probably the same as Moseroth. Deut. 10.6.

Moseroth (mō'sērōth), unidentified desert resting place of the Israelites. Num. 33.30,31.

Moses (mō'zĭs), Hebrew lawgiver, probably b. Egypt. The prototype of the prophets, he led his people in the 13th cent. B.C. out of bondage in Egypt to the edge of Canaan. The Bible narrative is the source of information on Moses' life. As an infant he was divinely protected, and as a young man he received a special calling at the burning bush. Moses lived in constant touch with God, who guided him in leading Israel out of Egypt and across the desert. God promulgated the Law through his mouth, not only the Ten Commandments and the criminal code, but the whole liturgical law as well. In his old age, when the Hebrews were at the Jordan River ready to cross, God gave Moses a view of the Promised Land from Mt. Pisgah; but he did not enter it, for he died and was buried in Moab. All this is told in the books of EXODUS, LEVITICUS, NUMBERS, and DEUTERONOMY. The authorship of these and Genesis (collectively called the Pentateuch) has been ascribed to Moses since earliest times; hence they are called the Books of Moses. The Law he promulgated is called the Mosaic law. Many critics deny the Mosaic authorship of the books. Moses, one of the great names of Hebrew history, is referred to repeatedly in the Bible. Examples of eulogies are in Ecclus. 45.1-5; Heb. 11.23-29. Among the PSEUDEPIGRAPHA there is an Assumption of Moses. See Martin Buber, *Moses* (1946, repr. 1969); Mordecai Roshwald and Miriam Roshwald, *Moses: Leader, Prophet, Man* (1969).

Moses, Bernard, 1846–1930, American historian, b. Burlington, Conn. From 1876 until his death he was professor of history and political science, actively and as professor emeritus, at the Univ. of California. He served (1900–1902) on the U.S. Philippine Commission and in 1910 was minister to Chile. An authority on colonial Spanish America, he wrote *The Establishment of Spanish Rule in America* (1898), *South America on the Eve of Emancipation* (1908), *The Spanish Dependencies in South America* (2 vol., 1914), and *The Intellectual Background of the Revolution in South America, 1810–1824* (1926).

Moses, Grandma (Anna Mary Robertson Moses), 1860–1961, American painter, b. Washington co., N.Y., self-taught. She lived the arduous life of a farm wife, first in the Shenandoah Valley and later at Eagle Bridge, near Hoosick Falls, N.Y. In her late 70s, too frail to do hard work, she began to paint. Her pictures—called American primitives—are simple, gay scenes of farm life that struck the popular fancy and became widely known through prints and Christmas cards. She painted such subjects as *The Old Oaken Bucket, Sugaring-Off,* and *Out for the Christmas Trees. Thanksgiving Turkey* is in the Metropolitan Museum. At the age of 100 she illustrated "'Twas the Night before Christmas" by Clement Moore (1962). See her autobiography (1952) and study by Otto Kallir (1973).

Moses, Robert, 1888–, U.S. public official, b. New Haven, Conn. He was appointed (1919) by Alfred E. Smith to the committee to study and revamp New York state government machinery, became (1924) chairman of the state council of parks, and served (1927–28) as New York secretary of state until disagreement with Gov. Franklin Delano Roosevelt forced him from that position. In 1933 he declined the Fusion nomination for mayor of New York City, and in 1934 he was, as Republican candidate for governor, defeated by Herbert H. Lehman. As New York City park commissioner (1934–60) and head of the Triborough Bridge and New York City Tunnel Authority (1946–68), as well as in other municipal offices, Moses was responsible for reorganizing the department of parks and for planning new and improved highways, parks, bridges, and beaches. His works include *Working for People* (1956). See R. A. Caro, *The Power Broker* (1974).

Moses Lake, city (1970 pop. 10,310), Grant co., central Wash., on Moses Lake; settled 1897, inc. 1938. A distributing and shipping point for the Columbia basin project, its chief products are sugar, potatoes, and milk; a huge sugar plant is there.

Moshi (mō'shē), city (1967 pop. 26,864), capital of Kilimanjaro prov., NE Tanzania, on the southern slope of Mt. Kilimanjaro, near Kenya. It is the center of a rich coffee-growing region and is an industrial, tourist, and transportation center, connected by rail with Tanga on the Indian Ocean. Manufactures include ginned cotton, cured coffee, beverages, and clothing. The original town, now called Old Moshi and located nearby, was the capital of a 19th-century kingdom of the Chagga people and became (late 19th cent.) an administrative center under the Germans. In the 20th cent. the British moved Moshi to its present site.

Moshoeshoe II (mōshoi'shoi), 1938–, king of Lesotho. His given name was Constantine Bereng Seeiso. Educated in Great Britain, he was paramount chief of Basutoland (1960–66) and then became king when Basutoland became independent as Lesotho in 1966. His reign was briefly interrupted by exile, but he returned in 1970.

Moskenstraumen (môsk'ənstrou"mən) or **Maelstrom** (māl'strəm), tidewater whirlpool in the Lofoten Islands, NW Norway. Formed when a strong tidal current flows through an irregular channel S of Moskenesøya island, it is c.2.5 mi (4 km) wide and may at its center reach a speed of 10 ft (3 m) per second. It is a danger to small ships and has been described with great imagination by Edgar Allan Poe and Jules Verne. The term *maelstrom* is applied to any whirlpool.

Moskva (məskvä'), river, c.310 mi (500 km) long, rising in the hills W of Moscow, in central European USSR, and meandering generally E past Mozhaisk and Moscow to join the Oka River near Kolomna. It is connected with the upper Volga River at Dubna by the Moscow-Volga Canal (80 mi/130 km long), built between 1932 and 1937.

Moslem: see MUSLIM.

Mosley, Sir Oswald Ernald (mōz'lē), 1896–, British fascist leader. He entered (1918) Parliament as a Conservative, became (1922) an independent, and then joined (1924) the Labour party. He was junior minister in the Labour government of 1929 but resigned (1930) when the cabinet rejected his economic proposals. In 1931 he founded another socialist party, the New party, but it received little support, and Mosley began to drift toward fascism. He organized (1932) the British Union of Fascists, modeled upon the German and Italian fascist parties. Married first to Lady Cynthia Curzon, daughter of Lord Curzon, in 1936 he married Diana Guinness, sister of the writers Jessica and Nancy Mitford. Diana and another sister, Unity Freeman-Mitford, were friends of Hitler. Until after the outbreak of World War II, Mosley conducted a speech-making campaign of vilification and abuse, directed largely against the Jews. In 1940 he and his wife were interned. They were released in 1943. After the war Mosley attempted to revive his movement. As an unsuccessful candidate in the election of 1959 he called for an end to non-white immigration. See his autobiography, *My Life* (1968); D. R. Shermer, *Black Shirts: Fascism in Britain* (1971). Mosley's son Nicholas Mosley (Lord Ravensdale), b. 1923, is a novelist; his works include *Accident* (1964) and *Natalie Natalia* (1971).

mosque (mŏsk), building for worship used by members of the Muslim faith. Islam is little dependent upon ritual, and in the very beginning, when Muhammad arrived in Medina (A.D. 622), his house and courtyard became the place where the faithful gathered for prayer. After the Prophet's death and as the legions of Islam spread throughout the Middle East almost any edifice was used as a place of prayer and thus became a primitive mosque. In Syria, Christian churches served as mosques, and in Persia, Zoroastrian fire temples were used. The basic elements of a mosque are a place large enough for the congregation to assemble, especially on Friday, the Muslim sabbath, and some orientation so that the faithful may pray in the direction of Mecca; this direction is called the *qibla* and is marked by a mihrab, which usually takes the form of a decorated niche. In later ages mihrabs became quite elaborate; they are decorated with wooden fretwork in Morocco, with carved and pierced marble in Syria and Iraq, and with lusterware tiles bearing quotations from the Koran in Persia. Among other elements, a mosque may include a mimbar, a pulpit which is entered by a flight of steps and stands next to the mihrab; a *maqsura,* an enclosed space around the mihrab, generally set apart by lacy screens, in which the caliph, sultan, or governor prays; a MINARET, a tower, usually built at one or more corners of the mosque, from which the call to prayer is sounded; a *sahn,* a courtyard, surrounded by *riwaqs,* colonnaded or arcaded porticoes with wells or fountains for the necessary ablutions before prayer; and space for a madrasa, a school which often includes libraries and living quarters for teachers and pupils. Although all of the great mosques are resplendent with elaborate decorations, the prohibition against imitating God's works by creating living forms is always obeyed. Decorations are abstract, and geometric plant forms are so distant from their originals as to be unrecognizable. The early mosques of Syria and Egypt follow closely the primitive form, as in the mosque (begun 642) of Amr and that (879) of Ibn Tulun, both at Cairo. The first domical mosque, that of Omar (691) at Jerusalem, perhaps better known as the Dome of the Rock, follows an octagonal Byzantine plan, with a dome entirely of wood. Domed mosques were not commonly built, however, until some six centuries later. In the 14th cent. another type appeared, in which four arms roofed with pointed vaults form a cruciform plan about the central court. The arm towards Mecca, wider and deeper than the others, contains the mihrab. The finest example is the great mosque (1356) of Sultan Hasan at Cairo. The mosques of N Africa and Spain tended to be of the primitive type, as in the African mosque of Kairwan (late 7th cent.). The more important structure at Córdoba, Spain, was begun in 780 and enlarged in the 10th cent. until its prayer hall, with 16 rows of columns and arches, occupied an area greater than that of any Christian church. It became the Cathedral of Córdoba in 1238. Mosques of Persia inherited the Sassanian vaulting tradition and surface decoration with gorgeous ceramics. They thus possess a distinctive character in their pointed bulbous domes, lofty pointed portals, and magnificent polychrome tiles. In the 15th and 16th cent. the colonnaded prayer halls were replaced by large, square, domed interiors, sometimes surrounded by lower vaulted side aisles, as in the Blue Mosque at Tabriz (1437–68). This structure, of essentially Byzantine plan, is sheathed with incomparable blue ceramics. The imperial mosque at Isfahan (1585–1612) had four impressive porticoes on the court, and its main prayer hall, crowned by a bulbous dome and with a porch having an enormous pointed arch flanked by slender minarets, represents the climax of Persian mosque design. When the Turks took Constantinople (1453) they used the great Byzantine Church HAGIA SOPHIA as a mosque, and later employed it as a model for Islamic religious structures. To the great open plan of Hagia Sophia with its dominant dome, they added smaller domes, half domes, buttresses, and minarets and used Persian tiles and rather garish painted decoration for interiors. Thus they achieved at Constantinople such superb monuments as the mosque (1550–57) of Suleiman I, the Magnificent, by the architect Sinan, and the huge Ahmediyeh mosque (1608–14) of Ahmed I. Indian mosques betray their Persian origin in the prevalence of bulbous domes, round minarets, and great portals with pointed arches, although the traditional Persian tile sheathing is largely restricted to interiors. The use of stone and marble for exteriors, however, lends them a solid monumentality rarely seen in other Moslem styles, while colored stones inlaid against the white marble add touches of vivid beauty. During the Mogul dynasty, particularly under the brilliant reign of Shah Jahan (1627–58), mosques of surprising grandeur were erected. Among the finest Mogul examples are the huge mosque with its superb domes and entrance at Fatehpur Sikri (1556–1605); the three-domed Pearl Mosque at Agra (1646–53), famous for its simple plan and delicate inlays; and the Jama Masjid [great mosque] at Delhi, the largest in India. For a further discussion of the architectural development of the mosque, see ISLAMIC ART AND ARCHITECTURE; MOGUL ART AND ARCHITECTURE; MOORISH ART AND ARCHITECTURE; PERSIAN ART AND ARCHITECTURE.

Mosquera, Tomás Cipriano de (tōmäs' sĕprēä'nō thā mōskä'rä), 1798–1878, Colombian general and president. He first gained attention by his service in the war against Spain. As president (1845–49), he began as a conservative but became more liberal, sponsoring numerous reforms and encouraging the nation's material growth. After the conservatives gained control in 1856, Mosquera led a successful revolt (1860–62) that resulted (1863) in a federalist United States of Colombia. He served as provisional president until 1864. Domineering, unscrupulous, and violently emotional, he was feared and mistrusted even by his adherents, but he was, nonetheless, a vigorous leader. Although again elected (1866) president, he was imprisoned (1867), tried, and banished. He went to Peru, but returned later to become governor and senator of Cauca.

Mosquitia, region, Central America: see MOSQUITO COAST.

mosquito (məskē'tō), small, long-legged INSECT of the order Diptera, the true FLIES. The females of most species have piercing and sucking mouth parts and apparently they must feed at least once upon mammalian blood before their eggs can develop properly. The males may have beaks, or probosces, but cannot pierce, and they feed upon fruit and plant juices. The female produces the characteristic whining sound by vibrating thin horny membranes on the thorax. The eggs are laid singly or glued together to form rafts, usually in stagnant water in ponds, pools, open containers, and other aquatic habitats—the particular type of habitat depending on the species. The aquatic larvae, or wrigglers, pass through four larval stages, feeding on microscopic animal and plant life. Except in the genus *Anopheles,* the wriggler has an air tube near the end of the abdomen and makes frequent trips to the surface to use it as a supplement to the gills. The pupa, or tumbler, shaped like a question mark, takes no food but surfaces often to breathe through air tubes on its thorax. One method of mosquito control is the spreading of oily substances on infested water, which prevents access to air and suffocates the pupae. In summer the life cycle may take only two weeks, resulting in several generations a year in some species. During the blood meals the females may either acquire or transmit various disease organisms. Many species of *Anopheles* mosquitoes, recognizable by their tilted resting position, carry the protozoan parasites that cause MALARIA; species of the genus *Aedes* transmit the viruses responsible for yellow fever, jungle yellow fever, and DENGUE FEVER; and in the S United States and in the tropics, members of the genus *Culex,* to which the common house mosquito belongs, are vectors of filariasis, the infection by a filarial worm that causes ELEPHANTIASIS, and human ENCEPHALITIS. Mosquitoes have become adapted to extremes of climate and are found far north of the Arctic Circle, where they winter as larvae frozen in the ice. Dragonflies, damselflies, and several insectivorous birds are the natural enemies of the adults; the wrigglers are eaten in large quantities by small fishes and aquatic insects. Control of these major insect pests by other than natural means poses many problems; the long-range harmful effects of many insecticides, e.g., DDT, are very serious, and swamp drainage tends to upset the balance of nature in addition to eliminating the mosquito. Mosquitoes are classified in the phylum ARTHROPODA, class Insecta, order Diptera, family Culicidae. See bulletins of the U.S. Dept. of Agriculture.

Mosquito Coast or **Mosquitia** (məskē'tēə, mōskētē'ä), region, east coast of Nicaragua and Honduras. The name is derived from the Mosquito or Miskitto Indians, remnants of the CHOROTEGA. Never exactly delimited, the region is a belt c.40 mi (60 km) wide extending from the San Juan River N into NE Honduras. It is sultry and swampy, rising to low hills in the west. Banana cultivation is the main economic activity. The population is of mixed Indian-black African ancestry. In the early colonial period English and Dutch buccaneers preyed on Spanish shipping from coastal bases, and English loggers exploited the forest products. England established a protective kingdom at BLUEFIELDS in 1678. Jamaican Negroes were brought in to increase the labor supply. In 1848 the British claimed and took SAN JUAN DEL NORTE to offset U.S. interest in a transisthmian route to California. Nicaragua protested the seizure. The Clayton-Bulwer Treaty (1850) between the United States and Great Britain checked British expansion, but relinquishment of the coast was delayed until a separate treaty was concluded with Nicaragua (1860), which established the autonomy of the so-called Mosquito Kingdom. In 1894, José Santos ZELAYA ended the anomalous position of the territory by forcibly incorporating it into Nicaragua. The northern part, however, was awarded to Honduras in 1960 by the International Court of Justice, thus ending a long-standing dispute between the two countries.

Moss (môs), city (1970 pop. 25,210), capital of Østfold co., SE Norway, a port on the Oslofjord. It is a commercial, industrial, and tourist center, with shipyards and sawmills. On Aug. 14, 1814, the convention establishing the personal union of Sweden and Norway was signed there.

moss, any species of the class Bryopsida, in which the LIVERWORTS are sometimes included. Mosses and liverworts together comprise the division BRYOPHYTA, the first green land plants to develop in the process of evolution. It is believed that they evolved from certain very primitive vascular plants and have not given rise to any other type of plant. Their rootlike rhizomes and leaflike processes lack the vascular structure (xylem and phloem) of the true roots, stems, and leaves found in higher plants. Although limited to moist habitats because they require water for fertilization, bryophytes are usually extremely hardy and grow everywhere except in the sea. Mosses, the more complex class structurally, usually grow vertically rather than horizontally, like the liverworts. The green moss plant visible to the naked eye, seldom over 6 in. (15.2 cm) in height, is the gametophyte generation (see REPRODUCTION). Except for the commercially valuable SPHAGNUM or peat moss, mosses are of little direct importance to man. They are of some value in soil formation and filling in of barren habitats (e.g., dried lakes) prior to the growth of higher plants and also provide food for certain animals. Unrelated plants sharing the name moss include the CLUB MOSS, flowering moss, or pyxie (of the DIAPENSIA family), Irish moss, or carrageen (see ALGAE), reindeer moss (a LICHEN), and SPANISH MOSS. Mosses are classified in the division Bryophyta, class Bryopsida. See A. J. Grout, *Moss Flora of North America* (3 vol., 1928–39, repr. 1972).

moss agate: see AGATE.

Mossamedes (mōsä'mədĕs), town (1960 pop. 7,963), SW Angola, a port on the Atlantic Ocean. Iron ore is the leading export; sisal, cotton, tobacco, frozen meat, hides, and skins are also significant. The name is also spelled Moçâmedes.

moss animal, common name applied to members of the phylum ECTOPROCTA.

Mossi (mŏs'ē), African Negro people, numbering about 2 million, mostly in Upper Volta. From A.D. c.1000 the Mossi were organized into several kingdoms, one of which has continued to the present day. Despite long and intimate contact with Muslims, the Mossi have retained their ancient traditional religion, which has a strong emphasis on ancestor worship. See P. B. Hammond, *Yatenga* (1966).

Most, Johann Joseph (mōst), 1846–1906, German anarchist. A bookbinder by trade, he served as editor of socialist papers in Germany and Austria. His publications were suppressed, and he was frequently imprisoned for his public denunciation of religion, patriotism, and accepted moral standards. After sitting (1874–78) in the German Reichstag, he

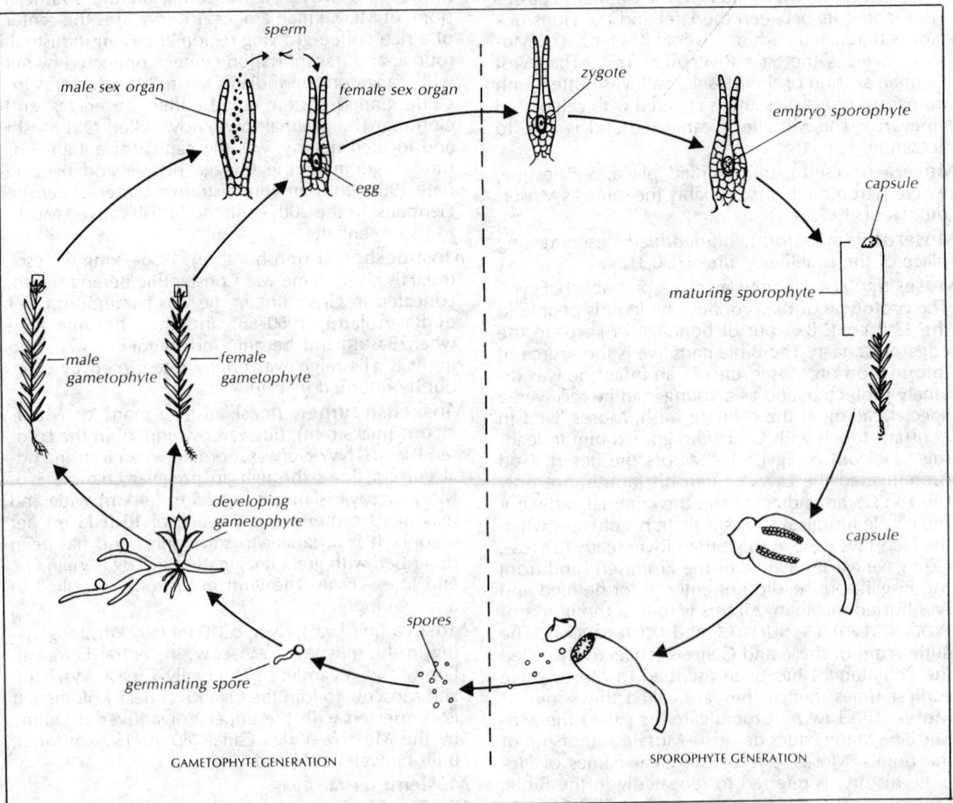

Life cycle of a moss: A germinating spore forms a transitory branching structure on the soil surface, which develops into the conspicuous gametophyte, the familiar moss plant. Eggs and sperm are formed in sex organs at the tips of the gametophytes. A fertilized egg develops into a sporophyte, a structure anchored on the gametophyte and dependent on it for nutrition. Spores are produced in the capsule of the mature sporophyte.

moved to France and then to England, where he served a 16-month prison term for glorifying the assassination of Russia's Alexander II. He emigrated (1882) to the United States and became a leader in the American anarchist movement. He was imprisoned a number of times for his activities, until he drifted away from anarchist politics.

Most (môst), Ger. *Brüx*, city (1970 pop. 54,875), NW Czechoslovakia, in Bohemia, near the East German border. It is a railway junction and industrial city in a lignite-mining area and has pipelines that carry gas to Prague. Chemicals, steel, and ceramics are the major products of Most. The city, whose history dates at least to the 11th cent., has several medieval churches and an old town hall.

Mostaganem (mōs"tägänĕm'), city (1966 pop. 63,297), capital of Mostaganem dept., NW Algeria, a port on the Mediterranean Sea. It was founded in the 11th cent. and reached its commercial height in the 16th cent. under the Turks. Its population had declined to about 3,000 when the French arrived in 1833. Wine, grain, meat, and wool are exported.

Mostar (mô'stär), city (1971 pop. 89,405), SW Yugoslavia, in Bosnia and Hercegovina, on the Neretva River. The chief city of Hercegovina, it has industries that produce tobacco, wine, and aluminum products. Bauxite and lignite are mined nearby. Known in 1442, it became (16th cent.) the chief Turkish administrative and commercial center in Hercegovina. It passed to Austria in 1878 and to Yugoslavia in 1918. The city has a 16th-century Turkish stone bridge and numerous Turkish mosques and old houses.

Mostel, Zero (mŏs"tĕl'), 1915–, American actor, b. New York City as Samuel Joel Mostel. Mostel made his Broadway debut in *Keep 'Em Laughing* (1942). He is particularly adept at profound yet comic character roles. His major stage appearances include *Ulysses in Nighttown* (1958 and 1974), *Rhinoceros* (1961; film, 1973), *A Funny Thing Happened on the Way to the Forum* (1962; film, 1966), and *Fiddler on the Roof* (1964). Mostel's other films include *The Producers* (1968). See his *Zero by Mostel* (1965).

most-favored-nation clause, provision in a commercial treaty binding the signatories to extend to each other benefits equal to those accorded any third state. The purpose of the clause is to insure equal commercial opportunities, especially with regard to import duties and freedom of investment. Such agreements are generally reciprocal, although in the late 19th and early 20th cent. unilateral most-favored-nation clauses were imposed on Asian nations by the more powerful Western states (see OPEN DOOR). Today tariff and trade agreements are negotiated simultaneously by all interested parties through the GENERAL AGREEMENT ON TARIFFS AND TRADE (GATT). Such a wide exchange of concessions is intended to promote FREE TRADE. There has been increasing criticism, however, of the principle of equality of trading opportunity on the grounds that freer trade benefits the economically strongest countries. GATT members have recognized in principle that the most-favored-nation rule should be relaxed to accommodate the needs of developing countries, and the UN Conference on Trade and Development (est. 1964) has sought to promote agreements by which the developed countries extend preferential treatment to the exports of the developing countries. Another challenge to the most-favored-nation principle has been posed by regional trading groups such as the Common Market, which have lowered or completely eliminated tariffs among the members while maintaining tariff walls between member nations and the rest of the world.

Mosul (mō'səl, mōsōōl'), Arab. *al Mawsil*, city (1965 pop. 243,311), provincial capital, N Iraq, on the Tigris River, opposite the ruins of Nineveh. It is the largest city in N Iraq and the second largest city in the country. Trade in agricultural goods and exploitation of oil are the two main occupations of the inhabitants. While most of the city people are Arabs, the surrounding region is peopled by Kurds. Mosul was the chief city of N Mesopotamia from the 8th to 13th cent., when it was devastated by the Mongols. The city remained poor and shabby through its occupation by the Persians (1508) and the Turks (1534–1918). Under the British occupation and mandate (1918–32) it regained its stature as the chief city of the region. Its possession by Iraq was disputed by Turkey (1923–25) but was confirmed by the League of Nations (1926). The city is the seat of Mosul Univ. and a center of Nestorian Christianity.

Motagua (mōtä'gwä), river, c.250 mi (400 km) long, rising in S central Guatemala and flowing NE to the Gulf of Honduras. The longest river within Guatemala, it waters a valley where hemp and bananas are raised. The trans-Guatamala railroad follows the valley.

Motala (mōō'tä"lä), city (1970 pop. 28,904), Östergötland co., S Sweden, on Lake Vättern and on the Göta Canal. It is an important lake port and an industrial center. Manufactures include locomotives and radio and television sets. The city has a powerful radio transmitter and a hydroelectric power plant.

motel, public lodging establishment, for automobile travelers. Motels have traditionally differed from hotels in that the former have facilities for free parking on the premises, are seldom more than three stories high, and offer occupants direct access to rooms without having to pass through a lobby. Motels are also generally smaller, farther away from urban areas, and offer fewer services than hotels. The distinction between motels and hotels, however, is very difficult to make, especially in the case of the so-called motor hotels, which combine the characteristics of both types of establishment. Motels can be seen as logical heirs to the earlier American public houses. Just as the inn was suited to 18th-century horse travel, and the hotel was suited to 19th-century railroad travel, the modern motel is suited to mass automobile travel on mid-20th-century expressways. Motels now surpass hotels in total number of establishments, accounting for well over 60% of all public lodging places.

motet (mōtĕt'), name for the outstanding type of musical composition of the 13th cent. and for a different type that originated in the Renaissance. The 13th-century motet, a creation (c.1200) of the school of Notre-Dame de Paris, was a polyphonic composition based on a TENOR that was a fragment of plainsong (or, later, of any type of melody, sacred or secular) arranged in a brief, reiterated rhythmic pattern called an *ordo*. It existed side by side but was distinct from the conductus, an earlier development of choral composition, which was not based on preexisting liturgical chants and which employed several voice parts in a type of harmony. The motet's original text, sometimes only a word or two, was kept, but the tenor may have been played on instruments. The second part, called *motetus* [from Fr. *mot*=word], had its own text, usually sacred and in Latin but by the second half of the century sometimes secular and in French. The third voice, the triplum, had still another text, and very often the motet combined a triplum that was a French love song and a *motetus* that was a Latin hymn to the Virgin Mary. The outgrowth of this early motet was the isorhythmic motet of the late 13th and the 14th cent. It employed a recurring rhythmic pattern called a *talea*, longer than an *ordo* and not restricted to the tenor part. Of the 23 extant motets of Guillaume de MACHAUT (c.1300–c.1377), an outstanding 14th-century composer, 20 are isorhythmic. Isorhythmic technique was not confined to the motet and persisted into the mid-15th cent. The Renaissance motet had but one text, in Latin, and was a polyphonic, unaccompanied composition. It had usually from four to six voices and was free from the 13th-century rhythmic rigidity. Cultivated by composers of the Flemish school, it had spread throughout Europe by the middle of the 15th cent. Outstanding composers are Josquin Desprez and Orlando di Lasso of the Flemish school; the Italians Andrea Gabrieli, Giovanni Gabrieli, and Palestrina; the Spaniard Tomás Luis de Victoria; and the Englishmen Thomas Tallis and William Byrd. In the baroque era the greatest motets were written in Germany to German texts. The *Symphoniae Sacrae* of Heinrich Schütz include many motets in various styles, with the addition of solo voices and instrumental accompaniment. The peak is reached in the six motets of Bach, which are thought to have had some continuo accompaniment. Since Bach's time the term *motet* has been applied to almost any kind of sacred choral polyphony but usually refers to unaccompanied Latin motets for use in Roman Catholic services. Many anthems in English, however, have been designated motets by their composers. See F. Matthiassen, *The Style of the Early Motet* (1966).

moth, any of the large and varied group of insects which, along with the BUTTERFLIES, make up the order Lepidoptera. The moths comprise the great majority of the 100,000 species of the order, and about 70 of its 80 families. The adult moth, like the butterfly, has sucking mouthparts, two compound eyes, and two pairs of wings that function as a single pair and are covered with flattened, dustlike scales. It is distinguished from butterflies by its stouter, usually hairy body and its unknobbed, often feathery antennae. Most moths are nocturnal in their habits, while butterflies are mostly diurnal. A moth flattens its wings against the surface on which it is resting, while a butterfly holds them horizontally. Moths range in size from species with a wingspread of ⅙ in. (2 mm) to the Atlas moth with a wingspread of 10 in. (25 cm). Many are protectively colored to match their backgrounds: their patterns may exactly resemble, for example, certain lichens or the bark of certain trees. Many others have large, eyelike markings on the hind wings that are thought to frighten potential predators. Moths undergo a complete metamorphosis (see INSECT), from egg through larva and pupa to adult. Moth larvae, or CATERPILLARS, are wingless and wormlike, with a row of simple eyes on either side of the body. They have chewing mouthparts and feed on leaves or other plant material. Many do great damage, such as the BEE MOTH, the CODLING MOTH, the GYPSY MOTH, the CLOTHES MOTH, and the CUTWORM. The pupa of most moths is protected by a cocoon, built by the larva just before pupating. The cocoon is often made wholly or largely of silk; the cocoon of the domesticated SILKWORM moth is the source of commercial silk. Some moths make a cocoon of bits of wood or of a leaf, glued together with silk; some pupate underground. During pupation the body form changes to that of the winged adult. Most adult moths feed on the nectar of flowers, and many plants depend on them for pollination. The short-lived adults of certain species do not eat at all. Among the large and beautiful moths of North America are the cecropia moth, largest of the E United States, and the pale green luna moth. Moths are classified in the phylum ARTHROPODA, class Insecta, order Lepidoptera.

Mother Carey's chicken: see PETREL.

mother goddess: see GREAT MOTHER OF THE GODS.

Mother Goose, name associated with NURSERY RHYMES. Most English nursery rhymes have been ascribed to Mother Goose. The origin of the name is still a matter of dispute. Some trace it to a French collection of tales by Charles Perrault (1697) that had the subtitle *Contes de ma mère L'Oye* [tales of mother goose]. This name has in turn been traced to Queen Goosefoot, Charlemagne's mother (see BERTRADA), who was a patron of children. Others claim an American origin in *Mother Goose's Melodies,* published 1719 in Boston by Thomas Fleet, whose mother-in-law was said to be Elizabeth Vergoose. A collection of Mother Goose rhymes was published by John Newbery in London in 1765. The subject matter of the rhymes has been linked by some scholars to actual events in English political history. See *The Annotated Mother Goose,* ed. by W. S. and Ceil Baring-Gould (1970); studies by K. E. Thomas (1930) and S. K. Abbey (1967).

Mother Lode, belt of gold-bearing quartz veins, central Calif., along the western foothills of the Sierra Nevada. The term is sometimes limited to a strip c.70 mi (110 km) long and from 1 to 6½ mi (1.6–10.5 km) wide, running NW from Mariposa. Popularly it is used to mean the gold-bearing area E of the Sacramento and San Joaquin rivers and W of the Sierra Nevada. The discovery of alluvial gold on the South Fork of the American River led to the 1848 gold rush. Mark Twain and Bret Harte helped make the Mother Lode famous.

mother-of-pearl or **nacre** (nā'kər), the iridescent substance that forms the lining of the shells of some fresh-water and some salt-water mollusks. Like the PEARL it is a secretion of the mantle, composed of alternate layers of calcium carbonate and conchiolin. Among the chief sources are the pearl oyster, found in warm and tropical seas, chiefly in the Orient; the fresh-water pearl mussel, which lives in many rivers of the United States and Europe; and the abalone of California, Japan, and other Pacific regions. Mother-of-pearl is used for buttons, for knife handles, for inlay work, and for many other purposes.

Motherwell, Robert, 1915–, American painter and writer, b. Aberdeen, Wash. Motherwell taught art at several colleges and during the early 1940s he became a cogent theoretician of ABSTRACT EXPRESSIONISM. He edited the series *Documents of Modern Art* (15 vol., 1944–61), and *Modern Artists in America* (1952). Motherwell's canvases are characterized by large, amorphous shapes, painted in strong, austere colors. One painting from his series *Elegy for the Spanish Republic* is in the Albright-Knox Art Gallery, Buffalo. He has also created numerous masterful collages. In 1958 he married the painter Helen FRANKENTHALER. Motherwell is the editor of *The Dada Painters and Poets* (1951) and *Documents of 20th-Century Art* (1971–).

Motherwell and Wishaw (wĭsh'ô), burgh (1971 pop. 74,184), Lanarkshire, S central Scotland. The two parts of the burgh were united in 1920. In a region of coal and iron, it is a center of steel and other heavy industry. There is a technical college. In 1975 the burgh became part of the Strathclyde region.

moth mullein, common name for the mullein *Verbascum blatteria,* a plant native to Europe and naturalized as a weed in the United States. It is a member of the family Scrophulariaceae (FIGWORT family).

motif (mōtēf'), in literature, term that denotes the recurrent presence of certain character types, objects, settings, or situations in diverse genres and periods of folklore and literature. Examples of motifs include swords, money, food, jewels, forests, oceans, castles, dungeons, tests of skill or wisdom, journeys, separations and reunions, chaos brought to order. Motifs are not restricted to literature. Hans von Wolzogen coined the term *leitmotiv* (Ger.,= guiding motive] to describe Richard Wagner's use of a recurring musical phrase to reinforce the emotional impact of characters, situations, and themes in his operas. The visual arts often rely on motifs to communicate deeper levels of meaning: The bison and deer painted on the walls of the caves at Lascaux represent both threat and survival, superior strength or speed, and food supply; the endlessly rocking cradle in D. W. Griffith's film *Intolerance* suggests rebirth and the inescapable frailties of the human condition (see SYMBOL; ARCHETYPE).

motif, in music: see MOTIVE.

motion, the change of position of one body with respect to another. The rate of change is the SPEED of the body. If the direction of motion is also given, then the VELOCITY of the body is determined; velocity is a VECTOR quantity, having both magnitude and direction, while speed is a scalar quantity, having only magnitude. Uniform motion is motion at a constant speed, usually either in a circle or in a straight line. Uniform linear motion can be described by a few simple equations. The distance s covered by a body moving with velocity v during a time t is given by $s=vt$. If the velocity is changing, either in direction or magnitude, the motion is said to be accelerated (see ACCELERATION). Uniformly accelerated motion is motion during which the acceleration remains constant. The average velocity during this time is one half the sum of the initial and final velocities. If a is the acceleration, v_o the original velocity, and v_f the final velocity, then the final velocity is given by $v_f=v_o+at$. The distance covered during this time is $s=v_ot+\frac{1}{2}at^2$. In uniform circular motion the speed is constant but the direction of motion is changing continuously. The acceleration causing this change, known as centripetal acceleration because it is always directed toward the center of the circular path, is given by $a=v^2/r$, where v is the speed and r is the radius of the circle. The relationship between FORCE and motion was expressed by Sir Isaac NEWTON in his three laws of motion: (1) a body at rest tends to remain at rest or a body in motion tends to remain in motion at a constant speed in a straight line unless acted on by an outside force, i.e., if the net unbalanced force is zero, then the acceleration is zero; (2) the acceleration a of a mass m by an unbalanced force F is directly proportional to the force and inversely proportional to the mass, or $a = F/m$; (3) for every action there is an equal and opposite reaction. The third law implies that the total momentum of a system of bodies not acted on by an external force remains constant (see CONSERVATION LAWS, in physics). Newton's laws of motion, together with his law of GRAVITATION, provide a satisfactory basis for the explanation of motion of ordinary macroscopic objects under ordinary conditions. However, when applied to extremely high speeds or extremely small objects, Newton's laws break down. Motion at speeds approaching the speed of LIGHT must be described by the theory of RELATIVITY. The equations derived from the theory of relativity reduce to Newton's when the speed of the object being described is very small compared to that of light. When the motions of extremely small objects (atoms and ELEMENTARY PARTICLES) are described, the wavelike properties of matter must be taken into account (see QUANTUM THEORY). The theory of relativity also resolves the question of absolute motion. When one speaks of an object as being in motion, such motion is usually in reference to another object which is considered at rest. Although a man sitting in a car is at rest with respect to the car, he and the car are both in motion with respect to the earth, and the earth is in motion with respect to the sun and the center of the galaxy. All these motions are relative. It was once thought that there existed a light-carrying medium, known as the luminiferous ETHER, which was in a state of absolute rest. Any object in motion with respect to this hypothetical frame of reference would be in absolute motion. The theory of relativity showed, however, that no such medium was necessary and that all motion could be treated as relative. See J. C. Maxwell, *Matter and Motion* (1877, repr. 1952).

motion picture camera: see under CAMERA.

motion picture photography or **cinematography,** photographic arts and techniques involved in making MOTION PICTURES. The motion picture camera (see under CAMERA) was developed from simple multi-image devices that, when spun or flipped, recorded the parts of a continuous movement. The camera photographed these parts of movements successively, and when the images were moved through the lens of a projector at a constant speed, they threw a moving image on a wall or screen. Among the foremost pioneers of the cinema was D. W. GRIFFITH, who gave the medium its first cohesive language of camera techniques. Prior to his innovations the camera had been used as a stationary recording device. The actors played their scenes before it as they had done before a theater audience. Griffith developed such subtle devices as the close-up, focusing on a hand, face, or object. By punctuating his scenes with close-ups, Griffith was able to heighten the emotional impact of his film and allow the camera a freedom of movement that has been further developed over succeeding decades. Cinematography is a collaborative effort coordinated by the director. Its history includes aesthetic elements, such as the close-up, and technological advances, such as the development of 3-D (three-dimensional cinematography) and Cinerama and CinemaScope (both wide-screen processes). Because they depended solely on visual perception, silent pictures brought the art of motion picture photography to a height it has seldom reached in sound films. Cutting, the reorganization of film footage by the removal of unwanted frames, was a silent film technique later used extensively in sound films. MONTAGE, the creative cutting of images that when juxtaposed form a meaning absent in the single images, was devised by Sergei M. EISENSTEIN in the Odessa massacre sequence in the classic film *The Battleship Potemkin* (1925). In this scene, image replaces image at a lightning pace, increasing the tension of the drama and creating a compelling picture of violence and terror. The German film industry prior to World War II also made significant contributions to cinema techniques. Joseph VON STERNBERG, Fritz LANG, and F. W. MURNAU concentrated on psychic and emotional states; by distorting objects and images they evolved a highly subjective film style in which the camera let the audience share the principal character's vantage point. This sort of subjectivity is particularly evident in Murnau's *The Last Laugh* (1924), which describes the grim transformations in the life of a hotel doorman. In Germany the development of an expressionist cinema coincided with the evolution of EXPRESSIONISM in painting and drama. Von Sternberg developed an approach in which he combined spectacular sets with soft focus to create a sense of fantasy and mystery. His film *The Devil Is a Woman* (1935), for example, is a dreamlike recreation of old Spain. From 1927, the creation of sound films posed the problem of incorporating a sound track into the wide-ranging visual repertoire of the silents. Smooth sound synchronization was eventually achieved by attaching the sound track tape directly to the film and recording both sound and image simultaneously. Orson Welles's *Citizen Kane* (1941) was a milestone among sound films. Of epic proportions, it was a superb showcase for numerous technical innovations. Welles and his cameraman, Gregg Toland, filmed scenes so that both floor and ceiling were visible; they accomplished this by setting the camera below floor level. This engendered a sense of containing the actors in a framework without diminishing the grandeur of their surroundings. With *Citizen Kane,* Welles created a language of cinematic drama that has been copied and adapted throughout the subsequent history of film. Technical developments in cinema of the color-film and wide-screen sort have developed more slowly than the purely imaginative enterprises of individual directors and their cameramen. The technology for color filming, for example, was developed during the 1920s, but the results were harsh and glaring. Despite all efforts color processes were not perfected until the 1930s and 40s, years after the introduction of sound. In the 1950s, 3-D was used but was generally restricted to adventure and science-fiction movies; after an initial ballyhoo the technique was abandoned. Split-screen techniques were used to fuse two different parts of a narrative. The extra wide screen was introduced in the 1950s. Cinerama involved a special camera; it shot film to be projected on a gigantic screen which partly surrounded the audience. The effect was meant to give the viewer the sensation of actually participating in the activity on the screen. At first it was used almost exclusively for travel films and other vehicles designed to show off the new technique. Cinerama productions were few and costly until the 1960s when serious work in this area began. In Stanley Kubrick's *2001: A Space Odyssey* (1968) the technique was exploited to convey the enormity of the universe. The wide-screen processes such as CinemaScope were much more extensively used, and they transformed the traditional square movie format into an imposing rectangular vista. Motion picture filming techniques have all been developed and refined during the past fifty years. A major proportion of credit for innovations in the medium belongs to cameramen and their technical assistants. The foremost American cameramen include Gregg Toland (*Tugboat Annie, Wuthering Heights, The Grapes of Wrath, Citizen Kane*), Charles Rosher (*Sunrise, The Yearling, Kiss Me Kate*), James Wong Howe (*The Thin Man, The Rose Tattoo, Picnic, Bell, Book, and Candle, Hud*), Lee Garmes (*Morocco, Shanghai Express, Duel in the Sun*), and Karl Freund (*The Last Laugh, Metropolis, Camille, The Good Earth*). The French directors of the 1960s' "new wave," including Alain Resnais, Louis Malle, François TRUFFAUT, and Jean-Luc GODARD, working within far smaller budgets than their American colleagues, evolved a particularly intimate camera style that was enormously influential. A startling, choppy sort of cinematography making frequent use of jump cutting, termed *cinéma vérité,* had a vogue in inexpensive productions during the 1960s. John Cassavetes made notable use of this stylistic approach in his films *Shadows* (1960) and *Faces* (1968). An intensely personal visual style has been the hallmark of cinematography in the past 20 years of filmmaking: Directors such as Alfred HITCHCOCK, Ingmar BERGMAN (working closely with his principal cameramen Gunnar Fischer and Sven Nykvist), Luis BUÑUEL, Ken Russell, and Michelangelo ANTONIONI have consistently produced movies in which a personal cinematographic style is a primary factor of their films' aesthetic success. See PHOTOGRAPHY, STILL. See S. M. Eisenstein, *Film Form and Film Sense* (tr. 1949, repr. separately 1969) and *Notes of a Film Director* (rev. ed. tr. 1970); H. M. Geduld, ed., *Film Makers on Film Making* (1967); Pauline Kael, *The Citizen Kane Book* (1971); R. L. Bare, *The Film Director: A Practical Guide to Motion Picture and Television Techniques* (1971).

motion pictures, movie-making as an art and an industry, including its production techniques, its creative artists, and the distribution and displaying of its products (see also MOTION PICTURE PHOTOGRAPHY; motion picture camera under CAMERA). Experiments in photographing movement had been made in both the United States and Europe well before the turn of the century with, at first, no realization of its technical and commercial possibilities. Serial photographs of racehorses in motion were obtained (c.1867) in California by Eadweard MUYBRIDGE and J. D. Isaacs by setting up a row of cameras with electrically operated shutters. The first motion pictures made with a single camera were by E. J. Marey, a French physician, in the 1880s, in the course of his study of motion. In 1889, Thomas Edison and his staff developed the kinetograph, a camera using rolls of coated celluloid film, and the Kinetoscope, a device for peep-show viewing. Marketed in 1893, the Kinetoscope became popular immediately in penny arcades. The rate of experimentation was accelerated. In France the LUMIÈRE brothers created the Cinématographe (1895). In the United States, projection machines, notably the Pantopticon and the Vitascope, were developed and first used in New York City in 1896. At first the screenings formed part of vaudeville shows and arcades, but in 1902 a Los Angeles shop that showed only moving pictures had great success; soon "movie houses" (converted shoprooms) sprang up all over the country. The first movie theater, complete with luxurious accessories and a piano, was built in Pittsburgh in 1905. A nickel was charged for admission, and the theater was called the nickelodeon. Movies developed simultaneously as a new art form and as an industry. They had enormous immediate appeal and were soon established as a medium for chronicling contemporary attitudes, fashions, and events. Early pictures were brief and amateurish. At first anything that moved was filmed, then everyday scenes and the crude beginnings of film drama. The camera was first used in a stationary position and later was panned from side to side or moved close to or away from the subject. There were no studios; because the early filmstocks were relatively insensitive, movies were shot in bright sunlight. Technical improvements were introduced as the potential of the medium for recording dramas was realized. The Frenchman George Méliés was the first to create cinematographic trick effects. He was also among the first to incorporate a plot line, artificially arranging his scenes to tell the story. His *Cinderella* (1900) and *A Trip to the Moon* (1902) were major innovative accomplishments. Edwin S. Porter, believing that the continuity of shots rather than the shots themselves was of primary significance, developed the principles of editing and those of dramatic contrast and parallel construction. He turned from Méliés's fantasies to the real world; with his *Great Train Robbery* (1903) a new era of film began. As business increased, production demands increased and competition grew. Cooperative experimentation changed into artistic and commercial rivalry, as various countries strove to perfect their newly organized cinema arts and industries. Later, with the evolution of sound films, language barriers forced each national industry to concentrate on its own development. See Peter Graham, *A Dictionary of the Cinema* (1964); Kenneth Macgowan, *Behind the Screen* (1965); André Bazin, *What Is Cinema?* (1967); Bosley Crowther, *The Great Films* (1967); Peter Cowie, ed., *Concise History of the Cinema* (2 vol., 1970); Gerald Mast, *A Short History of the Movies* (1971); David Shipman, *The Great Movie Stars* (2 vol.: 1970, 1972); David Robinson, *The History of World Cinema* (1973).

American Film. The American "movie factories," centered at first in the New York City area, were the scene of chaotic activity, with each director producing as many as two pictures a week. By 1908 a separation of crafts had developed, and actors, producers, cinematographers, writers, editors, and film laboratory technicians worked interdependently in a production effort overseen and coordinated by the director. Screen credits were unheard of; the profession was still not considered reputable. There were bitter disputes over patent rights. Companies holding essential patents formed, in 1909, the Motion Picture Patents Company, which attempted to keep unlicensed companies out of production and distribution. Many independents moved their operations to Los Angeles in order to be close to the Mexican border in case of injunction, and, after 1913, Hollywood, Calif., became the American movie capital. Films were at first sold outright to exhibitors; later they were distributed on a rental basis through film exchanges. In 1910 the "star system" came into being; the "fan letter" and the "fan magazine" appeared soon after. The era of lavish productions began with the Italian *Quo Vadis* (1913), a "spectacle" of nine reels that played for more than two hours. Directors of the day, D. W. GRIFFITH, Thomas Ince, Maurice Tourneur, J. Stuart Blackton, and Mack SENNETT, became known for the individual character of their films and were as famous as their stars, including Charlie CHAPLIN, Buster KEATON, Mary PICKFORD, Douglas FAIRBANKS, Marie DRESSLER, Lillian GISH, William S. HART, Greta GARBO, John Gilbert, Claudette COLBERT, Rudolph VALENTINO, Janet Gaynor, Ronald COLMAN, Clara Bow, Gloria SWANSON, Lon CHANEY, and Will ROGERS. During World War I the United States became dominant in the industry and the moving picture expanded into the realm of education and propaganda. In the postwar period the production genius of such men as Samuel GOLDWYN, Louis B. MAYER, Adolph Zukor, and Jesse L. Lasky, and the innovative talents of Cecil B. DE MILLE, Erich VON STROHEIM, and Ernst Lubitsch were dominant. The year 1926 brought experiments in sound effects and music, and in 1927 dialogue was successfully introduced in *The Jazz Singer* with Al Jolson; a year later the first all-talking picture, *Lights of New York,* was shown. With the talkies new directors achieved prominence—King Vidor, Joseph VON STERNBERG, Rouben Mamoulian, Frank Capra, and John FORD. Sound films gave a tremendous boost to the careers of some silent actors but destroyed many whose voices were not suited to recording. Among the most celebrated stars of the new era were Clark GABLE, Jean HARLOW, Marlene DIETRICH, Mae WEST, W. C. FIELDS, and the MARX BROTHERS. Stars were recruited from the stage as well as trained in the Hollywood studios. In its greatest years, from the 1930s until the early 1950s, Hollywood gave employment to a host of talented actors, foremost among whom were Ingrid BERGMAN, Joan CRAWFORD, Bette DAVIS, Katharine HEPBURN, Charles LAUGHTON, Barbara Stanwyck, William POWELL, Spencer TRACY, Humphrey BOGART, Leslie Howard, Gary COOPER, James STEWART, Cary GRANT, Irene Dunne, Edward G. ROBINSON, Henry FONDA, Gregory Peck, James CAGNEY, Judy GARLAND, Bob HOPE, James Mason, Fred ASTAIRE, and Gene KELLY. Producers and directors such as David O. SELZNICK, Darryl F. Zanuck, Mervyn LeRoy, William Wyler, George STEVENS, and Billy WILDER made significant contributions to cinematic art. Color had been achieved in early films by hand tinting, and since 1917 had been based on a red-green pattern. In 1932, Technicolor, a three-color process, was developed and seen for the first time in *La Cucaracha.* The medium had, after nickelodeon days, converted many legitimate theaters into movie houses. Later, during Hollywood's "golden age," thousands of sumptuous movie palaces were erected all over the United States, and drive-in movie theaters became popular outside urban centers. Since their inception the movies have always been termed an *industry,* with good reason. In 1938 there were more than 80 million single admissions per week (65% of the population). To meet the huge box-office demand, more than 500 films were produced that year. The industry in its heyday (1930–49) was managed by a number of omnipotent studios, including Metro-Goldwyn-Mayer, Warner Brothers, RKO, Paramount, Twentieth-Century Fox, and Universal. They produced endless cycles of films in imitation of a few successful original types. The range of themes included the criminal underworld, behind-the-scenes newspaper dramas, westerns, musicals, costume romances, character series such as the Charlie Chan films, prison stories, mysteries, comedies, and Broadway shows. Because of their enormous investments and gargantuan rewards (the film industry's gross income for 1946, its best year, was nearly $2 billion), the studios were encouraged to repeat conventionalized formula pictures. However, in the 1950s the overwhelming popularity of television began to eat into studio profits. In 1962 box-office receipts were only $900 million; by 1968 only 20 million people per week were going to a movie (10% of the population). Studios were forced by the Federal courts to yield the control of distribution and exhibition that they had maintained by means of massive conglomerate corporations. Independent distributors and theaters took a huge cut of the industry's income after World War II, and the great studios cut wages and laid off employees in a struggle to survive. To compete with television the studio heads strongly urged technological innovation. In the 1950s experiments abounded with wide-screen processes, such as CinemaScope and Cinerama; stereophonic sound systems; 3-D (three-dimensional cinematography); and even Aromarama, by which the audience was bombarded with scents appropriate to the film they were watching. Most of these gimmicky devices were expensive and short-lived. The 1950s and 60s, though less notable for fine films than the preceding decades, nevertheless provided vehicles for a few directors of major stature, including Elia KAZAN, John Frankenheimer, Stanley Kubrick, and Sidney Lumet, and for a great number of popular film stars, including Marlon BRANDO, Marilyn MONROE, Burt Lancaster, Montgomery Clift, Judy Holliday, James DEAN, Paul NEWMAN, Elizabeth TAYLOR, John WAYNE, Charlton Heston, Doris Day, George C. SCOTT, Audrey Hepburn, Sidney Poitier, and Shirley MacLaine. Eventually, c.1956, many studios were forced both to produce movies made especially for television, including commercials, and to sell their old films for television reruns. Numerous filmmakers, working independently of the decayed studio system, devoted themselves to making low-budget productions: films based on successful novels and plays; hero movies; and horror, science fiction, and rock 'n' roll stories. These new cycles diverged sharply from the silver-cloud romanticism and sentimentality of the studio productions and reflected a greatly changed American taste that preferred the depiction of a harsher reality and a more explicit sexuality. The trend away from the glamorous celebrity image that began in the 1960s gained momentum in the 70s. The few principal stars of these years include Jane Fonda (see under FONDA, HENRY), Barbra STREISAND, Dustin Hoffman, Steve McQueen, Woody Allen, and Liza Minelli (see under GARLAND, JUDY). Promising American directors of the 70s include Peter Bogdanovich, Roman Polanski, Francis Ford Coppola, Robert Altman, and William Friedkin. Accompanying the recession that began in 1974 was renewed public interest in movies. The motion picture industry was one of the very few American industries to declare substantial financial profits for the year 1974. The motion picture industry developed self-consciousness early: The Motion Picture Producers and Distributors of America, headed by William H. Hays, was established (1922) as a censorship board; the Hays Code, which dictated the moral standards to which all films had to comply, was for some 30 years restrictive of aesthetic vigor in the medium. In the late 1960s censorship was abandoned to a large extent, and definitions of pornography in specific films became a matter of state court decisions. Late in 1968 a voluntary, industry-wide classification code replaced the outmoded Production Code, which had been abandoned in 1966. The new Motion Picture Code and Rating Program was adopted to avoid a threatened state-controlled system. With the new code a film is given one of four ratings: G (general audiences, without restrictions), M (mature audiences, parental guidance advised), R (restricted audiences, no one younger than 16 admitted without a parent or guardian), and X (no one younger than 16 admitted). The age limit may be adjusted by individual state rulings. Since the system was instituted, R and X ratings have, in fact, been used as selling points by some filmmakers. The Academy of Motion Picture Arts and Sciences, formed in 1927, began the distribution in 1929 of their coveted ACADEMY AWARDS (called "Oscars" since 1931). See Gregory Battcock, *The New American Cinema* (1967); Roger Manvell, *New Cinema in the USA* (1968); Renata Adler, *A Year in the Dark* (1970); David Shipman, *The Great Movie Stars: The Golden Years* (1970); Paul Trent, *The Image Makers: Sixty Years of Hollywood Glamour* (1972); Penelope Gilliatt, *Unholy Fools* (1973); Charles Higham, *The Art of the American Film, 1900–1971* (1973); Pauline Kael, *I Lost It at the Movies* (1965), *Kiss Kiss Bang Bang* (1968), *Going Steady* (1970), *The Citizen Kane Book* (1971), and *Deeper into Movies* (1974).

British Film. Britain has produced some of the most illustrious talents in the history of film. Early efforts (c.1929) by the producer J. Arthur Rank to achieve a world market for British films were realized with the work of such postwar directors as Alfred HITCHCOCK, Carol REED, David Lean, and the Hungarian-born Alexander Korda. Their films were literate and often suspenseful and brought international fame to such actors as Laurence OLIVIER, Ralph RICHARDSON, John Mills, Paul SCOFIELD, Merle Oberon, and Michael REDGRAVE. Alec GUINNESS, Peter USTINOV, Peter Sellers, and Terry-Thomas created comedies that are sophisticated and singularly British in their sense of humor. Major British directors of the 1960s include the American-born Joseph LOSEY, Tony Richardson, Sidney Furie, and John Schlesinger. Among the great number of notable British actors of recent years are Dirk BOGARDE, Peter Finch, Michael Caine, Vanessa REDGRAVE, Stanley Baker, Glenda JACKSON, Richard BURTON, Julie Christie, Peter O'Toole, Maggie SMITH, Alan Bates, Claire Bloom, Albert Finney, Kenneth More, Michael York, Tom Courtenay, and Robert Shaw. See Roger Manvell, *New Cinema in Britain* (1969); Rachael Low, *The History of the British Film* (4 vol., 1973).

French Film. In the 1920s there was enormous creative film activity in France led by Louis Delluc and a group of directors around him—Abel Gance, Jean Epstein, and Germaine Dulac. Along with such directors as René CLAIR, Jean RENOIR, and Carl DREYER, they created films with an impressionistic and literary flavor. Later French films reflected first the optimism and then the despair of international events, as in Renoir's *Grand Illusion* (1937) and Marcel Carné's *Port of Shadows* (1938). In the postwar era H. G. Clouzot, René Clément, and Robert Bresson directed important films. In the late 1950s the "new wave" of young directors, including Alain Resnais, Louis Malle, François TRUFFAUT, and Jean-Luc GODARD, made innovations in cinematography and dramatic approach. Their efforts achieved a new cinematic intimacy and a relaxed mood. French film stars who have attained international acclaim include Jean GABIN, Arletty, Gérard Philipe, Brigitte Bardot, Jean-Paul BELMONDO, Jeanne MOREAU, Catherine Deneuve, Yves Montand, Simone Signoret, and Jean-Louis Trintignant. Among the foremost younger directors are Claude Chabrol, Eric Rohmer, and the Greek-born Costa-Gavras. The distinguished Spanish director-writer Luis BUÑUEL has done much of his major work in France since the 1920s. See Roy Armes, *The French Cinema since 1946* (2 vol., rev. ed. 1970); Georges Sadoul, *French Film* (1953, repr. 1972).

German Film. The great era of German cinema began in 1919 with Robert Wiene's *Cabinet of Dr. Caligari.*

It was written by Carl Mayer, who was among the most influential artists working in the German film industry in the 1920s. The films of this era were expressionist in style, paralleling developments in the other arts. Other notable directors, such as G. W. Pabst, F. W. MURNAU, Max OPHULS, and Fritz LANG, brought the medium to new heights of imaginative production. A decline set in c.1925 when Hollywood attracted many German directors, technicians, and actors to the United States. The advent of Hitler administered a death blow to the German motion picture industry in 1933. See D. S. Hull, *Film in the Third Reich* (1969); Roger Manvell and Heinrich Fraenkel, *The German Cinema* (1971); H. H. Wollenberg, *Fifty Years of German Film* (1948, repr. 1972).

Italian Film. The films of Roberto ROSSELLINI in the 1940s gave new impetus to the Italian cinema. Thereafter followed a cycle of exciting, compassionate, grimly realistic films from such directors as Vittorio De Sica, Luigi Zampa, Giuseppe de Santis, and Luchino Visconti. These films, usually concerned with social themes, were successful in Italy only after they had won a foreign market. In the 1950s, in order to win box-office appeal, a tendency to produce marketable and sensational movies diminished the reputation of Italian filmmakers. Quality and international acclaim were restored by Federico FELLINI, Michelangelo ANTONIONI, and Bernardo Bertolucci. Italian film stars who have won popularity abroad include Sophia LOREN, Marcello MASTROIANNI, Giulietta Masina, Monica Vitti, Raf Vallone, and Anna Magnani. See Gian Rondi, *Italian Cinema Today* (1965); Vernon Jarratt, *The Italian Cinema* (1951, repr. 1972); Pierre Leprohon, *The Italian Cinema* (tr. 1972).

Japanese Film. Since World War II films produced in the East have had an increasingly appreciative Western audience. Akira KUROSAWA's films, including *Rashomon, Seven Samurai,* and *Yojimbo,* are enormously popular action stories, in effect Japanese "westerns." Kurosawa's many productions, Kenju Mizoguchi's *Ugetsu,* and such delicately wrought works as *Tokyo Story* and *The Flavor of Green Tea over Rice* by Yasujiro Ozu brought worldwide acclaim to their directors and to Toshiro Mifune, who starred in many of Kurosawa's films. Noted for their imaginative use of camera and color techniques, Japanese films often combine elements of kabuki and samurai tradition with aspects of Western culture. See Donald Richie, *The Films of Akira Kurosawa* (1965) and *The Japanese Movie: An Illustrated History* (1966).

Russian Film. Dziga Vertov launched a weekly newsreel in 1922 urging new experiments in film technique, and Lev Kuleshov opened a cinema workshop to explore the psychological effects of film images. The result was the emergence of the Soviet epic films of the period 1925 to 1930. Encouraged by Lenin's belief that the film was of primary importance in the development of Soviet society, V. I. PUDOVKIN, Aleksandr DOVZHENKO, and especially Sergei EISENSTEIN made films based on Russian history. Their superbly photographed, intensely dramatic films are classics of cinematic art. Since World War II, Soviet filmmakers have generally produced rather stolid and heavy-handed films but have made major technical advances in cinematography and sound. See S. M. Eisenstein, *Film Form and Film Sense* (tr. 1949, repr. separately 1969) and *Notes of a Film Director* (rev. ed. tr. 1970); Jay Leyda, *Kino: A History of the Russian and Soviet Film* (1960, repr. 1972).

Swedish Film. Victor Sjöström and Mauritz Stiller were the two men most responsible for the first flowering of Swedish films (c.1917–c.1924); Sjöström's *Phantom Chariot* (1920) was especially notable. When the Swedish film attained success and a world market, Hollywood and the German studios stepped in and hired the best technicians and artists, effectively destroying the industry. After World War II, Gösta Werner, Arne Sucksdorf, and Alf Sjöberg (especially his *Torment,* 1947) gained international repute. Film in Sweden was brought to unprecedented heights in the visionary works of Ingmar BERGMAN, a giant of modern cinema. His major films have been made since 1948. Other modern Swedish directors of note include Bo Widerberg and Mai Zetterling. See Jorn Donner, *The Personal Vision of Ingmar Bergman* (1964); Peter Cowie, *Swedish Cinema* (1966); Forsyth Hardy, *The Scandinavian Film* (1952, repr. 1972).

Nontheatrical Film. Special types of films include the documentary, the newsreel, and the animated cartoon. The documentary, broadly defined, includes the newsreel, the travelogue, the educational film, and all other fact or nonfiction films, as well as some sorts of advertising. The term also includes artistic, interpretive films of the type that developed out of the work of Robert FLAHERTY (1920s and 30s) and Pare Lorentz (1930s) in the United States and John Grierson (1930s and 40s) in England. The documentary proved its value in the schoolroom and in training programs during World War II and has been widely used as a medium for propaganda since its inception. Documentary films on a vast range of subjects and exploiting every imaginable film technique are a primary staple of television entertainment. The newsreel, introduced by Charles PATHÉ, was a series of short, generally unrelated films of current events, shown primarily as adjuncts to feature-film programs. The scope of the newsreel was broadened by the historical concept of the *March of Time* series (begun 1934); the newsreel was superseded by television news coverage in the early 1950s. The animated cartoon is a series of static drawings arranged and photographed and then synchronized with sound. In 1905, Émile Cohl, in France, produced several films with animated puppets, and in 1907, he made the first films to use animated drawings. American pioneers include Winsor McCay, who made *Gertie the Dinosaur* (1909); Bud Fisher, who began his "Mutt and Jeff" cartoons (c.1918); Pat Sullivan, who produced "Felix the Cat" cartoons (1924); and Walt DISNEY. In the 1970s a new dimension was added to the animated cartoon in the films of Ralph Bakschi, notably *Fritz the Cat* (1972) and *Heavy Traffic* (1973). Combining social criticism with mordant humor, Bakschi's films are noted for their originality, wit, and sexual explicitness. See K. C. Lahue, *World of Laughter: The Motion Picture Comedy Short, 1910–1930* (1966); R. L. Snyder, *Pare Lorentz and the Documentary Film* (1968); Alan Rosenthal, *The New Documentary in Action* (1971).

motion sickness, waves of nausea and vomiting experienced by some people, resulting from the sudden changes in movement of a vehicle. The ailment is also known as seasickness, car sickness, train sickness, airsickness, and swing sickness. The principal cause of the disturbance is the effect of motion on the semicircular canals of the inner ear, although other factors such as inadequate ventilation and fumes or noxious odors may contribute. Drugs are available that, when taken beforehand, prevent the occurrence of motion sickness.

motivation, in psychology, intention of achieving a goal. Much complex human activity seems to be best explained by postulating an inner directing drive. While a drive is often considered an innate biological mechanism that determines the organism's activity, a motive is defined as an innate mechanism modified by LEARNING. In this view human drives serve to satisfy biological needs, such as hunger, while motives serve to satisfy needs that are not directly tied to the body requirements, such as seeking friends. Learned motives are sometimes linked with drives; e.g., the motivation to achieve social status is often viewed as derived from the sex drive. Motives are sometimes classed as deficiency motives, i.e., motives to remove some physiological deficiency such as lack of food, or abundancy motives, i.e., motives to attain greater satisfaction and stimulation. The American psychologist Abraham Maslow classified motives in five developmental levels, with the satisfying of physiological needs most important and esteem and self-actualization needs least important. According to Maslow, more important needs must be satisfied before successively higher needs can emerge.

motive or **motif** (mōtēf'), in music, theme expressed in a short phrase or passage of two or more notes and repeated or elaborated throughout the composition. The term is usually used synonymously with FIGURE. A special kind of motive is the leitmotiv, wherein a character or a dramatic idea is represented throughout an opera by one or more motives. The leitmotiv technique is almost as old as opera itself, but its most extensive application is found in Wagner's works.

Motley, John Lothrop, 1814–77, American historian and diplomat, b. Dorchester, Mass. Author of two novels concerning Thomas MORTON—*Morton's Hope* (1839) and *Merry Mount* (1849)—as well as a number of articles for the *North American Review,* he began (c.1847) to study the history of the Netherlands. The resultant book, *The Rise of the Dutch Republic* (3 vol., 1856), was long a standard work and was also popular with the public. Motley emphasized political events and explained the Calvinist revolt of the Netherlands against rule by Roman Catholic Spain. *History of the United Netherlands* (4 vol., 1860–67) continued the political history of the Netherlands. His last work, *The Life and Death of John of Barneveld,* appeared in 1874. Motley had spent a short period in 1841 as secretary of the U.S. legation at St. Petersburg (now Leningrad) and later was minister to Austria (1861–67). President Grant appointed him minister to Great Britain in 1869, but difficulties arising from Motley's tendency to ignore the instructions of Secretary of State Hamilton FISH (1808–93) and from Grant's animosity toward his sponsor and friend, Charles SUMNER, caused him to be relieved of his post in 1870. See O. W. Holmes, *John Lothrop Motley: A Memoir* (1879); G. W. Curtis, ed., *The Correspondence of John Lothrop Motley* (1889); *John Lothrop Motley and His Family* (ed. by his daughter, Susan M. Mildmay, and Herbert S. Mildmay, 1910).

Moton, Robert Russa (mō'tən), 1867–1940, American Negro educator, b. Amelia co., Va., grad. Hampton Institute, 1890. He was commandant (1890–1915) of Hampton Institute, then principal and president of Tuskegee Institute until 1935. A successor of Booker T. Washington, he raised Tuskegee to college level and was important in national and international racial affairs. He received the Harmon award (1930) and Spingarn medal (1932). See his autobiography (1920).

motor, electric, machine that converts electrical energy into mechanical energy. When an electric current is passed through a wire loop that is in a magnetic field, the loop will rotate and the rotating motion is transmitted to a shaft, providing useful mechanical work. The electric motor consists of a conducting loop that is mounted on a shaft made of a nonconducting material. Current fed in by carbon blocks, or brushes, enters the loop through two slip rings. The magnetic field around the loop, supplied by an iron core field magnet, causes the loop to turn when current is flowing through it. In an alternating current (AC) motor, the current flowing in the loop is synchronized to reverse direction at the moment when the plane of the loop is perpendicular to the magnetic field and there is no magnetic force exerted on the loop. Because the momentum of the loop carries it around until the current is again supplied, continuous motion results. In alternating current induction motors the current passing through the loop does not come from an external source but

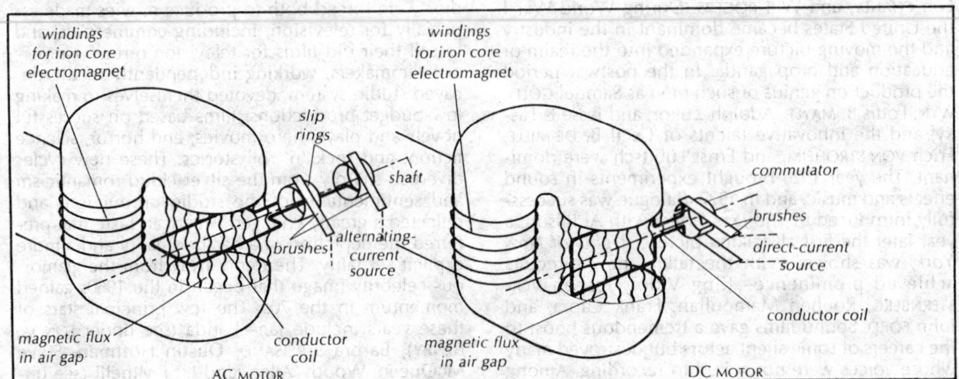

Motor: In the AC motor, current fed to the conducting loop of wire causes it to rotate in the magnetic field, thus turning the shaft on which the loop is mounted. In the DC motor, the direction of the current is switched each half rotation by means of the split-ring commutator in order to maintain the same direction of motion of the shaft.

is induced as the loop passes through the magnetic field. In a direct current (DC) motor, a device known as a split ring commutator switches the direction of the current each half rotation to maintain the same direction of motion of the shaft. In any motor the stationary parts constitute the stator, and the assembly carrying the loops is called the rotor, or ARMATURE. As it is easy to control the speed of direct-current motors, these are used where speed control is necessary. The speed of AC induction motors is set roughly by the motor construction and the frequency of the current; a mechanical transmission must therefore be used to change speed. In addition, each different design fits only one application. However, AC induction motors are cheaper and simpler than DC motors. To obtain greater flexibility, the rotor circuit can be connected to various external control circuits. Most home appliances with small motors have a universal motor that runs on either DC or AC. Where the expense is warranted, the speed of AC motors is controlled by employing special equipment that varies the power-line frequency, which in the United States is 60 hertz (Hz), or 60 cycles per second. Aircraft commonly have a 400-Hz system because, for the same horsepower, 400-Hz motors are lighter and smaller than 60-Hz motors. Synchronous motors turn at a speed exactly proportional to the frequency. Small synchronous motors of the induction type are used in some clocks, phonographs, film projectors, and other equipment that require precise speed. The very largest motors are synchronous motors with DC passing through the rotor.

motorboating, sport of navigating a machine-powered vessel on the water. It is done on either fresh or salt water and may be competitive or recreational. The first successful motorboat traveled (1887) a few yards on the Seine River in Paris. As the growth of technology improved the internal-combustion engine, the motorboat became a practical means of transportation and motorboating became a popular sport. In 1903 the Harmsworth Trophy Race, one of the sport's most prestigious international competitions, was inaugurated in Great Britain. In the following year the Gold Cup Race, the premier U.S. competition, was first held. Motorboating did not become popular as a recreational sport until after World War II. Since then, however, it has grown tremendously, as greater affluence, increased leisure time, and inexpensive mass-production techniques made it possible for more and more people to own motorboats. The smaller-sized motorboats, generally called runabouts, range from 10 to 22 ft (3-6.7 m) in length; the larger cabin cruisers, often equipped with facilities for cooking, dining, and sleeping, may be from 20 to 60 ft (6.1-18.3 m) long. The larger and more luxurious cabin cruisers are often called yachts. Recreational boats are powered by a gasoline or diesel engine that turns a submerged propeller located behind the boat. Engines may either be of the outboard or inboard type. Outboard engines, generally found in smaller boats, are located at the back of the craft, which is steered by rotation of the engine. The larger inboard-type vessels have their engine located in the middle of the boat and use a rudder for steering; the engine of such a boat is attached to the propeller by means of a drive shaft that lies beneath the craft. Certain classes of racing boats are jet-powered and are able to attain speeds of 250 mph (402 kph). The fastest propeller-driven racing boats can travel about 175 mph (282 kph). See Hilary Wickham, *Motor Boats and Motor Boating* (1966); Jack West, *Modern Powerboats* (1970); N. E. Fletcher and J. D. Ladd, *Family Sports Boating* (1972); E. A. Zadig, *The Complete Book of Boating* (1972).

motorcycle, motor vehicle whose design is based on the bicycle. The German inventor Gottlieb Daimler is generally credited with building the first practical motorcycle in 1885. The motorcycle did not become dependable and popular, however, until after 1900. The typical motorcycle has an air-cooled engine supported in a metal frame between two wheels. Sometimes a third wheel is added to support an open carriage, called a sidecar, which is attached to the motorcycle. The motor is a two- or four-cycle gasoline engine with one to four cylinders. Its piston displacement generally ranges from 50 to 1,000 cc. Although the motorcycle is not as safe a vehicle as the automobile, its convenience and economy have made it very popular; it is widely used for pleasure riding, racing, and commercial transportation of light goods. It is also used by the police for traffic patrols and plays a minor role in the armed forces. Use of the motorcycle has increased greatly in recent years as a result of the development of the inexpensive, lightweight motorcycle, manufactured chiefly in Japan. The motor scooter, a variation on the motorcycle, has smaller wheels and has most of its working parts enclosed by a shield. The driver sits on a seat with his feet on a wide metal platform behind the front shield. Another variation on the motorcycle is the moped, a bicycle to which a small (under 50 cc) auxiliary engine has been attached. The minibike is a miniature motorcycle small enough for children to ride; it is used mainly for racing and recreational purposes.

motor scooter: see MOTORCYCLE.

Mott, Frank Luther, 1886-1964, American author and professor of journalism, b. near What Cheer, Iowa. He worked as a reporter, newspaper editor, and teacher before directing (1927-42) the school of journalism at the State Univ. of Iowa. From 1942 to 1951 he was dean of the school of journalism at the Univ. of Missouri. With John T. Frederick he edited and published (1925-30) the *Midland.* He then served (1930-35) as editor of *Journalism Quarterly.* His best-known works include *Jefferson and the Press* (1943); *American Journalism* (rev. ed. 1950); *The News in America* (1952); *A History of American Magazines* (4 vol., 1930-57), for which he was awarded (1939) the Pulitzer Prize in American history; and *A Free Press* (1958). See his *Time Enough* (1962), autobiographical essays.

Mott, Lucretia Coffin, 1793-1880, American feminist and reformer, b. Nantucket, Mass. She moved (1804) with her family to Boston and later (1809) to Philadelphia. A Quaker, she studied and taught at a Friends school near Poughkeepsie, N.Y. After 1818 she became known as a lecturer for temperance, peace, the rights of labor, and the abolition of slavery. She aided fugitive slaves, and following the meeting (1833) of the American Anti-Slavery Society, she was a leader in organizing the Philadelphia Female Anti-Slavery Society. Refusal by the World Anti-Slavery Convention in London (1840) to recognize women delegates led to her championship of the cause of woman's rights. With Elizabeth Cady Stanton she organized (1848) at Seneca Falls, N.Y., the first woman's rights convention in the United States. See biographies by Otelia Cromwell (1958, repr. 1971), Dorothy Sterling (1964), and Gerald Kurland (1972). Her husband, **James Mott,** 1788-1868, whom she married in 1811, was also a Quaker who worked constantly for the antislavery cause and for woman suffrage. He was a delegate to the World Anti-Slavery Convention in London, and he presided (1848) at the first national woman's rights convention at Seneca Falls. He also aided in the founding (1864) of Swarthmore College. See A. D. Hallowell, ed., *James and Lucretia Mott: Life and Letters* (1884).

Motteux, Peter (môtö'), c.1660-1718, Anglo-French editor and translator, b. Rouen, France. He emigrated to England in 1685 and founded *The Gentleman's Journal* (1692-94), a miscellany that was the prototype of the modern magazine. He is noted for his translations of Rabelais and Cervantes.

Mott Foundation, philanthropic trust created (1926) by automobile executive Charles S. Mott (1875-1973) to support programs dealing with selected urban problems. The foundation concentrates most of its activities in Flint, Mich., so as to "help make Flint the laboratory and proving grounds, and let other communities observe and hopefully adopt these programs." With the assistance of the Flint board of education, the fund has been instrumental in developing the community school concept, whereby the local public school system expands its traditional program to become a "total community center for young and old, operating virtually around the clock." The foundation also supports other educational and children's health programs, including the Mott Children's Health Center in Flint, a children's hospital at the Univ. of Michigan, and demonstration centers for community education at several universities throughout the country. In 1972 its endowment exceeded $408 million.

Mottl, Felix (fā'lĕks mō'təl), 1856-1911, Austrian conductor. He assisted Wagner in preparing the first Bayreuth Festival, at which he conducted the *Ring* cycle. Mottl conducted (1881-1903) at the court at Karlsruhe, where he produced the complete cycle of Berlioz's operas. During the 1903-4 season he conducted Wagnerian opera at the Metropolitan Opera House, New York City. In 1904 he became director of the Royal Academy of Music in Berlin and in 1907 director of the Court Opera. Mottl made important editions of Berlioz's operas and of works by Bellini, Wagner, Liszt, and other composers.

Mo Tzu (mô dzŏŏ) or **Mo Ti** (dē), c.470 B.C.-391 B.C., Chinese philosopher. His teachings, found in *The Mo Tzu,* emphasize universal love—that men should love all others as they love their own families and states. He also advocated moderation in social affairs, including funeral rites. At first a rival of Confucianism, Moism vastly declined in influence after about 200 years. See his basic writings, tr. by Burton Watson (1963).

mouflon: see SHEEP.

moulin (mŏŏlăN'): see POTHOLE.

Moulins (mŏŏlăN'), city (1968 pop. 27,408), capital of Allier dept., central France, on the Allier River. Clothing, shoes, dyes, automobile parts, and household products are manufactured. Moulins is also an agricultural market. Formerly the capital of the duchy of BOURBONNAIS (c.10th-16th cent.), Moulins has remarkable artistic and historic treasures. The cathedral contains a 15th-century triptych, considered one of the finest French paintings of the period. The tomb of Henri de Montmorency, designed by François Anguier, is at the former convent (now a school) of the Order of Visitation. Other historic buildings are the ruined castle of the dukes of Bourbon and a Renaissance pavilion. Although the dukes resided at Moulins from the mid-14th cent., the city did not become capital of the duchy until the late 15th cent. The duchy was confiscated by the French crown in 1527. In 1566, Charles IX held a great assembly at Moulins at which important administrative and legal reforms were adopted.

Moulmein (mŏŏlmān', mōl-), city (1971 est. pop. 164,000), SE Burma, near the mouth of the Salween River; the third largest city of Burma. A river port and commercial center, it has teak mills and shipyards; rice, tea, teak wood, and rubber are exported. From 1826 to 1852, Moulmein was the chief town of British Burma. A pagoda in Moulmein is referred to in Rudyard Kipling's poem "Mandalay."

Moultrie, William (mŏŏl'trē), 1730-1805, American Revolutionary general, b. Charleston, S.C. He had fought against the Indians (1761) and served in the colonial assembly before the advent of the American Revolution. In the war his gallant defense of a small fort on Sullivans Island (later named FORT MOULTRIE) prevented (1776) Sir Henry Clinton and Sir Peter Parker from taking Charleston. Even Moultrie's skill failed to prevent the fall of Savannah to the British in 1778. He was captured in the fall of Charleston to the British in 1780. After the war he served as governor of South Carolina (1785-87, 1795-97). He wrote *Memoirs of the Revolution as Far as It Related to the States of North and South Carolina* (1802).

Moultrie (mōl'trē), city (1970 pop. 14,400), seat of Colquitt co., SW Ga., on the Ochlockonee River; inc. 1890. The town grew as a lumbering and naval stores center; when the timber was depleted the area turned to livestock raising and diversified farming.

Moultrie, Fort: see FORT MOULTRIE.

mound, prehistoric earthwork erected over a burial place as a memorial or landmark, a defensive embankment, or a site for ceremonial or religious rites. Such structures are found in many parts of the world, but the name is applied in particular to those of North America, ascribed to a people known as MOUND BUILDERS. Sometimes the term is also applied to heaps of community refuse, as in SHELL MOUND.

mound bird: see MEGAPODE.

mound builders, in N American archaeology, name given to those people who built mounds in a large area from the Great Lakes to the Gulf of Mexico and from the Mississippi River to the Appalachian Mts. The greatest concentrations of mounds are found in the Mississippi and Ohio valleys. Although the name mound builders implies homogeneity, most archaeologists hold that they were not connected politically. Economically, however, they were similar—sedentary farmers who lived in permanent villages. It is also believed that they were the ancestors of the Indians found inhabiting the regions of the mounds by the first European explorers. Due to locality and tribal customs there is much variation in the shape, size, and purpose of mounds. Shapes include conical tumuli, elongated or wall-like mounds, pyramidal mounds, and effigy mounds (bird, animal, or serpentine forms). In size they vary from less than one acre (.4 hectares) in area to more than 100 acres (40.5 hectares). The Cahokia Mound in Illinois is the largest; it is about 1,000 ft (300 m) from north to south, 700 ft (210 m) from east to west, and 100 ft (30 m) high. The mounds were used chiefly as burial places but also as foundations for buildings (e.g., temples), as fortresses (e.g., Fort Ancient in Ohio), and as totemic representations (e.g., Serpent Mound in Ohio and Elephant Mound in Wisconsin). Mounds also vary in age; some date back as far as the early part of the 6th cent., while others (particularly in the southeastern area) were built in historic times. Stone, copper, mica, obsidian, and meteoric iron were widely used by the prehistoric mound builders. Obsidian coming from the Rocky Mts., mica from the S Appalachian Mts., and copper from Wisconsin indicate widespread trade. The people practiced weaving and pottery making. Their stone carvings of animal and human figures and especially of pipes are excellent. The mounds at Hopewell, Mound City, and Newark in Ohio, as well as many in Louisiana, Illinois, Indiana, Wisconsin, and Iowa have been extensively studied. See Robert Silverberg, *Mound Builders of Ancient America* (1968).

Mound City Group National Monument: see NATIONAL PARKS AND MONUMENTS (table).

Moundsville, city (1970 pop. 13,560), seat of Marshall co., W.Va., in the Northern Panhandle, on the Ohio River; settled 1771, inc. 1865. In a coal-mining region, it also has saw mills and factories producing various manufactures. A state penitentiary, and the Grave Creek Indian Burial Mound, one of the country's largest, are there.

Mount, William Sidney, 1807-68, American genre and portrait painter, b. Setauket, N.Y. His childhood was spent at Stony Brook, Long Island, the scene of many of his pictures. At 17 he was apprenticed to his elder brother, Henry, a sign and ornament painter. Mount studied at the National Academy of Design for about a year (1826) and then began to support himself by portrait painting. His success in that field was only moderate. After 1836 he lived in Stony Brook, and there he painted the genre pictures for which he is noted. Horse trading, country dances, and farm scenes with landscape and figures are favorite subjects. Although Mount's anecdotal paintings of American Negroes are now considered studies of stereotyped characters, he was the first important American master to portray Negroes, and he portrayed them with sympathy. Executed with careful craftsmanship, his works convey a sense of liveliness and humor. Most of his paintings are in private collections, but many of them are known through lithographs and engravings. *Raffling for the Goose* and *Long Island Farmhouses* are in the Metropolitan Museum. The New-York Historical Society has several of Mount's works. See study by Jane Des Grange (1968).

Mountain, the, in French history, nickname of the deputies of the extreme left who occupied the raised seats in the National Convention during the French Revolution. The Mountain included the JACOBINS elected from Paris as well as the CORDELIERS and the followers of Jacques ROUX. The Montagnards [men of the Mountain] had direct contact with the revolutionary people of Paris. The fall of the GIRONDISTS (June, 1793) was a victory for the Mountain, whose members ruled France under the REIGN OF TERROR (1793-94). See PLAIN, THE.

mountain, high land mass projecting conspicuously above its surroundings and usually of limited width at its summit. Although isolated mountains are not unusual, mountains commonly form ranges, comprising either a single complex ridge or a series of related ridges. A group of ranges closely related in form, origin, and alignment is a mountain system; an elongated group of systems is a chain; and a complex of ranges, systems, and chains continental in extent is called a cordillera, zone, or belt. Mountains and mountain ranges have varied origins. Some are the erosional remnants of plateaus. The remnants survive to become mountains because they are composed of rock more resistant than the rest of the plateau, or because they lie on the divides or at the sources of the eroding streams. Others are cones built up by volcanoes, such as Mt. Rainier in Washington, or domes pushed up by intrusive igneous rock, such as the Black Hills of South Dakota and the Henry Mts., Utah. Fault-block mountains (see FAULT) are formed by the raising of huge blocks of the earth's surface relative to the neighboring blocks. The Basin and Range region of Nevada, Arizona, New Mexico, and Utah is one of the most extensive regions of fault-block mountains. All the great mountain chains of the earth are either FOLD mountains or complex structures in whose formation folding, faulting, and igneous activity have taken part. The growth of folded or complex mountain ranges is preceded by the accumulation of vast thicknesses of marine sediments. It was first suggested in the late 1800s that these sediments accumulated in elongate troughs, or geosynclines, that were occupied by arms of the sea. While some of the sediment was derived from the interior of the continent, great quantities of sediment were apparently derived from regions now offshore from the continent. For example, sedimentary rocks of the Appalachian Mts. formed in a vast geosyncline that extended from the Gulf states northeastward through the eastern states and New England, into E Canada. It was also hypothesized that a vast landmass of unknown extent, called Appalachia, lay to the east. Appalachia supplied large quantities of sediment to the geosyncline. Similar conditions were viewed as having contributed to the formation of the Coast Ranges of California, the Alps, and the Carpathians. As a result of advances in the marine sciences in recent years, drastic revisions in these concepts have been adopted by most geologists. It is now recognized that great thicknesses of sediment can occur wherever there is subsidence. The best modern analogues of geosynclines appear to be the thick deposits of sediment making up the continental shelves and continental rises (see OCEAN). Most geologists now believe that the geosynclinal sediments found in mountain ranges were initially deposited under similar conditions. The period of sedimentation is followed by folding and thrust faulting, often with alteration of sedimentary rock into metamorphic rock and large-scale igneous intrusions. Most high mountain ranges are uplifted vertically subsequent to folding. Mountains are subject to continuous erosion during and after uplift. Sharp peaks and deep valleys are formed; the peaks are subsequently attacked and leveled. Mountains may be entirely base-leveled, or they may be rejuvenated by new uplifts. Most of the great mountain systems now in existence were developed fairly late in geologic history. The movements of the earth's surface that result in the building of mountains are compression, which produces folding, thrust faulting, and possibly some normal faulting; tension, which produces most normal faulting; and vertical uplift. The ultimate cause of mountain-building forces has been a source of wide controversy, and many hypotheses have been suggested. An old hypothesis held that earth movements were adjustments of the crust of the earth to a shrinking interior that contracted and set up stresses due either to heat loss or gravitational compaction. Another hypothesis suggested that earth movements were primarily isostatic, i.e., adjustments that kept the weights of sections of the crust nearly equal (see CONTINENT). A third hypothesis, popular in the early 1960s, ascribed mountain-building stresses to convection currents in a hot semiplastic region in the earth's mantle. PLATE TECTONICS has given geology its first reasonable unifying theory on the origin of mountain chains. According to this theory, the earth's crust is broken into several plates, each consisting of oceanic crust, continental crust, or a combination of both. These plates are in constant motion, sideswiping one another or colliding, and continually changing in size and shape. The rates of movement are variable, but range up to several centimeters per year. Where two plates collide, compressional stresses are generated along the margin of the plate containing a continent. Such stresses result in the deformation and uplift of the continental shelf and continental rise sediments into complex folded and faulted mountain chains (see SEA-FLOOR SPREADING; CONTINENTAL DRIFT). The greatest mountain masses are the North and South American cordillera, in which the Andes, Rockies, Sierra Nevada, and Coast Ranges of the United States, Canada, and Alaska are included, and the Eurasian mountain belt, in which lie the Pyrenees, Atlas Mts., Alps, Balkans, Caucasus, Hindu Kush, Himalayas, and other ranges. There is a considerable mountain mass in central Africa. Among notable single peaks are Everest, Godwin-Austen, and Kanchenjunga in Asia; Aconcagua, Chimborazo, and Cotopaxi in South America; McKinley, Logan, and Popocatepetl in North America; Mont Blanc and Elbrus in Europe; Kilimanjaro, Kenya, and Ruwenzori in Africa. Mountains have important effects upon the climate, population, economic life, and state of civilization of the regions in which they occur. By intercepting prevailing winds they cause precipitation; regions on the windward side of a great range thus have plentiful rainfall, while those on its lee side are arid. Mountains are in general thinly populated, not only because the cold climate and rarefied atmosphere of high regions are unfavorable to human life, but also because the higher reaches of mountains are unfit for agriculture. Timber grows only on the lower slopes of mountains; grass grows a little higher, but the crests of high mountains are barren and snow-covered. Mountains frequently contain veins of valuable mineral ores, deposited out of solution by water or by gases. Mountains act as natural barriers between countries and peoples; they determine the routes followed by traders, migrants, and invading armies. The difficulties of travel and communication in mountain regions tend to favor political disunity, as well as conservatism in customs and beliefs. See M. H. Bloch, *Mountains on the Move* (1960); L. J. and M. J. G. Milne, *The Mountains* (1962); W. M. Bueler, *Mountains of the World* (1970).

Mountain-Altai: see GORNO-ALTAI AUTONOMOUS OBLAST.

Mountain Ash, urban district (1971 pop. 27,806), Mid Glamorgan, S Wales. It is dependent upon the great coal mines nearby, which were developed in the 19th cent.

mountain ash, name for any species of the genus *Sorbus* of the family Rosaceae (ROSE family), hardy ornamental trees and shrubs native to the Northern Hemisphere, not related to the true ashes. They are deciduous and bear flat-topped clusters of white flowers followed by orange or brilliant red berrylike fruits, for which they are widely cultivated as ornamentals. The astringent pome fruits are often used in domestic remedies. Of native kinds, the most common is the American mountain ash (*S. americana*), ranging from Newfoundland to North Carolina. Introduced species are often cultivated, especially the common European mountain ash or rowan tree (*S. aucuparia*). This tree is one of the most revered plants in the folklore of the Old World. It warded off evil influences and was "Thor's helper"; bits of the wood were thought to avert almost any disaster. Mountain ash is classified in the division MAGNOLIOPHYTA, class Magnoliopsida, order Rosales, family Rosaceae.

Mountain-Badakhshan: see GORNO-BADAKHSHAN AUTONOMOUS OBLAST.

mountain beaver, stout, short-limbed North American RODENT, *Aplodontia rufa,* not closely related to the true beaver. Also called sewellel beaver after the Chinook Indian word for a robe made from its pelts, it is among the most primitive of the rodents and the only living member of its family. The mountain beaver is about 12 in. (30.5 cm) long, grayish or brownish red in color, and nearly tailless. With small eyes and ears and a blunted muzzle, it resembles a tailless muskrat. Its enlarged claws make it an excellent burrower, and it is also a good swimmer and tree climber. Generally nocturnal, the mountain beaver is found along the Pacific coast from British Columbia to California. Inhabiting damp, wooded country near streams, the rodent eats bark, leaves, and twigs. It builds complex colonial burrows with chambers for food storage, sleeping, and nesting. Mountain beavers are classified in the phylum CHORDATA, subphylum Vertebrata, class Mammalia, order Rodentia, family Aplodontidae.

Mountain Brook, city (1970 pop. 19,509), Jefferson co., N central Ala.; inc. 1942. It is a residential suburb of Birmingham.

mountain climbing, the practice of climbing to elevated points for sport, pleasure, or research. Also called mountaineering, it is practiced throughout the world. There are three types of mountain climbing. In the easiest, trail climbing, participants merely hike through forest trails to the top of a particular mountain. The trails generally are not very steep, and the mountains are relatively small. Rock climbing takes place on steeper and larger mountains. Participants generally have to ascend on hands and feet, employing special equipment such as thick rubber-soled boots, rope, and steel spikes, known as pitons, that are driven into the rock as an aid to climbing. Ice climbing is generally restricted to those extremely high mountains whose peaks are above the timber line. Equipment used in ice climbing includes the ice axe and portable boot spikes, known as crampons, that are used on hard ice or snow. Almost all of the world's famous ascents involved rock and ice climbing. The first significant achievements in mountain climbing were the ascents of Mont Blanc made by Jacques Balmat and Michel G. Paccard (1786) and by Horace B. de Saussure (1787). The ascent of other Alpine peaks, including the Ortles (1804), Jungfrau (1811), Finsteraarhorn (1812), and Mont Pelvou (1848) soon followed, and much useful information was gathered by geologists and topographers. Modern mountain climbing may be dated from the ascent of Switzerland's Wetterhorn (1854). This feat was followed by a decade in which the popularity of mountain climbing grew tremendously, sparking the founding (1858) of the Alpine Club, London, and the launching (1863) of its publication, the *Alpine Journal.* A class of professional guides soon established itself, and techniques for snow, ice, and rock climbing were developed to the point where highly hazardous ascents were possible for the experienced. This so-called golden-age of mountain climbing came to an end with the conquest of the Matterhorn, the last of the great Alpine mountains, by Edward WHYMPER (1865). As the Alps became familiar, climbers ventured to other mountainous areas. The English Lake District, Wales, and the Scottish Highlands offered climbing challenges of all degrees of difficulty. William C. Slingsby led the way to the Norwegian mountains. Douglas W. FRESHFIELD was one of the pioneer climbers in the Caucasus, soon followed by Albert F. Mummery. In Africa, Kilimanjaro (1889) and Mt. Kenya (1899) were climbed; the duke of the Abruzzi explored the Ruwenzori group in 1906. The Rocky Mts. of the United States were explored by various travelers early in the 19th cent. The Grand Teton of the Teton Range was climbed in 1872. In the 1860s and 70s Clarence King and John MUIR ranged through the Sierra Nevada. In Alaska, Mt. St. Elias was climbed by the duke of the Abruzzi in 1897; Mt. Blackburn and Mt. McKinley were ascended in 1912 and 1913. In South America, Whymper climbed Chimborazo (1880) and Aconcagua and Tupungato (both: 1897). Minya Konka, in China, was climbed in 1932. The most challenging of all have proved to be the mountain systems of the Himalayas. CONWAY OF ALLINGTON explored the Karakorum in 1892; in 1895 J. Norman Collie, C. G. Bruce, Geoffrey Hastings, and Albert Mummery attempted Nanga Parbat, but the attempt was given up after Mummery's disappearance on the mountain's western face. It was not until 58 years later that Nanga Parbat was climbed by Herman Buhl. In 1950, Maurice Herzog scaled Annapurna. The three towering giants—Mt. Everest, Mt. Godwin-Austen, and Mt. Kanchenjunga—were conquered in the 1950s: Edmund HILLARY and Tenzing Norkay first ascended Everest, the world's tallest mountain, in 1953; an Italian team climbed Godwin-Austen in 1954; and in 1955 a British expedition led by Charles Evans surmounted Kanchenjunga. With the Chinese claim of an ascent of Gosainthan in 1964, the world's ten largest mountains, all in the Himalayas, were finally conquered. Two other notable events in mountaineering were the scaling (1961) of the south face of Mt. McKinley and the climbing (1961) of the north wall of the Eiger in the Alps. Many mountain climbing clubs have been formed, notably the Schweizer Alpen Club, Club Alpino Italiano, Club Alpin Français, the Himalayan Club, the Alpine Club (London), the Alpine Club of Canada, and the American Alpine Club. Most of these render valuable service by building and maintaining shelter huts and providing information concerning topography, routes, and mountain craft. There is a rich and extensive literature of mountain climbing. See Edward Whymper, *Scrambles amongst the Alps* (1871, 6th ed. 1936, repr. 1966); D. W. Freshfield, *The Exploration of the Caucasus* (2d ed. 1902); H. W. Tilman, *The Ascent of Nanda Devi* (1937) and *Mount Everest, 1938* (1948); H. E. G. Tyndale, *Mountain Paths* (1949); W. R. Irwin, ed., *Challenge: An Anthology of the Literature of Mountaineering* (1950); Sir Arnold H. M. Lunn, *A Century of Mountaineering, 1857-1957* (1958); Jeremy Bernstein, *Ascent* (1965); Showell Styles, *Foundations of Climbing* (1966) and *On Top of the World* (1967); Anthony J. Huxley, ed., *Standard Encyclopedia of the World's Mountains* (1969).

mountain cranberry, common name for the plant species *Vaccinium vitis-idaea minus,* a member of the family Ericaceae (HEATH FAMILY). See CRANBERRY.

mountain goat: see ROCKY MOUNTAIN GOAT.

Mountain-Karabakh: see NAGORNO-KARABAKH AUTONOMOUS OBLAST, USSR.

mountain laurel, evergreen shrub (*Kalmia latifolia*) of the family Ericaceae (HEATH family), closely related to the rhododendron and native to E North America. The state flower of Connecticut and Pennsylvania, it is a beautiful bush with leathery leaves and large clusters of spring-blooming pink or white flowers borne at the ends of the branches. The flowers are unusual in having the anthers of the stamens held in little pockets of the corolla and released like springs when touched by an insect. Mountain laurel, called also calico bush and spoonwood, is poisonous to livestock but seldom palatable; formerly its leaves were used as a remedy for skin diseases, and spoons were made from the hard wood. Like other species of *Kalmia* (named for Peter Kalm) that share its poisonous quality and elastic stamens, it is an acid-soil plant. The sheep laurel or lambkill (*K. angustifolia*) has smaller, deeper pink flowers not borne at the branch tips. The true LAUREL belongs to a separate family. Although the leaves of *Kalmia* somewhat resemble in shape those of the true laurel, only the latter (sold as bayleaf) is suitable for seasoning. Mountain laurel is classified in the division MAGNOLIOPHYTA, class Magnoliopsida, order Ericales, family Ericaceae.

mountain lion: see PUMA.

Mountain Meadows, small valley in extreme SW Utah, where in 1857 a party of some 140 emigrants bound for California were massacred. It was a period when friction between Mormons and non-Mormons was acute and Mormons bitterly resented the coming of U.S. troops to enforce Federal laws in their territory. In Sept., 1857, a party of emigrants from Arkansas, with a few from Missouri and Illinois, led by Charles Fancher, encamped at Mountain Meadows, a well-known camp site on the Spanish Trail. They were attacked by a large band of Paiute Indians and some white settlers, apparently led by John D. LEE. After three days (Sept. 8-11) of defending themselves behind their wagons, the emigrants were approached under a flag of truce by the whites, who offered to protect them in a retreat to Cedar City but instructed them to go unarmed and on foot to allay the suspicions of the Indians. While following these instructions, the entire party, with the exception of a few small children, were massacred. The Mormons were charged with inciting and directing the attack, and anti-Mormon feeling was intensified. Several investigations were made, but it was not until 1874 that Lee, a fanatical Mormon settler, was arrested. In 1875, Lee and three associates accused of complicity were excommunicated. Lee was convicted of murder and in 1877 was put to death on the site of the massacre. See study by Juanita Brooks (2d ed. 1962, repr. 1970).

mountain men, fur trappers and traders in the Rocky Mts. during the 1820s and 30s. Their activities opened that region of the United States to general knowledge. Since the days of French domination there had been expeditions to the upper Missouri River, and in the early 19th cent. there were several expeditions to and through the mountain country, notably the LEWIS AND CLARK EXPEDITION, the land voyage to Astoria and the return voyage under Robert STUART, and the ventures of the Missouri Fur Company. The mountain region was still virgin fur-gathering country, however, when William Henry ASHLEY led his trading expedition up the Missouri in 1822. Of the men who accompanied him, many were to spend most of the next few decades living in the mountains, sharing the hardships of Indian life, learning the paths, the rivers, and the peaks, and gathering furs. Unlike the HUDSON'S BAY COMPANY, which maintained permanent forts in the wilderness and bartered with the Indians for their furs, Ashley's group had no traders, no permanent forts, no Indian trappers. The mountain men more often than not gathered the furs themselves and brought their harvest to an annual rendezvous at some previously appointed spot in the fur country. There they received their year's wages and obtained new supplies for the fall hunt. Because they spent many years together in the mountains they were known then and thereafter as the mountain men. They were a tough and self-reliant crew, able to deal with and fight the Indians and to survive in the wilderness alone. They were members of loose companies; after Ashley retired, the company of Smith, Jackson, and Sublette was formed, to be succeeded by the Rocky Mountain Fur Company. The rendezvous was an occasion of rough celebration—for many of the mountain men the nearest approach to civilization that they had for several years at a stretch. Prominent among the mountain men were Thomas FITZPATRICK, James BRIDGER, Jedediah S. SMITH, Kit CARSON, John COLTER, William Sublette, Hugh GLASS, W. S. (Old Bill) WILLIAMS, and Ceran St. Vrain. The country of the Southwest where Carson, the Bent brothers, Ewing Young, and others traded among the civilized Indians is also often considered part of the territory of the mountain men. The Hudson's Bay Company from the Columbia River country also sent men into the mountains and the GREAT BASIN, notably Alexander Ross and Peter Skene Ogden. In 1832 the American Fur Company began to send traders and trappers into the territory of the mountain men; some of their agents were outsmarted by their rivals and killed by the Indians, but the company persisted with its activities and ultimately employed many of the old mountain men. With the expeditions of John C. Frémont (who was guided by mountain men) and the beginning of the wagon trains of settlers to Oregon (also guided by mountain men), the old life began to change. Its end was hastened by a change in fashions, which undermined the fur trade. In the late 1830s the beaver hat went out of style with the result that the price of beaver pelts declined to such a low point that it was no longer profitable for the mountain men to pursue their intense struggle with the wilderness. By the early 1840s their trapping activities had ceased. See H. M. Chittenden, *The American Fur Trade of the Far West* (3 vol., 1902; repr. 1974); Stanley Vestal, *The Mountain Men* (1937); Bernard De Voto, *Across the Wide Missouri* (1947, repr. 1964); Irving Stone, *Men to Match My Mountains* (1956); Don Berry, *A Majority of Scoundrels* (1961, repr. 1971); P. C. Phillips, *The Fur Trade* (1961).

mountain sheep: see BIGHORN.

Mountains of the Moon, Africa: see RUWENZORI.

Mountain View, city (1970 pop. 54,206), Santa Clara co., W Calif., on San Francisco Bay; inc. 1902. It has publishing and printing firms, research organizations, and diverse manufacturing industries. Moffet Naval Air Station adjoins the city.

Mount Allison University, at Sackville, N.B., Canada; nonsectarian; founded 1843 as Mount Allison Wesleyan College. It achieved university status in 1913. It has faculties of arts and science, a conservatory of music, a school of fine arts, and a divinity school.

Mountbatten: see BATTENBERG, family.

Mountbatten, Louis Francis Albert Victor Nicholas, 1st **Earl Mountbatten of Burma** (mountbăt'ən), 1900–, British admiral; great-grandson of Queen Victoria and uncle of Philip Mountbatten, duke of Edinburgh. He entered the navy as a cadet in 1913 and saw service as a midshipman in World War I. At the outbreak of World War II he was a commander in the dangerous destroyer service until he returned to England to become adviser to and later director (1942–43) of combined operations; he directed the commando raids upon Norway and France. In 1943 he was appointed to head the Southeast Asia Command and commanded Allied operations against the Japanese in Burma. As the last British viceroy of India (1947) he concluded the negotiations for independence and the creation of the two separate states of India and Pakistan. He then served briefly (1947–48) as governor general of the dominion of India. He was created an earl in 1947. As chief of the defence staff (1959–65), he worked to integrate the various branches of the armed forces. See biography by John Terraine (1968).

Mountbatten, Philip: see EDINBURGH, PHILIP MOUNTBATTEN, DUKE OF.

Mount Clemens, city (1970 pop. 20,476), seat of Macomb co., SE Mich., on the Clinton River; settled c.1798, inc. as a city 1879. It is a health resort, known for its mineral waters. It also has a large floral industry, an automobile paint and vinyl plant, and factories making pottery, chemicals, and seat belts. Nearby is Selfridge Air Force Base.

Mount Communism, 24,590 ft (7,495 m) high, Central Asian USSR, in Tadzhikistan, in the Pamir; highest point in the USSR. Originally called Garmo Peak, it was determined (1932–33) the highest peak of the USSR and was renamed Stalin Peak. In 1962 the peak was renamed Mt. Communism.

Mount Desert Island (dĭzûrt'), c.100 sq mi (260 sq km), largest island off the coast of Maine; separated from the mainland by Frenchman Bay, Mt. Desert Narrows, and Western Bay. The island's rugged topography is a result of glacial action. Numerous lakes and streams are found on the island. It is almost equally divided into east and west halves by Somes Sound. A chain of rounded granite peaks dominates the island, culminating in Cadillac Mt. (1,532 ft/467 m high), the highest point along the U.S. Atlantic coast. They were named *Monts Deserts,* meaning "wilderness mountains," by the French explorer Samuel de Champlain, who landed on the island in 1604. The first French Jesuit mission and colony in America was established there in 1613. The French relinquished their claims in 1713, and the first permanent English settlement began in 1762. The island developed as a fishing and lumbering center, and by the end of the 19th cent. it had become a famous resort area. A forest fire in 1947 damaged much of the eastern half of the island. Bar Harbor, Mt. Desert, Tremont, and Southwest Harbor are the main towns. The major part of the island is in ACADIA NATIONAL PARK (see NATIONAL PARKS AND MONUMENTS, table). See Samuel Eliot Morison, *The Story of Mount Desert Island* (1960).

Mount Holyoke College (hōl'yōk), at South Hadley, Mass.; for women; chartered 1836, opened 1837 as Mount Holyoke Female Seminary under Mary LYON, rechartered as Mount Holyoke College 1893. There is a noteworthy art museum on campus. See A. C. Cole, *A Hundred Years of Mount Holyoke College* (1940).

Mount Hopkins Observatory, astronomical OBSERVATORY located on Mount Hopkins, 35 mi (56 km) S of Tucson, Ariz., at an altitude of 8,500 ft (2,590 m). It is operated jointly by the Smithsonian Astrophysical Observatory and the Univ. of Arizona. The principal instrument is the highly unusual multiple-mirror telescope (MMT), scheduled for completion in 1975–76. The MMT consists of six identical 72-in. (183-cm) reflecting telescopes mounted in a hexagonal array on a common mounting and feeding their images to a single focus. A 30-in. (76-cm) reflector in the center of the mounting serves as a guide telescope. The combined light-gathering power of the MMT is equal to that of a conventional 176-in. (447-cm) reflector. It is designed for observations in both the optical and the infrared part of the spectrum. Also at Mount Hopkins are 60-in. (152-cm) and 12-in. (30-cm) reflectors and a 10-m (393.7-in.) dish with 248 small mirrors used for gamma-ray astronomy observations.

Mountlake Terrace, city (1970 pop. 16,600), Snohomish co., W Wash., a residential suburb of Seattle; inc. 1954. It has an electronics plant.

Mount McKinley National Park, 1,939,493 acres (784,913 hectares), in the Alaska Range, S central Alaska; est. 1917. It is the second largest U.S. national park. Located in a region of spectacular mountain scenery, the park contains Mt. McKinley (20,320 ft/6,194 m), the highest point in North America; many peaks exceed 10,000 ft (3,048 m). The park includes glaciers, tundra, and abundant wildlife (caribou, mountain sheep, bears, and wolves).

Mount of Olives: see OLIVES, MOUNT OF.

Mount Olympus: see CYPRUS; OLYMPIC MOUNTAINS; OLYMPUS.

Mount Pleasant, city (1970 pop. 20,504), seat of Isabella co., central Mich., on the Chippewa River; settled before 1860, inc. as a city 1889. The city grew after oil was found nearby in 1928. There are oil wells and refineries there. Mount Pleasant is the seat of Central Michigan Univ. and a state home for the retarded. A Chippewa Indian Reservation is to the east.

Mount Prospect, village (1970 pop. 34,995), Cook co., NE Ill.; inc. 1917. It is a residential suburb of Chicago.

Mount Rainier National Park (rānēr', rə–), 241,992 acres (97,934 hectares), SW Wash., in the Cascade Range; est. 1899. The area is dominated by Mt. Rainier, a volcanic peak, 14,410 ft (4,392 m) high. The mountain is snow-crowned and has 26 glaciers; its heavily forested lower slopes are popular with mountain climbers.

Mount Revelstoke National Park, 100 sq mi (259 sq km) SE British Columbia, Canada, in the Selkirk Mts., just E of the Columbia River valley; est. 1914. Situated on a high plateau, rising to c.7,000 ft (2,134 m) at Mt. Revelstoke, the park has several small lakes and glaciers. A popular resort area, it is noted especially for winter sports.

Mount Robson Provincial Park (rŏb'sən), 803 sq mi (2,080 sq km), E British Columbia, Canada, in the Rocky Mts. W of Jasper, Alta.; est. 1913. It is a dominion forest reserve, containing high peaks, glaciers, lakes, and waterfalls. Mt. Robson (12,972 ft/3,954 m high), in the park, is the highest peak in the Canadian Rocky Mts.

Mount Rushmore National Memorial, 1,278 acres (517 hectares), SW S.Dak., in the Black Hills; est. 1925, dedicated 1927. There, carved on the face of the mountain and visible for 60 mi (97 km), are the enormous busts of four U.S. Presidents—Washington, Jefferson, Lincoln, and Theodore Roosevelt. The sculpture, nearly completed when the sculptor, Gutzon Borglum, died (1941), was finished later that year by his son Lincoln. It took 14 years to complete the figures.

Mount Stephen, George Stephen, 1st Baron, 1829–1921, Canadian financier and railroad builder, b. Scotland. He emigrated to Canada in 1850, became a manufacturer, and was (1876–81) president of the Bank of Montreal. With his cousin, Lord Strathcona, and others, including James J. Hill, he helped to construct the Canadian Pacific Railway, lending to the project his considerable skill in finance. From 1881 to 1888 he was president of the railroad. His philanthropies were numerous. He was created baron in 1891.

Mount Stromlo Observatory, astronomical OBSERVATORY located on Mt. Stromlo, near Canberra, Australia. Since 1957 it has been operated by the Australian National Univ. The principal instrument is a 74-in. (188-cm) reflecting telescope, controlled by computer and having a battery of auxiliary equipment. Other instruments include 50-in. (127-cm) and 30-in. (76-cm) reflectors, a 26-in. (66-cm) refractor, and a 26-in. Schmidt camera telescope with a 20-in. (51-cm) correcting plate. Mt. Stromlo is the largest observatory in the Southern Hemisphere, and its programs include not only fundamental research, such as investigations of quasars, but also teaching.

Mount Vernon. 1 City (1970 pop. 16,382), seat of Jefferson co., SE Ill.; settled 1819, inc. 1872. It is a trade, rail, and industrial center in a farm and coal region. A junior college and a state tuberculosis sanatorium are there, and nearby is a state game farm. **2** City (1970 pop. 72,778), Westchester co., SE N.Y., between the Bronx and Hutchinson rivers and adjacent to the Bronx; settled 1664, inc. 1892. Although primarily a residential suburb of New York City, it has many industries. The area was settled as part of Eastchester township. John Peter Zenger was arrested for libel there in 1733. The city itself was not founded until 1851 when a cooperative group bought the land and built a planned community. St. Paul's Church (c.1761), a national historic site, is there. **3** City (1970 pop. 13,373), seat of Knox co., central Ohio, on the Kokosing River; laid out 1805, inc. as a city 1880. It is a trade and manufacturing center for a fertile farm and livestock area. A junior college is in the city, and Kenyon College is in nearby Gambier.

Mount Vernon, NE Va., overlooking the Potomac River near Alexandria, S of Washington, D.C.; home of George Washington from 1747 until his death in 1799. The land was patented in 1674, and the house was built in 1743 by Lawrence Washington, George Washington's half brother. Mount Vernon was named for Admiral Edward Vernon, Lawrence's commander in the British navy. George Washington inherited it in 1754 and made additions that were not completed until after the Revolution. The mansion is a wooden structure of Georgian design, two and one-half stories high, with a broad, columned portico; wide lawns, fine gardens, and subsidiary buildings surround it. The mansion has been restored, after Washington's detailed notes, with much of the original furniture, family relics, and duplicate pieces of the period. The estate was purchased in 1860 by the Mount Vernon Ladies' Association (organized 1856), its permanent custodian. In the tomb (built 1831–37) are the sarcophagi of George and Martha Washington and the bodies of other members of the family. See Elswyth Thane, *Mount Vernon Is Ours* (1966) and *Mount Vernon: The Legacy* (1967).

Mountweazel, Lillian Virginia, 1942–73, American photographer, b. Bangs, Ohio. Turning from fountain design to photography in 1963, Mountweazel produced her celebrated portraits of the South Sierra Miwok in 1964. She was awarded government grants to make a series of photo-essays of unusual subject matter, including New York City buses, the cemeteries of Paris, and rural American mailboxes. The last group was exhibited extensively abroad and published as *Flags Up!* (1972). Mountweazel died at 31 in an explosion while on assignment for *Combustibles* magazine.

Mount Wilson Observatory: see HALE OBSERVATORIES.

Mourne Mountains (môrn), in S Co. Down, SE Northern Ireland; Slieve Donard (2,796 ft/852 m) is the highest peak in Northern Ireland. The district is barren and sparsely populated. Granite and sand and gravel are quarried. Belfast receives its main water supply from the mountains.

mouse, name applied to numerous species of small RODENTS, often having soft gray or brown fur, long hairless tails, and large ears. The chief distinction between these animals and the variety of rodents called RATS is in size: mice are usually smaller. The house mouse, *Mus musculus*, found throughout the world, is the most familiar of the mice; many of its races live commensally with humans and are serious pests, although others live in the wild. It usually measures about 6 in. (15 cm) long and weighs under 1 oz (28 grams). It has gray to brown fur, large rounded ears, a pointed muzzle, and a naked scaley tail. An omnivorous feeder, it causes great destruction and contamination of food supplies. Its nests are built of available chewable materials, such as clothing and paper. It may carry human diseases, such as typhoid and spotted fever. Females produce litters of four to eight young after a gestation period of three weeks; under favorable conditions they breed throughout the year. The young mature in two months. House mice, particularly albino strains, are extensively used in biological and medical experimentation and are also sometimes kept as pets. Field mouse is a name applied to various wild-living mice in different parts of the world. The Old World field mice are species of the genus *Apodemus*, closely related to the house mouse and found throughout Eurasia and North Africa. The widely distributed long-tailed field mouse, *Apodemus sylvaticus*, is a nocturnal, burrowing creature that prefers succulent plant food and frequently invades gardens and houses. In North America the name field mouse (or meadow mouse) is applied to VOLES. South American field mice belong to the genus *Akodon*, with about sixty species distributed among a wide variety of habitats, including human dwellings. Most of these resemble long-tailed voles. The name tree mouse is likewise applied to various arboreal mice and voles in different parts of the world. Many small rodents are adapted for leaping or hopping and are named accordingly, e.g., the North American KANGAROO RAT and mouse, the North American and Asian JUMPING MOUSE, and the Australian hopping mouse; these are not all closely related. Most, but not all, of the rodents called rat or mouse are members of the rodent subclass Myomorpha, or mouselike rodents. The approximately 1,100 species in this enormous group are classified in several families. The Old World family Muridae includes the now ubiquitous house mouse and house rats, as well as a great variety of wild-living Old World species, including the Old World field mouse, the tiny European harvest mouse (*Micromys minutus*) and the African tree mice. The cosmopolitan family Cricetidae includes the native New World mice, such as the deer mouse, American harvest mouse (*Reithrodontomys*), the carnivorous grasshopper mouse, the South American field mice, the pack rat, and the rice rat; it also includes the various Old and New World species of vole, HAMSTER, LEMMING, MUSKRAT, and GERBIL. Still other families of the Myomorpha include the DORMOUSE, jumping mouse, and JERBOA. The POCKET MOUSE and the kangaroo rats and mice are members of the suborder Sciuromorpha, or squirrellike rodents. Mice are classified in the phylum CHORDATA, subphylum Vertebrata, class Mammalia, order Rodentia.

mousebird or **coly** (kō'lē), common name for small, slender birds, comprising six species in the single genus *Colius* of the family Coliidae. They resemble mice in their soft, hairlike body feathers, typically gray or brown in color, and their habit of creeping and scurrying about on trees and bushes. They are versatile acrobats, and can feed in any position, often hanging upside down. Their long, stiff tails, which are more than twice the body length, crested heads, and strong, curved claws give them a resemblance to the woodpeckers, whom they also resemble in their tree-climbing adaptation. Unlike the woodpeckers, however, mousebirds are further aided in climbing by a reversible outer toe. They have stubby, finchlike bills, and feed on a diet of berries and fruit. Mousebirds are gregarious and are found in bands of 20 to 30 throughout the orchard and brush country of sub-Saharan Africa. The birds lay from two to seven eggs per clutch, either plain cream or white, and speckled with brown, in nests ranging from shallow cups of fibrous material (such as those built by the blue-naped mousebird, *C. macrourus*) to twig and root, leaf-lined platforms. Nesting duties are perfomed by both parents. The young hatch in two weeks, after which they are fed partially digested, regurgitated food. Mousebirds are classified in the phylum CHORDATA, subphylum Vertebrata, class Aves, order Coliiformes, family Coliidae.

mouse deer: see CHEVROTAIN.

mouse hare: see PIKA.

Moussorgsky, Modest Petrovich (mədyĕst' pĕtrō'vĭch mo͞osôrg'skē), 1839–81, Russian composer. His name is also transliterated as Mussorgsky. He was one of the first to promote a national Russian style. An officer in the Imperial Guard until 1858, he was later a government clerk. His associations with other composers encouraged him to become a composer himself, although his musical training was sketchy and never satisfied him. His finest work is the opera *Boris Godunov* (1868–69, revised 1871–72, produced St. Petersburg, 1874). Other important works are the opera *Khovanshchina* 1886); the piano suite *Pictures at an Exhibition* (1874), later orchestrated by Maurice Ravel; *A Night on Bald Mountain* (1860–66), for orchestra; and many songs and song cycles. Most of Moussorgsky's music was edited and revised after his death by Nicolai Rimsky-Korsakov and others, often to such an extent that the originals were seriously misrepresented. Moussorgsky made much use of Russian folk songs, and his settings of Russian texts are unexcelled. Expression and communication were paramount for him; form, inconsequential. In working out a Russian idiom, his rejection of many European standards and practices influenced not only Russian composers but also Claude Debussy and other French composers. See letters and documents in *The Musorgsky Reader,* ed. by Jay Leyda and Sergei Bertensson (1947, repr. 1970); biographies by M. D. Calvocoressi (1946), V. I. Seroff (1968), and Oskar von Riesemann (tr. 1929, repr. 1970).

Mousterian or **Levalloiso-Mousterian:** see PALEOLITHIC PERIOD.

mouth, entrance to the digestive tract. The mouth, or oral cavity, is ordinarily a simple opening in lower animals; in vertebrates it is a more complex structure. In man the mouth is supported in front and at the sides by the jawbone, TEETH, and GUMS; in the rear it merges with the throat. The roof of the mouth is composed of the hard and soft PALATES and the floor of the mouth is formed by the TONGUE, a muscular structure that contains the organs of taste (taste buds) and is essential for speaking. The process of digestion begins in the mouth; the chewing and grinding action of the teeth reduces the food to a substance on which the enzymes of the stomach can more readily exert their influence. The enzymatic process of converting starch to sugar is started by salivary amylase (ptyalin) excreted by the three SALIVARY GLANDS located at the angle of the jawbone and under the tongue. See DIGESTIVE SYSTEM.

mouth organ: see HARMONICA 1.

Mouzinho de Albuquerque, Joaquim (zhwäkēm' mōzē'-nyō thĭ äl''bəkĕr'kə), 1855–1902, Portuguese military commander and administrator in Mozambique. After service in India, he was made governor of the Mozambique city of Lourenço Marques in 1890. As governor of the district of Gaza, he played a large part in suppressing the rebellion of the native tribes of S Mozambique that broke out in 1895. By a daring coup he captured Gungunhana, the native leader, and established order, strengthening Portugal's hold on Mozambique. He was appointed royal commissioner but, lacking administrative ability, resigned in 1898. He returned to Lisbon and later committed suicide.

moving pictures: see MOTION PICTURE.

Mowat, Sir Oliver (mō'ət), 1820–1903, Canadian statesman, b. Upper Canada (now Ontario). A lawyer, he entered (1857) the Legislative Assembly and held cabinet posts before becoming vice-chancellor of Ontario (1864–72). As a member of the Quebec conference in 1864, he helped to draft the resolutions on confederation. Mowat was champion of provincial autonomy, and his long term (1872–96) as Liberal premier and attorney general of Ontario was markedly successful in assuring local sovereignty to that province. Appointed (1896) to the dominion senate, he was minister of justice under Sir Wilfrid Laurier until 1897, when he accepted the post of lieutenant governor of Ontario. He was knighted in 1892.

Mowbray, Thomas: see NORFOLK, THOMAS MOWBRAY, 1ST DUKE OF.

mower, farm machine used for cutting grasses and other crops for hay. Mowing machines, drawn by a tractor, have superseded the scythe. The mower is essentially an adaptation of the REAPER, which has a far longer history. The first commercial mower was patented in 1847. Modern tractor mowers are distinguished largely according to the way the tractor is attached to them, e.g., trailing mowers, rear-mounted mowers, and side-mounted mowers. The lawn mower is a relatively small machine for cutting the grass of lawns and parks. It is propelled either by hand or by gasoline motors, as are the power mowers used for larger areas. See H. P. Smith, *Farm Machinery and Equipment* (5th ed. 1964); C. Culpin, *Farm Machinery* (8th ed. 1969).

Moza (mō'zə). **1** Son of Caleb. 1 Chron. 2.46. **2** Descendant of Saul. 1 Chron. 8.36,37.

Mozah (mō'zə), town, W of Jerusalem. It is identical with Qaluniya (Israel). Vespasian settled Roman legions here and called it Colonia Amasa. Joshua 18.26.

Mozambique (mō''zəmbēk'), country (1973 est. pop. 8,715,000), 302,328 sq mi (783,030 sq km), SE Africa, bordering on the Indian Ocean in the east, on South Africa and Swaziland in the south, on Rhodesia, Zambia, and Malawi in the west, and on Tanzania in the north. LOURENÇO MARQUES is the capital and largest city; other cities include BEIRA,

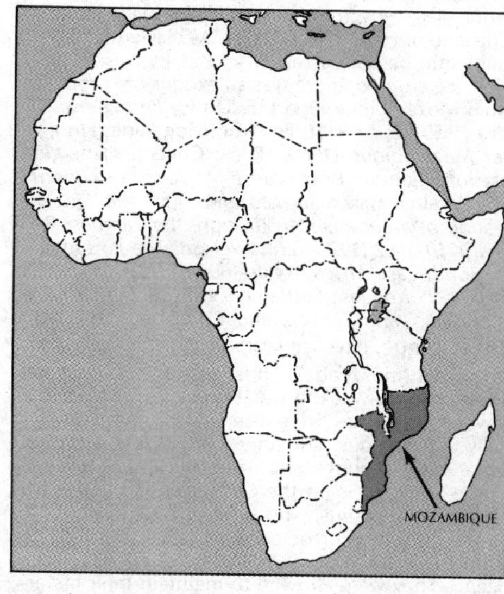

MOÇAMBIQUE, NAMPULA, Porto Amélia, QUELIMANE, Tete, Vila de Antonio Enes, and Vila Cabral. The Mozambique Channel (an arm of the Indian Ocean) separates the country from the island of Madagascar. Mozambique's c.1,600 mi (2,575 km) coastline is interrupted by the mouths of numerous rivers, notably the Ruvuma (which forms part of the boundary with Tanzania), Lúrio, Incomati (Komati), Lugela, Zambezi (which is navigable for c.290 mi/465 km within the territory), Revùe, Save (Sabi), and Limpopo. South of the Zambezi estuary the coastal belt is very narrow, and in the far north the coastline is made up of rocky cliffs. Along the northern coast are numerous islets and lagoons; in the far south is Delagoa Bay. The northern and central interior is mountainous; Monte Binga (7,992 ft/2,436 m), the country's loftiest point, is situated at the Rhodesian border W of Beira. About one third of Lake Nyasa falls within Mozambique's boundaries; Lake Chilwa (Lago Chirua) is at the border with Malawi. Much of the country is covered with savanna; there are also extensive hardwood forests, and palms grow widely along the coast and near rivers. More than 95% of the population is made up of black Africans, virtually all of whom speak a Bantu language. The principal ethnic groups are, in the north, the Yao, Makonde, and Makua; in the center, the Thonga, Chewa, Nyanja, and Sena; and in the south, the Shona and Tonga. Small numbers of Swahili live along the coast. In addition, before the agreement (1974) to grant independence was announced, there were about 170,000 whites (largely Portuguese), most of whom lived in urban areas; approximately 40,000 *mestiços,* or mulattoes (persons of mixed black African and white descent); and a small number of Asians (persons of Indian and Pakistani background) and Chinese. Most of the inhabitants of Mozambique follow traditional religious beliefs; in addition, there are about 1 million Christians (mostly Roman Catholic) and roughly 800,000 Muslims (most of whom live in the north). Mozambique is an overwhelming agricultural country, with the majority of its black African workers engaged in subsistence cultivation. Also, many black Africans grow cash crops on a part-time basis; about 150,000 work on plantations; and approximately 80,000 are employed as migratory laborers in South African mines. The principal food crops are maize, cassava, pulses, rice, potatoes, plantains, groundnuts, and sesame. Cotton (grown mainly in the north) and cashew nuts are the chief cash crops produced on private black African plots; cashew nuts also grow wild in most parts of Mozambique and are gathered by black Africans. The leading plantation crops are sugarcane, tea, copra, and sisal. Large numbers of cattle and goats are raised. There are small forestry and fishing industries. The territory's mineral wealth has not been determined fully, and mining is a minor factor in Mozambique's economy. Mozambique's rudimentary industrial plant is devoted largely to the processing of raw materials. In addition, refined petroleum, construction materials (particularly cement), steel, chemical fertilizer, clothing, and footwear are produced. Work on the first stage of the giant Cabora Bassa hydroelectric project (located on the Zambezi near Tete) was begun in 1969; when finished, the project will have the largest capacity for hydroelectric production (about 18 trillion kwh annually) in Africa and will greatly facilitate the expansion of industry in Mozambique as well as provide power to nearby countries. A smaller hydroelectric plant is situated at Chicamba Real (near Beira) on the Revùe River. The annual cost of Mozambique's imports is usually much higher than its earnings from foreign sales. The principal imports are machinery, foodstuffs, motor vehicles, crude petroleum and petroleum products, textiles, and metals; the chief exports are cotton, sugar, cashew nuts, tea, copra, and timber. Mozambique also derives considerable revenue from handling some of the foreign trade of nearby countries; goods are shipped on rail lines that terminate at the ports of Lourenço Marques, Beira, Nacala, and Lumbo (near Moçambique).

History. Bantu-speaking black Africans began to migrate into the region of Mozambique in the middle of the 1st millennium A.D. From 1000, Arab and Swahili traders settled along parts of the coast, notably at Sofala (near modern Beira), at Cuama (near the Zambezi estuary), and on the site of present-day Inhambane. The traders had contact with the interior, and Sofala was particularly noted as a gold- and ivory-exporting center closely linked with—and at times controlled by—Kilwa (on the coast of modern Tanzania). In 1498, Vasco da Gama, a Portuguese navigator en route around Africa to India, visited Quelimane and Moçambique. Between 1500 and 1502 Pedro Álvares Cabral and Sancho de Tovar, also Portuguese explorers, visited Sofala and Delagoa Bay. In 1505, the Portuguese under Francisco de Almeida occupied Moçambique, and Pedro de Anhaia established a Portuguese settlement at Sofala. The Portuguese also set up trading stations N of Cape Delgado (near the mouth of the Ruvuma), but their main influence (especially after 1600) in E Africa was in the Mozambique region. Between 1509 and 1512 António Fernandes traveled inland and visited the Mwanamutapa kingdom, which controlled the region between the Zambezi and Save rivers and was the source of much of the gold exported at Sofala. Soon after, Swahili traders resident in Mwanamutapa began to redirect the kingdom's gold trade away from Portuguese-controlled Sofala and toward more northern ports. Thus, Portugal became interested in directly controlling the interior. In 1531, posts were established inland at Sena and Tete on the Zambezi, and in 1544 a station was founded at Quelimane. In 1560 and 1561 Gonçalo da Silveira, a Portuguese Jesuit missionary, visited Mwanamutapa, where he quickly made converts, including King Nogomo Mupunzagato. However, the Swahili traders who lived there, fearing for their commercial position, persuaded Nogomo to have Silveira murdered. Between 1569 and 1572 an army of about 1,000 Portuguese under Francisco Barreto attempted to gain control of the interior, but Barreto and most of the soldiers died of disease at Sena. In 1574, an army of 400 men under Vasco Fernandes Homen marched into the interior from Sofala, but most of the men were killed in fighting with black Africans. In the late 16th and early 17th cent. the official Portuguese presence in the interior was limited to small trading colonies along the Zambezi. At the same time Portuguese adventurers began to establish control over large estates (called *prazos*), which resembled feudal kingdoms. They were ruled absolutely and often ruthlessly by their owners (called *prazeros*); black Africans were forced to work on plantations, and considerable slave-raiding was undertaken (especially after 1650). Some of the *prazeros* maintained private armies, and they were generally independent of the Portuguese crown to which they were theoretically subordinate. From about 1628 the Portuguese gained increasing influence in Mwanamutapa, and they became intimately involved in the civil wars that led to the demise of that kingdom by the end of the 17th cent. Mozambique was ruled as part of Goa in India until 1752, when it was given its own administration headed by a captain-general. Although the Portuguese helped introduce several American crops (notably maize and cashew nuts) that became staples of Mozambique's agriculture, the impact of their presence on black African society was mainly destructive. From the mid-18th to the mid-19th cent. large numbers of black Africans were exported as slaves, largely to the Mascarene Islands and to Brazil. In the 1820s and 1830s groups of Nguni-speaking people from S Africa invaded Mozambique; most of the Nguni continued northward into present-day Malawi and Tanzania, but one group, the Shangana, remained in S Mozambique, where they held effective control until the late 19th cent. From the mid-19th cent. to the late 1880s the *mestiço* Joaquim José da Cruz and his son António Nicente controlled trade along the lower Zambezi. Thus, when the scramble for African territory among the European powers began in the 1880s, the Portuguese government had only an insecure hold on Mozambique. Nevertheless, Portugal tried to increase its nominal holdings, partly in an attempt to connect by land its territory in Mozambique and in Angola (in SW Africa). Portuguese claims in present-day Rhodesia and Malawi were strongly opposed by the British, who in 1890 delivered an ultimatum to Portugal demanding that it withdraw from these regions. Portugal complied, and in 1891 a treaty establishing the boundaries between British and Portuguese holdings in SE Africa was negotiated. Beginning in the 1890s and ending only around 1920, the Portuguese established their authority in Mozambique by force of arms against determined black African resistance. Between 1895 and 1897 the Shangana were defeated; between 1897 and 1900 the Nyanja were conquered; in 1912 the Yao were pacified; and in 1917 control was established in extreme S Mozambique. In the 1890s several private companies were founded to develop and administer most of Mozambique. In 1910 the status of the territory was changed from province to colony. After the 1926 revolution in Portugal, the Portuguese government took a more direct interest in Mozambique. The companies lost the right to administer their regions, and at the same time the government furthered economic development by building railroads and by systematically forcing black Africans to work on white-owned land. Portuguese colonial policy was based on the egalitarian theory of "assimilation": if a black African became assimilated to Portuguese culture (i.e., if he was fluent in Portuguese, was Christian, and had a "good character"), he was to be given the same legal status as a white Portuguese. In practice, however, very few black Africans qualified for citizenship (partly because there were inadequate educational opportunities), and they were directed to work for whites or to grow export crops. In 1951 the status of Mozambique was changed to "overseas province" in a move designed to indicate to world opinion that the territory would have increased autonomy; in a similar move in 1972, Mozambique was declared to be a "self-governing state." In both instances, however, Portugal maintained firm control over the territory. Between 1961 and 1963 several laws (one of which abolished forced labor) were passed to improve the living conditions of the black Africans. At the same time, many African nations were becoming independent, and nationalist sentiment was growing in Mozambique. In 1962 several nationalist groups were united to form the Mozambique Liberation Front (Frelimo), headed by Eduardo Mondlane. The Portuguese adamantly refused to give the territory independence, and in 1964 Frelimo initiated guerrilla warfare in N Mozambique. In 1969, Mondlane was killed in Dar es Salaam; he was succeeded by Uria Simango (1969) and by Samora Moisès Machel (1970). By the early 1970s, Frelimo (which had a force of about 7,000 guerrillas) controlled much of central and N Mozambique and was engaged in often fierce fighting with the Portuguese (who maintained an army of about 60,000 in the territory). Frelimo's efficacy was hurt somewhat by internal dissension and by the defection of some of its leaders to the Portuguese side. Frelimo received aid from several foreign sources, including the government of Sweden (beginning in 1969). Roman Catholic missionaries accused the Portuguese of massacring about 400 inhabitants of the village of Wiriyamu (near Tete) in Dec., 1972; Portugal denied the charge. It was reported that beginning in mid-1973 Portugal had resettled about 1 million black Africans in fortified villages to insulate them from Frelimo activities. In April, 1974, the Roman Catholic bishop of Nampula (a white Portuguese) and 11 Roman Catholic missionaries were expelled from Mozambique for protesting the war against Frelimo. They (and also some high-level officers within the Portuguese army) held that peace in the territory could only be achieved by political means and not by using force. On April 25 the government of Portugal was overthrown by the military. The new regime (which favored self-determination for all of Portugal's colonies) made an effort to resolve the conflict in Mozambique by implementing a number of reforms, by releasing political prisoners, by calling for a cease-fire, and by entering (June) into negotiations with Frelimo. The talks resulted in a mutual cease-fire (July 29) and an agreement (Sept. 7) for Mozambique to become independent in June, 1975. In reaction to the agreement, a group of white rebels attempted to seize control of the Mozambique government but were quickly subdued by Portuguese and Frelimo troops. On Sept. 20 an interim black government took office with Joaquim Chissano of Frelimo as premier. As black rule of Mozambique became a reality and as increased racial violence erupted, there was an exodus of Europeans from Mozambique. See J. E. Duffy, *Portuguese Africa* (1959, repr. 1968); Eduardo Mondlane, *Struggle for Mozambique* (1969); R. H. Chilcote, *Emerging Nationalism in Portuguese Africa: Documents* (1972); Allen Isaacman, *Mozambique: The Africanization of a European Institution, the Zambesi Prazos, 1750–1902* (1972); Erik Axelson, *The Portuguese in South-East Africa, 1488–1600* (1973); M. D. D. Newitt, *Portuguese Settlement on the Zambesi: Exploration, Land Tenure, and Colonial Rule* (1973).

Mozambique, city: see MOÇAMBIQUE.

Mozarabs (mōzâr'əbz), Christians of Muslim Spain. Their position was the usual one of Christians and Jews in Islam: they were a separate community, locally autonomous, and they paid a special tax in place of the requirement made of Muslims to serve in the army. In Spain the Christians had their own rulers, called counts, who were directly responsible to the Muslim emir or caliph; their taxes, separate from those of Muslims, were collected by special agents. They were allowed to maintain their hierarchy (the primate of Spain being the archbishop of Toledo), and they used the Visigothic, not the Muslim, canon law. Their liturgy, called the Mozarabic rite, was like that of ancient Gaul. It is preserved only in chapels at Toledo and Salamanca. For one or two periods, notably in the 11th cent., the Mozarabs were persecuted. The chief Mozarab centers were Toledo, Seville, and Córdoba. The Christians were probably Arabic-speaking, and their culture, basically Romance-Visigothic, was heavily influenced by Muslim civilization. In turn, the Mozarabs greatly influenced modern Spanish culture.

Mozart, Wolfgang Amadeus (mōt'särt, Ger. vôlf'gäng ämädā'o͝os mō'tsärt), 1756–91, Austrian composer, b. Salzburg. Mozart represents one of the great peaks in the history of music. His works, written in almost every conceivable genre, combine luminous beauty of sound with classical grace and technical perfection. A remarkable prodigy, he was taught to play the harpsichord, violin, and organ by his father, Leopold, and began composing before he was five. When Mozart was six, he and his older sister, Marianne, were presented by their father in concerts at the court of the Empress Maria Theresa in Vienna and in the principal aristocratic households of central Europe, Paris, and London. His progress as a composer was amazing; by the age of 13 he had written concertos, sonatas, symphonies, a German operetta, *Bastien und Bastienne* (1768), and an Italian opera buffa, *La finta semplice* (1769). During a tour in Italy (1768–71) he absorbed Italian style, received great acclaim for his concerts in Rome and other major cities, and successfully produced his opera *Mitridate, re di Ponto* (1770). In 1771 he was appointed concertmaster to the archbishop of Salzburg; however, he was dissatisfied with his position and the restrictions placed on his work, and after six years he went on tour in search of a better post. He traveled with his mother, visiting numerous cities, including Munich, Mannheim (where he fell in love briefly with the singer Aloysia Weber), and Paris. Despite the successful performance in Paris of his Symphony in D (1778), known as the Paris Symphony, Mozart did not receive much attention there. After resuming his post at Salzburg in 1779, he composed *Idomeneo* (1781) for the Bavarian court. One of the best examples of 18th-century opera seria, it marks the first opera of Mozart's maturity. In the year of its production he resigned from the archbishop's service and moved to Vienna, where in 1782 he married Constanze Weber, the sister of Aloysia. Financial difficulties beset him almost immediately, since he was unable to secure a suitable position and had to earn his living by teaching and giving public concerts. In Vienna, Mozart met Haydn, and the two developed a long and warm friendship that benefited the work of each. Mozart's six string quartets (1782–85) dedicated to Haydn are testimony of his influence. *Die Entführung aus dem Serail* (*The Abduction from the Seraglio,* 1782), a Singspiel combining songs and German dialogue, brought Mozart some success. The Viennese court opera, however, was dominated by Italian tradition, and in his next operas Mozart turned to the style of the Italian opera buffa. With the librettist Lorenzo da Ponte he created the comic masterpiece *Le Nozze di Figaro* (*The Marriage of Figaro,* 1786) which, after a lukewarm reception in Vienna, made a sensation in Prague. From that city also came the commission that resulted in *Don Giovanni* (1787). Although it has come to be regarded as one of the most brilliant operas ever written, it was considered rather difficult by his public, which preferred his more frivolous works. At the death of Gluck (1787), Mozart succeeded him as chamber musician and court composer to Joseph II. His salary was far less than Gluck's had been, however, and his financial troubles persisted to the end of his life. An example of the elegant pieces written for social occasions is the serenade for strings, *Eine Kleine Nachtmusik* (1787). In the space of three months in 1788 Mozart composed his last three symphonies—No. 39 in E Flat, No. 40 in G Minor, and No. 41 in C, called the Jupiter Symphony. These display complete mastery of classical symphonic form as established by Haydn, and at the same time they express intense personal emotion distilled and elevated to a universal plane. In 1789 Mozart traveled to Berlin, where he was presented to King Frederick William II. Mozart's last three string quartets (1789–90) were written for the king, an accomplished cellist. Returning to Vienna, Mozart composed his clarinet quintet (1789); his last opera buffa, *Così fan tutte* (1790), and his last piano concerto, the Piano Concerto in B Flat (1791). In *Die Zauberflöte* (*The Magic Flute,* 1791), with libretto by the actor Emmanuel Schikaneder, Mozart returned to the Singspiel, bringing this form of light musical entertainment to a height of lyrical and symbolic art. Its composition was interrupted by a commission from a wealthy nobleman for a requiem mass and by the composition of *La Clemenza di Tito* (1791), an opera seria for the coronation of Leopold II as king of Bohemia. After the production of *Die Zauberflöte,* Mozart worked feverishly on the requiem, with the foreboding that it would commemorate his own death. He died at the age of 35 without finishing it; the work was completed by his pupil Franz Süssmayr. A thematic catalog of Mozart's works was made by Ludwig von Köchel and published in 1862, an edition revised by Alfred Einstein appearing in 1937. Mozart's works are usually identified by their numbers in this list, e.g., the Piano Concerto in B Flat, K.595. See his letters, ed. by Emily Anderson (tr., 2 vol., 2d ed. 1966); biographies by Eric Blom (rev. ed. 1937, repr. 1949), Alfred Einstein (4th ed. 1959), O. E. Deutsch (2d ed. 1965), and Otto Jahn (tr. 1891, 3 vol.; repr. 1970); studies on his quartets by T. F. Dunhill (1927), his operas by E. J. Dent (2d ed. 1947, repr. 1967), his symphonies by Georges de Saint-Foix (tr. 1947, repr. 1968); János Liebner, *Mozart on the Stage* (1972). Mozart's father, **Leopold Mozart,** 1719–87, besides being the teacher and promoter of his famous son, was a capable composer and author of *A Treatise on the Fundamental Problems of Violin Playing* (1756; tr. 1951), of interest today as a record of 18th-century musical practice.

Mozhaisk (məzhīsk'), city (1967 est. pop. 21,000), W central European USSR, on the Moskva River. It is a rail terminus and has clothing and brick factories. First mentioned in 1231, Mozhaisk was joined with Moscow principality in 1303 and became an important fortress and commercial center. The city was taken by the Germans on Oct. 15, 1941, in what marked their furthest advance directly W of Moscow. It was recaptured during the Soviet winter offensive of 1941–42.

Mrożek, Sławomir (slävô'mĕr mərô'zhĕk), 1930–, Polish dramatist and short-story writer. While working as a journalist for a Kraków newspaper, Mrożek began to write satirical short stories. His first collection, *Słon* (1957, tr. *The Elephant,* 1967) was an immediate success. In the late 1950s he abandoned journalism to write plays, the first of which, *Policja* [the police] (1958), was followed by eight short dramas. His first full-length work, *Tango* (tr. 1968) was staged in 1964 and performed throughout Europe. After the political crisis in 1968, Mrożek left Poland. His often satirical and macabre short stories are marked by extreme brevity. Mrożek's plays belong to the Theater of the Absurd and create their effect through illusion, distortion, and parody. See his *Six Plays* (tr. 1967), *The Ugupu Bird* (tr. 1968), and *Three Plays* (tr. 1972).

MSG: see GLUTAMIC ACID.

MSI: see INTEGRATED CIRCUIT.

Msta (əmstä'), river, c.280 mi (450 km) long, rising N of Vyshne Volochek, NW European USSR, and flowing generally NW into Lake Ilmen near Novgorod. Navigable in its lower course, it is included in the Vyshnevolotsk canal system.

Mtskhet (mətskhyĕt') or **Mtskheta** (-ə), town, SE European USSR, in Georgia, on the Kura River and the Georgian Military Road. It was the capital of ancient Iberia until the 6th cent. A.D., when the capital was moved to Tbilisi; Mtskhet remained the religious center of the country. The Sveti-Tskhoveli cathedral (11th cent.; destroyed by Tamerlane; rebuilt 15th cent.) contains the burial vaults of Georgian rulers. The Samtavro cathedral (11th cent.) was restored in 1903. In the hills near the town are ruins of the Dzhvari temple of the late 6th or early 7th cent.

Mtwara-Mikindani (əmtwä'rä-mēkēndä'nē), municipality (1967 pop. 20,413), capital of Mtwara prov., SE Tanzania, a port on the Indian Ocean. Cashew nuts and lime are processed. It is an export point for copper produced in Zambia.

Muallaqat (mo͞oäl"äkät'), Arabic anthology compiled by the scholar Hammad al Rawiya (d. c.775). It consists of seven (or, in some versions, nine or ten) odes, all by different poets of the 6th or early 7th cent. They are generally esteemed the finest of Arabic odes, and they present an unsurpassed picture of Bedouin life before Islam. The greatest Arabic poets are represented in the Muallaqat. The name also appears as Moallakat. See translation by A. J. Arberry (1957).

Muawiya (mo͞oä'wēä), d. 680, 1st UMAYYAD caliph (661–80), one of the greatest Muslim statesmen; son of Abu Sufyan, a Koreish tribesman of Mecca. He submitted to Islam the year of the surrender of Mecca and became Muhammad's secretary. Under Umar he became the very able governor of Syria. He struggled with ALI over the government of the empire and led in the deposition of HASAN. As caliph he made Islam an autocracy, retaining the old forms of self-government. He secured his domain against aggression by continual raids beyond its borders. Under him the Arabs became an obedient, flexible instrument of war. His policies ended the ancient hostility that long had separated the North and South Arabian tribes, thus making the Muslim empire the remarkably unified force that it was. Muawiya's administration was always tolerant, and he displayed an enlightened point of view in all his dealings. His name is also spelled Moawiyah.

Mucha, Alphonse (älfôNs' mo͝okh'ä), 1860–1939, Czech artist. Mucha's ART NOUVEAU style, characterized by twisting, swirling flower and hair motifs, set the style for poster art for a generation. He created celebrated posters for Sarah Bernhardt and designed sets and costumes for her plays. In his later works, primarily academic paintings, Mucha glorified the Slavic peoples. See biography by his son, Jiri Mucha (1966); his posters and photographs, ed. by Jiri Mucha et al. (1972); his graphic work, ed. by Jiri Mucha (1974).

mucilage (myo͞o'səlĭj), thick, glutinous substance, related to the natural gums, comprised usually of protein, polysaccharides, and uranides. It swells but does not dissolve in water. Mucilage is secreted by the seed covers of various plants, including marsh mallows and flaxes and certain seaweeds; it is the chief constituent of agar. In the plant it sometimes serves to check the loss of water, to facilitate seed dispersal, and to store food. It is used in medicine as an emollient and a demulcent. Mucilage is employed also as an adhesive, and the term is extended to include other slimy adhesives, especially solutions of gum, such as tragacanth mucilage.

mucin: see GLYCOPROTEIN.

muckrakers, name applied to American journalists, novelists, and critics who in the first decade of the 20th cent. attempted to expose the abuses of business and the corruption in politics. The term derives from the word *muckrake* used by President Theodore Roosevelt in a speech in 1906, in which he agreed with many of the charges of the muckrakers but asserted that some of their methods were sensational and irresponsible. He compared them to a character from Bunyan's *Pilgrim's Progress* who could look no way but downward with a muckrake in his hands and was interested only in raking the filth. Since the 1870s there had been recurrent efforts at reform in government, politics, and business, but it was not until the advent of the national mass-circulation magazines such as *McClure's, Everybody's,* and *Collier's* that the muckrakers were provided with sufficient funds for their investigations and with a large enough audience to arouse nationwide concern. All aspects of American life interested the muckrakers, the most famous of whom are Lincoln STEFFENS, Ida Tarbell, David Graham PHILLIPS, Ray Stannard BAKER, Samuel Hopkins ADAMS, and Upton SINCLAIR. In the early 1900s magazine articles that attacked trusts—including those of Charles E. Russell on the beef trust, Thomas Lawson on Amalgamated Copper, and Burton J. Hendrick on life insurance companies—did much to create public demand for regulation of the great combines. The muckraking movement lost support in about 1912. Historians agree that if it had not been for the revelations of the muckrakers the Progressive movement would not have received the popular support needed for effective reform. See Louis Filler, *Crusaders for American Liberalism* (1939); D. M. Chalmers, *The Social and Political Ideas of the Muckrakers* (1964); J. M. Harrison and H. H. Stein, ed., *Muckraking: Past, Present, and Future* (1974).

Muckross, Republic of Ireland: see KILLARNEY.

mucopolysaccharide (myo͞o"kəpŏlēsăk'ərīd), class of polysaccharide molecules composed of amino-sugars chemically linked into repeating units that give a linear unbranched polymeric compound. The monomeric amino-sugar constituents are ordinary monosaccharides that contain a nitrogen atom covalently bound to one of the ring carbons of the sugar portion. The nitrogen is, in turn, either bonded to two atoms of hydrogen (termed a primary amino-group) or to another carbon atom (hence, a substituted amino-group). Thus, the mucopolysaccharides are quite similar structurally to the more well-known animal and plant polysaccharides such as GLYCOGEN and STARCH. CHITIN is a particularly plentiful mucopolysaccharide and serves, like CELLULOSE, as a structural polysaccharide for many phyla of lower plants and animals. The shells of lobsters, crayfish, crabs, insects, and many other invertebrate organisms contain mostly chitin complexed with inorganic salts. The copepods, a group of microscopic marine organisms of the class Crustacea, alone are considered to synthesize about 10^9 tons of chitin per year. Chitin is probably the second most abundant organic compound on earth (the first being cellulose). HEPARIN, an anticoagulant used widely in the treatment of blood clotting disorders, such as pulmonary embolus, is a mucopolysaccharide. Another important compound of this class is hyaluronic acid, a molecule found universally in the connective tissues of animals and in their vitreous and synovial fluids. Hyaluronic acid in association with protein has been isolated from various organisms, and such complexes are thought to bind water in the cellular spaces, thus holding cells together in a jellylike matrix. In addition, such substances may provide the fluids of joints with lubricating and shock-absorbing qualities. Many other mucopolysaccharides are, like hyaluronic acid, associated with proteins, and are therefore also called GLYCOPROTEINS. The separation between mucopolysaccharides and glycoproteins is an arbitrary one, but the latter compounds are distinguished by their relative paucity of sugars.

Mudéjar (mo͞othā'här), name given to the MOORS who remained in Spain after the Christian reconquest but were not converted to Christianity, and to the style of Spanish architecture and decoration, strongly influenced by Moorish taste and workmanship, that they developed. In erecting Romanesque, Gothic, and Renaissance buildings, elements of Islamic art were used, achieving sometimes striking results. The dominant geometrical character, distinctly Oriental, emerged conspicuously in the accessory crafts—tilework, brickwork, wood carving, plaster carving, and ornamental metals. Even after the Muslims themselves were no longer employed, many of their contributions remained as an integral part of Spanish building. A particularly fine Mudéjar example is the Casa de Pilatos, of the early 16th cent., at Seville. See G. G. King, *Mudéjar* (1927).

mudflow: see LANDSLIDE.

mud hen: see RAIL.

mud puppy, common name for North American SALAMANDERS of the genus *Necturus,* found in rivers and streams throughout the E United States and SE Canada. The name derives from an erroneous belief that mud puppies bark. Like its relative, the European olm, the mud puppy exhibits NEOTENY, i.e., it reaches sexual maturity without losing its larval characteristics. Adults have lungs, characteristic of most adult salamanders, as well as gills, characteristic of larvae. Their short, sturdy limbs develop at an early stage. The mud puppy may reach a length of 12 in. (30 cm); it is reddish brown and black-spotted above and grayish below, with conspicuous bushy red gills at the sides of its head. It walks on river bottoms and feeds primarily on crayfish and aquatic plants. Mud puppies are classified in the phylum CHORDATA, subphylum Vertebrata, class Amphibia, order Urodela, family Proteidae.

mudskipper, name for several fishes of the genus *Periophthalmus,* of the GOBY family, found in coastal waters of the Indian and Pacific oceans. They live chiefly on mud flats and in brackish mangrove swamps and are adapted for remaining on dry land when the tide goes out. They have no special air-breathing organs, but absorb oxygen through the skin and gill chambers as long as these remain moist. When out of water, mudskippers use the fleshy bases of their pectoral fins for propulsion on the ground, and members of the larger species can skip faster than a person can move. The mudskipper's diet includes insects and small fish. About 8 in. (20 cm) long, it is olive brown, often with bluish markings. Its protruding, mobile eyes give it a froglike appearance. It is classified in the phylum CHORDATA, subphylum Vertebrata, class Osteichthyes, order Perciformes, family Gobiidae.

Mufaddaliyat (mo͞ofä"däleät') or **Mofaddaliyat** (mō-), great Arabic anthology compiled by the celebrated philologist Al Mufaddal ad-Dabbi (d. c.775). It contains 126 poems, some complete odes, others fragmentary. They are all of the Golden Age of Arabic poetry (500–650) and are the best collection of poems of that period by different authors. There are 67 authors, two of them Christian. The oldest poems in the collection date from c.500. The collection is a valuable source concerning pre-Islamic Arabian life. See tr. by Sir Charles Lyell (3 vol., 1921–24).

Muffat, Georg (gā'ôrk mo͞of'ät), 1645–1704, German organist and composer. Muffat studied in Italy with Arcangelo Corelli and Bernardo Pasquini. He also spent six years in Paris studying Jean Baptiste Lully's music. In 1690 he became *kapellmeister* at Passau. His compositions advanced the concerto grosso form and the art of writing for the organ.

muffler, in automobiles, device designed to reduce the noise from the exhaust of an internal combustion engine. When the exhaust gases from an internal combustion engine are released directly into the atmosphere, they create a loud noise, caused by the passage of the exhaust gases from the high pressure of the cylinder to the normal pressure of the atmosphere. To eliminate or tone down the noise, the gases are led through a pipe to a muffler. Typically a muffler consists of a tubular metal jacket containing perforated pipes and chambers through which the exhaust gases flow before entering the atmosphere. The pipes and chambers are arranged so that the noise from the exhaust gases is reflected back toward the engine or back and forth among the chambers, reducing greatly the amount of noise that is radiated into the environment.

mufti (mŭf'tē), in Muslim law, attorney who writes his opinion (*futwa*) on legal subjects for private clients or to assist judges in deciding cases. The recorded opinions of the muftis are a valuable source of information for the actual working of Muslim law as opposed to the abstract formulation. Only in the fields of marriage, divorce, and inheritance are the *futwas* binding precedents; on other subjects they might be set aside. In the Ottoman Empire the muftis were state officials, and the mufti of Constantinople was the highest of these. The British, who retained the institution in some Muslim areas under their control, gave to the office of HUSSEINI, the grand mufti of Jerusalem, great political importance.

Mufulira (mo͞ofo͞olē'rä), city (1972 est. pop., with suburbs, 124,100), N central Zambia, on the border with Zaïre. It is a copper-mining center, located on the COPPERBELT.

mugger: see CROCODILE.

Muggleton, Lodowicke, 1609–98, English religious leader, a journeyman tailor. With his cousin John Reeve, also a tailor, he founded a new sect, whose adherents were known as Muggletonians. In 1652, Muggleton and Reeve claimed to have been appointed by revelation as the two witnesses of Rev. 11.3, Reeve as the messenger and Muggleton as his mouthpiece in declaring a new spiritual dispensation. They denied the doctrine of the Trinity, teaching that God came on earth to die and left Elijah to be his vice regent in heaven. They held that God had a human body, that Eve was the incarnation of the evil spirit, and that the sun travels around the earth. Both Reeve and Muggleton were imprisoned (1653) for blasphemy; the former died in 1658. Their doctrines gained a number of adherents, and the sect did not die out until about the middle of the 19th cent. An autobiography of Muggleton is included in the posthumously published *Acts of the Witnesses* (1699). See *The Works of J. Reeve and L. Muggleton* (ed. by Joseph Frost and Isaac Frost, 3 vol., 1832).

Mughal: see MOGUL.

Mugodzhar Hills (mo͞ogəjär'), range, c.275 mi (440 km) long, Central Asian USSR, in Kazakhstan. The southern spur of the Urals, it forms the divide between the Caspian and the Aral basins. Its highest point is c.2,150 ft (660 m). There are coal, copper, nickel, and chrome deposits, and mining and small manufacturing are being developed.

mugwumps (mŭg'wŭmps"), slang term in U.S. political history for the Republicans who in 1884 deserted their party nominee, James G. BLAINE, to vote for the Democratic nominee, Grover CLEVELAND. See L. W. Peterson, *The Day of the Mugwump* (1961).

Muhammad (məhăm'əd) [Arab.,=praised], 570?–632, the Prophet of ISLAM, one of the great figures of history, b. Mecca; son of Abdallah ibn Abd-al-Muttalib and his wife Amina, both of the tribe of KURAISH, which ruled Mecca. Abdallah died soon after Muhammad's birth, and the boy was brought up by his uncle Abu Talib. When he was 24, Muhammad married Khadija, a wealthy widow much his senior, whom he seems to have loved dearly; he had no other wife in Khadija's lifetime. Khadija's daughter Fatima was the only child of Muhammad to have issue. Muhammad's position in the community was that of a wealthy merchant. When he was 40, he felt himself selected by God to be the Arab prophet of true religion, for the Arabs, unlike other nations, had hitherto had no prophet. In the cave of Mt. Hira, N of Mecca, he had a vision, in which he was commanded to preach. Thereafter throughout his life he continued to have revelations, many of which have been collected and recorded in the KORAN. His fundamental teachings were: there is one God; man must in all things submit to him; in this world nations have been amply punished for rejecting God's prophets, and heaven and hell are waiting for the present generation; the world will come to an end with a great judgment. He included as religious duties frequent prayer and alms-giving, and he forbade usury. In his first years Muhammad made few converts but many enemies. His first converts were Khadija, ALI (who became the husband of Fatima), and ABU BAKR. From about 620, Muhammad's affairs at Mecca were in crisis; the city was actively hostile, since much of its revenues depended on its pagan shrine, the KAABA, and an attack on the existing Arab religion was an attack on the prosperity of Mecca. While he was gaining only enemies at home, Muhammad's teaching was faring little better abroad; only at Yathrib did it make any headway, and on Yathrib depended the future of Islam. In the summer of 622 a plan was made at Mecca to murder Muhammad, but it was found out, and he escaped in the night from the city and made his way to Yathrib. From this event, the flight, or HEGIRA, of the Prophet (622), Islam counts its dates. Muhammad spent the rest of his life at Yathrib, henceforth called MEDINA, the City of the Prophet. At Medina he built his model theocratic state and from there ruled his rapidly growing empire. Muhammad's lawgiving at Medina is at least theoretically the law of Islam, and in its evolution over the next 10 years the history of the community at Medina is seen. Medina lies on the caravan route N of Mecca, and the Kuraishites of Mecca could not endure the thought of their outlawed relative taking vengeance on his native city by plundering their caravans. A pitched battle between Muhammad's men and the Meccans occurred at a place called Badr, and the ensuing victory of an inferior force from the poorer city over the men of Mecca gave Islam great prestige in SW Arabia. More than a year later the battle of Uhud was fought but with less fortunate results. By this time pagan Arabia had been converted, and the Prophet's missionaries, or legates, were active in the Eastern Empire, in Persia, and in Ethiopia. Muhammad's relations with the Jews and Christians of Arabia gradually worsened. Since he believed firmly in his position as last of the prophets and as successor of Jesus Christ, Muhammad seems at first to have expected that the Jews and Christians would welcome him and accept his revelations, but he was soon disappointed. Medina had a large Jewish population who controlled most of the wealth of the city, and they steadfastly refused to give their new ruler any kind of religious allegiance. Muhammad, after a long quarrel with them, appropriated much of their property, and his first actual conquest was the oasis of Khaibar, occupied by the Jews, in 628. At the same time his teaching became strictly condemnatory of the Jews. He never fell so far afoul of the Christians as of the Jews; but the failure of several missions among them made him distrustful of Christians as well as Jews. His renown increased, and in 629 he made a pilgrimage to Mecca without interference. There he won valuable converts, including Amr and Khalid (who had fought him at Uhud). In 630 he marched against Mecca, which fell without a fight. Arabia was won. Muhammad's private life—in particular his frequent marriages and the troubles of the harem—has received a vast, and perhaps disproportionate, amount of attention. His last favorite wife, AISHA, was able and devoted; he died in her arms June 8, 632. Islam has enshrouded Muhammad's life with a mass of legends and traditions (contained in the *Hadith*). He is considered by most Muslims to have been sinless. His name appears in various forms, two of the most important being Mohammed and the Turkish Mahomet. The biographies and accounts of Muhammad are many. Among recent ones are those by Tor Andrae (tr. 1936, repr. 1971), Essod Bey (tr. 1936), R.U.C. Bodley (1946, repr. 1968), J. B. Glubb (1970), and Maxime Rodinson (tr. 1971).

Muhammad I (Muhammad the Restorer), 1389?–1421, Ottoman sultan (1413–21), son of Beyazid I. By defeating his brothers he reunited most of his father's empire. He consolidated his authority and thus renewed Ottoman power. His son, Murad II, succeeded him.

Muhammad II (Muhammad the Conqueror), 1429–81, Ottoman sultan (1451–81), son and successor of Murad II. He is considered the true founder of the Ottoman Empire (Turkey). He completed the conquest of the Byzantine Empire by successfully storming (1453) Constantinople after a 50-day siege, for which he constructed the largest cannons the world had yet known. Byzantine Emperor CONSTANTINE XI fell in the heroic defense. Muhammad moved his capital from Adrianople to Constantinople and restored the greatness of that city by settling there the populations of other conquered towns. To Greek and Armenian citizens of Constantinople he granted the privileges that they were to enjoy throughout Ottoman rule, including the freedom to practice Orthodox Eastern Christianity. The Church of Hagia Sophia became a mosque. Muhammad then conquered the Balkan Peninsula, taking Greece, Bosnia, and several Venetian possessions in the Aegean islands. The khan of Crimea became his ally and vassal. However, his further advance was checked at Belgrade by John HUNYADI, in Albania by SCANDERBEG until 1478, and in Rhodes by the Knights Hospitalers under AUBUSSON. In Asia, Muhammad annexed the empire of Trebizond, ended most independent Turkish dynasties, and subdued the emirate of Karamania, putting to death its ruling family, who were Seljuk Turks. In 1480 he captured Otranto, in Italy, but the expedition had no results. Muhammad was a patron of learning and an accomplished linguist as well as a great commander. His son, Beyazid II, succeeded him. For a contemporary account of Muhammad II, see Kritoboulos, *A History of Mehmed the Conqueror* (tr. 1954).

Muhammad III, 1567–1603, Ottoman sultan (1595–1603), son and successor of Murad III to the throne of the Ottoman Empire (Turkey). Muhammad, who was a provisional governor under his father, was the last sultan to have any experience in public affairs before ascending the throne. He fought inconclusively in Hungary and in his last year lost Tabriz to Shah Abbas I of Persia. His son Ahmed I succeeded him.

Muhammad IV, 1641–92, Ottoman sultan (1648–87). He was proclaimed sultan of the Ottoman Empire (Turkey) by the corps of JANISSARIES after the deposition and murder of his father, Sultan İbrahim. Disorder and corruption continued until the KÖPRÜLÜ family obtained (1656) the office of grand vizier (chief executive officer) and restored order. However, the empire suffered severe setbacks. Algiers freed itself (1669) from Ottoman suzerainty. In 1683 the Turks, in alliance with the Hungarian THÖKÖLY, besieged Vienna but were repulsed by King John III of Poland. Turkish weakness being apparent, a Holy League was formed to carry the war into Ottoman territory. After the Turkish defeat (1687) at Mohacs by Charles V of Lorraine, Muhammad was deposed. His brother, Sulayman II, succeeded him.

Muhammad V, 1844–1918, Ottoman sultan (1909–18). He succeeded to the throne of the Ottoman Empire (Turkey) when the liberal Young Turk revolution of 1909 deposed his brother, Abd al-Hamid II. He exercised no actual power under the new constitution, and the administration was dominated by ENVER PASHA. During Muhammad's reign Turkey lost most of its remaining European possessions in the BALKAN WARS (1912–13) and lost Tripoli to Italy in 1911–12. Germany gained increasing influence over Turkish affairs, resuming the construction of the BAGHDAD RAILWAY in 1911. Muhammad sided with the Central Powers in World War I. He died shortly before the Turkish surrender and was succeeded by his brother, Muhammad VI.

Muhammad VI, 1861–1926, last Ottoman sultan (1918–22), brother and successor of Muhammad V. He became sultan of the Ottoman Empire (Turkey) near the end of World War I and soon capitulated to the Allies, who occupied Constantinople and sought to rule through him what remained of Turkey. He consented to the extremely harsh peace terms of the Allies (see SÈVRES, TREATY OF). In the meantime Kemal ATATÜRK gained control over Anatolia; after his victory over the Greeks he turned on Muhammad, who was deposed in 1922. The sultanate was abolished and the republic of Turkey established. Muhammad fled and died in exile. After his flight he was deposed as caliph, in which capacity he was succeeded by his cousin, Abd al-Majid. In 1924 the CALIPHATE was abolished and all members of the Ottoman house were exiled. Muhammad VI died at San Remo, Italy.

Muhammad V (Sidi Muhammad ben Youssef), 1910–61, king of Morocco (1957–61). He succeeded his father, Moulay Youssef, as sultan in 1927. An ardent nationalist, he was deposed and exiled (1953) by the French. After strong nationalist pressure, the French brought (1955) Muhammad ben Youssef from exile in Madagascar to France, where he was once again recognized as sultan. He obtained (1956) full recognition of Moroccan sovereignty from France and Spain, and in 1957 he took the title of king of Morocco. He was succeeded (1961) by his son, Moulay Hassan, who became Hassan II.

Muhammad, Elijah, 1897–, American black nationalist leader, b. near Sandersville, Ga. Originally named Elijah Poole, he left home at 16 and worked at various jobs. In 1923 he settled in Detroit and became an automobile assembly-line worker. In 1931 he became a follower of Wali Farad, or W. D. Fard, who had established a Temple of Islam in Detroit. When Farad disappeared in 1934, Poole (now renamed Muhammad) assumed leadership of the movement that was to become known as the BLACK MUSLIMS. He was imprisoned during World War II for encouraging resistance to the draft. Muhammad calls himself the "Messenger of Allah" and preaches that the only salvation for black people in the United States lies in withdrawal into an autonomous state. He retains almost autocratic control over his movement.

Muhammad Ahmad: see MAHDI.

Muhammad Ali, 1769?–1849, pasha of Egypt after 1805. He was a common soldier who rose by his military skill and political acumen. In 1799 he commanded a Turkish army in an unsuccessful attempt to drive Napoleon from Egypt. As pasha he was virtually independent of his nominal overlord, the Ottoman sultan. He modernized his armed forces and administration, created schools, and began many public works, particularly irrigation projects. The cost of these reforms bore heavily on the peasants without bringing them any benefits. In 1811 he exterminated the leaders of the MAMELUKES, who had ruled Egypt almost uninterruptedly since 1250. With his son, IBRAHIM PASHA, he conducted successful campaigns in Arabia against the Wahabis. In 1820 he sent armies to conquer the Sudan. He scored great successes fighting for the Ottoman sultan in Greece until the British, French, and Russians combined to defeat his fleet at Navarino in 1827. The sultan, Mahmud II, to win his intervention in the Greek revolt, had promised to make him governor of Syria. When the sultan refused to hand over the province, Muhammad Ali invaded Syria with great success. In 1839 he attacked his overlord in Asia Minor, but he was forced to desist when he lost the support of France and was threatened by united European opposition. In a compromise arrangement the Ottoman sultan made the governorship of Egypt hereditary in Muhammad's line. Toward the end of his life he became insane. See H. H. Dodwell, *The Founder of Modern Egypt* (1931).

Muhammad Ali, 1872–1925, shah of Persia (1906–9), son of MUZAFFAR AD-DIN Shah. Muhammad Ali, who was an opponent of constitutional government, began to rule at a critical period just after the constitution of 1906 had been granted. His struggle with the nationalists led to the bombing of the newly established parliament. He called in the aid of the Russians, who organized a Cossack brigade for him. His attempt to overthrow the constitutional government brought on two short civil wars (1908–9). Muhammad Ali was finally forced to abdicate in favor of his son AHMAD MIRZA. Later he attempted with Russian help to regain his throne, but he failed and afterward lived in exile in Russia.

Muhammad of Ghor, d. 1206, Afghan conqueror of N India. A brother of the sultan of Ghor, he was made governor of Ghazni in 1173 and from there launched a series of invasions of India. By 1186 he had conquered the Muslim principalities in the Punjab. He was severely defeated by the Rajputs under PRITHVI RAJ in 1191, but the following year he routed their army, and Delhi was captured. Muhammad's generals then overran Bihar and Bengal. He succeeded his brother as sultan in 1202 but was murdered in 1206. After his death his empire in N India fell apart and passed to his generals, one of whom founded the DELHI SULTANATE.

Muhammad Reza Shah Pahlevi (mo͞ohäm'mäd rĭzä shä pă'ləvē), 1919–, shah of Iran (1941–). Educated in Switzerland, he returned (1935) to Iran to attend the military academy in Teheran, where he learned several languages and became an accomplished sportsman. He ascended the throne in 1941, after his father, suspected of collaboration with the Germans, was deposed by British and Soviet troops. He narrowly escaped assassination (1949) by a member of the leftist Tudeh party, and in 1953 he briefly fled the country after a clash with the supporters of Muhammad Mussadegh. A moderate, the shah launched (1963) a reform program that included land redistribution to the peasants, the promotion of literacy, and the emancipation of women. After the departure of British forces from the Persian Gulf in the 1960s, the shah sought to transform Iran into the major military power of the area. Iran's position as one of the leading petroleum producers in the world has greatly strengthened the Shah's international position.

Muhammerah: see KHORRAMSHAHR, Iran.

Mühlberg (mül'bĕrkh), town, Leipzig dist., S East Germany, on the Elbe River. In 1547, Emperor Charles V defeated the SCHMALKALDIC LEAGUE there and captured Elector John Frederick I of Saxony.

Mühlenberg, Heinrich Melchior (mĕl'khēôr mü'lənbĕrk), 1711–87, American Lutheran clergyman, b. Germany, educated at Göttingen and at Halle. He arrived (1742) in Pennsylvania to serve as pastor of several congregations in and near Philadelphia, but he soon became the leader of all the Lutheran groups in the colonies. Often called the patriarch of Lutheranism in America, he organized (1748) the first Lutheran synod in the country. See his journals (3 vol., 1942–58); biography by W. J. Mann (1911). **John Peter Gabriel Muhlenberg** (mū'lənbûrg), 1746–1807, American clergyman, Revolutionary officer, and legislator, eldest son of Heinrich, was born in Trappe, Pa., and studied at Halle. Although he was raised a Lutheran and studied for the Lutheran ministry, he was ordained an Episcopalian to insure his legal status as a clergyman in Woodstock, Va. In 1776 he left his church in Woodstock to raise and lead a regiment in the American Revolution. Throughout the war he served with distinction, retiring (1783) as brevet major general. He entered political life in Pennsylvania and served three terms in the U.S. House of Representatives. **Frederick Augustus Conrad Muhlenberg,** 1750–1801, Lutheran clergyman and legislator, second son of Heinrich, also was born at Trappe, Pa., and educated at Halle. He was pastor of various churches in Pennsylvania and pastor (1773–76) of Christ (Lutheran) Church, New York City. Because of his sympathies with the Revolutionary cause, he left New York City (then under British occupation) and returned to Pennsylvania. Muhlenberg was a delegate (1779–80) to the Continental Congress and a member (1789–97) of the House of Representatives, twice serving as speaker. He cast the decisive vote on the appropriations bill that ensured the ratification of JAY'S TREATY. See P. A. W. Wallace, *The Muhlenbergs of Pennsylvania* (1950).

Muhlenberg, William Augustus (myo͞o'lənbûrg), 1796–1877, American Episcopal clergyman, hymn writer, and philanthropist, b. Philadelphia. He was a great-grandson of Heinrich Melchior Mühlenberg. Baptized in the Lutheran communion, he joined the Episcopal Church, in which he was ordained priest in 1820. In 1846, after pastorates in Lancaster, Pa., and Flushing, N.Y., he became rector of the Church of the Holy Communion, New York City. Muhlenberg helped found (1858) St. Luke's Hospital, of which he was first pastor and superintendent. He also founded St. Johnland, an industrial Christian settlement on Long Island. He was an influential leader in movements advancing Christian brotherhood and the unity of evangelical bodies throughout the world. Among his best-known hymns are *I Would Not Live Alway* and *Saviour, Who Thy Flock Art Feeding.* See biography by A. W. Skardon (1971).

Muhlenberg College, at Allentown, Pa.; Lutheran in America; coeducational; founded 1848 as Allentown Seminary, chartered 1864 as Allentown Collegiate Institute and Military Academy. The college adopted its present name in 1867.

Mühlhausen in Thüringen (mülhou'zən ĭn tür'ĭng-ən) or **Mühlhausen,** city (1970 pop. 45,385), Erfurt district, SW East Germany, on the Unstrut River. It is a major center for the manufacture of textiles and clothing. Other products include paper, machinery, and furniture. Barite is mined nearby. Fortified (10th cent.) by Henry I, Mühlhausen was a favorite residence of the German rulers. It was made a free imperial city in 1180 and later (13th cent.) joined the Hanseatic League. It became (16th cent.) an Anabaptist center and was dominated during the Peasants' War by Thomas Münzer, who was executed there in 1525. Mühlhausen changed hands several times before passing in 1815 to Prussia. Noteworthy structures of the city include several Gothic churches, a 17th-century city hall, medieval fortifications, and many houses dating from the 16th, 17th, and 18th cent.

Muir, Alexander (myo͝or), 1830–1906, Canadian song writer, b. Scotland. In 1867 he wrote the words and music for "The Maple Leaf Forever," which is regarded by many as the national hymn of Canada.

Muir, Edwin, 1887–1959, English author, b. Orkney, Scotland. He moved with his family to Glasgow in 1901, where he remained for 18 years. In 1919 he went to London and joined the staff on the *New Age.* During the early 1920s he traveled on the Continent, supporting himself chiefly with contributions to the *Freeman.* At the age of 35 he turned to writing poetry, producing such collections as *Chorus of the Newly Dead* (1926) and *The Labyrinth* (1949). However, it was not until his *Collected Poems* appeared in 1952 that Muir achieved recognition. A visionary poet, he sought in his personal, often dreamlike verse to understand the meaning of the spiritual universe. Muir is also well known as a literary critic. Included among his critical writings are *The Structure of the Novel* (1928), *The Present Age, from 1914* (1939), and *Essays on Literature and Society* (1949). His other works include translations of Kafka; three novels, *The Marionette* (1927), *The Three Brothers* (1931), and *Poor Tom* (1932); and an excellent autobiography, *The Story and the Fable* (1940), which later appeared in an enlarged edition, *An Autobiography* (1954). See his letters, ed. by P. H. Butter (1974); biography by P. H. Butter (1967); study by Elizabeth Huberman (1971).

Muir, John, 1838–1914, American naturalist, b. Dunbar, Scotland, studied at the Univ. of Wisconsin. He came to the United States in 1849 and settled in California in 1868. In recognition of his efforts as a conservationist and crusader for national parks and reservations, Muir Woods National Monument was named for him. He made extended trips throughout the country, often on foot; he also traveled in Alaska (discovering Muir glacier) and in Russia, India, and Australia. His books include *The Mountains of California* (1894), *The Story of My Boyhood and Youth* (1913), *Steep Trails* (1918). *John of the Mountains* (1938; ed. by L. M. Wolfe) contains his journals. See biography by W. F. Bade (2 vol., 1924, repr. 1972); study by Robert Silverberg (1972).

Muir Glacier: see GLACIER BAY NATIONAL MONUMENT.

Muir Woods National Monument: see NATIONAL PARKS AND MONUMENTS (table).

Mujibur Rahman (mo͞ojēbo͝or' rämän'), 1920–, East Pakistan (now Bangladesh) political leader, prime minister of Bangladesh (1972–), popularly known as Sheikh Mujib. During British rule he worked for Muslim rights, but after Pakistan gained its independence (1947) he became more concerned with East Pakistan, feeling that his people, the Bengalis, were unfairly dominated by West Pakistan. In 1949 he helped to found the AWAMI LEAGUE, Pakistan's first opposition party, of which he became general secretary (1953) and later president (1966). His opposition led to numerous prison terms, but he also held public office in East Pakistan and became a popular hero. The conflict between East and West Pakistan came to a head after the 1970 elections, in which Mujib's Awami League won a majority; Zulfikar Ali BHUTTO, leader of the major West Pakistan party, refused to agree to Mujib's demands for autonomy for East Pakistan. Further attempts at agreement failed, and civil war broke out in March, 1971, when Pakistani troops launched attacks in East Pakistan. Their terrorist campaign was initially successful, but, with the aid of India, East Pakistan, renamed Bangladesh, crushed the Pakistani army in late 1971 (see INDIA-PAKISTAN WARS). Mujib, who had been imprisoned in West Pakistan, was released in early 1972 and returned to assume the post of prime minister. He attempted to rebuild his devastated country and worked toward normalizing relations with Pakistan. In Jan., 1975, a constitutional change made Mujib president with dictatorial powers.

Mukachevo, Czech *Mukačevo* (both: mo͞o'kăchĕvô), Hung. *Munkács,* city (1969 est. pop. 61,000), extreme SW European USSR, in the Ukraine. It is a rail terminus and highway junction and has food, tobacco, beer, wine, furniture, textile, and timber industries. From the 9th to the 11th cent., Mukachevo was part of the Kievan state. Taken by the Hungarians in 1018, it became a dominion center of the Hungarian kings. It later (15th cent.) developed as a prominent trade and craft center. Part of the Transylvanian duchy from the 16th cent., Mukachevo then came under Austrian control and was made a key fortress of the Austro-Hungarian empire. Mukachevo passed to Czechoslovakia in 1919, was under German-Hungarian occupation from 1938 to 1944, and was ceded to the Ukrainian SSR in 1945. The city's architectural landmarks include a castle and a monastery (both 14th cent.) and a wooden church built in the Ukrainian architectural style (18th cent.).

Mukalla (məkä'lə, mo͞okăl'ə), town (1970 est. pop. 65,000), Southern Yemen, a port on the Gulf of Aden. It is the chief settlement of the Hadhramaut and the capital of the former sultanate of Qaiti. Fish products, tobacco, and coffee are exported.

Mukden: see SHEN-YANG, China.

Mukden Incident: see MANCHURIAN INCIDENT.

Mulatas (mo͞olä'täs), archipelago off the northeast coast of Panama. It consists of 332 coral islands. The inhabitants are almost pure-blooded aborigines of Carib origin; fishing and coconut gathering are the chief occupations. Protected by a treaty with the government of Panama, the Indians did not consent to scientific observation of their culture and visits of tourists until the late 1940s.

mulberry, common name for the Moraceae, a family of deciduous or evergreen trees and shrubs, often climbing, mostly of pantropical distribution, and characterized by milky sap. The related hemp family, whose plants do not contain latex, were formerly included in this family. The mulberry family is most important as the basis of the silkworm industry; silkworms feed on the leaves of the mulberries (genus *Morus*) and sometimes of the Osage orange (*Maclura pomifera*). Several genera bear edible fruit, e.g., *Morus, Ficus* (the fig genus), and *Artocarpus,* which includes the breadfruit and related species. Mulberry fruits are tender and juicy and resemble blackberries. The white mulberry (*M. alba*) has been cultivated in China since very early times. In the Middle Ages it began to replace the black mulberry (*M. nigra*), which had been grown by the Greeks and Romans and, from the 9th cent., by the people of N Europe for silkworm culture. Both the white and the red mulberry (*M. rubra,* native to North America) have been cultivated in America since colonial times, but the lack of cheap hand labor has prevented the establishment of a silkworm industry. In the South the fruit of *M. rubra* is made into wine and is considered a valuable agricultural and wildlife feed. In Greek legend the berries of the white mulberry turned red when its roots were bathed by the blood of the lovers Pyramis and Thisbe, who killed themselves. The Osage orange, also called bowwood because it was used by the Osage Indians to make bows, is a hardy tree native to the S central United States. Cultivated elsewhere, often as a hedge plant because of its spiny, impenetrable branches, it is a source of a flexible and durable

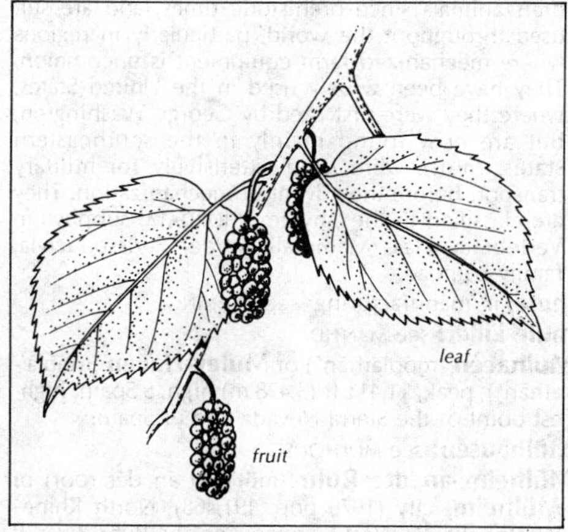

Red mulberry, Morus rubra

wood and of a yellow-orange dye, from the root bark, that is similar to the more widely used fustic (*Chlorophora tinctoria*). The heartwood of fustic yields a yellowish or olive dye, also called fustic, that has been used chiefly for dyeing woolens; it has largely been replaced by synthetic aniline dyes. In its native habitat of Central and South America, the fustic is also a timber tree. Fiber plants of the mulberry family include the paper mulberry (*Broussonetia papyrifera*) and the upas tree (*Antiaris toxicara*) of the Far East tropics, where the bast fiber is utilized for rough fabrics and for paper, often after a crude retting process. The latex of the upas [Malay,=poison tree] contains a potent drug used for arrow poison; the similarly employed strychnine tree of the logania family is sometimes also called upas. The breadfruit (*Artocarpus ultilis*) is cultivated as a staple food plant in the Pacific tropics and in the West Indies, where it was introduced from Polynesia in the late 18th cent.; the *Bounty* was carrying breadfruit plants to Jamaica when the famous mutiny occurred. Its wood, fiber, and latex are also variously utilized locally. The important FIG genus includes fruit trees, ornamentals (e.g., the rubber plant), and several species renowned in the religion and legends of India (e.g., the BANYAN and the BO TREE). The mulberry family is classified in the division MAGNOLIOPHYTA, class Magnoliopsida, order Urticales.

mulch, any material, usually organic, that is spread on the ground to protect the soil and the roots of plants from the effects of soil crusting, erosion, or freezing; it is also used to retard the growth of weeds. A mulch may be made of materials such as straw, sawdust, grass clippings, peat moss, leaves, or paper. For large areas under cultivation a tilled layer of soil serves the purpose of a mulch.

mule, hybrid offspring of a male donkey (see ASS) and a female HORSE, bred as a work animal. The name is also sometimes applied to the hinny, the offspring of a male horse and female donkey; hinnies are considered inferior to mules. The mule has many donkey characteristics—long ears, a. tufted tail, slender legs, small hooves, and a loud bray—but it resembles a horse in size and strength. Most mules weigh from 1,100 to 1,400 lb (500-640 kg). They lack the speed of horses, but are more surefooted and have great powers of endurance. Like donkeys, they are of a cautious and temperamental disposition and require expert handling to perform well. Both sexes are sterile. Mules have been bred as pack and draft animals since prehistoric times, and are still used throughout the world, particularly in regions where mechanized farm equipment is uncommon. They have been widely used in the United States, where they were first bred by George Washington, but are now found mainly in the southeastern states. Mules were used extensively for military transport before the advent of mechanization. They are classified in the phylum CHORDATA, subphylum Vertebrata, class Mammalia, order Perissodactyla, family Equidae.

mule, in manufacturing: see SPINNING.

mule killer: see MANTID.

Mulhacén (mo͞olāthän') or **Muley-Hacén** (mo͞olā'-äthän'), peak, 11,411 ft (3,478 m) high, S Spain; highest point of the Sierra Nevada and of Spain.

Mülhausen: see MULHOUSE.

Mülheim an der Ruhr (mül'hīm än dĕr ro͞or) or **Mülheim,** city (1970 pop. 191,468), North Rhine-Westphalia, W West Germany, on the Ruhr River. It is an industrial center of the RUHR district. The city formerly produced mainly coal and steel, but in the mid-20th cent. its products were diversified to include machinery, precision and optical instruments, clothing, and chemicals. Mülheim was chartered in 1808. There is a 12th-century castle in the city.

Mulholland, John (mŭl'hŏl"ənd), 1898-1970, American magician, b. Chicago, Ill. Mulholland came to be one of the most celebrated of stage performers of magic. Among his written works are *Quicker than the Eye* (1932), *Story of Magic* (1935), *The Art of Illusion* (1944), and *Book of Magic* (1963).

Mulhouse (mülo͞oz'), Ger. *Mülhausen*, city (1968 pop. 118,558), Haut-Rhin dept., E France, in Alsace, on the Ill River and the Rhône-Rhine canal. Cotton, wool, and clothing are the chief manufactures; machinery, chemicals, automobile parts, and steel pipes are also produced. Nearby are the only important potash mines in W Europe. Mulhouse became a free imperial city in the 13th cent. In 1515 it became an allied member (but not a canton) of the Swiss Confederation, and in 1586 it became a neutral republic. In 1798, Mulhouse voted to unite with France. After the Franco-Prussian War (1871), the city was made a part of Germany until 1918. Mulhouse has a 16th-century town hall and several narrow, winding streets and old houses.

Mull, island (1961 pop. 3,185), 351 sq mi (909 sq km), Argyllshire, NW Scotland, one of the Inner Hebrides, separated from the mainland by the Sound of Mull and the Firth of Lorn. The land is mountainous, rising from the deeply indented coast line to 3,169 ft (966 m) at Ben More. Mull has gardens and farms. Tobermory, a summer resort, is the chief town. A Spanish treasure galleon sank in its bay in 1588. There are several medieval castles. In 1975, Mull became part of the Stratclyde region.

Mullan, John, 1830-1909, American army officer and pioneer road builder, b. Norfolk, Va. After graduation (1852) from West Point, he helped (1853-55) to survey a route for a railroad from St. Paul, Minn., to the Pacific. Later he was (1855-58) in regular service in the army. From 1858 to 1863 he was engaged in building a military road from Fort Benton, Mont., at the head of navigation on the Missouri River, to Walla Walla, Wash. This road, known as the Mullan Wagon Road, was important in opening up the country to miners and settlers. His report (1863) to the Secretary of War and his *Miners' and Travelers' Guide* (1865) added greatly to the knowledge of the country. He resigned from the army in 1863 and after two unsuccessful commercial ventures took up the practice of law.

mullein: see FIGWORT.

Müller, Frederik Paludan: see PALUDAN-MÜLLER.

Müller, Friedrich Maximilian: see MÜLLER, MAX.

Müller, Hermann (hĕr'män mül'ər), 1876-1931, German statesman. A Social Democrat, he succeeded in 1919 to the post of German foreign minister and signed the Treaty of Versailles. He was chancellor in 1920 and again from 1928 to 1930. During the second tenure Germany accepted the KELLOGG-BRIAND PACT and the YOUNG PLAN. Largely because of the diplomatic efforts of Müller's foreign minister, Gustav STRESEMANN, the occupation of the Rhineland was ended in 1929. Müller's cabinet was the last parliamentary government of the Weimar Republic. He was succeeded by Heinrich BRÜNING.

Muller, Hermann Joseph (mŭl'ər), 1890-1967, American geneticist and educator, b. New York City, grad. Columbia (B.A., 1910; Ph.D., 1916). He taught (1915-18) at Rice Institute, Texas, at Columbia (1918-20), and at the Univ. of Texas from 1920 until he became senior geneticist (1933-37) of the Institute of Genetics in Moscow. In 1945 he became professor of zoology at Indiana Univ. His method for recognizing spontaneous gene MUTATION led to his discovery of a technique for artificially inducing mutations by means of X rays that has since had broad theoretical and practical application. For this discovery he was awarded the 1946 Nobel Prize in Physiology and Medicine. His writings include *Out of the Night* (1935), *Genetics, Medicine, and Man* (1947; written with others) and *Studies in Genetics* (1962), his selected papers. He also wrote articles on the biological effects of atomic radiation.

Müller, Johannes: see REGIOMONTANUS.

Müller, Johannes Peter (yōhän'əs pā'tər), 1801-58, German physiologist and anatomist. From 1833 until the end of his career he was professor at Berlin. He was famed as a teacher; for his extensive research in many fields, including embryology, general and microscopic pathology, biochemistry, comparative anatomy, psychology, and marine zoology; and for his theories on color vision and voice production. As a result of his experiments in neurology he proposed the law of specific energies, i.e., that each sensory nerve produces its own specific sensation (e.g., any stimulation to the optic nerve results in a sensation of light).

Müller, Johannes von (yōhä'nəs fən mül'ər), 1752-1809, Swiss historian. He spent much of his life in Germany, where he held political posts under the elector of Mainz, the king of Prussia, and King Jérôme Bonaparte of Westphalia. His patriotic history of Switzerland (5 vol., 1786-1808, in German), long since superseded, was hailed in its day with great enthusiasm. Evoking the past, Müller praised traditional institutions. He fully accepted the William Tell legend; from Müller's history Schiller drew the material for his drama.

Müller, Karl Otfried (kärl ôt'frēt'), 1797-1840, German classical scholar and archaeologist. He was professor of classics at the Univ. of Göttingen (1819-39), lecturing on art history, literature, mythology, and archaeology. His aim was to promote the study of Greek life as a whole, and his work helped to develop a new conception of Hellenism. In his writings he sought to relate classical civilization to the present. Müller was a pioneer in the research into the sources of Greek myths. His chief work was the *Geschichte hellenischer Stämme und Städte* [history of Hellenic origins and cities], of which he completed two volumes (1820, 1824). He published his *Manual of the Archaeology of Art* in 1830 (tr. 1847). His history of the literature of ancient Greece appeared in 1840. See J. E. Sandys, *A History of Classical Scholarship*, Vol. III (1908).

Müller, Max (Friedrich Maximilian Müller, Friedrich Max Müller, or Friedrich Max-Müller), 1823-1900, German philologist and Orientalist, b. Dessau; son of the poet Wilhelm Müller. After specializing in Sanskrit in Germany, he went to Oxford, where he lived for the remainder of his life. Müller did more than any other scholar to popularize philology and mythology, particularly in his lectures *Science of Language* (1861, 1863). He advanced the theory that myths originated from metaphors describing natural pnenomena. Greatly interested in comparative religion, he wrote works on Indian religion and philosophy, including the standard edition of the *Rig-Veda with Commentary* (6 vol., 1849-73). From c.1875 until his death Müller was engaged in his greatest work, the editing of *Sacred Books of the East* (51 vol.), being translations of important Oriental non-Christian religious writings. See his memoirs (tr. 1906); study by J. H. Voigt (1967).

mullet: see SILVERSIDES.

mullion (mŭl'yən), in architecture, a slender, upright intermediate member that subdivides an opening, as a division between panes of a window or between adjacent windows. Although the mullion occurs in some form in nearly all architectural styles, it is perhaps most characteristic of the elaborate Gothic systems of stone tracery, where, often exquisitely slender and contoured, it is used to divide the large windows into areas suitable for glazing.

Mull of Galloway (găl'əwā), headland, 239 ft (73 m) high, Wigtownshire, SW Scotland, the southernmost extremity of Scotland.

Mulock, Dinah Maria: see CRAIK, DINAH MARIA MULOCK.

Mulock, Sir William, 1844-1944, Canadian statesman and jurist, b. Ontario. A lawyer, he served (1882-1905) as a Liberal in the House of Commons. As postmaster general (1896-1905) in Wilfrid Laurier's cabinet, he was responsible for securing (1898) the adoption of penny postage within the British Empire, and in 1900 he became minister of labor. In 1905 he became chief justice of the exchequer division of Canada's supreme court. From 1923 to 1936 he was chief justice of Ontario. He was (1924-44) chancellor of the Univ. of Toronto. His longevity and his distinguished career won for him the title "Canada's grand old man." He was knighted in 1902.

Mulready, William (məlrĕd'ē), 1786-1863, Irish genre painter. He began as a drawing master and an illustrator of children's books. After 1809 he devoted himself to genre subjects and gained a considerable reputation. His popular paintings show the influences of Sir David Wilkie and of the Dutch school. Well-known examples are *The Sonnet* and *First Love* (both: Victoria and Albert Mus.) and *Snow Scene* (Tate Gall., London). Mulready illustrated Goldsmith's *Vicar of Wakefield.*

Multan (mo͞oltän'), city (1972 metropolitan area est. pop. 723,000), E central Pakistan, in the Punjab. It is an important road and rail junction, an agricultural center, and a market for textiles, leather goods, and other products. Its proximity to mountain passes into Afghanistan makes Multan a trading center for that country as well. The city's industries include metalworking, flour and oil milling, and the manufacture of cotton textiles, shoes, carpets, and glass. Multan is also known for its handicrafts, especially pottery and enamel work. One of the Indian subcontinent's oldest cities, Multan derives its name from an idol in the temple of the sun god, a shrine of the pre-Muslim period. The city was conquered (c.326 B.C.) by Alexander the Great, visited (A.D. 641) by the Chinese Buddhist scholar Hsüan-tsang, taken (8th cent.) by the Arabs, and captured by Muslim Turkish conqueror Mahmud of Ghazni in 1005 and by Tamerlane in 1398. In the 16th and 17th cent., Multan enjoyed peace under the early Mogul emperors. In 1818 the city was seized by Ranjit Singh, leader of the Sikhs. The British held it from 1848 until Pakistan achieved independence in 1947. Landmarks include an old fort containing the 14th-century tombs of two Muslim saints.

Multatuli: see DEKKER, EDUARD DOUWES.

multiple birth, bringing forth of more than one offspring at birth. Although many smaller mammals bear several young at a time, multiple births are relatively uncommon in man and other primates. Twinning, the process that leads to the production of more than one offspring, results in twins, and with decreasing frequency, triplets, quadruplets, quintuplets, and sextuplets. In the one-egg, or identical, type of twinning, a single fertilized ovum divides to form two complete organisms. Such twins are always of the same sex, are usually extraordinarily similar in physical appearance, and have identical blood group types. Twinning to form one-egg identical twins usually takes place early in pregnancy. If considerable development has taken place before the twinning occurs, there may be an incomplete separation of the two embryos resulting in conjoined offspring called SIAMESE TWINS. Fraternal twins are those that develop from two separate ova, each fertilized by a sperm. Fraternal twins may or may not be of the same sex and need not resemble each other more than do any other two offspring of the same parents. In the United States twins occur once in approximately 86 births. The incidence of multiple-egg births is partially genetically determined, varying according to race and family tendencies; and it is also influenced by external factors, i.e., the incidence increases with increasing age of the mother and the number of children she has already borne. One-egg, or identical, twinning occurs with the same frequency in all women, regardless of race, age, or other factors. There is evidence from comparative biology that deleterious factors in the environment of the newly fertilized ovum, such as a reduction in oxygen, increase the likelihood of one-egg twinning. FERTILITY DRUGS such as clomiphene, which are used when the cause of infertility is lack of released ova, sometimes cause several ova to be released and fertilized simultaneously. The use of these drugs has led to a recent rise in the incidence of multiple births, including quintuplets and sextuplets.

multiple sclerosis, chronic, slowly progressive disease of the central nervous system. Its cause is not known, but the symptoms result from a wasting of the nerve sheaths of the brain and spinal cord, particularly the white matter, resulting in irregular patches of degeneration. The onset of the disease is usually in the second or third decade of life, and its many symptoms affect almost every system of the body. There may be visual difficulties, emotional disturbances, speech disorders, convulsions, paralysis or numbness of various regions of the body, bladder disturbances, and muscular weakness. The symptoms have a tendency to disappear and return, sometimes at frequent intervals and sometimes after a remission of several years. The course of the disease is slow (survival being estimated at 27 years from onset of symptoms), and there is no specific treatment.

multiple star, in astronomy, system of more than two stars that orbit one another because of the interaction of their gravitational fields. Castor, in Gemini, is a multiple star that consists of a triple system, two components of which are spectroscopic binaries and the third an eclipsing binary—a total of six stars. See BINARY STAR.

multiplexing, in communication, technique whereby two or more independent messages, or information-bearing signals, are carried by a single common medium, or channel. When multiplexing is performed, two or more channels are combined into a single channel, or a single channel is divided into several subchannels. Many different types of multiplexing are possible. One type is frequency-division multiplexing, in which a single frequency channel is subdivided into two or more subchannels, each of which can then carry a smaller range of frequencies than could the original channel. Frequency-division multiplexing is used in television broadcasting, when audio and video signals share a single channel; in stereophonic FM radio broadcasting, when two audio signals share a single channel; and in microwave transmission of long-distance telephone calls, when 60 or more conversations are carried by a single microwave beam. A second type of multiplexing is time-division multiplexing, in which successive small time intervals are used for the transmission of messages over a single channel. Time-division multiplexing is often used in the construction of digital computers. When information can be stored into or retrieved from the computer's memory at a much greater rate than it can be supplied or used by an external device such as a card reader, printer, or teletype terminal, several such low-speed devices can share a single multiplexed data channel.

multiplication, fundamental operation in arithmetic and algebra, in which a number or numerical quantity is increased through successive ADDITIONS. Thus, if 5 is multiplied by 2, the result is the same as adding 5 and 5. Similarly, 7 multiplied by 4 is equivalent to 7+7+7+7. The number acted upon (i.e., 5 or 7) is called the multiplicand, and the number of times the multiplicand is to be used in the addition (2 or 4) is called the multiplier. The result is known as the product. Numbers that give a product when multiplied together are called factors of that product. The symbol of the operation is $\times$ or $\cdot$ and, in algebra, simple juxtaposition (e.g., xy means $x \times y$ or $x \cdot y$). Like addition, multiplication, in arithmetic and elementary algebra, obeys the ASSOCIATIVE LAW, the COMMUTATIVE LAW, and, in combination with addition, the DISTRIBUTIVE LAW. Multiplication in abstract algebra, as between vectors or other mathematical objects, does not always obey these rules. Quantities with unlike units may sometimes be multiplied, resulting in such units as foot-pounds, gram-centimeters, and kilowatt-hours. See also DIVISION.

Multscher, Hans (häns mo͝ol'chər), c.1400–1467, outstanding German sculptor and painter of the Swabian school of Ulm. Early in life he traveled to the Netherlands and Burgundy. Probably influenced by the work of Claus Sluter, he developed a powerfully realistic figural style in both painting and sculpture. About 1427 Multscher settled in Ulm. For the east facade of the town hall he carved figures of Charles the Great and equestrian statues of the kings of Poland and Bohemia. In 1437 he painted the *Wurzacher Altarpiece* (Berlin). He also worked on the famous altarpiece (1457) at Sterzing (now Vipiteno) in the Tyrol. For this work, a combination of painting and sculpture (now dispersed), he executed sculptures of the Virgin and saints, while the wings were painted by another artist.

Mulvian Bridge: see MILVIAN BRIDGE.

Mumford, Lewis, 1895–, American social philosopher; b. Flushing, N.Y.; educ. City College of New York, Columbia, New York Univ., and the New School for Social Research. A critic of the dehumanizing tendencies of modern technological civilization, Mumford argues that humanity's only hope lies in a return to human feelings and sensitivities and to moral values. In addition to social philosophy, his works cover such areas as architecture and city planning. He served as professor at Stanford, the Univ. of Pennsylvania, Massachusetts Institute of Technology, the Univ. of California at Berkeley, and other universities. Among his books are *Technics and Civilization* (1934), *The Culture of Cities* (1938), *The Condition of Man* (1944), *The Conduct of Life* (1951), *The Transformations of Man* (1956), *The City in History* (1961), and *Interpretations and Forecasts* (1973).

mumming play, form of drama developed in England in the early 17th cent., based on the legend of St. George and the dragon. The central theme of the play is the death and resurrection of the hero. The mumming play possibly evolved from some primitive folk celebration. However, it is most closely associated with the medieval sword dance, which symbolized the reawakening of the earth from the death of winter. During the Christmas season a few English villages still present the mumming play. See Alan Brody, *English Mummers and Their Plays* (1971).

mummy, dead human or animal body preserved by EMBALMING or by unusual natural conditions. As a rule mummies are from ancient times. The word is of Arabic derivation and refers primarily to the burials found in Egypt, where the practice of mummification was perfected over the centuries to an extreme of elaboration. Egyptian mummies more than 5,000 years old consist of hardly more than bones, skin, and hair, owing their preservation largely to the dry air of Upper Egypt. In humid Lower Egypt practically all mummies have perished. By the time of the New Kingdom the art of embalming had reached its height, and it is possible to determine fairly accurately how the great pharaohs appeared in life, e.g., Amenhotep II (in his tomb near Thebes), Thutmose III, Thutmose IV, Tutankhamen, Seti I, and Ramses II (all in Cairo). Mummification seems to be connected with a belief in life after death, the body being preserved so that the soul might return to it. The Egyptian method of preparing the body varied at different periods and also according to the wealth and importance of the person. At first only kings were mummified; later their courtiers and servants were also preserved to provide them with a retinue in the afterlife; even the meat offerings placed in the tomb for food were embalmed. Later in the period of Egyptian mummification, cats, dogs, cows, hawks, and other sacred animals were likewise embalmed. In other parts of the world, bodies preserved by various artificial means have been found in such widely separated places as the Aleutian Islands, the Canary Islands, and in the countries now composing what was the Inca civilization. The Inca dead were often entombed in coastal sands or in the high, arid caves of the Andes, where burials have been found in an excellent state of preservation. Natural mummification occurs in favorable soils and climates. Several intact human bodies dating from between 300 B.C. and A.D. 300 were found in the peat bogs of Jutland, Denmark. From the Middle Ages until the 18th cent. mummies were shipped from Egypt to Europe, where they were ground up and sold for medicinal purposes. See G. Elliot Smith and W. R. Dawson, *Egyptian Mummies* (1924); H. McCracken, *God's Frozen Children* (1930); R. A. Martain, *Mummies* (1945).

mumps (epidemic parotitis), acute contagious viral disease, manifesting itself chiefly in pain and swelling of the salivary glands, especially those at the angle of the jaw. Other symptoms are fever, a general feeling of illness, and pain on chewing or swallowing. Mumps most often affects children between the ages of 5 and 15, the incubation period being 14 to 21 days; the acute phase rarely lasts more than 3 days. The disease is usually more severe in adults, the most common complications being pain and swelling of the testes (in 25% of adult male patients) and swelling of the meninges that cover the brain and spinal cord (in about 30% of cases). Sterility resulting from involvement of the testes and fatalities from the meningoencephalitis occur in a small minority of male cases. Other possible complications include pancreatitis and involvement of the heart or thyroid. The ovaries are sometimes affected in females. Treatment consists mainly of bed rest and the administration of sedatives. A live virus vaccine has been developed that can be given to susceptible individuals over one year of age.

Mumtaz Mahal: see TAJ MAHAL.

Mun, Albert, comte de (älbĕr' kôNt də möN), 1841–1914, French Roman Catholic leader and politician. A monarchist at first, he later loyally supported the Third Republic. He was one of the few French Catholics of his day to attempt to implement the encyclical *Rerum novarum* (1891) issued by Pope LEO XIII, which dealt with the conditions of the working classes and the need for church action to remedy those conditions. Mun led in organizing associations of Catholic workers and advocating social reforms. A strong nationalist, he was bitterly hostile to Germany. See study by Miriam Lynch (1952).

Mun, Thomas (mŭn), 1571–1641, English writer on economics. A merchant in Italy and the Levant, he became (1615) a director in the East India Company. In his *Discourse of Trade from England unto the East Indies* (1621) he refuted claims that the company reduced the amount of bullion in England by exporting too much of it to India. He further defined his theory of the balance of trade in *Discourse on England's Treasure by Foreign Trade* (written 1630; pub. 1664). See E. A. J. Johnson, *Predecessors of Adam Smith: The Growth of British Economic Thought* (1937).

Munch, Andreas Peder (ändrä'äs pä'dər mo͝ongk), 1810–63, Norwegian historian and philologist. A principal figure in the Norwegian literary revival, he contributed an authoritative history of the Norwegian people, *Det norske folks historie* (8 vol., 1852–63). He maintained that the *Eddas* and sagas of Old Norse literature belonged to a purely Norwegian-Icelandic literature and not, as was generally supposed, to a common Scandinavian tradition. This view was later generally accepted.

Münch, Charles (shärl münsh), 1891–1968, French conductor, b. Alsace. Münch learned the violin from his father, then studied at the Strasbourg Conservatory, where he later taught and conducted (1925–32). After leading the Leipzig orchestra (1935–38), he was conductor of the orchestra of the Paris Conservatory (1938–46). He went to the United States in 1947, and for three seasons he appeared as guest conductor of the New York Philharmonic. Münch was conductor of the Boston Symphony Orchestra from 1949 until 1962. He was noted for his interpretations of modern French works. See his *I Am a Conductor* (1954, tr. 1955).

Munch, Edvard (ĕd'värt mo͝ongk), 1863-1944, Norwegian painter and graphic artist. He studied in Oslo and under Bonnat in Paris and traveled in Europe. In the 1890s he abandoned impressionism to portray from his profound sense of isolation the themes of death, fear, and anxiety. Munch said he heard "the scream of nature." To describe this, he developed an exciting, violent, and emotionally charged style that is recognized as being of primary importance in the birth of German EXPRESSIONISM. During the 1890s, Munch's most productive period, he made powerful and shocking woodcuts, developing a new technique of direct and forceful cutting that served to revive creative activity in this medium. Among his strongest and best-known works are *The Shriek* (1893), *The Kiss* (1895), and *Vampire*. Reaction to his stark, fearsome images caused the closing of an important Berlin exhibition of 1892. In 1909, after a severe mental illness, Munch returned from Germany to Norway, where he painted murals for the Univ. of Oslo and for an Oslo chocolate factory. His painting became brighter of palette and less introverted until the 1920s, when he again was moved to portray his dreadful anguish. Munch's work is in leading collections everywhere. See biography by Otto Benesch (tr. 1960); studies by Arve Moen (3 vol., 1956-58), Werner Timm (tr. 1969), J. P. Hodin (1972), and T. M. Messer (1973).

München, West Germany: see MUNICH.

München-Gladbach: see MÖNCHENGLADBACH, West Germany.

Muncie (mŭn'sē), city (1970 pop. 69,082), seat of Delaware co., E Ind., on the White River; inc. 1854. It is a trade, processing, and manufacturing center. The city is in a rich agricultural area that has dairying, livestock raising, and grain, soybean, fruit, and truck crops. Machine tools, metal goods, glass, electrical components, wire, and automotive and marine parts are among the many manufactures. The town was first established by the Delaware Indians and named for one of their tribes. White settlers were in the area before the land passed (1818) by treaty to the U.S. government. Industrialization came after the discovery (1886) of natural gas in the county. Muncie is the seat of Ball State Univ. It is the city pictured in the classic sociological community studies by Robert and Helen Lynd, *Middletown* (1929, repr. 1959) and *Middletown in Transition* (1937, repr. 1965).

Munda languages (mo͝on'də), group of languages generally regarded as a subfamily of the Southeast Asian family of languages. See SOUTHEAST ASIAN LANGUAGES.

Munday, Anthony, 1553-1633, English author, b. London. After spending his early years as an actor, he turned to writing. His literary output includes a number of plays (many written in collaboration), poems, pageants, several anti-Catholic pamphlets, and translations of popular French romances (including *Amadis de Gaul*). Among his plays are *John a Kent and John a Cumber* (c.1594) and two on the legend of Robin Hood, *The Downfall* and *Death of Robert, Earl of Huntington* (both 1601). See study by J. C. Turner (1928).

Mundelein, village (1970 pop. 16,128), Lake co., NE Ill.; founded 1835 as Mechanics Grove, inc. 1909. The name was changed in 1926 to honor George Cardinal Mundelein. Glass containers, labeling machines, and picture frames are made there. St. Mary of the Lake Seminary is located in Mundelein.

Münden (mün'dən) or **Hannoversch-Münden** (hänō'vərsh), town (1970 pop. 18,993), Lower Saxony, E West Germany, where the Fulda and Werra rivers flow together to form the Weser River. Its manufactures include machine tools, chemicals, and lead, aluminum, and rubber goods. Münden was founded in the late 12th cent. on the site of a Carolingian palace. Noteworthy structures of the picturesque town include the palace (renovated in the 16th cent. and now a museum), a stone bridge (built c.1400), a Renaissance-style town hall, and numerous half-timber houses.

Mungai, Njoroge (ənjərō'gä mo͝ong'gī), 1926-, government official in Kenya. He left private medical practice to become minister of health (1963-64), also serving as minister of internal security (1964-69) before becoming foreign affairs minister in 1969.

Munhall (mŭn'hôl), borough (1970 pop. 16,574), Allegheny co., SW Pa., an industrial suburb of Pittsburgh, on the Monongahela River; inc. 1901. Large steel and iron works are there. Munhall was a site of the HOMESTEAD STRIKE in 1892.

Muni, Paul (myo͞o'nē), 1895-1967, American actor, b. Austria, whose original name was Muni Weisenfreund. His parents brought him to the United States in 1902 and from 1903 to 1913 toured with him in vaudeville. Turning to the legitimate theater, he toured (1914-17) the Midwest and acted (1918-25) with the Yiddish Art Theatre in New York City. He began working in films in 1928 and won an Academy Award in 1936 for his performance in *The Life of Louis Pasteur.* An outstanding character actor, Muni's films include *The Life of Émile Zola* (1937), *The Good Earth* (1937), *Juarez* (1939), and *The Last Angry Man* (1959). In 1955 he appeared on Broadway in *Inherit the Wind.* See biography by M. B. Druxman (1974).

Munich (myo͞o'nĭk), Ger. *München* (mün'khən), city (1970 pop. 1,293,590), capital of Bavaria, S West Germany, on the Isar River near the Bavarian Alps. It is a commercial, industrial, transportation, communications, and cultural center. Its industries produce machinery, chemicals, pharmaceuticals, processed foods, precision and optical instruments, textiles, electrical appliances, and beer; vehicles and airplanes are assembled. The city is a major tourist and convention center and has radio, television, and film studios. Situated near a settlement (Munichen) that was established in Carolingian times, Munich was founded (1158) by Henry the Lion, duke of Saxony and of Bavaria. In 1255 it was chosen as the residence of the WITTELSBACH family, the dukes of Bavaria; it later became (1506) the capital of the dukedom. During the Thirty Years War, Munich was occupied (1632) by Gustavus II of Sweden. In 1806 the city was made capital of the kingdom of BAVARIA. Under the kings Louis I (1825-48), Maximilian II (1848-64), and Louis II (1864-86), Munich became a cultural and artistic center, and it played a leading role in the development of 19th- and 20th-century German painting. After World War I the city was the scene of considerable political unrest. National Socialism (Nazism) was founded there, and on Nov. 8, 1923, Adolf Hitler failed in his attempted Munich "beer-hall putsch"—a coup aimed at the Bavarian government. Despite this fiasco, Hitler made Munich the headquarters of the Nazi party, which in 1933 took control of the German national government. Michael Cardinal Faulhaber, the archbishop of Munich, was one of the few outspoken critics of the National Socialist regime. In Sept., 1938, the MUNICH PACT was signed in the city; in 1939, Hitler suppressed a Bavarian separatist plot there. Munich was badly damaged during World War II, but after 1945 it was extensively rebuilt and many modern buildings were constructed. Among the city's chief attractions are the Frauenkirche (Church of Our Lady), a twin-towered cathedral built from 1468 to 1488; the Renaissance-style St. Michael's Church (1583-97); the Theatinerkirche (17th-18th cent.), a baroque church; NYMPHENBURG castle (1664-1728), with a porcelain factory (founded 1747) and the nearby Amalienburg (1734-39), a small rococo hunting chateau; the new city hall (1867-1908); Propyläen (1846-62), a monumental neoclassic gate; and the large English Garden (laid out 1789-1832). The city also has several leading museums, including the Old Pinakothek (built 1826-36), which houses a distinguished collection of paintings; the Bavarian National Museum (built 1894-99); the Schackgalerie; the GLYPTOTHEK (built 1816-30); and the Deutsche Museum, which has wide-ranging exhibits on science, technology, and industry. The seat of an archbishop, Munich has a famous university (founded 1472 at Ingolstadt; transferred in 1802 to Landshut and in 1826 to Munich) in addition to a technical university, a conservatory of music, an opera, numerous theaters, and many publishing houses. Munich is also noted for its lively Fasching (Shrove Tuesday) and Oktoberfest (October festival) celebrations. The 1972 Olympic summer games were held (Aug.-Sept.) at Munich (except for the sailing and yachting events, held at Kiel). During the games 11 members of the Israeli Olympic team, 5 Palestinian guerrillas, and a West German policeman were killed in an attack by the guerrillas on the Israeli living quarters in the Olympic village and in a subsequent confrontation at a Munich airport.

Munich Pact, 1938. In the summer of 1938, Chancellor Hitler of Germany began openly to support the demands of Germans living in the Sudetenland (see SUDETES) of CZECHOSLOVAKIA for an improved status. In September, Hitler demanded self-determination for the Sudetenland. Disorders broke out in Czechoslovakia, and martial law was proclaimed. Meetings between Hitler and Prime Minister Neville CHAMBERLAIN of Great Britain, first at Berchtesgaden and then at Bad Godesberg, failed to achieve a satisfactory agreement. War seemed unavoidable. After appeals by President Franklin Delano Roosevelt and Benito Mussolini, a conference met at Munich (Sept. 29). Great Britain was represented by Chamberlain and Halifax, France by Edouard Daladier and Georges Bonnet, Italy by Mussolini and Galeazzo Ciano, Germany by Hitler and Ribbentrop. Neither Czechoslovakia nor the Soviet Union, which had offered aid to the threatened country under the terms of a 1935 treaty, was invited to the conference. England and France quickly surrendered to Hitler's demands, and the Munich Pact was signed Sept. 30 (but dated Sept. 29). It permitted immediate occupation by Germany of the Sudetenland, but also provided for plebiscites, which were never carried out. France and Britain guaranteed the new Czechoslovak boundaries. When Chamberlain arrived in London, he announced that he had secured "peace in our time." Abandoned by its allies, Czechoslovakia gave in to the terms, and President Beneš, the target of Hitler's most venomous attacks, resigned. Poland and Hungary, for whose minorities promises had been made at Munich, were allowed to seize, respectively, the TESCHEN district and parts of SLOVAKIA. The Munich Pact became a symbol of appeasement and shook the confidence of Eastern Europeans in the good faith of the Western democracies. World War II began about one year after its signing. See J. W. Wheeler-Bennett, *Munich: Prologue to Tragedy* (1948, repr. 1966); studies by Keith Eubank (1963), F. L. Loewenheim, ed. (1965), and D. E. Lee, ed. (1970).

municipal government: see CITY GOVERNMENT.

municipal home rule: see HOME RULE, MUNICIPAL.

municipal ownership: see PUBLIC OWNERSHIP.

Munk, Kaj (kī mo͝ongk), 1898-1944, Danish playwright, a clergyman. His ethical plays, traditional in form, led the Danish dramatic revival in the 1930s. Among them is *The Word* (1932), which deals with resurrection and faith. Munk, who attacked National Socialism in *He Sits by the Melting Pot* (1938) and *Niels Ebbesen* (1942, tr. 1944), was killed by the Nazis in the German occupation. A translation of his works appeared as *Five Plays* (1953).

Munkácsy, Mihály (mĭ'hälyə mo͞on'kächī), 1844-1909, Hungarian genre and historical painter, whose original name was Michael Lieb. In 1868 he went to Düsseldorf, where he painted *The Last Day of a Condemned Man,* which won him wide recognition. In 1872 he settled in Paris. From 1881 he painted chiefly religious and historical subjects in a highly dramatic style. His *Christ before Pilate* has been widely reproduced. Munkácsy's work is represented in the museums of Vienna, Philadelphia, and Chicago and in the Metropolitan Museum. See study by Geza Perneczky (1971).

Munkhafad al-Qattarah, basin, Egypt: see QATTARA DEPRESSION.

Munn vs. Illinois, case decided by the U.S. Supreme Court in 1876. Munn, a partner in a Chicago warehouse firm, had been found guilty by an Illinois court of violating the state laws providing for the fixing of maximum charges for storage of grain (see GRANGER MOVEMENT). He appealed, contending that the fixing of maximum rates constituted a taking of property without due process of law. The Supreme Court upheld the Granger laws, establishing as constitutional the principle of public regulation of private businesses involved in serving the public interest.

Muñoz Marín, Luis (lo͞oēs' mo͞onyōs' märēn'), 1898-, Puerto Rican political leader, governor of Puerto Rico (1949-65). He abandoned a career as poet and journalist in New York City to enter Puerto Rican politics. In 1938 he organized and headed the Popular Democratic party, campaigned vigorously for social and economic reform, and edited *La Democracia,* a San Juan daily founded by his father, Luis MUÑOZ RIVERA. The slogan "Bread, land, and liberty" won a large following among the poor. In 1948 he won the first free popular election for the governorship of Puerto Rico, and he was reelected in 1952 and 1956. A resourceful and energetic supporter of Commonwealth status for the island, he brought about the 1952 decision that proclaimed Puerto Rico an Associated Free State. In 1960 his election was opposed by the Roman Catholic Church in Puerto Rico, which denounced him for advocating the teaching of birth control; he was easily reelected despite the opposition. He consistently championed economic expansion in close cooperation with the United States. He did not run for reelection in 1964. See biographies by Thomas Aitken (1964) and T. G. Mathews (1967).

Muñoz Rivera, Luis (lwēs mo͞onyōs' rēvä'rä), 1859-1916, Puerto Rican journalist and nationalist. He founded *La Democracia,* a newspaper later edited by his son Luis MUÑOZ MARÍN. A leader in the campaign for independence from Spain, he obtained (1897) a charter, which was never put into effect, that granted some autonomy to Puerto Ricans. Heading the first Puerto Rican cabinet under U.S. occupation, Muñoz Rivera opposed military governorship and pleaded for greater self-government. Faced with bitter opposition in Puerto Rico, he moved to New York City and published the *Puerto Rico Herald,* which expounded the island's problems. As resident commissioner of Puerto Rico in Washington, D.C. (1910-16), he obtained U.S. citizenship for Puerto Ricans.

Munro, Dana Carleton, 1866-1933, American educator and historian, b. Bristol, R.I.; brother of Wilfred Harold Munro. After studying in Germany he was appointed (1893) an instructor in history at the Univ. of Pennsylvania. From 1902 to 1915 he was professor of European history at the Univ. of Wisconsin, and from 1915 to his death he was professor of medieval history at Princeton. An authority on the Crusades, he adopted a rigorous scientific method of research, basing all facts on references to contemporary sources. He wrote *A History of the Middle Ages* (1902), *A Source Book of Roman History* (1904), *The Middle Ages, 395-1272* (1921, rev. ed., *395-1500,* with R. J. Sontag, 1928), and *The Kingdom of the Crusaders* (1935). He translated and edited, with George C. Sellery, *Medieval Civilization: Selected Studies from European Authors* (1904, enl. ed. 1907).

Munro, Hector Hugh, pseud. **Saki** (säʹkē), 1870-1916, English author, b. Burma. He began his career writing political satires for the *Westminster Gazette.* From 1902 to 1908 he was a foreign correspondent for the Tory *Morning Post* and a contributor to other newspapers. He is best known for his witty, sometimes whimsical, often cynical and bizarre short stories; they are collected in *Reginald* (1904), *The Chronicles of Clovis* (1911), *Beasts and Super-Beasts* (1914), and other volumes. Included among his other works are two novels, *The Unbearable Bassington* (1912) and *When William Came* (1914). Munro was killed in France in World War I. See *The Short Stories of Saki,* ed. by Christopher Morley (1930); *The Novels and Plays of Saki* (1933, repr. 1971); biography by C. H. Gillen (1971); study by G. J. Spears (1963).

Munro, Wilfred Harold, 1849-1934, American historian and educator, b. Bristol, R.I.; brother of Dana Carleton Munro. From 1870 to 1871 he was a master at De Veaux College, Niagara Falls, N.Y., where he later (1881-89) served as president. After studying (1890-91) at the universities of Freiburg and Heidelberg, Munro became (1891) associate professor of history and director of university extension work at Brown. From 1899 until his retirement in 1911 he held the chair of European history there. In his lifetime Munro traveled widely. For many years president of the Rhode Island Historical Society, he was considered a foremost expert on Rhode Island history. His works include *The History of Bristol, R.I.* (1880), *Tales of an Old Sea Port* (1917), and *Among the Mormons in the Days of Brigham Young* (1927). He edited a 22-volume edition (1905-6, repr. 1968) of the works of W. H. Prescott.

Munsey, Frank Andrew (mŭnʹsē), 1854-1925, American publisher and author, b. Mercer, Maine. In 1882 he quit a telegraph operator's job in Maine to begin a career as publisher in New York City. He started the *Golden Argosy* (1882) as a juvenile magazine, for which he wrote serials himself, changed it to the *Argosy* for adults, and supplanted this with *Munsey's Magazine* (1889), the first 10-cent periodical. When one of his magazines failed, he scrapped it and started another; he thus disposed of *Godey's Magazine, All-Story Magazine,* and many others. Turning to newspapers, he bought the New York *Star* in 1891, renamed it the *Continent,* and made it a tabloid, probably New York's first, but it failed. Later, using the wealth he made from his magazines, from a chain of grocery stores, and from the financial operations of his trust company, he bought several newspapers, hoping to found a chain of them. However, he lost a great deal on the Boston *Journal* and the New York *Daily News.* The Washington *Times* and the Baltimore *Evening News* were among his successful papers. In 1916 he began buying papers to consolidate; for this he was sometimes called the executioner of newspapers. He merged the New York *Press* in the *Sun,* and in 1920 the unsuccessful *Sun* in the New York *Herald.* In 1924 he sold the *Herald* to the New York *Tribune,* having meanwhile renamed the *Evening Sun* the *Sun* and absorbed in it (1923) the *Globe and Commercial Advertiser.* His last purchase was that of the New York *Mail,* which he merged in his *Evening Telegram* in 1924. See biography by George Britt, *Forty Years, Forty Millions* (1935, repr. 1971).

Münster, Sebastian (sābäsʹtyän" münʹstər), 1489-1552, German scholar and geographer. He was a Franciscan monk but after the Reformation became a Protestant and taught at Heidelberg and at Basel, where he lived after 1536. A noted theologian and Hebraist, he edited the first Hebrew Bible produced (1534-35) by a German. His chief work is the *Cosmographia universalis* (1544), a descriptive geography standard for more than a century and translated into several languages.

Munster (mŭnʹstər), province (1971 pop. 880,018), 9,315 sq mi (24,126 sq km), SW Republic of Ireland. The largest of the Irish provinces, it comprises the counties of CLARE, CORK, KERRY, LIMERICK, TIPPERARY, and WATERFORD. One of the ancient kingdoms of Ireland, its control passed, after the Anglo-Norman invasion of Ireland, to the great families of the Fitzgeralds (earls of Desmond) and the Butlers (earls of Ormonde).

Münster (münʹstər), city (1970 pop. 198,371), North Rhine-Westphalia, W West Germany, a port and industrial center on the Dortmund-Ems Canal. Its manufactures include heavy machinery, textiles, metal products, and beer. The city is also a trade center for grain and lumber. Münster was founded (c.800) as a Carolingian episcopal see. Its bishops ruled a large part of Westphalia as princes of the Holy Roman Empire from the 12th cent. until 1803, when the bishopric was secularized. From the 14th cent. the city was a prominent member of the Hanseatic League, trading especially with England and Russia. In 1534-35 it was the scene of the Anabaptist experimental government under JOHN OF LEIDEN. In 1648 the Treaty of Münster was signed there (see WESTPHALIA, PEACE OF). Münster passed to Prussia in 1816 and became the capital of the province of Westphalia. It was severely damaged in World War II but was rebuilt after 1945. Münster still retains some of its medieval character. Its historical buildings include the cathedral (13th cent.), the Lambertikirche (14th-15th cent.), the Liebfrauenkirche (14th cent.), and several other churches, in addition to a baroque palace (1767-73), a Gothic city hall (14th cent.), and several gabled houses. The city is the seat of a university and contains the Westphalian state museum.

Munster, town (1970 pop. 16,514), Lake co., NW Ind. It is a primarily residential suburb in the industrialized Hammond-East Chicago area. There is some manufacturing.

Münsterberg, Hugo (mŭnʹstərbərg, mĭnʹ-), 1863-1916, American psychologist, b. Danzig, Ph.D. Univ. of Leipzig, 1885; M.D. Univ. of Heidelberg, 1887. At the instigation of William James he moved from Germany to Harvard to serve as professor of psychology (1892-1916), becoming director of the psychological laboratory in 1905. He pioneered in applied psychology and wrote many books on psychology and on American life and social problems. See biography by M. A. A. Münsterberg (1922, repr. 1973).

Muntenia: see WALACHIA.

muntjac: see DEER.

Münzer, Thomas (tōʹmäs münʹtsər), c.1489-1525, German Protestant reformer, generally linked with the ANABAPTISTS although he rejected baptism altogether. Münzer left his home and his position as a magistrate to join Martin Luther at Wittenberg in 1519, and he was a member of the delegation at the disputation with Johann Maier von ECK at Leipzig in the same year. His position soon diverged from Luther's as he became increasingly iconoclastic in theology and radical in political and social beliefs. Münzer claimed divine illumination, and while pastor (1520-23) at Zwickau he helped disturb affairs at Wittenberg with radical doctrine during the time that Luther was in retirement at the Wartburg. Münzer was ousted from Zwickau, from Allstedt (in Thuringia), and from Mühlhausen. Everywhere he went he aroused the dissatisfied peasantry and the workingmen of the towns. He proclaimed that God willed the overthrow of the social structure and the establishment of a simple, godly society, with community of property. At Mühlhausen he had worked with Heinrich Pfeiffer. When the Peasants' War broke out the two men succeeded in returning and taking over the Mühlhausen town council, and they set up a communistic theocracy. Upon the defeat of the peasant party, Münzer was beheaded. See biographical study by E. W. Gritsch (1967).

muon (myo͞oʹŏn), ELEMENTARY PARTICLE heavier than an ELECTRON but lighter than other particles having nonzero rest mass. The name *muon* is derived from mu meson, the former name of the particle. The muon was first observed in COSMIC RAYS by Carl D. Anderson and Seth Neddermeyer in 1936, the year after the existence of a particle of about the same mass had been predicted by Hideki Yukawa. However, the muon's behavior did not conform to that of Yukawa's MESON theory (which actually describes the PION, discovered more than 10 years later), and the muon is now classed as a LEPTON rather than a meson. The muon resembles the electron in every way except mass, the muon having 207 times the mass of the electron. Each particle is negatively charged and has a positively charged ANTIPARTICLE; each has half-integer spin and participates in the weak nuclear FORCE but not in the strong force; and each has an associated NEUTRINO and antineutrino. Muons are produced by the weak decay of pions into a muon and a muon antineutrino. The muon differs from the electron in that it is unstable, decaying with an average lifetime of 2.2×10^{-6} sec (2.2 microseconds) into an electron or positron and a pair of neutrinos, but this difference is related to the difference in mass; the electron is stable because there is no lighter particle into which it can decay. Muons can be substituted for electrons in orbit around the nucleus of an atom; the resulting atom is long-lived enough to exhibit behavior that further supports the close resemblance between the muon and the electron. The relationship between the muon and the electron has not been explained satisfactorily on theoretical grounds. Recent studies of muons have included the production of "muonic atoms" (ordinary atoms to which an orbiting muon is added) and muonium, which consists of an electron in orbit around a positive muon.

Muonio älv or **Muoniojoki,** river, Sweden and Finland: see TORNEÄLVEN, river.

Muppim (mupʹĭm), variant of SHUPHAM.

Mur (mo͝or), Hung. and Serbo-Croatian *Mura* (mo͞oʹrä), river, c.300 mi (480 km) long, rising in the Hohe Tauern, S central Austria. It flows NE to Bruck, where it receives the Mürz River, its chief tributary. Turning southeast, it flows past Graz (the head of navigation) and through NW Yugoslavia to the Drava River. The Mur forms part of the Austrian-Yugoslav and Yugoslav-Hungarian borders. Used for power production and the transportation of raw materials, the river has attracted many industries to its banks.

Murad I (mo͝orädʹ), 1326?-1389, Ottoman sultan (1362?-1389), son and successor of Orkhan to the throne of the Ottoman Empire (Turkey). Murad widened the Ottoman hold on European territory, conquering Macedonia and making Adrianople his residence. He granted Muslims sections of conquered lands as fiefs (see FEUDALISM). In 1373 he forced Byzantine Emperor JOHN V to pay tribute. Murad began the policy of compelling Christian youths to join the army corps known as the JANISSARIES. As a result of his victory at Kossovo, Serbia came under Ottoman rule. However, Murad was assassinated in his tent by a Serbian warrior as the fighting concluded. His son Beyazid I succeeded him. The name also appears as Amurath.

Murad II, 1403-51, Ottoman sultan (1421-51), son and successor of Muhammad I to the throne of the Ottoman Empire (Turkey). He was opposed at his accession by a pretender, Mustafa, who rapidly gained control over most of the Ottoman possessions in Europe. After defeating his rival, Murad unsuccessfully laid siege (1422) to Constantinople. In a war with Venice he seized (1430) Salonica, thus proving Ottoman naval power, and invaded Greece. In the north Murad fought the resistance led by John HUNYADI. Murad sought to retire from public life on several occasions, but each time was recalled by the pressure of events. In 1444 he won the great victory of Varna against the crusading forces led by King LADISLAUS III of Poland and Hungary. Murad was a patron of poetry and learning, and his court was a cultural center. His son Muhammad II succeeded him.

Murad III, 1546-95, Ottoman sultan (1574-95), son and successor of Selim II. He was dominated by his harem, and although his generals were successful against Persia, his reign marked the beginning of the decay of the Ottoman Empire (Turkey). His son Muhammad III succeeded him.

Murad IV, 1612?-1640, Ottoman sultan (1623-40), nephew and successor of MUSTAFA I. The last of the warrior-sultans of the Ottoman Empire (Turkey), he recovered (1638) Baghdad, which Shah Abbas I of

Persia had seized. On his victory he sent an order to murder his brother BEYAZID. Murad possessed prodigious strength and ruled with ruthless severity. The Greek patriarch Cyril LUCARIS was another of his victims. Murad was succeeded by his brother İbrahim (reigned 1640–48) and İbrahim's son Muhammad IV.

Murad V, 1840–1904, Ottoman sultan (1876), son of Abd al-Majid. He came to the throne of the Ottoman Empire (Turkey) when his uncle, ABD AL-AZIZ, was deposed, but he was soon declared insane and was succeeded by his brother, Abd al-Hamid II. His brief reign was dominated by MIDHAT PASHA.

Murad, river: see EUPHRATES, river.

Murano (mo͞orä'nō), suburb of Venice, NE Italy, on five small islands in the Lagoon of Venice. From the late 13th cent. it was the center of the Venetian glass industry, which reached a peak in the 16th cent. and was revived in the 19th cent. by Antonio Salviati. Today mirrors and optical instruments are also manufactured. With its old houses, canals, and bridges, Murano has the same quaint charm as Venice. Of note are a Venetian-Byzantine basilica (7th–12th cent.) and a museum of old and new Venetian glass.

Murasaki Shikibu (mo͞o"räsä'kē shē"kēbo͞o'), c.978–1031?, Japanese novelist, court figure at the height of the Heian period (795–1185). Known also as Lady Murasaki, she is celebrated as the author of the romantic novel *Genji-Monogatari* [tale of Genji], one of the first great works of fiction to be written in Japanese. It concerns the life of Prince Genji and his descendants and is a subtle delineation of a complex society. See Arthur Waley's excellent translation (1935, repr. 1960).

Murat, Joachim (zhōäshăN' mürä'), 1767–1815, marshal of France, king of Naples (1808–15). He left his theological studies to enter the army and fought in Egypt under Napoleon, whom he helped (1799) in the coup d'etat of 18 Brumaire. Having married (1800) Napoleon's sister Caroline BONAPARTE, he was made grand duke of Berg (1806) and in 1808 was chosen to succeed Joseph Bonaparte as king of Naples. A brilliant and dashing cavalry leader, Murat played an important part in Napoleon's victories, in the Russian campaign (1812), and in the battle of Leipzig (1813). After Leipzig, however, he reached (1814) an agreement with Austria in order to save his own throne. During the Hundred Days he deserted his new allies and again joined Napoleon. Defeated by the Austrians at Tolentino, he fled to Corsica after Napoleon's fall. In an attempt to regain Naples he was arrested and executed. See Hubert Cole, *The Murats* (1972).

Muratori, Ludovico Antonio (lo͞odōvē'kō äntô'nyō mo͞orätô'rē), 1672–1750, Italian historian, a Roman Catholic priest. One of the foremost scholars of his age, he was long archivist and ducal librarian at Modena. He discovered the *Muratorian Canon,* a scrap of early Christian literature (A.D. c.190) containing the earliest known list of the New Testament books. Muratori edited the important source collections *Rerum Italicarum scriptores* (28 vol., 1723–51) and *Antiquitates Italicae medii aevii* (6 vol., 1738–42). He also wrote a history (12 vol., 1744–49) of Italy from Christian times.

Murchison, Sir Roderick Impey (mûr'kĭsən), 1792–1871, British geologist. He served in the Napoleonic Wars but after the peace turned his attention to science. In the 1830s he undertook the investigation of previously undifferentiated rock strata in Wales and England; as a result of his researches he established the Silurian as a new geologic system and described it in *The Silurian System* (2 vol. in 1, 1839). With Adam Sedgwick he collaborated on the establishment of the Devonian system, and after carrying on an extended survey in Russia (1840–44) he also defined and named the Permian period. His last investigations were directed toward the geology of the Scottish Highlands. In 1846 he was knighted, and in 1855 he was appointed director general of the Geological Survey of Great Britain. Murchison endowed a chair of geology and mineralogy at the Univ. of Edinburgh. He revised and modified the material of his earlier work in *Siluria* (1854) and collaborated on the *Geology of Russia in Europe and the Ural Mountains* (1845). See biography by Sir Archibald Geikie (2 vol., 1875).

Murcia ((Span. mo͞or'thyä), region and former Moorish kingdom, SE Spain, on the Mediterranean Sea, comprising the present provinces of Albacete and Murcia. The area has a generally rugged terrain, except along its coastal plain, and it is one of the hottest and driest regions of Europe, resembling N Africa in climate and vegetation. However, an irrigation system (dating from Moorish times) and several fertile valleys (especially that of the Segura River) permit the growing of large crops of citrus and other fruits, vegetables, almonds, olives, and grapes. Hemp, esparto, and minerals (lead, silver, zinc) are exported. Sericulture, long a traditional occupation, has declined. The region was settled by the Carthaginians, who founded there (3d cent. B.C.) the port of Cartago Nova (modern Cartagena). It was taken (8th cent. A.D.) by the Moors and emerged as an independent kingdom after the fall (11th cent.) of the caliphate of Córdoba. Later occupied by the Almoravids and Almohads, the kingdom of Murcia also included parts of the modern provinces of Alicante and Almería. In 1243 it became a vassal state of Castile, which in 1266 annexed it outright.

Murcia, city (1970 pop. 243,759), capital of Murcia prov., SE Spain, on the Segura River. The city lies in one of the finest garden regions in Spain. The silk industry, a traditional occupation for many years, has declined. There are food-processing and other light industries. Lead, silver, sulfur, and iron are mined nearby. Murcia rose to prominence under the Moors, when it was for a time the capital of the independent kingdom of Murcia (see separate article). The Gothic cathedral (14th–15th cent.) and the episcopal palace are landmarks. Murcia is the see of a bishop and has a university (founded 1915). It suffered heavily in the civil war of 1936 to 1939.

murder, criminal HOMICIDE, usually distinguished from MANSLAUGHTER by the element of MALICE aforethought. The most direct case of malice aforethought occurs when at some time (no matter how recent) before actually accomplishing the homicidal act the slayer adopted the deliberate cold-blooded intent to commit it. Very often, however, the law presumes the existence of malice aforethought from the circumstances and it does not necessarily have to be proved directly. The most clear-cut case of this presumption of malice is when the killer by inadvertence slays some person other than his intended victim. Malice is presumed if the slayer intended only to inflict serious bodily injury or if he behaved with such reckless disregard of the safety of others as to betray a "depraved heart." Likewise a killing incidentally committed in the course of a FELONY (e.g., robbery or rape) is deemed murder; if the felony was accomplished by more than one person, all are equally guilty of the murder, not only the actual slayer. A killing that is incidental to a MISDEMEANOR, however, is treated as manslaughter. Many states prescribe various degrees of murder. Murder in the first degree generally is a calculated act of slaying and receives the severest penalty, often CAPITAL PUNISHMENT. In some states certain crimes that are defined as murder of a lower degree approximate more closely the definition of manslaughter in COMMON LAW. In a slaying it is frequently difficult to determine whether malice aforethought was present; consequently the governor of a state (or other chief executive) not infrequently uses his power of commutation of sentence to revoke the death penalty, and in some states the appellate courts automatically review all convictions of murder.

Murder, Inc., name given to the band of professional killers who operated (1930–40) throughout the United States as the enforcement arm of the Syndicate, composed of the national heads of ORGANIZED CRIME. Originally a gang of neighborhood thugs in Brooklyn, N.Y., they soon came to the attention of Louis (Lepke) Buchalter, a member of the Syndicate, who extended their activities to the national scene. With Albert Anastasia, allegedly the connection between the Troop, as the gunmen of Murder, Inc., were called, and the Syndicate, the band committed well over a hundred murders. They continued their criminal acts for years, allegedly protected by politicians, and it was not until the late 1930s with the investigations of Thomas E. Dewey that their existence came to public notice. Law-enforcement authorities led (1940–41) an assault on Murder, Inc.; it resulted in numerous convictions and several executions, including that of Louis (Lepke) Buchalter. However, the mysterious death of Abe (Kid Twist) Reles, chief killer of Murder, Inc., and the state's star witness, hampered the prosecution. See Burton Turkus and Sid Feder, *Murder, Inc.* (1951, repr. 1972).

Murdoch, Iris (Jean Iris Murdoch), 1919–, English novelist and philosopher, b. Dublin. In 1948 she was named lecturer in philosophy at Oxford, and in 1963 she was made an honorary fellow of St. Anne's College, Oxford. In 1956 she married John Oliver Bayley, the novelist and critic. Murdoch's novels, subtle, witty, convoluted, puzzling, and often wildly comic, have elicited widely differing critical interpretation. It is perhaps reasonable to say, however, that Murdoch views man as an "accidental" creature, thinking of himself as free but actually constricted by the boundaries of self, society, and the natural world. Although the plots of her novels are complex, involving innumerable characters in seemingly endless configurations and punctuated by extraordinary incidents, they often focus on an individual's discovery of his own lack of freedom and his lack of capacity for self-knowledge. Among her many novels are *The Flight from the Enchanter* (1956), *The Bell* (1958), *A Severed Head* (1961), *The Nice and the Good* (1968), *An Accidental Man* (1972), and *The Sacred and Profane Love Machine* (1974). Murdoch has worked on dramatizations of two of her novels, *A Severed Head* (1963, with J. B. Priestley), and *The Italian Girl* (1967, with James Sanders), and she has written a play, *The Servants and the Snow* (1970). She has also published *Sartre, Romantic Rationalist* (1953) and *The Sovereignty of Good* (1971). See studies by A. S. Byatt (1965), Peter Wolfe (1966), Rubin Rabinovitz (1969), and Frank Baldanza (1974).

Murdock, George Peter, 1897–, American anthropologist, b. Meriden, Conn., grad. Yale (B.A., 1919; Ph.D., 1925). He taught at Yale and later at the Univ. of Pittsburgh, becoming Mellon Professor of Anthropology there in 1960. He is noted for his work as head of Yale's Human Relations Area Files, where he attempted to classify and index the known cultures of the world.

Mureşul (mo͞o'rĕsho͞ol), Hung. *Maros* (mŏ'rôsh), river, c.470 mi (760 km) long, rising in the Carpathian Mts., N central Rumania. It flows generally west, past Deva and Arad, into S Hungary, where it joins the Tisza River at Szeged. It is navigable for small craft below Deva.

Muret (mürā'), town (1968 pop. 13,598), Haute-Garonne dept., S France. It is an agricultural market and produces foundry products, surgical instruments, and bricks. In 1213, Simon de Montfort, leader of the ALBIGENSIAN CRUSADE, defeated the nobles of S France at Muret, thus ending their independence. Muret has a 12th-century church and several 15th- and 16th-century houses.

Murfree, Mary Noailles: see CRADDOCK, CHARLES EGBERT.

Murfreesboro (mûr'frēzbûr"ə), city (1970 pop. 26,360), seat of Rutherford co., central Tenn., on Stones River; inc. 1817. It is the processing center of a dairy, livestock, and farm area, and its manufactures include electrical equipment, furniture, and rubber tires. Murfreesboro was the capital of Tennessee from 1819 to 1826. Andrew Jackson and Thomas Hart Benton practiced law there. The Civil War battle of Murfreesboro (or Stones River) was fought there (Dec. 31, 1862–Jan. 2, 1863). Confederate Gen. Braxton Bragg concentrated his army in Murfreesboro after retreating (Oct., 1862) from Kentucky. On Dec. 26 Union Gen. William Rosecrans moved from Nashville toward Chattanooga, and Bragg confronted him just N of Murfreesboro. Each planned to attack the other's right, but Bragg moved first and on Dec. 31 nearly routed the Union forces. After a day's lull, Rosecrans repulsed another attack with massive artillery fire. Both sides suffered heavy losses. On Jan. 3, Bragg retreated to Tullahoma and the Union army occupied Murfreesboro. Stones River National Battlefield (see NATIONAL PARKS AND MONUMENTS, table) commemorates the battle, and Civil War dead are buried in Stones River National Cemetery. Another historic attraction is Oakland Mansion, scene of the surrender (July, 1862) of a Federal garrison to Gen. N. B. Forrest. Middle Tennessee State Univ. is in Murfreesboro.

Murgab (mo͞orgäb'), river, 530 mi (853 km) long, rising in the Paropamisus range, NE Afghanistan, flowing NW into the USSR, through the Merv oasis, and disappearing into the Kara Kum desert, SE Turkmen SSR; it forms part of the Afghanistan-USSR border. With the Kusht, its main tributary, the river is an important source of water; irrigation dams are at Tashkepristroi and Iolotan. An alternate spelling is Morghab.

Murger, Henry (äNrē' mürzhĕr'), 1822–61, French poet and novelist. His *Scènes de la vie de Bohème* (1845–49; tr., 1905, 1930), like many of his works, is a romantic and sentimental account of the life of struggling writers and artists. It provided the story for Puccini's opera *La Bohème.* See biography by Robert Baldwick (1961).

muriate of potash: see POTASSIUM CHLORIDE.

muriatic acid: see HYDROGEN CHLORIDE.

Murieta, Joaquin: see MURRIETA or MURIETA, JOAQUIN.

Murillo, Bartolomé Estéban (bärtōlōmā' āstā'bän mōōrē'lyō), 1617?–1682, Spanish religious and portrait painter. He was born in Seville, where most of his life was spent. There, c.1645, he painted a series of 11 pictures of the history of the Franciscan order for a monastery. These brought him immediate fame, and for the remainder of his life he was the favorite painter of the wealthy and pious Andalusian capital. His early works show the influence of Zurbarán in the dramatic use of light and shadow. Murillo adapted several compositions from northern and Italian prints. Notable works of his early years include *St. Leander, St. Isidore, Vision of St. Anthony* (all: cathedral, Seville), *Birth of the Virgin* (Louvre), and his series for the Church of Santa María la Blanca. In 1660 he was instrumental in founding the Seville Academy, of which he shared the presidency with the younger Francisco de Herrera. From 1670 to 1682, Murillo painted many of his major religious works, including those for the Charity Hospital and for the Capuchin convent (Seville Mus.). These religious works, particularly the Madonnas, are noted for their sweetness of mood. In 1682, while working on the *Marriage of St. Catherine* for the Capuchin church of Cádiz, Murillo fell from a scaffold and died as a result of his injuries. Much modern critical opinion rates as Murillo's greatest works his fine portraits—e.g., *Don Andrés de Andrade y la Col* (Metropolitan Mus.) and *Knight of the Collar* (Prado)—and his naturalistic genre paintings, such as *Girl and Her Duenna* (National Gall., Washington, D.C.) and *Peasant Boy* (National Gall., London). While Murillo's work is best seen in Seville, fine examples are in the Prado and the Louvre, and in the New York, Detroit, Sarasota, and Cincinnati museums. See study by A. F. Calvert (1907).

Murmansk (mōōrmänsk'), city (1970 pop. 309,000), capital of Murmansk oblast, NW European USSR, on the Kola Gulf of the Barents Sea. The terminus of the NORTHEAST PASSAGE, it is a leading Soviet freight port, a naval base, and a base for fishing fleets and is the world's largest city N of the Arctic Circle. The port at Murmansk is ice free. The city is also a railroad terminus and is linked by rail with Moscow and Leningrad. Murmansk has fish canneries, shipyards, textile factories, breweries, and sawmills. Lumber, fish, and apatite are exported, and machinery and coal are imported. Murmansk was only a small village before World War I. The port and its rail line inland from Petrograd (now Leningrad) were built in 1915–16, when the Central Powers cut off the Russian Baltic and Black Sea supply routes. Allied forces occupied the Murmansk area from 1918 to 1920, during the Russian civil war. A major World War II supply base and port for Anglo-American convoys, Murmansk was bombarded by the Germans. The city has a polar research institute. Murmansk oblast, with rich apatite and nickel mines, was enlarged after World War II through the incorporation of former Finnish territories, notably Petsamo (PECHENGA).

Murnau, Friedrich W. (frē'drĭkh mōōr'nou), 1889–1931, German film director whose original name was Friedrich W. Plumpe. He began directing films in Germany in 1919 and went to Hollywood in 1927. Murnau's films are noted for their fluid camera work and for their use of the camera to depict states of mind. His best-known works are *Nosferatu* (1922), *The Last Laugh* (1924), *Fauste* (1926), and the American films *Sunrise* (1927), *Our Daily Bread* (1930), and *Tabu* (1931).

Murner, Thomas (tō'mäs mōōr'nər), 1475–1537, German satirist and Franciscan monk, b. Strasbourg. He was the most scurrilous writer of his time and spared almost no one in his satire. He attacked the clergy, even his own order, but when the Reformation became more radical, Murner turned against Luther. His most celebrated work is the pamphlet *Von dem grossen Lutherischen Narren: wie ihn Doktor Murner beschworen hat* [on the great Lutheran fool: how Dr. Murner exorcised him]. Murner's other works were inspired by Sebastian Brant's *Narrenschiff* [ship of fools] (1494).

Murom (mōō'rəm), city (1969 est. pop. 100,000), W central European USSR, on the Oka River. It is a port and a rail junction, with railroad repair shops and machinery, woodworking, and textile industries. First mentioned in the chronicles in 862, it became the capital of the Murom principality in the 12th cent. The city was ravaged by the Mongols in the 13th cent., and in 1393 it passed to the grand duchy of Moscow. In medieval times, Murom was an important trade center on the Oka-Volga water route. The city has a cathedral and some monasteries dating from the 16th and 17th cent.

Muroran (mōōrō'räN), city (1970 pop. 162,061), SW Hokkaido, Japan, on Uchiura Bay. It is a major industrial center and port, with iron, steel, and cement works and an oil refinery. Hot spring resorts are nearby.

Murphy, Charles Francis, 1858–1924, American political boss, b. New York City. He was the owner of many saloons in New York City and took a keen interest in Democratic politics. His services to Tammany Hall brought him a job as dock commissioner. After the retirement of Richard Croker, Murphy became (1902) boss of Tammany. He held control until his death, continued to build his political machine, and brought about the election of three New York City mayors—George B. McClellan, William Jay Gaynor, and John Francis Hylan—as well as three state governors. Extending his influence to state and national politics, he was instrumental in furthering the careers of Alfred E. Smith and Robert F. Wagner, Sr. See study by N. J. Weiss (1968).

Murphy, Frank, 1890–1949, American political figure, Associate Justice of the Supreme Court (1940–49), b. Harbor Beach, Mich. After serving as a U.S. attorney (1919–20) and as a judge of recorder's court (1923–30), he was elected mayor of Detroit in 1930. He resigned to become governor general (1933–35) and later (1935–36) U.S. high commissioner in the Philippine Islands. Elected governor of Michigan in 1936, his settlement of the automobile strike (1937) in Flint, Mich., made him a national figure. He was defeated for reelection in 1938. In Jan., 1939, Murphy, a New Deal Democrat, was appointed U.S. Attorney General and served until his appointment to the Supreme Court. For a short time in 1942 he left the bench to serve as an army officer. Justice Murphy's opinions reflected his ardent liberalism. See biography by J. W. Howard, Jr. (1968).

Murphy, William Parry, 1892–, American physician, b. Stoughton, Wis., M.D. Harvard, 1920. He taught at Harvard from 1923 and was associated with the Peter Bent Brigham Hospital, in Boston, from 1922. He made special studies of diabetes and diseases of the blood and particularly of the liver treatment for pernicious anemia. For his work on anemia he shared with G. H. Whipple and G. R. Minot the 1934 Nobel Prize in Physiology and Medicine. He wrote *Anemia in Practice* (1939).

Murphysboro (mûr'fēzbûr''ə), city (1970 pop. 10,013), seat of Jackson co., S Ill., on the Big Muddy River; inc. 1867. It is a trade and distributing center for a rich farm area. Shoes, clothing, and aluminum products are made. An apple festival is held there each September. There is a memorial to John A. Logan, who was born there, and a state park and a national forest are nearby.

Murray, Alexander Stuart, 1841–1904, Scottish archaeologist. He was assistant keeper (1867–86) and keeper (from 1886) of Greek and Roman antiquities at the British Museum. From 1894 to 1896 he was in charge of excavations in Cyprus. Among his writings are *Manual of Mythology* (1873, rev. ed. 1935), *Handbook of Greek Archaeology* (1892), *Terra-Cotta Sarcophagi* (1898), and *Excavations in Cyprus* (1900).

Murray, Lord George, 1694–1760, Scottish general. He took part in the risings of the JACOBITES in 1715, 1719, and 1745. Although he foresaw the hopelessness of the 1745 uprising, he was one of Charles Edward Stuart's ablest commanders in the rebellion, serving him in the victory of Prestonpans and in the retreat from the invasion of England. He opposed the strategy that led to the defeat at Culloden Moor (1746). After the battle, in which he commanded the right wing, he fled to Holland. See biography by Katherine Tomasson (1958).

Murray, Gilbert (George Gilbert Aimé Murray), 1866–1957, British classical scholar, b. Sydney, Australia. In 1908 Murray was appointed regius professor of Greek at Oxford. He is best known as a Greek scholar and especially as a translator of Greek drama. His translations were rendered in heroic rhymes to preserve the rhythm of the originals. Among his works are *History of Ancient Greek Literature* (1897), *The Rise of the Greek Epic* (1907), *Euripides and His Age* (1918), *The Classical Tradition in Poetry* (1927), and *Hellenism and the Modern World* (1953). Murray was active in the cause of world peace. He was chairman (1923–38) of the League of Nations Union and first president of the general council of the United Nations Association. He wrote several books about international politics, including *Liberality and Civilization* (1938). See Jean Smith and Arnold Toynbee, ed., *Gilbert Murray: An Unfinished Autobiography* (1960).

Murray, James, 1721?–94, British general, first civil governor of Canada, b. Scotland. He went to Canada as an army officer in 1757 and was prominent at the siege of Louisburg (1758) and in the crucial battle on the Plains of Abraham. Murray was given command of Quebec and withstood the efforts of the French. He was made military governor of Quebec and after the Treaty of Paris (1763) became (1764) the first civil governor of Canada, then called the Province of Quebec. His efforts to protect the French Canadians prepared the way for the Quebec Act (1774) and earned him the enmity of many of the English. Summoned (1766) to England to face charges of betraying British interests, he was vindicated. Although he continued in the governorship until 1768, he did not return to Canada. He remained in the army and reached the rank of full general (1783).

Murray, Sir James Augustus Henry, 1837–1915, English lexicographer. In 1879 he assumed the editorship of the *New English Dictionary* (the *Oxford English Dictionary*), which was his life's work (see DICTIONARY). Murray was a guiding force in this compilation, a triumph of modern scholarship, and its general plan and much of the work on details are to be credited to him. See M. M. Mathews, *A Survey of English Dictionaries* (1933).

Murray or **Moray, James Stuart,** 1st **earl of** (both: mûr'ē), 1531?–1570, Scottish nobleman. An illegitimate son of James V by a daughter of the earl of Mar, he was, therefore, half brother of MARY QUEEN OF SCOTS. Early a Protestant sympathizer, he joined the lords of the congregation in 1559 and was a leader of the opposition to the regent, MARY OF GUISE. After the return to Scotland of the young queen Mary (1561), he was her adviser, always favoring friendship with England and advocating religious reform. He opposed Mary's marriage (1565) to Lord DARNLEY and, after an abortive rebellion, fled to England. He returned (1566) immediately after the murder of David RIZZIO and was reconciled with Mary, who did not know that he had been involved in the murder conspiracy. When Mary was forced to abdicate in 1567, Murray was the only feasible candidate for regent. He made every effort to perpetuate Mary's incarceration and worked in the interests of the young king James VI, the English, and Protestantism. He was assassinated by a member of the Hamilton family. With John Knox, who wrote a panegyric on him, Murray was largely responsible for the success of the Scottish Reformation. See biography by Maurice Lee (1953, repr. 1971).

Murray, John, 2d **marquess** and 1st **duke of Atholl** (ăth'əl), 1660–1724, Scottish nobleman; son of the 2d earl and 1st marquess. A supporter of William III, he held high government posts in Scotland and was created duke in 1703. He successfully weathered a plot against him by Simon Fraser, Baron LOVAT, and James Douglas, 2d duke of QUEENSBERRY. A vigorous opponent of the union (1707) of England and Scotland, he was suspected of Jacobite leanings. Nonetheless, he supported the accession (1714) of George I (although he lost office) and remained loyal to the government during the Jacobite uprising of 1715.

Murray, John, 2d **earl** and 1st **marquess of Atholl,** 1635?–1703, Scottish nobleman. After the Restoration he held high offices in Scotland and was created marquess in 1676. He lost royal favor temporarily when he urged (1678) moderation in the measures against the COVENANTERS but fought vigorously against Archibald Campbell, 8th earl of ARGYLL in 1685. He was lukewarm to the accession (1688) of William III and allowed his troops to be used at Killiecrankie against the supporters of the new king.

Murray, John, 1741–1815, founder of the Universalist denomination in America, b. England. He was excommunicated by the Methodists after he had openly accepted Universalism as taught by James Relly (see UNIVERSALIST CHURCH IN AMERICA). Murray emigrated to America in 1770 where, after traveling as a Universalist preacher for four years in New Jersey, New York, and New England, he settled in Gloucester, Mass. He continued his preaching there and in nearby centers. In 1775, General Washington announced Murray's appointment as chaplain to the Rhode Island troops. He served as pastor of the newly organized Independent Church of Christ (1779) at Gloucester until he was called to the pastorate of the Universalist Society of Boston in 1793.

Murray, Lindley, 1745–1826, American grammarian, b. Pennsylvania. Murray practiced law until the Revolution, during which he acquired a fortune, and in 1784 went to live in England. A Quaker minister, he devoted his time to writing books on English grammar and religious essays. His most popular book was his *English Grammar* (1st ed. 1795), written for a Friends' school. It was the first standard English grammar and was tremendously popular.

Murray, Philip, 1886–1952, American labor leader, b. Blantyre, Scotland. He emigrated to the United States in 1902 and worked in the Pennsylvania coal mines. After he was discharged for fighting with a foreman, 600 miners struck, formed a local of the United Mine Workers of America (UMW), and elected (1904) Murray local president. A skillful negotiator, he rose to the vice presidency of the union by 1920. When the CIO was formed (see AMERICAN FEDERATION OF LABOR AND CONGRESS OF INDUSTRIAL ORGANIZATIONS), he became a CIO vice president and headed (1936) its successful steel workers' organizing campaign. He broke with John L. LEWIS, whom he succeeded as CIO president (1940). For supporting President Franklin Delano Roosevelt's reelection in 1940, Lewis forced Murray out of the UMW. (Lewis supported the Republican Wendell Willkie). However, Murray was elected president of the United Steel Workers of America in 1942 when that union was formed. Retaining the presidency of both the CIO and the United Steel Workers of America until his death, Murray was active in expelling (1949–50) Communist-dominated unions from the CIO.

Murray or **Moray, Thomas Randolph,** 1st **earl of** (both: mûr'ē), d. 1332, Scottish nobleman; nephew of ROBERT I. He joined Robert's revolt against Edward I of England in 1306 but was captured at the battle of Methven and forced to swear fealty to the English king. Recaptured (1308) by Sir James de DOUGLAS, he became one of Robert's strongest warriors and was created earl of Murray. In 1314 he captured Edinburgh Castle by a daring scaling operation and led a division at Bannockburn. He accompanied Edward BRUCE on his invasion of Ireland in 1315 and, with Douglas, led many raids into England, including the one in 1327 in which the young Edward III was nearly captured. He was a principal party in the negotiations that led to the Treaty of Northampton (1328), by which Edward recognized Robert I. He was regent (1331–32) of Scotland for the young David II.

Murray, William: see MANSFIELD, WILLIAM MURRAY, 1ST EARL OF.

Murray. 1 City (1970 pop. 13,537), seat of Calloway co., SW Ky., near the Tenn. line; inc. 1844. There are some manufacturing industries in the city, and agriculture and tourism are also important. Murray is located near five state parks and a recreational area operated by the Tennessee Valley Authority. Murray State Univ. is there. **2** City (1970 pop. 21,206), Salt Lake co., N central Utah; inc. 1903. It is a retail center with diverse manufacturing industries. The county fairgrounds are there.

Murray, principal river of Australia, 1,609 mi (2,589 km) long, rising in the Australian Alps, SE New South Wales, and flowing westward to form the New South Wales–Victoria boundary. It then flows southwest across South Australia state through Lake Alexandrina, a lagoon, into the Indian Ocean. It receives its main tributary, the Darling River, at Wentworth. The Murray-Darling watercourse is 2,911 mi (4,685 km) long but is of little use for navigation except in the lower reaches. Used primarily for irrigation, the Murray has numerous hydroelectric plants and reservoirs, including Hume Reservoir. The Murray and the Murrumbidgee, a tributary, receive most of the diverted water from the Snowy Mts. Hydroelectric Scheme. The Murray valley contains most of Australia's irrigated land; vines, fruits, and vegetables are grown.

Murray Bay, Canada: see LA MALBAIE.

murre (mör), common name for a group of diving birds of the same family as the AUK and the PUFFIN (family Alcidae) and including the guillemots. There are three species of murres, all about 18 in. (45 cm) long, brownish black above and white below. The common murre, *Uria aalge,* and the Brunnich's murre are found in the North Atlantic; the California murre is found in the Pacific. Murres are among the largest of the living members of the family. The smaller guillemots are also called sea pigeons. Murres eat small fish and crustaceans and lay their hard-shelled, pear-shaped eggs on bare rock. Murres return to the same breeding sites year after year. Both male and female incubate the single egg laid per season. Murres are classified in the phylum CHORDATA, subphylum Vertebrata, class Aves, order Charadriiformes, family Alcidae.

Mürren (mür'ən), village, Bern canton, S central Switzerland, in the Bernese Alps. It is a health and sports center with a splendid view of the Jungfrau and neighboring peaks.

Murrieta or **Murieta, Joaquín** (hwäkēn' mo͞oryä'tä), 1829?–1853, California bandit, b. Mexico. From 1849 to 1851 he mined in the California gold fields. After he and members of his family had been mistreated by American miners and driven from their claim, he became the leader of a band of desperadoes. For two years his robberies and murders terrorized California, until the legislature authorized Capt. Harry Love, deputy sheriff of Los Angeles co., to organize a company of mounted rangers to exterminate Murrieta's band. Surprised at his camp near Tulare Lake, Murrieta was shot, and most of his followers were killed or captured. Romanticization of his career began with the publication (1854) of John R. Ridge's *The Life and Adventures of Joaquín Murieta.*

Murrow, Edward Roscoe, 1908–65, American news broadcaster, b. Greensboro, N.C. He joined the Columbia Broadcasting System (CBS) in 1935 and became its European director two years later, assembling and training a news staff to cover the impending war. As a CBS war correspondent (1939–45) Murrow was noted for dramatic and accurate broadcasts from London during the battle of Britain. He served the network as vice president and director of public affairs (1945–47) and news analyst (1947–61), producing and broadcasting the popular *See It Now* and *Person to Person* programs on television. Murrow was director of the U.S. Information Agency from 1961 to 1964. See biography by Alexander Kendrick (1969).

Murrumbidgee (mərəmbĭj'ē), river, c.1,050 mi (1,690 km) long, rising in the Australian Alps, SE New South Wales, Australia, and flowing generally W to the Murray River on the Victoria border. Used extensively for irrigation, the river receives water from the Snowy Mountains Hydroelectric Scheme. Its valley is the most productive farming area in the Murray Basin; fruits, rice, and vegetables are grown. Burrinjuck Dam and hydroelectric station are on the river.

Murry, John Middleton, 1889–1957, English critic and editor. In 1919 he became editor of the *Athenaeum* and in 1923 founded his own review, the *Adelphi,* with which he was associated until 1948. He was friendly with many literary personalities, notably T. S. Eliot, D. H. Lawrence, and Virginia Woolf. His numerous books of criticism include *The Problem of Style* (1922); *Keats and Shakespeare* (1925); *Son of Woman* (1931), a biography of D. H. Lawrence; *William Blake* (1933); and *Jonathan Swift: A Critical Biography* (1954). Although he later altered his position on pacifism, he was the author of *The Necessity of Pacifism* (1937) and during World War II edited the pacifist journal *Peace News.* In 1913 he married Katherine MANSFIELD and after her death edited her journals and letters and collaborated in writing her biography (1933). His other works include *God* (1932) and *Christocracy* (1942), in which he discusses his mystical philosophy. See his autobiographical *Between Two Worlds* (1935); biographies by F. A. Lea (1959) and E. G. Griffin (1968).

Murten (mo͝or'tən), Fr. *Morat,* town (1970 pop. 4,256), Fribourg canton, W Switzerland, on the Lake of Murten. It is known chiefly as the scene of the defeat (1476) of Charles the Bold of Burgundy by the Swiss. Founded by the dukes of Zähringen in the 12th cent., Murten has preserved much of its historic architecture. It has a 13th-century castle, town walls (14th–15th cent.), and a 15th-century French Gothic church.

Murviedro, Spain: see SAGUNTO.

Murzuk: see MARZUQ, Libya.

Muş (mo͞osh), city (1970 pop. 23,511), capital of Muş prov., E Turkey. Grapes are grown nearby. Founded c.400 B.C., it was an important town of Armenia. Called Tarun by the Arabs, Muş was captured by the Seljuk Turks, the Mongols, and Tamerlane before being annexed by the Ottoman Empire in 1515.

Musa Dağı (mo͞o'sä däŭ'), peak, 4,445 ft (1,355 m) high, S Turkey, rising from the Mediterranean Sea, W of Antakya. The heroic resistance of the Armenians against the Turks at Musa Dağı in World War I is the subject of Franz Werfel's novel *The Forty Days of Musa Dagh.*

Musala (mo͞osälä'), mountain, 9,592 ft (2,924 m) high, SW Bulgaria. It is the highest peak of Bulgaria and of the Rhodope range.

Musashino (mo͞osä'shĭno͞o), city (1970 pop. 136,959), Tokyo Metropolis, E central Honshu, Japan, on the Sumida River. It is a suburb of Tokyo.

Muscat, Maskat, or **Masqat** (all: mŭs'kăt, mŭs'kət), city (1969 est. pop. 9,980), capital of Oman, SE Arabia, on the Gulf of Oman. It is flanked by rugged mountains. Muscat, which has a fine harbor, was seized by the Portuguese Afonso de Albuquerque in 1508 and kept by Portugal until 1648. Persian princes held it until 1741, when it became the capital of Oman. Dates, dried fish, and mother-of-pearl are exported, although much of Muscat's trade has been taken over by neighboring Matrah, which has better land communications.

Muscatine (mŭskətēn'), city (1970 pop. 22,405), seat of Muscatine co., SE Iowa, on the Mississippi River; inc. 1851. An early center of river traffic and lumbering, Muscatine today is the shipping and processing center of a rich agricultural area. Food products, grains, industrial alcohol, and vitamins are among the city's products. A junior college is there, and a state park is nearby.

muscle, the contractile tissue that effects the movement of the body. Muscle tissue is classified as striated, smooth, or cardiac, according to its structure and function. Striated, or skeletal, muscle, which is under conscious control, forms the bulk of the body's muscle tissue and gives the body its general shape. It is called striated because under the microscope it appears to be striped in alternating bands of light and dark. Smooth muscle, which lines most of the hollow organs of the body, is not under conscious control, but is regulated by the autonomic nervous system. Smooth muscle fibers are spindle-shaped, not obviously striated, and generally arranged in dense sheets. Smooth muscle lines the blood vessels, hair follicles, urinary tract, digestive tract, and genital tract. Its speed of contraction is slower than that of striated muscle, but it can remain contracted longer. Cardiac muscle is striated like skeletal muscle, but, like smooth muscle, is controlled involuntarily. It is found only in the heart, where it forms that organ's thick walls. The contractions of cardiac muscle are stimulated by a special clump of muscle tissue located on the heart itself, although the rate of contractions is subject to regulation by the autonomic nervous system. Skeletal muscles are attached (with some exceptions, such as the muscles of the tongue and pharynx) to the skeleton by means of tendons, usually in pairs that pull in opposite directions, e.g., the BICEPS (flexor) and TRICEPS (extensor) that move the forearm at the elbow. The end of the muscle attached to the bone that remains relatively fixed when the muscle contracts is called its origin, and the end attached to the bone that moves is called its insertion. For example, the point of origin of the biceps is on the scapula and humerus in the shoulder area; its insertion is on the radius of the forearm. The means by which all types of muscles contract is thought to be generally the same, although striated muscle has been studied most extensively. Striated muscles are composed of numerous cylindrically shaped bundles of cells called fibers, each enclosed in a sheath called the sarcolemma. Each muscle fiber contains several hundred to several thousand tightly packed strands called myofibrils that consist of alternating filaments of the protein substances ACTIN and MYOSIN. Actin and myosin interact before muscle contraction, forming the contractile material actomyosin. The energy required for muscle contraction comes from the breakdown of ADENOSINE TRIPHOSPHATE (ATP), a substance that is present in the cells and is formed during cellular RESPIRATION. A muscle fiber is stimulated to contract by electrical impulses from the nervous system. The point of contact between nerve and muscle is the myoneural juncture, where the chemical substance ACETYLCHOLINE is secreted, initiating the changes that cause the muscle to contract. During resting states some of the fibers in the musculature are maintained in a state of partial contraction, known as muscle tone. This permits muscles to contract quickly when stimulated without having to overcome the inertia of total relaxation.

Muscle Shoals, town (1970 pop. 6,907), Colbert co., NW Ala., on the Tennessee River opposite Florence; inc. 1923. It is the center of experimental development of phosphate and nitrate fertilizers and animal foods. Various products are made in the chemical works there, and the industrialization extends to Florence and other nearby towns. The river formerly descended at that point in a series of rapids called Muscle Shoals (more than 35 mi/56 km long with a drop of more than 130 ft/40 m). They were unnavigable, and early in the 19th cent. plans were made to construct a canal around them. However, a canal built by the state in the 1830s silted up and was abandoned. In 1890 a canal was successfully built by U.S. army engineers. In World War I a project for extracting nitrate was undertaken, but the nitrate works built in 1916 remained unused until the area was bought (1933) by the TENNESSEE VALLEY AUTHOR-

ITY. The building of Wilson Dam (1925) and of Wheeler Dam (1936) resulted in the submersion of the shoals.

muscovite: see MICA.

Muscovy: see MOSCOW, GRAND DUCHY OF.

Muscovy Company (mŭs'kəvē) or **Russia Company,** first major English joint-stock trading company. It began in 1553 as a group supporting exploration of a possible northeast passage to Asia. An expedition under Richard CHANCELLOR reached the White Sea, and Chancellor himself continued overland to Moscow. The company was chartered in 1555, with a monopoly on the newly opened Russian trade, and between 1562 and 1579 it financed expeditions to establish overland trade routes to Persia. In 1646, English merchants were excluded from Russia, but trade reopened on the restoration (1660) of Charles II, and the company was reorganized as a regulated company. It lost its monopoly, long a subject of political opposition, in 1698 but continued in existence until 1917. See T. S. Willan, *The Early History of the Russia Company* (1956, repr. 1968).

muscular dystrophy (dĭs'trōfē), chronic, progressive, wasting disease of the skeletal muscles. It usually occurs in more than one member of a family and is generally thought to be genetically determined, but its cause is unknown. The most common type of muscular dystrophy begins in early childhood, affects boys more often than girls, and is first noticed by a clumsiness in walking and a tendency to fall. In addition to changes in the leg muscles, there may be involvement of the pelvic and shoulder muscles, and in some instances, the heart muscles. In some cases the muscles are replaced by fatty tissue. Most patients are confined to a wheelchair by adolescence and die before adulthood. Another form of the disease, affecting both sexes equally, begins in adolescence and affects the muscles of the face, shoulders, and upper arms in its early stages. This form of the disease progresses more slowly and some patients may survive until middle age. There is no known treatment for muscular dystrophy. However, increased interest in the disease has led to a campaign in the United States for more funds for its study and the development of effective treatment.

Muses, in Greek mythology, patron goddesses of the arts, daughters of Zeus and Mnemosyne. Originally only three, they were later considered as nine. Calliope was the Muse of epic poetry and eloquence; Euterpe, of music or of lyric poetry; Erato, of the poetry of love; Polyhymnia (or Polymnia), of oratory or sacred poetry; Clio, of history; Melpomene, of tragedy; Thalia, of comedy; Terpsichore, of choral song and dance; Urania, of astronomy. Some say that Apollo was their leader. Early places of their worship were the district of Pieria, in Thessaly, where they were often called Pierides, and Mt. Helicon, in Boeotia. The springs of Castalia, Aganippe, and Hippocrene were sacred to them.

Museum of Fine Arts, Boston, chartered and incorporated (1870) after a decision by the Boston Athenaeum, Harvard Univ., and the Massachusetts Institute of Technology to pool their collections of art objects and house them in adequate public galleries. The first building was opened in 1876; the present one, designed by Guy Lowell, in 1909. The museum is supported entirely by private contributions and endowments. Its collection of art from India is thought to be the finest in the United States. The museum's collections of Chinese and Japanese art are outstanding. The Egyptian wing, housing the Way Collection, includes Old Kingdom sculpture unrivaled except in Cairo. The painting galleries are notable for many examples of Spanish art and are particularly strong in works by American artists; 18th-century portraitists, especially Copley and Stuart, are magnificently represented. The museum owns many canvases by John Singer Sargent as well as his mural decorations in the rotunda. The silver work of Paul Revere is shown in quantities unequaled elsewhere. There is also a rich collection of graphic art.

Museum of Modern Art, New York City, established and incorporated in 1929. It is privately supported. The founders were Mrs. John D. Rockefeller, Lillie P. Bliss, Mrs. W. Murray Crane, A. Conger Goodyear, Frank Crowninshield, and Paul J. Sachs; Goodyear served as its first president, and Alfred H. BARR, Jr., was appointed its first director. Operating at first in rented galleries, the museum has specialized in loan shows of contemporary European and American art. A start toward the permanent collection was made with the Lillie P. Bliss bequest, which included nine Cézannes and the Daumier *Washerwoman.* A permanent building was erected by Philip L. Goodwin in 1939 on ground donated by the Rockefellers, with a new wing added in 1962–63. The museum also has an outstanding department of photography, a reference library, and a film library. There are annual circulating exhibits, an art lending service, and art classes for nonprofessionals. The museum publishes a monthly *Art Calendar* and a quarterly *Bulletin,* as well as books on individual arts and artists in connection with exhibitions. Richard Oldenburg was appointed director in 1972. See catalog of paintings in the permanent collection by Helen Frank (1973).

Museum of Primitive Art, New York City, a privately supported institution, established in 1957. It is devoted entirely to the arts of the indigenous cultures of Africa, Oceania, and the Americas and to those art objects related to the early civilizations of Asia and Europe. The museum was founded by Nelson A. Rockefeller, who was elected its first president; Robert Goldwater was appointed director. The museum has a reference library and a photographic archive. It regularly issues catalogs and monographs in connection with exhibitions, and it sponsors a lecture series and loan exhibits.

Museum of the American Indian, Heye Foundation, New York City, devoted solely to the collection, preservation, and presentation of the culture of the aborigines of the Western Hemisphere. It was founded (1916) by Dr. George G. Heye and was opened to the public in 1922. The museum collection contains some 4 million objects. The pre-Columbian hall has a noted collection of art and artifacts from the civilizations of American Indians. The museum issues bulletins and monographs and conducts extensive fieldwork.

museums of art, institutions or buildings where works of art are kept for display or safekeeping. The word *museum* derives from the Greek *mouseion,* meaning temple to the works of the Muses. This article is chiefly concerned with museums of art in the Western Hemisphere.

North America and Mexico. In the United States the foremost repositories of art include, in New York City, the METROPOLITAN MUSEUM OF ART, the richest and most comprehensive American collection of world art (much of the museum's superb medieval collection is housed separately in the CLOISTERS); MUSEUM OF MODERN ART; Frick Collection, the dwelling and outstanding acquisitions of the industrialist Henry Clay Frick; WHITNEY MUSEUM OF AMERICAN ART; MUSEUM OF PRIMITIVE ART; GUGGENHEIM MUSEUM, exhibiting primarily the works of contemporary European and American artists; PIERPONT MORGAN LIBRARY, housing a vast number of important illuminated manuscripts; Hispanic Society Gallery; NEW-YORK HISTORICAL SOCIETY, noted for its 19th-century American paintings and Audubon collection; Brooklyn Museum, strong in Egyptian and American art; and the Brooklyn Institute of Arts and Sciences. In Boston the MUSEUM OF FINE ARTS houses a major collection of American paintings, including the largest number of works by Copley and Stuart in the nation and a magnificent collection of Oriental art; and the Gardner Museum (see under GARDNER, ISABELLA STEWART) holds a remarkable privately acquired collection in an unusual setting. In Cambridge, Mass., the Fogg Museum of Art of Harvard Univ. owns a great number of American works and has fine Italian art and graphic arts collections. Other collections of note in the E United States include the Albright-Knox Art Gallery (Buffalo, N.Y.); Worcester (Mass.) Art Museum; Wadsworth Athenaeum (Hartford, Conn.); Yale Gallery of Fine Arts (New Haven, Conn.); PENNSYLVANIA ACADEMY OF THE FINE ARTS and PHILADELPHIA MUSEUM OF ART, noted for its many works by Eakins (both: Philadelphia); Barnes Collection (Merion, Pa.), a superb private gallery of impressionist and post-impressionist works; Carnegie Institute (Pittsburgh); and the Walters Art Gallery (Baltimore). In Washington, D.C., the SMITHSONIAN INSTITUTION comprises four major galleries: the NATIONAL GALLERY OF ART, which houses the principal collection of the four; Freer Gallery of Art, notable for its many works by Whistler and its oriental art collection; National Collection of Fine Arts; and United States National Museum. The Corcoran Gallery of Art (see under CORCORAN, WILLIAM WILSON) and the Phillips Collection, both strong in American art, and the Hirshhorn Museum and Sculpture Garden, devoted to modern art, are also in Washington, D.C. In the Midwest and South the Cleveland Museum of Art, CINCINNATI ART MUSEUM, ART INSTITUTE OF CHICAGO, and the museums and galleries of Detroit, Columbus (Ohio), Toledo, Indianapolis, St. Louis, Minneapolis, Milwaukee, Kansas City (Mo.), and New Orleans are outstanding. The major collections in the West include the Gilcrease Institute (Tulsa, Okla.), Dallas Museum of Fine Arts, Huntington Library and Art Gallery (San Marino, Calif.), LOS ANGELES COUNTY MUSEUM, and the San Francisco Museum of Art. The National Gallery of Canada (Ottawa) holds that country's foremost public art collection. In Mexico City the major collections are the Palace of Fine Art and the magnificent new NATIONAL MUSEUM OF ANTHROPOLOGY, which houses a vast treasure of Mexican art and important archaeological discoveries as well as a superb ethnographic collection.

Great Britain. The richest British collections are housed in the BRITISH MUSEUM, VICTORIA AND ALBERT MUSEUM, NATIONAL GALLERY, NATIONAL PORTRAIT GALLERY, TATE GALLERY, Wallace Collection (see under WALLACE, SIR RICHARD), and Sir John Soane's Museum (all: London); Ashmolean Museum (Oxford); Fitzwilliam Museum (Cambridge); National Gallery of Ireland, National Museum of Ireland, and Trinity College Library (all: Dublin); and the Glasgow Art Galleries. In addition, the Royal Collection at Windsor Castle contains one of the finest treasures of art in the world.

Continental Europe. The major European museums and galleries include: Austria—Academy of Fine Arts, Art Historical Museum, Liechtenstein Gallery, Albertina, National Library, and the Czernin Collection (all: Vienna); Belgium—the Royal Museum of Fine Arts and the Old Museum (both: Brussels), and the Museum of Fine Arts (Antwerp); France—the LOUVRE, Museums of Modern Art, BIBLIOTHÈQUE NATIONALE, and CLUNY, Jeu de Paume, Rodin, Carnavalet, Petit-Palais, and Guimet museums (all: Paris), the Versailles Museum and the local institutions of Nantes, Chantilly, Marseilles, and other cities; Germany—a great number of German museums were destroyed during World War II. Most of the outstanding collections in Berlin and Munich were saved, and among the smaller surviving collections are those in the galleries of Augsburg, Cologne, Düsseldorf, Frankfurt-am-Main, Freiburg, Hanover, Leipzig, Nuremberg, Stuttgart, and Trier; Greece—Acropolis Museum, Byzantine Museum, and the National Archaeological Museum (all: Athens); Italy—UFFIZI, Pitti Palace, Academy art museum, and BARGELLO (all: Florence), the VATICAN, Lateran, Barberini, Farnese, and Borghese palaces (all: Rome), Academy of Fine Arts and Scuola de San Rocco (both: Venice), Brera Palace (Milan), Cathedral Museum (Siena), and National Museum (Naples); Netherlands—RIJKS MUSEUM (Amsterdam) and Mauritshuis (The Hague); Portugal—National Museum (Lisbon); Scandinavia—Royal Academy of Arts and National Museum (both: Copenhagen) and National Museum and State Historical Museum (both: Stockholm); Spain—PRADO, Armería, and El ESCORIAL (all: Madrid); and the El Greco Museum (Toledo); Switzerland—Swiss National Museum (Zurich) and Art Museum (Basel).

Middle East and Asia. In Egypt the Cairo Museum excels in the ancient art of that country, while in İstanbul, Turkey, the art of Babylon, Assyria, and Byzantium may be seen in the archaeological museums. The Tehran Museum and the Government Collections in Tehran hold many of the most important Persian art treasures. The Calcutta Museum exhibits the art of India. Among great Russian collections are those housed in the HERMITAGE (Leningrad) and the Tretyakov Gallery and Museum of Western Art (both: Moscow). In Japan in the National Museum (Tokyo), the Kyoto Museum, and the collections of Shoso-in and the National Museum (both: Nara), all periods of Japanese art are well represented. See Helmut Rauschenbusch, ed., *International Directory of Arts* (2 vol., 11th ed. 1971–72); *Museums of the World,* compiled by Eleanor Braun (1973); Kenneth Hudson and Ann Nicholls, *World Museums* (1974).

museums of science. Many early museums of science, e.g., the Ashmolean Museum (1683) at Oxford, originated from gifts of private collections. At first most exhibits consisted of classified and labeled geological or biological specimens. Later exhibition techniques have emphasized the grouping of specimens to illustrate origins, associations, and interrelationships. Exhibition devices include habitat groups, restorations, murals, dioramas, models, and key installations in feature exhibits. The illustration of abstract ideas in biology, e.g., evolution and heredity, was extended to physics and chemistry, long neglected in science museums. A pioneer in showing the principles of mechanics, light, heat, and sound was the Buffalo Museum of Natural Science. The modern science museum has a three-fold function—exhibition of collections, sponsoring of research, and education. Many museums provide cataloged reserve collections for students and undertake research and the publication of results; some participate in expeditions for research or for enlarging collections. Provisions for adult education include guided tours, lectures, and classes; museums cooperate with schools by providing loan exhibitions, special exhibits and tours for children, and story hours. Many museums now attempt to educate the public in the principles of ecology and wildlife and resource conservation. Outstanding in developing educational functions are the AMERICAN MUSEUM OF NATURAL HISTORY and the FIELD MUSEUM OF NATURAL HISTORY. Although most science museums cover the general field, there are many, including a number of university and college teaching museums, that specialize, notably in anthropology; one of these is the Heye Foundation, Museum of the American Indian, New York City. The establishment of the Adler Planetarium, Chicago (1930), the Fels Planetarium (1933) of the Franklin Institute, and the Hayden Planetarium (1935) of the American Museum of Natural History have stimulated science museums to deal with astronomy. Pioneers in the field of applied science include, in Europe, the Conservatoire des Arts et Métiers (the first industrial museum, est. 1799) and the Palais de la Découverte, both in Paris; the Science Museum, London; and the Deutsches Museum, Munich. In the United States are the Museum of Science and Industry, Chicago, and the Franklin Institute, Philadelphia. Many private companies have established their own museums, e.g., the glass museum in Corning, N.Y. Such private museums often have unique collections. The first of these, dating from 1916, was a button museum in Prague. A recent development in American science museums is the local trailside museums, most of them in national parks, whose establishment was stimulated by the success of Yosemite Museum (1921). Other notable specialized museums are the museums of oceanography in Monaco and in Berlin. Most of the principal countries of the world have national science museums or strong science collections in general museums. In London are the great natural history collection of the British Museum, housed in South Kensington, and the Museum of the Royal College of Surgeons, with its Hunterian Collection. Other noted science museums in Europe include Norway's Bergen Museum; the Royal Museum of Natural History, Stockholm; the National Museum, Copenhagen; the Rijks Museum, Leiden, noted for its departments of geology, mineralogy, and zoology; the University Museum, Amsterdam; the Natural History Museum, Vienna; the Natural History Museum (Jardin des Plantes), Paris; and the Museum of the Academy of Sciences, Leningrad. Germany has many excellent science museums in its cities and universities and many Italian universities are noted for their science collections. The chief cities of Australia, New Zealand, Africa, and Latin America are known for outstanding collections in local natural history and ethnology. Canada has notable collections, especially in Toronto, Ottawa, and Quebec. The U.S. National Museum is a bureau of the SMITHSONIAN INSTITUTION. There are many municipal and state museums of science. Universities and colleges that have notable museums include Harvard, with the Museum of Comparative Zoology (est. 1859 by Louis Agassiz, the earliest such collection in the United States) and the Peabody Museum of Archaeology and Ethnology; the Univ. of Chicago, with the Oriental Institute and the Walker Museum of Paleontology; and the Univ. of Pennsylvania, specializing in ethnology and archaeology, especially of the Americas and of Asia. In addition to those already mentioned, the Academy of Natural Sciences of Philadelphia (est. 1812) and the Boston Society of Natural History (est. 1830) are outstanding among American museums. In recent years there has been a trend to small special museums centering around limited fields of science or technology. Some are privately supported, others have been established by government agencies. Among them is the Dard Hunter Paper Museum (see HUNTER, DARD), which was established at the Massachusetts Institute of Technology in 1938 and moved to Appleton, Wis., in 1954; it embraces all aspects of paper making and of the use of paper. The American Museum of Atomic Energy opened in 1949 in Oak Ridge, Tenn. See BOTANICAL GARDEN. For American and Canadian museums see *The Official Museum Directory*, pub. by the American Association of Museums (1971); *Museums of the World*, comp. by Eleanor Braun (1973).

Mushi (mo͞o'shī), founder of a Levitical family. Ex. 6.19; Num. 3.20,33; 26.58; 1 Chron. 6.19,47; 23.21,23; 24.26,30.

Mushin (mo͞o'shĭn), city (1969 est. pop. 169,000), SW Nigeria, an industrial and residential suburb of Lagos. Manufactures include textiles, furniture, printed materials, metal products, plastics, milk products, and shoes. Motor vehicles are assembled. Mushin grew mainly after World War II, with the industrialization of the Lagos area.

mushroom, a type of basidium fungus characterized by spore-bearing gills on the underside of the umbrella- or cone-shaped cap. The name *toadstool* is popularly reserved for inedible or poisonous mushrooms, but this classification has no scientific basis. The only safe way of distinguishing between the edible and the poisonous forms is to learn to identify the individual species. Many poisonous mushrooms are of the genus *Amanita*, recognizable by the swollen bag (volva) at the base of the stalk. The genus includes the fly mushroom and the

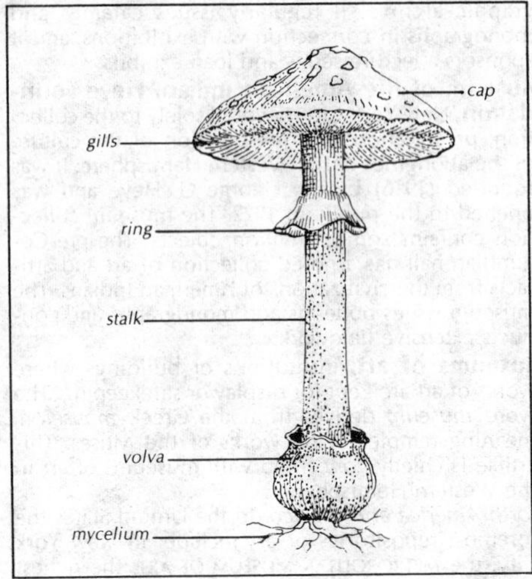

The poisonous mushroom Amanita

deadly amanita, or death angel. The use of edible mushrooms for food dates back at least to early Roman times. Originally a delicacy for the elite, mushrooms are now extensively grown on a commercial scale, especially strains of the field, or meadow, mushroom (*Agaricus campestris*). Their culture requires careful control of temperature and humidity. The bulk of the crop in the United States is grown near Philadelphia. In Europe more than 50 species of mushrooms are marketed. Although mushrooms contain some protein and minerals, they are largely composed of water and hence are of limited nutritive value. The TRUFFLE, PUFFBALL, and other edible fungi are sometimes also called mushrooms. In all cases the term *mushroom* is properly restricted to the plant's above-ground portion, which is the reproductive organ. Mushrooms are classified in the division FUNGI, class Basidiomycetes. See A. H. Smith, *The Mushroom Hunter's Field Guide* (1963); O. K. Miller, *Mushrooms of North America* (1972).

mushroom poisoning, fungal poisoning caused by ingestion of certain mushrooms, most commonly *Amanita phalloides* and other mushrooms of the genus. Symptoms, caused by toxic peptides, may include severe abdominal pain, vomiting, cold sweat, diarrhea, and excessive thirst; they appear 8 to 12 hours after ingestion. Damage occurs largely in the liver and kidneys. Some mushrooms contain substances that produce hallucinatory states, e.g., *Psilocybe mexicana* (see PSYCHOTOMIMETIC DRUG; ERGOT). Diseases caused by toxins, or poisons, from fungi, especially species of *Aspergillus* and *Fusarium,* are known as mycotoxicoses and are diseases of crops and livestock that cause significant economic losses. Occasional outbreaks of poisoning from eating canned mushrooms are not caused by poisonous mushrooms but by BOTULISM resulting from improper canning methods.

Musi (mo͞o'sē), river, c.325 mi (520 km) long, rising in the Pegunungan Barisan, S Sumatra, Indonesia. It flows SE to Palembang (head of oceangoing navigation), then northeast through the swampy coastal plain to the Bangka Strait. The Rawas River is its chief tributary. Rubber and a variety of tropical crops are raised in the valley.

Musial, Stanley Frank (myo͞o'zēəl), 1920–, American baseball player, b. Donora, Pa. At 17 he signed with the St. Louis Cardinals of the National League, and after three years in the minor leagues he joined (1941) the Cardinals. One of the great hitters of all time, Stan the Man, as Musial is known, won the National League batting championship seven times (1943, 1946, 1948, 1950–52, and 1957) and the league's most valuable player award three times (1943, 1946, and 1948). In 1963 he retired with a lifetime batting average of .331. He hit 475 home runs and holds the National League record for base hits (3,630). He was elected to the Baseball Hall of Fame in 1969.

music. For information on types of music see such articles as ABSOLUTE MUSIC; ALEATORY MUSIC; CHAMBER MUSIC; CHURCH MUSIC; COMPUTER MUSIC; ELECTRONIC MUSIC; JAZZ; PROGRAM MUSIC; ROCK MUSIC; and SERIAL MUSIC. In addition, see entries on the music of various nations and peoples, including AFRICAN NEGRO MUSIC; AMERICAN NEGRO SPIRITUALS; ARABIAN MUSIC; BALINESE MUSIC; CHINESE MUSIC; GREEK MUSIC; HINDU MUSIC; JAPANESE MUSIC; JAVANESE MUSIC; and JEWISH LITURGICAL MUSIC. The technical aspects of music, such as theory, notation, and tone, are treated in such general articles as THEORY and MUSICAL NOTATION, and in some more specific entries, including COUNTERPOINT; HARMONIC; HARMONY; KEY; MEASURE; MODE; MUSICOLOGY; NOTE; PITCH; POLYPHONY; RHYTHM; SCALE; SYNCOPATION; TABLATURE; TEMPERAMENT; TONALITY; TONE; TRANSPOSING INSTRUMENT; and TUNING SYSTEMS. There are numerous articles on various musical forms, including CANTATA; CONCERTO; MARCH; NOCTURNE; OPERA; ORATORIO; POLONAISE; SONATA; SONG; and SYMPHONY. In addition to such survey articles as CONCERT; CONDUCTING; MUSICAL INSTRUMENTS; MUSIC FESTIVALS; ORCHESTRA AND ORCHESTRATION, there are separate articles on musical instruments, treated singly, e.g., CLARINET; HARP; TRUMPET, or in groups, e.g., REED INSTRUMENT; STRINGED INSTRUMENT. In addition to the entry on VOICE, there are separate articles on ALTO; BARITONE; COUNTERTENOR; SOPRANO; and TENOR. Information on individual composers and performers can be found in biographical entries on composers, e.g. MONTEVERDI, CLAUDIO; PUCCINI, GIACOMO; and SCHUBERT, FRANZ PETER; musicians, e.g., BEIDERBECKE, BIX; GIESEKING, WALTER; RICHTER, SVIATOSLAV; and singers, e.g., DELLER, ALFRED; MERRILL, ROBERT; SEMBRICH, MARCELLA; and SINATRA, FRANK.

musical comedy: see MUSICALS.

musical glasses: see HARMONICA **2.**

musical instruments are classified in various ways, but the system devised in 1914 by Kurt Sachs and E. M. von Hornbostel has been accorded recognition by both anthropologists and musicologists because it is applicable not only to modern Western instruments but to primitive and exotic instruments as well. This system divides instruments into five main classes: idiophones, membranophones, aerophones, chordophones, and electrophones. Most idiophones, which are instruments made of a sonorous material needing no additional tension, and membranophones, whose sound is produced by the vibrations of a membrane stretched over a hollow resonator, are popularly grouped as PERCUSSION INSTRUMENTS; certain instruments, however, such as the JEW'S-HARP and the glass harmonica (see HARMONICA **2**), are idiophones, but are not percussion instruments. Aerophones are of two types: free aerophones, which include those REED INSTRUMENTS employing free reeds, and WIND INSTRUMENTS, which produce sound by means of an enclosed, vibrating column of air. Chordophones are STRINGED INSTRUMENTS. Electrophones, a development of the 20th cent., are of two types: those which simply add an electric amplifier to some existing instrument, e.g., the piano, guitar, or reed organ, and those whose sounds originate as electrical vibrations, e.g., the electric organ. See articles on individual instruments, e.g., DULCIMER. See Kurt Sachs, *The History of Musical Instruments* (1940); Karl Geiringer, *Musical Instruments* (1943); Alexander Buchner, *Musical Instruments: An Illustrated History* (rev. ed. 1973).

musical notation, symbols used to make a written record of musical sounds. Two different systems of letters were used to write down the instrumental and the vocal music of ancient Greece. In his five textbooks on music theory BOETHIUS (A.D. c.470–A.D. 525) applied the first 15 letters of the alphabet to the notes in use at the end of the Roman period. Notation of Gregorian chant was by means of neumes, which are thought to have been derived from symbols used in the Greek language to indicate pitch inflection. Neumes were certainly in use by the 6th cent., although the earliest extant manuscripts containing them are fragmentary ones from

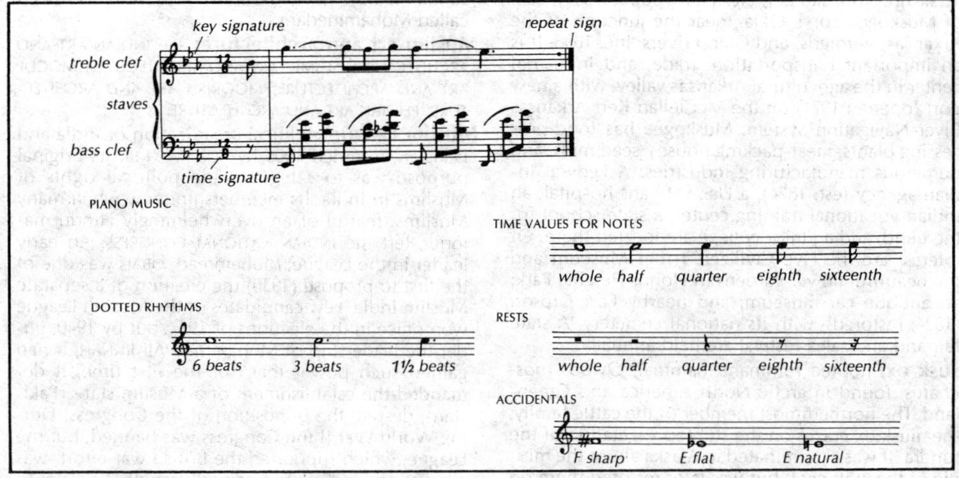

Musical notation

the 8th cent. These neumes indicated only the grouping of sounds in a given melody, evidently to recall to a singer the approximate shape of a melody already learned by ear. Heighted neumes, arranged above and below a line, made the intervals of a melody more discernible in 10th-century notation, and by the end of the 12th cent. the STAFF perfected by GUIDO D'AREZZO was in use. Guido placed letters on certain lines to indicate their pitch and thereby the pitch of the remaining lines and spaces. The letters evolved into the clef signs in use today—the G, or treble, clef; the F, or bass, clef; and the C clef, which was originally much used in vocal music and is now used mainly in scoring for certain instruments, such as the viola. The rhythm implied in plainsong notation is still the subject of controversy. Mensural notation, in which each note has a specific time value, became a necessity with the development of POLYPHONY. Certain neumes were selected to represent tones of long and short duration. In his *Ars cantus mensurabilis* (c.1280), Franco of Cologne, to standardize mensural notation, codified a set of rhythmic modes based on the metrical feet of poetry. In the 14th cent. Philippe de Vitry, author of *Ars nova*, which expands the system of Franco, freed music from the rigid system of the rhythmic modes. NOTES were divided into smaller fractions than halves. A staff of five lines for vocal music was adopted in France, and one of six lines in Italy; a four-line staff is still standard for plainsong. Red ink and black ink were used to indicate whether a note was to be divided into two or three units, and a dot was employed whose function was similar to that of the bar line, which today indicates the MEASURE. Signs for chromatic alteration of tones—the sharp to raise the tone a half step, or semitone, and the flat to lower it a half step—appear frequently in 14th-century music. These signs had assumed their present shapes by the end of the 17th cent. In the 15th cent. the round shape of notes replaced the old square or diamond shape, and time signatures replaced coloration to indicate whether notes of long duration were made up of two or three units. Today's time signature is a numerical fraction indicating the number of beats in a measure and the note value of the unit of beating. Instrumental music employed staves of varying numbers of lines until the 16th cent., when the five-line staff became the standard and ledger lines were invented to indicate pitches outside the compass of the staff. Expression signs and Italian terms (e.g., moderato) to indicate tempo and dynamics came into use in the 17th cent. The key signature originated early, in the form of one flat used to indicate that the mode employed had been transposed. Sharps were not generally used in signatures until the 17th cent. With the adoption of equal temperament (see TUNING SYSTEMS) and the major and minor modes, signatures indicating a major key or its relative minor became conventional. They assumed their present form during the baroque period. The solmization syllables (do, re, mi, etc.) of Guido d'Arezzo were the basis of a system of notation introduced into England in 1841 by John Curwen (1816–80) and much used there for the teaching of sight singing. English publishers usually print the tonic sol-fa notation above the staff notation in choral music. The advent of ALEATORY MUSIC has produced notation systems, varying from piece to piece, indicating only approximate pitch, duration, and dynamic relations. Notation for ELECTRONIC MUSIC is still not standardized but generally uses traditional reference symbols (staff and clef signs) in conjunction with specially adapted pitch and rhythm notation. For a system of notation of lute and keyboard music, see TABLATURE. See SCORE. See Willi Apel, *The Notation of Polyphonic Music, 900–1600* (5th ed. 1961); C. F. A. Williams, *The Story of Notation* (1903, repr. 1969); Erhard Karkoschka, *Notation in New Music* (1972); Gardner Read, *Music Notation* (3d ed. 1972).

musicals. Incorporating the songs and sketchy plots of OPERETTA with the topical numbers of the REVUE, musical comedy began in England at the end of the 19th cent. In the United States during World War I the colorful extravaganzas of George M. COHAN ushered in an era of patriotic and spectacular productions. Thereafter musical comedy flourished primarily in the United States. The songs were light and popular, and emphasis was placed on chorus dancing rather than on singing. Such stars as Lillian RUSSELL and DeWolf HOPPER were followed by Anna HELD, Marilyn Miller, Jack Donahue, Ray Bolger, Fred and Adele ASTAIRE, Gertrude LAWRENCE, Ethel MERMAN, Mary MARTIN, and Alfred DRAKE. Many of these graced the musicals of Irving BERLIN, Jerome KERN, Cole PORTER, Noel COWARD, George GERSHWIN, and Richard ROGERS and Lorenz HART. With the production in 1943 of Rogers and Hammerstein's *Oklahoma!*, musical comedy integrated music, song, and dance with a detailed plot. The later introduction of social problems and plots based on established literary works as in *West Side Story* (1957) by Leonard BERNSTEIN, and *My Fair Lady* (1956) by Alan Jay LERNER and Frederick Loewe, has caused such productions to be termed simply *musicals*. In the late 1960s the "rock musical" came into prominence with the production of *Hair* (1967). Variations of this style have included the religious *Jesus Christ, Superstar* (1971) and a rock music version of *Two Gentlemen of Verona* (1971). The popularity of musicals has created a new form of summer stock theater, the "music tent." The musical film has enjoyed popularity since the release of Jolson's *The Jazz Singer* in 1927. It developed from the Busby Berkeley spectacles of the 1930s to the scintillating gaiety and virtuosity of the Fred Astaire–Ginger Rogers comedies, to the operetta films of Jeanette MacDonald and Nelson Eddy, and the filmed biographies of musical celebrities. In the 1940s numerous romantic and patriotic musicals were produced. By the next decade musicals had come to depend heavily upon Broadway hits and previous film successes for subject matter. Outstanding among original musicals were *Top Hat* (1935), *An American in Paris* (1951), and *Singin' in the Rain* (1952). Noted singers and dancers that have appeared in film musicals include Judy GARLAND, Frank SINATRA, Gene KELLY, Mario Lanza, Howard Keel, Kathryn Grayson, Shirley Jones, Julie Andrews, and Barbra STREISAND. See studies by Lehman Engel (1967), David Ewen (rev. ed. 1970), Stanley Green (1971), and Alec Wilder (1972).

music festivals, series of performances separate from the normal concert season and often, but not always, organized around an idea or theme. Music festivals usually are held annually in the summer, sometimes in the open air. The concept has been traced as far back as the sixth-century B.C. Pythian Games at Delphi, which included musical competitions. In the Middle Ages competitive festivals were sponsored by guilds. The EISTEDDFOD in Wales is a direct descendant of medieval competitive festivals. Among the best-known music festivals with a specific theme held today are the BAYREUTH FESTIVAL, which features the operas of Wagner; the Munich and GLYNDEBOURNE FESTIVALS; the Darmstadt modern music festival; and the NEWPORT JAZZ FESTIVAL (now held in New York City). The SALZBURG FESTIVAL began (musically) as a Mozart festival; today, however, other composers are also performed; it is perhaps the outstanding example of a general classical music festival. Similar events are held in Aspen, Colo. (see ASPEN MUSIC FESTIVAL), Edinburgh, Spoleto (see SPOLETO FESTIVAL), and Bergen (Norway). The BERKSHIRE FESTIVAL at Tanglewood, near Lenox, Mass., features the Boston Symphony. The Saratoga (N.Y.) Festival of the Performing Arts features the Philadelphia Orchestra, the New York City Ballet, and popular-music performers. The festival idea has spread all over the world; Osaka began a festival of music and drama in 1958. In recent years festivals of rock music have frequently been held on a one-time basis. Two of the most famous were held at Monterey, Calif. (1967) and Woodstock, N.Y. (1969).

music-hall. In England, the Licensing Act of 1737 confined the production of legitimate plays to the two royal theaters—Drury Lane and Covent Garden; the demands for entertainment of the rising lower and middle classes were answered by song, dance, and acrobatics, and later by pantomime and comic skits and sketches provided by keepers of inns and taverns. The atmosphere, amidst eating and drinking, was boisterous and gay. Following the abolition (c.1843) of the royal theater patents, the rise of the music-hall as a separate place of variety entertainment was rapid. Personalities, such as the English Joseph Grimaldi, Dan Leno, Beatrice Lillie, Gracie Fields, and the French Yvette Guilbert, Maurice Chevalier, and Edith Piaf, became stars, beloved by their audiences. Like American vaudeville, the music-hall went into a decline with the coming of radio and motion pictures. See Diane Howard, *London Theatres and Music Halls, 1850–1950* (1971).

musicology, systematized study of music, particularly in the realm of historical research. The scholarly study of music of different historical periods was not practiced until the 18th cent., and few published efforts were rigorously researched. Notable exceptions include the works of two Englishmen, Charles Burney's *General History of Music* (1776–89) and J. Hawkins's *General History of the Science and Practice of Music* (1776). In the 19th cent. the general interest in antiquity induced curiosity in older music and the key problem of understanding obsolete forms of musical notation. François Joseph Fétis (1784–1871) and August Wilhelm Ambros (1816–76) were among the first to publish satisfactorily researched overviews of the development of Western music. Their inclusion of transcriptions of unknown medieval and Renaissance pieces is especially important. Today, the domain of musicology is defined by universities, where such study is centered, and includes study of acoustics, ethnomusicology, and aesthetics. Ironically, the study of musical compositions as such, as distinct from the study of data related to them, is not regarded as within the sphere of musicology but rather in the academically separate branch of study called music theory (see THEORY, in music).

Musil, Robert (rō'bĕrt mo͞o'zĭl), 1880–1942, Austrian novelist. His work, whose style has been compared to that of Proust, is marked by subtle psychological analysis. This is evident in the novel *Young Törless* (1906, tr. 1955) as well as in his chief work, *Der Mann ohne Eigenschaften* (3 vol., 1930–42; tr. *The Man without Qualities*, 1953–60). Many of his short stories have been translated and published in such posthumous collections as *Tonka and Other Stories* (tr. 1965) and *Three Short Stories* (1970). See studies by Burton Pike (1961, repr. 1971) and Lisa Appiqnanesi (1973).

musk, odorous substance secreted by an abdominal gland of the MUSK DEER, used in PERFUME as a scent and fixative. The gland, found only in males, grows to the size of a hen's egg; the secretion is reddish-brown, with a honeylike consistency and a strong odor that may function in the animal as a sexual attractant. After the pouch is cut the secretion hardens, assumes a blackish-brown color, and when dry becomes granular. In commerce the musk pouches are called "musk pods," and the dried secretion "musk grains." Usually a tincture of alcohol is made from the grains; this is then added to expensive perfumes. The chief constituent that gives musk its odor is the organic compound muscone. Musklike substances are also obtained from the MUSKRAT and the civet. Some plants yield oils which resemble musk; these include the seed of ambrette (*Hibiscus abelmoschos*) and the sumbul root (*Ferula sumbul*) of central Asia and Turkistan. A number of synthetic musklike products are now also used.

musk deer, small, antlerless deer, *Moschus moschiferus,* found in wet mountain forests from Siberia and Korea to the Himalayas. In summer it ranges up to 8,000 ft (2,400 m). It is from 20 to 24 in. (50–60 cm) high at the shoulder, with a brown coat, a pointed face, and large ears. The male has tusklike upper canine teeth curving down and backwards from the sides of the mouth, and a musk gland, called the pod, in the skin of the abdomen. Destruction of the animal for MUSK, which is used in perfume, has greatly reduced its numbers, and it has been exterminated in part of its range. It is classified in the phylum CHORDATA, subphylum Vertebrata, class Mammalia, order Artiodactyla, family Cervidae.

Muskegon (məskē'gən), city (1970 pop. 44,631), seat of Muskegon co., W Mich., on Lake Michigan; inc. as a city 1869. A port of entry, with a large landlocked harbor, the city is a car-ferry terminus and a shipping point for a farm, fruit, and industrial region. Among its many manufactures are automobile parts and engines, foundry products, pistons, bowling and billiard supplies, copper wire, gasoline pumps, and heavy machinery. Agriculture and tourism are also important. A fur-trading post was established there c.1810. The first sawmill was built in 1837, and the lumber industry thrived until 1890, when the city was swept by fire. A junior college is there, and two state parks are nearby.

Muskegon, river, 227 mi (365 km) long, rising in Houghton Lake, N central Mich., and flowing SW to Lake Michigan at Muskegon. At its mouth the river widens into **Muskegon Lake,** forming a harbor c.2.5 mi (4 km) wide and c.5.5 mi (8.9 km) long.

Muskegon Heights, city (1970 pop. 17,304), Muskegon co., W Mich., a suburb of Muskegon; inc. 1903. Piston rings, cranes, foundry castings, gasoline pumps, and office furniture are manufactured.

muskellunge: see PIKE.

musket: see SMALL ARMS.

Muskhelishvili, Nikolai Ivanovich (nyĭkəlī' ēvä'-nəvĭch mo͞os'hĕlē"shvēlē), 1891–, Soviet mathematician and mechanical engineer, grad. St. Petersburg Univ., 1914. From 1922 he taught at the Tiflis State Univ., where he influenced the establishment (1935) of the Tiflis Mathematical Institute. He was elected deputy to the Supreme Soviet for several terms; in 1939 he became a full member of the USSR Academy of Sciences. Muskhelishvili is best known for his research in integral equations and for his work in potential theory as applied to such problems as the torsion and bending of steel beams and the behavior of elastic materials. J. R. M. Radok translated into English his *Singular Integral Equations* (tr. 1953, 2d ed. 1961, repr. 1972) and *Some Basic Problems of the Mathematical Theory of Elasticity* (2d ed. 1963).

Muskie, Edmund Sixtus, 1914–, U.S. Senator (1959–), b. Rumford, Maine. A lawyer, he sat (1947–51) in the Maine legislature after serving in the navy in World War II. He later became (1955) Maine's first Democratic governor in 18 years and was elected to the U.S. Senate in 1958. He was reelected in 1964 and in 1970. In 1968, Muskie was the Democratic candidate for Vice President, sharing the ticket with Hubert Humphrey. The Democrats lost the election, but Muskie emerged as a leading contender for the 1972 Democratic nomination for President, to run against the incumbent, Richard M. Nixon. He ran in a number of primaries, but his candidacy foundered and in April, 1972, he announced that he would not campaign for any additional primaries. He remained in the race, however, withdrawing before the balloting was begun at the Democratic national convention. At the 1973 Senate hearings on the WATERGATE AFFAIR, evidence was offered that his campaign had been sabotaged by the Republican Committee to Reelect the President. See study by David Nevin (1972).

Muskingum (məskĭng'gəm), river, 111 mi (179 km) long, formed in NE Ohio, at Coshocton, by the union of the Walhonding and Tuscarawas rivers and flowing S through Zanesville, then SE to the Ohio River at Marietta. The Muskingum River system has extensive flood control projects. The canalized lower river is navigable. The upper river was a link in the Ohio and Erie Canal.

muskmelon: see MELON.

Muskogean (məskō'gēən), branch of North American Indian languages belonging to the Hokan-Siouan linguistic family, or stock, of North and Central America. See AMERICAN INDIAN LANGUAGES.

Muskogee (mŭskō'gē), city (1970 pop. 37,331), seat of Muskogee co., E Okla., near the junction of the Arkansas, Verdigris, and Grand rivers; inc. 1898. It is an important transportation, trade, and industrial center in the agricultural Arkansas valley, with a new port (opened 1971) on the McClellan-Kerr Arkansas River Navigation System. Muskogee has food-processing plants, meat-packing houses, seed mills, and numerous manufacturing industries. A Federal Indian agency (est. 1874), a U.S. veterans hospital, an Indian vocational training center, a state school for the blind, and a junior college are located there. Of interest are the Five Civilized Tribes Museum and the beautiful flower gardens in Honor Heights Park; an antique car museum; and nearby Fort Gibson (1824; restored), with its national cemetery. A state fair and an azalea festival are held annually.

musk ox, hoofed ruminant mammal, *Ovibos moschatus,* found in arctic North America and Greenland. The northernmost member of the cattle family, the musk ox grazes on the stunted vegetation of the tundra. It was exterminated in Alaska about the middle of the 19th cent. but was later restored there on Nunivak island. Its stoutly built body, about 4 ft (120 cm) at the shoulder in the male, is covered by a long, shaggy, brown to black coat, which conceals the short tail and the upper part of the short legs. The body has a musky odor. The horns are broad and flattened and nearly meet across the forehead at the base. They extend out from the sides of the head, curving downward and then upward in a hook. The hooves are very large and widely splayed, an adaptation to walking on snow. Musk oxen live in herds of 10 to 20 individuals in summer and up to 100 in winter. When in danger the herd forms a circle, horns pointing outward, with the young in the center. The chief enemy of the musk ox, besides the Indians and Eskimos who hunt it for flesh and fur, is the wolf. The musk ox is classified in the phylum CHORDATA, subphylum Vertebrata, class Mammalia, order Artiodactyla, family Bovidae.

muskrat, North American aquatic RODENT. The common muskrats, species of the genus *Ondatra,* are sometimes called by their American Indian name, musquash. They are found in marshes, quiet streams, and ponds through most of North America N of Mexico, but are absent from the extreme W and SE United States. A common muskrat resembles a large house rat with its tail flattened on either side; its hind feet are partially webbed between the toes. Its outer fur is shiny brown, and it has a dense undercoat. Its body length is 10 to 14 in. (25–36 cm), excluding 8 to 10 in. (20–25 cm) of tail. Its shoulder height is about 5 in. (13 cm), and its weight is 2 to 3 lb (0.9–1.4 kg). A solitary dweller, it may live in a burrow in a steep bank or a reed hut built in marshy shallows. Muskrat burrows are constructed above water level and are connected to an underwater entrance by a tunnel; huts are built with an underwater opening. Muskrats do not build dams or fell trees as do beavers. They swim by paddling with the hind feet, using the tail as a rudder. They feed on vegetation and aquatic animals; their chief enemy is the mink. Mating occurs in spring and summer. The gestation period is about 30 days and the female bears several litters of two to six young each season. Muskrat fur is much used commercially, chiefly for women's coats. It is often dyed to resemble more expensive furs and is sold under a variety of names, including *Hudson seal* and *river mink.* The secretion of the MUSK glands is used in making perfume. Introduced into Europe for its pelts, the muskrat became a serious pest because its tunneling below water level undermines canal banks and dike foundations. The round-tailed muskrat, or Florida water rat, *Neofiber alleni,* is found in swampy regions of Florida and SE Georgia. It dives and swims well, but is less aquatic then the common muskrat, spending much time on land. It is about 12 in. (30 cm) long, including the long, scaly tail. It is about 2 in. (5 cm) high at the shoulder, and weighs about ¾ lb (0.34 kg). Its feet are not webbed, and its tail is not flattened. Despite their greater size and longer tails, muskrats are closely related to VOLES. The water vole, *Arvicola,* found in most of Europe and N and W Asia, is an intermediate form; it is longer than other voles and in parts of its range leads an aquatic existance. Muskrats are classified in the phylum CHORDATA, subphylum Vertebrata, class Mammalia, order Rodentia, family Cricetidae.

Muslim (mŭz'lĭm) [Arab.,=one who surrenders (himself to God), an agent form of the verb of which ISLAM is a verbal noun], one who has embraced Islam, a follower of MUHAMMAD. The form *Moslem* is also common in English; the term *Mussulman* is now rarely used. Muslims have also been called Mohammedans.

Muslim art and architecture: see INDIAN ART AND ARCHITECTURE; ISLAMIC ART AND ARCHITECTURE; MOGUL ART AND ARCHITECTURE; MOORISH ART AND ARCHITECTURE; PERSIAN ART AND ARCHITECTURE.

Muslim League, political organization of India and Pakistan, founded 1906 by AGA KHAN III. Its original purpose was to safeguard the political rights of Muslims in India. Its membership grew when many Muslims, fearful of an overwhelmingly Hindu majority, left the INDIAN NATIONAL CONGRESS. An early leader in the League, Muhammad IQBAL, was one of the first to propose (1930) the creation of a separate Muslim India. Few candidates of the Muslim League won office in the elections of 1937, but by 1940, under the leadership of Muhammad Ali JINNAH, it had gained such power that, for the first time, it demanded the establishment of a Muslim state (Pakistan), despite the opposition of the Congress. During World War II the Congress was banned, but the League, which supported the British war effort, was allowed to function and gained strength. Its claim to represent the Muslims of India was vindicated when it won nearly all of the Muslim vote in the elections of 1946. In 1947, with the division of the Indian subcontinent, the Muslim League became the major political party of newly formed Pakistan. By 1953, however, dissensions within the League had led to the formation of several different political parties. Between 1958 and 1962, while martial law was in force under Muhammad AYUB KHAN, the League was officially defunct. Once martial law ended, the League reformed into two separate factions: the Convention Muslim League (under Ayub) and the Council Muslim League. This latter group joined a united front with other political parties in 1967 in opposition to the group led by Ayub. The Convention Muslim League ceased to exist when Ayub Khan resigned in 1969. The Council Muslim League, which had brought about the founding of Pakistan, was virtually eliminated from the political scene in the elections of 1970. See A. B. Rajput, *Muslim League, Yesterday and Today* (1948); Damodar P. Singhal, *Pakistan* (1972).

muslin, general name for plain woven fine white cottons for domestic use. It is believed that muslins were first made at Mosul (now a city of Iraq). They were widely made in India, from where they were first imported to England in the late 17th cent. Early muslins were often woven or embroidered with gold. Swiss muslin is a modern crisp, semitransparent fabric, either dyed or white, and sometimes figured. Certain sheetings are known as muslins. Bookbinders' muslin, made in Scotland, is fine and crisp.

Mussadegh, Muhammad (mo͞ohäm'mäd mo͞o'-sädāg), 1880–1967, Iranian political leader, prime minister of Iran (1951–53). He held a variety of government posts (1914–25) but retired to private life in protest against the shah's assumption of dictatorial powers in 1925. He returned to government (1944) as a member of parliament and quickly established himself as an opponent of foreign interference in Iranian affairs. He successfully fought Soviet attempts to exploit the oil fields of N Iran and led the movement to nationalize the British-owned Anglo-Iranian Oil Company. He became immensely popular, and after parliament passed his oil nationalization act (1951), the shah was forced to appoint him prime minister. Mussadegh's refusal to negotiate a settlement with the British alienated the shah and members of Iran's ruling class. A political crisis developed, and in Aug., 1953, Mussadegh's government was overthrown by the shah and his followers. After serving three years in prison, Mussadegh spent the rest of his life under house arrest.

mussel, edible freshwater or marine BIVALVE mollusk. Mussels are able to move slowly by means of the muscular foot. They feed and breathe by filtering water through extensible tubes called siphons; a large mussel filters 10 gal (38 liters) of water per day. The close-fitting shells protect the mussel from desiccation and enable it to live high up on the shore. Most marine mussels belong to the single family, Mytilidae. They are widespread and are especially abundant in cooler seas. They form extensive, crowded beds, anchoring themselves by the byssus, a secretion of strong threads. The blue mussel grows up to 3 in. (7.6 cm) and is common along the Atlantic coast; the smaller hooked mussel has a more southerly range. The horse mussel, found in deeper waters, grows to 6 in. (15 cm) in length. Freshwater mussels are chiefly of two kinds: the large, dark-shelled burrowing mussels, a source of pearls and of mother-of-pearl; and the tiny "fingernail clams" found on the bottoms of clear pools and brooks. Freshwater mussels (belonging to the family Unionidae), like the clam, pass through a parasitic larval state, living on the fins, gills, and bodies of fishes. The familiar jingle shells, delicate, shiny orange or yellow shells common on beaches, belong to the same order as the marine mussel. Mussels are classified in the phylum MOLLUSCA, class Pelecypoda, order Filibranchia.

Musset, Alfred de (Louis Charles Alfred de Musset) (älfrĕd' də müsā'), 1810–57, French romantic poet, dramatist, and fiction writer. His first collection of poems, *Contes d'Espagne et d'Italie* (1829), exhibited a strong Byronic influence. Four years later he went to Italy with George Sand, but his infatuation with her resulted in disillusionment. Most of his poems appeared first in *Revue des Deux Mondes;* they included such famous pieces as the gloomy "Rolla" (1833) and the exquisite love lyrics "La Nuit de mai," "La Nuit d'août," "La Nuit d'octobre," and "La Nuit de décembre" (1835–36). His poetry combined classic clarity with the passionate subjectivity of the romantics. Among his plays are *Fantasio* (1834) and a series of comedies based on proverbs, including *Il ne faut jurer de rien* (1834) and *On ne badine pas avec l'amour* (1836). He also wrote some brilliant *nouvelles,* but from 1840 he passed rapidly into decline. The autobiographical novel *Confession d'un enfant du siècle* (1836), gives an account of his affair with George Sand and reflects the disillusioned mood of many of his contemporaries. His correspondence with George Sand appeared in 1904, and his work was translated in *The Complete Writings of Alfred de Musset* (10 vol., 1905; rev. ed., 1907). See biographies by his brother, Paul de Musset (tr. 1877), Charlotte Haldane (1960), and H. D. Sedgwick (1931, repr. 1973).

Mussolini, Benito (bānē'tō mōōs-sōlē'nē), 1883–1945, Italian dictator and leader of the Fascist movement. His father, an ardent Socialist, was a blacksmith; his mother was a teacher. Mussolini taught briefly, lived (1902–4) in Switzerland to avoid military service, and in 1909 edited a Socialist paper in Trent (then in Austria). He was soon expelled as an agitator and in Milan became editor of the Socialist daily *Avanti.* In this period he advocated insurrection and authoritarian rule. Soon after World War I began, Mussolini turned nationalist and joined the pro-Allied interventionists. The Socialist party, which opposed all participation in nationalist wars, expelled him. He then founded his own daily, the *Popolo d'Italia,* which was subsidized by the French to encourage Italy's entry into the war on the side of the Allies. He joined (1915) the army and attained the rank of corporal. In the troubled postwar period (see ITALY), Mussolini organized his followers, mostly war veterans, in the *Fasci di combattimento,* who stood for aggressive nationalism, violently opposed the Communists and Socialists, and took for uniforms the black shirts of the followers of D'ANNUNZIO. Amid strikes, social unrest, and parliamentary breakdown, Mussolini preached forcible restoration of order and practiced terrorism with armed groups. In 1921 he was elected to parliament and the National Fascist party (see FASCISM) was officially organized. Backed by nationalists and propertied elements, in Oct., 1922, Mussolini sent the Fascists to march on Rome. King VICTOR EMMANUEL III permitted them to enter the city and called on Mussolini, who had remained in Milan, to form a cabinet. The new premier gradually transformed the government into a dictatorship. In 1924 the Socialist deputy MATTEOTTI was murdered. Opposition was put down by an efficient secret police and the Fascist militia. The press was regimented. Parliamentary government ended in 1928, and the state economy was reorganized along the lines of the Fascist CORPORATIVE STATE. Conflict between church and state was ended by the LATERAN TREATY (1929). Mussolini was called *Duce* [leader] by his followers; his official title was "head of the government," and he held, besides the premiership, as many portfolios as he saw fit. His ambition to restore ancient greatness found expression in grandiloquent slogans and speeches and in the erection of monumental buildings. The encouragement he gave to the already high Italian birth rate, his imperialistic designs, and his incitement of extreme nationalist groups created an explosive situation. Mussolini was at first cool to Adolf HITLER and opposed his designs on Austria. However, Mussolini's diplomatic isolation after his attack (1935) on ETHIOPIA led to a rapprochement with Germany. In 1936, Hitler and Mussolini aided Francisco FRANCO in the Spanish civil war; the Rome-Berlin AXIS was strengthened by a formal alliance (1939), which Mussolini's son-in-law and foreign minister, Galeazzo CIANO, helped to create. In 1938, Mussolini allowed Hitler to annex Austria and helped bring about the MUNICH PACT; in April, 1939, he ordered the occupation of Albania. Under German pressure, he inaugurated in Italy an anti-Semitic policy; it found little popular response. The Ethiopian and Spanish wars had diminished the Duce's popularity, and he did not enter World War II until France was falling in June, 1940. The failure of Italian arms in Greece and Africa and the imminent invasion by the Allies of the Italian mainland at last caused a rebellion within the Fascist party. In July, 1943, the Fascist grand council refused to support his policy—dictated by Hitler—and the king dismissed him and had him placed under arrest. He was freed two months later by a daring German rescue party and became head of the Fascist puppet government set up in N Italy by Hitler. On the German collapse (April, 1945) Mussolini was captured, tried in a summary court-martial, and shot with his mistress, Clara Petacci. Their bodies, brought to Milan, were hanged in a public square and buried in an unmarked grave. Mussolini's body was later removed, and in 1957 it was placed in his family's vault. Many of Mussolini's political speeches and pamphlets have been translated into English. His literary productions include *The Cardinal's Mistress* (tr., 1928) and *John Huss* (tr. 1929). *My Autobiography* (Eng. ed. 1939) is supplemented by *The Fall of Mussolini: His Own Story* (tr. ed. by Max Ascoli, 1948). See biographies by L. C. Fermi (1961), Richard Collier (1971), Max Gallo (tr. 1973), and by his widow, Rachele Mussolini (1974); study by Alan Cassels (1970).

Mussorgsky, Modest Petrovich: see MOUSSORGSKY.

Mussulman: see MUSLIM.

Mustafa I (mōōstäfä'), 1591–1639?, Ottoman sultan (1617–18, 1622–23), brother and successor of Ahmed I to the throne of the Ottoman Empire (Turkey). Set aside for incompetence, he was succeeded in 1618 by his nephew Osman II, who was executed in 1622. Mustafa, who was probably insane, returned to the throne only to be displaced by another nephew, Murad IV. During Mustafa's reign additional territory was lost to Persia.

Mustafa II, 1664–1703, Ottoman sultan (1695–1703), nephew and successor of Ahmed II. The grand vizier (chief executive officer) of the Ottoman Empire (Turkey), Husayn KÖPRÜLÜ, exercised the actual rule. The Turkish defeat (1697) at Senta by Prince Eugene of Savoy led to negotiations in 1699 (see KARLOWITZ, TREATY OF) that marked the end of the Turkish military threat to Europe. Mustafa II was succeeded by his brother, Ahmed III.

Mustafa III, 1717–73, Ottoman sultan (1757–73), son of Ahmed III. He succeeded his cousin Osman III to the throne of the Ottoman Empire (Turkey). The chief event of his reign was the war of 1768–74 with Russia (see RUSSO-TURKISH WARS), which ended disastrously for Turkey (see KUCHUK KAINARJI, TREATY OF). His brother Abd al-Hamid I succeeded him in Jan., 1774.

Mustafa IV, 1778–1808, Ottoman sultan (1807–8), son of Abd al-Hamid I. He was raised to the throne by the reactionary JANISSARIES who had deposed Mustafa's uncle, SELIM III, because they opposed his attempted reforms. When a Turkish army marched on the capital to restore Selim, Mustafa had him murdered, but the rebels killed Mustafa and placed his brother, Mahmud II, on the throne.

Mustafa or **Kara Mustafa** (kärä') [Turkish *kara*= black], d. 1683, Turkish grand vizier (chief executive officer) under Sultan Muhammad IV of the Ottoman Empire (Turkey). He succeeded his brother-in-law, Ahmed KÖPRÜLÜ. Ambitious and belligerent, he allied himself with the Hungarian rebels under THOKOLY against Holy Roman Emperor Leopold I and led the siege of VIENNA in 1683. His military incompetence facilitated the relief of Vienna by King John III of Poland, and the besieging army, including Mustafa, fled in panic. Mustafa suffered several routs during his retreat through Hungary and, having reached Belgrade, was ordered to commit suicide by the sultan.

Mustafa Kemal: see ATATÜRK, KEMAL.

Mustafa Nahas Pasha: see NAHAS PASHA.

mustang [Sp. *mesteño*= a stray], small feral HORSE of the W United States. Mustangs are descended from escaped Indian horses, which in turn were descended from horses of North African blood, brought to the New World by the Spanish c.1500. Mustangs have evolved their own distinguishing traits: They are small, swift, hardy, and intelligent—well suited to plains conditions. As ranching expanded in North America, cowboys began rounding up mustangs for use as cow ponies. Hence, in the terminology of ranchers, *mustang* often refers to a cow pony of feral stock, and the term *bronco* is used for an untamed mustang. A cayuse (after the Cayuse Indians of the NE United States) is a domestic Indian horse. Although the mustang, which has spent many generations in the wild, is somewhat different from the cayuse, the terms are sometimes used interchangeably. Cow ponies of mustang descent have been crossed with other breeds of horse, so that all horses of the W United States probably have mustang blood. The mustang, a variety of *Equus caballus,* is classified in the phylum CHORDATA, subphylum Vertebrata, class Mammalia, order Perissodactyla, family Equidae.

Mustapha. For persons thus named, see MUSTAFA.

mustard, common name for the Cruciferae, a large family chiefly of herbs of north temperate regions. The easily distinguished flowers of the Cruciferae have four petals arranged diagonally ("cruciform") and alternating with the four sepals. Most of the nearly 50 genera indigenous to the United States are found in the West. The family includes numerous weeds and wild flowers, e.g., PEPPERGRASS, TOOTHWORT, and SHEPHERD'S-PURSE. The Cruciferae, often rich in sulfur compounds and in vitamin C, include important food and condiment plants, many cultivated from ancient times. Especially important are the herbs of the genus *Brassica,* e.g., RAPE, rutabaga, TURNIP, mustard, and numerous varieties of the CABBAGE species. CRESS, WATERCRESS, HORSE-RADISH, and RADISH are also of this family. A few species are cultivated as ornamentals, e.g., CANDYTUFT, ROSE OF JERICHO, WALLFLOWER, and types of STOCK, ROCKET, and ALYSSUM. WOAD was formerly an important dye source. The herbs of the family that are called mustard are species of *Brassica* native to Europe and W Asia. Most important commercially are the black mustard (*B. nigra*) and white mustard (*B. alba*). These are yellow-flowered annuals naturalized in the United States; the black mustard is often a weed infesting grainfields, as is also the charlock, or wild mustard (*B. arvensis*). The black and the white mustard resemble each other and are used more or less similarly. They are cultivated for the seeds, which are ground and used as a condiment, usually mixed to a paste with vinegar or oil, sometimes with spices or with an admixture of starch to reduce the pungency. (The pungency of mustard does not develop until it is moistened.) These mustards are also grown as salad plants and for greens, as are the Indian, or leaf, mustard (*B. juncea*) and the Chinese mustard, or *pok-choi* (*B. chinensis*). The white mustard is used in some places as forage for sheep and as green manure. Black mustard has had several important medical uses, e.g., as counterirritant (in the form of a liniment or a plaster), as a stomach stimulant, and an emetic. Its seeds are more pungent than the white and yield a yellowish, biting oil (mustard oil) that has also been useful in medicine. The New Testament imagery of the mustard seed as a symbol of creative faith is sometimes identified with the black mustard, which in Palestine grows to a height of 10 or 12 ft (3–3.7 m), with branches frequented by birds (Mat. 13.31,32; Luke 13.19). Mustard is classified in the divison MAGNOLIOPHYTA, class Magnoliopsida, order Capparales, family Cruciferae.

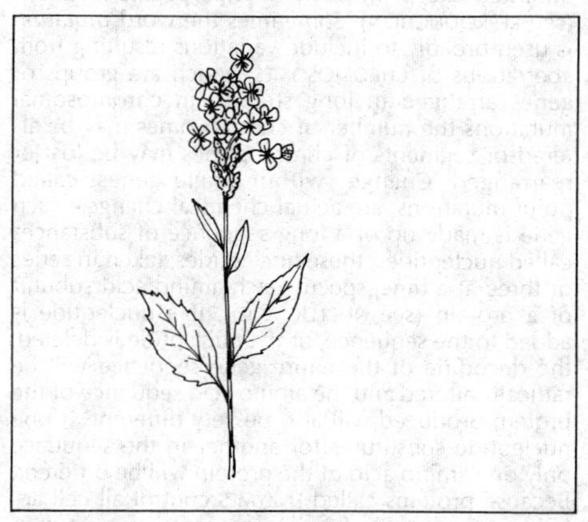

Black mustard, Brassica nigra

mustard gas, chemical compound used as a POISON GAS in World War I. The burning sensation it causes on contact with the skin is similar to that caused by oil from black mustard seeds. The compound is not a gas but a colorless, oily liquid with a somewhat sweet, agreeable odor; it boils at 217°C. A powerful vesicant, mustard gas causes severe blistering even in small quantities. Highly irritating to the eyes, it quickly causes conjunctivitis and blindness. If inhaled, it attacks the respiratory tract and lungs, causing pulmonary edema. Some effects of exposure to mustard gas are delayed up to 12 hr; death may result several days after exposure. Mustard gas was introduced by the Germans in warfare against the British at Ypres, Belgium, in July, 1917, and took a heavy toll of casualties. It is dispersed as an aerosol by a bursting shell. Chemically, mustard gas is a thioether, 2,2′-dichlorodiethyl sulfide, $(ClCH_2CH_2)_2S$. It can be prepared by reacting ethylene with sulfur monochloride, S_2Cl_2, or by other methods. Its vesicant property is readily destroyed either by oxidation or by chlorination (e.g., with bleaching powder).

mutagen: see MUTATION.

Mu-tan-chiang or **Mutankiang** (both: mo͞o-tänkyäng), city (1970 est. pop. 400,000), SE Heilungkiang prov., China. It is a railroad junction and a lumbering center in a rich timber region. Manufactures include wood pulp, paper, compound medicines, tires, aluminum, and cement. The city was formerly the capital of Sunkiang prov.

Mutankiang: see MU-TAN-CHIANG, China.

mutation, in biology, a sudden change in a GENE, or unit of hereditary material, that results in a new inheritable characteristic. In higher animals and many higher plants a mutation may be transmitted to future generations only if it occurs in germ, or sex cell, tissue; somatic, or body cell, mutations cannot be inherited except in plants that propagate asexually (see REPRODUCTION). Sometimes the word *mutation* is used broadly to include variations resulting from aberrations of CHROMOSOMES, which are groups of genes arranged in long strands; in chromosomal mutations the number of chromosomes may be altered or segments of chromosomes may be lost or rearranged. Changes within single genes, called point mutations, are actual chemical changes. Each gene is made up of a long sequence of substances called nucleotides; these nucleotides, taken in series of three at a time, specify each amino acid subunit of a protein (see NUCLEIC ACID). If a nucleotide is added to the sequence, or if a nucleotide is deleted, the decoding of the entire gene sequence will be radically altered and the amino acid sequence of the protein produced will also be very different. If one nucleotide substitutes for another in the sequence only one amino acid of the protein will be different. Because proteins called ENZYMES control all cell activities, a mutation affecting an enzyme can result in alteration of other cell components. A single gene mutation may have many effects if the enzyme it controls is involved in several metabolic processes. Many mutations are reversible, i.e., the mutant gene can revert to its previous form. Some genes are more unstable and susceptible to mutation than others, so that repeated mutations of corresponding genes in different individuals may occur, as in hemophilia. Experiments with various mutagens, the agents causing mutation, have shown that in many cases the gene itself is not destroyed but is simply altered. Mutations may be induced by exposure to ultraviolet rays and ionizing radiation from alpha, beta, gamma, and X rays, by extreme changes in temperature, and by certain chemicals such as nitrous acid, nitrogen mustard, and chemical substitutes for portions of the nucleotide subunits of genes. Drugs such as COLCHICINE double the normal number of chromosomes in a cell by interfering with the process of MITOSIS, or nonsexual cell division. Certain genes called mutator genes cause a high mutation rate of all genes in an organism; these genes may possibly cause production within the organism of chemical mutagens. In 1901 the observation of mutants, or sports, among evening primrose plants led the Dutch botanist Hugo de Vries to present his theory that new characteristics may appear suddenly and that these characteristics are inheritable; before this time it had been commonly accepted that evolution resulted from a gradual selection of favorable ACQUIRED CHARACTERISTICS. The work of de Vries and of subsequent investigators who demonstrated the distinction between mutation and environmental variations has shown the importance of mutation in the mechanism of EVOLUTION. H. J. Muller, an American geneticist, pioneered in inducing mutations by X-ray radiation (using the fruit fly, *Drosophila*) and developed a method of detecting invisible mutations (as opposed to observable ones) having lethal effects. Most mutations are lethal, since any change in the delicate balance of an organism having a high level of adaptation to its environment tends to be disruptive. Of the few positive mutations, most are of recessive traits that are neutral in their effect on the organism and so can be retained without inhibiting its growth or reproductive processes (see GENETICS). A change in the environment can encourage the survival of a dominant nonlethal mutation. Thus, hypothetically, a mutation caused in nature by the cumulative effect of ionizing radiation in the earth's atmosphere might, with a coincidental change in the environment, give rise to a new species; this process is now believed to be a chief agent in the process of evolution and in the extinction of species that fail to mutate in a changing environment.

Mutazilite: see ISLAM.

mute (myo͞ot), in music, device designed to diminish uniformly the loudness of a musical instrument. For example, a trumpet mute is cone-shaped and fits into the instrument's bell, and a violin mute is a wooden or rubber clamp that can be attached to the bridge.

Mutesa I (mo͞otā'sə), d. 1884, kabaka, or king, of Buganda (now in Uganda), c.1857–84. He brought Buganda to its height by increasing the autocratic powers of the kabaka, strengthening the army, improving the bureaucracy, and opening up trade, often in slaves, with Arab merchants. During his reign the first Europeans were admitted into Buganda.

Muth-labben (mŭth-lăb'ĕn), obscure word in the title of Ps. 9.

mutiny, concerted disobedient or seditious action by persons in military or naval service, or by sailors on commercial vessels. Mutiny may range from a combined refusal to obey orders to active revolt or going over to the enemy. In the armed forces it is one of the gravest crimes against military law. Mutiny may be committed on a private vessel whether it is at sea or in port. Two major naval mutinies occurred in Great Britain in 1797. The mutiny at Spithead, in which the enlisted men sent the officers ashore and ran the ships by committee, ended without violence or convictions. In the mutiny at Nore and Sheerness, however, the mutineers bombarded loyal ships and the ringleader, Richard Parker, was hanged. Many of the abuses in the navy—bad food, brutal discipline, withholding pay—were remedied as a consequence of this disaffection. Other well-known mutinies were the one aboard the BOUNTY and the INDIAN MUTINY of 1857–58. Mutinies tend to occur with some frequency in the armed forces of nations on the point of suffering defeat; thus, in 1918 the German navy mutinied at Kiel and the Austrian navy at Cattaro (now Kotor). A mutiny may be the signal for a revolution, as were the Russian mutinies in 1905 and 1917 at KRONSHTADT. See Conrad Gill, *The Naval Mutinies of 1797* (1913); G. E. Manwaring and Bonamy Dobrée, *The Floating Republic* (1938, repr. 1966); R. L. Hadfield, *Mutiny at Sea* (1938); Edmund Fuller, ed., *Mutiny* (1953).

Mutis, José Celestino (hōsā' thālĕstē'nō mo͞o'tēs), 1732–1808, Spanish naturalist and plant explorer. One of Linnaeus' first disciples in Spain, he went to South America and settled c.1760 in Bogotá. He collected plants, especially in the Andes, and introduced several into general use. His study of quinine, on which he wrote *El arcano de la quina* (1793), facilitated the colonization of malaria-ridden regions. Most of his monumentally planned work, *Flora de la Real Expedición Botánica del Nuevo Reino de Granada,* was left in manuscript and has been in the process of publication since 1954. Some of his voluminous correspondence with Linnaeus has been published in *A Selection of the Correspondence of Linnaeus,* comp. by Sir James Edward Smith (2 vol., 1821). Mutis was chiefly responsible for the creation of the Bogotá Observatory and gathered about him a group of scholars who made the university a renowned center of research. See his *Archivo Epistolar,* comp. by Guillermo Hernández de Alba (2 vol., 1968).

Mutsuhito: see MEIJI.

mutton, flesh of mature sheep prepared as food (as opposed to the flesh of young sheep, which is known as lamb). Mutton is deep red with firm, white fat. In Middle Eastern countries it is a staple meat, but in the West, with the exception of Great Britain, mutton and lamb comprise only a small proportion of the total meat consumption. In the United States the flesh of lambs six weeks to three months old is preferred. The cuts are leg, loin (chops and roasts), rack (rib chops and French chops), chuck, breast, and flank. The kidneys, heart, and sweetbreads are especially delicate.

Muttra, India: see MATHURA.

mutual fund, in finance, investment company or trust that has a very fluid capital stock. It is unique in that at any time it can sell or redeem any of its outstanding shares at net asset value (i.e., the price of a share equals total assets minus liabilities divided by the total number of shares). A mutual fund, also called an open-end investment company, owns the securities of several corporations and receives dividends on the shares that it holds. A closed-end investment company differs from an open-end company in that the number of shares is limited and the price of the shares may fluctuate above and below the net asset value. The earnings of a mutual fund are distributed to the holders of its shares. It is hoped that a loss on one holding will be made up by a gain on another. The holder of a mutual-fund share thus gains the advantage of diversification, which might ordinarily be beyond his means. Mutual funds, which provide skilled management for security holdings, may be classified as either common stock or balanced funds. Common stock funds mainly invest in common shares. Balanced funds, usually more conservative than common stock funds, invest in preferred stocks and bonds in addition to common issues. The forerunner of the modern mutual fund was established in Belgium in 1822, and the use of these closed-end investment companies soon spread to Great Britain and France. They became popular in the United States in the 1920s, but from the 1930s the open-end mutual fund became more popular. Mutual funds experienced a period of tremendous growth after World War II. See Hugh Bullock, *Story of Investment Companies* (1959); Harry Burton, *Investment and Unit Trusts in Britain and America* (1968); Stuart Mead, *Mutual Funds: A Guide for the Lay Investor* (1971).

Muybridge, Eadweard (ĕd'wərd mī'brĭj), 1830–1904, English photographer and student of animal locomotion. Muybridge changed his name from Edward James Muggeridge. A gifted and obsessed eccentric, he was a photographic innovator who left a vast and enormously varied body of work. In 1872 he made some experiments in photographing moving objects for the U.S. government. Afterwards he was engaged by Leland Stanford to record, with a series of sequential still cameras, the movements of a horse. He invented (1881) the zoöpraxiscope, which projected animated pictures on a screen, a forerunner of the motion picture. He wrote *The Horse in Motion* (1878) and *The Human Figure in Motion* (1901). His *Animals in Motion* (1899, repr. 1957) consists of 11 portfolios: thousands of pictures, of men, women, children, amputees, and many domestic and wild animals in action. This work was of considerable importance to artists. Muybridge murdered his wife's lover in 1874; the case was dismissed as justifiable homicide.

Muzaffarabad (mo͞ozŭf'fərăbäd″), town, NW Kashmir, at the confluence of the Jhelum and Neelam rivers. It is the chief city of Azad Kashmir, which is administered by Pakistan. Muzaffarabad is a trading center.

Muzaffar ad-Din (mo͞ozäf-fär' äd-dēn'), 1853–1907, shah of Persia (1896–1907), son of NASIR AD-DIN. A weak ruler, he borrowed money from Russia and failed to oppose the encroachments of Russia and Great Britain on Persian sovereignty. Much disaffection arose among the people. After the revolutionary outburst of 1906, he was forced to agree to the convocation of a national assembly. He died soon after signing the long-awaited liberal constitution. He was succeeded by Muhammad Ali.

Muzaffarnagar (mo͞ozŭf'fərănŭg″ər), town (1971 pop. 114,859), Uttar Pradesh state, N central India. It is the district administrative center of a wheat- and sugarcane-growing area.

Muzaffarpur (mo͞ozŭf'fərăpo͝or), city (1971 pop. 127,045), Bihar state, NE India, on the Gandak River. It is the district administrative center for a lichee- and mango-producing area and is the site of Bihar Univ.

Muziano, Girolamo (jērō'lămō mo͞otsyä'nō), c.1528–1592, Italian mannerist painter, also known as Girolamo Bressano. His large painting, *The Resurrection of Lazarus* (Pinacoteca, Vatican) gained him the friendship of Michelangelo. Muziano was noted for his landscapes, as well as for some mosaics for the Vatican that he designed with great finesse. He painted many historical compositions for the churches and palaces of Rome and was instrumental in the founding of St. Luke's Academy. He was also superintendent of the works of the Vatican under Gregory XIII.

Mv, former symbol of the element MENDELEVIUM, now Md.

MVD: see SECRET POLICE.

Mwanamutapa (mwä″nämōōtä′pä), former state, SE Africa. The Mwanamutapa empire, headed by a ruler of the same name, was founded c.1420 among the Karanga people (a subgroup of the Bantu-speaking Shona) and was centered at Great ZIMBABWE in present-day SE Rhodesia. The empire was ruled in pyramidal fashion, with the Mwanamutapa appointing regionally-based vassals. In about 1490 the empire split into two parts—Changamire in the south (including Great Zimbabwe) and Mwanamutapa in the north. The latter stretched from the Indian Ocean in the east to present-day central Zambia in the west and from central Rhodesia in the south to the Zambezi River in the north. An important source of gold and ivory, the area attracted Swahili traders from the east coast of Africa (in modern Tanzania). Beginning in the early 16th cent. Portuguese traders and soldiers from Mozambique established contact with the empire, and by the mid-17th cent. the Portuguese controlled Mwanamutapa, which continued to exist in nominal form until the late 19th cent. During this time, however, the social structure of the empire was severely dislocated by the ravages of slave traders.

Mwanza (mwän′zä), city (1967 pop. 34,861), capital of Mwanza prov., NW Tanzania, a port on Victoria Nyanza. Connected by rail with Dar-es-Salaam, the city handles much of Tanzania's trade with Kenya and Uganda, with which it is connected by boat. Industries include meat-packing, fishing, and the manufacture of textiles and soap. There is an institute for research in tropical diseases.

Mweru, Lake (mwā′rōō), c.70 mi (110 km) long and 30 mi (50 km) wide, alt. c.3,000 ft (910 m), central Africa, on the Zaïre-Zambia border. It is drained to the north by the Luvua River. The lake has large fisheries.

myasthenia gravis (mīəsthē′nēə grä′vĭs), chronic disorder of the muscles characterized by weakness and a tendency to tire easily. Its cause is not understood, but it is believed that the difficulty lies in the transmission of impulses from nerves to muscles. The disease is most common in young adults. The muscles of the neck, throat, lips, tongue, face, and eyes are primarily involved; those of the trunk and extremities are less frequently affected. Exertion quickly brings on difficulty in swallowing, chewing, and talking. The eyelids may droop, and there are visual disorders. Prolonged rest is likely to restore some of the muscle function; restricted activity at all times and complete rest during periods of aggravation of the illness are necessary. Treatment with drugs that temporarily strengthen muscles is helpful. Sudden inability to swallow or a respiratory crisis requires emergency treatment.

Mycale (mĭk′əlē), promontory, W Asia Minor, opposite Samós island. The center of the Ionian League was there, in the temple of Poseidon. In 479 B.C. the Greeks destroyed the Persian fleet at Mycale. This ended the Persian Wars for European Greece and began the rapid liberation of the Greeks of Asia Minor. Mycale, in modern Turkey, is called Samsun Daği. It was also known as Mt. Lydia.

Mycenae (mīsē′nē), ancient city of Greece, in Argolis. In historical times it had little importance and was usually dependent on Argos. Its significance is in its remote past as a center of MYCENAEAN CIVILIZATION. The famous Lion Gate, which led into the city, and the Treasury of Atreus, the largest of the beehive tombs outside the walls of the city, are the most notable of its ancient remains. See A. J. B. Wace, *Mycenae* (1949, repr. 1964); A. E. Samuel, *The Mycenaeans in History* (1966).

Mycenaean civilization (mīsēnē′ən), an ancient AEGEAN CIVILIZATION known from the excavations at MYCENAE and other sites. They were first undertaken by Heinrich SCHLIEMANN and others after 1876, and they helped to revise the early history of Greece. Divided into Early Helladic (c.2800–2000 B.C.), Middle Helladic (c.2000–1500 B.C.), and Late Helladic (c.1500–1100 B.C.) periods, the chronology roughly parallels that of the contemporary MINOAN CIVILIZATION. The Mycenaeans entered Greece from the north or northeast c.2000 B.C., displacing, seemingly without violence, the older Neolithic culture, which can be dated as early as 4000 B.C. These Indo-European Greek-speaking invaders brought with them advanced techniques in pottery, metallurgy, and architecture. Mercantile contact with Crete advanced and strongly influenced their culture, and by 1600 B.C., Mycenae had become a major center of the ancient world. The exact relationship of Mycenaean Greece to Crete between 1600 and 1400 B.C. is extremely complex, with both areas evidently competing for maritime control of the Mediterranean. After the violent destruction of Cnossus c.1400 B.C., Mycenae achieved supremacy, and much of the Minoan cultural tradition was transferred to the mainland. The Mycenaean commercial empire and consequent cultural influence lasted from 1400 to 1200 B.C., when the invasion of the DORIANS ushered in a period of decline for Greece. Events from 1100 to 900 B.C. are extremely obscure, but by the 9th cent. B.C. the centers of wealth and population showed a decisive shift. Although the Mycenaeans had certain innovations of their own, they drew much of their cultural inspiration from the Minoans. The great Mycenaean cities—Mycenae, Tiryns, Pylos, Thebes, Orchomenos—were noted for their heavy, complex fortifications and the massive, cyclopean quality of their masonry, while Minoan cities were totally unfortified. Mycenaean palaces were built around great halls called megara rather than around an open space as in Crete. Unlike the Cretans, the Mycenaeans were bearded and wore armor in battle. Their written language, preserved on numerous clay tablets from Pylos, Mycenae, and Cnossus, appears to be a form of archaic Greek linguistically related to ancient Cypriot. The presence of this script, known as Linear B, at Cnossus c.1500 B.C. indicates that Mycenaean Greeks had invaded and dominated Crete during the Late Minoan period before the final collapse c.1400 B.C. The works of Homer have been radically reevaluated since the archaeological discoveries of Mycenaean Greece. He is now considered to give admirable glimpses of the culture of the late Mycenaean civilization of the 12th cent. B.C. (see ACHAEANS). See William Taylour, *The Mycenaeans* (1964); A. E. Samuel, *The Mycenaeans in History* (1966); G. E. Mylonas, *Mycenae and the Mycenaean Age* (1966); W. A. McDonald, *Progress into the Past* (1967); John Chadwick, *The Decipherment of Linear B* (2d ed. 1968).

Mycerinus: see MENKAURE.

mycosis: see FUNGUS INFECTION.

Myers, Frederic William Henry (mī′ərz), 1843–1901, English essayist and poet. His works include the poem *St. Paul* (1867) and *Essays, Classical and Modern* (1883). He is well-known for his investigations of psychic phenomena in connection with the Society for Psychical Research, which he helped found in 1882, and for his *Human Personality and Its Survival of Bodily Death* (1903).

Myers, Gustavus, 1872–1942, American historian, b. Trenton, N.J. He worked on a number of newspapers and magazines in New York City, joined the Populist party and the Social Reform Club, and was a member (1907–12) of the Socialist party. Such books as *The History of Tammany Hall* (1901, rev. ed. 1917), *History of the Great American Fortunes* (3 vol., 1910, rev. ed. 1936), and *History of the Supreme Court of the United States* (1912) were detailed, realistic exposés through which Meyers made his reputation in the muckraking era of American literature. His other works include *History of Canadian Wealth* (1914), *America Strikes Back* (1935), *The Ending of Hereditary American Fortunes* (1939), and *History of Bigotry in the United States* (1943).

Myitkyina (myĭt′chĭnä), town (1964 est. pop. 14,000), N Burma, on the Irrawaddy River. The chief town of N Burma, it is a trade center (including teak and jade), the extreme northern terminus of a railroad line from Rangoon, and formerly an important town on the Ledo Road. In World War II its capture (Aug., 1944) by Allied troops after a siege of 78 days marked an important stage in the liberation of Burma from the Japanese.

Mykonos, Greece: see MÍKONOS.

Mylae (mĭ′lē), ancient port, NE Sicily, now MILAZZO. It was settled by colonists from Messina. Here in 260 B.C. the Romans in a newly built fleet were led to victory over the Carthaginians by the consul Caius Duilius in the First Punic War; it was Rome's first naval triumph. Mylae was (36 B.C.) the scene of a naval victory of Marcus Vipsanius Agrippa over Sextus Pompeius.

My Lai incident (mē lī), in the Vietnam War, a massacre of Vietnamese civilians by U.S. soldiers. On March 16, 1968, a unit of the U.S. army Americal division, led by Lt. William L. Calley, invaded the South Vietnamese hamlet of My Lai, an alleged Viet Cong stronghold. In the course of combat operations, unarmed civilians, including women and children, were shot to death (the final army estimate for the number killed was 347). The incident remained unknown to the American public until the autumn of 1969, when a series of letters by a former soldier to government officials forced the army to take action. Several soldiers and veterans were charged with murder, and a number of officers were accused of dereliction of duty for covering up the incident. Special investigations by the U.S. army and the House of Representatives concluded that a massacre had in fact taken place. Of the many soldiers originally charged, only five were court-martialed, and one, Lt. Calley, convicted. On March 29, 1971, he was found guilty of the premeditated murder of at least twenty-two Vietnamese civilians and sentenced to life imprisonment. In Sept., 1974, a Federal district court overturned the conviction. The army subsequently released Calley, but it appealed the court's decision. The My Lai incident aroused widespread controversy and contributed to growing disillusionment in the United States with the Vietnam War. In Nov., 1974, the U.S. army formally released a report on its investigation of the incident. See Richard Hammer, *The Court-Martial of Lt. Calley* (1971); S. M. Hersh, *Mylai 4* (1970) and *Cover-up* (1972).

Mylar, trademark for a type of polyester resin film that has especially good dimensional stability and high dielectric strength; the latter property allows it to be made in very thin layers as a dielectric in capacitors. Mylar can also be used as a base for magnetic tape.

Mymensingh (mī′mĕnsĭng), town (1961 est. pop. 53,300), N central Bangladesh, on an old channel of the Brahmaputra River. It is a trading center for rice, jute, sugarcane, oilseeds, tobacco, mustard, and pulses. Once noted for the manufacture of glass bangles, Mymensingh now has jute-pressing and electrical-supply industries. In the town are Ananda Mohan College (an affiliate of Dacca Univ.), an agricultural university, a veterinary training institute, and the Institute of Radiation Genetics and Plant Breeding.

myna or **mynah** (both: mī′nə), common name for a type of Asiatic STARLING found chiefly in India and Sri Lanka and known for its power of mimicry. Most familiar is the hill myna, *Gracula religiosa*, a large (12–15 in./30–38 cm), glossy black bird with yellow head wattles. It is a forest dweller and lives mostly on fruits. In the wild state its calls vary from low chuckles to loud whistles; when trained it is a better mimic than the parrot. The common myna of S Asia, genus *Acridotheres*, is smaller (10 in./25 cm) and not so good a mimic. The Papuan myna is found on the islands of the S Pacific. Mynas are classified in the phylum CHORDATA, subphylum Vertebrata, class Aves, order Passeriformes, family Sturnidae.

myoglobin (mī″əglō′bĭn), PROTEIN molecule isolated from the cells of vertebrate skeletal muscle that is both a structural and functional relative of HEMOGLOBIN, the oxygen-transport protein of the blood of higher animals. Myoglobin, which is composed of a single polypeptide chain of 153 AMINO ACID residues, has the ability to store oxygen by binding it to an iron atom; iron is part of myoglobin's essential chemical composition. The complete amino acid sequence of myoglobin has been determined; it is a relatively small protein with a molecular weight of approximately 17,000 grams per mole. The distribution of myoglobin among the higher animals is a reflection of its physiological function. It is found abundantly in the tissues of diving mammals, e.g., the whale, the seal, and the dolphin. High concentrations of myoglobin in these animals presumably allows them to store sufficient oxygen to remain under water for long periods. Myoglobin is found abundantly in man only in cardiac muscle, which, by virtue of its essential function, must possess the capacity for continued activity when environmental oxygen concentrations are low. Myoglobin has been investigated intensely and is the first protein molecule to have been completely described in terms of its three-dimensional geometry. This achievement won the British scientist John Kendrew a share in the 1962 Nobel Prize for Chemistry.

myopia: see NEARSIGHTEDNESS.

myosin (mī′əsĭn), one of the two major PROTEIN constituents of muscle. As isolated from muscle, myosin appears to be about 1,600 angstroms in length, with a relatively wide "head" attached to a 24-angstrom-wide rod. Its molecular weight is said to be about 480,000 grams per mole. Myosin is capable of splitting ADENOSINE TRIPHOSPHATE (ATP) into adenosine diphosphate (ADP) and phosphoric acid; this reaction is thought to provide the chemical energy necessary for muscle contraction. Myosin and ACTIN, the other major protein constituent of muscle, together form the myofibril, which in the presence of ATP is the fundamental contractile unit of muscle.

Myra (mī′rə), ancient city and seaport of Lycia, S Asia Minor (now S Turkey). The city was visited by Paul (Acts 27.5). It was the see of St. NICHOLAS. Ruins of a theater are on the acropolis.

Myrdal, Gunnar (gŭn'är mēr'däl), 1898–, Swedish economist, sociologist, and public official. A graduate (1927) of the Univ. of Stockholm, he became lecturer (1927) and professor (1931) of economics there. His *Crisis in the Population Question* (1934), written with his wife, Alva Myrdal, stimulated general welfare measures, which Myrdal helped to shape as a member (1933–38) of various government commissions. For the Carnegie Corp. of America he headed (1938–42) a study of blacks in America that resulted in the exhaustively detailed *An American Dilemma* (1944, new ed. 1962), written in collaboration with R. M. E. Sterner and Arnold Rose. It maintained that the racial problem in the United States was inextricably entwined with the democratic functioning of American society. Myrdal was Swedish secretary of commerce (1945–47) and executive secretary (1947–57) of the United Nations Economic Commission for Europe. In *Rich Lands and Poor* (1957) he advocated greater aid for the economic development of the poorer nations, and in *Asian Drama* (3 vol., 1968) he analyzed the social and economic factors affecting the governments of Asia. A foremost expert on the Swedish economy, he also wrote studies such as *The Cost of Living in Sweden, 1830–1930* (1933, tr. 1933). He shared the 1974 Nobel Prize in Economics. See also his *Challenge of World Poverty* (1970) and *Against the Stream* (1973).

myrobalan, name for the cherry PLUM and also for several Asiatic ALMOND trees.

Myron (mī'rən), fl. 5th cent. B.C., Greek sculptor. He is supposed to have been a pupil of Ageladas of Argos, but he worked largely in Athens. Sculpting in bronze, he was noted for his animals (of which no examples have survived) and for his athletes in action. His works are known through descriptions by ancient writers and two of them by copies, the *Discobolus* [Gr.,=discus thrower], the best copy of which is the Lancelotti *Discobolus* in Rome (Terme Mus.), and *Athena and Marsyas,* of which there are also Roman copies.

myrrh: see INCENSE-TREE.

myrtle, common name for the Myrtaceae, a family of shrubs and trees almost entirely of tropical regions, especially in America and Australia. The family is characterized by leaves (usually evergreen) containing aromatic volatile oils. Many have showy blossoms. Although of lesser importance in the United States, the family is of considerable economic value throughout the world for its timbers, gums and resins, oils, spices, and edible fruits. The true myrtle genus (*Myrtus*) is predominantly of the American tropics, but the classical myrtle (*M. communis*) is native to the Mediterranean area. It is a strongly scented bush whose glossy leaves and blue-black berries were made into wreaths for victors in the ancient Olympic games. (In America several unrelated plants are also called myrtles, e.g., the sand myrtle of the heath family, the periwinkles of the dogbane family, and several species of the bayberry family.) Among the many trees of the myrtle family yielding edible fruit, only the GUAVA (genus *Psidium*), native to tropical America, is grown commercially in the United States. The most important spice plants of the family are the CLOVE tree (*Syzygium aromaticum* or *Eugenia caryophyllata*), native to the Moluccas and the Spice Islands, and the tropical American *Pimenta* genus that includes the PIMENTO or allspice (*P. officinalis* or *dioica*) and the bay rum tree (*P. racemosa*), source of an oil used as an ingredient of BAY RUM. *Eucalyptus,* a large genus of evergreen shrubs and trees, is a characteristic component of the flora in its native Australia, where it is the leafy haunt and sole food source of the koala bear, often associated with it in story. Among its many common names are ironbark, bloodwood, and gum tree (a name also applied to many unrelated trees). Numerous species, especially the Tasmanian blue gum (*E. globulus*), are now naturalized in the W United States and have become the distinctive vegetation of many California areas that were previously treeless. In Australia several species are among the tallest trees known, e.g., *E. amygdalina regnans,* which reaches a height of over 300 ft (91 m). Eucalyptus trees are a valuable source of timber, of kinos (a resinous substance used in medicines and tanning), and of eucalyptol and other essential and medicinal oils. Some hardwood members of the myrtle family are among the many trees known as ironwood, e.g., *Eugenia confusa,* of Florida and tropical America. The myrtle family is classified in the division MAGNOLIOPHYTA, class Magnoliopsida, order Myrtales.

Mysia (mĭsh'ēə), ancient region, NW Asia Minor. It was N of Lydia and its coast faced Lesbos. Mysia was not a political unit, and it passed successively to Lydia, Persia, Macedon, Syria, Pergamum, and Rome. St. Paul passed through Mysia on his second missionary journey (Acts 16.7,8).

mysid shrimp: see SHRIMP.

Mysore: see KARNATAKA, state, India.

mysteries, in Greek and Roman religion, some important secret cults. The conventional religions of both Greeks and Romans were alike in consisting principally of propitiation and prayers for the good of the city-state, the tribe, or the family, and only secondarily of the person. In historical times the traditional rites in both Greece and Rome had become formalistic and barren of emotion. The individual sought a more emotional religion that would fulfill his desire for personal salvation and immortality. Secret societies were formed, usually headed by a priest or a hierophant. By the 5th cent. B.C. mysteries were an important part of the fabric of Hellenic life. Although the mystic rites were kept secret, it was known that they required elaborate initiations, including purification rites, beholding sacred objects, accepting occult knowledge, and acting out a sacred drama. Some mysteries were of foreign origin, such as the Middle Eastern cults of Cybele, Isis, and Mithra; some were embodied survivals of indigenous rites. The most important mystery cults in Greece were the Eleusinian, the Orphic, and the Andanian. Since the mystery deities were associated primarily with fertility, many scholars believe that these cults were based on unrecorded primitive fertility rites. The popularity of mystery cults spread in the Hellenistic age and still more widely in Roman times. See Lewis Farnell, *The Cults of the Greek States* (5 vol., 1896–1909); Eranos Yearbooks, *The Mysteries* (tr. 1955).

mystery play: see MIRACLE PLAY.

mystery story: see DETECTIVE STORY.

Mystic, Conn.: see STONINGTON.

Mystic. 1 River, c.10 mi (16 km) long, rising in SE Conn. and flowing S past Old Mystic and Mystic villages to the Long Island Sound. Mystic Seaport, a maritime museum, is at its mouth. **2** River, c.7 mi (11 km) long, rising in Mystic Lakes, E Mass., and flowing SE, past Medford, into Boston Harbor at Charlestown. Medford was one of the important early settlements on its banks.

mysticism (mĭs'tĭsĭzəm) [Gr.,=the practice of those who are initiated into the mysteries], the practice of putting oneself into, and remaining in, direct relation with GOD, the Absolute, or any unifying principle of life. Mysticism is inseparably linked with religion. Because of the nature of mysticism, firsthand objective studies of it are virtually impossible, and the student must confine himself to the accounts of mystics, autobiographical and biographical, or, as the mystics themselves say, he must experience for himself. The terms *mystic* and *mysticism* are used very broadly in English, being extended to mean magic, occultism, or the esoteric. There are certain common fallacies current about mysticism: that mystics are not "practical" and that they are revolutionary; on the contrary, many of the greatest mystics have been both intensely active as well as submissive to authority of whatever sort. Nor is the "solitary thinker" necessarily, or even usually, a mystic. There is no accepted explanation of mysticism, and few psychologists have interested themselves in its practice. William James studied the nature of mysticism but reached no conclusion that satisfied him. A significant philosophical evaluation of mysticism was made by Henri Bergson. There are two general tendencies in the speculation of mystics—to regard God as outside the soul, which rises to its God by successive stages, or to regard God as dwelling within the soul and to be found by delving deeper into one's own reality. The idea of transcendence, as held most firmly by mystics, is the kernel of the ancient mystical system, NEOPLATONISM, and of GNOSTICISM. Their explanation of the connection between God and man by emanation is epoch-making in the philosophy of contemplation. Among those who think of God, or the Supreme Reality, as being within the soul are the Quakers (see FRIENDS, RELIGIOUS SOCIETY OF) and the adherents of VEDANTA. The language of mysticism is always difficult and usually symbolic. This is readily seen in the Song of Songs in the Old Testament, in the book of Revelation in the New Testament, and in the writings of William Blake. The mystics of the Roman Catholic and of the Islamic traditions especially, have made use of a terminology borrowed from ordinary human love. A conventional analysis is as follows: The soul undergoes a purification (the purgative way), which leads to a feeling of illumination and greater love of God (the illuminative way); after a period the soul may be said to enter into mystical union with God (the unitive way), which begins with the consciousness that God is present to the soul; the soul progresses through a time of quiet and an ecstatic state to a final perfect state of union with God (spiritual marriage). Late in this process there is an experience (the dark night of the soul) wherein the contemplative finds himself completely deserted by God, by hope, and, indeed, even by the power to pray; it lasts sometimes for years. Visions, voices, ecstasies may accompany any or none of the states of contemplation before the final union. It is because of these external and nonessential manifestations that the erroneous idea has arisen that all enthusiastic and nonintellectual religious movements are necessarily mystical. The positive convictions of the mystic arise from the fact that they are based on what he must regard as objective reality directly perceived. Among the principal contemplatives of Christianity from post-Apostolic times to the Reformation are CLEMENT OF ALEXANDRIA, ORIGEN, St. AUGUSTINE, the false DIONYSIUS THE AREOPAGITE, CASSIAN, St. GREGORY I, ERIGENA, St. PETER DAMIAN, St. ANSELM, St. BERNARD OF CLAIRVAUX, St. Hildegard of Bingen, JOACHIM OF FLORIS, RICHARD OF SAINT VICTOR, HUGH OF SAINT VICTOR, HADEWIJCH, St. Gertrude, St. FRANCIS, JACOPONE DA TODI, St. BONAVENTURE, St. THOMAS AQUINAS, Ramon LULL, DANTE, ECKHART, TAULER, SUSO, RUYSBROECK, GROOTE, THOMAS À KEMPIS, NICHOLAS OF CUSA, ROLLE OF HAMPOLE, Walter HILTON, JULIANA OF NORWICH, Margery KEMPE, St. BRIDGET OF SWEDEN, St. CATHERINE OF SIENA, GERSON, St. BERNARDINE OF SIENA, and St. JOAN OF ARC. The Catholic tradition was continued by St. IGNATIUS OF LOYOLA, St. THERESA of Ávila, St. JOHN OF THE CROSS, St. FRANCIS OF SALES, and St. THERESA of Lisieux. Orders that have given their name to types of mysticism are CARMELITES, CARTHUSIANS, and CISTERCIANS. Among great Protestant mystics are Jakob BOEHME and George FOX, founder of Quakerism, the foremost Protestant mystical movement. In the 17th and 18th cent. much literature of the contemplative life was written by the METAPHYSICAL POETS and by Henry MORE, William LAW, and others. Extremes in post-Reformation mysticism are seen in Jansenism (see under JANSEN, CORNELIS) and in QUIETISM; and Emanuel SWEDENBORG may be regarded as a Protestant mystic. Also included in the mystic tradition were the Hermetic philosophers and the Alchemists. In Judaism the mystical tradition represented by the CABALA was continued in the modern HASIDISM. For Islamic mysticism, see SUFISM; al-GHAZALI; FARID AD-DIN ATTAR; Jalal ed-Din RUMI; Muin ad-Din Hasan CHISHTI; HAFIZ; JAMI; SADI. For Hindu mysticism, see VEDANTA; YOGA; Aurobindo GHOSE; Chinmoy GHOSE; Dayananda SARASWATI; RAMAKRISHNA; VIVEKANANDA; YOGANANDA. For Buddhism, see ZEN BUDDHISM; BUDDHA; MILAREPA; Daisetz SUZUKI. See also TAOISM. See R. M. Jones, *Studies in Mystical Religion* (1909, repr. 1970); Baron F. von Hügel, *The Mystical Element of Religion* (2d ed. 1923); S. N. Dasgupta, *Hindu Mysticism* (1927, repr. 1959); E. A. Peers, *Studies of the Spanish Mystics* (3 vol., 1927–60); Evelyn Underhill, *Mysticism* (rev. ed. 1930, repr. 1961); J. M. Clark, *The Great German Mystics* (1949); Jacques de Marquette, *Introduction to Comparative Mysticism* (1949); D. T. Suzuki, *Mysticism: Christian and Buddhist* (1957, repr. 1971); W. T. Stace, *Mysticism and Philosophy* (1960); R. C. Zaehner, *Hindu and Muslim Mysticism* (1960, repr. 1969); G. G. Scholem, *Major Trends in Jewish Mysticism* (3d ed. 1961); David Knowles, *The English Mystical Tradition* (1961); Elmer O'Brien, *Varieties of Mystical Experience* (1964); E. C. Butler, *Western Mysticism* (3d ed. 1967); L. H. Bridges, *American Mysticism* (1970).

mythology, term that literally means the telling of stories; it is also defined as the collective myths of a particular people and the scientific study of myths. A myth is a traditional story that usually occurs in a timeless past and involves supernatural elements. Myths are the products of prerational cultures and express serious concerns ranging from the creation of man and the universe to the evolution of political institutions or the assurance of agricultural fertility. The story concerned with the goddess PERSEPHONE, who spends four months in the underworld with Pluto and six months on the earth with her mother Demeter, is a myth explaining the changing seasons. Although there is no sharp line dividing myth and folktale, a myth is usually more serious, the folktale having greater entertainment function and dealing with social concerns of relative unimportance. In addition, the folktale places less emphasis on the supernatural, and more on narrative interest, which results in a more logical plot. Whereas myth tends to relate seemingly disconnected or irrational events, the folktale takes place in historical time. Its characters are less individually defined than in myth, and folktale heroes depend more on ingenuity and trickery than do mythological heroes. Thus the character Odysseus in Homer's *Odyssey* possesses many of the attributes of a folktale hero. Stories that can be roughly defined as folktales include "Cinderella," "Cupid and Psyche," the tales in the *Arabian Nights,* and the "Uncle Remus" stories. Two similar forms, legend and saga, are distinguished by their historical or quasi-historical nature. Legends are based on fact and concern an historical person, place, or incident. The story of Lady Godiva's naked ride through Coventry is a legend. Saga refers specifically to the prose tales of Norwegian and Icelandic kings, recorded in Iceland from the 12th to the 15th cent. There have been innumerable attempts to analyze and explicate myths, many of the explanations purporting to account for their apparent absurdity. The ancient Greeks developed allegorical interpretations of their own myths. Although this process was probably begun by Theagenes of Rhegium in the 6th cent. B.C., it was most fully developed by the Stoics, whose interpretations reduced the Greek gods to moral principles and natural elements (see STOICISM). EUHEMERUS considered the gods to have been renowned historical figures who, through the passage of time, became deified. Thus, mythological characters such as Zeus were considered to have been (at one time) men. A later allegorical interpretation, stemming from 18th-century study, states that at one time myths were invented by wise men to point out a truth, but that after a time myths were taken literally, e.g., Cronus who devoured his children is identified with the Greek word for time, which may be said to destroy whatever it brings into existence. The philological studies of myth by Max MÜLLER mark the beginning of serious modern mythology. Müller saw myths evolving out of corruptions of language. Therefore, what seems absurd in myth is the result of people forgetting or distorting the meanings of words, e.g., the phrase "sunrise follows the dawn," spoken in Greek could be interpreted as meaning Apollo pursues Daphne, the maiden of the Dawn. Other theories include the view that myth is the foreshadowing or corruption of the Scriptures; thus DEUCALION is another name for Noah. The animistic interpretation sees myths as developing from the improper separation between the human and nonhuman; animals, rocks, and stars are considered to be on a level of intelligence with people, and the dead are thought to inhabit the world of the living in spiritual form. Sir James FRAZER, whose epoch-making book *The Golden Bough* (1890) is a standard work on mythology, believed that all myths were originally connected with the idea of fertility in nature, with the birth, death and resurrection of vegetation as a constantly recurring motif. Other theories have more generally related myth to ritual or religious impulses by positing a common psychological or emotional basis. The anthropologist Bronislaw MALINOWSKI considered all myths to be validations of established behavior patterns and institutions within the society. Sigmund FREUD made a major contribution to the study of myth by relating the unconscious to myth and dream. Thus, the irrationality of myth arises from the same source as the disconnectedness of dream. Among 20th-century mythologers the theories of Mircea Eliade and Claude LÉVI-STRAUSS are significant. Eliade contends that myths are recited for the purpose of returning to the beginning of time when all things were initiated; by doing so, man can get back to the time of the original, successful creative act. Lévi-Strauss advocates interpreting myths on a structural basis. He dismisses the illogical in myth by denying the importance of content altogether. Ultimately, he believes that all myths are structural models of the mind's response to its world, and he contends that myths attempt to mediate between conflicting opposites such as nature and culture. While ancient Greek and Roman mythology is the best known of all such systems, great modern advances in the science of mythology have occurred since 19th-century scholars like James Frazer and Edward Burnett TYLOR became aware of the importance of myths of contemporary primitive cultures to the study of mythology in general. Studies of the myths of North and South American Indians, Australian aborigines, the peoples of S Africa, and other primitive peoples have demonstrated the remarkable similarity of myths of far different cultures. In addition these studies have effected a better understanding of classical mythology, which demonstrates points of contact with primitive totemistic myth while clearly displaying signs of rational refinement. Greek myth as we see it in Homer is an elaborate combination of mythical elements with legend and folktale. The Five Ages of Man described in Hesiod's *Theogeny* is a good example of mythic materials that have undergone a process of rational ordering. Other important mythologies are the Norse, which is less anthropomorphic than the Greek (see GERMANIC RELIGION); the Indian, or Vedic, which tends to be more abstract and other worldly than the Greek (see VEDA); the Egyptian, which is closely related to religious ritual (see EGYPTIAN RELIGION); and the Mesopotamian, which shares with the Greek mythology a strong concern with the relationship between life and death (see MIDDLE EASTERN RELIGIONS). Although there is no specific universal myth, there are many myths that occur in various cultures and ages. The flood myth is extremely common and is one of a group of myths that concern the destruction and recreation of the world or a particular society. While all cultures have myths of the creation of the world, these range from a god fashioning the earth from abstract chaos to a specific animal creating it from a handful of mud. Myths of cyclical destruction and creation are parallelled by myths of seasonal death and rebirth. In Greece the concern with renewed fertility was seasonal, whereas in certain other cultures (e.g., Mesopotamia) the concern was with longer periods of vegetative death through prolonged drought. The idea of a golden age is another common motif (e.g., Hesiod's Golden Age in the *Theogony* and the Garden of Eden in Christian thought). Man is here viewed as having degenerated from an earlier perfection. Myths of the millennium to come are also common, as are myths treating the origin of water or its retrieval from some being who has stolen it, and myths of the dead or the relation between the living and the dead. Myths also frequently deal with problems of social and political disorder, or with themes of nature as opposed to civilization. There have been many theories as to the reason for similarity in mythology. Carl JUNG believed that there is an inherent tendency in all people to form certain of the same mythic symbols. Tylor and Andrew LANG, on the other hand, thought that there is a certain stage of savage mentality that tends to produce similar myths. Another theory postulates mythic diffusion through travel, migration, and other forms of transcontinental communication. Whatever similarity exists in terms of theme or explicit content among various myths, today it is generally believed that the myths of each culture must be examined separately within the total cultural context. Our knowledge of the psychology of mythmaking people remains obscure, and myths function in a variety of ways within a single culture as well as differing in function from culture to culture. Myth has constantly been employed for the enrichment of literature since the time of Aeschylus and has been used by some of the major English poets (e.g., Milton, Shelley, Keats). Some great literary figures, notably William Blake, James Joyce, Franz Kafka, W. B. Yeats, T. S. Eliot, and Wallace Stevens have consciously constructed personal myths using the old materials and newly constructed symbols. Literary critics have therefore devoted much time to studying the significance of mythmaking and particular myths. See E. B. Tylor, *Primitive Culture* (2 vol., rev. ed. 1924); J. G. Frazer, *The Golden Bough* (3d ed., 13 vol., 1952); Otto Rank, *The Myth of the Birth of the Hero* (tr. 1952); Gertrude Jobes, *Dictionary of Mythology, Folklore and Symbols* (2 vol., 1961); Joseph Campbell, *The Masks of God* (4 vol., 1959–68); Thomas Bulfinch, *Mythology* (2d ed. 1970).

Mytilene, Greece: see MITILÍNI.

myxedema (mĭksədē'mə), condition associated with severe hypothyroidism and lack of thyroid hormone in the adult. In the child it is known as CRETINISM. Symptoms include a dry swelling of the skin, slowed speech and mental awareness, deepened voice, intolerance to cold, fatigue and weakness, and nonspecific degeneration of the heart. Most cases result from atrophy of the thyroid from unknown causes, although surgical removal or irradiation of the gland also precipitates the disorder. Myxedema is treated by administering thyroxine (thyroid hormone) or dried thyroid preparations.

Mzab (əmzäb'), stony, barren valley, Algeria, in the N Sahara. It was settled c.1000 by members of an austere Muslim sect, the Kharijites. The Mzabites dug wells, created date-palm oases, and built seven towns, united in a confederation. Their aptitude for trade made the area a caravan junction. France occupied the Mzab in 1853 and annexed it formally in 1882. Many Mzabite men spend several years in urban centers, amassing wealth as tradesmen. GHARDAÏA is the principal town of the region.

N

N, 14th letter of the ALPHABET. It is a usual symbol for a voiced alveolar (or dental) nasal, as in the English *not.* The diagraph *ng* represents a different sound, a voiced velar nasal, as in the English *sing.* The corresponding Greek letter is nu. In chemistry N is the symbol for the element NITROGEN.

Na, chemical symbol of the element SODIUM.

Naam (nā'ăm), son of Caleb. 1 Chron. 4.15.

Naamah (nā'əmə). **1** Daughter of Lamech. Gen. 4.22. **2** Mother of King Rehoboam. 1 Kings 14.21. **3** Unidentified town, SW Palestine. Joshua 15.41.

Naaman (nā'əmən). **1** Syrian captain whom Elisha cured miraculously of leprosy. 2 Kings 5. **2** Benjamite. Gen. 46.21; Num. 26.40; 1 Chron. 8.4.

Naamathite (nā'əməthīt), obscure epithet applied to Job's friend, Zophar. Job 2.11.

Naarah (nā'ārə, nāā'rə), wife of Ashur. 1 Chron. 4.5,6.

Naarai (nā'ārā, nāərā'ī), one of David's warriors. 1 Chron. 11.37. Paarai: 2 Sam. 23.35.

Naaran (nā'ərăn) or **Naarath** (-răth), unidentified town, central Palestine. Joshua 16.7; 1 Chron. 7.28.

Naashon (nā'əshŏn, nāăsh'ən) or **Naasson** (nā'əsŏn, nāăs'ən), same as NAHSHON.

Nabal (nā'bəl), wealthy sheep owner who resisted David's attempt at extortion. David's anger was appeased by the blandishments of ABIGAIL, Nabal's wife. 1 Sam. 25.

Nabataea (năb"ətē'ə), ancient kingdom of Arabia, south of Edom, in present-day Jordan. It flourished from the 4th cent. B.C. to A.D. 106, when it was conquered by Rome. The history of Nabataea consists mainly of the struggle to control the trade routes between the Orient and the Mediterranean. PETRA, the capital city, is noted for its unique rock-cut monuments, tombs, and temples. See study by J. I. Lawlor (1974).

Nabis (näbē') [from Heb.,=prophets], a group of artists in France active during the 1890s. Paul Sérusier and Maurice DENIS were the principal theorists of the group. Outstanding members were Édouard Vuillard, Pierre Bonnard, Aristide Maillol, and Félix Vallotton. The group held its first exhibition in 1892. Influenced by Gauguin, the Nabis developed a style characterized by flat areas of bold color and heavily outlined surface patterns. They were unified by their dislike of IMPRESSIONISM. Their work parallels to some degree the efforts of the contemporary symbolist poets. After a successful show in 1899, the group gradually disbanded. See study by Charles Chassé (tr. 1969).

Nablus (näblo͞os'), city (1967 est. pop. 47,000), W Jordan. It is the market center for a region where wheat and olives are grown and sheep and goats are grazed. Manufactures include soap made from olive oil and colorful shepherds' coats. The city is linked by highway with Jerusalem. Nablus, an ancient Canaanite town, has remains dating from c.2000 B.C., about the time when the city was held by Egypt. The Samaritans (see under SAMARIA) made it their capital and built a temple to rival that of Jerusalem. Nablus still has a small community of Samaritans. The city was destroyed (129 B.C.) by John Hyrcanus I. Under Hadrian it was rebuilt and named Neapolis, from which the present name derives. Nearby are the reputed sites of the tomb of Joseph and the well of Jacob. The city came under Israeli occupation following the Arab-Israeli War of 1967.

Nabokov, Vladimir (vlädē'mĭr näbô'kŏf), 1899–, Russian-American novelist. Born in St. Petersburg, Russia, of aristocratic parents, he emigrated to England after the Russian Revolution of 1917 and graduated from Cambridge in 1922. He moved to the United States in 1945. From 1948 to 1959 he was professor of Russian literature at Cornell Univ. He moved to Switzerland in 1959. An extraordinarily imaginative writer, Nabokov has often experimented with the form of the novel. Although his works are frequently obscure and puzzling—filled with grotesque incidents, word games, and literary allusions—they are always erudite, witty, and intriguing. Before 1940, Nabokov wrote in Russian under the name V. Sirin. Among his early novels are *Mary* (1926, tr. 1970), *King, Queen, Knave* (1928, tr. 1969), *Laughter in the Dark* (1932, tr. 1938), *Despair* (1936, tr. 1937, 1965), and *Invitation to a Beheading* (1938, tr. 1959). His first book in English was *The Real Life of Sebastian Knight* (1938). Nabokov's most famous work is undoubtedly *Lolita* (1958). The story of a middle-aged European intellectual's infatuation with a 12-year-old American "nymphet," *Lolita* has become something of a modern American classic. *Pale Fire* (1962) is a satirical fantasy consisting of a long poem and commentary written by a mad New England scholar who is the exiled king of a mythical Balkan country. *Ada or Ardor: A Family Chronicle* (1969) is a bizarre philosophical novel that is both the chronicle of a long incestuous love affair and a probe into the nature of time. Among Nabokov's other novels are *Bend Sinister* (1947), *Pnin* (1957), *Transparent Things* (1972), and *Look at the Harlequins!* (1974). He has also written volumes of poetry, such as *Poems and Problems* (1970); collections of short stories, including *Nine Stories* (1947), *Nabokov's Dozen* (1958), and *A Russian Beauty* (1973); a critical study of Gogol (1944); translations from the Russian; and several autobiographical volumes, notably *Speak, Memory* (1966). He has also achieved an international reputation as a lepidopterist. See studies by Andrew Field (1967), W. W. Rowe (1971), Douglas Fowler (1974); bibliography by Andrew Field (1973).

Nabonidus (năbənī'dəs), d. 538? B.C., last king of the Chaldaean dynasty of Babylonia. He was not of Nebuchadnezzar's family, and it is possible that he usurped the throne. He was absorbed in antiquarian and religious speculations, and he built temples while the state was left undefended. He was unpopular with both the priests and the people. When the Persian threat of Cyrus the Great grew strong, Nabonidus allied himself with Croesus of Lydia and Amasis II of Egypt, but to no avail. In 538? B.C. the kingdom fell to Cyrus with no resistance. Nabonidus' scholars preserved information valuable to modern archaeologists. Cuneiform records indicate that Belshazzar was Nabonidus' son and his coregent during the last years of Babylon.

Nabopolassar: see BABYLONIA.

Naboth (nā'bŏth), Jezreelite stoned to death because he would not let King Ahab have his vineyard. Elijah's curse on the royal family for their treatment of Naboth forecast the downfall of the dynasty. 1 Kings 21; 2 Kings 9.21–37.

Nabuchodonosor (năb"yo͝okədŏn'əsôr"), variant of NEBUCHADNEZZAR.

Nabuco, Joaquim (zhwäkēm' nəbo͞o' ko͞o), 1849–1910, Brazilian writer, abolitionist, and diplomat. A parliamentary deputy in imperial times, he was perhaps the strongest single force in bringing about the abolition of slavery (1888). He was prominent under the republic, serving as minister to Great Britain and as ambassador to the United States. A champion of Pan-Americanism, he presided over the Pan American Conference (1906). He is well known for his literary works, and his autobiography, *Minha formacao* [my formation] (1900), is a classic of its kind. See biography by his daughter, Carolina Nabuco, *The Life of Joaquim Nabuco* (tr. 1950, repr. 1969).

nacelle (nəsĕl'): see AIRPLANE.

Nachon (nā'kŏn), later PEREZ-UZZA.

Nachor (nā'kôr), variant of NAHOR.

Nachtigal, Gustav (go͝os'täf näkh'tēgäl), 1834–85, German explorer in Africa. He went (1869) on a mission for the king of Prussia to the sultan of Bornu. He visited the central Sahara region and reached Khartoum in 1874. In 1884 he annexed Togoland and the Cameroons for Germany.

Nacka (nä'kä), city (1970 pop. 27,384), Stockholm co., E Sweden, on the Baltic Sea, a suburb of Stockholm. It has radio and television stations and shipyards. Manufactures include steam turbines and processed food.

Nacogdoches (năk"ədō'chĭs), city (1970 pop. 22,544), seat of Nacogdoches co., E Texas, in a pine and hardwood forest area containing clays and sandy loams; settled 1779. Industries in this rapidly growing city include lumbering, clay refining, meat-packing, poultry raising and processing, and the manufacture of feed and fertilizer, brass valves, and wood products. Tourism is also important; the city is in the center of a large recreational area that contains the huge Sam Rayburn Reservoir and many lakes. A Spanish mission was founded there in 1716, but permanent settlers did not arrive until 1779. The settlement was an eastern bastion of the Spanish colony against the French in Louisiana. After the Louisiana Purchase it was twice (1812, 1819) seized by raiding expeditions from the United States. In 1820 about 100 American families were issued land grants there. Their settlement led to the FREDONIAN REBELLION in 1826. The city was active in the Texas Revolution (1835–36) and later developed into a market for cotton plantations. The state's first oil wells were drilled near the city in 1859. The remains of Nacogdoches Univ. (chartered in 1845) are on today's high school grounds. On the campus of Stephen F. Austin State Univ. is the Old Stone Fort, a Spanish presidio built in 1779. The home where Sam Houston joined the Roman Catholic Church is now a library and museum. Thomas J. Rusk also lived there. Four signers of the Texas Declaration of Independence are buried in the Oak Grove Cemetery.

nacre: see MOTHER-OF-PEARL.

NAD: see COENZYME.

Nadab (nā'dăb). **1** Aaron's eldest son, set apart for the priesthood. The exact nature of the transgression ("offering strange fire") for which he and his brother Abihu died is not clear. Ex. 6.23; 24; 28; Lev. 10; Num. 3.1–4; 26.61; 1 Chron. 6.3; 24.1–2. **2** King of Israel, son and successor of Jeroboam I. He was assassinated by BAASHA in the siege of Gibbethon. 1 Kings 15.25–31. **3** Descendant of Jerahmeel. 1 Chron. 2.28. **4** Benjamite. 1 Chron. 8.30.

Nadar (nädär'), pseud. of **Gaspard-Félix Tournachon** (gäspär'-fālĕks' to͞ornäshôN'), 1820–1910, French pioneer photographer and writer, b. Paris. Nadar opened a photographic studio in 1853 that became a meeting place for literary and artistic celebrities whose faces were captured in his superb portraits. He conceived the idea of mapmaking and surveying from a balloon, completing his first aerial photographs c.1858. Nadar invented the photo-essay, but his prose essays and novels brought him greater fame in his day than his photographs. His work is preserved in the Bibliothèque nationale.

Nadelman, Elie, 1882–1946, Polish-American sculptor, b. Warsaw. He spent some time in Paris and is said to have influenced Picasso. Before he settled (1914) in the United States his work was exhibited in New York City at the Armory Show in 1913. His sculptures of wood or metal have a smooth simplicity, and he worked inventively in a wide variety of styles. Probably his most famous bronze is *Man in the Open Air* (c.1915; Mus. of Modern Art, New York City), an urbane figure clad only in a small bow tie and bowler hat, in a pose slightly reminiscent of classical antiquity. Nadelman was comparatively unknown until interest in him was revived by a retrospective exhibition (1948) at the Museum of Modern Art. See biography by Lincoln Kirstein (1973).

Nader, Ralph, 1934–, U.S. consumer advocate, b. Winsted, Conn. Admitted to the bar in 1958, he practiced law in Connecticut and was a lecturer (1961–63) in history and government at the Univ. of Hartford. In 1965, Nader published *Unsafe at Any Speed*, a best-selling indictment of the auto industry and its poor safety standards. Largely through his influence, the U.S. Congress passed (1966) a stringent auto safety act. The leading U.S. advocate of consumer interests, Nader founded (1969) the Center for the Study of Responsive Law, an organization that, through carefully documented studies, exposed both corporate irresponsibility and the Federal government's failure to enforce regulatory legislation aimed at business. See biographies by R. F. Buckhorn (1972) and Charles McCarry (1972).

Nader Shah: see NADIR SHAH.

Nadezhdinsk: see SEROV, USSR.

Nadiad (nŭd'ēäd), city (1971 pop. 108,268), Gujurat state, W central India. It is a market for agricultural products. Metal utensils are made. The city formerly had walls and a moat.

nadir (nā'dər) [Arab.,=opposite], in astronomy, the point on the CELESTIAL SPHERE directly opposite the ZENITH, i.e., directly beneath the observer.

Nadir Shah or **Nader Shah** (both: nä'dēr shä), 1688–1747, shah of Iran (1736–47), sometimes considered the last of the great Asian conquerors. He was a member of the Afshar tribe. Although taken prisoner by the Uzbeks while he was still a child, he escaped and entered the service of the governor of Khurasan. There he earned a reputation for bravery. He then entered the service of Tahmasp, the son of Shah Sultan HUSAYN, who was asserting his claims against the Afghans under Mahmud, who had usurped the Persian throne. Nadir took the name Tahmasp Kuli Khan [Tahmasp's slave] and proceeded to win a series of battles against the Afghans. Decisively beaten, they retired to Kandahar, and Tahmasp was restored to the rule over Iran. Nadir, however, was the powerful figure of the realm. He warred against the Turks successfully, and when the shah turned victory to disaster by a conciliatory peace, Nadir in 1732 deposed him. Tahmasp's infant son Abbas III was placed on the throne with Nadir as regent. The conquests continued, and the western boundary was restored to what it had been before the Afghan invasions. In 1736 Nadir deposed Abbas and himself became shah, thus ending the rule of the Safavid dynasty. He attempted to weld Iran and the Ottoman Empire by unifying the Shiites and Sunnis. This led to much dissatisfaction in Shiite Iran, and the plan was discarded. In 1738-39 Nadir invaded Mogul India. He was brilliantly successful, taking and sacking Delhi and Lahore and carrying off vast treasure, including the Koh-i-noor diamond and the Peacock Throne. He also continued his conquests in other directions. Bukhara was subdued, and the limits of Iran were extended to the greatest that they had been since the days of the Sassanids. War with the Turks occupied his attention from 1743 to 1746. Nadir's later years were darkened by a turn toward tyranny, suspicion, and greed. So much did he fear opposition that he had his own son blinded. In 1747, during a campaign against rebellious Kurds, Nadir Shah was assassinated by officers of his own guard. Although the dynasty he founded, the Afshar dynasty (1736–49), was short-lived, Nadir is generally regarded as one of the greatest of all rulers of Persia. See study by Laurence Lockhart (1938, repr. 1973).

NADP: see COENZYME.

Naegeli, Karl Wilhelm von: see NÄGELI.

Naestved (nĕst'vĕth), city (1970 com. pop. 41,803), Storstrøm co., SE Denmark. It is a seaport, linked (since 1938) with the Karrebaek Fjord (an arm of the Store Baelt) by a 5-mi (8.1-km) canal. It is also an industrial center and a rail junction.

Nafa: see NAHA, Okinawa.

Näfels (nā'fəls), town (1970 pop. 3,739), Glarus canton, E central Switzerland. The town has a magnificent baroque palace.

Nafud (năfo͞od') or **Nefud** (nĕfo͞od'), desert area in the northern part of the Arabian Peninsula, occupying a great oval depression; 180 mi (290 km) long and 140 mi (225 km) wide. This area of red sand is surrounded by sandstone outcrops that have eroded into grotesque shapes. The Nafud is noted for its sudden violent winds, which have formed great crescent-shaped dunes, rising up to 600 ft (183 m). Rainfall occurs once or twice a year. In some lowland basins, especially those near the Hejaz Mts. (to the west), there are oases where dates, vegetables, barley, and fruits are raised. The Nafud is connected to the Rub al Khali, the great desert of S Arabia, by the Dahna, a corridor of gravel plains and sand dunes, 800 mi (1,287 km) long and 15 to 50 mi (24.1-80.5 km) wide.

Nagaland (nä'gəlănd), state (1971 pop. 515,561), 6,365 sq mi (16,485 sq km), NE India. Formerly called the Naga Hills–Tuensang area in Assam state, it became a separate state in 1961. It is a wild, forested, and undeveloped region bounded on the E by Burma. The region is inhabited by Nagas, a Tibeto-Burman tribe, who are largely animists and practice head hunting. There is a strong movement for independence, and the region has been the scene of several clashes between Indian troops and the Naga tribes. The state is governed by a chief minister and cabinet responsible to a bicameral legislature with one elected house. The states of Assam, Nagaland, Meahalaya, Manipur, and Tripura and the union territories of Mizoram and Arunachal Pradesh have a common governor appointed by the president of India.

Nagano (nägä'nō), city (1970 pop. 285,310), capital of Nagano prefecture, central Honshu, Japan, on the Tenryu River. It has printing, food-processing, machine-building, and textile-manufacturing industries. Nagano is also a religious center, the site of Zenkoji, a 7th-century Buddhist temple that houses statues sent from the king of Korea in 552. Nagano prefecture (1970 pop. 1,956,863), 5,261 sq mi (13,626 sq km) is known for its raw-silk industry.

Nagaoka (nägä'ôkä), city (1970 pop. 162,262), Niigata prefecture, central Honshu, Japan. An industrial center, it has oil refineries, chemical plants, engineering works, and machine-building factories. Nagaoka is also a distribution point for agricultural products.

Nagarjuna: see MADHYAMIKA.

Nagasaki (näg'äsä'kē), city (1970 pop. 421,055), capital of Nagasaki prefecture, W Kyushu, Japan, on Nagasaki Bay. It is one of Japan's leading ports. Shipbuilding is the chief industry; steelworks, collieries, fisheries, and electrical machinery plants are also important. Nagasaki's port, the first to receive Western trade, was known to Portuguese and Spanish traders before it was opened to the Dutch in 1567. After the Portuguese and Spanish merchants were forced to leave Japan in 1637, the Dutch traders were restricted (1641–1858) to De-Jima, an island in the harbor. Nagasaki was gradually reopened to general foreign trade during the 1850s. Long a center of Christianity, the city had until 1945 Japan's largest Roman Catholic cathedral. During World War II, on Aug. 9, 1945, Nagasaki became the target of the second atomic bomb ever detonated on a populated area; about 75,000 people were killed or wounded, and more than one third of the city was devastated. Among Nagasaki's landmarks is Glover Mansion, scene of Puccini's opera *Madama Butterfly.* Nagasaki prefecture (1970 pop. 1,569,984), 1,574 sq mi (4,077 sq km), is mainly agricultural. Raw-silk production is widespread, and coal is mined near Sasebo. Important cities are Nagasaki, Hirado, known for its fine porcelain ware, and Sasebo, the site of a large naval base. The prefecture includes the island of Goto-retto.

Nagel, Ernest, 1901–, American philosopher, b. Nove Mesto, Czechoslovakia, grad. College of the City of New York, 1923, and Columbia (Ph.D., 1930). His family emigrated to the United States in 1911. He joined (1931) the philosophy faculty of Columbia, where he became (1955) John Dewey professor of philosophy. Under the influence of his teacher, Morris R. Cohen, he was originally an advocate of logical realism, holding that the principles of logic represent the universal and eternal traits of nature. Later, however, he withdrew from this ontological position and developed an approach to logic and the philosophy of science that stressed abstract and functional aspects. Among his works are *An Introduction to Logic and Scientific Method* (with M. R. Cohen, 1934), *Sovereign Reason* (1954), *Logic without Metaphysics* (1957), *The Structure of Science: Problems in the Logic of Scientific Explanation* (1961), and *Observation and Theory in Science* (with others, 1971).

Nägeli or **Naegeli, Karl Wilhelm von** (both: kärl vĭl'hĕlm fən nā'gəlē), 1817–91, Swiss botanist. He was professor at the Univ. of Munich from 1858 and was noted especially for his work on plant cytology and development. He made studies of the process of division in pollen grains and in unicellular algae, and he determined the function of many plant parts, such as the antheridia and spermatozoids of ferns. In his studies of cells he made a distinction between the nuclear material and a mucous layer of living matter (protoplasm).

Nagercoil (nä'gərkoil), city (1971 pop. 141,207), Tamil Nadu state, S India. Nagercoil is the southernmost city in India. It is a district administrative center for a region where rice is grown and ilmenite and monazite are mined.

Nagge (năg'ē), in the Gospel genealogy. Luke 3.25.

Nagorno-Karabakh Autonomous Oblast (nəgôr'nə-kərəbäkh), autonomous region (1970 pop. 149,000), 1,699 sq mi (4,400 sq km), SE European USSR, in Azerbaijan, between the Caucasus and the Karabakh range. Stepanakert (the capital) and Shusha are the chief towns. The region has numerous mineral springs as well as deposits of polymetallic ore, lithographic stone, marble, and limestone. Farming and grazing are important and there are various light industries. The population of the oblast is mainly Armenian, with Russian, Azerbaijani, and Kurdish minorities. A part of Caucasian Albania called Artsakh, the area was taken by Armenia in the 1st cent. A.D. and by the Arabs in the 7th cent. The region was renamed Karabakh in the 13th cent. In the early 17th cent., it passed to the Persians, who permitted local autonomy, and in the mid-18th cent. the Karabakh khanate was formed. Karabakh alone was ceded to Russia in 1805; the khanate passed to the Russians by the Treaty of Gulistan in 1813. In 1822 the Karabakh khanate was dissolved and the area became a Russian province. The Nagorno-Karabakh (Mountain-Karabakh) Autonomous Oblast was established in 1923.

Nagoya (nä"gō'yä), city (1970 pop. 2,036,022), capital of Aichi prefecture, central Honshu, Japan, on Ise Bay. A major port, transportation hub, and industrial center, it has iron and steel works, textile mills, aircraft factories, automotive works, and chemical, plastics, and fertilizer plants. Fine porcelain, pottery, and cloisonné are also produced. The city has nine universities, of which Nagoya Imperial Univ. is the most famous. Nagoya has two famous shrines, the Atsuta (founded in the 2d cent.), where the sacred imperial sword is housed, and the Higashi Honganji, which was built in 1692. A fortress town in the 16th cent., Nagoya retains a castle built by Ieyasu in 1612 and reconstructed in 1959.

Nagpur (näg'po͝or), city (1971 pop. 866,144), Maharashtra state, central India, on the Nag River. Formerly the capital of Berar and Madyha Pradesh states, it is a transportation center and a leading industrial and commercial city. Founded in the 18th cent. as the capital of the Nagpur Mahratta kingdom, it passed in 1853 to the British.

Nagy, Imre (ĭm'rĕ nôj, nŏd'yə), 1895?–1958, Hungarian Communist leader. Nagy was a symbol of the 1956 Hungarian revolt against the Soviet Union. As an agricultural expert he held several government posts in postwar Hungary before serving (1953–55) as premier. His "new course" de-emphasized heavy industry, stopped forcible collectivization, and loosened police controls; he was increasingly critical of Soviet influence in Hungary. Denounced for Titoism, he was removed from office. His expulsion from the Hungarian Communist party in early 1956 was rescinded at the request of rioting students shortly before the Hungarian revolution began (see HUNGARY). Nagy was recalled as premier of the new government on Oct. 24, 1956. He took refuge in the Yugoslav embassy when the Soviets counterattacked (Nov. 4) and crushed the revolt. Leaving the embassy under a safe-conduct pledge, he was seized by Soviet police and was later returned to the custody of the new Hungarian regime headed by János KÁDÁR. His trial and execution were announced in 1958.

Nagykanizsa (nŏ'dyəkŏnĭ"zhŏ), city (1970 pop. 39,411), SW Hungary. It is an industrial center producing oil derricks and other heavy equipment, glass, and beer. There are oil fields nearby. Founded c.1300 as a fortress, Nagykanizsa was captured by the Turks in 1600. It has a museum, an 18th-century Franciscan church, and the ruins of the old fortress. The city is sometimes called Kanizsa.

Nagykőrös (nŏ'dyəkö'rösh), town (1970 pop. 25,785), central Hungary. It is the center of a fruit-growing region and has an old Reformed church, a college, and a town hall. The poet John Arany was born in Nagykőrös.

Nagyszombat: see TRNAVA, Czechoslovakia.

Naha (nä'hä), city (1970 pop. 276,380), on OKINAWA island, in the Ryukyu Islands, Japan. A port on the southwest coast, it is also the chief manufacturing center of the island. In 1853, Commodore Perry chose Naha as his first base for the penetration of Japan. The city was virtually destroyed during World War II. In 1945 it became the headquarters of the U.S. military governor of the Ryukyus, and when the island was returned to Japan in 1972, it became the capital of Okinawa prefecture. The name is also spelled Nafa and Nawa.

Nahalal, Nahallah (both: nā'həlăl) or **Nahalol** (-lŏl), city in N Palestine, part of the inheritance of the children of Zebulon. Joshua 19.15; 21.35; Judges 1.30.

Nahaliel (nāhăl'ēĕl), unidentified stream, entering the Dead Sea. Nearby was a desert camping place. Num. 21.19.

Naham (nā'hăm), name in a genealogy. 1 Chron. 4.19.

Nahamani (nāhăm'ənī), leader among the returned exiles. Neh. 7.7.

Nahanni National Park (nəhăn'ē), c.1,840 sq mi (4,770 sq km), SW Mackenzie dist., Northwest Territories, Canada, W of Fort Simpson; est. 1972. Located just E of the Yukon border, the park extends along the lower portion of the South Nahanni River. The river's spectacular course passes through three deep canyons and over Virginia Falls (c.300 ft/90 m high) and numerous rapids. A wilderness area, the park has hot springs and caves and a variety of plant and animal life.

Naharai (nā″hărā′ī) or **Nahari** (nā′hărī), armor-bearer of Joab. 2 Sam. 23.37; 1 Chron. 11.39.

Nahash (nā′hăsh). **1** Ammonite king whose cruelty caused his destruction by Saul. 1 Sam. 11,12. His successor was HANUN **1**. **2** Father of SHOBI, called Nahash of Rabbah, perhaps the same as **1**. **3** Father of ABIGAIL **2**.

Nahas Pasha (Mustafa Nahas Pasha) (nähäs′ pä′shä), 1876–1965, Egyptian statesman, leader (1927–52) of the WAFD party. He was premier five times between 1928 and 1952. During World War II the British forced (1942) King Farouk to appoint Nahas as head of a government favorable to the Allies. When he became premier for the last time (1951), he denounced the Anglo-Egyptian treaty of alliance, which he had signed as premier in 1936. Agitation against the British led to rioting in Cairo in Jan., 1952, and Nahas was dismissed by the king. After the king's abdication later in the year, Nahas supported the new Egyptian government, but he was subsequently forced to disband the Wafd. He and his wife were imprisoned in 1953. After their release in 1954 he retired into private life.

Nahath (nā′hăth). **1** Duke of Edom. Gen. 36.13,17; 1 Chron. 1.37. **2** Levite. 2 Chron. 31.13. **3** Ancestor of Samuel. 1 Chron. 6.26. Toah: 1 Chron. 6.34. Tohu: 1 Sam. 1.1.

Nahavand (nähävänd′), city (1966 pop. 24,000), Hamadan governorate, Kermanshah prov., W Iran. It is an agricultural trade center. Nahavand was the scene of a decisive victory of the Arabs over the Persians in 641 or 642. The name also appears as Nehavand and Nihavand.

Nahbi (nä′bī), one of the spies sent by Moses into Canaan. Num. 13.14.

Nahmanides (nämän′ĭdēz), 1194–c.1270, Jewish scholar, exegete, and cabalist, b. Spain. He wrote commentaries on the Old Testament and on the Talmud. A mystic, he rejected part of Maimonides' philosophy but recognized his greatness. He wrote an account of his disputation with the anti-Jewish agitator Pablo Christiani, which took place in the presence of King James I of Aragón. In 1267, Nahmanides settled in Palestine. He is also called Rabbi Moses Ben Nahman (abbreviated to Ramban). See Gershom Sholem, *Major Trends in Jewish Mysticism* (1946); C. B. Chavel, *Ramban: His Life and Teachings* (1960).

Nahor (nā′hôr). **1** Abraham's grandfather. Gen. 11.22–25. Nachor: Luke 3.34. **2** Abraham's brother. Gen. 22.20–23. Nachor: Joshua 24.2.

Nahshon (nä′shŏn), ancestor of David. Num. 1.7; Ruth 4.18–20; 1 Chron. 2.10. Naashon: Ex. 6.23. Naasson: Mat. 1.4; Luke 3.32.

Nahuatl: see NAHUATLAN; AMERICAN INDIAN LANGUAGES.

Nahuatlan (nä′wŏt″lən), group of languages of the Uto-Aztecan branch of the Aztec-Tanoan linguistic stock of North and Central America. A Nahuatlan language of great historical importance is Nahuatl, or Aztec. A descendant of the now extinct Aztec, the language of the ancient Aztec empire, Nahuatl is spoken today by more than 800,000 people, mainly in Mexico. Aztec is thought to have reached 5 million people in an area extending from Mexico to Panama. The Nahuatlan group also includes a number of other living languages, such as Pipil and Pochutla, and extinct tongues, among them Toltec, Chichimec, and Nahuatlato. See AMERICAN INDIAN LANGUAGES.

Nahuel Huapí (näwĕl′ wäpē′), lake, c.210 sq mi (540 sq km), in Río Negro and Neuquén provs., W central Argentina. The 45-mi (72-km) lake is drained northeastward by the Limay River. It is part of Nahuel Huapí National Park (est. 1934) and is a popular resort area.

Nahum (nā′əm, -həm), book of the Old Testament, 34th in the order of the Authorized Version, seventh of the books of the Minor Prophets. It is a prophecy of doom against Nineveh, capital of the Assyrian Empire, delivered by one Nahum the Elkoshite, who is otherwise unknown. One analysis of the book divides it into four poems, the first (an acrostic; 1.2–8) and second (1.9–2.1) on the awful power of God, and others (2.2–13 and 3) being eloquent descriptions of the destruction of the city. Nineveh fell in 612 B.C., and scholars differ as to whether the book was written before or after the event. For bibliography, see OLD TESTAMENT. See also A. O. Haldar, *Studies in the Book of Nahum* (1947); W. A. Maier, *The Book of Nahum* (1959).

naiad, in zoology: see INSECT.

naiads, in Greek mythology: see NYMPH.

Naidu, Sarojini (sərō′jĭnē nī′do͞o), 1879–1949, Indian poet and political leader. Born Sarojini Chattopadhyay, she was educated in Madras and at King's College, London, and Cambridge. In 1898 she married Dr. M. G. Naidu. Her poetry, originally published in three volumes—*The Golden Threshold* (1905), *The Bird of Time* (1912), and *The Broken Wing* (1915)—was written in English but deals, in a romantic vein, with Indian themes. It gained her an international reputation, and she was elected (1914) a fellow of the Royal Society of Literature. Her salon at the Taj Mahal Hotel in Bombay was a center of intellectual society. She was active in the Indian National Congress and in 1925 became its first woman president. Participation in passive disobedience campaigns brought her several jail sentences. She was a close associate of Mohandas Gandhi and served (1947–49) as governor of the United Provinces. See her verses collected in *The Sceptred Flute* (1928) and *The Feather of the Dawn* (1961); biography by Padmini Sengupta (1966).

nail, metal pin driven by force applied at one end into pieces of material, usually wood, to join them together. The strength of a nailed joint depends on the properties of the wood, the type and number of nails used, and the type of loads applied to the joint. When the nail is subjected to side loading, the strength of the nail itself also becomes important. Generally speaking, a nail holds better when driven across the grain of a wood than parallel with it and better in a hardwood than in a softwood. However, since a softwood has less tendency to split than a hardwood, more nails can be driven into it. Various means, such as texturing the surface of a nail or coating it with high-friction materials are used to increase its withdrawal resistance.

nail, in anatomy, the horny outgrowth shielding the tip of the finger and the toe in man and most other primates. The nail consists of dead cells pushed outward by dividing cells in the root, a fold of epidermis at the base of the nail (see SKIN). The hard material in nail cells is the tough protein material, keratin. If the root is destroyed, the nail ceases to grow. Otherwise, growth from root to tip is achieved in about four months. The small-celled and relatively bloodless tissue near the base of the nail forms a white, crescent-shaped spot called the lunula, or moon. No pigment occurs in nail cells, but since they are translucent, their appearance is pink because of blood vessels beneath. A painful inflammation (felon) of the fingertip may result from infection starting in a hangnail. Pressure from improperly fitting shoes may cause the large toenail to cut into the skin along its edges (the so-called ingrown toenail). Horny derivatives of the integument, homologous to the primate nail, have evolved into various structures in other animals, e.g., the hooves of horses and cattle and the claws of birds and reptiles.

Nain (nā′ĭn), village of Galilee, Palestine, SE of Nazareth. It is the modern Nein (Israel). Here Jesus raised a widow's son from the dead. Luke 7.11.

Naioth (nā′yŏth), unlocated dwelling place of the prophets (apparently N of Jerusalem), to which David fled. 1 Sam. 19–20.

Nairn (nârn), burgh (1971 pop. 8,038), county town of Nairnshire, N Scotland, at the mouth of the Nairn River on Moray Firth. It is a resort and fishing center with a good harbor. In 1975, Nairn became part of the Highland region.

Nairnshire (nârn′shĭr, -shər), county (1971 pop. 11,049), 163 sq mi (422 sq km), NE Scotland. NAIRN is the county town. The hilly southern section slopes to a fertile farm belt near the northern coast. The Nairn and the Findhorn are the chief rivers. Oats, barley, and potatoes are the staple crops. There are good livestock and dairy farms, and sheep graze on the southern uplands. Small industries are the processing of seaweed and granite and the manufacture of whiskey and bricks. The county was settled by Northern Picts and was part of the province of Moray before it came under the Scottish crown. CAWDOR Castle is the legendary scene of the murder of Duncan by Macbeth. In 1975, Nairnshire became part of the Highland region.

Nairobi (nīrō′bē), city (1970 est. pop. 535,200), capital of Kenya, S Kenya, in the E African highlands. A modern city with broad boulevards, Nairobi is Kenya's largest city and its administrative, communications, and economic center. It is the trade and distribution center for a productive agricultural area specializing in coffee and cattle. The chief manufactures are food products, beverages, construction materials, cigarettes, chemicals, textiles, clothing, glass, and furniture. The city is linked by road with the rest of Kenya and by railroad with MOMBASA (on the Indian Ocean coast), W Kenya, and Uganda. Although Nairobi is only 90 mi (145 km) south of the equator, it has a moderate climate, largely because of its high altitude (c.5,500 ft/1,680 m). Many tourists are attracted to Nairobi National Park, a large wildlife sanctuary on the city's outskirts, and to nearby scenic and hunting areas. Nairobi was founded in 1899 on the site of a waterhole of the pastoral MASAI as a railhead camp on the Mombasa-Uganda line. In 1905 it replaced Mombasa as the capital of the British East Africa Protectorate (1920–63, Kenya Colony). Nairobi became the center of the prosperous European-dominated highlands farming area. In the 1950s the "MAU MAU" rebellion flared among KIKUYU people near Nairobi; there were related disturbances in the city. The National Univ., several medical and technical schools, Coryndon Memorial Museum, which has collections on Kenya's prehistory and natural history, and the Sorsbie art gallery are in Nairobi, which is also the seat of the railway and airway corporations of the EAST AFRICAN COMMUNITY. The first All Africa Trade Fair, sponsored by the ORGANIZATION OF AFRICAN UNITY, was held there in 1972.

Naismith, James (nā′smĭth), 1861–1939, American athletic director, inventor (1891) of basketball, b. Almonte, Canada. While an instructor of physical education at the International YMCA Training School (now Springfield College) at Springfield, Mass., he originated basketball as a gymnasium sport. The game was originally played with a soccer ball and two peach bushel baskets, from which the game took its name. Twelve of the thirteen rules Naismith created are still basic to the game. Naismith was later (1898–1937) director of physical education at the Univ. of Kansas. See biography by B. L. Webb (1973).

Naivasha (nīvä′shä), lake, 12 mi (19.3 km) long and 9 mi (14.5 km) wide, W central Kenya, E Africa, in the Great Rift Valley. Located near Nairobi, the lake and the town of Naivasha are a popular resort. Fish, waterfowl, and hippopotamuses abound there.

Najaf: see AN NAJAF, Iraq.

Najafabad (näjäf″äbäd′), city (1971 est. pop. 46,000), Esfahan prov., W central Iran, near Esfahan. It is the trade center for an agricultural region noted for its pomegranates.

Najd, region, Arabia: see NEJD.

Nakatsu (näkä′tso͞o), city (1970 pop. 57,461), Oita prefecture, NE Kyushu, Japan, on the Suo Sea at the mouth of the Yamakuni River. It is a commercial center and port and was the residence of Yukichi Fukuzawa (1835–1901).

Nakhichevan (nəkhēchĭvän′yə), city (1970 pop. 33,000), capital of Nakhichevan Autonomous SSR, SE European USSR, in Azerbaijan. Its industries include food processing, wine making, cotton ginning, and the production of furniture, leather, and building materials. The ancient Naxuana, the city was ruled by Armenians, Persians, Arabs, Mongols, and Turks, became a flourishing Armenian trade center in the 15th cent., and was ceded by Persia to Russia by the Treaty of Turkmanchai (1828). In the 19th cent. it was an important trading post between Persia and Russia. Nakhichevan has Greek and Roman remains and two 12th-century mausoleums.

Nakhichevan Autonomous Soviet Socialist Republic, autonomous republic (1970 pop. 202,000), 2,124 sq mi (5,501 sq km), SE European USSR, in Azerbaijan, bordering on Iran and Turkey in the south. Nakhichevan (the capital), Ordubad, and Dzhulfa are the main cities. The lowlands are irrigated and produce cotton, tobacco, rice, winter wheat, and fruits. In the foothills grapes are grown for the wine industry, and silkworms are raised. There are salt, molybdenum, lead, and zinc deposits. The republic's industries include food processing, cotton cleaning, and the bottling of mineral water. The population consists mainly of Azerbaijani Turks, with Russian and Armenian minorities. The republic was founded in 1924.

Nakhodka (nəkhôt′kə), city (1970 pop. 104,000), Far Eastern USSR, c.20 mi (32 km) E of VLADIVOSTOK, on the Sea of Japan. A port city with fewer winter ice problems than Vladivostok, Nakhodka has assumed an increasingly large share of shipping from the Soviet Far East.

Nakhon Pathom (nä′kôn pätŭm′), town (1964 est. pop. 32,000), capital of Nakhon Pathom prov., SW Thailand, on the Mekong River. It is a transportation and commercial center on the Bangkok-Singapore

RR. Phra Pathom, the largest Buddhist stupa in Thailand, is there.

Nakhon Ratchasima (nä'kôn rächä'sĭmä") or **Korat** (kōrät'), city (1965 est. pop. 54,000), capital of Nakhon Ratchasima prov., S central Thailand, on the Mun River. Strategically located near the mountain pass leading from the central plain to NE Thailand, Nakhon Ratchasima is the administrative, economic, and transportation center of the Korat plateau. Copper deposits are nearby. Founded in the 17th cent., the city grew rapidly after the construction (1890) of the railroad from Bangkok.

Nakian, Reuben, (näk'yän), 1897–, American sculptor, b. College Point, New York. Nakian's work is characterized by bold, massive, rough-textured forms organically draped or leaning heavily against one another. Most are abstract portrayals of themes from classical mythology. The monumental *Rape of Lucrece* (1955–58; Mus. of Modern Art, New York City) is made of welded steel sheets and rods. Nakian's works are noted for spontaneous sensuality.

Naksh-i Rustam: see PERSEPOLIS.

Nakskov (näk'skou), city (1970 com. pop. 17,178), Storstrøm co., SE Denmark, a seaport at the head of Nakskov Fjord (an arm of the Langelands Baelt). It has large sugar refineries.

Nakuru (näkōō'rōō), city (1969 pop. 47,800), capital of Rift Valley prov., W central Kenya. Founded in the early 20th cent. as a center of European settlement, Nakuru is a growing commercial and industrial city. Manufactures include textiles, processed food, and pyrethrum extract. Nearby is Lake Nakuru (c.35 sq mi/90 sq km), noted for its flamingo haunts.

Nalanda, India: see BARAGAON.

Nalchik (näl'chĭk), city (1970 pop. 146,000), capital of the Kabardino-Balkar Autonomous Republic, S European USSR, on the northern slope of the Greater Caucasus. A health and tourist resort, it also has considerable industry, notably a molybdenum-tungsten mill. Nalchik was founded in 1817 as a Russian stronghold.

nalorphine (năl'ərfēn), derivative of MORPHINE that acts to reverse the effects of morphine and other NARCOTICS. It counteracts narcotic-induced nervous system and respiratory system depression but is not effective against depression induced by other sedatives such as BARBITURATES. Nalorphine and other narcotic antagonists are useful in reversing the effects of narcotic overdoses. Because nalorphine causes withdrawal symptoms in addicts, it is administered to apparent ex-addicts to determine if they have returned to drug use. Nalorphine is marketed under the trade name Nalline.

Namangan (nəmən-gän'), city (1970 pop. 175,000), capital of Namangan oblast, Central Asian USSR, in Uzbekistan, in the Fergana Basin. A center for the production of cotton and silk, it also has food-processing plants. Russian forces captured Namangan in 1875.

Namaqualand (nəmä'kwəlănd) or **Namaland** (nä'məlănd), region, c.150,000 sq mi (388,500 sq km), SW Africa. It extends from Windhoek, South West Africa, in the north to NW Cape Prov., Republic of South Africa, in the south and from the Namib Desert in the west to the Kalahari Desert in the east. The Orange River divides the region into Great Namaqualand (in South West Africa) and Little Namaqualand (in Cape Prov.). An arid region, Namaqualand is populated chiefly by the pastoral-agricultural Nama (Hottentots), who speak a KHOIKHOI language. Near the Atlantic Ocean are extensive alluvial diamond beds; copper is mined in Little Namaqualand. Karakul pelts are a major export of the region.

Namath, Joe (Joseph William Namath), 1943–, American football player, b. Beaver Falls, Pa. Namath's brilliance as a quarterback at the Univ. of Alabama earned him a three-year no-cut contract of $387,000 from the New York Jets before he had played one minute of professional football. Namath's high contract brought about all-out rivalry for new players between the National and American football leagues and ultimately produced a merger between the two. Although hampered by knee and shoulder injuries, Namath's career has been marked by excellence. He led the Jets to a victory in the 1969 Superbowl game and in 1967 passed for a total of 4,007 yards, a season's record. Candid, outspoken and controversial, he was nicknamed "Broadway Joe" for his fast and free lifestyle. He appeared in several motion pictures.

name. Personal identifying names are found in every known culture, and they often pass from one language to another. Hence the occurrence of Indian place names in America and the occurrence among American families of names of various linguistic origins (e.g., Roosevelt, Hoover, La Follette, La Guardia). The use of personal names apparently began at a very early stage in man's history, with single names of persons presumably coming into use earlier than double ones; in the Bible double names are mainly confined to those who have common forenames, e.g., Judas Barsabas and Mary Magdalen. Anglo-Saxon and Scandinavian names were generally formed of two common words, e.g., *Hrothgar* (Roger) meaning "fame-spear." English surnames developed in the late Middle Ages and, apart from patronymics (Adams, Jefferson, Jackson, Harrison), have a variety of origins; they come from places (Lincoln, Garfield, Cleveland), from trades (Tyler, Taylor), from personal traits (Stout, Black), and from the calendar (Noël, May). The Irish *Mac,* meaning "son," and *ua,* meaning "grandson," were attached to family and tribe names as *Mac, Mc,* or *M'* and *O'* (see O), respectively. The *O'* was apparently not used in Scotland. The Welsh, in translating their patronymic (*ap*=son of) settled on English forms ending in *s,* hence Welsh names such as Davis (from David) and Jones (from John). French *de,* when written separately, like German *von,* is deemed to mark a noble name. Spanish practice varies by country; one common usage gives a surname combining those of each parent, e.g., Serrano Y Domínguez or Serrano Domínguez, for one whose father was a Serrano and mother a Domínguez. In Russian the middle name consists of the father's forename with a patronymic suffix, e.g., *Nikolayevich.* In the Roman republic three names were used, the forename (*praenomen*), of which there were fewer than 20; the gens or tribe name (*nomen*); and finally the family name (*cognomen*); e.g., Caius Julius Caesar, or Caius of the Caesar family of the Julian gens. An additional name (*agnomen*) might be added, as a nickname or honor, e.g., Africanus, for victory in Africa, in the case of Scipio. In many cultures the name is of supernatural significance. Besides animistic commonplaces such as naming children after lucky men or wily animals, there are widespread taboo practices, such as not naming children after living relatives or changing the name on the death of a namesake or avoiding the name of a family totem. In some cultures the name given the child at birth is temporary and is replaced with another at puberty. A woman loses her family name and adopts that of her husband at the time of her marriage in most Western cultures. In the Judeo-Christian tradition the name has great significance, especially in the case of divine names; thus the Hebrews did not utter the name of God. Christians have traditionally baptized children with an appropriately Christian name, especially the name of a saint, henceforth the patron; an additional name is taken at confirmation. The Puritans discouraged the use of any but biblical first names. The practice of changing names by court action is commonly adopted in order to afford a clear record. See E. G. Withycombe, ed., *Oxford Dictionary of English Christian Names* (2d ed. 1950, repr. 1963); Elsdon Smith, *Dictionary of American Family Names* (1956) and *Personal Names: A Bibliography* (1952, repr. 1965); L. G. Pine, *The Story of Surnames* (1965); C. M. Yonge, *History of Christian Names* (rev. ed. 1966); W. O. Hassal, *History Through Surnames* (1967).

Namhoi: see FO-SHAN, China.

Namib (nä'mĭb), desert, c.800 mi (1,290 km) long and from 30 to 100 mi (50–160 km) wide, SW Africa, along the coast of South West Africa. It occupies a rocky platform between the Atlantic Ocean and the escarpment of the interior plateau. Isolated mountains rise from the desert and sand dunes cover its southern portion. It receives less than ½ in. (1.3 cm) of rain annually and is barren of vegetation. Tungsten, salt, and alluvial diamonds are mined.

Namibia: see SOUTH WEST AFRICA.

Namier, Sir Lewis Bernstein (nām'yər), 1888–1960, English historian, b. Poland. He attended the London School of Economics and Oxford and became professor at the Univ. of Manchester in 1931, teaching there until 1953. His greatest fame rests on his *Structure of Politics at the Accession of George III* (1929, 2d ed. 1957). By minute biographical examination of the members of several parliaments, Namier determined that politics in the mid-18th cent. was controlled by a series of small and fluid groups and that self-interest was as important as great issues in dictating political allegiance. His method, which came to be called Namierism, was adopted by other historians and led to much reevaluation of English history. The Namierites have been criticized by scholars who feel that their method is not suitable for most periods of English history. Namier's studies of Europe before World War II include *Diplomatic Prelude, 1938–1939* (1948), *Europe in Decay* (1950), and *In the Nazi Era* (1952). Among his other works is *1848: The Revolution of the Intellectuals* (1946). He was an active Zionist, and from 1929 to 1931 he was political secretary of the Jewish Agency for Palestine. He was knighted in 1952. See biography by his wife, Julia Namier (1971).

Nampa (năm'pə), city (1970 pop. 20,768), Canyon co., SW Idaho, in the fertile Treasure Valley; inc. 1890. It is the commercial, processing, and shipping center for an irrigated agricultural, orchard, and dairy region and is included in the Boise project. It has food and seed processing plants and a huge sugar factory. Camp trailers, mobile homes, tin cans, and wood products are also manufactured. Northwest Nazarene College is there, and a U.S. wildlife refuge is nearby.

Nampo (näm'pô), formerly **Chinnampo,** city, W North Korea, on Korea Bay. It is the port city for Pyongyang and is also a leading metallurgical center. Other industries include rice and flour milling.

Nampula (nămpōō'lə), city (1960 pop. 103,985), NE Mozambique. It is an agricultural trade center, located on the railroad connecting the seaports of Lumbo and Nacala with Malawi. Cement is manufactured.

Namsos (näm'sōs), town (1970 pop. 11,190), Nord-Trøndelag co., W Norway, a port at the mouth of the Namsen River on the Namsenfjord. In World War II, Namsos was the scene (1940) of heavy fighting between the British and the Germans.

Nam Tso, lake, Tibet: see NA-MU HU.

Na-mu Hu (nä-mōō hōō) or **Nam Tso** (näm tsō), salt lake, 950 sq mi (2,461 sq km), central Tibet, SW China. The largest lake in Tibet, it lies at an altitude of 15,180 ft (4,627 m).

Namur (nämür'), Flemish *Namen,* province (1970 pop. 380,561), S Belgium, bordering on France in the south. The chief cities are Namur (the capital) and Dinant. The province is generally hilly; it is drained by the Meuse, Sambre, and Lesse rivers and is traversed in the south by the Ardennes. It is largely agricultural; there are also extensive marble, chalk, and stone quarries; coal and iron mines; and glass and cutlery factories. The province, which is mainly French-speaking (see WALLOONS), includes the former county of Namur, part of the former prince-bishopric of Liège, and part of Hainaut.

Namur, Flemish *Namen,* city (1970 pop. 32,269), capital of Namur prov., S central Belgium, at the confluence of the Meuse and Sambre rivers. It is a commercial and industrial center and a rail junction. Manufactures include machinery, leather goods, and porcelain. It is also an episcopal see and a tourist spot. Namur was a Merovingian fortress (first mentioned in the 7th cent.) and later (10th cent.) became the seat of a county. The county fell to the counts of Flanders in 1262 and in 1421 was bought by Philip the Good of Burgundy. It later shared the history of the Austrian and Spanish Netherlands. Because of its strategic location, Namur was frequently besieged. In the War of the Grand Alliance it fell (1692) to the French but was retaken by the Dutch in 1695. The first Barrier Treaty (1709) gave the Netherlands the right to garrison Namur, a right confirmed by two further treaties (1713, 1715) supplementing the Peace of Utrecht. Refortified in 1887, it was part of the Belgian defenses on the Meuse at the start of World War I. Of note are the Church of St. Loup (17th cent.) and St. Aubain Cathedral (18th cent.).

Nanaimo (nənī'mō), city (1971 pop. 14,948), SW British Columbia, Canada, on Vancouver Island. It is a port, the base of a herring-fishing fleet, and the trade center for a farm and lumbering region. There are several sawmills and a large pulp-producing plant in the city.

Nana Sahib (nä'nä sä'hĭb), b. c.1821, leader in the Indian Mutiny, his real name was Dandhu Panch. The adopted son of the last peshwa (hereditary prime minister) of the Mahrattas, his request (1853) to the British to grant him the peshwa's title and pension was refused. In the outbreak (June, 1857) of the mutiny at Cawnpore (Kanpur) his men massacred the British garrison and colony. After suppression of the rebellion, he escaped to Nepal, where he probably died. See P. C. Gupta, *Nana Sahib and the Rising at Cawnpore* (1963).

Nan-ch'ang or **Nanchang** (both: nän-chäng), city (1970 est. pop. 900,000), capital of Kiangsi prov., China, on the Kan River, near the southern end of P'o-yang Lake. A major transportation center, it has a port, rail links to Shanghai, Chekiang, and Hunan, and an airport. It is a large economic and industrial center with machine shops, food-processing establishments, the country's largest integrated silk complex, and plants making fertilizer, tractors, cement, tires, and pharmaceuticals. An old walled city, Nan-ch'ang dates from the Sung dynasty (12th cent.), but it received its present name in the Ming dynasty. Nan-ch'ang is considered the birthplace of the People's Liberation Army. There, in 1927, a force of 30,000 Communist troops, led by CHU TEH, rose against the Kuomintang government and briefly established the first Soviet republic in China. Occupied by the Japanese (1939–45) in World War II, Nan-ch'ang was reoccupied by the Nationalists in 1945 but fell to the Communists in 1949. An agricultural institute and a medical college are in the city.

Nancheng: see HAN-CHUNG, China.

Nan-ching: see NANKING, China.

Nancy (näNsē'), city (1968 pop. 127,821), capital of Meurthe-et-Moselle dept., NE France, on the Meurthe River and the Marne-Rhine Canal. It is the administrative, economic, and educational center of LORRAINE. Situated at the edge of the huge Lorraine iron fields, Nancy is an industrial city manufacturing foundry products, boilers, electrical equipment, machine tools, and textiles. In the city are a noted fine arts museum, an academy of fine arts, and a large university (founded 1854). Nancy grew around a castle of the dukes of Lorraine and became the duchy capital in the 12th cent. In 1477, Charles the Bold of Burgundy was defeated and killed at the gates of Nancy by Swiss troops and the forces of René II of Lorraine. The major part of the center of Nancy, a model of urban planning and a gem of 18th-century architecture, was built during the liberal reign of Stanislaus I, duke of Lorraine (reigned 1738–66) and ex-king of Poland. Nancy passed to the French crown in 1766. In 1848 it was one of the first cities to proclaim the republic. From 1870 to 1873 it was occupied by the Germans following the Franco-Prussian War, and it was partially destroyed in World War I. Points of interest include the Place Stanislas, the Place de la Carrière, an 18th-century cathedral, and the 16th-century ducal palace. The Church of Cordeliers (15th cent.) houses the magnificent tombs of the princes of Lorraine.

Nanda Devi (nŭn'də dā'vē), peak, 25,645 ft (7,817 m) high, Uttar Pradesh state, N India, in the Himalayas. Except for some peaks in Kashmir, it is the highest point in India. Hindus believe that the goddess Nanda, wife of Siva, lives there. Nanda Kot, at an elevation of 22,538 ft (6,870 m), is said to be Nanda's "couch." The peak was scaled in 1936 by an Anglo-American expedition.

Nander (nän'dār), town (1971 pop. 126,400), Maharashtra state, S central India, on the Godavari River. Nander is a district administrative center and is known for its fine muslin. It is also a market for cattle, grain, and cotton. A fort built by the Moguls is nearby.

Nanga Parbat (nŭng'gə pŭr'bət), peak, 26,660 ft (8,126 m) high, in the Punjab Himalayas, W Kashmir; 7th-highest peak in the world. Six expeditions—almost all ending disastrously—were sent against it. A German-Austrian team led by Herman Buhl finally reached the peak in 1953.

Naniwa: see OSAKA, Japan.

Nanking (năn'kĭng') or **Nan-ching** (nän-jĭng) [southern capital], city (1970 est. pop. 2,000,000), capital of Kiangsu prov., E central China, in a bend of the Yangtze River. It has served at times in the past as capital of China. The second largest city in the region (after Shanghai), Nanking is at the intersection of three major railroad lines. Industry, which once centered around "nankeen" cloth (unbleached cotton goods), has been vigorously developed under the Communist government. The city now has an integrated iron-steel complex, an oil refinery, food-processing establishments, and some 600 plants making chemicals, textiles, cement, fertilizers, machinery, electronic equipment, optical instruments, photographic equipment, and trucks. Nanking has long been celebrated as a literary and political center. It was the capital of China from the 3d to the 6th cent. and again from 1368 to 1421. The Treaty of Nanking, signed in 1842 at the end of the Opium War, opened China to foreign trade. During the Taiping Rebellion insurgents held the city from 1853 to 1864. It was captured by the revolutionists in 1911, and in 1912 it became the capital of China's first president, Sun Yat-sen. When in 1927 the city fell to the Communists, the foreign residents fled to the protection of British and American warships on the Yangtze River. The Kuomintang under Chiang Kai-shek retook the city, and it became (1928) the regular Nationalist capital. In 1932 when the Japanese were threatening to attack the city, the government was temporarily removed to Lo-yang, and on Nov. 21, 1937, just before Nanking fell to the Japanese, it was moved to Chungking. The Japanese entry into the city, which was accompanied by widespread killing and brutality, became known as the "rape of Nanking." The Japanese established (1938) their puppet regime in Nanking. Chinese forces reoccupied the city Sept. 5, 1945, and the capitulation of the Japanese armies in China was signed there on Sept. 9. Nanking again fell to the Communists in April, 1949, and from 1950 until 1952, when it became the provincial capital, Nanking was administered as part of an autonomous region. The city is the seat of numerous institutions of higher learning, notably Nanking Univ. The Nanking Military Academy is there. The city is also noted for its large library, and both its astronomical observatory and its botanical gardens are among the largest in the country. The original city wall (70 ft/21 m high), most of which still stands, dates from the Ming dynasty and encircles most of the modern city. The tomb of the first Ming emperor is approached by an avenue lined with colossal images of men and animals. Also of interest are the tomb of Sun Yat-sen, a memorial to China's war dead (a steel pagoda), and the Taiping museum. A 4-mi (6.4 km), two-level railway and road bridge was completed across the Yangtze in 1968.

Nan Ling (nän lĭng), mountain range of Kwangtung, Hunan, and Kwangsi provs., S China; rises to c.6,900 ft (2,100 m). The Nan Ling form the geographical boundary between central and S China. They separate the Yangtze and Si drainage basins, protect S China from cold northern air masses, and divide the Cantonese civilization and linguistic area from that of N China. The mountains lie in parallel ridges that hinder north-south travel.

Nanni d'Antonio di Banco (nän'nē däntôn'yō dē bäng'kō), c.1384–1421, Florentine sculptor. After study with his father, Antonio di Banco, who worked on the cathedral of Florence, Nanni executed his major figural sculpture for the cathedral and the Church of Orsanmichele. He relied upon classical Roman models for elements of his basically Gothic figures. Many of his works stood as companions to works by DONATELLO.

Nan-ning (nän-nĭng), city (1970 est. pop. 375,000), capital of the Kwangsi Chuang Autonomous Region, S China, on the Si River in a fertile farming area. The city has a medium-sized integrated iron and steel complex, a sugar refinery, other food-processing plants, and factories making fertilizer, machine tools, cement, and farm machinery. The city is on the Hunan-Kwangsi RR to North Vietnam. A medical college and an agricultural institute are there.

Nanortalik (nänôkh'tälĭk), town (1969 pop. 1,281), in Nanortalik dist. (1969 pop. 2,885), SW Greenland, between Cape Farewell and Julianehåb. It is a fishing center.

Nan-p'ing (nän-pĭng) or **Yen-ping** (yĕn'-pĭng), city, N central Fukien prov., China, on the upper Min River. It has expanded from a regional market town to include cement, paper-product, chemical, and machine-tool manufacturing.

Nansei-shoto: see RYUKYU ISLANDS.

Nansen, Fridtjof (frĭt'yôf nän'sən), 1861–1930, Norwegian arctic explorer, scientist, statesman, and humanitarian. He made his first trip to the arctic regions on a sealer in 1882 and upon his return became curator of the natural history collection of the Bergen Museum. In 1888, with a party of five, he made a memorable journey across Greenland on skis, described in his *First Crossing of Greenland* (1890). Conceiving a startling and much-derided plan for reaching the North Pole by drifting in the ice across the polar basin, he sailed to the Arctic in 1893 in the *Fram,* especially designed to resist crushing by ice. The *Fram* was anchored in the ice pack at lat. 83° 59′ N, drifted northward to 85° 57′, and later (1896) returned safely (although without having reached the pole) to Norway, as Nansen had predicted, by way of Spitsbergen. In the meantime, Nansen had left the ship in 1895 and with F. H. Johansen set forth to complete the journey to the pole by sledge. They were, however, turned back by ice conditions at lat. 86° 14′ N, the northernmost point to have been reached by man at that time. When they were wintering (1895–96) on Franz Josef Land (now often called Fridtjof Nansen Land), members of the Jackson-Harmsworth expedition (see JACKSON, Frederick George) chanced upon them and sent them home in one of their ships. Nansen's arrival in Norway was followed eight days later by that of the *Fram,* under Otto Sverdrup. Although neither he nor his ship had reached the North Pole, his expedition gave the world much new valuable information about the Arctic Ocean and the arctic regions and made Nansen internationally famous. He had proved that a frozen sea lay around the Pole and filled the polar basin (see ARCTIC OCEAN). With his highly detailed information on oceanography, meteorology, diet, and nutrition, Nansen had laid the basis for all future arctic work. *Farthest North,* his account of this brilliant exploit, appeared in English translation in 1897, and the expedition's scientific material was published as *The Norwegian North Polar Expedition* (ed. by Nansen, 6 vol., 1900–1906). The Nansen Fund for scientific research was established in his honor. At the university in Christiania (now Oslo), he became professor of zoology (1897) and of oceanography (1908). Nansen's career as a statesman began in 1905, when he worked for the peaceful separation of Norway from Sweden; his efforts were rewarded by his appointment as Norway's first minister to Great Britain (1906–8). In 1901 he had become director of an international commission to study the sea, and he made (1910–14) several scientific journeys, mainly in the N Atlantic. In the years after World War I he added to his role of great explorer that of great humanitarian, becoming internationally renowned for his service to famine-stricken Russia as well as for his work in the repatriation of war prisoners. Appointed (1921) as League of Nations high commissioner for refugees, Nansen received the 1922 Nobel Peace Prize, and the League honored him by creating (1931) the Nansen International Office for Refugees, which won the 1938 Nobel Peace Prize. As a memorial to his father, Odd Nansen founded (1937) the Nansen Help to supplement the work of the Nansen International Office. The diversity of Fridtjof Nansen's interests is shown in his writings, which include *Eskimo Life* (1893), *Closing-Nets for Vertical Hauls and for Vertical Towing* (1915), *Russia & Peace* (1923), and *Armenia and the Near East* (1928). See biographies by his daughter, Liv (Nansen) Hoyer (1955), Edward Shackleton (1959), and J. M. Scott (1971); Per Vogt et al., *Nansen: Explorer, Scientist, Humanitarian* (1962).

Nanterre (näNtâr'), city (1968 pop. 90,632), capital of Hauts-de-Seine dept., N central France, on the right bank of the Seine River. It is an industrial center where metals, automobiles, electrical equipment, machine tools, and rolling stock are manufactured. In May, 1968, the Nanterre branch of the Univ. of Paris was the scene of student protests that spread to other areas and led to a national political crisis. The National Basilica of Ste Geneviève, with a 15th-century nave, is in Nanterre.

Nantes (näNt), city (1968 pop. 265,009), capital of Loire-Atlantique dept., W France, on the Loire River. It is an important industrial and shipping center with its ocean port at SAINT-NAZAIRE. Food products (especially biscuits), naval equipment, metals, dyes, clothing, bicycles, and agricultural equipment are the leading manufactures. The chief town of the Gallic tribe of the Namnetes, Nantes became an important trade and administrative center under the Romans. It was made an episcopal see in the 4th cent. Nantes was ravaged and held (843–936) by Norsemen and later (10th cent.) fell to the dukes of Brittany, who resided there until Brittany became part of France in 1524. During the French Revolution, Nantes was nearly stormed by royalist troops of the VENDÉE and was the scene of massacres by the revolutionaries in 1793. Nantes was a center of resistance to the German occupation in World War II, and its civilian population suffered ruthless reprisals. Points of interest include a 10th-century castle on the Loire and a 15th-century cathedral with tombs of dukes of Brittany. The Univ. of Nantes (founded 1460) is one of the city's many educational facilities.

Nantes, Edict of, 1598, decree promulgated at Nantes by King Henry IV to restore internal peace in France, which had been torn by the Wars of Religion; the edict defined the rights of the French Protestants (see HUGUENOTS). These included full liberty of conscience and private worship; liberty of public worship wherever it had previously been granted and its extension to numerous other localities and to estates of Protestant nobles; full civil rights including the right to hold public office; royal subsidies for Protestant schools; special courts, composed of Roman Catholic and Protestant judges, to judge cases involving Protestants; retention of the organization of the Protestant church in France; and Protestant control of some 200 cities then held by the Huguenots, including such strongholds as La Rochelle (see ROCHELLE, LA), with the king contributing to the maintenance of their garrisons and fortifications. The last condition, originally devised for an eight-year period but subsequently renewed, was to serve as guarantee to the Huguenots that their other rights would be respected; however, it gave French Protestantism a virtual state within a state and was incompatible with the centralizing policies of cardinals Richelieu and Mazarin and of Louis XIV. The fall (1628) of La Rochelle to Richelieu's army and the Peace of Alais (1629) marked the end of Huguenot political privileges. After 1665, Louis XIV was persuaded by his Roman Catholic advisers to embark on a policy of persecuting the Protestants. By a series of edicts that narrowly interpreted the Edict of Nantes, he reduced it to a scrap of paper. Finally, in 1685, he declared that the majority of Protestants had been converted to Catholicism and that the edict of 1598, having thus become superfluous, was revoked. No French Protestants were allowed to leave the country; those who openly remained Protestants were promised the right of private worship and freedom from molestation, but the promise was not kept. Thousands fled abroad to escape the system of DRAGONNADES, and several provinces were virtually depopulated. The revocation of the Edict of Nantes greatly weakened the French economy by driving out a highly skilled and industrious segment of the nation, and its ruthless application increased the detestation in which England and the Protestant German states held the French king. Its object—to make France a Catholic state—was fulfilled on paper only, for many secretly remained faithful to Protestantism, while the prestige of the Roman Catholic Church suffered as a result of Louis's intolerance. See W. J. Stankiewicz, *Politics and Religion in Seventeenth Century France* (1960).

Nanteuil, Robert (rōbĕr' näNtö'yə), 1623?–1678, French draftsman and engraver. His pastel portraits gained him popularity, and in 1658 Louis XIV made him draftsman to the royal cabinet. His 221 extant portrait engravings excel in the vivacity and precision of their characterization. Nanteuil was especially successful in creating a three-dimensional effect in his works. He made portraits of almost all the important personages at the court. Among the finest are the portraits of Jean Loret, Gilles Ménage, and the Marquis de Maisons. He made 11 portraits of Louis XIV and 14 of Mazarin.

Nanticoke (năn'tĭkōk), city (1970 pop. 14,632), Luzerne co., NE Pa., on the Susquehanna River; founded 1793, inc. as a city 1926. It is largely residential. Its manufactures include chemicals, clothing, and shoes. Nanticoke was formerly the heart of an anthracite-coal mining region, but mechanization and reduced mining operations have diminished the importance of coal to its economy.

Nantucket (năntŭk'ĭt), island, c.14 mi (23 km) long, from 3 to 6 mi (4.8–9.6 km) wide, SE Mass., lying c.25 mi (40 km) S of Cape Cod, from which it is separated by Nantucket Sound. Muskeget Channel is located between Nantucket and Martha's Vineyard to the west. Exhibiting evidence of glaciation (terminal moraine, outwash plain), Nantucket has sandy beaches and low, rolling hills composed of sand and gravel. It is sparsely vegetated; wild cranberries, heather, and wild roses predominate. Nantucket and the small adjacent islands constitute both Nantucket town and Nantucket co. Settled in 1659, the island was part of New York from 1660 to 1692, when it was ceded to Massachusetts. Nantucket was a major whaling port until the decline of the industry (c.1850), and it later developed into a well-known resort and artists' colony. The village of Nantucket is the trade center of the island and is known for its many old houses. The island has a whaling museum and an 18th-century windmill. The first U.S. lightship station (est. 1856) is located near Nantucket.

Nan-t'ung or **Nantung** (both: nän-tōōng), town (1970 est. pop. 300,000), N Kiangsu prov., E central China, on the Yangtze River, about 30 mi (50 km) from the East China Sea. The center of an important cotton-growing area, it is an old town that has become industrialized. Manufactures include textiles, cottonseed oil, processed foods, chemicals, machine tools, fertilizers, and trucks. Many industries are in the suburb of Tangkiacha. Nan-t'ung was called Tungchow until 1912. A medical college is there.

Naomi (nāō'mē, -mī, nā'ō-), in the Bible, Ruth's mother-in-law. Ruth 1.19,20.

Naoroji, Dadabhai (dä'dəbhī närō'jē), 1825–1917, Indian nationalist leader. The son of a Parsi priest, he distinguished himself academically at an early age and at 27 became professor of mathematics at Elphinstone Institution, Bombay. At 30 he left for England to start a career in business, but his real aim was to work for an improvement in British policies toward India. He was particularly concerned about the economic consequences of British rule for India, and he wrote and lectured extensively on the "drain" of wealth, or unilateral transfer of resources from India to Britain, which he regarded as the principal cause of Indian poverty. His writings on this subject, especially his classic study, *Poverty and Un-British Rule in India* (1901), played a major role in arousing and stimulating economic nationalism in India. Naoroji was active for over 60 years in Indian social and political causes. He was a founder of several organizations, including the East India Association and the Indian National Congress. He served three times as president of the Congress (1886, 1893, 1906). He was the first Indian to be elected a member of the British Parliament—in 1892, as a Liberal. As a member of Parliament he was instrumental in securing the appointment of a royal commission on Indian expenditure, the Welby Commission, and served on it as its sole Indian member. Naoroji was one of the first to proclaim the goal of self-government for India from the Congress platform. The younger generation of nationalist leaders, including such men as Gopal Krishna Gokhale and Mohandas K. Gandhi, regarded him as their mentor, and he was affectionately hailed as the Grand Old Man of India. See biography by R. P. Masani (1939).

naos (nā'ŏs), inner portion of a Greek temple, enclosed within walls and generally surrounded by colonnaded porticoes. In it stood the statue of the deity to whom the temple was consecrated. The naos was provided with a columned porch, typically only in front (pronaos) but often also at the back (opisthodomos). It was the prototype for the CELLA of the Roman temple.

Napa (năp'ə), city (1970 pop. 35,978), seat of Napa co., W Calif., on the Napa River; inc. 1872. Grapes and other fruits are grown in the adjacent Napa valley, which is well known for its wines. Napa's manufactures include concrete and steel products and leather goods. Napa College is there.

napalm (nā'päm), incendiary material developed during World War II by Harvard scientists cooperating with the U.S. army and used in bombs and flame throwers. Napalm is based on a mixture of gasoline, sometimes mixed with other petroleum fuels, and a thickening agent. The thickener, to which the term napalm was originally applied, turns the mixture into a thick jelly that flows under pressure, as when shot from a flame thrower, and sticks to a target as it burns. One of the first thickeners used was an aluminum soap (a salt of aluminum and certain fatty acids). Later thickeners have been based on polystyrene and similar polymers.

Napata (năpā'tə, -pä'-), ancient city of NUBIA, just below the Fourth Cataract of the NILE. From about the 8th cent. B.C., Napata was the capital of the kingdom of CUSH. Many great temples like those of Thebes were built here by TAHARKA (XXV dynasty). The Cushite capital was later moved (c.530 B.C.) to MEROË.

Naperville (nā'pərvĭl), city (1970 pop. 23,885), Du Page co., NE Ill., on the Du Page River, in a farm area; settled 1831–32, inc. as a city 1890. Naperville is the seat of North Central College and the Evangelical Theological Seminary.

Naphish (nā'fĭsh), son of Ishmael. Gen. 25.15; 1 Chron. 1.31. Nephish: 1 Chron. 5.19.

Naphtali (năf'təlī), son of Jacob and Bilhah and progenitor of one of the 12 tribes. The tribe's allotment lay NW of the Sea of Galilee. In its early days the tribe was warlike and its hero was BARAK. It was part of the kingdom of Israel and shared its fate. Gen. 30.7,8; 46.24; 49.21. Nephthalim: Mat. 4.13,15; Rev. 7.6.

naphtha (năp'thə, năf'-), term usually restricted to a class of colorless, volatile, flammable liquid hydrocarbon mixtures. Obtained as one of the more volatile fractions in the fractional distillation of PETROLEUM (when it is known as petroleum naphtha), in the fractional distillation of coal tar (coal-tar naphtha), and in a similar distillation of wood (wood naphtha), it is used widely as a solvent for various organic substances, such as fats and rubber, and in the making of varnish. Because of its dissolving property it is important as a cleaning fluid; it is also incorporated in certain laundry soaps. Coal-tar (aromatic) naphthas have greater solvent power than petroleum (aliphatic) naphthas. Originally the term *naphtha* designated a colorless flammable liquid obtained from the ground in Persia. Later it came to be applied to a number of other natural liquid substances having similar properties. Technically, gasoline and kerosine are considered naphthas.

naphthalene (năf'thəlēn''), colorless, crystalline, solid aromatic hydrocarbon with a pungent odor. It melts at 80°C, boils at 218°C, and sublimes upon heating. It is insoluble in water, somewhat soluble in ethanol, soluble in benzene, and very soluble in ether, chloroform, or carbon disulfide. Naphthalene is obtained from coal tar, a by-product of the coking of coal. It is used in mothballs and gives them their characteristic odor. From it are prepared derivatives that are used in the preparation of dyes and as insecticides and organic solvents. The molecular structure of naphthalene is that of two BENZENE rings fused together with two adjacent carbon atoms common to both rings.

naphthol (năf'thôl), $C_{10}H_7OH$, either of two crystalline monohydric alcohols. The naphthols are position ISOMERS, differing in the location of the HYDROXYL GROUP, —OH, on the carbon skeleton of NAPHTHALENE; α-naphthol is 1-hydroxynaphthalene and β-naphthol is 2-hydroxynaphthalene:

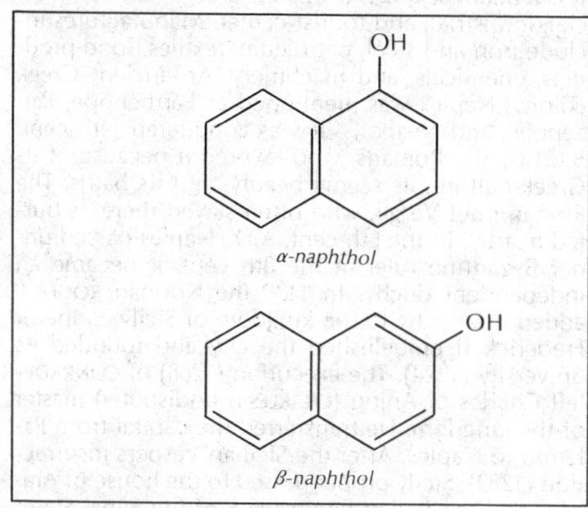

The naphthols have a number of similar properties. They melt at 95°C and 122°C and boil at 279°C and 285°C, respectively; both are soluble in alcohol and ether and slightly soluble in hot water. One way in which they differ is the form of their crystals—α-naphthol crystallizes in prisms and β-naphthol in plates. The naphthols are prepared by reacting naphthalene with sulfuric acid and hydrolyzing the resultant sulfate ester by heating it with sodium hydroxide solution. Both naphthols exhibit antiseptic properties. They are used in the synthesis of certain azo dyes and antioxidants for rubbers. Naphthol solutions are used in chemical analysis to detect the ferric ion; dissolved ferric ion turns an α-naphthol solution violet and turns a β-naphthol solution green.

Naphtuhim (năf'tōōhĭm), descendant of Noah. Gen. 10.13; 1 Chron. 1.11.

Napier, Sir Charles James (nā'pēr, nəpēr'), 1782–1853, British general; brother of Sir William Napier. He served with distinction in the Napoleonic Wars. Stationed (1822–30) on the Greek island of Cephalonia, he became acquainted with Lord Byron and was asked, although he declined, to command the Greek independence forces. As commander (1839–40) of the troops in N England, he exercised moderation in dealing with Chartist unrest. In 1841 Napier went to India, where he undertook the conquest (1843) of Sind. He served as governor of Sind until 1847. See biography by Rosamond Napier Lawrence (1952); H. T. Lambrick, *Sir Charles Napier and Sind* (1952).

Napier, John, 1550–1617, Scottish mathematician. He invented logarithms and wrote *Mirifici logarithmorum canonis descriptio* (1614), containing the first logarithmic table and the first use of the word *logarithm*. His *Rabdologiae* (1617) gives various methods for abbreviating arithmetical calculations. One method of multiplication uses a system of numbered rods called Napier's rods, or Napier's bones; this was a major improvement on the ancient system of counters then in use. In 1619, after Napier's death, his *Mirifici logarithmorum canonis constructio*, which gave the method of construction of his logarithms, was published by his son Robert and edited by Henry Briggs. Napier introduced the decimal point in writing numbers. Napier was also known as an outspoken exponent of the Protestant cause. His religious writings include *A Plaine Discovery of the Whole Revelation* (1593), the earliest Scottish interpretation of the scriptures.

Napier, Robert Cornelis, 1st **Baron Napier of Magdala,** 1810–90, British general. In the engineering service in India, he fought in the Sikh Wars

(1845–49) and took part in the relief of Lucknow (1857) during the Indian Mutiny. He was raised (1868) to the peerage following an expedition to Ethiopia in which he captured Magdala and compelled the release of British captives. He later acted as commander in chief in India (1870–76) and as governor of Gibraltar. See biography by his son, H. D. Napier (1927), and his letters (ed. by his son, 1936).

Napier, Sir William Francis Patrick, 1785–1860, British general and historian; brother of Sir Charles James Napier. He served in the Peninsular War and wrote a famous and still authoritative *History of the War in the Peninsula* (6 vol., 1828–40).

Napier (nā'pēər), city (1971 pop. 40,186), E central North Island, New Zealand, on Hawke Bay. It is a major wool-exporting port as well as a fishing port and wool market. Napier suffered a ruinous earthquake in 1931. It is the seat of an Anglican cathedral.

Naples, Ital. *Napoli,* city (1971 pop. 1,232,877), capital of Campania and of Naples prov., S central Italy, on the Bay of Naples, an arm of the Tyrrhenian Sea. It is a major seaport, with shipyards, and a commercial, industrial, and tourist center. Manufactures include iron and steel, petroleum, textiles, food products, chemicals, and machinery. An ancient Greek colony, Naples was mentioned as Parthenope, Palaepolis, and Neapolis. It was conquered (4th cent. B.C.) by the Romans, who favored it because of its Greek culture, its scenic beauty, and its baths. The Roman poet Vergil, who often stayed there, is buried nearby. In the 6th cent. A.D., Naples passed under Byzantine rule; in the 8th cent. it became an independent duchy. In 1139 the Norman ROGER II added the duchy to the kingdom of Sicily. Emperor Frederick II embellished the city and founded its university (1224). The execution (1268) of CONRADIN left Charles of Anjou (CHARLES I) undisputed master of the kingdom. He transferred the capital from Palermo to Naples. After the Sicilian Vespers insurrection (1282), Sicily proper passed to the house of Aragón, and the Italian peninsula S of the Papal States became known as the kingdom of Naples (see separate article). Naples was its capital until it fell to Garibaldi and was annexed to the kingdom of Sardinia (1860). The city suffered severe damage in World War II. Naples is beautifully situated at the base and on the slopes of the hills enclosing the Bay of Naples. The bay, dominated by Mt. Vesuvius, extends from Cape Misena in the north to the Sorrento peninsula in the south and is dotted with towns and villas. Near its entrance are the islands of Capri, Ischia, and Procida. Naples is a crowded and noisy city, famous for its songs, festivals, and gaiety. Especially interesting parts of the city are the Old Spacca Quarter (the heart of Old Naples) and the seaside Santa Lucia sector. Noteworthy structures in Naples include the Castel Nuovo (1282); the Castel dell'Ovo (rebuilt by the Angevins in 1274); the Renaissance-style Palazzo Cuomo (late 15th cent.); the large Carthusian Monastery of St. Martin (remodeled in the 16th and 17th cent.); the neoclassic Villa Floridiana, which houses a museum of porcelain, china, and Neopolitan paintings; the Church of Santa Chiara (Gothic, with 18th-century baroque additions), which contains the tombs of Robert the Wise and other Angevin kings; the Cathedral of St. Januarius (14th cent., with numerous later additions, including a 17th-century baroque chapel; the Royal Palace (early 17th cent.); and the Church of Santa Maria Donna Regina. Naples has several museums including the National Museum, which holds the Farnese collection and most of the objects excavated at nearby Pompeii and Herculaneum; the picture gallery, housed in Capodimonte palace; and the aquarium. As a musical center Naples reached its greatest brilliance in the 17th and 18th cent.; Alessandro and Domenico Scarlatti, Porpora, Pergolesi, Paisiello, and Cimarosa were among the representatives of the Neapolitan style. The Teatro San Carlo, a famous opera house, was opened in 1737. The city has a conservatory and several art academies. Near Naples is the Camaldulian Hermitage (founded 1585), from which there is an excellent view of the bay region.

Naples, resort city (1970 pop. 12,042), Collier co., SW Fla., on the Gulf of Mexico; inc. 1927. It is noted for its beach.

Naples, kingdom of, former state, occupying the Italian peninsula south of the former Papal States. It comprised roughly the present regions of CAMPANIA, ABRUZZI, MOLISE, BASILICATA, APULIA, and CALABRIA. Naples was the capital. In the 11th and 12th cent. the Normans under ROBERT GUISCARD and his successors seized S Italy from the Byzantines. The popes, however, claimed suzerainty over S Italy and were to play an important part in the history of Naples. In 1139, ROGER II, Guiscard's nephew, was invested by Innocent II with the kingdom of SICILY, including the Norman lands in S Italy. The last Norman king designated Constance, wife of Holy Roman Emperor Henry VI, as his heir and the kingdom passed successively to FREDERICK II, CONRAD IV, MANFRED, and CONRADIN of Hohenstaufen. Under them S Italy flowered, but in 1266 CHARLES I (Charles of Anjou), founder of the ANGEVIN dynasty, was invested with the crown by Pope Clement IV, who wished to drive the Hohenstaufen family from Italy. Charles lost Sicily in 1282 but retained his territories on the mainland, which came to be known as the kingdom of Naples. Refusing to give up their claim to Sicily, Charles and his successors warred with the house of Aragón, which held the island, until in 1373 Queen JOANNA I of Naples formally renounced her claim. During her reign began the struggle for succession between Charles of Durazzo (later CHARLES III of Naples) and Louis of Anjou (LOUIS I of Naples). The struggle was continued by their heirs. Charles's descendants, LANCELOT and JOANNA II, successfully defended their thrones despite papal support of their French rivals, but Joanna successively adopted as her heir ALFONSO V of Aragón and Louis III and RENÉ of Anjou, and the dynastic struggle was prolonged. Alfonso defeated René and in 1442 was invested with Naples by the pope. His successor in Naples, FERDINAND I (Ferrante), suppressed (1485) a conspiracy of the powerful feudal lords. Meanwhile the Angevin claim to Naples had passed to the French crown with the death (1486) of René's nephew, Charles of Maine. CHARLES VIII of France pressed the claim and in 1495 briefly seized Naples, thus starting the ITALIAN WARS between France and Spain. Louis XII, Charles's successor, temporarily joined forces with Spain and dethroned Frederick (1501), the last Aragonese king of Naples, but fell out with his allies, who defeated him. The Treaties of Blois (1504–5) gave Naples and Sicily to Spain, which for two centuries ruled the two kingdoms through viceroys—one at Palermo, one at Naples. Gonzalo FERNÁNDEZ DE CÓRDOBA was the first viceroy of Naples. Under Spain, S Italy became one of the most backward and exploited areas in Europe. Heavy taxation (from which the nobility and clergy were exempt) filled the Spanish treasury; agriculture suffered from the accumulation of huge estates by quarreling Italian and Spanish nobles and the church; famines were almost chronic; disease, superstition, and ignorance flourished. A popular revolt against these conditions, led by MASANIELLO, was crushed in 1648. In the War of the Spanish Succession the kingdom was occupied (1707) by Austria, which kept it by the terms of the Peace of Utrecht (1713; see UTRECHT, PEACE OF). During the War of the POLISH SUCCESSION, however, Don Carlos of Bourbon (later CHARLES III of Spain) reconquered Naples and Sicily. The Treaty of Vienna (1738) confirmed the conquest, and the two kingdoms became subsidiary to the Spanish crown, ruled in personal union by a cadet branch of the Spanish line of BOURBON. Naples then had its own dynasty, but conditions improved little. In 1798, Ferdinand IV and his queen, MARIE CAROLINE, fled from the French Revolutionary army. The PARTHENOPEAN REPUBLIC was set up (1799), but the Bourbons returned the same year with the help of the English under Lord NELSON. Reprisals were severe; Sir John ACTON, the queen's favorite, once more was supreme. In 1806 the French again drove out the royal couple, who fled to Sicily. Joseph BONAPARTE, made king of Naples by Napoleon I, was replaced in 1808 by Joachim MURAT. Murat's beneficent reforms were revoked after his fall and execution (1815) by Ferdinand, who was restored to the throne (Marie Caroline had died in 1814). In 1816, Ferdinand merged Sicily and Naples and styled himself FERDINAND I, king of the Two Sicilies. For the remaining history of Naples, annexed to Sardinia in 1860, see TWO SICILIES, KINGDOM OF THE. See Harold Acton, *The Bourbons of Naples (1734–1825)* (1956) and *The Last Bourbons of Naples 1825–61* (1961); Benedetto Croce, *History of the Kingdom of Naples* (1925, tr. 1970).

Naples, University of, at Naples, Italy; founded 1224; transferred to Salerno 1252 but returned to Naples 1258. It has faculties of law; economics and commerce; letters and philosophy; medicine; mathematics, physics, and natural sciences; pharmacy; engineering; architecture; agriculture; and veterinary medicine.

Napoleon I, 1769–1821, emperor of the French, b. Ajaccio, Corsica. The son of Carlo and Letizia Bonaparte (or Buonaparte; see under BONAPARTE), young Napoleon was sent (1779) to French military schools at Brienne and Paris, where his small stature won him the nickname "the Little Corporal." He received his commission in the artillery in 1785. After the outbreak of the French Revolution he took part in the Corsican uprising against Pasquale PAOLI. In 1793, Paoli forced the Bonapartes to leave the island. Returning to military duty in France, Bonaparte was associated with the Jacobins and first attracted notice by his distinguished part in dislodging the British from Toulon (1793); he was promoted to brigadier general and sent to the Italian front. Briefly under arrest in the Thermidorian reaction (1794; see THERMIDOR), he was released but remained out of favor. A political event was to reopen his career overnight. In Oct., 1795, the Convention was assailed by a Parisian mob (see VENDÉMIAIRE), and Paul BARRAS persuaded the Convention to place Bonaparte in command of the troops; Napoleon dispersed the mob with what he called "a whiff of grapeshot"—which killed about 100 insurgents. He was given command of the army of the interior. After drawing up a plan for an Italian campaign, he was, again with Barras's help, made commander in chief of the army of Italy. He left for Italy in March, 1796, after marrying Josephine de Beauharnais (see JOSEPHINE). Assuming command of a starving and ragged army, he succeeded within a short time in transforming it into a first-class fighting force. The brilliant success of his Italian campaign was based on three factors: his supply system, which he made virtually independent of the financially exhausted Directory by allowing the troops to live off the land; his reliance on speed and massed surprise attacks by small but compact units against the Austrian forces; and his magic influence over the morale of his soldiers. Napoleon swept across N Italy, forcing Sardinia to sign a separate peace in May, 1796. After his victory at Lodi (May 10), he entered Milan (May 14), laid siege to Mantua (July, 1796), and made a brief dash southward, obtaining favorable armistices from the king of Naples and the pope. After the great victories of Arcole (Nov., 1796) and Rivoli (Jan., 1797) and the fall of Mantua (Feb., 1797), Bonaparte began to cross the Alps toward Vienna. However, the slow advance of the northern French armies in Germany and the danger of being cut off in the rear caused him to arrange—without instructions from Paris—the truce of Leoben (April, 1797), complemented in October by the Treaty of CAMPO FORMIO. Now the idol of half of Europe, Bonaparte returned to France and drew up a plan to crush the British Empire by striking at Egypt and, ultimately, at India. The plan was supported by Charles Maurice de TALLEYRAND and by the directors, who were eager to rid themselves of the ambitious young general. Bonaparte sailed in May, 1798, succeeded in evading Horatio NELSON, and took Malta on the way to Egypt. Shortly after landing at Aboukir (Abu Qir), he won a brilliant victory over the Mamelukes in the battle of the Pyramids (July, 1798). His successes, however, were made useless when the French fleet was utterly destroyed (Aug. 1–2) by Nelson in Aboukir Bay. Turkey declared war on France. A French expedition to Syria was repelled at ACRE. Back in Egypt, Napoleon defeated Turkish forces attempting to land at Aboukir (July, 1799). Meanwhile, matters were going from bad to worse in Europe. The French were expelled from Italy by the forces of the Second Coalition (see FRENCH REVOLUTIONARY WARS), and at home the Directory faced bankruptcy. Unannounced, Napoleon returned to France, leaving General Kléber in charge of a hopeless situation in Egypt, and joined a conspiracy already hatched by Emmanuel SIEYÈS, one of the directors.

The Consulate. The Directory was overthrown by the coup d'etat of 18 BRUMAIRE (Nov. 9–10, 1799), and the CONSULATE was set up, with Bonaparte as first consul. The autocratic constitution of the year VIII was accepted by plebiscite. In effect, the constitution established the dictatorship of Bonaparte. Taking energetic measures, Bonaparte reorganized the administration under strong central control, stabilized the currency, established the Bank of France, and reformed the tax system. He made peace with the Roman Catholic Church by the CONCORDAT OF 1801 and reformed the legal system with the CODE NAPOLÉON. In 1800, Napoleon turned against the foreign foe, crossed the St. Bernard pass, and defeated (June 14) the Austrians at Marengo, Italy. With the Treaty of Lunéville (1801) with Austria and the Treaty of Amiens (1802) with Great Britain, the Second Coalition was ended and France became paramount on the Continent. Napoleon's ambition did not rest. In Aug., 1802, a plebiscite approved his becoming first consul for life; a modified constitution, that of the year X, came into force. In the same year he incorporated Piedmont into France. His continued intervention in Italy, Germany, the HELVETIC RE-

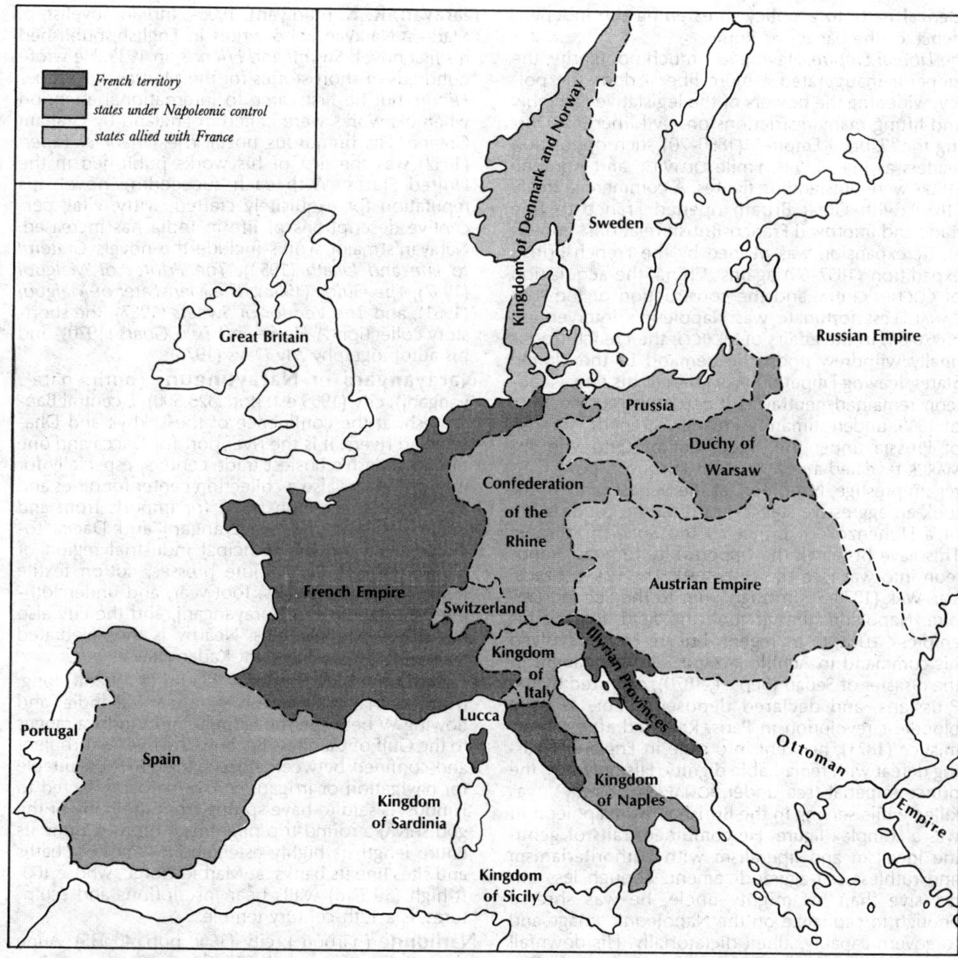

Napoleonic Europe (1812)

PUBLIC (Switzerland), and the Netherlands as well as his refusal to arrange a commercial treaty with Great Britain aroused British distrust. Britain failed to restore Malta to the Knights Hospitalers, as the Treaty of Amiens had stipulated. In May, 1803, Britain again declared war on France. Napoleon built up his army, apparently in order to invade England, but the invasion fleet he assembled (1803–5) was repeatedly struck by storms, and a major part of the French fleet was engaged in the disastrous expedition of Charles LECLERC to Haiti.

The Empire. While warfare languished, Napoleon took advantage of the plot of Georges CADOUDAL against his life, seized and executed the duc d'ENGHIEN, and had himself proclaimed emperor of the French by a subservient senate and tribunate (May, 1804). Confirmation by a plebiscite was a foregone conclusion, and on Dec. 2, in the Cathedral of Notre Dame, Napoleon took the crown from the hands of Pope Pius VII and set it on his own head. An imperial court and a nobility were created. The constitution of the year XII retained the features of the previous two constitutions, but its liberal provisions were gradually restricted. When Napoleon, in 1805, proclaimed himself king of Italy and annexed Genoa to France, a Third Coalition was formed against him by Great Britain, Austria, Russia, and Sweden. Napoleon crushed the Austrians at Ulm, occupied Vienna, and won (Dec. 2, 1805) his most brilliant victory over the combined Russians and Austrians at AUSTERLITZ. Austria, with the harsh Treaty of Pressburg (Dec. 26), was forced out of the coalition. Prussia, which entered the coalition late in 1806, was thoroughly defeated (Oct. 14) at Jena, and Napoleon entered Berlin in triumph. British sea power, however, had grown stronger than ever through Nelson's victory at TRAFALGAR (1805), and Napoleon resolved to defeat Britain by economic warfare. His CONTINENTAL SYSTEM was answered by the British ORDERS IN COUNCIL. On land, warfare with Russia continued. The indecisive battle at EYLAU (Feb. 8, 1807) was made good by Napoleon at Friedland (June 14), and Russia submitted. By the treaties of TILSIT (July, 1807), King Frederick William III of Prussia lost half of his territories and became a vassal to France; Russia recognized the Grand Duchy of Warsaw, created from Prussian territory, and other territorial changes. Sweden was defeated in 1808 with the help of Russia. With only Britain left in the field, Napoleon was now master of the Continent. The whole map of Europe was rearranged. The states of Germany had already been altered by the CONFEDERATION OF THE RHINE; Napoleon's allies, the electors of Bavaria, Württemberg, and Saxony, were made kings; the Holy Roman Empire was dissolved (1806); the kingdoms of Holland and Westphalia were created (1806 and 1807), with Napoleon's brothers Louis and Jérôme Bonaparte (see under BONAPARTE) occupying the thrones. Napoleon's stepson, Eugène de BEAUHARNAIS, was made (1805) viceroy of Italy, and a third brother, Joseph Bonaparte (see under BONAPARTE), became (1806) king of Naples. In 1808, Napoleon made Joseph king of Spain after obtaining the abdication of Charles IV and his son Ferdinand VII; in Naples, Joseph was replaced with Marshal Joachim MURAT, who was married to Napoleon's sister Caroline. Another Napoleonic marshal, Jean Bernadotte, became heir to the Swedish throne in 1810 (see CHARLES XIV). An attempt (1809) by Austria to reopen war against France was defeated at Wagram (July 6, 1809) and resulted in the cession of Illyria to France by the Treaty of Schönbrunn. The Papal States were declared annexed to France (1809), and when Pope PIUS VII replied with an excommunication, he was imprisoned and later was forced to sign an additional concordat. Napoleon secured an annulment of his marriage with Josephine, who was unable to bear him a child, and was married in March, 1810, to MARIE LOUISE, the daughter of the Austrian emperor Francis I (formerly Holy Roman Emperor Francis II). A son was born to them (the "king of Rome," later known as the duke of Reichstadt or NAPOLEON II), thus insuring the imperial succession.

Decline and Fall. Great Britain had never submitted, and the Continental System proved difficult to enforce. Napoleon's first signs of weakness appeared early in the PENINSULAR WAR (1808–14). The victory of 1809 over Austria had been costly, and the victory of Archduke CHARLES at Aspern (May, 1809), showed that the emperor was not invincible. Everywhere forces were gathering to cast off the Napoleonic yoke. Napoleon's decision to invade Russia marked the turning point of his career. His alliance with Czar ALEXANDER I, dating from the treaties of Tilsit and extended at the Congress of ERFURT (1808), was tenuous. When the czar rejected the Continental System, which was ruinous to Russia's economy, Napoleon gathered the largest army Europe had ever seen. The *Grande Armée*, some 500,000 strong, including troops of all the vassal and allied states, entered Russia in June, 1812. The Russian troops, under Mikhail KUTUZOV and Prince BARCLAY DE TOLLY, fell back, systematically devastating the land. After the indecisive battle of Borodino (Sept. 7), in which both sides suffered terrible losses, Napoleon entered Moscow (Sept. 14), where only a few thousand civilians had stayed behind. On Sept. 15, fires broke out all over Moscow; they ceased only on Sept. 19, leaving the city virtually destroyed. With his troops decimated, his prospective winter quarters burned down, his supply line overextended, and the Russian countryside and grain stores empty, Napoleon, after sending an unsuccessful plea to the czar for peace, began his fateful retreat on Oct. 19. Stalked by hunger, the *Grande Armée*, now only a fifth of its original strength, reached the Berezina River late in November. After the passage of that river, secured at a terrible sacrifice, the retreat became a rout. In December, Napoleon left his army and hastened to Paris to prepare French defenses. Of his allies, Prussia was the first to desert; a Prussian truce with the czar (Dec. 30) was followed by an alliance in Feb., 1813. Great Britain and Sweden joined the coalition, followed (Aug., 1813) by Austria, and the "War of Liberation" began. At the Battle of the Nations at LEIPZIG (Oct. 16–19), Napoleon was forced to retreat. In November the allies offered Napoleon peace if France would return to her natural boundaries, the Rhine and the Alps. Napoleon rejected the offer, and the allies continued their advance. They closed in on Paris, which fell to them on March 31, 1814. Napoleon abdicated, first in favor of his son and then unconditionally (April 11). He was exiled to Elba, which the allies gave him as a sovereign principality. His victors were still deliberating at the Congress of Vienna (see VIENNA, CONGRESS OF) when Napoleon, with a handful of followers, landed near Cannes (March 1, 1815). In the course of a triumphant march northward he once more rallied France behind him. King Louis XVIII fled, and Napoleon entered Paris (March 20), beginning his ephemeral rule of the HUNDRED DAYS. Attempting to reconstruct the empire, he liberalized the constitution, but his efforts were cut short when warfare began again. Napoleon was utterly crushed in the WATERLOO CAMPAIGN (June 12–18). He again abdicated and surrendered himself to a British warship, the *Bellerophon*, in the hope of finding asylum in England. Instead, he was shipped as a prisoner of war to the lonely island of SAINT HELENA, where he spent his remaining years quarreling with the British governor, Sir Hudson LOWE, talking with his ever-dwindling group of followers, and dictating his memoirs. After long suffering from cancer, he died May 5, 1821. The Napoleonic legend, the picture of a liberal conquerer spreading the French Revolution throughout Europe, was a potent factor in French history and helped make Napoleon's nephew emperor as Napoleon III. Estimates of Napoleon's place in history differ widely. He was beyond doubt one of the greatest conquerors in history. He also promoted the growth of liberalism through his valuable and lasting administrative and legal reforms. His changes in the map of Europe stimulated the movements for national unification. Although he made use of such ruthless police chiefs as Joseph FOUCHÉ and Anne SAVARY to suppress all opposition, he cannot be compared to 20th-century dictators such as Adolf Hitler. Besides the duke of Reichstadt, Napoleon had at least one other son, Comte Alexandre WALEWSKI. Napoleon's remains were ordered returned to France by Louis Philippe in 1840 and were entombed under the dome of the Invalides in Paris. More or less apocryphal sayings and anecdotes illustrating Napoleon's character and manners are as innumerable as the books written about him. A standard biography is that by August Fournier (tr. 1924); more recent are those by F. M. H. Markham (1963), R. B. Holtman (1967), J. M. Thompson (1952, repr. 1969), and Georges Lefebvre (2 vol., tr. 1969). See also the writings of Louis Madelin, J. H. Rose, Frédéric MASSON, Albert Vandal, Eugene Tarlé, Octave Aubry, and the bibliographies in their works; Napoleon's own memoirs, dictated to Emmanuel de LAS CASES and others; and his correspondence. Among the countless contemporary memoirs, those of P. P. de Ségur and A. A. L. de CAULAINCOURT are especially noteworthy.

Napoleon II, 1811–32, son of Napoleon I and MARIE LOUISE, known as the king of Rome (1811–14), as the prince of Parma (1814–18), and after that as the duke of Reichstadt. Napoleon's abdication in 1815 was in favor of his son, so that he was known to the Bonapartists as Napoleon II, although he never ruled. After 1815 he was a virtual prisoner in Austria, where he died of tuberculosis. In 1940 his remains were transferred, as a gift to France from Adolf Hitler, from Vienna to the dome of the Invalides in Paris, where he now rests beside his father. The pitiful life of the "Eaglet" is the subject of Edmond Rostand's drama *L'Aiglon*. See biography by André Castelot (tr. 1960).

Napoleon III (Louis Napoleon Bonaparte), 1808–73, emperor of the French (1852–70), son of Louis BONAPARTE, king of Holland. The nephew of Napoleon I, he spent his youth with his mother, Hortense de BEAUHARNAIS, in Switzerland and Germany and became a captain in the Swiss army. Animated by a mixture of liberalism and Bonapartism, he indulged (1830–31) in revolutionary activities in Italy. In 1836 he attempted a ludicrous military coup at Strasbourg and was exiled to the United States by the government of Louis Philippe. He managed to return to Switzerland, but French protests at his proximity finally caused him to depart (1838) for England. In 1840 he again attempted an insurrection, this time at Boulogne-sur-Mer. He was tried and sentenced to life imprisonment. Detained in the fortress of Ham, Somme dept., he wrote letters, pamphlets, and books, among them a mildly socialistic work on the extinction of pauperism. He made an easy escape in 1846, walking out disguised as a laborer, and went to England.

A Myth Fulfilled. After the FEBRUARY REVOLUTION of 1848 Louis Napoleon returned to France. He gathered a following, was elected to the national assembly, and in Dec., 1848, defeated Louis Eugène CAVAIGNAC in the presidential elections by an overwhelming majority. Although assisted by Cavaignac's unpopularity with the working classes, Louis Napoleon's success was largely due to his name. He vaguely promised support to all interests, and he evoked French nostalgia for the past Napoleonic glory. As president of the Second Republic, he was limited by law to one term. He soon began to strengthen his position and took special care to conciliate the powerful conservative forces. The strong Roman Catholic opposition was allayed by allowing (1849) a French army to restore Pope Pius IX to Rome and by assenting (1850) to an education bill, presented by Frédéric de Falloux, which greatly favored the church. After the defeat in the assembly in July, 1851, of a constitutional amendment that would have allowed the president to serve for more than one term, Louis Napoleon began plans for a coup d'état. The masterly coup of Dec. 2, 1851, was largely engineered by Louis Napoleon's half brother, the duc de MORNY. The legislative assembly was dissolved and its meeting place occupied by the army, universal suffrage was restored, and a plebiscite authorizing the revision of the constitution was announced. An attempted workers' uprising was brutally repressed. To assure a majority in the plebiscite, Morny used tactics of intimidation and strict electoral management. Victory would, in any case, have been the probable outcome. The Bonaparte name promised glory, order, and a possible solution of France's political division. The plebiscite registered overwhelming approval. The new constitution (Jan., 1852) gave the president dictatorial powers and created a council of state, a senate, and a legislative assembly subservient to the president. Subsequent decrees barred republicans from the ballot and throttled the press.

Emperor of the French. In Nov., 1852, a new plebiscite overwhelmingly approved the establishment of the Second Empire, and Louis Napoleon became Emperor Napoleon III. For eight years he continued to exercise dictatorial rule, tempered by rapid material progress. Railway building was encouraged; the rebuilding of Paris and other cities brought a construction boom; and the first French investment banks were authorized. Napoleon's foreign ventures were successful at first. The CRIMEAN WAR (1854–56) and the Congress of Paris (see PARIS, CONGRESS OF) restored French leadership on the Continent. Napoleon then turned toward Italy. A long-time supporter of Italian nationalism, he met the Sardinian premier Camillo CAVOUR at Plombières and secretly agreed on a joint campaign of France and Sardinia to expel Austria from Italy and to establish an Italian federation of four states under the presidency of the pope; France was to be compensated with Nice and Savoy. War broke out in 1859 (see RISORGIMENTO). However, after the costly victory of the French and Sardinians at SOLFERINO, Napoleon suddenly deserted his Italian ally and made a separate peace with Austria at VILLAFRANCA DI VERONA. His act was partly motivated by the opposition of the French clerical party to a policy threatening the independence of the papacy at Rome.

The Liberal Empire. Having lost much popularity, the emperor inaugurated a more liberal domestic policy, widening the powers of the legislative assembly and lifting many restrictions on civil liberties. During the "Liberal Empire" (1860–70) such opposition leaders as Jules FAVRE, Émile OLLIVIER, and Adolphe THIERS were outstanding figures. A commercial treaty (1860) with Great Britain opened France to free trade and improved Franco-British relations. Imperialistic expansion was pushed by the French-British expedition (1857–60) against China, the acquisition of COCHIN CHINA, and the construction of the SUEZ CANAL. Less fortunate was Napoleon's intervention (1861–67) in the affairs of MEXICO; the French troops finally withdrew upon the demand of the United States, leaving Emperor MAXIMILIAN to his fate. Napoleon remained neutral in the AUSTRO-PRUSSIAN WAR of 1866, underestimating Prussian strength. The rise of Prussia under the leadership of Otto von BISMARCK revealed a new rival for European power. To regain prestige, Napoleon, at the behest of advisers, took an aggressive stand regarding the candidature of a Hohenzollern prince to the Spanish throne. This gave Bismarck the opportunity to goad Napoleon into war (see EMS DISPATCH). The FRANCO-PRUSSIAN WAR (1870–71) brought ruin to the Second Empire. Napoleon himself took the field, leaving his empress, EUGÉNIE, as regent, but he early devolved his command to Achille BAZAINE. He was caught in the disaster of Sedan (Sept. 1, 1870), captured by the Prussians, and declared deposed (Sept. 4) by a bloodless revolution in Paris. Released after the armistice (1871), he went into exile in England, bearing defeat with remarkable dignity. His only son, the prince imperial (see under BONAPARTE, family), was killed while serving in the British army. Napoleon III was a complex figure. He combined traits of genuine idealism and liberalism with authoritarianism and ruthless self-aggrandizement. Though less impressive than his mighty uncle, he was shrewd enough to capitalize on the Napoleonic image and to govern capably, albeit dictatorially. His downfall came when he encountered the far more canny Bismarck.

Bibliography. See studies of the Second Empire by Pierre de La Gorce (7 vol., 1894–1905, in French), Émile Ollivier (18 vol., 1895–1918, in French), Philip Guedalla (2d ed. 1928), and J. M. Thompson (1954, repr. 1967); F. A. Simpson, *The Rise of Louis Napoleon* (new ed. 1925, repr. 1968) and *Louis Napoleon and the Recovery of France* (3d ed. 1951); Albert Guérard, *Napoleon III* (1943); D. H. Pinkney, *Napoleon III and the Rebuilding of Paris* (1958); J. P. T. Bury, *Napoleon III and the Second Empire* (1964); B. D. Gooch, *The Reign of Napoleon III* (1969); W. H. C. Smith, *Napoleon III* (1972).

Napoleonic Wars, 1803–15, the wars waged by or against France under Napoleon I. For a discussion of them see under NAPOLEON I.

Nara (nä'rä), city (1970 pop. 208,257), capital of Nara prefecture, S Honshu, Japan. An ancient cultural and religious center, it was founded in 706 by imperial decree and was modeled after Ch'ang-an, the capital of T'ang China. Nara was (710–84) the first permanent capital of Japan. The noted temple, Todai-ji, has a 53.5-ft-high (16.3 m) image of Buddha, said to be one of the largest bronze figures in the world. Nara Park, the largest (1,250 acres/506 hectares) city park in Japan, includes the celebrated Imperial Museum, which houses ancient art treasures and relics. Near the city is wooded Mt. Kasuga, the traditional home of the gods; its trees are never cut. Also nearby is Horyu-ji, founded in 607, the oldest Buddhist temple in Japan, with the grave of Jimmu, the first emperor. Nara prefecture (1970 pop. 930,073), 1,425 sq mi (3,691 sq km), is largely mountainous and its population centers in and around the capital.

naranjillo (näränhē'yō), large tropical subshrub (*Solanum quitoense*) of the family Solanaceae (NIGHTSHADE family), native to the Andes. Tomatolike fruits, orange-colored and leathery-skinned, grow along the large main stalk, sometimes 10 ft (21.3 m) high. Their juicy, flavorful, slightly acid pulp is much used locally for beverages and sherbets. The naranjillo, or lulo, became known to North Americans as a beverage at the 1939 New York World's Fair. Naranjillo is classified in the division MAGNOLIOPHYTA, class Magnoliopsida, order Polemoniales, family Solanaceae.

Narashino (närəshē'nō), city (1970 pop. 99,951), Chiba prefecture, E central Honshu, Japan, on Tokyo Bay. It is a newly developed suburb of Tokyo and has a large metals industry.

Narayan, R. K. (nərī'yän), 1906–, Indian novelist, b. Madras. Narayan, who writes in English, published his first novel, *Swami and Friends*, in 1935. He wrote hundreds of short stories for the Madras newspaper *Hindu*, but he first came to international attention when his works were hailed in England by Graham Greene. His humorous novel *The Financial Expert* (1952) was the first of his works published in the United States. With each succeeding novel, his reputation for exquisitely crafted, witty, vital, perceptive descriptions of life in India has increased. Narayan's major works include the novels *Grateful to Life and Death* (1953), *The Printer of Malgudi* (1957), *The Guide* (1958), *The Man-Eater of Malgudi* (1961), and *The Vendor of Sweets* (1967), the short-story collection *A Horse and Two Goats* (1970), and his autobiography *My Days* (1974).

Narayanganj or **Narayungunj** (both: närä'yəngənj), city (1969 est. pop. 326,500), E central Bangladesh, at the confluence of the Lakhya and Dhaleshwari rivers. It is the river port for Dacca and one of Bangladesh's busiest trade centers, especially for jute. The city is also a collection center for hides and skins and a reception point for imports from and exports to Calcutta. Narayanganj and Dacca together make up the principal industrial region of Bangladesh. There are jute presses, cotton textile mills, and leather, glass, footwear, and underclothing manufactures in Narayanganj, and the city also has ship repair facilities. Nearby is the celebrated shrine of the Muslim saint Kadam Rasul.

Narbada (nərbŭ'də), river, c.775 mi (1,250 km) long, rising in Madhya Pradesh state, central India, and flowing W between the Satpura and Vindhya ranges to the Gulf of Cambay. Because the river is turbulent and confined between steep banks, it is unsuitable for navigation or irrigation. The Narbada, sacred to Hindus, is said to have sprung from the body of the god SHIVA; a round-trip pilgrimage on foot along its entire length is highly esteemed. Many holy baths and sites line its banks; at Marble Gorge, whose 100-ft-high (30.5 m) walls bear inscriptions and sculptures, is a 12th-century temple.

Narbonne (närbôn'), city (1968 pop. 40,035), Aude dept., S France, near the Mediterranean coast. It is the commercial center of a wine-growing region and an industrial city producing sulfur, copper, and clothing. It was the first Roman colony established in Transalpine GAUL (118 B.C.) and was known as Narbo Martius; it later became the capital of the Roman province of Gallia Narbonensis. Narbonne was an archiepiscopal see from the 4th cent. until 1801. The city was occupied by the Visigoths in A.D. 413 and taken by the Saracens in 719 and the Franks in 759. It later became the seat of the viscounts of Narbonne, vassals of the counts of Toulouse, and was united to the French crown in 1507. Its port, silted up in 1320, brought great wealth to the city, especially during the Middle Ages. Narbonne was an important center of the Jews in the Middle Ages. Their expulsion (late 13th cent.) and the Black Death (1310), which is said to have taken 30,000 lives, were severe blows to the city's prosperity. In Narbonne are the remains of a Roman amphitheater and bridge, the splendid St. Just Cathedral (13th–14th cent.), and an archiepiscopal palace (13th cent.), now the town hall and museum.

narcissism (närsĭs'ĭzəm), Freudian term, drawn from the Greek myth of Narcissus, indicating an exclusive self-absorption. A normal stage in the development of children, it is called secondary narcissism when occurring after puberty; it indicates that the libido or sexual energy of the individual is directed exclusively toward himself and that, therefore, he is incapable of emotional relationships with others.

Narcissus, Roman whose household was partly Christian. Rom. 16.11.

Narcissus, d. A.D. 54, secretary of the Roman Emperor Claudius I. A freedman with great influence, he had a command in an expedition to Britain in A.D. 43. He revealed to Claudius the intrigue of MESSALINA and expedited her death (A.D. 48). The woman that Narcissus chose for Claudius' next wife was, however, passed over in favor of AGRIPPINA II, who was hostile to Narcissus. After Claudius' death she drove Narcissus to commit suicide. In the course of his lifetime Narcissus amassed a huge fortune.

Narcissus (närsĭs'əs), in Greek mythology, beautiful youth who refused all offers of love, including that of ECHO. As punishment for his indifference he was made to fall in love with his own image in a mountain pool. Unable to possess the image, he pined away and was turned into a flower.

narcissus: see AMARYLLIS.

narcosis (närkō'sĭs), state of stupor induced by drugs. The use of narcotics as a therapeutic aid in psychiatry is believed to have a history dating back to the use of opium for mental disorders by the early Egyptians. Prolonged narcosis was employed at the beginning of the 20th cent.; its chief value was the reduction of excitement and tension in the psychotic patient. J. S. Horsley introduced (1936) the term *narcoanalysis* for the use of narcotics to induce a trancelike state in which the patient talks freely and intensive psychotherapy may be applied. It was used with considerable success in treatment of acute combat psychoneuroses during World War II.

narcotic, any of a number of substances that have a depressant effect on the nervous system. The chief narcotic drugs are OPIUM, its constituents MORPHINE and CODEINE, and the morphine derivative HEROIN. In small doses narcotics have valuable medical uses, numbing the senses, relieving severe pain, and inducing sleep. They are also used preoperatively to relieve pain and anxiety. Common side effects include constipation, nausea, and allergic reactions. In large doses narcotics can be highly dangerous, causing stupor, coma, convulsions, or death. All narcotics are addictive; several morphine derivatives as well as chemically dissimilar narcotics that have been developed for medical use have fewer side effects and are less addictive than morphine, but they are also generally less potent. Unlike general anesthetics such as ETHER and CHLOROFORM, narcotics depress the respiratory center and in low doses relieve pain without inducing sleep. Respiratory depression occurs in newborns whose mothers have been given narcotics such as MEPERIDINE (Demerol) during labor. Narcotics differ from BARBITURATES and other SEDATIVES in that they have no anticonvulsant action; also, narcotics relieve pain, while sedatives do not. There have been nationally and internationally based attempts to control the production of narcotics and to limit their export and import to medical use only. Nevertheless, large quantities continue to be grown in India and in the "Golden Triangle" region of Burma, Thailand, and Laos, and a large illicit traffic in these substances continues. See DRUG ADDICTION AND DRUG ABUSE.

Narew (nä'rĕf), Rus. *Narev,* river, c.275 mi (440 km) long, rising in the Białowieza Forest, W European USSR, near the border with Poland. It flows generally NW through NE Poland past Łomża, the head of navigation, then SW to the Vistula River near Warsaw. The Western Bug and the Biebrza rivers are the chief tributaries. Canals connect the Narew's tributaries with the Neman and Pripyat rivers. During World Wars I and II, major battles took place along the Narew's banks.

Narezhny, Vasily Trofimovich (vəsē'lyē trəfē'məvĭch nərĕzh'nē), 1780–1825, Russian novelist. He was an important forerunner of Gogol in his realistic descriptions of Ukrainian and Cossack life. He is best known for the picaresque novel *The Russian Gil Blas* (1814).

narghile (när'gəlē"): see PIPE SMOKING.

Nariño, Antonio (äntō'nyō närē'nyō), 1765–1823, Colombian revolutionary. A liberal intellectual, Nariño was one of the first to foment revolution against Spain in South America. For secretly translating and distributing copies of *The Declaration of the Rights of Man* he was condemned to prison (1795), but escaped to France and then to England, returning (1797) to NEW GRANADA to continue secret agitation. Arrested, he was released, imprisoned again, and, after an escape, confined at Cartagena. He was freed by the revolutionaries and, returning to Bogotá, became (Sept., 1811) president of Cundinamarca, one of the independent states formed after the dissolution of the vice-royalty of New Granada. Advocating strong central government as the only way of preserving independence, Nariño was opposed by the military juntas of other states, which desired simply a loose federation. He was involved in civil wars with the federalists until he was granted dictatorial powers and succeeded in uniting the patriot forces to repel a royalist invasion. He drove the Spanish from Popayán, but was defeated (May, 1814) at Pasto. He surrendered himself but not his army and was later imprisoned for four years in Cádiz. He was released by Spanish revolutionaries in 1820 and returned to aid Simón BOLÍVAR, who made him vice president of the greater republic of Colombia (1821), but he resigned two months later. Often vilified for his stubborn adherence to his own opinions, Nariño was not recognized until many years later as one of the greatest and most self-sacrificing of the early advocates of independence. See biography by Thomas Blossom (1967).

Naroda (nä'rədə) or **Narodnaya Gora** (närôd'nəyə gō'rə) [Rus.,=people's mountain], peak, c.6,180 ft (1,880 m) high, NE European USSR, in the N Urals. It is the highest peak of the Urals.

narodniki (närôd'nĭkē), Russian populists, adherents of an agrarian socialist movement active from the 1860s to the end of the 19th century. Influenced by the writings of Alexander Herzen, the *narodniki* attempted to adapt socialist doctrine to Russian conditions; they envisaged a society in which sovereignty would rest with small self-governing economic units resembling the traditional Russian village commune and held together in a loose voluntary confederation replacing the state. The *narodniki* first went to the villages in 1874 to spread their doctrine among the peasants, but they were rejected. In 1876 they formed a secret society, known as Land and Liberty, to promote a mass revolutionary uprising. Expelled from the countryside by the police, they soon became dominated by the movement's terroristic wing, the People's Will, formed in 1879, which undertook several political assassinations; in 1881 a member of the group assassinated Czar ALEXANDER II. Thereafter populism declined. In 1901 the Socialist Revolutionary party was founded as the heir to the *narodniki* movement.

Narragansett Bay, arm of the Atlantic Ocean, 30 mi (48 km) long and from 3 to 12 mi (4.8–19 km) wide, deeply indenting the state of Rhode Island. Its many inlets provided harbors that were advantageous to colonial trade and later to resort development. At the head of the bay is Providence; Newport is at the entrance, on Rhode Island. Conanicut Island and Prudence Island are also in the bay. The 1938 and 1954 hurricanes swept up the bay, inflicting heavy damage along the shores.

Narragansett Indians, North American Indians whose language belongs to the Algonquian branch of the Algonquian-Wakashan linguistic stock (see AMERICAN INDIAN LANGUAGES). In the early 17th cent. they occupied most of Rhode Island, from Narragansett Bay on the east to the Pawcatuck River on the west. The Narragansett escaped the great pestilence of 1617 that swept through S New England, and the remnants of tribes who had suffered joined them for protection, making the Narragansett a powerful tribe. In 1636, CANONICUS, the Narragansett chief, sold Roger WILLIAMS land on which to settle. Williams gained great influence over the Narragansett, inducing them to become the allies of the Massachusetts colonists in the Pequot War (1637). The Narragansett in 1674 numbered some 5,000. The next year witnessed the outbreak of King Philip's War, which destroyed Indian power in S New England. The Narragansett shared the common fate. Their fort near the site of Kingston, R.I., was attacked (1675) by a colonial force under Josiah Winslow, and in that engagement, known as the Swamp Fight, the Narragansett under Canonchet lost almost a thousand men. The survivors migrated to the north and to the west, and a few joined the Mahican and the Abnaki; but a number of them returned and settled among the Niantic Indians near Charlestown, R.I., the combined group taking the Narragansett name. Their numbers steadily declined, and by 1832 there were 80 left. The Narragansett were of the Eastern Woodlands culture.

Narrows, the, strait: see NEW YORK BAY, N.Y.

Narses (när'sēz), c.478–c.573, Roman official and general, one of the eunuchs of the palace. He assisted in the suppression of the Nika riot (532) by bribing the Blues of the Circus (see BLUES AND GREENS) to return their allegiance to JUSTINIAN I. In 538 he was sent to Italy to cooperate with BELISARIUS; their dissensions delayed the campaign, and he was recalled. After the recall of Belisarius, Narses returned to Italy and completed the conquest, defeating (552) TOTILA. He defeated (554) an army of Franks and Alemanni at Capua. He was subsequently appointed exarch of Italy; however, his administration was unpopular, and he was recalled.

narthex (när'thĕks), entrance feature peculiar to early Christian and Byzantine churches, although also found in some Romanesque churches, especially in France and Italy. Usually extending across the entire west front of the building, it was a vestibule for the penitents and catechumens who were not admitted to the church proper. The narthex was either enclosed within the building (often separated from the nave by a mere screen of columns) or consisted of an exterior colonnaded or arcaded portico. In the latter case it was sometimes merely a continuation of the ATRIUM, as in a number of Italian basilical churches, including the original basilica (4th cent.) of St. Peter's Church, Rome. The inner narthex was particularly characteristic of the monastic churches, where admission was restricted. In churches having both types of narthex, as in HAGIA SOPHIA, Constantinople (originally a Christian church), the outer one is termed exonarthex. With the growth of unrestricted entry into the churches, the narthex served no further ritual purpose after the 13th cent. The deeply recessed portals of Gothic cathedrals are derivatives of the narthex.

Naruszewicz, Adam Stanislaw, (ä'däm stänēs'läf närōōshĕ'vĕch), 1733–96, Polish historian. A Jesuit, he became, after the suppression of his order, bishop of Smolensk (1788) and of Lutsk (1790). At the court of Stanislaus II he held a position similar to poet laureate. Naruszewicz organized extensive historical research in the archives and wrote a history (7 vol., 1780–1824) of the Polish nation. See study by Neomisa Rutkowska (1941).

Narva (när'və), city (1969 est. pop. 53,000), NW European USSR, in Estonia, on the left bank of the Narva River. A leading textile center, it also has machinery plants, sawmills, flax and jute factories, fisheries, and food-processing industries. The city is also an important producer of electric power. Founded by the Danes in 1223, Narva passed to the Livonian Knights in 1346 and was a member of the Hanseatic League. In 1492, Ivan III of Russia built the fortress Ivangorod on the right bank of the Narva, facing the Hermann fortress of the knights. After the dissolution (1561) of the Livonian Order, the city was first seized by the Russians, then taken (1581) by the Swedes; it continued to be contested by the two nations. In 1700, Charles XII of Sweden, with inferior forces, resoundingly defeated Peter I of Russia at Narva in the first great battle of the Northern War (1700–1721). Peter, however, captured the city in 1704, and it remained part of Russia until 1919, when it was incorporated into newly independent Estonia. German forces occupied the city in World War II. In 1945 all Estonian territory E of the Narva River, including Ivangorod fortress, was ceded to the USSR. The city is dominated by two old fortresses, and it has retained a 14th-century Eastern Orthodox cathedral (originally Roman Catholic), and a 17th-century town hall and exchange buildings. The population consists mostly of Russians.

Narva, river, c.50 mi (80 km) long, rising in Lake Chudskoye, NW European USSR, and flowing northeast past the city of Narva into the Gulf of Finland. It forms the border between the Estonian and Russian republics. The falls of the river supply power to the textile industry of Narva.

Narváez, Pánfilo de (pän'fēlō thā närvä'ĕth), c.1470–1528, Spanish conquistador. After service in Jamaica, he aided Diego de VELÁZQUEZ in conquering Cuba and was sent (1520) to Mexico by Velázquez to force CORTÉS into submission. Narváez's force was defeated, and he was captured and imprisoned. Released in 1521, he returned to Spain, and Charles V commissioned him to conquer and settle Florida. With five vessels and 600 men he sailed from Sanlúcar in June, 1527, and, after storms and desertions had cost the expedition much in time and men, he reached Florida (probably near Tampa Bay) in April, 1528. Narváez sent his ships on toward Mexico and then led 300 men inland to Apalachee (near the present-day Tallahassee) in a futile search for gold. Disappointed and much harassed by Indians, the Spanish turned back to the coast. There they built several crude vessels in which they set out for Mexico, but all except CABEZA DE VACA and three companions were lost off the coast of Texas or after landing among hostile Indians.

Narváez, Ramón María (rämōn' märē'ä), 1800–1868, Spanish general and statesman. He distinguished himself fighting for ISABELLA II against the Carlists (1834–39). When ESPARTERO rose to power (1840), Narváez joined the partisans of MARIA CHRISTINA in exile. He returned in 1843 to take part in Espartero's overthrow and was created duque de Valencia in 1845. As leader of the moderate conservatives, Narváez held the premiership, with only brief interruptions, from 1844 to 1851 and had several short ministries later (1856–57, 1864–65, and 1866–68). His authoritarian policies helped to provoke the uprising that soon after his death caused the downfall of Queen Isabella II.

Narvik (när'vĭk), city (1970 pop. 13,181), Nordland co., N Norway, an ice-free port on the Ofotfjord opposite the Lofoten Islands. It was founded (1887) as the Atlantic port for the Kiruna and Gällivare iron mines in Sweden and was known as Victoriahavn until 1898. The city is now a tourist center. In World War II, Narvik fell to the Germans when they invaded Norway on April 9, 1940. To prevent the Germans from using Narvik as a shipping base for

Swedish iron ore, a British expeditionary force briefly occupied (May 28–June 9, 1940) the port.

narwhal (när'wəl), a small arctic WHALE, *Monodon monoceros.* The males of this species, and an occasional female, bear a single, tightly spiraled tusk that measures up to 9 ft (2.7 m) in length. This tusk is an overgrown upper central incisor tooth, generally the one on the left. Very rarely do both incisors grow out in this manner; the animal is otherwise toothless. The narwhal is short-headed and virtually snoutless. When mature, it is mottled gray in color. Like its close relative the BELUGA, it lacks a dorsal fin, but it does have a long, low dorsal hump. The narwhal may reach a length of 20 ft (6.1 m), excluding the horn. It is found in the Arctic and N Atlantic oceans, occasionally as far south as Britain; narwhals usually travel in groups of 15 to 20 animals. The diet of narwhals consists chiefly of cuttlefisn and cod. Mating occurs in the summer, and after a gestation of 14 months the female gives birth to a single blue-gray calf measuring up to 5 ft (1.5 m). The calves are weaned at six months. Formerly hunted for its tusk, which was believed to have magical properties, the narwhal is now hunted primarily for oil. It is classified in the phylum CHORDATA, subphylum Vertebrata, class Mammalia, order Cetacea, family Monodontidae.

Naryn (nərĭn'), river, c.450 mi (720 km) long, rising in several branches in the Tien Shan mountain system, SW Kirghizia and SE Uzbekistan, Central Asian USSR. It flows generally W through the Fergana Valley where it joins with the Kara Darya to form the Syr Darya. Its lower course is used for irrigating a cotton-growing area. The city of **Naryn** (1970 est. pop. 21,000), SW Kirghizia, on the upper course of the river, at an altitude of 6,610 ft (2,015 m), is the center of a wheat-growing and sheep-grazing district.

Nasby, Petroleum V., pseud. of **David Ross Locke,** 1833–88, American journalist and satirist, b. Vestal, N.Y. Locke was editor of the Findlay, Ohio, *Jeffersonian* when he first became prominent by publishing (1861) in it the Nasby letters. The writer, Petroleum Vesuvius Nasby, was ostensibly an ignorant, violently prejudiced, proslavery sympathizer, and the letters, which caught the fancy of readers from Lincoln down, were of aid to the Union cause in the Civil War. The letters soon appeared in the Toledo *Blade,* of which Locke became editor and part owner in 1865. He subsequently wrote Nasby letters as satiric propaganda for other causes. The Nasby letters were collected in various volumes including *Swingen Round the Circle* (1866) and *The Nasby Letters* (1893). See biographies by Cyril Clemens (1936) and J. M. Harrison (1969).

Nasca: see NAZCA.

Nascimento, Edson Arantes do: see PELÉ.

Naseby (nāz'bē), village, Northamptonshire, central England, near Northampton. Nearby, on June 14, 1645, the parliamentarians under Sir Thomas Fairfax of Cameron and Oliver Cromwell defeated the royalists under Charles I and Prince Rupert in a decisive battle of the ENGLISH CIVIL WAR.

Nash, Beau (Richard Nash), 1674–1761, Englishman of fashion. As master of ceremonies at Bath he was the recognized leader of society. He maintained his luxurious mode of living by gambling until gaming was forbidden in 1745. He died a poor pensioner.

Nash, John, 1752–1835, English architect; pupil of Sir Robert Taylor. After enjoying an extensive practice in Wales, he began to work c.1792 in London. His capacities were greatest in town planning, and he is chiefly known for his boldly planned development of the Marylebone region of London. His scheme, as put into execution in 1818, comprehended Regent St., with its Quadrant, and Regent's Park, with its terraces and surrounding streets of formally designed town houses. Nash also designed the Haymarket theater and remodeled Buckingham Palace. He initiated the neoclassic Regency style and was responsible for the extensive use of stucco for the facades of city buildings. See studies by Sir John Summerson (2d ed. 1950) and Terence Davis (new ed. 1968, repr. 1973).

Nash, John Henry, 1871–1947, American printer and bibliophile, b. Woodbridge, Canada. After learning the printer's trade, he emigrated to the United States in 1894. He eventually became professor of typography at the Univ. of Oregon. Nash published finely-crafted editions of several works, including *The Divine Comedy* (1929), Benjamin Franklin's *Autobiography,* and the Vulgate (1932). He was famous for his collection of books with handmade bindings.

Nash, Ogden, 1902–1971, American poet, b. Rye, N.Y., studied at Harvard. He was popular for a wide assortment of immensely quotable verses, ranging from urbane satire to absurdity in their subject and rhyme. He also wrote plays and children's books. His collections include *Hard Lines* (1931), *I'm a Stranger Here Myself* (1938), *Selected Verse* (1946), *Versus* (1949), *The Private Dining Room* (1953), *You Can't Get There from Here* (1957), *Verses From 1929 On* (1959), *Everyone But Thee and Me* (1962), and *Bed Riddance* (1970).

Nash, Paul, 1889–1946, English painter and wood engraver. He studied at the Slade School of Art, London. Nash worked at the front as official artist in both World Wars. He helped to form Unit One, an English avant-garde group of artists and architects. Nash's paintings of the English landscape were imbued with a visionary and mystical atmosphere. His writings were published in one volume in 1949.

Nashe or **Nash, Thomas** (both: năsh), 1567–1601, English satirist. Very little is known of his life. Although his first publications appeared in 1589, it was not until *Pierce Penniless His Supplication to the Devil* (1592), a bitter satire on contemporary society, that his natural and vigorous style was fully developed. His ardent anti-Puritanism involved him in the Martin MARPRELATE CONTROVERSY, resulting in a scurrilous pamphlet battle with Richard and Gabriel Harvey in which Nashe produced some of his liveliest writing. *The Unfortunate Traveler* (1594), his best-known work, was a forerunner of the picaresque novel of adventure. His plays include a satirical masque, *Summer's Last Will and Testament* (1592); and a lost comedy written with Ben Jonson, *The Isle of Dogs* (1597), which caused the imprisonment of several persons, including Jonson himself, for "seditious and slanderous" language. See his works edited by R. B. McKerrow (5 vol., 1904–10); selected writings ed. by S. Wells (1964); study by G. R. Hibbard (1962).

Nashoba (năshō'bə), former community, SW Tenn., on the Wolf River near Memphis. It was founded by Frances Wright and others as a place in which Negro slaves, who were purchased especially for the purpose, might be educated for freedom. Influenced by the example of Robert Owen's cooperative colony at New Harmony, Ind., Frances Wright bought the land in 1825. She and the other trustees were impractical administrators, however, and the venture was unsuccessful from the beginning. The difficulties of pioneering were increased by the prevalence of swamp fever and by poor management during her frequent absences. The community was denounced as a center of free love and miscegenation and by 1829 was practically deserted by its white members. The following year the slaves were transported to Haiti.

Nashua (năsh'o͞oə), city (1970 pop. 55,820), seat of Hillsborough co., S N.H., on the Merrimack and Nashua rivers near the Mass. line; settled c.1655, inc. as a city 1853. Because of the availability of water power, Nashua developed (early 19th cent.) as a textile mill town. Its chief manufactures include electronic equipment, paper, shoes and leather, and machinery. It is the seat of Rivier College, New England Aeronautical Institute, a state vocational and technical college, and a junior college. The Federal Aviation Agency has a large traffic control center there.

Nashville, city (1970 pop. 447,877), state capital, coextensive with Davidson co., central Tenn., on the Cumberland River, in a fertile farm area; inc. as a city 1806, merged with Davidson co. 1963. It is a port of entry and an important commercial and industrial center. The city has railroad shops and factories making a great variety of manufactures including automobile glass, wearing apparel, footwear, food products, tires, and commercial, industrial, and agricultural chemicals. Nashville is noted for its music industry; it is a major recording center, especially for country music. It also has many publishing houses producing religious materials, school annuals, magazines, and telephone directories. Two large insurance companies have their headquarters in Nashville. The city was founded (1779) by a group of pioneers under James Robertson (who is buried there). Fort Nashborough was built on the banks of the river, and the next year 60 families arrived to settle the area. As the northern terminus of the Natchez Trace, the settlement developed early as a cotton center and river port and later as a railroad hub. It became permanent capital of the state in 1843. After the fall of FORT DONELSON in Feb., 1862, Nashville was abandoned to Union troops under D. C. Buell and became an important Union base for the remainder of the Civil War. Union Gen. G. H. Thomas won a decisive victory (Dec. 15–16, 1864) over J. B. Hood there. Sometimes called the "Athens of the South," Nashville has many buildings of classical design (including a replica of the Parthenon, built in 1897), and is a noted educational center. It is the seat of Vanderbilt Univ., Fisk Univ., Tennessee State Univ., the Univ. of Tennessee at Nashville, Meharry Medical College School of Medicine, George Peabody College for Teachers, Scarritt College for Christian Workers, David Lipscomb College, Belmont College, Free Will Baptist Bible College, a state technical institute, a junior college, and a state school for the blind. Among the points of interest are the capitol (designed by William Strickland; completed 1855), with the tomb of James K. Polk; the war memorial building, with museums; the country music hall of fame and museum; "Opryland, U.S.A." (a family entertainment complex); a replica of Fort Nashborough; and several old churches and antebellum homes. Nearby is the Hermitage, home of Andrew Jackson.

Nasik (nä'sĭk), town (1971 pop. 176,187), Maharashtra state, W central India. It is a center of brassware manufacture and cattle and poultry breeding. The ancient town of Panchavati, it is holy as the site of the Ramayana exile of the Hindu god Rama and Sita, his wife. Nasik is a district administrative headquarters. The Indian Currency Note Press and Military and Police Training College are there. Nearby are ancient Jain and Buddhist caves.

Nasir ad-Din (nä'sər äd-dēn), 1831?–1896, shah of Persia (1848–96). He and his able vizier, Mirza Taqi Khan, were responsible for shaking Persia from a long period of inertia. He traveled extensively in Europe and brought back many Western ideas, some of which he applied to the reorganization of the government. Nasir ad-Din Shah had ambitions to reclaim the old Persian territories to the east and made an effort to wrest Herat from Afghanistan, but British intervention put an end to his hopes and forced Persia to recognize the claim of Afghanistan. Nasir ad-Din Shah granted numerous concessions to the British, including the Reuter concession in 1872 and the Imperial Bank of Persia in 1889. BABISM arose during his reign. He wrote travel diaries, and his simple and pithy style influenced later Persian literature. In later years, he resisted demands for reforms. He was assassinated by one of his subjects and was succeeded by Muzaffar ad-Din.

Nasiriya: see AN NASIRIYAH, Iraq.

Naskapi Indians: see MONTAGNAIS AND NASKAPI INDIANS.

Nasmyth, Alexander (nā'smĭth), 1758–1840, Scottish landscape and portrait painter. His *Stirling Castle* (National Gall., London) is a good example of his simple, picturesque Scottish scenes. His portrait of Robert Burns is in the National Gallery of Edinburgh. His son and pupil, **Patrick Nasmyth,** 1787–1831, was a celebrated landscapist. His *At Penshurst, Kent* is in the Metropolitan Museum.

Nasmyth, Patrick: see NASMYTH, ALEXANDER.

Nasoreans: see MANDAEANS.

Nass (năs), river, 236 mi (380 km) long, rising in the Coast Mts., W British Columbia, Canada, and flowing SW to Portland Inlet of the Pacific Ocean. It is navigable for 25 mi (40 km) and has valuable salmon fisheries.

Nassau (nä'sou), former duchy, central West Germany, situated N and E of the Main and Rhine rivers. It is now mostly included in the state of Hesse, and partly in the state of Rhineland-Palatinate. Wiesbaden was the capital; other towns included the mineral spas of Bad Homburg, Bad Schwalbach, and Schlangenbad in the beautiful Taunus hills and Bad Ems on the Lahn River. The region takes its name from the small town of Nassau, on the Lahn E of Ems, where the original castle of the house of Nassau was built in the early 12th cent. by a count of Laurenburg. His descendants took the title count of Nassau. In 1255 the dynasty split into two main lines. The ruling line was called the Walramian line for Count Walram II; his younger brother, Otto, founded the Ottonian line. In 1806, Nassau, which had received some territorial additions, joined the Confederation of the Rhine and was raised to a duchy. In 1816 the territories belonging to the various branches of the Walramian line were united by Duke William (1816–39). His successor, Adolf, sided against Prussia in the Austro-Prussian War (1866) and as a result lost his duchy to Prussia. Nassau was then united with the former Electoral Hesse to form the Prussian province of Hesse-Nassau. Duke Adolf of Nassau, however, succeeded in 1890 to the grand duchy of Luxembourg, where his descendants continue to rule. The Ottonian line of Nassau acquired

(15th cent.) the lordship of Breda and settled in the Netherlands. It came into European prominence in the 16th cent. with William the Silent, who inherited the principality of Orange in S France and became stadtholder of the Netherlands. His sons, Maurice of Nassau and Frederick Henry, succeeded him as princes of Orange and as stadtholders; these titles then passed to Frederick Henry's son, William II of Orange, and to William's son William III, who also became king of England. William III died (1702) without direct heirs, and the principality of Orange (which had become purely titular) passed to John William Friso, of the collateral branch of Nassau-Dietz. His son, Prince William IV, became (1748) hereditary stadtholder of the Netherlands, and from him all subsequent rulers of the Netherlands (except Louis Bonaparte) are descended in direct line. The Dutch line of the Nassau family is known as the house of Orange.

Nassau (nă'sô), city (1970 pop. 101,503), capital of the BAHAMA ISLANDS. A port on New Providence island, it has a large and beautiful harbor and is the commercial and social center of the islands. Its warm, healthful climate and colorful atmosphere have made it a favorite winter resort. Formerly called Charles Towne, it was renamed Nassau in 1695. In the 18th cent. it was a rendezvous for pirates, among them Blackbeard. Three forts, Nassau (1697), Charlotte (1787-94), and Fincastle (1793), were built to ward off the numerous Spanish invasions. American revolutionists in 1776 captured and held it a short time.

Nassau, Fort: see FORT NASSAU.

Nasser, Gamal Abdal (gəmäl' ăb'dəl nä'sər), 1918-70, Egyptian army officer and political leader, first president of the republic of Egypt (1956-70). A revolutionary since youth, he was wounded by the police and expelled (1935) from secondary school in Cairo for leading an anti-British student demonstration. He attended (1937) law school and graduated from the Royal Military Academy in 1938. In 1942 he founded the secret Society of Free Officers, which fought against political corruption and foreign domination of Egypt. A major in the first Arab-Israeli war (1948), he was wounded in action. In July, 1952, he led the army coup that deposed King Farouk; Gen. Muhammad Naguib was the nominal head of the government, but Nasser held power through his control of the Revolutionary Command Committee. In 1954, following an attempt on Nasser's life, he arrested Naguib and became premier of Egypt. In 1956 he was, unopposed, elected president of the republic of Egypt. His nationalization of the Suez Canal precipitated (1956) a short-lived, abortive Anglo-French invasion. When Egypt and Syria merged (1958-61) to form the United Arab Republic, Nasser served as its president. An opponent of monarchal governments in the Middle East, he sent troops to assist (1962-67) Yemenite revolutionaries in their civil war with Saudi Arabian-backed royalists. In 1967 he precipitated war with Israel by dissolving UN peacekeeping forces in the Sinai and blockading the Israeli port of Elat. He resigned from office following Egypt's disastrous defeat, but massive demonstrations of support forced him to return to office immediately. During his period of rule, Nasser instituted a program of land reform and economic and social development, known as Arab socialism; the completion (1970) of the Aswan Dam was the crowning achievement of his regime. More than for his material accomplishments, however, Nasser achieved fame for leading the reestablishment of Arab national pride, seriously wounded by many decades of Western domination. In foreign affairs, he originally assumed a neutralist position, seeking support from both the East and the West to bolster his position in the Middle East. After his nation's military defeat in 1967, however, Nasser became increasingly dependent on the Soviet Union for military and economic aid. A pan-Arabist and advocate of Third-World unity, Nasser was probably the most important Arab leader of the 20th cent. See biographies by Wilton Wynn (1959), Joachim Josten (1960, repr. 1974), and Robert St. John (1960).

Nasser, Lake, c.1,550 sq mi (4,010 sq km), on the Nile River, SE Egypt and N Sudan. It extends c.350 mi (560 km) behind Aswan High Dam to the Second Cataract at Wadi Halfa (now submerged). The lake's rising waters forced more than 80,000 people to relocate and submerged many historic sites.

Nast, Thomas, 1840-1902, American caricaturist, illustrator, and painter, b. Landau, Germany. He was brought to the United States in 1846. He began his career as a draftsman for *Frank Leslie's Illustrated Newspaper* and *Harper's Weekly.* He was sent to England by the *New York Illustrated News,* served (1860) as artist correspondent in Garibaldi's campaign, contributing sketches to English, French, and American papers, and attracted wide attention with his cartoons of the Civil War, published in *Harper's Weekly.* He is best known for his clever and forceful political and personal cartoons, which were instrumental in breaking the corrupt Tweed Ring in New York City. It was Nast who created the tiger, the elephant, and the donkey as political symbols of Tammany Hall, the Republican party, and the Democratic party. Nast was also an illustrator of note and a painter in oil. He died at Guayaquil, Ecuador, where he was American consul general. See study by M. Keller (1968).

nastic movement, in botany, the movement of plant parts in response either to certain external stimuli or to internal growth stimuli. Nastic movements, which are generally slow, can be observed by time-lapse photography. Such movements as those of developing buds, which swell, open up, and eventually fall off, are examples of internally directed, or autonomic, nastic movements. The opening and closing movements of many flowers, and the responses of leaves to changes of temperature and light, are externally directed, or paratonic, nastic movements. Specialized plants, such as the insectivorous sundew, move in response to the touch and chemical stimuli of captured insects. Nastic movements are responses to stimuli that uniformly envelop the plant or else elicit a uniform response regardless of the direction they come from, whereas TROPISMS are movements in response to stimuli coming from one direction; geotropism, for example, is the response to gravity. The distinction between the two is sometimes unclear.

nasturtium (năstûr'shəm), any plant of the genus *Tropaeolum,* tropical American herbs (usually climbing) native to mountainous areas of South and Central America. Several species are cultivated in the United States as ornamentals for their yellow or red flowers, e.g., the common nasturtiums *(T. majus* and *T. minus)* and the canary-bird flower *(T. peregrinum).* These species have been hybridized. The plants are sometimes used for food, i.e., the tuberous roots, the seeds (pickled as capers), and the tart flowers and leaves (used in salads). Properly, *Nasturtium* is the botanical name for the water cresses, an unrelated genus of the family Cruciferae (MUSTARD family). Nasturtiums are classified in the division MAGNOLIOPHYTA, class Magnoliopsida, order Geraniales, family Tropaeolaceae.

Natal (nətăl'), province (1970 pop. 4,245,675), 33,578 sq mi (86,967 sq km), E South Africa, on the Indian Ocean. The capital is PIETERMARITZBURG; the largest city is DURBAN. Natal is bounded in the N by Mozambique and Swaziland and in the W by the Orange Free State and Lesotho. The province rises from a narrow (except in the north) coastal belt to an inland region fringed in the W by the Drakensberg Range, whose highest point in Natal is c.11,200 ft (3,410 m). The Tugela River flows W to E across central Natal. Sugar refining is the main industry. Sheep, cattle, citrus fruits, maize, sorghum, cotton, bananas, and pineapples are also raised. Industries, located mainly in and around Durban, include, besides sugar refineries, textile, clothing, rubber, fertilizer, paper, and food-processing plants, tanneries, and oil refineries. Natal produces considerable coal (especially coking coal) and timber. The province has a good rail network; Durban is one of South Africa's major ports. The main institutions of higher education are the Univ. of Natal (Durban and Pietermaritzburg) and the Univ. of Durban. Natal National Park in the Drakensberg Range includes falls (c.2,800 ft/850 m) of the Tugela River. In the early 19th cent. Natal was inhabited primarily by Bantu-speaking Zulu people. In the 1820s and 30s the British acquired much of Natal from the Zulu chiefs CHAKA and Dingane. BOER farmers arrived (see TREK) in 1837 and, after battles with the Zulu (notably the Boer victory over Dingane at Blood River in 1838), established (1838-39) a republic. In 1843, Britain annexed Natal to Cape Colony, and a Boer exodus followed. In 1856, Natal became a separate colony. Sugarcane cultivation began c.1860, and many Indians (mostly indentured laborers) came to work in the sugar industry. Many Indians remained in Natal as free men after their term of indenture expired; and by 1900 they outnumbered whites. In 1893, Natal was given internal self-government, and in 1910 it became a founding province of the Union of South Africa.

Natal (nətäl'), city (1970 pop. 264,567), capital of Rio Grande do Norte state, NE Brazil, just above the mouth of the Potengi River. Its port is important in the handling of coastal shipping and in the export of the state's tungsten. There is also some light industry in the city. Beautifully situated among white, palm-studded beaches, Natal is a modern city that has retained its colonial flavor. Natal [Port.,=Nativity] was founded on Christmas Day, 1599. It was occupied by the Dutch from 1633 to 1654 and in 1817 was briefly the seat of a republican government until it was suppressed by imperial authorities. It grew rapidly during World War II, when an airport was built for flights to Africa. Natal has several institutions of higher learning.

Natanya: see NETANYA, Israel.

Natashkwan (năt"ăshkwŏn', nətăsh'kwən), river, 241 mi (388 km) long, rising in S Labrador, Canada, and flowing S across E Que. to the Gulf of St. Lawrence. It is noted for trout and salmon fishing. Iron-bearing sands found along its banks are mined.

Natchez (năch'ĭz), city (1970 pop. 19,704), seat of Adams co., SW Miss., on bluffs above the Mississippi River; settled 1716, inc. 1803. It is the trade, shipping, and processing center for a cotton, livestock, and timber area where oil and natural gas are also found. One of the oldest towns on the Mississippi River, Natchez was founded in 1716 when Bienville established Fort Rosalie there, but Natchez Indians annihilated the garrison in 1729. The area passed to England (1763), to Spain (1779), and to the United States (1798). Natchez was capital of the Mississippi Territory from 1798 to 1802. Its strategic location at the junction of the Mississippi and the southern terminus of the Natchez Trace brought prosperity to the area. Natchez became a great river port and cultural center of the planter aristocracy before the Civil War. It served as state capital from 1817 to 1821. In the Civil War it was taken by Federal forces in 1863. The city has preserved its antebellum charm. Many of its historic homes are visited during the annual festival period in March and April. There is a junior college in Natchez. See R. G. Pishel, *Natchez: Museum City of the Old South* (rev. ed. 1959); William Johnson, *Natchez: The Ante-Bellum Diary of a Free Negro* (2 vol., 1951; repr. 1968).

Natchez Indians, North American Indians of the Hokan-Siouan linguistic stock (see AMERICAN INDIAN LANGUAGES). In the 17th cent. they lived in SW Mississippi near the present-day city of Natchez and numbered some 6,000. The Natchez were typical of the southeastern part of the Eastern Woodlands cultural area—sedentary, agricultural people, who had an elaborate form of sun worship. Their chief, ruler of a rigid class society, held absolute sway over the lives and property of his subjects. The Natchez were first visited by the French in 1682, and in 1716 and 1722 warfare broke out between the Natchez and the French. In 1729 the Natchez, angered at French encroachments, massacred the French at Fort Rosalie. The French, aided by the Choctaw, retaliated by attacking the Natchez villages and scattering the inhabitants. One small group settled near their former home, and a second crossed the Mississippi River into Louisiana; there they were again attacked (1731) by the French, who killed or captured many of them. Some 450 Natchez captives were sold into slavery. A third group, the largest, joined the Chickasaw. This group numbered some 700 in 1735. Other Natchez Indians settled with the Cherokee and the Creek. In the late 1960s a few Natchez still lived in Oklahoma. See R. S. Neitzel, *Archeology of the Fatherland Site* (1965).

Natchez Trace, road, from Natchez, Miss., to Nashville, Tenn., of great commercial and military importance from the 1780s to the 1830s. It grew from a series of Indian trails used in the 18th cent. by the French, English, and Spanish successively. At first traveled only N from Natchez to Nashville, because the American frontiersman could float his goods south to New Orleans by flatboat, it came to be used in both directions with U.S. expansion into the Old Southwest. It was made a post road in 1800 and was improved by the army. Andrew Jackson marched over the Trace to New Orleans in the War of 1812 and later used it in his Indian campaigns. With the coming of steamboat transportation, it passed into decline. The Natchez Trace Parkway memorializes and generally follows the old Natchez Trace. Meriwether Lewis and Ackia Battleground national monuments were disestablished and incorporated into Natchez Trace Parkway in 1961 (see NATIONAL PARKS AND MONUMENTS, table).

Natchitoches (năk'ĭtŏsh), city (1970 pop. 15,974), seat of Natchitoches parish, NW La.; inc. 1819. Its industry is centered on the production, processing, and shipping of farm products, chiefly cotton. The first permanent settlement in the Louisiana Purchase

Territory, Natchitoches was founded c.1714 as a French military and trading post. It was the dividing line between French and Spanish territory, and a royal highway ran from there to Mexico City. It was an important port on the Red River until the river changed its course in the early 1800s (the riverbed has since filled and is now known as Cane River Lake). The city was a center of operation during the Mexican War. It was occupied by the Union army during the Civil War. An historical tour of old homes and plantations every October attracts tourists. Northwestern State Univ. of Louisiana and a U.S. fish hatchery are there.

Nathan (nā'thən). **1** Prophet in the time of David and Solomon. With his parable of the ewe lamb he denounced David for his abduction of Bath-sheba. Later his advice saved the kingdom for Solomon. His account of the lives of David and Solomon was probably a main source for the Book of Samuel. 2 Sam. 7; 12; 1 Kings 1; 1 Chron. 29.29; 2 Chron. 9.29. **2** Son of David. 1 Chron. 3.5; 14.4; Luke 3.31. **3** Father of one of David's guard. 2 Sam. 23.36. **4** Brother of one of David's men. 1 Chron. 11.38. **5** Descendant of Jerahmeel. 1 Chron. 2.36. **6** Companion of Ezra. Ezra 8.16. **7** One who had a foreign wife. Ezra 10.39.

Nathan, George Jean, 1882–1958, American editor and drama critic, b. Fort Wayne, Ind. A member of the New York *Herald* staff, he departed to join H. L. Mencken in editing *Smart Set* (1914–23), which they made into a guide for the young American intellectual. In 1924 they founded the *American Mercury,* a magazine that fostered the most rebellious and lively in current literature and drama; for a decade the magazine was the arbiter of American literary taste. Nathan was himself primarily a critic of the drama, famous for the erudition and cynicism of his reviews. He was an early champion of several important playwrights, notably Eugene O'Neill. He was a founder and an editor (1932–35) of the *American Spectator,* and after 1943 he wrote a syndicated column for the New York *Journal-American.* His criticism appeared in many volumes: *Mr. George Jean Nathan Presents* (1917); *The Critic and the Drama* (1922); *The Testament of a Critic* (1931); *Since Ibsen* (1933); *The World of George Jean Nathan,* ed. by Charles Angoff (1952); and *The Magic Mirror,* edited by T. G. Curtiss (1960). He also set forth his philosophy of criticism in *Autobiography of an Attitude* (1925). See study by Constance Frick (1943, repr. 1971).

Nathanael (nəthăn'ēəl), disciple mentioned only in St. John's Gospel and plausibly identified with St. BARTHOLOMEW. John 1.45–51; 21.2.

Nathania: see NETANYA, Israel.

Nathan-melech (nā'thăn-mē'lĕk), chamberlain of Josiah. 2 Kings 23.11.

Natick (nā'tĭk), town (1970 pop. 31,057), Middlesex co., E Mass., a residential and industrial suburb of Boston, on Lake Cochituate; founded 1651 as a "praying Indian" village by John Eliot, settled by whites 1718, inc. 1781. Manufactures include shoes, electronic components, and clothing.

Nation, Carry Moore, 1846–1911, American temperance advocate, b. Garrard co., Ky. During her childhood her family moved a great deal, finally settling at Belton, Mo., where she married (1867) Charles Gloyd, a physician. She soon abandoned Gloyd when he became a hopeless alcoholic, and in 1877 she married David Nation, an itinerant minister and lawyer. A proponent of temperance for many years and convinced of her divine appointment to destroy the saloon, Carry Nation gained fame in 1900 while living in Kansas when she began to supplement public prayers and denunciation with the personal destruction of saloon liquor and property. (Although Kansas was a dry state at this time and saloons were illegal, there was little enforcement of prohibition laws.) From Kansas she traveled to New York and soon became a national figure for the temperance cause. She presented a formidable obstacle to anyone attempting to stop her; her size (6 ft, 175 lb) and her use of the hatchet to smash saloons became legendary. Nevertheless, she was often attacked and beaten badly and was arrested 30 times in her life. Because of her unorthodox tactics, most temperance organizations were hesitant to support her. She did, however, focus public attention on the cause of prohibition and helped to create a public mood favorable to the passage of the Eighteenth Amendment. Besides her temperance activities, she was also a forceful advocate of woman suffrage, although she received little support from suffrage organizations. See her autobiography, *The Use and Need of the Life of Carry Nation* (1904), and biographies by Herbert Asbury (1929), Carleton Beals (1962), and Robert L. Taylor (1966).

National Academy of Sciences, a private organization of leading American scientists and engineers devoted to the furtherance of science and its use for the general welfare. The Academy was founded in 1863; there are presently about 1,000 members. Members are elected in recognition of their distinguished and continuing achievements in original research. The Academy acts as an official adviser to the Federal government on matters of science and technology. Separate sections of the Academy represent all of the physical and biological sciences and many of the social sciences.

National Accelerator Laboratory (NAL), physical science research center located near Batavia, Ill. Construction, which started in Dec., 1968, was largely finished by 1973. Working under a contract with the U.S. Atomic Energy Commission, the Universities Research Association operates the laboratory. The Association is a corporation composed of over 50 major research-oriented universities. Work at the laboratory is devoted to the study of elementary particles, principally through the use of a particle accelerator called a proton synchrotron that is the world's largest basic scientific research instrument. Having the shape of a circular ring, it is 4 mi (6.5 km) in circumference. In it protons have been accelerated up to energies of 400 billion electron volts.

National Aeronautics and Space Administration (NASA), civilian agency of the U.S. Federal government with the mission of conducting research and developing operational programs in the areas of SPACE EXPLORATION, artificial satellites (see SATELLITE, ARTIFICIAL), and rocketry. NASA came into existence on Oct. 1, 1958, superseding the National Advisory Committee on Aeronautics (NACA), an agency that had been oriented primarily toward laboratory research. The emphasis at NASA was to be on the implementation of operational programs. While the NACA budget never exceeded $5 million and its staff never exceeded 500, the NASA annual budget eventually reached $5 billion. In 1966, NASA had a staff of 34,000, with 400,000 contract employees working directly on agency programs. The creation of NASA had been spurred by American unpreparedness at the time the Soviet Union launched (Oct. 4, 1957) the first artificial satellite (Sputnik). NASA took over the Langley, Ames, and Lewis Research Centers from NACA. Soon after its creation, NASA acquired from the U.S. army the Jet Propulsion Laboratory operated by the California Institute of Technology. Later, the Army Ballistic Missile Arsenal at Huntsville, Ala., was placed under NASA control The best-known NASA facilities are the Lyndon B. Johnson Space Center near Houston, Tex., where the Apollo and other manned flights were coordinated, and Cape Canaveral (formerly Cape Kennedy), where the launches actually took place. The construction of spacecraft and support equipment was fulfilled by a large number of contractors and subcontractors, including many of the giants of U.S. industry. The total cost of the Apollo project was $20 billion, very close to the original estimate. At the conclusion of the Apollo program, Federal funds for space exploration declined somewhat, but support still continues at a high level. See Richard Hirsch and J. J. Trento, *The National Aeronautics and Space Administration* (1973).

National Archives, official depository for records of the U.S. Federal government, established in 1934 by act of the Congress. Although displeasure concerning the method of keeping national records was voiced in Congress as early as 1810, the United States continued to entrust the records to the various agencies that had accumulated them. That practice resulted in much loss, confusion, deterioration, and destruction of documents. It was not until 1926 that Congress provided for the construction of a national archives building where Federal government records could be stored, assembled, and preserved. The congressional act of 1934 organized the National Archives to be administered by the archivist of the United States. Aided and advised by the National Archives Council, the archivist was charged with accepting and preserving the records of the three branches of the Federal government. The building to house them was completed in 1935. The National Archives has proved invaluable in facilitating the research of scholars, particularly in the field of American history. See Monro MacCloskey, *Our National Attic* (1968); H. G. Jones, *The Records of a Nation* (1969).

national assembly, name of a number of past and present constituent or legislative bodies. In France, under the constitutions of the Fourth and Fifth republics, the lower house of parliament has been called the national assembly. Usually, however, the name *national assembly* has been applied to provisional bodies. Often in times of crisis, when the old order dissolves through decay, war, or revolution, representatives of the people meet to work out a new order. Such was the case in the French Revolution, when members of the STATES-GENERAL proclaimed themselves (1789) a national assembly. The FEDERAL CONSTITUTIONAL CONVENTION of 1787 and the FRANKFURT PARLIAMENT of 1848–49 were national assemblies. At the end of the Franco-Prussian War of 1870–71, after the downfall of Napoleon III, France again elected a national assembly, which drew up the basic constitutional laws for the Third Republic. Under the Third Republic the name *national assembly* applied to joint sessions of the senate and the chamber of deputies. National assemblies framed the republican Weimar constitution of Germany in 1919 and the Bonn constitution for West Germany in 1948–49. For a list of some of the chief legislative bodies of the world, see LEGISLATURE.

National Association for the Advancement of Colored People (NAACP), organization composed mainly of American blacks, but with many white members, whose goal is the end of racial discrimination and segregation. The association was formed as the direct result of the lynching (1908) of two blacks in Springfield, Ill. The incident produced a wide response by white Northerners to a call by Mary W. Ovington, a white woman, for a conference to discuss ways of achieving political and social equality for blacks. This conference led to the formation (May, 1910) of the NAACP, headed by eight prominent Americans, seven white and one, William E. B. DU BOIS, black. The selection of Du Bois was significant, for he was a black who had rejected the policy of gradualism advocated by Booker T. WASHINGTON and demanded immediate equality for blacks. He became the editor of the association's periodical *The Crisis,* which reported progress or the lack of it in race relations around the world. The new organization grew so rapidly that by 1915 it was able to organize a partially successful boycott of the motion picture *The Birth of a Nation,* which portrayed blacks of the Reconstruction era in what was considered a distorted light. Most of the NAACP's early efforts were directed against LYNCHING. In this area it could claim considerable success. In 1911 there were 71 lynchings in the United States, with a black person the victim 63 times; by the 1950s so effective had NAACP action been that lynching virtually disappeared in the United States. Since its beginning, and with increased emphasis in the years since World War II, the NAACP has advocated nonviolent protests against discrimination and has disapproved of extremist black groups, many of which criticize the organization as passive. With a 1972 membership of 450,000 in 1,730 local branches, the association remains the most influential civil rights organization in the United States. The NAACP Legal Defense and Education Fund, an independent legal aid group, argues in court on behalf of the NAACP and other civil rights groups. Along with the NAACP, it was instrumental in helping to bring about the Supreme Court's ruling (1954) against segregated public education, in the landmark *Brown* vs. *Board of Education of Topeka* case. See R. L. Jack, *A History of the National Association for the Advancement of Colored People* (1943); Langston Hughes, *Fight for Freedom* (1962); B. J. Ross, *J. E. Spingarn and the Rise of the NAACP, 1911–1939* (1972).

national bank, in the United States, financial institution of a class authorized by Congress in acts of 1863 and 1864. The acts were intended to provide a way of marketing the large bond issues made necessary by the Civil War and to give circulation to a paper currency more trustworthy than the notes of state banks had proved to be. The act of 1864 authorized the formation of private banking corporations that were to invest a large part of their capital in bonds of the United States and that might then issue their notes as currency. The amount of the notes was not to exceed 90% of either the face value or the par value of the bonds, depending on which of the two was smaller. Subsequent acts modified the act of 1864 in various details, and the plan was changed fundamentally by the Federal Reserve Act of Dec. 23, 1913, which provided for the gradual substitution of Federal reserve notes and Federal reserve bank notes for national bank notes. The Federal Reserve Act also required all national banks to become members of the FEDERAL RESERVE SYSTEM. See bibliography under BANKING.

National Bureau of Standards, governmental agency within the U.S. Dept. of Commerce with the mission of strengthening and advancing the application of science and technology in the national interest and for public benefit. The Bureau was established by act of Congress on March 3, 1901; presently its headquarters are at Gaithersburg, Md., with additional facilities located at Boulder, Colo. The Bureau conducts research to provide a basis for the nation's physical measurement system; scientific and technological services for industry and government; a technical basis for equity in trade; and services to promote public safety. The results of this research are made available to potential users by an extensive publications program. Within the Bureau, the Institute for Materials Research investigates the properties of materials needed by industry, commerce, educational institutions, and government. The Institute for Applied Technology facilitates the use of available technology while also promoting innovation; of particular importance are the programs concerned with building codes and fire prevention. The Institute for Computer Sciences and Technology aids other governmental agencies in selection, acquisition, and effective use of automatic data-processing equipment. The Boulder installation comprises many divisions, among them: basic standards, time and frequency standards, cryogenics, electronics, and laboratory astrophysics. See D. M. Bates, W. H. Donnelly, and C. S. Sheldon, *National Bureau of Standards* (1971).

National Capital Parks: see NATIONAL PARKS AND MONUMENTS (table).

National City, city (1970 pop. 43,184), San Diego co., S Calif., on San Diego Bay; inc. 1887. Citrus fruits and vegetables are packed, and there are defense-related industries. The city also serves as the headquarters of the Pacific Reserve Fleet.

National Council of the Churches of Christ in the United States of America, cooperative agency of some 33 Protestant and Orthodox Eastern denominations, formed in 1950. Not a governing body, it promotes, through a number of activities, general spiritual welfare and interchurch cooperation. It has three principal divisions: Christian Life and Mission, Christian Education, and Overseas Ministries. There are also several commissions and offices. The agency has no authority over the internal activities of its constituent bodies, whose total membership exceeds 40 million. The council is the chief instrument of the ECUMENICAL MOVEMENT in the United States; its international counterpart is the WORLD COUNCIL OF CHURCHES. The National Council has its headquarters in New York City.

national debt: see DEBT, PUBLIC.

National Defense Education Act (NDEA), Federal legislation passed in 1958 providing aid to education in the United States at all levels, public and private. NDEA has been especially active in the advancement of education in science, mathematics, and modern foreign languages; but it has also provided aid in other areas, including technical education, area studies, geography, English as a second language, counseling and guidance, school libraries and librarianship, and educational media centers. The act provided institutions of higher education with 90% of capital funds for low-interest loans to students. NDEA also gave Federal support for improvement and change in elementary and secondary education. The act contains statutory prohibitions of Federal direction, supervision, or control over the curriculum, program of instruction, administration, or personnel of any educational institution.

National Education Association (NEA), organization of professional educators in the United States, with more than one million members. The NEA was founded (1857) as the National Teachers Association and was chartered by Congress in 1906. It is composed of 4 departments, 16 national affiliates, and 11 associated organizations, each representing an area of specialized interest. Its general aim is to promote the welfare of all professional educators, including both teachers and administrators. See E. B. Wesley, *NEA; the First Hundred Years* (1957).

National Forest System, federally-owned reserves, c.187,000,000 acres (75,680,000 hectares), administered by the Forest Service of the U.S. Dept. of Agriculture. The system is made up of 155 national forests and 19 national grasslands in 44 states, Puerto Rico, and the Virgin Islands. Most of the acreage is found in the Western states, with Alaska, Idaho, and California having the most extensive holdings. In the East, large national forests are in the Green, White, Allegheny, and Blue Ridge mts. The national grasslands are found on the Great Plains. By law the reserves must be used for timber production, watershed land, wildlife preservation, livestock grazing, mining, and recreation. In 1891, Congress authorized the President to set aside forest reserves; Yellowstone Park Timber Reserve (now Shoshone National Forest) in Wyoming was the first (1891) to be established. The forest reserves were administered by the General Land Office of the Dept. of the Interior until 1905, when they were transferred to the Forest Service. They were designated national forests in 1907. See FOREST. See Michael Frome, *The Forest Service* (1971); F. E. Wood and F. D. Wood, *Forests are for People* (1971); R. S. Gilmour, *Policy Making for the National Forests* (1971); publications of the Forest Service, U.S. Dept. of Agriculture, and the American Tree Association, Washington, D.C.

National Gallery, London, one of the permanent national art collections of Great Britain. Its building, in Greek style, stands in Trafalgar Square. It was designed and erected (1832–38) by William Wilkins and was shared for 30 years with the Royal Academy of Arts. In 1876 a new wing was added, designed by E. M. Barry. The nucleus of the collection was formed in 1824 with 38 pictures from J. J. Angerstein's collection. The gallery is rich in Italian paintings of the 15th and 16th cent. and has fine collections of French, Flemish, and Dutch masters. The National Portrait Gallery, whose collection dates from 1858, has adjoined the National Gallery since 1896. Originally controlled by the National Gallery, the TATE GALLERY attained complete independence in 1955 by an act of Parliament.

National Gallery of Art, Washington, D.C., a branch of the SMITHSONIAN INSTITUTION, established by act of Congress, March 24, 1937. Andrew W. MELLON donated funds for construction of the building as well as his own collection of 130 American portraits. The marble building was designed by John Russell Pope; it was opened in March, 1941. Other gifts to the gallery include Samuel H. Kress's collection of Italian masterpieces (1939) and the Joseph E. Widener Collection, the Chester Dale Collection, the Lessing J. Rosenwald collection of drawings and prints, the Edgar W. and Bernice C. Garbisch collection of 175 American naïve paintings (given since 1953); and the Paul Mellon collection of portraits of American Indians by George Catlin (given 1968). The gallery's paintings number more than 1,200. The collection is especially rich in Italian, French, and American works. The government turned over to the gallery the Index of American Design, consisting of about 20,000 drawings and watercolors illustrating the history of American crafts and folk art. See John Walker, *National Gallery of Art* (1963); Huntington Cairns and John Walker, ed., *A Pageant of Painting from the National Gallery of Art* (2 vol., 1966).

national grasslands: see NATIONAL FOREST SYSTEM.

National Guard, U.S. militia. The militia is authorized by the Constitution of the United States, which also defines the militia's functions and the Federal and state role. Article 1, Section 8, provides that Congress shall have the power to call forth "the Militia to execute the Laws of the Union, suppress insurrections and repel invasions." Congress was entrusted with organizing, arming, and disciplining the militia, but the appointment of officers and the training of the militia were reserved to the states. Further provisions were made in the Second Amendment. In peacetime the National Guard is placed under state jurisdiction and can be used by governors to quell local disturbances (e.g., the National Guard was called in during the Detroit and Newark riots of 1967). In times of war or other emergencies the National Guard is absorbed into the active service of the United States and the President is commander in chief. The National Guard was partially mobilized for the Korean War (1950–53) and the Berlin crisis of 1961. The National Guard's equipment and personnel are standardized to conform with U.S. army regulations. Enlistment is voluntary; compensation, paid by the Federal government, is given for periods of drill and field training. An air National Guard was formed in 1947.

National Institute of Arts and Letters, honorary academy of notable American artists, writers, and composers. Its membership is limited to 250 native or naturalized U.S. citizens. Founded (1898) for the furtherance of literature and the fine arts in America, the institute offers a number of prizes annually, including the Brunner Memorial Award in Architecture and the Gold Medal for excellence in the arts. Located in New York City, the institute also sponsors the American Academy of Arts and Letters (founded 1904), an organization of Americans of outstanding achievement in art, literature, or music. The academy's membership, limited to 50, is selected from its parent body. Awards given by the academy include the Howells Medal for the Novel (conferred every 5 years). It also purchases paintings by American artists for distribution to museums. The academy maintains a 14,000-volume library at its New York headquarters.

nationalism, political or social philosophy in which the welfare of the nation-state as an entity is considered paramount. Nationalism is basically a group state of mind or consciousness in which the individual believes his primary duty and loyalty to be to the nation-state. Often it implies a belief in national superiority and glorifies various national virtues. This love of nation may be overemphasized, and concern with one's own national self-interest to the exclusion of the rights of other nations may lead to international conflict. Nationalism is a comparatively recent phenomenon, generally considered to have been born with the French Revolution, but despite its short history, it has been extremely important in forming the bonds that hold modern nations together. Today it operates alongside the legal structure and supplements the formal institutions of society in providing much of the cohesiveness and order necessary for the existence of the modern nation-state. For people to express nationalism it is first necessary for them to conceive of themselves as belonging to a nation, that is, for them to somehow identify themselves with a large group of people, all of whom generally have something in common. The rise of centralized monarchies, which placed people under one rule and eliminated FEUDALISM, made this possible. The realization that they might possess a common history, religion, language, or race also aided people in forming a national identity. When both a common identity and a formal authority structure over a large territory (i.e., the state) exist, then nationalism becomes possible. In its first powerful manifestation in the French Revolution nationalism carried with it the notion of popular sovereignty, from which some have inferred that nationalism can occur only in democratic nations. However, this thesis is belied by the intense nationalism that characterized the German Empire and later Nazi Germany. Where nationalism arises, its specific form is the product of each particular nation's history.

Empire and Nation. Although nationalism is unique to the modern world, some of its elements can be traced throughout history. The first roots of nationalism are probably to be found in the ancient Hebrews, who conceived of themselves as both a chosen people, that is, a people as a whole superior to all other peoples, and a people with a common cultural history. The ancient Greeks also felt superior to all other peoples and moreover felt a sense of great loyalty to the political community. These feelings of cultural superiority (ethnocentrism), which are similar to nationalism, gave way to much more universal identifications with the foundation of the vast Roman Empire. The Christian Church also contributed to universalism through its teaching of the oneness of mankind. The tradition of universality did not die with the fall of the Roman Empire. A universal scholarly language and cultural heritage and a universal church still remained, and the Holy Roman Empire was based on universal concepts. But as strong centralized monarchies were built from petty feudal states, as regional languages and art forms were evolved, and as local economies widened, popular identification with these developments became increasingly strong. In areas such as Italy, which were not yet single nations, recurring invasions led such thinkers as Niccolò MACHIAVELLI to advocate national political federation. The religious wars of the Reformation set nation against nation, though the strongest loyalty continued to adhere to the sovereign rather than to the state. In the 16th and 17th cent. the nationalistic economic doctrine of MERCANTILISM appeared. The growth of the middle classes, their desire for political power, and the consequent development of democratic political theory were closely connected with the emergence of modern nationalism. The theorists of the French Revolution believed that men could establish a government dedicated to the equality and liberty of all people. To them the nation was inseparable from the people and for the first time in history men could create a government in accordance with the general will of the people. Although their aims were universal, they glorified the nation that would establish their aims, and nationalism found its first political expression.

The Nineteenth Century. It was in the 19th cent. that nationalism became a widespread and powerful force. During this time nationalism expressed itself in many areas as a drive for national unification or independence. The spirit of nationalism took an especially strong hold in Germany where thinkers such as Johann Gottfried von HERDER and Johann Gottlieb FICHTE had developed the idea of VOLK. However, the nationalism that inspired the German people to rise against the empire of NAPOLEON I was conservative, tradition-bound, and narrow rather than liberal, progressive, and universal. And when the fragmented Germany was finally unified as the German Empire in 1871, it was a highly authoritarian and militarist state. After many years of fighting, Italy also achieved national unification and freedom from foreign domination. However, certain areas inhabited by Italians (e.g., Trieste) were not included in the new state, and this gave rise to the problem of IRREDENTISM. In the United States, where nationalism had evinced itself in the doctrine of Manifest Destiny, national unity was maintained at the cost of the Civil War. In the latter half of the 19th cent., there were strong nationalist movements among the peoples subject to the supranational Austrian and Ottoman empires, as there were also in Ireland, under British rule, and in Poland, mostly under Russian rule. At the same time, however, with the emergence in Europe of strong, integrated nation-states, nationalism became increasingly a sentiment of conservatives. It was turned against such international movements as socialism, and it found outlet in pursuit of glory and empire (see IMPERIALISM). Nationalist conflicts had much to do with bringing on World War I.

The Twentieth Century. The early 20th cent. saw the establishment of many independent nations, especially through the peace treaties ending World War I. The Paris Peace Conference adopted the principal of national self-determination, a doctrine upheld by the League of Nations and later by the United Nations. While self-determination is a nationalist principle, it is also one that recognizes the basic equality of all nations, large or small, and in this sense it transcends a narrow nationalism that claims superiority for itself. It was exactly this latter type of nationalism, however, that arose in Nazi Germany, preaching the superiority of the so-called Aryan race and the need for the extermination of the Jews (see NATIONAL SOCIALISM). Italian FASCISM was in a similar manner based upon extreme nationalist sentiments. At the same time, Asian and African colonial territories, seeking to cast off imperial bonds, were developing nationalist movements. Perhaps the most famous of these was the INDIAN NATIONAL CONGRESS, which struggled for Indian independence for over 60 years. After World War II nationalism in Asia and Africa spread at such a fast pace that dozens of new "nations" were created from former colonial territorial holdings. These countries today face great problems in forging those elements necessary to establish stable nationhood. There is some question as to whether nationalism will remain a powerful force in world relations in the future. Growing interdependence and communications among nations have created an internationalism that is basically opposed to the restricted scope of nationalism. Such organizations as the United Nations, the European Common Market, the Pan-American Union, and pan-African movements stress cooperation and allegiance among nations. Although nationalism will undoubtedly retain some importance, its influence may decline with the strengthening of internationalism. See Carleton Hayes, *Historical Evolution of Modern Nationalism* (1931, repr. 1968); Hans Kohn, *The Idea of Nationalism* (1944, repr. 1967) and *Nationalism: Its Meaning and History* (rev. ed. 1965); E. H. Carr, *Nationalism and After* (1945); L. L. Snyder, *The Meaning of Nationalism* (1954, repr. 1968); Anthony Smith, *Theories of Nationalism* (1971).

nationality, in political theory, the quality of belonging to a nation, in the sense of a group united by various strong ties. Among the usual ties are membership in the same general community, common customs, culture, tradition, history, and language. While no one of these factors is essential, some must be present for cohesion to be strong enough to justify the term *nationality*. Used in this sense, nationality does not necessarily denote membership of a specific political state. There are many examples of nations divided between several states and of states composed of several nations and parts of nations. Thus not all Albanians live in Albania, and, on the other hand, Switzerland has citizens whose native languages are German, French, Italian, and Romansh. In political theory the belief that a state should be identical with a nation is called the "principle of nationalities," or, more commonly, "self-determination." This view is a typical expression of NATIONALISM; it was advanced partly as a means of solving the problem of the national MINORITY after World War I. Nationality in its specific legal sense is a very different concept; it is attachment to a state by a tie of allegiance. Nationals in this sense are fundamentally distinguished from aliens (see ALIEN) and in most, but not all, countries are identical with CITIZENS. Nationality gives the state the right to impose certain duties, especially military service. Some states will punish their nationals for crimes wherever committed; the United States, however, punishes only those crimes, except treason, that are committed within American territorial jurisdiction. States may tax the income and other assets of their nationals regardless of whether they reside abroad. The national owes duties to his government but is also entitled to diplomatic protection when in a foreign country. Such protection includes the assistance of consular officials when the national is accused of crime and the offering of refuge in emergencies. In many instances certain persons, particularly those who have undergone NATURALIZATION, will be regarded as nationals by two states at once. Such problems of dual nationality have been a frequent cause of international diplomatic disputes. See Paul Weis, *Nationality and Statelessness in International Law* (1956); Benjamin Akzin, *States and Nations* (1966); Cuthbert Joseph, *Nationality and Diplomatic Protection* (1969).

nationalization, acquisition and operation by a country of business enterprises formerly owned and operated by private individuals or corporations. State or local authorities have traditionally taken private property for such public purposes as the construction of roads, dams, or public buildings. Known as the right of eminent domain, this process is usually accompanied by the payment of compensation. By contrast, the concept of nationalization is a 20th cent. development that differs from eminent domain in motive and degree; it is done for the purpose of social and economic equality and is usually, although not always, applied as a principle of communistic or socialistic theories of society. The Communist states of Eastern Europe nationalized all industry and agriculture in the period following World War II. Under the Labour government of the period 1945 to 1951, Great Britain nationalized a number of important industries, including coal, steel, and transportation. In non-Communist countries it has been common practice to compensate the owners of nationalized properties, at least in part; however, in the Communist countries, where private ownership is opposed in principle, there usually has not been such compensation. Nationalization of foreign properties also occurs, especially in undeveloped nations, where there is often great resentment of foreign control of major industries. Instances of such nationalization include Mexico's seizure of oil properties owned by U.S. corporations (1938), Iran's nationalization of the Anglo-Iranian Oil Company (1951), the nationalization of the Suez Canal Company (1956) by the Egyptian government, and Chile's nationalization of its foreign-owned copper-mining industry (1971). Such expropriations raise complex problems of international law. In some cases disputes over nationalization are settled by adjudication, with the expropriated parties obtaining compensation for their former properties, if only in part. In other instances, where no compensation is offered, severe strain in international relations may arise. The International Court of Justice ruled (1952) in the Anglo-Iranian Oil Company dispute that a concession made by a state to a foreign corporation is not an international agreement and is subject to the law of the conceding state—a position indicating that investors must assume the risk of nationalization in the country in which they invest. The Afro-Asian group at the United Nations has insisted that the right to nationalize is implied by the principle of self-determination embodied in the UN Charter. See Konstantin Katsarov, *The Theory of Nationalization* (tr. 1964); Julius Margolis, ed., *Public Economics* (1969); G. L. Reid and Kevin Allen, *Nationalized Industries* (1970).

National Labor Relations Board (NLRB), independent agency of the U.S. government created under the National Labor Relations Act of 1935 (Wagner Act), and amended by the acts of 1947 (TAFT-HARTLEY LABOR ACT) and 1959 (LANDRUM-GRIFFIN ACT), which affirmed labor's right to organize and bargain collectively through representatives of their own choice or to refrain from such activities. The board of five members (appointed by the U.S. President with the approval of the Senate for five-year terms) is assisted by 31 regional directors. This board determines proper bargaining units, conducts elections for union representation, and investigates charges of unfair labor practices by the employer. Unfair practices include interference, coercion, or restraint in labor's self-organizational rights; interference with the formation of labor unions; encouraging or discouraging membership in a union; and refusal to bargain collectively with the duly chosen representative of his employees. The Wagner Act was validated by the Supreme Court in 1937. The NLRB functioned during World War II, but labor relations were mainly handled by the National War Labor Board (WLB), which existed from 1942 until 1945. A 12-man body, with the public, management, and labor equally represented, the WLB soon shifted from arbitration to formulating policies. With the passage in 1947 of the Taft-Hartley Labor Act (also known as the Labor-Management Relations Act), the NLRB was converted into a purely judicial body, with the prosecution of unfair labor practices transferred to a general counsel. The board's action was dependent upon the filing by the union chiefs of affidavits proving that they were not Communists and of complete financial data. The NLRB's field of investigation was extended to cover the following practices as unfair to employers: refusal to bargain collectively, coercing employers in the selection of their bargaining agency, persuading employers to discriminate against certain employees, and conducting secondary boycotts or jurisdictional strikes. In 1959 the Taft-Hartley Labor Act was amended by the Landrum-Griffin Act (also known as the Labor-Management Reporting and Disclosure Act) repealing the requirement that a union must file a non-Communist affidavit and a financial report in order to obtain a hearing before the NLRB. The act also gave the states permission to assume jurisdiction over cases that the NLRB declined, even when interstate commerce was involved. Organizational and recognition picketing (i.e., picketing of companies where another union is already recognized) were made unlawful, and the NLRB general counsel was required to seek an injunction against such picketing if a violation was proved. The Landrum-Griffin Act also affected policies of the board. It banned secondary boycott pressures and, with some exceptions, outlawed so-called hot-cargo agreements (i.e., express or implied contracts that prevent employers from doing business with persons declared off limits by unions). In 1967 the Supreme Court upheld a NLRB ruling that the hot-cargo amendment to the Landrum-Griffin Act could not be used to prevent workers from striking to protect their jobs. NLRB power was reduced (1970) when the Supreme Court ruled that the NLRB could not compel a company or a union to accept a collective bargaining agreement but could only umpire labor-management disputes.

National Museum of Anthropology, Mexico City. The present building, designed by Pedro Ramirez Vazquez and inspired by ancient Mexican architecture, was opened in 1964 and houses choice and extensive archeological remains of pre-Columbian Mexico. The exhibitions include studies of prehistoric animal life in Mexico and superb ethnological displays of the peoples of Mexico. Artifacts from Mayan and Aztec civilizations include a magnificent funerary mask of inlaid turquoise, serpentine, and shell mosaic (3d–8th cent. A.D.) discovered at Teotihuacán, and the vast Aztec round calendar in relief.

National Museum of the United States: see SMITHSONIAN INSTITUTION.

National Organization for Women (NOW), group founded (1966) to support "full equality for women in America in a truly equal partnership with men." Its founder and first president was feminist leader Betty Friedan, author of *The Feminine Mystique* (1963). Through a program of legislative lobbying, court litigation, and public demonstrations, NOW seeks to attain its major goal of ending sexual discrimination in employment. The largest women's rights group in the United States, it also supports the establishment of child-care centers for working mothers, legalized abortion, and paid maternity leave, as well as adoption of the equal rights amendment to the U.S. Constitution. NOW seeks the abolition of alimony laws and includes men in its membership. It consists of approximately 200 local chapters that are affiliated with the main office, located in Chicago.

national parks and monuments. The National Park Service, a bureau of the U.S. Dept. of the Interior, was established in 1916 to correlate the administration of 37 national parks and monuments under

NATIONAL PARKS

Name	Location	Date Autho- rized	Gross Area		Special Characteristics
			ACRES	HECTARES	
*Acadia	S Maine	1919	41,642	16,853	Mountain and coast scenery.
*Arches	E Utah	1929	82,953	33,571	Giant arches formed by erosion.
*Big Bend	W Texas	1935	708,221	286,617	Canyons and desert plain on the Rio Grande.
*Bryce Canyon	SW Utah	1923	36,010	14,573	Canyon with colored walls and rock formations.
*Canyonlands	SE Utah	1964	257,640	104,267	Rocks, spires, and mesas; Indian petroglyphs.
Capitol Reef	S Utah	1937	254,242	102,892	Highly colored sandstone cliffs dissected by gorges; named for a white, dome-shaped rock.
*Carlsbad Caverns	SE N.Mex.	1923	46,753	18,921	Great limestone caverns.
*Crater Lake	SW Oregon	1902	160,290	64,869	Blue lake in a crater.
*Everglades	S Fla.	1934	1,400,533	566,796	Subtropical wilderness.
*Glacier	NW Mont.	1910	1,013,101	410,002	Region of glaciers, forests, and lakes.
*Grand Canyon	NW Ariz.	1908	673,575	272,596	Great gorge of the Colorado River.
*Grand Teton	NW Wyo.	1929	310,443	125,636	Scenic portion of the Teton Range.
*Great Smoky Mountains	N.C., Tenn.	1926	516,626	209,079	Wild, beautiful area in the Great Smoky Mts.
*Guadalupe Mountains	W Texas	1966	81,077	32,812	Mountain region; contains a limestone fossil reef.
*Haleakala	Hawaii, on Maui	1960	27,283	11,041	Largest inactive crater in the world.
*Hawaii Volcanoes	Hawaii, on Hawaii	1916	229,616	92,926	Volcanic region.
*Hot Springs	Central Ark.	1921	3,535	1,431	Mineral springs.
*Isle Royale	NW Mich.	1931	539,341	218,271	Forested islands in Lake Superior.
Kings Canyon	E Calif.	1890	460,331	186,296	Canyons, peaks, sequoias. See SEQUOIA NATIONAL PARK.
*Lassen Volcanic	N Calif.	1907	106,934	43,276	Volcanic peaks and lava formations.
*Mammoth Cave	Central Ky.	1926	51,354	20,783	Extensive underground passages.
*Mesa Verde	SW Colo.	1906	52,074	21,074	Prehistoric cliff dwellings.
*Mount McKinley	Central Alaska	1917	1,939,493	784,913	Highest peak in North America.
*Mount Rainier	SW Wash.	1899	241,992	97,934	Volcanic peak and glaciers.
North Cascades	N Wash.	1968	505,000	204,373	Area of great alpine scenery in the Cascade Range; bisected by Ross Lake National Recreation Area.
*Olympic	NW Wash.	1938	896,599	362,854	Rain forests and glaciers in the OLYMPIC MOUNTAINS.
*Petrified Forest	E Ariz.	1906	94,189	38,118	Petrified logs; part of the Painted Desert.
Platt	S Okla.	1906	912	369	Cold mineral springs in the ARBUCKLE MOUNTAINS.
*Redwood	NW Calif.	1968	56,201	22,745	Coast redwood forests.
Rocky Mountain	Central Colo.	1915	262,191	106,109	Scenic ROCKY MOUNTAINS region on the continental divide; many high snow-capped peaks.
*Sequoia	E Calif.	1890	386,863	156,563	Groves of giant sequoias.
*Shenandoah	N Va.	1926	193,537	78,324	Forested region of the BLUE RIDGE mts.
*Virgin Islands	Virgin Islands, on St. John	1956	14,419	5,835	Unusual scenery, marine life, coral gardens; ruins of the Danish colony.
Voyageurs	N Minn.	1971	219,431	88,804	Scenic northern lakes region; interesting glacial features and history.
*Wind Cave	SW S.Dak.	1903	28,059	11,355	Limestone caverns in the Black Hills.
*Yellowstone	Wyo., Mont., Idaho	1872	2,221,773	899,152	Geysers, Yellowstone canyon, falls; first and largest U.S. national park.
*Yosemite	Central Calif.	1890	761,320	308,106	Mountain region with Yosemite Valley.
*Zion	SW Utah	1909	147,035	59,505	Multicolored canyon in a desert region.

NATIONAL MONUMENTS

Name	Location	Date Autho- rized	ACRES	HECTARES	Special Characteristics
Agate Fossil Beds	NW Nebr.	1965	3,050	1,234	World-famous quarries containing numerous well-preserved Miocene mammal fossils.
Alibates Flint Quarries and Texas Panhandle Pueblo Culture	NW Texas	1965	93	38	Flint quarries, first worked by Indians c.10,000 years ago; rich archaeological and historic area.
*Aztec Ruins	NW N.Mex.	1923	27	11	Ruins of a Pueblo Indian town.
Badlands	SW S.Dak.	1929	243,508	98,548	See BADLANDS.
Bandelier	N N.Mex.	1916	29,661	12,004	Ruins of prehistoric Pueblo Indian homes.
Biscayne	S Fla.	1968	95,064	38,472	Example of a living coral reef; includes part of BISCAYNE BAY.
Black Canyon of the Gunnison	W Colo.	1933	13,667	5,531	Deep, narrow canyon of the GUNNISON River, named for its dark-colored walls, which are always in shadow.
Booker T. Washington	Central Va.	1956	218	88	Birthplace and childhood home of Booker T. WASHINGTON.
Buck Island Reef	Virgin Islands, on Buck Island	1961	850	344	One of the finest marine gardens in the Caribbean; bird rookeries and grottoes.
Cabrillo	S Calif.	1913	123	50	Memorial to Juan Rodríguez CABRILLO.
*Canyon de Chelly	NE Ariz.	1931	83,840	33,930	Ruins of prehistoric Indian villages.
Capulin Mountain	NE N.Mex.	1916	775	314	Huge cinder cone of extinct volcano.
Casa Grande Ruins	S Ariz.	1892	473	191	Huge building built c.600 years ago in the ruins of an Indian pueblo.
Castillo de San Marcos	NE Fla.	1924	20	8	Old Spanish masonry fort in SAINT AUGUSTINE, Fla.
Castle Clinton	SE N.Y.	1946	1	.4	See BATTERY, THE.
Cedar Breaks	SW Utah	1933	6,155	2,491	Amphitheater (2,000 ft/610 m deep) formed by erosion.
Chaco Canyon	NW N.Mex.	1907	21,509	8,705	Ruins representing the highest point of PUEBLO INDIAN prehistoric civilization (A.D. 900–1000).
Channel Islands	SW Calif.	1938	18,167	7,352	Part of the SANTA BARBARA ISLANDS; sea lions, fossils.

* See separate article for additional information. For example, for Acadia, see ACADIA NATIONAL PARK.
† Not owned by the Federal government.
The following units were added to the National Parks System in 1974: John Day Fossil Beds National Monument, Oregon; Clara Barton National Historic Site, Maryland; Knife River Indian Villages National Historic Site, North Dakota; Martin Van Buren National Historic Site, New York; Springfield Armory National Historic Site, Massachusetts; Tuskegee Institute National Historic Site, Alabama; Boston National Historical Park, Massachusetts; Big Cypress National Preserve, Florida; Big Thicket National Preserve, Texas.

NATIONAL MONUMENTS (Continued)

Name	Location	Date Authorized	Gross Area ACRES	Gross Area HECTARES	Special Characteristics
Chiricahua	SE Ariz.	1924	10,645	4,308	Unusually shaped rock formations.
Colorado	W Colo.	1911	17,669	7,151	Huge monoliths and other unusual erosional features.
*Craters of the Moon	S Idaho	1924	53,545	21,670	Volcanic cones, craters, fissures, lava flows.
Custer Battlefield	SE Mont.	1879	765	310	Site of the Custer massacre. See LITTLE BIGHORN, river.
*Death Valley	Calif., Nev.	1933	1,907,760	772,070	Lowest point in North America; desert environment.
Devils Postpile	E Calif.	1911	798	323	Basaltic columns, some 60 ft (18 m) high.
*Devils Tower	NE Wyo.	1906	1,347	545	Volcanic rock tower; first national monument.
Dinosaur	Utah, Colo.	1915	206,663	83,637	Rich quarries of well-preserved fossils.
Effigy Mounds	NE Iowa	1949	1,468	594	Outstanding examples of Indian mounds.
El Morro	W N.Mex.	1906	1,279	518	Sandstone monolith with inscriptions of Spanish explorers and American pioneers.
Florissant Fossil Beds	Central Colo.	1969	5,992	2,425	Well-preserved insect, seed, and leaf fossils of the Oligocene period; petrified sequoia tree stumps.
Fort Frederica	SE Ga.	1936	250	101	Ruins of a fort built by James OGLETHORPE on one of the Sea Islands
Fort McHenry	N Md.	1925	43	17	Historic shrine; place where the *Star-spangled Banner* was written. See FORT MCHENRY.
Fort Jefferson	S Fla.	1935	47,125	19,071	In the Dry Tortugas Islands; the largest all-masonry fort in the Western Hemisphere; built 1846.
Fort Matanzas	NE Fla.	1924	299	121	Spanish fort in SAINT AUGUSTINE, Fla.
Fort Pulaski	SE Ga.	1924	5,517	2,233	Fort on Cockspur Island. See FORT PULASKI.
Fort Stanwix	Central N.Y.	1935	18	7	See FORT STANWIX.
Fort Sumter	SE S.C.	1948	34	14	Scene of the engagement that opened the Civil War. See FORT SUMTER.
Fort Union	NW N.Mex.	1954	721	292	Ruins of a U.S. army fort on the Santa Fe Trail.
Fossil Butte	W Wyo.	1972	3,178	1,286	Area containing Paleocene-Eocene fossil fish.
George Washington Birthplace	E Va.	1930	394	159	Estate and reconstructed mansion. See WAKEFIELD.
George Washington Carver	SW Mo.	1943	210	85	Birthplace and boyhood home of George Washington CARVER.
Gila Cliff Dwellings	SW N.Mex.	1907	533	216	Well-preserved dwellings built by the Pueblo Indians into a 150-ft (46-m) cliff.
*Glacier Bay	SE Alaska	1925	2,803,840	1,134,714	Glaciers, ice displays; largest unit of the National Park System.
Grand Canyon	NW Ariz.	1932	198,280	80,244	Part of the GRAND CANYON.
Grand Portage	NE Minn.	1951	710	287	9-mi (14-km) portage on the route to the Northwest used by explorers, missionaries, and fur traders.
Gran Quivira	Central N.Mex.	1909	611	247	Ruins of a Spanish mission and Indian pueblos.
Great Sand Dunes	S Colo.	1932	36,740	14,869	Large, high sand dunes in the Sangre de Cristo Mts.
Hohokam Pima	Central Ariz.	1972	1,555	629	Archaeological remains of the Hohokam culture.
Homestead	SE Nebr.	1936	195	79	Site of the first farm claimed under the HOMESTEAD ACT.
Hovenweep	Utah, Colo.	1923	505	204	Prehistoric Indian pueblos and cliff dwellings.
Jewel Cave	SW S.Dak.	1908	1,275	516	Limestone caves with chambers connected by narrow passages; in the Black Hills.
Joshua Tree	S Calif.	1936	558,184	225,897	Rare Joshua trees, or "praying plant"; named by Mormons because of upstretched arms.
*Katmai	SW Alaska	1918	2,792,137	1,129,978	Volcanic area; second largest unit of the National Park System.
Lava Beds	N Calif.	1925	46,239	18,713	Examples of volcanism; scene of Modoc Indian uprising.
Lehman Caves	E Nev.	1922	640	259	Honeycombed limestone caves; rock formations.
Marble Canyon	N Ariz.	1969	32,665	13,220	Canyon of the Colorado River with high vertical walls of red sandstone and white limestone.
*Montezuma Castle	Central Ariz.	1906	842	341	Well-preserved prehistoric cliff dwellings.
Mound City Group	S Ohio	1923	68	28	Prehistoric Indian mounds.
Muir Woods	W Calif.	1908	503	204	Grove of virgin redwood trees.
*Natural Bridges	SE Utah	1908	7,600	3,076	Three huge natural bridges.
Navajo	NE Ariz.	1909	360	146	Ruins of large cliff dwellings.
Ocmulgee	Central Ga.	1934	683	276	Remains of mounds and prehistoric towns.
Oregon Caves	SW Oregon	1909	480	194	Limestone caverns with four levels; rock formations.
Organ Pipe Cactus	S Ariz.	1937	330,874	133,905	Organ pipe cactus and other unique desert growth.
Pecos	N N.Mex.	1965	341	138	15th-century ruins of Pecos Pueblo, once the largest Indian settlement in the Southwest.
Pinnacles	W Calif.	1908	14,498	5,867	Rock spires from 500 to 1,200 ft (152–366 m) high; caves.
Pipe Spring	NW Ariz.	1923	40	16	Spring first visited by the Mormons; old fort.
Pipestone	SW Minn.	1937	283	114	Quarry that was a source for Indian peace pipes.
*Rainbow Bridge	S Utah	1910	160	65	Pink sandstone arch.
Russell Cave	NE Ala.	1961	310	125	Cave containing a nearly continuous archaeological record of human habitation from about 6000 B.C. to A.D. 1650.
Saguaro	SE Ariz.	1933	79,084	32,005	Saguaro, other cacti, varied desert growth.
Saint Croix Island	E Maine	1949	57	23	Commemorates the French settlement on the island in the SAINT CROIX River.
Scotts Bluff	W Nebr.	1919	3,084	1,248	Landmark on the Oregon Trail.
Statue of Liberty	SE N.Y.	1924	58	23	See LIBERTY, STATUE OF; ELLIS ISLAND.
Sunset Crater	N Ariz.	1930	3,040	1,230	Volcanic cinder cone with multicolored crater; lava flows; ice cave.
Timpanogos Cave	N Utah	1922	250	101	Limestone cavern on Mt. Timpanogos.

* See separate article for additional information. For example, for Acadia, see ACADIA NATIONAL PARK.
† Not owned by the Federal government.
The following units were added to the National Parks System in 1974: John Day Fossil Beds National Monument, Oregon; Clara Barton National Historic Site, Maryland; Knife River Indian Villages National Historic Site, North Dakota; Martin Van Buren National Historic Site, New York; Springfield Armory National Historic Site, Massachusetts; Tuskegee Institute National Historic Site, Alabama; Boston National Historical Park, Massachusetts; Big Cypress National Preserve, Florida; Big Thicket National Preserve, Texas.

NATIONAL MONUMENTS (Continued)

Name	Location	Date Autho-rized	Gross Area ACRES	HECTARES	Special Characteristics
Tonto	Central Ariz.	1907	1,120	453	Well-preserved 14th-century cliff dwellings built by the Salado Indians in the Salt River valley.
Tumacacori	S Ariz.	1908	10	4	Mission founded by Father Eusebio F. KINO; rebuilt by the Franciscans.
Tuzigoot	Central Ariz.	1939	43	17	Excavated ruins of a large Indian pueblo.
Walnut Canyon	N Ariz.	1915	1,879	760	12th-century Sinagua Indian cliff dwellings.
White Sands	S N.Mex.	1933	146,535	59,303	Wind-drifted gypsum sands.
Wupatki	N Ariz.	1924	35,233	14,259	Several prehistoric pueblos.
Yucca House	SW Colo.	1919	10	4	Remains of a prehistoric Indian village.

NATIONAL HISTORIC SITES

Name	Location	Date Autho-rized	ACRES	HECTARES	Special Characteristics
*Abraham Lincoln Birthplace	Central Ky.	1916	117	47	Traditional birthplace cabin in memorial building on site of Lincoln's birthplace.
Adams	E Mass.	1946	5	2	Home of Presidents John Adams and John Quincy Adams and other members of the family.
Allegheny Portage Railroad	SW Pa.	1964	767	310	Inclined-plane railroad that lifted passengers and cargoes of boats on the Pennsylvania Canal over the Allegheny Mts.
Andersonville	SW Ga.	1970	495	200	Civil War prison camp. See under ANDERSONVILLE.
Andrew Johnson	NE Tenn.	1935	17	7	Home, shop, and grave of President Andrew JOHNSON; site includes Andrew Johnson National Cemetery.
Bent's Old Fort	SE Colo.	1960	178	72	Fur-trading post, Indian rendezvous, and rest-station on the Santa Fe Trail; built c.1830 by Charles and William BENT. See BENT'S FORT.
Carl Sandburg Home	SW N.C.	1968	247	100	Farm home of author Carl SANDBURG.
†Chicago Portage Railroad	NE Ill.	1952	91	37	Portion of a portage discovered (1673) by Marquette and Jolliet; later used as a link between the Great Lakes and the Mississippi River.
†Chimney Rock	W Nebr.	1956	83	34	500-ft (150-m) landmark on the Oregon Trail.
Christiansted	Virgin Islands, on St. Croix	1952	27	11	Commemorates the Virgin Islands' colonial development, especially under Danish rule in the 18th and 19th cent.
†Dorchester Heights	E Mass.	1951	5	2	Site of American batteries that helped force the evacuation of British forces from Boston (1776) during the Revolution.
Edison	NE N.J.	1962	20	8	Buildings and equipment used by Thomas A. EDISON.
Eisenhower	S Pa.	1969	493	200	Home and farm of President Dwight D. EISENHOWER.
Ford's Theatre	Washington, D.C.	1970	.25	.1	Sites of President Abraham LINCOLN's assassination and death; includes the Lincoln Museum.
Fort Bowie	SE Ariz.	1964	1,060	429	Ruins of a fort (est. 1862) that was the base of military operations against GERONIMO and his followers.
Fort Davis	W Texas	1961	460	186	Key post in the defensive system of W Texas, guarding (1854–91) the San Antonio-El Paso road through the Davis Mts.; troops attached there fought the Comanche and Apache Indians.
*Fort Laramie	SE Wyo.	1938	563	228	Buildings of an old fort on the Oregon Trail.
Fort Larned	Central Kansas	1964	681	276	Protected the Santa Fe Trail; served as a military base during the Plains War (1860s) and later as an Indian Bureau administrative center.
Fort Point	W Calif.	1970	96	39	Largest brick and granite mid-19th-century coastal fortification on the west coast of North America.
Fort Raleigh	NE N.C.	1941	160	65	Site of the first attempted settlement by the English in North America. See ROANOKE ISLAND.
†Fort Scott	SE Kansas	1965	7	3	A historic area; commemorates historic events in Kansas prior to and during the Civil War.
Fort Smith	NW Ark.	1961	19	8	One of the first U.S. military posts in the Louisiana Purchase; maintained law and order in the Oklahoma Territory. See FORT SMITH, Ark.
Fort Union Trading Post	N.Dak., Mont.	1966	380	154	American Fur Company trading post. See FORT UNION.
Fort Vancouver	SW Wash.	1948	220	89	Site of a HUDSON'S BAY COMPANY post (1825–49) and later of a U.S. army fort.
†Gloria Dei	SE Pa.	1942	3	1	Second oldest Swedish church in the United States; founded 1677, present building erected c.1700.
Golden Spike	N Utah	1957	2,172	879	Site where the UNION PACIFIC RR and the Central Pacific RR joined to form the first transcontinental railroad.
Grant-Kohrs Ranch	W Mont.	1972	1,564	633	Headquarters of one of the largest 19th-century range ranches.
Hampton	NE Md.	1948	45	18	Late 18th-century Georgian mansion.
Herbert Hoover	E Iowa	1965	148	60	Birthplace, childhood home, and burial place of President Herbert HOOVER.
Home of Franklin D. Roosevelt	SE N.Y.	1944	188	76	Home, "Summer White House," and burial place of Franklin D. and Eleanor Roosevelt. See HYDE PARK.
Hopewell Village	SE Pa.	1938	848	343	Restored 19th-century iron-making village.
Hubbell Trading Post	NE Ariz.	1965	160	65	Example of a late 19th-century trading post in the Southwest.
†Jamestown	SE Va.	1940	21	8	Site of the first permanent English settlement in America. See JAMESTOWN, Va.
Jefferson National Expansion Memorial	E Mo.	1935	91	37	Area commemorating westward exploration and settlement; includes Gateway Arch. See SAINT LOUIS, Mo.
John Fitzgerald Kennedy	E Mass.	1967	.09	.04	Birthplace and early boyhood home of President John F. Kennedy.
John Muir	W Calif.	1964	9	4	John Muir House and Martínez Adobe, commemorating contributions of John MUIR to conservation and literature.

* See separate article for additional information. For example, for Acadia, see ACADIA NATIONAL PARK.
† Not owned by the Federal government.
The following units were added to the National Parks System in 1974: John Day Fossil Beds National Monument, Oregon; Clara Barton National Historic Site, Maryland; Knife River Indian Villages National Historic Site, North Dakota; Martin Van Buren National Historic Site, New York; Springfield Armory National Historic Site, Massachusetts; Tuskegee Institute National Historic Site, Alabama; Boston National Historical Park, Massachusetts; Big Cypress National Preserve, Florida; Big Thicket National Preserve, Texas.

NATIONAL HISTORIC SITES (Continued)

Name	Location	Date Authorized	Gross Area ACRES	Gross Area HECTARES	Special Characteristics
Lincoln Home	Central Ill.	1971	12	5	Only private home owned by Abraham Lincoln; he was living there when he was elected President.
Longfellow	E Mass.	1972	2	.8	Home of Henry Wadsworth LONGFELLOW (1837–82) in Cambridge; also George Washington's headquarters during the siege of Boston (1775–76).
Lyndon B. Johnson	SE Texas	1969	8	3	Sites of the birthplace and boyhood home of President Lyndon B. JOHNSON.
†McLoughlin House	NW Oregon	1941	.6	.24	Home of the fur trader Dr. John MCLOUGHLIN.
Pennsylvania Avenue	Washington, D.C.	1965	. . .	. . .	Portion of Pennsylvania Ave. and adjacent area between the Capitol and the White House.
Puukohola Heiau	Hawaii, on Hawaii	1972	77	31	Hill of Whale Temple built (1791) by King Kamehameha the Great; ruins of John Young's house.
Sagamore Hill	SE N.Y.	1962	85	34	Estate and Victorian-style home of President Theodore ROOSEVELT (1858–1919).
Saint-Gaudens	W N.H.	1964	86	35	Memorial to the American sculptor Augustus SAINT-GAUDENS; contains his home studios, gardens.
†Saint Paul's Church	SE N.Y.	1943	6	2	18th-century church associated with the events leading to the arrest of John Peter ZENGER; link in American architectural history.
St. Thomas	Virgin Islands, on St. Thomas	1960	2	.8	Fort Christian (1680), the oldest standing structure in the Virgin Islands and the center of early Danish settlement.
Salem Maritime	NE Mass.	1938	11	4	Wharf and buildings important during Salem's seafaring days.
†San Jose Mission	S Texas	1941	4	2	Restored Spanish frontier mission (est. 1720).
San Juan	NE Puerto Rico	1949	48	19	Oldest fortification within the limits of U.S. territory, built (16th cent.) by the Spanish to protect the harbor guarding the sea lanes to the New World.
Saugus Iron Works	E Mass.	1968	9	4	Reconstruction of the 17th-century Colonial ironworks.
The Mar-A-Lago	E Fla.	1969	17	7	Private mansion illustrating the affluent society's way of life in the 1920s.
Theodore Roosevelt Birthplace	SE N.Y.	1962	.11	.04	Birthplace and boyhood home of President Theodore ROOSEVELT.
Theodore Roosevelt Inaugural	W N.Y.	1966	1	.4	Ansley Wilcox House, where Theodore Roosevelt took the oath of office (1901) as President.
†Touro Synagogue	SE R.I.	1946	.2	.08	Fine example of Colonial architecture; one of the oldest synagogues in the country.
Vanderbilt Mansion	E N.Y.	1940	212	86	19th-century palatial Victorian residence of a grandson of Cornelius Vanderbilt.
Whitman Mission	SW Wash.	1936	98	40	Site of the mission of Dr. Marcus WHITMAN.
William Howard Taft	SW Ohio	1969	.78	.32	Birthplace and early home of President William Howard TAFT.

NATIONAL HISTORICAL PARKS

Name	Location	Date Authorized	Gross Area ACRES	Gross Area HECTARES	Special Characteristics
Appomattox Court House	S central Va.	1930	938	380	Site of Lee's surrender to Grant. See under APPOMATTOX, Va.
Chalmette	SE La.	1939	142	57	Scene of part of the battle of New Orleans in the War of 1812.
Chesapeake and Ohio Canal	D.C., Md., W.Va.	1938	20,239	8,191	See CHESAPEAKE AND OHIO CANAL.
City of Refuge	Hawaii, on Hawaii	1955	181	73	Ancient burial ground and place of refuge.
*Colonial	SE Va.	1930	9,430	3,816	Historic Yorktown, Jamestown, and Cape Henry. Colonial Parkway connects some sites with Williamsburg.
Cumberland Gap	Ky., Tenn., Va.	1940	20,176	8,165	Mountain pass of the Wilderness Road. See CUMBERLAND GAP.
George Rogers Clark	SW Ind.	1966	23	9	Memorial near the site of old Fort Sackville, seized from British by Gen. G. R. CLARK in 1779.
Harpers Ferry	Md., W.Va.	1944	1,530	619	See HARPERS FERRY.
Independence	SE Pa.	1948	22	9	Historic points of interest; site of the signing of the Declaration of Independence. See INDEPENDENCE HALL.
Minute Man	E Mass.	1959	750	304	Scene of fighting on the opening day of the Revolutionary War; includes North Bridge, Minute Man statue, Battle Road (see LEXINGTON AND CONCORD, BATTLES OF), and the home of Nathaniel HAWTHORNE.
*Morristown	N N.J.	1933	1,358	550	Site of military encampments during the Revolution; Washington's headquarters, 1779–80.
Nez Percé	NW Idaho	1965	3,000	1,214	22 sites that preserve and commemorate the history and culture of the Nez Percé Indians.
San Juan Island	NW Wash.	1966	1,752	789	Dedicated to the peaceful relationship between the United States, Britain, and Canada since the SAN JUAN BOUNDARY DISPUTE.
Saratoga	E N.Y.	1938	5,500	2,226	Scene of a famous battle in the Revolution. See SARATOGA CAMPAIGN.
Sitka	SE Alaska	1910	108	44	Site of the Tlingit Indians' defeat by Russian settlers in 1804. See SITKA.

NATIONAL MEMORIALS

Name	Location	Date Authorized	Gross Area ACRES	Gross Area HECTARES	Special Characteristics
Arkansas Post	SE Ark.	1960	305	123	Site of the first permanent French settlement in the lower Mississippi valley. See ARKANSAS POST.
*Arlington House	NE Va.	1925	3	1	Former home of the Custis and Lee families; memorial to Robert E. LEE.
Benjamin Franklin	SE Pa.	1972	.12	.05	Statue of Benjamin Franklin in the rotunda of the Franklin Institute.
Chamizal	W Texas	1966	55	22	Memorializes the peaceful settlement of the 99-year border dispute between the United States and Mexico.
Coronado	SE Ariz.	1952	2,834	1,147	Area near Francisco Vásquez de CORONADO's point of entry (1540) into the United States.

* See separate article for additional information. For example, for Acadia, see ACADIA NATIONAL PARK.
† Not owned by the Federal government.
The following units were added to the National Parks System in 1974: John Day Fossil Beds National Monument, Oregon; Clara Barton National Historic Site, Maryland; Knife River Indian Villages National Historic Site, North Dakota; Martin Van Buren National Historic Site, New York; Springfield Armory National Historic Site, Massachusetts; Tuskegee Institute National Historic Site, Alabama; Boston National Historical Park, Massachusetts; Big Cypress National Preserve, Florida; Big Thicket National Preserve, Texas.

Name	Location	Date Autho-rized	Gross Area ACRES	Gross Area HECTARES	Special Characteristics
NATIONAL MEMORIALS (Continued)					
De Soto	W Fla.	1948	30	12	Commemorates the landing (1539) of Hernando DE SOTO in Florida and his exploration of S United States.
Federal Hall	SE N.Y.	1939	.45	.18	Site of the first seat of the Federal government and George Washington's inauguration (1789).
Fort Caroline	NE Fla.	1950	128	52	Area overlooking the site of FORT CAROLINE.
Fort Clatsop	NW Oregon	1958	125	51	Site of the winter encampment of the LEWIS AND CLARK EXPEDITION.
Frederick Douglass Home	Washington, D.C.	1962	8	3	Home of Frederick DOUGLASS from 1877 to 1895.
General Grant	SE N.Y.	1958	.76	.31	Tomb of President Ulysses S. GRANT and his wife, Julia.
Hamilton Grange	SE N.Y.	1962	.71	.29	Home of Alexander HAMILTON.
Johnstown Flood	SE Pa.	1964	54	22	Memorializes the Johnstown flood of 1889. See JOHNSTOWN, Pa.
Lincoln Boyhood	SW Ind.	1962	200	81	Site of the farm where Abraham Lincoln was raised and the burial place of his mother, Mary Hanks Lincoln.
*Lincoln Memorial	Washington, D.C.	1911	164	66	Classical structure with a heroic statue of Lincoln.
*Mount Rushmore	SW S.Dak.	1925	1,278	517	Carvings of Washington, Jefferson, Lincoln, and Theodore Roosevelt on the granite face of Mt. Rushmore.
Perry's Victory and International Peace Memorial	N Ohio	1936	36	15	Scene of the victory near Put-in-Bay of Oliver H. PERRY in the War of 1812.
Roger Williams	E R.I.	1965	5	2	Memorial to Roger WILLIAMS, the founder of the Rhode Island colony and a religious freedom pioneer.
Thaddeus Kosciuszko	SE Pa.	1972	.01	.004	Commemorates the life and work of Thaddeus KOSCIUSZKO.
*Thomas Jefferson	Washington, D.C.	1934	18	7	Classical structure with a statue of Jefferson.
*Washington Monument	Washington, D.C.	1848	106	43	555-ft (169-m) high obelisk honoring Washington.
Wright Brothers	NE N.C.	1927	431	174	Scene of the first (1903) successful flight of Wilbur and Orville WRIGHT.
NATIONAL MEMORIAL PARK					
*Theodore Roosevelt	W N.Dak.	1947	70,436	28,505	Part of Roosevelt's Elkhorn Ranch; badlands along the Little Missouri River.
NATIONAL MILITARY PARKS					
Chickamauga and Chattanooga	Ga., Tenn.	1890	8,113	3,283	See CHATTANOOGA, Tenn.
Fort Donelson	NW Tenn.	1928	600	243	See FORT DONELSON.
Fredericksburg and Spotsylvania County Battlefields Memorial	NE Va.	1927	3,672	1,486	See FREDERICKSBURG, Va.
Gettysburg	S Pa.	1895	3,409	1,380	See GETTYSBURG, Pa.
Guilford Courthouse	N N.C.	1917	233	94	See GUILFORD COURTHOUSE, BATTLE OF.
Horseshoe Bend	E Ala.	1956	2,040	826	See HORSESHOE BEND.
Kings Mountain	N S.C.	1931	3,950	1,599	Site of an American victory over the British at a critical point during the Revolution (Oct. 7, 1780).
*Moores Creek	SE N.C.	1926	50	20	Site of a battle between patriots and Loyalists.
Pea Ridge	NW Ark.	1956	4,279	1,732	Site of the Civil War battle of Pea Ridge, which saved Missouri for the Union.
Shiloh	SW Tenn.	1894	3,702	1,498	Site of the Civil War battle of SHILOH.
Vicksburg	W Miss.	1899	1,741	705	Site of the VICKSBURG CAMPAIGN of the Civil War.
NATIONAL BATTLEFIELD PARKS					
Kennesaw Mountain	NW Ga.	1917	3,683	1,491	Site of Sherman's attack on the Confederate forces in the ATLANTA CAMPAIGN.
Manassas	NE Va.	1940	2,727	1,104	See BULL RUN.
Richmond	E Va.	1936	742	300	See RICHMOND, Va.
NATIONAL BATTLEFIELDS					
Big Hole	SW Mont.	1910	656	265	Scene of an attack by U.S. soldiers on Chief Joseph.
Cowpens	NW S.C.	1929	845	342	Site of an American militia victory over British infantry and cavalry forces in the Revolutionary War battle of Cowpens (Jan. 17, 1781).
Fort Necessity	SW Pa.	1931	500	202	See FORT NECESSITY.
Petersburg	SE Va.	1926	2,731	1,105	Scene of the Battle of the Crater and a 10-month Union campaign (1864–65) to seize PETERSBURG, Va., a railroad center supplying Richmond and General Lee.
Stones River	Central Tenn.	1927	331	134	See MURFREESBORO, Tenn.
Tupelo	NE Miss.	1929	2	.6	See TUPELO, Miss.
Wilson's Creek	SW Mo.	1960	1,728	699	Site of Civil War battle for control of Missouri (Aug. 10, 1861).
NATIONAL BATTLEFIELD SITES					
Antietam	Central Md.	1890	783	317	See ANTIETAM CAMPAIGN.
Brices Cross Roads	NE Miss.	1929	1	.4	Site of a rout of Union troops by Confederate cavalry under Gen. N. B. Forrest (June 10, 1864).

* See separate article for additional information. For example, for Acadia, see ACADIA NATIONAL PARK.
† Not owned by the Federal government.
The following units were added to the National Parks System in 1974: John Day Fossil Beds National Monument, Oregon; Clara Barton National Historic Site, Maryland; Knife River Indian Villages National Historic Site, North Dakota; Martin Van Buren National Historic Site, New York; Springfield Armory National Historic Site, Massachusetts; Tuskegee Institute National Historic Site, Alabama; Boston National Historical Park, Massachusetts; Big Cypress National Preserve, Florida; Big Thicket National Preserve, Texas.

NATIONAL CEMETERIES

Name	Location	Date Authorized	Gross Area ACRES	Gross Area HECTARES	Special Characteristics
Antietam (Sharpsburg)	Central Md.	c.1862	11	4	Civil War cemetery.
Battleground	Washington, D.C.	1864	1	.4	Civil War cemetery.
Fort Donelson (Dover)	NW Tenn.	c.1867	15	6	Civil War cemetery.
Fredericksburg	NE Va.	c.1865	12	5	Civil War cemetery.
Gettysburg	S Pa.	1863	21	8	Civil War cemetery; site of President Lincoln's GETTYSBURG ADDRESS.
Poplar Grove (Petersburg)	SE Va.	c.1866	9	4	Civil War cemetery
Shiloh (Pittsburg Landing)	SW Tenn.	c.1866	10	4	Civil War cemetery.
Stones River (Murfreesboro)	Central Tenn.	c.1865	20	8	Civil War cemetery.
Vicksburg	W Miss.	c.1865	118	48	Civil War cemetery.
Yorktown	SE Va.	c.1866	3	1	Civil War cemetery.

NATIONAL RECREATION AREAS

Name	Location	Date Authorized	Gross Area ACRES	Gross Area HECTARES	Special Characteristics
Amistad	S Texas	1965	65,000	26,301	U.S. part of Amistad Reservoir, on the Rio Grande.
Arbuckle	S Okla.	1965	8,851	3,582	See ARBUCKLE MOUNTAINS.
Bighorn Canyon	Mont., Wyo.	1964	122,623	49,626	Yellowstone Reservoir and spectacular Bighorn Canyon, on the BIGHORN River.
Coulee Dam	NE Wash.	1946	100,059	40,494	Franklin D. Roosevelt Lake, formed by the GRAND COULEE DAM in the Columbia River; interesting geology.
Curecanti	E Colo.	1965	41,103	16,634	Blue Mesa, Morrow Point, and Crystal reservoirs in the upper Black Canyon of the Gunnison.
Delaware Water Gap	N.J., Pa.	1965	68,826	27,854	Scenic DELAWARE WATER GAP.
Gateway	N.Y., N.J.	1972	26,172	10,592	Beaches, marshes, islands, and waters in and around New York City. One of the first two national urban recreation areas.
Glen Canyon	Ariz., Utah	1958	1,196,545	484,242	Lake Powell, formed by the GLEN CANYON DAM.
Golden Gate	W Calif.	1972	34,202	13,842	Offers a variety of recreation in and around San Francisco. One of the first two national urban recreation areas.
Lake Chelan	N Wash.	1968	62,000	25,091	Located in the Stehekin Valley and in the northern part of fjordlike Lake CHELAN.
Lake Mead	Ariz., Nev.	1936	1,936,978	783,895	Lake MEAD, formed by Hoover Dam, and Lake Mohave, formed by Davis Dam; the first national recreation area established by Congress.
Lake Meredith	NW Texas	1965	41,097	16,632	Includes Lake Meredith, on the Canadian River, a popular water sports area in the Southwest.
Ross Lake	N Wash.	1968	107,000	43,303	Extends along the Skagit River canyon; bisects North Cascades National Park.
Shadow Mountain	N Colo.	1952	18,240	7,382	Shadow Mountain Lake and Lake Granby; part of the Colorado-Big Thompson project.
Whiskeytown-Shasta-Trinity	N Calif.	1965	41,937	16,972	Reservoirs and forestland; the National Park Service runs the Whiskeytown unit, and the Forest Service administers the Shasta and Trinity units.

NATIONAL LAKESHORES

Name	Location	Date Authorized	Gross Area ACRES	Gross Area HECTARES	Special Characteristics
Apostle Islands	NW Wis.	1970	42,826	17,332	APOSTLE ISLANDS and a strip of the Bayfield Peninsula, on the south shore of Lake Superior.
Indiana Dunes	NW Ind.	1966	8,721	3,529	200-ft (60-m) sand dunes, beaches, and marshes along the south shore of Lake Michigan.
Pictured Rocks	N Mich.	1966	67,000	27,115	Sandstone cliffs, sand dunes, beaches, marshes, waterfalls, and inland lakes along Lake Superior; the first national lakeshore.
Sleeping Bear Dunes	W central Mich.	1970	71,068	28,761	Section of the Lake Michigan shoreline and the North and South Manitoulin islands; beaches, sand dunes, forests, and lakes.

NATIONAL SEASHORES

Name	Location	Date Authorized	Gross Area ACRES	Gross Area HECTARES	Special Characteristics
Assateague Island	Md., Va.	1965	39,630	16,038	35-mi (56-km) barrier island; beaches; wildlife refuge including the wild Chincoteague ponies.
Cape Cod	SE Mass.	1961	44,600	18,050	See CAPE COD.
Cape Hatteras	E N.C.	1937	28,500	11,534	The first national seashore. See under HATTERAS, CAPE.
Cape Lookout	E N.C.	1966	24,500	9,915	Three barrier islands with beaches, sand dunes, and salt marshes; Cape Lookout Lighthouse.
Cumberland Island	SE Ga.	1972	39,494	15,983	Largest island off Georgia; beaches, sand dunes, marshes, and lakes.
*Fire Island	SE N.Y.	1964	19,311	7,815	Barrier beach.
Gulf Islands	Fla., Miss.	1971	125,000	50,588	Historic forts and white sand beaches near Pensacola, Fla.; Fort Massachusetts and primitive offshore islands in S Miss.
Padre Island	S Texas	1962	133,918	54,197	See PADRE ISLAND, Texas.
*Point Reyes	W Calif.	1962	64,546	26,122	Coastal area with beaches and steep bluffs.

NATIONAL PARKWAYS

Name	Location	Date Authorized	Gross Area ACRES	Gross Area HECTARES	Special Characteristics
Baltimore-Washington	Central Md.	1950	2,431	984	Approach to the nation's capital from the northeast; includes Greenbelt Park, a natural woodland.

* See separate article for additional information. For example, for Acadia, see ACADIA NATIONAL PARK.
† Not owned by the Federal government.
The following units were added to the National Parks System in 1974: John Day Fossil Beds National Monument, Oregon; Clara Barton National Historic Site, Maryland; Knife River Indian Villages National Historic Site, North Dakota; Martin Van Buren National Historic Site, New York; Springfield Armory National Historic Site, Massachusetts; Tuskegee Institute National Historic Site, Alabama; Boston National Historical Park, Massachusetts; Big Cypress National Preserve, Florida; Big Thicket National Preserve, Texas.

Cross-references are indicated by SMALL CAPITALS.

Name	Location	Date Authorized	Gross Area ACRES	Gross Area HECTARES	Special Characteristics
NATIONAL PARKWAYS (Continued)					
Blue Ridge	Va., N.C.	1936	94,749	38,345	Scenic route in the BLUE RIDGE mts. between Shenandoah and Great Smoky Mts. national parks; many roadside parks, lookouts, and trails; the first national parkway.
George Washington Memorial	Va., Md.	1930	7,142	2,890	Parkway connecting landmarks associated with the life of George Washington along both sides of the Potomac River from Mt. Vernon to Great Falls, then south to Chain Bridge.
John D. Rockefeller, Jr., Memorial	NW Wyo.	1972	23,700	9,591	Scenic corridor between Yellowstone and Grand Teton national parks commemorating Rockefeller's role in the creation of many national parks.
Natchez Trace	Miss., Ala., Tenn.	1938	45,298	18,332	Parkway following the general location of the old trail known as NATCHEZ TRACE.
Suitland	Md., D.C.	1949	731	296	Landscaped parkway between Washington, D.C., and Suitland, Md. (Andrews Air Force Base).
NATIONAL SCENIC TRAIL					
Appalachian	Maine, N.H., Vt., Mass., Conn., N.Y., N.J., Pa., Md., W.Va., Va., N.C., Tenn., Ga.	1968	50,000	20,235	See APPALACHIAN TRAIL.
NATIONAL SCENIC RIVER					
Lower Saint Croix	Minn., Wis.	1972	7,845	3,175	Scenic lower course of the St. Croix River; part of the Wild and Scenic Rivers System.
NATIONAL SCENIC RIVERWAYS					
*Ozark	Mo.	1964	72,101	29,179	Scenic parts of the Current and Jacks Fork rivers; the first national scenic riverway.
Saint Croix	Minn., Wis.	1968	67,747	27,417	200 mi (320 km) of the St. Croix River and its Namekagon tributary; trails, camping, boating.
Wolf	Wis.	1968	5,516	2,232	Scenic 24-mi (38-km) stretch of fast water.
NATIONAL RIVER					
Buffalo	NW Ark.	1972	95,840	38,786	130-mi (209-km) stretch of the Buffalo River and its valley; the first national river.
INTERNATIONAL PARK					
†Roosevelt-Campobello	SW New Brunswick, Canada	1964	2,722	1,102	Summer home of President Franklin D. Roosevelt on CAMPOBELLO island; first international park to be administered by a joint U.S.-Canadian commission.
NATIONAL SCIENTIFIC RESERVE					
†Ice Age	Wis.	1964	32,500	13,153	Contains features of continental glaciation; first national scientific reserve.
NATIONAL CAPITAL PARKS					
National Capital Parks	D.C., Va., Md.	1790	7,054	2,855	More than 700 parks in and around Washington, D.C.
WHITE HOUSE					
*White House	Washington, D.C.	1943	18	7	Official residence of the President.
PARKS (other)					
Catoctin Mountain Park	NW Md.	1936	5,769	2,335	Campgrounds, trails, and scenic drive located in the Catoctin Mts.; Camp David, the presidential retreat, is there.
John F. Kennedy Center for the Performing Arts	Washington, D.C.	1958	17	7	Site of cultural performances in its theater, concert hall, and opera house.
Piscataway Park	S Md.	1961	1,059	429	Preserves the view from Mt. Vernon of the opposite shore of the Potomac River.
Prince William Forest Park	NE Va.	1936	18,572	7,516	Woodland with 89 species of trees in pure stands.
Theodore Roosevelt Island	Washington, D.C.	1932	88	36	Wilderness preserve in the Potomac River; a tribute to the "conservationist President."
Wolf Trap Farm Park for the Performing Arts	N Va.	1966	188	48	Set in a rolling, wooded landscaped area to provide artistic enjoyment and recreation; the first national park for the performing arts.

* See separate article for additional information. For example, for Acadia, see ACADIA NATIONAL PARK.
† Not owned by the Federal government.
The following units were added to the National Parks System in 1974: John Day Fossil Beds National Monument, Oregon; Clara Barton National Historic Site, Maryland; Knife River Indian Villages National Historic Site, North Dakota; Martin Van Buren National Historic Site, New York; Springfield Armory National Historic Site, Massachusetts; Tuskegee Institute National Historic Site, Alabama; Boston National Historical Park, Massachusetts; Big Cypress National Preserve, Florida; Big Thicket National Preserve, Texas.

the charge of the department. By 1975 it was administering the more than 300 areas of scenic, historic, or scientific interest that make up the National Park System. The areas are classified into natural, historical, recreational, and cultural groupings to facilitate park management and to identify areas by their prominent characteristics. The National Park Service has six regional headquarters—in Washington, D.C.; Philadelphia; Richmond, Va.; Omaha, Nebr.; Santa Fe, N.Mex.; and San Francisco. Instructed by an act of Congress to "conserve the natural and historic objects in such manner as will leave them unimpaired for the enjoyment of future generations," the National Park Service has great and varied responsibilities, directing a wide program of construction and of educational and protective work. Congress laid the foundation of the National Park System in 1872 when it established Yellowstone National Park "as a pleasuring ground for the benefit and enjoyment of the people." Congress accelerated expansion of the National Park System in 1906 with the passage of the Antiquities Act, which permitted the President to proclaim national historic landmarks, structures, and "other objects of historic and scientific interest" on Federal lands. Until 1925, when an act was passed authorizing acceptance of donated land, nearly all of the National Park System was carved out of public lands. In 1933 the National Park Service was given trusteeship over areas hitherto under the jurisdiction of the Agriculture and War Depts. Since then Congress has also authorized the preservation of significant historic sites and the establishment of national parkways, national seashores, national recreational areas, national lakeshores, national wild and scenic rivers, national scenic trails, and national preserves. See publications of the U.S. National Park Service; W. H. Matthews, *A Guide to the National Parks: Their Landscape and Geology* (1973).

National Radio Astronomy Observatory (NRAO), Federal observatory for RADIO ASTRONOMY, founded in 1956 and operated under contract with the National Science Foundation by Associated Universities, Inc., a group of nine major universities. The headquarters is at Green Bank, W.Va., where the antennas, or radio telescopes, include a paraboloid transit antenna 300 ft (91 m) in diameter (which is free to move only on a north-south line); a fully steerable 140-ft (43-m) paraboloid; an interferometer consisting of three steerable 85-ft (26-m) paraboloids; a horn-shaped antenna 120 ft (37 m) in length that is fixed in place; and two smaller, steerable paraboloids. At Kitt Peak, near Tucson, Ariz., the observatory has a 36-ft (11-m) steerable paraboloid, and in New Mexico the observatory plans to erect a combination of antennas known as VLA (Very Large Array), consisting of 27 parabolic dishes, each 82 ft (25 m) in diameter, mounted on a Y-shaped track and movable along the track. This project will require about ten years to build. Principal research programs of the NRAO include the study of galactic structure, extragalactic radio sources, molecules in space, pulsars, quasars, and the evolution of stars and galaxies.

National Reactor Testing Station: see ARGONNE NATIONAL LABORATORY.

National Recovery Administration (NRA), in U.S. history, administrative bureau established under the National Industrial Recovery Act of 1933. In response to President Franklin Delano Roosevelt's congressional message of May 17, 1933, Congress passed the National Industrial Recovery Act, an emergency measure designed to encourage industrial recovery and help combat widespread unemployment. The act called for industrial self-regulation and declared that codes of fair competition—for the protection of consumers, competitors, and employers—were to be drafted for the various industries of the country and were to be subject to public hearings. The administration was empowered to make voluntary agreements dealing with hours of work, rates of pay, and the fixing of prices. Employees were given the right to organize and bargain collectively and could not be required, as a condition of employment, to join or refrain from joining a labor organization. The NRA—by a separate executive order—was put into operation soon after the final approval of the act. President Roosevelt appointed (June, 1933) Hugh S. JOHNSON as administrator for industrial recovery. Until March, 1934, the NRA was engaged chiefly in the drawing up of industrial codes; a blanket code for all industries was adopted, and well over 500 codes of fair practice were adopted for the various industries. Patriotic appeals were made to the public, and firms were asked to display the Blue Eagle, an emblem signifying NRA participation. Attacked in certain quarters as authoritarian, the NRA did not last long enough to fully implement its policies. In May, 1935, in the case of the *Schechter Poultry Corp.* vs. *United States* the U.S. Supreme Court invalidated the compulsory-code system on the grounds that the NRA improperly delegated legislative powers to the executive and that the provisions of the poultry code did not constitute a regulation of interstate commerce. The NRA was extended in skeletonized form until Jan. 1, 1936. Many labor provisions of the NRA were reenacted in later legislation (see WAGES AND HOURS ACT and NATIONAL LABOR RELATIONS BOARD). See L. S. Lyon et al., *The National Recovery Administration* (1933, repr. 1972); C. L. Dearing et al., *The ABC of the NRA* (1934); C. A. Pearce, *NRA Trade Practice Programs* (1939).

National Republican party, in U.S. history, a short-lived political party opposed to Andrew JACKSON. In the election of 1828, which Jackson won overwhelmingly, some of the supporters of his opponent, President John Quincy Adams, called themselves National Republicans. It was under this name that, following the lead of the Anti-Masonic party, they held a national nominating convention at Baltimore in Dec., 1831, and chose Henry CLAY to oppose Jackson in the 1832 election. The adherents of the National Republican party constituted a mixture of industrialists, business leaders, farmers, laborers, and mechanics, who believed in Clay's program of high tariffs, internal improvements, and a national bank. The main issue of the campaign was Jackson's veto of the second BANK OF THE UNITED STATES. Clay was badly beaten, and by 1836 the National Republicans had combined with other groups opposed to Jackson to form the WHIG PARTY.

National Road, U.S. highway built in the early 19th cent. At the time of its construction, the National Road was the most ambitious road-building project ever undertaken in the United States. It finally extended from Cumberland, Md., to St. Louis and was the great highway of Western migration. Agitation for a road to the West began c.1800. Congress approved the route and appointed a committee to plan details in 1806. Contracts were given in 1811, but the War of 1812 intervened, and construction did not begin until 1815. The first section (called the Cumberland Road) was built of crushed stone. Opened in 1818, it ran from Cumberland to Wheeling, W.Va., following in part the Indian trail known as NEMACOLIN'S PATH. Largely through the efforts of Henry Clay it was continued (1825–33) westward through Ohio, using part of the road built by Ebenezer Zane. By this time the older part of the road was badly in need of repair. Control of the road was therefore turned over to the states through which it passed, where tolls for maintenance were collected. It was carried on to Vandalia, Ill., and finally to St. Louis. The old route became part of U.S. Highway 40. At points on the road copies of a statue called the *Madonna of the Trail* have been erected to honor the pioneer women who went West over the National Road. See Philip D. Jordan, *The National Road* (1948).

National Science Foundation (NSF), an independent agency in the executive branch of the U.S. Federal government concerned with promoting a national science policy by supporting basic research and education in science. The National Science Board is the policy-making body of the NSF. It consists of 25 members appointed by the President with the consent of Congress. Founded in 1950, the NSF has an operating staff numbering about 1,000, most of whom are administrators. NSF does not conduct research of its own. Rather it makes support grants to qualified educational and nonprofit institutions and awards fellowships to individual scientists, teachers, and students. The foundation supports projects in the mathematical, physical, medical, biological, social, and engineering sciences. It supports the development of improved science curriculum materials and fosters the interchange of scientific ideas nationally and internationally. Among the more important NSF programs (some continuing) are: International Geophysical Year; International Decade of Ocean Exploration; Global Atmospheric Research Program; Ocean Sediment Coring Program; and the Arctic and Antarctic Research Programs. Among the more important permanent NSF facilities are: National Center for Atmospheric Research (Boulder, Colo.), National Radio Astronomy Observatory (Green Bank, W.Va.), Kitt Peak National Observatory (Tucson, Ariz.), National Astronomy and Ionosphere Center (Arecibo, Puerto Rico), and Cero Tolo Inter-American Observatory (La Serena, Chile).

National Security Council, Federal executive council responsible for planning, coordinating, and evaluating the defense policies of the United States and also exercising general direction over the Central Intelligence Agency. Created in 1947 by the National Security Act, the National Security Council members are the President, the Vice President, the Secretary of State, the Secretary of Defense, and the Director of the Office of Emergency Preparedness. The council also has a civilian staff that is headed by an executive secretary appointed by the President.

National Socialism or **Nazism,** doctrines and policies of the National Socialist German Workers' party, which ruled Germany under Adolf HITLER from 1933 to 1945. In German the party name is Nationalsozialistische Deutsche Arbeiterpartei (NSDAP); members were first called Nazis as a derisive abbreviation.

The Rise of the Party. After World War I a number of extremist political groups arose in Germany, including the miniscule German Workers' party, whose spokesman was Gottfried Feder. Its program combined socialist economic ideas with rabid nationalism and opposition to democracy. The party early attracted a few disoriented war veterans, including Hermann GOERING, Rudolf HESS, and Hitler. After 1920 Hitler led the party; its name was changed, and he reorganized and reoriented it, stamping it with his own personality. By demagogic appeals to latent hatred and violence, through ANTI-SEMITISM, anti-Communist diatribes, and attacks on the Treaty of Versailles, the party gained a considerable following. Its inner councils were swelled by such frustrated intellectuals as P. J. GOEBBELS, and by the element of riffraff typified by Julius STREICHER, while its public adherents were heavily drawn from the depressed lower middle class. Hitler minimized the socialist features of the program. National Socialism made its appeal not to an economic class but rather to the insecure and power-hungry elements of society.

Ideology and Organization. Nazi ideology drew on the racist doctrines of the comte de GOBINEAU and Houston Stewart CHAMBERLAIN, on the nationalism of Heinrich von TREITSCHKE, and on the hero-cult of Friedrich NIETZSCHE, often transforming the ideas of these thinkers. Nazi dogma, partly articulated by Hitler in *Mein Kampf,* was elaborated by the fanatical Alfred ROSENBERG. Vague and mystical, it was not a system of well-defined principles but rather a glorification of prejudice and myth with elements of nihilism. Its mainstays were the doctrines of racial inequality and of adherence to the leader, or Führer; its constant theme was nationalist expansion. According to Nazi dogma, races could be scientifically classified as superior and inferior. The highest racial type was the Nordic, or Germanic, type of the "Aryan" race, while Negroes and Jews were at the bottom of the racial ladder. Intermarriage contributed to the deterioration of the superior race, and the Jews, knowing this, had furthered prostitution and seduction to defile the Germans. Consequently only small islands of the pure remained, but it was their destiny to govern their inferiors and, through scientific breeding, to extend the "master race" and limit inferior races. The Jews, however, obstructed the conquering path of the "master race." Marxism, international finance, and Freemasonry were all Jewish devices to dominate the world. Even Christianity was denounced by Rosenberg as a Jewish creation, but Hitler hedged on this point. International Jewry was blamed for the humiliation of Germany in the Treaty of Versailles (1919), and German Jewry was accused of betraying Germany in World War I. Nazi expansionism was linked to race in the geopolitical theories of Karl HAUSHOFER; from the degenerate Slavs in particular the Germans would wrest *Lebensraum* [living space]. The ruling "master race" itself was to be organized into an authoritarian pyramid, at the apex of which stood the infallible Führer. Strength and discipline were deified by the Nazis, and democracy was spurned as a depraved form of government that protected the weak and mediocre. Nazi ideology probably gave less strength to the movement than did its well-organized party structure. From Communism Hitler borrowed the cell system, and from Italian Fascism he took the uniformed party militia. The mass of the militia was the brown-shirted SA, the *Sturmabteilung* [storm troops]. The elite was the black-uniformed SS, the *Schutzstaffel* [security echelon], under Heinrich HIMMLER. The party had its own salute (the raised arm and the words *Heil Hitler!*), symbol (the swastika), and anthem (the *Horst Wessel Lied*).

The military trappings and mass demonstrations of the Nazis attracted many followers. For the coming to power of National Socialism and the history of Germany under its rule, see GERMANY.

Control of the State. After ousting the left wing of the party, represented by Gregor STRASSER, Hitler, once in power, secured his position by the "Blood Purge" (June, 1934) of SA leader Ernst ROEHM and others who might challenge him. Loyal Nazis were placed in positions of authority within the government and eventually came to control it. A corporative state was established in which labor lost all rights and was even regimented in its recreation by the "Strength through Joy" movement. Youth, schools, and the press came under repressive control. The books of "undesirable" authors were repeatedly burned. Germany was divided into party districts; the *Gauleiter* [district leader] in effect superseded the state government. The judicial system was reorganized, and special courts were established to deal with political offenses. Nazi ideology was enthroned as national law, and Nazi methods replaced rational legal procedure. Anti-Semitic legislation (the Nuremberg Laws) forbade intermarriage with Jews, deprived Jews of civil rights, and barred them from professions. Other laws similarly barred the Communists. A German Christian Church was set up to control Protestant churches; its chief opponent, Martin NIEMOELLER, was arrested. The Gestapo (see SECRET POLICE) tracked down political opponents, Jews, and other undesirables; their internment in CONCENTRATION CAMPS was often a prelude to their murder, particularly in the case of the Jews after the start of World War II. Medical "experiments," some of them conducted to prevent the reproduction of Jews and "misfits," maimed thousands more.

Nazism Outside Germany. In the period of German expansion the Nazis found many adherents outside Germany. In Austria the inclusion in the government of Nazi leader SEYSS-INQUART speeded Austrian annexation, and in Czechoslovakia the Sudete German party (see SUDETES) aided the absorption of that country by Germany. The party of Jacques Doriot in France, the Rexists in Belgium, the Iron Guard in Rumania, the Hungarian National Socialists, the Croatian Ustachi, and the German-American *Bund* in the United States were all affiliated to some extent with the Nazis. In World War II the Nazis imposed their system and dogma on Europe by force. Millions of Jews, Russians, Poles, and others were interned and exterminated; millions more were used for forced labor. Only the collapse of Germany's military might prevented the annihilation of the Jews and the complete subjugation of Europe. With the Allied victory National Socialism was outlawed in Germany. See Hermann Rauschning, *The Revolution of Nihilism* (tr. 1939); Franz Neumann, *Behemoth* (2d ed. 1944, repr. 1963); Eugen Kogon, *The Theory and Practice of Hell* (tr. 1950; repr. 1972); W. L. Shirer, *The Rise and Fall of the Third Reich* (1960); J. C. Fest, *The Face of the Third Reich* (tr. 1970); K. D. Bracher, *The German Dictatorship* (tr. by Jean Steinberg, 1970); Albert Speer, *Inside the Third Reich* (tr. 1970); Dietrich Orlov, *The History of the Nazi Party: 1933–1945* (1973).

National Theatre of Great Britain, a government-funded repertory company based in London. Although the idea for such a company originated in the 19th cent., the theater was not finally established until 1963, with Laurence OLIVIER appointed as director. Funding, first begun in 1908, was interrupted by the two world wars, but in 1949 the government granted £1 million to the project. Temporarily housed in the OLD VIC theater, the company's opening performance of *Hamlet* has been followed by outstanding productions of *Saint Joan, Uncle Vanya,* and *Othello,* among many classic and modern works.

National Trust, British association to preserve for the nation places of natural beauty or buildings of architectural or historic interest in the British Isles; founded 1894, chartered 1895. By act of Parliament (1907) the Trust was empowered to acquire land inalienably and to be exempt from duties on property given or willed. In 1934 the Trust received special powers to protect by covenant privately owned property. The owner retains such property and its income, but may neither build on it nor alter its use without permission.

National University, at Manila, the Philippines; English language; founded 1900 as Colegio filipino. Its present name was adopted in 1921. It has colleges of commerce, dentistry, pharmacy, education, liberal arts, engineering, and architecture.

National Youth Administration (NYA), former U.S. government agency established in 1935 within the Works Progress Administration; it was transferred in 1939 to the Federal Security Agency and was placed in 1942 under the War Manpower Commission. Created in a period of widespread unemployment as part of the New Deal program of President Franklin Delano Roosevelt, the NYA at first engaged in obtaining part-time work for unemployed youths. As unemployment decreased and war approached, emphasis was gradually shifted to training youths for war work until, early in 1942, all NYA activities not contributing to the war effort were dropped. Its activities ceased late in 1943.

Nation of Islam: see BLACK MUSLIMS.

Native American Church, religious cult of the Navaho Indians; it blends fundamentalist Christian elements and pan-Indian moral principles. The movement began among the Kiowa Indians about 1890 and, led by John Wilson (Big Moon), soon spread to other tribes. The sacramental food of the cult was peyote, a hallucinogenic cactus, and the group came to be known as peyotists. In 1918, peyotists from a number of tribes incorporated their movement as the Native American Church. In 1940 the cult was declared illegal by the Navaho Tribal Council, which saw it as a threat to Navaho culture and to Christianized Navahos. The church flourished underground, however, until 1967, when the tribe reversed its decision. Estimates of practicing membership in Arizona, New Mexico, and Utah, where the Navaho live, run from a third to 80% of the tribe.

nativism, in anthropology, social movement that proclaims the return to power of the natives of a colonized area and the resurgence of native culture, along with the decline of the colonizers. The term has also been used to refer to a widespread attitude in a society of a rejection of alien persons or culture. Nativism occurs within almost all areas of nonindustrial culture known to anthropologists. One of the earliest careful studies of nativism was that of James Mooney (1896), who studied the Ghost Dance among Indians of the W United States. In 1943, Ralph Linton published a brief paper on nativistic movements that served to establish the phenomenon as a special topic in anthropological studies of culture change.

NATO: see NORTH ATLANTIC TREATY ORGANIZATION.

natrium: Latin for SODIUM.

Natron, Lake (nā'trən), c.35 mi (60 km) long and 15 mi (20 km) wide, in the Great Rift Valley, E Africa, on the Kenya-Tanzania border. It has unexploited soda, salt, and magnesite deposits.

Nattier, Jean-Marc (zhäN-märk nätyā'), 1685–1766, French painter; son of the painter Marc Nattier and the miniaturist Marie Courtois. His early works include historical and mythological paintings as well as portraits of Peter the Great and Catherine I of Russia. From 1737 he exhibited portraits regularly at the salons and enjoyed the patronage of the Orléans family and the royal court. He usually portrayed his sitters in the guise of mythological characters and sought effects of graceful elegance at the expense of characterization. He is extensively represented in European museums. Typical of his works is the *Portrait of a Lady as Diana* (1756; Metropolitan Mus.).

Natufian: see NEOLITHIC PERIOD; MESOLITHIC PERIOD.

Natural Bridge, village (1970 est. pop. 600), Rockbridge co., W Va., in the Shenandoah valley; founded 1774. Nearby is the famous Natural Bridge over the gorge of Cedar Creek. It is a limestone arch 215 ft (66 m) high with a span of 90 ft (27 m) and was once owned by Thomas Jefferson, who built a cabin there for visitors and kept a guest book. Today a public highway crosses the bridge.

Natural Bridges National Monument, 7,600 acres (3,076 hectares), SE Utah; est. 1908. Located in an area of colored cliffs and box canyons, the monument contains three huge natural sandstone bridges: Owachomo (also called Rock Mound), 106 ft (32 m) high with a span of 180 ft (55 m); Kachina, 210 ft (64 m) high with a span of 206 ft (63 m); and Sipapu, 220 ft (67 m) high with a span of 268 ft (82 m).

natural childbirth: see BIRTH.

natural gas, natural mixture of gases found issuing from the ground or obtained from specially driven wells. The composition of natural gas varies in different localities. Its chief component, methane, usually makes up from 80% to 95%, the balance being composed of varying amounts of other HYDROCARBON compounds, carbon dioxide, nitrogen, hydrogen, carbon monoxide, helium, and sometimes other gases, such as hydrogen sulfide. Because of its flammability and high calorific value, natural gas is used extensively as an illuminant and a fuel. Although commonly associated with the production of petroleum, it is found also at a distance from such fields in sand, sandstone, and limestone deposits. Some geologists believe the gas to be a by-product or an end product of the evolution of petroleum, while others think it has a separate origin. Some of the hydrocarbons found in gasoline also occur as vapors in natural gas. By liquefying these hydrocarbons, gasoline can be obtained. Natural gas was known to the ancients but was considered by them to be a supernatural manifestation because, noticed only when ignited, it appeared as a mysterious fire bursting from fissures in the ground. One of the earliest attempts to harness it for economic use occurred in the early 19th cent. in Fredonia, N.Y. Toward the latter part of the century large industrial cities began to make use of natural gas, and pipelines were constructed to conduct the gas to these centers. In the early 1970s the U.S. yearly production of natural gas was over 20 trillion cu ft (5.6×10^{11} cu m); however, consumption was so great that imports were necessary and restrictions on the use of natural gas were being considered. **Liquefied natural gas,** or LNG, is natural gas that has been pressurized and cooled so as to liquefy it for convenience in shipping and storage. As its boiling point is very low, natural gas is not easy to liquefy or to maintain in the liquid state. It is only fairly recently that cryogenic, or extreme cold, technology has advanced to the point where the liquefaction of natural gas is commercially feasible. However, the weight of the containers necessary to confine LNG is considerable, limiting its usefulness. Some of the natural gas imported into the United States is carried as LNG in special tankers.

Natural History, American Museum of: see AMERICAN MUSEUM OF NATURAL HISTORY.

naturalism, in art, is a product of the interest in science prevalent in 19th-century Europe. The naturalist painters sought to render nature precisely as perceived without recourse to ideal forms. The life of the working people was a popular subject with the naturalists, particularly with J. F. MILLET and DAUMIER.

naturalism, in literature, an approach that proceeds from an analysis of reality in terms of natural forces, e.g., heredity, environment, physical drives. The chief literary theorist on naturalism was Émile ZOLA, who said in his essay *Le Roman expérimental* (1880) that the novelist should be like the scientist, examining dispassionately various phenomena in life and drawing indisputable conclusions. The naturalists tended to concern themselves with the harsh, often sordid, aspects of life. Notable naturalists include the Goncourt brothers, J. K. Huysmans, Maupassant, the English authors George Moore and George Gissing, and the American writers Theodore Dreiser, Frank Norris, Stephen Crane, James T. Farrell, and James Jones. In the drama, naturalism developed in the late 19th cent. By stressing photographic detail in scene design, costume, and acting technique, it attempted to abolish the artificial theatricality prominent in 19th-century theater. The movement was most closely associated with the Théâtre Libre (founded 1887) of André Antoine, with the Freie Bühne (founded 1889) of Otto Brahm, and with the Moscow Art Theatre (founded 1898) under the direction of Stanislavsky. Notable naturalistic dramatists include Becque, Brieux, Hauptmann, Tolstoy, and Gorky.

naturalism, in philosophy, in general a position that attempts to explain all phenomena and account for all values by means of strictly natural (as opposed to supernatural) categories. The particular meaning of naturalism varies with what is opposed to it. It is usually considered the opposite of idealism and is sometimes equated with empiricism or materialism; it is not easily distinguished from positivism. Naturalism limits itself to a search for causes and takes little account of reasons. Naturalism in the broad sense has been maintained in diverse forms by Aristotle, the Cynics, the Stoics, Giordano Bruno, Spinoza, Thomas Hobbes, Auguste Comte, Jean Jacques Rousseau, Friedrich Nietzsche, Karl Marx, William James, John Dewey, and Alfred North Whitehead. However, these philosophers differ widely on specific questions. Some, like Comte and Nietzsche, were professed atheists, while others accepted a god in pantheistic terms. Aristotle, James, and Dewey all attempted to explain phenomena in terms of biological processes of perception; Spinoza and the idealists tended instead to emphasize metaphysics; later thinkers of all schools have placed emphasis on unifying the scientific viewpoint with an all-encompassing reality. This amalgamation of science and an over-all explanation of the universe in naturalistic terms is the source of much of contemporary philosophic thought. See Marvin Farber, *Naturalism and Subjectivism* (1959); V. C. Punzo, *Reflective Naturalism* (1969).

naturalization, official act by which a person is made a national of a country other than his native one. In some countries naturalized persons do not necessarily become CITIZENS but may merely acquire a new NATIONALITY. There is no such limitation in the United States; the Fourteenth Amendment to the Constitution declares that "all persons born or naturalized in the United States" and subject to U.S. jurisdiction are citizens. Article 1, Section 8, of the Constitution gives Congress the power to enact uniform naturalization laws. These laws require the renunciation of previous national allegiance (see EXPATRIATION). Under the first American statute (1790) all unindentured white males who had lived in the United States for two years might become citizens. The period of residence was lengthened to five years in 1795 and, as a result of antiforeign feeling then prevalent, to 14 years in 1798. In 1802 it was reduced to five years, which remains the usual term. The McCarran-Walter Act (1952; amended, 1965) revised and recodified the whole body of immigration and naturalization regulations. By the terms of this act, declarations of intention two years before naturalization were eliminated, and naturalization could be granted 30 days after petitioning, following rigorous examination. The act introduced seditious behavior, discovery of fraud, and prolonged absences abroad as grounds for cancellation of naturalization, although the implementation of these provisions was limited by subsequent Supreme Court decisions. Ths act is administered by the Immigration and Naturalization Service of the Dept. of Justice. The petitioner for naturalization must meet several requirements, including the ability to read and speak English; in addition, he must swear to support the Constitution and must be adjudged of good moral character. The actual conferring of citizenship is in most cases the action of a Federal court. Since 1922 alien women do not become U.S. citizens by marrying a citizen or by the naturalization of their husbands. Children under 18, however, become citizens automatically on the naturalization of the head of the family, usually the father. The process of naturalization in some circumstances is shortened for members of the U.S. armed forces and for the wives of American citizens, and there are certain exceptions made by means of private immigration and naturalization bills passed by Congress. In addition to individual acts of naturalization, whole populations may be naturalized. An example is the conferring of citizenship at various times in U.S. history on the populace of Texas, Alaska, Hawaii, Puerto Rico, and the Virgin Islands. See IMMIGRATION. See F. G. Franklin, *The Legislative History of Naturalization in the United States* (1906, repr. 1969); D. H. Smith, *The Bureau of Naturalization* (1926, repr. 1973).

natural law, theory that some laws are basic and fundamental to human nature and are discoverable by human reason without reference to specific legislative enactments or judicial decisions. Natural law is opposed to positive law, which is man-made, conditioned by history, and subject to continuous change. The concept of natural law originated with the Greeks and received its most important formulation in STOICISM. The Stoics believed that the fundamental moral principles that underlay all the legal systems of different nations were reducible to the dictates of natural law. This idea became particularly important in Roman legal theory, which eventually came to recognize a common code regulating the conduct of all peoples and existing alongside the individual codes of specific places and times (see NATURAL RIGHTS). Christian philosophers such as St. THOMAS AQUINAS perpetuated this idea, asserting that natural law was common to all peoples—Christian and non-Christian alike—while adding that revealed law gave Christians an additional guide for their actions. In modern times, the theory of natural law became the chief basis for the development by Hugo GROTIUS of the theory of international law. In the 17th cent., such philosophers as Spinoza and G. W. von Leibniz interpreted natural law as the basis of ethics and morality; in the 18th cent. the teachings of Jean Jacques ROUSSEAU, especially as interpreted during the French Revolution, made natural law a basis for democratic and egalitarian principles. The influence of natural law theory declined greatly in the 19th cent. under the impact of POSITIVISM, EMPIRICISM, and MATERIALISM. In the 20th cent., such thinkers as Jacques MARITAIN saw in natural law a necessary intellectual opposition to totalitarian theories. See Jacques Maritain, *The Rights of Man and Natural Law* (1943, repr. 1971); Josef Fuchs, *Natural Law* (1965); Julius Stone, *Human Law and Human Justice* (1965).

natural resources, conservation of: see CONSERVATION OF NATURAL RESOURCES.

natural rights, political theory that maintains that an individual enters into society with certain basic rights and that no government can deny these rights. The modern idea of natural rights grew out of the ancient and medieval doctrines of NATURAL LAW, i.e., the belief that man, as a creature of nature and God, should live his life and organize his society on the basis of rules and precepts laid down by nature or God. With the growth of the idea of individualism, especially in the 17th cent., natural law doctrines were modified to stress the fact that the individual, because he is a natural being, has rights that cannot be violated by anyone or by any society. Perhaps the most famous formulation of this doctrine is found in the writings of John LOCKE. Locke assumed that men were by nature rational and good, and that they carried into political society the same rights they had enjoyed in earlier stages of society, foremost among them being freedom of worship, the right to a voice in their own government, and the right of property. Jean Jacques ROUSSEAU attempted to reconcile the natural rights of the individual with the need for social unity and cooperation through the idea of the SOCIAL CONTRACT. The most important elaboration of the idea of natural rights came in the North American colonies, however, where the writings of Thomas Jefferson, Samuel Adams, and Thomas PAINE made of the natural rights theory a powerful justification for revolution. The classic expressions of natural rights are the English Bill of Rights (1689), the American Declaration of Independence (1776), the French Declaration of the Rights of Man and the Citizen (1789), the first 10 amendments to the Constitution of the United States (known as the Bill of Rights, 1791), and the Universal Declaration of Human Rights of the United Nations (1948). See B. F. Wright, *American Interpretation of Natural Law* (1931, repr. 1962); Leo Strauss, *Natural Right and History* (1957); O. F. von Gierke, *Natural Law and the Theory of Society, 1500–1800* (1913, tr. 1934, repr. 1958); Julius Stone, *Human Law and Human Justice* (1965).

natural selection: see SELECTION.

Nau, Jacques Jean David (zhäk zhäN dävēd' nō), c.1630–1671, French pirate in the West Indies. He is also called François L'Olonnois. He went to the West Indies in 1650. Expelled in 1653 from the Spanish colony of Santo Domingo for buccaneering activities, he found refuge on Tortuga, fitted out a vessel, and began plundering Spanish possessions. His cruelty toward prisoners was bestial, and he was feared over the Spanish Main. In a fight with the Spanish in Campeche all his men were killed, but Nau, disguising himself, watched the celebration of his death and then escaped in a canoe with a few French fugitive slaves. Capturing a Spanish boat in a surprise attack off Cuba, he continued to plunder, sacking Maracaibo in 1667. Wrecked by a storm in the Gulf of Darien, Nau was killed by the Indians.

Naucalpan (noukäl'pän), city (1970 pop. 373,605), Mexico state, S central Mexico, on the Hondo River. It is an industrial extension of Mexico City.

Naucratis (nŏk'rətĭs), ancient city of Egypt, on the Canopic branch of the Nile, 45 mi (72 km) SE of Alexandria. It was probably given (7th cent. B.C.) by Psamtik to Greek colonists from Miletus and was the first Greek settlement in Egypt. The rise of Alexandria and the shifting of the Nile caused its decline. The site has been excavated, revealing pottery of a Greek type and ruins of Greek temples.

Naugatuck (nôg'ətŭk"), borough (1970 pop. 23,034), New Haven co., SW Conn., on both sides of the Naugatuck River; settled 1704, inc. 1844. Rubber products have been made since Henry Goodyear, brother of Charles, established a rubber plant there in 1843. Other manufactures are candy, machinery, iron castings, and electrical and metal products. Several buildings in Naugatuck were designed by McKim, Mead, and White.

Naugatuck, river, 65 mi (105 km) long, rising in NW Conn. and flowing S, past Waterbury, to the Housatonic River at Derby. Many manufacturing centers are along its course. In 1955 it overflowed its banks and caused considerable damage. Thomaston Dam (completed 1960), built for flood control, forms a reservoir on the river.

Nauheim: see BAD NAUHEIM, West Germany.

Naum (nā'əm), name in the Gospel genealogy. Luke 3.25.

Naumann, Friedrich (frē'drĭkh nou'män), 1860–1919, German political leader. A Lutheran pastor, he renounced (1894) the ministry to enter politics. He was a leading member of the Progressive party and worked to infuse this middle-class liberal party with social reformism. He was elected to the Reichstag (1907–12, 1913–18) and served as party leader. Naumann founded and edited the political weekly *Hilfe.* After the overthrow of the monarchy (Nov., 1918) he helped found the German Democratic party, which favored a democratic republic. Naumann was the author of *Mittel-Europa* (1915; tr. *Central Europe,* 1916), a significant work in the Pan-German movement.

Naumburg (noum'bŏŏrkh) or **Naumburg an der Saale** (-än dər zä'lə), city (1970 pop. 37,636), Halle district, S East Germany, on the Saale River. Manufactures of this industrial city include machine tools, processed food, textiles, and toys. Founded in the 11th cent., Naumburg developed as a trade center and joined the Hanseatic League. It passed to Saxony in 1564 and to Prussia in 1815. The city has retained parts of its medieval walls; a 16th-century city hall; and a beautiful cathedral (13th–14th cent.), with some of the finest sculptures of the German Gothic period.

Nauplia, Greece: see NÁVPLION.

Nauru (näoo'roo), atoll (1972 est. pop. 8,800), c.8 sq mi (20 sq km), central Pacific, just south of the equator and W of the GILBERT ISLANDS. Until 1968, when it became one of the world's smallest independent states, Nauru was administered by Australia under United Nations Trusteeship. Nauru is important for its high-grade phosphate deposits, on which the economies of Australia and New Zealand are heavily dependent. Almost 2,000,000 tons of phosphates are produced annually. After independence Nauru took control of the deposits from the British Phosphate Commission. Nauru was discovered in 1798 by the British and was annexed in 1888 by Germany. Occupied during World War I by Australian forces, it was placed (1920) under a League of Nations mandate to Australia. Throughout World War II the island was occupied by the Japanese. Nauru is a parliamentary republic with a president (Administrator), elected by the legislative council, and a small cabinet. Nauruans are predominantly Polynesian, with heavy intermixtures of Micronesian and Melanesian strains. Nauru was formerly called Pleasant Island.

nausea, sensation of discomfort, or queasiness, in the stomach. It may be caused by irritation of the stomach by food or drugs, unpleasant odors, overeating, fright, or psychological stress. It is usually relieved by vomiting. Nausea is frequently present during the early months of pregnancy, and it is a concomitant of motion sickness. However, nausea may also be the symptom of a serious illness; thus persistent nausea should receive medical attention.

Nausicaä (nôsĭk'ēə): see ODYSSEUS.

Nautical Almanac: see EPHEMERIS.

nautilus, CEPHALOPOD mollusk belonging to the sole surviving genus (*Nautilus*) of a subclass that flourished 200 million years ago, known as the nautiloids. The spirally coiled shell consists of a series of chambers; as the nautilus grows it secretes larger chambers, sealing off the old ones with thin septa. The animal lives in the largest and newest chamber, with a tubular elongation of the body, known as the siphuncle, extending through the septa to the apex of the shell. The siphuncle secretes gas in the empty chambers, giving the animal the buoyancy that permits it to swim, which it accomplishes by ejecting water through a funnel. The nautilus breathes by means of siphons; it feeds on crabs and other animals, which it catches with its long, slender tentacles (numbering more than 90) that encircle the mouth. There is a thickened area over the head, called the hood, or operculum, that acts as a protective lid when the animal withdraws into the shell. The nautilus lives in deep water in the S Pacific and Indian oceans. The PAPER NAUTILUS, which is not a true nautilus, is a close relative of the octopus, belonging to the order Octopoda. The true nautilus is classified in the phylum MOLLUSCA, class Cephalopoda, order Nautilida, family Nautilidae.

Nautilus: see SUBMARINE.

Navaho (nä'vəhō), language belonging to the ATHABASCAN branch of the Nadene linguistic family, or stock, of North America (including Mexico). See AMERICAN INDIAN LANGUAGES.

Navaho Indians or **Navajo Indians** (both: nä'vəhō), North American Indians whose language belongs to the ATHABASCAN branch of the Nadene linguistic stock (see AMERICAN INDIAN LANGUAGES). A migration from the North to the Southwest area is thought to have occurred in the past because of an affiliation with N Athabascan speakers; the Navaho settled among the Pueblo and also assimilated with the Shoshone and the Yuma both physically and culturally while keeping a distinct social group. The Navaho are a composite group with over 50 separate clans. In the 17th cent. they occupied the region between the San Juan and Little Colorado rivers in NE Arizona, but they ranged far outside that territory. The Navaho were a predatory tribe who (often in alliance with their relatives, the Apache) constantly raided the PUEBLO INDIANS and later the Spanish and Mexican settlements of New Mexico. When the Americans occupied (c.1846) New Mexico, the Navaho pillaged them. Punitive expeditions against the Navaho were only temporarily successful until Kit Carson, by destroying the Navaho's sheep, subdued them in 1863-64. A majority of them were imprisoned for four years at Fort Sumner in New Mexico. In 1868 they were released from prison and given a reservation of 3.5 million acres (1,416,000 hectares) in NE Arizona, NW New Mexico, and SE Utah and a new supply of sheep. The Navaho then numbered some 9,000. Since that date they have remained a peaceful and industrious people and have been steadily increasing in number. By the early 1970s, with some 120,000 Navahos on or adjacent to the reservation, they constituted the largest Indian tribe in the United States. Their reservation has grown to over 16 million acres (6,475,000 hectares), 2 million acres (809,400 hectares) of which they own jointly with the HOPI INDIANS. The Navaho were a nomadic tribe. In winter they lived in earth-covered lodges and in summer in brush shelters. They farmed (corn and beans), hunted (deer, elk, and antelope), and gathered wild vegetable products. After sheep were introduced (early 17th cent.) by the Spanish, sheep raising superseded hunting and farming. Thus the Navaho became a pastoral people. They have adopted many peaceful arts—from the Mexicans metalworking, from the Pueblo Indians weaving. They live in extended kin groups and traditional inheritance is through the mother's line; women have an important position in the society. Navaho religion is elaborate and complex, with many deities, songs, chants, and prayers, and numerous colorful ceremonies, such as the squaw dance and the night chant. The vast mythology includes a creation myth that states that Esdzanadkhi (probably Mother Earth) created man. The Navaho have also subscribed to the PEYOTE cult. In the 1930s the overgrazed and eroded grasslands of the Navaho Reservation caused the Federal government to reduce the tribe's sheep, cattle, and horses by as much as 50%. The government, having left the Indians without a means of support, began a program of irrigation projects, thus enabling them to turn to agriculture for a livelihood. But even farming can support only a fraction of the people, and as a result many have had to obtain their income off the reservation. The discovery of oil, gas, and other minerals has helped to increase the tribal income (now about $16 million per year)). See R. M. Underhill, *The Navahos* (1956); Clyde Kluckholn and Dorothea Leighton, *The Navaho* (rev. ed. 1962); L. R. Bailey, *The Long Walk: A History of the Navaho Wars, 1846-1868* (1964); Laura Gilpin, *The Enduring Navaho* (1968); J. U. Terrell, *The Navajos* (1970); James Downs, *The Navajo* (1972); Frank McNitt, *Navajo Wars* (1972).

Navajo Dam, 402 ft (123 m) high and 3,648 ft (1,112 m) long, NW N.Mex., on the San Juan River, near the Colo. line; built 1958-63 by the U.S. Bureau of Reclamation. The dam, a major unit of the Colorado River storage project, is among the largest earth-filled dams in the world. It regulates the flow of the San Juan River and provides flood control. Water impounded by the dam is used by the Navajo Indian irrigation project to irrigate c.110,000 acres (44,500 hectares) of land on the Navajo Indian Reservation.

Navajo National Monument: see NATIONAL PARKS AND MONUMENTS (table).

naval architecture, science of designing ships. A naval architect must consider especially the following factors: floatability, i.e., the ability of the ship to remain afloat while meeting the requirements of the vessel's service under normal and abnormal weather and water conditions or after being damaged by collision or grounding; strength sufficient to withstand loads for which the vessel is intended; stability, i.e., the capability of the vessel to return to an upright position after being inclined by wind, sea, or conditions of loading; speed, which is affected by the outline of the hull and the type of engines, boilers, and propellers; steering, i.e., the design of the rudder and the hull structure to effect efficient turning; living conditions, including adequate ventilation and other health and safety considerations; and the arrangement of the structure and equipment to facilitate handling of cargoes. Additional problems are faced in the design of warships. Heavy, concentrated loads in the form of gun turrets, the protective armor, and other factors make warship design a field in itself. The three principal plans made for the construction of a ship are the sheer plan, a profile of the ship, showing the outline of the intersection of a series of vertical longitudinal planes with the shell of the ship and including the location of the transverse bulkheads, decks, and main structures; the body plan, a view showing sections made by vertical transverse planes; and the half-breadth plan, indicating the outline of a series of horizontal longitudinal planes. In addition, innumerable general and detail drawings are made, which include all the internal and external equipment. J. P. Comstock, ed., *Principles of Naval Architecture* (1967); Ross Munro-Smith, *Applied Naval Architecture* (1967); T. C. Gillmer, *Modern Ship Design* (1970).

naval conferences, series of international assemblies, meeting to consider limitation of naval armaments, settlement of the rules of naval war, and allied issues. The **London Naval Conference** (1908-9), composed of delegates of 10 powers, resulted in the influential Declaration of London (see LONDON, DECLARATION OF). After World War I, U.S. President Harding called the **Washington Conference** (1921-22). Several treaties resulted. The Five-Power Treaty limited tonnage of aircraft carriers and capital ships and arranged for the United States, Great Britain, and France to scrap a number of ships. Agreement was reached on a ratio of capital ships for Great Britain, the United States, Japan, France, and Italy; the ratio was set at 5:5:3:1.67:1.67. Another five-power treaty made the rules of warfare applying to surface ships applicable also to submarines and outlawed the use of poison gas. In the Four-Power Treaty, France, Japan, Great Britain, and the United States agreed to respect each other's possessions in the Pacific. The status quo of naval fortifications in the W Pacific was to be maintained. Japan was to return Shantung to China, which was guaranteed territorial integrity and greater control over its tariff by two Nine-Power Treaties. The Washington Conference treaties were to remain in force until Dec. 31, 1936. The **Geneva Conference** (1927) failed to reach agreement on more comprehensive limits for warships. At the **London Conference** (1930), Japan won a 7:10:10 ratio with the United States and Great Britain in small cruisers and destroyers, remained at a 3:5:5 ratio with them in large cruisers, and won parity in submarines. France and Italy refused to take part in the new ratios, but, with the other three powers, agreed to defer further construction of capital ships. An escalator clause provided for naval expansion in case of any threat to national security by the naval building of a nonsignatory nation. The announcement in 1934 of Japan's intention to withdraw from the Washington Conference treaties resulted in another **London Conference** (1935). Japan withdrew from the conference when refused naval parity with the United States and Great Britain. These two powers and France signed (March 25, 1936) an agreement to limit cruisers and destroyers to 8,000 tons and capital ships to 35,000 tons. Reports of Japanese building in excess of 35,000 tons led to a revision (1938) of the treaty limits on the size of capital ships, and with the outbreak of World War II in 1939 the treaties were completely abandoned.

naval science: see STRATEGY AND TACTICS.

naval stores, term initially applied to the cordage, mask, resin, tar, and timber used in building wood sailing ships; it now designates the products obtained from the pine tree, e.g., pine oil, pitch, rosin, tar, and turpentine. These products fall into two classes, those obtained from living pines and those from dead pines. Most of the naval stores used in the world are produced in the SE United States and in France. Naval stores are now used largely in the manufacture of soap, paint, varnish, shoe polish, lubricants, linoleum, and roofing material.

Navan (năv'ən) or **An Uaimh,** urban district (1971 pop. 4,607), county town of Co. Meath, E Republic of Ireland, at the confluence of the Boyne and Blackwater rivers. It produces woolens and has sawmills. Clothing, furniture, and carpets are also made. There are remains of the old town walls. Nearby are some medieval ruins and Navan Mote, an imposing earthwork.

Navarino, battle of (nävärē'nō), 1827, naval battle resulting from the intervention of the European powers in the Greek War of Independence from the Ottoman Empire (Turkey). England, France, and Russia had demanded an armistice in the Greek-Turkish warfare. The Turks refused to bring the fighting to a halt, and the three European powers sent their fleets to stop Egyptian reinforcements for the Turks from landing in Greece. In Sept., 1827, a large Egyptian fleet, with troop transports, commanded by Ibrahim Pasha, landed at Navarino (now Pylos). The allied fleet commander, Admiral Sir Edward Codrington, persuaded Ibrahim to await further instructions from his father, Muhammad Ali of Egypt. When the Greeks continued operations, Ibrahim disregarded his agreement; thereupon the allied ships entered (Oct.) the harbor and destroyed the bottled-up Egyptian fleet. The destruction of the fleet helped bring about the withdrawal (1828) of Muhammad Ali from the war in Greece. See study by C. M. Woodhouse (1965).

Navarre (nəvär'), Span. *Navarra* (nävä'rä), province (1970 pop. 464,867), N Spain, bordering on France, between the W Pyrenees and the Ebro River. Pamplona is the capital. Navarre and the Basque Provinces together form the region of Vascongadas y Navarra. The beautiful mountain slopes have extensive cattle pastures and vast forests that yield hardwoods, which are economically important. The fertile valleys produce sugar beets, cereals, and vegetables; vineyards are important in the Ebro valley. The establishment of hydroelectric plants has permitted some industrial development. The population of Navarre is largely of Basque stock, and the early history of the region is that of the BASQUES. The pass of RONCESVALLES, which leads from France to Navarre, made the region strategically important early in its history. The Basques defended themselves successfully against the Moorish invaders as well as against the Franks; the domination of Charlemagne, who conquered Navarre in 778, was short-lived. In 824 the Basque chieftain Iñigo Aritza was chosen king of Pamplona, which was expanded under his successors and became known as the kingdom of Navarre. It reached its zenith under Sancho III (reigned 1000-1035), who married the heiress of Castile and ruled over nearly all of Christian Spain. On his death the Spanish kingdoms were again divided (into Navarre, Aragón, and Castile). The kingdom of Navarre then comprised the present province of Navarre, the Basque Provinces (which were later lost to Castile), and, N of the Pyrenees, the district called Lower Navarre, now a part of France. In 1234, Navarre passed through inheritance to the house of Champagne and in 1305 to King Philip IV of France. Navarre stayed with the French crown until the death (1328) of Charles IV, when it passed to Charles' niece, whose son, Charles II (Charles the Bad), played an important part in the Hundred Years War and in the French civil unrest of the time. In 1479, Navarre passed, through marriage, to the counts of Foix and then to the house of Albret. Ferdinand V (Ferdinand the Catholic), after defeating Jean d'Albret, annexed most of Navarre in 1515. The area N of the Pyrenees (Lower Navarre) remained an independent kingdom until it was incorporated (1589) into the French crown when Henry III of Navarre became King Henry IV of France. It was united with Béarn into a French province. Until the French Revolution the kings of France carried the additional title king of Navarre. Since the rest of Navarre was in Spanish hands, the kings of Spain also carried (until 1833) the title king of Navarre. During that period Navarre enjoyed a special status within the Spanish monarchy; it had its own cortes, taxation system, and separate customs laws. In 1833, Navarre sided with the CARLISTS but recognized Isabella II as queen in 1839.

Navarrete, Juan Fernández (hwän fārnän'dĕth nävärā'tā), 1526-79, Spanish religious painter, called El Mudo [the mute]. He studied in a monastery and later in Italy, perhaps with Titian. In 1568 he became court painter to Philip II, for whom he enriched the Escorial with eight fine altarpieces, among them *Nativity, Abraham and the Three Angels* (Escorial), and *Baptism* (now in the Prado). Through Navarrete, Venetian influence reached Spain. His later works combine sketchy distances with rich color and realistic foreground effects.

Navarrete, Martín Fernández de (mārtēn' fārnän'dĕth dā), 1765-1844, Spanish historian and hydrographer. Joining (1780) the Spanish navy, he entered (1796) the navy department and later established its hydrographic office. After Napoleon took Spain, Navarrete retired (1809). In 1823 he became director of the hydrographic office. In 1824 he was made director of the Royal Academy of History, which at his instigation and under his editorship began the great *Colección de documentos inéditos* (112 vol., 1842–95). This compilation of Spanish historical sources is especially valuable for information about the 16th cent. Navarrete is also famous for his collection (5 vol., 1825–37) of narratives of Spanish voyages of discovery of the late 15th and 16th cent.

nave (nāv), in general, all that part of a church that extends from the atrium to the altar and is intended exclusively for the laity. In a strictly architectural sense, however, the term indicates only the central aisle, excluding side aisles. The floor plan of a wide central portion with narrower aisles on either side existed in the typical HYPOSTYLE hall of Egyptian temples and later in the Roman civic basilicas. From the latter it passed into the churches of the early Middle Ages and gradually to Gothic cathedrals. The nave, in the developed Gothic style, became the main body of the structure, its vaulted roof borne high above the aisles on a slender masonry skeleton, transmitting its thrusts downward and outward through great piers and flying buttresses. Internally the piers, rising the full height of the nave walls to carry the ribs of the four-part vault or sexpartite vault, divided the walls into a series of bays in which three features, ground floor arcade, TRIFORIUM, and CLERESTORY, were evident, one above another.

navigable water, in the broadest sense, a stream or body of water that can be used for commercial transportation. When, as in the early common law, the term is restricted to waters affected by tides, it denotes only the open sea and tidal rivers. In most U.S. jurisdictions the definition tends to include any body of water that may be put to public use, e.g., streams that can be used only for logging and for small pleasure boats would still be considered navigable. In the United States each state determines what private use may be made of wholly intrastate navigable waters (see WATER RIGHTS), but the Federal government alone has authority over navigable interstate and international waters. In general, if the water is of restricted navigability, the right of public use is strictly confined to transporting goods; use of the water for irrigation, power, and the like is limited to the abutting landowners.

navigation, science and technology of finding the position and directing the course of vessels and aircraft. In ancient times, navigation must have been by the guidance of the sun and stars and landmarks along the coast. The Phoenicians were probably the most daring of the ancient navigators. They built large ships and traveled out of sight of land by day and by night. They probably circumnavigated Africa. The Vikings often carried birds, which were used to find land when no coast was visible. A bird would be released and its flight watched, since the bird on rising to a higher altitude might sight land and naturally would fly toward it. In England, Queen Elizabeth I did much to establish navigation laws, giving additional powers to Trinity House, a guild that had been created in 1514 for the piloting of ships and the regulation of British navigation. During this period the study of bodies of water, or hydrography, was given much attention, and harbors and the outlets of rivers were surveyed and buoyed. A tremendous advance in navigation had taken place with the introduction of the COMPASS. Early in the 15th cent. there was progress by the Portuguese under the leadership of Prince Henry the Navigator, who built an observatory and formulated tables of the declinations of the sun; collected a great amount of nautical information, which he placed in practical form; made charts; and sponsored expeditions that led to numerous discoveries. With the development of shipbuilding and the increase in knowledge of astronomy, there was increased use of instruments. The cross-staff was used to find latitude early in the 15th cent. It consisted of two pieces of wood, the cross at right angles to, and sliding on, the staff. At each end of the 26-in. (66-cm) cross a small hole was bored, and at the end of the staff a sight was fixed. To measure the altitude of a heavenly body, the instrument was sighted in that direction, and the cross was moved forward or back until the heavenly body appeared through the upper hole and the horizon through the lower. The altitude could then be read on a scale marked on the staff. Another device used for finding latitude was the astrolabe. Both were far from accurate. The navigating equipment carried by Columbus probably was simply a compass, a cross-staff, and a table of the sun's declination. Vasco da Gama on his first voyage around the Cape of Good Hope in 1497 used the astrolabe. The Flemish geographer G. K. Mercator's work in improving charts at the end of the 16th cent., the works of the Spanish scientist Martín Cortés during the same period, the determining of the earth's circumference, and the introduction of logarithms at the beginning of the 17th cent. by the Scottish mathematician John Napier were all factors that did much to advance the intricate science of navigation. However, up to the beginning of the 18th cent., while the quadrant was used to find latitude and the log line and half-minute glass employed to tell the distance traveled, the problem of finding the longitude had not been satisfactorily solved before the invention of the chronometer. The appearance of the Nautical Almanac (see EPHEMERIS) in 1767 was a great step forward in navigation, and the 19th cent. saw the development of books on navigation that far surpassed any earlier instructions, such as the standard book by Nathaniel Bowditch, an American mathematician. The system of dead reckoning, which was much refined, is the art of finding a position by calculating the point of departure (i.e., the last known point of latitude and longitude), the course (as shown by the compass), the speed and the distance traveled according to the log, and the time elapsed. The use of buoys and the making of careful charts made navigation easier, while the fixing of positions by sextant and astronomical charts was greatly improved. The next great revolution in navigation, however, waited until well into the 20th cent., when radio signals came into wide use. The development of RADAR, LORAN, and radio direction finding during World War II caused fundamental changes in navigational practice. See AIR NAVIGATION. See latest edition of *Bowditch's Practical Navigator.*

Navigation Acts, in English history, name given to certain parliamentary legislation, more properly called the British Acts of Trade. The acts were an outgrowth of MERCANTILISM, and followed principles laid down by Tudor and early Stuart trade regulations. They had as their purpose the expansion of the English carrying trade, the provision from the colonies of materials England could not produce, and the establishment of colonial markets for English manufactures. The rise of the Dutch carrying trade, which threatened to drive English shipping from the seas, was the immediate cause for the Navigation Act of 1651, and it in turn was a major cause of the First DUTCH WAR. It forbade the importation of plantation commodities of Asia, Africa, and America except in ships owned by Englishmen. European goods could be brought into England and English possessions only in ships belonging to Englishmen, to people of the country where the cargo was produced, or to people of the country receiving first shipment. This piece of Commonwealth legislation was substantially reenacted in the First Navigation Act of 1660 (confirmed 1661). The First Act enumerated such colonial articles as sugar, tobacco, cotton, and indigo; these were to be supplied only to England. This act was expanded and altered by the succeeding Navigation Acts of 1662, 1663, 1670, 1673, and by the Act to Prevent Frauds and Abuses of 1696. In the act of 1663 the important staple principle required that all foreign goods be shipped to the American colonies through English ports. In return for restrictions on manufacturing and the regulation of trade, colonial commodities were often given a monopoly of the English market and preferential tariff treatment. Thus Americans benefited when tobacco cultivation was made illegal within England, and British West Indian planters were aided by high duties on French sugar. But resentments developed. The Molasses Act of 1733, which raised duties on French West Indian sugar, angered Americans by forcing them to buy the more expensive British West Indian sugar. Extensive smuggling resulted. American historians disagree on whether or not the advantages of the acts outweighed the disadvantages from a colonial point of view. It is clear, however, that the acts hindered the development of manufacturing in the colonies and were a focus of the agitation preceding the American Revolution. Vigorous attempts to prevent smuggling in the American colonies after 1765 led to arbitrary seizures of ships and aroused hostility. The legislation had an unfavorable effect on the Channel Islands, Scotland (before the Act of Union of 1707), and especially Ireland, by excluding them from a preferential position within the system. Shaken by the American Revolution, the system, along with mercantilism, fell into decline. The acts were finally repealed in 1849. See studies by G. L. Beer (1907–13); L. A. Harper, *The English Navigation Laws* (1939, repr. 1964); *Cambridge History of the British Empire,* Vol. I (1929); O. M. Dickerson, *The Navigation Acts and the American Revolution* (1951, repr. 1974).

navigation satellite, artificial SATELLITE designed expressly to aid the navigation of sea and air traffic. The first navigation satellite of the Transit series was successfully launched on April 13, 1960. Based on the Doppler shift of signals received from Transit, a ship at sea can accurately determine its longitude and latitude. To be useful to commercial carriers, the signals sent by a navigation satellite must be strong enough to be received by the fairly simple electronics carried aboard ships. Transit's transmitter is powered by a system that generates electricity from nuclear isotopes. Communications and applications satellites also serve navigational purposes.

Navigators' Islands: see SAMOA.

Návpaktos (näf'päktôs) or **Naupactus** (nôpăk'təs), town (1971 pop. 8,170), central Greece, a port on the Gulf of Corinth near the Gulf of Pátrai. The town was captured by Athens in 456 B.C. and was an important Athenian naval base in the Peloponnesian War. It later declined but rose to commercial importance as part of the Byzantine Empire. Known also as Lepanto in medieval and modern times, it came under the rule of Venice in 1407 and under the Ottoman Turks in 1499. In 1571, Christian forces of Europe won a major naval battle over the Ottoman Empire near the town (see LEPANTO, BATTLE OF). In 1828, Greek insurgents took the town from Ottoman control.

Návplion (näf'plēôn) or **Nauplia** (nô'plēə), town (1971 pop. 9,281), capital of Argolís prefecture, S Greece, in the Peloponnesus, a port on the Gulf of Argolís. It is a commercial center that ships tobacco, cotton, and fruits. According to tradition, the town was founded by Nauplius, who was the father of Palamedes. In 1715, Návplion was captured by the Ottoman Turks from Venice. The town was taken in 1822 by the Greek insurgents and was (1830–34) the first capital of independent Greece. The revolt (1862) against King Otto I began there.

navy, originally, all ships of a nation, whether for war or commerce; the term *navy* now designates only such vessels as are built and maintained specifically for war. Navies were maintained by all the early Eastern nations bordering on the Mediterranean. The Greeks, the Romans, and the Italian states had navies of a similar nature. In the north the famous Viking ships were organized into small but effective fleets. It was to meet their attacks that Alfred the Great, in the 9th cent., organized a royal fleet and became the first to realize that a navy was essential to England. Henry VII, in the 16th cent., reorganized the royal navy and established dockyards, and the reign of Elizabeth I saw additional naval developments. France's navy originated with Louis IX in the mid-13th cent., and Spain, after the disaster of the Armada in 1588, rebuilt the Spanish navy, although Spain never again became a major sea power. In Russia, Peter I established a navy at the end of the 17th cent. In the same century the British royal navy became the strongest in the world, and it ruled the seas for 300 years. British naval power rested not so much on numbers or superior ship construction as on its professional class of officers. Although British naval superiority was challenged by other European powers, such as the Dutch and French, in the 17th, 18th, and 19th cent., Great Britain maintained its superiority. In the late 19th and early 20th cent. Germany, Italy, and Japan developed strong navies. A congressional vote of $100,000 in 1775 financed the beginning of the United States navy in the American Revolution, and in 1798 the Dept. of the Navy was established. The U.S. navy did not, however, attain any considerable size or strength until after 1800. In 1845, through the efforts of George Bancroft, the United States Naval Academy was opened. In the Civil War, the South for a time enjoyed great success in attacking Northern seaborne commerce, but in the end the South's vessels were driven from the seas by the Union navy. After the Civil War, U.S. naval power languished until the late 19th cent., when the appearance of Japan and Germany as major naval powers encouraged the United States to establish a strong navy, and during the Spanish-American War the United States emerged as the second strongest sea power of the world. It was at this time that modern naval weapons such as the torpedo, the rifled naval gun, and the SUBMARINE were developed. World War I was to a large extent a contest between the naval strengths of Britain and Germany. Germany lost its navy at the end of the war. After World War I naval tactics were revolutionized by the development of the airplane. Previously the decisive naval weapon had been the heavily gunned warship; the new decisive naval weapon was the aircraft carrier, whose superiority was made clear in World War II when U.S. carrier-based aircraft dominated the Pacific and did much to cripple German submarine strength in the Atlantic. At the end of World War II, Germany, Italy, and Japan were stripped of their navies, Britain was economically weakened, and the United States emerged with the strongest navy in the world. By the early 1970s the Soviet Union and the United States had the most powerful navies. The development of nuclear-powered vessels, together with nuclear weapons, has altered the role of the navy in a nation's STRATEGY AND TACTICS. See AIRCRAFT CARRIER; BATTLESHIP; CRUISER. See A. T. Mahan, *The Influence of Sea Power upon History* (1890, repr. 1970); David Cooney, *A Chronology of the U.S. Navy: 1775-1965* (1965); H. T. Lenton, *Warships of the British and Commonwealth Navies* (1966); L. W. Martin, *The Sea in Modern Strategy* (1967). Fletcher Pratt and H. E. Howe, *Compact History of the United States Navy* (rev. ed. 1967); D. J. Carrison, *The United States Navy* (1968); Clark Reynolds, *Command of the Sea* (1974).

Navy, United States Department of the: see DEFENSE, UNITED STATES DEPARTMENT OF.

Navy Island, in the Niagara River, just above Niagara Falls, S Ont., Canada. It is famous as the scene of the last stand made by William Lyon Mackenzie and some of his fellow rebels in the Upper Canadian Rebellion of 1837.

Nawa: see NAHA, Okinawa.

Náxos (năk'sôs, năk'sŏs), island (1971 pop. 14,201), c.160 sq mi (410 sq km), SE Greece, in the Aegean Sea; largest of the CYCLADES. Náxos (1971 pop. 2,892), the chief town, is on the western shore. The fertile island produces fruits, olive oil, and a noted white wine. It has been a source of white marble, emery, and granite since ancient times. Náxos is famous in mythology as the place where Theseus abandoned Ariadne. It was a center of the worship of Dionysius. The island was colonized by the Ionians and in 490 B.C. was captured and sacked by the Persians. It was a member of the DELIAN LEAGUE, but after an unsuccessful attempt to secede was captured (c.470 B.C.) and became a tributary to Athens. Náxos passed to Venice in 1207 and was the seat of a Venetian duchy until 1566, when it fell to the Ottoman Turks. It became part of independent Greece in 1829.

Naxuana: see NAKHICHEVAN, USSR.

Nayarit (näyärēt'), state (1970 pop. 547,992), 10,547 sq mi (27,317 sq km), W Mexico, on the Pacific Ocean. TEPIC is the capital. Mostly wild and rugged, Nayarit is broken by western spurs of the Sierra Madre Occidental. In the northeast are broad, tropical plains watered by the Santiago River, a continuation of the Lerma. Nayarit has two volcanoes. The volcanic soil, heavy rains, and altitude variations permit the cultivation of a variety of products of tropical and temperate agriculture—sugarcane, cotton, coffee, tobacco, and grains. Cattle raising is also important. Forest and mineral wealth on the mainland and on Las Tres Marías islands is almost unexploited. The state's coastal swamps are noted bird refuges. The Nayarit region was known to the Spanish early in the 16th cent., and one of its towns, Compostela (near Tepic), was the first capital of NUEVA GALICIA. Spain did not finally conquer the area until the early 17th cent., however. Shortly afterward, Nayarit became a dependency of Guadalajara and, upon Mexican independence, part of Jalisco. Continued turbulence led to Nayarit's separation as a territory in 1884. It became a state in 1917. The name Nayarit is given to pre-Columbian clay figurines, mostly grotesque, that are found in the vicinity.

Nayler, James, 1617?-1660, English Quaker leader. He served in the parliamentary army during the English civil war. In 1651 he became a Quaker and a disciple of George Fox, but gradually gathered a band of followers about himself. In 1656 he rode into Bristol, his followers crying "Holy, holy, holy, Lord God of Israel." Nayler's explanation that his disciples were worshiping the "Christ within him" rather than himself did not prevent a parliamentary trial (1656). He was sentenced to be pilloried, whipped, branded, and imprisoned. Nayler was author of a number of well-written religious pamphlets; his collected works were published in 1716. See biographies by M. R. Brailsford (1927) and Emilia Fogelklou (1931).

Nazarene (năz'ərēn), term used of early Christians. It alludes to Nazareth. Acts 24.5.

Nazarenes (năz'ərēnz), group of German artists of the early 19th cent., who attempted to revive Christian art. In 1809, J. F. Overbeck and Franz Pforr formed an art cooperative in Vienna called the Brotherhood of St. Luke. The group moved to Rome and established themselves in a disused monastery. They were joined by Philipp Veit, Peter von Cornelius, Schnorr von Carolsfeld, and Schadow-Godenhaus. They lived simply, devoting the mornings to household tasks and the afternoons to painting. Many of them collaborated on the frescoes in the Casa Bartholdy (1816-17; now in Berlin) and the Casino Massimo (1822-32, Rome). Using early Italian and late medieval German pictures as models, they worked within the limits of religious dogma and not from nature. Although their paintings were uncomfortably composed, poorly colored, and lacking in imagination, the Nazarenes exerted considerable influence in Germany and in England upon the PRE-RAPHAELITES.

Nazareth (năz'ərĭth), town, N Israel, in Galilee. As the home of Jesus Christ, it is a great pilgrimage and tourist center. Nazareth is also the trade center for an agricultural region. The town's manufactures include processed food, cigarettes, and pottery. Mineral water is bottled in Nazareth, and stone is quarried nearby. Nazareth is first mentioned in the New Testament, although its settlement antedates historic times. It was captured by Crusaders in 1099, taken by Saladin in 1187, and retaken in 1229 by Frederick II. In 1263, Muslims conquered Nazareth and massacred its Christian population. In 1517, Nazareth was annexed by the Ottoman Empire. The town was part of the British-administered Palestine mandate (1922-48) and was captured by Israeli forces in the 1948 War. The Basilica of the Annunciation and the Mosque of Peace are in Nazareth.

Nazarite [Heb. *nazir*=consecrated], in the Old Testament, a man dedicated to God. The Nazarite, after taking a special vow, abstained from intoxicating beverages, never cut his hair, and avoided corpses. An inadvertent breach of these rules called for purificatory rites. His vow was for a fixed term (though it could also be for life), at the end of which he was released. Samuel, the prophet, and Samson were Nazarites. The name is also spelled Nazirite.

Nazas (nä'säs), river, c.180 mi (290 km) long, rising in the Sierra Madre Occidental, Durango state, N Mexico, and flowing generally east to disappear into the ground near Torreón. During the wet season it usually inundates a vast desert basin and sometimes reaches Laguna de Mayran. With its control dams, it provides water for irrigating the Laguna dist.

Nazca or **Nasca** (both: näs'kä), ancient culture of the Nazca, Pisco, and Ica river valleys on the desert coast of S Peru. Flourishing during the first millennium A.D., the Nazca culture seems to have developed out of the PARACAS culture, and after 900 it was apparently under TIAHUANACO influence until the Inca conquered the region in the 15th cent. The Nazca excelled in the production of beautiful ceramics and textiles. Highly polished, expertly designed, and with polychrome painting, Nazca pottery is unlike that of other Peruvian cultures. Textiles show a multitude of weaving techniques and extraordinary skill in dyeing with several shades of the same color; both coastal cotton and highland alpaca wool were used. Aerial exploration of the arid tableland surrounding the Palpa valley has revealed a remarkable network of lines and trapezoids interspersed with giant animal figures of unmistakable Nazca origin; the animals were probably built to be seen by sky gods, and the lines are believed to be related to observations in astronomy. See P. A. Means, *Ancient Civilizations of the Andes* (1931); J. Alden Mason, *The Ancient Civilizations of Peru* (1957, rev. ed. 1964); G. H. S. Bushnell, *Peru* (1956, rev. ed. 1963); E. P. Lanning, *Peru before the Incas* (1967).

Naze, the, cape: see LINDESNES, Norway.

Nazi: see NATIONAL SOCIALISM.

Nazianzen: see GREGORY NAZIANZEN, SAINT.

Nazimova, Alla (nəzĭ'məvə), 1879-1945, Russian-American actress. She turned from music to the drama, studying with Stanislavsky and later appearing at the Moscow Art Theatre. In 1905 she emigrated to New York City and played Russian roles in her native tongue. She made her English-speaking debut (1906) in Ibsen's *Hedda Gabler* and thereafter became the foremost interpreter of Ibsen in the United States. In 1910 she took over the Thirty-Ninth Street Theatre, which was renamed the Nazimova. An actress of sensitivity and power, she gave memorable performances in Chekhov's *Cherry Orchard* (1928) and in O'Neill's *Mourning Becomes Electra* (1931). Her films include *Camille* (1921), *A Doll's House* (1922), and *The Bridge of San Luis Rey* (1944).

Nazism: see NATIONAL SOCIALISM.

Nazor, Vladimir, 1876-1949, Yugoslav poet and novelist, b. Croatia. Nazor's early career paralleled the emergence of the Young Croatian literary movement. His verses in *Croat Kings* (1912) established him as the great patriot poet of his homeland. *Istrian Tales* (1913) revealed his storytelling skill. By illuminating the personality of the South Slavs through tales of his native Croatia, he helped to create the Yugoslav national consciousness. In World War II he joined the partisans and wrote stirring appeals for national freedom.

Nb, chemical symbol of the element NIOBIUM.

Nd, chemical symbol of the element NEODYMIUM.

Ndebele: see MATABELE.

Ndjamena (ənjä'mänä), formerly **Fort-Lamy** (fôr-lämē'), city (1972 est. pop. 179,000), capital of Chad and of Chari-Baguirmi prefecture, SW Chad. It is a port on the Chari River and a transportation hub that lies on roads leading to Nigeria, Sudan, and the Central African Republic. Ndjamena is primarily an administrative center. It is also a major regional market for livestock, salt, dates, and grains. Meat processing is the chief industry. The city was founded as Fort-Lamy by the French in 1900 and named after Major L. J. M. Lamy, a French soldier and explorer who conquered much of the area. Its name was changed to Ndjamena in 1973. The city has schools of administration and veterinary medicine and an international airport.

Ndola (əndō'lä), city (1972 est. pop., with suburbs, 201,300), N central Zambia, near Zaïre. It is a commercial, mining, and manufacturing center, located on the COPPERBELT. Copper mining in Ndola long antedates the coming of the Europeans (c.1900). Manufactures include cement, footwear, and soap; motor vehicles are assembled. Ndola is the site of Northern Technical College (1964).

Ne, chemical symbol of the element NEON.

Neagh, Lough (lŏkh nā), lake, 153 sq mi (396 sq km), 18 mi (29 km) long and 11 mi (18 km) wide, central Northern Ireland. It is the largest freshwater body in the British Isles but is not a deep lake. Fed by the Upper Bann, Blackwater, and other streams and drained to the north by the Lower Bann, it is noted for pollan, trout, and eel fisheries. Mesolithic man is believed to have first appeared in Ireland (c.6000 B.C.) near the lake. According to a legend, quoted by Giraldus Cambrensis, the Norman-Welsh historian, and cited in Thomas Moore's "Let Erin Remember" (*Irish Melodies*), the lake occupies the site of a town which was flooded; buildings may sometimes be seen through the water.

Neagle, John, 1796-1865, American portrait painter, b. Boston. He was reared in Philadelphia, where he was apprentice to a coach painter. After travel in the West, he settled in Philadelphia and married the stepdaughter of Thomas Sully. He made a name for himself by his famous portrait *Pat Lyon at the Forge* (Pa. Acad. of the Fine Arts) in 1826. A skillful delineator of character, he was also a forceful draftsman and a fine colorist. There are works by him in the museums of Cleveland, Minneapolis, New Orleans, and New York City.

Neah (nē'ə), unidentified place, N Palestine. Joshua 19.13.

Neale, Sir John Ernest (nēl), 1890–, English historian. He was educated at the Univ. of Liverpool and London Univ. and was professor of English history at London Univ. from 1927 to 1956. He is considered the foremost authority on the political and constitutional history of the Elizabethan era. In *Queen Elizabeth* (1934) he presented the queen as an astute and judicious political leader. In *The Elizabethan House of Commons* (1949, rev. ed. 1963), following the method of Sir Lewis Namier, he showed the dominance of local, aristocratic, and semifeudal influences in elections to Elizabethan parliaments. Neale's other works include *Elizabeth I and Her Parliaments* (2 vol., 1953-57) and *Essays in Elizabethan History* (1958). He was knighted in 1955.

Neale, John Mason (nēl), 1818-66, English clergyman, historian, and hymn writer, grad. Trinity College, Cambridge, 1840. An enthusiastic supporter of the High Church movement, he was under the inhibition (i.e., not allowed to perform any ministerial duties) of his bishop from 1846 to 1863. From 1846 until his death he was warden of Sackville College, East Grinstead, Sussex, a charitable institution for the aged; there he wrote voluminously—history, theology, travel books, poems, hymns, and books for children. A nursing sisterhood which he had founded elsewhere was moved to East Grinstead in 1856 and continued there as St. Margaret's Sisterhood. He is best known for his numerous translations of Greek and Latin hymns. In 1859 appeared his translation of a sizable part of Bernard of Cluny's

De contemptu mundi, from which several of Neale's best-known hymns are taken. See A. G. Lough, *The Influence of John Mason Neale* (1962).

Neander, Johann August Wilhelm (yō'hän ou'gōōst vĭl'hĕlm näān'dər), 1789–1850, German theologian and church historian. Of Jewish parentage, he became a Lutheran (1806), changing his name from David Mendel. In 1813 he became professor of church history at the Univ. of Berlin. A disciple of Friedrich Schleiermacher, he was one of the leaders in the attempt to mediate between the rationalists and the extreme orthodox Lutheran theologians. He wrote many books, of which the best known is *Allgemeine Geschichte der christlichen Religion und Kirche* (11 vol., 1825–52; tr. *General History of the Christian Religion and Church,* 9 vol., 1847–55).

Neanderthal (näān'dərtäl''), small valley, W West Germany, E of Düsseldorf. In 1856 the remains of NEANDERTHAL MAN were discovered there.

Neanderthal man (nēăn'dərthôl''), an early form of man, generally considered of the species *Homo sapiens,* living during the last glacial period, between 100,000 and 40,000 years ago. Fossils of this type were first discovered in 1856 in Neanderthal, a valley in West Germany. Since then, many Neanderthal remains have been found in Europe, N Africa, the Middle East, and Siberia, with artifacts of the Mousterian culture (Middle PALEOLITHIC PERIOD). This culture included a variety of stone tools used in the hunting and processing of wild animals. The Neanderthals sometimes inhabited caves and used fire, and are the first people for whom we have evidence of burials and possible religious rites. Fossils of Neanderthal man have also been found in Java (Solo man) and Zambia (Rhodesian man). The classic, European Neanderthal probably evolved from earlier types such as Swanscombe man and Steinheim man, who had less extreme skeletal features. The classic Neanderthal had a large, thick skull with heavy brow ridges, a sloping forehead, a chinless jaw, and a brain size averaging 1,450 cc, somewhat larger than modern man. He was slightly over 5 ft (152 cm) tall and had a robust body. The relationship of Neanderthal man to modern man is uncertain. Some anthropologists believe that they were parallel lines evolving from an earlier common type. In Europe, there is no evidence of continuity between Neanderthal man and CRO-MAGNON MAN, who is physically and culturally distinct and appeared in Europe about 35,000 years ago, perhaps as an immigrant from another area. However, there is no evidence of contact between Neanderthal and Cro-Magnon and no reason to believe the former was exterminated by the latter, as has been proposed. From Mt. Carmel in Israel there is evidence of the evolution or interbreeding between Neanderthal and a modern type of man. Thus, whether Neanderthal man became extinct, or blended or evolved into modern man, there is little reason to exclude him from the species *Homo sapiens.* See MAN, PREHISTORIC. See W. E. LeGros Clark, *History of the Primates* (10th ed. 1970); Ashley Montagu, *Man: His First Two Million Years* (rev. ed. 1969).

Neapolis (nēăp'əlĭs) [Gr.,=new city], name of many cities in ancient Greek and Roman times. The most important is the modern NAPLES, Italy.

Nearchus (nēär'kəs), fl. 324 B.C., Macedonian general, b. Crete; friend of ALEXANDER THE GREAT. In 325 B.C., Alexander, about to leave India, had a fleet built in the Indus to transport part of the army home. Nearchus was put in command. They sailed up the Persian coast and rejoined (324 B.C.) Alexander at Susa in Persia. Nearchus' own account of this voyage, together with his description of India, is included in Arrian's *Indica.* See Arrianus Flavius, *Indica,* tr. by E. I. Robson, Vol II, *The Loeb Classical Library* (1933, repr. 1958).

Near Eastern religions: see MIDDLE EASTERN RELIGIONS.

Neariah (nē''ərī'ə). **1** One of David's line. 1 Chron. 3.22,23. **2** Son of Ishi, a Simeonite captain. 1 Chron. 4.42.

Near Islands: see ALEUTIAN ISLANDS.

nearsightedness, or myopia, defect of vision in which far objects appear blurred but near objects are seen clearly. Because the eyeball is too long or the refractive power of the eye's lens is too strong, the image is focused in front of the retina rather than upon it. Corrective EYEGLASSES with concave LENSES compensate for the refractive error and help to focus the image on the retina.

Neath (nēth), municipal borough (1971 pop. 28,568), West Glamorgan, S Wales, on the Neath River. It is a market and industrial town. Metallurgy is the main industry. There are ruins of Neath Abbey, founded c.1130.

neat's-foot oil, a pale yellow oil from the feet of neat (bovine) cattle. It has a peculiar odor. It is used in waterproofing and softening leather and as a lubricant for delicate machinery.

Nebai (nĕb'āī, nēbā'ī), signer of the covenant. Neh. 10.19.

Nebaioth (nēbā'yŏth), Arabian tribe living probably SE of Palestine, sometimes identified with the Nabataeans. Isa. 60.7.

Nebajoth (nēbā'jŏth), son of Ishmael. Gen. 25.13; 28.9; 36.3.

Neballat (nēbăl'ăt), Benjamite town, W central Palestine, NE of the present-day Lod (Israel). It was reoccupied after the return from captivity. Neh. 11.34.

Nebat (nē'băt), father of King Jeroboam I. 1 Kings 11.26.

Nebit-Dag (nyĭbēt'-däk), city (1970 pop. 56,000), Central Asian USSR, in Turkmenistan, at the southern foot of the Greater Balkhan range. On the Trans-Caspian RR, it is an industrial center of a region yielding oil and natural gas. The city was founded in 1933 and was called Nefte-Dag until the late 1930s.

Nebo (nē'bō). **1** Town of Moab, near Mt. Pisgah and S of Heshbon. Num. 32.3,38; 33.47; 1 Chron. 5.8; Isa. 15.2; Jer. 48.1,22. **2** City of Judah of postexilic times. Ezra 2.29; 10.43; Neh. 7.33. **3** Hebrew name for Babylonian god of knowledge, literature, and agriculture. Isa. 46.1.

Nebo, Mount, 2,625 ft (800 m) high, N Jordan. From there Moses viewed the Promised Land before his death. (Num. 21.20; 23.14; Deut. 3.27.)

Nebraska (nəbrăs'kə), state (1970 pop. 1,483,791), 77,227 sq mi (200,018 sq km), central United States, in the Great Plains region, admitted as the 37th state of the union in 1867. LINCOLN is the capital, and OMAHA is the largest city. The state is roughly rectangular, except in the northeast and the east where the border is formed by the irregular course of the Missouri River and in the southwest where the state of Colorado cuts out a squared corner. Elsewhere Nebraska is bounded by Wyoming on the west, by South Dakota on the north, by Iowa and Missouri on the east, and by Kansas on the south. The land rises more or less gradually from 840 ft (256 m) in the east to 5,300 ft (1,615 m) in the west. The great but shallow Platte River, formed in W Nebraska by

the junction of the North Platte and the South Platte, flows across the state from west to east to join the Missouri S of Omaha. The Platte and the Missouri, together with their tributaries, give Nebraska all-important water sources that are still essential to farming in this agrarian state. Underground water sources also furnish widespread irrigation. The river valleys have long provided routes westward, and today the transcontinental railroads and highways follow the valleys. From the Missouri westward over about half the state stretch undulating farm lands, where the fertile silt is underlaid by deep loess soil. Nebraska's population is concentrated there, many being farmers who produce grains for the market or for feeding hogs and dairy cattle. In this region also are Nebraska's two great cities—Omaha, one of the largest meat-packing and meat-processing centers in the world, and Lincoln, an important insurance center—as well as many of the state's larger towns. To the west and northwest the sand hills of Nebraska fan out, their wind-eroded contours now more or less stabilized by grass coverage. Cattle graze on the slopes and tablelands, protected in the severe winters by the sand bluffs and the valleys. The climate is severely continental throughout Nebraska, but averages for the state are almost meaningless, since there are great variations from place to place. A low of $-40°F$ ($-40°C$) in the winter is not unusual, and during the short intense summers temperatures may easily reach 110°F (43°C). Rainfall is almost twice as heavy in the east as in the west. Yet in the west along the river valleys the mixture of silt and sand is watered enough to yield abundantly to cultivation, even under semiarid conditions. Irrigation along the Platte and its tributaries has increased the sugar-beet crop, while on the southwest plateaus wheat farming flourishes. In the far west the land rises to the foothills of the Rocky Mts. and displays spectacular bedrock foundations. Mineral deposits of oil (discovered in Cheyenne co. in 1949–50), sand and gravel, and stone contribute to the state's economy, but agriculture remains the dominant occupational pursuit. To promote agriculture the Univ. of Nebraska maintains experimental agricultural stations throughout the state. A program of soil conservation has been developed, with a shelter belt running across the state to check the effect of wind erosion, and dryland-farming techniques have also been encouraged. Forest conservation is stressed, and the state has one of the nation's largest man-made forests. Nebraska's chief agricultural products are cattle, corn, hogs, and wheat. Nebraska ranked 4th among the states in cattle production in 1972. In addition to corn and wheat, other important crops grown are hay and sorghum grain. Nebraska's largest industry is food processing, which derives much of its raw materials from the state's farm products. The state has diversified its industries since World War II, and the manufacture of electrical machinery and chemical products, while secondary to food processing, is also important. Nebraska's soil has been used for farming since prehistoric times, but the Indians of the plains—notably the PAWNEE INDIANS—devoted themselves more to hunting the buffalo than to farming, since buffalo, as well as the pronghorn and lesser animals, were then abundant in the area. The Spanish explorer Francisco Vásquez de Coronado and his men were the first white men to visit the region. They probably came through Nebraska in 1541. The French also came and in the 18th cent. engaged in fur trading, but development began only after the area passed from France to the United States in the LOUISIANA PURCHASE of 1803. The LEWIS AND CLARK EXPEDITION (1804) and the explorations of Zebulon M. Pike (1806) as well as the later scientific explorations in W Nebraska of Stephen H. Long (1820) increased knowledge of the country, but the activities of the fur traders were more immediately valuable in terms of settlement. Manuel Lisa, a fur trader, probably established the first trading post in the Nebraska area in 1813. Bellevue, the first permanent settlement in Nebraska, first developed as a trading post. Steamboating on the Missouri River, initiated in 1819, brought much business to the river ports of Omaha and Brownville. Military posts, notably Fort Atkinson (1819–27), were founded to protect developing commerce from the Indians. The natural highway formed by the Platte valley, known to the earliest of fur traders, became deeply rutted in the 1840s and 50s by the wagons of the pioneers going west over the Oregon Trail and also the California Trail and the Mormon Trail. Nebraska settlers made money supplying the wagon trains with fresh mounts and pack animals as well as food. Nebraska became a territory after passage of the KANSAS-NEBRASKA ACT in 1854. The territory, which initially extended from lat. 40°N to the Canadian border, was firmly Northern and Republican in sympathy during the Civil War. In 1863 the territory was reduced to its present-day size by the creation of the territories of Dakota and Colorado. Congress passed an enabling act for statehood in 1864, but the original provision in the state constitution limiting the franchise to white men delayed statehood until 1867. In that year the Union Pacific RR was built across the state, and the land boom, already vigorous, became a rush. Farmers settled on free land obtained under the HOMESTEAD ACT of 1862, and E Nebraska took on a settled look. The population rose from 28,841 in 1860 to 122,993 in 1870. The Pawnee Indians were subdued in 1859, and by 1880 war with the Sioux and other Indian disturbances were over. With the coming of the railroads, cow towns, such as Ogalalla and Schuyler, were built up as shipping points on overland cattle trails. Buffalo Bill's Wild West Shows, commemorating the raucous days of cowboy, cattleman, and Indian scout, were opened in Nebraska in 1882. Farmers had long since been staking out homestead claims across the sand hills to the high plains, but ranches also prospered in the state. The ranchers, trying to preserve the open range, ruthlessly opposed the encroachment of the farmers, but the persistent farmers won. Many conservationists believe that much land was plowed under that should have been left with grass cover to prevent erosion in later dust storms. Nature was seldom kind to the people of Nebraska. Ranching was especially hard hit by the ruinous cold of the winter of 1880–81, and farmers were plagued by insect hordes from 1856 to 1875, by prairie fires, and by the recurrent droughts of the 1890s. Many farmers joined the GRANGER MOVEMENT in the lean 1870s and the Farmers' Alliances of the 1880s. In the 1890s many beleaguered farmers, faced with ruin and angry at the monopolistic practices of the railroads and the financiers, formed marketing and stock cooperatives and voiced their discontent by joining the POPULIST PARTY. The first national convention of the Populist party was held at Omaha in 1892, and Nebraska's most famous son, William Jennings Bryan, headed the Populist and Democratic tickets in the presidential election of 1896. Populists held the governorship of the state from 1895 to 1901. Improved conditions in the early 1900s caused Populism to decline in the state, and the return of prosperous days was marked by progressive legislation, the building of highways, and conservation measures. The flush of prosperity, largely caused by the demand for foodstuffs during World War I, was almost feverish. Overexpansion of credits and overconfidence made the depression of the 1920s and 30s all the more disastrous (see GREAT DEPRESSION). Many farmers were left destitute, and many were able to survive only because of the moratorium on farm debts in 1932. They received Federal aid in the desperate years of drought in the 1930s. Better weather and the huge food demands of World War II renewed prosperity in Nebraska. Since the war, efforts have continued to make the best use of the water supply, notably in such Federal plans as the MISSOURI RIVER BASIN PROJECT, a vast dam and water-diversion scheme. Nebraska's present constitution was adopted in 1875. The executive branch is headed by a governor elected for a four-year term. By constitutional amendment in 1934 the legislature was made unicameral, with 49 members elected on a nonpartisan basis for terms of four years. The legislature meets in the Nebraska capitol, which was designed by the architect Bertram Goodhue and rises majestically out of the Nebraska prairie. The state elects three Representatives and two Senators to the U.S. Congress and has five electoral votes in presidential elections. Although James Exon, a Democrat, was elected governor in 1970 (and re-elected in 1974), the state usually votes Republican. Among Nebraska's noted citizens have been the pioneer and historian Julius Sterling Morton, who originated Arbor Day for tree planting, and such immigrants as the Swiss Jules Sandoz, who made the sand hills bloom with fruit trees, and the German Henry A. Koenig, who introduced cultivation of the sugar beet to the Western plateaus. Willa Cather, a native of Nebraska, vividly recaptured the spirit of pioneer Nebraska in her novels *My Antonia* and *O Pioneers!* The self-reliant independence of the Populists and William Jennings Bryan was carried on by George W. Norris, who championed conservation of resources and the cause of the common man and who was largely responsible for the creation of the state's legislature. Points of interest to the traveler include Father Flanagan's Boys Town, near Omaha; the Oglala National Grassland; the Fort Niobrara National Wildlife Refuge, near Valentine; and the Homestead National Monument, near Beatrice. The pioneers' migration west over the Oregon Trail is commemorated by the Scotts Bluff National Monument and the Chimney Rock National Historic Site. Hundreds of fresh and alkali lakes in the state attract sportsmen and campers. The state's leading institution of higher education is the Univ. of Nebraska, mainly at Lincoln. See J. E. Weaver and W. J. Himmel, *The Environment of the Prairie* (1931); Federal Writers' Project, *Nebraska: A Guide to the Cornhusker State* (1939, repr. 1973); E. A. Whiseand, *This is Nebraska* (1941); Everett N. Dick, *The Sod-House Frontier* (1937); Virginia Faulkner, ed., *Roundup: A Nebraska Reader* (1957); J. C. Olson, *History of Nebraska* (2d ed. 1966, repr. 1974).

Nebraska, University of, mainly at Lincoln; land-grant and state supported; coeducational; chartered 1869, opened 1871. The university has an excellent archaeological museum and noted art galleries. The medical college, which conducts important cardiographic, cancer, and psychiatric research, is at Omaha. A school of agriculture is at Curtis.

Nebuchadnezzar (nĕb″əkədnĕz′ər), d. 562 B.C., king of Babylonia (c.605–562 B.C.), son and successor of Nabopolassar. In his father's reign he was sent to oppose the Egyptians, who were occupying W Syria and Palestine. At Carchemish he met and defeated (605 B.C.) Pharaoh NECHO, thus becoming the undisputed master of Western Asia. The sudden death of his father caused Nebuchadnezzar to return home to safeguard his inheritance, permitting Necho to escape to Egypt with part of his army. Three years later (601 B.C.) Necho defeated Nebuchadnezzar in battle. This event may have encouraged the Judaean revolt under JEHOIAKIM. Jehoiakim died shortly after the siege began and was succeeded by his son, Jehoiachin. In March, 597 B.C., Nebuchadnezzar crushed the revolt and carried off the young Jehoiachin and many of his nobles to Babylon. Nebuchadnezzar then placed the puppet king Zedekiah on the throne of Judaea. A new revolt occurred (588–587 B.C.) in Judaea. After a siege of about a year, Jerusalem was finally destroyed in 586 B.C. (see 2 Kings 25; Jer. 39). Nebuchadnezzar was a splendid builder, and BABYLON with its hanging gardens was then the greatest city of the ancient world. However, Babylon was shortly to fall under conquest when Nabonidus was king. The book of Daniel depicts Nebuchadnezzar as a conceited and domineering king and tells of his going mad and eating grass. See Jeremiah and 2 Kings 24. He is also called Nebuchadrezzar or Nebuchodonosor.

nebula (nĕb′yo͝olə) [Lat.,=mist], in astronomy, an immense body of highly rarefied gas and dust in the interstellar spaces of galaxies; this term was also applied to bodies later discovered to be galaxies, e.g., the so-called Great Nebula in the constellation Andromeda. At the start of the 19th cent. the English astronomer William Herschel concluded that, rather than being swarms of stars, nebulas were of a continuous fluid nature. In 1864, William Huggins confirmed this conclusion by determining that the spectra of nebulas are made of bright lines characteristic of radiating gases. Diffuse nebulas and planetary nebulas are two major classifications of these objects. Diffuse nebulas appear as light or dark clouds (called bright and dark nebulas), are irregular in shape, and range up to 100 light years in diameter. Some bright nebulas, composed primarily of hydrogen gas ionized by nearby hot blue-white stars, radiate their own light; they are called emission nebulas and are characterized by sharp spectral emission lines. Other bright nebulas, existing near cooler stars and not receiving the radiation necessary to make them luminous, reflect the starlight and are called reflection nebulas. Over 300 bright nebulas have been cataloged; prime examples are the ORION NEBULA, visible to the unaided eye, and the smaller North American Nebula. Dark nebulas are not close enough to stars either to absorb radiation and emit their own light or to reflect stellar light. They are detected as empty patches in a field of stars or as dark clouds obscuring part of a bright nebula in the background, as in the case of the Horsehead Nebula. Smaller bodies of dark nebulous matter having unusually high densities have been observed in some bright nebulous regions. Many astronomers believe that these bodies, called globules, are in the process of condensation and are the initial stages in the birth of stars. Planetary nebulas appear through the telescope as small disks with well-defined boundaries. Each consists of a shell of gaseous material surrounding a central hot star that emits radiation causing this material to glow. These shells measure about 20,000 AU in diameter (1 AU is the mean distance between the earth and the sun) and are slowly expanding, which suggests that they were expelled by the stars in nova and SUPERNOVA explosions; the CRAB NEBULA provides strong evidence for this belief. Over 400 planetary nebulas are known and are found at distances of 3,000 to 30,000 light years from the earth.

nebular hypothesis: see SOLAR SYSTEM.

Nebushasban (nĕb″yo͞oshăz′băn), official under Nebuchadnezzar. Jer. 39.13.

Nebuzaradan (nĕb″yo͞ozâr′ədăn), trusted official of Nebuchadnezzar. 2 Kings 25.8–20; Jer. 39.9–13; 40.1; 52.30.

Necessity, Fort: see FORT NECESSITY.

Nechako (nĭchăk′ō), river, 287 mi (462 km) long, rising in Tetachuck and Ootsa lakes, central British Columbia, Canada, and flowing NE, then E to the Fraser River at Prince George. Kenney Dam (325 ft/99 m high; completed 1952) and Kemano Dam (320 ft/98 m high; completed 1954) are among the highest dams in Canada. Kemano Dam, with a 1,670,000-kw capacity, is one of the world's largest hydroelectric generating plants.

Necho (nē′kō), fl. 670 B.C., lord of Saïs, Egypt. He was confirmed in his holding after the Assyrian conquest in 670; he was later taken to Nineveh in chains for plotting to revolt but was pardoned and restored. He probably fell opposing (663) the Nubian reconquest under Tanutamon. His son PSAMTIK founded the XXVI dynasty. His grandson and Psamtik's son, the pharaoh **Necho,** 609–593 B.C., took advantage of the confusion that followed the fall of Nineveh (612) to invade Palestine and Syria, both of which he took without difficulty. However, Necho's real objective was to reach Haran in time to assist the Assyrians who were under siege by the Babylonian king Nebuchadnezzar. King Josiah of Judah tried (609 B.C.) to stop him at Megiddo, but Josiah was defeated in battle and killed. Necho's failure to reach Haran resulted in the final defeat of Assyria. In 605, Necho fought with Nebuchadnezzar at Carchemish on the Euphrates and was thoroughly beaten. He fled to Egypt, where he remained for the rest of his life. He attempted to reexcavate the canal from the Nile to the Red Sea and also sent out a group of Phoenicians on a three-year expedition in which they were said to have circumnavigated Africa. The name also appears as Neco and Nechoh. See 2 Kings 23.29,33; 2 Chron. 35.20–23; 36.1–4; Jer. 46.2.

Neckar (nĕk′är), river, 228 mi (367 km) long, rising in the Black Forest, SW West Germany. It flows generally N past Tübingen, Stuttgart, and Heilbronn, then W past Heidelberg before joining the Rhine River at Mannheim. The Neckar is celebrated for its scenic charm; its hilly banks are covered with fine vineyards, orchards, and woods. It is navigable to Stuttgart and is connected to the Danube by a canal. There are more than 20 hydroelectric power plants on the river.

Necker, Jacques (zhäk nĕkĕr′), 1732–1804, French financier and statesman, b. Geneva, Switzerland. In 1750 he went to Paris and entered banking. He rose rapidly to importance, established a bank of his own, and became a director of the French East India Company. As a writer, Necker opposed the then fashionable PHYSIOCRATS and free traders; his eulogy on Jean Baptiste Colbert was lauded (1773) by the French Academy, and his *Essai sur la législation et le commerce des grains* (1775) criticized the free trade in grains advocated by A. R. J. TURGOT. In 1776, Necker, who had previously aided the government with loans, was made director of the treasury; in 1777 he was made director general of finances. He did not have the title controller general, because he was a foreigner and a Protestant. The salon of his wife, Suzanne Necker, exerted considerable influence. By measures of reform and retrenchment and by borrowing at high interest to finance the colonial cause in the American Revolution, he sought to restore the nation's financial position and gain popular confidence. In 1781 he published his *Compte rendu*, which stated that the government was in a sound financial position. He then demanded greater reform powers and was opposed by the comte de MAUREPAS, who resented his increased influence. He resigned and retired to St. Ouen. There he wrote the *Traité de l'administration des finances de la France* (1784). Returning to Paris in 1787, Necker was soon exiled from the city for having engaged in public controversy over financial policy with Charles Alexandre de CALONNE. In 1788, Louis XVI recalled Necker as director general of finances and minister of state. The populace acclaimed him, and he concurred with the recommendation that the States-General be summoned and reforms introduced. When his enemies at court again secured his dismissal in 1789, the populace, on July 14, stormed the Bastille in the first outbreak of violence of the French Revolution; Necker was once more recalled. His final resignation came in 1790. His last years were spent at "Coppet," his Swiss estate. His daughter, Germaine de STAËL, wrote *La Vie privée de M. Necker* (1804), and his grandson edited a collection of his writings (1820–21).

Necker, Suzanne (Curchod) (süzän′ kürshō′), 1739–94, French writer; wife of Jacques Necker and mother of Mme de Staël. Her salon was frequented by celebrated Frenchmen and foreign visitors. A hospital that she founded c.1776 is still in existence. Her writings on literary and moral subjects include *Des inhumations précipitées* (1790), *Réflexions sur le divorce* (1794), and miscellaneous collections published as *Mélanges* in 1798 and 1801.

necklace: see COLLAR; JEWELRY.

Neco: see NECHO.

necropolis: see CEMETERY.

nectar: see AMBROSIA.

nectarine (nĕk″tərēn′), name for a tree *(Prunus persica nectarina)* of the family Rosaceae (ROSE family) and for its fruit, a smooth-skinned variety of the peach. The nectarine is a classical example of bud variation (see MUTATION). The nectarine tree occasionally produces peaches, and the peach tree nectarines. In appearance, culture, and care the nectarine is almost identical to the peach. It is cultivated in north temperate zones of both hemispheres, in America chiefly in the mild Pacific coastal area. The nectarine has been known for at least 2,000 years; in the 16th cent. it was called the nut of Persia. Nectarines are classified in the division MAGNOLIOPHYTA, class Magnoliopsida, order Rosales, family Rosaceae.

Nedabiah (nĕd″əbī′ə), one of David's line. 1 Chron. 3.18.

Nederland (nē′dərlənd), city (1970 pop. 16,810), Jefferson co., SE Texas; founded by Dutch settlers as a rice-farming community in 1897, inc. 1940. Primarily a residential suburb between Beaumont and Port Arthur, it has two oil companies and has industries that produce butadiene, plastics, and synthetic rubber.

Needham (nēd′əm), town (1970 pop. 29,748), Norfolk co., E Mass., a suburb of Boston; founded 1680, set off from Dedham and inc. 1711. Although largely residential, textiles, paper products, electronic equipment, and other items are manufactured there.

needle, implement of metal or other material used to carry the thread in sewing and in various forms of needlework and manufacturing. The earliest needles were merely awls or punches. Stone, bone, ivory, and thorns, with or without an eye, were used by primitive peoples. The midrib of the palm is used in Africa, with the thread tied on. Much of the embroidery of antiquity must have required fine needles; China is supposed to have first used steel ones, and the Moors are credited with carrying them to the West. The needle-making trade was established in Nuremberg in the 14th cent. and in England in Elizabeth's reign. In 1656 the first needlemakers' guild was chartered. Manufacturing by machinery developed gradually. In 1785 the first steel rod was mechanically prepared; in 1826 eyes were drilled by stamping, and by 1870 the manufacture was mostly mechanical. Different kinds of steel are used for different needles, e.g., chromium and stainless steel for surgical and hypodermic uses. Over 250 kinds of needles are made, such as the pearl needles of India, bead needles for fine beadwork, and others for carpets, shoes, upholstery, sailmaking, knitting, and every type of sewing machine.

needlefish, common name for members of the family Belonidae, which comprises 50 species of elongated, surface-swimming predaceous fish abundant in warm seas. They have beaklike jaws armed with sharp teeth, giving them a superficial resemblance to the GAR; some needlefishes reach a length of 6 ft (1.8 m). The saltwater garfish, *Strongylura longirostris,* may be 4 ft (1.2 m) long but is usually smaller; it is found in Atlantic coastal waters and estuaries. Garfishes resemble twigs and are often mistaken for them when lying motionless at the surface of the water. They swim in small schools and occasionally leap clear of the water in their pursuit of smaller fish. The flesh is palatable, although the greenish bones make it repellent to some. Other species include the billfish and the houndfish, or agujon, an important food fish of Puerto Rico. The closely related halfbeaks, or balaos, family Hemiramphidae, smaller than needlefishes and with only the lower jaw extended, are a herbivorous family linking the needlefishes and the FLYING FISH. Needlefishes are classified in the phylum CHORDATA, subphylum Vertebrata, class Osteichthyes, order Beloniformes, family Belonidae.

needlepoint: see LACE.

Needles, the, England: see WIGHT, ISLE OF.

needlework, work done with a needle, either plain sewing, mending, or ornamental work such as EMBROIDERY, QUILTING, smocking, hemstitching, fagoting, some kinds of lacemaking (see LACE), patchwork, and appliqué. KNITTING, crocheting (see CROCHET WORK), netting, and tatting are also classified as needlework, being done with specialized needles or, as in netting and tatting, with shuttles. Many of the processes used are ancient, and some have several uses, such as the darning stitch employed in mending, embroidery, and lacemaking. Patchwork or appliqué, consisting of a cut or pieced design of one fabric applied to the surface of another, was used in ancient Egypt and India.

Neenah (nē′nə), city (1970 pop. 22,892), Winnebago co., E Wis., on Lake Winnebago at the mouth of the Fox River; settled c.1835 on the site of a Winnebago Indian village, inc. as a city 1873. Located in a dairy-farming region, Neenah, the Indian name for "water," is known, with its twin city Menasha, as a center for the manufacture of paper and paper products. Other leading industries make cans, foundry products, steel, paper-mill machinery, and wood products. Neenah's industrial development began c.1850 when flour mills serving the surrounding farming area were opened. In 1865 the paper industry was started. Places of interest include Doty Cabin, a replica of the home of James Duane Doty (2d governor of Wisconsin Territory), and the Bergstrom Art Center, with its antique-glass collection. Hydroelectric power is generated for Neenah and Menasha by falls of the Fox River. Lake Winnebago is a year-round recreation area.

Neer, Aert van der (ärt vän dĕr när), c.1603–77, Dutch landscape painter. Working mostly in Amsterdam, he excelled in painting unusual light effects, such as moonlight, sunsets, conflagrations, and glimmering light on snow and ice. His winter landscapes are among the best in Dutch art. He is well represented in many European galleries. The Metropolitan Museum has his *Sunset, The Farrier,* and *Landscape.* His son and pupil, **Eglon Hendrik van der Neer,** 1634–1703, was a genre, landscape, and portrait painter. He was court painter to the elector palatine in Düsseldorf. He excelled in painting luxurious interiors, hunting scenes, and mythological or biblical subjects in Dutch settings. His *Esther and Ahasuerus* (Uffizi) is characteristic of his work.

Neerwinden (närvĭn′dən), village, Liège prov., E Belgium. In the War of the Grand Alliance the French under Marshal Luxembourg defeated (1693) William III of England there. In the French Revolutionary Wars, a French defeat (1793) at Neerwinden resulted in the defection of General Dumouriez to the Austrians.

Nefertiti (nĕf″ərtē′tē) or **Nefretete** (nĕf″rĕtē′tē), fl. c.1372–1350 B.C., queen of ancient Egypt; wife of IKHNATON (XVIII dynasty) and aunt of Tutankhamen. She seems to have been divorced by Ikhnaton late in his reign. The exquisite limestone bust of Nefertiti (Berlin Mus.) has given rise to the tradition that she was one of the most beautiful women of antiquity.

Nefud: see NAFUD.

negative: see PHOTOGRAPHIC PROCESSING.

Negeri (nā′gərē) or **Negri Sembilan** (nā′grē sĕmbē′lən), state (1971 pop. 479,312), 2,590 sq mi (6,708 sq km), Malaysia, S Malay Peninsula, on the Strait of Malacca. The capital is SEREMBAN. Its principal rivers are the Linggi on the west and the Muar on the east. Copra, rubber, and rice are grown and exported; tin is mined and also exported. More than half the inhabitants are non-Malays (Chinese and Indians). The separate political existence of Negri Sembilan began in the 18th cent. After a considerable immigration of Minangkabaus from Sumatra, the Negri Sembilan [nine states] broke away (1777) from the sultanate of Riau and Johor to form a loose confederation. Each state was then practically independent. The British established their influence by making treaties with the separate states (1874–89) and by reforming them into a closer federation (1895). Negeri became one of the Federated Malay States (1896) and in 1948 became part of the Federation of Malaya. See MALAYSIA, FEDERATION OF.

Negev (nĕg′ĕv) or **Negeb** (nĕg′ĕb) [Heb.,=dry], hilly desert region of S Israel, c.5,140 sq mi (13,310 sq km), bordered by the Judaean Hills, the Wadi Arabah, the Sinai peninsula, and the narrow Mediterranean coastal plain; it comprises more than one half of Israel's land area. The Negev receives c.2 to 4 in. (5–10 cm) of rain annually. In the Beersheba basin, NW Negev, there are fertile loess deposits, but the region's aridity prevented cultivation until irrigation was provided by the National Water Carrier Project, which taps the Sea of Galilee. The Negev region also has a good mineral potential; copper, phosphates, and natural gas are already commercially extracted. In ancient times there were several prosperous cities along the principal wadis (watercourses) of the area; in modern times the Negev was the scene of much fighting between Egyptian and Israeli forces after the partition of Palestine in 1948. Many kibbutzim (see COLLECTIVE FARM) are located in the Negev; Beersheba and Arad are the chief cities in the region.

Neginah (nĕg′ĭnä), pl. **Neginoth** (nĕg′ĭnŏth), direction for the musical accompaniment of a psalm. Pss. 4, 6, 54, 55, 61, 67, 76.

negligence, in law, breach of an obligation to act with care. Inadvertent behavior characterizes negligence, whereas willful behavior characterizes wantonness. The obligation to act with care may arise out of a contract, as in the duty of a common carrier to exercise a high degree of care in preserving from injury goods or persons being transported. The law also supposes that persons in the ordinary course of conduct must take pains to avoid inflicting injuries on others or on themselves. In all noncontractual situations the standard applied to determine the existence of negligence is the presumptive behavior of the "reasonable, prudent man." Injury that results despite that degree of care or from circumstances beyond human control (see ACCIDENT and ACT OF GOD) is not compensable. It is usually the function of the jury to determine whether the act in question was negligent; on the other hand, in cases where due care must have been absent (e.g., when an automobile collapses on first being driven) the judge may apply the doctrine of *res ipsa loquitur* [Lat.,= the thing speaks for itself] and rule that there was negligence as a matter of law. Ordinarily if the plaintiff was guilty of contributory negligence, he may not recover damages; a typical case is that of a pedestrian who crosses a street without looking out for motorists and is hit by a vehicle. In the case supposed, if the motorist nevertheless sees the pedestrian and negligently fails to stop (i.e., if he has a "last clear chance" to avoid injury), he is nevertheless liable. Certain restrictions have been imposed on the right to recover damages for injury due to negligence. Quite often damages can only be collected if there was some physical impact; nervous suffering alone is usually insufficient unless the suffering led to a miscarriage. Damages are sometimes allowed for intentional interference with peace of mind (e.g., undue harassment by a bill collector). At common law the right to recover for negligence belonged to the injured party only; if he died before completion of his lawsuit or as a result of his injuries, his heirs might not recover. Today all jurisdictions have statutes that permit the heirs to bring suit both for the wrongful death and for the injuries to the deceased. Negligence claims are the chief source of current civil litigation; the bulk of cases arises from vehicular traffic. In the case of automobile accidents, however, negligence may become less important because of the adoption of NO-FAULT INSURANCE laws in many jurisdictions. Besides its civil aspects, negligence may also be criminal if it results in MANSLAUGHTER or if it is a serious breach of a public duty (e.g., carelessness by the engineer of a railroad train).

Negoiu (nĕgoi′o͞o), peak, 8,317 ft (2,535 m) high, central Rumania, NW of Cîmpulung; second highest peak of the Transylvanian Alps.

Negombo (nāgōm′bō), town (1968 est. pop. 53,000) W Sri Lanka (Ceylon), at the mouth of the Negombo Lagoon. Chiefly noted for its ceramics and brassware, it is also a fishing center and a market for coconut products and cinnamon. Many 17th-century Dutch buildings remain. Sri Lanka's major international airport is on the outskirts of Negombo.

negotiable instrument, bill of exchange, check, promissory note, or other written contract for payment that may serve as a substitute for money. It is simple in form and easy to transfer. Transfer of a negotiable instrument, accomplished by delivery or endorsement and delivery, gives the new holder of the contract the right to enforce fulfillment in his own name. Negotiable instruments made payable to bearer are transferred by delivery; those made payable to order are transferred by endorsement and delivery. Like COMMERCIAL PAPER, negotiable instruments were developed to meet the needs of trade. They are used by businessmen to facilitate long-distance transactions and to avoid the constant exchange of large amounts of cash.

Negri, Ada (ä′dä nĕ′grē), 1870–1945, Italian writer. Her first poems, *Fatalità* (1892, tr. *Fate and Other Poems,* 1898) voiced bitter protest against the state of the poor. Her passionate lyrics, developed in *Maternità* (1904) reached their climax in *Il libro di Mara* (1919). *Canti dell'isola* (1924) sang of the beauty of Capri. In her last years Negri took refuge in religion and her last volumes of poetry, *Vespertina* (1931) and *Il dono* (1936), express resignation and serenity. Her prose includes *Le solitarie* (1917), short stories, and the autobiographical novel *Stella mattutina* (1921, tr. *Morning Star,* 1930). She became the first woman member of the Italian Academy in 1940.

Negrillo: see PYGMY.

Negrín, Juan (hwän nāgrēn′), 1891–1956, Spanish statesman. A professor of physiology at the Univ. of Madrid, he was active in the Socialist party and was elected to the Cortes in 1931. After the SPANISH CIVIL WAR began (1936), Negrín was first finance minister and then premier (1937–39) of the republic. Dependent on the USSR for arms, he was unable to control Communist influence in the Republican army. He fled (1939) to France and then to England. He died in Paris.

Negrito: see PYGMY.

Negro, in American history, person of the Negroid grouping (as opposed to the Mongoloid and Caucasoid groupings) whose ancestors originated in Africa S of the Sahara. American Negroes, or blacks, number about 22 million, or 11% of the country's total population. For information about Negroid peoples in other parts of the world, mostly Africa, see such articles as BANTU, EWE, FULANI, HAUSA, HAYA, HERERO, IBO, KHOIKHOI, KIKUYU, MATABELE, MOSSI, PYGMY, SWAHILI, TUTSI, and YORUBA. For additional information pertaining to American Negroes, see CIVIL RIGHTS, INTEGRATION, and SLAVERY.

Slavery. Negroes have lived in the Americas since the early 16th cent., many having accompanied the early Spanish and Portuguese explorers to the New World. The year 1517, when Spanish colonizers were permitted to import 12 Negroes each, is said to mark the formal opening of the highly profitable Negro slave trade in the New World, and it has been estimated that by 1540 10,000 Negroes were being imported annually to the Spanish West Indies. In the 17th cent., after Spain lost all claim to exclusive control of the islands in the Caribbean, British West Indian planters began to import Negro slaves in great numbers to work the sugar plantations developed after 1640. Spain's colonies in South America and Portugal's colony of Brazil also provided important markets for the slave trade. Excluded from Africa by the papal arbitration of 1493, Spain granted to companies and individuals of various countries the privilege (known as the asiento) of bringing slaves to its colonies. The largest concentration of Negroes on the South American continent were found in the viceroyalty of New Granada (Panama, Colombia, Venezuela, and Ecuador) and in Portuguese Brazil. The influence of the Roman Catholic Church in Latin America, which encouraged the manumission of slaves, helps explain why slavery was abolished peaceably there in the 19th cent., in contrast to the epic struggle that accompanied its demise in the United States and Haiti. The first Negroes in what is now the United States came to Virginia in 1619 as indentured servants; a few Negroes even owned their own plantations. However, the English, in need of a source of labor, turned to the supply of Negroes available first in the West Indies and then directly in W Africa itself. With the success of tobacco planting, Negro slavery was sanctioned by law in Virginia in 1661 and in Maryland in 1663. The institution was the foundation of the economy in all the Southern colonies. The Northern colonies also had Negro slaves, mainly in the Hudson valley and in Pennsylvania. Although the Massachusetts Body of Liberties of 1641 banned bond slavery in the colony, the Puritans played a large role in fostering the institution in America through their activities in the slave trade. Boston, Newport, and other New England ports profited from the TRIANGULAR TRADE, and many slaves were kept in New England. All the colonies had codes or individual laws regulating the activities of Negroes. These were mildest in New England and most severe in the South, where the growth of the Negro population had alarmed the whites. Under the Virginia code, for example, slaves found guilty of murder or rape were hanged. Robbery and lesser offenses were punished by whipping, maiming, or branding. Southern fears of slave insurrections were well grounded, for many Negroes were not disposed to accept their bondage docilely. As early as 1663, Virginia Negroes conspired to rebel. Not until after the French and Indian War (1754–63), however, was there any considerable sentiment against slavery in America. The fact that one of the men killed in the Boston Massacre (1770), Crispus Attucks, was a runaway slave doubtless disturbed many a conscience, and in Massachusetts, at least, it became habit to denounce England and slavery in the same breath. Despite the fact that the efforts of Thomas Jefferson to have slavery condemned in the Declaration of Independence were unsuccessful, approximately 5,000 Negroes fought for the American Revolutionaries, and many distinguished themselves, notably Salem Poor in the Battle of Bunker Hill. The vast majority of black soldiers served alongside white soldiers, not in segregated fighting groups. After the war antislavery and manumission societies increased, and slavery was gradually abolished in the Northern states. The provision in the ORDINANCE OF 1787 barring slavery and involuntary servitude in the Northwest Territory marked a peak in postwar antislavery sentiment. Nevertheless, slavery was protected by the Constitution of the United States, under which three fifths of a state's slaves were counted towards its portion of the representation in Congress (Article 1, Section 2). The Constitution also recognized the public obligation to return fugitive slaves (Article 4, Section 2), but prohibited the slave trade after Jan., 1808 (Article 1, Section 9). Despite these constitutional guarantees, slavery slowly declined and might well have died a lingering death in the South had not the invention (1793) of the cotton gin radically changed economic conditions. The invention of the cotton gin spurred large-scale production of cotton, which required the labor of increasing numbers of slaves as new lands were quickly opened up westward to the Mississippi. It is with the cotton plantation that Negro slavery in the United States is especially associated. By 1830 there were more than 2 million slaves. At the bottom of the slave social order on a typically large cotton plantation were the field hands, who performed the backbreaking productive work of the plantation. They were often supervised by the overseer, who was apt to be responsible for much of the cruelty that existed under the system. Somewhat better off than the field slaves were the semiskilled workers—carpenters, blacksmiths, etc. At the top of the hierarchy were the house servants, better clothed and fed and with much less onerous duties than the field hands, whom they tended to view with contempt. Only the larger plantations had house servants, and their number came to be an indication of a planter's wealth. Religious activity among the Negroes was not opposed by whites so long as it did not challenge the institution of slavery. Early in the 18th cent. there were some slave congregations on the larger plantations and in the towns. In the 1830s, however, Negro preachers were outlawed in most states, and the slaves were more and more required to attend the churches of their masters. Religious instruction for the Negroes laid emphasis on obedience and subserviency, and the Southern churches became strong defenders of slavery. Despite widespread laws against teaching Negroes, many of the slaves did receive some education, and there were even a few schools for Negroes. Prominent Negroes in the United States prior to the Civil War included Sojourner TRUTH, an early civil rights advocate, David Walker, publisher of *Appeal* (a militant abolitionist pamphlet), and Phillis WHEATLEY, the poet. The economic interests of the slaveowner were often inimical to a stable family life for his slaves. Slave marriages were not usually accompanied with religious ceremony. Slave families were often broken up as the children were sold from their parents' home to different owners. This feature came to be viewed by many as the most vicious of the many outrages of the institution. That miscegenation (involving white males and Negro females almost exclusively) was widespread is well attested by the varied complexions of the mulattoes, quadroons, and other mixtures that came to abound. Sometimes slave owners would free their slaves by a last will and testament; in other cases slaves had their freedom bought for them by free Negroes. On the other hand, on rare occasions, there were free Negroes who owned slaves themselves. For the most part the free Negroes in the South lived in the larger towns, where they were hated and feared by the poor whites as economic competitors. Their situation was often less enviable than that of highly favored house slaves, for they were severely restricted in their movements and in other ways. Other slaves could dream of escape to the North, and thousands did escape, aided by the UNDERGROUND RAILROAD. The possibility of a general slave insurrection existed but none ever occurred, not even in the course of the Civil War when most able-bodied Southern white men were at the fighting fronts. Some of the most famous Negro rebels were Gabriel Prosser, who led a slave revolt in Virginia (1800), Denmark VESEY, a freeman of Charleston, S.C., whose elaborate plot (1822) was made known to the whites before it went into effect, and Nat TURNER, a Virginia slave, leader of the Southampton Insurrection (1831), which was quickly suppressed. The antislavery sentiment in the North, spurred on by the ABOLITIONISTS, began to reach crusading proportions. Some of the most prominent among Negro abolitionists were Frederick DOUGLASS, Josiah HENSON, Sojourner Truth, and Harriet TUBMAN. Slavery, particularly the question of its extension into the new Federal territories, had been a serious national political issue ever since the adoption of the MISSOURI COMPROMISE in 1820, and with the COMPROMISE OF 1850, which featured stricter FUGITIVE SLAVE LAWS, and the KANSAS-NEBRASKA ACT (1854), it became the dominant theme in politics (see also DRED SCOTT CASE).

From the Civil War to 1954. A new party, the Republican, was organized in part to oppose the further extension of slavery. When its candidate, Abraham Lincoln, was elected President in 1860, the Southern states seceded from the Union and the two sections were soon in arms against each other. More than 186,000 Negroes fought in the Union ranks in the Civil War, 93,000 of them coming from the Confederate states. They fought in segregated units and were mostly led by white officers, with some Negro noncommissioned officers. Lincoln's EMANCIPATION PROCLAMATION, while having no effect on Negroes of the border slave states, technically freed the slaves in the Confederacy. With the Union triumph in April, 1865, came the end of slavery for almost 4 million Negroes. The problems of adjusting to freedom for Negroes were compounded by their general lack of education. The Federal government established the FREEDMEN'S BUREAU to assist them, and the Republican party organized the UNION LEAGUE CLUBS to attempt to acquire their newly won and powerful vote. At the height of the radical Republican RECONSTRUCTION program for the South, Negroes began to exercise political power, with 16 serving in Congress between 1869 and 1880. Reaction to Reconstruction was expressed among white Southerners in such white supremacy organizations as the KU KLUX KLAN. The legislatures of Reconstruction, despite their corruption, did enact much sound social legislation, especially concerning public education. Economically, freedom left the Negro not much better off than he had been under slavery. The share-cropping system, which replaced the antebellum plantation, held Negroes, as well as the poor whites, in another kind of bondage. A crowning disappointment came in the 1880s and 1890s, when the Southern states, beginning with Mississippi, adopted new state constitutions that, in providing for the poll tax and education requirements for voting, effectively disfranchised the Negro despite the Fifteenth Amendment to the Constitution. These constitutions marked a triumph for white supremacy. Meanwhile the pattern of segregation had been firmly established when Tennessee enacted (1870) laws prohibiting the intermarriage of Negroes and whites and adopted (1875) the first of the JIM CROW LAWS. The rest of the South rapidly followed suit, and the new state constitutions firmly established the color line. In 1896 the U.S. Supreme Court ruled, in *Plessy* vs. *Ferguson,* that states had the right to segregate blacks and whites, so long as the accommodations were equal. Justice for the Negro was difficult to obtain, and when mob feeling was high, LYNCHING often resulted. The policy of segregation in the schools of the South became expensive, one that the region could ill afford, and its effect was noticed in the generally low level of Southern education. Despite all these handicaps and considering the short span of their free status, Negroes, under such leaders as Booker T. WASHINGTON of TUSKEGEE INSTITUTE, made some strides forward. Washington emphasized vocational and technical training for Negroes and insisted that their future was still in the South. But he was not disposed to protest disfranchisement and the abrogation of civil rights and was therefore roundly attacked by other Negro leaders, notably William E. B. DU BOIS. Many Negroes began to migrate to Northern cities, where they found work chiefly in domestic service and as laborers. In the North their status was, in general, improved. In the South there was also a movement from rural areas to the city. Negro churches often became the center of social activities, providing an important social service for Negroes. Although labor unions generally did not welcome Negro membership, the urban migration was peaceful except where Negroes were introduced as strikebreakers; in such cases riots often occurred. In World War I, when the supply of European laborers was cut off, the lack was supplied by importing large numbers of Negroes into the North where they entered the semiskilled occupations. In the cities of the North, Negroes crowded into such slumlike districts as HARLEM. Sanitary conditions were totally inadequate, and Negro mortality ran high above the average for the rest of the population. Many Northern whites resented this mass intrusion and the resultant competition in industry and in housing. Race rioting broke out in several places, one of the worst occurring in East St. Louis, Ill., in 1917; there was another in Chicago in 1919. In spite of the frequently wretched conditions under which Negroes lived, over 400,000 were called upon to serve in the armed forces during World War I. Negroes were voting in increasing numbers, even in some cases to the extent of controlling the election, while public schools, conveyances, and, to some degree, places of recreation and amusement were open to them. The scope of their activities in industry, business, the trades, and the professions was constantly widened. To this progress the NATIONAL ASSOCIATION FOR THE ADVANCEMENT OF COLORED PEOPLE (NAACP), organized in 1910, contributed much. In addition the National League on Urban Conditions Among Negroes (later known as the National URBAN LEAGUE) was founded in 1911. Others joined the Universal Negro Improvement Association founded after World War I by Marcus GARVEY, an organization advocating that Negroes return to Africa. Notable black Americans during the 1920s and 1930s include Mary McL. BETHUNE, George Washington CARVER, Countee CULLEN, Langston HUGHES, Joe LOUIS, Paul ROBESON, Walter Francis WHITE, and Richard WRIGHT. Until the 1930s most Negroes voted Republican in politics, but when Franklin Delano Roosevelt's New Deal brought them increased social and economic benefits they soon became one of the most important elements in the Democratic coalition. While more than one million Negroes were serving in the armed forces in World War II, the migration from the South to cities of the North was repeated; additionally, the rigid anti-Negro policy in industry was beginning to weaken. When industrial production skyrocketed even before the United States entered the war, Negro leaders headed by A. Philip RANDOLPH threatened a march on Washington unless job discrimination was ended. This was forestalled when, in 1941, President Roosevelt issued Executive Order 8802, which prohibited racial discrimination in the defense industries. The FAIR EMPLOYMENT PRACTICES COMMITTEE was set up to receive and investigate complaints, and although it had no punitive powers its very existence improved the employment status of Negroes. Many whites became resentful of the gains the Negroes were making, and this often led to tension between the races. A race riot in which 25 Negroes and 9 whites were killed shook Detroit in 1943. The racial tensions of the United States helped revive the Ku Klux Klan as it would produce the White Citizens Council in the 1950s. The emergence of new independent African nations after World War II gave impetus to an African Freedom movement. During World War II segregation continued in the armed forces, and in protest William H. Hastie, Negro civilian aide to the Secretary of War, resigned in 1943. However, the army had its first Negro general, Benjamin O. DAVIS, whose son, Benjamin O. DAVIS, Jr., commanded a highly praised Negro fighter group in the U.S. air force. The years following the war were heartening ones for American Negroes as they struggled to escape unequal treatment. Achievements of individuals such as Ralph J. BUNCHE in diplomacy, Jackie ROBINSON in major-league baseball, Althea GIBSON in tennis, Thurgood MARSHALL (later to become the first Negro to serve on the U.S. Supreme Court) in law, and Robert C. WEAVER in government were applauded by nearly all Americans. Important advances were made in the field of civil rights. In 1946, President Harry S. Truman appointed a Committee on Civil Rights, composed of distinguished blacks and whites, to inquire into the civil rights of minorities. The threat of a Southern filibuster cut off immediate action on civil rights, but during the Truman administration considerable progress was made toward integration of the armed forces, which was completely achieved by 1953.

The Civil Rights Movement and Beyond. A momentous decision was made in May, 1954, when the U.S. Supreme Court unanimously overturned the *Plessy* vs. *Ferguson* decision of 1896. The decision in *Brown* vs. *Board of Education of Topeka, Kansas* declared that "separate educational facilities are inherently unequal" and ordered all the nation's school systems desegregated. The following year Negroes in Montgomery, Ala., boycotted the bus lines in that city and forced desegregation of the facilities. Led by such figures as Martin Luther KING, Jr., of the Southern Christian Leadership Council (SCLC), picketing and boycotting soon spread to communities in the North and South. In 1957 the first Civil Rights Act since 1875 was passed by the U.S. Congress. Other organizations joined in the civil rights movement; college students in the South, both black and white, formed the Student Non-Violent Coordinating Committee (SNCC) and began sit-in demonstrations at segregated restaurants, while the Congress of Racial Equality (CORE) sent integrated buses into the South on what were known as freedom rides. In 1963 over 200,000 blacks and whites held a march in Washington, D.C., to demonstrate for racial equality. The following year, under the leadership of President Lyndon Baines Johnson, the U.S. Congress passed the most far-reaching Civil Rights Act in history, forbidding discrimination in public accommodations among other things. In 1965 the Voting Rights Act was enacted, a measure designed to protect Negro voting rights. Besides SCLC, SNCC, and CORE, Roy WILKINS of the NAACP and Whitney Young of the Urban League were active in seeking equal rights for Negroes. Other Negroes were making their mark on the U.S. culture, including Ralph ELLISON and James BALDWIN in literature, Lorraine Hansberry and Imamu Amiri Baraka (formerly LeRoi Jones) in drama, while blacks virtually dominated certain aspects of music and sports. Despite legal and cultural gains, other blacks had begun to advocate separation (notably the Black Muslims) or more militant action (notably the BLACK PANTHER PARTY under the leadership of Huey Newton and Eldridge Cleaver). Rioting had begun in 1964 in Rochester, N.Y.; Watts, a black ghetto in Los Angeles exploded in 1965 leaving 34 people dead. Other major riots followed in Detroit and Newark in 1967. SNCC, under Stokely Carmichael, had become more militant, dropping whites from membership. Martin Luther King, Jr., was assassinated in Memphis, Tenn., in 1968 setting off riots in over 125 U.S. cities. Nevertheless, President Johnson, in the aftermath, was able to encourage Congress to pass another Civil Rights Act, containing the broadest open-housing clause ever enacted into law. The momentum of the civil rights movement began to wane in the late 1960s as blacks turned their attention to economic issues, rather than legal or political ones. The early 1970s were characterized by the issue of achieving racial balance by busing school children, a measure bitterly opposed by many whites in the North and South. The Supreme Court ruled in 1972 that busing was legal for this purpose. Despite certain gains in the 1960s, the median income for Negroes in the early 1970s was still well below that for whites. The proportion of Negroes in urban ghettos continued to increase, with over 50% of the Negro population living in the central cities. As Negroes have gone through considerable cultural and political change in the 20th cent., so have the terms used to refer to them (by themselves and by whites). Early in the 20th cent. the term *colored* was considered desirable; later the term *Negro* found favor, while in the 1960s and early 1970s the terms *black* and *Afro-American* were generally considered more acceptable. For works written before 1928 see M. N. Work, *A Bibliography of the Negro in Africa and America* (1928, repr. 1970). For works written after 1928 see W. E. B. Du Bois, *Black Reconstruction* (1935, repr. 1966); Herbert Aptheker, *American Negro Slave Revolts* (1943, repr. 1963) and *Afro-American History* (1971); E. F. Frazier, *Black Bourgeoisie* (1957, repr. 1965); E. E. Thorpe, *The Mind of the Negro* (1961); Langston Hughes, *Fight for Freedom* (1962); Gunnar Myrdal et al., *An American Dilemma* (rev. ed. 1962); T. F. Gossett, *Race* (1963, repr. 1965); E. F. Frazier, *The Negro Church in America* (1963, repr. 1974); Larry Cuban, *The Negro in America* (1964); Ashley Montagu, *Man's Most Dangerous Myth* (4th ed. 1964); Thomas Pettigrew, *A Profile of the Negro American* (1964); C. E. Silberman, *Crisis in Black and White* (1964); K. B. Clark, *Dark Ghetto* (1965); E. K. Welsch, *The Negro in the United States* (1965); J. P. Davis, ed., *The American Negro Reference Book* (1966); C. V. Woodward, *The Strange Career of Jim Crow* (2d rev. ed. 1966); Stokely Carmichael and C. V. Hamilton, *Black Power* (1967); J. H. Franklin, *From Slavery to Freedom* (3d ed. 1967); J. H. Franklin and Isidore Starr, ed., *The Negro in Twentieth Century America* (1967, repr. 1969); Gilbert Osofsky, *Burden of Race* (1967); E. A. Salk, ed., *A Layman's Guide to Negro History* (1967); P. T. Drotning, *A Guide to Negro History in America* (1968) and *Black Heros in our Nation's History* (1970); Alan Conway, *The History of the Negro in the U.S.A.* (1968); D. W. Hoover, ed., *Understanding Negro History* (1968); LeRoi Jones and Larry Neal, ed., *Black Fire* (1968); W. D. Jordan, *White Over Black* (1968); *Report of the National Advisory Commission on Civil Disorders* (1968); I. J. Sloan, *The American Negro* (1968); Bryan Fulks, *Black Struggle* (1969); Floyd McKissick, *Three-Fifths of a Man* (1969); Alphonso Pinkney, *Black Americans* (1969); Benjamin Quarles, *The Negro in the Making of America* (1969); Florette Henri, *Bitter Victory: A History of Black Soldiers in World War I* (1970); August Meier, *From Plantation to Ghetto* (1970); E. W. Miller, *The Negro in America* (rev. ed. 1970); Jean Stein and George Plimpton, *American Journey* (1970); J. A. Alvarez, *From Reconstruction to Revolution* (1971); M. F. Berry, *Black Resistance, White Law* (1971); Edward Wakin, *Black Fighting Men in United States History* (1971); Houston Baker, *Long Black Song* (1972); Norman Coombs, *The Black Experience in America* (1972); C. V. Hamilton, ed., *The Black Experience in American Politics* (1973); Theodore Rosengarten, *All God's Dangers: The Life of Nate Shaw* (1974); A. E. Barbeau and Florette Henri, *The Unknown Soldiers: Black American Soldiers in World War I* (1974).

Negro, Río (rē'ō nä'grō), river, c.400 mi (640 km) long, formed in central Argentina by the confluence of the Neuquén and the Limay rivers, and flowing E across Río Negro prov. (N Patagonia) to the Atlantic Ocean. The river is used for irrigation.

Negro, Río, river, c.1,400 mi (2,250 km) long, rising as the Guainía River in E Colombia where it flows NE before turning south to form part of the Colombia-Venezuela border. It then flows SE through Amazonas state, Brazil, to the Amazon near Manaus. The river is filled with islands and has many secondary channels. Its main tributary is the Río Branco. The Río Negro is connected with the Orinoco basin by the Casiquiare, a natural canal. An important commercial channel (rubber and nuts are shipped on it), the Río Negro was discovered (1638) by Pedro Teixeira, a Portuguese explorer. The river was named for its black color, which results from vegetal debris, not sediment.

Negro, Río, principal river of Uruguay, c.500 mi (800 km) long, rising in S Brazil and flowing SW across central Uruguay to the Uruguay River. It traverses a sheep-raising region; there is agriculture along its lower course. On the river is Embalse del Río Negro (c.4,000 sq mi/10,360 sq km), the largest artificial lake in South America. It extends 87 mi (140 km) upstream from Rincón de Bonete, a hydroelectric dam (completed 1949) with a 128,000-kw capacity. Downstream from Bonete is Rincón de Baygorria (1960), with a 108,000-kw capacity.

Negropont, Greece: see ÉVVOIA.

Negros (nā'grōs), island (1970 est. pop. 2,300,000), 4,905 sq mi (12,704 sq km), one of the Visayan Islands, 4th largest of the Philippines, between Panay and Cebu. Although mountainous (Mt. Canloan, a volcano, rises to c.8,088 ft/2,465 m), Negros has extensive arable lowlands; they are intensively cultivated and densely populated. Negros is the sugar center of the Philippines; two thirds of the nation's sugarcane is grown there, and sugar processing is a major industry. The island is also a leading banana- and corn-producing region. It has coconut plantations, copper and coal deposits, and a lumber industry. Paper products are made from sugarcane residue.

Nehavend: see NAHAVAND, Iran.

Nehelamite (nēhĕl'əmīt), obscure epithet of the false prophet Shemaiah. Jer. 29.24–31.

Nehemiah (nē"əmī'ə). **1** Central figure of the book of Nehemiah: see EZRA. **2** One who returned from the Exile. Ezra 2.2; Neh. 7.7. **3** Worker on the wall. Neh. 3.16.

Nehemiah, book of the Bible: see EZRA.

Nehiloth (nē'hĭlŏth), in the title of Ps. 5, musical direction of unknown meaning.

Nehru, Jawaharlal (jəwähərläl' nä'rōō, nē'–), 1889–1964, Indian statesman, b. Allahabad; son of Motilal Nehru. Educated in England at Harrow and Cambridge, he was admitted to the English bar in 1912 and practiced law in India for several years. After the massacre at AMRITSAR (1919), he devoted himself to the struggle for India's freedom. His compelling oratory as well as his close association with Mohandas Gandhi contributed to making him a leader of the INDIAN NATIONAL CONGRESS, and in 1929 (the first of four times) he was elected its president. A leader of the radical wing of the Congress, Nehru spent most of the period from 1930 to 1936 in jail for conducting civil disobedience campaigns. About 1939 disharmony developed between him and Gandhi. Nehru, who had been influenced by a study of Marxism, opposed Gandhi's ideal of an agrarian society and advanced a program calling for the industrialization and socialization of India. This ideological conflict was further complicated by personal struggles among the political elite of the Congress. During World War II, however, Nehru and Gandhi were united in their opposition to aiding Great Britain unless India was immediately freed, and Nehru was imprisoned from Oct., 1942, to June, 1945. After his release, he participated in the negotiations that led to the creation of the two independent states of India and Pakistan in 1947. He became India's prime minister and minister of foreign affairs and led the country through the difficult early years of independence. The domestic problems of those years included the massive influx of Hindu refugees from Pakistan; the integration of the princely states into the new political structure (Hyderabad was incorporated by force in 1948, and Kashmir's accession caused the first India-Pakistan War, ending in the partition of the state); controversy and unrest associated with the reorganization of the states on a linguistic basis; and difficulties in Kerala, where a Communist government was elected in 1957 but dissolved by the central government in 1959. On the economic front the government launched a series of five-year plans with the declared goal of achieving a "socialist pattern of society." In foreign affairs Nehru adopted a policy of neutralism. He stressed the importance of the Afro-Asian bloc in international politics and became one of its leading spokesmen. He also opposed the formation of military alliances and urged a moratorium on all nuclear testing. Some observers felt that he lost stature as an advocate of peace by employing force in Kashmir and by seizing (1961) Goa from the Portuguese. It also appeared that he might be abandoning strict neutralism for a more pro-Western policy when he requested Western aid to defend India against Chinese border incursions in 1962. A politician and statesman of great skill, Nehru was enormously popular in India. He wrote voluminously, especially while in prison; his notable works include *Glimpses of World History* (1936) comprising letters to his daughter, and *The Discovery of India* (1946). See his autobiography, *Toward Freedom* (American ed. 1941, repr. 1958); studies by M. N. Das (1961) and W. E. A. Range (1961); biographies by F. R. Moraes (1956, repr. 1959 and 1964), Michael Brecher (1959, abr. ed. 1962) and Michael Edwardes (1971); B. R. Nanda, *The Nehrus* (1962); G. W. Tyson, *Nehru: The Years of Power* (1966).

Nehru, Motilal (mō'tĭləl), 1861-1931, Indian political leader, father of Jawaharlal Nehru. A successful attorney, he joined the Indian National Congress at his son's urging and served as its president in 1919. In 1923, however, he entered the national legislature as leader of the Swaraj [independence] party, formed to wreck the constitution by obstruction from within. After returning (1926) to the Congress party, he was chairman of an all-party commission to draft a constitution for India; its report (1928), which proposed dominion status for India and ruled out separate Hindu and Muslim electorates, was rejected by the radical Congress members, led by Jawaharlal Nehru, and by the Indian Muslim leaders. See his selected speeches, ed. by K. M. Panikkar and A. Pershad (1961); biographies by Bal Ram Nanda (1964) and Beatrice Lamb (1967).

Nehum (nē'həm), alternative name of REHUM **2.**

Nehushta (nēhŭsh'tə), mother of King Jehoiachin. 2 Kings 24.8.

Nehushtan (nēhŭsh'tăn), brazen serpent made by Moses. It was eventually worshiped by the Israelites, and Hezekiah destroyed it. Num. 21.9; 2 Kings 18.4.

Nei-chiang or **Neikiang** (both: nā-jēäng), city (1970 est. pop. 240,000), central Szechwan prov., China, on the To River. It is a port and railroad center with sugar-refining and food-processing industries.

Neidhart von Reuental (nīt'härt fən roi'əntäl), c.1180-c.1245, Bavarian court poet. With his bright, humorous lyrics of village and peasant life, he introduced a new rustic note to the songs of the courtly minnesingers.

Neiel (nē'yəl, nēĭ'əl), unidentified landmark, N Palestine. Joshua 19.27.

Neikiang: see NEI-CHIANG, China.

Neilson, William Allan (nēl'sən), 1869-1946, American educator, b. Scotland, M.A. Univ. of Edinburgh, 1891, Ph.D. Harvard, 1898. He taught English in Scotland and Canada and at Bryn Mawr and Columbia and served (1906-17) as professor of English at Harvard. From 1917 until his retirement in 1939 he was president of Smith. He was author of a number of critical works, editor of the Cambridge and Tudor editions of Shakespeare (1906, 1911), and editor in chief of the second edition (1934) of *Webster's New International Dictionary.* See M. F. Thorp, *Neilson of Smith* (1956).

Neisse (nīs'ə), two rivers of SW Poland. The **Glatzer Neisse** (glät'sər), Pol. *Nisa Kłodzka,* c.120 mi (190 km) long, rises in the Sudetes, SW Poland, and winds generally NE past Kłodzko to the Oder River near Brzeg. A large dam at Otmuchow serves hydroelectric and irrigation projects. The **Lausitzer Neisse** (lou'zĭt"sər) or **Lusatian Neisse** (lo͞osā'shən), Czech. *Lužická Nisa,* Pol. *Nisa Łużycka,* c.140 mi (230 km) long, rises in the Sudetes, NW Czechoslovakia, and flows generally N to the Oder River near Guben, East Germany. Since 1945 it has formed part of the border between East Germany and Poland. Görlitz, East Germany, is the chief city on the river. It is also known as Görlitzer Neisse.

Neith (nē'ĭth) or **Neit** (nēt), in Egyptian religion, goddess of hunting and war. Her cult was very popular during the XXVI dynasty, particularly at Saïs. She also assumed the attributes of a mother goddess and was frequently identified with Isis.

Nejd (nĕjd) or **Najd** (näjd), region, central Saudi Arabia. RIYADH, the country's capital and major city, is located there. The Nejd is a vast plateau from 2,500 to 5,000 ft (762-1,524 m) high. There is a chain of oasis settlements in the eastern section; elsewhere the area is roamed by nomadic Bedouins. The Nejd, the stronghold of the WAHABI movement, was gradually conquered (1899-1912) from Turkey by the Wahabi leader, Ibn Saud. From there he completed his conquest of the HEJAZ and Al Hasa. In 1932 the Nejd became part of his newly constituted domain, Saudi Arabia.

Nejef: see AN NAJAF, Iraq.

Nekeb: see ADAMI.

Nekhtnebf I (nĕkt"nĕb'əf), Gr. *Nectanebos I,* king of ancient Egypt (379-361 B.C.), founder of the XXX dynasty. By the gallant defense of the fortresses of the Nile delta and then of Memphis he saved his country from the Persian invasion of Pharnabazus in 374 B.C. This defeat of the Persians touched off a general revolt of the satraps of W Asia, which occupied Persia for the rest of his reign. He built splendid temples at Bubastis, Memphis, Abydos, Al Karnak, and Edfu. His son, Tachos, while invading Syria, was overthrown by **Nekhtnebf II** (reigned 359-343). Nekhtnebf II built an all-granite temple at Horbeit, a kiosk at Philae, bas-reliefs at Al Karnak, and statues at Abydos and Bubastis. Persia had now recovered its strength and bent all its efforts to reconquer Egypt. With Greek aid Nekhtnebf was able to resist the first attack in 351, but in 343, hopelessly outnumbered, he was defeated and fled.

Nekoda (nēkō'də), name of two families who returned from the Exile. Ezra 2.48,60; Neh. 7.50,62.

Nekrasov, Nikolai Alekseyevich (nyĭkəlī' əlyĭksyā'yəvĭch nyĭkrä'səf), 1821-77, Russian poet, editor, and publisher. Nekrasov began writing poetry when he was seven. Disowned by his brutal father for entering the university, he lived in poverty for many years. The critic Belinsky befriended him and thereafter Nekrasov had brilliant success as an editor and publisher during a period of severe censorship. He discovered and published Leo Tolstoy, Goncharov, and Dostoyevsky. He bought (1846) and edited Pushkin's literary review *The Contemporary,* making it the finest review of its day. Nekrasov sought to improve social conditions in Russia and his powerful verses were used as slogans by revolutionaries. He made original use of the prosaic diction and rhythms of peasant oral literature. His major works include *The Red-nosed Frost* (1863, tr. 1887), the tragic poem *Russian Women* (1867), and the satirical portrait of feudal Russia, *Who Is Happy in Russia?* (1873, tr. 1957). His literary collaborator for many years was his mistress, Avdotya Panaeva.

nekton: see MARINE BIOLOGY.

Nellore (nĕlōr'), city (1971 pop. 133,607), Andhra Pradesh state, SE India, on the Pennar River. Nellore is a district administrative center and a market for cotton and oilseed. It also has milling and processing industries.

Nelson, Byron (John Byron Nelson, Jr.), 1912-, American golfer, b. Fort Worth, Texas. In 1926 he began playing golf as a caddy, and in 1933 he entered upon his professional career. Nelson won the U.S. National Open title in 1939 and the Professional Golfers Association championship in 1940 and again in 1945.

Nelson, Horatio Nelson, Viscount, 1758-1805, British admiral. He entered the navy at the age of 12 and became a captain at the age of 20. He saw service in the West Indies, in the Baltic, and in Canada. During these years he became friendly with the duke of Clarence (later William IV) and married (1787) a widow, Frances Nisbet, in the West Indies. That same year he returned to England and remained inactive and somewhat in disfavor at the admiralty until Great Britain entered (1793) the FRENCH REVOLUTIONARY WARS, when he was given command of the British ship *Agamemnon.* Nelson served in the Mediterranean, fighting at Toulon and helping to capture Corsica. At Calvi he lost the sight of one eye. Under John JERVIS, later earl of St. Vincent, he was largely responsible, acting boldly and without orders, for the victory over the Spanish off Cape St. Vincent (1797). He was made a rear admiral by seniority and was created a knight of the Bath. In the unsuccessful British attempt (1797) to capture Santa Cruz de Tenerife, Nelson lost his right arm and was returned to England. Upon his return to service, he was sent on detached duty to find the French fleet. After a long pursuit the French fleet was destroyed in 1798 at Aboukir (the modern ABU QIR), stranding NAPOLEON I and the entire French army in Egypt. Nelson was showered with rewards and honors, but received only the comparatively modest title of Baron Nelson of the Nile. He was placed in command of a squadron assisting the kingdom of the Two Sicilies. Here he fell in love with Emma, Lady HAMILTON, the wife of the British ambassador, who became his mistress. After the French took possession of Naples (1799) and set up the PARTHENOPEAN REPUBLIC, Nelson blockaded the city. During his absence on one occasion, the royalist commander, Fabrizio RUFFO, made a generous peace with the Neapolitan republicans. But Nelson, on his return, annulled the treaty and executed the Neapolitan admiral, Francesco Caracciolo, for desertion to the French. When the British commander in chief in the Mediterranean ordered him to Minorca, Nelson refused to obey on the grounds that his presence in Naples was politically necessary, but it was suspected that he did not wish to leave Lady Hamilton. In 1800 he returned to England with the Hamiltons and soon separated (1801) from his wife. The same year, Lady Hamilton bore him a daughter, Horatia. Nelson contrived his appointment as second in command, under Sir Hyde Parker, of the fleet sent against the armed neutrality of the Baltic powers. He defeated (1801) the Danes at Copenhagen, ignoring Parker's order to cease action by putting his telescope to his blind eye and saying that he could not see the signal. He was made a viscount, returned to England, and was given command of the Channel fleet to repel an expected French invasion. During the interlude of peace (1802-3), he lived in the country with the Hamiltons. Upon the renewal of war (1803), Nelson was given command of the fleet in the Mediterranean and blockaded the French fleet at Toulon for 22 months. When the French finally escaped, he pursued the fleet across the Atlantic to the West Indies and back to Spain, where it took refuge with the Spanish fleet in Cadiz. On Oct. 21, 1805, the combined fleets ventured out of port, and found Nelson waiting for them off Cape TRAFALGAR. Before the battle he gave the famous signal, "England expects that every man will do his duty." He won his most spectacular victory but died in the action. The most famous of Britain's naval heroes, he is commemorated by the celebrated Nelson Column in Trafalgar Square, London. See biographies by Robert Southey (1813, latest ed. 1956), A. T. Mahan (1897, repr. 1968), C. S. Forester (1929), W. M. James (1948), Oliver Warner (1958), G. M. Bennett (1972), and Christopher Lloyd (1973).

Nelson, Knute (kəno͞ot'), 1843-1923, U.S. Senator (1895-1923), b. Voss, Norway. He was brought to the United States at the age of six, grew up on a Wisconsin farm, and served in the Union army in the Civil War. Admitted (1867) to the bar, he served (1868-69) in the Wisconsin legislature before moving to Minnesota, where he practiced law and entered Republican politics. After service (1875-78) in the Minnesota state senate, he was (1883-89) a U.S. Congressman and became (1893) governor of Minnesota. He resigned the governorship to serve in the U.S. Senate, where, dissenting from orthodox Republicanism, he favored a modified tariff, supported antitrust and income-tax legislation, backed U.S. membership in the League of Nations, and helped create the Dept. of Commerce and Labor. See biography by M. W. Odland (1926).

Nelson, Leonard, 1882-1927, German philosopher. On the faculty of the Univ. of Göttingen from 1909, he was interested in the use of critical method to establish a scientific foundation for philosophy and in the systematic development of philosophical ethics. Nelson viewed Immanuel Kant's *Critique of Pure Reason* as a treatise on method, and he further developed the thought of Jakob Friedrich Fries, the only post-Kantian who had adopted that approach. Nelson's work in the area of ethics proceeded from a faith in systematic, critical reasoning, on which the values of his system are based. His concern with ethical standards and the question of how human freedom could be reconciled with natural necessity led him to practical undertakings, including the formation of his own political organization and his own school for political education. Among his works that have been translated are *Socratic Method and Critical Philosophy* (1949), *System of Ethics* (1956), *Critique of Practical Reason* (1970), and *Progress and Regress in Philosophy: From Hume and Kant to Hegel and Fries* (1970).

Nelson, Robert, 1794-1873, Canadian rebel, b. Montreal; brother of Wolfred Nelson. Like his brother, he was a surgeon in the War of 1812, and with him he entered the Legislative Assembly of Lower Canada in 1827 as a supporter of Louis Joseph Papineau. Although Robert Nelson took no active part in the rebellion of 1837, after its collapse he organized in the United States a band of adventurers with whom he invaded Canada in 1838, proclaiming it a republic and himself president of the provisional government. The invasion was quickly put down, and Nelson fled to Vermont.

Nelson, Thomas, 1738–89, American Revolutionary general, signer of the Declaration of Independence, b. Yorktown, Va. He was a delegate to the Continental Congress (1775–77, 1779), commander (1777–81) of the Virginia militia in the Revolution, and governor (1781) of the state. Nelson lost his fortune aiding the Revolutionary cause and died impoverished.

Nelson, Wolfred, 1792–1863, Canadian rebel, b. Montreal. A brother of Robert Nelson, Wolfred served as a surgeon in the War of 1812. In 1827 he entered the Legislative Assembly of Lower Canada as a supporter of Louis Joseph Papineau. For his leading role in the rebellion of 1837, Nelson was banished (1838) to Bermuda; with the amnesty of 1843 he returned to Montreal, resumed his medical practice, and served again (1844–51) in the Legislative Assembly.

Nelson, city (1971 pop. 9,400), SE British Columbia, on the Kootenay River. It is a transportation and administrative center for a lumbering and farming region. The Notre Dame Univ. of Nelson is there.

Nelson, municipal borough (1971 pop. 31,225), Lancashire, N England. It has cotton and rayon factories and electrical-engineering works.

Nelson, city (1971 pop. 29,282), N South Island, New Zealand, at the head of Tasman Bay. It is a port with light industries. The Cawthron Institute for scientific research is in the city. Nelson has an Anglican cathedral.

Nelson, river, c.400 mi (640 km) long, issuing from the northeast end of Lake Winnipeg, central Man., Canada, and flowing NE to Hudson Bay at Port Nelson. With the Bow-South Saskatchewan-Saskatchewan river system, which enters NW Lake Winnipeg, the Nelson is part of a 1,600-mi (2,575-km) continuous stream from W Alberta to Hudson Bay. The Nelson is being developed to make use of its great hydroelectric power potential. Nickel-mining and -refining operations at Thompson use electricity generated by the river. Kettle Rapids Dam, the second largest hydroelectric facility in Canada, is on the river. The Nelson's mouth was discovered (1612) by Sir Thomas Button. The river was long followed by fur traders; from 1682 to 1957 the Hudson's Bay Company maintained a trading post at York Factory on Hudson Bay.

Nemacolin's Path (nĕm'əkō''lĭnz), Indian trail between the Potomac and the Monongahela rivers, going from the site of present-day Cumberland, Md., to the mouth of Redstone Creek (where Brownsville, Pa., now stands). It was blazed and cleared in 1749 or 1750 by Nemacolin, the Delaware Indian chief, and Thomas Cresap, a Maryland frontiersman. The path was of great military importance as the route of George Washington's first Western expedition and of Gen. Edward Braddock's expedition in the French and Indian War. It was known as Braddock's Road until the Cumberland Road or NATIONAL ROAD was built on the same route.

Neman (nyĕ'mən), Ger. *Memel,* Lithuanian *Nemanus,* Pol. *Niemen,* river, c.580 mi (930 km) long, rising in central Belorussia, W European USSR, SW of Minsk. It flows generally W to Grodno, then N and W through S Lithuania to form part of the Lithuania-Kaliningrad Oblast border before entering the Kursky Zalev of the Baltic Sea through a small delta. Kaunas and Sovetsk are large cities along its course. The Neman is navigable c.60 mi (100 km) above Grodno. The meeting of Napoleon I and Czar Alexander I, which resulted in the Treaty of Tilsit (1807), took place on a raft in the middle of the river.

Nematoda (nĕm''ətōd'ə), class of organisms, many important parasites, belonging to the phylum ASCHELMINTHES.

Nematomorpha (nĕm''ətəmôr'fə), class of organisms belonging to the phylum ASCHELMINTHES.

Némcová, Božena (bô'zhĕnä nĕm'kôvä), 1820–62, Czech novelist and storyteller. Němcová developed the regional tale, which she enhanced with an original prose style. Her work provided escape from a wretchedly poor and unhappy life. Her best-known novel is *Babička* (1855, tr. *The Grandmother,* 1891), a simple, moving portrait of Czech village life. Her other major works include *Mountain Village* (1856), *The Disobedient Kids and Other Tales* (tr. 1921), and *The Shepherd and the Dragon: Fairy Tales* (tr. 1930).

Nemea (nē'mēə, nĭmē'ə), city of ancient Greece, in N Argolis. At the temple of Zeus were held the Nemean games, which from 573 B.C. were one of the four Panhellenic festivals; the games were held in the second and fourth years of each Olympiad. Of Pindar's odes, 11 celebrate Nemean victories. The temple and palaestra have been excavated. Nemea is also the name of a river that formed the boundary of Corinth and Sicyon (near modern Sikión).

Nemean lion (nĭmē'ən), in Greek mythology, an enormous lion, said to be the offspring of Echidna and Typhon. It was invulnerable to all weapons until Hercules, in his first labor, strangled it with his bare hands. He then wore its pelt.

Nemerov, Howard (nĕm'ĕrôf), 1920–, American poet, novelist, and critic, b. New York City, grad. Harvard, 1941. He has taught at Bennington since 1948. Some of his poems, ranging in tone from light to philosophical, are collected in *Image and the Law* (1947) and *The Next Room of the Law* (1964). Nemerov's fiction deals with moral dilemmas, as in *The Melodramatists* (1949), a satirical depiction of a Boston family. See his *Journal of the Fictive Life* (1965) and *Reflexions on Poetry and Poetics* (1972).

Nemertinea (nĕmərtĭn'ēə), phylum of elongated, often flattened marine WORMS, sometimes called ribbon worms. There are 500 to 600 known species, ranging in size from a fraction of an inch to 90 ft (27 m). The most distinctive structure of the carnivorous ribbon worms is a proboscis that can be shot out to capture food. When not in use the proboscis is sheathed in a muscular tube that lies above the digestive tract. When everted, it can coil about the prey, entangling it in a sticky mucus that is sometimes toxic. In many species the proboscis is tipped with a sharp spike, or stylet, which pierces the prey continuously as the irritating secretions are poured on. The proboscis can also be used for defense or for burrowing into sand or mud. Annelid worms form the bulk of the nemertine diet, although mollusks and other marine animals are also eaten. A ciliated epidermis and several other anatomical structures that bear a close resemblance to those of flatworms (see PLATYHELMINTHES) are characteristic of ribbon worms; however, in the latter group they are generally more complex. The nemertine nervous system is similar to those in higher flatworms, but there is a greater concentration of nervous tissue in the brain and nerve cords. Most nemertines have sense organs, such as light-sensitive pigment cups, similar to those of the PLANARIAN flatworms. Nearly all species also have deep ciliated grooves in the head region in close association with the brain. The grooves are believed to have a chemoreceptive or endocrine function. Nemertinea is the most primitive phylum that has developed a closed circulatory system, in which the blood does not bathe the tissues, but is confined to vessels with distinct walls. Excretion is accomplished by tubules that are in intimate contact with the circulatory system. The nemertine digestive tract, in a departure from the blind gut of flatworms, has developed into a tube with an opening at both ends. The presence of a second, or anal, opening at the posterior end permits ingestion and egestion to occur simultaneously. Food is pushed through the digestive tract, and blood moves along the circulatory tubes by the undulating movement of the body-wall musculature, located below the epidermis. The larger worms also move about on the ocean floor by means of such muscle contractions. Smaller types glide along on epidermal cilia over trails of secreted mucus. In most species the sexes are separate. The eggs and sperm are usually shed into the water and fertilized externally. Many nemertines, like the planarians, are also capable of reproducing asexually by fragmentation of the body.

Nemesis (nĕm'ĭsĭs), in Greek religion, personification of the gods' retribution for violation of sacred law; the avenger. Sometimes she was said to be the goddess of good and ill fortune.

Nemi, Lake (nā'mē), Latin *Nemorensis lacus,* small picturesque crater lake, c.1 mi (1.6 km) long, in the Alban Hills, central Italy, SE of Rome. The sacred wood and the ruins of the celebrated temple of DIANA are there. Two pleasure ships of the Roman emperor Caligula that were lying at the bottom of Lake Nemi for almost 2,000 years were raised (1930–31) from the lake after its level had been lowered c.70 ft (21 m). No valuables were found, but objects interesting from the artistic and technical point of view were recovered. During World War II the ships were destroyed (1944) by the retreating German forces.

Nemirovich-Danchenko, Vladimir (vlədyĕ'mĭr nămĕrō'vĭch-dän'chĕngkō), 1859–1943, Russian stage director, cofounder and director of the MOSCOW ART THEATRE. Prior to his historical meeting with Constantin STANISLAVSKY in 1897, he was an actor, war correspondent, novelist, music and drama critic, and playwright. After publication of his last novel, *On the Steppes* (1897), he devoted all his efforts to the Moscow Art Theatre, whose influence was felt throughout Europe and the United States. See his autobiography (1936, repr. with new introd. by Joshua Logan, 1968).

Nemophila (nəmŏf'ələ): see WATERLEAF.

Nemours, Gaston de Foix, duc de: see FOIX, GASTON DE.

Nemours, Louis Charles Philippe Raphaël d'Orléans, duc de (lwē shärl fēlēp' räfäĕl' dôrlāäN' dük də nəmo͞or'), 1814–96, French prince; second son of King Louis Philippe. In 1831 he was offered the throne of Belgium, but Louis Philippe declined for him in order to avoid antagonizing Great Britain. He fought in Algeria and was active (1842–48) in the chamber of peers. After the February Revolution of 1848 he lived in England. He helped to effect a rapprochement between the legitimist pretender, the comte de Chambord, and the Orleanist pretender, his nephew Louis Philippe Albert d'Orléans. He returned to France in 1871.

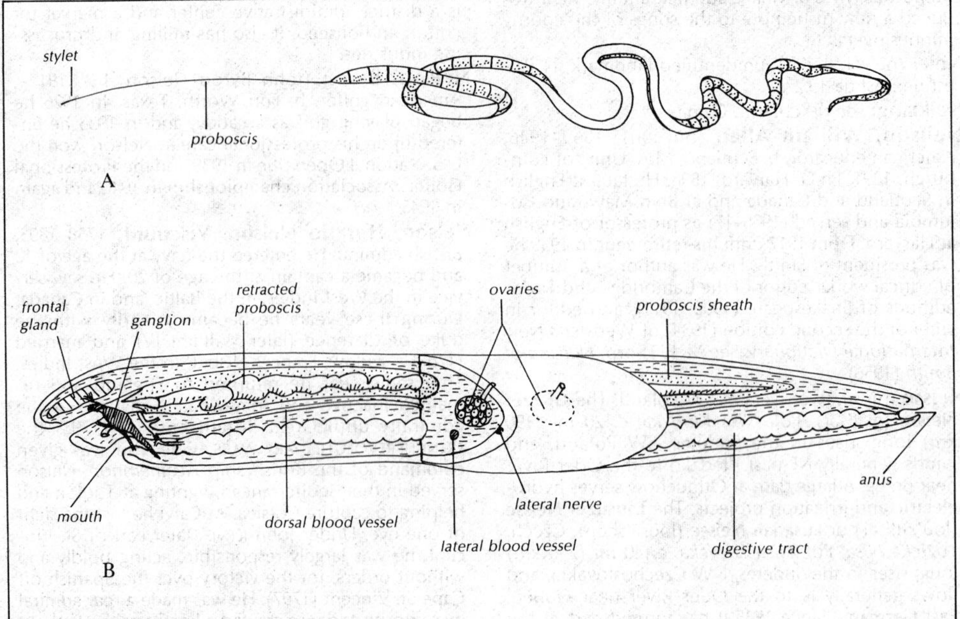

A. *Ribbon worm, representative of the phylum Nemertinea*
B. *Internal anatomy of a ribbon worm*

Nemuel (nĕmyo͝o'əl). **1** Descendant of Reuben. Num. 26.9. **2** See JEMUEL.

Nemunas: see NEMAN, river, USSR.

Nen: see NENE, river, England.

Nenagh (nē'nə, nē'năkh), urban district (1971 pop. 4,926), Co. Tipperary, S central Republic of Ireland. It is an agricultural market with varied manufactures. Nenagh Castle (c.1200) has a circular keep. The district also contains ruins of a Franciscan friary, founded in the 13th cent. and destroyed by Cromwell's forces in 1650.

Nen-chiang (nŭn-jēäng) or **Nunkiang** (no͞on-gēäng), former province (c.26,000 sq mi/67,340 sq km), NE China. The capital was Tsitsihar (Ch'i-ch'i-ha-erh). It was one of nine provinces established by the Nationalist government in Manchuria in 1945. However, since the Nationalists never gained effective control of Manchuria, the province existed only on paper. It was bordered on the S by the Sungari River and crossed by the Nonni (Nen Chiang); the soil in the valleys of these rivers is some of the most fertile in Manchuria. In 1950, Nen-chiang was absorbed by Heilungkiang prov.

Nen Chiang (nŭn jēäng) or **Nonni** (nôn'nē), river, 740 mi (1,191 km) long, rising in the I-lo-hu-li Shan, N Heilingkiang prov., NE China, and flowing south along the east side of the Great Khingan range to the Sungari River; forms part of the Heilungkiang-Kirin province border. Though frozen from November to April, the river and its valley form an important trade artery. It is navigable for shallow-draft vessels along most of its length; a railroad follows its valley.

Nene (nĕn, nēn) or **Nen** (nĕn), river, c.90 mi (140 km) long, rising in the Northampton Uplands, central England, and flowing NE past Northampton, Oundle, Peterborough, and Wisbech to the Wash. It has been made navigable to Peterborough and drains part of the Fens.

Nenets National Okrug (nyĕ'nyĭts), administrative division (1970 pop. 39,000), 68,224 sq mi (176,700 sq km), extreme NE European USSR. Formed in 1929, the okrug forms the northern part of Arkhangelsk oblast and extends along the tundra coast of the Barents, White, and Kara seas. Naryan-Mar, the capital, is a lumber port on the Pechora River. The okrug includes the northern section of the Pechora coal basin, with mines at Khalmer-Yu and along the Silova River. Reindeer raising, fishing, fur trapping, and seal hunting are the chief occupations. Fish canning, saw-milling, and hide processing are important. Cattle are grazed in meadows along the river banks. Many of the formerly nomadic Nentsy live in agricultural settlements and raise potatoes, cabbages, and turnips. The okrug's population consists mainly of Nentsy and Russians, with a Komi minority. The Nentsy, previously known as SAMOYEDES, speak a Finno-Ugric language and are either Orthodox Christians or animists. They were first mentioned in the 11th cent., became tributaries of the grand duchy of Moscow at the end of the 15th cent., and gained their independence in the 17th cent. after prolonged warfare.

Nenni, Pietro (pyĕ'trō nĕn'nē), 1891–, Italian journalist and political leader. He was imprisoned in 1911 for his participation in the protest movement against the Italo-Turkish war in Libya. He joined the Socialist party in 1921 and subsequently became Paris correspondent and later editor of the Socialist party newspaper *Avanti.* As an opponent of Fascism, he was forced to emigrate to France in 1926. He fought against the fascists in Spain during the Spanish civil war. In 1943 he was arrested by the Germans in Vichy France and then imprisoned in Italy. Released in August, 1943, he began to reorganize the Italian Socialist party, becoming its secretary general in 1944. He held that post until the formation (1966) of the Unified Socialist party, composed of Socialists and Democratic Socialists. Nenni was party president. The combined party fell apart in 1969. Nenni served in several postwar cabinets, as deputy prime minister or as minister of foreign affairs. In 1971 he ran unsuccessfully for president of Italy.

Nennius (nĕn'ēəs), fl. 796, Welsh writer, to whom is ascribed the *Historia Britonum.* He lived on the borders of Mercia and probably was a pupil of Elbod, bishop of Bangor. The *Historia* is a compilation containing much on the early history of Britain and the Anglo-Saxon invasions. Although some scholars think that it was compiled by Nennius from various works, most now agree that the history is a revision by Nennius of an older work. It is important chiefly for the study of early British legends, especially the ARTHURIAN LEGEND. There are several manuscripts in Latin and Irish. Among the many translations of the *Historia* is an excellent one by A. W. Wade-Evans (1938) of a Latin text.

neoclassicism: see CLASSICISM.

neodymium (nē"ōdĭm'ēəm), metallic chemical element; symbol Nd; at. no. 60; at. wt. 144.24; m.p. about 1010°C; b.p. about 3130°C; sp. gr. 7.004 at 20°C; valence +3. Neodymium is a lustrous silver-yellow metal. It is one of the RARE-EARTH METALS in the LANTHANIDE SERIES of group IIIb of the PERIODIC TABLE. It exists in two distinct forms (see ALLOTROPY); at room temperature it has a hexagonal crystalline structure, but when heated above about 800°C it assumes a face-centered cubic conformation with specific gravity about 6.8. The metal tarnishes in air; the coating formed does not protect the metal from further oxidation, so it must be stored away from contact with air. The oxide (neodymia, Nd_2O_3) is light blue. The metal is also attacked by water and by acids. Its salts form various red aqueous solutions. Neodymium is present in the minerals MONAZITE and bastnasite. The metal may be prepared from its halides by reduction. Neodymium is one of several metals in an alloy commonly used in cigarette lighter flints. Neodymium is used in coloring glasses. The earth didymia is a mixture of the oxides of neodymium and praseodymium. The lenses of goggles used by glassblowers are made with a didymium glass that absorbs the yellow sodium glare of the flame. Neodymium was discovered in 1885 by C. A. von Welsbach who separated Mosander's "didymium" into two components, the earths neodymia and praseodymia.

neo-impressionism: see POSTIMPRESSIONISM.

neo-Kantianism: see KANT, IMMANUEL.

Neolithic period or **New Stone Age.** The term *neolithic* is used, especially in archaeology and anthropology, to designate a stage of cultural evolution or technological development characterized by the use of stone tools, the existence of settled villages largely dependent on domesticated plants and animals, and the presence of such crafts as pottery and weaving. The time period and cultural content indicated by the term varies with the geographic location of the culture considered and with the particular criteria used by the individual scientist. The domestication of plants and animals usually distinguishes Neolithic culture from earlier PALEOLITHIC or MESOLITHIC hunting, fishing, and food-gathering cultures. The Mesolithic period in several areas shows a gradual transition from a food-collecting to a food-producing culture. The termination of the Neolithic period is marked by such innovations as the rise of urban civilization or the introduction of metal tools or writing. Again, the criteria vary with each case. The earliest known development of Neolithic culture was in SW Asia between 8000 B.C. and 6000 B.C. There the domestication of plants and animals was probably begun by the Mesolithic Natufian peoples, leading to the establishment of settled villages based on the cultivation of cereals, including wheat, barley, and millet, and the raising of cattle, sheep, goats, and pigs. In the Tigris and Euphrates river valleys, the Neolithic culture of the Middle East developed into the urban civilizations of the Bronze Age by 3500 B.C. Between 6000 B.C. and 2000 B.C. Neolithic culture spread through Europe, the Nile valley (Egypt), the Indus valley (India), and the Yellow River valley (N China). The formation of Neolithic cultures throughout the Old World resulted from a combination of local cultural developments with innovations diffused from the Middle East. In SE Asia, a distinct type of Neolithic culture involving rice cultivation developed, perhaps independently, before 2000 B.C. In the New World, the domestication of plants and animals occurred independently of Old World developments. By 1500 B.C., Neolithic cultures based on the cultivation of maize, beans, squash, and other plants were present in Mexico and South America, leading to the rise of the Inca and Aztec civilizations and spreading to other parts of the Americas by the time of European contact. The term *Neolithic* has also been used in anthropology to designate cultures of more contemporary primitive, independent farming communities. See V. G. Childe, *New Light on the Most Ancient East* (4th ed. 1953, repr. 1968); Grahame Clark and Stuart Piggott, *Prehistoric Societies* (1965); R. J. Braidwood, *Prehistoric Men* (7th ed. 1967); S. M. Cole, *The Neolithic Revolution* (4th ed. 1967).

neomycin (nē"ōmī'sĭn), broad spectrum ANTIBIOTIC effective against both gram positive and gram negative bacteria (see GRAM'S STAIN). It interferes with protein synthesis in sensitive bacterial cells such as species of *Proteus* and *Staphylococcus.* Neomycin is mainly used topically in the treatment of skin and mucous membrane infections, wounds, and burns. Although it is also used systemically, it is highly toxic. Neomycin was first isolated in 1949 by the American microbiologist Selman Waksman from a strain of the bacterial species *Streptomyces fradiae.*

neon (nē'ŏn) [Gr.,=new], gaseous chemical element; symbol Ne; at. no. 10; at. wt. 20.183; m.p. −248.67°C; b.p. −245.92°C; density 0.8999 grams per liter at STP (see separate article); valence 0. Neon is a colorless, odorless, and tasteless gas. It is one of the INERT GASES in group 0 of the PERIODIC TABLE; it does not form compounds in the normal chemical sense. A small amount of neon in a partially evacuated glass tube emits a bright reddish-orange glow while conducting electricity. Neon is a rare gas present in the atmosphere to a very limited extent. It is obtained as a by-product in the production of liquid air. The greatest commercial use of neon is in advertising signs (see LIGHTING). It is also used in high-intensity beacons, in some electron tubes, in Geiger counters, in automotive ignition timing lights, and in high-voltage warning indicators. It is used for particle detection in high-energy physics research. Neon finds use in LASERS both as a light-emitting agent and as a coolant. Liquid neon is a particularly good cryogenic refrigerant since it will absorb more heat without vaporizing than an equal volume of liquid helium or liquid hydrogen. Neon was discovered in 1898 by William RAMSAY and M. W. Travers.

neoplasm or **tumor,** new tissue composed of cells that grow in an abnormal way. Normal tissue is growth-limited, i.e., cell reproduction is equal to cell death. Feedback controls limit cell division after a certain number of cells have developed, allowing for tissue repair but not expansion. Tumor cells, lacking such feedback controls, proliferate, and monopolize body nutrients. Tumors may be benign or malignant. Benign tumors, differing from normal tissue in structure and excessive growth of cells, are rarely fatal. However, even benign tumors may grow large enough to interfere with normal function. Some benign uterine tumors, known to weigh as much as 50 lb (22.7 kg), displace adjacent organs, causing digestive and reproductive disorders. Benign tumors are usually treated by complete surgical removal. Cells of malignant tumors, i.e., CANCERS, have characteristics that differ from normal cells in other ways beside cell proliferation. Malignant cells resemble embryonic cells in that they are unspecialized. It has been suggested that formation of cancer tissue involves a regressive change of normal, specialized cells in which there is a loss of the biological controls on gene expression that normally keep cells specialized and growth-limited. Malignant cells are invasive, i.e., they infiltrate surrounding normal tissue; later, malignant cells metastasize, i.e., spread via blood and the lymph system to other sites. The methods used to treat cancer—surgery, IMMUNOSUPPRESSIVE DRUGS, and radiation—are not always curative. Both benign and malignant tumors are classified according to the type of tissue in which they are found. For example, fibromas are neoplasms of fibrous connective tissue, and melanomas are abnormal growths of pigment (melanin) cells. Malignant tumors originating from epithelial tissue, e.g., in skin, bronchi, and stomach, are termed carcinomas. Malignancies of epithelial glandular tissue such as are found in the breast, prostate, and colon, are known as adenocarcinomas. Malignant growths of connective tissue, e.g., muscle, cartilage, lymph tissue, and bone, are called sarcomas. Lymphomas are malignant forms of any of the white blood cell types resulting in various types of LEUKEMIA. A system has been devised to classify malignant tissue according to the degree of malignancy, from grade 1, barely malignant, to grade 4, highly malignant. In practice it is not always possible to determine the degree of malignancy or even whether the tissue is benign or malignant.

Neoplatonism (nē"ōplā'tənĭzəm), ancient mystical philosophy based on the doctrines of PLATO. Considered the last of the great pagan philosophies, it was developed by PLOTINUS (3d cent. A.D.). It has had a lasting influence on Western metaphysics and MYSTICISM, although its original form was much altered by the followers of Plotinus. Neoplatonism was a viable force from the middle of the 3d cent. to 529, when Justinian closed the Academy at Athens. Although Plotinus is the central figure of Neoplatonism, his teacher, Ammonius Saccus (175–242), a self-taught laborer of Alexandria, may have been the actual founder; however, no writings of Ammonius have survived. Plotinus left Egypt, settled in Rome in 244, and founded a school there. The enduring source of Neoplatonist thought is the *Enneads* of Plotinus, which were collected and published after his death by his student PORPHYRY, a Phoenician. Plotinus' purpose was to put into systematic form an idealistic philosophy and thus combat the trends of Stoicism and skepticism that had crept into interpretations of the philosophy of Plato. Plotinus rejected the dualism of two disparate realms of being (good and evil, material and transcendent, universal and particular) and set forth instead one vast order containing all the various levels and kinds of existence. At the center of the order is the One, an incomprehensible, all-sufficient unity. By the process of EMANATION the One gives rise to the Divine Mind or Logos [word], which contains all the forms, or living intelligences, of individuals. The content of the Divine Mind, therefore, constitutes a multiple reflection of the unitary perfection of the One. Below the divine mind is the World Soul, which links the intellectual and material worlds. These three transcendent realities, or hypostases (the One, the Divine Mind, and the World Soul) support the finite and visible world, which includes individual men and matter. Plotinus sometimes compared the One to a fountain, from which overflowed the lower levels of reality. The Neoplatonic cosmology also had religious overtones, for Plotinus believed that men potentially sought a life in which the individual soul would rise through contemplation to the level of intelligence (the Divine Mind) and then through mystic union would be absorbed in the One itself. Conversely, a privation of being or lack of desire toward the One was the cause of sin, which was held to be a negative quality (i.e., nonparticipation in the perfection of the One). There are thus two reciprocal movements in Neoplatonism: the metaphysical movement of emanation from the One, and the ethical or religious movement of reflective return to the One through contemplation of the forms of the Divine Mind. While Plotinus' thought was mystical (i.e., concerned with the infinite and invisible within the finite and visible world), his method was thoroughly rational, stemming from the logical and humanistic traditions of Greece. Many of his philosophical elements come from earlier philosophies; the existence of the One and the attendant theory of ideas were aspects of the later writings of Plato, particularly the *Timaeus*, and Stoicism had identified the World Soul with transcendent universal reason. What was distinctive in Plotinus' system was the unified, hierarchical structuring of these elements and the theory of emanation. The followers of Plotinus took divergent paths. Porphyry, who remained in Rome, made extensive use of allegory in expounding Plotinus' rationalistic thought and attacked Christianity in the name of Hellenic paganism. IAMBLICHUS taught in Rome for a time and then returned to Chalcis in Syria to found a Neoplatonic center there. At this center, and also at others in Athens and Alexandria, the mystical trends of the East, including divination, demonology, and astrology, were grafted onto the body of Neoplatonism. The central figures at the Athenian school were Plutarch the Younger (350-433) and PROCLUS, who came from Byzantium to become head of the Academy. The Athenian school culminated in Simplicius, a commentator on Aristotle, and Damascius, who tried to recover the original thought of Plotinus; they were the survivors of the Academy when it was closed in 529. The Alexandrian school of Neoplatonism, which included the woman philosopher HYPATIA, was more scholarly but less theological than its Syrian and Athenian counterparts and is important mainly for its commentaries on Aristotle. It survived into the 7th cent., and some Alexandrian Neoplatonists, notably Synesius, became Christians. Neoplatonism was an early influence on Christian thinkers. The Christian apologists CLEMENT OF ALEXANDRIA and ORIGEN had vied with the incipient Neoplatonic tradition for control of the Platonic heritage. The philosophy was firmly joined with Christianity by St. Augustine, who was a Neoplatonist before his conversion. It was through Neoplatonism that Augustine conceived of spirit as being immaterial and viewed evil as an unreal substance (in contradistinction to Manichaean doctrine). The writings of Pseudo-Dionysius (see DIONYSIUS THE AREOPAGITE) and BOETHIUS display Neoplatonic influences. In the Middle Ages, elements of Plotinus' thought can be found in St. Thomas Aquinas and John Scotus Erigena, particularly in the identification of the One with God and the Divine Mind with the angels. The system also influenced medieval Jewish and Arab philosophy. G. W. F. Hegel's metaphysics had Neoplatonic ingredients. Neoplatonic metaphysics and aesthetics influenced the German Romantics (see ROMANTICISM), the 17th-century English metaphysical poets, William Blake, and the CAMBRIDGE PLATONISTS. Many mystical movements in the West, including those of Meister Eckhardt and Jacob Boehme, owe something to the Neoplatonists. See Philip Merlan, *From Plotinus to Neoplatonism* (2d ed. 1960); R. T. Wallis, *Neoplatonism* (1972).

neoprene: see RUBBER.

Neoptolemus (nē″ŏptŏl′ĭməs), in Greek legend, son of Achilles. In the Trojan War he proved himself brave but cruel. He killed Priam at the altar of Zeus and threw Astyanax, son of Hector, from the wall of Troy. After the war he took Andromache as a slave to his kingdom in Epirus. Later he abandoned her for Hermione. He was killed at Delphi for an outrage he committed against the shrine. In Euripides' *Andromache*, Orestes murders him to win the love of Hermione. He was sometimes called Pyrrhus.

neo-Pythagoreanism: see PYTHAGORAS.

neo-scholasticism, philosophical viewpoint, prominent in the 19th and 20th cent., that sought to apply the doctrines of SCHOLASTICISM to contemporary political, economic, and social problems. It is often called neo-Thomism for its close links to St. THOMAS AQUINAS, but it is more properly called neo-scholasticism, as the movement encompassed the principles of other scholastics, such as DUNS SCOTUS. Jacques MARITAIN and Étienne GILSON were eminent neo-scholastics.

Neosho, river, c.460 mi (740 km) long, rising in E central Kansas and flowing SE into NE Okla. (where it is generally known as the Grand River) then south to join the Arkansas River near Muskogee, Okla. Pensacola Dam (which impounds the huge Lake of the Cherokees) and Fort Gibson dam and reservoir are in NE Oklahoma; there are several flood control units on the river in Kansas.

neostigmine (nē″ōstĭg′mēn,-mĭn), drug used to mimic the effects of stimulation of the parasympathetic NERVOUS SYSTEM. Along with several other drugs that have a similar mode of action, it inhibits the action of the enzyme cholinesterase, which destroys the substance ACETYLCHOLINE at nerve endings. Because neostigmine increases the effective concentration of acetylcholine, it causes such body changes as contraction of the pupils, increased activity of intestinal muscles, and increased secretion by the salivary and sweat glands. It will cause menstrual bleeding in a nonpregnant woman whose menstrual period is delayed, and it is therefore used as a pregnancy test. Neostigmine and related drugs are also used to diagnose and control the neuromuscular disease myasthenia gravis. Because neostigmine causes decreased fluid pressure in the eye it is used to treat certain types of glaucoma. The drug ATROPINE is sometimes given along with neostigmine to prevent the latter's side effects. EPHEDRINE often enhances the action of neostigmine.

neoteny (nēŏt′ənē), in biology, sexual maturity reached in the larval stage of an animal. When environmental conditions are such as to inhibit the completion of metamorphosis, e.g., when low temperature or lack of available iodine inhibit the action of the thyroid gland, the larval form may mature sexually, mate, and produce fertile eggs. If environmental conditions improve, neoteny is reversible; i.e., the larvae can complete metamorphosis and attain normal maturity. Neoteny commonly occurs in some salamanders (see AXOLOTL). In insects, reproduction in the larval stages is known as paedogenesis; it occurs in certain beetles and gall midges. In the midges, the daughter larvae produced within a mother larva consume the mother and escape; the process may continue for several generations.

neo-Thomism: see THOMAS AQUINAS, SAINT.

NEP: see NEW ECONOMIC POLICY.

Nepal (nəpôl′), independent kingdom (1973 est. pop. 11,600,000), c.54,000 sq mi (139,860 sq km), central Asia. KATMANDU is the capital. Landlocked and isolated by the Himalayas, Nepal is bordered on the W, S, and SE by India; on the E by Sikkim; and on the N by the Tibet region of China. Geographically, Nepal comprises three major areas. The south, known as the Terai, is a comparatively low region of cultivable land, swamps, and forests that provide valuable timber. In the north is the main section of the Himalayas, including Mt. Everest (29,028 ft/8,848 m), the world's highest peak. Nepal's major rivers, which rise in Tibet, rush through deep Himalayan gorges. Central Nepal, an area of moderately high mountains, contains the Katmandu valley, or Valley of Nepal, the country's most densely populated region and its administrative, economic, and cultural center. Nepal's railroads, connecting with lines in India, do not reach the valley, which is served by a bridgelike cable line. There are few modern highways. The population of Nepal represents a long intermingling of Mongolians, who migrated from the north (especially Tibet), and Indo-Aryans, who

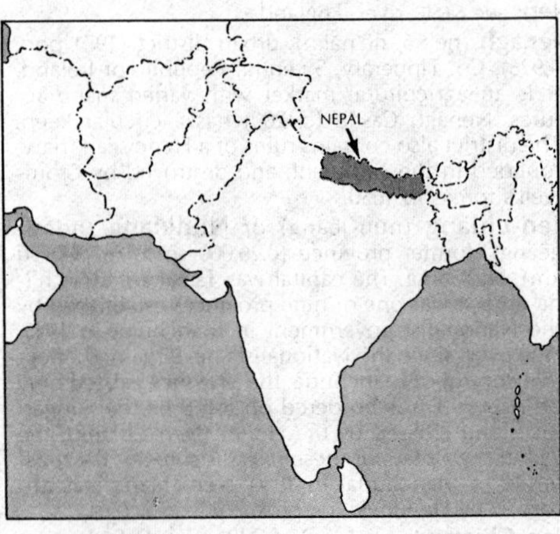

came from the Ganges plain in the south. The chief ethnic group, the Newars, were probably the original inhabitants of the Katmandu valley. Several ethnic groups are classified together as Bhotias; among them are the Sherpas, famous for guiding mountain-climbing expeditions, and the Gurkhas, a term sometimes loosely applied to the fighting castes, who achieved fame in the British Indian army and continue to serve as mercenaries in India's army and in the British overseas forces. Nepali, the country's official language, is of Sanskrit derivation and has similarities to Hindi. Tibeto-Burman languages, Munda languages, and various Indo-Aryan dialects are also spoken. Hinduism and Buddhism, particularly its Tibetan form (see TIBETAN BUDDHISM), coexist in Nepal, where tribal and caste distinctions are still important and Brahmans (the Hindu priestly class) retain great political influence. The royal family is Hindu. The overwhelming majority of Nepal's people engage in agriculture, which contributes about two thirds of the national income. In the Terai, the main agricultural region, rice is the chief crop; other food crops include pulses, wheat, barley, and oilseeds. Jute, tobacco, cotton, indigo, and opium are also grown in the Terai, whose forests provide sal wood and commercially valuable bamboo and rattan. In the lower mountain valleys, rice is produced during the summer, and wheat, barley, oilseeds, potatoes, and vegetables are grown in the winter. Corn, wheat, and potatoes are raised at higher altitudes, and terraced hillsides are also used for agriculture. Large quantities of medicinal herbs, grown on the Himalayan slopes, are sold worldwide. Livestock raising is second to farming in Nepal's economy; oxen predominate in the lower valleys, yaks in the higher, and sheep, goats, and poultry are plentiful everywhere. Transportation and communication difficulties have hindered the growth of industry and trade. Wood and metal handicrafts are important. Biratnagar and Birganj, in the Terai, are the main manufacturing towns; their products include cotton cloth, textiles, cigarettes, matches, furniture, shoes, stainless steel, sugar, processed rice, flour, oilseeds, and jute. Katmandu, a minor industrial center, has plywood, furniture, and mica-processing factories. Significant quantities of mica and small deposits of ochre, copper, iron, lignite, and cobalt are found in the hills of Nepal. Tourism is the chief source of foreign income (along with subsidies from the Indian government and Gurkha pensions). Religious shrines, especially Buddha's reputed birthplace at Lumbini, are the main attractions. Nepal's trade is overwhelmingly with India, and Great Britain is also an important trading partner. By the 4th cent. A.D. the Newars of the central Katmandu valley had apparently developed a flourishing Hindu-Buddhist culture. From the 8th-11th cent. many Buddhists fled to Nepal from India, which was being invaded by Muslims, and a group of Hindu Rajput warriors set up the principality of Gurkha just west of the Katmandu valley. Although a Newar dynasty, the Mallas, ruled the valley from the 14th-18th cent., there were internecine quarrels among local rulers. These were exploited by the Gurkha king Prithur Narayan Shah, who conquered the Katmandu valley in 1768. Gurkha armies seized territories far beyond the present-day Nepal; but their invasion of Tibet, over which China claimed sovereignty, was defeated in 1792 by Chinese forces. An ensuing peace treaty forced Nepal to pay China an annual tribute, which continued until 1910. Also in 1792, Nepal first entered into treaty relations with

Great Britain. Gurkha expansion into N India, however, led to a border war (1814–16) and to British victory over the Gurkhas, who were forced by treaty to retreat into roughly the present borders of Nepal and to receive a British envoy at Katmandu. The struggle for power among the Nepalese nobility culminated in 1846 with the rise to political dominance of the Rana family. Jung Bahadur Rana established a line of hereditary prime ministers, who controlled the government until 1950, and the Shah dynasty kings were mere figureheads. In 1854, Nepal again invaded Tibet, which was forced to pay tribute from then until 1953. Under the Ranas, Nepal was deliberately isolated from foreign influences; this policy helped to maintain independence during the colonial period but prevented economic and social modernization. Relations with Britain were cordial, however, and in 1923 a British-Nepalese treaty expressly affirmed Nepal's full sovereignty. Nepal supplied many troops for the British army in both world wars. The successful Indian movement for independence (1947) stimulated democratic sentiment in Nepal. The newly formed Congress party of Nepal precipitated a revolt in 1950 that forced the autocratic Ranas to share power in a new cabinet. King Tribhuvan Bir Bikram, who sympathized with the democratic movement, took temporary refuge in India and returned as a constitutional monarch. In 1959 a democratic constitution was promulgated, and parliamentary elections gave the Congress party a clear majority; the following year, however, King Mahendra (reigned 1952–72) cited alleged inefficiency and corruption in government as evidence that Nepal was not ready for Western-style democracy. He dissolved parliament, detained many political leaders, and in 1962 inaugurated a system of "basic democracy," based on the elected village council (panchayat) and working up to district and zonal panchayats and an indirectly elected national panchayat. The king, who must approve all panchayat legislation, is aided by a council of ministers appointed from members of the national panchayat and by an advisory state council. Political parties are banned. King Mahendra modernized Nepal through such programs as a land reform that distributed large holdings to landless families and a law removing the legal sanctions for caste discrimination. Crown Prince Birenda succeeded to the throne (1972) upon his father's death; like previous Nepalese monarchs, he married a member of the Rana family in order to insure political peace. Nepal has maintained a position of nonalignment in foreign affairs. It joined the United Nations in 1955. The following year a treaty recognized Chinese sovereignty over Tibet and officially terminated the century-old Tibetan tribute to Nepal; all Nepalese troops left Tibet in 1957. The Sino-Nepalese border treaty of 1961 defined Nepal's Himalayan frontier. India's geographical proximity, cultural affinity, and substantial economic aid renders it the most influential foreign power in Nepal; but charges that India had sheltered antiroyalist Nepalese politicians, in addition to the factor of China's growing power, caused friction with India in the late 1960s; in 1969, Nepal canceled an arms agreement with India and ordered the Indians to withdraw their military mission from Katmandu and their wireless operators from the Tibet-Nepal frontier. Meanwhile, Nepal has received U.S., Soviet, and Chinese economic assistance; a Chinese-financed highway linking Katmandu with Tibet is a particularly important aid project. See D. R. Regni, *Medieval Nepal* (4 vol., 1965–66), N. B. Thapa and D. P. Thapa, *Geography of Nepal* (enl. and rev. ed. 1969), I. R. Aryal and T. P. Dhungyal, *A New History of Nepal* (1970), Jeremy Bernstein, *The Wildest Dreams of Kew: A Profile of Nepal* (1970), Toni Hagen, *Nepal: The Kingdom in the Himalayas* (rev. ed. 1971), R. S. Chauhan, *The Political Development in Nepal, 1950–70* (1972).

Nepheg (nē'fĕg). **1** Descendant of Kohath. Ex. 6.21. **2** Son of David. 2 Sam. 5.15; 1 Chron. 3.7; 14.6.

Nephele: see ATHAMAS.

Nephilim (nĕfĭl'ĭm), Hebrew word of no known meaning retained in RV. It is translated "giants" in AV. Gen. 6.4; Num. 13.33.

Nephish (nē'fĭsh), variant of NAPHISH.

Nephishesim (nĕfĭsh'ēsĭm), family who returned from the Exile. Neh. 7.52. Nephusim: Ezra 2.50.

nephrite: see JADE.

nephritis (nəfrī'təs), inflammation of the KIDNEY. The disease can take several forms. Pyelonephritis is usually associated with a bacterial infection transmitted from the bladder or blood; it affects the renal pelvis and is treated with antibiotics. Glomerulonephritis, or Bright's disease, causes degenerative changes in the renal capillaries (glomeruli) and is believed to be an allergic response to infection elsewhere in the body, especially streptococcal infection. Symptoms include headache, mild fever, puffiness of the eyes and face, high blood pressure, and discoloration of the urine. Treatment includes bed rest and limiting the intake of water, sodium, and proteins; antibiotics are given to halt the streptococcal invasion. The disease occurs more frequently among the young. About 95% of patients recover from the acute phase of the disease; however, if glomerulonephritis becomes chronic, renal damage results after many years, causing kidney failure.

nephron: see URINARY SYSTEM.

nephrosis (nəfrō'səs), kidney disease characterized by lesions of the epithelial lining of the renal tubules, resulting in marked disturbance in the filtration function and the consequent appearance of large amounts of protein (albumin) in the urine (see URINARY SYSTEM). The nephrotic syndrome can result from a number of conditions including streptococcal infection in children leading to chronic glomerulonephritis, reaction to toxins, diabetes, collagen disease, and other end-stage kidney diseases. The major symptom is massive edema. Corticosteroid therapy has been successful in treating certain forms of the disease.

Nephthalim (nĕf'thəlĭm), variant of NAPHTALI.

Nephtoah (nĕftō'ə), fountain, on the border between Judah and Benjamin. The site is identified with the modern Me Neftoah (Israel). Joshua 15.9; 18.15.

Nephusim (nēfyo͞o'sĭm), variant of NEPHISHESIM.

Nepomuk, John of: see JOHN OF NEPOMUK, SAINT.

Nepos, Cornelius (nē'pŏs), c.100 B.C.–c.25 B.C., Roman historian. He was an intimate friend of Pomponius Atticus, Cicero, and Catullus. His only extant work is a collection of biographies, mostly from a lost larger work, *De viris illustribus* [on illustrious men]. The general method was to compare the lives of great Roman and non-Roman leaders. Nepos wrote in a popular manner in clear and simple Latin; his work was sometimes inaccurate, but significant in the history of biography writing.

Nepos, Julius, d. 480, Roman emperor of the West (474–80). The military governor of Dalmatia, he was appointed emperor of the West by Leo I, emperor of the East. A year later he was deposed by ORESTES, who raised his own son ROMULUS AUGUSTULUS to the throne. Julius Nepos, however, was still recognized in the East and in Gaul until his death in 480.

Neptune, in Roman religion, god of water. He was presumably an indigenous god of fertility, but in later times he was identified with the Greek POSEIDON, god of the sea. At his festival, the Neptunalia (July 23), arbors were dedicated to him.

Neptune, in astronomy, 8th planet from the sun at a mean distance of about 2.8 billion mi (4.5 billion km) with an orbit lying between those of Uranus and Pluto; its period of revolution is about 165 years. Neptune was discovered as the result of observed irregularities in the motion of Uranus and was the first planet to be discovered on the basis of theoretical calculations. J. C. Adams of England and U. J. Leverrier of France independently predicted the position of Neptune, and it was discovered by J. C. Galle in 1846, the day after he received Leverrier's prediction. Neptune has an equatorial diameter of about 27,700 mi (44,300 km), nearly four times that of the earth, and a mass about 17 times the earth's mass. It is much like Uranus and the other giant planets, with a thick atmosphere of hydrogen, helium, methane, and ammonia, a relatively low density, and a rapid period of rotation. The actual period is difficult to determine because of the lack of definite, recognizable surface features, but it is estimated to be 16 hr and to cause a polar flattening of about 2%. Neptune has two known natural satellites. The larger, Triton, was discovered in 1846, a month after the discovery of the planet itself; it has a diameter of about 2,300 mi (3,700 km), making it similar in size to the moon, and its motion is RETROGRADE, i.e., motion opposite that of the planet's rotation. The smaller satellite, Nereid, discovered in 1949, has a diameter of about 200 mi (320 km).

neptunium (nĕpto͞o'nēəm), radioactive chemical element; symbol Np; at. no. 93; mass no. of most stable isotope 237; m.p. about 640°C; b.p. estimated at 3900°C; sp. gr. 20.25 at 20°C; valence +3, +4, +5, or +6. Neptunium is a silvery radioactive metal. It is a member of the ACTINIDE SERIES in group IIIb of the PERIODIC TABLE. Neptunium has three distinct forms (see ALLOTROPY); the orthorhombic crystalline structure occurs at room temperature. Neptunium forms numerous chemical compounds. The element was discovered in 1940 by E. M. McMillan and P. H. Abelson, who produced neptunium-239 (half-life 2.3 days) by bombarding uranium with neutrons from a cyclotron at the Univ. of California at Berkeley. Neptunium, the first TRANSURANIUM ELEMENT, was named for the planet Neptune, which is beyond Uranus in the solar system. Neptunium is found in very small quantities in nature in association with uranium ores. There are 15 known isotopes of neptunium. Neptunium-237, the most stable, has a half-life of about 2 million years.

Ner (nûr), father of Abner. 1 Sam. 14.51.

Nerchinsk (nyĕr'chĭnsk), city, SE Siberian USSR. Founded in 1654, the city was a Russian outpost in the Far East from the 17th to the 19th cent. A Russo-Chinese border treaty signed at Nerchinsk in 1689 was the first treaty concluded between China and a European power; it granted the Transbaikalia area to Russia and left the Amur valley to China. The treaty also permitted Russian trading caravans to go to Peking; Nerchinsk became an important customs and trade center on the caravan route.

Nereid (nĭr'ēəd), in astronomy, one of the two known moons, or natural satellites, of NEPTUNE.

nereids: see NYMPH.

Nereus (nēr'o͞os, -ēəs), in Greek mythology, seagod. He was the son of Pontus and Gaea and the father of the nereids. A kindly, wise old man of the sea, Nereus could change into many shapes and had the power of prophecy.

Nereus (nē'rēəs), Roman Christian. Rom. 16.15.

Nergal (nûr'gäl, -gəl), ancient deity worshiped in Babylonia and Assyria. He was a god of the midsummer sun, of war, of the chase, and of the dead. He could be beneficent, but he was primarily associated with pestilence and destruction. According to the Old Testament, he originated in Cuth (2 Kings 17.30).

Nergal-sharezer (nûr'gäl-shərē'zər), one of the Babylonians who rescued Jeremiah from prison. He bore the title Rab-mag. He had the same name, and was perhaps the same person, as the Babylonian king Neriglissar. Jer. 39.3,13.

Neri (nē'rī), name in Luke's genealogy. Luke 3.27.

Neri, Filippo de': see PHILIP NERI, SAINT.

Neriah (nērī'ə), father of Baruch. Jer. 32.12; Baruch 1.1.

Nernst, Walther Hermann (väl'tər hĕr'män nĕrnst), 1864–1941, German physicist and chemist, a founder of modern physical chemistry. After doing outstanding research on osmotic pressure and electrochemistry, he turned to THERMODYNAMICS, establishing in 1906 a new tenet (often called the third law of thermodynamics) that dealt with the behavior of matter at temperatures approaching absolute zero. For his work in thermodynamics he won the 1920 Nobel Prize in Chemistry. He later specialized in electroacoustics and astrophysics. Nernst invented (1898) an electric metallic-filament lamp, a link between the carbon lamp and the incandescent lamp. His works include *Theoretical Chemistry from the Standpoint of Avogadro's Rule and Thermodynamics* (1893, 5th Eng. ed. 1923) and *The New Heat Theorem* (1918, tr. 1926). See biography by K. A. G. Mendelssohn (1973).

Nero (Nero Claudius Caesar)(nēr'ō), A.D. 37–A.D. 68, Roman emperor (A.D. 54–A.D. 68). He was originally named Lucius Domitius Ahenobarbus and was the son of Cneius Domitius Ahenobarbus (consul in A.D. 32) and of AGRIPPINA II, who was the great-granddaughter of Augustus. Agrippina married (A.D. 49) CLAUDIUS I and persuaded him to adopt Nero and make him the guardian of BRITANNICUS, Claudius' son; Octavia, Claudius' daughter, was given to Nero as his wife. On Claudius' death Nero was made emperor without difficulty. His chief advisers were SENECA and the head of the Praetorian Guard, Burrus; as long as they were in power, the government was fairly efficient. In A.D. 55, Agrippina saw the bonds of her domination of Nero loosening and intrigued in favor of Britannicus. Nero poisoned the boy. POPPAEA SABINA, the wife of his friend OTHO, became his mistress; according to rumor she was to blame for the worst of Nero's behavior. In A.D. 59 he murdered his mother and in A.D. 62, his wife. Burrus died in A.D. 62, and Seneca retired, leaving Nero without competent advisers. Half of Rome was burned in a fire (A.D. 64), intended (according to unjustified rumor) to serve as the backdrop for a recitation by Nero on the fall of Troy. Nero accused the Christians of starting the fire, and he began the first Roman persecution; according to Christian tradition this included among its victims St. Peter and

St. Paul. Nero rebuilt the city magnificently, laying out broad, regular streets and erecting a splendid palace. By then, however, he was hated, and in A.D. 65 there was a plot to make Caius Calpurnius Piso emperor. The detection of this plot began a string of violent deaths, e.g., of Seneca, Lucan, and Thrasea Paetus. Nero had ambitions to be a poet and artist, and he was an enthusiastic admirer of Greek culture; in A.D. 67 he visited Greece. In A.D. 68 a general in Gaul, Caius Julius Vindex, revolted unsuccessfully; then GALBA and Otho revolted, too. The Praetorian Guard joined this sedition, and Nero committed suicide. Among his last words were, "What an artist the world is losing in me!" His memory was publicly execrated. Nero was the last emperor of the family of Julius Caesar. See biographies by B. W. Henderson (1903, repr. 1968) and Michael Grant (1970).

Nero, Caius Claudius, fl. 216–201 B.C., Roman general in the Second Punic War. He defeated HASDRUBAL in the battle on the Metaurus (207 B.C.).

Neruda, Jan (yän nĕ'ro͝odä), 1834–91, Czech essayist and poet, b. Prague. His popular *Stories from Malá Strana* (1878), tales drawn from his childhood in Prague and satiric portraits of members of the Czech middle classes, exemplifies early Czech realism. Neruda's poetry in its simplicity and lyricism has been compared to the work of Heinrich Heine. His best-known poems are contained in *Ballads and Romances* and *Plain Themes* (both: 1883). His mature verse expresses his resignation to unhappiness.

Neruda, Pablo (pä'blō nāro͞o'thä), 1904–73, Chilean poet, diplomat, and Communist leader, whose original name was Neftalí Ricardo Reyes Basualto. Neruda's highly personal poetry brought him enormous acclaim. After 1927 he was in consular service in the Far East, Argentina, Mexico, and Europe. A surrealist, Neruda revitalized everyday expressions and employed bold metaphors in free verse. His evocative poems are filled with grief and despair and bespeak a quest for simplicity. They proclaim the dramatic Chilean landscape and rage against the exploitation of the Indian. In his writings and during his political career as a Chilean Communist party leader and diplomat, Neruda has exerted wide influence in Latin America. His many volumes of poetry include *Crepusculario* [twilight book] (1919), *Twenty Love Poems and One Song of Despair* (1924, tr. 1969), the surrealistic *Residence on Earth and Other Poems* (1933, tr. 1946), *Canto general* (1950), *Elementary Odes* (1954, tr. 1961), *Nuevas odas elementales* (1955), *A New Decade: 1958–1967* (tr. 1969), *Extravagaria* (1958, tr. 1974), *New Poems: 1968–1970* (tr. 1972), and *Toward the Splendid City* (tr. 1974). Neruda was awarded the 1971 Nobel Prize in Literature during his service as Chilean ambassador to France. Neruda died in Chile during the week of the 1973 military coup. See his *Early Poems* (tr. 1969) and *Selected Poems* (tr. 1970).

Nerva (Marcus Cocceius Nerva) (nûr'və), A.D. c.30–A.D. 98, Roman emperor (A.D. 96–A.D. 98). He had an honorable career as a statesman at Rome, and his reputation was blameless. At the death of DOMITIAN he was chosen emperor by the senate in a strong movement toward constitutionalism and senatorial influence and away from hereditary succession. Nerva was mild and unassuming; he reformed the land laws in favor of the poor, revised taxation, and tolerated the Christians. He was unable, however, to manage the Praetorian Guard, who were angered by the murder of their idol, Domitian. The elderly Nerva, seeing that a strong hand was needed, adopted TRAJAN and turned over the government to him. He died soon afterward. See B. W. Henderson, *Five Roman Emperors* (1927).

Nerval, Gérard de (zhārär' də nĕrväl'), 1808–55, French writer, an early romantic. His real name was Gérard Labrunie. His writings include translations of *Faust* (1828) and other German works; short stories, notably in *Les Filles du feu* (1854, partial tr. *Daughters of Fire*, 1922); travel sketches; and poems. *Les Chimères* (12 sonnets appended to *Les Filles du feu*) and *Aurélia*, his fantastic spiritual autobiography, which mirrors a life that ended in madness and probable suicide, have had some influence on modern surrealists. See his selected writings (tr. by Geoffrey Wagner, 1957); study by Norma Rinsler (1973).

nerve: see NERVOUS SYSTEM.

nerve gas, any of several POISON GASES intended for military use, e.g., TABUN, SARIN, SOMAN, and VX (see separate article). Nerve gases were first developed by Germany during World War II but were not used at that time. These gases generally cause death by asphyxiation, often preceded by such symptoms as blurred vision, excessive salivation, and convulsions. Physiologically, the toxic effect of nerve gases arises because they inactivate the enzyme cholinesterase, which normally controls the transmission of nerve impulses; the impulses continue without control, causing breakdown of respiration and other body functions. ATROPINE is an effective antidote against most nerve gases.

Nervi, Pier Luigi (pyĕr lwo͞oē'jē nĕr'vē), 1891–, Italian architectural engineer. Nervi is considered one of the foremost European architectural designers of the 20th cent. His first large work, the Giovanni Berta stadium at Florence (1930–32), won world acclaim for the daring and beauty of its cantilevered stairs and roof. Nervi experimented with prefabricated elements in the construction of the Italian air force base at Orbetello (1939). In the mid-1940s he developed *ferro-cemento*, a strong, light material composed of layers of steel mesh grouted together with concrete. With this material he was able to achieve complicated building units for vast and complex structures. His innovations made possible the intricate and beautiful buildings that have brought him world renown. Especially outstanding are his exposition halls at Turin (1949, 1950); the Gatti wool factory, Rome (1951–53); the railway station, Naples (1954); and three Olympic buildings in Rome (1956–59). Nervi has also collaborated in such projects as the headquarters of the UN Educational, Scientific, and Cultural Organization, Paris (1953–57), the office building of Pirelli, Milan (1955–59), and the George Washington Bridge bus station, New York City (1961–62). See his *New Structures* (tr. 1963) and *Aesthetics and Technology in Building* (tr. 1965); study by A. L. Huxtable (1960).

Nervii (nûr'vēī), ancient people of Belgica, GAUL. They revolted against the Romans and were crushed by Julius Caesar (57 B.C.). Their capital was Bagacum, the present-day Bavay, France.

Nervo, Amado (ämä'thō när'vō), 1870–1919, Mexican poet. Known as the "monk of poetry," he studied for the priesthood but abandoned it for writing. An intimate friend of Rubén Darío, he was a leading figure of MODERNISMO. His poetry is known for its simplicity and musical phrasing. Most of his verses deal with his inward world, where he sought peace from external torments. His major collections include *Serenidad* (1914), *Elevación* (1916), and *Plenitud* (1918). Nervo was a diplomat for several years and died during his service as Mexican minister to Uruguay. See E. T. Wellman, *Amado Nervo, Mexico's Religious Poet* (1937).

nervous system, network of specialized tissue that controls actions and reactions of the body and its adjustment to the environment. Virtually all of the METAZOA (multicelled animals) have at least a rudimentary nervous system. Invertebrate animals show varying degrees of complexity in their nervous systems, but it is in the vertebrate animals (phylum CHORDATA, subphylum Vertebrata) that the system reaches its greatest complexity. In vertebrates the system has two main divisions, the central and the peripheral nervous systems. The central nervous system consists of the BRAIN and SPINAL CORD. Linked to these are the cranial, spinal, and autonomic nerves, which, with their branches, constitute the peripheral nervous system. The brain may be compared to a computer and its memory banks, the spinal cord to the conducting cable for the computer's input and output, and the nerves to a circuit supplying input information to the cable and transmitting the output to muscles and organs. The nervous system is built up of nerve cells, called neurons, which are supported and protected by other cells. Of the 10 billion or so neurons making up the human nervous system, approximately half are found in the brain. From the cell body of a typical neuron extend one or more outgrowths (dendrites), threadlike structures that divide and subdivide into ever smaller branches. Another, usually longer structure called the axon also stretches from the cell body. It sometimes branches along its length but always branches at its microscopic tip. When the cell body of a neuron is chemically stimulated, it generates an impulse that passes from the axon of one neuron to the dendrite of another; the junction between axon and the dendrite is called a SYNAPSE. Such impulses carry information throughout the nervous system. So-called white matter in the central nervous system consists primarily of axons coated with light-colored myelin produced by certain neuroglial cells. Nerve cell bodies that are not coated with white matter are referred to as gray matter. Nonmyelinated axons that are outside the central nervous system are enclosed only in a tubelike neurilemma sheath composed of Schwann cells, which are necessary for nerve regeneration. Nerve fibers in the central nervous system cannot regenerate because they lack a neurilemma. There are regular intervals along peripheral axons where the myelin sheath is interrupted. These areas, called nodes of Ranvier, are the points between which nerve impulses, in myelinated fibers, jump, rather than pass, continuously along the fiber (as is the case in unmyelinated fibers). Transmission of impulses is faster in myelinated nerves, varying from about 3 to 300 ft (1–91 m) per sec. Both myelinated and unmyelinated dendrites and axons are termed nerve fibers; a nerve is a bundle of nerve fibers; a cluster of nerve cell bodies (neurons) on a peripheral nerve is called a ganglion. Neurons are located either in the brain, in the spinal cord, or in peripheral ganglia. Grouped and interconnected ganglia form a plexus, or nerve center. Sensory (afferent) nerve fibers deliver impulses from receptor terminals in the skin and organs to the central nervous system via the peripheral nervous system. Motor (efferent) fibers carry impulses from the central nervous system to effector terminals in muscles and glands via the peripheral system. The peripheral system has 12 pairs of cranial nerves: olfactory, optic, oculomotor, trochlear, trigeminal, abducent, facial, acoustic, glossopharyngeal, vagus, accessory, and hypoglossal. These have their origin in the brain and primarily control the activities of structures in the head and neck. The spinal nerves arise in the spinal cord, 31 pairs radiating to either side of the body: 8 cervical, 12 thoracic, 5 lumbar, 5 sacral, and 1 coccygeal. The autonomic nerves form a subsidiary system that regulates the iris of the eye and the smooth-muscle action of the heart, blood vessels, glands, lungs, stomach, colon, bladder, and other visceral organs not subject to willful control. The autonomic system contains only motor (efferent) nerves. Although its impulses originate in the central nervous system, it performs more or less automatically, without conscious intervention of higher brain centers. Because it is linked to those centers, however, the autonomic system is influenced by the emotions; for example, anger can increase the rate of heartbeat. All the fibers of the autonomic nervous system are motor channels, and their impulses arise from the nerve tissue itself, so that the organs they innervate (supply with nerves) perform more or less involuntarily and do not require stimulation to function. Autonomic nerves exit from the central nervous system as part of other peripheral nerves but branch from them to form two more subsystems: the sympathetic and parasympathetic nervous systems, the actions of which oppose each other. For example, sympathetic nerves cause arteries to contract while the parasympathetic nerves cause them to dilate. If the antagonistic action of the sympathetic and parasympathetic systems should lose its normal balance, better control can often be restored by the use of drugs to stimulate or inhibit nervous activity as the need may be. Certain plant derivatives, such as BELLADONNA, COCAINE, and CAF-

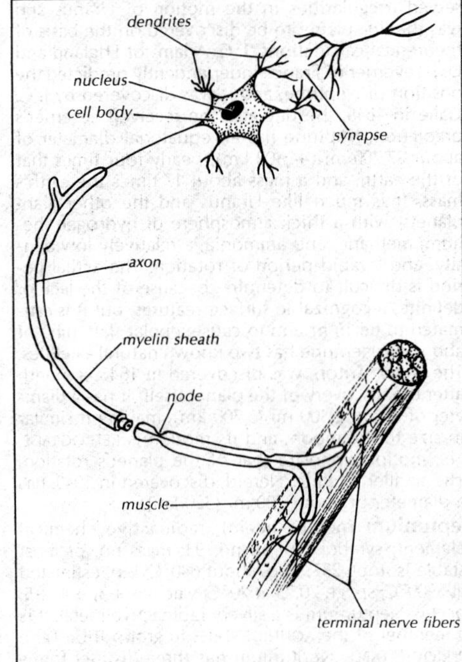

Nerve cell

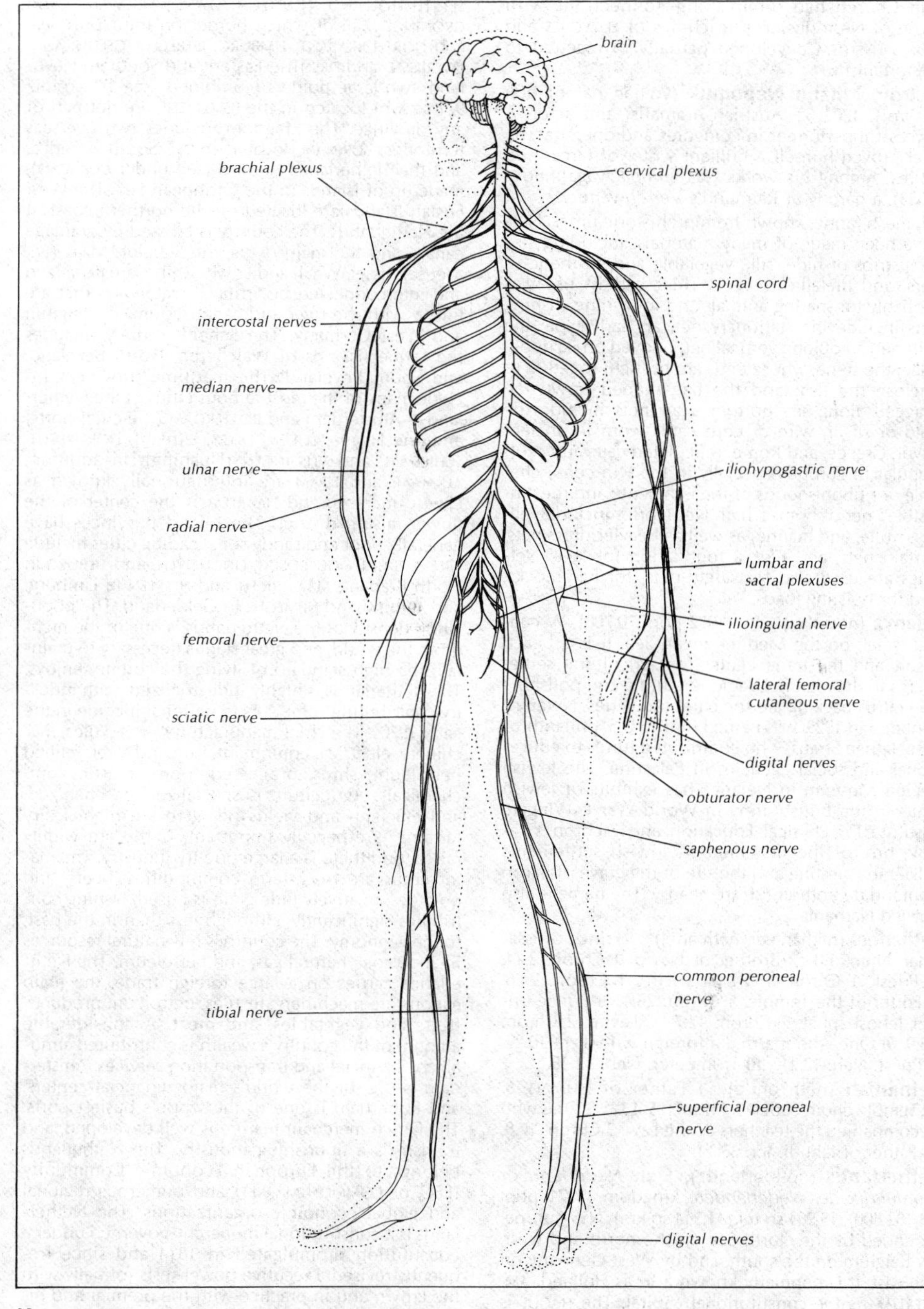

Nervous system.

FEINE, have a variety of stimulatory, inhibitory, and hallucinatory effects on the nervous system. Sympathetic impulses are conducted to the organs by two or more neurons. The cell body of the first lies within the central nervous system and that of the second in an external ganglion. Eighteen pairs of such ganglia interconnect by nerve fibers to form a double chain just outside the spine and running parallel to it. Parasympathetic impulses are also relayed by at least two neurons, but the cell body of the second lies near or within the target organ. In general, nerve function is dependent on both sensory and motor fibers, sensory stimulation evoking motor response. Even the autonomic system, while motor throughout, is activated by sensory impulses from receptors in the organ or muscle. Where especially sensitive areas or powerful stimuli are concerned, it is not always necessary for a sensory impulse to reach the brain in order to trigger motor response. A sensory neuron may link directly to a motor neuron at a synapse in the spinal cord, forming a reflex arc that performs automatically. Thus, tapping the tendon below the kneecap causes the leg to jerk involuntarily because the impulse provoked by the tap, after traveling to the spinal cord, travels directly back to the leg muscle. Such a response is called an involuntary reflex action. Commonly, the reflex arc includes one or more connector neurons that exert a modulating effect, allowing varying degrees of response, e.g., according to whether the stimulation is strong, weak, or prolonged. Reflex arcs are often linked with other arcs by nerve fibers in the spinal cord. Consequently a number of reflex muscle responses may be triggered simultaneously, as when a person shudders and jerks away from the touch of an insect. Links between the reflex arcs and higher centers enable the brain to identify a sensory stimulus, such as pain; to note the reflex response, such as withdrawal; and to inhibit that response, as when the arm is held steady against the prick of a hypodermic needle. Reflex patterns are inherited rather than learned, having evolved as involuntary survival mechanisms. But voluntary actions initiated in the brain may become reflex actions through continued association of a particular stimulus with a certain result. In such cases an alteration of impulse routes occurs that permits responses without mediation by higher nerve centers. Such responses are called conditioned reflexes, the most famous example being one of the experiments PAVLOV performed with dogs. After the dogs had learned to associate the provision of food with the sound of a bell, they salivated at the sound of the bell even when food was not offered. Habit formation and much of learning are dependent on conditioned reflexes. To illustrate, the brain of a student typist must coordinate sensory impulses from both the eyes and the muscles in order to direct his fingers to particular keys. After enough repetition the fingers automatically find and strike the proper keys even if the eyes are closed. The student has "learned" to type; that is, his typing has become a conditioned reflex. See E. C. Crosby et al., *Correlative Anatomy of the Nervous System* (1962); E. D. Gardner, *Fundamentals of Neurology* (5th ed. 1968); P. W. Nathan, *The Nervous System* (1969); Ian Cooke and Mack Lipkin, Jr., *Cellular Neurophysiology* (1972).

Nesconset (nĕskŏn'sĭt), uninc. village (1970 pop. 10,048), Suffolk co., SE N.Y., on Long Island.

Nesiotes: see CRITIUS.

Neskaupstaður (nĕs'köüpstä"thür), town (1969 est. pop. 1,500), extreme E Iceland, on the Mjóifjörður, an arm of the Norwegian Sea. It is the chief town of E Iceland and a fishing port with freezing plants and fish-meal factories. It was chartered in 1929.

Ness, Loch (lŏkh), lake, 22 mi (35 km) long, Inverness-shire, N central Scotland, in the Great Glen. More than 700 ft (213 m) deep and ice-free, it is fed by the Oich and other streams and drained by the Ness to the Moray Firth. It forms part of the Caledonian Canal. Since Dec., 1933, when newspapers published accounts of a "monster," 40 to 50 ft (12–15 m) long, said to have been seen in the loch, there have been several alleged sightings.

Nesselrode, Karl Robert, Count (kärl rō'bĕrt nyĕsĕlrô'dyĭ), 1780–1862, Russian statesman of German descent, b. Lisbon. He entered diplomatic service under Czar Alexander I, became state secretary in 1814, and attended the Congress of Vienna (1814–15). In 1816, he became Russian foreign minister, sharing influence with Count CAPO D'ISTRIA until the latter's retirement in 1822. Guiding Russian policy for 40 years, Nesselrode, a leading conservative statesman, favored the Holy Alliance and in 1849 dispatched Russian troops to help Austria crush the Hungarian revolt led by Louis KOSSUTH. His efforts to expand Russian influence in the E Mediterranean at the expense of Turkey and his miscalculations of British and French tolerance of this policy contributed decisively to the outbreak of the Crimean War. Nesselrode also served as chancellor from 1845 to 1856. His autobiography was published in 1866.

Nessus: see HERCULES.

nest, structure for the reception and incubation of the eggs of birds, reptiles, insects, and some fish or for the parturition of mammals, and also for the care of the young during their period of helplessness. Birds are the chief nest builders, exhibiting great variety and ingenuity among the different species. The type of nest depends on the environment and the condition of the young when hatched. Altricial birds, whose young are generally blind, naked, and helpless on hatching, usually build higher and more elaborate nests than do precocial birds, whose young have a downy covering and are able to move about and feed themselves soon after emerging from the egg. Most sea birds, shore birds, and game birds do not build real nests but lay their eggs directly on a rocky ledge or in a shallow depression scooped out of the earth or sand. Woodpeckers and parrots nest inside hollow trees, as do the Old World hornbills; the male hornbill seals the female into the cavity, leaving an aperture only large enough for him to feed her as she incubates the eggs. Sand martins and kingfishers dig tunnels into shore banks, with enlarged nesting chambers at the ends. The stork's nest is a simple platform of sticks, and the eagle's aerie, built in tree tops or on cliffs, may be 5 to 12 ft (1.5–3.7 m) in diameter; both birds add to their nests each year. As a general rule, the smaller the bird the more elaborate is the nest. Among passerine (perching) birds the male usually selects the feeding and nesting territory, while the female chooses the nest site. In many species the duties of nest building and incubating are shared. The nest is usually bowl-shaped and composed of twigs, grass, leaves, and (when available) bits of cloth and string; thrushes line their nests with clay. Intricately woven pendent arboreal nests give the American oriole its alternate name, *hangnest*; the Old World weaver birds' nests are similar, with one species building immense communal structures housing up to 600 birds. Swallows, ovenbirds, and flamingos build nests of mud cemented with saliva, and an Oriental swift builds its nest entirely of a salivary secretion (used to make bird's-nest soup by the Chinese). The turkeylike megapode, or mound bird, of Australia leaves its eggs in a pile of decaying vegetation, which provides the heat to incubate them; it is the only bird to share this nesting method with the reptiles. Among the insects, ants, bees, and wasps are well known for their nests. Some fish (e.g., the stickleback) build nests of weeds. Most rodents (e.g., mice and squirrels) are nesters; rabbits line their nests with down, as do ducks and geese. The den or lair of the larger mammals (e.g., wolves and lions) serves the same function as a nest.

Nestor (nĕs'tər), in Greek mythology, wise king of Pylos; son of Neleus and father of Antilochus. In the *Iliad,* Nestor went with the Greeks to the Trojan War, and although he had lived three generations he was still a vigorous warrior and a respected adviser. In the *Odyssey,* because of his piety and prudence, the gods allowed him to return unharmed to Pylos after the war.

Nestor (nĕs'tər), d. 1115?, Russian chronicler. A monk in a Kiev monastery, he wrote biographies of saints Boris and Gleb and of the prior of his monastery. Until recently the authorship of the *Russian Primary Chronicle,* also known as *The Tale of Bygone Years* and as the *Chronicle of Nestor,* was attributed to him. It is now believed that he was the author of one of its sources. See *Russian Primary Chronicle* (tr. by S. H. Cross, 1953, repr. 1968).

Nestorian Church, Christian community of Iraq, Iran, and Malabar, India. It represents the ancient church of Persia and is sometimes called the Assyrian (or East Syrian) Church. It numbers about 100,000, including emigrants to the United States. It has much in common with other Eastern rites. The liturgy (said in Syriac) is probably of the Antiochene family of liturgies; the rite is called Chaldean or Assyrian. The churches are not much ornamented, but the Nestorians offer great honors to the Cross. A unique feature of their worship is their "holy leaven," an altar bread they believe is derived from dough used at the Last Supper. The theology of the church is not precise, but there are traits of ancient Nestorianism—its members venerate Nestorius as a saint, they deny the Virgin the title Mother of God while otherwise honoring her highly, and they reject the ecumenical councils after the second. The ancient Persian church was the only one to espouse the cause of Nestorius; as a result it lost communion with the rest of Christendom. The head of the church, called the patriarch of the East, currently resides in the United States; the office is hereditary, from uncle to nephew. The church has relations with some Jacobites and some Anglicans. Among the Nestorians and outnumbering them lives a community in communion with the pope and called usually Chaldean Catholics. They have rite and practices in common with the Nestorians but have had a separate church organization since the 16th cent. The largest group using this rite is that of the Malabar Chaldean Catholics, who ultimately derive their Christianity from Syrian missions in India. The great period of expansion of the Nestorian church was from the 7th to the 10th cent.; there were missions to China and India. A famous monument in Sian, China, was put up (781) by Chinese Nestorians. The missions were destroyed and the church reduced by persecutions by the Chinese, the Hindus, and the Muslims. In the 19th and early 20th cent. there were terrible massacres of Nestorians and Chaldeans by Kurds and Turks. See W. C. Emhardt and G. M. Lamsa, *The Oldest Christian People* (1926, repr. 1970); Donald Attwater, *The Christian Churches of the East* (1947–48); John Joseph, *The Nestorians and Their Muslim Neighbors* (1961); Shirley Glubok *Digging in Assyria* (1970).

Nestorianism, heresy that held Jesus Christ to be two distinct persons, closely and inseparably united. In 428, Emperor Theodosius II named an abbot of Antioch, Nestorius (d. 451?), as patriarch of Constantinople. In that year Nestorius, who had been a pupil of THEODORE OF MOPSUESTIA, outraged the Christian world by opposing the use of the title Mother of God for the Virgin on the grounds that, while the Father begot Jesus as God, Mary bore him as a man. This view was contradicted by Cyril, patriarch of Alexandria, and both sides appealed to Pope Celestine I. The Council of Ephesus (see EPHESUS, COUNCIL OF) was convened in 431 to settle the matter. This council (reinforced by the Council of Chalcedon in 451) clarified orthodox Catholic doctrine, pronouncing that Jesus Christ, true God and true man, has two distinct natures that are inseparably joined in one person and partake of the one divine substance. Nestorius, deposed after the Council of Ephesus, was sent to Antioch, to Arabia, and finally to Egypt. A work believed to be by Nestorius, *Bazaar of Heraclides,* discovered c.1895, gives an account of the controversy. The patriarch of Antioch and his bishops, accusing Cyril of unscrupulous action, stayed out of communion with Alexandria until a compromise was reached in 433, but though the subject was discussed in 553 at the Council of Constantinople (see CONSTANTINOPLE, COUNCIL OF), Nestorianism was practically dead in the empire after 451. The doctrines that continued in the Nestorian Church had diminishing connections with those of Nestorius. The teachings of EUTYCHES and MONOPHYSITISM developed partially in reaction to Nestorianism.

Nestroy, Johann Nepomuk (yō'hăn nā'pōmo͝ok nĕs'troi), 1802–62, Austrian dramatist and actor. A successful performer in comedies and operettas, he later proved himself a brilliant writer of farces and satires. Among his works was *Lumpacivagabundus* (1833), a parody of Raimund's *Verschwender.*

net, mesh fabric, known from prehistoric times. Nets have been made of many materials, including sinews, strips of hide, silk, vegetable and synthetic fibers, and metallic threads. Their earliest use was probably for snaring animals and for fishing. Fishing nets include the stationary net, an early type; the drift net, an oblong vertical net, buoyed on its upper edge; the seine, whose ends are brought together to enclose the fish; and the bag-shaped trawl net, dragged along sea bottom. Hair nets include the gold or silver, wire or cord cauls worn in ancient Egypt, Greece, and Rome; reticulated caps and cauls popular in Europe especially in the 14th cent.; chenille or ribbon snoods of the 19th cent.; and the "invisible" net of human hair. Net fabrics include veilings, tulle, and maline, as well as heavier dress nets, curtain nets, and *filet,* a foundation for lace. Nettings are used also for safety nets, for hammocks, and for hoisting loads.

Netanya (nətän'yə), city (1972 pop. 70,700), W central Israel, on the Mediterranean Sea. It is a beach resort and the trade center for agricultural settlements in the region. Diamond cutting and polishing and citrus packing are the chief industries. Netanya, founded in 1929, was named for the U.S. philanthropist Nathan Straus, who contributed funds to educational and social agencies in Palestine. The Jewish Legion Museum in Netanya has exhibits of Jewish units in the British army in World War I. Wingate Institute for Physical Education and Zichron Ya'akov, one of the first modern Jewish settlements (1882) in Palestine and the site of the grave of Baron Edmond de Rothschild, are nearby. The name is also spelled Nathania.

Nethaneel (nēthăn'ēəl, nĕth'ənēl). **1** Prince of Issachar. Num. 1.8. **2** Brother of David. 1 Chron. 2.14. **3** Priest. 1 Chron. 15.24. **4** Levite. 1 Chron. 24.6. **5** Porter of the Temple. 1 Chron. 26.4. **6** Prince under Jehoshaphat. 2 Chron. 17.7. **7** Levite. 2 Chron. 35.9. **8** One who married a foreign wife. Ezra 10.22. **9** Priest. Neh. 12.21. **10** Trumpeter. Neh. 12.36.

Nethaniah (nĕth"ənī'ə). **1** Father of ISHMAEL **6.** **2** Temple choir leader. 1 Chron. 25.2,12. **3** One who accompanied the teachers of the Law. 2 Chron. 17.8. **4** Father of Jehudi. Jer. 36.14.

Netherlands (nĕ*th*'ərləndz), Dut. *Nederland* or *Koninkrijk der Nederlanden,* kingdom (1971 pop. 13,182,800), 15,963 sq mi (41,344 sq km), NW Europe, bounded by the North Sea on the north and west, by Belgium on the south, and by West Germany on the east. It is popularly known also as Holland. AMSTERDAM is the constitutional capital; The HAGUE is the seat of government. The country is mostly lowlying. About 40% of the land is situated below sea level and is made up of territory (mostly in the western part of the country) reclaimed from the sea since the 13th cent. and guarded by dunes and dikes. The Netherlands has 11 provinces: Zeeland,

SOUTH HOLLAND, NORTH HOLLAND, FRIESLAND, and GRONINGEN, all of which border on the North Sea; and NORTH BRABANT, LIMBURG, UTRECHT, GELDERLAND, OVERIJSSEL, and DRENTHE. Eastern and Southern Flevoland, two large polders (combined area 375 sq mi/ 971 sq km) located in the IJSSELMEER, are not part of any province. The kingdom includes two overseas territories, SURINAM, located in NE South America, and the Netherlands Antilles (see under CURAÇAO), made up of islands in the Caribbean Sea. The West Frisian Islands are located off the northern coast of the Netherlands. The country is crossed by drainage canals, and the main rivers, the Scheldt, Maas (Fr., *Meuse*), IJssel, Waal, and Lower Rhine, are canalized and interconnected by artificial waterways that are linked with the river and canal systems of Belgium and West Germany. The Scheldt estuary includes the former islands of Walcheren, North Beveland, and South Beveland. The maritime provinces include many of the most famous cities of the Netherlands—Amsterdam and ROTTERDAM (the chief ports) and The Hague, LEIDEN, DELFT, Utrecht, DORDRECHT, SCHIEDAM, and VLISSINGEN (Flushing). In addition, ALKMAAR and EDAM are internationally known as cheese markets, and HAARLEM is the center of the flower-raising district. The inland provinces have generally poor and sandy soil. Leading cities include BREDA, 'S HERTOGENBOSCH, EINDHOVEN, and TILBURG in North Brabant; MAASTRICHT and HEERLEN in Limburg; and ARNHEM and NIJMEGEN in Gelderland. The population density of the Netherlands is one of the highest in the world, and great skill is necessary to maintain the high standard of living the country enjoys. The Netherlands is highly industrialized, with industry contributing some 40% to national income in the early 1970s. The chief manufactures are textiles, machinery, electrical equipment, iron and steel, refined petroleum, ships, processed foods, plastics, and chemicals. Agriculture is specialized, mechanized, and efficient, and yields per acre are high. Dairy farming is especially important. Cattle are widely raised, and there is a large poultry industry. The major crops are truck-farm commodities, beets, and potatoes; relatively little grain is raised. Fishing contributes significantly, although less than in the past, to the economy. The country's few natural resources include coal, natural gas, and petroleum. The Netherlands carries on a large foreign trade; the main exports are machinery, textiles, petroleum products, fruits and vegetables, and meat. A considerable amount of the country's wealth is contributed annually by financial and transportation services. Amsterdam is one of the world's major financial centers, and Rotterdam is one of the world's busiest ports. The Dutch merchant marine is well developed, and tourism is a flourishing industry. The Netherlands belongs to the European Economic Community (EEC, or COMMON MARKET) and numerous regional and global economic organizations. The Netherlands is a constitutional monarchy governed under a constitution promulgated in 1814 and since frequently revised. Executive power rests formally with the crown and in practice with the premier and his cabinet. Legislative power is vested in the bicameral States-General. The deliberative upper, or first, chamber is elected by the 11 provincial estates, and the more powerful lower, or second, chamber is chosen by direct universal suffrage. The royal succession is settled on the house of Orange (see NASSAU); Queen JULIANA (reigned 1948–) is the present monarch. The royal house belongs to the Dutch Reformed Church. However, there is complete freedom of worship in the country, and each religious community receives a state subsidy. Roman Catholics, who nearly equal the Protestants in total adherents, are most numerous in the southern provinces. The archbishop of Utrecht is the Roman Catholic primate of the Netherlands. The country's four great public universities are at Leiden, Utrecht, Groningen, and Amsterdam. There is also a Catholic university at Nijmegen and a Calvinist university at Amsterdam. Specialized higher education is offered by technical schools at Delft, Eindhoven, and Enschede, and by the schools of economics at Rotterdam and Tilburg. Linguistic conformity to Dutch, the official language, is complete except in Friesland, where Frisian is spoken in places.

Rise and Revolt. One of the LOW COUNTRIES, the Netherlands did not have a unified history until the late 16th cent. The region west of the Rhine formed part of the Roman province of Lower Germany and was inhabited by the BATAVI; to the east of the Rhine were the Frisians. Nearly the entire area was taken (4th–8th cent.) by the Franks, and with the break-up of the Carolingian empire, most of it passed (9th cent.) to the east Frankish (i.e., German) kingdom and thus to the Holy Roman Empire. The counts of HOLLAND emerged as the most powerful medieval lords of the region, next to their southern neighbors, the dukes of Brabant and the counts of Flanders. In the 14th and 15th cent. Flanders, Holland, Zeeland, Gelderland, and Brabant passed to the powerful dukes of BURGUNDY, who thus controlled virtually all the Low Countries. Though the Dutch towns and ports were slower in their economic development than the great commercial and industrial centers of Flanders and Brabant, they began to rival them in the 15th cent. They nearly all belonged to the Hanseatic League, and they enjoyed vast autonomous privileges. In 1477, MARY OF BURGUNDY by the Great Privilege restored all the liberties of which her predecessors had deprived the provincial estates of the Low Countries. Her marriage to the Archduke Maximilian (later Emperor MAXIMILIAN I) brought the Low Countries into the house of Hapsburg. Emperor Charles V gave them (1555) to his son PHILIP II of Spain. By that time the northern provinces (i.e., the present Netherlands) had reached great economic prosperity. The inroads of Calvinism were helping to distinguish the Low Countries from Catholic Spain; the nobles, supported by many of the people for economic and religious reasons, demanded greater autonomy for the provinces and removal of the Spanish officials. Philip's attempt, first through Cardinal GRANVELLE and then through the duke of ALBA, to introduce the Spanish Inquisition and to reduce the Low Countries to a Spanish province met determined opposition among all classes of the population, Catholics and Protestants alike. The struggle for the independence of the Low Countries began (1562–66) in Flanders and Brabant. The northern provinces, under the leadership of WILLIAM THE SILENT, prince of Orange, early succeeded (1572–74) in expelling the Spanish garrisons. The Low Countries united under William in their struggle against Spain in the Pacification of GHENT (1576). Alessandro FARNESE, who in 1578 succeeded John of Austria as Spanish governor, eventually reconquered the southern provinces, which remained in Spanish possession (see NETHERLANDS, AUSTRIAN AND SPANISH) and were gradually reconverted to Catholicism. The river barriers were crucial in protecting the rebellion and the Protestant religion of the north. The seven northern provinces—Holland, Zeeland, Utrecht, Gelderland, Overijssel, Friesland, and Groningen—formed (1579) the Union of Utrecht and declared (1581) their independence. The struggle continued. William the Silent, assassinated in 1584, was succeeded as stadtholder (chief of state) by his son, MAURICE OF NASSAU, who was at first guided by Johan van OLDENBARNEVELDT. An English expedition under Robert Dudley, earl of LEICESTER, to aid the Dutch against Farnese, was ineffectual, but subsequently Maurice won important successes, and in 1609 a 12-year truce was concluded with SPINOLA, the Spanish commander.

The United Provinces. Fighting with Spain was resumed in the Thirty Years War (1618–48), at the end of which the independence of the United Provinces—as the independent Netherlands was called—was recognized in the Peace of Westphalia (1648). Spain also ceded North Brabant, with Breda, and part of Limburg, with Maastricht. While still struggling for their independence and while involved in the religious struggle between Calvinists and REMONSTRANTS, the Dutch laid the foundation of their commercial and colonial empire. The Dutch East India Company (see EAST INDIA COMPANY, DUTCH) was founded in 1602, the DUTCH WEST INDIA COMPANY in 1621. The decline of Antwerp under Spanish rule and the right (awarded to the Dutch in the Peace of Westphalia) to control the Scheldt estuary gave supremacy to the Dutch ports, particularly Amsterdam. Dutch merchants traded in every continent (they even enjoyed exclusive privileges in Japan), and a superior Dutch vessel, the flute, captured the major share of the world's carrying trade. The United Provinces opened their doors to religious refugees, notably to Portuguese and Spanish Jews and to French Huguenots; these contributed vastly to the immense prosperity of 17th-century Holland. With material wealth came a cultural golden age. Rembrandt, Vermeer, Jacob van Ruisdael, Frans Hals, and others carried DUTCH ART to its peak. The Univ. of LEIDEN won world fame; the philosophers Descartes and Spinoza and the jurist Grotius were active in the United Provinces. Prince FREDERICK HENRY, who had succeeded his brother Maurice in 1625 as stadtholder, was in turn succeeded by his son, Prince WILLIAM II, in 1647. His death in 1650 was the signal for the opponents of the hereditary privileges of the house of Orange to reassert the rights of the provinces and the States-General. Jan de WITT, the political leader of the estates of Holland (the most powerful of the seven provinces), was chosen (1652) grand pensionary of Holland and directed the fate of the Dutch republic for the following 20 years. To prevent Prince William III of Orange (son of William II) from regaining the authority of his father, de Witt by the Eternal Edict (1667) abolished the office of stadtholder in Holland and secured the virtual exclusion of the house of Orange from state affairs. De Witt's administration was largely taken up by the DUTCH WARS with England (1652–54, 1664–67), arising out of the first of the English NAVIGATION ACTS (1651) and the Dutch-English commercial rivalry. The Treaty of Breda (1667) was advantageous to the Netherlands, which gained trade privileges and had its possession of Surinam recognized. The Netherlands reached the peak of its political power when, by forming (1668) the TRIPLE ALLIANCE with Sweden and England, it forced Louis XIV of France to halt the War of Devolution against Spain. Louis XIV took revenge by starting (1672) the third of the Dutch Wars, in which the French overran the Netherlands. In defense, the Dutch opened their dikes and flooded the country, creating a watery barrier that was virtually impenetrable. De Witt sought to negotiate peace but was murdered (1672) by a mob of Orange followers. The stadtholderate was restored to WILLIAM III (after 1689 also king of England). The war devastated the provinces, but in the Treaty of Nijmegen (1678–79) the Dutch obtained important concessions from France. The Netherlands again fought Louis XIV in the War of the GRAND ALLIANCE (1688–97) and in the War of the SPANISH SUCCESSION. On the death (1702) of William III the stadtholderate was again suspended and the States-General resumed control of the government, but in 1747 the republican party lost power, and William IV of Orange became hereditary stadtholder. In the 18th cent. the relative commercial, military, and cultural positions of the United Provinces in Europe declined as those of England and France ascended. The Netherlands sided against England in the American Revolution and as a result lost several colonies at the Treaty of Paris of 1783 (see PARIS, TREATY OF). A patriotic movement by J. D. van der Capellen (1741–84) was beginning to popularize the vigorous ideas of the Enlightenment, and when in the French Revolutionary Wars the French overran (1794–95) the Netherlands, there was much popular approval. William V fled abroad, and the BATAVIAN REPUBLIC was set up (1795) under French protection. In 1806, Napoleon I established the Kingdom of Holland and made his brother Louis BONAPARTE its first king. Louis was deposed in 1810, and the kingdom was annexed by France. Although French rule was opportunistic, the French legal, financial, and educational reforms began a national revival in the Netherlands.

The Kingdom of the Netherlands. At the Congress of Vienna (1814–15) the former United Provinces and the former Austrian Netherlands were united under King WILLIAM I, son of William V of Orange. In 1830, however, the former Austrian provinces (Belgium), whose language, religion, and culture differed from those of the Dutch, rebelled against Dutch rule and declared their independence. A final agreement between Belgium and the Netherlands was reached only in 1839 (see LONDON CONFERENCE). William I was forced to abdicate in 1840 and was succeeded by WILLIAM II, under whom Jan THORBECKE introduced important constitutional reforms in 1848. Under WILLIAM III (1849–90) the Netherlands enjoyed a period of commercial expansion and internal development. The Industrial Revolution progressed rapidly after 1860. Trade unionism grew in the late 19th cent., and considerable national social-welfare legislation was passed. At the same time the country's cultural life flourished, led by the painter Vincent van Gogh, the writer Louis Couperus, and others. In 1890, Queen WILHELMINA began her reign of almost 60 years. The Netherlands was neutral in World War I. In 1927 a 20 mi- (32 km-) long dam was completed; it enclosed the Zuider Zee and thus created the IJsselmeer, a large freshwater lake. A number of large polders, including Eastern and Southern Flevoland and the Northeast Polder, have since been created in the IJsselmeer. In World War II, Germany invaded (May, 1940) the Netherlands without warning, crushed Dutch resistance, and wantonly destroyed Rotterdam. The queen and her government fled abroad. German occupation authorities, headed by Arthur Seyss-Inquart, established a reign of terror; underground resistance led to mass executions and deportations. Of the approximately 112,000 Dutch Jews, about 104,000 were deported to Poland by the Germans and exterminated. Allied airborne landings (1944) at Arnhem and Eindhoven liberated Zeeland, North Brabant, and Limburg provinces. The German collapse in May, 1945, was followed by the immediate return of the queen and the cabinet and by a relatively speedy recovery. The Netherlands became a charter member of the United Nations (1945) and in 1947 joined in a close alliance with Belgium and Luxembourg, which became (1958) the BENELUX ECONOMIC UNION. The country also participated actively in the EUROPEAN COMMUNITY, including the Common Market, and in 1949 joined the North Atlantic Treaty Organization (NATO). Queen Wilhelmina abdicated (1948) in favor of her daughter, Juliana, who continued to rule with a coalition cabinet dominated by the Catholic and Labor parties. In 1959 a new coalition excluding the Labor party was formed, and similar coalitions held power for most of the years into the 1970s. However, in mid-1973, after 164 days of negotiations following parliamentary elections in Nov., 1972 (in which the Catholics suffered considerable losses), a left-center coalition led by Joop den Uyl, head of the Labor party, came to power. The Netherlands gave Indonesia independence in 1949, and in 1962 relinquished Netherlands New Guinea (now IRIAN BARAT, a part of Indonesia). The Netherlands Antilles and Surinam were raised from colonial status to equality with the mother country in 1954. Despite the loss of the eastern empire and despite catastrophic floodings in the North Sea storms of 1953, the Dutch economy expanded in the 1950s and 60s. The industrial plant was enlarged significantly. After the 1953 floods the 25-year Delta Project was begun. By the early 1970s most of the river estuaries in SW Netherlands were sealed off and thus protected from the flood tide. As a result of the project Walcheren, North Beveland, and South Beveland were joined to the mainland and ceased to be islands. Considerable controversy surrounded the marriage (1966) of Crown Princess Beatrix to Claus von Amsberg, a former West German diplomat who had served in the German army in World War II. In 1967, Princess Beatrix gave birth to a son, Willem-Alexander, the first male heir in line of succession since 1884. In the early 1970s the Netherlands enjoyed material prosperity and considerable influence in European affairs. The country suffered considerably from a ban on the sale of crude petroleum imposed by Arab nations in the wake of the Arab-Israeli War of Oct., 1973, in retaliation for the Netherlands' traditional friendship with Israel; between late 1973 and early 1974 the government prohibited private motor vehicular traffic on Sunday, and gasoline was rationed. The crisis had eased somewhat by mid-1974, and the Arabs lifted the oil embargo in July. See P. J. Blok, *History of the People of the Netherlands* (5 vol., tr. 1898–1912, repr. 1970); Sacheverell Sitwell, *The Netherlands* (2d ed. 1955); Pieter Geyl, *The Revolt of the Netherlands* (2d ed. 1958) and *History of the Low Countries* (1964); Johan Gouldsblom, *Dutch Society* (1967); C. W. Wilson, *The Dutch Republic and the Civilization of the Seventeenth Century* (1968); Anthony Bailey, *The Light in Holland* (1970); A. M. Lambert, *The Making of the Dutch Landscape* (1971); W. Z. Shetter, *The Pillars of Society: Six Centuries of Civilization in the Netherlands* (1971).

Netherlands, Austrian and Spanish, that part of the Low Countries that, from 1482 until 1794, remained under the control of the imperial house of HAPSBURG. The area corresponds roughly to modern Belgium and Luxembourg. The Low Countries passed from the house of Burgundy to that of Hapsburg through the marriage (1477) of MARY OF BURGUNDY to Archduke Maximilian (later Emperor Maximilian I); their son Philip (later PHILIP I of Castile) inherited FLANDERS, BRABANT, ARTOIS, HAINAUT, the duchy of LUXEMBOURG, LIMBURG, HOLLAND, and Zeeland. His son, Emperor Charles V, added UTRECHT, GELDERLAND, OVERIJSSEL, FRIESLAND, and DRENTHE and in 1547 declared the entire Netherlands hereditary Hapsburg possessions. In 1555 he abdicated the Netherlands in favor of his son, PHILIP II of Spain. The provinces of the Netherlands retained their individual institutions and provincial estates and thus limited the powers of the Spanish governors at Brussels. The harsh regime of the duke of ALBA, who replaced (1567) Margaret of Parma as governor and suspended constitutional procedure, provoked the opposition of the Dutch and Flemish, led by William the Silent of Orange; Lamoral, count of Egmont; Hendrik, lord of Brederode; Marnix; and others. In 1576 the opposition united in the Pacification of GHENT. Despite the ruthless campaigns of Alba and his successors—Requesens, John of Austria (d. 1578), and the more diplomatic Alessandro Farnese—Spain recovered only the southern provinces while the seven United Provinces of the NETHERLANDS gained independence. The bloody struggle ruined the prosperous Flemish cities, particularly ANTWERP. Protestantism was extirpated in the Spanish Netherlands, and Belgium and Luxembourg remain to this day overwhelmingly Catholic. The provinces were a battleground in every major European war from the 17th cent. to World War II, but after each war their industry and commercial enterprise enabled them to recover quickly. Spain lost North Brabant and part of Limburg to the United Provinces at the Peace of Westphalia (1648); Artois and parts of Hainaut and of Luxembourg to France at the Peace of the Pyrenees (1659); and parts of Flanders (including Dunkirk and Lille) and of Hainaut to France in the treaties of Aix-la-Chapelle (1668) and Nijmegen (1678–79). The remaining Spanish possessions in the Low Countries were transferred (1714) to the Austrian branch of the Hapsburgs by the Peace of Utrecht. The bishopric of LIÈGE, an ecclesiastic principality, was not part of the Hapsburg possessions but was under Spanish and (after 1714) Austrian influence and shared the history of the neighboring provinces. After 1780, Emperor Joseph II ordered anticlerical reforms and measures for administrative and judicial centralization, which aroused the opposition of Catholic and conservative leaders as well as that of enlightened democrats. Finally, late in 1789, the States-General of the Austrian Netherlands declared Joseph deposed and proclaimed the republic of the United States of Belgium. Joseph's successor, Leopold II, succeeded in conciliating the States-General, which in 1790 elected his son Charles as hereditary grand duke. The Austrian recovery of Belgium was short-lived, for by 1794 the FRENCH REVOLUTIONARY WARS had brought the whole area under French control, and in 1797 it was formally ceded to France in the Treaty of Campo Formio. For the history of the area after its incorporation (1815) into the kingdom of the Netherlands, see BELGIUM and LUXEMBOURG, duchy.

Netherlands Antilles: see CURAÇAO.

Netherlands East Indies: see INDONESIA.

Netherlands New Guinea: see IRIAN BARAT.

Netherlands West Indies: see CURAÇAO.

Nethinim (nĕth'ĭnĭm), alien captives of the Jews who performed the humblest tasks of the temple. Their lot improved until in post-Exilic times they became the equals of other temple officials. Joshua 9.3–27; Ezra 2.43,58,70; 7.7,24; 8.17,20; Neh. 10.28.

Néthou, Pic de: see ANETO, PICO DE.

Netophah (nētō'fə), town, near Jerusalem, in ancient Palestine. Ezra 2.22; Neh. 7.26.

Netscher, Caspar (kăs'pär nĕch'ər), 1639–84, Dutch portrait and genre painter, b. Heidelberg. He moved to Holland, where he studied with Ter Borch. Netscher was especially adept in the rendering of fabrics. He painted portraits of many illustrious persons of his time, including those of William of Orange and Mary II of England and of Mme de Montespan. The Metropolitan Museum contains *The Card Party* and two portraits, and the Museum of Fine Arts, Boston, his *Boy Blowing Bubbles.*

Nettilling Lake (nĕch'ĭlĭng), freshwater lake, 1,956 sq mi (5,066 sq km), S Baffin Island, Franklin dist., Northwest Territories, Canada; one of the largest lakes entirely within Canada. It is located in an arctic lowland region and is fed by Amadjuak Lake and by numerous streams that drain the tundra. It empties through the Koukdjuak west into Foxe Basin. The lake is frozen most of the year.

nettle, common name for the Urticaceae, a family of fibrous herbs, small shrubs, and trees found chiefly in the tropics and subtropics. Several species of nettles are covered with small stinging hairs that on contact emit an irritant (formic acid) which produces a skin rash sometimes called urticaria (see HIVES). The tropical American genus *Urera* is very powerful and sometimes dangerous. Stinging nettles in the United States include species of *Urtica,* widely distributed, and *Laportea canadensis,* a characteristic plant of eastern forests. *L. gigas,* the Australian nettle tree, reaches 90 ft (27.4 m) in height. Various plants of the family supply fiber, e.g., ramie, or China grass (*Boehmeria nivea*), native to SE Asia. Its valuable fiber is extremely strong, silky, and durable, but very difficult to extract. Because of the high quality of its various products (e.g., fabric, paper, and cordage) it has been cultivated experimentally in the United States and other countries. The young foliage of many temperate nettles supplies edible greens. Various unrelated plants are sometimes also called nettles, e.g., the Old World nettle trees of the elm family and the prickly horse nettle of the nightshade family. The nettle family is classified in the division MAGNOLIOPHYTA, class Magnoliopsida, order Urticales.

Nettuno (nät-to͞o'nō), town (1971 pop. 24,776), in Latium, central Italy, on the Tyrrhenian Sea. It is an agricultural center and a seaside resort. With nearby ANZIO it was the site of an Allied landing (Jan. 22, 1944) in World War II.

network, electric, interconnection of electric devices such as generators, batteries, resistors, capacitors, inductors, rectifiers, and transistors. Fundamentally there is no difference between an ELECTRIC CIRCUIT and an electric network except that in common parlance a circuit is likely to be fairly simple, whereas there is no limit to the complexity of a network.

Netzahualcóyotl (nätsäwälkō'yōtəl), city (1970 pop. 571,035), Mexico state, S central Mexico. It is a communications center whose importance lies chiefly in its proximity to Mexico City.

Neubrandenburg (noibrän'dənbûrk"), city (1970 pop. 45,685), capital of Neubrandenburg dist., N East Germany, on the Tollensesee. Manufactures include machinery, chemicals, and food products. Founded in 1248 by the margraves of Brandenburg, Neubrandenburg passed to Mecklenburg in 1292.

Neuchâtel (nöshätĕl'), Ger. *Neuenburg,* canton (1970 pop. 169,173), 309 sq mi (800 sq km), NW Switzerland, in the Jura mts. It is a forested region with pastures. Cattle are raised, and cheese and wine are produced. Watches and cutlery—mainly manufactured at Le LOCLE and La CHAUX-DE-FONDS—and cotton goods are the primary industrial products. There are rich asphalt deposits. The population is mainly French-speaking and Protestant. A part of Burgundy by the 10th cent., Neuchâtel was later governed by counts under the Holy Roman Empire. The county passed (1504) to the French house of Orléans-Longueville and in 1648 became independent. In 1707 it chose Frederick I of Prussia as its prince. It remained an autonomous principality, although in 1815 it became a canton of the Swiss Confederation, with which it had been allied since the 15th cent. In 1848 a revolution abolished the monarchy within Neuchâtel, and in 1857, after some complications, the king of Prussia renounced his claim to the canton. Its capital, **Neuchâtel** (1970 pop. 38,784), has industries that produce watches, jewelry, machinery, and chocolate. The town still retains a medieval aspect with its numerous statues, fountains, and old structures. It has an old church (12th–13th cent.), a castle (12th–17th cent.), and a noted university (founded 1838). The town is on the northern shore of the **Lake of Neuchâtel,** 24 mi (39 km) long and 4 to 5 mi (6.4–8 km) wide, which borders on the cantons of Neuchâtel, Bern, Fribourg, and Vaud. The lake is surrounded by valuable vineyards and picturesque settlements. There are many remains of lake dwellings (see LA TÈNE).

Neue Sachlichkeit: see NEW OBJECTIVITY.

Neufahrwasser: see GDAŃSK, Poland.

Neu Hannover: see LAVONGAI.

Neuhausen am Rheinfall (noi'houzən äm rīn'fäl), town (1970 pop. 12,103), Schaffhausen canton, N Switzerland, on the right bank of the Rhine River. It is a manufacturing center adjoining the city of SCHAFFHAUSEN.

Neuhof, Theodor, Baron von (tā'ōdôr' bärōn' fən noi'hōf), 1694–1756, German adventurer, b. Metz, France. After a varied career as a soldier and a diplomat, he was persuaded by Corsicans rebelling against Genoese rule to become (1736) their king as Theodore I of Corsica. Driven from Corsica by the Genoese with French aid in 1738, he tried (1738, 1743) unsuccessfully to regain his throne. After 1749 he lived in poverty in England and was once released from debtors' prison through the influence of Horace Walpole. King Theodore figures grotesquely in Voltaire's *Candide.* See Aylmer Vallance, *The Summer King* (1956).

Neuilly, Treaty of (nöyē'), 1919, peace treaty concluded between the Allies and Bulgaria after World War I. It was signed at Neuilly-sur-Seine, France. Bulgaria ceded part of W Thrace to Greece and several border areas to Yugoslavia; S Dobruja was confirmed in Rumanian possession. Reparations were required, and the Bulgarian army was limited to 20,000 men.

Neuilly-sur-Seine (nöyē'-sür-sĕn), city (1968 pop. 71,215), Hauts-de-Seine dept., N central France. One of the wealthiest suburbs of Paris, Neuilly-sur-Seine also manufactures machines, boilers, and precision instruments. The American Hospital of Paris is there.

Neu Lauenberg: see DUKE OF YORK ISLANDS.

Neumann, Johann Balthasar (yō'hän bältäsär' noi'män), 1687–1753, German architect. He traveled (1718) in Austria and N Italy and studied (1723) in Paris. Neumann designed several palaces and churches in Würzburg, some of which were decorated by Tiepolo. In 1742 he began the planning of the most famous rococo church in Germany, that of Vierzehnheiligen, celebrated for the sumptuous architectural decoration of the interior within a series of oval spaces.

neume (no͞om), in music: see MUSICAL NOTATION.

Neu Mecklenburg: see NEW IRELAND.

Neumünster (noi'mün"stər), city (1970 pop. 86,013), Schleswig-Holstein, N West Germany. It is a transportation and industrial center; manufactures include machinery, textiles, and clothing. Known in the 12th cent., Neumünster was chartered in 1870.

Neunkirchen (noin'kĭr"khən), city (1971 pop. 10,900), Lower Austria province, E Austria, on the Schwarza River. Manufactures of this industrial city include metal goods, furniture, and building materials.

Neunkirchen, city (1970 pop. 43,743), Saarland, W West Germany. Manufactures include iron and steel, machinery, chemicals, and textiles. Neunkirchen was first mentioned in the 13th cent.

Neu Pommern: see NEW BRITAIN.

neuralgia (no͝oră'jə, nyo͝o–), acute paroxysmal pain along a peripheral sensory nerve. Unlike NEURITIS, there is no inflammation or degeneration of nerve tissue. Neuralgia occurs commonly in the area of the facial, or trigeminal, nerve and brings attacks of excruciating pain at varying intervals. Often no cause can be found for trigeminal neuralgia, and in severe cases deadening of the nerve with novocaine or alcohol, or even surgical interruption of the nerve, is necessary to bring relief. Neuralgia can be caused by such disturbances as diabetes, infections, diseases of the nervous system, anemia, and extreme cold. The pain may occur for many months after an attack of shingles (see HERPES ZOSTER), and it is one of the symptoms of syphilitic involvement of the central nervous system. In many cases, pain can be relieved by hot applications, drugs, and various kinds of physiotherapy.

neurasthenia (no͝or"əsthē'nēa), condition characterized by general lassitude, irritability, lack of concentration, worry, and hypochondria. The term was introduced into psychiatry in 1869 by G. M. Beard, American neurologist. Used by Freud to describe a fundamental disorder in mental functioning, the term was incorrectly applied to almost any psychoneurosis and has been largely abandoned.

Neurath, Constantin, Baron von (kôn'stäntēn bärōn' fən noi'rät"), 1873–1956, German diplomat. After holding numerous diplomatic posts, he was (1932–38) foreign minister under chancellors Franz von Papen and Kurt von Schleicher. A supporter of Adolf Hitler's foreign policy, he remained in office after Hitler took over the government. In 1938 he was dismissed in favor of Joachim von Ribbentrop. Following the German occupation of Czechoslovakia, Neurath was appointed (1939) "protector" of Bohemia and Moravia; however, he was considered too lenient in his treatment of the Czechs and was replaced by Reinhard Heydrich in 1941. At the Nuremberg war-crimes trial Neurath was sentenced (1946) to imprisonment for 15 years. In 1954 he was released because of illness; he died two years later.

neuritis (no͝orī'tĭs, nyo͝o–), inflammation of a peripheral nerve, often accompanied by degenerative changes in nervous tissue. The cause can be mechanical (injury, pressure), vascular (occlusion of a vessel or hemorrhage into nerve tissue), infectious (invasion by microorganisms), toxic (metallic or chemical poisoning, alcoholism), or metabolic (vitamin deficiencies, pernicious anemia). Symptoms of neuritis that arise from involvement of sensory nerves are tingling, burning, pin-and-needle sensations, or even loss of sensation. If motor nerves are involved, symptoms may range from a slight loss of muscle tone to paralysis. Since neuritis is regarded as a condition that results from a number of disorders, rather than a disease in itself, treatment is directed first at the underlying cause. See NEURALGIA.

neurology (no͝orŏl'əjē, nyo͝o–), study of the morphology, physiology, and pathology of the human nervous system. As researchers, neurologists carry on investigative and experimental work in such areas as conductivity, embryology, and the metabolism of nervous tissue. As practicing physicians, neurologists diagnose and treat diseases that involve the nervous system. Since the brain is an integral part of the nervous system, the domain of neurology overlaps with psychiatry. However, each remains a discrete medical specialty.

neuron, specialized cell in animals that, as a unit of the NERVOUS SYSTEM, carries information by receiving and transmitting electrical impulses.

neurosis: see PSYCHONEUROSIS.

Neusatz: see NOVI SAD, Yugoslavia.

Neusiedler Lake (noi'zēdlər), Ger. *Neusiedlersee,* Hung. *Fertő tó,* c.130 sq mi (340 sq km), on the Austria-Hungary border SE of Vienna. The lake's area and depth (average 5 ft/1.5 m) vary considerably with the seasons. The heavy growth of lake reeds supplies the Austrian cellulose industry. Carp fisheries are in the lake. Its lonely and desolate salt marshes attract a variety of wild life and have been protected since 1935. The Neusiedler region has noted resorts. There are remains of prehistoric lake dwellers in the vicinity.

Neuss (nois), city (1970 pop. 114,613), North Rhine-Westphalia, W West Germany. It is a rail junction and canal port, near the left bank of the Rhine opposite Düsseldorf. Its industries produce metal goods, heavy and light machinery, paper, and food products. Built on the site of a Roman camp called Novaesium, Neuss was chartered in the 12th cent. It belonged to the archbishopric of Cologne until the French Revolutionary Wars. In 1474–75, Charles the Bold of Burgundy, supporting the archbishop in a quarrel with the chapter of Neuss, unsuccessfully besieged the city for 11 months. It passed to Prussia in 1815. Noteworthy structures include the Romanesque Church of St. Quirinus (13th cent.), a city gate (13th cent.), and the city hall (17th–18th cent.).

Neustadt an der Weinstrasse (noi'shtät än dĕr vīn'shträsə), city (1970 pop. 50,909), Rhineland-Palatinate, W West Germany; chartered 1275. It is the center of the Rhenish Palatinate wine trade; manufactures include metal products and textiles. The city is also known as Neustadt an der Haardt.

Neustrelitz (noi"shtrā'lĭts), city (1970 pop. 27,788), Neubrandenburg district, N East Germany. It is a transportation center and has metalworks, publishing houses, and wood mills. Neustrelitz was founded (1733) as the capital of Mecklenburg-Strelitz after the earlier ducal residence at nearby Strelitz had burned down (1712).

Neustria (nōōs'trēə), western portion of the kingdom of the FRANKS in the 6th, 7th, and 8th cent., during the rule of the MEROVINGIANS. It comprised the Seine and Loire country and the region to the north; its principal towns were Soissons and Paris. The realm originated with the several partitions of the lands of CLOVIS I (d. 511) among his sons and grandsons during the 6th cent. The dynastic rivalry involved Neustria in almost constant warfare with the eastern portion of the Frankish kingdom, which became known as AUSTRASIA. The conflict culminated in the long and bitter war between Queen FREDEGUNDE of Neustria (d. 597) and Queen BRUNHILDA of Austrasia (d. 613). Neustria and Austrasia were reunited briefly by CLOTAIRE I, CLOTAIRE II, and DAGOBERT I. After Dagobert the kings sank to insignificance, while the mayors of the palace rose in power. In 687, PEPIN OF HERISTAL, mayor of the palace of the king of Austrasia, defeated his Neustrian rival and united Austrasia and Neustria. His descendants, the CAROLINGIANS, continued to rule the two realms, first as mayors and after 751 as kings.

Neutra, Richard Joseph (noi'trə, nōō'trə), 1892–1970, American architect, born and educated in Vienna. Although Neutra worked for a time with Eric Mendelsohn and later with Frank Lloyd Wright, after he opened his own practice in Los Angeles in 1926 he adhered to a more functionalist approach (see MODERN ARCHITECTURE). A notable early example (1929) is the Lovell "Health House," Los Angeles. His Corona Avenue School, Los Angeles (1935) reflects his interest in opening a structure directly into natural surroundings. Neutra planned several federal housing projects, including Channel Heights, San Pedro (1943). Among his later works are Research House II, Los Angeles (1967) and the Northridge Medical Arts Building, Calif. (1968). Neutra's many books include *Survival through Design* (1954), *World and Dwelling* (tr. 1962), and *Building with Nature* (1971). See his autobiography (1962); studies by Esther McCoy (1960) and Rupert Spade, ed. (1971).

Neutra: see NITRA, Czechoslovakia.

neutrality, in international law, status of a nation that refrains from participation in a war between other states and maintains an impartial attitude toward the belligerents. At the opening of hostilities a nonbelligerent state generally issues a proclamation of neutrality, which not only explains its international position but also serves as a warning to its own nationals, whom it declines to protect if they are penalized by a belligerent for committing an unneutral act. After the proclamation is issued it is the duty of the neutral power to observe strict impartiality in its relations with the warring nations. There must be no discrimination or preference. However, this is not always the reality, and the terms *benevolent* and *hostile,* when applied to neutrality, imply the sympathy of a neutral for one or other of the belligerents. The duty of the belligerent, on the other hand, is to respect neutral territory and neutral territorial waters (see WATERS, TERRITORIAL). Neutrality is perpetual when it is imposed upon a nation by treaty obligations. Though its sovereignty is thus limited, the state becomes inviolable. Switzerland, neutralized by the Congress of Vienna (1815), is an example of a perpetually neutral state. Temporary neutrality flows from the unlimited sovereignty of the state, which allows it freely to decide its position in time of war and voluntarily to abstain from participation. In medieval times, neutrality as a concept was impossible, for feudal obligations theoretically, at least, determined positions in any given conflict. However, the powerful states that later evolved were free to follow a policy of noninterference in the wars of neighboring nations. Maritime warfare gave great impetus to the development of neutrality laws. The objective of belligerents was to destroy the enemy's commerce; but nonbelligerents demanded freedom to trade impartially. A belligerent could not interfere too drastically with a neutral's trade, for fear that the noncombatant would become allied with the enemy; thus compromises were effected. Neutral states might trade, but under certain conditions and with certain exceptions. Neutral duties and rights, first recognized by the 14th-century *Consolato del mare* [tribunal of the sea], were codified or incorporated in treaties and thus became part of international law. While the Hanseatic League and the maritime cities of the Mediterranean had been able to demand respect for neutral rights, it was not until much later that the duties of neutrals were stressed. In 1780, and again in 1800, the Baltic powers formed a league of armed neutrality to resist by force British violation of neutral rights. George Washington in his neutrality proclamation (1793) not only insisted upon respect for American neutrality but also promised the fulfillment of its accompanying duties. The Declaration of Paris (1856) standardized certain laws of neutrality (see PARIS, DECLARATION OF); the Declaration of London (1909) codified certain principles of neutrality with regard to maritime law (see LONDON, DECLARATION OF). At the Second Hague Conference (1907) neutral rights and obligations were defined in two conventions. The general neutrality convention, after declaring neutral territory inviolable, laid down regulations for neutral states and listed acts that should not be regarded as favoring one of the belligerents. The convention on neutrality in naval war, which was fuller, elaborated upon the duties of neutrals but did not incorporate rules for CONTRABAND and BLOCKADE. In World Wars I and II, violations of neutrality by both sides were frequent, and attempts were made to justify the action by assertions that changed methods of warfare warranted changes in the observance of international law. When the League of Nations was established, it was generally recognized that member states could not be neutral in any dispute in which the League called upon them to intervene. The United States, which was not a member, asserted its intention to remain aloof from all wars and adopted (1935) the Neutrality Act. The United Nations, unlike the League, includes all the major world powers. Their obligations under the charter to restore and maintain the peace preclude neutrality, and states, such as Switzerland, which are committed to neutrality cannot become members. Nevertheless, during the Korean War many nations that did not participate in the conflict claimed the status of "nonbelligerents." The Geneva Conventions of 1949 provide a role for neutrals in the administration of prisoner-of-war agreements. The rules of neutrality of the air, though still uncodified, are generally accepted. They are based on land and sea rules and provide, among other things, that the air space of a neutral country is inviolable. See J. B. Oakes, *The Edge of Freedom* (1961); Roderick Ogley, *The Theory and Practice of Neutrality in the Twentieth Century* (1970); Nils Orrik, *The Decline of Neutrality, 1914–1941* (2d ed. 1971).

Neutrality Act, law passed by the U.S. Congress and signed by President Franklin Delano Roosevelt in Aug., 1935. It was designed to keep the United States out of a possible European war by banning shipment of war materiel to belligerents at the discretion of the President and by forbidding U.S. citizens from traveling on belligerent vessels except at their own risk. The demand for this legislation arose from the conviction of many Americans that U.S. entry into World War I had been a mistake. This conviction was strengthened by the well-publicized investigations of American war loans to the Allies by a Senate committee headed by Gerald P. NYE. The Neutrality Act was amended (Feb., 1936) to prohibit the granting of loans to belligerents, and later (Jan. and May, 1937) neutrality was extended to cover civil wars, a step inspired by the Spanish civil war. In Nov., 1939, the act was revised in favor of supplying warring nations on the "cash-and-carry" principle; but U.S. vessels were excluded from combat zones, and U.S. citizens were forbidden from sailing on belligerent vessels. These provisions were lifted by amendment in Nov., 1941, after the LEND-LEASE policy had been established. The act was thus practically out of operation even before American neutrality ended with Pearl Harbor.

neutralization, chemical reaction, according to the Arrhenius theory of ACIDS AND BASES, in which a water solution of acid is mixed with a water solution of base to form SALT and water; this reaction is complete only if the resulting solution has neither acidic nor basic properties. Such a solution is called a neutral solution. Complete neutralization can take place when a strong acid, such as hydrochloric acid, HCl, is mixed with a strong base, such as sodium hydroxide, NaOH. Strong acids and strong bases completely break up, or dissociate, into their constituent ions when they dissolve in water. In the case of hydrochloric acid, hydrogen ions, H^+, and chloride ions, Cl^-, are formed. In the case of sodium hydroxide, sodium ions, Na^+, and hydroxide ions, OH^-, are formed. The hydrogen and hydroxide ions readily unite to form water. If the number of hydrogen ions in the hydrochloric acid solution is equal to the number of hydroxide ions in the sodium hydroxide solution, complete neutralization occurs when the two solutions are mixed. The resulting solution contains sodium ions and chloride ions that unite when the water evaporates to form sodium chloride, common table salt. In a neutralization reaction in which either a weak acid or a weak base is used, only partial neutralization occurs. In a neutralization reaction in which both a weak acid and a weak base are used, complete neutralization can occur if the acid and the base are equally weak. The heat produced in the reaction between an acid and a base is called the heat of neutralization. When any strong acid is mixed with any strong base, the heat of neutralization is always about 13,700 calories for each EQUIVALENT WEIGHT of acid and base neutralized. See *p*H (separate article); TITRATION.

Neutral Nation, group of North American Indian tribes of the Iroquoian branch of the Hokan-Siouan linguistic stock (see AMERICAN INDIAN LANGUAGES). In the early 17th cent. they occupied the territory along the northern shore of Lake Erie. They then numbered some 12,000. Their culture was substantially that of the Eastern Woodlands area. Father Joseph Daillon visited them in 1626 and reported that their customs were very similar to those of the Huron Indians. The French gave the Neutral Nation its name because of its neutrality in the Iroquois-Huron wars. This neutrality, however, was short-lived, for when the remnants of the Huron joined (1649) them, the Iroquois Confederacy practically destroyed the Neutral Nation. A few survivors assimilated with the Seneca Indians. See G. K. Wright, *The Neutral Indians* (1963).

neutrino (nōōtrē'nō) [Ital.,=little neutral (particle)], massless ELEMENTARY PARTICLE emitted during the decay of certain other particles. The neutrino was first postulated in 1930 by Wolfgang Pauli in order to maintain the law of conservation of energy during beta decay (see CONSERVATION LAWS; RADIOACTIVITY). When a radioactive nucleus emits a beta particle (electron), the particle may have any energy from zero up to a certain maximum. Pauli suggested that when the beta particle has less than the maximum possible value, the remaining energy is carried away by an undetected particle, the neutrino. Its charge must be zero because a charged particle would easily be detected. Moreover, if it were charged, the law of conservation of charge would be violated during beta decay. The neutrino was named by Enrico Fermi to distinguish it from the neutron, discovered in 1932. Further studies showed that the neutrino was also necessary to maintain the conservation laws of momentum and spin. Like the electron, the neutrino is a LEPTON; it participates only in the weak decay of nuclear particles and has no role in the strong force binding nuclei together. Neutrinos are also emitted when a PION decays into a MUON and when a muon decays into an electron or positron. An energetic neutrino can induce the reverse of these reactions. The neutrino was not detected directly until 1956. In 1962 it was found that the neutrino associated with the muon is distinct from that associated with the electron. Each type of neutrino has its own antiparticle. Neutrinos are stable and can be destroyed only by the same processes through which they are created—particle decays involving the weak nuclear interaction.

neutrino astronomy, study of stars by means of their emission of NEUTRINOS, subatomic particles that result from nuclear reactions and are emitted by the star along with light. The light received from a star is emitted by the surface layers, which in turn absorb the light coming from the interior. Neutrinos, on the other hand, are absorbed only very weakly by matter and, once created by nuclear reactions in the stellar core, pass directly through the outer parts of the star. Thus neutrinos permit astronomers to look directly into the energy-producing core of a star. Their weak tendency to interact with matter also makes them very difficult to detect. Neutrino "observatories" are located in deep mines, where hundreds of feet of rock shield out the cosmic rays that would completely swamp the tiny effects due to neutrinos. The neutrinos pass as easily through the rock as they pass through the star. Because of its proximity, the sun is expected to be by far the most intense source of neutrinos and has been the initial object of study. Neutrino astronomy should eventually develop into an important means of gaining information concerning processes within stars and, in particular, of checking predictions that neutrino emission represents a very large loss of energy for many stars and therefore speeds stellar evolution.

neutrography: see NEUTRON.

neutron, uncharged ELEMENTARY PARTICLE of slightly greater mass than the PROTON. It was discovered by James Chadwick in 1932. The stable isotopes of all elements except hydrogen and helium contain a number of neutrons equal to or greater than the number of protons. The preponderance of neutrons becomes more marked for very heavy nuclei. A nucleus with an excess of neutrons is radioactive; the extra neutrons convert to protons by beta decay (see RADIOACTIVITY). In a nucleus the neutron can be stable, but a free neutron decays, on the average, in about 17 min (1,013 sec) into a proton, an electron, and an antineutrino. The fact that the neutron possesses a magnetic moment suggests that it has an internal structure of electric charge, although the net charge is zero. The electron-scattering experiments of Robert Hofstadter indicate that the neutron, like the proton, is surrounded by a cloud of PIONS; protons and neutrons are bound together in nuclei by the exchange of virtual pions. The neutron and the proton are regarded by physicists as two aspects or states of a single entity, the nucleon. The antineutron, the neutron's ANTIPARTICLE, was discovered in 1956. The neutron, like other particles, also possesses certain wave properties, as explained by the QUANTUM THEORY. The field of neutron optics is concerned with such topics as the DIFFRACTION and polarization of beams of neutrons. The formation of images using the techniques of neutron optics is known as neutrography. See D. J. Hughes, *Neutron Story* (1959); K. H. Beckurts and Karl Wirtz, *Neutron Physics* (tr. 1964).

neutron bomb: see HYDROGEN BOMB.

neutron star, extremely small, extremely dense celestial object comparable to the sun in mass but only a few kilometers in radius. The existence of neutron stars was predicted in 1939, and their nature was theoretically described based on the laws of physics. In the central core of a neutron star there are no stable atoms or nuclei; only ELEMENTARY PARTICLES can survive the extreme conditions of pressure and temperature. Surrounding the core is a fluid composed primarily of NEUTRONS squeezed in close contact. The fluid is encased in a rigid crystalline crust a few hundred meters thick. The outer gaseous atmosphere is probably only a few centimeters thick. The neutron star resembles a single giant NUCLEUS because the density everywhere except in the outer shell is as high as the density in the nuclei of ordinary matter. The only observational evidence of their existence to date is provided by the PULSARS, which are radio sources that fluctuate in intensity in a manner indicating that they might be rotating neutron stars.

Neuwied (noi'vēt"), city (1970 pop. 62,560), Rhineland-Palatinate, W West Germany, a port at the confluence of the Rhine and Wied rivers. Manufactures of this industrial city include building materials, steel, and machinery. Neuwied developed around a palace begun by Count Frederick III of Wied in 1648. There are Roman ruins nearby.

Neva (nē'və, Rus. nyĭvä'), river, 46 mi (74 km) long, NW European USSR, connecting Lake Ladoga with the Gulf of Finland, an inlet of the Baltic Sea. Leningrad is situated in its delta. The Neva is connected by canal systems with the Volga River and with the White Sea. It freezes in winter.

Nevada (nəvăd'ə, -vä-), state (1970 pop. 488,738), 110,540 sq mi (286,299 sq km), W United States, admitted as the 36th state of the Union in 1864. CARSON CITY is the capital; LAS VEGAS is the largest city, and RENO is also of importance. Nevada is bounded on the W by California, on the N by Oregon and Idaho, on the E by Utah, and on the SE by Arizona (with the Colorado River marking most of the border). Since S Nevada narrows down to almost a point, there is only a fragmentary border with Arizona on the south. Most of the state lies within the GREAT BASIN. The rivers in the southeast belong to the Colorado River system, while those of the extreme north drain into the Snake. Like the Humboldt, most Nevada rivers go nowhere, ending instead in desolate alkali sinks—except where they have been diverted for irrigation and reclamation. About half a

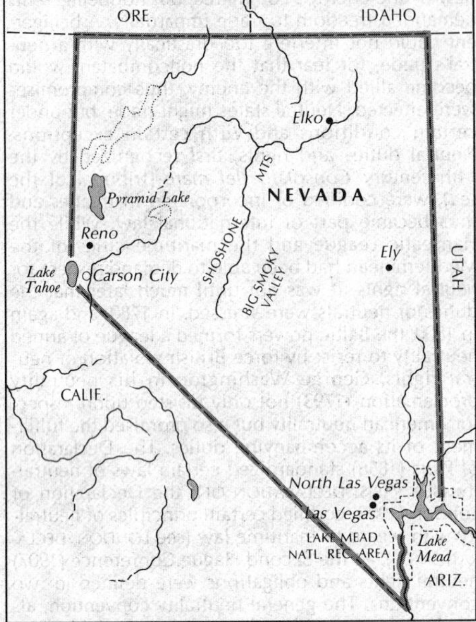

million acres (202,345 hectares) of land are being reclaimed by the Humboldt project, the Newlands project, and the Truckee River storage project. The alkali sinks and great arid stretches clothed with sagebrush and creosote bush typify Nevada's landscape. Its mountain chains generally run north and south, segmenting the state. On the California border stand the lofty Sierra Nevada [snowy range]. The days and nights in this dry country are generally clear, and the temperature varies with the season as well as the altitude. The mean elevation is c.5,500 ft (1,676 m). In the north and west the winters reach extreme cold, while in parts of the south the summers approach ovenlike heat. Many of the high plateau areas are excellent for grazing, and cattle and sheep raising is one of the important industries of the state. Because of the prevailing dryness and the steep slopes, agriculture is not highly developed, but is devoted mainly to growing hay and alfalfa as winter food for the cattle; however, wheat and barley are also grown. A considerable amount of the state's foodstuffs are imported. The population has been sparse since the time when the Paiute Indians and other tribes eked out a meager living from the land and the animals. The fortune of Nevada has been not in its land but in the almost incredible wealth below the surface of the land—lead, silver, gold, zinc, antimony, arsenic, and tungsten. In recent years the state has been a leading producer of copper, gold, sand and gravel, iron ore, and mercury. Petroleum was discovered in 1954. There is also some manufacturing; principal industries include the manufacture of stone, clay, and glass products, chemicals, food products, lumber, electrical machinery, and fabricated metals. In the 20th cent. resorts have been developed — notably at Reno, the leading commercial city as well as "the divorce capital of the world," and at Las Vegas, renowned for its gambling (legalized in 1931) and night life. Gambling taxes are a primary source of state revenue. The space-research industry, which began in the 1950s, declined in the late 1960s. In the 1770s several Spanish explorers came near the area of present-day Nevada; the report of Father Silvestre Vélez de Escalante on the forbidding aspects of the steep and dry "unknown land" discouraged further exploration. However, half a century later fur traders thrusting into the Rocky Mts. for beaver pelts publicized the region. Jedediah S. Smith came across S Nevada on his way to California in 1827. The following year Peter Skene Ogden, a Hudson's Bay Company man trading out of the Oregon country, entered NE Nevada. In 1828, Ogden discovered the Humboldt River. Joseph Walker in 1833–34 went along the Humboldt and crossed the Sierra Nevada to California. Later many wagon trains crossed Nevada on the way to California, especially during and after the gold rush of 1849; however, the difficult journey caused many tragic experiences like those of the DONNER party. Travelers going to California over the Old Spanish Trail also crossed S Nevada, and Las Vegas became a station on the route. With Kit Carson, John C. Frémont had explored much of the state between 1843 and 1845, and his reports gave the Federal government its first comprehensive information on the area, which the United States acquired from Mexico in the MEXICAN WAR. These accounts possibly aided Brigham Young when he was shepherding the Mormons west to build a new home in the mountains and valleys of Utah. When in 1850 the Federal government set up the Utah Territory, almost all of Nevada was included except the southern tip, which was then part of New Mexico. Trouble between the U.S. government and the Mormons led to an army campaign against the Mormons in 1857, and Brigham Young recalled most of the few Mormons who had settled in the region that is now Nevada back to Salt Lake City, the capital of the new Mormon commonwealth. Non-Mormons had been averse to settling in Mormon-dominated territory, but after gold was found in 1859 non-Mormons did come into the area. A rush from California began and multiplied manyfold as news of the COMSTOCK LODE silver strike spread. Most of the newcomers preferred to consider themselves as still being within California, and a political question was added to the general upheaval. Meanwhile, miners came helter-skelter, raising camps that grew overnight into such booming and raucous places as Virginia City. One of the newcomers, Mark Twain, left a vivid picture of these raw Nevada days in *Roughing It.* Partly to impose order on the lawless, wide-open mining towns, Congress made Nevada into a territory in 1861 as fortune hunters, the venturesome, and the curious poured in. The territory was then enlarged by increasing its eastern boundary by one degree of longitude in 1862. It was rushed into statehood in 1864, with Carson City as its capital. President Lincoln (in order to get more votes to pass the Thirteenth Amendment) had signed the proclamation even though the territory did not actually meet the population requirement for statehood. In 1866, Nevada acquired its present-day boundaries when the southern tip was added and more eastern land was gained from Utah. Communications with the East, which had been spectacularly but briefly maintained by the pony express, were firmly established by the completion of the transcontinental railroad in 1869. The state continued to be dependent on its precious ores, and its fate was affected by new strikes such as the "big bonanza" (1873), which enriched the silver kings, J. W. Mackay and J. G. Fair, and the discovery (1900) of silver deposits at Tonopah, of copper at Ely, and of gold at Goldfield (1902). Resting on such an undiversified base, the economy was (and still is) seriously shaken by mining depressions and by fluctuations in the market prices of the minerals. Naturally the political leaders of Nevada were vociferous in favor of the free coinage of silver. From the 1870s to the 1890s the people of Nevada were strong supporters of the "cheap money" advocates and were thus linked with the discontented farmers of the Middle West in favoring the Bland-Allison Act and the Sherman Silver Purchase Act (although both were considered insufficient measures). They enthusiastically endorsed the silver program of William Jennings Bryan and the Democrats in 1896, and even after its resounding defeat they continued to clamor for government purchase and coinage of silver. In the 20th cent. the Federal government has played an active role in Nevada. The Newlands Irrigation Project

(1907) was the nation's first irrigation project built by the Federal government. The HOOVER DAM was completed in 1936. The U.S. Atomic Energy Commission began conducting nuclear tests in Nevada at Frenchman Flat and Yucca Flat in the 1950s. Nevada's constitution was adopted in 1864. The legislature is composed of 20 senators elected for four-year terms and 40 assemblymen elected for two-year terms. The governor is elected for a four-year term. The state elects two U.S. Senators and one Representative; it has three electoral votes. Mike O'Callaghan, a Democrat, became governor in 1971 and was elected to a second term in 1974. Besides Reno and Las Vegas, there are many points of interest. Hoover Dam impounds Lake Mead, one of the largest artificial lakes in the world. Lake Mead Recreational Area has facilities for fishing, swimming, and boating. Other attractions include Lake Tahoe, on the Nevada-California line, Lehman Caves National Monument, Death Valley National Monument, and restored mining ghost towns like Virginia City. The state's leading institution of higher education is the Univ. of Nevada, at Reno. See Federal Writers' Project, *Nevada* (1940, repr. 1973); D. Morgan, *The Humboldt* (1943); O. Lewis, *The Silver Kings* (1947); R. G. Lillard, *Desert Challenge: An Interpretation of Nevada* (1942, repr. 1966); E. W. Billeb, *Mining Camp Days* (1968); W. S. Shepperson, *Retreat to Nevada* (1968); J. W. Hulse, *The Nevada Adventure* (rev. ed. 1969); R. R. Elliott, *History of Nevada* (1973).

Nevada, University of, mainly at Reno; land-grant and state supported; coeducational; chartered 1864, opened 1874 at Elko, moved 1886. It maintains the Mackay School of Mines and the Desert Research Institute. The university has a branch campus at Las Vegas.

Nevelson, Louise, 1900–, American sculptor, b. Kiev, Russia. Using odd pieces of wood, found objects, cast metal and other materials, Nevelson constructs huge walls or enclosed box arrangements of complex and rhythmic abstract shapes. These are covered entirely with black, white, or gold paint. The uniform tone gives her work a mysterious quality and emphasizes the structural importance of its shadows. Huge works such as *World* (1966; Detroit Inst. of Art) reflect a sense of total environment. Examples of Nevelson's work are in the Whitney Museum and Museum of Modern Art in New York City. See study by John Gordon (1967).

Nevers (nəvĕr'), city (1968 pop. 45,068), capital of Nièvre dept., central France, on the Loire and Nièvre rivers. It is the center of an iron and steel district and has important pottery and china industries. Other manufactures include metal and foundry products, mechanical and electrical equipment, refrigerators, chemicals, textiles, and printed matter. Nevers became the seat of a bishopric in the 6th cent. and was long the capital of the duchy and province of NIVERNAIS. Among the points of interest are the ducal palace (15th–16th cent.), now a courthouse; the Church of St. Étienne (11th cent.), a gem of Romanesque architecture; the cathedral (13th–16th cent.); and the Church of St. Bernadette-du-Banlay (1966). In the Convent of St. Gildard are the remains of St. Bernadette, who lived there from 1860 to 1879.

Neville, Charles: see WESTMORLAND, CHARLES NEVILLE, 6TH EARL OF.

Neville, Ralph: see WESTMORLAND, RALPH NEVILLE, 1ST EARL OF.

Neville, Richard: see WARWICK, RICHARD NEVILLE, EARL OF.

Nevin, Ethelbert Woodbridge, 1862–1901, American pianist and composer, b. Edgeworth, Pa., studied in Boston and in Germany. He made his debut as a pianist in Pittsburgh in 1886 but devoted most of his time to composition of songs and short, lyrical pieces. One song, *The Rosary* (1898), enjoyed great popularity. Other popular works are *Narcissus,* from the piano cycle *Water Scenes* (1891), and settings of Eugene Field's poems "Little Boy Blue" and "Wynken, Blynken, and Nod."

Nevin, John Williamson, 1803–86, American theologian and educator, b. near Strasburg, Pa., grad. Union College, 1821, and Princeton Theological Seminary, 1826. He was professor of biblical literature (1830–40) in Western Theological Seminary at Allegheny (now part of Pittsburgh), and from 1840 he taught theology at the German Reformed Church Seminary, Mercersburg, Pa. He served (1841–53) as acting president of Marshall College, which in 1853 became part of Franklin and Marshall College; there he was president from 1866 to 1876. His writings and teachings gave rise to what was called the Mercersburg theology. Among his works are *The Anxious Bench* (1843), *The Mystical Presence* (1846), and *Anti-Christ; or, The Spirit of Sect and Schism* (1848). See studies by Theodore Appel (1889, repr. 1969) and J. H. Nichols (1961).

Nevins, Allan, 1890–1971, American historian, b. Camp Point, Ill. After studying at the Univ. of Illinois, he followed a career in journalism until 1927. Teaching at Columbia from 1928, he became a full professor in 1931 and was made De Witt Clinton professor of American history in 1942. He retired in 1958, becoming a senior research associate of the Huntington Library. Nevins, one of the most prolific U.S. historians of the 20th cent., is noted for the exhaustive research and comprehensive treatment that characterize his wide range of historical writings. His masterful political biographies include *Grover Cleveland* (1932) and *Hamilton Fish* (1936), both of which won Pulitzer Prizes; *Frémont: Pathmarker of the West* (1939); and *Herbert H. Lehman and His Era* (1963). In works on the economic giants of America, among them *Abram S. Hewitt* (1935) and *Study in Power: John D. Rockefeller* (rev. ed. 1953), Nevins pointed out the role of the captains of industry in making America a world power. *The Ordeal of the Union* (1947–60), Nevins's six-volume history of the Civil War era from 1847 through 1863, is a comprehensive narrative of the age, covering social, economic, and political aspects. Among many other notable works are *Illinois* (1917), a history of the state university; *The Evening Post* (1922), an early work in the history of journalism; *The American States during and after the Revolution, 1775–1789* (1924), a valuable study of change in this period; *The Emergence of Modern America, 1865–1878* (1927), a social history; and *The Gateway to History* (1938, rev. ed. 1962), an introduction to historiography. The many papers edited by Nevins include the diaries of Philip Hone (1927), John Quincy Adams (1928), James K. Polk (1929), and George Templeton Strong (1952), as well as the letters of Grover Cleveland (1933). Nevins also established the Columbia oral history program, the first of its kind in the nation.

Nevis, British West Indies: see SAINT KITTS-NEVIS.

Nevis, Ben, peak: see BEN NEVIS, Scotland.

New, Harry Stewart, 1858–1937, U.S. Postmaster General (1923–29) and politician, b. Indianapolis. He was long connected (1878–1903) with the Indianapolis *Journal.* New was an Indiana state senator (1896–1900), chairman (1907–8) of the Republican National Committee, and served (1917–23) in the U.S. Senate, where he was a leader in the fight against the League of Nations. As Postmaster General under Warren G. Harding and Calvin Coolidge, New gave great stimulus to commercial aviation by giving contracts to private firms to carry airmail.

New Albany, city (1970 pop. 38,402), seat of Floyd co., S Ind., near the falls of the Ohio River opposite Louisville, Ky.; inc. 1819. It was a shipbuilding center in the 19th cent., and the riverboats *Robert E. Lee* and *Eclipse* were built there. Today the city's industries produce plywood, men's suits, machine parts, chemicals, and many other products. Two bridges link New Albany with Louisville. William Vaughn Moody lived in the city. Indiana Univ. Southeast is in nearby Jeffersonville.

New Alesund, town, Spitsbergen: see NY-ÅLESUND.

New Amsterdam, Dutch settlement at the mouth of the Hudson River and on the southern end of Manhattan island; est. 1624. It was the capital of the colony of New Netherland from 1626 to 1664, when it was captured by the British and renamed New York.

New Archangel, Alaska: see SITKA.

Newark, Ont.: see NIAGARA-ON-THE-LAKE.

Newark. 1 City (1970 pop. 27,153), Alameda co., W Calif., on the east side of San Francisco Bay; inc. 1955. **2** City (1970 pop. 21,078), New Castle co., NW Del.; settled before 1700, inc. 1852. The second-largest city in the state, it is the seat of the Univ. of Delaware. It has a huge automobile assembly plant, several research laboratories, and a variety of light manufactures. The only Revolutionary battle on Delaware soil was fought (Sept., 1777) at nearby Cooch's bridge. **3** City (1970 pop. 381,930), seat of Essex co., NE N.J., on the Passaic River and Newark Bay; settled 1666, inc. as a city 1836. It is a port of entry and the largest city in the state. Aided by its location only 8 mi (13 km) W of New York City, Newark is a major transportation, industrial, commercial, and manufacturing center. Its leather industry dates from the 17th cent., and its jewelry manufactures and insurance businesses were started in the early 19th cent. Among the city's many other products are beer, cutlery, electronic equipment, pharmaceuticals, fabricated metal items, and paints and varnishes. Newark International Airport is one of the world's busiest, and there is a seaport operated by the Port Authority of New York and New Jersey. Newark was settled (1666) by Puritans from Connecticut under the leadership of Robert Treat. It was the scene of Revolutionary skirmishes. The city's industrial growth began after the Revolution, aided by new inventions and the development of transportation facilities. The Morris Canal was opened in 1832, and the railroads arrived in 1834 and 1835. A flourishing shipping business resulted, and Newark became the industrial center of the area. In the late 19th cent. its industry was further developed, especially through the efforts of such men as Seth Boyden and J. W. Hyatt. Newark Port opened in 1915, and the city's shipbuilding played an important role in World War I. Newark's landmarks include Trinity Cathedral (1810, with the spire of a church built in 1743); the Sacred Heart Cathedral (begun 1898, completed 1953); the First Presbyterian Church (1791); the Newark Public Library (founded 1888), developed by John Cotton Dana; the Newark Museum (1909), founded by Dana; and the county courthouse (1906), designed by Cass Gilbert, with Gutzon Borglum's statue of Lincoln in front. Other points of interest include Borglum's large group *Wars of America* (1926) in Military Park (a Revolutionary War drilling ground and a Civil War tenting area) and many historic homes. Newark's educational institutions include Rutgers Univ. in Newark, Newark College of Engineering, the Seton Hall Univ. law school, a junior college, and a preparatory academy founded in 1774. Aaron Burr and Stephen Crane were born in Newark. **4** Village (1970 pop. 11,644), Wayne co., W central N.Y., on the Barge Canal, in a farm area. Food is processed, and jewelry, furniture, and cartons are manufactured. A state school for the mentally retarded is there. **5** City (1970 pop. 41,836), seat of Licking co., central Ohio, on the Licking River, in a livestock area; inc. 1826. It is a farm trade and processing center, a transportation hub, and an industrial city. Newark's outstanding group of Indian mounds attract many visitors. The Newark Earthworks State Memorials include three locations within the city's limits: the Great Circle; the Octagon Mound, with smaller mounds inside the octagon; and the Wright Earthworks. The Museum of Ohio Indian Art is there. A campus of Ohio State Univ. is in Newark.

New Bedford, city (1970 pop. 101,777), seat of Bristol co., SE Mass., at the mouth of the Acushnet River on Buzzard's Bay; settled 1640, set off from Dartmouth 1787, inc. as a city 1847. Formerly one of the world's greatest whaling ports, it has become a leading port for the fishing and scalloping industries. New Bedford also handles much transatlantic and intracoastal trade. During the Revolution the harbor was a haven for American privateers, prompting the British to invade and burn the town in 1778. The whaling industry boomed after the Revolution, reaching a peak in the 1850s. The first cotton-textile mill in the city dates from 1846, but the textile industry declined in the 1920s. Today New Bedford's manufactures include clothing, textiles, electrical machinery, electronic components, rubber products, and tools and dies. The Seamen's Bethel, described by Herman Melville in *Moby Dick*; the Bourne Whaling Museum; the Old Dartmouth Historical Society; Friends' Academy (1810); and the Swain School of Design are in New Bedford. The Free Public Library holds a large collection of material on whaling. There is a sizable Portuguese-speaking minority in the city.

New Berlin, city (1970 pop. 26,910), Waukesha co., SE Wis., a suburb of Milwaukee; founded 1840, inc. 1959. It is largely residential.

New Bern, city (1970 pop. 14,660), seat of Craven co., E N.C., a port and trading center at the junction of the Neuse and the Trent rivers; inc. 1723. Settled in 1710 by Swiss and German colonists under Baron Christopher de Graffenried and John Lawson, New Bern was the second town in North Carolina and an early colonial capital; in 1774 it was the seat of the first provincial convention. Notable among the old buildings is the beautiful Tryon Palace (1767–70), which was the colonial capitol and governor's mansion; it was badly burned in 1798 and was not reconstructed until the 1950s. In the Civil War the city was captured (March, 1862) by Union forces under Gen. S. E. Burnside.

Newberry, Truman Handy, 1864–1945, American naval officer and cabinet official, b. Detroit. He engaged in various financial enterprises and helped organize (1902) the Packard Motor Car Company. A founder and active member of Michigan state naval brigade, he served as lieutenant on the U.S.S. *Yosemite* in the Spanish-American War. He later was Assistant Secretary (1905-8) and Secretary (1908-9) of the Navy, and in World War I was assistant to the commandant of the Third Naval Dist. Newberry was elected Republican Senator from Michigan in 1918, but his conviction by a Michigan court of corruption in obtaining the nomination prevented him from taking his seat. The case was dismissed by the Supreme Court, a Senate committee exonerated him, and he entered the Senate in Jan., 1922. He resigned eleven months later.

Newberry, Walter Loomis, 1804-68, American merchant and banker, b. East Windsor (in the section now South Windsor), Conn. In 1822 he entered the shipping business with his brother Oliver in Buffalo, and in 1826 they went to Detroit, where they established a prosperous dry-goods business. In 1833 he moved to the newly established town of Chicago, where he had previously made extensive investments in real estate. He engaged in the commission business, prospered, and later entered banking and also became president of the Galena and Chicago Union RR. He was active in civic affairs, founded the Young Men's Library Association, and made numerous philanthropic gifts. His will provided for the founding and endowment of the **Newberry Library** in Chicago, a free reference library that specializes in the fields of history, literature, music, and philology and has gained an international reputation. It has a fine collection of Americana.

Newberry Library: see under NEWBERRY, WALTER LOOMIS.

Newbery, John, 1713-67, English publisher and bookseller. He established juvenile literature as an important branch of the publishing business. Included among his publications is *Little Goody Two Shoes* (1766). Although he published his books anonymously, it is assumed that he planned and wrote a number of them himself. In 1922 the Newbery medal was established by Frederic Melcher to be awarded to the most distinguished children's book of the year written by an American.

Newbolt, Sir Henry John, 1862-1938, English poet and historian. He is best remembered for his vigorous and imperialistic poems of the sea, collections of which include *Admirals All* (1897), *The Sailing of the Long Ships* (1902), and *Drake's Drum and Other Songs of the Sea* (1914). The centennial history *The Year of Trafalgar* (1905) established him as a naval historian. He was knighted in 1915. See his autobiography, *My World as in My Time* (1932).

New Braunfels (broun'fəlz), city (1970 pop. 17,859), seat of Comal co., S central Texas, on the Guadalupe River; inc. 1847. It has a big power plant and large textile industries. The city was founded (1845) by Prince Carl von Solms-Braunfels and settled by thousands of German immigrants. Today it retains many German civic and cultural features. Local attractions include a historical museum; Landa Park, which contains Comal springs, river, and lake; and the nearby natural bridge caverns.

New Brighton, village (1970 pop. 19,507), Ramsey co., SE Minn., a suburb of Minneapolis-Saint Paul; inc. 1891. It lies in a farming region that specializes in growing squash. Its manufactures include electronic equipment, pumps, and well screens. The village has a theological seminary.

New Britain, industrial city (1970 pop. 83,441), Hartford co., central Conn.; settled c.1686, inc. 1871. The tin shops and brassworks in the city were established in the 18th cent. New Britain became famous as the "Hardware City" because of its tool and household-hardware industry. Central Connecticut State College is there. Of interest are the city hall (1884) and a park designed by Frederick Law Olmsted in the center of the city. Elihu Burritt was born in New Britain.

New Britain, volcanic island (1970 est. pop. 154,000), c.14,600 sq mi (37,810 sq km), SW Pacific, largest island of the BISMARCK ARCHIPELAGO and part of Papua New Guinea. RABAUL is the chief town and port. The island is mountainous, with active volcanoes, hot springs, and peaks over 7,000 ft (2,130 m) high. There are many European plantations on New Britain; the major export is copra, and some copper, gold, iron, and coal are mined. Discovered and named by the English explorer William DAMPIER in 1700, New Britain became part of German New Guinea in 1884. Germany called it Neu Pommern (New Pomerania). In 1920 it was mandated to Australia by the League of Nations and in 1947 was made a UN trust territory under Australian control.

New Brunswick, province (1971 pop. 634,557), 27,985 sq mi (72,481 sq km), including 512 sq mi (1,326 sq km) of water surface, E Canada. FREDERICTON is the capital and the third largest city. The largest city is SAINT JOHN and the second largest is MONCTON. One of the Maritime Provinces, New Brunswick is bounded on the N by Chaleur Bay and Quebec prov.; on the E by the Gulf of St. Lawrence, Northumberland Strait, and Nova Scotia; on the S by the Bay of Fundy; and on the W by Maine. Its irregular coastline provides excellent facilities for fishing and shipping enterprises. Rivers cross the rolling countryside; they were the first means of transportation and are still important arteries of travel and commerce. The largest river, the St. John, crosses the province from northwest to southeast, and the Miramichi River flows northeasterly and drains the central lowlands. Most of the roads follow the river banks. Dairying thrives on fine pasturage, and the major crops are hay, clover, oats, potatoes, berries, and fruit. A careful conservation program maintains

a supply of second-growth hardwoods and softwoods; forests cover about three fourths of the total area, and lumbering is New Brunswick's most important industry. Great quantities of pulpwood and paper are produced, and the mills at Dalhousie on the north coast are among the largest in the world. Manufacturing has greatly expanded since World War II; in addition to wood items and pulp and paper, products include stoves and heating equipment, shoes, and confectionery. Industry is generally run by hydroelectric power, and fuel resources include coal and much untapped water power, which is being developed. In the northeast there are valuable deposits of lead, copper, silver, and pyrite. The major mineral product is zinc; mined in quantity since the late 1950s, it now accounts for half of all of New Brunswick's mineral income. New Brunswick's fisheries are among the most valuable in Canada, with a variety of freshwater and saltwater fish (cod, salmon, herring, and sardines) as well as shellfish (lobsters, oysters, and clams). Trade flows in and out of the ports of St. John and Moncton, facilitated by railroad connections throughout the province, eastward to Nova Scotia and westward to Quebec. New Brunswick derives considerable revenue from sportsmen and tourists. Its forests are still filled with bear, deer, and moose, and the rivers abound in trout and silver salmon. Easy accessibility from the United States has made Woodstock the gateway to the province. Permanent summer residences are concentrated around Passamaquoddy Bay. Natural attractions include the Grand Falls on the upper reaches of the St. John as well as the spectacular Fundy tides—the highest in the world, sometimes surging to over 50 ft (15 m). The tides in turn cause the Reversing Falls at St. John and the "Bore," a twice-daily tidal wave coming up the Petitcodiac River. They have also sculpted the famous Hopewell Rocks, another tourist attraction. The first white man said to have sailed along the New Brunswick coast was a Portuguese navigator, Estevão Gomes (1525), although there is evidence of Basque fishermen at an earlier date. Jacques Cartier landed at Point Escuminac in 1534 and skirted the shores of Miramichi Bay. The first white settlement was made in 1604 at the mouth of the St. Croix River by Champlain and the sieur de Monts. During this period, while France and England made conflicting territorial claims, the present province of Nova Scotia and the coast of New Brunswick were considered one region, called ACADIA by the French and Nova Scotia by the British. British control of this region was confirmed by the Peace of Utrecht (1713-14). Doubting the loyalty of the Acadians, the British expelled them in 1755, although many fled into the interior, which was still effectively controlled by the French. (Today about 40% of the people of New Brunswick are Acadians.) Great Britain gained possession of the rest of New Brunswick when it gained all of Canada after the French and Indian Wars (see PARIS, TREATY OF, 1763). When the population of New Brunswick was increased by many thousands of Loyalists who fled New England after the American Revolution, that area was organized (1784) into a separate colony. As trees were cut down for shipbuilding, the land was cleared for farming. By the middle of the 19th cent. lumbering and farming were extending into the interior, and St. John was a busy port and shipbuilding town. Dissatisfaction with the arbitrary rule of the provincial governor resulted in the achievement of responsible (or cabinet) government in 1849. In 1867, under the British North America Act, federation with the other provinces into the dominion of Canada was somewhat reluctantly accepted. At present the population is about equally distributed between farm, non-farm rural, and urban areas, although urbanization is noticeably increasing. In 1960, Louis J. Robichaud, leader of the Liberal party, was the first Acadian to become premier of New Brunswick. The Progressive Conservative party came into power in 1970, when Richard Bennett Hatfield became premier. New Brunswick sends 10 senators (appointed) and 10 representatives (elected) to the national parliament. The Univ. of New Brunswick is at Fredericton. See J. C. Webster, *A Historical Guide to New Brunswick* (1928); L. O. Thomas, *The Province of New Brunswick* (1930); A. C. Smith, *The Mosaic Province of New Brunswick* (1965); W. S. MacNutt, *New Brunswick: A History, 1784-1867* (1963) and *New Brunswick and its People* (1966).

New Brunswick, city (1970 pop. 41,885), seat of Middlesex co., central N.J., on the Raritan River; settled 1681, inc. as a city 1784. Originally developed as a commercial center (especially for collecting and shipping grain), New Brunswick now has large pharmaceutical-, medical-, and surgical-supply industries. The city is also an educational center, the seat of Rutgers Univ. and New Brunswick Theological Seminary. Washington, retreating from New York, stayed one week in New Brunswick in 1776. Joyce Kilmer was born there; his birthplace is now an American Legion post. Also in the city are the national headquarters of the Scouts of America. Nearby Camp Kilmer, a U.S. army reserve center, was an important base during World War II and the Korean War.

New Brunswick, University of, at Fredericton, N.B., Canada; nondenominational; provincially supported; coeducational; chartered and opened 1800 as the College of New Brunswick, called King's College by royal charter 1828, achieved university status 1859. The university has faculties of arts, education, engineering, forestry, law, nursing, and science, and a school of graduate studies.

Newburgh (no͞o'bərg, nyo͞o'-), city (1970 pop. 26,219), Orange co., SE N.Y., on the west bank of the Hudson River, opposite Beacon; settled 1709 by Palatines, inc. 1800. Once an important river port and whaling town, the city now has textile and garment industries. Other important manufactures are handbags, floor tile, and varied metal products. A major thermoelectric plant is in Newburgh. The city has many old houses, and the streets run sharply to the river. At Hasbrouck House (1750; now a museum), Washington made his headquarters from April, 1782, to Aug., 1783. It was in Newburgh that the Continental Army was disbanded. Mt. St. Mary College is in the city, and Ladycliff College is in nearby Highland Falls.

Newburn, urban district (1971 pop. 39,379), Northumberland, NE England, on the Tyne River. It is a coal-mining and industrial center. There is a 12th-century church in Newburn.

Newbury, municipal borough (1971 pop. 23,696), Berkshire, S central England. In a farming region, it trades in wool, malt, and farm products. Paper, furniture, and metal products are made. In the Middle Ages the town became an important textile-manufacturing center. The 16th-century cloth hall now contains a museum. Civil war battles were fought at Newbury in 1643 and 1644.

Newburyport, city (1970 pop. 15,807), a seat of Essex co., NE Mass., at the mouth of the Merrimack River; settled 1635, set off from Newbury and inc. 1764. Its silverware and rum industries date from colonial times. An early shipbuilding, whaling, and shipping center, it declined after Jefferson's Embargo of 1808 and the War of 1812, although ships continued to be built there through the clipper-ship era. Its many notable old houses include the Coffin House (c.1651), the Swett-Isley House (c.1671), and the Short House (c.1732). A fire in 1811 destroyed much of the village. William Lloyd Garrison and Francis Cabot Lowell were born in Newburyport.

New Caledonia, Fr. *Nouvelle Calédonie,* overseas territory of France (1971 est. pop. 113,680), South Pacific, c.700 mi (1,130 km) E of Australia. It comprises the island of New Caledonia, the ISLE OF PINES, the LOYALTY ISLANDS, Walpole Island, and the Huon, Chesterfield, and Belep groups; the total land area is 7,082 sq mi (18,342 sq km). The capital is NOUMÉA on New Caledonia island. The principal industries are the mining and refining of nickel, iron mining, and the production of coffee and copra. Cattle and poultry are raised, but many foodstuffs must still be imported from Australia. The government consists of a governor appointed by France, an elected territorial assembly, and a council. L'Union calédonienne, a largely indigenous party, controls the assembly. The inhabitants are largely Melanesians, with Polynesians in the outlying islands. Capt. James COOK sighted and named the main island in 1774; the French annexed it in 1853. New Caledonia island, the largest island of the territory (6,223 sq mi/16,118 sq km) is mountainous and temperate in climate. It is rich in mineral resources, especially nickel, iron, manganese, cobalt, gold, and silver. The island is densely forested in some places, but almost all the kauri pine that was once an important export has been cut down.

New Canaan (kā'nən), town (1970 pop. 17,455), Fairfield co., SW Conn.; settled c.1700, inc. 1801. It is mainly a residential town and summer resort. Dairy products are made, and there are tree nurseries.

New Castile, Spain: see CASTILE.

Newcastle, Thomas Pelham-Holles, duke of, 1693–1768, English politician, brother of Henry PELHAM. He inherited (1711) the estates of his uncle, John Holles, duke of Newcastle, adopted his name, and received (1715) his title. In 1724 he became secretary of state under Sir Robert WALPOLE, and he retained that position after Walpole's fall and through his brother's long ministry (1743–54). In 1754 he succeeded his brother as first lord of the treasury, or prime minister. His weak policy in the Seven Years War led to his resignation in 1756, but the next year he returned to power as nominal head of a coalition ministry with William Pitt, later 1st earl of CHATHAM. Forced (1762) out of office by George III's favorite, Lord Bute, he later served (1765) as lord privy seal under the marquess of Rockingham. Newcastle was ineffective and irresolute in his conduct of public affairs, but he wielded immense political influence through his clever use of patronage, helping to provide parliamentary majorities for Walpole, Pelham, and Pitt. See Basil Williams, *Carteret and Newcastle* (1943, repr. 1966); John B. Owen, *The Rise of the Pelhams* (1957, repr. 1971); R. A. Kelch, *Newcastle; A Duke without Money* (1974).

Newcastle, William Cavendish, duke of, 1593?–1676, English soldier and politician. Of great wealth, Cavendish became (1638) governor of the prince of Wales and a privy councilor. During the civil war he supplied financial and military aid to the royalist cause, raising, maintaining, and leading troops in the northern counties. He was at first successful, but part of his force was defeated at Winceby by Oliver Cromwell in 1643, and after his defeat with Prince Rupert at Marston Moor in 1644 he retired to the Continent. He returned to England with Charles II at the Restoration, having expended nearly £1,000,000 in the royalist cause. His estates were restored, and he was created duke of Newcastle in 1665. He engaged little in politics thereafter. Newcastle wrote several plays and books on horsemanship and was a lifelong patron of writers, among others Ben Jonson (who wrote two masques for the entertainment of Charles I at Newcastle's Welbeck estate in 1633 and 1634) and, later, John Dryden. His second wife, **Margaret (Lucas) Cavendish, duchess of Newcastle,** 1623?–1673, achieved contemporary notice for her poems, plays, essays, scientific treatises, letters, orations, and fantasies. Her biography of her husband (1667) was edited by C. H. Firth (1906). See H. T. E. Perry, *The First Duchess of Newcastle and Her Husband as Figures in Literary History* (1918); Douglas Grant, *Margaret the First* (1957).

Newcastle, city (1971 pop. 145,718; urban agglomeration pop. 249,962), New South Wales, SE Australia, on the Pacific Ocean. It is the center of the largest coal-mining area in the country and is a large port. Coal, wool, iron and steel, and wheat are exported. The city has steel mills and shipyards; chemicals, glass, fertilizer, and textiles are also produced. The first permanent settlement on the site was made in 1804. The Univ. of Newcastle, a branch of the Univ. of Sydney, is in the city. There is also an Anglican cathedral.

Newcastle, town (1971 pop. 6,460), E central N.B., Canada, on the Miramichi River. Located in a lumbering region, it has sawmills and a large pulp mill. Newcastle was the birthplace of the Canadian leader Peter Mitchell and was the boyhood home of Lord Beaverbrook.

New Castle. 1 City (1970 pop. 21,215), seat of Henry co., E Ind.; inc. 1839. It is a farm trade center, and its manufactures include auto and truck parts, doors, and metal products. A state rehabilitation hospital is there. The city has a number of prehistoric Indian mounds. Wilbur Wright's birthplace is nearby. **2** City (1970 pop. 38,559), seat of Lawrence co., W Pa., at the junction of the Shenango and Neshannock rivers, in a fertile farm area; inc. 1825. Coal, limestone, iron ore, and clay deposits found in the region contribute to the city's economy. Manufactures include bronze tools and parts, pottery and china, and rolling mill and steel plant equipment. The Hoyt Institute of Fine Arts is there, and two state parks are nearby.

Newcastle disease, acute viral disease of domestic poultry. Newcastle disease is characterized by sneezing, coughing, and the development of nervous signs. Affected birds may show tremors, circling, falling, twisting of the head and neck, or complete paralysis. Mortality is highest (reaching 90%) in very young birds. Adult mortality is very low. Egg production drops sharply and the eggs produced are of poor quality. Birds with nervous signs are permanently affected, but laying hens will usually return to their former level of production within four to eight weeks. The virus can also be transmitted to man, causing only a temporary conjunctivitis. The disease can be controlled by an attenuated vaccine that is added to the birds' drinking water.

Newcastle Harbour, Australia: see HUNTER, PORT.

Newcastle-under-Lyme, municipal borough (1971 pop. 76,970), Staffordshire, W central England, on the Lyme River. It is partly in the POTTERIES district. Among the industries are coal mining, and brick, tile, and clothing manufacturing. There are ruins of a castle built (12th cent., the "new castle" of the name) by Ranulf, earl of Chester. The 13th-century parish church was rebuilt in 1876 by Sir George Gilbert Scott. Chesterton, a section of the borough, has extensive Roman remains. Nearby is Keele Univ.

Newcastle upon Tyne, county borough (1971 pop. 222,153), county town of Northumberland, NE England, on the Tyne River. It is an important shipping and trade center. The famous coal-shipping industry began in the 13th cent., but coal exports were exceeded by wool exports until the 16th cent. There are many heavy industries in the area, and the city is one of the chief shipbuilding centers of England. Newcastle stands on the site of the Roman military station Pons Aelii, at Hadrian's Wall. Later the site was occupied by the Angles until the Norman conquest. In 1080, Robert II, duke of Normandy and eldest son of William the Conqueror, built a fortified castle from which the town took its name. The castle was besieged and repaired several times; the oldest parts now standing date from 1177. The town walls, of which traces and towers remain, are attributed to Edward I. For 10 months in 1646 Charles I was a prisoner in Newcastle. The Cathedral of St. Nicholas dates partly from the 14th cent.; there is a Roman Catholic cathedral designed by Pugin. There are several notable old buildings including Trinity Almshouse (1492). The Royal Grammar School was founded in the 16th cent. Among the many educational institutions are the Univ. of Newcastle upon Tyne, formerly King's College. In 1974, Newcastle upon Tyne became part of the new metropolitan county of Tyne and Wear.

Newcastle upon Tyne, University of, at Newcastle upon Tyne, England; established 1937 as King's College as a result of the merger of Armstrong College (1871) and the College of Medicine (1834) of the University of Durham. In 1963 the school gained university status. It has faculties of medicine, arts, science, appled science, economic and social studies, law, agriculture, and education.

New Church: see NEW JERUSALEM, CHURCH OF THE.

New City, uninc. village (1970 pop. 27,344), seat of Rockland co., SE N.Y., a suburb of New York City. Situated in a farming region, New City is mostly residential.

Newcomb, Simon, 1835–1909, American astronomer, b. Nova Scotia, grad. Lawrence Scientific School, Harvard, 1858. Living in the United States from 1853, he was appointed (1857) a computer on the *American Nautical Almanac* and later (1877–97) was its director. He was professor of mathematics in the U.S. navy from 1861 until his retirement in 1897, professor of mathematics and astronomy at Johns Hopkins from 1884 to 1894, and for several years editor of the *American Journal of Mathematics.* Newcomb participated in several eclipse expeditions and in 1882 went to the Cape of Good Hope to observe the transit of Venus. The record of many of his researches was published in the *Astronomical Papers of the American Ephemeris,* a series that he established in 1879. His investigations and computations of the orbits of six planets resulted in his tables of the planetary system, which were almost universally adopted by the observatories of the world. Newcomb urged the use of a common system of constants and fundamental stars by astronomers of all nations. A subject to which he devoted many years of study was the theory of the moon's motion. From the formulas he established it was possible to construct accurate lunar tables. His writings include a valuable early paper, *On the Secular Variations and Mutual Relations of the Orbits of the Asteroids* (1860) and *On the Motion of Hyperion* (1891). See his *Reminiscences of an Astronomer* (1903); study by L. M. Dunphy (1956).

Newcomb College: see TULANE UNIV. of Louisiana.

Newcomen, Thomas, 1663–1729, English inventor of an early atmospheric steam engine (c.1711). It was an improvement over an earlier engine patented (1698) by Thomas Savery, who shared the later patent with Newcomen. This improved engine was used successfully to pump water. See study by Lionel Rolt (1965).

New Deal, in U.S. history, term for the domestic reform program of the administration of Franklin Delano ROOSEVELT; it was first used by Roosevelt in his speech accepting the Democratic party nomination for President in 1932. The New Deal is generally considered to have consisted of two phases. The first phase (1933–34) attempted to provide recovery and relief from the GREAT DEPRESSION through programs of agricultural and business regulation, inflation, price stabilization, and public works. Meeting (1933) in special session, Congress established numerous emergency organizations, notably the NATIONAL RECOVERY ADMINISTRATION (NRA), the AGRICULTURAL ADJUSTMENT ADMINISTRATION (AAA), the CIVILIAN CONSERVATION CORPS, and the PUBLIC WORKS ADMINISTRATION. Congress also instituted farm relief, tightened banking and finance regulations, and founded the TENNESSEE VALLEY AUTHORITY. Later Democratic Congresses devoted themselves to expanding and modifying these laws. In 1934, Congress founded the SECURITIES AND EXCHANGE COMMISSION and the FEDERAL COMMUNICATIONS COMMISSION and passed the Trade Agreements Act, the National Housing Act, and various currency acts. The second phase of the New Deal (1935–41), while continuing with relief and recovery measures, provided for social and economic legislation to benefit the mass of working people. The SOCIAL SECURITY system was established in 1935, the year the NATIONAL YOUTH ADMINISTRATION and WORK PROJECTS ADMINISTRATION were set up. The WAGES AND HOURS ACT was passed in 1938. The Revenue Acts of 1935, 1936, and 1937 provided measures to democratize the Federal tax structure. A number of New Deal measures were invalidated by the Supreme Court, however; in 1935 the NRA was struck down and the following year the AAA was invalidated. The President unsuccessfully sought to reorganize the Supreme Court. Meanwhile, other laws were substituted for legislation that had been declared unconstitutional. The New Deal, which had received the endorsement of agrarian, liberal, and labor groups, met with increasing criticism. The speed of reform slackened after 1937, and there was growing Republican opposition to the huge public spending, high taxes, and centralization of power in the executive branch of government; within the Democratic party itself there was strong disapproval from the "old guard" and from disgruntled members of the BRAIN TRUST. As the prospect of war in Europe increased, the emphasis of government shifted to foreign affairs. There was little retreat from reform, however; at the end of World War II, most of the New Deal legislation was still intact. See Basil Rauch, *History of the New Deal 1933–1938* (1944); Arthur Schlesinger, Jr., *The Coming of the New Deal* (1959) and *The Politics of Upheaval* (1960); Morton Keller, ed., *The New Deal: What Was It?* (1963).

New Delhi (dĕl′ē), city (1971 pop. 292,857), capital of India, Delhi union territory, N central India, on the right bank of the Jumna River. Predominantly an administrative center, it was constructed between 1912 and 1929 to replace Calcutta as capital of British India; New Delhi was officially inaugurated in 1931. The city is also a transportation hub and trade center with textile mills, printing plants, and light industrial facilities. Designed by architects Sir Edwin Lutyens and Herbert Baker, New Delhi has broad, symmetrically aligned streets that provide vistas of historic monuments. Between the main government buildings a broad boulevard, the Raj Path, leads east to west from a massive war memorial arch (built 1921) through a great court to the resplendent sandstone and marble government house (formerly the viceroy's palace; now the residence of India's president). In the southern section of the city is the prayer ground where Mahatma Gandhi was assassinated (1948). In the west are Balmiki and Lakshminarayan temples, which Gandhi frequented. The city has a large sports stadium and numerous medical institutes.

New Democratic party (NDP), Canadian political party, founded in 1961 when the Co-operative Commonwealth Federation (CCF) reorganized itself and entered into close ties with Canadian labor unions, especially the Canadian Labor Congress (CLC). The CCF, formed in 1932, began as a largely W Canadian federation of farm, labor, and socialist groups with a democratic socialist program of increased welfare measures, moderate nationalization, and government economic planning. It had some success, especially in western provinces, and was the majority party in Saskatchewan (1944-64). The NDP has put less emphasis on specific socialist proposals in an attempt to broaden its appeal. Under the leadership of Thomas C. Douglas and, from 1971 to 1974, David Lewis, the party improved its showing in E Canada, but its main strength remained in the west, where, in the early 1970s, it formed provincial governments in Manitoba, Saskatchewan, and British Columbia. As a result of the 1972 elections, the NDP, with 31 seats in the federal House of Commons, held the balance of power between the major Liberal and Progressive Conservative parties and provided the Liberal Prime Minister Pierre Trudeau with his parliamentary majority. This situation ended in 1974, when the NDP lost half of its seats. See S. M. Lipset, *Agrarian Socialism* (2d ed. 1968); W. D. Young, *The Anatomy of a Party* (1969).

New Economic Policy (NEP), official economic reconstruction program of the USSR from 1921 to 1928. It replaced the economic policies of "war Communism" (1918–21), an emergency program established by Lenin during the civil war. War Communism had included forced requisition of grain, nationalization of all trade and industry, strict control of labor, payment in kind, and confiscation of financial capital. As a result of this program and of the ravages of the war, industrial and agricultural production declined sharply, and the population suffered severe deprivation. General unrest erupted in an insurrection in the Kronstadt naval base. At this time (March, 1921) Lenin introduced the NEP in order to revive the economy. The new program signified a return to a limited capitalist system. Forced requisition of grain was replaced by a specific tax in kind; peasants could retain excess produce and sell it for a profit. Smaller businesses were permitted to operate as private enterprises. Large industries remained under state control. They operated on the open market, but the state controlled the fixing of prices and the appointment of boards of directors. Private trade and wages were restored, and compulsory labor service was abolished. By 1928, the NEP had raised the Soviet national income above its prewar level. However, the NEP policies proved inadequate for expansion and were reversed (1928) by the first FIVE-YEAR PLAN. See A. G. Mazour, *Soviet Economic Development* (1967); Eugene Zaleski, *Planning for Economic Growth in the Soviet Union, 1918–1932* (tr. 1971); E. H. Carr and R. W. Davies, *Foundations of Planned Economy* (2 vol., 1971).

New England, name applied to the region comprising six states of the NE United States—MAINE, NEW HAMPSHIRE, VERMONT, MASSACHUSETTS, RHODE ISLAND, and CONNECTICUT. The region is thought to have been so named by Capt. John Smith because of its resemblance to the English coast (another source has it that Prince Charles, afterward Charles I, inserted the name on Smith's map of the country). Topographically it is partly cut off from the rest of the nation by the Appalachian Mts. on the west. From the Green Mts., the White Mts., and the Berkshire Hills, the land slopes gradually toward the Atlantic Ocean. Many short, swift rivers furnish waterpower. The Connecticut River is the region's longest river. Because of the generally poor soil, agriculture was never a major part of the region's economy. However, excellent harbors and nearby shallow banks teeming with fish made New England a fishing and commercial center. Shipbuilding was important until the end (mid-1800s) of the era of wooden ships. During the colonial period the region carried on a more extensive foreign commerce than the other British colonies and was therefore more affected by the passage of the British NAVIGATION ACTS. New England was the major center of the events leading up to the American Revolution, particularly after 1765, and was the scene of the opening engagements of the Revolution. The return of peace necessitated a reorganization of commerce, with the result that connections were made with the American Northwest and China. The War of 1812 had an adverse effect on the region's trade, and opposition to the war was so great that New England threatened secession (see ESSEX JUNTO; HARTFORD CONVENTION). After the war the growth of manufacturing (especially of cotton textiles) was rapid, and the region became highly industrialized. A large part of the great migration to the Northwest originated there. Agriculture dwindled with the growth of the West. Prior to the Civil War, the section furnished leaders for most of the social and humanitarian movements, and it has long been a leading literary (see AMERICAN LITERATURE) and educational center of the country. The geographic and early political conditions developed a New England type of British stock, generally referred to as Yankee; according to tradition, he has a genius for self-government, thrift, generosity to a cause considered worthy, and general resourcefulness. Numerically, the Yankees have been almost outstripped, especially in S New England, by numerous waves of immigrants from Europe. After World War II the character of New England industry changed. Traditional industries (e.g., shoe and textile) have been superseded by such modern industries as electronics. Tourism, long a source of income for the region, greatly increased, and people came to New England from all parts of the country for both winter and summer vacations. Stone quarrying, dairying, and potato farming are important. Boston has long been the chief urban center of New England. See the works of Van Wyck Brooks, Perry Miller, and Samuel E. Morison; W. B. Weeden, *Economic and Social History of New England, 1620–1789* (1890, repr. 1963); C. M. Andrews, *The Fathers of New England* ("Chronicles of America" series, Vol. VI, 1919); J. T. Adams, *The History of New England* (3 vol., 1923–27, repr. 1971); R. P. T. Coffin, *New England* (1951); Andrew Hepburn, *Guide to New England* (1969).

New England Confederation, union for "mutual safety and welfare" formed in 1643 by representatives of the colonies of Massachusetts Bay, Plymouth, Connecticut, and New Haven. They met in Boston and adopted a written constitution binding the colonies in a league as "The United Colonies of New England." The chief purpose of the league was coordination of defense and the settlement of boundary disputes; the internal affairs of each colony were to be left to its own management. Questions of war and peace and other matters of common concern were to be determined by a body of eight commissioners, two from each of the colonies. Six commissioners were required to form a working majority. Meetings of the board were to be held at least once a year. The burden of expense for war was to be levied against the four colonies in proportion to the male population of each between the ages of 16 and 60. The first experiment in federation in America, the league was based upon compromise. Its chief weaknesses lay in the inability of the commissioners to do much more than advise and in the petty rivalries among the colonies. Massachusetts Bay, having by far the largest population, had to furnish more fighting men and taxes than any other colony and felt aggrieved at not having more power in the confederation. In 1653, Massachusetts Bay flatly refused to undertake the war against the Dutch that the confederation planned. Maine and the Narragansett Bay settlements (Rhode Island) sought admission to the union but were refused on political and religious grounds. Shortly before New Haven was annexed (1665) to Connecticut, the regulations were changed so that the commissioners would meet once every three years, but the confederation gradually declined. It revived between 1675 and 1676 to undertake its most important task, completely breaking the power of the Indians of S New England in KING PHILIP'S WAR. With the revocation of the Massachusetts charter in 1684, the confederation was dissolved. See H. L. Osgood, *The American Colonies in the Seventeenth Century* (3 vol., 1904–7, repr. 1957).

New England Conservatory of Music, at Boston, Mass.; coeducational; est. 1867, chartered and opened 1870. It is closely associated with the Boston Symphony Orchestra and the Berkshire Music Center at Tanglewood. Jordan Hall, its main auditorium, is noted for recitals and performances by outstanding artists.

New England Primer, famous American school book, first published before 1690. Its compiler was Benjamin Harris, an English printer who emigrated to Boston. This was the book from which most of the children of colonial America learned to read. The letters of the alphabet were illustrated by rhymed couplets (e.g., "The idle Fool/Is whipt at School") and woodcuts; the lessons frequently contained moral texts based on the Old Testament. The book was reprinted many times, with various changes in text and even in title. Although it has been estimated that as many as 2 million were sold in the 18th cent., copies of the book are now rare. See P. L. Ford, ed., *The New England Primer* (1897, repr. 1962).

New Forest, densely wooded area and ancient royal hunting ground, Hampshire, S England, bounded by the Avon and Solent rivers and Southampton Water. William I organized the area in 1079 as a royal forest to provide revenue and timber. Since 1877 the Court of Verderers has administered the area as a public park. It presently consists of c.145 sq mi (380 km), of which 102 sq mi (264 sq km) belong to the crown and 44 sq mi (114 sq km) are wooded. The woods contain mostly oak and beech trees; there are extensive tracts of bog and heath, and about a fourth of the land is cultivated. Pigs, cattle, and ponies are raised. Lyndhurst and Ringwood are towns in the New Forest.

Newfoundland (nyo͞o′fənlənd, nyo͞ofənlănd′), province (1971 pop. 522,104), 156,185 sq mi (404,519 sq km), E Canada. It is sometimes called **Newfoundland and Labrador.** The province consists of the island of Newfoundland and adjacent islands (1971 pop. 493,938), 43,359 sq mi (112,300 sq km), and the mainland area of Labrador and adjacent islands (1971 pop. 28,166), 112,826 sq mi (292,219 sq km). The capital is ST. JOHN'S. Newfoundland island lies at the mouth of the Gulf of St. Lawrence and is bounded on the north, east, and south by the Atlantic Ocean and separated on the northwest from Labrador by the Strait of Belle Isle. Labrador, part of the LABRADOR-UNGAVA peninsula, forms the northeastern tip of the Canadian mainland. It is bounded on the east by the Atlantic Ocean down to the Strait of Belle Isle and on the south and west by Quebec. Cape Chidley, Labrador's northernmost point, is on the Hudson Strait. Newfoundland has a rocky, irregular coast, indented with numerous inlets. The major portion of the island is a plateau, with many lakes and marshes, and with forests covering less than half the area. Throughout the province the in-

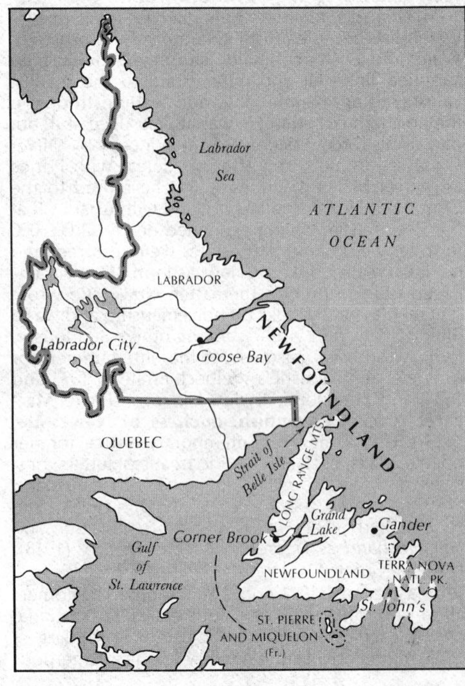

land wilderness has an abundance of fur-bearing animals, waterfowl, and fish, while caribou graze on the tundra of the northern wasteland. The cod-fishing area of the Grand Banks is probably the best in the world. Cod, lobster, herring, and salmon are caught throughout the coastal waters. The province has a generally cool and moist climate. In Labrador, the cold Labrador current, bringing temperatures below freezing eight months of the year, and the lack of transportation facilities have combined to retard economic development. However, Labrador is rich in mineral resources (iron, copper, graphite, nickel, zinc), timber, and waterpower. Exploitation of the tremendous iron reserves in the southwest lake district, begun in the 1950s, and the growth of the logging industry have brought new towns and roads. A giant hydroelectric project has been built at Churchill Falls. Mining is the main industry, and Newfoundland is the leading Canadian province in iron production. The processing of fish and the manufacture of wood products are also important. There are large pulp and paper mills at GRAND FALLS and CORNER BROOK, both on Newfoundland. Agriculture in the province is limited by the unfavorable soil and climate, and much of the food supply must be imported. Nearly half the population lives in St. John's or the surrounding Avalon Peninsula. Corner Brook is the second largest city. Most of the inhabitants are of English or Irish descent, but in Labrador there are small numbers of Indians and Eskimo. The Beothuk Indians on the island of Newfoundland died out in the 19th cent. Vikings visited the area c.1000 and briefly established a settlement on Newfoundland. A Portuguese, João Vaz Corte Real, sailed to Newfoundland in 1472, and after the two voyages of John Cabot at the end of the century, fishermen and explorers from several European countries came to the area. Sir Humphrey Gilbert claimed Newfoundland for England in 1583. The first settlers arrived in 1610. France contested England's claims and Newfoundland changed hands several times. The Treaty of Paris of 1763 definitively awarded Newfoundland and Labrador (where the French had established trading posts) to Great Britain, although France retained the fishing rights on the northwest coast of Newfoundland that had been granted by the Peace of Utrecht in 1713. In 1783 the "French Shore" was redefined to include the entire western coast. In the early 19th cent. the Hudson's Bay Company developed the fur trade, and this, together with the expansion of the fishing industry, led to increased immigration from Europe, particularly Ireland. Representative government was introduced in 1832 and parliamentary government in 1855. The port of Heart's Content became the western terminal of the transatlantic cable in 1866. In 1869 the voters of Newfoundland rejected union with Canada; in 1895, after a disastrous fire in St. John's and the failure of local banks, negotiations to join Canada resumed but were unsuccessful. Relatively little attention had been paid to Labrador, but in 1895 iron ore was discovered in the Grand Falls (now Churchill Falls) region. As part of the Anglo-French Entente Cordiale of 1904, France abandoned the French Shore. Possession of Labrador was disputed between Quebec and Newfoundland until 1927, when the British Privy Council demarcated the western boundary, enlarged its land area, and confirmed Newfoundland's title to it. During the economic depression of the 1930s, Britain suspended Newfoundland's self-government and assumed administrative and financial control. Actual authority was exercised by a joint commission of Newfoundlanders and British. During World War II, U.S. and Canadian military bases were established in Labrador and on Newfoundland. After the war Newfoundland voted to join Canada, and in 1949 it became Canada's tenth province. See A. B. Perlin, *The Story of Newfoundland* (1959); Dorothy Henderson, *The Heart of Newfoundland* (1965); G. W. S. J. Chadwick, *Newfoundland: Island into Province* (1967).

Newfoundland, breed of massive, powerful WORKING DOG developed in Newfoundland, probably in the 17th cent., and later perfected in England. It stands from 25 to 28 in. (63.5–71.1 cm) high at the shoulder and weighs from 110 to 150 lb (49.9–68.1 kg). Its dense, flat-lying coat is coarse and rather oily and is usually a dull jet black in color. The Landseer type of Newfoundland is one in which the color is other than solid black, the most frequent being black with white markings. The precise origin of the Newfoundland is obscure, but the most convincing evidence points to the crossbreeding of arctic and other dogs native to Newfoundland with the ship dogs of European fishermen. Specimens of the resulting breed, similar to the modern variety but smaller, were then brought to England, where their size and appearance were refined. The Newfoundland is an excellent water dog and has been used to rescue drowning people. It also has been a popular draft animal, particularly on its native island. Today it is raised for show competition and as a family companion, being especially gentle with children. See DOG.

Newfoundland and Labrador: see NEWFOUNDLAND, Canada.

New France: see CANADA.

New Galicia: see NUEVA GALICIA.

Newgate (nyōō'gĭt), former prison in the City of London, England, originally in the gatehouse of the principal west gate of London. Dating from the 12th cent. and burned by Wat Tyler's followers in 1381, it was rebuilt in the 15th cent. with funds bequeathed by Sir Richard Whittington. The great fire of 1666 damaged it, and the Gordon rioters partially burned it again in 1780. In the 19th cent. Newgate was a target of Elizabeth Fry's efforts to improve prison conditions. After 1868, executions were held within the prison rather than outside, where they had been attracting huge crowds of sensation-seekers. After 1880 the prison was used only for pre-trial detention, and in 1902 it was torn down.

New General Catalog or **NGC,** standard reference list of NEBULAS. It is based on the General Catalog, published in 1864, which included 2,500 nebulas cataloged by William Herschel and an additional 2,500 cataloged by his son, John Herschel. The General Catalog was combined with work of other observers and the resulting total of more than 7,800 entries was published as the New General Catalog of Nebulae by J. Dreyer in 1888. This work was updated by publication of two Index Catalogs (IC), in 1895 and 1910. More than 13,000 objects are listed in these works, of which more than 12,000 are extragalactic nebulas (galaxies). Some nebulas listed in the NGC are also listed in the MESSIER CATALOG, e.g., the Andromeda Galaxy is listed both as NGC 224 and as M31.

New Glasgow, town (1971 pop. 10,849), N N.S., Canada, on East River. It is an industrial town located in a coal region. Steel products are manufactured, and there is a large pulp mill nearby.

New Granada (grənä'də), former Spanish colony, N South America. It included at its greatest extent present Colombia, Ecuador, Panama, and Venezuela. Between 1499 and 1510 a host of conquerors explored the Caribbean coast of Panama and South America. After 1514, Pedro Arias de Ávila was successful in assuring permanent colonization of the isthmus of Panama. At Santa Marta (1525) and Cartagena (1533), Spanish control of the Colombian coast was firmly established, and in the next few years the northern hinterland was explored. German adventurers, notably Nikolaus Federmann, penetrated the Venezuelan and Colombian llanos between 1530 and 1546. By far the greatest of the conquerors was Gonzalo JIMÉNEZ DE QUESADA, who in 1536 ascended the Magdalena River, climbed the mighty Andean cordillera, where he subdued the powerful Chibcha (an advanced Indian civilization), and by 1538 had founded Santa Fé de Bogotá, later known simply as BOGOTÁ. He named the region El Nuevo Reino de Granada [the new realm of Granada]. During the next 10 years the conquest was virtually completed. No civil government was established in New Granada until 1549, when an audiencia, a body with both executive and judicial authority, was set up in Bogotá. To further stabilize colonial government, New Granada was made a presidency (an administrative and political division headed by a governor) in 1564, and the audiencia was relegated to its proper judicial functions. Loosely attached to the viceroyalty of Peru, the presidency came to include Panama, Venezuela, and most of Colombia. Disputes with—and the great distance from—Lima led to the creation (1717) of the viceroyalty of New Granada, comprising Colombia, Ecuador, Panama, and Venezuela. Later the captaincy general of Venezuela and the presidency of Quito were detached, creating a political division that was to survive the revolution against Spain and the efforts of Simón Bolívar to establish a republic of Greater Colombia. The struggle for independence began in 1810, and by 1830 Venezuela and Ecuador had seceded, and the remnant (Colombia and Panama), was renamed the Republic of New Granada. This became the Republic of Colombia in 1886, from which the present Panama seceded in 1903. See R. B. C. Graham, *The Conquest of New Granada* (1922, repr. 1967); C. R. Markham; *The Conquest of New Granada* (1912, repr. 1971); J. M. Henao and Gerardo Arrubla, *History of Colombia* (tr., 2 vol., 1938; repr. 1972).

New Guinea (gĭn'ē), island (1970 est. pop. 3,200,000), c.342,000 sq mi (885,780 sq km), SW Pacific, N of Australia; the world's second largest island after Greenland. Politically it is divided into two sections: the Indonesian province of Irian Barat (West Irian or West New Guinea; formerly Netherlands New Guinea) in the west; and the self-governing country of Papua New Guinea in the east. The island is c.1,500 mi (2,410 km) long and c.400 mi (640 km) wide at the center. Largely tropical, it has vast mountain ranges such as the Owen Stanley and the Bismarck mts.; Djaja Peak (16,503 ft/5,030 m) in Irian Barat is the highest point. The lower courses of the large rivers (the Fly, Sepik, Mamberamo, and Purari) are generally swampy, with a few grassy plains. The inhabitants of New Guinea are Melanesians, Negritos, and Papuans, some of whom, in the more inaccessible regions, still practice headhunting and cannibalism. The fauna, generally similar to that of Australia, consists largely of marsupials and monotremes, with venomous snakes among the reptiles. The island is known for its many unique species of butterflies and birds of paradise. There are mangrove and sandalwood forests; some timber is exported. Agriculture, largely for subsistence, forms the basis of New Guinea's economy. Sweet potatoes constitute the principal food crop. Agricultural products, some of which are grown on European-owned plantations and exported, include copra, cocoa, coffee, pyrethrum, sisal hemp, rubber, kapok, sago, sugarcane, coconuts, nutmeg, and tobacco. Pearl-shell culture and tortoise fishing are carried on along the coasts. Although some gold, silver, and manganese are mined and oil is extracted in Irian Barat, much of the area remains unexploited. New Guinea was probably first sighted by the Portuguese explorer Antonio d'Abreu in 1511 and was named for its resemblance to the Guinea coast of W Africa. During the next two centuries, the island was visited by Europeans from many nations. In 1828 the Dutch formally annexed the western half of the island, and in 1885 the British proclaimed a protectorate over the southeastern coast and the adjacent islands under the name of British New Guinea; in the same year, the Germans took possession of the northeast. Australia obtained control of British New Guinea in 1905 and renamed it the Territory of Papua. During World War I, Australian forces occupied the German-controlled region in the northeast, which was mandated to Australia by the League of Nations in 1920. Renamed the Territory of New Guinea, this area became a UN trust territory under Australian control after World War II. The island was the scene of bitter fighting between Japanese and Allied forces. In 1949 the territories of Papua and New Guinea were merged administratively, and in 1973 they were united into a self-governing country that was slated for complete independence from Australia sometime in the 1970s. Netherlands New Guinea was transferred to Indonesian administration in 1963 and became a province in 1969.

New Guinea, Territory of: see PAPUA NEW GUINEA.

Newham, borough (1971 pop. 235,700) of Greater London, SE England, on the Thames River. Newham was created in 1965 by the merger of the county boroughs of East Ham and West Ham, part of the metropolitan London borough of Woolwich, and part of the municipal borough of Barking. Newham is residential in the northeast. The Royal Docks and associated industries are in the south; chemical factories and railroad yards predominate in the northwest. Few buildings in the borough are more than a century old, because the area's growth stemmed largely from London's 19th-century industrial expansion. The southwest especially suffered from slum conditions; much of it was destroyed during World War II and was rebuilt in the 1960s. Joseph Lister and Gerard Manley Hopkins were born in West Ham.

New Hampshire, state (1970 pop. 737,681), 9,304 sq mi (24,097 sq km), NE United States, in New England, one of the Thirteen Colonies. It is bounded on the north by the Canadian province of Quebec, on the east by Maine and the Atlantic Ocean, on the south by Massachusetts, and on the west by the Connecticut River, which separates it from Vermont. CONCORD is the capital and third largest city; the largest city is MANCHESTER, followed by NASHUA. The continental ice sheet once covered the entire state and, in receding, scraped the mountains, peneplained the intervening upland areas, and rerouted the water courses into precipitous streams and beautiful lakes. Across the north central part of the state the residual White Mountains of the Appalachian chain form ranges abruptly broken by notches cut into their rocky walls. Between the Carter-Moriah Range and the Presidential Range in the east,

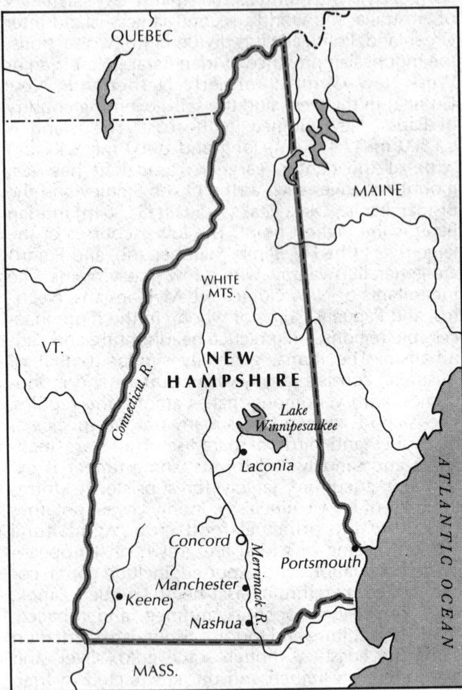

the Ellis River drops 80 ft (24 m) through Pinkham Notch. West of the Presidential Range (which includes Mt. Washington, highest peak in New England at 6,288 ft/1,917 m), the cascading courses of the Ammonoosuc and Saco rivers divide it from the Franconia Mountains at Crawford Notch. To the southwest Franconia Notch overlooks the famous Old Man of the Mountain, beneath which the Pemigewasset tumbles on its way to join the Merrimack. The northernmost gap, Dixville Notch, is surrounded by rocky pinnacles that look down upon a wild, fir-covered country abounding in lakes and streams. South of the mountains the lake and upland area is frequently interrupted by isolated peaks called "monadnocks" from the original Monadnock in SW New Hampshire. Practically every part of the state is within sight of, and identifies itself with, some peak. Along the coast the ocean tempers the climate, but inland there are great temperature extremes. Occasional high winds and violent storms roar through the narrow valleys and rebound off the rocky walls. Annual precipitation is about 40 in. (102 cm), with snowfall mounting to 8 ft (2.4 m) in the mountain regions. Intensive agriculture is hampered by the mountainous topography and by extensive areas of unfertile and stony soil, but seaward and westward the land surface declines to the broad valley of the Connecticut River, and the upper Connecticut valley (known as Coos country) is pleasantly pastoral. Farmers are helped by the cooperative marketing that has expanded since World War II. Their main sources of income are dairy products, eggs, cattle, and greenhouse products. Hay, apples, sweet corn, and potatoes are the chief crops. However, since the late 1800s manufacturing has been predominant. Based upon the percentage of population employed by industry, New Hampshire is one of the most industrialized states in the union. In recent years it has been the only New England state to gain in manufacturing employment; its unemployment rate is well below the national average. Industry is concentrated in the intervales of the rivers, where the abundant water power has been harnessed. Leading products are leather and leather goods (such as shoes and boots), electrical and other machinery, textiles and related products, and paper and paper products. Lumbering has been important since the first sawmill was built on the Salmon Falls River in 1631. The virgin forests of spruce, fir, and hardwoods that once covered the entire state have been logged off, but today second growth extends over much of the land, and the production of lumber, maple sugar, and pulp and paper are major industries, especially in the north. Printing and publishing are also important enterprises. The state's only port, Portsmouth, is situated on the estuary of the Piscataqua River. Its busy naval base, which has been building ships since 1800, is a commercial center in the state. Although New Hampshire has long been known as the Granite State, its large deposits of granite—used for building as early as 1623—are no longer extensively quarried. The use of steel and concrete in modern construction has greatly decreased the granite market. Today sand and gravel, stone, clays, and feldspar are the state's leading minerals. In 1962 the White Mts. were discovered to be an important potential source of thorium, an expensive nuclear fuel. Nevertheless, mineral production remains a minor factor in New Hampshire's economy. Second only to industry in economic importance is the year-round tourist trade. Modern transportation and improved highways have enabled more and more people to enjoy the state's beaches, mountains, and lakes. The largest lake, beautiful Winnipesaukee, is dotted with 274 inhabitable islands, while along the Atlantic shore 18 mi (29 km) of curving beaches (many state-owned) attract vacationists. Of the rugged Isles of Shoals off the coast, three belong to New Hampshire. Originally fishing colonies, they are now used largely as summer residences. In the winter skiers flock north, and the state has responded to the increasing popularity of winter sports by greatly expanding its facilities. When the snows melt, skiers are replaced by equally enthusiastic climbers. Native crafts such as wood carving, weaving, and pottery making have been revived to meet the tourist market. New Hampshire has 142 state parks and forests, and the White Mountains National Forest, which extends into Maine, has c.724,000 acres (293,000 hectares) in New Hampshire. The state's scenic beauty and serenity have long inspired writers and artists. Hawthorne, Whittier, and Longfellow summered in New Hampshire. Augustus Saint-Gaudens sculpted many of his finest works at the artist's colony at Cornish, and the MacDowell Colony at Peterborough is a summer haven for musicians, artists, and writers; their ranks have included E. A. Robinson and Thornton Wilder. The state is most intimately connected with the works of Robert Frost; Frost himself once said that there was not one of his poems "but has something in it of New Hampshire." The region was first explored by Martin Pring (1603) and Samuel de Champlain (1605). In 1620 the Council for New England, formerly the Plymouth Company, received a royal grant of land between lat. 40°N and 48°N. One of the Council's leaders, Sir Ferdinando Gorges, formed a partnership with Capt. John Mason and in 1622 obtained rights between the Merrimack and Kennebec rivers, then called the province of Maine. By a division Mason took (1629) the area between the Piscataqua and the Merrimack, naming it New Hampshire. The first permanent colony had been established at Dover some time before 1628. Portsmouth was founded by Anglican farmers and fishermen in 1630. In 1638 the Rev. John Wheelwright, banished from Massachusetts on a charge of antinomianism, founded Exeter; in the same year a Puritan group settled at Hampton. Thus at a time when theological doctrine was of great importance, three conflicting religious positions were represented in four towns. Through claims based on a misinterpretation of its charter, Massachusetts annexed S New Hampshire between 1641 and 1643. Although New Hampshire was proclaimed a royal colony in 1679, Massachusetts continued to press land claims until the two colonies finally agreed on the eastern and southern boundaries (1739–41). Although they were technically independent of each other, the crown habitually appointed a single man to govern both colonies until 1741, when Benning Wentworth was made the first governor of New Hampshire alone. Wentworth and his friends purchased the Mason rights in 1746 (see Masonian Proprietors under MASON, JOHN, 1586–1635), laying claim to lands E of the Hudson and thereby provoking a protracted controversy with New York (see NEW HAMPSHIRE GRANTS). Although a royal order in 1764 established the Connecticut River as the western boundary of New Hampshire, the dispute flared up again in the American Revolution and was only settled when Vermont became a state. The French and Indian Wars had prevented colonization of the inland areas, but once the hostile Indians were thoroughly defeated a land rush began. Lumber camps were set up and sawmills were built along the streams. The Scotch-Irish settlers had already initiated the textile industry by growing flax and weaving linen. By the time of the Revolution many of the inhabitants had tired of British rule and were eager for independence. In Dec., 1774, a band of patriots overpowered Fort William and Mary (later Fort Constitution) and secured the arms and ammunition for their cause. New Hampshire was the first colony to declare its independence from Great Britain and to establish its own government (Jan., 1776). In the American Revolution, Gen. John Stark and Gen. John Sullivan were among the notable New Hampshire men to serve the patriot cause. After the war an economic depression, marked by severe deflation, a shortage of currency, and unequal distribution of taxation, moved the people to open protest against the state legislature. Forces under General Sullivan put down the protest without bloodshed (1786). Largely through the efforts of John Langdon, New Hampshire became the ninth and last necessary state to ratify (1788) the new Constitution of the United States. The Federalists dominated political activity at first; the gradual rise to power of the Jeffersonians resulted in the DARTMOUTH COLLEGE CASE (1819), in which Daniel Webster, New Hampshire's famous native son, acted as counsel for the Federalist trustees of Dartmouth. In the same year New Hampshire abolished state support of the Congregational Church through the Toleration Act. New Hampshire's northern boundary was fixed in 1842 when the WEBSTER-ASHBURTON TREATY set the international line between Canada and the United States. The Democrats remained in political control until their inability to take a united antislavery stand brought about their decline. When Franklin Pierce, New Hampshire's only President of the United States (1853–57), tried to smooth over the slavery quarrel and unite his party, antislavery sentiment was strong enough to alienate many of his followers. During the Civil War, New Hampshire was a strong supporter of the Northern cause and contributed many troops to the Union forces. After the war its economy began to emerge as primarily industrial, and population growth was steady although never spectacular. The production of woolen and cotton goods and the manufacturing of shoes led all other enterprises. The forests were rapidly and ruthlessly exploited, but in 1911 a bill was passed to protect big rivers by creating forest reserves at their headwaters, and since that time numerous conservation measures have been enacted and large tracts of woodland have been placed under state and national ownership. The Great Depression of the 1930s severely dislocated the state's economy, especially in the one-industry towns. The effort made then to broaden economic activities has been continually intensified. The recent establishment of important new industries such as electronics has successfully counterbalanced the departure to other states of older industries such as textiles. New Hampshire's present constitution was adopted in 1784; it is the second oldest in the country. New Hampshire is the only state in which amendments to the constitution must be proposed by convention; once every seven years a popular vote determines the necessity for constitutional revision. The state's executive branch is headed by a governor and five powerful administrative officers called councillors. The governor is elected for a two-year term and is traditionally limited to two successive terms. Perhaps the most unusual feature of New Hampshire politics is the size of its bicameral legislature (General Court); it is one of the largest representative bodies in the Western world, with 24 senators and from 375 to 400 representatives, all elected for two years. The state elects two Senators and two Representatives to the U.S. Congress and has four electoral votes. The New Hampshire presidential primary is the first to be held in election years and has often forecast national trends or influenced important political decisions. Republicans have played the dominant role in New Hampshire politics since the Civil War, but the growth in population over the past 25 years has tended to strengthen the Democratic party, especially in the industrial cities. The first Democratic governor in 40 years was elected in 1962. Meldrim Thomson, Jr., a Republican, was elected governor in 1972 and was reelected in 1974. Among the state's more prominent institutions of higher learning are the Univ. of New Hampshire, at Durham, and Dartmouth College, at Hanover. See F. B. Sanborn, *New Hampshire* (1904); E. S. Stackpole, *History of New Hampshire* (5 vol., 1917); Federal Writers' Project, *New Hampshire: A Guide to the Granite State* (1938); Cornelius Weygandt, *The Heart of New Hampshire* (1944); James Squires, *The Granite State of the United States* (1956); K. W. Jennison, *New Hampshire* (1944, repr. 1961); W. H. Frye, *New Hampshire as a Royal Province* (1908, repr. 1970); R. F. Upton, *Revolutionary New Hampshire* (1936, repr. 1971); Jeremy Belknap, *The History of New Hampshire* (3 vol., 1784–92; repr. 1971), R. N. Hill, *Yankee Kingdom* (rev. ed. 1972).

New Hampshire, University of, at Durham; land-grant and state supported; coeducational; chartered

1866, opened 1868 as the state college of agriculture and mechanic arts, a division of Dartmouth College, at Hanover. It moved in 1892 and in 1923 became the Univ. of New Hampshire. In addition to agriculture and university extension services, it maintains agricultural and engineering experiment stations at Durham and forestry and agricultural development programs. In 1963 the state colleges at Keene and Plymouth became part of the university. The school has a noteworthy creative arts center.

New Hampshire chicken, dual-purpose breed of POULTRY that is no longer grown commercially. It is retained for its genetic input into modern breeding programs.

New Hampshire Grants, early name (1749–77) for Vermont, given because most of the early settlers came in under land grants from Benning Wentworth, the colonial governor of New Hampshire. Although the 1664 charter for New York set New York's eastern boundary at the Connecticut River, it was modified by Connecticut in 1683, and Massachusetts in 1749 (officially 1757), at a line 20 mi (32 km) E of the Hudson River (c.45 mi/70 km W of the Connecticut River). Governor Wentworth, assuming that the line would be carried farther north, proceeded without authority to issue a grant for the settlement of Bennington in 1747, and in the next few years he issued numerous grants in the region. New York protested the infringement, but the French and Indian Wars intervened, and it was not until after 1760 (when Wentworth had resumed making grants) that the matter was brought before British authorities. In 1763 a decision in New York's favor was rendered, but it was difficult to enforce. The speculators, who had the grants, and the settlers who came in under them, opposed the New York claims. The GREEN MOUNTAIN BOYS were organized, with resistance led by Ethan ALLEN. Violence resulted, and in 1777 the New Hampshire Grants declared themselves independent of both New York and New Hampshire; they entered the Union under the name of Vermont.

New Harmony, town (1970 pop. 971), Posey co., SW Ind., on the Wabash River; founded 1814 by the HARMONY SOCIETY under George Rapp. In 1825 the Harmonists sold their holdings to Robert Owen and moved to Economy, Pa., where their sect survived for another 78 years. Owen established a communistic colony in New Harmony that gained prominence as a cultural and scientific center and attracted many noted scientists, educators, and writers. Dissension arose, and in 1828 the community ceased to exist as a distinct enterprise, although the town remained an intellectual center. The nation's first kindergarten, first free public school, first free library, and first school with equal education for boys and girls were all established there. Today 25 old Rappite buildings remain. See G. B. Lockwood, *The New Harmony Communities* (1902, repr. 1971); K. J. Arndt, *George Rapp's Harmony Society, 1785–1847* (rev. ed. 1972).

New Haven, city (1970 pop. 137,707), New Haven co., S Conn., a port of entry where the Quinnipiac and other small rivers enter Long Island Sound; inc. 1784. Firearms and ammunition, prestressed concrete, shirts, tools, pyrotechnic devices, rubber products, and door locks are among the many manufactures. The city is an educational center, being the seat of YALE UNIVERSITY and its allied institutions and of Albertus Magnus College and Southern Connecticut State College. New Haven was founded in 1637–38 by Puritans led by Theophilus Eaton and John Davenport. It was one of the first planned communities in America and was the chief town of a colony that later included Milford, Guilford, Stamford, Branford, and Southold (on Long Island). Its government was theocratic; religion was a test for citizenship, and life was regulated by strict rules (see BLUE LAWS). In 1665 the colony was reluctantly united with Connecticut; it was joint capital with Hartford from 1701 to 1875. In the late 18th and early 19th cent. New Haven was a thriving port. Manufacturing grew, and New Haven firearms, hardware, and coaches and carriages became famous products. New Haven was raided by a British and Tory force in the American Revolution, and the port was blockaded during the War of 1812. The world's first commercial telephone exchange was established there in 1879. The city today centers upon a large public green, dating from 1680, on which stand three churches built between 1812 and 1816—Center and United churches (both Congregational) and Trinity Church (Episcopal). Many old buildings have been preserved, and there is a historic district. Landmarks in the city are two traprock cliffs—West Rock, with the Judges' Cave, and East Rock. Since the 1950s, New Haven has received national attention for its pioneering urban renewal projects. The nation's first antipoverty program began there in 1962. Despite these improvements, the city suffered a serious racial riot in 1967. A state mental health center is there. Noah Webster and Eli Whitney lived in New Haven and are buried in the city. See R. G. Osterweis, *Three Centuries of New Haven, 1638–1938* (1953); F. Powledge, *Model City* (1971).

New Hebrides (hĕb'rĭdēz), Fr. *Nouvelles Hébrides,* island group (1972 est. pop. 86,000), c. 5,700 sq mi (14,760 sq km), South Pacific, E of Australia. The islands are jointly governed by France and Great Britain. New Hebrides is a 450-mi (724-km) chain of 80 islands, of which the most important are ESPIRITU SANTO (the largest), EFATE, Malekula, Malo, Pentecost, and Tanna. The administrative center, Vila, is on Efate. The group is forested and mountainous, with the highest peak (c.6,195 ft/1,890 m) on Espiritu Santo. The chief industries are copra production, tuna fishing, manganese mining, and cattle raising. The economy is controlled by Australians, British, and French. The natives are predominantly Melanesians, with some Polynesians; there are also Chinese settlers and Vietnamese laborers. Because of the many mutually unintelligible native tongues, Pidgin English has become the lingua franca. The New Hebrides were discovered by the Portuguese navigator Pedro Fernandez de Queiros in 1606. Capt. James Cook made the first systematic exploration of the islands in 1774. English missionaries began arriving in the early 19th cent. With them came the "sandalwooders," who, once the local sources of sandalwood ran out, began kidnapping natives for the sugar and cotton plantations in Queensland, Australia. British attempts to halt the decimation of the native population met success in 1887, when the islands were placed under an Anglo-French naval commission. The commission was replaced by a condominium in 1906. Each power has sovereignty over its own nationals but no territorial sovereignty. Natives owe allegiance to neither Great Britain nor France. There is joint administration on all levels, with resident commissioners (representatives of the British and French high commissioners) stationed at various places in the island group.

New Hyde Park, village (1970 pop. 10,116), Nassau co., SE N.Y., on Long Island; inc. 1927. It is a residential community with some manufacturing. Thomas Dongan, a governor (1682–88) of colonial New York, lived there.

New Iberia, city (1970 pop. 30,147), seat of Iberia parish, S La., on Bayou Teche, which is connected to the Intracoastal Waterway by a canal; inc. 1836. It is a processing center for a sugarcane, oil, dairy, vegetable farm, rock salt, and fishing area. The city has carbon plants, salt mines, canneries, shipyards, and factories making microwave ovens and custom-built homes. Acadian refugees from Nova Scotia settled there beginning c.1765, and French is still spoken by many of the inhabitants. Numerous old houses are in the area; among them are "Justine" (1822) and "Shadows on the Teche" (1834), a classic example of Greek revival architecture. A sugarcane festival is held in New Iberia every September. Nearby are many wildlife refuges, sheltering a multitude of migratory birds.

Ne Win, U (o͞o nä wĭn), 1911–, Burmese soldier and political leader. His original name was Shu Maung, which he abandoned for Ne Win in 1941 when he was a member of the nationalist military group supported by the Japanese. He became commander of the Burmese Independence Army in 1943 and later campaigned against the Japanese. After independence from Great Britain was achieved in 1948, he became Indonesian defense minister. In 1958 he deposed his old associate, U NU, and took the office of prime minister. U Nu returned (1960–62) to office, but Ne Win removed him again, assuming the posts of prime minister and minister of defense. His transformation of Burma into a police state and his "Burmese Way to Socialism" failed to solve the country's pressing economic problems. Under the new constitution adopted (1974) Ne Win became president.

Newington, town (1970 pop. 26,037), Hartford co., central Conn., a suburb of Hartford; settled 1670, inc. 1871. Although chiefly residential, it has some manufacturing. A large tuberculosis sanatorium and a veterans hospital are in the town.

New Ireland, volcanic island (1970 pop. 50,600), c.3,340 sq mi (8,650 sq km), SW Pacific, in the BISMARCK ARCHIPELAGO, part of Papua New Guinea. New Ireland is largely mountainous, rising to c.4,000 ft (1,220 m). Much of the island is under cultivation, especially the east coast. Kavieng is the chief town and port. The island was first sighted in 1616 but until 1797 was thought to be part of New Britain, from which it is separated by a 20-mi (32-km) channel. The island was a German protectorate from 1884 to 1914 and was called Neu Mecklenburg (New Mecklenburg) by the Germans.

New Jersey, state (1970 pop. 7,168,164), 7,836 sq mi (20,295 sq km), E United States, one of the Middle Atlantic states and one of the Thirteen Colonies. The capital is TRENTON. Surrounded by water except along the 50 mi (80 km) of northern border with New York state, New Jersey is bounded on the east by the Hudson River, New York Bay, and the Atlantic Ocean and on the south and west by Delaware Bay and the Delaware River (which separate it from Delaware and Pennsylvania). The northern third of New Jersey lies within the Appalachian Highland region, where ridges running northeast and southwest shelter valleys containing pleasant streams and glacial lakes. Beyond the crest of wooded slopes are long-established farms given over to dairying and field crops. The Kittatinny Mts., with the state's highest elevations (up to 1,803 ft/550 m), stretch across the northwest corner of New Jersey from the

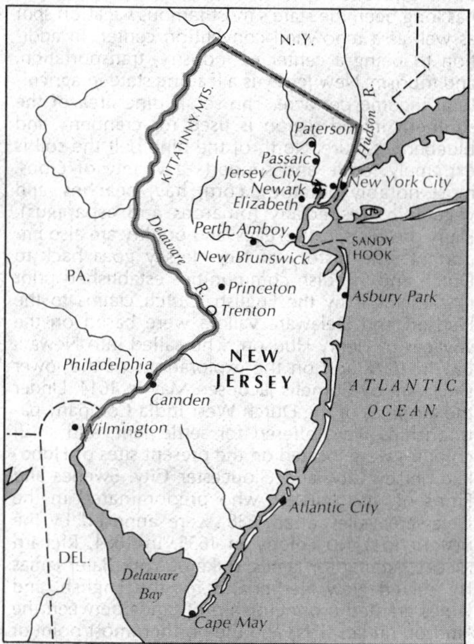

New York border to the spectacular DELAWARE WATER GAP. Southeast of the Highlands lie the Triassic lowlands or piedmont plains, extending from the northeastern border to Trenton and encompassing every major city of the state except CAMDEN and ATLANTIC CITY. The monotony of the lowlands is broken by ancient trap-rock ridges that extend to the Palisades of the Hudson, and many commuter towns are located along the wooded slopes. East of NEWARK and HACKENSACK acres of tidal marshes have been converted to industrial use. Drainage is provided by the state's major rivers, the Passaic, the Raritan, and the Hackensack. The busy lowlands give way in the south to the coastal plains, which cover more than half the state. The coast itself is highly developed as a resort area. Sandbars make large harbors impractical but provide 115 mi (185 km) of sheltered waterways that have made possible a superior combination of bay and ocean facilities. Only four states are smaller in size than New Jersey, yet New Jersey ranks eighth in the nation in population, a fact indicative of its economic importance. It is an industrial giant, a major transportation terminus, a long-established playground for summer vacationers, and a year-round commuter area pouring thousands daily into New York City and Philadelphia. The state is noted for its output of chemicals and pharmaceuticals, machinery, processed foods, and a host of other products, including electronic equipment and missile components. Rubber and textiles are also produced (notably at PATERSON and PASSAIC), as well as silk goods and synthetics. The hub of New Jersey industry is Newark, the largest city, but Camden, the largest Jersey port on the Delaware River, is also important. Although stone, zinc, and sand and gravel are the state's only native mineral resources of consequence, it is a center for copper smelting and refining as well as the nation's third largest producer of titanium concentrate. BAYONNE is the terminus of pipelines originating in Texas and Oklahoma, and there are oil refineries at LINDEN. A tremendous transportation system, concentrated in the industrial lowlands, funnels state products and a huge volume of interstate traffic to the seaports of Newark, HOBOKEN, JERSEY CITY, and PERTH AMBOY and to the New York area. New Jersey has a massive concentration of railroad trackage. Great highways like the Garden State Parkway, the New Jersey Turnpike, and the Pulaski Skyway are part of a network of toll roads and freeways. New Jersey is linked to Delaware and Pennsylvania by many bridges across the Delaware River. Traffic to and from New York is served by railway tunnels and by the facilities of the PORT AUTHORITY OF NEW YORK AND NEW JERSEY—the double-decked George Washington Bridge, the Lincoln and Holland vehicular tunnels, and three bridges to Staten Island. Airports are operated by many cities, and Newark airport (controlled by the Port Authority) ranks among the world's busiest. Shipping in New Jersey centers on the ports of the Hudson River and New York Bay area, with relatively minor seagoing traffic on the Delaware as far north as Trenton. Because of this extensive transportation network, New Jersey's ocean beaches, inland lakes, forests, and mountain areas have become the basis for a thriving vacation industry. Atlantic City in particular has long been the state's most famous vacation spot as well as a renowned convention center. In addition to being a center of industry, transportation, and tourism, New Jersey is a leading state in agricultural income per acre. The scrub pine area of the southern inland region is used for cranberry and blueberry culture. North of the pine belt the soil is extremely fertile and supports a variety of crops, most notably potatoes, corn, hay, peaches, and vegetables (especially tomatoes and asparagus). Dairy products, cattle, eggs, and poultry are also important. The history of New Jersey goes back to Dutch and Swedish communities established prior to settlement by the English. Dutch claims to the Hudson and Delaware valleys were based on the voyages of Henry Hudson, who sailed into Newark Bay in 1609, and on the explorations of the lower Delaware by Cornelis Jacobsen May in 1614. Under the auspices of the Dutch West India Company patroonships were offered for settlement, and small colonies were located on the present sites of Hoboken, Jersey City, and Gloucester City. Swedes and Finns of NEW SWEDEN, who predominated in the Delaware valley after 1638, were annexed by the NEW NETHERLAND colony in 1655. In 1664, Richard NICOLLS, acting for James, duke of York (later James II), seized New Netherland for the English, and James granted proprietorship of lands between the Hudson (at lat. 41°N) and the northernmost point of the Delaware to Lord John BERKELEY and Sir George CARTERET. Nicolls, unaware of the transaction, permitted New England religious dissenters to buy Indian land in the Elizabethtown and Monmouth purchases. Carteret and Berkeley encouraged settlement through a liberal charter, free land grants, and provisions for an appointed council and an elected assembly. New Jersey remained under proprietary rule until it was returned to the crown in 1702. During that period New Jersey's history was marked by land title disputes, dubious business transactions, and frequent changes of authority. Out of this confusion certain trends emerged, which were significant in the evolution of the area. The first trend stemmed from the fact that the original grants to Berkeley and Carteret divided the region in two. The split was further defined in the Quintipartite Deed of 1676, which divided the province into East and West Jersey; in 1680 the line was specified as running from Little Egg Harbor to the northernmost branch of the Delaware. Subsequent cultural and economic developments have preserved the tie between N New Jersey and New York, and S New Jersey and Philadelphia. The second trend, toward a popular flouting of constituted authority, appeared in protests against such proprietary demands as quitrents, and later in frequent refusals to submit to the dictates of royal governors. East Jersey was held by Carteret and governed by his cousin Philip CARTERET, until the former's death in 1680 (except for a brief period of Dutch reoccupation in 1673–74, after which Carteret lost the Elizabethtown and Monmouth purchases.) In 1681, William Penn and 11 other Quakers purchased East Jersey from Carteret's widow. Within a year ownership was extended to 12 other proprietors, and from that time the land was subdivided by sale, Scottish proprietors playing a major part in development. A board of proprietors was set up (1684) to assist in governmental affairs, and Perth Amboy became the capital. In West Jersey the Berkeley interests were sold in 1674 to John FENWICK, acting in partnership with Edward Byllynge, and the following year Fenwick and other Quakers founded a settlement at Salem. Financial difficulties resulted in the intervention of William Penn and other Quakers, who purchased the Fenwick rights (except those to Salem) in 1677 and held West Jersey jointly with Byllynge. A constitution was framed, and the first assembly met at the capital, Burlington, in 1681. The Byllynge title was bought by Dr. Daniel Coxe in 1687 and sold to the West Jersey Society in 1692. In both Jerseys confusion resulting from the unwieldy number of landowners together with widespread resentment against authority caused the proprietors to surrender voluntarily their governmental powers to the crown in 1702, although they retained their land rights. New Jersey's independence from New York was recognized, but authority was vested in the governor of New York until 1738, when Lewis MORRIS was appointed governor of New Jersey alone. Until Trenton became the capital in 1790, the legislature met in alternate years at Perth Amboy and Burlington. Under the royal governors the same problems persisted—land titles were in dispute and opposition to the proprietors culminated in riots in the 1740s. East Jersey took on the somber color of Calvinism, implanted by Scottish and New England settlers, while in West Jersey the Quakers soon developed a landed aristocracy with strong political and economic influence. Anti-British sentiment gradually spread from its stronghold in East Jersey throughout the colony and took shape in Committees of Correspondence. Though the Tory party was to prove strong enough to raise six Loyalist battalions, the patriot cause was generally accepted, and in June, 1776, the provincial congress adopted a constitution and declared New Jersey a state. Because of its strategic position, New Jersey was of major concern in the American Revolution. Washington's memorable Christmas attack on the Hessians at Trenton in 1776, followed by his victory at Princeton, restored the confidence of the patriots. In June, 1778, Washington fought another important battle in New Jersey, at Monmouth. Altogether, about 90 engagements were fought in the state, and Washington moved his army across it four times, wintering twice at MORRISTOWN. At the Federal Constitutional Convention in 1787, the delegates from New Jersey sponsored the cause of the smaller states and carried the plan for equal representation in the Senate. New Jersey was the third state to ratify (Dec., 1787) the Constitution of the United States. By this time New Jersey's population had grown from an estimated 15,000 in 1700 to approximately 184,000. Agriculture had been supplemented by considerable mining and processing of copper and iron and by the production of lumber, leather, and glass. During the next 50 years, a period of enormous economic expansion, the dominance of the landed aristocracy gave way to industrial growth and to a more democratic state government. The important textile industry, powered by the falls of the Passaic, was initiated at Paterson. Potteries, shoe factories, and brickworks were built. Roads were improved, the Morris Canal and the Delaware and Raritan canals were chartered, and the Camden and Amboy RR completed a line from New York to Philadelphia with monopoly privileges. Prior to the Civil War an era of reform resulted in the framing of a new state constitution (1844) in which property qualifications for suffrage were abolished, provisions were made for the popular election of the governor and the assemblymen, and a balance of power and responsibility was established among the executive, legislative, and judicial departments. In spite of some pro-Southern sentiment, New Jersey recruited its quota of regiments in the Civil War and gave valuable financial aid to the Union. The war demands proved lucrative for commerce and industry, and the expanding labor market attracted large numbers of European immigrants. By 1865 the pattern of the state's development was molded. Population and industry showed rapid and steady growth. Large economic interests grasped control of political power, giving rise to sporadic but unsustained popular movements for reform. The Camden and Amboy RR was transferred by lease to the Pennsylvania RR in 1871, and its monopolistic power was lessened by legislation opening the state to all rail lines and by the assessment and taxation of railroad properties. After the 1870s easy incorporation laws and low corporation tax rates attracted new trusts to incorporate through "dummy" offices in the state. There was much liberal sentiment against the power of "big business." A general reform movement sponsored by Woodrow WILSON when he was governor (1910–12) resulted in such legislation as the direct primary, a corrupt practices act, and the "Seven Sisters" acts for the regulation of trusts (later repealed). The state voted predominantly Democratic from the Civil War until 1896. Since that time it has frequently voted Republican in national elections, and in state politics it has often divided power between Democratic governors and Republican legislatures. The powerful political machine of Frank Hague, centered in Jersey City, wielded great influence in the Democratic party from 1913 to 1949, when it was defeated by insurgents within its ranks. In 1947 a new constitution was framed and accepted to replace the antiquated constitution of 1844. The liberal Bill of Rights was preserved and extended, governmental departments were streamlined, the cumbersome court system was simplified, the executive power was strengthened, and labor's right to organize and bargain collectively was recognized. In 1966 another convention was called to rewrite those portions of the 1947 constitution invalidated by application of the U.S. Supreme Court's "one man, one vote" rule to state legislatures. The convention drafted sweeping revisions, which were approved by the electorate in Nov., 1966. A six-day race riot in Newark in July, 1967, drew attention to the urgent need for social and political reform in many of the state's urban centers. The election of Kenneth A. Gibson as Newark's mayor in 1970 and in 1974 was considered an auspicious sign by many, but the legacy of corrupt machine politics remains a serious obstacle to change at all levels of government. During the early 1970s the state government proposed plans for massive urban renewal and economic development projects. The New Jersey legislature consists of a senate of 40 members, elected to serve four-year terms, and an assembly of 80 members, elected for two-year terms. The governor serves a four-year term and may be reelected once. Brendan Byrne, a Democrat, became governor in 1974. New Jersey sends 15 Representatives and 2 Senators to the U.S. Congress and has 17 electoral votes. In the important area of water resources and rights, New Jersey signed the DELAWARE RIVER BASIN COMPACT in 1961 with three other states and the Federal government. New Jersey's two best-known institutions of higher learning were established in the 18th cent.—Princeton Univ., at Princeton, as the College of New Jersey in 1746; and Rutgers Univ., mainly at New Brunswick, as Queen's College in 1766. Included among other New Jersey educational institutions are Fairleigh Dickinson Univ., with three campuses; Seton Hall Univ., mainly at South Orange; and Stevens Institute of Technology, at Hoboken. The Institute for Advanced Study, at Princeton, is one of the leading research centers of the country. See I. S. Kull, ed., *New Jersey: A History* (5 vol., 1930); H. E. Wildes, *The Delaware* (1940) and *Twin Rivers: The Raritan and the Passaic* (1943); J. E. Pomfret, *The Province of West New Jersey, 1609-1702* (1956) and *The Province of East New Jersey, 1609-1702* (1962); R. J. Vecoli, *The People of New Jersey* (1965); J. T. Cunningham, *This Is New Jersey* (new ed. 1968) and *Colonial New Jersey* (1971); J. S. Cawley and Margaret Cawley, *Exploring the Little Rivers of New Jersey* (3d ed. 1971); S. M. Groff, *New Jersey's Historic Houses* (1971); C. L. Lundin, *Cockpit of the Revolution* (1940, repr. 1972); Federal Writers' Project, *New Jersey: A Guide to Its Present and Past* (1939, repr. 1972); J. E. Pomfrett, *Colonial New Jersey* (1973).

New Jersey College for Women: see RUTGERS UNIV.

New Jerusalem, Church of the, or **New Church,** religious body instituted by the followers of Emanuel SWEDENBORG, who are generally called Swedenborgians. Knowledge of Swedenborg's teachings was spread in England largely by two clergymen, Thomas Hartley and John Clowes, and a printer, Robert Hindmarsh. The first public services of an organized congregation were held (1788) in London. In 1789 a general conference met. In the United States, Swedenborg's teachings were introduced (1784) by James Glen, member of a London society. A New Church society was formed (1792) in Baltimore, and in 1817 a general convention of the New Jerusalem in the United States of America was organized. In polity it is a modified episcopacy, with each society enjoying great freedom in administering its own affairs. A general convention is held annually. The teachings of the church stress individual self-realization through study of Swedenborg's interpretation of the Scriptures. In 1890 a number of members broke their connection with the general convention to form a separate organization, which in 1897 took the name "General Church of the New Jerusalem." This body regarded Swedenborg's theological writings as "the very Word of the Lord revealed at his second coming." See his theological works; Robert Hindmarsh, *Rise and Progress of the New Jerusalem Church* (1861); M. B. Block, *The New Church in the New World* (1932, repr. 1968); Helen Keller, *My Religion* (1960).

New Kensington, city (1970 pop. 20,312), Westmoreland co., SW Pa., on the Allegheny River, in a coal-mining area; laid out 1891 on the site of Fort Crawford (1778), inc. as a city 1933. Aluminum products, the chief manufacture, have been made there since 1892. A branch of Pennsylvania State Univ. is in New Kensington.

New Lanark, Scotland: see LANARK.

Newlands, Francis Griffith, 1848-1917, American legislator, b. Natchez, Miss. After practicing law in San Francisco from 1870, he moved (1888) to Nevada. He became well known for his interest in irrigation and reclamation and for his advocacy of free silver. He was (1893-1903) U.S. Congressman from Nevada and served (1903-17) as a Democrat in the U.S. Senate. He wrote the Newlands Act of 1913, concerning mediation and conciliation in labor controversies, and the Reclamation Act of 1902. He played an important role in the establishment of the Federal Trade Commission (1914) and in preparing the way for the Transportation Act of 1920. See M. F. Hudson, ed., *Francis G. Newlands: His Work* (1914); A. B. Darling, ed., *Public Papers of Francis G. Newlands* (2 vol., 1932).

Newlands, John Alexander Reina, 1838-98, British chemist. He studied at the Royal College of Chemistry in London and worked as an industrial chemist. Newlands prepared the first periodic table of elements arranged in the order of atomic weights and pointed out the "Law of Octaves," i.e., that every eighth element has similar properties. His idea was ridiculed by his colleagues but was vindicated five years later when the Russian chemist D. I. Mendeleev published a more developed form of the table.

Newlands project, on the Carson and Truckee rivers, W Nev.; one of the first projects built by the U.S. Bureau of Reclamation (1903-8). The project irrigates c.71,500 acres (28,935 hectares); grains and truck crops are grown and livestock is raised. Lahontan Dam (completed 1915) produces electricity for the project.

New Laws: see LAS CASAS, BARTOLOMÉ DE.

New London, city (1970 pop. 31,630), New London co., SE Conn., on the Thames River near its mouth on Long Island Sound; laid out 1646 by John Winthrop, inc. 1784. It is a deepwater port of entry, with shipbuilding, textile, and food-processing industries. A privateers' rendezvous during the Revolution, New London survived a partial burning by Benedict Arnold in 1781 and a British blockade during the War of 1812. The city reached the height of its maritime prosperity in the 19th cent., when it flourished as a shipping, shipbuilding, and whaling and sealing port. The last whaler ceased operations in 1909, and the excellent harbor is now used mainly by the U.S. navy as a submarine base and by yachtsmen and students of the United States Coast Guard Academy (located in the city). Annual Yale-Harvard boat races are held on the Thames. Connecticut College and a junior college are at New London; the city also has a whaling museum, an art museum, and many old buildings, including the Hempsted House (1678) and the old town mill (1650; built by John Winthrop). The New London Lighthouse (1760) was rebuilt in 1801. Old Fort Trumbull, built in 1849 on the site of a Revolutionary fort, now houses a U.S. navy underwater sound laboratory. Nathan Hale taught school in New London, and Richard Mansfield, Sarah Knight, and Bishop Samuel Seabury are buried there.

Newman, Barnett, 1905-71, American artist, b. New York City. A member of the New York school, Newman was one of the first to reject conventional notions of spatial composition in art. In his severe *Stations of the Cross* series (1958-66), he divided raw canvas vertically at intervals by black or white bands of various widths. In later color-field paintings (e.g., *Who's Afraid of Red, Yellow, and Blue IV?*, 1969-70) Newman used large areas of primary color as the sole source of visual and emotional impact. See study by Thomas B. Hess (1971).

Newman, Ernest, 1868-1959, English music critic. An instructor at Midland Institute, Birmingham (1903-05), he joined the staff of the Manchester *Guardian* in 1905, the Birmingham *Daily Post* in 1906, the London *Observer* in 1919, and *The Times* of London in 1920. Outstanding among his writings is his *Life of Richard Wagner* (4 vol., 1933-46). He translated Albert Schweitzer's *J. S. Bach* and Romain Rolland's *Beethoven the Creator* and wrote many important books on music.

Newman, John Henry, 1801-90, English churchman, cardinal of the Roman Catholic Church, one of the founders of the OXFORD MOVEMENT, b. London. He studied at Trinity College, Oxford, and held a fellowship at Oriel College, where he became tutor (1826) after his ordination (1824) in the Church of England. He was made vicar of St. Mary's, Oxford, in 1827 and was (1831-32) select preacher to the university. In 1832 he resigned his tutorship after a dispute over the religious duties of a tutor and went on a Mediterranean tour with Hurrell Froude. While he was on this trip he wrote "Lead, Kindly Light" and other hymns. After John KEBLE preached the celebrated sermon "National Apostasy" in the summer of 1833, Newman threw himself into the discussion that ensued and in September began the *Tracts for the Times*. These, joined with his sermons given at St. Mary's, provided constant guidance and inspiration to the Oxford movement. About 1840, Newman began to lose faith in the position he had taken, and an article by Nicholas WISEMAN led him to reconsider the Roman Catholic claims. In 1841 his Anglican career came to a crisis; in that year Newman published *Tract 90*, demonstrating that the Thirty-nine Articles, the formulary of faith of the Church of England, were consistent with Catholicism. It created a great outcry from Anglicans everywhere and a ban on the *Tracts for the Times* from the bishop of Oxford. Newman now went into retirement at Littlemore (a chapelry attached to St. Mary's), where he remained for more than a year, living with a group of men in a sort of monastic seclusion. He gave up his living in Sept., 1843, and in 1845 was received into the Roman Catholic Church. The chief literary products of Newman's retirement consisted of the *Essay on Miracles* and the *Essay on the Development of Christian Doctrine*. In 1846 he went to Rome, where he received ordination and a doctorate of divinity. He entered the Oratorians (see ORATORY, CONGREGATION OF THE) and came back to England (1847) filled with the idea of extending the church in England by means of the Oratory. After living at various places he settled at Edgbaston (on the outskirts of Birmingham); there, in the Oratory he founded, he remained the rest of his life. Newman's life was marked by several unpleasant public events, the first of these being a libel suit against him by an Italian ex-friar named Achilli. Newman lost the suit, but was later exonerated, and a great fund was publicly raised to defray the expense and the fine he had incurred. In 1854 the bishops of Ireland tried to found a Catholic university in Dublin and made Newman its head; he found himself in difficulties at once, and the ill-planned project was abandoned. Newman's theories appearing in his *Idea of a University Defined* (1873) were chiefly developed about this time; he believed that education should be moral training rather than instruction and proposed in token support of his position the founding of a Roman Catholic hall at Oxford to provide Catholics with the advantages of Catholicism and university training together. This (1858) was opposed by Henry MANNING and the English hierarchy, much to Newman's disappointment. Newman's reputation in England was greatly enhanced soon after this by one of the most celebrated incidents of his career, the controversy with Charles KINGSLEY. This began in 1864 when Kingsley remarked in a review that the Catholic clergy was not interested in the truth for its own sake. After several exchanges Newman published the *Apologia pro vita sua* (1864), a masterpiece of religious autobiography, undoubtedly its author's greatest work. A few years later an ambitious work of another kind appeared, the *Grammar of Assent* (1870), designing to set forth a sort of logic of religious belief. At this time Newman was involved in an annoying incident that gained more notice than its importance warranted; Newman, who opposed the enunciation at the time of the infallibility dogma, was quoted as denouncing those (including Cardinal Manning) who advocated its definition. He was misunderstood in England, and his enemies (Catholic and non-Catholic) spread rumors in Rome that he opposed the dogma itself. Newman lost favor with the papacy, and it was not until after the death of Pius IX that he regained papal support when Pius's successor, Leo XIII, created him cardinal (1879) at the general demand of English Catholicism. About the same time (1878) Trinity College, Oxford, gave him an honorary fellowship. Cardinal Newman spent his declining years at Edgbaston, loved and admired by his countrymen. Newman's misunderstanding with Manning nevertheless lasted over 30 years. The two cardinals were temperamentally poles apart; Newman had no interest in social reform and Manning no taste for theological controversy. Newman ranks as one of the masters of English prose; his style is simple, lucid, clear, and convincing. His poems, however, never gained a great reputation, except for *The Dream of Gerontius* (1866), which was later set to music by Sir Edward Elgar; and his religious novels, *Loss and Gain* (1848) and *Callista* (1856), are no longer read. For the collected editions of his works, Newman wrote refutations of his own Anglican writings, especially those dealing with Anglicanism as a *via media*. Newman's immediate influence was greatest c.1840, and many Anglicans entered the Roman Catholic Church at his inspiration. His essays retain their vitality and popularity. For selections from his writings, see Geoffrey Tillotson, ed., *Prose and Poetry* (1957); Henry Tristram, ed., *Autobiographical Writings* (1957) and *Catholic Sermons* (1957); James Collins, ed., *Philosophical Readings* (1961). The definitive biography is that of W. P. Ward (1927). See also biographies by Seán O'Faoláin (1952), Meriol Trevor (2 vol., 1962-63), and T. L. Sheridan (1967); studies by A. D. Culler (1955), J. H. Walgrave (tr. 1960), C. F. Harrold (1945, repr. 1966), and H. L. Weatherby (1973).

Newman, Paul, 1925-, American actor, b. Cleveland, Ohio. After performing for several years in television dramas, Newman appeared in numerous and varied films. His enduring, most popular characterization is that of an insolent, casual, and self-reliant anti-hero with a penchant for wry humor, seen in *The Hustler* (1961), *Hud* (1963), *Cool Hand Luke* (1967), *Butch Cassidy and the Sundance Kid* (1969), and *The Sting* (1973). His other notable films include two from plays by Tennessee Williams: *Cat on a Hot Tin Roof* (1959) and *Sweet Bird of Youth* (1962). Newman directed *Rachel Rachel* (1968), starring his wife, Joanne Woodward, and *Sometimes a Great Notion* (1971), in which he starred.

Newmarket, urban district (1971 pop. 12,934), West Suffolk, E England. It has been a racing center since early in the 17th cent. There are four principal races: the One Thousand Guineas, the Two Thousand Guineas, the Cambridgeshire, and the Cesarewitch. One of the courses on Newmarket Heath is crossed by an ancient earthwork known as the Devil's Dyke. In 1974, Newmarket became part of the new non-metropolitan county of Suffolk.

New Mexico, state (1970 pop. 1,016,000), 121,666 sq mi (315,115 sq km), SW United States, admitted to the Union in 1912 as the 47th state. The capital is SANTA FE, and the largest city is ALBUQUERQUE. The state is bounded on the N by Colorado, on the E by Oklahoma and Texas, on the S by Texas and Mexico, and on the W by Arizona. At its northwest corner,

four states (Arizona, Utah, Colorado, and New Mexico) meet at right angles—the only point in the United States where this occurs. New Mexico is roughly bisected by the Rio Grande and has an approximate mean altitude of 5,700 ft (1,737 m). The topography of the state is marked by broken mesas, wide deserts, heavily forested mountain wildernesses, and high, bare peaks. The mountain ranges, part of the Rocky Mts., rising to their greatest height (more than 13,000 ft/3,962 m) in the Sangre de Cristo Mts., are in broken groups, running north to south through central New Mexico and flanking the Rio Grande. In the southwest is the tumbled Gila Wilderness. Broad, semiarid plains, particularly prominent in S New Mexico, are covered with cactus, yucca, creosote bush, sagebrush, and desert grasses. Water is rare in these semiarid regions, where the scanty rainfall is subject to rapid evaporation. Because irrigation opportunities are few, most of the farmland is given over to grazing. There are many large ranches, and cattle and sheep graze year-round on the open range. The two notable rivers besides the Rio Grande—the Pecos and the San Juan—are used for some irrigation; the Carlsbad and Fort Sumner reclamation projects are on the Pecos, and the Tucumcari project is nearby. Other projects utilize the Colorado River basin; however, the Rio Grande, harnessed by the Elephant Butte Dam, remains the major irrigation source for the area of most extensive farming. Cotton lint, grown primarily in the irrigated regions, is a chief crop; in the regions that support dry farming, the major crops are hay, wheat, and sorghum grains. Dairy products are also very important. The harvest of piñon nuts, pinto beans, and chili—crops characteristic of New Mexico—is very picturesque. Much of the state's income is derived from its considerable mineral wealth. In 1972 the state ranked first nationally in the production of uranium ore, manganese ore, potash, salt, and perlite; third in copper ore; and fourth in natural gas, beryllium, and tin concentrates. Petroleum and coal are also found in large quantities. Silver and turquoise have been used in making Indian jewelry since long before the coming of the white man. About one fourth of the land is forested. Pinewood is the chief commercial wood. Millions of acres of the wild and beautiful country of New Mexico are under Federal control as national forests and monuments, and, together with the attractive climate of the state, make tourism a chief source of income. Best known of the state's attractions are the Carlsbad Caverns National Park and the Aztec Ruins National Monument. Thousands of tourists annually visit the White Sands, Bandelier, Capulin Mountain, Chaco Canyon, El Morro, Fort Union, Gila Cliff Dwellings, and Gran Quivira national monuments (see NATIONAL PARKS AND MONUMENTS, table). Use of the land and minerals goes back to the prehistoric time of the early Indian cultures in the Southwest that long preceded the flourishing sedentary civilization of the PUEBLO INDIANS that the Spanish found along the Rio Grande and its tributaries. Many of the Indian pueblos exist today much as they were in the 13th cent. Word of the pueblos reached the Spanish through Cabeza de Vaca, who may have wandered across S New Mexico between 1528 and 1536; they were enthusiastically identified by Fray Marcos de Niza as the fabulously rich Seven Cities of Cibola. A full-scale expedition (1540–42) to find the cities was dispatched from New Spain, under the leadership of Francisco Vásquez de Coronado. The treatment of the Indians by Coronado and his men led to the long-standing hostility between the Indians and the Spanish and made Spanish conquest of the land drawn-out and difficult. An attempt by missionaries to convert the Indians in 1581 led to the death of the friars who headed it. Antonio de Espejo, sent out on an expedition (1582–83) to find the friars, explored much of the country. His report of precious minerals and grazing lands led to the founding of the first regular colony at SAN JUAN by Juan de Oñate in 1598. Almost immediately he was faced with a serious revolt by the Indians of ACOMA, which he severely suppressed. In 1609, Pedro de Peralta was made governor of the "Kingdom and Provinces of New Mexico," and a year later he founded his capital at Santa Fe. The little colony did not prosper greatly, although some of the missions flourished and haciendas were founded. Subjecting the Indians to forced labor caused further trouble. The fierce APACHE INDIANS rose in 1676, and in 1680 came the great Pueblo revolt led by Popé. The Indians fell upon the Spanish and wiped out their settlements, and the survivors were driven entirely out of New Mexico. The Spanish did not return until the stern campaign of Diego de Vargas Zapata reestablished their control in 1692. In the 18th cent., despite sporadic Indian warfare, the development of ranching and of some farming and mining was more thorough, laying the foundations for the Spanish culture in New Mexico that still persists. About one third of the population today is of mixed Spanish descent (many of them, however, fairly recent immigrants from Mexico); until recently Spanish was an accepted official language, and in many isolated communities Spanish is still the dominant tongue. After the LOUISIANA PURCHASE in 1803, Spanish officials tried earnestly to prevent U.S. penetration. However, when Mexico achieved its independence from Spain in 1821, New Mexico became a province of Mexico, and trade was opened with the United States. By the following year the SANTA FE TRAIL was being traveled by the wagon trains of American traders. In 1841, after Texas was established as a republic, a group of Texans embarked on an expedition to assert Texan claims to part of New Mexico; they were captured and treated severely by the Mexican governor. Their treatment may have had some slight effect in bringing on the MEXICAN WAR. That war marked the coming of the Anglo-American culture to New Mexico. Stephen W. Kearny entered (1846) Santa Fe without opposition, and two years later the Treaty of GUADALUPE HIDALGO ceded New Mexico to the United States. The territory, which included Arizona and other territories, was enlarged by the GADSDEN PURCHASE (1853). A bid for statehood with an antislavery constitution was halted by the COMPROMISE OF 1850, which settled the Texas boundary question in New Mexico's favor and organized New Mexico as a territory without restriction on slavery. In the Civil War, New Mexico was at first occupied by Confederate troops from Texas, but was taken over by Union forces early in 1862. After the war and the withdrawal of the troops, the territory was plagued by conflict with the Apache and NAVAHO Indians. Indian troubles continued sporadically in New Mexico and Arizona (made a separate territory in 1863) until the Apache chief Geronimo surrendered in 1886. However, there were local troubles even after that time. Already the ranchers had taken over much of the grasslands. The coming of the SANTA FE RAILROAD in 1879 encouraged the great cattle boom of the '80s. There were typical cow towns, feuds among cattlemen as well as between cattlemen and the authorities (notably the Lincoln County War), and the activities of such outlaws as Billy the Kid. The cattlemen were unable to keep out the sheepherders and were overwhelmed by the homesteaders and squatters, who fenced in and plowed under the "sea of grass." Land claims gave rise to bitter quarrels among the homesteaders, the ranchers, and the old Spanish families, who made claims under the original grants. Despite overgrazing and reduction of lands, ranching survived and continues to be important together with the limited but scientifically controlled irrigated and dry farming. Statehood was granted in 1912. Pancho Villa raided Columbus, N. Mex., in March, 1916. In 1943 the U.S. government built LOS ALAMOS as a center for atomic research. The first atom bomb was exploded at the White Sands Proving Grounds in July, 1945. The growth of military establishments and atomic-energy centers has greatly contributed to the economic advance of New Mexico in recent years. In the early 1970s about one quarter of the personal income in the state came from government payrolls. The climate of the state and the increasing population have aided New Mexico's effort to attract new industries; manufacturing, centered especially around Albuquerque, includes food and mineral processing and the production of chemicals, electrical equipment, and ordnance. New Mexico is governed under the constitution of 1912. The legislature has a senate of 42 members elected for four-year terms and a house of representatives with 70 members elected for two-year terms. The governor is elected for four years. The state elects two U.S. Senators and two Representatives, and has four electoral votes. New Mexico has been generally Democratic in politics. Bruce King, a Democrat, became governor in 1970. Jerry Apodaca, also a Democrat, succeeded him in 1974. The clear, dry air and the startling and grandiose scenery have made the state a place of winter or year-round residence for those seeking health or a place of retirement. Many writers and artists have made their homes in communities such as Taos and Santa Fe. The Apache, Navaho, and Ute Indians live on Federal reservations within the state—the Navaho reservation, with over 16 million acres (6.5 million hectares), is the largest in the country—and the Pueblo Indians, settled, agricultural people, live in pueblos scattered throughout the state (for individual pueblos, see separate articles). The most prominent educational institution in the state is the Univ. of New Mexico, at Albuquerque. See M. H. Hall, *Sibley's New Mexico Campaign* (1960); Federal Writers' Project, *New Mexico: A Guide to a Colorful State* (1940, rev. ed. 1962); W. A. Beck, *New Mexico: A History of Four Centuries* (1962); E. Fergusson, *New Mexico: A Pageant of Three Peoples* (2d ed. 1964); A. K. Gregg, *New Mexico in the Nineteenth Century* (1968); R. W. Larson, *New Mexico's Quest for Statehood* (1968).

New Mexico, University of, mainly at Albuquerque; state supported; coeducational; chartered 1889, opened 1892. It maintains a two-year branch campus at Gallup, an extension center at Taos, and research centers at Los Alamos and Holloman Air Force Base missile development center. It conducts archaeological excavations throughout the state, and its anthropology museum has extensive collections in Southwest history.

New Mexico State University, at Las Cruces; land-grant and state supported; coeducational; chartered and opened 1889 as a college. It became a university in 1960. The school also has campuses at Alamogordo and Farmington, as well as two-year branches at Carlsbad and Grants It maintains statewide extension centers, experimental farms, and agricultural substations.

New Milford. **1** Town (1970 pop. 14,601), Litchfield co., W Conn., on the Housatonic River; inc. 1712. It is situated in a dairy-cattle and poultry region. Its manufactures include concentrated foods, paper products, brass and copper, electronic equipment, and precision instruments. The present town hall there is on the homesite of Roger Sherman, a drafter and signer of the Declaration of Independence. The Canterbury School is in New Milford. **2** Borough (1970 pop. 19,149), Bergen co., NE N.J., on the Hackensack River, a suburb of New York City; inc. 1922. It is primarily residential. New Milford was settled in 1695 by French Huguenots. One of the original homes still stands and another is preserved in replica. A French Huguenot cemetery is also in the borough. In 1776, George Washington's forces crossed the Hackensack River there during their retreat from Fort Lee to Trenton, N.J. Washington used the New Bridge Inn (still standing).

Newnan, city (1970 pop. 11,205), seat of Coweta co., W Ga., in a rich farm and livestock area; inc. 1828.

New Netherland, territory included in a commercial grant by the government of Holland to the DUTCH WEST INDIA COMPANY in 1621. Colonists were settled along the Hudson River region; in 1624 the first permanent settlement was established at Fort Orange (now Albany, N.Y.). The principal settlement in the tract after 1625 was New Amsterdam (later New York City) at the southern end of Manhattan island, which was purchased from the Indians in 1626. Colonization proceeded slowly, hampered by trouble with the Indians, poor administration, and rivalry with New England settlers. In 1664 the territory was taken by the English, who divided it into the two colonies of New York and New Jersey.

new objectivity (Ger. *Neue Sachlichkeit*), German art movement of the 1920s. The chief painters of the movement were George Grosz and Otto Dix, who were sometimes called verists. They created styles of bitter realism and protest that mirrored the disillusionment following World War I. New objectivity retained the intense emotionality of earlier movements in German art (see BRÜCKE and BLAUE REITER), but it abandoned the symbolism of EXPRESSIONISM for direct social commentary. Max Beckmann produced works in a related, though more philosophical, vein.

New Orleans (ôr'lēənz -lənz, ôrlēnz'), city (1970 pop. 593,471), seat of Orleans parish, SE La., between the Mississippi River and Lake Pontchartrain, 107 mi (172 km) by water from the river mouth; founded 1718 by the sieur de Bienville, inc. 1805. It was built within a great bend of the Mississippi (and is therefore called the Crescent City) on subtropical lowlands, now protected from flooding by levees. The river is crossed there by the Huey P. Long Bridge (completed 1935) and the Greater New Orleans Bridge (completed 1958), which is one of the largest cantilever bridges in the country. Lake Pontchartrain is spanned by a spectacular 24-mi (39-km) double causeway (opened 1957). The largest city in Louisiana and one of the largest in the South, New Orleans is a major U.S. port of entry. It has long been one of the busiest and most efficient international ports in the country, second only to New York in dollar value of foreign trade. Coffee, sugar, and bananas are among its imports (the coffee and banana wharves are tourist attractions); exports include oil, petrochemicals, rice, cotton, sulfur, and lumber. Coastwise traffic is heavy (the city is at the junction of the Intracoastal Waterway with the Mississippi River), and New Orleans is a major rail, highway, air, and river focus. It has an international airport. Its fine port (there are more than 62 mi/100 km of wharves) and the bountiful natural resources in the area have made the city one of the leading industrial centers in the South. Food processing is a major enterprise. The city has huge oil and chemical industries, great shipbuilding and repair yards, and plants manufacturing a wide variety of products. Most of the larger industries have been developed recently, but soon after the sieur de Bienville had the city platted in 1718 it took prominence as a port, and in 1722 it became the capital of the French colony. The transfer of Louisiana to Spain by the secret Treaty of Fontainebleau (1762) was confirmed by the Treaty of Paris (1763). New Orleans—deeply involved in the struggle for control of the Mississippi—was returned to French hands only briefly before passing to the United States with the Louisiana Purchase (1803). Nevertheless, the tone of the city's life was dominated by Creole culture until late in the 19th cent., and the French influence is still seen even today. After Andrew Jackson's victory over the British at New Orleans (Jan. 8, 1815) had written a postscript to the War of 1812, the westward movement in the United States carried the queen city of the Mississippi to almost fabulous heights as a port and market for cotton and slaves. New Orleans then was stamped with its lasting reputation for glamour, gay living, elegance, and wickedness. Then as now Negroes were a large element in the population, and they contributed to the exotic flavor of the city. Jazz had its origin in the late 19th cent. among the Negro musicians of New Orleans. The quadroon balls—sumptuous affairs attended by rich whites and their quadroon mistresses—disappeared with the Civil War, but Negro folkways and stories of voodoo magic persist into the 20th cent. The golden era ended when in the Civil War the city fell (1862) to Admiral David G. Farragut and suffered under the occupation by Union troops led by Benjamin F. Butler. New Orleans recovered from Reconstruction and passed through the end of the river-steamboat era to emerge as a modern city. Its past, however, is perhaps a greater factor than the warm, damp climate in attracting visitors and artists and writers. The picturesque French quarter (Vieux Carré) of the old city, north of broad Canal St., is a major tourist attraction. In the heart of the quarter is Jackson Square (the former Place d'Armes); fronting upon the square are the Cabildo (1795; formerly the government building, it now houses part of the Louisiana state museum); St. Louis Cathedral (1794); and other 18th- and 19th-century structures. Several world-famous restaurants, specializing in shrimp, oysters, and fish from nearby waters, uphold the New Orleans tradition of good living, and the annual Mardi Gras is perhaps the best-known festival in the United States. Also adding to the color of the city are the many parks, museums (including a jazz museum and the Isaac Delgado Museum of Art), and gardens. The city has two racetracks. Chalmette National Historical Park, site of the 1815 battle of New Orleans, is to the east (see NATIONAL PARKS AND MONUMENTS, table). New Orleans is also an educational center, the seat of Dillard Univ., Loyola Univ., Tulane Univ., Louisiana State Univ. in New Orleans, the Louisiana State Univ. Medical Center, Delgado Vocational-Technical Junior College, Our Lady of Holy Cross College, and several theological seminaries. The Tulane Univ. campus is the scene of the annual Sugar Bowl football game. A hurricane in Sept., 1965, left many people dead and millions of dollars of property damage. In April, 1973, when the Mississippi River rose to its highest recorded level in Louisiana, New Orleans was saved from inundation by the opening of spillways upstream that diverted much of the river's flow away from the city. The unusual life and history of the city have produced a literature, including the works of George W. Cable, Lafcadio Hearn, Grace Elizabeth King, Charles Gayarré, and Alcée Fortier. See also E. S. Basso, ed., *The World from Jackson Square* (1948); Harnett Kane, *Queen New Orleans* (1949); Federal Writers' Project, *New Orleans City Guide* (rev. ed. 1952); E. L. Tinker, *Creole City* (1953); T. K. Griffin, *New Orleans* (rev. ed. 1964); M. L. Christovich et al., comp., *New Orleans Architecture* (1971–72); L. V. Huber, *New Orleans: A Pictorial History* (1971).

New Philadelphia, city (1970 pop. 15,184), seat of Tuscarawas co., E Ohio, on the Tuscarawas River, in a coal and clay area; founded 1804, inc. 1833. Foundry products, machinery, and pottery are made. The Tuscarawas Regional Campus of Kent State Univ. is there. Nearby is the SCHOENBRUNN VILLAGE STATE MEMORIAL, a reconstruction of the first settlement in Ohio.

New Plymouth, city (1971 pop. 34,314), W central North Island, New Zealand, on the Tasman Sea. It is a port and has iron, copper-product, and other industries. Nearby is an oil field.

Newport, Christopher, 1565?–1617, English mariner, commander of early voyages to Virginia. He commanded a privateering expedition to the West Indies (1592) that returned to England with the Spanish vessel *Madre de Dios*, the richest prize ever taken by the Elizabethan privateers. He was employed by the London Company to command their expeditions to Virginia. On the first voyage he sailed from England with Capt. John Smith and other colonists in Dec., 1606, and arrived near the site of Jamestown in May, 1607. He returned to England in July and sailed again for the colony in October with the "first supply" of emigrants and provisions, reaching Jamestown in Jan., 1608, to find the colonists greatly reduced and in dissension. Later that year he brought the "second supply" from England and explored the country beyond the falls of the James River. On his fourth voyage from England (1609), Newport was wrecked on the Bermudas with Sir Thomas GATES and Sir George SOMERS and did not reach Virginia until May, 1610. In 1611 he made his last voyage to Virginia, taking Sir Thomas DALE to the colony. In his later years Newport made three voyages for the East India Company, dying at Bantam, in present Indonesia, on the last.

Newport. 1 Municipal borough (1971 pop. 22,286), administrative center of the Isle of Wight, S England. It is also a port and the commercial center of the island, with agricultural markets and light industry (plastics, soft drinks, and woodwork). In the 17th cent. King Charles I was imprisoned in nearby Carisbrooke Castle. The town grammar school dates from the early 17th cent. There are remains of a Roman villa in Newport. **2** County borough (1971 pop. 112,048), Monmouthshire, SE Wales, on the Usk River. It is the administrative center of the county. Newport has large steel works. Coal is exported, and iron ore is imported. Aircraft are made, and tin plate, iron, steel, aluminum, and other metal goods are manufactured. In 1839 Newport was the scene of Chartist riots. The Church of St. Woollos, partly Norman, is the cathedral of Monmouth diocese. There are three technical colleges. In 1974, Newport became part of the new nonmetropolitan county of Gwent.

Newport. 1 City (1970 pop. 25,998), seat of Campbell co., N Ky., on the Ohio River opposite Cincinnati and on the east bank of the Licking River opposite Covington; laid out 1791, inc. as a city 1835. It has a large steel-rolling mill, several clothing factories, a brewery, and a lumber mill. It was a station on the Underground Railroad. Various antivice crusades have started there. **2** City (1970 pop. 34,562), seat of Newport co., SE Rhode Island, on Aquidneck (also called Rhode) Island; settled 1639, inc. 1784. The economy of this historic city, a port of entry, revolves chiefly around the many naval installations there. Also important are the summer tourist industry, educational facilities, fishing, and agriculture. William Coddington and John Clarke founded Newport in 1639. Newport and Portsmouth united in 1640 and entered a permanent federation with Providence and Warwick in 1654. Shipbuilding, dating from 1646, and foreign commerce, especially trade in Negro slaves, pineapples, rum, and molasses, brought prosperity. The town early harbored refugees of various groups—Friends and Jews first arrived in the 1650s, and the Seventh-Day Baptists organized a church there in 1671. Jewish merchants contributed greatly to Newport's pre-Revolutionary prosperity, and it became the leading town of the colony. In the American Revolution the British occupied the town (1776–79); many buildings were destroyed, most of the citizens moved away, and Newport never fully regained its former economic prestige. It was replaced in importance by Providence, with which it was joint state capital until 1900. In the 19th cent. Newport developed as a fashionable resort of the very rich, and many palatial mansions were built. Outstanding tourist attractions are The Breakers, the former summer house of Cornelius Vanderbilt, including its stable, which houses a large horse-drawn carriage exhibit; Belcourt Castle; The Elms; Marble House; and Château-sur-Mer. Cliff Walk and Ocean Drive are known for their spectacular views of the ocean and the coastline. Of historic interest are the Wanton-Lyman-Hazard House (c.1675; scene of a Stamp Act riot in 1765); Trinity Church (1726); the beautiful old colony house or statehouse (1739); Touro Synagogue (1763), oldest in the country and since 1946 a national historic site; the Redwood Library and Athenaeum (1747); and the brick market house or city hall (1762). Newport is host to yacht races (including the America's Cup) and tennis tournaments (tennis was popularized there, and the National Tennis Hall of Fame is in the Newport casino). Notable jazz and folk music festivals were held there in the 1950s and 60s. The city is the seat of Salve Regina College, a junior college, and the Naval Academy Preparatory School. The U.S. navy base in Newport was closed in early 1974, creating great unemployment in the city. Newport was hard hit by hurricanes in 1938 and 1954; its historic waterfront is undergoing major redevelopment. Newport Bridge (1969) spans the east passage of Narragansett Bay, linking the city with Jamestown. Matthew Perry was born in Newport. See A. F. Downing and V. J. Scully, *The Architectural Heritage of Newport, Rhode Island, 1640–1915* (1952); M. M. Shea, *The Story of Colonial Newport* (1962); Earl Washburn, comp., *Newport Historic Guide* (3d ed. 1963).

Newport Beach, residential and resort city (1970 pop. 49,422), Orange co., S Calif., on Newport Bay and the Pacific Ocean; inc. 1906. It is a popular seaside resort and yachting center. Manufactures include electronic equipment, plastics, and fiberglass boats.

Newport Jazz Festival, annual summer music festival, originally held at Newport, R.I. Sponsored by Mr. and Mrs. Louis Lorillard and George Wein, the first performance was held in July, 1954. The festival brings together jazz lovers and great figures of the jazz world. It has presented such performers as Louis Armstrong, Dave Brubeck, and Billie Holliday as well as many European artists. Riots caused performance cancellations in 1960, 1969, and 1971, and in 1972 the festival was moved to New York City. Under Wein's direction the Newport Jazz Festival has expanded into a series of festivals held annually in the United States, Europe, Japan, and elsewhere.

Newport News, independent city (1970 pop. 138,177), SE Va., on the Virginia peninsula, at the mouth of the James River, off Hampton Roads, near Norfolk; inc. 1896. It is a major port for transatlantic and intracoastal shipping; commodities handled include coal, oil, tobacco, grain, and ores. Newport News is also one of the world's largest shipbuilding and repair centers. The U.S.S. *Enterprise II*, the first nuclear-powered aircraft carrier, was constructed there. Its manufactures include metal products, building materials, and processed seafood. Newport News was settled by Irish colonists c.1620 but did not grow appreciably until 1880, when it became the terminus of the Chesapeake and Ohio RR; the shipbuilding industry began in 1886. During the Civil War, the U.S. army captured Newport News and established a fortified base and prison camp. In 1862 the famous battle between the ironclad ships *Monitor* and *Merrimac* took place off Newport News. The city's points of interest include the Mariners Museum, the War Memorial Museum of Virginia, the Peninsula Junior Nature Museum and Planetarium, and the Victory Arch (1919, rebuilt 1962). Fort Eustis, with the Matthew Jones House (1660) on the fort's grounds, is there. Christopher Newport College is in the city.

New Providence, borough (1970 pop. 13,796), Union co., NE N.J.; settled c.1720, set off and inc. 1899. It is largely residential but has some light industry, research laboratories, and insurance-company offices. Roses are grown there commercially. Originally called Turkey Town, its name was changed to New Providence in 1778.

New Providence: see BAHAMA ISLANDS.

New Red Sandstone, name for the thick red layer of the Triassic formation in Great Britain (see TRIASSIC PERIOD). It is many thousands of feet thick and is composed chiefly of red sandstones, clays, and conglomerate; the red color and the occurrence of workable quantities of salt and gypsum suggest markedly arid conditions at the time of deposition.

New River, c.320 mi (510 km) long, rising in the Blue Ridge, NW N.C. It flows NE through SW Virginia, then NW into West Virginia where it joins with the Gauley River to form the Kanawha River. It is used extensively to generate electricity. Bluestone Dam (completed 1952), near Hinton, W.Va., provides flood control and power; its reservoir, the second largest in West Virginia, extends 36 mi (58 km) upstream.

New Rochelle (rōshĕl'), city (1970 pop. 75,385), Westchester co., SE N.Y., on Long Island Sound; settled by Huguenots 1688, inc. as a village 1858, as a city 1899. Although mainly a residential suburb of New York City, it has some light industry. The house where Thomas Paine lived has been preserved. Iona College and the College of New Rochelle are in the city.

New Romney (rŭm'nē), municipal borough (1971 pop. 3,414), Kent, SE England, in Romney Marsh. Until the sea receded it lay on the coast and was one of the CINQUE PORTS; many documents concerning the Cinque Ports are kept in the town guildhall. A famous sheep fair is held in New Romney in August. Of several ancient churches, only the partly Norman Church of St. Nicholas remains. Old Romney is a village farther inland.

Newry, urban district (1971 pop. 11,393), Co. Down, SE Northern Ireland, on the Clanrye River and the Newry Canal. It has canal connection with Carlingford Lough, the Bann River, and Lough Neagh. Newry is a seaport with linen mills, tobacco and food processing, and varied manufactures. In the 12th cent. Maurice McLoughlin, king of Ireland, founded an abbey on the site, around which the town grew; the abbey became in 1543 a collegiate church of secular priests and was later dissolved. The town's castle was taken by Edward Bruce in 1315; the duke of Berwick burned part of Newry in his retreat before the forces of the duke of Schomberg in 1689. Newry is the seat of the Roman Catholic bishop of Dromore and contains St. Patrick's parish church (1578), the first Protestant church built in Ireland.

news agency, local, national, international, or technical organization that gathers and distributes news, usually for newspapers, periodicals, and broadcasters. As early as the 1820s a news agency, the Association of Morning Newspapers, was formed in New York City to gather incoming reports from Europe. Other local news agencies sprang up, and by 1856 the General News Association—comprising many important New York City papers—was organized. Out of this agency emerged in the 1870s the New York Associated Press (AP), a cooperative news agency for the New York papers that sold copy to daily papers throughout the country; the United Press (UP) began in 1882. Ten years later these organizations were merged, but the same year a rival agency, the Associated Press of Illinois, was founded. In Europe three international agencies had arisen—Agence Havas of Paris (1835); the Reuter Telegram Company of London (1851), known simply as Reuters; and the Continental Telegraphen Compagnie of Berlin (1849), known as the Wolff Agency. These began as financial-data services for bankers but extended their coverage to world news. By 1866 national agencies were arising in many European countries; they covered and sold news locally only, relying on the major services for coverage and sales abroad. After the Associated Press of Illinois signed exchange contracts with the worldwide networks, the United Press went under (1897). In 1900 the Associated Press of Illinois, desiring to restrict its membership, reincorporated in New York state and was thereafter known as the Associated Press; in 1915, however, the United States forbade the agency to restrict its members' use of other services. A Supreme Court decision in 1945 ended the exclusion of members' competitors. In 1906, William Randolph Hearst founded the International News Service (INS), available to papers of other publishers as well as his own. The United Press Association, usually called United Press although there was no connection with the earlier organization, became an affiliate of the Scripps-Howard newspapers and sold reports to others. The AP, UP, and INS grew steadily, and by the 1930s their foreign operations freed them of dependence on the European agencies, which tended to reflect national viewpoints in political news. The agencies' treatment of news tended toward uniformity, and, in 1958, INS was merged with UP, forming United Press International (UPI). After World War II most Western agencies (except UP and INS) became cooperatives owned by their member publishers. Among these are Reuters and Agence France-Presse (the renamed Agence Havas). Notable cooperatives allied with Reuters include the Canadian Press, the Australian Associated Press, and the Press Trust of India. Government ownership of news agencies stems from 1915, when Germany established a service called Transocean to broadcast war propaganda. In 1918 the USSR founded Rosta, which in 1925 became Tass. Tass, an arm of the Council of Ministers of the RSFSR, serves as the local agency for that republic. In addition it is an international agency with jurisdiction over the agencies of the other Soviet republics. With the expansion of Soviet influence in Eastern Europe, the Balkan agencies allowed their ties with Western international services to dissolve, and they moved into the Tass system. Among the long-established agencies now in the Tass sphere are Polska Ajencja Prasowa of Poland, Magyar Tavirati Iroda of Hungary, and Agerpress of Rumania. Since 1915 news agencies have transmitted most copy over telephone wires to teletypewriters in newspaper offices. The late 1940s, however, brought the introduction of Teletypesetter machines, which receive stories from the agencies in the form of perforated paper tape. The tape is fed into typesetting machines, which it activates without the use of human operators. In using Teletypesetters to save labor, publishers have ceded to the agencies some of their editing prerogative, thereby standardizing usage and writing style in newspaper stories. Most news agencies also offer their clients photographs, news analyses, and special features; for radio and television stations they transmit newsbroadcast scripts. See Kent Cooper, *Barriers Down* (1942, repr. 1969); UNESCO, *News Agencies, Their Structure and Operation* (1953, repr. 1969); Victor Rosewater, *History of Cooperative News Gathering in the United States* (1930, repr. 1971).

New Sarum, England: see SALISBURY.

New School for Social Research, in New York City; coeducational; chartered and opened 1919 as a center for adult education. It has a two-year upper division liberal arts college (est. 1944) and a graduate school. A special program for freshmen was begun in 1972. The school's facilities also include the Human Relations Work Study Center, the Institute for Retired Professionals, and the Center for New York City Affairs. Emphasis is given to adult classes, particularly noncredit and highly specialized courses in social sciences and languages.

New Siberian Islands, Rus. *Novosibirskiye Ostrova,* archipelago, c.10,900 sq mi (28,200 sq km), N Siberian USSR, in the Arctic Ocean between the Laptev and East Siberian seas, part of the Yakut Autonomous Republic. The archipelago is separated into two groups by the Sannikov Strait. The northern group, the New Siberian or Anjou islands (c.8,200 sq mi/21,200 sq km) includes the Kotelny, Faddeyevsky, Novaya Sibir, and other smaller islands; the southern group consists of the LYAKHOV ISLANDS (c.2,700 sq mi/7,000 sq km). The De Long Islands, NE of Novaya Sibir, are also part of the archipelago. The islands are almost always covered by snow and ice and have a very scant tundra; ice dating from the Pleistocene Ice Age and intermingled with sediment is found there. The sparsely settled islands were discovered (1773) by Ivan Lyakhov, a Russian merchant. Mammoth fossils have been found (1870s) in the islands by the Swedish explorer Nils A. E. Nordenskjöld, as well as by Siberian fur and ivory hunters. The islands were neglected until 1927, when metereological stations were set up there.

New Smyrna Beach (smûr'nə), city (1970 pop. 10,580), Volusia co., NE Fla., on Indian River (a lagoon; part of the Intracoastal Waterway) and on Ponce de Leon Inlet of the Atlantic Ocean; inc. 1903. It is a center for citrus-fruit packing, and it has commercial fishing and seafood-processing industries and varied light manufacturing. It is also a tourist city, with 8 mi (11.3 km) of white sand beaches. A Spanish Franciscan mission was established there in 1696 on the site of an Indian village. Colonists arrived in 1767, but the settlement did not prosper until the advent of the railroad in the mid-19th cent. Of interest in the area are a huge Indian mound made of shells and artifacts, and the ruins of a Spanish fort (c.1565) and of a sugar mill (c.1830; burned by Seminoles). A U.S. coast guard station is on Ponce de Leon Inlet.

New South Wales, state (1970 est. pop. 4,567,000), 309,443 sq mi (801,457 sq km), SE Australia. It is bounded on the E by the Pacific Ocean. SYDNEY is the capital. The other principal urban centers are NEWCASTLE, LISMORE, WOLLONGONG, and BROKEN HILL. More than half the population live in the Sydney metropolitan area. Located in the temperate zone, the state has a generally favorable climate. There are four main geographic regions: the coastal lowlands; the eastern highlands, culminating in Mt. Kosciusko (7,314 ft/2,229 m), the highest peak of the Australian Alps and of Australia; the western slopes; and the western plains, which cover about two thirds of the state. The Murray River, which forms the greater part of the southern border, and its principal tributaries are important for the state's extensive irrigation systems. New South Wales is economically the most important state in Australia. The Sydney-Newcastle-Wollongong area is the greatest industrial region in the commonwealth, with steel the principal product. Agriculture is also important: Wheat, wool, and meat are produced, and there is considerable dairy farming. Tropical fruits and sugarcane are grown in the northeast. The state's rich mineral resources include coal, gold, iron, copper, silver, lead, and zinc. The area was first visited in 1770 by Capt. James Cook, who proclaimed British sovereignty over the east coast of Australia. Sydney, the first Australian settlement, was founded in 1788 as a prison farm. During the 1820s and 30s the character of New South Wales changed as the wool industry grew and the importation of convicts ceased. In the early 19th cent. the colony included Tasmania, South Australia, Victoria, Queensland, the Northern Territory, and New Zealand. These territories were separated and made colonies in their own right between 1825 and 1863. In 1901, New South Wales was federated as a state of the Commonwealth of Australia. The Australian Capital Territory (site of CANBERRA, the federal capital), an enclave in New South Wales, was ceded to the commonwealth in 1911. Jervis Bay, S of Sydney, became commonwealth territory in 1915. The nominal head of the state government is the governor, appointed by the British crown on advice of the cabinet; however, actual executive functions are exercised by the premier and cabinet, who are responsible to a bicameral state parliament.

New Spain: see MEXICO, republic.

newspaper, publication issued periodically, usually daily or weekly, to convey information and opinion about current events. The earliest recorded effort to inform the public of the news was the Roman *Acta diurna,* instituted by Julius Caesar and posted daily in public places. In China the first newspaper appeared in Peking in the 8th cent. In several German cities manuscript newssheets were issued in the 15th cent. The invention and spread of the printing press (1430–50) was the major factor in the early development of the newspaper. The Venetian government posted the *Notizie scritte* in 1556, for which readers paid a small coin (*gazetta*). In England in the 17th cent., journalism consisted chiefly of newsletters printed principally by Thomas Archer (1554–1630?), Nathaniel Butter (d. 1664), and Nicholas Bourne (fl. 1622). The London *Gazette,* founded (1665) in Oxford, is still published as a court journal. The first daily paper in England was the *Daily Courant* (1702). Thereafter many journals of opinion set a high standard of literary achievement in journalism—the *Review* (1704–13) of Daniel Defoe; the *Examiner* (1710–11) edited by Jonathan Swift; and the *Tatler* (1709–11) and the *Spectator* (1711–12) of Joseph Addison and Richard Steele. After John Wilkes's successful battle for greater freedom of the press, English newspapers began to reach the masses in the 19th cent. Today some 50,000 newspapers of many sorts are published. British papers have the largest circulations in the Western Hemisphere. Of several present-day London papers born in the 18th cent., *The Times,* founded in 1785 by John Walter, is internationally known. The Manchester *Guardian,* now printed in London, is internationally known as a forthright and independent journal. Other prominent London newspapers include the *Daily Express,* the *Daily Mail,* the *Daily Mirror,* and the *Daily Telegraph.* As in England, the continental newspaper developed in the 17th cent. One of the oldest papers, *Avisa Relation oder Zeitung,* appeared in Germany in 1609; the *Nieuwe Tijdingen* was published in Antwerp in 1616; the first French newspaper, the *Gazette,* was founded in 1631. Major French newspapers today include *Aube, Figaro, France-Soir, Monde,* and *Populaire.* Among newspapers of contemporary Germany are *Tagesspiegel* (Berlin), *Welt* (Hamburg), *Rheinische Merkur* (Coblenz), *Süddeutsche Zeitung* (Munich), *Frankfurter Allgemeine,* and *Frankfurter Rundschau.* Other well-known European newspapers include the *Irish Independent* (Dublin), *Popolo* (Rome), *Corriere della Sera* (Milan), *Osservatore romano* (Vatican), and *Neue Zürcher Zeitung* (Zürich). In 1965 Swedish daily newspapers numbered 119, reaching nearly 100 per cent of the adult population. In the USSR, *Pravda* and *Izvestia* are the daily official newspapers. Newspapers have played an important historical role as the organs of revolutionary propaganda. The most notable of such revolutionary newspapers was *Iskra,* founded by Lenin in Leipzig in 1900. In Asia the leading newspapers include *Jen Min Jih Pao* (Peking), *Asahi Shinbum* (Tokyo), the Hong Kong *Times,* the *Times of India* (Delhi), and the Manila *Times.* The Japanese daily papers have the third greatest circulation in the world. In the United States and several other democratic countries the press has evolved as a fourth estate, free from government authority and responsible to the public. A single number of a newssheet, *Publick Occurrences,* was issued in Boston in 1690 and was then suppressed by royal authority. John Campbell's Boston *News-Letter* endured from 1704 to 1776. Benjamin Franklin founded the *Pennsylvania Gazette* in 1728. Other colonial papers include the *American Weekly Mercury* (Philadelphia), the New York *Gazette,* and the *Maryland Gazette.* The first American daily, the *Pennsylvania Evening Post and Daily Advertiser,* appeared in Philadelphia in 1793. The *Independent Journal* (New York) carried the famous Federalist essays. Two rival political organs were Alexander Hamilton's *Gazette of the United States* and Thomas Jefferson's *National Gazette,* edited by Philip FRENEAU. The first New York daily newspaper was the *Minerva* (1793), edited by Noah Webster. Under other names it survived into the 20th cent. The New York *Evening Post,* for many years edited by William Cullen Bryant, was established in 1801. It is America's oldest newspaper with a continuous daily publication. William Lloyd Garrison made the *Liberator* a powerful organ for the abolitionists. The New York *Sun* (1833) achieved national fame under Charles A. DANA. The New York *Herald,* launched (1835) by James Gordon BENNETT, was famous for its foreign news coverage and later established a Paris edition. Horace GREELEY, one of the best-known figures in American journalism, was proprietor and editor of the New York *Tribune* from its inception in 1841 until 1872. The *Tribune* was influential in the Civil War period. The New York *Times* was founded (1851) by Henry J. Raymond, and under the supervision of Adolph S. OCHS it achieved worldwide coverage and circulation, which it has retained. The New York *World* became enormously influential after its purchase by Joseph PULITZER. Other major U.S. newspapers include the New York *Daily News* (one of the largest circulations in the world), the Providence *Journal,* the Baltimore *Sun,* the Washington *Post,* the Cleveland *Plain Dealer,* the St. Louis *Post-Dispatch,* the Chicago *Tribune,* the Nashville *Tennesseean,* the Kansas City *Star,* the Atlanta *Constitution,* the Los Angeles *Times,* the San Francisco *Chronicle,* the *Christian Science Monitor* (Boston), the Dallas *News,* the Philadelphia *Bulletin,* the Denver *Post,* and the New Orleans *Times-Picayune.* Among the foreign-language papers published in urban areas are *El Diário* in New York and the *Deutsche Zeitung* in Milwaukee. Several newspapers are oriented toward professional interests; *Variety* deals with show business and the *Wall Street Journal* is primarily concerned with commerce and finance. The 20th cent. has witnessed many newspaper consolidations. In England large newspaper-publishing empires were built up by Lords Rothermere, Northcliffe, and Beaverbrook. The great American syndicates were founded by Joseph Pulitzer, J. G. Bennett, William Randolph HEARST, F. A. MUNSEY, E. W. SCRIPPS, and the McCormick-Pattersons. The great city newspapers are read all over the country; small towns and rural districts usually have daily or weekly local papers made up largely of syndicated matter, with a page or two of local news and editorials. These local papers are frequently influential political organs. Since the invention of the telegraph, which enormously facilitated the rapid gathering of news, the great NEWS AGENCIES, such as Reuters in England, Havas in France, and Associated Press and United Press International in the United States, have sold their services to newspapers and to their associate members. Improvements in typesetting (e.g., the LINOTYPE) and in PRINTING (especially the web press), have made possible the publication of huge editions at great speed. Modern newspapers are supported primarily by the sale of advertising space, as they are sold at only a fraction of the cost of production. The extent to which the editorial policy of a paper is affected by the interests of its advertisers has been a subject of frequent controversy, as has the entire question of private ownership vs. public control of newspapers. In recent years newspapers have wielded vast influence through their controlling interests in other media, including radio and television. For discussion of newspaper censorship, see PRESS, FREEDOM OF THE. See also JOURNALISM and PERIODICAL. See R. E. Wolseley and L. R. Campbell, *Exploring Journalism* (3d ed. 1957); F. L. Mott, *American Journalism: a History, 1690–1960* (3d ed. 1962); J. C. Merrill, *The Elite Press: Great Newspapers of the World* (1968); A. K. MacDougall, *The Press* (1972); A. M. Lee, *The Daily Newspaper in America* (1937, repr. 1972).

Newstead Abbey (nyo͞o'stĭd, -stĕd), Nottinghamshire, central England, on the border of Sherwood Forest, between Nottingham and Mansfield. It was founded c.1170 by Henry II in atonement for the murder of Thomas à Becket. It was secularized and granted to Sir John Byron by Henry VIII. The poet Lord Byron lived at the abbey intermittently from 1806 to 1816. He sold it in 1818. His rooms are preserved as he left them.

New Stone Age: see NEOLITHIC PERIOD.

New Style dates: see CALENDAR.

New Sweden, Swedish colony (1638–55), on the Delaware River; included parts of what are now Pennsylvania, New Jersey, and Delaware. With the support of Swedish statesman Axel Oxenstierna, Admiral Klas Fleming (a Finn), and Peter Minuit (a Dutchman), the New Sweden Company was organized in Sweden in 1633. Two ships (the *Kalmar Nyckel* and the *Fogel Grip*), commanded by Minuit, reached the Delaware River in March, 1638. Minuit immediately bought land from the Indians and founded Fort Christina, where Wilmington, Del., now stands. In 1643, Tinicum Island became the colony's capital. About half of the colonists were Finns (Finland was then part of Sweden). Peter Stuyvesant, with a Dutch force larger than the population of New Sweden, took the little colony in 1655. A monument to the *Kalmar Nyckel* stands in Wilmington.

newt, name for members of a large SALAMANDER family, widely distributed in the Northern Hemisphere and including the common European salamanders. Newts are lizardlike in shape and are usually under 6 in. (15 cm) long including the slender tail. Some are brightly colored and secrete irritating substances. Like other salamanders, newts go through an aquatic, gilled larval stage. In some species the adults remain aquatic, although they lose their gills and breathe air; in others the adults are terrestrial, returning to water only to breed. Still other newts go through two adult stages: A terrestrial stage, during which they are called efts, is followed by a permanent aquatic stage. One such species is the common red-spotted newt (*Diemictylus viridescens*) of the E United States, known in its terrestrial stage as red eft. The 3-in. (7.5-cm) adult lays its eggs in spring on the stems and leaves of water plants. The greenish-brown larvae remain in the water for several months before emerging as efts, orange-red with a double row of black-ringed vermilion spots. The efts spend two or three years on land, hibernating in winter under leaves, and then return permanently to the water, becoming olive green and developing a broad swimming tail. Newts are classified in the phylum CHORDATA, subphylum Vertebrata, class Amphibia, order Urodela, family Salamandridae.

New Territories: see HONG KONG.

New Testament, the distinctively Christian portion of the BIBLE, consisting of 27 books of varying lengths dating from the earliest Christian period. The books were transmitted in Greek, or rather in *koiné,* a popular form of Greek, which was spoken in the biblical regions from the 4th cent. B.C. The works are, in the conventional order: 4 biographies of Jesus, namely, the Gospels of MATTHEW, MARK, LUKE, and JOHN; a history of apostolic missionary activity, the ACTS OF THE APOSTLES; 21 letters written in apostolic times, called epistles, named for their addressee or, in the case of the last 7, for their supposed author—ROMANS, First and Second CORINTHIANS, GALATIANS, EPHESIANS, PHILIPPIANS, COLOSSIANS, First and Second THESSALONIANS, First and Second TIMOTHY, TITUS, PHILEMON, HEBREWS, JAMES, First and Second PETER, First, Second, and Third JOHN, and JUDE; and finally a prophecy, the REVELATION, or Apocalypse. The books were not written in the same time or place, and each presents problems of date, composition, and, in some cases, authorship. The 27 books of the New Testament represent a portion only of early Christian literature (see PATRISTIC LITERATURE); there are other gospels, epistles, narratives, and prophecies, especially among the PSEUDEPIGRAPHA. The selection by the church of the New Testament books as being alone canonical (i.e., divinely inspired) took place slowly. The first canon was compiled by the heretic MARCION in the 2d cent. His selection, which was rejected by the church, pointed out the need for an established canon. The earliest extant orthodox list is the Muratorian Canon (A.D. c.190), which contains most of the books of the final New Testament. There was, however, dispute for some time over 7 books (Hebrews, James, Second Peter, Second and Third John, Jude, Revelation) that were finally included in the canon and over others (including the epistles of ST. IGNATIUS OF ANTIOCH, ST. CLEMENT I, and the Shepherd of HERMAS) that were in the end rejected. The present New Testament canon appears for the first time in the Festal Epistle of St. Athanasius (367). In the Reformation there was questioning of the canon, notably by Martin Luther, who rejected especially James, because of its disagreement with the Lutheran tenet of justification by faith alone. All major Christian churches use the same New Testament. See studies by D. J. Selby (1971), F. F. Bruce (1972), C. M. Connick (1972), W. G. Kümmel (tr. of 2d ed. 1972), Vincent Taylor (1972), and H. C. Kee et al. (3d ed. 1973).

New Thought, popular philosophical movement with religious implications; it affirms "the creative power of constructive thinking." A successor of New England TRANSCENDENTALISM, New Thought grew out of the healing practices of P. P. Quimby and the "mental science" of W. F. Evans, a Swedenborgian minister. From its initial emphasis on the healing of disease it developed into an intensely individualistic and optimistic philosophy of life and conduct. The name was adopted in the 1890s to indicate this broader interest. Annual national conventions were held from 1894, and in 1914 the International New Thought Alliance was formed, with branches in England, Australia, and elsewhere. Composed of many smaller groups, such as Divine Science, UNITY (until 1922), and Home of Truth, the alliance is held together by one central teaching, namely, that man through the constructive use of his mind can attain freedom, power, health, prosperity, and all good, molding his body as well as the circumstances of his life. The doctrine was widely popularized by such writers as O. S. Marden and Ralph Waldo Trine, especially in the latter's *In Tune with the Infinite* (1897). Beyond this unifying principle of the constructive power of the mind and the prevailing optimism of the movement, there are a great variety of diverse and often mutually contradictory ideas in New Thought. Individual New Thought leaders have employed concepts from every variety of idealistic, spiritualistic, pantheistic, cabalistic, and theosophical thought, as well as from Christianity. There are also frequent overtones of the mystical and occult in New Thought literature. See H. W. Dresser, *A History of the New Thought Movement* (1919); C. S. Braden, *Spirits in Rebellion: The Rise and Development of New Thought* (1963).

Newton, Alfred, 1829–1907, English zoologist, b. Geneva. He studied (1854–65) ornithology in Lapland, Iceland, the West Indies, and North America and in 1866 became the first professor of zoology and comparative anatomy at Cambridge. In 1900 he received the Royal Medal of the Royal Society and the Gold Medal of the Linnaean Society. His writings include *Zoology of Ancient Europe* (1862) and *Dictionary of Birds* (1893–96). Newton edited (1865–70) the review *Ibis.*

Newton, Gilbert Stuart, 1794–1835, English genre and portrait painter, b. Halifax, N.S., studied in Boston with his uncle Gilbert Stuart, and later abroad. He was greatly influenced by the 17th-century Dutch masters. Representative examples of his art are *Yorick and the Grisette; The Window* (National Gall., London); and *Deserted* (Metropolitan Mus.).

Newton, Sir Isaac, 1642–1727, English mathematician and natural philosopher (physicist), who is considered by many the greatest scientist that ever lived. He studied at Cambridge and was professor there from 1669 to 1701, succeeding his teacher Isaac Barrow as Lucasian professor of mathematics. His most important discoveries were made during the two-year period from 1664 to 66, when the university was closed and he retired to his hometown of Woolsthorpe. At that time he discovered the law of universal GRAVITATION, began to develop the CALCULUS, and discovered that white light is composed of all the colors of the SPECTRUM. These findings enabled him to make fundamental contributions to mathematics, astronomy, and theoretical and experimental physics. He summarized his discoveries in terrestrial and celestial mechanics in his *Philosophiae naturalis principia mathematica* [mathematical principles of natural philosophy] (1687), one of the greatest milestones in the history of science; in it he showed how his principle of universal gravitation provided an explanation both of falling bodies on the earth and of the motions of planets, comets, and other bodies in the heavens. The first part of the *Principia* is devoted to dynamics and includes Newton's three famous laws of MOTION; the second part to fluid motion and other topics; and the third part to the system of the world, i.e., the unification of terrestrial and celestial mechanics under the principle of gravitation and the explanation of KEPLER'S LAWS of planetary motion. Although Newton used the calculus to discover his results, he explained them in the *Principia* by use of older geometric methods. Newton's discoveries in optics were presented in his *Opticks* (1704), in which he elaborated his theory that LIGHT is composed of corpuscles, or particles. His corpuscular theory dominated optics until the early 19th cent., when it was replaced by the wave theory of light; the two theories were combined in the modern QUANTUM THEORY. Among his other accomplishments were his construction (1668) of a reflecting TELESCOPE and his anticipation of the calculus of variations, founded by Gottfried Leibniz and the Bernoullis. In later years Newton considered mathematics and physics a recreation and turned much of his energy toward alchemy, theology, and history, particularly problems of chronology. He was his university's representative in Parliament (1689-90, 1701-2) and was president of the Royal Society from 1703 until his death. He was made warden of the mint in 1696 and master in 1699, being knighted in 1705 in recognition of his services at the mint as much as for his scientific accomplishments. Although Newton was known as an open and generous person, at various times in his life he became involved in quarrels and controversies. The most notable was his dispute with Leibniz over which of them had first invented calculus; today they are jointly ascribed the honor. Five volumes of a seven-volume edition of Newton's correspondence (ed. by H. W. Turnbull and J. F. Scott, 1959-74) and six volumes of an eight-volume edition of his mathematical papers (ed. by D. H. Whiteside et al., 1967-74) have been published. See biographies by L. T. More (1934, repr. 1962), E. N. Andrade (1954, repr. 1965), J. D. North (1967), and F. E. Manuel (1968); F. E. Manuel, *Isaac Newton: Historian* (1963); John Herivel, *The Background to Newton's Principia* (1965); Alexandre Koyré, *Newtonian Studies* (1965); I. B. Cohen, *Introduction to Newton's Principia* (1971).

Newton, John, 1725-1807, English clergyman and hymn writer. Until 1755, his life was spent chiefly at sea. Then until 1760 he was surveyor of tides at Liverpool, using his leisure for the study of Greek, Hebrew, and theology. After being ordained he became curate of Olney, Buckinghamshire, in 1764. When William COWPER made his home in the parish, friendship and literary sympathy between the two men resulted in their publishing jointly the *Olney Hymns* (1779 and later eds.). Among the best known of Newton's hymns are "How Sweet the Name of Jesus Sounds" and "Glorious Things of Thee Are Spoken." From 1779 he was rector of St. Mary Woolnoth, London.

Newton. **1** City (1970 pop. 15,619), seat of Jasper co., central Iowa; inc. 1857. It is an industrial city where washing machines are produced. **2** City (1970 pop. 15,439), seat of Harvey co., S central Kansas, in a wheat area; inc. 1872. It is an important railroad division point with railroad shops and has a large mobile home industry. Farm equipment is also made. The Chisholm Trail passed through the site. In the early 1870s German Mennonites from Russia brought seed for what became the first hard winter wheat in Kansas. The city still has a large Mennonite population, and there is a monument to their ancestors. Bethel College is in North Newton. **3** City (1970 pop. 91,263), Middlesex co., E Mass., a suburb of Boston on the Charles River; settled before 1640, inc. as a city 1873. It comprises a large number of beautiful residential villages and several industrial villages. The city is the seat of Newton College, Mount Alvernia College, Andover Newton Theological School, and two junior colleges. Horace Mann, Nathaniel Hawthorne, Mary Baker Eddy, and Samuel Francis Smith lived in Newton.

newton, abbr. N, unit of FORCE in the MKS SYSTEM of units, which is based on the METRIC SYSTEM; it is the force that produces an acceleration of 1 meter per second per second when exerted on a mass of 1 kilogram. The newton is named for Sir Isaac Newton.

Newtonian focus: see TELESCOPE.

Newton's law of gravitation: see GRAVITATION.

Newton's laws of motion: see MOTION.

Newtontoppen: see SPITSBERGEN, island, Norway.

New Toronto (tərŏn'tō), part of metropolitan TORONTO, S Ont., Canada, on Lake Ontario.

Newtown, town (1970 pop. 16,942), Fairfield co., SW Conn., on the Housatonic; inc. 1711. Fabric rubber hose and plastic products are made. There are dairy and fruit farms in the area.

Newtownards (nyōōtənärdz'), municipal borough (1971 pop. 15,387), Co. Down, E Northern Ireland, near the head of Strangford Lough. There are textile and other industries in Newtownards. Walter de Burgh, earl of Ulster, founded a Dominican monastery there (now in ruins) in 1244.

new towns, planned urban communities in Great Britain, developed by long-term loans from the central government and first authorized by the New Towns Act of 1946. The chief purpose of the act was to reduce congestion in the great cities (or at least prevent its increase) through the creation of attractive, healthful urban units that would provide local employment for their residents. The idea goes back to the book by Ebenezer HOWARD on "garden cities" (1898). It was given impetus by the example of the "new towns" of LETCHWORTH (1903) and WELWYN GARDEN CITY (1919-20), both established with private capital. The act of 1946 empowered the government to designate areas (which might or might not already contain an existing municipality) as new towns, to appoint development corporations, and to approve their plans. New towns in Northern Ireland have development commissions, established and governed under a separate act (1965). Most of the 28 new towns were intended to alleviate the growth problems of Greater London, Manchester, Merseyside, Tyneside-Wearside, Birmingham and the Black Country, and Clydeside. New towns have also been designated to stimulate economic growth (CRAIGAVON) and to provide needed housing and community services for industrial areas (CORBY, GLENROTHES, CWMBRAN). More recently the instrument of the new town development corporation and the machinery of the new towns legislation have been used to decentralize population through the expansion of already large towns (PETERBOROUGH, NORTHAMPTON, and IPSWICH). Central Lancashire New Town, designated in 1970, represents yet another variation, the "clustertown." The area is comparatively large, containing a county borough (PRESTON) and two other towns (Leyland and CHORLEY). Its total population of some 250,000 is projected to increase to 435,000 by 1993. Its purpose is to relieve congestion in Liverpool and Manchester and create a more balanced distribution of economic growth for Lancashire. See Sir Frederic Osborn and Arnold Whettick, *The New Towns* (2d rev. ed. 1969); Hazel Evans, ed., *New Towns: The British Experience* (1972).

New Ulm (ŭlm), city (1970 pop. 13,051), seat of Brown co., S Minn., at the confluence of the Minnesota and Cottonwood rivers; inc. as a city 1876. New Ulm, a processing and trade center for a grain and cattle region, has a huge rye mill. The city's manufactures include dairy products, flour, beer, tools, textiles, electronic equipment, and mobile homes. New Ulm was settled in 1854 by Germans, who named it after Ulm, Germany. In 1862, C. E. Flandrau, then a justice of the Minnesota supreme court, led the defense of the city during a Sioux Indian uprising. New Ulm has a 102-ft- (31-m-) high bronze statue of Arminius (Hermann), a German leader of the 1st cent.

New Waterford, town (1971 pop. 9,579), on NE Cape Breton Island, N.S., Canada, NE of Sydney. It is chiefly a coal-mining center.

New Westminster, city (1971 pop. 42,835), SW British Columbia, Canada, on the Fraser River, part of metropolitan Vancouver. Founded in 1859 as Queensborough, it was the capital of British Columbia until Victoria was made capital after the union of British Columbia and Vancouver Island in 1866. New Westminster is a year-round port, with an excellent harbor that is the base of the Fraser River fishing fleet and a shipping point for grain, lumber, minerals, and canned goods. Among the city's industries are salmon, fruit, and vegetable canneries; foundries; oil refineries; paper, lumber, and flour mills; and meat-packing plants. Columbia and St. Louis colleges are in the city, as are Anglican and Roman Catholic cathedrals.

New Windsor, England: see WINDSOR.

New Year's Day. Among ancient peoples the first day of the year frequently corresponded to the vernal or autumnal equinox, or to the summer or winter solstice. In the Middle Ages it was celebrated among Christians usually on March 25. After the adoption of the Gregorian calendar that began in 1582, the day was observed on the first of January. The Jewish New Year is the first day of Tishri, which falls some time in September or in early October. The Chinese New Year (between Jan. 10 and Feb. 19 of the Gregorian calendar) is the most important of their festivals. The Muslim New Year falls on the first day of Muharram.

New York, state (1970 pop. 18,241,266), 49,576 sq mi (128,402 sq km), E United States, one of the Middle Atlantic states and one of the Thirteen Colonies. New York is known as the Empire State. ALBANY is the capital; NEW YORK City is the largest city. The state, irregular in shape, is bounded on the north by the Canadian provinces of Quebec and Ontario, with the Saint Lawrence River and Lake Ontario marking the Ontario border. In the northwest the Niagara River, with magnificently scenic NIAGARA FALLS, forms the border with Ontario between Lake Ontario and Lake Erie. Lake Erie itself and a minute portion of Pennsylvania constitute the rest of the western border. Pennsylvania and New Jersey are to the south, except where the state extends into the Atlantic Ocean at New York City and Long Island. To the east, New York borders on Connecticut, Massachusetts, and Vermont. Lake Champlain, stretching past the Canadian border, is part of the boundary with Vermont; it is also the chief northern feature of the great valley (including the Hudson River and its west tributary, the Mohawk River) that dominates all E New York. The Hudson is noted for its beauty, as are Lake Champlain and neighboring Lake George, which have many resorts. West of the lakes are the wild and rugged Adirondack Mts., another major vacationland, with woods in the north and sports and health centers like Lake Placid and Saranac Lake. Mt. Marcy (5,344 ft/1,629 m), the highest point in the state, is in the Adirondacks near Lake Placid. The rest of NE New York is hilly, sloping gradually to the valleys of the St. Lawrence and Lake Ontario. The Mohawk River, which flows from Rome to the Hudson, is part of the NEW YORK STATE BARGE CANAL, a major route to the Great Lakes and the midwestern United States. Most of the southern part of the state is on the Allegheny plateau, which rises in the SE to the Catskill Mts., an area that attracts many vacationers from New York City and its environs. New York City, in turn, attracts multitudes of tourists from all over the world. The western extension of the state to Lakes Ontario and Erie is hilly land with many bodies of water, notably Oneida Lake and the celebrated Finger Lakes. The western region has resorts as well as large industrial cities such as BUFFALO on Lake Erie, ROCHESTER on Lake Ontario, SYRACUSE, UTICA, and in the south, BINGHAMTON. The western section is drained by the Allegheny River and rivers of the Susquehanna and Delaware systems. The DELAWARE RIVER BASIN COMPACT, signed in 1961 by New York, New Jersey, Pennsylvania, Delaware, and the Federal government, regulates the utilization of water of the Delaware system. SCHENECTADY, Albany, and New York City are the major industrial cities of the lower Mohawk and the Hudson; most of the other river towns have factories and trade in manufactured goods as well as farm products. Except in the mountain regions, the areas between cities are rich agriculturally. The Finger Lakes region has apple orchards; in 1973 New York along with Washington state led the nation in apple production. New York has vineyards and is famous for its champagnes. Other areas of the state produce diverse crops, especially grains, truck crops, hay, and potatoes (grown in great quantity on E Long Island); New York ranks third, after Wisconsin and California, as a milk producer. The farmers of New York constitute an important element of the population, forming the backbone of conservative upstate as opposed to more liberal metropolitan New York City and, to a lesser degree, the other industrial cities. The state has mineral resources—emery, garnet, talc, titanium concentrate, zinc, lead, salt, gypsum, stone, sand and gravel, iron ore, petroleum, and natural gas—but most of its great industries depend on imported raw materials. The state has a complex system of railroads, air routes, and modern highways, notably the New York State Thruway, which serve industry. The rivers and the New York State Barge Canal, an improvement of the old ERIE CANAL, also carry much freight, although they are not as important as they once were. Ocean shipping is handled by the great port of New York City and by Buffalo, made accessible to oceangoing shipping by the SAINT LAWRENCE SEAWAY, which opened in 1959. Hydroelectricity for N New York is produced by the St. Lawrence power project and by the Niagara power project, which began producing in 1961. New York is the nation's chief manufacturing state and, by virtue of New York City, its commercial and financial leader as well. Its manufactures, which are extremely diverse, include wearing apparel, food products, machinery, chemicals, paper, electrical equipment (notably at Schenectady), optical instruments and cameras (Rochester), and transportation equipment. Printing and publishing, mass communications, advertising, and entertainment are among New York City's notable industries. Long Island has aircraft plants and Brookhaven National Laboratory, an atomic energy testing and research center. Many cities throughout the state are noted for their specialities—e.g., Gloversville for gloves and Amsterdam for rugs and carpets. Commercial fishing is pursued in Lakes Erie and Ontario and in the waters around Long Island. The state has c.14,500 acres (5,870 hectares) of forest, but forestry is not a major industry. Before Europeans began to arrive in the 16th cent., New York was inhabited mainly by Algonquian- and Iroquoian-speaking Indians. The Algonquians, including the Mohegan, Leni-Lenape, and Wappinger tribes, lived chiefly in the Hudson valley and on Long Island. The Iroquoians, living in the central and western parts of the state, included the Cayuga, Mohawk, Oneida, Onondaga, and Seneca tribes, who joined c.1570 to form the IROQUOIS CONFEDERACY. The state was first approached by Europeans from two directions, W from the sea and S from Canada. Giovanni da Verrazano, a Florentine in the service of France, visited (1524) the great harbor of New York Bay but did little exploring. In 1609, Samuel de Champlain, a Frenchman, went down Lake Champlain from Canada, and Henry Hudson, an Englishman in the service of the Dutch, went up the Hudson nearly to Albany. The French from Canada continued to penetrate N and W New York, and valiant missionaries like St. Isaac Jogues and the other Jesuit Martyrs of North America tried to convert the Indians to Christianity in the 17th cent. However, the French, who had allied themselves with the Huron Indians of Ontario, came up against the uncompromising hostility of the Iroquois Confederacy, which dominated W New York. The Dutch early claimed the Hudson region, and the Dutch West India Company (chartered in 1621, organized in 1623) planted (1624) their colony of New Netherland, with its chief settlements at New Amsterdam on the lower tip of present-day Manhattan island (purchased in 1626 from the Canarsie Indians for trinkets worth about $24) and at Fort Nassau, later called Fort Orange (present-day Albany). To increase the slow pace of colonization the Dutch set up the patroon system in 1629, thus establishing the landholding aristocracy that became the hallmark of colonial New York. The little colony did not thrive under its governors, who included Peter Minuit, Wouter Van Twiller, and Willem Kieft. Minuit, in disgust, went over to Swedish service, and the colony of New Sweden, founded by Minuit in 1637 along the Delaware River south of the Dutch settlements, was viewed by the Dutch as an intrusion. The last and most able of the Dutch administrators, Peter Stuyvesant (in office 1647-64), captured New Sweden for the Dutch in 1655. Stuyvesant also reorganized the insecure little settlement of New Amsterdam, making himself very unpopular by his high-handed ways, especially against religious dissenters. He was unable to meet the threat of the English, who had been penetrating Long Island and SE New York ever since Lion Gardiner came in 1639. The English, claiming the whole region on the basis of the explorations of John Cabot, made good their claim in the Second Dutch War (1664-67). In 1664 an English fleet sailed into the harbor of New Amsterdam, and Stuyvesant capitulated without a struggle. New Netherland then became the colonies of New York and New Jersey, granted by King Charles II to his brother, the duke of York (later James II). Except for brief recapture (1673-74) by the Dutch, New York remained English until the American Revolution. Richard Nicolls was the first English administrator, and transition from Dutch rule was accomplished peacefully, with the Dutch settlers sharing in the limited self-government established under the Duke's Laws. After the early days of the colony, the popular governor Thomas Dongan (1683-88) put New York on a firm basis and began to establish the alliance of the English with the Iroquois, which later played an important part in New York history. The attempt in 1688 to combine New York and New Jersey with New England under the rule of Sir Edmund Andros was a failure, and that imperious governor managed to turn almost all the colonists against him. When news arrived of the Glorious Revolution (1688) and the overthrow (1689) of Andros by Bostonians, the rebellious New York City merchant Jacob Leisler gained sufficient popular support to grasp brief (1689-91) control of the provincial government and run it in the interest of the popular antiaristocratic party, establishing a representative assembly on his own authority. Leisler's government was overthrown by royal authority, and he was executed for treason. After this the rift continued to widen between the great landholders and the small farmers and artisans, who were allied with the increasingly powerful merchant group. A representative government was again set up, this time by the crown, and in the 18th cent. it extended its power and influence. Although dominated by a small group of landed and mercantile families (the DeLanceys, Schuylers, Philipses, and Beekmans), it made possible compromise between provincial interests and royal orders. The trial and acquittal (1735) of John Peter Zenger, which established truth as sufficient defense in a libel suit, was a landmark in the development of freedom of the press. The threat of the French was continuous, and New York was involved in a number of the French and Indian Wars (1689-1763). The friendship of Sir William Johnson with some of the Iroquois aided the British in the warfare and also opened part of central New York to settlers, mainly from the British Isles. Raids and counterraids of the wars and

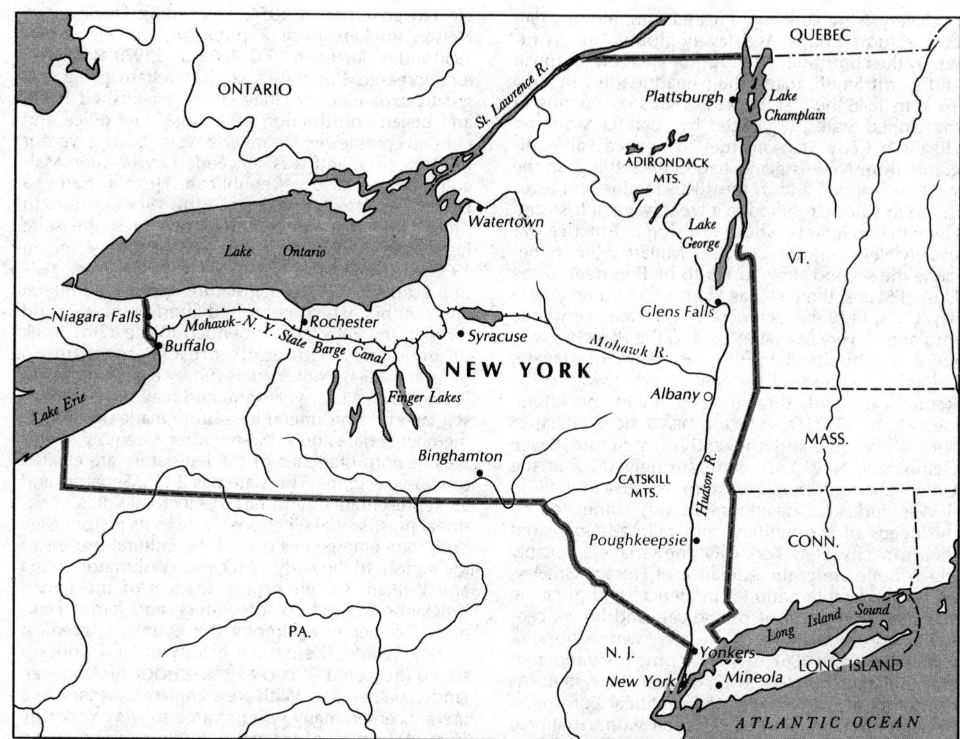

sporadic Indian massacres hindered growth, however, and much of W New York remained unsettled by colonists throughout the 18th cent. Slowly, however, the colony, with its busy shipping and fishing fleets, its expanding farms, and its first college (King's College, founded in 1754, now Columbia Univ.), was beginning to establish its own identity, separate from that of England. Colonial self-assertiveness grew after the warfare with the French ended; there was considerable objection to the restrictive commercial laws, and the Navigation Acts were flouted by smuggling. When the Stamp Act was passed, New York was a leader of the opposition, and the Stamp Act Congress met (1765) in New York City. The policies of Lt. Gov. Cadwallader Colden, who did not oppose the Stamp Act, occasioned considerable complaint, and unrest grew. When trouble flared into the American Revolution, New Yorkers were divided. Many, especially among the great landholders, were Loyalists. To draw a strict parallel between the social classes and the patriotic sentiments of the people would be misleading, however, for sometimes it was the poor farmer who was a Loyalist while the lord of a manor was a patriot. About one third of all the military engagements of the American Revolution took place in New York state. The first major military action in the state was the capture (May, 1775) of Ticonderoga by Ethan Allen and his Green Mountain Boys and Benedict Arnold. Crown Point was also taken. In Aug., 1776, however, George Washington was unable to hold lower New York against the British under Gen. William Howe and lost the battle of Long Island, as he did the succeeding actions at Harlem Heights (Sept. 16) and White Plains (Oct. 28). The British invested New York City and held it to the war's end. The state had, however, declared independence and functioned with Kingston as its capital, George Clinton as its first governor, and John Jay as its first chief justice. New York was in 1777 the key to the overall British campaign plan, which was directed toward taking the entire state and thus separating New England from the South. This failed finally (Oct., 1777) in the battles near the present-day resort of Saratoga Springs (see SARATOGA CAMPAIGN), generally considered as the decisive action of the war, partly because France was now persuaded to join the war on the side of the Colonies. The British alliance with the Iroquois was at this point turned against the patriots. Sir Guy Johnson, John Butler and his Rangers, and the Indians kept the frontier in turmoil. The most striking incident was the wanton massacre at Cherry Hill (1778). However, John Sullivan and James Clinton led a successful punitive expedition in 1779 that quieted W New York. For the rest of the war there was more or less of a stalemate, with the British occupying New York City, the patriots holding most of the rest of the state, and Westchester co. disputed ground. In 1780, Benedict Arnold failed in his attempt to betray West Point. By the end of the war many Loyalists had left New York; the emigrants included former large landowners whose holdings had been seized by the legislature. After the war speculation in W New York land (some newly acquired by quieting Massachusetts claims) rose to dizzying heights. The Holland Land Company, for example, took over the vast holdings of Robert Morris. The eastern boundary of the state was established after long wrangles and violence when Vermont was admitted as a state in 1791. The influence of Alexander Hamilton was paramount in bringing New York to accept (1788) the Constitution of the United States at a convention in Poughkeepsie. Other leaders, however, mostly from the landed aristocracy (such as John Jay and Gouverneur Morris), were also powerful. Hamilton, Jay, and James Madison wrote THE FEDERALIST, a series of essays, to promote ratification. New York City was briefly (1789-90) the capital of the new nation and was also the state capital until 1797, when Albany succeeded it. Political dissension between the Federalists and the Jeffersonians was particularly keen in New York state, and Aaron Burr had much to do with swinging the state to Jefferson. George Clinton (governor 1777-95; 1801-04) and his nephew, De Witt Clinton (governor 1817-22, 1825-28), were prominent in public affairs. From the 1780s increased commerce (somewhat slowed by the Embargo Act of 1807) and industry, especially textile milling, marked the turn away from the old, primarily agricultural, order. It was on the Hudson that Robert Fulton demonstrated (1807) his steamboat. In the War of 1812, New York saw action in 1813-14, with the British capture of Fort Niagara and particularly with the brilliant naval victory of Thomas Macdonough over the British on Lake Champlain at Plattsburgh. The state continued its development, which was quickened and broadened by the building of the Erie Canal. The canal, completed in 1825, and railroad lines constructed (from 1831) parallel to it made New York the major East-West commercial route in the 19th cent. and helped to account for the growth and prosperity of the port of New York. Cities along the canal (Buffalo, Syracuse, Rome, Utica, and Schenectady) prospered. Albany grew, and New York City, whose first bank had been established by Hamilton in 1784, became the financial capital of the nation. New constitutions broadened the suffrage in 1821 and again in 1846; slavery was abolished in 1827. Politics was largely controlled from the 1820s to the 40s by the ALBANY REGENCY, which favored farmers, artisans, and small businessmen. Martin Van Buren was the regency's chief figure. The regency's control was challenged by the business-oriented Whigs, led by Thurlow Weed and William H. Seward, and by the ANTI-MASONIC PARTY. The rise of tension between the reform-minded LOCOFOCOS and the TAMMANY organization in New York City weakened the Democratic party in the 1830s. After the panic of 1837, Seward was governor (1839-52), and his Whig program included internal improvements, educational reform, and opposition to slavery. New York was a leader in numerous 19th cent. reform groups. Antislavery groups, underwritten by the contributions of Arthur and Lewis Tappan and Gerrit Smith, made their headquarters in New York. In 1848 the first woman's rights convention in the United States, organized by Lucretia Mott and Elizabeth Cady Stanton, met in Seneca Falls. Migrants from New England had been settling on the western frontier, and in the 1840s famine and revolution in Europe resulted in a great wave of Irish and German immigrants, whose first stop in America was usually New York City. In 1850, Millard Fillmore became the second New Yorker to be President of the United States; the first was Martin Van Buren (1837–41). The split of the Democrats over the slavery issue into anti-slavery BARNBURNERS and the HUNKERS, who were not opposed to the extension of slavery, helped pave the way for New York's swing to the Republicans and Abraham Lincoln in the fateful election of 1860. Despite the DRAFT RIOTS (1863) in New York City and the activities of the Peace Democrats, New York state strongly favored the Union and contributed much to its cause in the Civil War. Industrial development was stimulated by the needs of the military, and railroads increased their capacity. New York City's newspapers, notably the *Tribune* under the guidance of Horace Greeley, had considerable national influence, and after the war the publication of periodicals and books centered more and more in the city, whose libraries expanded. From 1867 to 1869, Cornelius Vanderbilt consolidated the New York Central RR system. As economic growth accelerated, political corruption became rampant. Samuel J. Tilden won a national reputation in 1871 for prosecuting the Tweed Ring of New York City, headed by William Marcy Tweed, but Tammany soon recovered much of its prestige and influence as the Democratic city organization. The Republican party also had bosses, notably Roscoe Conkling and Thomas Collier Platt, and the split between Democratic New York City and Republican upstate widened. Chester A. Arthur (1881–85) and Grover Cleveland (1885–89, 1893–97) were New Yorkers who served as Presidents of the United States in the late 19th cent. The inpoufing after 1880 of immigrants from Ireland, Italy, and Eastern Europe brought workers for the old industries, which were expanding, and for the new ones, including the electrical and chemical industries, which were being established. Labor conditions worsened but were challenged by the growing labor movement, whose targets included sweatshops (particularly notorious in New York City). MUCKRAKERS were particularly vociferous in New York in the late 19th and early 20th cent. Service as New York City police commissioner and then as reforming governor of New York helped Theodore Roosevelt establish the national reputation that sent him to the vice presidency and then to the White House (1901–9). Charles Evans Hughes, who later became a Republican presidential candidate, Secretary of State, and Chief Justice of the U.S. Supreme Court, also entered national politics as an effective reforming governor of New York (1907–10). A fire in 1911 at the Triangle Shirt Waist Company in New York City that killed 140 workers resulted in the passage of some early labor laws like the Widowed Mothers Pension Act. The Democrats returned to power in the state in 1912, and subsequently New York seesawed from one party to the other. The reform programs continued to gain ground, however, and Democratic state administrations between World War I and II—those of Alfred E. Smith (1918–20, 1922–28), Franklin D. Roosevelt (1928–32), and Herbert H. Lehman (1932–42)—presided over a wide variety of reform measures. The reform programs emphasized public works, conservation, reorganization of state finances, social welfare, and extensive labor laws. Four years after Smith's defeat in the 1928 presidential election, Roosevelt went to the White House. Lehman followed Roosevelt's national NEW DEAL program by instituting the Little New Deal in New York state. At the same time Fiorello LaGuardia, Republican mayor of New York City (1934–45), enthusiastically supported Roosevelt's social and economic reforms. The Republican party returned to power in the state in 1942 with the election of Thomas E. Dewey as governor (reelected 1946, 1950). Dewey had the immense task of coordinating state activities with national efforts in World War II, which strained New York's resources to the utmost. He also built upon the reforms of his predecessors, extending social and antidiscrimination legislation, and won a reputation for effectiveness that made him twice (1944 and 1948) the Republican presidential nominee. W. Averell Harriman, a Democrat, was elected governor in 1954, succeeding Dewey, and Nelson Rockefeller, a Republican, was elected in 1958 and reelected in 1962, 1966, and 1970. Rockefeller increased the state's social welfare programs, greatly expanded the State Univ. (established 1948), and began construction of a large state-office and cultural complex in Albany. He resigned as governor in Dec., 1973, and was succeeded by Lt.-Gov. Malcolm Wilson, also a Republican. Hugh J. Carey, a Democrat, defeated Wilson in the 1974 election. In order to increase government revenues, the state legislature in 1966 approved a state lottery and in 1970 sanctioned the New York City Off-Track Betting Corp. In 1971 the legislature approved a liberal abortion bill, which permitted abortion on demand through the 24th (later amended to the 12th) week of pregnancy. Under its present constitution (adopted 1894), New York is run by a governor, who is elected to a four-year term and may succeed himself, and by a bicameral legislature made up of a 60-member Senate and a 150-member Assembly. Members of both branches of the legislature are elected to two-year terms. The state has 2 U.S. Senators and 39 Representatives and has 41 electoral votes in national presidential elections. Early in its history New York state emerged as one of the cultural leaders of the nation. In the early 19th cent. Washington Irving and William Cullen Bryant, leaders of the famed Knickerbocker School of writers, and James Fenimore Cooper were among the country's foremost literary figures. The natural beauty of New York inspired the noted HUDSON RIVER SCHOOL of American landscape painters. With New England's decline as a literary center, many writers came to New York City from other parts of the nation, helping to make it a literary and publishing center and the cultural heart of the country. Apart from New York City (see separate articles for educational and cultural institutions in New York City and its boroughs), the institutions of higher education in the state include Alfred Univ., Bard College, Colgate Univ., Cornell Univ., Hobart College, Long Island Univ., Rensselaer Polytechnic Institute, Sarah Lawrence College, Skidmore College, State Univ. of New York, Syracuse Univ., U.S. Military Academy, Univ. of Rochester, Vassar College, and Wells College. In addition to the great forest preserves of the Adirondack and Catskill mts., New York has many state parks, among which Jones Beach State Park and Allegany State Park are well known. Part of Fire Island is a national seashore. The racetrack and mineral waters of SARATOGA SPRINGS make it both a pleasure and health resort, and the Thousand Islands are popular with summer vacationers. Among the several places of historic interest in the state under Federal administration (see NATIONAL PARKS AND MONUMENTS, table) are those at HYDE PARK, with the burial place of Eleanor and Franklin D. Roosevelt, and the Vanderbilt Mansion. See A. C. Flick, *A History of The State of New York* (10 vol., 1933–37; repr. 10 vol. in 5, 1962); D. M. Ellis, *New York: The Empire State* (1964); J. H. Thomson, ed., *The Geography of New York State* (1966); D. M. Ellis, *A History of New York State* (1967); Federal Writers' Project, *New York: A Guide To The Empire State* (rev. ed. 1946, repr. 1970); Edmund Wilson, *Upstate: Records and Recollections of Northern New York* (1971); William Smith, *The History of The Province of New York,* ed. by M. Karnmen (1972).

New York, city (1970 pop. 7,895,563), area with water surface c.365 sq mi (950 sq km), SE N.Y., largest city in the United States and one of the three largest in the world, on New York Bay at the mouth of the Hudson River. It comprises five boroughs, each coextensive with a county: Manhattan (New York co.), the heart of the city, an island; the Bronx (Bronx co.), on the mainland, NE of Manhattan and separated from it by the Harlem River; Queens (Queens co.), on Long Island, E of Manhattan across the East River; Brooklyn (Kings co.), also on Long Island, on the East River adjoining Queens and on New York Bay; and Richmond (Richmond co.), on Staten Island, SW of Manhattan and separated from it by Upper Bay. The metropolitan area (1970 est. pop. 11,600,000) encompasses parts of SE New York state, NE New Jersey, and SW Connecticut and includes both industrial and residential areas. Many thousands of suburban commuters arrive daily in Manhattan, adding their numbers to the already teeming population of the bustling city. New York, with its fine deep-water harbor, is the largest port in the United States and one of the leading ports in the world. It is the trade center of the nation and the financial center of the entire world. Manufacturing—primarily of small but highly diverse types—accounts for a large but declining amount of employment. Clothing and other apparel, such as furs; chemicals; metal products; and processed foods are some of the principal manufactures. New York is also the principle center of U.S. television and radio broadcasting, book publishing, and other mass communications. The most celebrated newspaper is the New York *Times*. New York attracts many business and professional conventions. It was the site of two World's Fairs (1939–40; 1964–65). The city is served by three major airports: John F. Kennedy International Airport and LaGuardia Airport, both in Queens, and Newark International Airport, in New Jersey. Railroads converge upon New York from all points, giving quick access to outlying areas. Millions of tourists visit the city each year. To newcomers, the city seems filled with feverish movement. With its vast cultural and educational resources, famous shops and restaurants, places of entertainment (including many of the nation's legitimate theaters), striking and diversified architecture (including the EMPIRE STATE BUILDING and the two World Trade Center buildings), colorful ethnic neighborhoods, parks and botanical gardens, and rich historical background, New York is almost unparalleled. Since the 19th cent. it has been for the United States the symbol of ambition, luxury, and sin. Some of its streets and neighborhoods have become accepted symbols throughout the nation. WALL STREET means big finance; BROADWAY, the theater; FIFTH AVENUE, many fine shops; Seventh Avenue, the women's-garment manufacturing district and fur-processing area; Greenwich Village—now somewhat anachronistically, for parts have become fashionable residential areas—the refuge of poets and artists who abandon all for art. (By the early 1970s the artist colony had shifted to SoHo.) Since the mid-19th cent., various waves of migration have marked the neighborhoods. The new immigrants clung together in poor neighborhoods, then in better parts of the city, then separated. Yet they left remnants of their culture—Armenian restaurants, Hungarian clubs, and the like. Yorkville, for example, still has many German restaurants; Chinatown persists about Mott and Doyer streets. The newest immigrants are blacks, who moved into Harlem and other areas after 1910, and Puerto Ricans and other Hispanic-Americans, who grew numerous after 1940. They have further widened the already broad spectrum of New York City life.

History. Although Giovanni da Verrazano may have been the first European to explore the region, and Henry Hudson certainly visited the area, it was with Dutch settlements on Manhattan and Long Island that the city truly began to emerge. In 1624 the colony of NEW NETHERLAND was established, with the town of NEW AMSTERDAM on the lower tip of Manhattan as its capital. Peter Minuit of the DUTCH WEST INDIA COMPANY supposedly bought the island from its Indian inhabitants for about $24 worth of trinkets (the sale was completed in 1626). Under the Dutch, schools were opened and the Dutch Reformed Church was established. In 1664 the English, at war with the Netherlands (see DUTCH WARS), seized the colony for the duke of York, for whom it was renamed. Peter Stuyvesant was replaced by Richard Nicolls as governor, and New York became the capital of the British province of New York. The Dutch returned to power only briefly (1673–74). A liberal charter was granted under Thomas Dongan in 1686 and remained in effect for many years. English rule was not, however, without dissension, and the autocratic rule of British governors was one of the causes of an insurrection that broke out in 1689 under the leadership of Jacob Leisler. The insurrection was put down in 1691 by British authorities. In 1741 there was further violence when an alleged plot by Negro slaves to burn New York was ruthlessly suppressed, and about 30 Negroes were killed or tortured. Meanwhile, despite these outbreaks, New York was growing, and its expanding commerce was attracting settlers from many nations. The first newspaper, the New York *Gazette,* appeared in 1725, and 10 years later the trial of John Peter Zenger helped to establish the principle of a free press. Kings College (now Columbia University) was founded in 1754. New York was active in the colonial opposition to British measures after trouble in 1765 over the STAMP ACT. As revolutionary sentiments increased, the New York SONS OF LIBERTY forced (1775) Gov. William Tryon and the British colonial government from the city. Although many New Yorkers were Loyalists, Continental forces commanded by George Washington defended (1776) the city. After the patriot defeat in the battle of Long Island (see LONG ISLAND, BATTLE OF) and the succeeding actions at Harlem Heights and White Plains, Washington gave up New York, and the British occupied the city until the end of the war for independence. Under the British occupation two mysterious fires (1776 and 1778) destroyed a large part of the city. After the Revolution, New York was briefly (1789-90) the first capital of the United States and was the state capital until 1797. President Washington was inaugurated (April 30, 1789) at Federal Hall, where the Subtreasury Building now stands. New development was marked by such events as the beginning of the stock exchange and the foundation of the Bank of New York under Alexander Hamilton. By 1790, New York was the largest city in the United States, with over 33,000 inhabitants; by 1800 the number had risen to 60,515. In 1811 plans were adopted for the laying out of New York's streets on a grid pattern. The opening of the Erie Canal (1825), which made New York the seaboard gateway for the Great Lakes region, was of tremendous importance to the city, ushering in another era of commercial expansion and ending the competition for dominance with Boston and Philadelphia. The New York and Harlem RR was built in 1832. The fire of 1835, one of a series of disastrous conflagrations, destroyed much of the Old Dutch town, but it brought about new building laws and the construction of the Croton water system. By 1840, New York had become the leading port of the nation. During the Civil War the majority of New Yorkers, under the leadership of Gov. Horatio Seymour, supported the Union. However, in 1863 the DRAFT RIOTS broke out in protest against the Federal Conscription Act. Extensive immigration had begun before the Civil War, and after 1865, with the acceleration of industrial development, another wave of immigration began and reached its height in the late 19th and early 20th cent. Immigrants from various lands settled in distinct ethnic neighborhoods, and these, although lending interest and diversity to the city's culture, generally developed into crowded slums, such as Hell's Kitchen and the Five Points of the lower East Side. In addition, the newcomers were often the victims of political and economic exploitation. Municipal politics was dominated by TAMMANY and the Tweed Ring, led by W. M. Tweed. The first of many scandalous disclosures about the city's political life came in 1871, leading to Tweed's downfall. Until 1874, when portions of Westchester were annexed, the city's boundaries were those of present-day Manhattan. With the adoption of a new charter in 1898, New York became Greater New York, a metropolis of five boroughs—New York City was split into the present Manhattan and Bronx boroughs, and the independent city of Brooklyn was annexed, as were Queens co. and Staten Island. The Flatiron Building (1902) foreshadowed the skyscrapers that today give Manhattan its famed skyline, and the first subway (1904) was the forerunner of the present far-reaching system of rapid transit. New York in the 20th cent. has been served by such mayors as Seth Low, William J. Gaynor, John Purroy Mitchel, James J. Walker (whose resignation was brought about by the Seabury investigation), Fiorello H. LaGuardia, Robert F. Wagner, Jr., John V. Lindsay, and Abraham D. Beame. In the 1930s, Thomas E. Dewey led an assault on MURDER, INC. and organized crime, earning a national reputation for "racket busting." The need for regional planning resulted in the zoning legislation of 1916 and the formation of such bodies as the Port of New York Authority (1921; now the PORT AUTHORITY OF NEW YORK AND NEW JERSEY), the Regional Plan Association (1929), the Municipal Housing Authority (1934), and the City Planning Commission (1938). In the period following World War II, New York suffered from the urban problems that are common to most large cities in the United States. The transportation system, especially the subways, seemed increasingly unable to handle the vast numbers of commuters and visitors to the city. The public-school system became more and more pressed for funds and new facilities. Housing for the poor posed a serious ever-present problem. In the 1960s the city experienced race riots, as did many other large urban areas in the country. Crime rose, and pollution of the air and water created potential health problems. During summers New Yorkers became accustomed to inadequate supplies of electrical power to meet everyday needs. Common to solving the problems was the increasing need for revenues, met in part by state and Federal aid.

Points of interest and educational and cultural facilities. The city's many bridges include the GEORGE WASHINGTON BRIDGE, BROOKLYN BRIDGE, Henry Hudson Bridge, Triborough Bridge, the Bronx-Whitestone Bridge, the Throgs Neck Bridge, and the VERRAZANO-NARROWS BRIDGE, which opened in 1964. The Holland Tunnel (the first vehicular tunnel under the Hudson) and the Lincoln Tunnel link Manhattan with New Jersey. The Queens-Midtown Tunnel and the Brooklyn-Battery Tunnel, both under the East River, connect Manhattan with W Long Island. The new Queens-Manhattan subway tunnel and the proposed Second Avenue subway are two of a series of additional traffic links and arteries planned to meet the city's ever-expanding transportation needs. Islands in the East River include Roosevelt Island, Rikers Island (site of a city penitentiary), and Randalls Island (with Downing Stadium). In New York Bay are LIBERTY ISLAND (with the Statue of LIBERTY); GOVERNORS ISLAND; and ELLIS ISLAND, which along with Castle Garden (see BATTERY, THE) served as the point of entry for many immigrants. New York City is the seat of the UNITED NATIONS. It is also a cultural capital and the most influential arbiter of taste in the entire nation. LINCOLN CENTER FOR THE PERFORMING ARTS is a complex of buildings housing the METROPOLITAN OPERA COMPANY, the NEW YORK PHILHARMONIC-SYMPHONY ORCHESTRA, the New York City Ballet, the New York City Opera, the JUILLIARD SCHOOL, the Vivian Beaumont Theatre and Library Building, as well as the law school of Fordham University. Also in the city are Carnegie Hall and New York City Center, featuring performances by visiting musical and theatrical companies. Among the best known of the city's many museums and scientific collections are the METROPOLITAN MUSEUM OF ART, the MUSEUM OF MODERN ART, the Solomon R. Guggenheim Museum (designed by Frank Lloyd Wright), the Frick Collection (housed in the Frick mansion), the Whitney Museum of American Art, the MUSEUM OF PRIMITIVE ART, the Museum of the City of New York, the AMERICAN MUSEUM OF NATURAL HISTORY (with the Hayden Planetarium), the museum and library of the New-York Historical Society, and the Brooklyn Museum (see BROOKLYN INSTITUTE OF ARTS AND SCIENCES). The NEW YORK PUBLIC LIBRARY, one of the largest in the United States, is the administrative hub for many smaller public libraries. Major educational institutions include City Univ. of New York (see NEW YORK, CITY UNIVERSITY OF), COLUMBIA UNIVERSITY, COOPER UNION, FORDHAM UNIVERSITY, General Theological Seminary, Jewish Theological Seminary, NEW SCHOOL FOR SOCIAL RESEARCH, NEW YORK UNIVERSITY, and UNION THEOLOGICAL SEMINARY. A center for medical treatment and research, New York has more than 130 hospitals and several medical schools. Noted hospitals include BELLEVUE HOSPITAL, Mt. Sinai Hospital, Columbia-Presbyterian Medical Center, and New York Hospital. Among New York's noted houses of worship are Trinity Church, St. Paul's Chapel (dedicated 1776), SAINT PATRICK'S CATHEDRAL, the Cathedral of St. John the Divine (see SAINT JOHN THE DIVINE, CATHEDRAL OF), Riverside Church, and Temple Emanu-El. New York's parks and recreation centers include parts of Gateway National Recreation Area (see NATIONAL PARKS AND MONUMENTS, table); CENTRAL PARK, the Battery, Washington Square Park, Riverside Park, and Fort Tryon Park (with the CLOISTERS) in Manhattan; the New York Zoological Park (Bronx Zoo), the New York Botanical Garden, and Van Cortlandt Park in the Bronx; and CONEY ISLAND (with boardwalks, beaches, and an aquarium) and Prospect Park in Brooklyn. Sports events are held at Madison Square Garden in Manhattan, Yankee Stadium in the Bronx, and Shea Stadium in Queens. Among the many other places of interest are ROCKEFELLER CENTER; GREENWICH VILLAGE, with its cafés and restaurants; and TIMES SQUARE, with its garish lights and theaters. Even the BOWERY, once noted for its saloons and dance halls and now mainly for its derelicts, still holds an attraction for tourists. Of historic interest are Fraunces Tavern (built 1719), where Washington said farewell to his officers after the Revolution; Gracie Mansion (built late 18th cent.), now the official residence of the mayor; the Edgar Allen Poe Cottage; and Grant's Tomb. See separate articles on the boroughs. See A. Nevins and J. A. Krout, ed., *The Greater City: New York, 1898–1948* (1948); S. E. Lyman, *The Story of New York: An Informal History* (1964); V. S. Pritchett, *New York Proclaimed* (Am. ed. 1965); E. R. Ellis, *The Epic of New York City* (1966); I. N. Phelps Stokes, *The Iconography of Manhattan Island* (6 vol., 1915–28, repr. 1967); Federal Writers' Project, *New York City Guide* (rev. ed. 1972); E. Barlow, *The Forests and Wetlands of New York City* (1971); N. Silver, *Lost New York* (1971); J. A. Kouwenhoven, *Columbia Historical Portrait of New York* (1953, repr. 1972).

New York, City University of, at New York City; organized in 1929 as the College of the City of New York, expanded and renamed 1961. It includes BARUCH COLLEGE, BROOKLYN COLLEGE, CITY COLLEGE, LEHMAN COLLEGE, HUNTER COLLEGE, JOHN JAY COLLEGE OF CRIMINAL JUSTICE, QUEENS COLLEGE, Richmond College, York College, and several two-year community colleges in the various boroughs. The university is city and state supported. Residents of New York City are admitted tuition free to the undergraduate program. The headquarters for the university's graduate division is in Manhattan.

New York, State University of, est. 1948 by the amalgamation under one board of trustees of 29 state-supported institutions. It now comprises all state-supported institutions of higher education, with the exception of the senior colleges of the City University of New York. The university consists of over 70 units throughout the state, including 4 university centers (at Albany; Binghamton; Stony Brook; and Buffalo, formerly the Univ. of Buffalo), 2 medical centers, 13 colleges of arts and sciences, 2 specialized colleges, 6 two-year agricultural and technical colleges, 5 statutory colleges, and 38 community colleges. Graduate work at the doctoral level is offered at 12 campuses, at the master's level at 22 campuses. University-wide research programs include the Atmospheric Sciences Research Center and the Center for International Studies and World Affairs (with headquarters at Albany), the Institute for Theoretical Physics and the Marine Sciences Research Center (Stony Brook), and the Western New York Nuclear Research Center and the Center for Immunology (Buffalo).

New York, University of the State of, chartered 1784. It consists of all secondary and higher educational institutions incorporated in the state and other institutions, organizations, and agencies for education. The university is empowered to promote and investigate education in the state; to charter, register, and inspect educational institutions; to license certain professional practitioners; to certify teachers and librarians; and to apportion state financial assistance to public educational institutions. It is governed by a board of regents, which consists of 15 members elected by the state legislature; the board administers the State Regents Examinations, which are given to high school students throughout the state.

New York Bay, arm of the Atlantic Ocean at the mouth of the Hudson River, SE N.Y. and NE N.J., enclosed by the shores of NE New Jersey, E Staten Island, S Manhattan, and W Long Island (Brooklyn) and opening on the SE to the Atlantic Ocean between Sandy Hook, N.J., and Rockaway Point, N.Y. It is a sheltered deep harbor able to accommodate the largest ships. The tidal range of the bay is very small and it is ice-free. New York Bay is divided into Upper and Lower Bay, which are connected by the Narrows, a strait (c.3 mi/4.8 km long; 1 mi/1.6 km wide) separating Staten Island from Brooklyn. The Verrazano-Narrows Bridge spans the strait between Fort Wadsworth and Fort Hamilton. Upper Bay, c.5.5 mi (8.8 km) in diameter, is joined to Newark Bay (to the west) by Kill Van Kull and to Long Island Sound by the East River. It is one of the world's busiest harbors with extensive port facilities on all shores (see PORT AUTHORITY OF NEW YORK AND NEW JERSEY). Ellis and Liberty islands (both part of Statue of Liberty National Monument) and Governors Island (site of Fort Jay) are in Upper Bay. Ferries cross the bay from Staten Island to Manhattan. The larger Lower Bay, which includes Raritan Bay on the west and Gravesend Bay on the northeast is joined to Newark Bay by Arthur Kill. Jamaica Bay is an eastern extension of Lower Bay. Sections of Lower Bay's shoreline are part of Gateway National Recreation Area. Ambrose Channel, federally maintained, crosses Sandy Hook bar at the bay's entrance and extends north to the piers of Upper Bay, where it is 2,000 ft (610 m) wide. Giovanni da Verrazano, the Italian explorer, was the first European to enter (1524) the bay. Henry Hudson later explored it (1609) and claimed the region for the Dutch East India Company. An English colony replaced the Dutch colony in 1664.

New York Central RR, formed in 1853 by the consolidation of many small New York state railroads. In 1867, Cornelius Vanderbilt became president of the railroad and, through a series of mergers, formed the New York Central and Hudson River RR Company, linking New York City with Buffalo. Vanderbilt continued to expand his railroad empire through financial maneuvers, and in the 20th cent. New York Central trains reached as far west as St. Louis, with trunk lines in six states. In 1914 the railroad reverted to its original name. By 1930, having absorbed other large railroads, the New York Central was one of the leading railroads connecting the Eastern seaboard with Midwestern cities. The only railroad having freight connections into Manhattan, it was an important factor in New York City's food supply. The New York Central was responsible for many technological innovations, including the first sleeping car, the first high-powered brakes, and the first centralized traffic-control system. In 1968, after a long legal battle that reached the U.S. Supreme Court, the New York Central and the Pennsylvania railroads merged to form the Penn Central Company. At the time of merger, the New York Central operated in 11 states and 2 Canadian provinces.

New York City Ballet, one of the foremost American dance companies of the 20th cent. It was founded by Lincoln KIRSTEIN and George BALANCHINE as the Ballet Society in 1946. In 1948 the company took its present name and began regular performances at the New York City Center. It moved to the New York State Theater at Lincoln Center for the Performing Arts in 1964. Under Balanchine's direction the company developed a distinctly American style of dancing, combining Italian, French, and Russian traditions with an austere emotional control and flair for musicality. The company's works have ranged from the intensely dramatic *Age of Anxiety* (1950) and the highly comic *Souvenirs* (1955) to the formal abstractions of *Agon* (1958) and the lavish theatricality of *A Midsummer Night's Dream* (1962). Balanchine has been closely identified with the company's development, although other outstanding choreographers, including Jerome ROBBINS, have created works for it. Its roster of exceptional performers has included Maria TALLCHIEF, Melissa Hayden, André EGLEVSKY, Todd Bolender, Suzanne Farrell, Edward VILLELLA, and Jacques d'AMBOISE. The company has toured extensively throughout the United States and abroad. See study by Lincoln Kirstein (1973).

New-York Historical Society, New York City. Founded in 1804, the society is a repository of art, artifacts, and literature relating to American, especially New York, history. Among its celebrated permanent collections are 435 watercolors by John James Audubon for his engraved folio volumes, *The Birds of America,* and American paintings from colonial times through the 19th cent. The society's educational programs include changing exhibitions of American cultural subjects, lectures by noted scholars and historians, and a large library facility providing extensive material to scholars on early America.

New York, New Haven, and Hartford RR, commonly called the New Haven RR; inc. 1872. Between 1872 and 1920, when dozens of small railroads were completed under the direction of financier John P. Morgan and company president Charles S. Mellen, the railroad's holdings were vastly expanded to include c.2,000 mi (3,220 km) of tracks throughout New England, intercity electric railroads, steamship lines, and public utilities. In 1913, the New Haven faced financial catastrophe, and in 1914 the railroad's operations were investigated by the Interstate Commerce Commission. Hurt by the growth of automobile and truck transportation and by the depression of the 1930s, the New Haven went bankrupt. It prospered during World War II under new management but collapsed in the late 1950s because of unprofitable passenger service. In 1968 the railroad, having been reorganized, merged with the newly formed Penn Central Company.

New York Philharmonic-Symphony Orchestra, oldest symphony orchestra in the United States. Its present name derives from the merger (1928) of the New York Philharmonic Orchestra with the New York Symphony Orchestra. The Philharmonic Society of New York was formed in 1842 and gave its first concert that year. Ureli C. Hill, its first president, was also one of its conductors and violinists. The first permanent conductor, Carl Bergmann, was appointed in 1865. Other important conductors were Leopold Damrosch (1876-77), Theodore Thomas (1877-78; 1879-91), Anton Seidl (1891-98), Walter Damrosch (1902-3), Gustav Mahler (1909-11), and Joseph Stransky (1911-23). In 1921 the Philharmonic merged with the National Symphony Orchestra, whose conductor, J. W. Mengelberg, remained with the Philharmonic until 1930. After engagements as guest conductor, Wilhelm Furtwängler was appointed (1925) permanent conductor. Arturo Toscanini was his successor (1927-36). The New York Symphony Orchestra—the other component of the merged Philharmonic-Symphony—was founded by Leopold Damrosch in 1878 and conducted by him until 1885. His son Walter, who succeeded him, pioneered the performance of new works and brought symphonic music to many American communities for the first time. In 1920 this orchestra toured Europe, the first American group to do so. After the merger Toscanini conducted until he was succeeded by John Barbirolli (1937-43), Artur Rodzinsky (1943-47), Leopold Stokowski (1949-50), and Dmitri Mitropoulos (1949-57). Leonard Bernstein became musical director in 1958, retiring in 1969. He was succeeded by Pierre Boulez in 1971. Now commonly known as the New York Philharmonic, the orchestra plays summer concerts of a more popular nature in Central Park in New York. It has made many recordings and toured in North and South America, Europe, and the USSR. In 1962 it moved into Philharmonic Hall, now Avery Fisher Hall, at LINCOLN CENTER FOR THE PERFORMING ARTS. See John Erskine, *The Philharmonic-Symphony Society of New York* (1943); Howard Shanet, *Philharmonia: A History of New York's Orchestra* (1974).

New York Pro Musica (New York Pro Musica Antiqua), vocal and instrumental ensemble, founded in New York City in 1952 by Noah Greenberg. The group performed music of the era 1200 to 1700. Since early composers did not usually score their music, the group researched and reconstructed much of the music it performed. Instruments such as the SACKBUT, SHAWM, CRUMHORN, zinke, viola da gamba, and portative organ were also restored or constructed. The ensemble was famous for its annual production of the *Play of Daniel,* a medieval music drama. It also performed works by such composers as Henry Purcell, Orlando di Lasso, and Palestrina, and their contemporaries. For several reasons, including financial pressures, the group disbanded in 1974.

New York Public Library, free library supported by private endowments and gifts and by the city and state of New York, chartered in 1895. It is the largest library in the world, being a depository of all books printed in the United States as well as a great research and branch library circulation system. A bequest (1848) of John Jacob Astor left $400,000 for a reference library, which was chartered in 1849, constructed on Lafayette Place, and opened to the public in 1854. J. G. Cogswell, superintendent (1848-61), compiled the first catalog. The Lenox Library (chartered 1870; opened 1876) on Fifth Ave. at 70th St. was the gift of the book collector James LENOX; it, too, was strictly a reference library. The will of S. J. Tilden established the Tilden Trust (chartered 1887) for the maintenance of a free reading room. After extended litigation, the sum of about $2 million was made available in 1892. An act consolidating the Astor and Lenox libraries and the Tilden Trust was passed in 1895. J. S. BILLINGS was appointed first director of the library. In 1897, New York City agreed to build and equip a central building on the site of the Croton reservoir on Fifth Ave. between 40th and 42d St. and to provide for its maintenance and repair. The building, designed by Thomas Hastings and J. M. Carrère, was completed in 1911. A circulation department was formed in 1901 by the absorption of the 11 branches of the New York Free Circulating Library founded in 1878 by teachers of a Grace Church sewing class and chartered in 1880. In 1901, Andrew Carnegie gave more than $5 million for buildings for circulation branches, provided the city would give the land and guarantee maintenance. From this fund, 39 Carnegie branches have been built. The branch system also absorbed several independently endowed circulating libraries including the Harlem Library, the Washington Heights Library, the Aguilar Free Library (Jewish; four branches), and the Cathedral Library (Roman Catholic; five branches). A circulating and reference branch devoted entirely to the performing arts is located at LINCOLN CENTER FOR THE PERFORMING ARTS. A new midtown branch was opened in 1970 at 8 E 40th St. in Manhattan. In 1974 the department had 83 branches and six bookmobiles in the boroughs of Manhattan, the Bronx, and Richmond; Queens and Brooklyn have independent systems. The central building houses the reference collection of books, pamphlets, records, films, and other materials; the executive offices for both reference and circulation departments; an art gallery; a photograph-lending library; a library for the blind and physically handicapped; and one branch with circulating materials for all age levels. In 1973 the total number of volumes, excluding reference books, in all branches was 3,281,248. Noncirculating reference works numbered 496,577. Circulating materials other than books numbered 5,180,371. The total circulation figure of all materials in all branches was 10,686,286 items. In the fiscal year 1972-73 the total expenditure by the library system for books alone was $1,707,000 and for other materials, $578,000. The library has especially fine collections on Americana, art, economics, folklore, music, black history and literature, New York City, Jewish history, and Semitic languages. It has an excellent newspaper collection and is an important collector and holder of prints, manuscripts, first editions, and rare books, including the Berg collection of English and American literature. See histories by H. M. Lydenberg (1923, repr. 1972) and Phyllis Dain (1972).

New York School of Social Work: see COLUMBIA UNIV.

New York State Barge Canal, waterway system, 525 mi (845 km) long, traversing New York state and connecting the Great Lakes with the Hudson River and Lake Champlain. The canal, a modification and improvement of the old ERIE CANAL, was authorized (1903) by public vote, was begun in 1905, and was completed in 1918. Its main sections are the Erie Canal, extending from Troy to Tonawanda; the Champlain Canal, joining the Erie Canal at Waterford and extending north (via the Hudson as far as Fort Edward) to Whitehall on Lake Champlain; the Oswego Canal, connecting the Erie Canal with Oswego on Lake Ontario; and the Cayuga and Seneca Canal, joining the Erie Canal with Cayuga and Seneca lakes. The Barge Canal (12 ft/3.7 m deep), with 57 electrically operated locks, accommodates 2,000-ton vessels and is toll free. Pleasure craft are the most numerous vessels on the canal.

New York Times Company vs. Sullivan, case decided in 1964 by the U.S. Supreme Court. In 1960 the *Times* ran a fund-raising advertisement signed by civil rights leaders that criticized, among other things, certain actions of the Montgomery, Ala., police department. Some facts were incorrect. Although no names were mentioned, L. B. Sullivan, Montgomery's police commissioner, sued the *Times* for libel and won $500,000 in an Alabama court. The newspaper appealed. At issue was the protection given press criticism of the official conduct of public officials. In overturning the lower court's ruling, the Supreme Court held that debate on public issues would be inhibited if officials could recover for honest error that produced false defamatory statements. The court limited the right of recovery to public officials who could prove actual malice (i.e., that the newspaper knew the statement was false or acted in reckless disregard of the truth).

New York University, mainly in New York City; coeducational; chartered 1831, opened 1832 as the Univ. of the City of New York, renamed 1896. It comprises 13 schools and colleges, maintaining four main centers (including the Medical Center) in the city, as well as the Institute of Environmental Medicine at Sterling Forest, N.Y. Its research units also include the Courant Institute of Mathematical Sciences, the Institute of Rehabilitation Medicine, and the Institute of Finance. New York Univ. conducts programs in Spain, France, and Puerto Rico. Among its other facilities in the city are Town Hall (a concert hall operated by the university since 1958), and a well-known fine arts center.

New Zealand (zē'lənd), country (1971 pop. 2,860,-475), 103,736 sq mi (268,676 sq km), in the S Pacific Ocean. The capital is WELLINGTON. New Zealand comprises NORTH ISLAND and SOUTH ISLAND (the two principal islands), STEWART ISLAND, and the CHATHAM ISLANDS. Small outlying islands belonging to New Zealand are the Auckland Islands, the Kermadec Islands, Campbell Island, the Antipodes, Three Kings Island, Bounty Island, Snares Island, and Solander Island. Dependencies are the Tokelau Islands, Niue Island, and Ross Dependency. The Cook Islands, internally self-governing, are "free associates" of New Zealand. North Island is known for its active volcanic mountains, its hot springs, and its mineral deposits. The country's most important river (the Waikato) and largest lake (Taupo) are both on North Island. On South Island, the massive Southern Alps extend almost the entire length of the island, and in the southwest are many beautiful fjords. The largest areas of virgin forest are in the southern and northern extremities of South Island. Among the unusual

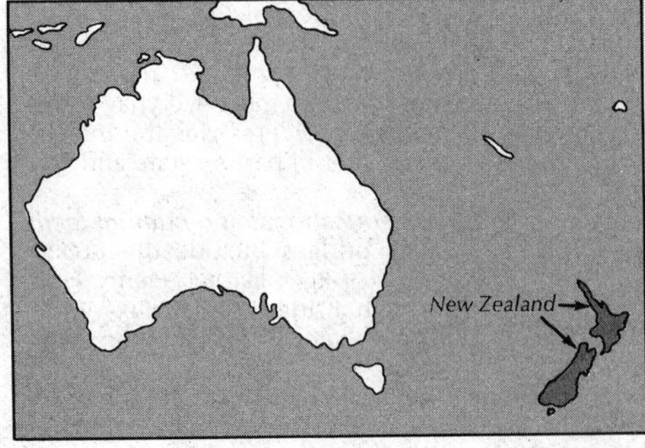

animals native to New Zealand are the kiwi, the albatross, certain varieties of parrot, the tuatara (survivor of a prehistoric order of reptiles, Rhynchocephalia), and poisonous spiders; there are no land snakes. Large oyster beds are found in the Foveaux Strait between Stewart Island and South Island. Extensive areas of New Zealand have been set aside as national parks, the most impressive being Tongariro, Tasman, and Fiordland parks. In addition to Wellington, the principal cities are AUCKLAND (the leading port), CHRISTCHURCH, DUNEDIN, LOWER HUTT, and INVERCARGILL. More than 40% of the population live in urban areas. Agriculture is the mainstay of the economy, although industry employs a larger number of people. The principal exports are dairy products, meat, and wool. Other important products include wheat, fruits, and kauri gum. Small amounts of coal, gold, iron, and oil are also produced. Food processing is the largest manufacturing industry; and there is a variety of small light-manufacturing industries. The Dutch navigator, A. J. Tasman, was the first European to reach New Zealand, which was already inhabited by Polynesian Maoris. Of the present Maori population of about 225,000, most live on North Island, largely in the hot springs district. New Zealand was visited by Capt. James Cook four times between 1769 and 1777. The first missionary, Samuel MARSDEN, arrived in 1814. Between 1792 and 1840, Englishmen made several unsuccessful attempts to found a colony. In 1840 the first permanent settlement was made at Wellington by a group sent by the New Zealand Company and led by Edward Gibbon Wakefield. In that year the Treaty of Waitangi guaranteed to the Maoris the full possession of their land in exchange for their recognition of the sovereignty of the British crown. Nevertheless, the white settlers continued until 1870 to wage bloody battles against the Maoris over land. Originally part of the New South Wales colony of Australia, New Zealand was made a separate colony in 1841. In 1852 the British Parliament granted it self-government, and by the Statute of Westminster of 1931 the colony became completely independent (although the New Zealand Parliament did not confirm the statute until 1947, preferring instead to have Great Britain conduct its foreign affairs). New Zealand has been a leader in progressive social legislation. It was the first country to grant (1893) women over 21 the right to vote. A comprehensive social security system was begun in 1898 with the enactment of an old age pension law. New Zealand sent troops to aid the U.S. war effort in South Vietnam in the 1960s. The New Zealand government consists of the governor general (representing the British crown), a prime minister and cabinet (the effective executive), and a unicameral parliament. The chief political parties are the Labour and the National. New Zealand is a member of the Commonwealth of Nations, the United Nations, and the Southeast Asia Treaty Organization. There are universities at Auckland, Hamilton, Wellington, Palmerston North, Christchurch, and Dunedin. New Zealand has no established religion; the three largest denominations are Anglican, Presbyterian, and Roman Catholic. See John Forster, *Social Process in New Zealand* (1969); K. B. Cumberland and J. S. Whitelaw, *New Zealand* (1970); R. M. Lockley, *Man Against Nature* (1970); Keith Sinclair, *A History of New Zealand* (rev. ed. 1970).

New Zealand literature. New Zealand has produced only a few writers known outside its own islands: Among them are Katherine MANSFIELD, short-story writer; Sylvia ASHTON-WARNER, novelist and teacher; Hector Bolitho, biographer; Eileen Duggan, Catholic poet; Kenneth Sisam, scholar; "G. B. Lancaster" (born in Tasmania), historical novelist; Dame Ngaio MARSH, writer of detective fiction; and Janet FRAME, novelist. Other 20th-century writers who have attained recognition outside New Zealand are Errol Brathwaite, Ian Cross, Maurice Duggan, O. E. Middleton, Frank Sargeson, and Maurice Shadbolt. From such 19th-century writers as Alfred Domett and Samuel BUTLER to present-day students of Maori culture and of New Zealand government, authors from outside New Zealand have found fascinating subject matter there. See histories of New Zealand literature by Alan Mulgan (1943), J. C. Reid (1946), and G. A. Wilkes and J. C. Reid (1970); Joan Stevens, *The New Zealand Novel, 1860–1965* (2d ed. 1966); H. W. Rhodes, *New Zealand Fiction since 1945* (1968); V. J. O'Sullivan, ed., *An Anthology of Twentieth-Century New Zealand Poetry* (1970).

New Zealand spinach, succulent annual (*Tetragonia expansa*) of Australia, New Zealand, Japan, and S South America, grown for the edible leaves. The plant grows prostrate, often spreading to cover several feet. It is cooked like spinach. It is in the same family as the ICE PLANT. New Zealand spinach is classified in the division MAGNOLIOPHYTA, class Magnoliopsida, order Caryophyllales, family Aizoaceae.

Nexø, Martin Andersen: see ANDERSEN NEXØ.

Ney, Elisabeth or **Elisabet** (nī), 1833–1907, German-American sculptor, b. Münster. After studying sculpture at Munich and Berlin, she traveled widely and executed busts of King George V of Hanover, Garibaldi, and Bismarck. She emigrated to America in 1870, living and working in Texas, where she made statues of Stephen F. Austin, Samuel Houston, and other prominent Texans. See biography by J. I. Fortune and Jean Burton (1943); Vernon Loggins, *Two Romantics and Their Ideal Life* (1946).

Ney, Michel (mēshĕl' nā), 1769–1815, marshal of France. Called "the bravest of the brave" by Napoleon I, Ney, a cooper's son from Saarlouis, rapidly rose to glory in the French Revolution. He distinguished himself in the campaigns of 1794 and 1795, commanded the army of the Rhine briefly in 1799, seized Elchingen (1805), and conquered Tyrol. His assistance was decisive in Napoleon's victory at Friedland. Ney's greatest feat was his defense of the rear in the retreat from Moscow in 1812. He was created Duke of Elchingen and prince of Moskowa by Napoleon. Later, Ney was one of the generals who urged Napoleon to abdicate after Leipzig. Ney was raised (1814) to the peerage by Louis XVIII. On Napoleon's return from exile in Elba, Ney promised the king that he would stop Napoleon on his march to Paris, but instead he joined Napoleon and commanded in the WATERLOO CAMPAIGN. He was condemned for treason by the house of peers and shot. See biography by J. T. Foster (1968).

Neyagawa (nāyägä'wä), city (1970 pop. 206,961), Osaka prefecture, SW Honshu, Japan, on the Shinyodo River. It is a suburb of Osaka.

Neyshabur (nāshäbo͝or'), city (1966 pop. 33,482), Khorasan prov., NE Iran. It is the trade center for a farm region where cotton, fruit, and grain are grown. Manufactures of the city include food products and leather goods; turquoise is mined nearby. Neyshabur was founded by the Sassanid ruler Shapur I in the 3d cent. A.D. and was rebuilt (4th cent.) by Shapur II. The city became one of the foremost cities of Persia. Under the Seljuk Turks (11th–12th cent.) is was made into an important cultural center; several colleges were founded there by Nizam al-Mulk. Al-Ghazali, the noted philosopher of the 11th–12th cent., studied in Neyshabur, and his famous contemporary Omar Khayyam, the poet and mathematician, was born in the city and is buried there. The tomb of Omar was rebuilt in 1934. Near Neyshabur archaeologists have made important finds of glazed pottery and stucco work from the 9th and 10th cent. The city is also known as Nishapur.

Nezhin (nyĕ'zhĭn), city (1969 est. pop. 58,000), S central European USSR, in the Ukraine, on the Oster River. It is a rail terminus on the main Moscow-Kiev line and an agricultural trade center. Industries include engineering, food processing, and the manufacture of machinery, railroad cars, lacquers, paints, clothing, building materials, and whaling equipment. Known in the 11th cent., the city was the center of the Nezhin Ukrainian Cossack regiment from 1649 to 1782. It became an important trading center in the 17th and 18th cent. after Greek merchants received permission from hetman Chmielnicki to settle there in 1657.

Neziah (nēzī'ə), family of Nethinim returned from the Exile. Ezra 2.54; Neh. 7.56.

Nezib (nē'zĭb), city, SW Palestine, NW of Hebron. Joshua 15.43.

Nez Percé Indians (nĕz pûrs, nā pĕrsā'), [Fr.,= pierced nose], North American Indians whose language belongs to the Sahaptin-Chinook branch of the Penutian linguistic stock (see AMERICAN INDIAN LANGUAGES). Also called the Sahaptin, or Shahaptin, they were given the name "Nez Percé" by the French because some of them wore nose pendants; however, this custom does not seem to have been widespread among them. They were typical of the Plateau area, fishing for salmon and gathering camas, cowish, and other roots. After the introduction of the horse (c.1700) they became noted horse breeders and adopted many Plains area traits, including buffalo hunts. In 1805, when visted by Lewis and Clark, they were occupying a large region in W Idaho, NE Oregon, and SE Washington. In the 1830s the Nez Percé, then numbering some 6,000, attracted national attention by sending emissaries to St. Louis to ask for books and teachers. Their request attracted to the Pacific Northwest missionaries who played an important role in opening the region to settlement. The Nez Percé ceded (1855) a large part of their territory to the United States. The gold rushes in the 1860s and 1870s, however, brought large numbers of miners and settlers onto their lands, and a treaty of cession was fraudulently extracted (1863) from part of the tribe. This led to the uprising under Chief JOSEPH in 1877. By the early 1970s, about 1,500 Nez Percé lived on a reservation in Idaho. See H. J. Spinder, *The Nez Percé Indians* (1908, repr. 1974); Theodore Mathieson, *The Nez Percé War* (1964); A. M. Josephy, Jr., *The Nez Percé Indians and the Opening of the Northwest* (1965, abr. ed. 1971); M. H. Brown, *The Flight of the Nez Percé* (1966, repr. 1972); Deward Walker, *Conflict and Schism in Nez Percé Acculturation* (1968).

Nez Percé National Historical Park: see NATIONAL PARKS AND MONUMENTS (table).

Ngami, Lake (əng-gä'mē, ng–), reedy marsh, c.40 mi (60 km) long and from 4 to 8 mi (6.4–12.9 km) wide, NW Botswana. During the Pleistocene epoch, the lake covered an extensive area. Since the late 1880s, when papyrus growth blocked the mouth of its main tributary, the lake has greatly shrunk in size; it now intermittently receives water from the Okavango River. David Livingstone, the Scottish missionary and explorer, was the first European to visit (1849) the lake.

Ngo Dinh Diem: see DIEM, NGO DINH.

Ngouabi, Marien (ən-gwä'bē), 1938–, president of the People's Republic of the Congo (1969–). A soldier, he became chief of the general staff and head of the National Revolutionary Council, which removed Alphonse Massamba-Debat from office in 1968. As head of state from 1969 he established an authoritarian regime that crushed opposition elements.

Nguyen Cao Ky: see KY, NGUYEN CAO.

Nguyen Thi Binh: see BINH, NGUYEN THI.

Nguyen Van Thieu: see THIEU, NGUYEN VAN.

Nha Trang (nä träng), city (1968 est. pop. 102,000), E central South Vietnam, a commercial port on the South China Sea. It has an important fishing industry. On the highway and railroad from Saigon north to the demarcation line, it was the site of a major U.S. military base in the Vietnam War; the base extended 15 mi (24 km) south to the harbor of Cam Ranh Bay. The city has a commercial airport.

Ni, chemical symbol of the element NICKEL.

niacin: see COENZYME; VITAMIN.

niacinamide: see VITAMIN.

Niagara, Ont.: see NIAGARA-ON-THE-LAKE.

Niagara, river, 34 mi (55 km) long, issuing from Lake Erie between Buffalo, N.Y., and Fort Erie, Ont., Canada. It flows north around Grand Island (American) and over NIAGARA FALLS to Lake Ontario; the river forms part of the U.S.-Canadian border. The upper section of the river is navigable for c.20 mi (30 km) to a series of rapids above the falls; in its last 7 mi (11 km) it is again navigable, from Lewiston, N.Y., to Lake Ontario. The New York State Barge Canal enters the river at Tonawanda, N.Y.; the Welland Canal, on the Ontario side, is a lake-freighter route around the falls. Hydroelectric power is generated by diverting water from the river above Niagara Falls to generating plants. Many bridges cross the Niagara River, notably Peace Bridge (1927); bridges linking Grand Island with both shores (1935); Rainbow Bridge (1941) below the falls; and American Rapids Bridge (1960), linking Goat Island with the mainland.

Niagara, Fort: see FORT NIAGARA.

Niagara Falls, city (1971 pop. 67,163), S Ont., Canada, on the Niagara River opposite Niagara Falls, N.Y. Formerly called Clifton, it is a port of entry and an important industrial city, the home of Canadian factories for many well-known U.S. firms. Electric power is supplied by the falls. Between the city and the falls and along the gorge below the falls is Queen Victoria Park.

Niagara Falls, city (1970 pop. 85,615), Niagara co., W N.Y., at the great falls of the Niagara River; inc. 1892. Tourism is one of its oldest industries, and there are many state parks in the area, including New York State Niagara Reservation. The city is also a port of entry; its manufactures include chemical and mechanical products, rocket parts, and food products. One of the world's first hydroelectric power plants was built there; it was replaced between 1963 and 1965 by a plant capable of producing 2,100,000 kw. Settled by Indians, the site was occupied by the French in the 1680s, captured by the British in 1759, and settled by Americans in 1805. Lost to the British during the War of 1812, it was regained by the United States after the Treaty of Ghent in Dec., 1814.

Several bridges span the river to Canada. Niagara Univ. and a junior college are there.

Niagara Falls, in the Niagara River, W N.Y. and S Ont., Canada; one of the most famous spectacles in North America. The falls are on the international line between the cities of Niagara Falls, N.Y., and Niagara Falls, Ont. Goat Island splits the cataract into the American Falls (167 ft/51 m high and 1,060 ft/323 m wide) and the Horseshoe, or Canadian, Falls (158 ft/48 m high and 2,600 ft/792 m wide). The falls were formed c.10,000 years ago as the retreating glaciers exposed the Niagara escarpment, thus permitting the waters of Lake Erie to flow north, over the scarp, to Lake Ontario. The escarpment has been gradually eroded back toward Lake Erie, a process that has formed the Niagara Gorge (c.7 mi/11 km long); the Whirlpool Rapids and the Whirlpool are there. Horseshoe Falls is eroding upstream at a faster rate than the American Falls because of the greater volume of water passing over it. A great rock slide occurred (1954) at the American Falls and formed a huge talus slope at its base. Water was diverted from the American Falls for several months in 1969 by the U.S. Corps of Engineers to study the bedrock and to remove some of the talus. International agreements control the diversion of water for hydroelectric power; weirs divert part of the flow above the deeper Canadian Falls to supplement the flow in the shallower American Falls. Hydroelectric-power developments were authorized under the Niagara Diversion Treaty (1950), which stipulated a minimum flow to be reserved for the falls and the equal division of the remaining flow between the United States and Canada. In the United States the project was undertaken by the Power Authority of the State of New York. Water is diverted from the river above the upper rapids into underground conduits (46 ft/14 m wide and 66 ft/20 m high). It is then conveyed overland, dropping 314 ft (96 m) to a point below the lower rapids where, as it returns to the river, the water passes through turbines that power 13 generators of the Robert Moses Niagara Power Plant (1,950,000-kw capacity; opened 1961), the largest non-Federal hydroelectric plant in the United States and one of the world's largest power stations. Associated with the New York hydroelectric-power project is the construction in the area of new roads, bridges, and parks. In Canada the project was undertaken by the Hydro-Electric Power Commission of Ontario. Water is diverted from the river above the falls and is fed into the Sir Adam Beck Generating Stations (1,775,000 kw; 1954) by way of a series of tunnels and canals. The governments of the United States and Canada also control the appearance of the surrounding area, much of which has been included in parks since 1885. The earliest written description of the falls is that of Louis Hennepin (in *Nouvelle Découverte,* 1697), who was with the expedition of Robert Cavalier, sieur de La Salle, the French explorer, in 1678. Historical and natural history material relating to the region is in the Niagara Falls Museum in the city of Niagara Falls, N.Y.

Niagara-on-the-Lake or **Niagara,** town (1971 pop. 12,552), S Ont., Canada, on Lake Ontario at the mouth of the Niagara River. It was settled (1784) by American LOYALISTS and in 1792 Lieutenant Governor Simcoe made the town the capital of Upper Canada, renaming it Newark. The legislature met there until 1796. Fort George, built (1796–99) to defend the settlement, was taken in 1813 by the United States but retaken in the same year. The town is officially called Niagara-on-the-Lake to distinguish it from the Canadian and U.S. cities of Niagara Falls.

Niamey (nyämā'), city (1970 est. pop. 70,000), capital of Niger and its Niamey dept., SW Niger, a port on the Niger River. Niamey is Niger's largest city and its administrative and economic center. Much of its importance stems from its location on the Niger River at the crossroads of the country's two main highways. The city is the trade center for an agricultural region that specializes in growing groundnuts. Manufactures include bricks, food products, beverages, ceramic goods, cement, and shoes. Niamey was a small town when the French colonized the area in the late 19th cent., but it grew after it became the capital of Niger in 1926. It is the site of the National School of Administration (1963) and the National Museum, which has ethnological and zoological collections.

Nias (nē'äs), volcanic island (1961 pop. 314,829), 1,569 sq mi (4,064 sq km), Indonesia, in the Indian Ocean, off Sumatra. The chief town is Gunungsitoli. Rice and other food crops are grown, livestock are raised, and there is hunting and fishing. Native handicraft is highly developed; megalithic shrines dot the land. The Dutch began trading there in 1669. The island is subject to severe earthquakes.

Nibelungen (nē'bəlo͝ong"ən) or **Nibelungs,** in Germanic myth and literature, an evil family possessing a magic hoard of gold. The hoard is accursed. The **Nibelungenlied** (-lēt") [song of the Nibelungen] is a long Middle High German epic by a south German poet of the early 13th cent. It includes pagan legends and traditions but is patently the product of a Christian, courtly world. The story is set in Worms, capital of Burgundy, and at the court of Etzel (Attila the Hun). The warrior Siegfried, having won the Nibelung hoard, marries Kriemhild and captures the Icelandic Queen Brunhild for Kriemhild's brother King Gunther. Brunhild contrives Siegfried's death at the hands of Gunther's henchman Hagen, who takes the treasure and buries it in the Rhine. The rest of the poem recounts Kriemhild's vengeance. She marries Etzel and has a child by him. Lulled into security, Gunther accepts her invitation and visits her with his court, including Hagen. The poem ends with general slaughter and holocaust, which only Etzel and a few others survive. Although marred by stylistic flaws, the Nibelungenlied contains fine delineations of character, especially of Kriemhild, Siegfried, and Hagen. Its great strength lies in its acute depiction of the Germanic ideas of fate and loyalty to the chief. There are many English translations, e.g., by D. G. Mowatt (1962) and F. G. Ryder (1962). See studies by D. G. Mowatt and H. Sacker (1967) and H. Bekker (1971). **Der Ring des Nibelungen** [the ring of the Nibelungs] is an operatic tetralogy by Richard Wagner, comprising the four operas *Das Rheingold, Die Walküre, Siegfried,* and *Die Götterdämmerung.* The complete cycle was first produced in Bayreuth in 1876. It was based largely on Scandinavian legends from the VOLSUNGASAGA, on the Icelandic *Poetic Edda,* and on the Nibelungenlied. See studies by A. E. Dickinson (1926) and F. E. Winkler (1964).

Nibhaz (nĭb'hăz), deity worshiped in Samaria by the captive Avites. 2 Kings 17.31.

Nibshan (nĭb'shăn), unidentified desert place, S Palestine. Joshua 15.62.

Nicaea (nīsē'ə), city of Bithnyia, N Asia Minor, built in the 4th cent. B.C. by Antigonus I as Antigonia and renamed Nicaea by Lysimachus for his wife. It flourished under the Romans and was the scene of the ecumenical council called in A.D. 325 by Constantine I. Another council held in 787 sanctioned the devotional use of images. The city, captured by the Turks in 1078 and by the Crusaders in 1097, passed finally to the Turks in 1330. It is sometimes called Nice. The modern İznik, Turkey, is on the site.

Nicaea, empire of, 1204–61. In 1204 the armies of the Fourth Crusade set up the Latin Empire of Constantinople, but the Crusaders' influence did not extend over the entire Byzantine Empire. Several Greek successor states, chief among them the empire of Nicaea, sprang up (see also EPIRUS, DESPOTATE OF; TREBIZOND, EMPIRE OF). The empire of Nicaea preserved the continuity of emperors, patriarchs, and institutions of Byzantium. Founded by THEODORE I (Theodore Lascaris) in NW Asia Minor, with Nicaea as its capital, it played the decisive part in reuniting the Byzantine Empire. Theodore I and his successors of the LASCARIS family expanded their domains, defeated their neighbors to the south, the Seljuk Turks, and in alliance with IVAN II of Bulgaria weakened their chief rivals, the despots of Epirus. They successfully warred against the Latins, and when the Mongol invasions weakened the Turks of Iconium, Nicaea became supreme in Asia Minor. MICHAEL VIII (Michael Palaeologus), who usurped the throne of Nicaea in 1259, captured Constantinople from the Latins and restored (1261) the Byzantine Empire.

Nicaea, First Council of, 325, 1st ecumenical council, convened by Roman Emperor Constantine the Great to solve the problems raised by ARIANISM. It has been said that 318 persons attended, but a more likely number is 225, including every Eastern bishop of importance, four Western bishops (among them HOSIUS of Córdoba, president of the council), and two papal legates. The chief figures at the council were ARIUS and his opponent, ATHANASIUS. The council adopted, as a test of faith, a formula that seems to have been based on a simple baptismal creed presented possibly by Eusebius of Caesarea; this was not, however, the Nicene Creed as we have it today (see CREED). The formula included the word *homoousion* [consubstantial], which was used concerning the Son and the Father. The word, suggested probably by Hosius, became the touchstone of orthodoxy and the bugbear of Arianism, for it established the divinity and the equality of the Son in the Trinity. The creed was accepted by all the bishops except two, who were banished along with Arius to Illyricum. The council ruled on other questions as well, attempting to standardize the date of Easter, undertaking to reform the clergy, and granting patriarchal authority to the bishop of Alexandria. The First Council of Nicaea was significant as the model and the original of ecumenical councils. The test it adopted provided a universal statement of faith in place of the earlier and varying baptismal formulas.

Nicaea, Second Council of, 787, 7th ecumenical council, convened by Byzantine Empress IRENE. Called to refute ICONOCLASM, the council declared that images ought to be venerated (but not worshiped) and ordered them restored in churches. Practically the only Western delegates were the papal legates, but popes have confirmed the conciliar canons. It is the last council accepted by both the Roman Catholic Church and the Orthodox Eastern Church as ecumenical.

Nicanor (nīkā'nôr), one of the seven deacons. Acts 6.5.

Nicaragua (nĭkärä'gwä), republic (1970 pop. 1,974,924), 49,579 sq mi (128,410 sq km), Central America. The capital is MANAGUA. Nicaragua, the most sparsely populated nation in Central America, is bordered on the N and NW by Honduras, on the E by the Caribbean Sea, on the S by Costa Rica, and on the SW by the Pacific Ocean. There are four main geographic areas. The northwestern highlands have peaks as high as 8,000 ft (2,440 m). On the Caribbean is the torrid MOSQUITO COAST, with the historic port of BLUEFIELDS. A lowland belt running northwest to southeast contains lakes Managua and Nicaragua. The fourth region is a narrow volcanic belt squeezed between the lakes and the Pacific; in this region the productive wealth and the population (almost entirely mestizo) are concentrated. CORINTO, on the Pacific, is the chief port. Agriculture employs nearly two thirds of the work force and accounts for nearly one third of the gross national product. The chief commercial crops are coffee, cotton, and sugar-cane; these, together with meat, are the largest exports. Timber and gold are also exported. The principal manufactured goods are chemicals, textiles, and processed foods. The population is overwhelmingly Roman Catholic. There are universities at LEÓN and Managua. The country probably takes its name from Nicarao, an Indian cacique defeated in 1522 by the Spanish under Gil González de Ávila. In 1524, Francisco FERNÁNDEZ DE CÓRDOBA founded

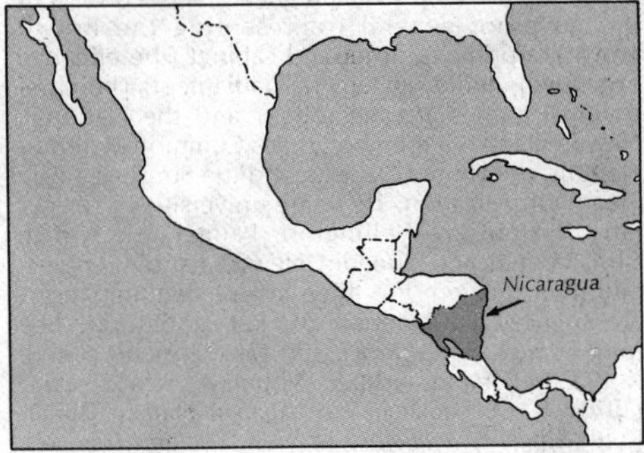

León and GRANADA. León became the political and intellectual capital, Granada the stronghold of the aristocracy. Under Spanish rule Nicaragua was part of the captaincy general of Guatemala. After declaring independence from Spain (1821), Nicaragua was briefly part of the Mexican Empire of Agustín de Iturbide and then (1825–38) a member of the CENTRAL AMERICAN FEDERATION. Nicaraguan politics were wracked by conflict between Liberals and Conservatives, centered respectively in León and Granada; Managua was founded as the capital in 1855 as a compromise. British influence had been established along the east coast in the 17th cent., and in 1848 the British seizure of SAN JUAN DEL NORTE opened a period of conflict over control of the Mosquito Coast. The United States was interested in a transisthmian canal (see NICARAGUA CANAL), and its interest was heightened by the discovery of gold in California. In 1851, Cornelius VANDERBILT opened a transisthmian route through Nicaragua for the gold seekers. The CLAYTON-BULWER TREATY (1850) settled some of the issues between Great Britain and the United States concerning the proposed canal, but Nicaragua remained in a state of disorder that culminated in the temporary triumph (1855–57) of the filibuster William WALKER. After Walker's defeat there was a long period of quiet under Conservative control until the Liberal leader, José Santos ZELAYA, became president in 1894. He instituted a vigorous dictatorship, extended Nicaraguan authority over the Mosquito Coast, promoted economic development, and interfered in the affairs of neighboring countries. His financial dealings with Britain aroused the apprehension of the United States and helped bring about his downfall (1909). In 1912, U.S. marines were landed to support the provisional president, Adolfo Díaz, in a civil war. The Bryan-Chamorro Treaty, giving the United States exclusive rights for a Nicaraguan canal and other privileges, was ratified in 1916. (It was terminated in 1970.) The Liberals opposed the U.S. intervention, and there was guerrilla warfare against the U.S.-supported regime for years. American occupation ended in 1925 but resumed the next year, when Emiliano CHAMORRO attempted to seize power. Augusto César SANDINO was a leader of the anti-American forces. The U.S. diplomat Henry L. Stimson succeeded in getting most factions to agree (1927) to binding elections, although Sandino continued to fight. The marines were withdrawn in 1933. Three years later Anastasio SOMOZA emerged as the strong man in Nicaragua. He officially became president in 1937 and ruled for 20 years. In the 1947 elections a new president was chosen, but he was ousted by Somoza after less than a month in office. Nicaragua virtually became Somoza's private estate; the regime aroused much criticism among liberal groups in Latin America. Under Somoza relations with other Central American republics were poor. In 1960 a boundary dispute with Honduras was decided against Nicaragua by the International Court of Justice. Somoza was assassinated in 1956, and his son Luis Somoza Debayle became president. Another son, Anastasio Somoza Debayle, headed the armed forces. René Schick Gutiérrez was chosen by the Somoza family to be elected president in 1963. After his death in 1966, Lorenzo Guerrero, the vice president, succeeded. Anastasio Somoza Debayle was elected president in 1967. In Aug., 1971, following an agreement between the ruling National Liberal party (NLP) and the opposition Conservative party, the national assembly voted to abrogate the 1950 constitution. A constitutional assembly selected a three-man governing council to run the country until new presidential elections were held. Although Somoza resigned from office in May, 1972, handing power to the governing council, he retained effective control of the country as head of the armed forces, leader of the NLP, and, after the earthquake (Dec., 1972) that devasted Managua, as director of the emergency relief operations. Somoza resigned from the armed forces in Feb., 1974, to become a presidential candidate and easily won the September elections. In the early 1970s sporadic terrorism and guerrilla incidents were directed against the Somoza regime. See Neill Macaulay, *The Sandino Affair* (1967); William Kamman, *A Search for Stability: United States Diplomacy Toward Nicaragua, 1925–1933* (1968); Rafael de Nogales y Méndez, *The Looting of Nicaragua* (1928, repr. 1970); J. M. Ryan et al., *Area Handbook for Nicaragua* (1970); D. I. Folkman, *The Nicaragua Route* (1972); H. K. Meyer, *Historical Dictionary of Nicaragua* (1972); William Walker, *The War in Nicaragua* (1860, repr. 1972).

Nicaragua, Lake, 3,089 sq mi (8,001 sq km), c.100 mi (160 km) long and up to 45 mi (72 km) wide, SW Nicaragua; the largest lake of Central America. It is drained into the Caribbean Sea by the San Juan River. Lake Nicaragua, along with Lake Managua (which drains into it from the northwest), occupies part of the Nicaragua Depression, an extensive lowland region stretching across the isthmus. Once part of the sea, the lake was formed when the land rose. There are several islands in the lake (the largest is Isla de Ometepe); and small volcanoes rise above its surface. The fresh water of Lake Nicaragua contains fish usually associated with salt water, including tuna and sharks, which have adapted to the environmental change. The lake is a transportation route; Granada is its chief port. Located only 110 ft (34 m) above sea level, the lake reaches a depth of 84 ft (26 m). It was to be an important link in the proposed NICARAGUA CANAL.

Nicaragua Canal, proposed waterway between the Atlantic and the Pacific oceans. It would be 172.8 mi (278 km) long and would generally follow the San Juan River, then go through Lake Nicaragua near the southern shore and across the narrow isthmus of Rivas to the Pacific Ocean. First proposed by Henry Clay, the U.S. Secretary of State in 1826, the route was an important factor in negotiation of the CLAYTON-BULWER TREATY (1850). In later times the route has been considered as an adjunct to the Panama Canal; it would shorten the water distance between New York and San Francisco by nearly 500 mi (805 km). Under the Bryan-Chamorro Treaty (1916), the United States paid Nicaragua $3 million for an option in perpetuity and free of taxation, including 99-year leases to the Corn Islands and a site for a naval base on the Gulf of Fonseca. Costa Rica protested that Costa Rican rights to the San Juan River had been infringed, and El Salvador maintained that the proposed naval base affected both it and Honduras. Both protests were upheld by the Central American Court of Justice. The court rulings were ignored by Nicaragua and the United States. The action was bitterly criticized by Latin Americans and others as an example of U.S. imperialism.

Niccoli, Niccolò de' (nēk-kōlō' dā nēk'kōlē), 1363–1437, Italian humanist. One of the distinguished Florentine scholars in Cosimo de' Medici's circle, he wrote little but is remembered for his important collection of Greek and Latin manuscripts. He devoted his time and fortune (as well as funds provided by Cosimo) to this collection, now the nucleus of the Laurentian library in Florence.

Niccolò d'Arezzo: see NICCOLÒ DI PIERO LAMBERTI.

Niccolò di Piero Lamberti (nēk-kōlō' dē pyā'rō lämbĕr'tē), c.1370–1451, Italian sculptor and architect of the early Renaissance, sometimes called Niccolò d'Arezzo. He worked mostly in Florence on decorations for the cathedral and for the Church of Orsanmichele and in Venice on the facade of St. Mark's.

Nice (nēs), city (1968 pop. 325,400), capital of Alpes-Maritimes dept., SE France, on the Mediterranean Sea. Nice is the most famous resort on the French Riviera. Although the economy depends mainly on the tourist trade, the electronics industry as well as other manufactures are important. The port of Nice handles both commercial and tourist traffic. The Carnival of Nice marks the height of the city's festival season. Probably a Greek colony (*Nikaia*, or *Nicaea* in Latin) established in the 5th cent. B.C., Nice became an episcopal see in the 4th cent. A.D. It was pillaged and burned by the SARACENS in 859 and 880. In the 13th and 14th cent. the city belonged to the counts of Provence and Savoy. In 1543 the united forces of Francis I and Barbarossa attacked and burned Nice. It was annexed to France in 1793, restored to Sardinia in 1814, and again ceded to France in 1860 after a plebiscite. At the beginning of the French Revolution the city was a haven for Royalist émigrés. Nice has several churches dating from the 12th through the 17th cent.

Nicene Creed: see CREED.

Nicephorus, Saint (nīsĕf'ərəs), 758?–829?, patriarch of Constantinople (806–15), Byzantine historian and theologian. St. Nicephorus attended the Second Council of Nicaea as lay representative of the emperor. His appointment by Emperor Nicephorus I to the patriarchate while he was still a layman aroused the anger of the monastic party under St. Theodore of Studium, but the quarrel was quieted. St. Nicephorus opposed ICONOCLASM and secured a pledge of orthodoxy from Emperor MICHAEL I. Michael's successor, LEO V, however, insisted that the patriarch modify his views, but Nicephorus refused and was deposed and exiled. In his exile he wrote a brief narrative of Byzantine history from 602 to 769 and several tracts against iconoclasm. Feast: March 13.

Nicephorus I, d. 811, Byzantine emperor (802–11). He was minister of finance under Empress IRENE, whom he deposed and succeeded. He improved the state of the treasury, revised the taxes of all classes, and vigorously asserted the imperial authority over the church. This policy and his appointment of St. Nicephorus to the patriarchate of Constantinople precipitated a conflict with THEODORE OF STUDIUM, whom he exiled in 809. Nicephorus consolidated Byzantine strength in the Balkans. He was killed while fighting the Bulgars and was succeeded briefly by his son Stauracius and then by his son-in-law, Michael I.

Nicephorus II (Nicephorus Phocas) (fō'kəs), c.912–969, Byzantine emperor (963–69). He was a successful general under Constantine VII and Romanus II. On Romanus' death (963) he married the emperor's widow, Theophano, and was proclaimed emperor by his troops. He left the aristocracy its estates and took property from the monasteries. The heavy taxes he imposed to support his military ventures against the Arabs and the Bulgars caused much discontent. His downfall and murder, however, were the result of a palace intrigue between Theophano and her lover, John Tzimisces. Tzimisces succeeded to the throne as JOHN I.

niche: see ECOLOGY.

Nichinan (nēchēnän'), city (1970 pop. 53,288), Miyazaki prefecture, SE Kyushu, Japan, on the Pacific Ocean. It is an important fishing port and manufacturing center for paper pulp and paper products.

Nicholas, Saint, patron of children and sailors, of Greece, Sicily, and Russia, and of many other places and persons. Little is known of him, but he is traditionally identified as a 4th-century bishop of Myra in Asia Minor. His relics were stolen from Myra in the Middle Ages and taken to Bari, Italy. St. Nicholas is the subject of many legends. He is credited with restoring to life three boys who had been chopped up and pickled in salt by a butcher. Another famous story concerns his giving three bags of gold to the daughters of a poor man and thus saving them from lives of prostitution. Later tradition transformed the bags into three gold balls, which became the symbol of pawnbrokers. In the Netherlands and elsewhere St. Nicholas's feast (Dec. 6) is a children's holiday, appropriate for gifts. The English in colonial New York adopted from the Dutch the now unrecognizable saint, calling him Santa Claus (a contraction of the Dutch *Sint Nikolaas*). They moved his feast day to the English gift holiday, Christmas. The career and qualities attributed to Santa Claus are all recently acquired.

Nicholas I, Saint (Nicholas the Great), c.825–867, pope (858–67), a Roman; successor of Benedict III. He was a vigorous and politically active pope who arbitrated both temporal and religious disputes. His decisions often set important precedents, as when the pope upheld the right of the bishop of Soissons to appeal to Rome against his superior, Archbishop HINCMAR. Much of his pontificate was concerned with preventing the proposed divorce of LOTHAIR of Lotharingia, who wished to remarry. Even when Holy Roman Emperor Louis II occupied Rome, the pope refused to yield. In the end he forced Lothair to reinstate his wife. Nicholas challenged the right of PHOTIUS to occupy the see of Constantinople and attempted to have St. IGNATIUS OF CONSTANTINOPLE restored to it. St. Nicholas worked with Boris I to introduce Roman ecclesiastical jurisdiction in Bulgaria, which had recently been converted by the Byzantines. A letter from the pope to Boris is extant. He was succeeded by Adrian II. Feast: Nov. 13.

Nicholas III, d. 1280, pope (1277–80), a Roman named Giovanni Gaetano Orsini; successor of John XXI. As a cardinal he made a great reputation in diplomacy, and he was a close confidant of popes for 30 years. He was elected pope after a six-month delay. Nicholas's principal efforts were directed to rendering the Holy See free of civil interference; he was most successful in obtaining renunciation by Rudolf I (Rudolf of Hapsburg) of all control over the Romagna. By passing laws preventing non-Romans from obtaining privileges in Rome, he quietly frustrated the ambitions of Charles I, king of Naples, to dominate central Italy. He was the first pope in a century to live regularly in Rome, and he has been called the founder of the Vatican. He was succeeded by Martin IV.

Nicholas V, antipope (1328–30); see RAINALDUCCI, PIETRO.

Nicholas V, 1397–1455, pope (1447–55), an Italian named Tommaso Parentucelli, b. probably Sarzana, Liguria; successor of Eugene IV. From Eugene IV he inherited the antipapal enactments of the Council of Basel (see BASEL, COUNCIL OF). By a conciliatory policy Nicholas gained the Concordat of Vienna (1448) with Holy Roman Emperor FREDERICK III. It undid much of the damage to papal authority, and the following year the council and the antipope, Felix V, submitted to Nicholas. In 1450 a splendid jubilee marked the schism's end. To further church reform, the pope sent (1450) Nicholas of Cusa to Germany. Pope Nicholas was renowned for learning and piety; he established the papacy as a patron of the humanities and was a founder of the Vatican Library. Lorenzo VALLA benefited from his generosity. A plot on his life and the fall (1453) of Constantinople to the Ottoman Turks clouded his last days. He was succeeded by Calixtus III.

Nicholas I, 1796–1855, czar of Russia (1825–55), third son of Paul I. His brother and predecessor, Alexander I, died childless (1825). Constantine, Paul's second son, was next in succession but had secretly renounced (1822) the throne after marrying a Polish aristocrat. This secrecy resulted in confusion at Alexander's death and touched off the Decembrist uprising, a rebellion against Nicholas, which he crushed on the first day of his reign. Nicholas strove to serve his country's best interests as he saw them, but his methods were dictatorial, paternalistic, and often inadequate. One important achievement, however, was the codification (1832–33) of existing Russian law. A few measures attempted to limit the landlords' powers over their serfs, and the condition of peasants belonging to the state was improved. Industry progressed somewhat; the first Russian railroad was completed in 1838. Efforts were made to stabilize the ruble and reduce the growing national debt. The motto "autocracy, orthodoxy, and nationality," expressing the principles applied to a new system of education, was also used by Nicholas in suppressing liberal thought, controlling the universities, increasing censorship, persecuting religious and national minorities, and strengthening the secret police. Intellectual life was in ferment, the revolutionary movement took form, and the two schools of thought held by SLAVOPHILES AND WESTERNIZERS emerged. With PUSHKIN, LERMONTOV, and GOGOL a golden age in literature began. Under Nicholas, Russia gained control of part of Armenia and the Caspian Sea after a war with Persia (1826–28). A war with Turkey (1828–29; see RUSSO-TURKISH WARS) gave Russia the eastern coast of the Black Sea and the mouth of the Danube. Nicholas brutally suppressed the uprising (1830–31) in POLAND and abrogated the Polish constitution and Polish autonomy. In 1849 he helped Austria crush the revolution in Hungary. His attempts to dominate Turkey led to the disastrous CRIMEAN WAR (1853–56). He was succeeded by his son Alexander II. See biography by Constantin de Grunwald (1946, tr. 1954); I. G. Golovin, *Russia under the Autocrat Nicholas I* (1846, repr. 1970).

Nicholas II, 1868–1918, last czar of Russia (1894–1917), son of Alexander III and Maria Feodorovna. He was educated by private tutors and the reactionary POBYEDONOSTZEV. Alexander III gave his son little training in affairs of state, and Nicholas proved to be a charming but ineffective and easily influenced ruler. In 1894 he married Princess Alix of Hesse (ALEXANDRA FEODOROVNA). Soon after his accession Nicholas stated that he intended to maintain the autocratic system. He continued the suppression of opposition, the persecution of religious minorities, and the Russification of the borderlands. Revolutionary movements were growing rapidly. The Social Democratic Labor party (later divided by BOLSHEVISM AND MENSHEVISM) was founded in 1898; the SOCIALIST REVOLUTIONARY PARTY was formed in 1901; the liberals pressed for constitutional government. In foreign affairs, Nicholas initiated the first of the HAGUE CONFERENCES and supported an aggressive policy in the Far East. The humiliating outcome of the RUSSO-JAPANESE WAR (1904–5) resulted in the peasant revolts, industrial strikes, and violent outbreaks known as the Revolution of 1905. In Jan., 1905, a crowd of workers who had come peaceably to petition the czar were fired upon in front of the Winter Palace; the government's action on that "Bloody Sunday" proved fateful. After the general strike of Oct., 1905, Count WITTE, who soon became premier, induced Nicholas to sign a manifesto promising representative government and basic civil liberties. An elective DUMA and an upper chamber were set up, but neither the extreme revolutionaries nor the czar were seriously disposed to uphold the parliament. Nicholas soon curtailed the Duma and dismissed Witte in 1906, replacing him with I. A. Goremykin and then with P. A. STOLYPIN. The outbreak in 1914 of World War I briefly swept aside internal conflict. In 1915, Nicholas took over the command of the army from Grand Duke Nicholas and left the czarina in virtual control at home. This act led to a constant stream of resignations from the ministers; their posts were filled by the sycophants of Alexandra, who was completely dominated by RASPUTIN until his murder in 1916. Discontent at home spread, the army tired of war, the food situation deteriorated, the government tottered, and in March, 1917, Nicholas was forced to abdicate (see RUSSIAN REVOLUTION). He was held first in the Czarskoye Selo palace, then near Tobolsk. The advance, in July, 1918, of counterrevolutionary forces caused the soviet of Ekaterinburg (now Sverdlovsk) to fear that Nicholas might be liberated; after a secret meeting a death sentence was passed on the czar and his family, who were shot in a cellar at Ekaterinburg on the night of July 16. Their bodies were burned. Nicholas's vague mysticism, limited intelligence, and submission to sinister influences made him particularly unfit to cope with the events that led to his tragic end. See C. E. Vulliamy, ed., *The Letters of the Tsar to the Tsaritsa* (tr. 1929) and E. J. Bing, ed., *The Secret Letters of the Last Tsar* (tr. 1938); Michael Florinsky, *The End of the Russian Empire* (1931); Sir Bernard Pares, *The Fall of the Russian Monarchy* (1939); Noble Frankland, *Imperial Tragedy* (1961); Victor Alexandrov, *The End of the Romanovs* (1966); R. K. Massie, *Nicholas and Alexandra* (1967).

Nicholas I, 1841–1921, prince (1860–1910) and king (1910–18) of Montenegro, successor of his uncle, Danilo II. In 1862, after a series of frontier incidents, Nicholas was forced into war with the Ottoman Empire (Turkey). Despite heroic resistance he had to conclude an unfavorable peace. He then reorganized his army. Although he rivaled Serbia for leadership of the South Slavs, in 1876 he allied himself with Serbia, intervened in favor of the rebels in Bosnia and Hercegovina, declared war on the Turks, and waged a successful campaign in Hercegovina. Russia's entrance (1877) into the war assured him of success. The Treaty of SAN STEFANO (1878) trebled the size of Montenegro; the final boundaries adopted at the Congress of Berlin reduced the Montenegrin gains but gave access to the Adriatic Sea. Montenegro was recognized as fully independent, and, in 1910, Nicholas proclaimed himself king. He sided with Serbia in World War I but sought (1915) a separate peace with the Central Powers after his troops had been routed. When Montenegro was occupied by Austrian troops, he fled the country. In exile, he resisted the proposed union of Montenegro with Serbia under a Serbian king and as a result was deposed (1918) by a national assembly, which proclaimed the union. Nicholas succeeded in marrying his five daughters into the ruling houses of Europe, including those of Italy, Russia, and Serbia.

Nicholas (Nikolai Nikolayevich) (nyĭkəlī' nyĭkəlī'əvĭch), 1856–1929, Russian grand duke and army officer; first cousin of Czar Alexander III and grandson of Czar Nicholas I. He served in the Russo-Turkish War of 1877–78. During the Revolution of 1905, he refused the czar's request that he become military dictator, thus forcing Nicholas to accept Count Witte's plan for an elective national assembly. Nicholas was made commander in chief of the Russian armies at the outbreak of World War I. In 1915 Czar Nicholas II, influenced by the czarina and Rasputin, relieved him of his post and took over the command himself. Grand Duke Nicholas was made commander in the Caucasus, where he won successes against the Turks until the February Revolution of 1917 deprived him of his command. He left Russia in 1919 and settled in France.

Nicholas II Land: see SEVERNAYA ZEMLYA, USSR.

Nicholas of Cusa (Nicolaus Cusanus), 1401?–1464, German humanist, scientist, statesman, and philosopher, from 1448 cardinal of the Roman Catholic Church. The son of a fisherman, Nicholas was educated at Deventer, Heidelberg, Padua, Rome, and Cologne. He became bishop of Brixon (Bressanone) in 1450 and instituted widespread, though temporary, reforms of the monasteries. As papal legate he traveled throughout Europe preaching and negotiating diplomatic affairs for the Holy See. Nicholas' greatest achievements were in science and philosophy. His researches and writings formed major advances in Renaissance mathematics, astronomy, and mysticism. He held, before the time of Copernicus and Newton, that the nearly spherical earth revolves on its axis about the sun and that the stars are other worlds. He described the Gregorian calendar reform in detail, before it occurred. In mathematics Nicholas propounded significant concepts of the infinitesimal and contributed to modern relativity theory. His mystical religious philosophy was set forth in his essays *De Docta Ignorantia* [of learned ignorance] (1440, tr. 1954), *De Conjuncturis Libri Duo,* and *De Visio Dei* [vision of God] (1453, tr. 1928). It anticipated the direction of growth of Renaissance conjecture concerning the nature of man and his relationship to the cosmos. See studies by Morimichi Watanabe (1963) and F. H. Burgevin (1969).

Nicholls, Francis Redding Tillou, 1834–1912, American politician, b. Donaldsonville, La. At the outbreak of the Civil War he helped organize a company of Confederate volunteers and through active service rose to the rank of major general. He resumed his former law practice after the war and in 1876 was nominated for governor by the Democrats in a desperate effort to end the carpetbag rule in Louisiana. He was thus involved in the disputed state and presidential election returns of 1876 and shared in negotiations that placed him in the governorship and swung the electoral votes to Rutherford B. HAYES. A conservative, Nicholls served with ability. He retired to private life in 1881 but in 1887 ran for governor again as the foe of the notorious Louisiana Lottery. The destruction of the lottery was the chief event of his second administration. He was (1892–1911) a state supreme court justice.

Nichols, Jeannette Paddock, 1890–, American historian, b. Rochelle, Ill. She received her Ph.D. from Columbia in 1923 and taught there (1919–21) and at Wesleyan College (1922–23). In 1957 she became a professor at the Univ. of Pennsylvania. She wrote a history of Alaska (1924) and *Twentieth Century United States* (1943). She edited, with J. G. Randall, *Democracy in the Middle West, 1840–1940* (1941), and she wrote several books in conjuncton with her husband, the historian **Roy Franklin Nichols** 1896–1973, b. Newark, N.J., who also received his Ph.D. from Columbia in 1923. He taught there from 1922 to 1925 before going (1925) to the Univ. of Pennsylvania, where he became a full professor (1930) and dean of the graduate school (1952). Among his books are *The Democratic Machine, 1850–1854* (1923); *Franklin Pierce, Young Hickory of the Granite Hills* (1931); *Religion and American Democracy* (1959); *The Stakes of Power, 1845–1877* (1961); and *The Invention of the American Political Parties* (1967). With his wife he wrote *The Growth of American Democracy* (1939) and *The Republic of the United States: A History* (1942). He received the Pulitzer Prize in history for *The Disruption of American Democracy* (1948), a detailed analysis of U.S. political history immediately preceding the Civil War dealing in particular with the breakup of the Democratic party. See his autobiography, *A Historian's Progress* (1968).

Nicholson, Ben, 1894–, English painter; son of Sir William Nicholson. Nicholson's geometric abstractions of landscapes and still lifes are discreetly colored and lyrically expressed. In works such as *Relief* (1939; Mus. of Modern Art, New York City) Nicholson developed the purism of de STIJL with great elegance. His paintings are in many collections, including the museums of Minneapolis, Detroit, Philadelphia, New York City, and Washington, D.C. He was married to the painter Winifred Dacre and later to the sculptor Barbara HEPWORTH. See his *Drawings, Paintings and Reliefs, 1911–1968* (1969); study by Charles Harrison (1969, repr. 1972).

Nicholson, Francis, 1655–1728, British colonial administrator in North America. Lieutenant governor under Sir Edmund ANDROS, he fled (1689) to England during the revolt in New York led by Jacob LEISLER. He returned (1690) to America as lieutenant governor of Virginia and was later governor of Maryland (1694–98) and governor of Virginia (1698–1705). *A Modest Answer to a Malicious Libel* (1704) is a defense of his conduct in quarrels in Virginia. In 1709 Nicholson led an expedition against Port Royal (now Annapolis Royal, N.S.) and the next year successfully occupied the town, recording his experiences in the *Journal of an Expedition . . . for the Reduction of Port Royal* (1711). He was named (1713) governor of Nova Scotia, but his term of office ended on the death of Queen Anne in 1714. He was (1720–25) royal governor of South Carolina. During all his administrations he actively promoted education and the Church of England.

Nicholson, James, c.1736–1804, American naval officer, b. Chestertown, Md.; brother of Samuel Nicholson. During the American Revolution, Nicholson, appointed (1776) a captain in the Continental navy, was senior officer after the dismissal of Esek Hopkins in 1778. While awaiting the *Virginia,* his first command, Nicholson and his crew fought at the battle of Trenton (Dec., 1776). In attempting to elude the British blockade of Chesapeake Bay, the *Virginia* ran aground and was captured (1778), although Nicholson escaped. His next ship, the *Trumbull,* held the *Watt* to a draw in 1780, but in 1781 it was captured by superior British forces. Nicholson later lived in New York City, where he was active as a Jeffersonian in politics.

Nicholson, James William Augustus, 1821–87, American naval officer, b. Dedham, Mass.; grandson of Samuel Nicholson. He was appointed a midshipman in 1838, served under Commodore Perry in the Far East (1853), and took part in the attempt to relieve Fort Sumter (1861) that precipitated the Civil War. During the war he commanded ships in the successful Union assaults on Port Royal, S.C., Jacksonville, and other Florida coastal cities and on Mobile Bay. He was retired in 1883 with the rank of rear admiral.

Nicholson, Samuel, 1743–1811, American naval officer, b. Maryland. The brother of James Nicholson, he served in the Continental navy during the American Revolution, making many successful captures. He was commissioned (1794) captain in the new U.S. navy, superintended the construction of the *Constitution,* and on her completion in 1798 (at the time of American-French difficulties) cruised the Atlantic in search of French ships.

Nicholson, Sir William, 1872–1949, English woodcut artist, illustrator, and painter. The striking contrasts of black and white of his woodcutting technique were used to great effect on posters, on which he collaborated with his brother-in-law James Pryde. They became known as the Beggerstaff Brothers. Nicholson illustrated many books and his woodcut portraits, verging sometimes on caricature, cover a large segment of London society. He was knighted in 1936. His work is represented in the Tate Gallery, London.

Nicias (nĭsh'ēəs), d. 413 B.C., Athenian political leader and general. After Pericles' death he emerged as the primary rival of Cleon and his war party. He was a moderate democrat, not an oligarch, and he wanted peace with Sparta. In 421 he arranged the Peace of Nicias. When the expedition to Syracuse was urged by ALCIBIADES, Nicias tried to discourage it, but Athens nevertheless made him commander, along with Alcibiades and Lamachus. Alcibiades was soon recalled, and Lamachus died, leaving the expedition in Nicias's care. Nicias vacillated in his policies in the siege. When the Spartan Gylippus arrived, and only retreat from Syracuse was feasible, Nicias refused to allow a retreat until it was too late. The Athenian fleet and expedition were shortly overwhelmed by the Syracusans, and Nicias was captured in a hasty retreat on land and subsequently executed.

nickel, metallic chemical element; symbol Ni; at. no. 28; at. wt. 58.71; m.p. about 1453°C; b.p. about 2732°C; sp. gr. 8.902 at 25°C; valence 0, +1, +2, +3, or +4. Nickel is a hard, malleable, ductile, lustrous, silver-white metal with a face-centered cubic crystalline structure. It takes a high polish. In its magnetic properties and chemical activity it resembles iron and cobalt, the elements preceding it in group VIII of the PERIODIC TABLE. It is a fairly good conductor of heat and electricity. In its familiar compounds nickel is bivalent, although it assumes other valences. It also forms a number of complex compounds. Most nickel compounds are blue or green. Nickel dissolves slowly in dilute acids but, like iron, becomes passive when treated with nitric acid. Finely divided nickel adsorbs hydrogen. Commercially, the most important compound is the sulfate, which is used in electroplating, as a mordant in dyeing, in preparation of other nickel compounds, and in paints, varnishes, and ceramics. The nickel oxides are also important; they are used in ceramic glazes, in glass manufacture, in the preparation of alloys, and in the Edison BATTERY. Pure wrought nickel in the form of sheets and wire has many uses. Finely divided nickel is used as a catalyst, e.g., in the hydrogenation of oils. Nickel is used as a protective and ornamental coating for less corrosion resistant metals, especially iron and steel; it is applied by electroplating and by other methods (see PLATING). It is used in the nickel-cadmium storage battery. The major use of nickel is in the preparation of alloys. The chief attributes of nickel alloys are strength, ductility, and resistance to corrosion and heat. Many stainless STEELS contain nickel. Nickel steels are used in safes and armor plate. Alloys of nickel and copper are widely used, e.g., Monel metal, nickel bronze, and nickel silver. The so-called German silver is a nickel-copper alloy. Nickel-copper alloys are used in coinage; the American "nickel" coin is about one-fourth nickel. Constantan is a nickel-copper alloy used in thermocouples. Other alloys of nickel include nickel-chromium alloys (such as Nichrome) used for electric heating elements; alloys of aluminum, nickel, cobalt, and iron (such as Alnico) used to make magnets; and alloys of nickel, chromium, and cobalt used structurally in jet engines. Nickel occurs in a number of minerals; its chief ores are PENTLANDITE and PYRRHOTITE (nickel-iron sulfides) and GARNIERITE (nickel-magnesium silicate). Nickel is present in most meteorites. It is also found in trace amounts in plants and animals. The chief production of nickel is from the sulfide ores mined near Sudbury, Ont., Canada. Nickel sulfide ores are concentrated by the FLOTATION PROCESS, then smelted or roasted to partially convert them to the oxide form, and further treated in a Bessemer converter to form a matte. The metal is separated from copper and other metals present in the Bessemer matte by electrorefining or chemical methods (see Mond process under MOND, LUDWIG). The end product is in the form of nickel cathodes, pellets, or powder. Nickel was discovered in 1751 by A. F. Cronstedt in kupfernickel (niccolite), a copper-colored nickel arsenide mineral.

Nicklaus, Jack William, 1940–, American golfer, b. Columbus, Ohio. He began playing golf at the age of 10 and before becoming a professional in late 1961 was considered by many the greatest amateur golfer since Bobby Jones. In his first year as a professional in 1962 he defeated Arnold Palmer in the U.S. Open and won the first World Series of Golf. Capable of hitting drives in excess of 300 yards, Nicklaus won the Masters four times and the U.S. Open three times. In Dec., 1973, he became the first golfer to exceed $2 million in career earnings.

Niclaes, Hendrik: see FAMILISTS.

Nicobar Islands, India: see ANDAMAN AND NICOBAR ISLANDS.

Nicodemus (nĭk″ədē'məs), member of the Sanhedrin interested in Jesus. He helped St. Joseph of Arimathea to bury Him. John 3.1–21; 7.50,51; 19.39–42. Among the PSEUDEPIGRAPHA is a Gospel of Nicodemus.

Nicolai, Otto (ô'tō nēkōlä'ē, nē'kōlī), 1810–49, German composer. His opera *Il Templario* (1840), after Scott's *Ivanhoe*, was successful, but his masterpiece was the comic opera *The Merry Wives of Windsor* (1849). He founded (1842) the Philharmonic Concerts, Vienna, for the purpose of presenting adequate performances of Beethoven's music.

Nicolas (nĭk'ōləs), one of the seven deacons. He was a proselyte from Antioch. Acts 6.5.

Nicolay, John George (nĭk'əlā), 1832–1901, biographer of Lincoln, b. Bavaria. In 1837 he was brought to the United States, and his family settled in Pike co., Ill. He worked on the Pittsfield, Ill., *Free Press* and was its editor and owner from 1854 to 1856. In 1860 he and his close friend, John Hay, became private secretaries to Abraham Lincoln and continued as such during his presidency. In 1890 Nicolay and Hay brought out their *Abraham Lincoln: a History* (10 vol.), which had been planned since 1861. It is the authorized biography, and though biased by hero worship and a sometimes excessive respect for conventions, it is a basic historical work for study of the period. Hay and Nicolay also edited Lincoln's complete works. See biography by his daughter, Helen Nicolay (1949).

Nicole, Pierre (pyĕr nēkôl'), 1625–95, French Jansenist writer. He studied and taught at Port-Royal abbey, the center of Jansenism (see under JANSEN, CORNELIS). One of his pupils there was Racine. He worked with Pascal on the *Provinciales*. His chief writings in his mission of popularizing Jansenism were two series of epistolary essays, *Les Visionnaires* and *Lettres sur l'hérésie imaginaire*. In 1679 he fled with Antoine ARNAULD to Belgium, but he became reconciled with the authorities and returned to Paris in 1683. Subsequently he led in the attack on quietism.

Nicolet, Jean (zhäN nēkôlā'), 1598?–1642, French explorer in the Old Northwest. He came to New France with Samuel de Champlain in 1618. In 1634, under the direction of Champlain, he took a notable voyage west in search of the Northwest Passage, exploring Lake Michigan, Green Bay, and the Fox River. He was drowned on a trip to Trois Rivières.

Nicolle, Charles Jules Henri (shärl zhül äNrē' nēkôl'), 1866–1936, French physician and microbiologist. He worked with P. P. É. Roux in Paris and was director of the Pasteur Institute in Tunis from 1903 and professor at the Collège de France, Paris, from 1932. He worked on various diseases, including whooping cough, measles, trachoma, and influenza, and demonstrated (1909) the transmission of typhus by the body louse. For his work on typhus he received the 1928 Nobel Prize in Physiology and Medicine.

Nicolls, Richard, 1624–72, first English governor of New York, b. Bedfordshire, England. He served in the English civil war as a royalist and followed the Stuarts into exile, where he entered the service of the duke of York (later King James II). In 1664, Charles II laid claim to the Dutch colony in America and gave it to the duke of York, who appointed Nicolls governor. Nicolls and his followers took New Amsterdam from the Dutch with little difficulty. Despite his arbitrary powers, he was an effective ruler of the English colony, renamed New York. He balanced the interests of the English and Dutch settlers and brought about a gradual transition to English institutions. He issued the legal code known as the Duke's Laws in 1665. After his resignation (1667) Nicolls returned to England and was killed at the naval battle of Southwold Bay in the third Dutch War.

Nicol prism (nĭk'əl), optical device invented (1828) by William Nicol of Edinburgh. It consists essentially of a crystal of calcite, or ICELAND SPAR, that is cut at an angle into two equal pieces and joined together again with Canada balsam. An ordinary beam of light entering the crystal undergoes double refraction, i.e., is split into two parts, each of which is affected in a different way. One of these parts, the so-called ordinary ray, undergoes total reflection at the Canada-balsam joint and is turned off from its course to pass out at one side of the crystal. The other ray, the extraordinary ray, passes on through the crystal. By means of this device a beam of light can be polarized (see POLARIZATION OF LIGHT) or a beam of polarized light can be subjected to analysis. The principle involved has been applied to the microscope in the illumination of the field.

Nicolson, Sir Harold, 1886–1968, English biographer, historian, and diplomat, b. Tehran, Iran. Educated at Oxford, he entered the foreign office in 1909, and, until his resignation 20 years later, he represented the British government in various parts of the world. His work at the Paris Peace Conference (1919) prompted the study *Peacemaking, 1919* (1933) and stimulated an interest in diplomacy that is reflected in *Diplomacy* (1939) and *The Evolution of Diplomatic Method* (1954, 3d ed. 1963). He served in the House of Commons from 1935 to 1945 and was knighted in 1953. Among the subjects of his skillful and sympathetic biographies are Paul Verlaine (1921), Tennyson (1923), Byron (1924), Swinburne (1926), Curzon (1934), Dwight Morrow (1935), King George V (1953), and Sainte-Beuve (1957). Other works include *The Congress of Vienna* (1946), *Good Behaviour* (1956), *The Age of Reason* (1961), and *Kings, Courts, and Monarchy* (1962). He was married to the novelist Vita Sackville-West. See his diaries and letters, ed. by his son, Nigel Nicolson (3 vol., 1966–68); Nigel Nicolson, *Portrait of a Marriage* (1973).

Nicolson, Marjorie Hope, 1894–, American educator, b. Yonkers, N.Y., grad. Univ. of Michigan (B.A., 1914; M.A., 1918) and Yale (Ph.D., 1920). She was dean and professor at Smith from 1929 to 1941, when she became the first woman professor on the graduate faculties of Columbia. She remained there until 1962, serving her last eight years as chairman of the graduate department of English and Comparative Literature. She was a member of the Institute for Advanced Study at Princeton (1963–68). An authority on 17th-century literature and thought, she is the author of *The Breaking of the Circle* (1950), *Science and Imagination* (1956), *Mountain Gloom and Mountain Glory* (1959), *A Reader's Guide to Milton* (1963), *Pepys' Diary and the New Science* (1965), and *This Long Disease, My Life* (1968).

Nicomedia (nĭkōmē'dēə), ancient city, NW Asia Minor, near the Bosphorus, in present-day Turkey. Refounded (264 B.C.) by Nicomedes I of Bithynia to replace Astacus as his capital, it flourished for centuries. The Goths sacked the city in A.D. 258. Diocletian chose it for the eastern imperial capital, but it was soon superseded by Byzantium (Constantinople). The modern city on its site is İzmit.

Nicopolis (nĭkŏp'əlĭs, nī–) [Gr.,=city of victory], ancient city, NW Greece, in Epirus. It was founded by Octavian (later Augustus) to celebrate the victory (31 B.C.) at Actium, which is nearby. The city largely eclipsed Ambracia. It is mentioned by St. Paul (Titus 3.12). Its ruins are near the modern Préveza.

Nicosia (nĭkəsē'ə), Gr. *Levkosia,* Turkish *Lefkoşa,* city (1971 est. pop. 117,000), capital of Cyprus, on the Pedieos River in the central plain of the island. It is also the center of an administrative district. Nicosia, the country's largest city, is an agricultural trade center and has textile, brandy, cigarette, leather, pottery, and other manufactures. Known as Ledra or Ledrae in antiquity, it was the residence of the LUSIGNAN kings of Cyprus from 1192, became a Venetian possession in 1489, and fell to the Turks in 1571. The tombs of the Lusignans are in the former Church of St. Sophia (13th cent.), now a mosque. There also are remnants of the Venetian fortifications and museums with notable collections of antiquities. Nicosia was the scene of bitter strife in the period just prior to Cypriot independence (1960) and after the Turkish invasion of Cyprus (1974). The name is also spelled Nikosia.

nicotiana (nĭkō″shēā'nə) [see NICOTINE], any plant of the genus *Nicotiana* of the family Solanaceae (NIGHTSHADE family). Most species are herbs native to tropical America, although there are a few North and South American species and one Australian species. Many are cultivated for their fragrant trumpet-shaped flowers, which usually open at night. Commercial TOBACCO is obtained chiefly from the leaves of *Nicotiana tabacum*. The smaller plant cultivated and smoked by the Indians of E United States before the arrival of white men is *N. rustica*. It and other nicotianas are used for making insecticides as well as for smoking. Nicotiana is classified in the division MAGNOLIOPHYTA, class Magnoliopsida, order Polemoniales, family Solanaceae.

nicotinamide (nĭk″ətĭn′əmīd): see VITAMIN.

nicotinamide adenine dinucleotide and **nicotinamide adenine dinucleotide phosphate:** see COENZYME.

nicotine, $C_{10}H_{14}N_2$, poisonous, colorless, oily liquid ALKALOID with a pungent odor and an acrid taste. It turns brown on exposure to air. Dissolved in water, it is widely used as an insecticide. It is extremely poisonous to man because it interferes with the nervous system, causing respiratory failure and general paralysis. A very small dose, less than 50 mg, proves fatal within a few minutes. Nicotine occurs in the leaves of the tobacco plant, and some nicotine is present in tobacco smoke, although much of that present in tobacco is converted by combustion to less harmful products.

nicotinic acid: see COENZYME; VITAMIN.

Nicoya, Gulf of (nēkō′yä), inlet of the Pacific Ocean, Central America, between the Nicoya Peninsula and the northwest mainland of Costa Rica. The catch from the fine fishing in the gulf is canned at Puntarenas. The village of Nicoya on the peninsula was probably the first Spanish settlement (c.1530) in Costa Rica.

Nidaros: see TRONDHEIM, Norway.

Nidwalden: see UNTERWALDEN, Switzerland.

Niebuhr, Barthold Georg (bär′tôlt gā′ôrkh nē′bo͝or), 1776–1831, German historian, b. Copenhagen; son of Karsten Niebuhr. He served in the Danish and, after 1806, in the Prussian civil service, took part in the foundation of the Univ. of Berlin, and was (1816–23) Prussian ambassador to the Holy See. From 1823 to his death he taught at the Univ. of Bonn. Niebuhr's history of Rome (3 vol., 1811–32; tr. 3 vol., 1828–42) may be said to have inaugurated modern scientific historical method. Niebuhr related individual events to the political and social institutions of ancient Rome; he sought to recreate the past in terms understandable to the modern reader. An admirer of the Roman republic, he favored agrarianism as the basis of a well-balanced state. He regarded Prussia as a modern parallel of the Roman state and advocated Prussian leadership in the unification of Germany. His liberalism was antirevolutionary, and he was sympathetic to reforms instituted from above. See his translated *Collected Lectures* (8 vol., 1852–53); Antoine Guilland, *Modern Germany and Her Historians* (tr. 1915, repr. 1970).

Niebuhr, Helmut Richard, 1894–1962, American theologian, b. Wright City, Mo., grad. Elmhurst College (Ill.), 1912, and Eden Theological Seminary, 1915, M.A. Washington Univ., 1917, B.D. Yale Divinity School, 1923, Ph.D. Yale, 1924. He was the younger brother of Reinhold Niebuhr. He was ordained (1916) a minister in the Evangelical and Reformed Church and for a short time was a pastor in St. Louis. Niebuhr then taught (1919–22 and 1927–31) at Eden Theological Seminary and served (1924–27) as president of Elmhurst College. In 1931 he joined the faculty of Yale Divinity School and in 1954 was named Sterling professor of theology and Christian ethics at Yale Univ. Niebuhr was early influenced by the work of Kierkegaard and Barth; later, however, he turned his attention to the personal nature of man's relationship to God and advocated a reworking of Christianity in the light of the 20th cent. Among his works are *Social Sources of Denominationalism* (1929), *The Kingdom of God in America* (1937), *The Meaning of Revelation* (1941), *Christ and Culture* (1951), *The Purpose of the Church and Its Ministry* (1956), and *Radical Monotheism and Western Culture* (1960). See studies by Paul Ramsay, ed. (1959), J. D. Godsey (1970), Libertus Hoedermaker (1971), and J. W. Fowler (1974).

Niebuhr, Karsten (kär′stən), 1733–1815, German traveler in Arabia. He was sole survivor of a party of five (of whom the best known was Peter Forskal, a Swedish naturalist) sent by Frederick V of Denmark to explore Arabia (1761–63). From Mocha, Niebuhr sailed for India, returning to Europe by way of the Persian Gulf and the Tigris River, through Palestine, Syria, and Constantinople (1767). He wrote several accounts of his travels.

Niebuhr, Reinhold (rīn′hōld nē′bo͝or), 1892–1971, American religious and social thinker, b. Wright City, Mo. A graduate of Yale Divinity School, he served (1915–28) as pastor of Bethel Evangelical Church in Detroit, where he became deeply interested in social problems. In 1928 he began teaching at Union Theological Seminary, becoming professor of applied Christianity in 1930; he remained in this post until his retirement in 1960. In the early 1930s he shed his liberal Protestant hopes for the church's moral rule of society and became a political activist and a Socialist. A prolific writer, he urged—notably in *Moral Man and Immoral Society* (1932), *Christianity and Power Politics* (1940), and *The Nature and Destiny of Man* (2 vol., 1941–43)—clerical interest in social reforms as well as the beliefs that men are sinners, that society is ruled by self-interest, and that history is characterized by irony, not progress. After World War II, he dropped much of his social radicalism and preached "conservative realism." In his later works, such as *Faith and History* (1949), Niebuhr argued for balances of interests and defended Christianity as the world view that best explains the heights and barbarisms of human behavior. In *A Nation So Conceived* (1963) he analyzed aspects of the American character. He also wrote *Man's Nature and his Communities* (1965), *Faith and Politics* (ed. by R. H. Stone 1968), and *The Democratic Experience* (with P. E. Sigmund, 1969). See biography by R. H. Stone (1972); studies by C. W. Kegley et al., ed. (1956), H. P. Odegard (1956, repr. 1972), and June Bingham (1961, repr. 1972).

Niederle, Lubor (lü′bôr nē′dərlě), 1865–1944, Czech archaeologist and ethnographer, an authority on the origin and early civilization of the Slavs. He based his studies on archaeological findings, supplemented by historical, philological, and ethnographical information. His major work, *Slavonic Antiquities* (4 vol., 1901–25, in Czech), was partially translated into French as *Manuel de l'antiquité slave* (2 vol., 1923–26).

Niel, Adolphe (ädôlf′ nyĕl), 1802–69, marshal of France under Napoleon III. He served with the corps of engineers in the Algerian campaigns, in the French intervention against the Roman republic (1849), in the Crimean War, and in the Italian war of 1859. Becoming minister of war in 1867, he started a program of farseeing military reform that was generally abandoned after his death.

niello (nēĕl′ō) [Ital. from Latin *nigellus*=blackish], black metallic alloy of sulfur, copper, silver, and usually lead, used as an inlay on engraved metal. The metal surface is brushed with a borax solution as a flux, dusted with powdered niello, then heated. After cooling, the surface is scraped and shows a black pattern in the incised lines. Pulling a paper proof of the design in order to make corrections before inlaying is said to have been the start of printing from an engraved plate. The Egyptians are credited with originating niello decoration, which was practiced in classical times, spread throughout Europe during the Middle Ages, and came into high repute in the 15th cent. with the work of the Florentine goldsmith FINIGUERRA.

Nielsen, Carl, 1865–1931, Danish composer. Nielsen was a pupil of Niels Gade at the Royal Conservatory in Copenhagen. Considered Denmark's foremost composer, he is known internationally, primarily for his six symphonies. Nielsen also composed one concerto apiece for flute, clarinet, and violin; two operas; a woodwind quintet; four string quartets; songs; incidental music; and many other chamber, choral, and piano pieces. His orchestral writing is extremely dense in texture. His music is frequently polyphonic. Although he never abandoned tonality, he built works from contrasting key centers, so that they give little sense of a tonic key. Nielsen's books include *Living Music* (1953) and *My Childhood* (1953). See studies by Robert Simpson (1952 and 1965).

Niembsch Edler von Strehlenau, Nikolaus: see LENAU, NIKOLAUS.

Niemcewicz, Julian Ursyn (yo͞ol′yän o͞or′sĭn nyĕmtsĕ′vĕch), 1757–1841, Polish writer and patriot. A member of the Polish diet, he fought under Kosciusko in the insurrection of 1794 and with him was imprisoned in St. Petersburg. After going with Kosciusko to the United States he returned (1807) to Poland to become the secretary of the senate. In the insurrection of 1831 he failed to obtain Western aid for Poland, and he died, an exile, in Paris. Though not a great literary talent, he wrote historical and political plays, satires, novels, and poems that were important polemics in the cause of Polish liberation. His adaptations of Western themes greatly enriched Polish literature.

Niemen: see NEMAN, river, USSR.

Niemeyer (Soares), Oscar (o͞oskär′ nē′mīər so͞oä′rəs), 1907–, Brazilian architect. Influenced by Le Corbusier, Niemeyer developed an architecture noted for its daring conception and purity of line. He was one of the chief collaborators in the design of the ministry of education in Rio de Janeiro (1937–43). With Lúcio COSTA and P. L. Wiener, Niemeyer designed the Brazilian Pavilion for the New York World's Fair in 1939. For Pampulha, in Belo Horizonte, he planned several major buildings. In 1947 he collaborated on the design for the UN headquarters in New York City. Niemeyer directed the creation of the new capital, Brasília (1950–60) within Costa's master plan. His remarkable original work on this project brought him enormous acclaim. He designed several large structures (e.g., the Boavista Bank, Rio de Janeiro, 1946), and residences (e.g., the House Tremaine, Santa Barbara, Calif., 1947). See biographical studies by Stamo Papadaki (1960) and Rupert Spade, ed. (1971).

Niemoeller or **Niemöller, Martin** (both: mär′tĭn nē′mölər), 1892–, German Protestant churchman. He studied theology after distinguishing himself as a submarine commander in World War I. Though at first a supporter of National Socialism, Niemoeller (then a pastor at Berlin-Dahlem) preached courageously against the neopagan tendencies of the Hitler regime after it came into power in 1933. He attacked Hitler's creation of a "German Christian Church" and became the leader of the German pastors' emergency league and of the CONFESSING CHURCH which was subsequently organized. Briefly arrested in 1937, he was imprisoned again from 1938 until his liberation (1945) by the Allies. After his release Niemoeller became (1947) church president (the equivalent of bishop) of the Evangelical Church in Hesse-Nassau, with his seat at Wiesbaden, and founded (1948) a cooperative council of all German Protestant churches, of which he became president. Among his writings are his autobiography, *Vom U-Boot zur Kanzel* [From U-boat to pulpit] (1934). See biographies by C. S. Davidson (1959) and Dietmar Schmidt (tr. 1959); Marlene Maertens, ed., *The Challenge to the Church* (1965).

Nien Rebellion (nē′ĕn), uprising that occurred against the Ch'ing dynasty of China. Bands [Chinese,=*nien*] of antigovernment rebels in the south part of the North China Plain (between the Yangtze and Hwai rivers) coalesced in 1853 as government strength weakened in the face of the TAIPING REBELLION (1850–64). The Nien employed guerrilla tactics and swift cavalry movement but lacked a coherent ideology and strong central leadership. Faced with the greater Taiping challenge, the Ch'ing made little headway against the Nien. Finally in 1868, the Nien received a series of shattering blows from armies led by LI HUNG-CHANG and TSO TSUNG-T'ANG, and the rebellion was brought to an end. See study by Chiang Siang-tseh (1954).

Niepce, Joseph Nicéphore (zhôzĕf′ nēsāfôr′ nyĕps), 1765–1833, French chemist, who originated a process of photography (see PHOTOGRAPHY, STILL). From 1829 he worked with Louis Daguerre, who perfected the process after the death of Niepce. A nephew, **Claude Felix Abel Niepce de Saint-Victor,** 1805–70, also a chemist, was the first to use albumen in photography and also produced photographic engravings on steel.

Nietzsche, Friedrich Wilhelm (frē′drĭkh vĭl′hĕlm nē′chə), 1844–1900, German philosopher, b. Röcken, Prussia. The son of a clergyman, Nietzsche studied Greek and Latin at Bonn and Leipzig and was appointed to the chair of classical philology at Basel in 1869. In his early years he was friendly with the composer Richard Wagner, although later he was to turn against him. Nervous disturbances and eye trouble forced Nietzsche to leave Basel in 1879; he moved from place to place in a vain effort to improve his health until 1889, when he became hopelessly insane. Nietzsche was not a systematic philosopher but rather a moralist who passionately rejected Western bourgeois civilization. He regarded Christian civilization as decadent, and in place of its "slave morality" he looked to the superman, the creator of a new heroic morality that would consciously affirm life and the life values. That superman would represent the highest passion and creativity and would live at a level of experience beyond the conventional standards of good and evil. His creative "will to power" would set him off from "the herd" of inferior humanity. Nietzsche's thought had widespread influence but was of particular importance in Germany. Apologists for Nazism seized on much of his writing as a philosophical justification for their doctrines of national and racial superiority and their despisal of political democracy and equality. Most scholars regard this as a perversion of Nietzsche's thought, pointing to his strong individualism and his contempt for the state, especially the German state. Among his most famous works are *The Birth of Tragedy* (1872, tr. 1910); *Thus Spake Zarathustra* (1883–91, tr. 1909, 1930), and *Beyond Good and Evil* (1886, tr. 1907). See his selected letters ed. by Christopher Middleton (1969); biographies by C. K. Brinton (1941, repr. 1965), H. A. Reyburn (1948, repr. 1973), and Ivo Frenzel (1967); studies by R. J. Hollingdale (1965 and 1973), W. A. Kaufmann (3d ed. 1968), Rose Pfefler (1972), R. C. Solomon, ed. (1973), and J. T. Wilcox (1974).

Nieuwpoort or **Nieuport** (both: nē'o͞opôrt), town (1970 pop. 8,273), West Flanders prov., W Belgium, on the North Sea at the mouth of the Yser River. It is a fishing port, an industrial center, and a beach resort. The site of a strong fortress, Nieuwpoort suffered heavily in the many wars of the Low Countries and was almost completely destroyed by the Germans in World War I.

Nièvre (nyĕ'vrə), department (1968 pop. 247,702), central France. NEVERS is the capital.

Niflheim (nē'fəlhīm"), in Norse mythology, lowest region of the underworld. A land of mist and cold, Niflheim was sometimes called the home of the dead. See also HEL.

Nigel (nī'jəl), town (1970 pop. 33,850), Transvaal, NE South Africa. Gold mining and processing are the main industries. The town is also a regional commercial center. Founded in 1909 and named for Nigel MacLeish, a prominent gold miner, the town is the site of Sub-Nigel, formerly one of the world's richest gold mines.

Niger (nī'jər), in the Bible: see SIMEON **4.**

Niger (nī'jər), republic (1973 est. pop. 4,300,000), 489,189 sq mi (1,267,000 sq km), W Africa, bordering on Upper Volta and Mali in the west, on Algeria and Libya in the north, on Chad in the east, and on Nigeria and Dahomey in the south. NIAMEY is the country's capital and its largest city; other cities include MARADI, TAHOUA, and ZINDER. Niger is extremely arid except along the Niger River in the southwest and near the border with Nigeria in the south, where there are strips of savanna. Most of the rest of the country is either semidesert or part of the Sahara. In N central Niger are the Aïr mts. (average elevation: 3,000 ft/910 m; maximum elevation: c.5,900 ft/1,800 m), which receive slightly more rainfall than the surrounding desert. The inhabitants of Niger are black Africans. The main ethnic groups are the HAUSA (who make up about 55% of the population), the closely related Djerma and Songhai (together 24%), the FULANI (11%), and the Tuareg (3%). The great majority of the population is rural and lives in the south. About 85% of the people are Muslim, and most of the rest follow traditional religious beliefs. The country's official language is French. The economy of Niger is overwhelmingly agricultural, with about 90% of its work force engaged in farming (largely of a subsistence type). The Hausa, Djerma, and Songhai are mainly sedentary farmers, and the Fulani and Tuareg are principally nomadic and seminomadic pastoralists. The leading farm crops are millet, sorghum, cassava, groundnuts, rice, cotton, sugarcane, and dates (grown in oases in the desert). Large numbers of poultry, goats, cattle, sheep, and camels are raised. Most of the country's few manufactures are basic consumer goods such as processed food, beverages, footwear, and radios. In addition, groundnut oil, ginned cotton, and construction materials (mainly bricks and cement) are produced. In the early 1970s large high-grade uranium ore deposits at Arlit (Arhli) in the Aïr mts. began to be worked by a Franco-Niger company, and a uranium-ore concentrating plant was opened. Small quantities of cassiterite (tin ore), low-grade iron ore, gypsum, phosphates, natron, and salt also are extracted in the country. There is a small but growing fishing industry, operating mainly in the Niger River and in Lake Chad (in the southeast). Niger has a very limited transportation network; there is no railroad, and most of the country's all-weather roads are confined to the south and southwest. A major road also runs N from Zinder, through Agadès (in the Aïr mts.), and on into Algeria. Niger is landlocked and has only poor access to the sea. The annual cost of Niger's imports usually is considerably higher than the value of its exports. The leading imports are textiles and clothing, machinery, foodstuffs, motor vehicles, and petroleum products; the chief exports are groundnuts and groundnut products, live cattle, cotton, and uranium. The principal trade partners are France, West Germany, Ivory Coast, and Dahomey. In 1974, Niger became a charter member of the West African Economic Community, which linked six former French territories.

History. Numerous Neolithic remains have been found in the desert areas of Niger. The region was probably known to the Egyptians before the beginning of recorded history; Ptolemy later wrote of Roman expeditions to the Aïr mts. In the 11th cent. A.D., Tuareg migrated from the desert to the Aïr region, where they later (c.1300) established a state centered at Agadès (Agadez). Agadès was situated on a major trans-Saharan caravan route that connected N Africa with present-day N Nigeria. In E Niger, Bilma, a salt-mining center, was on another

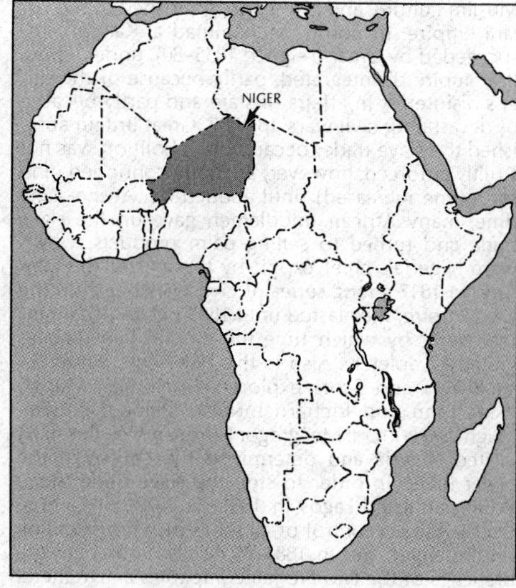

important trans-Saharan route that linked N Africa with the state of BORNU (located in present-day NE Nigeria). In the 14th cent. the Hausa (most of whom lived in what is now N Nigeria) founded several city-states in S Niger. In the early 16th cent. much of W and central Niger came under the SONGHAI empire (centered at Gao on the Niger River in present-day Mali), and after the fall of Songhai at the end of the 16th cent. E and central Niger passed to Bornu. In the 17th cent. the Djerma people settled in SW Niger near the Niger River. In the early 19th cent. Fulani gained control of S Niger as a result of the holy war waged against the Hausa by the Muslim reformer Usuman dan Fodio. At the Conference of Berlin (1884-85) the territory of Niger was placed within the French sphere of influence. The French established several military posts in S Niger in the late 1890s, but did not occupy Agadès until 1904 because of concerted Tuareg resistance. In 1900, Niger was made a military territory within Upper Senegal-Niger, and in 1922 it was constituted a separate colony within FRENCH WEST AFRICA. Zinder was the colony's capital until 1926, when it was replaced by Niamey. The French generally governed through existing political structures and did not alter substantially the institutions of the country; they undertook little economic development and provided few new educational opportunities. National political activity began in 1946, when Niger received its own assembly under the constitution establishing the FRENCH UNION. The first important political organization was the Niger Progressive party (PPN), a part of the *Rassemblement démocratique africain* (which had branches in most French West African territories). In the mid-1950s a leftist party (later called Sawaba) headed by Bakary Djibo became predominant in the colony. However, when it unsuccessfully campaigned for complete independence from France in a 1958 referendum, the PPN (which favored autonomy for Niger within the FRENCH COMMUNITY) regained power. Niger achieved full independence on Aug. 3, 1960, and Hamani Diori, the leader of the PPN, became its first president; he was reelected president in 1965 and 1970. In the early years of independence, sporadic terrorist campaigns were waged by the outlawed Sawaba party (most of whose members lived in exile); in the late 1960s Sawaba disbanded, and many of its former adherents were granted amnesty by Diori. Otherwise, Niger enjoyed political stability, despite its weak economy and occasional ethnic conflicts (especially between the Tuareg and the central government); the PPN maintained firm control of the country's 50-member unicameral national assembly. Close ties were retained with France, which gave Niger considerable aid. The country was severely affected by the Sahelian drought that began in 1968 and was continuing unabated in 1974; much of its livestock died and crop production fell drastically. In April, 1974, Diori was overthrown in a military coup led by Lt.-Col. Seyni Kountche, who charged that Diori's government had handled the drought situation inadequately and had allowed corruption. See Pierre Bonardi, *La République du Niger* (1960); Edmond Séré de Rivières, *Histoire du Niger* (1965); Pierre Donaint and François Lancrenon, *Le Niger* (1972).

Niger (nī'jər), great river of W Africa, c.2,600 mi (4,180 km) long, rising on the Fouta Djallon plateau, SW Republic of Guinea, and flowing NE through Guinea and into the Mali Republic. In central Mali the Niger forms its vast inland delta (c.30,000 sq mi/ 77,700 sq km), a maze of channels and shallow lakes. An irrigation project in the delta, begun by the French in the 1930s and including a large dam at Sansanding (1941), has opened more than 100,000 acres (40,470 hectares) to farming, especially rice cultivation. Just below Timbuktu, Mali, the Niger begins a great bend, flowing first E and then SE out of Mali, through the Republic of Niger (where it forms part of the border with Dahomey), and into Nigeria. At Lokoja, central Nigeria, the BENUE, its chief tributary, joins the Niger, which then flows south, emptying through a great delta into the Gulf of Guinea. The delta (c.14,000 sq mi/36,260 sq km)—the largest in Africa—is characterized by swamps, lagoons, and navigable channels. The region is a major source of palm oil and petroleum. Major towns in the delta are PORT HARCOURT and BONNY. Much of the Niger is seasonally navigable, and below LOKOJA it is open to ships virtually all year. The Niger is a major source of fish, especially perch and tiger fish. A hydroelectric and irrigation project, centered around the Kainji dam (1968), is located on the Niger near Jebba, Nigeria. The upper Niger region was an important part of the former empires of MALI and SONGHAI. The course of the Niger long puzzled Western geographers; only from 1795 to 1797 did Mungo PARK, the Scots explorer, correctly establish the eastern flow of the upper Niger, and it was not until 1830 that Richard and John LANDER, English explorers, proved that the river emptied into the Gulf of Guinea. The water level of the Niger was substantially lowered as a result of the long-term W African drought that began in the late 1960s and was continuing unabated in 1974.

Nigeria, Federation of (nījĭr'ēə), republic (1973 est. pop. 79,800,000), 356,667 sq mi (923,768 sq km), W Africa, bordering on the Gulf of Guinea (an arm of the Atlantic Ocean) in the south, on Dahomey in the west, on Niger in the northwest and north, on Chad in the northeast, and on Cameroon in the east. The country is divided into 12 states. LAGOS is the capital and largest city; other major cities include ABA, ABEOKUTA, ADO, BENIN, EDE, ENUGU, IBADAN, IFE, ILESHA, ILORIN, IWO, KADUNA, KANO, MAIDUGURI, MUSHIN, OGBOMOSHO, ONITSHA, OSHOGBO, PORT HARCOURT, and ZARIA. The Niger River and its tributaries (including the Benue, Kaduna, and Kebbi rivers) drain most of the country. Nigeria has a 500-mile (800-km) coastline, for the most part made up of sandy beaches, behind which lies a belt of mangrove swamps and lagoons that averages 10 mi (16 km) in width but increases to c.60 mi (100 km) wide in the great Niger delta in the east. North of the coastal lowlands is a broad hilly region, with rainforest in the south and covered with savanna in the north. Behind the hills is the great plateau of Nigeria (average elevation 2,000 ft/610 m), a region of plains covered largely with savanna but merging into scrubland in the north. Greater altitudes are attained on the Bauchi and Jos plateaus in the center and in the Adamawa Massif (which continues into Cameroon) in the east, where Nigeria's highest point (c.6,700 ft/2,040 m) is located. The inhabitants of Nigeria are black Africans, who are divided into about 250 ethnic groups. Four of these groups—the HAUSA (about 14,550,000 in 1972) and FULANI (about 6,920,000) in the north, the YORUBA (about 12,460,000) in the southwest, and the IBO (about 12,460,000) in the southeast—together make up approximately 67% of the population. Other peoples include the Kanuri, Nupe, and Tiv of the north, the Edo of the south, and the Ibibio-Efik and Ijaw of the southeast. English and Hausa are official languages. About 47% of the population, living mostly in the north, are Muslim; about 35%, living almost exclusively in the south, are Christian; and the rest follow traditional beliefs. The economy of Nigeria is mainly agricultural, with about 70% of the work force engaged in farming (much of which is of a subsistence type). The chief crops grown in the north are sorghum, millet, soybeans, groundnuts, and cotton; the principal agricultural commodities produced in the south are maize, yams, rice, palm products, cacao, and rubber. In addition, large numbers of poultry, goats, sheep, and cattle are raised in the country. Petroleum is the leading mineral produced in Nigeria; it is found in the Niger delta and offshore in the bights of Benin and Biafra. Petroleum production on an appreciable scale began in the later 1950s, and in the early 70s it was by far the leading earner of foreign exchange. The low-sulfur content of much of Nigeria's petroleum makes it especially desirable in a pollution-conscious world. Other minerals extracted include tin, coal, limestone, salt, columbite, tantalite, low-grade iron ore, and gold. Industry in Nigeria is largely confined to the processing of agricultural goods and to the manufacturing of basic consumer goods, such as clothing, soap, tobacco products, and furniture. Other manufactures include refined petroleum, cement, and metal goods. In addition, numerous traditional craftsmen produce woven goods, pottery, metal objects, and carved wood and ivory. Nigeria's road and rail systems are constructed basically along north-south lines; the country's chief seaports are Lagos, WARRI, Port Harcourt, and CALABAR. Mainly because of its growing petroleum shipments, Nigeria usually earns more from exports than it spends on imports. Other important exports include groundnuts, palm products, cacao, and tin ore. The main imports are machinery, chemicals, textiles, motor vehicles, and manufactured consumer goods. The leading trade partners are Great Britain, the United States, the Netherlands, and France.

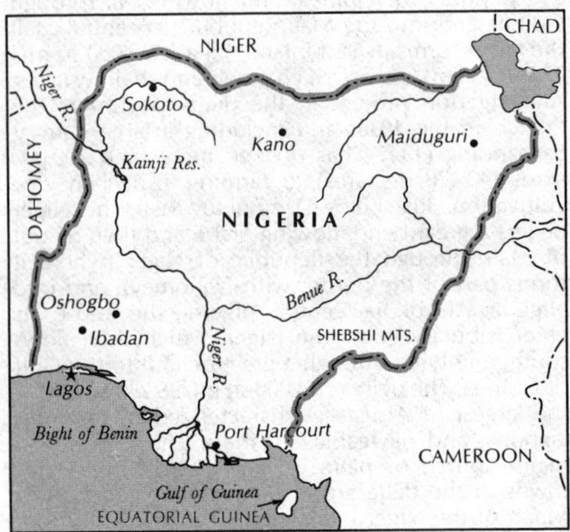

History. Little is known of the earliest history of Nigeria. By c.2000 B.C. most of the country was sparsely inhabited by persons who had a rudimentary knowledge of raising domesticated food plants and of herding animals. From c.800 B.C. to A.D. c.200 the neolithic Nok culture (named for the town where archaeological findings first were made) flourished on the Jos Plateau; the Nok people made fine terracotta sculptures and probably knew how to work tin and iron. The first important centralized state to influence Nigeria was Kanem-Bornu, which probably was founded in the 8th cent., to the north of Lake Chad (outside modern Nigeria). In the 11th cent., by which time its rulers had been converted to Islam, Kanem-Bornu expanded south of Lake Chad into present-day Nigeria, and in the late 15th cent. its capital was moved there. Beginning in the 11th cent. seven independent Hausa city-states were founded in N Nigeria—Biram, Daura, Gobir, Kano, KATSINA, Rano, and Zaria. Kano and Katsina competed for the lucrative trans-Saharan trade with Kanem-Bornu, and for a time had to pay tribute to it. In the early 16th cent. all of Hausaland was briefly controlled by the Songhai Empire. However, in the late 16th cent., Kanem-Bornu replaced Songhai as the leading power in N Nigeria, and the Hausa states regained their autonomy. In southwest Nigeria two Yoruba states—Oyo and Benin—had developed by the 14th cent.; the rulers of both states traced their origins to Ife, renowned for its naturalistic terra-cotta and brass sculpture. Benin was the leading state in the 15th cent. but began to decline in the 17th cent., and by the 18th cent. Oyo controlled Yorubaland and also Dahomey. The Ibo people in the southeast lived in small communities. In the late 15th cent. Portuguese navigators became the first Europeans to visit Nigeria. They soon began to purchase slaves and agricultural produce from coastal middlemen; the slaves had been captured further inland by the middlemen. The Portuguese were followed by British, French, and Dutch traders. Among the Ibo and Ibibio a number of city-states were established by individuals who had become wealthy by engaging in the slave trade; these included BONNY, Owome, and Okrika. There were major internal changes in Nigeria in the 19th cent. In 1804, Usuman dan Fodio (1754–1817), a Fulani and a pious Muslim, began a jihad [Arab.,=holy war] to reform the practice of Islam in the north. He soon conquered the Hausa city-states, but Bornu, led by Muhammad al-Kanemi (also a Muslim reformer) until 1835, maintained its independence. In 1817, Usuman dan Fodio's son, Muhammad Bello (d.1837) established a state centered at SOKOTO, which controlled most of N Nigeria until the coming of the British (1900–1906). Under both Usuman dan Fodio and Muhammad Bello, Muslim culture, and also trade, flourished in the Fulani empire. In Bornu, Muhammad al-Kanemi was succeeded by Umar (reigned 1835–80), under whom the empire disintegrated, partly because of the ruler's disinterest in affairs of state and partly because of devastating civil wars. In 1807, Great Britain abolished the slave trade; because the abolition was not strictly enforced, however, the trade continued (and for a time increased) until about 1875. At the same time, many African middlemen gave up the slave trade and turned to selling palm products, which were Nigeria's chief export by the end of the century. In 1817 a long series of civil wars began in the Oyo Empire; they lasted until 1893 (when Britain intervened), by which time the empire had disintegrated completely. Also in the 19th cent., a number of British and Scots explorers (including Mungo PARK, John and Richard LANDER, Dixon Denham, Hugh CLAPPERTON, Macgregor Laird, and W. B. BAIKIE) visited Nigeria and determined the course of the Niger River. In order to stop the slave trade there, Britain annexed Lagos in 1861. In 1879, Sir George GOLDIE gained control of all the British firms trading on the Niger, and in 1884–85 he also took over the branches of the two French companies active there. In the early 1880s he signed treaties with numerous African leaders, including the sultan of Sokoto. Largely because of Goldie's efforts, Great Britain was able to claim S Nigeria at the Conference of Berlin (see BERLIN, CONFERENCE OF) held in 1884–85. In the following years, the British established their rule in SW Nigeria, partly by signing treaties (as in the Lagos hinterland) and partly by using force (as at Benin in 1897). Jaja, a leading African trader based at OPOBO in the Niger delta and strongly opposed to European competition, was captured in 1897 by Harry Johnston, a British official, and deported. Goldie's firm, given (1886) a British royal charter, as the Royal Niger Company, to administer the Niger River and N Nigeria, antagonized Europeans and Africans alike by its monopoly of trade on the Niger; in addition, it was not sufficiently powerful to gain effective control over N Nigeria, which was also sought by the French. Therefore, in 1900 its charter was revoked and British forces under Frederick LUGARD began to conquer the north, taking Sokoto in 1903. By 1906 Britain controlled Nigeria, which was divided into the Colony (i.e., Lagos) and Protectorate of Southern Nigeria and the Protectorate of Northern Nigeria. In 1914 the two regions were amalgamated and the Colony and Protectorate of Nigeria was established. The administration of Nigeria was based on a system devised by Lugard and called "indirect rule"; under this system, Britain ruled through existing political institutions rather than by using a wholly new administrative network. In some areas (especially the southeast) new African officials (resembling the traditional rulers in other parts of the country) were set up; in most cases they were not accepted by the mass of the people and were able to rule only because British power stood behind them. All important decisions were made by the British governor, and the African rulers, partly by being associated with the colonialists, soon lost most of their traditional authority over their subjects. Under the British, Nigeria's economy grew considerably; railroads and roads were built and the production of cash crops, such as palm nuts and kernels, cacao, cotton, and groundnuts, was encouraged. The country became more urbanized as Lagos, Ibadan, Kano, Onitsha, and other cities grew in size and importance. From 1922, African representatives from Lagos and Calabar were elected to the legislative council of Southern Nigeria; they constituted only a small minority, and Africans otherwise continued to have no role in the higher levels of government. Self-help groups organized on ethnic lines were established in the cities and occasionally (as in Aba in 1929) discontent with colonial rule flared into open protest. A small Western-educated elite developed in Lagos and a few other southern cities. In 1947, Great Britain promulgated a constitution that gave the traditional authorities a greater voice in national affairs. The Western-educated elite was excluded, and, led by Herbert Macaulay and Nnamdi AZIKIWE, its members vigorously denounced the constitution. As a result, a new constitution, providing for elected representation on a regional basis, was instituted in 1951. Three major political parties emerged—the National Council of Nigeria and the Cameroons (NCNC; from 1960 known as the National Convention of Nigerian Citizens), led by Azikiwe and largely based among the Ibo; the Action Group, led by Obafemi AWOLOWO and with a mostly Yoruba membership; and the Northern People's Congress (NPC), led by Ahmadu Bello and based in the north. The constitution proved unworkable by 1952, and a new one, solidifying the division of Nigeria into three regions (Eastern, Western, and Northern) plus the Federal Territory of Lagos, came into force in 1954. In 1956 the Eastern and Western regions became internally self-governing, and the Northern region achieved this status in 1959. With Nigerian independence scheduled for 1960, elections were held in 1959; no party won a majority, and the NPC combined with the NCNC to form a government. Nigeria attained independence on Oct. 1, 1960, with Abubakar Tafawa BALEWA of the NPC as prime minister and Azikiwe of the NCNC as governor-general; when Nigeria became a republic in 1963, Azikiwe was made president. The first years of independence were characterized by severe conflicts within and between regions. In the Western region, a bloc of the Action Group split off (1962) under S. I. Akintola to form the Nigerian National Democratic party (NNDP); in 1963 the Mid-Western region (whose population was mostly Edo) was formed from a part of the Eastern region. In 1964 there was great controversy over the 1963 population census, which the NCNC claimed overestimated the number of inhabitants in the Northern region and thus gave it undue representation in the federal parliament. (There was a similar dispute following the 1973 census.) National elections late in 1964 were hotly contested, with an NPC-NNDP coalition (called the National Alliance) emerging victorious. In Oct., 1965, elections in the Western region were marred by widespread irregularities. In Jan., 1966, Ibo army officers staged a successful coup d'etat, which resulted in the deaths of Federal Prime Minister Balewa, Northern Prime Minister Ahmadu Bello, and Western Prime Minister S. I. Akintola. Maj. Gen. Johnson T. U. Aguiyi-Ironsi, an Ibo, became head of a military government and suspended the national and regional constitutions. His attempts to abolish the regions and establish a centralized state brought a violent reaction in the north. In July, 1966, a coup led by Hausa army officers ousted Ironsi (who was killed) and placed Lt. Col. Yakubu GOWON at the head of a new military regime. In Sept., 1966, many Ibos living in the north were massacred. Gowon attempted to start Nigeria along the road to civilian government but met determined resistance from the Ibos, who were becoming increasingly fearful of their position within Nigeria. In May, 1967, the Eastern parliament gave Lt. Col. Chukwuemeka O. OJUKWU, the region's leader, authority to declare the region an independent republic. Gowon proclaimed a state of emergency, and, as a gesture to the Ibos, redivided Nigeria into 12 states (including one, the East-Central state, that comprised most of the Ibo people). However, on May 30, Ojukwu proclaimed the independent Republic of BIAFRA, and in July fighting broke out between Biafra and Nigeria. Biafra made some advances early in the war, but soon federal forces gained the initiative and, after much suffering, Biafra capitulated on Jan. 15, 1970, and the secession ended. The early 1970s were marked by reconstruction in areas that were formerly part of Biafra, by the gradual reintegration of Ibos into national life, and by a slow return to civilian rule (which Gowon promised would be completed by 1976). Spurred by the booming petroleum industry, the Nigerian economy quickly recovered from the effects of the civil war and made impressive advances, although inflation, high unemployment, a decline in the world price of peanuts and cocoa, and drought caused problems. The prolonged drought that desiccated the Sahel region of Africa began to have a profound effect on semi-arid N Nigeria in late 1973; thousands of head of livestock died, farming suffered, and the fishing industry on Lake Chad collapsed as the lake shrank in size. As a result, there was a migration of peoples into the less arid areas and into the cities of the south. See S. O. Biobaku, *The Egba and Their Neighbors* (1957); J. S. Coleman, *Nigeria: Background to Nationalism* (1958); K. Onwuka Dike, *Trade and Politics in the Niger Delta, 1830–85* (1959); G. I. Jones, *Trading States of the Oil Rivers* (1963); J. F. A. Ajayi and Robert Smith, *Yoruba Warfare in the Nineteenth Century* (1964); E. A. Ayandele, *The Missionary Impact on Modern Nigeria, 1842–1914* (1966); S. J. Hogben and A. H. M. Kirk-Greene, *The Emigrants of Northern Nigeria* (1966); R. K. Udo, *Geographical Regions of Nigeria* (1970); C. K. Eicher and C. Liedholm, ed., *Growth and Development of the Nigerian Economy* (1970); S. K. Painter-Brick,

Nigerian Politics and Military Rule: Prelude to Civil War (1970); Sir Alan Burns, *History of Nigeria* (rev. ed. 1972); Michael Crowder, *The Story of Nigeria* (3d ed. 1973); S. O. Biobaku, ed., *Sources of Yoruba History* (1973).

night blindness, inability to see normally in subdued light. It is usually a result of vitamin A deficiency. The rod cells, one of two light-sensitive areas of the retina of the EYE, are impaired in their capacity to produce a chemical compound called rhodopsin, or visual purple, that is necessary for the perception of objects in dim light. Consequently, the visual threshold, or the minimum intensity of light necessary for sight, is greatly increased. Folk medicine has long recognized the role of the ingestion of liver in alleviating the condition, but it was not until the first quarter of the 20th cent. that vitamin A was identified as the crucial element. Treatment of night blindness consists of the oral or intravenous administration of vitamin A.

night-blooming cereus: see CACTUS.

night crawler: see EARTHWORM.

nighthawk: see GOATSUCKER.

Nightingale, Florence, 1820–1910, English nurse, the founder of modern nursing, b. Florence, Italy. Her life was dedicated to one purpose, care of the sick and of the war wounded. In 1844 she began to visit hospitals; in 1850 she spent some time with the nursing Sisters of St. Vincent de Paul in Alexandria; and a year later she studied at the institute for Protestant deaconesses in Kaiserswerth, Germany. Her goal was set, and in 1854 she organized a unit of 38 woman nurses for service in the Crimean War. By the end of the war she had become a legend. With the testimonial fund collected for her war services she established (1860) the Nightingale School and Home for training nurses at St. Thomas's Hospital, London. She was called "the Lady with the Lamp" because she believed that a nurse's care was never ceasing, night or day. Florence Nightingale was the first woman to be given the British Order of Merit (1907). After her death the Crimean Monument, Waterloo Place, London, was erected in her honor in 1915, and in 1934 the Florence Nightingale International Foundation was inaugurated. She had taught that nursing was a noble profession for women, and she made it so. She wrote *Notes . . . on Hospital Administration* (1857), *Notes on Hospitals* (1859), *Notes on Nursing* (1860), and *Notes on Nursing for the Labouring Classes* (1861). See biography by Cecil Woodham-Smith (1950); Lytton Strachey, *Eminent Victorians* (1918, repr. 1967).

nightingale, common name for a migratory Old World bird of the family Turdidae (thrush family), celebrated for its vocal powers. The common nightingale of England and Western Europe, *Luscinia megarhynchos*, is about 6½ in. (16.3 cm) long, reddish-brown above and grayish-white below. It winters in Africa and reaches England about mid-April. Its famous song is delivered only by the male during the breeding season, at any time of day or night. A larger species is found in Eastern Europe. The bulbul, a prodigious songster of Persian literature, was once thought to be a nightingale but has been identified with another family; the Virginia nightingale is a grosbeak; and the Pekin, or Japanese, nightingale belongs to the babbler family. Nightingales are classified in the phylum CHORDATA, subphylum Vertebrata, class Aves, order Passeriformes, family Turdidae.

nightjar, common name for birds also known as GOATSUCKERS.

night school: see VOCATIONAL EDUCATION.

nightshade, common name for the Solanaceae, a family of herbs, shrubs, and a few trees of warm regions, chiefly tropical and South American. Many are climbing or creeping types, and rank-smelling foliage is typical of many species. The odor is due to the presence of various alkaloids (including SCOPOLAMINE, NICOTINE, and ATROPINE), chemicals that have been used medicinally since ancient times as stimulants, narcotics and pain relievers, poisons, and antidotes for such agents as opium and snake venom. The chief drug plants of the family are BELLADONNA, or deadly nightshade (*Atropa belladonna*), HENBANE (*Hyoscyamus niger*), MANDRAKE (*Mandragora officinum*), JIMSON WEED (*Datura stramonium*), and TOBACCO (*Nicotiana tabacum*). Only the last two are indigenous to the Americas. The Old World species have figured prominently in herbals and in the magic potions of alchemy. The family also includes several important food plants, e.g., the POTATO (*Solanum tuberosum*), the TOMATO (*Lycopersicon esculentum*), the red PEPPER, or pimiento (species of *Capsicum*), and the EGGPLANT (*Solanum melongea*), the only one native to the Old World. Species of SALPIGLOSSIS, PETUNIA, BUTTERFLY FLOWER, and the genus *Solanum* are among the members of the family

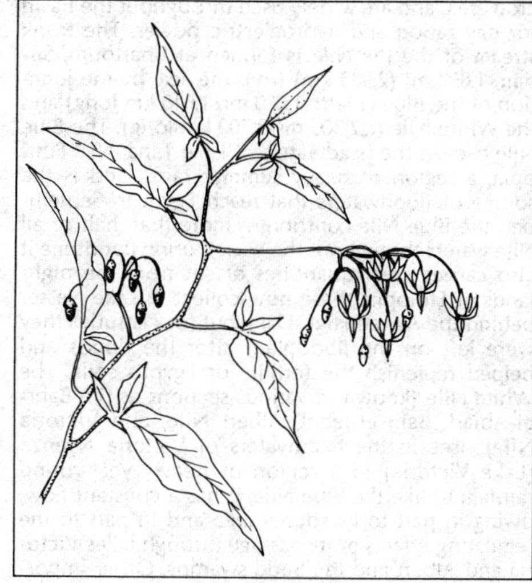

Nightshade, Solanum dulcamara

cultivated as ornamentals. The name nightshade is commonly restricted to members of the *Solanum*, characterized by white or purplish star-shaped flowers and decorative orange berries; among the better known species are the BITTERSWEET, or woody nightshade (*S. dulcamara*), the buffalo bur (*S. rostratum*), the horse, or bull, nettle (*S. carolinense*), the Jerusalem cherry (*S. pseudocapsicum*), and the black nightshade (*S. niger*). The buffalo bur, originally native to the Western plains, and the horse nettle, native to the Southeast, are straggly, prickly plants which are now naturalized over most of the United States and often become pests. The berries of the horse nettle (not a true NETTLE botanically) have been used medicinally. Leaves of the buffalo bur served as food for the Colorado POTATO BEETLE before the advent of the cultivated potato in its vicinity. Both plants are sometimes called SANDBUR, properly the name for a prickly grass. The Jerusalem cherry, probably of Old World origin, is a house plant popular for its scarlet berries. The black nightshade was named for the dull black color of its berries, unusual for the genus; it is native to Europe but naturalized throughout the United States, where it is now one of the most common species of *Solanum* found growing wild. Because its leaves may be poisonous, it is sometimes called deadly nightshade, properly the name for the belladonna, which is not found wild in America. Nightshades are classified in the division MAGNOLIOPHYTA, class Magnoliopsida, order Polemoniales, family Solanaceae.

nihilism (nī'əlĭzəm), theory of revolution popular among Russian extremists until the fall of the czarist government (1917); the theory was given its name by Ivan Turgenev in his novel *Fathers and Sons* (1861). Nihilism stressed the need to destroy existing economic and social institutions, whatever the projected nature of the better order for which the destruction was to prepare. Nihilists were not without constructive programs, but agreement on these was not essential to the immediate objective, destruction. Direct action, such as assassination and arson, was characteristic. Such acts were not necessarily directed by any central authority. Small groups and even individuals were encouraged to plan and execute terroristic acts independently. The assassination of Czar Alexander II was one result of such terrorist activities. The constructive programs published by nihilists include the establishing of a parliamentary government; the programs were on the whole moderate in comparison with the revolutionary measures of 1917. Nihilism was too diffuse and negative to persist as a movement and gradually gave way to other philosophies of revolt; it remained, however, an element in later Russian thought. See Ronald Hingley, *Nihilists* (1967); Stanley Rosen, *Nihilism: A Philosophical Essay* (1969); Michael Novak, *The Experience of Nothingness* (1970).

Niigata (nē'gätä), city (1970 pop. 383,869), capital of Niigata prefecture, N Honshu, Japan, on the Sea of Japan at the mouth of the Shinano River. It is the main port for the west coast of Honshu, with exports of oil, machinery, and textiles. Niigata has an important chemical industry based on the area's coal and natural gas deposits. The city is traversed by many canals and is the site of one of the largest flower farms in the Orient. Niigata was opened to foreign trade in 1869. Niigata prefecture (1970 pop. 2,360,982), 4,856 sq mi (12,577 sq km), yields petroleum, gold, silver, raw silk, and farm products.

Niihama (nē'hämä), city (1970 pop. 126,033), Ehime prefecture, N Shikoku, Japan. It is a commercial and fishing port and a manufacturing and mining center.

Niihau (nē'hou), island (1970 pop. 237), 70 sq mi (181 sq km), in Kauai co., Hawaii, W of Kauai island. It is mostly arid lowland, rising to 1,281 ft (390 m) at Paniau Mt. Niihau is suitable only for cattle grazing, and the island, privately owned since 1864 when it was purchased from the Hawaiian kingdom by an American family, is operated as a ranch.

Niitsu (nē'tso͞o), city (1970 pop. 57,089), Niigata prefecture, W central Honshu, Japan. It is a center for mechanical and chemical industries in an oil- and natural gas-producing region.

Niiza (nē'zä), city (1970 pop. 77,704), Saitama prefecture, E central Honshu, Japan, on the Yonase River. It is a suburb of Tokyo.

Nijinsky, Vaslav (vəsläf' nyĭzhĕn'skē), 1890–1950, Russian ballet dancer and choreographer. In 1900 he entered the Imperial Ballet School, St. Petersburg, and made his debut in 1907. He traveled to Paris (1909) and, as premier danseur in Diaghilev's Ballet Russe, was the first to dance *Petrouchka, Les Sylphides, Scheherazade*, and *The Spectre of the Rose*, all choreographed by Fokine, and *The Afternoon of a Faun* (1912), *Le Sacre du Printemps* (1913), and *Till Eulenspiegel* (1916), which he himself choreographed. Nijinsky, often considered the greatest male dancer of the 20th cent., was noted for his jeté and elevation. His relationship with Diaghilev was stormy, ending bitterly when the dancer married. Nijinsky's career was abruptly terminated by insanity (1919). He lived in retirement in England and Switzerland until he died. See his diary, ed. by his wife, Romola Nijinska (1936, rev. ed. 1963); biographies by Romola Nijinska (1933 and 1952, repr. 1968) and Richard Buckle (1971). His sister, **Bronislava Nijinska** (brônē'slɑvə nyĭzhĕn'skə), 1891–1972, was also a noted dancer and choreographer with Diaghilev. Her ballets *Les Biches* and *Les Noces* are frequently performed.

Nijmegen (nī'mā''gən), city (1971 pop. 150,185), Gelderland prov., E Netherlands, on the Waal River, near the West German border. It is a rail and water transportation point and an industrial center. Its manufactures include metal products, paper, clothing, and soap. One of the oldest cities in the Netherlands, Nijmegen was founded in Roman times and flourished under Charlemagne (8th–early 9th cent.). It was chartered in 1184, became a free imperial city, and later joined the Hanseatic League. It subscribed (1579) to the Union of Utrecht, formed as a defensive measure against Philip II of Spain. The treaties of Nijmegen (1678–79), which ended the Dutch War (1672–78) of Louis XIV of France, were signed there (see DUTCH WARS). In World War II Allied airborne troops wrested (Sept., 1944) Nijmegen from the Germans but failed to rescue the troops caught at Arnhem. Nijmegen has a 13th-century church (the Groote Kerk), a 16th-century town hall, a 17th-century weighhouse, and the remains of a palace built (c.777) by Charlemagne and rebuilt by Frederick Barbarossa in 1165. It is the seat of the Catholic Univ. of Nijmegen (founded 1923). The city is known in French as Nimègue and in German as Nimwegen.

Nike (nī'kē), in Greek mythology, goddess of victory, daughter of Pallas and Styx. Often an attendant of Zeus or Athena, she also presided over all contests, athletic as well as military. She was a popular subject in art, usually represented as winged and bearing a wreath or palm branch. The *Victory* (or *Nike*) *of Samothrace* (Louvre) is one of the finest extant Greek sculptures. The Romans identified Nike with Victoria.

Nikisch, Arthur (är'to͝or nē'kĭsh), 1855–1922, Hungarian conductor and violinist, grad. Vienna Conservatory, 1873. He played in Wagner's orchestra at the dedication of the Festspielhaus at Bayreuth and with the Vienna court orchestra. In 1878 he became conductor of the Leipzig Opera, remaining until 1889, when he became conductor of the Boston Symphony Orchestra. He conducted (1893–95) the Budapest Opera and afterward was conductor of the Leipzig Gewandhaus and the Berlin Philharmonic until his death.

Nikko (nĕk'kō), town (1970 pop. 28,502), Tochigi prefecture, central Honshu, Japan, in Nikko National Park. It is a tourist resort and religious center, famous for its ornate temples and shrines, dating from the Yedo period (1600–1868) and notable for rich coloring. Within the shrine of Ieyasu is the Yomeimon (Gate of Sunlight), perhaps the most beautiful gate in Japan. The park is noted for its mountain scenery, waterfalls, and cryptomeria forests. Nikko has Buddhist as well as Shinto shrines.

Nikolais, Alwin, 1912–, American dancer and choreographer, b. Southington, Conn. Nikolais became director of his own dance company in New York City in 1949. He makes ingenious use of colors, lighting, and sound as integral parts of such abstract and exhilarating dance works as *Kaleidoscope* (1956) and *Illusion* (1961). Many of his works have been presented on television in the United States.

Nikolayev (nyĭkəlä'yəf), city (1970 pop. 331,000), capital of Nikolayev oblast, S European USSR, in the Ukraine, at the confluence of the Bug and Ingul rivers and on the bank of the Dnepr-Bug estuary. A major seaport and rail junction, Nikolayev exports grain, iron, and manganese. It has shipyards, machinery plants, and cast iron works. Founded in 1784 as a fortress near the site of the ancient Greek colony of Olbia, the city was named Nikolayev in 1788 when it became a shipbuilding center.

Nikolsburg: see MIKULOV, Czechoslovakia.

Nikolsk-Ussuriski: see USSURIYSK, USSR.

Nikon (nē'kōn), 1605–81, Russian churchman, patriarch of the Russian Orthodox Church (1652–66). Widely known as a reformer, he accepted the patriarchate on the condition that he would be obeyed in everything. He undertook at once a reform of church discipline and ritual with a view to purging accretions and eccentricities from the Russian rites. His reforms, particularly his introduction of a new prayer book (1654), created a schism in the church and inspired the formation of a major opposition sect, the RASKOLNIKI, who retained the older usages banned by Nikon. Heterodox sects such as the DUKHOBORS formed and attached themselves to the Raskolniki to avoid persecution. By 1658, Nikon had aroused sufficiently powerful opposition to bring about his banishment, and in 1666 he was deposed and degraded. He was a figure unique in Russian church history, for he opposed any interference by the state in church affairs and considered the two institutions to be distinct and separate. His reforms were maintained after his disgrace.

Nikopol (nĕkô'pôl), town (1963 est. pop. 5,800), N Bulgaria, a port on the Danube River bordering Rumania. Farming, viticulture, and fishing are the chief occupations. Nikopol has one of the world's major sources of manganese; most of the ore is sent by water or rail to the Ukraine. The town's industries also include steel rolling, flour milling, tanning, shipbuilding, and the manufacture of construction materials. Founded in 629 by Byzantine emperor Heraclius, Nikopol (then Nicopolis) became a flourishing trade and cultural center of the second Bulgarian kingdom. In 1396 at Nikopol the Ottoman Turks under Bayazid I defeated an army of crusaders led by King Sigismund of Hungary (later Emperor SIGISMUND). The Turkish victory removed the last serious obstacle to a Turkish advance on Christian Europe. However, when Tamerlane defeated Bayazid (1402), Europe gained a respite. The Turks strongly fortified Nikopol, which was strategically important during the Russo-Turkish wars (18th–19th cent.), but the city later declined.

Nikopol (nyĭkô'pəl), city (1970 pop. 125,000), S European USSR, in the Ukraine, on the Dnepr River. It is a rail terminus and the industrial center of one of the world's richest manganese-mining areas. The city has steel and machinery plants, shipyards, flour mills, and food-processing and brewing industries. Nikopol stands on the site of one of the earliest trade routes and strategic crossing points over the Dnepr. The city was founded in the 18th cent. on the site of a fortified camp of the Zaporozhe Cossacks. Manganese production at Nikopol became important in the 19th cent.

Nikosia, Cyprus: see NICOSIA.

Nikšić (nĕk'shĭch), town (1971 pop. 66,810), SW Yugoslavia, in Montenegro. It is the commercial center of an agricultural region. Founded in the early Middle Ages, Nikšić was under Turkish rule until 1878, when it passed to Montenegro. The town has a Byzantine cathedral (the gift of Nicholas II of Russia) and a Roman bridge.

Nile, longest river in the world, c.4,160 mi (6,695 km) long from its remotest headstream, the Luvironza River in Burundi, central Africa, to its delta on the Mediterranean Sea, NE Egypt. The Nile flows northward and drains c.1,100,000 sq mi (2,850,000 sq km), about one tenth of Africa, including parts of Egypt, Sudan, Ethiopia, Kenya, Uganda, Rwanda, Burundi, and Zaïre. Its waters support practically all agriculture in the most densely populated parts of Egypt, furnish water for more than 20% of Sudan's total crop area, and are widely used throughout the basin for navigation and hydroelectric power. The trunk stream of the the Nile is formed at Khartoum, Sudan, 1,857 mi (2,988 km) from the sea, by the junction of the Blue Nile (c.1,000 mi/1,610 km long) and the White Nile (c.2,300 mi/3,700 km long). The Blue Nile rises in the headwaters of Lake Tana, NW Ethiopia, a region of heavy summer rains, and is the source of floodwaters that reach Egypt in September; the Blue Nile contributes more than half of all Nile waters throughout the year. During floodtime it also carries great quantities of silt from the highlands of Ethiopia; these now collect in Lake Nasser behind the Aswan High Dam, but for centuries they were left on the floodplain after the floods and helped replenish the fertility of Egypt's soils. The White Nile (known in various sections as the Bahr-el-Abiad, Bahr-el-Jebel, Albert Nile, and Victoria Nile) rises in the headwaters of Victoria Nyanza (Lake Victoria) in a region of heavy, year-round rainfall; unlike the Blue Nile, it has a constant flow, owing in part to its source area and in part to the regulating effects of its passage through lakes Victoria and Albert and the Sudd swamps. Other important tributaries of the Nile are the Atbara and Sobat rivers. The Gezira, or "island," formed between the Blue Nile and the White Nile as they come together at Khartoum is Sudan's principal agricultural area and the only large tract of land outside Egypt irrigated with Nile waters. From Khartoum to the Egyptian border at Wadi Halfa (now submerged) and on to Aswan in Egypt, the Nile occupies a narrow entrenched valley with little floodplain for cultivation; in this stretch it is interrupted by six cataracts (rapids). From Aswan the river flows north 550 mi (885 km) to Cairo, bordered by a floodplain that gradually widens to c.12 mi (20 km); irrigated by the river, this intensively cultivated valley contrasts with the barren desert on either side. North of Cairo is the great Nile delta (c.100 mi/160 km long and up to 115 mi/185 km wide), which contains 60% of Egypt's cultivated land and extensive areas of swamps and shallow lakes. Two distributaries, the Damietta (Dumyat) on the east and the Rosetta (Rashid) on the west, each c.150 mi (240 km) long, carry the river's remaining water (after irrigation) to the Mediterranean Sea. Regular steamship service is maintained on the Nile between Alexandria (reached by canal) and Aswan; the Blue Nile is navigable June through December from Suki (above Sennar Dam) to Roseires Dam; the White Nile is navigable all year between Khartoum and Juba in Sudan, and between Nimule and Murchison Falls on the Victoria Nile. The use of the Nile for irrigation, now regulated by the Nile Waters Treaty of 1959, dates back to at least 4000 B.C. in Egypt. The traditional system of basin irrigation—in which Nile floods were trapped in shallow basins and a cool season crop of wheat or barley was grown in soaked and silt-replenished soil—has been replaced in the last 150 years by a system of perennial irrigation and the production of two or three crops a year, including cotton, sugarcane, and peanuts. The delta barrages, just below Cairo, channel water into a system of feeder canals for the delta, and other barrages at Isna, Asyut, and Nag Hammadi keep the level of the Nile high enough all year for perennial irrigation in the valley of Upper Egypt; the Idfina Barrage on the Rosetta prevents infiltration by the sea at low water. Nile water is also used for irrigation in the Fayyum Basin. The Aswan Dam (completed 1902 and raised twice since then) was the first dam built on the Nile to store part of the autumn flood for later use; it has a storage capacity of 5 billion cu m and is now supplemented by the Aswan High Dam (completed 1971), 5 mi (8 km) upstream, with a storage capacity of 48 billion cu m, sufficient (with existing dams) to hold back the entire flood for later use. Construction of the Aswan High Dam has added c.1,800,000 acres (728,500 hectares) of irrigated land to Egypt's cultivable area and converted c.730,000 acres (295,400 hectares) from basin to perennial irrigation. Other important storage dams, all outside Egypt, but built with Egypt's help or cooperation, are the Owen Falls Dam (1954) and Jebel Aulia Dam (1937) on the White Nile; the Sennar (1927) and Roseires (1966) on the Blue Nile; and the Kashm-el-Girba Dam (1964) on the Atbara River. A number of other schemes to increase the available waters of the Nile have been proposed from time to time; they include the Equatorial Nile Project, or Jonglei Diversion Canal, to carry the White Nile around the Sudd and reduce evaporation losses; the construction of a dam at Lake Tana on the Blue Nile; and the construction of dams at Nimule on the Bahr-el-Jebel, on the Albert Nile, and below Lake Kyoga on the Victoria Nile. The source of the Nile and its life-giving floods was a mystery for centuries. Ptolemy held that the source was the "Mountains of the Moon," and the search for these and for the origin of the Nile attracted much attention in the 18th and 19th cent. James Bruce, the Scottish explorer, identified (1770) Lake Tana as the source of the Blue Nile, and John Speke, the British explorer, is credited with the identification (1861–62) of Lake Victoria and Ripon Falls as the source of the White Nile. See Elliot Elisofon, *The Nile* (1964); Bruce Brander, *The River Nile* (2d ed. 1968); Alan Moorhead, *The White Nile* (rev. ed. 1971) and *The Blue Nile* (rev. ed. 1972).

Nile, battle of the: see ABU QIR.

Niles, Hezekiah, 1777–1839, American journalist, b. Jefferis's Ford, Pa. Editor (1805–11) of the Baltimore *Evening Post* and founder (1811) of *Niles' Weekly Register*, he was one of the most influential journalists of his day. Devoted primarily to politics, *Niles' Weekly Register* is considered an important source for the history of the period.

Niles. 1 Village (1970 pop. 31,432), Cook co., NE Ill., a suburb adjacent to Chicago, on the Chicago River; settled 1832, inc. 1899. It has large plants making duplicating machines, electronic equipment, and tools and dies. The village has a replica (half size) of the leaning tower of Pisa. Niles College of Loyola Univ. is there. **2** City (1970 pop. 12,988), Berrien co., SW Mich., on the St. Joseph River, in a farm and fruit area; inc. 1829. It was the site of a Jesuit Mission (1690) and of Fort St. Joseph, built by the French (1697). The fort fell to the British (1761), to the Indians (Pontiac's Rebellion, 1763), and to the Spanish and Indians (1780, 1781); it was later abandoned. Permanent settlement began in 1827, and as a station on the stagecoach route between Detroit and Chicago, Niles grew as a commercial and industrial center. Ring Lardner was born there. **3** City (1970 pop. 21,581), Trumbull co., NE Ohio, on the Mahoning River; settled 1806, inc. as a city 1895. It is an iron and steel center. The city has a memorial to President William McKinley, who was born in Niles.

nilgai: see ANTELOPE.

Nilgiri Hills, India: see GHATS.

Nilotes (nī'lō'tēz), people of E Africa who speak Nilotic languages. Among these are the Nuer and the Masai. The most prominent Nilotic ethnic groups live in S Sudan, N Uganda, and N Kenya. Originally from E Sudan, they migrated south centuries ago. Farmers and herders, they became primarily pastoralists in their new lands. The Nilotes are noted for their tall stature. Some Nilotic peoples, such as the Masai, are dedicated to their traditional life and have resisted intrusions by European culture.

Nilsson, Birgit (bĭr'gĭt nĭl'sən), 1918–, Swedish soprano. Her powerful voice first came to international attention at the Munich Opera, where she was heard (1954–55) as Brünnhilde in Wagner's *Die Walküre* and in the title role in Strauss's *Salome*. In 1959 she made her debut at the Metropolitan Opera in New York City as Isolde. Although she is particularly noted for Wagnerian roles, Nilsson has also performed in the Italian repertoire, notably as Turandot and Aïda.

nimbostratus: see CLOUD.

nimbus (nĭm'bəs), in art, the luminous disk or circle or other indication of light around the head of a sacred personage. It was used in Buddhist and other Oriental art and by the early Greeks and Romans to designate gods and heroes and appeared in Christian art in the 5th cent. Although usually a circle or disk, the nimbus has various forms—triangular for God the Father; a circle with a cross for Christ; a square for a living person; a disk or circle for a saint, with sometimes a band of small stars for the Virgin Mary. In stained glass Christ and the Virgin were often represented surrounded by an ovoid light called a *vesica piscis* [Lat., = fish bladder]. (See ICONOGRAPHY.) The square form was symbolic of the material world; the circle symbolized spiritual perfection and eternal blessedness; and the triangle represented eternity and the Trinity. The nimbus is usually of gold and may have a clearly defined outline or the light may be diffused, radiating from the head in lines that melt into the picture. The term *aureole* may denote a crown or radiance around the head or it may be an oval used as a background for the whole body. When nimbus and aureole are combined for one figure, the illumination is called a glory. An almond-shaped glory is a mandorla. Halo is a nontechnical term to denote either a disk behind the head or a circle surrounding it.

nimbus, in meteorology, low, dark, formless CLOUD covering the entire sky, from which rain or snow is steadily falling. The term is usually applied to any cloud from which rain descends. Modifications are cumulonimbus, fractonimbus (ragged, broken nimbus), and nimbostratus.

Nimègue: see NIJMEGEN.

Nimeiry, Muhammad Gaafur al- (mo͞ohäm'mäd gäfo͞or'äl-nĭmĕr'ē), 1930–, Sudanese army officer and politician. Early active in the Sudanese nationalist movement, he was temporarily expelled from high school (1948) after leading a student strike against British rule. He attended military college and served in the army, where he rose to the rank of colonel. In 1969 he led a group of leftist army officers in a coup against the civilian government of Muhammad Ahmad Mahgoub. Nimeiry established himself as president and later (1972) as prime minister. In 1972, Nimeiry signed a truce with secessionist forces in S Sudan, thus ending some 17 years of civil war.

Nîmes (nēm), city (1968 pop. 129,866), capital of Gard dept., S France, in Cévennes. Its products include machinery, textiles and clothing, and tinware. An old Gallic town, it became Roman c.120 B.C. As Nemausus it was an important city, one of the finest of Narbonensis province (see GAUL). United to the French crown in 1258, it later became a stronghold of the Huguenots but suffered greatly from the revocation of the Edict of Nantes (1685). Nîmes is famous for its remarkable collection of Roman relics. The magnificent Roman arena (1st cent. A.D.), seating up to 24,000, is still in use. The well-preserved Maison Carée [square house], a Roman temple (1st or 2d cent. A.D.), one of the finest examples of Roman architecture, houses a museum of Roman antiquities. Other Roman relics are the temple of Diana (2d cent. A.D.), a watchtower, and the nearby PONT DU GARD.

Nimitz, Chester William (nĭm'ĭts), 1885–1966, American admiral, b. Fredericksburg, Texas. A graduate of Annapolis, he was chief of staff to the commander of the submarine force of the Atlantic Fleet in World War I. In 1939, he was made chief of the Bureau of Navigation, and, after the attack on Pearl Harbor, he succeeded (1941) Husband E. Kimmel as commander of the Pacific Fleet. Admiral Nimitz headed the naval fighting forces in the Pacific throughout World War II. In Dec., 1944, he was made admiral of the fleet (five-star admiral) and a year later succeeded Ernest J. King as chief of naval operations. After he retired (Dec., 1947) from the navy, he headed (1949) the United Nations commission in the dispute over Kashmir. See E. P. Hoyt, *How They Won the War in the Pacific* (1970).

Nimrah: see BETH-NIMRAH.

Nimrim, stream, perhaps the Wadi Numeirah, flowing into the southeastern end of the Dead Sea. Isa. 15.6; Jer. 48.34.

Nimrod, descendant of Cush who is recorded as a mighty hunter. Gen. 10.8; 1 Chron. 1.10.

Nimrud: see CALAH.

Nimshi (nĭm'shī), grandfather of Jehu. 1 Kings 19.16; 2 Kings 9.2,14; called father of Jehu. 2 Kings 9.20; 2 Chron. 22.7.

Nimwegen: see NIJMEGEN.

Nin, Anaïs (ənī'ĭs nĭn, nēn), 1903–, American writer, b. Paris. The daughter of the Spanish composer Joaquin Nin, she was brought to the United States at nine. She was an early patient of JUNG, and a concern with the subconscious is found in all her works. Her fiction, noted for its poetic style and searching portraits of women, includes the novels *Winter of Artiface* (1939) and *A Spy in the House of Love* (1954) and the short-story collection *Ladders to Fire* (1946). She has also published portions of her diaries, her correspondence with Henry MILLER (1965), and various critical works, including *The Novel of the Future* (1970).

ninebark, any plant of the genus *Physocarpus* of the family Rosaceae (ROSE family). Ninebarks are North American (one is Asian) deciduous, hardy, spring-blooming shrubs, with thin bark which peels off in many layers. The most common American species is *P. opulifolius,* found along rocky streams E of the Rockies. Ninebarks are similar to the closely related spiraeas and are also cultivated as ornamentals. Ninebarks are classified in the division MAGNOLIOPHYTA, class Magnoliopsida, order Rosales, family Rosaceae.

Nine-Power Treaty: see NAVAL CONFERENCES.

Nineveh (nĭn'əvə), ancient city, capital of the Assyrian Empire, on the Tigris River opposite the site of modern Mosul, Iraq. A shaft dug at Nineveh has yielded a pottery sequence that can be equated with the earliest cultural development in N Mesopotamia. The old capital, Assur, was replaced by Calah, which seems to have been replaced by Nineveh. Nineveh was thereafter generally the capital, although Sargon built Dur Sharrukin (Khorsabad) as his capital. Nineveh reached its full glory under SENNACHERIB and ASSURBANIPAL. It continued to be the leader of the ancient world until it fell to a coalition of Babylonians, Medes, and Scythians in 612 B.C. and the Assyrian Empire came to an end. Excavations, begun in the middle of the 19th cent., have revealed an Assyrian city wall with a perimeter of c.7.5 mi (12 km). The palaces of Sennacherib and Assurbanipal, containing magnificent sculptures, have been discovered, as well as Assurbanipal's library, including over 20,000 cuneiform tablets. The city is mentioned often in the Bible. The book of Nahum tells of its fall. Gen. 10.11; Zeph. 2.13; Mat. 12.41; Luke 11.30. See R. C. Thompson, *A Century of Exploration at Nineveh* (1929); Shirley Glubok, ed. *Digging in Assyria* (1970).

Ninghsia Hui Autonomous Region (nĭng'shyä' hwē), autonomous region (1968 est. pop. 2,000,000), c.105,800 sq mi (247,000 sq km), N China. The capital is YING-CH'UAN. Ninghsia is part of the Inner Mongolian plateau, and desert and grazing land make up most of the area. Extensive land reclamation and irrigation projects, however, have increased cultivation, pushing the nomadic herdsmen north or forcing them to change their life styles. The southeast section, through which the Huang Ho (Yellow River) flows, is the best agricultural land. Wheat, kaoliang, rice, beans, fruit, and vegetables are grown. Wools, furs, hides, and rugs are exported, and there is some gold and silver mining. Desert lakes yield salt and soda. The chief cities—Ying-ch'uan, Wu-chung, and Shih-tsui-shan—are all on the Huang Ho. Other towns are merely stations on the camel caravan routes, which are still important avenues of trade. One railroad, linking Lan-chou with Pao-t'ou, crosses the region. The Chinese population is chiefly confined to the south; the rest of the area is inhabited by Hui and Mongols. Formerly a province, Ninghsia was incorporated into Kansu in 1954 but was detached and reconstituted as an autonomous region for the Hui people in 1958. In 1969, Ninghsia Hui received a part of the Inner Mongolian Autonomous Region. Ninghsia Univ. is in Ying-ch'uan.

Ninghsien: see NING-PO, China.

Ning-po or **Ningpo** (nĭng-pô), city (1970 est. pop. 350,000), NE Chekiang prov., SE China, at the confluence of the Yung (or Ning-po) and Yao rivers. Situated at the terminus of the E Chekiang RR, it is one of China's leading fishing ports. Industries, in addition to fishing, include salt panning, food canning, and the production of textiles. Long a center of culture and religion, Ning-po has many temples and Buddhist monasteries. The present site of Ning-po has been occupied since the 8th cent. A.D., and during the Ming dynasty it was known as Ching-yuan. From 1433 to 1549 it served as the port of entry for Japanese missions to the Chinese court. The Portuguese, who had established a trading settlement there in the 16th cent., called the city Liampo. In the Opium War (1841), British forces occupied the city. The Treaty of Nanking (1842), which ended hostilities, made Ning-po a treaty port. The city was known as Ninghsien from 1911 to 1949.

Ninon de Lenclos: see LENCLOS, NINON DE.

Niobe (nī'ōbē), in Greek mythology, queen of Thebes, wife of Amphion and daughter of Tantalus. The mother of six sons and six daughters, she boasted of her fruitfulness, saying that Leto had only two children. Apollo and Artemis, angry at this insult to their mother, killed all Niobe's children. Crying inconsolably, she fled to Mt. Sipylus. There Zeus turned her into a stone image that wept perpetually.

niobium (nīō'bēəm), metallic chemical element; symbol Nb; at. no. 41; at. wt. 92.906; m.p. about 2470°C; b.p. 4927°C; sp. gr. 8.57 at 20°C; valence +2, +3, +4, or +5. Niobium is a rare, soft, malleable, ductile, gray-white metal with a body-centered cubic crystalline structure. In its physical and chemical properties it resembles TANTALUM, the element below it in group Vb of the PERIODIC TABLE. At normal temperatures it is insoluble in solutions of most acids or alkalies. It reacts readily at high temperatures with oxygen, carbon, the halogens, nitrogen, and sulfur; it must be placed in a protective atmosphere when processed. It forms four oxides; the pentoxide, Nb_2O_5, is the basis of a series of salts called niobates. Niobium is important in the production of high-temperature-resistant alloys and special stainless steels; large amounts of niobium have been used in the U.S. space program. Niobium carbide is used in cutting tools. Although the name *niobium* has been officially adopted by the International Union of Pure and Applied Chemistry and is used by chemists, the name *columbium* (Cb) is used by many metallurgists and commercial producers of the metal. Niobium is widely distributed in nature; it is about one and a half times as abundant as lead. It occurs in the minerals columbite and tantalite, together with tantalum. Separating niobium and tantalum is difficult. The element was discovered in 1801 by Charles Hatchett and first isolated in 1864 by C. W. Blomstrand.

Niobrara (nīəbrâr'ə), river, c.430 mi (690 km) long, rising in the High Plains, E Wyo., and flowing E across N Nebraska to the Missouri River on Nebraska's northeast border. The Mirage Flats irrigation project uses water impounded by Box Butte Dam (completed 1946) to irrigate c.35,000 acres (14,160 hectares).

Nioro (nyō'rō), town (1967 est. pop. 11,000), W Mali. The market center for an agricultural region where millet, cotton, and gum arabic are produced, Nioro has a cotton ginning and treatment plant. Cattle raising is also important, and the town has an experimental station for raising Karakul sheep. In the 16th cent. Nioro, located at the convergence of several trade routes, was part of the SONGHAI empire. By the early 17th cent. it was able to form the independent state of Kaarta. In 1854 the state fell to Al-hajj Umar, the militant Muslim reformer, and in 1891 Nioro was taken by the French.

Niort (nyôr), city (1968 pop. 50,079), capital of Deux-Sèvres dept., W France, in Poitou. An old agricultural marketplace, it now has plywood, chemical, metallurgy, clothing, tobacco, and printing industries. Niort was originally a Gallo-Roman town called Novioritum. During the 16th and 17th cent. it was a stronghold of the HUGUENOTS. Of the old fortress (12th–13th cent.), two huge towers remain; there are also several fine Renaissance buildings, including a town hall (16th cent.) and a church (15th–17th cent.).

Nipigon, Lake (nĭp'ĭgŏn), c.1,870 sq mi (4,840 sq km), central Ont., Canada. It has many islands. Its outlet, the Nipigon River (40 mi/64 km long) flows south, past the logging town of Nipigon, into Lake Superior.

Nipissing, Lake (nĭp'ĭsĭng), c.350 sq mi (910 sq km), S Ont., Canada, between the Ottawa River and Georgian Bay. It extends west from the city of North Bay and is drained SW by the French River c.50 mi (80 km) to Georgian Bay.

Nippon (nĭp'ŏn, nĭpŏn'), name for Japan, derived from Dai Nippon, meaning Great Japan. The expression comes from the Chinese ideograph for the place where the sun comes from, or Land of the Rising Sun. The term Nipponism has come to imply an extreme Japanese nationalism.

Nippur (nĭpo͝or'), ancient city of Babylonia, a N Sumerian settlement on the Euphrates. It was the seat of the important cult of the god Enlil, or Bel. Excavations at Nippur have yielded the remains of several temples that date from the middle of the 3d millennium B.C. and were later rebuilt and restored many times. Over 40,000 clay tablets found there serve as a primary source of information on Sumerian civilization. Assurbanipal erected a ziggurat in Nippur. Relics of the Persian and Parthian periods have also been unearthed at the site.

Niriz, lake: see BAKHTEGAN.

nirvana (nērvä'nə), in BUDDHISM, JAINISM, and HINDUISM, a state of supreme liberation and bliss, contrasted to *samsara* or bondage in the repeating cycle of death and rebirth. The word in Sanskrit refers to the going out of a flame once its fuel has been consumed; it thus suggests both the end of suffering and the cessation of desires that perpetuate bondage. Epithets of nirvana in Buddhism include "the free," "the immortal," and "the unconditioned." Nirvana is attainable in life, and the death of one who has attained it is termed *parinirvana,* or complete nirvana. This has often been interpreted as annihilation, but in fact the Buddhist scriptures say that the state of the enlightened man beyond death cannot be described. Nirvana in the different Indian traditions is achieved by moral discipline and the practice of YOGA leading to the extinction of all attachment and ignorance. See also KARMA.

Niš or **Nish** (both: nēsh), city (1971 pop. 193,320), E Yugoslavia, in Serbia, on the Nišava River. An important railway and industrial center, it has industries that manufacture machinery, leather and tobacco products, and armaments. The Roman Naissus, it was the site of a victory (A.D. 269) of Claudius II over the Ostrogoths and was the birthplace of Constantine I (Constantine the Great). In 441 it was destroyed by the Huns but was rebuilt (6th cent.) by Emperor Justinian I. In the Middle Ages the city passed back and forth between the Bulgarian and Serbian empires. The Turks captured it c.1386, were defeated there in 1443 by John Hunyadi, and recaptured it again in 1456. It became (until 1878) their most important military stronghold in the Balkans. It passed to Serbia in 1878. The city retains a medieval fortress that dominates the S Morava valley. The Tower of Skulls (Serbo-Croatian *Cele Kula*) was built to commemorate the Serbs massacred by the Turks in the uprising of 1809.

Nisa, rivers: see NEISSE, rivers of Poland.

Nishapur, Iran: see NEYSHABUR.

Nishinomiya (nē″shēnō′mēä), city (1970 pop. 376,763), Hyogo prefecture, S Honshu, Japan, on Osaka Bay. It produces a famous sake. Nishinomiya is a resort, as well as the site of several temples that were founded in the 7th and 8th cent. Kobe Women's College is in the city.

Nishio (nēshē′ō), city (1970 pop. 75,193), Aichi prefecture, central Honshu, Japan. It is an agricultural market and manufacturing center for textiles and sake.

Nisibin, Turkey: see NUSAYBIN.

Nisqualli Indians (nĭz′kwälē), North American Indians whose language belongs to the Salishan branch of the Algonquian-Wakashan linguistic stock (see AMERICAN INDIAN LANGUAGES). In the early 19th cent. they lived on the Nisqually River in Washington. Their culture was essentially that of the Northwest Coast area; they fished for salmon, lived in large wooden houses, and were expert at wood carving. In 1854 they signed the Medicine Creek Treaty, which set aside a small reservation for them in W central Washington. The Nisqualli took part in the Indian uprisings of 1858. By the early 1970s the reservation population was about 200. See M. W. Smith, *The Puyallup-Nisqually* (1940, repr., 1969).

Nisroch (nĭs′rŏk), Assyrian god in whose temple Sennacherib was worshiping when he was assassinated. 2 Kings 19.37; Isa. 37.38.

niter or **nitre:** see POTASSIUM NITRATE.

Niterói (nētəroi′), city (1970 pop. 324,367), capital of Rio de Janeiro state, SE Brazil, on Guanabara Bay opposite the city of Rio de Janeiro. It is a residential suburb of Rio, and many of its citizens commute to work across the bay. Niterói is also an important industrial center. Foodstuffs, transportation equipment, textiles, pharmaceuticals, and metals are the principal products. The area was settled by Indians in 1573 on land granted by the king of Portugal. The city's name derives from the Indian word *Nyteroi* meaning "hidden water." By 1819 the Indian community was extinct, and in 1835 Niterói became the provincial capital.

niton: see RADON.

Nitra (nyĭ′trä), Ger. *Neutra,* Hung. *Nyitra,* city (1970 pop. 45,908), S Czechoslovakia, in Slovakia, on the Nitra River, a tributary of the Danube. It is an agricultural market center and has sugar refineries, breweries, and food-processing industries. Dating from Roman times, Nitra was important from the 9th cent. onward as a religious center and fortress. It became a free city by royal decree in 1248 and was made a Roman Catholic bishopric in 1288. Nitra's bishopric church and a castle (founded c.830) are the oldest structures in Slovakia. The city also has an agricultural college.

nitrate, chemical compound containing the nitrate (NO_3) RADICAL. Nitrates are salts or esters of NITRIC ACID, HNO_3, formed by replacing the hydrogen with a metal (e.g., sodium or potassium) or a radical (e.g., ammonium or ethyl). Some important inorganic nitrates are POTASSIUM NITRATE (KNO_3), SODIUM NITRATE ($NaNO_3$), SILVER NITRATE ($AgNO_3$), and AMMONIUM NITRATE (NH_4NO_3). Calcium nitrate is used in fertilizers; barium and strontium nitrates are used to color fireworks and signal flares; bismuth nitrate is used in making pharmaceuticals. Nearly all metal nitrates are readily soluble in water; for this reason they are often used when a water soluble salt of a metal is needed. The presence of nitrates in the soil is of great importance, since it is from these compounds that plants obtain the nitrogen necessary for their growth. Nitrogen-fixing bacteria are important in keeping the soil supplied with nitrates. Organic nitrates are esters formed by reaction of nitric acid with the hydroxyl ($-OH$) group in an alcohol. NITROGLYCERIN is the trinitrate of glycerol; guncotton is a nitrate of CELLULOSE. In chemical analysis, a test for nitrates involves the addition of a solution of ferrous sulfate to the substance to be tested, followed by the addition (without mixing) of a few drops of concentrated sulfuric acid; the presence of a nitrate is indicated by the formation of a brown ring—of $Fe(NO)^{+2}$ complex ion—where the sulfuric acid contacts the test mixture.

nitric acid, chemical compound, HNO_3, colorless, highly corrosive, poisonous liquid that gives off choking fumes in moist air. It is miscible with water in all proportions. It forms an azeotrope (constant-boiling mixture) that has the composition 68% nitric acid and 32% water and that boils at 120.5°C. The nitric acid of commerce is typically a solution of 52% to 68% nitric acid in water. More concentrated solutions are available. Solutions containing over 86% nitric acid are commonly called fuming nitric acid; they often have a reddish-brown color from dissolved nitrogen oxides. Nitric acid is a strong oxidizing agent. It ionizes readily in solution, forming a good conductor of electricity. It reacts with metals, oxides, and hydroxides, forming NITRATE salts. Chief uses of nitric acid are in the preparation of fertilizers, e.g., AMMONIUM NITRATE, and explosives. It is also used in the manufacture of chemicals, e.g., in making dyes. It is produced chiefly by oxidation of ammonia (the OSTWALD PROCESS). Small amounts are produced by the treatment of SODIUM NITRATE with sulfuric acid. Nitric acid was known to the alchemists as *aqua fortis;* the name is used in commerce for impure grades of it. AQUA REGIA is a mixture of nitric and hydrochloric acids.

nitrifying bacteria: see NITROGEN CYCLE.

nitrile: see RUBBER.

nitrobenzene, $C_6H_5NO_2$, very poisonous, flammable, pale yellow, liquid aromatic compound with an odor like that of bitter almonds. It is sometimes called oil of mirbane. Nitrobenzene melts at 5.7°C, boils at 211°C, is only slightly soluble in water, but is very soluble in ethanol, ether, and benzene. It is prepared by treating benzene with a mixture of nitric and sulfuric acids; in the resulting nitration reaction, one hydrogen in the benzene molecule is replaced with a nitro group, NO_2. The major use of nitrobenzene is in the production of ANILINE, commercially the most important amine; nitrobenzene is heated with iron and dilute hydrochloric acid, and the resulting anilinium chloride is treated with sodium carbonate to release aniline.

nitrocellulose, nitric acid ESTER of CELLULOSE (a glucose polymer). It is usually formed by the action of a mixture of nitric and sulfuric acids on purified cotton or wood pulp. The extent of nitration and degradation (breaking down) of the cellulose is carefully controlled in order to obtain the desired product. When cotton is treated so that nearly all of the hydroxyl groups of the cellulose molecule are esterified, but with little or no degradation of the molecular structure, the nitrocellulose formed is called guncotton. Guncotton resembles cotton in its appearance. Extremely flammable, it explodes when detonated and is used in the manufacture of explosives. Guncotton is insoluble in such common solvents as water, chloroform, ether, and ethanol. If the nitration is not carried to completion (the point at which about two thirds of the hydroxyl groups are esterified), the soluble cellulose nitrate PYROXYLIN is formed.

nitrogen (nī′trəjən), gaseous chemical element; symbol N; at. no. 7; at. wt. 14.0067; m.p. −210°C; b.p. −196°C; density 1.25 grams per liter at STP; valence principally −3, +3, or +5. Nitrogen is a colorless, odorless, tasteless diatomic gas. It is found in group Va of the PERIODIC TABLE. It does not burn, does not support combustion, and is only slightly soluble in water. It is relatively inactive chemically, but many of its compounds display marked reactivity. At high temperatures it reacts with some of the other elements to form nitrides. Nitrogen has several oxides. NITROUS OXIDE, N_2O, is a gas used as an anesthetic; it is often called laughing gas. Nitric oxide, NO, is a gas used in the manufacture of sulfuric acid; in air it forms nitrogen dioxide, NO_2, a poisonous reddish-brown gas. Nitrogen trioxide, N_2O_3, is unstable at ordinary temperatures. Nitrogen pentoxide, N_2O_5, forms nitric aicd when dissolved in water. Important compounds of nitrogen include NITRIC ACID, AMMONIA, many EXPLOSIVES, CYANIDES, FERTILIZERS, and the PROTEINS. Many organic compounds contain nitrogen. Nitrogen for industrial use is produced largely by the fractional distillation of liquid air. Nitrogen is used to some extent for filling light bulbs, in thermometers, and generally anywhere a relatively inert atmosphere is needed. The chief importance of the element lies in its compounds. The expression "nitrogen fixation" refers to the extraction of the element from the atmosphere by its combination with other elements to form compounds. This is accomplished commercially in several ways. In the HABER PROCESS, nitrogen is reacted with hydrogen to form ammonia; in the cyanamide process, nitrogen is reacted with calcium carbide at high temperatures to form calcium cyanamide; in the arc process, nitrogen is reacted with oxygen in an electric arc to form nitrogen oxides. Nitrogen is abundant in the atmosphere; it is about 78% (by volume) of dry air. Nitrogen is present in the protoplasm of all living matter; it and its compounds are necessary for the continuation of life (see NITROGEN CYCLE). Nitrogen is present in foods and is important in the human diet. Nitrogen was discovered by Daniel Rutherford in 1772, although K. W. Scheele and others were studying phlogisticated air (air from which the oxygen had been removed, usually by combustion). Lavoisier was the first to treat phlogisticated air as a separate element, which he called *azote.* The term *nitrogen* was first used by J. A. Chaptal in 1790. This early "nitrogen" was later shown by John Strutt, or Lord Rayleigh, and William Ramsay to contain argon; Henry Cavendish had shown in 1785 that there was an unreactive gas other than nitrogen present in air.

nitrogen cycle, the continuous flow of nitrogen through the BIOSPHERE by the processes of nitrogen fixation, ammonification (decay), nitrification, and denitrification. Nitrogen is vital to all living matter, both plant and animal; it is an essential constituent of amino acids, which form proteins, which in turn build protoplasm. Although the earth's atmosphere is 78% nitrogen, free gaseous nitrogen cannot be utilized by animals or by higher plants. To enter living systems, nitrogen must first be "fixed" (combined with oxygen or hydrogen) into compounds that plants can utilize, such as nitrates or ammonia. A certain amount of atmospheric nitrogen is fixed by lightning and by some blue-green algae. But the great bulk of nitrogen fixation is performed by soil bacteria of two kinds: those that live free in the soil and those that live enclosed in nodules in the roots of certain leguminous plants (e.g., alfalfa, peas, beans, clover, soy beans, and peanuts). Among the free-living forms are species of *Clostridium,* discovered c.1893 by Sergei WINOGRADSKY, and *Azotobacter,* discovered c.1901 by M. W. Beijerinck. Both *Clostridium* and *Azotobacter* are generally present in agricultural soils, and both are saprophytes, i.e., they use the energy from decaying organic matter in the soil to fuel cell processes, including nitrogen fixation. Bacteria that live in the roots of LEGUMES are of the genus *Rhizobium,* first isolated c.1888 by Beijerinck. These rod-shaped, motile bacteria enter the roots chiefly through the root hairs and then work their way to the inner root tissues. There they stimulate the growth of tumorlike nodules. Within the nodules the bacteria develop into branched forms called bacteroids, which live in a symbiotic (mutually beneficial) relationship with the green plant. The bacteroids take carbohydrates from the plant for energy to fix nitrogen and synthesize amino acids; the plants take the amino acids elaborated in the nodule to build plant tissue. Animals in turn consume the plants and convert plant protein into animal protein. *Rhizobia* can be found free-living in the soil, but they cannot fix nitrogen in the free state, nor can the legume root fix nitrogen without *Rhizobia.* The exact biochemistry of nitrogen fixation within the nodule is not yet understood. It is estimated that more than 300 lbs of nitrogen per acre (340 kg per hectare) can be fixed by fields of alfalfa and other legumes. After a harvest legume roots left in the soil decay, returning organic nitrogen compounds to the soil for uptake by the next generation of plants. For this reason, crop rotation in which a leguminous crop is alternated with a nonleguminous one is a common practice for maintaining soil fertility. Decomposing animal remains and animal wastes also return organic nitrogen to the soil as ammonia. Many different kinds of decay microorganisms participate in ammonification. The nitrifying bacteria of the genus *Nitrosomonas* oxidize the ammonia to nitrites, and *Nitrobacter* oxidize the nitrites to nitrates. The nitrates can then be taken up again by the green plant. The cycle of fixation-decay-nitrification-fixation can proceed indefinitely without any nitrogen being returned to a gaseous state. But still another group of microorganisms, the denitrifying bacteria, can reduce nitrates all the way to molecular nitrogen. Denitrification occurs only in the absence of oxygen and is not common in well-cultivated soils. Nitrogen fixation can also be accomplished artificially by various

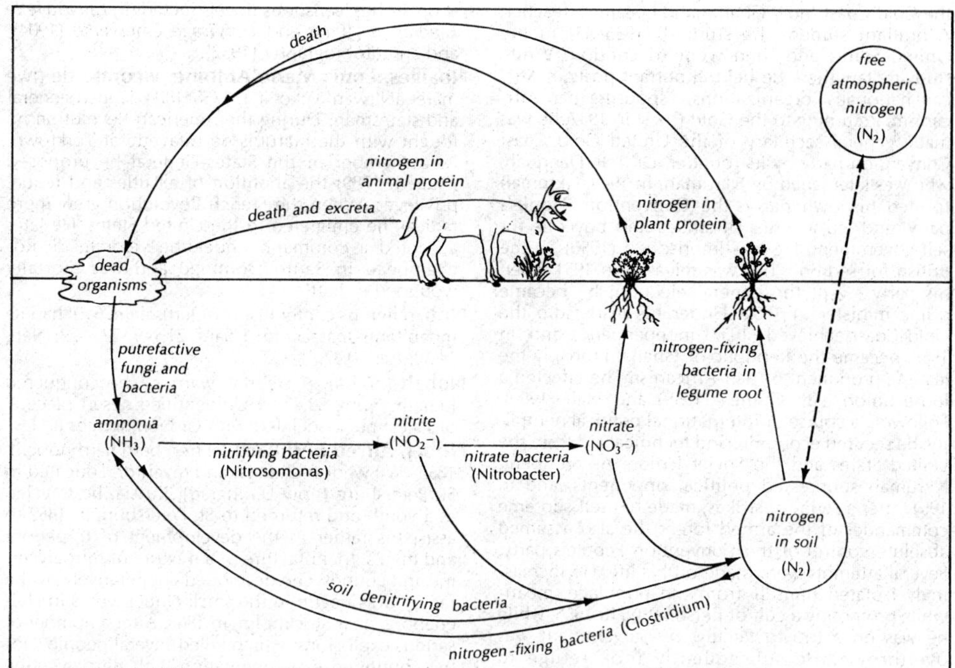

Nitrogen cycle

methods (see NITROGEN). Man annually fixes vast amounts of nitrogen for industrial purposes and for use as fertilizer. Unfortunately, large-scale legume cultivation and artificial fixation may be upsetting the natural nitrogen cycle in the biosphere. There is some question whether natural denitrification can keep pace with fixation. For one thing, run-off of nitrate fertilizer can cause EUTROPHICATION of lakes and streams (see WATER POLLUTION) and can foul drinking supplies. Another environmental problem is that inorganic fertilizers tend to depress legume fixation. As a consequence, root tissue remaining after harvest is poorer and thus more fertilizer must be applied the following year.

nitrogen-fixing bacteria: see NITROGEN CYCLE.

nitrogen mustard, any of various poisonous compounds originally developed for military use (see POISON GAS). Like mustard gas and lewisite, it is a vesicant (blistering agent). In the form of its crystalline hydrochloride it is used as a drug in the treatment of cancerlike diseases such as leukemia, Hodgkin's disease, and some tumors. Nitrogen mustards cause mutations in the genetic material of cells, thereby disrupting mitosis, or cell division. Cells vary in their susceptibility to the nitrogen mustards, with rapidly proliferating tumor and cancer cells most sensitive; bone marrow, which produces red blood cells, is also sensitive, and depression of red blood cell production is a frequent side effect of nitrogen mustard therapy. The nitrogen mustards also suppress the immune response (see IMMUNITY).

nitroglycerin (nī''trōglĭs'ərĭn), $C_3H_5N_3O_9$, colorless, oily, highly explosive liquid. It is the nitric acid triester of GLYCEROL and is more correctly called glycerol trinitrate. It is insoluble in water but soluble in ether, acetone, benzene, and chloroform. An unstable compound, nitroglycerin decomposes with explosive violence when heated or jarred. It is mixed with an absorbent material to form DYNAMITE (which is not so sensitive to slight shocks) and is also used as a component of smokeless powder. Nitroglycerin was discovered (c.1847) by the Italian chemist Ascanio Sobrero and was first produced commercially by Alfred NOBEL. It is used medicinally to provide temporary relief from the symptoms of angina pectoris.

nitro group, in chemistry, FUNCTIONAL GROUP that consists of a nitrogen atom joined to two oxygen atoms. Compounds that contain a nitro group, e.g., picric acid and trinitrotoluene (TNT), are called nitro compounds; many nitro compounds are unstable and are used as explosives. As a result of the chemical bonding in the nitro group, the nitrogen atom is positively charged and each oxygen atom has a partial negative charge. For this reason the nitro group has a powerful attraction for electrons. Many of the chemical reactions of nitro compounds are due to this ELECTRONEGATIVITY of the nitro group.

nitrous oxide or **nitrogen (I) oxide,** chemical compound, N_2O, a colorless gas with a sweetish taste and odor. Its density is 1.977 grams per liter at STP. It is soluble in water, alcohol, ether, and other solvents. Although it does not burn, it supports combustion since it decomposes into oxygen and nitrogen when heated. The gas is prepared commercially by the thermal decomposition of ammonium nitrate, NH_4NO_3, at about 240°C to produce nitrous oxide and water; the reaction must be carefully controlled to prevent explosive decomposition of the nitrous oxide. The gas is purified, liquified by compressing and cooling it, and stored in metal cylinders. A major use of nitrous oxide is in anesthesia, e.g., in dentistry. It is commonly called laughing gas since it produces euphoria and mirth when inhaled in small amounts. It is also used in making certain canned pressurized foods, e.g., instant whipped cream. Nitrous oxide was discovered (1772) by Joseph Priestley, who called it "diminished nitrous air"; he prepared it from "nitrous air" (nitric oxide, NO) by treatment with iron powder or a mixture of iron and sulfur powders. Its properties were further studied (1799) by Sir Humphry DAVY.

Nitti, Francesco Saverio (frănchās'kō sävā'rēō nēt'tē), 1868–1953, Italian premier and economist. A professor of economics at the Univ. of Naples, he entered parliament in 1904 and was minister of agriculture (1911–14) and of finance (1917–19). In 1919 he became premier, but internal difficulties and criticism of his foreign policy caused his resignation in 1920. Nitti lived in exile during the Fascist period, returned after World War II, and with Benedetto Croce and former premier ORLANDO formed the right-wing Democratic Union party. He wrote economic and political studies.

Niue (nēō͞o'ä), coral island (1971 est. pop. 5,100), c.100 sq mi (260 sq km), South Pacific, a territory of New Zealand. The island has fertile soil and exports copra and bananas. Alofi is the chief town. Niue is also known as Savage Island.

Nivelle, Robert Georges (rôbĕr' zhôrzh nēvĕl'), 1856–1924, French general. His services in World War I gained him the post of chief assistant to General Pétain at VERDUN, and he was later given the command of the Verdun sector. He succeeded (1916) General Joffre as commander in chief of the French armies, but the signal failure of the 1917 Aisne offensive lost him the post; he was given a command in North Africa.

Nivelles (nēvĕl'), Flemish *Nijvel,* city (1970 pop. 16,126), Brabant prov., central Belgium. It is an industrial center and a rail junction. Manufactures include machinery, paper, and railroad equipment. Of note are a 7th-century convent and a Romanesque church (11th cent; rebuilt in the 18th cent.).

Nivernais (nēvĕrnā'), region and former province, central France. It roughly coincides with Nièvre dept. Drained by the Loire and the Yonne, it is a hilly plateau, rising to the Morvan mts. in the east. It has metallurgical, chemical, and livestock industries. Nevers is its chief town and historic capital. A county after the 10th cent., it passed (1384) through inheritance to Philip the Bold of Burgundy, and later, as a duchy, passed (1565) through a complicated succession to the house of GONZAGA. Cardinal Mazarin bought (1659) the title, which remained with his family even after Louis XIV incorporated (1669) Nivernais into the royal domain.

nix or **nixie,** in Germanic mythology, water sprite. The nixes could assume various shapes, most frequently as half human and half fish. They could do favors for humans, particularly in teaching them bewitching music, but for the most part they were treacherous and malignant.

Nixon, Richard Milhous, 1913–, 37th President of the United States (1969–74), b. Yorba Linda, Calif. A graduate of Whittier College and Duke Univ. law school, he practiced law in Whittier, Calif., from 1937 to 1942, was briefly with the Office of Emergency Management, and served during World War II with the navy in the South Pacific. In 1946, without professional political experience, he was elected to Congress as a Republican. In the House of Representatives he became nationally known for his work on the House Committee on Un-American Activities (renamed the House Internal Security Committee in 1969), where he was credited with forcing the famous confrontation between Alger HISS and Whittaker CHAMBERS, thus precipitating the perjury case against Hiss. In 1950 he was elected to the U.S. Senate after a particularly bitter electoral campaign. In the Senate, Nixon denounced President Truman's policy in Asia, supported Gen. Douglas MacArthur's proposal to expand the Korean War, and attacked the Democratic administration as favorable to socialism. He was elected to the vice presidency on the Republican ticket with Dwight D. Eisenhower in 1952. As Vice President, Nixon was kept closely informed of administration policy and played an important role in government affairs. He made frequent official trips abroad, notably in 1958 to South America, where he faced a hostile demonstration in Venezuela, and in 1959 to the USSR, where he engaged in a much-publicized informal debate with Premier Nikita Khrushchev. Nixon received the Republican presidential nomination in 1960 with only a minimum of opposition and campaigned in support of the Eisenhower administration policies. He was defeated but gained almost as much of the popular vote as the successful John F. Kennedy. Nixon returned to politics in 1962, winning the Republican nomination for governor of California. After losing the election he returned to the practice of law. In 1968 Nixon again won the Republican nomination for president; Spiro T. AGNEW was his running mate. In a low-key campaign, Nixon promised to bring peace with honor in Vietnam and to unite a nation deeply divided by the Vietnam War and the racial crisis. He defeated his two opponents, Hubert H. Humphrey and George C. Wallace, but won only a plurality of the popular vote. As President, Nixon began the phased withdrawal of U.S. troops from South Vietnam. He achieved (1973) a cease-fire accord with North Vietnam, but only after he had ordered invasions of Cambodia (1970) and Laos (1971) and the saturation bombing of North Vietnam. In other areas of foreign policy, Nixon eased cold war tensions. He initiated strategic arms limitation talks with the Soviet Union in 1969 and visited (1972) the People's Republic of China. At home, Nixon reversed many of the social and economic welfare policies of President Lyndon B. Johnson. He vetoed much new health, education, and welfare legislation and impounded congressionally approved funds for domestic programs that he opposed. Nixon's Southern strategy, through which he hoped to woo the South into the Republican party, led him to weaken the Federal government's commitment to racial equality and to sponsor antibusing legislation in Congress. Nixon's first term in office was also beset by economic troubles. A severe recession and serious inflation brought about the imposition (1971) of a wide-reaching system of wage and price controls. Despite these problems, Nixon and Agnew easily won reelection in 1972; widespread popular distrust of his Democratic opponent, Senator George S. McGovern, brought Nixon a landslide victory. (Agnew was forced to resign in 1973, however, on charges of corruption that began when he was Baltimore county executive, and Gerald R. FORD was nominated by Nixon and confirmed by Congress to succeed Agnew.) Soon after his reelection Nixon's popularity plummeted as the growing revelations of the WATERGATE AFFAIR indicated pervasive corruption in his administration, and there was widespread criticism of the amount of government money spent on his private residences. Further problems ensued when the Internal Revenue Service (IRS) found that Nixon's donation of papers to the Federal government, which had been taken as a deduction on his

Federal income tax returns, had been made after a law went into effect disallowing such deductions. The IRS assessed (1974) Nixon for the back taxes plus interest. Many public officials and private citizens had already begun to question Nixon's fitness to remain in office, and in 1974 the House of Representatives initiated impeachment proceedings. The House Committee on the Judiciary, which conducted the impeachment inquiry, subpoenaed Nixon's tape-recorded conversations relating to the Watergate affair and finally received (April 30) transcripts of most, but not all, of the tapes. Nixon also released transcripts of these conversations to the public, continuing to profess noninvolvement in the Watergate coverup despite growing evidence to the contrary. Meanwhile, Watergate special prosecutor Leon Jaworski subpoenaed tapes that had been previously requested but that were not among those included in the transcripts. Nixon refused to relinquish these, basing his refusal on claims of "executive privilege," i.e., the confidentiality of executive communications whose release might endanger national security. On July 24, 1974, the Supreme Court ruled that President Nixon must surrender these tapes to Jaworski. The House Judiciary Committee had already completed its investigations and subsequently recommended (July 27–30) three articles of impeachment against the President, charging him with obstruction of justice in the investigation of the break-in at the Democratic national headquarters in the Watergate apartment complex; abuse of power through misuse of the Internal Revenue Service for political purposes, illegal wiretapping, establishment of a private investigative unit that engaged in unlawful activities, and interference with the lawful activities of the Federal Bureau of Investigation (FBI), the Central Intelligence Agency, the Dept. of Justice, and other government bodies; and failure to comply with subpoenas issued by the House Judiciary Committee. On Aug. 5, Nixon made public the transcripts of three conversations covered by the Supreme Court ruling, and admitted that he had, six days after the Watergate break-in, ordered the FBI to halt its investigation of the burglary. Nixon's revelation provoked widespread calls for his resignation; finally, responding to pressure from his closest advisers, he resigned on Aug. 9, the first U.S. President ever to do so. He left the White House immediately and returned to his estate in San Clemente, Calif. His successor, Gerald Ford, granted him a full pardon for any illegal acts that he might have committed while President, thus quashing the possibility of criminal proceedings against the former President. Subsequently, four of his close associates, including John Mitchell, H. R. Haldeman, and John Ehrlichman, were convicted (Jan. 1, 1975) on charges arising from the affair. See his *Six Crises* (1962); biographies by Earl Mazo (1959, rev. ed. with Stephen Hess, 1968), Garry Wills (1970), Bruce Mazlish (1972), and Frank Mankiewicz (1973); John Osborne, *The Nixon Watch* (5 vol., 1970–74); Jules Witcover, *The Resurrection of President Nixon* (1970); Rowland Evans and R. D. Novak, *Nixon in the White House* (1971); Henry Brandon, *The Retreat of American Power* (1973); A. M. Jones, ed., *U.S. Foreign Policy in a Changing World: The Nixon Administration, 1969–1973* (1973).

Niza, Marcos de: see MARCOS DE NIZA.

Nizam: see HYDERABAD, India.

Nizamabad (nĭzäm'äbäd), town (1971 pop. 114,868), Adhra Pradesh state, S central India. It is a district administrative center and a market for grain, sugar, and vegetable oil. The district is irrigated by the Nizamsagar hydroelectric project.

Nizhnevartovsk (nyĕzh"nyĭvär'təfsk), city (1970 est. pop. 50,000), N Siberian USSR. The discovery of a huge oilfield at nearby Lake Samotlor in 1965 quickly transformed the small village of Nizhnevartovsk into an oil center. The field is said to be one of the world's largest. Soviet planners envisage the city as a major hub in the developing oil industry of W Siberia.

Nizhni Tagil (nyēzh'nyē təgēl'), city (1970 pop. 378,000), E European USSR, in the central Urals, on the Tagil River. A leading metallurgical and heavy industry center, it uses the ore from deposits at Kachkanar and on Mount Vysokaya. Railroad cars, machinery, and chemicals are manufactured, and copper, iron, and gold are mined in the district. Nizhni Tagil was founded in 1725.

Nizhny Novgorod: see GORKY, USSR.

Nkrumah, Kwame (kwä'mä nkro͞o'mä), 1909–1972, African political leader, prime minister (1957–60) and president (1960–66) of Ghana. The son of a goldsmith, he was educated at mission schools in the Gold Coast (now Ghana) and became a teacher. A brilliant student, he studied (1935–45) in the United States and then went to London. While studying law there he held important posts in African nationalist organizations, espousing pan-Africanism. Returning to the Gold Coast in 1947, he was made general secretary of the United Gold Coast Convention party by its founder, Dr. J. B. Danquah, who was later jailed by Nkrumah. In 1949, Nkrumah formed his own party, the Convention People's party, and led a series of strikes and boycotts for self-government. He was imprisoned (1950) by the British for sedition, but was released in 1951 when his party swept the general election; he became prime minister in 1952. Under his leadership the Gold Coast achieved (1957) independence and, in 1960, became the Republic of Ghana. Probably the leading proponent of pan-Africanism, he effected a loose union with Guinea (1959) and Mali (1960). Following a course of international political neutrality, he secured economic and technical aid from the United States and the Soviet Union. As president, Nkrumah suppressed political opponents, and in 1961, after a series of strikes, made himself supreme commander of the armed forces; he also assumed absolute control of the Convention People's party. Several attempts were made on his life. He increasingly isolated himself from the populace, meanwhile promoting a cult of personality. In 1966, while he was on a trip to Peking, his government was overthrown. He subsequently took refuge in Guinea. See his autobiography (1957); biographies by Genoveva Marais (1972) and Basil Davidson (1974); study by H. L. Bretton (1967).

NKVD: see SECRET POLICE.

NMR: see MAGNETIC RESONANCE.

No (nō), biblical name for Thebes, Egypt. Jer. 46.25; Ezek. 30.14–16; Nahum 3.8.

No (nō), lake, S central Sudan, in the swampy SUDD region. It is formed by the flood waters of the WHITE NILE and varies in size seasonally. Its maximum area is c.40 sq mi (100 sq km). Much papyrus grows in the lake.

No, chemical symbol of the element NOBELIUM.

no: see ORIENTAL DRAMA.

Noadiah (nōədī'ə). **1** Levite. Ezra 8.33. **2** Prophetess. Neh. 6.14.

Noah (nō'ə) or **Noe** (nō'ē), in the Bible, the builder of the ARK. He alone of men was deemed by God to be worth saving, and it was at divine direction that he built the ship that saved human and animal life from the DELUGE. After the flood God established a covenant with Noah. Noah's sons, Shem, Ham, and Japheth, are eponymous ancestors of races as mankind is divided in the Bible. The flood story in the GILGAMESH epic has many similarities to the story of Noah. Gen. 6–10; 1 Chron. 1.4; Ecclus. 44.17–18; Ezek. 14.14, 20; Mat. 24.37; Luke 3.36; 17.26; Heb. 11.7. The name appears also among the daughters of ZELOPHEHAD.

Noah, Mordecai Manuel (môr'dĭkī), 1785–1851, American journalist and politician, b. Philadelphia. He became a journalist in Charleston, S.C., and gave ardent support to the War of 1812. As a special agent to Algiers, he helped secure (1813–15) the release of the American prisoners held by Algerian pirates. He returned to the United States, held public offices in New York City, founded and edited many newspapers, including the New York *Enquirer* and the *Evening Star,* and wrote plays. His plays include *She Would Be a Soldier* (1819) and *The Grecian Captive* (1822). Becoming acutely conscious of the problems of the Jewish people, Noah unsuccessfully attempted to buy Grand Island in the Niagara River as a city of refuge for the Jews of the world. See biography by Isaac Goldberg (1936).

Noailles, Adrien Maurice, duc de (ädrēäN' mōrēs' dük də nōī'yə), 1678–1766, marshal of France. He fought in the War of the Spanish Succession and was head of the finance council under the regent Philippe II d'Orléans. He distinguished himself in the War of the Polish Succession and the War of the Austrian Succession and exercised considerable influence on the development of French foreign policy.

Noailles, Anna Élisabeth de Brancovan, comtesse de (änä' ālēzābĕt' də bräNkôväN' kôNtĕs'), 1876–1933, French poet, daughter of a noble Rumanian family. She was renowned for the brilliant gatherings at her home. Her turbulent romantic lyrics of love and nature, many of which appeared in the *Revue des Deux Mondes,* were gathered in *Le Cœur innombrable* (1901), *L'Ombre des jours* (1902), and *Poèmes d'enfance* (1928). She also wrote short stories, sensuous novels including *La Nouvelle Espérance* (1903) and *Le Visage émerveillé* (1904), and an autobiography (1932).

Noailles, Louis Marie Antoine, vicomte de (lwē märē' äN'twän' vēkôNt'), 1756–1804, French general and statesman. During the American Revolution he fought with the marquis de Lafayette at Yorktown. As a member of the States-General he proposed (Aug. 4, 1789) the abolition of all titles and feudal privileges. When the French Revolution grew more radical, he emigrated to the United States. He later accepted a command under the vicomte de Rochambeau in Santo Domingo and was mortally wounded in battle.

Nob, religious center just N of Jerusalem. Saul had its inhabitants massacred. 1 Sam. 21.1–9; 22.6–23; Neh. 11.32; Isa. 10.32.

Nobah (nō'bə). **1** Hebrew warrior who conquered Kenath. Num. 32.42. **2** Unidentified desert place, E of Palestine, associated with Gideon. Judges 8.11.

Nobel, Alfred Bernhard (äl'frĕd bĕrn'härd nōbĕl'), 1833–96, Swedish chemist and inventor. Educated in St. Petersburg (now Leningrad), Russia, he traveled as a youth and returned to St. Petersburg in 1852 to assist his father in the development of torpedoes and mines. Manufacture of a mixture of nitroglycerine and gunpowder, developed cooperatively by the family, was begun in the small Nobel works in Heleneborg, near Stockholm, in 1863. After a number of serious explosions, which killed several people, Nobel continued experimentation with nitroglycerine in order to find a safer explosive. In 1866 he perfected a combination of nitroglycerine and kieselguhr, a diatomaceous earth, to which he gave the name dynamite. His other inventions include an explosive gelatin more powerful than dynamite and the smokeless powder Ballistite. Nobel, who inclined toward pacifism, had long had reservations about his family's industry, and he developed strong misgivings about the potential uses of his own invention. On his death in San Remo, Italy, he left a fund from the interest of which annual awards, called NOBEL PRIZES, were to be given for work in physics, chemistry, physiology and medicine, and literature, and toward the promotion of international peace. See biography by Henrick Schück and others, *Nobel: The Man and His Prizes* (3d ed. 1972).

nobelium (nōbē'lēəm), artificially produced radioactive chemical element; symbol No; at. no. 102; mass no. of most stable isotope 255; m.p., b.p., and density unknown; valence +2 or +3. Nobelium is one of the synthetic radioactive TRANSURANIUM ELEMENTS; it is a member of the ACTINIDE SERIES in group IIIb of the PERIODIC TABLE. It was first produced and detected in April, 1958, by A. Ghiorso, T. Sikkeland, J. R. Walton, and G. T. SEABORG at the Univ. of California at Berkeley; they used a heavy-ion linear accelerator to bombard a mixture of curium-244 and curium-246 with carbon-12 ions, producing nobelium-254 (half-life 55 sec). The name of the element was originally suggested by scientists at the Nobel Institute of Physics, who in 1957 reported synthesis of an isotope of the element; although the name was adopted, it was later shown that the element could not have the properties they reported. Seven isotopes of the element are known; the most stable isotope, nobelium-255, has a 3-min half-life.

Nobel Prize, award given for outstanding achievement in physics, chemistry, physiology and medicine, peace, literature, or economics. The awards were established by the will of Alfred NOBEL, who left a fund to provide annual prizes in the first five areas listed above. These prizes were first given in 1901. A prize in economics was established in 1968 from funds provided by the Swedish national bank, Sveriges Riksbank, and was first awarded in 1969. Each prize consists of a gold medal, a sum of money, and a diploma with the citation of award. The amount of money available for each prize varies from year to year; in 1972 it was about $100,000. The Nobel Prizes are awarded without regard to nationality; the judges are, by the terms of Nobel's will, the Royal Swedish Academy of Science, the Swedish Royal Caroline Medico-Surgical Institute, the Swedish Academy, and a committee elected by the Norwegian parliament. The awards are made on Dec. 10, the anniversary of Nobel's death, the Peace Prize being presented in Oslo and the others in Stockholm. A prize is sometimes shared; several times the Nobel Peace Prize has been given to an organization. There may be one or more years in which a prize or prizes may not be awarded; this has happened most often with the Peace Prize. A table of those who have been designated to receive the prizes accompanies this article.

NOBEL PRIZES

Year	Peace	Chemistry	Physics	Physiology and Medicine	Literature	Economics
1901	J. H. Dunant Frédéric Passy	J. H. van't Hoff	W. C. Roentgen	E. A. von Behring	R. F. A. Sully-Prudhomme	
1902	Élie Ducommun C. A. Gobat	Emil Fischer	H. A. Lorentz Pieter Zeeman	Sir Ronald Ross	Theodor Mommsen	
1903	Sir William R. Cremer	S. A. Arrhenius	A. H. Becquerel Pierre Curie Marie S. Curie	N. R. Finsen	Bjørnstjerne Bjørnson	
1904	Institute of International Law	Sir William Ramsay	J. W. S. Rayleigh	Ivan P. Pavlov	Frédéric Mistral José Echegaray	
1905	Baroness Bertha von Suttner	Adolf von Baeyer	Philipp Lenard	Robert Koch	Henryk Sienkiewicz	
1906	Theodore Roosevelt	Henri Moissan	Sir Joseph Thomson	Camillo Golgi S. Ramón y Cajal	Giosuè Carducci	
1907	E. T. Moneta Louis Renault	Eduard Buchner	A. A. Michelson	C. L. A. Laveran	Rudyard Kipling	
1908	K. P. Arnoldson Fredrik Bajer	Sir Ernest Rutherford	Gabriel Lippman	Paul Ehrlich Élie Metchnikoff	R. C. Eucken	
1909	Auguste Beernaert P. H. B. Estournelles de Constant	Wilhelm Ostwald	Guglielmo Marconi C. F. Braun	Emil T. Kocher	Selma Lagerlöf	
1910	International Peace Bureau	Otto Wallach	J. D. van der Waals	Albrecht Kossel	Paul Heyse	
1911	T. M. C. Asser A. H. Fried	Marie S. Curie	Wilhelm Wien	Allvar Gullstrand	Maurice Maeterlinck	
1912	Elihu Root	Victor Grignard Paul Sabatier	N. G. Dalen	Alexis Carrel	Gerhart Hauptmann	
1913	Henri La Fontaine	Alfred Werner	Heike Kamerlingh Onnes	C. R. Richet	Sir Rabindranath Tagore	
1914		T. W. Richards	Max von Laue	Robert Barany		
1915		Richard Willstätter	Sir William H. Bragg Sir William L. Bragg		Romain Rolland	
1916					Verner von Heidenstam	
1917	International Red Cross		C. G. Barkla		K. A. Gjellerup Henrik Pontoppidan	
1918		Fritz Haber	Max Planck			
1919	Woodrow Wilson		Johannes Stark	Jules Bordet	C. F. G. Spitteler	
1920	Léon Bourgeois	Walther Nernst	C. E. Guillaume	S. A. S. Krogh	Knut Hamsun	
1921	Hjalmar Branting C. L. Lange	Frederick Soddy	Albert Einstein		Anatole France	
1922	Fridtjof Nansen	F. W. Aston	N. H. D. Bohr	A. V. Hill Otto Meyerhof	Jacinto Benavente y Martínez	
1923		Fritz Pregl	Robert A. Millikan	Sir Frederick G. Banting J. J. R. Macleod	W. B. Yeats	
1924			K. M. G. Siegbahn	Willem Einthoven	W. S. Reymont	
1925	Sir Austen Chamberlain Charles G. Dawes	Richard Zsigmondy	James Franck Gustav Hertz		G. B. Shaw	
1926	Aristide Briand Gustav Stresemann	Theodor Svedberg	J. B. Perrin	Johannes Fibiger	Grazia Deledda	
1927	F. É. Buisson Ludwig Quidde	Heinrich Wieland	A. H. Compton C. T. R. Wilson	Julius Wagner-Jauregg	Henri Bergson	
1928		Adolf Windaus	Sir Owen W. Richardson	C. J. H. Nicolle	Sigrid Undset	
1929	Frank B. Kellogg	Sir Arthur Harden Hans von Euler-Chelpin	L. V. de Broglie	Christian Eijkman Sir Frederick G. Hopkins	Thomas Mann	
1930	Nathan Soderblom	Hans Fischer	Sir Chandrasekhara V. Raman	Karl Landsteiner	Sinclair Lewis	
1931	Jane Addams Nicholas Murray Butler	Carl Bosch Friedrich Bergius		Otto H. Warburg	E. A. Karlfeldt	
1932		Irving Langmuir	Werner Heisenberg	E. D. Adrian Sir Charles Sherrington	John Galsworthy	
1933	Sir Norman Angell		P. A. M. Dirac Erwin Schrödinger	Thomas H. Morgan	I. A. Bunin	
1934	Arthur Henderson	Harold C. Urey		G. H. Whipple G. R. Minot W. P. Murphy	Luigi Pirandello	
1935	Carl von Ossietzky	Frédéric Joliot-Curie Irène Joliot-Curie	Sir James Chadwick	Hans Spemann		

NOBEL PRIZES (Continued)						
Year	Peace	Chemistry	Physics	Physiology and Medicine	Literature	Economics
1936	Carlos Saavedra Lamas	P. J. W. Debye	C. D. Anderson V. F. Hess	Sir Henry H. Dale Otto Loewi	Eugene O'Neill	
1937	E. A. R. Cecil, Viscount	Sir Walter N. Haworth Paul Karrer	C. J. Davisson Sir George P. Thomson	Albert von Szent-Gyorgyi	Roger Martin du Gard	
1938	Nansen International Office for Refugees		Enrico Fermi	Corneille Heymans	Pearl S. Buck	
1939		Adolf Butenandt Leopold Ruzicka	E. O. Lawrence	Gerhard Domagk	F. E. Sillanpää	
1940						
1941						
1942						
1943		Georg von Hevesy	Otto Stern	E. A. Doisy Henrik Dam		
1944	International Red Cross	Otto Hahn	I. I. Rabi	Joseph Erlanger H. S. Gasser	J. V. Jensen	
1945	Cordell Hull	A. I. Virtanen	Wolfgang Pauli	Sir Alexander Fleming E. B. Chain Sir Howard W. Florey	Gabriela Mistral	
1946	J. R. Mott Emily G. Balch	J. B. Sumner J. H. Northrop W. M. Stanley	P. W. Bridgman	H. J. Muller	Hermann Hesse	
1947	American Friends Service Committee and Friends Service Council	Sir Robert Robinson	Sir Edward V. Appleton	C. F. Cori Gerty T. Cori B. A. Houssay	André Gide	
1948		Arne Tiselius	P. M. S. Blackett	Paul H. Mueller	T. S. Eliot	
1949	John Boyd Orr, Baron	W. F. Giauque	Hideki Yukawa	W. R. Hess Egas Moniz	William Faulkner	
1950	Ralph J. Bunche	Otto Diels Kurt Alder	C. F. Powell	Philip S. Hench Edward C. Kendall Tadeus Reichstein	Bertrand Russell, Earl Russell	
1951	Léon Jouhaux	Edwin M. McMillan Glenn T. Seaborg	Sir John D. Cockcroft Ernest T. S. Walton	Max Theiler	Pär F. Lagerkvist	
1952	Albert Schweitzer	A. J. P. Martin R. L. M. Synge	Felix Bloch E. M. Purcell	S. A. Waksman	François Mauriac	
1953	George C. Marshall	Hermann Staudinger	Frits Zernike	F. A. Lipmann Sir Hans A. Krebs	Sir Winston L. S. Churchill	
1954	Office of the United Nations High Commissioner for Refugees	Linus C. Pauling	Max Born Walther Bothe	J. F. Enders F. C. Robbins T. H. Weller	Ernest Hemingway	
1955		Vincent du Vigneaud	Willis E. Lamb, Jr. Polykarp Kusch	A. H. T. Theorell	Halldór K. Laxness	
1956		Sir Cyril N. Hinshelwood Nikolai N. Semenov	W. B. Shockley W. H. Brattain John Bardeen	D. W. Richards, Jr. A. F. Cournand Werner Forssmann	Juan Ramón Jiménez	
1957	Lester B. Pearson	Sir Alexander R. Todd	Tsung-Dao Lee Chen Ning Yang	Daniele Bovet	Albert Camus	
1958	Georges Henri Pire	Frederick Sanger	P. A. Cherenkov Igor Y. Tamm Ilya M. Frank	Joshua Lederberg G. W. Beadle E. L. Tatum	Boris L. Pasternak	
1959	Philip J. Noel-Baker	Jaroslav Heyrovsky	Emilio Segrè Owen Chamberlain	Severo Ochoa Arthur Kornberg	Salvatore Quasimodo	
1960	Albert J. Luthuli	W. F. Libby	D. A. Glaser	Sir Macfarlane Burnet P. B. Medawar	Alexis St.-L. Léger	
1961	Dag Hammarskjöld	Melvin Calvin	Robert Hofstadter R. L. Moessbauer	Georg von Bekesy	Ivo Andrić	
1962	Linus C. Pauling	M. F. Perutz J. C. Kendrew	L. D. Landau	J. D. Watson F. H. C. Crick M. H. F. Wilkins	John Steinbeck	
1963	International Committee of the Red Cross League of Red Cross Societies	Giulio Natta Karl Ziegler	Eugene Paul Wigner Maria Goeppert Mayer J. Hans D. Jensen	Sir John Carew Eccles Alan Lloyd Hodgkin Andrew Fielding Huxley	George Seferis	
1964	Martin Luther King, Jr.	Dorothy Mary Crowfoot Hodgkin	Charles Hard Townes Nikolai Gennadiyevich Basov Alexander Mikhailovich Prokhorov	Konrad E. Bloch Feodor Lynen	Jean Paul Sartre	

NOBEL PRIZES (Continued)

Year	Peace	Chemistry	Physics	Physiology and Medicine	Literature	Economics
1965	United Nations International Children's Emergency Fund	Robert Burns Woodward	Richard Phillips Feynman Shinichiro Tomonaga Julian Seymour Schwinger	François Jacob André Lwoff Jacques Monod	M. A. Sholokhov	
1966		Robert S. Mulliken	Alfred Kastler	Francis Peyton Rous Charles Brenton Huggins	S. Y. Agnon Nelly Sachs	
1967		Manfred Eigen Ronald George Wreyford Norrish George Porter	Hans Albrecht Bethe	Ragnar Granit Haldan Keffer Hartline George Wald	Miguel Angel Asturias	
1968	René Cassin	Lars Onsager	Luis W. Alvarez	Robert W. Holley H. Gobind Khorana Marshall W. Nirenberg	Yasunari Kawabata	
1969	International Labor Organization	Derek H. R. Barton Odd Hassel	Murray Gell-Mann	Max Delbrück Alfred D. Hershey Salvador E. Luria	Samuel Beckett	Ragnar Frisch Jan Tinbergen
1970	Norman E. Borlaug	Luis Federico Leloir	Louis Eugène Néel Hans Olof Alfven	Julius Axelrod Bernard Katz Ulf von Euler	Alexandr I. Solzhenitsyn	Paul A. Samuelson
1971	Willy Brandt	Gerhard Herzberg	Dennis Gabor	Earl W. Sutherland	Pablo Neruda	Simon Kuznets
1972		Stanford Moore William Howard Stein Christian B. Anfinsen	John Bardeen Leon N. Cooper John Robert Schreiffer	Gerald M. Edelman Rodney R. Porter	Heinrich Böll	Sir John R. Hicks Kenneth J. Arrow
1973	Henry A. Kissinger Le Duc Tho	Ernst Otto Fischer Geoffrey Wilkinson	Leo Esaki Ivar Giaever Brian D. Josephson	Konrad Lorenz Nikolaas Tinbergen Karl von Frisch	Patrick White	Wassily Leontief
1974	Sean MacBride Eisaku Sato	Paul J. Flory	Martin Ryle Antony Hewish	Albert Claude George Emil Palade Christian de Duve	Eyvind Johnson Harry Martinson	Gunnar Myrdal Friedrich A. von Hayek

Nobeoka (nōbāō'kä), city (1970 pop. 128,292), Miyazaki prefecture, E Kyushu, Japan, on the mouth of the Gokase River. It is a commercial and fishing port and a production center for chemicals, foodstuffs, and textiles.

Nobili, Roberto de, 1577–1656, Italian Jesuit missionary. He was ordained in Rome in 1603 after seven years' training in Naples and sailed the following year for India with a group of Portuguese missionaries. For his unconventional adoption of Hindu customs, he was censured by the authorities in 1610 and compelled to petition an inquisition headed by the archbishop of Goa for approval of his methods. Until his work was again permitted (1623), de Nobili wrote many religious books, including Sanskrit translations of Christian writings.

noble gas: see INERT GAS.

Nobunaga (Nobunaga Oda) (nōbo͞onä'gä ōdä'), 1534–82, Japanese military commander. The son of a DAIMYŌ, Nobunaga greatly expanded his father's holdings, becoming master of three provinces near present-day Nagoya. The emperor secretly appealed to him for help, and Nobunaga, acting in the emperor's name, became (1568) dictator of central Japan. Though he restored the ousted shōgun (Nobunaga's ancestry made him ineligible for the title), the real power was his and, aided by his general HIDEYOSHI Toyotomi and his ally IEYASU, he unified all Japan except the extreme north and west. He broke the temporal power of the great Buddhist sects by destroying their armies. He was one of the first Japanese commanders to supply his foot-soldiers with muskets. The early Jesuits in Japan gained Nobunaga's respect and, thereby, his permission to preach. Under his rule, free trade was encouraged and an era of castle building began. He was murdered by one of his discontented generals before the unification of all Japan, a task that was completed by Hideyoshi and Ieyasu.

nocardiosis: see FUNGUS INFECTION.

nocturne (nŏk'tûrn) [Fr.,=night piece], in music, romantic instrumental piece, free in form and usually reflective or languid in character. John Field wrote the first nocturnes, influencing Chopin in the writing of his 19 nocturnes for piano.

Nod, Land of, in the Bible, the refuge of Cain somewhere E of Eden. Gen. 4.16.

Noda (nō'dä), city (1970 pop. 66,641), Chiba prefecture, E central Honshu, Japan, on the Edo River. It is a commercial and industrial center.

Nodab (nō'dăb), name of a tribe at war with the Jews. 1 Chron. 5.19.

noddy, tropical tern including five species in the genus *Anous.* The name noddy is said to derive from their easy familiarity with man. Noddies are web-footed seabirds with long wings (though shorter than those of most terns) and pointed, tapering bills. They are highly gregarious, especially during the breeding season. Of the five species, two are nearly all black in plumage (*A. stolidus* and *A. galapagoensis*) and one is white. The dark-plumaged noddy tern (*A. stolidus*) is the most common of all noddies. It is found throughout the S Atlantic. It does not dive for food as do most terns but rather feeds on surface-dwelling animals. It typically nests on bushes or low trees but will also build its twig nest on seaweed or even bare ground. It lays a single egg per clutch. The white fairy tern (*A. albus*) is distributed more widely throughout tropical seas. It lays its single egg on a tree branch or rock ledge, to which the newly hatched young clings by its remarkably powerful claws. *A. albivittus* and *A. leucocapillus* are the two intermediately colored species. Noddies are classified in the phylum CHORDATA, subphylum Vertebrata, class Aves, order Charadriiformes, family Laridae.

node, in astronomy, point at which the ORBIT of a body crosses a reference plane. One reference plane that is often used is the plane of the earth's orbit around the sun (ECLIPTIC). Since the moon's orbit has an INCLINATION of 5°9′ to the plane of the ecliptic, there are two nodes in the moon's orbit around the earth; the point where the moon in its orbit crosses from south of the ecliptic plane to north of it is called the ascending node, and the point where it crosses from north to south is called the descending node. A line connecting two nodes is called a line of nodes. The lunar nodes are the points where the moon's line of nodes, when extended, strike the CELESTIAL SPHERE. The lunar nodes regress (move westward along the ecliptic) due to PERTURBATIONS from the other bodies in the solar system, e.g., the sun and planets. Another reference plane that can be used to define nodes is the plane of the earth's equator, which is also the plane of the CELESTIAL EQUATOR. There are two nodes in the sun's apparent orbit around the earth. The ascending node, when the sun appears to cross the celestial equator from south to north, is the vernal EQUINOX; the descending node is the autumnal equinox. Perturbations like those that cause regression of the lunar nodes cause the PRECESSION OF THE EQUINOXES.

nodes of Ranvier: see NERVOUS SYSTEM.

Nodier, Charles (shärl nôdyā'), 1780–1844, French poet. From 1824 he was librarian of the Bibliothèque de l'Arsenal in Paris. His salon was the nucleus of the beginning romantic movement and was frequented by such men as Hugo, Sainte-Beuve, and Dumas père. His best works are the imaginative tales *Trilby; ou, Le Lutin d'Argail* (1822) and *La Fée aux miettes* (1832). See bibliography by S. F. Bell (1971); study by Hilda Nelson (1972).

nodule: see CONCRETION.

Noe (nō'ē), variant of NOAH.

Noé, Amédée de: see CHAM.

no-fault insurance, type of indemnity plan, usually applied to automobile coverage, in which those injured in an accident receive direct payment from the company with which they themselves are insured. Originated (1947) in Saskatchewan, Canada, no-fault insurance eliminates the need for accident victims to establish another's liability, or fault, through a civil lawsuit. Lawyers' groups oppose no-fault, saying that it limits the citizen's right to sue. Supporters say that it leads to quicker settlement of accident claims and lower premium rates than the traditional tort liability system. The first comprehensive no-fault plan in the United States was adopted (1971) in Massachusetts. Since then the system has spread to other states. Virtually all no-fault plans contain provisions for liability lawsuits in cases of serious injury.

Nogah (nō'gə), son of David. 1 Chron. 3.7; 14.6.

Nogales (nōgä'lās), city (1970 pop. 56,865), Sonora state, NW Mexico, on the Arizona border, contiguous to Nogales, Ariz. The northern terminus of Mexico's west coast railroad and national highway, Nogales derives its importance chiefly from international trade. A brief but bloody border dispute led to the city's occupation by Americans from Nogales, Ariz., in 1918.

Nogaret, Guillaume de (gēyōm' də nôgărā'), 1265?–1313, French statesman. A jurist, he was a member of the royal council of King Philip IV. During Philip's conflict with Pope BONIFACE VIII concerning papal authority, Nogaret was prominent in denouncing the pope. In 1303 he led the French troops sent to kidnap Boniface at Anagni. Although Nogaret made the pope his prisoner, he was forced to release him when the populace rose in within Boniface's defense. Boniface died (Oct., 1303) within a month, and his successor issued a papal bull (1304) against Nogaret. He finally obtained absolution in 1311. Philip made him keeper of the seal and he was instrumental in the attack on the KNIGHTS TEMPLARS.

Nogi, Maresuke (mără'so͞okä nō'gē), 1849–1912, Japanese general. Made a lieutenant general in 1895, he became governor-general of Taiwan. He was the hero of the capture of Port Arthur in the RUSSO-JAPA-

NESE WAR and was honored as a model of loyalty when he committed HARA-KIRI to follow the Meiji emperor into death.

Noginsk (nəgĕnsk'), city (1970 pop. 104,000), central European USSR, on the Klyazma River. It is a major textile center, processing cotton, silk, and wool. Founded in the 16th cent. as Rogozhi, the city was later called Bogorodsk; it was renamed Noginsk in 1930.

Noguchi, Hideyo (hēdä'yō nōgōō'chē), 1876–1928, Japanese bacteriologist, grad. Tokyo Medical College, 1897. He came to the United States c.1900 to work with Simon Flexner at the Univ. of Pennsylvania and in 1904 joined the Rockefeller Institute (now Rockefeller Univ.) staff. He made important studies of snake venoms, of smallpox and yellow-fever vaccines, and of the laboratory diagnosis of trachoma. He isolated (1913) the *Treponema pallidum* from a syphilis patient, proving that this spirochete was the cause of syphilis; he also developed a skin test for syphilis. He died of yellow fever in Accra, Ghana, where he had been studying that disease. His writings include *Action of Snake Venom upon Cold-Blooded Animals* (1904) and *Laboratory Diagnosis of Syphilis* (rev. ed. 1923). See biography by Gustav Eckstein (1931).

Noguchi, Isamu (ēsä'mōō nōgōō'chē), 1904–, American sculptor, b. Los Angeles. A student of Gutzon Borglum, Noguchi won Guggenheim fellowships (1927 and 1928) permitting him to study in Paris under Brancusi. Although he has created much independent sculpture and numerous striking stage settings for the Martha Graham dance company, he is best known for his abstract sculptures designed as adjuncts to architecture. An example of this highly integrated environmental work is his massive red cube designed for the Marine Midland Bank building, New York City. Noguchi has created many playgrounds and stone sculpture gardens; he designed a notable garden in Mexico City and for UNESCO in Paris (1958). His entrance for the new Museum of Modern Art, Tokyo, was completed in 1969. He is the author of *A Sculptor's World* (1968). See studies by Shuzo Takiguchi and others (1953) and John Gordon (1968).

Noguchi, Yone (Yonejiro Noguchi) (yō'nā nō'gōōchē; yō"näjĭrō'), 1875–1947, Japanese poet and critic of Japanese art and poetry. Noguchi traveled and lectured in the United States and England. He later taught English literature at Keio Univ. in Tokyo. Writing in English as well as in Japanese, he helped to stimulate Western interest in many Japanese artists. His *Selected Poems,* written in English, appeared in 1921. Noguchi's other works include *Japan and America* (1921) and *Harunobu* (1940).

Nohah (nō'hä), son of Benjamin. 1 Chron. 8.2.

noh drama: see ORIENTAL DRAMA.

noise, electrical, unwanted electrical currents or voltages that interfere with the operation of electronic systems. Electrical noise limits the sensitivity of radio receiving systems and, when present at high enough levels, may cause false outputs from digital circuits. In radio receivers it is important that the noise produced by amplifiers, especially early-stage amplifiers, be kept as low as possible. Random noise originates when a current flows through a conductor that has resistance and is above absolute zero in temperature. It also arises in electron tubes and semiconductor devices, as well as from atmospheric disturbances and radiation from space (see STATIC). Nonrandom noise originates from the operation of other systems, e.g., automotive ignition systems, and from interfering signals.

noise pollution, man-created noise harmful to health or welfare. Transportation vehicles are the worst offenders, with aircraft, railroad stock, trucks, buses, automobiles, and motorcycles all producing excessive noise. Construction equipment, e.g., jackhammers, riveters, and bulldozers, is a second prolific noise producer. Noise intensity is measured in DECIBEL units. The decibel scale is logarithmic; each 10-decibel increase represents a 10-fold increase in noise intensity. Human perception of loudness also conforms to a logarithmic scale; a 10-decibel increase is perceived as roughly a doubling of loudness. Thus 30 decibels is 10 times more intense than 20 decibels and sounds twice as loud; 40 decibels is 100 times more intense than 20 and sounds 4 times as loud; 80 decibels is a million times more intense than 20 and sounds 64 times as loud. Distance diminishes the effective decibel level reaching the ear. Thus moderate auto traffic at a distance of 100 ft (30 m) rates about 50 decibels. To the driver with his car window open or a pedestrian on the sidewalk, the same traffic rates about 70 decibels; that is, it sounds 4 times louder. At a distance of 2,000 ft (600 m), the noise of a jet takeoff reaches about 110 decibels—approximately the same as a riveting machine or auto horn only 3 ft (1 m) away. Subjected to 45 decibels of noise, the average person cannot sleep. At 120 decibels the ear registers pain; hearing damage begins at a much lower level, about 85 decibels. Federal estimates indicate that some 80 million (or more than one in three) Americans are continually harassed by noise pollution, 40 million to a degree endangering health, with 16 million already suffering noise-induced hearing loss. There is evidence that among young Americans hearing sensitivity is decreasing year by year because of exposure to excessive noise. Apart from hearing loss, such noise can cause lack of sleep, irritability, heartburn, indigestion, ulcers, high blood pressure, and possibly heart disease. One burst of noise, as from a passing truck, is known to alter endocrine, neurological, and cardiovascular functions in many individuals; prolonged or frequent exposure to such noise tends to make the physiological disturbances chronic. In addition, noise-induced stress creates severe tension in daily living and contributes to mental illness. Noise is now recognized as a controllable pollutant that can yield to abatement technology. In the United States the Noise Control Act of 1972 empowers the Environmental Protection Agency to determine the limits of noise required to protect public health and welfare; to set noise emission standards for major sources of noise in the environment, including transportation equipment and facilities, construction equipment, and electrical machinery; and to recommend regulations for controlling aircraft noise and sonic booms, statistically a nuisance to some 40 million persons. The law further requires that consumer goods be labeled with their noise-generating characteristics so that buyers may select quieter equipment.

Nokia (nō'kēä), town (1970 pop. 19,459), SW Finland, on Lake Näsijärvi. It is an industrial community where wood and rubber products are manufactured.

Nol, Lon: see LON NOL.

Nola (nô'lä), town (1971 pop. 26,666), in Campania, S Italy. It is an agricultural center with food-processing industries. An Etruscan stronghold as early as 500 B.C., Nola flourished after passing (c.316 B.C.) to Rome and was an important center of early Christianity. Nearby are Roman ruins (an amphitheater and tombs) and an old cemetery where Christian martyrs are buried. Augustus died at Nola in A.D. 14.

Noland, Kenneth, 1924–, American painter, b. Asheville, N.C. Noland first experimented with bands of pure color in bull's-eye and chevron motifs and horizontal parallel stripes. He emphasized the flatness of his canvas by staining paint into raw canvas and using uniform color values. In his work color itself is the subject. Later paintings treat plaid designs with muted color bands of varied width.

Nolde, Emil (ā'mēl nôl'də), 1867–1956, German expressionist painter and graphic artist. His original name was Emil Hansen. After teaching in Switzerland (1892–98), Nolde traveled through Europe and in 1906 joined the BRÜCKE group of German expressionists. Nolde's explosively colored paintings were continually refused by the Berlin secession group. In protest Nolde wrote an open letter to Max LEIBERMANN, president of the secession, and thereby started a bitter controversy. In 1911 he helped found the New Secession. Nolde's most powerful work was his exploration of the supernatural (demonic heads, mystic appearances, and religious images). His woodcut *The Prophet* (1912; National Gall. of Art, Washington, D.C.) is a terrible, savage image of pain. He painted bold, arresting landscapes and applied his expressionist technique to produce notable oils and watercolors of flowers (e.g., *Flowers,* Mus. of Modern Art, New York City). His masklike portraits conjure up a world of primitive emotions. Violent, clashing colors are combined with exaggerated distortions of shape. Among of his well-known paintings are *Christ among the Children* (Mus. of Modern Art, New York City) and *Ripe Sunflowers* (Inst. of Arts, Detroit). Nolde's work was condemned and largely confiscated by the Nazi regime. See his *Unpainted Pictures,* ed. by Werner Haftmann (tr. 1965, rev. ed. 1972) and *Landscapes,* ed. by Martin Urban (tr. 1970); studies by Werner Haftmann (tr. 1959) and Peter Selz (1963).

Nolichucky (nŏl"ĭchŭk'ē, nŏl'ĭchŭk"ē), river, c.150 mi (240 km) long, rising in the Blue Ridge, W N.C., and flowing NW and W to the French Broad River W of Greeneville, Tenn. A power dam impounds Davy Crockett Lake SW of Greeneville. The first settlement on the river was made in 1772. John Sevier, first governor of Tennessee, was nicknamed Nolichucky Jack; David Crockett was born at Limestone on the Nolichucky.

Nollekens, Joseph (nŏl'ĭkənz), 1737–1823, English sculptor, b. London. He studied in Rome and in 1770 returned to London, where he became the most fashionable portrait sculptor of his day. Among his famous busts are those of George III, the younger Pitt, Charles James Fox (1792, private coll.), Laurence Sterne (1766, National Portrait Gall., London), and Benjamin West. His numerous statues and groups in marble include *Cupid and Psyche* and *Bacchus.*

Nollet, Jean Antoine (zhäN äNtwän' nôlā'), 1700–1770, French clergyman, experimental physicist, and leading member of the Paris Academy of Science. He constructed one of the first electrometers and developed a theory of electrical attraction and repulsion that supposed the existence of a continuous flow of electrical matter between charged bodies. Nollet was the first professor of experimental physics at the Univ. of Paris.

nomad (nō'măd"), one of a group of people without fixed habitation. Wandering herdsmen living in tents still occupy sections of Asia, and the hunting groups of the Far North, including the Eskimo, still predominate in much of the arctic and subarctic regions; parts of Africa are also peopled with nomadic groups. Although nomadism has been a way of life for many groups, it is on the decline. Besides the herdsmen and the hunters and fishers, there are nomadic groups that move about in search of wild plants as food in season (such as the kamas bulb formerly sought by the Indians of the Pacific Northwest and the wild rice gathered in the Great Lakes region). Peoples who move seasonally but have permanent homes for part of the year are said to be seminomadic, and there have been seminomadic peoples of various types throughout history. The nomadic groups are generally organized in tribal units, and usually the adult males are closely knit into war bands, in order to establish territorial rights over the area within which a group migrates. The incursions of nomads into settled civilizations marked the early history of ancient Egypt and Babylonia and reached their height with the great Mongol invasions of W Asia and Europe in the 13th, 14th, and early 15th cent., notably under Jenghiz Khan and Tamerlane. Formerly efforts were made to generalize about nomads and find a common denominator among such diverse cultures as those of the North American Indian hunter, the Bedouin of Arabia, and the roving gypsies, but these have largely been abandoned in favor of studying each culture as a unit. Even the idea that nomadism represents a transition from the Neolithic hunter to the sedentary farmer is not accepted as valid. There are instances of peoples who have abandoned farming and have become nomads, e.g., some of the Indians of the Great Plains who forsook their farms to hunt bison, after the horse had been introduced.

Nome (nōm), city (1970 pop. 2,488), W Alaska, on the southern side of Seward Peninsula, on Norton Sound; founded c.1898, when gold was discovered on the beach there. It is the commercial and supply center for NW Alaska, with an airport and steamer connections to Seattle. Major economic mainstays are tourism, fishing, and fur trapping. The city is a center of Eskimo handicrafts. Oil deposits have been found in the area. Nome was a great gold rush town from 1899 to 1903; it attracted some 20,000 prospectors, but many died or left because of the hardships. Dredging, which replaced older methods of mining, ceased in 1962. A U.S. air force base is there. The city is the scene of an annual fair and the All-Alaska Championship Dog Race. Cape Nome lies to the southeast.

nomenclature, biological: see CLASSIFICATION.

nominalism, in philosophy, a theory of the relation between universals and particulars. Nominalism gained its name in the Middle Ages, when it was contrasted with REALISM. The problem arises because in order to perceive a particular object as a particular thing, say a table, we must have a prior notion of table. Does this prior notion then have an independent existence? Nominalism says that it does not, that is just a name for a group. Nominalism is appropriate to materialist and empirical philosophy and hence has been popular in modern thought. See R. A. Eberle, *Nominalistic Systems* (1970).

nominative (nŏm'ĭnətĭv), [Lat.,=naming], in Latin grammar, the CASE usually employed for the NOUN that is the subject of the sentence. The term is used in the grammar of languages with Latinlike features, but the case may in fact have different functions.

Nomura, Kichisaburo (kēchēsäbo͞orō' nō'mo͞o"rä), 1877–1964, Japanese admiral and diplomat. A graduate of the Japanese naval academy, he commanded troops at Shanghai in 1932, was made a full admiral in 1933, and resigned from active service in 1937. He was (1939) foreign minister before being appointed (1940) ambassador to the United States. He and a special envoy, Kurusu, were carrying on negotiations in Washington when Japan attacked Pearl Harbor. After World War II, Nomura denied that he knew beforehand of the attack.

Non, in the Bible, variant of NUN.

nonconformists, in religion, those who refuse to conform to the requirements (in doctrine or discipline) of an established church. The term is applied especially to Protestant dissenters from the Church of England. Nonconformity in England appeared not long after the Reformation in the secession from the Established Church of such small groups as the Brownists (see BROWNE, ROBERT) and, a little later, the PILGRIMS. Most of those, however, who objected to the Elizabethan church settlement did not at first intend to secede; their hope was rather to reshape the Established Church (see PURITANISM). The conflicts thus engendered within the Church of England were a major factor leading to the English civil war. After the victory of the Puritan party in that war, a Presbyterian church establishment was adopted (1646), but in that period also the separatists, or INDEPENDENTS, gained a stronger foothold. The restoration (1660) of the monarchy also brought the restoration of episcopacy and harsh legislation against the Puritans (see CLARENDON CODE). The Act of Uniformity (1662) made a distinct split unavoidable, since it required episcopal ordination for all ministers. As a result, nearly 2,000 clergymen left the Established Church. Significant nonconformity dates from that time. The term *dissenter* similarly came into use, particularly after the Toleration Act (1689), in which reference was made to the "Protestant Dissenters." Presbyterians, Congregationalists, Baptists, Quakers, Unitarians, and Methodists are among the nonconforming denominations in England. In Scotland, where the established church is Presbyterian, the Anglicans, or Episcopalians, are among the nonconformists. In recent usage, churches independent of the established or state church in both England and Scotland are often called Free Churches. See Champlin Burrage, *The Early English Dissenters* (1912); Horton Davies, *The English Free Churches* (1952).

Nones: see CALENDAR.

Nonesuch Press, private press founded in London in 1922 by Francis Meynell and David Garnett. Unlike most private presses, Nonesuch designs the books it publishes on its own small press but has production done by selected commercial firms. Nonesuch Press has followed a policy of publishing only books that are not in print or that exist in inadequate editions or translations. Among its noted publications are the collected works of William Congreve (1923), the works of William Wycherly (1924), and a translation of *Don Quixote* (1930). It has also published books by Milton, Dryden, Dickens, Tennyson, and Conrad.

non-Euclidean geometry, branch of GEOMETRY in which the postulate of Euclidean geometry allowing one and only one line parallel to a given line through a given external point is replaced either by one allowing two parallels through the point or by one allowing no parallels. The first case leads to the hyperbolic geometry developed by the Russian N. I. Lobachevsky in 1826 and independently by the Hungarian Janos Bolyai in 1832; the second to the elliptic geometry developed by the German Bernhard Riemann in 1854. The results of these two types of non-Euclidean geometry are identical with those of Euclidean geometry in every respect except those propositions involving parallel lines, either explicitly or implicitly (as in the theorem for the sum of the angles of a triangle). In hyperbolic geometry the two rays extending out in either direction from a point *P* and not meeting a line *L* are considered distinct parallels to *L*; among the results of this geometry is the theorem that the sum of the angles of a triangle is less than 180°. One surprising result is that there is a finite upper limit on the area of a triangle, this maximum corresponding to a triangle all of whose sides are parallel and all of whose angles are zero. In elliptic geometry there are no parallels to a given line *L* through an external point *P*, and the sum of the angles of a triangle is greater than 180°. Riemann's geometry is called elliptic because a line in the plane described by this geometry has no point at infinity, where parallels may intersect it, just as an ellipse has no asymptotes. An idea of the geometry on such a plane is obtained by considering the geometry on the surface of a sphere, which is a special case of an ellipsoid. The shortest distance between two points on a sphere is not a straight line but an arc of a great circle (a circle dividing the sphere exactly in half). Since any two great circles always meet (in not one but two points, on opposite sides of the sphere), no parallel lines are possible. The angles of a triangle formed by arcs of three great circles always add up to more than 180°, as can be seen by considering such a triangle on the earth's surface bounded by a portion of the equator and two meridians of longitude connecting its end points to one of the poles (the two angles at the equator are each 90°, so the amount by which the sum of the angles exceeds 180° is determined by the angle at which the meridians meet at the pole). The type of non-Euclidean geometry proposed by Lobachevsky is called hyperbolic because a line in the hyperbolic plane has two points at infinity, just as a hyperbola has two asymptotes. The analogy used in considering this geometry involves the lines and figures drawn on a saddle-shaped surface. What distinguishes the plane of Euclidean geometry from the surface of a sphere or a saddle surface is the curvature of each (see DIFFERENTIAL GEOMETRY); the plane has zero curvature, the surface of a sphere and other surfaces described by Riemann's geometry have positive curvature, and the saddle surface and other surfaces described by Lobachevsky's geometry have negative curvature. Similarly, in three dimensions the spaces corresponding to these three types of geometry also have zero, positive, or negative curvature, respectively. As to which of these systems is a valid description of our own three-dimensional space (or four-dimensional space-time), the choice can be made only on the basis of measurements made over very large, cosmological distances of a billion light-years or more, for the differences between a Euclidean universe of zero curvature and a non-Euclidean universe of very small positive or negative curvature are too small to be detected from ordinary measurements. One interesting feature of a universe described by Riemann's geometry is that it is finite but unbounded; straight lines ultimately form closed curves, so that a ray of light could eventually return to its source. See COSMOLOGY; RELATIVITY. See D. M. Y. Sommerville, *Bibliography of Non-Euclidean Geometry* (1911, repr. 1960); H. S. M. Coxeter, *Non-Euclidean Geometry* (5th ed. 1965).

Nonimportation Act: see EMBARGO ACT OF 1807.

nonintercourse, in international law, refusal of a state to engage in diplomatic or commercial relations with another state. It is a hostile act of retaliation for some wrong and is intended to effect redress. Since nations normally have diplomatic and commercial intercourse, nonintercourse may in some circumstances be a threat of war.

Nonintercourse Act: see EMBARGO ACT OF 1807.

Nonius, Petrus: see NUNES, PEDRO.

nonjurors [from Latin,=not swearing], those English and Scottish clergymen who refused to break their oath of allegiance to James II and take the oath to William III after the GLORIOUS REVOLUTION of 1688. They upheld the principles of hereditary succession and the divine right of kings, and their refusal to recognize William as king led to their removal from office. In England, the original nonjurors included William SANCROFT, archbishop of Canterbury, some bishops, and about 400 other members of the clergy; and their ranks were later augmented by those who refused (1714) to take the oath of allegiance to George I. In Scotland, most of the Episcopal clergy became nonjurors when their church was disestablished (1690) in favor of Presbyterianism. Many nonjurors were active in the rising of the JACOBITES in 1715, despite their doctrine of nonresistance to established authority. Later their numbers dwindled, however, and their attention turned to theology. Their high standard of thought was notable and influential in its day. The BANGORIAN CONTROVERSY, in which nonjuror William LAW was prominent, precipitated the prorogation of the convocation of the Church of England in 1717. The exiled Stuart pretenders continued to appoint nonjuring bishops, including Jeremy COLLIER, preserving the nonjuring episcopal succession until 1805.

nonmetal, chemical ELEMENT possessing certain properties by which it is distinguished from a METAL. In general, this distinction is drawn on the basis that a nonmetal tends to accept electrons and form negative IONS and that its oxide is acidic. Nonmetals are poor conductors of heat and electricity (see CONDUCTION) and do not have the luster of metals. Arsenic, antimony, selenium, and tellurium exhibit both nonmetallic and metallic properties and are called metalloids. Unlike the metals, which are all solids (with the exception of mercury) under ordinary conditions of temperature and pressure, the nonmetals appear in all three states. Argon, chlorine, fluorine, helium, hydrogen, krypton, neon, nitrogen, oxygen, and xenon are normally gases. Bromine is a liquid. Boron, carbon, iodine, phosphorus, silicon, and sulfur are solids. Certain of them, e.g., boron, carbon, iodine, silicon, and sulfur, form crystals, as do the metals. In hardness they vary considerably. Carbon in its allotropic form, the diamond, is the hardest element known. With the exception of carbon, sulfur, nitrogen, oxygen, and the inert gases—argon, helium, krypton, neon, and xenon—the nonmetals do not occur uncombined in nature, but exist in numerous relatively abundant compounds, among which are the oxides, halides (binary halogen compounds), sulfides, carbonates, nitrates, phosphates, silicates, and sulfates. With a few exceptions, the nonmetallic elements are important chiefly for their compounds. For the properties and uses of specific nonmetals, see the separate articles on these elements.

Nonni, river, China: see NEN CHIANG.

Nonnus (nŏn'əs), fl. 5th cent.?, Greek poet, b. Panopolis, Egypt. His extant epic, *Dionysiaca* (in 48 books), a collection of legends about Dionysus, has innovations in meter that predict the later accentual versification. He is probably also the author of a hexameter version of the Gospel of St. John.

Nono, Luigi (lo͞oē'jē nô'nō), 1924–, Italian composer, b. Venice. Nono studied with Hermann Scherchen and Bruno Maderna. He adopted the 12-tone method of composition (see SERIAL MUSIC), and his first major work, the *Canonic Variations* (1950), is based on a tone row from Arnold Schoenberg's *Ode to Napoleon*. (Nono's wife is Schoenberg's daughter.) Several of Nono's works are overtly political. Examples are the antifascist opera *Intolerance* (1960); *A Specter Rises over Europe* (1971), a setting of *The Communist Manifesto*; and *Voices Destroying Walls*, for chorus and orchestra, which is performed with a machine gun pointed at the audience. In recent years Nono has written electronic music. *The Forest is Young and Vital* (1966) is for singers and tape.

Nonpartisan League, in U.S. history, political pressure group of farmers and workers organized in 1915 and led by a former socialist, Arthur C. Townley, who believed that the solution to the farmers' troubles lay in united political action. Feeding on agrarian discontent with falling prices and political boss rule, the Nonpartisan League spread through the Western wheat belt from Wisconsin to Washington and to the Southwest; its greatest strength was in Minnesota and the Dakotas. The group demanded state-owned grain elevators, flour mills, and packing houses as well as low-cost public housing for farmers and workers. Although it was not a political party in the usual sense, it exercised its power by endorsing and even nominating candidates of the major parties. It never attracted support from industrial workers, and other means for expressing the farmers' desires opened. After World War I it declined sharply, although it retained prominence in some areas, particularly North Dakota. See R. L. Morlan, *Political Prairie Fire* (1955).

nonsporting dog, classification used by breeders and kennel clubs to designate dogs that may formerly have been bred to hunt or work but that are now raised chiefly as house pets and companions. The following nine breeds are registered as nonsporting dogs by the American Kennel Club: BOSTON TERRIER, BULLDOG, CHOW CHOW, DALMATIAN, FRENCH BULLDOG, KEESHOND, LHASA APSO, POODLE, and SCHIPPERKE.

nonsusceptibility: see IMMUNITY.

Noot, Jan van der (yän vän dĕr nōt), b. 1539 or 1540, d. 1595?, Flemish poet. He wrote sonnets, odes, and other pieces in imitation of Petrarch and especially of Ronsard.

Nootka Indians (no͝ot'kə), North American Indians whose language belongs to the Wakashan branch of the Algonquian-Wakashan linguistic stock (see AMERICAN INDIAN LANGUAGES). The Nootka proper are a small group on the west coast of Vancouver Island, British Columbia, but the name is often given to the Aht Confederacy, which includes more than 20 tribes. Nootka culture was fundamentally that of the Northwest Coast area; they fished for salmon, lived in long wooden houses, and created elaborate totem poles. The so-called Nootka hats of woven fiber were common among other tribes of this area. With the exception of the Makah and a few of their neighbors, they were the only Indians on the Pacific coast who hunted whales.

Nootka Sound, inlet of the Pacific Ocean and natural harbor on the west coast of Vancouver Island, SW British Columbia, Canada, lying between the mainland and Nootka Island (206 sq mi/534 sq km). The mouth of the sound was sighted (1774) by Juan Pérez, the Spanish explorer. The sound itself was discovered by Capt. James Cook (1778), who was the first European to land in that region. John Meares, the British explorer, established a trading post on Nootka Sound in 1788. Its seizure by Spaniards in 1789 became the subject of a controversy between Spain and England over claims in the region. The Nootka Convention (1790) resolved the dispute and opened the N Pacific coast to British settlement.

Noph (nŏf), biblical name of Memphis, Egypt. Isa. 19.13; Jer. 2.16; 44.1; 46.14,19; Ezek. 30.13,16.

Nophah (nō'fə), unidentified place, apparently NE of the Dead Sea. Num. 21.30. The text is uncertain; possibly it is not a place name.

Noranda (nərăn'də), city (1971 pop. 10,741), SW Que., Canada. Together with its twin city, ROUYN, it is the center of a gold-, copper-, and zinc-mining region. Noranda is the site of a large smelter.

Norco, city (1970 pop. 14,511), Riverside co., S Calif.; inc. 1964. Norco is in a farm region of the Santa Ana mountain plains. Poultry and eggs are the city's major products. Its industries are associated with those of adjacent Corona. A U.S. naval hospital is nearby.

Nord (nôr), department (1968 pop. 2,417,899), N France, bordering on the North Sea and Belgium. LILLE is the capital.

Nordau, Max Simon (mäks zē'môn nôr'dou), 1849–1923, Hungarian writer and physician. Nordau wrote in German. Of his several controversial works, the best remembered is the novel *Degeneration* (2 vol., 1892–93; tr. 1895), in which he sought to establish a relationship between the rise of urban civilization and the decline of moral and aesthetic standards. Nordau was a prominent Zionist and in 1903 barely escaped assassination for his Zionist activities. See biography by Anna and Maxa Nordau (tr. 1943); study by Meir Ben-Horin (1956).

Nordaustlandet (nôr"ôst'lä'nə, no͞o"-) or **North East Land,** second largest island of Svalbard, 5,610 sq mi (14,530 sq km), in the Arctic Ocean NE of Spitsbergen. It is covered by an ice cap (c.1,600 ft/490 m high) that slopes eastward into the sea. The island was discovered (1613) by Thomas Marmaduke and was explored (1873) by Nils Nordenskjöld; a British expedition charted it in 1935–36.

Nordenskjöld, Nils Adolf Erik, Baron (nĭls ä'dôlf ā'rĭk no͞or'dənshöld), 1832–1901, Swedish geologist and arctic explorer, first to navigate the Northeast Passage, b. Finland. He served as geologist on several expeditions to Spitsbergen under Otto Torrell, the noted Swedish geologist, on one of which he found plant fossils of the Tertiary period. From 1864 he commanded a series of expeditions in the course of which he mapped Spitsbergen, reached (1868) lat. 81°42'N (the highest then attained), made a journey (1870) on the inland ice of Greenland, and at Spitsbergen (1872–73) gathered extensive zoological and botanical collections. After 1872 he became interested in discovering the Northeast Passage as a possible route of trade. He reached Novaya Zemlya, crossed the Kara Sea, and ascended (1875) the Yenisei River, which he explored again in 1876. After these reconnoitering trips, he set out in the *Vega* in 1878, rounded Cape Chelyuskin, but was stopped by ice at the entrance to Bering Strait. In 1879 he passed East Cape and sailed into the Bering Sea (northward extension of the Pacific). He completed the trip to China and returned to Sweden in 1880 and was created baron. In 1883 he penetrated for about 75 mi (120 km) the great ice barrier E of Greenland and in 1890 paid his sixth visit to Spitsbergen. During the last twenty years of his life Nordenskjöld wrote several valuable books on geography, cartography, and travel. Among his translated works is *The Voyage of the Vega* (1881). His *Facsimile-Atlas* (1889) and *Periplus* (1897) are especially interesting for their collections of early maps, charts, and geographical documents. See *The Arctic Voyages of Adolf Erik Nordenskiöld* (ed. by Alexander Leslie, 1879). His nephew, **Nils Otto Gustaf Nordenskjöld**, 1869–1928, was a geographer and explorer. He headed an expedition to Patagonia (1895–97) and later explored the Klondike and Alaska (1898) and Greenland (1900). From 1901 to 1904 he commanded an expedition to the Antarctic that yielded important geographical results. He became professor of geography at the Univ. of Göteborg in 1905.

Nordfjord (nôr'fyôr", no͞or'fyo͞or"), inlet, c.50 mi (80 km) long, Sogn og Fjordane co., SW Norway. To the south, between Nordfjord and Sognafjord, is Jostedalsbreen glacier. The Nordfjord's several branches, cutting deeply into the mountains and celebrated for their scenery, are favored tourist spots.

Nordhausen (nôrt'hou"zən), city (1970 pop. 44,505), Erfurt district, W East Germany, at the southern foot of the Harz mts. It is an industrial center and rail junction. Manufactures include cotton and linen textiles, clothing, heavy machinery, and construction materials. Nearby are potash mines. Known in the early 10th cent., Nordhausen was chartered in the 12th cent. and was a free imperial city from 1253 to 1803. In 1815 it passed to Prussia. The city was severely damaged in World War II. Noteworthy buildings include the cathedral (12th–13th cent.) and the late Gothic city hall.

Nordhoff, Charles (nôrd'hŏf), 1830–1901, American journalist and author, b. Westphalia. In 1835 he emigrated with his family to Cincinnati. His service (1844–47) in the navy, and later on whaling and fishing ships, provided literary material for his books *Nine Years a Sailor* (1857) and *Stories of the Island World* (1857). He wrote for the New York *Evening Post* (1858–71), part of the time as editor, and was Washington correspondent (1874–90) for the New York *Herald*. A leading political commentator of his day, Nordhoff was the author of such works as *Communistic Societies in the United States* (1875) and *The Cotton States in the Spring and Summer of 1875* (1876). His grandson, **Charles Bernard Nordhoff** (1887–1947), was coauthor with J. N. Hall of *Mutiny on the Bounty* (1932), *Men Against the Sea* (1933), *Pitcairn's Island* (1934), and other works.

Nordica, Lillian (nôr'dĭkə), 1859–1914, American soprano, b. Farmington, Maine, as Lillian Norton. She studied in Milan, where she made her operatic debut in 1879. She sang in St. Petersburg, Paris, and London and in 1883 made her debut at the Academy of Music, New York City, and in 1890 at the Metropolitan Opera. Although most famous for Wagnerian roles, added to her repertory in 1894 when she sang at Bayreuth, she was equally capable in such florid roles as that of Marguerite in *Faust*.

Nordic Council, international consultative body, created in 1952 by Denmark, Iceland, Norway, and Sweden. Finland joined the council in 1955. The council may take up any problem of joint interest except matters of defense. Among its accomplishments are the abolition of visas, the creation of a common labor market, mutual recognition of academic degrees, and mutual law enforcement.

Nordic race: see RACE.

Nordkapp, promontory: see NORTH CAPE, Norway.

Nordkyn, Cape (nôr'chün, no͞or'-) or **Kinnarodden** (chĭ'närôd"ən), northernmost point of the European mainland, Finnmark co., N Norway, E of North Cape, at lat. 71°8' N.

Nordland (nôr'län, no͞or'-), county (1972 est. pop. 241,000), 14,798 sq mi (38,327 sq km), N central Norway, bordering on the Norwegian Sea in the west and on Sweden in the east. The chief towns are Bodø (the capital), Mo, and Narvik. The county has many fjords and approximately 600 islands, including the Lofoten and the Vesterålen groups. Fishing, mining (iron, lead, and zinc), and livestock raising are the main occupations. In addition copper is mined and processed at Sulitjelma.

Nördlingen (nört'lĭngən), town (1970 pop. 14,692), Bavaria, S West Germany. It is a manufacturing center and a rail junction. Historically a Swabian town, Nördlingen was founded in the 9th cent. and became a free imperial city c.1217. In the Thirty Years War an imperial army under Gallas defeated (1634) troops at Nördlingen led by Duke Bernhard of Saxe-Weimar; the victory by the imperial side was a major reason for France's entry into the war in 1635. In 1645 the town was the scene of a German defeat at the hands of French troops under Condé. It passed to Bavaria in 1803. The picturesque town retains its walls (14th–16th cent.), a town hall (14th cent.), the late-Gothic Church of St. George (1427–1505), and numerous 16th- and 17th-century houses.

Nord-Trøndelag (nôr-trön'dəläg, no͞or'-), county (1972 est. pop. 119,000), 8,673 sq mi (22,463 sq km), central Norway, N of the Trondheimsfjord and bordering on the Atlantic Ocean in the west. The chief towns are Steinkjer (the capital), Namsos, and Levanger. The economy is based on farming, fishing, mining, and the manufacture of forest products.

Nore (nôr), river, c.70 mi (110 km) long, rising in NE Co. Tipperary, Republic of Ireland. It flows northeast, then southeast through a rich agricultural region to the Barrow River near New Ross. The Nore valley is noted for its scenic beauty.

Nore, the, sandbank in the Thames estuary, SE England, 3 mi (4.8 km) E of Sheerness. At the east end is Nore Lightship. The name is also applied to part of the Thames estuary, a famous anchorage. A mutiny in the British fleet there, shortly after the SPITHEAD mutiny in 1797, failed to achieve its goals of a more equitable division of prize money and an end to brutality. Richard Parker, its leader, was executed.

norepinephrine (nôr"ĕpĭnĕf'rən), organic compound, the major neurotransmitter substance of that part of the NERVOUS SYSTEM consisting of the postganglionic sympathetic nerves. When an impulse traveling along a nerve cell in this system reaches the end of the cell, it stimulates the cell to secrete norepinephrine, which diffuses to a receptor site on the target organ, resulting in the sympathetic response typical of the particular organ involved. This function is exactly analogous to that of ACETYLCHOLINE, the neurotransmitter substance of the rest of the nervous system. Norepinephrine is found in substantial quantities in the medulla of the ADRENAL GLAND, where it can evidently be released into the blood stream as a HORMONE. Norepinephrine accounts for 10% to 30% of the hormone in the adrenal medulla, the rest consisting chiefly of EPINEPHRINE. Norepinephrine is structurally identical to epinephrine, except that one methyl group of epinephrine is replaced by a hydrogen atom in norepinephrine. When acting as a hormone, norepinephrine slows the heart rate and increases both the systolic and diastolic blood pressures, mostly by increasing the resistance to blood flow in capillaries far removed from the heart. The hormone has other actions as well, but in almost all cases it can be shown to have effects different from those of epinephrine. Norepinephrine is synthesized in the body from the amino acid TYROSINE. It had been proposed many times as a neurotransmitter during the early half of the 20th cent., but the first convincing demonstration that the postganglionic sympathetic neurotransmitter was indeed norepinephrine was made in 1946.

Norfolk, Hugh Bigod, 1st **earl of:** see BIGOD, HUGH, 1ST EARL OF NORFOLK.

Norfolk, John Howard, 1st **duke of,** 1430?–1485, English nobleman. The grandson of Thomas Mowbray, 1st duke of Norfolk, he held considerable estates in Norfolk. A faithful adherent of the house of York in the Wars of the Roses, he was made sheriff of Norfolk and Suffolk by Edward IV and entrusted with diplomatic missions. He later supported Richard III, who in 1483 made him the 1st duke of Norfolk of the HOWARD family (the Mowbray line having died out in 1476) and earl marshal of England. Norfolk was killed at the battle of Bosworth.

Norfolk, Thomas Howard, 2d **duke of,** 1443–1524, English nobleman, son of John Howard, 1st duke of Norfolk. He fought at the battle of Bosworth (1485) in which his father was killed. He himself was captured, attainted, and placed in the Tower of London. He was released (1489) by Henry VII and restored to the earldom of Surrey, which he had received in 1483, but not to the dukedom of Norfolk. He was entrusted by Henry VII with the care of the northern borders and in 1501 was made lord treasurer. Recognized as the leading general in England, he commanded the army that defeated (1513) the Scots at Flodden and was created (1514) duke of Norfolk. Although an influential member of Henry VIII's privy council, he was gradually forced to relinquish much of his power to the ascending Thomas Wolsey. He served as guardian of the realm during Henry's absence in 1520. In 1521, acting as lord high steward, he was compelled to sentence his friend Edward STAFFORD, 3d duke of Buckingham, to death.

Norfolk, Thomas Howard, 3d **duke of,** 1473–1554, English nobleman, prominent in the reign of HENRY VIII; son of Thomas Howard, the 2d duke. He married (1495) a daughter of Edward IV and thus became brother-in-law to Henry VII. He fought (1513) against the Scots at Flodden and became (1514) earl of Surrey when his father was made duke of Norfolk. After his first wife's death he married Elizabeth, daughter of Edward Stafford, 3d duke of Buckingham. He served (1520–21) as lord lieutenant of Ireland. Succeeding his father as lord high treasurer in 1522 and as duke of Norfolk in 1524, Norfolk led the opposition to Thomas, Cardinal Wolsey. He supported Henry VIII's divorce from Katharine of Aragón and his marriage (1533) to Norfolk's niece Anne Boleyn. Later he presided (1536) at the trial and execution of Anne. Although Norfolk conducted the campaign against the Pilgrimage of Grace (1536), he remained Catholic. He was an enemy of Thomas CROMWELL and instrumental in bringing about his fall (1540). After the execution in 1542 of another of his nieces, Catherine HOWARD, Henry's fifth queen, Norfolk's influence waned, and he was forced back into the position of a mere military commander. In 1546 he and his son Henry Howard, earl of Surrey, were charged with treason. Surrey was executed, but Norfolk was saved by the death of the king. He was released (1553) from prison on the accession of Mary I and restored to his dukedom. He led the forces against the rebellion (1554) of Sir Thomas Wyatt, the younger.

Norfolk, Thomas Howard, 4th **duke of,** 1536–72, English nobleman, son of Henry Howard, earl of Surrey. He succeeded his grandfather, the 3d duke, in 1554. He was favored by Queen Elizabeth I, although he was jealous of the larger measure of confidence she placed in Robert Dudley, earl of Leicester. Norfolk commanded the English forces that intervened in Scotland in 1559–60 and in 1568 was chief of the commission that inquired into Scottish affairs after the flight of MARY QUEEN OF SCOTS to England. A widower, he conducted secret negotiations for Mary's hand. Elizabeth heard of the project, however, and forbade it, and Norfolk was imprisoned (1569–70). On his release Norfolk was drawn into the plot of Ridolfi, agent of Philip II of Spain, who was planning a Spanish invasion and the dethronement of Elizabeth. The plot was discovered, Norfolk was imprisoned (1571) in the Tower of London, tried, and beheaded.

Norfolk, Thomas Mowbray, 1st **duke of,** c.1366–1399, English nobleman. He was created earl of Nottingham in 1383, and in 1385 he was made earl marshal of England for life. He joined Thomas of Woodstock, duke of GLOUCESTER, and the other baronial opponents of RICHARD II in 1387 and was one of the five lords appellant who "appealed" (i.e., accused) the king's favorites of treason and secured their conviction in the Merciless Parliament of 1388. After Richard regained control in 1389, however, he was conciliatory to Nottingham, who accompanied him to Ireland in 1394. In 1397, Nottingham aided the king in bringing to trial his former associates, Gloucester and the earls of Arundel and Warwick. Gloucester was placed in his custody, and he was possibly responsible for his murder. Although created duke of Norfolk in 1397, he began to fear that the king might turn on him and confided in the other remaining lord appellant, the duke of Hereford (later HENRY IV). A dispute arose between Norfolk and Hereford when Hereford told the king of Norfolk's suspicions, and trial by combat was proposed. At the last moment, however, Richard intervened and banished both from the country, Norfolk for life. He died in Italy.

Norfolk (nôr'fək), county (1971 pop. 616,427), 2,054 sq mi (5,320 sq km), E England. The county town is NORWICH. The region is one of flat, fertile farmlands, with a long, low coast bordering on the North Sea and the Wash. The principal rivers are the Ouse, the Bure, the Yare and its tributary the Wensum, and the Waveney. A series of connected shallow lakes, known as the Broads, occupies the eastern portion of the county. Norfolk produces excellent cereal and root crops and supports extensive breeding of cattle and poultry. Fishing, the manufacture of agricultural machinery, and light industries are also important. There are numerous vestiges of habitation dating from prehistoric times. After the Anglo-Saxon invasion of England, Norfolk became a part of the kingdom of EAST ANGLIA, the home of the "north folk" of that region, whence its name. In 1974, Norfolk was reorganized as a nonmetropolitan county, and a small area of NE East Suffolk was added to it.

Norfolk (**1, 2** nôr'fək; **2** nôr'fôk"). **1** City (1970 pop. 16,607), Madison co., NE Nebr., on the Elkhorn River; inc. 1881. A trade and railroad center in a fertile farming region, it has a livestock market, feed mills, creameries, bottling companies, and meat-packing and food-processing plants. Norfolk is the site of a junior college and a state mental hospital. **2** City (1970 pop. 307,951), independent and in no county, SE Va., on the Elizabeth River and the southern side of Hampton Roads; founded 1682, inc. as a city 1845. The largest city in the state, it is a port of entry and a major commercial, industrial, shipping, and distribution center. With Portsmouth and Newport News, it forms the Port of Hampton Roads, one of the best natural harbors in the world. The city has 50 mi (80 km) of waterfront and an extensive maritime trade; quantities of coal, grain, tobacco, seafood, and farm products are exported. Industries include shipbuilding, meat and seafood processing, automobile assembling, and the manufacture of fertilizers, farm implements, chemicals, textiles, and peanut oil. Norfolk is also a major military center; with Portsmouth the city forms an extensive naval complex. The headquarters of the 5th Naval Dist., the Atlantic Fleet, the 2d Fleet, and the Supreme Allied Command are there. The huge operating base (largest in the United States) includes a major naval air station, a supply center, and numerous other facilities. The Norfolk navy yard is in Portsmouth. A rallying point for Tory forces at the start of the American Revolution, Norfolk was attacked (1776) by Americans and in the ensuing battle caught fire and was nearly destroyed. In the Civil War it was first a Confederate naval base; the battle between the *Monitor* and the *Merrimack* was fought in Hampton Roads. Norfolk fell to Union forces in May, 1862, and was occupied by them throughout the rest of the war. Of interest in the city are St. Paul's Church (1738; only building to survive the burning of 1776); Fort Norfolk (1794); the Gen. Douglas MacArthur Memorial, where the general is buried; and many old homes. Norfolk is the seat of Old Dominion Univ., Norfolk State College, and Virginia Wesleyan College. The Chesapeake Bay Bridge-Tunnel links Norfolk with the Delmarva Peninsula, and the Hampton Roads Bridge-Tunnel links it with Hampton, Va.

Norfolk Island (nôr'fək), island (1970 est. pop. 1,380), 13 sq mi (34 sq km), South Pacific, a territory of Australia, c.1,035 mi (1,670 km) NE of Sydney. A resort, Norfolk has luxuriant vegetation and is known for its pine trees. Bean and palm seeds are exported, and livestock is raised. Discovered in 1774 by Capt. James COOK, the island was claimed by Great Britain in the hope that the pines would provide masts for the navy. When the wood proved unsatisfactory, Norfolk was made into a prison island (1788–1855). In 1856 the prisoners were removed and some of the descendants of the *Bounty* mutineers were moved to Norfolk from Pitcairn Island. Norfolk Island was annexed to Tasmania in 1844, became a dependency of New South Wales in 1896, and was transferred to the Commonwealth of Australia in 1913. See study by Merval Hoare (1971).

Norfolk Island pine: see MONKEY-PUZZLE TREE.

Noricum (nŏr'ĭkəm), province of the Roman Empire. It corresponded roughly to modern Austria S of the Danube and W of Vienna. It was bordered on the west by Rhaetia and on the east by Pannonia. Noricum was incorporated into the Roman Empire in 16 B.C. It prospered as a frontier colony for centuries, then declined and was overrun by German tribes in the 5th cent.

Norilsk (nərēlsk'), city (1970 pop. 135,000), Krasnoyarsk Kray, N Siberian USSR. The northernmost major city in the Soviet Union and the world's second largest city (after Murmansk) above the Arctic Circle, Norilsk is the center of a region where nickel, copper, cobalt, platinum, and coal are mined. A railroad links Norilsk with the Yenisei port of DUDINKA, from where ores are shipped via the Northern Sea Route to the European USSR. Founded in 1935, Norilsk was reportedly the site of forced labor camps during the Stalin era.

norm, authoritative rule or standard by which something is judged and on that basis approved or disapproved. Examples of norms include standards of right and wrong, beauty and ugliness, and truth and falsehood. Several fields of philosophy, especially ETHICS, AESTHETICS, and LOGIC, concern themselves with the evaluation and application of such rules.

Normal, town (1970 pop. 26,396), McLean co., central Ill.; inc. 1865. It lies in a productive farming area noted especially for fruits and nursery stock. Paper products are manufactured in Normal. The town originally grew around Illinois State Univ. (1857; formerly called Illinois State Normal Univ.), which remains a major contributor to its economy.

normality, in chemistry: see CONCENTRATION.

normal school: see TEACHER TRAINING.

Norman, Montagu Collet, 1st **Baron Norman of St. Clere,** 1871–1950, English financier. He was governor of the Bank of England from 1920 to 1944, a tenure of office that broke all tradition. He long favored the gold standard, first supporting its retention and later its return. Norman was raised to the peerage in 1944. See biographies by Sir Henry Clay (1957) and Andrew Boyle (1968).

Norman, city (1970 pop. 52,117), seat of Cleveland co., central Okla.; inc. 1891. Air conditioners, packaged foods, and airplanes are among the city's manufactures. Norman is the seat of the Univ. of Oklahoma.

Norman architecture, term applied to the buildings erected by the Normans in all lands that fell under their dominion. It is used not only in England and N France, but also in S Italy (Apulia) and in Sicily. The Norman buildings in England and France were largely Romanesque, chiefly based upon the ROMANESQUE ARCHITECTURE of Lombardy in Italy. Churches, abbeys, and castles, the principal works, showed massive proportions, sparsely adorned masonry, and a frequent use of the round arch. The development of the style was confined chiefly to the period from 1066 to 1154, a period of tremendous building activity. Arising in Normandy, the style was quickly introduced into England, superseding the Saxon. It first appeared at Westminster Abbey, where only the foundations remain. In England and Normandy there was a closely parallel development. The great French works include the ruined abbey of Jumièges, near Rouen, the beginnings of the great fortified abbey of Mont-Saint-Michel, and the two abbeys at Caen that were founded by William the Conqueror, all belonging to the middle and late 11th cent. The greatest activity, however, was in England, where after 1070 the Normans built hundreds of parish churches and commenced most of the great cathedrals. All underwent later restorations; the only intact early Norman design is the small St. John's Chapel (c.1087), built by William the Conqueror, in the Tower of London. In both England and Normandy church plans were cruciform. Over the crossing of nave and transepts was a prominent square tower, one of the most effective Norman features. Blind arcades, sometimes with interlacing arches, were the common adornment for walls. Moldings carved with the beakhead, zigzag, or chevron, or alternating lozenges are especially identified with the style. Increased skill and the adoption of the chisel resulted in grotesque sculptured animal forms and in the sculptured reliefs of the tympanums over doorways. Certain elements of Anglo-Norman construction pointed toward the development of GOTHIC ARCHITECTURE. Whereas in early Norman buildings wooden roofs prevailed, the cathedral at Durham (commenced 1093) was the first to employ a ribbed vault system with pointed arches (the nave was finished c.1133). Other great English cathedrals tended away from the early massiveness of wall construction and showed an increasing verticality, including those at Winchester (begun 1079), Ely (1083–1109) and Peterborough (begun 1118). The austere grandeur of the English and French Norman style was modified in S Italy and especially in Sicily by the mingling of Byzantine and Arabic elements. See A. W. Clapham, *English Romanesque Architecture after the Conquest* (Vol. II, 1934); D. F. Renn, *Norman Castles in Britain* (1970).

Norman Conquest, period in English history following the defeat (1066) of King HAROLD of England by William, duke of Normandy, who became WILLIAM I of England. The conquest was formerly thought to have brought about broad changes in all phases of English life. More recently historians have stressed the continuity of English law, institutions, and customs, but the subject remains one of controversy. The initial military conquest of England was quick and brutal. The members of the Anglo-Saxon upper class who were not killed in the battle of Hastings were almost all involved in the rebellion from 1068 to 1070 and were either killed or deprived of their lands. Thus a Norman aristocracy was superimposed on the English, and the new elite brought with it Norman feudal customs (see FEUDALISM), which were reinforced by the need for cohesion and mutual military support among the fairly small group of conquerors. Thus the rebellions among the Norman barons were minor and short-lived, the interests of stability being paramount. To consolidate his position William used the existing Anglo-Saxon administrative system, which functioned as part of a centralized monarchical tradition. It was this tradition, as adapted by the Normans, that gave English feudalism its uniquely cohesive nature. There was little change in the administrative and judicial systems during the Norman period (usually defined as ending with the accession of the Plantagenet Henry II in 1154) and later developments were not in the nature of Norman superimpositions. William I's archbishop of Canterbury, LANFRANC, established a separate system of canon law courts, effectively asserted the supremacy of his archdiocese, and brought the English church into closer contact with developments in Europe, particularly with the reforms of Pope Gregory VII. The Norman kings, however, successfully resisted papal encroachment on their control over episcopal appointments. The period saw many churches and castles built, the latter chiefly on the south and east coasts and on the Welsh and Scottish borders (see NORMAN ARCHITECTURE). Norman French became the language of the court and upper classes, and of literature, and had great effect on the development of the ENGLISH LANGUAGE. See G. W. S. Barrow, *Feudal Britain* (1956, repr. 1965); D. J. A. Matthew, *The Norman Conquest* (1966); D. C. Douglas, *The Norman Achievement, 1050-1100* (1969); F. M. Stenton, *The First Century of English Feudalism, 1066-1166* (2d ed. 1961) and *Anglo-Saxon England* (3d ed. 1971).

Normandy (nôr'məndē), Fr. *Normandie* (nôrmäNdē'), region and former province, NW France, bordering on the English Channel. It now includes five departments—Manche, Calvados, Eure, Seine-Maritime, and Orne. Normandy is a region of flat farmland, forests, and gentle hills. The economy is based on cattle raising, fishing, and tourism. In ROUEN (the historic capital), Le Havre (see HAVRE, LE), and CHERBOURG there are also shipbuilding, metalworking, oil-refining, and textile industries. Normandy has outstanding beach resorts, notably Deauville, Granville, and Étretat. It is known too for its many old fairs and festivals. MONT-SAINT-MICHEL lies off the coast where Normandy and Brittany meet. Part of ancient GAUL, the region was conquered by Julius Caesar and became part of the province of Lugdunensis. It was Christianized in the 3d cent. and conquered by the Franks in the 5th cent. Repeatedly devastated (9th cent.) by the Norsemen, it finally was ceded (911) to their chief, Rollo, 1st duke of Normandy, by Charles III (Charles the Simple) of France. The Norsemen (or Normans), for whom the region was named, soon accepted Christianity. Rollo's successors acquired neighboring territories in a series of wars. In 1066, Duke William (William the Conqueror), son of Robert I, invaded England, where he became king as William I. The succession in Normandy, disputed among William's sons (Robert II of Normandy and William II and Henry I of England), passed to England after the battle of Tinchebrai (1106), in which Henry defeated Robert. In 1144, Geoffrey IV of Anjou conquered Normandy; his son, Henry Plantagenet (later Henry II of England), was invested (1151) with the duchy by King Stephen of England. It was by this series of events that branches of the Angevin dynasty came to rule England, as well as vast territories in France, Sicily, and S Italy, where the Normans had begun to establish colonies in the 11th cent. Normandy was joined to France in 1204 after the invasion and conquest by Philip II. Normandy was again devastated during the Hundred Years War (1337-1453). The Treaty of Brétigny (1360) confirmed Normandy as a French possession, but Henry V of England invaded the region and conquered it once more. With the exception of the larger Channel Islands, Normandy was permanently restored to France in 1450, and in 1499, Louis XII established a provincial PARLEMENT for Normandy at Rouen. The Protestants made great headway in Normandy in the 16th cent., and there were bitter battles between Catholics and HUGUENOTS. Louis XIV sought to complete the assimilation of Normandy into France, and in 1654 the provincial estates were suppressed. The revocation of the Edict of Nantes (1685) led to a mass migration of Huguenots from Normandy and a grave economic setback for the region. In the 18th cent., however, prosperity returned. In 1790 the province, with others in France, was abolished and replaced by the present-day departments. The region was the scene of the Allied invasion (1944) of Europe in World War II.

Normandy campaign, June to Aug., 1944, in World War II. The Allied invasion of the European continent through Normandy began about 12:15 A.M. on June 6, 1944 (D day). The plan, known as Operation Overlord, had been prepared since 1943; supreme command over its execution was entrusted to Gen. Dwight D. Eisenhower. In May, 1944, tactical bombing was begun in order to destroy German communications in N France. Just after midnight on June 6, British and American airborne forces landed behind the German coastal fortifications known as the Atlantic Wall. They were followed after daybreak by the seaborne troops of the U.S. 1st Army and British 2d Army. Field Marshal B. L. Montgomery was in command of the Allied land forces. Some 4,000 transports, 800 warships, and innumerable small craft, under Admiral Sir B. H. Ramsay, supported the invasion, and more than 11,000 aircraft, under Air Chief Marshal Sir Trafford Leigh-Mallory, formed a protective umbrella. While naval guns and Allied bombers assaulted the beach fortifications, the men swarmed ashore. At the base of the Cotentin peninsula the U.S. forces established two beachheads—Utah Beach, W of the Vire River, and Omaha Beach, E of the Vire, the scene of the fiercest fighting. British troops, who had landed near Bayeux on three beaches called Gold, Juno, and Sword, advanced quickly but were stopped before Caen. On June 12 the fusion of the Allied beachheads was complete. The German commander, Field Marshal Gerd von Rundstedt, found that Allied air strength prevented use of his reserves. U.S. forces under Gen. Omar N. Bradley cut off the Cotentin peninsula (June 18), and Cherbourg surrendered on June 27. The Americans then swung south. After difficult fighting in easily defendable "hedgerow" country they captured (July 18) the vital communications center of Saint-Lô, cutting off the German force under Field Marshal Erwin Rommel. The U.S. 3d Army under Gen. George S. Patton was thrown into the battle and broke through the German left flank at Avranches. Patton raced into Brittany and S to the Loire, swinging east to outflank Paris. A German attempt to cut the U.S. forces in two at Avranches was foiled (Aug. 7-11). The British had taken Caen on July 9, but they were again halted by a massive German tank concentration. They resumed their offensive in August and captured Falaise on Aug. 16. Between them and the U.S. forces driving north from Argentan the major part of the German 7th Army was caught in the "Falaise pocket" and was wiped out by Aug. 23, opening the way for the Allies to overrun N France. See G. A. Harrison, *Cross Channel Attack* (1951); Cornelius Ryan, *The Longest Day* (1959, repr. 1967); Alexander McKee, *Last Round Against Rommel* (1964); A. A. Mitchie, *The Invasion of Europe* (1964); Army Times Ed., *D-Day, the Great-est Invasion* (1969).

Norman Isles, Great Britain: see CHANNEL ISLANDS.

Normans, designation for the Northmen, or NORSEMEN, who conquered Normandy in the 10th cent. and adopted Christianity and the customs and language of France. Abandoning piracy and raiding, they adopted regular commerce and gave much impetus to European trade. They soon lost all connection with their original Scandinavian homeland, but they retained their craving for adventure, expansion, and enrichment. In 1066 the NORMAN CONQUEST of England made the duke of Normandy king of England as WILLIAM I (William the Conqueror). The Norman nobility displaced the Anglo-Saxon nobility of England. Early in the 11th cent. bands of Norman adventurers appeared in S Italy, where at first they aided the local nobles in their rebellion against Byzantine rule. A steady stream of land-hungry Norman nobles, under the pretext of expelling the Greeks, proceeded to take over the land. Most remarkable among these adventurers were the numerous sons of Tancred de Hauteville. One of these, William Iron Arm, became lord of APULIA in 1043; he was succeeded by his brother Drogo and by another brother, Humphrey, who defeated (1053) Pope Leo IX, when the pope attempted to enforce papal rights in S Italy. In 1059, Humphrey's brother and successor ROBERT GUISCARD was invested by Pope Nicholas II with duchies of Apulia and Calabria and the island of Sicily, which was yet to be conquered. He completed the Norman conquest of S Italy; another brother, ROGER I, conquered Sicily, and in 1130 Roger's son, ROGER II, set up the kingdom of SICILY, which included the island and the Norman possessions in S Italy. The Normans soon adopted Italian speech and customs. Their ambitious plans against the Byzantine Empire were a factor in bringing about the CRUSADES, in which they at first played an important part. The medieval Normans were notable for the great authority given their dukes; for their enthusiasm for conquest; and for their economic and social penetration of conquered areas. Wherever the Normans went, NORMAN ARCHITECTURE left its traces. See Edmund Curtis, *Roger of Sicily and the Normans in Lower Italy* (1912); C. H. Haskins, *The Normans in European History* (1915, repr. 1966) and *Norman Institutions* (1918, repr. 1960); J. J. C. Norwich, *The Normans in the South, 1016-1130* (1967) and *The Kingdom in the Sun, 1130-1194* (1970).

Norman Wells, village, W Mackenzie dist., Northwest Territories, Canada, on the Mackenzie River, W of Great Bear Lake. It is the center of an oil region.

Norns, the Norse Fates. Like the Fates of Greek mythology, the Norns spun and wove the web of life. Belief in the Norns was of great importance in Germanic religion and life. It was said that no one, not even the gods, could escape their fate. The Norns were usually three in number—Urth or Wyrd (the past), Verthandi (the present), and Skuld (the future). The three weird sisters of destiny in Shakespeare's *Macbeth* are probably Scottish equivalents of the Norns.

Norodom Sihanouk (nōrōdŭm' sĭhənŭk'), 1922-, king of Cambodia (1941-55). Norodom was educated in Saigon and Paris and was elected king by a royal council in 1941. During the Japanese occupation of Cambodia he was held a virtual prisoner. After the war he adopted (1947) a constitution that made Cambodia a limited monarchy and achieved (1949) some autonomy for his country within the French Union. Following the first elections (1950), however, Norodom dissolved the assembly and ruled by decree. He became prime minister as well as king in 1951 and appointed a cabinet made up largely of members of the royal family. In 1953 he went into voluntary exile when France rejected his demand for complete independence. In 1955 he abdicated the throne in favor of his father, Norodom Suramarit, but retained the premiership and control of the Popular Socialist Community party, which he had founded. As premier he took Cambodia out of the French Union. After his father's death (1960) he again became head of state, although not king. Initially professing neutrality in foreign affairs, he broke (1965) diplomatic relations with the United States in retaliation for Cambodian casualties resulting from South Vietnamese and U.S. incursions into Cambodia in the Vietnam War. In March, 1970, while on a trip to Moscow, Sihanouk was overthrown by a rightist coup d'etat protesting his policy of allowing Viet Cong and North Vietnamese troops to use Cambodian territory. He set up a government in exile in Peking. In 1973 his memoirs, *My War With the CIA*, were published. See Jean Lacouture, *The Demigods* (tr. 1970).

Norrell, Norman: see under FASHION.

Norridge, village (1970 pop. 17,020), Cook co., NE Ill., a residential suburb of Chicago; inc. 1940.

Norris, Charles Gilman: see NORRIS, FRANK.

Norris, Edwin, 1795-1872, English philologist. Norris wrote a number of articles on little-known languages of Asia and Africa. His most important work was his uncompleted *Assyrian Dictionary* (3 vol., 1868-72), which is a landmark in the history of CUNEIFORM lexicography.

Norris, Frank (Benjamin Franklin Norris), 1870-1902, American novelist, b. Chicago. After studying in Paris and at the Univ. of California (1890-94), he entered Harvard, where he wrote *McTeague* (1899), a proletarian novel influenced by the experimental NATURALISM of Zola. His most impressive work was his proposed trilogy, "The Epic of Wheat," of which only two parts were written—*The Octopus* (1901), depicting the brutal struggle between the wheat farmers and the railroad, and *The Pit* (1903), dealing with the anarchic speculation on the Chicago grain market. Norris spent several years as a war correspondent in South Africa (1895-96) and Cuba (1898). *The Responsibilities of the Novelist* (1903), a collection of essays, contains his idealistic views on the role of the writer. See study by W. B. Dillingham (1969). His brother **Charles Gilman Norris,** 1881-1945, b. Chicago, grad. Univ. of California, 1903, was the author of a number of naturalistic novels on American life, including *Salt* (1917), *Brass* (1921), *Bread* (1923), *Seed* (1930), and *Flint* (1944).

Norris, George William, 1861-1944, American legislator, b. Sandusky co., Ohio. After admission to the bar in 1883, he moved (1885) to Furnas co., Nebr., where he practiced law and was prosecuting attorney and then (1895-1902) judge of the district court. From 1903 to 1913 he served in the U.S. House of Representatives. A liberal Republican, Norris secured (1910), through an alliance of insurgent Republicans with Democrats, the passage of a resolution that reformed the House rules and wrested absolute control from the speaker of the House, Joseph B. CANNON. Elected (1912) to the U.S. Senate, he opposed President Wilson's foreign policy, voted against U.S. participation in World War I, and denounced the Treaty of Versailles. He was at constant odds with the Coolidge administration, backed (1928) Democrat Alfred E. Smith for President, and favored President Franklin Delano Roosevelt's domestic and foreign policies. Norris was read out of the Republican party and became (1936) an independent. He was author (1932) of the Twentieth Amendment to the Constitution, which abolished the "lame duck" session of Congress and changed the date of the presidential inauguration. He sponsored (1932) the Norris-La Guardia Act, which forbade the use of injunctions in labor disputes to prevent strikes, boycotts, or picketing. An advocate of government water power development, he fathered the bills that created (1933) the Tennessee Valley Authority. He also supported farm relief measures. After serving 30 years in the Senate, he was defeated for reelection in 1942. His *Fighting Liberal* (1945, repr. 1961) is autobiographical. See biographies by Alfred Lief (1939) and N. L. Zucker (1966); studies by Richard Lowitt (1963 and 1971).

Norris, John, 1657-1711, English clergyman and philosopher. As the most prominent follower of Malebranche he wrote, in exposition of that philosopher's system, *An Essay towards the Theory of the Ideal or Intelligible World* (1701-4). Previously he had been one of the earliest critics of Locke's *Essay on Human Understanding.* His writings also show a decided Platonic influence. Among his works are *A Collection of Miscellanies* (1687) and *An Account of Reason and Faith* (1697). See F. I. MacKinnon, *The Philosophy of John Norris* (1910).

Norris, Kathleen, 1880-1966, American novelist, b. San Francisco; wife of Charles G. Norris. Her first success, *Mother* (1911), was followed by over 80 sentimental novels. *Certain People of Importance* (1922) is perhaps her most ambitious work.

Norris Dam: see TENNESSEE VALLEY AUTHORITY.

Norristown, borough (1970 pop. 38,169), seat of Montgomery co., SE Pa., on the Schuylkill River; settled c.1712, laid out 1784, inc. 1812. It is a regional trade center. Its manufactures include clothing, woolen textiles, metal products (especially tubing), electrical machinery, and asbestos products. The borough is named for Isaac Norris (1671-1735), a Quaker merchant and a mayor of Philadelphia, who in 1704 bought a large tract of land there from his friend William Penn. Gen. Winfield Scott Hancock, a commander during the Civil War and Democratic candidate for President in 1880, was born in Norristown and is buried there. The County Historical Society there is noted for its collection of local folk art. The Norristown Hospital for the Insane is in the borough. Valley Forge is nearby.

Norrköping (nôr'chö"pĭng), city (1970 pop. 107,948), Östergötland co., SE Sweden, a seaport at the head of the Bråviken, a narrow inlet of the Baltic Sea. Sweden's fourth largest city, it is a commercial, industrial, and transportation center. A major textile center, it also has industries producing paper, rubber, furniture, electrical goods, and processed food. Norrköping was founded in the 14th cent. and was burned (1719) by the Russians in the Northern War. However, it has retained many old buildings, including Hedvig's Church (17th cent.).

Norrland: see SWEDEN.

Norse, another name for the North Germanic, or Scandinavian, group of the Germanic subfamily of the Indo-European family of languages (see GERMANIC LANGUAGES). The modern Norse languages—Danish, Faeroese, Icelandic, Norwegian, and Swedish—all stem from an earlier form of Norse known as Old Norse. Now extinct, Old Norse was the language spoken by the Germanic tribes living in Scandinavia before A.D. 1000. It was first written in RUNES, some examples of which go back to the 3d cent. A.D., but later the Roman alphabet was used. The earliest extant Old Norse manuscripts in the Roman alphabet are from the 12th cent. Old Norse is also noteworthy as the language of the Eddas and sagas (see OLD NORSE LITERATURE; ICELANDIC LITERATURE). See Eric V. Garden, *An Introduction to Old Norse* (2d ed. 1957).

Norse literature: see OLD NORSE LITERATURE.

Norsemen, name given to the Scandinavian VIKINGS who raided and settled on the coasts of the European continent in the 9th and 10th cent. They are also referred to as Northmen or Normans. Recent research indicates that Norse raids of Western Europe may have been known in the early Middle Ages. Among the causes of the great influx (9th cent.) of Norsemen to the coasts of NW Germany, the Low Countries, France, and Spain were lust for wealth and power, search for adventure, and the attempt of King HAROLD I of Norway to subjugate the independent nobles of his land, thereby forcing them to look to foreign conquests. The impact of the Norse invasions was particularly lasting in N France. The invaders, whose major raids began c.843, sailed up the French rivers, particularly the Seine, and repeatedly attacked, looted, and burned such cities as Rouen and Paris. Their actions threatened to plunge France back into the barbarism from which it was just emerging. The Norsemen gradually established settlements, generally at the river mouths; thus they constantly threatened to renew their river raids, and they ruined French commerce and navigation. In 911, ROLLO, one of their leaders, was invested by King CHARLES III (Charles the Simple) with the duchy of NORMANDY, originally the territory around Rouen. Rollo's successors considerably expanded their territory and were only nominal vassals of the French kings. The Norsemen accepted Christianity, adopted French law and speech, and continued in history under the name of NORMANS. The name of Normandy itself and several Norman place names are survivals of the Norse period. The Norsemen did not differ essentially from the other Vikings, who were known as Danes in ENGLAND and as VARANGIANS in Russia. See T. D. Kendrick, *A History of the Vikings* (1930, repr. 1968); E. C. Oxenstierna, *The Norsemen* (tr. 1965) and *The World of the Norsemen* (tr. 1968).

Norse religion: see GERMANIC RELIGION.

Norstad, Lauris, 1907-, U.S. air force general, b. Minneapolis. A graduate of West Point, in World War II he headed the 12th Air Force in North Africa and was director of operations for the Allied air forces in the Mediterranean. After a variety of postwar assignments, he was sent to Germany in 1950 as commander of U.S. air forces in Europe and in 1951 became commander in chief of U.S. and Allied air forces in Central Europe. Norstad became (1952) the youngest four-star general in U.S. history. Deputy air commander for the North Atlantic Treaty Organization (1953-56), he was supreme allied commander in Europe from 1956 to 1963.

North, Christopher, pseud. of **John Wilson,** 1785-1854, Scottish author. Among the first contributors to *Blackwood's Magazine,* he joined the staff in 1817 and quickly became one of its chief critical writers. His Tory sympathies gained him the chair of moral philosophy (1820-51) at the Univ. of Edinburgh. His best-known work is in the *Noctes Ambrosianae,* an occasional discursive feature of *Blackwood's* to which he contributed the majority of the articles. See memoir by his daughter, Mary Gordon (1863).

North, Sir Dudley, 1641-91, English merchant and economist. Agent for the Turkey Company in Constantinople from 1662 to 1680, he returned to England a wealthy man and was commissioner of the customs and of the treasury under Charles II and James II. He was one of the earliest proponents of free trade in his pamphlets, *Discourses upon Trade* (1691, ed. by J. H. Hollander, 1935).

North, Frederick North, 8th Baron, 1732-92, British statesman, best known as Lord North. He entered Parliament in 1754 and became a junior lord of the treasury (1759), privy councilor (1766), and chancellor of the exchequer (1767). In 1770, North, who had proved himself an able parliamentarian, was appointed prime minister; the support of GEORGE III kept him in that office for 12 years. North was a capable administrator, who introduced financial reforms and began reform of the East India Company with the Regulating Act of 1772. However, he is chiefly remembered for his incompetent colonial policies. His stern response to the Boston Tea Party (see INTOLERABLE ACTS) helped unite the American colonists against England. After the outbreak of the American Revolution, North offered to resign, but since no acceptable replacement could be found, he remained in office until after news of the British surrender at Yorktown. In 1783 he formed a coalition with his former opponent, the Whig Charles James FOX, but George III secured its collapse by the defeat of Fox's East India bill. For the remainder of his career North supported the opposition against William Pitt, but he was forced to retire from active political life when his sight failed. He succeeded his father to the earldom of Guilford two years before his death. See biography by A. C. Valentine (2 vol., 1967); C. R. Ritcheson, *British Politics and the American Revolution* (1954).

North, Roger, 1653-1734, English biographer. A lawyer, he wrote excellent biographies of his brothers: Francis North, Lord Guilford, Keeper of the Great Seal (1742); Dudley North, a merchant (1744); and John North, master of Trinity College, Cambridge (1744). He is also noted for his *Autobiography* (1887).

North, Sir Thomas, 1535?-1601?, English translator. He is famous for his translation of Plutarch, entitled *Lives of the Noble Grecians and Romans* (1579), which he made from the French of Jacques Amyot. This work, ornate but vivid, was a source for many of Shakespeare's plays, among them *Antony and Cleopatra* and *Julius Caesar,* and was a major influence in the development of Elizabethan prose.

North Adams, city (1970 pop. 19,195), Berkshire co., NW Mass., in the Berkshire Hills, on the Hoosic River near the Vt. border; settled c.1737, set off from Adams and inc. 1878. It is a commercial and industrial center in a summer resort and winter ski area. Manufactures include electronic and electrical components, paper products, and chemicals.

North Africa, campaigns in. Italy's entrance into World War II (June 10, 1940) made N Africa an active theater in which control of the Suez Canal and the Mediterranean Sea was contested. Active fighting began with the rapid Italian occupation of British Somaliland in Aug., 1940. The desert war in the north started in September and for more than two years thereafter seesawed between NE Libya and NW Egypt. The almost uniformly level terrain along the coast allowed tanks and aircraft to play dominant roles. Temporary success was always won by the side that first was able to build up air and armored strength, but for a long time neither side could achieve decisive victory. The first of three Axis drives into Egypt was launched (Sept. 12, 1940) from Libya by Marshal Rodolfo Graziani's Italian forces. By Sept. 17 the Italian drive reached Sidi Barani (c.60 mi/97 km inside Egypt) and then stalled. On Dec. 9, 1940, the British under Gen. Archibald P. Wavell began a surprise counterattack with numerically inferior forces and chased Graziani c.500 mi (805 km) along the coast of Cyrenaica to El Agheila (Feb. 8, 1941). The collapse of the Italian army forced Germany to reinforce its ally with the Afrika Korps under Gen. Erwin Rommel. The British had cut their strength to send troops to Greece, and in April Rommel was able to drive them back to the border of Egypt. The Australian garrison at TOBRUK in Libya managed to hold out. Gen. Claude Auchinleck replaced Wavell. With the new British 8th Army, he attacked and pushed Rommel back to El Agheila (Jan., 1942). A German counterattack forced the British once again to abandon Bengasi. Auchinleck set up a defense line at El Gazala, N of Bir Hacheim, c.100 mi (160 km) within Libya. Rommel moved against this line on May 26, 1942. At Knightsbridge (June 13), the British lost 230 out of 300 tanks. Auchinleck retreated c.250 mi (400 km) into Egypt where he dug in along a 35-mi (56-km) line from El Alamein on the coast to the Qattara Depression (an impassable badland), only c.70 mi (112 km) from Alexandria. This time, Tobruk fell on June 21. Both sides now raced to build up strength. Gen. Sir Harold Alexander replaced Auchinleck, and Gen. Bernard L. Montgomery took direct command of the 8th Army. Rommel's attempt to break through failed. On Oct. 23, 1942, the greatly reinforced British forces launched their own offensive (for an account of the fighting, see ALAMEIN). To save his forces Rommel began one of the longest sustained retreats in history. Frustrating British attempts to engage him, he abandoned Tripoli, which fell to the British on Jan. 23, 1943. Rommel ended his retreat only when he took up a defensive position along the Mareth Line in S Tunisia. Meanwhile, American and British forces landed (night of Nov. 7-8, 1942) at Algiers, Oran, and Casablanca, thus occupying the territory to the west of Rommel. Under the command of Gen. Dwight D. Eisenhower, Allied forces pushed toward Tunisia. The Germans, however, rushed reinforcements from Italy. Axis forces in Tunisia now faced the British 8th Army in the south, Eisenhower's force on the west, and the Free French in the southwest; but the hilly terrain favored the defense. German counterattacks in Tunisia pushed west through Faid Pass (Feb. 14, 1943) and KASSERINE PASS (a week later), from which they were dislodged only after heavy fighting. In the south the Allies forced Rommel from the Mareth Line and moved up the coast to take Sousse in April. At the beginning of May, the Axis defense crumbled, and on May 7, 1943, the Americans took Bizerta and the British took Tunis. About a quarter of a million Axis soldiers capitulated on May 12. In E Africa the fighting had earlier resulted in complete British victory; by 1942, Italian and British Somaliland, Eritrea, and Ethiopia were reconquered. See John Strawson, *Battle for North Africa* (1969).

North America, third largest continent (1971 est. pop. 327,000,000), c.9,400,000 sq mi (24,346,000 sq km), the northern of the two continents of the Western Hemisphere. North America is usually considered to include all of the mainland and related offshore islands lying N of the Isthmus of Panama (which connects it with South America); however, other definitions exclude CENTRAL AMERICA (1971 est. pop. 19,000,000), 202,200 sq mi (523,698 sq km) and the Caribbean islands (1971 est. pop. 26,000,000), c.91,000 sq mi (235,690 sq km). The term "Anglo-America" is frequently used in reference to CANADA and the UNITED STATES combined, while the term "Middle America" is used to describe the region including MEXICO and the republics of Central America. GREENLAND, the French islands of St. Pierre and Miquelon (off Canada), and Hawaii (formerly considered part of Oceania) are categorized as parts of North America. The continent is bounded on the north by the Arctic Ocean, on the west by the Pacific Ocean and the Bering Sea, and on the east by the Atlantic Ocean, the Gulf of Mexico, and the Caribbean Sea. Its coastline is long and irregular. Hudson Bay is by far the largest body of water indenting the continent; others include the Gulf of St. Lawrence and the Gulf of California. There are numerous islands off the continent's coasts; the Arctic Ar-

chipelago, the West Indies, the Alexander Archipelago, and the Aleutian Islands are the principal groups. Mt. McKinley (20,320 ft/6,194 m), Alaska, is the highest point on the continent; the lowest point (282 ft/86 m below sea level) is in Death Valley, Calif. The Red Rock-Missouri-Mississippi river system (c.3,740 mi/6,020 km long) is the longest of North America. Together with the Ohio River and numerous other tributaries, it drains most of S central North America and forms the world's greatest inland waterway system. Other major rivers include the Colorado, Columbia, Delaware, Mackenzie, Nelson, Rio Grande, St. Lawrence, Susquehanna, and Yukon. Lake Superior (31,820 sq mi/82,414 sq km), the westernmost of the GREAT LAKES, is the continent's largest lake. The SAINT LAWRENCE SEAWAY, which utilizes the St. Lawrence River and the Great Lakes, enables ocean-going vessels to penetrate into the heart of North America. Physiographically, the Anglo-American section of the continent may be divided into five major regions: the CANADIAN SHIELD, a geologically stable area of ancient rock that occupies most of the northeastern quadrant, including Greenland; the APPALACHIAN MTS., a geologically old and eroded system that extends from Newfoundland to Alabama; the Coastal Plain, a belt of lowlands widening to the south that extends from S New England to Mexico; the Central Plains, which extend down the middle of the continent from the Mackenzie valley to the Gulf Coastal Plain and include the Great Plains on the west and the agriculturally productive Central Lowland on the east; and the North American Cordillera, a complex belt of geologically young mountains and associated plateaus and basins, which extend from Alaska into Mexico and include two orogenic belts—the PACIFIC MARGIN on the west and the ROCKY MTS. on the east—separated by a system of intermontane plateaus and basins. The Coastal Plain and the main belts of the North American Cordillera continue south into Mexico (where the Mexican Plateau, bordered by the Sierra Madre Oriental and the Sierra Madre Occidental, is considered a continuation of the intermontane system) to join the Transverse Volcanic Range, a zone of high and active volcanic peaks S of Mexico City. There the predominantly north-south structural lines of Anglo-America and N Mexico and the predominantly east-west structural lines of Central and Caribbean America come together. North America, extending to within 10° of latitude of both the Equator and the North Pole, embraces every climatic zone, from tropical rainforest and savanna on the lowlands of Central America to areas of permanent ice cap in central Greenland. Subarctic and tundra climates prevail in N Canada and N Alaska, and desert and semiarid conditions are found in interior regions cut off by high mountains from rain-bearing westerly winds. However, a high proportion of the continent has temperate climates very favorable to settlement and agriculture. During the Ice Age of the Pleistocene epoch, a continental ice sheet, centered on Hudson Bay (the floor of which is slowly rebounding after being depressed by the great weight of the ice), covered most of N North America; glaciers descended the slopes of the Rocky Mts. and those of the Pacific Margin. Extensive glacial lakes, such as BONNEVILLE, LAHONTAN, AGASSIZ, and Algonquin, were formed by glacial meltwater; their remnants are still visible in the GREAT BASIN and along the edge of the Canadian Shield in the form of the GREAT SALT LAKE, the Great Lakes, and the large lakes of W central Canada. The first human inhabitants of North America were of Asian origin; they crossed over to Alaska from NE Asia more than 48,000 years ago, moved southward along the Pacific coast, and then eastward. European discovery and settlement of North America dates from the 10th cent., when Norsemen settled (986) in Greenland. Although evidence is fragmentary, they probably reached E Canada c.1000 at the latest. Of greater impact on the subsequent history of the continent were Christopher Columbus's discovery of the Bahamas in 1492 and later landings in the West Indies and Central America, and John Cabot's explorations of E Canada (1497), which established English claims to the continent. Spanish and French expeditions also explored much of North America. Today, the population of Canada and the United States is largely of European and African origin and is highly urbanized (about 74% live in urban areas); much of the population is centered in large conurbations and coalescing urban belts along the southern margin of Canada and in the northeastern quadrant of the United States around the Great Lakes and along the Atlantic coast. Mexico's population, about 60% mestizo (of mixed European and Indian origin), is moderately urbanized (about 59%) and clusters around Mexico City. People of European descent are a minority in most Central American and Caribbean countries, and the population outside the capital cities is largely rural. The largest urban agglomerations on the continent are New York City, Mexico City, Los Angeles, and Chicago. North America's extensive agricultural lands (especially in Canada and the United States) are a result of the interrelationship of favorable climatic conditions, fertile soils, and technology. Irrigation has turned arid and semiarid regions into fertile oases. North America produces most of the world's corn, meat, cotton, soybeans, tobacco, and wheat, along with a variety of other food and industrial raw material crops. Mineral resources are also abundant; the large variety includes coal, iron ore, bauxite, copper, natural gas, petroleum, mercury, nickel, potash, and silver. Much of North America's great hydroelectric potential is being developed; many of the world's largest hydroelectric power plants are located in North America. The factories of North America provide an abundance of basic and manufactured products that provide a high standard of living for the people of Canada and the United States. See R. C. West and J. P. Augelli, *Middle America: Its Lands and Peoples* (1966); T. H. Clark and C. W. Stearn, *The Geological Evolution of North America* (1968); J. W. Watson, *North America: Its Countries and Regions* (2d ed. 1968); O. P. Starkey and J. L. Robinson, *The Anglo-American Realm* (1969); J. H. Paterson, *North America: A Geography of Canada and the United States* (4th ed. 1970); W. P. Cumming et al., *The Discovery of North America* (1972).

North American Indian art, diverse traditional arts of native North Americans. These arts were a significant part of the everyday lives of their creators. In each region at least one art form seems to have been developed especially well in response to the environment, the ideology and way of life, the availability of materials, and contact with other groups with whom particularly valued items could be traded. In all regions animal skins were worked, and stone provided the basic tools, including arrowheads, spear points, knives, and axes. Ritual surrounded the making of much of the art. The later Indian cultures of the Eastern Woodlands (such as the Seneca, Cherokee, and Iroquois) practiced agriculture, along with hunting, fishing, and gathering of wild foods. They made pottery and baskets, quill- and beadwork, birch-bark utensils, and particularly fine plaited sashes. The Seneca excelled at carved wood ritual masks. The mainstay of life for the Indians of the Plains (such as the Blackfoot, Crow, and Sioux) was the buffalo, whose skin, both rawhide and tanned, was used for clothing, containers, tepee covers, and shields. These were often painted or decorated with beads and porcupine-quill embroidery. Featherwork, of which the familiar "war bonnet" is a prime example, was lavish. The peoples of the Subarctic region (including the Northern Athabascan region) subsisted by hunting, fishing, and gathering. They made beaded skin garments as well as bark containers and canoes. The Eskimo of the Arctic survived in virtual isolation by hunting and fishing; their skin and fur garments were elaborately tailored. They carved fine sculptures of Arctic animal life (including seals, walruses, and polar bears) and hunting motifs, using stone, ivory, and bone, and their ceremonial masks were particularly sensitive. The subjects of their work were chosen from their extensive mythology as well as their everyday experience. On the Northwest Coast, where salmon fishing provided the main source of food, the Indians (Tlingit, Haida, Kwakiutl) lived in settled villages. These groups developed elaborate woodcarving techniques used to fabricate houses, huge dugout canoes, totem poles and other heraldic and ritual posts, as well as outstanding masks, bowls, and ladles. Human and animal figures were stylized to abstraction in this work. In addition, they made superb basketry and clothing by twining, and metalwork weapons and jewelry. The Canadian Indians of the Subarctic (e.g., Cree, Beaver, Sekani, Yellowknife) were fishermen and hunters and lived much like the groups of the Northwest Coast. They made tools of birch bark and wood and decorated their clothing, canoes, and dwellings (tepees and movable bark houses) with designs worked in paint, quills, and moosehair. California, Great Basin, and Plateau groups (Pomo, Nez-Percé, Paiute), who settled in villages, lived by gathering, hunting, and some fishing. They developed basketry, especially in N and Central California, as a highly refined art. Using a great variety of materials these Indians created a large number of basketry forms and techniques to make such items as baby carriers, collecting and winnowing baskets, fish weirs, and hats. As cooking and serving containers, the baskets were watertight. They also fashioned ceremonial and "gift" baskets imbued with religious significance. Featherwork was much used for headdresses, capes, skirts, and mantles, in dance costumes, and as decoration, together with beads, on baskets. In the Southwest the Indians generally practiced agriculture and lived in settled villages. Here pottery making, particularly of jars and bowls, is still a highly developed art with a rich tradition extending back to pre-Columbian times. An art of strong, graphic, geometric design developed for pottery decoration. In this region cotton was cultivated to be spun into yarn, and a backstrap loom with heddles was used prior to European contact. The Spaniards brought sheep which the Navaho adopted and whose wool they began to use in weaving, developing rugs and blankets that are in great demand today. Many designs for blankets were adapted from the ritual sand-painting art at which the Navahos excelled. The Hopi and Zuñi developed the brilliantly carved and ornamented kachina dolls to represent living spirits. These are greatly valued by collectors. After the Spanish conquest, silverworking evolved among the Southwestern Pueblo groups, especially among the Navaho, Zuñi, and Hopi, who perfected it to the level of fine art, largely as jewelry. Art for its own sake was apparently of little concern to most tribes. Standards of beauty were usually based on traditional notions, not on innovation or experimentation away from the cultural norm. One of the remarkable aspects of North American Indian art is the cleverness with which a variety of materials were combined to create a single object. The time, labor, and patience required to prepare many of their artifacts is of a magnitude that is difficult for modern man to conceive. That beyond the most basic preparation of materials there was also a desire to decorate beautifully bespeaks man's needs beyond the utilitarian. In recent years the works of the ever-diminishing number of North American Indian craftsmen have come greatly into vogue, commanding ever-higher prices. Among the most sought-after articles are works of jewelry, Eskimo sculpture, textiles of the Southwestern groups, kachina dolls, and beaded work. Museums with major collections of North American Indian art include: American Museum of Natural History, New York City; Field Museum of Natural History, Chicago; Milwaukee Public Museum, Milwaukee; Museum of the American Indian, New York City; National Museum of Canada, Ottawa; Peabody Museum of Archaeology and Ethnology, Harvard University, Cambridge; Portland Art Museum, Portland (Ore.); Provincial Museum, Victoria, British Columbia; Robert H. Lowie Museum of Anthropology, University of California, Berkeley; Southwest Museum, Los Angeles; U.S. National Museum, Smithsonian Institution, Washington, D.C. See Miguel Covarrubias, *The Eagle, the Jaguar, and the Serpent* (1954); Erna Siebert, *North American Indian Art* (tr. 1967); Frederick Dockstader, *Indian Art in America* (3d ed. 1968); C. L. Tanner, *Southwest Indian Craft Arts* (1968); O. T. Mason, *Aboriginal Indian Basketry* (1970); A. H. Whiteford, *North American Indian Arts* (1970).

North American Indian music. The music of the North American Indians is primarily a vocal art, usually choral, although some tribes favor solo singing. Indian music is entirely melodic; there is no harmony and no polyphony, although there is occasional antiphonal singing between soloist and chorus. Indian melody is, in general, characterized by a descending melodic figure; its rhythm is irregular. Not only is there no conception of absolute pitch, but intonation is uncertain. This uncertainty is the result of the Indian's distinctive method of voice production, involving muscular tension in the vocal apparatus and making possible frequent strong accents and glissandos. Singing is nearly always accompanied, at least by drums. Drums and rattles are the chief percussion instruments and are of various types. The wind instruments are mainly flutes and whistles. For the Indian, song is the chief means of communicating with the supernatural powers, and music is seldom performed for its own sake; definite results, such as the bringing of rain, success in battle, or the curing of the sick, are expected from music. There are three classes of songs—traditional songs, which are handed down from generation to generation; ceremonial and medicine songs; and modern songs, which show the influence of European culture. Songs of the second group are supposed to have been received by their owners in dreams. Songs of heroes are often old songs, adapted to the occasion with the insertion of the new hero's name. The love songs often associated with Indian music are influenced by the music of the white man and are regarded as degenerate by many Indians. See NORTH AMERICAN INDIAN ART; NORTH AMERICAN INDIAN LANGUAGES. See Frances Densmore, *The American Indians and Their Music* (rev. ed. 1936); Charles Kaywood, *A Bibliography of North American Folklore and Folksong* (1951); Charles Hofman, *American Indians Sing* (1967); and many books by Frances Densmore on music of individual tribes (most repr. 1972).

North American Nebula, bright diffuse nebula in the northern constellation Cygnus about 1000 light-years away; cataloged as NGC 7000. It has a configuration resembling parts of Canada and the United States, including the Gulf of Mexico, Mexico, and Central America.

Northampton, Henry Howard, earl of (nôrthămp'tən), 1540-1614, English courtier; son of the poet, Henry Howard, earl of Surrey; member of the powerful HOWARD family. His public career under Elizabeth I was marked by a charge of intrigue with Mary Queen of Scots and imprisonment (1583-85) for suspected heresy and treason. He attached himself to Robert Devereux, 2d earl of Essex, at the height of that nobleman's ascendancy, as well as to Essex's enemy, Robert Cecil (later earl of Salisbury). James I made Howard a privy councilor (1603), earl of Northampton (1604), and lord privy seal (1608). He became (1612) the king's principal minister on Salisbury's death. He supported the divorce of his grandniece, Frances Howard, from the 3d earl of Essex, and was responsible for the imprisonment of Sir Thomas OVERBURY, although presumably not for his murder.

Northampton, county borough (1971 pop. 126,608), county town of Northamptonshire, central England, on the Nene River. Shoemaking has long been the chief industry; engineering is second (roller bearings, earth-moving equipment, and motor vehicle components). Northampton was an important settlement of the Angles and of the Danes, and its Norman castle was the scene of parliaments from the 12th to the 14th cent. and of many sieges. In 1460, Henry VI was defeated by the Yorkists in Northampton (see ROSES, WARS OF THE). In 1675 much of the town was destroyed by fire. There are Roman and ancient British remains in the vicinity. The Church of St. Giles has a Norman doorway; All Saints' has a 14th-century tower; St. Peter's (12th cent.) has a Norman interior; and there is a Roman Catholic cathedral designed by Pujin. The 12th-century St. Sepulchre's is one of the four round churches in England. St. John's Hospital was founded in 1138. One of the few remaining Eleanor Crosses (see ELEANOR OF CASTILE) is near Northampton, at Hardingstone.

Northampton (nôrth″hămp'tən, nôr″thămp'tən), city (1970 pop. 29,664), seat of Hampshire co., W Mass., on the Connecticut River; inc. as a town 1656, as a city 1883. Cutlery, brushes, dinnerware, wire, optical devices, plastic products, and caskets are made in Northampton. It is the seat of Smith College and has a junior college, Clarke School for the Deaf, a veterans hospital, and a state mental hospital. Calvin Coolidge lived in Northampton and was mayor of the city. His papers and mementos are preserved in the Forbes Library. Jonathan Edwards was pastor there, and Dr. Sylvester Graham lived and is buried in the city. Historic Deerfield, the home of Deerfield Academy and the site of many old homes, is nearby. A wildlife sanctuary is also in the area.

Northamptonshire (nôrthămp'tənshĭr) or **Northants** (nôrth-hănts'), county (1971 pop. 467,843), 914 sq mi (2,367 sq km), central England. The county town is NORTHAMPTON. The county is undulating agricultural country, devoted to pasture and forests. The principal river is the Nene. A large ironstone field underlies the north central part of the county. Corby has iron and steel works. Northampton has long been a center of boot and shoe manufacture. Ermine Street and Watling Street, Roman roads, crossed the county. In Anglo-Saxon times the area was part of the kingdom of MERCIA and was probably organized as a shire in Danish times. In 1974, Northamptonshire was reorganized as a nonmetropolitan county.

North Andover (ăn'dōvər), town (1970 pop. 16,284), Essex co., NE Mass., on the Merrimack River, in a dairy and farm area; settled c.1644, set off from Andover and inc. 1855. A former textile town, its manufactures include telephone equipment, chemicals, plastics, and textile machinery. It is the seat of Merrimack College, Brooks Preparatory School, and a Boston Univ. theology center. Samuel Phillips and Anne and Simon Bradstreet lived there. The beautiful spring-fed Lake Cochichewick is nearby.

Northants, England: see NORTHAMPTONSHIRE.

North Arlington, borough (1970 pop. 18,096), Bergen co., NE N.J., a residential and industrial suburb of Newark, on the Passaic River; settled 1700s, inc. 1896.

North Atlantic Drift, warm ocean current in the northern part of the Atlantic Ocean. It is a continuation of the GULF STREAM, the merging point being at lat. 40°N and long. 60°W. Off the British Isles it splits into two branches, one going south as the Canary Current and the other going north along the coast of W and N Europe, where it exerts considerable influence upon the climate as far as the north coast of W USSR.

North Atlantic Treaty Organization (NATO), established under the North Atlantic Treaty, signed in Washington, D.C., on April 4, 1949, by the foreign ministers of Belgium, Canada, Denmark, France, Great Britain, Iceland, Italy, Luxembourg, the Netherlands, Norway, Portugal, and the United States. Greece and Turkey entered the alliance in 1952, and West Germany (the Federal Republic of Germany) entered in 1955. NATO maintains headquarters in Brussels, Belgium. The treaty, one of the major Western countermeasures in the COLD WAR against the threat of aggression by the Soviet Union, was aimed at safeguarding the freedom of the Atlantic community. Considering an armed attack on any member an attack against them all, the treaty provided for collective self-defense in accordance with Article 51 of the United Nations Charter. The treaty was also designed to encourage political, economic, and social cooperation. The organization was reorganized and centralized in 1952. NATO's highest organ, the North Atlantic Council, may meet on several levels—heads of government, ministers, or permanent representatives. The council determines policy and supervises the work of the many civilian and military agencies of NATO. The chairman of the council is the secretary general of NATO. Under the North Atlantic Council is the Military Committee, which may meet at the level of chiefs of staff or of permanent representatives. Its executive agency, with headquarters in Washington, D.C., is composed of representatives of the chiefs of staff of all member countries except France, which withdrew (1966) from the Military Committee while remaining a member of the Council. Iceland is represented by a civilian because it has no military establishment. The strategic area covered by the North Atlantic Treaty is divided among three commands and a regional planning group. The European Command is under the Supreme Allied Commander Europe (SACEUR) and covers the area from the North Cape to the Mediterranean Sea and from the eastern border of Turkey to the Atlantic Ocean. SACEUR directs the NATO forces assigned to his command, prepares and coordinates plans for defense, and, in time of war, would control all land, sea, and air operations in the European Command. The Atlantic Command is headed by the Supreme Allied Commander Atlantic (SACLANT), with headquarters at Norfolk, Va.; it covers the area from the North Pole to the Tropic of Cancer and from the coast of North America to the coasts of Africa and Europe. There is also a Channel Command, responsible for covering the English Channel and the southern area of the North Sea. The Canada-United States Regional Planning Group coordinates the defense of North America with the overall operations of NATO. See Lord Hastings Ismay, *NATO: The First Five Years, 1949-1954* (1954); Paul Henri Spaak, *Why NATO?* (1959); André Beaufre, *NATO and Europe* (1966); James Huntley, *The NATO Story* (1969).

North Attleboro (ă'təlbərə), industrial town (1970 pop. 18,665), Bristol co., SE Mass., near the R.I. line; settled 1669, set off from Attleboro and inc. 1887. Jewelry has been made there since 1807. The Woodcock tavern dates from 1670. A fish hatchery is nearby.

North Augusta, city (1970 pop. 12,883), Aiken co., SW S.C., on the Savannah River opposite Augusta, Ga.; settled c.1860, inc. 1906. Located in a dairy-farming and poultry-raising region, it is mostly residential. Veneer, bricks and tiles, paper products, and textiles are manufactured there. Many local people are employed at the Atomic Energy Commission's nearby Savannah River Plant and in Augusta, Ga.

North Australia: see NORTHERN TERRITORY, Australia.

North Battleford, city (1971 pop. 12,698), W Sask., Canada, at the confluence of the North Saskatchewan and Battle rivers, opposite Battleford. It is the service and distributing center for NW Saskatchewan, with grain elevators, cold-storage plants, and tanneries.

North Bay, city (1971 pop. 49,187), SE Ont., Canada, on Lake Nipissing. It is the transportation and commercial center of lumbering and mining districts and an outfitting point for hunting and fishing parties. Mining equipment is manufactured there.

North Bellmore, uninc. town (1970 pop. 22,893), Nassau co., SE N.Y., on Long Island.

North Belmont, uninc. town (1970 pop. 10,759), Gaston co., S N.C., on the Catawba River.

North Borneo or **British North Borneo:** see SABAH, Malaysia.

North Brabant (brəbănt'), Dutch *Noordbrabant* (nōrt″brăbănt'), province (1971 pop. 1,819,400), c.1,920 sq mi (4,970 sq km), S Netherlands, bordering on Belgium in the south and on West Germany in the east. The capital is 's Hertogenbosch (Den Bosch); other cities include Tilburg, Eindhoven, and Breda. The province has fertile soil near the Maas (Meuse), which is its northern boundary, but elsewhere is made up mostly of sandy heathland. Wheat and sugar beets are grown, cattle are raised, and dairying is pursued. Among the chief manufactures of the province are textiles, motor vehicles, electrical appliances, shoes, and pharmaceuticals. The history of the province was that of Brabant (see BRABANT, DUCHY OF) until the late 16th cent., when the Dutch revolted against the harsh Spanish rule. As a result of the Spanish reconquest of the larger part of the duchy, Brabant was divided by the Peace of Westphalia (1648) between the Spanish (later Austrian) Netherlands and the United Provinces of the Netherlands. North Brabant, the smaller part occupied by the United Provinces, remained Catholic. It was administered by the United Provinces as a territory and was not granted a seat in the States-General. In 1795, North Brabant became a province of the Netherlands.

North Braddock, borough (1970 pop. 10,838), Allegheny co., W Pa., a suburb of Pittsburgh, on the Monongahela River; inc. 1897. Andrew Carnegie's first steel plant was built there in 1875. The borough was the site of Gen. Edward Braddock's defeat in the French and Indian War and of a mass meeting of farmers instituting the WHISKEY REBELLION.

North Branford, town (1970 pop. 10,778), New Haven co., S Conn., on the Branford River; settled c.1680, inc. 1831. A large traprock quarry is there, and there is some light industry.

Northbridge, town (1970 pop. 11,795), Worcester co., S Mass., on the Blackstone River; settled 1704, set off from Uxbridge and inc. 1772. It includes the textile-producing village of Whitinsville.

Northbrook, village (1970 pop. 27,297), Cook co., NE Ill., a suburb of Chicago; settled 1836. It was incorporated as Shermerville in 1901 and was reincorporated as Northbrook in 1923. It is largely residential, but has some industry and research laboratories and is an insurance center. Originally a farming community, Northbrook developed industry after the coming of a railroad in 1871. Botanical gardens and a forest preserve are just east of the village.

North Canadian, river, 760 mi (1,223 km) long, rising in NE N.Mex., and flowing SE through Okla. to join the Canadian River in the Eufaula reservoir, E Okla. Federal dams and reservoirs on the river and its tributary, Wolf Creek, are part of the Arkansas River basin project for flood control and other purposes.

North Canton, city (1970 pop. 15,228), Stark co., NE Ohio, a suburb of Canton; settled c.1815, inc. as a city 1961. Vacuum cleaners and industrial die castings are among the city's manufactures.

North Cape or **Nordkapp** (nōr'käp), promontory, rising steeply c.1,000 ft (300 m) from the Arctic Ocean, near but not at the north end of Magerøya island, Finnmark co., N Norway. Although Magerøya is separated by a narrow channel from the mainland, North Cape, at lat. 71° 10′ N, is considered to be the northernmost important point of the European continent. The northernmost point actually situated on the mainland is Cape Nordkyn. The North Cape is a traditional stop for tourist steamers.

North Carolina, state (1970 pop. 5,082,059), 52,586 sq mi (136,198 sq km), SE United States, one of the Thirteen Colonies. RALEIGH is the capital and the fourth largest city. The largest cities are CHARLOTTE, GREENSBORO, and WINSTON-SALEM. The state is bounded on the N by Virginia, on the E by the Atlantic Ocean, on the S by South Carolina and Georgia, and on the W by Tennessee. Serving as a buffer against the Atlantic is a long chain of islands, with constantly shifting sand dunes, from which project three famous capes—Hatteras, Lookout, and Fear. Between the islands and the shore line stretch the lagoons—Albemarle Sound and Pamlico Sound are the largest—that receive the Chowan, Roanoke, Tar, and Neuse rivers as well as Cape Fear River (WILMINGTON, the chief port, is at the head of its broad

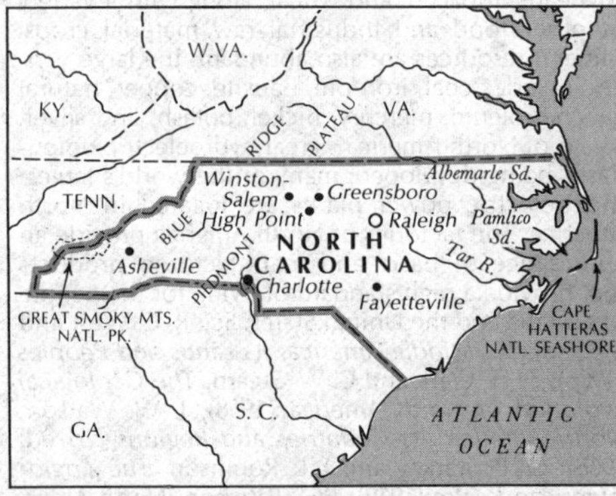

estuary). The mainland bordering the sounds is low, flat tidewater country, often swampy, even beyond the Dismal Swamp. In the upper coastal plain the land rises gradually from the tidewater level, reaching 500 ft (152 m) at the fall line. There begins the Piedmont, a rolling hill country with many swift streams such as the Broad River; the Catawba, or Wateree; and the Yadkin, or Pee Dee, with its three large dams. The hydroelectric power these rivers generate has made this a great manufacturing area, and the Piedmont supports most of the state's population and has its largest cities. At the western edge of the Piedmont the land rises abruptly in the Blue Ridge, then dips down to several basins, and rises again in the Great Smoky Mts. ASHEVILLE is the metropolis of this mountain region, with Mt. Mitchell (6,684 ft/2,037 m) the highest peak E of the Mississippi River. The French Broad River, the Watauga, and other rivers rising W of the Blue Ridge flow into the Mississippi system, almost all via the Tennessee River. North Carolina, in the warm temperate zone, has a mild, generally uniform climate, and the rainfall is abundant and well distributed. The state leads the nation in the production of tobacco, textiles, and furniture. It grows 40% of all U.S. tobacco, and while this accounts for most of its agricultural income, the continuing trend has been toward diversification. Broilers (North Carolina ranks fourth in their production), dairy items, corn, soybeans, peanuts, hogs, and eggs are also important. Plentiful forests supply the thriving furniture and lumber industries. North Carolina has long been a major textile manufacturer, producing cotton, knit, synthetic, and silk goods. Other leading manufactures are electrical machinery and chemicals. The state also has mineral resources: it leads the nation in the production of feldspar, mica, and lithium materials; is second in olivine and crushed granite, third in talc, and fourth in asbestos, clays, and phosphate rock. There are valuable coastal fisheries, with shrimp, menhaden, and crabs the principal catches. North Carolina's congenial climate, its many miles of beaches, and its spectacularly beautiful mountains, attract large numbers of visitors and vacationers each year. Chief among the tourist attractions are the Cape Hatteras National Seashore, the Cape Lookout National Seashore, the Blue Ridge Parkway, and the Great Smoky Mts. National Park. Wildlife abounds in the national forests (the state has four) and in the Dismal Swamp. Places of historic interest include Fort Raleigh National Historic Site, on Roanoke Island; the Wright Brothers National Memorial, at Kitty Hawk; Carl Sandburg Home National Historic Site, at Flatrock; and Guilford Courthouse and Moores Creek national military parks. One of the largest military reservations in the nation is at Fort Bragg, near Fayetteville, and the huge U.S. Marine Corps amphibious training base is at Camp Lejeune, near the mouth of the New River. North Carolina's treacherous coast was explored by Verrazano in 1524, and possibly by some Spanish navigators. In the 1580s, Sir Walter Raleigh attempted unsuccessfully to establish a colony on one of the islands (see ROANOKE ISLAND). The first permanent settlements were made (c.1653) around Albemarle Sound by colonials from Virginia. Meanwhile, Charles I of England had granted (1629) the territory S of Virginia between the 36th and 31st parallels (named Carolina in the king's honor) to Sir Robert Heath. Heath did not exploit his grant, and it was declared void in 1663. Charles II reassigned the territory to eight court favorites, who became the "true and absolute Lords Proprietors" of Carolina. In 1664, Sir William Berkeley, governor of Virginia and one of the proprietors, appointed a governor for the province, which after 1691 was known as North Carolina. Deputy governors, appointed from Charleston, S.C., ruled North Carolina from 1691 to 1711. Their failure to provide a stable and efficient government severely retarded the growth of the colony. By 1700 there were only some 4,000 people, predominantly of English stock, along Albemarle Sound. There, with the help of indentured servants and Negro and Indian slaves, they raised tobacco, corn, and livestock, mostly on small farms. Naval stores were the chief manufacture. The people were semi-isolated; only vessels of light draft could negotiate the narrow and shallow passages through the island barriers, and communication by land was almost impossible, except with Virginia, and even then swamps and forests made it difficult. There was, however, some trade (not only with Virginia but also with New England and Bermuda), and by 1711, when North Carolina was made a separate colony with its own governor, there were three towns—Bath, Edenton, and New Bern. The destructive war with the Tuscarora Indians broke out that year. The Tuscarora were defeated, and in 1714 the remnants of the tribe moved north to join the Iroquois Confederacy. A long, bitter boundary dispute with Virginia was partially settled in 1728 when a joint commission ran the boundary line 240 mi (386 km) inland. One of the Virginia commissioners, William Byrd, a cultured but prejudiced gentleman, remarked in his *History of the Dividing Line* that North Carolinians were quarrelsome and lazy. Although Anglicanism had been made the state religion in 1715, visiting clergymen also deplored the irreligious, unrestrained character of the people, always ready to oppose proprietary demands, few as they were. When the British government became dissatisfied with the work of the proprietors, North Carolina was made (1729) a royal colony. Thereafter the region developed more rapidly. The Indians were gradually pushed back over the Appalachians as the Piedmont was increasingly occupied. Germans and Scotch-Irish followed the valleys down from Pennsylvania, and Highland Scots settled along the Cape Fear River. These varied racial elements, in addition to smaller groups of Swiss, French, and Welsh who had migrated to the region earlier in the century, gradually amalgamated. There has been little foreign immigration since colonial days, and North Carolina's white population is now largely homogeneous. In 1768 the back-country farmers, justifiably enraged by the excessive taxes imposed by a legislature dominated by the eastern aristocracy, organized the REGULATOR MOVEMENT in an attempt to effect reforms. The insurgents were suppressed at Alamance in 1771 by the provincial militia led by Gov. William Tryon, who executed seven of the Regulators. After the outbreak of the American Revolution, royal authority collapsed. A provisional government was set up, the disputed MECKLENBURG DECLARATION OF INDEPENDENCE was allegedly promulgated (May, 1775), and the provincial congress instructed (April 12, 1776) the colony's delegates to the Continental Congress to support complete independence from Britain. Most Loyalists, including Highland Scots, fled North Carolina after their defeat (Feb. 27, 1776) at the battle of Moores Creek Bridge near Wilmington. The British, however, did not give up hope of Tory assistance in the state until their failure in the CAROLINA CAMPAIGN (1780–81). The designation of North Carolinians as "Tar Heels" was said to have originated during that campaign when patriotic citizens poured tar into a stream across which Cornwallis's men retreated, and the British emerged with the substance sticking to their heels. Settlements had been established beyond the mountains before the Revolution (see WATAUGA ASSOCIATION and TRANSYLVANIA COMPANY) and were increased after the war. In 1784, North Carolina ceded its western lands to the United States, spurring the transmontane people to organize a new, short-lived government (see FRANKLIN, STATE OF). Within the year North Carolina repealed the act ceding the land; however, the cession was reenacted in 1789, and that territory became (1796) the state of Tennessee. North Carolina opposed a strong central government and did not ratify the Constitution until Nov., 1789, months after the new U.S. government had begun to function. Little social and economic progress was made under the state's undemocratic constitution (framed in 1776), which largely served the interests of the politically dominant, tidewater planter aristocracy, and North Carolina appeared to be on the verge of revolution. In 1835, however, the western part of the state, now its most populous section, finally succeeded in enacting a constitution that abolished the property and religious qualifications for voting and holding office (except for Jews) and provided for the popular election of governors. In the same year began the final forced removal of most of the CHEROKEE INDIANS; but to check the steady, voluntary migration of whites, internal improvements, especially the building of railroads and plank roads, were effected. The Public School Law (1839) inaugurated free education, and other important reforms were instituted. The period of progress continued until the Civil War. Few North Carolinians held Negro slaves, and considerable antislavery sentiment existed until the 1830s, when the organized agitation of Northern abolitionists began, provoking a defensive reaction that North Carolinians shared with most Southerners. Yet it was a native of the state, Hinton Rowan Helper, who made the most notable southern contribution to antislavery literature. Not until President Lincoln's call for troops after the firing on Fort Sumter did the state secede and join (May, 1861) the Confederacy. The coast was ideal for blockade-running, and the last important Confederate port to fall (Jan., 1865) was Wilmington (see FORT FISHER). Gov. Zebulon B. Vance zealously defended the state's rights against what he considered encroachments by the Confederate government. Although many small engagements were fought on North Carolina soil, the state was not seriously invaded until almost the end of the war when Gen. William Sherman and his huge army moved north from Georgia. After engagements at Averasboro and Bentonville in March, 1865, Confederate Gen. J. E. Johnston surrendered (April 26, 1865) to Sherman near Durham; next to Lee's capitulation at Appomatox, it was the largest (and almost the last) surrender of the war. In May, 1865, President Johnson applied his plan of Reconstruction to the state. The radical Republicans in Congress, however, adopted their own scheme in 1867, and the Carolinas, organized as the second military district, were again occupied by Federal troops. The Reconstruction constitution of 1868 abolished slavery, removed all religious tests for holding office, and provided for the popular election of all state and county officials. In 1871 the legislature, with conservatives again in control, impeached and convicted Gov. William H. Holden. The often maligned period of Reconstruction actually saw the beginning of the modern state, with a tremendous rise in industry in the Piedmont. Increased use of tobacco in the Civil War stimulated the growth of tobacco manufacturing, first centered at Durham, and the introduction of the cigarette-making machine in the early 1880s was an immense boon to the industry, creating tobacco barons such as James B. Duke and R. J. Reynolds. Agriculture, however, was in a critical condition. The old plantation system was replaced by farm tenancy, which long remained the dominant system of holding land (in the early 1970s at least one quarter of the farms were still being operated by tenants). Much farm property was destroyed, credit was lacking, and transportation broke down. The nation-wide agrarian revolt reached North Carolina in the GRANGER MOVEMENT (1875), the Farmers' Alliance (1887), and the POPULIST PARTY, which united with the Republicans to carry the state elections in 1894 and 1896. However, the Fusionists were blamed for the rise of Negro control in many tidewater towns and counties, and in the election of 1898, when the Red Shirts, like the Ku Klux Klan of Reconstruction days, were active, the Democrats regained control. The turn of the century marked the beginning of a new progressive era, typified by the successful airplane experiments of the Wright Brothers near Kitty Hawk. The crusade for public education for both races led by Gov. Charles B. Aycock, elected in 1900, achieved wide results, and new interest was created in developing the state's agricultural and industrial resources. But one old pattern was strengthened when a suffrage amendment, the "grandfather clause" assuring white supremacy, was added (1900) to the state constitution. Since World War I the state government has increasingly followed a policy of consolidation and centralization, taking over the public school system and the supervision of county finance and roads. A huge highway development program, begun by the counties in 1921, was assumed by the state (1931) when the counties could no longer meet the costs. Expenditures for higher education were greatly increased, and the three major state educational institutions were merged into a greater Univ. of North Carolina. Industrialization burgeoned after World War II, and in the 1950s the value of manufactured goods surpassed that of agriculture for the first time. In that period, and especially in the administration of Gov. Luther H. Hodges, over $1 billion in new industry was established, making North Carolina the leading industrial state of the South. This industrialization continued during the 1960s and early 1970s, increasing at a rate unmatched by any other Southern state. North Carolina, more than many other Southern states, was able to make a peaceful adjustment to INTEGRATION in the public schools following the Supreme Court's desegregation ruling in 1954. North Carolina's first constitution was adopted in 1776. Its present constitution dates from 1868 but was thoroughly revised in 1875–76 as a result of Reconstruction experiences; it has been amended many times since. The state's executive branch is headed by a governor elected for a four-year term and not permitted immediate reelection. North Carolina's bicameral general assembly has a senate with 50 members and a house with 120 members, all elected for two-year terms. The state elects 2 Senators and 11 Representatives to the U.S. Congress and has 13 electoral votes. It has been strongly Democratic since Reconstruction times, but it bolted in 1928 to vote against Alfred E. Smith and again in 1968 and 1972 to vote for Richard M. Nixon; James Holshouser, Jr., a Republican, was elected governor in 1972. In addition to the Univ. of North Carolina, the state's notable institutions of higher learning include Duke Univ., at Durham; East Carolina Univ., at Greenville; Appalachian State Univ., at Boone; and Wake Forest Univ., at Winston-Salem. See Federal Writers' Project, *The North Carolina Guide*, ed. by B. P. Robinson (rev. ed. 1955); S. H. Hobbs, *North Carolina: An Economic and Social Profile* (1958); J. H. Wheeler, ed., *Historical Sketches of North Carolina from 1584 to 1851* (from original records, 1964); John Brickell, *The Natural History of North Carolina* (1737, repr. 1969); H. T. Lefler and A. R. Newsome, *North Carolina: The History of a Southern State* (3d ed. 1973); H. T. Lefler and W. S. Powell, *Colonial North Carolina: A History* (1973).

North Carolina, University of, mainly at Chapel Hill; state supported; coeducational; chartered 1789, opened 1795, the first state college to open as a university. In 1931 the North Carolina State College of Agriculture and Engineering (founded 1887, opened 1889) at Raleigh, the Woman's College of the Univ. of North Carolina (founded 1891, opened 1892) at Greensboro, and the Univ. of North Carolina at Chapel Hill were consolidated under the present name. The university also has campuses at Asheville, Charlotte, and Wilmington. A leading Southern university, it has a noted university press and institutes for research in folklore, the natural sciences, fisheries, statistics, and Latin American studies. There is a noteworthy art center and a planetarium, and the university library has an outstanding collection of North Caroliniana. See Archibald Henderson, *The Campus of the First State University* (1949); L. R. Wilson, *The University of North Carolina, 1900–1930* (1957); Phillips Russell, *These Old Stone Walls* (1972).

North Carolina Agricultural and Technical State University, at Greensboro; land-grant and state supported; coeducational; opened 1890, est. 1891.

North Cascades National Park: see NATIONAL PARKS AND MONUMENTS (table).

North Channel, strait, c.75 mi (120 km) long, between Northern Ireland and Scotland, connecting the Irish Sea with the Atlantic Ocean. It is 13 mi (21 km) across at its narrowest point.

North Chicago, industrial city (1970 pop. 47,275), Lake co., NE Ill.; inc. 1909. Its economy is closely intertwined with the neighboring city of Waukegan, which has a good harbor on Lake Michigan. Pharmaceuticals, chemicals, and iron, steel, and wood products are among the many manufactures. A sit-down strike at a steel plant there in 1937 led to a U.S. Supreme Court decision (1939) ruling sit-down strikes illegal. Adjacent to the city is the Great Lakes Naval Base.

North China Plain: see HUANG HO.

Northcliffe, Alfred Charles William Harmsworth, Viscount, 1865–1922, British journalist, b. Ireland. He was the one of the most spectacular of popular journalists and newspaper publishers in the history of the British press. Beginning his career as a free-lance contributor to popular periodicals, he launched in 1888 his first independent effort, *Answers to Correspondents,* a weekly of informative tidbits. With his brother Harold (later Viscount Rothermere) as his financial administrator, he increased the circulation of his magazine in five years to more than a million copies a week. Other publications were gradually acquired that formed the basis for what became the world's largest periodical combine, the Amalgamated Press. In 1894, Northcliffe bought the London *Evening News,* launching his career in newspaper publishing. Continuing to popularize, he inaugurated such specialties as woman's columns, serials, and social gossip in this and in later papers that he founded—the *Daily Mail* in 1896 and the *Daily Mirror* in 1903. He gained control of the dying *Times* in 1908, putting it back on its feet with changes in make-up and editorial policy; *The Times* was sold to Lord Astor after Northcliffe's death. His newspaper campaigns during World War I, particularly those concerning faulty munitions, national conscription, and food rationing, were determining factors in England's conduct of the war, and his support of Lloyd George in 1916 was instrumental in bringing the downfall of the Asquith government. He was made a viscount in 1917. See biographies by Reginald Pound and Geoffrey Harmsworth (1960) and H. H. Fyfe (1930, repr. 1969); Paul Ferris, *The House of Northcliffe* (1972).

North College Hill, city (1970 pop. 12,363), Hamilton co., SW Ohio, a suburb of Cincinnati; inc. as a city 1940. It is mostly residential. The Clovernook Home for the Blind there has a braille printing shop. North College Hill also has a Revolutionary War cemetery.

Northcote, James (nôrth'kət), 1746–1831, English historical and portrait painter. He worked as assistant to Reynolds and studied at the Royal Academy. From 1777 to 1780 he studied in Italy and on his return painted a series of pictures for Boydell's Shakespeare Gallery, including the well-known *Murder of the Princes in the Tower* (1791; now destroyed). Northcote was the author of biographies of Sir Joshua Reynolds (1813) and of Titian (1830).

North Dakota, state (1970 pop. 617,761), 70,665 sq mi (183,022 sq km), N central United States, admitted to the Union in 1889 simultaneously with South Dakota (they are the 39th and 40th states). BISMARCK, on the eastern bank of the Missouri River, is the capital; FARGO, GRAND FORKS, and MINOT are other large cities. North Dakota is bounded on the N by the Canadian provinces of Saskatchewan and Mani-

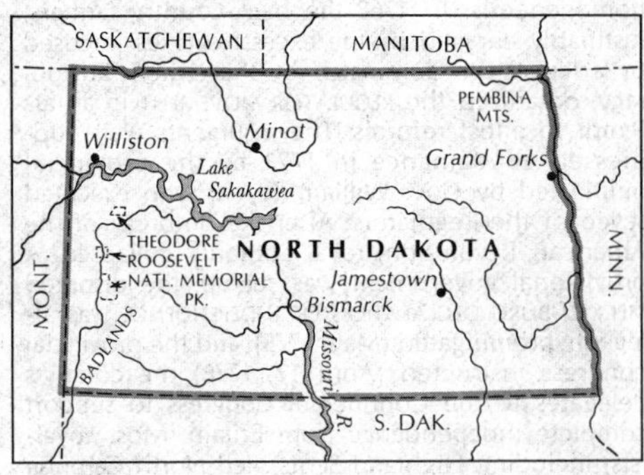

toba, on the E by the Red River, which separates it from Minnesota, on the S by South Dakota, and on the W by Montana. Situated in the geographical center of North America, North Dakota is subject to the extremes and vagaries of a continental climate. Semiarid conditions prevail in the western half of the state, but in the east an average annual rainfall of 22 in. (55 cm), much of it falling in the crop-growing months of spring and summer, enables the rich soil to yield abundantly. North Dakota is one of the most rural states in the nation (the 1970 census classified only 44.3% of its population as urban); the cities and towns supply the needs of neighboring farms, and industry is largely devoted to the processing of agricultural products. The eastern half of the state is in the central lowlands, a belt of black earth covered in spring by the soft green of quickly sprouting grain and later by the bronze of flowering wheat or the blue of flax. Along the banks of the Red River there is a wedge of land, c.40 mi (60 km) wide at the Canadian border and tapering to 10 mi (16 km) in the south, that is the floor of the former glacier Lake Agassiz. Treeless, except along the riversides, and without rocks, this flat land was transformed into the bonanza wheat fields of the 1870s and 80s, with farms ranging in size from 3,000 to 65,000 acres (1,200–26,000 hectares). Today the average farm in the Red River valley is about 450 acres (180 hectares; the state average is about 1,000 acres/400 hectares), and its major crop, wheat, is varied with such crops as flax and seed potatoes. To the west of the valley a series of escarpments rises some 300 ft (91 m) to meet the drift prairies, where rolling hills, scattered lakes, and occasional moraines form a pleasant and fertile countryside. The productivity of the soil makes North Dakota a leader in wheat, flaxseed, barley, rye, and oats. However, cattle and cattle products exceed all the crops except wheat in income earned. In the western part of the state a combination of unfavorable topography and scant rainfall precludes intensive cultivation except in the river valleys. An area some 50 mi (80 km) E of the Missouri River is a farm and grazing belt, divided from the drift prairies by the Missouri escarpment. Westward from the Missouri rolls an irregular plateau, covered with short prairie grasses and cut by deep coulees. Where wind and rain have eroded the hillsides there are unusual formations of sand and clay, glowing in yellows, reds, browns, and grays. Along the Little Missouri this section is called the Badlands, so named because the region (once described as "hell with the fires out") was difficult to traverse in early days. Situated there, where from 1883 to 1886 the young Theodore Roosevelt spent part of each year ranching, are the three units of the Theodore Roosevelt National Memorial Park. On the plateau cattle graze, finding shelter in the many ravines, and large ranges are an economic necessity; during the heavy snows only radio and television relieve the isolation of prairie life. In the northwestern area of the state oil was discovered in 1951, and petroleum is now North Dakota's leading mineral product, ahead of lignite, sand, and gravel. There are about 2,000 producing oil wells. Refineries are in Williston, Mandan, Dickinson, McGregor, and Tioga; there are also natural gas fields. Underlying the western counties are lignite reserves estimated at 350 billion tons, a large part of the nation's coal reserves. In close proximity to the lignite beds are fine deposits of clay of such varied types that they serve as both construction and pottery materials. Despite mineral production and some manufacturing, however, agriculture continues to be North Dakota's principal pursuit, and the processing of grain, meat, and dairy products is vital to such cities as Fargo, Grand Forks, Minot, and Bismarck. The Missouri and the Red River, once the major transportation routes, are more important now for their irrigation potential. Several dams have been built, notably Garrison Dam, and a number of Federal reclamation projects have been completed as part of the Missouri River basin project. There has also been reforestation. The first farmers in the region of whom there is definite knowledge were the Mandan Indians. They were found tilling the soil on the banks of the Missouri in 1738 by the French explorer Pierre de la Vérendrye. Other agricultural tribes were the Arikara and the Hidatsa. Seminomadic and nomadic tribes were the Cheyenne, Cree, Sioux, Assiniboin, Crow, and Ojibwa (Chippewa). Vérendrye's two sons, continuing their father's search for a westward route to India, revisited the area in 1742. Subsequent explorations were concerned with the fur trade. With the LOUISIANA PURCHASE of 1803 the northwestern half of North Dakota became part of the United States. The southeastern half was acquired from Great Britain in 1818 when the international line with Canada was fixed at the 49th parallel. Earlier the LEWIS AND CLARK EXPEDITION had wintered (1804–5) with the Mandan Indians, and the NORTH WEST COMPANY and the HUDSON'S BAY COMPANY had established trading posts in the Red River valley. These ventures introduced an industry that dominated the region for more than half a century. Within that era the buffalo vanished from the plains and the beaver from the rivers. From its post at Fort Union, established in 1828, John Jacob Astor's American Fur Company gradually gained monopolistic control for a time over the trade of the region. Supply and transport were greatly facilitated when a paddlewheel steamer, the *Yellowstone,* inaugurated steamboat travel on the turbulent upper Missouri in 1832. Additional transportation was provided by the supply caravans of Red River carts, which went westward across the Minnesota prairies and returned to the Mississippi loaded with valuable pelts. The first attempt at agricultural colonization was made at Pembina in 1812 by a group of settlers under the auspices of the earl of Selkirk (see RED RIVER SETTLEMENT), but the first permanent farming community was not established until 1851 when another group settled at Pembina. This was still the only farm settlement in the future state when Dakota Territory was organized in 1861 to include what eventually became present-day North Dakota, South Dakota, Montana, and Wyoming. Several military posts had been established starting in 1857 to protect travelers and railroad workers from Indians. Even when free land was opened in 1863 and the Northern Pacific RR was chartered in 1864 a preoccupation with the Civil War and the eruption of Indian discontent into open warfare prevented any appreciable settlement. Gen. Alfred H. Sully joined Gen. Henry H. Sibley of Minnesota in retributive campaigns against the Sioux Indians in 1863–66. A treaty was signed in 1868. In 1876, after gold was discovered on Indian land in the Black Hills, the unwillingness of the whites to respect treaty agreements led to further war with the Indians, and the force of George A. Custer was annihilated at the battle of the Little Bighorn in present-day Montana. Ultimately, however, the Sioux under Chief Sitting Bull fled to Canada, where they surrendered voluntarily; they were returned to reservations in the United States. The first cattle ranch in North Dakota was established in 1878. With the construction of railroads in the 1870s and 80s, thousands of European immigrants, principally Scandinavians, Germans, and Czechs, arrived. They worked the land on their own homesteads or on the large Eastern-financed bonanza wheat fields of the low central prairies. Borrowing the idea from Europe, they founded agricultural cooperatives. Local politics was rapidly reduced to a struggle between the agrarian groups and the corporate interests. Alexander McKenzie of the Northern Pacific was for many years the most important figure in the state. Republicans held the elective offices. Agrarian groups formed the Farmers' Alliance and in 1892, three years after North Dakota had achieved statehood, the Farmers' Alliance combined with the Democrats and Populists to elect Eli Shortridge, a Populist, as governor. Later, when the success of the La Follette Progressives in Wisconsin encouraged the growth of the Republican Progressive movement in North Dakota, a fusion with the Democrats elected "Honest John" Burke as governor for three terms (1906–12). Much of the agrarian discontent was focused on marketing practices of the large grain interests. Although many small cooperative grain elevators were established, they did not prove effective, and the farmers pressed for state-owned grain elevators. When this movement failed in the legislature of 1915, the NONPARTISAN LEAGUE, directed in North Dakota by Arthur C. Townley, was organized on a platform that included state ownership of terminal elevators and flour mills, state inspection of grain and grain dockage, relief of farm improvements from taxation, and rural credit banks operated at cost. Working primarily with the Republican party because it was the majority party in North Dakota, the league captured the state legislature in 1919 and proceeded to enact virtually its entire platform. This included the establishment of an industrial commission to manage state-owned enterprises and the creation of the Bank of North Dakota to handle public funds and provide low-cost rural credit. The right of recall was also enacted, by which voters could remove an elected official. The reforms were disappointing in operation. Dissension arose within the league, and the Independent Voters Association was organized to represent the conservative Republican position. The industrial commission was accused of maladministration, and the provision of recall was exercised three times, the first against Gov. L. J. Frazier in 1921. William Langer, who had been active with both the Nonpartisan League and the Independent Voters Association, was elected governor in 1932 running as a Nonpartisan. Langer was convicted on a Federal charge of misconduct in office in 1934, although the conviction was later reversed. Langer again became governor in 1936, running as an individual candidate and not on the ticket of either party; subsequently he was elected to the U.S. Senate four times. Although the majority of North Dakota's voters are Republican, the occasional alignment of a faction with other parties makes elections exciting and uncertain. In the 1960s, Democrats Quenton Burdick and William L. Guy were elected to the U.S. Senate and governorship, respectively. In 1973, Arthur A. Link, also a Democrat, became governor. The state is governed under the 1889 constitution. The legislature consists of 51 senators elected to four-year terms and 102 representatives elected to two-year terms. The governor is elected for a four-year term. North Dakota elects two U.S. Senators and one Representative; it has three electoral votes. With such attractions as the Badlands, the International Peace Garden on the Canadian border, and recreational facilities provided by reservoirs (resulting from dam building in the 1950s), tourism has become North Dakota's third-ranking source of income, behind agriculture and mineral production. The state's institutions of higher education include the Univ. of North Dakota, at Grand Forks; North Dakota State Univ. of Agriculture and Applied Science, at Fargo; Jamestown College, at Jamestown; and several other colleges and junior colleges. See Edna LaMoore Waldo, *Dakota: An Informal Study of Territorial Days* (2d ed. 1936); Federal Writers' Project, *North Dakota: A Guide to the North Prairie State* (1938, rev. ed. 1950); H. E. Briggs, *Frontiers of the Northwest* (1940); M. E. Kazeck, *North Dakota* (1956); E. B. Robinson, *History of North Dakota* (1966).

North Dakota, University of, at Grand Forks; state supported; coeducational; chartered 1883, opened 1884. It has a special program in fuel technology and conducts noted research in biochemistry and cancer. There is a two-year branch at Williston.

North Dakota State University of Agriculture and Applied Science, at Fargo; land-grant and state supported; coeducational; chartered and opened 1890 as North Dakota Agricultural College, renamed 1960. The agricultural experiment station center is there. The university has branches throughout the state, including an institute of forestry at Bottineau.

North Downs: see DOWNS, NORTH, chalk hills, England.

Northeast Boundary Dispute, controversy between the United States and Great Britain concerning the Maine–New Brunswick boundary. The treaty of 1783 ending the American Revolution had described the northeastern boundary of the United States as running due north from the source of the St. Croix River to the highlands dividing the St. Lawrence River tributaries and the Atlantic Ocean, and along those highlands to the northwesternmost head of the Connecticut River. Disputes over that definition lasted almost 60 years. The identity of the St. Croix was decided (1798) by a commission created by Jay's Treaty (1794). However, as no mountain range existed between the Atlantic and St. Lawrence systems, the question was submitted to arbitration, in accordance with the Treaty of Ghent (1814). The king of the Netherlands, as arbitrator, designated the St. John River as the boundary (1831), but this decision was not accepted by the United States. In 1839 the dispute led to the so-called AROOSTOOK WAR, a conflict between inhabitants of New Brunswick and Maine, which produced strained relations between the United States and Great Britain. The long-standing controversy was ended with the WEBSTER-ASHBURTON TREATY (1842), which set the boundary practically according to the line proposed by the king of the Netherlands, with the United States receiving the larger portion of the disputed area.

Northeastern University, at Boston, Mass.; coeducational; founded 1898. It is noted for its work-study programs. The university maintains research projects in business, science, social science, pharmacy, and engineering. There is a branch campus in Burlington.

North-East Frontier Agency, India: see ARUNACHAL PRADESH.

North East Land, island, Svalbard: see NORDAUSTLANDET.

Northeast Passage, water route along the northern coast of Europe and Asia, between the Atlantic and Pacific oceans. Beginning in the 15th cent., efforts were made to find a new all-water route to India and China. Most of these attempts were directed at seeking a NORTHWEST PASSAGE. However, English, Dutch, and Russian navigators did try to seek a northeast route by sailing along the northern coast of Russia and far into the arctic seas. In the 1550s, English ships made the first attempt to find the passage. Willem Barentz, the Dutch navigator, made several futile voyages in the 1590s, as did Henry Hudson in the early 17th cent. The decline of Dutch shipping in the 1700s left the exploration mainly to the Russians; among the men sent out was Vitus Bering, who explored the eastern part of the passage. The Russian Great Northern Expedition (1733–43) explored most of the coast of N Siberia. The Northeast Passage was not, however, traversed by anyone until Nils A. E. Nordenskjöld of Sweden accomplished the feat in 1878–79. In the early 1900s, icebreakers sailed through the passage, and in the 1930s the Northern Sea Route, a shipping lane, was established by the USSR. Since World War II the USSR has maintained a regular highway for shipping along this passage through the development of new ports and the exploitation of resources in the interior. A fleet of Soviet icebreakers, aided by aerial reconnaissance and by radio weather stations, keeps the route navigable from June to October. The Northern Sea Route cuts the distance between Soviet Atlantic and Pacific ports in half.

Northern Cross: see CYGNUS.

Northern Crown: see CORONA BOREALIS.

Northern Dvina: see DVINA (Northern Dvina).

Northern Expedition, in modern Chinese history, the military campaign by which the KUOMINTANG party overthrew the WARLORD-backed Peking government and established a new government at Nanking. At the outset of the campaign in July, 1926, the Kuomintang controlled only Kwangtung and Kwangsi provs. It was allied with the smaller Communist party and was receiving aid from the Soviet Union. Communist activists spread out across SE China, fomenting strikes and thereby weakening the enemy's rear. By March, 1927, the Kuomintang armies (swelled by the defection of intact enemy units) had pushed back the warlord armies of WU P'EI-FU and Sun Ch'uan-fang and had taken all of SE China including the economic centers of Wuhan and Shanghai. At this point, a struggle broke out between the right-wing Kuomintang commander in chief, CHIANG KAI-SHEK, and the left-wing-controlled provisional government at Wuhan under WANG CHING-WEI. Arguing that Communist activities were socially and economically disruptive and would slow the primary task of political unification under the Kuomintang, Chiang launched a purge of Communists. When he was stripped of command (April, 1927), Chiang formed a rival regime at Nanking. Finally, in July, 1927, the Wuhan government also broke with the Communists, and in Feb., 1928, the two factions reunited at Nanking under Chiang's leadership. The Kuomintang renewed the offensive against the remaining northern forces (notably the army of CHANG TSO-LIN) Peking was taken by the Kuomintang in June, 1928, and the national government was moved to Nanking. See Liu Chih-pu, *A Military History of Modern China, 1924–1949* (1956, repr. 1972); H. R. Isaacs, *The Tragedy of the Chinese Revolution* (2d rev. ed. 1966).

Northern Illinois University, mainly at De Kalb, Ill.; est. 1895 as a normal school, became (1921) Northern Illinois State Teachers College, gained university status in 1957. The Lorado Taft Field campus, near the city of Oregon, offers practical work in the life sciences.

Northern Ireland: see IRELAND, NORTHERN.

Northern Land: see SEVERNAYA ZEMLYA, USSR.

northern lights: see AURORA BOREALIS.

Northern Pacific Railway, American rail line, following the northern route from Duluth and St. Paul, Minn., to Seattle, Wash., and Portland, Oregon. It is now part of the Burlington Northern Railroad, one of the four major railways in the W United States. The Northern Pacific Railway Company was chartered by special act of Congress in 1864, and construction was begun in 1870. Jay Cooke at first managed the enterprise, but after the Panic of 1873 the railroad company went into bankruptcy. Under the leadership of Henry Billard, the Northern Pacific was opened in 1883 from Ashland, Wis., to Portland, Oregon. In 1901 there was a spectacular financial contest between the interests of E. H. Harriman and those of James HILL and J. P. Morgan for control of the Northern Pacific. The Hill-Morgan group secured control, but an agreement between the two groups resulted in the organization of the Northern Securities Company, a giant holding company that controlled the Northern Pacific, the Great Northern, and the Chicago, Burlington & Quincy. When the trust was dissolved (1904) as a violation of the Sherman Antitrust Act, the Hill-Morgan interests came into control of the Northern Pacific. In spite of the breakup of the Northern Securities Company, a proposal for a very similar merger was made by a consultant for the Interstate Commerce Commission in 1921. The plan was never acted upon, but 40 years later the Northern Pacific again asked for permission to merge with the Great Northern and the Burlington lines. Finally, in 1970 the Supreme Court approved the consolidation. The huge Burlington Northern Railroad has assets of nearly $3 billion and an estimated annual operating revenue of some $800 million. Its 25,000 mi (40,000 km) of track extend from the Pacific Northwest E to the Great Lakes and S to the Gulf of Mexico. In addition, the company owns or has mineral rights to 8.4 million acres (3.4 million hectares) of Western land.

Northern Rhodesia: see ZAMBIA.

Northern Sea Route, USSR: see NORTHEAST PASSAGE.

Northern Territory, territory (1970 est. pop. 71,400), 520,280 sq mi (1,347,525 sq km), N central Australia. It is bounded on the N by the Timor Sea, the Arafura Sea, and the Gulf of Carpentaria. DARWIN is the territorial capital. In the north are lowlands, in the southeast are low plains sloping toward the Lake Eyre depression, and in the southwest are the MacDonald Ranges. The main rivers are the Victoria, Daly, Adelaide, and Roper, all of which drain into the northern seas. The climate in the north is tropical, with a monsoon season; the south becomes colder and drier as the elevation rises. About three fourths of the population live in the Darwin and Alice Springs metropolitan areas. Some 20,000 aborigines live in Northern Territory on 15 reservations with a total area of 94,000 sq mi (243,460 sq km); the Arnhem Land preserve is the largest. The territory's economic development has been accelerating in recent years. Gold is worked to a very small extent; uranium, bauxite, manganese, iron, lead, and zinc deposits are increasingly exploited. Stockbreeding, encouraged by government development projects, is the major rural activity. There is very little farming in the territory. Peanuts, pearl shell, and trepang are the principal exports. Northern Territory's first settlement was established at Port Essington in 1824, in an attempt to forestall French colonization. The settlement failed, and permanent settlement did not resume until 1869. Northern Territory was part of New South Wales from 1825 to 1863 and of South Australia from 1863 to 1911. Transferred to direct rule by the commonwealth in 1911, it was divided into two territories in 1926 but was reunited in 1931. The territorial government consists of an administrator, appointed by the commonwealth, and an advisory council. Northern Territory elects a member with full voting rights to the commonwealth House of Representatives.

Northern War, 1700–1721, general European conflict, fought in N and E Europe at the same time that the War of the SPANISH SUCCESSION was fought in the west and the south. It arose chiefly from the desire of the neighbors of Sweden to break Swedish supremacy in the Baltic area, and from the conflicting ambitions of PETER I of Russia and CHARLES XII of Sweden. Many other interests were involved, however. Although there was no direct link between the Northern War and the War of the Spanish Succession, Sweden generally received the diplomatic support of France, and England supported Russia early in the war, but withdrew support later. The outbreak of the war was preceded by the alliance (1699) of Peter I, FREDERICK IV of Denmark, and AUGUSTUS II of Poland (who was also elector of Saxony) against Charles XII, whose youth and inexperience they hoped would make him an easy victim. The war began with the invasion of Swedish Livonia by the Poles and of ducal Schleswig (which had rebelled against Danish rule with Swedish support) by the Danes. The bold and unexpected landing of Charles XII in Zealand threatened Copenhagen and forced Denmark out of the war (1700). Charles then turned his attention to the east; late in 1700 he routed a much superior Russian force at Narva and relieved Riga, which the Poles were besieging. Invading Poland, Charles took Warsaw and Cracow (1702), secured the election of STANISLAUS I as king of Poland (1704), followed Augustus into Saxony, and forced him to break his alliance with Russia and to recognize Stanislaus as king by the Treaty of Altranstädt (1706). While Charles was victorious in Poland, however, Peter I occupied Ingermanland and part of Livonia. Resuming (1707) his campaign against Russia, Charles invaded the Ukraine, where MAZEPA had promised to foment an anti-Russian uprising. Mazepa's project failed, and the Swedes, cut off from reinforcements and in need of a stronghold, laid siege to the fortress of Poltava. There a superior Russian army utterly defeated (1709) the Swedes, and Charles with a handful of men retired to Bessarabia, on Turkish territory. His intrigues at Constantinople induced the sultan to declare war on Russia (1710). Peter I, allied with Prince Constantine BRANCOVAN of Walachia and Prince Demetrius Cantemir of Moldavia, invaded these two vassal principalities of Turkey and entered Jassy, but he soon found himself outnumbered and consented (1711) to the disadvantageous Treaty of the Pruth (see RUSSO-TURKISH WARS). While Charles was stubbornly refusing to leave Turkey, Augustus II took advantage of his plight; he invaded (1709) Poland and expelled Stanislaus I, while Peter I completed the conquest of Swedish Livonia, Ingermanland, and Karelia. Frederick IV of Denmark also resumed the war, seized ducal Schleswig, and conquered the Swedish duchies of Bremen and Verden in Germany, which he sold to Hanover on condition that Hanover join in the war against Sweden. Swedish Pomerania was taken by the Poles, and Prussia, fishing in troubled waters, seized Stettin. In 1714, Charles XII returned to Sweden. Undaunted by the coalition of Russia, Denmark, Poland, Saxony, Hanover, and Prussia, he began military operations in Norway (then ruled by Denmark), where he was fatally shot in 1718. His successor, Ulrica Leonora, and her husband, Frederick I of Sweden, began peace negotiations. Peace was made with all enemies but Russia in the treaties of Stockholm and Frederiksborg (1719-20). Augustus II of Poland restored all his conquests; Hanover retained the duchies of Bremen and Verden, but paid a large indemnity; Prussia received Stettin and part of W Pomerania, the rest reverting to Sweden; Denmark restored its conquests for a payment, but Sweden permitted the union of ducal Schleswig with royal Schleswig under the Danish crown and renounced Swedish exemption from customs duties in the Sound. By the Treaty of Nystad with Russia (1721) Sweden ceded Livonia (including Estonia), part of Karelia, and Ingermanland, but retained Finland. The lasting results of the Northern War were the waning of Swedish power, the establishment of Russia as a major power of Europe, with its "window" on the Baltic Sea, and the decay of Poland. See Leonard Cooper, *Many Roads to Moscow* (1968).

Northfield, city (1970 pop. 10,235), Rice co., SE Minn., near Minneapolis-St. Paul, on the Cannon River; inc. 1875. It is the trade center for a dairy and farming region. Northfield's manufactures include plastic, wood, food, and electrical products, and woodworking and conveyor machinery. Color film is processed, packaged, and printed. On Sept. 7, 1876, Jesse and Frank James and their bandit gang attempted a bank robbery there. In the ensuing gun battle several gang members and two Northfield citizens were killed; the robbery attempt failed. The gang broke up after the capture of several of its members. Each September, Northfield celebrates the famous event by holding a festival during which the robbery attempt is reenacted. Carleton College, St. Olaf College, and the Laura Baker School for retarded children are in Northfield. Numerous lakes, used for recreational purposes, are nearby.

Northfleet, urban district (1971 pop. 26,679), Kent, SE England. Shipbuilding and the production of cement and paper are the main industries. Huggens College is in Northfleet. In the center of town is a Roman Catholic church built by Sir George Scott.

North Fork, river, c.100 mi (160 km) long, rising in the Ozarks, S Mo., and flowing S, into N Ark., to the White River. Near its mouth is Norfolk Dam (completed 1944), which impounds Norfolk Lake. The dam's power plant has a 70,000-kw capacity.

North German Confederation, 1867-71, alliance of 22 German states N of the Main River. Dominated by Prussia, it replaced the GERMAN CONFEDERATION and included the states that had supported Prussia in the Austro-Prussian War (1866). The South German states, notably Bavaria, Baden, Württemberg, and the grand duchy of Hesse, though excluded from the confederation, were nevertheless closely bound to it through their membership in the ZOLLVEREIN. Prepared in broad outline by Otto von BISMARCK, the constitution of the confederation, when adopted by the members, provided for a federal council (Bundesrat), composed of deputies from the states, and a lower house (Reichstag), elected by direct manhood suffrage. Prussia exercised predominant influence in both bodies. Executive power was vested in the president—the king of Prussia—who appointed the federal chancellor (as it turned out, Bismarck). The states retained their own governments, but the military forces were controlled by the federal government. In 1871 this constitution was adopted, with some changes, by the German Empire, which replaced the confederation.

North Haven, town (1970 pop. 22,194), New Haven co., S Conn., on the Quinnipiac River; settled c.1650, set off from New Haven 1786. Although chiefly residential, it has some manufactures.

North Highlands, uninc. town (1970 pop. 31,854), Sacramento co., N central Calif., a residential suburb of Sacramento, in the Sacramento valley.

North Holland, Dutch *Noordholland* (nōrt″hô′lănt), province (1971 pop. 2,260,000), c.1,080 sq mi (2,800 sq km), NW Netherlands, a peninsula between the North Sea in the west and the IJsselmeer in the east. The province includes several of the West Frisian islands. Haarlem is the capital; other cities include Amsterdam, Hilversum, IJmuiden, Den Helder, and Zaandam. North Holland is largely made up of low-lying fenland. It is drained by numerous small rivers and canals and is protected by dikes. There are many picturesque drawbridges, windmills, and tulip fields. Since the 1940s manufacturing has formed the backbone of the province's economy. Agriculture, cattle raising, flower growing, cheese production, fishing, and foreign trade are also important sources of wealth. For the history of the province, see HOLLAND.

North Island (1971 pop. 2,051,363), 44,281 sq mi (114,688 sq km), New Zealand. It is the smaller but more populous of the two principal islands of the country. The principal cities are WELLINGTON, capital of New Zealand, and AUCKLAND. Separated from South Island by Cook Strait, North Island is irregularly shaped with a long peninsula projecting northwest. There are volcanic mountains, the highest being Ruapehu (9,175 ft/2,797 m) and Mt. Egmont (8,260 ft/2,518 m). Its largest river, the Waikato is the most important river of New Zealand, draining Lake Taupo, the country's largest lake. The island contains most of New Zealand's dairy and wine industries. Oil, iron, and coal are found there. Near the center of the island is a hot springs resort area.

North Kingstown (kĭng′stən, kĭngz′toun″), town (1970 pop. 29,793), Washington co., S central R.I., on Narragansett Bay; inc. as Kings Towne 1674, divided into North Kingstown and South Kingstown 1723. North Kingstown includes Quonset Point and the villages of Allentown, Davisville, Saunderstown, and Wickford. The site of North Kingstown was settled in 1641 by Roger Williams, founder of Providence, R.I. North Kingstown is a regional trade center and fishing port and attracts many tourists. Its manufactures include machine tools, primary metals, printed materials, chemicals, plastics, and textiles. Points of interest in North Kingstown include Smith's Castle (1678), now a museum containing 18th- and 19th-century American furnishings; Casey House (1725), which retains the bullet holes made during skirmishes between British troops and minutemen during the Revolutionary War; Old Narragansett Church (1707); the birthplace (now a museum) of Gilbert Stuart (1755-1828), the portrait painter; and South County Museum, containing antiques and collections of early New England firearms, vehicles, and furniture. The Wickford Art Festival and an Indian powwow are held every summer. Narragansett Bay is used for recreational boating and fishing.

Northlake, city (1970 pop. 14,212), Cook and Du Page counties, NE Ill., near Chicago; inc. 1949. Its varied manufactures include food, electrical, and paper products. St. John Vianney Roman Catholic Church, which is shaped like a fish, has the largest mosaic-tile mural in the Western Hemisphere.

North Las Vegas, city (1970 pop. 36,216), Clark co., SE Nev., a residential suburb of Las Vegas; inc. 1946. The Garden of Cities there features trees and plants from cities throughout the United States. Part of Nellis Air Force Base is within city limits.

North Little Rock, city (1970 pop. 60,040), Pulaski co., central Ark., on the Arkansas River opposite Little Rock; settled c.1856, inc. as a city 1903. North Little Rock lies in a cotton, rice, soybean, dairy-cattle, and truck-farm area. Its manufactures include food products, lumber and preserved wood, insecticides and fertilizers, nonwoven fabric, metal products, and mattresses. There are large railroad repair shops. In the early 19th cent. the discovery of a small silver vein drew settlers to the area, which was called Silver City in the futile hope that more silver would be found. Most of the area later became part of Little Rock, but in 1903 local citizens pushed a bill through the Arkansas legislature permitting a part of Little Rock to secede and join the small village of North Little Rock. In 1906 the name was changed to Argenta in a further attempt to disassociate the city from Little Rock, but in 1917 it was renamed North Little Rock. Camp Joseph T. Robinson, a U.S. army facility, and Fort Roots veterans hospital are nearby.

Northmen: see NORSEMEN.

North Merrick, uninc. residential village (1970 pop. 13,650), Nassau co., SE N.Y., on Long Island.

North Miami, city (1970 pop. 34,767), Dade co., SE Fla., a suburb of Miami, on Biscayne Bay; inc. 1926. It is mainly a residential and resort city. Its manufactures include boats, wooden furniture, and aluminum products. A local movie studio is noted for its underwater film productions. The city is linked with Miami Beach by a causeway. In the early 1970s North Miami built Interama, a large cultural, educational, and recreational complex that was designated as a site for the U.S. bicentennial celebration (1976). Interama includes a state university. A campus of Miami-Dade Junior College is just outside North Miami.

North Miami Beach, resort city (1970 pop. 30,723), Dade co., SE Fla., on the Atlantic coast; inc. 1931.

North Minch, strait: see MINCH, Scotland.

North New Hyde Park, uninc. town (1970 pop. 17,945), Nassau co., SE N.Y., on Long Island.

North Olmsted (ŏm′stĕd), city (1970 pop. 34,861), Cuyahoga co., NE Ohio, a suburb of Cleveland; inc. as a city 1951. It is mainly residential; the chief industry produces printed materials. The first U.S. municipal bus line began operations in the city in 1931.

North Ossetia: see OSSETIA, USSR.

North Plainfield, residential borough (1970 pop. 21,796), Somerset co., NE N.J.; settled 1736, inc. 1885. A Revolutionary War cemetery is there.

North Platte (plăt), city (1970 pop. 19,447), seat of Lincoln co., W central Nebr., at the confluence of the North Platte and South Platte rivers; inc. 1873. It is a processing and shipping point for grain and livestock. It has meat-packing plants and a railroad repair shop. Nearby are Scouts Rest Ranch (formerly a home of Buffalo Bill, who lived in North Platte for 30 years), Fort McPherson National Cemetery, a Univ. of Nebraska experimental station, and a state fish hatchery. There is an annual rodeo in the city.

North Platte, river, c.680 mi (1,090 km) long, rising in the Park Range, N Colo., and flowing in a great bend N through SE Wyo., then east across the plains of W central Nebr. to join the South Platte River at North Platte city and form the Platte River. The North Platte project and the Kendrick project utilize the North Platte's water for power and irrigation. Kingsley Dam (170 ft/52 m high and 3.4 mi/5.5 km long; completed 1942) near Ogallala, Nebr., is one of many dams on the river; it impounds the largest lake in Nebraska. The valley of the North Platte, followed by the Overland Trail, was a chief route used by westward moving pioneers; Fort Laramie National Historic Site is on the river near the mouth of the Laramie River.

North Platte project, unit of the U.S. Bureau of Reclamation, in the North Platte River valley, W Nebr. and E Wyo. It supplies hydroelectric power to many towns and industries and provides irrigation for c.335,000 acres (135,570 hectares) of land extending 111 mi (179 km) along the valley from Guernsey, Wyo., to below Bridgeport, Nebr. Among the project's dams and reservoirs are Guernsey Reservoir, formed by Guernsey Dam (completed 1927), and Pathfinder Reservoir, created by Pathfinder Dam (completed 1909). There are also several large dams on the branches of the North Platte. The power system of the project (6,500-kw capacity) has been integrated with the Missouri River basin project.

North Pole, northern end of the earth's axis, lat. 90° and long. 0°. It is distinguished from the north MAGNETIC POLE. The North Pole was first reached (1909) by U.S. explorer Robert E. Peary. See also ARCTIC REGIONS.

North Providence, town (1970 pop. 24,337), Providence co., NE R.I.; set off from Providence and inc. 1765. Once a large textile town, it is now mainly suburban. A major portion of Rhode Island College is within the town's limits.

North Reading (rĕd'ĭng), residential town (1970 pop. 11,264), Middlesex co., NE Mass., on the Ipswich River; settled 1651, set off from Reading and inc. 1853.

North Rhine-Westphalia (nôrth rīn-wĕstfāl'yə), Ger. *Nordrhein-Westfalen* (nôrt'rīn-vĕst"fä'lən), state (1970 pop. 16,914,000), 13,111 sq mi (33,957 sq km), W West Germany. Düsseldorf is the capital. The state is bounded by Belgium and the Netherlands in the west, Lower Saxony in the north and east, Hesse in the southeast, and Rhineland-Palatinate in the south. Situated in the lower Rhine plain, North Rhine-Westphalia includes the Teutoburg Forest and the Rothaargebirge. It is drained by the Rhine, Ruhr, Wupper, Lippe, and Ems rivers. A highly industrialized state, it contains the largest industrial concentration in Europe (see RUHR district) and has excellent transportation facilities. Its manufactures include chemicals, machines, processed foods, textiles, clothing, and iron and steel. North Rhine-Westphalia is also the most populous state in West Germany and has numerous large cities, including Aachen, Cologne, Düsseldorf, Duisburg, Essen, Dortmund, Remscheid, Oberhausen, and Wuppertal. There are universities at Bielefeld, Bochum, Bonn, Dortmund, Düsseldorf, Cologne, and Münster. The state was formed in 1946 through the union of the former Prussian province of WESTPHALIA, the northern part of the former Prussian RHINE PROVINCE, and the former state of LIPPE. It possesses little historic unity as yet.

North Richland Hills, town (1970 pop. 16,514), Tarrant co., N Texas, a residential suburb of Fort Worth; inc. 1953.

North Riding, England: see YORKSHIRE.

North Royalton, city (1970 pop. 12,807), Cuyahoga co., NE Ohio, a suburb of Cleveland; settled 1811, inc. as a village 1927, as a city 1960. A dairy-processing and sawmilling center in the 19th cent., North Royalton is now encouraging new industries to locate there.

North Saint Paul, village (1970 pop. 11,950), Ramsey co., SE Minn., a suburb of St. Paul, in a lake resort region; inc. 1888. Conveyor systems and masonry products are manufactured there.

North Saskatchewan: see SASKATCHEWAN, river.

North Schleswig: see SCHLESWIG, duchy.

North Sea, arm of the Atlantic Ocean, c.222,000 sq mi (574,980 sq km), c.600 mi (1,000 km) long and c.400 mi (640 km) wide, NW of Central Europe. It washes the shores of Great Britain, Norway, Denmark, West Germany, the Netherlands, Belgium, and the northern tip of France. In the south the Strait of Dover connects it with the English Channel. The North Sea is deepest (c.2,165 ft/660 m) along the coast of Norway and contains several shallows, the largest of which is the Dogger Bank, midway between England and Denmark. The cod and herring fisheries of the North Sea are of great value. In 1970 oil was discovered under the sea floor.

North Shields, England: see TYNEMOUTH.

North Slope, Alaska: see ALASKA NORTH SLOPE.

North Star: see POLARIS.

North Sydney, town (1971 pop. 8,604), NE Cape Breton Island, N.S., Canada, on Sydney Harbour. It is the coal-shipping port for the nearby Sydney Mines and a winter base for the Cape Breton fisheries.

North Texas State University, at Denton, Texas; coeducational; est. 1890 as a normal school, became North Texas State Normal College in 1899, became North Texas State Teachers College in 1923. In 1949 the school's name was changed to North Texas State College, and in 1961 the school gained university status. Its music library is one of the largest in the United States. The university consists of colleges of arts and sciences, business administration, and education as well as a graduate school and schools of home economics, library and informational sciences, and music.

North Tonawanda (tŏnəwŏn'də), industrial and commercial city (1970 pop. 36,012), Niagara co., W N.Y., on the Niagara River at the terminus of the Barge Canal; settled c.1802, inc. as a city 1897.

Northumberland, Algernon Percy, 10th **earl of** (nôrthŭm'bərlənd), 1602-68, English nobleman. He was created Baron Percy in 1626 and succeeded his father as earl in 1632. Charles I in 1638 made him lord high admiral of England and in 1639 gave him command of the expedition against Scotland, which he was forced to relinquish because of illness. Disagreeing with the king's policy, he gradually moved over to the parliamentary party. His support gave Parliament an important advantage, for it thus gained control of most of the fleet. Northumberland, a leader of the peace party, twice engaged in unsuccessful negotiations with Charles on behalf of Parliament, opposed the king's trial, and was given custody of Charles's younger children. He took no active part in affairs under the Commonwealth or after the Restoration, although he held several offices after 1660.

Northumberland, Henry Percy, 1st **earl of,** 1342-1408, English nobleman. He fought in France in the Hundred Years War, became warden of the Scottish Marches, and was a supporter of John WYCLIF. Created earl of Northumberland by Richard II in 1377, he and his son Sir Henry PERCY (Hotspur) were engaged in constant warfare with the Scots. He was a leading supporter of Henry of Lancaster (Henry IV) in the usurpation of 1399, but with his brother, Thomas Percy, earl of WORCESTER, and Hotspur, Northumberland revolted against the king in 1403. He submitted after the death of his son at the battle of Shrewsbury in the same year. By 1405, however, he was plotting again with OWEN GLENDOWER and, after fleeing to Scotland and France, invaded (1408) England from the north with the expectation of recruiting followers. He was slain and his forces were defeated at Bramham Moor.

Northumberland, Henry Percy, 4th **earl of,** 1446-89, English nobleman. When his father, the 3d earl, was killed fighting in the Lancastrian army at Towton (1461), he was imprisoned by Edward IV and the earldom forfeited. He was released in 1469, restored to the earldom in 1470, and served the Yorkist monarch. Although Northumberland accepted lands and offices from Richard III, he withheld his men in the battle at Bosworth (1485) and submitted to the earl of Richmond, who was crowned Henry VII. Northumberland was killed by rebels in Yorkshire.

Northumberland, Hugh Percy, 2d **duke of,** 1742-1817, British general. He fought on the Continent in the Seven Years War and, although he disapproved of the war against the colonists in America, served there (1774-77) as a lieutenant general. He covered the bloody British retreat from Concord to Charlestown after the battle of Lexington and took part in the attack on Fort Washington. Recalled at his own request, following disputes with Gen. William Howe, he was made a general in 1793.

Northumberland, John Dudley, duke of, 1502?-1553, English statesman. The son of Edmund Dudley, minister of Henry VII, John was restored to his inheritance in 1512 after his father's attainder and execution (1510). Rising by means of his military ability, he became Viscount Lisle, warden of the Scottish Marches (1542), and lord high admiral (1543). Named as one of the executors of Henry VIII's will, he helped Edward Seymour, later duke of SOMERSET, become protector of the young EDWARD VI, while he himself was created earl of Warwick and lord high chamberlain. Cooperative and politic, he dissembled his plans for power while distinguishing himself in the field; he took part (1547) in the victory over the Scots at Pinkie and suppressed (1549) the rebellion of Robert KETT. By never actually committing himself and by playing on both Catholic and Protestant sympathies, he finally formed a coalition against Somerset, deposing him in 1549 and having him executed in 1552. Of little religious conviction himself, he then posed as a firm Protestant to increase his power over Edward VI and ruthlessly advanced the Reformation for political ends. He made himself duke of Northumberland in 1551. In a desperate plan to perpetuate his power, he convinced the dying Edward that the latter's sister Mary should be excluded from the succession as a Catholic, and he browbeat the council into proclaiming Lady Jane GREY, his daughter-in-law, as queen when the monarch died (1553). Unpopular with the people, he was deserted by his army and forced to surrender to Queen Mary I. He was condemned for high treason and was executed. See biography by B. L. Beer (1974); J. D. Mackie, *The Earlier Tudors* (1952); W. K. Jordan, *Edward VI: The Threshold of Power* (1970).

Northumberland, Thomas Percy, 7th **earl of,** 1528-72, English nobleman. He was the nephew and heir of the childless 6th earl but did not succeed on the latter's death (1537) because his father had been attainted for participation in the Pilgrimage of Grace (1536). He finally received the title from Queen Mary I in 1557 and was entrusted with the protection of the Scottish borders, but he lost this position after the accession of the Protestant Elizabeth I. In conjunction with the earl of WESTMORLAND he plotted (1569) with the Spanish to restore Roman Catholicism to England and to release Mary Queen of Scots. They gathered an army, but it was defeated (1569). Northumberland was captured by the Scots, ransomed (1572) to the English, and beheaded.

Northumberland (nôrthŭm'bərlənd), county (1971 pop. 794,975), 2,019 sq mi (5,229 sq km), NE England. The county town is NEWCASTLE UPON TYNE. Northernmost of the English counties, it is separated from Scotland by the Cheviot Hills and the Tweed River, and borders on the North Sea. The terrain is level along the rugged coast line and hilly in the interior, where high moorlands alternate with fertile valleys. Other rivers are the Tyne, the Derwent, the Wansbeck, the Till, the Alno, and the Coquet. The southeast of the county is heavily populated and industrialized. Chief industries are coal mining, shipping, and ship building and repairing. Sheep and cattle are raised. HADRIAN'S WALL was built in Roman times. In the 6th cent. the Angles established themselves in the region, which later became the kingdom of NORTHUMBRIA. The area suffered severely during the border wars between England and Scotland. In 1974, Northumberland was reorganized as a nonmetropolitan county; a small but populous area in the southeast (including Newcastle upon Tyne) became part of the new metropolitan county of Tyne and Wear.

Northumberland Strait, arm of the Gulf of St. Lawrence, c.200 mi (320 km) long and from 9 to 30 mi (14.5-48 km) wide, separating Prince Edward Island from New Brunswick and Nova Scotia.

Northumbria, kingdom of (nôrthŭm'brēə), one of the Anglo-Saxon kingdoms in England. It was originally composed of two independent kingdoms divided by the Tees River, Bernicia (including modern E Scotland, Berwick, Roxburgh, E Northumberland, and Durham) and Deira (including the North and East Ridings of Yorkshire), both settled by invading Angles c.500. Sparse records tell of a King Ida of Bernicia and a King Ælli or Ælle of Deira in the middle of the 6th cent. Æthelfrith of Bernicia (593-616) united the kingdoms to form Northumbria and added Scottish and Welsh territory. He was defeated by Edwin of Deira (616-32), who accepted (627) Roman Christianity and established Northumbrian supremacy in England. Edwin was killed by Cadwallon of the Welsh kingdom of Gwynned, an ally of Penda of MERCIA and, after a year of anarchy, was succeeded by Oswald of Bernicia (633-41), who brought in St. Aidan to introduce Celtic Christianity. Oswald was killed by Penda. Under Oswald's successors, Osiu (641-70) and Ecgfrith (670-85), Northumbria's power gradually declined as that of Mercia increased. Osiu, however, established the Roman Church over the Celtic Church at the Synod of Whitby (663). The late 7th and 8th cent. saw almost constant political discord but also the golden age of the Church, arts, scholarship, and literature in Northumbria. The invading Danes with their smashing victory at York in 867 soon wrecked all culture. They occupied S Northumbria, and the Angles were able to keep only a small kingdom stretching from the Tees N to the Firth of Forth; however, all Northumbria acknowledged Edward the Elder of Wessex as overlord in 920. The conquering Canute (1015) and his successors installed Danish earls, of whom Siward (d. 1055) was the last and most powerful. The Northumbrians expelled his successor, Tostig, in 1065. He was replaced by Morcar, the brother of Edwin, earl of Mercia. The next year Tostig returned with Harold Hardrada of Norway and beat Morcar and Edwin at Fulford, but Harold II of England came north and defeated the invaders.

North Valley Stream, uninc. residential town (1970 pop. 14,881), Nassau co., SE N.Y., on Long Island.

North Vancouver, city (1971 pop. 31,847), SW British Columbia, Canada, on Burrard Inlet of the Strait of Georgia, opposite Vancouver, of which it is a suburb. Shipbuilding, woodworking, and chemical manufacturing are the chief industries.

North Vietnam: see VIETNAM.

Northwest Boundary Dispute: see OREGON, state; SAN JUAN BOUNDARY DISPUTE.

North West Company, fur-trading organization in North America in the late 18th and early 19th cent.; it was composed of Montreal trading firms and fur traders. After the conquest of Canada by the British, which was formalized by the Treaty of Paris in 1763, the French traders from Montreal and the COUREURS DE BOIS were gradually more or less supplanted in the fur trade by Scotsmen. Many of these new traders allied themselves with the French already in the country, and vigorous partnerships sprang up. The Montreal men continued to contest control of the trade in the North with the HUDSON'S BAY COMPANY, and they extended trade to the West rapidly and efficiently. There were, however, too many conflicting interests in the fields, and the competition not only took all profit out of the trade but also led to bloodshed. The Montreal merchants who supplied the traders and the traders themselves sought to do away with some of the evils by forming in 1779 a company of sorts; this was later renewed, then abandoned. A new effort was made when a number of Montreal merchants under the leadership of Simon McTavish made an agreement in the winter of 1783-84 that created a company called the North West Company. There was some dissension, and the firm of Gregory and McLeod put up strong opposition. It was not until 1787 that a stable combination was reached. The stockholders were the trading companies of Montreal (which had many interests besides the fur trade and retained their separate existence) and the "wintering partners," the men who did all the actual trading for fur with the Indians. The traders were, for the most part, active and aggressive, and they made much more headway than the Hudson's Bay Company men. The Northwesters, as they were called, broke new territory for the trade in the West and did not hesitate to try to take the trade even in the vicinity of Hudson Bay. The older company was stirred into some action, and there was an increasingly sharp rivalry. This was not serious, however, until after the Hudson's Bay Company passed under the dominance of Lord SELKIRK. The younger company, meanwhile, was split by dissension, brought on chiefly by the hostility between two important figures in the company, McTavish and Sir Alexander MACKENZIE. Mackenzie became (1802) the chief figure in a rival company created c.1798 and usually called the XY Company. This opposition disappeared after the death of McTavish in 1804; Mackenzie's men were reunited with the Northwesters. To the North West Company is due some of the glory of Mackenzie's earlier voyages to the Arctic (1789) and Pacific (1792-93) oceans. The geographer David THOMPSON was in the company's employ when he did most of his valuable work, and other explorers, such as Alexander HENRY, the younger, were Northwesters. The company pushed its business into the territory of the United States and met with little opposition except from John Jacob ASTOR. The Southwest Company, established in 1811, was practically, although not actually, a combination of Astor and North West Company interests; this was disrupted by the War of 1812. On the Pacific Northwest coast, which was largely explored by Northwesters, Astor was also a rival, but the American post, Astoria (see ASTORIA **3**), was sold to the North West Company during the War of 1812 by Astor employees sympathetic to the British; however, it helped establish a U.S. claim to the Pacific Northwest. After 1810 the rivalry between the North West Company and Hudson's Bay Company grew in intensity and became a problem for the British government. The conflict over the RED RIVER SETTLEMENT led to virtual warfare between the companies, and the final solution was the union of the two companies in 1821. The name of the older company was kept and there was no longer a North West Company. In the united company, however, the personnel was predominantly of the Northwestern stamp, and the spirit of the company was that of the vigorous North West Company. See G. C. Davidson, *The North West Company* (1918, repr. 1967); H. A. Innis, *The Fur Trade in Canada* (1930, repr. 1962); W. S. Wallace, ed., *Documents Relating to the North West Company* (1934, repr. 1968); M. E. W. Campbell, *The North West Company* (1957); Gabriel Franchère, *Adventure at Astoria, 1810-1814* (tr. 1967).

Northwestern University, mainly at Evanston, Ill.; coeducational; chartered 1851, opened 1855 by Methodists. In 1873 it absorbed Evanston College for Ladies. Notable on the Evanston campus are Dearborn Observatory, the Technological Institute, and the theater department. The Deering library includes a noted collection of first- and limited-edition books on contemporary English and American literature. The schools of medicine, dentistry, and law are at Chicago.

North-West Frontier Province, province and historic region (1969 est. pop. 10,937,000), c.41,000 sq mi (106,200 sq km), NW Pakistan, bounded on the N and W by Afghanistan. PESHAWAR is the capital. An area of high, barren mountains dissected by fertile valleys, it is predominantly agricultural. Wheat is the chief crop; barley, sugarcane, tobacco, cotton, and fruit trees are also cultivated, and livestock is raised. Irrigation works, notably the Warsak project on the Kabul River, supplement the scanty rainfall. Mineral resources include iron, copper, marble, rock salt, gypsum, antimony, and coal. There are some mountain forests. Food processing, cotton and wool milling, papermaking, and the production of cigarettes, textiles, chemicals, and fertilizer are the main industries; handicrafts also flourish. Fierce pastoral Pathan tribes inhabit the countryside. The region has been historically and strategically influenced by its proximity to the Khyber Pass, through which came invaders from central Asia. Alexander the Great conquered the region c.326 B.C., but his garrisons were routed by Chandragupta, founder of the MAURYA empire of India. In the early centuries A.D., Kanishka and his Kushan dynasty ruled the area. The Pathans arrived in the 7th cent., and by the 10th cent. conquerors from Afghanistan had made Islam the dominant religion. Under local Pathan rulers from the late 12th cent. until Babur annexed it to his Mogul empire, the region paid nominal allegiance to the Moguls in the 16th and 17th cent. After Nadir Shah's invasion (1738), it became a feudatory of the Afghan Durrani kingdom. The Sikhs later held the area, which passed to Great Britain in 1849. The British maintained large military forces and paid heavy subsidies to pacify the rebellious Pathan tribes, separated the region from the North-West Provinces of India in 1901 and constituted the North-West Frontier Province, whose people voted to join newly independent Pakistan in 1947. From 1955 to 1970 the North-West Frontier Province was a section of the consolidated province of West Pakistan. The region has been restive because of the Pushtunistan controversy (see PATHAN). See study by Arthur Swinson (1967).

Northwest Mounted Police: see ROYAL CANADIAN MOUNTED POLICE.

Northwest Ordinance: see ORDINANCE OF 1787.

Northwest Passage, water routes through the Arctic Archipelago, N Canada, and along the northern coast of Alaska between the Pacific and Atlantic oceans. Even though the explorers of the 16th cent. demonstrated that the American continents were a true barrier to a short route to the Orient, there still remained hope that a natural passage would be found leading directly through the barrier. During the same period, the idea of reaching China and India by sailing over the North Pole or by sailing through a passage north of Europe and Asia—the Northeast Passage—also became popular. However, the Northwest Passage remained the most important goal, and the search for the passage continued even though at that time such a route had no commercial value. Sir Martin Frobisher, the English explorer, was the first European to explore (1576-78) the eastern approaches of the passage. John Davis also explored (1585-87) this area, and in 1610 Henry Hudson sailed north and discovered Hudson Bay while seeking a short route to the Orient. Soon afterward, William Baffin, an English explorer, discovered (1616) Baffin Bay, through which the passage was finally discovered. English statesmen and merchants, anxious to have the passage found, encouraged exploration. Luke Fox and Thomas James made (1831-32) voyages into Hudson Bay. Although one of the avowed goals of Hudson's Bay Company was to find the Northwest Passage, little was accomplished until a century after its charter, when Samuel Hearne, a British explorer with the company, went overland as far west as the Coppermine River (1771-72) and demonstrated that there was no short passage to the western sea. The British government offered prizes for achievements in northern exploration, and Captain James Cook was inspired to make the first attempt at navigating the passage from the west. He died before he could accomplish anything. However, the British, Spanish, and Americans pushed explorations on the Pacific coast; and the explorations of the Russians about Kamchatka and Alaska, together with the voyages of Alexander Mackenzie, the Canadian explorer, had now shown the contours of the continental barrier. Wars between Britain and France interrupted the search for the Northwest Passage, and when resumed after the wars the explorations were made in the interests of science, not commerce. The desire to extend man's knowledge was the chief motive in arctic exploration after the expeditions of British explorers John Ross and David Buchan were sent out in 1818. Ross's later voyages, and those of Sir William Edward Parry, F. W. Beechey, Sir George Back, Thomas Simpson, and Sir John Franklin pushed forward the knowledge of arctic regions and of the Northwest Passage. The last tragic expedition of Franklin indirectly had more effect than any other voyage, because of the many expeditions sent out to discover his fate. In his expedition (1850-54), Robert J. Le M. McClure penetrated the passage from the west along the northern coast of the continent and by a land expedition reached Viscount Melville Sound, which had been reached (1819-20) by Parry from the east. The actual existence of the Northwest Passage had been proved, and the long search was over. It was many years, however, before a transit of the passage was made. This feat, which had been attempted by so many men, was first accomplished (1903-6) by the Norwegian explorer Roald Amundsen. Interest in the Northwest Passage slackened until the 1960s, when oil was discovered in N Alaska and there was a desire for a short water route to transport oil to the east coast of the United States. In 1969, the SS *Manhattan,* an ice-breaking tanker, became the first commercial ship to transit the Northwest Passage. See L. H. Neatby, *In Quest of the Northwest Passage* (1958); E. S. Dodge, *Northwest by Sea* (1961); R. J. McClure, *The Discovery of the North-West Passage* (1856, repr. 1969); Bern Keating, *The Northwest Passage* (1970).

Northwest Territories, region (1971 pop. 34,807), 1,304,903 sq mi (3,379,699 sq km), NW Canada. The Northwest Territories lie W of Hudson Bay, N of lat. 60°N, and E of Yukon, and occupy more than one third of Canada's area. YELLOWKNIFE has been the territorial capital since 1967; before 1967 the government was conducted from Ottawa. The region is divided into three administrative districts—Keewatin, W of Hudson Bay and including the islands in Hudson Strait, Hudson Bay, and James Bay; Mackenzie, E of Yukon; and Franklin in the northern section, consisting of the ARCTIC ARCHIPELAGO and the Boothia and Melville peninsulas. Geographically, the region is separated by the tree line, which runs roughly northwest to southeast, from the Mackenzie River delta in the Arctic Ocean to the Churchill harbor area on Hudson Bay. The TUNDRAS extend over much of the north and east; there the Eskimos and Indians derive their small incomes from trapping fur and obtain many necessities from fish, seals, reindeer, and caribou. Most of the development of the Northwest Territories has taken place in Mackenzie dist., an area well covered with soft woods and rich in minerals. In this district are two of the largest lakes in the world, Great Slave and Great Bear. Eastward from these lakes the geology of the region is that of the CANADIAN SHIELD. Great Slave and Great Bear lakes are linked to the Arctic Ocean by one of the world's longest rivers, the Mackenzie, which runs 2,635 mi (4,241 km) from its source in British Columbia. Agriculture in the Northwest Territories is virtually impossible except for limited cultivation south of the Mackenzie River region. Government agriculture experimental stations, however, are at Fort Simpson and Yellowknife. Trapping, the region's oldest industry, ranks third after mining and fishing. A thriving commercial fishing industry, based on whitefish and lake trout, is centered on the village of Hay River, on Great Slave Lake. Minerals are now the Territories' most valuable natural resource. Leading minerals are lead and zinc, both mined at Pine Point on Great Slave Lake. Oil is pumped and refined at Fort Norman and Norman Wells on the Mackenzie River; gold is being produced in increasing quantities at Yellowknife and on the Snare River; copper is extracted on the Coppermine River and in Keewatin near Hudson Bay; and exceptionally high-grade iron ore has been discovered on Baffin Island. The region also has tungsten, silver, cadmium, and nickel deposits. Important hydroelectric developments are on the Yellowknife and Snare rivers. Transportation and communication in the Northwest Territories are difficult. Long winters close the rivers to navigation for all but two months of the year. Despite the Great Slave Railway and the Mackenzie highway system, which links Alberta to the Great Slave area, most commerce, supply, and travel continue to be air-

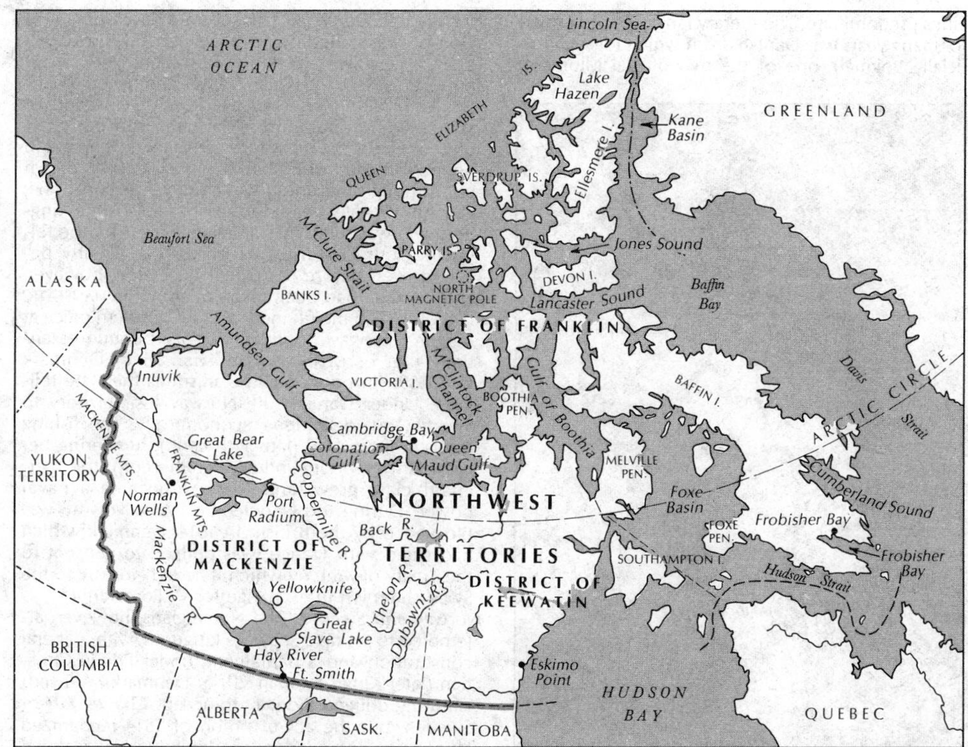

borne. An extensive northern roads program, first announced in 1966, was expected to help open up the area when completed, and there are now extensive telecommunications services. Sir Martin Frobisher was the first in a long line of courageous explorers to touch some part of the area, but it was Henry Hudson who discovered the gateway to the Northwest (Hudson Bay) in 1610. For several decades the Hudson's Bay Company sent out trader-explorers through the northern sea lanes and coast, and in 1771 Samuel Hearne descended the Coppermine River. In 1789, Alexander Mackenzie, exploring for the North West Company, journeyed to the mouth of the Mackenzie River. Sir John Franklin made scientific expeditions to the Arctic Northwest in the first half of the 19th cent., obtaining valuable geographical data. The area that is now the Northwest Territories was part of the vast lands sold by the Hudson's Bay Company to the new Canadian confederation in 1870. Some of those lands were added to the provinces of Quebec and Ontario. The province of Manitoba was carved from them in 1870, and Alberta and Saskatchewan in 1905. The present boundaries of the Northwest Territories were set in 1912. Today the territory is administered by a commissioner and a 14-member council sitting in Yellowknife, backed up by the Royal Canadian Mounted Police. The government operates a school system, and, with the aid of scattered missions throughout the vast region, provides extensive health and welfare services. The Territories are represented in the Canadian Parliament by one elected representative in the House of Commons. With its valuable minerals and their strategic importance, enhanced by transpolar navigation, the region continues to present major challenges in every field of human endeavor. The Northwest Territories are the site of the Nahanni and Baffin Islands national parks (both est. 1972). See C. A. Dawson, ed., *The New Northwest* (1947); L. Roberts, *The Mackenzie* (1949); P. R. Calder, *Men against the Frozen North* (1958); R. A. Phillips, *Canada: The Story of the Yukon and Northwest Territories* (1966); K. J. Rea, *Political Economy of the North* (1968).

Northwest Territory, first possession of the United States, comprising the geographical region known as the Old Northwest, S and W of the Great Lakes, NW of the Ohio River, and E of the Mississippi River, including the present states of Ohio, Ind., Ill., Mich., Wis., and part of Minn. Men from New France began to penetrate this rich fur country in the 17th cent.; in 1634, the French explorer Jean Nicolet became the first to enter the region. He was followed by explorers and traders—Radisson and Groseilliers, Duluth, La Salle, Jolliet, Perrot, and Cadillac—as well as by missionaries such as Jogues, Dablon, and Marquette. The Great Lakes region was controlled by a few widely scattered French posts, such as Kaskaskia, Vincennes, Prairie du Chien, and Green Bay; links were established between the Northwest settlements and those in French Louisiana (St. Louis, New Orleans). The two chief posts of the Old Northwest were Detroit and Mackinac (Michilimackinac), but French influence spread among the Indian tribes east to the Iroquois country. In the 18th cent. the Northwest was coveted not only by the British colonists in Canada, but also by those in the American seaboard colonies, who organized the OHIO COMPANY in 1747 for the purpose of extending the Virginia settlements westward. At the same time, the French sought to strengthen their hold on the Northwest by building forts. The clash of British and French interests culminated in the expedition led by George Washington that resulted in the loss of Fort Necessity and the outbreak of the last of the FRENCH AND INDIAN WARS. The wars ended in 1763 with the Treaty of Paris, by which the British obtained Canada and the Old Northwest. Almost immediately after the British took over, Pontiac, an Ottawa Indian chief, led an uprising against them. The Indians were somewhat appeased by the British Proclamation of 1763 that closed the region W of the Allegheny Mts. to white settlement in an attempt to protect the Indian fur trade and lands; but this action caused resentment among the American frontiersmen and contributed to the American Revolution. The mysterious machinations of Robert Rogers, an American frontiersman, further endangered the British hold on the Old Northwest. During the Revolutionary War, an expedition led by the American general George Rogers Clark penetrated deep into the region in 1778–79, in one of the most daring and valuable exploits of the war. The Old Northwest, which became U.S. territory in 1783 by the Treaty of Paris ending the Revolution, soon became one of the most pressing problems before the U.S. Congress. The four so-called landed states—Virginia, Massachusetts, New York, and Connecticut—claimed portions of the Old Northwest, while states with no western land claims, especially Maryland, argued that if the claims of the landed states were recognized, the wealth and population of the other states would be attracted to the western lands. The final solution was the cession of all the lands to the U.S. government, which was thus greatly strengthened; New York made its cession in 1780, Virginia in 1784, Massachusetts in 1785, and Connecticut in 1786. Two reserves were kept, the Virginia Military District and the Connecticut WESTERN RESERVE in Ohio. The Ordinance of 1787 set up the machinery for the organization of territories and the admission of states. Its terms prohibited slavery in the Northwest Territory, encouraged free public education, and guaranteed religious freedom and trial by jury. The OHIO COMPANY OF ASSOCIATES, the most active force in early colonization, was followed by later companies that brought settlers into the territory. But British traders opposed American expansion, and the Indians were hostile. A series of Indian campaigns culminated in 1794, when the American general Anthony Wayne won a victory at Fallen Timbers; his victory was solidified by the Greenville Treaty of 1795. Meanwhile, JAY'S TREATY and subsequent negotiations smoothed out some of the British-American difficulties. The Northwest posts were transferred to Americans in 1796, although British influence remained strong among the Indians. Settlers poured into the southern part of the Territory, and in 1799 a legislature was organized. In 1800 the western part was split off as Indiana Territory, and by 1802 the eastern portion was populated enough to seek admission as a state; it was admitted as Ohio in 1803. Other territories were then formed—Michigan in 1805, Illinois in 1809, and Wisconsin in 1836. The British traders, however, wanted the Northwest set aside as Indian land. Indian unrest led Tecumseh and Shawnee Prophet to seek a permanent foothold for the natives. Some Western Americans, meanwhile, sought to extend the Northwest to Canada. The quarrel over the Northwest was a major cause of the WAR OF 1812. The Treaty of Ghent (see GHENT, TREATY OF), which ended the war, solved the problem of the Northwest. Despite opposition from British merchants in the region, Great Britain irrevocably gave the Northwest to the United States. See John A. Caruso, *The Great Lakes Frontier* (1961); W. Havighurst, *Land of Promise* (1946) and *The Heartland* (1962); F. S. Philbrick, *The Rise of the West* (1965); H. N. Scheiber, *The Old Northwest* (1969); H. Bird, *War for the West* (1971).

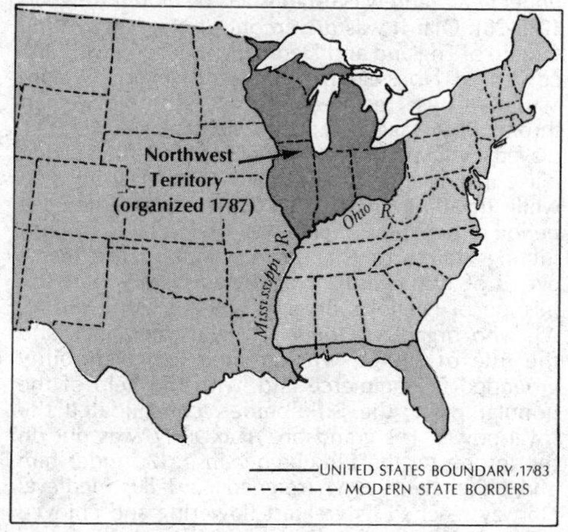

Northwest Territory

Northwich (nôrth'wĭch), urban district (1971 pop. 18,109), Cheshire, W central England, at the confluence of the Weaver and Dane rivers. Northwich has long been the center of England's salt production, but the manufacture of chemicals is now its leading occupation. It was the site of a Roman station. The rock-salt fields have been used since before the Christian era. The library and salt museum are noteworthy.

North Yorkshire, nonmetropolitan county (1972 est. pop. 629,000), N England, created under the Local Government Act of 1972 (effective 1974). It is composed of the county borough of YORK, and parts of the former counties of YORKSHIRE (North Riding, East Riding, and West Riding).

Norton, Caroline Elizabeth Sarah (Sheridan), 1808–77, English author; granddaughter of Richard Brinsley Sheridan. She gained more renown for her eventful life than for her writings. Her husband George Norton's divorce suit, with Lord Melbourne as correspondent, caused a sensation in its time. Although Norton lost the suit, he was given custody of their children and allowed to collect his wife's literary earnings. Her writings included poems and novels; however, she is best-remembered for *English Laws for Women in the Nineteenth Century* (1854) and *A Letter to the Queen* (1855), both of which helped bring about improvement of the status of married women in England. See biography by Alice Acland (1948).

Norton, Charles Eliot, 1827–1908, American scholar and teacher, b. Cambridge, Mass., grad. Harvard, 1846. As professor of the history of art at Harvard (1875–98) and as a man of letters he had a stimulating influence on his time. He edited (1864–68), with James Russell Lowell, the *North American Review* and was a founder (1865) of the *Nation.* Of his several scholarly works, the most notable were his Italian studies and his prose translation (3 vol., 1891–92) of Dante. See his letters (1913); study by Kermit Vanderbilt (1959).

Norton, city (1970 pop. 12,308), Summit co., NE Ohio, a residential suburb of Akron.

Norton Sound, inlet of the Bering Sea, c.150 mi (240 km) long and 125 mi (200 km) across at its widest point, W Alaska, S of the Seward Peninsula. Norton Bay is its northeast arm. Nome is on the north shore and the Yukon River flows into the sound from the south. It is navigable from May to October.

Norumbega (nôrəmbĕg'ə), name vaguely used, especially on European maps of the 16th and 17th cent., to indicate a region, a river, or a city on the east coast of North America. Fabulous tales were told of the city, but its location and its identity are uncertain. Probably the word is an Indian version of the old form of Norway. In the late 19th cent., Professor E. N. Horsford revived interest in the matter by identifying Norumbega as the site of a Norse settlement in America, claiming to have discovered its position on the Charles River at Watertown, Mass. No conclusive results have been reached on the matter, and it is generally considered that Norumbega is purely mythical. See R. H. Ramsay, *No Longer on the Map* (1972).

Norwalk (nôr'wôk"). **1** City (1970 pop. 91,827), Los Angeles co., S Calif.; settled in the 1850s, inc. 1957. Cerritos College, a state mental hospital, and the county's largest public library are there. **2** City (1970 pop. 79,113), Fairfield co., SW Conn., at the mouth of the Norwalk River, on Long Island Sound; settled 1640, inc. 1913. Electronic and electrical equipment, pumps, and food products are manufactured, and aircraft research is carried on. Norwalk was burned by the British in the Revolution. It has a junior college, a state technical college, and an amateur symphony orchestra. The city includes numerous small islands in the harbor and the village of Silvermine, an artists' colony. **3** City (1970 pop. 13,386), seat of Huron co., N Ohio; inc. 1881. It is a trade and processing center for a farm area, with factories that make rubber products, packaging materials, and machine parts. The city was settled (c.1817) by "Fire Sufferers" from Norwalk, Conn., whose homes had been burned by the British in the Revolution.

Norway, Nor. *Norge,* kingdom (1973 est. pop. 3,960,000), 125,181 sq mi (324,219 sq km), N Europe, occupying the western part of the Scandinavian peninsula. OSLO is the capital. Extending from the Skagerrak c.1,100 mi (1,770 km) NE to North Cape on the Arctic Ocean, the country forms a narrow mountainous strip along the North Sea and the Atlantic Ocean, which in Norway is also called the Norwegian Sea. It has a long land frontier with Sweden and in the north borders on Finland and the USSR. The coastline, c.1,700 mi (2,740 km) long, is fringed with islands (notably the Lofoten islands and Vesterålen) and is deeply indented by numerous fjords. Sognafjord, Hardangerfjord, Nordfjord, and Oslofjord are among the largest and best known. From the coast the land rises sharply to high plateaus such as Dovrefjell and the Hardangervidda. Galdhøpiggen, in the Jotunheimen range, is the high point (8,098 ft/2,468 m); west of it lies Jostedalsbreen, the largest glacier field in Europe. The mountains and plateaus are intersected by fertile valleys, such as Gudbrandsdalen, and by rapid rivers, which furnish hydroelectric power and are used for logging. The Glåma, in the south, is the most important river. Most of the population is concentrated along the southern coast and valleys, where the chief cities—Oslo, BERGEN, STAVANGER, KRISTIANSAND, and DRAMMEN—are located. Farther north along the coast is TRONDHEIM, and in the extreme north are NARVIK, TROMSØ, and HAMMERFEST. The beautiful Norwegian fjords and the midnight sun of the far north attract many tourists. Because of the North Atlantic Drift, Norway has a mild and humid climate for a northern country. Almost three quarters of the land is unproductive; less than 4% is under cultivation. The vast mountain pastures are used for the grazing of cattle and sheep, and, in the north, for reindeer raising. About one quarter of Norway is forested; timber is the chief natural resource and is the basis for one of the main industries. The chief industries are shipping and trading. The great Norwegian merchant fleet carries a large part of the world's trade. Fishing (notably of cod, herring, and mackerel) is important, and fresh, canned, and salted fish from Norway are exported to the entire world. Norway has also long had a whaling fleet. The pulp and paper, electrochemical, and electrometallurgical industries are important to the economy. Mineral resources include pyrites and iron ore, which are heavily mined, and some coal, copper, zinc, and lead. Nickel, aluminum, ferroalloys, and semifinished steel are produced. The majority of Norwegians are of Scandinavian stock, but in the northern county of FINNMARK, Lapps and Finns predominate. The literary language of Norway for many years was Danish, from which Rigsmål (officially Bokmål), one of the two official idioms of

Norway, is derived (see NORWEGIAN LANGUAGE and NORWEGIAN LITERATURE). Landsmål (officially Nynorsk), the other official idiom, is similar. Frequent spelling reforms account for the variation in Norwegian place names. Norway is a constitutional monarchy; the legislative power is vested in the parliament or Storting. The two main parties are the moderately socialist Labor party and the pro-free enterprise Conservative party; there are also five other parties. Administratively the country is divided into 18 rural counties (Nor. *fylker*) and the Oslo district. The outlying possessions of Norway are Svalbard and Jan Mayen in the Arctic Ocean and Bouvet and Peter I islands in the S Atlantic; Norway has claims in Antarctica. The Lutheran Church is the state church, but all other religions enjoy freedom of worship. The king nominates the nine bishops and other clergy of the Lutheran Church. The educational level in Norway is very high; the leading universities are in Oslo (founded 1811) and Bergen (founded 1946).

Medieval Norway. The history of Norway before the age of the VIKINGS is indistinct from that of the rest of Scandinavia. In the 9th cent. the country was still divided among the numerous petty kings of the *fylker.* HAROLD I, of the Yngling or Scilfing dynasty (which claimed descent from one of the old Norse gods), defeated the petty kings (c.900) and conquered the Shetlands and the Orkneys, but failed to establish permanent unity. Harold's campaigns drove many nobles and their followers to settle in Iceland and France. In the next two centuries Norsemen raided widely in W Europe and established the Norse duchy of Normandy. Harold himself concentrated on developing a dynasty; before he died (c.935) the country was divided among his sons, but one of them, HAAKON I, defeated (c.935) his brothers and temporarily reunited the kingdom. Christianity, brought by English missionaries, gained a foothold under OLAF I and was established by OLAF II (reigned 1015–28). Olaf II was driven out of Norway by King Canute of England and Denmark, in league with discontented Norwegian nobles; however, his son, MAGNUS I, was restored (1035) to the Norwegian throne. Both Magnus and his successor, HAROLD III, played a vital part in the complex events then taking place in England and Denmark. After Harold died while invading England (1066), Norway entered a period of decline and civil war, precipitated by conflicting claims to the throne. Among the major events of 12th-century Norwegian history were the mission of Nicholas Breakspear (later Pope ADRIAN IV), who organized the Norwegian hierarchy, and the rule of SVERRE, who created a new nobility grounded in commerce and, with the help of the popular party, the Birkebeiner, consolidated the royal power. His grandson, HAAKON IV, was put on the throne by the Birkebeiner in 1217; under him and under MAGNUS VI (reigned 1263–80) medieval Norway reached its greatest flowering and enjoyed peace and prosperity. During this time Iceland and Greenland recognized Norwegian rule.

Norway and Denmark. The separate development of Norway was halted by the accession (1319) of MAGNUS VII, who was also king of Sweden. He was unpopular in Norway, which he was compelled to surrender (1343) to his son, Haakon VI, husband of MARGARET of Denmark. Margaret subsequently united the rule of Norway, Sweden, and Denmark in her person and in 1397 had the KALMAR UNION drawn up. Although the union was strictly a personal one, Norway virtually ceased to exist as a separate kingdom and was ruled by Danish governors for the following four centuries. Its power had greatly declined even before Margaret's accession, however, and its trade had been taken over by the HANSEATIC LEAGUE, which maintained its chief northern office at Bergen. Norway's political history became essentially that of DENMARK. Christian III of Denmark (1535–59) introduced Lutheranism as the state religion. Under Danish rule Norway lost territory to Sweden but developed economically. The fishing industry flourished (late 17th cent.), lumbering became an important industry (18th cent.), the merchant class grew, and Norway became a naval power. During the Napoleonic Wars, Norway was blockaded by the British. In 1814, Denmark, which had sided with France, was obliged to consent to the Treaty of Kiel, by which it ceded Norway to the Swedish crown in exchange for W Pomerania.

Norway and Sweden. The Norwegians, however, attempted to set up a separate kingdom, with a liberal constitution and a parliament, under Prince Christian (later King Christian VIII of Denmark). A Swedish army obliged Norway to accept Charles XIII of Sweden, but the act of union of 1814 recognized Norway as an independent kingdom, in personal union with Sweden, with its own constitution and parliament. Despite some Swedish concessions to growing Norwegian nationalism, Swedish-Norwegian relations were strained throughout the 19th cent. Johan SVERDRUP, the Liberal leader, succeeded in making the ministry responsible to parliament despite royal opposition (1884), but other problems remained. The Norwegian interest in obtaining greater participation in foreign policy came to a crisis in the late 19th cent. over the issue of a separate Norwegian consular service, justified by the spectacular growth of Norwegian shipping and commercial interests. Finally, in 1905, the Storting declared the dissolution of the union and the deposition of Oscar II. Sweden acquiesced after a plebiscite showed Norwegians nearly unanimously in favor of separation; in a second vote Norway chose to become a monarchy, and parliament elected the second son of Frederick VIII of Denmark king of Norway as HAAKON VII.

Modern Norway. Two important features in Norwegian history of the late 19th and early 20th cent. were the large-scale emigration to the United States and the great arctic and antarctic explorations by such notable men as Fridtjof Nansen and Roald Amundsen. Three outstanding cultural figures of the period were Edvard GRIEG, Henrik IBSEN, and Edvard MUNCH. In World War I, Norway remained neutral. The industrial development of Norway, spurred by the harnessing of water power, contributed to the rise of the Labor (socialist) party, which has predominated in Norwegian politics since 1927. In the 1930s much social welfare legislation was passed, including public health and housing measures, old age pensions, aid to the disabled, and unemployment insurance. Norway attempted to remain neutral in World War II, but in April, 1940, German troops invaded, and, in a short time nearly the whole country was in German hands. King Haakon and his cabinet set up a government in exile in London, and the Norwegian merchant fleet was of vital assistance to the Allies throughout the war. Despite the attempts of Vidkun QUISLING to promote collaboration with the Germans, the people of Norway defied the occupation forces. German troops remained in Norway until the war ended in May, 1945. Although half of the Norwegian fleet was sunk during the war, Norway quickly recovered its commercial position. Postwar economic policy included a degree of socialization and measures such as permanent price, interest, and dividend controls. Norway was one of the original members of the United Nations (the Norwegian Trygvie Lie was the first UN Secretary-General), and it became a member of NATO in 1949. King OLAF V succeeded to the throne in 1957 as the second king of independent Norway. Norway joined the EFTA (see INTERNATIONAL GOVERNMENTAL ORGANIZATIONS) in 1959. Norwegian voters rejected membership in the Common Market in 1972, but trade agreements with the market were made the next year. Between 1965 and 1971 the Labor party was out of power for the first time since 1936. See F. N. Stagg, *North Norway* (1952), *The Heart of Norway* (1953), *West Norway* (1954), and *East Norway* (1956); Anders Hagen, *Norway* (tr. 1967); Michael Drake, *Population and Society in Norway, 1735-1865* (1969); Knut Gjerset, *History of the Norwegian People* (1932, repr. 1969); John Midgaard, *A Brief History of Norway* (2d ed. 1969); P. S. Andersen, *Vikings of the West: The Expansion of Norway in the Early Middle Ages* (1971); R. G. Popperwell, *Norway* (1972); T. K. Derry, *A Short History of Norway* (2d ed. 1968) and *A History of Modern Norway, 1814-1972* (1973).

Norway rat: see RAT.

Norwegian elkhound, breed of compact HOUND whose origins in Norway go back more than 5,000 years. It stands about 19 in. (48.3 cm) high at the shoulder and weighs between 40 and 50 lb (18.1-22.7 kg). Its thick, close-lying, gray coat is composed of a soft, woolly undercoat and a coarse outercoat. The elkhound was used by the Vikings as a herder of flocks and hunter of such game as elk, bears, mountain lions, and lynx. Still used to hunt elk today, it locates its quarry by scent and then leads the hunter to it. In the United States it is kept as a pet and watchdog. See DOG.

Norwegian language, member of the North Germanic, or Scandinavian, group of the Germanic subfamily of the INDO-EUROPEAN family of languages. It is spoken by about 3,500,000 people in Norway and by an additional 700,000 in the United States. Norwegian is a daughter language of Old Norse (see GERMANIC LANGUAGES; NORSE language). Today there are two official forms of Norwegian: *bokmål* [book language] and *nynorsk* [new Norwegian]. *Bokmål,* also called *riksmål* [national language] and Dano-Norwegian, was greatly influenced by Danish, which was the dominant language of officialdom when Norway was under Danish rule (1397-1814). The language of the cities, the official and professional classes, and literature, *bokmål* came to differ greatly from the Norwegian spoken by the common people. Since 1905, however, orthographical and grammatical reforms by the government have brought *bokmål* closer to the popular form of Norwegian. *Nynorsk,* also known as *landsmål* [country language], stems from the native Norwegian dialects that evolved from Old Norse (uninfluenced by Danish), and it is therefore very different from *bokmål.* Developed by Ivar Aasen, *nynorsk* was introduced by him in 1853 as part of a nationalistic desire to have a purely Norwegian language for the country. It is based on rural dialects and spoken principally in rural areas. Both *bokmål* and *nynorsk* are employed by the government, the schools, and the mass media, but *bokmål* is by far the more widely used of the two, especially in education and literature. Some efforts have been made to fuse the two forms of Norwegian into one common Norwegian tongue called *samnorsk* [common Norwegian], and there is hope that this can be accomplished. Norwegian grammar is fairly simple. The form of the noun is changed only to indicate possession and the plural, and personal inflection of the verb has been discarded. Like Swedish, Norwegian uses pitch accents, but to a lesser degree. The pitch accents give the language a musical quality and are sometimes employed to distinguish the meanings of homonyms. Norwegian employs the Roman alphabet, which was introduced in Norway in the 11th cent. and to which three characters, *æ, ø,* and *å,* have been added. See K. G. Chapman, *Icelandic-Norwegian Linguistic Relationships* (1962); E. I. Haugen and K. G. Chapman, *Spoken Norwegian* (1964); E. I. Haugen, *Language Conflict and Language Planning: The Case of Modern Norwegian* (1966).

Norwegian literature early flourished as OLD NORSE LITERATURE. In 1380, Norway was united with Denmark, and Danish culture began a long dominance in Norway; Norwegian culture sank to its nadir in the 16th cent. as Danish became the written language. The works of Absolon Beyer (1528-75), in Norwegian and Latin, reveal a new humanism. In the 17th cent. few works other than the poems and histories of Petter Dass were free of arid learning, excessive adornment, and latinization. Rationalist and neo-classic concepts of the Enlightenment were popularized by Ludvig HOLBERG in the early 18th cent. when a nationalist strain was also apparent. Norwegian independence from Denmark, gained in 1814, was a vital stimulus to literature. The mutual antagonism of the literary figures Henrik WERGELAND and J. S. WELHAVEN introduced a literary struggle between the national and the cosmopolitan. The folk collections of Jørgen MOE and P. C. ASBJØRNSEN re-created a cultural tradition, and by 1850 Ivar Aasen had developed the *landsmål* language to replace Danish *riksmål;* it linked peasant dialects and the tongue of the sagas to contemporary literature. National romanticism reigned at mid-century, but the novels of Camilla COLLETT foreshadowed the great realist movement. By the 1870s, Henrik IBSEN and Bjørnstjerne BJØRNSON had opened the mainstream of realism and had emerged as titans of world drama. Chief novelists of the realist school were Jonas LIE and Alexander KIELLAND, Kristian Elster, Hans Jaeger, and Arne GARBORG. The neo-romantic movement of the 1890s called forth the imaginative brillance of Knut HAMSUN, the psychologically oriented novels of Hans Kinck (1865-1926), and the lyric verse of Nils Vogt. Idealism marked the social dramas of Gunnar HEIBERG. Many different themes and styles prevailed in the era after World War I. Johan BOJER, Peter Egge (1869-1959), and Olav DUUN wrote novels of Norwegian life, and the Nobel laureate Sigrid UNDSET gained stature for her novels of ethics and religion. Radical credos were expressed in the plays of Hilge Krog (1889-1962) and poems of Arnulf Øverland. Sigurd HOEL gained acclaim as an outstanding satirist; Herman WILDENVEY remained the lyricist of Norway. The hopes and fears of the times were reflected in the verse and drama of Nordahl Grieg (1902-43). There was no significant literary achievement in Norway during World War II. The war experience and post-war anxieties were explored in the novels of Odd Bang-Hansen, in the experimental work of Kåre Holt, and in the poetry of Halldis Vesaas, Claes Gill, and Jan-Magnus Bruheim. See histories by Harald Beyer (tr. 1957), and Theodore Jorgenson (1933, repr. 1970); B. W. Downs, *Modern Norwegian Literature* (1966).

Norwegian Sea, part of the Atlantic Ocean, NW of Norway, between the Greenland Sea and the North Sea. It is separated from the Atlantic by a submarine ridge. The warm Norwegian Current gives the sea generally ice-free conditions.

Norwich (nôr'ĭj, -ĭch), county borough (1971 pop. 121,688), county town of Norfolk, E England, on the Wensum River just above its confluence with the Yare. It is a market center for cattle and grain. Farm machinery, textiles, chocolate, shoes, and mustard are among its manufactures. Since the 11th cent. Norwich has been a leading provincial city. It was sacked by the Danes in the 11th cent. and scourged by the Black Death in 1348. Norwich was the scene of events in Wat Tyler's rebellion of 1381 and in the uprising under Robert Kett in 1549. There are many medieval churches and a great cathedral founded in 1096 by the first bishop of Norwich. Norwich Castle, part of which dates from Norman times, was made into a museum for collections of natural history and local antiquities in 1894. It also houses paintings of the 18th- and 19th-century Norwich school of artists. There are many other old buildings, including St. Giles's Hospital (13th cent.), Suckling House (14th cent.), Strangers Hall (15th cent.; now a museum), the guildhall (15th cent.), and St. Andrew's Hall (15th cent.; formerly a Dominican church). The Maddermarket Theatre, a reconstruction of a Shakespearean theater, has a permanent amateur company. The Norwich grammar school dates from the 13th cent. Norwich is the cultural center of the county; triennial music festivals have been held since 1824. It is the seat of the Univ. of East Anglia (1963). Harriet Martineau was born in Norwich.

Norwich (nôr'wĭch, -ĭch), industrial city (1970 pop. 41,739), SE Conn., seat of New London co., on hilly ground, where the Yantic and Shetucket form the Thames; settled 1659, inc. 1784, town and city consolidated 1952. It has various manufacturing industries. The last great battle between the Mohegans and Narragansetts took place on that site in 1643, and the Indian chiefs are buried there. Norwich was a leading colonial industrial city; Thomas Danforth began making pewterware there in 1733. The city was also the birthplace of Benedict Arnold. The many historic structures include the Leffingwell Inn (1675) and the home of Samuel Huntington, who practiced law in the city. A state technical college and a state hospital are there.

Norwich terrier, breed of small, sturdy TERRIER developed in England in the second half of the 19th cent. It stands about 10 in. (25.4 cm) high at the shoulder and weighs about 11 lb (4.9 kg). The harsh, straight coat lies close to the body and is weather-resistant. It may be red, red wheaten, black and tan, or grizzle in color. The Norwich was originally bred as a compact hunter for work on rats and rabbits. Very soon after the Norwich made its debut as a new breed, owning one became a fad at Cambridge Univ. This early popularity did much to insure the permanence of the breed, as a number of students went on to raise the Norwich after they graduated. Today it is kept chiefly as a pet. See DOG.

Norwich University, at Northfield, Vt.; private military college; founded 1819, opened 1820 at Norwich, Vt.; chartered under present name 1834, moved 1866. Its programs are primarily in liberal arts and engineering.

Norwood. 1 Uninc. town (1970 pop. 14,973), Dade co., SE Fla., a residential suburb of Miami. **2** Town (1970 pop. 30,815), Norfolk co., E Mass.; settled 1678, set off from Dedham and Walpole and inc. 1872. It is chiefly residential. **3** City (1970 pop. 30,420), Hamilton co., SW Ohio, a suburb of Cincinnati; settled early 1800s, inc. 1888. It has varied light industries.

nose, organ of breathing and of smell. The external nose, composed of bone and cartilage, is the most prominent feature of the face. The internal nose is a hollow structure above the roof of the mouth, divided by the septum into two nasal cavities that extend from the nostrils to the PHARYNX. The mucous membrane that lines the nasal cavities is covered with fine hairs that help to filter dust and impurities from the air before it reaches the lungs; the air is also moistened as it passes over the sticky nasal membrane. There are three horizontal folds on the walls of the nasal cavities, called the conchae. The uppermost concha is densely supplied with capillaries that warm the air passing over them to near body temperature. High in the nasal cavity is a small tract of mucous membrane containing the nerve cell endings of the olfactory nerve, which imparts the sense of smell. Therefore, inflammation of the nasal mucous membranes, which commonly accompanies colds and other infections, not only obstructs breathing but also impairs the sense of smell.

nosebleed, nasal hemorrhage occurring as the result of local injury or disturbance. Most nosebleeds are not serious and occur when one of the small veins of the septum (the partition between the nostrils) ruptures. These will usually stop in a few minutes without treatment, or will cease when pressure is applied to the nose. A nosebleed may also occur in association with infections, heart failure, high blood pressure, arteriosclerosis, scurvy, leukemia, hemophilia, and other disorders. To control a more serious nosebleed, the subject should lie down and apply cold compresses to the nose; packing the nasal passages with cotton may help. Persistent nosebleeds should be brought to the attention of a physician.

no-see-um: see MIDGE.

Noske, Gustav (gōōs'täf nôs'kə), 1868-1946, German politician, a Social Democrat. A former member of the Reichstag, he was in charge of the armed forces after the republican revolution of Nov., 1918, and was minister of defense in 1919-20. In these capacities he ruthlessly suppressed radical uprisings throughout Germany, notably the insurrection of the Communist SPARTACUS PARTY. He was forced to resign after the abortive monarchist Kapp Putsch (1920), because many Social Democrats felt that he had encouraged counterrevolutionary activity through his alliance with the army against radicals. Noske became governor of Hanover in 1920 but was dismissed (1933) by the National Socialists, who otherwise left him unmolested until 1944, when he was arrested on suspicion of having shared in the attempt on Hitler's life. He was released in 1945 by Soviet troops.

Nostradamus (nŏs"trədā'məs), 1503-66, French astrologer and physician, whose real name was Michel de Nostredame. He is reputed to have effected remarkable cures during outbreaks of the plague in S France. His rhymed prophecies under the title *Centuries* (1555) gained him the favor of the French court. Obscure and symbolic, the predictions have been subject to many interpretations. See Erika Cheetham, ed. and tr., *Prophecies on World Events by Nostradamus* (1974).

notation: see ARITHMETIC and MUSICAL NOTATION.

note, in business: see PROMISSORY NOTE.

note, in MUSICAL NOTATION, symbol placed on or between the lines of a staff to indicate the pitch and the relative duration of the tone to be produced by voice or instrument. The largest note value in common use in the United States is the whole note, an elliptical outline. Its value is halved by the addition of a stem. A solid note with a stem is the quarter note, the most usual metric unit in modern notation. The eighth note resembles the quarter note, with the addition of a flag at the end of the stem; with each flag added, the value of the note is again halved. European music printing makes use of the breve, whose value is twice that of the whole note.

For each note value, there is a rest of corresponding value; rests are named in the same way as notes, e.g., whole rest, half rest.

Noteć (nô'tĕch), river, c.270 mi (430 km) long, NW Poland. It rises S of Inowrocław and flows generally W into the Warta River near Gorzów Wielkopolski. The Noteć is connected by the Bydgoszcz Canal with the Vistula River and is navigable for almost its entire length.

Notker Balbulus (nōt'kər băl'byŏŏləs), c.840–912, German monk and scholar, abbot of St. Gall (from 890). He composed liturgical poetry and music. Notker's life of Charlemagne preserves much of the matter of the Charlemagne legend. While Notker was abbot of St. Gall patristic studies were encouraged and the library was enriched.

Notker Labeo (lä'bēō), c.950–1022, German monk, teacher at St. Gall. He translated into Old High German Boethius' *Consolations of Philosophy,* Capella's *Marriage of Mercury and Philology,* Pope Gregory I's *Morals,* and Aristotle's *Categories.* Notker was one of the founders of German vernacular literature.

Noto (nō'tō), peninsula, c.45 mi (70 km) long and from 6 to 17 mi (9.6–27 km) wide, Ishikawa prefecture, W central Honshu, Japan, between the Sea of Japan and Toyama Bay. The rugged peninsula has a deeply indented east coast. Farming, lumbering and fishing are major economic activities.

notochord (nō'təkôrd"), in biology, supporting rod running most of the length of animals of the phylum CHORDATA and present at varying times in the life cycle. Composed of large cells packed within a firm connective tissue sheath, the notochord lies between the neural tube (spinal cord) and the gut. The division of the phylum Chordata into subphyla is based on the structure of the notochord and the time of life in which it is present: In the subphylum Urochordata (tunicates) the notochord characterizes the larval, swimming, stage of the animals and does not extend into the head; in the subphylum Cephalochordata (lancelets) the notochord extends to the extreme tip of the head in both young and adults; and in the subphylum Vertebrata the notochord becomes surrounded by skeletal vertebrae during embryonic development—in higher vertebrates it is present in the early embryo only and is later completely replaced by the vertebrae.

Notodden (nō'tô"dən), town (1970 pop. 13,320), Telemark co., SE Norway. The world's first nitrate factory was built there in 1905. Today, the town also has paper mills, iron foundries, and several large hydroelectric stations. Nearby at Hedal is the largest Norwegian stave church (c.1250).

Notre Dame, University of (nō'tər dām, nō'trə), at Notre Dame, Ind., near South Bend; Roman Catholic; est. (for men) and opened 1842, chartered 1844. It has a noted law school and computing center as well as laboratories for research in botany, radiation, geology, metallurgy, and engineering. It also operates important research institutes in the humanities; notable is the Jacques Maritain Philosophical Center. The university maintains an outstanding library system. For many years the school had a cooperative program with nearby St. Mary's College (est. 1844 as St. Mary's Academy, chartered 1850 at Bertrand, Mich., moved and chartered 1855; for women); in 1971 the university agreed to merge with the college to form one coeducational institution.

Notre Dame Bay, arm of the Atlantic Ocean, c.40 mi (60 km) long and 50 mi (80 km) wide, E N.F., Canada. The Exploit River empties into it. The bay has an irregular shoreline and contains many islands; Fogo Island is east of the bay. There are numerous fishing settlements along the coast, many of which have fish-processing plants; Botwood is the chief town and port.

Notre-Dame de Paris (nô'trə-däm də pärē') [Fr.,= Our Lady of Paris], cathedral church of Paris, a noble achievement of early Gothic architecture in France. It stands upon the Île de la Cité, a small island in the Seine, where originally stood several pagan altars. In the 6th cent. or before, a Christian church was built on the site, later replaced by two churches. Both were in ruins by the 12th cent., when Maurice de Sully demolished them in order to erect a vast cathedral suitable to the needs of the city. The cornerstone was laid in 1163 by Pope Alexander III. The high altar was consecrated 20 years later, and the nave was completed except for the roofing in 1196. However, in 1230 the nave was reconstructed and the present flying buttresses were added. Soon after, chapels were installed between the buttresses, which radically altered not only the plan but the entire aesthetic of the building. The towers were finished c.1245, but the building was not completed until the beginning of the 14th cent. Among the master builders are the names Jehan de Chelles, Pierre de Montreuil, Pierre de Chelles, and Jehan Rave. The plan consists of a wide central nave rising 110 ft (34 m) high and flanked by double aisles, with a transept of slight projection from the main body. The aisles continue around the east end, which, with the projecting chapels, forms a chevet. Three sculptured portals are deeply recessed in the majestic west front. Above them a row of sculptures in niches extends across the facade, and over this, in the center, is the huge traceried rose window. In the French Revolution rioters converted the cathedral into a "Temple of Reason" and destroyed the sculptures of the west facade. Skillful restorations were begun in 1845 by Viollet-le-Duc.

Notre Dame Mountains, section of the Appalachian system, extending c.500 mi (800 km) from the Green Mts. of Vermont into the Gaspé Peninsula, Canada. Worn low by erosion, the ancient mountains have an average elevation of c.2,000 ft (610 m).

Nott, Eliphalet (ĭlĭf'əlĭt), 1773–1866, American educator, inventor, and clergyman, b. Ashford, Conn. In 1804, Nott became president of Union College, a post he held for 62 years; he initiated an extensive building program and introduced a scientific course as an alternative to the traditional classical curriculum. He published a number of pamphlets on slavery, temperance, and education and contributed to science by his experiments with heat. Nott was granted over 30 patents and was the inventor of the first anthracite coal base-burner stove. See Codman Hislop, *Eliphalet Nott* (1971); G. P. Schmidt, *The Old Time College President* (1930).

Nottaway (nŏt'əwā), river, c.140 mi (230 km) long, issuing from Mattagami Lake, W Que., Canada, and flowing NW into S James Bay. It is noted for sturgeon. The Waswanipi River (c.195 mi/310 km long) is its chief headstream.

Nottingham, Charles Howard, 1st **earl of** (nŏt'-ĭngəm), 1536–1624, English nobleman. A member of one of the branches of the HOWARD family, he succeeded his father as Baron Howard of Effingham in 1573. He was first cousin to Queen Elizabeth I, to whom he rendered distinguished service—military, naval, and civil. Appointed (1585) lord high admiral, he commanded the English fleet that defeated the Spanish Armada (1588) and shared command (with the 2d earl of Essex) of the expedition against Cádiz (1596). He was created (1597) earl of Nottingham and in 1599 was given command of both land and sea forces. Nottingham continued his service under James I, remaining lord high admiral until 1619.

Nottingham, Daniel Finch, 2d **earl of,** 1647–1730, English politician, son of Heneage Finch, the 1st earl. A staunch supporter of the Church of England, he disapproved of James II's pro-Roman Catholic policies, although he remained loyal to him as king. He accepted the Glorious Revolution, however, and became secretary of state (1689–93) under William III. Holding that religious penalties for dissenters detracted from the integrity of the Anglican church, he pressed for the Toleration Act (1689). On the other hand, he favored civil disabilities for dissenters and long advocated a bill against occasional conformity (i.e., the practice of many dissenters of qualifying for office by merely occasionally receiving communion in the Church of England). In 1711, Nottingham made a bargain with the Whig leaders to oppose Tory proposals for peace in the War of the Spanish Succession in return for their support of his bill against occasional conformity. President of the council on the accession (1714) of George I, he retired in 1716 because he opposed the severe treatment meted out to some of the Jacobite rebels of 1715. In 1729 he inherited the earldom of Winchilsea, which title then became united with that of Nottingham. See Henry Horwitz, *Revolution Politicks* (1968).

Nottingham, Heneage Finch, 1st **earl of** (hĕn'ĭj), 1621–82, lord chancellor of England. He took no part in the politics of the English civil war, but in 1660 he entered Parliament and became solicitor general, serving as prosecutor at the trial of the regicides. He became attorney general in 1670 and lord chancellor in 1675. He was created earl of Nottingham in 1681. In an age of corruption he added to his reputation as an able lawyer that of a statesman of integrity. He is remembered by lawyers for his just and systematic administration of equity.

Nottingham, Thomas Mowbray, earl of: see NORFOLK, THOMAS MOWBRAY, 1ST DUKE OF.

Nottingham, county borough (1971 pop. 299,758), county town of Nottinghamshire, central England, on the Trent River. It is a center of rail and road transportation. The most important industries are the manufacture of lace, hosiery, cotton, and silk. The long-established textile industry greatly profited from the inventions of Hargreaves and Arkwright. Coal, cigarettes, pharmaceuticals, bicycles, and electronic equipment are among Nottingham's many other products. In the 9th cent. it was one of the Danish Five Boroughs. In the 12th cent. much of the city was destroyed by fire. Parliaments were held in Nottingham in 1334, 1337, and 1357. In 1642 the town was the scene of the raising of the standard of Charles I, marking the beginning of the civil war. Early in the 19th cent. LUDDITES were active in the city. The present castle (17th cent.) overlooking the Trent River was burned in 1831 during Reform Bill riots, was restored in 1878, and now houses an art museum. The earlier Norman castle on the same site was once the prison of David II of Scotland and the headquarters of Richard III before the battle of Bosworth Field. Other features of interest are the council house in the market place, a modern Roman Catholic cathedral (designed by A. W. N. Pugin), the 16th-century grammar school (now a high school), the Univ. of Nottingham (1948), and St. Peter's Church, part of which dates from the 12th cent. According to tradition Robin Hood was born in Nottingham. William Booth, founder of the Salvation Army, was born there in 1829.

Nottingham, University of, at Nottingham, England; established 1881 as University College, Nottingham. It received its charter as a university in 1948. It has faculties of agricultural science, arts, applied science, education, law and social sciences, medicine, and pure science.

Nottinghamshire (nŏt'ĭng-əmshĭr) county (1971 pop. 974,640), 843 sq mi (2,183 sq km), central England. The county town is NOTTINGHAM. The land, partially reclaimed fenland, is low-lying and fertile. An area of moors devoted to pasturage, in the south, is known as the Wolds. The principal river is the Trent. SHERWOOD FOREST, with its legends of Robin Hood, includes the Dukeries, a district noted for its splendid estates. Cereal crops and sugar beets are grown. Dairying is extensive, and sheep are also raised. The Nottinghamshire coal fields, with Nottingham, MANSFIELD, and WORKSOP the chief mining centers, extend along the western border. There are small oil fields at Egmanton and Bothamsell. The mineral wealth also includes limestone, sandstone, and gravel. Hosiery, clothing, bicycles, lace, and other products are manufactured. The county was a part of the Anglo-Saxon kingdom of MERCIA. It was there that Charles I unfurled his banner (1642) and marked the beginning of the civil war. Scrooby, the home of William Brewster, was the cradle of the Pilgrims. In 1974, Nottinghamshire was reorganized as a nonmetropolitan county; a small area in the northwest was assigned to the new metropolitan county of South Yorkshire.

Notus: see EOS.

Nouakchott (nwäkshôt'), city (1972 est. pop. 37,000), capital of the Islamic Republic of Mauritania and its Nouakchott dist., W Mauritania, a port on the Atlantic Ocean. Nouakchott was a small village until 1957, when it was chosen as the capital of Mauritania. A large-scale construction program began in 1958. Today Nouakchott is Mauritania's largest city and its administrative center. Its ocean port, which is c.4 mi (6.4 km) from the city proper, has modern storage facilities, especially for petroleum. Handicrafts are made, and light industry is carried on in the city. Nouakchott is located on a major highway and has an international airport. Some historians believe that nearby stood the ribat (monastery) from which the Muslim ALMORAVIDS set out on their conquests of Africa and Spain in the 11th cent.

Noue, François de La: see LA NOUE, FRANÇOIS DE.

Nouméa (nōōmāä'), town (1971 est. pop. 58,000), chief port and capital of the French overseas territory of NEW CALEDONIA, on New Caledonia island, South Pacific. The site of a U.S. airfield in World War II, it is an important air base on transpacific flight routes. Nouméa has many modern office buildings and is the seat of the South Pacific Commission, an international body formed in 1947 to promote the economic and social welfare of island people. The town was a French penal colony from 1864 to 1897.

noumenon (nōō'mənŏn"), in the philosophical system of Immanuel KANT, the "thing-in-itself"; it is the opposite of PHENOMENON, or the thing that appears to us. Noumena, which have an existence alone and are the basic realities behind all sensory experience, are conceived by reason and are therefore thinkable but not knowable. An example of a noumenon is the superego, which lies beyond the limit of possible experience.

noun [Lat.,=name], in English, PART OF SPEECH of vast semantic range. It can be used to name a person, place, thing, idea, or time. It generally functions as subject, object, or indirect object of the verb in the sentence, and may be distinguished by a number of formal criteria. A noun may be recognized by INFLECTION (e.g., *-'s* and *-s*) or by derivation (e.g., *-ness*, *-ity*, and *-tion*). Most languages have a major form class composed of words referring to persons, animals, and objects; but the Latin type of noun declension, with its CASE system, is unusual outside a few families of languages.

nova: see SUPERNOVA.

Novalis (nōvä'lĭs), pseud. of **Friederich von Hardenberg** (frē'drĭkh fən här'dənbĕrk), 1772-1801, German poet. He studied philosophy under Schiller, Schlegel, and Fichte and was especially influenced by Fichte. He later studied geology. Novalis was one of the great German romantics; his chief work was the novel *Heinrich von Ofterdingen* (1802), unfinished at the time of his early death from tuberculosis. It tells the story of a legendary minnesinger, whose wanderings and search for a "blue flower" became symbols of German romantic poetry. Novalis's grief at the death (1797) of his young love, Sophie von Kühn, found expression in a volume of beautiful and deeply religious lyrics, *Hymns to the Night* (1800, tr. 1889, 1948), and in the hymns translated as *Devotional Songs* (1802?). *Christendom or Europe* (1826, tr. 1844) is an exposition of his Roman Catholicism. See study by Bruce Haywood (1959).

Nova Lisboa (nô'və lĕzhbō'ə), city (1969 est. pop. 50,000), W central Angola. The chief town of inland Angola, Nova Lisboa stands on a high plateau and serves as a road, rail, and air transport hub and as a commercial and shipping center for a rich agricultural region. Its railway repair shops are among the largest in Africa. Nova Lisboa exports grain, rice, hides, skins, and fruit. Milling and the production of lime are carried on in the city. Nova Lisboa was founded in 1912 as Huambo.

Novara (nōvä'rä), city (1971 pop. 100,555), capital of Novara prov., Piedmont, N Italy. It is an agricultural and industrial center and a rail junction. Manufactures include textiles, chemicals, machinery, and printed materials. It is a major market for rice. Several battles were fought (1500, 1513) near Novara during the ITALIAN WARS. At Novara, in March, 1849, the Austrians under Radetzky defeated the Piedmontese under Charles Albert (see RISORGIMENTO). The Church of San Gaudenzio (16th-17th cent.) has an impressive campanile (19th cent.).

Nova Scotia (nō'və skō'shə) [Lat.,=new Scotland], province (1971 pop. 788,960), 21,425 sq mi (55,491 sq km), E Canada. One of the MARITIME PROVINCES, it comprises a mainland peninsula and the adjacent Cape Breton Island. The capital is the port of HALIFAX; other important cities are SYDNEY, GLACE BAY, DARTMOUTH, TRURO, and NEW GLASGOW. It is bounded on the N by the Gulf of St. Lawrence, on the E and S by the Atlantic Ocean, and on the W by New Brunswick, from which it is largely separated by the Bay of Fundy. The climate is moderate and the rainfall abundant. The east coast is rocky, with numerous bays and coves, and is dotted with many charming fishing villages. Off the beautiful south shore is Sable Island, called the graveyard of the Atlantic; on the west coast huge Fundy tides wash the shores. There is considerable mining activity in Nova Scotia. Coal is mined principally in the Sydney-Glace Bay area of Cape Breton Island. Gypsum, barite, and salt are also mined. Fishing is next in importance. Fleets operate on the continental shelf edging the coast or move out to the Grand Banks. Cod, lobster, and haddock are the biggest catch. Inland, the forests yield spruce lumber, and the province's industries produce much pulp and paper. In the northwest there is dairying, and the region of Annapolis and Cornwallis supports valuable apple orchards. There are also important hay, grain, fruit, and vegetable crops. The bay lowlands, reclaimed by dikes in the 17th cent., are very productive. The iron and steel industry is centered at Sydney, and the province has a variety of manufacturing industries, including fish- and food-processing. In addition to its all-year port facilities, Halifax is a railroad terminus and a center of shipbuilding and sugar refining. The rivers of Nova Scotia have a number of small hydroelectric stations that help support the economy. A system of railroads and highways interlaces the province, providing an additional lure to tourists attracted by the charms of the rural and coastal countryside. Frequently visited historical spots include the Alexander Graham Bell Museum at Banneck, the Shrine of Evangeline at Grand Pré, and the town of Annapolis Royal, site of the first permanent Canadian settlement (1610). Cape Breton Island (est. 1936) and Kejimkujik (est. 1968) national parks are in Nova Scotia. Sportsmen are attracted by abundant game and all types of fishing, and some of the best sailing on the continent. Two Algonquian tribes, the Abnaki and the Micmac, inhabited the area before white men arrived. John Cabot may have landed (1497) on the tip of Cape Breton Island; European fishermen were already making regular stops during their yearly expeditions. An unsuccessful French settlement was made in 1605 at Port Royal (now Annapolis Royal). In 1610 the French succeeded at the same site. For the next century and a half France and England contested bitterly for colonial rights to ACADIA, which included present-day Nova Scotia, New Brunswick, and Prince Edward Island. In 1621 Sir William Alexander obtained a patent from James I for the colonization of Acadia. Control alternated between France and England through several wars and treaties. Under the Peace of Utrecht (1713-14), the Nova Scotia peninsula was restored to England, although Cape Breton Island was retained by the French. Hostilities were renewed in 1744. During the French and Indian War (1755-63), a tragic incident was the expulsion of the French Acadians—described by Longfellow in *Evangeline.* The Treaty of Paris (1763) gave all of French North America to England. Prince Edward Island, joined to Nova Scotia in 1763, became separate in 1769. With the influx (c.1784) of UNITED EMPIRE LOYALISTS, additional settlement occurred. In 1784 New Brunswick and Cape Breton also became separate colonies; Cape Breton rejoined Nova Scotia in 1820. During the early 19th cent. thousands of Scots and Irish emigrated to Nova Scotia. Under the leadership of Joseph Howe, Nova Scotia became the first colony to achieve (1848) responsible (or cabinet) government. It acceded to the Canadian confederation as one of the four original members in 1867 after considerable difficulty over economic arrangements. Nova Scotia has pioneered in Canadian history with the first newspaper (Halifax Gazette, 1752), the first printing press (1751), and the first university (King's College, Windsor, 1788-89). See J. M. Beck, *The Government of Nova Scotia* (1957); W. S. McNutt, *The Atlantic Provinces* (1965); J. B. Brebner, *New England's Outpost* (1927, repr. 1974) and *The Neutral Yankees of Nova Scotia* (1937, repr. 1970); T. B. Akins, comp., *Acadia and Nova Scotia* (1869, repr. 1972).

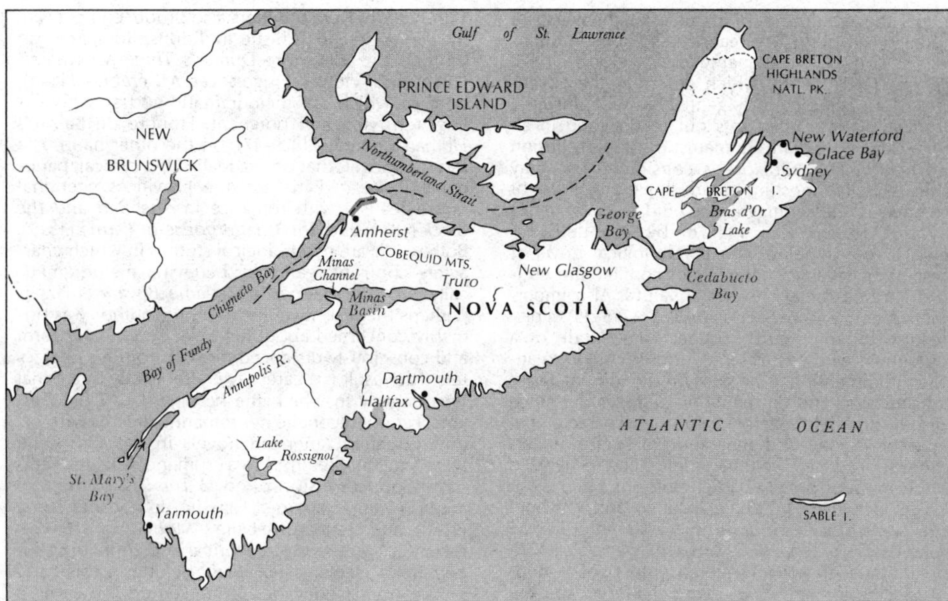

Nova Sofala (nô'və sōōfä'lə), city, SE Mozambique, on Mozambique Channel. An early Arab trading post, it was settled by the Portuguese in 1505, when a fort was built. Nova Sofala was the starting point for expeditions into the mineral-rich hinterland.

Novatian (nōvā'shən), fl. 250, Roman priest, antipope (from 251), and theologian. He opposed the election of St. Cornelius as pope and set himself up instead. He gained followers throughout the empire because of his espousal of the old doctrine of MONTANISM that those fallen from grace were barred from the church forever. At the instigation of St. Cyprian of Carthage, who was himself quite strict on readmission to the church, virtually the whole church recognized Cornelius and repudiated Novatian and his followers, who maintained their own hierarchy for two or three centuries. After 325 their distinction was almost solely historical in significance, for the sect was merged with DONATISM. Novatian's chief work, *On the Trinity,* which was written as a refutation of the Gnostics, the Theodotians, and the Sabellians, was later regarded as an orthodox expression of ante-Nicene doctrine, except for the last chapter, which anticipated Arianism.

Novato (nōvä'tō), residential city (1970 pop. 31,006), Marin co., W Calif., on San Pablo Bay; inc. 1960.

Novaya Zemlya (nô"vīə zĭmlyä'), archipelago, c.35,000 sq mi (90,650 sq km), in the Arctic Ocean between the Barents and Kara seas, NW USSR. It consists of two main islands (separated by Matochkin Strait) and many smaller ones. The mountains of Novaya Zemlya, rising to c.3,500 ft (1,070 m), are a continuation of the Urals. In the north the archipelago is glaciated and is covered by arctic desert; the southern part is tundra. Copper, lead, zinc, and asphaltite are found there. Fishing, sealing, and trapping are the chief occupations of the region's small population, which lives mainly along the western coast. The islands have been used by the Russians for thermonuclear testing. Discovered by Novgorodians in the 11th or 12th cent., the islands were sighted by explorers searching for the Northeast Passage in the 1500s. Since the mid-1800s Russians have explored Novaya Zemlya and built settlements and scientific stations.

novel, in modern literary usage, a sustained work of prose fiction a volume or more in length. It is distinguished from the SHORT STORY and the fictional sketch, which are necessarily brief.

History of the Novel. Although the novel has a place in the literatures of all nations, this article will concentrate on the evolution of the novel in England, France, the Soviet Union, and the United States. The term *novel* is derived from *novella*, Italian for a compact, realistic, often ribald prose tale popular in the Renaissance and best exemplified by the stories in Giovanni Boccaccio's *Decameron* (1348-53). The novel can, therefore, be considered a work of imagination that is grounded in reality. On the other hand, during the Middle Ages a popular literary form was the romance, a type of tale that describes the adventures, both natural and supernatural, of such figures of legend as the Trojan heroes, Alexander the Great, and King Arthur and his knights. Thus, the modern novel is rooted in two traditions, the mimetic and the fantastic, or the realistic and the romantic. Indeed, the conflict between romantic dreams and harsh reality has been the theme of many great novels. The historical development of the novel continually reflects the dual tradition. Among its precursors Petronius' *Satyricon* (1st cent. A.D.) presents a vivid portrait of life in Nero's Rome while satirizing the corruption there, whereas the *Metamorphoses* (2d cent. A.D.) of Lucius Apuleius describes the fantastic adventures of a young man who is transformed into an ass; *Daphnis and Chloë* (3d cent. A.D.), attributed to Longus, is a love story about a goatherd and a shepherdess, while the *Thousand and One Nights* (10th-11th cent.) is a collection of stories that often tell of magic or supernatural happenings; and *Tale of Genji* (11th cent.), by Lady Murasaki, depicts Japanese court life, whereas *Amadis of Gaul* (13th or 14th cent.) recounts the fabulous exploits of a knight who is a model of chivalry. The realistic and romantic tendencies converge in Cervantes's *Don Quixote de la Mancha* (1605, 1615), which describes the adventures of an aging country gentleman who, inspired by chivalric romances, sets out to do good in an ugly world. A brilliant, humanistic study of illusion and reality, *Don Quixote* is considered by many critics to be the most important single progenitor of the novel. Of lesser magnitude but lasting influence is *The Princess of Cleves* (1678), by Mme de La Fayette; a forerunner of the psychological novel, it presents believable characters in conflict and criticizes shifting social and moral values. Also important is Alain René Le Sage's *Gil Blas* (1715-35), a picaresque [Span. *picaro*=rogue, knave] tale of a young man who passes rapidly from one job to another, commenting as he goes on the idiosyncrasies of his masters and on the world at large. This story, episodic and held together by a single character, became the model for a generation of English writers who first produced what has come to be recognized as the modern novel. Daniel Defoe is famous for *Robinson Crusoe* (1719), a detailed and convincingly realistic account of the successful efforts of an island castaway to survive, and *Moll Flanders* (1722), which relates the picaresque adventures of a good-natured harlot and thief. Samuel Richardson extended the influence of the form over its middle-class audience with his epistolary novels: *Pamela* (1740), about the rewards of virtue, and *Clarissa* (1747-48), about the evils of a fall from virtue. Meant to offer instruction in letter writing as well as in moral conduct, these works emphasize character rather than action. However, both elements are present in Henry Fielding's *Tom Jones* (1749). This novel was the first to present a full portrait of ordinary English life, including a none-too-perfect but likable hero; in addition the work included critical comments by the author on the nature of the novel. Each of the 18th-century novels mentioned is essentially realistic, and each has, at one time or another, been designated the first novel in English. Against this mainstream, with its emphasis on external reality, stands Laurence Sterne's *Tristram Shandy* (1760-67), a rambling nine-volume novel replete with blank pages, digressions, chapters in reverse order, and unconventional punctuation, all of which combine to reveal an internal, psychological reality based on John Locke's theory of the association of ideas; psychological reality would resurface as a fictional preoccupation early in the 20th cent. The novel became the dominant form of literature in the 19th cent., which produced many works that are considered milestones in the development of the form. In Britain, Sir Walter Scott's *Waverley* (1814), about the 1745 Jacobite rising behind Charles Edward Stuart, inaugurated the historical novel. Jane Austen's *Pride and Prejudice* (1813) and *Emma* (1816), contemplating and satirizing life among a small group of country gentry in Regency England, initiated the highly structured and polished novel of manners. A variant with a wider scope is William Makepeace Thackeray's *Vanity Fair* (1847-48), which anatomizes and satirizes London society. The serialization of novels in various periodicals brought the form an ever-expanding audience. Particularly popular were the works of Charles Dickens, including *Oliver Twist* (1839) and *David Copperfield* (1850). Readers were drawn by Dickens's sympathetic, melodramatic, and humorous delineation of a world peopled with characters of all social classes, and by his condemnation of various social abuses. Further portraits of English society appear in Anthony Trollope's Barsetshire novels, which scrutinize clerical life in a small, rural town, and George Eliot's *Silas Marner* (1861) and *Middlemarch* (1871-72), which treat the lives of ordinary people in provincial towns with humanity and a strong moral sense. George Meredith's *Ordeal of Richard Feverel* (1859) and *The Egoist* (1879) are analytical tragicomedies set in high social circles. The conflict between man and nature is stressed in Thomas Hardy's *Return of the Native* (1878) and *Tess of the D'Urbervilles* (1891). Although the great English novels of the 19th cent. were predominantly realistic, novels of fantasy and romance formed a literary undercurrent. Charlotte Brontë's *Jane Eyre* (1847) and Emily Brontë's *Wuthering Heights* (1847) each present imaginative, passionate visions of human love. Robert Louis Stevenson revived the adventure tale and the horror story in *Treasure Island* (1883) and *The Strange Case of Dr. Jekyll and Mr. Hyde* (1886). Horror and adventure were combined in the novels of Joseph Conrad, notably *Lord Jim* (1900) and *Heart of Darkness* (1902), both works achieving high levels of stylistic and psychological sophistication. Major 19th-century French writers also produced novels in the romantic and realistic traditions. Romance can be found in Alexandre Dumas's *Three Musketeers* (1844) and Victory Hugo's *Les Misérables* (1844), both of which are melodramatic and swashbuckling, terrifying and poignant. Honoré de Balzac's *Human Comedy* (1829-47), on the other hand, is a series of novels that offer a realistic, if cynical, panorama of life in Paris and the provinces. Stendhal mixed realism with romance in *The Red and the Black* (1831) and *The Charterhouse of Parma* (1839). Both works are psychological studies in which characters confront reality by behaving melodramatically. Gustave Flaubert's *Madame Bovary* (1857) is perhaps the first novel in which the author was primarily concerned about his work as a literary form and consciously distanced himself from his characters. The result is a carefully crafted study of a banal love tragedy in which the heroine, like Don Quixote, cannot reconcile her romantic dreams with ordinary reality. American novels in the 19th cent. were explicitly referred to as romances. James Fenimore Cooper's historical novel *The Last of the Mohicans* (1826), Nathaniel Hawthorne's *Scarlet Letter* (1850), and Herman Melville's *Moby-Dick* (1851)—the latter two heavily allegorical and containing supernatural elements—properly belong in this category. In the last decades of the century, however, a shift toward realism occurred. Mark Twain's *Adventures of Huckleberry Finn* (1883), a revival of the picaresque novel, is romantic in its Mississippi River setting but realistic in its satirical attack on religious hypocrisy and racial persecution. By the end of the century Henry James had brought his moral vision and powers of psychological observation to the novel in numerous works, including *The Portrait of a Lady* (1881), *The Spoils of Poynton* (1897), and *The Ambassadors* (1903). These novels are not only masterpieces of realism but also—in their carefully crafted form, experimental point of view, and superb style—supreme examples of the novel as a literary genre. A lesser figure, William Dean Howells, realistically portrayed a marriage and divorce in *A Modern Instance* (1882) and the newly rich classes in *The Rise of Silas Lapham* (1885). In the 19th cent. Russian novelists quickly gained world reputations for their powerful statements of human and cosmic problems. If Leo Tolstoy's *War and Peace* (1865-69) is a God-centered novel, Feodor Dostoyevsky's *Crime and Punishment* (1866) can be considered a God-haunted one. World War I and its attendant disillusion with 19th-century values radically altered the nature of the novel. In search of greater freedom of expression English writers like E. M. Forster in *Howard's End* (1910), D. H. Lawrence in *Sons and Lovers* (1913), and James Joyce in *Ulysses* (1922) described more explicitly than ever before the conflict between human intellect and human sexuality. Joyce, along with Dorothy Richardson in *Pilgrimage* (1915-38) and Virginia Woolf in *Mrs. Dalloway* (1925) and *To the Lighthouse* (1927), carried Freud's discovery of the unconscious into art by attempting to portray human thought and emotion through the STREAM OF CONSCIOUSNESS technique. Like Sterne these writers were concerned with inner rather than outer reality. In the United States the profound postwar dislocation of values is evident in such novels as *The Great Gatsby* (1925), by F. Scott Fitzgerald, about a romantic bootlegger whose version of the American dream of success is shattered by a corrupt reality; *The Sun Also Rises* (1926), by Ernest Hemingway, concerning a group of disillusioned expatriots in Europe who find meaning only in immediate physical experience; and *The Sound and the Fury* (1929), by William Faulkner, about the disintegration of a once-proud Southern family. An even more profound dislocation occurred in the years following World War II. To many American novelists the atrocities of the Nazi regime, the specter of the atom bomb, the tensions of the cold war, the horrors of the war in Vietnam, the assassinations and riots of the 1960s, and the political corruption of the 70s rendered so-called reality terrifyingly unreal and made the realistic novel obsolete. And so, again, there was a switch toward the fantastic. Novelists such as John Hawkes, William Burroughs, and Kurt Vonnegut wrote darkly surreal fantasies, while Philip Roth and Norman Mailer produced brutal satires of American life and Joyce Carol Oates wrote fictive studies of violence in America. The 20th-century novel in France is distinguished primarily by Marcel Proust's *Remembrance of Things Past* (1913-27), a monumental novel in seven parts that is at once an inquiry into the meaning of experience, a study of the development of an artist, and a detailed portrait of life within a particular segment of French society. Also important are Jean-Paul Sartre's *Nausea* (1938) and Albert Camus's *The Stranger* (1942), both fictional explications of EXISTENTIALISM. In the late 1950s there appeared in France the so-called new novel, in which traditional elements such as plot, characterization, and rational ordering of time and space are abandoned and replaced by flashbacks, slow motion, magnification of objects, and a scenario format, all of which produce a mutant—the novel influenced by films. New novelists include Michel Butor, Alain Robbe-Grillet, Marguerite Duras, and Nathalie Sarraute. After the 1917 Revolution, the novel in the Soviet Union either avoided offending the Communist party or, by reflecting a dissenting outlook, avoided publication in the USSR. Mikhail Sholokhov's epic series about the Don Cossacks, including *And Quiet Flows the Don* (1934), met the first qualification; Boris Pasternak's *Dr. Zhivago* (1957), about life in Russia from 1903 to 1929, and Aleksandr Solzhenitsyn's *Cancer Ward* (1968) and *First Circle* (1968), both realistic, powerful accounts of life under Stalin's regime, met the second and were published outside the Soviet Union.

Types of Novel. For convenience in analyzing the forms, critics often place novels in categories that encompass years of historical development. An early and prevalent type was the picaresque novel, in which the protagonist, a social underdog, has a series of episodic adventures in which he sees much of the world around him and comments satirically upon it. Variations of this type include, in addition to those already mentioned, Saul Bellow's *Adventures of Augie March* (1953) and Thornton Wilder's *Theophilus North* (1973). Notable examples of the epistolary novel are *Dangerous Connections* (1782), by Pierre Laclos, a study in depravity made all the more devastating because the characters' evil is revealed obliquely through their correspondence, and *The Documents in the Case* (1930), by Dorothy L. Sayers, in which a crime and its solution are revealed through letters. The historical novel embraces not only the event-filled romances of Scott, Cooper, and Kenneth Roberts, but also works that strive to convey the essence of life in a certain time and place, such as Sigrid Undset's *Kristin Lavransdatter* (1920-22), about life in medieval Norway, and Mary Renault's *Mask of Apollo* (1966), set in ancient Greece. Closely related to the historical novel is the social novel, which presents a panoramic picture of an entire age. Balzac's *Human Comedy* and Tolstoy's *War and Peace* became models for those that followed, including *U.S.A.* (1937), by John Dos Passos. The naturalistic novel studies the effect of heredity and environment on human beings. Emile Zola's series, *The Rougon-Macquarts* (1871-93) influenced Arnold Bennett's novels of the "Five Towns," which treat life in the potteries in the English midlands; other novels that can be called naturalistic are *The Four Horsemen of the Apocalypse* (1918), by Vicente Blasco Ibáñez, and *An American Tragedy* (1925), by Theodore Dreiser. A derivative of the social novel is the regional novel, which delineates the life of people in a particular place—focusing on customs and speech—to demonstrate how environment influences its inhabitants. Notable examples of this genre are Hardy's "Wessex novels" and William Faulkner's novels set in Yoknapatawpha County. The novels of Ignazio Silone, notably *Bread and Wine* (1936), are both social and regional—in a small Italian village Silone reveals a microcosm of Mussolini's Italy. Further classifications include novels of the soil—stark stories of people living close to the earth like Ole Rølvaag's *Giants in the Earth* (1927); novels of the sea such as Richard Henry Dana's *Two Years before the Mast* (1840); and novels of the air like Antoine de St. Exupéry's *Night Flight* (1931). Novels that treat themes of creation, judgment, and redemption are often called metaphysical novels; famous examples include Franz Kafka's *The Castle* (1926), Georges Bernanos's *Diary of a Country Priest* (1936), and Graham Greene's *Heart of the Matter* (1948). The German *Bildungsroman* [formation novel], *Erziehungsroman* [education novel] and *Künstlerroman* [artist novel] make useful distinctions among works like Thomas Mann's *Magic Mountain* (1924), Colette's *Claudine* series (1900-1903), and Joyce's *Portrait of the Artist as a Young Man* (1915) respectively. Taken together, they can be called novels of initiation. So can Proust's *Remembrance of Things Past*, but because of its extensive analysis of the minds and hearts of a large cast of characters it can also be placed with such disparate works as *Demian* (1919), by Herman Hesse, *The Catcher in the Rye* (1951), by J. D. Salinger, and *Thousand Cranes* (tr. 1956), by Yasunari Kawabata, in the ranks of the psychological novel. The tradition of the novel of manners, with its emphasis on the conventions of a particular group of people in a particular time and place, persists in such works as Edith Wharton's *Age of Innocence* (1920), John O'Hara's *Butterfield 8* (1935), and John Updike's *Couples* (1967). Although classification of novels is helpful in indicating the breadth and diversity of the form, the great novel transcends such categorization, existing as a complete, many-faceted world in itself.

Point of View. Critics have also classified the numerous experiments at reader manipulation carried on by novelists who relate their stories from different points of view. The omniscient point of view is that of the all-knowing author who is also the narrator. Thus Fielding's voice is heard in *Tom Jones* as is that of Dickens in *A Tale of Two Cities* (1859). Point of view can be limited in a variety of ways. Indeed, much of the development of the novel in the 20th cent. involved such limitation. And as the importance of point of view increased, the importance of plot diminished. In *The Golden Bowl* (1904), James used a narrator-observer who filters the events and emotional climate of the story for the reader, but whose own knowledge of other characters' motives and of the outcome of events is restricted. Since he talks about others, he uses the third person. For *Remembrance of Things Past,* Proust created a narrator-participant who analyzes the lifelong development of his own intellectual, emotional, and aesthetic faculties in the first person. In *Ulysses,* Joyce composed interior monologues for his characters, which ran simultaneously with their ordinary conversation with other people. Faulkner's *Sound and the Fury* is told from the point of view, successively, of an idiot, a neurotic, and an egoist. More recently, the French new novelists like Butor in *The Modification* (1957) have experimented with the second person narrative, which creates a deliberate, unexpected yet not unpleasant tension for the reader who wonders whether the narrator is addressing him or talking to himself. See DETECTIVE STORY; SCIENCE FICTION; separate entries on the authors mentioned in the article. See Henry James, *The Future of the Novel* (ed. by Leon Edel, 1956); F. R. Leavis, *The Great Tradition* (1948, repr. 1964); E. M. Forster, *Aspects of the Novel* (1927, repr. 1966); Percy Lubbock, *The Craft of Fiction* (1957, repr. 1966); Anthony Burgess, *The Novel Now: A Guide to Contemporary Fiction* (1967); Philip Stevick, ed., *The Theory of the Novel* (1967); D. I. Grossvogel, *Limits of the Novel* (1968); Edwin Muir, *The Structure of the Novel* (1929, repr. 1969); David Goldknopf, *The Life of the Novel* (1972); György Lukács, *The Theory of the Novel* (tr. 1973); see also E. A. Baker, *The History of the English Novel* (10 vol., 1950; Vol. XI by Lionel Stevenson, 1967); C. C. van Doren, *The American Novel, 1789–1939* (rev. ed. 1955); R. V. Chase, *The American Novel and Its Tradition* (1957); Martin Turnell, *The Novel in France* (1951, repr. 1958); D. E. Maxwell, *American Fiction* (1963); Roy Pascal, *The German Novel* (1956, repr. 1965); Henri Peyre, *French Novelists of Today* (1967); Arnold Kettle, *An Introduction to the English Novel* (rev. ed., 2 vol. in 1, 1968); H. M. Waidson, *The Modern German Novel, 1945–1965* (2d ed. 1971); A. F. Boyd, *Aspects of the Russian Novel* (1972).

novella: see NOVEL.

Novels: see CORPUS JURIS CIVILIS.

November: see MONTH.

novena (nōvē'nə) [Lat.,=a group of nine], in the Roman Catholic Church, primarily a series of public or private prayers extending over nine consecutive days, especially nine days preceding a feast. They often carry an INDULGENCE. More rarely, a novena extends over any nine days, as nine consecutive Mondays or nine first Fridays of the month. By extension, especially in America, the term is used for a regular series of prayers, e.g., a "perpetual novena" occurring every Friday. Novenas are made especially in honor of the saints to ask their intercession for certain benefits. They are frequent in honor of the Virgin Mary (under her various aspects, e.g., Our Lady of Sorrows), of St. Joseph, of St. Anne, of St. Anthony, and of other saints whose cults are popular, and they are said for the repose of the souls in purgatory. Widespread public novenas are those of Pentecost (beginning the Saturday after Ascension), of the Assumption (Aug. 7–15), of the Immaculate Conception (Nov. 30–Dec. 8), and the "novena of grace," in honor of St. Francis Xavier (March 3–11). Public novenas must be approved by the church authorities. The practice of novenas is very ancient in the Western Church, and the idea was probably borrowed from Roman paganism.

Novgorod (nôv'gərət), city (1970 pop. 128,000), capital of Novgorod oblast, NW European USSR, on the Volkhov River near the point where it leaves Lake Ilmen. Novgorod's industries produce china, furniture, bricks, and wood and food products. It is one of the oldest Russian cities, believed to have been founded in antiquity by the Slovenes. A major commercial and cultural center of medieval Europe, it lay on the chief trade routes of Eastern Europe. Rurik, who is said to have founded the Russian state in 862, was invited by the inhabitants of Novgorod to rule them. Culturally, the city was the equal of Kiev; the bulk of ancient manuscripts originated in Novgorod. The capital was transferred to Kiev by Oleg in 886, but Novgorod remained the chief center of foreign trade, obtaining self-government in 997 and achieving independence from Kiev in 1136, when it became the capital of an independent republic—Sovereign Great Novgorod, an area that embraced the whole of N Russia to the Urals. Novgorod was governed by a popular assembly or *veche* that elected—and often exiled—the dukes. Although they held supreme military and judicial powers, the dukes had no legislative or administrative functions; these powers were vested in elected magistrates. However, the popular assemblies were disorderly, and power was gradually obtained by the aristocracy. The strength of the republic rested on its economic prosperity. Situated on the great trade route to the Volga valley, it became, with London, Bruges, and Bergen, one of the four chief trade centers of the HANSEATIC LEAGUE. German merchants had a colony in Novgorod. Furs, hides, wax, honey, flax, and tar were the chief exports. Cloth and metals were imported from Europe and corn from central Russia. Transit trade with the Orient reached a great volume. The enterprising merchants of Novgorod extended the power of the republic over the entire north of Russia, levied tribute even beyond the Urals, and founded many colonies. The citizens of Novgorod repulsed the attacks of the Teutonic Knights and Livonian Knights and of the Swedes and escaped the Mongol invasion. At its height, in the 14th cent., its population rose to c.400,000. Its colorful splendor during that period, its hundreds of churches, its great shops and arsenals, its huge fairs, have furnished rich themes for later Russian art and folklore. However, the 14th cent. also witnessed the start of Novgorod's long struggle with Moscow for supremacy. Internecine disputes among the republic's leaders weakened it in the face of growing Muscovite strength. Although it became a vassal of Moscow after the Muscovite invasions in 1456 and 1470, Novgorod was allowed to retain its self-government. It was not until 1478 that it came under Moscow's complete control and lost its freedom. Novgorod retained its commercial position until St. Petersburg (now Leningrad) was built in 1703. The magnificent architectural monuments of Novgorod earned it the name the "museum city" until World War II, when it was held by the Germans (1941–44) and suffered great damage. Chief among the losses was the 12th-century kremlin, on the left river bank, containing the Cathedral of St. Sophia (founded 1045). On the right bank, the former commercial center, were numerous medieval churches and a museum of old Russian art. Many of the damaged buildings have been restored, but their frescoes are lost forever.

Novibazar: see NOVI PAZAR, Yugoslavia.

Novikov, Nikolai Ivanovich (nyĭkəlī' ēvä'nəvĭch nô'vĕkəf), 1744–1818, Russian journalist and publisher. In 1769, with the *Drone,* he started the vogue of the satirical magazine modeled on Addison's *Spectator.* This and subsequent journals were halted by Catherine II in 1774 because of their sharp attacks on serious social injustice. He published several other short-lived satirical journals and huge numbers of books designed to spread enlightenment at a modest price, and again was stopped by imperial order. Novikov was imprisoned (1792–96) for affiliation with the Rosicrucian Order of Freemasons. Released a broken man, he retired to study mysticism in seclusion.

Novi Ligure (nō'vē lē'gōōrā), town (1971 pop. 32,213), Piedmont, NW Italy. It is an industrial center and transportation junction. At Novi Ligure in 1799 the Austrian and Russian forces under Suvarov defeated the French under Joubert, who was killed.

Novi Pazar (nô''vē päzär'), town (1971 pop. 64,454), E Yugoslavia, in Serbia, on the Raška River. It is a trade and industrial center where textiles, carpets, and copper ware are produced. Known as Raška or Rashka in the 9th cent., it was the capital of Serbia from the 12th to the 14th cent. It was captured by the Turks in 1456 and became an important trade center and the seat of the Turkish sanjak [district] of Novibazar (an older spelling). The sanjak of Novibazar was occupied by Austria from 1879 to 1908, but remained under Turkish civil administration until 1913, when it passed to Serbia. It became part of Yugoslavia after World War I. The town retains much of its Turkish architecture.

Novi Sad (nô'vē säd), Ger. *Neusatz,* Hung. *Újvidék,* city (1971 pop. 214,048), NE Yugoslavia, in Serbia, on the Danube River. The capital of the Vojvodina region and an industrial center and port, it has industries that produce agricultural machinery, electrical equipment, and munitions. Known in the 16th cent., it rapidly developed as a commercial center, became an Orthodox episcopal see, and was made (1748) a royal free city of Austria-Hungary. In the 18th and early 19th cent. Novi Sad was the center of the Serbian literary revival. It was incorporated into Yugoslavia in 1918. The city has a Greek Orthodox church, a university, and numerous cultural facilities.

Novocain (nō'vəkān''), trade name for the anesthetic PROCAINE.

Novocherkassk (nô''vəchĭrkäsk'), city (1970 pop. 162,000), SE European USSR, on the Aksai River (the right tributary of the Don). It manufactures locomotives, machine tools, mining and building equipment, electrical apparatus, oil field machinery, and chemicals. Founded in 1805, it remained the administrative center of the Don Cossacks until 1920. Novocherkassk was the site of the hetman's palace and has a Don Cossack historical museum.

Novokuznetsk (nô'vōkōōz''nĕtsk), city (1970 pop. 499,000), S central Siberian USSR, on the Tom River. Iron, steel, mining equipment, chemicals, aluminum, and iron alloys are produced. The old town of Kuznetsk was founded by Cossacks in 1617 and was a trading center until the 20th cent. It was developed in the 1930s as Stalinsk, an iron and steel center of the Kuznetsk Basin, and was merged with its newer industrial section in 1932. The name Novokuznetsk dates from 1961.

Novomoskovsk (nô''vəməskôfsk'), city (1970 pop. 134,000), W central European USSR. An industrial center in the Moscow coal basin, it has coal mines and chemical plants. Founded in 1930 as Bobriki, the city was renamed Stalinogorsk in 1934 and Novomoskovsk in 1961.

Novonikolayevsk: see NOVOSIBIRSK, USSR.

Novorossiysk or **Novorossiisk** (both: nô''vərəsēsk'), city (1970 pop. 133,000), Krasnodar Kray, SE European USSR, on the Black Sea. A major port and a naval base, it exports grain, has shipyards, and is a major center of the Soviet cement industry. The city stands on the site of a Genoese colony (13th–14th cent.) and of a Turkish fortress, captured by the Russians in 1808. The present city was founded in 1838, and the first cement factory was opened in 1882. Before 1914 it was one of the important grain-exporting cities of Russia. The city was held (1919–20) by the White forces during the Russian civil war.

Novosibirsk (nô''vəsĭbērsk'), city (1970 pop. 1,161,000), capital of Novosibirsk oblast, S Siberian USSR, on the Ob River and the Trans-Siberian RR. It is a large river, rail, and air transportation hub and is the leading industrial center of Siberia. Novosibirsk has machine, textile, chemical, and metallurgical industries. Founded as Novonikolayevsk in 1893, during the construction of the Trans-Siberian RR, it grew as a trade center and was renamed in 1925. Its growth is largely due to the proximity of the KUZNETSK BASIN. The Siberian branch of the Academy of Sciences of the USSR is in Novosibirsk. There is a hydroelectric power station on the Ob above the city. The region forming Novosibirsk oblast (which includes the BARABA STEPPE) is predominantly agricultural, although there is coal mining to the east.

Novosibirskiye Ostrova, USSR: see NEW SIBERIAN ISLANDS.

Novotný, Antonín (än'tônyēn nô'vôtnē), 1904–75, Czechoslovakian Communist leader. A founding member (1921) of the Communist party, he participated (1948) in the Communist seizure of power and became first secretary of the party in 1953. In 1957 he became president of Czechoslovakia, thus uniting the two top national posts. Novotný's regime was characterized by repression, bureaucracy, and economic stagnation. A liberal majority, led by Alexander DUBČEK, coalesced against him and in Jan., 1968, Novotný was replaced as first secretary by Dubček. Later that year he was forced to resign from the presidency.

Novy Margelan: see FERGANA, USSR.

Novy Urgench: see URGENCH, USSR.

Nowa Huta: see KRAKÓW, Poland.

Nowy Port: see GDANSK, Poland.

Nowy Sącz (nô'vĭ sôNch'), Ger. *Neu-Sandez,* city (1970 pop. 41,103), SE Poland, on the Dunajec. It is a railway junction and industrial center producing machinery, agricultural tools, chemicals, and footwear. There are deposits of lignite and petroleum in the vicinity. Chartered in 1298, it passed to Austria in 1772 and was included in Poland in 1919. The city has several old churches; its 14th-century palace was destroyed in World War II.

Noyes, Alfred (noiz), 1880–1958, English poet, best known for his poems "The Highwayman" and "The Barrel-Organ." His first volume of verse, *Loom of Years,* appeared in 1902. It was followed by such poems as the epic *Drake* (1908) and the colorful *Tales of the Mermaid Tavern* (1913). From 1914 to 1923, Noyes was professor of English literature at Princeton. In 1925, Noyes converted to Roman Catholicism; *The Unknown God* (1934) is an account of his conversion. His later writings include *The Torch Bearers* (1922–30), a trilogy in verse on man's scientific accomplishments; *The Sun Cure* (1929), a novel; and a biography of Voltaire (1938). His collected poems were published in 1950. Noyes was a literary conservative who adhered to traditional models in the structure and substance of his poetry. His poems, highly colored and romantic, are often marred by sentimentality. See his autobiography, *Two Worlds for Memory* (1953); biography by Walter Jerrold (1930).

Noyes, John Humphrey, 1811–86, American reformer, founder of the ONEIDA COMMUNITY, b. Brattleboro, Vt. He studied theology at Yale but lost his license to preach because of his "perfectionist" doctrine. This took its name from Mat. 5.48 and was based on the belief that man's innate sinlessness could be regained through communion with Christ. At Putney, Vt., he formed (1839) a society of Bible communists, later called Perfectionists. In 1846 they began the practice of complex marriage, a form of polygamy, but this so aroused their neighbors that Noyes was forced to flee. In 1848 he established another community at Oneida, N.Y. (and later a branch at Wallingford, Conn.), where he developed his religious and social experiments in communal living. By 1879 internal dissension had arisen and outside hostility became so strong that Noyes went to Canada, where he spent the rest of his life. His writings include *The Berean* (1847, repr. 1969) and many pamphlets. See George W. Noyes, comp., *Religious Experience of John Humphrey Noyes* (1923, repr. 1971) and *John Humphrey Noyes: the Putney Community* (1931); R. A. Parker, *A Yankee Saint* (1935); Pierrepont B. Noyes, *My Father's House* (1937); C. N. Robertson, ed., *Oneida Community* (1970).

Noyon (nwäyôN'), town (1968 pop. 11,863), Oise dept., N France. It has foundries; metalworks; and machine, asbestos, clothing, furniture, and food-processing industries. In 768 at Noyon, Charlemagne was crowned king of the Franks. France and Spain signed a treaty there in 1516 (see ITALIAN WARS). The town was devastated in both World Wars, but the Cathedral of Notre Dame (12th–13th cent.) has survived. The house where John Calvin was born is now a museum.

Np, chemical symbol of element NEPTUNIUM.

Nu, U (o͞o no͞o), 1907–, Burmese political leader, prime minister of Burma (1948–56, 1957–58, 1960–62). A nationalist, he was expelled by the British authorities from the Univ. of Rangoon law school in 1936 for his political activities. He taught school and then became a leader of the Burmese nationalist movement; he assumed the nationalist title Thakin [lord or master] and was known as Thakin Nu until he attained the honorific U. In 1942, with the growing threat of a Japanese invasion, he was imprisoned by the British. Released after the Japanese occupied Burma, he served as foreign minister in the puppet cabinet while organizing an anti-Japanese guerrilla force. After the war he helped secure (1948) Burma's independence from Britain and was (1948–56) its first premier. He resigned in 1956, returned to power in 1957, but was forced to yield to the army, led by General Ne Win, in 1958. He was reelected in 1960 but in 1962 was deposed and arrested by Ne Win. Released in 1966, he organized (1969) and led from exile in Thailand a movement opposing Ne Win. In 1973 he was forced to leave Thailand and went to the United States. A devout Buddhist, he was long the popular spiritual leader of his country. Among his works are *The People Win Through* (1951), *An Asian Speaks* (1955), and *Burma under the Japanese* (1954). See Richard Butwell, *U Nu of Burma* (1963, repr. 1969).

Nubia (no͞o'bēə), ancient state of NE Africa. At the height of its political power Nubia extended, from north to south, from the First Cataract of the Nile (near Aswan, Egypt) to Khartoum, in the Sudan. It early came under the influence of the pharaohs, and in the 20th cent. B.C. Seti I completed the occupation of the area. Many centuries later Egypt itself was ruled (8th and 7th cent. B.C.) by conquering Nubians of the CUSH (Kush) kingdom. Later, after the Assyrians expelled (c.667 B.C.) Tirhakah from Egypt, the Cushite capital was moved (c.530) from NAPATA to MEROË. Meroë fell (c.350) to the Ethiopians and was abandoned. The region then came under the sway of the Nobatae, a Negro tribe that mixed with the indigenous stock and formed a powerful kingdom with its capital at Dongola. The kingdom was converted to Christianity in the 6th cent. A.D Joined with the Christian kingdom of Ethiopia, it long resisted Muslim encroachment, but in the 14th cent. it finally collapsed. Nubia was then broken up into many petty states. Muhammad Ali of Egypt conquered (1820–22) Nubia, and in the late 19th cent. much of the area was held by supporters of the MAHDI. See A. J. Arkell, *A History of the Sudan to A. D. 1821* (1955).

Nubian Desert, eastern region of the Sahara Desert, c.157,000 sq mi (407,000 sq km), NE Republic of Sudan, NE Africa, between the Nile and the Red Sea. The arid region, largely a sandstone plateau, has numerous wadis flowing toward (but never reaching) the Nile, whose great bends are entrenched in the western part of the region.

nuclear disarmament: see DISARMAMENT, NUCLEAR.

nuclear energy, the energy stored in the NUCLEUS of an atom and released through fission, fusion, or RADIOACTIVITY. In these processes a small amount of MATTER is converted to ENERGY according to the relationship $E = mc^2$, where E is energy, m is mass, and c is the speed of light (see RELATIVITY). The release of nuclear energy is associated with changes from less stable to more stable nuclei and produces far more energy for a given mass of fuel than any other source of energy. In fission processes, a fissionable nucleus absorbs a neutron, becomes unstable, and splits into two nearly equal nuclei. In fusion processes, two nuclei combine to form a single, heavier nucleus. The most stable nuclei—those with the highest binding energies per nucleon holding their components together—are in the middle range of atomic weights, with the maximum stability at weights near 60. Thus, fission, which produces two lighter fragments, occurs for very heavy nuclei, while fusion occurs for the lightest nuclei. The process of nuclear fission was discovered in 1938 by Otto Hahn and Fritz Strassmann and was explained in early 1939 by Lise Meitner and Otto Frisch. The fissionable ISOTOPE of uranium, U-235, can be split by bombarding it with a slow, or thermal, neutron. (Slow neutrons are called "thermal" because their average kinetic energies are about the same as those of the molecules of air at ordinary temperatures.) The atomic numbers of the nuclei resulting from the fission add up to 92, which is the atomic number of uranium. A number of pairs of product nuclei are possible, with the most frequently produced fragments being krypton and barium. Since this reaction also releases an average of 2.5 neutrons, a CHAIN REACTION is possible, provided at least one neutron per fission is captured by another nucleus and causes a second fission. In an ATOMIC BOMB, the number is greater than 1 and the reaction increases rapidly to an explosion. In a NUCLEAR REACTOR, where the chain reaction is controlled, the number of neutrons producing additional fission must be exactly 1.0 in order to maintain a steady flow of energy. Uranium-235, which occurs naturally as one part in 140 in a natural mixture of uranium isotopes, is not the only material fissionable by thermal neutrons. Uranium-233 and plutonium-239 can also be used but must be produced artificially. Uranium-233 is produced from thorium-232, which absorbs a neutron and then undergoes beta decay. Plutonium-239 is produced in a similar manner from uranium-238, which is the most common isotope of natural uranium. The average energy released by the fission of uranium-235 is 200 million electron volts, and that released by uranium-233 and plutonium-239 is comparable. Fission can also occur spontaneously, but the time required for a heavy nucleus to decay spontaneously by fission (10 million billion years in the case of uranium-238) is so long that induced fission by thermal neutrons is the only practical application of nuclear fission. However, spontaneous fission of uranium can be used in the DATING of very old rock samples. The development of nuclear energy from fission reactions began with the program to produce atomic weapons in the United States. Early work was carried out at several universities, and the first sustained nuclear chain reaction was achieved at the Univ. of Chicago in 1942 by a group under Enrico Fermi. Later the weapons themselves were developed at Los Alamos, N. Mex., under the direction of J. Robert Oppenheimer (see MANHATTAN PROJECT). Nuclear fusion, on the other hand, although it was known theoretically in the 1930s as the process by which the sun and most other stars radiate their great output of energy, was not achieved by man until the 1950s. Fusion reactions are also known as thermonuclear reactions because the temperatures required to initiate them are more than 1,000,000°C. In the HYDROGEN BOMB, such temperatures are provided by the detonation of a fission bomb. The energy released during fusion is even greater than that released during fission. Moreover, the fuel for fusion reactions, hydrogen, is readily available in large amounts, and there is no release of radioactive byproducts. In stars ordinary hydrogen, whose nucleus consists of a single proton, is the fuel for the reaction and is fused to form helium through a complex cycle of reactions (see NUCLEOSYNTHESIS). This reaction takes place too slowly, however, to be of practical use on the earth. The heavier isotopes of hydrogen—DEUTERIUM and TRITIUM—have much faster fusion reactions. For sustained, controlled fusion reactions, a fission bomb obviously cannot be used to trigger the reaction. The difficulties of controlled fusion center on the containment of the nuclear fuel at the extremely high temperatures necessary for fusion for a time long enough to allow the reaction to take place. For deuterium-tritium fusion, this time is about 0.1 sec. At such temperatures the fuel is no longer in one of the ordinary STATES OF MATTER but is instead a PLASMA, consisting of a mixture of electrons and charged atoms. Obviously, no solid container could hold such a hot mixture; therefore, containment attempts have been based on the electrical and magnetic properties of a plasma, using magnetic fields to form a "magnetic bottle." Another method has used LASER beams aimed at tiny pellets of fusion fuel. Once practical

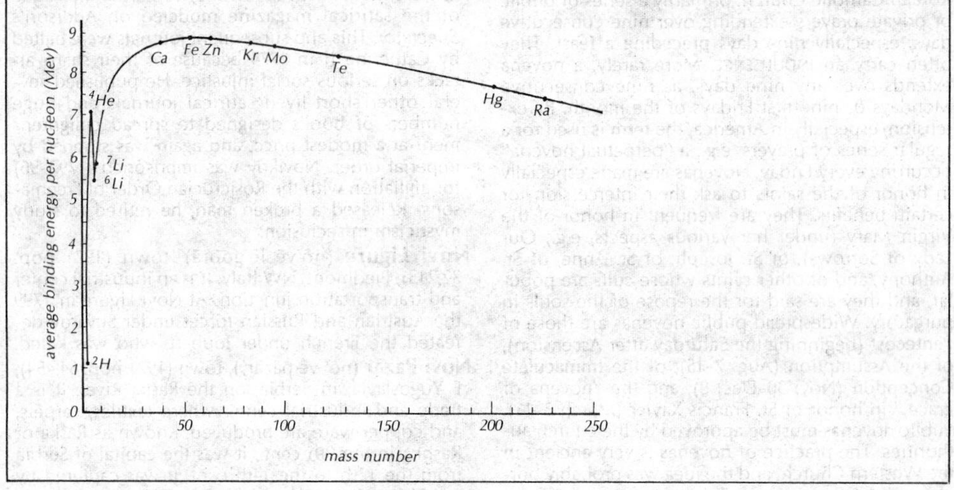

Graph of binding energy per nucleon as a function of mass number

controlled fusion is achieved, it will have great advantages over fission as a source of energy. Deuterium is relatively easy to obtain, since it constitutes a small percentage of the hydrogen in water and can be separated by electrolysis, in contrast to the complex and expensive methods required to extract uranium-235 from its sources. Yet the most pressing problem of nuclear energy is not the technological difficulties that must be overcome to provide large quantities of this energy for peaceful uses but the threat to the continued existence of the human race posed by the vast stockpiles of nuclear weapons held by the major national governments (see DISARMAMENT, NUCLEAR). See Irene D. Jaworski and Alexander Joseph, *Atomic Energy* (1961); C. N. Martin, *The Atom: Friend or Foe* (1962); Samuel Glasstone, *Sourcebook on Atomic Energy* (3d ed. 1967); Harry Foreman, ed., *Nuclear Power and the Public* (1970); Irving Adler, *Atomic Energy* (1971); Richard C. Lewis, *Nuclear Power Rebellion: Citizen vs. the Atomic Industrial Establishment* (1972).

nuclear magnetic resonance: see MAGNETIC RESONANCE.

nuclear physics, study of the components, structure, and behavior of the NUCLEUS of the atom. It is especially concerned with the nature of matter and with NUCLEAR ENERGY. The subject is commonly divided into three fields: low-energy nuclear physics, the study of RADIOACTIVITY; medium-energy nuclear physics, the study of the force between nuclear particles; and high-energy nuclear physics, the study of the transformations among subatomic particles in reactions produced in a PARTICLE ACCELERATOR. See ELEMENTARY PARTICLES.

nuclear reactor, device for producing controlled release of NUCLEAR ENERGY. A fission reactor consists basically of a mass of fissionable material usually

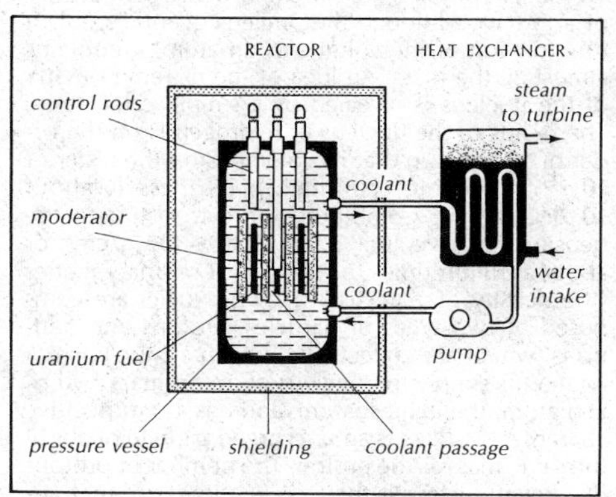

Power reactor system

encased in shielding and provided with devices to regulate the rate of fission and an exchange system to extract the heat energy produced. Reactors can be used for research or for power production. A research reactor is designed to produce various beams of radiation for experimental application; the heat produced is a waste product and is dissipated as efficiently as possible. In a power reactor the heat produced is of primary importance for use in driving conventional heat engines; the beams of radiation are controlled by shielding. A reactor is so constructed that fission of atomic nuclei produces a self-sustaining nuclear CHAIN REACTION, in which the neutrons produced are able to split other nuclei. A chain reaction can be produced in a reactor by using uranium or plutonium in which the concentration of fissionable isotopes has been artificially increased. Even though the neutrons move at high velocities, the enriched fissionable isotope captures enough neutrons to make possible a self-sustaining chain reaction. In this type of reactor the neutrons carrying on the chain reaction are fast neutrons. A chain reaction can also be accomplished in a reactor by employing a substance called a moderator to retard the neutrons so that they may be more easily captured by the fissionable atoms. The neutrons carrying on the chain reaction in this type of reactor are slow (or thermal) neutrons. Substances that can be used as moderators include graphite, beryllium, and heavy water (DEUTERIUM oxide). The moderator surrounds or is mixed with the fissionable fuel elements in the core of the reactor. A nuclear reactor is sometimes called an atomic pile because a reactor using graphite as a moderator consists of a pile of graphite blocks with rods of uranium fuel inserted into it. Reactors in which the uranium rods are immersed in a bath of heavy water are often referred to as "swimming-pool" reactors. Reactors of these types, in which discrete fuel elements are surrounded by a moderator, are called heterogeneous reactors. If the fissionable fuel elements are intimately mixed with a moderator, the system is called a homogeneous reactor (e.g., a reactor having a core of a liquid uranium compound dissolved in heavy water). The breeder reactor is a special type used to produce more fissionable atoms than it consumes. It must first be primed with certain isotopes of uranium or plutonium that release more neutrons than are needed to continue the chain reaction at a constant rate. In an ordinary reactor, any surplus neutrons are absorbed in nonfissionable control rods made of a substance, such as boron or cadmium, that readily absorbs neutrons. In a breeder reactor, however, these surplus neutrons are used to transmute certain nonfissionable atoms into fissionable atoms. Thorium (Th-232) can be converted by neutron bombardment into fissionable U-233. Similarly, U-238, the most common isotope of uranium, can be converted by neutron bombardment into fissionable plutonium-239. These transmutations have made possible the large-scale production of atomic energy. The excess nuclear fuel produced can be extracted and used in other reactors or in nuclear weapons. The heat energy released by fission in a reactor heats a liquid or gas coolant that circulates in and out of the reactor core, usually becoming radioactive. Outside the core, the coolant circulates through a heat exchanger where the heat is transferred to another medium. This second medium, nonradioactive since it has not circulated in the reactor core, carries the heat away from the reactor. This heat energy can be dissipated or it can be used to drive conventional heat engines that generate usable power. Atomic power stations are now in service in various parts of the world, including the United States, the USSR, and Great Britain. Submarines and surface ships propelled by nuclear reactors are in operation, and adaptation of nuclear reactors for use in rockets, aircraft, and locomotives is in progress. The design of nuclear fusion reactors, which are still in the experimental stage, differs considerably from that of fission reactors. In a fusion reactor, the principal problem is the containment of the PLASMA fuel, which must be at a temperature of millions of degrees in order to initiate the reaction. Magnetic fields have been used in several ways to hold the plasmas in a "magnetic bottle." Once their development reaches a practical stage of application, it is expected that fusion reactors will have many advantages over fission reactors. See *Reactor Handbook*, ed. by C. R. Tipton, Jr., et al. (4 vol., 2d ed. 1960–64); G. I. Bell, *Nuclear Reactor Theory* (1970).

nuclear structure: see NUCLEUS.

nuclear test-ban treaty: see DISARMAMENT, NUCLEAR.

nucleic acid, any of a group of organic substances, found in the chromosomes of living cells and viruses, that play an important role in the storage and replication of hereditary information and in protein synthesis. In most organisms, nucleic acids occur in combination with proteins; the combined substances are called nucleoproteins. Nucleic acid molecules are complex chains of varying length. The two chief types of nucleic acids are DNA (des- or deoxyribonucleic acid), found mainly in the nuclei of normal cells, and RNA (ribonucleic acid), found mostly in the cytoplasm but also in small amounts in the nuclei, nucleoli, and chromosomes. A substance that he called nuclein (now known as DNA) was isolated in 1869 by Friedrich Miescher, but it was only recently that research revealed its significance as the material of which the GENE is composed, and thus its function as the chemical bearer of hereditary characteristics. The amount of RNA varies from cell to cell, but the amount of DNA is constant for all typical cells of any given species of plant or animal, no matter what the size or function of that cell. This amount doubles as the chromosomes replicate themselves before cell division takes place (see MITOSIS); in the ovum and sperm the amount is half that in the body cells (see MEIOSIS). The chemical and physical properties of DNA suit it for both replication and transfer of information. Each DNA molecule is a long two-stranded chain. The chains are made up of subunits called nucleotides, each containing a sugar (deoxyribose), a phosphate group, and one of four nitrogenous bases, adenine, guanine, thymine, and cytosine, denoted A, G, T, and C respectively. The information carried by genes is coded in sequences of nucleotides, which correspond to sequences of amino acids in the polypeptide chains of proteins. In 1953 the molecular biologists J. D. Watson, an American, and F. H. Crick, an Englishman, proposed that the two DNA strands were coiled into a double helix. In this model each nucleotide subunit along one strand is connected to a nucleotide subunit on the other strand by hydro-

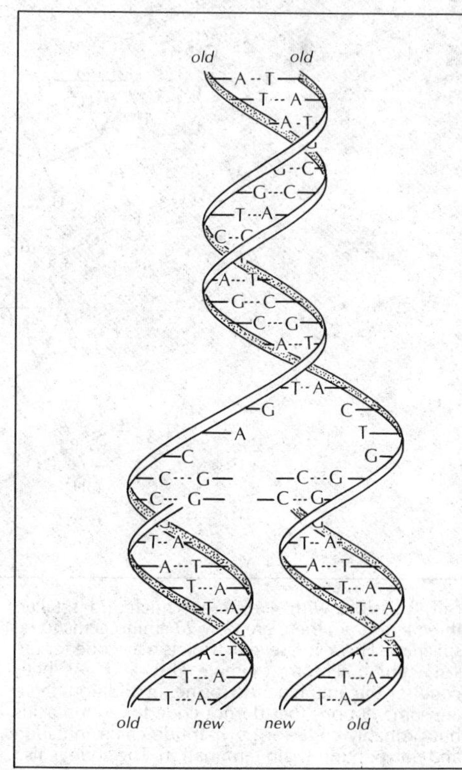

Replication of strands of DNA

gen bonds between the base portions of the nucleotides. The fact that adenine only bonds with thymine (A—T) and guanine only bonds with cytosine (G—C) determines that the strands will be complementary, i.e., that for every adenine on one strand there will be a thymine on the other strand. All four nucleotides occur on a single strand. It is the property of complementarity between strands that insures that DNA can be replicated, i.e., that identical copies can be made in order to be transmitted to the next generation. In order to be expressed as protein, the genetic information must be carried to the protein-synthesizing machinery of the cell, which is usually in the cell's cytoplasm (see CELL). One form of RNA mediates this process. RNA is similar to DNA, but contains the sugar ribose instead of deoxyribose, and the base uracil (U) instead of thymine. To initiate the process of information transfer, one strand of the double-stranded DNA chain serves as a template for the synthesis of a single strand of RNA that is complementary to the DNA strand. This process is called transcription, and—like all steps in protein synthesis—it is mediated by enzymes. The newly synthesized RNA, called messenger RNA, or mRNA, moves quickly to bodies in the cytoplasm called ribosomes. Each ribosome is the site of synthesis of a polypeptide chain. Clusters of ribosomes, called polyribosomes, or polysomes, attach to the mRNA so that many polypeptide chains are synthesized from the same mRNA. Ribosomes are composed of noninformational ribonucleic acid bound to a protein. The nucleotide sequence of the mRNA is translated into the amino acid sequence of a protein by adaptor molecules composed of a third type of RNA called transfer RNA, or tRNA. There are at least 20 different species of tRNA, with each species binding one of the 20 amino acids. In protein synthesis, a nucleotide sequence along the mRNA does not specify an amino acid directly; rather, it specifies a particular species of tRNA. For example, in coding for the amino acid tyrosine, a nucleotide sequence of mRNA is complementary to a portion of a tyrosine-tRNA molecule. As each specified tRNA associates with its complementary space on the mRNA, the tRNA releases its amino acid, which is added onto the lengthening protein chain. When the protein chain is complete, it is released from the ribosome site. The particular sequence of amino acids in each polypeptide chain is determined by the genetic code. Starting at one end of the mRNA strand, each 3-nucleotide sequence, or codon, specifies one amino acid, and a series of such codons specifies a polypeptide chain. Although a "vocabulary" of 64 words, or specifications, is theoreti-

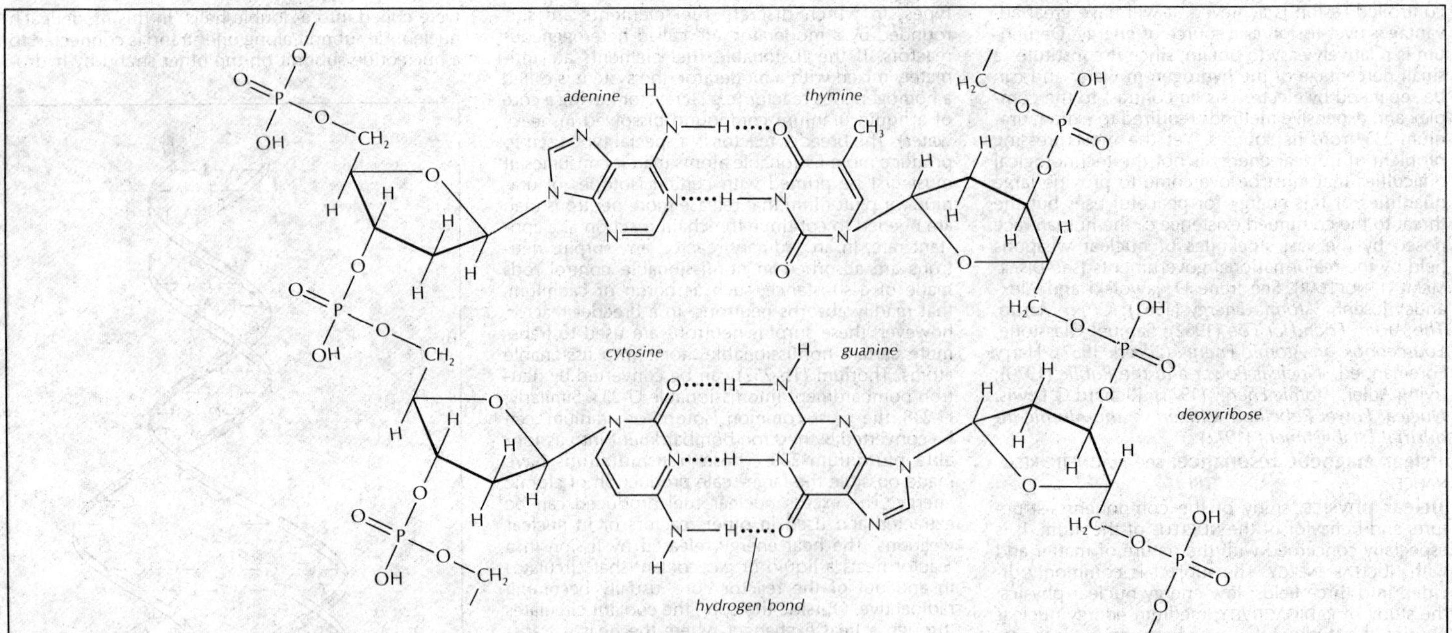

DNA showing pairing of bases

cally possible with 4 different nucleotides taken three at a time, there are only 20 amino acids to be specified. However, several triplets may code for the same amino acid; for example, UAU and UAC both code for the amino acid tyrosine. In addition, there are some codons that do not code for amino acids but probably code for polypeptide chain initiation and polypeptide chain termination. The code is also nonoverlapping; i.e., a nucleotide in one codon is never part of either adjacent codon. Although the code seems to be universal in all living organisms, the sequences of the nucleotides, determining the structure of all of an organism's proteins, vary according to the species and the individual. The determination of the mechanism of protein synthesis has been seen as a step toward increased understanding of many genetic processes, including MUTATION and regulation of cell metabolism. Some mutagens, or mutation-inducing agents, cause the substitution of one nucleotide for another in an mRNA strand; other mutagens cause deletion or addition of nucleotides. Decoding, or reading, of such strands will be radically altered. Metabolic regulation has been studied to determine how the genes that control enzyme synthesis can be switched on or off when certain substances are present. For example, in the process known as induction, bacteria synthesize the enzyme β-galactosidase only when lactose is present. Induction has been linked to the activity at a so-called operator site on a chromosome. When the operator site is open, the genes it controls function freely; when it is blocked, as by a repressor molecule, the genes it controls also do not function. Gene expression and control and the function of cellular components are studied in the science of molecular biology. RNA was first synthesized in 1955. In 1965 the nucleotide sequence of tRNA was determined, and in 1967 the synthesis of biologically active DNA was achieved. See Isaac Asimov, *The Genetic Code* (1963); J. D. Watson, *The Double Helix: A Personal Account of the Discovery of the Structure of DNA* (1968); J. N. Davidson, *The Biochemistry of the Nucleic Acids* (7th ed. 1972).

nucleolus: see CELL.

nucleon, term applying to both the PROTON and the NEUTRON, the two constituents of atomic nuclei. The nucleon may be considered a single fundamental particle, of which the proton and the neutron are two different states. See ATOM; ELEMENTARY PARTICLES.

nucleoprotein: see NUCLEIC ACID.

nucleosynthesis, in astronomy, production of all the chemical ELEMENTS from the simplest element, hydrogen, by thermonuclear reactions within stars (see NUCLEUS; NUCLEAR ENERGY). A star obtains its energy by fusing together light nuclei to form heavier nuclei; in this process, mass (m) is converted into energy (E) in accordance with Einstein's formula, $E=mc^2$, in which c is the speed of light. The reactions are initiated by the high temperatures (about 14 million degrees Celsius) at the center of the star. In the course of producing nuclear energy, the star synthesizes all the elements of the PERIODIC TABLE from its initial composition of mostly hydrogen and a small amount of helium. The first step is the fusion of four hydrogen nuclei to make one helium nucleus. This "hydrogen-burning" phase supplies energy to stars on the main sequence of the HERTZSPRUNG-RUSSELL DIAGRAM. There are two chains of reactions by which the conversion of hydrogen to helium is effected: the proton-proton cycle and the carbon-nitrogen-oxygen cycle. They were both first studied and proposed as sources of stellar energy by H. Bethe and C. von Weizsäcker. In the proton-proton cycle, two hydrogen nuclei (protons) are fused and one of these protons is converted to a neutron by beta decay (see RADIOACTIVITY) to make a deuterium nucleus (one proton and one neutron). Then a third proton is added to deuterium to form the light ISOTOPE of helium, helium-3. When two helium-3 nuclei collide, they form a nucleus of ordinary helium, helium-4 (two protons and two neutrons), and release two protons. This last step releases considerable energy. The carbon-nitrogen-oxygen cycle requires minute traces of carbon as a catalyst. Four protons are added, one by one, to a carbon nucleus to form a succession of excited (unstable) nuclei of carbon, nitrogen, and oxygen. The intermediate nuclei shed their excess electric charge via beta decay and the final oxygen nucleus spontaneously splits into the original carbon nucleus and a helium-4 nucleus, releasing energy. The net effect is again the combination of four hydrogen nuclei to form one helium-4 nucleus; the carbon is free to begin the cycle over again. The proton-proton cycle operates in less massive and luminous stars like the sun, while the carbon-nitrogen-oxygen cycle (which speeds up dramatically at higher temperatures) dominates in more massive and luminous stars. After the bulk of a star's hydrogen has been converted to helium by either of these processes, sufficiently high temperatures are eventually reached to initiate "helium-burning" by the triple-alpha process; in this process, three helium nuclei (alpha particles) are fused to make a carbon nucleus. By successive additions of helium nuclei, the heavier elements through iron-56 are built up. The elements whose atomic weights are not multiples of four are created by side reactions that involve neutrons. Because iron-56 is the most stable of the elements, it is very difficult to add an extra helium nucleus to it. However, iron-56 will readily capture a neutron to form the less stable isotope, iron-57. From iron-57, the elements through bismuth-209 can be synthesized. The elements more massive than bismuth-209 are radioactive; that is, they spontaneously break apart. However, during a SUPERNOVA, an extremely intense flux of neutrons is generated and nuclear reactions proceed so rapidly that the radioactive elements do not have enough time to decay, resulting in the rapid creation of the radioactive elements up to and beyond uranium.

nucleotide (no͞o'klēətīd", nyo͞o'-), organic substance formed by the combination of phosphoric acid, the sugars RIBOSE or deoxyribose, and either a PURINE or a PYRIMIDINE base. Phosphoric acid groups may be attached either directly to the sugar by ester linkages, or by anhydride linkages to phosphoric acid groups in the nucleotide; the sugar is in turn attached to the base by a glycosidic bond. The most important nucleotides are those derived from the bases ADENINE, GUANINE, CYTOSINE, THYMINE, and URACIL.

nucleus: see ATOM; CELL, in biology.

nucleus, in physics, the extremely dense central core of an ATOM. Although the nucleus occupies only a tiny fraction of the volume of an atom, it contains almost all the mass. An idea of the extreme DENSITY of the nucleus is revealed by a simple calculation. The radius of the nucleus of hydrogen is on the order of 10^{-12} cm so that its volume is on the order of 10^{-36} cm^3 (cubic centimeter); its mass is about 10^{-24} g (gram). Combining these to estimate the density, we have 10^{-24} g/10^{-36} cm^3 $\sim 10^{12}$ g/cm^3, or about a trillion times the density of ordinary matter (the density of water is 1 g/cm^3). Nuclei are composed of two types of particles, protons and neutrons, which are collectively known as nucleons. A PROTON is simply the nucleus of an ordinary hydrogen atom, the lightest atom, and has a unit positive charge. A NEUTRON is an uncharged particle of about the same mass as the proton. The number of protons in a given nucleus is the atomic number of that nucleus and determines which chemical ELEMENT the nucleus will constitute when surrounded by electrons. The total number of protons and neutrons together in a nucleus is the atomic mass number of the nucleus. Two nuclei may have the same atomic number but different mass numbers, thus constituting different forms, or ISOTOPES, of the same element. The mass number of a given isotope is the nearest whole number to the ATOMIC WEIGHT of that isotope and is approximately equal to the atomic weight (in the case of carbon-12, exactly equal). A nucleus may be represented conveniently by the chemical symbol for the element together with a subscript and superscript for the atomic number and mass number. The nucleus of ordinary hydrogen, i.e., the proton, is represented by $^{1}_{1}H$, an alpha particle (helium nucleus) is $^{4}_{2}He$, the most common isotope of chlorine is $^{35}_{17}Cl$, and the uranium isotope used in the atomic bomb is $^{235}_{92}U$. Nuclear reactions involving changes in atomic number or mass number can be expressed easily using this notation. For example, the first artificially produced nuclear reaction involved bombarding a nitrogen nucleus with alpha particles and resulted in an isotope of oxygen with the release of a proton: $^{4}_{2}He+^{14}_{7}N\rightarrow^{17}_{8}O+^{1}_{1}H$. Note that the total of the atomic numbers on the left is equal to the total on the right (i.e., $2+7=8+1$), and similarly for the mass numbers ($4+14=17+1$). Alpha particles also played an important role in the discovery of the nucleus itself in 1911. Following the discovery of RADIOACTIVITY by Becquerel in 1896, Ernest Rutherford identified the three types of radiation given off by natural radioactive substances and named them alpha, beta, and gamma. He later used alpha rays (helium nuclei) to bombard a thin target of gold foil and found that, although most of the alpha particles passed directly through the foil, a few were deflected by large amounts. By a quantitative analysis of his experimental results, he was able to propose the existence of the nucleus and estimate its size and charge. After the discovery of the neutron in 1932, physicists turned their attention to the understanding of the strong FORCE that binds protons and neutrons together in nuclei. This force must be great enough to overcome the considerable repulsive force existing between several protons because of their electrical charge. The force is so strong that it binds them into the smallest possible volume. It must exist between nucleons without regard to their charge, since it acts equally on protons and neutrons, and it must not extend very far away from the nucleons (i.e., it must be a short-range force), since it has negligible effect on protons or neutrons outside the nucleus. In 1935, Hideki Yukawa proposed a theory that this nuclear "glue" was produced by the exchange of a particle between nucleons, just as the electromagnetic force is produced by the exchange of a PHOTON between charged particles. The range of a force is dependent on the mass of the particle carrying the force; the greater the mass of the particle, the shorter the range of the force. The range of the electromagnetic force is infinite because the mass of the photon is zero. From the known range of the nuclear force, Yukawa estimated the mass of the hypothetical carrier of the nuclear force to be about 200 times that of the electron. Given the name MESON because its mass is between that of the electron and those of the nucleons, this particle was finally observed in 1947 and is now called the pi meson, or PION, to distinguish it from other mesons that were discovered (see ELEMENTARY PARTICLES). Both the proton and the neutron are surrounded by a cloud of pions given off and reabsorbed again within an incredibly short interval of time. Certain other mesons are assumed to be created and destroyed in this way as well, all such particles being termed "virtual" because they exist in violation of the law of conservation of energy (see CONSERVATION LAWS) for a very short span of time allowed by the UNCERTAINTY PRINCIPLE. When nuclear masses are measured, it is found that the mass is always less than the sum of the masses of the individual nucleons bound in the nucleus. The difference between the nuclear mass and the sum of the individual masses is known as the mass defect and is due to the fact that some of the mass must be converted to energy in order to make the nucleus stable. This nuclear binding energy is related to the mass defect by the famous formula from RELATIVITY, $E = mc^2$, where E is energy, m is mass, and c is the speed of light. As expected, the binding energy of a nucleus increases with increasing mass number. A more interesting property of a nucleus is the binding energy per nucleon, found by dividing the binding energy by the mass number. The average binding energy per nucleon is observed to increase rapidly with increasing mass number up to a mass number of about 60, then to decrease rather slowly with higher mass numbers. Thus, nuclei with mass numbers around 60 are the most stable, and those of very small or very large mass numbers are the least stable. Two important phenomena result from this property of nuclei. Nuclear fission is the spontaneous splitting of a nucleus of large mass number into two nearly equal nuclei whose mass numbers are in the most stable range. Nuclear fusion, on the other hand, is the combining of two light nuclei to form a heavier single nucleus, again with an increase in the average binding energy per nucleon. In both cases, the change to a more stable final state is accompanied by the release of a large amount of energy per unit mass of the reacting materials as compared to the energy released in chemical reactions (see NUCLEAR ENERGY). Not all nucleons are bound with the same energy in a given nucleus. Individual differences must be explained in terms of a model for the internal structure of a nucleus. Several models have evolved that fit certain aspects of nuclear behavior, but no single model has successfully described all aspects. One model is based on the fact that certain properties of a nucleus are similar to those of a drop of incompressible liquid. For example, the LATENT HEAT of vaporization (the energy required to break the drop up into molecules) is proportional to the mass of the drop; analogously, the binding energy of a nucleus, which must be supplied in order to fragment the nucleus into its component nucleons, is proportional to the mass number of the nucleus. The liquid-drop model has been particularly successful in explaining details of the fission process and in evolving a formula for the mass of a particular nucleus as a function of its atomic number and mass number, the so-called semiempirical mass formula. Another model is the Fermi gas model, which treats the nucleons as if they were particles of a gas restricted by the Pauli EXCLUSION PRINCIPLE, which allows only two particles of opposite spin to occupy a particular energy level described by the QUANTUM THEORY. These particle pairs will fill the lowest energy levels first, then successively higher ones, so that the "gas" is one of minimum energy. There are actually two independent Fermi gases, one of protons and one of neutrons. The tendency of nucleons to occupy the lowest possible energy level explains why there is a tendency for the numbers of protons and neutrons to be nearly equal in lighter nuclei. In heavier nuclei the effect of the larger number of charges from the protons raises the energy of the protons, with the result that there are more neutrons than protons (for uranium-235, for example, there are 143 neutrons and only 92 protons). The pairing of nucleons in energy levels also helps to explain the tendency of nuclei to have even numbers of both protons and neutrons. Neither the liquid-drop model nor the Fermi gas model, however, can explain the exceptional stability of nuclei having certain values for either the number of protons or the number of neutrons, or both. These so-called magic numbers are 2, 8, 20, 28, 50, 82, and 126. Because of the similarity between this phenomenon and the stability of the noble gases, which have certain numbers of electrons that are bound in closed "shells," a shell model was suggested for the nucleus. There are major differences, however, between the electrons in an atom and the nucleons in a nucleus. First, the nucleus provides a force center for the electrons of an atom, while the nucleus itself has no single force center. Second, there are two different types of nucleons. Third, the assumption of independent particle motion made in the case of electrons is not as easily made for nucleons. The liquid-drop model is in fact based on the assumption of strong forces between the nucleons that considerably constrain their motion. However, these difficulties were solved and a good explanation of the magic numbers achieved on the basis of the shell model, which included the assumption of strong coupling between the spin angular momentum of a nucleon and its orbital angular momentum. Various attempts have been made, with partial success, to construct a model incorporating the best features of both the liquid-drop model and the shell model. See George Gamow, *The Atom and Its Nucleus* (1961); H. A. Bethe and Philip Morrison, *Elementary Nuclear Theory* (2d ed. 1956).

nudibranch: see SEA SLUG.

Nueva Galicia (nwä'vä gälē'syä), Spanish colonial administrative region, W Mexico, comprising roughly the present states of Jalisco and Nayarit with S Sinaloa. Conquered (1529–31) by Nuño de GUZMÁN and later governed by Francisco Vásquez de Coronado, the territory was the scene of the MIXTÓN WAR in 1541. In 1548 it was given its own audiencia at Guadalajara. Nominally subject to the viceroy of New Spain, it was essentially a separate administration controlled from Spain, and it came to be known after the creation (1563) of a presidential office of its own as the presidency of Nueva Galicia. Its independent character, however, declined as in the colonial era authority was more and more centralized in Mexico City.

Nueva San Salvador: see SANTA TECLA, El Salvador.

Nuevitas (nwāvē'täs), city (1970 pop. 20,734), Camagüey prov., E Cuba, on the Guincho peninsula on the north coast. Nuevitas is sheltered by a huge harbor, has two auxiliary ports, and is a major shipping point for Cuban sugar; it also serves as a road and rail terminus. Chromium is mined nearby. The large bay was discovered by Columbus in 1492. Founded in 1775, the city was moved to its present site in 1828.

Nuevo Laredo (nwā'vō lärā'thō), city (1970 pop. 150,922), Tamaulipas state, NE Mexico, across the Rio Grande from Laredo, Texas. Linked with the United States by automobile and railroad bridges, Nuevo Laredo is the northern terminus of the national railroad and the Inter-American Highway, as well as the chief point of entry for U.S. tourists driving to Mexico. It is also a center of international trade and the distribution point for an agricultural (mainly cotton) and livestock-raising area. Founded in 1755, the city was part of Laredo until the end of the Mexican War in 1848. Nuevo Laredo played a role in the Mexican revolution of 1910 and was burned extensively in 1914.

Nuevo León (nwā'vō lāōn'), state (1970 pop. 1,653,-808), 25,136 sq mi (65,102 sq km), N Mexico. MONTERREY is the capital. The southern and western parts of the state are traversed by the Sierra Madre Oriental, but some of the extreme western portions lie within the vast, semiarid basin lands of N Mexico, which are cultivable under irrigation. Much of the north is arid cactus country, but to the east, where the plains sweep down toward the lowlands of Tamaulipas and are crossed by several large rivers, the land is suitable to agriculture. Grains, sugarcane, cotton, and maguey are grown. Nuevo León is a leading national producer of iron, steel, and chemicals; other manufactures include beer and other beverages and textiles. Road and rail connections within the state are excellent. The population is predominantly white and mestizo; there are very few Indians. Nuevo León enjoys one of the highest living standards in Mexico. The area was explored and settled by the Spanish in the late 16th cent. Nuevo León became a state in 1824. It was occupied by U.S. troops during the Mexican War, amid fierce resistance.

Nuffield, William Richard Morris, 1st **Viscount** (nŭf'ēld), 1877–1963, English automobile manufacturer and philanthropist. Beginning his career as the proprietor of a bicycle shop, he later became a manufacturer of motorcycles and, in 1912, of automobiles. The Morris cars quickly became one of the biggest mass-production industries in Great Britain, and Morris became known as the "British Ford." During World War II, Morris, who was created Viscount Nuffield in 1938, engaged in the manufacture of aircraft. At the time of his death his philanthropic bequests amounted to over £30 million, the largest part of which was directed to research in medicine and social services, notably at Oxford, where Nuffield College is named in his honor.

Nuffield Radio Astronomy Observatory: see JODRELL BANK EXPERIMENTAL STATION.

nuisance, in law, an act that, without legal justification, interferes with safety, comfort, or the use of property. A private nuisance (e.g., erecting a wall that shuts off a neighbor's light) is one that affects one or a few persons, while a public nuisance (e.g., conducting a disorderly house) affects many persons. In some cases the victim of a private nuisance may abate it (e.g., tear down the wall). Damages are available to a party who suffers from a private nuisance or who is especially injured by a public nuisance, and courts will issue injunctions against continuing nuisances. Since public nuisances are injurious to the community, they may be prosecuted as crimes. Nuisance is a flexible legal category. Thus, while a slaughterhouse is lawful in a manufacturing district, it may be a nuisance in a residential quarter. Activities, such as operating blast furnaces, once deemed nuisances, are now recognized as indispensable and lawful.

Nukha: see SHEKI, USSR.

Nukualofa (no͞o"kwälō'fä), town (1966 pop. 15,685), capital and chief port of the Kingdom of Tonga, on the northern coast of Tongatabu island. The royal palace and government buildings are in Nukualofa.

Nuku Hiva (no͞o'ko͞o' hē'vä), volcanic island, 127 sq mi (329 sq km), South Pacific, largest of the MARQUESAS ISLANDS, FRENCH POLYNESIA. The island is fertile, with well-watered valleys; its highest point is c.4,000 ft (1,220 m). There are eight harbors, the best of which is Taiohae Bay on the southern coast. Copra is the chief export. The village of Taiohae was the capital of the Marquesas Islands until the French takeover.

Nukus (no͞oko͞os'), city (1970 pop. 74,000), capital of Karakalpak Autonomous Republic, Central Asian USSR, in Uzbekistan, in the Khorezm oasis and on the Amu Darya River. It has alfalfa and food-processing industries and is a center for repairing machines and motors.

nullification, in U.S. history, a doctrine expounded by the advocates of extreme STATES' RIGHTS. It held that states have the right to declare null and void any Federal law that they deem unconstitutional. The doctrine was based on the theory that the Union is a voluntary compact of states and that the Federal government has no right to exercise powers not specifically assigned to it by the U.S. Constitution. The KENTUCKY AND VIRGINIA RESOLUTIONS declared (1799) nullification to be the rightful remedy by the states for all unauthorized acts done under the pretext of the Constitution. A closely reasoned reinforcement to the doctrine of nullification was set forth—in response to the tariff of 1828, which favored Northern interests at the expense of the South—by John C. CALHOUN in his South Carolina Exposition (1828). The strong pro-Union stand of President Jackson brought forth further remonstrances from Southern leaders. After enactment of the tariff act of 1832 South Carolina called a state convention, which passed (1832) the ordinance of nullification. This ordinance declared the tariff laws null and void, and a series of enactments in South Carolina put the state in a position to resist by force any attempt of the Federal government to carry the tariff act into operation. President Jackson in reply dramatically issued a strong proclamation against the nullifiers, and a FORCE BILL was introduced into the U.S. Senate to give the President authority to use the armed forces if necessary to execute the laws. Jackson, however, felt that the South had a real grievance and, behind his show of force, encouraged friends of compromise, led by Henry Clay, to prepare a bill that the South would accept. This compromise tariff was rushed through Congress, and after its passage (1833) the South Carolina state convention reassembled and formally rescinded the ordinance nullifying the tariff acts. To preserve its prerogative it adopted a new ordinance nullifying the force bill. But the issue was not pressed further until the election of Abraham Lincoln, when the doctrine of SECESSION was brought to the foreground. See C. S. Boucher, *The Nullification Controversy in South Carolina* (1916, repr. 1968); C. M. Wiltse, *John C. Calhoun: Nullifier, 1829–1839* (1949); W. W. Freehling, ed., *The Nullification Era* (1967).

nullity of marriage, in law, an unlawful marriage that is either void or voidable because of conditions existing at the time of the marriage. A bigamous or incestuous marriage, for example, is void, and there is no need to bring a suit to obtain a DECREE declaring it void. However, a decree is necessary to annul voidable marriages. Grounds, generally specified by statute, include fraud or duress preventing legal consent to the marriage and sexual impotence of one spouse that existed at the time the marriage was contracted and that was unknown to the other spouse. The results of nullity of marriage are different from those of DIVORCE. A decree of nullity declares, in effect, that the parties never were married, and at one time it absolved them from all obligations to each other. Today, however, statutes in some states have mitigated the results of annulment, e.g., by making children of the void marriage legitimate and by permitting alimony. See HUSBAND AND WIFE.

Numantia (no͞omăn'shə), ancient settlement, Spain, near the Durius (now Douro) River and north of modern Soria. Numantia played a central role in the Celtiberian resistance to Roman conquest. Its inhabitants withstood repeated Roman attacks from the time of Cato the Elder's campaign (195 B.C.) until Scipio Aemilianus finally took the city in 133 B.C., after an eight-month blockade, thus completing the conquest of Spain. Archaeologists have uncovered the remains of Roman camps and evidence of settlement dating back to the Bronze Age.

Numa Pompilius (no͞o'mə pŏmpĭl'ēəs), legendary king of Rome, successor to Romulus. He was known for his wisdom and piety and enjoyed a long and peaceful reign. His consort, the nymph Egeria, was said to have aided him in his rule. The origin of Roman ceremonial law and religious rites was ascribed to him.

numbat (nŭm'băt), small MARSUPIAL, of SW Australia, also known as the marsupial anteater. The numbat, *Myrmecobius fasciatus*, resembles a squirrel in size and general appearance, but is adapted for eating insects, with a pointed snout and a long, cylindrical tongue covered with a sticky secretion. The body is brown with white transverse stripes and the tail is bushy. The numbat lives in eucalyptus forests and feeds chiefly on termites, which it finds in fallen branches and under litter. It sleeps by night in a den in a hollow log. Like other marsupials, numbats give birth to very undeveloped young, which crawl to the mother's teats and remain attached to them for several months; unlike most marsupials, however, numbats do not have pouches surrounding the teats. Numbats are classified in the phylum CHORDATA, subphylum Vertebrata, class Mammalia, order Marsupialia, family Dasyuridae.

number, entity describing the magnitude or position of a mathematical object or extensions of these concepts. Cardinal numbers describe the size of a collection of objects; two such collections have the same (cardinal) number of objects if their members can be matched in a one-to-one correspondence. Ordinal numbers refer to position relative to an ordering, as first, second, third, etc. The finite cardinal and ordinal numbers are called the natural numbers and are represented by the symbols 1, 2, 3, 4, etc. Both types can be generalized to infinite collections, but in this case an essential distinction occurs that requires a different notation for the two types (see TRANSFINITE NUMBER). To the natural numbers one adjoins their negatives and zero to form the integers. The ratios a/b of the integers, where a and b are integers and $b\neq0$, constitute the rational numbers; the integers are those rational numbers for which $b=1$. The rational numbers may also be represented by repeating decimals; e.g., $1/2=0.5000\ldots$, $2/3=0.6666\ldots$, $2/7=0.285714285714\ldots$ (see DECIMAL SYSTEM). The real numbers are those representable by an infinite decimal expansion, which may be repeating or nonrepeating; they are in a one-to-one correspondence with the points on a straight line and are sometimes referred to as the continuum. Real numbers that have a nonrepeating decimal expansion are called irrational, i.e., they cannot be represented by any ratio of integers. The Greeks knew of the existence of irrational numbers through geometry; e.g., $\sqrt{2}$ is the length of the hypotenuse of a right triangle whose legs are both of unit length. The proof that $\sqrt{2}$ is unable to be represented by such a ratio was the first proof of the existence of irrational numbers, and it caused tremendous upheaval in the mathematical thinking of that time. Another type of number, the imaginary number, was discovered through algebra; the roots $-\sqrt{-3}$ and $+\sqrt{-3}$ of the equation $x^2+3=0$ are examples of this type. The root of a negative number has no meaning in the set of real numbers; however, its value can be represented by a line by choosing as a unit $i=\sqrt{-1}$. The imaginary number $\sqrt{-3}$ can then be expressed as $\sqrt{-3}=\sqrt{3\cdot(-1)}=\sqrt{3}\cdot\sqrt{-1}=\sqrt{3}i$. Numbers of the form $z=x+yi$, where x and y are real, such as $8+7i$ (or $8+7\sqrt{-1}$), are called complex numbers; x is called the real part of z and yi the imaginary part. The real numbers are thus complex numbers with $y=0$; e.g., the real number 4 can be expressed as the complex number $4+0i$. The complex numbers are in a one-to-one correspondence with the points of a plane, with one axis defining the real parts of the numbers and one axis defining the imaginary parts. Mathematicians have extended this concept even further, as in QUATERNIONS. A number z is called algebraic if it is the root of a polynomial equation $z^n+a_{n-1}z^{n-1}+\ldots+a_1z+a_00$, where the coefficients $a_0, a_1, \ldots, a_{n-1}$ are all rational; if z cannot be a root of such an equation, it is said to be transcendental. The number $\sqrt{2}$ is algebraic because it is a root of the equation $z^2+2=0$; similarly, i, a root of $z^2+1=0$, is also algebraic. However, F. Lindemann showed (1882) that π is transcendental, and using this fact he proved the impossibility of "squaring the circle" by straight edge and compass alone (see famous GEOMETRIC PROBLEMS OF ANTIQUITY). The number e has also been found to be transcendental, although it still remains unknown whether $e+\pi$ is transcendental.

number-average molecular weight: see MOLECULAR WEIGHT.

Numbers, book of the Old Testament, fourth of the five books of the Law (the Pentateuch or Torah) ascribed by tradition to Moses. It continues the narrative of Exodus in the journey of the Jews from Egypt to the Promised Land—Leviticus is parenthetical in the account. Numbers begins at Sinai and ends in Moab on the eve of the entry into Palestine. The geographical detail of the journey (10–21) is bare, and only the main lines can be discerned. The book contains incidental legislation. Its events include two censuses (1;26), whence the title; the sending of spies to reconnoiter the Promised Land (10;13); the emergence of Joshua and Caleb as leaders (14); the rebellion of Korah, Dathan, and Abiram (16); the curse of Balaam turned into a blessing (22–24); and the apostasy at Shittim punished by Phinehas (25). For critical views of the composition of Numbers and bibliography, see OLD TESTAMENT.

number theory, branch of mathematics concerned with the properties of the integers (the numbers $0,1,-1,2,-2,3,-3,\ldots$). An important area in number theory is the analysis of prime numbers. A prime number is an integer $p>1$ divisible only by 1 and p; the first few primes are 2, 3, 5, 7, 11, 13, 17, and 19. Integers that have other divisors are called composite; examples are 4, 6, 8, 9, 10, 12, ... The fundamental theorem of arithmetic, the unique factorization theorem, asserts that any positive integer a is a product ($a=p_1\cdot p_2\cdot p_3\cdot\cdot\cdot p_n$) of primes that are unique except for the order in which they are listed; e.g., the number 20 is the product $20=2\cdot2\cdot5$, and it is unique (disregarding order) since 20 has this and only this product of primes. This theorem was known to the Greek mathematician Euclid, who proved that there are infinitely many primes. Analytic number theory has given a further refinement of Euclid's theorem by determining a function that measures how densely the primes are distributed among all integers. Twin primes are primes having a difference of 2, such as (3,5) and (11,13). It is still unknown whether there are infinitely many twin primes. Another unsolved problem of number theory is posed by Fermat's equation $x^n\cdot y^n=z^n$. Pierre de Fermat, a 17th-century French mathematician, claimed to have proved that when n is greater than 2, there are no positive integers x, y, and z that satisfy the equation. However, the proof, if it exists, has never been found. The modern theory of numbers made its first great advances through the work of Leonhard Euler, C. F. Gauss, and Fermat. It remains a major area of mathematical research, to which the most sophisticated mathematical tools have been applied. See Trygve Nagell, *Introduction to Number Theory* (2d ed. 1964); I. M. Niven and H. S. Zuckerman, *An Introduction to the Theory of Numbers* (3d ed. 1972).

numeral, symbol denoting NUMBER. The decimal system is believed to have originated in counting on the fingers, using both hands as the most convenient method. Arabic numerals are 1, 2, 3, 4, ... Roman numerals are I, II, III, IV, ... Both the Arabic and the Roman symbols are believed to be related to this method: 1 or I is one finger, 2 or II is two fingers, and 3 or III is three fingers. The word "digit" is from the Latin *digitus*, meaning "finger." Some of the symbols are less easily explained, but V seems to be the open hand, and X seems to be two open hands. The Roman system has no symbol for zero, and in the Arabic system zero is much more recent than the other symbols. The Maya, who were skilled in mathematics, had a symbol for zero. The symbols called Arabic were learned from Arabs by Europeans, but they apparently originated in India. Some languages show traces of reckoning by units of 20: the toes as well as the fingers may have been used in counting.

numeration, in mathematics, process of designating NUMBERS according to any particular system; the number designations are in turn called numerals. In any system of numeration, a base number must be specified, and groupings are then made by powers of the base number. The position of a numeral in a grouping indicates which power of the base it is to be multiplied by. The most widely used system of numeration is the DECIMAL SYSTEM, which uses base 10. Thus, in the decimal system, the numeral 342 means $(3\times10^2)+(4\times10^1)+(2\times10^0)$, or $300+40+2$. The BINARY SYSTEM uses base 2 and is important because of its application to modern computers. Whereas the decimal system uses the ten digits 0,1,2,3,4,5,6,7,8,9, the binary system uses only the two digits 0,1. In the binary system, the numeral 111, for example, means $(1\times2^2)+(1\times2^1)+(1\times2^0)$, i.e., $4+2+1$, or 7, in the decimal system. The decimal numeral 7 and the binary numeral 111 are thus designations for the same number. The duodecimal system uses 12 as a base and has some advantages arising from the fact that 12 is divisible by four different numbers—2,3,4,6—other than 1 and 12 itself. The base 12 requires the use of 12 different digits. Thus, in addition to the digits 0,1,2,3,4,5,6,7,8,9, the symbols X (called "dek") and E (called "el") to represent the numbers 10 and 11 have been suggested by the Duodecimal Society of America. The duodecimal numeral 24E, for example, means $(2\times12^2)+(4\times12^1)+(11\times12^0)$, i.e., $(2\times144)+(4\times12)+(11\times1)$, or 347, in the decimal system. The decimal, binary, and duodecimal systems of numeration constitute only three examples. The ancient Babylonians used a system of base 60, which still survives in our smaller divisions both of time and of angle, i.e., minutes and seconds. In general, any integer n greater than one can be used as the base of a numeration system, and the system will employ n different digits.

Numidia (no͞omĭd'ēə), ancient country of NW Africa, very roughly the modern ALGERIA. It was part of the Carthaginian empire until MASINISSA, ruler of E Numidia, allied himself (c.206 B.C.) with Rome in the PUNIC WARS. After the Roman victory over Carthage led to peace in 201 B.C., Masinissa was awarded rule of all Numidia. This began Numidia's most flourishing period, culturally and politically. Numidia's encroachments on reviving Carthage furnished Rome with a pretext for the Third Punic War (149–146 B.C.). Masinissa's successor was Micipsa (148–118 B.C.), one of whose heirs, JUGURTHA, brought on a fatal war with Rome. Later, in the Roman civil war, King JUBA I sided with Pompey, and Numidia lost (46 B.C.) all independence with Julius Caesar's victory. Juba II was favored by the Romans as a subject prince, and the region subsequently flourished for several centuries. Numidia was invaded by the Vandals in the 5th cent. A.D. and by the Arabs in the 8th cent. The main urban centers of ancient Numidia were Cirta (now Constantine) and Hippo Regius.

numismatics (no͞o"mĭzmăt'ĭks, –mĭs–), collection and study of coins, medals, and related objects as works of art and as sources of information. The COIN and the MEDAL preserve old forms of writing, portraits of eminent persons, and reproductions of lost works of art; they also assist in the study of early customs, in ascertaining dates, and in clarifying economic status and trade relations. In the past many valuable coin collections were assembled by individuals; in the 20th cent., however, public museums have been responsible for building the largest collections. The largest coin market in the world is in London. See J. A. MacKay, *Value in Coins and Medals* (1968); John Porteous, *Coins in History* (1969); Burton Hobson and Robert Obojski, *Illustrated Encyclopedia of World Coins* (1970); C. J. Andrews, *Fell's International Coin Book* (5th ed. 1973); Charles French, *American Guide to U.S. Coins* (annual ed.).

Nun, father of Joshua. Joshua 1.1. Non: 1 Chron. 7.27.

nun: see MONASTICISM.

Nun'Álvares Pereira: see PEREIRA, NUN'ÁLVARES.

Nunc dimittis (nŭngk dĭmĭt'ĭs) [Lat.,=now thou dismissest], prayer of Simeon (Luke 2.29–32). It begins, "Lord, now lettest thou thy servant to depart in peace, according to thy word." It is an evening hymn, sung in the Roman compline and the evening prayer of Anglican churches.

nuncio, apostolic (nŭn'shēō), resident LEGATE of the Holy See at the capital of a temporal government. Nuncios are in most of the principal countries of Europe and Latin America, but there are none in the United States, Great Britain, or the USSR. In some countries the nuncio is by courtesy made the "dean" of the diplomatic corps. Ministers of the second class are called apostolic internuncios.

Nuneaton (nənē'tən), municipal borough (1971 pop. 66,979), Warwickshire, central England. There are coal mines in the vicinity, and iron goods, hats, and cotton, silk, rayon, and woolen textiles are manufactured. There are remains of the 12th-century nunnery that gave Nuneaton its name. George Eliot was born in the borough.

Nunes, Pedro (pĕ'drōō nōō'nəsh), Lat. *Petrus Nonius,* 1502–1578, Portuguese mathematician, geographer, and writer on navigation and geometry. He was the first (1534) to demonstrate an instrument for measuring angles and was the reputed inventor of the rhumb line. He became royal cosmographer in 1529. From 1544 to 1562 he was professor of mathematics at Coimbra. Two of his works are *De crepusculis* (1542) and *De arte atque ratione navigandi* (1546).

Núñez, Rafael (räfäāl' nōō'nyās), 1825–94, president of Colombia (1880–82, 1884–94). After a term as a liberal, he was reelected and became increasingly conservative. A new constitution created the centralized Republic of Colombia in 1886.

Núñez Cabeza de Vaca, Álvar: see CABEZA DE VACA, ÁLVAR NÚÑEZ.

Núñez Vela, Blasco (blä'skō nōō'nyās vā'lä), d. 1546, first viceroy of Peru (1544–46). Sent to replace VACA DE CASTRO and to enforce the New Laws of Bartolomé de LAS CASAS, he had a violent, short career. He antagonized all in command and either ordered a murder or committed it himself. He was arrested and put on a ship for Spain, but landed at Tumbez, was defeated by Gonzalo PIZARRO, and was executed.

Nunivak (nōō'nĭvăk), island, c.1,700 sq mi (4,400 sq km), off W Alaska, in the Bering Sea. Fogbound most of the year, Nunivak is covered with low vegetation and has a small Eskimo population engaged in hunting and fishing. Reindeer and musk oxen have been introduced. The island was discovered in 1821 by Russian explorers.

Nunkiang: see NEN-CHIANG, China.

Nur ad-Din (nōōr ăd-dēn), 1118–74, ruler of Syria. He was the son of the conqueror Zengi, or Zangi, and he succeeded to power in 1145. He defeated the Seljuk Turks in Asia Minor and fought on somewhat better than equal terms with Baldwin III of Jerusalem. His lieutenant Shirkuh barely forestalled the forces of Baldwin's successor, Amalric I, in occupying Egypt. Nur ad-Din built hospitals and caravansaries and was notable for his rule of temperance and justice. Aroused by the independent actions of SALADIN, Shirkuh's successor, Nur ad-Din was about to invade Egypt at the time of his death.

Nuremberg (nōōr'əmbərg), Ger. *Nürnberg* (nürn'bĕrk"), city (1970 pop. 473,555), Bavaria, S West Germany, on the Pegnitz River. One of the great historic cities of Germany, Nuremberg is now an important commercial, industrial, and transportation center. Its manufactures include electrical equipment, heavy machinery, precision instruments, chemicals, textiles, printed materials, beer, and liquor. Homemade toys and fine gingerbread (Ger. *Lebkuchen*) are traditional export items. First mentioned in 1050, Nuremberg received a charter in 1219 and was made a free imperial city by the end of the 13th cent. The city was independent of the burgraviate of Nuremberg, which included a large part of Franconia and which came (1192) under the control of the Hohenzollern family. Nuremberg soon became, with Augsburg, one of the two great trade centers on the route from Italy to N Europe. The cultural flowering of Nuremberg in the 15th and 16th cent. made it the center of the German Renaissance. Among the artists who were born or lived there, Albrecht Dürer was the greatest; others, such as the sculptors Adam Kraft, Veit Stoss, and Peter Vischer and the painter and woodcarver Michael Wolgemut, adorned the city with their works, which brought together the Italian Renaissance and the German Gothic traditions. The city was also an early center of humanism, science, printing, and mechanical invention. The scholars W. Pirkheimer and C. Celtes lectured in the city, A. Koberger set up a printing press and Regiomontanus an observatory, and the first pocket watches, known as Nuremberg eggs, were made there c.1500. An interest in culture on the part of the prosperous artisan class found expression in the contests of the meistersingers (mastersingers), among whom the shoemaker-poet Hans Sachs (1494–1576) was the most prominent. In 1525, Nuremberg accepted the Reformation, and the religious Peace of Nuremberg, by which the Lutherans gained important concessions, was signed there (1532). In the Thirty Years War, Gustavus II was besieged (1632) in Nuremberg by Wallenstein. The city declined after the war and recovered its importance only in the 19th cent. when it grew as an industrial center. In 1806, Nuremberg passed to Bavaria. The first German railroad, from Nuremberg to nearby Fürth, was opened in 1835. After Adolf Hitler came to power, Nuremberg was made a national shrine by the National Socialists (Nazis), who held their annual party congresses nearby from 1933 through 1938. The city was the home of the Nazi leader Julius Streicher and became a center of anti-Semitic propaganda. At the party congress of 1935 the so-called Nuremberg Laws were promulgated; they deprived German Jews of civic rights, forbade intermarriage between Jews and non-Jews, and deprived persons of partly Jewish descent of certain rights. Until 1945, Nuremberg was the site of roughly half the total German production of airplane, submarine, and tank engines; as a consequence, the city was heavily bombed by the Allies during World War II and was largely destroyed. After the war, Nuremberg was the seat of the international tribunal for war crimes. Since 1945 much of the city's architectural beauty has been restored. Among the historic buildings are the churches of St. Sebald (1225–73), St. Lorenz (13th–14th cent.), St. Jacob (14th cent.), and Our Lady (1352–61); the Hohenzollern castle (11th–16th cent.); the old city hall (1616–22); and the house (now a museum) where Albrecht Dürer lived from 1509 to 1528. A large portion of the city walls (14th–17th cent.) still stands. Nuremberg is the site of the German National Museum (founded 1852), a part of the Univ. of Erlangen-Nuremberg, and a museum of transportation.

Nureyev, Rudolf (nōōrĕ'yĕf), 1938–, Soviet ballet dancer, b. Ufa, Bashkir Republic, USSR. Nureyev studied in Ufa and in Leningrad, and in 1958 he became a soloist with the Kirov Ballet, Leningrad. In 1961 he defected from the Soviet Union while on tour in Paris. Nureyev is regarded by many as the leading classical ballet dancer of his generation. He is noted for his overpowering stage presence and his exceptionally athletic skill and fiery grace. His major roles include the leads in *La Bayadère, Les Sylphides, Giselle, Swan Lake, Romeo and Juliet, Le Corsaire, Raymonda,* and *Sleeping Beauty.* As guest artist with the Royal Ballet, London, and elsewhere he has appeared with many celebrated ballerinas, most notably as partner to Margot Fonteyn. He has also revised and staged several ballets, including the Marius Petipa version of *Don Quixote* (1966). Nureyev has also danced in a number of works by modern-dance choreographers including Glen Tetley and Paul Taylor.

Nurhaci (nōōr'hächē), 1559–1626, Manchu national founder. He consolidated the MANCHU tribes under his control and founded the administration that later ruled China as the CH'ING dynasty (1644–1912). His greatest achievement was the creation of the BANNER SYSTEM of military organization that welded the Manchu nation and its early Mongol and Chinese adherents into an efficient war machine. In 1618 he attacked the MING forces and took part of Liaotung. Further victories followed, and in 1625 he moved the Manchu capital to Mukden (Shen-yang). During this later period, Nurhaci developed a civil administration with the help of captured Chinese officials. The further sinicization of the Manchu administration under his son and successor, Abahai, paved the way for the Manchu conquest of China.

Nuristan (nōōrĭstăn') [Persian,=land of light or the enlightened], region on the southern slopes of the Hindu Kush, NE Afghanistan, bordered on the E by Pakistan. Formerly called Kafiristan [land of the infidels], it is inhabited by an ethnically distinctive people (numbering about 60,000), who practiced animism until their forcible conversion to Islam in 1895–96. Inhabiting relatively isolated villages in deep, narrow mountain valleys, they grow wheat, barley, millet, peas, wine grapes, and other fruit and raise livestock (chiefly goats). A special artisan caste specializes in woodcarving, pottery making, weaving, and metalwork. The Nuristanis, divided into several tribes, speak Dardic dialects (often mutually unintelligible) belonging to a distinct branch of the Indo-European language family.

Nurmi, Paavo (pä'vō nōōr'mē), 1897–1973, Finnish track star. Between 1920 and 1932 he set 20 world running records and won nine Olympic gold medals. His Olympic victories included the 10,000-meter run and the cross-country event at Antwerp in 1920, the 1,500-meter and 5,000-meter and cross-country runs at Paris in 1924, and the 10,000-meter run at Amsterdam in 1928. In addition, he won three gold medals in team events. He was disqualified from the 1932 Olympic games because of violations of the amateur athletic code; he later became wealthy as a sporting goods merchant.

Nürnberg, West Germany: see NUREMBERG.

nursery, in horticulture, an establishment or area for the propagation, breeding, and early cultivation of plants. In North America the term *nursery* originally specified a place where hardy woody plants, especially fruit trees, were started; but as the market for and interest in new varieties of garden plants increased, nurseries broadened their province to include the cultivation and development of all types of plants, including tropical varieties and annuals, and their sale either as seedlings ready for planting or as seeds. The modern nursery, staffed by horticulture experts and equipped with facilities for both experimental and mass production, supplies home gardeners, flower and fruit growers, farmers, and foresters with seeds and seedlings of specified qualities. Under nursery conditions varieties of plants have been bred that have greater yields and are hardier, longer blooming, and more disease resistant than those grown in the ordinary farm or garden, where controlled selection and hybridization would be tedious if not impossible. Grafting and budding are also commonly used by nurseries to produce superior plants. Until the advent of artificial irrigation and the use of vast greenhouses to control temperature, nurseries depended on natural conditions for success—as did the bulb nurseries of Holland, which were long famous for flowers and ornamental plants.

nursery rhymes, verses, generally brief and usually anonymous, for children. The best-known examples are in English and date mostly from the 17th cent. A popular type of rhyme is used in "counting-out" games, e.g., "Eenie, meenie, minie, mo." The subject matter of the rhymes has been linked by some scholars to actual events in English political history. Most famous of nursery rhymes is the MOTHER GOOSE collection. See *Oxford Dictionary of Nursery Rhymes,* ed. by Iona and Peter Opie (1952); studies by Lima Eckenstein (1906, repr. 1968) and Henry Bett (1924, repr. 1973).

nursery school, educational institution for children from two to four years of age. It is distinguishable from a DAY NURSERY in that it serves children of both working and nonworking parents, rarely receives public funds, and has as its primary objective to promote the social and educational adjustment of children, rather than to provide a daytime child-care service. The first nursery schools were opened in London in 1907. Pioneers in nursery school work in the United States were the State Univ. of Iowa; Teachers College, Columbia Univ.; Smith; and Vassar. Early American nursery schools were often sponsored by and affiliated with local universities. The Eliot Pearson School (opened in the 1920s as the Ruggles Street Nursery) is one of the oldest schools of its type and is still affiliated with Tufts Univ. Few public school systems include nursery education; the facilities offered are chiefly private, philanthropic, or cooperative. See H. M. Christianson, *The Nursery School: Adventure in Learning and Living* (1961); K. H. Read, *The Nursery School* (5th ed. 1971).

nursing, science of providing continuous care for ill people. While nursing as an occupation has always existed, it is only in fairly recent years that it has developed as a profession. In ancient times, when medical lore was associated with good or evil spirits, the sick were usually cared for in temples and houses of worship. In the early Christian era, nursing duties were undertaken by certain women in the church, their services being extended to patients in their homes. These women had no real training as we know it today, but experience taught them some valuable skills, especially in the use of herbs and drugs, and some gained fame as the physicians of their era. In later centuries, however, nursing duties for the most part fell to ignorant and disreputable women. In the 17th cent., St. Vincent de Paul began to encourage women to undertake some form of training for their work, but there was no real hospital training school for nurses until one was established in Kaiserwerth, Germany, in 1846. There, Florence Nightingale received the training that later enabled her to establish at St. Thomas's Hospital in London, the first school designed primarily to train nurses rather than to provide nursing service for the hospital. Similar schools were established in 1873 in New York City, New Haven, and Boston. Since then nursing has become one of the most important professions open to women (and to a lesser extent to men). Nursing candidates must prepare themselves by a rigorous course of training that includes a thorough grounding in anatomy, physiology, pharmacology, the cause and treatment of disease, the intricacies of nutrition and diet, surgical skills, and a variety of techniques pertaining to the proper care of the patient. Many nurses prepare themselves for specialized work, such as the care of newborn infants, maternity patients, or the mentally ill, or for duties in the operating room. Training for a career as a registered nurse can be met by three possible programs of study: a two-year course at a junior college, a three-year hospital course, or a four-year degree program at a college or university. Emphasis on collegiate education for nurses is on the upsurge because greater knowledge is required to apply the latest methods of diagnosis and therapy. Training by any of the above methods includes both classroom study and actual hospital practice, and the graduate must still be examined and licensed by the state. This applies also to women in religious orders who train and work as nursing sisters. In addition to duties in the hospital or in the home there are many fields open to the professional nurse, such as the Red Cross, the military services, public health agencies, industry, teaching, and missionary work in remote areas of the world. Recently, the acute shortage of nursing personnel has been lessening. However, the demand for qualified professionals is still great, especially for teaching and administration in nursing schools. The age limits and educational requirements for practical nurses are less stringent, and the period of training is much shorter (usually one year). Sufficient training is given to such women to enable them to care for and feed patients, administer medication, and perform other routine duties, thereby releasing the registered nurse for the more technical aspects of the profession. In many areas practical nurses are also examined and licensed by the state. See G. J. and H. J. Griffin, ed., *Jensen's History and Trends of Professional Nursing* (6th ed. 1969); other histories by I. M. Stewart and A. L. Austin (5th ed. 1962) and J. A. Dolan (12th ed. 1968); E. K. Spalding and L. E. Notter, *Professional Nursing* (7th ed. 1965); E. V. Fuerst and LuVerne Wolff, *Fundamentals of Nursing* (4th ed. 1969).

Nusatenggara: see SUNDA ISLANDS, Indonesia.

Nusaybin (no͞osĭbĭn') or **Nisibin** (nē'sĭbēn), town (1970 pop. 13,941), SE Turkey, near the Syrian border. It is a commercial and transportation center. It has ruins of the ancient Nisibis, the residence of early (2d cent. B.C.–1st cent. A.D.) Armenian kings. In early Christian times it was a center of Nestorianism. In 1839 the Egyptians defeated the Turks at Nusaybin.

nut, in botany, a dry one-seeded FRUIT which is indehiscent (i.e., does not split open along a definite seam at maturity). Among the true nuts are the acorn, chestnut, and hazelnut. Commonly the word *nut* is used for any seed or fruit having an edible kernel surrounded by a hard or brittle covering. Thus the peanut pod is actually a legume, the Brazil nut is a seed enclosed with others in a capsule, and the almond is part of a drupe, a type of fruit that includes olives and peaches. Others that are not botanically true nuts are the cashew, coconut, litchi, pecan, pistachio, and walnut. Nuts have long been recognized and gathered as a valuable contribution to the diet. Most nuts have a high content of oil; in addition they may contain substantial amounts of protein, carbohydrate, minerals, and vitamins. Although nuts were originally harvested from wild trees, this century has seen the increasing cultivation of nut orchards—especially in warmer climates—for commercial production both for food and for by-products. See J. G. Woodroof, *Tree Nuts* (2 vol., 1967); R. A. Jaynes, ed., *Handbook of North American Nut Trees* (rev. ed. 1973).

Nut (no͝ot, nŭt), in Egyptian religion, sky-goddess. She was the sister-wife of the earth-god Geb, to whom she bore Osiris, Isis, Set, and Nephthys. She was sometimes represented with her hands and feet on the earth and the curve of her body forming the vault of heaven.

nutation, in astronomy, a slight wobbling motion of the earth's axis. The causes of nutation are similar to those of the PRECESSION OF THE EQUINOXES, involving the varying attraction of the MOON on the earth's equatorial bulge. However, the period of the motion is only 18.6 years, the same as that of the precession of the moon's nodes, as opposed to the nearly 26,000-year period of the precession of the equinoxes. Nutation was discovered by the English astronomer James Bradley in 1728 but was not explained until 20 years later.

nutcracker, common name for a small crow of the genus *Nucifraga* in the family Corvidae (crow family). The Old World nutcracker (*N. caryocatactes*) is found throughout the colder regions of Europe, including high mountain forests. Its plumage is chocolate brown, speckled with white. With its strong, conical beak, it feeds omnivorously on a diet of conifer seeds, nuts, small buds, and insects. In a squirrellike fashion, it stores seeds during the summer and fall against the winter's snow, and has a remarkable ability to relocate its cache exactly, even though covered with snow. Clark's nutcracker (*N. columbians*), pale gray with black and white wings, is found throughout W North America, and is similar in its habits and choice of habitat to *N. caryocatactes.* It somewhat resembles a stout-billed mockingbird. Like most crows, nutcrackers are intelligent and aggressive birds. They are highly gregarious, and their flocks show a complex social organization. Their young are born blind and helpless. Nutcrackers are classified in the phylum CHORDATA, subphylum Vertebrata, class Aves, order Passeriformes, family Corvidae.

nutgall: see GALL.

nuthatch (nŭt'hăch), common name applied to a number of Old and New World species of small birds of the genus *Sitta,* related to the titmouse and the creeper. The name refers to its habit of wedging nuts into crevices in trees and pecking them open. Nuthatches are unique in that they climb down tree trunks headfirst in their search for insects and spiders. Unlike the creepers, the nuthatches have straight bills and do not use their short tail feathers as a prop. Nuthatches are classified in the phylum CHORDATA, subphylum Vertebrata, class Aves, order Passeriformes, family Sittidae.

Nutley, town (1970 pop. 31,913), Essex co., NE N.J., a residential suburb of Newark, on the Passaic River; settled 1680, inc. 1902. Pharmaceuticals, textiles, and paper products are made. After the Civil War the town was a center for writers and artists. Annie Oakley lived in Nutley.

nutmeg, evergreen tree (*Myristica fragrans*) native to the Moluccas but now cultivated elsewhere in the tropics and to a limited extent in S Florida. The fruit is the source of two spices of commercial value: whole or ground nutmeg, from the inner seed; and mace, from the fibrous aril (seed covering) that separates the seed from its thick outer husk. It also supplies butters and an essential oil used in medicines, toilet preparations, and dentifrices. Other trees of the *Myristica* genus, also called nutmegs, are of a limited use commercially; a wax is prepared from several American species. Connecticut is called the Nutmeg State in reference to the wooden nutmegs reputedly made there. Nutmeg is classified in the division MAGNOLIOPHYTA, class Magnoliopsida, order Magnoliales, family Myristicaceae.

nutria (no͞o'trēə) or **coypu** (koi'po͞o), aquatic RODENT, *Myocastor coypus,* of South America, introduced in the S United States for its fur, which is similar to that of beaver but not as thick or durable. The nutria resembles a small beaver with a ratlike tail. It is up to 25 in. (64 cm) long, excluding the 15-in. (38-cm) sparsely haired, round tail; it has large reddish incisor teeth and partially webbed hind feet. The outer fur is long, coarse, and brown; it is the soft, gray undercoat that is valued commercially. Descendants of nutrias escaped from fur farms are now found in much of the United States, especially in swampy regions. They build burrows in banks with the entrances above water level and feed on aquatic vegetation, competing with the native muskrat for food. Nutrias have also established themselves successfully in Europe. They are classified in the phylum CHORDATA, subphylum Vertebrata, class Mammalia, order Rodentia, family Capromyidae.

nutrition, study of the materials that nourish an organism and of the manner in which the separate components are used for maintenance, repair, growth, and reproduction. Nutrition is achieved in various ways by different forms of life. Plants that contain the green pigment CHLOROPHYLL can synthesize their food from inorganic substances in the process called PHOTOSYNTHESIS. Organisms such as plants that can thus manufacture complex organic compounds from simple inorganic nutrients are termed autotrophic. Organisms that must obtain "prefabricated" organic compounds from their environment are heterotrophic, and these include the fungi, some other plants, and animals. Heterotrophic plants may be saprophytic (obtaining nutrients from dead organisms) or parasitic (obtaining nutrients from living organisms while living on or in them). Heterotrophic animals may be parasites, herbivores (plant-eaters), carnivores (meat-eaters), or omnivores (obtaining nutrition from both plants and animals). Man, an omnivore, requires food substances to supply the components necessary to build tissues, to repair tissues as they wear out and die, to keep the body in good working condition, and to supply fuel for energy; those food substances fall chiefly into three major groups: proteins, carbohydrates, and fats. PROTEIN in the diet provides AMINO ACIDS for forming body proteins, including the structural proteins for building and repairing tissues, and the enzymes for carrying out the metabolic processes. A body that is in the process of building itself (such as that of a growing child or an adult recovering from illness) will need a greater proportion of protein to weight than one that is fully grown and utilizes protein merely for repair of worn-out tissues. The average adult requires 1 gram of protein per kilogram of body weight per day; children may require two to three times this amount. Good sources of protein are meat, fish, eggs, legumes (e.g., peas, beans, and lentils), milk, and cheese. CARBOHYDRATES (starches and sugars) provide a readily available energy source. They are also converted by the body to GLYCOGEN and fat, the storage forms of calories for energy, and to some of the amino acids used in protein synthesis. Carbohydrates also supply the bulk in the diet. They make up 25% to 50% of the calories in a well-balanced diet; 1 gram of carbohydrate supplies about 4 calories. Cereals, fruits, vegetables, syrups, and sugar are good sources of carbohydrates. Fats (see FATS AND OILS) in the diet provide a concentrated source of energy; 1 gram of fat supplies about 9 calories. Fats in the body, in addition to acting as a source of stored energy, supply physical protection and insulation for tissues and form important portions of cell membrane structure. Fats also aid in the absorption of the fat-soluble vitamins (vitamins A, D, E, and K) from the intestine. Milk, butter, meat, and oils are important sources of fat. To keep the body functioning properly it is necessary to have, in addition to the basic foods, a sufficient intake of accessory substances such as VITAMINS, minerals, and enough water to carry nutrients to the tissues and waste products away from them. Vitamins function as COENZYMES in important body processes and must be entirely supplied in the diet. A large number of minerals are required, some in trace amounts and others, such as calcium and iron, in relatively large amounts. Milk and cheese are excellent sources of calcium; liver, meat, and egg yolks are good sources of iron. Minerals are vital to the development of teeth and bones (calcium, phosphorus, and fluoride) and to the functioning of a number of the body's metabolic systems. Iron is a necessary part of hemoglobin in the blood; various metals are required in many enzymes; sodium and potassium are essential to maintenance of fluid balance and functioning of the nervous system; and iodine is required for thyroid hormone. Good nutrition is reflected not only in the growth and function of the body but also in its appearance. The eyes, skin, hair, and teeth indicate whether body nourishment is good or poor. A poorly nourished child will fail to grow properly; a poorly nourished adult will have a decreased resistance to infection and disease. A diet deficient in proteins causes a disease called kwashiorkor in children; a diet deficient in both protein and calories results in marasmus, with lethargy, abdominal enlargement, and wasting—the classical malnutrition syndrome. Poor nutrition may result from excesses in the diet as well as deficiencies; excess of certain vitamins or minerals can produce disease states, and excess of carbohydrates or fat can result in obesity. For good nutrition a person should eat a well-balanced diet, that is, one that provides an adequate amount of each of the classes of nutrients each day, furnishing at the same time an adequate but not excessive number of calories for the body's energy needs. Children require relatively larger amounts of nutrients and calories because of their rapid growth. Generally a well-balanced diet includes at least one serving daily from each of the following groups: milk and milk products, meat and meat substitutes (including eggs and legumes), vegetables and fruits, and breads and cereals. Specialized diets are useful in the treatment of certain disease states; the most common is a low-calorie diet to produce weight loss in obese persons. A diet low in PHENYLALANINE is used to treat PHENYLKETONURIA. A diet low in CHOLESTEROL and saturated fats seems to be useful in the treatment and possibly in the prevention of heart disease. Elimination of certain foods from the diet may be necessary to control allergies in some individuals. In addition, special diets are often followed by various religious groups. In all cases, however, specialized diets must provide all classes of essential nutrients in adequate amounts to maintain health in adults and support growth in children. See H. A. Guthrie, *Introductory Nutrition* (2d ed. 1971); P. S. Howe, *Basic Nutrition in Health and Disease* (5th ed. 1971); M. V. Krause and M. A. Hunscher, *Food, Nutrition and Diet Therapy* (5th ed. 1972); M. T. Arlin, *The Science of Nutrition* (1972).

Nuttall, George Henry Falkiner, 1862–1937, American-British bacteriologist, b. San Francisco, M.D. Univ. of California, 1884, Ph.D. Univ. of Göttingen, 1890. In 1899 he became associated with Cambridge Univ., where he was professor of biology from 1906. He contributed much to the knowledge of parasites and of insect carriers of diseases. He organized the Molteno Institute for Research in Parasitology at Cambridge and directed it from 1921. Nuttall established (1901) and edited the *Journal of Hygiene* and also founded (1908) and edited *Parasitology.* His writings include *Blood Immunity and Blood Relationship* (1904); he was a coauthor of *The Bacteriology of Diphtheria* (1908).

Nuttall, Thomas, 1786–1859, American naturalist, b. England. He was a pioneer in American paleontology and was curator (1822–32) of the Harvard botanical garden. He accompanied several scientific expeditions to the Mississippi and Missouri valleys and the Pacific coast and published his findings in *The Genera of North American Plants* (2 vol., 1818) and *A Manual of the Ornithology of the United States and of Canada* (1832). In 1842 he returned to England. He also wrote an account of his travels (1819) into the Arkansas territory. See study by J. E. Graustein (1967).

Nuuanu Pali (no͞o-ä'no͞o pä'lē), sheer cliff and mountain pass, alt. 1,200 ft (366 m), Koolau Range, SE Oahu island, Hawaii. The pass is the principal route between Honolulu and E Oahu.

Nuwara Eliya (no͝ov'ərə ā'lĭyə, no͝orā'lēə), town (1963 pop. 19,988), S Sri Lanka (Ceylon). A hill resort and health center in a tea-growing area, it was first settled in 1827 by the British. According to legend, Sita, the wife of Rama, hero of the Sanskrit epic *Ramayana,* was imprisoned near Nuwara Eliya.

nux vomica (nŭks vŏm'əkə), bitter-tasting drug obtained from the poisonous seeds of *Strychnos nux-vomica,* a tree that grows in Sri Lanka, India, and N Australia. The dried seeds contain STRYCHNINE and brucine, both colorless crystalline alkaloids, as well as sugar, acid, and oil. In the past nux vomica was used as a tonic in the form of a tincture, or alcoholic solution, but it is not used in modern medicine. In minute quantities it has a powerful peristaltic action on the intestines and in larger doses causes convulsions and death.

Nuzi (no͞o'zē), site near Kirkuk, N Iraq. Thousands of clay tablets unearthed there bear inscriptions said to have been made by the Horims (or Horites) of the Bible. The tablets, which are in Akkadian, reveal much about ancient laws and customs.

nyala: see BUSHBUCK.

Ny-Ålesund (nü"-ô'ləso͞on) [New Alesund], town, on Kongsfjorden, NW Spitsbergen island, Svalbard. It is a coal-mining settlement. Ny-Ålesund was (1926) the base of polar flights by Richard Byrd, in an airplane, and by Roald Amundsen, who, with Lincoln Ellsworth and Umberto Nobile, flew from there to Alaska in the dirigible *Norge.*

nyanza (nĭăn'zə, nē–), a BANTU LANGUAGE word for lake. The word is commonly used with some E African lakes, e.g., VICTORIA NYANZA and ALBERT NYANZA.

Nyasa, Lake (nīăs'ə), or **Lake Malawi** (məlä'wē), Port. *Niassa,* c.11,600 sq mi (30,040 sq km), c.360 mi (580 km) long and from 15 to 50 mi (24–80 km) wide, E central Africa, in the GREAT RIFT VALLEY. Lake Nyasa, the third largest lake in Africa, is bordered by Tanzania in the north and northeast, by Mozambique in the east, and by Malawi in the south and west. The lake is bounded by steep mountains, except in the south. Its main tributary is the Ruhuhu River in the northeast; the Shiré (in the south), a tributary of the Zambezi, is the lake's sole outlet. There is regular steamship service on the lake. First discovered by the Portuguese explorer Caspar Boccaro c.1616, Lake Nyasa was visited and named by the Scottish missionary David LIVINGSTONE in 1859.

Nyasaland: see MALAWI.

Nyaya (nyä'yə): see INDIAN PHILOSOPHY.

Nyborg (nü'bôr), city (1970 com. pop. 17,775), Fyn co., S central Denmark, a seaport at the head of Nybord Fjord (an arm of the Store Baelt). It is an industrial center, with shipyards and plants manufacturing textiles and tobacco products. In Nyborg castle (built c.1170; now in ruins) Eric V granted (1282) the first Danish constitution.

Nye, Edgar Wilson (nī), known as **Bill Nye,** 1850–96, American humorist and journalist, b. Shirley Mills, Maine. He lived in Wisconsin from 1852 to 1876, when he went to Wyoming. There he was admitted to the bar and became a judge. He founded and edited (1881–84) the Laramie *Boomerang* and contributed to it humorous comments and yarns of frontier life, which were collected in *Bill Nye and Boomerang* (1881), *Forty Liars and Other Lies* (1882), and *Baled Hay* (1884). In 1886 he moved to New York City, where he wrote for the *World* and gave lyceum recitals, some of them with James Whitcomb Riley. Among his later works are the comical *Bill Nye's History of the United States* (1894) and *Bill Nye's History of England* (1896) and the play *The Cadi* (1891). See *Bill Nye: His Own Life Story* (comp. by his son, F. W. Nye, 1926); his letters (ed. by N. O. Rush, 1951).

Nye, Gerald Prentice, 1892–1971, U.S. Senator (1925–45), b. Hortonville, Wis. After settling (1915) in North Dakota he devoted himself to country journalism. A progressive Republican, he was appointed to fill an unexpired term in the U.S. Senate; he remained there until defeated for reelection in 1944. As Senator, he headed the committee that investigated (1934–36) the role played by U.S. businessmen in the American entrance into World War I. An outspoken isolationist, he fathered the Neutrality Act. See study by W. S. Cole (1962).

Nyerere, Julius Kambarage (käm"bərä'gä nĭ"ərā'rā), 1921–, African political leader, 1st president (1964–) of Tanzania, formerly Tanganyika. The son of a chief, he alternated study at Makerere College (Uganda) and the Univ. of Edinburgh with teaching in mission schools. He founded (1954) the Tanganyika African National Union, a political party, and as its representative in the legislative council, he was leader of the opposition. Nyerere became chief minister after the 1960 elections, and when Tanganyika attained independence (1961) he was its first prime minister. When Tanganyika became (1962) a republic, Nyerere was elected first president. He was the architect of the union (1964) of Tanganyika and Zanzibar into a republic, as Tanzania, and he brought it (1967) into the East African Community, a customs union with Uganda and Kenya. See biography by W. E. Smith (1971).

Nyíregyháza (nyē'rĕjhä"zŏ), city (1970 pop. 70,640), NE Hungary. It is a county administrative center, a road and rail junction, and the market for an extensive agricultural region. Known in the 13th cent., the city was destroyed during the Turkish occupation (16th cent.) of Hungary but was rebuilt in the 18th cent. Its museum contains gold relics dating from Avar times.

Nyitra: see NITRA, Czechoslovakia.

Nykøbing (nü'kö"bĭng), name of several places in Denmark. **1** City (1970 com. pop. 25,870), capital of Storstrøm co., SE Denmark, on Falster Island and on the Guldborg Sund, connected by bridge with Lolland. It is a seaport and has sugar refineries, breweries, and textile mills. Of note are a Gothic church (until 1532 a Franciscan monastery) and the ruins of a 12th-century castle. **2** Town (1970 pop. 9,066), Viborg co., NW Denmark, on Mors Island and on the Limfjørd. It has a large iron foundry, oyster fisheries, and textile and tobacco industries. **3** Town (1970 com. pop. 6,157), Vestsjaelland co., E central Denmark, a seaport on the Isefjord. It is an industrial center and a popular summer resort with fine beaches. The town has sawmills, machine shops, breweries, and dairy industries.

Nyköping (nü'chö"pĭng), city (1970 pop. 37,716), capital of Södermanland co., SE Sweden, a port on the Baltic Sea. It is a commercial and industrial center. An atomic research center is nearby. Nyköping was founded in the 13th cent. on the site of a former trading town. It was destroyed by fire in 1665, was rebuilt, and was sacked by the Russians in 1719. Historic structures in the city include St. Nicholas Church (13th–18th cent.), the city hall (17th cent.), and ruins of Nyköpingshus castle (13th cent.).

nylon, synthetic thermoplastic material characterized by strength, elasticity, resistance to abrasion and chemicals, low moisture absorbency, and capacity to be permanently set by heat. After 10 years of research E. I. du Pont de Nemours & Company introduced nylon in 1938 as monofilaments for bristles and in 1940 as multifilament yarn for hosiery. Nylon is now manufactured also in the form of sheets, coatings, and molded plastics and used in a variety of products, including fabrics, surgical sutures, thread, insulating wire coverings, mosquito netting and screening, gears and bearings, rope, and tire cords. There are a variety of nylons, all being polyamides frequently made from diamines and dicarboxylic acids. The most generally useful of these is nylon (66), made from hexamethylene amine and adipic acid.

nymph (nĭmf), in Greek mythology, female divinity associated with various natural objects. It is uncertain whether they were immortal or merely long-lived. There was an infinite variety of nymphs. Some represented various localities, e.g., acheloids, or nymphs of the River Achelous; others were identified with the part of nature in which they dwelled, e.g., oreads, or mountain nymphs; and still others were associated with a particular function of nature, e.g., hamadryads, or tree nymphs, whose lives began and ended with that of a particular tree. Nymphs were represented as young, beautiful, musical, amorous, and gentle, although some were associated with the wilder aspects of nature and were akin to satyrs; others were vengeful and capable of destruction, as in the story of DAPHNE. Other important nymphs were naiads, nymphs of streams, rivers, and lakes; nereids, daughters of Nereus, who lived in the depths of the Mediterranean Sea; dryads, tree nymphs; and oceanids, 3,000 ocean nymphs who were the daughters of Oceanus. ARETHUSA, THETIS, CALYPSO, and ECHO were famous nymphs. The nymphs' cult was widespread in Greece.

nymph, in zoology: see INSECT.

Nymphas (nĭm'fəs), Christian of Laodicea. Col. 4.15.

Nymphenburg (nüm'fənbo͝orkh), group of châteaus and a large park, Munich, Bavaria, S West Germany. The main building is the Nymphenburg château (built 1664–1728), which belonged to the dukes (later kings) of Bavaria. Also noteworthy is Amalienburg (1734–39), a small baroque hunting château designed by François de Cuvilliés. A famous porcelain factory was founded at Nymphenburg in 1747. By the Treaty of Nymphenburg (1741) Spain promised Charles Albert of Bavaria (see CHARLES VII, emperor) its support in his attempt to secure the imperial election.

Nyslott, Finland: see SAVONLINNA.

Nyssa (nĭs'ə), name of several ancient cities devoted to the worship of Dionysus. The best known of them is a town of Cappadocia, Asia Minor, near the Halys (now the Kizil Irmak) River. It was the residence of St. Gregory of Nyssa.

Nystad: see UUSIKAUPUNKI, Finland.

Nystad, Treaty of: see NORTHERN WAR.

nystagmus (nĭstăg'məs), rhythmical, jerky or rolling movements of the eyes. Nystagmus occurs normally following rotation of the head; the eyes move slowly in counterrotational direction in an attempt to focus on a fixed spot, followed by rapid movement back. Abnormal nystagmus often results from a disorder in the nerve signals to the muscles of the eyeballs. Overstimulation of eyeball muscles, precipitated by signals from the inner ear, is known as vestibular nystagmus. The condition may also be associated with other nervous system disorders, such as delirium resulting from illness, tumors, or multiple sclerosis. Other causative factors include eye fatigue, watching rapidly moving scenery as when riding in a train, and, in children, some types of crossed eyes. Treatment is directed toward the underlying abnormal condition.

O

O, 15th letter of the ALPHABET. It is a usual symbol for a mid-back, rounded vowel, rather like the first part of *oi.* Such a vowel was represented by omicron [Gr., = little *o*], its formal and positional correspondent in the Greek alphabet. English ō is a diphthong of ŏ and *w.* In chemistry O is the symbol of the element OXYGEN. In surnames O' is derived from the Irish patronymic system; e.g., O'Neill meant "grandson of Niall," probably referring originally to Niall Glundubh, high king of Ireland, 915–19 (see NAME).

Oahe Dam (ōwä'hē), major unit of the Missouri River basin project, 242 ft (74 m) high and 9,360 ft (2,853 m) long, on the Missouri River, central S.Dak., near Pierre; built 1948–63 by the U.S. Corps of Engineers. The reservoir impounded by the dam extends c.250 mi (400 km) upstream and has the third largest capacity in the United States. The dam provides power (595,000-kw capacity), flood control, improvement of navigation, and irrigation.

Oahu (ōä'ho͞o), island (1970 pop. 629,145), 593 sq mi (1,536 sq km), third largest and chief island of Hawaii, part of Honolulu co., between Molokai and Kauai. Oahu is composed of two parallel mountain ranges (Waianae and Koolau) that are separated by a rolling plain dissected by deep gorges; Mt. Kaala (4,040 ft/1,231 m) is the island's highest peak. Oahu has no active volcanoes, but there are many extinct craters, among them Diamond Head, Koko Head, and Punchbowl. Pearl Harbor indents the island's southern coast. Honolulu, the state capital and the economic center of Hawaii, is on the highly urbanized southern coast of Oahu. Manoa Valley is the site of the Univ. of Hawaii, Punahou Academy, and the Mid-Pacific Institute. The island is an important defense area that includes the headquarters of the U.S. Pacific Command and the Pearl Harbor naval base. There are many bathing beaches (including Waikiki), some of which have coral gardens. Large pineapple and sugarcane plantations cover the rural areas of the island, and their products form Oahu's chief agricultural exports. Dairy farming and fishing are also important economic activities.

oak, any tree or shrub of the genus *Quercus* of the family Fagaceae (BEECH family). The genus includes about 300 species, found chiefly in north temperate zones and also in Polynesia. The more southerly species, ranging into the tropics, are usually evergreen. Oaks are cultivated for ornament and are prized as the major source of hardwood lumber. The wood is durable, tough, and attractively grained; it is especially valued in shipbuilding and construction and for flooring, furniture, railroad ties, barrels, tool handles, and veneer (particularly highly burled oak). The oaks are commonly divided into two groups, the black (or red) and the white. The former (e.g., the scarlet, pin, Spanish, willow, laurel, and shingle oaks) are characterized by leaves with sharp-tipped lobes and by acorns that mature in two years. The white oaks (e.g., the white, post, bur, cork, and holly oaks) are characterized by smooth-lobed leaves and acorns that mature in one year. *Q. alba,* the white oak, is the most important timber tree of the oak genus. Lumber-yielding species of chestnut (genus *Castanea*) are included in the white oak group when the term is used as a timber classification. The live oaks, evergreen species common in the S and SW United States, are sometimes considered a separate group. The bark of some oaks is employed in medicine, in tanning, and for dyes; that of the CORK OAK supplies the cork of commerce. The GALLS caused by certain insects are utilized commercially. The Mediterranean kermes oak (*Q. coccifera*) is host to the KERMES insect, source of the world's oldest dyestuff. Acorns, the fruit of oak trees, have long been employed as a source of hog feed, tannin (chiefly from valonia, the acorn cup of the Turkish oak, *Q. aegilops*), oil, and especially food. Acorns were one of the most important foods of the North American forest Indians; they were pulverized, leached to extract the bitter taste, and then cooked in various ways. Acorns have also been used as food in other regions where they are native. A symbol of strength, the oak has been revered for both historical and mythological associations. It was the favorite of Jove and Thor and especially sacred to the druids. St. Louis administered justice under an oak, and the CHARTER OAK is legendary in America. Several unrelated plants are also called oak, e.g., the Jerusalem oak (a lobe-leaved annual of the goosefoot family) and the poison oak of the sumac family (see POISON IVY). Oaks are classified in the division MAGNOLIOPHYTA, class Magnoliopsida, order Fagales, family Fagaceae.

Oak Creek, city (1970 pop. 13,928), Milwaukee co., SE Wis., a suburb of Milwaukee, on Lake Michigan; inc. 1955. Electronic equipment, heavy machinery, aluminum products, and glues are made there.

Oak Forest, village (1970 pop. 17,870), Cook co., NE Ill., a residential suburb of Chicago, in a diversified farming area; inc. 1947.

Oakland. 1 City (1970 pop. 361,561), seat of Alameda co., W Calif., on the eastern side of San Francisco Bay; inc. 1852. A containerized shipping port and a major rail terminus, it has shipyards, chemical plants, glassworks, and food-processing establishments. The spectacular San Francisco-Oakland Bay Bridge was opened in 1936, and several tunnels connect Oakland with other nearby cities. Oakland is the headquarters and hub of the Bay Area Rapid Transit, a 75-mi (121-km), three-county rapid transit system that began operation in 1972. The city has an international airport. Of interest are the new Oakland Museum, Chabot Observatory, the Morcom Rose Garden, and Jack London Square (a restaurant and entertainment area). The city has a symphony orchestra, fine parks, a state arboretum, a children's amusement park, and a zoo. It is the seat of Mills College, Holy Names College, California College of Arts and Crafts, and two junior colleges. St. Mary's College is nearby. A large U.S. naval supply center and a U.S. army terminal and depot are in the city. The Oakland-Alameda County Coliseum and Arena is the home of the city's major league professional baseball, football, and ice hockey teams. Jack London lived in Oakland. **2** Residential borough (1970 pop. 14,420), Bergen co., NE N.J.; settled early 1700s, inc. 1902.

Oakland Park, city (1970 pop. 16,261), Broward co., SE Fla., on the Atlantic coast.

Oak Lawn, village (1970 pop. 60,305), Cook co., NE Ill., a suburb of Chicago; inc. 1909. It is chiefly residential with some light manufacturing industries. Products include metal work, machine tools and parts, kitchen cabinets, musical instruments, and school supplies.

Oakley, Annie, 1860–1926, American theatrical performer, b. Darke co., Ohio. Her original name was Phoebe Anne Oakley Mozee. From childhood on she was a "dead shot" with a rifle. She defeated in contest the noted marksman and vaudeville star Frank E. Butler, who subsequently married her and became her manager and assistant. As a major attraction (1885–1902) of Buffalo Bill's Wild West Show she performed remarkable feats of marksmanship. In 1901 she was partially paralyzed in a railroad accident but continued to delight audiences with her brilliant shooting for 20 years. See biography by Walter Havighurst (1954).

Oak Park. 1 Village (1970 pop. 62,511), Cook co., NE Ill., a residential suburb adjacent to Chicago; settled 1833, inc. 1901. Some 25 houses in the village were designed by Frank Lloyd Wright, who lived there. Ernest Hemingway was born in Oak Park. **2** City (1970 pop. 36,762), Oakland co., SE Mich., a suburb of Detroit; inc. 1927. It is chiefly residential, but there is some industry.

Oak Ridge, city (1970 pop. 28,319), Anderson and Roane counties, E Tenn., on Black Oak Ridge and the Clinch River; founded by the U.S. government 1942, inc. as an independent city 1959. Many activities in the fields of atomic energy and nuclear physics are pursued; manufactures include complex nuclear instruments, electronic instrumentation, irradiated products, and nuclear fuel. The site was chosen (1942) for what was then called the Clinton Engineer Works, and the city was built by the Federal government to house the workers who developed the uranium-235 and plutonium-239 for the atomic bomb. The existence and purpose of the community were kept secret from most of the country until the summer of 1945. The project was under the control of the Atomic Energy Commission, but the city has since (1955–59) been turned over to its residents. The former Clinton National Laboratory for nuclear research became (1948) the Oak Ridge National Laboratory. The Oak Ridge Institute of Nuclear Studies (1948), composed of many sponsoring educational institutions, and the Univ. of Tennessee Biomedical Science graduate school are also there. Tourist attractions include the American Museum of Atomic Energy; a nearby nuclear graphite reactor; the K-25 overlook, from which can be seen the Oak Ridge gaseous diffusion plant; and an arboretum.

Oakwood, city (1970 pop. 10,095), Montgomery co., SW Ohio, a residential suburb adjacent to Dayton; inc. 1907.

oasis (ōā'sĭs), fertile area in the desert. Oases are to be found where there is enough moisture to permit the growth of vegetation. The water may come up to the surface in springs, or it may be collected and retained in mountain hollows. In the Sahara there are mountains of sufficient height to cause occasional precipitation, which is the reason for many oases in that region. The creation of oases by artificial irrigation in desert areas has been successfully performed, especially in parts of Israel. Oases vary considerably in size. They range from a pond with a group of date palms to oasis cities with extended agricultural cultivations.

Oates, Joyce Carol, 1938–, American novelist, b. Lockport, N.Y., grad. Syracuse Univ. (B.A., 1960); Univ. of Wisconsin (M.A., 1961). Since 1967 she has taught English at the Univ. of Windsor in Ontario, Canada. Oates writes about contemporary American life, which she sees as defined by violence. She is particularly concerned with human psychology and the connection between violence and love. Although her novels have been labeled gothic, the violence in them is neither mysterious nor necessarily dramatic; it occurs randomly, as in everyday life. Her characters are ordinary, inarticulate people, who endure and then sublimate the terrible things that happen to them. For example, in the second chapter of *them,* Loretta Wendell awakes to find her lover bleeding and dead beside her, shot by her brother; she calls a policeman who rapes her and disposes of the body; eventually Loretta marries the policeman and, in later years, cares for her brother. Unlike such writers as Barthelme and Vonnegut who have turned to fantasy to express the horror of modern life, Oates writes realistically, often rooting her novels in current events. There is, however, always a strong surrealist element in her works. Her novels include *With Shuddering Fall* (1964); *A Garden of Earthly Delights* (1967), *Expensive People* (1968), and *them* (1969), a trilogy; *Wonderland* (1971); and *Do With Me What You Will* (1973). She has also published volumes of short stories, poems, and literary criticism.

Oates, Titus, 1649–1705, English conspirator. An Anglican priest whose whole career was marked with intrigue and scandal, he joined forces with one Israel Tonge to invent the story of the Popish Plot of 1678. Oates, who had been briefly a convert to Roman Catholicism, claimed that there was a Jesuit-guided plan to assassinate Charles II and to hasten the succession of the Catholic James, duke of York (later James II). The account was completely fabricated, and Oates, examined by the privy council, would perhaps have been immediately exposed had not treasonous letters from Edward Coleman, secretary of the duchess of York, to the French Jesuit, François La Chaise, been discovered as a result of his accusations. The unexplained death of Sir Edmund Berry Godfrey, the judge to whom Tonge and Oates first told their story, was attributed without evidence to the Catholics, and three innocent men were hanged for it. A frenzy of anti-Catholic hatred swept through England, resulting in the judicial murder of a number of Roman Catholic peers and commoners and in the arrest and persecution of many others.

Oates enjoyed temporary eminence and even accused Queen Catherine of plotting to poison the king. In 1685, Oates was convicted of perjury, severely flogged, and imprisoned. Under William III he was released and pensioned. See John Kenyon, *The Popish Plot* (1972).

oath, vocal affirmation of the truth of one's statements, made by appealing to a deity. From the earliest days of human history, calling upon the gods of a community to witness the truth of a statement or the solemnity of a promise has been commonly practiced. The force of the oath depended on the belief that supernatural powers would punish falsehood spoken under oath or the violation of a promise. The oath thus performed wide legal and quasi-legal functions. It was the basis of the medieval process of COMPURGATION. It is still used in legal proceedings today; thus a jury is sworn in, and a witness takes an oath before testifying. In modern times the force of the oath is strengthened by punishment for PERJURY. Some difficulties have arisen in cases of atheists or of persons with religious scruples against oath taking (e.g., Quakers), but statutes have now generally been modified so that a witness may affirm his intention to tell the truth without appealing to a deity; the witness, of course, may still be punished for perjury if he fails to tell the truth. The main classes of oaths are the assertory oath, which concerns past or present facts, and the promissory oath, which refers to future conduct (such as that taken by an alien upon naturalization or by a high government official on assuming office).

oats, cereal plants of the genus *Avena* of the family Gramineae (GRASS family). Most species are annuals of moist temperate regions. The early history of oats is obscure, but domestication is considered to be recent compared to that of the other grains—perhaps c.2500 B.C. During the Bronze Age, the time when horses were first used as draft animals, oats were widely grown in N Europe but were apparently still uncultivated by the civilizations around the Mediterranean. Of the oats now grown commercially, less than 5% is for human consumption, chiefly in the form of rolled oats or oatmeal for breakfast foods; they do not contain the glutenous type of protein necessary for making bread. The chief value of oats remains as a pasturage and hay crop, especially for horses. They have a high nutritive value; a spirited horse is said to "feel his oats." Oats are valuable also in crop rotation and have various industrial uses. Oat hulls are a source of FURFURAL, and oat flour is used as a food preservative in ice cream and other dairy products. Oat straw is preferred by farmers for animal bedding. Diseases such as cereal rusts and smuts (see DISEASES OF PLANTS) cause a heavy annual crop loss, but disease-resistant varieties of oats are being developed. Oats rival corn and wheat as a leading grain crop in the United States (the country of highest production), Canada, N Europe, and the Soviet Union. The common cultivated species (*A. sativa*), native to Eurasia, is no longer found growing wild. Like wheat, it is broadly classified into spring and winter types, depending upon the season of planting. Oats are classified in the division MAGNOLIOPHYTA, class Liliatae, order Cyperales, family Gramineae.

Oaxaca (wähä'kä), state (1970 pop. 2,011,946), 36,375 sq mi (94,211 sq km), S Mexico, on the Pacific Ocean and its arm, the Gulf of Tehuantepec. OAXACA is the capital. The state is almost entirely dominated by the Sierra Madre del Sur; there are deep, tortuous valleys in the south and broad, open, semiarid valleys and plateaus in the north. Except on the west and the north the periphery of the state is tropical. The climate of the interior is generally temperate and healthful. Fertile valleys make agriculture the principal economic activity; sugarcane, coffee (of which Oaxaca is a leading national producer), tobacco, cereals, and tropical and semitropical fruits are grown. Stock raising is also important. Oaxaca's reportedly extensive mineral deposits remain largely unexploited. The state has flour mills and manufactures textiles of cotton, wool, and pita fiber, as well as sarapes, pottery, leather goods, and beverages. Despite the existence of several good highways, inadequate communications remain the chief barrier to the state's industrialization. Oaxaca is the most thoroughly Indian of Mexico's states, with its population predominantly MIXTEC and ZAPOTEC. There are famous archaeological sites at MITLA and MONTE ALBÁN.

Oaxaca, city (1970 pop. 98,000), capital of Oaxaca state, S Mexico. Situated in a valley encircled by low mountains, Oaxaca is a commercial and tourist center with gardens and many fine examples of colonial church architecture. The church and monastery of Santo Domingo is a national monument. Oaxaca is noted for hand-wrought gold and silver filigree, pottery, and sarapes that rank among the finest in Mexico. The chief city of S Mexico, Oaxaca is linked with the federal capital by rail and the Inter-American Highway. The city is subject to severe earthquakes. According to Aztec tradition, Oaxaca was founded as Huasyacac in 1486, during the brief ascendancy of the Aztec over the Mixtec and Zapotec Indians. Prominent in the Mexican revolution against Spain, the city also joined in the War of the Reform and in resistance to the French intervention. Porfirio Díaz and Benito Juárez were born in Oaxaca.

Ob (ôp), river, c.2,300 mi (3,700 km) long, W Siberian USSR. With the Irtysh River, its chief tributary, it is c.3,460 mi (5,600 km) long and is the world's fourth longest river. Formed by the junction of the Biya and Katun rivers (both of which rise in the Altai range) SW of Biysk, the upper Ob flows NW, then NE past Barnaul and Novosibirsk through the W Siberian lowlands to be joined by the Tom River. The middle Ob flows northwest through the swampy forests in the Tomsk and Narym regions and then is joined by the Chulym, Ket, and Irtysh rivers. The lower Ob consists of the Great Ob and the Small Ob and flows N, then E into Ob Bay, an estuary and shallow arm (c.500 mi/800 km long and 35–50 mi/56–80 km wide) of the Arctic Ocean between the Yamal and Gyda peninsulas. The width of the Ob increases downstream to c.25 mi (40 km) near its mouth. The valley of the middle Ob is subject to flooding each spring as the thaw occurs in the upper Ob basin before the ice in the lower course of the Ob has melted. Although frozen from five to six months of the year, the Ob is an important trade and transport route; Novosibirsk, Barnaul, Kamenna-Obi, and Mogochin are the chief ports. There is a large hydroelectric power station at Novosibirsk. The Ob is rich in sturgeon, salmon, and carp. There are major deposits of oil and natural gas in the basin of the middle and lower Ob.

Obadiah (ō"bədī'ə). **1** Prophet, author of the book of OBADIAH. **2** Ahab's major-domo. 1 Kings 18.3–16. **3** Descendant of David. 1 Chron. 3.21. **4** Issacharite. 1 Chron. 7.3. **5** Benjamite. 1 Chron. 8.38. **6** One of David's mighty men. 1 Chron. 12.9. **7** Prince under Jehoshaphat. 2 Chron. 17.7. **8** Repairer of the Temple. 2 Chron. 34.12. **9, 10, 11** Israelites who returned from the Exile. Ezra 8.9; Neh. 10.5; 12.25. **12** Father of ISHMAIAH. **13** Same as ABDA **2.**

Obadiah or **Abdias** (ăbdī'əs), book of the Old Testament, 31st in the order of the Authorized Version, fourth and shortest of the books of the Minor Prophets. The prophet is otherwise unknown and has been dated from the 8th to the 6th cent. B.C. The book has only 21 verses. The prophecy calls down doom on Edom, who had gloated over the misfortune of Israel, and says that Israel will triumph in the judgment. Verses 1–9 are closely paralleled in Jer. 49.7–22, and verse 17 is apparently quoted in Joel 2.32. See J. D. Watts, *Obadiah* (1969).

Obaidallah: see FATIMID.

Obal (ō'băl), son of Joktan. Gen. 10.28. Ebal: 1 Chron. 1.22.

Oban (ō'bən), burgh (1971 pop. 6,910), Argyllshire, W Scotland, on the Firth of Lorne. A port and seaside resort, its circular bay is an excellent yacht basin. The Argyllshire Highland Games are held there each September. Near the ruins of Dunollie Castle, a 12th-century fortress, is a great rock called the Dog Stone, to which the Gaelic hero Fingal is said to have chained his giant dog Bran. In 1975, Oban became part of the Strathclyde region.

obbligato (ŏbləgä'tō) [Ital.,=obligatory], in music, originally a term by which a composer indicated that a certain part was indispensable to the music. Obbligato was thus the direction opposite to ad libitum [Lat.,=at will], which indicated that the part so marked was unessential and might be omitted. Misunderstanding of the term *obbligato*, however, resulted in a reversal of its meaning; when a violin part, for example, is added to a song it is called a violin obbligato, whereas it may be a superfluous ornament for which ad libitum would be a more precise direction.

Obdorsk: see SALEKHARD, USSR.

Obed (ō'bĕd). **1** David's grandfather. Ruth 4.21,22; 1 Chron. 2.12; Mat. 1.5; Luke 3.32. **2** One of David's mighty men. 1 Chron. 11.47. **3** Jerahmeelite. 1 Chron. 2.37,38. **4** Father of AZARIAH **18. 5** Gatekeeper at the Temple. 1 Chron. 26.7.

Obed-edom (ō'bĕd-ē'dŏm), Levite in whose house the Ark of the Covenant was kept. 2 Sam. 6.10; 1 Chron. 13.13; 15.18,21,24; 16.5,38; 26.4,8,15; 2 Chron. 25.24.

Obeid, El: see AL UBAYYID, Sudan.

obelisk (ŏb'əlĭsk), slender four-sided tapering monument, usually hewn of a single great piece of stone, terminating in a pointed or pyramidal top. Among the ancient Egyptians these monoliths were commonly of red granite from Syene and were dedicated to the sun god. They were placed in pairs before the temples, one on either side of the portal. The greatest number erected in any one place was in Heliopolis, but eventually almost every temple entrance was flanked by a pair of them. Down each of the four faces, in most cases, ran a line of deeply incised hieroglyphs and representations, setting forth the names and titles of the Pharaoh. The cap, or pyramidion, was sometimes sheathed with copper or other metal. Obelisks of colossal size were first raised in the XII dynasty. Of those still standing in Egypt, one remains at Heliopolis and two at Al Karnak, one from the time of Thutmose I and one of Queen Hatshepsut which is estimated to be 97.5 ft (29.7 m) high. Many of the historic shafts have been carried from Egypt, notably one of the reign of Ramses II from Luxor, now in the Place de la Concorde, Paris, and CLEOPATRA'S NEEDLES in London and New York. Others are in Rome and Florence. In the United States two familiar structures of obelisk form (though not monoliths) are the Washington and the Bunker Hill monuments.

Oberalp (ō'bər-älp), Alpine pass, 6,733 ft (2,052 m) high, between Grisons and Uri cantons, S central Switzerland. Oberalpsee, a small lake, is nearby, and the Alpine peak Oberalpstock, 10,926 ft (3,330 m) high, is northeast of the pass.

Oberammergau (ō"bəräm'ərgou), town (1970 est. pop. 4,700), Bavaria, S West Germany, in the Bavarian Alps. It has been a noted center of woodcarving since the 12th cent. Oberammergau is famous for the PASSION PLAY performed there every 10 years (last in 1970), originally (1634) in fulfillment of a vow made during a plague in 1633. Tourism is the town's major source of income. There are numerous fresco-decorated houses and a rococo church.

Oberhausen (ō'bərhou"zən), city (1970 pop. 246,736), North Rhine-Westphalia, W West Germany, an industrial center of the RUHR district. It is a port on the Rhine-Herne Canal and a rail junction. Manufactures include iron and steel, machinery, and chemicals. The first German steam engine was built in Sterkrade, now a district of Oberhausen, in 1814. Oberhausen was chartered in 1874.

Oberholtzer, Ellis Paxson (ō'bərhōlt"sər), 1868–1936, American historian, b. Chester co., Pa. He studied abroad at several universities and for a number of years worked on various Philadelphia newspapers. His doctoral thesis, *The Referendum in America* (1893), became widely known. He edited the *Manufacturer* (1896–1900) and the "American Crisis Biographies," and from 1915 to 1921 he was secretary of the Pennsylvania State Board of Motion Picture Censors. Besides such books on Philadelphia history as *The Literary History of Philadelphia* (1906) and *Philadelphia: A History of the City and Its People* (4 vol., 1912), his works include biographies of Robert Morris (1902) and Jay Cooke (1907) and a history of the United States (5 vol., 1917–37).

Oberland, Bernese: see BERN, Switzerland.

Oberlin, Jean Frédéric (zhäN frādārĕk' ôbĕrlăN'), 1740–1826, Alsatian Lutheran clergyman. He was appointed in 1767 to a pastorate in Ban-de-la-Roche, Bas-Rhin dept., France. Oberlin improved the district by introducing cotton manufacture, new agricultural methods, and good roads and by founding a savings bank, a model orphanage, and five schools. Oberlin College, Ohio, was named for him. See biography by Marshall Dawson (1934).

Oberlin College, at Oberlin, Ohio; coeducational; opened 1833 as Oberlin Collegiate Institute, became Oberlin College in 1850. It includes a college of arts and sciences and a well-known conservatory of music. One of the first colleges to have coeducational classes, Oberlin College was also a center of abolitionism. The early faculty was made up largely of New England Congregationalists, and Oberlin Theology is a modified form of Calvinism emphasizing the doctrine of free will (see FINNEY, CHARLES GRANDISON).

Oberon (ō'bərŏn"), in astronomy, one of the five known moons, or natural satellites, of URANUS.

obesity, condition resulting from excessive storage of fat in the body. Obesity is considered a serious health hazard. It predisposes the individual to many disorders, such as diabetes and heart disease, it shortens the life span, and it complicates childbirth and surgery. Occasionally there may be a physiological cause for obesity such as a glandular malfunction (in the pituitary, thyroid, or adrenal cortex) or a disorder of the hypothalamus (the area at the base of the brain). However, in the vast majority of cases, the cause is overeating. More calories are taken in than are required for energy, and the excess food is stored in the body as fat. There are several causes of overeating. Excessive eating established by the family and cultural environment during childhood may become a lifelong habit. Most often, the cause is related in some degree to psychological distress. For example, the obese person may be nervous or unhappy and may substitute food for some other gratification that is missed in life. Insufficient exercise can be a contributing factor; the less active the person, the fewer calories needed to maintain normal body weight. If obesity does not have a physiological cause, the only way to correct it is to reduce the amount of food taken in. A weight of more than 10% above what is normal for the individual (according to standard age, height, and weight tables) is considered to indicate a state of obesity. The professional help of a physician is often necessary to determine the extent of the obesity and to prescribe an appropriate diet. However, since the reasons for overeating are commonly related to psychological problems, it is difficult to establish proper eating habits permanently if the underlying emotional problem is left unchanged.

Obil (ō'bĭl), keeper of David's camels. He was an Ishmaelite. 1 Chron. 27.30.

oblast (ŏ'blăst, ŏ'-, Rus. ô'bləstyə) [Rus.,=region], administrative and territorial division in the USSR. Oblasts in which the majority of the population is of a nationality different from that of the constituent republic in which they are included generally enjoy autonomous status. The boundaries of oblasts are usually based on economic and administrative considerations; as a result, oblasts vary considerably in size and population.

obliquity of the ecliptic: see INCLINATION.

oboe (ō'bō, ō'boi) [Ital., from Fr. *hautbois*] or **hautboy** (ō'boi, hō'-), woodwind instrument of conical bore, its mouthpiece having a double reed. The instruments possessing these general characteristics may be referred to as the oboe family, which includes the ENGLISH HORN, the BASSOON, and the CONTRABASSOON or double bassoon. The oboe was developed in the mid-17th cent. in France from various older double-reed instruments, which the oboe, with its greater expressive and dynamic range, largely displaced by the 18th cent. It was soon used in the orchestra, possibly as early as 1657, and was

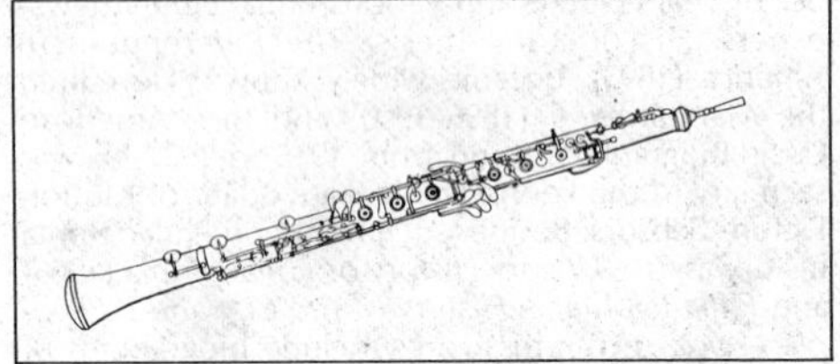

Oboe

the principal orchestral woodwind throughout most of the 18th cent., the flute and clarinet gaining an equal footing only late in the century. It was also a favorite solo instrument, and it has an extensive solo and chamber-music literature from the baroque and early classical periods. In the 19th cent., although retaining its importance in the orchestra, it was rarely employed for solo purposes. In the 20th cent. its solo use has increased. It was gradually improved mechanically, notably in the 19th cent., and the Conservatory model, developed in France, is most used now. The *oboe d'amore,* pitched a third lower than the oboe, was much used in the baroque era, especially by J. S. Bach. It fell into disuse thereafter, but has been revived in the 20th cent. Its tone is less brilliant than that of the oboe. The *oboe da caccia* is an early version of the English horn, pitched a fifth lower than the oboe and therefore a transposing instrument. Oboes of this size were known by 1665, and Purcell scored for one in his *Dioclesian* (1691). A curved form, often with the present instrument's characteristic bulbous bell, appeared in the 18th cent. and was employed occasionally by Bach, Haydn, and Mozart. See also SHAWM.

Obote, Apollo Milton (ōbō'tā), 1925–, president of Uganda (1966–71). Milton Obote was a trade union organizer in Kenya before returning to Uganda, where he became (1957) a member of the legislative council and founded (1960) the Uganda People's Congress. Prime minister from 1962 to 1966, he led a revolution and installed himself as president in 1966. Obote was overthrown by Idi AMIN in 1971 and fled to Tanzania, where he tried to organize anti-Amin forces.

Oboth (ō'bŏth), unidentified desert encampment, S of the Dead Sea. Num. 21.10; 33.43,44.

Obrecht, Jacob (yä'kōp ō'brĕkht), c.1450–1505, Flemish composer. Obrecht was ordained as a priest in 1480. He wrote an early four-part setting of the St. Matthew Passion. His sacred music combined the polyphony of Johannes Ockeghem with folk elements. Obrecht was a victim of the plague.

Obregón, Álvaro (äl'värō ōbrāgōn'), 1880–1928, Mexican general and president (1920–24). A planter in Sonora, he supported Francisco I. MADERO in the revolution against Porfirio Díaz. In 1913, Obregón joined Venustiano CARRANZA in the overthrow of Victoriano Huerta and later was commander against the opponents of Carranza, especially Francisco VILLA. One of the most enlightened generals in the revolution, he was for a time Carranza's minister of war. When the latter attempted to perpetuate himself in power, Obregón promptly led a successful revolt (1920). After the provisional administration of Adolfo de la HUERTA, Obregón became president. The revolutionary program became official during his administration and advanced out of confusion and blood into a recognizable if not thoroughgoing system of agrarian and labor reforms; peonage was still rampant. The most significant achievement of the Obregón regime was the educational program advanced by José VASCONCELOS. The United States delay (until 1923) in recognizing his regime was due mainly to proclamations by certain self-styled radicals urging, among other things, the nationalization of oil deposits. Obregón was involved in a long, bitter quarrel with the church. His government was gravely challenged when de la Huerta was persuaded by opponents of Plutarco Elías CALLES, Obregón's presidential candidate, to lead a revolt (1923–24). In 1928, Obregón was again chosen president, but before taking office he was assassinated by a fanatical Roman Catholic. He wrote *Ocho mil kilómetros en campaña* (1917), recollections of his campaigns.

Obrenović or **Obrenovich** (both: ōbrĕ'nəvĭch), Serbian dynasty. Its founder, Miloš Obrenović (see MILOŠ), was the first modern Serbian ruler. The murder (1817) of Karageorge (Karadjordje), probably at Miloš's instigation, started the long feud between the Obrenović and the Karadjordjević families. Miloš's son MICHAEL, prince of Serbia, was assassinated in 1868. His successor, Prince MILAN, was proclaimed king of Serbia in 1882. Milan's son ALEXANDER, king of Serbia, the last ruling Obrenović, was assassinated in 1903; on his death the Karadjordjević dynasty again came into power.

Obrenovich: see OBRENOVIĆ.

O'Brien, Conor Cruise, 1917–, Irish author and diplomat. Educated at Trinity College, Dublin, he entered the department of external affairs of Ireland in 1944 and served as a counselor in Paris (1955–56) and as a member of the Irish delegation to the United Nations (1956–60). He left the diplomatic service after representing (1961) the UN secretary general in Katanga (now Shaba) and was vice chancellor of the Univ. of Ghana (1962–65) and a professor at New York Univ. (1965–69). Since 1969 he has been a Labour member of the Irish parliament, the Dáil. He became minister of posts and telegraphs in 1973. Among his works are *Parnell and His Party, 1880–1890* (1957, repr. 1964), *To Katanga and Back* (1962, repr. 1966), *Writers and Politics* (1965), *Power and Consciousness* (1969), and *States of Ireland* (1972).

O'Brien, Lawrence Francis, 1917–, U.S. Postmaster General (1965–68), b. Springfield, Mass. Active in public relations and real estate in Springfield, he began organizing political campaigns for John F. Kennedy in the early 1950s. The national director of organization for the Kennedy-Johnson presidential campaign in 1960, he served both President Kennedy and President Lyndon B. Johnson as Special Assistant for Congressional Relations. In 1965 he became Postmaster General. He resigned in April, 1968. Later that year, he became Democratic national chairman. After the unsuccessful 1968 Democratic presidential campaign, he gave up the post, but he became chairman again in 1970. Replaced during the 1972 campaign, he helped run George McGovern's unsuccessful bid for the presidency. See his *No Final Victories: a Life in Politics* (1974).

O'Brien, William, 1852–1928, Irish journalist and political leader. He became (1881) editor of a newspaper, *United Ireland,* which championed the Irish agrarian cause (see IRISH LAND QUESTION). Imprisoned in the same year, he wrote, at the behest of Charles PARNELL, the famous *No Rent Manifesto.* He sat in the British Parliament (1883–95, 1900–1918), initiated the United Irish League (1898), which helped to reunite the pro- and anti-Parnell factions of the nationalist movement, and helped shape the Wyndham Land Act of 1903. Later he founded the All-for-Ireland League, advocating a more conciliatory policy toward Britain. He wrote *Recollections* (1905), *Evening Memories* (1920), and *The Irish Revolution* (1923); his letters were edited by his wife, S. F. O'Brien, as *Golden Memories* (2 vol., 1929). See biography by Michael MacDonaugh (1928).

O'Brien, William Smith, 1803–64, Irish revolutionary. He entered Parliament from Ireland in 1828 and worked for Catholic Emancipation, Irish poor relief, and state support of the Irish Catholic clergy. O'Brien's political opinions moved steadily to the left. At first he opposed the agitation of Daniel O'CONNELL to repeal the parliamentary union of Great Britain and Ireland, believing that the British Parliament would grant some relief to Ireland, but in 1843 he joined the Repeal Association and rapidly became O'Connell's second in the Irish nationalist struggle. O'Brien's group, called Young Ireland, became convinced that only direct action would free Ireland, and in 1846, with John MITCHEL, Thomas Francis MEAGHER, and Charles Gavan DUFFY, O'Brien seceded from O'Connell's association to form the Irish Confederation. The aggravation of the famine and Mitchel's arrest and conviction in 1848 determined them to rise against the government. The revolt was abortive, and the only engagement was an attempt to attack a police detachment in Co. Tipperary. O'Brien was arrested and sentenced to death for treason, but the sentence was commuted to transportation to Tasmania. He received a full pardon in 1856. Afterward he returned to Ireland and traveled on the Continent and in America, but he was no longer politically active. See Denis Gwynn, *Young Ireland and 1848* (1949).

obscenity, in law, anything that tends to corrupt public morals by its indecency. The words *obscenity* and *obscene* are not, however, technical legal terms and are not susceptible of exact definition, since the moral concepts that the terms connote vary from time to time and also from place to place. The meaning may also vary according to the context in which it is used, although usually it relates to sexual impurity. In the 1950s the U.S. Supreme Court began to relax rules prohibiting the possession, sale, and distribution of obscene material, often called pornography, but in 1973 that trend was reversed. The court ruled that material that appealed to prurient interest in sex and that did not have serious literary, artistic, political, or scientific value could be banned as obscene. It ruled that a national definition of obscenity was not necessary and, therefore, that communities could develop local standards within the court's guidelines. The decision on whether material falls within a definition of obscene is usually made by a jury. See H. M. Clor, *Obscenity and Public Morality* (1969).

observatory, scientific facility especially equipped to detect and record naturally occurring scientific phenomena. Although geological and meteorological observatories exist, the term is generally applied to astronomical observatories. Early civilizations, such as those of Babylonia, China, and Egypt, recognized the regular and periodic nature of heavenly motions and established primitive observatories to maintain astronomical records. The main purposes of these early observatories were to regulate the calendar and predict the changes of season. Because it was believed that unusual occurrences, such as comets and eclipses, foretold future events on earth, the early observatories also served a religious function, and most of the ancient astronomers were priests. Later observatories were established to compile accurate star charts and an annual ephemeris that would be of use to navigators in determining longitude at sea. The instruments in use before the invention of the telescope include the SEXTANT, quadrant, ASTROLABE, and armillary sphere. These are all calibrated sighting devices for determining the angular positions of stars and planets. The armillary sphere was the most sophisticated of these instruments. It was composed of a number of rings corresponding to great circles on the celestial sphere and was used to determine both the right ascension and the declination of a star. The last great observatory of the pretelescopic era was built by Tycho Brahe at Uranienborg, on the island of Ven, Denmark. The invention of the TELESCOPE in the early 17th cent. revolutionized observational astronomy in two ways. First, the positions and motions of celestial bodies could be measured much more accurately with telescopes than with the earlier instruments. Such data provided a source of precise time signals. Second, the telescope could be used to analyze the physical nature of celestial bodies themselves. Until the 19th cent., telescopic images were inspected visually by highly trained observers who made drawings of what they saw. The development of dry-plate photography, which permitted long exposure times, however, offered a much more sensitive method of recording images. Perhaps the most valuable use of the telescope is in connection with the spectroscopic study of starlight. The total light from a star is separated into its various wavelengths (see SPECTRUM), and the intensity of each is measured. The temperature and chemical composition of stars can be obtained by this method, as well as information about stellar motion and magnetic fields. In addition to spectrographs and photometers, an observatory is often equipped with comparator microscopes and densitometers for measuring the spectra recorded on photographic plates. Observatories specializing in solar astronomy usually have coronographs and spectroheliographs. Atmospheric limitations on telescopic observations include weather conditions, air turbulence, air glow, and any source of extraneous illumination. To minimize such conditions optical observatories are generally located at high altitudes in sparsely populated areas. A recent development is the extension of astronomical observations to wavelengths outside the visible spectrum. Most important has been the development of RADIO ASTRONOMY, the study of radio waves emitted by celestial bodies. The ideal location for an observatory is beyond the earth's atmosphere. Several artificial SATELLITES have been equipped with telescopes for infrared, visible, ultraviolet, and X-ray observations. Skylab was a manned orbiting space observatory (see SPACE EXPLORATION). The world's oldest major observatory is the ROYAL GREENWICH OBSERVATORY, now located at Herstmonceux, England. Important modern observatories in the United States include the HALE OBSERVATORIES, on Mt. Wilson and Palomar Mt., Calif.; KITT PEAK NATIONAL OBSERVATORY, in Arizona; LICK OBSERVATORY, in California; LOWELL OBSERVATORY, in Arizona; MCDONALD OBSERVATORY, in Texas; MAUNA KEA OBSERVATORY, in Hawaii; MOUNT HOPKINS OBSERVATORY, in Arizona; UNITED STATES NAVAL OBSERVATORY, in Washington, D.C.; and YERKES OBSERVATORY, in Wisconsin. Foreign observatories include the Crimean Astrophysical Observatory, in the USSR; CERRO TOLOLO INTER-AMERICAN OBSERVATORY and the EUROPEAN SOUTHERN OBSERVATORY, both in Chile; PULKOVO, in the USSR; and MOUNT STROMLO OBSERVATORY and SIDING SPRING OBSERVATORY, both in Australia. Important radio observatories include ARECIBO IONOSPHERIC OBSERVATORY, in Puerto Rico; JODRELL BANK EXPERIMENTAL STATION, in England; and the NATIONAL RADIO ASTRONOMY OBSERVATORY, in Green Bank, W.Va.

obsidian (ŏbsĭd'ēən), a volcanic GLASS, homogeneous in texture and having a low water content, with a vitreous luster and a conchoidal fracture. The color is commonly black, but may be some shade of red or brown, and cut sections sometimes appear to be green. Like other volcanic glasses, obsidian is a LAVA that has cooled too quickly for the contained minerals to crystallize. In chemical composition it is rich in silica and similar to granite. It is favored by primitive peoples for knives, arrowheads, spearheads, and other weapons and tools.

obstetrics (ŏbstĕ'trĭks), branch of medicine specializing in treatment of women during PREGNANCY and childbirth (see BIRTH). The care of women during childbirth was originally in the hands of women (see MIDWIFERY), but in the 16th cent. physicians grew interested in the field. Progress in the medical and surgical sciences in general was reflected in increasing improvements in obstetrical skills. Of special importance were the invention of the delivery forceps by Peter Chamberlen in the 17th cent. and the introduction of anesthesia in the 19th cent. The adoption of antiseptic methods according to the theories of Joseph Lister and Ignaz Semmelweis reduced the incidence of infection in childbirth and made possible successful cesarean section when surgical removal of the infant from the uterus became necessary. Modern obstetrical care includes treatment of the diseases and abnormalities of pregnancy and care of the mother for a period of time after delivery (postnatal period). Obstetrics is often combined with GYNECOLOGY as a medical specialty.

Obuasi (ōbwä'sē), town (1970 pop. 22,818), S central Ghana. Highly concentrated gold ore is mined, and there are gold-extraction plants. Gold was mined in Obuasi by black Africans as early as the 17th cent. From the late 1890s it was developed by Europeans into a modern mining town.

Obwalden: see UNTERWALDEN, Switzerland.

Ocala (ōkăl'ə), city (1970 pop. 22,583), seat of Marion co., N central Fla.; inc. 1868. It is a trade, processing, and transportation hub for a major citrus region also known for its thoroughbred horses, cattle, lumber, phosphatic limestone, and fuller's earth. Manufactures include wood products, clothing, concrete goods, and fabricated metalware. Ocala is also a resort city; fish and game abound in the many nearby lakes and streams and in Ocala National Forest. The site was selected (1846) for the county seat and named for the Indian village Ocali (visited by De Soto in 1539), which had been nearby. Tourist attractions include Six Gun Territory, a replica of a frontier town; and Silver Springs, adjacent to the city. A junior college is in Ocala.

ocarina (ŏkərē'nə), musical wind instrument with eight finger holes, rather egg-shaped, and made of metal or terra-cotta. It was invented in the late 19th cent. in Italy and is popular with amateurs for its relative simplicity and low cost. It is occasionally called a "sweet potato" because of its shape.

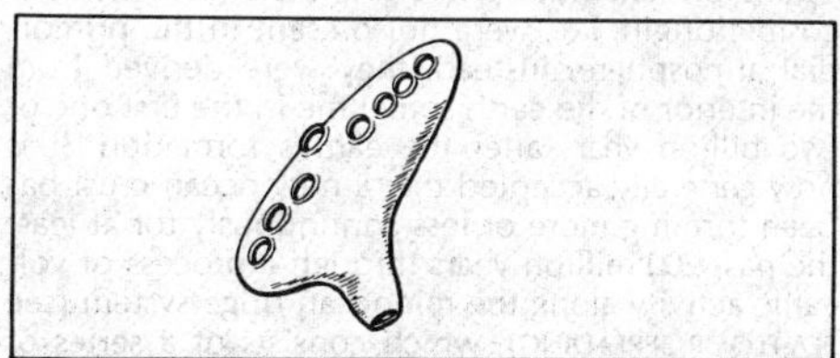

Ocarina

O'Casey, Sean (shôn), 1884–1964, Irish dramatist, one of the great figures of the Irish literary renaissance. A Protestant, he grew up in the slum district of Dublin and was active in various socialist movements and in the rebellions for Irish independence. His first plays, *The Shadow of a Gunman* (1923), *Juno and the Paycock* (1924), and *The Plough and the Stars* (1926), were performed by the Abbey Players with great success. These grim, satiric, and often violent tragicomedies are usually considered O'Casey's most brilliant works. They all treat aspects of the Irish movement for independence, and they are not always kind to the Irish people. *The Plough and the Stars* touched off a riot in the theater, and after this event O'Casey left Ireland for England, never to return. His later plays, more experimental and expressionistic, include *The Silver Tassie* (rejected by the Abbey Theatre in 1928, but successfully produced in London and New York in 1929), *Within the Gates* (1934), *Purple Dust* (1940), *Red Roses for Me* (1942), and *The Bishop's Bonfire* (1955). All of O'Casey's plays exhibit a mastery of language and an unsentimental sympathy for the poor. His six autobiographical volumes—*I Knock at the Door* (1939), *Pictures in the Hallway* (1942), *Drums under the Windows* (1945), *Inishfallen, Fare Thee Well* (1949), *Rose and Crown* (1952), and *Sunset and Evening Star* (1954)—were collectively published as *Mirror in My House* (2 vol., 1956). He also wrote a book of drama criticism, *The Green Crow* (1956). His collected plays appeared in four volumes in 1949–51. See biographies by M. B. Marguiles (1970) and by his wife, Eileen O'Casey (1972); studies by Robert Hogan (1960) and David Krause (1960).

Occam, William of: see WILLIAM OF OCCAM.

occasionalism, metaphysical doctrine that denies that finite things have any active power and asserts that God is the only cause, whereas physical events and mental states are only occasions for God's action. It was formulated in the 17th cent. by Arnold Geulincx and developed by Nicolas Malebranche. The theory was intended to resolve the problem of interaction in general, and of that between mind (immaterial) and body (material) in particular, which was posed by the dualism of René Descartes.

Occidental College, at Los Angeles, Calif.; United Presbyterian; coeducational; chartered 1887. The school maintains a cooperative engineering program with Columbia and the California Institute of Technology.

Occleve, Thomas: see HOCCLEVE, THOMAS.

Occom or **Occum, Samson** (both: ŏk'əm), 1723–92, American Indian clergyman, b. near Norwich, Conn. He became one of the first pupils of Eleazer WHEELOCK, and in 1749 he went to Long Island, N.Y., to serve the Montauk Indians as pastor and schoolmaster. Occom was ordained in 1759, and later he went (1766) to England to help raise the funds used to establish Dartmouth College.

occultation (ŏk"əltā'shən), in astronomy, eclipse of one celestial body by another, e.g., when the moon lies between a star and the earth. Occultations of stars by the moon have great importance in astronomy. Since stellar positions are very accurately known, the time and position of an occultation can be used to determine the position of the moon. Alternatively, an observer can determine his LONGITUDE by comparing the time at which he observes an occultation with a table listing the GREENWICH MEAN TIME at which the occultation occurs.

occultism (əkŭl'tĭzəm), belief in supernatural sciences or powers, such as magic, astrology, alchemy, theosophy, and spiritism, either for the purpose of enlarging man's powers, of protecting him from evil forces, or of predicting the future. All the so-called natural sciences were in a sense occult in their beginnings; most early scientists were considered magicians or sorcerers because of the mystery attending their investigations. In the modern world occultism has centered in small groups that seek to perpetuate secret knowledge and rites alleged to be derived from the ancients.

occupational disease, illness incurred because of the conditions or environment of employment. Unlike accidents, some time usually elapses between exposure to the cause and development of symptoms. In some instances, symptoms of disease may not become evident for 20 years or more. Among environmental causes are subjection to extremes of temperature (leading to heatstroke or frostbite), unusual dampness (causing diseases of the respiratory tract, skin, or muscles and joints) or changes in atmospheric pressure (causing DECOMPRESSION SICKNESS, or the bends) and exposure to infrared or ultraviolet rays or those emanating from radium and other radioactive substances. The modern widespread use of X ray, radium, and materials involved in the production of nuclear power has led to an especial awareness of the dangers of RADIATION SICKNESS. Careful checking of equipment and the proper protection of all personnel working with such equipment is mandatory. In addition there are hundreds of industries in which metal dusts, chemical substances, and unusual exposure to infective substances constitute occupational hazards. The most common of the dust-inspired disorders are the lung diseases caused by silica, asbestos, beryllium, bauxite, and iron ore (see PNEUMOCONIOSIS) to which miners, granite workers, and many others are exposed. Fumes, smoke, and toxic liquids from a great number of chemicals are other occupational dangers. Carbon monoxide, carbon tetrachloride, chlorine, creosote, cyanides, dinitrobenzene, mercury, lead, phosphorus, and nitrous chloride are but a few of the substances that on entering through the skin, respiratory tract, or digestive tract cause serious and often fatal illness. Occupational hazards result also from infective sources. Persons who come into contact with infected animals in a living or deceased state are in danger of acquiring such diseases as ANTHRAX and TULAREMIA. Doctors, nurses, and other hospital personnel are prime targets for the tuberculosis bacillus and for many other infectious organisms. Recognition of the effects of working under deleterious conditions and with harmful substances has resulted in protection of workers in many fields. Legislation to prevent or limit the occurrence of occupational disease dates from the Factory Act in England in 1802. Many occupational abuses have been redressed by legislation in the United States, and workmen's compensation takes care, by a system of insurance, of those who incur occupational diseases. See Paul Brodeur, *Expendable Americans* (1974), and Rachel Scott, *Muscle and Blood* (1974).

ocean, interconnected mass of water covering 70.78% of the surface of the earth, often called the world ocean. It is subdivided into four major units that are separated from each other by the continental masses. The Antarctic Ocean is sometimes considered a separate ocean, extending from the shores of Antarctica northward to c.40°S lat. The Atlantic, Indian, and Pacific oceans extend northward from Antarctica as huge "gulfs" separating the continents. The Arctic Ocean, nearly landlocked by Eurasia and North America and nearly circular in outline, caps the north polar region. The major oceans are further subdivided into smaller regions loosely called seas, gulfs, or bays. Some of these seas, such as the Sargasso Sea of the North Atlantic Ocean, are only vaguely defined, while others, such as the Mediterranean Sea or the Black Sea, are almost totally surrounded by land areas. Large and totally landlocked saltwater bodies, such as the Caspian Sea and Salton Sea, are actually salt lakes. Whenever possible, the boundaries between oceans are designated by the continental land masses bordering them or by ridges in the ocean floor, which also serve as geographic boundaries. Where these features are absent (such as the ill-defined northern boundary of the Antarctic Ocean), the boundary is somewhat arbitrarily fixed by fluctuating zones of opposing currents that act as partial barriers to the mixing of waters between the two adjacent oceans. The oceans are not uniformly distributed on the face of the earth. Continents and ocean basins tend to be antipodal with respect to one another, i.e., continents are found on the opposite side of the earth from ocean basins. For example, Antarctica is antipodal to the Arctic Ocean; Europe is opposed by the South Pacific Ocean. Furthermore, over two thirds of the earth's land area is found in the Northern Hemisphere, while the oceans comprise over 80% of the Southern Hemisphere. The world ocean has an area of about 361 million sq km (139,400,000 sq mi), an average depth of about 3,730 m (12,230 ft), and a total volume of about 1,347,000,000 cu km (322,280,000 cu mi). Each cubic mile of sea water weighs approximately 4.7 billion tons and holds 166 million tons of dissolved solids. The average temperature of the oceans is 3.9°C (39°F). The oceans hold the answers to many important questions about the development of the earth and the history of life on earth. For instance, within the rocks and sediment of the ocean floors the geological history of the earth is recorded. Fossils in this sediment record a portion of the biological history of the earth at least back to the Jurassic period, which ended about 140,000,000 years ago. The first appearance of life on the earth is thought to have occurred in the oceans 2 or 3 billion years ago. Throughout his history man has been directly or indirectly influenced by the oceans. They serve as a source of food and valuable minerals and provide a place for both recreation and waste disposal. Increasingly, man is turning to the oceans for his food supply either by direct consumption or indirectly by harvesting fish that is then processed for livestock feed. It has been estimated that as much as 10% of man's protein intake comes from the oceans. Nevertheless, the food-producing potential of the oceans is only partly realized. Other biological products of the oceans are also commercially used. For example, pearls taken from oysters are used in jewelry, and shells are widely used as a source of building material. Ocean water is processed to extract commercially valuable minerals such as salt, bromine, and magnesium. Although nearly 60 valuable chemical elements have been found dissolved in ocean water, most are in such dilute concentrations that commercial extraction is not yet profitable. In a few arid regions of the world, such as Ascension Island, Kuwait, and Israel, ocean water is desalinated to produce fresh water. The shallow continental shelves have been exploited as a source of sands and gravels. In addition, extensive deposits of petroleum-bearing sands have been exploited in offshore areas, particularly along the Gulf and California coasts of the United States and in the Persian Gulf. Manganese nodules on the deep ocean floor are formed by the precipitation of manganese oxides and other metallic salts around a nucleus of rock or shell. These nodules represent a potentially rich and extensive resource and considerable research is currently being conducted to explore nodule mining and metallic extraction techniques. Ocean water may prove to be a limitless source of energy in the event that nuclear fusion reactors are developed, since the oceans contain great quantities of deuterium. The oceans are becoming more important for recreational use, as each year more people are attracted to the sports of swimming, fishing, scuba diving, boating, and waterskiing. The oceans are also becoming more polluted because those who use them for recreational and commercial purposes are disposing of more and more wastes there (see WATER POLLUTION). The atmosphere affects the oceans and is in turn influenced by them. The action of winds blowing over the ocean surface creates waves and the great current systems of the oceans. When winds are strong enough to produce spray and whitecaps, tiny droplets of ocean water are thrown up into the atmosphere where some evaporate, leaving microscopic grains of salt buoyed by the turbulence of the air. These tiny particles may become nuclei for the condensation of water vapor to form fogs and clouds. In turn, the oceans act upon the atmosphere—in ways not clearly understood—to influence and modify the world's climate and weather systems. When water evaporates, heat is removed from the oceans and stored in the atmosphere by the molecules of water vapor. When condensation occurs, this stored heat is released to the atmosphere to develop the mechanical energy of its motion. The atmosphere obtains nearly half of its energy for circulation from the condensation of evaporated ocean water. Because the oceans have an extremely high thermal capacity when compared to the atmosphere, the ocean temperatures fluctuate seasonally much less than the atmospheric temperature. For the same reason, when air blows over the water, its temperature tends to come to the temperature of the water rather than vice versa. Thus maritime climates are generally less variable than regions in the interiors of the continents. The relationships are not simple. The pattern of atmospheric circulation largely determines the pattern of oceanic surface circulation, which in turn determines the location and amount of heat that is released to the atmosphere. Also, the pattern of atmospheric circulation determines in part the location of clouds, which influences the locations of heating of the ocean surface. It now appears that the waters making up the present oceans and the gases that make up the present atmosphere of the earth were not of cosmic origin, i.e., were not present in the primordial atmosphere. Instead, they were derived from the interior of the earth sometime in the first one or two billion years after the earth's formation. It is now generally accepted that a new ocean crust has been forming more or less continuously for at least the past 200 million years through a process of volcanic activity along the midocean ridge system (see SEA-FLOOR SPREADING), which consists of a series of underwater mountains. On the basis of present knowledge it seems highly probable that all ocean waters and atmospheric gases were gradually released by the separation of these volatile components from the silicate rocks of the crust and upper mantle through volcanic activity. (Molten lava is known to contain appreciable amounts of water and other volatiles that are released upon solidification.) With the passage of time, water released by volcanic activity gradually filled oceanic depressions. Virtually all continents are surrounded by a gently sloping submerged plain called the continental shelf, which is an underwater extension of the coastal plain. Changes in sea level have alternatingly exposed and inundated portions of the continental shelf. Continental shelves vary in width from almost zero up to the 1,500-km-wide (930-mi) Siberian shelf in the Arctic Ocean. They average 78 km (48 mi) in width. The edge of the shelf occurs at a depth that ranges from 20 to 550 m (66 to 1,800 ft), averaging 130 m (430 ft). The shelves consist of vast deposits of sands, muds, and gravels, overlying crystalline rocks or vast thicknesses of consolidated sedimentary rocks. Although there is a great variation in shelf features, nonglaciated shelves are usually exceptionally flat, with seaward slopes averaging on the order of 205 m per km (10 ft per mi), or less than 1° of slope. The edge of the shelf, called the shelf break, is marked by an abrupt increase in slope to an average of about 4°. The continental shelves are the regions of the oceans best known and most exploited by commercial venture. It is this region where virtually all of the petroleum, commercial sand and gravel deposits, and fishery resources are found. It is also the locus of waste dumping. The continental slopes begin at the shelf break and plunge downward to the great depths of the ocean basin proper. Deep submarine canyons, some comparable in size to the Grand Canyon of the Colorado River, are sometimes found cutting across the shelf and slope, often extending from the mouths of terrestrial rivers. The Congo, Amazon, Ganges, and Hudson rivers all have submarine canyon extensions. It is assumed that submarine canyons on the continental shelf were initially carved during periods of lower sea level in the course of the ice ages. Their continental slope extensions were carved and more recently modified by turbidity currents—subsea "landslides" of a dense slurry of water and sediment. Many continental slopes end in gently sloping, smooth-surfaced features called continental rises. The continental rises usually have an inclination of less than ½°. They have been found to consist of thick deposits of sediment, presumably deposited as a result of slumping and turbidity currents carrying sediment off the shelf and slope. The continental shelf, slope, and rise together are called the continental margin. The deep ocean floor begins at the seaward edge of the continental rise or marginal trench, if one is present, and extends seaward to the base of the underwater midocean mountains. Many relief features of great importance are present in this region. Vast abyssal plains cover significant portions of the deep ocean basin. Such plains are occasionally broken by low, oval-shaped abyssal hills. The abyssal plains cover about 30% of the Atlantic and nearly 75% of the Pacific ocean floors. They are among the flattest portions of the earth's crust and appear to be formed by the deposition of fine sediment carried by turbidity currents that have covered and smoothed out irregularities in the ocean floor. One of the most significant features of the ocean basins is the midocean ridge. First discovered in the Atlantic Ocean on the CHALLENGER EXPEDITION, its relief features were further investigated during the German *Meteor* expedition of 1925–26. By the early 1960s it had been confirmed that the Mid-Atlantic Ridge was only part of a continuous feature that extended 55,000 km (34,000 mi) through the Atlantic, Indian, South Pacific, and Arctic oceans. The ridge is a broad bulge in the ocean floor that rises 1 to 3 km (0.6–2 mi) above the adjacent abyssal plains. It has a variable width averaging more than 1,500 km (c.900 mi). It is crossed by a number of fracture zones (transform FAULTS) and displays a deep rift 37 to 48 km (23–30 mi) wide and about 1.6 km (1 mi) deep at its very crest. One of the most surprising findings of the early oceanographers was that the deepest parts of the oceans were not in the centers, as they had expected, but were in fact quite close to the margins of continents, particularly in the Pacific Ocean. Further exploration showed that these deeps were located in long V-shaped trenches bordering the seaward edge of volcanic island arcs. These trenches are one of the most striking features of the Pacific floor. Trenches virtually encircle the rim of the Pacific basin. The trenches have lengths of thousands of kilometers, are generally hundreds of kilometers wide, and extend 3 to 4 km (1.9–2.5 mi) deeper than the surrounding ocean floor. The greatest ocean depth has been sounded in the Challenger Deep of the Marianas Trench, a distance of 11,033 m (36,198 ft) below sea level. One of the most unique and intriguing aspects of ocean water is its salinity, or dissolved salt content. The measurement of salinity is essentially the determination of the amount of dissolved salts in 1 kg of ocean water and is expressed in parts per thousand (0/00). Ocean salinities commonly range between 33 0/00 to 38 0/00, with an average of about 35 0/00. Thirty-five parts per thousand salinity is equivalent to 3.5% by weight. Six elements constitute over 90% of the total salts dissolved in the oceans (chlorine, sodium, magnesium, sulfur, calcium, and potassium). Pressure in the ocean waters increases with increasing depth due to the weight of the overlying water. The pressure increases at the rate of 1 atmosphere for every 10 m (33 ft) of depth (1 atm = 15 lb per sq in. or 1,016 dynes per sq cm). The surface circulation of the oceans is intimately tied to the prevailing wind circulation of the atmosphere (see WIND). As the planetary winds flow across the water, frictional stresses are set up which push huge rivers of water in their path. The general pattern of these surface currents is a nearly closed system of currents, called gyres, which are approximately centered on the HORSE LATITUDES (about 30° latitude in both hemispheres). Major circulation of water in these gyres is clockwise in the Northern Hemisphere and counterclockwise in the Southern Hemisphere. In the North Pacific and North Atlantic oceans, smaller counterclockwise gyres are developed partly due to the presence of the continents. These are centered on about 50°N lat. The most dominant current in the Southern Ocean is the West Wind Drift, which circles Antarctica in an easterly direction. The northern and southern hemispheric gyres are divided by an eastward flowing equatorial countercurrent, which essentially follows the belt of the doldrums. This countercurrent is caused by the return flow of water piled up along the eastward portion of the equatorial seas, and its return flow is uninhibited by the weak and erratic winds of the doldrums. Analysis of current records shows that a number of major currents, such as the Gulf Stream, have strong fast-moving currents beneath them trending in the opposite direction to the surface current. Such undercurrents, or countercurrents, appear to be as important and pervasive as the surface currents. In 1952 the Cromwell current was found flowing eastward beneath the south equatorial current of the Pacific. In 1961 a similar current was discovered in the Atlantic. Thermohaline circulation refers to the deep-water circulation of the oceans and is primarily caused by differences in density between the waters of different regions. It is mainly a convection process where cold, dense water formed in the polar regions sinks and flows slowly toward the equator. Most of the deep water acquires its characteristics in the Antarctic region and in the Norwegian Sea. Antarctic bottom water is the densest and coldest water in the ocean depths. It forms and sinks just off the continental slope of Antarctica and drifts slowly along the bottom as far as the middle North Atlantic Ocean, where it merges with other water. The circulation of ocean waters is vitally important in dispersing heat energy around the globe. In general, heat flows poleward in the surface currents, while the displaced cold water flows equatorward in deeper ocean layers. The marine environment is divided into two major realms, the benthic and the pelagic, based upon the ecological characteristics and marine life associated with them. The benthic realm refers to the floor of the oceans, extending from the high tide line to the greatest ocean depths. The organisms that live in or on the bottom are called benthos. The benthic realm is subdivided on the basis of depth into the littoral zone, which extends from high tide to a depth of about 200 m (660 ft), and the deep-sea realm. The benthic life forms are both sessile (attached) and motile (mobile). They are distributed from nearshore littoral regions to the ocean depths and play an important role in the food chain. Some benthonic life forms live by predation, others sift organic matter from the water, and others scavenge the bottom for organic debris that has settled there. Benthonic plants can live only in the euphotic zone, the uppermost 100–200 m (330 to 660 ft) of the ocean, where sunlight penetrates. Benthonic animals that live below the euphotic zone must depend on the rain of organic debris from above to supply their food needs, and thus the deep regions of the benthic realm are not highly populated. The pelagic realm consists of all of the ocean water covering the benthic realm. It is divided horizontally into the neritic, or fertile nearshore, province and the oceanic province. Vertically it is divided into the euphotic zone and the aphotic (without sunlight) zone. Drifting, free-floating organisms, called plankton, and organisms with poor mobile ability populate the euphotic zone. Most plankton are microscopic or near-microscopic in size. Phytoplanton are floating plants, such as diatoms, dinoflagellates, coccolithopores, and blue-green algae. Zooplankton are floating animals of the sea and rely on the phytoplankton as food sources. Foraminifera and radiolaria are the dominant protozoan zooplankton that secrete tests (shells) that are incorporated into the sediment of the ocean floor. Many juvenile forms of swimmers (such as shrimp) or bottom dwellers (such as barnacles) pass through a planktonic phase. Marine organisms capable of self-locomotion are called nektonic life forms. Fish, squid, and whales are examples of marine nekton. See MARINE BIOLOGY; OCEANOGRAPHY; TIDE. See also Rachel Carson, *The Sea Around Us* (1961); Leonard Engel, *The Sea* (1961); John Bardach, *Harvest of the Sea* (1968); J. R. Moore, ed., *Oceanography: Readings From Scientific American* (1971); M. G. Gross, *Oceanography* (1972); Richard Perry, *The Unknown Ocean* (1972).

Ocean City, city (1970 pop. 10,575), Cape May co., SE N.J., a resort on the Atlantic coast; inc. 1897. Ocean City is an 8-mi-long (13-km) island between the Atlantic Ocean and Great Egg Harbor Bay; it is linked to the mainland by a 2-mi (3.2-km) causeway.

Oceania (ōshēăn'ēə, -ā'nēə) or **Oceanica** (ōshēăn'ĭkə), collective name for the approximately 25,000 islands of the Pacific, usually excluding such nontropical areas as the Ryukyu and Aleutian islands and Japan, as well as Formosa, Indonesia, and the Philippines, whose populations are more closely related to mainland Asia. Oceania is generally considered synonomous with the South Sea Islands and is divided ethnologically into MELANESIA, MICRONESIA, and POLYNESIA. The total population of the islands is about 1.2 million, of which some 20% are Asians and 7% Europeans. Only a few thousand of the islands have been named.

Oceanian languages, aboriginal languages spoken in the region known as OCEANIA. If Oceania is restricted to the Melanesian, Micronesian, and Polynesian islands, the indigenous tongues spoken on these islands belong for the most part to the Malayo-Polynesian family of languages (see MALAYO-POLYNESIAN LANGUAGES). Papuan languages are spoken on the island of New Guinea, which is sometimes considered a part of Melanesia. The Papuan languages are native to 2 million people of New Guinea. They are not, so far as is known, related to the Malayo-Polynesian linguistic family or, for that matter, to any other family of languages. More research is needed to discover how the various Papuan tongues are related to one another and also how many of them there are. Currently, their number is estimated at about 150 languages. When the area of Oceania is extended to include Australia and Malaysia, indigenous languages of the Australian group spoken in Australia (see AUSTRALIAN LANGUAGES) may be added to the Malayo-Polynesian stock (predominating in Malaysia as well as in Melanesia, Micronesia, and Polynesia) as tongues of this region. The term "Oceanic languages" amounts, in fact, to a geographical rather than a linguistic classification.

Oceanic art, works produced by the island peoples of the S and NW Pacific, including Melanesia (New Guinea and the islands to its north and east), Micronesia (Marianas, Caroline, Marshall, and Gilbert islands), and Polynesia (Hawaii, New Zealand, and Easter Island). Melanesian art possesses an ecstatic and colorful quality that is unique in Oceanic art. Wood carvings and ritual masks, the best studied of Melanesian artifacts, are brilliantly colored and dramatically sexual in nature. Each object was designed to serve a ritual purpose. Created for a specific use, it was not meant to endure for posterity. These works were decorated with reference to a complex mythology the significance of which is largely lost to Western interpretation. Particular aspects of Melanesian art had an enormous impact on European artists, including Max Ernst and Constantin Brancusi (Sepik River style), Alberto Giacometti and Henry Moore (New Ireland style), during the period from 1915 to 1940, but the great variety of Melanesian styles has remained unknown and poorly represented in European and American collections. Among the principal styles familiar in the West are the symmetrical scrollwork carvings and symbolic barkcloth paintings of the Geelvinck Bay area of W New Guinea; the carved drums and ritual figures and polychromed pottery of the Sepik River peoples, as well as their round and beaked masks, displaying strong emotional and erotic symbolism; the carved bird and spiral motifs and superbly decorated canoe prow boards of the Massim area of SE New Guinea; the severe ceremonial carved objects with mother-of-pearl inlay characteristic of the Solomon and Admiralty islands; and the extraordinary heraldic stone sculptures and decorated boards (*malanggan*) with complicated motifs from folklore produced by the people of New Ireland. These are but a few examples of the tremendously varied and as yet little understood treasures of design created by these peoples to be casually discarded once they have fulfilled their ceremonial function. In comparison to Melanesian arts, the objects produced by the Micronesians are streamlined, highly finished, executed with astonishing precision, and almost coldly functional. The designs developed by these peoples show a highly evolved respect for natural materials, which are scarce. Their objects are spare, smooth, and totally distinctive. Among their most elegant works are canoes with clean, graceful lines, expansive houses, and sparsely decorated cult objects. Rows of figures placed on Mortlock Atoll illustrate mythological events and were thought to protect the islanders from typhoons. Very little Polynesian art survived the influx of Western missionaries who mutilated and destroyed an art they considered pornographic and idolatrous. Among the Polynesian works that remain in museum collections are the characteristic greenish pottery of Fiji, remarkable examples of Hawaiian featherwork, exquisite mats woven in Samoa, wooden and stone ritual sculptures from the smaller islands, and pendants carved in jadeite from New Zealand. These peoples, unlike the Melanesians, intended to create enduring works of art. The artist was limited by strict, formal conventions peculiar to the traditions of his island; nevertheless many produced works that revealed great creative imagination within the stylized form. The few surviving Hawaiian works attest to a strong tradition of sculptural wood carving without surface decoration. Highly decorative printed bark-cloth thickly figured with geometric patterns are typical of Fiji, and this powerful geometry extended to much of the ornamental carved work throughout W and central Polynesia. The Maori of New Zealand excelled at surface decoration of curvilinear design. They employed spiral motifs in intricate combinations, even in tatooing the human face. After death such tatooed faces were often preserved on their dried skulls as ritual objects. The Maori also made spectacular carved ceremonial canoes and houses and produced fine textiles with complex woven designs. The Marquesas islanders developed the tatoo into a fine art with which they covered the entire body. On Easter Island an acute scarcity of wood resulted in the development of an economical carving technique of great precision and beauty. The far more abundant reddish stone, tufa, was carved to create gargantuan, expressive human figures, weighing as much as 20 tons. Most Polynesian work was vividly painted or feathered, but this coloring has been lost, as has the ritual significance of the extraordinary motifs employed. See Maurice Leenhardt, *Arts of the Oceanic Peoples* (tr. 1950); Herbert Tischner, *Oceanic Art* (1954); Douglas Newton, *Art Styles of the Papuan Gulf* (1961); Alfred Bühler et al., *The Art of the South Sea Islands* (1962); Jean Guiart, *The Arts of the South Pacific* (1963); K. M. Trowell and Hans Nevermann, *African and Oceanic Art* (1968); C. A. Schmitz, *Oceanic Art* (1971).

oceanids: see NYMPH.

Ocean Island, also known as **Banaba** (bənä'bə), island (1968 pop. 2,192), 2.2 sq mi (5.7 sq km), central Pacific, a part of the British colony of the GILBERT AND ELLICE ISLANDS. The island was discovered by the British in 1804, annexed in 1900, and was the administrative capital of the colony until World War II. The inhabitants are largely Micronesians. Ocean Island has important phosphate deposits mined by the British Phosphate Commission, but the deposits are expected to be depleted by about 1980.

oceanography, study of the sea. It integrates the marine applications of geography, geology, physics, chemistry, marine biology, and meteorology. Oceanography as a comprehensive study dates from the Challenger expedition (1872–76), directed by the naturalists C. W. Thomson, a Scot, and John Murray, a Canadian. The term oceanography became current through reports of the expedition edited by Murray, who later became a leader in the study of ocean sediment. The success of the Challenger expedition and the importance of a knowledge of the sea to shipping, fisheries, the laying of telegraph cables, and climatological studies led many nations to send out expeditions. Universities and private individuals, as well as governments, have established institutions for the study of the ocean; there exist today about 250 such institutions. One of the earliest was the marine biological station at Naples (founded 1872), which stimulated the founding of many other seaside stations, some of which, e.g., the Scripps Institution of Oceanography at La Jolla, Calif., have enlarged their activities to include all fields of oceanographic research. Other notable institutions in the field include the Oceanographic Museum at Monaco (1910); the biological station of the Univ. of Oslo; the Woods Hole Oceanographic Institution at Woods Hole, Mass. (1930); and the Lamont-Doherty Geological Observatory of Columbia Univ. The first international oceanographic organization was the International Council for the Exploration of the Sea (1901); in 1955 UNESCO set up an advisory committee on marine science. Projects such as Conshelf, under the direction of Jacques Cousteau, Sealab, under the auspices of the U.S. navy, and Tektite, a cooperative venture of the U.S. Dept. of the Interior and the National Aeronautics and Space Administration, have established temporary stations on the continental shelf and ocean bottom to see whether a human can live and work in a watery home for extended periods. Modern deep-diving equipment has been improved to permit descents to very great depths; a U.S. bathyscaphe, Trieste II, descended to 35,800 ft (11,000 m) in the Marianas Trench in 1960. Deep-diving craft (see SUBMERSIBLE) prove invaluable for direct observation of the deep ocean bottom and for studying marine life. In 1966 the U.S. Congress created a National Council for Marine Resources and Engineering Development charged with exploring all aspects of ocean development. Congress also authorized the National Science Foundation to sponsor sea-grant colleges in a fashion analogous to the Dept. of Agriculture's sponsorship of land-grant colleges. The Mohole Project, which had planned to penetrate to the earth's mantle, was terminated by Congressional action; however, preliminary success of Mohole drilling provided impetus for construction of the deep-sea drilling vessel *Glomar Challenger*, which began a program to obtain drill cores of the deep ocean floor (see DEEP SEA DRILLING PROJECT). Many ocean phenomena, such as currents and waves, are still incompletely understood. See Jacques Cousteau, *The Silent World* (1953); Robert Cowen, *The Frontiers of the Sea* (1960); Albert Defant, *Physical Oceanography* (1961); Jerome Williams, *Oceanography* (1962); M. G. Gross, *Oceanography, A View of the Earth* (1972); R. R. Ward, *Into the Ocean World* (1974).

ocean perch: see ROCKFISH.

Oceanside. 1 City (1970 pop. 40,494), San Diego co., S Calif., on the Gulf of Santa Catalina; inc. 1888. It is a commercial and trading center for a rich inland farm area and for nearby Camp Pendleton, a huge U.S. marine corps amphibious base. The city has a large flower and bulb industry, and its principal manufactures are electric and electronic components. Deep-sea fishing and tourism are also important. A junior college is in the city, and nearby is San Luis Rey Mission (founded 1798). **2** Uninc. resort city (1970 pop. 35,028), Nassau co., SE N.Y., on the south shore of Long Island.

Oceanus (ōsē'ənəs), in Greek mythology. **1** Circular stream that flows around the edge of the earth. The sun and moon rise from and descend into this stream; it is the source of all rivers. **2** Personification of the circular stream described above. He was the Titan son of Uranus and Gaea, the husband of Tethys, and the father of the river-gods and the sea nymphs (or oceanids). He was conceived of as a powerful but kindly old man. Some legends say that Dione was also the daughter of Oceanus and Tethys.

ocellus (pl. ocelli): see EYE.

ocelot, medium-sized cat, *Felis pardalis,* of Central and South America. It is occasionally found as far N as Texas. The ocelot has a yellow-brown coat with black spots, rings, and stripes. It is about 30 in. (76 cm) long, not including the 14-in. (35-cm) tail, stands about 16 in. (41 cm) high at the shoulder, and weighs up to 35 lb (18 kg). Ocelots live in forests, where they hunt, mainly on the ground, both by day and by night. They prey on birds, snakes, and small mammals. The female gives birth to twins. Ocelots are hunted for their pelts, which are used for coats and trim. They are able to be tamed and are sometimes kept as pets. They are classified in the phylum CHORDATA, subphylum Vertebrata, class Mammalia, order Carnivora, family Felidae.

Ochakov (əchä'kəf), city, SW European USSR, on the Dnepr-Bug estuary and on the Black Sea. It is the center of an agricultural district and a seaport with fishing industries. In the 7th and 6th cent. B.C., there were several Greek colonies in the area, and Ochakov is on the site of the ancient Greek city of Alektor. In 1492 a Crimean khan built a fortress called Kara-Kermen there. When the Turks took control of it, they renamed it Ochakov. In the 16th and 17th cent., the Ukrainian Cossacks attacked the Turks at Ochakov. The city fell to the Russians (1788) during the Russo-Turkish War from 1787 to 1792. In the Crimean War it was occupied (1855) by the allies. Ochakov is near the site of the ancient Greek colony of Olbia.

ocher (ō'kər), mixture of varying proportions of iron oxide and clay, used as a PIGMENT. It occurs naturally as yellow ocher (yellow or yellow-brown in color), the iron oxide being limonite, or as red ocher, the iron oxide being hematite. Ocher grades into sienna, a yellow-brown pigment containing a higher percentage of iron ore than ocher as well as some manganese dioxide; sienna grades into umber, which is darker brown and contains a higher percentage of manganese dioxide. Burnt sienna is brown or bright red; burnt umber is a darker brown than umber. Ocher is produced in the United States, in France (French ocher being of a very high grade), and in some other parts of Europe. Italy is a leading producer of sienna and umber, and Cyprus of umber.

Ochino, Bernardino (bārnärdē'nō ōkē'nō), 1487–1564, Italian religious reformer. Ochino was a Capuchin friar, a popular preacher, and vicar general of the Capuchins in 1538 and 1541. Influenced by Juan de VALDÉS and his circle in Naples, Ochino turned to belief in justification by faith alone, gave up his belief in monastic vows, and adopted an independent Protestantism. In 1542 he fled from the Roman Inquisition to Geneva, where he was well received by Calvin. After two years there he went to England, where he was highly respected until the accession of Mary I, when he returned to Switzerland and became (1555) pastor at Zürich. There he rejected such Calvinist doctrines as predestination. Expelled from the Swiss cantons in 1563 by the Calvinists, he spent his last year in Germany and Poland.

Ochoa, Severo (sāvā'rō ōchō'ä), 1905–, American biochemist and educator, b. Spain, M.D. Univ. of Madrid, 1929. After teaching at the universities of Madrid, Heidelberg, and Oxford, he came to the United States in 1940. In 1954 he was appointed chairman of the department of biochemistry at New York Univ. He became an American citizen in 1956. With Arthur Kornberg he received the 1959 Nobel Prize in Physiology and Medicine for the synthesis of ribonucleic acid (RNA) and deoxyribonucleic acid (DNA), organic compounds that carry hereditary qualities in all reproduction.

Ocho Rios (ō'chō rē'ōs), town, NE Jamaica, on the Caribbean Sea. It is a major tourist center, as well as a commercial port that exports mainly bauxite.

Ochrida: see OHRID, Yugoslavia.

Ochs, Adolph S. (ōks), 1858–1935, American newspaper publisher, b. Cincinnati. Starting as a newsboy in Knoxville, Tenn., he became a printer's apprentice, compositor, and, in 1878, publisher of the Chattanooga *Times.* In 1896 he acquired the then failing New York *Times* and made it one of the greatest newspapers in the world. He also controlled the Philadelphia *Times* and the Philadelphia *Public Ledger,* which he merged and in 1913 sold to Cyrus H. K. Curtis. Unlike the sensational journalists of his day, Ochs stressed nonpartisan, almost clinical news reporting. From 1900 until his death he was a member of the executive committee and a director of the Associated Press. See G. W. Johnson, *An Honorable Titan* (1946, repr. 1970).

Ockeghem, Johannes (yōhän'əs ŏk'əgĕm), c.1425–1495, Flemish composer. Ockeghem is thought to have been a pupil of Gilles Binchois and was definitely taught by Guillaume Dufay. He himself taught Josquin Desprez. He served three kings of France—Charles VII, Louis XI, and Charles VIII— and died at Tours. Considered the leader of the second generation of Flemish composers, he made highly influential contributions to imitative counterpoint in sacred music.

Ockham, William of: see WILLIAM OF OCCAM.

Ocmulgee (ōkmŭl'gē), river, c.255 mi (410 km) long, formed SE of Atlanta, NW Ga., by the confluence of the Yellow, South, and Alcovy rivers. It flows SE past Macon to join the Oconee River and form the Altamaha River near Lumber City. The river passes the remains of prehistoric Indian villages preserved in Ocmulgee National Monument.

Ocmulgee National Monument: see NATIONAL PARKS AND MONUMENTS (table).

Oconee (ōkō'nē), river, 282 mi (454 km) long, rising in the Appalachian Mts., N Ga., and flowing SE to the Ocmulgee River to form the Altamaha River. Sinclair Dam (completed 1953) and Furman Shoals Dam (completed 1953) are on the Oconee.

O'Connell, Daniel, 1775–1847, Irish political leader. He is known as the Liberator. Admitted to the Irish bar in 1798, O'Connell built up a lucrative law practice. Gradually he became involved in the Irish fight for CATHOLIC EMANCIPATION; his abilities as a speaker, organizer, and leader soon advanced him to the uncontested command of the movement. In 1823 he founded the Catholic Association, a formidable and powerful agitation society, which despite English restrictive measures became a great national force. The pressure on Parliament was brought to a head by O'Connell's election in 1828 to a seat in the House of Commons (permitted by the repeal of the Test Act), despite his inability as a Catholic to take the oaths required to sit in Parliament. Alarmed, the government was obliged to pass (1829) the Catholic Emancipation Act. In Parliament, O'Connell supported the Whigs and the reform cause. He supported repeal of the parliamentary union of Great Britain and Ireland, forming a new agitation society to replace each one suppressed by the government. O'Connell worked indefatigably for the reform of the existing government of Ireland and for the abolition of compulsory support of the Church of Ireland. In 1841, O'Connell became the first Catholic lord mayor of Dublin since the time of James II. In 1843 he was indicted for creating disaffection; he was declared guilty and imprisoned, but the sentence was overturned (1844) by the House of Lords. Favoring constitutional methods, O'Connell lost support in the 1840s to nationalists who preferred revolutionary means to end the union and to solve the IRISH LAND QUESTION. He also lost followers who resented his Catholic sectarianism. The secession of the Young Ireland group from his Repeal Association signified his declining authority. Ordered to seek a change for his health, he set out for Italy, where he died. O'Connell's eminence as a leader and creator of national feeling and unity greatly affected the history of Ireland. See M. R. O'Connell, ed., *Correspondence of Daniel O'Connell* (1973); Robert Dunlop, *Daniel O'Connell and the Revival of National Life in Ireland* (1900); A. D. Macintyre, *The Liberator: Daniel O'Connell and the Irish Party* (1965); biographies by Sean O'Faolain (1938) and Denis Gwynn (1947).

O'Connor, Feargus (fûr'gəs), 1794–1855, Irish Chartist leader. Elected to the Parliament of 1832 as a supporter of Daniel O'CONNELL; he soon quarreled with O'Connell and was forced out of Parliament in 1835. Thereafter he devoted himself chiefly to the English radical movement. In 1837 he founded a paper, the *Northern Star,* which developed into the foremost organ of CHARTISM. O'Connor quickly became a leader of the Chartists and, for more than a decade, played a major role in their conventions. But his advocacy of physical force created difficulties with the government and disunity within the movement. In 1846 he began a land distribution scheme that came to be known as the National Land Company. Reelected to Parliament in 1847, he organized the demonstration of 1848 that presented the third Chartist petition to Parliament. The disclosure that many of the petition signatures were falsified and the bankruptcy of his land company discredited him completely. In 1852 he was declared insane. See biography by Donald Read and Eric Glasgow (1961).

O'Connor, Flannery (Mary Flannery O'Connor), 1925–64, American author, b. Savannah, Ga., grad. Women's College of Georgia (A.B., 1945), State University of Iowa (M.F.A., 1947). As a writer, O'Connor is highly regarded for her bizarre imagination, uncompromising moral vision, and superb literary style. Combining the grotesque and the gothic, her fiction treats contemporary Southern life in terms of stark, brutal comedy and violent tragedy. Her characters, although often deformed in both body and spirit, are impelled toward redemption. All of O'Connor's fiction reflects her strong Roman Catholic faith. *Wise Blood* (1952) and *The Violent Bear It Away* (1960) are novels focusing on religious fanaticism; *A Good Man Is Hard To Find* (1955) and *Everything That Rises Must Converge* (1965) are short-story collections. Her *Collected Stories* was published in 1971. O'Connor was the victim of a type of lupus and spent the last ten years of her life as an invalid, writing and raising peacocks on her mother's farm near Milledgeville, Ga. She died in 1964 at 39. See her *Mystery and Manners,* ed. by Sally and Robert Fitzgerald (1969); studies by Josephine Hendin (1970) and Kathleen Feeley (1972).

O'Connor, Frank, 1903–66, Irish short-story writer, whose name originally was Michael O'Donovan. He was a librarian in Dublin and later a director of the Abbey Theatre (1936–39). O'Connor is noted primarily for his short stories—witty, tender, and penetrating studies of Irish life. He also published poetry, critical works, and volumes of Irish history. See his autobiography, *An Only Child* (1961).

O'Connor, Rory or **Roderick,** 1116?–1198, last high king of Ireland. He became king of Connaught in 1156 and seized the high kingship in 1166. His ascendancy was brief, however, for his quarrel with DERMOT MCMURROUGH, who brought the English to Ireland, led to Rory's submission as vassal to Henry II of England by the Treaty of Windsor (1175). O'Connor remained king of Connaught and nominal high king, but his power declined and he retired to a monastery before his death.

O'Connor, Thomas Power, 1848–1929, Irish journalist and politician, known as Tay Pay [i.e., T. P.] O'Connor. In 1879 he won public notice for his hostile biography of Benjamin Disraeli. In Parliament he represented Galway (1880–85), then Liverpool until his death, achieving the longest record of unbroken parliamentary service in his era. O'Connor supported the cause of Irish HOME RULE through numerous essays and articles, through the newspapers that he founded, including the *Star,* the *Sun,* and the *Weekly Sun,* and through fund-raising tours in the United States (1881–82, 1918). His most important books were *The Parnell Movement* (1886) and *Memoirs of an Old Parliamentarian* (1929). See biography by H. H. Fyfe (1934).

Ocran (ŏk'răn), father of a chief Asherite. Num. 1.13; 2.27; 7.72,77; 10.26.

octahedron: see POLYHEDRON.

octane number, figure of merit representing the resistance of GASOLINE to premature detonation when exposed to heat and pressure in the combustion chamber of an internal-combustion engine. Such detonation is wasteful of the energy in the fuel and potentially damaging to the engine; premature detonation is indicated by knocking or pinging noises that occur as the engine operates. If an engine running on a particular gasoline makes such noises, they can be lessened or eliminated by using a gasoline with a higher octane number. The octane number of a sample of fuel is determined by burning the gasoline in an engine under controlled conditions, e.g., of spark timing, compression, engine speed, and load, until a standard level of knock occurs. The engine is next operated on a fuel blended from a form of isooctane that is very resistant to knocking and a form of heptane that knocks very easily. When a blend is found that duplicates the knocking intensity of the sample under test, the percentage of isooctane by volume in the blended sample is taken as the octane number of the fuel. Octane numbers higher than 100 are found by measuring the amount of tetraethyl lead that must be added to pure isooctane to duplicate the knocking of a sample fuel. At present three systems of octane rating are used in the United States. Two of these, the research octane and motor octane numbers, are determined by burning the gasoline in an engine under different, but specified, conditions. Usually the motor octane number is lower than the research octane. The third octane rating, which Federal regulations require on commercial gasoline pumps, is an average of research octane and motor octane. Under this system a regular grade gasoline has an octane number of about 90 and a premium grade between 95 and 96. Most American-made cars that were built in the 1971 model year or later can use regular gasoline. To prevent knocking, premium grade gasoline must be used in many cars built before 1971 and in some new cars that have high-performance engines.

octave (ŏk'tĭv) [Lat.,=eighth], in music, the perfect INTERVAL between the 1st and 8th tones of the diatonic scale. The upper note of an octave has a frequency of vibration twice that of the lower, and in modern Western notation the two have the same letter name. The octave is the first overtone (see HARMONIC). The range of the male voice is roughly an octave below that of the female; men and women supposedly singing in UNISON actually sing in octaves.

Octavia (ŏktā'vēə). **1** d. 11 B.C., Roman matron, sister of Emperor AUGUSTUS and wife of Marc ANTONY, her second husband. She was distinguished for her beauty and virtue and for some years helped in maintaining peace between her brother and her husband. Antony fell in love with CLEOPATRA, and after his war with Augustus began, he divorced (32 B.C.) Octavia. After his death, she reared his children by Fulvia (his first wife) and by Cleopatra, as well as her own. **2** A.D. 42–A.D. 62, Roman matron, daughter of Emperor Claudius I and MESSALINA and wife of NERO, whom she married in A.D. 53. Nero deserted her for Poppaea and divorced her. She was falsely accused of adultery, banished to Pandateria, an island in the Bay of Naples, and put to death. She is the subject of *Octavia*, a unique contemporaneous tragedy, erroneously attributed to Seneca.

Octavian and **Octavius:** see AUGUSTUS.

October: see MONTH.

October Revolution, 1917, in Russian history: see RUSSIAN REVOLUTION.

octopus, CEPHALOPOD mollusk having no shell, eight muscular arms or tentacles, a pouch-shaped body, and two large, highly developed eyes. The prey (crabs, lobsters, and other shellfish) is seized by the sucker-bearing arms and pulled into the web of tissue at the base of the arms, paralyzed and partially digested by a poisonous salivary secretion, and chewed by the horny, beaklike jaws and the radula, or tooth ribbon. Octopuses move by pulling themselves along with their arms or by forcibly expelling water through the funnel or siphon in the manner of their near relative, the squid. Sometimes they construct barricades of large stones; most hide in rocky crevices at the approach of danger or cloud the water by ejecting dark "ink" from the ink sac. They also change color (from pinkish to brown) according to mood and environment, sometimes exhibiting rapid waves of color changes that sweep over the body. The 3-ft (91-cm) American devilfish is found off Florida and in the West Indies; a smaller species that reaches only 2 in. (5 cm) is found N of Cape Cod. The common octopus of the Mediterranean and the Atlantic occasionally reaches 10 ft (3 m) in length; the giant octopus of the Pacific may have a diameter of over 30 ft (9 m). Octopuses reproduce sexually. One of the arms of the male is modified into a sexual organ that deposits spermatophores in the mantle cavity of the female. The eggs are encased in capsules and attached to a rock, where the female guards them. The young hatch directly, without a larval stage. Octopus is eaten in many parts of the world. Octopuses are classified in the phylum MOLLUSCA, class Cephalopoda, order Octopoda, family Octopodidae, genus *Octopus.*

Oda Nobunaga: see NOBUNAGA.

Odda, village: see HARDANGERFJORD.

ode, elaborate and stately lyric poem of some length. The ode dates back to the Greek choral songs that were sung and danced at public events and celebrations. The Greek odes of Pindar, which were modeled on the choral odes of Greek drama, were poems of praise or glorification. They were arranged in stanzas patterned in sets of three—a strophe and an antistrophe, which had an identical metrical scheme, and an epode, which had a structure of its own. The ode of the Roman poets Horace and Catullus employed the simpler and more personal lyric form of Sappho, Anacreon, and Alcaeus (see LYRIC). The ode in later European literature was conditioned by both the Pindaric and the Horatian forms. During the Renaissance the ode was revived in Italy by Gabriello Chiabrera and in France most successfully by Ronsard. Ronsard imitated Pindar in odes on public events and Horace in more personal odes. Horatian odes also influenced the 17th-century English poets, especially Ben Jonson, Robert Herrick, and Andrew Marvell. Milton's ode "On the Morning of Christ's Nativity" (1629) shows the influence of Pindar, as do the poems written for public occasions by his contemporary Abraham Cowley. However, the Cowleyan (or irregular) ode, originated by Cowley, disregarded the complicated metrical and stanzaic structure of the Pindaric form and employed freely altering stanzas and varying lines. In general the odes of the 19th-century romantic poets—Keats, Shelley, Coleridge—and of such later poets as Swinburne and Hopkins tend to be much freer in form and subject matter than the classical ode. Notable examples of the three kinds of ode are: Pindaric ode, e.g., Thomas Gray's "The Progress of Poesy"; Horatian ode, e.g., Keats's "To Autumn"; Cowleyan ode, e.g., Wordsworth's "Ode: Intimations of Immortality." Although the ode has been seldom used in the 20th cent., Allen Tate in "Ode on the Confederate Dead" and Wallace Stevens in "The Idea of Order at Key West," made successful, and highly personal, use of the form. See studies by Carol Maddison (1960), G. N. Shuster (1965), Robert Shafer (1918, repr. 1966), and J. D. Jump (1974).

Oded (ō'dĕd). **1** Father of the prophet Azariah. 2 Chron. 15.1. **2** Prophet who interceded for captive Judahites. 2 Chron. 28.9.

Odenathus, Septimius (sĕptĭm'ēəs ōdĭnā'thəs), d. 267, king of Palmyra. His family (the Septimii) had dominated PALMYRA for many years, and Odenathus by his policy of cooperation with Rome raised his state to its zenith. As a Roman general he warred against Shapur I of Persia after the defeat of VALERIAN. He won (260) a resounding victory over Shapur for Emperor Gallienus and drove the Persians back until he threatened Ctesiphon. He also put down (261) an insurrection against Gallienus in Emesa. Odenathus' main interest was to protect Palmyra's trade with the East against the Persians. He willingly permitted his state (including Syria, NW Mesopotamia, and W Armenia) to be autonomous within the Roman Empire. He and his eldest son were murdered, and soon after his death his second wife, the beautiful and ambitious ZENOBIA, brought Palmyra to ruin.

Ödenburg: see SOPRON, Hungary.

Odense (ō'thənsə), city (1970 com. pop. 164,935), capital of Fyn co., S central Denmark, a seaport linked by canal with the Odense Fjord (an arm of the Kattegat). Denmark's third largest city, it is an important commercial, industrial, and cultural center and a rail junction. There are large shipyards and plants manufacturing metal goods, motor vehicles, machinery, dairy products, and processed food. Founded in the 10th cent., Odense is one of the oldest cities of N Europe. It has been an episcopal see since 1020. Of note in the city are a 12th-century church and the 13th-century Cathedral of St. Knud, one of the finest examples of Danish Gothic architecture. Odense has several colleges and a university. The house of the writer Han Christian Andersen, who was born in Odense in 1805, is now a museum.

Odenwald (ō'dənvält), hilly, forested region, S central West Germany, bordering on the Neckar and Main rivers and the Rhine plain. Its highest point (2,055 ft/626 m) is the Katzenbuckel. Fruit and grapes are grown in the western and southern regions, and there are porphyry quarries.

Oder (ō'dər), Czech and Pol. *Odra*, river, 562 mi (904 km) long; the second longest river of Poland. It rises in the E Sudetes, N central Czechoslovakia, and flows generally NW through SW Poland, then N along the Poland–East Germany border to the Baltic Sea N of Szczecin, Poland. The Warta and the Lausitzer Neisse rivers are its chief tributaries. There are power dams on the Oder's headwaters in Czechoslovakia. Navigable from Racibórz, Poland, the Oder is an important waterway of Central and Eastern Europe, connecting the industrial region of Silesia with the sea. Barges on the river carry iron, coal, and coke. The Oder is linked by canals with the Spree and Elbe rivers; the Warta connects it with the Vistula River. Wrocław, Frankfurt an der Oder, and Szczecin are the chief cities on the Oder.

Oder-Neisse line, frontier established in 1945 between Germany and Poland; it followed the Oder and W Neisse rivers from the Baltic Sea to the Czechoslovak border. The boundary, desired by most Poles at the expense of Germany, came about as a result of agreements between the Soviet Union, Great Britain, and the United States at the Yalta and Potsdam conferences in 1945. The Soviet leader Joseph Stalin endorsed the Oder-Neisse line partly as a compensation for the Polish eastern territories that the USSR had annexed and partly under pressure from the USSR-sponsored Polish government. Although the boundary was originally opposed by the United States and Great Britain because it would make Poland excessively dependent upon the Soviet Union, they sanctioned it informally at Yalta in Feb., 1945. After disputed territories, including the former free city of Danzig (now Gdansk), had been in effect incorporated into Poland and their German population largely expelled, the Potsdam Conference of Aug., 1945, recognized the line as Poland's western frontier pending a peace treaty with Germany. In the absence of such a treaty, an agreement between the German Democratic Republic (East Germany) and Poland recognized the line as the permanent frontier in 1950. The West German government recognized it in 1971.

Odessa (ōdĕs'ə, Rus. ədyĕ'sə), city (1970 pop. 892,000), capital of Odessa oblast, SW European USSR, in the Ukraine, a port on Odessa Bay of the Black Sea. The third largest Ukrainian city after Kiev and Kharkov, Odessa is an important rail junction and highway hub and one of the USSR's major industrial, cultural, scientific, and resort centers. Grain, sugar, machinery, coal, petroleum products, cement, metals, jute, and timber are the chief items of trade at the port of Odessa, which is the leading Soviet Black Sea port and is kept open all year with the aid of icebreakers. Odessa is also a naval base and the home port of a fishing and an antarctic whaling fleet. The city's industries include shipbuilding, oil refining, machine building, metalworking, food processing, and the manufacture of chemicals, machine tools, movie equipment, clothing, and products made of wood, jute, and silk. Large health resorts are located nearby. Ukrainians, Russians, Jews, and Greeks predominate in Odessa's cosmopolitan population. The city is said to occupy the site of an ancient Miletian Greek colony (Odessos, Ordyssos, or Ordas) that disappeared between the 3d and 4th cent. In the 14th cent. the site, then under Lithuanian control, became a Crimean Tatar fortress and trade center called Khadzhi-Bei. In 1764 it passed to the Turks, who built a fortress (Yenu-Duniya) to protect the harbor. It was captured by the Russians in 1789. By the Treaty of Jassy in 1792, Turkey ceded the region between the Dnestr and the Bug (including Odessa) to Russia, which rebuilt Odessa as a fort, commercial port, and naval base. The city that developed around the fort grew rapidly as the chief grain-exporting center of the Ukraine; its importance was further enhanced with the coming of the railroad in the second half of the 19th cent. It was a free port from 1819 to 1849, and in 1866 it was linked by rail with Kiev, Kharkov, and the Rumanian city of Jassy. Industrialization began in the latter part of the 19th cent. Odessa was a center of emigré Greek and Bulgarian patriots, of the Ukrainian cultural and national movement, of Jewish culture, and of the labor movement and social democracy. The city's first workers' organization was founded in 1875. Odessa was the scene in 1905 of the workers' outbreak led by sailors from the battleship *Potemkin.* When Turkey closed the Dardanelles to the Allies in World War I, the port of Odessa was also closed and was later bombarded by the Turkish fleet. Following the 1917 Bolshevik Revolution, the city was successively occupied by the Central Powers, the French, the Reds, and the Whites until the Red Army definitively took it from General DENIKIN in 1920 and united it with the Ukrainian SSR. Odessa suffered greatly in the famine of 1921–22 after the Russian civil war. Despite a heroic defense during World War II, the city fell to German and Rumanian forces in Oct., 1941. It was under Rumanian administration as the capital of Transnistra until its liberation (April, 1944) by the Soviet Army. Many buildings were ruined and approximately 280,000 civilians (mostly Jews) were reportedly massacred or deported during the Axis powers' occupation. Odessa has a university (est. 1865), an opera and ballet theater (1809), a historical museum (1825), a municipal library (1830), an astronomical observatory (1871), an opera house (1883-87), and a picture gallery (1898).

Odessa (ōdĕs'ə), city (1970 pop. 78,380), seat of Ector co., W Texas; founded 1881, inc. 1927. Great oil deposits to the south changed Odessa from a small ranch town into a large oil center with refineries and plants producing fuels, carbon black, chemicals, plastics, synthetic rubber, industrial gas, and oilfield equipment. The region is underlaid with potash deposits. The airport between Midland and Odessa handles much transcontinental and international traffic. A junior college is in the city. Nearby is a large meteor crater.

Odets, Clifford (ōdĕts'), 1906-63, American dramatist, b. Philadelphia. After graduating from high school he became an actor and in 1931 joined the GROUP THEATRE. Turning his attention from acting to playwriting, Odets soon came to be regarded as the most gifted of the American social-protest dramatists of the 1930s. His first work for the Group, *Waiting for Lefty* (1935), a somewhat Marxian drama of the awakening and insurgency of the impoverished working classes, aroused immediate international attention. *Awake and Sing* (1935), his first full-length play and considered to be his best work, compassionately portrays the struggles and rebellion of a financially destitute Jewish family. Other plays include *Till the Day I Die* (1935), *Paradise Lost* (1935), *Golden Boy* (1937), and *Clash by Night* (1942). Odets spent many years in Hollywood writing film scripts. In his later plays he turned from social drama to rather turgid and self-conscious dramas of the individual, such as *The Big Knife* (1949), *The Country Girl* (1950), and *The Flowering Peach* (1954). See biographical studies by Edward Murray (1968) and G. C. Weales (1971).

Odin, Norse god: see WODEN.

Odinga, Oginga (ōgĭng'gä ōdĭng'gä), 1911–, Kenyan political leader. A Luo, he was active in the Kenyan independence movement and later became (1960) vice president of the Kenya African National Union (KANU). After Kenya became a republic in 1964 Odinga served as vice president. He came into increasing conflict with President Jomo Kenyatta, however, and in 1966 was ousted as party vice president. He later resigned as Kenya's vice president and headed an opposition political party, the Kenya Peoples Union. Arrested after antigovernment rioting in 1969 and accused of seeking Soviet aid, he was finally released in 1971 as part of Kenyatta's attempt to appease the Luo. Shortly afterward he rejoined KANU. See his autobiography, *Not Yet Uhuru* (1967).

Odo, count of Paris, French king: see EUDES.

Odoacer (ōdōā'sər) or **Odovacar** (-vā'kər), c.435-493, chieftain of the Heruli, the Sciri, and the Rugii (see GERMANS). He and his troops were mercenaries in the service of Rome, but in 476 the Heruli revolted and proclaimed Odoacer their king. Odoacer defeated the Roman general ORESTES at Piacenza, took Ravenna (the West Roman capital), and deposed ROMULUS AUGUSTULUS, last Roman emperor of the West (until the coronation in 800 of Charlemagne). The date 476 is often accepted as the end of the West Roman Empire. However, Odoacer's action made little difference in the status of Western Rome, which had long been prey to the barbarian armies; the emperors had been mere puppets. Emperor ZENO of the East, considering himself heir to the West Roman Empire, reluctantly recognized Odoacer's authority over Italy and granted him the title of patrician. The Roman administration of Italy continued to function under Odoacer, who retained the chief officers of state. In 488, Zeno sent THEODORIC THE GREAT, king of the Ostrogoths, into Italy to expel Odoacer. Several times defeated, Odoacer consented (493) to a treaty by which he was to share his authority with Theodoric. Invited to a banquet by Theodoric, Odoacer and his son and chief officers were treacherously assassinated; thus Theodoric made himself master of Italy.

odometer (ōdŏm'ĭtər), instrument provided in an automotive vehicle to indicate the total number of miles that have been traveled. The odometer generally shares a housing with the vehicle's SPEEDOMETER and is driven by a cable that the two share. When the vehicle is in motion, this cable moves a series of gears in the odometer, turning a set of numbered drums that count the miles traveled. These drums can usually indicate up to 99,999.9 mi. Some odometers, called trip meters, are manually resettable to zero; these are used to measure the lengths of individual trips. Odometers are often equipped with means for indicating if they have been tampered with, i.e., set back to make it appear that a vehicle has traveled fewer miles than it actually has. An instrument similar in design and function to the automotive odometer may be fitted to a bicycle.

O'Donnell, Hugh Roe, 1571?-1602, Irish chieftain and ruler of Tyrconnel (modern Donegal), known as Red Hugh. His father tended to favor the English, who left him free to continue the traditional O'Donnell struggle with the O'Neills, until Hugh was taken hostage by the English for his father's loyalty and imprisoned (1587-92). On his escape his father resigned the clan leadership to him, and Hugh led a rising against the British (1594-1601). Successful at first, and aided by Spain, he enlarged his own territories but gradually lost control over the other nobles who resented his personal ambition. He was defeated, with Hugh O'Neill, 2d earl of TYRONE, at Kinsale (1601) and fled to Spain, where he died.

O'Donnell, Leopoldo (lāōpōl'dō ōthō'nĕl), 1809-67, Spanish general and statesman; member of a branch of the Irish O'Donnells of Tyrconnel. He fought successfully for ISABELLA II against the Carlists. When ESPARTERO seized (1840) power in Spain, O'Donnell went into exile with MARIA CHRISTINA. He failed in an attempted coup against Espartero in 1841. After Espartero's fall, O'Donnell was governor of Cuba (1844-48). In 1854 he led a military revolt and, assisted by a popular uprising in Madrid, overthrew the government of Maria Christina. He then served as war minister under Espartero, whom he ousted (1856), and was several times premier (1856, 1858-63, 1865-66). As the leader of the Liberal Union party, which he had founded, O'Donnell followed a more or less moderate policy. He took command in the successful Spanish campaign (1859-60) in Morocco and after the capture of Tetuán was given the title duque de Tetuán. In 1866 his harsh repression of an uprising organized by Gen. Juan Prim led to O'Donnell's dismissal.

O'Donojú, Juan (hwän ōthōnōhōō'), d. 1821, Spanish colonial administrator. He distinguished himself in the army and became captain general of Andalusia. Sent out (1821) as captain general and acting viceroy of New Spain, he found all Mexico, except a few towns, in the control of the revolutionists under ITURBIDE. He signed the Treaty of Córdoba, conceding most of the revolutionary demands, and became a member of the board of regents in Mexico. He died before the treaty was disavowed by Spain.

Odovacar: see ODOACER.

Odra: see ODER, river, Poland and Czechoslovakia.

Odría, Manuel (mänōōĕl' ōdrē'ä), 1897-1974, president of Peru (1948-56). A conservative general, he became army chief of staff in 1946 and seized power (1948) after leading an anti-APRA coup that forced Víctor Raúl HAYA DE LA TORRE to seek asylum. He was legally elected president in 1950. With dictatorial methods, some brutal, he consolidated his power and instituted extensive economic reforms. In 1956, Odría permitted an election and went into temporary voluntary exile when Manuel Prado was chosen as president. Odría ran unsuccessfully for president in 1962.

Odum, Howard Washington (ō'dəm), 1884-1954, American sociologist, b. Bethlehem, Ga., grad. Emory College, 1904, Ph.D. Clark Univ., 1909, and Ph.D. Columbia, 1910. In 1920 he became professor of sociology at the Univ. of North Carolina and was director of its school of public welfare (1920-32) and of its Institute for Research in Social Science (1924-44). A member of the North Carolina state planning board after 1935, he also served on many other state and regional committees. By far the most important of his works was *Southern Regions of the United States* (1936), a thorough and highly influential study. He also contributed much to literature on folk music and on regional and racial sociology. Odum wrote a trilogy of novels on the life of a wandering Negro: *Rainbow round My Shoulder* (1928), *Wings on My Feet* (1929), and *Cold Blue Moon* (1931).

Odysseus (ōdĭs'ēəs), Lat. *Ulysses* (yōōlĭs'ēz), in Greek mythology, son and successor of King Laertes of Ithaca. A leader of Greek forces during the Trojan War, Odysseus was noted (as in the *Iliad*) for his cunning strategy and his wise counsel. In post-Homeric legend, however, he was pictured as a wily, lying, and evil man. He avoided service in the Trojan War by feigning madness—until exposed by Palamedes, whom he later treacherously caused to be executed. The legends of Odysseus' wanderings, some of which stem from pre-Homeric times, have been used throughout literature, most notably in the *Odyssey*. See Edith Hamilton, *Mythology* (1942, repr. 1971).

Odyssey (ŏd'ĭsē): see HOMER.

OECD: see INTERNATIONAL GOVERNMENTAL ORGANIZATIONS.

Oecolampadius, Johannes (yōhän'əs ökōlämpä'-dēōōs, ĕk''əlămpā'dēəs), 1482-1531, German Protestant reformer, associate of Huldreich ZWINGLI in the Reformation in Switzerland. He was in 1516 a preacher at Basel, where he worked with Erasmus on his *New Testament*. In 1520 he preached in Augsburg, then for a time was in a convent at Altmünster. Martin Luther's teachings won his interest, and in 1522 he acted as chaplain among reformers under Franz von Sickingen at Ebernburg and then returned to Basel to devote himself to the work of the Reformation. He agreed with the views of Zwingli on the nature of the Eucharist, defending this position against Luther in the Colloquy of Marburg, 1529, while Zwingli disputed the question with Melanchthon. See biographies by J. J. Herzog (1843) and K. R. Hagenbach (1859); Williston Walker, *The Reformation* (1900).

Oedipus (ĕd'ĭpəs, ē'dĭ-), in Greek legend, son of Laius, king of Thebes, and his wife, Jocasta. Laius had been warned by an oracle that he was fated to be killed by his own son; he therefore abandoned Oedipus on a mountainside. The baby, however, was rescued by a shepherd and brought to the king of Corinth, who adopted him. When Oedipus was grown, he learned from the Delphic oracle that he would kill his father and marry his mother. He fled Corinth to escape this fate, believing his foster parents to be his real parents. At a crossroad he encountered Laius, quarreled with him, and killed him. He continued on to Thebes, where the SPHINX was killing all who could not solve her riddle. Oedipus answered it correctly and so won the widowed queen's hand. The prophecy was thus fulfilled. Two sons, Polynices and Eteocles, and two daughters, Antigone and Ismene, were born to the unwittingly incestuous pair. When a plague descended on Thebes, an oracle declared that the only way to rid the land of its pollution was to expel the murderer of Laius. Through a series of painful revelations, brilliantly dramatized by Sophocles in *Oedipus Rex*, the king learned the truth and in an agony of horror blinded himself. According to Homer, Oedipus continued to reign over Thebes until he was killed in battle; but the more common version is that he was exiled by Creon, Jocasta's brother, and his sons battled for the throne (see SEVEN AGAINST THEBES). In Sophocles' *Oedipus at Colonus*, Oedipus is guided in his later wanderings by his faithful daughter, Antigone.

Oedipus complex, Freudian term, drawn from the myth of OEDIPUS, designating attraction on the part of the child toward the parent of the opposite sex and rivalry and hostility toward the parent of its own. It occurs during the phallic stage of the psycho-sexual development of the personality, approximately years three to five. Resolution of the Oedipus complex is believed to occur by IDENTIFICATION with the parent of the same sex and by the renunciation of sexual interest in the parent of the opposite sex. Freud considered this complex the cornerstone of the superego and the nucleus of all human relationships. Many psychiatrists, while acknowledging the significance of the Oedipal relationships to personality development in our culture, ascribe love and attraction toward one parent and hatred and antagonism toward the other not necessarily to sexual rivalry but to resentment of parental authoritarian power.

Oehlenschläger, Adam Gottlob (ä'däm gŏt'lōb ö'lənshlāgər), 1779-1850, Danish romantic poet and dramatist. Oehlenschläger turned for themes to the sagas and to Scandinavian history; he is known as the national poet of Denmark. His poem "Golden Horns" (1802) is an original and creative treatment of myth. Other works include lyrics, epics, and a series of historical plays, the best known of which, *Hakon Jarl* (1807), describes the decline of heathenism in Scandinavia. Other dramas are *Axel and Valborg* (1809) and *Helge* (1814). In 1829, Oehlenschläger was crowned Scandinavian poet laureate.

Oeneus (ē'nēəs), in Greek mythology, king of Calydon and father of MELEAGER. When Oeneus forgot to dedicate the fruits of his first crop to Artemis, she terrorized his kingdom with a wild boar, which was killed in the Calydonian hunt.

Oenone (ēnō'nē), in Greek mythology, nymph skilled in the art of healing. Paris loved her, but later deserted her for Helen. Oenone, in revenge, sent their son, Corythus, to guide the Greeks to Troy. When Paris lay mortally wounded, he asked her to heal him but she refused. After learning of his death, she committed suicide.

Oenothera (ēnəthĭr'ə): see EVENING PRIMROSE.

Oersted, Hans Christian, Dan. *Ørsted* (häns krĭs'-tyän ör'stĭth), 1777–1851, Danish physicist and chemist. He was professor at Copenhagen from 1806. His discovery (1819) that a magnetic needle is deflected at right angles to a conductor carrying an electric current established a relationship between magnetism and electricity and initiated the study of electromagnetism. He was the first to isolate aluminum (1825). The unit of magnetic field strength is named for him.

Oeta (ē'tə), Gr. *Oiti,* mountain range, central Greece, stretching c.15 mi (25 km) W from Thermopylae on the Gulf of Lamía. Mt. Oeta (c.7,060 ft/2,150 m) is the highest peak. In legend Hercules died there on a pyre after being poisoned by Nessus' robe.

O'Faoláin, Seán (shôn ōfăl'ən), 1900–, Irish writer. The relation of the individual to society is often the theme of his novels and stories. He frequently writes about Ireland, analyzing the nation's agony in adjusting past history with present reality. O'Faoláin is probably best known for his short stories, collected in such volumes as *Midsummer Night Madness* (1932), *The Man Who Invented Sin* (1948), *The Heat of the Sun* (1966), and *The Talking Trees* (1971). Among his novels are *A Nest of Simple Folk* (1933) and *Come Back to Erin* (1940). His nonfiction works include biographies of De Valera (1933) and Daniel O'Connell (1938) and several studies of Ireland, notably *Song of Ireland* (1943) and *The Irish* (1948). See study by Maurice Harmon (1967).

Ofen: see BUDAPEST, Hungary.

Ofen (ō'fən), Alpine pass, 7,070 ft (2,155 m) high, Grisons canton, E Switzerland. The Ofen Pass Road links the Engadine Valley with the Italian Tyrol.

Offa (ŏf'ə), d. 796, king of Mercia (757–96). He succeeded Æthelbald to the throne, but it was some years before he attained the power of his predecessor. Gradually he asserted his overlordship in Kent and then Sussex, and by 774 his charters styled him *rex Anglorum* [king of the English]. He restricted Cynewulf, king of Wessex, to the area S of the Thames and in 794 had Ethelbert, king of the East Angles, beheaded and thereafter ruled his kingdom. In time the rulers of Wessex and Northumbria became his sons-in-law. In 786 the pope sent two legates to him, and by 788 Offa had set up an independent archbishopric of Litchfield, thus wresting control of the churches in Mercia from the hostile archbishop of Canterbury. He introduced a new coinage in the form of the silver penny, which for centuries was to be the basis of the English currency. Offa had sufficient standing in Europe to negotiate with Charlemagne as an equal; and, although they quarreled over a proposed marriage of their children, they signed (796) a commercial treaty, the first recorded in English history. At some time between 784 and 796 the earthwork known as OFFA'S DYKE was built between Wales and Mercia. Offa's laws, now lost, were used by King Alfred in his codification. The Offa referred to in *Beowulf* and other Anglo-Saxon heroic poetry was not the king of Mercia, but a king of the Angles on the Continent, probably at the end of the 4th cent. See F. M. Stenton, *Anglo-Saxon England* (3d ed. 1971).

Offaly (ŏf'əlē), county (1971 pop. 51,834), 771 sq mi (1,997 sq km), central Republic of Ireland. The county town is TULLAMORE. A part of the central plain of Ireland, the county is for the most part flat, and sections are covered by the Bog of Allen. The Slieve Bloom Mts. are on the southeastern border. The Shannon, the chief river, forms much of the western border. Other rivers are the Brosna and Blackwater. Agriculture is the chief occupation; cattle, pigs, and poultry are bred in considerable quantity. Grains and potatoes are grown. Among the light industries is distilling. With adjacent areas, the region formed the kingdom of Offaly in ancient Ireland. It was known as King's County until the establishment of the Irish Free State. At CLONMACNOISE are the ruins of one of the greatest religious centers of early Ireland.

Offa's Dyke, ancient entrenchment of W England and E Wales, from the Dee estuary to near the estuary of the Wye River. It was built in the 8th cent. by Offa, king of MERCIA, as a barrier against the Welsh and lies mainly along the England-Wales boundary. Watt's Dyke, a similar work, roughly parallels a section of Offa's at a distance of c.2 mi (3.2 km). Parts of the dikes are well preserved.

Offenbach, Jacques Levy (ô'fənbäk, Fr. zhäk lāvē' ôfĕnbäk'), 1819–80, French composer, b. Cologne. The son of a cantor, he went to Paris to study at the conservatory and in 1849 became a conductor at the Théâtre Français. The most successful composer of French operettas, he wrote more than 100 of them, the most successful of which perhaps was *Orphée aux enfers* (1858). Others include *La Belle Hélène* (1864), *La Vie parisienne* (1866), *Barbe-bleue* (1866), *La Grande Duchesse de Gérolstein* (1867), and *La Périchole* (1868). Witty, fresh, gay, and cleverly orchestrated, they were immensely popular during the Second Empire, which they often satirized. Offenbach's one serious opera, *Les Contes d'Hoffmann* (*Tales of Hoffmann,* 1881), after E. T. A. Hoffmann, was his masterpiece. Unfinished at his death, the opera was produced posthumously, and in 1951 it was made into a motion picture combining opera and ballet. See his *Orpheus in America* (tr. 1957); biography by A. Moss (1954).

Offenbach am Main (ôf'ənbäkh äm mīn) or **Offenbach,** city (1970 pop. 117,306), Hesse, central West Germany, on the Main River. It is an industrial center long famous for the manufacture of leather goods; chemicals, metal products, and machinery are also produced. Offenbach was first mentioned in the late 10th cent.; it passed to the counts of Isenburg in the 15th cent. and was annexed by Hesse-Darmstadt in 1816. A Renaissance-style palace (1564–78) and museums of leathercraft, typography, and graphics are located in the city.

offertory [Lat.,=offering], in the Roman Catholic MASS and in derived liturgical forms, the preparation of bread and wine on the altar and their formal offering to God. It takes place after the gospel and the creed and before the preface. A short psalm verse from Scriptures is appointed to be said or sung at the beginning; it varies from day to day. This is called the offertory verse. From ancient times it has been customary to collect the alms of the worshipers about the time of the offertory, hence the term has been transferred to the collection taken up in nonliturgical services in Protestant churches and to the music played or sung during the collection. The choice of this selection is usually left to the musicians of the church, and in many Protestant churches the offertory is the choir's principal musical selection in the service.

Office of Price Administration (OPA), U.S. Federal agency in World War II, established to prevent wartime inflation. The OPA issued (April, 1942) a general maximum-price regulation that made prices charged in March, 1942, the ceiling prices for most commodities. Ceilings were also imposed on residential rents. These regulations were gradually modified and extended by OPA administrators—notably Leon HENDERSON (1941–42), Prentiss H. Brown (1943), and Chester B. BOWLES (1943–46)—until almost 90% of the retail food prices were frozen. Prices continued to rise, however, and new drives to secure compliance resulted; ultimately the OPA succeeded in keeping consumer prices relatively stable during the remaining war years. Besides controlling prices, the OPA was also empowered to ration scarce consumer goods in wartime. Tires, automobiles, sugar, gasoline, fuel oil, coffee, meats, and processed foods were ultimately rationed. At the end of the war rationing was abandoned, and price controls were gradually abolished. The agency was finally disbanded in 1947.

Office of Strategic Services (OSS), U.S. World War II agency created in 1942 under the jurisdiction of the Joint Chiefs of Staff for the purpose of obtaining information about enemy nations and of sabotaging their war potential and morale. Headed by William H. Donovan, the OSS comprised personnel from all the branches of the armed forces as well as civilians. Although the "cloak and dagger" section gained the most publicity after the war, some of the most valuable work was done by the research and analysis section. Behind enemy lines, the OSS acted as a liaison with the underground in Nazi-dominated countries. The OSS was disbanded in 1945. Later many of its functions were assumed by the Central Intelligence Agency. See Stewart Alsop and Tom Bradon, *Sub Rosa: The O.S.S. and American Espionage* (1946, repr. 1964); R. H. Smith, *OSS* (1972).

Office of War Information (OWI), U.S. World War II agency, created in 1942 to consolidate government information services. The OWI absorbed the functions of the Office of Facts and Figures, the Office of Government Reports, the division of information of the Office for Emergency Management, and the foreign information service of the Coordinator of Information. Elmer DAVIS was named director. Besides coordinating the release of war news for domestic use, the office established an overseas branch, under Robert E. SHERWOOD, which launched a huge information and propaganda campaign abroad. Congressional opposition to the domestic operations of the OWI resulted in increasingly curtailed funds, and by 1944 the OWI operated mostly in the foreign field, contributing to undermining enemy morale. The agency was abolished in 1945, and its foreign functions were transferred to the Dept. of State. See Wallace Carroll, *Persuade or Perish* (1948).

Offner, Richard, 1889–1965, American art historian, b. Vienna, studied at Harvard, Ph.D. Univ. of Vienna, 1914. An outstanding authority on Italian art of the 13th and 14th cent., he taught at New York Univ. from 1923 to 1957. He wrote *A Critical and Historical Corpus of Florentine Painting* (1930–69), his major, multivolumed work. *Italian Primitives at Yale University* (1927) and *Studies in Florentine Painting* (1927) are other writings.

offset: see PRINTING.

Offutt Air Force Base, U.S. military installation, 1,907 acres (772 hectares), E Neb., S of Omaha; est. 1896 as Fort Crook, an army base. Converted to an airbase in the early 1900s and renamed in 1924, it is now the headquarters of the Strategic Air Command. The Nebraska Museum of Aerospace History is on the base.

O'Flaherty, Liam (lē'əm ōflă'hərtē), 1897–, Irish novelist, b. Aran Islands, Co. Galway. Many of his novels have an almost naturalistic realism. Always compassionately interested in the common man, he wrote psychological novels of troubled individuals, such as *The Informer* (1925), successfully filmed; *The Black Soul* (1924), *Mr. Gilhooley* (1926), and *The Assassin* (1928). *Famine* (1937), *Land* (1946), and *Insurrection* (1951) are novels of 19th-century Ireland. He has also written notable short stories, as well as autobiographical works, *Two Years* (1930) and *Shame the Devil* (1934). See studies by John Zneimer (1970) and J. H. O'Brien (1973).

Og (ŏg), giant king of Bashan conquered by the Israelites. Deut. 3.1–13.

Ogaden (ōgä'dän), region, Harar prov., SE Ethiopia, bordering on the Somali Democratic Republic. It is an arid region, inhabited mainly by Somali pastoral nomads. The region was conquered by Menelik II of Ethiopia in 1891. A clash (Dec. 5, 1934) between Italian and Ethiopian troops at the watering hole of Walwal in Ogaden was used as a pretext by Italy to begin a war (1935–36) against Ethiopia. Since 1960, Somali nationalists have demanded the union of Ogaden with the Somali Democratic Republic, and there have been violent clashes over the precise boundaries of Ogaden.

Ogasawara-gunto: see BONIN ISLANDS.

Ogbomosho (ōbōō'môshô, ŏgbōmō'shō), city (1971 est. pop. 387,000), SW Nigeria. It is the trade center for a farming region. Cotton cloth is woven. Ogbomosho was founded in the 17th cent. It resisted FULANI invasions in the early 19th cent. and grew by absorbing refugees from towns destroyed by the Fulani. A teachers college is in the city.

Ogden, city (1970 pop. 69,478), seat of Weber co., N Utah, at the confluence of the Ogden and Weber rivers; inc. 1851. Aerospace industries, Hill Air Force Base, and the Ogden Defense Depot are the major employers. The site of a trading post in the 1820s, the area was settled by Mormons in 1847. Weber State College; a state industrial school; and two Mormon tabernacles are in Ogden. The city is surrounded by mountains; major ski resorts are in the area, including Snow Basin at nearby Mt. Ogden.

Ogden, river, 35 mi (56 km) long, rising in the Wasatch Range in N Utah, and flowing SW to join the Weber River at Ogden. The river has been used for irrigation for nearly a century, and it now irrigates c.23,000 acres (9,300 hectares). The Ogden-Brigham Canal (c.20 mi/30 km long) carries water N to Brigham. Pineview Dam, completed by the Bureau of Reclamation in 1937, is at the head of Ogden Canyon. The headwater region of the Ogden is a winter sports area.

Ogdensburg, city (1970 pop. 14,544), St. Lawrence co., N N.Y., on the St. Lawrence River at the mouth of the Oswegatchie, in a resort area, opposite Prescott, Ont. (with which it is connected by an international bridge); settled by French missionaries and trappers 1749, inc. as a city 1868. In the city are a junior college and an art gallery with works of Frederic Remington, who lived in Ogdensburg.

Ogé, Vincent (văNsäN' ōzhā'), c.1750–1791, Haitian revolutionist and national hero. A free mulatto, well educated and comparatively wealthy, he was sent to plead before the National Assembly at the outbreak of the French Revolution for the concession of civil rights to free mulattoes and for the emancipation of slaves in Haiti. Failing in his mission, he returned to Haiti in 1790 and, when the French governor refused to remove restrictions, headed an insurrection. Defeated, Ogé was tried, convicted of treason, and broken on the wheel.

ogham, ogam, or **ogum** (all: ŏg'əm, ō'əm), ancient Celtic alphabet of one of the Irish runic languages. It was used by the druids and abandoned after the first few centuries of the Christian era. The ogham RUNES remain only in gravestone INSCRIPTIONS found mostly in W Ireland and also in England, Scotland, and the Shetland Islands. The origin of ogham is uncertain; it contained 25 letters formed of straight lines and may have been adapted from a SIGN LANGUAGE. A treatise on ogham, *The Book of Ballymote* (15 cent.), confirms that it was a secret, ritualistic language. See R. A. Macalister, *The Secret Languages of Ireland* (1937).

Ogier the Dane (ō'jēər, ōzhyā'), in the CHANSONS DE GESTE, a paladin of Charlemagne. Although his military feats save emperor and kingdom, he is for a time at odds with Charlemagne. In some versions Morgan le Fay takes him to Avalon, from where he returns after 200 years to save France. As Holger, or Olger, Danske he is a popular Danish hero.

Oglala Sioux: see SIOUX INDIANS.

Oglesby, Richard James (ō'gəlzbē), 1824–99, Union general in the American Civil War and Illinois political leader, b. Oldham co., Ky. He moved to Decatur, Ill., where he became a lawyer. Oglesby fought in the Mexican War and went to California in the gold rush, but in 1851 he resumed his practice in Decatur. In the Civil War he rose to be a major general of volunteers. He fought under Ulysses S. Grant at Belmont and Fort Donelson and was severely wounded at Corinth (1862). Resigning his commission in 1864, he served as governor of Illinois (1865–69, 1873), U.S. Senator (1873–79), and again governor (1885–89). Oglesby, Ill., was named for him.

Oglethorpe, James Edward (ō'gəlthôrp), 1696–1785, English general and philanthropist, founder of the American colony of GEORGIA. He had some military experience before being elected (1722) to the House of Commons, where he held a seat for 32 years. As chairman of a parliamentary committee investigating penal conditions, Oglethorpe became interested in the plight of the debtor classes. The need for a buffer colony between South Carolina and the Spanish in Florida admirably fitted his proposal to establish an asylum for debtors. He and 19 associates were granted (June, 1732) a charter, to expire in 21 years, making them trustees of the colony of Georgia. Early in 1733, Oglethorpe, leading 116 carefully selected colonists, reached Charleston, S.C., and on Feb. 12, 1733, he founded Savannah. After establishing friendly relations with the Yamacraw, a branch of the Creek Indians, who ceded their land for settlement, he set about perfecting the colony's defense against the Spanish, building forts and instituting a system of military training. On a visit to England (1734–35) Oglethorpe obtained new regulations banning rum and slavery in the colony, which aroused opposition. He returned to Georgia with John WESLEY and Charles WESLEY. England declared war on Spain in 1739, and in 1740, Oglethorpe led an unsuccessful expedition against St. Augustine. However, near Fort Frederica on St. Simons Island, Oglethorpe defeated the Spanish in the battle of Bloody Marsh (June 9, 1742), thereby assuring Georgia's survival. A second unsuccessful assault on St. Augustine (1743) and the displeasure of some of the colonists with his rigid management led to his recall to England. The charges brought against him were dismissed, but he never returned to Georgia. In his later years he was an intimate of the literary circle gathered around Samuel Johnson. See *Letters from General Oglethorpe*, collected by the Georgia Historical Society (1873); biographies by L. F. Church (1932), A. A. Ettinger (1936, repr. 1968), and J. G. Vaeth (1968).

Ogoki (ōgō'kē), river, c.300 mi (480 km) long, rising in lakes W of Lake Nipigon, W central Ont., Canada, and flowing NE to the Albany River. A dam at Waboose Rapids forms a reservoir (45 mi/72 km long), which drains to the south into Lake Nipigon.

Ogooué or **Ogowe** (both: ōgōwā'), river, c.560 mi (900 km) long, rising on the Batéké Plateau, SW Congo Republic. It flows NW and W across Gabon to the Gulf of Guinea, near Port-Gentil, where it forms a large delta. Navigable for most of its length, the river is the chief economic artery of Gabon. Savorgnan de Brazza, the French explorer, charted the Ogooué's course in 1880.

O'Gorman, Juan (hwän), 1905–, Mexican architect. Trained by Villagran Garcia, O'Gorman produced designs adapting the INTERNATIONAL STYLE to Mexican requirements. O'Gorman's most notable work is the University Library, Mexico City (1952), with its elaborate, fantastic mosaic facade.

Ogowe: see OGOOUÉ, river, Africa.

OGPU: see SECRET POLICE.

O'Grady, Standish, 1846–1928, Irish author and historian. A leader in the IRISH LITERARY RENAISSANCE, he followed his *History of Ireland* (1878–80) with English versions of the heroic legends of Ireland. The best are probably his volumes about CUCHULAIN (1892–1917; repr. 1920).

O'Grady, Standish Hayes, 1832–1915, Irish scholar. His great work was the *Silva Gadelica* (1892), a collection of old Irish tales. He also translated heroic stories from the Gaelic and began a catalogue of the Irish manuscripts in the British Museum, thus laying a foundation for the later scholars of the Celtic renaissance.

Ogyges (ŏj'ĭjēz), in Greek mythology, ancient king of Boeotia or Attica. It was in his reign that the Ogygian flood, a vast and destructive deluge, occurred. The adjective Ogygian, derived from his name, means ancient.

Ogygia (ōjĭj'ēə): see CALYPSO.

Ohad (ō'hăd), one of the sons of Simeon. Gen. 46.10; Ex. 6.15.

O'Hara, John, 1905–70, American novelist and short story writer, b. Pottsville, Pa. He worked as a newspaper reporter and later as a screen writer before the appearance of his first novel, *Appointment in Samarra* (1934). The book, an immediate success, began O'Hara's long career as a highly commercial and popular writer. Among his other novels are *Butterfield 8* (1935), *Pal Joey* (1940; musical comedy adaptation, 1941), *A Rage to Live* (1949), *Ten North Frederick* (1955), *From the Terrace* (1958), *The Lockwood Concern* (1965), and *The Ewings* (1972). O'Hara has been called a photographic, acid observer of American urban life. Some critics believe his best work is in his collections of short stories, which include *The Doctor's Son* (1935), *Hellbox* (1947), *Assembly* (1961), *The Cape Cod Lighter* (1962), *The Horse Knows the Way* (1964), and *Good Samaritan and Other Stories* (1974). See biography by Finis Farr (1973).

Ohel (ō'hĕl), one of Zerubbabel's sons. 1 Chron. 3.20.

O. Henry, pseud. of **William Sydney Porter,** 1862–1910, American short-story writer, b. Greensboro, N.C. He went to Texas in 1882 and worked at various jobs—as teller in an Austin bank (1891–94) and as a newspaperman for the Houston *Post.* In 1898 an unexplained shortage in the Austin bank was charged to him. Although many people believed him innocent, he fled to the Honduras but returned to be with his wife, who was fatally ill. He eventually served three years in prison, where he first started writing short stories. Upon his release he settled in New York City and became a highly successful and prolific contributor to various magazines. His short, simple stories are noted for their careful plotting, ironic coincidences, and surprise endings. Although his stories have been criticized as shallow and contrived, O. Henry did catch the color and movement of the city and evidenced a genuine sympathy for ordinary people. His approximately 300 stories are collected in *Cabbages and Kings* (1904), *The Four Million* (1906), *The Voice of the City* (1908), *Options* (1909), and others. See biographies by Gerald Langford (1957) and Richard O'Connor (1970); study by Joseph Gallegly (1970); bibliography by P. S. Clarkson (1938).

O'Higgins, Ambrosio (ōhĭg'ĭnz, Span. ämbrō'syō ōē'gēns), 1720?–1801, Spanish colonial administrator, b. Ballinary, Co. Sligo, Ireland. Educated at Cádiz, Spain, under the care of his uncle, who was a Jesuit, he went to South America as a trader. After an adventurous career he so distinguished himself in campaigns against the Araucanian Indians that he was appointed (1789) governor of Chile. He was later made marquis of Osorno and served capably as viceroy (1796–1801) of Peru. Bernardo O'Higgins was his son.

O'Higgins, Bernardo (bĕrnär'thō), 1778–1842, South American revolutionary and ruler (1817–23) of Chile; illegitimate son of Ambrosio O'Higgins. He was chosen in 1813 to replace José Miguel CARRERA as revolutionary leader. After the loss at RANCAGUA, O'Higgins fled with the remnant of his army to Argentina, where he joined forces with SAN MARTIN. Returning to Chile in 1817, San Martín and O'Higgins defeated the Spaniards at CHACABUCO. O'Higgins was named supreme director of Chile, whose independence he proclaimed on Feb. 12, 1818. His financial, political, and social reforms aroused much opposition, and in 1823 he was deposed and exiled to Peru, where he remained until his death. See biographies by Jay Kinsbruner (1968) and Stephen Clissold (1969).

Ohio, state (1970 pop. 10,652,017), 41,222 sq mi (106,765 sq km), N United States, in the Great Lakes region of the Middle West, admitted as the 17th state of the Union in 1803. COLUMBUS is the capital and the second largest city. The largest city is CLEVELAND. Other major cities are CINCINNATI, TOLEDO, and AKRON. The Ohio River, from which the state takes its name, separates it in the SE from West Virginia and in the S from Kentucky; Ohio is bounded on the W by Indiana, on the N by Michigan and Lake Erie, and on the E (N of the Ohio River) by Pennsylvania. From the dunes on Lake Erie to the gorge-cut plateau along the Ohio River, the land is fairly flat, with some pleasant rolling country and in the southeast rugged little hills leading to the mountains of West Virginia. Before the coming of the white man Ohio was covered with many square miles of virgin forest, but today only vestiges of the trees that helped to build the many cities remain. The state is highly industrialized. Yet it continues to draw from the earth: it leads the nation in the production of

lime, is second in the production of clays, and ranks third in the production of salt, sand and gravel, and stone. It also ranks high in the exploitation of coal. The land supports rich farms, especially where the soil was improved ages ago by glacier-ground limestone. Although most of the working population is engaged in industry and most of the state's income is derived from commerce and manufacturing, Ohio has extensive farms and large amounts of corn, soybeans, hay, wheat, cattle, hogs, and dairy items are produced. Railroads and highways crisscross the state, bearing a tremendous traffic of raw materials and manufactures. The Lake Erie ports—Toledo, Cleveland, and Sandusky—handle much iron and copper ore, coal, oil, and finished materials (including steel and automobile parts). Since the opening of the SAINT LAWRENCE SEAWAY (1959) these ports have been exporting the products of Ohio directly overseas. The state has many manufacturing centers, with an emphasis on heavy industry. Its leading products are transportation equipment, primary and fabricated metals, machinery, and plastic and rubber goods (Akron is world famous as a major rubber center). In prehistoric times Ohio was inhabited by the MOUND BUILDERS, many of whose mounds are preserved in state parks and in the Mound City Group National Monument. Before the arrival of Europeans, E Ohio was the scene of bloody Indian warfare when the Iroquois exterminated (1655) the Erie Indians. In addition to the Iroquois, other Indians soon prominent in the region were the Miami, the Shawnee, and the Ottawa. La Salle began his explorations of the Ohio valley in 1669 and claimed the entire area for France. The Ohio River became a magnet for fur traders and landseekers, and the British, moving in (see OHIO COMPANY), hotly contested the French claims. Rivalry for control of the forks of the Ohio River led to the outbreak (1754) of the last of the FRENCH AND INDIAN WARS. The defeat of the French gave the land to the British, but British possession was disturbed by PONTIAC'S REBELLION and the Indian flare-ups that followed. An expedition under

Henry Bouquet was sent (1763) to restore order. In an effort to prevent further Indian troubles, the British government issued a proclamation (1763) forbidding white settlement W of the Appalachian Mts. Then in 1774, with the QUEBEC ACT, the British placed the region between the Ohio River and the Great Lakes within the boundaries of Canada. The colonists' resentment over these acts contributed to the discontent that led to the American Revolution. In that war George Rogers Clark conducted military operations in the Ohio country. Ohio was part of the vast area ceded to the United States by the Treaty of Paris (1783; see PARIS, TREATY OF). Conflicting claims to land in that area made by Connecticut, Massachusetts, and Virginia were settled by relinquishment of almost all of the claims (see WESTERN RESERVE) and the organization of the Old Northwest by the ORDINANCE OF 1787. Ohio was the first region developed under the provisions of that ordinance, with the activities of the OHIO COMPANY OF ASSOCIATES promoted by Rufus Putnam and Manasseh Cutler. Marietta, founded in 1788, was the first permanent American settlement in the Old Northwest. In the years that followed, various land companies were formed, and settlers poured in from the east, down the Ohio on flatboats and barges, or across the mountains by wagon—their numbers varying with conditions but steadily expanding the population. The Indians, supported by the British, resisted American settlement. They successfully opposed campaigns led by Josiah Harmar and Arthur St. Clair but were decisively defeated by Anthony Wayne in the battle of FALLEN TIMBERS (1794). The British thereafter (1796) withdrew their outposts from the Northwest under the terms of JAY'S TREATY, and the area was pacified. Ohio became a territory in 1799. General St. Clair, as the first governor, ruled in an arbitrary fashion that made Ohioans for many years afterward distrustful of all government. In 1802 a state convention drafted a constitution, and in 1803 Ohio entered the Union, with Chillicothe as its capital. Columbus became the permanent capital in 1816. In the War of 1812 the Americans lost many of the first battles of the war in the Old Northwest and their military frontier was pushed back to the Ohio River. Two British attacks on Ohio soil were successfully resisted: one against Fort Meigs at the mouth of the Maumee River and another against Fort Stephenson on the Sandusky. The area was further secured with O. H. Perry's naval victory on Lake Erie near Put-in-Bay, Ohio, and W. H. Harrison's victory in the battle of the Thames on Canadian soil. After the war Ohio's growth was spurred by the building of the Erie Canal, other canals, and toll roads. Ohio's society of small farms exported their produce down the Ohio and the Mississippi rivers to St. Louis and New Orleans. In 1837, Ohio won a territorial struggle with Michigan usually called the Toledo War. The Loan Law, adopted in the Panic of 1837, encouraged railroad and industrial development. Railroads gradually succeeded canals, preparing the way for the industrial expansion that followed the Civil War. In the war most Ohioans were sympathetic with the Union, and the state contributed many soldiers to the Union army. Native sons such as Joshua R. Giddings, Salmon P. Chase, and Edwin M. Stanton, had long been prominent opponents of slavery. Nevertheless, the Peace Democrats, the KNIGHTS OF THE GOLDEN CIRCLE, and the COPPERHEADS were very active; Clement L. Vallandigham drew many votes in the gubernatorial election of 1863. Ohio was the scene of the northernmost penetration of Confederate forces in the war—the famous raid (1863) of John Hunt Morgan, which terrorized the people of the countryside until Morgan and most of his men were finally captured in the southeast corner of the state. After the Civil War industrial development increased rapidly when the shipment of ore from the upper Great Lakes region was intensified and the development of the petroleum industry in NE Ohio shifted the center of economic activity from the banks of the Ohio River to the shores of Lake Erie, particularly around Cleveland. Immigrants began to swell the population, and huge fortunes were made. Ohio became very important politically. The state contributed seven American presidents: Ulysses S. Grant, Rutherford B. Hayes, James A. Garfield, Benjamin Harrison, William McKinley, W. H. Taft, and Warren G. Harding. Big business and politics became entwined as in the relations of Marcus A. Hanna and McKinley. City bosses such as George B. Cox bore out this pattern. The state as a whole was for many years steadily Republican, despite the rise of organized labor in the late 19th cent. and considerable labor strife. In the 1890s the reforming mayor of Toledo, Samuel "Golden Rule" Jones, won national fame for his espousal of city ownership of municipal utilities. Floods in the many rivers flowing to the Ohio and in the Ohio River itself have long been a problem; a devastating flood in 1913 led to the establishment of the Miami valley conservation project. Continuing long-term state and Federal projects have improved locks and dams along the entire length of the Ohio and its tributaries, for navigation as well as flood control purposes. Both farms and industries in Ohio were hard hit by the Great Depression that began in 1929. In the 1930s the state was wracked by major strikes such as the sit-down strikes in Akron (1935–36) and the so-called Little Steel strike (1937). World War II brought great prosperity to Ohio, but labor strife was later resumed, as in the steel strikes of 1949 and 1959. Industrialization has continued, and Ohio has become an important center for industrial research, with Nela Park near Cleveland and Battelle Memorial Institute in Columbus being among the more notable research centers. There are also important rubber research laboratories in Akron. Ohio's cultural development has been marked by the fame achieved by the Cleveland and Cincinnati symphony orchestras and by the unusually large number of institutions of higher learning located in the state. Among them are Antioch College, at Yellow Springs; Bowling Green State Univ., at Bowling Green; Case Western Reserve Univ. (formerly Western Reserve Univ. and Case Institute of Technology), at Cleveland; Kent State Univ., at Kent; Kenyon College, at Gambier; Miami Univ., at Oxford; Oberlin College, at Oberlin; the Ohio State Univ., at Columbus; Ohio Univ., at Athens; Ohio Wesleyan Univ., at Delaware; Univ. of Cincinnati; Univ. of Toledo; and a large number of other state and private institutions. Ohio's present constitution was adopted in 1851. It has been amended many times, most notably in 1912 after a constitutional convention and the adoption of 33 changes, including many progressive labor provisions and such measures as initiative, referendum, and the direct primary. The state's executive branch is headed by a governor elected for a four-year term and permitted two successive terms. Ohio's bicameral general assembly has a senate with 33 members, elected for four-year terms (half each two years) and a house with 99 members elected for two-year terms. The state elects 2 Senators and 23 Representatives to the U.S. Congress and has 25 electoral votes in presidential elections. Republicans have played a more dominant role than Democrats in Ohio politics since the Civil War, but the Democratic party is strong and the state has often supported Democratic candidates. John J. Gilligan, a Democrat, was elected governor in 1970. In 1974, James A. Rhodes, a Republican who had been governor from 1962 to 1970, was again elected chief executive. See E. H. Roseboom and L. Roseboom, *Towboat River* (1948); D. W. Bowman, *Pathway of Progress; A Short History of Ohio* (1951); Walter Havighurst, *The Heartland: Ohio, Indiana, Illinois* (1962); G. Izant, *Ohio Scenes and Citizens* (1964); E. H. Roseboom and F. P. Weisenburger, *A History of Ohio* (rev. ed. 1967); K. W. Wheeler, *For the Union* (1968); F. A. Bonadio, *North of Reconstruction: Ohio Politics, 1865–1870* (1970); Federal Writers' Project, *Ohio Guide* (1940, repr. 1973).

Ohio, river, 981 mi (1,579 km) long, formed by the confluence of the Allegheny and Monongahela rivers in W Pa., at Pittsburgh; it flows generally northwest, then southwest and west to enter the Mississippi River at Cairo, Ill. The Ohio's course follows a portion of the southern edge of the region covered by continental ice during the Pleistocene epoch; glacial meltwater probably cut its original channel. The river is a major tributary of the Mississippi and supplies more water to it than does the Missouri River. The Ohio River basin covers c.204,000 sq mi (528,400 sq km); the chief tributaries are the Tennessee, Cumberland, Wabash, Kentucky, and Muskingum. The Ohio is prone to spring flooding, and extensive flood control and protection devices have been constructed along the river and its tributaries. These devices also improve the river's navigability; a 9-ft (2.7-m) channel is maintained along its entire length. A system of modern locks and dams, constructed since 1955 to replace older structures, speeds the transit of barges and pleasure craft; a canal (first opened in 1830) at Louisville bypasses the Falls of the Ohio, a 2¼-mi (3.6-km) long series of rapids having a 24-ft (7-m) drop. Coal and lignite account for more than half of all cargoes moved on the river; other leading commodities include sand and gravel, gasoline, and basic chemicals. The principal river ports are Huntington, W. Va., Cincinnati, Louisville, and Pittsburgh. The Ohio River basin is one of the most populated and industrialized regions of the United States. Eight states (Ill., Ind., Ky., N.Y., Ohio, Pa., Va., and W.Va.) affected by the river's pollution from factory wastes, runoff from coal mines, and discharge of raw municipal sewage ratified (1948) the Ohio River Valley Sanitation Compact; some results of their cleanup efforts are discernible, and the river now supports marinas and other recreational facilities and good fishing for carp, sunfish, and bass. The French explorer La Salle reportedly reached the Ohio River in 1669, but there was no significant interest in the valley until the French and the British began to struggle for control of the river in the 1750s. An early settlement was established at the forks of the Ohio (modern Pittsburgh) by the OHIO COMPANY of Virginia in 1749, but it was captured by the French in 1754 and the unfinished Fort Prince George was renamed Fort Duquesne; it was recaptured by the British and renamed Fort Pitt in 1758. At the end of the French and Indian Wars, Britain gained control of the river by the treaty of 1763, but settlement of the area was prohibited. Britain ceded the region to the United States at the end of the Revolutionary War (1783), and it was opened to settlement by the Ordinance of 1787, which established the Northwest Territory. Thereafter, until the opening of the Erie Canal in 1825, the Ohio River was the principal route to the newly opened West and the principal means of transporting to market the region's growing output from farms, factories, and coal mines. Traffic declined on the river after the railroads were built in the mid-1800s, but it began to revive after World War II. The new locks and dams and improvements in the channel of the river are expected to bring more traffic. See Writers' Program, *The Beautiful River* (1940); R. E. Banta, *The Ohio* (1949); Walter Havighurst, *River to the West* (1970).

Ohio and Erie Canal, former waterway of Ohio, 307 mi (494 km) long, between Lake Erie at Cleveland and the Ohio River at Portsmouth; built 1825–32. It utilized part of the courses of the Cuyahoga, Muskingum, and Scioto rivers and had 49 locks. It flourished as a means of transporting freight until the advent of the railroad era in the 1850s. The canal was responsible for the growth of cities along its route, especially Cleveland, Akron, and Columbus.

Ohio Company, organization formed (1747) to extend settlements of Virginia westward. The members were mostly Virginia planters interested in land speculation and the fur trade. A royal charter (1749) granted the members 200,000 acres around the forks of the Ohio River, and in 1750 the company employed Christopher GIST to explore the Ohio valley. The first organized group to develop the region W of the Alleghenies, the company embarked on vigorous British colonial activity. The company's colonizing activities, however, were viewed by the French as a challenge to their claim to this region. The immediate rivalry helped to bring on the final French and Indian War. Later the Ohio Company merged its interests with another land company, but the American Revolution obstructed its plans. See K. P. Bailey, *The Ohio Company of Virginia and the Westward Movement, 1748–1792* (1939); A. P. James, *The Ohio Company* (1959).

Ohio Company of Associates, organization for the purchase and settlement of lands on the Ohio River, founded at Boston in 1786. Its organizers were a group of New England men, most of them former American Revolutionary army officers. In July, 1787, one of the directors, Dr. Manasseh CUTLER, was sent to New York to a meeting of Congress to negotiate the land purchase. There he shrewdly allied himself with a group of New York speculators led by William DUER, secretary of the U.S. Treasury Board. Congress desperately needed revenue, and the prospect of selling large tracts of land in Ohio hastened its passage of the Northwest ORDINANCE OF 1787. In order to conclude the matter quickly, Cutler suggested the appointment of Gen. Arthur St. Clair, then president of Congress, as governor of the Northwest Territory. On Oct. 27 two contracts were signed by Cutler and Winthrop Sargent, secretary of the Ohio Company. The first gave to the company 1,780,000 acres (720,340 hectares) of land at the confluence of the Ohio and Muskingum rivers for a payment of $1 million in government securities, then worth about 12¢ specie to the dollar. The contract also provided that one section of land in every township be devoted to the maintenance of public schools, another section be set apart for religious uses, and two entire townships be reserved for a university. The second contract, made for William Duer, gave to the Scioto Company (as Duer and his associates were known) the option to buy 5,000,000 acres (2,023,428 hectares) of land on the Ohio and Scioto rivers. The Scioto Company's scheme was purely speculative and its contract lapsed before any land was purchased. The Ohio Company, however, had a genuine plan of settlement. In April, 1788, Gen. Rufus PUTNAM, one of the directors, began settlement of the company's land and laid out Marietta. In 1796 the company divided its shares and ceased to be a significant land company.

Ohio State University, at Columbus; land-grant and state supported; coeducational; chartered 1870, opened 1873 as Ohio Agricultural and Mechanical College, renamed 1878. Branch campuses are at Lima, Mansfield, Marion, and Newark. The university maintains extensive scientific programs and facilities, as well as notable research programs in literature, medicine, the social sciences, computer technology, engineering, and agriculture. Its library houses many important collections relating to American literature and history, religion, geology, and linguistics. In collaboration with Ohio Wesleyan Univ., it operates the Perkins Observatory near Delaware, Ohio, and the Perkins 72-in. (1.8-m) telescope near Flagstaff, Ariz.

Ohio University, mainly at Athens; state supported; coeducational; chartered 1804, opened 1809 as the first college in the Old Northwest. There are branch campuses at St. Clairsville, Chillicothe, Lancaster, Portsmouth, and Zanesville. Its facilities include a noted university museum and a library that houses a special collection relating to the history of the Northwest Territory.

Ohio Wesleyan University, at Delaware, Ohio; United Methodist; coeducational; chartered 1842, opened 1844. In 1877 it absorbed Ohio Wesleyan Female College (founded 1853). The university, in cooperation with Ohio State Univ., operates the Perkins Observatory, an important center for astronomical research.

Ohm, Georg Simon (gā'ôrkh zē'môn ōm), 1787–1854, German physicist. He was professor at Munich from 1852. His study of electric current led to his formulation of the law now known as Ohm's law. The unit of electrical resistance was named for him. He also made studies in acoustics and in crystal interference. His writings include *The Galvanic Current Investigated Mathematically* (1827, tr. 1891).

ohm [for G. S. Ohm], symbol Ω, unit of electrical resistance, defined as the resistance to the flow of a steady electric current offered by a column of mercury 14.4521 grams in mass with a length of 1.06300 m and with an invariant cross-sectional area, when at a temperature of 0°C. The megohm (1,000,000 ohms) and the milliohm (.001 ohm) are units derived from the ohm.

ohmmeter (ōm'mē"tər), instrument used to measure the electrical RESISTANCE of a conductor. It is usually included in a single package with a VOLTMETER, and often an AMMETER. In normal usage, the ohmmeter operates by using the voltmeter to measure a voltage drop, then converting this reading into a corresponding resistance reading through OHM'S LAW. If the current is known, the voltage drop across the unknown resistance may be read to give the resistance directly. If the current is not known, or if it is not possible to measure the voltage across the unknown directly, reading the voltage drop across a known resistance in the same circuit will give the current, and once this voltage is subtracted from the total drop for the circuit, the voltage drop across the unknown, and thus its resistance, may be found.

Ohm's law [for G. S. Ohm], law stating that the electric current i flowing through a given resistance r is equal to the applied voltage v divided by the resistance, or $i=v/r$. For general application to alternating-current circuits where inductances and capacitances as well as resistances may be present, the law must be amended to $i=v/z$, where z is IMPEDANCE. There are conductors in which the current that flows is not proportional to the applied voltage. These do not follow this law and are called nonohmic conductors.

Ohrid (ō'khrēd), **Ochrida,** or **Okhrida** (both: ŏ'krĭdə), town (1971 pop, 54,037), extreme S Yugoslavia, in Macedonia, on a rock above Lake Ohrid, on the Yugoslav-Albanian frontier. Macedonia's chief resort, it is a tourist and commercial center, as well as a railroad terminus. Fishing, tanning, sericulture, and the manufacture of silk textiles are also economically important. Ohrid stands on or near the site of the Greek colony of Lychnidos, founded in the 3d cent. B.C. It was captured by the Romans in A.D. 168 and became a major trade center and an early episcopal see. In the 9th cent. Ohrid was incorporated into the first Bulgarian empire, and in the 10th cent. it became the seat of the Bulgarian patriarchate and flourished as the political and cultural center of Bulgaria. Traditionally a Slavic cultural center, Ohrid served as a conduit of Christianity into other Slav-inhabited areas. After Ohrid's reconquest in 1018 by the Byzantine Empire, the patriarchate was abolished; but the town remained a metropolitan see. Ohrid was captured by the Serbs in 1334 and fell to the Turks in 1394. It was briefly reconquered by the Albanian hero Scanderbeg in the 15th cent. During World War I, Ohrid was taken by Serbian troops; after the war, it was joined to Yugoslavia. Bulgarian forces held the town during World War II, but it was then restored to Yugoslavia. Ohrid's numerous ancient churches and other historical relics include the cathedrals of St. Sophia (9th cent.) and St. Clement (1299), both with medieval frescoes; two 14th-century churches; and the walls and towers of the former Turkish citadel. The town is also noted for its museums, galleries, fishing institute, and other educational facilities.

Ohrid, Lake, Albanian *Ohrit,* deepest lake of the Balkans, c.130 sq mi (340 sq km), on the Yugoslav-Albanian border. It is connected with Lake Prepa by underground channels and is drained to the north by the Drin River. On its shores stand several monasteries, notably that of St. Naum (10th cent.).

Ohthere (ōthĕr'ə), fl. 880, Norse explorer. His account of his voyage around the North Cape, along Lapland, and into the White Sea was incorporated by Alfred the Great in the introduction to his Anglo-Saxon translation of Orosius' universal history and was requoted by Hakluyt in his *Principal Navigations.* Another voyage of Ohthere southward along the Norwegian coast and to Denmark furnished additional information on the geography of N Europe.

oil beetle: see BLISTER BEETLE.

oilbird, common name for an owllike, cave-dwelling bird, *Steatornis caripensis,* belonging to the family Steatornithidae. It spends its days in dark caves, maneuvering by means of a batlike sonar device, or echo-locator, found in its ears. The oilbird emits a clicking sound at an audible frequency of 7,000 cycles per sec, unlike the bat's cry, which is supersonic. Hence the pulsations of the oilbird can be easily detected by the human ear while the bird is in flight. For night-flying, the bird depends upon its large, highly light-sensitive eyes. Oilbirds, also called guacheros [Sp.,=one who cries], are found throughout N South America and on the island of Trinidad. As much as 13 in. (33 cm) in body length, with wingspans up to 3 ft (91 cm), they are rich brown in color with black bars and scattered white spots. They have powerful, hooked beaks surrounded by stiff, whiskerlike hairs. The beaks are used to pluck fruit while the bird hovers in the air; it never perches. Oilbirds are also the only nocturnal, fruit-eating birds. They nest in large colonies on high, rocky cave ledges, often a good distance into the cave. The female lays two to four eggs per clutch, which hatch in about 33 days. Their naked young are fed on rich, oily fruits and become grotesquely fat, reaching twice the adult weight at their maximum size. They lose this "baby fat" when their feathers begin to grow in. In the past, baby oilbirds were captured, and their fat boiled down for torch oil, hence their name. Oilbirds are classified in the phylum CHORDATA, subphylum Vertebrata, class Aves, order Caprimulgiformes, family Steatornithidae.

Oil City, city (1970 pop. 15,033), Venango co., NW Pa., on the Allegheny River; inc. 1871. The city was founded after Edwin L. Drake struck oil nearby in 1859. Today it is a major refining and shipping center for the state's oil industry and a producer of oil-field equipment. It is also a financial and banking center for NW Pennsylvania. A junior college is there. Bountiful fish and game in the area attract sportsmen.

oilcloth, originally, cloth treated with oil or other substances so as to be waterproof and used for fishermen's and sailors' wear, for coach robes and covers, and later as a floor covering, called floorcloth. Subsequently it was made of heavy canvas, jute, or burlap, sized with glue, and coated with a thick oil paint, several coats being used and successively rubbed down with pumice stone. It was machine printed, dried in a drying room, varnished, and rolled. LINOLEUM and various kinds of vinyl products have superseded oilcloth as a floor covering. A variety of oilcloth fabrics is now produced for wall, table, and shelf coverings, for raincoats, and for many small wares.

oil gas, any of a group of fuel gases produced from oil by exposing it to high temperatures. High-Btu oil gas is so called because of its high heating value; it is often used to supplement natural gas during periods of high demand. Refinery oil gases are produced as by-products during normal heat treatment in oil refining. Their chief use is in the heating of refinery equipment. Typically, oil gas consists of methane, ethane, propane, butane, and some of their derivatives.

oil of bitter almond: see BENZALDEHYDE.

oil of vitriol: see SULFURIC ACID.

oil of wintergreen: see SALICYLIC ACID.

oils, term commonly used to indicate a variety of greasy, fluid substances that are, in general, viscous liquids at ordinary temperatures, less dense than water, insoluble in water but soluble in alcohol and ether, and flammable. These substances, however, differ so much among themselves in chemical composition that, in chemistry, their classification in one group is not practical and is employed only in a general way in accordance with popular usage. PETROLEUM and substances obtained from it, which are mixtures of HYDROCARBONS, are classed together, because of their origin, as mineral oils. They are widely used as fuels, illuminants, and lubricants. Distinguished from these in that they are obtained from animals and plants and are mixtures of carbon-hydrogen-oxygen compounds are the fatty oils or fixed oils. There is fundamentally no difference between fatty oils and fats (see FATS AND OILS). Such oils are used extensively as lubricants and in the making of SOAP. Depending upon their ability to oxidize when exposed to the atmosphere and form a thin, skinlike layer over substances upon which they are spread, the fixed, or fatty, oils are classed as drying or nondrying oils. The drying oils, e.g., linseed, hempseed, and poppy seed oil, are used in making paints and varnishes. On the other hand, such vegetable oils as olive, rapeseed, and castor oil and such animal oils as lard oil and neat's-foot oil do not possess this property and fall into the nondrying group. Another large and varied group of oils is recognized, the ESSENTIAL OILS or volatile oils, which occur in plants but differ from the fixed, or fatty, oils in that they are volatile. In general, they give to the plant in which they are found its characteristic odor, flavor, or other properties peculiar to it.

oil spill: see WATER POLLUTION.

oilstone: see WHETSTONE.

Oirat Autonomous Oblast or **Oirot Autonomous Oblast:** see GORNO-ALTAI AUTONOMOUS OBLAST, USSR.

Oise (wäz), department (1968 pop. 540,988), N France, in Picardy. BEAUVAIS is the capital.

Oise, river, 186 mi (299 km) long, rising in the Ardennes mts., S Belgium, and flowing through N France generally SW past Compiègne to join the Seine River near Pontoise. Navigable for most of its length, the Oise is an important transportation route; canals link it with the Aisne and Sambre rivers.

Oisin: see OSSIAN.

Oistrakh, David Feodorovich (oi'sträk), 1908–74, Russian violinist, b. Odessa. Encouraged by his father, an amateur violinist, he began to study his instrument at the age of five. He graduated from the Odessa conservatory in 1926 and launched a brilliant concert career. In the late 1930s he was appointed professor at the Moscow conservatory and won the Stalin Prize. His concert tours in Europe and in America (after 1955) and his celebrated recordings of works by Brahms, Beethoven, Tchaikovsky, and the modern Soviet composers met with great success. Oistrakh was internationally esteemed as one of the towering violinists of his day. His son and pupil, Igor (1931–), is a virtuoso violinist.

Oita (ō'ētä), city (1970 pop. 260,576), capital of Oita prefecture, NE Kyushu, Japan, a port on Beppu Bay. It is a rail hub, a manufacturing center, and a distribution point for agricultural products. Oita was an important castle town in the 16th cent. and traded with the Portuguese. Oita prefecture (1970 pop. 1,155,623), 2,447 sq mi (6,338 sq km), is mountainous, rising to 5,850 ft (1,783 m) in Mt. Kuju. Gold, silver, and tin are mined.

Ojeda, Alonso de (älōn'sō thā ōhā'thä), c.1466–1515?, Spanish conquistador. He joined Columbus on his second voyage and in 1499—at first accompanied by VESPUCCI—explored the northeastern coast of South America. In 1508 he was made governor of territories of N South America. Near present Cartagena he was defeated by the Indians and virtually rescued by Diego de Nicuesa. Again he had trouble with the Indians and, leaving his men under the command of Francisco PIZARRO, sought aid in Hispaniola. He reached Cuba, but his actions after arrival are obscure. His men abandoned the colony and were picked up not far from Cartagena by ENCISO.

Ojibwa Indians (ōjĭb'wā", -wə) or **Chippewa Indians** (chĭp'əwā", -wə), group of North American Indians whose language belongs to the Algonquian branch of the Algonquian-Wakashan linguistic stock (see AMERICAN INDIAN LANGUAGES). In the mid-17th cent., when visited by Father Claude Jean ALLOUEZ, they occupied the shores of Lake Superior. They were constantly at war with the Sioux and the Fox over possession of the rich fields of wild rice in this region. When the Ojibwa received (c.1690) firearms from the French, they drove the Fox from N Wisconsin. They then turned against the Sioux, compelling the Sioux to cross the Mississippi River. The Ojibwa continued their expansion W across Minnesota and North Dakota until they reached the Turtle Mts. in N central North Dakota. This group became the Plains Ojibwa. In 1736 the Ojibwa obtained their first foothold E of Lake Superior, and after a series of engagements with the Iroquois, they obtained the peninsula between Lake Huron and Lake Erie. Thus by the mid-18th cent. the Ojibwa controlled a large area, from the eastern shore of Lake Huron in the east to the Turtle Mts. in the west. The Ojibwa, one of the largest tribes N of Mexico, then numbered some 25,000. They were allied with the French in the French and Indian Wars, and with the British in the War of 1812. After the War of 1812 they made a treaty with the United States, and since that time they have lived on reservations in Michigan, Wisconsin, Minnesota, and North Dakota. The Ojibwa, except for the Plains Ojibwa, were a fairly sedentary people who depended for food on fishing, hunting (deer), farming (corn and squash), and the gathering of wild rice. They obtained and used maple sugar and smoked kinnikinnick. The characteristic dwelling was the wigwam. The Ojibwa had a unique form of picture writing that was intimately connected with the religious and magico-medical rites of the Midewiwin society. Their name also occurs as Ojibway and Chippeway, but they are not to be confused with the CHIPEWYAN INDIANS. Presently the Ojibwa number some 50,000 in the United States and Canada. See Frances Densmore, *Chippewa Customs* (1929, repr. 1970); Ruth Landes, *Ojibwa Sociology* (1937, repr. 1969) and *Ojibwa Woman* (1938, repr. 1971); Harold Hickerson, *The Chippewa and Their Neighbors* (1970).

Ojos del Salado (ō'hōs thĕl sälä'thō), peak, 22,539 ft (6,870 m) high, on the border between Argentina and Chile, in the Andes. It is the second highest of the Andean peaks. In 1956 a Chilean expedition reported its height to be 23,239 ft (7,083 m), thus making it greater than Aconcagua and therefore the tallest peak in the Western Hemisphere, but this report has been unconfirmed.

Ojukwu, Chukwuemeka Odumegwu (chŏŏk"-wōōämā'kä ōdōōmäg'wä ōjōōk'wä), 1933–, Nigerian general and secessionist. Of Ibo background, he joined (1957) the Nigerian army and rose to become (1966–67) military governor of E Nigeria. That region seceded (1967) from Nigeria as the Republic of BIAFRA, with Ojukwu as head of state. He held office during the bloody war (1967–70) between Biafra and Nigeria and then went into exile in the Ivory Coast upon Biafra's defeat.

Oka (ō'kə), village, S Que., Canada, on the north shore of the Lake of the Two Mountains (a widening of the Ottawa) and SW of Montreal. It is noted as the site of a Trappist monastery and farm (est. 1881), where Oka cheese is made. Columbium is mined. An agricultural institute there is affiliated with the Univ. of Montreal.

Oka (əkä'), river, c.925 mi (1,490 km) long, rising S of Orel, central European USSR. It flows N past Orel and Kaluga, E past Serpukhov, Kolomna, and Ryazan, and then NE past Murom to join the Volga River at Gorky. It is navigable by large vessels below Kolomna, c.550 mi (890 km) upstream, and traverses densely populated agricultural and industrial areas. Among its tributaries are the Moskva, the Klyazma, and the Moksha.

Oka, river, c.600 mi (970 km) long, rising in the Sayan Mts., Buryat Autonomous Republic, S central Siberian USSR. It flows N through Irkutsk oblast to join the Angara River below Bratsk. The lower Oka valley is flooded by waters impounded behind Bratsk Dam.

Okada, Keisuke (kä'sōōkā ōkä'dä), 1862–1952, Japanese statesman and admiral. He was (1927–29, 1932–34) minister of the navy before serving (1934–36) as premier. He resigned the premiership after the abortive military coup of Feb., 1936, in which he narrowly escaped assassination. At the close of World War II, he was a key figure in pressing for a compromise peace.

Okanagan Lake (ōkənä'gən), 69 mi (111 km) long and from 2 to 4 mi (3.2–6.4 km) wide, S British Columbia, Canada. It drains southward through the Okanagan River. The lake is in a prosperous fruit-growing region.

Okanogan Indians or **Okinagan Indians** (both: ōkənä'gən), confederation of North American Indians of the Salishan branch of the Algonquian-Wakashan linguistic stock (see AMERICAN INDIAN LANGUAGES). In the late 18th cent. they numbered some 2,500. In the early 19th cent. they occupied an area extending from the west side of the Okanagan River in Washington N to British Columbia. In winter the Okanogan lived in semisubterranean earth lodges and in summer in mat or bark lodges. They fished, hunted, and gathered roots and berries. The Okanogan land claims were never adjusted. Today they live in British Columbia and, with the Colville (a related tribe), on the Colville Reservation in Washington.

okapi (ōkă'pē), nocturnal ruminant mammal, *Okapia johnstoni,* of the GIRAFFE family. It inhabits the almost sunless rain forests of the upper Congo and feeds on leaves. Its shape is reminiscent of a giraffe's, but it is smaller, with a much shorter neck. It is deep reddish brown with black and white zebra-striped legs. Its head is giraffelike and in the male bears blunt skin-covered horns. The okapi was unknown to zoologists until the beginning of the 20th cent. It is classified in the phylum CHORDATA, subphylum Vertebrata, class Mammalia, order Artiodactyla, family Giraffidae.

Okara (ōkä'rə), city (1972 metropolitan area est. pop. 142,000), N central Pakistan. It is a market for food grains, oilseed, and cotton. There is also a factory for spinning and weaving cotton.

Okavango (ōkəväng'gō) or **Kubango** (kōōbäng'-gō), Port. *Cubango,* river, c.1,000 mi (1,610 km) long, rising in the highlands of central Angola, W central Africa, and flowing southeast, across the Caprivi Strip, to the Okavango Swamp, N Botswana. It forms part of the Angola–South West Africa border. The Okavango Swamp (c.4,000 sq mi/10,360 sq km) occupies a depression that contained a large prehistoric lake. The northern part of the swamp has papyrus growth and is wet throughout the year; the rest of the swamp fills with water as the seasonal cycle progresses.

Okayama (ōkä'yämä), city (1970 pop. 375,106), capital of Okayama prefecture, SW Honshu, Japan, on an inlet of the Inland Sea. It is a railroad hub, an industrial center, and an important market for peaches and fancy matting. Stoneware, cotton textiles, machinery, chemicals, and rubber goods are produced in Okayama. The city has a 16th-century feudal castle, an 18th-century park, and a medical university. Okayama prefecture (1970 pop. 1,707,014), 2,721 sq mi (7,047 sq km), has an oil refinery and other industries.

Okeechobee, Lake (ō"kēchō'bē), c.700 sq mi (1,810 sq km), SE Fla., N of the Everglades; third largest freshwater lake and fourth largest lake wholly within the United States. It is c.35 mi (60 km) long and up to 25 mi (40 km) wide, with a maximum depth of 15 ft (4.6 m). The Kissimmee River is its chief source and the Caloosahatchee River its main outlet. In reclaiming the Everglades and adjacent lands, many canals (also used for transportation) were built extending from the southern part of the lake, itself a link in the Okeechobee Waterway. A levee, built after the disastrous hurricane of 1926, rims the lake's southern shore and protects the region from flood waters. The levees and canals have impeded the flow of water from the lake into the Everglades, which now suffers from saltwater intrusion. The drained lands bordering the lake produce vegetables and sugarcane. West of the lake, cattle are raised. Okeechobee Battlefield National Historic Landmark, the site of a large battle (1837) during the Seminole Wars, is nearby.

Okeechobee Waterway or **Cross-Florida Waterway,** 155 mi (249 km) long, across S Fla., from Stuart on the Atlantic Ocean to Fort Myers on the Gulf of Mexico. Its main segments are the St. Lucia Canal, Lake Okeechobee, Lake Hicpochee, and Caloosahatchee River. The shallow (6 ft/1.8 m) waterway has four locks and is used by small commercial and pleasure craft. It is also an outlet for the flood waters of Lake Okeechobee.

O'Keeffe, Georgia (ōkēf'), 1887–, American painter, b. Sun Prairie, Wis. After working briefly as a commercial artist in Chicago, O'Keeffe abandoned painting until she began the study of abstract design with A. W. Dow at Columbia Univ. Teachers College. Thereafter she taught art in Texas. Her work was first exhibited in 1916 at the 291 Gallery of Alfred STIEGLITZ, whom she married in 1924. Immaculate, sculptural, organic forms painted in strong, clear colors predominate in her works. Having lived much of her life in New Mexico, O'Keeffe employs numerous Southwestern motifs such as bleached bones, barren, rolling hills, clouds, and desert blooms. *Cow's Skull, Red, White, and Blue* (1931; Metropolitan Mus.) is a characteristic work. Her pristine abstract designs carry strong elements of sexual symbolism—especially her flower paintings, the most personal of her works. Using a photographic close-up technique, she reveals the exquisite recesses of calla lilies, orchids, and hollyhocks. Her later works are more purely abstract. O'Keeffe is represented nationally in major museums. See her collected drawings (1968); studies by D. C. Rich (1943) and Lloyd Goodrich and Doris Bry (1970).

Okefenokee Swamp (ō"kəfənōk', -nō'kē), c.600 sq mi (1,550 sq km), c.40 mi (60 km) long and averaging 20 mi (32 km) in width, SE Ga., extending into N Fla. It is a saucer-shaped depression with low ridges and small islands rising above the water and vegetation cover. It abounds in varied wildlife, and is drained by the Suwanee and St. Marys rivers. In Georgia the swamp makes up most of the Okefenokee National Wildlife Refuge (est. 1937).

Okeghem, Jean d': see OCKEGHEM, JOHANNES.

Okhotsk, Sea of (ōkōtsk'), Rus. *Okhotskoye More,* 590,000 sq mi (1,528,100 sq km), northwest arm of the Pacific Ocean, W of the Kamchatka peninsula and the Kuril Islands. It is connected with the Sea of Japan by Tatar and La Pérouse straits and with the Pacific Ocean by passages through the Kuril Islands. The sea is generally less than 5,000 ft (1,524 m) deep; its deepest point, near the Kuriles, is 11,033 ft (3,363 m). The sea is icebound from November to June and has frequent heavy fogs. Fishing and crabbing are carried on off W Kamchatka peninsula. Magadan and Korsakov, in the Soviet Union, are the largest ports.

Okhrida: see OHRID, Yugoslavia.

Okinawa (ō"kĭnä'wä), island (1965 pop. 812,339), 454 sq mi (1,176 sq km) W Pacific Ocean, SW of Kyushu; a part of Okinawa prefecture, Japan. It is the largest of the Okinawa Islands in the RYUKYU ISLANDS archipelago. NAHA is the largest city and chief port. Okinawa is a long, narrow, irregularly-shaped island of volcanic origin with coral formations in the southern part. The northern part is mountainous, rising to 1,657 ft (505 m), and has a dense vegetation cover. Most of the island's population is located in the south. Okinawa has a humid subtropical climate. Sugarcane, sweet potatoes, and rice are grown and fishing is important. There is some light industry in Naha. Okinawa was the scene of the last great U.S. amphibious campaign in World War II. U.S. army and marine forces landed there on April 1, 1945 and fought one of the bloodiest campaigns of the war, while the navy offshore suffered heavy damage in resisting attacks by suicide planes (see KAMIKAZE). The Japanese garrison, having lost 103,000 of its 120,000 men, ended organized resistance on June 21, 1945. U.S. casualties were 48,000, one fourth listed as dead. Okinawa was placed in Aug., 1945, under a U.S. military governor and remained under U.S. control until May, 1972, when it was returned to Japan. U.S. military bases were allowed to remain on the island. See James Belote and William Belote, *Typhoon of Steel: The Battle for Okinawa* (1970).

Oklahoma (ōkləhō'mə), state (1970 pop. 2,559,253), 69,919 sq mi (181,090 sq km), SW United States, admitted as the 46th state of the Union in 1907. OKLAHOMA CITY is the capital, and the other large city is TULSA. The state is bounded on the north by Kansas and on the east by Missouri and Arkansas; the Red River marks the southern border with Texas except in the west, where the Texas Panhandle thrusts north and reduces Oklahoma to a thin panhandle bounded in the west by New Mexico and touching Colorado in the north. The high, short-grass plains of W Oklahoma are part of the GREAT PLAINS and, like the rest of that area, are frozen by north winds in the winter and baked by soaring heat in the summer. There are wide grazing lands and broad wheat fields. The plains are broken here and there, notably by Black Mesa in the Panhandle and by the Wichita Mts. in the southwest, but the general slope is downward to the east, and central and E Oklahoma is mostly prairie, rising in the northeast to the Ozark Mts. and in the southeast to the Ouachita Mts. The

rivers that flow from west to east across the state—the Arkansas and its tributaries, the Cimarron and the Canadian (with the North Canadian) in the north, the Red River with the Washita and other tributaries in the south—are much more prominent in the east. Formerly the major crop of Oklahoma was cotton, but now wheat is the leading cash crop; however, income from livestock exceeds that from crops. Many minerals are found in the state, including coal, but the mineral that has given the state its wealth is oil. After the first well was drilled in 1888, the petroleum industry grew by fits and starts to enormous proportions, and Oklahoma City and Tulsa are among the great natural gas and petroleum centers (the two are often found together) of the world. Many of Oklahoma's factories process raw materials found in the state. There is also an important aviation industry. Oklahoma has a rich Indian heritage. The Indian population is exceeded only by that of Arizona; in 1970 there were almost 65,000 Indians in Oklahoma. Several Indian cultures, some highly advanced materially, existed in the area before the first European visited there in 1541. Francisco Coronado almost certainly crossed Oklahoma in that year in his search for Quivira, and Hernando De Soto may have visited E Oklahoma. Later Juan de Oñate passed through W Oklahoma, and some other Spanish explorers and traders and French traders from Louisiana visited the region, but there was no development of the area. The Indians roamed over the land, tribes of the Plains cultures—Osage, Kiowa, Comanche, and Apache—in the west, and the Wichita and other relatively sedentary tribes farther east. It is asserted that the first European trading post was established at Salina by the Chouteau family of St. Louis before the territory was transferred to the United States by the LOUISIANA PURCHASE in 1803, but the land remained in control of the sparse and nomadic Indian population. For the most part only traders, official explorers (notably Stephen H. Long), and scientific and curious travelers (among them Washington Irving and George Catlin) came into the present-day state. In 1819 the Adams-Onís Treaty with Spain defined Oklahoma as the southwestern boundary of the United States. After the War of 1812 the U.S. government invited the Cherokee Indians of Georgia and Tennessee to move into the area, and a few had come to settle before intense white pressure for their lands, with the approval of President Andrew Jackson, forced the Cherokee Indians and the others of the Five Civilized Tribes (the Choctaw, the Chickasaw, the Creek, and the Seminole) to abandon their old homes E of the Mississippi and to take up residence in what was to become the INDIAN TERRITORY. Their tragic removal is known as the Trail of Tears. They settled on the hills and little prairies of the eastern section and built separate organized states and communities. The Cherokee particularly had a highly Europeanized culture, with a written language, invented by their great leader Sequoyah, and highly developed institutions. Some of these Indians were slaveholders and ran their agriculture on the traditional Southern plantation pattern; others were small farmers. The Five Civilized Tribes clashed briefly with the Plains Indians, particularly the Osage, but they were for a time free from white interference, and they were able to establish a civilization that strongly affected the whole history of the region. The troubles of the whites did not, however, long escape them, and the Civil War was a major disaster. Although no major battle of the war was fought in present-day Oklahoma, there were innumerable skirmishes. Most Indians allied themselves with the Confederacy, but Unionist disaffection was widespread, and individual violence was so prevalent that many fled, leaving their farms to desolation. As a punishment for taking the Confederate side the Five Civilized Tribes lost the western part of the Indian Territory, and the Federal government began assigning lands there to such landless eastern tribes as the Delaware and the Shawnee, as well as to nomadic Plains tribes, who caused much trouble before they were subdued and settled on reservations. The territory was victimized by lawlessness and served as a hideout for white outlaws. After the establishment of a Federal court at Fort Smith, Isaac Parker became famous as the hanging judge. Immediately after the Civil War the long drives of cattle from Texas to the Kansas railroad began to cross Oklahoma, traveling over the cattle trails that became part of Western folklore. The best known is perhaps the CHISHOLM TRAIL. The cattle were fattened on the virgin ranges of Oklahoma, and cattlemen began to look on the grasslands with speculative and covetous eyes. The first railroad to cross Oklahoma was built between 1870 and 1872, and thereafter it was not possible to keep white settlers out. They came despite laws and Indian treaties, and by the '80s there was a strong admixture of whites. Ranches were developed, too, nominally owned by Indians, but actually controlled by white cattlemen and their cowboys; the region took on a tinge of the Old West of the cattle frontier, a tinge that it has never wholly lost. In the '80s, land-hungry frontier farmers, the boomers, agitated to obtain the "unassigned" lands in the western section—the lands not given to any Indian tribe. The agitation succeeded, and a large strip was opened for settlement with much fanfare on April 22, 1889. Prospective settlers lined up on the territorial border, and at high noon they were allowed to cross on a "run" to compete in finding and claiming the best lands. Those who illegally entered ahead of the set time were the sooners. Later other strips of territory were opened, and settlers poured in from the Middle West and the South. These exciting days of the opening of the region were described by Edna Ferber in her novel *Cimarron.* The western section of what is now the state of Oklahoma became the Oklahoma Territory in 1890; it included the Panhandle, that tiny strip of territory that, taken from Texas by the Compromise of 1850, had become a no-man's-land where settlers came in undisturbed. In 1893 the DAWES COMMISSION was appointed to implement a policy of dividing the tribal lands into individual holdings; the Indians resisted, but the policy was finally enforced in 1906. The wide lands of the Indian Territory were thus made available to white men. The Civilized Tribes made the best of a poor bargain, and the Indian Territory and Oklahoma Territory were united in 1907 to form the state of Oklahoma, with a constitution that included provision for initiative and referendum. Already the oil boom had reached major proportions, and the young state was on the verge of great economic development. At the same time, cotton, wheat, and corn were major money crops, and cattle-land holdings, although shrinking, were still enormous. In World War I the great demand for farm products brought an agricultural boom to the state, but in the 1920s the state fell upon hard times. Recurrent drought burned the wheat in the fields, and overplanting, overgrazing, and unscientific cropping aided the weather in making NW Oklahoma part of the DUST BOWL of the 1930s. Farm tenancy increased in the 1920s, and in both the east and west the farms tended more and more to be held by large interests and to be consolidated in large blocks. A great number of tenant farmers were compelled to leave their dust-stricken farms and went west as migrant laborers; the tragic plight of these Okies is the theme of John Steinbeck's *Grapes of Wrath.* With the return of sparse rains, however, and with increasing care in selecting crops and in conserving and utilizing water and soil resources, much of the Dust Bowl was again made into productive farm land. The demands for food in World War II and Federal price supports for agricultural products after the war aided farm prosperity. Large state and Federal programs for conserving the water of rivers and for supplying irrigation have resulted in the construction of many large dams and reservoirs, such as the reservoir impounded by Fort Gibson Dam on the Grand River, resulting in improved agricultural conditions and creating new recreation areas. (For more detailed information on irrigation projects, see separate articles on the rivers of Oklahoma.) Platt National Park, the site of extensive mineral springs, and Arbuckle National Recreation Area are in S Oklahoma. In 1971, the opening of the Oklahoma portion of the Arkansas River Navigation System gave the cities of Muskogee and Tulsa direct access to the sea. During the 1920s two governors, John C. Walton and Henry S. Johnston, were impeached. Prohibition, in effect since statehood, was repealed in 1959. A judicial scandal in the 1960s resulted in a thorough reform of the judicial system. The original 1907 constitution is still in effect. Oklahoma has a legislature of 48 senators and 99 representatives, both elected for two-year terms. The governor is elected for a four-year term. The state elects two U.S. Senators and six Representatives and has eight electoral votes. In statewide politics Oklahoma has been consistently Democratic, although earlier in the century there were strong third-party movements. In 1962 the Republicans elected a governor for the first time. Richard Nixon carried the state in 1960, 1968, and 1972. In 1974, David L. Boren, a Democrat, was elected governor. The most important institutions of higher learning in the state are the Univ. of Oklahoma and Oklahoma State Univ. See Federal Writers' Project, *Oklahoma: A Guide to the Sooner State* (1941, rev. ed. 1957); E. E. Dale and M. L. Wardell, *History of Oklahoma* (1948); V. E. Harlow and Gene Aldrich, *Oklahoma: Its Origins and Development* (rev. ed. 1955); C. Osborn, *Oklahoma Comes of Age* (1965); A. M. Gibson, *Oklahoma; A History of Five Centuries* (1965); V. E. Harlow, *Oklahoma History* (5th ed. 1967); E. C. McReynolds, *Oklahoma: A History of the Sooner State* (rev. ed. 1971); Alice Marriott and C. K. Rachlin, *Oklahoma* (1973).

Oklahoma, University of, mainly at Norman, state supported; coeducational; chartered 1890, opened 1892. The schools of medicine and nursing, with hospitals and a research foundation, are at Oklahoma City. At Lake Texoma is a biological research station.

Oklahoma Agricultural and Mechanical College: see OKLAHOMA STATE UNIV.

Oklahoma City (1970 pop. 368,856), state capital, and seat of Oklahoma co., central Okla., on the North Canadian River; inc. 1890. It is an important livestock market, the state's wholesale and distributing center, and a farm trade and processing point. Oil is a major product; the city is situated in the middle of an oil field (opened 1928), and there are wells even on the capitol grounds. The city has large stockyards and meat-packing houses, grain mills, and cotton-processing plants. The nearby Tinker Air Force Base, a logistics center with one of the world's largest air depots, is an important source of civilian employment. Oklahoma City was settled overnight in a land rush after the area was opened to homesteaders on April 22, 1889. It became the state capital in 1910. The second largest city in land area in the United States (650 sq mi/1,683 sq km), it extends into three counties and has many parks. Of interest are the capitol, the state historical museum, the National Cowboy Hall of Fame and Western Heritage Center, the state fair park, the civic center buildings and monuments, a theater complex, a new convention center, the state library, the Oklahoma Health Sciences Center, and a zoo. Educational institutions include Oklahoma City Univ., Oklahoma Christian College, the medical school of the Univ. of Oklahoma, and several junior colleges. The city has a symphony orchestra.

Oklahoma State University, at Stillwater; land-grant and state supported; coeducational; chartered 1890, opened 1891 as Oklahoma Agricultural and Mechanical College, renamed 1957. There are technical branches at Oklahoma City and Okmulgee.

Okmulgee (ōk"mŭl'gē), city (1970 pop. 15,180), seat of Okmulgee co., E central Okla., in an oil and farm area; inc. 1900. It is an agricultural processing center and has two large glass plants and an oil refinery. It was founded on the site of the Creek capital (1868–1907) and boomed with the discovery of oil in 1907. An old Creek Indian council house (1878) is on the town square. A state technical school is in Okmulgee and nearby are an Indian mission (1882) and Lake Okmulgee.

Okolona (ōkəlō'nə), town (1970 pop. 17,643), Jefferson co., NW Ky., a suburb of Louisville.

okra: see MALLOW.

okrug (ō'kro͝og, Rus. ô'kro͞ok) [Rus.,=area], administrative division in the USSR. There are only national okrugs in existence at present. They form the lowest type of autonomous unit in the Soviet "ladder of nationalities." Okrugs are sparsely settled ethnic minority areas that are smaller than a kray (territory), and that usually have populations of less than 100,000. National okrugs have a local council and one representative in the Soviet of Nationalities of the Supreme Soviet of the USSR. There are ten national okrugs, all for the peoples of Siberia and the far North (Aga Buryat, Komi-Permyak, Koryak, Nenets, Taymyr, Ust-Orodynski Buryat, Khanty-Mansi, Chukotsk, Evenki, and Yamalo-Nenets); all were formed between 1929 and 1937. Originally conceived by sympathetic ethnographers as a kind of reservation, the national okrugs have become an instrument for integrating the lives of the natives into the Soviet system.

Okubo, Toshimichi (tō"shēmē'chē ō'kōōbō), 1830–78, Japanese statesman. A major figure in the Meiji restoration, he was influential in introducing Western ideas to Japan. He supported the emperor against the shogun and worked to eliminate feudalism. A powerful figure in the new government, he put down (1873) the party favoring war with Korea. In 1874 he became home minister and sponsored a military expedition to Taiwan. After the Satsuma rebellion of 1877 (see SAIGO, TAKAMORI), in which he took the government side, he was assassinated, presumably by a fellow clansman of Satsuma. See biography by Masakaza Iwata (1964).

Okuma, Shigenobu (shēgā'nōbōō ō'kōōmä), 1838–1922, Japanese statesman. He was an early supporter of the emperor and entered the Meiji government as finance minister in 1869. In 1876 he had the annual stipends of the former feudal aristocracy changed to payments in lump sums, with great saving for the state. His power in the government grew steadily, and by 1881 he was the only oligarch able or inclined to challenge the conservative and autocratic ideals of Hirobumi ITO. In 1881, Okuma publicly urged the government to set up a parliament and embarrassed the Ito clique by exposing their fraudulent scheme to sell government assets in Hokkaido. The oligarchs, fearing growing popular support for Okuma, persuaded the emperor to oust him. Okuma founded (1882) a reform party called the Kaishinto (a forerunner of the Minseito) and agitated for parliamentary government. However, Okuma's connections with the Mitsubishi business interests (see ZAIBATSU) were publicized, and his prestige, and that of democratic government, declined. As foreign minister (1888–89), he negotiated to revise the unequal treaties with the Western powers, which limited Japan's tariff autonomy and permitted extraterritoriality for Europeans. The bomb of a terrorist who opposed the Japanese government's attempt to find a compromise cost Okuma a leg. He again served as foreign minister in 1896 and 1897, and during this period the unequal clauses in the treaties were finally eliminated. In 1898 he and ITAGAKI merged their parties to form the Kenseito (Constitutional party). During his second premiership (1914–16) the army was expanded, and Japan, entering World War I on the Allied side, seized Kiaochow and presented China with the TWENTY-ONE DEMANDS.

Olaf I (Olaf Tryggvason) (ō'läf trüg'väsōn), c.963–1000, king of Norway (995–1000), great-grandson of Harold I. His early life of exile and slavery is surrounded with romantic legend, and little is definitely known of it. He aided his father-in-law, the duke of Poland, in war and took part in harrying the English coast. He may have been present at the famous battle of MALDON. Later converted to Christianity, he made peace (c.994) with the English. In 995, Olaf went to Norway, overthrew Haakon, and became king. He undertook the conversion of Norway to Christianity by force and by persuasion. He commissioned Lief Ericsson to carry Christianity to Greenland. Olaf died during his defeat at the naval battle of Svolder. The victors, King Sweyn of Denmark and King Olaf of Sweden, divided Norway.

Olaf II (Saint Olaf), c.995–1030, king of Norway (1015–28). He is also called Olaf the Stout or Olaf the Fat. He spent part of his early life in England and helped Æthelred fight the Danes. He was converted to Christianity, and when he returned (1015) to Norway he zealously tried to Christianize the country. He established himself by defeating Earl Sweyn, and then he proceeded to unify the country politically and to establish the new religion. He antagonized the nobles by employing men of humbler birth as royal officials. When CANUTE of England and Denmark asserted his right to the overlordship of Norway, many nobles deserted Olaf for the Dane. Olaf attacked Denmark, but the expedition ended in a fruitless naval battle. In 1028, Olaf defeated a leading noble, but the murder of the vanquished man by one of Olaf's men led to a powerful insurrection. Olaf fled to Russia, and Canute became king with Earl Haakon as viceroy. After Haakon was drowned at sea, Canute's son, Sweyn, was named king. Olaf made an attempt to regain his kingdom in 1030, only to lose his life in the battle of Stiklestad. He came to be considered the patron saint of Norway. Harold III was his half brother, Magnus I his son. Feast: July 29.

Olaf V, 1903–, king of Norway (1957–), son and successor of Haakon VII. In 1929 he married Princess Martha of Sweden (d. 1954). Following the German invasion of Norway, Olaf took an active part in the struggle for liberation. He assumed supreme command of the Norwegian forces in 1944 and returned to Norway in 1945. His son Harald (Harold) is heir to the throne.

Olaf Guthfrithson (gūth'frĭth"sən), d. 941, Norse king of Dublin (934–41). His father, Guthfrith, king of Dublin and of York, had been driven out of England by ATHELSTAN in 927. Olaf led (937) his allies, Constantine of Scotland and Owen of Strathclyde, against Athelstan in the battle of Brunanburh and was severely defeated. He returned to Ireland, but after Athelstan's death he invaded (939) York. A treaty between Olaf and King EDMUND, successor of Athelstan, gave Olaf control over Northumbria and part of Mercia. His successor, **Olaf Sihtricson** (sĭt'rĭk"sən), d. 981, often called Olaf Cuaran, was expelled from Northumbria by Edmund in 944. He returned to rule in Ireland, where he was in 980 defeated at the battle of Tara. He died a penitent at the monastery of Iona.

Olafsfjörður (ō'läfsfyör"thür), town, N Iceland, near the mouth of the Eyjafjörður. It is a fishing port.

Öland (ō'länd), narrow island (1969 est. pop. 26,750), 520 sq mi (1,347 sq km), Kalmar co., SE Sweden, in the Baltic Sea, separated from mainland Sweden by the Kalmarsund. Borgholm is the chief town; there are many summer resorts on the island. Sugar beets, cereals, and vegetables are grown, and cattle are raised. The island also has some industries and a fishing fleet. Öland has numerous monuments dating from the Stone Age and was first mentioned in the 8th cent. It has often been a battleground in the frequent wars among the Scandinavian countries.

Olathe (ōlā'thē), city (1970 pop. 17,917), seat of Johnson co., NE Kansas, near Kansas City; inc. 1858. Its manufactures include aircraft communication and guidance systems, batteries, machinery, and plastic components. The city's name is derived from the Shawnee Indian word for *beautiful*.

Olbers, Heinrich Wilhelm Matthäus (hīn'rĭkh vĭl'hĕlm mätē'ōōs ôl'bərs), 1758–1840, German physician and astronomer. He originated (1797) the first satisfactory method for calculating the orbits of comets, but despite the fame it brought him, he remained an amateur astronomer and became a physician. However, he continued his research on comets and discovered several. He was the first to detect the comet of 1815 (Olbers's comet, period 72.7 years). He also discovered two asteroids, Pallas (1802) and Vesta (1807). Considering their orbits and those of the other asteroids then known, he concluded that they are fragments of a disrupted planet that had formerly revolved around the sun.

Olbia (ŏl'bēə), Ionic Greek colony of Miletus, founded at the beginning of the 6th cent. B.C. It is on the right bank of the Bug River between Nikolayev and Ochakov, S central Ukrainian SSR. The leading Milesian colony and later a republic, its economy centered around handicrafts and trade. Its prosperity resulted especially from the exportation of wheat. The period of its flowering was from the 6th cent. B.C. to the 3d cent. B.C. In the 2d cent. B.C., Olbia was incorporated into the Scythian state of the Crimea. About the middle of the 1st cent. B.C., Olbia was invaded by the Getae and others. By the end of the 6th cent. life in Olbia came to a standstill. Excavations have unearthed towers and city gates from the Hellenic period and parts of a fortified wall and a temple of Apollo from the Roman period.

Olcay, Osman (ōsmän' ōljī'), 1924–, Turkish diplomat. He joined the ministry of foreign affairs in 1945 and quickly rose in the diplomatic service. From 1954 to 1963 he was involved in North Atlantic Treaty Organization (NATO) affairs. He was ambassador to Finland (1964–66), and to India and Ceylon (1966–68), deputy secretary general of NATO at Brussels (1969–71), and foreign minister (1971). In 1972 he was made Turkey's permanent representative at the United Nations.

old age: see GERIATRICS.

old-age pension: see PENSION; SOCIAL SECURITY.

Oldbury: see WARLEY.

Old Castile, Spain: see CASTILE.

Oldcastle, Sir John, 1378?–1417, English leader of LOLLARDRY. He married the heiress of Lord Cobham in 1408 and was known as "the good Lord Cobham." Under the rule of Henry IV he performed valuable military service, especially in Wales, where he became a friend of the prince of Wales (later Henry V). His devotion to the teachings of John WYCLIF brought upon him in 1413 condemnation for heresy. Oldcastle escaped from the Tower of London and was active in Lollard conspiracies until 1417, when he was captured and condemned. He was executed by hanging over a slow fire.

Old Catholics, Christian denomination, established by German clergy and laymen who separated themselves from the Roman Catholic Church when they rejected (1870) the decrees of the Vatican Council, especially the dogma of the infallibility of the pope. The Old Catholic movement began publicly with a meeting of professors at Nuremberg in 1870 under the leadership of Johann Joseph Ignaz von DÖLLINGER. By 1874 a new church had been established with a bishop consecrated by a Dutch Jansenist bishop. It rejected communion with the pope and many Roman Catholic doctrines and practices. The church was greatly influenced by Protestantism, and although the Roman ritual was retained (in German), priests were allowed to marry, and confession was made optional. National churches are found in many countries including the Netherlands, West Germany, Central Europe, and the United States; total membership is estimated at about 1 million. See C. B. Moss, *The Old Catholic Movement* (2d ed. 1964).

Old Church Slavonic: see CHURCH SLAVONIC.

Oldenbarneveldt, Johan van (yōhän' vän ôl"dənbär'nəvĕlt), 1547–1619, Dutch statesman. He aided WILLIAM THE SILENT in the struggle for Dutch independence from Spain and opposed the dictatorial policy set by Robert Dudley, earl of LEICESTER, chosen by the States-General as governor general in 1586. After Leicester's departure (1587) he helped to concentrate military power in the hands of MAURICE OF NASSAU. Made permanent advocate of Holland in 1586, Oldenbarneveldt controlled the civil affairs of the United Provinces (in which Holland was prominent). He represented the patrician manufacturing and commercial oligarchies that ruled Amsterdam, Rotterdam, and Dordrecht; and during his administration Dutch commerce expanded spectacularly, and the Dutch East India Company was founded. He negotiated (1609) a 12-year truce with Spain, despite the objections of Maurice of Nassau, and thus secured virtual recognition of Dutch independence. As leader of the party favoring control of state affairs by the States-General, Oldenbarneveldt was increasingly opposed by the party of the nobles and the house of Orange. This conflict was aggravated by the fierce struggle of the REMONSTRANTS and the strict Calvinists; in this quarrel, Oldenbarneveldt and Maurice of Nassau found themselves in opposing camps. In 1618, Maurice, determined to crush the Remonstrants, convoked the Synod of Dort, which condemned their doctrine. Oldenbarneveldt was arrested and, after a highly irregular trial for treason, was sentenced to death. His execution was a judicial murder brought about by his personal enemies; no incriminating evidence has ever been found against Oldenbarneveldt, who was one of the ablest and most patriotic statesmen in the history of the Dutch.

Oldenburg, Claes, 1929–, Swedish-American artist, b. Stockholm. A leader of the POP ART movement, Oldenburg explores the ironic and humorous aspects of common objects that he grossly distorts in scale and shape. He is noted for his soft sculptures of stuffed cloth and his giant objects (e.g., *Giant Saw, Hard Version*, 1969; Vancouver Art Gall.). His giant monument, *Lipstick*, was erected at Yale in 1969. His work is represented in the Museum of Modern Art and Whitney Museum, both in New York City. See study by Barbara Rose (1970).

Oldenburg (ôl'dənbōōrkh), former state, NW West Germany. It is now included in the state of LOWER SAXONY. The city of Oldenburg was the capital. The former state consisted of three widely separated divisions. The largest of these, Oldenburg proper, now forms the district of Oldenburg, stretching S from the North Sea, W of the Weser River; the two other divisions, both very small, were BIRKENFELD and the district (but not the city) of LÜBECK. Oldenburg proper is a low-lying, fertile, and marshy land. The history of Oldenburg is mainly of dynastic significance. Originally a part of Saxony, the county of Oldenburg came into prominence in the 12th cent., when the counts became princes of the empire. In 1448, Count Christian became king of Denmark as Christian I, while his younger brother, Gerard, and his successors continued to rule Oldenburg. On the extinction (1667) of the German line, Oldenburg passed (1676) to Christian V of Denmark (direct descendant of Christian I). In 1773, Christian VII exchanged Oldenburg for ducal HOLSTEIN with Grand Duke (later Emperor) Paul I of Russia, heir of the Danish cadet line of Holstein-Gottorp. Paul gave Oldenburg to his maternal great uncle, Frederick Augustus of Holstein-Gottorp, bishop of Lübeck, who assumed (1777) the ducal title. Peter I of Oldenburg, nephew and successor of Frederick Augustus, lost his duchy to Napoleon I but recovered Oldenburg and the bishopric of Lübeck in 1813 and subsequently acquired Birkenfeld and obtained the title grand duke. A member of the German Confederation from 1815, Oldenburg sided (1866) with Prussia in the Austro-Prussian War and joined (1871) the German Empire. The last grand duke abdicated in 1918, and Oldenburg joined the Weimar Republic.

Oldenburg, city (1970 pop. 130,852), Lower Saxony, NW West Germany, on the Hunte River and the Küstenkanal (Coast Canal). It is a rail junction, transshipment point, agricultural market, and industrial center. Manufactures include machinery, glass, chemicals, and textiles. Oldenburg was first mentioned in 1108 and was chartered in 1345. It was the seat of the counts of Oldenburg until 1667, when it passed, with the county, to Denmark. From 1777 to 1918 it served as the residence of the dukes (later grand dukes) of Oldenburg. Noteworthy buildings include the former ducal palace (17th–18th cent.) and the Gothic Lambertikirche, a church built in the 13th cent. (rebuilt 18th–19th cent.).

Old English: see TYPE; ENGLISH LANGUAGE; ANGLO-SAXON LITERATURE.

old English sheepdog, breed of large, wiry WORKING DOG developed in England in the early 19th cent. It stands from 21 to 25 in. (53.3–63.5 cm) high at the shoulder and weighs from 55 to 65 lb (24.9–29.5 kg). Its double coat is composed of dense, water-resistant underhairs and a profuse, harsh, curl-free outercoat. It may be any shade of gray, grizzle, blue, or blue-merle, with or without white. The tail is bobbed to approximately 1½ in. (3.8 cm). The old English sheepdog was originally raised in W England as a drover of sheep and cattle. Today it is popular as a farm dog and show dog and as a pet. See DOG.

Old Faithful, geyser: see YELLOWSTONE NATIONAL PARK.

Oldfield, Anne, 1683–1730, English actress. The successor of Mrs. Bracegirdle, she first won acclaim in 1704 for her brilliant portrayal of Lady Modish in Colley Cibber's *Careless Husband.* She had a triumphant career in both tragedy and comedy, being noted for her majestic and powerful style. Her portrayal of Jane Shore in Rowe's drama was particularly admired. She is buried in Westminster Abbey.

Oldham, John (ōl'dəm), c.1600–1636, colonist in New England, b. England. A trader, he emigrated to Plymouth in 1623 but was banished (1624) because of his opposition to the strict government. Later he was involved in establishing the unsuccessful settlement on Cape Ann (1626), several of the settlements in the Massachusetts Bay colony, and Wethersfield, Conn. His murder by the Pequot Indians on Block Island was one of the events leading to the Pequot War (1637).

Oldham, John, 1653–83, English poet and satirist. His best-known works are the ironical *Satires against the Jesuits* (1681) and *A Satire against Virtue* (1679). He was much admired by Dryden, who wrote the beautiful "To the Memory of Mr. Oldham," included in Oldham's collected works (1684).

Oldham, county borough (1971 pop. 105,705), Lancashire, NW England. It is a center of cotton spinning and has numerous mills, foundries, and engineering works. There is coal in the vicinity. The town hall, the art gallery, the museum, and Alexandra Park are noteworthy. There is a 17th-century grammar school and a College of Further Education. In 1974, Oldham became part of the new metropolitan county of Greater Manchester.

Old Hundred: see DOXOLOGY.

Old Ironsides: see CONSTITUTION, ship.

Old Lyme (līm), residential and resort town (1970 pop. 4,964), New London co., SE Conn., on Long Island Sound, at the mouth of the Connecticut River; settled c.1655, inc. 1855. Its fine old houses built by sea captains have attracted many artists to the town. The Congregational Church (1817; burned in 1909, but carefully restored) has been portrayed by Childe Hassam.

Oldman, river, c.250 mi (400 km) long, rising in the Rocky Mts., SW Alta., Canada, and flowing generally E past Lethbridge to join the Bow River W of Medicine Hat and form the South Saskatchewan River. The Belly River is its chief tributary. The Oldman flows through a farming region; wheat and sugar beets are the main crops. Bituminous coal is mined along the river.

Old Man of the Mountain, in Islamic history: see ASSASSIN.

Old Man of the Mountain, N. H.: see FRANCONIA MOUNTAINS.

old-man's-beard, name for several plants, among them a CLEMATIS and a SAXIFRAGE.

Old Norse literature, the literature of the Northmen, or Norsemen, c.850–c.1350. It survives mainly in Icelandic writings, for little medieval vernacular literature remains from Norway, Sweden, or Denmark. The Norwegians who settled Iceland late in the 9th cent. brought with them a body of oral mythological poetry that flourished there in a sturdy, seafaring world removed from the warring mainland. The first great period, which lasted until c.1100, was oral, as writing was not introduced until well after the establishment of Christianity (c.1000). From c.1100 to c.1350 both the oral poetry and new compositions were set down. The conscious, clear prose style that developed for both saga and history antedates that of all other modern European literatures except Gaelic. In the later 13th cent., with Iceland's loss of independence to Norway, literary activity declined and had virtually disappeared a century later. The surviving body of literature can best be discussed as consisting of several types. Eddic writings (see EDDA) were condensations of ancient lays, in alliterative verse (see ALLITERATION), on old gods and heroes. Also composed in alliterative verse, but more complex and artificial in form, was scaldic poetry, which flourished in Norway about the 10th cent., reaching its height slightly later in Iceland. Comprising poems of praise, triumph, lamentation, and love, it is subjective in approach and highly mannered in technique. Intricate metrical schemes are meticulously observed, and diction is polished to the point of preciousness, especially in the incessant use of the kenning (a metaphoric substituted phrase, e.g., "ship-road" for "sea"), found also in ANGLO-SAXON LITERATURE. As the scalds became a group apart, and only the initiated could understand their highly allusive verse, SNORRI STURLUSON was prompted to write the *Prose Edda* (c.1222) as a text of scaldic poetry, in a vain attempt to promote and preserve the old techniques. As scaldic poetry declined, new forms rose to replace it, among them the ballad and the sacred hymn. A new rhymed verse developed, somewhat analogous to that in MIDDLE ENGLISH LITERATURE and used for much the same purpose—translation and paraphrase of foreign ROMANCES. The bulk of medieval Norse literature, and the most readable today, survives in the form of SAGAS, that is, prose narratives, sometimes interspersed with verse, which relate the lives of legendary or historical figures with objectivity and skillful characterization and which reflect the old Icelandic devotion to personal honor and family. Historical writing of the 11th and 12th cent. is also noteworthy. In this field Snorri Sturluson contributed his *Heimskringla.* Ari Thorgilsson produced *Islendingabok* (c.1125), an account of the island's history, an abridged version of which has survived. He was probably partly responsible also for the *Landnamabok,* a topographical and genealogical account of Iceland; other works by Thorgilsson have been lost. Finally, all the Scandinavian countries produced medieval ballads, but these were not written down until much later. There remain numerous unsolved problems concerning oral composition, transmission of origins and influences, and dating. See studies by H. R. Davidson (1943, repr. 1968) and L. M. Hollander (1945, repr. 1968); Stefan Einarsson, *A History of Icelandic Literature* (1957); *Old Norse Literature and Mythology,* ed. by E. C. Polomé (1969).

Old Northwest: see NORTHWEST TERRITORY.

Old Orchard Beach, town (1970 pop. 5,404), York co., SW Maine, on the Atlantic coast; settled c.1631, inc. 1883. For many years a popular resort, it has a beach and amusement facilities. There was a trading post nearby before 1630.

Old Pretender: see STUART, JAMES FRANCIS EDWARD.

Old Red Sandstone, series of red and brown sandstones and shales deposited in Wales and Scotland and in England near the Welsh and Scottish borders in the DEVONIAN PERIOD of geologic time. The Old Red Sandstone, in contrast to the typical formations of the Devonian, is largely a continental formation, laid down in fresh water and on land as a result of the erosion of the highlands of the SILURIAN PERIOD. It is very thick in Scotland and contains a large assemblage of fossils, particularly of the Devonian fishes, in a remarkable state of preservation. The Old Red Sandstone was correlated with the marine Devonian by the British geologists Rodney Murchison and Adam Sedgwick. Popular interest in the formation and its fossils was created largely by the work of the Scottish geologist Hugh Miller.

Olds, town (1971 pop. 3,376), S Alta., Canada, N of Calgary, in a stock, dairy, and wheat-farming region. It has grain elevators and is the seat of a provincial agricultural school.

Old Sarum (sâr'əm), site of a former city, Wiltshire, S England, just N of SALISBURY (New Sarum). Excavations in the mound on which the settlement stood have revealed remains of an ancient British camp, the Roman station Sorbiodunum, a still later Saxon town, and a Norman town. The seat of the bishopric, moved to Old Sarum from Sherborne in 1075, was transferred to Salisbury in 1220, and Old Sarum's great cathedral was torn down, parts of it being used in the construction of the cathedral at Salisbury. At Old Sarum the Use of Sarum, a ritual adopted in S England, was compiled. Old Sarum was important until strife between the men of the castle and garrison and the men of the religious institution caused the removal of the see to the new site and the decay of the old city; shortage of water and exposure to winds may also have been causes of its decline. The "rotten borough" of Old Sarum continued to be represented in Parliament until the Reform Bill of 1832 was passed.

Old Stone Age: see PALEOLITHIC PERIOD.

Old Style dates: see CALENDAR.

Old Testament, Christian name for the Hebrew Bible, which serves as the first portion of the Christian Bible (c.f. NEW TESTAMENT). It consists of a varying number of books, given in varying order. The contemporary Jewish reckoning is as follows: (1) the TORAH or Law, the five books of the Pentateuch, i.e., Genesis, Exodus, Leviticus, Numbers, and Deuteronomy; (2) the Prophets, consisting of Joshua, Judges, First and Second Samuel, First and Second Kings, Isaiah, Jeremiah, Ezekiel, and the Twelve (or Minor) Prophets; (3) the Writings (Hagiographa), a heterogeneous group to which belong (a) Psalms, Proverbs, and Job, (b) the Scrolls (*Megillot*), consisting of the Song of Solomon (Song of Songs), Ruth, Lamentations, Ecclesiastes, and Esther, (c) Daniel, Ezra, Nehemiah, and First and Second Chronicles. The canon of the Jews as it stands was adopted A.D. c.100; the traditional order and the extant Hebrew texts all derive from one Hebrew source of the first centuries of the Christian era, the MASORA; the origin of the Masoretic version is unknown. The Old Testament long used in the Christian church was derived not from the Masoretic but from an entirely different text. The SEPTUAGINT, a Hellenistic Jewish translation into Greek about the 3d cent. B.C., became the Old Testament of Christianity, and later translations were made from it or patterned after it. The canon of the Septuagint was entirely different from that of the Masora. The Latin Bible found its official form in the VULGATE, the work of St. Jerome; this largely agreed with the list of books of the Septuagint, and the list and order of the Vulgate was the canon accepted by the Western Church; this is also called the Western canon. At the Reformation the English Protestants withdrew recognition of the canonicity of those portions of the Old Testament that appeared in the Western canon but not in the Masoretic canon, considering them (the deuterocanonical books) suitable for instruction but not as necessarily inspired; this position had been suggested in earlier times by St. Jerome. To set them clearly apart from the works considered inspired, the Authorized Version (AV; see BIBLE) translators put them together in an appendix to the Old Testament, which they entitled APOCRYPHA. Thus the Reformed canon became exactly like the Masoretic, with a difference of order—AV retaining the Western order. The difference between the Western and the Reformed canon is seen by comparing the AV with the Douay version (representing the Western canon). The following are the books of the Old Testament (AV), the names in parentheses being usual names in the Douay when it differs from that in AV, those in italics being the books appearing in Douay and not in AV: Genesis, Exodus, Leviticus, Numbers, Deuteronomy, Joshua (Josue), Judges, Ruth, First and Second Samuel (First and Second Kings), First and Second Kings (Third and Fourth Kings), First and Second Chronicles (First and Second Paralipomenon), Ezra (First Esdras), Nehemiah (Second Esdras), *Tobias, Judith,* Esther, Job, Psalms, Proverbs, Ecclesiastes, Song of Solomon

(Canticle of Canticles), *Wisdom, Ecclesiasticus,* Isaiah (Isaias), Jeremiah (Jeremias), Lamentations, *Baruch,* Ezekiel (Ezechiel), Daniel, Hosea (Osee), Joel, Amos, Obadiah (Abdias), Jonah (Jonas), Micah (Micheas), Nahum, Habakkuk (Habacuc), Zephaniah (Sophonias), Haggia (Aggeus), Zechariah (Zacharias), Malachi (Malachias), First and Second *Maccabees.* The critical study of the Old Testament is called HIGHER CRITICISM when dealing with literary-historical problems and lower criticism when dealing with questions of a purely textual nature. Chronology and authorship present great difficulties. So far as historical dating is concerned, many systems have been devised. Before the 1st millennium B.C. there is little likelihood of any outside source against which to check biblical chronology, but from the time of David it is possible to devise a chronology with some checks from nonbiblical sources. Of the various chronological systems none is sure; no single system is accepted by more than a few historians. The authorship of the books of the Old Testament is known from tradition and internal evidence. The books from Genesis to Nehemiah (except Ruth) present similar problems and are usually grouped together in considering authorship. The higher criticism of the mid-19th cent. assaulted the traditions about the Bible, its text, and its very credibility. Of no books was this truer than of the so-called "historical" books. With the turn of the century there was begun a gradual recession from the extreme stand, because archaeological finds tended to support rather than to impugn the veracity of the narratives. The following expresses to some extent the opinion of a less extreme criticism: In the 10th cent. B. C. the first of a series of editors collected materials from earlier traditional folkloric and historical records (i.e., both oral and written sources) to compose a narrative of the history of the Hebrews. Stemming from differing traditions originating among those living in what was later the northern kingdom of Israel and those in the southern kingdom of Judah, we can trace two dominant compilations, known as the E and the J, respectively. These were combined by a Judaean some time after the fall of the northern kingdom and are to be found inextricably associated in Genesis, Exodus, Numbers, Joshua, Judges, and First and Second Samuel. According to scholars, this combined JE narrative is the bulk of the earlier Old Testament, and it is unreliable in that it consists in the rewriting or rearranging of old traditions rather than in anything that the authors knew at first hand. To Deuteronomy critics assign a late 7th-century (B.C.) authorship, considering the "finding of the Law" a pious fable. Deuteronomy, they believe, was written for a specific purpose—to provide a written law for the people. Leviticus was, according to some scholars, composed soon after 570 B.C. by a man (called H) in close sympathy with the aspirations of Ezekiel. Deuteronomy is not the only book representing the group that sponsored the reforms, for most of First and Second Kings is said to have been composed by persons of the same point of view. These "Deuteronomists," according to this thesis, used old sources and pointed their moral constantly. One of the principal sources of the first six books, in the higher criticism, is called P or Priestly Code. This, the product of the legalistic atmosphere of the first postexilic period, is seen in parts of all the first six books, but most notably in Numbers. P, with D (Deuteronomy), JE, and H, then, make up the first and oldest portion of the Bible. The books of Chronicles and of Ezra and Nehemiah are, according to the critics, not history at all, but a long moral account of the Jews, showing the rewards for goodness and the retribution for evil. The author of these four books, called the Chronicler, is put in the late 4th cent. B.C. The lateness of date of composition is, generally, the chief matter of difference between the higher critics and other biblical critics. See also DEAD SEA SCROLLS and BIBLICAL ARCHAEOLOGY. See C. A. Briggs, *General Introduction to the Study of Holy Scripture* (rev. ed. 1900, repr. 1970); S. R. Driver, *An Introduction to the Literature of the Old Testament* (rev. ed. 1913, repr. 1961); W. F. Albright, *From the Stone Age to Christianity* (1940, repr. 1967); Aage Bentzen, *Introduction to the Old Testament* (2d ed. 1952, repr. 1967); R. H. Pfeiffer, *The Books of the Old Testament* (1957, repr. 1965); C. H. Gordon, *The World of the Old Testament* (1958); J. A. Brewer, *The Literature of the Old Testament* (3d ed. rev. 1962); R. C. Dentan, *Preface to Old Testament Theology* (rev. ed. 1963); H. F. Hahn, *Old Testament in Modern Research* (rev. ed. 1966).

Old Vic, London theater, opened in 1914 by Lilian Baylis as a Shakespearean repertory company. *The Taming of the Shrew* was its first production, and by 1923 the entire works of Shakespeare had been presented. Since Baylis's death in 1937 the theater has continued to flourish as the home of Shakespeare and of other classic revivals and as the training ground for many an accomplished actor. Since 1963 it became the temporary home of the NATIONAL THEATRE OF GREAT BRITAIN.

Olean (ōˈlēănˈˈ), city (1970 pop. 19,169), Cattaraugus co., W N.Y., on the Allegheny River near the Pa. line; settled 1804, inc. 1893. Manufactures include diesel engines, compressors, tile, plastics, and electrical and electronic parts. St. Bonaventure Univ. and Seminary are nearby. Ski resorts and a state park are in the area.

oleander: see DOGBANE.

oleaster (ōˈˈlēăsˈtər), common name for members of the Elaeagnaceae, a family principally of shrubs with leathery leaves and a dense covering of glistening hairs. Most members of the family are steppe and rock plants of the Northern Hemisphere; a few species are indigenous to the United States. Several are cultivated as hardy ornamental shrubs, especially the buffalo berry (*Shepherdia argentea*), whose edible fruits were gathered by Indians and by the Alaskan Eskimos; the common oleasters (*Elaeagnus augustifolia* and related species); and the sea buckthorn (*Hippophaë rhamnoides*), a native of the Old World. Oleaster is classified in the division MAGNOLIOPHYTA, class Magnoliopsida, order Myrtales.

olefin (ōˈləfĭn) or **olefin series:** see ALKENE.

Oleg (ōˈleg, Rus. ôlĕkˈ), d. c.912, founder of Kievan Russia. Succeeding his kinsman RURIK as leader of the VARANGIANS at Novgorod, Oleg led forth his retainers to seize Kiev (c.879). He made Kiev his capital and set about uniting the Slavic tribes along the Volkhov-Dnepr waterway, freeing them from the overlordship of the Khazars. Oleg concluded commercial treaties with the Byzantine Empire in 907 and 911, making trade with the empire a major factor in the Kievan economy and opening the path for Greek Christian cultural penetration. Oleg was succeeded by IGOR.

Olekma (əlyĕkˈmə), river, c.820 mi (1,320 km) long, rising in the Yablonovy range, SE Siberian USSR. It flows N through Amursk oblast and the Yakut Autonomous Republic to the Lena River below Olekminsk.

Olenek (əlyĭnyôkˈ), river, c.1,350 mi (2,200 km) long, rising in the central Siberian plateau, Krasnoyarsk Kray, E Siberian USSR. It winds E then N through NW Yakut Autonomous Republic to the Laptev Sea. It is navigable for c.600 mi (970 km) upstream and abounds in fish.

oleomargarine: see MARGARINE.

Oléron (ôlārôNˈ), island (est. pop. 15,000), 68 sq mi (176 sq km), Charente-Maritime dept., W France, in the Bay of Biscay. It is an oystering, farming, and ranching area and a summer vacation spot. The Law of Olérón (see MARITIME LAW), promulgated by Louis IX, was named after the island. Oléron was a stronghold of Protestantism in the 16th cent. A bridge (1966) links it with the mainland.

oleum: see SULFURIC ACID.

oligarchy (ŏlˈəgärkē) [Gr.,= rule by the few], rule by a few members of a community or group. When referring to governments, the classical definition of oligarchy, as given for example by Aristotle, is of government by a few, usually the rich, for their own advantage. It is compared with both ARISTOCRACY, which is defined as government by a few chosen for their virtue and ruling for the general good, and various forms of DEMOCRACY, or rule by the people. In practice, however, almost all governments, whatever their form, are run by a small minority of members. From this perspective, the major distinction between oligarchy and democracy is made on the basis of the degree of effective and regularized consent by the majority of members to such minority rule and the extent and type of barriers impeding those who attempt to join this ruling group.

Oligocene epoch (ŏlˈəgōsēnˈˈ), third epoch of the TERTIARY PERIOD in the CENOZOIC ERA of geologic time. More of North America was dry land during the Oligocene than in the preceding EOCENE EPOCH. The Gulf Coast was flooded, but the Atlantic coast N of South Carolina became emergent; the principal formation of the Gulf district was the Vicksburg limestone. The Pacific coast, like the more northern Atlantic coast, was largely elevated; erosion led to the deposition of the Oligocene portion of three sediments (the Sespe conglomerate, sandstone, and shale), which contains red beds like those of the Permian period. Over large areas of W Nebraska and NE Colorado and parts of Wyoming and the Dakotas, great erosion of the Rockies was responsible for the White River clays and sands, which are noted for the mammalian fossils that are widely exposed in the badlands of these states. Late in the Oligocene, the John Day deposits of volcanic ash, notable for their included fossils, were formed in Oregon. In S Europe, the formations are somewhat similar to those of the Eocene; a sandstone and shale formation, the Flysch, was laid down in regions adjacent to mountain systems. The Alpine mountain building episode reached peak intensity as Africa further impinged against the Eurasian plate (see PLATE TECTONICS). Arabia split away from Africa along the Red Sea rift at this time also. In the middle Oligocene a sea extended over N Europe from as far east as the Urals and was connected with the greater Mediterranean through the present Rhine valley. There are extensive deposits of Oligocene lignite in Germany, indicating swamp conditions either before or during the flood, and the Alsatian potash, salt, and gypsum are Oligocene. During the Oligocene there was considerable volcanic activity in central Europe, Scotland, Ireland, and Iceland, as well as in the San Juan Mts. of Colorado and the Absaroka Mts. of Wyoming where in Yellowstone National Park remnants of this volcanism remains. The life of the Oligocene was marked in Europe and North America by the virtual disappearance of the archaic mammals of the Paleocene. True carnivores—ancestral dogs, cats, and saber-toothed animals—made their appearance, along with beavers, mice, rabbits, and squirrels. A more highly developed type of horse, giant hogs, and camels were other new arrivals. The titanotheres—mammals remotely related to the horse and the rhinoceros—evolved to types of great size, then died out. The brontotherium, which appeared in North America, was the largest mammal to ever live on that continent. Running, aquatic, and true rhinoceroses developed. The earliest elephant and a primitive anthropoid ape appeared in Africa. The climate of the Oligocene was mild and temperate in North America.

oligopoly: see MONOPOLY.

oligosaccharide: see CARBOHYDRATE.

Ólimbos: see OLYMPUS, mountains, Greece.

Olinda (ōōlēnˈdə), city (1970 pop. 196,471), Pernambuco state, E Brazil, on the Atlantic Ocean. Founded in 1537, it was captured by the Dutch in the 1630s and burned to the ground. The rebuilt city served as a provincial capital until 1827. Olinda's reputation as a center of learning dates from 1796, when a Jesuit seminary was founded there.

Oliphant, Laurence (ŏlˈĭfənt), 1829–88, British author, b. Capetown, South Africa. Although he wrote some valuable travel books, he is probably best remembered for his fascinating life. The son of a judge, he became a lawyer and later secretary to Lord ELGIN. He was a correspondent for the London *Times* during the Crimean War, went with Elgin to China, was an associate of Garibaldi, and traveled all over the world. In 1867 he became a disciple of Thomas Lake HARRIS in a religious community at Brocton, N.Y. His writings include several travel books, notably *A Journey to Katmandu* (1852); two novels, *Piccadilly* (1866) and *Altiora Peto* (1883); an autobiography, *Episodes in a Life of Adventure* (1887); and *Scientific Religion* (1888). He and his first wife, Alice Le Strange, wrote a curious book, *Sympneumata: Evolutionary Forces Now Active in Man* (1885), inspired by Harris and supposedly dictated by a spirit. After Alice's death Oliphant married (1888) Rosamond Dale Owen, granddaughter of Robert Owen. They established a colony of Jews in Palestine. See her *My Perilous Life in Palestine* (1928); biography by his cousin, Margaret Oliphant (1891); study by V. and R. A. Colby (1966).

Oliphant, Margaret Oliphant (Wilson), 1828–97, Scottish author. She was widowed at the age of 31 and subsequently supported her own three children and her brother and his family. Astonishingly prolific, she wrote many novels, including a series about life in a Scottish village called *Chronicles of Carlingford* (1863–76); the best novels in the series were *Salem Chapel* and *Miss Marjoribanks.* She wrote guidebooks; semihistorical works, such as *The Makers of Modern Rome* (1895); and biographies of Sheridan (1883) and her cousin Laurence Oliphant (1891), among others. See her *Days of My Life* (1857), and her autobiography (1899).

Olisipo: see LISBON, Portugal.

Olitski, Jules (ōlĭtˈskē), 1922–, American painter, b. Russia. Although considered a color-field painter (see POST-PAINTERLY ABSTRACTION), Olitski produces works that are freer and less severe than many of those associated with the movement. Using a spray gun, he covers large canvases with several layers of varied pastel colors, creating a soft, atmospheric effect. See study by Kenneth Moffett (1973).

Oliva, Peace of (ōlē'və, -vä), 1660, treaty signed at Oliva (now a suburb of Gdańsk) by Poland and Sweden. John II of Poland renounced the theoretical claim of his line to the Swedish crown, which his father, Sigismund III, had in practice lost in 1599. Poland furthermore confirmed Sweden in possession of N Livonia. Frederick William, elector of Brandenburg, was recognized in full sovereignty over Prussia (later known as East Prussia) but in turn confirmed Pomerelia (later West Prussia) as Polish.

Olivares, Gaspar de Guzmán, conde-duque de (gäspär' dā gōōthmän' kōn'dā-dōō'kā dā ōlēvä'rās), 1587–1645, Spanish statesman. He was appointed chief minister on the accession (1621) of PHILIP IV, over whom he had earlier gained influence. Honest and hardworking, he fought corruption at the court, prosecuted the unscrupulous ministers of Philip III, and endeavored to restrict the privileges and landed wealth of the church. He did not, however, repudiate Spanish subservience to Austria, and Spain became involved more widely in the THIRTY YEARS WAR, resuming the war with the Netherlands (1621) and entering conflicts in Italy. Olivares's centralizing policy within Spain led to an uprising, supported by France, in Catalonia and to the secession (1640) of Portugal. To obtain funds for his campaigns he resorted to oppressive measures. His unpopularity led to his fall in 1643. Olivares was a patron of the arts and literature and encouraged the painters Rubens, Velázquez, and Murillo and the writers Lope de Vega and Quevedo y Villegas.

olive, common name for the Oleaceae, a family of trees and shrubs (including climbing forms) of warm temperate climates and of the Old World tropics, especially Asia and the East Indies. Many are popular ornamentals, particularly the LILAC (*Syringa*), true JASMINE (*Jasminum*), PRIVET (*Ligustrum*), and FORSYTHIA genera; of these only the last has species native to the United States. Several indigenous species of ASH (*Fraxinus*) are valuable for timber in North America. The true olive (*Olea europaea*) is the source of the fruit also called olive and of olive oil; it is the most commercially important member of the family. The olive tree, a small evergreen, has been cultivated since the beginning of historical times in its native Asia Minor. Its cultivation spread very early to all the Mediterranean countries, and this is still the chief area of production. It is now grown also in Australia, S Africa, Mexico, and California, where it was introduced (c.1769) at the San Diego mission by Spanish missionaries. The mission olive of today, one of the best varieties for both pickling and oil, was developed from the trees grown at the mission. The several hundred horticultural varieties of olives, many cultivated since ancient times, differ in appearance, flavor, and oil content. Some varieties have been developed especially for oil extraction, the chief use of the fruit. Of the eating olives, green olives are picked when full-grown but unripe, and are often pitted and stuffed with pimientos or anchovies. Ripe olives, usually purplish black, are richer in oil. Both green and ripe olives are treated with lye to remove the bitter quality and then packed in brine. Olive wood, hard and close-grained, is used for cabinetwork and furniture. According to Greek mythology the olive was Athena's gift to mankind, and Athens was named in her honor for this gift. The olive branch has been the symbol of peace since before Christian times, because the oil could be used both to heal human ills and to calm troubled waters. The first vegetation seen by Noah after the Deluge was the branch of olive brought back by the dove, and a dove bearing an olive branch has also been used in art as a symbol of peace. Olives are classified in the division MAGNOLIOPHYTA, class Magnoliopsida, order Scrophulariales, family Oleaceae.

olive oil, clear, bland, yellowish oil expressed from the olive. Oil makes up about 25% of the whole ripe fruit. Olive oil was used in the ancient world for lighting, in the preparation of food, and as an anointing oil for both ritual and cosmetic purposes. It is produced mainly in the Mediterranean Sea area, i.e., Algeria, Greece, Italy, Morocco, Portugal, Spain, Tunisia, and Turkey. Although olive oil occupies a relatively minor place in world food consumption, it is an essential commodity for those regions where the olive is grown. However, it has, in recent years, become a stronger export item, and several international agreements have been signed since 1959 to protect the olive oil market. The yield of oil varies with the climate, cultivation, and variety of olive. For the finest, or virgin oil, the fruit is gathered before it is fully ripened, peeled, and subjected to gentle pressure without heat. Ripe fruit yields more oil of a less perfect flavor. A second pressure yields lesser grades of commercial edible oil; then the pulp may be mixed with water to produce technical oils, used in industrial processes. Finally a solvent may be used to obtain the lowest grade. Machine manipulation removes pits and crushes by hydraulic pressure. Edible oil may vary in color from clear white to a golden yellow or a yellowish green. The oil is separated from the juice by settling and is washed, filtered, and aged. For use in cold climates it is now often clarified by removing the stearin, or solid part of the fat. It may be extensively adulterated by the addition of such oils as cottonseed, sesame, and others, but laws in the United States require that it be labeled as salad oil if it contains foreign ingredients. Olive oil contains a large proportion of easily digested fats. The principal fat in the diet of countries where it has long been cultivated, olive oil is often used in place of cream and butter and as a salad oil and cooking fat. Although olive oil is chiefly used as a food or in food preservation, it has other uses; it is used in textile soaps, certain pharmaceuticals, and cosmetics.

Oliver, Andrew, 1706–74, lieutenant governor of colonial Massachusetts (1771–73), b. Boston. Oliver was elected to the provincial council in 1746 and later served as secretary of the province. His acceptance of the post of stamp officer after the passage of the Stamp Act led to violent demonstrations against him, which forced him to resign the office. He became lieutenant governor in 1771, but popular indignation against him broke out again in 1773 as the result of the discovery of private letters he and Gov. Thomas HUTCHINSON had written to England criticizing the colonists and recommending coercive measures.

Oliver or **Olivier, Isaac** (ŏlĭv'ēər), 1556?–1617, English miniature painter. Oliver was a worthy follower of Hilliard as miniature painter to Elizabeth's court. His work, more naturalistic than Hilliard's, is to be seen in the British and the Victoria and Albert museums, London, and in the Cleveland Museum. His son and pupil, **Peter Oliver,** c.1594–1648?, was also an important miniaturist. He painted numerous watercolor copies of old masters, most of which are now in Windsor Castle.

Oliver, King (Joseph Oliver), 1885–1938, American jazz musician, b. Abend, La. Oliver began his professional career in 1904 with the Onward Brass Band. After playing with leading bands in New Orleans and establishing himself as a master cornetist, he moved to Chicago in 1918. From 1920 to 1923 he led the Creole Jazz Band, which became the greatest exponent of the New Orleans, or "Dixieland," jazz idiom. Oliver's style was noted for its bursting, exuberant power and its great range. He strongly influenced Louis ARMSTRONG. See M. T. Williams, *King Oliver* (1961).

Olives, Mount of, or **Olivet** (ŏl'ĭvĕt), ridge, E of Jerusalem, mentioned in the Old Testament as the scene of David's flight from the city, Ezekiel's theophany, and Zechariah's prophecy, and in the New Testament as a frequent resort of Jesus and the scene of his Ascension. The principal hill of the mount is often called "the Ascension." Bethany and Bethphage lie near its foot, and the garden of Gethsemane is on the western slope. 2 Sam. 15.30; Ezek. 11.23; Zech. 14.4; Mat. 21.1; Acts 1.12.

Olivier, Isaac: see OLIVER, ISAAC.

Olivier, Laurence Kerr, Baron Olivier of Brighton, 1907–, English actor, director, and producer. Olivier is often referred to as the greatest actor of the 20th cent. He made his stage debut at Stratford-on-Avon in 1922 and soon achieved renown through his work with the Old Vic company. Noted for his remarkable versatility, he has been brillantly successful in the classics, in modern realistic plays, and in comedy. After 1930 he made a number of outstanding films including *Wuthering Heights* (1939), *Rebecca* (1940), *Pride and Prejudice* (1940), *Henry V* (1944), *Richard III* (1956), *The Entertainer* (1960), *Othello* (1965), *Three Sisters* (1970), and, for television, *Long Day's Journey into Night* (1973) and *The Merchant of Venice* (1974). In 1948 he won an Academy Award for his portrayal of Hamlet in the film that he also produced and directed. In 1962, Olivier was appointed director of the National Theatre of England. Under his direction it has mounted many distinguished productions and become one of the finest repertory companies in the world. Olivier was knighted in 1947 and in 1970 was created a life peer, the first actor to be so honored. He is married to the actress Joan Plowright. See Felix Barker, *The Oliviers* (1953); *Olivier*, a collection of memoirs by his friends, ed. by Logan Gourlay (1973). Olivier was often co-starred on stage and screen with his second wife, **Vivien Leigh,** 1913–67, whose best-known films include *Gone with the Wind* (1939), *Waterloo Bridge* (1940), *Lady Hamilton* (with Olivier as Nelson, 1941), and *A Streetcar Named Desire* (1951). For the first and last films named she won an Academy Award.

Olivier, Sydney Haldane Olivier, 1st Baron, 1859–1943, British colonial administrator. Olivier was interested throughout his life in socialism and was one of the first members of the FABIAN SOCIETY, contributing to the famous *Fabian Essays* (1889). He was colonial secretary in Jamaica from 1899 to 1904 and later governor of the island (1907–13). In 1924 he was secretary of state for India during Ramsay MacDonald's brief Labour government and was raised to the peerage. A number of his works deal with colonial questions, among them *White Capital and Coloured Labour* (1906, rev. ed. 1927) and *The Anatomy of African Misery* (1927). See his letters and selected writings (ed. with a memoir by Margaret Olivier, 1948).

olivine (ŏlĭv'ēn), an iron-magnesium silicate mineral, $(Mg,Fe)_2SiO_4$, crystallizing in the orthorhombic system. It is a common constituent of silica-poor igneous rocks; dunite consists almost entirely of olivine, and peridotite consists of olivine admixed with pyroxene. It also occurs in lunar rocks and meteorites. It has a characteristic yellow-green to olive-green color, hence the name. Transparent olivine of good color can be cut into attractive gemstones; the gem form is known as peridot. The principal sources of gem-quality olivine are St. John's Island in the Red Sea, Burma, and Arizona. Magnesium-rich olivine has a very high melting point and is used in the manufacture of refractories. It was formerly called chrysolite.

Ollivant, Alfred, 1874–1927, English novelist. He wrote the classic dog story *Bob, Son of Battle* (1898), published in England as *Owd Bob*. Other works include *The Gentleman* (1908), *The Royal Road* (1912), *Boy Woodburn* (1917), and *Tomorrow* (1927).

Ollivier, Émile (āmēl' ôlēvyā'), 1825–1913, French statesman, a leading figure in the "Liberal Empire" of Napoleon III. Widely known as a brilliant lawyer, he was elected to the legislature in 1857. He and Jules FAVRE were the chief figures of the liberal opposition that sought to gain reforms by constitutional means. After 1863, Ollivier cooperated with the duc de MORNY to gain liberal concessions from Napoleon and gradually drew away from his republican colleagues to lead a new liberal group supporting cooperation with the government. Growing public discontent led Napoleon to call on Ollivier to form a ministry, and the Ollivier ministry was organized in Jan., 1870. The new ministry instituted sweeping constitutional reforms, transforming the empire into a parliamentary regime. Unfortunately, the dispute over the Hohenzollern succession in Spain soon erupted into hostilities in the FRANCO-PRUSSIAN WAR. Although Ollivier was initially opposed to war, he endorsed the final decision to declare war on Prussia. Replaced as premier (Aug., 1870), Ollivier went to Italy. He returned to France after three years and spent his later life writing historical and political books, many of them in defense of his ministry. His major collection is *L'Empire libéral* (18 vol., 1895–1918). See his *Journal, 1846–1869* (1961, in French); biography by Theodore Zeldin (1963).

olm: see MUD PUPPY.

Olmec (ŏl'mĕk), term for the culture of ancient Mexican Indian peoples of the tropical lowlands of the present-day states of Veracruz and Tabasco. The Olmecan period is tentatively dated from c.500 B.C. to A.D. 1150. The earliest evidences at La Venta (Tabasco) and Tres Zapotes (Veracruz) show a highly developed agricultural civilization. The Olmec left behind huge sculptured heads, carved of basalt and sometimes weighing over 20 tons. The bar and dot system of recording time was in use, and, if the earliest date (31 B.C.) is correctly deciphered, Olmec use antedates the earliest definitely known date (A.D. 320) of the Maya, who are often credited with having originated the system. The Olmec influenced the cultures of the ZAPOTEC, the MIXTEC, and the TOLTEC. See Ignacio Bernal, *The Olmec World* (tr. 1969).

Olmsted or **Olmstead, Frederick Law,** 1822–1903, American landscape architect and writer, b. Hartford, Conn. He first attained fame for accounts of his travels in the South in the early 1850s, in which he painted vivid pictures of slaveholding society—*A*

Journey in the Seaboard Slave States (1856), *A Journey through Texas* (1857), *A Journey in the Back Country* (1860), and *Journeys and Explorations in the Cotton Kingdom* (1861). His *Walks and Talks of an American Farmer in England* had already appeared in 1852. When Central Park in New York City was projected, he and Calvert Vaux prepared the plan that was accepted, and Olmsted superintended its execution. The well-planned park was a new departure, which was developed by Olmsted in other cities, e.g., Prospect Park, Brooklyn, N.Y.; South Park, Chicago; Mt. Royal Park, Montreal; and park systems in Buffalo and Boston. Perhaps his most spectacular achievement was the laying out of the grounds (afterward Jackson Park) in Chicago for the World's Columbian Exposition in 1893. He also took an interest in the creation of state and national parks and in city planning. See his *Forty Years of Landscape Architecture: Central Park,* ed. by F. L. Olmsted, Jr., and Theodora Kimball (1928, repr. 1973); biography by L. W. Roper (1974); studies by J. G. Fabos et al. (1968) and Elizabeth Barlow (1972). His son, **Frederick Law Olmsted** or **Olmstead,** 1870–1957, b. Staten Island, N.Y., grad. Harvard, 1894, was also a landscape architect and city planner. He studied with his father and began practice in 1895. He taught (1900–1914) Harvard's first course in landscape architecture. As a city planner he served on many committees and government boards. In 1901 he was influential in the plan for beautifying Washington, D.C.

Olmütz: see OLOMOUC, Czechoslovakia.

Olney, Jesse, 1798–1872, American geographer and teacher. His *Practical System of Modern Geography* (1828), a standard work for decades, revolutionized the teaching of geography; his method was to familiarize the student with his own environment and then progress to the study of more distant places. He served in the Connecticut legislature for eight terms, was elected state comptroller in 1867, and wrote textbooks and a volume of poetry.

Olney, Richard, 1835–1917, American cabinet member, b. Oxford, Mass. He was a successful Boston lawyer and had served briefly in the state legislature before President Cleveland appointed him to his cabinet. As Attorney General (1893–95), he obtained an injunction against the strikers in the PULLMAN STRIKE of 1894; under it Eugene V. DEBS was held in contempt of court. Olney also persuaded Cleveland to send in troops to break the strike, ostensibly to prevent interference with the mails, although Gov. John P. ALTGELD declared troops unnecessary. In 1895, Olney became Secretary of State. He played a vigorous part in the negotiations with the British over the VENEZUELA BOUNDARY DISPUTE. In the course of the talks he stated flatly that the United States is "practically sovereign on this continent, and its fiat is law upon the subjects to which it confines its interposition." This principle was later supported by Theodore Roosevelt as a corollary of the MONROE DOCTRINE. See biography by Henry James (1923, repr. 1971); study by G. G. Eggert (1974).

Olomouc (ô'lômōts), Ger. *Olmütz,* city (1970 pop. 79,931), N central Czechoslovakia, in Moravia, on the Morava River. Olomouc is an industrial city, with factories producing steel, machinery, electrical equipment, and food products, especially candy and chocolate. An ancient town, it was once the leading city of Moravia and was strongly fortified. In 1242, Wenceslaus II of Bohemia defeated the Mongol invaders there. Also at Olomouc, in 1469, Matthias Corvinus, king of Hungary, had himself crowned king of Bohemia. The city was held by the Swedes from 1642 to 1650. In 1758, Frederick II besieged it unsuccessfully. An agreement between Austria and Prussia was signed there (1850), dissolving the German Union under Prussia's presidency and restoring the German Confederation, headed by Austria. Prussia smarted under the "humiliation of Olmütz" until 1866, when it defeated Austria in war. Present-day landmarks include the Cathedral of St. Wenceslaus (begun 12th cent.), the city hall (rebuilt 13th cent.), and two Gothic churches. Also in the city are a university (founded 1566), the Cyril-Methodius theological faculty, and several libraries. The Marquis de Lafayette was once imprisoned in Olomouc's fortress. Today there are lovely parks and gardens where the fortress formerly stood.

Ólonos, Mount: see ERYMANTHOS, mountains, Greece.

Olson, Charles, 1910–70, American critic and poet, b. Worcester, Mass., grad. Harvard (B.A., 1932; M.A., 1933). His literary reputation was established with *Call Me Ishmael* (1947), a study of the influence of Shakespeare and other writers on Melville's *Moby Dick.* Later he became noted as a poet. Olson wrote what he called "projective" (open) verse, which he believed transmitted energy from the past to the reader. His works include *The Maximus Poems* (1960 and 1968), *Casual Mythology* (1969), and *Poetry and Truth* (1971).

Olson, Floyd Bjornstjerne, 1891–1936, American lawyer and politician, b. Minneapolis. In his early life he was an itinerant laborer and for a time belonged to the Industrial Workers of the World. He studied law at the Univ. of Minnesota and at the Northwestern College of Law in Minneapolis and in 1915 was admitted to the bar. As county attorney (1920–30) of Hennepin co., he brought about an investigation of graft in the Minneapolis city council. Elected governor of Minnesota three times (1930, 1932, and 1934) on the Farmer-Labor ticket, Olson won national attention in 1933 by threatening to declare martial law and confiscate private wealth unless the legislature enacted relief measures to deal with depression conditions. A strong supporter of the New Deal, he led in the repeal of the Minnesota newspaper "gag" laws, ordered a two-year moratorium on mortgage foreclosures of farms, secured relief for the unemployed, and openly sided with labor in a series of strikes that occurred after 1934. See biography by G. H. Mayer (1951).

Olsztyn (ôl'shtĭn), Ger. *Allenstein,* city (1970 pop. 94,119), N Poland. It is a trade, manufacturing, and railroad center. Founded (1348) by the Teutonic Knights, who built its impressive castle, it was ceded to Poland in 1466 and to Prussia in 1772. The city was retained by Germany after a plebiscite in 1920. It suffered heavy damage in World War II and reverted to Poland in 1945.

Olten (ôl'tən), town (1970 pop. 21,209), Solothurn canton, N Switzerland, on the Aare River. It is an important rail center and has manufactures of aluminumware, shoes, and chemicals.

Oltenia: see WALACHIA.

Olympas (ōlĭm'pəs), Christian at Rome. Rom. 16.15.

Olympia, city (1970 pop. 23,111), state capital, and seat of Thurston co., W Wash., at the southern tip of Puget Sound, on Budd Inlet; inc. 1859. It is a port of entry. Lumber products and beer are manufactured and there are oyster fisheries. Settled in 1846, it was made capital of the newly created Washington Territory in 1853. Of interest are a state historical museum, the state library, the fine old capitol building (1893), and the newer, imposing group of white sandstone capitol buildings. A local attraction is the annual salmon run from Budd Inlet into Capitol Lake. St. Martin's College and Evergreen State College are there, and an Indian reservation and a state park are nearby. The Olympic Mts. may be seen to the north, and Mt. Rainier to the east.

Olympia, important center of the worship of Zeus in ancient Greece, in Elis near the Alpheus (now Alfiós) River. It was the scene of the OLYMPIC GAMES. The great temple of Zeus, which was situated between the Cladeus and Alpheus rivers, was especially celebrated for the ivory, gold-adorned statue of Zeus by Phidias—one of the SEVEN WONDERS OF THE WORLD. Excavation, which revealed the great temple, also uncovered the Hermes of Praxiteles, several other temples within the sacred enclosure (called the Altis), and the stadium.

Olympiad, unit of a chronological ERA of ancient Greece, a four-year period, each one beginning with the OLYMPIC GAMES. TIMAEUS (c.356–c.260 B.C.) of Sicily was the first to use, as a check on chronology, the list of victors kept in the gymnasium at Olympia. The first Olympiad was reckoned to have begun in 776 B.C.

Olympian, in Greek religion, one of the 12 important gods who succeeded the Titans as rulers of the universe. The divine family of the Olympians was headed by Zeus, who ruled the heavens and earth, and his queen, Hera. Zeus' brothers, Poseidon and Hades (also called Pluto), ruled the sea and underworld respectively. The divine children were Ares, Hermes, Apollo, Hephaestus, Athena, Aphrodite, and Artemis. It was said that Zeus' sister Hestia, who was also an Olympian, resigned her place to Dionysus. The Olympians, whose honors and attributes have come down to us almost entirely through Homer and Hesiod, lived in majestic splendor on Mt. Olympus. Similar to human beings in both physical appearance and character traits, the gods feasted on ambrosia and nectar and took special delight in their mortal loves. About the 6th cent. B.C. the Olympian gods began to yield in importance to the mystery cults (see MYSTERIES).

Olympias, d. 316 B.C., wife of PHILIP II of Macedon and mother of ALEXANDER THE GREAT. She did not get on well with Philip, who had other wives, but the story that she murdered him is probably false. She reputedly had great influence in molding her son and in giving him an interest in mysticism and in art. Her violent ambitions plunged her into quarrels with Antipater, whom Alexander had left as regent in Macedonia, and after Alexander's death she tried to forestall CASSANDER, Antipater's son, in Macedonia. He in turn besieged her in Pydna on the Gulf of Thessaloníki, and after her capture he ordered her execution.

Olympic elk: see WAPITI.

Olympic games, principal athletic meeting of ancient Greece, and, in modern times, series of international amateur sports contests. The ancient Greek games were held in the summer once every four years at Olympia in honor of Zeus. According to tradition, the competitions were initiated in 776 B.C., when the first OLYMPIAD began. They were the greatest festival in the Greek world from the 6th cent. B.C. and were at their height in the 5th and 4th cent. B.C. However, they became more and more professionalized until in the Roman period they provoked much censure. They were eventually discontinued by Emperor Theodosius I of Rome at the end of the 4th cent. A.D. Among the Greeks, the games were nationalistic in spirit and states were said to have been prouder of Olympic victories than of winning battles. Women, foreigners, slaves, and dishonored persons were forbidden to compete. Contestants were required to train faithfully for 10 months before the games, had to remain 30 days under the eyes of the people of Elis, who had charge of the regulation of the games, and had to take an oath that they had faithfully observed training before participating in the events. At first, Olympic games were confined to running; Coroebus was the official winner of the foot race in 776 B.C. Over a period of time many new events were added—the long run (720 B.C.), when the loin cloth was abandoned and athletes began appearing naked; the PENTATHLON (708 B.C.); boxing (688 B.C.); chariot racing (680 B.C.); the pancratium (648 B.C.), involving boxing and wrestling contests for boys (632 B.C.); and the foot race with armor (580 B.C.). Greek women, forbidden not only to participate in but also to watch the Olympic games, held games of their own, called Heraea, said to have been founded by Hippodameia. Those were also held every four years but had fewer events. Known to have been conducted as early as the 6th cent. B.C., the Heraea games were discontinued about the time the Romans conquered Greece. The winners of the Olympics (and of the Heraea) were crowned with chaplets of wild olive, and in their home city-states the male champions were also awarded many valuable gifts and privileges. A list of Olympic winners from 776 B.C. to A.D. 217 was drawn up by Julius Africanus and was preserved by Eusebius. The glory of the Olympic games was heightened by the introductory procession, the call of the trumpet, religious festivities, and banquets. The poetry of PINDAR celebrates the athletic triumphs at Olympia. Pausanias also wrote on the Olympics. The modern revival of the Olympic games is due in a large measure to the efforts of Pierre, baron de Coubertin, of France. They were first held, appropriately enough, in Athens in 1896, but that meeting and the ones that followed at Paris (1900) and at St. Louis (1904) were hampered by lack of sufficient organization and the absence of worldwide representation. The fact that the meeting at St. Louis attracted few but American competitors led to a special unofficial meet in 1906 at Athens under Greek auspices. The first successful meet was held at London in 1908. Successive Olympic games were held at Stockholm (1912), Antwerp (1920), Paris (1924), Amsterdam (1928), Los Angeles (1932), Berlin (1936), London (1948), Helsinki (1952), Melbourne (1956), Rome (1960), Tokyo (1964), Mexico City (1968), and Munich (1972). World War I prevented the Olympic meeting of 1916, and World War II brought about the cancellation of the 1940 and 1944 meetings. The number of entrants, of competing nations, and of athletic events has gradually increased. To the traditional TRACK AND FIELD ATHLETICS, which includes the DECATHLON and pentathlon, were added a host of games and sports—cycling, swimming, shooting, fencing, volleyball, rowing, water polo, basketball, field hockey, canoeing, equestrian sports, soccer, yachting, weight lifting, boxing, gymnastics, and wrestling. Olympic events for women made their first appearance in 1912 and since then have become increasingly important. A separate series of winter-sports Olympic meets was originated (1924) at Chamonix, France. Successive winter Olympic meets were held at St. Moritz, Switzerland (1928), Lake Placid, N.Y. (1932), Garmisch-Partenkirchen, Germany (1936), again at St. Moritz (1948), Oslo, Norway (1952), Cortina, Italy (1956), Squaw Valley, Calif. (1960), Innsbruck, Austria (1964), Grenoble, France (1968), and Sapporo, Japan (1972). The winter games include ice hockey, bobsledding, skiing, and speed and figure skating. Although Olympic events are officially won only by individuals, nations often attempt to assign political significance to the Olympic feats of their citizens. An unofficial system of national-team scoring is popular, and great prestige is often attached to placing high in those ratings. Politics has influenced the Olympic games in other ways, from the propagandistic showmanship of the Nazis in Berlin (1936) to the exclusion of Rhodesia from the Munich games (1972) because of pressure from many black African nations. However, the most savage example of politics affecting the Olympics occurred in Munich (1972), when nine Israeli athletes were kidnapped and subsequently killed by Arab terrorists. The Olympic games are controlled and general policies are set up by the International Olympic Committee to which each participating nation sends at least one delegate. Individual nations have their own Olympic committees to control and regulate Olympic trial meets, to supervise the activities of their national Olympic organization, and to ensure that contestants do not violate the AMATEUR code. See Heintz Schobel, *Ancient Olympic Games* (tr. 1966); Richard Schaap, *Illustrated History of the Olympics* (rev. ed. 1967); Robert Bateman, *The Book of the Olympic Games* (1968); John Kieran and Arthur Daley, *The Story of the Olympic Games, 776 B.C.–1972 A.D.* (1973).

Olympic Mountains, highest part of the COAST RANGES, on the Olympic Peninsula, NW Wash. Mt. Olympus (7,965 ft/2,427 m) is the highest point in the mountains, which are composed mainly of sedimentary rock. The west side of the mountains is in one of the areas of greatest precipitation in the United States, with an annual rainfall of 130 in. (330 cm); the northeast side is in one of the driest areas on the West Coast. On the upper slopes are 60 small glaciers fed by heavy winter snows. The greater part of the Olympic Mts. is included in **Olympic National Park** (est. 1938). Rugged mountains, alpine meadows, coniferous rain forests, glaciers, lakes, and streams characterize this area. The national park includes a 50-mi (80-km) stretch of shoreline along the Pacific Ocean that contains scenic seascapes and wildlife sanctuaries.

Olympio, Sylvanus (sĭlvän'əs ōlĭmpē'ə), 1902–63, African political leader, president of Togo from 1961 to 1963. He was active in trade before entering politics and helped bring about Togo's independence from France. Before Togo became a republic in 1960, he was premier and minister of finance and justice. He was assassinated in a coup in 1963 by a group of ex-soldiers.

Olympus (ōlĭm'pəs), Gr. *Ólimbos,* mountain range, c.25 mi (40 km) long, N Greece, on the border of Thessaly and Macedonia, near the Aegean coast. It rises to c.9,570 ft (2,920 m) at Mt. Olympus, the highest point in Greece. The peak was first ascended in 1913. In Greek mythology the summit, shut from the sight of men on earth by clouds, was the home of the OLYMPIAN gods. Later the name Olympus was given to the remote heavenly palace of the gods.

Olympus, Mount: see CYPRUS; OLYMPIC MTS.; OLYMPUS.

Olynthus (ōlĭn'thəs), ancient city of Greece, on the peninsula of Chalcidice (now Khalkidhikí), NE of Potidaea. A league of Chalcidic cities grew up in the late 5th cent. B.C., and Olynthus, as the head of this Chalcidian League, vigorously opposed the threats of Athens and Sparta. Athens captured the city and held it for a brief time. In 379 B.C., Sparta defeated Olynthus and dissolved the league, which was, however, re-formed after the fall of Sparta. Olynthus had been allied with PHILIP II of Macedon against Athens, but, fearing Philip's power, sought Athenian aid. Philip attacked, and Demosthenes in his Olynthiac orations eloquently urged his fellow Athenians to aid the threatened city. Philip destroyed (348 B.C.) the city despite Athenian aid. Excavations at Olynthus have revealed the layout of the city. See Mabel Gude, *A History of Olynthus* (1933); D. M. Robinson et al., *Excavations at Olynthus* (13 vol., 1929–50).

Om (ôm), in Hinduism and Buddhism, a mystic word or MANTRA. *Om* is regarded as the syllable of the supreme Reality and is sometimes called "the mother of mantras." It is often found at the beginning of prayers, mantras, and scriptures as a word of invocation and adoration. In Hinduism its three Sanskrit letters (transliterated *a, u,* and *m*) symbolize the trinity of the gods Brahma the creator, Vishnu the preserver, and Shiva the destroyer of the universe. In Buddhism it stands at the beginning of the famous mantra, "Om mani padme hum" [hail, the jewel in the lotus].

Omagh (ō'mä), urban district (1971 pop. 27,998), county town of Co. Tyrone, W Northern Ireland, on the Strule River. It is a farm market. Dairy products are processed and shirts are manufactured there. The Royal Inniskelling Fusiliers are barracked in Omagh.

Omagua (ōmä'gwä, –wä), legendary land of treasure. It is comparable to EL DORADO and was sought by the Spanish conquistadors.

Omaha (ō'məhä, –hô), city (1970 pop. 346,929), seat of Douglas co., E Nebr., on the west bank of the Missouri River; inc. 1857. The largest city in the state, it is a busy port of entry and a major transportation center. Located in the heart of the country's great farming region, it is one of the largest livestock markets and meat-processing centers in the world and a market for agricultural products. Much of the city's industry is devoted to food processing. Among its many manufactures are farm machinery, fertilizers, computer components, telephone equipment, furniture, clothing, insecticides, soap, cans, chemicals, paints, and airplane and automobile parts. Omaha is the home of many insurance companies and a center for medical treatment and research. Founded when the Nebraska Territory was opened to settlement in 1854, it grew as a supply point for westward migration and became a thriving transportation and industrial center after the arrival of the railroad in 1869. It was the territorial capital from 1855 to 1867. A world's fair, the Trans-Mississippi and International Exhibition, was held there in 1898. The city has fine park and school systems and is the seat of Creighton Univ., the Univ. of Nebraska at Omaha, and the College of St. Mary. Of interest are the Joslyn Art Museum, an aerospace museum, a Mormon cemetery, and Fontenelle Forest. Fort Omaha (built 1868) now serves as headquarters of the naval reserve training command. Boys Town is to the west, and Offutt Air Force Base, headquarters of the Strategic Air Command, is to the south.

Omaha Indians, North American Indians whose language belongs to the Siouan branch of the Hokan-Siouan linguistic stock (see AMERICAN INDIAN LANGUAGES). They, with the Ponca, migrated from the Ohio valley to the confluence of the Missouri and the Mississippi rivers and from there to Iowa. At the mouth of the Niobrara River in Nebraska they separated from the Ponca. The Omaha moved farther up the Missouri River, but after an outbreak (1802) of smallpox, which considerably reduced their population, they moved to NE Nebraska. A typical tribe of the Plains area, they lived in earth lodges in the winter and tepees in the summer. The Omaha were organized into a rather elaborate class system. They warred intermittently against the Sioux. In 1854 the Omaha ceded all their lands W of the Missouri River to the United States and moved to Dakota co., Nebr. In 1865 they sold part of their reservation to the United States for the use of the Winnebago. An act of 1882 granted the Omaha the right to own land individually; in the early 1970s some 1,400 continued to live on the Omaha Reservation. See Alice Fletcher, *A Study of Omaha Indian Music* (1893); Alice Fletcher and Francis La Flesche, *The Omaha Tribe* (1907); R. F. Fortune, *Omaha Secret Societies* (1932).

O'Mahony, John (ōmă'hənē), 1816–77, Irish patriot. He attended Trinity College, Dublin, and became a proficient Irish scholar. After taking part in the unsuccessful Young Ireland rebellion of 1848, he fled to France and from there to the United States, where he was a founder and organizer of the FENIAN MOVEMENT.

O'Malley, Frank Ward, 1875–1932, American newspaperman, b. Pittston, Pa. As reporter (1906–19) for the New York *Sun* he was especially noted for his stories of humor and pathos. Among his books is *The Swiss Family O'Malley* (1928).

Oman, Sir Charles William Chadwick (ō'mən), 1860–1946, British historian, b. India, educated at Oxford under William Stubbs. He was a foremost military historian; his most notable works are *A History of the Art of War in the Middle Ages* (1898, rev. ed. 1953); its companion study, *A History of the Art of War in the Sixteenth Century* (1937); and his exhaustive *History of the Peninsular War* (7 vol., 1902–30). His *History of Greece* (1888) and *History of England before the Norman Conquest* (1910, 8th ed. 1937) are standard works, but almost entirely concerned with political and military history. He was a member of Parliament (1919–35) for Oxford Univ. and was knighted in 1920.

Oman (ōmän'), sultanate (1970 est. pop. 750,000), c.82,000 sq mi (212,380 sq km), SE Arabian peninsula, on the Gulf of Oman and the Arabian Sea. It was formerly known as Muscat and Oman. It is bordered on the W by Southern Yemen and Saudi Arabia and on the N by the United Arab Emirates, which separate the major portion of the sultanate from a small area on the Strait of Hormuz. The capital is MUSCAT; the largest town is Matrah (1960 pop. 14,119). For the most part, Oman comprises a narrow coastal plain backed by hill ranges and an interior desert plateau. The highest point is Jebel Sham (c.9,900 ft/3,018 m). In the extreme north dates are cultivated, and in the southwest there is an abundance of sugarcane and cattle. Fishing is an important industry. The major product, however, is oil, which began to

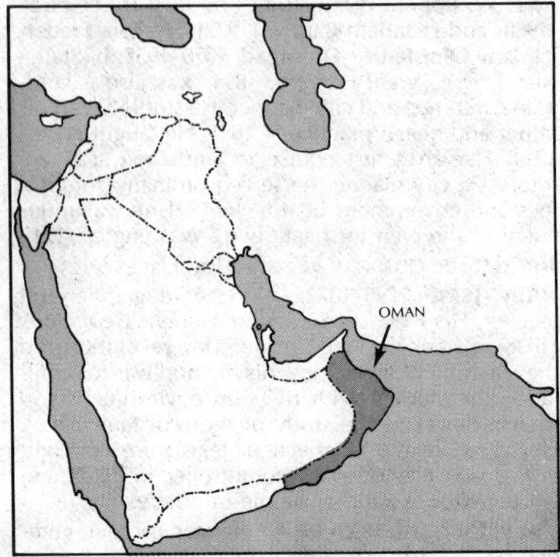

be exported in 1967. The inhabitants are mostly Arabs; there are minorities of Indians, Negroes, and Baluchis. Much of the coast of Oman was controlled by Portugal from 1508 to 1659, when Turkey took possession. The Turks were driven out in 1741 by Ahmad ibn Said of Yemen, who founded the present royal line. In the late 18th cent. Oman began its close ties with Great Britain, which have continued to the present. In the early 19th cent. Oman was the most powerful state in Arabia, controlling Zanzibar and much of the coast of Iran and Baluchistan. Zanzibar was lost in 1856, and the last Omani hold on the Baluchistan coast, Gwadar, was ceded to Pakistan in 1958. The sultan of Oman has had frequent clashes with the imam (leader) of the interior tribes. In 1957 the tribes revolted but were suppressed with British aid. Several Arab countries supporting the imam charged in the 1960s that the sultan's regime was oppressive and that the British were exercising colonial influence in Oman. In 1965 the United Nations called for the elimination of British influence there. In 1970 sultan Said bin Timur was deposed by his son, Qabus bin Said. Qabus promised to use oil revenues for modernization. Rebel activity continued, however, particularly in Dhofar, in the south, where a Chinese-aided liberation front was strong. Oman joined the United Nations and the Arab League in 1971. The sultan exercises absolute power. See R. G. Landen, *Oman Since 1856* (1967); Salīl ibn Ruzaik, *History of the Imâms and Seyyids of Oman* (1871, repr. 1967); Wendell Phillips, *Oman, A History* (1968, repr. 1972).

Omar: see UMAR, caliph.

Omar (ō'mär), duke of Edom. Gen. 36.11,15.

Omar Khayyam (kīäm'), fl. 11th cent., Persian poet and mathematician, b. Nishapur. He was called Khayyam [tentmaker] probably because of his father's occupation. The details of his life are mostly conjectural, but he was well educated and became celebrated as the outstanding mathematician of his time. As astronomer to Sultan Malik Shah, he was one of a group that undertook to reform the calendar. Their work led to the adoption of a new era, the so-called Jalalian or Seljuk era, beginning March 15, 1079. Although he wrote a number of important mathematical studies, Omar's fame as a scientist has been greatly eclipsed by the popularity of his *Rubaiyat,* epigrammatic verse quatrains, first noticed in the Occident c.1700. The work was generally unknown until sometime after a freely paraphrased English translation of them was first published by Edward FITZGERALD in 1859. Since that date a number of other translations have been made in English and in other languages. FitzGerald omitted many of the quatrains (which were independent and unconnected) and rearranged them into a unity expressing Omar's hedonistic philosophy; it is, however, impossible to establish definitely that many of the nearly 500 quatrains attributed to Omar are really his work. The verses have been offered in literally hundreds of editions. See A. J. Arberry, *Omar Khayyam* (1952); study by Ali Dashti (tr. 1972).

Ombos (ŏm'bŏs), ancient city, S Egypt, on the Nile, S of Idfu. It was strategically located on top of a hill. The city attained great importance under the Ptolemies, who built there a mighty temple complex dedicated to the crocodile-headed god Suchos and the falcon-headed Haroeris.

ombú (ōmbōō'), large evergreen tree (*Phytolacca dioica*) of the pampas of Argentina and Uruguay. It has an umbrellalike spread of foliage; the trunk may attain a girth of 40 to 50 ft (12.2–15.2 m). The tree grows rapidly. Its wood is spongy and soft enough to be cut with a knife. Venerated by the gauchos as an ancient and mystic plant, the ombú is the only tree native to the pampas, where it presents a solitary and distinctive aspect and provides welcome shade. Because the sap is poisonous, the ombú is not browsed by cattle and is immune to locusts and other pests. The dark, glossy leaves are sometimes used locally for a brew. The ombú is of the same genus as the North American POKEWEED. It is planted as a shade tree in S California. Ombú is classified in the division MAGNOLIOPHYTA, class Magnoliopsida, order Caryophyllales, family Phytolaccaceae.

ombudsman (ăm'bədzmən) [Swed.,=agent or representative], public official appointed to deal with individual complaints against government acts. The office originated in Sweden in 1809 when the Swedish legislature created a *riksdagens justitieombudsman*, or parliamentary agent of justice, and in the 20th cent. it has been adopted by a number of countries. As a government agent serving as an intermediary between citizens and the government bureaucracy, the ombudsman is usually independent, impartial, universally accessible, and empowered only to recommend. In the United States the term *ombudsman* has been used more widely to describe any machinery adopted by private organizations (e.g., large business corporations and universities) as well as by government to investigate complaints of administrative abuses. In 1969, Hawaii became the first of many American states to appoint an ombudsman. See studies by Walter Gelhorn (1966), S. V. Anderson, ed. (1968) and Geoffrey Sawyer (2d ed. 1968).

Omdurman (ŏmdərmăn'), Arab. *Umm Durman*, city (1969 est. pop. 232,000), central Sudan, on the White Nile opposite Khartoum. It is the largest city and chief commercial center of Sudan and part of a tri-city metropolitan area (with Khartoum and Khartoum North) that forms the country's industrial and cultural heart. Industries include leather tanning and furniture and pottery making. In 1884 the Mahdi made his military headquarters at the village of Omdurman. After the Mahdist forces destroyed Khartoum (1885), the Mahdi's successor, Khalifa Addallah, made Omdurman his capital, and the city grew rapidly as the site of the Mahdi's tomb. The battle of Karari, which took place (1898) near Omdurman, marked the defeat of the Mahdist state in the Sudan by the Anglo-Egyptian army of Lord Kitchener. Although most of the city was destroyed after the battle, the Mahdi's tomb has been restored and embellished. The Khalifa's former residence is now a museum. See Philip Ziegler, *Omdurman* (1974).

O'Meara, Barry Edward (ōmä'rə), 1786–1836, Irish physician. A surgeon in the British navy, he attended the exiled French emperor Napoleon I on St. Helena and became involved in a feud with Napoleon's custodian, Sir Hudson LOWE, whom he charged with mistreatment of Napoleon. O'Meara was forced to return to England. See his *Napoleon in Exile* (1822).

O-mei or **Omei** (both: ō-mā), peak, c.10,000 ft (3,050 m) high, SW Szechwan prov., central China. With many Buddhist images and temples and monasteries, it is one of China's sacred peaks.

omen, sign or augury believed to foreshadow the future. Almost any occurrence can be interpreted as an omen. The typical omen was a natural phenomenon, such as a meteor, an eclipse, or the flight of birds. Among the Greeks and Romans the interpretation of omens was a major part of religious life and required trained priests, such as the Roman augur, to explain the meaning of the signs. Belief in omens still survives in superstitions concerning such things as black cats, nightmares, unlucky days, and breaking mirrors.

Omicron Ceti: see MIRA.

omnibus: see BUS.

omnivore: see CARNIVORE.

Omphale (ŏm'fəlē''): see HERCULES.

omphalos (ŏm'fəlŏs), in Greek and Roman religion, navel-shaped stone used in the rites of many cults. The most famous omphalos was at Delphi; it was supposed to mark the center of the earth.

Omri (ŏm'rī). **1** King of Israel. He was a general in the army of Elah, and on the king's death at the hands of ZIMRI **1**, Omri proclaimed himself king. Soon after this Zimri killed himself. Omri defeated Tibni, a pretender, and moved his capital from Tirzah to Samaria, thenceforth the chief city of Israel. Omri is mentioned on the Moabite stone and on Assyrian inscriptions, which call Israel "the land of Omri." Omri was in close touch with the Syrian petty kingdoms, and his son Ahab's marriage with Jezebel was a result of this alliance. 1 Kings 16.16–28; 20.34. **2** Benjamite. 1 Chron. 7.8. **3** Judahite. 1 Chron. 9.4. **4** Issacharite. 1 Chron. 27.18.

Omsk (ômsk), city (1970 pop. 821,000), capital of Omsk oblast, W Siberian USSR, at the confluence of the Irtysh and Om rivers and on the Trans-Siberian RR. It is a major river port and produces agricultural machinery and railway equipment. There are also oil refineries, grain mills, and textile plants. Founded as a fortress in 1716, Omsk became a major transportation and administrative center in the 19th cent. During the civil war that followed the Revolution of 1917, Omsk served as headquarters of the anti-Bolshevik armed forces of Admiral A. V. Kolchak.

Omuta (ō'mōōtä) or **Omuda** (-dä), city (1970 pop. 175,143), Fukuoka prefecture, W Kyushu, Japan, a port on the Amakusa Sea. Coal is exported, and there is a large chemical industry.

On (ŏn). **1** Reubenite conspirator in Korah's revolt. Num. 16.1,2. **2** The Egyptian Heliopolis.

Oña, Pedro de (pā'thrō thā ō'nyä), 1570?–1643, Chilean poet. Having been born in Latin America, he is considered Chile's first national poet. His poetry is both epic and religious. Inspired by LA ARAVCANA, by Alonso de ERCILLA Y ZÚÑIGA, he wrote the epic *Arauco domado* (1596; tr. *Arauco Tamed*, 1948). Other works include *El vasauro* (1635), a religious poem, and *El Ignacio de Cantabria* (1639), a pious work celebrating St. IGNATIUS OF LOYOLA.

onager (ŏn'əjər) or **Persian wild ass,** wild ASS of Central Asia, *Equus hemonius onager*. One of the several races of Asian wild ass (*E. hemonius*), it formerly ranged widely across S Russia, Iran, and Afghanistan. A small, slenderly built animal, it stands about 4 ft (120 cm) high at the shoulder. Its back and legs are rusty brown and its belly white. It has a black tail tuft, a short, stiff black mane, and a black spinal stripe lined with white on either side. For many centuries it was hunted for sport by the Persian nobility, and young onagers were captured for the breeding of riding animals. Owing to the swiftness and endurance of the onager, relatively few animals were captured by traditional methods. However, since the invention of modern firearms and automobiles, the animals have been extensively slaughtered for their flesh and hides. They survive in the USSR only on the Badkhys reserve and are greatly reduced in numbers elsewhere. The continued existence of the race is in doubt. The onager is classified in the phylum CHORDATA, subphylum Vertebrata, class Mammalia, order Perissodactyla, family Equidae.

Onam (ō'nəm). **1** Horite. Gen. 36.23; 1 Chron. 1.40. **2** Judahite. 1 Chron. 2.26,28.

Onan (ō'nən), Judah's son whose evasion of his obligation to his brother's widow caused his death. Gen. 38.

Onassis, Aristotle Socrates (âr''ĭstŏt'əl sŏk'rətēz ōnăs'ĭs), 1906?–, Greek shipowner and financier, b. Turkey. Leaving Turkey after the Turkish defeat of Greek forces at Smyrna (1922), he revived the family tobacco business in Argentina. In 1925 he received Argentinian and Greek citizenship. Onassis purchased his first ships in the early 1930s and later in the decade became the first Greek shipowner to enter the tanker business. In 1946 he married the daughter of the influential Greek shipowner Stavros Livanos, and he later became the brother-in-law of Stavros Niarchos, another Greek shipowner; together the three men formed the most powerful shipping clan in the world. Later, however, considerable rivalry developed among them. After divorcing (1961) his first wife, he gained special prominence in the United States through his marriage (1968) to Jacqueline Bouvier Kennedy, widow of President John F. Kennedy. A controversial figure in world finance, Onassis was formerly the principal stockholder of the company that controlled the Monte Carlo casino. He was also the founder (1957) of Olympic Airways of Greece. See biography by Christian Cafaris and Jacques Harvey (tr. 1972).

Onassis, Jacqueline Bouvier, 1929–, b. Southampton, N.Y. Of a socially prominent family, she worked (1951–53) as a journalist and photographer before marrying (1953) John F. Kennedy. As first lady (1961–63), Jacqueline Kennedy planned and conducted the restoration of the White House and had Congress declare the White House a national museum. After the assassination of President Kennedy, she returned to private life and later married (1968) the Greek shipping magnate Aristotle Onassis. See biography by R. T. Harding and A. L. Holmes (1966); M. B. Gallagher, *My Life with Jacqueline Kennedy* (1969); M. V. Thayer, *Jacqueline Kennedy: The White House Years* (1971).

Oñate, Juan de (hwän dā ōnyä'tā), fl. 1595-1614, Spanish explorer in the American Southwest, possibly b. New Spain. The expedition of Antonio de Espejo had awakened interest in the northern territories, and in 1595 Oñate entered into a contract with the viceroy to conquer and settle New Mexico. Political changes hampered his actions, but in 1598 he led an expedition north. Oñate took possession of New Mexico for the Spanish king and established a settlement at San Juan. He was immediately faced by an Indian revolt at Acoma, which he put down severely. In 1601, Oñate, in search of QUIVIRA, led an expedition across present Oklahoma to the plains around Wichita, Kansas, then returned, unsuccessful, to New Mexico, where discontent was rife among the colonists. Anxious to find a route to the South Sea, he led (1605) an expedition westward, reached the Colorado River, and went down it to the Gulf of California before turning back to his colony. He sought to resign as governor in 1607 but had to remain until he was relieved (1609) by a new governor. The officials of New Spain were disappointed that he had found no ready wealth, and Oñate was tried on charges of misconduct in office. Convicted in 1614, he later sought a pardon, which was granted before 1624. One of his lieutenants, Gaspar de Villagrá, celebrated Oñate's deeds in *Historia de la Nueva México*, but his real achievements in founding and exploring a broad new realm did not receive the deserved recognition. See study by G. P. Hammond and Agaptio Rey (1953).

Oncken, Hermann (hĕr'män ông'kən), 1869-1946, German historian. He taught at the universities of Heidelberg, Munich, Chicago, and (1928–35) Berlin. He was forced to retire because of his opposition to the Nazi regime. Among his chief works are *Napoleon III and the Rhine* (1926, tr. 1928, repr. 1967) and a history (1933) of Germany from 1870 to World War I. His other writings include essays and excellent biographies of Ferdinand Lassalle (1904) and of Rudolf von Bennigsen (1910). Oncken also edited diplomatic documents dating from 1858 to 1871.

Oncken, Wilhelm (vĭl'hĕlm), 1838–1905, German historian. He taught at the Univ. of Giessen after 1866. A typical liberal national of the 19th cent., Oncken regarded history as a means of national political education. His early field was Greek history, but he later concentrated on the history of the Prussian state and of German unification. He edited a cooperative history, the *Allgemeine Geschichte in Einzeldarstellungen* [general history in its special phases] (45 vol., 1876–93), which became a standard household fixture for the educated German family. Several of Oncken's own volumes were included in the collection.

Ondo (ŏn'dō), city (1969 est. pop. 86,000), SW Nigeria. It is the market center for a cacao and timber producing region and has rice mills and sawmills. Formerly the capital of a YORUBA kingdom, Ondo came under British protection in 1893.

Onega (ōnē'gə, ōnā'-, Rus. ŭnyä'gŭ), river, c.260 mi (420 km) long, rising in Lake Lacha, NW European USSR, and flowing N into the Onega Gulf of the White Sea, SW of Arkhangelsk. It is navigable (May-November) except for the rapids in its middle course.

Onega, Lake, Finnish *Ääninen*, Rus. *Onezhskoye Ozero*, lake, c.3,800 sq mi (9,800 sq km), NW European USSR, in Karelia, between Lake Ladoga and the White Sea. The second largest lake in Europe, it is c.150 mi (240 km) long with a maximum width of c.60 mi (100 km) and a maximum depth of c.360 ft (110 m). The lake is located on the heavily glaciated Baltic Shield. Its shores are low and sandy in the south, rocky and indented in the north. It is frozen from November to May. The lake receives the Vytegra and the Vodla rivers and drains SW through the Svir River into Lake Ladoga. The Baltic-White Sea Canal has its southern terminus at Povenets on the lake's northern shore. Petrozavodsk is the chief city and port on Lake Onega. Parallel to the southern shore of the lake runs the **Onega Canal,** 45 mi (72 km) long, which joins the Svir and Vytegra rivers and forms part of the Volga-Baltic Waterway.

Oneida (ōnī'də), city (1970 pop. 11,677), Madison co., central N.Y.; inc. 1901. It has milk-processing plants and factories manufacturing paper and plastic products. Nearby was the **Oneida Community,** a religious society of Perfectionists that was established (1848) by John Humphrey Noyes. Members of the sect held all property in common and practiced complex marriage and common care of the children. The community prospered by making steel traps and silverware. In 1881 it was reorganized as a joint stock company, and the social experiments were abandoned. See M. L. Carden, *Oneida: Utopian Community to Modern Corporation* (1969).

Oneida Indians: see IROQUOIS CONFEDERACY.

Oneida Lake, c.80 sq mi (210 sq km), 22 mi (35 km) long and 1 to 5 mi (1.6–8.1 km) wide, central N.Y., NE of Syracuse. The New York State Barge Canal links the eastern end of the lake with the Mohawk River and also follows part of the Oneida River, which flows from the western end of the lake c.20 mi (30 km) into the Oswego River.

O'Neill, Eugene (Gladstone), 1888–1953, American dramatist, b. New York City. Widely acknowledged as America's greatest playwright, O'Neill brought to the U.S. stage its first serious native drama. He was the son of James O'Neill, a popular romantic actor noted for his portrayal of the Count of Monte Cristo. Young O'Neill, his mother, and his older brother lived an unsettled life traveling with James on tour. The mother became a drug addict, the brother an alcoholic. The tortured relationships in his family haunted O'Neill all his life and are reflected in many of his plays. O'Neill's early education was received in boarding schools. He entered Princeton in 1906 but remained there only a year. During the next few years he did a great variety of things—prospected for gold, traveled as a seaman on voyages to South America and South Africa, worked as a newspaper reporter—experiences that familiarized him with the life of sailors, stevedores, and the outcasts of society that populate many of his plays. In 1912, O'Neill was stricken with tuberculosis and spent six months in a sanatorium. During this period of enforced leisure he reconsidered his mode of life and decided to become a playwright. In the next two years he wrote 11 one-act and two long plays. He studied with George Pierce BAKER at Harvard in 1914–15, and in the summer of the following year he began his association with the PROVINCETOWN PLAYERS, a theatrical group that produced many of his one-act plays, including *Bound East for Cardiff* (1916), *The Long Voyage Home* (1917), and *The Moon of the Caribbees* (1918). With the production in 1920 of *Beyond the Horizon* (Pulitzer Prize), the first of his full-length plays to be acted, O'Neill's reputation as a dramatist was established. *Beyond the Horizon,* a grim domestic drama set in New England, was followed by *Diff'rent* (1920); *The Emperor Jones* (1920), an expressionist drama about the disintegration of a Negro dictator; and *Anna Christie* (1921; Pulitzer Prize), which concerns a waterfront prostitute's efforts to redeem herself. In 1922 came *The Hairy Ape,* an experimental, surrealistic play depicting the spiritual agony of a stoker who has lost his harmony with the world. After several "ambitious" failures, O'Neill's first great play, *Desire under the Elms* (1924), was produced; set in 19th-century New England, it dramatizes the impassioned battle for dominance between a hard, puritanical father and his sensitive son. O'Neill's next important work, *The Great God Brown* (1926), is a complicated, symbolic play about modern man's futile struggle to identify himself with nature. The nine-act drama, *Strange Interlude* (1928; Pulitzer Prize), a Freudian character study of an emotionally sterile woman, utilized Elizabethan asides to produce the effect of STREAM OF CONSCIOUSNESS. His other plays of the period include *Marco Millions* (1928), *Lazarus Laughed* (1928), and *Dynamo* (1929). In 1931, O'Neill's great trilogy *Mourning Becomes Electra* was produced. Set in post-Civil War New England, it is a retelling of the ancient Greek story of the murder of AGAMEMNON by his wife Clytemnestra, and the revenge and guilt of their children Orestes and Electra. In this, as in all his major plays, O'Neill depicts tormented characters endeavoring to comprehend their destiny. His only comedy, *Ah, Wilderness!,* a nostalgic play of youth's awakening, appeared in 1933. After *Days Without End* (1934), no new O'Neill play was performed until 1946, when *The Iceman Cometh* was produced. Considered by many critics to be his greatest work, *The Iceman Cometh* is the drama of a group of wasted, drunken outcasts who are stripped of their illusions by a misguided, guilt-ridden savior. In 1947, *A Moon for the Misbegotten,* about the tragic, frustrated love between an alcoholic and a farm woman, was produced. It was not well received, but a revival of the play in 1973 was extraordinarily successful. O'Neill's last years were tragic: Two of his three marriages ended in divorce; his eldest son committed suicide, and he renounced his daughter Oona when, at 18, she married the actor Charlie Chaplin, a man her father's age; O'Neill himself contracted a crippling disease that made him unable to write. At his death O'Neill left several important plays in manuscript, including the autobiographical masterpiece, *Long Day's Journey into Night* (produced 1956; Pulitzer Prize), and two parts of an unfinished cycle of plays using American history as a background—*A Touch of the Poet* (first U.S. production, 1958) and *More Stately Mansions* (first U.S. production, 1967). Although many of O'Neill's plays are uneven in composition and suffer from frequently clumsy experimentation with theatrical and thematic innovations, his work as a whole gives striking evidence of a deeply poetic and tragic artist. In 1936, O'Neill was awarded the Nobel Prize in literature. See biographies by Louis Sheaffer (2 vol., 1968–73) and Arthur and Barbara Gelb (rev. ed. 1974); studies by Oscar Cargill et al. (1961) and Travis Bogard (1972).

O'Neill, Hugh: see TYRONE, HUGH O'NEILL, 2D EARL OF.

O'Neill, Margaret (Peggy O'Neill), c.1796–1879, wife of John Henry EATON, U.S. Secretary of War under President Andrew Jackson. She was the daughter of a Washington tavern keeper and married John Timberlake, a purser in the U.S. navy. After his death, she became (1829) the wife of Eaton, who soon afterwards entered the cabinet. The wives of the other cabinet members refused to accord her social recognition because of the alleged intimacy between Major Eaton and Peggy O'Neill before their marriage and because of her humble birth. President Jackson, a close friend of Eaton, tried in vain to ensure Peggy Eaton a place in society. The attempt almost disrupted the cabinet and worsened the relations between the President and the Vice President, John C. CALHOUN, whose wife was a social leader. As a result, Jackson transferred his favor to Martin VAN BUREN, who as a widower was better able than others to recognize Mrs. Eaton. She was well received at the court of Spain, to which her husband was appointed minister in 1836, and was a social favorite in London and Paris. Her maiden name is also recorded by historians as O'Neale and O'Neil. See biography by Leon Phillips (1974).

O'Neill, Owen Roe, 1590?–1649, Irish chieftain. Nephew of Hugh O'Neill, 2d earl of TYRONE, he left Ireland after the "flight of the earls" in 1607 and spent 30 years in the Spanish army, serving notably at Arras (1640). He returned to Ireland in 1642, superseded his kinsman Sir Phelim O'Neill as leader of the O'Neill clan, and for the next seven years led the Roman Catholic faction in the intermittently successful rebellion against English authority. O'Neill's death removed the only Irish general who might have been capable of resisting Oliver Cromwell.

O'Neill, Shane, 1530?–1567, Irish chieftain. The eldest son of Con O'Neill, 1st earl of Tyrone, he carried on a bitter feud with his father after Con accepted Henry VIII's nomination of Con's illegitimate son, Matthew, as baron of Dungannon and heir to the O'Neill title. Shane's agents murdered Matthew in 1558, but when Con died in 1559, the English recognized Matthew's eldest son, Brian, as his successor. In 1562, after the murder of Brian, Shane reached a compromise with Queen Elizabeth I in London and was acknowledged as chieftain of Tyrone. Upon his return to Ireland, however, he plunged anew into tribal warfare against his rivals in Ulster. He claimed to be serving Elizabeth in his successful campaign (1564–65) against the MacDonnells, Scottish immigrants on the coast of Antrim. Later, however, he directed his raids and depredations against the English. Defeated by the O'Donnells at Letterkenny, he fled and sought refuge with his former enemies, the MacDonnells, who murdered him.

O'Neill, Terence Marne O'Neill, Baron, 1914–, Ulster Unionist politician. A member of one of the oldest Protestant families in Ireland, he entered the Northern Ireland Parliament in 1946. He served as minister of finance (1956–63) and prime minister (1963–69). Regarded as one of the most liberal Unionists, he personally favored the broadening of Roman Catholic civil rights, although his party did not. His main concern was improving the economy of the province; his government stressed industrial expansion, training facilities for skilled trades, and the development of tourism, with considerable success. His formal meetings with Irish Prime Minister John Lynch were regarded as too compromising by right wing Unionists, and the gradual increase in prosperity did not satisfy Roman Catholic grievances. After failing to win a mandate for moderation in the elections of Feb., 1969, he resigned. He was made a life peer in 1970.

Oneonta (ōnēŏn'tə), city (1970 pop. 16,030), Otsego co., E central N.Y., on the Susquehanna River, in a farm area of the Catskills; settled c.1780, inc. as a city 1909. Oneonta grew after the coming of the railroad in 1865. Although no longer an important rail center, its railroad shops are still major employers. Feed and grain, apparel, truck bodies, and electronic items are among the local manufactures. The State Univ. College at Oneonta and Hartwick College are there. Many Indian artifacts have been found in the area.

Onesimus (ōnĕs'ĭməs), runaway slave about whom Paul wrote the epistle to PHILEMON. See also Col. 4.9.

Onesiphorus (ŏn″ĕsĭf'ərəs), man whom Paul praised highly for hospitality and kindness. 2 Tim. 1.16–18.

Onganía, Juan Carlos (hwän kär'lōs ōngänē'ä), 1914–, president of Argentina (1966–70). He served (1963–65) as commander in chief of the army and in 1962 led a revolt within the army that purged the extreme right-wing faction. He was established in the presidency by the military junta that deposed President Illia. Operating under a new charter that abolished political parties, dissolved congress, and gave the president both executive and legislative powers, he integrated the armed forces and the government and attempted to force moral and educational reform. His authoritarian measures aroused opposition, and his position was further eroded by soaring inflation and widespread labor and student unrest. In June, 1970, Onganía was deposed by the military junta, which installed Gen. Roberto Levingston in his place.

onion, plant of the family Liliaceae (LILY family), of the same genus (*Allium*) as the chive (*A. schoenoprasum*), garlic (*A. sativum*), leek (*A. porrum*), and shallot (*A. ascalonium*). These plants are characterized by an edible bulb composed of food-storage leaves that are rich in sugar and a pungent oil, the source of its strong taste. The above-ground green leaves, typically long and tubular, are also eaten. All these species are believed to be native to SW Asia and are known to have been cultivated since ancient times. The onion (*A. cepa*), no longer found wild, is a biennial now grown in many varieties throughout the world as a table vegetable. Common varieties include the strong-flavored red onion, the milder yellow onion, and the bland white onion. Pearl onions are small white onions used for pickling. The large Spanish and Bermuda onions have a delicate flavor. The onion was grown extensively by the ancient Egyptians, in whose writings it is mentioned, and was later spread by the Spanish colonists. The more pungent garlic, a perennial, has a bulb consisting of small bulbils called cloves. This part is most often used in cooking, chiefly as flavoring; garlic is especially popular in the Mediterranean region and the Far East. Garlic oil has been used medicinally as a stimulant; the Romans fed it to slaves and soldiers. The shallot (supposedly introduced to Europe from Ascalon, or Ashqelon, by the Crusaders, hence the botanical name) is a perennial with clusters of small onionlike bulbs. It and the more familiar leek, a biennial with a small single bulb, are both commonly used whole in salads, as asparaguslike cooked vegetables, and in soups and stews. The leek, cultivated in ancient Egypt and probably introduced to England by the Romans, is the floral emblem of the Welsh, who adorn their hats with its leaves on St. David's Day. *Scallion* is a popular term for any edible *Allium* with a reduced bulb, especially the leek and shallot. The Welsh onion (*A. fistulosum*) is a leeklike plant popular in the Orient. The chive, today found wild in Italy and Greece, is a hardy perennial sometimes used as an ornamental border plant. For flavoring, its leaves are the most desirable portion. Several species of *Allium* are native to North America, chiefly in the West, where the edible types were collected by Indians.

Because of the disagreeable odor and taste imparted to the milk of cows that feed upon them, some species are considered weeds, especially the common wild garlic, *A. vineale*, naturalized from Europe. Onion is classified in the division MAGNOLIOPHYTA, class Liliatae, order Liliales, family Liliaceae.

Onions, C. T. (Charles Talbut Onions), 1873–1965, English philologist, lexicographer, author, and editor. After a post with British Naval Intelligence in World War I, he held a fellowship at Magdalen College, Oxford, and from 1927 to 1949 was a reader at Oxford. Onions served as coeditor of the *Oxford English Dictionary* until its completion in 1933. He also edited the two-volume *Shorter Oxford English Dictionary* (1933, 1936, 1945) and was preparing the one-volume *Oxford Dictionary of English* when he died. His other works include *An Advanced English Syntax* (1904) and *A Shakespeare Glossary* (1911).

Onitsha (ōnĭch'ə), city (1969 est. pop. 189,100), SE Nigeria, a port on the Niger River. The city's manufactures include textiles, beverages, shoes, lumber, phonograph records, and printed materials. Fishing and canoe-building are traditional local industries. Onitsha is the northern limit of year-round navigation on the Niger and is an important entrepôt linking traders from the Niger delta with the upper Niger and Benue rivers and with a wide region of E Nigeria. A road bridge (built 1965) across the Niger at Onitsha is a vital link between E and W Nigeria. Onitsha was probably founded in the 16th cent. by immigrants from BENIN. In the 17th cent. IBO tribesmen arrived. In 1857 a British trading station and a Christian mission were established in the city, and in 1884 Onitsha came under British protection.

Onkelos (ŏng'kəlŏs), 2d cent. A.D., translator of the Hebrew Bible into Aramaic, his work later being given the title Targum Onkelos (see TARGUM). A proselyte, he gained the respect of the leading Hebrew scholars of his day. His translation became almost as authoritative a text as the Pentateuch itself.

Onnes, Heike Kamerlingh: see KAMERLINGH ONNES, HEIKE.

Ono (ō'nō), town, W central Palestine, the modern Qiryat Ono (Israel), E of Tel Aviv. 1 Chron. 8.12; Ezra 2.33; Neh. 7.37.

onomatopoeia (ŏn"əmăt"əpē'ə) [Gr.,=word-making], in language, the representation of a sound by an imitation thereof; e.g., the cat *mews*. Poets often convey the meaning of a verse through its very sound. For example, in "Song of the Lotus-Eaters" Tennyson indicates the slow, sensuous, and langorous life of the Lotus-Eaters by the sound of the words he uses to describe the land in which they live:

Here are cool mosses deep,
And through the moss the ivies creep,
And in the stream the long-leaved flowers weep,
And from the craggy ledge the poppy hangs in sleep.

Onomatopoeia can also represent harsh and unpleasant sounds, as in Browning's "Meeting at Night":

A tap at the pane, the quick sharp scratch
And blue spurt of a lighted match.

Onomichi (ōnō'mēchē), city (1970 pop. 101,364), Hiroshima prefecture, SW Honshu, Japan, on the Inland Sea. It is a shipping center and the site of several Buddhist temples, notably that of Senko-ji (10th cent.).

Onondaga Indians: see IROQUOIS CONFEDERACY.

Onondaga Lake (ŏnəndä'gə, -dô'-), brackish lake, 5 mi (8 km) long and 1 mi (1.6 km) wide, central N.Y., NW of Syracuse. In 1654, Father LeMoyne, a missionary, was taken to salt springs along the lake shore by the Onondaga Indians. He showed them how to obtain salt from the water by boiling it. In 1795 the lake was purchased from the Indians by New York state for its salt resources. The Salt Museum on the lakeshore near Liverpool contains relics of the early salt industry, which thrived in the mid-19th century.

Onslow, George, 1784–1853, French composer. Onslow studied piano in London and composition in Paris. Although he wrote symphonies, comic operas, and various chamber works, he is remembered principally for his 34 string quintets and 36 string quartets. His *Bullet Quintet* (No. 15) is a musical rendition of the hunting accident that left him partially deaf for life.

Ontario (ŏntâr'ēō), province (1971 pop. 7,703,106), 412,582 sq mi (1,068,587 sq km), E central Canada. TORONTO, the second largest city in Canada, is the capital; other important cities are OTTAWA (the capital of Canada), HAMILTON, WINDSOR, LONDON, and THUNDER BAY. Ontario, the second largest Canadian province, is the most productive in terms of mining and industrial and agricultural output. It is bounded on the N by Hudson Bay and James Bay; on the E by Quebec; on the S by the St. Lawrence River, lakes Ontario, Erie, Huron, and Superior, and by the United States; and on the W by Manitoba. The province has three main geographic regions. In the western and central portion is the Canadian Shield, a region of mineral-rich rock covered with forests and broken by a labyrinth of rivers and lakes. In the north is the Hudson Bay Lowlands bordering on Hudson and James bays, an area consisting mainly of marshes, swampland, and forest. In the south and east is the Great Lakes-St. Lawrence lowlands, where nine tenths of the population lives and where industry and agriculture are concentrated. Climate varies among the regions. The far north has subarctic conditions, while the west has a temperate climate. Around the Great Lakes the weather is moderate and summers are longer than in other parts of the province. The St. Lawrence River gives Ontario access to the Atlantic. Other important rivers are the Ottawa (which forms part of the boundary with Quebec), the St. Clair, the Detroit, and the St. Marys. Several of the province's rivers are used to generate hydroelectric power, among them the Niagara, with its famous falls. The most important economic activity in Ontario is manufacturing, and the Toronto-Hamilton region is the most highly industrialized section of the province. Major industrial products include transportation equipment, foods and beverages, metals and metal products, electrical goods, machinery, chemicals, and paper products. Agriculture is also important, with cattle, dairy products, and hogs producing the most income. Other major crops are corn, wheat, potatoes, and soybeans. On the shores of the eastern Great Lakes are orchards and tobacco plantations. Mining is important in the Canadian Shield region, where iron ore, copper, zinc, gold, silver, and uranium are found. The area around Sudbury is particularly rich in copper and nickel. Ontario is also a major producer of lumber and pulp and paper. People of British ancestry make up about two thirds of the province's population, and one tenth are French. Ontario has four national parks and numerous tourist attractions, two of the most notable being Niagara Falls and the annual Shakespeare Festival at Stratford. Among the province's institutions of higher education are the Univ. of Toronto, the Univ. of Ottawa, McMaster Univ., Queen's Univ., and the Univ. of Western Ontario. Before the arrival of the white man the area of Ontario was inhabited by several Indian tribes, the largest of which was the Huron. Étienne Brulé explored southern Ontario in 1610–12. Henry Hudson sailed into Hudson Bay in 1611 and claimed the region for England. Within a few years Samuel de Champlain reached (1615) the eastern shores of Lake Huron, and French explorers, missionaries, and trappers had established posts at several points. However, settlement was long hindered by the hostility of the Iroquois Indians. In the late 17th cent. the British established trading posts in the Hudson Bay area, and the Anglo-French struggle for control of Ontario began. The conflict was resolved by the Treaty of Paris of 1763, which gave Great Britain all of France's mainland North American territory. In 1774 the British attached Ontario to QUEBEC, which had a predominantly French culture. When many pro-British Loyalists migrated to Ontario after the American Revolution, the desire for institutions and a government separate from those of Quebec grew. The Constitutional Act of 1791 split Quebec into Lower Canada (present-day Quebec) and Upper Canada (present-day Ontario), with the Ottawa River as the dividing line. During the War of 1812, Americans raided Upper Canada and burned Toronto (1813). After the war many English, Scottish, and Irish settlers came to the colony. Conflict developed between the conservative, aristocratic governing group, known as the Family Compact, and the reformers and radicals led by William Lyon MACKENZIE. The radicals staged an armed uprising in 1837 but were easily suppressed. However, the rebellion occurred at the same time as a revolt in Lower Canada, and the British government sent over Lord Durham (see DURHAM, JOHN GEORGE LAMBTON) to study the situation in the North American colonies. He recommended the reunion of the two colonies (to place the French of Quebec in a minority) and the granting of self-government. Accordingly Upper and Lower Canada were joined in 1841 and became known, respectively, as Canada West and Canada East. Parliamentary self-government was not granted until 1849. However, conflict between French and English made the united province unworkable, and in 1867 when the confederation of Canada was formed, Ontario and Quebec became separate provinces. With the construction of the transcontinental railroad in the 1880s, settlement increased in western Canada and Ontario's commerce and industry flourished. The exploitation of the minerals in the Canadian Shield region began in the early

20th cent. The main political parties in Ontario are the Liberals, who held power during the late 19th cent., and the Conservatives, who have governed from 1905 to the present (with the exception of two interludes between 1919–23 and 1934–43). The New Democrats, a socialist party formerly known as the Cooperative Commonwealth Federation, was formed during the depression. See Fred Landon, *Western Ontario and the American Frontier* (1941, repr. 1970); Dean Fink, comp., *Life in Upper Canada, 1781–1841* (1971); G. P. Glazebrook, *Life in Ontario* (1968, repr. 1971); R. L. Gentilcore, ed., *Ontario* (1972); Jacob Spelt, *Urban Development in South Central Ontario* (1972); J. V. Wright, *Ontario Prehistory* (1972).

Ontario, city (1970 pop. 64,118), San Bernardino co., SE Calif., near Los Angeles, in a region of vineyards; inc. 1891. Citrus fruits are grown. Also important to the economy are the manufacture of iron products, clothing, and mobile homes and the overhauling of jet engines. Founded in 1882, the city is the site of Ontario Motor Speedway, Chaffey College, and an international airport.

Ontario, Lake, 7,540 sq mi (19,529 sq km), 193 mi (311 km) long and 53 mi (85 km) at its greatest width, between SE Ont., Canada, and NW N.Y.; smallest and lowest of the Great Lakes. It has a surface elevation of 246 ft (75 m) above sea level and a maximum depth of 778 ft (237 m). Lake Ontario is fed chiefly by the waters of Lake Erie by way of the Niagara River; other tributaries are the Genesee, Oswego, and Black rivers in New York and the Trent River in Ontario. The lake is drained to the northeast by the St. Lawrence River. Oceangoing vessels reach the lake through the St. Lawrence Seaway and use the Welland Canal to bypass Niagara Falls and reach Lake Erie; smaller craft (mostly pleasure boats) can travel the Rideau Canal between Kingston and Ottawa, and the Trent Canal between the Bay of Quinte and Georgian Bay. Navigation on the lake is not usually impeded by ice in winter. The chief Canadian lakeshore cities are St. Catherines, Hamilton, Toronto, Oshawa, and Kingston; on the south shore are Rochester and Oswego, N.Y. Commercial fishing is important, but pollution and infestation of lampreys have reduced the value of the catch. A U.S.-Canadian pact (1972) established that water quality would be improved and further pollution ended. Recreational facilities are provided at state and provincial parks. The first European to see (1615) Lake Ontario was Étienne Brulé, the French explorer; later that year Samuel de Champlain visited it.

ontogeny: see BIOGENETIC LAW.

ontology: see METAPHYSICS.

Onychophora (ŏn″əkŏf′ərə), small phylum with about 70 species of animals that are often called "missing links" between annelids (phylum ANNELIDA) and arthropods (phylum ARTHROPODA). The thin cuticle and wormlike form of onychophorans are reminiscent of annelids, while the tracheal system and details of embryonic development foreshadow similar developments in arthropods. The unsegmented, stumpy legs with arthropodlike claws are unique. Onychophorans live inconspicuously in surface litter and under fallen logs, where humidity is high and protection against drying is greatest. Ancient onychophorans were marine. Modern species live in widely scattered wet, warm to temperate habitats in South Africa, Central America, and New Zealand, suggesting a much wider distribution of terrestrial forms in the past. The 10 genera are often referred to collectively as *Peripatus.*

onyx (ŏn′ĭks), variety of cryptocrystalline QUARTZ, differing from AGATE only in that the bands of which it is composed are parallel and regular. Its appearance is most striking when the bands are of sharply contrasting colors; black and white specimens are often used for cameos. Onyx was used in Roman times for vases and cups. SARDONYX contains onyx and carnelian or sard. "Onyx marble," "Mexican onyx," and "Oriental alabaster" are terms applied to TRAVERTINE.

oolite (ō′əlīt, ō′ō-), rock composed of small concretions, usually of calcium carbonate, containing a nucleus and clearly defined concentric shells. In the British Isles oolitic limestone is characteristic of the middle and upper Jurassic, which was formerly termed the Oolite on this account.

Oost, Jacob van (yä′kōp vän ōst), the elder, 1601–71, Flemish portrait and religious painter, b. Bruges. He spent most of his life in Bruges, with the exception of several years in Rome, where he was a pupil of Annibale Carracci. A follower also of Rubens and Caravaggio, he developed a vigorous and realistic style. There are various pictures by van Oost in the churches of Bruges; *Resurrection* and *Descent from the Cross* are in the cathedral. His son and pupil, **Jacob van Oost,** the younger, 1637–1713, settled in Lille, where he continued his father's tradition. Much of his work remains in the churches and museums of that city.

Oostende (ōstĕn′də), Fr. *Ostende,* city (1970 pop. 71,227), West Flanders prov., W Belgium, on the North Sea. It is a major commercial and fishing port, connected by canals with Bruges and Ghent. It is also an industrial center and a seaside resort. Manufactures include processed food, ships, and chemicals. A port by the time of the First Crusade (11th cent.), Oostende was fortified (1583) by William the Silent and played a leading role in the Dutch struggle for independence. The city was taken (1604) by the Spaniards under Spinola after a three-year siege in which it was almost totally destroyed, was sacked again in 1745 by the French, and suffered heavy Allied bombardment in World War II. From the mid-19th cent. to World War I it was one of Europe's most fashionable social centers. The city is also known as Ostend.

Ootacamund (o͞o′təkəmŭnd″), town (1971 pop. 63,003), Tamil Nadu state, SW India, in the Nilgiri Hills. At an altitude of c.7,000 ft (2,130 m), the town is the most famous hot-weather resort in S India. It is also a district administrative center and a market for tea, coffee, teak, and sandalwood. There are tea plantations, a munitions factory, and breweries in Ootacamund. See Mollie Panter-Downes, *Ooty Preserved* (1967).

OPA: see OFFICE OF PRICE ADMINISTRATION.

opal (ō′pəl), a mineral consisting of poorly crystalline to amorphous silica, $SiO_2 \cdot nH_2O$; the water content is quite variable but usually ranges from 3% to 10%. Common opal is usually colorless or white, but it may be gray, brown, yellow, or red; the color is due to fine-grained impurities. Opal is formed at low temperatures from silica-bearing waters and can occur in fissures and cavities of any rock type. Precious, or gem, opal has a rich iridescence and remarkable play of changing colors, usually in red, green, and blue. This is the result of a specific internal structure consisting of regularly packed uniform spheres of amorphous silica a few tenths of a micron in diameter; sphere diameter and refractive index determine the range of colors displayed. The greater part of the world's supply of precious opal comes from the Coober Pedy and Andamooka fields in South Australia. The original source, known in Roman times, was near Cervenica in Czechoslovakia. Precious opal has also been mined in Honduras, Mexico, and the Virgin Valley in Nevada. Fire opal is a bright red transparent or translucent opal that may or may not show a play of color.

Opa-Locka (ō′pə-lŏk′ə), city (1970 pop. 11,902), Dade co., SE Fla.; inc. 1926. Diverse industrial plants are in the city, and the large county airport is nearby. A U.S. coast guard station is located at the airport, and Opa-Locka has many aviation training schools. Its city hall is patterned after a Moorish castle, and other buildings are also of unusual Arabian architecture.

op art (ŏp), movement that developed in the United States and Europe in the mid-1960s. Its practitioners sought to produce a purely optical art stripped of all but perceptual associations. Vibrating colors, concentric circles, and pulsating moiré patterns were characteristic of op works by Victor Vasarely, Richard Anuszkiewicz, Bridget RILEY, Ad REINHARDT, and Kenneth NOLAND. A comprehensive exhibition of op art, entitled "The Responsive Eye," was organized by the Museum of Modern Art, New York City, in 1965.

Opava (ō′pävä), Ger. *Troppau,* city (1970 pop. 50,194), N central Czechoslovakia, in Moravia, on the Opava River and near the Polish border. A prosperous market center in a fertile agricultural region, it has food-processing plants and industries producing machinery, mining equipment, metal goods, textiles, pharmaceuticals, and timber. The city is also a road and rail hub. Opava was founded in the 12th cent. and later became the capital of Austrian Silesia. In 1820 representatives of the European great powers met there, at the Congress of Troppau, to discuss problems arising after the settlement of the Napoleonic Wars. City landmarks include a 15th-century cathedral built by the Teutonic Knights, the 15th-century Church of St. George, and a 17th-century Jesuit foundation.

Opelika (ōpəlī′kə), city (1970 pop. 19,027), seat of Lee co., E Ala., near the Chattahoochee River, in a farm area; inc. 1854. It is a trade center, with textile, lumber, and metallurgical industries.

Opelousas (ŏpəlo͞o′səs), city (1970 pop. 20,387), seat of St. Landry parish, S central La.; inc. 1821. Its industries are based chiefly on the agricultural products and livestock of the surrounding region. Opelousas still retains some of its early French and Spanish flavor, and many antebellum structures remain. It was founded c.1765 by French traders and served (1863) as state capital for a period during the Civil War. James Bowie lived there and his house is now a museum.

open-chain compound: see ALIPHATIC COMPOUND.

open cluster, see STAR CLUSTER.

Open Door, maintenance in a certain territory of equal commercial and industrial rights for the nationals of all countries. As a specific policy, it was first advanced by the United States, but it was rooted in the typical MOST-FAVORED-NATION CLAUSE of the treaties concluded with China after the OPIUM WAR (1839–42). Although the Open Door is generally associated with China, it also received recognition at the Berlin Conference of 1885, which declared that no power could levy preferential duties in the Congo basin. The United States had become a Far Eastern power through the acquisition of the Philippine Islands, and when the partition of China by the European powers and Japan seemed imminent, the U.S. government strove to preserve equal industrial and commercial privileges. Secretary of State John Hay sent (1899) notes to the major powers (France, Germany, Great Britain, Italy, Japan, and Russia), asking them to declare formally that they would uphold Chinese territorial and administrative integrity and would not interfere with the free use of the treaty ports within their spheres of influence in China. In replying, each nation evaded Hay's request, taking the position that it could not commit itself until the other nations had complied. However, in March, 1900, Hay announced that the powers had granted consent to his request. Only Japan challenged this declaration and the Open Door became an international policy. After the BOXER UPRISING, Hay dispatched (1900) a similar circular note. Two years later, the U.S. government protested that Russian encroachment in MANCHURIA was a violation of the Open Door. When Japanese replaced Russian influence in S Manchuria after the Russo-Japanese War (1904–5) the Japanese and U.S. governments pledged to maintain a policy of equality in Manchuria. In finance, American efforts to preserve the Open Door led (1909) to the formation of an international banking consortium through which all Chinese railroad loans would be made. The United States withdrew in 1913, asserting that the consortium violated Chinese administrative integrity. The next violation of the Open Door policy occurred in 1915, when Japan presented to China the TWENTY-ONE DEMANDS. That incident led (1917) to another exchange of notes between the United States and Japan in which there were renewed assurances that the Open Door would be respected, but that the United States recognized Japan's special interests in China. The Open Door principle had been further weakened by a series of secret treaties (1917) between Japan and the Allies, which promised Japan the German possessions in China. The increasing disregard of the Open Door was a main reason for the convocation of the Conference on the Limitation of Armament (1921–22) in Washington, D.C. As a result of the conference, the Nine-Power Treaty, guaranteeing the integrity and independence of China and reaffirming the Open Door principle, was signed by the United States, Great Britain, Japan, France, Italy, the Netherlands, Portugal, China, and Belgium. With the Japanese seizure (1931) of Manchuria and the creation of Manchukuo, the Open Door received its greatest reverse. After World War II, China's position as a sovereign state was recognized. No nation, therefore, had the right or capacity to carve out spheres of influence or to attempt to exclude other states from trade, and the Open Door policy ceased to exist. See G. Z. Wood, *The Genesis of the Open Door Policy in China* (1921); M. J. Bau, *The Open Door Doctrine in Relation to China* (1923); C. S. Campbell, *Special Business Interests and the Open Door Policy* (1951); William L. Tung, *China and the Foreign Powers* (1970).

open education, also known as open classroom, type of educational reform. The central tenet of this informal system is that children want to learn and will do so naturally if left to their own initiative. The open classroom is marked by decentralized learning areas, freedom of movement from area to area and even from room to room, group and individual student activities, and unstructured periods of study.

Open education is concerned with erasing the formalized roles of student and teacher; instruction itself is rarely given to more than two or three pupils at a time and the same material is hardly ever presented to the class as a whole. Growing out of principles developed at British infant and junior schools, it first became popular in American elementary schools during the late 1960s. Many of its ideas were enunciated earlier by those involved in the PROGRESSIVE EDUCATION movement. See Herbert R. Kohl, *The Open Classroom* (1969); *Open Education,* ed. by Ewald B. Nyquist and Gene R. Hawes (1972).

open-end investment company: see MUTUAL FUND.

open enrollment, a policy of admitting to college all high school graduates in an effort to provide a higher education for all who desire it. To critics it means an inevitable lowering of standards as a considerable effort must be devoted to development of basic skills. The most ambitious programs of open enrollment in the United States have been undertaken in California and New York City. Under California's system, codified in 1960, high school graduates in the top eighth of their class may attend a Univ. of California campus. Those in the top third qualify for a state college. All the rest may attend a two-year junior college. New York City's plan, begun in 1970, guarantees every high school graduate, academic or vocational, a tuition-free place in a city college.

open-hearth process: see STEEL.

open shop: see CLOSED SHOP AND OPEN SHOP.

Open University, at Walton, Buckinghamshire, England; founded 1969. In 1971 a teaching program was begun that consists of correspondence courses integrated with television and radio broadcasts, residential summer schools, and a counseling and tutorial service that operates through a network of local study centers. Students (about 40,000) are usually over 21, working full-time, and studying in their spare time. The university has faculties of arts, educational sciences, mathematics, science, social sciences, and technology.

Opéra (ôpärä'), chief opera house of Paris, on the Place de l'Opéra, one of the main crossroads on the right bank of the Seine. Designed by J. L. C. GARNIER, it was built between 1861 and 1875. One of the largest and most sumptuous theaters in the world, it has a smaller seating capacity than many lesser houses, because its huge stage and foyers and its famous grand staircase take up much of the room. The Paris Opéra has been copied, on a reduced scale, by many opera houses throughout the world. The home of grand opera in the 19th cent., it has retained its musical reputation as one of the world's foremost houses. Its corps de ballet is particularly famous. On the facade of the Opéra is the masterwork of the sculptor J. B. Carpeaux, *The Dance.*

opera, drama set to music. The LIBRETTO may be serious or comic, although neither form necessarily excludes elements of the other. Opera differs from OPERETTA in its musical complexity and usually in its subject matter. It differs also from ORATORIO, which is customarily based on a religious subject and is given without scenery, costumes, or stage action. Although both opera and operetta may have spoken dialogue, in opera the dialogue usually has musical accompaniment, such as the harpsichord continuo in the operas of Mozart and Rossini. More often, the music in opera is continuous, with set pieces such as solos, duets, trios, quartets, etc., and choral pieces designed to dramatize the action and display the particular vocal skills of the principal singers. For example, the last act trio from Gounod's *Faust* gives Mephistopheles (bass), Faust (tenor), and Marguerite (soprano) excellent opportunity to display their vocal talents singly and then weave their voices in ensemble singing as the two men vie for the soul of Marguerite, who is intent on salvation. The artificial conventions of opera—dialogue that is sung rather than spoken and the somewhat exaggerated style of acting—are mostly overcome by the composer's music.

Early Opera in Italy, France, England, and Germany. Although musical drama, such as *The Play of Daniel* (12th cent.), had previously existed, it was in the year 1600 that opera came into being. Opera began in Florence, Italy, fostered by the *camerata* [society], a group of scholars, philosophers, and amateur musicians that included the librettist Ottavio Rinuccini (1562–1621) and the composers Vincenzo Galilei, Emilio del Cavaliere (c.1550–1602), Jacopo Peri, and Giulio Caccini. It was their aim to promote the principle of monodic musical declamation, i.e., a single melodic line with little or no accompaniment that emulated the style of ancient Greek drama; accordingly, the earliest operas took their plots from mythology, the legend of Orpheus and Eurydice being one of the most popular. The early composers referred to their work as dramma per musica [drama through music], and operas of the 17th and 18th cent., based on myth, lofty in tone, with much pageantry and elaborate arias, became known as opera seria. Although fragments of Jacopo Peri's *Dafne* (c.1597) exist, the same composer's *Euridice* (1600), set to verse by Ottavio Rinuccini, is generally considered the first opera. Development of BAROQUE opera occurred at Rome and Venice. In 1632 appeared the work that established Roman opera, *Sant' Alessio,* by Stefano Landi (c.1590–c.1625), with a libretto by Giulio Rospigliosi (later Pope Clement IX). Landi modified the strict declamatory style of the Florentines with formal devices: The RECITATIVE and ARIA became clearly differentiated, and more prominent use was made of choruses and instrumental form. Also, the libretto included comic scenes, which had had no part in earlier operas. However, it was not until the appearance of Claudio Monteverdi in Venice that baroque opera reached its peak, and the art form that began as entertainment for the aristocracy became available to popular audiences. In 1637 the first public opera house in the world opened in Venice, and by 1700 at least 16 more theaters were built and hundreds of operas produced. At the Venetian public opera house two of Monteverdi's best-known works, the early *La Favola d'Orfeo* (*The Tale of Orpheus,* 1607) and *L'Incoronazione di Poppea* (*The Coronation of Poppea,* 1642), were performed. Monteverdi's influence was considerable, for he may be said to be responsible for the introduction of bel canto and buffo styles. He also reflected the moods and dramatic vividness of the opera, and his work became a model for the operatic composers who followed. With the next generation of Venetian composers, headed by Marcantonio Cesti (1623–69) and Pietro Francesco Cavalli, an international style developed, and local schools disappeared. The recitative diminished in musical interest in favor of the aria, the chorus gave way to the virtuoso soloist, and the Renaissance interest in antiquities was superseded by a trend toward comedy and parody. Alessandro Stradella, a forerunner of the 18th-century Neapolitan school, wrote operas in this style. The official existence of French opera began in 1669 with the establishment of the Académie royale de Musique, which was taken over by Jean Baptiste Lully in 1672 after the bankruptcy of its founders. Italian opera, the pastoral, French classical tragedy, and the *ballet de cour* (see BALLET) were the antecedents of French opera. Lully introduced his audience to grand-scale entertainment: lavish stage settings and scenery in addition to ballets, choruses, and long disquisitions on love and glory. His operas were divided into five acts and a prologue. The operas of Jean Philippe Rameau followed the tradition established by Lully, but were less successful. Two of his works, however, *Les Indes galantes* (*The Gallant Indies,* 1735) and *Castor et Pollux* (1737), have music surpassing their librettos. The Neapolitans also had opera seria, notably in the works of Alessandro Scarlatti, but they added another element to the art in the form of opera buffa. Comedy had already made its appearance in opera, mainly in the form of brief interludes, or intermezzi (see INTERMEZZO), that were played between the acts of opera seria. Now it came into its own, with such works as Giovanni Battista Pergolesi's *La serva padrona* (*The Servant as Mistress,* 1733), Giovanni Paisiello's (1740–1816) *Il Barbiere di Siviglia* (*The Barber of Seville,* 1782), and Domenico Cimarosa's *Il matrimonio segreto* (*The Secret Marriage,* 1792). The characters were from commedia dell'arte, the subject matter satirical and earthy, replacing the staid classical heroism of earlier operas. There was no spoken dialogue. The first English opera was *The Siege of Rhodes,* with a text by poet laureate Sir William D'Avenant, in 1656. The MASQUE was the true antecedent of English opera, and John Blow's *Venus and Adonis* (c.1685) was actually an opera. The one great English opera of the 17th cent. was *Dido and Aeneas* (1689), by Henry Purcell, after whose death England succumbed completely to Italian opera. The reigning "English" composer was a German who had completely absorbed the Neapolitan Italian style, George Frideric Handel. Although best-known as the composer of the oratorio *Messiah,* Handel spent most of his musical energy between 1705 and 1738 in composing operas. His first opera in England was *Rinaldo* (1711), an instant success, and among the many other operas he composed are *Giulio Cesare* (1724), *Rodelinda* (1725), and *Alcina* (1735). Handel's operas featured castrati (see CASTRATO), who had great popularity, and who were beginning to dominate opera, sometimes forcing composers to write around them, adding music that had little or nothing to do with the plot. Coincident with Handel's efforts at establishing Italian opera in England were the attempts of native talent to produce an English musical theatrical form. The result was *The Begger's Opera* (1728), with a libretto by the poet John Gay and music composed partly by John Christopher Pepusch; *The Beggar's Opera* inaugurated the form of ballad opera that satirized Italian opera and contemporary politics and eventually led to the singspiel, the German comic opera with spoken dialogue, that was to reach it highest development in the works of Wolfgang Amadeus Mozart. Although the early court opera of Germany showed preference for the Italian school—Frederick the Great is said to have compared German singing to the neighing of horses—in the 18th cent. German composers began to turn their attention to singspiel. Georg Philipp Telemann had anticipated the technique of Pergolesi's *La serva padrona* in his *Pimpione* (1725), a comic opera with only two characters. In the same vein is Johann Christian Standfuss's (?–1756) *Der Teufel ist Los* (*The Devil to Pay,* 1752), an unpretentious composition written in the simple style of folk melody. However, it was Mozart's *Die Entfürhung aus dem Serail* (*The Abduction from the Seraglio,* 1782) that fully established singspiel in Vienna, the international music capital. Singspiel had now become fused with Italian aria-oriented opera. Throughout the 17th and 18th cent., Italian opera seria continued to dominate the musical scene. It was not until the works of Christoph Willibald von Gluck that the course of opera took a new turn. In a letter to the Grand Duke Leopold of Tuscany, Gluck stated his principal aim: "I sought to restrict music to its true function, namely to serve poetry by means of expression—and the situations which make up the plot—without interrupting the action. . ." He accomplished that aim with *Orfeo ed Euridice* (1762) and *Alceste* (1767). The unity of drama and music was continued by Mozart, who presents characters familiar to every age, with all the virtues and foibles of the human race. Goethe compared him with Shakespeare; underlying Mozart's panorama of characters is music of the utmost humor, drama, delicacy, and charm. His major librettist was Lorenzo da Ponte (1749–1838), who produced texts for three of Mozart's greatest works: *Le Nozze di Figaro* (*The Marriage of Figaro,* 1786), *Don Giovanni* (1787), and *Così fan tutte* (*Women are Like That,* 1790). In *La clemenza di Tito* (1791) Mozart used the work of Pietro Metastasio for his libretto. Metastasio, who had come to Vienna in 1730, was one of the most influential librettists of his day. Many of his librettos were used several times by various composers, including Handel and Gluck. The libretto for Mozart's last great opera *Die Zauberflöte* (*The Magic Flute,* 1791) was written by Emmanuel Schikaneder (1751–1812).

Opera in the 19th Cent. Hero worship, a return to nature, idealism, and fantasy are elements of late 18th-century romanticism that found their way into 19th-century German opera. Ludwig van Beethoven's only opera, *Fidelio* (1805, rev. 1814), is set against the background of personal freedom versus political tyranny. But it was Mozart's *Die Zauberflöte,* which rested on the foundations of singspiel, that was really the point of departure for German romantic opera—for E. T. A. Hoffmann's *Undine* (1816) and Carl Maria von Weber's *Der Freischütz* (1821) and *Oberon* (1826). These operas, although somewhat limited in melodic invention, fused in their plots the natural and the supernatural and paved the way for the grandiose music dramas of Richard Wagner, who also wrote his own librettos. Wagner's early operas, such as *Rienzi* (1842), based on Edward Bulwer-Lytton's novel of the same name, and *Der Fliegende Holländer* (*The Flying Dutchman,* 1843) are Italian-style operas, with arias, duets, trios, and choral pieces. In the romantic tradition, he turned to medieval lore for *Tannhäuser* (1845) and to tales of chivalry and knighthood for *Lohengrin* (1850), *Tristan und Isolde* (1865), and *Parsifal* (1882). *Die Meistersinger von Nürnberg* (1868), Wagner's only comic opera, used the real-life cobbler and poet Hans Sachs as the central character. The set pieces of the Italian school were put aside in favor of leitmotifs (leading motifs) that were used to identify individual characters and situations and present a flow of music, at times almost symphonic in nature, that was uninterrupted by recitative. The culmination of this technique was *Der Ring des Ni-*

belungen (*The Ring of the Nibelungs*), a tetralogy composed of *Das Rheingold* (1869); *Die Walküre* (1870); *Siegfried* (1876); and *Götterdämmerung* (1876). After the French Revolution (1789), spectacular and melodramatic operas became popular. Outstanding examples are by Luigi Cherubini, Étienne Nicolas Méhul, Jean François Lesueur, and Gasparo Spontini. Extensive use was made of plots involving rescue. Paris had now become the center of operatic activity, and the performance there of Daniel François Esprit Auber's *La Muette de Portici* (*The Mute Girl of Portici*, 1828), also known after its hero as *Masaniello*, Gioacchino Rossini's *Guillaume Tell* (*William Tell*, 1829), Giacomo Meyerbeer's *Robert le Diable* (1831), and Jacques Halévy's *La Juive* (*The Jewess*, 1835) established grand opera, of which Meyerbeer's works were the outstanding examples, featuring historical subjects with pointed reference to contemporary issues, religious elements, and violent passions. The influence of French grand opera was enormous, reaching even to the early works of Wagner and Verdi. Hector Berlioz's masterpiece *Les Troyens* (*The Trojans*, 1890), while owing nothing to Meyerbeer, may also be considered grand opera. Opéra comique (distinguished from grand opera in that it had spoken dialogue) in the middle of the 19th cent. took two directions, leading on the one hand toward operetta and on the other toward a more serious, lyrical opera. Of that genre Ambroise Thomas, Charles Gounod, Georges Bizet, Léo Delibes, and Jules Massenet were the chief composers. Gounod's *Faust* (1859) and Bizet's *Carmen* (1875), two of the most popular French operas ever written, actually had spoken dialogue in their original versions, but this qualification for works given at the Opéra Comique Theater was ultimately dropped. The operas of Emmanuel Chabrier and Vincent d'Indy show the influence of Wagner, while Gustave Charpentier's *Louise* (1900) is representative of naturalism. Perhaps the most complete realization of the ideals that had marked French opera from its beginning was Claude Debussy's *Pelléas et Mélisande* (1902). During this period Italian opera remained relatively independent of both the Parisian style and the later Wagner music drama. In Italy, the voice remained master of the orchestra, and melody, presented with clarity and directness, ruled out overly polyphonic writing. The early masters of melody were Rossini, Donizetti, and Bellini. An introduction, a formal aria displaying bel canto singing, i.e., smoothness of vocal line with flawless phrasing and high notes, sometimes followed by a cabaletta (a rapid passage requiring precision singing), were the foundations of their operas. Rossini's *L'Italiana in Algeri (The Italian Girl in Algiers*, 1813) and *Il Barbiere di Siviglia* (1816) are just two of his comic operas that provide sparkling melodies, brilliant arias and ensembles, and fast-moving plots. Gaetano Donizetti wrote tragedies (for example, *Lucia di Lammermoor*, 1835) and a trilogy on the queens Elizabeth I, Mary Stuart, and Anne Boleyn that gave the soprano lead exquisite scenes and arias for displaying her ability at coloratura singing. His two comic operas *L'Elisir d'Amore* (1832) and *Don Pasquale* (1843) are in the same bubbling melodic vein of the best of Rossini. Vincenzo Bellini also gave his leading ladies splendid arias combining dramatic and coloratura techniques, such as those in *Norma* (1831) and *I Puritani* (1835); nor did he, Rossini, or Donizetti slight the male voices, writing parts that enabled them to display astonishing vocal versatility. The dominant composer of the period, however, was Giuseppe Verdi, whose operas epitomized the lyric-dramatic style of the Italian school. Verdi's operas are usually classified by periods—early, middle, late. Of the early period, *Nabucco* (*Nebuchadnezzar*, 1842) was his first success. The middle period contains three undisputed masterpieces: *Rigoletto* (1851, based on Victor Hugo's drama *The King's Jester*), *Il Trovatore* (*The Troubador*, 1853), and *La Traviata* (1853, based on Alexandre Dumas' play *Camille*). All are characterized by Verdi's trademark: magnificent, sustained melodies in the standard forms of aria, recitative, and choral numbers. The work initiating Verdi's third period was *Aïda* (1871). All his life Verdi searched for the ideal libretto and finally found two in his last operas. The tragic *Otello* (1887) and the comic *Falstaff* (1893), based on plays by Shakespeare with librettos by Arrigo Boito, brought new dimensions to operatic music, the melodic outpouring vividly emphasizing the plight of the jealousy-mad Otello and the humor of the larger-than-life comic figure of Falstaff. Verdi also wrote two operas for the Paris Opéra: *Les Vêpres siciliennes* (*The Sicilian Vespers*, 1855) and *Don Carlos* (1867). Toward the end of the 19th cent. the verismo style came into being, which attempted to show the seamier side of life while still cast in the musical tradition of Italian opera. Of these, Pietro Mascagni's *Cavalleria Rusticana* (*Rustic Chivalry*, 1890) and Ruggiero Leoncavallo's *I Pagliacci* (*The Clowns*, 1892), are prime examples. Of Verdi's successors in Italy, the only one who approached his genius was Giacomo Puccini. His simple, lyrical melodies, at times criticized for being overly sentimental, underline the tragic fates of his fragile heroines. *Manon Lescaut* (1893) and *La Bohème* (1896) were Puccini's first two triumphs, and both brought him international fame. *Tosca* (1900), based on a melodrama by Victorien Sardou, was another instant success, but *Madama Butterfly* (1904) failed when it was first performed, only to become a hit when revised a few months after its premiere. The suggestion that Puccini write on an American theme resulted in *La Fanciulla del West* (*The Girl of the Golden West*, 1910). Although not the overwhelming success of his previous operas, *La Fanciulla* had harmonic textures that were a departure from his earlier work and anticipated the music of Puccini's last opera, *Turandot* (1926). The 19th cent. also saw the beginning of Russian opera, marked by the nonnational romanticism of Peter Ilyich Tchaikovsky in *Eugene Onegin* (1879), after Pushkin's poem, and *The Queen of Spades* (1890). On the other hand, Mikhail Glinka in *A Life for the Czar* (1836) and *Russlan and Ludmilla* (1842), Aleksandr Dargomijsky in *Russalka* (1856), and Modest Moussorgsky in his masterpiece *Boris Godunov* (1874), turned to Russian history and literature to produce strictly national operas. Nicolai Rimsky-Korsakov added the dimension of folklore and fantasy in *May Night* (1880), *The Snow Maiden* (1881), and in his last opera, *The Golden Cockerel* (1909).

20th-century Opera. In the early part of the 20th cent. the foremost operatic composer was Richard Strauss. Although influenced by Wagner, he composed operas with rich and stunning orchestrations, often using dissonant harmonies and abandoning tonality to emphasize the humor or drama of a scene. Among his most successful operas are *Salomé* (1905), *Elektra* (1909), *Der Rosenkavalier* (1911), *Ariadne auf Naxos* (1912), and the allegorical *Die Frau ohne Schatten* (*The Woman without a Shadow*, 1919). After World War I a period of innovation began that has continued to the present day. Alban Berg's *Wozzeck* (1925) and *Lulu* (unfinished, 1937) have been the most enduring of early atonal operas; Arnold Schoenberg's serial work *Moses and Aaron* (unfinished, 1932) had successful revivals in the United States in the 1960s. Paul Hindemith's *Mathis der Maler* (1938), dealing with the life of the painter Mathias Grünewald, represents the trend of the 1930s toward lavishly staged, moralistic epics. Operatic composers who have emerged since World War II include Gian-Carlo Menotti, Samuel Barber, Alberto Ginastera, and Hans Werner Henze. The former two have composed in traditional musical idiom, such as Menotti's *The Medium* (1946), *The Consul* (1950), and *Amahl and the Night Visitors* (written for television, 1951) and Barber's *Vanessa* (1957) and *Antony and Cleopatra* (1966). Henze's *The Young Lord* (1965) and Ginastera's *Bomarzo* (1964) and *Beatrix Cenci* (1971) have been highly innovative and controversial. Operas by the Americans Douglas Moore and Carlisle Floyd have used American history, legend, and folk music, as reflected in Moore's *The Ballad of Baby Doe* (1956) and Floyd's *Susannah* (1955). The most internationally accepted post-World War II composer of operas is the Englishman Benjamin Britten. His first operatic success was *Peter Grimes* (1945), followed by *The Rape of Lucretia* (1946). Britten's other works include *Billy Budd* (after Melville's story, 1951), *The Turn of the Screw* (after Henry James's story, 1954), *A Midsummer Night's Dream* (1960), and *Death in Venice* (after the novella by Thomas Mann, 1973). Britten's operas are cast in traditional musical and dramatic form. Owing to indifference to new works on the part of the opera-going public and most major opera houses, plus the financial burden incurred in staging a new work, many composers in the 1960s and 70s turned to community and college opera workshops to produce their works. See articles on individual composers, e.g., WAGNER, VERDI.

Bibliography. See Wallace Brockway and Herbert Weinstock, *The World of Opera* (1962); E. J. Dent, *Opera* (rev. ed. 1965); D. J. Grout, *A Short History of Opera* (2d ed. 1965); Herbert Graf, *Opera for the People* (2d ed. 1969); R. G. Pauly, *Music and the Theater: An Introduction to Opera* (1970); Joseph Wechsberg, *The Opera* (1972); Leslie Orrey, *A Concise History of Opera* (1973). For studies of librettos see P. J. Smith, *The Tenth Muse* (1971) and A. H. Drummond, *American Opera Librettos* (1973). For books containing summaries of opera plots, see M. J. Cross, *Complete Stories of the Great Operas* (1952) and *More Stories of the Great Operas* (1971) and *The Victor Book of the Opera* (13th ed., ed. by H. W. Simon, 1968).

opera glass: see BINOCULAR.

operational amplifier, AMPLIFIER whose output voltage is proportional to the negative of its input voltage and that boosts the amplitude of an input signal many times, i.e., has a very high gain. It is usually connected so that part of the output is fed back to the input. Operational amplifiers were originally developed to be used in synthesizing mathematical operations in analog COMPUTERS, hence their name. Because of recent advances in semiconductor technology, they have become available as integrated circuits. They are widely used when a closely controlled amount of gain or some form of signal processing is necessary in an electronic system.

operetta (ŏpərĕt'ə), type of light opera with a frivolous, sentimental story, often employing parody and satire and containing both spoken dialogue and much light, pleasant music. In the early 19th-century *opéras comiques* of Boieldieu, Auber, and Adolphe Adam, there was a growing tendency toward sophistication, preparing the way for Offenbach, who during the Second Empire created the operetta. The distinction between the operetta and the lighter examples of *opéra comique* that immediately preceded it is hard to draw; in general the *opéra comique* makes some appeal to the sentiments, while the French operetta attempts only to amuse. The Viennese operetta, dating from c.1870, did not have the excellent librettists that the French enjoyed; the operettas of Johann Strauss the younger suffered from this defect. Those of Suppé owe much of their virtue to Offenbach's influence. Less distinguished are the products of the early 20th cent., represented by the works of Franz Lehár and Oscar Straus. The immortal operettas of W. S. Gilbert and Sir Arthur Sullivan were to London of the 1880s what Offenbach's works had been to Paris 20 years earlier. The noteworthy composers in American operetta are Victor Herbert and Reginald de Koven. After World War I operettas gradually gave way to musical comedies (see MUSICALS).

operon, in molecular biology, site on a chromosome containing genes that control protein synthesis (structural genes) together with a gene that determines whether the structural genes function or not (operator gene). See NUCLEIC ACID.

Ophel (ō'fəl), hill in ancient Jerusalem. It was the dwelling place of Nethinim. 2 Chron. 27.3; 33.14; Neh. 11.21.

ophicleide (ŏf'ĭklīd) [Gr.,=serpent with keys], brass wind musical instrument of relatively wide conical bore, largest of the keyed BUGLES; invented in 1817

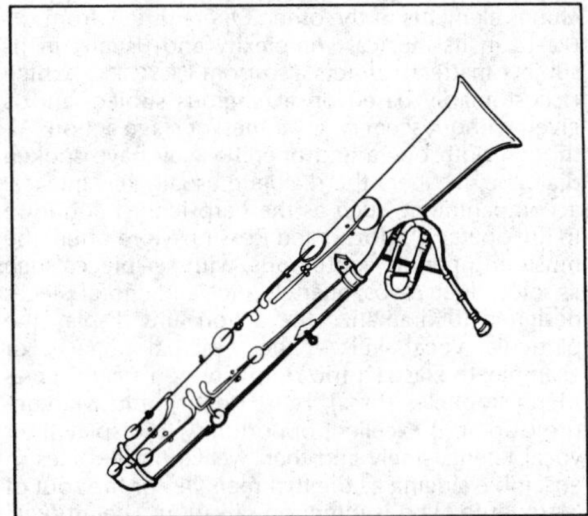

Ophicleide

by Jean-Hilaire Asté of Paris. It had from 8 to 11 keys and a full, loud tone; since its intonation was deficient, however, it was soon displaced in the orchestra by the bass tuba. Many composers scored for it before the tuba was available.

Ophion (ōfī'ən), in Greek mythology, a huge serpent. According to the Pelasgian creation myth, he ruled the world with his mother, Eurynome, before the reign of Cronus. When he became unruly, Eurynome banished him to the underworld.

Ophir (ō'fər). **1** Seaport or region, frequently mentioned in the Old Testament, from which the ships of Solomon brought fine gold in great quantity. Sandalwood, precious stones, ivory, apes, and peacocks were also part of the triennial cargo. The location of Ophir is unknown. It has been variously identified with NE Africa, SE Arabia, and India, but the present tendency is to identify it with SW Arabia (the modern Yemen) and possibly the neighboring African coast. 1 Kings 9.28; 10.11; 22.48; 1 Chron. 29.4; 2 Chron. 8.18; 9.10; Job 22.24; 28.16; Ps. 45.9; Isa. 13.12. **2** Son of Joktan. Gen. 10.29; 1 Chron. 1.23.

Ophites (ŏ'fīts) [Gr.,=believers in the serpent], group of Gnostic sects notorious for extreme cultism and inverted morality. Certain of these sects were known as Naasseni. Almost all that is known of Ophitism has been gleaned from St. Irenaeus, Origen, and other writers opposed to GNOSTICISM. The Ophites carried to extremes the teaching of MARCION that an essential hostility exists between the God of the Old Testament and the God of the New Testament. The Ophites held that the Old Testament villains were actually heroes and revered Cain, the Sodomites, and the Egyptians. Specially worshiped was the serpent, as the creature in Eden that tried to give Adam and Eve the knowledge withheld from them by Jehovah. Much of the serpent worship and the occult ritualism was probably symbolic of certain esoteric knowledge. The Ophites acknowledged Jesus as the savior, but rejected the importance of the crucifixion; Christ came to reveal gnosis (knowledge), not to die for men's sins. One Ophitic hymn, the *Hymn of the Naasenes,* survives. See Ernesto Buonaiuti, *Gnostic Fragments* (1924); R. M. Grant, *Gnosticism and Early Christianity* (1959, rev. ed. 1966).

Ophni (ŏf'nī), unidentified town, E central Palestine, allotted to Benjamin. Joshua 18.24.

Ophrah (ŏf'rə). **1** Judahite. 1 Chron. 4.14. **2** Benjamite town, central Palestine, the modern et-Taiyiba (Jordan), NE of Bethel. Joshua 18.23; 1 Sam. 13.17. **3** Home town of Gideon, not identified. Judges 6.11,24; 8.27,32; 9.5.

ophthalmia neonatorum: see CONJUNCTIVITIS.

ophthalmology (ŏf"thălmŏl'əjē), branch of medicine specializing in the anatomy, function, and diseases of the EYE. In a broad sense it includes infection and other disorders of the eye, surgery, refraction, orthoptics, prevention of blindness, and care of the blind. An important contributor to the evolution of self-illuminating diagnostic instruments was Allvar Gullstrand of Sweden. He devised the slit-lamp (which illuminates the interior of the eye with an intense beam of light) in 1911. He improved the stationary OPHTHALMOSCOPE (instrument for viewing the interior of the eye) in 1912; portable ophthalmoscopes were developed later. Other instruments used in ophthalmology include the tonometer, a device for determining the fluid pressure in the eye, and the ophthalmometer, an instrument for measuring the eye's dimensions, capacity, and refractive errors. The sulfa drugs, antibiotics, and cortisone products have played an important role in the cure of highly destructive eye infections. Advances in surgery of the eye have saved or restored the sight of many who in former years were doomed to certain blindness. Procedures for cataract removal are constantly being improved. Operation for detached retina, originally devised by Jules Gonin of Switzerland, has also undergone improvement. Ramon Castroviejo of New York was largely responsible for the development of corneal transplantation—use of corneas of the deceased to restore sight to the living. Great advances have been made in preventive measures: routine examination of school children for eye infections and refractive errors; periodic tonometric readings to detect glaucoma in older persons; regulation of lighting conditions in occupational establishments; and strict inspection of immigrants for contagious eye infections.

ophthalmoscope (ŏfthăl'məskōp"), instrument used for examining the inner structure of the EYE. The device was invented by the German physiologist H. L. F. von Helmholtz in 1851. His model consisted of three plates of glass pressed together and mounted on a handle at a 45° angle. A light was placed beside the subject whose eyes were to be examined. Some light passed through the plates, but some was reflected back into the eye. The form of the instrument now in general use consists of a concave mirror and a battery-powered light source within a tubular handle. Sighting is through a single or binocular eyepiece. The ophthalmoscope is equipped with a rotating disc of lenses to permit observation of the eye at varying depths and magnifications. Examination of the eye may be enhanced by administering drugs to dilate the pupil.

opiate drug, any of a group of drugs derived from OPIUM that are NARCOTICS. Used medically to relieve pain and induce sleep, they include CODEINE, MORPHINE, and the morphine derivative HEROIN. Sometimes included in the group are certain synthetic drugs that have morphinelike pharmacological action.

Opie, John, 1761–1807, English portrait and historical painter. Opie showed a remarkable talent as a young man. He became the protégé of the poet John Wolcot, and enjoyed a brief popularity as a fashionable portrait painter in the Reynolds tradition. In 1786 he began a series of seven pictures for Boydell's Shakespeare Gallery. His portrait of Mary Wollstonecraft is in the National Portrait Gallery, London. See Ada Earland, *John Opie and His Circle* (1911).

Opitz, Martin (mär'tĭn ō'pĭts), 1597–1639, leader of the Silesian school of German poetry. His influence as poet, critic, and metrical reformer was widely recognized during his time; he was ennobled as Opitz von Boberfeld by Emperor Ferdinand II in Vienna. Opitz's poems, written during the THIRTY YEARS WAR, reflect shifting religious and worldly loyalties; *Lob des Krieges-Gottes* [in praise of the god of war] preceded only briefly *Trost Gedichte in Widerwertigkeit des Krieges* [comfort poems in troubled war times] (1633). Opitz's greatest contribution to the literary arts was his *Buch von der deutschen Poeterey* [book on German poetry] (1624). His translation of Rinuccini's *Dafne* became the libretto for the first German opera. See study by Bernhard Ulmer (1971).

opium, substance derived by collecting and drying the milky juice in the unripe seed pods of the opium POPPY (*Papaver somniferum*). Opium varies in color from yellow to dark brown and has a characteristic odor and a bitter taste. Its chief active principle is the alkaloid MORPHINE, a NARCOTIC. Other constituents are the alkaloids CODEINE, PAPAVERINE, and noscapine (narcotine); HEROIN is synthesized from morphine. Opium and its various constituents exert effects upon the body ranging from analgesia, or insensitivity to pain, to narcosis, or depressed physiological activity leading to stupor. Morphine, heroin, and codeine are addicting drugs; papaverine and narcotine are not. A tincture of opium is called LAUDANUM; PAREGORIC is a mixture of opium, alcohol, and camphor. The medicinal properties of opium have been known from the earliest times, and it was used as a narcotic in Sumerian and European cultures at least as early as 4000 B.C. The drug was introduced into India by the Muslims and its use spread to China; the practice of opium smoking was brought to the United States by Chinese immigrants. Large quantities of opium are still grown in India, Pakistan, Afghanistan, parts of South America, and a geographical region encompassing parts of Burma, Laos, and Thailand. Despite laws and agreements to control its use, a worldwide illicit opium traffic persists. See DRUG ADDICTION AND DRUG ABUSE.

Opium War, 1839–42, conflict between Great Britain and China. Great Britain, seeking to end the restrictions imposed by China on foreign trade, found a pretext for action when, in 1839, China took action to enforce its prohibition of opium importing. Opium belonging to British merchants was destroyed at Canton, and the British responded by attacking several coastal cities. China, unable to withstand modern arms, was easily defeated. The Treaty of Nanking (1842) provided that the ports of Canton, Amoy, Foochow, Ningpo, and Shanghai should be open to British trade and residence; in addition Hong Kong was ceded to the British. Within a few years other Western powers received commercial and residential privileges, and the foreign "occupation"' of China began. In 1856 a second war broke out following the Chinese seizure of a British-registered ship, the *Arrow,* in Canton. British and French troops took Canton and Tientsin and compelled the Chinese to accept the treaties of Tientsin (1858), to which France, Russia, and the United States were also party. China agreed to open 11 more ports, permit foreign legations in Peking, sanction Christian missionary activity, and legalize the importation of opium. China's subsequent attempt to block the entry of diplomats into Peking led to a renewal of the war in 1859. This time the British and French occupied Peking and burnt the imperial summer palace. The Peking conventions of 1860, by which China was forced to make additional concessions, concluded the hostilities. See P. C. Kuo, *A Critical Study of the First Anglo-Chinese War* (1934); Maurice Collis, *Foreign Mud* (1946, repr 1964); Arthur Waley, *The Opium War through Chinese Eyes* (1958, repr. 1968); Hsin-Pao Chang, *Commissioner Lin and the Opium War* (1964).

Opobo (ŏpō'bō), town, SE Nigeria, in the Niger River delta. It is a palm oil collection center and has fishing and boatbuilding industries. Opobo was founded in 1869 by a group of immigrants from nearby BONNY led by JAJA, a middleman in the palm oil trade with Europeans. Opobo prospered, but Jaja antagonized the Europeans by hampering their trade. Jaja was deported by the British in 1887, after which Opobo declined.

Opole (ôpô'lĕ), Ger. *Oppeln,* city (1970 pop. 122,075), S Poland, on the Oder River. A river port and rail junction, it is also an important trade center; with manufactures of cement, metals, and furniture. Originally a Slavic settlement, it was the seat (1163–1532) of the dukes of Opole of the PIAST dynasty. The duchy passed (1532) to the house of Hapsburg and (1742) to Prussia. It was the capital (1919–45) of the Prussian province of Upper Silesia. In the city are the churches of St. Adalbert (10th cent.) and of the Holy Cross (14th cent.).

Oporto (ōōpôr'tō), Port. *Pôrto,* city (1970 pop. 310,437), capital of Porto dist. and Douro Litoral, NW Portugal, near the mouth of the Douro River. It is the second city of Portugal (Lisbon is the largest) and an important Atlantic port. Its outer harbor is at LEIXÕES. Oporto's most famous export is port wine, to which the city gives its name, but cork, fruits, olive oil, and building materials are also exported. Cotton, silk, and wool textiles are milled, clothing and leather goods are made, and there are other manufactures. The ancient settlement, probably of pre-Roman origin, was known as Cale and later as Portus Cale. Oporto was captured by the Moors in 716 and retaken in 1092. The centuries of war depopulated the town. HENRY OF BURGUNDY secured the title of duke of Portucalense in the 11th cent., and Oporto thus gave its name to the state that became a kingdom. It was for some time the chief city, although not the capital, of little Portugal. Wine exports increased after the Methuen Treaty (1703) with England. The creation by the marquês de Pombal of a wine monopoly brought the "tipplers' revolt" (1757) in Oporto. After the French conquest of Portugal in the Peninsular War, Oporto was the first city to revolt (1808). It was retaken by the French but liberated (1809) by Wellington. In 1832, in the Miguelist Wars, Dom Pedro I of Brazil long withstood a siege of the city by his brother, Dom Miguel. Oporto was later a center of republican thought, and in 1891 an abortive republican government was set up there. The city's most conspicuous landmark is the Torre dos Clérigos, a baroque tower; also noteworthy are the Romanesque cathedral, and the two-storied Dom Luis bridge (1881–87), which spans the Douro.

opossum (əpŏs'əm, pŏs'-), name for several MARSUPIALS, or pouched mammals, of the family Didelphidae, native to Central and South America, with one species extending N to the United States. With the exception of an obscure group found in South American forests, opossums are the only living marsupials outside the Australia-New Guinea region. Extremely abundant despite the encroachment of civilization, and apparently little changed over millions of years, they owe their success to their adaptability, omnivorous diet, and rapid reproductive rate. Opossums are more or less arboreal, nocturnal animals, with long noses, naked ears and prehensile tails, and opposable hind toes tipped with flat pads. They eat small animals, eggs, insects, and fruit. The common, or Virginia, opossum, *Didelphis marsupialis,* ranges from Argentina to the N United States; it is found mostly in wooded areas and is common in the SE United States. The common opossum resembles a large rat, with a white face and long, coarse fur of mixed white-tipped and black-tipped hairs. It spends time both in trees and on the ground and makes nests of leaves, usually in holes in trees. When frightened it goes into a state of collapse; this involuntary "playing possum" sometimes saves it from predators, who lose interest in an apparently dead animal. The female usually has the typical marsupial pouch, although it is absent in some of the South American species. The 6 to 18 young are born after a gestation of 12 days and weigh 1/15 oz. (1.9 grams); they crawl through the mother's fur to the pouch where they are carried and nursed for three months. After emerging, they ride on the mother's back, clinging to her fur or tail with their own tails. Because it raids domestic poultry and corn, the opossum is hunted in the South as a pest, as well as for food and sport. Among the other opossum species are the tiny mouse opossums (*Marmosa* species) and the yapok, or water opossum (*Chironectes* *minimus*), which has webbed feet and leads a semiaquatic existence. The yapok ranges from Guatemala to Brazil. Opossums are classified in the phylum CHORDATA, subphylum Vertebrata, class Mammalia, order Marsupialia, family Didelphidae. See study by J. F. Keefe (1967).

Oppeln: see OPOLE, Poland.

Oppenheimer, J. Robert (ŏp'ənhī"mər), 1904–67, American physicist, b. New York City, grad. Harvard (B.A., 1925), Ph.D. Univ. of Göttingen, 1927. He taught at the Univ. of California and the California Institute of Technology from 1929 (as professor from 1936) until his appointment in 1947 as director of the Institute for Advanced Study at Princeton, N.J. His early work was concerned with the quantum theory and nuclear physics. With Max Born he contributed to the quantum theory of molecules, and later (1930) he published an important paper on the nature of antiparticles, which had been predicted but not yet detected. As director of the atomic-energy research project at Los Alamos, N.Mex., from 1942 to 1945, Oppenheimer made important contributions to the development of atomic energy for military purposes. After the atomic bomb was used against Japan, Oppenheimer became one of the foremost proponents of civilian and international control of atomic energy; he was chairman of the general advisory committee of the U.S. Atomic Energy Commission from 1946 to 1952 and consultant to the American delegate to the UN Atomic Energy Committee. He strongly opposed the development of the hydrogen bomb in 1949 on both technical and moral grounds. In 1953 he was suspended by the Atomic Energy Commission as an alleged security risk. His case stirred wide controversy. In Oct., 1954, he was unanimously reelected director of the Institute for Advanced Study. In addition to his contributions as a theoretical physicist and an administrator, Oppenheimer achieved a reputation as one of the outstanding teachers of his generation; he left a lasting influence both at California and at Princeton. His book *Science and the Common Understanding* was published in 1954. See I. I. Rabi et al., *Oppenheimer* (1969); John Major, *The Oppenheimer Hearing* (1971); P. M. Stern and H. P. Green, *The Oppenheimer Case* (1971).

Opper, Frederick Burr, 1857–1937, American cartoonist and illustrator, b. Madison, Ohio. He began as a contributor to comic papers and was associated with Frank Leslie's publications for three years, with *Puck* for 18 years, and with the New York *Journal.* His work is characterized by extreme simplicity, vigor, and humor. He illustrated the works of Mark Twain, Bill Nye, Eugene Field, and Finley P. Dunne and wrote and illustrated *Happy Hooligan* (1902), *Our Antediluvian Ancestors* (1902), *Alphonse and Gaston* (1902), and *John Bull* (1903).

Oppian (ŏp'ēən), fl. 2d cent., Greek poet. He is the author of a didactic poem (in five books of hexameters) on fishing called *Halieutica.* Two other poems, formerly attributed to Oppian, are now believed to be by other writers—*Cynegitica* (on hunting), perhaps by another poet named Oppian, and *Ixeutica* (on birdcatching).

Oppland (ôp'län), county (1972 est. pop. 174,000), 9,773 sq mi (25,312 sq km), S central Norway. The chief towns are Lillehammer (the capital) and Gjovik. The county is traversed from northwest to southeast by the Gudbrandsdalen valley. Farming and lumbering are the main occupations. The northern section is mountainous.

Opportunity, uninc. town (1970 pop. 16,604), Spokane co., E Wash., a residential suburb of Spokane.

opportunity school: see ILLITERACY.

opposition, in astronomy, alignment of two celestial bodies on opposite sides of the sky as viewed from earth. Opposition of the moon or planets is often determined in reference to the sun. Only the superior planets, whose orbits lie outside that of the earth, can be in opposition to the sun. When a planet is in opposition to the sun, its ELONGATION is 180°, it exhibits RETROGRADE MOTION, and its PHASE is full. This is a good time to observe a planet, since it rises when the sun sets and is visible throughout the night, setting as the sun rises.

Ops (ŏps), in Roman religion, goddess of harvests. She was the wife of Saturn, by whom she bore Jupiter and Juno. At her festivals, the Opiconsivia and the Opalia, held in August and December, respectively, she was worshiped as a goddess of sowing and reaping and was associated with Consus, god of crops. She was later identified with the Greek RHEA.

opsonization: see IMMUNITY.

optative: see MOOD.

optical density: see REFRACTION.

optical double: see BINARY STAR.

optical rotation: see POLARIZATION OF LIGHT.

optical sensing, in general, any method by which information that occurs as variations in the intensity, or some other property, of light is translated into an electric signal. This is usually accomplished by the use of various photoelectric devices. In one method, known as optical character recognition, a computer is given the capability of "reading" printed characters. Reflected or transmitted light from the character strikes an array of photoelectric cells, which effectively dissect it into light and dark areas. By analysis of these areas the computer is able to recognize the character, with some tolerance for less than perfect and uniform printing. Optical sensing is also used in various pattern-recognition systems, e.g., in military reconnaissance and astronomical observation; it is also used in photographic development, to enhance detail and contrast. See GRAPHIC TERMINAL.

optician, filler of prescriptions for and dispenser of corrective lenses. An optician transcribes the prescription of an optometrist (see OPTOMETRY) or ophthalmologist (see OPHTHALMOLOGY) into instructions for laboratory mechanics or he may grind the lenses himself. He fits and adjusts the lenses to his client and makes suggestions as to the selection of frames. Increasingly, opticians have taken over the task of fitting contact lenses as well as EYEGLASSES. Some states require that lab technicians and retail merchandisers be licensed opticians. Requirements may be met through academic training or through a laboratory apprenticeship.

optic nerve: see VISION.

optics, scientific study of LIGHT. Physical optics is concerned with the genesis, nature, and properties of light; physiological optics with the part light plays in VISION; and geometrical optics with the geometry involved in the REFLECTION and REFRACTION of light as encountered in the study of the MIRROR and the LENS.

optometry (ŏptŏm'ətrē), eye care specialty concerned with eye examination, determination of visual abnormalities, and the prescription of lenses and other corrective measures. The principal concern of early optometrists was the prescription of corrective lenses for defects of vision due to refractive error. However, modern optometry includes the fitting of contact lenses and of telescopic eyeglasses as an aid to the near-blind, as well as the field of orthoptics, i.e., the practice of strengthening the eye muscles and improving their coordination by eye exercises. Prescriptions for corrective lenses provided by an optometrist are often brought to an OPTICIAN who grinds and fits the lenses. Optometrists are also trained to recognize diseases of the eye; when indicated, medical treatment is then referred to an ophthalmologist, a physician who specializes in disorders of the eye (see OPHTHALMOLOGY). The word *optometry* came into use in 1904 with the organization of the American Optometric Association. Until this time people bought eyeglasses from traveling vendors whose activities were not supervised. With the passage of optometry laws, this method of dispensing glasses was prohibited. Optometrists must now fulfill certain educational requirements and be examined and licensed by the state. Some of the schools of optometry in the United States are affiliated with colleges or universities. An optometry degree follows a four-year or five-year course in preoptometry and optometry.

opus (ō'pəs) [Lat.,=work], in music, term used in cataloging a composer's works, designating either a single composition or a group published together or considered a unit. Opus numbers assigned by the composer are of greater value than those assigned by the publisher. Beethoven was the first composer whose use of opus numbers was consistent enough to be of value.

Opus Dei (ō'pəs dā'ē) [Lat.,=work of God], Roman Catholic lay order, particularly influential in Spain. The order was founded in 1928 by a wealthy lawyer turned priest, José María Escriva de Balaguer, who objected to the liberal atmosphere at the Univ. of Madrid. It gained national importance after the Spanish civil war, gradually extending its influence over education, the press, and financial institutions, and receiving government support. In the 1950s and 60s it replaced the FALANGE as the most important conservative political and religious force in Spain, but its influence declined in the early 1970s. Among some 22,000 members (who take revocable vows of poverty, chastity, and obedience, to serve God in worldly vocations) are cabinet ministers and other government officials and many of the country's professional, intellectual, and business elite. The movement seeks to promote traditional Christian values and Spanish nationalism and to suppress liberalism and immorality. Recognized (1950) by the Vatican as a secular institute, Opus Dei now has branches in other countries, including the United States.

oracle, in Greek religion, priest or priestess who imparted the response of a god to a human questioner. The word is also used to refer to the response itself and to the shrine of a god. Every oracular shrine had a fixed method of divination. Many observed signs, such as the motion of objects dropped into a spring, the movement of birds, or the rustle of leaves. Often dreams were interpreted. A later and popular method involved the use of entranced persons whose ecstatic cries were interpreted by trained attendants. Before an oracle was questioned consultants underwent rites of purification and sacrifice. There were many established oracles in ancient Greece, the most famous being those of Zeus at DODONA and of Apollo at DELPHI. Other oracular shrines were located in Syria, Egypt, and Italy.

oracle bones, bones used for divination by the Chinese during the SHANG dynasty (traditionally c.1766 B.C.–c.1122 B.C.). Along with contemporary inscriptions on bronze vessels, these records of divination, which were incised on the shoulder blades of animals (mainly oxen) and on turtle shells, contain the earliest form of Chinese writing. In addition to being an important source for understanding the development of written Chinese, they tell a great deal about Shang society. Questions asked by the diviners concerned such matters as sacrifices, weather, war, hunting, travel, and luck. The bones were heated to produce cracks from which "yes" or "no" answers were somehow derived. A small number of oracle bones have the answer and the eventual outcome inscribed. Discovered in the ruins of the Shang capital of Anyang in the late 19th cent., they were first sold as so-called dragon bones to be ground up for use in Chinese medicinal compounds and only received the attention of scholars in the 1920s.

Oradea (orä'dyä) or **Oradea-Mare** (-mä'rĕ), Hung. *Nagyvárad,* Ger. *Grosswardein,* city (1970 est. pop. 138,000), W Rumania, in Crişana-Maramureş, near the Hungarian border. It is the marketing and shipping center for a livestock and agricultural region. Oradea is also an important industrial city. There are health resorts nearby. The city was made (1083) the seat of a Roman Catholic bishop by King Ladislaus I of Hungary. Destroyed (1241) by the Tatars, it was rebuilt in the 15th cent. Oradea was held by the Turks from 1660 to 1692. Hungary ceded it (1919) to Rumania after World War I, but Hungarian forces occupied the city during World War II. About half the population is Magyar. Oradea is the seat of an Orthodox Eastern bishop. Most of the city's architecture is baroque, dating from the reign of Maria Theresa.

Öraefajökull (ö'rīväyö"kütəl), mountain, SE Iceland, rising from the Vatnajökull glacier. Öraefajökull is an ice-covered, three-peaked volcano. The largest of its four recorded eruptions occurred in 1362; all have been destructive, owing to the devastating floods caused by melting ice. Its highest peak, Hvannadalshnúkur (6,950 ft/2,118 m), is also the highest point in Iceland.

Oraibi (ōrī'bē), pueblo, N Ariz., on a mesa N of Winslow. It was built c.1150 and was discovered in 1540 by Pedro de Tovar, a lieutenant of Coronado. The mission of San Francisco, established on the site in 1629, was destroyed in the Pueblo revolt of 1680. Oraibi was long the most important pueblo of the HOPI INDIANS, but because of economic disturbances and internal dissension many of the inhabitants left in 1907 to form the pueblos of Hotevila and Bakavi. Oraibi is now little more than a ruin. See Mischa Titiev, *Old Oraibi: A Study of the Hopi Indians of the Third Mesa* (1944, repr. 1967).

Oran (ôräN'), city (1966 pop. 328,257), capital of Oran dept., NW Algeria, a port on the Gulf of Oran of the Mediterranean Sea. One of the country's leading ports, it ships wheat, wine, alcohol, vegetables, meat, wool, cigarettes, and iron ore. The city, surrounded by vineyards and market gardens, is a commercial, industrial, and financial center. The site of modern Oran has been inhabited since prehistoric times, but the city's founding is generally attributed to Moorish Andalusian traders in the 10th cent. Oran's subsequent prosperity, based on commerce, was interrupted when the Moors began to engage in piracy, thus provoking reprisals from Spain. Spanish forces captured and fortified the city in 1509 and held it until the Turks arrived in 1708. Spain recovered Oran in 1732. The city was successfully besieged (1791) by the district governor of Mascara and was made a provincial capital of the Ottoman Empire. French troops captured Oran in 1831 and began to develop it as a naval base, along with nearby MERS-EL-KEBIR. The building of the port and the construction of railroads linking Oran with the interior made the city the economic capital of W Algeria in the late 19th cent. Oran, held by Vichy France during World War II, fell to the Allied forces in Nov., 1942. Civil strife ravaged the city in the late 1950s: the French terrorist OAS (Secret Army Organization) and the Algerian nationalist FLN (Front for National Liberation) perpetuated violence against civilians. There followed a general exodus of the European population, which had been the largest, proportionally, of any North African city. Oran consists of a modern, French-style section and an old Spanish-type quarter with a casbah (fortress) and an 18th-century mosque. The city provided the setting for Albert Camus's novel *The Plague*.

Orange (ôräNzh'), town (1968 pop. 25,630), Vaucluse dept., SE France. An agricultural market center, the town also produces refined sugar, pâtés, preserves, wool, and shoes. Tourism is also important. Orange was an earldom probably founded by Charlemagne. It became the capital of a principality (12th cent.) and was passed from family to family and eventually (1554), through inheritance, to William the Silent, of the house of Nassau. Among William's descendants were William III of England and the ruling family of the Netherlands. Orange was conquered (1672) by Louis XIV and confirmed in French possession by the Treaty of RYSWICK (1697) and the Peace of UTRECHT (1713), although the title remained with the Dutch princes of Orange. The town has important Roman ruins, notably a triumphal arch (1st cent. A.D.) and an amphitheater (c.120 A.D.) which is still in use.

Orange. **1** City (1970 pop. 77,365), Orange co., S Calif.; inc. 1888. Citrus fruits are packed and processed, and rubber products, doors, and industrial furnaces are manufactured. Chapman College is there. **2** Town (1970 pop. 13,524), New Haven co., SW Conn., a residential suburb of New Haven, on the Housatonic; settled 1720, set off from Milford 1822, inc. 1921. Tools, furniture, and clothing are made. The first house (1720) still stands. **3** City (1970 pop. 32,566), Essex co., NE N.J.; settled c.1675, set off from Newark 1806, inc. as a city 1872. Orange and the surrounding municipalities of East Orange, West Orange, South Orange, and Maplewood are known as "The Oranges," a single suburb of Newark and New York City. Although chiefly residential, Orange has plants making office machines, clothing, aircraft parts, and pharmaceuticals. **4** City (1970 pop. 24,457), seat of Orange co., SE Texas, a deep-water port on the Sabine River at its junction with the Intracoastal Waterway; settled c.1800, inc. 1858. In the wet, lush country of the Gulf Coast, it is a port of entry, with shipyards, oil and gas wells, and major petrochemical plants. The U.S. navy has a "mothball fleet" there.

orange, name for a tree of the family Rutaceae (RUE, or orange, family), native to China and Indochina, and for its fruit, the most important fresh fruit of international commerce. Its physical characteristics (especially the rich citric acid and vitamin content of the fruit) and history of cultivation are similar to those of the other types of CITRUS FRUITS, all of which are species of *Citrus*. Columbus brought the orange to the West Indies, and it is known that orange trees were well established in Florida before 1565 and were growing in California by 1800. The orange now grows in the warm parts of all continents. Flowers and fruits in all stages of development are on the tree throughout the year, although a large portion of the fruits ripen at one time. The orange is attacked by many insects and fungus diseases and is quite sensitive to frost. If the fruits are picked when still "green" (though fully mature), they must undergo a bleaching or degreening process to bring out the orange or yellow color in their rinds. Some oranges are artificially colored before marketing. Among the commercially important species of oranges are the sweet, or common, orange (*C. sinensis*), which furnishes most of the varieties for commercial growing, including the Baiá, or Washington, navel (a winter orange) and the Valencia (a summer orange); the sour, or Seville, orange (*C. aurantium*), which is grown in the United States chiefly as understock on which to bud sweet orange varieties, although in Europe its fruit is much used in marmalade; the king orange (*C. nobilis* or *reticulata*), which includes the "kid glove," or loose-rind, group of mandarin oranges and tangerines; and the Satsuma varieties, known for their hardiness. Oranges hybridize freely. The citrange is a cross between the inedible trifoliate orange (*C. trifoliata*) and a sweet orange variety; the tangelo is produced by crossing a tangerine and a grapefruit. Most oranges, like other citrus fruits, are consumed fresh or made into juice. The fruit and rind are also much used in MARMALADE, preserves, flavoring, and confections. Some varieties yield perfume. The flower is a favorite for bridal decoration and is the state flower of Florida. The yellow wood, which is hard and close-grained, is manufactured into small articles. Orange is classified in the division MAGNOLIOPHYTA, class Magnoliopsida, order Sapindales, family Rutaceae.

Orangeburg, city (1970 pop. 13,252), seat of Orangeburg co., central S.C., on the North Fork of the Edisto River; settled 1732, inc. as a city 1883. It is the trade and processing center of a cotton area and has large textile and garment industries. Tools, office machines, wood, and chemicals are also made there. The second oldest township in the state, Orangeburg was a planned settlement established by German-Swiss immigrants who had free grants of land. Today it is the seat of South Carolina State College and Claflin College. Points of interest include the beautiful Edisto gardens and the Donald Bruce House (c.1735). A U.S. fish hatchery, an aircraft and automobile museum, and a state park are nearby.

Orange Free State, province (1970 pop. 1,715,589), 49,866 sq mi (129,153 sq km), E central South Africa. BLOEMFONTEIN is the capital and largest city; other important cities include Bethlehem and Kroonstad. The province is chiefly a plateau, rising gradually from c.4,000 ft (1,220 m) in the west to c.6,000 ft (1,830 m) in the east; there are higher elevations in the Drakensberg Range in the southeast. The economy is mainly agricultural; maize, sorghum, potatoes, wheat, sheep, and cattle are raised. Gold mining is also important, and uranium oxide, diamonds, and coal are mined. Synthetic rubber, fertilizers, plastics, textiles, and processed foods are manufactured, and oil is refined from coal. Bloemfontein is the province's road and rail hub. The Univ. of the Orange Free State in Bloemfontein is the chief institution of higher education. In the early 19th cent. the sparsely populated Orange Free State was inhabited mainly by the Bantu-speaking Tswana people. BOER farmers entered the territory from the 1820s; after 1835 their immigration accelerated (see TREK). In 1848 the British, who then held Cape Colony and Natal, annexed the region as the Orange River Sovereignty. After conflicts with the Boers and failure to establish an orderly administration, Britain, by the Bloemfontein Convention (1854), granted the territory independence as the Orange Free State. With the increased tension following the raid into the TRANSVAAL (1895–96), led by L. S. Jameson, the Free State was drawn into the conflict between Britons and Boers that resulted in the SOUTH AFRICAN WAR (1899–1902). The British again annexed the Free State, as the Orange River Colony, in 1900. In 1907 the colony was granted self-government, and in 1910 it became a founding province of the Union of South Africa.

Orangemen, members of the Loyal Orange Institution, a Protestant Irish society founded and largely flourishing in the province of Ulster, or Northern Ireland. It was established (1795) to maintain the Protestant ascendancy in Ireland in the face of the rising agitation for Catholic Emancipation. Its name is taken from the family name of King William III of England, who defeated King James II in the battle of the Boyne in 1690. July 12, the anniversary of this victory, is the principal holiday of the order, on which the members wear orange-colored flowers and orange sashes and march in parades. Branches of the society, with somewhat different aims, have been formed elsewhere.

Orange River, chief river of S Africa, c.1,300 mi (2,090 km) long, rising in the Maluti Mts., N Lesotho. It flows SW through Lesotho, then meanders northwest and west through central Republic of South Africa, forming the boundary between Orange Free State and Cape Prov. and part of the South Africa–South West Africa line before entering the Atlantic Ocean at Oranjemund. The Vaal River is its chief tributary. The lower Orange River flows through the southern part of the Kalahari and Namib deserts; in very dry years it does not reach the sea. At the mouth of the river are rich alluvial diamond beds. Shoals, falls (Aughrabies Falls is 400 ft/122 m high), irregular flow, and a sandbar at its mouth limit navigation, but the river is used extensively for irrigation. The Orange River Project, a 30-year scheme begun in the early 1960s, will bring c.750,000 acres (305,000 hectares) of land under irrigation and provide hydroelectric power and municipal water supplies. The Hendrik Verwoerd Dam (completed 1972) is the project's principal unit. Dams and tunnels in the upper Orange basin will divert water to the Fish and Sunday rivers in S Cape Prov.

orangutan (ōrăng'o͞otăn), an APE, *Pongo pygmaeus*, found in the swampy coastal forests of Borneo and Sumatra. Highly specialized for arboreal life, it usually travels through the trees by swinging slowly and deliberately from branch to branch. It rarely descends to the ground, where it walks awkwardly on all fours. Adult males are about 4½ ft (1.4 m) tall and weigh about 150 lbs (68 kg). Their arms are extremely long, the span sometimes exceeding 7 ft (2.1 m). Their legs are short and bowed; the heelbone is absent. The body is rather rotund and is covered with long reddish fur. The face of a young orangutan is quite like that of a human; the name means "forest person" in Malay. Old males sometimes develop cheek expansions and enormous vocal sacs. Orangutans travel about in small groups; at night they sleep in individual nests constructed in the forks of trees. Their diet is principally vegetarian and they are especially fond of durian fruit. Orangutans are classified in the phylum CHORDATA, subphylum Vertebrata, class Mammalia, order Primates, family Pongidae.

Oranienbaum: see LOMONOSOV, USSR.

Oranienburg (ōrä'nyənbo͝orkh), city (1970 pop. 20,442), Potsdam district, central East Germany, on the Havel River. It is a center of a fruit-growing region. Manufactures include chemicals, machinery, and processed food. Oranienburg was the site of one of the earliest CONCENTRATION CAMPS (est. 1933) set up by the National Socialist (Nazi) regime.

oratorio (ôrətôr'ēō), musical composition employing chorus, orchestra, and soloists and usually, but not necessarily, a setting of a sacred libretto without stage action or scenery. The immediate forerunner of oratorio, Emilio del Cavaliere's sacred opera *La rappresentazione di anima e di corpo* applied the techniques of the newly created opera to the *sacra rappresentazione*, the Italian mystery play. Cavaliere's work was performed in 1600 in one of the buildings known as the oratories of St. PHILIP NERI. Soon afterward there developed the *oratorio volgare*, also in Italian, which employed a *testo*, or narrator, to advance the action of the story. By c.1640 the term *oratorio* had come to stand for the work itself rather than the place in which it was given, and 10 years later the Latin oratorio was given definitive form in the works of Giacomo CARISSIMI. His style was carried to France by his pupil Marc Antoine Charpentier, but the oratorio did not flourish there. Carissimi's influence is also discernible in the oratorios of Heinrich SCHÜTZ and of Handel. After Carissimi the only outstanding Italian oratorios are those of his pupil Alessandro Scarlatti, of which 14 are known. Scarlatti included RECITATIVE with developed arias in works that greatly resembled opera. Pietro METASTASIO wrote a number of oratorios, several of which were set more than once. In Germany settings of the Passion assumed greater importance than the true oratorio, but the oratorios of Schütz are equalled only by those of J. S. Bach and Handel. Handel inaugurated the English oratorio, and his *Messiah*, although atypical among his own usually epic oratorios, became the prototype for the works of many later composers. Haydn's two great oratorios show the influence of Handel. Mendelssohn's highly dramatic *Elijah* and *St. Paul* exerted a strong influence, particularly in England, where the oratorio enjoyed great vogue throughout the 19th cent. A long succession of mediocre works, including several popular examples by Sir Arthur Sullivan, was followed by the more notable ones of Elgar and Walford Davies. Wagner, Liszt, Dvořák, Berlioz, and Franck all wrote romantic oratorios. In the 20th cent. Honegger's *King David* (1921) and *Dance of the Dead* (1940), Stravinsky's opera-oratorio *Oedipus Rex* (1927), Hindemith's *Das Unaufhörliche* (1931), William Walton's *Belshazzar's Feast* (1931), and Britten's *War Requiem* (1961) are noteworthy. See G. P. Upton, *The Standard Oratorios* (1888); P. M. Young, *The Oratorios of Handel* (1949).

oratory, the art of swaying an audience by eloquent speech. In ancient Greece and Rome oratory was included under the term *rhetoric*, which meant the art of composing as well as delivering a speech. Oratory first appeared in the law courts of Athens and soon became important in all areas of life. It was taught by the Sophists. The Ten Attic Orators (listed by Alexandrine critics) were Antiphon, Andocides, Lysias, Isocrates, Isaeus, Aeschines, Demosthenes, Lycurgus, Hyperides, and Dinarchus. Classic Rome's great orators were Cato the Elder, Mark Antony, and Cicero. The theory of rhetoric was discussed by Aristotle and Quintilian; and three main classes of oratory were later designated by classical rhetoricians: (a) deliberative—to persuade an audience (such as a legislature) to approve or disapprove a matter of public policy; (b) forensic—to achieve (as in a trial) condemnation or approval for a man's actions; (c) epideictic—"display rhetoric" used on ceremonial occasions. Rhetoric was included in the medieval liberal arts curriculum. In subsequent centuries oratory was utilized in three main areas of public life—politics, religion, and law. During the Middle Ages, the Renaissance, and the Reformation, oratory was generally confined to the church, which produced such soul-searing orators as Savanorola, Martin Luther, John Calvin, and John Knox. With the development of parliaments in the 18th cent., great political orators appeared—Charles James Fox, Edmund Burke, Henry Gratten, and Daniel O'Connell in England and Ireland; Patrick Henry and James Otis in the United States; and Danton and Mirabeau in France. Because these politicians usually spoke to men of their own class and education, their orations were often complex and erudite, abounding in classical allusions. In the 19th cent., the rise of Methodism and evangelical religions produced great preachers like John Wesley and George Whitefield who addressed a wide audience of diverse classes of people. Their sermons, replete with biblical allusions and appeals to the emotions, profoundly influenced the oratorical style of many politicians. Famous 19th cent. orators included Disraeli and John Bright in England, Charles Stewart Parnell in Ireland, Lamartine in France, Ferdinand Lasalle in Germany, Louis Kossuth in Hungary, and Joseph Mazzini in Italy. Great American orators included Abraham Lincoln, Henry Clay, John C. Calhoun, Daniel Webster, Stephen Douglas, and Henry Ward Beecher. In the 20th cent., orators made frequent use of the "catch phrase" (e.g., William Jennings Bryan's "cross of gold" speech). Noted orators in the first half of the 20th cent. were Bryan, Eugene Debs, Susan B. Anthony, and Woodrow Wilson in the United States, Lenin and Trotsky in Russia, and David Lloyd George and Winston Churchill in England. The bombastic oratorical style of Hitler and Mussolini, inevitably associated with their discredited political ideologies, brought grandiloquent oratory into disrepute. The advent of radio forced oratory to become more intimate and conversational, as in the "fireside chats" of President Franklin D. Roosevelt. Television forced additional demands on the orator (or, as he came to be called, the *public speaker*)—he not only had to sound good, he also had to look good. Still, most politicians, notably Adlai E. Stevenson and John F. Kennedy, succeeded in utilizing the ubiquitous television camera to heighten the impact of their speeches. The particular effectiveness of great oratory was movingly demonstrated in 1963 when the civil rights leader Martin Luther King delivered his "I have a dream" speech to an audience of 200,000 people in Washington, D.C., and to millions more listening to him on radio and watching him on television.

Oratory, Congregation of the [Lat. abbr., *Cong. Orat.*], in the Roman Catholic Church, association of secular priests organized into independent communities according to the rule written by St. PHILIP NERI. The purpose of the oratory is to raise the religious standards of the locale. To do this they employ three means—prayer, especially the solemn performance of the liturgy; the sacraments, especially the confessional; and preaching, every oratory having daily sermons. Confessions are heard at all times. The best-known oratory of the English-speaking world is probably that of John Henry Newman, who introduced it to England as a means of extending the church there. An oratory was established in the United States in 1961.

orbit, in astronomy, path in space described by a body revolving about a second, larger body where the motion of the orbiting body is dominated by their mutual gravitational attraction. Within the solar system, planets and comets orbit the sun and satellites orbit the planets. From earliest times, astronomers assumed that the orbits in which the planets moved were circular; yet, the numerous catalogs of measurements compiled especially during the 16th cent. did not fit this theory. At the beginning of the 17th cent., Johannes Kepler stated three laws of planetary motion that explained the observed data: the orbit of each planet is an ellipse with the sun at one focus; the speed of a planet varies in such a way that an imaginary line drawn from the planet to the sun sweeps out equal areas in

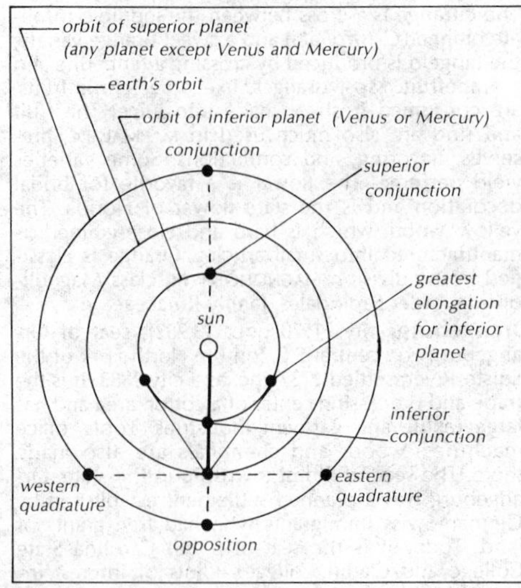

Important points in a planet's orbit as seen from the earth

equal amounts of time; and the ratio of the squares of the periods of revolution of any two planets is equal to the ratio of the cubes of their average distances from the sun. After the laws of planetary motion were established, astronomers developed the means of determining the size, shape, and relative position in space of a planet's orbit. The size and shape of an orbit are specified by its semimajor axis and by its eccentricity. The semimajor axis is a length equal to half the greatest diameter of the orbit. The eccentricity is the distance of the sun from the center of the orbit divided by the length of the orbit's semimajor axis; this value is a measure of how elliptical the orbit is. The position of the orbit in space, relative to the earth, is determined by three factors: (1) the INCLINATION, or tilt, of the plane of the planet's orbit to the plane of the earth's orbit (the ecliptic); (2) the longitude of the planet's ascending node (the point where the planet cuts the ecliptic moving from south to north); and (3) the longitude of the planet's perihelion point (point at which it is nearest the sun; see APSIS). These five quantities, which determine the size, shape, and position of a planet's orbit, are known as the orbital elements. If only the sun influenced the planet in its orbit, then by knowing the orbital elements plus its position at some particular time, one could calculate its position at any later time. However, the gravitational attractions of bodies other than the sun cause PERTURBATIONS in the planet's motions that can make the orbit shift, or precess, in space or can cause the planet to wobble slightly. Once these perturbations have been calculated one can closely determine its position for any future date over long periods of time. Modern methods for computing the orbit of a planet or other body have been refined from methods developed by Newton, Laplace, and Gauss, in which all the needed quantities are acquired from three separate observations of the planet's apparent position. These laws of planetary orbits also apply to the orbits of comets and natural satellites and to those of artificial satellites and space probes. The orbits of comets are so elongated that they are nearly parabolic (see PARABOLA); when the orbit of a newly discovered comet is calculated, it is first assumed to be a parabola and then corrected to its actual shape. Natural satellites that are close to their primaries tend to have nearly circular orbits in the same plane as that of the planet's equator, while more distant satellites may have quite eccentric orbits with large inclinations to the planet's equatorial plane. All of the planets and most of the satellites in the solar system move in the same direction in their orbits, counterclockwise as viewed from the north celestial pole; some satellites, however, have RETROGRADE MOTION, i.e., they revolve in a clockwise direction. The reason for this anomaly in the motions of satellites is not yet understood.

Orcades: see ORKNEY, Scotland.

Orcagna (ōrkä'nyä) or **Arcagnolo** (ärkä'nyōlō), c.1308–1368, Florentine painter, sculptor, and architect, whose original name was Andrea di Cione. He was one of the leading artists of his day. According to Vasari, he studied sculpture under Andrea Pisano. In 1343 he enrolled in St. Luke's Guild as a painter. The only extant authenticated painting is his famous altarpiece in the Strozzi Chapel of Santa Maria Novella, Florence. An awesome work, it represents *Christ in Glory with Saints Thomas and Peter.* In his painting he reverted to the Byzantine remote and monumental figural type. He usually worked in collaboration with his brothers Nardo, Jacopo, and Matteo di Cione. They were all strongly influenced by Giotto. Fragments of the *Prophets* by Orcagna and his assistants have come to light in Santa Maria Novella, as well as portions of his *Triumph of Death, Last Judgment,* and *Hell* in the Church of Santa Croce. In 1355 he was appointed chief architect of Orsanmichele in Florence, for which he executed an elaborate marble tabernacle depicting *The Death and Assumption of the Virgin.* In 1359 he became chief architect of the cathedral at Orvieto and designed a mosaic for the facade. See Millard Meiss, *Painting in Florence and Siena after the Black Death* (1951, repr. 1964).

orchard, generally an area on which fruit or nut trees are planted and cultivated. The words *grove* and *plantation* are often used when the fruits are tropical, e.g., a "citrus grove" or a "banana plantation." The distinction among the three terms arises from common usage rather than definition. The orchard of ancient times was a pleasure garden of formal design, often adorned with fountains and statuary. Today orchards are more commonly commercial ventures, sometimes covering many acres. Machinery is now often used for cultivating, spraying, picking, and packing. The ground beneath the trees may be kept clear or cover crops may be grown, or the two practices may alternate. In young orchards it is usually possible to grow vegetables and berry fruits as cover crops in the rows between the trees, thus helping maintenance costs until the trees begin to bear.

orchard grass or **cocksfoot,** widely distributed perennial grass (*Dactylis glomerata*) native to Eurasia and N Africa and extensively naturalized in the United States. It is cultivated as a hay grass more tolerant of drought and shade than timothy but less winter-hardy. A variety with silvery-striped leaves is grown as an ornamental. Orchard grass is classified in the division MAGNOLIOPHYTA, class Magnoliopsida, order Cyperales, family Gramineae.

orchestra and orchestration. An orchestra is a musical ensemble, under the direction of a conductor, employing four classes of instruments: strings, woodwinds, brass, and percussion. The strings, except the harp, have several players for each part, the others usually only one. The strings are the bowed violin, viola, violoncello (or cello), double bass, and the plucked harp; the woodwinds are the flute, oboe, English horn, clarinet, and bassoon, all of which appear in more than one size; the brass are French horn, trumpet, trombone, and tuba; the percussion are kettledrums, snare and bass drums, cymbals, triangle, and xylophone, to name only a few of the most frequently used. The strings are the most important section of the orchestra; they are the most versatile and flexible and play almost continuously in most scores. The woodwinds are next in importance; they add color to the string sound and in some passages carry the melody. Of the brass, the French horn is the most useful, since it blends equally well with the woodwinds or the other brasses. The trumpets, trombones, and tuba are the "heavy artillery" of the orchestra; playing loudly, they provide a dynamic climax, but they are also effective in subdued passages as a group or individually. The percussion instruments are used to emphasize rhythm. The kettledrums are most important, blending best with the rest of the orchestra and also being tunable to a definite pitch. The others stand out so prominently that they are most effective when used sparingly. The harp is principally a color instrument and does not share the importance of the bowed strings. The piano and organ occasionally are used as orchestral instruments, apart from their role as soloists in concertos. The orchestra in the modern sense of the word did not exist before the 17th cent. Previous instrumental ensemble music was chamber music, except for occasional ceremonies when as many instruments as were available would be massed together. Until well into the 17th cent. there was little thought of specifying what instrument should play a part; any available instrument with the proper range was used. The first known example of orchestration, scoring for specific instruments, occurs in Giovanni Gabrieli's *Sacrae Symphoniae* (1597). Monteverdi's *Orfeo* (1607), one of the first operas, demands a large and varied group of instruments—all, in fact, that were available to him through his patron. During the 17th cent. the violin family displaced the VIOLS, except

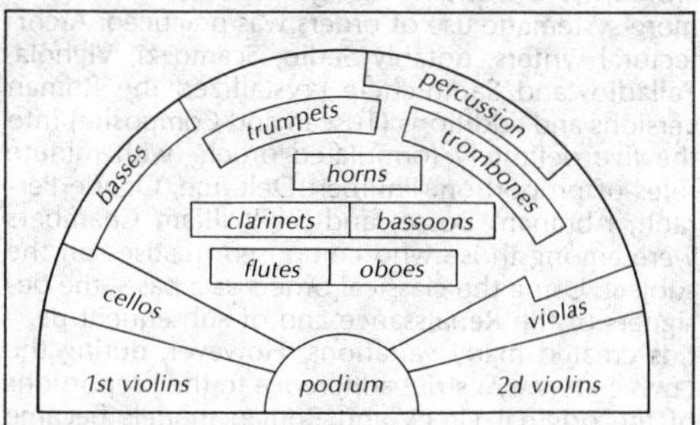

Typical seating plan of a symphony orchestra

the double-bass viol, as the principal strings of the orchestra. By the end of the century a division into four parts had become standard: first and second violins, violas, and violoncellos, with the double basses playing the cello part an octave lower. (Not until the 19th cent. did the cellos and basses frequently have different parts to play.) Woodwinds appeared in the earliest orchestras, though infrequently and subordinate to the strings—usually two oboes and a bassoon, with flutes sometimes replacing the oboes. The flutes were established as regular orchestra members, playing together with the oboes, only late in the 18th cent. The trumpets, inseparable from the kettledrums through the 17th and 18th cent., were used occasionally in the 17th cent. and became standard in the orchestra by about 1700. The French horn was fully accepted by 1750. The trombone was used in church music even before the 17th cent. and occasionally in opera thereafter; it did not become a regular member of the symphony orchestra until after 1800. Throughout the baroque period and into the second half of the 18th cent., the basso continuo was an integral part of the scoring and required that a harpsichord or some other chord-playing instrument fill in the harmonies above the FIGURED BASS. The treble and bass were strongly emphasized, while the middle parts were often left to the continuo alone. The orchestra was rather small at this time; Bach had as few as 18 players for his larger church works, and Handel usually used about 30. During the latter half of the 18th cent. the classical orchestra was gradually established through the disuse of the continuo and the acceptance of the clarinet. The abandonment of the continuo led to much greater independence in the string parts, which now had to fill the harmony unaided; instead of both violin parts doubling the melody and the violas, cellos, and basses doubling the bass, there were now four distinct parts. The clarinet, like the flute, first appeared as an alternate for the oboe, but in the late works of Haydn and Mozart the orchestra was standardized, with pairs of flutes, oboes, clarinets, bassoons, French horns, trumpets, and kettledrums in addition to the strings. All the wind instruments, especially the woodwinds, could carry the melody, providing desired changes of color. In the 19th cent., beginning in the works of Beethoven, the brass took an increasingly prominent place. The trombone was used regularly, while the invention of the valve in 1813 soon made the horn and trumpet completely chromatic. All the brass thus became melody instruments, instantly available in the most remote keys. The horn section was increased to four early in the century, and the introduction of the tuba (c.1835–50) gave the brass a dependable contrabass register it had previously lacked. The woodwinds also were improved mechanically in the 19th cent., greatly enlarging their technical capabilities. Throughout the century the string section was expanded to balance the increasing numbers of wind players. The scores of Mozart and Beethoven generally required an orchestra of about 40; those of Weber and early Wagner called for about 55; Wagner's *Ring* cycle (1854–74) called for about 110; and Strauss's *Elektra* for 115. Hector Berlioz was highly influential in the 19th cent. in increasing awareness of orchestral color and in encouraging the use of a larger orchestra; his *Traité d'orchestration*, a fundamental work of its kind, envisioned an ideal orchestra of 465. After the climax of orchestral bulk in the works of Wagner, Mahler, Strauss, and several others, composers reacted against orchestral gigantism, first in the IMPRESSIONISM of Debussy and his followers. They still used a large orchestra, but more restrainedly, making more distinctive use of the instruments and largely avoiding massive sonorities. Stravinsky's *Rite of Spring* (1913) illustrates the early 20th-century interest in diverse instrumental combinations and original exploitation of the instruments' capabilities. The composers of the 20th cent. in general have continued exploring novel uses of instruments and have preferred a moderate-sized orchestra. Seventy-five to ninety players suffice for most 20th-century scores; a reduced, or chamber, orchestra of classical or baroque dimensions has also been much used. In this century the percussion section is used more prominently; new instruments have been devised and the playing of old ones varied. Some important orchestras may be mentioned: the Leipzig Gewandhaus-Konzerte, not called by that name until later, began in 1743; the Philharmonic Society, London, was established in 1813; the Société des Concerts du Conservatoire, Paris, in 1828; the Wiener Philharmonische Konzerte, Vienna, began in 1842; the Berlin Philharmonisches Orchester was established in 1882. Among the oldest American orchestras still in existence are the New York Philharmonic Society (founded 1842; merged into the New York Philharmonic-Symphony Orchestra in 1928), the St. Louis Symphony (1880), the Boston Symphony Orchestra (1881), the Chicago Symphony (1891), the Cincinnati Symphony (1895), and the Philadelphia Orchestra (1900). See articles on individual American orchestras; e.g., PHILADELPHIA ORCHESTRA. For orchestra, see Ebenezer Prout, *The Orchestra* (2 vol., 1899); Paul Bekker, *The Orchestra* (1963); Philip Hart, *Orpheus in the New World: the Symphony Orchestra as an American Cultural Institution* (1973). For orchestration, see Cecil Forsyth, *Orchestration* (1936); Walter Piston, *Orchestration* (1955); Kent Kennan, *Technique of Orchestration* (2d ed. 1970).

orchid, popular name for members of the Orchidaceae, a family of perennial herbs widely distributed in both hemispheres. The unusually large family (of some 450 genera and an estimated 10,000 to 15,000 species) includes terrestrial, epiphytic (see AIR PLANT), and saprophytic (see PARASITE) genera. Although the latter may sometimes lack chlorophyll, none are actually parasitic. Orchids grow most abundantly in tropical and subtropical forests, where they are largely epiphytic; however, the greatest number of genera are temperate, thriving in

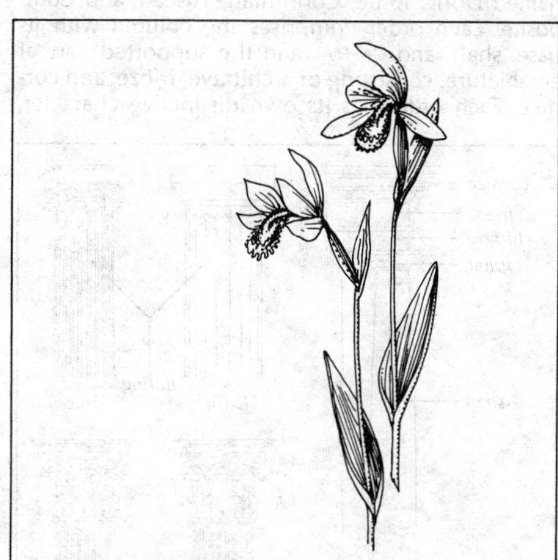

Rose pogonia, Pogonia ophioglossoides, *a member of the orchid family*

all kinds of shaded habitats except excessively dry or cold ones. Most temperate orchids and all those of arctic regions are terrestrial. This family of monocotyledonous plants has evolved from prototypes of the lily and amaryllis family and is noteworthy for the wide variety of its highly specialized and curiously modified forms. Epiphytic types have a stem swollen at the base to form a pseudobulb (for food storage) and pendulous aerial roots adapted for water absorption and sometimes containing chlorophyll to make photosynthesis possible. In terrestrial types a symbiotic relationship often exists between the roots and filamentous fungi (mycorrhiza). Horticulturists have found that the presence of certain fungi is necessary for the germination of the minute seeds. Orchid pollen occurs as mealy or waxen lumps of tiny pollen grains, highly varied in form. The flowers characteristically consist of three petals and three petallike sepals, the central sepal modified into a conspicuous lip (labellum) specialized to secrete nectar that attracts insects. Most of the diverse forms of orchid flowers are apparently complicated adaptations for pollination by specific insects, e.g., the enormous waxflower of Africa, which has a labellum over a foot long and is pollinated by a moth with a tongue of equal length. The saclike labellum of the lady's-slipper serves the same function by forcing the insect to brush against the anther and the stigma (male and female organs) while procuring nectar. Orchids are among the most highly prized of ornamental plants. In Mexico the flowers are used symbolically by the natives; each one conveys a sentiment associated with different ceremonies or religious figures. From the time that orchids were first imported from the Bahamas to the British Isles (in the early 18th cent.) these flowers have been cultivated for their commercial value and have been successfully hybridized and variegated. Today the expensive orchid of the florists' trade is usually the large cattleya; species of this genus (*Cattleya*) are epiphytic plants native to tropical America. Hawaii has become a major center for commercial orchid culture. A species of the *Vanilla* genus, also of tropical America, is important economically as the source of natural VANILLA flavoring. Among the other cultivated orchids are several of the terrestrial rein orchids (genus *Habenaria*) and many epiphytic tropical genera, e.g., the Asian *Dendrobium*, with pendant clusters of flowers; *Epidendrum*, represented in the SE United States by the greenfly orchid; and *Odontoglossum*, indigenous to the Andes mts. About 140 species of orchid are native to North America, usually as bog plants or flowers of moist woodlands and meadows. Species of lady's-slipper, or moccasin flower (*Cypripedium*) [Lat.,=slipper of Venus], include the pink-blossomed common, or stemless, lady's-slipper (*C. acaule*) and the showy lady's-slipper (*C. reginae*), both of the northeast, and varieties of the yellow lady's-slipper (*C. calceolus*), which grow in all but the warmest regions of the continent. Other terrestrial genera that grow as American wild flowers are the fringe orchids (*Blephariglottis*); the small-blossomed twayblades (species of *Liparis* and *Listera*); the pogonias, or beardflowers (*Pogonia*); the wild pinks, or swamp rose orchids (*Arethusa*), of northeastern sphagnum bogs; the grass pinks (*Limodorum*) of eastern bogs and meadows; the ladies'-tresses, or pearl-twists (*Spiranthes*), with a distinctive spiral arrangement of yellowish or white flowers; the evergreen rattlesnake plantains (*Goodyera*); and the orchises (species of *Orchis, Habenaria,* and other genera). The coralroots (*Corallorhiza*), named for the corallike branching of their underground rhizomes, are a nongreen saprophytic genus which includes some North American species. Because orchids are characteristically slow-growing and difficult to seed, excessive picking and futile attempts to transplant have depleted native species in some areas. The orchid family is classified in the division MAGNOLIOPHYTA, class Liliatae, order Orchidales. See R. T. Northen, *Home Orchid Growing* (3d ed. 1970); M. A. Reinikka, *A History of the Orchid* (1972).

orchil: see ARCHIL.

Orchomenus (ôrkŏm'ĭnəs), ancient city of Boeotia, central Greece, NW of Lake Copaïs. After 1600 B.C. it was an important center of the Mycenaean civilization. In later times the city was eclipsed by Thebes. Near Orchomenus, Sulla won (85 B.C.) a significant victory over Archelaus, general of MITHRADATES VI. Excavations on the site have been extensive. There was another Orchomenus in Arcadia, NW of Mantinea.

Orcus (ôr'kəs): see PLUTO.

Ord, Edward Otho Cresap, 1818–83, Union general in the American Civil War, b. Cumberland, Md. He commanded a brigade in Virginia (1861–62), was promoted to major general of volunteers, and fought at Iuka and Corinth, Miss. (1862). In the last stage of the Vicksburg campaign (1863), Ord led the 13th Corps. Returning to the Virginia theater in 1864, he served briefly as commander in the Shenandoah valley, and in the final operations against Robert E. Lee he led successively the 8th Corps, the 18th Corps, and the Army of the James. Ord commanded various departments after the war. In 1881 he was made a major general on the retired list.

ordeal, ancient legal custom whereby an accused person was required to perform a test, the outcome of which decided the person's guilt or innocence. By an ordeal, appeal was made to divine authority to decide the guilt or innocence of one accused of a crime or to choose between disputants. This custom was known to ancient peoples as well as to those of fairly advanced material culture. Until recent times the ordeal was practiced in many parts of Asia and Africa. In the early Middle Ages it was widely used to settle legal questions in Western Europe. In England it was a regular form of trial and persisted until trial by JURY became common. Forms of the ordeal varied with the locality and with the nature of the crime. The ordeal by fire—walking through fire or putting the hand into a flame—was common, and there were other fiery ordeals, such as walking on hot plowshares or plunging the hand into molten metal. Usually it was believed that if the accused was innocent God would spare him. Commonly there was a lapse of several days before the injuries were inspected; then someone considered a competent judge decided from the severity of the injuries as to innocence or guilt. One form of ordeal, the trial by water, was that used to determine whether or not an accused woman was a witch. The woman was bound and cast into water that had been blessed. If the water rejected her—i.e., if she floated—she was considered guilty. If the water received her, she was considered innocent. A common form of ordeal in contentions between two parties was the submission to some trial of chance, e.g., casting LOTS. Allied to this in spirit was the DUEL, which supposedly worked on the principle that God would favor the cause of the righteous in the battle. The trial by battle or by combat (sometimes called a judicial duel or wager of battle) was a recognized procedure in the Middle Ages. It was introduced from France to England after the Norman Conquest. In this trial, one of the contending parties issued a wager of battle, or challenge. Both parties under oath declared their assertions truthful; a duel was fought, and the victor was awarded the decision. In case one of the parties was a woman, a child, or a feeble man, he or she could be represented by a champion, i.e., a knight who was a relative or who had agreed to fight. As time went on a class of professional champions arose. The Roman Catholic Church from early times disapproved of the ordeal despite its apparently religious aspect, and in 1215 it categorically forbade the clergy to take part in such ceremonies.

order, in taxonomy: see CLASSIFICATION.

Ordericus Vitalis (ôrdĕr'ĭkəs vĭtăl'ĭs), 1075–c.1143, Norman monk and chronicler, b. England. He spent most of his life in Saint-Évroul in Normandy. His *Ecclesiastical History* (4 vol., tr. 1853–56; repr. 1968), a universal history to 1143, is valuable for a study of the Normans in England, France, and Italy and for the history of his own times.

Order of American Knights: see KNIGHTS OF THE GOLDEN CIRCLE.

orders, holy [from Lat. *ordo,*=rank], in Christianity, the traditional degrees of the clergy, conferred by the Sacrament of Holy Order. The episcopacy, priesthood or presbyterate, and diaconate were in general use in Christian churches in the 2d cent. In the Roman Catholic tradition a development, beginning in the 3d cent. and culminating in the Middle Ages, resulted in a division of orders into major (priesthood, including episcopacy, diaconate, and subdiaconate) and minor (acolyte, exorcist, lector, and porter), with a special rite of introduction into the clerical state called TONSURE. The minor orders and the major orders of subdiaconate and diaconate were largely ceremonial, considered steps to priestly ordination, and were taken by those who intended to be ordained to the priesthood. A considerable revision of that schema was undertaken in the present century under the direction of Pope Paul VI. In 1967 the diaconate was restored as an independent order with its own ministry (e.g., preaching, baptizing, distributing Holy Communion), and married men began to be received into this order. In 1972 tonsure, minor orders, and subdiaconate were abolished, and a rite of admission to candidacy to the diaconate and priesthood took their place. As a result the Roman Catholic Church, like the Church of England, has three orders—bishop, priest, deacon—and, like the Orthodox Eastern churches, it has permanent deacons who serve in local parishes and assist the priests. For various Protestant clerical systems, see MINISTRY. Traditionally in the West, the episcopacy has the plenitude of priestly power. Archbishops, patriarchs, and the pope are bishops. Bishops alone have the power to ordain to major orders. In the Roman Catholic Church the ordination to the priesthood is considered a SACRAMENT, conferring on the recipient the power to celebrate the eucharist and marking him with an indelible character. Like the sacraments of baptism and confirmation, ordination is never repeated. The rite entails the laying on of hands and the recitation of the prayer beginning "Receive the Holy Spirit." Priests are required to take an oath of obedience to the bishop or superior and a promise of CELIBACY (already taken at diaconate by those intending to be priests); they are also bound to recite the divine office, the traditional daily prayer of the priest. The diaconate was instituted in the primitive church for the distribution of alms and other material duties. (Acts 6.1–6.) The main administrative life of the Roman Catholic Church is conducted by bishops and their priests called secular clergy; priests who are members of religious orders are called regular clergy (see MONASTICISM). Monsignor and cardinal are honorary titles and are not identified with any particular office; they are not considered orders. See APOSTOLIC SUCCESSION; CARDINAL. See also P. Palmer, *Sacraments of Healing and of Vocation* (1963); D. N. Power, *Ministers of Christ* (1969); P. Bradshaw, *The Anglican Ordinal* (1971); C. R. Meyer, *Man of God* (1974).

orders in council, in British government, orders given by the sovereign on the advice of all or some of the members of the privy council, without the prior consent of Parliament. Orders in council, first so named in the 18th cent., are based either on royal prerogative or on statutory authority. The prerogative allows an order in council to be used to ratify a treaty, to declare the end of a state of war, or to appoint civil service commissioners, but as a vehicle of royal power such an order no longer has any utility. Orders in council are authorized by statute in situations where a possible emergency is contemplated in which routine legislative procedure might be too cumbersome. The order is recommended to the sovereign by the government official responsible, and there is generally a provision for subsequent parliamentary ratification. The most important use of this administrative device has been in time of war. The economic blockade of European ports during the Napoleonic Wars was accomplished by means of orders in council, and they were also used in World Wars I and II, particularly in reference to foreign trade and domestic economic regulation. Among possible current uses are the declaration of a state of emergency, the dissolution of government departments and the redistribution of governmental functions, and the issuance of an extradition order.

orders of architecture. In classical styles of architecture the various columnar types fall, in general, into the five so-called classical orders, which are named Doric, Ionic, Corinthian, Tuscan, and Composite. Each order comprises the column with its base, shaft, and CAPITAL and the supported part or entablature, consisting of architrave, frieze, and cornice. Each order has its own distinctive character,

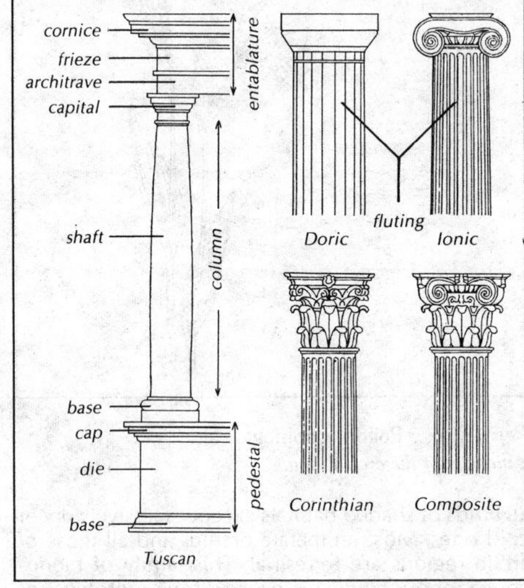

Orders of architecture

both as to relative proportions and as to the detail of its different parts. The entablature height is generally about one quarter that of the column; a pedestal, when used, is about one third the height of the column. For the DORIC ORDER, the IONIC ORDER, and the CORINTHIAN ORDER, originally developed by the Greeks, the Roman writer Vitruvius attempted to formulate the proportionings of their parts. In Greece the Doric was the earliest order to develop, and it was used for the PARTHENON and for most temples. The Corinthian was little used until the Romans adapted it. They employed it more than they did any other order and introduced brackets, or modillions, in its cornice. The Roman orders made greater use of ornament than the Greek, and their column proportions were more slender. In the 15th cent. Alberti revived an interest in the work of Vitruvius. At the same time, architects made drawings of Roman ruins and applied the Roman orders rather arbitrarily to building design. In the 16th cent. a more systematic use of orders was practiced. Architectural writers, notably Serlio, Scamozzi, Vignola, Palladio, and Sanmichele crystallized the Roman versions and additions (Tuscan and Composite) into the five definitely formulated orders, with minute rules of proportion. Philibert Delorme, Claude Perrault, Abraham Bosse, and Sir William Chambers were among those who composed treatises on the subject. Using the classical orders as a basis, the designers of the Renaissance and of subsequent periods created many variations. However, during the CLASSIC REVIVAL, a strict adherence to the proportions of the original Greek and Roman models became the rule.

Ordinance of 1787, adopted by the Congress of Confederation for the government of the Western territories ceded to the United States by the states. It created the Northwest Territory and is frequently called the Northwest Ordinance. It was based on the ordinance of 1784, drafted by Thomas Jefferson, which provided for dividing the region into numerous territories. The 1784 ordinance never went into effect. In 1785 an ordinance was passed providing for division and sale of the lands. Subsequently, the application of the OHIO COMPANY OF ASSOCIATES to purchase a large tract of land in the region forced Congress to act on political administration for the area. The able leaders of the company, Rufus PUTNAM and Manasseh CUTLER, were influential in the drafting of the ordinance, which was passed July 13, 1787. It set up a government in the region N of the Ohio River. A territorial governor, a secretary, and three judges were to be appointed by Congress, which would retain control until the population reached 5,000 voting citizens, when an elected legislature would be set up and the territory would obtain a nonvoting representative in the U.S. House of Representatives. When any portion of the territory reached a population of 60,000 or more, it could apply for admission to the Union as a state according to conditions laid down in the ordinance; there were to be not less than three or more than five states created out of the region (five were ultimately created). The ordinance also provided that no man born in the Northwest Territory should be a slave, that no law should ever be passed there that would impair the obligation of contract, that the fundamental rights and religious freedom be observed, and that education be promoted. The ordinance was the most significant achievement of Congress under the Articles of Confederation. It set the form by which subsequent Western territories were created and later admitted into the Union as states and marked the beginning of Western expansion of the United States.

ordinate: see CARTESIAN COORDINATES.

ordination: see MINISTRY; ORDERS, HOLY.

Ordos (ôr'dōs), Mandarin *Ehr-de-szu,* sandy desert plateau region, c.35,000 sq mi (90,650 sq km), Inner Mongolian Autonomous Region, N China; almost encircled by the great northern bend of the Huang Ho. The Great Wall of China separates the Ordos from the fertile loess land to the south and east. The desert receives less than 10 in. (25 cm) of rain annually, mainly in the form of thunderstorms. The region has many salt lakes and intermittent streams. Large soda deposits are mined. The alkaline soil supports some grasslands, and nomadic Mongol herdsmen raise sheep and goats; some oasis-farming is also practiced. A project to rebuild hundreds of miles of old irrigation canals was begun in 1954 as part of a general Huang Ho basin scheme.

Ordovician period (ôrdəvĭsh'ən) [from the Ordovices, ancient tribe of N Wales], second period of the PALEOZOIC ERA of geologic time (see GEOLOGIC ERAS, table). It was similar to the preceding CAMBRIAN PERIOD, with shallow seas spread for most of the time over the British Isles, Scandinavia, the Baltic region, the Mediterranean region, a large part of Siberia, and much of North America. The Ordovician rocks are chiefly sedimentary. Because of the restricted area and low elevation of the solid land, which set limits to erosion, marine sediments that make up a large part of the Ordovician system consist chiefly of limestone; shale and sandstone are less conspicuous. The Ordovician of North America can best be studied in New York state. In the Early, or Lower, Ordovician epoch, also called the Canadian epoch, the waters spread over the Appalachian area and deposited the Beekmantown limestone, then withdrew generally, to return and deposit the

Chazy limestone of the lower Middle Ordovician, also known as the Champlainian epoch. In the interval between Beekmantown time and Chazy time, large areas, chiefly outside of New York, were apparently covered with wind-blown sand which became the St. Peter sandstone. In the Middle Ordovician the sea spread over North America to a greater extent than in any other period and laid down the Trenton limestone, which in its eastern section is overlaid or intercalated with the Utica mud shale. In the east, increased erosion of the land subsequently led to the deposition of other shales, which became more and more sandy toward the end of the period. The Upper Ordovician, or Cincinnatian, of the west saw the formation of different series of shales, one of them, the Richmond, laid down by a second great Ordovician flood. The close of the Ordovician was marked by more general earth disturbances than the close of the Cambrian. The Taconian disturbance created a chain of fold mountains extending from Newfoundland to New Jersey and was accompanied by volcanic activity. Among the important economic resources of the Ordovician strata are oil, natural gas, the lead and zinc of Wisconsin, Iowa, and Illinois, the "Portland cement rock" of Pennsylvania and New Jersey, Vermont marble, and the calcium phosphate of the Tennessee limestone. The Ordovician seas were rich in animal life. The most characteristic invertebrates were the minute graptolites, other numerous forms being brachiopods, bryozoans, and trilobites. Some cystoids and crinoids appeared; there were a few corals and many cephalopods. Especially noteworthy was the appearance of a few primitive, fishlike vertebrates.

Ordu (ôrdo͞o'), city (1970 pop. 38,522), capital of Ordu prov., N Turkey, a port on the Black Sea. Hazelnuts are grown and exported. It is the site of Cotyora, founded by Greek colonists, c.500 B.C.

Ordzhonikidze (ərjənyĭkē'dzĭ), city (1970 pop. 236,000), capital of the North Ossetian Autonomous Soviet Socialist Republic, SE European USSR, on the Terek River and at the northern foot of the Caucasus. It is the starting point of the Georgian Military Road as well as an industrial center with an electric zinc smelter and lead and silver refineries; it also has chemical plants, food-processing factories, and industries producing chemicals, motors, tractor equipment, clothing, and textiles. The population is Russian, Ossetian, Armenian, and Georgian. Founded in 1784 as a fortress during the Russian conquest of the Caucasian region, it was long the military and political center of Russia in the Caucasus and was named Vladikavkaz. It was made the capital of the Gorskaya (Mountain People's) ASSR in 1921, which in 1936 became the North Ossetian ASSR. It was renamed Ordzhonikidze in 1932, Dzaudzhikau in 1944, and again Ordzhonikidze in 1954. The famous Kazbek Peak rises just above the city. There is a university in Ordzhonikidze.

ore, metal-bearing mineral mass that can be profitably mined. Nearly all rock deposits contain some metallic minerals, but in many cases the concentration of metal is too low to justify MINING the ore. Ores are usually found concentrated in deposits with a definite gradation of metal concentration from the ore to the surrounding rock. The ore often occurs in veins, which are ore-filled fissures in the rock. The veins vary in thickness from only fractions of an inch to several hundred feet. Minerals with no commercial value, called gangue minerals, are usually found mixed with the ore in the vein. Some veins are buried deep within the ground, but others lie close to the surface. Veins of ore exposed to weathering are often eroded and redeposited in placers and alluvial deposits, e.g., ore-bearing stream and lake gravels or beach sands. Some ores are simple chemical compounds, while others are chemically complex MINERALS. Important ores of ALUMINUM, IRON, MANGANESE, and TIN are oxides; important ores of ANTIMONY, COPPER, LEAD, MERCURY, NICKEL, SILVER, and ZINC are sulfides. Some metals, called native metals, occur uncombined in nature, e.g., copper, GOLD, PLATINUM, and silver. The recovery of metals from their ores is one area of the field of METALLURGY.

oreads (ōr'ēăd"): see NYMPH.

Oreb (ō'rĕb), Midianite prince defeated by Gideon. Judges 7.25; 8.3; Ps. 83.11; Isa. 10.26.

Örebro (örəbro͞o'), city (1970 pop. 99,844), capital of Örebro co., S central Sweden, W of Lake Hjälmaren. It is a commercial, industrial, and transportation center. Manufactures include shoes, paper, and processed food. Known since the 11th cent., it was the site of 15 national diets, notably the one in 1529, which brought the Reformation to Sweden, and the one in 1810, which elected Bernadotte (late CHARLES XIV) crown prince of Sweden and Norway.

oregano (ərĕg'ənō), name for several herbs used for flavoring food. A plant of the family Labiatae (MINT family), *Origanum vulgare,* also called Spanish thyme and wild marjoram, is the usual source for the spice sold as oregano in the Mediterranean countries and in the United States. Its flavor is similar to that of MARJORAM but slightly less sweet. In Spain and Italy many other *Origanum* species are also grown as oregano. A related herb (*Coleus amboinicius*) of the same family, called *suganda* in its native Indomalaysia, is known as oregano in the Philippines and Mexico, where it is a popular flavoring. Several other herbs also provide spices called oregano, e.g., species of *Lippia* and *Lantana* of the vervain family. In all cases the flavoring is made from the dried herbage. Oregano is classified in the division MAGNOLIOPHYTA, class Magnoliopsida, order Lamiales, family Labiatae.

Oregon (ŏr'ĭgən, -gŏn), state (1970 pop. 2,091,385), 96,981 sq mi (251,181 sq km), NW United States, in the Pacific Northwest, admitted 1859 as the 33d state. SALEM is the capital and the third largest city; the largest city is PORTLAND, followed by EUGENE. Oregon is bounded on the N by Washington, from which it is largely separated by the Columbia River; on the E by Idaho, with the Snake River forming the boundary in the northern half; on the S by Nevada and California; and on the W by the Pacific Ocean. The state's contrasting physical features are characterized by great forested mountain slopes and treeless basins, rushing rivers and barren playas, lush valleys and extensive wastelands. The major determinant for these unusual climatic differences is the Cascade Range, a rugged mountain chain running north to south c.100 mi (160 km) inland. As the eastward-moving air masses, warmed by the Japanese Current and heavy with moisture from the Pacific

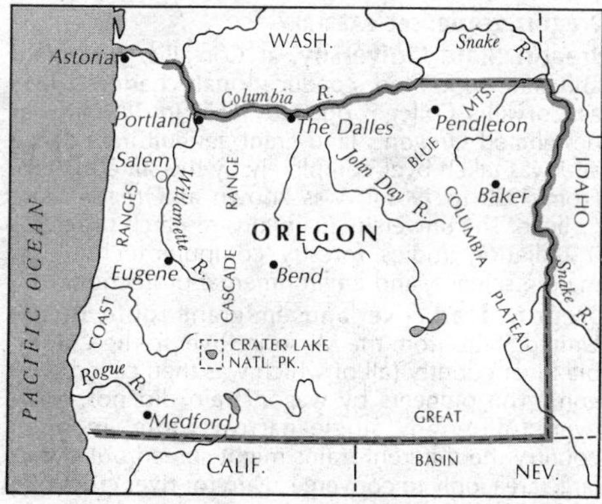

Ocean, rise and meet the cooler mountain temperatures, rain is precipitated over the western third of Oregon. Dry air and continental climate prevail over the eastern two thirds of the state. The western shoreline (c.300 mi/480 km) is bordered by narrow coastal plains of sandy beaches, luxuriant pastures, and occasional jutting promontories. About 25 mi (40 km) inland, the rugged Coast Range rises to heights of 4,000 ft (1,220 m) to serve as the western wall of the Willamette valley. In the valley, where the navigable Willamette flows through miles of rolling farmlands into the Columbia River, lies the agricultural, commercial, and industrial center of the state. Portland, whose metropolitan area contains nearly half the state's population, straddles the Willamette near its junction with the Columbia. Salem and Eugene lie southward in the valley, which is sealed off by the low range of the Calapooya Mts. The snow-capped peaks of the Cascades are on the east, with beautiful Mt. Hood rising to the state's highest elevation (11,235 ft/3,424 m). Mighty stands of timber, many of them protected as national forests, cover the slopes. Eastward the Cascades level out into plateaus drained in the north by the Deschutes and the John Day rivers. To the south a variegated pattern of marshland and mountain merges in the east into the semiarid Great Basin. There, little vegetation grows, and the absence of potable water makes habitation difficult. North of this area rise the pine-covered Blue Mts. and Wallowa Mts., which in some places extend to the Snake River to form precipitous gorges. Other parts of the region where the Snake cuts through the plateau are more level and have been made productive through irrigation. Oregon's irrigation projects include the Deschutes, the Umatilla, and the Vale; the Klamath, shared with California; and the Boise and the Owyhee, shared with Idaho. The state's major sources of farm income are cattle (huge herds graze on the plateaus of the Cascades), dairy items, wheat, and greenhouse products. Chief crops in terms of quantity produced are hay, wheat, potatoes, and barley. In 1970, Oregon was the nation's leading producer of snap beans, peppermint, and sweet cherries (orchards are particularly numerous in the N Willamette valley), and the second largest producer of broccoli and strawberries. The state's 30,739,000 acres (12,440,000 hectares) of rich forestlands (about one half the area of the state) comprise the country's greatest reserves of standing timber; huge areas have been set aside for conservation. Oregon has been the nation's foremost lumber state since 1950; it produces about 25% of the nation's lumber and about 70% of its plywood; wood processing is Oregon's major industry. Douglas fir predominates in the Cascades and western pine in the eastern regions. Other major products are food, paper and paper items, machinery, and fabricated metals. Printing and publishing are important businesses. Abundant, cheap electric power is supplied by numerous dams, most notably those on the Columbia River—Bonneville Dam, The Dalles Dam, and McNary Dam. The John Day Dam, when completed, will be the second largest hydroelectric generator in the country. The many dams also aid in flood control and navigation. The Bonneville Dam enables large vessels to travel far inland, and although river traffic is not as vital as formerly, the Columbia River cities still serve as transport centers for a vast hinterland to the east. Oregon's river resources are one of its greatest assets. Its salmon-fishing industry, centered around Astoria, is one of the world's largest; other catches are tuna and crabs. Although mining is still underdeveloped, Oregon leads the nation in the production of nickel. Sand and gravel, stone, and cement are also major sources of mineral income. Oregon's beautiful ocean beaches, lakes, and mountains draw thousands of visitors annually, making tourism the state's third largest industry (the second is agriculture). Major attractions are the Oregon Caves National Monument, Fort Clatsop National Memorial, and McLoughlin House National Historic Site; Crater Lake National Park is a vacationer's paradise (see NATIONAL PARKS AND MONUMENTS, table). There are 13 national forests, 1 national grassland, and more than 220 state parks. Initial interest in the region was aroused by the search for the NORTHWEST PASSAGE. Spanish seamen skirted the Pacific coast from the 16th to the 18th cent., hoping to claim the area. The English may first have arrived in the person of Sir Francis Drake, who sailed along the coast in 1579, possibly as far as Oregon. Two centuries later, in 1778, Capt. James Cook, seeking the award of £20,000 for the discovery of the Northwest Passage, charted some of the coastline. By this time the Russians were pushing southward from posts in Alaska and the British fur companies were exploring the West. Oregon's furs promised to become an important factor in the rapidly expanding China trade, and the Oregon coast was soon active with the vessels of several nations engaged in fur trade with the Indians. British captains, among them John Meares and George Vancouver, made the coastal area known, but it was an American, Robert Gray, who first sailed up the Columbia River (1792), thus establishing U.S. claim to the areas that it drained. Canadian traders of the North West Company were approaching the Columbia River country when the overland Lewis and Clark expedition arrived in 1805. David Thompson was already making his way to the lower river when John Jacob Astor's agents (in the Pacific Fur Company) founded Astoria, the first permanent settlement in the Oregon country. In the War of 1812 the post was sold (1813) to the NORTH WEST COMPANY, but in 1818 a treaty provided for 10 years of joint rights for the United States and Great Britain in Oregon (i.e., the whole Columbia River area). This agreement was later extended. The North West Company merged with the HUDSON'S BAY COMPANY in 1821, and soon the region was dominated by the Hudson's Bay men, under the patriarchal guidance of Dr. John McLoughlin at Fort Vancouver. American influence in the area was heralded by the arrival of Jedediah S. Smith, while other MOUNTAIN MEN were rivaling the Hudson's Bay men on the southeastern edge of the region. Hall J. Kelley founded the American Society for Encouraging the Settlement of the Oregon Territory in 1829, and one of his disciples, Nathaniel J. Wyeth, attempted to set up a permanent Columbia River post. Both men were sheltered by McLoughlin, as were the missionaries, whose numbers increased after the arrival of Marcus Whitman in 1836. Whitman and his associates went into what is now Washington and Idaho, but other missionaries settled in the Willamette valley itself. They were the harbingers of the "great migration" westward over the OREGON TRAIL beginning with enormous wagon trains in 1842 and 1843. Trouble between the settlers and the British followed. The Americans, under such leaders as Jesse Applegate, set out to form their own government, and although little stock is now given the story of how Marcus Whitman "saved" Oregon by his transcontinental journey, Americans were nevertheless fired to demands for the ousting of the British from the whole of the Columbia River country up to lat. 54°40'N; one of the slogans of the 1844 election was "Fifty-four forty or fight." War with Britain was a threat momentarily, but diplomacy prevailed. In 1846 the boundary was set at the line of lat. 49°N. Soon afterward the country was shocked by the massacre of Marcus Whitman and other settlers at the hands of the Indians, and it was partly as a measure of protection that the Oregon Territory was created in 1848, embracing the area W of the Rockies from the 42d to the 49th parallel. The area was reduced with the creation of the Washington Territory in 1853, and Oregon became a state in 1859 with a constitution that prohibited slaveholding, but which also forbade free Negroes from entering the state. Although the California gold rush caused a temporary exodus of settlers, it also brought a new market for Oregon's goods, and the Oregon gold strike that followed attracted some permanent settlement to the eastern hills and valleys. Wheat farming prospered and in 1867–68 a surplus crop was shipped to England—the beginning of Oregon's great wheat export trade. Cattle and sheep were driven up from California to graze on the tall grass of the semiarid plateaus, and soon cattle barons, such as Henry Miller, acquired huge herds. They dominated the industry until the late 19th cent., when sheepmen and homesteaders succeeded in reducing the cattle range. The '50s, '60s, and '70s were plagued by Indian uprisings, but by 1880 Indian troubles were over, and the next few decades brought increasing settlement and internal improvements. During the '80s, and largely under the management of Henry Villard of the Northern Pacific RR, transcontinental rail lines were completed to the coast and down the Willamette valley into California, bringing new trade and stimulating the beginnings of manufacture. Lumbering, which had long been important, became a leading industry. Seemingly almost overnight logging camps and sawmills were built in the western foothills. The huge stands of Douglas fir and cedar brought fortunes to the lumbering kings, and the threat to natural resources led ultimately to the creation of national forests. By the time of the Lewis and Clark Centennial Exposition at Portland in 1905, less than 50 years after statehood had been gained, the frontier era had passed. Most of the feuding on the eastern plateaus was over, and cattle and sheep grazed peacefully on fenced-in ranges. In spring the Willamette valley was abloom with fruit blossoms, and the river cities were busy with trade and industry. Politically, Oregon has been steadily conservative and the Republican party has remained strong, despite Democratic victories by Franklin Roosevelt and Lyndon Johnson. Dissidents from conservatism have often shown surprising strength, however (as seen in the political career of Wayne Morse), and Oregon has been a leader in social and political reforms. It was the first state, for example, to institute initiative, referendum, and recall; to ease the laws governing the use of marijuana; and to initiate a ban against nonrecyclable containers. Several issues have divided conservative and liberal thought sharply. One has been the question of minority groups. In the 1880s the influx of Chinese threatened the labor market and brought violent anti-Chinese sentiment, and in the 20th cent. there was opposition to the Japanese. Feeling against minorities has never been universal, however, and large groups have vigorously opposed it. In the 1930s one of the most disputed issues was the question of public or private development of power. Today, however, it has to be recognized that the Federal power and irrigation projects have had a profound effect on the economy of the entire Pacific Northwest. Many acres have been opened to irrigated farming, and the tremendous industrial expansion of World War II was to a large extent dependent on Bonneville power. Oregon still operates under its original constitution, drawn and ratified in 1857. Its executive branch is headed by a governor elected for a four-year term. Its bicameral legislature has a senate with 30 members elected for four-year terms and an assembly with 60 members elected for two years. The state elects 2 Senators and 4 Representatives to the U.S. Congress and has 6 electoral votes. Robert Straub, a Democrat, was elected governor in 1974. Among the state's more prominent institutions of higher learning are the Univ. of Oregon, at Eugene; Oregon State Univ. at Corvallis; Reed College, and the Univ. of Portland, at Portland; and Willamette Univ. at Salem. The old standard history of Oregon was that written for Hubert Howe BANCROFT by Francis Fuller Victor (1886–88). See C. L. Skinner, *Adventurers of Oregon* (1920); Nancy Wilson Ross, *Farthest Reach* (1941); H. M. Corning, *Dictionary of Oregon History* (1956); S. N. Dicken, *Oregon Geography* (4th ed. 1965); D. O. Johansen and C. M. Gates, *Empire of the Columbia: A History of the Pacific Northwest* (2d ed. 1967); D. A. Watson and R. L. Allen, *Oregon Economic and Trade Structure* (1969); Ray Atkeson, *Oregon Coast* (1972); Federal Writers' Project, *Oregon: End of the Trail* (1940, repr. 1973).

Oregon, city (1970 pop. 16,563), Lucas co., NW Ohio, a suburb adjacent to Toledo, on Lake Erie; inc. 1958. It is a port with railroad-owned and -operated docks. The city has industries producing oil, chemicals, and wire products. About two thirds of the city's area is open farmland. The chief crops are tomatoes, soybeans, greenhouse vegetables, fruits, and grains.

Oregon, University of, mainly at Eugene; state supported; coeducational; chartered 1872, opened 1876. The medical, dental and nursing schools are at Portland. The university has institutes for research in molecular biology, theoretical science, marine biology, community studies, and industrial and labor relations as well as a center for environmental studies. It has a notable art museum with an important Oriental collection and a museum of natural history that contains collections in anthropology and zoology.

Oregon Caves National Monument: see NATIONAL PARKS AND MONUMENTS (table).

Oregon grape: see BARBERRY.

Oregon State University, at Corvallis; land-grant and state supported; coeducational; chartered 1858 as Corvallis College, opened 1865. In 1868 it was designated Oregon's land-grant agricultural college and was taken over completely by the state in 1885. From 1920 to 1961 it was known as Oregon State College. The university maintains research programs in radiation studies, forestry, computer technology, marine science, and environmental protection.

Oregon Trail, overland emigrant route in the United States from the Missouri River to the Columbia River country (all of which was then called Oregon). The pioneers by wagon train did not, however, follow any single narrow route. In open country the different trains might spread out over a large area, only to converge again for river crossings, mountain passes, and other natural constrictions. In time many cutoffs and alternate routes also developed. They originated at various places on the Missouri, although Independence and Westport (now part of Kansas City, Mo.) were favorite starting points, and St. Joseph had some popularity. Those starting from Independence followed the same route as the SANTA FE TRAIL for some 40 mi (64 km), then turned NW to the Platte and generally followed that river to the junction of the North Platte and the South Platte. Crossing the South Platte, the main trail followed the North Platte to Fort Laramie, then to the present Casper, Wyo., and through the mountains by the broad, level South Pass to the basin of the Colorado River. The travelers then went SW to Fort Bridger, from which the Mormon Trail continued SW to the Great Salt Lake, while the Oregon Trail went northwest across a divide to FORT HALL, on the Snake River. It then went along the Snake River. The California Trail branched off to the southwest, but the Oregon Trail continued to FORT BOISE. From that point the travelers had to make the hard climb over the Blue Mts. Once the mountains were crossed, paths diverged somewhat, although many, if not most, went to Fort Walla Walla before proceeding down the south bank of the Columbia River to the Willamette valley, where the early settlement centered. The end of the trail shifted as settlement spread. The MOUNTAIN MEN were chiefly responsible for making the route known, and Thomas FITZPATRICK and James BRIDGER were known as guides. Capt. Benjamin de Bonneville first took wagons over South Pass in 1832. The first genuine emigrant train was that led by John Bidwell in 1841, half of which went to California, the rest proceeding from Fort Hall to Oregon on horses and mules. The first train of emigrants to reach Oregon was that led by Elijah WHITE in 1842. In 1843 occurred the "great emigration" of more than 900 persons and more than 1,000 head of stock. Four trains made the journey in 1844, and by 1845 the emigrants reached a total of over 3,000. Although it took the average emigrant train six months to traverse the c.2,000-mi (3,200-km) trail, the trail continued in use for many years. Travel upon the trail gradually declined with the coming of the railroads, and it was abandoned in the 1870s. The classic by Francis Parkman, *The Oregon Trail*, actually concerns only the eastern part of the trail. See Federal Writers' Project, *The Oregon Trail* (1939, repr. 1972); F. B. Coons, *The Trail to Oregon* (1954); J. R. Gregg, *A History of the Oregon Trail, Santa Fe Trail, and Other Trails* (1955); D. S. Lavender, *Westward Vision* (1963).

Orekhovo-Zuyevo (əryĕ'khəvə-zo͞o'yĭvə), city (1970 pop. 120,000), W central European USSR, on the Klyazma River. There is a large textile industry (dating from the 18th cent.) and a major chemical industry.

Orel (əryôl'), city (1970 pop. 232,000), capital of Orel oblast, central European USSR, on the Oka River. It is a large railroad junction, an agricultural trade center, and an industrial city producing machinery, textiles, construction equipment, automobile parts, and clothing. It was founded in 1564 by Ivan IV as a fortified settlement to protect the southern border of Muscovy from Crimean Tatar attacks. In the 18th and 19th cent. it was a large trade center. Orel was (1919) the northernmost point reached by Denikin's White Army in the Russian civil war. The city was almost totally destroyed in World War II. The house of the author Turgenev, who was born in Orel, is now a museum.

Orellana, Francisco de (fränthēs'kō thā ōrälyä'nä), d. c.1546, Spanish explorer of the Amazon River. He took part in the conquest of Peru and was a lieutenant of Gonzalo Pizarro on the expedition that started into the interior of South America in 1538. At the Napo River his detachment was separated from the rest of the expedition, and he floated down the length of the Amazon in one of the most improbable successful voyages in history, arriving at its mouth in Aug., 1541. His tales of female warriors (possibly a mistaken impression of long-haired male warriors) gave the river its name. He died in a subsequent attempt to explore the river from its mouth. See H. C. Heaton and B. T. Lee, ed., *The Discovery of the Amazon* (tr. 1934, repr. 1970), an eyewitness account by Gaspar de Carvajal.

Orem (ôr'əm), city (1970 pop. 25,729), Utah co., N central Utah, near Provo; settled 1861, inc. 1919. Orem is located in an irrigated truck-farming and fruit-growing area. It has a large steel mill; other manufactures include electronic components, skis, and canned foods.

Ore Mountains: see ERZGEBIRGE.

Oren (ō'rĕn), descendant of Judah. 1 Chron. 2.25.

Orenburg (əryĭnbo͝ork'), formerly **Chkalov** (chkä'ləf), city (1970 pop. 345,000), capital of Orenburg oblast, Central Asian USSR, on the Ural River. A rail junction on the Trans-Caspian RR, it is a major food-processing and agricultural machine center. Other industries produce machines and machine tools, elevator equipment, leather goods, clothing, and silk. Founded in 1735 as a fortress, Orenburg resisted (1773–74) a siege by Pugachev. It became a center for Russian trade with Kazakhstan and central Asia. It was called Chkalov, in honor of the aviator, from 1938 to 1957.

Orense (ōrän'sā), city (1970 pop. 73,379), capital of Orense prov., NW Spain, in Galicia, on the Miño River. It is the center of an agricultural region with extensive vineyards. There are some light industries. A Roman settlement, it reached its greatest importance as the capital of the kings of the Suebi (5th–6th cent.). It has a fine 12th-century bridge and a Gothic cathedral, frequently restored. There are hot sulfur springs, known since Roman times.

Oreopithecus (ôr"ēōpĭth'əkəs, -pĭthē'kəs), extinct group of apes whose fossils have been found in Italy. It has some similarities to later ancestors of man, probably as a result of parallel evolution. Although related to predecessors of modern apes and man, it is generally classed in a family by itself.

Orestes (ōrĕst'ēz), d. 476, Roman general. With the help of barbarians he deposed (475) the Roman emperor of the West, Julius Nepos, and raised his own son, ROMULUS AUGUSTULUS, to the throne. The next year the barbarians under ODOACER revolted; Orestes was killed at Piacenza, and his son was deposed.

Orestes, in Greek mythology, the only son of Clytemnestra and Agamemnon and brother of Electra and Iphigenia. After the slaying of Agamemnon by Clytemnestra and Aegisthus, Orestes, still a boy, was sent to live in exile. Since it was the duty of the senior male in the house to punish the murderers, Orestes was commanded by Apollo to avenge the crime. With the assistance of Electra and his friend Pylades, who accompanied him in all his adventures, he killed his mother and her lover. After this matricide he was haunted by the Furies (Erinyes) until he reached Athens. He was tried and acquitted by the Areopagus, the tribunal of Athenian judges. Not all the Furies, however, accepted the verdict; and, to win full expiation from his crime, he was told to steal the sacred image of Artemis from Tauris. At Tauris he was reunited with Iphigenia and with her assistance stole the image and safely returned to Greece. It is said that he later married Hermione, the daughter of Menelaus and Helen. In the *Oresteia*, Aeschylus dramatized his vengeance and expiation. The story was also used by Sophocles and Euripides.

Orestia, Turkey: see EDIRNE.

Øresund (örəsŭnd′) or **the Sound,** Swed. *Öresund*, c.45 mi (70 km) long, strait between the Danish island of Sjaelland and Sweden, connecting the Kattegat with the Baltic Sea, to which it is the deepest channel. Between Hälsingborg and Helsingør it is only 2.5 mi (4 km) wide. Copenhagen and Malmö are on the Øresund. A strategic passage, control of the strait was long contested between Denmark and Sweden.

Orff, Carl (ôrf), 1895–, German composer and educator. After studying at the Academy of Music at Munich, he helped to found the Günter School there in 1924. As a composer Orff wished to simplify music, to return to its primitive components. He attempted to adapt old monodic forms to modern tastes, employing dissonant counterpoint and vigorous rhythms. His most famous work is the *Carmina Burana* (1937), a scenic oratorio derived from a group of medieval poems in German and Latin (see also GOLIARDIC SONGS). This oratorio forms part of a trilogy that includes *Catulli Carmina* (1943), a scenic cantata based on the works of Catullus; and *Trionfo di Afrodite* (1953). Orff's other works include the operas *Der Mond* [the moon] (1939) and *Die Kluge* [the wise woman] (1943). Since 1960 he has been head of the Orff School for Music in Munich. His work in music education has attracted a considerable following in the United States.

Orford, Robert Walpole, 1st **earl of:** see WALPOLE, ROBERT, 1ST EARL OF ORFORD.

organ, musical wind instrument in which sound is produced by one or more sets of pipes, each pipe producing only one pitch by means of a mechanically produced or electrically controlled wind supply. Ktesibios of Alexandria, in the 3d cent. B.C., invented the *hydraulos*, in which water pressure was used to stabilize the wind supply. The pipes were arranged in rows upon the wind chest and the air was permitted to enter any pipe at will by means of wooden sliders. The *hydraulos* was the prevailing organ for several centuries and reappeared at intervals throughout the Middle Ages. Evidence of the first purely pneumatic organ is found on an obelisk erected at Byzantium before A.D. 393. Byzantium became the center of organ building in the Middle Ages, and in 757 Constantine V presented a Byzantine organ to Pepin the Short. This is the earliest positive evidence of the appearance of the organ in Western Europe. By the 10th cent., however, organ building had made considerable progress in Germany and England. The organ built c.950 in Winchester Cathedral is said to have had 400 pipes and 26 bellows and required two players and 70 men to operate the bellows. The keyboard, or manual, was a creation of the 13th cent., making possible the performance of more complex music. The earliest extant music written specifically for organ, dating from the early 14th cent., gives evidence that by then the manuals of the organ had full chromatic scales, at least in the middle registers. Organs in the Middle Ages already had several ranks of pipes, each key causing a number of pipes to sound simultaneously. All were diapasons, or principals, the pipes of timbre characteristic only of the organ, and the various pipes controlled by one key were tuned to the fundamental and several harmonics of a given tone. The 15th cent. saw considerable development of the organ, particularly in Germany and Flanders. It became possible to sound single pipes from a rank through the use of stops. Mutation and mixture stops that produce a HARMONIC of the unison pitch came to be used in combination with the unison to vary tone color. Solo stops imitative of other instruments, mainly flute and reed pipes, were added, and the pedal became standard. Until the 19th cent., Italy and England preferred an organ with no pedals. It was the Flemish and German builders who developed the organ of distinctive and contrasting timbres, and the peak in organ building was reached in the German organ of the baroque, as described by Michael Praetorius in his *Syntagma musicum* (1618). The greatest organ builder, perhaps of all time, was Gottfried Silbermann (1683–1753) of Dresden. His organs produced a light, transparent tone, ideal for the performance of the great baroque polyphonic music. After this period the art of organ building degenerated, and the organ lost its place in the center of musical life. The 19th-century desire for a highly expressive organ led to the obscuring of diapason tone by the large number of stops imitative of orchestral tone and to the common employment of the swell and the crescendo pedal. The swell involves enclosing one or more divisions of the organ in a wooden box on one side of which are shutters opened or closed by means of a swell pedal; the crescendo pedal, when gradually opened or closed, adds or takes off stops one by one. The early 20th cent. saw the electrification of the mechanical parts of the organ, ending the trend toward monstrous size and overwhelming power. In the early 20th cent., however, Albert Schweitzer was active in the preservation and restoration of many fine old organs, and there was a movement back to the ideals of Silbermann. In the United States, Walter Holtkamp, beginning in 1932, and G. Donald Harrison, in 1935, became the leading figures in this movement. Harrison designed many organs suitable for the performance of music of all periods. The organ repertory is vast and varied. The great organ masterpieces of the 17th and 18th cent. include works by John Bull, Handel, Jan Sweelinck, Girolamo Frescobaldi, and Dietrich Buxtehude. In the compositions of J. S. Bach. the capabilities of the organ found their most magnificent expression. See W. L. Sumner, *The Organ* (3d ed. 1962); Harold Gleason, *Methods of Organ Playing* (5th ed. 1962); C. F. Williams, *The Story of the Organ* (1903, repr. 1972).

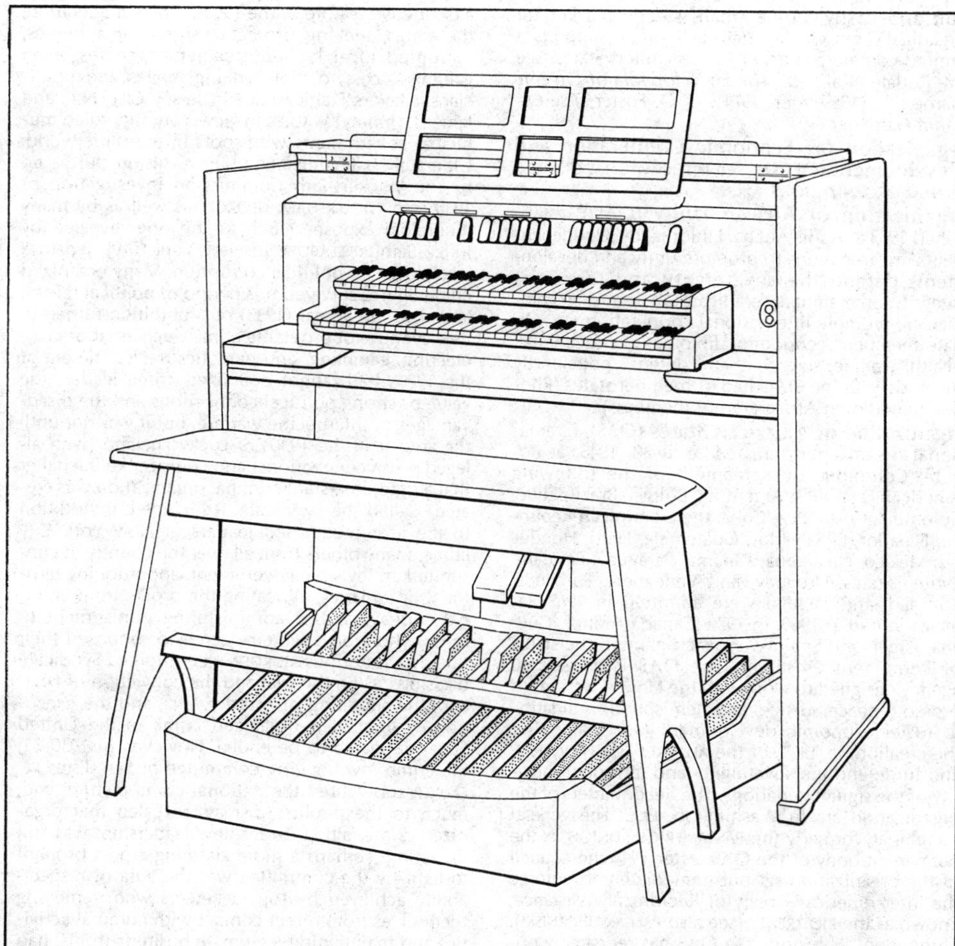

Organ

organic chemistry, branch of CHEMISTRY dealing with the compounds of carbon. Of all the elements, carbon forms the greatest number of different compounds; moreover, compounds that contain carbon are about one hundred times more numerous than compounds that do not. Organic chemistry is of vital importance to the petrochemical, pharmaceutical, and textile industries, where a prime concern is the synthesis of new organic molecules and POLYMERS. Compounds containing only hydrogen and carbon, of which there are many thousands, are called HYDROCARBONS; the simplest is METHANE (CH_4). In general, a particular type of organic compound, such as an ALCOHOL, ALDEHYDE, ETHER, or KETONE, is identified by the presence of a characteristic FUNCTIONAL GROUP of atoms. The functional group is the part of the molecule most responsible for its particular chemical nature. Organic compounds containing nitrogen are of great importance in BIOCHEMISTRY. They generally contain the amine group (NH_2). Molecules containing both the NH_2 and COOH groups are called AMINO ACIDS and are the building blocks of proteins.

organic food, food raised without chemical fertilizers or pesticides and processed without the various additives commonly used in commercial food processing. Proponents of organic food claim that it is healthier and more nutritious and that it tastes better. The principal objection to organic food is that chemical fertilizing and the use of chemical pesticides and herbicides are economically fundamental to the mass-production, highly-mechanized technology that underlies the whole agricultural revolution. Bulky organic fertilizers are inefficient to handle both in transportation from their source and in applying to the fields. Furthermore, organic farming requires more manual labor and attention, thereby increasing costs. In the United States, organic food in the early 1970s became almost a billion-dollar-a-year industry.

organic gardening, the practice of raising plants—especially fruits and vegetables, but ornamentals as well—without the use of synthetic pesticides or fertilizers. In the United States, as elsewhere, awareness of the environmental damage and threats to health (see POLLUTION; ENVIRONMENTALISM) caused by DDT, dieldrin, and other INSECTICIDES and by the excessive use of chemical fertilizers has fostered interest in organic gardening, particularly among home gardeners. Organic gardeners use short-lived, biodegradable pest-killers and prefer manure for fertilizer. Organic farming on a large scale is both difficult and costly, but a small, steady market for organically grown, or "natural," foods supports a limited commercial effort in the United States. See J. I. Rodale et al., ed., *The Encyclopedia of Organic Gardening* (1959, repr. 1971); C. O. Foster, *The Organic Gardener* (1972).

Organization for Economic Cooperation and Development (OECD): see INTERNATIONAL GOVERNMENTAL ORGANIZATIONS.

Organization of African Unity (OAU), established 1963 at Addis Ababa, Ethiopia, by 32 independent African nations to promote unity and development; defend the sovereignty and territorial integrity of members; eradicate all forms of colonialism; promote international cooperation; coordinate members' economic, diplomatic, educational, health, welfare, scientific, and defense policies. By the mid-1970s the OAU had 41 member states (Rhodesia and South Africa are not members).

Organization of American States (OAS), international organization, created April 30, 1948, at Bogotá, Colombia, by agreement of the following American republics: Argentina, Bolivia, Brazil, Chile, Colombia, Costa Rica, Cuba, the Dominican Republic, Ecuador, El Salvador, Guatemala, Haiti, Honduras, Mexico, Nicaragua, Panama, Paraguay, Peru, the United States, Uruguay, and Venezuela. Barbados, Trinidad, and Tobago were admitted in 1967; Jamaica joined in 1969. In 1970, Canada, France, Guyana, Israel, and Spain were each granted the status of Permanent Observer. The OAS is a regional agency designed to work with the United Nations to promote peace, justice, and hemispheric solidarity, to foster economic development (especially after the creation, in 1961, of the ALLIANCE FOR PROGRESS), and to defend the sovereignty and territorial integrity of the signatory nations. The headquarters of the organization are in Washington, D.C. The general secretariat, formerly the PAN AMERICAN UNION, is the permanent body of the OAS. After 1948 the council of the organization set out immediately to enforce the Inter-American Treaty of Reciprocal Assistance, known as the RIO TREATY (see also PAN AMERICANISM). Throughout its history, the OAS has repeatedly opposed unilateral intervention in the affairs of member countries, e.g., at its meetings held in Caracas (1954), Santiago (1959), San José (1960), and Bogotá (1960). However, the OAS itself approved (1965) the U.S. intervention in the Dominican Republic's civil war. Among the many conflicts handled by the council were those between Costa Rica and Nicaragua (1948, 1949, and 1955), when the Nicaraguan regime of Anastasio Somoza was censured for aiding the attempted overthrow of the Costa Rican regime of José Figueres; the conflicts between the Dominican dictator Rafael Trujillo Molina and Haiti, Cuba, Guatemala, and Venezuela (1949, 1950, and 1960); the Haiti-Dominican Republic dispute in 1963; the Panama-United States conflict over control of the Panama Canal in 1964; and the Honduras-El Salvador dispute in 1969. A continuing problem for the OAS has been its relationship with Cuba since that country established (1959) a Communist government. In 1962, Cuba was formally expelled from the organization, and two years later a trade boycott was imposed, Cuba being charged with the attempted subversion of other OAS countries. However, by the early 1970s, Chile and Peru had begun to trade with Cuba again and the future of the boycott was in doubt. See studies by O. C. Stoetzer (tr. 1965) and Margaret Ball (1969).

organized crime, criminal activities that are organized and coordinated on a national scale, often with international connections. The folklore of the United States is replete with tales of outlaw bands, and in this sense organized crime is not new. However, the romantic tradition of the daring desperadoes, particularly Jesse James, Cole Younger, and, later, Baby Face Nelson and John Dillinger, has been superseded by the grim reality of the corporate criminal organization. Firmly rooted in the social structure, it is protected by corrupt politicians and high-powered legal advice and derives astronomical profits from such public vices as GAMBLING, PROSTITUTION, and the illicit use of narcotics. The organized-crime syndicate in the United States is a product of the PROHIBITION era of the early 20th cent. The efforts of Federal officials to enforce the unpopular Volstead Act (see under VOLSTEAD, Andrew Joseph) of 1920 resulted in the growth of highly organized bootlegging rings, with nationwide and, often, international contacts. However, though loose alliances were joined among such groups as the Al CAPONE mob of Chicago, the Detroit Purple gang, and the Owney Madden ring of New York City, gang wars were commonplace, and gangland killing was a distinctive feature of the 1920s. Once in operation, the gangs, seeking protection for their activities, corrupted local law-enforcement agencies, even gaining access to high-ranking judges and politicians. Mayors Frank HAGUE in Jersey City, N.J., and James J. (Jimmy) WALKER in New York City ruled municipal governments with roots in the underworld. Ultimately a feeling of public revulsion, furthered by the Wickersham Commission investigation of 1930 (see WICKERSHAM, GEORGE) as well as by many municipal exposés (such as the one revealed by Judge Samuel SEABURY in New York City), led to a crackdown on political corruption. Many organized crime figures survived this period of political reform and after the repeal (1933) of prohibition turned to new avenues of profitable crime, such as labor racketeering, gambling, and narcotics traffic. The era of the 1920s had taught organized crime leaders the value of strong political connections and the disadvantages of internecine warfare, but it was not until the advent in the 1930s of Lucky Luciano (with alleged MAFIA connections) and Louis Lepke Buchalter that a tight, interstate criminal organization was created. Called the Syndicate, it included, in addition to the aforementioned leaders of New York City crime, many others from all over the country. It constituted an invisible government, apportioning territorial boundaries, allocating the profits from criminal endeavors, and administering punishment to those who violated their decrees or opposed their rule. The notorious MURDER, INC., enforced Syndicate decisions. With the trial and the conviction of Luciano, the smashing of Murder, Inc., and the execution of Buchalter, organized crime in the United States appeared to be ended. However, in 1950–51, the crime investigating committee of Sen. Estes KEFAUVER spotlighted the national crime picture, and, much to the public's dismay, revealed that organized crime, albeit under new leadership, was still operating. Perhaps a more alarming aspect brought to light by the committee was the aura of respectability achieved by top racketeers who, removing themselves from direct contact with criminal activities and maintaining legitimate business fronts, had managed to insulate themselves from criminal prosecution. The Kefauver investigation led to a flurry of law-enforcement activity, particularly attempts to deport foreign-born crime kings, and the public believed that the situation was once more under control. This complacency was shattered in Nov., 1957, when a routine police check in remote Apalachin, N.Y., uncovered a convention of gangland leaders from all over the United States and abroad. The resulting rash of investigations, while once again revealing the power and extensive operations of organized crime, even more dramatically exposed the inadequacy and inability of local law-enforcement agencies to cope with organized crime. The extent to which organized crime succeeds in the United States was evident in the President's Commission on Law Enforcement and Administration of Justice report in 1967; it estimated that twice as much money is made by organized crime as by all other types of criminality combined. See Gus Taylor, *Organized Crime in America* (1962); Hank Messick, *The Silent Syndicate* (1966); U.S. President's Commission on Law Enforcement and Administration of Justice, *Task Force Report: Organized Crime* (1967); Donald Cressey, *Theft of the Nation* (1969); Ralph Salerno, *The Crime Confederation* (1969); Hank Messick and Burt Goldblatt, *The Mobs and the Mafia* (1972); Francis Ianni, *Black Mafia* (1974).

Organ Pipe Cactus National Monument: see NATIONAL PARKS AND MONUMENTS (table).

organum (ôr'gənəm), in music, compositional technique, developed in Europe during the 10th cent., in which each note of Gregorian chant melody was doubled by another note. In the earliest examples, called parallel organum, the doubling interval was constant, usually the lower fourth or fifth. In the 12th cent., composers began to use constantly changing doubling intervals; the resulting compositions had two independent melodies and can be considered the beginning of polyphonic music.

Orhan: see ORKHAN.

Oribe, Manuel (mänwĕl' ōrē'bā), d. 1857, president of Uruguay (1834–38). After serving with José Gervasio Artigas, he became one of the Thirty-three Immortals who raised the standard of independence under Juan LAVALLEJA. He succeeded Fructuoso RIVERA as president and became friendly with the Argentine dictator, Juan Manuel de ROSAS. He lost the support of Rivera, who revolted (1836) and forced him to resign (1838). With the help of Lavalleja and Rosas, the exiled Oribe began the long civil war that nearly destroyed Uruguay. It was marked especially by the eight-year siege (1843–51) of Montevideo, but a combined force of Brazilians, rebellious Argentines under URQUIZA, and the besieged (the Colorados) finally defeated Oribe's party (the Blancos).

oribi: see ANTELOPE.

oriel (ôr'ēəl), projecting or bay window in an upper story, supported on brackets, corbels, or an engaged column. It is usually polygonal or curved in plan, sometimes rectangular, and often rises through two or more stories. It is most characteristic of the late medieval and early Renaissance period in England, where it was a favorite feature in civic and domestic buildings, but it is also found in France and Germany during the same period. It occurs frequently over entrances. The term is often loosely but incorrectly applied to any bay window.

Oriental drama. Of the three major Oriental dramas—Sanskrit, Chinese, Japanese—the oldest is Sanskrit, although the dates of its origin are uncertain.

Sanskrit drama. Sanskrit drama is part of Sanskrit literature, the classical literature of India, which flourished from about 1500 B.C. to about A.D. 1100. The earliest extant critical work on Sanskrit drama is attributed to Bharata, the legendary formulator of the dramatic art in India. That work, the *Na ya-sastra* (c.2d cent. A.D.) is relatively late but could be a reworking of a much earlier version. References to the drama and to dramatic criticism in the work of the grammarian PANINI constitute a more certain indication of an early date for Sanskrit drama. The earliest-known Sanskrit playwright was Bhasa (c.3d cent. A.D.) while among the most renowned were KALIDASA, Bhavabhuti (c.8th cent. A.D.), and King HARSHA. Few Sanskrit plays survive, perhaps due to the limited size of their exclusively aristocratic audience as well as to their antiquity. The plays were performed in palaces and, as in all Oriental drama, the performances were highly stylized in terms of gesture and costume, and music and dance played a significant part in them. To the Westerner, Sanskrit plays would probably seem overladen with religious and supernatural elements. However, they are also firmly grounded in the real world, which often forms a positive contrast to the negative aspects of the supernatural; the plays of Kalidasa convey a sense of the natural world with a fine simplicity, whereas those of Bhavabhuti depict a more grandiose nature. It is undoubtedly the religious influence, however, which explains the happy endings occurring in all Sanskrit drama. Love and heroism are the two most common sources of emotion in the plays, although there is a frequent infusion of a sense of wonder produced by the supernatural elements. Indeed, some plays are almost totally concerned with the supernatural (Kalidasa's *Vikramorvasi*) while others treat political and historical topics (Kalidasa's *Malavikagnimitra*). Another type is represented by *Mrcchakatika*, attributed to the legendary King Sudraka, which concerns ordinary people and is profuse in exciting, melodramatic incident. Sanskrit drama later developed into a didactic form of religious allegory represented by the *Prabodhacandrodaya* of Krsnamisra (11th cent.). The language of Sanskrit drama alternates between prose and lyric poetry. Since SANSKRIT is a literary language, it is used only by important characters; inferior characters speak in the vernacular known as Prakrit.

Chinese drama. The classical Chinese theater developed during the Yüan dynasty (1260–1328). Springing from story cycles made familiar by professional storytellers, Yüan plays relied for their appeal on romantic or sentimental plots. During the Ming dynasty (1368–1644) the drama utilized the plots of popular novels. Until the 19th cent., Chinese drama was not spoken; it was a mixture of music and declamation. Like the Sanskrit, Chinese drama avoids TRAGEDY as that term is understood in the West. However, it is frequently infused with pathos, often involving the deaths of women. Although acting style, character types, stage properties, and other external features of Chinese drama are highly conventionalized, there is great narrative freedom in the plays themselves. Often they are replete with Confucian ethical precepts, propounded with rigid didacticism. Many of the plays, however, embody a Taoist mysticism that runs counter to Confucian influence. Chinese drama is more social and less concerned with romantic love than is the Sanskrit. Family and country are frequently regarded as of more importance than the individual. In contrast to the Sanskrit, Chinese drama was written for a popular audience, and dramatic performances took place in virtually every village. There are many Chinese plays extant, ranging in mood from pathos to farce.

Among the masterpieces of Chinese drama are *The Injustice Suffered by Tou F* by Kuan Han-ch'ing, *The Western Chamber* by Wang Shi-fu, and *The Orphan of the House of Chao* by Chi Chun-hsaing (all 12th-15th cent.); *The Peony Pavilion* by T'ang Hsien-tsu (16th cent.); and *The Palace of Long Life* by Hung Sheng (17th cent.). In the West, Chinese drama is regarded as an entertainment rather than a serious art form. There are several reasons for this judgment: first, the formlessness of Chinese plays, as, for example, Hung Sheng's *Palace of Eternal Youth* (1688), a play in 49 scenes without any act divisions; second, the spectacular nature of Chinese drama, which relies heavily on music, song, acrobatics, mimicry, and costuming; and third, the preponderance of stock characters, such as the comic drunk, in Chinese drama. Perhaps the basic difficulty for Westerners is the fact that in Chinese drama no attempt is made at realism; props and scenery are symbolic (for instance, a flag represents an army); the property man is present on stage; characters at times directly address the audience. Also, often only parts of plays are performed, or, scenes are performed in arbitrary sequence. Since the early 19th cent. the Peking opera has been the dominant force in the Chinese theater. After World War I, a realistic, spoken drama, patterned after Western plays, developed, but since the establishment of the People's Republic of China in 1949 the theater (except on Taiwan) has devoted itself to political propaganda.

Japanese drama. The Japanese No (or Noh) drama stands in stark contrast to both the Sanskrit and the Chinese. The No plays are very short, virtually plotless, and tragic in mood. Performances of No plays are highly stylized, and they move at an extremely slow pace, often stretching a text of two or three hundred lines into an hour-long stage play. Such performances integrate singing, speech, instrumental music (three drums and a flute), dancing, and mime into a unity in which no single element dominates. A particularly striking feature of the performances is the use of wooden masks by the principal character, women characters, and old people. The No drama was developed in the 14th cent., bringing together elements from the earlier *sarugaku* [monkey music] and *dengaku* [rustic music]. Its invention is attributed to Kanami Kiyotsugu (1333–1384), while his son Zeami Motokiyo (1363–1443) brought the No to its peak of refinement. Zeami was also a playwright who produced such classics of the No drama as *The Well-Curb* and *The Lady Aoi*. There may have been thousands of No plays written, but only about 250 are still performed. The language of the No is highly concise and symbolical. Quotations from Chinese and Japanese poetry are included to give the works a traditional basis and, in addition, are often central to the theme. The setting is usually limited to a single place of extreme importance to the main character. The plays center around a single character called the *shite*. Of secondary importance is the *waki*, who is often a priest and who serves as a foil to the *shite*. Both the *shite* and the *waki* have one or two attendants. There is also a chorus whose sole function is to sing. Frequently the chorus sings the lines appropriate for the *shite*, while he dances or mimes the action. It is common for characters to speak lines that seem meant for another character or to finish up another character's speech; finally, a character may speak of himself in the third person. The effect of these devices is to objectify and universalize what otherwise is a highly emotional and personalized experience. The usual form of the play is to present two manifestations of the *shite*. In the first part the *shite* presents a false or disguised appearance. In the second part he presents his true or spiritual self. The No stage is a plain platform about 20 ft (6 m) square with a walkway leading from the back of the stage to the greenroom. The musicians are placed at the back of the stage, and the chorus is on the right. The positions of all characters are very precisely set, as is the stylized movement on stage. Developing about the same time as the No was a type of short farce known as the *Kyogen*. The *Kyogen* are placed between No plays as comic relief. They do not use music, take about 20 min to perform, and are very broad in their humor. In the 16th and 17th cent. two forms of drama developed in Japan that have since far surpassed the aristocratic and difficult No drama in popularity; they are the *Ningyo-shibai* [marionettes] and the Kabuki. Both show similarities to the No in their integration of movement, music, and language. Also, like the No, the *Kabuki* uses only male actors, even for female roles. However, both the *Ningyo-shibai* and Kabuki place greater emphasis on excitement and conflict in the plot. The Kabuki uses more characters than the No, is characterized by much action on the stage as opposed to the stately, slow movement of the No, and avoids the use of recondite symbolism and allusion that frequently make the No a puzzle. The most popular play in the Kabuki repertoire is a revenge play entitled *The Treasury of Loyal Retainers*. The *Ningyo-shibai* reached its peak in the 18th cent. with the work of the playwright Monzaemon CHIKAMATSU. One interesting facet of the Kabuki stage, perhaps reflecting its popular origins, is the walkway (*hanamichi*), which extends from the stage into the audience to the back of the auditorium. The Kabuki, both in classical and modernized form, continues to be popular in Japan today while the No is restricted to a very few theatrical groups and is often obscure even to Japanese. In the 20th cent. the Japanese have produced many Western plays, but their influence on Japanese drama has not yet been significant. The contemporary novelist Yukio Mishima wrote some No plays which, with their modern setting and pessimism, are far different in spirit than the originals. For further information see also SANSKRIT LITERATURE; CHINESE LITERATURE; JAPANESE LITERATURE; and DRAMA, WESTERN. See A. B. Keith, *The Sanskrit Drama* (1926); Faubion Bowers, *Japanese Theatre* (1952); Earle Ernst, *The Kabuki Theatre* (1956); Arthur Waley, ed., *The Nō Plays of Japan* (1922, repr. 1957); A. C. Scott, *The Classical Theatre of China* (1957); L. C. Arlington and Harold Acton, ed., *Famous Chinese Plays* (tr. 1937, repr. 1963); H. W. Wells, *The Classical Drama of India* (1963) and *The Classical Drama of the Orient* (1965); Masakatsu Gunji, *Kabuki* (tr. 1969); and Donald Keene, ed., *Twenty Plays of the No Theatre* (tr. 1970); L. C. Pronko, *Guide to Japanese Drama* (1973).

Orientale, region, Zaïre: see HAUT-ZAÏRE.

Oriental music. The oldest musical culture of the Orient is CHINESE MUSIC, the principal source of JAPANESE MUSIC. The music of Siam is similar to JAVANESE MUSIC, from which BALINESE MUSIC is derived. Also closely related are HINDU MUSIC and ARABIAN MUSIC.

orientation, in architecture, the disposition of the parts of a building with reference to the points of the compass. From remote antiquity the traditional belief in the efficacy of religious ceremonials performed at dawn toward the rising sun has influenced the orientation of temples and other sacred structures. In Mesopotamia and Egypt, in Mayan Central America, even at Stonehenge in England, entrances and other important architectural features were designed to point toward the east; the temples of Greece and Rome often, though not invariably, faced the rising sun. In medieval Europe and, consequently, in modern Europe and the Americas, it became customary to have the congregation and the priest at the altar facing east. So strong was this custom that "west front" came to be a generic term for the facade of a church. Some churches were so built that a central line of the axis of the church pointed exactly to the rising sun on the day of the saint for whom the church was named. Such orientation was, however, by no means universal. St. Peter's at Rome, continuing an earlier tradition, faces in the opposite direction. Important secular buildings in the West often face toward the cardinal points of the compass, and the gridiron pattern of a city's streets is frequently so laid out. Practical problems also govern orientations. The disposition of a building in relation to the prevailing wind or to the sun has long been an important consideration in construction. Early commentators on the problem were Xenophon and Vitruvius. Examples of the concern for climatological orientation can be found in ancient Rome, where there were laws regarding the placement and heights of buildings, or in Puebla, Mexico, where in 1554 the streets were planned so that winds would not sweep through the city. Although orientation in accordance with climatic conditions was in many instances ignored in the 19th cent., modern architects have considered it and have tended to design their buildings accordingly. See J. E. Aronin, *Climate and Architecture* (1953).

Oriente (ōryän'tā), province (1970 pop. 2,998,972), SE Cuba, the easternmost province of Cuba. SANTIAGO DE CUBA is the capital. The largest, most populous, and one of the wealthiest of Cuban provinces, Oriente is characterized by important mountain ranges (notably the Sierra Maestra, which contains Cuba's highest point, Pico Turquino) and by numerous large bays (including GUANTANAMO) along the coast. The Cauto and other long rivers run through the province. Principal crops are bananas, coffee, and cacao. The mining of copper and nickel is important, and Oriente prov. is worldfamous for its liquor industry. Oriente was the site of the first settlement in Cuba and the launching point for the Spanish conquest of the island in the early 16th cent. It has played a key role in the fighting during all of Cuba's political upheavals. Major provincial cities, besides Santiago de Cuba, are Guantanamo, HOLGUÍN, and MANZANILLO.

Origen (ôr'ĭjĭn), 185?–254?, Christian philosopher and scholar. His full name was Origines Adamantius, and he was born in Egypt, probably in Alexandria. When he was quite young, his father was martyred. At the age of 18, Origen became head of the catechetical school of Alexandria, where he had studied under CLEMENT OF ALEXANDRIA. In the 28 years of his labors in Alexandria, Origen became famed for his teaching (for which he accepted no money) and wrote prodigiously. A stern ascetic, he castrated himself out of zeal for purity. Hence he was not ordained a priest, but he was permitted to preach while on journeys to Rome, Caesarea, and Jerusalem. His interpretation of the Scriptures in preaching and lecturing won him wide acclaim. Later (c.230) the bishops of Jerusalem and Caesarea ordained him, but Demetrius, his own bishop, ordered him deposed and banished from Alexandria. In Caesarea, Origen founded (231) a new school that became even more illustrious than the one in Alexandria. Among his students was St. Gregory Thaumaturgus. In the persecution (c.250) of Decius, Origen was imprisoned, tortured, and pilloried; this experience probably caused his death some time after his release. Learned in Greek philosophy, he was a most erudite and profound biblical scholar as well. According to St. Jerome he wrote 800 works. Extant are letters, apologies, and exegeses. His critical edition of the Bible, the *Hexapla*, is famous in the history of textual criticism; this was a parallel edition of six Hebrew and two Greek versions. None of these remains in its original form. Origen's system of theology is given in his *De principiis* [on first principles], known through a Latin version of Rufinus. The chief of his apologies is *Contra Celsum* [against Celsus]. Origen attempted to synthesize the fundamental principles of Greek philosophy, particularly those of NEOPLATONISM and Stoicism, with the Christianity of creed and Scripture so as to prove the Christian view of the universe to be compatible with Greek thought. Before St. Augustine, Origen was the most influential theologian in the church. His threefold plan of interpreting Scripture (literal, ethical, and allegorical) influenced subsequent exegetical works. In spite of Origen's fame as an apologist for Christianity, there was question as to his orthodoxy. His somewhat recondite blending of pagan philosophy with Christian theology led to his condemnation by Justinian in the Monophysite controversy. There is good reason to believe that he was often the victim of misquotation and unfair interpretation. See G. W. Butterworth, tr., *Origen on First Principles* (1936); R. B. Tollinton, tr., *Selections from the Commentaries and Homilies of Origen* (1929); Jean Daniélou, *Origen* (tr. 1955).

original sin, in Christian theology, the SIN OF ADAM, by which all mankind fell from divine GRACE. In effect it is the fundamentally graceless nature of man requiring redemption to save it. The purpose of BAPTISM is to wash away original sin and to restore man to his innocent state, but even after baptism original sin leaves a tendency to sin.

Orillia (ōrĭl'ēə), town (1971 pop. 24,040), SE Ont., on Lake Couchiching. Manufactures include industrial machinery, household appliances, and industrial rubber products. It is also a summer resort. A monument to Champlain, erected in 1925, commemorates his explorations. Stephen Leacock had a summer home there.

Orinase (ôr'ĭnās), trade name for the drug tolbutamide, used to control the type of DIABETES that occurs in mature individuals. Orinase and chemically similar ANTIDIABETIC DRUGS are sulfonamide derivatives, but unlike other sulfonamides, or SULFA DRUGS, they do not have antibacterial properties. They are believed to stimulate the production of the sugar-regulating substance INSULIN in the beta cells of the PANCREAS, and are not used where the pancreas is incapable of producing insulin. Orinase is mainly prescribed for older patients with a mild diabetic condition that is not controllable by diet alone. It is also used to diagnose mild forms of diabetes and some pancreatic tumors. The usefulness of Orinase-type drugs is currently debated.

Orinoco (ōrēnō'kō), river of Venezuela, estimated to be from 1,500 to 1,700 mi (2,410–2,735 km) long. Rising near Mt. Délgado Chalbaud in the Guiana Highlands, S Venezuela, the Orinoco flows in a wide arc through tropical rain forests and savannas (llanos), forming part of the Venezuela-Colombia border, and enters the Atlantic Ocean through a large marshy delta (c.7,800 sq mi/20,200 sq km) in NE Venezuela. One of South America's longest rivers, it and its branches drain an extensive basin; the Apure River is its chief tributary. The Orinoco is joined to the Amazon system by the Casiquiare, a natural canal. The huge flow of the Orinoco varies markedly with the season. Divided into upper and lower courses by the Ature and Maipures cataracts, the river is navigable for most of its length. Dredging permits oceangoing vessels to reach Ciudad Bolívar, c.270 mi (435 km) upstream; a high suspension bridge crosses the river there. Ciudad Guyana, which developed in an industrial zone in the late 1960s, is the principal city on the river. Christopher Columbus probably discovered the mouth of the Orinoco in 1498, and Lope de Aguirre, the Spanish adventurer, seems to have traveled most of its length in 1560. In 1799, Alexander von Humboldt, the German naturalist, explored the upper reaches, but it was not until 1944 that an aerial expedition sighted the source area in the remote highlands. Further explorations in 1951 and 1956 located two rivulets now considered the headwaters. See Hector Acebes, *Orinoco Adventure* (1954).

oriole, common name applied to various perching birds of the Old (family Oriolidae) and New (family Icteridae) Worlds. The European orioles are allied to the crows, while the American orioles, of the hangnest group, belong to the blackbird and meadowlark family. Old World orioles are found in forests and are large birds (8–12 in./20–30 cm). They are swift fliers. Orioles have clear calls and some are very good mimics. Mainly insectivorous, the Old World orioles also eat fruits, mainly berries. These orioles build cup-shaped nests in which to lay their clutches of two to five eggs. Both sexes incubate the eggs. The golden oriole of Europe is a beautiful orange-yellow bird with black wings and tail that ranges from England to Siberia and winters in Africa. The related mango bird inhabits India, and allied species are found in Africa and Australia. The black-naped oriole, *Oriolus chinensis,* is a black and yellow bird found from India to the Philippines. The New World orioles are considerably smaller than the Old World birds. In the male Baltimore oriole of E North America the head, throat, shoulders, wings, and tail are black and the rest of the plumage is orange. Its nest, a deep, woven bag, is suspended from the tip of a high branch. New World orioles also feed chiefly on insects and fruit. In the orchard oriole, chestnut replaces the brilliant orange of the Baltimore oriole. Bullock's oriole, of W North America, has orange markings on the head. New World orioles lay four to six eggs per clutch and both sexes incubate the eggs. Orioles are classified in the phylum CHORDATA, subphylum Vertebrata, class Aves, order Passeriformes, families Icteridae (New World orioles) and Oriolidae (Old World orioles).

Orion (ōrī'ən), in Greek mythology, Boeotian hunter. When Oenopion delayed giving his daughter Merope to him, Orion, when drunk, violated her. Oenopion then blinded him, but his vision was restored by the rays of the sun. The story of Orion's death has many versions. Some state he offended Artemis, who killed him. Others say that he became her favorite hunting companion, but offended Apollo, who loosed a giant scorpion to chase Orion into the sea. Apollo then tricked Artemis into shooting Orion. When she discovered what she had done, she gave way to her grief and immortalized her companion and the scorpion by placing them in the heavens as constellations.

Orion, in astronomy, CONSTELLATION located on the celestial equator. It is one of the most conspicuous and easily recognizable constellations in the entire sky. From ancient times it has been mentioned in the literature of many peoples and is traditionally depicted as the figure of a warrior. Four bright stars form a quadrangle marking his shoulders and feet; brilliant red BETELGEUSE (Alpha Orionis) at his right shoulder, BELLATRIX (Gamma Orionis) at his left shoulder, and dazzling RIGEL (Beta Orionis) at his left foot are all among the 25 brightest stars in the sky, while Saiph (Kappa Orionis) at the right foot is of second magnitude. Three bright second-magnitude stars form a belt almost along the celestial equator; hanging from the belt is a sword of dimmer stars and including the famous Great Nebula (M42). Orion reaches its highest point in the evening sky in late January.

Orion Nebula, bright diffuse NEBULA in the constellation Orion; also known as the Great Nebula of Orion and cataloged as M42 or NGC 1976. It is located near the middle of the "sword" hanging from Orion's "belt" of stars. Its central bright region is about 1° in diameter and it has a total extension of 3°. It is about 1,600 light-years distant and 60 light-years in diameter. The nebula is an enormous cloud of gas surrounding several stars, of which the most prominent is Theta Orionis. To the naked eye the nebula appears to be a faint star but becomes a vague patch of light when viewed through binoculars. The bright region is divided into two sections, the northeast portion being cataloged separately as M43 or NGC 1982.

Orissa (ərĭs'ə, ō-), state (1971 pop. 21,934,827), 60,162 sq mi (155,820 sq km), E India, on the Bay of Bengal. BHUBANESWAR is the capital. The relatively unindented coastline (c.200 mi/320 km long) lacks good ports, and the state depends mainly upon agriculture and fishing for its livelihood. The narrow, level coastal strip, including the delta of the Mahanadi River, is exceedingly fertile. Rainfall is heavy and regular, and two crops of rice (by far the most important food) are grown annually. Sugarcane, tobacco, and jute are also raised. In the south are the Eastern Ghats, which yield valuable timber, and in the north are deposits of iron, manganese, coal, and mica. A canal system links the Mahanadi River with the Hooghly River in West Bengal. The dense population, mainly concentrated in Bhubaneswar, Cuttack, Berhampur, and Puri, is Oriya-speaking. The interior of Orissa, inhabited largely by Munda-speaking aborigines, is hilly and mountainous. In ancient times the region of Orissa was the center of the strong Kalinga kingdom, although it was temporarily conquered (c.250 B.C.) by Asoka and held for almost a century by the Mauryas. With the gradual decline of Kalinga, several Hindu dynasties arose and built famous temples at Bhubaneswar, Puri, and Konarak. After long resistance to the Muslims, the region was finally overcome (1568) by Afghan invaders and soon after passed to the Mogul empire. In 1803 it was conquered by the British. The coastal section, which was made (1912) part of Bihar and Orissa Province, became in 1936 the separate province of Orissa. In 1948 and 1949 the area of Orissa was almost doubled and the population was increased by a third with the addition of 24 former princely states. In 1950, Orissa became a constituent state of India. It is governed by a chief minister and cabinet responsible to an elected unicameral legislature and by a governor appointed by the president of India.

Oriya (ôrē'yə), language belonging to the Indic group of the Indo-Iranian subfamily of the Indo-European family of languages. See INDO-IRANIAN LANGUAGES.

Orizaba (ōrēsä'bä), city (1970 pop. 92,728), Veracruz state, E central Mexico. It is the commercial center of a prosperous bean, citrus, and tropical fruit growing region. The development of water power has stimulated manufacturing industries, especially cotton and wool textile factories. A favorite resort of Emperor Maximilian, Orizaba has remained a popular vacation spot. Mineral springs are nearby, and the majestic cone of Mt. Orizaba rises in the distance. The city is also a cultural center noted for its fine-arts institute. The federal school in Orizaba houses murals by José Clemente Orozco. In 1862, Benito Juárez, seeking to forestall foreign intervention in Mexican affairs, called a conference at Orizaba of foreign representatives; his efforts failed. French forces subsequently used the city as a base for their invasion of Mexico.

Orizaba, peak, 18,700 ft (5,700 m) high, in the Cordillera de Anáhuas, E Mexico, on the Veracruz-Puebla border. It is the highest peak in Mexico and the third-highest in North America. This snow-capped volcano, called Citlaltépetl in Aztec times, is inactive; the last eruption occurred in 1687. The peak was first climbed in 1848.

Orkhan (ôrkhän'), 1288?–1362?, Ottoman sultan (1326–1362?), son and successor of OSMAN I as leader of the Ottoman Turks. He defeated Byzantine Emperor Andronicus III and conquered large parts of Asia Minor, including Nicaea and İzmit. In 1345 the Ottomans first crosssd into Europe to aid Byzantine Emperor JOHN VI (John Cantacuzene). Orkhan married John's daughter Theodora. Orkhan crossed the Dardanelles two more times, assisting John against Stephen Dushan of Serbia and gaining for the Ottomans a foothold in Europe. He left a well-organized state to his son and successor, Murad I. Orkhan was the first Ottoman ruler to assume the title of sultan.

Orkhon (ôr'kŏn, ôr-khŏn'), river, c.300 mi (480 km) long, rising in the Khangai mts., N central Mongolian People's Republic, and flowing east, then north, past the site of ancient Karakorum, and then north-east to join the Selenga River just S of the USSR border. It is navigable for shallow-draft vessels only during July and August. The Orkhon Inscriptions, discovered in 1889 by the Russian explorer N. M. Yadrinstev near the site of ancient Karakorum, date from the 8th cent. They comprise minor Chinese texts and the oldest known material in a Turkic language. They were studied in 1891 by the Russian turkologist V. V. Radlov and were deciphered by the Danish philologist Vilhelm Thomsen in 1896.

Orkney, county (1971 pop. 17,075), 376 sq mi (974 sq km), N Scotland, consisting of the **Orkney Islands,** an archipelago of about 70 islands in the Atlantic Ocean and the North Sea, N of Caithness across the Pentland Firth. Less than half the islands are inhabited. Mainland (Pomona), the largest, has KIRKWALL, the county town, and STROMNESS. Other large islands are HOY, South Ronaldsay, Stronsay, Sanday, Westray, and Rousay. The climate is mild, windy, and wet. Orkney is one of Scotland's richest farming counties. Beef cattle and eggs are the most important produce. Sheep and pigs are also raised. Some fishing, mainly for lobster, is carried on in Scapa Flow and in the north. Orkney was settled by Picts. There were Viking invasions in the 8th cent. From 875 to 1231 it was a Viking earldom under the Norwegian crown. Details of this period are recounted in the *Orkneyinga Saga*, a Norse epic of the time. In 1231, Orkney passed to the Scottish earls of Angus on the death of the last Viking earl. It became a possession of the Scottish crown in 1472 in trust for the undelivered dowry of Margaret of Norway on her marriage to James III (1469), but the long Norse occupation left marked Scandinavian traces in the people and their culture. James V visited Kirkwall in 1540 and made Orkney a county. SCAPA FLOW, S of Mainland, was Britain's major naval base in World Wars I and II. Orkney has many prehistoric relics. Stone Age villages have been unearthed at SKARA BRAE on Mainland and a broch (prehistoric fort) at Rinyo on Rousay. Other relics are the burial chambers at MAESHOWE and the standing stones at STENNESS.

Orlando: see ROLAND.

Orlando, Vittorio Emanuele (vēt-tô'rēō ämänwĕ'lā ōrlän'dō), 1860–1952, Italian statesman and jurist. He held several cabinet posts from 1903 to 1917 and was premier from 1917 to 1919. As one of the Big Four (Georges Clemenceau, David Lloyd George, Orlando, and Woodrow Wilson) at the Paris Peace Conference in 1919, he demanded the fulfillment of the secret Treaty of London of 1915, by which the Allies had promised Italy ample territorial compensation in Dalmatia for its entry into World War I. Meeting stubborn opposition from Wilson and failing to secure British or French support, he dramatically left the conference in April, 1919, but returned in May. Even then no solution satisfactory to Italy was found; Orlando resigned and was succeeded as premier by Francesco Nitti. Opposing Fascism, Orlando gave up (1925) his seat in parliament and devoted himself to teaching and writing. After the fall of Mussolini in 1943, he became, with Benedetto Croce and Nitti, a leader of the conservative Democratic Union. From 1948 until his death he was a senator. See Robert Lansing, *The Big Four and Others of the Peace Conference* (1921).

Orlando (ôrlăn'dō), city (1970 pop. 99,006), seat of Orange co., central Fla., in a lake region; inc. 1875. It has resort activities and is the trade and shipping center for a citrus-fruit and vegetable area. It also has aerospace and electronic industries. Orlando was settled near Fort Gatlin, a post established (c.1837) during the Seminole War. Florida Technological Univ., Valencia Junior College, McCoy Air Force Base, and two naval training centers are there. Of interest are Eola Park, on the shores of Lake Eola in downtown Orlando, botanical gardens, a museum, and a planetarium. Walt Disney World is nearby.

Orléanais (ôrlāänā'), region and former province, N central France, on both sides of the Loire River. ORLÉANS, the historic capital, CHARTRES, and BLOIS are the chief cities. The region includes Loiret, Loir-et-Cher, and parts of Eure-et-Loir and Yonne depts. BEAUCE in the north, Little Beauce in the west, and Gâtinais in the east are rich agricultural districts; the large ancient forest of Orléans (northeast of the city) occupies the center of the region. The fertile Loire valley yields fruits, vegetables, and grapes and is dotted by many fine châteaux, notably Blois and CHAMBORD. South of the Loire bend is the swampy Sologne Plain, which has been considerably improved by drainage. The nucleus of the Orléanais has been part of the royal domain since the time of

Hugh Capet (10th cent.); see CAPETIANS. Although Orléanais is one of the areas of France least affected by Roman civilization, there are abundant ruins of fortresses and churches from the Carolingian period (c.7th cent.).

Orléans (ôrlääN'), family name of two branches of the French royal line. The house of Valois-Orléans was founded by Louis, duc d'Orléans (see separate article), whose assassination (1407) caused the civil war between ARMAGNACS AND BURGUNDIANS. This house ascended the French throne (1498) in the person of Louis XII, who died without male issue. Gaston, brother of Louis XIII, was made duke of Orléans (see separate article), but died without a male heir. The modern house of Bourbon-Orléans was founded by **Philippe I, duc d'Orléans,** 1640-1701, a brother of King Louis XIV. A notorious libertine, he was excluded from participation in state affairs, though he fought in the Dutch War and won the victory of Cassel (1677). He married (1661) HENRIETTA OF ENGLAND and, after her death, ELIZABETH CHARLOTTE OF BAVARIA (1671). His son, **Philippe II, duc d'Orléans,** 1674-1723, regent of France (1715-23) during the minority of Louis XV, distinguished himself in the War of the Grand Alliance and in the War of the Spanish Succession. He was known for his cynicism and immorality. The will of King Louis XIV, which made him president of the regency council, severely restricted his authority, but he had the will annulled. His rule was marked by a resurgence of the noble elements subdued by Louis XIV. Councils of state, comprising the higher nobility, were formed, but they failed, and government by ministers, or secretaries of state, was restored. To deal with the financial crisis, Orléans called on John LAW, who established a royal bank. But Law's financial schemes collapsed in 1720. Foreign affairs under the regency were conducted by Guillaume DUBOIS. Orléans concluded the QUADRUPLE ALLIANCE of 1718 and made war on Spain (1719-20). Social life during his regency reached an apex of licentiousness. See W. H. Lewis, *The Scandalous Regent* (1961). The ambitions of the regent and his descendants ultimately brought the house of Orléans into open opposition to the ruling house. The regent's great-grandson, Louis Philippe Joseph, duc d'Orléans, called Philippe Égalité (see separate article), supported the French Revolution. His adherents, the Orleanists, who sought a compromise between the monarchical and the revolutionary principles, came into power by the July Revolution of 1830 and put Philippe Égalité's son LOUIS PHILIPPE on the French throne. Representatives of the capitalist upper bourgeoisie, the Orleanists limited their definition of revolutionary liberty to the middle class. After the fall of Louis Philippe (1848), they continued to support the claims of his descendants, the Orleanist pretenders, who returned from exile after the fall of Napoleon III (1871). Their prospects, though high under the presidency of Marshal MacMahon, dwindled steadily, especially after the Third Republic exiled all pretenders in 1886. Louis Philippe's eldest son, **Ferdinand Philippe Louis Charles Henri, duc d'Orléans,** 1810-42, took part in the French expedition to Belgium (1831-32) and in the Algerian wars (1835-40). His unfinished *Campagnes de l'armée d'Afrique, 1835-39,* was published in 1870. He died in a carriage accident. His eldest son, **Louis Philippe Albert d'Orléans, comte de Paris,** 1838-94, went to the United States after his candidacy for the throne had failed in 1848 and fought in the Civil War under General McClellan. Back in France in 1871, he was Orleanist pretender but relinquished his rights to the legitimist pretender, Henri de CHAMBORD (1873). After Chambord's death (1883), he became head of the entire house of Bourbon. In 1886 he was exiled by the law against pretenders. He was the author of *History of the Civil War in America* (tr., 4 vol., 1875-88) and other works. He died in England. His brother, **Robert Philippe Louis Eugène Ferdinand d'Orléans, duc de Chartres,** 1840-1910, also fought in the American Civil War. In the Franco-Prussian War he served in the French army under the name Robert le Fort. After 1871 he fought in the Algerian wars, but he also was exiled in 1886. Owing to his brother's renunciation of his claims, the duke of Chartres was regarded by many Orleanists as pretender from 1873 to 1883. **Louis Philippe Robert, duc d'Orléans,** 1869-1926, succeeded his father, Louis Philippe Albert, comte de Paris, as pretender in 1894. Born and educated in England, he served (1888-89) in the Indian army. An explorer, he left accounts of his wide travels. He died childless, and his pretensions to the French throne passed to his cousin Jean d'Orléans, duc de Guise, son of the duke of Chartres, and his heirs.

Orléans, Charles, duc d' (shärl dük dôrlääN'), 1391-1465, French prince and poet; nephew of King Charles VI. After the assassination of his father, Louis d'ORLÉANS, he became (1407) titular head of the Armagnacs (see ARMAGNACS AND BURGUNDIANS). After the English invasion of France in 1415, Charles was captured at the battle of Agincourt and remained in captivity in England until 1440, when he was ransomed. In retirement at Blois, he devoted the rest of his life to writing verse and to the society of literary men. Among his poems, which are remarkable for their polish and charm, is the rondeau, "Le temps a laissié son manteau" [the season has shed its cloak]. There are translations of his poems by Andrew Lang, W. E. Henley, and Ezra Pound. Charles's son was King Louis XII. See biography by Enid McLeod (1970).

Orléans, Gaston, duc d' (gästôN'), 1608-60, son of King Henry IV and Marie de' Medici, younger brother of Louis XIII. He took part in many of the conspiracies of the great nobles against Louis XIII's minister, Cardinal Richelieu and several times fled from France. Although Gaston was pardoned after each revolt, his associates did not fare so well; the younger Henri de MONTMORENCY and the marquis de CINQ MARS were executed. After the death (1643) of Louis XIII, Gaston became lieutenant general of France and successfully campaigned against the Spanish. For his leading part in the FRONDE he was exiled (1652) to Blois. Gaston was the father of Mlle de MONTPENSIER.

Orléans, Henrietta Anne, duchesse d': see HENRIETTA OF ENGLAND.

Orléans, Henri Philippe Marie, prince d' (äNrē' fēlēp' märē' präNs'), 1867-1901, French explorer and author, b. England; son of Robert, duke of Chartres. After a journey (1889) from Siberia to Siam, by way of Tibet, and a visit (1892) to SE Africa, he left (1895) Hanoi, to complete the earlier work of M. J. F. Garnier on the Mekong River in Indochina. He traveled as far as the Brahmaputra, established the fact that the Salween originates in Tibet, and also discovered the source of the Irrawaddy. His accounts of his travels include *Around Tonkin and Siam* (1894, tr. 1894) and *From Tonkin to India* (1897, tr. 1898).

Orléans, Louis, duc d' (lwē), 1372-1407, brother of King CHARLES VI of France, whose chief counselor he was from 1388 to 1392. After 1392, when Charles VI suffered his first attack of insanity, Louis became involved in a long struggle for control with his uncle, PHILIP THE BOLD of Burgundy, and with Philip's successor, JOHN THE FEARLESS. Unpopular because of his extravagance, he was treacherously murdered by John's order in 1407. His death precipitated the civil war between ARMAGNACS AND BURGUNDIANS.

Orléans, Louis Philippe Joseph, duc d' (lwē fēlēp' zhôzĕf'), known as **Philippe Égalité** (ägälētā'), 1747-93, French revolutionist; great-grandson of Philippe II, duc d'Orléans (see ORLÉANS, family) and great-great-great-grandson of King Louis XIII. First duke of Montpensier and then duke of Chartres, he succeeded his father as duke of Orléans in 1785. A libertine, he squandered his immense wealth, then, to recoup his fortune, lined the gardens of his Palais Royal with shops. The gardens became a gathering point for the popular elements of Paris. He became a leader of the discontented faction, and at the Assembly of the Notables (1787) he was briefly exiled for protesting the king's attempt to force the Parlement of Paris to consent to taxation. As a deputy to the States-General (1789), he was one of the liberal nobles who joined the third estate (June 25, 1789). After incurring blame for disturbances in the capital, he accepted a mission (Oct., 1789-July, 1790) to England. His liberal views were suspected of cloaking an ambition to become constitutional monarch, and as the revolution progressed he lost the confidence of both republicans and royalists. After exchanging his title for the name Citizen Égalité, he was elected to the National Convention (Sept., 1792), where he joined the MOUNTAIN and voted for the execution of King Louis XVI. When his eldest son deserted to the enemy with General DUMOURIEZ, Philippe Égalité was arrested (April, 1793). He was guillotined (November) during the Reign of Terror. His son became King LOUIS PHILIPPE.

Orléans, city (1968 pop. 100,134), capital of Loiret dept., N central France, on the Loire River. A commercial and transportation center, it has food-processing, tobacco, machine-building, electrical, pharmaceutical, chemical, and textile industries. The old city is surrounded by sprawling modern suburbs. Orléans was first known as Genabum, a commercial city of the Carnutes, a Celtic tribe. The city revolted against Julius Caesar (52 B.C.), was burned, and was rebuilt and called Aurelianum. Unsuccessfully attacked by Attila the Hun (451), it was taken by Clovis I (498), after which it became (511) the capital of the Frankish kingdom of Orléans. The kingdom was united with Neustria in the 7th cent. Under the Capetians, the first kings of France, the city became (10th cent.), after Paris, the principal residence of the French kings. Orléans, with the surrounding province, the ORLÉANAIS, constituted part of the small nucleus of the royal domain, and it was several times given in appanage as a duchy to the eldest brother of the king of France and to his descendants (see ORLÉANS, family). The siege of Orléans (1428-29) by the English threatened to bring all of France under England's rule, and its lifting by Joan of Arc turned the tide of the Hundred Years War (1337-1453). In the Wars of Religion (16th cent.) the city was briefly the headquarters of the HUGUENOTS and was besieged in 1563 by Catholic forces. Orléans remained in Catholic hands until the Edict of NANTES (1598). During the 17th and 18th cent. the city was a prosperous industrial and commercial center, and its university (founded 14th cent.) was famous throughout Europe. The advent of railroads in the 19th cent. somewhat reduced the city's importance as a trade center dependent on the Loire River port. Orléans was severely damaged during the German invasion of France in 1940, and many irreplaceable historic buildings were destroyed. Several fine structures remain, including the Cathedral of Sainte-Croix, rebuilt (17th-19th cent.) after its destruction by the Huguenots in 1568; and the Renaissance town hall, where Francis II died in 1560. The feast of Joan of Arc is celebrated in Orléans with particular splendor each May.

Orléans, Île d' (ēl dôrlääN'), or **Orléans Island** (ôrlääN', ôr'lēənz), 20 mi (32 km) long and 5 mi (8 km) wide, S Que., Canada, in the St. Lawrence NE of Quebec. It is connected with the mainland by a highway bridge. Settled (1651) by the French, it was the site of one of Wolfe's camps in his attack on Quebec in 1759. It is a popular tourist attraction. Potatoes, strawberries, cheese, and poultry are the chief products of the island.

Orléansville: see EL ASNAM, Algeria.

Orley, Bernard van (bĕr'närt vän ôr'lī), or **Barend van Orley** (bä'rənt), c.1491-1542, Flemish painter. In 1515 he was settled in Brussels, where he became court painter to Margaret of Austria, regent of the Netherlands, and to her successor, Mary of Hungary. Influenced by Dürer and Raphael, van Orley may have gone to Italy or known of Raphael's tapestry cartoons. In any case, an unmistakable Italianate influence is apparent in his work. Among his paintings are *Holy Family* (Louvre); a triptych, *The Tribulations of Job* (Brussels); *Crucifixion* (Rotterdam); and *The Last Judgment* (Antwerp). Van Orley also executed designs for stained glass and tapestries, an example of the latter being the *Hunts of Maximilian* (Louvre).

Orlon, trademark for an acrylic fiber made in filament or staple form. Orlon is resistant to sunlight and atmospheric gases, which makes it ideal for awnings, curtains, and other outdoor uses. It is also characterized by stability, little or no shrinkage in fabrics, a soft, warm feel, and good drapability. The filaments have a high tensile strength that is almost as good when wet as dry. The fibers have good elasticity and low moisture absorption. Orlon is resistant to chemicals, chiefly acids, and it has the ability to withstand high temperatures, which makes it suitable for various industrial uses. Other uses for the filament include evening wear, sports fabrics, and rainwear fabric. The staple fiber is used in bulky suiting fabric, overcoatings and topcoatings, dress fabrics, knitted wear, and washable woven sportswear.

Orlov, Aleksey Grigoryevich, Count (əlyĭksyā' grĭgôr'yəvĭch, ərlôf'), 1737-1808, Russian nobleman; brother of Grigori G. Orlov. He and his brother headed the conspiracy to put CATHERINE II on the throne of Russia. It is alleged that he was the actual murderer of PETER III. He distinguished himself in the Russo-Turkish War of 1768-74.

Orlov, Grigori Grigoryevich, Count (grĭgô'rē), 1734-83, Russian nobleman. One of the first lovers of CATHERINE II, he and his brother led the conspiracy that deposed PETER III and put her on the throne. Although the empress was deeply in love with him and owed her power to him more than to any other man, his position as a favorite at Catherine's court did not give him a decisive voice in state affairs. He was later supplanted by other favorites, notably Potemkin. Catherine gave him high military posts but did not act on his scheme for the emancipation of the serfs.

Orly (ôrlē′), city (1968 pop. 30,571), Val-de-Marne dept., N central France, a suburb SE of Paris. It is the site of Orly Field, one of the chief airports of Paris.

Ormandy, Eugene (ôr′məndē), 1899–, American conductor, b. Budapest. At the age of five Ormandy entered the Budapest Conservatory, where he studied the violin. Graduating in 1914, he became a member of the faculty. In 1921 he came to the United States, working as violinist, concertmaster, and later conductor of the Capitol Theatre Orchestra, New York City. After a successful guest appearance with the Philadelphia Orchestra, he was appointed conductor of the Minneapolis Symphony Orchestra in 1931. In 1936 he became associate conductor of the Philadelphia Orchestra and its permanent conductor and music director in 1938. Ormandy was known for superb romantic interpretations, excelling in works by Beethoven and 19th-century masters.

Ormazd (ôr′məzd): see ZOROASTRIANISM.

Ormerod, Eleanor Anne (ôr′mərŏd), 1828–1901, English economic entomologist. She aided the Royal Horticultural Society in forming a collection of insect farm pests and was awarded the Flora medal. Her *Notes for Observations on Injurious Insects* (1877), initiated the *Annual Series of Reports on Injurious Insects and Farm Pests.* She was the first woman fellow (1878) of the Meteorological Society, consulting entomologist to the Royal Agricultural Society, and lecturer at the Royal Agricultural College. Her works include *A Manual of Injurious Insects with Methods of Prevention* (1881) and *Text Book of Agricultural Entomology* (1892). See her autobiography (1904).

ormolu (ôr′məlo͞o), finish used on metal to imitate gold. It is employed chiefly for furniture mountings. The term originally applied to a coating of ground gold and was extended to alloys of copper and zinc. Ormolu mountings were characteristic of 18th-century furniture and attained their highest artistic and technical development in France, especially in the work of Charles Cressent, Pierre Gouthière, and Jacques Caffieri. Ormolu was produced on a large scale in England, with Matthew Boulton the chief manufacturer. Workmanship deteriorated in the 19th cent.

Ormond Beach, resort and residential city (1970 pop. 14,063), Volusia co., NE Fla., on Halifax River (a lagoon) and the Atlantic Ocean; inc. 1880. It was founded (1873) as a health resort and was the winter home of several famous people, including John D. Rockefeller, who died there in 1937.

Ormonde, James Butler, 12th **earl** and 1st **duke of,** 1610–88, Irish statesman, most powerful royalist influence in Ireland during the ENGLISH CIVIL WAR. A ward of the crown after the death (1619) of his father, Viscount Thurles, he was brought up a Protestant and in 1629 married the heiress of the earl of Desmond. He succeeded his grandfather as earl of Ormonde in 1633. In Ireland from 1633, Ormonde gained the favor of Thomas Wentworth, (later 1st earl of STRAFFORD). He was placed (1640) in command of the army in Ireland after Strafford's return to England. As lieutenant general, he fought the Irish rebels in 1641 and, although greatly hampered by the Irish lords justices, defeated the rebels at Killsalghen and Kilrush. He was made a marquess in 1642, again defeated (1643) the rebels, and, under orders from Charles I, concluded the treaty of "cessation," placing most of Ireland in the hands of the Confederate Catholics. Ormonde then dispatched forces to the king in England and was appointed (1644) lord lieutenant of Ireland. In this position he skillfully maintained himself against both the Catholic rebels and the Protestant adherents of the English Parliament. In 1647, however, he made terms with Parliament in order to restore peace in Ireland and gave up his office. He joined (1648) the queen and Prince Charles in Paris, but in 1649 he returned to Ireland and proclaimed the prince as King Charles II. Leaving the island again at the insistence of Charles, he commissioned (1650) the earl of CLANRICARDE as his deputy. Ormonde represented Charles in the negotiations preceding the Restoration, and after 1660 he was given numerous offices and titles, including privy councilor, lord high steward of England, earl of Brecknock (in the English peerage), and duke of Ormonde (Irish; also English in 1682). Again lord lieutenant of Ireland, he worked to promote Irish trade and to effect the complicated business of restoration of property. He was unpopular with the Restoration court, especially with the 2d duke of BUCKINGHAM, who apparently instigated (1669) an unsuccessful attempt on Ormonde's life. Ormonde was removed (1669) as lord lieutenant but was restored to office in 1677. Because of his mild anti-Catholic measures at the time of the Popish Plot (see OATES, TITUS), he was attacked by the 1st earl of SHAFTESBURY. He was again removed from the lord lieutenancy in 1684 as a result of intrigue. Thereafter he emerged from retirement only to oppose James II's attempt to dispense with the anti-Catholic laws. In an age of complex loyalties, Ormonde directed his considerable talents to the support of the Stuarts, except when opposition to Parliament seemed hopeless. He survived his son, the earl of Ossory, and was succeeded by his grandson. See biographies by Thomas Carte (6 vol., 1851) and Lady Burghclere (2 vol., 1912).

Ormonde, James Butler, 2d **duke of,** 1665–1745, Irish soldier. He was the son of Thomas Butler, earl of Ossory, and grandson of the Ist duke, whom he succeeded in 1688. A staunch Tory and popular military figure, he supported the cause of William of Orange (William III) and fought in the battle of the Boyne (1690). Early in the War of the Spanish Succession he commanded (1702) land forces in the fruitless expedition against Cádiz. Later, as lord lieutenant of Ireland (1703–6, 1710–13) and as the duke of Marlborough's successor (1711) in command of the forces, he appeared to be one of the most powerful men in the kingdom. He became involved, however, in the plot to prevent the accession of George I, and in 1715 he was impeached. Fleeing to France, he was attainted, took part in the risings of the Jacobites in 1715 and 1719, and spent the rest of his life in exile.

Ormonde, James Butler, 5th **earl of,** 1420–61, Irish nobleman. He was knighted in his youth by Henry VI of England and was created earl of Wiltshire in 1449. He succeeded to the earldom of Ormonde in 1453. A staunch Lancastrian, he was made deputy (1451) and then viceroy (1453) of Ireland and lord high treasurer of England (1455). In the Wars of the Roses, he fought at St. Albans, Wakefield, and Mortimer's Cross, and, after being captured at Towton, was executed by the Yorkists.

Ormonde, Thomas Butler, 10th **earl of,** 1532–1614, Irish nobleman. Brought up at the English court, he was the first of his family to embrace Protestantism. He succeeded to the earldom of Ormonde in 1546, and in 1554 he went to Ireland, where he tried to mediate between the Irish and their English rulers. He became involved in a bitter quarrel in Munster with Gerald Fitzgerald, 15th earl of DESMOND, the representative of the traditional enemies of the Ormondes, as a result of which Desmond was imprisoned. Ormonde was at the court of Elizabeth I (1565–69) and returned to Ireland only because his presence there was essential to maintain order. When Desmond (who had been released in 1573) rose in rebellion in 1579, Ormonde was made military governor of Munster and led the fight against the Desmond faction until the rebellious earl was captured and slain (1583). In 1588, Ormonde helped to capture the survivors of the Spanish Armada on the coast of Ireland, and in 1597 he was made lieutenant general of Ireland and supported the English troops against Hugh O'Neill, 2d earl of TYRONE. In 1612 he became vice admiral of Ireland.

Ormskirk, urban district (1971 pop. 27, 618), Lancashire, N England. It is a market town. Silk and cotton textiles and metal goods are made. The church, with an embattled tower, contains the burial chapel of the earls of Derby. Nearby are ruins of Burscough Abbey (12th cent.). There is a teacher training college.

Ormulum: see ORRMULUM.

Ormuz, Iran: see HORMOZ.

Ormuzd (ôr′məzd): see ZOROASTRIANISM.

ornament, in architecture, decorative detail enhancing structures. Structural ornament, an integral part of the framework, includes the shaping and placement of the BUTTRESS, CORNICE, MOLDING, ceiling, and ROOF and the CAPITAL and other elements of the column, as well as the use of building materials of contrasting color or texture. Applied ornament embraces the adornment of structural members with statuary, carving, molding, paint, inlay, mosaic, and facings. The design of ornament has followed the artistic development of various eras, reaching the height of exuberance during the baroque. See DECORATIVE ARTS and articles on the architecture of individual countries and periods, e.g., EGYPTIAN ARCHITECTURE and GOTHIC ARCHITECTURE AND ART. See A. D. F. Hamlin, *A History of Ornament* (2 vol., 1916–23); Joan Evans, *Style in Ornament* (1950).

ornament, in music, notes added to a melodic line for the purpose of embellishment or decoration, often called graces. Ornamentation was practiced as early as the Middle Ages by the singers of plainsong, and the practice seems to have reached its height in the baroque era. Treatises were written and attempts made to standardize practices. Symbols were adopted as a kind of shorthand for the notation of some ornaments, others were written out in complete notation, and still others were left to the discretion of the solo performer—often the composer himself. Since the baroque era, composers have attempted to indicate their intentions regarding ornaments in precise notation. In the 20th cent. the tendency has been toward a minimum of ornamentation; however, the same period has seen extensive research to make possible the performance of baroque music in the manner of the baroque era.

Ornan (ôr′năn), same as ARAUNAH.

Orne (ôrn), department (1968 pop. 288,524), NW France, in Normandy and part of Perche. ALENÇON is the capital.

ornithopter (ôr′nəthŏp″tər): see FLIGHT.

Oromocto (ôrōmŏk′tō), town (1971 pop. 11,427), S central N.B., Canada, on the St. John River. The town developed because of its proximity to Camp Gagetown, the largest (436 sq mi/1,129 sq km) military camp in Canada.

Oronsay (ô′rənsā, ŏ′rənzā), island, 3 sq mi (7.8 sq km), Argyllshire, NW Scotland, one of the Inner Hebrides. The island contains ruins of a 14th-century priory, a sculptured cross from 1510, and many carved stones unearthed (1882) from Viking graves. Oronsay is separated from Colonsay by a narrow sound.

Orontes (ōrŏn′tēs), river, c.250 mi (400 km) long, rising in the northern part of the Al Biqa valley, Lebanon, and flowing generally N through Syria, then W into S Turkey and into the Mediterranean Sea; celebrated because of the antiquity of settlement along its banks. The river is unnavigable but is important for irrigation, especially in Syria. Marshes on its middle course have been drained and the land reclaimed for farming. On its lower course, the river has cut below the surrounding plain, and it is noted for remarkable water wheels, from 20 to 70 ft (6–21 m) in diameter, at Hims and Hamah; the wheels, turned by the current, lift water onto the plains.

Orosius, Paulus (ōrō′shēəs), c.385–420, Iberian priest, theologian, and historian, b. Tarragona, Spain or Braga, Portugal. He went to see St. Augustine (c.413) and wrote, on request, a summary of the errors of Priscillian and of Origen. Augustine then sent him to Palestine to warn St. Jerome of the menace of Pelagianism. Unable to return to Spain, which was overrun by the Vandals, Orosius remained in Africa, where he completed the *Seven Books of History against the Pagans* (tr. by I. W. Raymond, 1936), which had been undertaken to continue the thrust of Augustine's *City of God.* The work became a kind of textbook of universal history for the Middle Ages; it treats world history as a concrete proof of the apocalyptic visions of the Bible. King Alfred translated it into Anglo-Saxon.

Oroville Dam, 770 ft (235 m) high and 7,600 ft (2,317 m) long, on the Feather River, N Calif., near Oroville; highest dam in the United States. The largest unit of the Feather River project, the dam was built (1957–68) to provide electric power, drinking water, and irrigation for central and S California.

Orozco, José Clemente (hōsā′ klāmān′tā ōrō′skō), 1883–1949, Mexican muralist, genre painter, and lithographer, grad. Mexican National Agricultural School. He became an architectural draftsman and in 1908 turned to painting. With Rivera he led the Mexican renaissance. His work is bold in execution and deals compassionately with social themes, especially with man versus machine. From 1917 to 1919 and from 1927 to 1934, Orozco was in the United States. Much of his work is true fresco painting, executed directly on the wet plaster, such as his mural painting in the New School for Social Research, New York City. His work in the United States also includes *Prometheus* (Frary Hall, Pomona College, Calif.) and *Epic of Culture in the New World* (Baker Library, Dartmouth College). There are several fine mural paintings in Mexico, such as those at Guadalajara in the university, the governor's palace, and the orphanage chapel. See catalog by Jon Hopkins (1967); autobiography (tr. 1962); MacKinley Helm, *Man of Fire* (1953, repr. 1971); study by Alma Reed (1956).

Orpah (ôr′pə), sister-in-law of Ruth. Ruth 1.4,14.

Orpen, Sir William, 1878–1931, British portrait and genre painter, b. Ireland. He is best known for his scenes of Irish daily life, his paintings and sketches of life at the front in World War I, and his portraits. His paintings *Myself and Venus* (Carnegie Inst., Pittsburgh) and *Leading the Life in the West* (Metropolitan Mus.) are characteristic of his work. Orpen was knighted in 1918. Although not a profound talent, he was the most popular painter of his day.

orphan: see CHILDREN, DEPENDENT; ADOPTION; FOUNDLING HOSPITAL; GUARDIAN AND WARD.

Orpheus (ôr'fēəs, ôr'fyo͞os), in Greek mythology, celebrated Thracian musician. He was the son of Calliope by Apollo or, according to another legend, by Oeagrus, a king of Thrace. Supposedly, the music of his lyre was so beautiful that when he played, wild beasts were soothed, trees danced, and rivers stood still. Orpheus married the nymph Eurydice. When ARISTAEUS tried to violate her, she fled, was bitten by a snake, and died. Orpheus descended to Hades searching for her. He was granted the chance to regain Eurydice if he could refrain from looking at her until he had led her back to sunlight. Orpheus could not resist, and Eurydice vanished forever. Grieving inconsolably, he became a recluse and wandered for many years. According to some legends, he became a devoted follower of Dionysus and introduced that god's cult in many places, but the women of Thrace, offended by his inattention, tore him to pieces. Another legend says that Orpheus taught the Thracian men to worship the sun (Apollo) above all other gods; in revenge Dionysus caused the wives of the Thracian men to murder their husbands and tear Orpheus to pieces. It was said that his head was thrown into the river Hebrus and floated, still singing, into the sea to the island of Lesbos, where an oracle of Orpheus was established. He was celebrated in the Orphic Mysteries.

Orphic Mysteries or **Orphism,** religious cult of ancient Greece, prominent in the 6th cent. B.C. According to legend Orpheus founded these MYSTERIES and was the author of the sacred poems from which the Orphic doctrines were drawn. The rites were based on the myth of Dionysus Zagreus, the son of Zeus and Persephone. When Zeus proposed to make Zagreus the ruler of the universe, the Titans were so enraged that they dismembered the boy and devoured him. Athena saved Zagreus' heart and gave it to Zeus, who thereupon swallowed the heart (from which was born the second Dionysus Zagreus) and destroyed the Titans with lightning. From the ashes of the Titans sprang the human race, who were part divine (Dionysus) and part evil (Titan). This double aspect of man's nature, the Dionysian and the Titanic, is essential to the understanding of Orphism. The Orphics affirmed the divine origin of the soul, but it was through initiation into the Orphic Mysteries and through the process of transmigration that the soul could be liberated from its Titanic inheritance and could achieve eternal blessedness. Orphism stressed a strict standard of ethical and moral conduct. Initiates purified themselves and adopted ascetic practices (e.g., abstinence from eating animal flesh) for the purpose of purging evil and cultivating the Dionysian side of the human character. See W. C. Guthrie, *Orpheus and Greek Religion* (rev. ed. 1953, repr. 1967).

orphism, a short-lived movement in art founded in 1912 by Robert DELAUNAY, Frank KUPKA, the DUCHAMP brothers, and Roger de la Fresnaye. Apollinaire coined the term *orphism* to describe the lyrical, shimmering chromatic effects that these painters sought to introduce into the drier aesthetic of CUBISM. Moving toward pure abstraction, the orphists saw painting as sensation. For a time their number included Léger, Picabia, Chagall, and Gliezes. The movement influenced the German BLAUE REITER group and the American synchromists Stanton MACDONALD-WRIGHT and Morgan RUSSELL.

orpine (ôr'pĭn): see STONECROP.

Orr, Bobby (Robert Orr), 1948–, Canadian hockey player. He began skating at the age of 4 and was discovered by the Boston Bruins of the National Hockey League at age 12. He began playing with the Bruins in 1966 and revitalized the team. A skater, passer, and shooter of exceptional talent, and a remarkably high scorer for a defenseman, Orr earned a reputation as a vigorous and audacious competitor.

Orr, James Lawrence, 1822–73, American politician, b. Craytonville, S.C. He served in the South Carolina legislature (1844–48) and in the U.S. House of Representatives (1849–59), where he was (1857–59) speaker. Orr opposed secession during the 1850s but followed his state into the Confederacy after Abraham Lincoln was elected President in 1860. After brief military service, he was elected (Dec. 1861) to the Confederate senate, where he held office throughout the Civil War. He was elected governor of South Carolina in 1866. Orr, at first a supporter of President Andrew Johnson's Reconstruction plan, became a radical Republican when it became clear that the radical Republicans were dominant. He was appointed (Dec. 1872) minister to Russia, where he died.

Orrefors (ôrəfôrs',-fôsh'), town, Kronoberg co., SE Sweden. It is noted for the manufacture of fine crystal and glassware. Simon Gate and Edward Hald, who made Orrefors famous, were outstanding engravers of glassware, and their work is represented in numerous collections. The town has a museum of glass.

Orrery, Charles Boyle, 4th **earl of** (ŏr'ərē), 1676–1731, English nobleman; grandson of the 1st earl of Orrery. He succeeded his brother as earl in 1703. A supporter of Sir William TEMPLE in his controversy with Richard BENTLEY over modern and antique scholarship, Orrery edited (1695) *The Epistles of Phalaris.* The issue was satirized—and made famous—by Jonathan SWIFT in his *Battle of the Books.* Orrery rose to the rank of major general (1709) in the War of the Spanish Succession, and assisted in the negotiation of the Peace of Utrecht (1713–14). He was a patron of the inventor George Graham, who designed the PLANETARIUM called the orrery.

Orrery, Roger Boyle, 1st **earl of,** 1621–79, Irish statesman and writer; son of Richard Boyle, 1st earl of Cork. Created (1627) Baron Broghill, he studied at Trinity College, Dublin, traveled abroad, and served against the Irish rebels in 1641. Although a royalist, he served in the parliamentary army after 1647. He later became involved in a plot to restore Charles II, but Oliver Cromwell personally intervened to persuade him to serve the Commonwealth. He helped restore order in Ireland, received large grants of land, and served in the parliaments of 1654 and 1656 and as lord president of the council in Scotland. When the restoration of Charles II seemed inevitable, he crossed to Ireland and helped secure it for the king. He was made earl of Orrery (1660) and a lord justice, served in the Parliament of 1661, and was lord president of Munster until 1668. A friend and patron of the writers of his age, Orrery also wrote rhymed-verse tragedies, among them *Henry the Fifth* (1668), *Mustapha* (1668), and *The Black Prince* (1669); a romance, *Parthenissa* (1654–65); and a military treatise (1676). See preface by W. S. Clark to his edition (2 vol., 1937) of Orrery's dramatic works; study by K. M. Lynch (1965).

orrisroot: see IRIS.

Orrmulum or **Ormulum** (both: ôrm'yo͝oləm), Middle English collection of homilies on the Gospels, in verse, comprising about 10,000 lines in all. The collection was written c.1200 by Orrm (or Orrmin), an Augustinian canon of Lincolnshire. Because the author had his own system of spelling and because the manuscript is probably in his own handwriting, the *Orrmulum* is of great importance for the study of Middle English phonology.

Orrum, Eilley: see BOWERS, EILLEY ORRUM.

Ors, Eugenio d' (āo͞ohā'nyō dôrs), 1882–1954, Spanish writer. His works include *Glosari,* brief essays in which he attempted to relate passing events to aesthetic and intellectual concepts; a novel in Catalan (1912); and *El secreto de la filosofia* (1947). He also wrote much on art. He was an early supporter of Franco.

Orsay, Alfred Guillaume Gabriel, count d' (ălfrĕd' gēyōm' găbrēĕl', dôrsā'), 1801–52, French dandy. The son of a Bonapartist general, he went to England in 1821, where he met Marguerite, countess of BLESSINGTON, and her husband. In 1827, D'Orsay married Blessington's daughter, but the union was unsuccessful. After Blessington's death D'Orsay and Marguerite became the center of a fashionable artistic and literary circle in London. D'Orsay was long the authority on matters of taste in English society. In 1849, to escape his creditors, he fled to Paris.

Orsha (ôr'shə), city (1970 pop. 101,000), W central European USSR, a port at the confluence of the Dnepr and Orshitsa rivers. One of Belorussia's leading rail and water transport junctions and industrial centers, Orsha is the starting point of shipping on the Dnepr. The city's industries include machine building, metalworking, food processing, and the production of machine tools, reinforced concrete, silicone, and linen. First mentioned as Rsha in 1067, the city passed to Lithuania in the 13th cent. It was an important Polish fortress and trade center from the 16th cent. until its annexation by Russia in 1772, during the first partition of Poland.

Orsini (ōrsē'nē), powerful Roman family that included three popes and numerous other churchmen, soldiers and statesmen. The eponymous ancestor was one Ursus. Giacinto Orsini, who became Pope Celestine III in 1191, founded the family's greatness. Matteo Rosso Orsini was elected a Roman senator in 1241, and in 1277 Giovanni Gaetano Orsini ascended the papal throne as Nicholas III. The long rivalry between the Guelph Orsini family (see GUELPHS AND GHIBELLINES) and the Ghibelline COLONNA family lasted until the early 16th cent. and often plunged Rome into anarchy. The Orsini were made princes of the Holy Roman Empire in the 17th cent. Among the prominent members of the family were Lorenzo Orsini (d. 1536), who defended (1527) Rome and the Castel Sant' Angelo against the troops of Holy Roman Emperor Charles V; the princesse des URSINS; and Pietro Francesco Orsini, who became Pope Benedict XIII in 1724. Representatives of the family are still living.

Orsini, Felice (fālē'chā), 1819–58, Italian patriot who attempted to assassinate the French emperor Napoleon III. He was a follower of Mazzini in the movement for Italian unification. As a young man he became an active revolutionary in the Papal States and in Tuscany. He was jailed (1855–56) by the Austrians for his activities but escaped. In 1857 he broke with Mazzini, and in 1858 he made an attempt on the life of Napoleon III, whom he held responsible for the failure of the Italian revolutions of 1848–49. Although ably defended by Jules Favre, he was executed. His act, designed to arouse world interest in the Italian cause, influenced Napoleon's decision to intervene in favor of Italian unification. See biography by M. S. J. Packe (1958).

Orsk (ôrsk), city (1970 pop. 225,000), Orenburg oblast, in the foothills of the S Ural Mts., E European USSR, on the Ural River. It is the center of the Orsk-Khalilovo industrial area, which has rich iron, copper, nickel, and coal deposits. There are metallurgical plants, machine works, and oil refineries. Orsk was founded in 1735.

Ortegal, Cape (ôrtāgäl'), NW Spain, in Galicia, extending into the Atlantic. It is usually considered the southwestern limit of the Bay of Biscay.

Ortega y Gasset, José (hōsā' ôrtā'gä ē gäsĕt'), 1883–1955, Spanish essayist and philosopher. He studied in Germany and was influenced by neo-Kantian thought. He called his philosophy the metaphysics of vital reason, and he sought to establish the ultimate reality in which all else was rooted. In 1910 he became a professor of metaphysics at the Univ. of Madrid. In *Meditaciones del Quijote* (1914) and *España invertebrada* (1921) he compared Germanic and Mediterranean cultures. *The Modern Theme* (1923, tr. 1931) is one of his best philosophical books. Many of the essays in *El Espectador* (8 vol., 1916–34) first appeared in the *Revista de Occidente,* a review he founded (1923) and directed. But it was with *The Revolt of the Masses* (1929, tr. 1932) that Ortega gained international fame. He held that unless the masses can be directed by an intellectual minority, chaos will result. Although he supported the republic, he fled at the outbreak (1936) of the civil war, first to France and then to Argentina. After World War II he returned to Madrid, where he founded the Institute of Humanities. His other collections translated into English include *Toward a Philosophy of History* (1941), *The Mission of the University* (1944), *Concord and Liberty* (1946), *The Dehumanization of Art* (1948), *Man and People* (1957), and *Man and Crisis* (1958). See biographies by Harold Raley (1971) and Franz Niedermayer (1973).

Ortelius, Abraham (ôrtē'lyəs), 1527–98, Flemish geographer, of German origin. Next to his contemporary Mercator, he is the greatest of the 16th-century Flemish school of geography. He traveled with Mercator in 1560 and was inspired by him to begin his chief work, *Theatrum orbis terrarum* (1570), the first modern atlas of the world. The first edition of this atlas contained 53 maps, in part compiled from maps of 87 cartographers; the 1587 edition had 103 maps. Ortelius was made geographer to Philip II of Spain in 1575. He produced a number of other geographic works, of which one of the best known is the *Thesaurus geographicus* (1587).

orthoclase feldspar: see FELDSPAR.

orthodontics: see DENTISTRY.

Orthodox Eastern Church, community of Christian churches whose chief strength is in the Middle East and E Europe. Their members number over 123 million worldwide. The Orthodox agree doctrinally in accepting as ecumenical the first seven councils (see COUNCIL, ECUMENICAL) and in rejecting the jurisdiction of the bishop of Rome (the pope). This repudiation of the papal claims is the principal point dividing the Orthodox from Roman Catholics. Eastern Christians who have returned to communion with the pope are called Eastern Catholics, or Uniates; in every respect apart from this obedience to Rome, they resemble their Orthodox counterparts. This use of the terms *Catholic* (obeying the pope) and *Orthodox* (belonging to one of the Orthodox churches) is not technical, for both groups call themselves both Catholic and Orthodox (see CATHOLIC CHURCH). The word *Orthodox* became a favorite at the time of the overthrow (753) of iconoclasm in Constantinople. Orthodox acceptance of the seven councils entails exclusion from their communion, on grounds of heresy, of the Nestorian, Jacobite, Coptic, and Armenian churches; it also involves holding a sacramental doctrine of grace *ex opere operato* (see GRACE) and of veneration of the Virgin Mary, two points differentiating the Orthodox from Protestants. The ritual that developed at the patriarchate of Constantinople—known as the Byzantine rite—gradually replaced other local rites in the Orthodox East, and after the 13th cent. became, with local variations and translations, the standard of Orthodox worship. It is sometimes called the Greek rite, because the original language was Greek, but the LITURGY was adapted into Slavonic, Arabic, Estonian, and many other languages. The liturgy is not usually celebrated daily as in the West, and it is always sung. Leavened bread is used in the Eucharist, and communion is given to laymen in both kinds (i.e., both bread and wine) with a spoon. Infants receive communion and confirmation. The other sacraments are similar to those of the Latin rite, except in details; e.g., confirmation is conferred by priests. The frequency of confession varies in the different autocephalous (i.e., self-governing) churches. The church buildings are generally square, with a solid sanctuary screen covered with icons (*iconostasis*) (for the style, see BYZANTINE ART AND ARCHITECTURE). The parish priests may marry; monks and bishops may not. The old mode of government was the patriarchate (see PATRIARCH), but now for the most part the churches, all of which are autocephalous, are each governed by a holy synod, a board of bishops and laymen, often appointed by the government; where the head of the church is called patriarch, he is often only the moderator of the synod. The number of Orthodox churches recognizing one another as such is indefinite because of the fluid state of the relations of Orthodox bishops in countries to which communicants have emigrated. The four ancient patriarchates enjoy highest prestige. The patriarchate of Constantinople, having the primacy of honor after Rome, was set up when the Eastern capital was established; it included Asia Minor and the Balkan Peninsula. From the time of JUSTINIAN I the emperor controlled the patriarch absolutely. The patriarch was freer under the Turks, who gave him civil and religious jurisdiction over all the Orthodox within the Turkish Empire. The patriarch of Constantinople never quite succeeded in establishing jurisdiction in the East comparable to that of the pope in the West. First the Russians, then the Greeks and the Balkan countries set up autonomous churches, always opposed by the patriarch, especially in the case of Bulgaria. In republican Turkey the patriarch rules a remnant only; some Orthodox in the United States recognize his jurisdiction. The Orthodox patriarchates of Alexandria and Antioch are minority churches (for the corresponding separated churches, see COPT; JACOBITE CHURCH), as is the patriarchate of Jerusalem. The patriarch represents Orthodox interests in the shrines. There are many churches apart from those directly under the patriarchs. A unique, ancient church is that of Mt. Sinai, made up of the monastery of St. Catherine and its subject houses. The archbishop is also abbot. The monastic community of Mt. Athos in Greece is of special interest. There are seven national churches, each the traditional patriotic church of the people. The Church of Cyprus has been autonomous since the Council of Ephesus. The Church of Georgia is also ancient. In the 19th cent. it was absorbed by the Russian church but in 1917 resumed its autonomy. The ruler is called catholicus. The Russian Orthodox Church, for centuries the largest of Orthodox churches, was headed first by the metropolitan of Kiev, under Constantinople. The see was moved to Moscow, and in 1589 a new patriarchate was set up, under the czar. The language of the ritual is OLD CHURCH SLAVONIC. In 1721, Peter the Great (Peter I) abolished the patriarchate and established a synod, which he controlled through its lay procurator. In 1917 the patriarchate was revived, just before the Bolshevik Revolution began the weakening of the whole church structure. In the disturbances of the revolution many priests and bishops were killed or exiled. Churches were plundered of their sacred vessels, and seminaries were closed. In World War II, however, the government consented (1943) to the reopening of churches and to the election of a patriarch (the first since 1925). The new patriarch and his successors have been loyal to the Communist government. As the Soviet Union annexed lands after 1939, the local Orthodox churches disappeared; the same was true of Catholic churches of the Eastern rites, and thus it was announced that the Byzantine-rite Catholics of Ukraine and Ruthenia had united with the Russian Orthodox. The autocephalous Church of Greece dates from the Greek War of Independence. It is the state church and legally much favored. The Serbian patriarch (at Belgrade) heads the Church of Yugoslavia, which is made up almost wholly of Serbs. This church has suffered restrictions from the Communist government. The Church of Bulgaria was severed from communion by the ancient patriarchates in the 19th cent., but the Russian church recognized it. Its ruler is an exarch. The Rumanian Orthodox Church has a patriarch at Bucharest; it was probably the most carefully organized of Orthodox churches. After 1945 the government announced that the Roman Catholic dioceses of the Rumanian rite had been annexed by the Orthodox church. Other Orthodox churches are minority denominations of recent creation. The Albanian Orthodox Church suffered considerably under Italian rule during World War II, as well as under Communist rule since then. The Orthodox churches of Finland and of Poland, founded after World War I, lost most of their members when the eastern sections of the countries were repossessed by the Soviet Union in World War II. The Japanese Orthodox Church became autonomous under government pressure (1939); it had its origin in a Russian mission founded in 1860. There are a number of autonomous Orthodox groups that began in emigration. Thus in the United States there have been separate hierarchies of Greeks, Russians, and others, sometimes in communion with each other. There have been many efforts to establish a single American Orthodox church. In 1950 several Eastern Orthodox denominations joined with Protestant groups in the formation of the National Council of the Churches of Christ in the United States of America; almost all Orthodox churches in America are now members. The relations between the Orthodox and the Western Church have been full of misunderstandings, which became grave as political and cultural ties loosened after the 5th cent. There were breaks between Constantinople and Rome in the 9th cent. (see PHOTIUS) and in 1054 (see LEO IX, SAINT), but the main obstacle to reconciliation was the conduct of the Crusades, especially the Fourth Crusade (when the Crusaders seized Constantinople), since the whole of Western Christendom, most of all the pope, was inevitably blamed. In 1274 there was an attempt at reunion (Second Council of Lyons), and in 1439 another (see FERRARA-FLORENCE, COUNCIL OF); the second was repudiated (1472) by Constantinople. In the Middle Ages the points at issue, besides the papal authority, were matters of worship and discipline, not of belief; the addition of a phrase (*filioque*) to the Nicene Creed (see CREED **1**) proved not to involve doctrine at all. There have been fractional reunions, notably the Union of Brest-Litvosk (1595) of Ukrainians, who retained their hierarchy and rites. A synthetization of Orthodox and Protestant beliefs was unsuccessfully attempted in the 17th cent. by Patriarch Cyril LUCARIS. In the 19th cent. began the cultivation of cordial relations between Anglicans and Orthodox, and official exchanges between them have become frequent. In 1962 several observers from the Orthodox churches attended the second Council of the Vatican (see VATICAN COUNCIL, SECOND) convened by Pope John XXIII. The following year the Orthodox churches (with the exception of the Greek church) agreed to open a dialogue with Rome on equal terms. See S. N. Bulgakov, *The Orthodox Church* (1935, repr. 1964); A. A. King, *The Rites of Eastern Christendom* (2 vol., 1950, repr. 1962); R. M. French, *The Eastern Orthodox Church* (1951, repr. 1961); Donald Attwater, *The Christian Churches of the East* (2 vol., rev. ed. 1961); Jean Meyendorff, *The Orthodox Church, Its Past and Its Role in the World Today* (tr. 1962); Ernst Benz, *The Eastern Orthodox Church, Its Thought and Life* (tr. 1963); Alexander Schmemann, *The Historical Road of Eastern Orthodoxy* (tr. 1963); Timothy Ware, *The Orthodox Church* (1964); John Paraskevas and Frederick Reinstein, *The Eastern Orthodox Church* (1969).

orthopedics (ôrthəpē'dĭks), medical specialty concerned with deformities, injuries, and diseases of the bones, joints, ligaments, tendons, and muscles. Most of the early advances in orthopedics were made by practicing physicians, many of them surgeons, to correct deformities such as clubfoot and to provide supports for broken or diseased bones. The first institute for correcting skeletal deformities was opened in Switzerland in the 18th cent. The development of bone grafting, the advent of surgical methods for treating fractures, and other advances led to the recognition of orthopedics as a distinct medical specialty by 1920. Clubfoot, the aftereffects of poliomyelitis, fractures, spinal deformities, and arthritic disorders are among the conditions that require the attention of an orthopedist. Treatment provided by an orthopedist may include manipulation, the fitting of braces or other appliances, exercising, and surgery.

Ortles (ôrt'lās), range of the Ötztal Alps, in Trentino-Alto Adige, N Italy. It has many glaciers. Ortles peak, 12,792 ft (3,899 m) high, the highest peak, was first ascended in 1804.

Orton, Arthur: see TICHBORNE CASE.

Ortona (ōrtô'nä), town (1971 pop. 20,894), Abruzzi, central Italy, on the Adriatic Sea. Now a small fishing port and a seaside resort, it was a major port from the 11th cent. to 1447, when its fleet and arsenal were destroyed by the Venetians. The 12th-century cathedral (now restored) and the Aragonese castle (15th cent.) were heavily damaged in World War II.

Ortygia: see SYRACUSE, Italy.

Oruro (ōrōō'rō), city (1962 est. pop. 87,000), capital of Oruro dept., W Bolivia. It is Bolivia's third largest city and its railroad center. Oruro's economy is based on exploitation of the region's mineral resources—silver, wolfram, copper, and especially tin. Because of the altitude (12,159 ft/3,706 m), agriculture is almost nonexistent. Oruro was founded in 1595 to exploit the rich silver deposits nearby. When silver production declined in the 19th cent., it became almost a ghost town. It expanded with the development of other mineral resources.

Orvieto (ōrvyĕ'tō), city (1971 pop. 23,158), in Umbria, central Italy, on the Poglia River. Situated at the top of a rocky hill, it is a tourist and pilgrimage center. Orvieto is probably located on the site of the Etruscan town of VOLSINII (sacked by the Romans in 280 B.C.), which was later rebuilt as Urbs Vetus. It became a free commune by the 12th cent. but was later at the mercy of indigenous and foreign tyrants until it passed to the popes in 1448. There are notable Romanesque, Gothic, and Renaissance buildings in Orvieto, but the fame of the city is due mainly to its beautiful cathedral (begun in 1290). The cathedral's white and black marble facade is decorated with delicate sculptures and colorful mosaics, and the Chapel of San Brizio, inside, has frescoes by Fra Angelico and by Luca Signorelli, whose powerful scenes of the Apocalypse inspired Michelangelo. The city also has a well (200 ft/61 m deep) dug in rock (completed 1537).

Orwell, George, pseud. of **Eric Arthur Blair,** 1903–50, British novelist and essayist, b. India. He is best remembered for his satirical novels, *Animal Farm* and *Nineteen Eighty-Four.* After attending Eton, he served (1922–27) with the Indian imperial police in Burma. He returned to Europe in 1927, living penuriously in Paris and later in London. In 1936 he fought with the Republicans in the Spanish civil war and was seriously wounded. His writings—particularly such early works as *Down and Out in Paris and London* (1933), *Burmese Days* (1934), *The Road to Wigan Pier* (1937), and *Homage to Catalonia* (1938)—are highly autobiographical. All of Orwell's works, however, are concerned with the sociopolitical conditions of his time, notably with the problem of human freedom. *Animal Farm* (1946) is a witty, satirical fable about the failure of communism, and *Nineteen Eighty-Four* (1949), is a prophetic novel describing the dehumanization of man in a mechanistic, totalitarian world. Orwell's other novels include *A Clergyman's Daughter* (1935), *Keep the Aspidistra Flying* (1936), and *Coming Up for Air* (1940). The master of a superb, lucid prose style, Orwell wrote many literary essays, which some critics find superior to his novels. His volumes of essays include *Dickens, Dali and Others* (1946), *Shooting an Elephant* (1950), and the *Collected Essays, Journalism and Letters of George Orwell* (4 vols., 1968). See studies by George Woodcock (1966), Raymond Williams (1971), and Roberta Kalechofsky (1973); Peter Stansky and William Abrahams, *The Unknown Orwell* (1972).

oryx (ôr'ĭks), name for several small, horselike ANTELOPES, genus *Oryx*, found in deserts and arid scrublands of Africa and Arabia. They feed on grasses and scrub and can go without water for long periods. Oryxes are light in color with dark patches on the face and legs. They have slight shoulder humps, tufted tails, and straight or slightly curved slender horns that point backward. The common oryx (*O. gazella*) ranges from S Africa along the east coast to Tanzania. It is beige with black or brown markings. The variety found in the southern part of this range has extremely long horns and is known as the gemsbok; a large male gemsbok stands more than 4 ft (120 cm) at the shoulder and weighs up to 450 lb (200 kg). The E African variety is smaller, with shorter horns, and is called the beisa. The white, or scimitar-horned, oryx (*O. tao*) of the N African deserts has long, back-curved horns; it is nearly white with chestnut markings. The Arabian, or Beatrix, oryx (*O. leucoryx*) is the smallest oryx, standing up to 40 in. (100 cm) high. It is white with dark brown and black markings. The Arabian oryxes once ranged over the deserts of SW Asia and were hunted by nomads for flesh and hides. However, they have been nearly exterminated in the 20th cent. by hunting from automobiles. A small population survives in Oman, and a number are breeding successfully in zoos. The oryx is classified in the phylum CHORDATA, subphylum Vertebrata, class Mammalia, order Artiodactyla, family Bovidae.

Os, chemical symbol of the element OSMIUM.

Osage, river, c.360 mi (580 km) long, formed by the confluence of the Marais des Cygnes and the Little Osage rivers, W Mo. It flows NE to join the Missouri River near Jefferson City. Bagnell Dam (172,000-kw capacity; completed 1931) across the Osage River impounds the Lake of the Ozarks, the largest lake in the state. The power produced there is consumed mainly by St. Louis. The Osage River basin project provides for flood control, power production, and recreation.

Osage Indians (ō'sāj, ōsāj'), North American Indians whose language belongs to the Siouan branch of the Hokan-Siouan linguistic stock (see AMERICAN INDIAN LANGUAGES). In prehistoric times they lived with the Kansa, the Ponca, the Omaha, and the Quapaw in the Ohio valley, but by 1673 they had migrated to the vicinity of the Osage River in Missouri. They often conducted war against other Indians, and in the early 18th cent. allied themselves with the French against surrounding tribes, such as the Illinois. The Osage had a typical Plains area culture. One distinctive trait, however, was the tribal division between the Wazhazhe, or meat eaters, and the Tsishu, or vegetarians. In 1802, according to Lewis and Clark, three groups constituted the Osage—the Great Osage, on the Osage River, the Little Osage, farther up the same river, and the Arkansas band, on the Vermilion River, a tributary of the Arkansas. They then numbered some 5,500. By a series of treaties begun in 1810 the Osage ceded to the United States their extensive territory in Missouri, Arkansas, and Oklahoma, and they moved to a reservation in N central Oklahoma. They have since been given the right to own their land individually. The discovery of oil on their reservation land, plus their landholdings, have combined to make the Osage the wealthiest Indians in the United States. In the early 1970s the Osage numbered some 5,000. See Francis La Flesche, *The Osage Tribe* (1921, repr. 1970) and *War Ceremony and Peace Ceremony of the Osage Indians* (1939); J. J. Mathews, *The Osages, Children of the Middle Waters* (1961); W. D. Baird, *The Osage People* (1972).

Osage orange: see MULBERRY.

Osaka (ō'säkä), city (1970 pop. 2,980,409), capital of Osaka prefecture, S Honshu, Japan, on Osaka Bay, at the mouth of the Yodo River. One of Japan's largest cities and principal industrial and commercial centers, Osaka is the focal point of a chain of industrial cities (called the *Hanshin* or *Kinki*) stretching to Kobe, an alternate port for Osaka. Food processing, printing, and the manufacture of steel, chemicals, and textiles are among the chief industries. The city is also a major port and transportation hub. An educational and cultural center, Osaka is known for its puppet and other theaters and for Osaka Univ. and Kansai Univ. Its parks and gardens are noted for their beauty. Landmarks include the Buddhist temple of Shitennoji, founded in 593, and Temmangu, a Shinto shrine founded in 949. As Naniwa, the city was the site of imperial palaces as early as the 4th cent. Its importance as a commercial center dates from the 16th cent., when it became Hideyoshi's seat and grew to be Japan's leading trade center. Hideyoshi's huge castle, reconstructed in 1931, still dominates the city. Osaka prefecture (1970 pop. 7,620,331), c.700 sq mi (1,810 sq km), has a rugged interior and a flat and fertile coast.

O Salutaris Hostia (săl″yōōtâr'ĭs, sä″lōōtä'rĭs) [Lat.,=O saving victim], hymn to the Host, one of the two hymns regularly sung at the Benediction of the Blessed Sacrament in the Roman Catholic Church. The other hymn is *Tantum ergo* (see PANGE LINGUA). *O Salutaris* is really the last two stanzas of a Corpus Christi hymn, *Verbum supernum prodiens*, probably written by St. Thomas Aquinas.

Osawatomie (ō″səwŏt'əmē, ŏs″ə-), city (1970 pop. 4,294), Miami co., E Kansas, on the Marais des Cygnes River; founded 1855 by the New England Emigrant Aid Company, inc. 1883. It is a farm trade center in an area of oil and natural gas fields. The town, once a station on the Underground Railroad, has a memorial park that contains the cabin where John Brown lived in 1856. A marble shaft commemorates the battle in which five of Brown's men were killed.

Osborn, Henry Fairfield, 1857–1935, American paleontologist and geologist, b. Fairfield, Conn. He was professor of comparative anatomy (1883–90) at Princeton, and professor of biology (1891–96) and of zoology (1896–1910) at Columbia, where he was also dean of the faculty of pure science (1892–95). From 1891 he was associated with the American Museum of Natural History and formed one of the world's foremost collections of vertebrate fossils. Under his presidency (1908–33) the museum's scientific staff, facilities, and endowments were greatly expanded. He joined the U.S. Geological Survey as vertebrate paleontologist in 1900 and became (1924) senior geologist. His voluminous writings include general works on evolution and over 500 technical papers on paleontology.

Osborne, Dorothy, later **Lady Temple** (ŏz'bərn), 1627–95, English letter writer. The daughter of a royalist, she became engaged to Sir William Temple against the wishes of her family. Her letters to Temple, both through their long engagement and after their marriage in 1655, show her as a woman of wit, learning, and strong character, and form an excellent picture of the period. See edition of her letters (1928); study by Lord David Cecil (1948).

Osborne, John, 1929–, English dramatist. He began his theatrical career as an actor and playwright in provincial English repertory theaters. Osborne's plays usually focus on an individual character and the sheer force of his language rather than on action. His first commercial success was *Look Back in Anger* (1956), concerning a restless and vociferous young man of the working class who is at war with himself and society; it became the seminal work for the so-called ANGRY YOUNG MEN. His other plays depict, although with less vehemence, the frustration of living in a futureless, dying world that is fraught with false values. Among Osborne's later plays are *The Entertainer* (1957), *Epitaph for George Dillon* (with Anthony Creighton, 1958), *Luther* (1961), *Inadmissible Evidence* (1964), *A Patriot for Me* (1965), *Time Present* (1968), and *A Place Calling Itself Home* (1973). He also wrote the screenplay for *Tom Jones* (1963), the film version of Fielding's novel.

Osborne, Thomas Burr, 1859–1929, American chemist, b. New Haven, Conn., grad. Yale, 1881. From 1886 he was with the Connecticut Agricultural Experiment Station. An authority on nutrition, especially proteins, he wrote *Proteins of the Wheat Kernel* (1907) and *The Vegetable Proteins* (1909, rev. ed. 1924).

Osborne, Thomas Mott, 1859–1926, American prison reformer, b. Auburn, N.Y., grad. Harvard, 1884. As chairman (1913) of the state commission on prison reform he became a voluntary prisoner in the Auburn penitentiary in order to learn conditions at first hand. *Within Prison Walls* (1914) records his experiences. At Sing Sing Prison, where he was warden (1914–15), he instituted a system of self-government for the inmates. The program aroused political hostility, and he resigned after a trial for misconduct although he was acquitted. From 1917 to 1920 he was commandant of the U.S. naval prison at Portsmouth, N.H. He maintained that prisons should educate rather than punish. His views are expressed in *Society and Prisons* (1916, repr. 1972) and *Prisons and Common Sense* (1924). See biography by R. W. Chamberlain (1935, repr. 1972); study by Frank Tannenbaum (1933).

Osborne House, a favorite residence of Queen Victoria, near East Cowes, on the Isle of Wight, S England. The queen died there in 1901. The state apartments are open to the public.

Oscan (ŏs'kən), extinct language belonging to the Italic subfamily of the Indo-European family of languages. See ITALIC LANGUAGES.

Oscar I, 1799–1859, king of Sweden and Norway (1844–59), son and successor of Charles XIV. His reign was one of social and economic advance. His book on the reform of criminal law and prisons had wide influence. Oscar was succeeded by his elder son, Charles XV.

Oscar II, 1829–1907, king of Sweden (1872–1907) and Norway (1872–1905), younger son of Oscar I. He succeeded his brother, Charles XV. He refused to concede to Norway its own consular representation, thus increasing the tension between Norway and the crown. In 1905, Norway completely severed its union with Sweden, and Oscar relinquished the Norwegian throne. During the later part of his reign, Swedish industry made great progress. Oscar was a man of culture and an able musician and writer. His best-known work is a life of Charles XII. His son Gustavus V succeeded him.

Osceola (ŏsēō'lə, ō-), c. 1800–1838, leader of the SEMINOLE INDIANS. He was also called Powell, the surname of his supposed white father. In the early 1830s, Osceola was living close to Fort King, near the site of Ocala, Fla. Although not a chief, he rose to a position of prominence among the Seminole and led the young warriors who denounced the treaties of 1832 and 1833, which provided for the removal of the Indians to the West. In Dec., 1835, Osceola's warriors killed Wiley Thompson, the Indian agent in charge of the removal. U.S. troops under General Jesup drove his band southward into the Everglades, but Osceola, skillfully using guerrilla tactics, resisted capture. Fighting ceased early in 1837, only to break out again in June. Overtures for peace were sent to Osceola, and he agreed to meet with Jesup in St. Augustine under a flag of truce. Jesup, never intending to discuss peace, had Osceola seized and imprisoned at Fort Moultrie, S.C., where he died shortly afterward. See study by William and Ellen Hartley (1973).

oscillating universe: see COSMOLOGY.

oscillator (ŏs'əlā″tər), device whose output signal, in the absence of any input signal, varies regularly with time. Although various types of oscillator exist (e.g., mechanical oscillators such as the pendulum-escapement system of a clock and electromechanical oscillators such as a buzzer) the term is usually reserved for electronic oscillators. An oscillator generally consists of an AMPLIFIER having part of its output returned to the input by means of a FEEDBACK loop; the necessary and sufficient condition for oscillation is that the signal, in passing from input to output and back to input via the feedback loop, arrive at the input with no change in amplitude or phase. If this condition is met for only a single frequency, the output is a pure sine wave; if it is met for more than one frequency, the output is a complex wave. Some oscillators are designed to operate under certain conditions so that the output is a square wave, a triangular wave, or a pulse. In some cases, a very stable mechanical oscillator, such as a specially prepared quartz crystal, may be coupled to an electronic oscillator to enhance its frequency stability.

oscilloscope (əsĭl'əskōp″), electronic device used to produce visual displays corresponding to electrical signals. Displays of such nonelectrical phenomena as the variations of a sound's intensity can be made if the phenomena are converted into electrical signals. The display is formed by a moving dot on the screen of a CATHODE-RAY TUBE. For most applications horizontal deflecting circuits move the dot in a repetitive cycle from left to right, and then, very quickly, back to its starting position to begin the next sweep. If during this process the vertical deflecting circuits move the dot up and down in response to the variations of the signal to be observed, a wavelike picture of the signal appears on the screen. An oscilloscope is one of the most valuable tools of an engineer or electronics technician.

Osee (ōsē'), variant of HOSEA.

Ösel: see SAREMA, island, USSR.

Osgood, Herbert Levi, 1855–1918, American historian, b. Canton, Maine. He taught at Worcester Academy (1877–79) and Brooklyn High School (1883–89). From 1890 to 1896 he was adjunct professor and, after 1896, professor of history at Columbia. A recognized authority on American colonial history, he wrote *The American Colonies in the Seventeenth Century* (3 vol., 1904–7) and *The American Colonies in the Eighteenth Century* (4 vol., 1924), which deal mainly with the origin and development of English-American political institutions. He also wrote *Socialism and Anarchism* (1889). He edited *Minutes of the Common Council of the City of New York, 1675–1776* (8 vol., 1905) and contributed to the *Political Science Quarterly*, of which he was an editor (1891–1918), and the *American Historical Review*. See biography by his son-in-law, Dixon Ryan Fox (1924, repr. 1973).

Osh (ôsh), city (1970 pop. 120,000), capital of Osh oblast, Central Asian USSR, in Kirghizia, in the Fergana Valley. One of the oldest settlements of Central Asia, Osh was for centuries a major silk-production center, strategically situated on a trade route to India. The old Oriental city adjoins the larger modern section. The Tash-Sulayman [Solomon's throne], an odd-shaped rock, was once a place of Muslim pilgrimage.

O'Shaughnessy, Arthur William Edgar (ōshôn'əsē), 1844–81, English poet and naturalist. He was a member of the zoological department of the British Museum. He wrote four volumes of poetry—*Epic of Women* (1870), *Lays of France* (1872), *Music and Moonlight* (1874), and *Songs of a Worker* (1881)—which all reveal the influence of D. G. Rossetti. One ode, beginning, "We are the music-makers," is his best-known poem.

Oshawa (ŏsh'əwə), city (1971 pop. 91,587), SE Ont., Canada, on Lake Ontario. The production of automobiles, begun in 1907, is the leading industry. Many other products are made, notably leather goods. The town is on the site of a French trading post; there is now an automobile museum.

Oshea (ōshē'ə), variant of JOSHUA.

O-shima (ō-shē'mä), island, c.35 sq mi (90 sq km), near the entrance to Tokyo Bay, E Japan. The largest and most northerly of the Izu-shichito group, it is the site of volcanic Mt. Mihara (2,477 ft/7,550 m). Agriculture and fishing are chief activities there. It is a recreation area for Tokyo. The island was visited (17th cent.) by Maarten Vries, the Dutch navigator.

Oshkosh (ŏsh'kŏsh"), city (1970 pop. 53,221), seat of Winnebago co., E Wis., on Lake Winnebago, where the Upper Fox River enters; inc. 1846. It is a resort center and has varied manufacturing industries. Father Allouez visited the site in 1670; French explorers traveled there in the 18th cent.; and a French fur-trading post was set up in the early 19th cent. Oshkosh grew as a lumber town. The downtown area was destroyed by fire in 1875. A branch of the Univ. of Wisconsin is there.

Oshogbo (ōshōb'bō), city (1969 est. pop. 242,000), SW Nigeria, on the Oshun River. Primarily a farming and commercial city, it has cotton gins, a traditional textiles industry, and cigarette factories. The city is also a road and rail junction, and has an airport. Oshogbo was probably founded in the 17th cent. as a town in the YORUBA kingdom of Ijesha (see ILESHA). In 1839 it was the site of a decisive battle in which IBADAN, a Yoruba city-state, defeated ILORIN, an expansionist FULANI state, thus halting Ilorin's southward advance. An influx of refugees after the battle swelled Oshogbo's population.

Osiander, Andreas (ändrā'äs ōzēän'dər), 1498–1552, German reformer. His original name was Hosemann or Heiligmann. Ordained a priest in 1520, Osiander joined the cause of the Reformation in 1522. He supported Martin Luther vigorously, participating in the Marburg Conference (1529), the Diet of Augsburg (1530), and the signing of the Schmalkaldic Articles (1537). Frequently during controversies the coarseness and violence of his language aroused personal enmity. In 1548, Osiander's refusal to agree to the Augsburg Interim made it necessary for him to leave Nuremberg, and he joined the theological faculty at the new Univ. of Königsberg. Osiander's mystical interpretation of the Lutheran doctrine of justification by faith led to a disagreement with his colleagues that subsequently involved the whole German Evangelical Church.

osier (ō'zhər): see WILLOW.

Osijek (ō'sēyĕk), Ger. *Esseg*, Hung. *Eszék*, city (1971 pop. 143,109), N Yugoslavia, in Croatia, on the Drava River. The chief city of Slavonia, it is a river port and industrial center. Metal and wood items, textiles, and furniture are among its industrial products. Osijek grew around a castle built in 1091 on the site of the Roman colony and fortress of Mursa. It became an early episcopal see and was under Turkish rule from 1526 to 1687. It was later part of Austria-Hungary and passed to Yugoslavia in 1918.

Osipenko: see BERDYANSK, USSR.

Osiris (ōsī'rĭs), in EGYPTIAN RELIGION, legendary ruler of predynastic Egypt and god of the underworld. He was the son of the sky goddess Nut and the earth god Geb. The great benefactor of mankind, Osiris brought to the people knowledge of agriculture and civilization. In a famous myth he was treacherously slain by his evil brother Set, who cut his body into 14 pieces and spread the fragments throughout Egypt. Thereupon, Isis, sister and wife of Osiris, sought and found his scattered body. She buried the pieces, making each burial place a sacred spot. According to another legend Isis did not bury Osiris, but collected the pieces of her dead husband and miraculously brought him back to life. Osiris' son Horus later killed Set and became the new king of Egypt, while Osiris became ruler and judge of the underworld. The worship of Osiris, like that of the sun god Ra, was one of the great cults of ancient Egypt. It gradually spread throughout the Mediterranean world and, with that of Isis and Horus, was especially vital during the time of the Roman Empire. Identified variously with the waters of the Nile, the grain of the earth, the moon, and the sun, Osiris was the great symbol of the creative forces of nature and the imperishability of life. He was commonly represented as swathed in mummy wrappings, wearing the crown of Upper Egypt (a dome-shaped hat with a papyrus tuft) and holding a whip and a crook. See J. G. Frazer, *Adonis, Attis, Osiris* (1907, new ed. 1961); E. A. W. Budge, *Osiris* (1911, new ed. 1961, repr. 1973); J. G. Griffiths, *The Origins of Osiris* (1966).

Oskaloosa (ŏskəlōō' sə), city (1970 pop. 11,224), seat of Mahaska co., SE Iowa, on the North and South Skunk rivers; inc. 1852. It is the trade and processing center of a rich farm and livestock area. Coal has been mined there for over 100 years; a huge strip mine is still in operation. Manufactures include farm equipment, trousers, fire hydrants, and feeds and seeds. A small fort was established there in 1835 and it became a post on a much traveled westward trail. The city was settled (1844) by Quakers. William Penn College is there. The city has a pioneer farm and an annual regional fair.

Oskarshamn (ôs"kärs-hä'mən), city (1970 pop. 20,942), Kalmar co., SE Sweden, a seaport on the Kalmarsund (an arm of the Baltic Sea); chartered 1856. Manufactures of this industrial center include processed copper, paper, and machinery.

Osler, Sir William (ō'slər), 1849–1919, Canadian physician, M.D. McGill Univ., 1872. Renowned as a physician and as a medical historian, he was also the most brilliant and influential teacher of medicine in his day. He was professor at McGill (1875–84), the Univ. of Pennsylvania (1884–89), Johns Hopkins (1889–1904), and Oxford (from 1905). In 1911 he was knighted. His many medical observations include those on blood platelets and on the abnormally high red blood cell count in polycythemia. He wrote *The Principles and Practice of Medicine* (1892), one of the most prestigious medical textbooks in modern times, often revised, and *A Concise History of Medicine* (1919). See *Aphorisms from His Bedside Teachings and Writings* (W. B. Bean, ed., 1950); biographies by Harvey Cushing (1925) and E. G. Reid (1931).

Oslo (ŏŏs'lōō); city (1970 pop. 481,548), capital of Norway, of Akershus co., and of Oslo co. (175 sq mi/453 sq km), SE Norway, at the head of the Oslofjord (a deep inlet of the Skagerrak). Oslo is Norway's largest city, its main port, and its chief commercial, industrial, and transportation center. Manufactures include ships, processed food, textiles, forest products, machines, and printed materials. Founded c.1050 by Harold III, Oslo became (1299) the national capital. In the 14th cent. it came under the dominance of the HANSEATIC LEAGUE. After a great fire (1624), the city was rebuilt by Christian IV and was renamed Christiania (or Kristiania); in 1925 the name Oslo again became official. The city's modern growth dates from the late 19th cent., when it also replaced Bergen as the main city in Norway. In World War II, Oslo fell (April 9, 1940) to the Germans, and it was occupied until the surrender (May, 1945) of the German forces in Norway. The neighboring industrial commune of Aker was incorporated into Oslo in 1948. Today, Oslo is a modern city in design and construction, and its government has fostered contemporary art in a number of impressive public projects. Among these are the 150 sculptural groups by Gustav VIGELAND in the famous Frogner Park. The city's chief public buildings include the royal palace (1848), the Storting (parliament), and the city hall (1950), which was decorated by many Norwegian artists. Surviving medieval structures include the Akerskirke (12th cent.) and the Akershus fortress (13th cent.), and there are ruins of the Cathedral of St. Hallvard, the first cathedral of Oslo. The Univ. of Oslo (founded 1811), the national theater (1899), the national gallery, a Nobel Institute, and a college of architecture are among the city's cultural institutions. In addition, the Folk Museum has reconstructions of old Norwegian timber houses and of a 12th-century stave church, and the Kon-Tiki Museum has mementos of Thor Heyerdahl's trip (1947) across the Pacific Ocean. The forested hills surrounding Oslo are popular excursion points; the annual Holmenkollen ski meet nearby attracts an international group of skiers. The 1952 Olympic winter games were held at Oslo. Drøbak, further south on the Oslofjord, is a winter port of Oslo and a summer resort.

Osman, caliph: see UTHMAN.

Osman I (ōsmän') or **Othman I** (ōthmän'), 1259–1326, leader of the Ottoman TURKS and founder of the dynasty that established and ruled the OTTOMAN EMPIRE (Turkey). The Osmanli or Ottoman Turks derive their name from Osman. He proclaimed (1290) his independence from his overlord, the Seljuk Turks, upon the collapse of their empire. Aided by an influx of Muslim warriors, he expanded his state in NW Asia Minor at the expense of the petty Christian lords who were his neighbors. He nevertheless inaugurated a policy of religious tolerance. Just before his death in 1326, his son and successor, ORKHAN, took the city of Bursa from the Byzantines.

Osman Nuri Pasha (ōsmän' nōōrē' päshä'), 1837–1900, Turkish general. He fought in the Crimean War of 1854–56 and in Lebanon, Crete, and Arabia in the 1860s and 70s. He was made *muşir* [marshal] for his successes (1876) in Serbia. In the Russo-Turkish War of 1877–78 he gallantly defended Pleven in Bulgaria but was ultimately forced to surrender to the Russians. He served almost continuously as war minister from 1878 to 1885.

Osmeña, Sergio (sār'hēō ōsmā'nyä), 1878–1961, Filipino statesman, b. Cebu island. He served as provincial governor of Cebu and as first speaker (1907–22) of the Philippine assembly. After service in the Philippine senate (1922–35), he was elected vice president of the new Philippine Commonwealth established in 1935. In March, 1942, he fled with President Manuel Quezon as the islands fell completely to the Japanese. After Quezon's death (1944) Osmeña became president of the government-in-exile, returning to the Philippines with U.S. invasion forces in Oct., 1944. In the 1946 presidential election he was defeated by Manuel Roxas.

osmium (ŏz'mēəm), metallic chemical element; symbol Os; at. no. 76; at. wt. 190.2; m.p. about 3000°C; b.p. about 5000°C; sp. gr. 22.48 at 20°C; valence usually +3, +4, +6, or +8. Osmium is a very hard, brittle, lustrous bluish-white metal with a close-packed hexagonal crystalline structure. It immediately precedes iridium in group VIII of the PERIODIC TABLE. Although the measured density of osmium is greater than that of any other element, calculations based on crystal structure indicate that iridium may be more dense. Osmium does not oxidize readily in air except when heated or in powdered form; it then forms the unpleasant smelling, highly toxic tetroxide, OsO_4. The tetroxide is used in microscopy as a stain, in fingerprint detection, and as a catalyst. Osmium is not affected by common acids but is oxidized to the tetroxide by hot nitric acid, hot sulfuric acid, or aqua regia. Osmium reacts with fluorine or chlorine gas at high temperatures to give the tetrafluoride or tetrachloride. In addition to the valences noted above, osmium assumes other valences between 0 and +8 in various compounds. Osmium is found in platinum ores and in the mineral osmiridium. It is recovered commercially as a by-product of the refining of nickel ores mined near Sudbury, Ont., Canada. The metal is used largely for the production of hard alloys for use in fountain pen points, phonograph needles, and instrument bearings. Osmium was discovered by Smithson Tennant in 1804 in a residue left after dissolving crude platinum in aqua regia.

osmosis (ŏzmō'sĭs), transfer of a liquid solvent through a semipermeable membrane that does not allow dissolved solids (solutes) to pass. Osmosis refers only to transfer of solvent; transfer of solute is called DIALYSIS. In either case the direction of transfer is from the area of higher concentration of the material transferred to the area of lower concentration. This spontaneous migration of a material from a region of higher concentration to a region of lower concentration is called DIFFUSION. If a vessel is separated into two compartments by a semipermeable membrane, both compartments are filled to the same level with a solvent, and solute is added to one side, osmosis will occur; and the level of the liquid on the side containing the solute will rise. If an external pressure is exerted on the side containing the solute, the transfer of solvent can be stopped and even reversed (reverse osmosis). The minimum pressure necessary to stop solvent transfer is called the osmotic pressure. Since the osmotic pressure is related to the concentration of solute particles, there is a mathematical relationship between osmotic pressure, freezing-point depression, and boiling-point elevation. Properties such as osmotic pressure, freezing point, and boiling point, which depend on the number of particles present rather than on their size or chemical nature, are called colligative properties. For dilute solutions the mathematical relationship between the osmotic pressure, temperature, and concentration of solute is much like the relation between pressure, temperature, and volume in an IDEAL GAS. A number of theories explaining osmotic pressure by analogy to gases have been devised, but most have been discarded in favor of thermodynamic interpretations using such concepts as the entropy of dilution. Osmosis and dialysis are of prime importance in living organisms, where they influence the distribution of nutrients and the release of metabolic waste products. In plants osmosis is at least partially responsible for the absorption of soil water by root hairs and for the elevation of the liquid to the leaves of the plant. Two solutions separated by a semipermeable membrane are said to be isotonic if no osmosis occurs. If osmosis occurs, transfer of solvent is from the hypotonic solution to the hypertonic solution, which has the higher osmotic pressure. Living cells of both plants and animals are enclosed by a semipermeable membrane called the cell membrane, which regulates the flow of liquids and of dissolved solids and gases into and out of the cell. The membrane forms a selective barrier between the cell and its environment; not all substances can pass through the membrane with equal facility. Without this selectivity, the substances necessary to the life of the cell would diffuse uniformly into the cell's surroundings, and toxic materials from the surroundings would enter the cell. If blood cells (or other cells) are placed in contact with an isotonic solution, they will neither shrink nor swell. If the solution is hypertonic, the cells will lose water and shrink (plasmolyze). If the solution is hypotonic (or if pure solvent is used) the cells will swell; the osmotic pressure that is developed may even be great enough to rupture the cell membrane. Plants wilt when watered with saltwater or treated with too much fertilizer, since the soil around their roots then becomes hypertonic. Saltwater from the ocean is hypertonic to the cells of the human body; the drinking of ocean water dehydrates body tissues instead of quenching thirst.

Osnabrück (ŏs″näbrük′), city (1970 pop. 143,905), Lower Saxony, N West Germany, on the Hase River, linked by canal with the Midland Canal. It is an inland port, a rail junction, and an industrial center, with iron and steel mills, machinery plants, and factories that manufacture textiles, paper, and motor vehicles. Located on the site of an ancient Saxon settlement, Osnabrück was made (783) an episcopal see by Charlemagne. The city became a member of the Hanseatic League and a center of the linen trade. It accepted the Reformation in 1543; however, the cathedral remained Catholic, and under the Peace of Westphalia (see WESTPHALIA, PEACE OF)—one of whose treaties was signed (Aug., 1648) in the Osnabrück city hall—the see was occupied alternately by Catholic and Lutheran bishops. The bishopric of Osnabrück was secularized in 1803, and the city passed (1815) to Hanover at the Congress of Vienna. The Catholic diocese was restored in 1857. Osnabrück was badly damaged in World War II. Noteworthy buildings include the three-towered cathedral (begun 783, burned down 1254; rebuilt in Romanesque style with Gothic additions); the Gothic Church of St. Mary (c.1300); and the city hall (1487–1512). Osnabrück also contains a teachers college (housed in a 17th-century palace) and a museum.

Osnappar: see ASSURBANIPAL.

Osorio, Oscar (ōskär′ ōsō′ryō), 1910–69, president of El Salvador (1950–56). A peasant farmer, he joined the army and rose to the rank of major. As a member of the junta that seized power in 1948, he served as provisional executive until his election in 1950. Under his rule, the country's first social security legislation was enacted, a more liberal constitution was adopted, housing was improved, and labor unions were legalized. Osorio was succeeded (1956) by his hand-picked successor, Lt. Col. José María Lemus.

Osorno (ōsōr′nō), city (1970 pop. 105,793), capital of Osorno prov., S central Chile, in the heart of the lake district. Osorno is chiefly an agricultural processing and distributing center. Founded in 1553, it was later destroyed by the Araucanian Indians and was reestablished in 1796 by order of Ambrosio O'Higgins. An influx of immigrants in the latter half of the 19th cent. has given Osorno the atmosphere of a German town.

osprey (ŏs′prē), common name for a bird of prey related to the hawk and the New World vulture and found near water in most parts of the world. The American osprey, or fish hawk, *Pandion haliaetus,* has white underparts and a wingspread of 5 to 6 ft (152 to 183 cm). It feeds solely on live fish and is usually seen hovering over the water, into which it plunges feet first to grasp its prey. Ospreys are classified in the phylum CHORDATA, subphylum Vertebrata, class Aves, order Falconiformes, family Pandionidae.

Osroene (ŏsrōē′nē), ancient kingdom of NW Mesopotamia, in present-day SE Turkey and NE Syria. EDESSA was its capital. It broke away (2d cent. B.C.) from the Seleucid empire and formed a separate kingdom. It came under Roman rule late in the 2d cent. A.D.

Oss (ôs), city (1971 pop. 41,047), North Brabant prov., S Netherlands; chartered 1399. It is an industrial center; manufactures include meat products, chemicals, and pharmaceuticals.

Óssa (ô′sä), peak, c.6,490 ft (1,980 m) high, NE Thessaly, N Greece. According to legend the ALOADAE piled Mt. Pelion on Óssa when they stormed Olympus.

Ossetia (ŏsē′shə, Rus. əsyĕ′tēə), region of the central Caucasus, S European USSR. On the northern slope is the North Ossetian Autonomous Soviet Socialist Republic (1970 pop. 552,000), 3,100 sq mi (8,029 sq km), in the Russian Republic; Ordzhonikidze is the capital. This region extends north beyond the Terek River. On the southern slope is the South Ossetian Autonomous Oblast (1970 pop. 99,000), 1,500 sq mi (3,885 sq km), in Georgia; Tskhinvali is its capital. The oblast extends southward almost to the Kura River. Both sections of Ossetia have valleys that produce fruit, wine, grain, and cotton. Lumbering and livestock raising are important in the mountains. North Ossetia has lead, silver, zinc, and oil deposits and nonferrous metallurgical, oil-extracting, and food-processing industries. The Ossetians, an Iranian-speaking people, are mainly Sunnite Muslims in the north and Eastern Orthodox Christians in the south, where Georgian culture prevails. They are descended from medieval Alans. During the 17th cent. the northern Ossetians were subject to Karbada princelings. From the 18th cent. they came under strong Russian influence, and between 1801 and 1806 all of Ossetian territory was annexed to Russia. Ossetian art work includes wood, stone, and silver carving.

Ossetian Military Road, highway, c.170 mi (270 km) long, across the Caucasus, S European USSR, linking Kutaisi with Alagir. It crosses the Caucasian crest as a trail through the pass at Mamison.

Ossian (ŏsh′ən) or **Oisin** (əshēn′), legendary Gaelic poet, supposedly the son of FINN MAC CUMHAIL, hero of a cycle of tales and poems that place his deeds of valor in the 3d cent. A.D. These traditional tales were preserved in Ireland and in the Scottish Highlands, with Ossian as the bard who sang of the exploits of Finn and his Fenian cohorts. A later cycle of Ossianic poetry centered on Cuchulain, another traditional hero. Ossian is generally represented as an old, blind man who had outlived both his father and his son. The name is remembered by most people in connection with James MACPHERSON, who published translations of two poems that he said had been written by Ossian; scholars subsequently proved that they were actually a combination of traditional Gaelic poems and original verses by Macpherson himself.See James Macpherson, *The Poems of Ossian* (1805, repr. 1974).

Ossietzky, Carl von (fən ôsyĕt′skē), 1889–1938, German pacifist. He was a leader of the peace movement in Germany after World War I and was editor of the antimilitarist weekly *Weltbühne* from 1927. Ossietzky was imprisoned (1932) for articles in the *Weltbühne* exposing secret rearmament in Germany. After Adolf Hitler's rise to power in 1933, Ossietzky was sent to a concentration camp. Suffering from tuberculosis, he was removed (1936) to a prison hospital shortly before the announcement that he had been awarded the 1935 Nobel Peace Prize. The German government protested and barred all Germans from future acceptance of a Nobel Prize. Still imprisoned, Ossietzky died two years later.

Ossining (ŏs′ənĭng), village (1970 pop. 21,659), Westchester co., SE N.Y., on the Hudson River; settled c.1750, inc. 1813 as Sing Sing, renamed 1901. Fine wire, surgical instruments, heart pumps, and maps are among the village's manufactures. Ossining is the site of Sing Sing state prison (built 1825–28). This prison was long known for its extreme discipline, but under Thomas Mott Osborne and Lewis Edward Lawes notable reforms were introduced. Maryknoll, the headquarters of the Catholic Foreign Mission Society, is near the village.

Ossoli, Marchesa: see FULLER, MARGARET.

Ossory, Thomas Butler, earl of (ŏs′ərē), 1634–80, Irish nobleman; son of James Butler, 12th earl and 1st duke of Ormonde. Created earl of Ossory in 1662, he was made (1665) lieutenant general in Ireland and often acted as deputy lord lieutenant there for his father. He distinguished himself in naval engagements (1666, 1672) against the Dutch and was made rear admiral in 1673. He carried (1674) to the prince of Orange (later William III) the offer of marriage with Princess Mary and commanded (1677–78) British troops in Flanders.

Ossory, ancient kingdom of Ireland, the borders of which are now largely traced by those of the Roman Catholic episcopal see of Ossory, including Kilkenny and parts of Co. Offaly and Co. Laoighis. An independent state on the borders of Leinster and Munster, its overlordship was long disputed. It became part of Leinster under the Normans in the 12th cent., and by the middle of the 14th cent. had become part of the earldom of Ormonde, held by the Butler family.

Ostade, Adriaen van (ä′drēän vän ô′städə), 1610–85, Dutch genre painter, b. Haarlem. Trained in the studio of Frans Hals, he was strongly influenced by his fellow student Adriaen Brouwer. Van Ostade created good-humored depictions of village and peasant life, in which the figures are lively in expression and action. Later, under the influence of Rembrandt, he used a warmer palette and deeper chiaroscuro (high contrast) effects. His work after 1650 was refined, the color and light skillfully balanced. In addition to his more than 1,000 oils, van Ostade executed about 50 graphic works and supplied figures for many other artists' landscapes. He is represented in important collections throughout Europe and the United States. Among his many notable works are *Peasants in an Inn* (The Hague); *The Drinker* (Louvre); *The Smoker* (Antwerp); and *The Old Fiddler* (Metropolitan Mus.). His brother and pupil, **Isaak van Ostade,** 1621–49, painted at first in close imitation of his brother, but his interest in landscape led to paintings of a more pastoral character. He created many fine winter landscapes.

Ostend: see OOSTENDE, Belgium.

Ostend Manifesto, document drawn up in Oct., 1854, at Ostend, Belgium, by James BUCHANAN, American minister to Great Britain, John Y. MASON, minister to France, and Pierre SOULÉ, minister to Spain. William L. MARCY, Secretary of State under President Pierce, instructed Soulé to try to buy Cuba from Spain, but Soulé antagonized the Spanish by his political intrigues and aggressive threats (he issued an unwarranted ultimatum to the Spanish government on the BLACK WARRIOR affair). Pierce then ordered a conference of the three diplomats in Europe, all proslavery Democrats, at Ostend. The resulting manifesto strongly suggested that the United States should take Cuba by force if Spain refused to sell. Southerners, who had long feared that Cuba might become an independent black republic, applauded the document, but it was vigorously denounced by the free-soil press as a plot to extend slavery. Marcy immediately repudiated it for the U.S. government.

osteomyelitis (ŏs″tēōmī″əlī′tĭs), infection of the bone and bone marrow. Direct infection of bone usually occurs through open fractures, penetrating wounds, or surgical operations. Infecting microorganisms may also reach the bone via the bloodstream, the most common means of bone infection in children. Osteomyelitis is characterized by pain, high fever, and formation of an ABSCESS at the site of infection. Infection may be caused by a variety of microorganisms, including staphylococci, streptococci, and other pathogenic bacteria. Unless treated vigorously with ANTIBIOTICS and sometimes surgery, bone destruction may result.

osteopathy (ŏstēŏp′əthē), practice of therapy based on manipulation of bones and muscles. This school of medicine, founded by A. T. STILL in 1874, maintains that the normal body produces forces necessary to fight disease and that most ailments are due to "structural derangement" of the body. Frequent slight strains are held to be capable of causing misalignment of bones and various other conditions of the muscle tissue and cartilage, all of which are termed "lesions," and treatment is directed toward correction of these conditions. The first school of osteopathy was founded at Kirksville, Mo., in 1892. Certain other colleges in the United States are accredited by the American Osteopathic Association to give the required four-year course of training and to grant the degree of D.O. (Doctor of Osteopathy). These colleges give a complete course of instruction in conventional medicine as well as in osteopathic theory and practice. Osteopaths are licensed to practice medicine, including surgery and the prescription of drugs, throughout most of the United States; however, they often specialize in treating bone and muscle conditions that are responsive to osteopathic methods. See E. R. Booth, *History of Osteopathy and Twentieth-Century Medical Practice* (1924); E. H. Bean, *The Spirit of Osteopathy* (1956); J. M. Hoag, *Osteopathic Medicine* (1969).

Osterman, Andrei Ivanovich, Count (əndrā' ēvä'nəvĭch əstyĭrmän'), 1686–1747, Russian statesman, b. Germany. His original name was Heinrich Johann Friedrich Ostermann. Under Czar Peter I he held various positions in the diplomatic service. He was made baron for his role in negotiating the Treaty of Nystad, which ended (1721) the Russo-Swedish NORTHERN WAR. Under Czarina Catherine I, Osterman directed Russian foreign policy and was a member of the privy council. A master court intriguer, he was able to maintain his powerful position under the three rulers who followed Catherine. He shrewdly sided with Czarina Anna upon her accession in 1730 against the privy council's attempt to limit her powers. He negotiated an end to the War of the Polish Succession (1733–35) and the Russo-Turkish War of 1736–39. During the brief regency of ANNA LEOPOLDOVNA, Osterman was the virtual ruler of Russia. After Elizabeth seized (1741) power, Osterman was sentenced to death but then was reprieved and exiled to Siberia.

Östersund (östərsŭnd'), city (1970 pop. 27,320), capital of Jämtland co., central Sweden, on Lake Storsjön; founded 1786. It is a commercial, industrial, and transportation center.

Østfold (öst'fôl''), county (1972 est. pop. 224,000), 1,614 sq mi (4,180 sq km), SE Norway, between the Oslofjord in the west and the Swedish border in the east. Moss is the capital. The county's productive farms produce much grain, vegetables, and dairy goods. The area around the lower Glåma River is one of the important industrial centers in Norway. Timber is floated down the Glåma from the Østerdalen valley for processing. The region of Østfold has been important in the cultural and military history of Norway and includes numerous prehistoric remains.

Ostia (ŏs'tēə), ancient city of Italy, at the mouth of the Tiber. It was founded (4th cent. B.C.) as a protection for Rome, then developed (from the 1st cent. B.C.) as a Roman port, rivaling Puteoli. Augustus, Claudius I, Trajan, and Hadrian expanded the city and harbor. From the 3d cent. A.D. the city began to decline. The ruins, of great archaeological interest, rival those of Pompeii in showing the layout of an ancient Italian city.

ostinato: see GROUND BASS.

ostracism (ŏs'trəsĭz''əm), ancient Athenian method of banishing a public figure. It was introduced after the fall of the family of PISISTRATUS. Each year the assembly took a preliminary vote to decide whether a vote of ostracism should be held. If a majority approved holding an ostracism, a day was set for the voting. When the polling took place, each voter put into an urn a potsherd (*ostrakon*) marked with the name of a person he wished ostracized. The man named on the most *ostraka* was exiled, unless fewer than 6,000 votes were cast (some authorities believe that a total of 6,000 votes was necessary to ostracize a person). The exile lasted normally 10 years with no confiscation. ARISTIDES, CIMON, and others were recalled before 10 years were up. The last ostracism was probably that of Hyperbolus (416? B.C.), a demagogue of humble origin. Other cities used ostracism also. Numerous *ostraka* have been found in modern excavations, many bearing the names of Aristides and Themistocles.

Ostrava (ô'strävä), formerly **Moravská Ostrava** (mô'räfskä), Ger. *Mährisch Ostrau*, city (1970 pop. 278,737), N central Czechoslovakia, in Moravia, near the junction of the Oder and Ostravice rivers. It is the heart of the Ostrava-Karviná industrial and mining region, the most heavily industrialized area of Czechoslovakia. Anthracite and bituminous coal, iron and steel, rolling stock, machinery, and ship and bridge parts are the major products of the city, which also has a large chemical industry. One of Czechoslovakia's largest cities, Ostrava is a regional administrative center, a road and rail hub, and the site of several hydroelectric stations. It was well known as a small town in the Middle Ages and later became important because of its strategic location guarding the Moravian Gate, the entrance to the Moravian lowlands. The city's industrial prominence dates from the late 19th cent., after the opening of its first coal mine and the coming of the railroad. German forces occupied Ostrava from 1939 to 1945. The city is a cultural and educational center, noted especially for its college of mining and metallurgy.

ostrich, common name for a large flightless bird (*Struthio camelus)* of Africa and parts of SW Asia, allied to the rhea, the EMU and the extinct MOA. It is the largest of living birds; some males reach a height of 8 ft (244 cm) and weigh from 200 to 300 lb (90–135 kg). The ostrich runs at great speed with wings outspread. The inner of the two toes on each foot is much the larger and bears most of the bird's weight. The ostrich kicks when angered and can inflict serious injury. In both sexes the head, neck, and thighs are bare or scantily feathered. The male is glossy black with beautiful long white plumes on the wings and tail. The female is a dull grayish brown. Usually the polygamous male has from two to six females in his flock. The cock scoops out a hollow for the eggs, which weigh nearly 3 lb (1.35 kg) each. One of the females incubates the eggs during the day, and the cock takes over at night. During the 19th-century vogue for ostrich plumes, farms were established in South Africa and later in North America, Australia, and Europe; after World War I fashions changed and the industry collapsed. Ostriches are classified in the phylum CHORDATA, subphylum Vertebrata, class Aves, order Struthioniformes, family Struthionidae.

Ostrogoths (East Goths), division of the Goths, one of the most important groups of the GERMANS. According to their own unproven tradition, the ancestors of the Goths were the Gotar of S SWEDEN. By the 3d cent. A.D., the Goths settled in the region N of the Black Sea. They split into two divisions, their names reflecting the areas in which they settled; the Ostrogoths settled in the Ukraine, while the VISIGOTHS, or West Goths, moved further west of them. By c.375 the Huns conquered the Ostrogothic kingdom ruled by ERMANARIC, which extended from the Dniester River, north and east to the headwaters of the Volga River. The Ostrogoths were subject to the Huns until the death (453) of ATTILA, when they settled in Pannonia (roughly modern Hungary) as allies of the Byzantine (East Roman) empire. The Ostrogoths, who had long elected their rulers, chose (471) THEODORIC THE GREAT as king. A turbulent ally, the Byzantine emperor, ZENO, commissioned Theodoric to reconquer Italy from ODOACER. The Ostrogoths entered Italy in 488, defeated and slew (493) Odoacer, and set up the Ostrogothic kingdom of ITALY, with Ravenna as their capital. After Theodoric's death (526) his daughter AMALASUNTHA was regent for her son Athalric. She placed herself under the protection of the Byzantine emperor JUSTINIAN I. Her murder (535) served as pretext for Justinian to send BELISARIUS to reconquer Italy. He crushed the Ostrogothic kingdom, but on his recall (541) the Ostrogoths rebelled under the leadership of TOTILA. In 552 the Byzantine general NARSES defeated Totila, who fell in battle. As a result, the Ostrogoths lost their national identity, and the hegemony over Italy passed to Byzantium and shortly afterward to the Lombards. Under the Ostrogothic kings, the culture of late antiquity was revived by Boethius and Cassiodorus; Dionysius Exiguus compiled church law; and Saint Benedict laid the basis of Western monasticism. Roman law and institutions were for the most part maintained; however, the Ostrogoths were resented as aliens by the Italians, from whom they differed not only in culture but also in religion, since they were Arians. See Thomas Hodgkin, *Italy and Her Invaders,* Vol. I–III (2d ed. 1892–96, repr. 1967).

Ostrołeka (ôstrôlĕ'kä), Rus. *Ostrolenka*, town (1970 pop. 22,000), NE Poland, on the Narew River. It is a railway junction and a manufacturing center where pulp and paper, lumber, and bricks are produced. Chartered in 1427, it passed to Prussia in 1795 and to Russia in 1815. It reverted to Poland in 1920. The town has several churches built in the 14th and 17th cent.

Ostrovsky, Aleksandr Nikolayevich (əlyĭksän'dər nyĭkəlī'yəvĭch əstrôf'skē), 1823–86, Russian dramatist. Ostrovsky's first play, *The Bankrupt* (1847; reworked as *It's a Family Affair*, 1850), was widely read but was banned from the stage. He left a government clerical post in 1851 to devote his time to writing. Most of his more than 50 plays deal with the merchant or petty-official classes and the conflicts within their patriarchal families. All but eight of his works were written in blank verse, using colloquial language. Ostrovsky's masterpiece is *The Storm* (1860), the tragedy of a woman driven to suicide. The play is the basis for Janáček's opera *Katia Kabanova.* Ostrovsky's popular play *Poverty Is No Crime* (1854) concerns a marriage of convenience. Rimsky-Korsakov used his *Snow Maiden* (1873) as the libretto of an opera and Tchaikovsky drew upon several plays by Ostrovsky as inspiration for musical works. The playwright's major works have been translated into English.

Ostrovsky, Nikolai Alekseyevich (nyĭkəlī' əlyĭksyā'-yəvĭch), 1904–36, Soviet novelist. He wrote the popular political and autobiographical novel *The Making of a Hero* (1936, tr. 1937) and also one volume of an unfinished novel, *Born of the Storm* (1937, tr. 1939). Ostrovsky was paralyzed and blind after 1927.

Ostwald, Wilhelm (vĭl'hĕlm ôst'vält), 1853–1932, German physical chemist and natural philosopher, b. Riga, Latvia. He was professor of chemistry and director of the chemical laboratory (1886–1906) at the Univ. of Leipzig. He received the 1909 Nobel Prize in Chemistry for his work on catalysis and his investigations into the fundamental principles governing equilibrium and rates of reaction. He also did outstanding work on color. He wrote *Colour Science* (1923, tr. 1931) and many textbooks. Ostwald originated the Ostwald process for preparing nitric acid. Ammonia mixed with air is heated and led over a catalyst (platinum). It reacts with the oxygen to form nitric oxide, which is then oxidized to nitrogen dioxide; this in turn reacts with water to form nitric acid.

O'Sullivan, Timothy H., c.1840–1882, American pioneer photographer, b. New York City. O'Sullivan worked in Matthew Brady's first New York gallery and on the battlefronts of the Civil War. He made photographs for the 40th-parallel surveys (1867–69) and the first underground mine pictures, at the Comstock Lode. Most of his views made for the Wheeler Colorado River expedition were lost fighting the rapids. In 1873, O'Sullivan photographed the ecology and the civilizations of the Arizona and New Mexico deserts. He was appointed chief photographer to the treasury department in 1880. See biography by J. D. Horan (1966).

O'Sullivan Dam, Wash.: see COLUMBIA BASIN PROJECT.

Osuna, Pedro Téllez Girón, duque de (pā'thrō tā'lyāth hērōn' dōō'kā thā ōsōō'nä), 1579–1624, Spanish general and administrator. As viceroy of Sicily (1611–16) and of Naples (1616–20), he arrogated power to himself and fought the Turks and Barbary pirates. In 1617, suspecting Venetian anti-Spanish activities, he defeated a Venetian fleet in the Adriatic. In 1618 the Venetians accused him of plotting to overthrow the Venetian republic and Osuna was recalled (1620) to Spain and imprisoned (1621). Historians disagree on whether there was an actual conspiracy.

Oswald, Saint, d. 641, king of Northumbria (633–41), son of AETHELFRITH. In exile during the reign of EDWIN, Oswald and his brother OSWY became Christians. After Edwin's death Oswald defeated (633) Cadwallon, king of North Wales, and recovered his father's kingdom. He brought from Iona a group of Scottish monks, led by St. Aidan, who established their base at Lindisfarne (see HOLY ISLAND) and introduced Celtic Christianity to Northumbria. Oswald was for a time the strongest ruler in England, being acknowledged overlord of Wessex and other southern kingdoms. Killed in battle by PENDA of Mercia, he came to be revered as a Christian martyr. Feast: Aug. 5 in the Roman martyrology; Aug. 9 in Britain.

Oswald, Lee Harvey, 1939–63, presumed assassin of John F. Kennedy, b. New Orleans. Oswald spent most of his boyhood in Fort Worth, Texas. Later, he attended a Dallas high school, and on leaving school, enlisted (1956) in the Marines and served until 1959. An avowed Marxist, he went to the Soviet Union in 1959, declaring his intention (never fulfilled) of renouncing American and obtaining Russian citizenship. In 1962 he returned to the United States, bringing his Russian wife and young daughter. In succeeding months, Oswald moved around the country, finally coming back to Dallas, where, in Oct., 1963, he obtained a job at the Texas State

School Book Depository. From that building the shots were fired that took President Kennedy's life on Nov. 22, 1963. Oswald fled the scene. Later, a policeman trying to accost him was shot and killed before Oswald was seized and charged. On Nov. 24, while in police hands, Oswald was murdered by a nightclub proprietor, Jack Ruby. In 1964 the WARREN COMMISSION held Oswald to be the sole assassin.

Oswego (ŏswē'gō), city (1970 pop. 23,844), seat of Oswego co., N Central N.Y., on Lake Ontario and the Oswego River; founded 1722, inc. as a city 1848. The largest U.S. port on Lake Ontario, it is a port of entry and a northern terminus of the Barge Canal. The city's manufactures include aluminum, textiles, and paper products. A trading post established there after the English founded Oswego (1722) became a vital outlet for the Albany fur trade. The strategic location prompted the building of Fort Oswego (1727), Fort George (1755), and present Fort Ontario (1755; an active U.S. army post until 1946, and a state historic site since 1951). These fortifications were much contested in the colonial wars. The city's importance as a lake port came with the completion of the Barge Canal (1917) and the St. Lawrence Seaway (1959). It is the seat of State Univ. College of Arts and Science at Oswego. James Fenimore Cooper's novel *The Pathfinder* is laid in the Oswego River valley.

Oswego, river, 23 mi (37 km) long, formed by the confluence of the Oneida and the Seneca rivers, central N.Y., NW of Syracuse and flowing NW to Lake Ontario at Oswego. It is a part of the state's barge-transportation system.

Oswego tea: see BEE BALM.

Oswestry (ŏz'wĕstrē, -wəs-), rural district (1971 pop. 30,320), Shropshire, W central England. It is a market town with plastics, clothing, and printing industries. The district is named for St. Oswald, a Northumbrian king who was killed there in a battle (7th cent.) against King Penda of Mercia. The poet Wilfred Owen was born in Oswestry. In 1974, Oswestry became part of the new nonmetropolitan county of Salop.

Oświęcim (ôshvyĕN'chĕm), Ger. *Auschwitz,* town (1970 pop. 39,600), SE Poland. It is a railway junction and industrial center producing chemicals, leather, and agricultural implements. There are coal deposits in the vicinity. In World War II the Germans organized a CONCENTRATION CAMP system there, consisting of 3 main and 30 forced-labor camps. At the Brzezinka (Ger. *Birkenau)* extermination camp about 4,000,000 prisoners, mostly Jews, were annihilated.

Oswy or **Oswiu** (both: ŏz'wē), d. 670, king of Northumbria. He succeeded (641) his brother OSWALD in Bernicia only, Deira (the other part of Northumbria) having become a dependency of Mercia. However, when he killed PENDA of Mercia at the battle of Winwæd (654), he not only made himself ruler of all Northumbria but gained actual possession of Mercia and overlordship of the southern English kingdoms. He lost Mercia again to Penda's son Wulfhere in 657. Oswy continued the conversion of England to Celtic Christianity (see CELTIC CHURCH), sending missionaries to Mercia and Essex. To resolve the differences between the Celtic and Roman usages of the church in England, the king called the Synod of WHITBY (663), at which he gave his decision in favor of the Roman party.

Otaru (ōtä'ro͞o), city (1970 pop. 191,850), SW Hokkaido, Japan, on Ishikari Bay. It is the main coal-exporting port of the island and a center of herring fisheries.

Otfried von Weissenburg (ôt'frēt fən vī'-sənbo͝orkh), 9th-century German monk and poet; pupil of Rabanus Maurus Magnentius. His *Liber Evangeliorum* (863–71) is a counterpart in Old High German to the 9th-century Old Saxon HELIAND. Otfried's gospel tales are versified in a meter derived from Latin, and he is the first German poet known to have used end rhymes.

Othman: see UTHMAN.

Othman I: see OSMAN I.

Othni (ŏth'nī), son of Shemaiah. 1 Chron. 26.7.

Othniel (ŏth'nēĕl), first judge of Israel after the death of Joshua. For capturing a city he was given as wife Caleb's daughter Achsah. Joshua 15.17; Judges 3.9–11.

Otho. For German rulers thus named, see OTTO.

Otho, Marcus Salvius (ō'thō), A.D. 32–A.D. 69, Roman emperor (Jan.–April, A.D. 69). He was a friend of NERO, and his wife, Poppaea Sabina, became Nero's mistress; Otho was repaid (A.D. 58) with the province of Lusitania. In A.D. 68 he joined the revolt of GALBA against Nero, but on Galba's accession Otho formed a conspiracy. Galba was killed, and Otho made himself emperor. Meanwhile VITELLIUS had been proclaimed emperor at Cologne and was on his way to Rome. Otho was defeated in N Italy and killed himself. See B. W. Henderson, *Civil War and Rebellion in the Roman Empire, 68–70 A.D.* (1908).

Otis, Bass, 1784–1861, American portrait painter and mezzotint engraver, b. Bridgewater, Mass. He probably produced the first lithograph in America, a portrait of the Rev. Abner Kneeland, in a volume of his lectures (1818). Otis practiced portrait painting in New York City and Philadelphia, reproducing some of his works in mezzotint. Among his best-known likenesses are those of Thomas Jefferson, Stephen Girard, and James Madison. His only known genre composition, *Interior of a Smithy,* is in the Pennsylvania Academy of the Fine Arts.

Otis, Elisha Graves, 1811–61, American inventor, b. Halifax, Vt. From his invention (1852) of an automatic safety device to prevent the fall of hoisting machinery he developed the first passenger elevator (1857). The invention of the elevator was of great importance to architecture because it permitted the building of skyscrapers.

Otis, Harrison Gray, 1765–1848, American political leader, b. Boston; nephew of James Otis. He practiced law in Boston, and was elected (1795) to the Massachusetts legislature. A staunch Federalist, he served (1797–1801) in Congress and was again a member of the state legislature from 1802 to 1817. In 1814 he was a leader of the HARTFORD CONVENTION and subsequently defended that meeting. Otis was a U.S. Senator (1817–22) and mayor of Boston (1829–31). He published *Letters Developing the Character and Views of the Hartford Convention* (1820) and *Otis' Letters in Defence of the Hartford Convention* (1824). See biographical study by S. E. Morison (1913, repr. 1969).

Otis, Harrison Gray, 1837–1917, American soldier and journalist, b. Marietta, Ohio. He was (1860) a member of the Republican national convention that nominated Abraham Lincoln for President, served with distinction in the Civil War, and, as brigadier general, participated (1898) in the Spanish-American War. In 1886 he acquired control of the Los Angeles *Times,* a newspaper that under his management became bitterly opposed to organized labor. His newspaper plant was dynamited in 1910, and two union laborers were convicted of the crime.

Otis, James, 1725–83, American colonial political leader, b. Barnstable co., Mass. A lawyer first in Plymouth and then in Boston, he won great distinction and served (1756–61) as advocate general of the vice admiralty court. He resigned to oppose the issuing of writs of assistance by the superior court of Massachusetts; the writs, which authorized customs officials to search for smuggled goods, were virtually general search warrants. Arguing eloquently before the court, Otis claimed that the writs violated the natural rights of the colonials as Englishmen and that any act of Parliament violating those rights was void. Otis lost the case but soon became the leader of the radical wing of the colonial opposition to British measures. He was elected (1761) to the colonial assembly and was made head (1764) of the Massachusetts committee of correspondence. In his speeches and pamphlets, Otis defined and defended colonial rights. He proposed and participated in the Stamp Act Congress (see STAMP ACT), and his ideas were used in the protests drafted by that body. Hated by the conservatives, his election (1766) as speaker of the assembly was vetoed by the royal governor. After the passage of the Townshend Acts (1767) Otis helped Samuel Adams draft the Massachusetts circular letter to the other colonies denouncing the acts. In 1769, Otis was struck on the head during a quarrel with a commissioner of customs. He subsequently became insane and took no further part in political affairs. See C. F. Mullett, ed., *Some Political Writings of James Otis* (1929); biography by William Tudor (1823, repr. 1970).

Oto Indians (ō'tō), North American Indians, also called the Otoe, whose language belongs to the Siouan branch of the Hokan-Siouan linguistic stock (see AMERICAN INDIAN LANGUAGES). At one time, with the Iowa and the Missouri, they formed part of the Winnebago nation, N of the Great Lakes. The Oto with the Missouri left the nation, but after a quarrel the Oto separated from the Missouri and settled in S Minnesota. Constantly beset by overpowering enemies, they were driven south and joined the Pawnee near the mouth of the Platte River. In 1880–82 the Oto migrated to Oklahoma. The Oto had a Plains area type of culture. Today they live, with the Missouri, on a reservation in N central Oklahoma, where they number some 1,000. See B. B. Chapman, *The Otoes and the Missourias* (1965).

Otomí (ōtōmē'), a Macro-Otomanguean language spoken by American Indians of W central Mexico. See AMERICAN INDIAN LANGUAGES.

otosclerosis: see DEAFNESS.

Otranto (ô'träntō), town (1971 pop. 4,163), in Apulia, extreme S Italy, on the Strait of Otranto, which links the Adriatic and Ionian seas. It is a small fishing port and a seaside resort. Originally a Greek settlement, Otranto became an important port under the Romans. Later ruled by the Byzantines and the Normans, it never recovered from its devastation (1480) by the Turks. Of note are an 11th-century cathedral (restored 17th–18th cent.), with a fine mosaic floor (12th cent.), and the ruins of an imposing Aragonese castle (15th cent.) that provided the setting of Horace Walpole's Gothic novel, *The Castle of Otranto.*

Otsego Lake, c.9 mi (14.5 km) long, E central N.Y., SE of Utica, in a resort region. A branch of the Susquehanna River issues from its southern end at Cooperstown. The lake is the Glimmerglass of James Fenimore Cooper's tales.

Otsu (ō'tso͞o), city (1970 pop. 171,739), capital of Shiga prefecture, S Honshu, Japan. It is a tourist center and a port for excursion steamers on Lake Biwa. Nylon, cotton yarn, textiles, polypropylene, electrical appliances, precision instruments, and machinery are among the city's industrial products. A former imperial seat (2d and 7th cent.), Otsu is the site of Miidera, a 7th-century Buddhist temple, and of the grave of Basho, the famous poet.

ottava rima (ōtä'və rē'mə): see PENTAMETER.

Ottawa (ŏt'əwə), city (1971 pop. 302,341; est. metropolitan pop. 450,000), capital of Canada, SE Ont., at the confluence of the Ottawa and Rideau rivers. HULL, Que., just across the Ottawa at the mouth of the Gatineau River, forms part of the metropolitan area. The Rideau Canal separates the city into upper and lower towns; along its banks and those of the rivers are many landscaped drives as well as much of the city's land area, which totals 1,500 acres (607 hectares). Ottawa is not primarily an industrial center; however, it has industries that produce, among other goods, paper and paper products, printed materials, telecommunications equipment, and electrical products. The area's industries utilize the hydroelectric power of the Ottawa (Chaudière Falls) and Gatineau valleys. Ottawa proper was founded in 1827 by Col. John By, an engineer in charge of construction of the Rideau Canal. At first called Bytown, the present name was adopted in 1854. In 1858, Ottawa was chosen by Queen Victoria to be the capital of the United Provinces of Canada, and in 1867 it became capital of the Dominion of Canada. The government buildings, built between 1859 and 1865, were burned in 1916 but were immediately rebuilt on an enlarged scale. Other notable buildings are Rideau Hall, the residence of the governor general, the Anglican and Roman Catholic cathedrals, the National Museum, the National Art Gallery, the National Arts Centre, the Dominion Observatory, and the Royal Mint. Ottawa Univ., Carlton Univ., and St. Patrick College are in the city. About one third of the population is French speaking. See H. J. Walker, *The Ottawa Story* (1953); Blodwen Davies, *Ottawa: Portrait of a Capital* (1954); Wilfrid Eggleston, *The Queen's Choice* (1961); R. B. Haig, *Ottawa* (1970).

Ottawa. 1 City (1970 pop. 18,716), seat of La Salle co., N central Ill., at the confluence of the Fox and Illinois rivers, in a fertile farm area; inc. as a city 1853. Rich deposits of silica in the area are used in the production of glass and sand products. The city has a marble manufacturing industry; other products are machines, tools, and plastic products. Points of interest include the site of the first Lincoln-Douglas debate (1858) and Fort Johnson (1832). Several state parks are in the area, and scenic attractions along the rivers draw many visitors. **2** City (1970 pop. 11,036), seat of Franklin co., E Kansas, on the Marais des Cygnes River; inc. 1867. The rail and industrial center of a farm area, its industries produce mobile homes, plastic products, clothing, cabinets, and building blocks. The city is named for the Ottawa Indians, who moved there (1832) after ceding their Ohio lands to the United States; they were subsequently removed (1867) to Oklahoma. Ottawa Univ. is in the city.

Ottawa, river, c.700 mi (1,130 km) long, largest tributary of the St. Lawrence River, Canada. It rises in the Laurentian Highlands, SW Que., and flows generally W through La Vérendrye Provincial Park to Lake Timiskaming, then SE forming part of the Quebec-

Ontario border, past Ottawa, and into the St. Lawrence River near Montreal. Its lower course has several expansions, known as the Allumetter, Chats, and Deschênes lakes and Lake of the Two Mountains. Among its chief tributaries are the Gatineau, Lièvre and Coulonge rivers. Hydroelectric power stations at La Cave, Des Joachims, Bryson, Chenaux, Chats, Chaudière Falls, and Carillion have a combined generating capacity of about 1.5 million kw. The river is navigable for large vessels as far as Ottawa; it is connected with Lake Ontario by the Rideau Canal system. There is some farming in the valley below Pembroke, but lumbering is the chief industry along the lower river. The region along the river between Montreal and Ottawa is one of the most populated of Canada. Samuel de Champlain, the French explorer, was the first European to visit (1613–15) the valley; the river, known then as the Grand River, later became an important highway for fur traders and missionaries.

Ottawa, University of, at Ottawa, Ont., Canada; bilingual; provincially supported; founded 1848 as the College of Bytown. It became the Univ. of Ottawa in 1866. It has faculties of arts, canon law, psychology, education, pure and applied science, law, medicine, theology, philosophy, and social sciences and schools of graduate studies, library science, nursing, hospital administration, and physical education and recreation.

Ottawa Indians, North American Indians whose language belongs to the Algonquian branch of the Algonquian-Wakashan linguistic stock (see AMERICAN INDIAN LANGUAGES). According to tradition the Ottawa, the Ojibwa, and the Potawatami were originally one family, dwelling N of the Great Lakes; after the separation, some of the Ottawa settled on Manitoulin Island in Lake Huron and along the shores of Georgian Bay. In 1615, when noted by Samuel de Champlain, many of them lived near the mouth of French River on Georgian Bay. The Ottawa, known as great traders, claimed the Ottawa River region and controlled trade with the French on that river. They allied themselves with the French and the Huron. Their alliance with the Huron, however, made them the enemies of the Iroquois, who forced them to flee to the islands off Green Bay. After a few years some moved on to Keweenaw Bay in Lake Superior, while another section joined the Huron and went to the Mississippi near Lake Pepin. From there the Sioux drove them northward to Chequamegon Bay in N Wisconsin. Promised protection by the French, the Ottawa returned (1670) to Manitoulin Island, where the mission of St. Simon was established among them. Next they joined the Huron at Mackinac in Michigan, and soon after they dispersed over a wide area. The Ottawa were active in the Indian wars of the Old Northwest; PONTIAC was an Ottawa Indian. Part of the Ottawa are settled on Walpole Island in Lake St. Clair, part are on Manitoulin Island, while others have settled in Kansas, Oklahoma, and Michigan. The Ottawa were of the Eastern Woodlands cultural area. They had a well-developed creation myth that stated that they were descended from three families: the Michabou, or Great Hare, the Namepich, or Carp, and the Bear's Paw. See A. S. Blackbird, *History of the Ottawa and Chippewa Indians of Michigan* (1897).

otter, name for a number of aquatic, carnivorous mammals of the WEASEL family, found on all continents except Australia. The common river otters of Eurasia and the Americas are species of the genus *Lutra*. The North American river otter, *L. canadensis*, ranges from N Alaska and Canada to the S United States. Its slender body is 2½ to 3 ft (76–91 cm) long, excluding the 12-in. (30-cm), heavy tail; it weighs from 10 to 25 lb (4–10 kg). It has thick, glossy brown fur, which is commercially valuable. The head is flattened, the legs are short, and the hind feet are webbed. An agile swimmer, it fishes in streams and lakes, along the banks of which it makes its burrow. It also eats frogs, crayfish, and other water animals. Although it spends most of its time in water, it makes overland trips on occasion. The otter is a social and playful animal; groups have been seen playing "follow the leader," sliding down mudbanks, or tobogganing in the snow, apparently for the sake of pleasure. Of the freshwater otters, the South American giant otter, *Pteronura brasiliensis*, is the most highly modified for aquatic life. Its highly streamlined body is up to 7 ft (213 cm) long, the tail is keeled, and the feet are short, webbed, and nearly useless on land. Its mouth is set under the muzzle, like that of a shark. Hunted extensively for its fur, the giant otter may be in danger of extinction over much of its range. Otters of other genera are found in Africa and SE Asia. The sea otter, *Enhydra lutris*, found in and around the kelp beds of the N Pacific, is the only exclusively marine species, although river otters sometimes enter the ocean at the mouths of rivers. The sea otter swims on its back and in this position carries its cub and eats its meals of abalone, crab, and sea urchin, sometimes using a rock to smash open the shells. Relentless hunting of the animal led to its near extinction; however, it is now protected by international agreement. Otters are classified in the phylum CHORDATA, subphylum Vertebrata, class Mammalia, order Carnivora, family Mustelidae. See Ed Park, *The World of the Otter* (1972).

Otter, Peaks of, two peaks, W central Va., in the Blue Ridge, W of Lynchburg. The one, Flat Top, is 4,004 ft (1,220 m) high; the other, Sharp Top, 3,870 ft (1,180 m). They are in Moses H. Cone Memorial Park, a section of the Blue Ridge National Parkway.

Otterbein, Philip William (ŏt'ərbīn"), 1726–1813, German-American clergyman, a founder of the United Brethren in Christ. After pastoral work in Germany, he emigrated (1752) to America as a missionary of the German Reformed Church. In association with Martin BOEHM, whom he met c.1768, he carried on successful evangelistic work, mainly in the German settlements of Pennsylvania and Maryland. His influence was widespread, especially after he became pastor of an independent congregation in Baltimore known as the Evangelical Reformed Church. While remaining a member of the German Reformed Church, Otterbein played a leading role with Boehm and a small group of lay preachers in laying the foundations (1789) of a denomination to be known as the United Brethren in Christ (later the EVANGELICAL UNITED BRETHREN CHURCH), of which he and Boehm were elected bishops in 1800. Otterbein College is named for him.

Otterburn, village, Northumberland, N England. It was the scene of a victory (1388) of the Scots over the English. The engagement, in which Sir Henry Percy was taken captive, is the subject of the English ballad "Chevy Chase" and the Scots ballad "Otterburn."

otterhound, breed of large HOUND developed in England over centuries. It stands about 25 in. (63.5 cm) high at the shoulder and weighs up to 65 lb (29.5 kg). The water-repellent double coat is composed of hard, oily outer hairs and a thick, woolly undercoat. It is usually colored white and blue, but it may also be various shades of tan or black and tan. During the latter half of the 19th cent., when the hunting of otters in England was at its peak, as many as 20 packs of otterhounds regularly worked the countryside and riverbanks. Today it is still used as a hunter, frequently for raccoon, but is more often kept as a farm dog and pet. See DOG.

Otto I or **Otto the Great,** 912–73, Holy Roman emperor (962–73) and German king (936–73), son and successor of Henry I of Germany. He is often regarded as the founder of the HOLY ROMAN EMPIRE. Boldly developing the policies that his father had begun, Otto brought the Middle Kingdom of the Carolingian LOTHAIR I (see VERDUN, TREATY OF), including Italy, Burgundy, and LOTHARINGIA, under German influence and broke the independence of the duchies. The rebellions of Otto's brother, Henry, and of Duke EBERHARD of Franconia were ended by the battle of Andernach (939) and Henry's submission (941). King Louis IV of France, hoping to gain Lotharingia, had assisted the rebels, and Otto campaigned against him (940) with HUGH THE GREAT; in 942, however, Otto and Louis reached an agreement, and Otto helped Louis to defeat Hugh (950). In 951, Otto invaded Italy, taking advantage of an appeal from the widowed Italian queen, ADELAIDE, who was about to be forced into a marriage with the son of BERENGAR II. Defeating Berengar, Otto assumed the title king of the Lombards, married Adelaide, and returned to Germany, where Berengar eventually paid him homage. In Germany another revolt was brewing. Rivalry and jealousy among the dukes, particularly against Otto's brother, Henry, whom he had made duke of Bavaria in 947, resulted in a rebellion in 953 led by CONRAD THE RED and Otto's son Duke Ludolf of Swabia. New attacks by the Magyars ended the rebellion and forced the dukes to form a united front against the invaders, who were defeated (955) in the Lechfeld. Otto had already begun to counter the ducal power by creating the "Ottonian system," entailing close alliance between the crown and the higher prelates. An important exponent of the alliance was his brother and chief adviser, St. BRUNO, archbishop of Cologne, whom Otto made duke of Lotharingia. Meanwhile, in Italy, Berengar II resumed his aggression. Pope JOHN XII appealed to Otto, who entered Rome and was crowned emperor early in 962, reviving the imperial title of the Carolingians and legitimizing the German kings' claim to the Middle Kingdom; Otto thus linked the destinies of Italy and Germany. John soon found the emperor too powerful and, while Otto was campaigning against Berengar, secretly negotiated with Otto's enemies. Otto hastened back to Rome (963), deposed John, and installed a new pope, Leo VIII. The Romans, seeing all independence lost, rose in 964 and restored John, but John died the same year and Otto reinstated Leo. Otto's campaign (966–72) to gain control over S Italy was unsuccessful, but a minor diplomatic triumph was scored in 972 when Emperor John I of Byzantium gave a Greek princess in marriage to Otto's son and successor, Otto II.

Otto II, 955–83, Holy Roman emperor (973–83) and German king (961–83), son and successor of Otto I. He was crowned joint emperor in 967. Shortly after his father died Otto faced a rebellion by his cousin, Henry the Wrangler, duke of Bavaria, who coveted the crown. Otto defeated and deposed Henry (976), at the same time making Austria, CARINTHIA, and the Nordgau virtually independent of Bavaria. During this period he also repulsed a Danish attack. In 978, Otto invaded France in retaliation for the French king Lothair's attempt to conquer Lorraine; the inconclusive war ended in 980. Campaigning in Italy (981–82), Otto was, after some initial success, disastrously defeated by the Arabs in S Italy. In 983 he held a diet of German and Italian nobles at Verona, where he had his son Otto III elected German king. Meanwhile, the Danes and the Slavs were again attacking his German lands, but Otto died suddenly before he could act. Regarding Germany and Italy as a united realm, Otto II felt his position as emperor more keenly than his role as German king. His failure in Italy greatly weakened the imperial prestige.

Otto III, 980–1002, Holy Roman Emperor (996–1002) and German king (983–1002), son of Holy Roman Emperor Otto II and the Byzantine princess Theophano. On Otto's accession Henry the Wrangler, the deposed duke of Bavaria, attempted to become his guardian and then to obtain the crown, but the plot was frustrated and Henry was forced to abandon it, although he was restored in Bavaria. Instead, Theophano was regent until her death in 991 and Otto's grandmother Adelaide succeeded her until 994. Otto established his cousin Bruno in the vacant papacy as Gregory V (996) and restored him (998) after his expulsion by a Roman revolt. After Gregory's death (999), Otto installed his tutor Gerbert of Aurillac as pope (see SYLVESTER II). His pilgrimage (1000) to the grave of his friend St. ADALBERT gave him the opportunity to strengthen the influence of his "ecclesiastical empire" against Germany's eastern neighbors. Possessed of brilliant talents and remarkably well educated, Otto III was alternately swayed by extreme asceticism and by ideas of his high position as the scion of both the Western and the Eastern imperial houses. In 998 he settled in Rome, hoping to make this the seat of his empire, which would include German, Italian, and Slavic lands. He tried unsuccessfully to establish a permanent imperial administration. In 1001 discontented Romans rioted and forced Otto to flee the city. He was planning to attack Rome when he died. Otto was succeeded by HENRY II, son of Henry the Wrangler.

Otto IV, 1175?–1218, Holy Roman emperor (1209–15) and German king, son of HENRY THE LION, duke of Saxony. He was brought up at the court of his uncle King Richard I of England, who secured his election (1198) as antiking to PHILIP OF SWABIA after the death of Holy Roman Emperor HENRY VI. Civil war in Germany ensued. The murder of Philip (June, 1208), who had just been recognized by Pope INNOCENT III as king, although not Otto's work, revived his cause; he won over the princes by submitting to a new election (Nov., 1208). By the charter of Speyer (March, 1209), Otto confirmed his earlier acknowledgment (1201) of the papacy's rights to the Papal States and his promise of aid in upholding papal suzerainty over Sicily. He also conceded the freedom of episcopal elections and the unrestricted right of appeal to the pope. However, no sooner was he crowned emperor (Oct., 1209) at Rome than he reverted to the Hohenstaufen policy of dominance over Italy. He seized (1210) the lands left to the church by MATILDA of Tuscany. Only when he invaded Apulia and prepared to attack Sicily, however, did Innocent III excommunicate him (1210). Prompted by the pope and by King Philip II of France, some of the German nobles revolted and elected the Hohenstaufen, Frederick of Sicily (later

Holy Roman Emperor FREDERICK II), as king. In the ensuing war Otto was supported by the nobles of the Lower Rhine and of the northeast, as well as by his uncle King John of England, but he was defeated (1214) at Bouvines by Philip II of France. The pope declared him deposed in 1215.

Otto I, 1848–1916, king of Bavaria (1886–1913). Although incurably insane after 1872, he succeeded his brother King Louis II under the regency of his uncle Luitpold (1886–1912) and Luitpold's son Louis (1912–13). In 1913, Otto was deposed by an act of parliament, and the regent became king as Louis III.

Otto I, 1815–67, first king of the Hellenes (1833–62). The second son of King Louis I of Bavaria, he was chosen (1832) by a conference of European powers at London to rule newly independent GREECE. He ascended the throne under a highly unpopular regency of Bavarians. A military coup (1843) forced a constitution on the king. His authority was further weakened when Greece sought to attack Turkey in 1854 after the outbreak of the Crimean War; France and Britain as a result occupied the port of Piraeus (Piraiévs). The king's attempts to discard the constitution led to another military revolt (1862) and to his deposition. In 1863 the Greeks chose a Danish prince to become their king as George I.

Otto, 1912–, Austrian archduke and former pretender to the Austro-Hungarian throne, son of Emperor Charles I and Empress Zita. After World War II began, he went to the United States and made an unsuccessful attempt to form an Austrian legion to fight Germany. Returning to Europe in 1946, he remained in exile. In 1961, he relinquished his claims to the throne and subsequently visited Austria. An author and lecturer, he wrote *The Social Order of Tomorrow* (1957, tr. 1959) and a biography of the emperor Charles V (tr. 1970).

Otto, Frei (frī), 1925–, German architect. Most notable for his tensile and pneumatic structures, Otto is among the first major architects to experiment with lightweight design. He is a noted designer of exhibition tents and sports arenas. Otto has also experimented with pneumatic membranes stabilized and maintained by means of air and gas pressure. Structures built with these membranes are used for oil-storage tanks, grain silos, and greenhouses. Otto has also designed a pneumatic covering for an arctic city of 45,000 inhabitants.

Otto, Nikolaus August (nē'kōlous ou'go͝ost ô'tō), 1832–91, German engineer. He was coinventor (1867) of an internal-combustion engine, and he devised (1876) the four-stroke Otto cycle, which was widely adopted for automobile, airplane, and other motors.

Ottocar I (ŏt'əkär) or **Přemysl Ottocar I** (pərzhĕm'ĭsəl ôt'ôkär), d. 1230, duke (1197–98) and king (1198–1230) of Bohemia. The struggle within the Holy Roman Empire for the imperial crown enabled Ottocar to obtain (1198) from PHILIP OF SWABIA the royal title. Holy Roman Emperor Frederick II confirmed the title (1212) and the election (1216) of Ottocar's son (later Wenceslaus I) as his successor. In 1221, Ottocar was forced to surrender disciplinary rights over the clergy to the bishop of Prague, but retained control over secular church affairs.

Ottocar II or **Přemysl Ottocar II,** c.1230–1278, king of Bohemia (1253–78), son and successor of Wenceslaus I. Ottocar shrewdly exploited the disorders of the great interregnum in the HOLY ROMAN EMPIRE to build an empire reaching from Bohemia to the Adriatic. He won (1251) the duchy of Austria by election, marriage, and conquest and became involved in a long war over Styria with BELA IV of Hungary; after defeating (1260) Bela, he added Styria to his possessions and, having procured the annulment of his first marriage, married a Hungarian princess. In 1269 he acquired, through diplomacy, Carinthia, Carniola, and Istria. Thus Ottocar's domains included most of the later Hapsburg crownlands. Ottocar sought the German crown in 1273, but his unprecedented power made him unpopular with the electors. RUDOLF I of Hapsburg was elected Holy Roman emperor. Ottocar, who contested the election, was declared deprived of his dominions by the Diet of Regensburg (1274) and was placed by Rudolf under the ban of the empire (1275). In 1276, yielding to a powerful German-Hungarian coalition headed by Rudolf, Ottocar surrendered all but Bohemia and Moravia, with which he was reinvested by Rudolf. However, Ottocar's revived ambitions and Rudolf's interference in Bohemian affairs provoked a new war. Ottocar was defeated and killed on the MARCHFELD in a fierce battle against Germans and Hungarians. He was succeeded by his son, WENCESLAUS II. Ottocar greatly encouraged the growth and independence of the towns, thereby earning the reproach of favoring the Germans (most numerous in the towns) over the Czechs, and he sought to reduce the power of the great nobles. An astute diplomat, he was also a courageous warrior. He helped to conquer East Prussia from the pagan Prussians and founded the city of Königsberg (now Kaliningrad).

Ottoman Empire (ŏt'əmən), vast state founded in the late 13th cent. by the Ottoman or Osmanli TURKS (the last of the Turkish peoples to invade the Near East) and ruled by the descendants of Osman I until its dissolution in 1918. It was the greatest of the modern states. Modern TURKEY formed only part of the empire, but the terms "Turkey" and "Ottoman Empire" were often used interchangeably. The Ottoman state began as one of many small Turkish states that emerged in Asia Minor during the breakdown of the empire of the Seljuk Turks. The Ottoman Turks began to absorb the other states, and during the reign (1451–81) of Muhammad II they ended all other local Turkish dynasties. The early phase of Ottoman expansion took place under Osman I, ORKHAN, MURAD I, and BEYAZID I at the expense of the Byzantine Empire, Bulgaria, and Serbia. BURSA fell in 1326, and Adrianople (the modern EDIRNE) in 1361; each in turn became the capital of the empire. The great Ottoman victories of KOSSOVO (1389) and NIKOPOL (1396) placed large parts of the Balkan Peninsula under Ottoman rule and awakened Europe to the Ottoman danger. The Ottoman siege of Constantinople was lifted at the appearance of TAMERLANE, who defeated and captured Beyazid in 1402. The Ottomans, however, soon rallied.

The Period of Great Expansion. Their empire, reunited by MUHAMMAD I, expanded victoriously under Muhammad's successors MURAD II and MUHAMMAD II. The victory (1444) at VARNA over a crusading army led by Ladislaus III of Poland was followed in 1453 by the capture of CONSTANTINOPLE. Within a century the Ottomans had changed from a nomadic horde to the heirs of the most ancient surviving empire of Europe. Their success was due partly to the weakness and disunity of their adversaries, partly to their excellent and far superior military organization. Their army comprised numerous Christians—not only conscripts, who were organized as the corps of JANISSARIES, but also volunteers. Turkish expansion reached its peak in the 16th cent. under SELIM I and SULAYMAN I (Sulayman the Magnificent). The Hungarian defeat (1526) at MOHACS prepared the way for the capture (1541) of Buda and the absorption of the major part of HUNGARY by the Ottoman Empire; TRANSYLVANIA became a tributary principality, as did WALACHIA and MOLDAVIA. The Asiatic borders of the empire were pushed deep into Persia and Arabia. Selim I defeated the Mamelukes of EGYPT and SYRIA, took Cairo in 1517, and assumed the succession to the CALIPHATE. ALGIERS was taken in 1518, and Mediterranean commerce was threatened by corsairs, such as BARBAROSSA, who sailed under Turkish auspices. Most of the Venetian and other Latin possessions in GREECE also fell to the sultans. During the reign of Sulayman I began (1535) the traditional friendship between France and Turkey, directed against Hapsburg Austria and Spain. Sulayman reorganized the Turkish judicial system, and his reign saw the flowering of Turkish literature, art, and architecture. In theory, the sultan of the Ottoman state, who was also the caliph, was answerable only to God. In practice his prerogatives were limited by the spirit of Muslim canonical law (*sheriat*), and he usually shared his authority with the chief preserver (*sheyhülislam*) of the *sheriat* and the grand vizier (chief executive officer). In the progressive decay that followed Sulayman's death, the clergy (*ulema*) and the Janissaries gained power and exercised a profound, corrupting influence. The first serious blow by Europe to the empire was the naval defeat of Lepanto (1571; see LEPANTO, BATTLE OF), inflicted on the fleet of SELIM II by the Spanish and Venetians under John of Austria. However, MURAD IV in the 17th cent. temporarily restored Turkish military prestige by his victory (1638) over Persia. CRETE was conquered from Venice, and in 1683 a huge Turkish army under Grand Vizier Kara MUSTAFA surrounded Vienna. The relief of Vienna by JOHN III of Poland and the subsequent campaigns of CHARLES V of Lorraine, LOUIS OF BADEN, and EUGENE OF SAVOY ended in negotiations in 1699 (see KARLOWITZ, TREATY OF), which cost Turkey Hungary and other territories, and from which the disintegration of the Ottoman Empire may be dated.

Decline of the Empire. Economically, socially, and militarily, Turkey remained a medieval state, unaffected by the developments in the rest of Europe. Turkish domination over the northern part of Africa (except Tripoli and Egypt) was never well defined or effective, and the eastern border was inconstant, shifting according to frequent wars with Persia. Of the vassal princes, only the khans of CRIMEA were generally loyal. The sultans themselves had sunk into indolence and depravity. Until the ascension (1603) of Ahmad I, the succession to the throne was habitually contested by all the sons of the deceased sultan, and it was the patriotic duty of the victor to kill his rivals in order to restore order. Although this practice was barbarous, when it ceased other problems arose. The eldest male member of the family was recognized as the heir-designate, but to prevent threats to the sultan the imperial prince was denied any involvement in public affairs and was kept in luxurious imprisonment. When the prince finally ascended the throne, he was often alcoholic or lunatic. The actual rule was usually exercised by the grand viziers, many of whom were able men (notably those of the KÖPRÜLÜ family). However, palace intrigues tended to disrupt the administration and frequently led to the dismissal of the grand vizier, habitually announced by the presentation of the bowstring, with which the minister was supposed to commit suicide. The sultans themselves often were the creatures of the JANISSARIES, whose favor was purchased by large gifts at the ascension of a sultan. One of the most nefarious aspects of the court of Constantinople (known as the Seraglio and the Sublime Porte) was the all-pervading corruption and bribery that had been raised to a system of administration. The pashas and hospodars (governors) who administered the provinces and vassal states purchased their posts at exorbitant prices. They recovered their fortunes by extorting still larger sums from their subjects. The peasantry was thus reduced

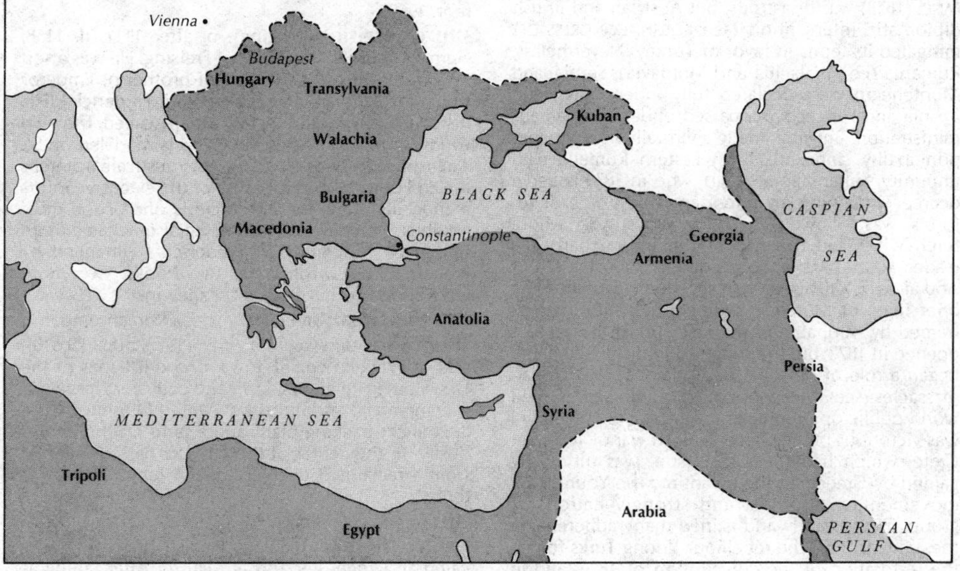

Ottoman Empire (c.1683)

to abject misery. Besides exacting taxes and tributes, the Ottoman government took little interest in its provinces. A positive feature in Ottoman administration was the religious toleration generally extended to all non-Muslims. According to the millet system, members of various religious minorities were grouped into communities (millets) that were autonomous in spiritual and in certain administrative and judicial matters. This, however, did not prevent occasional massacres and discriminatory fiscal practices. In Constantinople the Greeks and Armenians held a privileged status and were very influential in commerce and politics. Some of the highest administrative offices were held by Greek families, known as Phanariots (see under PHANAR). The despotic system of government was mitigated only by the observance of Muslim law. The breakup of the state gained impetus with the RUSSO-TURKISH WARS in the 18th cent. The treaties of Kuchuk-Kainarji (1774), Jassy (1792), and Bucharest (1812) cost Turkey the northern and northeastern coasts of the Black Sea. Egypt was only temporarily lost to Napoleon's army, but the Greek War of Independence and its sequels, the Russo-Turkish War of 1828–29 (see ADRIANOPLE, TREATY OF), and the war with MUHAMMAD ALI of Egypt resulted in the loss of Greece and Egypt, the protectorate of Russia over Moldavia and Walachia, and the semi-independence of Serbia. Drastic reforms were introduced in the late 18th and early 19th cent. by SELIM III and MAHMUD II, but they came too late. By the 19th cent. Turkey was known as the Sick Man of Europe.

Europe and the End of the Empire. The disintegration of the Ottoman Empire was regarded by the Western European statesmen as a threat to the general peace and became a major problem in European relations (see EASTERN QUESTION). The European powers had a large economic stake in the empire owing to the system of capitulations (privileges accorded to foreign diplomats and traders). Treaties of capitulation were signed with France (1535), England (1579), the Netherlands (1598), Russia (1768), and Austria (1780), and finally with Italy and Germany in the 19th cent. The Ottoman Empire thus gradually lost its economic independence. It was unable to control its own customs tariffs, and the resulting influx of foreign manufactured goods greatly harmed the native industries, which were still carried on by artisans. Equally disastrous were the influx of foreign capital and the huge loans obtained by the Turkish government from abroad, which brought Turkey under total financial dependency. The Ottoman Bank, founded in 1856, was the state bank, but it was in the hands of English and French capital. Public works and industrial exploitation were furthered by foreign capital, but the profits went, naturally, abroad. The Ottoman public debt reached staggering heights. Although Turkey was theoretically among the victors in the CRIMEAN WAR, it emerged from the war economically exhausted. The Congress of Paris (1856) recognized the independence and integrity of the Ottoman Empire, but this event marked the confirmation of the empire's dependency rather than of its rights as a European power. The rebellion (1875) of BOSNIA AND HERCEGOVINA precipitated the Russo-Turkish War of 1877–78, in which Turkey was defeated despite its surprisingly vigorous stand. The Treaty of SAN STEFANO (1878) was disastrous, but Austrian and British diplomatic intervention (see BERLIN, CONGRESS OF) mitigated its terms in favor of Turkey. Nevertheless, Rumania (i.e., Walachia and Moldavia), Serbia, and Montenegro were declared fully independent and Bosnia and Hercegovina passed under Austrian administration. Bulgaria, made a virtually independent principality, annexed (1885) Eastern Rumelia with impunity. Sultan ABD-AL MAJID, who in 1839 issued a decree containing an important body of civil reforms, was followed (1861) by ABD AL-AZIZ, whose reign witnessed the rise of the liberal party. Its leader, MIDHAT PASHA, succeeded in deposing (1876) Abd al-Aziz. ABD AL-HAMID II acceded (1876) after the brief reign of Murad V. A liberal constitution was framed by Midhat, and the first Turkish parliament opened in 1877, but the sultan soon dismissed it and began a rule of personal despotism. The Armenian massacres (see ARMENIA) of the late 19th cent. turned world public opinion against Turkey. Abd al-Hamid was victorious in the Greco-Turkish war of 1897, but Crete, which had been the issue, was ultimately gained by Greece. In the meantime the Young Turk movement, a reformist and strongly nationalist group, grew steadily and gained many adherents in the army. In 1908 the rebellious Young Turks forced the restoration of the constitution of 1876, and in 1909 the parliament deposed the sultan and put MUHAMMAD V on the throne. Taking advantage of the Young Turk revolution, Bulgaria proclaimed its full independence and Austria-Hungary annexed Bosnia and Hercegovina in 1908, while disorders broke out in Albania and Arabia. A war with Italy (1911–12) resulted in the loss of Libya; and in the two successive BALKAN WARS (1912–13), Turkey lost nearly its entire territory in Europe to Bulgaria, Serbia, Greece, and newly independent Albania. The nationalism of the Young Turks, whose leader ENVER PASHA gained virtual dictatorial power by a coup d'etat in 1913, antagonized the remaining minorities in the empire. The outbreak of World War I found Turkey solidly lined up with the Central Powers. From the time of the revolution of 1908–9, Germany had obtained increasing influence over Ottoman affairs. The BAGHDAD RAILWAY was built by German interests, and the Turkish armed forces were reorganized and trained by German officers. Russia was the first nation to declare war on Turkey in Nov., 1914. The United States merely severed (1917) relations with Turkey, but was not at war with the country. Turkish troops were successful against the Allies in the GALLIPOLI CAMPAIGN (1915), while fighting in the Caucasus and Mesopotamia was long indecisive. In 1917, however, British forces occupied Baghdad and Jerusalem. Arabia rose against Turkish rule, and in 1918, Turkish resistance collapsed both in Asia and Europe. An armistice was concluded in October, and the Ottoman Empire came to an end. The Treaty of Sèvres (see SÈVRES, TREATY OF) confirmed its dissolution. With the victory of the Turkish nationalists, who had refused to accept the peace terms and who overthrew the sultan in 1922, the history of modern Turkey began. See P. Wittek, *The Rise of The Ottoman Empire* (1938); S. Mardin, *The Genesis of Young Ottoman Thought* (1962); R. H. Davison, *Reform in the Ottoman Empire, 1856–1876* (1963); W. S. Vuchinich, *Ottoman Empire: Its Record and Legacy* (1965); W. Miller, *The Ottoman Empire and its Successors, 1801–1927* (rev. ed. 1936, repr. 1966); L. Cassels, *The Struggle for the Ottoman Empire, 1717–1740* (1968); Halil Inalcik, *The Ottoman Empire: The Classical Age, 1300–1600* (tr. 1973).

Ottonian art (ŏtō'nēən), art produced (c.900–1050) in the East Frankish kingdom of Germany known, after the emperors Otto (936–1002), as the Ottonian kingdom. Influenced by Byzantine and Carolingian forms, Ottonian basilicas, such as St. Michael at Hildesheim (1001–36), are simple, blocklike, symmetrical structures with wide aisles and vast expanses of bare wall. Ottonian religious sculpture is monumental in scale and executed with clear, round forms and highly expressive facial features. The wooden *Gero Crucifix* (969–76; Cologne Cathedral) reflects a humanitarian concern for the sufferings of Christ. Sophisticated relief bronzes were cast for the cathedral doors at Hildesheim (1015). Ottonian manuscript illumination was superbly developed; produced at several flourishing artistic centers, including Regensburg and Fulda, it combined Carolingian and Byzantine influences. Manuscripts such as the *Gospel Book of Otto II* are two-dimensional, figural, and linear, incorporating much gold leaf to emphasize the picture surface. See John Beckwith, *Early Medieval Art* (1964); Magnus Backes and Regine Dölling, *Art of the Dark Ages* (tr. 1969); Adolph Goldschmidt, *German Illumination* (2 vol., tr. 1928; repr. 1969).

Otto of Freising (frī'zĭng), b. after 1111, d. 1158, German chronicler, bishop of Freising. He was a son of Leopold III of Austria, a half brother of Emperor Conrad III, and an uncle of Emperor Frederick I. His history of the world to 1146, usually called *The Two Cities* (tr. by C. C. Mierow, 1928), is modeled on St. Augustine's *City of God* and pessimistically foretells the end of the world. Because of the extensive information included, the chronicle is one of the most notable of medieval histories. He also began a more optimistic biography of Frederick I (financed by Frederick) but wrote only two books; two more were added by his assistant, Rahewin.

Otto the Great: see OTTO I, Holy Roman emperor.

Ottumwa (ŏtŭm'wə, ō-), city (1970 pop. 29,610), seat of Wapello co., SE Iowa, on both banks of the Des Moines River, in a farm and coal area; inc. 1851. A commercial and industrial center, Ottumwa has a large meat-packing plant and a farm machinery industry. In the center of the city is a park developed from a reclaimed river bottom. A junior college is there.

Otus (ō'təs): see ALOADAE.

Otway, Thomas, 1652–85, English dramatist, educated at Winchester and at Oxford. After failing as an actor, he turned to writing for the stage. His first play, *Alcibiades,* was produced in 1675 with the actress Elizabeth Barry, and Otway fell passionately in love with her. His next play, the rhymed heroic tragedy *Don Carlos* (1672), was a huge success. In 1676 he produced an adaptation of Racine, called *Titus and Berenice,* and of Molière, called *The Cheats of Scapin.* After a brief career in the army, occasioned perhaps by his frustrated love for Mrs. Barry, he returned to the theater to write his two greatest plays—the blank-verse tragedies *The Orphan* (1680) and *Venice Preserved* (1682). Both plays are noted for their economy of plot and their simple yet powerful portrayal of the course of human passion. In all his plays Otway brought a sentimental pathos and romantic beauty to the formal manner of the Restoration heroic tragedy. He died in poverty at the age of 33. See biography by R. G. Ham (1931, repr. 1969); studies by A. M. Taylor (1950) and Edgar Schumacher (1924, repr. 1970).

Ötztal Alps (öts'täl), mountain group, in the Tyrol, W Austria, S of the Inn River. It rises to 12,380 ft (3,773 m) in the Wildspitze, the highest peak in the Tyrol. The village of Obergurgl is a skiing resort and a starting point for mountain climbing.

ouabain: see DIGITALIS.

Ouachita (wô'shĭtô"), river, c.600 mi (970 km) long, rising in the Ouachita Mts., W Ark. It flows east, southeast, and south through a rich cotton-producing region of S Arkansas and NE Louisiana and into the Red River system. It is joined by the Tensas River at Jonesville, La., below which it is called the Black River. Hot Springs, Ark., and Monroe, La., are the largest cities on the river. The river is navigable for shallow-draft vessels below Arkadelphia. Three dams in the river near Hot Springs—Remmel (completed 1925), Carpenter (1931), and Blakeley Mountain (1955)—impound respectively Lake Catherine, Lake Hamilton, and Lake Ouachita (63 sq mi/101 sq km, Arkansas' largest). The hydroelectric-power plant at Blakeley Mountain Dam has a 75,000-kw capacity. The lakes, part of a Federal flood-control project, are the center of a popular recreation area.

Ouachita Mountains, range of east-west ridges between the Arkansas and Red rivers, extending c.200 mi (320 km) from central Ark. into SE Okla. Magazine Mt. (c.2,800 ft/850 m high) is the tallest peak. The Ouachita Mts. are geologically considered offshoots of the Appalachian Mts. They are composed of strongly folded and faulted sedimentary rocks. There is a whetstone industry near Hot Springs, Ark. Mineral springs, lakes, and extensive wooded areas attract tourists. Several parts of the region have been set aside as public parks or forest reservations.

Ouagadougou or **Wagadugu** (both: wägədōō'-gōō), city (1970 est. pop. 115,500), capital of Upper Volta. It is the nation's largest city and its administrative, communications, and economic center. Ouagadougou is also the trade and distribution center for an agricultural region whose main crop is peanuts. The city's industry is limited to handicrafts and the processing of food and beverages. It has an international airport, rail connections with Abidjan, Ivory Coast, and road links with Niamey, Niger. Ouagadougou was founded in the late 11th cent. as the capital of a MOSSI empire ruled by the *moro naba* [ruler of the world]. It remained a center of Mossi power until 1896, when French forces captured it.

ouakari: see MONKEY.

Ouargla (wär'glä), town and oasis (1966 pop. 18,206), E Algeria. It is the administrative center of a well-watered oasis at the junction of several Saharan desert caravan routes. Ouargla lies in the heart of a palm grove numbering more than 500,000 productive trees. The Hassi Messaoud oil fields are nearby. The oasis was settled A.D. c.1000 by Muslims of the Kharijite sect, who were fleeing religious persecution. It became a small city-state which, from the 16th cent., paid tribute to the Turks. The town was conquered by French forces in 1853. It has a museum of Sahara desert life. An alternate spelling is Wargla.

Ouchy (ōōshē'), village, Vaud canton, W Switzerland, on the Lake of Geneva. It is the port and shorefront of LAUSANNE. Ouchy is a resort and was at times the residence of Shelley and Byron.

Oud, Jacobus Johannes Pieter (yäkō'bəs yōhä'nəs pē'tər out), 1890–1963, Dutch architect. Oud's interest in abstract painting led him to conceive of buildings composed in terms of pure planes. With several painters, including Mondrian and Theo van Doesburg, he became associated with the influential STIJL group, helping to establish its journal. From 1918 to 1933, Oud was official architect of Rotterdam and devoted himself to the production of extensive housing groups. Using reinforced concrete, he developed severely simplified forms in such dwellings as the workingmen's colony at Oud-Mathenesse (1921–22) and at the Hook of Holland (1926). His later works reveal a greater interest in ornamentation, e.g., the Shell Building at the Hague (1938) and the Children's House at Arnhem (1952–60). See study by K. Wiekart (tr. 1965).

Oudenaarde (ou″dənär'də), Fr. *Audenarde,* town (1970 pop. 26,615), East Flanders prov., W Belgium, on the Scheldt River. It is a textile center and a rail junction. At Oudenaarde, in 1708, the allies under Marlborough and Eugene of Savoy defeated the French under the dukes of Burgundy and of Vendôme in the War of the Spanish Succession. Oudenaarde has a Gothic town hall (16th cent.).

Oudh (oud), historic region of N central India, now part of the state of Uttar Pradesh. Its early history centers around the ancient kingdom of Kosala, which had Ajodhya as capital. The region passed under Gupta rule in the 4th cent. A.D. and later it became (11th–12th cent.) the center of the Rajput state of Kanauj. In the 13th cent. it was conquered by the legions of the Delhi Sultanate. It became (16th cent.) a province of the Mogul empire, and was subsequently governed by the nawabs of Oudh from their capitals of Faizabad (1724–75) and Lucknow (1775–1856). The annexation (1856) of Oudh as a British province was a major cause of the Indian Mutiny (1857–58). In 1877, Oudh was joined with the presidency of Agra to form the United Provinces, now the constituent state of Uttar Pradesh.

Oudh, town, India: see AJODHYA.

Oudinot, Nicolas Charles (nĕkôlä' shärl o͞odēnō'), 1767–1847, French soldier. A veteran of the French Revolutionary and Napoleonic Wars, he was created marshal of France (1809) and duke of Reggio (1810) by Napoleon I. He served as governor of Holland from 1810 to 1812. After Napoleon's first abdication Oudinot gave his support to Louis XVIII. He commanded the national guard during the HUNDRED DAYS, and for his support of Louis XVIII he was made a peer of France. Later, he participated in the Spanish expedition of 1823.

Oudjda: see OUJDA, Morocco.

Oudry, Jean Baptiste (zhäN bätēst' o͞odrē'), 1686–1755, French animal painter. A pupil of Largillière, he became court painter to Louis XV, recording the king's hunts in his paintings and tapestry designs. He was also director of the Beauvais and the Gobelin tapestry works. He is known for his illustrations of La Fontaine's *Fables.* His work, to be seen in museums throughout Europe, is characterized by the use of brilliant color. Typical of his work are *Ducks Resting in Sunshine* and *Dogs Guarding Dead Game* (Metropolitan Mus.)

Ouessant: see USHANT.

Ougrée (o͞ogrā'), city (1970 pop. 20,574), Liège prov., E Belgium, on the Meuse River, a suburb of Liège. It is a center of heavy industry.

Ouida (wē'də), pseud. of **Louise de la Ramée** (də lä rəmā'), 1839–1908, English novelist. She was a prolific writer of flamboyant, romantic tales, the best of which are *Under Two Flags* (1867), *Moths* (1880), and *In Maremma* (1882). Her stories for children include *Two Little Wooden Shoes* (1874), *Bimbi* (1882), and the well-known *Dog of Flanders* (1872).

Ouidah (wē'dä), town (1967 est. pop. 19,887), S Dahomey, a port on the Gulf of Guinea. Palm products, copra, coffee, and citrus fruit, which are processed nearby, are shipped from Ouidah. Fishing as well as curing and drying is carried on in the town. Ouidah is linked by rail with Cotonou and by road with Lomé, Togo. It was the capital of a small state founded about the 16th cent. From the early 17th cent., Portuguese, French, and Dutch traders were intermittently active at Ouidah, whose name was derived by Europeans from a nearby Portuguese fort called St. John of Adjuda. In the 18th and early 19th cent. Ouidah was an important export point for black African slaves. In the 1840s the French established a substantial trade with Ouidah, exchanging textiles, guns, and gunpowder for palm oil and ivory. The town was annexed by France in 1886. Ouidah has a Portuguese fort (1788) that contains a museum. The name of the town is also spelled Whydah.

Oujda or **Oudjda** (both: o͞ojdä'), Arab. *Ujda,* city (1970 est. pop. 160,000), NE Morocco, near the Algerian border. It is a railroad junction, agricultural market, and commercial center. It was occupied by the French in 1844, 1859, and 1907.

Oulu (ō'lo͞o), Swed. *Uleåborg,* city (1970 pop. 87,244), capital of Oulu prov., W central Finland, at the mouth of the Oulu River on the Gulf of Bothnia. It is a seaport and has metal shops, leather plants, and wood-processing and other industries. The city grew around a castle founded in 1590, was chartered in 1610, and became (19th cent.) an important commercial center. The Univ. of Oulu was founded in 1959.

ounce, in zoology: see LEOPARD.

ounce: see ENGLISH UNITS OF MEASUREMENT.

Our Father: see LORD'S PRAYER.

Ourique (ōrē'kə), town (1970 pop. 3,482), Beja dist., S Portugal, in Baixo Alentejo. Although tradition says Alfonso I defeated the Moors there in 1139, the battle of Ourique was actually fought at some undetermined place nearby.

Ouro Prêto (ō'ro͞o prā'to͞o) [Port.,=black gold], city (1970 pop. 46,166), Minas Gerais state, E Brazil. Founded as Vila Rica in the gold rush near the end of the 17th cent., it became a prosperous 18th-century mining town, a cultural center, and the chief seat of the abortive move for independence led by TIRADENTES. The city declined as the mines lost importance but remained the capital of Minas until 1897, when it was superseded by Belo Horizonte. Since 1933 the city has been a national historic site, preserving the 18th-century atmosphere of narrow, twisting, cobbled streets, the colonial mint and treasury, the old houses, the theater (oldest in South America), the governor's mansion, and the old churches, most notably the Church of São Francisco, decorated with the magnificent carvings of Aleijadinho. A mining school (est. 1875) is in Ouro Prêto.

Ourthe (o͝ort), river, c.100 mi (160 km) long, rising in the Ardennes mts., E Belgium, and flowing generally north to join the Meuse River at Liège. Its valley provides one of the few passages between the Meuse valley and the S Ardennes.

Ouse (o͞oz). **1** or **Great Ouse,** river, c.155 mi (250 km) long, rising in the Northampton Highlands, Northamptonshire, S central England. The Great Ouse flows generally NE past Bedford and Ely to the Wash near King's Lynn, Norfolk, and drains the E Midlands and the W Fens. It is navigable for two thirds of its length. **2** River, c.60 mi (100 km) long, formed by the confluence of the Ure and Swale rivers near Boroughbridge, North Yorkshire, NE England. It flows generally SE past York to join with the Trent River and form the Humber River. All of its chief tributaries rise in the Pennines. Navigable to York, the Ouse is an important commercial waterway.

Outer Barrier, series of sandy barrier islands or offshore bars, extending c.75 mi (120 km) along the south shore of Long Island, SE N.Y., from Rockaway Beach at the west to the east end of Shinnecock Bay and separating a series of lagoons (Great South Bay, Moriches Bay, and Shinnecock Bay) from the Atlantic Ocean. East Rockaway, Jones, Fire Island, Moriches, and Shinnecock inlets pierce the barrier, forming the narrow, sandy islands. The resort communities of Atlantic Beach, Long Beach, and Westhampton Beach; and Fire Island National Seashore, Jones Beach State Park and other recreational areas are found there. The sparsely settled and largely undeveloped low-lying islands suffer from wave erosion. During storms they are sometimes inundated and pierced.

Outer Hebrides, Scotland: see HEBRIDES, THE.

Outer Mongolia: see MONGOLIAN PEOPLE'S REPUBLIC.

outer space: see SPACE EXPLORATION.

outrigger, canoe-type vessel with a wood or bamboo float attached to the side of the craft and extending out over the water. The term *outrigger* also refers to the float itself. The craft is used throughout the South Pacific, although its greatest development has probably come in Sri Lanka (Ceylon), where traders may load up to 30 tons of cargo into a single vessel. Designed for speed and stability, the outrigger is usually propelled by sail or paddle. Certain sailing outriggers can attain speeds in excess of 20 knots (23 mi/37 km per hr). An outrigger is usually sailed with the float facing the wind, providing a counterweight against capsizing. It becomes dangerous, however, when the float is on the leeward side. To solve this problem, double outriggers, or canoes with an outrigger float on each side, are also used.

Ouwe, Hartmann von: see HARTMANN VON AUE.

ovalbumin: see ALBUMIN; GLYCOPROTEIN.

Ovando Candia, Alfredo (älfrā'thō ōvän'dō kän'dēä), 1918–, president of Bolivia (1965–66, 1969–70). Commander in chief of the Bolivian armed forces, he was co-president with René BARRIENTOS ORTUÑO in 1965. He served as interim president after Barrientos resigned the co-presidency early in 1966, then stepped aside when Barrientos was elected president in July. He personally directed the campaign against the Cuban-backed guerrillas under Ernesto "Che" GUEVARA. Ovando seized the presidency in Sept., 1969. As president, he nationalized the U.S. controlled oil industry. His regime was weakened by economic problems and by continual conflicts between left and right. He was ousted in Oct., 1970, but served as ambassador to Spain under President Juan José Torres. He retired from the army in 1971.

ovary, ductless gland of the female in which the ova (female reproductive cells) are produced. In vertebrate animals the ovary also secretes the sex hormones ESTROGEN and PROGESTERONE, which control the development of the sexual organs and the secondary sexual characteristics. The interaction between the GONADOTROPIC HORMONES from the PITUITARY GLAND and the sex hormones from the ovary controls the monthly cycle in humans of ovulation and MENSTRUATION. There are two ovaries in the human, held in place on each side of the uterus by a membrane; each ovary is about the size of an almond. About 500,000 immature eggs are present in the cortex of the ovary at birth. Starting at puberty, eggs mature successively, and one breaks through the ovarian wall about every 28 days in the process known as ovulation, which continues until menopause, or cessation of reproductive functioning in the female. After its release from the ovary, the ovum passes into the oviduct (fallopian tube) and into the uterus. If the ovum is fertilized by the sperm (male reproductive cell), pregnancy ensues (see REPRODUCTIVE SYSTEM). In flowering plants the part of the pistil containing the ova is called the ovary; the ripened ovary is the fruit.

ovenbird, common name for a member of the family Furnariidae, primitive passerine birds, which build elaborate, domed nests of clay or dig tunnels in the ground to lay their eggs. Ovenbirds are most common in South America, where most are forest dwellers, although a few species are found on the coast and some high in the Andes. The North American ovenbird is not a member of this group, but is a WARBLER. True ovenbirds are classified in the phylum CHORDATA, subphylum Vertebrata, class Aves, order Passeriformes, family Furnariidae.

Overbeck, Johann Friedrich (yō'hän frē'drĭkh ō'vərbĕk), 1789–1869, German religious painter. Expelled from the Vienna Academy because of his opposition to its classicism, he went to Rome and with Peter von Cornelius, Veit, Schadow-Godenhaus, and others, formed the group known as the NAZARENES. His first real successes were his frescoes for the Casa Bartholdy (now in Berlin) and for the Villa Massimo. Among his notable paintings are *Christ's Entry into Jerusalem* and *Christ's Agony in the Garden.* Overbeck sought to make his art serve religion. His influence was due more to the purity of his doctrine than to the power of his work, which is often lacking in pictorial appeal and in color.

Overbury, Sir Thomas, 1581–1613, English author and courtier. He was a friend and adviser to Robert Carr, an Oxford acquaintance. The two quarreled violently when Overbury disapproved of Carr's marriage to Frances Howard, divorced wife of the earl of Essex. Overbury's hostility was so marked that the Howard family brought pressure to bear, and James I had Overbury imprisoned in the Tower, where he was slowly poisoned. Carr and Frances Howard were convicted of his murder, but their lives were spared by the king. Overbury was a notable writer of brief informal essays describing a type or an individual. His best-known sketch in verse, *A Wife* (1614), outlines his conception of the ideal wife. See studies by W. J. Paylor (1936), W. L. McElwee (1952), and M. A. de Ford (1960).

Overijssel (ō″vərī'səl), province (1971 pop. 933,000), c.1,500 sq mi (3,885 sq km), E central Netherlands, between the IJsselmeer in the west and West Germany in the east. Zwolle is the capital; other cities include Almelo, Deventer, Enschede, Kampen, and Zutphen. The province is drained by the IJssel River and by several canals. It is generally sandy but supports extensive stock raising and dairying. The province's chief manufactures include textiles, clothing, and machinery. The lordship of Overijssel belonged in the Middle Ages to the bishop of Utrecht, but was sold (1527) to Emperor Charles V. It joined (1579) the Union of Utrecht and became one of the United Provs. of the Netherlands.

Overland, city (1970 pop. 24,949), St. Louis co., E Mo., a suburb of St. Louis; inc. 1939.

Overland Park, city (1970 pop. 76,034), Johnson co., NE Kansas, a residential suburb of Kansas City; inc. 1960.

Overland Trail, any of several trails of westward migration in the United States. The term is sometimes used to mean all the trails westward from the Missouri to the Pacific and sometimes for the central trails only. Particularly, the term has been applied to a southern alternate route of the OREGON TRAIL. It branched from the parent trail at the junction of the North Platte and South Platte rivers and followed the South Platte to present Julesburg, where it left the river and went overland to the North Platte, rejoining the parent trail east of Fort Laramie. The term is also particularly applied to a route to California that went west from Fort Bridger to the Great Salt Lake (thus duplicating in part the Mormon Trail), then on to Sutter's Fort in California; it was much used by California-bound immigrants. See Richard Dunlop, *Great Trails of the West* (1970); Herbert Eaton, *The Overland Trail to California in 1852* (1973).

Overlea, uninc. town (1970 pop. 13,086), Baltimore co., N Md., a residential suburb of Baltimore.

over-the-counter, method of buying and selling securities outside the organized stock exchange. Unlike an organized stock exchange, the over-the-counter market is composed of thousands of far-flung dealers who negotiate most transactions by telephone and telegraph. For the most part, dealers purchase stocks for their own account and sell them to customers at a markup over wholesale prices. Over-the-counter trading represents the single largest securities market in the United States today; it includes almost all U.S. government securities and municipal and corporate bonds, as well as most commercial bank and insurance company stocks. The National Association of Securities Dealers (established 1939) regulates the trade practices of more than 4,000 over-the-counter dealers. There is no fixed fee schedule for over-the-counter dealers, and only since the late 1940s have bid-and-asked prices been published regularly.

overture, instrumental musical composition written as an introduction to an opera, ballet, oratorio, musical, or play. The earliest Italian opera overtures were simply pieces of orchestral music and were called *sinfonie*. Jean Baptiste Lully standardized the French overture, using an opening section in pompous chordal style and dotted rhythms followed by a fugal section. This type of overture was much imitated, an example being the overture to Handel's *Messiah*. In some of the 17th-century Neapolitan operas, to some extent in Jean Philippe Rameau's operas and most notably in Gluck's, the overture began to foreshadow what was to come in the work's tunes. In many 19th-century operas and 20th-century musicals the overture is simply a potpourri of the work's tunes. The concert overture, a composition in one movement that may be in any of a variety of styles, arose in the 19th cent.; the overtures of Brahms, Mendelssohn, and Beethoven are outstanding.

Ovid (Publius Ovidius Naso) (ŏv′ĭd), 43 B.C.–A.D. 18, Latin poet, b. Sulmo (present-day Sulmona), in the Apennines. Although trained for the law, he preferred the company of the literary coterie at Rome. He enjoyed early and widespread fame as a poet and was known to the emperor Augustus. In A.D. 8, for no known reason, he was abruptly exiled to Tomis, a Black Sea outpost, S of the Danube, where he later died. The poems of Ovid fall into three groups—erotic poems, mythological poems, and poems of exile. His verse, with the exception of the *Metamorphoses* and a fragment (*Halieutica*) is in elegiacs, which are of unmatched perfection. The love poems include *Amores* [loves], 49 short poems, many of which extol the charms of the poet's mistress Corinna, probably a synthesis of several women; *Epistulae heroidum* [letters from heroines], an imaginary series written by ancient heroines to their absent lovers; *Ars amatoria* [art of love], didactic, in three books, with complete instructions on how to acquire and keep a lover. In the mythological category is the *Metamorphoses*, a masterpiece and perhaps Ovid's greatest work. Written in hexameters, it is a collection of myths linked together with such consummate skill that the whole is artistically harmonious. The *Fasti*, also a mythological poem, contains six books on the days of the year from January to June, giving the myths, legends, and notable events called to mind on each day. As a source for religious antiquities, it is especially valuable. The poems of exile include *Tristia* [sorrows], five books of short poems, conveying the poet's despair in his first five years of exile and his supplications for mercy, and the *Epistulae ex Ponto* [letters from the Black Sea], in four books, addressed to friends in Rome, showing somewhat abated poetic power. Ovid wrote poetry to give pleasure; therefore he is not for readers who insist upon moral lessons or lofty edification. No other Latin poet wrote so naturally in verse or with such sustained wit. Unsurpassed as a storyteller, he was also an expert on the ways of women. A major influence in European literature, Ovid was also a primary source of inspiration for the artists of the Renaissance and the baroque. The *Metamorphoses* was translated during this period by A. Golding (1567), George Sandys (1632), and John Dryden (1700). See modern verse translations by R. Humphries (1955 and 1958) and H. Gregory (1964); studies by L. P. Wilkinson (1955 and 1962), H. F. Fränkel (1945, repr. 1969), Brooks Otis (1966, repr. 1971), and J. W. Binns, ed. (1973).

oviduct: see FALLOPIAN TUBE.

Oviedo (ōvyā′thō), city (1970 pop. 154,117), capital of Oviedo prov. (coextensive with the region of Asturias) NW Spain, near the great mining district of the Cantabrian Mts. Oviedo is one of the most important industrial centers of Spain; ordnance, firearms, gunpowder, textiles, and many other products are manufactured. Founded c.760, Oviedo flourished in the 9th cent. as the capital of the Asturian kings but lost much of its importance after the capital was transferred to León early in the 10th cent. The cathedral, begun in 1388, contains the tombs of the Asturian kings and has a high square tower. Adjoining it is the Camara Santa (9th and 11th cent.), which housed the cathedral's store of sacred relics and treasures, famous over all Spain. The Univ. of Oviedo was founded in 1604. The city suffered severely during the revolt of the Asturian miners in 1934 and in a siege during the civil war. A new quarter has since been built on the southwest side of the city.

Ovoca: see AVOCA, river, Ireland.

ovolo (ō′vəlō″): see MOLDING.

ovum (ō′vəm), in biology, specialized plant or animal sex cell, also called the egg, or egg cell. It is the female sex cell, or female gamete; the male gamete is the SPERM. In higher animals the ovum differs from the sperm in that it is larger and is nonmotile, a smooth sphere or oval lacking the flagellum of the sperm. Like that of the sperm, its nucleus contains the chromosomes, which bear the hereditary material of the parent. A gamete, ovum or sperm, contains half the number of chromosomes found in the body cells of the parent, i.e., the gamete is haploid. In animals, ova contain stored food called the yolk, the amount of which varies in different species, depending on the length of time required for the embryo to become self-sufficient in obtaining nourishment outside the egg. Ova are produced in the OVARY of the female; they are formed from reproductive cells (called primordial germ cells) in a process called oogenesis. In this maturation process a germ cell builds up its food supply and then undergoes a series of cell divisions (called MEIOSIS), by which the number of chromosomes in the mature ovum is reduced by half. In oogenesis in animals only one of the four cells formed by meiotic division is functional. In this ovum all the yolk from the original cell is collected; the three other, yolkless, cells are called polar bodies and never develop further. Maturation also occurs in the formation of sperm (spermatogenesis), but in spermatogenesis, in contrast to oogenesis, all four of the cells formed by meiotic division are functional. The union of mature sperm and ovum, each bearing half the normal number of chromosomes, results in a single cell (the zygote) with a full number of chromosomes. The zygote undergoes a series of cell divisions (see MITOSIS) producing a multicellular EMBRYO and finally a mature individual. In all sexually reproducing animals the production and maturation of the ovum, its FERTILIZATION, and its early embryonic development are essentially identical. In plants that reproduce sexually the pattern is similar. In the mosses and ferns the egg cells are formed in special organs called archegonia and are fertilized by sperm that are commonly flagellated and motile like those of animals. In flowering plants the ovary is situated in the base of the PISTIL of the flower. After fertilization by a sperm contained in a pollen grain, the zygote develops into the embryo, contained in the seed. The term *ovum* is usually restricted to the single female sex cell, but the term *egg*, in its common use to indicate a bird's egg, refers to a more complex structure, only part of which is produced in the ovary of the bird. The ovum of such an egg is a cell swollen with yolk material. The rest of the egg—e.g., the jelly mass surrounding amphibian eggs, and the shell, membranes, and egg white, or albumen, of bird eggs—is not cellular and is secreted around the ovum as it passes down the oviduct. The development of a new individual from an unfertilized ovum is called PARTHENOGENESIS. The study of the ovum is included in the science of embryology.

Owain Gwynedd (ō′wän gwĭn′ĕth), d. 1170, prince of North Wales (1137–70). During the troubled reign of King Stephen of England, Owain and other Welsh princes were able to reoccupy much territory earlier wrested from them by the Anglo-Normans. Henry II of England invaded North Wales in 1157 and, though his expedition was a military failure, compelled Owain to do homage. In 1165, however, Owain inspired a general Welsh revolt, and the English army that attempted to quell it was forced to turn back because of bad weather and short supplies. Owain continued to expand his possessions and enjoyed independence until his death.

Owatonna (ōwətŏn′ə), city (1970 pop. 15,341), seat of Steele co., SE Minn.; inc. 1854. It has many diversified industries and is the home of numerous business firms. A bank designed by Louis Sullivan was built there in 1908. A state park is nearby.

Owen, John, 1616–83, English Puritan divine and theologian. In the civil war Owen supported the parliamentary cause. Oliver Cromwell took him as chaplain to Ireland and Scotland and had him appointed (1651) dean of Christ Church, Oxford, and vice chancellor (1652) of the university. He lost his posts after the Restoration. He was called to the presidency of Harvard, but he declined. Owen's writings include devotional literature and treatises against Arminianism and Socinianism. His works were edited by Thomas Russell (with a biography by William Orme, 28 vol., 1826) and by W. H. Goold (with a biography by Andrew Thomson, 24 vol., 1850–55). See James Moffatt, *The Golden Book of John Owen* (1904); Reginald Kirby, *Threefold Bond* (1936).

Owen, Sir Richard, 1804–92, English zoologist and comparative anatomist. He studied medicine in Edinburgh and in 1827 joined the staff of the Hunterian museum of the Royal College of Surgeons, where he was first Hunterian professor of comparative anatomy and physiology (1836–56) and also conservator. As superintendent (1856–83) of the natural history department of the British Museum, he organized its removal to South Kensington. Owen's contributions to science were many and important. Although he opposed the theory of evolution, he introduced the important concepts of homology and analogy of animal structure, using his extensive findings in paleontology. His monumental work was the *Descriptive and Illustrated Catalogue of the Physiological Series of Comparative Anatomy* (5 vol., 1833–40). See biography by his grandson R. S. Owen (1894, repr. 1970).

Owen, Robert, 1771–1858, British social reformer and socialist, pioneer in the cooperative movement. The son of a saddler, he had little formal education but was a zealous reader. At the age of 10 he began working in the textile business and by 1794 had become a successful cotton manufacturer in Manchester. In 1800 he moved to New Lanark, Scotland, where he had bought, with others, the mills of David Dale (whose daughter he married). There he reconstructed the community into a model industrial town with good housing and sanitation, nonprofit stores, schools, and excellent working conditions. Mill profits increased. The New Lanark experiment became famous in England and abroad, and Owen's ideas spread. He instigated the reform that resulted in the passage of the Factory Act of 1819—a watered down version of his proposals, but still a landmark in social reform. He also proposed the formation of self-sufficient cooperative agricultural-industrial communities. One such community, called NEW HARMONY, was established (1825) in Indiana but failed after numerous disagreements among its members. Professing a disbelief in religion (1817) and calling for the transformation of society rather than its reform (1820), Owen gradually lost much of his former upper-class support but was embraced by the working classes. After his return (1829) from the United States he became involved in the trade union movement and advocated the merging of unions with cooperative societies. Soon, however, the government took repressive action, and many workers responded by proclaiming the need for class struggle. Believing in the peaceful reordering of society, Owen ended his association with trade unionism and spent the last 25 years of his life writing and lecturing on his beliefs on education, marriage, and religion. Throughout his life Owen based his social programs on the idea that individual character is molded by environment and can be improved in a society based upon cooperation. Chief among his extensive writings are *New View of Society; or, Essays on the Formation of Character* (3 vol., 1813-14, *Report to the County of Lanark* (1821), and his autobiography (1857-58, repr. 1970). See biographies by Frank Podmore (1907, repr. 1971), G. D. H. Cole (3d ed. 1966), R. H. Harvey (1949), and M. I. Cole (1953, repr. 1969); studies by Arthur Morton (1962); John Butts, ed. (1971), and R. G. Garnett (1973).

Owen, Robert Dale, 1801-77, American social reformer, b. Scotland; son of Robert Owen. He studied at his father's New Lanark school and in Switzerland. In 1825 he went to NEW HARMONY, Ind. There he met Frances WRIGHT, with whom he established (1829) in New York City the *Free Enquirer*, a paper opposing organized religion and urging wide social changes. In this and in his *Moral Physiology* (1830) Owen publicly advocated birth control for the first time in the United States. He later became active in Indiana and U.S. politics. As a member of Congress (1843-47) he was instrumental in the founding of the Smithsonian Institution. When the Indiana constitution was revised in 1850, Owen secured an extension of property rights for married women and state provision for public schools. He served (1853-58) as U.S. minister to Naples, where he became a spiritualist. After his return to the United States he strongly advocated the emancipation of slaves and helped investigate the condition of the freedmen. His writings include *An Outline of the System of Education at New Lanark* (1824), *Hints on Public Architecture* (1849), *The Wrong of Slavery* (1864), *The Debatable Land between This World and the Next* (1872), a novel, a play, and numerous pamphlets. See the autobiography of his early years, *Threading My Way* (1874); biographies by R. W. Leopold (1940, repr. 1969) and Eleanor Pancoast and A. E. Lincoln (1940).

Owen, Ruth Bryan: see ROHDE, RUTH BRYAN.

Owen, Wilfred, 1893-1918, English poet, b. Oswestry, Shropshire. He served as a company commander in the Artist's Rifles during World War I and was killed in France on Nov. 4, 1918, one week before the armistice. Owen's poetic theme, the horror and pity of war, is set forth in strong verse that transfigured traditional meters and diction. Nine of these poems are the basis of the text of Benjamin Britten's *War Requiem* (1962). Although Owen had worked on poems while living in France between 1913 and 1918, he never published. While on sick leave from the front in a Scottish hospital, he met the poet Sigfried SASSOON, who encouraged him to publish in magazines. He did, but these efforts were cut short by his return to the front. Two years after his death Sassoon arranged for the publication of 24 poems (1920). See his collected poems (1931, 1963, and 1973); collected letters, ed. by his brother, Harold, and John Bell (1967); biography by Arthur Orrmont (1972); study by G. M. White (1969).

Owen Falls, on the Victoria Nile, SE Uganda, near Jinja, site of Owen Falls Dam. The dam, which submerged the waterfall, controls the discharge from Lake Victoria (c.2 mi/3.2 km upstream) into the Nile basin and supplies hydroelectricity to Uganda and Kenya.

Owen Glendower (glĕn'dou"ər, glĕndou'ər), 1359?-1416?, Welsh national leader. A scion of the princes of Powys, he was also claimant through his mother to the lands of Rhys ap Gruffydd; he was thus one of the most powerful lords in Wales. After studying law in London and fighting in the English army, he returned to Wales. In 1400 he emerged as the leader of a revolt against English rule. The immediate occasion was a quarrel with his neighbor Lord Grey of Ruthin, an English border baron; but deeper causes of the national upheaval that followed lay in Welsh antagonism toward their English overlords, Welsh resentment of unjust English laws and administration, and widespread economic discontent. Owen, proclaimed (1400) prince of Wales by his followers, kept the revolt against HENRY IV of England burning for years. In 1402 he captured Sir Edmund de MORTIMER, whose nephew the 5th earl of March had a claim to the English throne, and secured his support. He then allied himself with the discontented Percy family (Sir Henry PERCY; his father, Henry Percy, 1st earl of NORTHUMBERLAND; and Thomas Percy, earl of WORCESTER). The defeat of the Percys at the battle of Shrewsbury in 1403 (in which Owen did not take part), was only a temporary setback for the Welsh leader. The following year he displayed his skill as a daring guerrilla fighter by capturing the key castles of Aberystwyth and Harlech. He was recognized by Charles VI of France, with whom he made (1404) an alliance, and summoned (1405) his own parliament. However, the failure of an expedition from France on his behalf (1405-6) weakened him, and the recapture by the English of Aberystwyth (1408) and Harlech (1409) left him powerless. He disappeared into the mountains and refused to take advantage of the general amnesty offered by Henry V. See biographies by J. E. Lloyd (1931) and Glanmor Williams (1966).

Owens, Jesse, 1913-, U.S. track star, b. Alabama. He is also called John Cleveland Owens, although his original name is said to be simply J. C. Owens. After his family moved to Cleveland he excelled at track and field events in high school. He won the broad-jump titles at the outdoor (1933-34) and indoor (1934-35) meets of the National Amateur Athletic Union, and while on the track team of Ohio State Univ., Owens broke (1935-36) several world records at broad jumping, hurdle racing, and flat racing. At the 1936 Olympic games in Berlin, Jesse Owens, a Negro on the U.S. team, astounded the world and upset Hitler's "Aryan" theories by equaling the world mark (10.3 sec) in the 100-meter race, by breaking world records in the 200-meter race (20.7 sec) and in the broad jump (26 ft 5⁵⁄₁₆ in./8.07 m) and by winning also (along with Ralph Metcalfe) the 400-meter relay race. His records lasted for more than 20 years. Owens later participated in professional exhibitions and in various business enterprises. He was secretary of the Illinois Athletic commission until 1955 and later became active in the Illinois youth commission. In 1970 he published the semiautobiographical *Blackthink: My Life as Black Man and White Man* .

Owens, river, c.120 mi (190 km) long, rising in the Sierra Nevada, E Calif., SE of Yosemite National Park and flowing southeast, nominally to enter Owens Lake (now dry), near Mt. Whitney. At a point c.45 mi (70 km) NW of Owens Lake, an aqueduct diverts the river's water to Los Angeles; water that is not diverted flows on to Owens Lake, where it evaporates.

Owensboro, city (1970 pop. 50,329), seat of Daviess co., W Ky., on the Ohio River; settled c.1800, inc. as a city 1866. It is an important tobacco market and a shipping point for a farm and oil region. Its varied manufactures include radio tubes, whiskey, chemicals, electrical equipment, steel, cigars, and furniture. Owensboro is the seat of Kentucky Wesleyan College and Brescia College.

Owen Sound, city (1971 pop. 18,469), SE Ont., Canada, on Owen Sound. It is a port and railroad terminal in a farming region, and it has large grain elevators. There are printing and other industries.

Owen Stanley Range, mountain chain, c.300 mi (480 km) long, SE Papua New Guinea, on New Guinea island. It rises to Mt. Victoria (13,363 ft/4,073 m). The region, drained by several small rivers, is largely jungle.

OWI: see OFFICE OF WAR INFORMATION.

owl, common name for nocturnal birds of prey found on all continents. Owls superficially resemble short-necked hawks, except that their eyes are directed forward and are surrounded by disks of radiating feathers. This peculiarity lends them an appearance of studious intelligence, and the owl has long been used as a symbol of wisdom. Although owls are able to see in daylight, their eyes are especially adapted to seeing in partial darkness, and most owls spend the day sleeping in caves, hollow trees, and other secluded places. Their plumage is so soft and fluffy that they are almost noiseless in flight. The order (Strigiformes) of owls is divided into two families; the barn owls (family Tytonidae), with heart-shaped faces, are one, and the typical owls (family Strigidae) compose the other. Owls feed on rodents, toads and frogs, insects, and small birds; like the hawks, they regurgitate pellets of indigestible matter. The elf and saw-whet owls of the SW United States and the pygmy owl of the Old World are only 6 in. (15 cm) long, while the eagle owl of Eurasia, the hawk owl of Australia, the great horned owl of North America (*Bubo virginianus*), and the snowy and great gray owls of the Arctic reach 2 ft (61 cm) with wingspreads of 4 to 5 ft (1.2 to 1.5 m). Many owls usurp the deserted nests of other birds, especially hawks; the burrowing owl of the New World lives in deserted prairie-dog burrows or digs its own. The barred owl has a familiar four-hoot call; the screech owl, misnamed for a similar European species, has a mournful descending cry. The long-eared owl is found in North America; the short-eared owl is ubiquitous. The tawny owl is common in England. Owls are classified in the phylum CHORDATA, subphylum Vertebrata, class Aves, order Strigiformes, families Tytonidae and Strigidae. See J. A. Burton, ed., *Owls of the World* (1974).

Owl and the Nightingale, The, Middle English poem written probably by Nicholas de Guildford of Dorsetshire about the beginning of the 13th cent. Written in 2,000 lines of octosyllabic couplets, it describes a debate between the sober owl and the merry nightingale as to their respective merits. The allegory may represent the argument between asceticism and pleasure, philosophy and art, or the older didactic poetry and the newer secular love poetry. Conversational diction, humor, and dramatic touches make this poem one of the best of the period.

Owo (ō'wō), city (1969 est. pop. 93,000), S Nigeria. It is primarily a farming and commercial city, located in an area producing cacao and timber. Owo was the capital of a YORUBA state of the same name that was founded in the 14th cent. Owo came under British protection in 1893.

Owosso (ōwŏs'ō), city (1970 pop. 17,179), Shiawassee co., S Mich., on the Shiawassee River; inc. 1859. Thomas E. Dewey was born in the city.

Owyhee (ōwī'ē, -hē), river, c.300 mi (480 km) long, rising in several branches in SW Idaho, N Nev., and SE Oregon and flowing N across NE Oregon to the Snake River; named in 1826 for two Hawaiian employees of the Hudson Bay Company who were killed by Indians. After gold and silver were discovered in the region in 1863, there were many mining camps along the river. The Owyhee reclamation project of the U.S. Bureau of Reclamation irrigates c.118,000 acres (47,750 hectares) W of the Snake River. The project is contiguous and closely associated with the BOISE PROJECT. Owyhee Dam forms a reservoir 52 mi (84 km) long.

ox: see CATTLE.

oxalic acid (ŏksăl'ĭk) or **ethanedioic acid** (ĕth"-āndīō'ĭk), HO_2CCO_2H, a colorless, crystalline organic carboxylic acid that melts at 189°C with sublimation. Oxalic acid and oxalate salts are poisonous. Oxalic acid is found in many plants, e.g., sorrel and rhubarb, usually as its calcium or potassium salts. Oxalic acid is the only possible compound in which two CARBOXYL GROUPS are joined directly; for this reason oxalic acid is one of the strongest organic acids. Unlike other carboxylic acids (except FORMIC ACID), it is readily oxidized; this makes it useful as a reducing agent for photography, bleaching, and ink removal. Oxalic acid is usually prepared by heating sodium formate with sodium hydroxide to form sodium oxalate, which is converted to calcium oxalate and treated with sulfuric acid to obtain free oxalic acid.

oxalis (ŏk'səlĭs) or **wood sorrel,** any species of the plant genus *Oxalis*. Most of the cultivated kinds are tropical herbs used as window plants. The leaves are usually cloverlike and respond to darkness with "sleep" movements by folding back their leaflets. Several species grow wild in North America, including the white wood sorrel (*O. acetosella*), widely distributed in the north temperate zone and one of the plants identified as the SHAMROCK. This and, to a lesser extent, other species have long been used for salads and greens because of their pleasantly acid taste; these species contain OXALIC ACID. Although species of *Oxalis* are called sorrels, the genus is unrelated to the true sorrel, or dock (genus *Rumex*), of the buckwheat family. Oxalis is classified in the division MAGNOLIOPHYTA, class Magnoliopsida, order Sapindales, family Oxalidaceae.

oxbow lake, stagnant lake formed in an abandoned riverbed when a river cuts through the neck of one of its meanders, or loops, characteristic of the course of rivers of low current. The cutoff meander is rapidly closed at both ends by river silt deposits. Without outlet and usually without inlet, the oxbow lake often becomes a marsh or swamp and is finally filled in through siltation and the growth of vegetation.

Oxelösund (ŏŏk"səlösŭnd'), city (1970 pop. 15,085), Södermanland co., SE Sweden, a port on the Baltic Sea; chartered 1950. It is an industrial center, a resort, and a major export point for iron ore. Manufactures include iron and steel and glassware.

Oxenstierna, Count Axel Gustafsson, 1583-1654, Swedish statesman. Named chancellor in 1612, he was the actual administrator of Sweden because GUSTAVUS II was continually occupied with foreign campaigns. Oxenstierna also organized the conquered territories, skillfully managed financial affairs, and aided Gustavus's wars by his diplomacy. In 1629 he arranged a favorable truce with Poland, freeing the army for the campaign in Germany. Habitually cautious, he opposed Sweden's entry into the THIRTY YEARS WAR, but he acceded to the king's wishes and devoted his energies to keeping supplies and troops at the command of the king. After the death (1632) of Gustavus II at Lützen, the diet granted Oxenstierna full control of Swedish affairs in Germany. At a congress at Heilbronn (1633), he managed to weld the German Protestant princes into some semblance of unity. The Swedish defeat at Nördlingen (1634) forced Oxenstierna to solicit direct assistance from France. From Cardinal Richelieu he secured enlarged subsidies and the open entry (1635) of France into the conflict. As the dominant member of the council of regency in the minority of CHRISTINA and virtual ruler of Sweden (1632–44), he followed a cautious foreign policy and distinguished himself by his great program of reforms, including commercial, administrative, and social improvements. He was the author of the constitution of 1634, which centralized administration. He planned and directed the war against Denmark (1643–45) and brought it to a successful conclusion in the Peace of Bromsebro, by which Sweden gained several Danish provinces. Clashes between Oxenstierna and the young queen led to the decline of his power. He himself took no part in the negotiations of the Peace of Westphalia (1648), but his son was one of the Swedish representatives. Oxenstierna opposed the abdication of Christina in 1654, but for the short remainder of his life he served Charles X well in attempts to rehabilitate Sweden financially.

oxeye, name for several plants, e.g., the oxeye DAISY and BLACK-EYED SUSAN, but particularly for two genera: *Heliopsis,* native to North America, and *Buphthalmum,* native to Europe and W Asia but cultivated elsewhere. Both are perennials of the family Compositae (COMPOSITE family) and are grown as ornamentals for their showy yellow heads. Oxeyes are classified in the division MAGNOLIOPHYTA, class Magnoliopsida, order Asterales, family Compositae.

Oxford, Edward de Vere, 17th **earl of,** 1550–1604, English poet, b. Castle Heddingham, Essex, educated at Queens' and St. John's colleges, Cambridge. He traveled in Italy, acted in and produced plays, and was one of the court circle of writers. On the theory that he wrote Shakespeare's plays, see studies by E. T. Clark (1937) and L. P. Bénézet (1958). See his poems (ed. by J. T. Looney, 1921).

Oxford, Robert Harley, 1st **earl of:** see HARLEY, ROBERT, 1ST EARL OF OXFORD.

Oxford, county borough (1971 pop. 108,564), county town of Oxfordshire, S central England. In addition to its importance as the seat of OXFORD UNIVERSITY, Oxford has significant industries, including the manufacture of automobiles and steel products. A trading town and frontier fort, it was raided by Danes in the 10th and 11th cent. By the 12th cent. it was the site of a castle, an abbey, and the university. It had foundations of several orders, including the Dominicans and the Gray Friars. During the 13th cent. there were frequent conflicts between the town and the university in which the university, with the support of the church and the king, was usually victorious. During the civil wars Oxford was the royalist headquarters; it was besieged but not damaged by the parliamentarians. Among its famous historic buildings (apart from the colleges) are the Radcliffe Camera (1737), the Observatory (1772), and Sheldonian Theatre (designed by Christopher Wren); the churches of St. Mary the Virgin (13th cent.) and St. Michael (11th cent.); and several old inns. The chapel (12th cent.) of Christ Church College is also the cathedral church of the city. The ASHMOLEAN MUSEUM and the BODLEIAN LIBRARY are notable. Besides the university, Ruskin College (1899), and Magdalen College School (c.1480), a public school, are in Oxford.

Oxford. 1 Town (1970 pop. 10,345), Worcester co., S Mass.; settled 1687 by French Protestants, inc. 1693. It is chiefly residential, with some light manufacturing. Clara Barton was born in the town. **2** City (1970 pop. 13,846), seat of Lafayette co., N central Miss.; inc. 1837. It is principally a university town, the seat of the Univ. of Mississippi ("Ole Miss"). Household appliances, motors, clothing, and lumber products are manufactured in the city. Oxford was the home of the novelist William Faulkner and the setting for some of his works. The Mary Buie Museum there houses one of the largest doll collections in the United States. An annual pilgrimage takes tourists to the many antebellum buildings in the area. A national forest is nearby. In 1962, Oxford was the scene of rioting and conflict when the first black student was enrolled in the university. **3** Village (1970 pop. 15,868), Butler co., SW Ohio, near the Ind. line, in a farm area; laid out 1810, inc. 1830. It is a residential college town, the seat of Miami Univ. and The Western College. There are many old houses. Nearby are a state park and a pioneer farm (1835; now a museum).

Oxford, Provisions of: see PROVISIONS OF OXFORD.

Oxford and Asquith, Herbert Henry Asquith, 1st **earl of,** 1852–1928, British statesman. Of a middle-class family, he attended Oxford, became a barrister in London in 1876, and was elected to Parliament as a Liberal in 1886. He attracted attention as junior counsel for Charles PARNELL before the Parnell Commission of 1889 and was home secretary (1892–95) in William Gladstone's last ministry. After the outbreak (1899) of the South African War, Asquith was associated with the so-called Liberal imperialists, who favored the war and proposed that the Liberals adopt a generally more aggressive foreign policy. His powerful championship of the traditional Liberal free-trade policy was an important factor in bringing the party back to power in 1905. He was chancellor of the exchequer under Sir Henry Campbell-Bannerman and succeeded him as prime minister in 1908. In the next six years Asquith's government put through an advanced program of social welfare legislation, including old age pensions (1908) and unemployment insurance (1911). It also embarked on a program of naval expansion to match Germany's. To finance both programs, Asquith's chancellor of the exchequer, David LLOYD GEORGE, introduced (1909) a radical budget that was rejected by the House of Lords. This caused a constitutional crisis. After two general elections (Jan. and Dec., 1910), Asquith secured passage of the Parliament Act of 1911, which stripped the House of Lords of its veto power (see PARLIAMENT). In 1912, Asquith renewed Liberal efforts to establish Irish HOME RULE, a course that provoked a violent reaction from Protestants in Ulster, who were firmly supported by the Conservative party. Ireland appeared to be on the verge of civil war but the outbreak (1914) of World War I forestalled it. Having brought Great Britain into the war, Asquith proved a less than successful wartime leader. In 1915 he formed a coalition government with the Conservatives, but conflicts within the cabinet, continued reverses in the field, and a virulent campaign waged against him by the newspapers of Lord NORTHCLIFFE made his position increasingly difficult. At the end of 1916 a complicated intrigue on the part of Lloyd George and the Conservative leaders resulted in Asquith's resignation. He remained leader of the declining LIBERAL PARTY until 1926, having been raised to the peerage in 1925. See his *Occasional Addresses, 1893–1916* (1918, repr. 1969), *Speeches* (1927); biographies by J. A. Spender and Cyril Asquith (2 vol., 1932) and Roy Jenkins (1964, repr. 1967); Winston Churchill, *Great Contemporaries* (rev. ed. 1938, repr. 1959). Asquith's second wife, **Margot (Tennant) Asquith, countess of Oxford and Asquith,** 1864–1945, whom he married in 1894, was prominent in London society and noted for her wit. Her frank autobiography (1920–22) created a minor sensation. She wrote a novel and several volumes of personal reminiscence, including *Places and Persons* (1925), *More Memories* (1933), and *Off the Record* (1944).

Oxford Group: see BUCHMAN, FRANK N. D.

Oxford movement, religious movement begun in 1833 by Anglican clergymen at Oxford Univ. to renew the Church of England (see ENGLAND, CHURCH OF) by reviving certain Roman Catholic doctrines and rituals. This attempt to stir the Established Church into new life arose among a group of spiritual leaders in Oriel College, Oxford. Prominent among them were John Henry NEWMAN, John KEBLE, Richard Hurrell Froude, Charles Marriott, and later Edward Bouverie PUSEY and Richard William CHURCH. In July of 1833, Keble preached a sermon, *On the National Apostasy,* which Newman held to be the actual opening of the movement. A few days later a meeting was held at Hadleigh, Suffolk, in the rectory house of Hugh James Rose, "the Cambridge originator of the Oxford movement," and a resolution was made to uphold "the apostolic succession and the integrity of the Prayer-Book." Newman, who felt that extensive popularizing was more effective than organization, immediately launched a series of pamphlets, *Tracts for the Times.* Later, Keble and Pusey joined him, and their group became known as the Tractarians. To the tracts was added *The Library of the Father of the Holy Catholic Church,* translations from patristic writings, to encourage a return to the beliefs and customs of the first centuries of the church. The Tractarians preached Anglicanism as a via media between Roman Catholicism and evangelicalism. Newman became the acknowledged leader in answering critics and advocating the restoration of practices abandoned in the Church of England since the Reformation. When the Tractarians attacked Renn Dickson Hampden, a follower of Richard Whately, the liberals, led by Dr. Thomas Arnold, opposed them openly. After 1834, Pusey was influential in the movement, adding force and dignity to the controversial manner and emphasizing the observance of ritual. Opponents dubbed the movement "Puseyism." Within the movement itself, a Romanizing party developed under William George WARD, Frederick William FABER and others, and it was partly to counter them that Newman wrote his celebrated *Tract 90* on the Thirty-nine Articles, which aroused a storm of opposition and brought the series to an end (1841). The movement lost valuable supporters to Roman Catholicism, including Newman, and Henry Edward MANNING. The movement to Roman Catholicism was opposed by Pusey, under whose leadership the majority remained loyal to the Church of England. Under Pusey the movement advanced beyond its academic beginning and became an effective vehicle for ecclesiastical and, later, social reform. The Oxford movement stressed higher standards of worship, and particularly in the later period many changes were made in the church services, e.g., beautification of churches, intonation of services, the wearing of vestments, and emphasis on hymn singing. Every effort to revive ceremonial customs aroused a storm of excitement and opposition leading at times to rioting. This violence culminated in 1860 at St. George's-in-the East, London. Because attention was centered upon the forms of expression in the churches, especially between 1857 and 1871, the followers of the Oxford movement became known as ritualists. Anglo-Catholicism was another name for the movement as its supporters tried to secure in the Established Church recognition of ancient Catholic liturgy and doctrine. The changes desired by the ritualists caused much public agitation and litigation between 1850 and 1890. In 1874 the Public Worship Regulation Act was passed by Parliament, avowedly to "put down Ritualism." On the part of churchmen the struggle was fought in resistance to secular authority in spiritual affairs. No Anglo-Catholic could recognize the mandates of a purely parliamentary court, such as the judicial committee of the privy council, which, although it lacked spiritual authority, was the supreme court of ecclesiastical appeal. The last imprisonment for refusal to admit its authority was made in 1887, after which such resistance was respected as reasonable. Among the means for renewing deep and personal devotion to the teachings of the Bible, Keble, Newman, and especially Pusey, sought to develop religious community life. Sisterhoods were founded, the first in 1845. They became centers of charitable and social work of importance. Communities for men were fewer and expanded less rapidly. In later years the followers of the movement have placed increasing emphasis on the responsibility of Christians in the life of society and have given much attention to social problems. This social concern led to the foundation of the Christian Social Union in 1889 under Brooke Foss Westcott and Henry Scott Holland. The Oxford movement has exerted a great influence, doctrinally, spiritually, and liturgically not only on the Church of England, but also throughout the Anglican Communion. See R. W. Church, *The Oxford Movement* (1891, rev. ed. 1970, ed. by Geoffrey Best and John Clive); S. L. Ollard, *A Short History of the Oxford Movement* (1915); C. P. S. Clarke, *The Oxford Movement and After* (1932); Geoffrey Faber, *Oxford Apostles* (1934, repr. 1954); Owen Chadwick, *The Mind of the Oxford Movement* (1960); E. R. Fairweather, *The Oxford Movement* (1964); M. R. O'Connell, *The Oxford Conspirators* (1969); Raymond Chapman, *Faith and Revolt* (1970). For studies of the rise of the religious orders, see A. M. Allchin, *The Silent Rebellion* (1958) and P. F. Anson, *The Call of the Cloister* (1955). On the Christian Social Union and similar movements, see M. B. Reckitt, *Maurice to Temple* (1947).

Oxford sheep, relatively large-bodied, hornless breed developed in England using crosses between Hampshire and Cotswold sheep. The breed was selected for size and productivity. It has not had widespread popularity in the United States.

Oxfordshire or **Oxon,** county (1971 pop. 380,814), 749 sq mi (1,940 sq km), S central England. The county town is OXFORD. The terrain is generally flat except for a branch of the Chiltern Hills in the southeast. The county is drained by the Thames River (or Isis as it is sometimes locally called) and its affluents, the Windrush, the Evenlode, the Cherwell, and the Thame. The chief occupation is farming (wheat, barley, and oats), with some dairying and sheep raising. Ironstone and limestone are found. Oxford is the industrial center (automobiles and steel products). In the Middle Ages Oxfordshire was a part of the Anglo-Saxon kingdom of MERCIA. During the English civil war it was a stronghold of royalist resistance. Near Woodstock, rich in historical associations, is BLENHEIM PARK. In 1974, Oxfordshire was reorganized as a nonmetropolitan county.

Oxford University, at Oxford, England. It had its beginnings in the early 12th cent. in groups of young scholars who gathered around the learned monks and teachers of the town. Although University College and Balliol had been founded earlier, the system of residential colleges began with Merton College (1264). Consisting of a corporation of scholars and masters, having its own statutes, property, buildings, and customs, the medieval college maintained almost complete autonomy within the university, as it does today. The present colleges, with their dates of founding, include University (1249), Balliol (1263), Merton (1264), St. Edmund Hall (1269), Exeter (1314), Oriel (1326), Queen's (1340), New (1379), Lincoln (1427), All Souls (1437), Magdalen (1458; pronounced môd'lĭn), Brasenose (1509; pronounced brāz'nōz), Corpus Christi (1516), Christ Church (1546), Trinity (1554), St. John's (1555), Jesus (1571), Wadham (1610, charter received 1612), Pembroke (1624), Worcester (1714), Keble (1871), Hertford (1874), and St. Antony's (1948, charter received 1953). The women's colleges are Lady Margaret Hall (1878), Somerville (1879), St. Hugh's (1886), St. Hilda's (1893), and St. Anne's (1952). Nuffield (1937, charter received 1958) is a postgraduate college of men and women for research in social studies. Women first received degrees in 1920, but they were not admitted to full university status until 1959. Oxford's faculties include theology, law, medicine, literae humaniores, modern history, English language and literature, modern languages, Oriental studies, mathematics, physical sciences, music, psychological studies, and anthropology and geography. The university was a leading center of learning throughout the Middle Ages; such scholars as Roger Bacon, Duns Scotus, John Wyclif, and Bishop Grosseteste were associated with it. It has maintained an outstanding reputation especially in the classics, in theology, and in political science. The Oxford Union is a world famous debating society. The Ashmolean Museum (see under ASHMOLE, ELIAS) and the BODLEIAN LIBRARY are notable features of the university. A large sum was left for scholarships for foreign students by Cecil RHODES. Instruction at Oxford is by lectures and the tutorial system, by which each student writes a weekly paper on a prescribed subject and discusses it with his tutor. Until 1948 the university had two representatives in Parliament. The Oxford Univ. Press was established by 1478. See C. E. Mallet, *History of the University of Oxford* (3 vol., 1924–27, repr. 1968); Felix Markham, *Oxford* (1967); J. P. V. D. Balsdon, *Oxford Now and Then* (1970).

oxidases, in biochemistry, enzymes that catalyze reactions that directly involve molecular oxygen (see OXIDATION AND REDUCTION). CYTOCHROMES are oxidases with iron-containing groups with the structure of heme (see COENZYME); they are involved in cellular RESPIRATION and PHOSPHORYLATION. Copper-containing oxidases catalyze a variety of biological oxidations including oxidation of catechol to quinone.

oxidation and reduction, complementary chemical reactions characterized by the loss or gain, respectively, of one or more electrons by an atom or molecule. Originally the term *oxidation* was used to refer to a reaction in which oxygen combined with an element or compound, e.g., the reaction of magnesium with oxygen to form magnesium oxide or the combination of carbon monoxide with oxygen to form carbon dioxide. Similarly, *reduction* referred to a decrease in the amount of oxygen in a substance or its complete removal, e.g., the reaction of cupric oxide and hydrogen to form copper and water. When an atom or molecule combines with oxygen, it tends to give up electrons to the oxygen in forming a CHEMICAL BOND. Similarly, when it loses oxygen, it tends to gain electrons. Such changes are now described in terms of changes in the oxidation number, or oxidation state, of the atom or molecule (see VALENCE). Thus, oxidation has come to be defined as a loss of electrons or an increase in oxidation number, while reduction is defined as a gain of electrons or a decrease in oxidation number, whether or not oxygen itself is actually involved in the reaction. In the formation of magnesium oxide from magnesium and oxygen, the magnesium atoms have lost two electrons, or the oxidation number has increased from zero to +2. This is also true when magnesium reacts with chlorine to form magnesium chloride. In solution, ferrous iron (oxidation number +2) may be oxidized to ferric iron (oxidation number +3) by the loss of an electron. In the reduction of cupric oxide the oxidation number of copper has changed from +2 to zero by the gain of two electrons. The two processes, oxidation and reduction, occur simultaneously and in chemically equivalent quantities. In the formation of magnesium chloride, for every magnesium atom oxidized by a loss of two electrons, two chlorine atoms are reduced by a gain of one electron each. Oxidation-reduction reactions, called also redox reactions, are most simply balanced in the form of chemical equations by arranging the quantities of the substances involved so that the number of electrons lost by one substance is equaled by the number gained by another substance. In such reactions, the substance losing electrons (undergoing oxidation) is said to be an electron donor, or reductant, since its lost electrons are given to and reduce the other substance. Conversely, the substance that is gaining electrons (undergoing reduction) is said to be an electron acceptor, or oxidant. Common reductants (substances readily oxidized) are the active metals, hydrogen, hydrogen sulfide, carbon, carbon monoxide, and sulfurous acid. Common oxidants (substances readily reduced) include the halogens (especially fluorine and chlorine), oxygen, ozone, potassium permanganate, potassium dichromate, nitric acid, and concentrated sulfuric acid. Some substances are capable of acting either as reductants or as oxidants, e.g., hydrogen peroxide and nitrous acid. The CORROSION of metals is a naturally occurring redox reaction. Industrially, many redox reactions are of great importance: COMBUSTION of fuels; ELECTROLYSIS (oxidation occurs at the anode and reduction at the cathode); and metallurgical processes in which free metals are obtained from their ores.

oxidation number or **oxidation state:** see VALENCE.

oxidative phosphorylation: see PHOSPHORYLATION.

oxide, chemical compound containing OXYGEN and one other chemical ELEMENT. Oxides are widely and abundantly distributed in nature. Water is the oxide of hydrogen. Silicon dioxide is the major component of sand and quartz. Carbon dioxide is given off during respiration by animals and plants. Carbon monoxide, sulfur dioxide, and oxides of nitrogen are among the waste gases of gasoline-burning internal combustion engines. Nitrous oxide is an oxide of nitrogen often called laughing gas. Many of the metals form oxides. Some metal oxides, e.g., those of iron, aluminum, tin, and zinc, are important as ores. Litharge and red lead are lead oxides used as pigments in paint. A number of elements, e.g., arsenic, carbon, manganese, nitrogen, phosphorus, and sulfur, combine with oxygen to form more than one oxide. The inert gases do not form oxides. The halogens and inactive metals do not combine directly with oxygen, but their oxides can be formed by indirect methods. Oxides are usually named according to the number of oxygen atoms present in a molecule, e.g., monoxide (or simply oxide), dioxide, trioxide. In a molecule of carbon monoxide, CO, for example, there is one oxygen atom; in carbon dioxide, CO_2, there are two; and in phosphorus pentoxide, P_2O_5, there are five. Oxides are commonly classified as acidic or basic oxides or anhydrides. Sulfur trioxide is an acid anhydride; it reacts with water to form sulfuric acid. Phosphorus pentoxide reacts vigorously with water to form phosphoric acid. Many metal oxides react with water to form alkaline hydroxides; e.g., calcium oxide (lime) reacts with water to form calcium hydroxide (slaked lime). Some metal oxides do not react with water but are basic in that they react with an acid to form a salt and water. Others exhibit AMPHOTERISM; i.e., they react with both acids and bases. Still others are neutral and nonreactive.

Oxnam, Garfield Bromley, 1891–1963, American Methodist bishop, b. Sonora, Calif., grad. Univ. of Southern California (B.A., 1913) and Boston Univ., 1915. He was ordained in 1916. After teaching at the Univ. of Southern California (1919–23) and at Boston Univ. (1927–28), he was (1928–36) president of DePauw Univ. In 1936 he was elected bishop of his denomination. After serving as resident bishop in the Omaha, Boston, and New York areas, he was assigned to the Washington (D.C.) area in 1952. From 1948 to 1954 he was president of the World Council of Churches. A liberal on social problems, he wrote *Preaching in a Revolutionary Age* (1944), *I Protest* (1954), and *A Testament of Faith* (1958). See biography by R. G. Smith (1953).

Oxnard, city (1970 pop. 71,225), Ventura co., S Calif., on the Pacific coast; inc. 1903. Its economy, formerly based on agriculture, mining, and nearby military bases, has been broadened to include large industrial and commercial operations. A navy missile range is at nearby Point Mugu. Oxnard is the gateway for visitors to the Santa Barbara Islands and to Los Padres National Forest.

Oxon, England: see OXFORDSHIRE.

oxpecker, common name for an African starling of the genus *Buphagus.* Aslo known as tickbirds, oxpeckers have very short legs and sharp claws, which aid them in perching on the backs of large mammals, both wild and domesticated. They are paid no heed to by the animal host, and only the elephant seems not to tolerate them. Oxpeckers use their broad, thick, laterally flattened beaks to pick at and feed on skin parasites such as ticks and embedded larvae. They also pick at scabs, often opening and enlarging wounds, and probably obtain their main nourishment from the blood from these wounds rather than from the ticks. Although these birds are valuable from the standpoint of ridding domesticated animals of ticks, they also feed on tick-free game and become debilitating parasites themselves. Nevertheless, they protect wild game from danger by setting up rattling cries, which alert the animals to the presence of predators. There are two species of oxpeckers, both about 9 in. (23 cm) long, with brown plumage and lacking distinctive markings. The slightly larger yellow-billed oxpecker (*B. africanus*), found from Senegal to Ethiopia and Natal, has a yellow, red-tipped bill, while that of the purely African red-billed oxpecker (*B. erythrorhychus*) is totally red. Oxpeckers are so highly adapted to life on their hosts that even courtship behavior and copulation occur upon the host animal's back. The hair of the animal is used to line the bird's nest, built usually in a tree by the yellow-billed oxpecker or a rock-hole by the red-billed. Females lay three to five white to pale blue, brown-spotted eggs per clutch. Oxpeckers are classified in the phylum CHORDATA, subphylum Vertebrata, class Aves, order Passeriformes, family Sturnidae.

Oxus: see AMU DARYA.

oxyacetylene torch (ŏk″sēəsĕt'əlēn), tool that mixes and burns oxygen and acetylene to produce an extremely hot flame. This torch can be used for cutting steel and for welding iron and various other metals. The temperature of the flame can reach as high as 6300°F (3480°C).

oxygen, gaseous chemical element; symbol O; at. no. 8; at. wt. 15.9994; m.p. −218.4°C; b.p. −183°C; density 1.429 grams per liter at STP; valence −2. Oxygen is a colorless, odorless, tasteless gas; it is the first member of group VIa of the PERIODIC TABLE. It is denser than air and only slightly soluble in water. A poor conductor of heat and electricity, oxygen supports combustion but does not burn. Normal atmospheric oxygen is a diatomic gas (O_2) with molecular weight 31.9988. OZONE is a highly reactive triatomic (O_3) allotrope of oxygen (see ALLOTROPY). When cooled below its boiling point oxygen becomes a pale blue liquid; when cooled still further the liquid solidifies, retaining its color. Oxygen is paramagnetic in its solid, liquid, and gaseous forms. Although eight isotopes of oxygen are known, atmospheric oxygen is a mixture of the three isotopes with mass numbers 16, 17, and 18. Oxygen is extremely active chemically, forming compounds with almost all of the elements except the inert gases. The common reaction in which it unites with another substance is called oxidation (see OXIDATION AND REDUCTION). The burning of substances in air is rapid oxidation or COMBUSTION. The RESPIRATION of animals and plants is a form of oxidation essential to the liberation of the energy stored in such food materials as carbohydrates and fats. The rusting of iron and the corrosion of many metals results from the action of the oxygen in the air. Oxygen unites directly with a number of other elements to form OXIDES. It is a constituent of many acids and of hydroxides, carbohydrates, proteins, fats and oils, alcohols, cellulose, and numerous other compounds such as the carbonates, chlorates, nitrates and nitrites, phosphates and phosphites, and sulphates and sulphites. Oxygen is the most abundant element on earth, constituting about half of the total material of its surface. Most of this oxygen is combined in the form of silicates, oxides and water. It makes up about 90% of water, two thirds of the human body and one fifth by volume of air. It is found in the sun, and has a role in the stellar carbon cycle (see NUCLEOSYNTHESIS). Oxygen is prepared for commercial use by the liquefaction and fractional distillation of air and more expensively by the electrolysis of water; it is stored and transported under high pressure in steel cylinders. It can also be obtained by heating certain of its compounds, such as barium peroxide, potassium chlorate, and the red oxide of mercury. Oxygen is of great importance in the chemical and the iron and steel industries. Its major use is in steel production, for example in the BESSEMER PROCESS. The OXYACETYLENE TORCH is another important industrial application. Oxygen is utilized in medicine in the treatment of respiratory diseases and is mixed with other gases for respiration in submarines, high-flying aircraft, and spacecraft. Liquid oxygen is used as an oxidizer in the fuel systems of large rockets. The existence and properties of oxygen had been noted by many scientists before the announcement of its isolation by Priestley in 1774. Scheele had also succeeded in preparing oxygen from a number of substances, but publication of his findings was delayed until after that of Priestley's. As a result, Priestley and Scheele are credited with the discovery of the element independently. The fact that the gas is a component of the atmosphere was finally and definitely established by Lavoisier a few years later. In 1929, W. F. Giaque and H. L. Johnston announced the discovery of two isotopes of oxygen, of mass numbers 17 and 18. Oxygen was formerly the official standard for the ATOMIC WEIGHTS of elements. The chemists used natural oxygen, a mixture of three isotopes, to which the value of 16 was assigned while the physicists assigned the value of 16 specifically to the oxygen isotope 16. In 1961 carbon-12 replaced oxygen as the standard.

oxygen tent, device used to maintain a patient in an oxygen-rich environment. The oxygen tent is composed of a clear plastic sheet suspended over the bed and tucked beneath the mattress to provide an almost airtight compartment. The oxygen supply and temperature are controlled by means of gauges. Zippers on the sides of the tent provide access to the patient. The device is particularly useful in the treatment of heart and lung disorders that limit the body's supply of oxygen and thus necessitate a higher concentration of the gas than is normally present in the air.

oxy group (ŏk'sē), in chemistry, FUNCTIONAL GROUP that consists of an oxygen atom joined by single bonds to two separate ALKYL GROUPS or ARYL GROUPS. It is the functional group of ethers.

Oxyrhynchus (ŏk″sĭrĭng'kəs), excavation site, Upper Egypt, W of the Nile and now the village of Behnesa. Some of the largest finds of papyruses have been made (1896–97, 1906–7) there. The papyruses, ranging in date from the 1st cent. B.C. to the 10th cent. A.D., are partly Ptolemaic, but chiefly Roman and Byzantine. Most of the inscriptions are in Greek. Many of the papyruses contain lost literary works by famous Greek authors as well as many theological and legal texts and documents. The town that was here is known only from the papyruses, which tell of a Greek colony first and a Christian monastic center later.

oxytocin (ŏksĭtō'sĭn), HORMONE released from the posterior lobe of the PITUITARY GLAND that facilitates uterine contractions and the milk-ejection reflex. The structure of oxytocin, a cyclic PEPTIDE consisting of nine amino acids, was determined in 1953; in that same year it was confirmed that a synthetic peptide of the reported structure had biological activity. There is evidence that both oxytocin and ANTIDIURETIC HORMONE (two very similar peptides) are biosynthesized in the hypothalamus of the brain and travel down neuronal axons to the posterior pituitary, where they accumulate prior to release. Stimuli that elicit the release of oxytocin include childbirth, suckling, and coitus; the uterine contractions that result may facilitate either childbirth or the ascent of spermatozoa through the fallopian tubes. The milk-ejection response occurs only in females immediately after childbirth. The role of oxytocin in males is unknown.

Oyama, Iwao (ēwä'ō ō'yämä), 1842–1916, Japanese field marshal. A native of Satsuma and a follower of Okubo Toshimichi, he worked to overthrow the Tokugawa shogunate and restore the emperor. Made acting war minister in 1876, he was instrumental in putting down the Satsuma rebellion of 1877. In the First Sino-Japanese War he captured Port Arthur and Weihaiwei, and in the Russo-Japanese War he was commander in Manchuria. As war minister in several cabinets and as chief of staff he upheld the autocratic power of the oligarchs (see GENRO) against democratic encroachments. Oyama was given the rank of prince for his military accomplishments, and on his death he was awarded a state funeral.

Oyo (ôyô'), city (1969 est. pop. 130,000), SW Nigeria. It is primarily a farming town, producing tobacco, yams, and cassava. Traditional artisans make textiles and leather goods and carve utensils from shells of the calabash gourd. Oyo was founded c.1835 as the successor of Old Oyo (Katunga), the capital of the YORUBA empire of Oyo, which was destroyed in the Yoruba civil wars of the early 19th cent. Oyo is about 100 mi (161 km) S of Old Oyo. The city came under British protection in 1893.

oyster, edible BIVALVE mollusk found in beds in shallow, warm waters of all oceans. The shell is made up of two valves, the upper one flat and the lower convex, with variable outlines and a rough outer surface. Since the oyster spends most of its life (except for the free-swimming larval stage) attached—having fused its valve with a sticky substance to a substratum of shells, rocks, or roots—the foot is rudimentary. In some species the sexes are separate and the eggs are laid and fertilized in the water; in others the animal is hermaphroditic and the eggs are retained with the shell. Only a small proportion of the millions of eggs laid survive. Large numbers of the free-swimming larvae, called veligers, are consumed by fish and other animals. After the oyster becomes sessile, it is victimized by oyster drills, starfish, and other enemies. Most species are too small for food, but the American, or common, oyster reaches a length of 2 to 6 in. (5–15 cm). These oysters are harvested in artificial beds on both coasts of the United States: on the Atlantic especially in the regions of the Delaware and Chesapeake bays and in the waters off Long Island, in the Gulf Coast off Louisiana, in the Pacific off the state of Washington. Prepared beds are usually seeded with veligers or young sessile oysters called spats. In warm waters they mature in 1½ years; in cooler waters the period of growth is about 4 to 5 years. They are usually transplanted several times before harvest to enhance their food supply and stimulate growth. The wing and the pearl oysters are widespread in warmer seas; there is one eastern and one western species of each in American waters. The great pearl oyster, from which the PEARL is obtained, is a large (12-in./30.5-cm) tropical species. Oysters are classified in the phylum MOLLUSCA, class Pelecypoda, order Filibranchia, family Ostreidae.

Oyster Bay, uninc. area (1970 pop. 6,822) of the Town of Oyster Bay, Nassau co., SE N.Y., on N Long Island, on Long Island Sound; settled 1653. It is chiefly residential. Nearby is Theodore Roosevelt's estate, "Sagamore Hill," which was made a national shrine in 1953 and a national historic site in 1963. Also of interest in Oyster Bay are several 18th-century homes and the Theodore Roosevelt memorial bird sanctuary (owned by the National Audubon Society), which adjoins Roosevelt's grave.

oyster catcher, common name for members of the family Haematopodidae, ploverlike shorebirds, cosmopolitan in distribution. Their distinctive red bills are long, blunt, and flattened, efficient for catching and opening the oysters, mussels, and clams on which they feed. They are noisy birds, larger (21 in./52 cm) and more brightly marked than most other shorebirds. Species found in America are the black, European, and Frazer's oyster catchers of the genus *Haematopus.* Oyster catchers nest in shallow, debris-lined cavities in the sand. They lay two to four eggs per clutch, and both male and female share incubation duties. Oyster catchers are classified in the phylum CHORDATA, subphylum Vertebrata, class Aves, order Charadriiformes, family Haematopodidae.

oyster plant, name for several plants, among them the SALSIFY.

Ozaki, Yukio (yo͞o'kyō ōzä'kē), 1859–1954, Japanese statesman, the outstanding liberal of modern Japan. A newspaper editor, he helped Okuma form the Kaishinto (Progressive party) in 1881. He was a member of the Seiyukai in 1900 and its leader in 1913; he later joined (1921) the Kenseikai. Ozaki was elected to every diet from 1890 to 1952. A severe critic of the oligarchs, he fought for universal manhood suffrage, opposed Japanese militarist policy in China and Manchuria, and after 1945 urged reconstruction of Japan on a democratic basis. He was jailed during both World Wars. His strong ties to the West were symbolized by his famed gift of cherry trees to Washington, D.C., and by his many trips abroad.

Ozanam, Antoine Frédéric (äNtwän' frādārēk' ōzänäm'), 1813–53, French Roman Catholic scholar. In 1831 he first achieved notice with his pamphlet against the Saint-Simonians. In Paris (1839), where he went to study, he met Chateaubriand, Lacordaire, Ampère, and other leaders of Catholic thought. In 1833 he helped found a charitable organization that was to become the worldwide St. Vincent de Paul Society. A scholar of law and literature, he was also one of the chief leaders of his time in Catholic social theory. His works, which had great influence in Germany and Italy, cover a wide range of material, mostly on medieval literature, thought, and history; his notable history of the Franks emphasizes the role of the church in transmitting Roman civilization to the barbarian cultures of the West.

Ozark (ō'zärk), city (1970 pop. 13,555), seat of Dale co., SE Ala., in a timber and farm area; settled 1820, inc. 1870. Textiles, wearing apparel, and farm equipment are made. An institute of aviation technology is located there, and U.S. Fort Rucker, the army's aviation center, is nearby.

Ozark Mountains, Mo.: see OZARKS, THE.

Ozark National Scenic Riverways, 72,101 acres (29,179 hectares), along the Current and Jacks Fork rivers, SE Mo.; est. 1964 as the first national riverway. Many springs flow into the rivers; Big Springs is one of the largest single-outlet springs in the United States. Many large caves with interesting dripstone formations are found along the rivers. Forests cover about 75% of the riverways. Wildlife and fish are abundant in the area.

Ozarks, Lake of the, man-made lake, 93 sq mi (241 sq km), c.130 mi (210 km) long, central Mo., largest reservoir in the state; created by the impounding of the Osage River by Bagnell Dam. Its irregular 1,375-mi (2,213-km) shoreline is included in Lake of the Ozarks State Park, the largest recreational area in Missouri.

Ozarks, the, or **Ozark Plateau,** upland region, actually a dissected plateau, c.50,000 sq mi (129,500 sq km), chiefly in S Mo. and N Ark., but partly in Oklahoma and Kansas, between the Arkansas and Missouri rivers. The Ozarks, which rise from the surrounding plains, are locally referred to as mountains. Composed of igneous rock overlain by limestone and dolomite, the ancient land form has been worn down by erosion. Summits (knobs) are found wherever there is a resistant rock outcrop; the Boston Mts. are the highest and most rugged section, with several peaks more than 2,000 ft (610 m) high. The Ozarks are rich in lead and zinc, and there are good fruit-growing areas. Subsistence farming and household crafts are found in the more isolated regions. The Ozarks have several large lakes that were created by dams across the White and Black rivers; the dams generate electricity. The scenic Ozarks, with forests, streams, and mineral springs, are a popular tourist region.

Ozawa, Seiji (sä'jē ōzä'wä), 1935–, Japanese conductor. A graduate of the Toho School of Music, Ozawa won competitions in Europe and the United States and, as a result, was hired by the New York Philharmonic as an assistant conductor in 1961. He was director of the Toronto Symphony Orchestra from 1965 to 1970 and in 1970 was named director of the San Francisco Symphony Orchestra. Ozawa is the first Japanese conductor to gain recognition in the West. Interested in performing unfamiliar works, he is noted for the clarity, sensitivity, and precision of his technique. He has performed as guest conductor with the world's major orchestras. In 1973 he was named music director of the Boston Symphony Orchestra.

Ózd (ōzd), city (1970 pop. 38,637), NE Hungary, near the Czechoslovak border. It is an industrial center with ironworks, steelworks, and lignite mines.

Ozem (ō'zĕm). **1** Brother of David. 1 Chron. 2.15. **2** Descendant of Hezron. 1 Chron. 2.25.

Ozenfant, Amédée (ämādā' ōzäNfäN'), 1886–1966, French art theorist and painter. He criticized the cubists after 1912 for creating a merely decorative art form. Ozenfant advocated a disciplined geometry known as purism. With Le Corbusier he wrote *Après le cubisme* (1918) and *La peinture moderne* (1927). His painting *The Vases* is in the Museum of Modern Art, New York City. Ozenfant's book *Foundations of Modern Art* (1931) is well-known.

Ozias (ōzī'əs) [Gr., = Heb. Uzziah]. **1** Same as UZZIAH **1.** **2** Ruler of Bethulia at the time of Judith. Judith 6–10; 13–16.

Ozni (ŏz′nī), same as EZBON **1.**

ozocerite (ōzō′kərīt, -sərīt, ō″zōsēr′īt) or **ozokerite** (ōzō′kərīt) [Gr.,=wax smelling], waxy solid substance. It occurs in various parts of the world in rock deposits. In order to extract ozocerite, the rock is crushed and then treated with hot water, which melts the ozocerite. When refined it appears on the market as ceresin, a colorless waxy solid that is employed as a substitute for beeswax and also as an adulterant. Ozocerite is used in the manufacture of candles and of various composite hard-rubber substitutes, for making polishes, and in electrotyping. Chemically, it is a mixture of hydrocarbons; it is classed as a crude paraffin and called, consequently, mineral wax. Ozocerite ranges in color from white or colorless (when pure) to yellow, brown, or black and sometimes greenish.

ozone (ō′zōn), an allotropic form of the chemical element OXYGEN (see ALLOTROPY). Pure ozone is an unstable, faintly bluish gas with a characteristic fresh, penetrating odor. The gas has a density of 2.144 grams per liter at STP (see separate article). Below its boiling point (−112°C) ozone is a dark blue liquid; below its melting point (−193°C) it is a blue-black crystalline solid. Ozone is triatomic oxygen, O_3, and has a molecular weight of 47.9982 atomic mass units (amu). It is the most chemically active form of oxygen. It is formed in the ozone layer of the stratosphere by the action of solar ultraviolet light on oxygen. Although it is only present in this layer to an extent of about 10 parts per million, ozone is important because its formation prevents most ultraviolet and other high-energy radiation, which is harmful to life, from penetrating to the earth's surface. Ultraviolet light is absorbed when its strikes an ozone molecule; the molecule is split into atomic and diatomic oxygen: O_3+ ultraviolet light $\rightarrow O+O_2$. Later, in the presence of a catalyst, the atomic and diatomic oxygen reunite to form ozone. Some environmental scientists fear that certain man-made pollutants (e.g., nitric oxide, NO) may interfere with this delicate balance of reactions that maintains the ozone's concentration, possibly leading to a drastic depletion of stratospheric ozone. Ozone is also formed when an electric discharge passes through air; for example, it is formed by lightning and by some electric motors and generators. Ozone is produced commercially by passing dry air between two concentric-tube or plate electrodes connected to an alternating high voltage; this is called the silent electric discharge method. Ozone is used commercially as a disinfectant and decontaminant for air and water, and as a bleaching agent for waxes, oils, and other organic compounds. The major commercial use is in the production by ozonolysis of azelaic acid (used in making plastics); it is also used in the synthesis of cortisone and certain synthetic sex hormones. Ozonization, the reaction of ozone with the double or triple bonds of unsaturated organic molecules, is useful in determining the structure of organic compounds.

ozonosphere (ōzō′nəsfēr″): see ATMOSPHERE.

P

P, 16th letter of the ALPHABET, representing the voiceless bilabial stop. It corresponds to Greek pi, but in form it looks like Greek rho (see R). For the technical use of P in higher criticism, see OLD TESTAMENT. In chemistry P is the symbol of the element PHOSPHORUS.

Pa, chemical symbol of the element PROTACTINIUM.

Paarai (pā'ārā, pāərā'ī), same as NAARAI.

Paardeberg (pär'dəbərg, -bĕrk), historic location, Orange Free State, Republic of South Africa. In Feb., 1900, during the South African War, Gen. Piet Cronje and his Boer troops were forced to surrender to the British army at Paardeberg.

Paarl (pärl), town (1970 pop. 48,585), Cape prov., S South Africa, on the Berg River. It is the center of South Africa's wine industry and of a tobacco-growing region. Canned foods, jams, textiles, and cigarettes are important products. Paarl was founded in 1687 by Dutch farmers, and in 1690 French Huguenots settled there. It is the site of a teachers college and of a commercial college.

Paasikivi, Juho Kusti (yōō'hō kōōs'tē pä'sĭkĭv"ē), 1870–1956, president of Finland (1946–56). He entered the Finnish parliament in 1907 and was minister of finance in 1908–9. After Finland proclaimed full independence from the Soviet Union, Paasikivi was briefly premier (1918), and in 1920 he negotiated the peace treaty with the USSR at Dorpat. In subsequent years he devoted himself mainly to his banking firm. He took part in the unsuccessful negotiations that preceded the Finnish-Russian War of 1939–40 and headed the Finnish peace delegation to the USSR in 1940. He apparently won favor with the Soviet government and with Stalin, and he opposed the Finnish declaration of war on the Soviet Union in 1941. Paasikivi headed the Finnish delegation at the armistice negotiations in 1944. In 1945 he was elected president of Finland after Mannerheim's resignation and took office in 1946. In foreign policy he avoided friction with the USSR. Reelected in 1950 by an anti-Communist coalition, he resigned in 1956 because of poor health and was succeeded as president by Urho Kekkonen.

Pabianice (päbyänē'tsĕ), city (1970 pop. 62,275), central Poland. A textile center, it also has industries producing chemicals, machine tools, and electric bulbs. Founded in the 13th cent., the city passed to Prussia in 1793 and to Russia in 1815. It reverted to Poland in 1919. Its industrial development began about 1830 when the first textile mills were established in the city. Pabianice has a small castle and a 16th-century church.

Pablos, Juan (hwän pä'blōs), d. 1561?, printer in Spanish America. Pablos printed in Mexico City the first book known to have been printed in the Western Hemisphere. It was a religious manual, *Breve y más compendiosa doctrina christiana en lengua mexicana y castellana* [a brief and greatly abridged Christian doctrine in the Mexican and Castilian languages]. It appeared in 1539, a full century before the appearance of the *Bay Psalm Book,* the first book printed within the present boundaries of the United States. Pablos was an Italian, a native of Brescia in Lombardy, and went to Mexico in 1539 as the agent of Juan Cromberger, a printer of Seville. He continued to print books with the Cromberger mark after Cromberger's death (1540), but in 1548 he began to print in his own name and continued to do so until 1560. See also MARTÍN, ESTEBAN.

Pabna (pŭb'nä), town (1961 est. pop. 40,800), W Bangladesh, on the Ichamati River. It is noted for handloom products and hosiery. The Hindu temple of Jor Bangla and a college affiliated with Rajshahi Univ. are located in Pabna.

Paca, William (pā'kə, păk'ə), 1740–99, political leader in the American Revolution, signer of the Declaration of Independence, b. near Abingdon, Md. A lawyer and Maryland legislator, he served (1774–79) in the Continental Congress. Paca was governor of Maryland from 1782 to 1785 and was also a judge of state courts and of a U.S. district court.

Pachacamac (pä"chäkämäk'), ruins of a walled Indian city, Peru, about 25 mi (40 km) SE of Lima near the present-day village of La Mamacoma. Built before the time of the Incas in one of the irrigable valleys of the coastal desert, Pachacamac is noted for its great pyramidal temple and for the remains of polychrome frescoes adorning its adobe walls. Culturally and chronologically it is related to CHANCAY and other centers of the Cuismancu empire. At the time of the Spanish conquest it was a major Inca shrine; Pizarro is said to have destroyed a shrine and taken away a quantity of silver and gold in 1523.

Pacheco, Francisco (fränthēs'kō pächā'kō), c.1564–1654, Spanish portrait and religious painter. Although fine examples of his work are in the galleries of Madrid and Seville, he is best known as the instructor and father-in-law of Velázquez and as the author of *Arte de la pintura* (1649), which contains interesting data on his great contemporaries.

Pacheco Areco, Jorge (hôr'hā pächā'kō ärā'kō), 1920–, president of Uruguay (1967–72). A newspaper editor, he became vice president of Uruguay in March, 1967, and succeeded to the presidency upon the death (Dec., 1967) of President Oscar Gestido. Facing staggering problems of inflation, domestic unrest, and guerrilla terrorism, he declared a state of emergency, instituted wage and price controls, prohibited strikes, and imposed a press censorship. He steadfastly refused to negotiate with the TUPAMAROS, and waged a vigorous military campaign against them. In 1971, after ignoring the legislature's repeal of the state of emergency, he was impeached by the lower house; the senate was still considering the impeachment bill when Pacheco ran for reelection (Nov., 1971) along with a proposed constitutional amendment to permit a president to succeed himself. The voters rejected the amendment, and Juan M. Bordaberry succeeded to the presidency (1972). Pacheco was appointed ambassador to Spain.

Pacher, Michael (mĭkh'äĕl pä'khər), c.1435–1498, German religious painter and probably a wood carver, a native of the Tyrol. He painted figures reminiscent of the art of Mantegna, whose work Pacher must have seen on a trip to N Italy. His few known works are chiefly altarpieces, composed on a monumental scale and distinguished for their beauty of workmanship. His masterpiece is the great altarpiece in the village church of St. Wolfgang, Salzkammergut, Austria, executed c.1480 and consisting of a beautifully carved centerpiece in late Gothic style with four wings, painted with scenes from the lives of Christ and St. Wolfgang. See study by Nicolò Rasmo (tr. 1971).

Pachmann, Vladimir de (vlədyē'mĭr də päkh'män), 1848–1933, Russian pianist, studied with his father, a violinist, and at the Vienna Conservatory. He devoted himself almost exclusively to playing Chopin's smaller piano pieces, and he was known as a colorful, eccentric performer.

Pachuca de Soto (pächōō'kä thā sō'tō), city (1970 pop. 84,543), capital of Hidalgo state, central Mexico, at the head of a ravine surrounded by foothills of the Sierra Madre Oriental. Pachuca, one of Mexico's oldest and most famous mining towns, was founded in 1534 on the site of an ancient Toltec city. The region is extremely rich in ore deposits, especially silver, which has been mined since Aztec times. Pachuca is also a cultural and educational center, with a university, a meteorological observatory, and a noted school of mining and metallurgy. Landmarks include a 16th-century convent and church and La Caja, built in 1670 as a storehouse to hold the royal tribute.

Pachysandra (păk"ĭsăn'drə): see BOX.

Pacific, War of the, 1879–84, war between Chile and the allied nations, Peru and Bolivia; also called the Chile-Peruvian War. The trouble began when President Hilarión DAZA of Bolivia rescinded (Feb., 1879) the contract that had given a Chilean company the right to exploit nitrate deposits in Atacama, a province of Bolivia. In reprisal Chile took the port of Antofagasta, and two weeks later war was formally acknowledged. Peru, bound since 1873 by a defensive alliance to Bolivia, refused to promise to remain neutral, and Chile declared war on Peru. At the end of 1879, Chile had not only won Atacama and the Peruvian province of Tarapacá, but by the capture of *Huáscar*, a Peruvian ironclad warship, had gained control of the sea. Although the presidents of Peru and Bolivia, Mariano Ignacio PRADO and Hilarión Daza, respectively, were replaced by other leaders, no change occurred in the war; by coordinated sea and land attacks the Chilean conquest continued. During 1880, Chilean forces took Tacna and Arica and, after an invasion by sea and the victories of Chorillos and Miraflores (Jan., 1881), made a triumphal entry into Lima. Although the Peruvian leader Andrés Avelino CÁCERES, aided by Miguel IGLESIAS, gallantly fought a guerrilla campaign, Peru and Bolivia were thoroughly vanquished. The Treaty of Ancón (Oct., 1883) restored peace between Peru and Chile; a truce at Valparaíso (April, 1884) was signed between Bolivia and Chile, but a definitive treaty was not agreed upon until 1904. Chile acquired Atacama, Bolivia's only coastal territory, now called Antofagasta. Peru also had to cede Tarapacá to Chile and surrendered control of the provinces of Tacna and Arica, their disposition to be decided by plebiscite after 10 years. This provision led to the TACNA-ARICA CONTROVERSY.

Pacifica, residential city (1970 pop. 36,020), San Mateo co., W Calif., on the Pacific coast; inc. 1957. A Nike missile base is there.

Pacific Grove, residential and resort city (1970 pop. 13,505), Monterey co., W central Calif., on a point where Monterey Bay meets the Pacific Ocean; inc. 1889. Among the natural attractions of the area are the millions of Monarch butterflies that arrive each fall to spend the winter. Stanford Univ. has a marine laboratory there. Nearby Point Pinos Lighthouse has been in operation since 1855.

Pacific Islands, Trust Territory of the (1970 pop. 90,940), consisting of the CAROLINE ISLANDS, the MARSHALL ISLANDS, and the MARIANAS ISLANDS, held by the United States under United Nations trusteeship. The territory, covering a vast area of the Pacific, includes more than 2,000 islands and islets. The combined land area is 717 sq mi (1,857 sq km). The inhabitants are virtually all Micronesians. The islands were acquired by Germany but were seized by Japan in 1914. In 1922, they were mandated to Japan by the League of Nations. During World War II the islands were occupied (1944) by U.S. forces and administered by the naval government on Guam. In 1947 the United Nations approved U.S. trusteeship of the islands, and their affairs were placed under the administration of the U.S. Dept. of the Interior. There is an appointed governor and an elected territorial congress, consisting of a house of representatives and a senate. For administrative purposes, the three main island groups are divided into six districts—PALAU, YAP, TRUK, PONAPE, Marshall Islands, and Marianas Islands—each sending two members to the senate. The headquarters of the trust territory is on SAIPAN, to which it was moved from Guam (part of the Marianas Islands but not of the trust territory) in 1962. The islands' only significant exports are copra and fish.

Pacific Margin, western section of the great North American Cordillera, W United States and W Canada, stretching from SW Alaska to S Calif. It is composed of a central lowland region (Central Valley, Willamette valley, Puget Sound lowlands) flanked by the COAST RANGES on the west and the SIERRA NEVADA, CASCADE RANGE, COAST MTS., and ALASKA RANGE on the east.

Pacific Ocean, largest and deepest ocean, c.70,000,000 sq mi (181,300,000 sq km), occupying about one third of the earth's surface; named by the Spanish explorer, Ferdinand Magellan; the southern part is also known as the South Sea. It extends from the arctic to antarctic regions between North and South American on the east and Asia and Australia on the west. It is connected with the Arctic Ocean by the Bering Strait; with the Atlantic Ocean by the Drake Passage, Straits of Magellan, and the Panama Canal;

and with the Indian Ocean by passages in the Malay Archipelago and between Australia and Antarctica. Its maximum length is c.9,000 mi (14,500 km), and its greatest width c.11,000 mi (17,700 km), between the Isthmus of Panama and the Malay Peninsula. The principal arms of the Pacific Ocean are (in the north) the Bering Sea; (in the east) the Gulf of California; (in the south) Ross Sea; and (in the west) the Sea of Okhotsk, the Sea of Japan, and the Yellow, East China, South China, Philippine, Coral, and Tasman seas. Along the E Pacific shore, generally, the coast rises abruptly from a deep sea floor to mountain heights on land, and there is a narrow continental shelf. The Asian coast is generally low and indented and is fringed with islands rising from a wide continental shelf. A series of volcanoes, the Circum-Pacific Ring of Fire, rims the Pacific basin. The approximately 20,000 islands in the Pacific Ocean are concentrated in the south and west. Most of the larger islands are structurally part of the continent and rise from the continental shelf; these include the Japanese island arc, the Malay Archipelago, and the islands of NW North America and SW South America. Scattered around the Pacific and rising from the ocean floor are high volcanic islands (such as the Hawaiian Islands) and low coral islands (such as those of OCEANIA). Few large rivers drain into the Pacific Ocean; the largest are the Columbia of North America and the Huang Ho and Yangtze of China. The floor of the Pacific Ocean, which has an average depth of c.14,000 ft (4,300 m), is largely a deep sea plain. The greatest known depth (36,198 ft/11,033 m) is in the Challenger Deep in the Marinas Trench c.250 mi (400 km) SW of Guam. Rising from the plain are swells (many of which are volcanic), seamounts, and guyots; the extensive Albatross Plateau covers most of the SE and E central Pacific basin. Huge whirls, formed by the major ocean currents, are found roughly north and south of the equator; the Equatorial Counter Current separates them. The northern whirl is formed by the North Equatorial Current, Japan Current, North Pacific Drift, and California Current; the southern whirl is formed by the South Equatorial Current, East Australian Current, West Wind Drift, and Peruvian (or Humboldt) Current. There are many branch and feeder currents that help to constantly circulate ocean water of differing temperatures and salinities. The Pacific islands of the south and west were populated by Asian migrants who crossed long distances of open sea in primitive boats. European travelers including Marco Polo had reported an ocean off Asia, and in the late 15th cent. trading ships had sailed around Africa to the western rim of the Pacific, but recognition of the Pacific as distinct from the Atlantic Ocean dates from Balboa's sighting of its eastern shore (1513). Magellan's crossing of the Philippines (1520–21) initiated a series of explorations, including those of Drake, Tasman, Dampier, Cook, Bering, and Vancouver, which by the end of the 18th cent. had disclosed the coastline and the major islands. In the 16th cent. supremacy in the Pacific area was shared by Spain and Portugal. The English and the Dutch established footholds in the 17th cent., France and Russia in the 18th, and Germany, Japan, and the United States in the 19th. Sealers and whalers sailed the Pacific from the late 18th cent., and Yankee clippers entered Pacific trade in the early 19th cent. The principal commercial fishing areas in the Pacific are found in the shallower waters of the continental shelf; salmon, halibut, herring, sardines, and tuna are the chief catch. Most of the trans-Pacific sea-lanes pass through the Hawaiian Islands; the chief Pacific ports are San Francisco, Los Angeles, Seattle, Tokyo-Yokohama, Hong Kong, Shanghai, Manila, and Sydney. Since the 1950s many of the South Pacific islands have become tourist centers. The international date line passes through the Pacific Ocean. See Gardner Soule, *The Greatest Depths* (1970); E. S. Dodge, *Beyond the Capes: Pacific Exploration from Captain Cook to the Challenger, 1776–1877* (1971); John Gilbert, *Charting the Vast Pacific* (1971).

Pacific Rim National Park, 60 sq mi (155 sq km), along the west coast of Vancouver Island, near Ucluelet, SE British Columbia, Canada; est. 1971. The park includes Long Beach, several islands, the historic Life Saving Trail, and a variety of marine life.

Pacific scandal, 1873, a major event in Canadian political history. Charges were made in Parliament that the Conservative administration of Sir John A. MACDONALD had accepted campaign funds from Sir Hugh ALLAN in return for a promise to award Allan's syndicate the contract to build the Canadian Pacific Railway. Macdonald's statement that the contract and the contributions were unconnected was received with skepticism. Donald A. Smith (later Lord STRATHCONA) broke with Macdonald over the crisis and through his publicly expressed lack of confidence in Macdonald was partly responsible for the Conservative administration's downfall. The government was forced to resign because of the scandal, and the Conservative party was badly defeated in the ensuing elections.

pacifism, advocacy of opposition to war through individual or collective action against militarism. Although complete, enduring peace is the goal of all pacifism, the methods of achieving it differ. Some groups oppose international war but advocate revolution for suppressed nationalities; others are willing to support defensive but not offensive war; others oppose all war, but believe in maintaining a police force; still others believe in no coercive or disciplinary force at all. One of the strongest motivations in the promotion of peace has been religion, the objection to war being, in general, based on the belief that the willful taking of human life is wrong. The Eastern religions, especially Buddhism, decry war and advocate nonresistance, and there has been a strong pacifistic element in Judaism and Christianity. The Sermon on the Mount contains an exhortation to peace. The church generally voiced opposition to war as such (with the notable exception of the Crusades); in the Middle Ages, the TRUCE OF GOD was the outcome of ecclesiastical attempts to halt private warfare. Some later sects—especially the Anabaptists, Quakers, Moravians, Dukhobors, and Mennonites—have elevated nonresistance to a doctrinal position. Another motivating force in pacifism has been humanitarianism and the humanitarian outrage at the destruction caused by war. Economic motives have also played a part in pacifist arguments; the pacifists condemn the economic waste of war, which they claim is avoidable. International cooperation and pacifism are closely connected and pacifists usually advocate international agreements as a way to insure peace. Pacifism is also closely connected with movements for international disarmament. Modern pacifism began early in the 19th cent., with peace societies being formed in New York (1815), in Massachusetts (1815), and in Great Britain (1816). Other countries followed the lead; societies were established in France and Switzerland not long afterward. In 1828, William LADD, one of the early pacifists, welded the many local societies that had been established in the United States into the American Peace Society. More radical pacifists came to the fore, and the peace movement in the United States became connected with other causes under the leadership of such men as Elihu Burritt and William Lloyd GARRISON; but Garrison later abandoned his pacifism and advocated war to end slavery. The first international peace congress met in London in 1843, marking the first attempt to organize on an international scale. Both the Mexican War and the Crimean War checked development temporarily, and the Civil War completely destroyed for the moment the peace movement in the United States. After the Civil War, the movement reappeared in new forms, influenced strongly by the internationalists. The efforts of Frédéric Passy in France and of Sir William Randal Cremer in Great Britain led to the foundation of the Inter-Parliamentary Union in 1892. The International Peace Bureau was founded at Bern, Switzerland, in 1892. The award of the Nobel Peace Prize (see NOBEL, ALFRED BERNHARD) did much to encourage pacifist thought. Even the Franco-Prussian and Spanish-American wars did not check the spread of peace agitation. But the peace societies, the international organizations, and the Hague Conferences, were all powerless to check the rush of events to World War I. Although the percentage of CONSCIENTIOUS OBJECTORS was small, after the war the peace movement reappeared with greater vigor than before, and, in spite of increased nationalism throughout the world, a concerted effort toward peace was made not only in the peace congresses but also in such agitation as the pacifist resolution (1933) of the Students' Union at Oxford. During the 1920s and early 30s pacifism enjoyed an upsurge; the doctrine of nonresistance as applied in India by Mohandas K. GANDHI gained attention and respect for the movement. The hopes placed in the League of Nations, however, failed to materialize, and some pacifists placed their trust in isolationism and appeasement as events led to World War II. This time the number of conscientious objectors in the United States and Great Britain was larger than in World War I. After World War II, broken international contacts were again restored; a world pacifist conference projected for 1949 in India was postponed because of the assassination of Gandhi. At its meeting in 1948, the World Council of Churches was unable to reach agreement in regard to pacifism and the church. Although pacifists were not very active in the United States during the Korean War in the early 1950s, this was not the case during the Vietnam War in the 1960s and early 70s; pacifists and other antiwar groups joined together for several major protest marches in Washington, D.C., and other cities. The presence of ardent pacifists among the prominent figures in the literary and artistic worlds had an effect in spreading the aims of the movement. The writings of Bertha von Suttner and of Ludwig Quidde demonstrate how pacifism may be espoused in fictional writing. Apart from such statesmen as Aristide Briand, William Jennings Bryan, Frank Kellogg, and Ramsay MacDonald, among other notable names in pacifism are Leo Tolstoy, Jane Addams, Élie Ducommun, Guglielmo Ferrero, Albert Gobat, Alfred H. Love, David Starr Jordan, Sir Norman Angell, Nicholas Murray Butler, Philip Noel-Baker, Bertrand Russell, Martin Luther King, Jr., A. J. Muste, Staughton Lynd, and Dr. Benjamin Spock. Among the many agencies and associations that have been organized for the advancement of world peace, aside from those already mentioned, are the Carnegie Endowment for International Peace, War Resisters International, and World Council of Peace. Recent pacifist movements have tended to concentrate their efforts on urging unilateral or multilateral disarmament and the cessation of nuclear testing. A slight beginning toward those aims was realized in 1972 when an agreement was signed between the Soviet Union and the United States that would limit future production of missiles. See Sidney Spencer, *Pacifism in Theory and Practice* (1926); G. F. Hershberger, *War, Peace, and Nonresistance* (rev. ed. 1953); G. H. MacGregor, *New Testament Basis of Pacifism* (rev. ed. 1958); G. C. Zahn, *An Alternative to War* (1963); David Martin, *Pacifism: An Historical and Sociological Study* (1965); Peter Brock, *Pacifism in the United States* (1968) and *Twentieth-Century Pacifism* (1970).

packaging, containment and packing prior to sale with the primary purpose of facilitating the purchase and use of a product. Before 1800 packaging was restricted almost entirely to containment for shipping, with minimum levels of protection and preservation. Grocery bags, for example, were known in the 17th cent.; however, it was not until the 19th cent. that practical bag-making machinery was developed. That century saw the emergence of metal cans (1810), setup boxes (1844), folding cartons (1879), and the Owens bottle machine (1899). Early in the 20th cent., marketing-oriented packaging began to evolve. Branding, quality, storage and handling, and point-of-sale display became important attributes. Today, packaging has become a major medium of advertising and marketing.

Packer, Asa, 1805–79, American industrialist, b. Groton, Conn. He acquired coal lands in Pennsylvania, constructed canal locks on the Lehigh Canal, and became wealthy operating coal-carrying boats along the canal. A county judge for several years, Packer was also a Democratic member of Congress (1853–57). He promoted the Lehigh Valley RR and donated (1866) money and land for the building of Lehigh Univ. See biography by M. C. Stuart (1938).

packing industry: see MEAT-PACKING.

pack rat, RODENT of the genus *Neotoma,* of North and Central America, noted for its habit of collecting bright, shiny objects and leaving other objects, such as nuts or pebbles, in their place; also called trade rat or wood rat. Most common in the southern and western parts of the United States, but found as far south as Nicaragua, the pack rat stores the objects it collects to decorate its nest. The rodent may reach a length of 18 in. (45.7 cm) including tail, has soft brown fur, and resembles a squirrel with large ears. It eats nuts, berries, seeds, twigs, and roots. Its nest is a large stick structure built in a sheltered area. The desert species adorns its nest with bits of cactus, turning it into an impenetrable fortress. A litter is born after a gestation period of 33 to 39 days and contains from two to six young. Pack rats are classified in the phylum CHORDATA, subphylum Vertebrata, class Mammalia, order Rodentia, family Cricetidae.

Pactolus (păktō'ləs), small river of ancient Lydia, W central Asia Minor (now Turkey), joining the Hermus (modern Gediz) after passing Sardis. It was famous for the gold washed from its sands, a source of wealth to the kings of Lydia.

Padan-aram (pā'dən-ā'răm), that part of ARAM that lay in the Euphrates valley. Gen. 28.2,5,7; 31.18; 33.18; 35.9,26; 46.15. Padan: Gen. 48.7. Aram-naharaim in title of Ps. 60; homeland of the Hebrew patriarchs.

Padang (pädäng'), town (1961 pop. 143,699), capital of West Sumatra prov., on W Sumatra, Indonesia, on the Indian Ocean at the mouth of the small Padang River. An important port, it has a large trade in coffee, copra, rubber, spices, tobacco, and cement, which are shipped principally from its outport, Telukbayur. Padang is the principal outlet for the important Ombilin coalfields. In the area are a huge cement plant and several textile mills. The town has an airport and is the seat of Andalas Univ.

Paddington, London, England: see WESTMINSTER, CITY OF.

paddlefish, large freshwater fish, *Polyodon spathula,* of the Mississippi valley, also called spoonbill or duckbill and named for its flattened, paddle-shaped snout. The largest specimens weigh well over 150 lb (67.5 kg) and reach 6 ft (183 cm) in length. The snout may be a third of the length of the body; it is equipped with sense organs that assist the fish in finding its prey of small crustaceans, which it strains out with gill rakers (see GILL). Paddlefishes are primitive; unlike most modern fishes, they have skins with reduced scales, almost wholly cartilaginous skeletons, and upturned tail fins. They are uniform leaden gray in color. Valued as food fish, their greenish black eggs are mixed with those of the closely related STURGEON for CAVIAR. A Chinese species found in the Yangtze River is said to grow to 20 ft (610 cm). Paddlefishes are classified in the phylum CHORDATA, subphylum Vertebrata, class Osteichthyes, order Acipenseriformes, family Polyodontidae.

pademelon: see KANGAROO.

Paderborn (pä"dərbôrn'), city (1970 pop. 66,829), North Rhine-Westphalia, N central West Germany. It is an agricultural market and industrial center; manufactures include chemicals, machinery, and textiles. Paderborn was made (805) an episcopal see by Charlemagne, who convened several imperial diets there. The city grew rapidly in the 11th cent. and in the 13th cent. joined the Hanseatic League. Its bishops ruled a large district as princes of the Holy Roman Empire until the bishopric was secularized in 1803 and passed to Prussia. The Catholic diocese was reinstated in 1821 and was raised to an archdiocese in 1930. Paderborn was badly damaged in World War II. Noteworthy buildings include the cathedral (11th–13th cent.) and a city hall (1613–20) in late-Renaissance style. There is a theological school, which held university status from 1614 to 1819.

Paderewski, Ignace Jan (păd"ərĕf'skē, Pol. ēnyäs'-yän pädĕrĕf'skē), 1860–1941, Polish pianist, composer, and statesman; studied at the Warsaw Conservatory and later with Theodor Leschetizky. Following debuts in Vienna (1887) and Paris (1888), his brilliant, sensitive playing won him world-wide popularity exceeding that of any performer since Franz Liszt. In 1891 he made the first of many concert tours of the United States. An ardent patriot, he briefly headed Polish governments in 1919 and 1940–41 (the latter in exile). He amassed a large fortune, most of which he donated to the service of Poland and the benefit of needy musicians and Jewish refugees. Paderewski died shortly after returning to the United States to plead Poland's cause once again. In addition to the famous Minuet in G for piano, his works include some orchestral music, an opera, a cantata, a violin sonata, and piano pieces and songs. He established (1900) the Paderewski Fund to forward musical composition in the United States. See his memoirs, ed. by Mary Lawton (1938); biographies by Charles Phillips (1934) and Antoni Gronowicz (1943).

Padilla, Ezequiel (äsākyĕl'pä*th*ē'yä), 1890–1971, Mexican political leader. A revolutionary under Pancho Villa, he studied law in New York City. He served as secretary of public education (1928–30) and helped found Mexico's modern school system. As foreign minister (1940–45) during World War II, he was a leader at hemispheric conferences and a forceful proponent of inter-American solidarity; he was a signer of the Charter of the United Nations at San Francisco (1945). He ran unsuccessfully for president in 1946 and was elected senator in 1964.

Padilla, Juan de (hwän dā pä*th*ē'lyä), c.1490–1521, Spanish revolutionary leader in the war of the *comuneros* [municipalities] against Holy Roman Emperor CHARLES V. Charles's conduct and his foreign advisers offended Spanish national feeling and led to a rising in Toledo under Padilla's leadership (1520). Soon other Castilian cities rose and joined Toledo in a Santa Junta [holy league]. Padilla sought to legitimize the junta by securing the support of Charles's mad mother, JOANNA, but the movement soon degenerated into class warfare. Padilla's army was defeated at Villalar (April, 1521), and he was executed.

Padon (pā'dŏn), ancestor of a family that returned from Exile. Ezra 2.44; Neh. 7.47.

Padre Island, low, sandy island, c.115 mi (185 km) long, less than 3 mi (4.8 km) wide, S Texas; longest barrier beach in the United States. It is characterized by large, irregular sand dunes, sparse vegetation, and a strong prevailing wind off the gulf. Padre Island was discovered and charted in 1519 by the Spanish explorer Alfonso Alvarez de Pineda. It became infamous as a ship's graveyard; during a hurricane in 1553, most of a Spanish treasure fleet of 20 ships broke up on the island. Padre Nicholas Balli, for whom the island was named, founded the Santa Cruz Ranch c.1800; cattle have been almost continuously raised on the island. **Padre Island National Seashore** is located in the undeveloped central part of the island, where more than 350 kinds of birds, and many small animals, reptiles, and varied marine life are found (see NATIONAL PARKS AND MONUMENTS, table).

Padua (păd'yo͞oə), Ital. *Padova,* city (1971 pop. 231,152), capital of Padova prov., in Venetia, NE Italy, connected by canal with the Brenta, Adige, and Po rivers. It is an agricultural, commercial, and industrial center and a rail junction. Manufactures include machinery, motor vehicles, leather goods, and processed food. Called Patavium by the Romans, it was second to Rome in wealth. The city was destroyed by the Lombards in A.D. 601 but recovered quickly. Except for a 20-year period of rule by Ezzelino da Romano, Padua was from the 12th to the 14th cent. a free commune of great political and economic importance. It subdued neighboring cities and became an artistic center, where Giotto painted his masterpiece, a series of frescoes (1304–6) in the Capella degli Scrovegni. Under the rule of the munificent Carrara family (1318–1405) and under the domination of Venice (1405–1797), Padua continued to flourish. Mantegna (1431–1506), a native of Padua, produced much work there; parts of frescoes executed by him are preserved in the 13th-century Eremitani church. Other notable structures in the city include the six-domed basilica of St. Anthony (1232–1307), whose high altar is adorned with bronzes by Donatello; the bronze equestrian statue of *Gattamelata* (a Venetian general), also by Donatello, in the square of the basilica; the classical cathedral; and the law courts. The Univ. of Padua, the oldest in Italy after that of Bologna, was founded in 1222 by teachers and students who had fled from Bologna. Now centered in Il Bo palace, the university established the first anatomy hall (well preserved) in Europe in 1594. Galileo taught (1592–1610) at the university, and Dante, Petrarch, and Tasso were students there.

Paducah (pədyo͞o'kə, -do͞o'-), city (1970 pop. 31,627), seat of McCracken co., SW Ky., on the Ohio River at the mouth of the Tennessee River; inc. as a city 1856. It is an important tobacco market, a farm trade and shipping point, and a river port. It also has railroad shops, boat yards, and a shoe factory. During the Civil War, Paducah was held for the Union (1861) by Grant, and in 1864 it was the objective of a raid by Nathan Forrest. The city suffered serious floods in 1884, 1913, and 1937. Of interest is the city hall, designed by Edward Durrell Stone. A junior college is in the city.

Padus: see PO, river.

Paean (pē'ən), in Greek mythology, divine physician of the gods. Paean apparently became an epithet for Apollo, the healer. The paean, a hymn of praise to Apollo and often to other gods, was sung as a prayer for safety or deliverance at battles and other important occasions.

paedogenesis: see NEOTENY.

Paeligni (pēlĭg'nī), ancient people of central Italy, related to other Oscan-speaking groups, e.g., the Samnites, whom they joined in unsuccessful resistance to Roman hegemony (c.305 B.C.).

Paeonius (pēō'nēəs), Gr. *Paionios,* fl. 5th cent. B.C., Greek sculptor from Mende in Thrace. An inscription on the triangular base of the statue of Nike (Victory) at Olympia states that Paeonius made it. This figure is a contemporary version of the bronze original whose base was found at Delphi. It is so much farther advanced in style and execution than the pediment sculptures for the temple of Zeus, Olympia, that modern authorities doubt the statement of Pausanias attributing those of the eastern end of the pediment to this sculptor. The Nike was dedicated by the Messenians and Naupactians, probably to commemorate the siege of Sphacteria in 424 B.C.

Pães, Sidónio: see PAIS, SIDONIO.

Paestum (pĕst'əm), ancient city of Lucania, S Italy. It was a colony of the Greek city of Sybaris (c.600 B.C.) and was first named Posidonia. It flourished with the rest of MAGNA GRAECIA through the 6th cent. B.C. The Romans took the city in 273 B.C.; they called it Paestum. The ruins, near the present Pesto, include some of the finest and best-preserved Doric temples in existence.

Paetus: see THRASEA PAETUS.

Páez, José Antonio (hōsā' äntō'nyō pä'ās), 1790–1873, Venezuelan revolutionist, president, and caudillo. He boldly led (1810–19) a band of *llaneros* [plainsmen] in skillful guerrilla warfare against the Spanish, aided Simón BOLÍVAR at the battle of Carabobo (1821), and drove (1823) the Spanish from their last Venezuelan stronghold at Puerto Cabello. He led the separatist movement that disrupted Bolívar's Colombian republic and was the first president of Venezuela (1831–35). A conservative oligarch and exponent of personalism, he served again (1839–43), dominating the nation until 1847. Páez commanded unsuccessful revolutions in 1848 and 1849 against José T. MONAGAS, his own choice for president, and was exiled (1850–58). He returned and in 1861 became supreme dictator. Two years later he again went into exile. He died in New York City. See biography by R. B. Cunninghame Graham (1929, repr. 1970).

Páez, Pedro (pā'*th*rō pä'āth), 1564–1622, Spanish Jesuit missionary. He preached in Goa, India, was enslaved for seven years in Sana, Yemen, and in 1603 arrived in Ethiopia. He rapidly learned Amharic and converted the Ethiopian royal family from Coptic Christianity to Roman Catholicism.

Pag (päg), Ital. *Pago,* island (101 sq mi/262 sq km), in the Adriatic, off the Dalmatian coast, W Yugoslavia. Noted for its fine embroidery and lace, it also has vineyards, a fishing industry, and bauxite deposits. The chief village is Pag, a resort on the eastern coast; it has a palace and a cathedral from Venetian times.

Pagan (pəgän'), ruined city, Myingyan prov., central Burma, on the Irrawaddy River. Covering an area c.40 sq mi (100 sq km), it is one of the great archaeological treasures of Southeast Asia and a holy place of pilgrimage. Founded c.849, it became in the 11th cent. the seat of King Anawratha, who introduced Buddhism into upper Burma. Under his rule and that of his descendants, Pagan was adorned with thousands of Buddhist shrines and temples, principally in stone and brick. Occupied by the Mongols in 1287, Pagan was sacked and burned by the Shans in 1299. The thousands of surviving temples, pagodas, and monasteries are massive and imposing structures, built with a knowledge of the true arch and showing strong Indian influence.

Paganini, Niccolò (nēkōlō' pägänē'nē), 1782–1840, Italian violinist, whose virtuosity became a legend. He extended the compass of the violin by his use of harmonics, perfected the use of double and triple stops, and revived the practice of *scordatura,* the diverse tunings of the strings. Paganini made his debut as a child prodigy in 1793 at Genoa, his birthplace. In 1801 he retired to a villa in Tuscany and did not resume his concerts until 1805, when he became court violinist to the princess of Lucca. After he left (1813) her court, his success in Milan carried his fame throughout Europe. His retirement in 1835 was followed by the loss of his voice and, later, by death from cancer of the larynx. Paganini composed numerous pieces, most of them bravura variations for violin. Among the few compositions published during his lifetime are the 24 caprices for violin that were adapted for piano by both Schumann and Liszt. See biographies by J. Pulver (1970) and S. S. Stratton (1971).

Page, Thomas Nelson, 1853–1922, American author and diplomat, b. Hanover co., Va. His novels and stories are sentimental idealizations of the Old South. Among his novels are *On Newfound River* (1891) and *Red Rock* (1898); his volumes of stories include *In Ole Virginia* (1887) and *The Burial of the Guns* (1894). *Italy and the World War* (1920) is the record of his years as ambassador to Italy (1913–19).

Page, Walter Hines, 1855–1918, American journalist and diplomat, b. Cary, N.C. He became (1880) a reporter for the St. Joseph (Mo.) *Gazette* and wrote a series of articles on the problems of the South. In 1883 he secured control of the Raleigh (N.C.) *State Chronicle* and crusaded for reforms in Southern agriculture, education, and industry. He was editor of the *Forum* (1890–95) and then of the *Atlantic Monthly* (1896–99). After he became (1899) a partner in the publishing firm of Doubleday, Page and Company, he founded (1900) the magazine *World's Work,* which he edited until he was appointed (1913) U.S. ambassador to Great Britain by President Woodrow Wilson. He did much to improve Anglo-American relations, but his outspoken sympathetic attitude toward the Allied cause in World War I brought a rift between him and Wilson, who was striving to maintain strict American neutrality. See study by Ross Gregory (1970).

Page, William, 1811–85, American historical and portrait painter, b. Albany, N.Y., studied with S. F. B. Morse and at the National Academy of Design. Among his best-known works are *Farragut's Triumphal Entry into Mobile Bay* (presented to Grand Duke Alexis of Russia, 1871) and *Ruth and Naomi* (N.Y. Historical Society). Influenced by Emerson, Page was probably closer to the ideas of transcendentalism than any other American painter. He believed that art was the earthly counterpart of the divine creative process. In Italy from 1850 to 1857, he constructed a system of body proportions inspired by classical antiquity. He also devised color theories. Page is highly esteemed for his portraits, which are simply and poetically rendered. A portrait of his wife, Sophie, is in the Detroit Institute of Arts. See monograph by Joshua Taylor (1957).

pageant, modern dramatic spectacle celebrating a special occasion or an event in the history of a locality. In medieval times the word *pageant* had meant the wagon or the movable stage on which one scene of a mystery or MIRACLE PLAY was performed. The pageant was built on wheels and consisted of two rooms, the lower one being used as a dressing room and the upper used as a stage. The word also referred to the complex wooden machine-structures built for the Tudor MASQUE. The modern form of the pageant came into general use in England and America since the production, in 1905, of L. N. Parker's Sherborne pageant in England. Pageants include such celebrations as the Mardi Gras and annual local festivals.

Paget, Sir James (păj'ĭt), 1814–99, British surgeon and pathologist. He taught and practiced at St. Bartholomew's Hospital, London, and cataloged the museums of St. Bartholomew's and of the Royal College of Surgeons. He was a skilled diagnostician and an authority on diseases of the bones and joints. His works include *Lectures on Tumours* (1851) and *Lectures on Surgical Pathology* (1853).

Pagiel (pā'gēĕl, pāgī'əl), Asherite chief. Num. 1.13; 2.27; 7.72,77; 10.26.

Pagnol, Marcel (märsĕl' pänyôl'), 1895–1974, French dramatist and film director. His trilogy of sentimental comedies set on the Marseilles waterfront—*Marius* (1929), *Fanny* (1931), and *César* (1936)—have been widely translated and adapted. The trilogy was also filmed with Pagnol writing the screenplays for all three segments (1931, 1932, 1934) and directing the last segment, *César.* Among the other films he directed are *The Well-Digger's Daughter* (1940) and *Letters from My Windmill* (1955). *Merlusse* (1935, tr. 1937), an original script for a film, embodies Pagnol's theories of the film art. His other works include the plays *Judas* (1956) and *Angèle* (1970), as well as several autobiographical volumes. See his memoir, *The Days Were Too Short* (tr. 1960).

pagoda (pəgō'də), name given in the East to a variety of buildings of tower form that are usually part of a temple or monastery group and serve as shrines. Those of India (see STUPA) are chiefly pyramidal structures of masonry, tapering to an apex and elaborately adorned with carving and sculpture. In China the pagoda, derived from India, is one of the

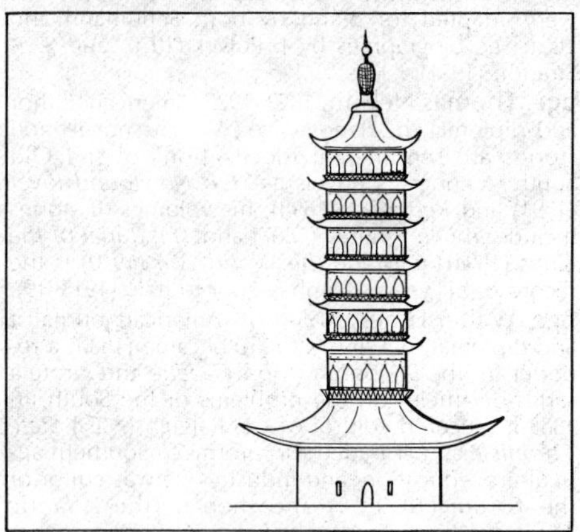

Pagoda

most characteristic architectural types and in general is devoted to sacred usage. Octagonal, hexagonal, or square in plan, they are built in superimposed stories, sometimes as many as 15; from each story projects an upward-curving tiled roof. The material most commonly used is brick, often faced with slabs of glazed and colored tile. A few date back to the T'ang dynasty (A.D. 618–906). In Japan the pagodas were introduced from China with Buddhism. They are usually square in plan and five stories high, each story having its projecting roof. Generally made of wood, they exhibit superb carpentry craftsmanship. The Horyu-ji tower near Nara, of the 7th cent., is a noted example.

Pago Pago (päng'ō päng'ō, päng'gō päng'gō), village (1970 pop. 2,451) and capital of American SAMOA, on the Southern shore of TUTUILA island. Pago Pago has an excellent, landlocked harbor and is the only port of call in American Samoa. From 1878 to 1951 it was a coaling and repair station for the U.S. navy. Just south of the town is the Pago Pago International Airport. The name also appears as Pangopango.

Pahang (pəhŭng', -hăng'), state (1971 pop. 503,131), 13,920 sq mi (36,053 sq km), Malaysia, S Malay Peninsula, on the South China Sea. It is the largest state of West Malaysia. The capital is Kuala Lipis. The region is mostly covered with dense jungle and has a mountainous interior. It is drained by the Pahang River (c.285 mi/460 km long), the chief river of the Malay Peninsula. Rubber, rice, and coconuts are produced, and gold and tin are mined. Over half the population is Malay, but there is a large Chinese minority. Before the 16th cent. Pahang was the vassal state of the various powers that in turn dominated the Malay Peninsula. After the fall of Malacca (1511), Pahang formed part of the sultanate of Riau and Johor (except in the 17th cent. when it was captured by Acheh) until its own rulers established themselves as independent sovereigns in the 19th cent. Pahang became a British protectorate in 1888 and in 1896 became one of the Federated Malay States. In 1948 it joined the Federation of Malaya. See MALAYSIA, FEDERATION OF.

Pahari (pəhä'rē), languages or dialects of the Indic group of the Indo-Iranian subfamily of the Indo-European family of languages. See INDO-IRANIAN LANGUAGES.

Pahath-moab (pā'hăth-mō'ăb), chief house of Judah. Ezra 2.6; 8.4; 10.30; Neh. 3.11; 7.11; 10.14.

Pahlavi language (pä'ləvē") or **Pehlevi language** (pā'-), member of the Iranian group of the Indo-Iranian subfamily of the Indo-European family of languages. Pahlavi is the form of the Persian language that followed Old Persian and preceded Modern Persian. Also called Middle Persian, it was used during the Sassanid, or Sassanian, rule of Persia (3d to 7th cent. A.D.). See INDO-IRANIAN LANGUAGES.

Pahlevi: see REZA SHAH PAHLEVI; MUHAMMAD REZA SHAH PAHLEVI.

Pahlevi, Iran: see BANDAR-E PAHLAVI.

pahoehoe: see LAVA.

Pai (pä'ī), variant of PAU.

Paignton: see TORBAY.

Päijänne (pă'ēyăn'nä), lake c.560 sq mi (1,450 sq km), S central Finland, stretching c.85 mi (130 km) from Lahti, the chief port, N to Jyväskylä. One of the largest lakes of the Finnish plateau, it consists of several long rocky basins dotted with numerous islands. The Kymijoki drains it into the Gulf of Finland. Lake steamers and lumber rafts utilize the waterway.

pain, unpleasant or hurtful sensation resulting from stimulation of nerve endings. The stimulus is carried by nerve fibers to the spinal cord and then to the brain, where the nerve impulse is interpreted as pain. The excessive stimulation of nerve endings during pain is attributed to tissue damage, and in this sense pain has protective value, serving as a danger signal of disease and often facilitating diagnosis. Unlike other sensory experiences, e.g., response to touch or cold, pain may be modified by sedatives and analgesics or, if unusually severe, by narcotics. If sedatives do not suffice and if the cause of the pain cannot be removed or treated, severing a nerve in the pain pathway may bring relief. Pain is occasionally felt not only at the site of stimulation but in other parts of the body supplied by nerves in the same sensory path; for example, the pain of angina pectoris or coronary thrombosis may extend to the left arm. This phenomenon is known as referred pain. Subjective or hysterical pain originates in the sensory centers of the brain without stimulation of the nerves at the site of the pain.

Paine, Albert Bigelow, 1861–1937, American author, b. New Bedford, Mass. He is best remembered as the author of the authorized biography of Mark Twain (3 vol., 1912) and as the editor of Twain's letters (1917). Among his other works are several children's books, including *The Hollow Tree* and *The Arkansas Bear* (both 1898); a novel, *The Great White Way* (1901); and a biography of Thomas Nast (1904).

Paine, John Knowles, 1839–1906, American composer, organist, and educator, b. Portland, Maine, studied in Berlin. In 1862 he began to teach music at Harvard and held (from 1875) the first chair of music in an American university. His compositions, romantic and programmatic in style, were received enthusiastically in his day, and he won fame abroad, both as organist and composer. His opera *Azara* (1901), for which he was also the librettist, was given only a concert performance, and few of his orchestral works are heard today. His fame rests on his pioneer work in music education, and many of his pupils were among the prominent composers of the generation succeeding him.

Paine, Robert Treat, 1731–1814, political figure in the American Revolution, signer of the Declaration of Independence, b. Boston, Mass. He served briefly as a chaplain in the French and Indian War but gave up the ministry for law. In 1770 he conducted the prosecution of the British troops indicted for murder in the BOSTON MASSACRE. Paine was a member of the Continental Congress (1774–78) and in 1775 was sent (with John Langdon and Robert R. Livingston) on an unsuccessful mission to win Canada to the Revolutionary cause. Paine later served as attorney general of Massachusetts and then (1790–1804) as state supreme court justice.

Paine, Thomas, 1737–1809, Anglo-American political theorist and writer, b. Thetford, Norfolk, England. He was the son of a Quaker. An excise officer, he was dismissed from the service after leading (1772) agitation for higher salaries. Paine emigrated to America in 1774, bearing letters of introduction from Benjamin Franklin, who was then in England. He soon became involved in the clashes between England and the American colonies and published the enormously successful pamphlet *Common Sense* (Jan., 1776), in which he argued that the colonies had outgrown any need for English domination and should be given independence. In Dec., 1776, Paine wrote the first of a series of 16 pamphlets called *The Crisis* (1776–83). These essays were widely distributed and did much to encourage the patriot cause throughout the American Revolution. After the war he returned to his farm in New Rochelle, N.Y. In 1787 he went to England and while there wrote *The Rights of Man* (2 parts, 1791 and 1792), which defended the French Revolution in reply to Edmund Burke's *Reflections on the Revolution in France.* Its basic premises were that there are natural rights common to all men and that only democratic institutions are able to guarantee these rights. Paine's attack on English institutions led to his prosecution for treason and subsequent flight to Paris (1792). There, as a member of the National Convention, he took a significant part in French affairs. During the Reign of Terror he was imprisoned by the Jacobins from Dec., 1793, to Nov., 1794. During this time he wrote his famous deistic, antibiblical work *The Age of Reason* (2 parts, 1794 and 1795), which alienated many people. His diatribe against George Washington, *Letter to Washington* (1796), added more fuel to the persisting resentment against him. When Paine returned to the United States in 1802, he was practically ostracized; he died in poverty seven years later. An idealist, a radical, and a master rhetorician, Paine wrote and lived with a keen sense of urgency and excitement. See his writings ed. by M. D. Conway (1894–96, repr. 1969) and representative selections ed. by H. H. Clark (1944, repr. 1961); biographies by D. F. Hawke (1974) and Audrey Williamson (1974).

Painesville, city (1970 pop. 16,536), seat of Lake co., NE Ohio, on the Grand River, in a farm area; laid out c.1805, inc. as a city 1902. It has railroad shops and plants that manufacture chemicals and machinery. The city is the seat of Lake Erie College.

Painlevé, Paul (pōl păNləvā'), 1863–1933, French statesman and mathematician. A mathematical prodigy when a child, he entered on a career devoted to science. He was a professor at the Sorbonne and the École Polytechnique when the Dreyfus Affair aroused his interest in politics. He entered on his political career as a leftist deputy (1910). In World War I he held several cabinet posts and was briefly premier in 1917. He was premier once more in 1925, succeeding Herriot, and was minister of war (1925–29) and minister of aviation (1930–31, 1932–33). In mathematics, Painlevé ranked among the best minds of his time; his contribution was particularly important in the field of differential equations. He published numerous writings on mathematics, astronomy, mechanics, philosophy, and politics.

paint, mixture of a PIGMENT and a binding medium, usually thinned with a solvent to form a liquid vehicle. The term includes LACQUER, Portland cement paint, printing ink, calcimine, and whitewash. Paint is used to decorate or protect surfaces and is generally applied in thin coats which dry (by evaporation or by oxidation of the vehicle) to an adhesive film. Industrial finishes are usually applied by spraying or immersion and are often hardened by baking. Pigments, finely ground, impart color (including black and white) and affect the consistency, crack resistance, and flow characteristics of paint. They may be manipulated to produce glossy, satin, or flat finishes. Oil paints are pigments dispersed in a DRYING OIL. One of the oldest oil vehicles, and still the commonest, is LINSEED OIL; castor, tung, and other vegetable oils and fish oil are also employed. The oils are diluted with a thinner, usually TURPENTINE; metallic salts that catalyze oxidation of the oil may be added to increase the rate of drying. For water paints, the vehicle is a mixture of water with a binder such as glue or casein. Enamel paints contain VARNISH and usually dry to a hard, glossy finish. Industrial lacquers (widely used on automobiles and furniture) are valued for rapid drying to a hard finish. The vehicle is commonly PYROXYLIN in an organic solvent. Luminous paint contains a phosphorescent substance, generally a metallic sulphide. See C. R. Martens, *Technology of Paints, Varnishes, and Lacquers* (1968).

painted cup: see FIGWORT.

Painted Desert, badlands on the northeastern bank of the Little Colorado River, NE Ariz., stretching c.200 mi (320 km) SE from the Grand Canyon; includes Petrified Forest National Park. Striking bands of color result from irregularly eroded layers of red and yellow sediment and bentonite clay.

painted tongue: see SALPIGLOSSIS.

Painter, William, 1540?–1594, English translator. His *Palace of Pleasure* (1566–67)—a collection of translations from Boccaccio, the *Heptameron,* and many other sources—was drawn upon by Shakespeare and other Elizabethan dramatists.

painter, animal: see PUMA.

paint horse: see PINTO HORSE.

painting, direct application of pigment to a surface to produce by tones of color or of light and dark some representation or decorative arrangement of natural or imagined forms. The materials of the surface, or ground; the pigments employed; the binder, or medium, in which the color is mixed; and its diluting agent are all used by the painter to produce the desired effects in such common techniques as FRESCO, WATERCOLOR, oil, distemper, gouache, TEMPERA, and ENCAUSTIC. In addition to these, painting properly embraces many other techniques ordinarily associated with DRAWING, a term that is often used to refer to the linear aspects of the same art. But if painting and drawing are not always clearly distinguishable from each other, both are to be distinguished from the print, in which the design is not produced directly but is transferred from another surface to that which it decorates. While the print may be one of many identical works, the painting or drawing is always unique. Painting has been freely combined with many other arts, including sculpture, architecture, and, in the modern era, photography. In ancient Greece and medieval Europe most buildings and sculptures were painted; nearly all of the ancient decoration has been lost, but some works from Egypt have preserved their coloring and give us an insight into the importance such an art can assume. The art of painting in China was linked from the 1st cent. A.D. with the development of the Buddhist faith. From the 7th cent. subject matter in Oriental painting roughly approximated that of Western art. The early Christian and then the Byzantine artists established iconographic and stylistic prototypes in wall painting and manuscript ILLUMINATION that remained the basis for Christian art (see ICONOGRAPHY). Highly spiritualized in concept, the medieval painting tradition gave way to a more worldly orientation with the development of Renaissance art. The murals of Giotto became a vehicle for the expression of new and living ideas and sentiments. At the height of the Renaissance a large proportion of the works were decorations of walls and altarpieces, which were necessarily conceived in terms of their part in a larger decorative whole and their appeal for a large public. The greatest masterpieces of Raphael and Michelangelo and of the Florentine masters are generally public works of this character. The same period, however, saw the rise of the separate easel painting and the first use of oil on canvas. Simultaneously are found the beginnings of GENRE and other secular themes and the elaboration of PORTRAITURE. Basing their art on the technical contributions of the Renaissance, e.g., the study of PERSPECTIVE and anatomy, the baroque masters added a virtuosity of execution and a style of unparalleled drama. From the age of the rococo, painting tended in the direction of greater intimacy. It is noteworthy, for example, that many of the masterpieces of the 19th cent., and particularly of IMPRESSIONISM, are small easel paintings suitable for the private home. The same period saw the rise of the large public gallery with both temporary and permanent exhibitions, an institution greatly expanded in the 20th cent. Today the reawakened interest in mural painting and the contributions of painting to such arts as the motion picture have led some to believe that a return to a greater emphasis on the public functions of the art is taking place. Such a view can find support in the notable influence of contemporary abstract painting in the fields of industrial and architectural design. But the art also continues to enjoy undiminished popularity in the home and gallery. Painting has had a long and glorious world history as an independent art. From Giotto to Picasso and from Ma Yuan to Hokusai, painting has never ceased to produce great exponents who have expressed not merely the taste but the aspirations, the concepts of space, form, and color, and the philosophy of their respective periods. See articles on individual painters, e.g., RUBENS; countries, e.g., DUTCH ART; periods, e.g., RENAISSANCE ART AND ARCHITECTURE; techniques, e.g., ENCAUSTIC. See D. M. Robb, *The Harper History of Painting* (1951); H. W. Janson, *Standard Treasury of the World's Great Paintings* (1960); Michael Levey, *A Concise History of Painting* (1962); H. L. C. Jaffé, ed., *20,000 Years of World Painting* (1967); Ralph Mayer, *Artist's Handbook of Materials and Techniques* (3d ed. 1970).

Pais or **Pães, Sidónio** (sĕdô'nyo͝o päNsh), 1872–1918, Portuguese dictator. After service in the army he was a professor of mathematics at the Univ. of Coimbra and a leader in establishing the republic in 1910. He held several cabinet posts and was minister in Berlin until Portugal entered World War I (1916). In Dec., 1917, Pais overthrew the democratic regime and made himself president. He exercised dictatorial powers that foreshadowed the Carmona and Salazar regime. He was assassinated in Dec., 1918.

Paisiello, Giovanni (jōvän'nē päēzyĕl'lō), 1740–1816, Italian composer. Paisiello served in St. Petersburg at the court of Catherine II from 1776 to 1784. He was also briefly Napoleon's *maître de chapelle*. Paisiello composed over 100 operas, church music, symphonies, piano concertos, and other works. His opera *The Barber of Seville* (1782) was so popular that for a time it hindered the success of Rossini's work of the same name. Paisiello's music is characterized by considerable melodic charm.

Paisley, Ian, 1926–, Northern Irish religious and political leader. A leading protagonist of militant Protestantism against Roman Catholicism in Northern Ireland, Paisley was ordained in the Presbyterian Church in 1946. In 1951, however, he broke away from Presbyterianism to found his own sect, the Free Presbyterian Church of Ulster, noted for its virulent antiecumenism. In the late 1960s he led numerous anti-Catholic marches, and was jailed in 1966 and again in 1969 for heading demonstrations that ended in rioting. Running on a platform to end all reforms intended to help the Catholic minority, he was elected to the Northern Irish Parliament in April, 1970, and to the British House of Commons in June, 1970. After the British government suspended the Northern Irish Parliament in March, 1972, Paisley called for the total integration of Northern Ireland into the United Kingdom and condemned the constitutional arrangements made for a new assembly and power sharing between Protestants and Catholics. He was elected (June, 1973) to the new assembly, but he and other militant Protestants withdrew from it in Jan., 1974. He supported the strike by the Protestant workers that brought the collapse (May, 1974) of the new coalition executive council and the reimposition of direct British rule. Paisley retained his seat in the House of Commons in the elections of February and October, 1974.

Paisley (pāz'lē), burgh (1971 pop. 95,344), Renfrewshire, W Scotland, on the White Cart Water, a stream. The county administrative offices are in Paisley. It has a thriving textile industry and is among the world's largest producers of thread. Other manufactures are boilers, chemicals, and soap. Patterned Paisley shawls were famous in the 19th cent. Paisley Priory (1163), later an abbey, holds the tombs of several members of Scottish royalty. It was burned by the English in 1307. The present building dates from the 15th cent. In 1975, Paisley became part of the Strathclyde region.

Paiute Indians (pīo͞ot'), two distinct groups of North American Indians speaking languages belonging to the Shoshonean group of the Uto-Aztecan branch of the Aztec-Tanoan linguistic stock (see AMERICAN INDIAN LANGUAGES). The Northern Paiute ranged over central and E California, W Nevada, and E Oregon. The Southern Paiute occupied NW Arizona, SE California, S Nevada, and S Utah. The Northern Paiute were more warlike than their southern relatives; they fought the miners and the settlers during the 1860s, and a considerable part of them joined the Bannock in the war of 1878. The Southern Paiute are often called the Digger Indians because they subsisted on root digging. In general the Paiute of the Great Basin area subsisted by hunting, fishing, and digging for roots. They lived in small round huts (wickiups) that were covered with tule rushes. It was among the Paiute that the GHOST DANCE religion, which was to be of much significance on the frontier in the 1890s, first appeared (c.1870). The Indian messiah, WOVOKA, was a Paiute. Today the Paiute number some 4,000 on reservations in Arizona, California, Nevada, and Oregon. The name is also spelled Piute. See J. H. Steward, *Ethnography of the Owens Valley Paiute* (1933); O. C. Stewart, *Northern Paiute Bands* (1939); M. M. Wheat, *Survival Arts of the Primitive Paiutes* (1967).

Pajou, Augustin (ōgüstăN' päzho͞o'), 1730–1809, French sculptor. He won the Prix de Rome at the age of 18 and began a long career of royal commissions. He is noted for the elegance of his decorative work, particularly of the Opéra, Versailles (1768–70). His best works are his portrait busts, among which are those of Pascal; Descartes (Institut, Paris); and Buffon and Mme Du Barry (both: Louvre).

Pakenham, Sir Edward Michael (păk'ənəm), 1778–1815, British general. He entered the army in 1794 and served in the wars against Napoleon I, emperor of France. He distinguished himself in the Peninsular War at Salamanco in 1812. During the War of 1812 with the United States, he commanded British forces in the battle of New Orleans; it was the last engagement of the war, fought on Jan. 8, 1815, after peace had been signed at Ghent. Andrew JACKSON led the American troops, who won a decisive victory over the British. Pakenham was killed.

Pakhoi: see PEI-HAI, China.

Pakistan (păk'ĭstăn", päkĭstän'), republic (1972 est. pop. 64,890,000), 310,403 sq mi (803,944 sq km), S Asia. ISLAMABAD is the capital. Pakistan formerly consisted of two regions—West Pakistan and East Pakistan—located in the northwestern and northeastern corners of the Indian subcontinent and separated from each other by more than 1,000 mi (1,610 km) of India; East Pakistan became the independent state of BANGLADESH following the 1971 civil war. Pakistan

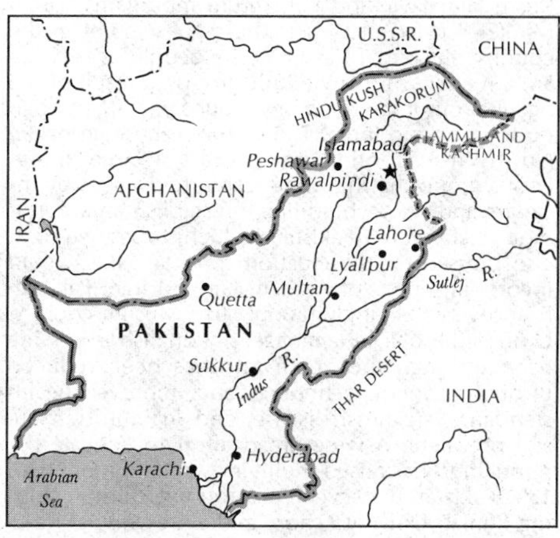

is bordered by India on the east, the Arabian Sea on the south, Iran on the southwest, and Afghanistan on the west and north; in the northeast is the disputed territory (with India) of Jammu and Kashmir (see KASHMIR), of which the part occupied by Pakistan borders on China. Pakistan is composed of four provinces—BALUCHISTAN, NORTH-WEST FRONTIER PROVINCE, PUNJAB, and SIND, all of which closely coincide with the historic regions—and a federal district that is the site of the capital. The country has a generally hot and dry climate, with desert conditions prevailing throughout most of the area. Along the western border and in a section of the north are semiarid steppelands; a subtropical climate with marked summer rainfall is found in a small section of the northeast along the Himalayan foothills; and a mountain climate that varies with altitude is found in the north. The Indus is the chief river of Pakistan and is the nation's lifeline. It flows the length of the country and is fed by the combined waters of the five rivers of Punjab—the Chenab, Jhelum, Ravi, Beas, and Sutlej. Along the Indus and its tributaries are found most of Pakistan's population, its chief agricultural areas, and its major hydroelectric power stations. Pakistan may be divided into four geographic regions—the plateau of W Pakistan, the plains of E Pakistan, the hills of NW Pakistan, and the mountains of N Pakistan. The plateau region of W Pakistan, which is roughly coextensive with Baluchistan prov., is an arid region with relatively wetter conditions in its northern sections. Numerous low mountain ranges rise from the plateau, and the Nal and Dasht rivers are the largest streams. Large portions of the region are unfit for agriculture, and although some cotton is raised, nomadic sheep grazing is the principal activity. Coal, chromite, and natural gas are found in this area, and fishing and salt trading are carried on along the rugged Makran coast. QUETTA, the chief city, is an important railroad center on the line between Afghanistan and the Indus valley. East of the plateau region are the extensive alluvial plains of E Pakistan, through which flow the Indus and its tributaries. The region, closely coinciding with Sind and Punjab provs., is hot and dry and is occupied in its eastern part by the Thar Desert. Extensive irrigation facilities, fed by the waters of the Indus system, make the Indus basin the agricultural heartland of Pakistan. A variety of crops (especially wheat, rice, and cotton) are raised there. The Indus delta, however, is not fertile and supports little agriculture. The irrigated portions of the plain are densely populated, being the site of many of Pakistan's principal cities, including KARACHI (the nation's chief port), LAHORE, LYALLPUR, HYDERABAD, and MULTAN. The higher parts of the plain, in the north, as in the vicinity of Lahore, have a favorable subtropical climate and have become Pakistan's resort center. In 1973, c.20,000 sq mi (51,800 sq km) of Punjab and Sind provs. were inundated by flood waters from the Indus; homes and crops were destroyed and the death toll was high. In NW Pakistan, occupying about two thirds of North-West Frontier Province, is a region of low hills and plateaus interspersed with fertile valleys. The elevation of the region tempers the arid climate. It is a predominantly agricultural area, with wheat the chief crop; fruit trees and livestock are also raised. Oil and coal are the chief minerals, although a variety of other minerals are found in small amounts. PESHAWAR and RAWALPINDI, the largest cities of this area, are major manufacturing centers. In the northern section of the North-West Frontier Province and in the Pakistani-occupied sector of Kashmir are the rugged ranges and the high, snow-capped mountains of the Hindu Kush, Himalaya, and Karakorum mountains; Tirich Mir (25,236 ft/7,692 m) is the highest point in the country outside of Kashmir. The people of Pakistan are a mixture of many ethnic groups, a result of the occupation of the region by groups passing through on their way to India. The PATHAN tribesmen of the North-West Frontier Province are a large, indigenous group that has long resisted advances by invaders and who would like to establish an autonomous state within Pakistan. Baluchi tribesmen have also pressed for the creation of a state that would incorporate parts of Afghanistan and Iran. Pakistan is an overwhelmingly (about 90%) Muslim country. Urdu is the official language, but English is in wide use. Although the death rate has been reduced through modern technology and improved health standards, sickness, disease, and malnutrition are still prevalent. A widespread effort to educate the population has raised the literacy rate to more than 15%. Pakistan has several major universities, including Punjab Univ. at Lahore and Sind Univ. at Karachi. Agriculture is the mainstay of Pakistan's economy, employing some 70% of the population. Wheat, rice, cotton, sugarcane, and tobacco are the chief crops. Most of Pakistan's agricultural output comes from the Indus basin. The country is not self-sufficient in food, even though vast irrigation schemes have extended farming into arid areas, and fertilizers and new varieties of crops have increased yields. Pakistan's rapidly increasing industrial base is able to supply most of the country's needs in consumer goods. The country's natural resources provide materials for such industries as textile production (the biggest earner of foreign exchange), oil refining, metal processing, and cement and fertilizer production. Since the mid-1950s electric power output has greatly increased, mainly because of the development of hydroelectric power potential and the use of nuclear power plants. Pakistan's chief imports are machinery, food, manufactured goods, and mineral fuels. The chief trading partners are the United States, Great Britain, Japan, and West Germany. Pakistan is governed by the constitution of April, 1973, which provides for a federal parliamentary form of government. There is a bicameral Parliament whose 210 members in the National Assembly and 63 members in the Senate (14 from each province, 5 from federally administered tribal areas, and 2 from the federal capital) are elected by popular vote. The president is the head of state, and the prime minister, in whom most power is vested, is the chief executive. Each province has its own legislative assembly whose members are elected by direct popular vote, a provincial governor appointed by the president, and a chief minister elected by the legislative assembly. There is an independent judicial branch of government.

Early History. The northwest of the Indian subcontinent, which now constitutes Pakistan, lies athwart the historic invasion routes through the Khyber, Gumal, and Bolan passes from central Asia to the heartland of India, and for thousands of years invaders and adventurers swept down upon the settlements there. The earliest known culture in the area was the prehistoric INDUS VALLEY CIVILIZATION, which flourished until it was overrun by Aryan invaders c.1500 B.C. The Aryans were followed by the Persians of the Achaemenid empire, who by c.500 B.C. reached the Indus River. Alexander the Great, conqueror of the Persian empire, invaded the Punjab in 326 B.C. The Seleucid empire, heir to Alexander's Indian conquest, was checked by the Mauryas, who by 305 B.C. occupied the Indus plain and much of Afghanistan. After the fall of the Mauryas (2d cent. B.C.) the Indo-Greek Bactrian kingdom rose to power, but was in turn overrun (c.97 B.C.) by Scythian nomads called Saka and then by the Parthians (A.D. c.7). The Parthians, of Persian stock, were replaced by the Kushans; the Kushan KANISHKA ruled (2d cent. A.D.) all of what is now Pakistan from his capital at Peshawar. In 712, the Muslim Arabs appeared in force and conquered Sind, and by 900 they controlled most of NW India. They were followed by the Ghaznavid and Ghorid Turks. The first Turki invaders reached Bengal c.1200 and an important Muslim center was established there, principally through conversion of the Hindus. Although the northeast of the Indian subcontinent (now Bangladesh) remained, with interruptions, part of a united Mogul empire in India from the early 16th cent. to 1857, the northwest changed hands many times before it became (1857) part of imperial British India. It was overrun by Persians in the late 1730s; by the Afghans, who held Sind and the Punjab during the latter half of the 18th cent.; and by the Sikhs, who rose to power in the Punjab under Ranjit Singh (1780-1839). The British attempted to subdue the anarchic northwest during the First Afghan War (1839-42) and succeeded in conquering Sind in 1843 and the Punjab in 1849. The turbulence of the region was intensified by the fierce forays of Baluchi and Pathan tribesmen from the mountainous hinterlands. The British occupied Quetta in 1876 and again attempted to conquer the tribesmen in the Second Afghan War (1878-80) but were still unsuccessful. With the creation of the North-West Frontier Province in 1901, the British shifted from a policy of conquest to one of containment. Unlike previous settlers in India, the Muslim immigrants were not absorbed into Hindu society. Their ranks were augmented by the millions of Hindus who had been converted to Islam during the declining years of the Mogul empire; there was cultural interchange between Hindu and Muslim, but no homogeneity emerged. After the Indian Mutiny (1857), a rising Hindu middle class began to assume dominant positions in industry, education, the professions, and the civil service. Although, in these early decades of the Indian National Congress, vigorous efforts were made to include Muslims in the nationalist movement, concern for Muslim political rights led to the formation of the MUSLIM LEAGUE in 1906; in the ensuing years Hindu-Muslim conflict became increasingly acute. The idea of a Muslim nation, distinct from Hindu India, was introduced in 1930 by the poet Muhammad IQBAL and was ardently supported by a group of Indian Muslim students in England, who were the first to use the name Pakistan [land of the pure, from the Urdu *pak,* = pure and *stan,* = land]. It gained wide support in 1940 when the Muslim League, led by Muhammad Ali JINNAH, demanded the establishment of a Muslim state in the areas of India where Muslims were in the majority. The league received nearly all of the Muslim vote in the 1946 elections, and Britain, faced with a united Muslim voice, reluctantly agreed to the formation of Pakistan as a separate dominion under the provisions of the Indian Independence Act, which went into effect on Aug. 15, 1947.

Independence and After. Jinnah became the governor-general of the new nation and LIAQUAT ALI KHAN the first prime minister. While India inherited most of the British administrative machinery, Pakistan had to start with practically nothing; records and Muslim administrators were transferred from New Delhi to a chaotic, makeshift capital at Karachi. Moreover, an autumn of violence and slaughter among Hindus and Muslims came between independence and the task of developing the new nation. Disturbances in Delhi were only a prelude to the slaughter in the Punjab, where the Gurdaspur district had been partitioned to give India access to Kashmir. Although there was some violence in Calcutta, the efforts of Mohandas K. Gandhi prevented widespread killing in partitioned Bengal. The communal strife took more than a million lives; 7.5 million Muslim refugees fled to both parts of Pakistan from India, and 10 million Hindus left Pakistan for India. Disputes between India and Pakistan arose also over the princely states of Junagadh, Hyderabad, and Kashmir. In the first two, Muslim rulers held sway over a Hindu majority but India forcibly joined both states to the Union, dismissing the wishes of the rulers and basing its claims instead on the wishes of the people and the facts of geography. In Kashmir the situation was precisely the opposite; a Hindu ruler held sway over a Muslim majority in a country that was geographically and economically tied to West Pakistan. The ruler signed over Kashmir to India in Oct., 1947, but Pakistan refused to accept the move. Fighting broke out (see INDIA-PAKISTAN WARS) and continued until Jan., 1948, when India and Pakistan both appealed to the United Nations, each accusing the other of aggression. A cease-fire was agreed upon and a temporary demarcation line partitioned (1949) the disputed state. In the meantime Pakistan faced serious internal problems. A liberal statement of constitutional principles was promulgated in 1949, but parts of the proposed constitution ran into orthodox Muslim opposition. On Oct. 16, 1951, Prime Minister Liaquat Ali Khan was assassinated by an Afghan fanatic. His death left a leadership void that prime ministers Khwaja Nazimuddin (1951-53) and Muhammad Ali (1953-55) and governor-general Ghulam Muhammad (1951-55) failed to fill. In East Bengal, which had more than half of the nation's population, there was increasing dissatisfaction with the federal government in West Pakistan. In 1954, faced with growing crises, the government dissolved the constituent assembly and declared a state of emergency. In 1955, the existing provinces and princely states of West Pakistan were merged into a single province made up of 12 divisions, and the name of East Bengal was changed to East Pakistan, thus giving it at least the appearance of parity with West Pakistan. In Feb., 1956, a new constitution was finally adopted, and Pakistan formally became a republic within the British Commonwealth; Gen. Iskander Mirza became the first president. Economic conditions remained precarious, even though large shipments of grain from the United States after 1953 had helped to relieve famine. In foreign relations, Pakistan's conflict with India over Kashmir remained unresolved, and Afghanistan continued its agitation for the formation of an autonomous Pushtunistan nation made up of the Pathan tribesmen along the northwest frontier. Pakistan joined the Southeast Asia Treaty Organization in 1954 and the Central Treaty Organization in 1955. After 1956 the threat to the stability of the Pakistan government gradually increased, stemming from continuing economic difficulties, frequent cabinet crises, and widespread political corruption. Finally, in Oct., 1958, President Mirza abrogated the constitution and granted power to the army under Gen. Muhammad AYUB KHAN. Ayub subsequently assumed presidential powers (in 1960 he was elected to a five-year term), abolishing the office of prime minister and ruling by decree. Under the dictatorship, a vigorous land reform and economic development program was begun, and a new constitution, which provided for a federal Islamic republic with two provinces (East and West Pakistan) and two official languages (Bengali and Urdu), went into effect in 1962. The new city of Islamabad, N of Rawalpindi (which had been interim capital since 1959), became the national capital, and DACCA, in East Pakistan, became the legislative capital. In 1965, Ayub was reelected and a national assembly of 156 members—with East and West Pakistan each allocated 75 seats, and 6 seats reserved for women, who had previously been denied the vote under Islamic strictures—was elected. A treaty with India governing the use of the waters of the Indus basin was signed (1961) but no agreement has been reached with regard to the waters of the Ganges. Communal strife was constantly present in the subcontinent—in Jan., 1961, several thousand Muslims were massacred in Madhya Pradesh state in India, and there were reprisals in Pakistan; in 1962 there was further communal conflict in Bengal. Diplomatic relations between Pakistan and Afghanistan were severed (1961-63) after some border clashes and continued Afghan agitation, supported by the USSR, for an independent Pushtunistan. A series of conferences on Kashmir was held (Dec., 1962-Feb., 1963) between India and Pakistan following the Chinese assault (Oct., 1962) on India; both nations offered important concessions and solution of the long-standing dispute seemed imminent. However, Pakistan then signed a bilateral border agreement with China that involved the boundaries of the disputed state, and relations with India again became strained. Pakistan's continuing conflict with India over Kashmir erupted in fighting (April-June, 1965) in the Rann of Kutch region of NW India and SE West Pakistan and in an outbreak of warfare (August-September) in Kashmir. Some improvement in relations between the two countries came in 1966, when President Ayub Khan and Prime Minister Lal Bahadur Shastri of India reached an accord in the Declaration of Tashkent at a meeting sponsored by the USSR. Despite the accord, however, the basic dispute over Kashmir remained unsettled. In an effort to gain support in the conflict with India, Pakistan somewhat modified its pro-Western policy after 1963 by establishing closer relations with Communist countries, especially with China, by taking a neutral position on some international issues, and by joining the Regional Cooperation for Development Program of SW Asian nations. East Pakistan's long-standing discontent with the federal government was expressed in 1966 by a movement for increased autonomy, supported by a general strike. Following disastrous riots in late 1968 and early 1969, Ayub resigned and handed the government over to Gen. Agha Muhammad YAHYA KHAN, the head of the army, who then declared martial law. The first direct universal voting since independence was held in Dec., 1970, to elect a National Assembly that would draft a new constitution and restore federal parliamentary government. The AWAMI LEAGUE, under Sheik MUJIBUR RAHMAN, in a campaign for full autonomy in East Pakistan, won an overwhelming majority in the National Assembly by taking 153 of the 163 seats allotted to East Pakistan.

The opening session of the National Assembly, scheduled to meet in Dacca in Mar., 1971, was twice postponed by Yahya, who then canceled the election results, banned the Awami League, and imprisoned Sheik Mujib in West Pakistan on charges of treason. East Pakistan delcared its independence as Bangladesh on Mar. 26, 1971, but was then placed under martial law and occupied by the Pakistani army, which was composed entirely of troops from West Pakistan. In the ensuing civil war, some 10 million refugees fled to India and hundreds of thousands of civilians were killed. India supported Bangladesh and on Dec. 3, 1971, sent troops into East Pakistan. Following a two-week war between Pakistan and India, in which fighting also broke out along the India-West Pakistan border, Pakistani troops in East Pakistan surrendered (Dec. 16) and a cease-fire was declared on all fronts. Following Pakistan's defeat, Zulfikar Ali BHUTTO, the deputy premier and foreign minister, took absolute control in West Pakistan. Sheik Mujib was released from prison and eventually allowed to return to Bangladesh. Relations with India remained strained over the issue of the more than 90,000 Pakistani soldiers who had surrendered after the civil war and become prisoners-of-war, over Pakistan's refusal to recognize Bangladesh, and over Bangladesh's declared intention to bring to trial some Pakistani soldiers on war-crimes charges. A summit meeting held in Simla, India, in July, 1972, resulted in an easing of tensions and an agreement to settle differences between the two nations peacefully. Demarcation of the truce line in Kashmir was finally completed in Dec., 1972. In Aug., 1973, India and Pakistan reached an agreement on the release of Pakistani prisoners-of-war and the exchange of hostage populations in India, Pakistan, and Bangladesh—especially of the Bengalis in Pakistan and the Biharis in Bangladesh. Bhutto recognized Bangladesh in Feb., 1974, prior to the start of a world Islamic summit conference in Lahore. See O. H. Spate et al., *India and Pakistan: A General and Regional Geography* (3d ed. 1967), K. B. Sayeed, *Pakistan: The Formative Phase, 1857-1948* (2d ed. 1968), David Loshak, *Pakistan Crisis* (1971), R. F. Nyrop et al., *Area Handbook for Pakistan* (1971), W. N. Brown, *The United States and India, Pakistan, Bangladesh* (3d ed. 1972), Herbert Feldman, *From Crisis to Crisis: Pakistan 1962-1969* (1972), Rounaq Jahan, *Pakistan: Failure in National Integration* (1972), S. M. Burke, *Pakistan's Foreign Policy: An Historical Analysis* (1973).

Pakokku (pəkō'ko͞o), town (1962 est. pop. 157,000), central Burma, a port on the Irrawaddy River. It is a trading and shipping center. Pakokku grew in importance after the British occupation in the 19th cent. Nearby are the Yenangyaung oil fields, which have been in operation since the 1870s; the facilities were destroyed in World War II but have since been rebuilt. Pakokku was occupied by Communist rebels in 1949 and was held until 1955, when it was liberated by government forces.

Pakow: see P'ING-CH'ÜAN, China.

Palacio Valdés, Armando (ärmän'dō pälä'thyō väldās'), 1853-1938, Spanish novelist and critic. He began his career with critical writings, but his reputation rests on his realistic novels, characterized by an optimistic view of life. *La aldea perdida* [the lost village] (1911) and *La hermana San Sulpicio* (1889, tr. *The Joy of Captain Ribot,* 1900) are considered the best of these. A collection of his short stories appeared in English translation in 1935.

Palacký, František (frän'tyĭshĕk pä'lätskē), 1798-1876, Czech nationalist and historian, b. Moravia. Regarded as the father of the modern Czech nation, Palacký played a leading role in the Czech cultural and national revival in the 1820s, '30s, and '40s. During the revolution of 1848, he presided over the first Pan-Slav Congress (see PAN-SLAVISM) at Prague. He advocated Czech autonomy within a strong Austrian Empire as the best protection against German and Russian pressure. His paraphrase of Voltaire—"If the Austrian Empire did not exist, it would have to be invented"—remains famous. After the suppression of the liberal and nationalist uprisings of 1848 in the Austrian Empire, Palacký became disillusioned. He withdrew from political activity until 1861, when he became a deputy to the Austrian parliament. With the introduction (1867) of Austrian centralizing policies, he worked for complete Czech independence. Palacký was an advocate of enlightenment and education, rather than revolution. Strongly influenced by Immanuel Kant and J. J. Rousseau, he visualized the Czech nation as a bearer of the democratic ideal. His influence on the thinking of later national leaders, such as Thomas G. MASARYK, was enormous. In his *Geschichte Böhmens* [history of Bohemia] (in German, 5 vol., 1836-67; in Czech, 5 vol., 1848-76), he viewed Czech history as a constant struggle between Germans and Slavs. This monumental work of scholarship strongly influenced the burgeoning Czech national consciousness. See study by J. F. Zacek (1970).

Palaemon (pəlē'mŏn), in Greek mythology, seagod. He was the protector of ships, and in his honor the ISTHMIAN GAMES were celebrated. As a mortal he was called Melicertes. He became a seagod when he and his mother, INO, leaped into the sea to escape the murderous frenzy of his father, Athamas. Palaemon was identified with the Roman god Portunus.

palaeo-. For words beginning thus, see also PALEO-.

Palaeologus (pālēŏl'əgəs), Greek dynasty that ruled the Byzantine Empire from its restoration in 1261 to its final conquest by the Turks in 1453. The first emperor was MICHAEL VIII, restorer of the empire. He was succeeded by ANDRONICUS II (reigned 1282-1328) and ANDRONICUS III (reigned 1328-41). JOHN V acceded in 1341, but was kept from the throne until 1354 by John VI (John Cantacuzene) and from 1376 until 1379 by his son, Andronicus IV. At his death (1391) MANUEL II succeeded and ruled until 1425; he had to share his rule with JOHN VII after 1399. Manuel's sons JOHN VIII (reigned 1425-48) and Constantine XI (reigned 1449-53) succeeded him. Constantine XI was killed when the Turks stormed Constantinople. Branches of the Palaeologus family survived in various European countries. One branch ruled the Italian marquisate of Montferrat from the 14th cent. until the family's extinction in 1536. Distinguished for their erudition, the Palaeologi helped the Greek people to retain their cultural identity after their conquest by the Ottoman Turks. As statesmen they had to contend with the pressure of the Turks and with the reluctance of Western Europe to come to the aid of the Orthodox Greeks. Their rule marked the high point of feudalism, partitions of the empire, and internal conflict between religious and secular groups.

Palafox, José de (hōsā' thā päläfôkh'), 1776?-1847, Spanish general in the PENINSULAR WAR, celebrated for his heroic defense of Saragossa. Elected captain general of Aragón in 1808, he held Saragossa against the French with an improvised garrison of citizens and peasants. Though the French breached the city walls, his forces held out behind street barricades from June to Aug., 1808, when the French withdrew. In Dec., 1808, the French under Lannes again besieged the city. Palafox surrendered only in Feb., 1809, after three weeks of street fighting. He was held a prisoner in France until 1813. Palafox commanded the royal guards during the uprisings of 1820-23 against Ferdinand VII, but he lost his post because of his stand in favor of the liberal constitution. He later commanded the loyal troops against the Carlists and was created duque de Saragossa.

Palaihnihan Indians: see PIT RIVER INDIANS.

Palal (pā'lăl), worker on the wall of Jerusalem. Neh. 3.25.

Palamas, Kostes (kôstĕs' pälämäs'), 1859-1943, Greek poet. He studied at the Univ. of Athens of which he later was secretary for many years. Except in his early work, he wrote in demotic or vernacular Greek and translated into this idiom the New Testament and the works of various European writers. His own verse is considered more intellectual than lyric, although his lament *Taphos* (1898) is an exception. A versatile writer, he produced epics, lyrics, plays, short stories, and criticism. Many of his 30 volumes have been translated into English, among them a lyric drama *Trisevyene* (1903, tr. *Royal Blossom,* 1923) and a volume of poetry, *Life Unshakeable* (1904, partial tr. 1919, 1921). See study by Thanasis Maskaleris (1972).

Palamedes (păləmē'dēz), in Greek mythology, crafty Greek hero of the Trojan War. Because he had exposed Odysseus when he tried to evade going to war, Odysseus falsely accused him of treachery, produced erroneous evidence, and had him executed. Some say that Agamemnon and Diomed, because Palamedes advocated peace, aided Odysseus. Palamedes was credited with many inventions, including numbers, measures, and the alphabet.

palate (păl'ĭt), roof of the mouth. The front part or hard palate, formed by the upper maxillary bones and the palate bones, separates the mouth from the nasal cavity. The back portion, or soft palate, consists of muscular tissue forming a partial partition between the mouth and the throat. A small conelike projection, the uvula, hangs from the middle of the soft palate. The soft palate and uvula move upward during swallowing or sucking, preventing food from entering the nasopharynx. Both the hard and soft portions of the palate are lined with mucous membrane containing numerous glands that lubricate the mouth and throat. If the sides of the bony palate fail to come together during embryonic development an opening, or cleft, remains along the midline. This condition, known as cleft palate, is repaired surgically in early infancy. See DIGESTIVE SYSTEM.

Palatinate (pəlăt'ĭnāt"), Ger. *Pfalz,* two regions of West Germany. They are related historically, but not geographically. The Rhenish or Lower Palatinate (Ger. *Rheinpfalz* or *Niederpfalz*), often called simply the Palatinate, is a district (c.2,100 sq mi/5,440 sq km) of the state of RHINELAND-PALATINATE. The Rhenish Palatinate extends from the left bank of the Rhine and borders in the S on France and in the W on the Saarland and Luxembourg. Neustadt an der Weinstrasse is the capital; Ludwigshafen, Kaiserslautern, Pirmasens, and Speyer are the chief cities. It is a rich agricultural region, famed for its wines. The Upper Palatinate (Ger. *Oberpfalz*) is a district (c.3,725 sq mi/9,650 sq km) of NE Bavaria, separated in the east from Czechoslovakia by the Bohemian Forest. REGENSBURG is the capital. Agriculture and cattle raising are the chief occupations. The name of the two regions came from the office known as count palatine, a title used in the Roman, Byzantine, and Holy Roman empires and elsewhere, notably in England, Hungary, and Poland; the rights of office varied, but in general the palatine had superior judicial functions and enjoyed privileges superior to those of other nobles. Emperor Frederick I bestowed (1156) the title count palatine on his half-brother Conrad, who was in possession of territories on both sides of the Rhine. More extensive than the present Rhenish Palatinate, these territories also included the northern part of modern Baden (but not the bishopric of Speyer and other enclaves in the palatine lands W of the Rhine). When Conrad's line died out, the Palatinate passed (1214) to the Bavarian WITTELSBACH dynasty. The Wittelsbachs enlarged their holdings along the Bohemian border, which were constituted as the Upper Palatinate; and from the 14th cent. until 1777 the Wittelsbach holdings were split between the two main lines of the family, with the senior line holding the two palatinates and the junior line holding Bavaria. The electoral vote (see ELECTORS) alternated at first between the two lines, but was settled (1356) by the Golden Bull on the counts palatine, henceforth known as electors palatine. Their territories were called the Electoral Palatinate (Ger. *Kurpfalz*). Elector RUPERT became emperor in 1400. After his death the Palatinate line divided into several collateral branches, which held territories of their own. The direct line was succeeded to (1559) by the counts palatine of Simmern, who in turn were succeeded by the dukes palatine of Neuburg (1685) and the counts palatine of Sulzbach (1742). The Rhenish Palatinate flourished in the 15th and 16th cent., and its capital, HEIDELBERG, was a center of the German Renaissance and Reformation. The election (1619) of Elector Frederick V (see FREDERICK THE WINTER KING) as king of Bohemia precipitated the Thirty Years War, in which the Palatinate was ravaged both by the imperial forces under Tilly and by the Protestant army under Mansfeld. The Upper Palatinate and the electoral vote were taken from Frederick and transferred to Bavaria, but at the Peace of Westphalia (1648) a new vote was created for Frederick's successor, Charles Louis. The Palatinate-Neuburg line acquired (1666) the contested duchies of Jülich and Berg but, after its accession (1685) to the Electoral Palatinate, became involved in the War of the Grand Alliance with Louis XIV, who ordered the devastation (1688-89) of the Rhenish Palatinate. In 1720 the capital was transferred to MANNHEIM. The demise (1777) of the Bavarian line united all Wittelsbach lands except the duchy of ZWEIBRÜCKEN under Elector Charles Theodore. After the War of the BAVARIAN SUCCESSION (1778-79) the succession to Bavaria, the Palatinate, and Jülich and Berg was settled on the Palatinate-Birkenfeld line, which held Zweibrücken. However, by the time Duke Maximilian of Zweibrücken acceded (1799), the palatine lands W of the Rhine had been conquered by France in the French Revolutionary Wars. In 1803, Maximilian ceded the palatine lands E of the Rhine to Baden, Hesse-Darmstadt, and Nassau, but in 1806 he became king of a much-enlarged Bavaria, and at the Congress of Vienna (1815) he recovered part of the Rhenish Palatinate W of the Rhine, including Speyer and other enclaves. Several districts, however, were awarded to Prussia, Hesse, and Oldenburg. The Upper Palatinate was increased by the addition of Regensburg, which replaced Amberg as capital. Both the Rhenish and the Upper Palatinate became integral parts of Bavaria. After World War II the Rhenish Palatinate became (1946) a district of the newly created state of Rhineland-Palatinate.

Palatine (păl'ətīn), village (1970 pop. 25,904), Cook co., NE Ill.; inc. 1869. Safety equipment, machine tools, and industrial adhesives are the chief manufactures. A junior college is there.

Palatine, hill: see *Rome before Augustus* and *Roman Empire* under ROME.

Palau (pälou'), island group (1970 pop. 11,210), c.192 sq mi (497 sq km), W Pacific, in the W CAROLINE ISLANDS. Palau is one of six administrative districts of the U.S. Trust Territory of the Pacific Islands (see PACIFIC ISLANDS, TRUST TERRITORY OF THE). Palau consists of about 200 islands and islets, of which Babelthuap, Koror (the administrative center of the group), Arakabesan, and Malakal are the most important. Trochus shells and scrap metal are the only notable exports. Spain held the islands for about 300 years before selling them to Germany in 1899. Japan seized them in 1914 and was given a mandate over them by the League of Nations in 1920. A major Japanese naval base in World War II, Palau was seized by U.S. forces in 1944. Palau is sometimes spelled Pelew.

Palawan (pälä'wän), island (1970 pop. 232,322), 4,550 sq mi (11,785 sq km), 5th largest of the Philippines, N of Borneo and between the Sulu Archipelago and the South China Sea. Lumbering is an important industry on Palawan; it is a leading wood-products manufacturing area. There is little arable land, but subsistence farming is carried on. The island has important mercury and chromite deposits as well as commercial crocodile grounds. Many of its inhabitants are MOROS. During World War II, it was the site of a Japanese massacre of American prisoners.

Pale, in Irish history, that district of indefinite and varying limits around Dublin, in which English law prevailed before the complete subjugation of Ireland to English rule. The term was first used in the 14th cent. to designate what had previously been called English land. Outlying districts were styled the marches, or border lands. In the time of Henry VIII the Pale extended N from Dublin to Dundalk and c.20 mi (32 km) inland from the coast. It disappeared in the ensuing years as the English control of the whole of Ireland was made effective. There was another English Pale in France, comprising Calais and the surrounding area, until 1558. In Russia the Pale designated those regions in which Jews were allowed to live. The Jewish Pale was established in 1792, when it comprised the areas annexed from Poland in the first partition. The area was extended (partly as a result of further annexations), but even within the Pale the Jewish population was subjected to many restrictions. Most of these were in force until the Russian Revolution of 1917.

Palembang (pälĕmbäng'), city (1961 pop. 474,971), capital of South Sumatra province., on SE Sumatra, Indonesia. It is a deepwater port on both banks of the Musi River, one of the largest cities on the island, and the trade and shipping center for the S Sumatra oil fields. Rubber, coffee, and coal are also exported. There are large oil refineries, rubber plants, textile mills, fertilizer factories, and food-processing plants. Palembang in the 8th cent. was the capital of the powerful Hindu-Sumatran kingdom of Sri Vijaya. The Dutch began trading there in 1617, and later it was intermittently under British rule. The sultanate of Palembang was abolished by the Dutch in 1825. Sriwidjaja State Univ. is in the city.

Palencia (pälān'thēä), city (1970 pop. 58,370), capital of Palencia prov., N central Spain, in León. An industrial center with iron foundries, textile mills, and chemical plants, it was formerly noted for its woolen industry. Palencia was occupied by the Romans and sacked (6th cent.) by the Visigoths. It was recovered from the Moors in the 10th cent. and was in the 12th and 13th cent. a favorite residence of the kings of León. The first university in Spain was founded there (1212 or 1214) but was removed to Salamanca in 1238. There is a notable Gothic cathedral (14th–16th cent.) containing a fine collection of old Flemish tapestries and paintings by El Greco.

Palenque (päläng'kĕ), ancient city of the MAYA in Chiapas, S Mexico, in the Usumacinta valley. Its architectural elegance, adapted to tropical and topographical conditions, was a high point in the art of the Classic period. Stucco sculpturing and low-relief paneling reached their highest expression at Palenque. The Temple of Inscriptions, noted for its hieroglyphic tablets, is one of the best-preserved Mayan temples. Entablatures sloping inward and roofs slanting back to give a mansard effect show the great range of architectural concepts among the Maya.

Paleocene epoch (pā'lēəsēn"), first epoch of the TERTIARY PERIOD in the CENOZOIC ERA of geologic time. In W North America, the uplift of the Rocky Mts. that marked the end of the Mesozoic era continued throughout the Paleocene, and the Cretaceous inland seas gradually withdrew from the Great Plains area and central and SW California. In Montana and Wyoming the Fort Union shales and sandstones, laid down during this epoch, are noteworthy because they overlie undeformed upper Cretaceous sediments, thus recording the demise of the dinosaurs and the rise of mammals. Except for part of N France, Europe was largely emergent, i.e., raised above water. During this epoch, Greenland is thought to have split away from North America, opening a passage between the Atlantic and Arctic oceans.

paleography (pālēŏg'rəfē) [Gr.,=early writing], term generally meaning all study and interpretation of old ways of recording language. In a narrower sense, it excludes epigraphy (the study of inscriptions) and includes only the writing that is done on such materials as wax, papyrus, parchment, and paper. In Western Europe and in regions that have adopted Western European ways of writing, letters of all kinds—capital and lower case, roman, italic, black letter, and script—are derived from the capital letters of Roman inscriptions. From these "square" capitals developed less severe capitals called "rustic" and also letters called "uncial," with more curves than capitals have. The uncial M, for example, substitutes curves for the two angles at the top, as the lower-case letter does. Capitals and uncials are called majuscules and are distinguished from minuscules, the lower-case letters. The lower-case letters established themselves definitely in Alcuin's school at Tours in the time of Charlemagne. Letters of the kind preferred in that school are known as Carolingian, or Caroline, minuscules. Efforts to make letters ornate led to the development of black letter, no longer in use except in relatively few German printed books. Letters of this ornate kind, with many angles and with heavy shading, are sometimes called gothic—a term that is ambiguous, since it is used by printers for very simple letters without serifs. In type, italic letters were introduced by ALDUS MANUTIUS; they are said to have been suggested by the handwriting of Petrarch. As the Spencerian script of the 19th cent. enables us to give an approximate date for a document written in it, so one skilled in the history of handwriting can often assign a place and a date to a document of earlier times. It is sometimes possible to identify the writer of a document and to distinguish forgeries from authentic documents. Specialists devote themselves also to the many forms of writing not derived from Roman capitals, such as Greek, Arabic, and Chinese. See also ALPHABET; CALLIGRAPHY; CUNEIFORM; WRITING; INSCRIPTION; HIEROGLYPHIC. See Stanley Morison, *Politics and Script* (1972).

Paleolithic art, art of the most recent ice-age. Present study and knowledge of this art is largely confined to works discovered at more than 150 sites in W Europe, particularly to the magnificent cave paintings in N Spain and the Dordogne valley of SW France. Most of the these works were produced during two vast, overlapping periods. The Aurignacio-Perigordian (c.14,000–c.13,500 B.C.) includes the powerful Lascaux paintings, the outdoor sculpture at Laussel, and the several small female figurines, known as Venuses, found at several sites. The second period, the Solutreo-Magdalenian (c.14,000–c.9500 B.C.), includes the murals at Rouffignac and Niaux and the ceiling of the cave at Altamira, Spain, the Magdalenian's crowning masterpiece. Both of the great cave complexes were discovered by accident—Altamira in 1879, Lascaux in 1940. The painting styles, known as Franco-Cantabrian and ascribed to CRO-MAGNON MAN, embrace a variety of techniques including painting with fingers, sticks, pads of fur or moss; daubing; dotting; sketching with colored materials and charcoal; and spray painting through hollow bone or by mouth. Several pigments were used, and foreshortening and shadowing were skillfully employed. Images were often crowded close to and on top of each other, sometimes with obvious respect for previously applied paintings. Irregular surfaces were decorated in relief. Separate styles, presumably from different eras, can be discerned, 13 at Lascaux alone. In most Paleolithic caves animal figures (mainly horses, bison, cattle, and hinds) predominate, suggesting that the art may have had ritual significance related to hunting; there are few group or hunting scenes, however, and human figures are extremely rare. Drawn with vitality and the elegance of great simplicity, the animals are the masterworks of prehistoric art and are of an accuracy that provides invaluable evidence to paleozoologists. The Lascaux cave was closed when the paintings began to deteriorate. Some of Lascaux's painted rooms show no signs of human habitation and may have been used for ritual. Engravings on soft stone, bone, and ivory, as well as low reliefs and a few freestanding sculptures, have been found in or near many of these caves. Another style predominates in E Spain and bears a strong resemblance to the ROCK CARVINGS AND PAINTINGS of N and S Africa. The pictures, drawn chiefly in silhouette, are found on the walls of shallow rock shelters and are usually small; they depict human as well as animal figures in scenes of hunting, fighting, ceremonial, ritual, and domestic activities. This art seems to have reached its peak in the Mesolithic period. A third style, largely of Aurignacian origin, ranges from France to W Siberia and consists almost entirely of small sculptured figures of animals and human beings. The latter are chiefly female, often abnormally voluptuous, and are generally regarded as fertility goddesses; one of the most famous is the Venus of Willendorf, Austria. See AFRICAN ART and PALEOLITHIC PERIOD. See studies by Paolo Graziosi (tr. 1960), T. G. E. Powell (1966), André Leroi-Gourhan (tr. 1967), P. M. Grand (1967), and N. K. Sandars (1968).

Paleolithic period (pā"lēəlĭth'ĭk, -lēō-, păl-) or **Old Stone Age,** the earliest period of human development and the longest phase of mankind's history. It is approximately coextensive with the Pleistocene geologic epoch, beginning about 2 million years ago and ending in various places between 40,000 and 10,000 years ago, when it was succeeded by the MESOLITHIC PERIOD. By far the most outstanding feature of the Paleolithic period was the evolution of man from an apelike creature, or near man, to true *Homo sapiens* (see MAN, PREHISTORIC). This development was exceedingly slow and continued through the three successive divisions of the period, the Lower, Middle, and Upper Paleolithic. The most abundant remains of Paleolithic cultures are a variety of stone tools whose distinct characteristics provide the basis for a system of classification containing several toolmaking traditions or industries. The oldest recognizable tools made by members of the family of man are simple stone choppers, such as those discovered at Olduvai Gorge in Tanzania. These tools may have been made over 1 million years ago by AUSTRALOPITHECUS, ancestor of modern man. Fractured stones called eoliths have been considered the earliest tools, but it is impossible to distinguish man-made from naturally produced modifications in such stones. Lower Paleolithic stone industries of the early species of man called HOMO ERECTUS include the Choukoutienian of China and the Clactonian, Chellean-Abbevillian, Acheulian and Levalloisian represented at various sites in Europe, Africa, and Asia, from 100,000 to 500,000 years ago. Stone tools of this period are of the core type, made by chipping the stone to form a cutting edge, or of the flake type, fashioned from fragments struck off a stone. Hand axes were the typical tool of these early men who were hunters and food-gatherers. The Middle Paleolithic period includes the Mousterian culture, often associated with NEANDERTHAL MAN, an early form of man, living between 40,000 and 100,000 years ago. Neanderthal remains are often found in caves with evidence of the use of fire. Neanderthals were hunters of prehistoric mammals, and their cultural remains, though unearthed chiefly in Europe, have been found also in N Africa, Palestine, and Siberia. Stone tools of this period are of the flake tradition, and bone implements, such as needles, indicate that crudely sewn furs and skins were used as body covering. Since the dead were painted before burial, a kind of primitive religion may have been practiced. In the Upper Paleolithic period, Neanderthal man disappears and is replaced by a variety of *Homo sapiens* such as CRO-MAGNON MAN and Grimaldi man. This, the flowering of the Paleolithic period, saw an astonishing number of human cultures, such as the Aurignacian, Gravettian, Perigordian, Solutrean, and Magdalenian, rise and develop in the Old World. The beginnings of communal hunting and extensive fishing are found here, as is the first conclusive evidence of belief systems centering on magic and the supernatural. Pit houses, the first man-made shelters, were built, sewn clothing was worn, and sculpture and painting originated. Tools were of great variety, including flint and obsidian blades and projectile points. It is probable that the people of the Aurignacian culture migrated to Europe after developing their distinctive culture elsewhere, perhaps in Asia. Their stone tools are finely worked, and they made a typical figure-eight-shaped blade. They also used bone, horn, and ivory and made necklaces and other personal ornaments. They carved the so-called Venus figures, ritual statuettes of bone, and made outline drawings on cave walls. The hunters of the Solutrean phase of the Upper Paleolithic entered Europe from the east and ousted many of their Aurignacian predecessors. The Solutrean wrought extremely fine spearheads, shaped like a laurel leaf. The wild horse was their chief quarry. The Solutrean as well as remnants of the Aurignacian were replaced by the Magdalenian, the final, and perhaps most impressive, phase of the Paleolithic period. Here artifacts reflect a society made up of communities of fishermen and reindeer hunters. Surviving Magdalenian tools, which range from tiny microliths to implements of great length and fineness, indicate an advanced technique. Weapons were highly refined and varied, the ATLATL first came into use, and along the southern edge of the ice sheet boats and harpoons were developed. However, the crowning achievement of the Magdalenian was its cave paintings, the culmination of PALEOLITHIC ART. See L. S. B. Leakey, *Adam's Ancestors* (4th ed. 1960); M. C. Burkitt, *The Old Stone Age (4th ed. 1963);* Kenneth P. Oakley, *Man the Tool-Maker* (5th ed. 1963); François Bordes, *The Old Stone Age* (tr. 1968).

paleomagnetism, study of the intensity and orientation of the earth's magnetic field as preserved in the magnetic orientation of certain minerals found in rocks formed throughout geologic time. Paleomagnetic studies of rocks and ocean sediment have demonstrated that the orientation of the earth's magnetic field has frequently alternated over geologic time. Periods of "normal" polarity (e.g., when the north-seeking end of the compass needle points toward the present north magnetic pole, as it does today) have alternated with periods of "reversed" polarity (when the north-seeking end of the compass needle points southward). The cause of these magnetic "flip-flops" is not clearly understood. Studies of paleomagnetism are possible because some of the minerals that make up rocks—notably magnetite—become permanently magnetized by the earth's magnetic field at the time of their formation. For example, igneous rocks are formed when hot liquid material from below the earth's surface solidifies; when the susceptible minerals in the rocks cool below a certain temperature, they become magnetized parallel to the earth's magnetic field. Even minerals made up of crystals that grow at low temperatures can acquire magnetization. As the crystals grow, they acquire the same magnetic orientation as the field in which they are growing. Also, when magnetized minerals become disaggregated from their parent rocks by erosion and are carried into a sedimentary basin, they will tend to align themselves parallel to the earth's magnetic field as they settle in still water. When the deposit into which they settle hardens into rock, the magnetization will be fixed. Geophysicists have been able to trace changes in the orientation of the earth's magnetic field through geologic time by carefully collecting rock specimens of different ages and determining the alignment of their magnetic fields. That technique has provided a timetable for periods of normal and reversed polarity, showing 171 reversals in the earth's magnetic field in the past 76 million years. Paleomagnetic studies of the ocean floor have been of decisive importance in establishing the modern theories of CONTINENTAL DRIFT and SEA-FLOOR SPREADING.

paleontology (pā"lēantŏl'əjē) [Gr.,= study of early beings], science of the life of past geologic periods based on fossil remains. Although paleontology deals with early forms of life, it is usually treated as a part of geology rather than of biology, as the environment of the animals and plants with which it deals cannot be properly understood and reconstructed without knowledge of the age, structure, and composition of the rocks in which their remains are found. Paleontology is further united to geology because fossil evidence is much used for the establishment of the ages of rock strata. Micropaleontology, the study of microscopic fossils, is especially important for the recognition of subsurface strata in drilling for petroleum. Just as biology is commonly divided into botany and zoology, so paleontology is often divided into paleobotany (paleophytology) and paleozoology. Paleontology as a science separate from geology dates from the 19th cent., especially from the work of French naturalist Georges Cuvier on fossils. It received a great stimulus from the publication of the evolutionary hypothesis of Charles Darwin. See Kai Petersen, *Prehistoric Life on Earth* (1961); Theodore Delevoryas, *Morphology and Evolution of Fossil Plants* (1962); J. R. Beerbower, *Search for the Past* (2d ed. 1968); U. N. Lanham, *The Bone Hunters* (1973).

Paleosiberian languages (pā"lēōsībēr'ēən), also called Paleoasiatic or Hyperborean languages, family of languages spoken by about 20,000 indigenous inhabitants of Siberia. Of these, most live in extreme NE Siberia, and fewer than 1,000 live farther W near the Yenisei River. Only a few languages survive of this once extensive family, which formerly was spread over a considerable area of N Asia. Among the Paleosiberian languages still in use are Chukchi, Koryak, Kamchadal, Yukaghir, and Gilyak. These tongues have characteristics that recall a number of AMERICAN INDIAN LANGUAGES. For example, they are polysynthetic. In a polysynthetic language, a number of word elements are joined together to form a composite word that functions like a sentence in Indo-European languages. Most Paleosiberian languages did not have their own writing system in the past. Today their scripts are all based on the Cyrillic alphabet. See Roman Jakobson et. al., *Paleosiberian Peoples and Languages* (1957).

Paleozoic era (pā"lēəzō'ĭk), 3d major division of geologic time (see GEOLOGIC ERAS, table). It is subdivided into six periods, the first being the CAMBRIAN PERIOD. During the long hiatus between the late PRECAMBRIAN and early Paleozoic eras most of the evidence of the earth's early history was destroyed by erosion. From the beginning of the Paleozoic, shallow seas began to encroach on the continents, which had already assumed the general forms they were to have throughout the era. In North America, the era began with submerged geosynclines, or downward thrusts of the earth's crust, occupying the eastern, southeastern, and western sides of the continent, while the interior was dry land. As the era proceeded, the marginal seas periodically washed over the stable interior, leaving sedimentary deposits to mark their incursions. During the early part of the era, the area of exposed Precambrian foundation rocks, or shield, in central Canada was eroding, supplying sediment to the geosynclines from the interior. Beginning in the ORDOVICIAN PERIOD, mountain building intermittently proceeded in the eastern part of the Appalachian geosyncline throughout the rest of the era, bringing new sediments to the geosyncline from the east. Mountain-building processes created the Taconic range in the Ordovician, and later, the Acadian, or Older Appalachian, range in the DEVONIAN PERIOD. Sediments washing from the Acadian Mts. flooded the western part of the Appalachian geosyncline, filling it and forming the famous coal swamps of the CARBONIFEROUS PERIOD. Throughout the PERMIAN PERIOD uplift of the Appalachians totally destroyed the geosyncline as a sedimentary basin, and this region was never again inundated by vast marginal seas. Paleoclimatic studies in agreement with inferences based on glacial deposits found in early Paleozoic rocks indicate that central Africa was most likely in the polar regions during the early Paleozoic. Modern geophysical theory suggests that the Paleozoic mountain-building episodes were caused by the convergent motions of crustal plates containing the American and Afro-Eurasian continents. The most noteworthy feature of Paleozoic life is the sudden appearance of nearly all of the invertebrate animal phyla in great abundance at the beginning of the Cambrian. A few primitive fishlike vertebrates appeared in the Ordovician, scorpions in the SILURIAN period, amphibians in the Devonian, and reptiles in the Carboniferous. Reptiles increased in number and in variety during the Permian. The plant life of the Paleozoic era reached its climax in the Carboniferous and was much contracted in the Permian. A typical estimate for the length of the Paleozoic era is 375 million years, making it considerably shorter than the Precambrian.

Palermo (pälĕr'mō), Lat. *Panormus,* city (1971 pop. 650,645), capital of Palermo prov. and of Sicily, NW Sicily, Italy, on the Tyrrhenian Sea. Situated on the edge of the Conca d'Oro (Golden Conch Shell), a beautiful and fertile plain, it is Sicily's largest city and chief seaport. Manufactures include textiles, food products, chemicals, and cement. There are also shipyards in the city. An ancient Phoenician community founded between the 8th and 6th cent. B.C., it later became a Carthaginian military base and was conquered by the Romans in 254 B.C.-253 B.C. Palermo was under Byzantine rule from A.D. 535 to A.D. 831, when it fell to the Arabs, who held it until 1072. The city's prosperity dates from the Arab domination and continued when, under the Normans, it served (1072-1194) as the capital of the kingdom of Sicily. Under King Roger II (1130-54) and later under Emperor Frederick II (1220-50), Palermo attained its main artistic, cultural, and commercial flowering. The French Angevin dynasty transferred the capital to Naples; its misrule led to the SICILIAN VESPERS insurrection (1282), which began in Palermo. The city is rich in works of art; Byzantine, Arab, and Norman influence are blended in many buildings. Points of interest include the Arab-Norman Palatine Chapel (1130-40), located in the large palace of the Normans (today also the seat of the Sicilian parliament); the cathedral (founded in the late 12th cent.), which contains the tombs of Frederick II and other rulers; the Church of St. John of the Hermits (1132); the Palazzo Abbatellis (15th cent.), which houses the National Gallery of Sicily; the Gothic Palazzo Chiaramonte (1307); and the Capuchin catacombs. The city has a university.

Palermo stone, ancient Egyptian stone of black diorite engraved toward the end of the 5th dynasty (2565-2420 B.C.) and containing the earliest extant annals. The stone is only a small fragment of what was once a large slab. It is a hieroglyphic list of the kings of ancient Egypt before and after Menes, with regnal years and notations of events, and also includes such information as the height of the flooding of the Nile in various years. The stone was so named because it is housed in a museum in Palermo, Italy; small pieces of the stone are also in Cairo and in London.

Palés Matos, Luis (lwēs pälās' mä'tōs), 1898-1959, Puerto Rican poet and essayist. Palés Matos was an outstanding exponent of Afro-Antillean poetry, which by use of African intonations, dance rhythms, and colorful suggestion evokes the speech and the life of the West Indian Negro. His later poetry, blending satire and lyrical terseness, covered a broad range of themes. A major collection of his work is *Poesías, 1915-1956* (1957).

Palestine (păl'əstīn), historic region on the eastern shore of the Mediterranean Sea, comprising parts of modern Israel, Jordan, and Egypt; also known as the Holy Land. The name is derived from a word meaning "land of the Philistines." This article discusses mainly the physical geography and the history of Palestine until the United Nations took up the Palestine problem in 1947; for the economy and later history, see ISRAEL and JORDAN. In the Bible, Palestine is called Canaan before the invasion of Joshua; the usual Hebrew name is Eretz Israel [land of Israel]. Palestine is the Holy Land of Jews, having been promised to them by God; of Christians because it was the scene of Jesus' life; and of Muslims because they consider Islam to be the heir of Judaism and Christianity and because Jerusalem is the site, according to Muslim tradition, of Muhammad's ascent to heaven. Its boundaries, never constant, always included at least the land between the Mediterranean and the Jordan River. So defined, the region is c.140 mi (225 km) long and c.30 to c.70 mi (50-115 km) wide. Outside these bounds were such biblical lands as EDOM, GILEAD, MOAB, and Hauran. The British mandate of Palestine (1920-48) included also the Negev, a c.100-mile-long (160-km) desert stretching S to the Gulf of Aqaba. From east to west, Palestine proper comprises three geographic zones: the depression—northernmost extension of the Great Rift Valley—in which lie the Jordan River, Lake Hula, the Sea of Galilee (Lake Tiberias), the Dead Sea, and the Arabah, a dry valley S of the Dead Sea; a ridge rising steeply to the west of this cleft; and a coastal plain c.12 mi (20 km) wide. In N Palestine the ridge is interrupted by the Plain of Esdraelon (Jezreel) and the connecting valley of Bet Shean (Beisan), the most fertile part of the region. The highland area to the north is called GALILEE, its chief centers being ZEFAT and NAZARETH, near which rises Mt. Tabor. To the south of the Plain of Esdraelon the broad ridge stretches unbroken to the Negev. First there are the hills of SAMARIA, with northward prongs (to the east Gilboa and to the west Mt. Carmel) fronting on the Bay of Acre. The center of Samaria is NABLUS, which lies between Mt. Ebal and Mt. Gerizim. The mountains of JUDAEA are W of the Dead Sea. In Judaea are JERUSALEM, BETHLEHEM, and HEBRON. Well to the south, in the Negev, lies BEERSHEBA. The towns of the coastal plain are AKKO (Acre), HAIFA, NETANYA, and the twin cities of TEL AVIV-JAFFA. Near Tel Aviv are PETAH TIQWA, LOD, RAMLA, and REHOVOT. To the south is GAZA. The various sections of the plain are named the Valley of Zebulun or Plain of Acre, S of Akko; Sharon, S of Mt. Carmel; and the Shephelah, or Philistia, in the extreme south. Agriculture in the Jordan valley centers around Lake Hula and the Sea of Galilee. The chief town is TIBERIAS. Farther south the valley is too narrow to be of much use, except for providing water power, and there is only one city, JERICHO, E of Jerusalem. The surface—c.1,300 ft (400 m) below sea level—of the Dead Sea, into which the Jordan empties, is the lowest spot on the earth's surface. At the start of the Zionist colonization of Palestine in the late 19th cent., the rural people were Arab peasants (fellahin). Most of the population were Muslims, but in the urban areas there were important groups of Christians (at Nazareth, Bethlehem, and Jerusalem) and of Jews (at Zefat, Tiberias, Jerusalem, Jericho, and Hebron). The Holy Land derives its special character from being a place of pilgrimage. Shrines, shared in common by several religions, cluster most numerously about Jerusalem, Bethlehem, Nazareth, and Hebron. The earliest known inhabitants of Palestine were of the same group as the Neanderthal inhabitants of Europe. By the 4th millennium B.C. they were herders and farmers. It was in the 3rd millennium that most of the towns known in historic times came into existence. They became centers of trade for Egyptian and Babylonian goods. During the 2d millennium, Palestine was ruled by the Hyksos and by the Egyptians. Toward the end of this period Moses led the Hebrew people (see JEWS) out of Egypt, across the Sinai, and into Palestine. Around 1200 B.C., the Philistines invaded the southern coastland and established a powerful kingdom (see PHILISTIA). The Hebrews were subject to the Philistines until c.1000 B.C., when an independent Hebrew kingdom was established under SAUL, who was succeeded by DAVID and then by SOLOMON. After the expansionist reign of Solomon (c.950 B.C.), the kingdom broke up into two states, Israel, with its capital at Samaria, and Judah, under the house of David, with its capital at Jerusalem. The two kingdoms were later conquered by expanding Mesopotamian states, Israel by ASSYRIA (c.720 B.C.) and Judah by BABYLONIA (586 B.C.). In 539 B.C. the Persians conquered the Babylonians. The Jewish Temple, destroyed by the Babylonians, was rebuilt (516 B.C.). Under Persian rule Palestine enjoyed considerable autonomy. Alexander the Great of Macedon, conquered Palestine in 333 B.C. His successors, the Ptolemies and Seleucids, contested for Palestine. The attempt of the Seleucid ANTIOCHUS IV (Antiochus Epiphanes) to impose Hellenism brought a Jewish revolt under the MACCABEES, who set up a new Jewish state in 142 B.C. The state lasted until 63 B.C., when Pompey conquered Palestine for Rome. Palestine at the time of Christ was ruled by puppet kings of the Romans, the Herods (see HEROD). When the Jews revolted in A.D. 66, the Romans destroyed the Temple (A.D. 70). Another revolt between A.D. 132 and A.D. 135 was also suppressed (see BAR KOKBA, SIMON), Jericho and Bethlehem were destroyed, and the Jews were barred from Jerusalem. When Emperor Constantine converted to Christianity (312), Palestine became a center of Christian pilgrimage. Many Jews left the region, thus reducing the Jewish population. Palestine in the next few centuries generally enjoyed peace and prosperity until it was conquered in 614 by the Persians. It was recovered briefly by the Byzantine Romans, but fell to the Muslim Arabs under caliph Umar by the year 640. At this time (during the Umayyad rule), the importance of Palestine as a holy place for Muslims was emphasized, and in 691 the Dome of the Rock was erected on the site of the Temple of Solomon, which is claimed by Muslims to have been the halting station of the Prophet Muhammad on his journey to heaven. Close to the Dome, the Aqsa mosque was built. In 750, Palestine passed to the Abbasid caliphate, and this period was marked by unrest between factions that favored the Umayyads and those who preferred the new rulers. In the 9th cent., Palestine was conquered by the Fatimid dynasty, which had risen to power in North Africa. The Fatimids had many enemies—the Seljuks, Karmatians, Byzantines, and Bedouins—and Palestine became a battlefield. Under the Fatimid caliph al Hakim (996–1021), the Christians and Jews were harshly suppressed, and many churches were destroyed. In 1099, Palestine was captured by the Crusaders (see CRUSADES), who established the Latin Kingdom of Jerusalem. The Crusaders were defeated by SALADIN at the battle of Hittin (1187), and the Latin Kingdom was ended; they were finally driven out of Palestine by the Mamelukes in 1291. Under Mameluke rule Palestine declined. In 1516 the Mamelukes were beaten by the Ottoman Turks. The first three centuries of Ottoman rule isolated Palestine from outside influence. In 1831, Muhammad Ali, the Egyptian viceroy nominally subject to the Ottoman sultan, occupied Palestine. Under him and his son the region was opened to European influence. Ottoman control was reasserted in 1840, but Western influence continued. Among the many European settlements established, the most significant in the long run were those of Jews. Russian Jews were the first to come (1882). In the late 19th cent. the Zionist movement was founded (see ZIONISM) with the goal of establishing a Jewish homeland in Palestine. Dozens of Zionist colonies were founded there. At the same time Arab nationalism was developing in the Middle East in opposion to Turkish rule. In World War I the British, with Arab aid, gained control of Palestine. In the Balfour Declaration (1917) they promised Zionist leaders to aid the establishment of a Jewish "national home" in Palestine, with due regard for the rights of non-Jewish Palestinians. The British had also promised Arab leaders to support the creation of independent Arab states. The Arabs believed Palestine was among these, an intention that the British later denied. In 1919 there were about 568,000 Muslim Arabs, 74,000 Christians, and 58,000 Jews in Palestine. The first Arab anti-Zionist riots occurred in Palestine in 1920. The League of Nations approved the British mandate in 1922, although the actual administration of the area had begun in 1920. As part of the mandate Britain was given the responsibility for aiding the Jewish homeland and fostering Jewish immigration there. The British stressed that their policy to aid the homeland did not intend to make all Palestine the homeland, but that such a home should exist within Palestine and that there were economic limits to how many immigrants should be admitted (1922 White Paper). In the 1920s, Jewish immigration was slight, but the Jewish communities made great economic progress. In 1929 there was serious Jewish-Arab violence occasioned by a clash at the Wailing Wall in Jerusalem. A British report found that Arabs feared the economic and political consequences of continued Jewish immigration with its attendant land purchases. Zionists were angered when a new White Paper (1930) urged limiting immigration, but they were placated by Prime Minister Ramsay MacDonald (1931). The rise of Nazism in Europe during the 1930s led to a great increase in immigration. Whereas there were about 5,000 immigrants authorized in 1932, about 62,000 were authorized in 1935. Arabs conducted strikes and boycotts; a general strike in 1936, organized by Haj Amin al Husayni, mufti of Jerusalem, lasted six months. Some Arabs acquired weapons and formed a guerrilla force. The Peel commission (1937), finding British promises to Zionists and Arabs irreconcilable, declared the mandate unworkable and recommended the partition of Palestine into Jewish, Arab, and British (largely the holy places) mandatory states. The Zionists reluctantly approved partition, but the Arabs rejected it, objecting particularly to the proposal that the Arab population be forcibly transferred out of the proposed Jewish state. The British dropped the partition idea and announced a new policy (1939 White Paper). Fifteen thousand Jews a year would be allowed in for the next five years, after which Jewish immigration would be subject to Arab acquiescence; Jewish land purchases were to be restricted; and within 10 years an independent, binational Palestine would be established. The Zionists were shocked by what they considered a betrayal of the Balfour Declaration. The Arabs also rejected the plan, demanding instead the immediate creation of an Arab Palestine, the prohibition of further immigration, and a review of the status of all Jewish immigrants since 1918. The outbreak of World War II prevented the implementation of the plan, except for the restriction on land transfers. The Zionists and most Arabs supported Britain in the war (although Haj Amin al Husayni was in Germany and negotiated Palestine's future with Hitler), but tension inside Palestine increased. The Haganah, a secret armed group organized by the Jewish Agency, and the Irgun and the Stern Gang, terrorist groups, were active. British officials were killed by the terrorists. The horrible plight of European Jewry led influential forces in the United States to lobby for support of an independent Jewish state. President Truman requested that Britain permit the admission of 100,000 Jews. Illegal immigration, involving many survivors of Hitler's death camps, took place on a large scale. The independent Arab states organized the Arab League to exert internationally what pressure they could against the Zionists. An Anglo-American commission recommended (1946) that Britain continue administering Palestine, rescind the land transfer restrictions, and admit 100,000 Jews, and that the underground Jewish armed groups be disbanded. A plan for autonomy for Jews and Arabs within Palestine was discussed at a London conference (1947) of British, Arabs, and Zionists, but no agreement could be reached. The British, declaring their mandate unworkable and despairing of finding a solution, turned the Palestine problem over to the United Nations (Feb., 1947). At this time there were about 1,091,000 Muslim Arabs, 614,000 Jews, and 146,000 Christians in Palestine. See Guy Le Strange, *Palestine under the Moslems* (tr. 1965); G. A. Smith, *The Historical Geography of the Holy Land* (1930, repr. 1966); Michael Avi-Yonah, *A History of the Holy Land* (tr. 1969); Esco Foundation for Palestine, *Palestine: A Study of Jewish, Arab, and British Policies* (2 vol., 1947, repr. 1970); K. M. Kenyon, *Archaeology in the Holy Land* (3d ed. 1970); J. W. Parkes, *The Emergence of the Jewish Problem, 1878–1939* (1946, repr. 1970) and *Whose Lands? A History of the Peoples of Palestine* (1971); Abraham Schalit, ed., *The Hellenistic Age: Political History of Jewish Palestine from 332 B.C.E. to 67 B.C.E.* (1972); Doreen Ingrams, *Palestine Papers, 1917–1922* (1973).

Palestine (păl'əstēn), city (1970 pop. 14,525), seat of Anderson co., E Texas; inc. 1871. It is a market, processing, and rail center for a rich oil area and for the truck crops, livestock, and other produce of the rolling red hills. It has railroad repair shops, meat-packing plants, and factories that make glass products, cleansers, clay tile, and fabricated metal. The National Center for Atmospheric Research is there. The city has many old Victorian homes.

Palestine Liberation Organization (PLO), coordinating council for Palestinian refugee organizations, founded (1964) at the first Arab summit meeting. Mainly composed of guerrilla groups, the PLO is dominated by Al Fatah, the largest such group, whose leader, Yasir ARAFAT, has been chairman of the PLO since 1968. Other groups in the PLO include the Syrian-backed Al Saiqa and the Marxist-oriented Popular Front for the Liberation of Palestine (PFLP). The PLO is committed to the dissolution of Israel, mainly through the use of armed force. Since its founding, the organization has sponsored innumerable guerrilla raids on Israeli civilian and military targets. However, the PLO has disclaimed responsibility for many of the Palestinian movement's more spectacular acts of terror, such as the massacre of 11 Israeli participants at the 1972 Olympic games. With headquarters in Cairo, the PLO has been accorded the status of a government-in-exile by the Arab League. The PLO received UN recognition on Oct. 14, 1974; and a government in exile was recognized by the other Arab nations for a future Palestinian state, to be formed from land regained from Israel along the west bank of the Jordan River.

Palestrina, Giovanni Pierluigi da (jōvän'nē pyārlōōē'jē pä"lästrē'nä), c.1525–1594, Italian composer whose family name was Pierluigi; b. Palestrina, from which he took his name. Called "the first Catholic Church musician," Palestrina represents with Lasso the culmination of Renaissance music. In 1544 he was appointed choirmaster at the cathedral in his native town. In 1550 the bishop of Palestrina became Pope Julius III and appointed (1551) Palestrina master of the Julian Chapel Choir. Palestrina's first book of masses appeared in 1554, dedicated to the pope. From 1555 to 1560 he was choirmaster of the Cathedral of St. John Lateran, for which he wrote his *Lamentations*, and from 1561 to 1566 he was choirmaster of Saint Mary Major. After several years in the private service of Ippolito II, Cardinal d'Este, he returned in 1571 to the Vatican to resume leadership of the Julian Chapel Choir. He was undisputed master of the mass, of which he wrote 105 for four, five, six, and eight voice parts. Best known is his *Missa Papae Marcelli*. He also wrote madrigals, motets, magnificats, offertories, litanies, and settings of the Song of Songs. See biographies by E. M. King (1965), T. C. Day (1969), and J. Roche (1971).

Palestrina (pälāstrē'nä), town (1971 pop. 11,432), in Latium, central Italy. It is an agricultural market. It is located on the site of Praeneste, a town founded by c.800 B.C. and later destroyed (and rebuilt) by the Romans in the 1st cent. B.C. Of note are the ruins of a temple of Fortuna (8th cent. B.C.), celebrated for its oracles, and a 12th-century cathedral. The composer Palestrina was born there (c.1525).

Paley, William, 1743–1805, English theologian. Ordained in 1767, he lectured on moral philosophy at

Christ's College, Cambridge. He was made a prebendary of the cathedral church of Carlisle in 1780, and he became archdeacon of the diocese in 1782 and chancellor in 1785. In that year he published *Principles of Moral and Political Philosophy.* He wrote *Horae Paulinae* (1790), in proof that the New Testament is not "a cunningly devised fable," and *A View of the Evidences of Christianity* (1794), for which he is celebrated. *Natural Theology; or, Evidences of the Existence and Attributes of the Deity* (1802) achieved great popularity. In 1825 a complete edition of his writings was published by his son, Edmund Paley.

Palghat (pälgôt'), town (1971 pop. 95,765), Kerala state, SW India. It commands the Palghat Gap, the major pass through the Western Ghats. Palghat, of great strategic importance in the British wars with Hyder Ali, is now a district administrative headquarters and a trading and transportation center.

Palgrave, Sir Francis (păl'grāv, pôl'-), 1788–1861, English historian. His antiquarian interests led him to edit with scrupulous accuracy and to publish a number of historical records, such as the *Rotuli Curiae Regis* (1835), and to stress their importance as materials for historical writing. He was knighted in 1832, and he was from 1838 the official head of the Public Record Office. He wrote in the medieval field, emphasizing legal history and the continuity of the Roman tradition in English development. One of his best works was his *History of Normandy and England* (4 vol., 1851–64). R. H. I. Palgrave edited his father's *Collected Historical Works* (10 vol., 1919–22).

Palgrave, Francis Turner, 1824–97, English poet and anthologist; oldest son of Sir Francis Palgrave. Educated at Oxford, where he began his lifelong friendship with Tennyson, he was an official in the government education department until he became professor of poetry (1885–95) at Oxford. He is remembered as the editor of a famous anthology, *The Golden Treasury of the Best Songs and Lyrical Poems in the English Language* (1861). Its revised version and his many other anthologies were also popular. Of his own verse, *The Visions of England* (1881) and a few hymns are the best. See biography by G. F. Palgrave (1899).

Palgrave, Sir Robert Harry Inglis, 1827–1919, English banker and economist; son of Sir Francis Palgrave. He edited (1877–83) the *Economist,* wrote several books on economics, and served (1885) on the government commission on the depression of trade and industry, but he is best known as editor of *The Dictionary of Political Economy* (3 vol., 1894–99; appendix, 1908; rev. ed. by Henry Higgs, 1923–26).

Pali (pä'lē), language belonging to the Indic group of the Indo-Iranian subfamily of the Indo-European family of languages. Some scholars classify it as a PRAKRIT, or vernacular dialect of classical SANSKRIT. Pali, a tongue of the Middle Indic period (see INDO-IRANIAN languages) in which the Buddhist scriptures or canon (*Tipitaka*) were composed, became the main literary language of the Buddhists. As the number of Buddhists in India declined, Pali ceased to be employed in that country. The Buddhists of Ceylon, Burma, and Thailand, however, still use Pali as a liturgical language. See Wilhelm Geiger, *Pali Literature and Language* (tr., rev. ed. 1968).

Pa-li-ch'iao (pä-lē-chou) or **Palikao** (pä'lē'kou'), village, Hopeh prov., China, near Peking. There, in 1860, a British and French force that had recently occupied Tientsin defeated a Chinese army and invested Peking. China agreed to all Western demands, including the payment of indemnities and the acceptance of foreign diplomats at the imperial court in Peking. The occupying forces were then withdrawn.

Palikao, Charles Guillaume Cousin-Montauban, comte de (shärl gēyōm' kōōzăN'-môNtōbäN' kôNt də pälēkäō'), 1796–1878, French general. He commanded (1860) the French forces in China; his title was bestowed after his victory at Palichiao near Peking. At the start of the Franco-Prussian War he replaced (Aug., 1870) Ollivier as premier under the regency of Empress Eugénie. The capture of Napoleon III at Sedan was followed by the overthrow of the Second Empire in a bloodless revolution at Paris, and Palikao fled to Belgium.

Palikao: see PA-LI-CH'IAO, China.

Pali literature (pä'lē), sacred literature of BUDDHISM. The texts in the Pali canon are the earliest and most complete Buddhist sources, and they now represent the teachings of the Hinayana branch of the religion. Pali, the language in which the canon is written, is a Prakrit (vernacular dialect) of classical Sanskrit (see PRAKRIT LITERATURE). *Pali* means "scriptural text." The literature, originally oral, began to be set down soon after the death of the Buddha in 483 B.C.; the canon was codified c.250 B.C. under ASOKA. However, its various parts date from different periods. The canon is generally called the *Tipitaka* [threefold basket]; the name refers to the baskets passed from hand to hand by construction workers, and is thus a metaphor for the passing on of tradition. The first part, the *Vinayapitaka* [basket of discipline], contains rules for Buddhist monks; it was kept secret from laymen. The *Suttapitaka,* or *Sutrapitaka* [basket of teaching], is divided into five *nikayas* [collections]. The first four, containing discourses and verse statements of varying lengths and forms, are the main authority for the doctrines of early Buddhism. The fifth *nikaya* is a miscellany of anecdotes and dialogues. Ananda, Buddha's cousin and his most devoted disciple, figures in some of the dialogues. Some of the anecdotes in the fifth *nikaya* are related to the *Avadanas* [stories of great deeds] found in the Sanskrit literature of the Mahayana branch of Buddhism. The *Jatakas,* fables of former births of the Buddha in various animal forms, occur also in the fifth *nikaya.* The third basket, and final section, is the *Abhidhammapitaka* [basket of metaphysics], mainly an analytical and methodological elaboration of the previous *pitakas.* Probably the best-known work in the Pali canon is the *Dhammapada* [path of the law], an anthology of maxims arranged in 423 stanzas. Of the noncanonical works, the *Milindapanha* [the questions of Milinda] is outstanding. It describes the dialogue between the Indo-Bactrian king Menander (Milinda) and a Buddhist sage. After the decline of Buddhist influence in India, Pali literature was preserved in Ceylon (now Sri Lanka), and there a vast body of commentary and elaboration of the canon developed. The most notable writer of Pali in later times was Buddhaghosha, who flourished in the 5th cent. Pali is still written in Sri Lanka and to a lesser extent in SE Asia. The Pali Text Society, founded in London in 1882, has published several hundred volumes of texts as well as English translations of Pali literature. See Moriz Winternitz, *A History of Indian Literature* (3 vol., 1927–63); S. C. Banerji, *An Introduction to Pali Literature* (1964); Wilhelm Geiger, *Pali Literature and Language* (tr., rev. ed. 1968).

palimpsest (păl'ĭmpsĕst"): see MANUSCRIPT.

palindrome: see ANAGRAM.

Palisades, cliffs along the west bank of the Hudson River, NE N.J. and SE N.Y., extending from the region N of Jersey City, N.J., to the vicinity of Piermont, N.Y., with a general altitude of from 350 ft to 550 ft (107–168 m). The Palisades, rising vertically from close to the water's edge, are the margin of a sill of diabase, formed by the intrusion of molten material, which hardened into a great sheet. Slow cooling developed the columnar structure; uplift and faulting occurred, it is believed, at the close of the Triassic period, and centuries of erosion exposed the cliffs. A large part of the most scenic section, lying N of Fort Lee, N.J., is embraced in the **Palisades Interstate Park** (c.47,000 acres/19,000 hectares). The park, lying along the west bank of the river, includes a chain of hilly, wooded recreational areas between Fort Lee, N.J., and Newburgh, N.Y. There are scenic roads, trails for hikers, campgrounds, and facilities for winter and summer sports.

Palisades Park, residential borough (1970 pop. 13,351), Bergen co., NE N.J.; inc. 1899.

Palissy, Bernard (bĕrnär' pälēsē'), c.1510–c.1589, French potter. For 16 years he worked in vain to imitate white-glazed pottery (probably Chinese), even burning his furniture to fire his kilns. He succeeded in producing a widely imitated pottery, Palissy ware, admired for smooth glazes in richly colored enamels. He was appointed (c.1562) royal potter to Catherine de' Medici and created platters, ewers, and other ornamented pottery for the French court. He is noted for pieces reproducing scriptural and mythological subjects in low relief and for his rustic pieces decorated with sharply modeled forms copied from nature—notably reptiles, insects, and plants. He gave (c.1575–1584) public lectures on natural history. A writer of outstanding ability on a diversity of topics, including religion, chemistry, mineralogy, philosophy, and agriculture, he published two collections of discourses—*Recepte véritable* (1563) and *Discours admirables* (1580). Many of his views on nature have been confirmed by scientists. In 1588 he was sent, as a Huguenot, to the Bastille, where he died.

Palk Strait (pôk, pôlk), 40 to 85 mi (64–137 km) wide, between India and Sri Lanka (Ceylon). It is studded with shoal reefs called Adam's Bridge and by small islands off the Jaffna peninsula. The strait's treacherous waters are avoided by most ships. A train-ferry crosses the strait.

Palladio, Andrea (ändrĕ'ä päl-lä'dēō), 1508–80, Italian architect of the Renaissance, whose original name was Andrea di Pietro. He studied in Vicenza, and later in Rome he examined the remains of Roman architecture. The measured drawings he made of these were published with compositions of his own and, based on the treatise of Vitruvius, a description of practical systems of design and proportioning. This famous work, *I quattro libri dell' architectura* (1570, tr. *The Four Books of Architecture,* 1716), was reissued many times. His buildings, chiefly town palaces and villas, were executed mostly in Vicenza and its vicinity. Usually they were made of humble materials that contrasted with their formal classicism. Palladio's first important work (begun 1549) was to rebuild the medieval town hall, the basilica at Vicenza. He designed arches supported on minor columns and framed between larger engaged columns. Each of these arch-and-column compositions formed what is termed a "Palladian motif" and was much imitated. The characteristic facade of many of Palladio's country houses displayed the classic temple front—superimposed pilasters or columns or often a colossal order two stories in height and supported by a rusticated ground story. Generally in his buildings he systematized the ground plan, designing a central hall around which other rooms were grouped in absolute symmetry. Among his famous houses (built in the 1550s and 1560s) are the Villa Rotunda (overlooking Vicenza), the Chiericati Palace and the Valmarana Palace (both: Vicenza), and the Villa Barbaro (Maser). At Venice he adapted the classical motif to three church facades, in his designs for San Francesco della Vigna, San Giorgio Maggiore, and Il Redentore. Just before his death Palladio planned the Teatro Olimpico, in which he incorporated a permanent scenic background, built in architectural perspective. His books and his buildings exerted an unparalleled influence on European and American architecture. In the 17th cent., Inigo Jones imported into England Palladio's classic grandeur of design, influencing profoundly the course of English architecture. Subsequently, William Kent, Colin Campbell, Sir Christopher Wren, Sir William Chambers, and others created a great body of works termed Palladian. In the United States his influence can be seen in the manor houses of southern plantations, e.g., Thomas Jefferson's residence Monticello. See S. Semenzato, *The Rotunda of Andrea Palladio* (tr. 1970); Rudolf Wittkower, *Palladio and Palladianism* (1974).

Palladium (pəlā'dēəm), in Greek religion, sacred image kept in the temple of Athena at Troy. It was either an image of Athena or an image made by Athena of her unfortunate playmate Pallas (see PALLAS **1**). According to legend, the image was sent by Zeus to Dardanus, the founder of Troy, and it was believed that the city could not be taken while it possessed the Palladium. Thus during the Trojan War two Greeks, Diomed and Odysseus, stole it. Another legend says that during the sack of Troy, Ajax the Lesser carried it off. The Romans, who later claimed to have the true Palladium in their temple of the vestal virgins, said that Aeneas took it when he fled Troy. But many cities, including Argos, Athens, and Luceria, owned such images, all of which came to be known as Palladia.

palladium [from Gr. *Pallas,* goddess of wisdom], metallic chemical element; symbol Pd; at. no. 46; at. wt. 106.4; m.p. 1552°C; b.p. about 3000°C; sp. gr. 12.02 at 20°C; valence +2, +3, or +4. Palladium is a lustrous silver-white metal with a face-centered cubic crystalline structure. Directly above platinum, it is one of the platinum metals in group VIII of the PERIODIC TABLE. It is strongly resistant to corrosion in air and to the action of acids (except nitric acid) at ordinary temperatures. However, it is attacked by hot acids, and it dissolves in aqua regia. It forms many compounds, including oxides, chlorides, fluorides, sulfides, phosphides, and several complex salts. Palladium has a great ability to absorb hydrogen; when finely divided, one volume of palladium absorbs as many as 900 volumes of the gas. When heated, it allows hydrogen to diffuse rapidly through it; it is thus used to purify hydrogen gas. Palladium is found in nature with platinum minerals and in association with the nickel ores mined near Sudbury, Ont., Canada. Because of its corrosion resistance, a major use of palladium is in alloys used in low voltage electrical contacts. Palladium is used extensively in jewelry-making in certain alloys called "white gold." It may be alloyed with platinum or substituted for it. It is used in watch bearings, springs, and balance wheels and also for mirrors in scientific instruments. For use in dentistry it is alloyed with silver, gold, and copper. In chemistry it is a catalyst in sulfuric acid manufacture and in hydrogenation processes. Palladium salts are used in electroplating. Although palladium is not as abundant as platinum, it is less expensive. Palladium was discovered in 1803 by W. H. WOLLASTON.

Palladius, Saint (pəlā'dēəs), d. 431, first bishop of Ireland. Probably of Gallo-Roman origin, Palladius was sent (431) by Pope Celestine I to proselytize among the Irish. He built three churches but met with much opposition and left the same year. He is the forerunner of St. Patrick, who succeeded him in his work. Feast: July 7.

Palladius, fl. 4th cent. A.D., Roman author. He was a specialist on agriculture and possessed estates in both Italy and Sardinia. Palladius wrote a 14-volume treatise on farming that was well known in the Middle Ages. Most of the work is in prose and gives detailed instructions for a typical year on an average farm. The 14th book, on growing trees, is in elegaic verse. Although authorship of a 15th book, also in verse, is uncertain, it is attributed to Palladius.

Pallas, Peter Simon (pä'tər zē'môn pä'läs), 1741–1811, German naturalist and explorer. He became (1768) professor at the Academy of Sciences, St. Petersburg. In 1769, Pallas was a member of an expedition to observe the transit of Venus, and until 1774 he explored the upper Amur, the Caspian Sea, and the Ural and Altai mts., collecting valuable specimens in natural history. Pallas published (1771–76) an account of the journey and also wrote on natural history and on Bering's discoveries.

Pallas, in astronomy, 2d ASTEROID to be discovered. It was found in 1802 by H. Olbers. The second-largest asteroid, it has a diameter of c.300 mi (480 km). Its orbit has a semimajor axis of 2.78 ASTRONOMICAL UNITS and a period of 1,684 days.

Pallas (păl'əs), in classical mythology. **1** Name given to Athena after she killed either a youthful playmate named Pallas or, in some legends, the giant Pallas. **2** Goatish giant killed by Athena when he tried to rape her. **3** Titan, son of Creus and Eurybia, husband of Styx, and father of Nike. **4** In Vergil's *Aeneid,* son of Evander and an ally of Aenas.

Pallava (pəlä'vä), S Indian dynasty that established its capital at KANCHIPURAM in the 4th cent. A.D. Of obscure origin, it grew wealthy and strong and is most noted for its patronage of Dravidian architecture, especially for the so-called Seven Pagodas of MAHABALIPURAM. The Pallavas engaged in constant warfare with the CHALUKYAS of Badami and were finally eclipsed by the CHOLA kings in the 8th cent.

pallium (păl'ēəm), vestment proper to the pope, who confers it on archbishops in token of their union with and obedience to him. It is a band of cloth worn around the neck and has a 2-in. (5.1-cm) pendant hanging down in both front and back. There are six black crosses on the pallium. It is woven of wool from two lambs presented to the pope at the Church of St. Agnes on her feast day. Certain liturgical functions, such as ordination, require the use of the pallium, and an archbishop may not perform those until he has received it. The pallium is as old as the 6th cent.

Pall Mall (pĕl mĕl, păl măl), street in the City of Westminster borough, London, England. It is the main thoroughfare of St. James's district. St. James's Palace, Marlborough House, and a number of private clubs are on Pall Mall. The name derives from the game pall mall or paille maille, which was played in front of the palace in the 17th cent.

Pallu (păl'yo͞o), son of Reuben. Ex. 6.14; Num. 26.5,8; 1 Chron. 5.3. Phallu: Gen. 46.9. See PELETH **1.**

palm, common name for members of the Palmae, a large family of chiefly tropical trees, shrubs, and vines. Most species are trees, characterized by a crown of compound leaves, called fronds, terminating a tall, woody, unbranched stem. The fruits, covered with a tough fleshy, fibrous, or leathery outer layer, usually contain a large amount of endosperm (stored food). Although the palms are of limited use in the United States and other temperate areas, their economic importance in all tropical regions is second only to that of the grasses. Members of the family often furnish food, shelter, clothing, and other necessities of life for entire populations; an ancient Hindu song about the Palmyra palm (*Borassus flabelliformis*) of India enumerates 801 uses for the plant. Among the most important palms providing food and other products are the COCONUT, DATE, and SAGO. Palm sugar (jaggery) is obtained from the sap of several palms, e.g., species of *Phoenix, Cocos, Arenga* (in India), and *Raphia* (in Africa). Palm TODDY, or wine, is made especially in Africa and the Orient. The fruit of the BETEL palm provides the world's most-used masticatory. CARNAUBA wax is obtained from a Brazilian species. Among the important palm fibers are RAFFIA and RATTAN. *Daemonorops draco* yields DRAGON'S BLOOD, a resin. Another palm-fruit product, TAGUA, is used as a substitute for ivory. Species native to the United States include the tall royal palm of Florida and Cuba (usually *Roystonea regia* in Florida) and the California fan palm (*Washingtonia filifera*) of the Southwest and Mexico, much planted as an avenue ornamental. The PALMETTO PALM is the characteristic underbrush plant of the SE United States. Cabbage palm is a name applied to several species whose young heads of tender leaves are cooked as vegetables; these include the coconut palm, a royal palm (*R. oleracea*), and the cabbage palmetto (*Sabal palmetto*). The largest known plant seed, enclosed in a fruit weighing up to 40 lb (18 kg), is borne by *Lodoicea maldivica,* a palm of the Seychelles, sometimes called the

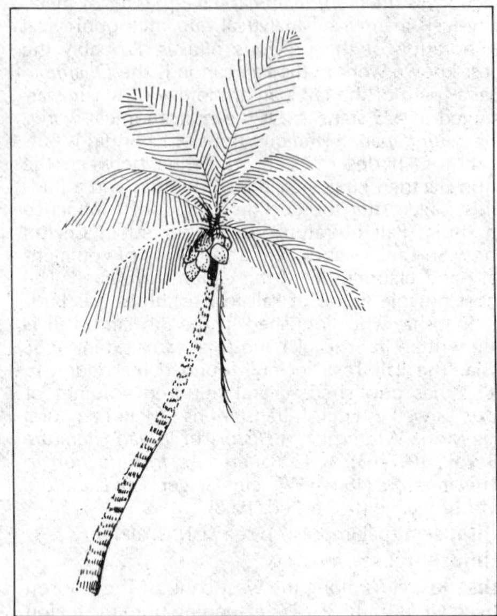

Coconut palm, Cocos nucifera

Seychelles nut palm or the double coconut. **Palm oil** is the fat pressed from the fibrous flesh of the fruit of many palms, principally the coconut palm, the African oil palm (*Elaeis guineensis*), and the babassu palm (*Orbignya oleifera*), and other South American species. Commercial palm oils are used chiefly for soaps and candles and also for lubricants, margarine, fuel, feed (chiefly the caked residue remaining after the oil has been expressed), and many other purposes. In the tropics much of the palm oil produced (often by crude extraction methods) is consumed locally. The total output of palm oil equals that of all other nondrying oils combined. The palm family is classified in the division MAGNOLIOPHYTA, class Liliatae, order Arecales.

Palma, Jacopo (yä'kōpō päl'mä), c.1480–1528, Venetian painter, called Palma Vecchio. He formed his style under the influence of Giovanni Bellini, Titian, and Giorgione and ranks as one of the foremost masters of his school. His pictures are notable for their brilliant coloring and lighting and for their idyllic landscape backgrounds. He is also known for his portraits of women, of which there is a splendid series in the Liechtenstein Gallery, Vienna. He left more than 40 unfinished works, which were completed by his numerous pupils. Among the most important of Palma Vecchio's works are many of his favorite subject, *Sacra Conversazione* (the Madonna and Child with saints), examples of which are in Naples, Vienna, and Venice; an altarpiece, with a figure of St. Barbara (Church of Santa Maria Formosa, Venice); *The Virgin Enthroned* (Church of San Stefano, Vicenza); *Christ and the Adulteress* and *St. Peter Enthroned* (Venice Acad.); *Adoration of the Shepherds* (Louvre); portraits in the National Gallery, London; and *St. Peter Presenting a Worshiper to the Infant Christ* (Palazzo Colonna, Rome). His grandnephew **Jacopo Palma,** 1544–1628, Venetian painter, called Palma Giovane, formed his style by studying the works of Titian, Tintoretto, and the great masters of Rome. He was a facile technician and an excellent colorist. Examples of his art are *The Last Judgment* and *The Savior Adored by Two Doges* (ducal palace, Venice); *St. Catherine Rescued from the Wheel* (Church of the Frari, Venice); and *Madonna with Saints* (Naples). See Joseph A. Crowe, *History of Painting in North Italy,* (3 vol., 1912, repr. 1972).

Palma, Ricardo (rēkär'thō), 1833–1919, Peruvian scholar and author. Palma abandoned an active early career as a naval officer, journalist, and politician to achieve note as a historian with a book on the Inquisition in Lima (1863). After the War of the Pacific (1879–84) he was in charge of rebuilding the destroyed national library. He made it one of the finest libraries in South America and served as its director for many years. Palma, however, won enduring fame and a unique place in Spanish American letters as the creator of a new genre, the *tradición,* or historical anecdote. Part fiction and part historical reconstruction, these sketches and stories about colonial Peru are permeated by wit, love of the past, and all-encompassing imagination. They were published in a long series of volumes, *Tradiciones peruanas* (1872–1910); some have been translated into English under the title *The Knights of the Cape* (ed. by Harriet de Onís, 1945). See study by S. L. Arora (1966).

Palma, Tomás Estrada: see ESTRADA PALMA, TOMÁS.

Palma or **Palma de Mallorca** (päl'mä thā mälyôr'kä), city (1970 pop. 234,098), capital of MAJORCA island and of Baleares prov., Spain, on the Bay of Palma. It is the chief port and commercial center of the BALEARIC ISLANDS. Picturesquely situated along the bay and into the surrounding hills, it is one of Europe's most renowned resorts. (There is an international airport.) Craft industries supplement the tourism. Stone Age remains have been found. The imposing Gothic cathedral, founded after James I of Aragón wrested (1229) Palma from the Moors, was finished only in the 17th cent. Nearby are the Castillo della Almudaina (once a Moorish palace), and the 15th-century Lonja [exchange]. There are several ancient churches, notably that of San Francisco (13th cent.), and fine private homes. The former royal palace of Bellver, c.2 mi (3.2 km) W of Palma, is a good example of 14th-century military architecture. During the civil war of 1936–39, Palma was an important naval and air base of the Insurgents.

Palmas, Las (läs päl'mäs), city (1970 pop. 287,038), capital of Las Palmas prov., Spain, on Grand Canary. The harbor nearby, at Puerto de la Luz, is the chief port of the Canary Islands and the busiest in Spain. Industries include fishing, fish processing, and tourism. The city was founded in 1478; still standing is a house where Columbus stayed in 1492.

Palma Soriano (päl'mä sōryä'nō), city (1970 pop. 41,188), Oriente prov., SE Cuba, in the Cauto River valley. It is a road and rail hub and the commercial and processing center for a rich coffee and sugarcane area. Palma Soriano emerged in the early 19th cent. as the heart of a coffee-growing zone developed by French emigrants from Haiti.

Palm Beach, town (1970 pop. 9,086), Palm Beach co., SE Fla., on a barrier beach between the Atlantic Ocean and Lake Worth (a lagoon); inc. 1911. It is a well-known resort, with many fine estates and luxurious hotels. In the winter its population expands to more than 30,000. It was settled during the 1870s. After the arrival of Henry M. Flagler in 1893, Palm Beach was rapidly developed. Of interest today are the Henry Morrison Flagler Museum, the Cluett Memorial Gardens, and the Four Arts Gardens.

Palme, Olof (o͞o'lôf päl'mə), 1927–, Swedish political leader, prime minister of Sweden (1969–). Sven Olof Joachim Palme joined the Social Democratic party in 1952 and entered parliament shortly afterward. He served (1954–63) as private secretary and counsel to Prime Minister Tage Erlander and then held several ministerial posts. In 1969, Palme succeeded Erlander as chairman of the Social Democratic party and soon as prime minister. In 1971, Palme led Sweden's rejection of a bid for membership in the Common Market as not compatible with a policy of Swedish neutrality. Although the 1973 general election resulted in a tie in the Riksdag between Palme's Social Democrats and the non-Socialist bloc, the prime minister remained in office. In foreign affairs, Palme's criticism of U.S. policy in Indochina led to a diplomatic rift with the United States, which ended in 1974.

Palmer, Alexander Mitchell (pä'mər), 1872–1936, American politician, b. Moosehead, Pa. Admitted (1893) to the bar, he built up a large law practice, became a leader in the state Democratic party, and served (1909–15) in Congress. In 1912, Palmer helped swing the Democratic convention to nominate

Woodrow Wilson for President. He was appointed (1913) judge of the U.S. Court of Claims and then (1917) alien property custodian. As U.S. Attorney General (1919-21), he initiated the notorious "Palmer Raids," in which some 3,000 allegedly subversive aliens were rounded up for deportation. Ultimately only a few hundred were deported; the vast majority were released. See R. K. Murray, *Red Scare: A Study in National Hysteria, 1919-1920* (1955); Stanley Coben, *A. Mitchell Palmer: Politician* (1963, repr. 1972).

Palmer, Alice Freeman, 1855-1902, American educator, b. Broome co., N.Y., grad. Univ. of Michigan, 1876. She was one of the leading early proponents of higher education for women in the United States. In 1879 she became head of the history department at Wellesley College, later serving as president (1881-87) and as trustee (from 1888). In 1887 she married George Herbert Palmer. A member of the Massachusetts state board of education after 1889, she was also dean of women at the Univ. of Chicago (1892-95), a director of the World's Columbian Exposition, and twice president of the Association of Collegiate Alumnae (American Association of University Women). See *An Academic Courtship: Letters of Alice Freeman Palmer and George Herbert Palmer, 1886-1887* (1940); biography by her husband G. H. Palmer (1908).

Palmer, Arnold, 1929-, American golfer, b. Latrobe, Pa. Palmer, the son of a professional golfer, early became proficient at the sport and as a youth won three regional titles. He turned professional after winning the 1954 U.S. amateur championship, and in 1955 he won the Canadian Open. He won the Masters tournament in 1958, 1960, 1962, and 1964, becoming its first four-time winner; the U.S. Open in 1960; and the British Open in 1961 and 1962. In 1967 he became the first professional to win more than a million dollars in prize money.

Palmer, Daniel David, 1845-1913, American founder of chiropractic, b. near Toronto, Canada. He practiced and taught CHIROPRACTIC, chiefly in Davenport, Iowa. His work was carried on and extended by his son, Bartlett J. Palmer.

Palmer, Erastus Dow, 1817-1904, American sculptor, b. Pompey, N.Y., self-taught. A carpenter in his youth, he spent his leisure time cutting cameos. He progressed to carving bas-reliefs and then figures in the round. His first full-length figure, *The Indian Girl,* and his most famous sculpture, *The White Captive,* are in the Metropolitan Museum. In his rendering of figures he followed the classical ideal.

Palmer, Frederick, 1873-1958, American writer and war correspondent, b. Pleasantville, Pa. He began war reporting in the Greco-Turkish War of 1896-97 and reached the height of his fame as a correspondent during World War I. In World War II he was with the British army in France and with the American army in Europe and the Pacific. His writings include novels, biographies, and many books based on his experiences. See his *With My Own Eyes* (1933).

Palmer, George Herbert, 1842-1933, American educator, philosopher, and author, b. Boston, grad. Harvard, 1864, and Andover Theological Seminary, 1870, studied (1867-69) in Europe. He became tutor in Greek at Harvard in 1870, assistant professor of philosophy in 1873, professor of philosophy in 1883, and professor of natural religion, moral philosophy, and civil polity in 1889. From 1913 he was professor emeritus and overseer (1913-1919). He was the first at Harvard to abandon the textbook and recitation method of teaching philosophy and to work out his own system of ideas in lectures. His works on literature include *The Life and Works of George Herbert* (1905); translations of the *Odyssey* and Sophocles' *Antigone;* and on philosophy, *The Field of Ethics* (1901) and *Altruism: Its Nature and Varieties* (1919). He also wrote a biography (1908) of his second wife, Alice Freeman Palmer, his own autobiography (1930), and a number of essays on education and other topics.

Palmer, Nathaniel Brown, 1799-1877, American sea captain and antarctic explorer, b. Stonington, Conn. While on a whaling voyage (1820-21) in the South Shetlands, he commanded the *Hero* on an exploring trip to the south and came back with a report that he had sighted land. Hence the name Palmer Land for the peninsula later named Graham Land by the British and known as PALMER PENINSULA, Graham Land, or Graham Coast. On this expedition Palmer also discovered the South Orkney Islands. He was well known as a commander and designer of clipper ships. See biography by J. R. Spears (1922).

Palmer, Ray, 1808-87, American Congregational clergyman and hymn writer, b. Little Compton, R.I., grad. Yale, 1830. He held pastorates in Bath, Maine (1835-50), and Albany, N.Y. (1850-66). He is remembered chiefly for the hymn "My Faith Looks up to Thee" (1830), a worldwide favorite, for which Lowell Mason wrote the tune *Olivet.*

Palmer, Samuel, 1805-81, English landscape watercolorist, etcher, and mystic. Under the influence of William Blake he produced a series of remarkable visionary drawings in sepia of moonlit landscapes. Palmer is also known for his Italian and English landscapes in watercolor, his illustrations of Spenser and Milton, his translations of Vergil's *Eclogues,* and his etchings. He is represented in the National Gallery and the Victoria and Albert Museum, both in London. See study by Raymond Lister (1969).

Palmer, town (1970 pop. 11,680), Hampden co., S Mass.; settled 1716, inc. 1775. It is an industrial and trade center; its manufactures include automobile parts, and metal, paper, and wire products. The town includes the villages of Palmer, Three Rivers, Thorndike, and Bondsville. Numerous ski areas and state parks are in the area.

palmer: see PILGRIM.

Palmerston, Henry John Temple, 3d Viscount, 1784-1865, British statesman. His viscountcy, to which he succeeded in 1802, was in the Irish peerage and therefore did not prevent him from entering the House of Commons in 1807. Initially a Tory, he served (1809-28) as secretary of war, but he differed with his party over his advocacy of parliamentary reform and joined (1830) the Whig government of the 2d Earl Grey as foreign minister. A firm believer in liberal constitutionalism, Palmerston was instrumental in securing the independence of Belgium (1830-31), and in 1834 he formed a quadruple alliance with France, Spain, and Portugal to help the Iberian countries put down rebellions aimed at restoring absolutist rule. He also organized the joint intervention with Russia, Austria, Prussia, and a reluctant France to prevent the disintegration of the Ottoman Empire as a result of the revolt of MUHAMMAD ALI of Egypt (1839-41). He was in opposition during Sir Robert Peel's administration (1841-46) but returned to the foreign office under Lord John Russell. Palmerston was an impulsive man who often acted without consultation; during his second period as foreign secretary he succeeded in offending not only foreign powers but also his colleagues and Queen Victoria. He quarreled with France in the affair of the Spanish Marriages (1846; see ISABELLA II), gave encouragement to the European revolutionaries of 1848, and in 1850 caused widespread outrage by blockading Greece in order to secure compensation for Don Pacifico, a Portuguese merchant claiming British citizenship, whose house in Athens had been destroyed in a riot. Finally his unofficial and unauthorized approval of the coup d'etat in France by Napoleon III led to his dismissal in 1851. Nevertheless he became home secretary in 1852 and in 1855 succeeded the 4th earl of Aberdeen as prime minister. His vigorous prosecution of the CRIMEAN WAR increased his already great popularity, as did the effective suppression of the INDIAN MUTINY, and although he lost office in 1858, he returned to power in 1859 and remained prime minister until his death. His attitude greatly facilitated the progress of the Italian RISORGIMENTO and the proclamation (1861) of the kingdom of Italy, but his attempt (1864) to help the Danes in the SCHLESWIG-HOLSTEIN question was unsuccessful. He maintained British neutrality in the American Civil War, despite his sympathy for the South and despite the irritating TRENT AFFAIR. Palmerston was not much interested in internal affairs, but he did firmly oppose further parliamentary reform. His diplomacy, reckless and domineering though it frequently was, usually served to advance British prestige. See biographies by H. Lytton Bulwer and Evelyn Ashley (5 vol., 1870-76), W. B. Pemberton (1954), Donald Southgate (1966), and J. G. Ridley (1970); study by C. K. Webster (2 vol., 1951; repr. 1969).

Palmerston North, city (1971 pop. 51,893), S North Island, New Zealand. It is a transportation and farm-marketing center with diverse industries. Massey Univ. was founded in the city in 1964.

palmetto palm or **palmetto** (pălmĕt'ō) [Span., = little palm], common name for PALM trees of the genera *Sabal* and *Serenoa,* ranging from the sandy pinelands of the S United States to Colombia. *Sabal palmetto,* the common native palm of the Southeastern states, is one of the trees called cabbage palm; it has an erect stem and fan-shaped leaves that are edible when young. Palmetto wood is used for pilings and the leaves for thatch. In cooler climates the palmetto is often grown as a greenhouse ornamental. South Carolina, where the tree is indigenous, is sometimes called the Palmetto State. Palmetto palms are classified in the division MAGNOLIOPHYTA, class Liliatae, order Arecales, family Palmae.

Palmira (pälmē'rä), city (1968 est. pop. 119,200), W Colombia, on the Pan American Highway. An agricultural center in the Cauca valley, Palmira is known as the "agricultural capital of Colombia." It gave its name to the tobacco of the region. Sugarcane, coffee, rice, and corn are also grown. The city was founded in 1705.

palmistry, form of DIVINATION based on a study of the hand and palm. It was practiced throughout much of the ancient world and still survives today. Significance concerning human destiny is read into all the characteristics of the hand—shape, size, hardness, and dryness, as well as the number, depth, and length of the lines of the palm.

palmitin (păl'mətĭn), fat that is the TRIGLYCERIDE of palmitic acid, $CH_3(CH_2)_{14}CO_2H$, i.e., the tripalmitate ester of glycerol. It is a white crystalline solid at ordinary temperatures, insoluble in water but soluble in ethanol and ether. When it is heated with an alkali (a process called saponification), a SOAP is produced. Palmitin and other palmitate esters occur abundantly in palm oil, lard, and tallow and also in olive oil, cottonseed oil, and butter—in fact, in most FATS AND OILS.

palm oil: see PALM.

Palm Springs, city (1970 pop. 20,936), Riverside co., S Calif.; founded 1876, inc. 1938. It is a verdant desert oasis and a fashionable resort. It was known to the Spanish as early as 1774 as Agua Caliente because of its hot springs. By 1872 it was a regular stop on the stagecoach run between Prescott, Ariz., and Los Angeles. Nearby are Mt. San Jacinto, with a cable run almost to the top, and Palm Canyon, containing forests of Washingtonia palms estimated to be over 1,000 years old. Also in the area are the Joshua Tree National Monument, a state park, a junior college, and a marine corps base.

Palm Sunday, in the Christian calendar, the Sunday before EASTER, sixth and last Sunday in LENT, and the first day of HOLY WEEK. It recalls the entry of Jesus into Jerusalem riding upon an ass, when the people shouted "Hosanna" and scattered palms in his path. In the Western Church, ceremonies of the day are the blessing and distribution of crosses made from palm leaves and the recitation of one of the three synoptic accounts of the Passion. Many wear crosses made of the palm.

Palmyra (pălmī'rə), ancient city of central Syria. A small modern village known as Tudmur is on the site. An oasis N of the Syrian Desert, 130 mi (209 km) NE of Damascus, Palmyra was important in Syrian-Babylonian trade by the 1st cent. B.C. Tradition says it was founded by Solomon, and it appears in the Bible as Tadmor [city of palms] 2 Chron. 8.4; however, this reference probably represents a confusion with Tamur in Palestine. Palmyra became of true importance only after Roman control was established (A.D. c.30). Local tribes vied for control, which fell to the Septimii by the 3d cent. A.D. Septimius ODENATHUS built Palmyra into a strong autonomous state that practically embraced the Eastern Empire, including Syria, NW Mesopotamia, and W Armenia. After his death his widow, ZENOBIA, briefly expanded the territory, but her ambition brought on (A.D. 272) an attack by Aurelian, who was victorious and partly destroyed (273) the city. In decline, Palmyra was taken by the Arabs and sacked by Tamerlane. It fell into ruins, and even the ruins were forgotten until the 17th cent. The great temple dedicated to Baal and other remains show the Oriental splendor of Palmyra at its prime.

Palmyra, uninhabited atoll (2 sq mi/5.2 sq km), central Pacific, one of the LINE ISLANDS, c.1,100 mi (1,770 km) SW of Honolulu. Discovered (1802) by Americans, and later claimed by the Hawaiian kingdom (1862) and Great Britain (1889), it was annexed by the United States in 1898. Palmyra was under the jurisdiction of the city and county of Honolulu until Hawaii was granted statehood in 1959. The atoll is now under the control of the U.S. Dept. of the Interior.

Palmyra palm: see PALM.

Palo Alto (păl'ō ăl'tō), city (1970 pop. 56,181), Santa Clara co., W Calif.; inc. 1894. Nearby Stanford is the seat of Stanford Univ. Although primarily residential, Palo Alto has an electronics industry. A local attraction is "El Palo Alto," a tree that is more than 1,000 years old.

Palo Alto, locality not far from Brownsville, Texas, where the first battle of the MEXICAN WAR was fought on May 8, 1846. American troops under Gen. Zachary Taylor defeated a Mexican force led by Gen. Mariano Arista, who retreated to Resaca de la Palma.

Palomar, Mount (păl'ōmär), peak, 6,126 ft (1,867 m) high, S Calif., NE of San Diego, in Cleveland National Forest. It is the site of **Mount Palomar Observatory,** operated jointly by the California Institute of Technology and Carnegie-Mellon Univ. It has the world's largest reflecting telescope (200 in./508 cm). Smog from nearby S California urban areas has reduced visibility from the observatory.

Palomar Observatory: see HALE OBSERVATORIES.

Palomino de Castro y Velasco, Acislo Antonio (äthēs'lō äntō'nyō pälōmē'nō thā kä'strō ē väläs'kō), 1655–1726, Spanish historical painter and writer on art, called the Spanish Vasari. He painted frescoes and easel pictures in Valencia, Córdoba, and Granada, but he is famous chiefly for his history of art, *El museo pictórico y escala óptica* (3 vol., 1715–24), which contains a wealth of biographical material concerning Spanish artists of the 16th and 17th cent. It was summarized and translated into English (1739).

palomino horse, American LIGHT HORSE that, contrary to popular opinion, is not a breed but a color type. The palomino is a characteristic golden, creamy tan, with an almost white mane and tail. White stripes on the face and white stockings are common. This coloring occurs in several breeds of light horse. Palominos were probably first selected for their beautiful color in Spain. They accompanied the conquistadors to the New World, where they were perpetuated by early Mexican horse breeders. They were discovered by Americans in California during the Mexican-American War, and are now popular parade and show horses; fanciers in the United States are trying to establish the palomino as a breed. Palominos have Arabian or Thoroughbred features, stand about 15 hands (60 in./150 cm) high, and weigh about 1,100 lb (500 kg).

Palos de la Frontera (pä'lōs dä lä frōntä'rä), town (1970 pop. 4,390), Huelva prov., SW Spain, in Andalusia, on the Tinto River near its mouth. From its port (now silted up), Columbus sailed on his first voyage of discovery (1492), returning and reembarking in 1493. Cortés landed there in 1528 after his conquest of Mexico.

Palos Verdes Estates (păl'əs vûr'dēz), city (1970 pop. 13,631), Los Angeles co., S Calif.; inc. 1939. It is a residential community.

palpitation (păl"pĭtā'shən), abnormal heartbeat that is often associated with a sensation of fluttering or thumping. The normal heartbeat is not noticeable to the individual. Palpitation may be a symptom of organic heart disease or of other body disorders such as an overactive thyroid gland or anemia. In healthy persons palpitation can be brought on by undue exertion, shock, excitement, or stimulants.

Palsgrave, John (pălz'grāv, pôlz'-), d. 1554, English scholar, educated at Oxford and at the Univ. of Paris. Palsgrave was tutor to Henry VIII's daughter Mary (later Mary I), who used her influence in his behalf after he had taken holy orders. His most important work was his *Lesclarcissement de la langue francoyse* (1530), written to instruct the English in the rules of French grammar. It has value today chiefly as a source of information about transitional stages of the English language of that period.

palsy: see PARALYSIS.

Palti (păl'tī), one of the 12 spies. Num. 13.9.

Paltiel (păl'tĭəl), prince of Issachar. Num. 34.26.

Paltite (păl'tīt): see BETH-PALET.

Paludan-Müller, Frederik (frĭ'thərĭk pä'lo͞othänmü'lər), 1809–76, Danish poet. In Denmark he is widely regarded as a peer of Kierkegaard and Hans Christian Andersen. Among his earlier works are *The Dancer* (1833) and *Cupid and Psyche* (1834). His masterpiece, the partly autobiographical poem *Adam Homo* (3 parts, 1841–48), deals with the duality of man's personality, the emptiness of social ambition, and the saving force of selfless love.

Palus Maeotis: see AZOV, SEA OF, USSR.

Pamir (pəmēr', pä-) or **Pamirs,** mountainous region of central Asia, located mainly in the Tadzhik SSR and extending into NE Afghanistan and SW Sinkiang, China; called the "roof of the world." Many peaks rise to more than 20,000 ft (6,096 m); Mount Communism (24,590 ft/7,495 m) and Lenin Peak (23,508 ft/7,165 m) are the highest peaks in the Pamir and the USSR. The region forms a geologic structural knot from which the great Tien Shan, Karakorum, Kunlun, and Hindu Kush mountain systems radiate. Snow-capped throughout the year, the Pamir experiences long cold winters and cool summers. Annual precipitation is c.5 in. (12.7 cm), which supports grasslands but few trees. Several large glaciers, including the 144-mi-long (231-km) Murghab Valley glacier, are in the Pamir. Coal is mined in the W Pamir, but nomadic sheep herding in the upland meadows is the main economic activity. Terak Pass, used by Italian traveler Marco Polo on his way to China in 1271, is one of several high passes used by routes passing through the Pamir. The French explorer Pierre Bonvalot made the first north-south crossing of the Pamir in 1886.

Pamlico Sound (păm'lĭkō), lagoon, 80 mi (129 km) long and 15 to 30 mi (24–48 km) wide, E N.C., separated from the Atlantic Ocean by a row of low, sandy barrier islands; largest lagoon along the U.S. East Coast. It receives the Neuse and Pamlico rivers and is linked on the N with Albemarle Sound. Cape Hatteras National Seashore is located on the barrier islands. Fish, oysters, and waterfowl abound.

Pampa (păm'pə), city (1970 pop. 21,726), seat of Gray co., extreme N Texas. This cow town on the Panhandle plains still ships cattle and wheat and packs meat, but discovery of oil and gas has also made it an industrial center with refineries, carbon-black plants, and other oil-based industries. Heavy machinery, earth-moving equipment, and steel are among its many manufactures.

pampas (păm'pəz, Span. päm'päs), wide, flat, grassy plains of temperate S South America, c.300,000 sq mi (777,000 sq km), particularly in Argentina and extending into Uruguay. Although the region gradually rises to the west, it appears mostly level. Precipitation decreases from east to west. Trees are found only along watercourses. Covered by grasses whose height varies with the amount of rainfall received, the soil of the pampas is very fertile and supports a thriving pastoral and farming economy. The **Pampa,** c.250,000 sq mi (647,500 sq km), of central and N Argentina embraces parts of the provinces of Buenos Aires, Santa Fe, Córdoba, and La Pampa. Cattle was first introduced to the region by the Portuguese in the 1550s. Throughout the colonial period under Spain, only a small part of the Pampa was used; economic activity was practically restricted to primitive stock raising for the exportation of hides, tallow, and jerked beef. Herds of cattle roamed freely over the Pampa and the GAUCHO, the Argentine cowboy, was the region's dominant figure in the 18th and early 19th cent. A new economic era was initiated in the second half of the 19th cent., when a growing European market for agricultural products (along with new technology for the shipment of food products) brought immigrant farmers (mostly Italian, Spanish, French and German) to the Pampa. They spread westward with the expansion of the railroad that was built to link the increasing number of ranches with the coast. Settlement spread into the interior and land was brought under the plow as unfriendly Indians were driven out of the region and the gaucho yielded to the farmer. In the 20th cent. agriculture remains the chief economic activity of the Pampa; livestock grazing and wheat growing are found in the drier W Pampa while corn and other grains along with dairying and truck crops are found in the more humid E Pampa. In the seaboard cities of Buenos Aires, La Plata, and Bahía Blanca and in the river ports of Rosario and Santa Fe are the only considerable industries; meat-packing and food processing are important. The region has a dense transportation network focused on Buenos Aires. The Pampa contains most of Argentina's population.

pampas grass, any species of the genus *Cortaderia,* tall South American plants of the family Gramineae (GRASS family) cultivated in warm climates for ornament. The common pampas grass (*C. argentea* or *selloana*) is a perennial with a cluster of long narrow drooping leaf blades. The male and female flowers are borne on separate plants; the ones which bear the female flowers have large, silvery, plumelike panicles which are sold for decorative purposes. Pampas grass is classified in the division MAGNOLIOPHYTA, class Liliatae, order Cyperales, family Gramineae.

Pampeluna, Spain: see PAMPLONA.

pamphlet, short unbound or paper-bound book. Its maximum size has varied from 64 to 96 pages. The pamphlet gained popularity as an instrument of religious or political controversy, giving the author and reader full benefit of freedom of the press. Relatively inexpensive to purchaser and publisher, it is less complicated to publish and therefore can be more timely than a hard-cover book. Several examples of this generally ephemeral literary form have proved to have permanent value (e.g., works by John Milton and Thomas Paine), and have been reprinted separately or in collections, such as the *Harleian Miscellany* (1744–46). See also CHAPBOOK.

Pamphylia (pămfĭl'ēə), ancient region of S Asia Minor, on the coast between Lycia and Cilicia, in present S Turkey. Its chief cities were Attalia, Side, and Perga. Pamphylia was not a political unit, except in the provincial administration of Rome, to which it passed after the surrender (188 B.C.) of ANTIOCHUS III.

Pamplona (pämplō'nä), city (1970 pop. 147,168), capital of Spanish Navarre, N Spain, on the Arga River. It is an important communications, agricultural, and industrial center, manufacturing kitchenware and chemicals. An ancient city of the Basques, it was repeatedly captured (5th–9th cent.) by the Visigoths, the Franks, and the Moors, but none of the conquerors—not even Charlemagne, who took it in 778 and razed its walls—exercised control for long. In 824 the Basque kingdom of Pamplona, later called the kingdom of Navarre, was founded. Pamplona remained the capital of Navarre until 1512, when Ferdinand V united the major part of Navarre with Castile. It is still surrounded by old walls and fortifications and has retained its Gothic cathedral (14th–15th cent.). In the Peninsular War, Pamplona was taken (1808) by the French and (1813) by the English. The celebration of the feast of San Fermin, described in Hemingway's *The Sun Also Rises,* is marked by running bulls through the streets of the city to the bullring. The Univ. of Navarre (1952) is in Pamplona. An older spelling is Pampeluna.

Pan (păn), in Greek religion, pastoral god of fertility. He was worshiped principally in Arcadia, and one legend states that he was the son of Hermes, another Arcadian god. Pan was supposed to make flocks fertile; when he did not, his image was flogged to stimulate him. He was depicted as a merry, ugly man with the horns, ears, and legs of a goat. Occasionally ill-tempered, he loved to frighten unwary travelers (hence the word *panic*). All his myths deal with amorous affairs. In a famous tale he pursued the nymph Syrinx, but before she was overtaken her sister nymphs changed her into a reed. Thus Pan plays the reed, or syrinx, in memory of her. Later, when Pan was worshiped in other parts of Greece and in Rome, he became associated with the Greek Dionysus and identified with the Roman Faunus, both gods of fertility.

Pan-Africanism, general term for various movements in Africa that have as their common goal the unity of Africans and the elimination of colonialism and white supremacy from the continent. However, on the scope and meaning of Pan-Africanism, including such matters as leadership, political orientation, and national as opposed to regional interests, they are widely, often bitterly divided. One catalyst for the rapid and widespread development of Pan-Africanism was the colonization of the continent by European powers in the late 19th cent. The First Pan-African Congress, convened in London in 1900, was followed by others in Paris (1919), London and Brussels (1921), London and Lisbon (1923), and New York City (1927). These congresses, organized chiefly by W. E. B. DuBois and attended by the North American and West Indian Negro intelligentsia, did not propose immediate African independence; they favored gradual self-government and interracialism. In 1944 several African organizations in London joined to form the Pan-African Federation, which for the first time demanded African autonomy and independence. The Federation convened (1945) in Manchester the Sixth Pan-African Congress, which included such future political figures as Jomo Kenyatta from Kenya, Kwame Nkrumah from the Gold Coast, Chief S. L. Akintola from Nigeria, Wallace Johnson from Sierra Leone, and Dr. Ralph Armattoe from Togo. While at the Manchester congress, Nkrumah founded the West African National Secretariat to promote a so-called United States of Africa. Pan-Africanism as an intergovernmental movement was launched in 1958 with the First Conference of Independent African States in Accra, Ghana. Ghana and Liberia were the only sub-Saharan countries represented; the remainder, Egypt, Tunisia, Libya, Sudan, and Morocco, were Arab and Muslim. Thereafter, as independence was achieved by more African states, various organizations and alliances came into being, each with its own interpretation of the future course of Pan-Africanism. Some of these attempts were as follows: the Union of African States (1960), the African States of the Casablanca Charter (1961), the African and

Malagasy Union (1961), and the Organization of Inter-African and Malagasy States (1962). By the early 1970s there were two major Pan-African groupings: the African-Malagasy-Mauritius Common Organization (OCAM), founded in 1964, an economic association composed of 10 French-speaking African states, and the ORGANIZATION OF AFRICAN UNITY (OAU), founded in 1963 and containing 41 members by 1972. See Tom Mboya, *Freedom and After* (1963); Colin Legum, *Pan-Africanism* (rev. ed. 1965); R. H. Green and K. G. V. Krishna, *Economic Cooperation in Africa* (1967); Jon Woronoff, *Organizing African Unity* (1970); Immanuel Geiss, *The Pan-African Movement* (1974).

Panaji, India: see GOA, DAMAN, AND DIU.

Panama (păn'əmä''), Span. *Panamá,* republic (1970 pop. 1,428,082), 29,209 sq mi (75,650 sq km), occupying the Isthmus of Panama, which connects Central and South America. To the west and east of Panama respectively are Costa Rica and Colombia; the PANAMA CANAL ZONE bisects the country. The capital and largest city is PANAMA City. In the west are rugged mountains (Chiriquí is 11,410 ft/3,478 m high) of volcanic origin, which yield in the middle of the country to low hills; there is a low mountain range in the east. Lowlands line both the Caribbean and Pacific coasts and there are numerous offshore islands. The climate is generally tropical with abundant rainfall. Vast forest reserves are virtually untouched, especially on the Caribbean side. There are indications of valuable copper deposits. Only about a quarter of the land is used for agriculture. On the upland savannas cattle are grazed and subsistence crops (notably rice), sugarcane, cocoa, and coffee are grown. Bananas are grown on the Pacific coast. The country has various light industries. Bananas are

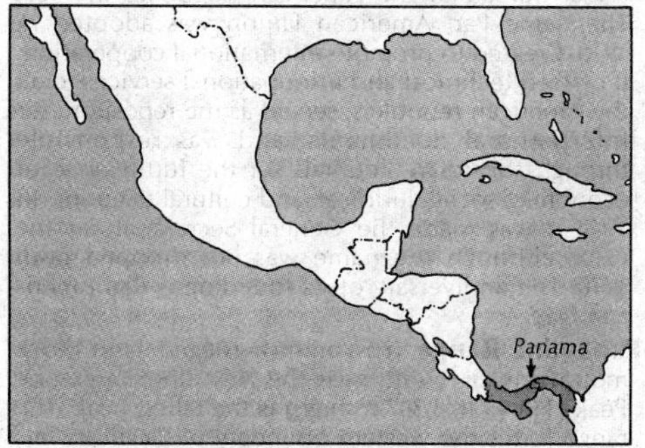

the leading export, followed by shrimp and fish products, sugar, and coffee. Manufactured goods, raw materials, and foodstuffs are imported. Much of the trade is with the United States. In 1968 the per capita national income was $507. Half the population is urban, and many of the urban workers are employed in the Panama Canal Zone. COLÓN, a major port, is the second largest city, and DAVID is the third largest city. The last ethnic breakdown of the population was made in 1940; it reported that 12% were white, 14.5% Negro, and 72% mixed. Spanish is the official language, and the population is almost entirely Roman Catholic. There are two universities in the country. The coast of Panama was first sighted in 1501 by the Spaniard Rodrigo de Bastidas, and Columbus dropped anchor off the present-day PORTOBELO in 1502. Martín Fernández de ENCISO and Diego de Niuesa failed in their efforts at colonization in DARIEN. Vasco Núñez de BALBOA became governor of the region, and in 1513 he made his momentous voyage across the isthmus to the Pacific, thus highlighting the dominant factor in the nation's history—the short distance from sea to sea. Under the governorship of Pedro Arias de Ávila, Panama City was founded (1519). Soon the isthmus became the route by which the treasures of the Inca empire were transferred to Spain, attracting the unwelcome attention of English buccaneers—such as Sir Francis Drake, William Parker, Sir Henry Morgan, and Edward Vernon—who swooped down on the gold-bearing galleons and the treasures of Portobelo. Panama was subordinated to the viceroyalty of Peru and remained in this status until 1717, when it was transferred to New Granada. Attempts at Scottish settlement in the DARIEN SCHEME of the 17th cent. failed wretchedly. With the decline of the Spanish Empire, Panama lost much of its importance in the carrying trade. It became a part of independent Colombia in 1821. Its significance as a crossroad was enhanced again when U.S. settlers bound for Oregon and the goldfields of California passed through Panama. W. H. Aspinall built (1848–55) the Panama RR, and the question of a canal across the isthmus became paramount. The project ultimately led to a revolution against Colombian sovereignty and the establishment of Panama as a separate republic (see PANAMA CANAL). The new state, proclaimed in Nov., 1903, was under the aegis of the United States, and the canal and American interests in it became the determinants of Panama's history. The Hay-Bunau-Varilla Treaty with the United States established the U.S.-controlled Canal Zone and authorized U.S. intervention in Panamanian affairs if necessary to protect the zone. The internal politics of the republic have been stormy, with frequent changes of administration. U.S. forces were landed in 1908, 1912, and 1918. A controversial figure in Panamanian politics has been Arnulfo ARIAS. Elected president in 1940, he was ousted a year later for being pro-Fascist. He seized power in 1949 but was overthrown in 1951. José Antonio Remón, elected in 1952, was assassinated in 1955; Ernesto de la Guardia, Jr., inaugurated the following year, survived disturbances in 1958 and 1959. In the meantime, a new canal treaty was concluded in 1955, as nationalist agitation developed in Panama over the Canal Zone issue. In 1958 and again in 1960 further steps were taken to assuage Panamanian discontent by establishing uniform wages and employment opportunities in the Canal Zone and by reaffirming Panama's titular sovereignty over the zone. Roberto F. Chiari, a conservative landowner, was elected president in 1960. Marco A. Robles defeated Arias for the presidency in 1964. When U.S. high school students illegally displayed an American flag in the Canal Zone (Jan., 1964), serious riots broke out. Diplomatic relations between Panama and the United States were briefly suspended. New treaties were negotiated (1967), providing for Panamanian sovereignty over the Canal Zone, joint operation of the canal, and possible construction of a new, sea-level canal, but Panama refused to ratify them (1970). In the latter part of 1973, Panama and the United States began a new series of negotiations aimed at resolving the conflict over the canal and the Canal Zone and in early 1974 both countries agreed in principle for the first time to the eventual end of U.S. jurisdiction there. Arias was again elected president in Oct., 1968, but was deposed 11 days later in a military coup. Gen. Omar Torrijos Herrera emerged as the dominant figure shortly thereafter. In 1969 all political parties were abolished. A 505-member assembly was elected in 1972 and wrote a new constitution, but General Torrijos was given executive power for six more years, after which the new constitution was scheduled to go into effect. See L. L. Pippin, *The Remón Era: An Analysis of a Decade of Events in Panama, 1947–1957* (1964); D. A. Howarth, *Panama: Four Hundred Years of Dreams and Cruelty* (1966); J. G. Niemeier, *The Panama Story* (1968); B. C. Hedrick and A. K. Hedrick, *Historical Dictionary of Panama* (1970); G. A. Mellander, *The United States in Panamanian Politics: The Intriguing Formative Years* (1971); T. E. Weil et al., *Area Handbook for Panama* (1972). See also bibliography under PANAMA CANAL.

Panama, city (1970 est. pop. 420,000), central Panama, capital and largest city of Panama, on the Gulf of Panama, bounded on the west by the Panama Canal Zone. Founded in 1519 by Pedro Arias de Ávila, the city flourished in early colonial times as the Pacific port of transshipment of Andean riches to Spain. After it was destroyed in 1671 by Sir Henry Morgan, it was refounded (1673) 5 mi (8.1 km) west on a rocky peninsula. The city declined as the Andean sources of gold disappeared but revived briefly during the California gold rush and the building (1848–55) of the trans-Panama railroad. Construction of the Panama Canal brought assured prosperity, and American sanitary measures and disease control made Panama a clean and healthful tropical city. The political, social, and cultural nucleus of the nation, it expanded rapidly after World War II into a polyglot metropolis, boasting new residential districts, improved recreational facilities, and such educational centers as the Univ. of Panama (founded 1935), important because of its inter-American organization and curriculum. Panama city is no longer a port; commerce is handled through neighboring Balboa. It has shoe, textile, and beverage industries.

Panama Canal, waterway across the Isthmus of Panama, connecting the Atlantic (by way of the Caribbean Sea) and Pacific oceans, built by the United States (1904–14) on territory leased in perpetuity from the republic of Panama. The canal, running S and SE from Limón Bay at Colón on the Atlantic to the Bay of Panama at Balboa on the Pacific, is 40 mi (64 km) long from shore to shore and 51 mi (82 km) long between channel entrances. The Pacific terminus is 27 mi (43 km) east of the Caribbean terminus. The minimum depth is 41 ft (12.5 m). From Limón Bay a ship is raised by Gatun Locks (a set of three) to an elevation 85 ft (25.9 m) above sea level, traverses Gatun Lake, then crosses the Continental Divide through Gaillard (formerly Culebra) Cut and is lowered by Pedro Miguel Lock to Miraflores Lake and then by the Miraflores Locks (a set of two) to sea level. Passage requires 7 to 8 hr. The average tidal range on the Atlantic side is less than a foot (30.4 cm); that on the Pacific side is 12.6 ft (3.8 m). Building an interoceanic canal was suggested early in Spanish colonial times. The United States, interested since the late 18th cent. in trading voyages to the coast of the Pacific Northwest, became much concerned with plans for a canal after settlers had begun to pour into Oregon and California. Active negotiations led in 1846 to a treaty, by which the republic of New Granada (consisting of present-day Panama and Colombia) granted the United States transit rights across the Isthmus of Panama in return for a guarantee of the neutrality and sovereignty of New Granada. After the United States had acquired (1848) California and the gold rush had begun, the isthmus gained more importance, and the trans-Panama RR was built (1848–55) with U.S. capital. At the same time, interest in an alternate route, the NICARAGUA CANAL, was strong in both Great Britain and the United States. Rivalry between the two countries was ended by the CLAYTON-BULWER TREATY (1850), which guaranteed that neither power should have exclusive rights or threaten the neutrality of an interoceanic route. In the 1870s and 80s the United States tried unsuccessfully to induce Great Britain to abrogate or amend the Clayton-Bulwer Treaty. After the United States acquired territory in the Caribbean and in the Pacific as a result of the Spanish-American War (1899), U.S. control over an isthmian canal began to seem imperative. Following protracted negotiations a U.S.-British agreement (see HAY-PAUNCEFOTE TREATIES) was made in 1901, giving the United States the right to build, and by implication fortify, an isthmian canal. It was then necessary for Congress to choose between Nicaragua or Panama as the route for the canal. Meanwhile a concession for building a sea-level canal in Panama (granted 1878) had been acquired by a French company under Ferdinand de Lesseps. Work was begun in 1881, but poor planning, disease among the workers, construction troubles, and inadequate financing drove the company into bankruptcy in 1889. Amid charges of corruption and mismanagement, French courts transferred (1894) the rights and assets to a new company. Although the alternate Nicaragua route was favored by the United States, an American representative of the French company, William Nelson Cromwell, began working vigorously to interest the United States in the Panama route, and Philippe Bunau-Varilla, a leading figure in the new company, devoted himself to the cause. When a U.S. commission recommended in 1901 a canal through Nicaragua, Bunau-Varilla persuaded the French directors to reduce the price of the company's rights and gained the support of Mark Hanna and later of the new President, Theodore Roosevelt. The commission reversed its recommendation, and Congress authorized purchase of the French company's rights and construction of the Panama Canal. The HAY-HERRÁN TREATY, signed (Jan., 1903) with Colombia, would have given the United States a strip of land across the Isthmus of Panama in return for an initial cash payment of $10 million and an annuity of $250,000, but the Colombian senate refused to ratify. An insurrection, involving Bunau-Varilla and other proponents of the canal as well as natives, was encouraged by the United States, and Panama rose in revolt on Nov. 3, 1903, declaring itself independent of Colombia. Invoking the treaty of 1846, the United States sent an American warship to Panama, and its presence prevented Colombian troops from quelling the outbreak. The new republic was formally recognized three days later, and on Nov. 17 the Hay-Bunau-Varilla Treaty was signed, granting to the United States, in return for the same terms offered Colombia, exclusive control of a canal zone in perpetuity, other sites necessary for defense, and sanitary control of Panama city and Colón. Colombia's efforts to secure redress for the loss of Panama later resulted in ratification of a treaty (1921) by which the United States paid Colombia $25 million and Colombia recognized the independence of Panama. Construction of a lock canal was decided on in 1906. The first three years were spent in the development of construction facilities, surveys, and disease control. The eradication of malaria and yellow fever, directed by Col. William Gorgas, was a notable achievement. Most of the actual construction work was supervised by Col. G. W. Goethals. The canal was informally opened August 15, 1914; formal dedication took place on July 12, 1920. The total cost was $336,650,000, and c.240 million cu yd (184 million cu m) of earth were evacuated. Madden Dam, which stores additional water for the locks, was completed in 1935. In 1939 treaty amendments increased Panama's annuity to $434,000 (retroactive to 1934 to offset dollar devaluation), provided for a transisthmian highway, and (at Panama's insistence) abrogated the U.S. guarantee of the neutrality and sovereignty of Panama. Although in the same year Congress authorized construction of a third set of locks, World War II intervened, and the plans were shelved. In 1955 the annuity was raised to $1,930,000, and the United States undertook to build a high-level bridge (completed 1962) over the Pacific side of the canal. The Gaillard Cut was widened in 1969 to permit two-way traffic. The very largest modern merchant and warships, however, cannot pass through the canal. In the 1960s there was increasing agitation in Panama to achieve greater Panamanian control over the canal. In 1965 the United States agreed to recognize Panama's sovereignty over the Canal Zone. A new treaty was negotiated in 1967 but was not ratified by Panama. See Philippe Bunau-Varilla, *Panama: The Creation, Destruction, and Resurrection* (1914); G. W. Goethals, *The Panama Canal: An Engineering Treatise* (1916); I. J. Klette, *From Atlantic to Pacific* (1967); M. P. DuVal, *And the Mountains Will Move: The Story of the Building of the Panama Canal* (1947, repr. 1968); D. B. Chidsey, *The Panama Canal* (1970); D. G. Payne, *The Impossible Dream* (1972); J. P. Speller, *The Panama Canal: Heart of America's Security* (1972).

Panama Canal Zone, area within Panama (1970 pop. 44,198), 553 sq mi (1,432 sq km), administered by the United States under a 1903 treaty (with later amendments) with Panama. The zone extends 5 mi (8.1 km) on either side of the Panama Canal. About three quarters of the civilian population are U.S. citizens. Cristóbal, Balboa (Caribbean and Pacific ports, respectively), and Ancon are the chief towns. The zone is administered by a governor appointed by the President of the United States. The governor is also the president of the Panama Canal Company.

Panama City, city (1970 pop. 32,096), seat of Bay co., NW Fla., on St. Andrews Bay; inc. 1909. A Gulf Coast resort with amusement parks and excellent fishing, it is also a port of entry. The city's industries produce paper, clothing, chemicals, and plastics. A junior college is there, and Tyndall Air Force Base and the U.S. Navy Mine Defense Laboratory are nearby.

panama-hat palm, perennial herb (*Carludovica palmata*) growing wild throughout the American tropics. Despite its frondlike leaves it is not a true palm. The leaves are used to weave Panama hats, an industry centered in Ecuador. The plant is classified in the division MAGNOLIOPHYTA, class Liliatae, order Arecales, family Cyclanthaceae.

Pan-American games, amateur athletic competition among representatives of countries in the Western Hemisphere. The competition, held every four years, is patterned after the OLYMPIC GAMES and is held in different host cities. The first Pan-American games, originally planned for 1942, were delayed by World War II and were not held until 1951. Competition is in track and field, swimming, water polo, baseball, basketball, boxing, cycling, fencing, gymnastics, pentathlon, shooting, weight lifting, wrestling, rowing, soccer, polo, equestrian events, tennis, volleyball, and yachting.

Pan American Highway, projected system of roads, c.16,000 mi (25,750 km) long, to link the nations of the Western Hemisphere. Suggested at the Fifth International Conference of American States (1923), the system (except for a gap between the Panama Canal and NW Colombia) is complete and extends from Alaska to Chile. A section called the INTER-AMERICAN HIGHWAY, between the United States and the Panama Canal, is popular with tourists driving to Mexico. The highway has many branches that connect with large cities off the main north-south route. Climatic zones along the highway vary from lush jungle to cold mountain passes nearly 15,000 ft (4,572 m) high. The scenery is often spectacular, and the highway crosses many picturesque localities. The system is far from uniform; some stretches are passable only during the dry season, and in several regions driving is occasionally hazardous. In the late 1960s much of the highway was improved.

Pan-Americanism, movement toward commercial, social, economic, military, and political cooperation among the 21 republics of North, Central, and South America. The struggle for independence after 1810 among the Latin American nations evoked a sense of unity, especially in South America where, under Simón BOLÍVAR in the north and José de SAN MARTÍN in the south, there were cooperative efforts. Francisco MORAZÁN briefly headed a CENTRAL AMERICAN FEDERATION. The United States was looked upon as a model, and recognition of the new republics was a part of U.S. foreign policy. Henry Clay and Thomas Jefferson set forth the principles of Pan-Americanism in the early 1800s, and soon afterward the United States declared through the MONROE DOCTRINE a new policy with regard to interference by European nations in the affairs of the Western Hemisphere. The policy, at first welcomed even though it established a U.S. hegemony, later came to be regarded by many Latin American nations as a mask for U.S. imperialistic ambitions. In the early 20th cent., U.S. manipulation to secure the PANAMA CANAL and its intervention in the affairs of other Latin American states, combined to create deep resentment in Latin America toward the United States. In the 19th cent., Latin American military nationalism came to the fore. Venezuela and Ecuador withdrew (1830) from Greater Colombia; the Central American Federation collapsed (1838); Argentina and Brazil fought continually over Uruguay, and then all three combined in the War of the Triple Alliance (1865–70) to defeat Paraguay; and in the War of the Pacific (1879–83), Chile defeated Peru and Bolivia. However, during this same period Pan-Americanism existed in the form of a series of Inter-American Conferences—Panama (1826), Lima (1847), Santiago (1856), and Lima (1864). The main object of those meetings was to provide for a common defense. The first of the modern Pan-American Conferences was held (1889–90) in Washington, D. C., with all nations represented except the Dominican Republic. Treaties for arbitration of disputes and adjustment of tariffs were adopted, and the Commercial Bureau of the American Republics, which became the PAN AMERICAN UNION, was established. Subsequent meetings were held in various Latin American cities. In general, the issues discussed were those introduced at the first conference. While the concepts under consideration were usually slow to take concrete form, there was marked progress in the codification of international law, acceptance of peace machinery, and creation of scientific and social agencies. Troubles, however, continued to flare. A major war was fought (1932–35) between Bolivia and Paraguay over the Chaco. Strained relations between the United States and Panama were temporarily resolved after a new treaty was signed (1936), which, although still restricting Panama's sovereignty in various ways, specifically ended the right of intervention hitherto possessed by the United States. With the administration of Franklin Delano Roosevelt a policy of determined cordiality toward Latin America—the "Good Neighbor" policy—bore fruit. As World War II approached, the nations of the Western Hemisphere drew closer together. Conferences held in 1936 and 1938 provided for consultation in case of outside threat. Accordingly, after the outbreak of World War II the Inter-American Neutrality Conference was held (1939) in Panama. A conference of foreign ministers at Havana produced (1940) the Act of Havana, declaring against changes of sovereignty in the Western Hemisphere. Most of the Latin American nations (with the notable exception of Argentina) supported or actually joined the Allies after the Japanese attack on Pearl Harbor. A significant step was taken at the Inter-American Conference on the Problems of War and Peace in Mexico City in 1945. The Act of Chapultepec, adopted there by 20 republics, called for joint action in repelling any aggression against an American state; the significant point was that this was to operate in cases of aggression by an American as well as by a non-American state. Its acceptance by Argentina established machinery to enforce peace in the Western Hemisphere. This was formalized by the Inter-American Treaty of Reciprocal Assistance (the RIO TREATY). In other fields, too, cooperation advanced, as in commercial and financial matters (e.g., the Inter-American Bank). As a consequence of the growing awareness of interdependence the Bogotá Conference of 1948 produced the ORGANIZATION OF AMERICAN STATES (OAS) to promote hemispheric unity. In the late 1950s the United States took steps toward an international price agreement on agricultural products and minerals, a measure long advocated by Latin American republics plagued by one-product economies. The Inter-American Development Bank began operations early in 1960. Since 1959 the most persistent problem facing the inter-American system has been the establishment of a Communist government in Cuba. Fidel Castro's zeal for supporting Communist guerrilla forces in other Latin American countries led, in 1962, to Cuba's expulsion from the inter-American system by the OAS. The vote, however, was not unanimous; Argentina, Bolivia, Brazil, Chile, Ecuador, and Mexico abstained. In the fall of 1962 the Latin American nations backed the United States in its decision to blockade Cuba as a consequence of the establishment of missile bases in several parts of the island. With the introduction of the ALLIANCE FOR PROGRESS in 1961, the United States attempted a long-term plan of economic assistance. In partial recognition of the weakness of this program, the Declaration of the Presidents of America was signed (1967) in Punta del Este, Uruguay, expressing commitment to Latin American economic integration, i.e., the creation of a common market (see CENTRAL AMERICAN COMMON MARKET; LATIN AMERICAN FREE TRADE ASSOCIATION). See J. L. Lockey, *Pan Americanism: Its Beginnings* (1920, repr. 1970); S. G. Inman, *Problems in Pan Americanism* (1925); C. H. Haring, *South America Looks at the United States* (1928); W. S. Robertson, *History of Latin America* (3d ed. 1943); Arthur P. Whitaker, *The Western Hemisphere Idea, Its Rise and Decline* (1954, repr. 1965); Alonso Aguilar, *Pan-Americanism from Monroe to the Present* (1965); Richard B. Gray, ed., *Latin America and the United States in the 1970s* (1971).

Pan American Union, former name for the General Secretariat of the ORGANIZATION OF AMERICAN STATES (OAS). It was founded (1889–90) at the first of the modern Inter-American Conferences (see PAN-AMERICANISM) as the Commercial Bureau of the American Republics and changed to the International Bureau of the American Republics in 1902. The name Pan American Union was adopted in 1910. Created to promote international cooperation, it offered technical and informational services to all the American republics, served as the repository for international documents, and was responsible through subsidiary councils for the furtherance of economic, social, juridical, and cultural relations. In 1948 it was made the General Secretariat for the OAS, although the name was not dropped until 1970. The anniversary of its founding is Pan American Day.

Panamint Range (păn'əmĭnt), rugged fault-block mountains, SE Calif., near the Nev. line. Telescope Peak (11,045 ft/3,367 m high) is the tallest peak. The range forms the western boundary of Death Valley; to the west of the range is Panamint Valley.

Pan-Arabism, general term for the movement toward political unification among the Arab nations of the Middle East. Since the 13th cent., when the Ottoman Turks rose to power and ended Arab dominance in the world of Islam, there have been stirrings among ARABS for reunification as a means of returning to power. However, Pan-Arabism as a viable force is a product of the 20th cent. and arose in part as a reaction to the Pan-Islamic movement sponsored by the Turks. The political bankruptcy of the Pan-Islamic movement was demonstrated in World War I when the Turkish caliph unsuccessfully called (1914) for a jihad (holy war) by all Muslims against the Christian allies. The ideals of secular Pan-Arabism, however, proved stronger. At the start of World War I, France and Great Britain, seeking allies against the German-Turkish alliance, encouraged the cause of Arab nationalism under the leadership of the Hashimite Sharif Husein, a descendant of the Prophet. As ruler of Mecca and a religious leader of Islam, he had great influence in the Arab world, an influence that continued with his two sons, Abdullah and Faisal. From the 1930s, hostility toward Zionist aims in Palestine was a major rallying point for Arab nationalists. The movement found official expression after World War II in the ARAB LEAGUE and in such unification attempts as the Arab Federation (1958), the United Arab Republic, the Arab Union, the Federation of Arab Emirates, and the Arab Federation (1970). The principal instrument of Pan-Arabism in the early 1960s was the Ba'ath (Arab Renaissance) political party, which was active in most Arab states, notably Egypt, Iraq, Jordan, Lebanon, Saudi Arabia, Syria, and Yemen. The party's ideals were Arab unity and socialism as expressed by Gamal Abdal NASSER. The defeat of the Arabs in the Arab-Israeli War of 1967 and the death (1970) of Nasser appeared to set back the cause of Pan-Arabism. In the early 1970s a projected merger between Egypt and Libya came to nought. However, during and following the 1973 Arab-Israeli War the Arab states showed new cohesion in their use of oil as a major economic and political weapon in international affairs. See George Antonius, *The Arab Awakening* (1946, repr. 1965); F. A. Sayegh, *Arab Unity* (1938, repr. 1958); Eugene M. Fisher and M. Cherif Bassiouni, *Storm over the Arab World* (1972).

Panathenaea (păn″ăthēnē′ə), in Greek religion, festival celebrated annually at Athens in honor of Athena. It included athletic and musical contests, poetic recitations, and sacrifices. At the end of the festivities a grand procession carried a richly embroidered peplos to the Acropolis as a present to Athena.

Panay (pänī′), island (1970 pop. 2,116,545), 4,446 sq mi (11,515 sq km), one of the Visayan Islands, 6th largest of the Philippines, NW of Negros. Primarily agricultural with extensive lowlands, it is a major rice and corn producing area. There are also sugar-processing, lumbering, and fishing industries. Horses are bred in the mountainous interior.

pancake, thin, flat cake, made of batter and baked on a griddle or fried in a pan. Pancakes, probably the oldest form of bread, are known in different forms throughout the world. The relative ease of baking on hot stoves or on a griddle has resulted in a variety of pancakes. Old English batter was mixed with ale. German and French pancakes, leavened by eggs and much beating, are baked very thin and served with jam or jelly. The French crêpe suzette is folded or rolled and heated in a sauce of butter, sugar, citrus juice, and liqueur. Russian blintzes, usually prepared with buckwheat, are thin, crisp pancakes, and commonly served with caviar and sour cream or folded over and filled with cream cheese or jam. Mexico has its tortilla, which is often served folded over a bean or meat filling and topped by tomato sauce (see TACO). In the United States pancakes are sometimes called battercakes, griddlecakes, or flapjacks and are usually leavened with baking powder or baking soda and are served with syrup. A pioneer favorite, still surviving in some localities, is the buckwheat cake.

Pančevo (pän′chĕvō), city (1971 pop. 110,433), NE Yugoslavia, in the Vojvodina region of Serbia, on the Tamiš River near its confluence with the Danube. A river port, it has industries that produce aircraft, electrical equipment, and glass. There is a fine old church containing valuable paintings and other works of Serbian religious art.

Panchatantra (pŭn″chətŭn′trə) [Sanskrit,=five treatises], anonymous collection of animal fables in SANSKRIT LITERATURE, probably compiled before A.D. 500 (see BIDPAI). The work, derived from Buddhistic sources, was intended as a manual for the instruction of sons of the royalty. The fables are in prose, with interspersions of aphoristic verse. The stories in the *Panchatantra* appear to have entered European literature circuitously through an Arabic version (A.D. c.750) of the translation into Syriac of the Pahlavi (literary Persian) translation (A.D. c.550) from the original. A variant spelling is *Pancatantra*. See the translation from the Sanskrit by A. W. Ryder (1925, repr. 1956).

Panchen Lama: see TIBETAN BUDDHISM.

pancreas (păn′krēəs), glandular organ that secretes digestive enzymes and hormones. In man, the pancreas is a yellowish organ about 7 in. (17.8 cm) long and 1.5 in. (3.8 cm) wide. It lies crosswise beneath the stomach and is connected to the small intestine at the DUODENUM (see DIGESTIVE SYSTEM). Most of the pancreatic tissue consists of grapelike clusters of cells that produce a clear fluid (pancreatic juice) that flows into the duodenum through a common duct along with bile from the liver. Occasionally the pancreatic duct enters the intestine separately. Pancreatic juice contains three important digestive enzymes: trypsin, amylase, and lipase, that, along with the enzymes secreted by the intestinal lining, complete the digestion of proteins, carbohydrates, and fats, respectively. Scattered among the enzyme-producing cells of the pancreas are small groups of endocrine cells, called the islets of Langerhans, that secrete two hormones, insulin and glucagon. These hormones are secreted directly into the bloodstream and, together, they regulate the level of glucose in the blood. Insulin lowers the blood sugar level and increases the amount of glycogen (stored carbohydrate) in the liver. Glucagon has the opposite action, i.e., it raises the level of blood sugar and lowers the amount of stored glycogen. Failure of the insulin-secreting cells to function properly results in DIABETES.

pancreatic juice, secretions of the exocrine portion of the PANCREAS into the small intestine. The juice contains a number of important digestive ENZYMES, including TRYPSIN, CHYMOTRYPSIN, carboxypeptidase, LIPASE, and AMYLASE. Pancreatic juice is alkaline in nature because of a high concentration of bicarbonate ions; this helps to neutralize the acidic GASTRIC JUICE from the stomach. Secretion of pancreatic juice is stimulated by hormones of the duodenum, such as secretin and cholecystokinin, and by nervous impulses through the vagus nerve.

panda, name for two nocturnal Asian mammals of the RACCOON family: the red panda, *Ailurus fulgens,* and the giant panda, *Ailuropoda melanoleuca.* The red panda, also known as lesser panda and cat bear, is found at high elevations in the Himalayas and the mountains of W China and N Burma. It resembles a raccoon but has a longer body and tail and a more rounded head. It is about 3.5 ft (105 cm) in total length and weighs about 12 lb (5.5 kg). The very thick fur is rust color to deep chestnut, with black on the under parts, limbs, and ears; there are dark eye patches on the white face. The red panda spends much of its time in trees but feeds on the ground, eating nuts, roots, and other plant matter. The giant panda superficially resembles a bear, although it is anatomically more like a raccoon. The body is chiefly white, and the limbs are brownish black, with the dark color extending up over the shoulder. The ears and eye patches are black. Adults weigh from 200 to 300 lb (90–140 kg) and are from 4.5 to 5 ft (140–150 cm) long with a 5-in. (13-cm) tail. Giant pandas live in restricted areas of the high mountain bamboo forests of central China; their diet consists almost entirely of bamboo shoots. Rare in the wild, they breed poorly in captivity. There are about 20 specimens in zoos, mostly in China; in 1972 a pair of giant pandas were sent from the Peking Zoo to the Washington (D.C.) National Zoo, in exchange for two musk oxen. Giant pandas are protected by law in China. Pandas are classified in the phylum CHORDATA, subphylum Vertebrata, class Mammalia, order Carnivora, family Procyonidae.

Pandarus (păn′dərəs), in Greek legend, a Trojan warrior. In the Trojan War (as recounted in Homer's *Iliad*) he broke the truce by wounding Menelaus and soon after was killed by Diomed. In the medieval romance of Troilus and Cressida, Pandarus is the name of the lascivious intermediary between the lovers. The word *pander* is derived from the latter story.

Pandean pipes: see PANPIPES.

Pandects: see CORPUS JURIS CIVILIS.

Pandemos (păndē′mŏs): see APHRODITE.

Pandharpur (pŭn′dərpo͝or), town (1971 pop. 53,634), Maharashtra state, W India, on the Bhima River. Many Hindu pilgrims attend the festivals held three times a year at the temple of Vishnu.

Pandit, Vijaya Lakshmi (vĭjī′ə läk′shmē pŭn′dĭt), 1900–, Indian diplomat, sister of Jawaharlal Nehru. She played an active role in the Indian National Congress before Indian independence and was several times imprisoned. She was leader of the Indian delegation to the United Nations (1946–51), ambassador to the Soviet Union (1947–49) and to the United States (1949–51), president of the UN General Assembly (1953–54), and India's high commissioner to the United Kingdom (1955–61). From 1962 to 1964 she was governor of Maharashtra. See biography by R. D. Andrews (1967).

Pando, José Manuel (hōsā′ mänwĕl′ pän′dō), 1848?–1917, Bolivian statesman, president of Bolivia (1899–1904). He earned military fame in the War of the Pacific, and in 1898 he joined the revolutionary junta that overthrew the conservative regime in 1899. The result was a liberal government under Pando, with the capital at La Paz instead of Sucre. In his administration financial reforms were accomplished, but trouble with Brazil over Acre resulted in the loss (1903) of that region, with the only solace the promise of the Madeira-Mamoré RR as an outlet for E Bolivia. The groundwork was laid for the settlement of the boundary with Chile, which took place in the administration of Ismael Montes.

Pandora (păn″dôr′ə), in Greek mythology, first woman on earth. Zeus ordered Hephaestus to create her as vengeance upon man and his benefactor, Prometheus. The gods endowed her with every charm, together with curiosity and deceit. Zeus sent her as a wife to Epimetheus, Prometheus' simple brother, and gave her a box that he forbade her to open. Despite Prometheus' warnings, Epimetheus allowed her to open the box and let out all the evils that have since afflicted man. Hope alone remained inside the box.

Pandulf (păn′dŭlf″), Ital. *Pandolfo,* d. 1226, Italian churchman. He was first sent to England in 1211 by Pope INNOCENT III on an unsuccessful mission to settle the pope's dispute with King JOHN. In 1213 he again went to England as papal legate to receive John's submission to the pope, and the next year he collected papal revenues in England. After being superseded in 1214 for a short time, he returned to England, where he was elected (1215) bishop of Norwich. He remained loyal to John throughout the Magna Carta negotiations and aided royal efforts to revoke the charter. Pandulf was again superseded but returned to England in 1218 as papal legate. He exerted great political power, becoming, in effect, regent (1219–21) in the minority of Henry III until Stephen LANGTON (archbishop of Canterbury) secured his recall. Pandulf's administration was severe but efficient. After resigning his legateship, he was consecrated bishop of Norwich in 1222. See F. A. Gasquet, *Henry the Third and the Church* (1905).

Paneth, Friedrich Adolf (frē′drĭkh ä′dôlf pä′nĕt), 1887–1958, Austrian chemist. He was educated at Vienna, Munich, and Glasgow. He held a number of teaching posts in Germany until he was forced into exile in England in 1933. After World War II he returned to Germany as director of the Max Planck Institute for Chemistry at Mainz. Among Paneth's contributions to the study of radioactivity was the demonstration that lead and radium-D, a product of the radioactive decay of radium, are chemically inseparable, a fact which led him to develop, with Georg von Hevesy, the technique of isotopic labelling (see ISOTOPE). Their work laid the foundation of modern radioactive tracer techniques.

Pangaea: see CONTINENTAL DRIFT.

Pangalos, Theodore (päng′gälôs), 1878–1952, Greek general and politician. He was instrumental in the overthrow (1922) of King Constantine I and initially supported the republic (1924). In June, 1925, he seized power, and in Jan., 1926, he suspended the constitution and assumed dictatorial powers, causing Paul Kondouriotis to resign as president and securing his own election to this post in April, 1926. Pangalos was overthrown in turn (Aug., 1926) by George Kondylis, who recalled Kondouriotis. Pangalos was imprisoned until 1928 and then in 1930 was deported to Kérkira (Corfu) for two years because of his involvement in new plots.

Pange lingua (pän′jä lĭng′gwä) [Lat.,=sing, O tongue], Corpus Christi hymn of the Roman Catholic Church, written by St. Thomas Aquinas. It is used on various occasions in honor of the Sacrament; the last two stanzas, called, as a separate hymn, *Tantum ergo,* are sung at Benediction of the Blessed Sacrament. *Pange lingua* has six stanzas of six alternately rhymed trochaic lines, alternately of eight and seven syllables. Its first line and its meter are taken from the 6th-century *Pange lingua* of Venantius Fortunatus.

Pan-Germanism, German nationalist doctrine aiming at the union of all German-speaking peoples under German rule. Pan-Germanists considered that not only the German groups in neighboring countries, such as Austria, Czechoslovakia, Poland, Switzerland, and Alsace, but even distant German-speaking groups such as Volga Germans, Baltic Germans, Transylvanian Germans, and German-Americans were linked by a blood tie to their fatherland. The doctrine originated in the late 19th cent. as an instrument of German imperialistic expansion. In 1893 the *Alldeutscher Verbund* (Pan-German League) was founded. The Pan-Germans became particularly vocal after Germany's defeat in World War I had deprived it of some border territories and its colonies. National Socialism appropriated Pan-Germanism; by the annexation of Austria and of German-speaking parts of Czechoslovakia in 1938 and by German conquests in Europe during World War II, Adolf Hitler nearly succeeded for a time in making the Pan-German program a reality.

Pangnirtung (păng″nərtŭng′), trading post, E Baffin Island, Franklin dist., Northwest Territories, Canada. It is a post of the Royal Canadian Mounted Police.

pangolin (păng-gō′lĭn), armored, toothless mammal of tropical Asia and Africa. Pangolins range in length from 3 to 6 ft (90–180 cm) including the long, broad tail. Their snouts are narrow and pointed. The body is low to the ground and is covered with large, triangular, overlapping scales on the back, the sides, the outer sides of the limbs, and the entire tail. The belly is covered with sparse hair. When threatened, the animal rolls into a ball and erects the scales, points upward, so that it resembles a large pinecone. It also secretes a foul-smelling liquid. Pangolins, also called scaly anteaters, break open logs with their large, powerful claws and use their exceedingly long, slender tongues to lap up the insects on which they feed. Members of some species are tree dwellers and have prehensile, or grasping, tails; others are terrestrial. Pangolins are not closely related to any other living mammals, and their ancestry is not known. There are seven species, all of the genus *Manis.* They constitute the family Manidae and the order Pholidota of the phylum CHORDATA, subphylum Vertebrata, class Mammalia.

Pangopango: see PAGO PAGO.

panhandle, in geography, a strip of land projecting from the main body of an area and shaped like the handle of a pan, such as the panhandles of West Virginia, Texas, and Alaska.

panic, crisis in financial and economic conditions, marked by public loss of confidence in the financial structure. Panics are characterized by a general rush of investors to convert their assets into cash, with runs on banks and a rapid fall of the securities market. Bank failures and bankruptcies naturally follow. Afterward recovery may be quick or gradual. Students of economic cycles have paid much attention to the process of panics, but without definitive result. Perhaps the earliest panic of modern capitalism occurred during 1720 in France and England. Known as the "Mississippi Bubble," it was touched off by wild speculation in the stock of John Law's colonizing company (see MISSISSIPPI SCHEME). The first real panic in the United State came in 1819, after the War of 1812 and after credit for Western expansion had been overextended. That of 1837 was much more severe; it was brought on partly by banking instability and by President Andrew Jackson's suppression of the Bank of the United States, but mainly by irresponsible financial operations in Western lands. The crisis of 1857 was partly caused by massive European speculation in American railroads. Thus, when the panic struck it affected both Europe and the United States. In 1869 stock manipulations brought on the panic known as BLACK FRIDAY. In 1873 there was a financial crisis in Vienna, as well as an American panic marking the bitter contest between agrarians (see POPULIST PARTY), caught by overextended credit, and the financial interests. That conflict continued and was again reflected in the crisis that came in the Panic of 1907. No great panic occurred again until 1929, when the stock market crash precipitated a worldwide financial crisis. Confidence was not restored until after 1933, and the effects of the panic were felt throughout the GREAT DEPRESSION of the 1930s. From 1929 to 1974, the western nations did not experience any panics, although there were a number of business booms and recessions. See C. A. Collman, *Our Mysterious Panics, 1830–1930* (1931, repr. 1968); G. W. Van Vleck, *The Panic of 1857* (1943, repr. 1967); M. N. Rothbard, *The Panic of 1819* (1962, repr. 1973); Robert Sobel, *Panic on Wall Street* (1968).

Panihati (pänēhä'tē), city (1971 pop. 148,121), West Bengal state, NE India, on the Hooghly River. It is a suburb of Calcutta.

Panini (pä'nēnē), fl. c.400 B.C., Indian grammarian. His *Ashtādhyāyī* [eight books] (tr. 1891) is one of the earliest works of descriptive linguistics and is also the first individually authored treatise on Sanskrit. Each of its 3,995 rules governing roots and suffixes is introduced in a *sutra,* a concise aphorism. The *Ashtādhyāyī* also contains valuable historical, social, and geographical information. It is still used in the Brahmanic schools in India. See his *Ashtādhyāyī,* ed. by Srīśa Chandra Vasu (tr. 1962); studies by Theodor Goldstuecher (1860, repr. 1965) and Vidyaniwas Misra (1966).

Panini, Giovanni Paolo: see PANNINI, GIOVANNI PAOLO.

Panipat (pä'nēpət), town (1971 pop. 88,017), Haryana state, NW India, on the Western Jumna Canal. It has sugar-processing plants and blanket and brassware industries. On a plain astride the easiest route from Afghanistan to central India, Panipat has seen several great battles. In 1526, Babur defeated the Delhi Sultanate there, thus paving the way for the formation of the Mogul empire. In 1556, Akbar defeated the Afghans at Panipat and thus secured Mogul rule. In 1761, Panipat was the site of an Afghan victory over the Mahrattas.

Panizzi, Sir Anthony (pänēt'sē), 1797–1879, British librarian, b. Italy. A political exile, Panizzi settled in England in 1823 and was naturalized in 1832. He was associated with the British Museum library as assistant librarian (1831–37), keeper of printed books (1837–56), and chief librarian (1856–67). His 91 rules (1839) became the basis of the museum's catalog. Panizzi designed the circular reading room and the galleries of the library and enforced the act requiring deposition at the museum of copies of books copyrighted in Great Britain. He was influential in obtaining for the museum considerable Parliamentary support as well as the bequest of the Grenville library in 1846. His celebrated edition of Boiardo's *Orlando Innamorato* and Ariosto's *Orlando Furioso* (9 vol.) was published from 1830 to 1834. Panizzi was knighted in 1869. See biographies by Edward Miller (1967) and L. A. Fagan (2d ed. 1970).

Panj, river: see AMU DARYA.

Panjim, India: see GOA, DAMAN, AND DIU.

Panjnad, river, Pakistan: see SUTLEJ.

Pankhurst, Emmeline Goulden, 1858–1928, British woman suffragist. Disappointed in the disinterest in women's suffrage shown by the Liberal party, the Fabian Society, and the Independent Labour party, she founded (1903) her own movement, the Women's Social and Political Union. Using spectacular militant means to further their cause, the members of her movement were frequently arrested. Arrested and imprisoned herself in 1912, she went on a hunger strike and soon gained release. Arrested again in 1913 she was released once more after a hunger strike, but imprisoned upon her recovery according to the provisions of the newly passed "Cat and Mouse" Act (Prisoners, Temporary Discharge for Health, Act; 1913). This pattern repeated itself 12 times in the following 12 months. On the outbreak of World War I, however, the government granted her a full release, and she turned her powers of leadership from the suffragist movement to the war effort. After the war she moved to Canada and her work for women's rights virtually ceased. Upon her return to England in 1926 she was a nationally revered figure. She died while standing for election to Parliament as a Conservative candidate two years later. A statue in her memory stands at Westminster. See her autobiography, *My Own Story* (1914, repr. 1970), and the biography by her daughter E. Sylvia Pankhurst (1936, repr. 1969); Ray Strachey, *The Cause* (1928, repr. 1969); Dudley Barker, *Prominent Edwardians* (1969). Her oldest daughter, **Christabel Pankhurst,** 1880–1958, was also a suffragist. Educated for the bar but refused admittance because of her sex, she later became an evangelist. In 1936 she was made a Dame of the British Empire. The youngest daughter, **Sylvia Pankhurst,** 1882–1960, created a sensation by opposing marriage as an institution and defending unmarried mothers; she carried her theories into practice by bearing an illegitimate son in 1927. She later was active in the cause of Ethiopian independence. Her writings include *The Suffragette Movement* (1931) and *Ethiopia, A Cultural History* (1935), in addition to the biography of her mother (1936). See David J. K. Mitchell, *The Fighting Pankhursts* (1967).

Pankow (päng'kō), district of East Berlin, E central East Germany, on the Panke River, bordering on West Berlin. It is an industrial center and the seat of the East German government. Pankow is known for its gardens, castles, and large parks.

Panmunjom (păn''mo͝onjŏm'), village, N South Korea. It lies south of the 38th parallel, the military demarcation line that partitions Korea. In the Korean War the truce negotiations, begun at nearby KAESONG, were moved in Oct., 1951, to Panmunjom, where the truce was signed on July 27, 1953.

Pannag (păn'ăg), unidentified article in the trade between Palestine and Tyre. Ezek. 27.17.

Pannini, or **Panini, Giovanni Paolo** (jōvän'nē pä'ōlō pänēn'nē, pänē'nē), 1691–1765, Italian painter. Pannini abandoned the study of architecture for painting, becoming famed for his broad cityscapes, or *vidute.* His commemorative paintings of public events work tiny human figures into vast urban settings. In his paintings of ruins (e.g., *Roman Ruins,* Mus. di Capodimonte, Naples), he combined the landmarks of ancient and Renaissance Rome.

Pannonia (pănō'nēə), ancient Roman province, central Europe, southwest of the Danube, including parts of modern Austria, Hungary, and Yugoslavia. Its natives, the warlike Pannonians, were Illyrians. Their final subjugation by Rome took place in A.D. 9. Pannonia was divided A.D. c.103 into the provinces of Upper Pannonia and Lower Pannonia. Important centers were Carnuntum, Vindobona (Vienna), Aquincum (Budapest), and Sirmium. Pannonia was abandoned by the Romans after 395.

Panofsky, Erwin (pănŏf'skē), 1892–1968, American art historian, b. Germany, Ph.D. Univ. of Freiburg, 1914. After teaching (1921–33) at the Univ. of Hamburg and serving as professor of fine arts at New York Univ., he joined (1935) the faculty at the Institute for Advanced Study, Princeton, N.J. His writings are among the most important of the 20th cent. in art history. Panofsky contributed studies, particularly in the realm of iconography, of the medieval, Renaissance, mannerist, and baroque periods. He is admired for his immense erudition, his discoveries, and his profound observations, laced with touches of humor. Among his principal works in English are *Studies in Iconology* (1939, 2d ed. 1962), *Albrecht Dürer* (1943, 4th ed. 1955), *Early Netherlandish Painting* (1953), and *Renaissance and Renascenses in Western Art* (2d ed. 1965). Other writings include *The Codex Huygens and Leonardo da Vinci's Art Theory* (1940), *Abbot Suger on the Abbey Church of St.-Denis and Its Art Treasures* (1946), *Gothic Architecture and Scholasticism* (1951), *Galileo as a Critic of the Arts* (1954), *Meaning in the Visual Arts* (1955), *Correggio's Camera di San Paolo* (1961), *Tomb Sculpture* (1964), *Idea: A Concept in Art Theory* (1924, tr. 1968), and *Problems in Titian, Mostly Iconographic* (1969)

Panormus (pənôr'məs), ancient name of PALERMO, Italy. Another Panormus was a port of Asia Minor, on the south shore of the Propontis (now the Sea of Marmara). It is the modern Turkish Bandirma, formerly also called Panderma.

panpipes, Pandean pipes (păndē'ən), or **syrinx** (sĭr'ĭngks), musical wind instrument, consisting of graduated tubes closed at one end and fastened together. The player holds the instrument vertically

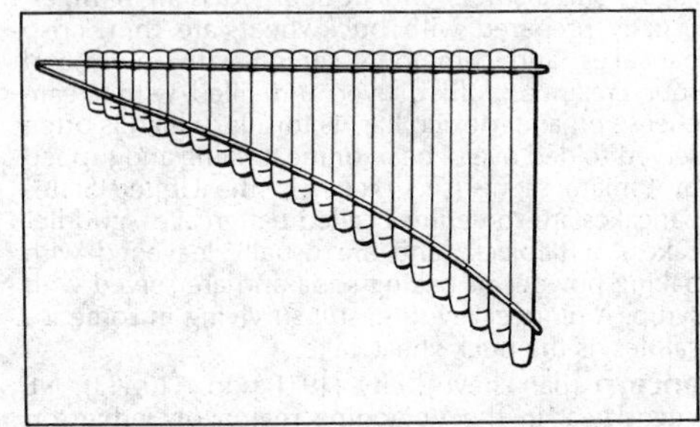

Panpipes

and blows into the open end of the tube; each tube has its own pitch. Of Chinese origin, the instrument was known to the Greeks (who connected its origin with the legend of the god PAN and the nymph Syrinx who was changed into reeds). It survives in some parts of Europe and South America.

Pan-Slavism, theory and movement intended to promote the political or cultural unity of all SLAVS. Advocated by various individuals from the 17th cent., it developed as an intellectual and cultural movement in the 19th cent. It was stimulated by the rise of romanticism and nationalism, and it grew with the awakening of the Slavs within the Austrian and Ottoman (Turkish) empires. Slavic historians, philologists, and anthropologists, influenced by Johann Gottfried von Herder, helped spread a national consciousness among the Slavs, and some dreamed of a unified Slavic culture to replace an allegedly declining Latin-German culture. The first Pan-Slav Congress, held at Prague in 1848 and presided over by František PALACKÝ, was confined to the Slavs under Austrian rule and was anti-Russian. The humiliating defeat suffered by Russia in the Crimean War (1853–56) helped transform a vague, romantic Russian Slavophilism into a militant and nationalistic Russian Pan-Slavism. Prominent among the Russian Pan-Slav publicists were Rotislav Andreyevich Fadeyev and Nikolai Yakovlevich Danilevsk[illegible] Fadeyev claimed that it was Russia's mission to li[illegible]erate the Slavs from Austrian and Ottoman domination by war and to form a Russian-dominated Slavic federation. Danilevsky predicted a long conflict between Russia and the rest of Europe, to be followed by a federation of states including the Greeks, Magyars, and Rumanians as well as the Slavs. In the reign of Czar Alexander II, the foreign minister, Aleksandr Gorchakov, opposed Pan-Slav aspirations, although many officials were Pan-Slavist. Pressures from the Pan-Slavs probably helped provoke the Russo-Turkish War of 1877–78 but afterward declined. In the decade preceding World War I, Pan-Slav agitation again increased and played a role in the growing conflict between Russia and Austria in the Balkan peninsula, where the Serbs opposed Austria. In 1908, Russia was forced to allow Austrian annexation of Bosnia and Hercegovina, but in 1914 Russia supported Serbia in the crisis that began World War I. After the Bolsheviks triumphed in the Russian Revolution of 1917, the Soviet government renounced Pan-Slavism. In World War II, however,

Pan-Slavist slogans were revived to facilitate Slavic and Communist dominance of Eastern European countries. Both in the 19th and 20th cent. Pan-Slav aspirations were limited by the conflicting political and economic hopes of the various groups of Slavs. See M. B. Petrovich, *The Emergence of Russian Pan-Slavism, 1856–1870* (1956); Hans Kohn, *Pan-Slavism* (2d ed., 1960).

pansy: see VIOLET.

Pantaleoni, Maffeo (mäf-fĕ'ō päntälāō'nē), 1857–1924, Italian economist and politician. He was finance minister in Gabriele D'Annunzio's government at Fiume (1919), one of the first senators named by Benito Mussolini, and a delegate (1923) to the League of Nations. In *Pure Economics* (1889, tr. 1898, repr. 1957), Pantaleoni made a distinguished contribution to the theory of marginal utility. He also did notable work in statistics and finance.

Pantaloon: see COMMEDIA DELL' ARTE.

pantanal (pəntənäl'), lowland region of SW Mato Grosso state, Brazil, between the Paraguay River and the western edge of the Brazilian Plateau. Although subject to annual flooding, it is not a marshland; the water is not stagnant, and there is no malaria. The pantanal completely dries out at the end of the six-month rainy season, leaving lush grasslands that are used for cattle grazing.

Pantelleria (păn'tāl-lārē'ä), volcanic island, 32 sq mi (83 sq km), S Italy, in the Mediterranean Sea between Sicily and Tunisia. Sweet wine, capers, raisins, and dried figs are exported. A colony of the Phoenicians and then of the Carthaginians, it passed to the Romans in 217 B.C. The island was later taken by the Arabs (8th cent. A.D.) and by the Normans (12th cent.). Because of its strategic location, it was strongly fortified by Italy in the 20th cent. During World War II, Pantelleria was bombed into surrender by the Allies in 1943. On the island are extinct cones (the highest rising to 2,743 ft/836 m), numerous fumaroles, and hot mineral springs.

pantheism (păn'thēĭzəm) [Gr. *pan*=all, *theos*=God], name used to denote any system of belief or speculation that includes the teaching "God is all, and all is God." Pantheism, in other words, identifies the universe with God or God with the universe. The term is thought to have been employed first by John TOLAND in the 18th cent., but pantheistic views are of very great antiquity. While all pantheism is monistic, it is expressed in different ways according to what is meant by the one whole that gathers up in itself all that exists, or what is meant by God. If the pantheist starts with the belief that the one great reality, eternal and infinite, is God, he sees everything finite and temporal as but some part of God. There is nothing separate or distinct from God, for God is the universe. If, on the other hand, the conception taken as the foundation of the system is that the great inclusive unity is the world itself, or the universe, God is swallowed up in that unity, which may be designated nature. Some forms of pantheism have had their beginnings in religion; others have been based upon a philosophic, scientific, or poetic point of view. Noteworthy among the religious forms is HINDUISM, in which the only reality, the supreme unity, is Brahman. This conception is closely connected with the idea of EMANATION. Pantheism had a place in the speculations of some Greek philosophers. XENOPHANES taught that the one God could know no motion or change. The conception of Parmenides left no room for development or ethical meaning. STOICISM gave a more definite expression to pantheistic doctrine, emphasizing the identity of God and the world. There is pantheism in the teachings of the Neoplatonists and of such Christian philosophers as ERIGENA and such mystics as ECKHART and BOEHME. The writings of Giordano BRUNO of the 16th cent. carried such weight as to influence the development of modern thought, especially through Spinoza, in whose monistic system pantheism receives its most complete and precise expression. In it God is the unlimited, all-inclusive substance, the first cause of the universe, with innumerable attributes, two of which, thinking and extension, are capable of being perceived. Pantheism of a kind can be traced in the idealistic philosophy of Fichte and Schelling, Hegel and SCHLEIERMACHER. Together with MYSTICISM, it fills a large place in literature, particularly in the poetry of nature.

pantheon (păn'thēŏn", -thēən), term applied originally to a temple to all the gods. The **Pantheon** at Rome was built by Agrippa in 27 B.C., destroyed, and rebuilt in the 2d cent. by Hadrian. Remarkably well preserved, it is mainly of brick with a great hemispherical dome whose supporting walls are set in concrete. In 609 it was converted into a Christian church consecrated to Santa Maria dei Martiri. The term is now applied to a monument in which illustrious dead are buried. The **Panthéon** (päNtāôN') in Paris was designed by J. G. Soufflot and was begun in 1764; the dome was completed (1781) after his death. An earlier church on the site was dedicated to St. Geneviève. The Panthéon was several times secularized and reconsecrated, becoming finally a mausoleum for illustrious Frenchmen.

panther, name commonly applied to the LEOPARD, especially to a black leopard. It is also used locally to designate various other cats including the JAGUAR and the PUMA. In animal systematics the generic name *Panthera* is given to all the big roaring cats: the LION, TIGER, leopard, snow leopard, and jaguar.

Pantin (päNtăN'), suburb NE of Paris (1968 pop. 47,714), Seine-Saint-Denis dept., N central France, on the Canal d'Ourcq. There is considerable timber trade through the canal. Pantin, an industrial town, also has large flour mills. Its manufactures include foundry products, chemicals, cigarettes, and processed foods.

Pantoja de la Cruz, Juan (hwän päntō'hä thā lä krōōth), 1553–1608, Spanish portrait painter, court painter to Philip II and Philip III; pupil and follower of Alonzo Sánchez Coello. The Prado contains beautiful examples of his severe portraiture and also a fine *Nativity.*

pantomime or **mime** (păn'təmīm) [Gr.,=all in mimic], silent form of the drama in which the story is developed by movement, gesture, and facial expression. It is known to have existed among the Chinese, Persians, Hebrews, and Egyptians and has been observed in many other cultures. Pantomime was popular in ancient Rome, where it was often explained by songs or simple action. The traditional characters of pantomime take their origin in the Italian COMMEDIA DELL' ARTE of the 16th cent. English pantomime, originated by John RICH, was more PAGEANT than pantomime, and in 1818, when J. R. Planche began his extravaganzas with "speaking openings," pantomime in England became a dramatic spectacle with songs and speeches. Joseph GRIMALDI and Jean Gaspard DEBURAU were famous pantomime stars of the 19th cent. In silent pictures, Charlie CHAPLIN made his name as a great pantomime actor. Marcel MARCEAU has revived the tradition in France. See Charles Aubert, *Art of Pantomime* (1927, repr. 1969); Joan Lawson, *Mime* (1957, repr. 1973).

pantone: see PRINTING.

pantothenic acid (păn'təthĕn'ĭk): see COENZYME; VITAMIN.

Pánuco (pä'nōōkō), river, c.315 mi (510 km) long, rising as the Santa María River in San Luis Potosí state, N central Mexico, and flowing generally east to empty into the Gulf of Mexico near Tampico. It is navigable for c.200 mi (322 km). Tributaries, including the Moctezuma, drain, sometimes by artificial means, the ANÁHUAC region.

Panzini, Alfredo (älfrē'dō päntsē'nē), 1863–1939, Italian novelist and lexicographer; pupil of Giosuè Carducci. He taught in secondary schools. His genial, popular novels include *Libro dei morti* [book of the dead] (1893), *Santippe* (1914), *Io cerco moglie* (1920, tr. *Wanted—a Wife,* 1922), and *Il diavolo nella mia libreria* [the devil in my library] (1920). His modern dictionary, which included slang, went through many editions. He also wrote historical works. Some of his short stories are translated in F. M. Guercio, *Anthology of Contemporary Italian Prose* (1931).

Pao-chi or **Paoki** (both: bou-jē), city (1970 est. pop. 275,000), SW Shensi prov., China, on the Wei River. On the Lunghai RR, it is an important junction point for the line to Ch'eng-tu, in Szechwan prov. It is also a newly flourishing industrial center with manufactures of textiles and paper.

Paoki: see PAO-CHI, China.

Paoking: see SHAO-YANG, China.

Paoli, Pasquale (päskwä'lā pä'ōlē), 1725–1807, Corsican patriot. He shared the exile (1739–55) of his father, Giacinto Paoli, a supporter of Baron NEUHOF ("King Theodore") against the Genoese, who ruled the island. In 1755 he returned to Corsica, led a revolt against the Genoese, and was chosen president under a republican constitution. His capital was at Corte. He governed with wide powers, but respected the constitution. Material prosperity, public order, and education were greatly furthered. In 1768, Genoa, despairing of reducing the island to submission, sold Corsica to France. Paoli fought brilliantly against the superior forces of the French, but in 1769 he was decisively defeated and fled to England, where his popularity was great. James Boswell, who had corresponded with him and visited him in Corsica, introduced him into the circle of Samuel Johnson. After the outbreak of the French Revolution, Paoli was appointed (1791) governor of Corsica. He subscribed to the liberal revolutionary principles, but opposed the radical turn the French Revolution took and, especially, the centralizing policy of the Revolutionary government. Accused (1793) of counterrevolutionary activities and summoned to Paris, he proclaimed the independence of Corsica and solicited British aid. With the help of Admiral Hood the French were defeated (1794). The pro-French party was banished and the Corsican national assembly (*consulta*) declared the island a British protectorate and chose an English governor. Paoli, who favored independence and who had hoped to be appointed viceroy, was disappointed when POZZO DI BORGO became chief of the Corsican council of state. Paoli went to England in 1795 and remained there until his death. After his departure the islanders rose against the British and in 1796 drove them out with French help. See James Boswell, *Boswell on the Grand Tour,* ed. by Frank Brady and F. A. Pottle (1955); P. A. Thrasher, *Pasquale Paoli* (1970).

Pao-ting or **Paoting** (both: bou-dĭng), city (1970 est. pop. 350,000), central Hopeh prov., China. It is a port on the Fu River and an agricultural distribution center, with food-processing industries. Chemicals, fertilizer, cotton cloth, synthetic fibers, and medicines are also manufactured. Pao-ting was the capital of Hopeh prov. until 1958. A medical college and an agricultural institute are in the city. Pao-ting was formerly called Tsingyuan.

Pao-t'ou or **Paotow** (both: bou-tō), city (1970 est. pop. 800,000), Inner Mongolian Autonomous Region, China. A port and major trade center on the Huang Ho (Yellow River), it is connected by rail with Peking, Lan-chou, the Mongolian People's Republic, and the USSR. Vigorous industrialization in recent years has made it a major manufacturing center. Iron and coal are mined in the vicinity, and the city has a large integrated iron and steel complex as well as sugar refineries, textile mills, and plants making motor vehicles, chemicals, fertilizers, and aluminum. Two nuclear reactors are nearby.

Paotow: see PAO-T'OU, China.

Pápa (pä'pŏ), town (1970 pop. 27,775), W Hungary, in a grain- and beet-growing area. It is an industrial town; cotton spinning, tobacco processing, and the manufacture of textiles and electric appliances are the major industries. Pápa has several churches, a Protestant theological college, and an 18th-century château built by Count Maurice Esterházy.

papacy (pā'pəsē), office of the pope, head of the Roman Catholic Church. He is pope by reason of being bishop of Rome and thus, according to Roman Catholic belief, successor in the see of Rome (the Holy See) to its first bishop, St. PETER. The pope therefore claims to be the shepherd of all Christians and representative (vicar or vicegerent) of Christ. This claim, that of the Petrine supremacy, is not acknowledged outside the Roman Catholic Church. That church further holds that God will not permit the pope to make an error in a solemn official declaration concerning a matter of faith or morality (see INFALLIBILITY). The pope is also patriarch of the West; the great majority, although not all, of the Christians recognizing his authority as pope are also under his authority as PATRIARCH. This question of areas of authority is practical only with regard to some of the Eastern-rite patriarchs who may, for example, appoint bishops without papal confirmation. The pope lives generally in Rome, of which a tiny portion (the Vatican City) is politically independent and under his rule; the pope is thus head of a state and owes no political allegiance (see VATICAN; ROME; CARDINAL; PAPAL ELECTION). For the ecclesiastical framework, the teaching, the history, and the geographical distribution of the church, see ROMAN CATHOLIC CHURCH. See also CHRISTIANITY.

The Papacy in the Early Church. There is no unequivocal evidence about the status of the pope in the earliest days of the church. That he was accorded special honor as the successor of St. Peter is acknowledged, but whereas Roman Catholic historians hold that the peculiar position of the Holy See was recognized and accorded authority, non-Catholic historians in general contend that the bishop of Rome was accorded honor over the other bishops, not authority. As missionaries sent directly from the city founded new churches throughout the West, more and more reverence was given to the pope. The Roman church was being enriched with gifts by

CHRONOLOGY OF POPES

In the following list, the date of election, rather than of consecration, is given. Before St. Victor I (189), dates may err by one year. Antipopes—i.e., those men whose elections have been declared uncanonical—are indicated.

St. PETER, d. 64? or 67?
St. LINUS, 67?–76?
St. CLETUS, or Anacletus, 76?–88?
St. CLEMENT I, 88?–97?
St. Evaristus, 97?–105?
St. Alexander I, 105?–115?
St. Sixtus I, 115?–125?
St. Telesphorus, 125?–136?
St. Hyginus, 136?–140?
St. Pius I, 140?–155?
St. Anicetus, 155?–166?
St. Soter, 166?–175?
St. Eleutherius, 175?–189?
St. Victor I, 189–99
St. Zephyrinus, 199–217
St. CALIXTUS I, 217–22
antipope: St. HIPPOLYTUS, 217–35
St. Urban I, 222–30
St. Pontian, 230–35
St. Anterus, 235–36
St. FABIAN, 236–50
St. CORNELIUS, 251–53
antipope: Novatian, 251
St. Lucius I, 253–54
St. Stephen I, 254–57
St. Sixtus II, 257–58
St. Dionysius, 259–68
St. Felix I, 269–74
St. Eutychian, 275–83
St. Caius, 283–96
St. Marcellinus, 296–304
St. Marcellus I, c.308–309
St. Eusebius, 309–c.310
St. Miltiades, or Melchiades, 311–14
St. SYLVESTER I, 314–35
St. Marcus, 336
St. JULIUS I, 337–52
LIBERIUS, 352–66
antipope: FELIX, 355–65
St. DAMASUS I, 366–84
antipope: Ursinus, 366–67
St. Siricius, 384–99
St. Anastasius I, 399–401
St. INNOCENT I, 401–17
St. Zosimus, 417–18
St. Boniface I, 418–22
antipope: Eulalius, 418–19
St. CELESTINE I, 422–32
St. Sixtus III, 432–40
St. Leo I, 440–61
St. Hilary, 461–68
St. Simplicius, 468–83
St. Felix III (or II), 483–92
St. GELASIUS I, 492–96
Anastasius II, 496–98
St. Symmachus, 498–514
antipope: Lawrence, 498–505
St. Hormisdas, 514–23
St. John I, 523–26
St. Felix IV (or III), 526–30
Boniface II, 530–32
pope or antipope: Dioscurus, 530
John II, 533–35
St. Agapetus I, 535–36
St. SILVERIUS, 536–37
VIGILIUS, 537–55
Pelagius I, 556–61
John III, 561–74
Benedict I, 575–79
Pelagius II, 579–90
St. GREGORY I, 590–604
Sabinian, 604–6
Boniface III, 607
St. Boniface IV, 608–15
St. Deusdedit, or Adeodatus I, 615–18
Boniface V, 619–25
HONORIUS I, 625–38
Severinus, 640
John IV, 640–42
Theodore I, 642–49
St. MARTIN I, 649–55
St. Eugene I, 654–57
St. Vitalian, 657–72
Adeodatus II, 672–76
Donus, 676–78
St. Agatho, 678–81
St. Leo II, 682–83
St. Benedict II, 684–85
John V, 685–86
Conon, 686–87
antipope: Theodore, 687
antipope: Paschal, 687
St. Sergius I, 687–701
John VI, 701–5
John VII, 705–7
Sisinnius, 708
Constantine, 708–15
St. GREGORY II, 715–31
St. Gregory III, 731–41
St. ZACHARIAS, 741–52
Stephen II, 752 (never consecrated)
STEPHEN II (or III), 752–57
St. Paul I, 757–67
antipope: Constantine, 767–69
antipope: Philip, 768
Stephen III (or IV), 768–72
ADRIAN I, 772–95
St. LEO III, 795–816
Stephen IV (or V), 816–17
St. Paschal I, 817–24
Eugene II, 824–27
Valentine, 827
Gregory IV, 827–44
antipope: John, 844
Sergius II, 844–47
St. LEO IV, 847–55
Benedict III, 855–58
antipope: Anastasius, 855
St. NICHOLAS I, 858–67
Adrian II, 867–72
JOHN VIII, 872–82
Marinus I, 882–84
St. Adrian III, 884–85
Stephen V (or VI), 885–91
FORMOSUS, 891–96
Boniface VI, 896
Stephen VI (or VII), 896–97
Romanus, 897
Theodore II, 897
John IX, 898–900
Benedict IV, 900–903
Leo V, 903
antipope: Christopher, 903–4
Sergius III, 904–11
Anastasius III, 911–13
Lando, 913–14
John X, 914–28
Leo VI, 928
Stephen VII (or VIII), 928–31
John XI, 931–35
Leo VII, 936–39
Stephen VIII (or IX), 939–42
Marinus II, 942–46
Agapetus II, 946–55
JOHN XII, 955–64
Leo VIII, 963–65, or Benedict V, 964–66 (*one of these was an antipope*)
John XIII, 965–72
Benedict VI, 973–74
antipope: Boniface VII, 974, 984–85
Benedict VII, 974–83
John XIV, 983–84
John XV, 985–96
Gregory V, 996–99
antipope: John XVI, 997–98
SYLVESTER II, 999–1003
John XVII, 1003
John XVIII, 1004–9
Sergius IV, 1009–12
Benedict VIII, 1012–24
antipope: Gregory, 1012
John XIX, 1024–32
Benedict IX, 1032–44
Sylvester III, 1045
Benedict IX, 1045
Gregory VI, 1045–46
Clement II, 1046–47
Benedict IX, 1047–48
Damasus II, 1048
St. LEO IX, 1049–54
Victor II, 1055–57
Stephen IX (or X), 1057–58
antipope: Benedict X, 1058–59
Nicholas II, 1059–61
Alexander II, 1061–73
antipope: Honorius II, 1061–72
St. GREGORY VII, 1073–85
antipope: Clement III, 1080–1100 (see GUIBERT OF RAVENNA)
Victor III, 1086–87
URBAN II, 1088–99
PASCHAL II, 1099–1118
antipope: Theodoric, 1100
antipope: Albert, 1102
antipope: Sylvester IV, 1105–11
Gelasius II, 1118–19
antipope: Gregory VIII, 1118–21
CALIXTUS II, 1119–24
HONORIUS II, 1124–30
antipope: Celestine II, 1124
INNOCENT II, 1130–43
antipope: Anacletus II, 1130–38
antipope: Victor IV, 1138
Celestine II, 1143–44
Lucius II, 1144–45
EUGENE III, 1145–53
Anastasius IV, 1153–54
ADRIAN IV, 1154–59
ALEXANDER III, 1159–81
antipope: Victor IV, 1159–64
antipope: Paschal III, 1164–68
antipope: Calixtus III, 1168–78
antipope: Innocent III, 1179–80
LUCIUS III, 1181–85
Urban III, 1185–87
Gregory VIII, 1187
Clement III, 1187–91
Celestine III, 1191–98
INNOCENT III, 1198–1216
HONORIUS III, 1216–27
GREGORY IX, 1227–41
Celestine IV, 1241
INNOCENT IV, 1243–54
Alexander IV, 1254–61
URBAN IV, 1261–64
CLEMENT IV, 1265–68
Gregory X, 1271–76
INNOCENT V, 1276
Adrian V, 1276
JOHN XXI, 1276–77
NICHOLAS III, 1277–80
MARTIN IV, 1281–85
Honorius IV, 1285–87
Nicholas IV, 1288–92
St. CELESTINE V, 1294
BONIFACE VIII, 1294–1303
BENEDICT XI, 1303–4
CLEMENT V, 1304–14
JOHN XXII, 1316–34
antipope: Nicholas V, 1328–30 (see RAINALDUCCI, PIETRO)
Benedict XII, 1334–42
CLEMENT VI, 1342–52
INNOCENT VI, 1352–62
URBAN V, 1362–70
GREGORY XI, 1370–78

The Great Schism, 1378–1417

Roman Line
URBAN VI, 1378–89
BONIFACE IX, 1389–1404
Innocent VII, 1404–6
GREGORY XII, 1406–15

Avignon Line
antipope: Clement VII, 1378–94 (see ROBERT OF GENEVA)
antipope: Benedict XIII, 1394–1423 (see LUNA, PEDRO DE)
antipope: Clement VII, 1423–29
antipope: Benedict XIV, 1425–30

Pisan Line
antipope: Alexander V, 1409–10
antipope: John XXIII, 1410–15 (see COSSA, BALDASSARRE)

MARTIN V, 1417–31
EUGENE IV, 1431–47
antipope: Felix V, 1439–49 (see AMADEUS VIII)
NICHOLAS V, 1447–55
CALIXTUS III, 1455–58
PIUS II, 1458–64
PAUL II, 1464–71
SIXTUS IV, 1471–84
INNOCENT VIII, 1484–92
ALEXANDER VI, 1492–1503
Pius III, 1503
JULIUS II, 1503–13
LEO X, 1513–21
ADRIAN VI, 1522–23
CLEMENT VII, 1523–34
PAUL III, 1534–49
Julius III, 1550–55
Marcellus II, 1555
PAUL IV, 1555–59
PIUS IV, 1559–65
St. PIUS V, 1566–72
GREGORY XIII, 1572–85
SIXTUS V, 1585–90
Urban VII, 1590
Gregory XIV, 1590–91
Innocent IX, 1591
CLEMENT VIII, 1592–1605
Leo XI, 1605
PAUL V, 1605–21
Gregory XV, 1621–23
URBAN VIII, 1623–44
Innocent X, 1644–55
Alexander VII, 1655–67
Clement IX, 1667–69
Clement X, 1670–76
INNOCENT XI, 1676–89
Alexander VIII, 1689–91
INNOCENT XII, 1691–1700
CLEMENT XI, 1700–21
Innocent XIII, 1721–24
Benedict XIII, 1724–30
Clement XII, 1730–40
BENEDICT XIV, 1740–58
Clement XIII, 1758–69
CLEMENT XIV, 1769–74
PIUS VI, 1775–99
PIUS VII, 1800–23
Leo XII, 1823–29
Pius VIII, 1829–30
GREGORY XVI, 1831–46
PIUS IX, 1846–78
LEO XIII, 1878–1903
St. PIUS X, 1903–14
BENEDICT XV, 1914–22
PIUS XI, 1922–39
PIUS XII, 1939–58
JOHN XXIII, 1958–63
PAUL VI, 1963–

converts, and it supported struggling young churches everywhere and supplied funds for charitable foundations all over Italy. As the political power of the city of Rome declined, the pope inherited some of the Roman emperor's position as symbol and defender of civilization. The combination of assurance and intrepidity in dealing with barbarian attacks and rulers of emerging states in this period (300–700) was a mark of the great popes—saints Julius I, Innocent I, Leo I, Gregory I, and Martin I. The papacy gained prestige in the West and was powerful in doctrinal disputes, especially in the struggles over ARIANISM, MONOPHYSITISM, and MONOTHELETISM.

The Papacy in the Middle Ages. A fateful event for the papacy was the donation of lands made to the pope by the Frankish king Pepin the Short in 756. The papacy had already been given lands (since the 4th cent.), but it was the Donation of Pepin that came to be considered the real as well as the symbolic founding of the PAPAL STATES. The pope thus became a powerful lay prince as well as an ecclesiastical ruler. This intermingling of powers was a determining condition in the struggle between CHURCH AND STATE that was a main theme in the history of the West in the Middle Ages. Strong lay princes attempted to direct the church just as the pope tried to establish secular as well as spiritual supremacy over the rulers. A central point at issue was INVESTITURE, but the conflict was far wider and deeper. Although all in the West recognized that Christendom was under one pope, that recognition had little bearing on the question of papal supremacy in secular affairs. By crowning (800) Charlemagne, Leo III at once sponsored the empire and sanctioned the creation of a state which, as the HOLY

ROMAN EMPIRE, was to be the chief antagonist of the papacy for centuries. The papacy reached a high point of corruption in the 10th cent., when the Holy See was cynically bought and sold, but it was redeemed in the 11th cent. by the sweeping Hildebrandine reform initiated and carried through by the forceful Gregory VII. From that time forward the relative power of the papacy in quarrels with the emperor and with the kings of England, France, Naples, and Spain depended largely upon the successes of individual popes and individual rulers. Pope Alexander III was pitted against Holy Roman Emperor Frederick I and against King Henry II of England, and Pope Innocent III, despite opposition by Emperor Otto IV and Emperor Frederick II, made himself virtual arbiter of the West. Innocent's reign (1198–1216) marked the zenith of papal secular power. Decline set in immediately. A century later Boniface VIII, an able canon lawyer, proved himself no match for the ruthless king of France, Philip IV. Pope Clement V in 1309 deserted Rome for Avignon and the domination of France. During the so-called Babylonian captivity (1309–78) all the popes were French, all lived at Avignon, and all were under the control of the French kings. Pope Gregory XI—acting partly on the advice of St. Catherine of Siena and St. Bridget of Sweden—moved the papacy back to Rome. But the church was immediately plunged into the disorder of the Great SCHISM (1378–1417). There were two or even three rival popes at a time (in later determination of true succession, those claimants ruled out of the succession are called antipopes). The schism ended in the Council of Constance (see CONSTANCE, COUNCIL OF). Since then, apart from the abortive revolt at the Council of Basel (see BASEL, COUNCIL OF), there has been no schism in the papacy. The pope had little real power outside Italy, and no 15th-century pope was prepared to attempt serious reform, which would have required challenging the vested interests of bishops, cardinals, and princes. Indeed, in the 15th cent. the papal court made Rome a brilliant Renaissance capital, enriched by some of the finest art of the West. The Renaissance popes, however, were little distinguished from other princes in the extravagance and immorality of their courts.

The Papacy in the Reformation. This corruption provided a background for the Protestant REFORMATION. Martin Luther and his colleagues were entering upon a basic theological revolution. They denounced the whole accepted view of God's relation to man and began a movement that still continues to advance with broadening effects. Corruption did, however, have an effect in alienating many followers of the established church. Within the church itself reformation began in earnest with the election (1534) of Paul III, first of a series of popes who carried out a reconstruction of church life in the Catholic Reformation (see REFORMATION, CATHOLIC). The Council of Trent (1545–47, 1551–52, 1562–63; see TRENT, COUNCIL OF) undertook to lay out the new definitions and regulations that reconstructed the church, including the papacy. The other major work of the 16th-century popes was the new development of foreign missions, which, as in ancient times, enhanced papal prestige. Of the several orders concerned with reform and missions, the Jesuits (see JESUS, SOCIETY OF) were the best known. The 16th cent. also saw the stabilization of the Papal States as they would remain until the 19th cent.

The Papacy in the 18th and 19th Centuries. The papacy continued to be plagued by another problem, one that reform had (of necessity) left untouched. This was the position in the church of the rulers of largely Roman Catholic states. Once one of these Catholic princes, whether devout or notoriously immoral, was sure of his power, he determined to include the church within it (e.g., insisting on the deciding voice in selecting the clergy). The kings of Spain even conducted their own Inquisition. It was accepted that Catholic rulers should hold a veto in papal elections. By the 18th cent. every Catholic prince was at odds with the papacy. Spain had the longest record of this sort, lasting into the 20th cent. In France the triumphant Bourbons developed GALLICANISM as a theory to justify their ecclesiastical pretensions; Louis XIV was its chief proponent, but the revolutionists of 1790 used it (in the Civil Constitution of the Clergy, banned by Pius VI), and so did Napoleon I as soon as he had signed the CONCORDAT OF 1801. Most extreme, and least enduring, were the schemes of Holy Roman Emperor JOSEPH II. In the 18th cent. the papacy seemed doomed; its weakness became a spectacle when Clement XIV was forced into suppressing the Jesuits, the only group in the church consistently loyal to the pope. Early in the 19th cent., when Pius VII tried to protect the sanctity of the Holy See, Napoleon had him ignominiously imprisoned. After the fall of Napoleon, with the increasing decline of the old absolutist states, the papacy imperceptibly gained. Papal opposition to the reunification of Italy deepened the suspicious dislike of most liberals for the papacy. The loss (1870) of the Papal States proved in the end a blessing for the papacy, although it took 60 years to solve the Roman Question—the problem of assuring the pope nonnational status in a nationally organized world (see LATERAN TREATY). The First VATICAN COUNCIL enunciated the doctrine of papal infallibility in 1870. In the modern world, the popes no longer faced trouble with Catholic princes but did engage in struggles with secular states over anticlerical or specifically anti-Catholic legislation (e.g., Otto von Bismarck's KULTURKAMPF in Germany and the anticlericalism in France, Portugal, and Mexico) or overt attacks on all religion.

The Papacy in the 20th Century. The popes at the end of the 19th cent. turned more toward pure spiritual and moral leadership in a tangled world. The growth of Catholicism in areas outside Europe tended to make the pope more and more the single unifying force in the church and therefore fundamentally an international element. A singular succession of dynamic popes strengthened this effect; Leo XIII, Pius X, Benedict XV, Pius XI, Pius XII, John XXIII, and Paul VI have all striven to reorient the church in the modern world, to combat secularism, and to extend morality in social relations. The social encyclical of Leo XIII, *Rerum Novarum* (1891), was echoed in the encyclical of Pius XI, *Quadragesimo Anno* (1931), reinforced and restated by John XXIII in *Mater et Magistra* (1961), and reaffirmed once again by Paul VI in *Populorum Progressio* (1967). The recommendations made in these encyclicals are international in scope, and the international prestige of the papacy has been increased by its steady advocacy of peace and its aid to the oppressed and destitute of the world. Politically, the role of the papacy has been more controversial. Pius XII was criticized by some for not condemning more strongly the Nazi regime in Germany (especially in its persecution of the Jews); these critics suggest that he was far more implacably hostile to Communism. The encouragement of greater lay participation in the church itself (e.g., approval of the liturgical movement), fostering of the varied contributions of the parts of the church, desire to unite all Christians, encouragement of the "progressive" renewal within the church itself—all these came to the fore when Pope John XXIII convened the Second VATICAN COUNCIL. The efforts of the council, under the close direction of John XXIII and Paul VI, to renew the spiritual and organizational life of the church had the paradoxical effect of increasing challenges to papal authority. The council's stress on the collegiality of bishops and pope in the rule of the universal church led to the establishment of national conferences of bishops, a step that tended to disrupt the direct exercise of papal authority over individual bishops and increase the autonomy of local churches. Following the council there arose discussions among Catholic theologians of the limits of papal jurisdiction and infallibility. Paul VI attempted to uphold the primacy of the papal teaching office in his reassertion, in the encyclical *Humanae Vitae* (1968), of the traditional doctrine prohibiting artificial birth control; his attempt was met with subtle evasion by some of the national conferences of bishops and by open defiance by some priests and theologians. At the same time he carried on the initiatives of his predecessor, John, in the areas of ecumenical contacts with Protestant and Orthodox Eastern leaders and of rapprochement with the Communist governments of Eastern Europe; implemented a policy of shared authority by regularly convoking advisory synods whose membership is composed chiefly of elected representatives of the national conferences of bishops; carried out a reorganization of the Roman curia, the central bureaucracy of the church; and continued the interest of the popes of the 20th cent. in international peace and justice.

Bibliography. For general works dealing with the papacy, see bibliography under ROMAN CATHOLIC CHURCH. Monumental histories of the papacy in limited periods have been written by the Catholic Ludwig von Pastor and by the non-Catholics Mandell Creighton and H. K. Mann. See J. B. Bury, *A History of the Papacy in the Nineteenth Century* (1930, repr. 1964); Paolo Brezzi, *The Papacy: Its Origins and Historical Evolution* (tr. 1958); Wladimir d'Ormesson, *The Papacy* (tr. 1959); Eric John, ed., *The Popes: A Concise Biographical History* (1964); Geoffrey Barraclough, *The Medieval Papacy* (1968); Peter Nichols, *The Politics of the Vatican* (1968); Walter Ullmann, *The Growth of Papal Government in the Middle Ages* (3d ed. 1970); Ludwig von Hertling, *Communio: Church and Papacy in Early Christianity* (tr. 1972).

Papadopoulos, George (pä"pədŏp'əlĭs), 1919–, Greek colonel and political leader. A career army officer, he became prominent as the leader and strongman of the military junta that seized power in Greece in April, 1967. At first Papadopoulos took the post of minister to the premier, but following King Constantine II's abortive coup in Dec., 1967, he assumed the premiership; he also resigned his army commission. Ruling by decree, Papadopoulos imprisoned many opponents and thwarted several attempts to overthrow him, especially that by naval officers in May, 1973. He narrowly missed assassination in Aug., 1968. In March, 1972, Papadopoulos assumed the post of regent; in June, 1973, he established a republic and assumed the presidency. He was overthrown by a military junta in Nov., 1973.

Papago Indians (păp'əgō, pä'–), North American Indians speaking a language that belongs to the Uto-Aztecan branch of the Aztec-Tanoan linguistic stock (see AMERICAN INDIAN LANGUAGES) and that is closely related to that of their neighbors, the PIMA Indians. The ancestors of both the Pima and the Papago were the Hohokam peoples. They were a semisedentary tribe who farmed corn, beans, and cotton and gathered wild vegetable products (e.g., the beans of the mesquite and the fruit of the giant cactus); although farming remains the major economic activity of the Papagos, many are engaged in cattle raising. The Papago suffered dreadful oppressions from their enemy, the Apache. The Papago were early visited by Spanish missionaries, including Father Eusebio Kino in 1694. In the 1860s the Papago joined with the Pima and Maricopa and helped the United States force a peace with the Apache. By an executive act of 1874 the United States created a reservation for them in S Arizona. By the early 1970s there were about 11,000 Papago living in S Arizona and N Sonora, Mexico. See R. M. Underhill, *Social Organization of the Papago Indians* (1939, repr. 1969); W. H. Kelly, *The Papago Indians of Arizona* (1963); Jack Waddell, *Papago Indians at Work* (1969).

Papagos, Alexander (pä'pägôs), 1883–1955, Greek soldier and political leader. Commissioned an officer in the Greek army in 1906, he rose rapidly through the ranks. In 1935 he became minister of war, and the following year he was made army chief of staff. He was commander in chief of the Greek army in World War II. Later he directed (1949) the successful struggle against the Communist rebels, and by 1950 he had become field marshal and head of the armed forces. He resigned in May, 1950, and shortly afterward formed the conservative Greek Rally party. In 1952 he became prime minister, serving until his death in Oct., 1955. He strengthened Greek ties with the West and developed the country's economy. He concluded the 1954 alliance with Yugoslavia and Turkey and improved Greek relations with Bulgaria and Albania.

papain: see PAPAYA.

papal election, election of the pope by the college of cardinals meeting in secret conclave in the Sistine Chapel not less than 15 nor more than 18 days after the death of the previous pontiff. The election is by secret ballot; Pius XII fixed the electoral majority at two thirds plus one vote. The election itself confers on the new pope full jurisdiction; no further formality is necessary. The elected pope may decline; if so, the balloting resumes. The secrecy of the conclave is assured by shutting off the cardinals completely from the outside world, and at one time expedition was encouraged by severe restriction of the cardinals' diet after a few days. After each session the paper ballots are burned; if the vote is inconclusive straw is added to produce black smoke. Thus, white smoke signifies that a new pope has been chosen. Theoretically any adult male Roman Catholic is eligible, but long-standing practice limits the candidates to cardinals; the last non-Italian elected was Adrian VI, a Netherlander, in 1522. In the vacancy of the Holy See the entire college of cardinals holds the papal jurisdiction, but its powers are extremely limited. The popes were at first elected like other bishops, by the clergy and laity of the diocese; serious political interference was discouraged in 769 by the exclusion of laymen from papal election. The election was limited (1059) to the cardinals by Nicholas II; the conclave was set up (1274) in its modern form by Gregory X. Decrees by Pius XII in

1945 and John XXIII in 1962 now fix the regulations for papal elections.

Papal States, Ital. *Lo Stato della Chiesa,* from 754 to 1870 an independent territory under the temporal rule of the popes, also called the States of the Church and the Pontifical States. The territory varied in size at different times; in 1859 it included c.16,000 sq mi (41,440 sq km) extending north-south on the Italian peninsula, from the Adriatic Sea and lower course of the Po River to the Tyrrhenian Sea, thus including the present regions of Latium, Umbria, Marche, and eastern Emilia-Romagna. The nucleus of the states consisted of endowments given to the popes from the 4th cent. in and around Rome, in other areas of the Italian mainland, and in Sicily, Sardinia, and other lands; these came to be called the Patrimony of St. Peter. The popes gradually lost their more distant lands, but in the duchy of Rome papal power became stronger and increasingly independent of the Eastern emperors and of the other states in Italy. In 754 (confirmed 756), PEPIN THE SHORT gave to Pope Stephen II the exarchate of RAVENNA and the Pentapolis. (Like Pope Zacharias, Pope Stephen II had recognized Pepin as rightful king of the Franks, and Pepin now needed papal assistance against the Lombards.) Over these vast territories the popes were long unable to exercise effective temporal sovereignty. In 774, Charlemagne confirmed the donation of his father, Pepin the Short; moreover, to give the papal claim to temporal power greater antiquity, the so-called Donation of Constantine (see CONSTANTINE, DONATION OF) to Pope Sylvester I was forged. On its basis later popes also claimed suzerainty over Naples, Sicily, and Sardinia. In 1115, Countess MATILDA of Tuscany, by leaving her territories to the church, helped to precipitate a long struggle between popes and emperors. In Rome itself, the popes' temporal power, almost nonexistent in the 10th cent., remained greatly limited until the 14th cent. by the interference of the emperors, by the power of the nobles, and by the ambitions of the commune of Rome, which contended that its authority also extended over the Papal States. In the 13th and 14th cent., the emperors renounced their claims to the duchy of Spoleto, the ROMAGNA, and the March of Ancona; however, the free communes and petty tyrannies that dominated these regions long resisted effective papal control. The Comtat Venaissin, a papal possession in S France until 1791 (though not a part of the Papal States), was acquired in 1274; in 1309, Avignon became the seat of the popes. From 1309 to 1417, during the "Babylonian Captivity" at Avignon and the Great Schism, the Papal States were in chaotic condition, only temporarily relieved by the efforts of Cardinal ALBORNOZ. Actual control by the papacy of its territories began in the 16th cent., when Cesare BORGIA, son of Pope Alexander VI, conquered the petty states of the Romagna and Marche; after his fall (1503) most of them passed directly under papal rule. In the early 16th cent., Pope JULIUS II consolidated papal power by abolishing local autonomies and by participating effectively in the ITALIAN WARS. The last principalities to lose their autonomy to the popes were Ferrara (1598) and Urbino (1631). The duchy of Castro was added in 1649. PARMA and Piacenza were alienated (1545) through the nepotism of Pope Paul III. After the Catholic Reformation (16th cent.) the spiritual power of the papacy grew while its political power waned. Papal troops, mostly Swiss and other mercenaries, offered almost no resistance to the French invaders under Napoleon Bonaparte in 1796. PIUS VI and his successor, PIUS VII, saw their states curtailed, occupied, and twice abolished between 1796 and 1814. The Congress of Vienna fully restored (1815) the states of the papacy and placed them under Austrian protection. Conspiracies and revolutions (notably of 1831 and 1848-49) characterized the following decades. PIUS IX was liberal at his accession and granted his states a constitution, but the events of 1848 turned him against the revolutionists. During the RISORGIMENTO, only French intervention at Rome prevented the total absorption of the Papal States. After the Austrians left (1859) Bologna and the Romagna, both united (1860) with the kingdom of Sardinia, as did Marche and Umbria. Giuseppe GARIBALDI invaded the remaining Papal States twice but was prevented from taking Rome—in 1862 by the intervention of Victor Emmanuel II of Italy, in 1867 by Napoleon III. The fall of Napoleon permitted Victor Emmanuel to seize Rome in 1870. However, Pius IX refused to recognize the loss of temporal power and became a "prisoner" in the Vatican; his successors followed his example. The so-called Roman Question was only resolved in 1929 by the LATERAN TREATY, which, among other things, established the Vatican City (see under VATICAN). For bibliography, see PAPACY. See L. M. Duchesne, *The Beginnings of the Temporal Sovereignty of the Popes, A.D. 754-1073* (1898, tr. 1908); D. P. Waley, *The Papal State under Martin V* (1958); Peter Partner, *The Lands of St. Peter: The Papal State in the Middle Ages and the Early Renaissance* (1972).

Papandreou, George (pä"pəndrā'o͞o), 1888-1968, Greek political leader. As a young man he became involved in antiroyalist politics, serving as a member of parliament and interior minister (1923) before being exiled in 1926. Upon his return he served in several government posts, but he was again exiled in 1936 by the Greek dictator John Metaxas. Papandreou was active in the Greek resistance in World War II and headed (1944-45) the government-in-exile. A staunch anti-Communist, he served (1946-52) in a number of Social Democratic cabinets and formed (1961) the liberal Center Union party. After his party won a majority in the elections of Feb., 1964, he became premier. In July, 1965, he was dismissed by King Constantine II following a dispute over control of the ministry of defense and the ASPIDA affair. After the military coup by George Papadopoulos in April, 1967, Papandreou was arrested and then placed sporadically under house detention until his death. His son, **Andreas Papandreou,** 1919-, was educated in Greece and the United States and became a naturalized U.S. citizen in 1944. He taught economics at several American universities. In the early 1960s he returned to Greece, became active in politics, and won a seat in parliament. He then served as deputy economics coordination minister in the Center Union government of his father. In 1965 he was accused of being the political leader of the leftist Aspida movement; he was indicted but not tried. Imprisoned in April, 1967, by the Papadopoulos government, Papandreou was freed in the amnesty of Dec., 1967, and went into exile abroad, forming the anti-Papadopoulos Pan-Hellenic Liberation Movement (PAK). After the fall of the military dictatorship, he returned (Aug., 1974) to Greece and formed a new Socialist party, which won about 13.5% of the vote in the election of Nov., 1974. He is the author of numerous books, including *Competition and its Regulation* (with J. T. Wheeler, 1954), *Democracy at Gunpoint: The Greek Front* (1970), and *Paternalistic Capitalism* (1972).

Papantla (päpän'tlä), town (1970 pop. 94,623), Veracruz state, E central Mexico. It is known for the nearby ruins of Tajín, thought to be the remains of a pre-Columbian civilization (fl. 400?-900?) known as Classic Veracruz. The most impressive relic is a spectacular pyramid in seven rectangular tiers, lined with niches that contained small idols. Tajín style is characterized by carved stone objects of unusual shape and unknown use.

papaverine (pəpăv'ərēn), alkaloid found in OPIUM that acts as a muscle relaxant and vasodilator. It is used to relieve irregularities in the contraction of heart muscle. Relaxing the smooth muscle of the larger blood vessels, the drug is also used to increase the blood supply to the brain and in the treatment of some types of blood clot formation.

papaya (pəpī'ə), soft-stemmed tree *(Carica papaya)* of tropical America resembling a palm with a crown of palmately lobed leaves. It is cultivated for its melonlike yellow fruits eaten raw or cooked and, more recently, for the juice which has become a commercial item. The juice contains the enzyme papain, somewhat similar to pepsin and digestant in action; the enzyme is used in commercial meat tenderizers. The papaya is also called melon tree and pawpaw. In the Caribbean area the fruit is called *fruta bomba.* The papaya is classified in the division MAGNOLIOPHYTA, class Magnoliopsida, order Violales, family Caricaceae.

Papeete (päpā-ā'tā), town (1971 est. pop. 24,000), capital of TAHITI and of FRENCH POLYNESIA, South Pacific. A port on the NW coast of Tahiti, Papeete ships copra, vanilla, and mother-of-pearl. The town has an important French nuclear laboratory and an international airport.

Papen, Franz von (fränts fən pä'pən), 1879-1969, German politician. Appointed (1913) military attaché to the German embassy in Washington, he was implicated in espionage activities that led (1915) the U.S. government to request his recall. He subsequently served in Turkey during World War I and, after the war, entered politics. He was (1921-32) a member of the Catholic Center party in the Prussian parliament. Although a political unknown, he was chosen (June, 1932) by President Paul von Hindenburg to succeed Heinrich Brüning as German chancellor in the hope that he could obtain support from right and center. He was, however, expelled from his party for accepting this post, and his cabinet won support only from a minority on the right. In seeking to weaken the left, he contributed to the rise of the National Socialists (Nazis), chiefly by lifting (June) the ban on their militia. In July he suspended the Prussian government and ousted its Socialist premier. Two successive elections failed to bring Papen substantial support in the Reichstag, and when he submitted his formal resignation after the elections of Nov., 1932, it was accepted. Kurt von SCHLEICHER succeeded him as chancellor, but Papen remained a close confidant of Hindenburg and sought to return to power through an alliance with the Nazis. He succeeded in bringing Adolf HITLER to power and was appointed vice chancellor in the new cabinet. Although Hitler soon eliminated his conservative allies from the cabinet, Papen continued to serve the Hitler regime, even after several of his close associates were murdered in the "blood purge" of June, 1934. As German minister to Vienna, he helped to prepare the German annexation of Austria (1938). From 1939 to 1944 he was ambassador to Turkey. Papen was acquitted (1946) by the Nuremberg war crimes tribunal. A sentence to eight years' hard labor imposed (1947) by a German "denazification" court was rescinded in 1949. His memoirs appeared in 1952 (tr. 1953).

paper, thin, flat sheet or tissue made usually from plant fiber but also from rags and other fibrous materials. It is used principally for printing and writing upon but has many other applications. The term also includes various types of PAPERBOARD, such as cardboard and wallboard. Paper is believed to have been invented by Ts'ai Lun c.105 in China, where it reached an advanced state of development. Chinese paper was a mixture of bark and hemp. Papermaking spread to Japan c.610 and to Samarkand c.751, whence it was introduced by the Arabs into Egypt c.900 and by the Moors into Spain at Játiva c.1150. Mills were established in Italy c.1276; in France, c.1348; in Germany, 1390; and in England, 1495. European paper was usually made of flax and hemp. Primitive bark paper had been made in Mexico and Central America in pre-Columbian times. Paper was first produced in the American colonies in 1690 by William Rittenhouse at Germantown. A quarter to a third of most new paper is made from waste paper. The body of paper is made up of matted cellulose fibers—since c.1860 derived principally from wood. Rags, mostly cotton cuttings from textile and garment factories, are used to make fine stationery and for such purposes as cigarette paper. For other special papers, or where wood is not available, manufacturers may use pressed sugarcane, bamboo, manila rope, cereal straws, esparto grass, and other fibers. Most paper, however is made from wood pulp. Mechanical pulp, or groundwood, prepared by grinding the wood, is used to make newsprint, tissue, towel, and other inexpensive papers. Lignin, which holds the fibers together, remains in the paper and turns yellow in sunlight. Chemical pulp is almost pure cellulose and is prepared from wood chips boiled under pressure with any of three chemicals—soda, sulfite, or sulfate—to dissolve the lignin binder and leave mostly cellulose fiber. Large quantities of water are used in the manufacture of paper, and the quality of the finished product is considerably affected by the quality of the water used. For this reason, the water is often chemically treated before it is used in the papermaking process. Wood pulp is washed, bleached, screened, and beaten, and then is blended to achieve the characteristics required by the intended use. The pulp, suspended in water, is poured over a wire screen in one of two machines that differ mainly in the form of the screen: a belt screen is used in the Fourdrinier machine and a cylindrical one in the cylinder machine. As water drains through the screen, a layer of fibers forms, which in the Fourdrinier is shaken to turn the fibers in different directions so that they mat. A wet felt belt pressed against the screen picks up the paper for feeding through sets of drying rollers. During this stage a rubber roller may be used to imprint a watermark. At the end of the process the paper is passed through a calender (stack of iron rollers), which presses the paper and smooths its surface. Fillers—chiefly clay or starch—are used to improve the printing, texture, and wet and dry strength of paper and to produce other special properties. Book paper is any kind of printing paper except newsprint. For the best reproduction of illustrations, especially halftones, book paper is coated with a layer of mineral pigment, usually clay, mixed with an adhesive. All writing papers are "sized"; i.e., a water-resistant substance such as rosin is added to the pulp to prevent the spreading of writing ink. Hanging paper, or wallpaper, is soft and bulky; it is rosin-sized for water resistance and coated to take a printed design. Bag and wrapping papers are made of kraft paper, the product of the sulfate process, because of its strength. See J. P. Casey, *Pulp and Paper* (rev. ed., 3 vol., 1960–61); K. W. Britt, ed., *Handbook of Pulp and Paper Technology* (1970).

paper birch: see BIRCH.

paperboard, material similiar in shape and composition to PAPER, but generally thicker, stronger, and more rigid. Paper machines, e.g., Fourdrinier machines, are used to make sheets of paperboard. Sometimes these machine-made sheets are pasted to each other or to paper sheets to build up special thicknesses. The function of a particular type of paperboard is often indicated by its name, e.g., *boxboard.* Paperboard can be made into a wide variety of items, including folding cartons, advertising displays, electrical insulators, and coasters.

paper nautilus, pelagic, surface-dwelling CEPHALOPOD mollusk of the genus *Argonauta.* Like the closely related octopus, the paper nautilus has a rounded body, eight tentacles, and no fins. It is so named for the beautiful papery shell, up to 8 in. (20 cm) long, that surrounds the female while she broods her eggs. This structure, actually a calcareous egg case, is secreted by the tips of the female's two greatly expanded dorsal tentacles prior to egg laying. After she deposits her eggs in the floating egg case, the female takes shelter in it herself; she is usually found with her head and tentacles protruding from the opening, but she retreats deeper inside if disturbed. The much smaller male, which lacks the modified dorsal tentacles, often shares the shell of a female. It was once believed that the paper nautilus, or argonaut, uses the expanded tentacles, extended from the shell, as a sail. The true nautilus (genus *Nautilus*) belongs to a different cephalopod order. The paper nautilus is classified in the phylum MOLLUSCA, class Cephalopoda, order Octopoda.

Paphlagonia (păf″ləgō′nēə), ancient country of N Asia Minor, between Bithynia and Pontus on the Black Sea coast, in modern Turkey. A mountainous district with the Halys as its chief river, Paphlagonia had a string of Greek colonies (including Sinope) along its coast. It was not a political unit and was annexed and occupied by the kings of Bithynia and Pontus respectively. It was won (63 B.C.) by the Romans.

Paphos (pā′fŏs), two ancient cities, SW Cyprus, on the coast. Old Paphos was probably founded in the Mycenaean period by colonists from Greece or Phoenicia. Modern excavations have revealed ruins dating from 3000 B.C. New Paphos, now Baffo, was 10 mi (16 km) to the northwest. An important seaport, it was the capital of Cyprus from the middle of the Hellenistic period until the time of Constantine. In the Bible, Paphos is the scene of the miraculous blinding of a sorcerer (Acts 13.6–13).

Papias (pā′pēəs), fl. A.D. 130, early Christian theologian, Apostolic Father of the Church, said to have been bishop of Hieropolis and a friend of St. Polycarp. Papias' five-volume work, *Oracles; or, Explanations of the Sayings of the Lord,* survives only in fragments quoted by Eusebius of Caesarea and St. Irenaeus. These are valuable sources for the history of the church.

papier-mâché (pā′pər-məshā′), art material made of paper strips soaked in a binder of starch or flour paste; it dries into a firm, hard substance. Papier-mâché is widely used in the production of decorative objects and sculptures of great lightness, delicacy, and strength.

papillon (păp′əlŏn″), breed of TOY DOG whose origins are obscure but whose widespread existence in Europe is attested to as early as the 17th cent. It stands from 8 to 11 in. (20.3–27.9 cm) high at the shoulder and weighs from 5 to 11 lb (2.3–5 kg). Its long, straight, abundant coat is fine and silky and forms a fringe of longer hair on the ears, chest, back of legs, and tail. Believed to have developed from a now extinct dwarf Belgian spaniel, the papillon derives its name, which means "butterfly" in French, from the unique appearance of its obliquely set, wing-shaped ears. The papillon was very fashionable as a lapdog in the courts of Europe. Today it is raised as a companion and house pet. See DOG.

Papin, Denis (dənē′ päpăN′), 1647–1712?, French physicist and inventor. He was an assistant of Christian Huygens and of Robert Boyle and was professor of mathematics at the Univ. of Marburg (1687–96). He invented (1679) a steam digester (forerunner of the autoclave), a vessel in which the boiling point of water is raised by an increase in steam pressure; this device demonstrated the influence of atmospheric pressure on boiling points. His other inventions include a safety valve (for the digester), a condensing pump, an air gun, and a paddle-wheel boat. A pioneer in the development of the steam engine, he devised in 1690 a pump with a piston raised by steam.

Papineau, Louis Joseph (lwē zhôsĕf′ päpēnō′), 1786–1871, French Canadian political leader and insurgent, b. Montreal. After serving as an officer in the War of 1812, he entered (1814) the Legislative Assembly of Lower Canada (Quebec), of which he was (1815–37) speaker. Eloquent and able, he soon became leader of the French Canadian Reform party. His hostility to the British government in Canada, whose measures he considered unfair to the French Canadians, inflamed some of his followers, the Patriotes, to open rebellion in 1837; shortly afterward a rebellion incited by William Lyon Mackenzie broke out in Upper Canada (Ontario). Papineau took no active part in the uprisings but fled to the United States, where he sought assistance for the Canadian colonial cause. Failing in his effort, he went to France. He received full amnesty in 1844 and returned to Canada in 1845. He reentered politics and again sat (1848–54) in the Canadian legislative assembly, but he never regained his former influence. See biographies by A. D. De Celles (in "Makers of Canada" series, Vol. V, 1926) and Fernand Guellet (1961).

Papinian (Aemilius Papinianus) (pəpĭn′ēən), d. 212, Roman jurist. He was a close friend of the Roman emperor Septimius SEVERUS, under whom he was *libellorum magister* [master of the rolls] and later Praetorian prefect; but Severus' son CARACALLA had Papinian put to death for reasons that are obscure. Papinian was a jurist of enormous erudition, perhaps the greatest figure in ROMAN LAW, and a stern moralist. A constitution of Theodosius II and Valentinian (426) reflects the Roman attitude toward him: five jurists (and the authors whom they quoted) were set up as the sole authorities to be cited—Paulus, Gaius, Ulpian, Modestinus, and Papinian. If they were not unanimous the majority was to prevail, but, in case of equal division, the opinion of Papinian was to decide. His chief works were *Quaestiones* (37 books), *Responsa* (19 books), *Definitiones* (2 books), and *De adulteriis* (2 books). They are known through quotations in the Theodosian Code and in the Digest of the CORPUS JURIS CIVILIS. See H. F. Jolowicz, *Roman Foundations of Modern Law* (1957).

Papp, Joseph, 1921–, American theatrical director and producer, b. New York City. Papp, a major influence in American theater, founded the nonprofit New York Shakespeare Festival in 1954. He has sought to make Shakespeare's works and other fine plays available to large numbers of New Yorkers. In 1957 the city granted him use of a site in Central Park for free productions of Shakespeare. Persevering and energetic, Papp also obtained (1967) from the city the Astor Library Building, where he has produced works by new playwrights in the Public Theater. He has also produced a number of Broadway plays, including Jason Miller's *That Championship Season,* and has directed many off-Broadway productions. His Central Park productions of a musical version of *Two Gentlemen of Verona* (1971) and *Much Ado About Nothing* (1972) were both so successful that they were given extended runs on Broadway.

Pappenheim, Gottfried Heinrich, Graf zu (gôt′frēt hīn′rĭkh gräf tsōō pä′pənhīm), 1594–1632, German military leader, imperial field marshal in the THIRTY YEARS WAR. A convert to Roman Catholicism, he became a counselor in the service of the Holy Roman emperor, but soon abandoned this position for a military career. In the early stages of the Thirty Years War he fought with Duke Maximilian I of Bavaria and the Catholic League, and he distinguished himself against the Protestant Union under FREDERICK THE WINTER KING at the battle of White Mt. (1620). He entered the imperial service in 1623. On May 20, 1631, he led the assault against the Protestant city of Magdeburg, which was sacked and virtually destroyed by his troops. Pappenheim was defeated (September) with Baron von TILLY by the Swedish king, Gustavus Adolphus (GUSTAVUS II), at Breitenfeld, but his cavalry was later effective in raids on small bands of Swedish troops. Fighting under the imperial commander Albrecht von WALLENSTEIN, he was mortally wounded at Lutzen.

Pappus (păp′əs), fl. c.300, Greek mathematician of Alexandria. He recorded and enlarged on the results of his predecessors, including Euclid and Apollonius of Perga, in his *Mathematical Collection* (8 books; date conjectural). The six and a half extant books, edited and translated into Latin by Commandinus (1588), stimulated a revival of geometry in the 17th cent.; Descartes expounded several of his problems. The collection was reedited by Frederick Hultsch (1876–78). Pappus' other works include a commentary on Ptolemy's *Almagest.* See T. L. Heath, *A Manual of Greek Mathematics* (1931).

paprika: see PEPPER.

Pap test or **Papanicolaou test** (păp″ənē′kəlou), medical procedure used to detect cancer of the uterine cervix. A scraping, or smear, is taken from the surface of the vagina or cervix and is prepared on a slide and stained for microscopic examination. The cells' appearance determines whether they are normal, suspicious, or cancerous. Although the test is 80% to 95% reliable, results termed suspicious may indicate infection or some abnormal condition other than cancer. The smear technique is also used to detect cancer of other tissues, e.g., in the bladder. The Pap test was developed by G. N. Papanicolaou and H. F. Traut in 1943.

Papua, Territory of: see PAPUA NEW GUINEA.

Papua New Guinea (păp′yōōə, gĭn′ē), country (1966 pop. 2,184,836), 183,540 sq mi (475,369 sq km), SW Pacific, encompassing the eastern half of the island of NEW GUINEA, as well as the BISMARCK ARCHIPELAGO, the TROBRIAND ISLANDS, SAMARAI Island, Woodlark Island, D'ENTRECASTEAUX ISLANDS, the LOUISIADE ARCHIPELAGO, and the northernmost Solomon Islands of Buka and BOUGAINVILLE. The capital is PORT MORESBY; other important cities include RABAUL, LAE, MADANG, Alexishafen, and Finschhafen. Papua New Guinea is a wild, rugged region, with limited communications. Agriculture is the mainstay of the economy. Sweet potatoes constitute the main food crop. Agricultural exports (notably coconut products, rubber, coffee, cocoa, and tea) generally represent the surplus from subsistence farming and the crops from European-owned plantations. Timber is also exported. Silver, manganese, copper, and gold are mined, but the gold reserves have steadily declined. Pearl-shell and tortoise fisheries dot the coast. Exploration for oil is underway. The native population is Melanesian. Although some 500 different languages are spoken in the region, pidgin English has become the *lingua franca.* The Univ. of Papua and New Guinea opened in 1966. Papua, the southern section of the country, was annexed by Queensland in 1883 and the following year became a British protectorate called British New Guinea. It passed to Australia in 1905 as the Territory of Papua. The northern section of the country formed part of German New Guinea from 1884 to 1914 and was called Kaiser-Wilhelmsland. Occupied by Australian forces during World War I, it was mandated to Australia by the League of Nations in 1920 and became known as the Territory of New Guinea. Australian rule was reconfirmed by the United Nations in 1947. In 1949 the territories of Papua and New Guinea were merged administratively, but they remained constitutionally distinct. They were combined on Dec. 1, 1973, as the self-governing country of Papua New Guinea, with Australia retaining control of defense and foreign relations. The country was slated for complete independence sometime during the 1970s. The first months of independence were characterized by the emergence of a separatist movement among Papuans, who feared New Guinean domination in the new state.

papyrus (pəpī′rəs), a sedge (*Cyperus papyrus*), now almost extinct in Egypt but so universally used there in antiquity as to be the hieroglyphic symbol for Lower Egypt and a common motif in art. The roots were used as fuel; the pith was eaten. The stem was employed for sandals, boats, twine, boxes, mats, sails, cloth and most notably as a writing material (used in Egypt until the introduction of paper there in the 8th cent. and exported throughout the Mediterranean world). This writing material, which was also called papyrus, was formed into sheets by laying lengthwise slices of the sedge side by side in two layers at right angles and pressing them together with an adhesive probably composed of their own juices and Nile water. The sheets were glued end to end and rolled on wooden rods to form manuscripts. Many examples have been recovered, especially in Egypt, and have furnished valuable literary and historical matter in Greek and other languages. The science of papyrology is concerned with the study of these documents. Papyrus is classified in the division MAGNOLIOPHYTA, class Liliatae, order Cyperales, family Cyperaceae.

Pará (pərä′), state (1970 pop. 2,161,316), 474,896 sq mi (1,229,981 sq km), N Brazil, in the lower Amazon

River basin bordering on the Guianas and the Atlantic Ocean. BELÉM is the capital. The hot, humid region is drained by the Amazon and its numerous tributaries. The state includes the island of MARAJÓ as well as several other islands of the Amazon delta. Mostly covered with rain forest, Pará has not been extensively developed, and the chief means of transportation is by river steamer. Brazil nuts, rubber, jute, medicinal plants, tropical hardwoods, and pepper are the principal products. The small manufacturing sector makes food products, pharmaceuticals, textiles, and rubber goods. The nearly constant rainfall has eroded soils to the point where conventional agriculture is almost impossible. The Portuguese settled in the area in the first decades of the 17th cent. in order to keep out the English, French, and Dutch. In the 18th cent. there was moderate sugar, rum, and coffee production; most of the labor force was made up of enslaved Indians. The region suffered during the 19th-century struggle for independence. The rubber industry grew rapidly in the mid-19th cent. but declined in the early 1900s. The pepper, jute, and legume plantations along the coast were established during the early 20th cent. by Japanese immigrants. The abundance of rivers has made Pará a great haven for smugglers. The state government consists of an elected governor and bicameral legislature.

Pará, city: see BELÉM.

Pará, river, c.200 mi (320 km) long, N Brazil. It is actually the southeastern arm or estuary of the Amazon, divided from the rest of the river by Marajó island. It receives the waters of the Tocantins River. The port of Belém is on the right bank.

***para*-aminobenzoic acid** (pâr'ə-əmē'nōbĕnzō'ĭk): see VITAMIN.

parable, in the Bible, term used in the Gospels not only for short illustrative narratives, but for figurative statements as well. Mat. 13; Mark 3.23; Luke 21.29-33. Old Testament parables include the ewe lamb (2 Sam. 12.1-4) and the unproductive vineyard (Isa. 5.1-7). The parables of Jesus include the barren fig tree (Luke 13.6-9); the drawnet (Mat. 13.47-50); the Good Samaritan (Luke 10.29-37); the great supper (Luke 14.15-24); the hidden treasure (Mat. 13.44); the importunate friend (Luke 11.5-8); the laborers in the vineyard (Mat. 20.1-16); the leaven (Mat. 13.33; Luke 13.20,21); the lost piece of silver (Luke 15.8-10); the lost sheep (Mat. 18.12-14; Luke 15.3-7); the marriage feast (Mat. 22.1-14); the mustard seed (Mat. 13.31,32; Mark 4.30-32; Luke 13.18,19); the pearl of great price (Mat. 13.45,46); the Pharisee and the publican (Luke 18.9-14); the pounds (Luke 19.11-27); the prodigal son (Luke 15.11-32); the rich fool (Luke 12.16-21); the rich man and Lazarus (Luke 16.19-31); the seed growing secretly (Mark 4.26-29); the sower (Mat. 13.3-9,18-23; Mark 4.3-9,14-20; Luke 8.4-15); the talents (Mat. 25.14-30); the tares (Mat. 13.24-30,36-43); the ten virgins (Mat. 25.1-13); the two debtors (Luke 7.40-50); the two sons (Mat. 21.28-32); the unjust judge (Luke 18.1-8); the unjust steward (Luke 16.1-8); the unmerciful servant (Mat. 18.23-35); the wicked husbandmen (Mat. 21.33-45; Mark 12.1-12; Luke 20.9-19). In the TALMUD there are many parables. See Joachim Jeremias, *Rediscovering the Parables* (1966); G. A. Buttrick, *The Parables of Jesus* (1973).

parabola (pərăb'ələ), plane curve consisting of all points equidistant from a given fixed point (focus) and a given fixed line (directrix). It is the CONIC SECTION cut by a plane parallel to one of the elements of the cone. The axis of a parabola is the line through the focus perpendicular to the directrix. The vertex is the point at which the axis intersects the curve. The *latus rectum* is the chord through the focus perpendicular to the axis. Examples of this curve are the path of a projectile and the shape of the cross section of a parallel beam reflector. The curve of the cable of a suspension bridge very closely approximates a parabola.

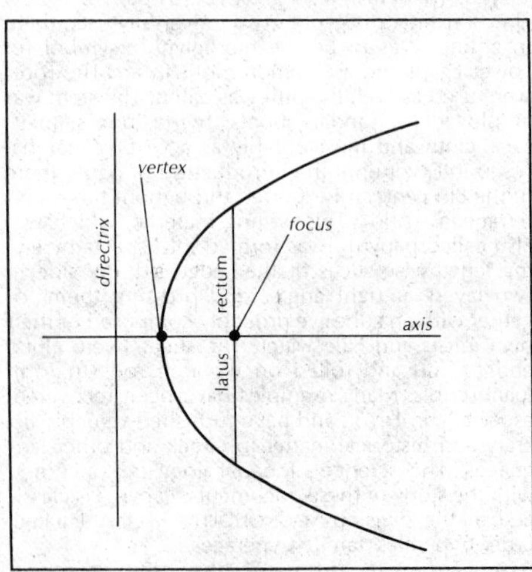

Parabola

Paracas (pärä'käs), Indian culture of ancient Peru. Named after the Paracas peninsula on the south coast, where their remains were first found, the Paracas produced resin-painted pottery and textiles, but little is known of their way of life. They were probably influenced by the earlier culture centered around Chavín de Huántar.

Paracel Islands (päräsĕl'), Chin. *Hsi-sha* or *Sisha,* group of low coral islands and reefs in the South China Sea, c.175 mi (280 km) SE of Hainan island. They are rich in guano and are thought to be underlain by oil deposits. Prior to World War II the islands were part of French Indochina and served as a weather station. During the war they were occupied by Japan but passed to China in 1945. The islands are also claimed by the South Vietnamese, who manned the weather station and a small garrison there until 1974, when they were attacked and driven from the islands by Chinese armed forces.

Paracelsus, Philippus Aureolus (fĭlĭp'əs ôrēō'ləs părəsĕl'səs), 1493?-1541, Swiss physician and alchemist. His original name was Theophrastus Bombastus von Hohenheim. He traveled widely, acquiring knowledge of alchemy, chemistry, and metallurgy, and although his egotism and his contempt for traditional theories earned him the enmity of his learned contemporaries, he gained wide popularity among the people (he lectured and wrote in German rather than Latin) and had great influence in his own and succeeding centuries. In Salzburg, where he died, a statue was erected to him in 1752. His thought was colored by the fantastic philosophies of his time, but he firmly opposed the humoral theory of disease championed by Galen; advocated the use of specific remedies for specific diseases, introducing many chemicals (e.g., laudanum, mercury, sulfur, iron, and arsenic) into use as medicines; and noted relationships such as the hereditary pattern in syphilis and the association of cretinism with endemic goiter and of paralysis with head injuries. He wrote numerous medical and occult works containing a curious mixture of sound observation and mystical jargon. His work *On Diseases of Miners* was the first study devoted to an occupational disease. See *Four Treatises of Theophrastus von Hohenheim* (ed. by H. E. Sigerist, 1941); studies by Sidney Rosen (1959) and A. G. Debus (1966).

parachute, umbrellalike device designed to retard the descent of a falling body by creating drag as it passes through the air. The development of modern aircraft has led to many experiments in the aerodynamic problems of parachute design, with the result that the parachute of today is a highly efficient instrument. It must permit slow descent, must be highly stable, have little weight and a small area, and must retain its shape and maintain its balance in descent. Usually it is constructed from a flexible material; when extended, it takes the form of an umbrella from which a series of cords converge downward to a harness strapped to the user. It can be folded into a small package—a task requiring a high degree of skill—and thus can be easily carried aboard an aircraft or strapped onto a man's body. Before the parachute can be opened the user must be clear of the aircraft in order to avoid entanglement, or fouling. The harness must be easily detachable when the earth's surface is reached, since the parachutist might be drowned or dragged along the ground. The rate of descent for a man-carrying parachute is about 18 ft (5.5 m) per sec. A French aeronaut, Jean Pierre Blanchard, claimed the invention of the parachute in 1785, and the first successful parachute descent from a great height was made in 1797 by the French aeronaut Jacques Garnerin, who dropped 3,000 ft (920 m) from a balloon. One of the most important uses of parachutes is as an escape system for persons aboard aircraft unable to land safely. Modern military jet aircraft are provided with ejection seats that shoot the pilot free of his craft and automatically release a parachute when the pilot is at a safe altitude. In addition, airborne military units and their equipment sometimes descend from transport planes by parachutes. In recent years, parachute jumping for sport, known as skydiving, has become popular. Parachutes are also used as braking devices for rockets, space vehicles, airplanes, and high-speed surface vehicles. See study by Bud Settick (1971).

Paraclete (pâr'əklēt), title of the HOLY GHOST, often translated as "Comforter" or "Advocate." John 14.16,26; 15.26; 16.7; 1 John 2.1.

Paradise: see EDEN, GARDEN OF; HEAVEN.

Paradise, uninc. town (1970 pop. 14,539), Butte co., N central Calif., in the foothills of the Sierra Nevada range. It is mainly residential. Gold was discovered nearby in 1859.

paradise fish, brilliantly colored freshwater Oriental fish, *Macropodus opercularis,* often kept in aquariums. The males reach a length of 3 in. (7.6 cm) and turn reddish with blue bars during mating season. Fantastic varieties with greatly extended and modified fins and tails have been developed. The roundtailed paradise fish *Macropodus chinensis* is a close relative. Paradise fish are classified in the phylum CHORDATA, subphylum Vertebrata, class Osteichthyes, order Perciformes, family Belontiidae.

paradox, statement that appears self-contradictory but actually has a basis in truth, e.g., Oscar Wilde's "Ignorance is like a delicate fruit; touch it and the bloom is gone." Many of the so-called New Critics maintain that paradox is not just a rhetorical or illustrative device but a basic aspect of all poetic language.

paraffin, white, more-or-less translucent, odorless, tasteless, waxy solid. It melts between 47°C and 65°C and is insoluble in water but soluble in ether, benzene, and certain esters. Paraffin is unaffected by most common chemical reagents but burns readily in air. Obtained from petroleum during refining, it is used in candles, for coating paper, and for various other purposes. Chemically, paraffin is a mixture of high-molecular-weight ALKANES, i.e., saturated HYDROCARBONS with the general formula C_nH_{2n+2}, where *n* is an integer between 22 and 27.

paraffin series: see ALKANE.

paraformaldehyde: see FORMALDEHYDE.

Paragould (pâr'əgo͞old), city (1970 pop. 10,639), seat of Greene co., NE Ark.; inc. 1882. The processing and trade center of an agricultural region, the city also has railroad shops and a wide variety of manufactures, including shoes, shirts, electric motors, and automobile parts.

Paraguay (pâr'əgwā, -gwī, Span. parägwī'), republic (1970 pop. 2,395,614), 157,047 sq mi (406,752 sq km), S central South America. The capital is ASUNCIÓN. Bolivia and Paraguay are the two landlocked nations of the continent. Paraguay is enclosed by Bolivia, Brazil, and Argentina. The eastern part of the country, between the Paraguay and Paraná rivers, where most of the population live, is a lowland, rising in the east and north to a plateau region. The Paraná, S of the Iguaçu River (with its magnificent falls), separates Paraguay from Argentina. The Paraguay River also forms a border with Argentina from its confluence with the Paraná N to the Pilcomayo River. The section W of the Paraguay River is a dry plain, part of the CHACO. Cattle are raised and QUEBRACHO is found in the woodlands of the Chaco Boreal. More than half of Paraguay's labor force are engaged in agriculture and forestry; less than 15% work in industry and mining. The principal crops are rice, corn, soybeans, wheat, cotton, and tobacco. Orange groves furnish a large part of the world's supply of petitgrain, used in perfumes and flavorings. MATÉ (Paraguay tea) is used domestically and is also exported. Livestock plays an important role in the economy. In addition to quebracho, hardwoods and cedars are commercially exploited. Meat-packing, vegetable-oil processing, and textile manufacturing are the main industries. Sandstone, clay, and limestone are found. The leading exports are meats, timber, and oils. The leading imports are foodstuffs, vehicles and machinery, chemicals, and fuels. The United States, Argentina, and West Germany are the main trade partners. Customs duties furnish an important part of Paraguay's revenues. All the important cities are in the east. Besides Asunción, they are VILLARRICA, Concepción, and ENCARNACIÓN. River transportation is a vital supplement to Paraguay's inadequate roads and railroads. The population is largely mestizo, a mixture of Spanish and GUARANÍ INDIAN strains. There has been considerable emigration to neighboring countries, especially Argentina. Spanish is the official language, but Guaraní is widely spoken. The Jesuit missions (the REDUCTIONS, active from the late 16th to the 18th cent.) made it possible for the Guaraní culture to blend with the Spanish. In later days European immigrants—German, Italian, and French, with some Irish and Scots—added new elements to the distinctive civilization of Paraguay. The country's arts and handicrafts reflect the various strains. A notable musical contribution, for example, is the *guaranía*, a form developed from native melodies by José Asunción

Flores during the Chaco War. Nanduti (spider web) lace is the most famous Paraguayan handicraft. The isolated Indian groups that live in the Chaco and elsewhere have little part in the national life. The established religion is Roman Catholicism. Most of the small number of Protestants are Mennonites. Illiteracy is a major problem. There are two universities, National (1890) and Catholic (1960), both in Asunción. Paraguay is governed under a 1967 constitution. The president, popularly elected, serves a five-year term. The legislature has two houses, a 30-member senate and a 60-member chamber of deputies. The two main parties, both conservative, are the National Republican Association-Colorado party, which has governed since 1948, and the Radical Liberal party (PLR). Other small groups are the Liberal party, a splinter of the PLR; the reformist Febreista Revolutionary party; the leftist Christian Democratic party; and the Communist party, which is outlawed. European influence in Paraguay began with the early explorations of the Río de la Plata. Juan Díaz de SOLÍS was the first to come (1516), and Sebastian Cabot followed him (1527) to the Paraguay River, which was thought to offer access to Peru. One of the main reasons for the voyages (c.1535) of Juan de AYOLAS and Domingo Martínez de IRALA was to seek a way across the continent. A colony grew up, as Asunción became the nucleus of the La Plata region. Irala dominated the colony until his death (1556 or 1557) and clashed with Álvar Núñez CABEZA DE VACA. At the end of the 16th cent. Hernando ARIAS DE SAAVEDRA, called Hernandarias, became governor of Río de la Plata prov., of which Paraguay was a part; it was through his efforts that the administrations of present Argentina and Paraguay were separated (1617). The Jesuit missions were founded in the days of Hernandarias (most of them in the trans-Paraná area, now in Argentina). Real independence from Spain was asserted when in 1721 José de Antequera led the COMUNEROS of Asunción in a successful revolt and governed independently for some 10 years. In 1776 the region was made part of the viceroyalty of the Río de la Plata. Manuel Belgrano was unsuccessful in carrying the Argentinian revolution against Spain into Paraguay in 1810, but the next year the colonial officials there were quietly overthrown. In 1814 the first of the three great dictators who were to mold Paraguay came to power. He was José Gaspar Rodríguez FRANCIA, the incorruptible, harsh, and autocratic dictator known as *El Supremo*, who kept Paraguay in the palm of his hand until his death in 1840. He was succeeded by another dictator, Carlos Antonio LÓPEZ, who held absolute power from 1844 to 1862. His son, Francisco Solano LÓPEZ, succeeded him and brought on disaster by involving Paraguay in war with Brazil, Argentina, and Uruguay (1865–70; see TRIPLE ALLIANCE, WAR OF THE). The Paraguayans fought heroically and sustained the loss of more than half the population. Recovery from the catastrophe was slow, and the desperate state of the economy was matched by political confusion, as warring caudillos established short-lived dictatorships. Nevertheless, in the late 19th and early 20th cent. conditions improved. Trade increased as Paraguayan products found markets, immigration was encouraged, and farming and modest little industries prospered fitfully. The unsettled boundary with Bolivia, however, turned from an irritation into a threat, and in 1932 Paraguay plunged into another major war—the CHACO War, which lasted until 1935. From it the little country emerged victorious but exhausted. The rapid succession of governments afterward was broken by the years when Higinio MORÍNIGO was in power (1940–48). Signs of recovery from the Chaco War appeared in improvements in education, public health, and roads, but the oppressive dictatorship of Morínigo was challenged by numerous uprisings. He was overthrown in 1948, and the country was again subjected to a series of short-lived governments. Gen. Alfredo STROESSNER engineered a successful coup in 1954. Stroessner repeatedly suppressed opposition. He was reelected in 1958 and 1963. The 1967 constitution permitted him to be reelected again in 1968 and 1973. Starting in the late 1960s, churchmen and students sporadically protested the government's repressive character. In 1973, Paraguay and Brazil agreed to build a huge hydroelectric project on the Paraná River at Itaipú. See George Pendle, *Paraguay* (3d ed. 1967); E. A. Hopkins et al., *Paraguay, 1852 and 1968* (1968); R. B. Cunninghame Graham, *A Vanished Arcadia* (1901, repr. 1968); T. E. Weil et al., *Area Handbook for Paraguay* (1972); J. R. Gorham, ed., *Paraguay: Ecological Essays* (1973); C. J. Kolinski, *Independence or Death: The Story of the Paraguayan War* (1965) and *Historical Dictionary of Paraguay* (1973); C. A. Washburn, *The History of Paraguay* (1871, repr. 1973).

Paraguay, river, c.1,300 mi (2,090 km) long, rising in the highlands of central Mato Grosso state, Brazil. Flowing generally southward, it forms the border between Brazil and Paraguay in the PANTANAL, then crosses the center of Paraguay, dividing the Gran Chaco from E Paraguay. Two large tributaries, the Pilcomayo and the Bermejo rivers, join it from the west. Below the Pilcomayo, the Paraguay River flows SW to the Paraná River, forming part of the Paraguay-Argentina border. Navigable for most of its course, the Paraguay River is one of the major arteries of the Río de la Plata system, with its chief port at Asunción, Paraguay.

Paraguay tea: see MATÉ.

Parah (pā′rə), Benjamite city. Joshua 18.23.

Paraíba (pərēˊbə), state (1970 pop. 2,384,615), 21,765 sq mi (56,371 sq km), NE Brazil, on the Atlantic Ocean. The capital is JOÃO PESSOA. The state extends inland from the Atlantic to the semiarid plateau of the interior (the SERTÃO). The economy is largely agricultural; although cattle-breeding remains the principal activity, more and more pastures have been given over to cultivation, with agave, cotton, sugarcane, and sisal as the chief crops. Industrialization has been hampered by the scarcity of hydroelectric power, but the state produces textiles, salt, food products, and metals (chiefly tin and scheelite). Fishing and the production of vegetable oil and cement are increasingly important. Prior to the arrival of the Portuguese in the late 16th cent., the region was densely settled by numerous Indian tribes. The area's colonization took more than 70 years to complete because of Indian hostility. By the early 17th cent. Paraíba was an important and prosperous captaincy, but this prosperity was interrupted by the Dutch occupation (1634–54), more Indian uprisings, and an epidemic of yellow fever in 1686. The first nationalist uprising in the area occurred in 1710. Throughout the 19th cent. economic development was impeded by continual outbreaks of violence and by the abolition of slavery. Not until the 1930s was some economic stability achieved. Frequent droughts have led to great migrations from the countryside to the cities. The state government consists of an elected governor and bicameral legislature.

Paraíba or **Paraíba do Sul** (do͞o so͞ol), river, c.650 mi (1,050 km) long, rising as the Paraitinga in the Serra do Mar, São Paulo state, SE Brazil. It flows southwesterly to a point NE of São Paulo city where it makes a hairpin turn and continues in a northeasterly direction through the state of Rio de Janeiro to the Atlantic Ocean near Campos. Below Três Rios it flows through a gorge on the Rio de Janeiro-Minas Gerais border. Its beautiful valley forms a rich agricultural region (site of Brazil's first commercial coffee plantation) as well as a major industrial center of Brazil.

parakeet or **parrakeet,** common name for a widespread group of small PARROTS, native to the Indo-Malayan region and popular as cage birds. Parakeets have long, pointed tails, unlike the chunky lovebirds with which they are sometimes confused. The budgerigar, also called the shell, zebra, or grass, parakeet (*Melopsittacus undulatus*), is the best known of the true parakeets. The wild budgerigar of Australia is usually green or blue with black-and-yellow markings; as a cage bird, however, it has been bred in white and yellow. The hanging parakeet sleeps upside down like a bat. The extinct Carolina parakeet was the only parrot native to the United States. It was 12 in. (30 cm) long with a yellow-green body and orange-red head. It was sought as a cage bird and for its plumage and also killed as a destroyer of fruit and grain crops. Parakeets are classified in the phylum CHORDATA, subphylum Vertebrata, class Aves, order Psittaciformes, family Psittacidae.

Parakou (pâr″əko͞o′), town (1967 est. pop. 20,000), capital of Borgou dept., central Dahomey. It is the trade center for a cotton, grain, and livestock-raising area. Located at the head of the railroad from Cotonou, it is the distribution center for N Dahomey and Niger. Parakou has an airstrip and a textile research center.

Parakrama Bahu I (pärăk′rəmə bä′ro͞o), fl. 12th cent., Sinhalese king of Ceylon (1153–86). He was the first to unite the island under one rule after Chola invaders were driven out in the late 11th cent. He made his capital at Pollonarrua, which became a great cultural center, and encouraged the construction of a highly efficient irrigation system that helped to make the island prosperous. After securing his hold on Ceylon, he invaded S India and sailed to Burma with an army.

paraldehyde, nervous system DEPRESSANT similar to alcohol in its effects and used as a SEDATIVE. A colorless flammable liquid with a disagreeable odor, paraldehyde produces sleep for up to 12 hr. with little or no muscle, heart, or respiratory depression. It is often given to alcoholics having delirium tremens, to induce sleep, and is also used to calm psychiatric patients. Like alcohol and other depressants it is addictive (see DRUG ADDICTION AND DRUG ABUSE). Paraldehyde is also used in the manufacture of synthetic resins, as a preservative, and in preparing leather. It is produced by treating acetaldehyde with a small amount of sulfuric acid.

Paralipomenon: see CHRONICLES.

parallax (pâr′əlăks), any alteration in the relative apparent positions of objects produced by a shift in the position of the observer. In astronomy the term is used for several techniques for determining distance. Trigonometric parallax is the apparent displacement of a nearby star against the background of more distant stars resulting from the motion of the earth in its orbit around the sun. Formally, the parallax of a star is the angle at the star that is subtended by the mean distance between the earth and the sun. A shift in the angular position of a star will be greatest when observed at intervals of six months (see accompanying diagram); this makes the parallax equal to the value of one half of the semiannual displacement of the star. If a star's parallax can be measured, it then determines the distance to the star. A unit of stellar measurement is the PARSEC; it is the distance at which a star would have a parallax of one second of arc and is equivalent to 206,265 times the distance from the earth to the sun, or about 3.3 light-years. A star's distance d in parsecs is the reciprocal of its parallax p (or $d = 1/p$). The first stellar parallax was measured in 1838 by Friedrich Bessel for the star 61 Cygni. Its parallax of 0.3 places it at a distance of 3.3 parsecs or about 11 light-years. The technique of stellar parallax is useful for stars within 100 parsecs. Spectroscopic parallax is the most widely used technique for determining the distances of stars that are too distant for their stellar parallaxes to be measured. From the analysis of a star's SPECTRUM, its position on the HERTZSPRUNG-RUSSELL DIAGRAM is determined. This diagram correlates the SPECTRAL CLASS of the star with its absolute MAGNITUDE. By comparing the absolute magnitude to its apparent brightness, the star's distance is calculated. Dynamical parallax is a method for determining the distance to a visual BINARY STAR. The angular diameter of the orbit of the stars around each other and their apparent brightness are observed. By applying KEPLER'S LAWS and the MASS-LUMINOSITY relation, the distance of the binary star can be determined. Geocentric parallax is a technique similar to stellar par-

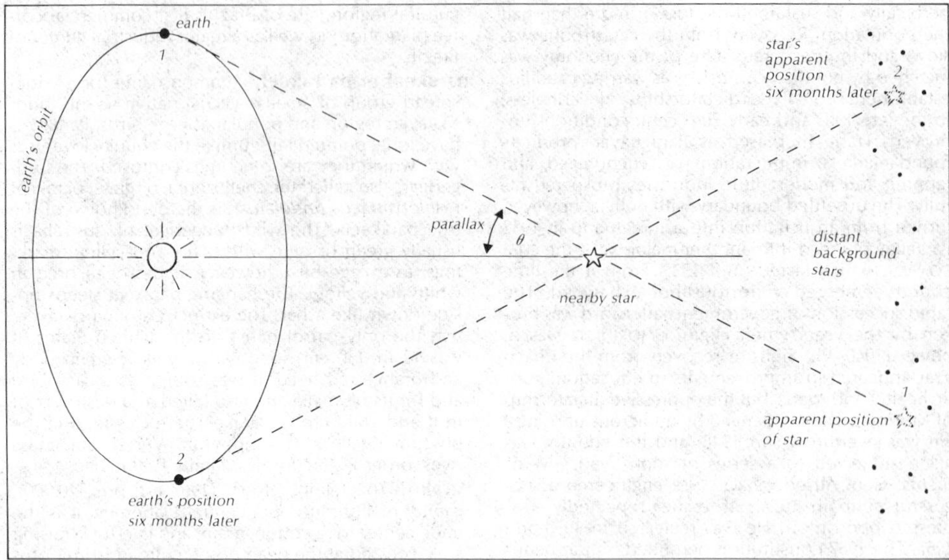

The trigonometric parallax of a star, expressed by the angle θ, is a measure of its apparent motion against the background of more distant stars as a result of the earth's motions in its orbit around the sun. Measurements are made at two points six months apart.

allax, which uses the diameter of the earth rather than the diameter of its orbit as a baseline. Because this baseline is relatively small, the technique is useful only for close celestial objects such as the moon or the asteroids.

parallel circuit: see ELECTRIC CIRCUIT.

parallel of latitude: see LATITUDE.

parallelogram, closed plane figure bounded by four line segments, or sides, with opposite pairs of sides parallel and equal in length. The rhombus, rectangle, and square are special types of parallelograms. Any side of a parallelogram is a base; an altitude is the perpendicular distance from a base to the opposite parallel side. The area of a parallelogram is equal to the product of the lengths of its base and altitude. The diagonals of a parallelogram, connecting opposite vertices, bisect one another; either diagonal divides the parallelogram into two congruent triangles.

paralysis or **palsy** (pôl'zē), complete loss or impairment of the ability to use voluntary muscles, usually as the result of a disorder of the nervous system. The nervous tissue that is injured may be in the brain, the spinal cord, or in the muscles themselves. Accordingly there may be general paralysis, involvement of only one side (hemiplegia), paralysis on both sides at one level (paraplegia), or localized paralysis in a small group of nerves or muscles. The cause of paralysis may be any injury that tears or compresses the nerves; it may be hemorrhage, tumor, infection (diphtheria, poliomyelitis, syphilis), or substances toxic to nerve tissue such as lead or alcohol. One of the most frequent causes of paralysis is stroke, in which hemorrhage, thrombosis, or obstruction of a cerebral vessel interferes with nerve function. Another disorder in which tremor is one of the main symptoms is PARKINSONISM. Cerebral palsy is due to an injury of brain motor tissue before or during birth. Partial or complete paralysis often accompanies multiple sclerosis.

paramagnetic resonance: see MAGNETIC RESONANCE.

paramagnetism: see MAGNETISM.

Paramaribo (păr"əmăr'ĭbō), city (1964 pop. 11,000), capital of Surinam, on the Surinam River, 17 mi (27 km) from the Atlantic Ocean. It exports bauxite, sugarcane, rice, cacao, coffee, rum, and tropical woods. Paramaribo has a museum, a cathedral, and canals that are reminiscent of the Netherlands. It is connected with the interior by a single railroad. The area was settled by the British from Barbados in 1630, and in 1650 the city became the capital of the new English colony. Paramaribo changed hands often between the British and Dutch but finally came under Dutch rule in 1815. The inhabitants are a mixture of Oriental, Indian, Negro, and Dutch.

paramecium (parəmē'sĭəm), unicellular animal, genus *Paramecium,* of the ciliate class of PROTOZOA, found in fresh water throughout the world. The paramecium has a stiff outer covering which gives it a permanent slipper shape. It swims rapidly by coordinated wavelike beats of its many cilia, short, hairlike projections of the cell. A paramecium normally moves forward in a corkscrew fashion but is capable of reversing direction when it encounters adverse conditions. This trial-and-error behavior (backing up and then continuing forward in a slightly different direction until an optimum path is found) is conspicuous when the animal is observed through a microscope. Paramecia and other ciliates are the most complex of all single-celled organisms. The paramecium has an external oral groove lined with cilia and leading to a mouth pore and gullet; food is digested in food vacuoles. There are also an anal pore, two contractile vacuoles that regulate the water content of the cell, and two nuclei. The larger nucleus, or macronucleus, is thought to regulate most cell functions, while the smaller nucleus, or micronucleus, is involved in reproduction. Paramecia feed on smaller organisms, such as bacteria. They usually reproduce asexually, by cell division. In certain strains sexual reproduction sometimes occurs; two individuals unite (conjugate) at the oral grooves and exchange portions of the micronuclei, after which each individual divides. Paramecia are classified in the phylum Protozoa, class Ciliophora, subclass Holotricha.

Paramount, city (1970 pop. 34,734), Los Angeles co., S Calif.; inc. 1957. Originally a dairy region, it has become highly industrialized since the 1950s. It has an oil refinery and industries that produce metal and plastic products, automotive parts, sports equipment, and furniture.

Paramus (pərăm'əs), borough (1970 pop. 28,381), Bergen co., NE N.J.; settled 1668, inc. 1922. It is a large retail-trade center. An early Dutch church and a junior college are there.

Paran (pā'răn), desert, the eastern region of the Sinai peninsula, SE of Kadesh. Ishmael settled there, and it was also the first resting place of the Israelites after Sinai and the refuge of David when Samuel died. Gen. 21.21; Num. 10.12; 13.3,26; 1 Sam. 25.1. El-paran: Gen. 14.6. See also Deut. 1.1; 33.2; 1 Kings 11.18; Hab. 3.3.

Paraná (pərənä'), state (1970 pop. 6,936,743), 77,048 sq mi (199,554 sq km), S Brazil, on the borders of Paraguay and Argentina and on the Atlantic Ocean. The capital is CURITIBA.

Paraná (päränä'), city (1970 pop. 189,537), capital of Entre Ríos prov., NE Argentina, a port on the Paraná River. It is the center of a grain and cattle district; there is an agricultural school nearby. Founded in 1730, Paraná was the capital of the Argentine confederation from 1853 to 1862. Points of interest include a cathedral and a provincial museum.

Paraná, river, c.2,000 mi (3,200 km) long, formed by the junction of the Paranaíba and the Rio Grande, SE Brazil. It has the second largest drainage system in South America. It flows generally southwest to its confluence with the Paraguay River, forming the southern border of Paraguay, then S and E through NE Argentina to join the Uruguay River in a huge delta at the head of the Río de la Plata. The lower Paraná is hampered by shifting channels, sandbars, and fluctuating river flow, and is subject to flooding. The Brazilian stretch flows in a deep bed and is broken by many waterfalls. The Paraná is the principal commercial artery of interior SE South America. Navigable for oceangoing vessels (via a dredged channel) to Rosario and Santa Fe in Argentina, the Paraná accommodates river craft to the Iguaçu River. A bridge over the river at Foz do Iguaçu links Brazil and Paraguay. The Paraná was first ascended (1526) by Sebastian Cabot, the English explorer in the service of Spain.

Paranaguá (pərənəgwä'), city (1970 pop. 52,173), Paraná state, SE Brazil, on the Atlantic Ocean. It is the port for CURITIBA, to which it is linked by rail and highway. Founded c.1600, the city has fine port facilities and has become increasingly important with the shift of coffee cultivation S from São Paulo state. A modern highway connects Paranaguá with Asunción, the capital of Paraguay.

Paranaíba (pərənīē'bə), river, c.500 mi (800 km) long, rising in W Minas Gerais state, Brazil. It flows generally westward through an agricultural region before joining the Rio Grande to form the PARANÁ. Diamonds are washed along its course.

paranoia (pâr"ənoi'ə), chronic functional PSYCHOSIS of insidious development characterized by persistent, unalterable, systematized, logically reasoned DELUSIONS, or false beliefs, commonly of persecution and grandeur. The term *paranoia* was first used by Karl L. Kahlbaum, the German psychiatrist, in 1863 to designate various persecutory and grandiose states. In the former case the paranoiac creates a complex delusional system that purports to show that people want to hurt him; in the latter, he sees himself as an exalted person with a mission of great importance to accomplish. The paranoiac may pursue a successful career. General demeanor, talk, and emotional and behavioral reactions remain unaltered except as influenced by delusional beliefs that eventually become the guiding motives of the paranoiac's life. Most paranoids are harmless, but occasionally a paranoid psychotic may decide to solve his problems in a violent way. The paranoid who is not psychotic is usually hostile and defensive without good reason, and tends to blame the environment for what is really dissatisfaction with self. In paranoid SCHIZOPHRENIA the patient develops delusional systems, often accompanied by HALLUCINATIONS, that control his behavior; as with other types of schizophrenia, there is deterioration in judgment, emotional organization, and perception of reality. The paranoid response is the DEFENSE MECHANISM of projection carried to excess.

Paranthropus (pârăn'thrəpəs): see AUSTRALOPITHECUS.

paraplegia (pâr"əplē'jēə), paralysis of the lower part of the body, commonly affecting both legs and often internal organs below the waist. Paraplegia is caused by an injury or disease that damages the spinal cord, and consequently always affects both sides of the body. The extent of the paralysis depends on the level of the spinal cord at which the damage occurs. For example, damage to the lowest area of the cord may result only in paralysis of the legs, whereas damage farther up on the cord causes possible loss of control over the muscles of the bladder and rectum as well. Most frequently the cause is an injury that either completely severs the spinal cord or damages some of the nervous tissue in the cord. Such damage could result from broken vertebrae that press against the cord. Diseases that cause paraplegia include spinal tuberculosis, syphilis, spinal tumors, multiple sclerosis, and poliomyelitis. Sometimes when the disease is treated and cured, the paralysis disappears, but usually the nerve damage is irreparable and paralysis is permanent. Treatment of paraplegia is aimed at helping to compensate for the paralysis by means of mechanical devices and through psychological and physical therapy.

parapsychology, study of mental phenomena not explainable by accepted principles of science. The use of scientific discipline in the investigation of paranormal and supernormal phenomena is comparatively modern, having its inception with the foundation (1882) in London of the Society for Psychical Research. Early efforts were to dissociate psychical phenomena from spiritualism and superstition and particularly to investigate mediums and their claims of evoking spirits or apparitions. The society also studied automatic writing, levitation, and ectoplasmic and poltergeist activities. One of its principal founders, Frederic William Henry Myers, summed up the society's early efforts in *Human Personality and Its Survival of Bodily Death* (1903). An American Society for Psychical Research was also founded; James Hervey Hyslop was a major figure in it. Considerable experimentation has been carried on over the years, perhaps the best-known being that of Joseph Banks Rhine at Duke Univ. Most study has been given to the area of extrasensory perception, or ESP, a term originated by Rhine to include telepathy, clairvoyance, and precognition. The Duke Univ. laboratory has also investigated psychokinesis, or PK, the direct exercise of mental influence on matter. In Great Britain the work of Whately Carington and Samuel George Soal has paralleled that of Rhine. The most common technique used has been card guessing and picture guessing. Although positive conclusions have been claimed by scientists of repute, the methods and results are highly criticized by many. There has been increasing interest in parapsychology, with research being conducted in Europe, the Soviet Union, and the United States. See Whately Carington, *Telepathy: Thought Transference* (3d ed. 1946); J. B. Rhine, *Reach of the Mind* (1947, repr. 1961); C. D. Broad, *Religion, Philosophy and Psychical Research* (1953); J. G. Pratt, *Parapsychology: An Insider's View of ESP* (1964, repr. 1966); L. E. Rhine, *ESP in Life and Lab* (1967); Alan Gauld, *The Founders of Psychical Research* (1968); Allan Angoff, ed., *The Psychic Force* (1970); J. B. Rhine, ed., *Progress in Parapsychology* (1971).

Pará rubber tree (pärä'), large tree (*Hevea brasiliensis*) of the family Euphorbiaceae (SPURGE family), native to tropical South America and the source of the greatest amount and finest quality of natural RUBBER. The yellow or white latex from which rubber is made occurs in numerous vessels in the bark, especially in the inner layers. The tree is tapped by making careful incisions, as deep as possible without injuring the tree's growth, in a lefthand spiral of 30° around the trunk, for the latex vessels spiral to the right at an angle of about 30° from the horizontal. The latex is collected in small cups and then treated—usually by coagulating it with acid, pressing it free of water, and drying the resultant sheets in a smokehouse to ready them for shipment. The size of the tree, the quality of the latex, and the number of taps possible varies with individual trees; the quantity of latex increases with the age of the tree, which may grow to a height of over 100 ft (30 m). The trees are tapped throughout the year, usually in the early morning, when the latex flow is greatest. Sometimes other trees that yield latex are also called Pará rubber trees. Pará rubber trees are classified in the division MAGNOLIOPHYTA, class Magnoliopsida, order Euphorbiales, family Euphorbiaceae.

parasite, plant or animal that at some stage of its existence obtains its nourishment from another living organism called the host. Parasites may or may not harm the host, but they never benefit it. They include members of many plant and animal groups, and nearly all living things are at some time hosts to parasitic forms. Many bacteria are parasitic on external and internal body surfaces; some of these invade the inner tissues and cause disease (e.g., typhoid fever, tuberculosis, and some types of pneumonia). Parasitic plants cause great losses among food crops and trees (see DISEASES OF PLANTS). Parasites are more prevalent in the animal kingdom; most are invertebrates, chiefly worms, e.g., the FLUKE, TAPEWORM, and trichina (see TRICHINOSIS); arthropods, e.g., the FLEA and LOUSE; and protozoans. Among the protozoan parasites that cause human disease are *Amoeba* (or *Entamoeba*) *histolytica*, the cause of amebic dysentery and liver abscess, and the several species of *Plasmodium* responsible for the three main types of malaria. Most parasites are obligate; i.e., they are unable to survive apart from their hosts. Often this is because in the course of evolution they have lost various of the organs necessary to live as independent units. Many parasites also have extremely specialized reproductive systems and complex life cycles, involving more than one host. Some higher plants and animals are parasitic, e.g., the dodders (vines of the morning-glory family) and the cuckoo, which lays its eggs in the nests of other birds. Organisms that obtain their nourishment from dead organic matter are called saprophytes, e.g., mushrooms. An epiphyte, or AIR PLANT, although it lives in association with another plant, is not a parasite. See also SYMBIOSIS. See T. W. M. Cameron, *Parasites and Parasitism* (1956); J. G. Baer, *Animal Parasites* (1971).

parasitism: see PARASITE.

parasol: see UMBRELLA.

parasympathetic nervous system: see NERVOUS SYSTEM.

parathion: see INSECTICIDE.

parathormone: see PARATHYROID HORMONE.

parathyroid glands (pâr"əthī'roid), four small endocrine bodies, located behind the thyroid gland, that govern calcium and phosphorus metabolism. These four masses of tissue (each about the size of a pea) are difficult to distinguish from the thyroid and are often embedded in it. Consequently, before their significance was known they were sometimes accidently removed during thyroid surgery, causing a deficiency in parathormone, the parathyroid hormone. Parathormone increases the concentration of calcium ions in the blood, with accompanying bone absorption and increased reabsorption of calcium ions by the kidneys. The hormone's effect on phosphate ion concentration is the opposite, i.e., phosphate ion concentration in the bloodstream decreases as a result of increased phosphate excretion by the kidneys. Excessive secretion of parathormone, e.g., caused by tumor of the parathyroid glands, is a serious disorder, for excessive blood calcium can cause kidney stones and long-term weakening of the bones. Undersecretion of parathormone, which can be caused by congenital and metabolic disorders, results in too little calcium in the bloodstream, and too much phosphorus. The result is tetany, i.e., violent muscle spasms.

parathyroid hormone or **parathormone,** a HORMONE secreted by the PARATHYROID GLANDS that regulates the METABOLISM of calcium and phosphate in the body. It has been purified extensively and appears to be a protein containing 83 amino acid residues, a sequence of which about 33 to 35 are necessary for biological activity. Parathyroid hormone acts to raise the extracellular calcium concentration, that is, the concentration of calcium ions in the spaces between the cells of the body and in the blood plasma; it promotes the absorption of calcium by the intestine, mobilizes calcium salts from the bones, and increases the tendency of the kidney to recover calcium from the urine. The hormone also enhances both the excretion of phosphate by the kidneys and its uptake by the cells. This removes phosphate, which tends to form a relatively insoluble salt with calcium, from the extracellular spaces, allowing more calcium to remain in solution. Calcium is intimately involved not only in the formation of bone, but also in the functioning of the nervous system; thus hypoparathyroidism, the disease associated with a deficiency in parathyroid hormone secretion, is characterized by muscle spasms leading eventually to generalized convulsions and various psychiatric symptoms. This condition is sometimes successfully treated by the administration of the hormone. Hyperparathyroidism, the result of oversecretion of the hormone, often leads to the resorption of bone and can only be treated by the surgical removal of portions of the parathyroid glands.

paratyphoid: see SALMONELLOSIS.

Paray-le-Monial (pärā'-lə-mônyäl'), town (1968 pop. 11,077), Saône-et-Loire dept., E central France. Ceramics and hosiery are produced. In the 17th cent. St. Margaret Mary founded the cult of the Sacred Heart of Jesus there. With the growth of the cult in the 19th cent. Paray-le-Monial became second only to LOURDES as a pilgrimage site in France. The town's Romanesque Church of Notre Dame dates from the 12th cent.

Parazoa: see PORIFERA.

Parbar (pär'bär), part of the Temple at Jerusalem. 1 Chron. 26.18.

Parcae (pär'sē): see FATES.

parcel post, sending of packages through the mail service. At the congress of the Universal Postal Union in Paris in 1878, an international parcel-post system was established. The British parcel-post bill, passed in 1882, put into effect the following year domestic, colonial, and foreign services. Various other countries established such systems; the United States entered into conventions with other governments to convey parcels sent into the country but delayed instituting a domestic service until the Parcel Post Act of 1912. A water route for parcel post was started in 1917, and a fleet of trucks was put into operation in the East the next year. Parcel-post delivery on rural routes was established in 1919, making it possible for farmers to ship eggs and other produce direct to the consumer. Small animals that do not require food or water while in transit are accepted as parcel post. Extra fees provide for the special handling, insurance, and special delivery of parcels. In 1948 an air parcel-post service was established. Under treaty arrangements the United States is able to exchange parcel post with most countries of the world.

Parcheesi: see BACKGAMMON.

parchment, untanned skins of animals, especially of the sheep, calf, and goat, prepared for use as a writing material. The name is a corruption of Pergamum, the ancient city of Asia Minor where preparation of parchment suitable for use on both sides was achieved in the 2d cent. B.C. Parchment, which is more durable than papyrus and susceptible of being folded into book form, very gradually superseded papyrus. In Europe it gave way to paper for use in books only after the advent of printing. The skins were soaked in water, treated with lime to loosen the hair, scraped, washed, stretched, and dried, and then rubbed with chalk and pumice stone. A fine grade prepared from the skin of the calf or kid became known as vellum, a name applied during the Middle Ages to any parchment used in manuscripts. For important manuscripts vellum was often dyed purple. Parchment is still used for certain documents and diplomas, for bookbindings and lampshades, and for the heads of drums, tambourines, and banjos. Vegetable parchment is paper treated to make it tough, translucent, and impervious to water.

Pardo, Manuel (mänwĕl' pär'dō), 1834–78, president of Peru (1872–76). After assisting José BALTA in establishing a constitutional government, Pardo succeeded him as president. To recover from the monetary ruin brought on Peru by the Balta regime, he advocated financial and administrative reforms. His term is chiefly noted for the signing (1873) of the treaty of alliance with Bolivia that led to war with Chile (see PACIFIC, WAR OF THE) in 1879. Later, because of his opposition to militarism, he was assassinated by a soldier. He is remembered for his benevolence and humanitarianism and especially for his services during the yellow-fever epidemic of 1867.

Pardo Bazán, Emilia, condesa de (āmē'lyä kōndā'sä dā pär'thō bäthän'), 1852–1921, Spanish novelist and critic. Her biography of St. Francis of Assisi appeared the same year as her controversial work, *La cuestión palpitante* (1883), a critical analysis of Zola's naturalism. Her many novels introduced naturalism into Spanish literature. Among those about social decay in her native Galicia are *El cisne de Vilamorta* (1885, tr. *The Swan of Vilamorta, 1891*); *Los pazos de Ulloa* (1886); and its sequel, *La madre naturaleza* (1887), generally considered her masterpiece.

pardon, in law, exemption from punishment for a criminal conviction granted by the grace of the executive of a government. A general pardon to a class of persons guilty of the same offense (e.g., insurrection) is an AMNESTY. A pardon (at least in the United States) absolutely terminates criminal liability, including any restrictions that result from a criminal conviction (though the pardoned person is not exonerated from the civil liability that his action may have incurred). A pardon is thus to be distinguished from alleviation of punishment (such as COMMUTATION OF SENTENCE, REPRIEVE, and PAROLE), which does not nullify the conviction and all of its effects. The Constitution of the United States gives the President power to grant reprieves and pardons for all Federal crimes, but he may not release a person from the effects of impeachment. In most of the states the governor has nearly the same power in respect to state crimes. Usually, the governor may not pardon those convicted of treason or criminal contempt of court. In canon law the pardon is the absolution granted in PENANCE; in the Middle Ages the word was used commonly to mean an INDULGENCE (hence pardoner, a dispenser of indulgences).

Pardubice (pär'do͝obĭtsĕ), Ger. *Pardubitz*, city (1970 pop. 71,774), N central Czechoslovakia, in Bohemia, on the Elbe River. Its chief economic activities are oil refining and chemical manufacturing. The city has many notable Gothic and Renaissance buildings. Horse races are often held there.

Paré, Ambroise (äNbrwäz' pärā'), c.1510–1590, French surgeon. Serving in the army, he revived the use of ligature instead of cautery with boiling oil and continued to devise and champion more humane treatments in medicine. He promoted the use of artificial limbs and introduced podalic version in childbirth, i.e., the manipulation of the fetus so that it is delivered feet first. He was surgeon to four kings of France, and his works were widely translated. See study by J. F. Malgaigne (tr. 1965); bibliography of his works by Janet Doe (1937).

Paredes y Arrillaga, Mariano (märyä'nō pärā'thās ē ärēyä'gä), 1797–1849, Mexican general and president (1846). A leader of the ultraconservatives, he helped to put Antonio López de Santa Anna into the presidency in 1841 but soon opposed him. In 1845, Paredes led a revolt against José Joaquín HERRERA, charging that Herrera was compromising the honor of Mexico by negotiating with the United States concerning Texas. When Paredes came to power he plunged the country into the Mexican War. Although he was made president, Mexico was in a state of anarchy, and the return of Santa Anna destroyed the hopes of Paredes, who went into exile (1847). Later he led an unsuccessful revolution.

paregoric (pâr″əgôr′ĭk), alcoholic solution of opium and camphor first prepared in the 18th cent. Because of the constipating effect of opium, paregoric has been used to control diarrhea. It was formerly a constituent of many cough elixirs.

Pareja, Juan de (hwän dā pärā′hä), c. 1610–70, Spanish religious and portrait painter, of Moorish origin. Pareja was the lifelong assistant of Velázquez. His paintings show originality and an impetuous baroque temper. An outstanding work, the *Calling of St. Matthew,* may be seen in the Prado.

Parent, Étienne (ātyĕn′ päräN′), 1801–74, French Canadian journalist and government official, b. Quebec prov. As editor of the *Canadien* he had a commanding position in French Canadian journalism and inspired many French Canadian writers. Parent took no active part in the rebellion of 1837, but he was briefly imprisoned for his attacks on the government. After the union of Upper and Lower Canada he was elected to the assembly. From 1847 to 1867 he was assistant secretary of Lower Canada and in 1867 he was acting assistant secretary of state for Canada.

parent and child, legal relationship that confers certain rights and duties on parent and child. The parents are ordinarily obliged to support the child, and they usually have the right to his custody. In earlier times the father's right was superior to that of the mother, but today courts favor either the mother or whichever parent is better suited to rear the child. In case of DIVORCE custody may be granted to either parent or divided between them. When neither parent is fit to perform his duties, custody may be awarded to other persons or to institutions. The mother of an illegitimate child has the right to his custody, but the father usually must contribute to the child's support. Whoever has the lawful custody of a child has the right to correct or punish him if the means used are not excessive. At common law parents had no right to support by a child, even though they were destitute and infirm. In the United States, that rule has, however, been changed by statute in many states. The parents are entitled to a minor child's services, and consequently to his earnings, if the child lives with them and is supported by them; and if their child is injured through negligence, they may bring suit for loss of his services. In law, emancipation is the dissolution of the parent-child relation. It may occur if the parents abandon the child, or at the parents' option (but usually not before the child is 18 years old), or when the child marries or attains majority. See GUARDIAN AND WARD; ADOPTION; LEGITIMATION. For the sociological and psychological aspects of the relationship, see FAMILY. See H. I. Clarke, *Social Legislation* (2d ed. 1957); H. H. Clark, Jr., *The Law of Domestic Relations in the United States* (1968).

parent education, movement to help parents' understanding of the problems of child life at home and in the school. Much parent education is carried on through the channels of adult education, both formally and informally. The Child Study Association (founded 1888) and the National Congress of Parents and Teachers (founded 1897) are active in disseminating literature and promoting discussion groups. The latter organization also sponsors local parent-teacher associations (PTAs) at over 45,000 schools in the United States. See publications of the Child Study Association and the National Congress of Parents and Teachers. See Sidonie M. Gruenberg, *Parents' Guide to Everyday Problems of Boys and Girls* (1958); Aline S. Auerbach, *Trends and Techniques in Parent Education* (1961); Evelyn Pickarts and Jean Fargo, *Parent Education* (1971).

parenthesis: see PUNCTUATION.

Pares, Sir Bernard, 1867–1949, English historian, authority on Russia. Educated at Cambridge, he made many trips to Russia. In World War I he was British attaché with the Russian army and attached to the British embassy in Petrograd. He was knighted in 1919. From 1922 to 1939 he was director of Slavonic studies at the Univ. of London. Pares, though not sympathetic to Stalinism, endeavored to improve Soviet-British relations. His comprehensive *History of Russia* (1926; definitive ed., 1955) was long unsurpassed as a text, and his *Fall of the Russian Monarchy* (1935) remains a standard work. See his autobiography, *A Wandering Student* (1948).

Pareto, Vilfredo (vēlfrĕ′dō pärĕ′tō), 1848–1923, Italian economist and sociologist, b. Paris, of an exiled noble family that returned to Italy in 1858. He studied mathematics and engineering in Turin and worked as an engineer for many years, meanwhile becoming increasingly interested in social and economic problems. His economic writings won him (1893) a professorship of political economy at the Univ. of Lausanne. His notable contribution in applying mathematics to economic theory is found especially in *Cours d'économie politique* (1896–97). In his sociological studies he sought to differentiate the rational and nonrational factors in social action. He used that concept as the basis for his theory of the cyclical development and fall of governing elite groups. His chief work in sociology, *Trattato di sociologia generale* (1916), has been translated as *Mind and Society* (4 vol., 1935). See G. C. Homans and C. P. Curtis, Jr., *An Introduction to Pareto: His Sociology* (1934, repr. 1970); study by Franz Borkenau (1936); J. H. Meisel, ed., *Pareto and Mosca* (1965).

parhelion: see HALO.

pariah (pərī′ə), a native of India of extremely low CASTE. Pariah castes, of which there are several hundred, are ordinarily so abhorred that physical contact with their members is considered ritually polluting; thus, a frequently used synonym is *untouchable.* Pariahs are not, as is sometimes stated, outcasts, this term being reserved for individuals who have been ostracized for serious violations of caste rules. The British government in India applied the term "scheduled castes" to the pariahs, and Mahatma Gandhi, who did much to help them, named them Harijans (Children of God). This latter term has all but replaced the name *pariah* in popular Indian usage. Since 1947, when India gained independence, the government of India has tried to improve the status of the pariahs; however, widespread discrimination still exists.

Parian marble: see PÁROS.

Parícutin (pärē′ko͞otēn), active volcano, c.8,200 ft (2,500 m) high, Michoacán state, W central Mexico. In one of the most spectacular eruptions of modern times, Parícutin burst forth from a cornfield on Feb. 20, 1943, and grew discontinuously until 1952, spewing forth over a billion tons of lava. It buried the town of San Juan Parangaricutiro and the village of Parícutin, whence its name. The cone (c.2,000 ft/610 m high) is a remarkable example of volcanic growth, and its development was closely studied by international scientific teams.

parimutuel betting (păr″ĭmyo͞o′tyo͞oĕl), system of cooperative wagering invented (c.1870) in France by Pierre Oller. According to the system, the total amount of money bet on a race (the pool) is divided among the holders of winning tickets, after deductions for tax and racetrack expenses. The uniqueness of parimutuel betting lies in the fact that the gambling public itself makes the payoff odds (e.g., if many people have bet on the actual winner of a contest then the payoff will be low, simply because the pool must be divided among many winners). Parimutuel wagering is the accepted betting procedure at major horse-racing tracks throughout the world. It is also used in greyhound racing and for jai alai games in the United States. Considered a major deterrent to illegal bookmaking, the modern parimutuel system depends on high-speed electronic calculating machines, known as totalizators, to record and display up-to-the-minute betting patterns.

Parini, Giuseppe (jo͞ozĕp′pā pärē′nē), 1729–99, Italian poet, a priest and teacher. He was a professor and a superintendent of schools in Milan; a liberal, Parini became (1796) a government official in the Napoleonic occupation. Best known of his verse is *The Day* (4 parts, 1763–1804; tr. 1927), a mock-didactic poem that satirizes the arrogance and depravity of the nobility. Parini's style was polished and reminiscent of classical Latin; he was widely emulated during the national revival. He also wrote lyrics, a drama, critical essays, and dialogues.

Paris, Louis Philippe Albert d'Orléans, comte de: see ORLÉANS, family.

Paris, Matthew: see MATTHEW OF PARIS.

Paris, Paulin (Alexis Paulin Paris) (pōlăN′ pärēs′), 1800–1881, French scholar. He was noted for his research in medieval French literature and for initiating the systematic study of Romance philology. His studies include *Les Manuscrits françois de la Bibliothèque du Roi* (7 vol., 1836–48) and *Les Romans de la Table ronde* (5 vol., 1868–77). His son, **Bruno Paulin Gaston Paris** (1839–1903), was a noted Romance philologist. Carrying on the work his father began, he edited the *Révue critique,* founded the journal *Romania,* and wrote critical and historical works on literature.

Paris (pâr′ĭs, Fr. pärē′), city (1968 pop. 2,590,771; metropolitan area pop. 8,196,746), N central France, capital of the country, on the Seine River. It is the commercial and industrial focus of France and a cultural and intellectual center of international renown. The city possesses an indefinable unity of atmosphere that has fascinated writers, poets, and painters for centuries. Paris is sometimes called the City of Light in tribute to its intellectual preeminence as well as to its beautiful appearance. Situated in the center of the Paris basin (see ÎLE-DE-FRANCE), and only 90 mi (145 km) from the English Channel, the city handles a great volume of shipping. Orly, Le Bourget, and Charles de Gaulle airports (the latter opened in 1974) and the seven major railroad stations make Paris one of the great transportation centers of western Europe. The Paris *metro* (subway) was built in 1900. The city has a great many newspapers, four radio stations, and three television channels. Elegant stores and hotels, lavish night clubs, theaters, and gourmet restaurants help make tourism the biggest industry in Paris. Other leading industries manufacture luxury articles, high-fashion clothing, perfume, and jewelry. Heavy industry, notably automobile manufacture, is located in the suburbs. About one quarter of the French labor force is concentrated in the Paris area. Paris is divided into 20 *arrondissements* (boroughs), each of which has a justice of the peace and an appointed mayor. An elected council has only advisory powers. Effective power resides with the prefect of the city, who is appointed by the national government. The region of Paris consists legally of the city and seven departments of France, headed by a regional prefect. Paris is divided into roughly equal sections by the Seine. On the right (northern) bank are the BOIS DE BOULOGNE, ARC DE TRIOMPHE, BIBLIOTHÈQUE NATIONALE, ÉLYSÉE Palace, Place de la CONCORDE, OPÉRA, COMÉDIE FRANÇAISE, LOUVRE, Palais de Chaillot, CHAMPS ÉLYSÉES, and the other great streets and boulevards. In the eastern part of the right bank is the Place de la BASTILLE; to the north is MONTMARTRE, the highest area in Paris, topped by the Church of SACRÉ-CŒUR. Much of the right bank, which has many of the most fashionable streets and shops, has a stately, formal air. At night many of its famous monuments and boulevards are floodlit. The left bank, with the SORBONNE, the FRENCH ACADEMY, the Panthéon (see under PANTHEON), the LUXEMBOURG PALACE and Gardens, the Chamber of Deputies, the QUAI D'ORSAY, and the Hotel des INVALIDES, is the governmental and to a large extent the intellectual section. The old Latin Quarter, for nearly a thousand years the preserve of university students and faculty; the Faubourg Saint-Germain section, at once aristocratic and a haven for students and artists (the celebrated Café des Deux Magots and Café de Flore are there); and MONTPARNASSE are the most celebrated left-bank districts. The Eiffel Tower, chief landmark of Paris, stands by the Seine on the Champ-de-Mars. The historical nucleus of Paris is the Île de la Cité, a small boat-shaped island largely occupied by the huge Palais de Justice and the Cathedral of Notre Dame de Paris. It is connected with the smaller Île Saint-Louis, occupied by elegant houses of the 17th and 18th cent. Characteristic of Paris are the tree-lined quays along the Seine (famed, on the left bank, for their innumerable open-air bookstalls), the historic bridges that span the Seine, and the vast tree-lined boulevards that replaced the city walls. Skyscrapers, apartment complexes, and highways have been added to the Paris scene in recent years. Julius Caesar conquered Paris in 52 B.C. It was then a fishing village, called Lutetia Parisiorum (the Parisii were a Gallic tribe), on the Île de la Cité. Under the Romans the town spread to the left bank and acquired considerable importance under the later emperors. The vast catacombs under Montparnasse and the baths (now in the Cluny Mus.) remain from the Roman period. Legend says that St. DENIS, first bishop of Paris, was martyred on Montmartre (hence the name) and that in the 5th cent. St. Geneviève, the patron saint of Paris, preserved the city from destruction by the Huns. On several occasions in its early history Paris was threatened by barbarian and Norman invasions, which at times drove the inhabitants back to the Île de la Cité. Clovis I and several other Merovingian kings made Paris their capital; under Charlemagne it became a center of learning. In 987, Hugh Capet, count of Paris, became king of France. The Capetians firmly established Paris as the French capital. The city grew as the power of the French kings increased. In the 11th cent. the city spread to the right bank. During the next two centuries—the reign of Philip Augustus (1180–1223) is especially notable for the growth of Paris—streets were paved and the city walls enlarged; the first Louvre (a fortress) and several churches, including Notre Dame, were constructed or begun; and the schools on the left bank were organized into the Univ. of Paris. One of them, the Sorbonne, became a fountainhead of theological learning with Albertus Magnus and St. Thomas Aquinas among its scholars. The university community constituted an autonomous borough; another was formed on the right bank by merchants ruled by their own provost. In 1358, under the leadership of the merchant provost Étienne Marcel, Paris first assumed the role of an independent commune and rebelled against the dauphin (later Charles V). During the period of the Hundred Years War the city suffered civil strife (see ARMAGNACS AND BURGUNDIANS), occupation by the English (1419-36), famine, and the Black Death. The Renaissance reached Paris in the 16th cent. during the reign of Francis I (1515-47). At this time the Louvre was transformed from a fortress to a Renaissance palace. In the Wars of Religion (1562-98), Parisian Catholics, who were in the great majority, took part in the massacre of St. Bartholomew's Day (1572), forced Henry III to leave the city on the Day of Barricades (1588), and accepted Henry IV only after his conversion (1593) to Catholicism. Cardinal Richelieu, Louis XIII's minister, established the French Academy and built the Palais Royal and the Luxembourg Palace. During the FRONDE, Paris once again defied the royal authority. Louis XIV, distrustful of the Parisians, transferred (1682) his court to Versailles. Parisian industries profited from the lavishness of Versailles; the specialization in luxury goods dates from that time. J. H. Mansart under Louis XIV and François Mansart, J. G. Soufflot, and J. A. Gabriel under Louis XV created some of the most majestic prospects of modern Paris. During the late 17th and the 18th cent. Paris acquired further glory as the scene of many of France's greatest cultural achievements: the plays of Molière, Racine, and Corneille; the music of Lully, Rameau, and Gluck; the paintings of Watteau, Fragonard, and Boucher; and the salons where many of the *philosophes* of the ENLIGHTENMENT gathered. At the same time, growing industries had resulted in the creation of new classes—the bourgeoisie and proletariat—concentrated in such suburbs (*faubourgs*) as Saint-Antoine and Saint-Denis; in the opening events of the FRENCH REVOLUTION, city mobs stormed the Bastille (July, 1789) and hauled the royal family from Versailles to Paris (October, 1789). Throughout the turbulent period of the Revolution the city played a central role. Napoleon (emperor, 1804-15) began a large construction program (including the building of the Arc de Triomphe, the Vendôme Column, and the arcaded Rue de Rivoli) and enriched the city's museums with artworks removed from conquered cities. In the course of his downfall Paris was occupied twice by enemy armies (1814, 1815). In the first half of the 19th cent. Paris grew rapidly. In 1801 it had 547,000 people; in 1817, 714,000; in 1841, 935,000; and in 1861, 1,696,000. The revolutions of July, 1830, and February, 1848, both essentially Parisian events, had repercussions throughout Europe. Culturally, the city was at various times the home or host of most of the great European figures of the age. Balzac, Hugo, Chopin, Berlioz, Liszt, Wagner, Delacroix, Ingres, and Daumier were a few of the outstanding personalities. The grand outline of modern Paris was the work of Baron Georges HAUSSMANN, who was appointed prefect by Napoleon III. The great avenues, boulevards, and parks are his work. During the Franco-Prussian War (1870-71), Paris was besieged for four months by the Germans and then surrendered. After the Germans withdrew, Parisian workers rebelled against the French government and established the COMMUNE OF PARIS, which was bloodily suppressed. With the establishment of the Third French Republic and relative stability, Paris became the great industrial and transportation center it is today. Two epochal events in modern cultural history that took place in Paris were the first exhibition of impressionist painting (1874) and the premiere of Stravinsky's *Sacre du Printemps* (1913). In World War I the Germans failed to reach Paris. After 1919 the outermost city fortifications were replaced by housing developments, including the Cité Universitaire, which houses thousands of students. During the 1920s, Paris was home to many disillusioned artists and writers from the United States and elsewhere. German troops occupied Paris during World War II from June 14, 1940, to Aug. 25, 1944. The city was not seriously damaged by the war. Paris was the headquarters of NATO from 1950 to 1967; it is also the headquarters of UNESCO. A program of cleaning the city's major buildings and monuments was completed in the 1960s. The city was the scene in May, 1968, of serious disorders, beginning with a student strike, that nearly toppled the Fifth Republic. In 1969, Les Halles, Paris's famous central market, called by Zola the "belly" of Paris, was dismantled. Paris was the site of the Vietnam peace negotiations (1968-73). See Janet Flanner, *Paris Journal* (2 vol., 1965-71) and *Paris was Yesterday, 1925-39* (1972); Maurice Kessel, *The History of Paris, From Caesar to Saint Louis* (tr. 1969); Leon Bernard, *The Emerging City: Paris in the Age of Louis XIV* (1970); André Chastel, *Paris* (tr. 1971); Pierre Couperie, *Paris Through the Ages* (tr. 1971); Maurice Guerrini, *Napoleon and Paris: Thirty Years of History* (tr. and abr. 1971); D. H. Pinkney, *Napoleon III and the Rebuilding of Paris* (1972).

Paris (pâr'ĭs), city (1970 pop. 23,441), seat of Lamar co., E Texas, in the Red River valley; settled 1824. It is a processing center for the rich farms of the blackland region. There are various manufactures. The city was rebuilt after its destruction by fire in 1916. A junior college is there, and many lakes are in the vicinity.

Paris or **Alexander,** in Greek mythology, son of Priam and Hecuba and brother of Hector. Because it was prophesied that he would cause the destruction of Troy, Paris was abandoned on Mt. Ida, but there he was raised by shepherds and loved by the nymph OENONE. Later he returned to Troy, where he was welcomed by Priam. Paris was chosen to settle a dispute among the goddesses Hera, Athena, and Aphrodite, all of whom claimed possession of the apple of discord, a golden fruit inscribed "to the fairest." It had been thrown among the guests at the wedding of Peleus and Thetis by Eris, who sought revenge because she had not been invited. Hera tried to bribe Paris with royal greatness and riches, and Athena offered him success in war, but Paris awarded the apple to Aphrodite, who promised him Helen, the most beautiful of women. With Aphrodite's help he abducted Helen from King Menelaus of Sparta; thus he brought on the Trojan War. In the war Paris killed Achilles, but was himself fatally wounded by Philoctetes.

Paris, Congress of, 1856, conference held by representatives of France, Great Britain, the Ottoman Empire (Turkey), Sardinia, Russia, Austria, and Prussia to negotiate the peace after the CRIMEAN WAR. In the Treaty of Paris (March 30, 1856), Russia agreed to the neutralization of the Black Sea, which was to be closed to war vessels and opened to the merchant marines of all nations. The Danubian principalities (Moldavia and Walachia, after 1859 called RUMANIA) were recognized as quasi-independent states under Turkish suzerainty; to them Russia ceded the left bank of the mouth of the DANUBE and part of Bessarabia. The lower Danube was placed under an international commission. The boundaries of Russia and Turkey in Asia were restored to their prewar limits (to the detriment of Russia). The Ottoman Empire became a member of the European concert, and its integrity was guaranteed; the sultan in turn promised to improve the status of his Christian subjects. Several principles of international law were adopted by the congress in the Declaration of Paris. The provisions of the treaty were altered (1878) by the Congress of Berlin. See C. D. Hazen et al., *Three Peace Congresses of the Nineteenth Century* (1917).

Paris, Declaration of, 1856, agreement concerning the rules of maritime warfare, issued at the Congress of Paris. It was the first major attempt to codify the international law of the sea. Conflicting methods used in dealing with property at sea had demonstrated the need for uniformity, while the respect paid to neutral rights in the Crimean War indicated that common principles of action would be accepted by the great powers. Four principles were enunciated by the declaration: PRIVATEERING would no longer be considered legal; a neutral flag would protect the goods of an enemy, except for CONTRABAND of war; neutral goods, with the exception of contraband of war, would not be liable to capture when under the enemy's flag; a BLOCKADE would be binding only if it prevented access to the coast of the enemy. At first the United States refused to accept the declaration, claiming that privateers were necessary if a nation did not have a strong navy. However, the United States accepted the declaration during the Civil War and the Spanish-American War. At the beginning of World War I prize courts recognized the declaration, but submarine warfare and extensive lists of contraband negated its principles. Part of its aims were restated in 1909 in the Declaration of London, but technological advances made many of its provisions inapplicable in 20th-century warfare.

Paris, Pact of: see KELLOGG-BRIAND PACT.

Paris, Treaty of, any of several important treaties, signed at or near Paris, France. The Treaty of Paris of Feb. 10, **1763,** was signed by Great Britain, France, and Spain; together with the treaty of HUBERTUSBURG, it terminated the SEVEN YEARS WAR. France lost its possessions on the North American continent by ceding Canada and all its territories E of the Mississippi to Great Britain, and by ceding W Louisiana to its ally, Spain, in compensation for Florida, which Spain yielded to Great Britain. France retained the islands of St. Pierre and Miquelon and recovered Guadeloupe and Martinique in the West Indies from Great Britain, in exchange for which it ceded Grenada and the Grenadines to the English. In East India, the French were permitted to return to their posts, but they were forbidden to maintain troops or build forts in Bengal; India thus virtually passed to Great Britain. In Africa, France yielded Senegal to Great Britain. Cuba and the Philippines were restored to Spain. In Europe, the French and Spanish returned Minorca to Great Britain, and France withdrew its troops from Germany. From this treaty dated the colonial and maritime supremacy of Great Britain. By the Treaty of Paris of Sept. 3, **1783,** Great Britain formally acknowledged the independence of the United States, and the warring European powers, Britain against France and Spain, with the Dutch as armed neutrals, effected a large-scale peace settlement. The preliminary Anglo-American articles (which went unchanged) were signed on Nov. 30, 1782, after months of tortuous negotiations, in which the chief American plenipotentiaries, John Adams, Benjamin Franklin, and John Jay, acquitted themselves so well that their achievement has been labeled "the greatest triumph in the history of American diplomacy." France and Spain signed separate preliminary articles with Great Britain on Jan. 20, 1783, and the Dutch and British signed theirs on Sept. 2, 1783. These preliminary agreements (except the Anglo-Dutch one, which was not ratified by both powers until June, 1784) were signed as definitive treaties on Sept. 3, 1783. The Anglo-American settlement fixed the boundaries of the United States. In the Northeast the line extended from the source of the St. Croix River due north to the highlands separating the rivers flowing to the Atlantic from those draining into the St. Lawrence River, thence with the highlands to lat. 45°N, and then along the 45th parallel to the St. Lawrence. From there the northern boundary followed a line midway through contiguous rivers and lakes (especially the Great Lakes) to the northwest corner of the Lake of the Woods, thence "due west" to the sources of the Mississippi (which were not then known). The Mississippi, south to lat. 31°N, was made the western boundary. On the south the line followed the 31st parallel E to the Chattahoochee River and its junction with the Flint River, then took a straight line to the mouth of the St. Marys River, and from there to the Atlantic. The navigation of the Mississippi was to be open to the citizens of both nations. Another section of the treaty granted Americans fishing rights off Newfoundland and the privilege of curing fish in the uninhabited parts of Labrador, Nova Scotia, and the Magdalen Islands, but not in Newfoundland. A third part provided that creditors of either side would be unimpeded in the collection of lawful debts. In a fourth section the American government promised to recommend to the several states that they repeal their confiscation laws, provide for restitution of confiscated property to British subjects, and take no further proceedings against the Loyalists. In the treaty with France, Britain relinquished the restrictions that had been imposed on the French naval port of Dunkirk, but aside from minor adjustments in the West Indies and Africa, the territorial dispositions made in the Treaty of Paris of 1763 were generally continued. Spain, however, in its treaty with Britain, reacquired the Floridas in America and the island of Minorca in the Mediterranean, while the British retained Gibraltar. The Treaty of Paris of May 30, **1814,** was concluded between France on the one hand and Great Britain, Russia, Austria, and Prussia on the other after the first abdication of Napoleon I. France was confined to its boundaries of 1792. No indemnity was exacted, and England returned all the French colonies save Tobago, St. Lucia, and Mauritius. Britain also kept Malta. A general conference was to be called for the territorial settlement in Europe (see VIENNA, CONGRESS OF). The leniency of the treaty to defeated France was chiefly due to the diplomatic skill of TALLEYRAND, who had engineered the restoration of Louis XVIII on the French throne. After Napoleon's return, his defeat at Waterloo, and his second abdication, a new peace treaty was signed at Paris on Nov. 20, **1815.** This treaty was much sterner than the first. France was reduced to the boundary of 1790, was required to pay 700 million francs in reparations, and was made to pay for the maintenance of an Allied army of occupation in NE France, which was to remain for a maximum of five years. All the provisions of the treaty of 1814 not expressly revoked were to remain binding, as was the Final Act of the Congress of Vienna. On the same day Great Britain, Russia, Austria, and Prussia renewed the QUADRUPLE ALLIANCE. For the Treaty of Paris of **1856,** see PARIS, CONGRESS OF. For the Treaty of Paris of **1898,** see SPANISH-AMERICAN WAR. After World War I several treaties were signed in 1919 and 1920 in or near Paris (see VERSAILLES, TREATY OF; SAINT-GERMAIN, TREATY OF; NEUILLY, TREATY OF; TRIANON, TREATY OF; SÈVRES, TREATY OF). Again, after World War II, peace treaties were signed in Paris in 1947 between the Allies and ITALY, RUMANIA, HUNGARY, BULGARIA, and FINLAND. Each treaty is a separate document.

Paris, University of, at Paris, France; founded 12th cent., confirmed 1215 by papal bull. It was suppressed during the French Revolution and replaced in 1808 by an academy of the Université Impériale. In 1890 it was reestablished as a university. In 1970 it was divided into 13 universities. The new universities are state institutions enjoying academic and financial autonomy, operated under the jurisdiction of the minister of education and financed by the state.

Paris green, also called Schweinfurt green, an extremely poisonous, bright green powder that was formerly used extensively as a pigment (e.g., in wallpaper) and that is sometimes used as an insecticide or to kill plant fungi; it must be used with great caution because of its poisonous nature. Chemically it is a copper acetoarsenite that may be prepared from arsenic trioxide and copper acetate.

Paris Pacts, four international agreements signed in Paris on Oct. 23, 1954, to establish a new international status for West Germany. Since the end of World War II, West Germany had been occupied by Allied forces and lacked its own means of defense. By 1950 fear of possible Soviet aggression in Europe had convinced many that West Germany should be rearmed. However, the prospect of a rearmed and once again powerful Germany caused adverse reactions in France. To prevent autonomous German power, France suggested (1951) the establishment of a European Defense Community (EDC) in which all the West European nations would combine their armies to form a unitary European force under joint command. Unstable political conditions in France, however, caused the plan for the EDC to be rejected by the French National Assembly in Aug., 1954. At a conference held in London in Sept.–Oct., 1954, the foreign ministers of Belgium, Canada, France, Great Britain, Italy, Luxembourg, the Netherlands, the United States, and West Germany reached agreement on an alternative to the EDC, and this plan was implemented by the four Paris treaties. The first treaty ended the occupation of West Germany and restored its full sovereignty, while providing for Allied troops to remain in the country. By the second agreement, the Brussels Treaty of 1948 was expanded to include West Germany and Italy, thereby creating the Western European Union (see INTERNATIONAL GOVERNMENTAL ORGANIZATIONS). Signed by the Brussels powers (Belgium, France, Great Britain, Luxembourg, and the Netherlands) and by West Germany and Italy, this agreement allowed West Germany to start upon a limited rearmament program, although it banned that nation's development of certain weapons, such as large warships and nuclear devices. In the third pact West Germany was accepted into the North Atlantic Treaty Organization (NATO) by a protocol signed by the 14 NATO members and West Germany. The fourth pact was a Franco-German agreement providing for a "European status" for the SAARLAND. This agreement, however, was rejected by the Saarlanders in a popular referendum, as a result of which the Saarland later became a West German state.

Paris Peace Conference, 1919: see VERSAILLES, TREATY OF.

parity or **space parity,** in physics, quantity that refers to the relationship between an object or process and the image that it can produce in a mirror. For example, any right-handed object will produce a mirror-image counterpart that is identical to it in every way except that the mirror image is left-handed. A moving particle that spins in a clockwise manner, as would a right-handed screw advancing through space, will possess a mirror-image particle that is identical to it in every way except that it spins counterclockwise, as would a left-handed screw advancing through space. The law of conservation of parity implies that every real object or process has a mirror image that can also exist and that obeys the same physical laws. Although this concept has little significance in classical physics, it is of great importance in atomic and nuclear physics. From this law scientists inferred that all ELEMENTARY PARTICLES and their interactions possessed mirror image counterparts that also exist. However, in 1956 C. N. Yang and T. D. Lee published a paper in which they argued that parity was not conserved in weak interactions. Their conjecture was verified the same year by C. S. Wu and co-workers at the U.S. National Bureau of Standards and other institutions in an experiment involving beta decay (see RADIOACTIVITY). Parity is still conserved in the strong nuclear interactions and in the electromagnetic interactions. Formally, parity, P, is a quantity that expresses the behavior of the wave function of any system of particles when the spatial coordinates x, y, z, of the wave function are reflected through the origin to $-x$, $-y$, $-z$ (see QUANTUM THEORY). This mathematical operation is called the parity, or space-inversion, operation. See also SYMMETRY.

Park, Mungo, 1771–1806, British explorer in Africa, b. Selkirk, Scotland. After serving as a surgeon with the East India Company, he was employed by the African Association to explore the course of the Niger River. Traveling NE from the Gambia River, he reached the Niger at Segu and proceeded 300 mi (483 km) upstream to Bamako. On his return to England he published *Travels in the Interior Districts of Africa* (1799). He was sent (1805) by the government to trace the Niger to its mouth, but at Bussa he and his party were attacked in their canoes by natives and Park was drowned. See Joseph Thomson, *Mungo Park and the River Niger* (1890, repr. 1970); S. L. Gwynn, *Mungo Park and the Quest of the Niger* (1934).

Park, Rosemary, 1907–, American educator, b. Andover, Mass., grad. Radcliffe (B.A., 1928; M.A., 1929), Univ. of Cologne (Ph.D., 1934). She was instructor in German (1930–32) and acting dean of freshmen (1934–35) at Wheaton College. From 1935 to 1947 she taught at Connecticut College, becoming professor in 1946, academic dean (1946–47), and president (1947–62). From 1962 to 1967 she was president of Barnard College. She was vice chancellor of the Univ. of California at Los Angeles from 1967 to 1970 and then professor of education there.

Park Chung Hee (pärk chŭng hē), 1917–, president (1963–) of the Republic of Korea (South Korea). Starting (1940) his military career in the Japanese army, he joined the new South Korean army after the establishment of Korean independence at the end of World War II and rose through the ranks. In 1961 he was a member of the military junta that overthrew the civilian government. He became chairman of the junta government and in 1963 was elected president. He was reelected in 1967 and again in 1971, having amended (1969) the constitution to allow himself a third successive term. Although his government made some economic progress, it became more dictatorial over the years. In 1972, Park declared martial law, allegedly to institute revitalizing reforms, and again altered the constitution to give himself almost unlimited power. Despite demands for democratic government, censorship, political repression, and torture of political prisoners increased. In Aug., 1974, Park's wife was killed during an assassination attempt against him.

Parker, Alton Brooks, 1852–1926, American jurist, U.S. presidential candidate (1904), b. Cortland, N.Y. He practiced law in Kingston, N.Y., and was (1877–85) surrogate of Ulster co., N.Y. He became important in state Democratic politics and successfully managed (1885) the campaign of David B. Hill for governor of New York. Parker served as justice of the New York supreme court (1885–89) and of the New York court of appeals (1889–92) before he was elected (1897) chief justice of the appellate division of the state supreme court. As a jurist he became noted for his liberal decisions in labor cases. He resigned as chief justice after receiving (1904) the Democratic party nomination for the U.S. presidency. Division within the party over the currency issue and the popularity of Theodore Roosevelt helped make Parker's defeat overwhelming. Returning to law practice, he defended the American Federation of Labor in the DANBURY HATTERS' CASE and served as counsel for the prosecution in the impeachment of Gov. William Sulzer.

Parker, Charlie "Bird" (Charles Christopher Parker, Jr.), 1920–55, American musician and composer, b. Kansas City, Kansas. He began playing alto saxophone in 1931, and after shifting from one band to another he met Dizzy Gillespie in New York City. They formed a quartet, which in 1945 made the first bop, or bebop, records and thus became the leaders of the bop movement in JAZZ. Parker's brilliant improvisations, noted for their power and beauty, soon earned the admiration of innumerable musicians. He composed several instrumental quartets and made many recordings. For many years Parker was addicted to drugs, which hastened his death. See biographies by Max Harrison (1961) and Ross Russell (1973).

Parker, Dorothy (Rothschild), 1893–1967, American short-story and verse writer, b. West End, N.J. While serving as drama critic for *Vanity Fair* (1916–17) and book critic for the *New Yorker* (1927), she gained an almost legendary reputation for her sardonic wit. Her first volume of poetry, *Enough Rope* (1926) brought her fame, and she followed it with such volumes as *Death and Taxes* (1931) and *Not So Deep as a Well* (1936). Although decidedly light and often flippant, Parker's satiric verse is carefully crafted and stunningly concise. Her short stories satirizing aspects of modern life are witty, wry, and often poignant. "Big Blond" is probably her best-known story. Collections of stories include *Laments for the Living* (1930) and *Here Lies* (1939). Her *Collected Stories* was published in 1942 and her *Collected Poetry* in 1944. She collaborated with Arnaud d'Usseau on the play *Ladies of the Corridor* (1953). See biography by John Keats (1970).

Parker, Francis Wayland, 1837–1902, American educator, b. Bedford, N.H. At the age of 16 he began his first job as a teacher in New Hampshire. After serving with the Union army in the Civil War, he returned to teaching and became head of a normal school in Dayton, Ohio. In 1872 he traveled to Germany to study the new methods of pedagogy being developed there, particularly those based on the theories of Johann HERBART. Upon his return to the United States (1875), Parker served for five years as superintendent of schools in Quincy, Mass. There he originated what came to be called the Quincy movement, emphasizing such elements of progressive education as group activities, the teaching of science, informal methods of instruction, and the elimination of rigid discipline. He extended these practices as a supervisor (1880–83) of schools in Boston, as principal (1883–99) of the Cook County Normal School, Chicago, and as founder and principal (1899–1901) of the Chicago Institute, which became part of the school of education of the Univ. of Chicago. His pioneering work led to improvements in curriculums and teacher training. See biographies by Ida C. Heffron (1934), Franklin Parker (1960), and J. K. Campbell (1967).

Parker, Sir Gilbert, 1862–1932, Canadian novelist, b. Ontario. His novels and collections of tales usually deal either with the history of Canada or with England and the empire. Among his works are *Pierre and His People* (1892), *The Seats of the Mighty* (1896), and *The Promised Land* (1928). He moved to England in 1889 and from 1900 to 1918 served in Parliament.

Parker, Horatio William, 1863–1919, American composer, b. Auburndale, Mass.; pupil of Rheinberger in Munich. He was an organist and choirmaster in Boston and New York City and taught at the National Conservatory, New York. In 1894, Parker became the first chairman of the music department at Yale, a position he held until his death. He composed for the stage, for orchestra, and for organ, but he is remembered as a writer of church music in the style of late German romanticism. See biography by his daughter, Isabelle Semler (1942, repr. 1973).

Parker, Sir Hyde, 1739–1807, British admiral. In the American Revolution he broke (1776) the defenses of the Hudson River at New York City—an exploit for which he was knighted in 1779. He later held commands in the Mediterranean, Jamaica, and the North Sea in the French Revolutionary and Napoleonic wars. Horatio NELSON was Parker's second in command at the great victory of Copenhagen (1801); his failure to observe Parker's signal to cease fighting is a famous incident in naval history. Nelson soon replaced Parker.

Parker, Isaac Charles, 1838–96, American frontier judge, b. Belmont co., Ohio. Self-taught in law, Parker began practice in St. Joseph, Mo., in 1859. He was elected to the U.S. House of Representatives in 1870 as a Republican. Parker was appointed (1875) judge of the western district of Arkansas, an unruly area that included in its jurisdiction the Indian Territory. He became known as a "hanging judge" because of the many death sentences he meted out. However, Parker's rigorous justice helped bring law and order to the area. See biographies by Fred Harrington (1951) and Homer Croy (1952); Glenn Shirley, *Law West of Fort Smith* (1957, repr. 1968).

Parker, Matthew, 1504–75, English prelate, archbishop of Canterbury. At Cambridge he was influenced by the writings of Martin Luther and other reformers. In 1535 he was appointed chaplain to Anne Boleyn and in 1537 to Henry VIII. In 1544, Parker became master of Corpus Christi College, Cambridge, to which he later left his fine collection of ancient manuscripts, and in 1545 he was made vice chancellor of Cambridge. Under Edward VI he was presented with the deanery of Lincoln, but after the accession of Mary I, who deprived him of his preferments, he lived in obscurity until he was called (1559) by Elizabeth I to the see of Canterbury. He courageously undertook the primate's responsibilities in a time of change and peculiar difficulty, sustaining a distinctly Anglican position between extreme Protestantism and Roman Catholicism. In 1562 he revised the Thirty-nine Articles. He supervised (1563–68) the preparation of the Bishops' Bible, published anonymously *De antiquitate Britannicae ecclesiae* (1572), and is also noted for his editions of the works of Matthew of Paris and other chroniclers. See biographies by John Strype (new ed., 3 vol., 1821, repr. 1973), E. C. Pearce (1925), E. W. Perry (1940), and V. J. K. Brook (1962).

Parker, Quanah, c.1852–1911, American Indian chief, b. Texas; son of a Comanche Indian chief, Peta Nocone, and Cynthia Ann Parker, a survivor of a massacre. In 1867 he became chief of the Comanche Indians and until 1875 led raids on frontier settlements. After his defeat and surrender he adjusted to the white civilization and promoted housing, agriculture, and education for Indians. A successful businessman in Oklahoma and Texas, he was believed at one time to be the wealthiest Indian in the United States. See. C. L. Jackson, *Quanah Parker, Last Chief of the Comanches* (1963).

Parker, Theodore, 1810–60, American theologian and social reformer, b. Lexington, Mass. He graduated from Harvard Divinity School in 1836 and was pastor (1837–46) of the Spring Street Unitarian Church, West Roxbury, Mass. The liberalism that he presented in Boston in 1841 and amplified in his scholarly *Discourse of Matters Pertaining to Religion* (1842) was then so radical that the Boston Unitarian clergy withdrew from him, although he remained a member of their association. He was one of the transcendentalists, contributed to the *Dial,* and edited (1847–50) the *Massachusetts Quarterly Review.* In 1845 he became preacher of the Twenty-eighth Congregational Society of Boston. His congregation grew to 7,000. In addition he lectured at lyceums throughout the country and was a leader in antislavery and other reform activities. In 1859 ill health forced him to retire, and he died in Florence. After his death Parker's works were widely read, and his once radical views gained acceptance. The best edition of his works is the Centenary (15 vol., 1907–13). See John Weiss, *The Life and Correspondence of Theodore Parker* (1864, repr. 1969); biographies by O. B. Frothingham (1874) and H. S. Commager (1936, repr. 1960); J. W. Chadwick, *Theodore Parker, Preacher and Reformer* (1900, repr. 1971); John E. Dirks, *The Critical Theology of Theodore Parker* (1948, repr. 1970).

Parker Dam, at the Ariz.-Calif. line, on the Colorado River; completed 1938. It is 320 ft (98 m) high and 856 ft (261 m) long. It impounds water for Los Angeles and other coastal cities, has a power plant (120,000-kw capacity), and supplies some water for irrigation. It also diverts water to Arizona.

Parkersburg, city (1970 pop. 44,208), seat of Wood co., NW W.Va., at the confluence of the Little Kanawha and the Ohio rivers; settled 1785, inc. 1820. An industrial and shipping center in a coal region, it has industries producing synthetic fibers, plastics, and glass. Two junior colleges are there. Nearby, in the Ohio River, is historic Blennerhassett Island.

Parkes, Sir Henry, 1815–96, Australian political leader, b. England. He emigrated to Australia in 1839 and later founded a newspaper, the *Empire,* to advocate responsible government and an end to the transporting of criminals to Australia. He served (1854–61) in the legislative council and then in the assembly of New South Wales. Returning (1863) from a two-year mission to England in the interests of immigration, he secured, as colonial secretary of New South Wales (1866–68), the passage of the first education act. From 1872 to 1891 he dominated provincial politics, serving several times as prime minister. Free trade, civil service reform, public works, and the federation of the Australian colonies were his constant concerns. See biography by C. E. Lyne (1897).

Parkes, town (1971 pop. 8,849), New South Wales, SE Australia. It is the site of a radiotelescope (opened 1961) capable of receiving radio waves from a distance of 1 billion light-years.

Parkes process: see SILVER.

Park Forest, village (1970 pop. 30,638), Cook and Will counties, NE Ill., a residential suburb of Chicago; inc. 1949.

Parkhurst, Charles Henry, 1842–1933, American clergyman and reformer, b. Framingham, Mass., grad. Amherst 1866, and studied theology at Halle and Leipzig. He was pastor of the Congregational Church at Lenox, Mass. (1874–80), and of the Madison Square Presbyterian Church, New York City (1880–1918). Becoming interested in municipal affairs and having been elected (1891) president of the Society for the Prevention of Crime, Parkhurst inaugurated a campaign against Tammany Hall, personally collecting evidences of corruption to substantiate his charges. The campaign led to the appointment of the Lexow committee to investigate conditions and to the defeat of Tammany and the election of a reform mayor in 1894. Parkhurst's writings include *Our Fight with Tammany* (1895, repr. 1970) and *My Forty Years in New York* (1923).

Parkinsonism, degenerative brain disorder first described by the English surgeon James Parkinson in 1817. Causes include head injury, encephalitis, syphilis, carbon monoxide poisoning, and cerebral arteriosclerosis. Sometimes there is no apparent cause; in such cases physicians call the condition Parkinson's disease. The disorder is also termed paralysis agitans, or shaking palsy. The typical Parkinson symptoms usually begin in middle to later life with trembling of the lips and hands, loss of facial expression, and muscular rigidity. As the malady progresses it may bring on body tremors, particularly in muscles at rest. Movements become slow and difficult. Walking degrades to a shuffle with arm swing lacking and back bent forward. After many years physical incapacity may occur, but Parkinsonism is not painful nor does it impair mental ability. Surgery can alleviate some tremors, and physical therapy may help mobility. Antihistamines, atropine sulfate, and the drug L-DOPA are useful in treatment.

Parkman, Francis, 1823–93, American historian, b. Boston. In 1846, Parkman started his journey along the Oregon Trail, both to improve his health and to study the Indians. He lived for a time with a band of Sioux and mixed freely with hunters, trappers, and other frontiersmen. On his return to Boston he collapsed physically and moved to Brattleboro, Vt. There Parkman dictated to his cousin *The Oregon Trail,* published in book form as *The California and Oregon Trail* (1849); the shorter title was resumed in later editions. His nervous affliction and his extreme weakness of sight made it necessary that books and manuscripts be read to him and that he take notes with the aid of a special wire frame. Despite this he labored on his *History of the Conspiracy of Pontiac* (1851). He grew worse for a time, and temporarily had to abandon his historical work. To keep himself occupied he wrote a novel, *Vassall Morton* (1856), which was not successful. Following a trip to Paris in 1858 to seek medical aid, he was for several years unable to continue his historical researches. He took up the study of horticulture and became an expert in the field, retaining his interest throughout his life; in 1866, *The Book of Roses* was published, and from 1871 to 1872 he was professor of horticulture at Harvard. His studies of the history of Canada and the early Northwest were eventually resumed, however, resulting in *Pioneers of France in the New World* (1865), *The Jesuits in North America in the Seventeenth Century* (1867), *The Discovery of the Great West* (1869; 11th and later editions pub. as *La Salle and the Discovery of the Great West*), *The Old Régime in Canada* (1874), *Count Frontenac and New France under Louis XIV* (1877), *Montcalm and Wolfe* (1884), and *A Half-Century of Conflict* (1892). Parkman served for a time as overseer of Harvard and later as a fellow of the Harvard Corp. (1875–88). He was a founder of the Archaeological Institute of America (1879) and was president of the Massachusetts Horticultural Society (1875–78). Despite the severe physical handicaps that beset him, Parkman's superior literary gifts, combined with his careful historical research, gained him wide contemporary prominence and established his name among the great historians of America. His work showed both anti-Catholic and antidemocratic prejudices, but it usually managed to combine accuracy and vigor of expression. There are several editions of Parkman's complete works. His journals were edited by Mason Wade (1947) and his letters by Wilbur R. Jacobs (1960). See biographies and studies by C. H. Farnham (1901, repr. 1969), H. O. Sedgwick (1904), Mason Wade (1942), O. A. Pease (1953, repr. 1968), and R. L. Gale (1974).

Park Range, part of the Rocky Mts., central Colo. and S Wyo., extending N from the Colorado River. Mt. Lincoln (14,284 ft/4,354 m) is the highest peak.

Park Ridge, city (1970 pop. 42,614), Cook co., NE Ill., a suburb adjacent to Chicago, on the Des Plaines River; inc. 1873. It is chiefly residential; several national and international corporations have their headquarters there. O'Hare International Airport is nearby.

Parkville, uninc. city (1970 pop. 33,897, including Carney), Baltimore co., N Md., a residential suburb of Baltimore.

parlement (pär'ləmənt, Fr. pärləmäN'), in French history, the chief judicial body under the *ancien régime.* Originally there was only the Parlement of Paris, which grew out of the feudal Curia Regis [king's court] and may be said to have had a separate existence from the reign of Louis IX (1226–70). Provincial parlements, similar in organization but less extensive in jurisdictional authority, were established from the 15th cent. onward. In 1789 there were, besides the Parlement of Paris, provincial parlements at Aix-en-Provence, Arras, Besançon, Bordeaux, Colmar, Dijon, Douai, Grenoble, Metz, Nancy, Pau, Rennes, Rouen, and Toulouse. The parlement consisted of a number of separate chambers: the central pleading chamber, called the *Grand-Chambre;* the *Chambre des Requêtes* (to deal with petitions) and the *Chambre des Enquêtes* (to handle inquests); the *Chambre de la Tournelle* (to settle criminal cases); and finally the *Chambre de l'Édit* (to process Huguenot affairs), which was active only in the 16th and 17th cent. Composed at first of bourgeois judges who obtained vacant seats by election or co-optation, the law courts increasingly became strongholds of an hereditary caste of magistrates. As early as the 14th cent. seats were bought, although the *premier président,* or parlement head, could only be a royal nominee. Despite several attempts to suppress venality, French monarchs, notably Louis XIV, actually encouraged the trend toward saleable judgeships and even attached titles of nobility to them in order to raise funds. At first the duties of the parlement were strictly judicial, but it gradually gained considerable political power through its function of registering all royal edicts and letters patent before they became law. The "right of remonstrance" empowered the parlement to point out any breach of monarchic tradition and thus provided a substantive check on capricious royal authority. The king, however, could force registration if he ordered a special *lettre de jussion* [peremptory order] or if he held a *lit de justice,* a solemn meeting of the parlement with the king in personal attendance. Moreover, the parlement lacked any right of political initiative. Its own moves were often dictated by the entrenched selfish interests of its almost exclusively noble members. From the late 16th cent. onward the parlements systematically opposed royal reform measures. They joined the FRONDE (1648–53), the abortive aristocratic revolution against Cardinal Mazarin. A century later in the parlements protests against a tax on all income from property, including offices such as judgeships, aroused such an uproar that the project eventually collapsed. In the decade after the conclusion (1763) of the Seven Years War, the continuance of wartime taxes was vigorously opposed by the parlements. Through his chancellor, René de MAUPEOU, Louis XV attempted to centralize political control by abolishing the parlements (1771) and substituting law courts that had no influence over policy. The new judicial system eliminated the sale of magistracies, judges becoming appointive salaried officials. After Louis XV's death (1774), however, Louis XVI pacified the privileged classes by restoring the old parlements. Thereafter clashes over taxation between the crown and the parlements gained momentum. In 1787 and 1788 the Parlement of Paris and the provincial parlements successfully opposed the fiscal reforms proposed by Archbishop LOMÉNIE DE BRIENNE to save France from bankruptcy; they claimed that only the three estates of the kingdom gathered in the States-General possessed the authority to pass on new taxes. In May, 1789, Louis

XVI finally summoned the States-General, a move that started the French Revolution. As bastions of reaction and privilege, the parlements were among the first institutions to be abolished in the early days of the Revolution. See J. H. Shennan, *The Parlement of Paris* (1968).

Parliament, legislative assembly of the United Kingdom of Great Britain and Northern Ireland. Over the centuries it has become more than a legislative body; it is the sovereign power of Great Britain, whereas the monarch remains sovereign in name only. Parliament consists, technically, of the monarch, the House of Commons, and the House of Lords, but the word in common usage refers to the members of the two houses or, more usually, to Commons alone. Parliament is housed in WESTMINSTER PALACE. The powers of the House of Lords have been negligible since 1911. The great power of the House of Commons lies, historically, in its control of government finances. The House of Lords is composed of the hereditary peers of the realm, life peers, 16 representative Scottish peers, and 26 Anglican prelates. Although there are about 1,000 eligible members, only a small fraction of that number choose to sit in the House. Commons is a democratically elected body of 635 members: 516 from England, 36 from Wales, 71 from Scotland, and 12 from Northern Ireland. The presiding officer is the speaker, who is elected by the members of the party in power. The prime minister must, by modern tradition, be a member of Commons; all other ministers of the CABINET may be from either house. The two-party system is a feature of British parliamentary government. The party elected to a majority chooses the prime minister—the executive head of government—and the minority party functions in Parliament as "Her Majesty's loyal Opposition." When the government party is unable to obtain a parliamentary majority on important issues, it is obliged to call a general election for a new Parliament. Elections are mandatory every five years, but the government may call for more frequent elections whenever it wishes. Unlike the U.S. system, there is no clear separation of legislative and executive branches of the government; the executive branch is, in effect, a committee of the legislature. The British Parliament has had great influence as a model for legislative bodies in other democratic countries.

The Origins of Parliament. There was no historical continuity between the Anglo-Saxon witenagemot and the British Parliament. In the 13th cent. occurred the first steps that were eventually to produce the modern institution through a long, slow process of evolution, working in many lines and drawing upon a variety of existing institutions and customs. The Curia Regis, the king's feudal council to which he summoned his tenants in chief, the great barons, and the great prelates, was the kernel from which Parliament and, more specifically, the House of Lords developed. The Curia Regis, more commonly called the great council, had merely quasi-legislative powers and was primarily a judicial and executive body. The development of the heritable right of certain barons (the peerage) to be summoned to the council, originally composed at the king's will, was not at all secure until the mid-14th cent., and even then was far from inviolable. The House of Commons originated in the 13th cent. in the occasional convocation of representatives of other social classes of the state—knights and burgesses—usually to report the "consent" of the counties and towns to taxes imposed by the king. Its meetings were often held in conjunction with a meeting of the great council, for the early 13th cent. recognized no constitutional difference between the two bodies; the formalization of Parliament as a distinct organ of government took at least another century to complete. During the Barons' War, Simon de MONTFORT summoned representatives of the counties, towns, and lesser clergy in an attempt to gain support from the middle classes. His famous Parliament of 1265 included two representative burgesses from each borough and four knights from each shire, admitted, at least theoretically, to full standing with the great council. Although Edward III's so-called Model Parliament of 1295 (which contained prelates, magnates, two knights from each county, two burgesses from each town, and representatives of the lower clergy) seemed to formalize a representative principle of composition, great irregularities of membership in fact continued well into the 14th cent. Nor did the division of Parliament into two houses coalesce until the 14th cent. Before the middle of the century the clerical representatives withdrew to their own convocations, leaving only two estates in Parliament (in contrast to the French States-General). The knights of the shires, who, as a minor landholding aristocracy, might have associated themselves with the great barons in the House of Lords, nevertheless felt their true interest to lie with the burgesses, and with the burgesses developed that corporate sense that marked the House of Commons by the end of the century.

The Growth of Parliamentary Sovereignty. The constitutional position of Parliament was at first undifferentiated from that of the great council. Large assemblies were called only occasionally, to support the king's requests for revenue and other important matters of policy, but not to legislate or "consent to taxation" in the modern sense. In the 14th cent., Parliament began to gain greater control over grants of revenue to the king. From Parliament's judicial authority (derived, through the Lords, from the judicial powers of the great council) to consider petitions for the redress of grievances and to submit such petitions to the king, developed the practice of withholding financial supplies until the king accepted and acted on the petitions. Statute legislation arose as the petition form was gradually replaced by the drafting of bills sent to the king and ultimately enacted by Commons, Lords, and king together. Impeachment of the king's ministers, another means for securing control over administrative policy, also derived from Parliament's judicial authority and was first used late in the 14th cent. In the 15th cent., through these devices, Parliament wielded wide administrative and legislative powers. In addition a strong self-consciousness on the part of its members led to claims of parliamentary "privilege," notably freedom from arrest and freedom of debate. With the growth of a stronger monarchy under the Yorkists and especially under the Tudors, Parliament became essentially an instrument of the monarch's will. The House of Lords with its chancellor and the House of Commons with its speaker appeared in their modern form in the 16th cent. The English Reformation greatly increased the powers of Parliament because it was through the nominal agency of Parliament that the Church of England was established. Yet throughout the Tudor period Parliament's legislative supremacy was challenged by the crown's legislative authority through the privy council, a descendant of part of the old feudal council. With the accession (1603) of the Stuart kings, inept in their dealings with Parliament after the wily Tudors, Parliament was able to exercise its claims, drawing on precedents established but not exploited over the preceding 200 years. In the course of the ENGLISH CIVIL WAR, Parliament voiced demands not only for collateral power but for actual sovereignty. Although under Oliver Cromwell and the Protectorate, parliamentary authority was reduced to a mere travesty, the Restoration brought Parliament back into power—secure in its claims to legislative supremacy, to full authority over taxation and expenditures, and to a voice in public policy through partial control (by impeachment) over the king's choice of ministers. Charles II set about learning to manage Parliament, rather than opposing or circumventing it. James II's refusal to do so led to the GLORIOUS REVOLUTION of 1688, which permanently affirmed parliamentary sovereignty and forced William III to accept great limitations on the powers of the crown. During the reign of Queen Anne even the royal veto on legislation disappeared.

The Ascendancy of Commons. Despite a general division into Whig and Tory parties toward the end of the 17th cent., political groupings in Parliament were more inclined to form about a particular personality or issue. Although members had considerable freedom to make temporary political alliances without regard to their constituencies, control over members was exercised by the ministry and the crown through patronage, which rested on the purchase of parliamentary seats and tight control over a narrow electorate. As members were paid no salaries, private wealth and liberal patronage were prerequisites to a seat in Commons; as a result, Parliament represented only the propertied upper classes, and private legislation took precedence over public acts throughout the 18th cent. The parliamentary skills of Sir Robert WALPOLE, in many respects the first prime minister, both signified and contributed to the growing importance of Commons. The crown retained the theoretical power to appoint a ministry of its choice, but the resignation (1782) of George III's minister Lord North established, once and for all, a tendency that had developed gradually since the Glorious Revolution—that the prime minister could not function without the support and confidence of the House of Commons. The complexion of Parliament changed rapidly after 1800. The union (1800) of Ireland and England dissolved the Irish Parliament and added to the British Parliament 100 Irish members, who functioned as an important political bloc throughout the 19th cent. With the appearance of powerful new classes created by the Industrial Revolution and with the currency of democratic doctrines grew demands for extension of suffrage, reform of flagrant abuses of patronage, and reorganization of the entire representative basis of Commons. The first step was achieved by the great REFORM BILL of 1832, followed by the Reform Bills of 1867 and 1884 and the eventual establishment of universal suffrage by the REPRESENTATION OF THE PEOPLE ACTS in the 20th cent. Parliamentary committees, appointed to investigate social conditions and recommend legislation, played an enlarged role. The tendency toward consolidation of parties was accelerated as public opinion became a factor in elections free from patronage. Although the Liberals and the Conservatives were known to stand for certain general policies, it was not until near the end of the 19th cent. that William E. Gladstone began the practice of making national campaign tours to pledge the party to a program for the coming Parliament. With the development of the party caucus, at about the same time, freedom of action by individual members was reduced. By the late 19th cent. members of working-class origin (later organized into the Labour party) were being elected to the House of Commons. Concomitantly, the class represented in the House of Lords began to lose power in the national social structure, and through long conflict with the Commons, particularly on matters of social legislation, the House of Lords itself was weakened. Commons was at first able to intimidate Lords by threatening the creation of enough new peers to override any opposition by the upper house. The contest over the financial bill of 1909 finally led Commons to a more drastic solution. The Parliament Act of 1911 stripped the House of Lords of its veto power on money bills, and on other bills provided that a measure should become law after being passed by Commons even if vetoed by Lords, if two years had elapsed from the time the bill was first introduced. The Parliament Act of 1949 reduced the period to one year. The 1911 act also provided for the payment of salaries to members, thus opening participation to representatives of all classes. Party discipline became increasingly strong as the 20th cent. progressed, to the extent that a member may be ejected from the parliamentary party if he does not vote the party line on specified issues. Long periods of service in Commons are now almost requisite in the climb to ministerial status. The rise of socialism in Great Britain after World War II did not greatly affect parliamentary structure, although increased delegation of important functions to civil service authorities reduced Parliament's immediate control of many governmental processes. See A. F. Pollard, *The Evolution of Parliament* (2d ed. 1926, repr. 1964); G. B. Adams, *Constitutional History of England* (rev. ed. 1935, repr. 1963); K. R. Mackenzie, *The English Parliament* (1950, repr. 1963); W. I. Jennings, *Parliament* (2d ed. 1957, repr. 1969); G. F. M. Campion, *An Introduction to the Procedure of the House of Commons* (3d ed. 1958); B. D. Lyon, *The Constitutional and Legal History of Medieval England* (1960); Ronald Butt, *The Powers of Parliament* (1967); E. B. Fryde and Edward Miller, ed., *Historical Studies of the English Parliament* (2 vol., 1970); G. D. Sayles, *The King's Parliament of England* (1974).

parliamentary law, rules under which deliberative bodies conduct their proceedings. In English-speaking countries these are based on the practice of the British Parliament, chiefly in the House of Commons. British parliamentary law is conventional, rather than statutory, including traditions and precedents as well as the Standing Orders of the House. Thomas Jefferson, when presiding over the U.S. Senate, prepared a manual of parliamentary law based on the practice of the House of Commons, and this practice has generally been followed in the House of Representatives as well. *Robert's Rules of Order,* first compiled by Henry Martyn ROBERT in 1876 and drawn from the usages of all three bodies, is the usually accepted authority on parliamentary law in the United States. Parliamentary law includes the rules necessary for the efficient and equitable conduct of business by an assembly. In Britain the effective interpreter of parliamentary law is the speaker of the House of Commons; in the United States the role is shared by the speaker of the House and the president of the Senate, who are partisan figures, unlike their British counterpart. See H. A. Bosmajian, ed., *Readings in Parliamentary Procedure* (1968); H. E. Hellman, *Parliamentary Procedure* (1968).

Parma, Alessandro Farnese, duca di: see FARNESE, ALESSANDRO.

Parma (pär'mä), city (1971 pop. 174,655), capital of Parma prov., in Emilia-Romagna, N Italy, on the Parma River and on the Aemilian Way. It is an agricultural market and an industrial center. Manufactures include textiles, watches, footwear, and fertilizer. Parmesan cheese is also produced. Parma was the site of a Roman colony (founded 183 B.C.) and became a free commune by the 12th cent. It later was ruled by outside powers (particularly Milan and France) and in 1513 was added to the Papal States by Pope Julius II. In 1545, Pope Paul III created the duchy of Parma and Piacenza, a substantial territory, and bestowed it on his son, Pier Luigi Farnese, whose descendants ruled it (with interruptions) until 1731. The duchy then passed, through the female line, to the Spanish Bourbons; the cadet line of Bourbon-Parma began in 1748. It was displaced in 1802, when Napoleon I annexed the duchy to France. The Congress of Vienna (1814–15) awarded it to Marie Louise, who ruled it from 1816 to 1847; it was then restored to the Bourbons. In 1860 the duchy was incorporated into the kingdom of Sardinia. The Parma school of painting flourished there in the 16th cent.; its leading artists were Correggio (who executed frescoes for the Convent of St. Paul and for the Romanesque cathedral) and Parmigiano. Points of interest in the city include an octagonal Romanesque baptistry (13th cent.); the garden palace (1560); and the Palazzo della Pilotta (1583–1622; damaged in World War II), which contains the National Museum of Antiquities, the National Gallery, and the Farnese Theatre. Parma was a center of learning in the Middle Ages and has a university.

Parma, city (1970 pop. 100,216), Cuyahoga co., NE Ohio, a suburb of Cleveland; settled 1816, inc. 1924. It is chiefly residential, but there is a large industrial research center. A junior college is in the city.

Parma Heights, city (1970 pop. 27,192), Cuyahoga co., NE Ohio, a residential suburb of Cleveland; settled 1818, set off from Parma and inc. 1912. It is surrounded on three sides by Parma, and the two cities share the same school system and other municipal facilities.

Parmashta (pärmăsh'tə), one of Haman's sons. Esther 9.9.

Parmenas (pär'mĕnəs), one of the seven deacons. He is said to have died a martyr at Philippi. Acts 6.5.

Parmenides (pärmĕn'ĭdēz), b. c.515 B.C., Greek philosopher of Elea, leading figure of the ELEATIC SCHOOL. Parmenides' great contribution to philosophy was the method of reasoned proof for assertions. Parmenides began his argument with the assertion that being is the material substance of which the universe is composed and argued that it was the sole and eternal reality. With this as a premise he proceeded to destroy by his dialectic argument the possibility of generation, destruction, change, and motion. All change and motion are illusions of the senses. Since being is spatially extended and is all that exists, there is no empty space, and motion is therefore impossible. Only fragments of his work have survived. See *Parmenides* (text, tr., commentary, and critical essays by Leonardo Tarán, 1965); study by A. P. Mourelatos (1970).

Parmenion (pärmē'nēən), d. 330 B.C., Macedonian general. He served under PHILIP II. On Philip's death Parmenion was largely responsible for the adherence of the army in Asia to ALEXANDER THE GREAT. He and the young king were warm friends, and at Issus and Gaugamela in Asia Minor, Parmenion commanded the left wing while Alexander himself led the right. When Alexander was pushing eastward in Persia, he left Parmenion to govern Media (now in Iran). While the king was in Drangiana (330 B.C.), a treason plot was discovered that seemed to implicate Philotas, Parmenion's son. Despite his innocence in this affair, Parmenion was killed at Alexander's command.

Parmesan cheese (pär'məzən, -zôn"), very hard, sharp-flavored, skim-milk cheese. Originally made in the area around Parma, Italy, it is now produced elsewhere in Italy and in other parts of the world. Most often used grated, it is an important ingredient in Italian cooking.

Parmigiano (pärmējä'nō) or **Parmigianino** (-jänē'nō), 1503–40, Italian painter and etcher, one of the most sensitive mannerist artists. His real name was Francesco Mazzola. The name Parmigiano is derived from his birthplace, Parma. His early paintings show the pervasive influence of Correggio. These include *The Marriage of St. Catherine* (Parma Gall.) and the frescoes in San Giovanni Evangelista. He was in Rome for a few years, but had to flee during the sack of the city in 1527. He went to Bologna where he painted an altarpiece, *Madonna and Child with St. Margaret and Other Saints.* One of his most curious works is a painting of himself seen in the distorted reflection of a convex mirror (Vienna). In 1531 he returned to Parma and spent the last years of his life painting frescoes in Santa Maria della Steccata. His style is noted for its remarkable grace and sensuality and for his elongated figures. Among his important works are the *Vision of St. Jerome* (National Gall., London); *Madonna dal Collo Lungo* (Pitti Palace, Florence); and the *Legend of Diane and Acteon* (Rocca di Fontanellato, near Parma). He was one of the first artists to use the technique of etching. Through this medium, his style became influential in Italy and N Europe. See A. E. Popham, *Catalogue of the Drawings of Parmigianino* (3 vol., 1971); study by Sydney Freedberg (1950, repr. 1971).

Parnach (pär'năk), Zebulunite. Num. 34.25.

Parnaíba (pərnīē'bə), river c.800 mi (1,290 km) long, rising in the highlands of NE Brazil. It flows generally north, forming the boundary between Maranhão and Piauí states, and enters the Atlantic Ocean through a delta near the town of Parnaíba, which is the shipping center for the valley; Teresina is the chief upstream city. The river is filled with rapids.

Parnassians (pärnăs'ēənz), group of 19th-century French poets, so called from their journal the *Parnasse contemporain.* Issued from 1866 to 1876, it included poems of Leconte de Lisle, Banville, Sully-Prudhomme, Verlaine, and J. M. de Heredia (1842–1905). The Parnassians were influenced by Théophile GAUTIER and his doctrine of art for art's sake. In reaction to the looser forms of romantic poetry, they strove for exact and faultless workmanship, selecting exotic and classical subjects which they treated with rigidity of form and emotional detachment.

Parnassós (pärnəsôs'), mountain, c.8,060 ft (2,460 m) high, Phocis, central Greece. In ancient Greece it was sacred to Apollo, Dionysus, and the Muses. The fountain of Castalia was on its slopes; at the foot of the mountain lay Delphi. Corycian Cave is located between Delphi and the summit. Bauxite is mined on the slopes.

Parnell, Charles Stewart (pär'nəl, pärnĕl'), 1846–91, Irish nationalist leader. The son of a Protestant landowner, he attached himself to the HOME RULE movement of Isaac Butt and was elected to the British Parliament in 1875. He quickly developed an obstructionist policy in Parliament, where his filibusters gave the Irish contingent a prominence far beyond its numbers. Although these tactics lost him the approval of Butt, they brought him the support of the militant FENIAN MOVEMENT. Joining the Fenians in their agitation against the Irish land laws, Parnell became president of the National Land League (see IRISH LAND QUESTION) in 1879. He encouraged the use of the boycott as a means of bringing pressure on the landlords and their agents, but the agitation also produced much violence, and the harsh Coercion Bill of 1881 was passed (over Parnell's opposition) to check it. In 1881, Parnell started *United Ireland,* a paper in support of the Land League, edited by William O'BRIEN. Arrested for his activities and put in Kilmainham jail, Parnell directed O'Brien to compose a manifesto against rent payment. Parnell's popularity increased, and he came to be referred to as the "uncrowned king of Ireland." He was released (1882) by the so-called Kilmainham treaty, by which the government agreed to settle the question of arrears in land rent if Parnell would help check violence against landlords. The PHOENIX PARK MURDERS of 1882 shocked Parnell as much as they did the English, but the Irish leader opposed the coercive Crimes Act that followed and was therefore charged with encouraging terrorism. Nonetheless, he retained the confidence of his followers both in Ireland and in America, where the fact that he was a grandson of the American naval hero Charles Stewart added to his appeal. In 1885 the Liberals' threat to renew the Crimes Act of 1882 led Parnell to throw the Irish vote to the Tories and thus bring down the government of William GLADSTONE. It was, however, an uncomfortable alliance, and in 1886 Parnell swung back to the Liberals, who returned to power. Gladstone then introduced in Parliament the first Home Rule Bill (1886), but the Liberal party split on the issue, and Gladstone's government fell again. In 1887, the London *Times* printed a series of hostile articles called "Parnellism and Crime," ending with a facsimile letter, purporting to carry Parnell's signature and apologizing for his denunciation of the Phoenix Park murders. A special commission found (1889) that the letter had been forged; and, although some of Parnell's activities were censured, he and his associates were exonerated. In 1889, Parnell was named as correspondent in a divorce suit brought by one of Parnell's colleagues, Captain O'Shea, against his wife, Katharine. Adultery was proved, the divorce granted (1890), and in 1891, Parnell married Katharine. The episode ruined his political influence; he was denounced both by the English liberals and by the Roman Catholic hierarchy in Ireland, and the Irish nationalists split into Parnellites and anti-Parnellites. His efforts to reunite the party failed and broke his health. Haughty and sensitive, Parnell was only a mediocre orator. Nevertheless, he possessed a marked personal fascination and was a shrewd political and parliamentary tactician. He succeeded in uniting the moderate and militant Irish nationalists in the drive for land reform and Home Rule and brought the Irish question to the forefront in British politics. See biographies by R. B. O'Brien (2 vol., 1898, repr. 1968), St. John Ervine (1925), and William O'Brien (1926); studies by C. C. O'Brien (1954, rev. ed. 1957), F. S. L. Lyons (1960), Jules Abels (1966), and Michael Hurst (1968).

Parnell, Thomas, 1679–1718, Irish poet, b. Dublin. Educated at Trinity College, Dublin, he was archdeacon of Clogher from 1706. He was a friend of Pope and Swift and a member of the Scriblerus Club. His poems, published posthumously by Pope, include "The Night-Piece on Death" and "Hymn to Contentment." He also wrote the introductory essay to Pope's *Iliad.*

Parnu (pär'nōō), Ger. *Pernau,* city (1967 est. pop. 42,000), W European USSR, in Estonia, on the Gulf of Riga. A seaport, it exports timber and flax and is also a beach and health resort. It was founded c.1250 by the Livonian Knights and became a city of the Hanseatic League. After the dissolution (1561) of the Livonian Order it was contested by Sweden, Russia, and Poland. Peter I of Russia took it from the Swedes in 1710, and its cession was confirmed by Sweden in 1721. Parnu was incorporated into newly independent Estonia in 1918. It is called Pyarnu in Russian.

parochial school (pərō'kēəl), school supported by a church. In the United States such schools are maintained by a number of denominations, including Lutherans and Seventh-Day Adventists, but the most numerous are those attached to Roman Catholic parishes. The Catholic parochial school system developed in the 19th cent. as a response to what was then seen as Protestant domination of the public school system in the United States. A group of American bishops met in the Third Plenary Council of Baltimore (1884) to plan for the establishment of a comprehensive parochial school system. Local churches were directed to establish elementary schools for the education of the parish children. In time a number of secondary, or high, schools, supported by a diocese and encompassing a number of parish schools, were also established. Both the elementary and secondary schools developed a religious curriculum emphasizing Catholic doctrine along with a secular curriculum very similar to that of the public schools. During the middle of the 20th cent., much of parochial education's traditional structure began to change. The ecumenical spirit generated by the Second Vatican Council (1962–65) convinced many Roman Catholics that the religious education of the parochial school was somewhat too separatist. Moreover, parochial schools suffered from the criticism that public schools provided a better secular education at less cost. Because of such criticisms, parochial schools were forced to hire lay teachers. Although the overwhelming majority of parochial school teachers were traditionally members of religious orders, laymen came to account for an increasingly larger proportion of the faculty (40% in 1970). But whereas those in orders usually receive little more than subsistence for their services, lay teachers generally demand salary parity with their public school counterparts. The result has been severe financial problems for many Roman Catholic schools. In the five-year period from 1965 to 1969 approximately 900 parish schools were closed; in the same period, the Catholic school population dropped by half a million. Although parochial schools still account for the bulk of the attendance at private schools in the United States, their loss of students and their financial difficulties have forced them to seek aid from public sources. Opponents of such aid, however, maintain that government financial assistance to any religious institution is unconstitutional. On the Federal level the problem has been dealt with by the "child-benefit theory." Under that form of compromise, aid is dispensed to the students of parochial schools, rather than to the schools themselves; the constitutional provision against aid to religious institutions is thereby circumvented. See Neil McCluskey, *Catholic Education Faces Its Future* (1968); Russell Shaw and Richard Hurley, eds., *Trends and Issues in Catholic Education* (1969); Harold Buetow, *Of Singular Benefit: The Story of U.S. Catholic Education* (1970).

parody, mocking imitation in verse or prose of a literary work. The following poem by Robert Southey was parodied by Lewis Carroll:

"You are old, Father William," the young man cried;
"The few locks which are left you are gray;
You are hale, Father William—a hearty old man;
Now tell me the reason, I pray."
"In the days of my youth," Father William replied;
"I remembered that youth would fly fast,
And abused not my health and my vigor at first,
That I never might need them at last."
Southey, "The Old Man's Comforts and how he gained them"

"You are old, Father William," the young man said,
"And your hair has turned very white,
And yet you incessantly stand on your head—
Do you think at your age it is right?"
"In my youth," Father William replied to his son,
"I feared it might injure the brain;
But now that I'm perfectly sure I have none,
Why I do it again and again."
Carroll, "Father William"

Parodies have existed since literature began. Aristophanes brilliantly parodied the plays of Euripides; Cervantes's *Don Quixote* (1605–15) parodies chivalric romances; Henry Fielding's novel *Joseph Andrews* (1742) parodies Samuel Richardson's moral novel *Pamela* (1740); and Max Beerbohm's *A Christmas Garland* (1912) wickedly parodies such authors as Kipling, Conrad, and Henry James. Noted 20th-century parodists include Ogden Nash, S. J. Perelman, Robert Benchley, James Thurber, E. B. White, and Woody Allen.

parole (pərōl'), in criminal law, release from prison of a convict before the expiration of his term on condition that his activities be restricted and that he report regularly to an officer. The convict generally remains under sentence, and the restrictions (as of residence, occupation, type of associates) and the supervision are intended to prevent a relapse into crime. Any violation of parole may result in return to imprisonment. The procedure of parole is regulated by statute in the jurisdictions of the United States. It is less often administered directly by the executive than it is by a board or officer with the power to release a convict after he has served the minimum of an indeterminate SENTENCE. Parole is designed to give the prisoner a chance to readjust and to expedite the process of rehabilitation. In military law, a parole is the promise by a prisoner of war on being released from confinement that he will remain in a stipulated place, not attempt to escape, and not take up arms again in the current hostilities against the forces that captured him. See David Dressler, *Practice and Theory of Probation and Parole* (1959).

Paropamisus (pâr"əpăm'ĭsəs, -pəmī'səs), mountain range, N Afghanistan, stretching c.300 mi (480 km) W from the Hindu Kush toward the Elburz mts. in Iran; rises to c.11,000 ft (3,350 m). Silver and lead crystal deposits are found there. The MURGAB and Hari Rud rivers rise in the Paropamisus, which is also called Safid Kuh.

Páros (pä'rôs, pâr'ŏs), island (1971 pop. 6,776), c.81 sq mi (210 sq km), SE Greece, in the Aegean Sea; one of the CYCLADES. The main town is Páros (1971 pop. 1,955). The land slopes to the coast from Mt. Hagios Ilias (c.2,500 ft/760 m high). Wine, tobacco, figs, and grains are produced on the island. The beautiful white, semitransparent Parian marble, used by sculptors and architects as early as the 6th cent. B.C., is quarried on the mountain. Páros was settled by Ionians and became a maritime power and a center of Aegean trade. In the 7th cent. B.C. it established colonies in THÁSOS and on the Sea of Marmara. During the Persian Wars, Athens accused Páros of aiding the Persians and captured the island in 479 B.C. Páros was held by the Ottoman Turks from 1537 to 1832, when it joined Greece. Two marble fragments of a great historical inscription, called the Parian Chronicle, have been found on the island. The chronicle was set up after 263 B.C., its terminal date. The larger fragment (covering 1581–354 B.C.) is one of the Arundel Marbles, housed at Oxford, England; the smaller (covering 356–299 B.C.) is in a museum on Páros.

Parosh (pā'rŏsh), ancestor of a Jewish family. Ezra 2.3; 10.25; Neh. 3.25; 7.8; 10.14. Pharosh: Ezra 8.3.

parotid glands: see SALIVARY GLANDS.

Parow (părou'), town (1970 pop. 60,146), Cape Prov., SW South Africa, near Cape Town. It is an industrial center whose manufactures include printed materials, processed timber, and metal goods.

Parr, Catherine, 1512–48, sixth queen consort of Henry VIII of England. She was the daughter of Sir Thomas Parr, an officeholder at the court, and had been twice widowed before Henry made her his wife in 1543. She exerted a beneficent influence over the aging king, interceding in behalf of Henry's daughters, Mary and Elizabeth (whom she helped to educate), and served for a time as queen regent (1544). At one point Catherine's Protestant sympathies placed her in danger, but she lived to become queen dowager and to wield considerable power at the start of the reign of Henry's son, Edward VI. She married (1547) Baron SEYMOUR OF SUDELEY but died in childbirth the next year. See biography by Anthony Martienssen (1974).

Parr, Thomas, 1483?–1635, English centenarian, known as Old Parr. His birth date is unauthenticated, and the chief sources of information about him are a pamphlet by the poet John Taylor entitled *The Olde, Olde, Very Olde Man* (1635) and an account by the distinguished physician William Harvey, who examined him after his death in London. Thomas Howard, 2d earl of Arundel, had brought Parr from Parr's native Shropshire to present him to Charles I, and according to Harvey, the old man died from the effects of change of climate. The alleged 152-year-old was buried in Westminster Abbey.

Parra, Nicanor (nĕkänōr' pä'rä), 1914–, Chilean poet. A poet who is also a professor of mathematics and physics, his works are influenced by existential philosophy. Notes of humor and satire mitigate the disillusion and anguish expressed in his poetry. His works include *Cancionero sin nombre* [poetry without name] (1937), *Poemas y antipoemas* (1954; tr. *Poems and Antipoems*, 1967), *Versos de salón* [parlor verses] (1962), *Canciones rusas* [Russian songs] (1967), and *Emergency Poems* (tr. 1972).

parrakeet: see PARAKEET.

Parral: see HIDALGO DEL PARRAL, Mexico.

Parramatta (pâr"əmăt'ə), city (1971 pop. 110,717), New South Wales, SE Australia, a suburb of Sydney, on the Parramatta River. It has an automobile parts industry. Founded in 1788, it is the second oldest settlement in Australia.

Parras de la Fuente (pä'räs dā lä fwān'tā), city (1970 pop. 32,664), Coahuila state, N Mexico. It is a road and rail junction located in a well-watered valley of a semiarid region. Parras, an agricultural center, has orchards and vineyards that make the city famous for wines and brandies. Cattle raising and cotton and flour milling are also important. In 1846, during the Mexican War, Parras was held by U.S. troops. French forces were defeated there (1866) in the French intervention.

Parrhasius (pərā'shēəs), fl. c.400 B.C., Greek painter. He was born in Ephesus but settled in Athens and is classed with the Attic painters. One of the greatest painters of Greece, a contemporary and rival of Zeuxis, he is credited by ancient writers with having been the first painter to attain perfect symmetry and correct proportions in his figures. Among the most celebrated of his numerous works were an allegorical painting, *Demos,* personifying the Athenian democracy, and *Theseus.* All his works have perished and are known only through descriptions by classical writers.

Parrington, Vernon Louis, 1871–1929, American scholar, b. Aurora, Ill. Professor of English at the Univ. of Washington (1908–29), he is famous for his economic interpretation of American literature, *Main Currents in American Thought* (3 vol., 1927–30), which had a great influence on subsequent literary criticism. He was awarded (1928) a Pulitzer Prize in history for the first two volumes. See Richard Hofstadter, *Progressive Historians* (1968).

Parrish, Maxfield, 1870–1966, American painter and illustrator, b. Philadelphia; pupil of Howard Pyle. He is known for his original and highly decorative posters, magazine covers, and book illustrations and for his murals, including decorations for the building of the Curtis Publishing Company in Philadelphia. His glowing colors, especially the blues, are characteristic. He illustrated Washington Irving's *"Knickerbocker" History of New York,* Eugene Field's *Poems of Childhood, The Arabian Nights,* Kenneth Grahame's *Golden Age* and *Dream Days,* and many other volumes. See biographies by P. W. Sheeter (1973) and Coy Ludwig (1973).

Parris Island: see SEA ISLANDS.

parrot, common name for members of the order Psittaciformes, comprising 315 species of colorful birds, pantropical in distribution, including the PARAKEET. Parrots have large heads and short necks, strong feet with two toes in front and two in back (facilitating climbing and grasping), and strong, thick bills, with the larger hooked upper mandible hinged to the bones of the head. They are arboreal, feeding on seeds and fruits—except the kea (*Nestor notabilis*) of New Zealand, which is a scavenger in winter. Although they belong to a different order, parrots have certain affinities to pigeons and cuckoos; like them, they feed their young by regurgitation, and they have swellings (ceres) at the base of the nostrils. Usually their voices are harsh, but the thick, fleshy tongue and special voice apparatus permit a wide range of articulations, and some species can be taught to imitate the human voice. The best mimics are the African gray parrots, *Psittacus erithacus,* and the Amazons, genus *Amazona.* In size parrots range from the 3½-in. (8.7-cm) pygmy parrot of the South Pacific to the 40-in. (100-cm) Amazon of South America, while in build they vary from the stocky lovebirds, e.g., the masked lovebird (*Agapornis personata*), to the slender lories, e.g., the black-capped lory (*Lorius domicella*) and the cockatoo. Their plumage is brilliant, the bodies solid green, yellow, red, white, or black with contrasting red, yellow, or blue on the head, wings, and tail. The cockatoos, crested parrots native to the Australian region, may be pink, white with yellow or scarlet crests, or dark-plumaged, like the great black, or palm, cockatoo, *Probosciger aterrimus.* They eat insects and are also able to crack extremely hard nuts. The smaller cockateels are gray with yellow heads. The large, long-tailed macaws are found in the rain forests of Central and South America. The species are named for their gaudy colors, e.g., the scarlet (*Ara macao*), gold-and-blue (*A. ararauna*), and red-and-green macaws. In captivity adult macaws may be vicious. In the wild they travel in pairs. The small Old World parrots known as lovebirds are so named for the apparent fondness of the mates for one another. The Australasian lory and smaller lorikeet (*Trichoglossus haematodus*) feed on fruits and nectar. Parrots are long-lived, and many are popular as cage birds. Care should be exercised, however, by selecting birds with known histories, since even apparently healthy birds may be carriers of infectious PSITTACOSIS, or parrot fever. Parrots are classified in the phylum CHORDATA, subphylum Vertebrata, class Aves, order Psittaciformes, family Psittacidae. See study by J. M. Corshaw (1973).

parrot fever: see PSITTACOSIS.

parrotfish, common name for a member of the large family Scaridae, colorful reef fishes of warm seas, resembling the WRASSES but of a larger size. Parrotfishes, also called pollyfishes, are so named for their powerful cutting-edged beaks, formed of fused incisorlike jaw teeth. With these they scrape from the surface of coral, algae, polyps, and other small plant and animal life upon which they feed. Parrotfishes also have a set of grinding teeth, located in the throat in front of the esophagus, with which they further break up their food to prepare it for the action of digestive enzymes. Common in Florida waters are the rainbow parrotfish, *Scarus guacamaia,* the largest (up to 3 ft/91 cm) of the family; the red and blue parrotfishes; and the oldwife. Parrotfishes are not valued in the United States as food except in Hawaii, where they are very popular and were once taboo (to be touched only by royalty). Parrotfishes occasionally cause a nervous reaction in humans, fatal to a small percentage of consumers; such fish poisoning (see CIGUATERA) is inexplicably caused by over 300 other species. Parrotfishes are classified in the phylum CHORDATA, subphylum Vertebrata, class Osteichthyes, order Perciformes, family Scaridae.

Parrot's Beak, region of SE Cambodia indenting S South Vietnam. During the Vietnam War, it was a staging ground for Communist forces against the Saigon government. In April, 1970, U.S. and South Vietnamese forces entered the region in an effort to destroy the sanctuary.

Parrsboro, town (1971 pop. 1,807), N N.S., Canada, a port on the north shore of Minas Basin of the Bay of Fundy. It is an export point for lumber and plywood.

Parry, Sir William Edward (pă'rē), 1790–1855, British arctic explorer and rear admiral. He entered the navy at 13 and made his first voyage to the Arctic under Sir John Ross in 1818 in search of the NORTHWEST PASSAGE. He was then put in command of the *Hecla* and the *Griper* in an expedition (1819–20) to hunt for the passage. F. W. Beechey was a member of the party. Parry sailed westward through Lancaster Sound and discovered and named Melville Island and others of the Parry Islands, as well as naming Barrow Strait. Two other unsuccessful attempts were made (1821–23, 1824–25) to find the Northwest Passage, in the course of which FURY AND HECLA STRAIT was discovered and new information about the arctic regions was disclosed. By discovering the entrance to the passage and the way to the north magnetic pole, Parry had also found important whaling grounds. In 1827 he made an attempt to reach the North Pole by sledge from Spitsbergen, attaining lat. 82° 45′ N, but was forced to turn back mainly by the fatigue of his exploring party. He published three journals describing his quest for the passage as well as a narrative of his attempt to reach the pole.

Parry Islands: see QUEEN ELIZABETH ISLANDS, Canada.

Parry Sound, town (1971 pop. 5,842), S Ont., Canada, on Parry Sound, an inlet of Georgian Bay of Lake Huron. It is an active port and the center of a popular vacation area.

Pars, ancient province, Iran: see FARS.

parsec (pär'sĕc) [*par*allax + *sec*ond], in astronomy, basic unit of length for measuring interstellar and intergalactic distances, equal to 206,265 times the distance from the earth to the sun, 3.26 light-years, or 3.08 × 10^{13} km (about 19 million million mi). The distance in parsecs of an object from the earth is the reciprocal of the PARALLAX of the object. The nearest star, Proxima Centauri, has a parallax of 0.″763 of arc and a distance of about 1.31 parsecs.

Parsees: see PARSIS.

Parshandatha (pärshăn'dəthə), one of Haman's sons. Esther 9.7.

Parsifal (pär'sĭfäl), figure of ARTHURIAN LEGEND also known as Sir Percivale, who is in turn a later form of a hero of Celtic myth. The name originally occurs as Pryderi, an alternative name of Gwry in *Pwyll Prince of Dyved,* a tale in the MABINOGION. Gwry is the original of Gawain, and in the later Percivale stories Gawain appears, often fulfilling the same role as the hero. The great feature of the Percivale cycle is the Holy GRAIL, and Welsh sources connect this sacred talisman with Percivale, who finds the Grail. CHRÉTIEN DE TROYES is the author of the first great artistic treatment of the theme; in Chrétien's unfinished poem Percivale finds the Grail at the Fisher King's castle and heals the king. The *Parzival* of WOLFRAM VON ESCHENBACH is one of the greatest medieval poems. Drawn largely from Chrétien, von Eschenbach's story is highly spiritualized and appears essentially in the form used by Richard Wagner in his music drama *Parsifal.* In the *Morte d'Arthur* of Sir Thomas MALORY, Percivale is admitted to the Grail with Galahad and Bors. See R. S. Loomis, *Arthurian Tradition & Chrétien de Troyes* (1949) and *Arthurian Literature in the Middle Ages* (1959).

Parsis or **Parsees** (both: pär'sēz, pärsēz'), religious community of India, practicing ZOROASTRIANISM. The Parsis (numbering about 120,000) are concentrated in Maharashtra and Gujarat states, especially in Bombay. Their ancestors migrated from Iran in the 8th cent. to avoid Muslim persecution. They use the ancient Pahlavi scriptures and are faithful to much of the Zoroastrian dogma. The Parsis deny the frequent assertion that they worship fire; rather they reverence fire (along with other aspects of nature) as manifestations of the divinity of Ahura Mazdah. To avoid contaminating fire, earth, or water, the Parsis dispose of their dead by exposing the bodies in "towers of silence" (circular structures some 20 ft/6 m high surrounding a stone courtyard) where vultures devour them. The community is closely unified, and schools established by the wealthier members make the Parsis one of the best-educated groups of India. Their economic importance is far greater than their small numbers would indicate. The huge Tata industrial empire bears the name of one of India's most famous Parsi families.

parsley, Mediterranean aromatic herb (*Petroselinum sativa* or *Apium petroselinum*) of the family Umbelliferae (CARROT family), cultivated since the days of the Romans for its foliage, used in cookery as a seasoning and garnish. In ancient times parsley was also used for chaplets and as a funeral decoration. Hamburg parsley is a variety grown for its edible root. Parsley is widely cultivated throughout the United States, chiefly in Louisiana. Parsley is classified in the division MAGNOLIOPHYTA, class Magnoliopsida, order Umbellales, family Umbelliferae.

Parsnip, river, c.150 mi (240 km) long, rising in central British Columbia, Canada, and flowing northwest to join the Finlay River at Williston Lake and form the Peace River. Discovered by Sir Alexander Mackenzie in 1793, it became, with the Peace River, an important fur-trade route.

parsnip, garden plant (*Pastinaca sativa*) of the family Umbelliferae (CARROT family), native to the Old World. It has been cultivated since Roman times for its long, fleshy, edible root. Wine and beer have also been made from it. The wild form has become naturalized in North America, often proving a bad pest. Parsnip is a biennial but is cultivated as an annual. The root can be left in the ground all winter without deterioration. It is also used as livestock feed. Parsnip is classified in the division MAGNOLIOPHYTA, class Magnoliopsida, order Umbellales, family Umbelliferae.

Parsons, Sir Charles Algernon, 1854–1931, British engineer. He invented a revolutionary steam turbine that bears his name. His first turbines were constructed to drive generators to produce electricity. In 1897, Parsons constructed the *Turbinia,* the first vessel to be propelled by turbines. The ship's amazing speed immediately claimed attention and led to the construction of many turbine-propelled warships for the British navy. Parsons also invented a device for improving phonographs, pioneered in aviation, and produced a nonskid device for automobile tires.

Parsons, Robert: see PERSONS, ROBERT.

Parsons, Talcott, 1902–, American sociologist, b. Colorado Springs, Colo., educated at Amherst College (B.A., 1924), London School of Economics, and Univ. of Heidelberg (Ph.D., 1927). He was on the faculty at Harvard from 1927 until his retirement in 1974. The work that brought him international renown was his attempt to construct a single theoretical framework within which general and specific characteristics of societies could be systematically classified; it is known as structural-functional theory. Among his writings are *The Structure of Social Action* (1937), *The Social System* (1951), *Structure and Process in Modern Societies* (1960), *Social Structure and Personality* (1964), *Societies* (1966), *Sociological Theory and Modern Society* (1967), and *Politics and Social Structure* (1969). See studies by W. C. Mitchell (1967) and Herman Turk and R. L. Simpson, ed. (1971).

Parsons, Theophilus, 1750–1813, American jurist, b. Byfield, Mass. One of the leading lawyers in New England, he was an outstanding member of the ESSEX JUNTO, which opposed (1778) the state constitution as framed by the legislature. As a delegate to the subsequent state constitutional convention (1780) he helped to frame a new constitution. A supporter of the Constitution of the United States, he urged its ratification by Massachusetts (1788). He was chief justice of Massachusetts from 1806 until his death. His son **Theophilus Parsons,** 1797–1882, also a lawyer, was born in Newburyport, Mass. A professor of law at Harvard, he wrote many law manuals. He was converted to Swedenborgianism and wrote several religious works.

Parsons, William: see ROSSE, WILLIAM PARSONS, 3D EARL OF.

Parsons, city (1970 pop. 13,015), Labette co., SE Kansas; inc. 1871. It is a shipping point for dairy products, grain, and livestock. There are various manufacturing industries. A junior college is there.

Partch, Harry, 1901–74, American composer, b. Oakland, Calif. Partch was a highly individualistic, largely self-taught composer. He developed a theory of "corporeal" music based on "harmonized spoken words," exemplified in works such as *Account of the Normandy Invasion by an American Glider Pilot.* The piece is based on a recording of the pilot's recollections. Partch also wrote music based on newsboy cries and hobo experiences. Another of his innovations was the division of the octave into a 43-note scale. He designed and built instruments to play music composed from this scale. Partch wrote several stage works, including, in 1952, music for William Butler Yeats's adaptation of Sophocles' *Oedipus.*

parthenogenesis (pär"thənōjĕn'əsĭs) [Gr.,=virgin birth], in biology, a form of reproduction in which the ovum develops into a new individual without fertilization. Natural parthenogenesis has been observed in many lower animals (it is characteristic of the rotifers), especially insects, e.g., the APHID. In many social insects, such as the honeybee and the ant, the unfertilized eggs give rise to the male drones and the fertilized eggs to the female workers and queens. The phenomenon of parthenogenesis was discovered in the 18th cent. by Charles Bonnet. In 1900, Jacques Loeb accomplished the first clear case of artificial parthenogenesis when he pricked unfertilized frog eggs with a needle and found that in some cases normal embryonic development ensued. Artificial parthenogenesis has since been achieved in almost all major groups of animals, although it usually results in incomplete and abnormal development. Numerous mechanical and chemical agents have been used to stimulate unfertilized eggs. In 1936, Gregory Pincus induced parthenogenesis in mammalian (rabbit) eggs by temperature change and chemical agents. No successful experiments with human parthenogenesis have been reported. The phenomenon is rarer among plants (where it is called parthenocarpy) than among animals. The existence of this process in so many forms suggests that all the factors necessary for early embryonic development are present in the ovum and that the sperm serves only to activate or initiate embryonic growth.

Parthenon (pär'thənŏn) [Gr.,=the virgin's place], temple sacred to Athena, on the ACROPOLIS at Athens. Built under Pericles between 447 B.C. and 432 B.C., it is the culminating masterpiece of Greek architecture. ICTINUS and CALLICRATES were the architects and PHIDIAS supervised the sculpture. The temple is peripteral, with 8 Doric columns at each end and 17 on the flanks (46 in all); it stands upon a stylobate three steps high. The body of the building comprised a cella and behind it an inner chamber (the Parthenon proper), which gave the temple its name. At front and rear, within the outer colonnade, were two porticoes, the pronaos and opisthodomos, respectively, with six columns each. Within the cella a Doric colonnade two tiers high supported the roof timbers and divided the space into a lofty central nave bounded by an aisle on three sides. Toward the west end of this nave stood the *Athena Parthenos,* the colossal gold and ivory statue by Phidias dedicated c.438 and destroyed in antiquity. The inner chamber, to the west, apparently served as treasury and was entered through a large western doorway. The pediments terminating the roof at each end of the building were ornamented with sculptured groups depicting the birth of Athena on the eastern end and the contest between Athena and Poseidon on the western end. The upper part of the cella walls and the friezes above the porticoes formed a continuous band of sculpture around the building, representing the Panathenaic procession held every fourth year in homage to the goddess. Of the 525 ft (160 m) of this sculptured frieze, 335 ft (102 m) still exists. The western portion is still in place; the greater part of the remainder, removed by Lord Elgin, is in the British Museum (see ELGIN MARBLES). In the 6th cent. the Parthenon became a Christian church, with the addition of an apse at the east end. It next served as a mosque, and a minaret was added to it. In 1687, in the Venetian attack on Athens, it was used as a powder magazine by the Turks and the entire center portion was destroyed by an explosion. The beauty of the Parthenon began to be appreciated in the 18th cent., and in 1762 measured drawings by James Stuart and Nicholas Revett gave strong impetus to the CLASSIC REVIVAL. After the end of Turkish control (1830), intensive archaeological study of the Parthenon commenced. Numerous attempts have since been made to establish the mathematical or geometrical basis supposedly employed in producing the design's high perfection. Restoration work is still being done. See studies by P. E. Corbett (1959) and R. Carpenter (1970).

Parthenopaeus (pär"thənōpē'əs): see SEVEN AGAINST THEBES.

Parthenopean Republic (pär"thənōpē'ən) [from *Parthenope,* an ancient name of Naples], state set up in Naples in Jan., 1799, by the French Revolutionary army under General CHAMPIONNET and by liberal Neapolitans after the flight of King Ferdinand IV (later FERDINAND I of the Two Sicilies). In 1798, Ferdinand had joined the Second Coalition against the French Revolution (see FRENCH REVOLUTIONARY WARS). His army was unable to halt the French, and Naples was conquered. In February, Cardinal Ruffo, at the head of royalist troops, landed in Calabria and attempted to oust the French. Military reverses in N Italy prompted the evacuation by the French of Naples in May, and in June the republic fell. Admiral Horatio NELSON, whose role in the victory was crucial, ignored Cardinal Ruffo's generous convention with the surrendering revolutionists and started the brutal reprisals that were continued by the restored king.

Parthia (pär'thēə), ancient country of Asia, SE of the Caspian Sea. In its narrowest limits it consisted of a mountainous region intersected with fertile valleys, lying S of Hyrcania and corresponding roughly to the modern Persian province of Khurasan. It was included in the Assyrian and Persian empires, the Macedonian empire of Alexander the Great, and the Syrian empire. The Parthians, mentioned in Acts 2.9, were famous horsemen and archers and may have been of Scythian stock. In 250 B. C., led by Arsaces, they freed themselves from the rule of the Seleucidae and founded the Parthian empire. At its height, in the 1st cent. B.C., this empire extended from the Euphrates across Afghanistan to the Indus and from the Oxus to the Indian Ocean. Defeating Marcus Licinius Crassus in 53 B.C., the Parthians threatened Syria and Asia Minor, but they were turned back by Ventidius in 39-38 B.C. Then began the decline of the empire, which in A.D. 226 was conquered by Ardashir I (Artaxerxes), the founder of the Persian dynasty of the Sassanidae. The chief Parthian cities were Ecbatana, Seleucia, Ctesiphon, and Hecatompylos. Such expressions as "a Parthian shot" were suggested by the Parthian ruse in which mounted men used their arrows effectively while in simulated flight. See N. C. Debevoise, *A Political History of Parthia* (1938, repr. 1968); P. B. Lozinski, *The Original Homeland of the Parthians* (1959); M. A. R. Colledge, *The Parthians* (1967).

particle accelerator, apparatus used in nuclear physics to produce beams of energetic charged particles and to direct them against various targets. Such machines, popularly called atom smashers, are needed to penetrate the atomic NUCLEUS in studies of its structure and of the forces that hold it together. Besides pure research, accelerators have practical applications in medicine and industry, most notably in the production of radioisotopes. There are many types of accelerator designs, although all have certain features in common. Only charged particles (most commonly protons and electrons; less often deuterons, alpha particles, and heavy ions) can be artificially accelerated; therefore, the first stage of any accelerator is an ION source to produce the charged particles from a neutral gas. All accelerators use electric fields (steady, alternating, or induced) to speed up particles; most use magnetic fields to contain and focus the beam. In linear

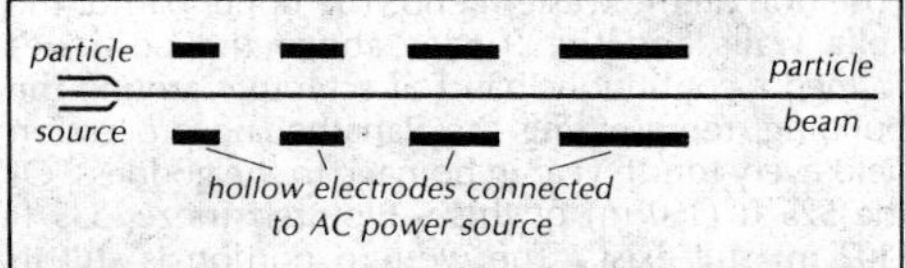

Linear accelerator (LINAC)

accelerators the particle path is a straight line; in other machines, of which the cyclotron is the prototype, a magnetic field is used to bend the particles in a circular or spiral path. The early linear accelerators used high voltage to produce high-energy particles; a large static electric charge was built up, which produced an electric field along the length of an evacuated tube, and the particles acquired energy as they moved through the electric field. The Cockcroft-Walton accelerator produced high voltage by charging a bank of capacitors in parallel and then connecting them in series, thereby adding up their separate voltages. The Van de Graaff accelerator achieved the high voltage by using a continuously recharged moving belt to deliver charge to a high-voltage terminal consisting of a hollow metal sphere. Today these two electrostatic machines are used in low-energy studies of nuclear structure and in the injection of particles into larger, more powerful machines. Linear accelerators can be used to produce higher energies, but this requires increasing their length. In order to reach high energy without prohibitively long paths, E. O. Lawrence proposed (1932) that particles could be accelerated to high energies in a small space by making them travel in a circular or nearly circular path. In the cyclotron, which he invented, a cylindrical magnet bends the particle trajectories into a circular path whose radius depends on the mass of the particles, their velocity, and the strength of the magnetic field. The particles are accelerated within a hollow, circular, metal box that is split in half to form two sections, each in the shape of the capital letter *D*. A radio-frequency electric field is impressed across the gap between the *D*'s so that every time a particle crosses the gap, the polarity of the *D*'s is reversed and the particle gets an accelerating "kick." The key to the simplicity of the cyclotron is that the period of revolution of a particle remains the same as the radius of the path increases because of the increase in velocity. Thus, the alternating electric field stays in step with the

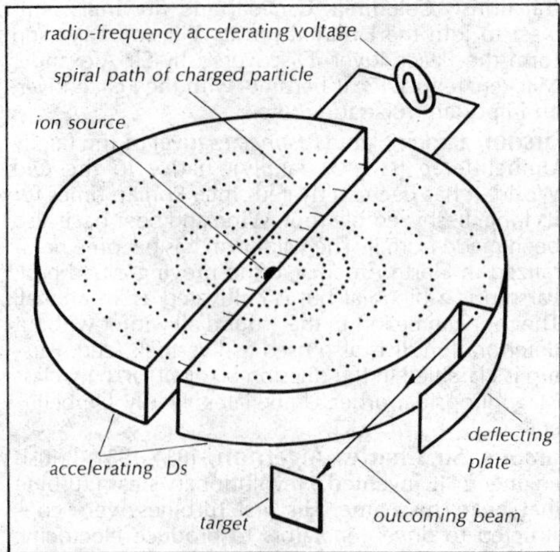

Cyclotron: As the charged particles move faster, they spiral out to the edge of the Ds.

particles as they spiral outward from the center of the cyclotron to its circumference. However, according to the theory of relativity the mass of a particle increases as its velocity approaches the speed of light; hence, very energetic, high-velocity particles will have greater mass and thus less acceleration, with the result that they will not remain in step with the field. For protons, the maximum energy attainable with an ordinary cyclotron is about 10 million electron-volts—in nuclear physics energies are commonly measured in millions (MEV) or billions (BEV) of ELECTRON-VOLTS (EV). Two approaches exist for exceeding the relativistic limit for cyclotrons. In the synchrocyclotron, the frequency of the accelerating electric field steadily decreases to match the decreasing angular velocity of the protons. In the isochronous cyclotron, the magnet is constructed so the magnetic field is stronger near the circumference than at the center, thus compensating for the mass increase and maintaining a constant frequency of revolution. The first synchrocyclotron, built at the Univ. of California at Berkeley in 1946, reached energies high enough to create PIONS, thus inaugurating the laboratory study of the MESON family of ELEMENTARY PARTICLES. Further progress in physics required energies in the BEV range, which led to the development of the synchrotron. In this device, a ring of magnets surrounds a doughnut-shaped vacuum tank. The magnetic field rises in step with the proton velocities, thus keeping them moving in a circle of nearly constant radius, instead of the widening spiral of the cyclotron. The entire center section of the magnet is eliminated, making it possible to build rings with diameters measured in miles. Particles must be injected into a synchrotron from another accelerator. The first proton synchrotron was the cosmotron at Brookhaven (N.Y.) National Laboratory, which began operation in 1952 and eventually attained an energy of 3 BEV. The 6.2-BEV synchrotron (the bevatron) at the Lawrence Radiation Laboratory, Univ. of California at Berkeley, was used to discover the antiproton (see ANTIPARTICLE). The 500-BEV synchrotron at the Fermi National Accelerator Laboratory at Batavia, Ill., was the most powerful accelerator in the world as of 1973. The synchrotron can be used to accelerate electrons but is inefficient. An electron moves much faster than a proton of the same energy and hence loses much more energy in SYNCHROTRON RADIATION. A circular machine used to accelerate electrons is the betatron, invented by Donald Kerst in 1939. Electrons are injected into a doughnut-shaped vacuum chamber that surrounds a magnetic field. The magnetic field is steadily increased, inducing a tangential electric field that accelerates the electrons (see ELECTROMAGNETIC INDUCTION). Linear accelerators, in which there is very little radiation loss, are the most powerful and efficient electron accelerators; the largest of these, the Stanford Univ. linear accelerator (SLAC), completed in 1957, is 2 mi (3.2 km) long and produces 20-BEV electrons. New linear machines differ from earlier electrostatic machines in that they use electric fields alternating at radio frequencies to accelerate the particles, instead of using high voltage. The acceleration tube has segments that are charged alternately positive and negative. When a group of particles passes through the tube, it is repelled by the segment it has left and is attracted by the segment it is approaching. Thus the final energy is attained by a series of pushes and pulls. Recently, linear accelerators have been used to accelerate heavy ions such as carbon, neon, and nitrogen. Other recent developments are the meson factories and the clashing-beams accelerators. A meson factory (the largest is at the Los Alamos, N. Mex., Scientific Laboratory) operates at conventional energies, usually below 1 BEV, but produces much more intense beams than previous accelerators; this makes it possible to repeat early experiments much more accurately. A clashing-beams machine is really a double accelerator that causes two separate beams to collide, either head-on or at a grazing angle. Because of relativistic effects, producing the same reactions with a conventional accelerator would require a single beam hitting a stationary target with much more than twice the energy of either of the colliding beams. A majority of the world's particle accelerators are situated in the United States, either at major universities or national laboratories. In Europe the principal facility is the European Center for Nuclear Research (CERN) in Geneva, Switzerland; in the Soviet Union important installations exist at Dubna and Serpukhov.

particle board: see COMPOSITION BOARD.

particle detector: see DETECTOR, in physics.

particles, elementary: see ELEMENTARY PARTICLES.

part of speech, in traditional English GRAMMAR, any one of about eight major classes of words, based on the parts of speech of ancient Greek and Latin. The parts of speech are NOUN, VERB, ADJECTIVE, ADVERB, INTERJECTION, PREPOSITION, CONJUNCTION, and PRONOUN. Some grammarians add articles and numerals. These word classes have traditional definitions in grammar books, i.e., "a noun is the name of a person, place, or thing" without reference to grammatical function. By this strict definition the word *toy* would be a noun in the sentence "The toy is under the tree" and in the sentence "It is a toy dog." However, an alternate method of defining parts of speech is in terms of the structural features and distribution patterns within a sentence. Thus *toy* would constitute a different part of speech in each of the above sentences since the word functions in different environments in each sentence, i.e., as a subject and as a modifier. Some English parts of speech (nouns, verbs, etc.) are productive classes allowing new members; others, with functional rather than lexical meaning (prepositions, articles, conjunctions) are nonproductive, having a limited number of members. See also INFLECTION. See Leonard Bloomfield, *Language* (1933); Charles Fries, *The Structure of English* (1952); W. Nelson Francis, *The Structure of American English* (1958); Otto Jespersen, *The Philosophy of Grammar* (1965); F. R. Palmer, *Grammar* (1971).

Parton, James, 1822-91, American biographer, b. England. He came to the United States in 1827. In 1848 he joined the staff of N. P. Willis's *Home Journal* in New York City. In 1856 he married Sara Payson Willis, also a writer. His biographical writing began with the very successful *Life of Horace Greeley* (1855) and was followed by biographies of Aaron Burr (1857), Andrew Jackson (1859-60), John Jacob Astor (1865), and others.

Partridge, Sir Bernard, 1861-1945, English caricaturist and illustrator. He was principal cartoonist for *Punch* from 1891 until his death. Partridge began his career by designing stained glass and painting watercolors, but he is best known as an illustrator.

partridge, common name applied to various henlike birds of several families. The true partridges of the Old World are members of the pheasant family (Phasianidae); the common European or Hungarian species has been successfully introduced in parts of North America. In some areas of the United States the name partridge is applied to the ruffed GROUSE, the BOBWHITE, and the plumed QUAIL; in Europe the South American tinamou is called a partridge. The gray partridge, *Perdix perdix*, is an Old World bird of about 1 to 1½ ft (30-45 cm). True partridges are classified in the phylum CHORDATA, subphylum Vertebrata, class Aves, order Galliformes, family Phasianidae.

partridgeberry: see MADDER.

Parts of Holland: see LINCOLNSHIRE.

Parts of Kesteven: see LINCOLNSHIRE.

Parts of Lindsey: see LINCOLNSHIRE.

party, political, organization whose aim is to gain control of the government apparatus, usually through the election of its candidates to public office. Political parties take many forms, but their main functions are similar: to supply personnel for government positions; to organize these personnel around the formation and implementation of public policy; and to serve in a mediating role between individuals and their government. Political parties are as old as organized political systems. For example, many of the ancient Greek city-states had organized, competitive parties. Political parties have been organized for various reasons: to support a particular political figure, to advance a particular policy or a general ideological stand, to aid politically certain groups or sections of society, or merely to combine for short-term political advantage. Political parties have also been organized in various ways; in some, control is exercised by a small central elite, either elected or self-perpetuating, while in others, power is decentralized, with candidate picking and decision making spread among local party units. The modern mass political party has taken shape in the last century, along with the rise of democratic ideology, universal suffrage, nationalism, and more effective means of communication. Such a party is commonly categorized by the type of party system in which it operates. In a noncompetitive or one-party system, the party is often employed as part of the governing apparatus, with the functions of maintaining public support for the regime, encouraging popular participation in government programs, and alerting the government to changes in public opinion. In competitive systems, a distinction may be made between two-party systems, which seem to encourage a party strategy of moderation and compromise aimed at obtaining a majority vote, and multiparty systems, where there is less compromise and where a party's strategy emphasizes retaining the support of its core voters. In general, however, the structure and behavior of a particular country's political parties depends most heavily on the country's political and cultural history. See V. O. Key, *Politics, Parties and Pressure Groups* (5th ed. 1964); Joseph LaPalombara and Myron Weiner, *Political Parties and Political Development* (1966); Maurice Duverger, *Political Parties* (3d ed. 1967); S. M. Lipset and Stein Rokkan, ed., *Party Systems and Voter Alignments* (1967); L. D. Epstein, *Political Parties in Western Democracies* (1967).

Paruah (păr'yo͞oə, păryo͞o'ə), father of one of Solomon's stewards. 1 Kings 4.17.

Parvaim (pärvā'ĭm), unknown region whence came gold for the Temple. 2 Chron. 3.6.

Pasach (pā'săk), Asherite chief. 1 Chron. 7.33.

Pasadena (păs''ədē'nə). **1** City (1970 pop. 112,981), Los Angeles co., S Calif., at the base of the San Gabriel Mts.; inc. 1866. Among the city's many manufactures are cosmetics, electronic equipment and systems, ceramics, plastics, and aircraft and missile components. Pasadena is the scene of the annual Tournament of Roses and of the postseason college football game held (Jan. 1) in the famous Rose Bowl (seating 100,000 spectators). The city is also the seat of the California Institute of Technology (with its noted NASA jet propulsion laboratory), Pasadena College, Pacific Oaks College, and a junior college. It has a symphony orchestra, a community playhouse, the Huntington Library and Art Gallery, four museums, and several gardens noted for their rare flora. Mt. Wilson and Mt. Lowe observatories are nearby. **2** City (1970 pop. 89,277), Harris co., S Texas, on the Houston ship channel; inc. 1928. It is an industrial suburb of Houston located in a highly productive oil area. The city has oil refineries, chemical plants, iron and steel works, paper and grain mills, food-processing establishments, and factories making oil field equipment, machinery and tools, building materials, paint, and clothing. The Lyndon B. Johnson Manned Space Center is just south, on Clear Lake. The city was founded (1895) and named for Pasadena, California. The site was very near the old San Jacinto battlefield (April, 1836); the San Jacinto Monument (built 1936–39; 570 ft/174 m high) commemorates the event. Also of interest is the U.S.S. *Texas,* moored at the battleground. The city has a junior college and holds an annual rodeo.

pasan: see GOAT.

Pasargadae (pəsär'gədē), capital of ancient Persia under Cyrus the Great. Its ruins lie 54 mi (87 km) by road NE of Persepolis, in present Iran. The buildings of Cyrus include a temple in the form of a tower; the remains of his palace; and his tomb, a structure of white stone 18 ft (5.5 m) high, on a massive base. According to Greek historians, Alexander the Great found Cyrus' tomb already rifled, and he sealed its entrance. The tomb has long since been reopened. The Muslims attribute the ruins to Solomon. The name also appears as Parsagarda.

Pascagoula (păskəgo͞o'lə), city (1970 pop. 27,264), seat of Jackson co., extreme SE Miss. A port of entry on Mississippi Sound at the mouth of the Pascagoula River, it is a resort and a fishing and shipbuilding center, with paper mills, an oil refinery, and factories producing chemicals and pet foods. It grew around the "Old Spanish Fort," built in 1718 and still extant. Large quantities of lumber were shipped in the late 19th cent. A junior college is in nearby Gautier.

Pascal, Blaise (blĕz päskäl'), 1623–62, French scientist and religious philosopher. Studying under the direction of his father, a civil servant, Pascal showed great precocity, especially in mathematics and science. Before he was 16 he wrote a paper on conic sections which won the respect of the mathematicians of Paris; at 19 he invented a calculating machine. Credited with founding the modern theory of probability, Pascal also discovered the properties of the cycloid and contributed to the advance of differential calculus. In physics his experiments increased knowledge of atmospheric pressure through barometric measurements and of the equilibrium of fluids (see PASCAL'S LAW). As a young man, Pascal came under the influence of Jansenism, and in 1651 his sister Jacqueline, who had also embraced Jansenist beliefs, entered the convent at Port-Royal, the center of the movement. As a result of the death of his father and of his own narrow escape from death, Pascal turned much of his attention to religion. When Antoine Arnauld, a noted Jansenist, was attacked by the Jesuits, Pascal championed him in his *Lettre escrite à un provincial* (1656). Those *Provincial Letters,* rendered into Latin, quickly circulated throughout Europe, and they still hold a leading place in the literature of polite irony. Pascal's religious writings were posthumously published as *Pensées de M. Pascal sur la religion et sur quelques autres sujets* (1670). For a modern edition see *Thoughts: An Apology for Christianity* (tr. 1955). In the *Pensées,* famous both as a religious and philosophical classic, Pascal states his belief in the inadequacy of reason to solve man's difficulties or to satisfy his hopes. He preached instead the final necessity of mystic faith for true understanding of the universe and its meaning to man. See biography by Jean Mesnard (tr. 1969); studies by F. T. Fletcher (1954), J. H. Broome (1966), Émile Cailliet (1944; repr. 1973), and Roger Hazelton (1974).

Pascal's law [for Blaise Pascal], states that pressure applied to a confined fluid at any point is transmitted undiminished throughout the fluid in all directions and acts upon every part of the confining vessel at right angles to its interior surfaces and equally upon equal areas. Practical applications of the law are seen in hydraulic machines.

Paschal II (păs'kəl) [Lat.,=of Easter], d. 1118, pope (1099–1118), an Italian (b. near Ravenna) named Ranieri; successor of Urban II. He was a Cluniac monk and, as a reformer, was made a cardinal by Pope Gregory VII. He was a loyal supporter of Urban II as well. His reign began auspiciously. Philip I of France was reconciled with the church (1104), St. Anselm was victor in his struggle in England, and the First Crusade was a great success. Difficulties with the Holy Roman emperor were continual, however, chiefly over the question of INVESTITURE. HENRY IV was deposed by his son HENRY V, with whom Paschal was allied. Henry V, however, proved no less strongly anti-investiture. He invaded Italy in 1110; negotiations between emperor and pope failed, and the emperor captured Paschal, who was compelled to surrender the papal position on investitures. Once freed, however, and encouraged by clerical protests, the pope reaffirmed the legislation against lay investiture in 1112 and 1116. The name is also spelled Pascal. He was succeeded by Gelasius II.

Paschen series (pä'shən): see SPECTRUM.

Pascin, Jules (zhül päskăN'), 1885–1930, American painter, b. Bulgaria. Born Julius Pincas, he moved to Paris in 1905. He acquired American citizenship in 1914. Essentially a draftsman, belonging to no one school, he portrayed, with flickering line and opalescent tone, the heavy sensuality of his female models. *Young Woman in Red* (1924; Musée d'Art Moderne, Paris) is characteristic. Pascin was a colorful and generous character in bohemian Parisian society. Two years after he returned to Paris he committed suicide. See his sketchbook, ed. by J. P. Leeper (1964); biography by Alfred Werner (1962); study by Gaston Diehl (1968).

Pasco, city (1970 pop. 13,920), seat of Franklin co., SE Wash., on the Columbia River near its confluence with the Snake and Yakima rivers. It is a trade and shipping center for the Columbia basin project; its industries manufacture paper, container board, and machine parts. Pasco was an early railroad division point. With Kennewick and Richland it forms a tri-city area that grew during World War II, when the Atomic Energy Commission's Hanford Works were constructed nearby. The completion (1956) of the McNary Dam extended Columbia River navigation to the mouth of the Snake River, thus making Pasco an inland port. A junior college is in the city.

Pascoli, Giovanni (jōvän'nē pä'skōlē), 1855–1912, Italian poet. Pascoli's childhood was marked by a series of tragedies: the deaths of his parents and of five of his brothers and sisters. A radical in his student days at the Univ. of Bologna, he was subdued by imprisonment (1879) for his political activities. After completing his studies he taught classics, succeeding Giosuè Carducci as professor of literature at Bologna in 1905. His tender poetry, written in pastoral style, won him international fame; many verses were inspired by memories of his family. Also seeing his mission as the chronicling of Italy's glory, he wrote of historical and patriotic subjects, earning D'Annunzio's epithet "the last son of Vergil." His works include *Carmina* (in Latin, 1914); the more mystical *Myricae* (1891–1903); and the patriotic *Odi e inni* (1906). Pascoli remains one of Italy's best-loved poets. He was also an essayist of distinction. See translations of his poems by A. M. Abbott (1927) and G. S. Purkis (1938, text ed. 1958).

Pas-dammim, varient of EPHES-DAMMIM.

Pas-de-Calais (pä-də-kālā'), department (1968 pop. 1,397,159), N France, on the Strait of Dover. ARRAS is the capital.

Pas-de-Calais: see DOVER, STRAIT OF.

Paseah (pəsē'ə). **1** Name in an obscure genealogy. 1 Chron. 4.12. **2** Family returned with Zerubbabel. Ezra 2.49; Neh. 3.6. Phaseah: Neh. 7.51.

pasha, highest honorary title in official usage in the Ottoman Empire and with slight variation in the states formed from its territories, where it is sometimes still employed (although Turkey formally abolished it in 1934 and Egypt in 1953). The designation, which is a personal rather than a hereditary distinction, was given under the Ottoman rulers to individuals of both civilian and military status, notably ministers, provincial governors, and army officers.

Pashitch, Nikola: see PAŠIĆ, NIKOLA.

Pashto: see PUSHTU.

Pashur (pā'shər). **1** Official who mistreated Jeremiah. Jer. 20.3. **2** Messenger to Jeremiah from the king. Jer. 21.1; 38.1. He is probably the ancestor of a post-Exilic priestly family. 1 Chron. 9.12; Ezra 2.38; Neh. 7.41; 11.12. **3** Father of a contemporary of Jeremiah. Jer. 38.1. **4** Priest. Neh. 10.3.

Pašić or **Pashitch, Nikola** (both: nē'kôlä pä'shĭch), 1845?–1926, Serbian statesman. After studying engineering, he became interested in politics and was elected (1878) to the Serbian parliament. In 1881 he founded the Radical party, which he led for the rest of his life. An opponent of the government of King Milan, he lived in exile from 1883 to 1889. After his return, he was (1891–92) premier of Serbia for the first of many times. Exiled (1899) by King Alexander, he returned to power after the accession (1903) of Peter I and virtually controlled Serbia in the years preceding World War I. Strongly pro-Russian and advocating the creation of a greater Serbia, he adopted a violently anti-Austrian policy after the annexation by Austria of BOSNIA AND HERCEGOVINA. The Austrian government accused him (1914), with cause, of having possessed knowledge of the plot against Archduke FRANCIS FERDINAND, whose assassination precipitated World War I. Pašić led Serbia throughout the war and in 1917 negotiated the union of Serbs, Croats, and Slovenes (see YUGOSLAVIA). He was an important figure at the Paris Peace Conference and was premier of Yugoslavia for most of the time from 1921 until his death. Favoring a greater Serbia in which Serbia would control the other sections through a centralized administration, he met bitter opposition from Stjepan RADIĆ in Croatia. Pašić and his party grew increasingly conservative in the latter part of his career. See Carlo Sforza, *Fifty Years of War and Diplomacy in the Balkans* (1940).

Pasig (pä'sĭg), river, 14 mi (23 km) long, SW Luzon, the Philippines. Flowing through Manila, it drains Laguna de Bay northwest to Manila Bay. Though small, the Pasig River is commercially important.

Pasiphaë (pəsĭf'əē''): see MINOS.

Paskevich, Ivan Feodorovich (ēvän' fyô'dərəvĭch pəskyĕ'vĭch), 1782–1856, Russian army officer and administrator. He fought in the Napoleonic Wars, was created count of Erivan after conquering (1827) Persian Armenia in the war with Persia (1826–28), and became field marshal after his successful campaign in the Russo-Turkish War of 1828–29. After the Polish insurrection of 1830, Paskevich captured Warsaw from the rebels (1831) and was made prince of Warsaw and viceroy of Poland by Czar Nicholas I. Brutal and authoritarian, he followed Nicholas's policy for the Russification of Poland. In 1849 he led the Russian troops that went to the aid of Austria against the Hungarian insurrectionists. In the Crimean War (1854–56), he commanded the army of the Danube.

Pasoeroean: see PASURUAN, Indonesia.

Pasolini, Pier Paolo (pyĕr pä'ōlō päsōlē'nē), 1922–, Italian writer and film director. A former Roman Catholic and Marxist, Pasolini brings to his writings and films a combination of religious and social consciousness. His early works, including the novel *Ragazzi di vita* (1957) and the film *Accatone* (1961), deal with the grim effects of poverty and squalor. Pasolini uses a popular Roman dialect in his novels, being opposed to traditional literary language, which he feels is imposed by the ruling classes. His major films include *The Gospel According to St. Matthew* (1964), *The Hawks and the Sparrows* (1966), *Oedipus Rex* (1967), *Teorema* (1968), and *Medea* (1970). All of his works are aimed at political and social reform.

pasqueflower (păsk'–), name for two similar perennials of the family Ranunculaceae (BUTTERCUP family). The Old World pasqueflower (*Anemone pulsatilla*) was so named because it blossoms during the Easter season. The American pasqueflower (*A. patens*), named for its resemblance to the European species, is a bluish open-bell-shaped wild flower of the prairie regions of North America. As a herald of spring and a symbol of old age (from the silvery heads of feathery seeds), the plant has been made the subject of Indian song and legend. It is the floral emblem of South Dakota. Patches of the flowers on their short, furry stems give an appearance of haze; for this reason the plant in the Great Plains region is called prairie smoke. Other names for the American variety are gosling flower, sandflower, windflower, wild crocus, and anemone. It contains a poison and is an irritant when fresh; the crushed leaves were applied by Indians as a counterirritant in cases of rheumatism and neuralgia. The pasqueflowers were formerly considered a separate genus (*Pulsatilla*) from the related true anemones. Pasqueflowers are classified in the division MAGNOLIOPHYTA, class Magnoliopsida, order Ranunculales, family Ranunculaceae.

Pasquier, Étienne (ātyĕn' päkyā'), 1529–1615, French jurist and man of letters. After study under Jacques Cujas, Pasquier began his legal career in 1549. Always a confirmed advocate of GALLICANISM, in 1565 he pleaded a famous case for the Univ. of Paris against the Jesuits. In 1585 he became advocate general of a division of the Parlement of Paris. Pasquier's most notable book, *Recherches de la France,* a learned work on French history and literature, reflected the tendency of the humanists to write in the vernacular rather than in Latin. See biography by L. C. Keating (1972).

pass, opening or way by which a natural or artificial barrier can be crossed. The term *pass* is usually applied to a relatively narrow passage through a mountainous region. A pass, like an isthmus, may have great strategic and economic importance; the history of a nation has often been determined by its success or failure in defending a pass, and land trade routes must necessarily cross passes. In the Alps, SAINT BERNARD, SIMPLON, and SAINT GOTTHARD are important; in the Caucasus, DARYAL is traversed by a great military road; in Asia, KHYBER PASS into India and the passes of the Himalayas, KARAKORUM, and other ranges are important.

passacaglia: see CHACONNE AND PASSACAGLIA.

Passaic (pəsā'ĭk), city (1970 pop. 55,124), Passaic co., NE N.J., a port on the Passaic River; settled 1678 by Dutch traders as Acquackanonk, named Passaic 1854, inc. as a city 1873. Formerly a great textile center, it now has highly diversified industries. The city has been the scene of considerable labor unrest; an Industrial Workers of the World strike occurred in 1912, and an important strike in protest against a wage cut and involving the right of assembly occurred in 1926.

Passaic, river, c.80 mi (130 km) long, rising near Morristown, NE N.J., and flowing with a winding course NE then S past several industrial towns to Newark Bay. It is navigable by large vessels to the rapids above Passaic. At Paterson is the Great Falls of the Passaic (70 ft/21.3 m high), a national natural landmark. The river's power aided the growth of industry in NE New Jersey.

Passamaquoddy Bay (păsəməkwŏd'ē), inlet of the Bay of Fundy, between Maine and New Brunswick, at the mouth of the St. Croix River. Most of it (including Campobello island) is within Canada's border. New Brunswick towns in the vicinity are St. Andrews and St. George; Maine towns are Eastport and Lubec (at the bay's entrance). A large hydroelectric project (frequently called the Quoddy project), which planned to make use of the bay's great tidal range and began (1935) in the U.S. sector with funds from the Public Works Administration, was suspended after Congress refused funds in 1936. An attempt to revive the project in the late 1950s failed.

Passamaquoddy Indians: see ABNAKI INDIANS or ABENAKI INDIANS.

Passarowitz, Treaty of (päsä'rōvĭts), 1718, peace treaty signed at Pozarevac (Ger. *Passarowitz*), E Serbia, Yugoslavia. It was concluded between the Ottoman Empire (Turkey) on the one side and Austria and Venice on the other. In the preceding war (1714–18) the Turks had been successful against the Venetians in Greece and Crete but had been defeated in 1716 at Petrovaradin by Prince EUGENE OF SAVOY, who in 1717 also stormed Belgrade. Eugene's victories represented a triumph for Austria, and the treaty reflected the military situation. Turkey lost the Banat of Temesvar, N Serbia (including Belgrade), N Bosnia, and Lesser Walachia to Austria. Venice lost all its possessions in the Peloponnesus and on Crete to Turkey, retaining only the Ionian Islands and the Dalmation coast. Belgrade and Lesser Walachia were recovered again by Turkey at the Treaty of Belgrade in 1739.

Passau (päs'ou), city (1970 pop. 30,700), Bavaria, SE West Germany, at the confluence of the Danube, Inn, and Ilz rivers, near the border with Austria. It is a river port, rail junction, and industrial center; manufactures include machinery, textiles, optical equipment, and printed materials. A Roman frontier outpost known as Castra Batava, Passau was made (738–39) an episcopal see by St. Boniface. The bishops of Passau were temporal lords of a substantial territory until 1803, when the bishopric was secularized and awarded to Bavaria; the diocese was restored in 1817. The Treaty of Passau (1552) was negotiated there between Maurice of Saxony and King (later Emperor) Ferdinand I, who represented his brother, Emperor Charles V; it secured the release of the captive Protestant princes and helped pave the way for the religious peace of 1555 (see AUGSBURG, PEACE OF). Noteworthy buildings in Passau include the cathedral (15th–17th cent.), which has one of the world's largest church organs; the Gothic city hall (begun 1398); the baroque episcopal palace; the Oberhaus fortress (13th–16th cent.); and a former Benedictine monastery (founded in the 8th cent.). There are also many fine houses and fountains in the Bavarian baroque style.

passenger pigeon: see PIGEON.

Passion cycle, in art, the depiction of the last events in the life of Christ. The Passion was a favorite subject of medieval and Renaissance artists and was considered the most ambitious of projects. The scenes depicted generally include the entry of Christ into Jerusalem, the washing of his feet, the Last Supper, the Agony in the garden, the betrayal, the denial of Peter, Christ before Pilate, the flagellation, the mocking of Christ, the road to Calvary, the 14 Stations of the Cross (developed in the 14th cent. as a separate Crucifixion cycle), the Deposition, the Pietà (or Lamentation), and the Entombment. The scenes may be represented singly, as in Michelangelo's *Pietà,* or as a suite, as in Giotto's frescoes in the Arena Chapel at Padua. The artists' interpretations of what was to be represented in each scene were strictly circumscribed by convention and were usually limited to biblical descriptions of the events.

passionflower, any plant of the genus *Passiflora,* mostly tropical American vines having pulpy fruits. Some species are grown in greenhouses for their large, unusual flowers of various colors; those seen by early Spanish settlers were interpreted as symbolic of the Crucifixion (whence the name), the 10 petals and sepals, fringed corona, five stamens, three styles, and coiling tendrils representing in order the 10 faithful apostles, crown of thorns, wounds, nails, and scourges. The most common native North American species (*P. incarnata*), ranging as far north as Missouri and Pennsylvania, has purple-and-white flowers and edible egg-shaped fruits called maypops. Several species of the large-fruited granadillas are cultivated commercially in the tropics for fruit, flavoring, and beverages. Passionflowers are classified in the division MAGNOLIOPHYTA, class Magnoliopsida, order Violales, family Passifloraceae.

Passionists: see PAUL OF THE CROSS, SAINT.

passion music, choral music whose text depicts events immediately surrounding the crucifixion of Christ. The earliest passions, composed from the 9th to the 14th cent., were monophonic and employed the actual biblical text of one of the four Evangelists. Polyphonic passions originated in England in the 15th cent. After the Reformation, free poetry was added to passion texts. Orchestral accompaniment was used during the baroque period. The passion music of J. S. Bach represents the culmination of the genre. See Basil Smallman, *The Background of Passion Music* (2d ed. 1970).

Passion play, genre of the MIRACLE PLAY that has survived from the Middle Ages into modern times. Its subject is the suffering, death, and resurrection of Jesus. The passion play was first given in Latin. By the 13th cent. parts of it included German verses, and 200 years later the entire play was performed in German. Toward the end of the 15th cent. these plays had become far more secular in content, having been degraded, in a religious sense, through their contact with carnival plays. Their production was forbidden by ecclesiastical authorities and only a few were revived after the Catholic Reformation. The chief survival among the Passion plays is the one performed at Oberammergau in the Bavarian Alps. This entirely amateur performance has been given every 10 years (with only three interruptions caused by war) since 1634, in fulfillment, it is said, of a vow that was made during a plague. In a few Latin American countries and in the United States passion plays are very occasionally performed. See M. J. Utting, *The Passion Play of Oberammergau* (1936).

passive: see VOICE.

Passover, one of the most important and elaborate of the Jewish festivals. Its celebration begins on the evening of the 14th of Nisan (first month of the religious calendar, corresponding to March-April) and lasts seven days in Israel, eight days in the Diaspora (although Reform Jews observe a seven-day period). Numerous theories have been advanced in explanation of its original significance, which has become obscured by the association it later acquired with the Exodus. In pre-Mosaic times it may have been a spring festival only, but in its present observance by Orthodox Jews, who celebrate it in commemoration of their deliverance from the yoke of Egypt, that significance has been practically forgotten. In the ceremonial evening meal (called Seder), which is conducted on the first evening in Israel and by Reform Jews, and on the first and second evenings by all other observant Jews in the Diaspora, various special dishes symbolizing the hardships of the Israelites during their bondage in Egypt are served; the narrative of the Exodus, the *Haggadah,* is recited; and praise is given for the deliverance. Only unleavened bread (matzoth) may be eaten throughout the period of the festival, in memory of the fact that the Jews, hastening from Egypt, had no time to leaven their bread. Tradition also requires that special sets of cooking utensils and dishes, uncontaminated by use during the rest of the year, be used throughout the festival. In ancient Israel the paschal lamb (see AGNUS DEI) was slaughtered on the eve of Passover, a practice retained today by the Samaritans. The Christian feast of Easter is calculated from the Pasch, or Passover. See T. H. Gaster, *Passover: Its History and Traditions* (1949, repr. 1962); Philip Goodman, ed., *The Passover Anthology* (1961).

Passy, Frédéric (frādārĕk' päsē'), 1822–1912, French economist, winner (1901, with J. H. Dunant) of the first Nobel Peace Prize. He studied law but abandoned it for journalism and the study of economics and problems of peace. In 1867 he founded the International League for Permanent Peace, later known as the French Society of the Friends of Peace; he served as its general secretary until 1889, when, in association with Sir William R. Cremer, he founded the Inter-Parliamentary Union of Arbitration. He was a member of the chamber of deputies from 1874 to 1889. His best-known work is *Historique du mouvement de la paix* (1904). The phonetician Paul Edouard Passy (1859–1940) was his son.

pastel (păstĕl'), artists' medium of chalk and pigment, tempered with weak gum water and usually molded in the form of sticks; also a work done in this medium. Pastel was in use in Italy in the 15th cent. and is doubtless much older. It was introduced into 18th-century France by the Venetian artist Rosalba Carriera. The medium was then used by such masters as Maurice Quentin de La Tour and Vigée-

Lebrun, and in the 19th cent. by Degas, Manet, Toulouse-Lautrec, Whistler, and Cassatt. In the 20th cent. Matisse was a master of pastel. Pastels are often classified as paintings, although the medium lends itself to the more direct and spontaneous approach of drawing.

Pasternak, Boris Leonidovich (păs'tərnăk", Rus. bərēs' lyä"ənyĕ'dəvĭch pəstyĭrnäk'), 1890–1960, Russian poet and translator. Pasternak became an international symbol of the incorruptible moral courage of an artist in conflict with his political environment. The son of the celebrated painter Leonid Pasternak and the concert pianist Rosa Kaufman, both of Jewish descent, Pasternak was greatly influenced by the composer Scriabin and by Leo Tolstoy, both family friends. He turned from music to philosophy, which he studied in Germany (1912–14). Pasternak published his first book of poems, *The Twin in the Clouds,* in 1914. *Over the Barriers* (1916) and *My Sister, Life* (1917, pub. 1922) established his reputation as a major poet. His poetic style, lyrical, sensual, and passionate, is imbued with fresh imagery and brilliant metaphor. His early work fused elements from futurist and symbolist techniques with his own dynamic innovations. Pasternak at first embraced the promise of the Revolution of 1917, but he came to abhor the ensuing Bolshevik restrictions on artistic freedom. He wrote two long narrative poems, *Spektorsky* (1926) and *The Year 1905* (1927). His collection of five short stories includes "The Childhood of Lovers" (1924), a complex and perceptive portrayal of a young girl. The brief autobiographical work *Safe Conduct* (1931) and the collection of poetry *Second Birth* (1932) were his last original works for many years. During the purges of the 1930s, Pasternak came under severe critical attack and, unable to publish his own poetry, devoted himself to making superb translations of classic works by Goethe, Shakespeare, and others. His survival of the purges is attributed to his translations of Georgian poets admired by Stalin. In his silence Pasternak became the hero of Russian intellectuals. His very rare public appearances were greeted with wild rejoicing. During World War II he published two new collections, *On Early Trains* (1942) and *The Terrestrial Expanse* (1945), simpler in style, which brought him fresh censure. After Stalin's death Pasternak began work on the novel *Doctor Zhivago* (Eng. tr. 1958; Rus. text pub. in the United States, 1959), his masterpiece in the great tradition of the Russian epic. The life of the physician and poet Yuri Zhivago, like Pasternak's own, is closely identified with the exalted and tragic upheavals of 20th-century Russia. Expressing the celebration of life characteristic of its author, the novel offended Soviet authorities by its insights into Communist society and its strain of Christian idealism. Denied publication in the USSR, it was first published in Italy in 1957 despite serious efforts to repress it. It soon became the object of unrestrained international acclaim. Pasternak was awarded the 1958 Nobel Prize in Literature, which he joyfully accepted. He was forced by immediate and unbearable pressures, including the threat of continued persecution of his intimate friend and collaborator, Olga Ivinskaya, to retract his acceptance. He pleaded to be allowed to remain in his beloved motherland. Expelled from the Soviet Writers Union, he lived in virtual exile in an artists' community near Moscow. See his *Collected Prose Works* (tr. 1945); *Selected Writings* (tr. 1958), which includes the autobiographical *Safe Conduct* (1931); *I Remember: Sketch for an Autobiography* (tr. 1959); translations of his poetry by Eugene Kayden (1959) and George Reavey (1959); his *Letters to Georgian Friends* (tr. 1965); studies by Robert Conquest (1962), M. F. and Paul Rowland (1967), and J. W. Dyck (1972).

Pasteur, Louis (păstûr', Fr. lwē pästör'), 1822–95, French chemist. He taught at Dijon, Strasbourg, and Lille, and in Paris at the École normale supérieure and the Sorbonne (1867–89). His early research consisted of chemical studies of the tartrates, in which he discovered (1848) molecular dissymmetry. He then began work on fermentation, which had important results. His experiments with BACTERIA conclusively disproved (1862) the theory of spontaneous generation and led to the germ theory of infection. His work on wine, vinegar, and beer resulted in the development of the process of PASTEURIZATION. Of great economic value also was his solution for the control of silkworm disease, his study of chicken cholera, and his technique of vaccination against ANTHRAX, which was successfully administered against RABIES in 1885. In 1888 the Pasteur Institute was founded in Paris, with Pasteur as its director, to continue work on hydrophobia and to provide a teaching and research center on virulent and contagious diseases. See biographies by his son-in-law, René Vallery-Radot (1920, repr. 1960), R. J. Dubos (1950 and 1960), Jacques Nicolle (1961), and Hilaire Cuny (tr. 1965).

pasteurization (păs"chŏŏrĭzā'shən, -rīzā'shən) [for Louis Pasteur], partial sterilization of liquids, especially of milk, wine, and beer, to destroy disease-causing and other undesirable organisms. Milk is pasteurized by heating it to about 145°F (63°C) for 30 min, followed by rapid cooling to below 50°F (10°C), at which temperature it is stored. The harmless lactic acid bacteria survive the process, but if the milk is not kept cold, they multiply rapidly and cause it to turn sour.

pastiche (păstēsh', pä-), work of art that combines themes and styles from various sources in such a way as to appear obviously derivative. Pastiches are frequently passed off as works by the artists from whom the motifs and figures were taken.

Pasto (pä'stō), city (1968 est. pop. 87,800), alt. 8,510 ft (2,594 m), capital of Nariña dept., SW Colombia. It is a distributing and processing center for the agricultural products of the surrounding region. Varnish and woolen goods are produced in the city. Founded in 1539, Pasto was a royalist city in the revolution against Spain and changed hands several times. Antonio NARIÑO was defeated at Pasto by the Spanish in 1814. Occupied for a short period in 1831 by Ecuadorian forces, Pasto was the scene of the treaty (1832) by which Colombia (then called New Granada) and Ecuador became separate states. The city retains a colonial appearance, with narrow streets and many old churches.

Paston Letters, collection of personal and business correspondence, mostly among members of the Paston family of Norfolk, England. The letters cover the years from 1422 to 1529, together with deeds and other documents. The family was at that time actively acquiring land and properties in the area, some of it by questionable means, including the estates of Sir John FASTOLF. The collection forms an indispensable source for the history, manners, morals, habits, customs, and moneys of the people of England at the close of the Middle Ages. A portion of the letters was published by James Fenn in 1787 and 1789, but the original manuscripts disappeared and doubt of their authenticity grew. However, they were rediscovered after 1865, with additional material. A definitive edition was edited by James Gairdner (1904), and a volume of selections edited with an introduction by Norman Davis was published in 1958.

Pastor, Ludwig, Freiherr von (lŏŏt'vĭkh frī'hĕr fən päs'tôr), 1854–1928, German historian. The author of the monumental and authoritative *History of the Popes from the Close of the Middle Ages* (40 vol., tr. 1891–1953), he combined a Roman Catholic bias with the most painstaking scholarship and erudition. He was privileged with access to the secret archives of the Vatican, and his history, largely based on hitherto unused documents, supersedes all previous histories of the popes. Pastor's theme is that the shortcomings of the papacy have reflected flaws of the age. Although not an unqualified defender of Catholicism, he has been criticized for lack of objectivity. He was Austrian minister to the Vatican from 1921.

Pastor, Tony, c.1837–1908, American theater manager, b. New York City. Pastor appeared on the stage from childhood and became an experienced acrobat, dancer, and singer. He opened his first theater at 444 Broadway, New York City, in 1861. Thereafter he opened two more Broadway theaters, and in 1881 began presenting shows at his best-known playhouse on 14th St. In these establishments Pastor introduced many performers who became famous (notably Lillian Russell) and presented vaudeville suitable for a mixed audience. See biography by Parker Zellers (1971).

pastoral, literary work in which shepherd life is presented in a conventionalized manner. In this convention the purity and simplicity of shepherd life is contrasted with the corruption and artificiality of the court or the city. The pastoral is found in poetry, drama, and fiction, and many subjects, such as love, death, religion, and politics, have been presented in pastoral settings. The earliest pastoral poetry of which there is record was written by the Greek poet Theocritus in the 3d cent. B.C. It is in his idyls, which celebrate the beauty and simplicity of rustic life in Sicily, that the well-known pastoral characters Daphnis, Lycidas, Corydon, and Amaryllis are first encountered. Theocritus was followed by Bion and Moschus in the 2d cent. B.C. and by Vergil, whose *Bucolics* appeared in 37 B.C. In these polished and literary verses, which were later called eclogues, Vergil describes an imaginary Arcadia in which the pastoral scenes are allegorical; they celebrate the greatness of Rome, express thanks to the emperor, and prophesy a golden age. In the 3d cent. A.D. a Greek poet, probably Longus, wrote *Daphnis and Chloë,* a pastoral romance that also infiltrated European literature. The pastoral eclogue enjoyed a revival during the Renaissance. Vergil's *Bucolics* were translated in the 15th cent. in Italy, and pastoral eclogues were written by Dante, Petrarch, and Boccaccio. The most elaborate pastoral romance was the *Arcadia* by Jacopo Sannazaro, written partly in prose and partly in verse. Poliziano's *Orfeo* (c.1471) is one of the earliest pastoral dramas. In France the *pastourelle*—a short poem in dialogue in which a minstrel courts a shepherdess—appeared as early as the 14th cent. and is exemplified in *Le Jeu de Robin et de Marion,* a play by Adam de La Halle. In English literature the pastoral is a familiar feature of Renaissance poetry. Sir Philip Sidney's *Arcadia* (1590) is an epic story in pastoral dress. In *The Shepheardes Calender* (1579) Edmund Spenser used the pastoral as a vehicle for political and religious discussion; and many of the love lyrics of Shakespeare, Ben Jonson, and Michael Drayton have a pastoral setting. Christopher Marlowe's "The Passionate Shepherd to His Love" is one of the most famous pastoral lyrics. Milton's philosophical and deeply felt "Lycidas" is a great pastoral elegy. In drama well-known examples of the pastoral are Shakespeare's *As You Like It,* the shearers' feast in *A Winter's Tale,* and Milton's masque *Comus.* Although poets, novelists, and dramatists of the 19th and 20th cent. have used pastoral settings to express the contrast of simplicity and innocence with the artificiality of the city, they have seldom employed the pastoral conventions of Theocritus and Vergil. Outstanding exceptions are Shelley's *Adonais* and Matthew Arnold's *Thyrsis,* both splendid pastoral elegies, and poets such as Wordsworth and Robert Frost, because of their rural subject matter, have also been referred to as "pastoral" poets. In 1935 the English poet and critic William Empson published *Some Versions of the Pastoral,* in which he defines the pastoral as the putting of the complex into the simple, ignoring the conventionalized bucolic setting as superficial; he then designates various literary works, from *Alice's Adventures in Wonderland* to the proletarian novel, as offshoots of the pastoral. In music, the pastorale is a piece imitating the simple music of shepherds. "He Shall Feed His Flock" from Handel's *Messiah* and Beethoven's Pastoral Symphony are superb examples of the pastorale. See the anthology ed. by T. P. Harrison (1939, repr. 1968); studies by J. F. A. Heath-Stubby (1969), H. E. Toliver (1971), and Laurence Lerner (1972).

Pastoral Epistles: name for the epistles of TIMOTHY and TITUS.

Pastrana Borrero, Misael (mēsäĕl' pästrä'nä bōr-rā'rō), 1923–, president of Colombia (1970–74). A lawyer and businessman and a member of the Conservative party, he served in the ministries of two liberal presidents in the 1960s and was (1968–69) ambassador to the United States. He succeeded Carlos Lleras Restrepo as president, narrowly defeating the former dictator Gustavo Rojas Pinilla. He continued his predecessor's social and economic reforms, noticeably strengthening the economy. He was succeeded by Alfonso López Michelsen, a liberal.

pastry, general name for baked articles of food made of paste or having paste as a necessary ingredient. The name is also used for the paste itself. The essential elements of paste are flour, liquid (usually milk or water, sometimes beaten egg), and shortening. The making of pastry was known to the ancient Greeks and Romans, but its modern development in the Western world dates from the late 18th cent. Pastry is classed according to the amount of shortening used and the method of blending it with the flour as plain, flaky, and puff pastry. Plain pastry is used to cover meat or fruit pies; flaky pastry, which requires more shortening than plain, is used in strudels and the Turkish baklava. Puff pastry is used in the making of cream puffs and éclairs.

pasture, land used for grazing livestock. Land unsuited for cultivation, e.g., hilly or stony land, may be used as pasture. Tilled land and meadow may be pastured after the crops are removed. Pastures that have been overgrazed and in which such soil-improving practices as liming, fertilizing, and seeding have been neglected lose a part of the feed nutrients required by livestock. Good management of pastures also calls for rotation of animals, because the composition of manure, which affects the nutrients in the soil, varies with the kind of animal being grazed, and also because different animals graze on different species of pasturage plants. Among other requirements are a sufficient water supply, trees to provide shade, and eradication of weeds. Most forage plants seeded in pastures are types of GRASS or CLOVER. Many are suitable not only for grazing but also for cutting and storage as HAY. See also RANGE.

Pasuruan or **Pasoeroean** (both: pä"so͞oro͞oän'), city (1961 pop. 63,408), E Java, Indonesia, on Madura Strait. A port, it exports sugar, rubber, coffee, and fish. The city has shipyards, sugar and rice mills, and various factories.

Patagonia (pätägō'nyä), region, c.300,000 sq mi (777,000 sq km), primarily in S Argentina, S of the Río Colorado and E of the Andes, but including extreme SE Chile and N Tierra del Fuego. Patagonia, except for the far southern plains, the sub-Andean region, and the Andes, is a vast, wind-swept semiarid plateau, sloping gently toward the east and terminating in cliffs along the Atlantic Ocean. Crossing from the Andes to the Atlantic are transverse valleys, some cradling rivers. Although most of the water courses are intermittently dry, some rivers (Río Negro, the Chubut, the Santa Cruz, and the Gallegos) are perennial. The sub-Andean region in the west contains numerous lakes (Nahuel Huapí, Buenos Aires, Viedma, and Argentino) fed by glaciers; it also has some deep, fertile valleys. Subantarctic conditions prevail in the far south. Until recently sheep raising (mainly for wool) was the major industry of Patagonia, but oil production, particularly around Neuquen, Río Gallegos, and Comodoro Rivadavia (the region's largest city), has become very important. There are coal deposits in the upper Río Gallegos valley, and iron ore deposits at Sierra Grande. Tourist resorts in the lake region are very popular. Cattle are raised, and agriculture is practiced in irrigated oases along the Río Negro and the Chubut. A rich field for the paleontologist, Patagonia has been visited by many scientific expeditions since the days of Charles Darwin. Of the original inhabitants, the Tehuelches (the "Patagonian giants") are the most important. Among the native animals are the guanaco, the rhea, the puma, and the deer. Probably first visited (1501) by Amerigo Vespucci, the Patagonian coast was explored (1520) by Ferdinand Magellan. Settlements were attempted in the 16th and 17th cent., but the inhospitable country and natives discouraged colonization. It was not until after Julio A. Roca, an Argentine general, campaigned against the Indians that Argentine ranchers began entering the territory in the late 19th cent. Chileans had been coming in for some time, and despite efforts to exclude them during and after the Argentine-Chilean boundary dispute in the early 20th cent., many continued to immigrate. Many Europeans, including many British, took up ranches. Making up more than a third of Argentine territory and still sparsely populated, Patagonia is a vast natural reserve, and settlement has steadily increased. Studies have revealed the presence of vast untapped mineral wealth. See *Reports of the Princeton University Expeditions to Patagonia* (1901–32); Bailey Willis, *A Yanqui in Patagonia* (1947); W. H. Hudson, *Idle Days in Patagonia* (new ed. 1954); E. E. Shipton, *Land of Tempest: Travels in Patagonia* (1963); Mollie Robertson, *The Sand, the Wind and the Sierras: Days in Patagonia* (1964).

Patakos, Stylianos (stēlyä'nôs pätäkôs'), 1912–, Greek general and political leader. Patakos, a Cretan, entered the Greek army in 1937 and rose through the ranks. In April, 1967, he was one of the leaders of the military coup headed by George PAPADOPOULOS, and served as interior and security minister. In Dec., 1967, after King Constantine II's abortive countercoup, he also became deputy premier; at the same time he resigned his army commission. Patakos later lost (1971) his ministerial post, but he retained the deputy premiership. He was temporary interior minister from May to Oct., 1973. Patakos fell from power with the overthrow of the Papadopoulos government in Nov., 1973.

Patan (pät'ən) or **Lalitpur** (ləlĭt'po͝or), city (1971 pop. 148,735), central Nepal, in the Katmandu valley, c.4,000 ft (1,220 m) above sea level. Agriculture and grazing are important in the surrounding area, and wool and leather are exported. The city is the center of the Banra sect of goldsmiths and silversmiths. Founded in the 7th cent., Patan is the oldest of Nepal's chief cities. It was the capital of a Nepali kingdom from the 17th cent. until captured and plundered by the Gurkhas under Prithvi Narayan Shah in 1768. Its decline continued with the rise in importance of Katmandu. According to legend, the Indian Maurya emperor Asoka visited the area c.250 B.C. and built the four stupas that still stand on the four sides of Patan.

Patani: see PATTANI, Thailand.

Patañjali: see YOGA.

Patapsco (pətăp'skō), river, c.65 mi (100 km) long, formed in central Md. by the confluence of the North Branch (c.45 mi/70 km long) and the South Branch and flowing SE into Chesapeake Bay at Baltimore. The lower river is tidal and forms a wide estuary on which Baltimore's harbor installations and industrial suburbs (including Sparrows Point) are located. The Baltimore Harbor Tunnel (c.6,300 ft/1,920 m long; opened 1957) carries vehicular traffic under the estuary.

Patara (păt'ərə), ancient Mediterranean port of Lycia, S Asia Minor (now Turkey). It was a Dorian colony. St. Paul visited Patara (Acts 21.1).

Pa-ta Shan-jen: see CHU TA.

Patay (pätā'), village (1968 pop. 1,948), Loiret dept., N central France. At Patay, in 1429, Joan of Arc defeated the English—one of the most serious English defeats in the Hundred Years War.

Patchen, Kenneth, 1911–72, American poet and novelist, b. Niles, Ohio. His writings, characterized by complete freedom of form, embrace genres as diverse as satire, fantasy, and metaphysical love poetry. His early verse—*Before the Brave* (1936) and *First Will & Testament* (1939)—places him with the social protest writers of the '30s. Among his many later collections are *Red Wine & Yellow Hair* (1949), *Because It Is* (1960), and *Hallelujah Anyway* (1967). During the 1950s he initiated the practice of reading poetry to a jazz accompaniment. His prose works include *The Journal of Albion Moonlight* (1941) and the satirical *Memoirs of a Shy Pornographer* (1945). Many of his works are illustrated by his own drawings.

Patchogue (păch'äg", -ôg"), village (1970 pop. 11,582), Suffolk co., SE N.Y., on Long Island, on Great South Bay; inc. 1893. A resort area, it has some light manufacturing.

patchouli or **patchouly** (both: păch'o͝olē, pəcho͞o'lē), fragrant shrubby East Indian plant (*Pogostemon patchouli*) of the family Labiatae (MINT family). It is the source of a perfume oil, also called patchouli, distilled from the leaves. Patchouli is classified in the division MAGNOLIOPHYTA, class Magnoliopsida, order Lamiales, family Labiatae.

Patel, Vallabhbhai (vŭl"ləb-bä'ē pətĕl'), 1875–1950, Indian political leader. He was admitted (1913) to the bar in England and set up a lucrative practice in India. In 1915 he met Mohandas Gandhi and within a short time became one of his closest associates, a staunch nationalist and a supporter of the Indian National Congress. A talented organizer, he successfully directed the civil-disobedience campaigns of the 1920s and 30s; several times he suffered imprisonment. He was mayor of Ahmedabad (1924–28) and was elected (1931) president of the Indian National Congress. In 1942 he was imprisoned, with other Congress leaders, for refusing to support the British war effort in World War II. After his release (1945), he initiated a purge of Communists (who had supported the war) from the Congress. Patel played an important role in the negotiations that led to independence and the partition of the subcontinent into the two states of India and Pakistan. In 1947 he was made deputy prime minister of India and minister of state affairs. Holding these offices until his death, he effected the complex and difficult feat of integrating the many princely states into the new Indian political structure. See his *Correspondence, 1945–50,* ed. by Durga Das (Vol. I, 1971); biographies by N. D. Parikh (tr., 2 vol., 1953–56) and L. N. Sarin (1972).

patella (pətĕl'ə): see KNEECAP.

Patenier, Joachim de: see PATINIR, JOACHIM DE.

patent, in law, governmental grant of some privilege, property, or authority. Today patent refers to the granting to the inventor of a useful product or process the privilege to exclude others from making his invention. *Patent* is also the term for the conveyance of PUBLIC LANDS to an individual. Patents developed out of the medieval institution of allowing monopolistic control over useful goods in order to encourage their sale and distribution; the authority was contained in letters patent (meaning open, i.e., public). The corrupt sale of such privileges and the consequent increase in the price of necessities led in England to the Statute of Monopolies (1623), which abolished all monopolies except those of inventors in their inventions. The U.S. Constitution (Article 1, Section 8) authorizes Congress to enact patent legislation; the first such law was enacted April 10, 1790. In 1836, Congress created the U.S. Patent Office and established the basic principles of American patent law. Comprehensive revision of that law occurred in 1870 and in 1952. In the United States any process or device may be patented if it is novel and useful and if plans and a working model are supplied. In all countries patents are valid for a limited term only (17 years in the United States); this limit ordinarily secures a profit to the inventor for a reasonable period yet will not permanently deprive the public of the free use of the invention. The American law was designed to encourage the maximum inventiveness. Unlike many European countries where the rights to patents are limited so as to make innovations in industry easier, the United States imposes no tax on the maintenance of patents, nor does it require the patentee to permit the use of his invention on pain of losing his patent. Although there have been many independent inventors in the United States, most important patents today are the property of large corporations capable of exploiting them. Injurious practices, such as withholding beneficial patents that might make obsolete some widely used product or process, have developed. Other practices, such as acquiring all patents in a given field and granting manufacturing licenses only to firms that promise to refrain from effective competition, have been repeatedly attacked by the Federal government under the antitrust laws (see TRUST). Difficulties have also developed in the effective and equitable regulation of patents taken out by foreigners. See F. L. Vaughan, *The United States Patent System: Legal and Economic Conflicts in American Patent History* (1956); B. W. Bugbee, *Genesis of American Patent and Copyright Law* (1967).

patent medicine, packaged DRUGS that can be obtained without prescription; the term was formerly used to describe quack remedies sold by peddlers. Patent, or proprietary, medicines are advertised to the public by trade name, purport to be effective against minor disorders and symptoms, and are packaged with directions for use. ANTISEPTICS, ANALGESICS, some SEDATIVES, LAXATIVES, and ANTACIDS, cold and cough medicines, and various skin preparations are included in the group. Sale of proprietary medicines is regulated by the Food and Drug Administration, which evaluates preparations as to their safety and effectiveness.

Pater, Walter Horatio (pā'tər), 1839–94, English essayist and critic. In 1864 he was elected a fellow of Brasenose College, Oxford, and he subsequently led an austere and uneventful life. Pater believed that the ideal life consisted of cultivating an appreciation for the beautiful and the profound. His first work, *Studies in the History of the Renaissance* (1873), established his reputation. Then followed his masterpiece, *Marius the Epicurean* (1885), a study of the intellectual and spiritual development of a young Roman in the time of Marcus Aurelius. His other works include *Imaginary Portraits* (1887); *Appreciations* (1889); *Plato and Platonism* (1893); *The Child in the House* (1894); and two posthumous publications, *Greek Studies* (1895) and *Gaston de Latour* (1896). His style is noted for its precision, subtlety, and refinement. See the biography by Thomas Wright (2 vol., 1907; repr. 1969); study by Richmond Crinkley (1970).

Paternò (pätärnô'), city (1971 pop. 45,530), E Sicily, Italy, at the foot of Mt. Etna, probably the ancient HYBLA. It is an agricultural market and a food-processing center.

paternoster: see LORD'S PRAYER.

Paterson, William, 1658–1719, British financier. By the time of the Glorious Revolution of 1688 (which he supported) he had acquired considerable wealth and influence through foreign trade. In 1691 he was the chief projector of the plan to establish the BANK OF ENGLAND, which finally came into being in 1694. Paterson served as a director from 1694 to 1695. In 1695 he proposed to the Scottish Parliament the famous but ill-fated DARIEN SCHEME. Subsequently he devoted several years to carrying out that plan and accompanied the expedition of 1698 to Darien. Paterson advised William III on economic, financial, and state affairs, and he strongly advocated the union of Scotland and England. Paterson strenuously argued for free trade and was a recognized authority in later years. His writings were edited by Saxe Bannister (3 vol., 1859). See biography by Saxe Bannister (1858); J. S. Barbour, *William Paterson and the Darien Company* (1927).

Paterson, William, 1745–1806, American political leader and jurist, b. Co. Antrim, Ireland. He emigrated to America as a child. Raised in New Jersey, he practiced law there and was attorney general (1776–83) of the state before he became a delegate to the FEDERAL CONSTITUTIONAL CONVENTION (1787). He was prominent as a champion of the rights of the small states; he set forth the New Jersey, or small state, plan (sometimes called the Paterson plan). He later played a prominent part in state and national life as U.S. Senator (1789–90), governor of New Jersey (1791–93), and Associate Justice of the U.S. Supreme Court (1793–1806). See biography by G. S. Wood (1933).

Paterson, city (1970 pop. 144,824), seat of Passaic co., NE N.J., at the falls of the Passaic River; inc. 1851. Founded in 1791 by Alexander Hamilton and others of the Society for Establishing Useful Manufactures, Paterson was a planned attempt to promote industrial independence in the newly-formed United States. In 1792 and 1794 cotton-spinning mills, forerunners of the city's textile industry, were established. In 1835, Samuel Colt began his manufacture of the Colt revolver. Shortly thereafter the silk industry was established, beginning a silk boom which would earn Paterson the appellation "Silk City of the World." The iron industry, which initially supplied Paterson with textile machinery, was producing locomotives in great numbers by 1880. After World War I, the aeronautics industry moved to Paterson. Industrial diversification has steadily increased. Today Paterson is the third-largest city in the state. The silk industry is gone, but textiles and transportation equipment are still manufactured, and there is a large garment industry. Among the many other manufactures are electronic equipment, paper and food products, fabricated metals, rubber, and plastics. Paterson has suffered many of the urban problems that plague large cities. During the first half of the 20th cent., notably in 1912–13, 1933, and 1936, many bitter strikes arose from bad labor conditions in the silk industry. More recently Paterson has attracted large numbers of immigrants, and the shortage of housing has become a major problem. Today about one third of the population is Spanish-speaking. Of special interest is the historic district that centers around the roaring falls of the river. Designated a national historic site in 1970, it is a unique display of industrial history, with old cobblestone streets and stone bridges; the abandoned houses of workmen and mill owners; and a great variety of industrial works, including several locomotive factories (one dating back to 1830), the Colt gun factory (1835), and historic spinning mills and waterworks. Also of interest are the public-library building, designed by Henry Bacon and a museum that has natural-history and Indian collections and contains the model submarine built by John P. Holland.

Pathan (pətän'), group of seminomadic peoples consisting of over 60 tribes, numbering 5 million in Afghanistan and 4 million in Pakistan. They are noted as fierce fighters, and throughout history they have offered strong resistance to invaders. The British attempted to subdue the Pathans in a series of punitive expeditions in the late 19th and early 20th cent. but were finally forced to offer them a semiautonomous area (see NORTH-WEST FRONTIER PROVINCE) between the border of British India and that of Afghanistan. After the creation of Pakistan in 1947, the new nation annexed the Pathan border regions, and a Pathan independence movement, called the Redshirts, was born. In the early 1950s, Afghanistan supported Pathan ambitions for the creation of an independent Pushtunistan (also called Pakhtunistan or Pakhtoonistan) in the border areas of West Pakistan. Several border clashes and ruptures of diplomatic relations between Afghanistan and Pakistan ensued. In the early 1970s thousands of armed Pathan tribesmen pressed for increased autonomy within Pakistan, even demanding independence after the secession of Bangladesh (East Pakistan). The Pathans are Muslims and speak Pushtu. They are also known as Pakhtuns, Pashtuns, Pushtuns, and Pakhtoons. See O. K. Caroe, *The Pathans, 550 B.C.–A.D. 1957* (1958, repr. 1965); J. W. Spain, *People of the Khyber* (1963), *The Pathan Borderland* (1963), and *The Way of the Pathans* (2d ed. 1973).

Pathé, Charles (păthā', Fr. shärl pätā'), 1873–1957, French photographer. He was the first to present (c.1909) the newsreel as a regular attraction at a theater in Paris. In 1910 he introduced the newsreel to the United States; thereafter the Pathé News Reel became an international product.

pathology, study of the cause of DISEASE and the modifications in function and changes in structure produced in any organ or part of the body by disease. The changes in tissue include degeneration, atrophy, hypertrophy, and inflammation. The microscope is an important factor in detecting tissue changes, especially in the examination of small sections of tissue removed for diagnosis (biopsy); for this reason real progress in pathology was not made until the 19th cent. X-ray films and testing of body fluids for abnormal composition are other diagnostic techniques. Experimental and comparative pathology are branches of the science. See E. R. Long, *A History of Pathology* (1962, repr. 1965); W. A. Anderson and T. M. Scotti, *Synopsis of Pathology* (8th ed. 1972); L. V. Crowley, *Introductory Concepts in Pathology* (1972).

Pathros (păth'rŏs), biblical name of Upper Egypt. It is mentioned as a place where Hebrews lived. The inhabitants are Pathrusim. Gen. 10.14; Isa. 11.11; Jer. 44.1,15; Ezek. 29.14; 30.14.

Patiala and East Punjab States Union (pətēä'lə, pənjäb'), former union of states, 10,099 sq mi (26,156 sq km), NW India. The capital was Patiala (1971 pop. 151,903). Comprising six former princely states, it was the only area in India in which the Sikhs had a majority. It was merged with Punjab state in 1956.

Patience: see PEARL, THE.

patience: see SOLITAIRE.

patina (păt'ənə), coating of carbonate of copper on articles of copper or bronze, formed after long exposure to a moist atmosphere or burial in the earth. Although commonly green, patina varies in color and consistency; it may be red, brown, black, blue, or gray, or it may be smooth, glossy, or crusty. It may be imitated by a number of oxidation processes. The term has been extended to include the film formed on metals, pottery, marble, and other materials by exposure and to the mellow surface acquired by furniture with time and waxing.

Patinir, Patenier, or **Patiner, Joachim de** (all: yō'ākhĭm də pätĭnēr'), d. 1524, Flemish landscape and religious painter. He probably studied with Gerard David in Bruges. In 1515 he was a member of the painters' guild in Antwerp, where he spent the remainder of his life. In 1521 his friend Dürer attended his second wedding and painted his portrait. Patinir was the first Flemish painter to regard himself primarily as a landscape painter. While small figures supply the theme of his pictures, they were sometimes painted by other artists. His immense vistas, painted with a limpid and meticulous clarity, have a serene lyricism. Among the best are *The Flight into Egypt* (Antwerp); *The Rest on the Flight into Egypt* (Prado); *The Baptism of Christ* (Vienna); *St. John at Patmos* (National Gall., London); and *Rest by the Way* (Minneapolis Inst. of Arts). The Metropolitan Museum has a fine triptych. See study by R. A. Koch (1968).

Patiño, Simón Ituri (sēmōn' ētōō'rē pätē'nyō), 1868–1947, Bolivian capitalist. He owned rich tin mines in Bolivia and invested his enormous fortune, thought to have been among the world's largest, in other financial enterprises. Called the Tin King, Patiño exerted considerable influence on his country's governmental policies, though he spent most of the latter half of his life abroad. Many of his Bolivian holdings were nationalized after the revolution of 1952. See biography by John Hewlett (1947).

Patkul, Johann Reinhold von (yō'hän rīn'hôlt fən pät'kōōl), 1660–1707, Livonian nobleman. He incurred the wrath of Charles XI of Sweden by championing the rights of the Livonian gentry and fled abroad to escape punishment. In 1698, Patkul entered the service of Augustus II of Poland and Saxony. He inspired Augustus's scheme to wrest Livonia from Sweden and reunite it with Poland and was instrumental in forming the anti-Swedish alliance of Poland, Denmark, and Russia that led (1700) to the NORTHERN WAR. He held high commands in the war, but when Augustus II made peace with Sweden at Altranstädt (1706) he delivered Patkul to Charles XII, who had him broken on the wheel.

Patmore, Coventry Kersey Dighton, 1823–96, English poet. Patmore's first poetry, published in 1844, led to an assistant librarianship (1846–65) at the British Museum. His principal works are *The Angel in the House* (in 4 books, 1854, 1856, 1860, 1863), a long poem that exalts the sanctity of married love (Patmore himself was happily married three times), and *The Unknown Eros* (1877), a series of odes reflecting the spiritual change effected by his conversion (1864) to Roman Catholicism. In 1878, *Tamerton Church Tower and Other Poems* (1853) was reprinted with *Amelia* and included the "Essay on English Metrical Law." Although Patmore's early poetry seems insipid and sentimental, his later work is bolder, more ornate, and more profound. See his collected poems (ed. by Frederick Page, 1949) and *Memoirs and Correspondence* (ed. by Basil Champneys, 1900–1901); studies by E. J. Oliver (1956), J. C. Reid (1957), and Osbert Burdett (1921, repr. 1973).

Pátmos (pät'môs, păt'məs), island (1971 pop. 2,432), c.13 sq mi (34 sq km), SE Greece, in the Aegean Sea; one of the DODECANESE, near Turkey. On the island, according to Rev. 1.9, the exiled St. John the Divine wrote the Revelation. The Monastery of St. John, founded there in the 11th cent. to commemorate his exile, holds a valuable manuscript collection.

Patna (păt'nə, pŭt'–), city (1971 pop. 474,349), capital of Bihar state, NE India, on the Ganges River. It is the hub of a rice-growing region and is an administrative and commercial center. The ancient Pataliputra, it was an imperial city during the Mauryan (c.325–185 B.C.) and Gupta (c.320–545 A.D.) eras. Asoka (270–230 B.C.) built a large palace there, and numerous ruins of the period remain. The Univ. of Patna was opened in 1917.

Paton, Alan (pā'tən), 1903–, South African novelist. A devoted leader in the struggle to end the oppression of the South African Negro, he served (1935–47) as principal of the Diepkloof Reformatory (near Johannesburg) for delinquent boys, where he instituted many reforms. After the publication of his first novel, *Cry, the Beloved Country* (1948), he became active in South African political affairs. He helped form the Liberal Association of South Africa, which later emerged as a political party. Paton's fiction, written with simplicity and compassion, reflects the deep conflicts that exist in South Africa today. His second novel, *Too Late the Phalarope,* appeared in 1953, and *Tales from a Troubled Land,* a collection of short stories, in 1961. Among his other works are *South Africa in Transition* (1956); *Hope for South Africa* (1958); *The Long View* (1968), a volume of essays; and *For You Departed* (1969), a memoir and tribute to his wife. Maxwell Anderson's play *Lost in the Stars* (1948) was based on *Cry, the Beloved Country.*

Patos, Lagoa dos (ləgô'ə dōōs pä'tōōs) [Port.,=lake of the ducks], shallow tidal lagoon, c.150 mi (240 km) long and up to 30 mi (48 km) wide, Rio Grande do Sul state, SE Brazil. A wide sandbar separates it from the Atlantic Ocean. Pôrto Alegre, at the head of the lagoon, is connected with Rio Grande and the sea by a dredged shipping channel. The lagoon is an important fishing ground. Rice is grown along the western shoreline.

Pátrai (pä'trā) or **Patras** (pətrăs', păt'rəs), Lat. *Patrae,* city (1971 pop. 111,607), capital of Akhaía prefecture, central Greece, in the Peloponnesus. It is a port on the Gulf of Pátrai, which connects the Gulf of Corinth with the Ionian Sea. Pátrai is a commercial, industrial, and transportation center that ships currants, tobacco, wine, olive oil, and sheepskins. It was allied with Athens in the Peloponnesian War and became (3d cent. B.C.) a leading member of the Second ACHAEAN LEAGUE. It led a revolt against the Macedonians in 218 B.C. but sank into insignificance before the Roman conquest (146 B.C.) of Greece; it was revived (late 1st cent. B.C.) as a Roman military colony by Augustus and soon flourished as a port. The city was conquered by the French nobleman Geoffroi I de Villehardouin in 1205 and was included in the Latin principality of Achaia. Pátrai was captured by the Ottoman Turks in 1458, passed to Venice in 1687, and was retaken by the Turks in 1715. The city was destroyed (1821) in the Greek War of Independence and was rebuilt on a rectangular pattern by Count Capo d'Istria in 1829. A university is there.

Patras, Greece: see PÁTRAI.

patriarch (pā'trēärk), in biblical tradition, one of the antediluvian progenitors of the race as given in Genesis (e.g., Seth) or one of the ancestors of the Jews (e.g., Abraham, Isaac, Jacob, and, sometimes, the sons of Jacob). The Testaments of the Twelve Patriarchs is the name of one of the PSEUDEPIGRAPHA.

patriarch, in Christian churches, title of certain exalted bishops, implying authority over a number of other bishops. There were originally three patriarchates: the West, held by the bishop of Rome (the pope; see PAPACY), Alexandria, and Antioch. To these were added Constantinople (381) and Jerusalem (451). To the West belonged everything W of the Balkans and Cyrene, and Constantinople ruled most of the Byzantine Empire. Syria and Mesopotamia were under Antioch, Palestine under Jerusalem, and Egypt under Alexandria. The triumph of Monophysitism in Egypt and Syria (5th–6th cent.) created new churches. Since then the three Orthodox patriarchs in Asia have had small, minority jurisdictions; they abandoned (12th cent.) their local rites in favor of the Byzantine. Besides the five ancient patriarchates there are a number of others. In communion with the pope there are 11: the Latin-rite patriarch of Jerusalem, who is bishop of local Latin-rite Catholics (the purely titular Latin-rite patriarchates of Constantinople, Alexandria, and Antioch were abolished in 1964); six who are heads of Eastern rites, having generally full patriarchal powers and not usually resident in their official sees, namely, Alexandria (Coptic rite), Antioch (three: Syrian rite, Melchite, and Maronite), Babylon (Chaldean rite; see NESTORIAN CHURCH), and Cilicia (Armenian rite); finally, in the Western Church the title patriarch is conferred, purely as an honor, on four prelates, the archbishop of Goa (patriarch of the East Indies), the archbishop of Lisbon, the archbishop of Venice, and the patriarch of the West Indies (normally Spanish). In the Russian Orthodox Church the czar set up (1580) a patriarch of Moscow; the title was abolished (1721) by Peter the Great and revived in 1917 (see ORTHODOX EASTERN CHURCH). The Orthodox archbishops of Belgrade and of Bucharest are called patriarchs. Besides all these there are a Coptic patriarch of Alexandria, a Jacobite patriarch of Antioch, a Nestorian patriarch, and four Armenian patriarchs (of Echmiadzin, Sis, Jersualem, and Constantinople).

patrician (pətrĭsh'ən) [Lat.,=of the fathers], member of the privileged class of ancient Rome. Two distinct classes appear to have come into being at the beginning of the republic; the PLEBS became the clientes [clients], who had no legal rights and looked to the patricians as their protectors or patroni [patrons]. Only the patricians held public office, whether civil or religious. From the 6th cent. B.C. the plebs struggled constantly for political equality until, by the 3d cent. B.C., the only offices reserved to the patricians were the civil office of interrex and some priestly offices. The increasing number of plebs in office together with patricians gave rise to the nobiles, an aristocracy of ruling families of both classes. Caesar and Augustus promoted plebs to the patrician class. Later, the term *patrician* became a title of honor. External marks of a patrician were a distinctive tunic and a shoe adorned with an ivory crescent. The Julian gens (to which Caesar belonged) was perhaps the most illustrious of patrician families.

Patrick, Saint, c.385-461, Christian missionary, the Apostle of Ireland, b. Bannavem Taberniae, (an unknown place in Britain, possibly near the Severn or in Pembroke). The facts of his life are largely obscured by legend. He belonged to a Christian family of Roman citizenship. Captured when barely 16 by Irish marauders and enslaved, he worked for six years as a herdsman on the slopes of Slemish (near Ballymena, Co. Antrim) or of Croaghpatrick or (most likely) of both. Then, in response to a voice, he escaped and embarked for Gaul. He spent some years wandering on the Continent and probably visited the Monastery of St. Martin at Marmoutier. He entered the monastery at Lérins and received the tonsure. He returned c.413 to his native Britain and lived for some years with relatives. During this time he had a vision that called him to return to Ireland to Christianize it. Accordingly, he returned to Europe (c.419) to perfect himself as a missionary. The next 12 years were spent in study at Auxerre. In 431, St. PALLADIUS, first missionary bishop sent to Ireland, died; Patrick was consecrated (432) in his place by St. GERMANUS OF AUXERRE. That winter Patrick landed near Saul and remained until spring, when he went to Tara and gained his first major converts. He defied the pagan priests of Tara by kindling the Easter fire on Slane, a nearby hill. This challenge to paganism created at first indignation, and subsequently respect, in the court of the high king. Tara became Patrick's headquarters, and with a band of followers he converted successively Meath, Leitrim, Cavan, and W Ireland. Further details of his missions are only generally known. In 444 or 445, with the approval of Pope St. Leo I, Patrick established his archiepiscopal see at Armagh. St. Patrick's mission was successful; Ireland was almost entirely Christian by the time of his death. He understood and wisely preserved the social structure of the country, converting the people tribe by tribe. Out of his hierarchy, organized by tribal units, developed the Celtic abbot-bishop system. At Patrick's instance, the traditional laws of Ireland were codified. Patrick modified them to harmonize with Christian practice, and he mitigated the harsher ones, particularly those that dealt with slaves and taxation of the poor. He introduced the Roman alphabet. In 457 he retired to Saul, where he died. He was buried in Downpatrick, which was a great European shrine until its destruction by the English government in 1539. Also enshrined to him is Croaghpatrick. Patrick's connection with SAINT PATRICK'S PURGATORY in Lough Derg is undoubtedly only legendary. The prime source for Patrick's life is the *Confessions,* a moving apology for his life and work written during his last years. Some years earlier he had written the *Letter to the Soldiers of Coroticus.* This is an angry appeal to raiders, supposedly Roman-British Christians, to repudiate their ruler Coroticus for his bloody raid on Ireland, and to return the women taken captive. St. Patrick was probably the author of the *Lorica* (or *Breastplate*) *of St. Patrick,* also called *The Cry of the Deer* (in Irish, *Fáed Fíada*), a mystic poem of faith, written in Irish and Latin. St. Patrick was one of the most successful missionaries in history. His personality is said to have been unusually winning. Feast: March 17. See Ludwig Bieler, ed., *Works of Saint Patrick* (1953); biographies by J. B. Bury (1905) and Paul Gallico (1958); study by R. P. C. Hanson (1968).

Patrimony of Saint Peter: see PAPAL STATES.

Patripassians: see MONARCHIANISM.

patristic literature, Christian writings of the first few centuries. They are chiefly in Greek and Latin; there is analogous writing in Syriac and in Armenian. The first period of patristic literature (1st-2d cent.) includes the works of St. CLEMENT I, St. IGNATIUS OF ANTIOCH, St. POLYCARP, and PAPIAS, the writing known as the Shepherd of Hermas (see HERMAS, SHEPHERD OF), the DIDACHE, and the first Christian PSEUDEPIGRAPHA. The writers of the 3d cent., often called the ante-Nicene Fathers, are principally St. JUSTIN MARTYR, CLEMENT OF ALEXANDRIA, St. IRENAEUS, ORIGEN, TERTULLIAN, and St. CYPRIAN. The last two of these are the earliest Fathers to write in Latin. As Christianity established itself, the interest shifted from apologetics to the new theological questions and to sermons and exegesis of Scripture. In the 4th and 5th cent. the number of writers increased greatly. The chief writers in Greek were EUSEBIUS OF CAESAREA, St. GREGORY NAZIANZEN, St. GREGORY OF NYSSA, St. BASIL THE GREAT, St. JOHN CHRYSOSTOM, St. Cyril (of Jerusalem), St. CYRIL (of Alexandria), and St. ATHANASIUS. Among the Latin Fathers were St. HILARY OF POITIERS, St. AMBROSE, St. AUGUSTINE, St. JEROME (who set a standard for later Latin in the Vulgate), CASSIAN, SALVIAN, St. HILARY OF ARLES, St. CAESARIUS OF ARLES, and St. GREGORY OF TOURS. The list in the West is closed conventionally with St. GREGORY, although St. Bernard of Clairvaux is often called the last of the Fathers. The canon of Greek Fathers is closed with St. JOHN OF DAMASCUS. There is a monumental collection of the Fathers (to Innocent III in the West and to the fall of Constantinople in the East) by Jacques Paul MIGNE; the Greek texts are accompanied by Latin translations. There are several collections of the Fathers in English, including new editions recently undertaken, and innumerable individual translations.

Patrobas (păt'rəbăs), Christian. Rom. 16.14.

Patroclus (pətrō'kləs): see ACHILLES.

patron [Lat.,=like a father], one who lends influential support to some person, cause, art, or institution. Patronage existed in various ancient cultures but was primarily a Roman institution. In Roman law the lord was *patronus* (protector or defender) in relation to his freedmen and to others, known as his clients, whom he represented in the senate and before tribunals. Roman communities and provinces chose a respected citizen as patron to defend their interests against the central government. Under the Roman Empire the term was applied to persons like MAECENAS who supported artists and writers, and thus the present idea of patronage developed. Perhaps the most munificent patronage occurred in Italy during the RENAISSANCE under patrons such as the MEDICI, the SFORZA, and many popes. FRANCIS I of France and his sister MARGARET OF NAVARRE were distinguished patrons of art and letters; a famous English patron was Lord CHESTERFIELD. Since ancient times Christians have honored patron saints as tutelary guardians of persons, institutions, places, and crafts. The patron saint of England is St. George or Edward the Confessor; of Ireland, St. Patrick; of Scotland, St. Andrew; of the United States (among Roman Catholics), Our Lady of the Immaculate Conception; and of children, St. Nicholas.

Patrons of Husbandry: see GRANGER MOVEMENT.

patroon (pətrōōn') [Dutch,=patron or employer], in American history, the name given to a Dutch landowner in New Netherland who exerted manorial rights in colonial times. To encourage emigration of Dutch farmers to America, the Dutch West India Company, by a 1629 charter, granted large estates (16 mi/26 km of land along navigable rivers or 8 mi/13 km on each shore and extending inland as far as it proved convenient) to members of the company who would establish settlements of 50 persons within four years. These company members, called patroons, were granted many privileges that were feudal in nature—the right to hold land as a perpetual grant, the right to establish civil and criminal courts, and the right to appoint local officers. Settlers were exempt from public taxes for a decade, but they were specifically required to pay the patroon in money, goods, or services. Manufacturing was prohibited under heavy penalty, and commerce was restricted to a great extent. Before long several estates were established along the Delaware, Connecticut, and Hudson rivers. In 1640 the charter was revised by the Dutch West India Company; the size of the land grants was halved, manufacturing was permitted, and all Dutch inhabitants in good standing could obtain estates. Indian raids, mismanagement, and insufficient cooperation from the Dutch West India Company, however, caused the patroons to fail. The only patroonship that succeeded was Rensselaerswyck, a large estate on the Hudson, which remained in the hands of the Van Rensselaer family until the middle of the 19th cent. After New Netherland came under English control in 1664, the patroon system continued and underwent few changes until 1775, when patroons became proprietors of estates. Some characteristics of feudal tenure did remain, and this condition brought about increasing tension between landlord and tenant in New York state until the ANTIRENT WAR (1839-46) brought about important modifications. See S. G. Nissenson, *Patroon's Domain* (1937, repr. 1973).

Patroon painters, group of portraitists active in colonial New York from 1715 to 1730. Their work embodied the first clearly American style. The Patroon painters served the Dutch families of New York, painting full or three-quarter-length figures, often gesturing and placed within an architectural setting. Animal and floral motifs were common in their works.

Pattani or **Patani** (both: pät'tänē'), city (1964 est. pop. 20,000), capital of Pattani prov., S Thailand, on the east coast of the Malay Peninsula, near the mouth of the Gulf of Siam. It is a port and the center of a region producing most of the spices grown in Thailand, as well as rubber and coconuts. Tin is mined and smelted, and salt is extracted in the city. The people are for the most part Malay Muslims. Pattani was a seat of the Sailendra power during the Sailendra domination of the Malay Peninsula and later was the center of a Malay state, which was drawn into the Thai orbit. With Ayutthaya, it was one of the first places in Siam opened to the Portuguese in the 16th cent. At first bound only by tenuous links of suzerainty to the courts of Ayutthaya and Bangkok, against which it was several times in revolt, Pattani was reduced to provincial status in the 19th cent.

pattern recognition: see OPTICAL SENSING.

Patterson, family of American journalists. **Robert Wilson Patterson,** 1850-1910, b. Chicago, grad. Williams, 1871, became (1871) a reporter on the Chicago *Times* and after 1873 was attached to the Chicago *Tribune.* He married Elinor Medill, the daughter of Joseph MEDILL. After being successively assistant night editor, Washington correspondent, editorial writer, and managing editor, he became, upon the death of his father-in-law in 1899, editor in chief of the newspaper, a position he held until his death. His son, **Joseph Medill Patterson,** 1879-1946, b. Chicago, worked (1901-5) on the staff of the Chicago *Tribune,* was elected (1903) to the Illinois legislature, and served (1905-6) as commissioner of public works in Chicago. His earlier socialistic views—recorded in the novels, plays, and articles that he wrote—gradually faded away after 1910, when he returned to the staff of the *Tribune.* By 1914, Patterson gained part control of the *Tribune,* which was managed by his cousins, Joseph Medill McCormick and Robert Rutherford MCCORMICK, and he remained as its coeditor until 1925. He served in France in World War I, and upon his return to the United States he founded (1919) in New York City the *Daily News*—the first successful tabloid in the country. By sensationalizing sex and crime and by extensive use of photography, Patterson gave his newspaper the top circulation in the United States. In 1925 he relinquished his holdings in the Chicago *Tribune* and then continued to expand the operations of the *Daily News* syndicate. He supported President Franklin D. Roosevelt until 1940, after which Patterson's isolationist viewpoint caused him to attack the Democratic administration. His sister, **Eleanor Medill Patterson,** 1884-1948, b. Chicago, also was a newspaper editor. She inherited an interest in the Chicago *Tribune* and became attached to the New York *Daily News.* In 1930 she became editor of the Hearst syndicate's Washington *Herald,* which she leased, together with the Washington *Times,* in 1937. Two years later she purchased the two newspapers and merged them into the Washington *Times-Herald.* "Cissy" Patterson became well-known for her spectacular news presentation. Under the name of Eleanor M. Gizycka she wrote the books *Glass Houses* (1926) and *Fall Flight* (1928). See biographies by P. F. Healy (1966) and R. A. Hoge (1966). Joseph Medill Patterson's daughter, **Alicia Patterson,** 1906–63, b. Chicago, joined the *Daily News* as a reporter in 1927. In 1939, in conjunction with her husband, Henry Guggenheim, she founded *Newsday* in Garden City, New York. She patterned her paper after her father's tabloid but remained a firm supporter of President Franklin D. Roosevelt and a strong internationalist. See J. W. Tebbel, *An American Dynasty* (1947, repr. 1968).

Patterson, Elizabeth, 1785–1879, American wife of Jérôme BONAPARTE, b. Baltimore. On a visit to America, Jérôme Bonaparte, brother of Napoleon Bonaparte, met and married her (1803). Jérôme was a minor, and Napoleon refused to recognize the marriage. When Jérôme returned (1805) to France, his wife was forbidden to land and went to England, where her son, Jerome Napoleon Bonaparte, was born. Napoleon issued (1806) a state decree of annulment for his brother, and Elizabeth Patterson was given a large annual pension. See E. L. Didier, *Life and Letters of Mme Bonaparte* (1879); C. E. N. Macartney and J. G. Dorrance, *The Bonapartes in America* (1939); Sidney Mitchell, *A Family Lawsuit* (1958).

Patterson, Floyd, 1935–, American boxer, b. near Waco, N.C. He was brought up in Brooklyn, N.Y. and was sent to the Wiltwyck School for Boys at Esopus, N.Y., a correctional institution, where he first began to box. As an amateur he won 40 of 44 fights, climaxing his career by winning (1952) the Olympic middleweight championship. He then turned professional and lost only one fight (a disputed decision in 1954) before he became, at the age of 21, the youngest man to win the heavyweight title; he succeeded Rocky Marciano, who had retired, by defeating (1956) Archie Moore. He successfully defended his title four times before losing it to Ingemar Johansson, of Sweden, in 1959. Patterson knocked out Johansson one year later to become the first man ever to regain the heavyweight title. Patterson also knocked out Johansson in their third fight (1961). In Sept., 1962, Patterson lost the championship to Sonny Liston by a first-round knockout. Despite the defeat Patterson remained a vigorous competitor and continued to box into the early 1970s. See his autobiography, *Victory over Myself* (1962).

Patti, Adelina (ădəlē'nə păt'ē), 1843–1919, coloratura soprano, b. Madrid, of Italian parents. She was trained in New York City, where she made her debut in 1859, thereafter singing with great acclaim in London, Paris, and Milan. In 1881 she returned to the United States and became the most popular and best-paid singer of her day. Her sisters, Carlotta and Amalia, followed her to the operatic stage, and her brother, Carlo, conducted opera in New Orleans, St. Louis, and New York.

Patton, George Smith, Jr., 1885–1945, American general, b. San Gabriel, Calif. A graduate of West Point (1909), he served in World War I and was wounded while commanding a tank brigade in France. Subsequently he served in the cavalry and the tank corps. In World War II he commanded (1942–43) a corps in North Africa and the 7th Army in Sicily. Despite a brilliant record, a much-publicized incident (Patton slapped a soldier suffering from battle fatigue) cost him his command and delayed until Aug., 1944, promotion to the permanent rank of major general. Early in 1944 he was given command of the 3d Army, which spearheaded the spectacular sweep of U.S. forces from Normandy through Brittany and N France, relieved Bastogne in Dec., 1944 (see BATTLE OF THE BULGE), crossed the Rhine (March, 1945), and raced across S Germany into Czechoslovakia. As military governor of Bavaria, he was criticized for leniency to Nazis and was removed (Oct., 1945) to take charge of the U.S. 15th Army. Patton was fatally injured in an automobile accident in Germany. See his autobiography, *War as I Knew It* (1947); biographies by H. H. Semmes (1955) and Fred Ayer, Jr. (1971); study by Herbert Essame (1974); Martin Blumenson, ed., *The Patton Papers* (Vol. I, 1972).

Patuxent (pətŭk'sənt), river, c.100 mi (160 km) long, rising in central Md. and flowing SE to Chesapeake Bay. Its estuary is a deepwater anchorage, and the river has important oyster beds.

Pátzcuaro (pät'skwärō), lake, c.100 sq mi (260 sq km) Michoacán state, W Mexico. Its indented shores, dotted with Tarascan Indian villages, green islands, and the curious native sailboats help make Lake Pátzcuaro popular as a resort. The lake is rich in fish. Pátzcuaro is the chief town on the lake.

Patzinaks: see PECHENEGS.

Pau (pā'yōō), unlocated capital city of an Edomite king. Gen. 36.39. It appears as Pai in 1 Chron. 1.50.

Pau (pō), city (1968 pop. 76,227), capital of Pyrénées-Atlantiques dept., SW France, at the foot of the Pyrenees. It is a major year-round tourist center, renowned for its scenery. It has metallurgical and wool industries, and shoes and clothing are manufactured. Founded in the 11th cent., it became the capital of BÉARN in the 15th cent. and the residence of the kings of NAVARRE in 1512. Henry IV was born in its château. Its university was founded in 1724.

Paul, Saint, d. A.D. 64? or 67?, the apostle to the Gentiles, b. Tarsus, Asia Minor. He was a Jew. His father was a Roman citizen, probably of some means, and Paul was a tentmaker by trade. His Jewish name was Saul. He was educated in Jerusalem, where he studied under Gamaliel and became a zealous nationalist; he was probably a Pharisee. The chronology of St. Paul's life is difficult, but there is general agreement (within a few years) on almost all details. The hypothetical dates given here are according to one chronological system. The sources for St. Paul's life are the Acts of the Apostles, in which he is the dominating figure, and the Pauline Epistles. The value of the latter depends on the extent to which they are accepted as genuinely written by the apostle. Romans, First and Second Corinthians, Galatians, Philippians, Colossians, First Thessalonians, and Philemon are undoubted; Ephesians and Second Thessalonians are accepted by all but a few critics; First and Second Timothy and Titus are generally considered to be in their present form of late provenance; finally, Hebrews was not written by St. Paul himself. His first known contact with Christianity is his approving presence at the martyrdom of St. Stephen. Soon after this he got a commission from the chief priest to go to Damascus to help suppress Christianity there (A.D. 33). As he approached Damascus he suddenly saw a blinding light and heard Jesus ask, "Why persecutest thou me?" Paul was temporarily blinded and was led into Damascus, where he was found (on the Lord's direction) by the disciple Ananias. On regaining his sight, Paul was baptized and immediately began preaching. (Acts 8.1–3; 9.1–30; 22.3–21; 26.9–23; Gal. 1.12–15.) Paul spent the next 13 years learning the faith, part of the time living in seclusion in the Arabian desert. He visited Jerusalem probably twice (A.D. 37, 44) and dwelt at Tarsus and Antioch for some time. (Acts 11.) From Antioch, Paul set out on his first missionary journey (Acts 13–14.27; A.D. 47–49), on which he was accompanied by St. Barnabas and for a time by St. Mark. In general the method was to go from city to city preaching in synagogues and in market places. Churches were set up, and as soon as the little Christian groups seemed strong enough the apostle and his companions would move on. On the first mission they went to Cyprus, thence across to Perga in Pamphylia. From Perga they moved N to Antioch of Pisidia, then in a southerly turn east of the mountains via Iconium and Lystra to Derbe. They then returned over their course to the Pamphylian coast and shipped from Attalia back to Antioch. About A.D. 50 there was a council of the apostles at Jerusalem to discuss whether Gentile Christians should be circumcised, i.e., whether Christianity was to be a Jewish sect. St. Paul opposed the Judaistic group vigorously, and the council decided against them. (Acts 15; Gal. 2.) On his second mission (Acts 15.36–18.22; A.D. 50–53) Paul, having quarreled with Barnabas, was accompanied by Silas. They went north by land from Jerusalem to Galatia via Lystra. Thence they moved W across Asia Minor to Troas, on the Aegean Sea. On visits to Philippi and Salonica they founded two churches that were to become great. After halting at Beroea in Thessaly they sailed to Athens, where Paul delivered his famous address on the "unknown god" in the market. (Acts 17.16–34.) From Athens, Paul went to Corinth. In the course of a long stay there he wrote First and Second Thessalonians (A.D. 52). Possibly about this time he also wrote his letter to the Galatians, although some scholars think this was the earliest of the epistles (written from Antioch), while others believe it was written later from Ephesus. At length Paul sailed to Caesarea in Palestine and visited Jerusalem again. He spent some time in Antioch. The third missionary journey of St. Paul (Acts 18.23–21.26; A.D. 53–57) took him to Galatia, then Phrygia, and over to Ephesus. His two-and-a-half-year stay in Ephesus was one of the most fruitful periods of his life; in this time he wrote his two letters to the Corinthians (A.D. c.56). By way of Macedonia he went to Corinth to help the Christians there. He probably wrote the Epistle to the Romans in Corinth. Thence he returned to Ephesus and finally to Jerusalem. This was his last visit to the Holy City (A.D. 57–59), for soon after he arrived he was arrested for provoking a riot. After being held prisoner for two years and after hearings before the council of priests, before the Roman procurator Felix and his successor Festus, before Herod Agrippa II, and again before Festus, he appealed to Rome on his citizen's right. So he was sent to Rome under guard. (Acts 21.27–28.31.) On the way they were shipwrecked on Malta but finally landed at Puteoli (Puzzuoli). Paul was imprisoned (A.D. 60) in Rome but was allowed to conduct his ministry among the Roman Christians and Jews who visited him. Of his final fate tradition says that he was beheaded south of the city, near the Ostian Way, probably during the persecution of Nero. A lesser tradition claims that Paul was released after his first imprisonment and that he went East again, and perhaps also to Spain, before his martyrdom. Some scholars believe that Paul was executed after his initial imprisonment, probably A.D. 62. St. Paul's tomb and shrine are at the Roman basilica of St. Paul's Without the Walls. St. Paul's figure dominates the apostolic age, and his epistles have left a tremendous impress on Christianity. The first Christian theological writing is found in them, where it is characterized rather by spiritual fervor than by systematic analysis. St. Paul became a fountainhead of Christian doctrine, and countless interpretations have been given of his teachings. Thus, Roman Catholic theology leans upon him at all times, and Martin Luther derived from the Epistle to the Romans his principle of justification by faith alone. There can be no doubt that Paul's interpretation of the life, death, and resurrection of Jesus, his doctrine of the church as the mystical body of Christ, his teaching on law and grace, and his view of justification have been decisive in the formation of the Christian faith. The feast of St. Peter and St. Paul, June 29, is one of the principal days of the church calendar; the conversion of St. Paul is commemorated Jan. 25. See biography by John Pollock (1969); Roman Catholic studies by Robert Sencourt (1948) and Amédée Brunot (tr. 1959); Protestant studies by Martin Dibelius (tr. 1953, repr. 1959) and William Barclay (1958); James Kallas, *The Satanward View* (1966); Günther Bornkamm, *Paul* (tr. 1971).

Paul II, 1417–71, pope (1464–71), a Venetian named Pietro Barbo; successor of Pius II. He was a nephew of Eugene IV. A Renaissance pope, he patronized printing, beautified and improved Rome, and collected antiquities. Paul, like Pius II, was involved in struggles with the Bohemian George of Podebrad and with Louis XI of France. He was succeeded by Sixtus IV.

Paul III, 1468–1549, pope (1534–49), a Roman named Alessandro Farnese; successor of Clement VII. He was created cardinal by Alexander VI, and his influence increased steadily. One of the most astute diplomats in the church, he directed his efforts chiefly in aid of the reforming party. With his election a new era in the papacy opened, for the Catholic Reformation (see REFORMATION, CATHOLIC) began. Paul favored a new council to reconcile the Protestants and reform the church. After elaborate preparations, countless intrigues, and several false starts the Council of Trent (see TRENT, COUNCIL OF) convened (1545). At his accession Paul appointed a special commission, made up of the most ardent reformers; this commission was valuable to the council for the information it had on actual conditions in Rome. Paul also patronized the newly founded Jesuits (see JESUS, SOCIETY OF), the great agents of the Catholic Reformation. The pope's interest in art was very great: he founded the Farnese Palace, had Michelangelo continue the decoration of the Sistine Chapel, and rebuilt and repaved many streets in Rome. He was succeeded by Julius III.

Paul IV, 1476–1559, pope (1555–59), a Neapolitan named Gian Pietro Carafa; successor of Marcellus II. First superior of the Theatines (see CAJETAN, SAINT), he was sternly ascetic. A leading reformer, he organized the Inquisition set up by Paul III. As pope, he labored to purify the clergy and abolish corruption and worldliness from the papal court, thus promoting reform (see REFORMATION, CATHOLIC). By his extreme views he alienated Catholic rulers. He repudiated the settlement between Mary I of England and Reginald Cardinal POLE, and he later declared Elizabeth I illegitimate and unfit to be queen. He was succeeded by Pius IV.

Paul V, 1552–1621, pope (1605–21), a Roman named Camillo Borghese; successor of Leo XI. He was created cardinal (1596) by Clement VIII and was renowned for his knowledge of canon law. On his election as pope he set out at once to restore all the prerogatives the papacy had ever enjoyed. He soon quarreled with Venice, where clergymen were tried by civil courts and churches could not be built without government consent. In the dispute Paolo Sarpi led the Venetian side and cardinals Baronius and Bellarmine the cause of the Holy See. In 1606 the pope put Venice under interdict, but the Venetian clergy refused to obey. The quarrel ended in 1607 with a Venetian victory. Paul also had a disagreement with France over GALLICANISM and with James I of England over oaths of allegiance. He added to the Vatican Library. His chapel in the Church of Santa Maria Maggiore, Rome, is famous. He was succeeded by Gregory XV.

Paul VI, 1897–, pope (1963–), an Italian (b. Concesio, near Brescia) named Giovanni Battista Montini; successor of John XXIII. The son of a prominent newspaper editor, he was ordained in 1920. Later he did advanced studies in Rome and entered (1922) the Vatican secretariat of state, in which he served for 32 years. After 1944, when Pius XII acted as his own secretary of state, Montini became especially influential as one of the two prosecretaries on whom the pope relied. As archbishop of Milan (1954–63) he showed particular concern with social problems and worked to improve relations between workers and employers. He was created a cardinal in 1958. Elected pope in June, 1963, Paul immediately demonstrated his intention of continuing the reforms of his predecessor, John XXIII. He reconvened the Second Vatican Council (see VATICAN COUNCIL, SECOND) and supervised the carrying out of many of its reforms, such as the vernacularization and reform of the liturgy. With the aim of continuing the work of the council after it ended, he instituted an international synod of bishops, and bishops were instructed to set up councils of priests in their own dioceses. In addition, considerable powers of dispensation were devolved from the Roman Curia onto the bishops, the rules on fasting and abstinence were relaxed, and some of the restrictions on intermarriage were lifted. A commission on canon law revision was also established. In 1964, Paul VI made a pilgrimage to the Holy Land; he was the first pope in over 150 years to leave Italy. That historic journey was followed by trips to India (1964), the United States (1965), where he addressed the United Nations, and other parts of the world, including Africa (1969) and Southeast Asia (1970). Relations between the Vatican and the Communist world were improved; Communist leaders visited the Vatican for the first time, and in 1971 Cardinal MINDSZENTY, whose presence in the U.S. embassy in Budapest had long bedeviled church-state relations in Hungary, was finally persuaded to go to Rome. The broader international outlook of the Vatican under Paul VI was matched by a new ecumenism. The pope met with the leaders of other churches and addressed (1969) the World Council of Churches, and limited doctrinal agreements were reached with the Anglicans and Lutherans. Such accords, however, did not represent any modification of the papal claim to spiritual leadership of the whole Christian Church, nor of the doctrine of papal infallibility. In fact, Pope Paul issued frequent reassertions of papal primacy in the face of growing dissent within the Roman Catholic Church itself. In 1968, in the encyclical *Humanae Vitae,* Paul reaffirmed the church's long-standing ban on contraception. The encyclical, a disappointment to many liberals within the church, raised a storm of protest, and many national hierarchies openly modified the statement. In the ferment that ensued, liberals also raised questions about priestly celibacy, divorce, and the role of women in the church—all issues on which Paul upheld the traditional position of the church. The dispute developed into a real contest of strength between the Vatican and the Dutch hierarchy in particular, which in 1970 endorsed the marriage of priests and the admission of women into the priesthood. The synod of bishops in 1971 supported the pope's stand on priestly celibacy, but a sizable minority were opposed. It appeared that despite Pope Paul's frequent warnings against dissent, challenges to papal authority would continue to occur. At the synod of bishops of 1974, assembled to discuss "evangelization in the modern world," Pope Paul disapproved the bishops' proposal for greater autonomy for the local churches. See his *Christian in the Material World* (tr. 1963), *Dialogues* (tr. 1964), *The Church* (tr. 1964), *The Pope Speaks* (tr. 1968); biography by W. E. Barrett (1964).

Paul I, 1754–1801, czar of Russia (1796–1801), son and successor of Catherine II. His mother disliked him intensely and sought on several occasions to change the succession to his disadvantage. During Catherine's lifetime Paul opposed her domestic policy, which strengthened the nobility, and her expansionist foreign policy. Upon his accession he introduced a law of succession based on primogeniture to strengthen the autocracy against the nobility. Paul rescinded many of the nobles' rights, limited the power of the imperial guards, and attempted to place limits on the nobility's exploitation of their serfs. He encouraged trade and industry and attempted to modernize the armed forces. His erratic conduct and whimsical application of petty regulations, however, caused great discontent. He prohibited foreign travel, certain types of dress, and the importation of Western books and music. In foreign policy, Paul joined (1798) the second coalition against France, but withdrew from the coalition the next year. He formed an armed neutrality league of Russia, Denmark, Sweden, and Prussia to counter English interference in neutral shipping, and he ordered an abortive invasion of India. Dissatisfaction with his rule, particularly among the nobles and military officers, led to a conspiracy against Paul, and he was murdered. His son and successor, Alexander I, knew of the conspiracy but did not participate in the murder. See biographies by Kazimierz Waliszewski (1913, repr. 1969) and M. E. Almedirgen (1959).

Paul, 1901–64, king of the Hellenes (1947–64), brother and successor of George II. He married (1938) Princess Frederika of Brunswick. During Paul's reign Greece followed a pro-Western policy, and the CYPRUS question was temporarily resolved. Paul was succeeded by his son, Constantine II.

Paul, Jean: see RICHTER, JOHANN PAUL FRIEDRICH.

Paul-Boncour, Joseph (zhôzĕf' pōl-bôNko͞or'), 1873–1972, French statesman. Although a Socialist, he remained independent of party ties from 1931 to 1945. He was permanent French delegate to the League of Nations (1932–36), was briefly premier (1932–33), and held several cabinet posts, notably the foreign ministry (1933–34, 1936, 1938). He voted (1940) against granting full powers to Marshal Pétain. In 1945 he was a delegate to the conference at San Francisco to draw up a charter for the United Nations. Paul-Boncour long advocated disarmament and an international police force as the sole effective means of preserving peace. His personal *Recollections of the Third Republic* (tr. 1958) is a political memoir.

Paulding, James Kirke, 1778–1860, American author and public official, Secretary of the Navy under Van Buren, b. near Millbrook, N.Y. He collaborated with Washington Irving and William Irving in producing the periodical *Salmagundi.* In addition, he wrote a number of satirical works, including *John Bull in America* (1825); some 70 tales and several novels, of which the most successful were *Koningsmarke* (1823) and *The Dutchman's Fireside* (1831); and a popular life of George Washington. See his letters (ed. by R. M. Aderman, 1962).

Pauli, Wolfgang (vôlf'gäng pou'lē), 1900–1958, Austro-American physicist, b. Vienna. He studied first with A. Sommerfeld at Munich and then with Niels Bohr at Copenhagen. After lecturing (1923–28) at the Univ. of Hamburg, Pauli was appointed professor at the Federal Institute of Technology, Zürich, which became famous under his direction. In the United States he was a member (1935–36, 1940–46) of the Institute for Advanced Study at Princeton. In 1946 he became a U.S. citizen. He divided his later years between Princeton and Zürich. He was awarded the 1945 Nobel Prize in Physics for his enunciation (1925) of the Pauli EXCLUSION PRINCIPLE, fundamental to quantum mechanics, according to which no two electrons in an atom may be in the same quantum state. It was later found that certain other particles also are governed by the principle. Among his many other achievements was the postulation of the existence of the NEUTRINO (1931), almost a quarter century before it was directly observed in 1955.

Paulicians (pôlĭsh'ənz), Christian heretical sect. The sect developed in Armenia from obscure origins and is first mentioned in the middle of the 6th cent., where it is associated with NESTORIANISM. The teachings of the Paulicians seem to show some gnostic influence, possibly that of MARCION or PAUL OF SAMOSATA, from whom they may have taken their name, and many of the adherents leaned toward ADOPTIONISM. They rejected the sacraments but nevertheless considered baptism of the greatest importance. They were iconoclasts and rejected extreme asceticism. By the 7th cent. the sect spread to the eastern provinces of the Byzantine Empire, where it met with strong persecution. The Council of Dvin (719) brought on new persecutions of the Paulicians in Armenia, but the permissive Isaurian emperors allowed them to flourish and even settled them as allies in Thrace. Renewed persecution caused them to side with the Muslims against Byzantium. By 844, at the height of its power, the sect established a Paulician state at Tephrike (present-day Divriğü, Turkey) under the leadership of Karbeas, or Corbeas. In 871 the Byzantine emperor Basil I ended the power of this state and the survivors fled to Syria and Armenia. In 970 the Paulicians in Syria were deported to the Balkans, where they combined with the BOGOMILS. Those in Armenia became identified with a minor sect, the Tondrakeci. They ceased to be a threat after the 11th cent. and did not survive to modern times. See N. G. Garsoïan, *The Paulician Heresy* (1968).

Pauling, Linus Carl, 1901–, American chemist, b. Portland, Oregon. He is one of the few recipients of two Nobel Prizes, winning the chemistry award in 1954 and the peace prize in 1962. His scientific career has centered around the California Institute of Technology, where he received his doctorate in 1925 and became professor of chemistry in 1931 after a period of study abroad with Arnold Sommerfeld, Niels Bohr, and Erwin Schrödinger. He was among the first to apply the QUANTUM THEORY to calculations of molecular structures; his book *The Nature of the Chemical Bond* (1939, 3d ed. 1960) is still the classic in the field. He developed the concept of resonance to explain covalent bonds in certain organic compounds (see CHEMICAL BOND). His later work concerned molecular biology; using physical techniques, he determined the three-dimensional structures of many antitoxins, amino acids, and proteins. He was the first recipient of two honors awarded by the American Chemical Society: the Langmuir prize (1931) and the Lewis medal (1951). Outside of his scientific work, Pauling has taken a vital interest in public affairs, especially the movement for world disarmament. His *No More War* (1958) is a plea for international peace. In addition to receiving the Nobel Peace Prize, he was among seven awarded the 1968–69 International Lenin Peace Prize. He has also championed the use of large quantities (megadoses) of vitamin C for controlling the common cold, and the use of chemotherapy in general for the cure of mental diseases such as schizophrenia.

Paulinus, Saint (pôlī'nəs), d. 644, Italian missionary, bishop of York (625–33). He was a Roman monk who went to England with the mission of St. AUGUSTINE OF CANTERBURY in 601. For some years he worked in Kent, then went as archbishop to Northumbria. Paulinus succeeded temporarily in converting Northumbria and Lindsey; he was forced to flee to Rochester when paganism returned with King Penda after King Edwin's death. He is sometimes considered the first archbishop of York.

Paulinus or **Suetonius Paulinus** (Caius Suetonius Paulinus) (swētō'nēəs), d. after A.D. 69, Roman general. Under Claudius I he was stationed (A.D. 42) in Mauretania, and he advanced inland past the Atlas Mts. In A.D. 59 he had the command in Britain. While on a campaign to reduce the druid stronghold of Mona (Anglesey), in A.D. 61, he was recalled to S Britain by the uprising of BOADICEA, who defeated the ninth legion and took Verulamium (St. Albans) and Londinium (London). Paulinus suppressed the revolt. After Nero's death he led the troops of OTHO against VITELLIUS, but the victorious Vitellius pardoned him (A.D. 69).

Paulist Fathers, American society of Roman Catholic priests, officially named the Society of Missionary Priests of St. Paul the Apostle (Latin abbr., C.S.P.). It was founded (1858) by Isaac HECKER, who envisioned a group of priests who would work for the conversion of Americans in ways appropriate to American life. The community has remained very small, and all its activities besides preaching are specialized. The Paulists engage in printing, mainly of pamphlets; have founded radio programs; and have built an excellent choir. Their monthly, the *Catholic World,* founded by Father Hecker, was one of the first serious U.S. Catholic journals. The rule of the

Paulist Fathers is based on that of the Redemptorists. See J. M. Gillis, *The Paulists* (1932).

Paul Knutson (no͞ot'sən, kənoo͞t'-), fl. 1354-64, Norse leader, alleged to have explored America. In 1354 or 1355, King Magnus of Norway directed Knutson to conduct an expedition to insure the continuance of Christianity in Greenland, where settlers were reported to have defected from the faith. Although there is no Norwegian evidence that Knutson undertook an expedition, believers in the voyage think that he sailed in 1355 and returned in 1363 or 1364.

Paullus, Aemilius (Lucius Aemilius Paullus Macedonicus) (ēmĭl'ēəs), c.229-160 B.C., Roman general. He was curule aedile (193 B.C.), praetor (191), and consul (182). In his consulship he conquered the Inguani, a Ligurian people. The Macedonian war between Rome and King PERSEUS had dragged on since 171; Paullus, in response to the general demand, accepted (168) a second consulship to fight in Macedonia. Capturing the king near Pydna, he set up the country as a Roman dominion; he also sacked Epirus. His name is sometimes spelled Paulus. Plutarch wrote his life.

Paulo Afonso Falls, Brazil: see SÃO FRANCISCO.

Paul of Aegina (ējī'nə), 7th cent.?, Greek physician. His only extant work is a medical history in seven books; it was translated into English, with a commentary by Francis Adams (3 vol., 1844-47). The sixth book, a treatise on surgery, influenced European and Arabic surgery in the Middle Ages.

Paul of Samosata (səmŏs'ətə), fl. 260-72, Syrian Christian theologian, heretical patriarch of Antioch. He was a friend and high official of ZENOBIA of Palmyra. Paul enounced a dynamic MONARCHIANISM, denying the three Persons of the Trinity. He taught that the Logos came to dwell in Jesus at baptism, but that Jesus possessed no extraordinary nature above other men, the Logos being entirely an attribute of God. Paul was repeatedly challenged and finally excommunicated (269), but he continued to function as bishop under Zenobia's protection until the Romans took Palmyra (272). His influence on Arius and Nestorius was considerable, but his supposed connection with the PAULICIANS is disputed. See ADOPTIONISM.

Paul of the Cross, Saint, 1694-1775, Italian, religious founder of the PASSIONISTS. His original name was Paolo Francesco Danei. He had visions calling him to found a new order and received papal permission in 1725. He was ordained in 1727. His order, intended to revive Christian life by emphasis on the Passion, is vigorous and widespread. Feast: April 28. See biography by Charles Almeras (tr. 1960).

Paulsen, Friedrich (frē'drĭkh poul'sən), 1846-1908, German neo-Kantian philosopher and educator. He was for many years a professor at Berlin. His philosophy was animistic and was chiefly influenced by Gustav FECHNER. Paulsen's major works include *System of Ethics* (1889, tr. 1899) and *Introduction to Philosophy* (1892, tr. 1895), which clearly shows his affiliations with Fechner. One of Paulsen's educational works of great importance is known in English as *German Education, Past and Present* (1907). See his autobiography (tr. and ed. by Theodor Lorenz, 1938).

Paul the Deacon, c.725-799?, Lombard historian. He received a good education, probably at Pavia, and he learned Latin thoroughly and some Greek. He lived at Monte Cassino and at Charlemagne's court. His first work was a continuation of the Roman history of Eutropius through Justinian. He also wrote a history of the diocese of Metz, a source for information about the early family of Charlemagne. Paul's chief work is a history of the Lombards, drawn from sources now lost, covering the last half of the 6th, the 7th, and the first half of the 8th cent. It is one of the oldest histories of a Germanic nation by a German. He also wrote homilies, poems, and a commentary on the Benedictine rule. He is frequently called by his Latin name, Paulus Diaconus.

Paulus (Julius Paulus) (pôl'əs), fl. c.200, Roman jurist. He was extremely prolific and is thought to have written some 300 books. His surviving work displays keen analysis of the opinions of other jurists and trenchant expression of his own views. Paulus was held in great respect; almost one sixth of the *Digest* of the CORPUS JURIS CIVILIS consists of his work, and he was one of the five jurists whose opinions were made authoritative in 426 by a constitution of Theodosius II and Valentinian (see PAPINIAN).

Paulus, Aemilius: see PAULLUS, AEMILIUS.

Paulus, Friedrich (frē'drĭkh pou'lo͝os), 1890-1957, German field marshal. He commanded the army at the siege of Stalingrad and was raised to marshal's rank several hours before his surrender (Jan., 1943) to the Russians. In captivity he joined the Russian-sponsored National Committee for a Free Germany and appealed to the Germans to surrender. Released in 1953, he lived in East Germany until his death.

Paulus Diaconus: see PAUL THE DEACON.

Paumotu: see TUAMOTU ISLANDS.

Pauncefote of Preston, Julian Pauncefote, 1st Baron (pôns'fo͝ot), 1828-1902, British diplomat. He served in various positions in the colonies before becoming (1882) permanent undersecretary for foreign affairs. As minister (ambassador after 1893) to Washington from 1889 until his death, Pauncefote dealt successfully with the problems concerning seal fishing in the Bering Sea, the Venezuela Boundary Dispute, and the Panama Canal question, which was readjusted by the HAY-PAUNCEFOTE TREATIES (1899-1901). He preserved friendly relations between Great Britain and the United States during the Spanish-American War and in 1899, as senior British delegate to the First Hague Conference, was a leading figure in the formation of a permanent tribunal of arbitration. He was created baron in 1899. See biography by R. B. Mowat (1929).

pauperism: see POOR LAW.

Pausanias (pôsā'nēəs), d. c.470 B.C., Spartan general; nephew of King Leonidas. He was the victorious commander at Plataea (479) near Thebes in the Persian Wars and followed up the battle with expeditions to Cyprus and Byzantium. From Byzantium he was called home to face a very circumstantial charge of treasonable negotiations with Persia; he was acquitted (c.475). The accusation was repeated several years later, and he was acquitted again, only to be accused (this time probably justly) of planning a coup at Sparta, in collaboration with the exiled THEMISTOCLES. To escape arrest he took sanctuary in a temple, where he was left to starve.

Pausanias, fl. A.D. 174, traveler and geographer, probably b. Lydia. His *Description of Greece* is an invaluable source for the topography, monuments, and legends of ancient Greece. There are translations by J. G. Frazer and W. H. S. Jones. See also J. G. Frazer, *Maps and Plans to Illustrate Pausanias' Description of Greece* (1930).

Pausias (pô'shēəs), fl. 1st half of 4th cent. B.C., Greek painter. He was celebrated for his decorative paintings, particularly in ENCAUSTIC, a method which he is said to have invented. His most famous single work, *A Sacrifice*, containing an admirably foreshortened and modeled figure of a bull, was preserved until late Roman times in the portico of Pompey's temple in Rome.

pavement, the wearing surface of a road, street, or sidewalk. Parts of Babylon and Rome are believed to have been paved, and the streets of Pompeii were covered with lava blocks; ROMAN ROADS were noted for their durable stone paving. Cobblestones were commonly used from late medieval times into the 19th cent. A pavement known as macadam road, introduced in England in the 19th cent., was used to cover many of the dirt roads then in existence. Commonly used today, it consists basically of compacted layers of small stones cemented into a hard surface by means of stone dust and water (water-bound macadam). Other paving surfaces include concrete, penetration macadam and bituminous-mixed macadam, sheet asphalt, bituminous concrete, and brick, wood, or stone-block pavements. Desirable qualities in pavements include durability, smoothness, quietness, ease of cleaning, and a non-slippery surface. The requirements conflict to a degree, so no one material is ideal in all respects. The subgrade, or natural soil on which the pavement rests, must be cut and shaped to suit the thickness and form of paving and rolled to ensure equal compression. Formerly a foundation of sand-covered earth was considered adequate; today a CONCRETE road slab is commonly used as a foundation for a sheet or block wearing surface. The foundation, like the surface, must be crowned, or slightly arched, for rapid shedding of water or, in the case of walks, sloped toward the gutter. Concrete foundations and surfaces must be provided with expansion joints. The first concrete pavement in the United States was laid in Bellefontaine, Ohio, in 1894; after 1900 the use of concrete increased enormously, mainly to meet the heavy demands of motor traffic. A bituminous macadam pavement made by the penetration method consists of a macadam road on which is poured a bituminous material that penetrates at least 2 in. (5 cm) and forms an impervious binder. For a bituminous-mixed macadam pavement, a heated mixture of stones or crushed rock and bituminous binder is spread on a macadam surface and rolled into a compact mass. A sheet asphalt pavement is built in three courses, a foundation course, a binder course, and a wearing course. The foundation is sometimes of cement concrete 4 to 12 in. (10.2-30.5 cm) thick. The binder course, whose function is to prevent creepage of the upper course, is composed of broken stone and asphalt cement. The wearing surface is a mixture of fine sand, filler, and asphalt cement. Each course is applied hot and is then thoroughly rolled. A bituminous concrete pavement consists of a mixture of graded stone and sand, filler, and a binder of asphalt cement. In a brick pavement a 1-in. (2.5-cm) bedding of sand, cement mortar, or mastic is laid between bricks and foundation. The bricks must be rolled and the joints filled with a cement grout or a bituminous filler. For a monolithic brick pavement, the brick is laid directly on a freshly poured concrete base and rolled before the concrete has set. Wood blocks were popular in the 19th cent. At first round or hexagonal blocks were laid closely together. These were superseded by rectangular blocks, preferably of long-leaf yellow pine treated with a preservative and laid with the grain vertical; joints were closed with a hot bituminous filler. Stone-block pavement, an ancient type, is adapted to locations subject to heavy wear. For ornamental pavements, see MOSAIC; TILE.

Pavese, Cesare (chā'zārā pävĕ'sā), 1908-50, Italian novelist, poet, and translator. A major literary figure in postwar Italy, Pavese brought American influence to Italian literature through his translations. He himself was strongly influenced by Melville. Pavese's flight from the Fascists and subsequent imprisonment were reflected in his writings, which dealt with social struggle and revealed his sympathy for the oppressed. His major works include *Il Compagno* [the comrade] (1948), *Tra Donne Sole* (1948; tr. *Among Women Only*, 1953), *La luna e i falò* (1950; tr. *The Moon and the Bonfire*, 1952), and *Il diavolo sulle colline* (1959; tr. *The Devil in the Hills*, 1960). Pavese's recurrent theme in these novels is the search of urban man, who is caught in continually changing situations, for permanence and stability. See his *Selected Works* (tr. 1969) and *American Literature: Essays and Opinions* (tr. 1970).

Pavia (pävē'ä), city (1971 pop. 86,872), capital of Pavia prov., Lombardy, N Italy, on the Ticino River near its confluence with the Po. Pavia has long been an agricultural center and is now also an industrial and transportation center. Manufactures include textiles, machinery, and food products. Known as Ticinum in Roman times, it was an important stronghold of the empire and later served as the capital of the Lombard kings. From the 9th to the 12th cent. the Italian kings, and several German kings, received the Iron Crown of Lombardy at Pavia. In the 12th cent. the city became a free commune, loyal, however, to the emperor. It was the last Lombard city to fall to the VISCONTI (1359), who built most of the cathedral and started the construction of the CERTOSA DI PAVIA, a Carthusian monastery. Pavia suffered heavily during the Italian wars, and near there, in 1525, Emperor Charles V defeated and captured Francis I of France. The city came successively under Spanish, French, and Austrian domination, and was liberated in 1859. Among Pavia's notable structures, besides the cathedral, are the Romanesque St. Michael's Church (12th cent.); the Lombard-Romanesque St. Peter's Church (12th cent.), where St. Augustine is buried; and the large Castello Visconteo (14th-15th cent.). There is a university, which was established (1361) around a celebrated law school (founded in the 9th cent.).

Pavlov, Ivan Petrovich (ēvän' pĕtrô'vĭch päv'ləf), 1849-1936, Russian physiologist and experimental psychologist. He was professor at the military medical academy and director of the physiology department at the Institute for Experimental Medicine, Leningrad, from 1890. Pavlov was a skillful ambidextrous surgeon; using dogs as experimental animals, he established fistulas from various parts of the digestive tract by which he obtained secretions of the salivary glands, pancreas, and liver without disturbing the nerve and blood supply. For his work on the physiology of the digestive glands he received the 1904 Nobel Prize in Physiology and Medicine. Using the same technique to create an artificial exterior pouch of the stomach, he experimented on nervous stimulation of gastric secretions and thus discovered the conditioned reflex (see BEHAVIORISM), which has had widespread influence in neurology and psychology. He also demonstrated that specific areas in the cerebral cortex are concerned with specific reflexes and based on these findings a mechanistic theory of human behavior that found political favor;

in 1935 the government built a laboratory for him. His chief work was *Conditioned Reflexes* (1926, tr. 1927). See biography by B. P. Babkin (1949); studies by Erwin Strauss (1963), Hilaire Cuny (tr. 1965), and I. P. Frolov (tr. 1937, repr. 1970).

Pavlova, Anna Matveyevna (pävlō'və, Rus. än'nə mətvyä'əvnə päv'ləvə), 1881–1931, Russian ballerina. In 1892 she entered the Imperial Ballet School, St. Petersburg. She made her debut in 1899 at the Maryinsky Theatre, but it was only after tours to Scandinavia (1907) and to Berlin and Vienna (1908) that she gained fame. In Paris, Pavlova danced (1909) with Nijinsky in Diaghilev's Ballet Russe; she made her American debut in 1910. Thereafter, until her death, she toured extensively with her own company, working for the first year in partnership with Mikhail Mordkin. Pavlova, considered the greatest ballerina of her time, excelled in *Giselle, Chopiniana,* and especially in *The Dying Swan,* choreographed for her by Michel FOKINE. Her repertoire included 23 ballets and 80 divertissements. Pavlova's perfect classical technique and ethereal quality brought her universal acclaim. See biographies by Victor Dandré (1932), C. W. Beaumont (1932), A. H. Franks et al. (1956), and Oleg Kerensky (1973).

Pavlovsk (päv'ləfsk), town, NW European USSR, a summer resort near Leningrad. Founded by Catherine the Great in 1777, it was named for Czar Paul I, for whose country estate it was intended. In 1796 it became the royal summer residence, and in the 19th cent. it also served as a summer residence for the nobility of St. Petersburg (now Leningrad). Pavlovsk contains English gardens, villas, mansions, a palace (1782–86) in the Russian classical style, several park pavilions (1780–83), the Pil tower (1795–97), and the mausoleum of Paul I (early 19th cent.). From 1838 until the Bolshevik Revolution, Pavlovsk was the scene of symphonic concerts conducted by Johann Strauss, Aleksandr Glazunov, and other famous musicians. Heavily damaged during World War II, the buildings at Pavlovsk have been largely reconstructed.

pawl: see RATCHET AND PAWL.

pawnbroker, one who makes loans on personal effects that are left as security. The practice of pawnbroking is ancient, as is recognition of the danger it involves of oppressing the poor. In fact, the Bible provides the poor with a number of safeguards against oppression from their creditors. According to Ex. 22.25–27 and Deut. 24, 6, 12, 13, 17, pawnbrokers may not practice usury, may not take necessities of life as security, and in general must not take as a pledge any article whose loss would severely injure the borrower. In the Middle Ages, Christians generally were forbidden by the church to lend money at INTEREST, and pawnbroking was left largely to the Jews as one of the few means of a livelihood open to them. Lombards also engaged extensively in moneylending, however, and in London, the financial center is still called Lombard St. The three gold balls that are the pawnbroker's sign may have derived from the Medici coat of arms. In some Latin American and European nations pawnshops are operated under religious, charitable, or municipal auspices. The most famous such pawnshop is Vienna's Dorotheum, founded (1707) by Emperor Joseph I and still run by the state to provide the poor with easy credit at low rates of interest. In Great Britain and in American states, pawnbroking is regulated by usury laws. Pawnshops are predominantly found in low-income areas, where residents are often unable to establish other types of credit.

Pawnee Indians (pônē'), North American Indians whose language belongs to the Caddoan branch of the Hokan-Siouan linguistic stock (see AMERICAN INDIAN LANGUAGES). At one time the Pawnee lived in what is now Texas, but by 1541, when Coronado visited Quivira, they seem to have been settled in the valley of the Platte River in S Nebraska. By the early 18th cent. the Pawnee had divided into four groups—the Skidi or Wolf, the Grand, the Republican, and the Tapage (or Noisy). They then numbered some 10,000. By the time French traders settled (c.1750) among them, the Pawnee had extended their territory to the Republican River in N Kansas and the Niobrara River in N Nebraska. In 1806, Spanish soldiers visited the Pawnee just before the arrival of the expedition of Zebulon M. Pike. In material culture the Pawnee resembled other Indians of the Plains area but they had an elaborate set of myths and rituals. Their supreme god was Tirawa (the sun), who with Mother Earth conceived Morning Star. Morning Star was the rising and dying god of vegetation. The Pawnee periodically sacrificed a young woman to Morning Star. This custom, one of the few examples of human sacrifice N of Mexico, was, however, ended by the great Pawnee chief Pitalesharo (b. c.1797). The Pawnee were hostile to the Sioux and the Cheyenne although friendly toward the Oto. They were fierce fighters, but they never warred against the United States, even when treated unjustly by the government. In fact the Pawnee provided scouts for the U.S. army in the Indian wars, as well as protecting the Union Pacific RR from the depredations of other Indians. Pawnee population was reduced by wars with the Sioux and by the smallpox and cholera epidemics of the 1830s and 1840s. By a series of treaties begun early in the 19th cent. the Pawnee ceded all of their land in Nebraska and in 1876 moved to a reservation in Oklahoma, where they were granted the right to own their land individually. In the early 1970s some 700 Pawnee lived on or near their reservation in Oklahoma. See Ralph Linton, *The Sacrifice to the Morning Star by the Skidi Pawnee* (1922); Waldo Wedel, *An Introduction to Pawnee Archeology* (1936); Gene Weltfish, *The Lost Universe* (1965); G. E. Hyde, *The Pawnee Indians* (rev. ed. 1973).

pawpaw: see CUSTARD-APPLE; PAPAYA.

Pawtucket (pətŭk'ĭt), city (1970 pop. 76,984), Providence co., NE R.I., on the Blackstone River at Pawtucket Falls; settled 1671, inc. 1885 after the eastern section (which was part of Massachusetts until 1862) was merged with the western section into a Rhode Island town. The third largest city in the state, Pawtucket has been a textile center since Samuel Slater built the nation's first successful water-powered cotton mill there in 1793. Among the city's many other manufactures are industrial fasteners, jewelry, Christmas ornaments, paper, and tires. The area, deeded to Roger Williams in 1638, was a haven for religious freedom in New England. Its industrial possibilities were early realized. Pawtucket's first settler was an ironworker who established (1671) a forge at the falls. Metalworks and sawmills sprang up, and after Slater erected his cotton mill on the banks of the river, the textile industry boomed. After World War II, when much textile manufacturing moved south, Pawtucket shared the decline of many New England towns, but in the late 1950s its industries were revitalized with state aid. Two major urban renewal programs have greatly modernized the area. The city's chief point of interest is the 1793 Slater mill, now a museum. Many tourist and recreational sites are in the area, including the Narragansett Racetrack.

Pax (păks), in Roman religion, goddess of Peace. Vespasian erected a temple to her at Rome. Her attributes were similar to those of the Greek Irene, the olive branch and the horn of plenty.

Paxoí (päksē') or **Paxos** (păk'səs), island (1971 pop. 2,227), c.7 sq mi (18 sq km), NW Greece, in the Ionian Sea; one of the Ionian Islands. Olive oil, citrus fruits, and almonds are produced.

Paxton, Sir Joseph, 1803–65, English architect, noted for his use of glass and iron in a proto-modern manner. Beginning his career as a gardener and estate manager, he then built two greenhouses at Chatsworth, Derbyshire, for the duke of Devonshire. The first was the great conservatory (1836–40); the second was a smaller building, designed to protect the Victoria Regia water lily. This work served as a model for the CRYSTAL PALACE, built for the Great Exhibition of 1851. He was knighted for the success of this design.

Payne, Peter, c.1380–1455, English religious leader. He espoused Wyclifite views while studying at Oxford and was forced to leave. He went to Prague (c.1416) and became a member of the extreme party of HUSSITES. At the Council of Basel he was (1433) one of their spokesmen and one of the most unyielding. In the Hussite Wars that followed he joined the Taborites. He left Prague in 1437 but was imprisoned in 1439. Ransomed, he is said to have been in Tabor when the fortress was captured.

Payne, Sereno Elisha (sərē'nō), 1843–1914, American legislator, b. Hamilton, N.Y. He was admitted to the bar (1866), practiced at Auburn, N.Y., and was active in Republican politics. He served (1883–87, 1889–1914) in Congress and was long a member of the Committee on Ways and Means, becoming chairman in 1899. Payne, a staunch though not extreme protectionist, was active in fostering Republican tariff legislation. He helped draft the McKinley Tariff Act (1890), the Dingley Act (1897), and the PAYNE-ALDRICH TARIFF ACT (1909).

Payne-Aldrich Tariff Act, 1909, passed by the U.S. Congress. It was the first change in tariff laws since the Dingley Act of 1897; the issue had been ignored by President Theodore Roosevelt. The Republican platform of 1908 pledged revision of the tariff downward, and to this end President Taft called (1909) Congress into special session. The House promptly passed a tariff bill, sponsored by Sereno E. PAYNE, which called for some reduced rates. The Senate substituted a bill, fathered by Nelson W. ALDRICH, which made fewer downward revisions and increased numerous rates. After a sustained attack on the Aldrich Bill by a group of insurgent Republicans in the Senate, a compromise bill was adopted, which somewhat moderated the high rates of the Aldrich bill; the measure was immediately signed by Taft. It lowered 650 tariff schedules, raised 220, and left 1,150 unchanged. Although the Payne-Aldrich Tariff Act was less aggressively protectionist than the McKinley Tariff Act (1890) and the later Dingley Act, it was, nevertheless, protectionist.

Paysandú (pīsändōō'), city (1963 pop. 52,472), capital of Paysandú dept., W Uruguay, a port on the Uruguay River. It is the commercial center for a rich stock-raising and farming district. In the city are meat-packing plants. The harbor, one of the last navigable points on the river, is a major loading station. Paysandú was settled in 1772 by a missionary and his Christianized Indian followers.

Paz, Octavio (oktä'vyō päs'), 1914–, Mexican poet and critic. Paz's books—revealing depth of insight, elegance, and erudition—place him among the ablest writers of his generation. His later works include the poetry collections *La estación violenta* (1956), *Piedra de sol* (1957), *Alternating Current* (tr. 1973), *Configurations* (tr. 1971), and *Early Poems: 1935–1955* (tr. 1974); the volumes of essays *The Labyrinth of Solitude* (tr. 1963), *The Other Mexico* (tr. 1972), and *The Bow and the Lyre* (tr. 1973); *El arco y la lira* (1956), a volume of criticism; and studies of Claude Lévi-Strauss (tr. 1970) and Marcel Duchamp (tr. 1970). In 1971–72 Paz delivered the Charles Eliot Norton lectures at Harvard; they are collected in *Children of the Mire: Modern Poetry from Romanticism to the Avant-Garde* (1974). See Ivar Ivask, ed., *The Perpetual Present* (1974).

Pazardzhik (päzärjĭk'), city (1968 est. pop. 59,500), S central Bulgaria, on the Maritsa River. Pazardzhik, a commercial center, was under Turkish rule from the 15th to the 19th cent. It has an agricultural college and an old church with a fine collection of icons.

Paz Estenssoro, Victor (vēktōr' päs āstānsō'rō), 1907–, president of Bolivia (1952–56, 1960–64). An attorney and economist, he was a founder (1941) of the National Revolutionary Movement (MNR). He helped lead the revolt that brought the party into power in 1943, but he was forced to flee to Argentina in 1946. While in exile he was elected (1951) president of Bolivia. The army annulled the election, provoking a bloody but successful MNR revolt (April, 1952), which gave Paz the presidency. Paz immediately launched a program of revolutionary measures. He expropriated the largest tin mines and improved the lot of the Indians by granting them suffrage and instituting land, educational, and welfare reforms. Prohibited a second consecutive term by the constitution, he was succeeded (1956) by his vice president, Hernán Siles Zuazo. Paz was reelected president in 1960, at which time he was faced with a deteriorating economy and a growing rift within the MNR. He aroused considerable opposition by amending the constitution to permit his reelection in 1964, and although he was reelected, both the right and the left factions bolted his party. In Nov., 1964, Paz was ousted by a military coup. He later settled in Peru, returning to Bolivia in 1971. Resuming leadership of the MNR, he cooperated with the newly formed military government until Dec., 1973, when he withdrew the MNR from the government. Shortly afterward Paz was deported to Paraguay.

Pázmány, Peter (päz'mänyə), 1570–1637, Hungarian churchman, cardinal of the Roman Catholic Church. Of a Calvinist family, he was converted to Catholicism in 1583, entered the Society of Jesus in 1587, and rose to become cardinal and prince primate of Hungary. He won back many Hungarians to the Catholic faith. He founded educational and monastic institutions. Pázmány was one of the great figures of the Catholic Reformation.

Pazzi conspiracy (pät'tsē), 1478, plot against Lorenzo de' MEDICI (Lorenzo il Magnifico) and his brother Giuliano, designed to end the hegemony of the Medici in the Florentine state and to enlarge papal territory. It was instigated by Pope SIXTUS IV, his nephew Gerolamo Riario, Archbishop Salviati, and members of the Pazzi family, a wealthy Florentine family who rivaled the Medici. Actually, the Pazzi were tools in the conspiracy, which aimed not only at the death of the Medici, but at the elevation of Riario to power in Florence. Details of the plot were worked out by Salviati and the Pazzi while Riario and the pope remained in Rome. On April 26, during High Mass at the cathedral, Giuliano de' Medici was stabbed to death, while Lorenzo escaped with a wound. The enraged Florentines seized and killed the conspirators. The Medici remained firmly entrenched in power.

Pb, chemical symbol of the element LEAD.

PCB: see POLYCHLORINATED BIPHENYL.

Pd, chemical symbol of the element PALLADIUM.

pea, hardy, annual, climbing leguminous plant (*Pisum sativum*) of the family Leguminosae (PULSE family), grown for food by man at least since the early Bronze Age and no longer known in the wild form. It is cultivated everywhere in home gardens and on a large scale commercially for canning. The round seed, borne in a pod, is a highly nutritious food, having a large protein content. The pod, too, of the varieties known as sugar peas can be eaten, and the whole plant is grown for forage; the vines of garden varieties are also used for feeding stock. In New England many gardeners plant them on April 19, the anniversary of the battle of Lexington—hoping to have their first peas by the Fourth of July, when according to traditional use they accompany salmon on the menu. Split peas are obtained from the field pea (var. *arvense*), grown also for forage and as a green manure. About three quarters of the total world crop of the field pea variety is grown in China; much is used for stock feed. It is believed that peas were long grown only for use as pea meal, dried peas, or forage. Using peas as a green table vegetable began in the late Middle Ages, and the garden varieties were developed subsequently. The garden pea is renowned as the plant with which Gregor Mendel conducted the experiments that initiated the science of genetics. The CHICK-PEA and the SWEET PEA belong to different genera. Peas are classified in the division MAGNOLIOPHYTA, class Magnoliopsida, order Rosales, family Leguminosae.

Peabody, Elizabeth Palmer, 1804-94, American educator, lecturer, and reformer, b. Billerica, Mass. The Peabody family moved (c.1809) to Salem, where the father began practicing dentistry. Of the three Peabody sisters, the second, Mary, married Horace Mann, and the youngest, Sophia, married Nathaniel Hawthorne. Elizabeth, after a period as governess in Hallowell, Maine, with her sister Mary established a school for girls in what is now Brookline, Mass. Although she was an inspired teacher, she was a poor businesswoman, and her ventures were short-lived. After giving up this school she wrote a series of history textbooks and became a successful lecturer on history. She assisted Bronson Alcott in his Temple School and recounted his educational theories in *Record of a School* (1835). Her path crossed those of most of the great New Englanders of her day—Emerson, William Ellery Channing, and many others. The bookshop she opened in Boston in 1840 was a literary center. Margaret Fuller held her conversation classes there, and Elizabeth soon found herself a publisher as well as a bookseller; the transcendental magazine, the *Dial,* pamphlets of the Anti-Slavery Society, and several of Hawthorne's early works were published by her. Of a projected periodical, *Aesthetic Papers,* only one number appeared, in 1849. After closing her bookshop she traveled about, lecturing and selling historical charts. An ardent abolitionist, Elizabeth went to Richmond in 1859 to plead unsuccessfully with the governor of Virginia for the life of one of John Brown's aides at Harpers Ferry. In 1861 she opened in Boston one of the first kindergartens in the country. With her sister Mary she wrote *Moral Culture of Infancy and Kindergarten Guide* (1866). She studied Froebel's methods in Germany in 1867-68, and on her return she established a Froebel Union and opened the first kindergarten training school in the country. From then on kindergarten training was the cause that took her traveling about the country. After her death a settlement, Elizabeth Peabody House, was established as a memorial. See L. H. Tharp, *The Peabody Sisters of Salem* (1950); study by R. M. Baylor (1965).

Peabody, Endicott, 1857-1944, American educator, b. Salem, Mass., grad. Cheltenham College, 1876, LL.B. Cambridge, 1880. Ordained (1885) in the Protestant Episcopal Church, Peabody had founded in 1884 the Groton School, Groton, Mass., modeled on the English public schools. He was its headmaster until he retired in 1940. See biography by F. D. Ashburn (1944).

Peabody, George, 1795-1869, American financier and philanthropist, b. South Danvers (now Peabody), Mass. At the age of 11 he was apprenticed to a grocer, and later (1814) he became a partner in a dry-goods firm in Georgetown, D.C. (now in Washington, D.C.). This firm moved to Baltimore, and he established branches in New York City and Philadelphia. While on a business trip to London, Peabody negotiated (1837) a large British loan that helped save the finances of the state of Maryland, but he refused a commission for his services. Peabody settled (1837) permanently in London; there he set up a brokerage business that became increasingly prosperous. He used his influence to better Anglo-American relations and financed the exhibition of American products at the Crystal Palace exhibition. Prominent among Peabody's philanthropies were large funds given for tenement clearance in London and the Peabody Education Fund of more than $2,000,000, to promote education in the South (partly used for the George Peabody College for Teachers, in Nashville, Tenn.). He also contributed to museums, universities, and libraries throughout the United States and endowed the archaeological museum of Harvard and the museum of physical sciences at Yale. See biography by Franklin Parker (1971).

Peabody, George Foster, 1852-1938, American banker and philanthropist, b. Columbus, Ga. Successful early in life as a banker and organizer of railroads and utility companies, he retired (1906) from business to devote himself to philanthropy and public service. He became a trustee of many colleges and universities in the United States and fought for the furtherance of education for Negroes. See biography by E. L. Ware (1951).

Peabody, city (1970 pop. 48,080), Essex co., NE Mass., a suburb of Boston, on the Danvers River; settled c.1633, inc. as South Danvers 1855, name changed 1868. Its tanning industry dates from early in the 18th cent. Leather goods, chemicals, electronic equipment, and machine tools are also produced. The Peabody Institute library contains much of the memorabilia of George Peabody, the philanthropist, for whom the city was named. There are many old houses there.

Peace, river, 945 mi (1,521 km) long, formed by the junction of the Finlay and Parsnip rivers at Williston Lake, N central British Columbia, Canada. It flows east through the Rocky Mts., then generally northeast across N Alberta and onto the Northern Plains where it meanders to the Slave River at Lake Athabasca. From the head of the Finlay River the Peace River is 1,195 mi (1,923 km) long; it is one of the chief headstreams of the Mackenzie River. At the mouth of the Peace River is Wood Buffalo National Park. The valley of the middle Peace is fertile, with wheat the chief crop; it is the northernmost commercially important agricultural region of Canada. Large natural gas reserves are tapped along the river; oil, coal, salt, and gypsum deposits are also worked. Near Hudson Hope, British Columbia, W. A. C. Bennett Dam (625 ft/191 m high; opened 1967) impounds Williston Lake (680 sq mi/1,761 sq km). The dam's power plant (present generating capacity 1.2 million kw) will have a 2.3 million-kw capacity when completed. It will be the third largest hydroelectric facility in Canada and one of the largest in the world. Most of its output will be used by Vancouver. The Peace River was probably discovered (1775-78) by Peter Pond, the American fur trader, and was first explored (1792-93) by Sir Alexander Mackenzie, the Canadian explorer. It was long an important route of fur traders. Settlement in the valley began in the early 1900s.

peace congresses, multinational meetings to achieve or preserve peace and to prevent wars. Although philosophical and religious PACIFISM is almost as old as war itself, organized efforts to outlaw war date only from the middle of the 19th cent. The term "peace congress" is applied to a meeting of diplomats to end specific wars by peace treaties, as well as to an international gathering convened to urge measures for preventing future wars. International efforts toward peace have concentrated on the following lines: the urging of international ARBITRATION and MEDIATION in disputes between nations; creation of an international organization, such as the League of Nations or the United Nations; development and codification of international law; extending the use and scope of the INTERNATIONAL COURT OF JUSTICE and endowing it with the necessary authority to enforce its decisions; and general disarmament by all nations. The first international peace congress was held in London in 1843. Proposals were made for a congress of nations and for international arbitration; military education was denounced, propaganda against war was urged, and the control of the manufacture and sale of arms and munitions was advocated. The second congress, known as the Universal Peace Congress, met in Brussels in 1848 and was followed by a series of such meetings—Paris, 1849; Frankfurt, 1850; and London, 1851. For a time, international peace agitation was interrupted, first by the Crimean War and then by the U.S. Civil War. In 1867, Charles Lemonnier convened a peace congress in Geneva known as the International League of Peace and Liberty; after the Franco-Prussian War (1870-71) it reconvened (1873) in Brussels, and David Dudley Field's *Proposals for an International Code* formed the basis of discussion. In the Western Hemisphere the first Pan-American Conference met in 1889-90 (see PAN-AMERICANISM). Meeting at the World's Columbian Exposition in Chicago in 1893, the Universal Peace Congress, which had resumed in 1889, discussed plans for an International Court of Arbitration. The court became a reality in 1899 when it was established at The Hague by the first of the HAGUE CONFERENCES. The Second Hague Conference (1907) was concerned, like the first, with arbitration and disarmament. By 1914 the court (see HAGUE TRIBUNAL) had successfully arbitrated 14 international disputes, but the outbreak of World War I disrupted the activities of all peace congresses, and it was not until 1919 that they were able to resume their work. It took another two years before the peace proposals of the 19th cent., incorporated in the Treaty of Versailles, bore fruit in the creation of two international organizations, the LEAGUE OF NATIONS at Geneva and the Permanent Court of International Justice (see WORLD COURT) at The Hague. After 1919 the chief international peace congresses were the annual meetings at Brussels of the International Federation of League of Nations Societies, which concerned themselves increasingly with disarmament. Throughout the 1920s peace congresses concentrated on urging countries to reduce their armed forces, and they influenced the holding of NAVAL CONFERENCES at Washington, D.C. (1921-22) and London (1930). A series of bilateral and multilateral disarmament conferences finally led to the KELLOGG-BRIAND PACT, signed (1928) by 15 nations who renounced war as an instrument of national policy. However, within three years Japan (a signatory to the pact) launched its undeclared war against Manchuria, and in 1935, Italy (another signatory) invaded Ethiopia; this was followed shortly by Germany's invasion (1939) of Poland and World War II. The horrors of that conflict, with its aftermath of economic and social chaos and the invention of nuclear weapons, intensified worldwide movements for peace through the UNITED NATIONS and increased the determination that the new international organization would succeed where the defunct League of Nations had failed. By the early 1970s there were several international peace organizations with the common goal of world peace. Some of the most prominent ones are the Christian Peace Conference (founded 1958), the International Confederation for Disarmament and Peace (founded 1964), the International Peace Bureau (founded 1892 and reorganized 1962; it serves as the operative agency for the World Union of Peace Organizations), the International Peace Research Association (founded 1964), the International Union of Peace Societies (founded 1891 and reconstituted in 1961), and the World Council of Peace (founded 1950). See A. C. F. Beales, *The History of Peace* (1931); D. S. Cheever and F. H. Haviland, *Organizing for Peace* (1954); G. F. Nuttall, *Christian Pacifism in History* (1958); R. S. Baker, *Woodrow Wilson and World Settlement* (1960); F. A. Hinsley, *Power and the Pursuit of Peace* (1963).

Peace Corps, agency of the U.S. government, whose purpose is to assist underdeveloped countries in meeting their needs for trained manpower. The Peace Corps was established in 1961 by an executive order of President Kennedy; Congress approved it as a permanent agency within the Dept. of State the same year. Peace Corps volunteers serve for two-year periods. Currently over 300 skills are offered in such areas as agriculture; the teaching of languages, mathematics, and science; vocational training; business and public administration; and natural resource development. In 1971 the Peace Corps was transferred to ACTION, an independent agency designed to coordinate several Federal volunteer programs. See Robert Carey, *The Peace Corps* (1970); B. K. Ashdoranner, *A Moment in History: The First Ten Years of the Peace Corps* (1971).

peace pipe: see CALUMET.

peach, fruit tree (*Prunus persica*) of the family Rosaceae (ROSE family) having decorative pink blossoms and a juicy, sweet drupe fruit. The peach appears to have originated in China, where it was mentioned in literature several centuries before Christ. It was introduced into Persia before Christian times and was spread by the Romans throughout Europe. Several of its horticultural varieties were brought by the Spanish to North America, where it became naturalized as far north as Pennsylvania by the late 17th cent. The numerous varieties of peaches under cultivation are generally distinguished as clingstone or freestone; the latter include the famous Elberta peach. The NECTARINE is a smooth-skinned peach with both freestone and clingstone varieties. In the United States commercial peach production centers in California and in the S Atlantic states. Elsewhere the peach is cultivated in S Europe, Africa, Japan, and Australia. The tree is prey to frost and is attacked by various fungi, virus diseases, and insect pests, against all of which careful precautions must be taken by growers. Purple-leaved and double-flowering forms are cultivated as ornamentals. In China where the flower is much used in decoration it is considered a symbol of longevity. The peach is closely related to other species of *Prunus*—e.g., the cherry, plum, and almond—of which Darwin thought the peach was an ancient variety. Peaches are classified in the division MAGNOLIOPHYTA, class Magnoliopsida, order Rosales, family Rosaceae.

Peacham, Henry, 1576?–1643?, English author, b. Hertfordshire, educated at Cambridge. *The Compleat Gentleman* (1622), his best-known work, offers his formula for the ideal Englishman. Among his other writings is a treatise on art, *The Gentleman's Exercise* (1607).

Peach Tree Creek: see ATLANTA CAMPAIGN.

Peacock, Reginald: see PECOCK, REGINALD.

Peacock, Thomas Love, 1785–1866, English novelist and poet. He was employed by the East India Company from 1819 to 1856, serving as its chief examiner the final 20 years. Peacock's novels, comic and delightfully satirical, parody the intellectual modes and pretenses of his age. *Nightmare Abbey* (1818), his best-known work, satirizes the English romantic movement and contains characters based on Coleridge, Byron, and Shelley. Other novels include *Headlong Hall* (1816), *Melincourt* (1817), *Maid Marian* (1822), *Crotchet Castle* (1831), and *Gryll Grange* (1860). Peacock's best poems—lyrics and drinking songs—are interspersed in his novels. He was one of Shelley's most intimate friends, and after the famous poet's death Peacock was his literary executor. See his works (ed. by H. F. B. Brett-Smith and C. E. Jones, 10 vol., 1924–34); biography by C. Van Doren (1911, repr. 1966).

peacock or **peafowl,** large bird of the genus *Pavo,* in the PHEASANT family, native to E Asia. There are two main species, the common (*Pavo cristatus*), and the Javanese (*P. musticus*) peacocks, both found in deep forest where they travel in small flocks. A third type, the Congo peacock, was discovered recently in Africa. Unusual peacocks are the Argus pheasant, with eyelike spots on its secondary flight feathers, and the white peacock, thought to be a mutation of the common peafowl. When the term *peafowl* is used, *peacock* then refers to the male of a species and *peahen* to the female. During courtship the crested male common peacock displays his elongated upper tail coverts—a magnificent green and gold erectile train adorned with blue-green "eyes"—before the duller-plumaged peahen. The peacock is well known as an ornamental bird, though it is quarrelsome and does not mix well with other domestic animals. The peacock figures in the Bible and in Greek and Roman myth, where it appears as the favorite bird of the goddess Hera, or Juno, and the bird was known to the pharaohs of Egypt and to 14th-century Europe, where it was roasted and served in its own plumage. Peafowl fly well despite their size, and roost in trees at night. Peacocks are classified in the phylum CHORDATA, subphylum Vertebrata, class Aves, order Galliformes, family Phasianidae.

Peacock Throne: see DELHI.

peafowl: see PEACOCK.

Peak District or **The Peak,** dissected plateau, c.30 mi (50 km) long and 22 mi (35 km) wide, Derbyshire, central England, forming the southern extremity of the Pennines. Kinderscout (2,088 ft/636 m) is the highest peak. Dovedale and Wyedale are the region's major valleys. Peak District has many caves including Peak Cavern and Speedwell. Peak District National Park (c.500 sq mi/1,295 sq km) was established in 1951.

Peaks of Otter, Va.: see OTTER, PEAKS OF.

Peale, Charles Willson (pēl), 1741–1827, American portrait painter, naturalist, and inventor, b. Queen Annes co., Md. Apprenticed to a saddler in Annapolis, he became at 20 his own master and taught himself various other trades—watchmaking, silversmithing, upholstery, and sign painting. Forced into bankruptcy, he fled to Boston, where he worked for a short time in Copley's studio. He returned to Annapolis to paint portraits of its wealthy citizens, a group of whom sent (1766) him to study with Benjamin West in London. Upon his return to America he established himself in Philadelphia in 1776. The earliest known portrait of Washington (1772; Washington and Lee Univ.) was painted by Peale. Of the many he painted of Washington, seven were from life. Peale served as a captain of volunteers in the Revolution, painting, when he could, portraits of military leaders. His group *Washington, Lafayette, and Tench Tilghman* hangs in the chamber of the house of delegates, Annapolis. Other portraits of Washington are in the Brooklyn Museum; the Metropolitan Museum; Princeton University; and the National Gallery of Art, Washington, D.C. After Copley's departure for England, Peale was the most popular portrait painter in the country. In 1779 he was elected to the Pennsylvania legislature and was politically active for several years. In 1784 he established what was known as "Peale's Museum," which was moved to Independence Hall in 1802. Besides a series of portraits of eminent Americans by Peale and his son Rembrandt, it contained a number of Indian relics, waxworks dummies, and specimens of natural history. He invented his own system of taxidermy and was a century ahead of his time in his concept of placing each animal in a simulated natural environment. In 1801 he formed the first scientific expedition in American history. From a New York state farm, he exhumed the skeleton of a mastodon, assembling and restoring the remains for his museum. Two major paintings of his later years underscore his scientific interests, *Exhuming the Mastodon* (1806–8; Peale Museum, Baltimore) and *The Artist in His Studio* (1822; Pa. Acad. of the Fine Arts). He was instrumental in founding (1805) the Pennsylvania Academy of the Fine Arts and taught there for a number of years. During his lifetime he painted a galaxy of historical figures, including Washington, Martha Washington, Franklin, Jefferson, Hamilton, John Paul Jones, John Hancock, and John Adams. Evidence of his versatility are his numerous inventions: a velocipede, new types of eyeglasses, false teeth, and the polygraph. On the polygraph he collaborated with Thomas Jefferson. See biography by C. C. Sellers (1969). His brother **James Peale,** 1749–1831, b. Chestertown, Md., painted portraits, particularly miniatures. There is a portrait of Washington by him in the New-York Historical Society and another in Independence Hall. Of Charles Willson Peale's 17 children, 4 became painters—**Titian Peale,** 1799–1885, animal painter, b. Philadelphia; **Rubens Peale,** 1784–1865, still-life painter, b. Bucks co., Pa.; **Raphaelle Peale,** 1774–1825, still-life and portrait painter, b. Annapolis, Md., known chiefly for *After the Bath* (Nelson Gall.-Atkins Mus., Kansas City, Mo.); and **Rembrandt Peale,** 1778–1860, portrait and historical painter, b. Bucks co., Pa. Rembrandt Peale practiced for several years in Charleston, S.C., became a pupil of Benjamin West in London, and visited Paris, where he painted many eminent Frenchmen. In 1810 he settled in Philadelphia, devoting himself chiefly to portraiture. He was one of the original members of the National Academy of Design and succeeded (1825) John Trumbull as president of the American Academy of Fine Arts. A clever lithographer, he also lectured on natural history and wrote several books. Examples of his portraits of Washington and other famous personages may be seen at the New-York Historical Society; Independence Hall, Philadelphia; the Metropolitan Museum; and the Museum of Fine Arts, Boston. His large allegory *The Court of Death* is in the Detroit Institute of Art. See studies by C. C. Sellers (2 vol., 1947) and (1952); C. H. Elam, ed., *The Peale Family* (1967).

peanut, name for a low, annual leguminous plant (*Arachis hypogaea*) of the family Leguminosae (PULSE family) and for its edible seeds. Native to South America and cultivated there by pre-Columbian Indians, the peanut was brought to North America in the slave-trade days by way of Africa, where it is said to have been introduced by early explorers. In the United States it has been extensively cultivated only since the late 19th cent. It is now grown in most tropical, subtropical, and temperate regions, especially in India and China (the major world producers), W Africa, and the SE United States. The seeds—peanuts—are eaten fresh or roasted and are used in cookery and confectionery. They are ground for peanut butter, an important article of commerce, and also yield an oil used for margarine, cooking oil, soap manufacture, and industrial purposes. The herbage is used for hay, the residue from oil extraction (called peanut-oil cakes) for stock feed, and the whole plant, left in the ground, as pasturage for swine. Peanut crops are usually harvested by hand except in the United States. Europe is the chief importer and processor, especially for oil manufacture. In the United States the amount of the crop converted to oil depends on the demand for whole peanuts; it is usually only 15% to 20%. Because of its numerous uses (George Washington CARVER developed several hundred), high protein content, and adaptability to varying demand, the peanut is an advantageous agricultural crop. There are two types of peanut plant—bunch nuts and vine, or trailing, nuts—named for the way the plants grow. The peanut plant is unusual for its habit of geocarpy: when the pod starts to form, it is pushed into the ground by the elongation of its stalk and matures underground. Other names for the peanut are goober, pinder, earthnut, groundnut, and ground pea. Peanuts are classified in the division MAGNOLIOPHYTA, class Magnoliopsida, order Rosales, family Leguminosae.

pear, name for a fruit tree of the genus *Pyrus* of the family Rosaceae (ROSE family) and for its fruit, a pome. The common pear (*P. communis*) is one of the earliest cultivated of fruit trees, both in its native W Asia and in Europe. Most of the pear strains grown for their sweet and juicy fruit are varieties of *P. communis* or of its hybrids with other species of *Pyrus*—usually *P. pyrifolia,* known as the Japanese, Chinese, or sand pear and indigenous to China. The main use of the sand pear today is as a rootstock in pear orchards; the related quince is used for the same purpose. Pear strains with fruit of really good eating quality were not developed until the 18th and 19th cent. in N Europe, whence almost all the present successful varieties (e.g., the Bartlett and Seckel) grown in the United States (chiefly on the Pacific coast and in the Great Lakes area) were directly imported. European production is far greater—especially in Germany, France, and Switzerland, where much of the crop is used for making pear cider (perry). Pears are also cultivated on a large scale in Japan, Turkey, Argentina, and Australia. They are usually sold fresh or canned; some are dried. Several varieties of the common pear and of other species—e.g., the small, white-foliaged snow pear (*P. nivalis*)—are cultivated as ornamentals, and pear wood, hard and dense, is used to a limited extent in cabinetmaking. The pear tree and its fruit are similar to the closely related apple (considered by some botanists to be of the same genus) in characteristics and in method of cultivation, but the tree is somewhat less hardy and the fruit more perishable. Pear or fire blight is the tree's most serious disease; it is also attacked by several insect pests. Pears are classified in the division MAGNOLIOPHYTA, class Magnoliopsida, order Rosales, family Rosaceae.

pear, prickly: see CACTUS.

Pea Ridge, chain of hills, NW Ark., where the Civil War battle of Pea Ridge (or Elkhorn Tavern) was fought March 6–8, 1862. Earl Van Dorn, leading a large Confederate command, which included Sterling Price's retreating Missouri forces and Ben McCulloch's army, attacked the strongly entrenched Union army under Samuel Ryan Curtis. The Confederate wings, becoming separated, were crushed on successive days. Pea Ridge was the first decisive victory won by the Union army W of the Mississippi; not until Price's raid (1864) did the Confederates again try to carry the war to Missouri in force.

Pea Ridge National Military Park: see NATIONAL PARKS AND MONUMENTS (table).

Pearl, Raymond, 1879–1940, American biologist, b. Farmington, N.H., B.A. Dartmouth, 1899, Ph.D. Univ. of Michigan, 1902. He studied abroad under Karl Pearson and others and headed (1907–18) the biology department of the Maine agricultural experiment station. From 1918 he was associated with Johns Hopkins Univ. He is known for his statistical studies of population growth, of mortality, birth rates, and longevity, and of human fertility. Besides founding and editing *Human Biology* and *Quarterly Review of Biology,* he wrote many books, including *Introduction to Medical Biometry and Statistics* (1923), *The Biology of Population Growth* (1925), *Alcohol and Longevity* (1926), and *The Natural History of Population* (1939).

Pearl, river, China: see CANTON, river.

Pearl, river, 485 mi (781 km) long, rising in E Miss. and flowing S to Lake Borgne, an inlet of the Gulf of Mexico; its lower section (116 mi/187 km) forms the Miss.-La. boundary. Above Jackson, Miss., the Pearl's largest city, is Ross Barnet Reservoir, one of the state's chief water storage areas. The lower Pearl valley accounts for about one half of U.S. tung-oil production.

pearl, hard, rounded secretion formed inside the shell of certain bivalve mollusks, used as a gem. It is secreted by the epithelial cells of the mantle, a curtain of tissue between the shell and body mass, and is deposited in successive layers around an irritating object such as a parasite or grain of sand that gets caught in the soft tissue of the mollusk. The pearl is built up of layers of aragonite or calcite (crystalline forms of calcium carbonate) held together by conchiolin (a horny organic substance); its composition is identical to that of the MOTHER-OF-PEARL, or nacre, that forms the interior layer of the mollusk shell. Pearls may be round, pear-shaped, button-shaped, or irregular (baroque) and are valued in that order. Pearls found attached to the inner surface of the shell are known as blister pearls. The best pearls are usually white, sometimes with a creamy or pinkish tinge, but may be tinted with yellow, green, blue, brown, or black. Black pearls, because of their rarity, are often highly valued. The unique luster, or orient, of pearls depends upon the reflection and refraction of light from the translucent layers and is finer in proportion as the layers are thinner and more numerous. The iridescence which some pearls display is caused by the overlapping of successive layers, which breaks up light falling on the surface. Pearls are not cut or polished like other gems. They are very soft and are injured by acids and heat; as organic products, they are subject to decay. Commercially valuable pearls are obtained from the pearl oyster (especially of the genus *Pinctata*) and from the freshwater pearl mussel (genus *Unio*). The largest natural pearl center is the Persian Gulf, which is said to produce the finest saltwater pearls. Other important sources are the coasts of India, China, Japan, Australia, the Sulu Archipelago, various Pacific islands, Venezuela, and Central America, and the rivers of Europe and North America. In ancient times the Red Sea was an important source. Nearly all of the world's supply of cultured pearls is produced by the Japanese, who have perfected the techniques of pearl cultivation. Pearls are commonly produced by placing a small mother-of-pearl bead enclosed in a piece of mantle tissue in the body of the oyster. The oysters are then placed in cages that are suspended into sheltered bays for the period of time (up to 4 years) required for pearl formation. See Joan Dickinson, *The Book of Pearls* (1968).

Pearl, The, one of four Middle English alliterative poems, all contained in a manuscript of c.1400, composed in the West Midland dialect, almost certainly by the same anonymous author, who flourished c.1370–1390. *The Pearl* is usually explained as an elegy for the poet's young daughter; in an allegorical vision of singular beauty he sees her as a maiden in paradise and becomes reconciled to her death. The second and third poems, *Cleanness* (or *Purity*) and *Patience,* are homiletic poems on those virtues. *Sir Gawain and the Green Knight,* the fourth poem, which relates a fabulous adventure of GAWAIN, is perhaps the most brilliantly conceived of all Arthurian romances. If single authorship is accepted, the artistry displayed in this poem and in *The Pearl* make the so-called *Pearl*-poet in some respects a rival to Chaucer. A fifth poem, *St. Erkenwald,* is attributed by some authorities to the same anonymous author. For translations of the first, fourth, and fifth poems and for bibliography, see R. S. Loomis and Rudolph Willard, ed., *Medieval English Verse and Prose* (1948); study by Ian Bishop (1968).

pearl ash: see POTASSIUM CARBONATE.

Pearl Harbor, land-locked harbor, on the southern coast of Oahu island, Hawaii, W of Honolulu; one of the largest and best natural harbors in the E Pacific Ocean. In the Pearl Harbor vicinity are many U.S. military installations, including the chief U.S. Pacific naval base, Hickam Air Force Base, Pearl Harbor Naval Air Station, and Camp H. M. Smith, headquarters of the U.S. Pacific Command. The United States first gained rights there in 1887, when the Hawaiian monarchy granted permission for the maintenance of a coaling and repair station. After the United States annexed Hawaii in 1900, Pearl Harbor was made a naval base. Harbor improvements and fortifications were later added, especially after the signing of the Berlin Pact in 1940 by the Axis nations. On Dec. 7, 1941, while negotiations were going on with Japanese representatives in Washington, Japanese carrier-based planes swept in without warning over Oahu and attacked (7:55 A.M. local time) the bulk of the U.S. Pacific fleet, moored in Pearl Harbor. Nineteen naval vessels, including eight battleships, were sunk or severely damaged; 188 U.S. aircraft were destroyed. Military casualties were 2,280 killed and 1,109 wounded; 68 civilians were also killed. On Dec. 8, the United States declared war on Japan. There were many charges of negligence against those responsible for Pearl Harbor's defense. A special investigatory commission appointed by President Franklin D. Roosevelt accused the army and navy commanders at Hawaii of dereliction of duty in a report on Jan. 24, 1942. Later army and navy investigations concluded that no valid grounds existed for court-martial. A joint congressional committee, formed in Sept., 1945, absolved the army and navy commanders in a formal report to Congress on July 16, 1946, but censured the War Dept. and the Dept. of the Navy. Pearl Harbor is now a national historic landmark; a memorial has been built over the sunken hulk of the USS *Arizona*.

Pearl River, uninc. village (1970 pop. 17,146), Rockland co., SE N.Y., near the N.J. line, a residential suburb of New York City.

Pears, Peter, 1910–, English tenor. Pears studied at the Royal College of Music and became a member of the Sadler's Wells Opera and the English Opera Group. In 1948 he made his Covent Garden debut. He has worked closely with Benjamin Britten since 1946. Together they have made a number of international tours, presenting works by Britten and other English composers. Pears has sung many premieres of Britten operas, including *Peter Grimes, Billy Budd, Gloriana,* and *The Turn of the Screw.* In 1974 he made his Metropolitan Opera debut singing Aschenbach in Britten's opera *Death in Venice*, based on the novella by Thomas Mann.

Pearse, Patrick Henry (pērs), 1879–1916, Irish educator and patriot. He was educated for the law but early in his career made himself part of the Gaelic movement in Ireland. Pearse was active in the work of the Gaelic League and edited its journal, *An Claidheamh Soluis.* He founded the influential bilingual St. Enda's School near Dublin. He joined (1913) the Irish Volunteers and commanded the Irish forces in the Easter Rebellion of 1916. Upon his surrender he was tried by court-martial in England and promptly executed. His stories, poems, and plays were collected in 1917, his political writings and speeches in 1922. See biographies by Louis Le-Roux (tr. by Desmond Ryan, 1932), and R. J. Porter (1973).

Pearson, Sir Cyril Arthur (pēr'sən), 1866–1921, English publisher. He founded and directed the periodicals *Pearson's Weekly, Pearson's Magazine,* and *The Lady's Magazine* and the London *Daily Express* (1900). Eventually he controlled a number of newspapers in various English cities. An ardent supporter of Joseph Chamberlain's tariff-reform movement, he organized the Tariff Reform League in 1903. In 1910 he was forced to relinquish directing his newspaper interests because of failing eyesight. He devoted himself thereafter to the cause of the blind and founded St. Dunstan's training center for soldiers blinded in World War I. He wrote *Victory over Blindness* (1919). See biography by Sidney Dark (1922).

Pearson, Drew, 1897–1969, American journalist and radio commentator, b. Evanston, Ill. He traveled around the world as a correspondent before joining the Baltimore *Sun* in 1926. Pearson gained national prominence with his syndicated column, "Washington Merry-Go-Round," which he began with Robert S. Allen in 1932 and later wrote with Jack ANDERSON. The column featured sensational exposés of government figures. Pearson's books include *The Case Against Congress* (1968) and a novel, *The Senator* (1968). See his diaries, ed. by Tyler Abell (1974); biography by Oliver Pilat (1973).

Pearson, John, 1613–86, English prelate and scholar. He was a royalist chaplain (1645) in the civil war, but during Cromwell's regime he lived quietly in London. His *Exposition of the Creed* (1659), based on sermons he delivered at St. Clement's, Eastcheap, reveals Pearson's remarkable knowledge, especially of the Church Fathers; with many notes, it has long been a standard work. After the Restoration, Pearson became master of Jesus College, Cambridge (1660), Margaret professor of divinity (1661), master of Trinity College (1662), and bishop of Chester (1673). His *Vindiciae epistolarum S. Ignatii* (1672), defending the genuineness of the letters of St. Ignatius of Antioch, was later confirmed.

Pearson, Karl, 1857–1936, English scientist. He studied law, taught geometry and applied mathematics and mechanics, and in 1911 became professor of eugenics at the Univ. of London and director of the eugenics laboratory. A disciple of Francis Galton, he applied statistical methods to the study of biological problems (especially evolution and heredity), a science he called biometrics. He founded and edited *Biometrika* and was author of many works including *The Grammar of Science* (1892), *Chances of Death* (2 vol., 1897), and a biography of Francis Galton (3 vol., 1914–30). See biography by E. S. Pearson (1938); study by C. C. Riddle (1958).

Pearson, Lester Bowles, 1897–1972, Canadian diplomat and political leader, b. Ontario prov. He served in the Canadian army in World War I. Pearson taught history at the Univ. of Toronto from 1924 to 1928 and then joined the Canadian diplomatic service. After serving (1928–35) as a first secretary in the department of external affairs, he was attached (1935–41) to the London office of the Canadian high commissioner; he later held (1941–44) various consular posts. He was Canada's senior adviser at the Dumbarton Oaks (1944) and San Francisco (1945) conferences that led to the establishment of the United Nations, and he headed Canada's UN delegation. As chairman of the UN political and security committee in 1947, he played a decisive role in mediating the Palestinian crisis. From 1948, when he entered Parliament as a Liberal, to 1957 Pearson was minister of external affairs and took a leading part in British Commonwealth affairs and the formation of the North Atlantic Treaty Organization. Pearson, one of the most respected members of the UN General Assembly, received the 1957 Nobel Peace Prize for his work on behalf of the United Nations in resolving the 1956 Arab-Israeli war. In 1958 he became head of the Liberal party and leader of the opposition. He led his party to a gain of 46 seats in the 1962 elections and succeeded John G. Diefenbaker as prime minister in early 1963. He retired as prime minister in 1968. He also served (1951–58) as chancellor of Victoria Univ. in Toronto. Among his books are *Democracy in World Politics* (1955), *Diplomacy in the Nuclear Age* (1959), and *Words and Occasions* (1970). See his memoirs (2 vol., 1972–73); biography by J. R. Beal (1964).

Peary, Robert Edwin (pēr'ē), 1856–1920, American arctic explorer, discoverer of the North Pole, b. Cresson, Pa. In 1881 he entered the U.S. navy as a civil engineer and for several years served in Nicaragua, where he was engaged in making surveys for the Nicaragua Canal. He became interested in arctic exploration and made a trip to the interior of Greenland in 1886; later (1891–92), having secured a leave of absence from the navy, he led an expedition to Greenland for scientific study and exploration. Important ethnological and meteorological observations were recorded, a long sled journey to the northeast coast of Greenland was made, Peary Land was explored, and the insularity and approximate northerly extension of Greenland were confirmed. New expeditions continued the work in 1893–95, and in two summer voyages (1896, 1897) Peary brought back to the United States his noted meteorites. These trips showed that arctic exploration could be conducted economically and without the loss of life. An account of his arctic experiences appeared in *Northward over the "Great Ice"* (1898). Granted another leave of absence from naval duty, he again led an expedition (1898–1902), this time to search for the North Pole. He was only able to reach lat. 84° 17′ N, but he made important surveys of Ellesmere Land and a study of the surface and drift of the polar ice pack. His *Nearest the Pole* (1907) recorded the events of his 1905-6 expedition, when he attained lat. 87° 6′ N, which was only c.174 mi (280 km) from his objective. With courage and will undaunted by disappointment and by harsh arctic experiences, he set out (1908) for his last and successful quest for the North Pole. From Ellesmere Island, Peary, accompanied by a servant and four Eskimos, made a final dash for the pole, which he reached on April 6, 1909. He announced that he had achieved his goal, but on his return he learned of the prior claim of Dr. Frederick A. COOK, who had been ship's surgeon on Peary's expedition of 1891–92. An extremely bitter controversy followed. Although Cook fought to the end of his life, not without some support, to substantiate his claim, Congress recognized Peary's achievement (which later scientific investigation has also verified) and offered him its thanks in 1911, the year in which he was retired from the navy with the rank of rear admiral. See his *North Pole* (1910) and *Secrets of Polar Travel* (1917); biographies by W. H. Hobbs (1936) and J. E.

Weems (1967); D. B. MacMillan, *How Peary Reached the Pole* (1934). Peary's wife, **Josephine Diebitsch Peary,** 1863–1955, accompanied him on several of his expeditions and gave birth in the arctic to Peary's daughter, Marie Ahnighito Peary. His wife published her experiences in *My Arctic Journal* (1893).

Peary Land, peninsula, N Greenland, extending into the Arctic Ocean. It terminates in Cape Bridgman in the northeast and Cape Morris Jesup in the north, the most northerly point of land yet discovered. The area is mountainous (rising to c.6,400 ft/1,950 m) and is free of the inland icecap. Sparse vegetation supports musk oxen and caribou. The peninsula is named for Robert E. Peary who first explored it in his expedition of 1891–92.

Peasants' Revolt: see TYLER, WAT.

Peasants' War, 1524–26, rising of the German peasants and the poorer classes of the towns, particularly in Franconia, Swabia, and Thuringia. It was the climax of a series of local revolts that dated from the 15th cent. Although most of the peasants' demands were economic or political rather than religious, the Reformation sparked the explosion. When the peasants heard the church attacked by Martin LUTHER and other reformers and listened to traveling preachers expound such doctrines as the priesthood of all believers, they concluded that their cause had divine support and that their grievances would be redressed. At Stühlingen, near the Swiss border, a revolt broke out in 1524. The peasants of Swabia and Franconia organized armies, and within a year the war spread over W and S Germany. Aid was given by some discontented nobles, such as Florian Geyer, Götz von BERLICHINGEN, and Ulrich I, dispossessed duke of WÜRTTEMBERG, as well as by large numbers of townsmen. A program called the Twelve Articles of the Peasantry listed among the demands liberty to choose their own pastors, relief from the lesser tithes, abolition of serfdom, the right to fish and hunt, restoration of inclosed common lands, abolition of death duties, impartiality of the courts, and restriction of the demands of landlords to their just feudal dues. These articles were modified variously to suit local conditions. Some atrocities by the peasants (e.g., the massacre of Weinsberg) marked the war, but those committed by their enemies were worse. The revolt received the blessing of the Swiss reformer Huldreich Zwingli and in Thuringia was led by the radical Anabaptist leader Thomas MÜNZER. Martin Luther, however, condemned the revolt, thus contributing to its eventual defeat. Lacking unity and firm leadership, the peasant forces were crushed (1525) largely by the army of the SWABIAN LEAGUE. It is estimated that 100,000 peasants were killed. In Austria, where the revolt continued until 1526, the peasants won some concessions, but in most areas they suffered continued or increased restrictions and had to pay tribute. The peasants' defeat dissuaded further attempts by the peasantry to improve their social and political position.

peat, soil material consisting of partially decomposed organic matter; found in swamps and bogs in various parts of the temperate zone. It is formed by the slow decay of successive layers of aquatic and semiaquatic plants, e.g., sedges, reeds, rushes, and mosses. One of the principal types of peat is moss peat, derived primarily from sphagnum moss; it is used in agriculture as poultry and stable litters as well as a mulch, a soil conditioner, and an acidifying agent; it is also used in industry as an insulating material. Another type of peat is fuel peat, which is most widely used in regions where coal and wood are scarce, e.g., Ireland, Scandinavia, and parts of the Soviet Union. Peat is the earliest stage of transition from compressed plant growth to the formation of coal. Large deposits of peat in the United States are found in Michigan, California, and the Florida Everglades.

peat moss: see SPHAGNUM.

Peć (pĕch), town (1971 pop. 90,386), S Yugoslavia, in Serbia, in the Kossovo-Metohija region. A trade center, it has industries that produce jewelry, carpets, and small arms. Stephen Dušan in 1346 made Peć the seat of the Orthodox patriarchs of Serbia, who resided there until 1766. The town is noted for its 13th-century patriarchal cathedral and several Turkish mosques and houses.

pecan: see HICKORY.

peccary (pĕk'ərē), small, wild pig, genus *Tayassu*, the only pig native to the Americas. Although similar in appearance to Old World pigs, peccaries are classified in a family of their own because of anatomical differences. Peccaries have downward-curved tusks with which they fight ferociously when threatened. They have large heads and long snouts; both sexes have scent glands on the rump. There are two peccary species. The collared peccary, or javelina, *Tayassu tajacu*, is the more common, ranging from the SW United States to Argentina and inhabiting many types of country, from tropical swamps to dry scrub regions. It is about 20 in. (50 cm) high at the shoulder and weighs about 50 lb (23 kg); it has grizzled gray-black hair marked with a white neck band and an erectile mane on the neck. Collared peccaries move about in small family groups, eating roots, fruits, insects, worms, and reptiles. The white-lipped peccary, *T. albirostris*, is found in smaller numbers in forests from S Mexico to N Argentina. Reddish brown to black, with white lips and cheeks, it is somewhat larger than the collared peccary and more predacious in its habits. White-lipped peccaries move about in large herds foraging for food and hunting small mammals. Peccaries are classified in the phylum CHORDATA, subphylum Vertebrata, class Mammalia, order Artiodactyla, family Tayassuidae.

Pechenegs (pĕchənĕgz') or **Patzinaks** (pätsĭnäks'), nomadic people of the Turkic family. Their original home is not known, but in the 8th and 9th cent. they inhabited the region between the lower Volga and the Urals. Pushed west (c.889) by the Khazars and Cumans, they drove the Magyars before them and settled in S Ukraine on the banks of the Dnepr. They long harassed Kievan Russia and even threatened (934) Constantinople. After unsuccessfully besieging Kiev (968) and killing the Kievan duke Sviatoslav (972), they were defeated (1036) by Yaroslav and moved to the plains of the lower Danube. Attacked (1064) by the Cumans, many Pechenegs were slain or absorbed. After once more besieging Constantinople (c.1091), they were virtually annihilated by Emperor Alexius I. Later there were significant communities of Pechenegs in Hungary.

Pechenga (pyĕ'chĭn-gə), Finnish *Petsamo*, town, NW European USSR, an ice-free port at the head of Pechenga Fjord on the Barents Sea and near the Norwegian border. It is also the northern terminus of an Arctic highway. Pechenga serves as the base for a fishing (notably herring) fleet. Located in an important nickel-, copper-, and uranium-mining region, the town has an ore refinery. Pechenga was known in the 16th cent. as a Muscovite foreign trading port. Ceded by Russia to Finland in 1920, it was a supply base in the German-Finnish drive on MURMANSK during World War II. The town was seized by the Russians and transferred to them by the Russo-Finnish armistice of 1944.

Pechora (pyĭchô'rə), river, c.1,120 mi (1,800 km) long, rising in the N Urals, N European USSR. It flows generally north through the forest and tundra regions of the Komi Autonomous Republic and the Nenets National Okrug into Pechora Bay (an inlet of the Barents Sea), forming a vast delta at Naryan-Mar. It is navigable for c.470 mi (760 km) upstream in summer and for c.1,040 mi (1,670 km) in spring and autumn. The important Pechora coal basin extends eastward to Vorkuta from the middle course of the river. The Pechora is used for fishing and lumber transport.

Pechstein, Max (mäks pĕkh'shtīn), 1881–1955, German expressionist painter and graphic artist. Early contact with the art of Van Gogh stimulated his development toward expressionism. In 1906, Pechstein joined the BRÜCKE group. His work, less intense and more decorative than that of the other members of the group, gained wide popularity. In 1914 he went to the South Seas, a trip which inspired his *Palau Triptych* and other works.

peck: see ENGLISH UNITS OF MEASUREMENT.

Peckham, Rufus Wheeler (pĕk'əm), 1838–1909, Associate Justice of the U.S. Supreme Court (1895–1909), b. Albany, N.Y. Admitted (1859) to the bar, he became a leading Albany lawyer and was prominent in local Democratic politics. He served on the state supreme court (1883–86) and the state court of appeals (1886–95) before being appointed by President Cleveland to the U.S. Supreme Court. A zealous defender of property rights, he ruled in the famous case of *Lochner* vs. *New York* (1905) that a minimum hours law was unconstitutional.

Pecock or **Peacock, Reginald** (pē'kŏk), c.1395–c.1460, English bishop and writer. He obtained the bishopric of St. Asaph in 1444 and transferred to Chichester in 1450. A learned, active, and controversial figure, Pecock is important as one of the first English writers to use the vernacular. He is the author of the *Repressor of Over-much Blaming of the Clergy* (c.1455), against the Lollards, and of other works. Because his religious views opposed the conventional theological thought of the time, he was accused of heresy and had to make public abjuration and resign his bishopric.

Pecos (pā'kəs), city (1970 pop. 12,682), seat of Reeves co., W Texas, on the Pecos River; inc. 1903. It is an important railroad and highway junction and the market for an extensive ranch and farm area irrigated by water pumped from underground or supplied by the Red Bluff Dam on the Pecos. It is also a sulfur, gas, and oil center. There are cattle feed lots, vegetable-packing houses, large automotive proving grounds, and a garment industry. Pecos was founded in the 1880s as a cow town at a crossing of the river. The annual rodeo, held there since 1883, was the world's first. Of interest is a Judge Roy Bean museum.

Pecos, river, 926 mi (1,480 km) long, rising in N N.Mex. near the Truchas peaks and flowing SE across E N.Mex. and W Texas to the Rio Grande; drains c.38,300 sq mi (99,200 sq km). In New Mexico, dams at Alamogordo, Avalon, and McMillan serve the Carlsbad reclamation project (est. 1906), which irrigates c.25,000 acres (10,120 hectares); in W Texas, Red Bluff Dam forms a reservoir on the Pecos. Long-standing interstate disputes about water use were settled in 1949, when a Federal bill provided for a compact between New Mexico and Texas. Near Pecos, N.Mex., is Pecos National Monument (see NATIONAL PARKS AND MONUMENTS, table), which encloses the ruins of Pecos pueblo. In the heyday of ranching in W Texas, "west of the Pecos" was the term for the distinct and rugged region of the western tip of the state.

Pecos National Monument: see NATIONAL PARKS AND MONUMENTS (table).

Pécs (pāch), Ger. *Fünfkirchen*, city (1970 pop. 145,307), SW Hungary, near the Yugoslav border. A county administrative seat and a railroad hub, Pécs is the industrial center of Hungary's chief coal-mining region. Coke, metals, agricultural machinery, tobacco, and leather goods are produced in the city, which is also famous for its pottery. There are extensive vineyards in the surrounding area. One of Hungary's oldest cities, Pécs was the site of a Celtic settlement and became the capital of the Roman province of Lower Pannonia under Emperor Hadrian. It was first known as Sopianae and later as Quinque Ecclesiae [Lat.,=five churches], from which the German name Fünfkirchen derived. In 1009 the city was made an episcopal see by St. Stephen, and in 1367 Louis I established the first Hungarian university there. Pécs was under Turkish rule from 1543 to 1686. Many German miners and colonists settled there during the 18th cent., and in 1780 it became a free city. The 11th-century cathedral (rebuilt in the late 19th cent.) is the most notable historic building in Pécs; the city also has an episcopal palace, a Turkish minaret, and several churches that were formerly mosques.

pecten: see SCALLOP.

pectin, any of a group of white, amorphous, complex CARBOHYDRATES that occur in ripe fruits and certain vegetables. Fruits rich in pectin are the peach, apple, currant, loganberry, and plum. Protopectin, present in unripe fruits, is converted to pectin as the fruit ripens. Pectin forms a colloidal solution in water and gels on cooling. When fruits are cooked with the correct amount of sugar and when the acidity is optimum and the amount of pectin present is sufficient, jams and jellies can be made. In overripe fruits the pectin becomes pectic acid, which does not form jelly with sugar solutions. Commercial preparations of pectin are available for jelly making.

Peculiar People, an alternate rendering for the biblical phrase "chosen people" (of Israel), applied to numerous Protestant dissenting sects such as the Plumstead peculiars. This group, founded in London in 1838 by John Banyard, refused medical treatment as an article of faith.

Pedahel (pĕd'əhĕl, pĕdā'hĕl), Naphtalite chief. Num. 34.28.

Pedahzur (pēdā'zər), Manassite. Num. 1.10; 2.20; 7.54.

Pedaiah (pēdā'yə, pē"dəī'yə). **1** Manassite. 1 Chron. 27.20. **2** Grandfather of Jehoiakim. 2 Kings 23.36. **3** Father of Zerubbabel. 1 Chron. 3.18,19. **4** Repairer of the wall. Neh. 3.25. **5** Assistant of Ezra. Neh. 8.4. **6** Benjamite. Neh. 11.7. **7** One of Nehemiah's treasurers. Neh. 13.13. The last four may not all be separate persons.

peddler or **hawker,** itinerant vendor of small goods. In rural America he carried his pack or drove a horse and cart from door to door. While the importance of the peddler to the small American community declined considerably with the growth of automobile transportation and mail-order houses, his role in certain sections of the Asian and African markets has remained important. See R. L. Wright, *Hawkers and Walkers in Early America* (1927, repr. 1965); J. R. Dolan, *Yankee Peddlers of Early America* (1964).

pediatrics (pēdēă'trĭks), branch of medicine specializing in the care of children and the treatment of childhood diseases. Pediatricians are concerned to a large extent with preventive medicine, for although they treat ordinary diseases and disorders that occur in the young, the emphasis is on watchful care against abnormality due to poor nutrition and hygiene and on immunization against the more devastating infections that beset children. Such attention is reflected in the better development and health of young people as well as in the dwindling mortality rates in infectious disease. Some surgeons specialize in pediatric surgery, in recognition of the fact that operating on young tissue and small organs requires particular skill and experience.

pediment, in architecture, the triangular gable end on a building of classic type or a similar form used decoratively. It consists of the TYMPANUM, or triangular wall surface, enclosed below by the horizontal cornice and above by the raking cornice, which follows the slope of the roof. In Greek architecture the pediment usually contained sculpture when used with the Doric order; however, this was not generally true with the Ionic order. In the Roman and Renaissance styles it was used also as a purely decorative motif, chiefly over doors and windows; the upper profile of the pediment was sometimes of segmental shape. In later Renaissance and baroque design the pediment often took on fantastic shapes, notably in the variants of the broken pediment, in which the two sides of the raking cornice do not join and the central space is filled with ornamental devices. First used by the Romans, the form was revived by Michelangelo and used by a host of later architects. The scrolled broken pediment was a favorite in American Colonial work, especially in doorways and over mantels.

Broken pediment

Eastern pediment of the temple of Zeus at Olympia

pedodontics: see DENTISTRY.

Pedrarias: see ARIAS DE ÁVILA, PEDRO.

Pedro. For Spanish and Portuguese rulers thus named, see PETER.

Pedro I (Dom Pedro de Alcântara) (pä'drō), 1798–1834, first emperor of Brazil (1822–31); son of John VI of Portugal. Dom Pedro was a child when the Portuguese royal family, fleeing from Napoleon's conquering French army, left Portugal for Brazil. He grew up in Rio de Janeiro, and when King John returned (1821) to Portugal, Dom Pedro remained as regent in Brazil. The situation of the colony, which had been the center of empire during the royal residence, was a sensitive one, and attempts by the Portuguese to reduce Brazil again to subordinate status caused dissatisfaction. Heeding his Brazilian advisers, especially José BONIFÁCIO, Pedro decided to defy the government in Lisbon. On Sept. 7, 1882, he issued the *Grito do Ipiranga,* which declared Brazil a separate empire. In 1824 he granted Brazil its first constitution. His popularity, however, was soon undermined by his arbitrary political measures, by his notorious private life, and by his preoccupation with Portuguese affairs. When John VI died in 1826, Dom Pedro was recognized as Peter IV of Portugal. However, he conceded the Portuguese crown to his daughter, MARIA II, on condition that she marry her uncle Dom MIGUEL and that Dom Miguel accept a constitutional charter for Portugal. Dom Miguel agreed but in 1828 seized the rule for himself and set up an absolute regime. Meanwhile, Dom Pedro's inability to cope with growing problems in Brazil led him to abdicate (1831) in favor of his son, Pedro II. He left for Europe, joined the Portuguese liberals who had established themselves in the Azores, and in 1832 proceeded with a small fleet to Oporto. In the Miguelist Wars he withstood the siege of Oporto by Dom Miguel. An English sea force fighting for Dom Pedro and Maria II defeated the Miguelist fleet, and Maria was restored to the throne. Dom Pedro died in the same year. See Sergio Correa da Costa, *Every Inch a King* (tr. 1949, 2d ed. 1964); C. H. Haring, *Empire in Brazil* (1958, repr. 1968).

Pedro II (Dom Pedro II de Alcântara), 1825–91, emperor of Brazil (1831–89). He succeeded under a regency when his father, Pedro I, abdicated. Because of their dislike for the regency, the liberals had him declared of age in 1840. His long reign was, after some rebellions at its start, a period of internal peace and material progress marred only by wars against nations to the south. Brazil aided Justo José de URQUIZA in the war (1851–52) against Juan Manuel de ROSAS, at the same time taking part in Uruguayan affairs in support of Venancio Flores. Later Brazil was joined with Argentina and Uruguay in the War of the Triple Alliance against Paraguay (1865–70). Although the undermining effects of these wars eventually contributed to the downfall of the empire, Pedro II's long reign was marked by a steady increase of immigration, produce, and wealth. The genial emperor was personally extremely popular, but the economic and political tendencies of his time betrayed him. In 1850 the slave trade was prohibited; in 1871 a law was passed providing for gradual emancipation; in 1888, when Pedro was in Europe, a law abolishing slavery was signed by his daughter ISABEL. This antagonized the rich planters, who had been the mainstay of the empire. The government had also alienated the military and some of the clerical support. Discontent was widespread, and in 1889 a quiet revolution led by Manuel Deodoro da FONSECA overturned the empire. Pedro was exiled and spent the remainder of his life in Europe. See biographies by M. W. Williams (1937, repr. 1966) and Harry Bernstein (1973); study by C. W. Simmons (1966); C. H. Haring, *Empire in Brazil* (1958).

Peebles, burgh (1971 pop. 5,881), county town of Peeblesshire, S Scotland, at the confluence of Eddleston Water and the Tweed River. It is a mountain resort and a farm market with woolen mills. There are ruins of a 13th-century church and castle. In 1975, Peebles became part of the Borders region.

Peeblesshire (pē'bəlz-shĭr) or **Tweeddale,** county (1971 pop. 13,675), 347 sq mi (899 sq km), SE Scotland. PEEBLES is the county town. The county is hilly, reaching 2,754 ft (839 m) in the southern uplands, and is drained by the Tweed River. The textile mills at Peebles and Innerleithen are the largest employers. Beef cattle and sheep are raised. In 1975, Peeblesshire became part of the Borders region.

Pee Dee or **Great Pee Dee,** river, c.435 mi (700 km) long, rising in the Blue Ridge, W N.C., and flowing NE then SE to Winyah Bay, S.C. It is called the Yadkin until it is joined by the Uharie River W of Troy, N.C. Several hydroelectric power plants are on the river in North Carolina.

Peekskill, city (1970 pop. 19,283), Westchester co., SE N.Y., on the Hudson River; settled 1665, inc. as a village 1816, as a city 1940. Clothing, optical instruments, lighting fixtures, and office equipment are manufactured there. Peekskill was a prominent trade center after the Revolutionary War. Peter Cooper and Henry Ward Beecher were born there. St. Peter's Church, dedicated in 1767, has been restored. A huge state military reservation is situated across Annsville creek from Peekskill, and Camp Smith, a center for national guard, police, and F.B.I. training, is there.

Peel, Sir Robert, 1788–1850, British statesman. The son of a rich cotton manufacturer, whose baronetcy he inherited in 1830, Peel entered Parliament as a Tory in 1809. He served (1812–18) as chief secretary for Ireland, where he maintained order by the establishment of a police force and consistently opposed Irish demands for CATHOLIC EMANCIPATION. In 1819 he was chairman of the parliamentary currency committee that recommended and secured Britain's return to the gold standard. As home secretary (1822–27, 1828–30) Peel succeeded in reforming the criminal laws and established (1829) the London police force, whose members came to be called Peelers or Bobbies. Early in his career Peel scrupulously defended Tory interests, but he gradually came to believe in the need for change. The first sign of a modified outlook was in his sponsorship (1829) of the bill enabling Roman Catholics to sit in the House of Commons. In opposing parliamentary reform he recovered some of the Tory support that he lost by this position, and after the REFORM BILL of 1832 had passed despite his opposition, he rallied the party and was prime minister for a brief term (1834–35). In 1834, however, Peel made the election speech known as the Tamworth manifesto, in which he explained that his party accepted the Reform Bill and would work for further changes but "without infringing on established rights." This statement came to be regarded as the manifesto for the CONSERVATIVE PARTY now emerging, under Peel's leadership, from the old Tory party. Among the able young men who rallied around Peel were William Ewart GLADSTONE and Benjamin DISRAELI. Peel was asked to form a cabinet in 1839 but declined when the young Queen VICTORIA refused to make requested changes in her household. He returned to power in 1841, however, and the reshaped party attitudes were very apparent in his new ministry, which introduced an income tax and a revised system of banking control, gave aid to the Irish Catholic Church, and attempted Irish land reform. Of far greater importance were the virtual abandonment of custom duties and the repeal of the CORN LAWS. Peel had formerly defended these laws, which protected Tory agricultural interests, but he was impressed by the arguments of Richard COBDEN against them and convinced by the disastrous effect of the potato famine in Ireland. The laws were repealed in June, 1846, but Peel's action split his party, and he resigned from office after a tactical defeat within the same month. Much abused as an apostate during his lifetime, Peel is now recognized as a practical statesman of forward-looking views and great courage. His memoirs were posthumously published (1856). His correspondence and private letters were edited by C. S. Parker (3 vol., 1891–99) and later by George Peel (1920). See biographies by G. Kitson Clark (1936), Tresham Lever (1942), and Norman Gash (2 vol., 1961 and 1972); study by G. Kitson Clark (2d ed. 1964).

Peele, George, 1558?–1597?, English playwright, educated at Oxford. He experimented in a variety of forms, including the pageant, history, pastoral, comedy, and melodrama, but his best-known work is *The Old Wives Tale* (1595), a frolicsome piece that infuses a depiction of ordinary English life with elements of folklore and romance. His other extant plays include *The Arraignment of Paris* (1584), *Edward I* (1593), *The Battle of Alcazar* (1594), and *The Love of King David and Fair Bethsabe* (1599). Peele was one of the "university wits," a group of poets and playwrights that included Marlowe, Nashe, and Robert Greene. See his life and works, ed. by C. T. Prouty (3 vol., 1952–70); biographies by D. H. Horne (1952) and G. K. Hunter (1968).

Peel Island, Japan: see BONIN ISLAND.

peeper: see TREE FROG.

peepul (pē'pəl): see BO TREE.

Peerce, Jan, 1904–, American tenor, b. New York City as Jacob Pincus Perelmuth. As a young man he began a career in medicine and studied the violin, but his vocal gift led to singing engagements in synagogues during the Jewish high holidays. He began singing in 1932 in Radio City Music Hall and later was discovered by Arturo Toscanini, who chose him to be a soloist in a performance of Beethoven's Ninth Symphony. Peerce made his operatic debut in Philadelphia in 1938, singing the Duke in Verdi's *Rigoletto.* In 1941 he made his debut with the Metropolitan Opera as Alfredo in Verdi's *La Traviata.* He soon became a leading tenor there in the French and Italian repertoire.

peewee: see FLYCATCHER.

Pegasus (pĕg'əsəs), in astronomy, northern CONSTELLATION lying SW of Andromeda and SE of Cygnus. It is named for the mythological winged horse Pegasus. The constellation is easily recognized by the Great Square formed by the bright stars Markab (Alpha Pegasi) at the southwest corner, Scheat (Beta Pegasi) at the northwest corner, Algenib (Gamma Pegasi) at the southeast corner, and Alpheratz in Andromeda at the northeast corner. The constellation reaches its highest point in the evening sky in October.

Pegasus, in Greek mythology, winged horse. He sprang full-grown from the neck of the dying Gorgon Medusa. With a slash of his hoof, he created the Hippocrene, a sacred spring of the Muses on Mt. Helicon. Hence, he has often been associated with the arts, especially poetry. Pegasus was captured by BELLEROPHON, who rode him through many adventures.

pegmatite: see GRANITE.

Pegu (pĕgōō'), city (1953 pop. 47,387), capital of Pegu div., S Burma, on the Pegu River. It is a port and railway junction. Founded c.825 by the Mons, it became their capital when their king, Binnya U, established his palace there. Pegu was the center of one of the three chief states of Burma from the 14th to the late 15th cent.; in the 16th cent. it was the capital of a united Burmese kingdom. After it was destroyed in 1564 and again in 1599, the Burmese moved their capital to Ava. In the 18th cent. the Talaings rebelled against the Burmese and set up their capital at Pegu; it was destroyed by the Burmese in 1757, but was later rebuilt as the center of a Burmese province. The city and province came under British rule in 1852. The city has many temples, of which the most impressive is the Shwe Maw Daw Pagoda.

Péguy, Charles (shärl pāgē'), 1873–1914, French poet and writer. Of a poor working family, he won scholarships and made a brilliant record as a student. He left the École normale supérieure to devote himself to the cause of socialism. He was, however, individual in his views, and he broke with the socialist party. In 1900 he founded the *Cahiers de la quinzaine,* a periodical in which he published his own works and those of other young writers. Through his life he worked passionately for justice, truth, and the good of the common man and the world. He was the outstanding Roman Catholic supporter of Dreyfus in the Dreyfus Affair, and his polemics against injustice were fiery. Though formally he was often at odds with the church, he is among the foremost modern Catholic writers. He sought to infuse spirituality into every aspect of life. His great poem *Le Mystère de la charité de Jeanne d'Arc* (1910, tr. by Julian Green 1950) expresses his ideal of the spiritual in action. His repetitive chantlike verse has great power. Others of his long works are *Le Porche du mystère de la deuxième virtu* (1911) and *Eve* (1913). He was killed at the battle of the Marne in World War I. Translations of his works appear in *Basic Verities* (1943) and *Men and Saints* (1944), both translated by Ann and Julian Green; Julian Green also translated some of Péguy's religious poetry in *God Speaks* (1945). See studies by Marjorie Villiers (1965), Nelly Jussem-Wilson (1965), and H. A. Schmitt (1967).

Peham: see BEHAM.

Pehlevi language: see PAHLAVI LANGUAGE.

Pehpiao: see PEI-P'IAO, China.

Pei, Ieoh Ming (pā), 1917–, Chinese-American architect, b. Canton, China. Pei emigrated to the United States in 1935 and worked for the National Defense Research Committee from 1943 to 1945. He taught at Harvard from 1945 to 1948, when he joined Webb and Knapp, Inc., and designed such projects as Zeckendorf Plaza and Mile High Center in Denver and Place Ville Marie in Montreal. He established I. M. Pei and Associates in 1955. In his works structure and environment are carefully integrated. Among his later notable works are the Earth Science Building (1964) and the Chemical Building (1970) at the Massachusetts Institute of Technology, the John F. Kennedy Memorial Library at Harvard, Tunghai Univ. at Taiwan, the Pane Mellon Arts Center and Choate School complex in Wallingford, Conn., the Herbert Museum of Art at Cornell Univ., Kips Bay Plaza and University Plaza in New York City, and such renewal projects as the Society Hill redevelopment in Philadelphia (1964). Pei drew the master plan for the Government Center in Boston.

Pei (pā, bā), river, c.200 mi (320 km) long, formed by the union of two headstreams in the Nan Ling mts., N Kwangtung prov., S China. It flows S into the Si River, E of Canton, to form the Canton River delta. Its entire course is navigable and was once an important north-south route; a road and railway now follow its valley. The name is also spelled Pei-chiang.

Pei-chiang, river, China: see PEI.

Pei-hai (bā-hī) or **Pakhoi** (bäk'hoi'), town (1970 est. pop. 175,000), Kwangsi Chuang Autonomous Region, SE China, a port on the Gulf of Tonkin. The chief pearl grounds of China are in the waters near Pei-hai. The town became a treaty port in 1877.

Pei-p'iao or **Pehpiao** (both: bā-pyou), town, Liaoning prov., China. It is a coal-mining center.

Peiping: see PEKING.

Peipus, Lake: see CHUDSKOYE, LAKE, USSR.

Peirce, Benjamin, 1809–80, American mathematician and astronomer, b. Salem, Mass., grad. Harvard, 1829. From 1833 he was a professor at Harvard; he helped establish the Harvard Observatory and was an organizer of the Dudley Observatory, Albany, N.Y. In the field of mechanics he made studies of the forms of elastic sacs containing fluids. From 1867 to 1874 he was superintendent of the U.S. Coast Survey. His fundamental contributions to mathematics were collected as *Linear Associative Algebra* (1870). He also wrote *A System of Analytic Mechanics* (1855).

Peirce, Charles Sanders (pûrs), 1839–1914, American philosopher, b. Cambridge, Mass., grad. Harvard, 1859; son of Benjamin Peirce. Except for occasional lectures he rejected the regimen of academic life and was in government service with the Geodetic Survey for many years. Regarding logic as the beginning of all philosophical study, Peirce felt that the meaning of an idea was to be found in an examination of the consequences to which the idea would lead. This principle was published in 1878 in *Popular Science Monthly,* using the term PRAGMATISM, which was later used by William James with acknowledgment. The influence of Peirce is clearly seen in the works of Josiah Royce and John Dewey, but recognition of his importance was delayed because of the scarcity of published works. He left many fragmentary manuscripts, but the only book published during his lifetime was *Photometric Researches* (1878). After his death his major essays were edited by M. R. Cohen in *Chance, Love, and Logic* (1923). See his collected papers (8 vol., 1931–58); studies by Justus Buchler (1939, repr. 1966), M. G. Murphey (1961), R. J. Bernstein, ed. (1965), and J. K. Feibleman (1970).

Peirithoüs: see PIRITHOÜS.

Peisistratus: see PISISTRATUS.

Peixoto, Floriano (flōrēä'nō pāshō'tō), 1842–95, Brazilian marshal and statesman, president of Brazil (1891–94). He took part in the establishment of the republic and was chosen vice president under Manuel Deodoro da Fonseca. When the president resigned in the face of a revolution, Peixoto succeeded to the presidency (Nov., 1891). He ruled dictatorially amid widespread dissension, putting down a naval revolt in 1893 and maintaining himself in power until the election of 1894, when he was defeated. In spite of his unpopularity, the "Iron Marshal" by his firmness consolidated the new republican government.

Pekah (pē'kə), king of Israel. He was a general under King Pekahiah and murdered him for the throne. As the head of an anti-Assyrian coalition, he went to war with Ahaz of Judah. Ahaz requested and received help from Tiglath-pileser III, and as a result Pekah lost the northern and eastern parts of his kingdom to Assyria. His successor was Hoshea. 2 Kings 15.25–37; 16.1,5.

Pekahiah (pē"kəhī'ə), King of Israel, son and successor of Menahem. His reign was ended by his murder at the hands of his general Pekah. 2 Kings 15.22–26.

Pekalongan (pĕk"älông'gän), city (1961 pop. 851,224), N central Java, Indonesia, on the Java Sea. It is a textile and batik center and the principal port for central Java; sugar, rubber, and tea are exported. A Dutch fort there was built in 1753.

Pekin (pē'kĭn), city (1970 pop. 31,375), seat of Tazewell co., central Ill., a port on the Illinois River; inc. 1839. A processing, rail, and shipping point in a grain, livestock, and coal area, Pekin has a large food industry. Corn products, cereals, liquor, yeast, and malt are produced.

Peking (pē-kĭng, pā-), city (1970 est. pop. 8,000,000), capital of the People's Republic of China. It is in central Hopeh prov., but constitutes an independent unit (6,564 sq mi/17,000 sq km) administered directly by the national government. The second largest city in China (after Shanghai), Peking is the political, cultural, financial, educational, and transportation center of the country. Under the Communist government it has also become a great industrial area, the heart of a vast complex of textile mills, iron and steel works, railroad repair shops, machine shops, chemical plants, and factories manufacturing heavy machinery, electronic equipment, aircraft, plastics, synthetic fibers, and rolling stock. It is a rail hub, receiving lines from all sections of the country and linked directly with North Vietnam and, through both Mongolia and Manchuria, with the USSR. It has air connections with all major Chinese cities and with numerous foreign countries. Since 723 B.C. several cities, bearing various names, have existed at this site. The nucleus of the present city was Kublai Khan's capital, Cambuluc (constructed 1260–90). Under the name Peking [Chin.,=northern capital] the city was the capital of China from 1421 until 1911. The gateway to Mongolia and Manchuria, it was often the prize of contending armies. In 1860, Great Britain and France captured it after the battle of Pa-li-ch'iao and forced the Chinese government to concede the Legation Quarter for foreign settlements. This cession was among the factors responsible for the Boxer Rebellion (1900), in which the foreign colony was besieged until relieved by a combined expeditionary force of American, Japanese, and European troops. The foreign powers exacted a treaty that provided for the permanent garrisoning of foreign troops in Peking. Repeatedly the city changed hands during the civil wars that followed the establishment of the Chinese Republic in 1911–12. From 1912 to 1927, Peking, Canton, and Han-k'ou alternated as centers of government. In 1928, when the seat of government was transferred to Nanking [Chin.,=southern capital], the name Peiping [Chin.,=northern peace] was adopted. Japan occupied the city after the famous Marco Polo Bridge incident in 1937 (see SINO-JAPANESE WAR, SECOND). The Japanese made the city the capital of a puppet state. With the end of World War II and the abolition of the last foreign concessions (1946), the city was entirely restored to Chinese sovereignty. In Jan., 1949, it fell to the Communists, who later that year designated it the capital of the newly founded People's Republic of China and restored the name Peking. Peking in the main consists of two formerly walled districts, the Outer or Chinese City and the Inner or Tatar City. The 25 mi (40 km) of ramparts and monumental gates that once surrounded the cities have been razed by the Communist government and replaced by wide avenues to aid the traffic flow. Within the Tatar City is the Forbidden City (formerly the emperor's residence), the Imperial City (where his retinue was housed), and the Legation Quarter. The Imperial City is now the seat of the Communist government. On the southern edge of the Tatar City is the T'ien An Men Square, which contains the monument to the heroes of the revolution, the Great Hall of the People, and the museum of history and revolution. Celebrations held in the square include May Day and the founding date (Oct. 1) of the People's Republic. Peking is known for its artificial lakes and for its parks and temples. It contains many of the greatest examples of architecture of the Ming and Ch'ing dynasties as well as remains from earlier times. The Temple of Heaven (15th cent.) is set in a large park and has a massive altar of white marble before which the emperors prayed at the summer solstice. In the temple of Confucius, built by Kublai Khan, are guarded incised boulders that date from the Chou dynasty. An ancient astronomical observatory, once used by

Catholic missionaries, still functions. The Forbidden City, now a vast museum, contains the imperial palaces (two groups of three each) and smaller palaces, all replete with art treasures. Just outside Peking, rivaling the beauties within, is the imperial summer palace with its lovely parks. After 1949, Peking began to spread well beyond its two core cities, and hundreds of new buildings, hotels, and cultural centers now dot the suburbs. A subway was completed in 1969. Peking has an opera, a ballet, and the impressive national library. It is the seat of many learned societies, research organizations, and academies of fine arts, drama, dance, and music. The more than 25 institutions of higher learning include Peking Univ., the People's Univ. of China, China Univ. of Science and Technology, Tsinghua Univ., the Peking Institute of Foreign Languages, two medical colleges, and many technical and scientific schools. The Peking zoo is famous for its collection of pandas. The Workers' Stadium is the scene of the Pan-Chinese games, held every four years. In addition to the many tourist attractions in the city, the Great Wall and the gigantic Ming tombs are easily accessible. At nearby Chou-k'ou-tien were discovered several fossil bones of *Sinanthropus pekingensis,* or Peking man, an early example of prehistoric man. See Roderick MacFarquhar, *The Forbidden City* (1972); Odile Cail, *Peking* (rev. ed. 1973).

Pekingese (pē″kĭnēz′), breed of small TOY DOG developed over many centuries in China. It stands from 6 to 9 in. (15.3–22.9 cm) high at the shoulder and weighs from 6 to 14 lb (2.7–6.4 kg). The long, straight, soft coat forms a ruff around the neck and fringes of feathery hair on the ears, legs, and tail. It may be any color. The Pekingese is believed to have existed in its present form as early as the 8th cent., when it was kept as a palace dog by the Chinese emperors. For centuries its breeding was closely guarded by the court; the punishment for stealing a Pekingese was death. When the imperial palace at Peking was invaded by the British in 1860, several of these royal dogs were taken and subsequently introduced into the West. Today the Pekingese is a very popular companion and house pet. See DOG.

Peking man: see HOMO ERECTUS.

Peking University, at Peking, People's Republic of China; founded 1952, incorporating the former Univ. of Peking (est. 1898), Tsinghun Univ. (est. 1928), and Yenching Univ. (est. 1919). It has faculties of mathematics and mechanical engineering, physics, chemistry, biology, geography, history, Chinese languages and literature, Russian language and literature, Oriental languages, Western languages and literature, philosophy, economics, law, and library science.

Pekod (pē′kŏd), designation of a group of people, presumably Babylonian. Jer. 50.21.

Pelagianism (pəlā′jənĭzəm), Christian heretical sect that rose in the 5th cent. to challenge St. Augustine's conceptions of GRACE and PREDESTINATION. The doctrine was advanced by the celebrated monk and theologian, Pelagius (c.355–c.425). He was probably born in Britain. After studying Roman and Greek law and rhetoric and later theology in England and Rome, he preached in Africa and Palestine, attracting able followers, such as Celestius and Julian of Eclannum. Pelagius thought that St. AUGUSTINE was excessively pessimistic in his view that man, in his sinful nature, must rely totally upon grace for salvation. Instead Pelagius taught that men have a natural capacity to reject evil and seek God, that Christ's admonition, "Be ye perfect," presupposes this capacity, and that grace, therefore, is simply the natural ability men have received from God to seek and to serve God. Pelagius rejected the doctrine of original sin; he taught that children are born innocent of the sin of Adam. Baptism, accordingly, ceased to be understood as a regenerative sacrament. Pelagius challenged the very function of the church, claiming that the law as well as the gospel can lead one to heaven and that pagans had been able to enter heaven by virtue of their moral actions before the coming of Christ. The church fought Pelagianism from the time that Celestius was denied ordination in 411. In 415, Augustine warned St. Jerome in Palestine that Pelagius was propagating a dangerous heresy there, and Jerome acted to prevent its spread in the East. Pelagianism was condemned by East and West at the Council of Ephesus (431). A compromise doctrine, Semi-Pelagianism, became popular in the 5th and 6th cent. in France, Britain, and Ireland. Semi-Pelagians taught that although grace was necessary for salvation, men could, apart from grace, desire the gift of salvation, and that they could, of themselves, freely accept and persevere in grace. Semi-Pelagians also rejected the Augustinian doctrine of predestination and held that God willed the salvation of all men equally. At the instance of St. Caesarius of Arles, Semi-Pelagianism was condemned at the Council of Orange (529). By the end of the 6th cent., Pelagianism disappeared as an organized heresy, but the questions of free will, predestination, and grace raised by Pelagianism have been the subject of theological controversy ever since (see MOLINA, LUIS; ARMINIUS, JACOBUS). Pelagius' *Expositions of Thirteen Epistles of St. Paul* were edited in English by Alexander Souter (3 vol., 1922–31). See B. B. Warfield, *Studies in Tertullian and Augustine* (1930, repr. 1970); John Ferguson, *Pelagius, a Historical and Theological Study* (1957); J. E. Chisholm, *The Pseudo-Augustinian Hypomnesticon Against the Pelagians and Celestinans* (vol. I, 1967).

pelagic zone: see OCEAN.

Pelaiah (pĕl″ā′ə). **1** Descendant of David. 1 Chron. 3.24. **2** Expounder of the Law. Neh. 8.7; 10.10.

Pelaliah (pĕl″əlī′ə), ancestor of Adaiah the priest. Neh. 11.12.

Pelatiah (pĕl″ətī′ə). **1** Zerubbabel's grandson. 1 Chron. 3.21. **2** Simeonite captain. 1 Chron. 4.42. **3** Signer of the Covenant. Neh. 10.22.

Pelayo (pālä′yō), d. 737, first king (c.718–737) of Asturias. He was elected king by the tribesmen of Asturias and by Visigothic leaders who had escaped Tarik. His victory over the Moors at Covadonga sometime between 718 and 725 marked the beginning of Christian resistance to the Moorish conquerors. Accounts of Pelayo are largely legendary.

Pele (pä′lā), Hawaiian goddess of the volcano. Her traditional home is Halemaumau, the fire pit of Kilauea crater on the island of Hawaii.

Pelé (pālā′), 1940–, Brazilian soccer (football) player. His real name is Edson Arantes do Nascimento. Perhaps the greatest player in the history of soccer, Pelé began playing at the age of 5 and joined the Santos at 16. Playing inside left forward, he led his team to numerous championships and the Brazilian national team to world championships in 1958, 1962, and 1970. He holds every scoring record in Brazil, and in international matches he scored an average of one goal per game. His playing style is marked by superb ball control and great tactical ability. The world's highest paid athlete, he has scored over 1,000 goals. In 1971 he retired from the Brazilian national team but continued to play with the Santos. He announced in October, 1974, that he would retire from the Santos at the end of the 1974 season.

Pelecypoda: see BIVALVE.

Pelée (pəlā′), volcano, 4,429 ft (1,350 m) high, on N Martinique island, French West Indies. On May 8, 1902, the day after the eruption of SOUFRIÈRE on St. Vincent, Pelée also erupted, engulfing SAINT-PIERRE at its base and killing c.40,000 people in the city and adjacent area. Because the chemical composition of the volcanic ash prevents plant life, the thick layer deposited over a wide expanse is almost complete wasteland. Pelée also erupted in 1792 and 1851. See Gordon Thomas and M. M. Witts, *The Day the World Ended* (1969).

Pelee, Point: see POINT PELEE, Ont., Canada.

Pelee Island (pē′lē), 18 sq mi (47 sq km), S Ont., Canada, in W Lake Erie. Scudder is the chief town. Ferry service connects the island with the Canadian and U.S. mainland. Middle Island off S Pelee is the southernmost point of Canada.

Peleg (pē′lĕg), ancestor of David. Gen. 10.25; 11.16. Phalec: Luke 3.35.

Pelet (pē′lĕt). **1** Name in an obscure genealogy. 1 Chron. 2.47. **2** Benjamite leader with David. 1 Chron. 12.3.

Peleth (pē′lĕth). **1** Reubenite, perhaps the same as PALLU. Num. 16.1. **2** Son of Jonathan. 1 Chron. 2.33.

Pelethites: see CHERETHITES AND PELETHITES.

Peleus (pē′lēəs, -ləs), in Greek mythology, son of Aeacus and the father of Achilles by Thetis. He and his brother Telamon killed their half-brother Phocus and were exiled from Aegina. After taking part in the Calydonian hunt, Peleus went to Iolcus, where he killed King ACASTUS and Acastus' wife because they had once tried to murder him.

Pelew: see PALAU.

Pelham, Henry (pĕl′əm), 1696–1754, British statesman; brother of Thomas Pelham-Holles, duke of NEWCASTLE. He entered Parliament in 1717 and served Sir Robert Walpole as secretary for war (1724–30) and paymaster-general (1730–43). In 1743 he became head of a Whig ministry that was to last until 1754. His administration concluded the Treaty of Aix-la-Chapelle (1748), ending the War of the Austrian Succession; it also reorganized and reduced the national debt and reformed (1752) the calendar. See William Coxe, *Memoirs of the Administration of the Right Honourable Henry Pelham* (1829, repr. 1971); study by J. W. Wilkes (1964).

Pelham, Peter (pĕl′əm), c.1695–1751, American engraver and painter, b. England; stepfather of John Singleton Copley. After studying and practicing in England, Pelham settled (c.1728) in Boston. He produced engravings of Cotton Mather and Increase Mather based on his own paintings. He also conducted a school.

Pelias (pē′lēăs), in Greek mythology, usurper of the throne of Iolcus. He was the son of Tyro and Poseidon and the twin brother of Neleus. After his birth his mother married Cretheus, king of Iolcus, and gave birth to Aeson. After Cretheus' death Pelias seized power, killed (or imprisoned) Aeson, and exiled Neleus. Later MEDEA, hoping to restore JASON as rightful successor to the throne, tricked the daughters of Pelias into murdering him.

pelican, common name for a large, gregarious aquatic bird of warm regions, allied to the cormorants and gannets. Pelicans are heavy-bodied, long-necked birds with large, flat bills. They are graceful swimmers and fliers, often seen flying in long lines or circling at great heights. Fish are stored in a deep expansible pouch below the lower mandible; the young feed from the pouch and throat. The white pelican, *Pelecanus onocrotalus,* of North America ranges from the NW United States to the Gulf and Florida coasts. It is about 5 ft (152.5 cm) long with a wingspread of 8 to 10 ft (244–300.5 cm). Both sexes have white plumage with black primary wing feathers. The white pelican scoops fish into its pouch as it swims; the smaller brown pelican, *P. occidentalis,* dives from the air for its prey. The eastern brown pelican of the SE United States and tropical America and the California brown pelican are strictly ocean birds. The spectacled pelican is found in Australia and New Guinea. There are several Old World species. Pelicans are classified in the phylum CHORDATA, subphylum Vertebrata, class Aves, order Pelecaniformes, family Pelecanidae.

pelican flower: see BIRTHWORT.

Pelion (pē′lēən), Gr. *Pílion,* mountain, 5,252 ft (1,601 m) high, N Greece, E Thessaly, on the Aegean coast. In ancient legend, the centaur CHIRON lived on the mountain and the ALOADAE piled Pelion on Mt. Óssa.

Pella (pĕl′ə), ancient city of Greek Macedonia, about 24 mi (39 km) NW of Thessalonica (now Thessaloníki). It became the capital of the Macedonian kingdom in the 4th cent. B.C. It prospered under Macedonian rule but declined after the Roman conquest of Macedonia (168 B.C.). Alexander the Great was born at Pella. Modern excavations have revealed many ancient buildings.

pellagra (pəlăg′rə), deficiency disease due to a lack of niacin (nicotinic acid), one of the components of the B complex vitamins in the diet. Niacin is plentiful in yeast, organ meats, peanuts, and wheat germ. The disease manifests itself in lesions of the skin and mucous membrane, diarrhea and other gastrointestinal symptoms, neurological derangement, and mental confusion. It is most common in areas where the diet consists mainly of corn, which, unlike other grains, lacks niacin as well as the amino acid tryptophan, which the body uses to synthesize the vitamin. Treatment includes large doses of niacin and the institution of a proper diet to prevent recurrences.

Pellan, Alfred (älfrĕd′ pĕläN′), 1906–, Canadian painter, b. Quebec. Pellan sold his painting *Corner of Old Quebec* to the National Gallery, Ottawa, when he was 16. He lived in Paris from 1926 until 1940, when he returned to Canada. Influenced by cubism and surrealism, Pellan became in turn a guiding force for younger Canadian artists when his work was exhibited in Montreal in 1940. He has painted murals for many art galleries (e.g., Winnipeg Art Gallery, 1968) and public buildings, and his work has frequently been exhibited internationally. See study by D. W. Buchanan and Paul Gladu (1960).

Pelleas, Sir: see ARTHURIAN LEGEND.

Pelletier, Pierre Joseph (pyĕr zhôzĕf′ pĕlətyā′), 1788–1842, French chemist. With J. B. Caventou, he was cofounder of alkaloid chemistry and codiscoverer of quinine, strychnine, brucine, and other alkaloids. He also isolated such other substances as picrotoxin, caffeine, and piperine. He was especially noted for his introduction of new methods of generating organic substances.

Pellico, Silvio (sĕl′vyō pĕl′lēkō), 1789–1854, Italian dramatic poet. His principal work is *Francesca da Rimini* (1815, tr. 1856). Imprisoned for eight years by the Austrians as a Carbonarist (see CARBONARI), he wrote a candid and moving account of his prison life, *Le mie prigioni* (1832, tr. *My Prisons*, 1833), which created widespread sympathy for the RISORGIMENTO movement.

Pelly, river, c.330 mi (530 km) long, rising W of the Mackenzie Mts., S central Yukon Territory, Canada, and flowing generally northwest to join the Yukon River at Fort Selkirk. The Pelly receives the Ross and Macmillan rivers. It was discovered (1840) by Robert Campbell of the Hudson's Bay Company.

Pelonite (pĕl'ənīt), obscure epithet of two of David's mighty men. Comparison with the parallel passages suggests that it stands for Gilonite (see GILOH) in 1 Chron. 11.36 and for Paltite (see BETH-PALET) in 1 Chron. 11.27; 27.10.

Pelopidas (pĭlŏp'ĭdəs), d. 364 B.C., Theban general. When the Spartans seized the citadel of Thebes (now Thívai) in 382, he fled to Athens and prepared the coup that recovered the city (379). He fostered and commanded the Sacred Band, an elite corps that sparked the Theban victories against Sparta at Tegyra (375) and Leuctra (371). Under Epaminondas he joined in the invasion (370–369) of the Peloponnesus. On an expedition into Macedonia (368) he was captured by the Thessalian Alexander of Pherae, but Epaminondas rescued him. Pelopidas went the next year to Persia as ambassador to Artaxerxes. He was killed at the hour of victory in a battle with the Thessalians at Cynoscephalae (now Khalkodhónion hills). Plutarch wrote his life.

Peloponnesian League: see SPARTA.

Peloponnesian War (pĕl'əpənē'zhən), 431–404 B.C., decisive struggle in ancient Greece between Athens and Sparta. It ruined Athens. The rivalry between Athens and Sparta was of long standing, in spite of well-differentiated spheres of interest. The Athenian empire was a maritime domain (see DELIAN LEAGUE) consisting of the Aegean, the shores of Chalcidice (now Khalkidhikí), Callipolis (modern Gallipoli), Byzantium, and many Black Sea colonies; for grain Athens was dependent on Thrace and the Black Sea. Sparta had a land empire. Its center was the Peloponnesus, but since Corinth and Thebes were Spartan allies, much of Greece was under its control. Most Greek cities, aside from Sparta, had for years seen vigorous struggles between oligarchic and democratic parties. Athens under Pericles (from 445 B.C.) had become a model of Greek democracy, with a regular foreign policy of intervention to help local democrats. The Spartans favored oligarchies like their own. As a result most cities, including Athens, had pro-Spartan minorities when the democrats had power and pro-Athenian minorities otherwise. The two empires were unstable at best, for Sparta and Athens were equally ruthless, governing their dependencies for profit and with cold-blooded brutality; hence the subject cities were always ready for revolt. It was a basic military fact that well-walled Athens could be beaten only by a fleet, and Sparta could be taken only by full-scale invasion. At the start, however, Athens had a small land army and Sparta a navy that was no match for that of Athens; still, the great Delian treasury at Athens was a significant advantage, and throughout the war a consciousness of weakness led Sparta to repeated efforts for peace. The war began after sharp contests between Athens and Corinth over Corcyra (now Kérkira) (433) and Potidaea (432). The first important action was the initial invasion of Attica by a Spartan army in 431. Pericles brought the rural population within the walls, which included a passage to the harbor at Piraeus (now Piraiévs). The Athenian fleet began raids, reduced (430 or 429) rebellious Potidaea, won (429) victories off Naupactus (now Návpaktos), and suppressed (428) a revolt in Lesbos. Meanwhile a plague (perhaps bubonic) wiped out (430–428) probably a quarter of the population of Athens, and Pericles died. His successor was CLEON. Sparta took (427) the long-besieged Plataea, an Athenian ally, but suffered a real defeat when Athens established (425) a base at Pylos in Spartan territory and captured Sphacteria (now Sfaktiriá) island along with an important Spartan contingent. Sparta suggested peace and was refused. The Spartan leader Brasidas now brilliantly surprised Athens with a campaign in NE Greece, taking (424) Athenian cities, including Olynthus and Amphipolis. Fighting went on over these even after an armistice (423) and ended in a decisive Spartan victory at Amphipolis, in which Brasidas and Cleon were both killed (422). The new Athenian leader, NICIAS, now arranged a peace (421); despite its terms, it actually froze the situation. At Athens the respite saw the rise of ALCIBIADES as a rival of Nicias. Alcibiades assisted the revolt of a coalition against Sparta in the Peloponnesus; however, the rebels were defeated (418) at MANTINEA; he also led (416) the sack of neutral Melos (now Mílos), which had refused to join the Athenian coalition. In the same year an embassy from Segesta, Sicily, came to ask Athenian help against its enemy city, Selinus. As Selinus was an ally of powerful Syracuse, Athens was undecided as to whether to become involved with Syracuse. The proponents of the invasion of Sicily, led by Alcibiades and dazzled by the prospect of imperial acquisition, won. In the greatest expeditionary force a Greek city had ever assembled, Alcibiades and Nicias both had (415) commands, but before the attack on Syracuse had begun, Alcibiades was recalled to Athens to face a charge of sacrilege. He fled to Sparta; at his advice the Spartans set up a permanent base at Decelea in Attica and sent a military expert, Gylippus, to Syracuse. The incompetent Nicias lost his chance to surprise Syracuse and had to have large reinforcements, and after two years his force was wiped out (413). For Athens the loss of men and ships was irretrievable, and all Greece knew it; soon Persia was financing a Spartan fleet. Alcibiades sailed it across the Aegean, and there was (412) a general revolt of Athenian dependencies. At Athens the Four Hundred, an oligarchic council, managed (411) a short-lived coup, and Alcibiades, who had quit the Spartans, received (410) an Athenian command. The Spartans had been invading the Hellespont (now Dardanelles) and had been beaten off Abydos (411); now Alcibiades destroyed their fleet at Cyzicus (410). Sparta sought a truce, but in vain. But the able new Spartan admiral, LYSANDER, built (407) a fleet with Persian aid and won a naval battle off Notium. This Athenian setback was used by the rivals of Alcibiades to drive (407 or 406) him from Athens for good. The Athenians won one more victory at Arginusae, near Lesbos, in 406 and again declined an offer of peace. The next year Lysander took a fleet to the Hellespont and wiped out the Athenian navy (at AEGOSPOTAMOS, 405). Master of the seas, Lysander sailed to Piraeus; there was an army of Spartan allies on the land side. Thus besieged by sea and land, Athens capitulated in 404. Corinth and Thebes wanted to destroy Athens, but the Spartans refused. Lysander installed an oligarchic government (the Thirty Tyrants). Athens was never again so important a political factor as before. For about 30 years afterward Sparta was the main power in Greece. The primary source for the Peloponnesian War (to 411) is THUCYDIDES; Xenophon's *Hellenica* is an inferior sequel. See also G. W. Henderson, *The Great War between Athens and Sparta* (1926); Donald Kagan, *The Outbreak of the Peloponnesian War* (1969).

Peloponnesus (pĕl"əpənē'səs) or **Pelopónnisos** (pâ"lôpô'nyēsôs), formerly **Morea** (mōrē'ə), peninsula (1971 pop. 986,912), c.8,300 sq mi (21,500 sq km), S Greece. It is linked with central Greece by the Isthmus of Corinth, and it is washed by the Aegean Sea on the east and southeast, by the Ionian Sea on the southwest and west, and by the gulfs of Pátrai and Corinth on the north. Its deeply indented south coast terminates in Cape Matapan. Mainly mountainous, the region includes the Taygetus, Kyllene, and Erímanthos mts. The Evrótas, and Alfiós are the chief rivers. Predominately agricultural and pastoral, the Peloponnesus produces currants, grapes, figs, citrus fruit, olives, tobacco, and wheat. The most fertile parts of the peninsula are the coastal strips in the north and west. Sheep and goat raising, textile manufacturing, fishing, and sericulture are major sources of income. There are deposits of pyrite, manganese, lignite, and chromium. The peninsula attracts many tourists; the port cities of Pátrai, Corinth, Kalámai, and Návplion are the main modern centers of the Peloponnesus. The chief ancient divisions of the Peloponnesus were Elis, Achaea, Argolis, and the city-state of CORINTH in the north; Arcadia in the center; and Lacedaemonia (comprising MESSENIA and Laconia) in the south. SPARTA, Corinth, ARGOS, and MEGALOPOLIS were among its chief cities in ancient times. Originally populated by Leleges and Pelasgians (said to have been the builders of MYCENAE and TIRYNS), the peninsula was later occupied by the ACHAEANS and then by the DORIANS, who dominated the Peloponnesus in historic times. With the exception of Achaea and Argos, the whole peninsula participated in the Persian Wars (500–449 B.C.). At the time of the Peloponnesian War (5th cent. B.C.) almost the entire peninsula was dominated by Sparta. Spartan hegemony, which after the defeat of Athens extended over all Greece, was broken in the 4th cent. B.C. by Epaminondas of Thebes, who thus prepared the way for the establishment of Macedonian supremacy over the Peloponnesus by Philip II of Macedon. The Second ACHAEAN LEAGUE, unable to shake off the Macedonian yoke, was ended in 146 B.C. by the Roman conquest of the Peloponnesus. Under Roman and Byzantine rule the Peloponnesus was reduced to provincial status and in the centuries that followed was repeatedly raided and invaded by Slavs, Bulgars, and Petchenegs. When, in 1204, the leaders of the Fourth Crusade established the Latin Empire of Constantinople (see CONSTANTINOPLE, LATIN EMPIRE OF), the French Villehardouin family received the principality of Achaia or Achaea (i.e., the Peloponnesus) as fief, except for several ports, which passed to Venice. A French feudal state was created and enjoyed a period of great prosperity and chivalrous culture under the Villehardouin princes. Many castles remain to show the unique mixture of French feudal culture and Hellenistic civilization that flourished in the Peloponnesus in the 13th cent. After the death (1278) of William of Villehardouin, the last prince, the principality passed first to the Angevin dynasty of Naples (by marriage), later to various nobles, and in 1383 to a body of Navarrese soldier-adventurers. Meanwhile the Byzantine Greeks were gradually recovering a good part of the peninsula, and in 1432 they achieved complete control. Their triumph, however, was short-lived, for by 1460 Sultan Muhammad II had conquered the peninsula and annexed it to the Ottoman Empire. In the Turko-Venetian Wars from the 15th cent. until the Treaty of Passarowitz (1718), Venice held parts of the Peloponnesus at various times and the entire peninsula from 1687 to 1715. As a result of the Greek War of Independence (1821–29) the peninsula passed to independent Greece.

Pelops (pē'lŏps), in Greek mythology, son of Tantalus. He was murdered by his father, who served his flesh at a banquet for the gods. The gods recognized this abominable trick, punished Tantalus and restored Pelops, giving him an ivory shoulder to replace the one Demeter had unwittingly eaten. He won his wife, Hippodamia, by defeating her father, King Oenomaus of Pisa, in a chariot race. To ensure victory Pelops not only used a winged chariot given to him by Poseidon, but he bribed Myrtilus, Oenomaus' charioteer, to betray his master. After winning the race Pelops would not pay Myrtilus his reward. Instead, he threw him into the sea. Before drowning, the charioteer cursed the house of Pelops, and misfortunes fell on the sons of Pelops, Atreus and Thyestes. The Peloponnesus peninsula was named for Pelops.

pelota (pəlō'tə): see JAI ALAI.

Pelotas (pəlô'təsh), city (1970 pop. 208,017), Rio Grande do Sul state, S Brazil, an inland port on the São Gonçalo canal. It is a major export point for the stock-raising region of S Rio Grande do Sul and is a transfer point for ocean-to-lake shipping. The city is Brazil's main producer of dried beef. Lard, shoes, furniture, candles, and soap are also manufactured. Pelotas was settled in the late 18th cent. by colonists from the Azores. It expanded in the 19th cent. with the growth of the dried-beef industry.

Peltier effect (pĕl'tyā): see THERMOELECTRICITY.

Pelusium (pĭlo͞o'shēəm), ancient city of Egypt, on the easternmost branch of the Nile (long since silted up) and c.20 mi (30 km) E of modern Port Said. It was especially important as a frontier fortress against attacks from the east. The Assyrians under Sennacherib were supposedly struck by pestilence at Pelusium, and in 525 B.C. the Persians under Cambyses overthrew Psamtik III there. There are Roman remains on the site. It is mentioned in the Bible under the name Sin (Ezek. 30.15,16).

pelvis, bony, basin-shaped structure that supports the organs of the lower abdomen. It receives the weight of the upper body and distributes it to the legs; it also forms the base for numerous muscle attachments. In the human pelvis there are two large HIP bones, each consisting of three fused bones, the illium, ischium, and pubis. The hip bones form a ring around a central cavity. The fused terminal segments of the spine, known as the sacrum and coccyx, connect the hip bones at the back of the central cavity; a fibrous band connects them at the front. In women the pelvis is wider and has a larger capacity than in men, a condition that reflects the child-bearing function in women. See SKELETON.

Pemba (pĕm'bə), island (1967 pop. 164,321), c.380 sq mi (980 sq km), NE Tanzania, in the Indian Ocean just off the E African mainland. Wete (the capital of Pemba region), Chake Chake, and Mkoani are the main towns. The island is the world's leading producer of cloves. Coconuts are also exported, and fishing is an important industry. The inhabitants of Pemba are black Africans, many of whom are partly descended from traders from the Persian Gulf region who settled on the island beginning in the 10th cent. The Portuguese occupied the island in the 16th cent. but were displaced by Omani Arabs in 1698. In 1822 the island was conquered by Sayyid Said (later the sultan of Zanzibar) from the rulers of Mombasa. Along with Zanzibar, Pemba passed under British rule in 1890, became independent in 1963, and merged with Tanganyika to form Tanzania in 1964.

Pemberton, John Clifford, 1814–81, Confederate general in the American Civil War, b. Philadelphia. He served in the Seminole and Mexican wars and at various frontier posts. He resigned from the U.S. army in April, 1861, and in June became a Confederate brigadier general. Pemberton was made a lieutenant general in Oct., 1862, and was assigned to command the region about Vicksburg. However, he was defeated by Ulysses S. Grant in the VICKSBURG CAMPAIGN and surrendered on July 4, 1863. After his exchange he resigned his lieutenant generalcy (May, 1864) and served as a colonel of ordnance for the rest of the war. See biography by J. C. Pemberton (1942).

Pembroke, Aymer de Valence, earl of (pĕm'bro͝ok), d. 1324, English nobleman; nephew of Aymer of Valence, bishop of Winchester. He succeeded his father, William, half brother of Henry III, as earl of Pembroke in 1296. Sent by Edward I to suppress the Scottish uprising, he defeated ROBERT I at Methven (1306) but was himself defeated at Loudon Hill (1307). Under EDWARD II he was one of the lords ordainers, appointed to limit the king's power. Disgusted by the murder (1312) of Piers Gaveston, the royal favorite, Pembroke switched his support to the king. He fought for Edward at Bannockburn (1314). By 1318 he had organized a moderate royalist group of barons, which mediated successfully between the king and the rebellious barons until displaced (1322) by Hugh le Despenser, the elder, and his son. Pembroke died suddenly on a diplomatic mission to France. See study by J. R. S. Phillips (1972).

Pembroke, Mary Herbert, countess of, 1561–1621; sister of Sir Philip Sidney. His *Arcadia* was written for her, and after his death she prepared it and his other works for publication. Patron of a number of poets, including Daniel, Spenser, and Jonson, she formed with them a literary coterie—the Pembroke circle—dedicated to continuing the literary ideals of Sidney.

Pembroke, Richard de Clare, 2d **earl of,** d. 1176, English nobleman, also known as Richard Strongbow. Having gone through his inheritance, he went (1170) to Ireland at the request of the hard-pressed DERMOT MCMURROUGH, king of Leinster. Strongbow subdued much of E Ireland, including Dublin, in victories over Rory O'CONNOR, king of Connaught, and married Dermot's daughter. Henry II of England, although he had given permission for the earl's expedition, visited him in 1171 to claim the rich coastal cities and to receive Strongbow's homage for the fief of the interior of Leinster. Pembroke fought for Henry in Normandy and was rewarded by a grant of additional territory in Ireland. He then returned to Ireland as the king's governor. Badly defeated (1174) at Thurles, he was engaged in almost continuous fighting against the Irish until his death.

Pembroke, William Herbert, 3d **earl of,** 1580–1630, English courtier and patron of letters. Son of Mary Herbert, countess of PEMBROKE, and nephew of Sir Philip Sidney, he was tutored by the poet Samuel Daniel and succeeded his father to the earldom in 1601. Prominent at court, he became (1611) a privy councilor and served as lord chamberlain of the royal household (1615–25) and lord steward (1626–30). He also furthered the exploration and colonization of America. Shakespeare's First Folio (1623) was dedicated to him and his brother, and he has been doubtfully identified with the "Mr. W. H." mentioned in the publisher's dedication of the 1609 edition of the Sonnets. Pembroke College, Oxford, was named in his honor while he was chancellor of the university (1617–30).

Pembroke, William Marshal, 1st **earl of,** d. 1219, English nobleman. He became (1170) a guardian of Prince Henry, eldest son of Henry II, and supported him in his abortive rebellion (1173–74) against his father. After the prince's death (1183), however, he went on crusade for the king. Upon the accession (1189) of Richard I, Marshal married Isabella, heiress of Richard de Clare, 2d earl of Pembroke, and took her titles, thereby becoming 1st earl of Pembroke in the Marshal line. During Richard I's absence from England, Marshal supported the king's brother JOHN against William of LONGCHAMP but helped thwart John's 1193 rebellion. Once John became king, however, the earl supported him and was one of his counselors at Runnymede. Elected regent for the young Henry III by the barons in 1216, Marshal successfully waged war against the invading Prince Louis (later Louis VIII) of France and by a firm policy toward recalcitrant barons secured a relatively stable kingdom. See Sidney Painter, *William Marshal* (1933, repr. 1967).

Pembroke (pĕm'brōk), town (1971 pop. 16,544), SE Ont., Canada, NW of Ottawa, on the Ottawa River. It is a lumbering center and also has steel and electric-products factories.

Pembroke, town (1970 pop. 11,193), Plymouth co., SE Mass., in an area of dairy and truck farms; settled 1650, set off from Duxbury 1712.

Pembroke (pĕm'bro͝ok), municipal borough (1971 pop. 14,092), SW Wales, on an inlet of Milford Haven bay. The town is an agricultural market with tourism, ship repairing, and light industries; it was formerly the site of several military bases. Pembroke contains a 10th-century priory and 12th-century castle. Henry VII was born there. In 1974, Pembroke became part of the new nonmetropolitan county of Dyfed.

Pembroke College, Providence, R.I.: see BROWN UNIV.

Pembroke Pines, city (1970 pop. 15,520), Broward co., SE Fla., a residential suburb of the Hollywood area; inc. 1961.

Pembrokeshire (pĕm'bro͝okshĭr), county (1971 pop. 97,295), 614 sq mi (1,590 sq km), SW Wales. The county town is HAVERFORDWEST. The coastline is severe and greatly indented, as at St. Bride's Bay and Milford Haven. Rolling hills and fertile valleys dominate the terrain. The Prescelly Hills are in the north and northeast. Chief rivers are the East and West Cleddau. The principal occupations are potato, poultry, and dairy farming. MILFORD HAVEN is an important oil port. Other towns are PEMBROKE and Tenby. Pembrokeshire is rich in megalithic remains. The region was harried by the Norsemen in the early Middle Ages and conquered by the Normans in the 11th cent. In the 12th cent. Flemish settlers were brought into the district. The cathedral at SAINT DAVID'S is one of the major ecclesiastical monuments of Wales. In 1974, Pembrokeshire became part of the new nonmetropolitan county of Dyfed.

Pembroke Welsh corgi, breed of short-legged, hardy WORKING DOG thought to have been introduced into South Wales by Flemish immigrants in the early 12th cent. It stands from 10 to 12 in. (25.4–30.5 cm) high at the shoulder and weighs from 18 to 24 lb (8.2–10.9 kg). Its dense, straight, medium-length coat may be solid red, sable, fawn, or black and tan, or any of these colors marked with white on the neck, chest, and legs. Although originally of entirely separate stock and markedly different appearance, the Pembroke and the Cardigan Welsh corgi have grown very close in type due to the crossing of the breeds begun in the early 19th cent. The Pembroke can be distinguished from the Cardigan by its shorter body and its stubby tail. Originally bred for herding cattle and horses, today the Pembroke is gaining popularity as a house pet. See DOG.

pemmican (pĕm'ĭkən), a travel food of the North American Indian. Slices of lean venison or buffalo meat were sun dried, pounded to a paste, and packed with melted fat in rawhide bags. Dried currants or wild berries were sometimes included in the paste. Pacific coast Indians used a similar fish compound.

pen, pointed implement used in writing or drawing to apply INK or a similar colored fluid to any surface, such as paper. Various kinds of pens have been used since ancient times. Reeds that were slit or frayed at the end were used in antiquity; similar pens, usually made of bamboo, are commonly employed in the Orient today. In ancient Greece and Rome much writing was done by scratching the wax coating of a tablet with a stylus, or style—a pointed implement whose blunt end was used to make erasures by smoothing the wax. Quills were introduced early in the Middle Ages and continued to be the main writing device until the mid-19th cent. Plucked from live birds (usually geese), the quills were treated with heat and shaped with a penknife, and they required frequent sharpening. Although metal pens were known to the Romans, and a few had been made in Europe in the 18th cent., a cheap, efficient slip-in nib did not come into common use until Josiah Mason improved existing models and began large-scale production in 1828 at Birmingham, England. The fountain pen, which feeds ink to the pen point from a reservoir, was first successfully produced on a commercial scale in the 1880s. The ball-point pen, introduced c.1944, offered several advantages over the fountain pen. Tipped with a ball bearing that rolls a gelatinous instant-drying ink onto paper, the ball-point pen contains a longer-lasting supply of ink than the fountain pen and is less likely to leak. Although soft-tip pens had been used in ancient times (the Egyptians made soft-tip pens from rushes c.4000 B.C., and the Chinese later used hair-tip pens), it was not until the 1950s that felt-tip markers came into fairly common use in the United States. By the 1960s felt-tip markers had been largely replaced by fiber-tip markers. These are made of such materials as nylon and plastic, are available in a wide variety of colors, and are capable of marking any surface, including plastic and glass.

Peñalara, Pico de: see GUADARRAMA, SIERRA DE.

Penal Laws, in British history, term generally applied to the body of discriminatory and oppressive legislation directed chiefly against Roman Catholics but also against Protestant nonconformists. This series of laws grew out of the English Reformation and specifically from those acts that established royal supremacy in the Church of England (see ENGLAND, CHURCH OF) in the reigns of Henry VIII and Elizabeth I. Under Henry VIII and Edward VI civil disabilities were imposed on those who remained in communion with Rome, so denying the king's spiritual headship. Elizabeth I made it impossible for Catholics to hold civil offices and imposed severe penalties upon Catholics who persisted in recognizing papal authority. Fines and prison sentences were prescribed for all who did not attend Anglican services, and the celebration of the Mass was forbidden under severe penalties. The excommunication (1570) of Elizabeth by Pope Pius V, the Catholic plots to place MARY QUEEN OF SCOTS on the English throne, and the attempted Spanish invasion by the ARMADA roused the government and public opinion to an intensely anti-Catholic pitch, and the Penal Laws were extended. Jesuits and other priests were expelled (1585) from England under penalty of treason, and harboring or aiding priests was declared a capital offense. Although a number of Catholics (e.g., Edmund CAMPION) were executed for treason, these laws were never thoroughly administered except against prominent people who refused to conform. Under James I the GUNPOWDER PLOT resulted in added severity, but the official attitude softened after 1618, as James sought friendly relations with Spain. Charles I's wife, Henrietta Maria, was a Catholic, and her position made easy some open disregard of the restrictive laws. In the ENGLISH CIVIL WAR the Catholics sided with the king, and Oliver Cromwell punished them, along with royalist Anglicans, by wide confiscations, but few were executed. After the Restoration of Charles II, Parliament passed the series of laws known as the CLARENDON CODE (1661–65) and the TEST ACT (1673), which required holders of public office to take various oaths of loyalty and to receive the sacrament of the Church of England. These laws penalized Protestant NONCONFORMISTS as well as Roman Catholics. However, the Protestant dissenters continued in their vehement anti-Catholicism and formed the backbone of the WHIG party, which coalesced in the attempt to exclude the Catholic James, duke of York (later James II) from the succession to the throne. The anti-Catholic movement culminated in the overthrow of James II in the GLORIOUS REVOLUTION (1688), and the Bill of Rights (1689) and the Act of SETTLEMENT (1701) excluded the Catholic branch of the house of Stuart from the throne. A Toleration Act (1689) relieved the Protestant nonconformists of many of their disabilities (although they remained excluded from office), but the Catholics were now subjected to new laws limiting their property and means of education. The JACOBITES, in their attempts to restore the Catholic Stuarts, kept the politico-religious issue of Roman Catholicism alive until 1745. By this time the relatively small number of Catholics remaining in England and Scotland made the anti-Catholic laws there a minor issue, but CATHOLIC EMANCIPATION was delayed until 1829.

Penal Laws in Ireland. In Ireland, however, where the population was predominantly Roman Catholic and the Glorious Revolution had been vigorously resisted, the Penal Laws were extended and made extremely oppressive during the 18th cent. After the Treaty of Limerick (1691), the Irish Parliament, filled with Protestant landowners and controlled from England, enacted a penal code that secured and enlarged the landlords' holdings and degraded and impoverished the Irish Catholics. As a result of these harsh laws, which were for the most part rigidly enforced, Catholics could neither teach their children nor send them abroad; persons of property could not enter into mixed marriages; Catholic property was inherited equally among the sons unless one was a Protestant, in which case he received all; a Catholic could not inherit property if there was any Protestant heir; a Catholic could not possess arms or a horse worth more than £5; Catholics could not hold leases for more than 31 years, and they could not make a profit greater than a third of their rent. The hierarchy of the Catholic Church was banished or suppressed, and Catholics could not hold seats in the Irish Parliament (1692), hold public office, vote (1727), or practice law. Cases against Catholics were tried without juries, and bounties were given to informers against them. Under these restrictions many able Irishmen left the country, and regard for the law declined; even Protestants assisted their Catholic friends in evasion. In the latter half of the 18th cent., with the decline of religious fervor in England and the need for Irish aid in foreign wars, there was a general mitigation of the treatment of Catholics in Ireland, and the long process of Catholic Emancipation began. See Brian Magee, *The English Recusants* (1938); E. I. Watkin, *Roman Catholicism in England from the Reformation to 1950* (1957).

penance (pĕn'əns), SACRAMENT of the Roman Catholic and Orthodox Eastern churches. By it the penitent (the person receiving the sacrament) is absolved of his sins by his confessor (the person hearing the confession and conferring the sacrament). Every Catholic is required to confess all his mortal (serious) sins before receiving communion and at least once a year. He need confess only the sins he has committed since baptism or since his last confession. To make the sacrament valid the confessor must be a priest or a bishop and the penitent must have contrition for his sins and a firm purpose of amendment. Sins inadvertently forgotten after a careful examination of conscience are included in the absolution. The confessor before giving absolution may admonish the sinner, and he imposes a penance (a punishment for guilt, usually consisting of some prayers). The penitent is required to make restitution for injuries to others. According to a canon of the Council of Trent, Jesus instituted this sacrament when he first appeared to the disciples after the resurrection (John 20.19–23). Following the Second Vatican Council, the Roman Catholic Church introduced the liturgy for a new communal penitential service, during which the individual has the opportunity to confess privately to a priest. Absolution is still granted on an individual basis only. In the Eastern churches confession is required before communion, but there has been no development of moral theology or of casuistry comparable to that of the West. The priest acts in the sacrament only as an instrument of God, who forgives sins by the sacrament.

Penang: see PINANG, Malaysia.

Penarth (pĕnärth'), urban district (1971 pop. 23,965), South Glamorgan, S Wales. A suburb of Cardiff and a seaside resort, it also has cement works and is a coal port. Turner House Art Gallery is in Penarth.

penates (pənā'tēz), in Roman religion, household gods, primarily guardians of the storeroom. Theirs was the chief cult of every Roman household, especially in early times. They were worshiped in connection with the LARES and, as guardians of the hearth, with Vesta. Every household was said to possess images of the penates, to whom offerings were made before each meal. Penates were also public gods, protectors of the community and state.

Pen-ch'i or **Penki** (both: bŭn-chē), city (1970 est. pop. 750,000), S Liaoning prov., China. It is an important heavy industrial center with rich iron and coal mines. Founded as a metallurgical center in 1915, it lies on the railroad from Shen-yang (Mukden) to North Korea.

pencil, pointed implement used in writing or drawing to apply graphite or a similar colored solid to any surface, especially paper. From prehistoric times lumps of colored earth or chalk were used as markers. The Egyptians ruled lines with metallic lead, as did medieval monks. The so-called lead pencil—a rod of graphite encased in wood—came into use in the 16th cent. From the late 18th cent. pulverized graphite was mixed with clay to bind it and to provide different degrees of hardness—the more clay, the harder the pencil. Today the mixture is forced through dies, cut to the required length, and kilnfired. The rods are laid in grooves of a thin board, a similar board is placed over them, and the wood is shaped into pencils, usually of round or hexagonal cross section. Pencils are also manufactured with cores of colored pigments mixed with clay and wax and of other materials. Mechanical pencils are commonly made of metal or plastic, the cores (or leads) being advanced by operating a screw mechanism or a propel-repel ejector mechanism.

Penck, Albrecht (äl'brĕkht pĕngk), 1858–1945, German geographer and geologist. He was professor at the Univ. of Vienna (1885–1906) and at the Univ. of Berlin (1906–26) and was director (1906–22) of the institutes of oceanography and of geography, Berlin. He is noted for his study of glaciation (especially in the Alps), for his pioneer classification of land forms, and for his work in the development of modern regional geography. Outstanding among his many works is *Morphologie der Erdoberfläche* [morphology of the earth's surface] (1894, rev. ed. 1928).

Pencz, Georg (gā'ôrkh pĕnts), c.1500–1550, German painter and engraver of the Nuremberg school. He probably studied with Dürer in Nuremberg. He was banished in 1525 but soon returned. Pencz is thought to have visited Italy and to have worked with Raimondi. The influence of Italian mannerism is evident in his work. Of his paintings the best are portraits, such as those of Marshal Schirmer (Nuremberg); Erhard Schwetzer and his wife (Berlin); and *Young Man* (Vienna). As an engraver he ranks among the best of the German "Little Masters." Notable prints include *Six Triumphs of Petrarch;* portrait of John Frederick I, elector of Saxony; and *Life of Christ* (26 plates).

Penda, d. 654, king of Mercia (c.632–654). A noble of the Mercian royal house, he fought (629) the king of Wessex for lands along the Severn River. He then allied himself with Cadwallon of Wales, defeated (632) EDWIN of Northumbria, and made himself king of Mercia. A great fighting king, he was the central figure in the history of Anglo-Saxon England for nearly a generation thereafter. He defeated and slew (641) OSWALD of Northumbria and extended his power over Wessex and East Anglia. His Greater Mercia included all the Midlands. However, he still had an enemy in the new king of Northumbria, OSWY; Penda attacked him in 654 and was killed in the battle. Penda himself remained heathen, but at the time of his son Peada's marriage he consented to that son's Christian baptism. Eight of Penda's descendants ruled Mercia, beginning with his son Wulfhere.

Pend d'Oreille Indians (pŏndərā') [Fr., = earring], North American Indians whose language belongs to the Salishan branch of the Algonquian-Wakashan linguistic stock (see AMERICAN INDIAN LANGUAGES). They are also known as the Kalispel Indians. The name Pend d'Oreille is derived from their custom of wearing shell earrings. In the early 19th cent. the Kalispel or Pend d'Oreille occupied NW Montana, N Idaho, and NE Washington. They then numbered some 1,600. Their culture was similar to that of the Spokan and other tribes of the Plateau area. Today the Pend d'Oreille live on reservations in Montana and Washington. In Washington they live with the Colville; in Montana, with the Flatheads.

Pendelikón (pĕntĕlĭkôn') or **Pentelicus** (pĕntĕ'lĭkəs), mountain, c.3,670 ft (1,120 m) high, central Greece, NE of Athens. The white marble quarried there was used for many buildings of ancient Athens. Marble is still taken from the region.

pendentive, in architecture, a constructive device permitting the placing of a circular dome over a square room or an elliptical dome over a rectangular room. The pendentives, which are triangular segments of a sphere, taper to points at the bottom and spread at the top to establish the continuous circular or elliptical base needed for the dome. In masonry the pendentives thus receive the weight of the dome, concentrating it at the four corners where it can be received by the piers beneath. Prior to the pendentive's development, the device of corbeling or the use of the SQUINCH in the corners of a room had been employed. The first attempts at pendentives were made by the Romans, but full achievement of the form was reached only by the Byzantines in Hagia Sophia at Constantinople (6th cent.). Pendentives were commonly used in Renaissance and baroque churches, with a drum often inserted between the dome and pendentives.

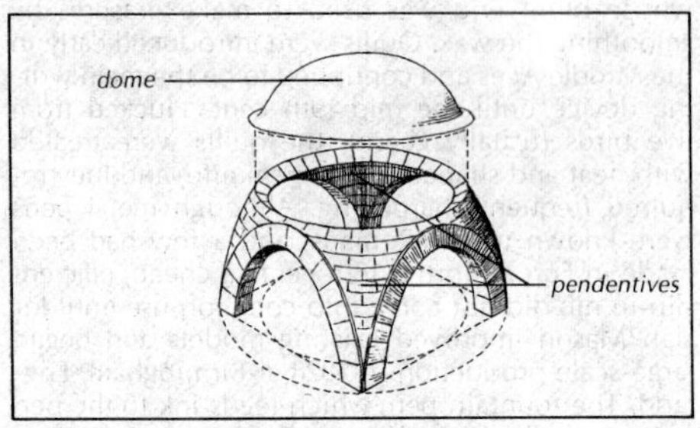

Pendentives

Penderecki, Krzysztof (kshĭsh'tôf pändĕrĕts'kē), 1933–, Polish composer. Penderecki studied at the Superior School of Music in Kraków. His music is characterized by unusual sonorities. He has devised his own system of notation to convey the effects desired. Penderecki's works include the *Threnody in Memory of the Victims of Hiroshima* (1960), a concerto for five-stringed violin (1967–68), *Utrenja* [morning prayer] (1970), and the *St. Luke Passion* (1963–66).

Pendergast, Thomas Joseph, 1872–1945, American political boss, b. St. Joseph, Mo. After holding minor political offices (1899–1910) in Kansas City, Mo., he became the acknowledged Democratic leader in city and state. Harry S. Truman entered politics under his aegis. In 1939, Pendergast was convicted of income-tax evasions, and his political machine was broken. Paroled (1940) from Leavenworth on condition that he abstain from political activity for five years, he later faced sentence for criminal contempt of court, but the U.S. Supreme Court reversed (1943) the decision against him under the statute of limitations. See study by L. W. Dorsett (1968).

Pendlebury, John Devitt Stringfellow, 1904–41, British archaeologist. He participated in expeditions to Macedonia (1928) and Tel el Amarna (1928–29 and 1930–36). From 1930 to 1934 he was curator of the site of Cnossus, and was later British vice consul at Candia, Crete. His writings include *Tell el-Amarna* (1935) and *The Archaeology of Crete* (1939).

Pendleton, Edmund, 1721–1803, American jurist and political leader in the American Revolution, b. Caroline co., Va. He began law practice in 1741 and was elected (1752) to the Virginia house of burgesses, where, although a leading conservative, he became an outstanding opponent of British colonial policies. Pendleton was a member of the Virginia committee of correspondence, delegate to the First Continental Congress (1774–75), head of the Virginia committee of safety (1775), and president of the convention (1776) that adopted his resolution instructing Virginia delegates to the Continental Congress to propose independence from Britain. After independence he was elected speaker of the new house of delegates. With Thomas Jefferson and George Wythe he completed (1779) the revision of the state's laws and was president of the court of appeals from 1779 to 1789 and of the reorganized supreme court of appeals from 1789 till his death. In 1788 he presided over the state convention that ratified the Federal Constitution. See his letters and papers ed. by D. J. Mays (2 vol., 1967); biography by Mays (2 vol., 1952).

Pendleton, George Hunt, 1825–89, American political leader, b. Cincinnati. He was admitted to the Ohio bar in 1847 and served (1854–56) in the state senate. He was an antiwar Democrat in the House of Representatives (1857–65) and vice presidential candidate on the unsuccessful Democratic ticket headed by Gen. George B. McClellan in the Civil War election of 1864. Pendleton advocated the so-called Ohio Idea—to pay in greenbacks those government bonds not specifying payment in specie (see GREENBACK); this stand probably cost him the Democratic presidential nomination in 1868. After running unsuccessfully for the governorship of Ohio in 1869, he was president of the Kentucky Central RR until 1879, when he returned to Congress as U.S. Senator from Ohio. He secured the adoption (1883) of legislation introducing competitive examinations in the CIVIL SERVICE. For this and for his support of other reform measures the Democratic party in Ohio denied him renomination. In 1885, President Cleveland appointed him minister to Germany, which post he held until his death.

Pendleton, city (1970 pop. 13,197), seat of Umatilla co., NE Oregon, on the Umatilla River, in the foothills of the Blue Mts.; founded 1869 on the old Oregon Trail, inc. 1889. A distribution and trade center for an extensive wheat, livestock, and timber region, Pendleton also has woolen and pine mills. It is the headquarters for Umatilla National Forest and Umatilla Indian Reservation. The annual Pendleton Roundup is held in September. A junior college, an agricultural experiment station of Oregon State Univ., and a state hospital are there.

Pendleton, Camp: see OCEANSIDE, Calif.

Pend Oreille Lake (pŏn"dərā'), 148 sq mi (383 sq km), 65 mi (105 km) long, and 1,200 ft (366 m) deep,

N Idaho; largest lake in Idaho and one of the largest and deepest lakes in the United States. Fed by the Clark Fork, and drained by the Pend Oreille River, the lake, with the surrounding national forests, is a place of beauty and a landmark in a farming, lumbering, and mining region.

Pendragon, Uther: see ARTHURIAN LEGEND.

pendulum, a mass, called a bob, suspended from a fixed point so that it can swing in an arc determined by its momentum and the force of gravity. The length of a pendulum is the distance from the point of suspension to the center of gravity of the bob (see CENTER OF MASS). Chance observation of a swinging church lamp led Galileo to find that a pendulum made every swing in the same time, independent of the size of the arc. He used this discovery in measuring time in his astronomical studies. His experiments showed that the longer the pendulum, the longer is the time of its swing. Christiaan HUYGENS determined an exact relation between the length of the pendulum and the time of vibration when the arc of swing is small. He arrived at the formula $T = 2\pi\sqrt{l/g}$, where T is the period, or time for one complete swing, l is the length, g is the acceleration of gravity (see GRAVITATION), and $\pi =$ 3.14 . . . (See HARMONIC MOTION). In 1673, Huygens devised a practicable means of making a pendulum control the speed with which a clock mechanism runs. This impetus to clockmaking resulted not only in the development of many types of clock, such as the "wag at the wall," the grandfather clock, and the banjo clock, but also in the application of pendulum control to other mechanisms. Metal pendulums are lengthened by heat; to counteract the effect of temperature changes, compensation pendulums have been devised, many of them operating by the opposite expansion of different metals in compound rods. Forces acting on the bob affect its swing. Since gravity varies from place to place, the pendulum has been used to determine the shape and mass of the earth by measuring the intensity of gravity. In the seismograph (see SEISMOLOGY), a pendulum registers the direction of an earthquake. In 1851, J. B. L. FOUCAULT demonstrated the rotation of the earth by suspending in the Panthéon in Paris a 200-ft (61-km) pendulum that traced its path in sand on the floor. The pendulum continued to vibrate in a single plane as the earth rotated underneath it, thus leaving a series of traces in the sand in all directions. A pendulum made to swing in a circle, describing a cone, is called a conical pendulum. In the torsion pendulum the bob vibrates by twisting and untwisting, as in the balance wheel of a watch.

Penelope (pənĕl'əpē), in Greek mythology, wife of Odysseus and the mother of Telemachus. In Homer's *Odyssey* she is pictured as a chaste and faithful wife. When Odysseus was away, she was surrounded by suitors who tried to persuade her that he would never return. She agreed to choose another husband when she finished weaving her father-in-law's shroud, but this was never done, for she unraveled by night what she wove by day. At last her strategem was discovered, and the suitors were enraged. She promised to marry the man who could bend her husband's great bow. None of the suitors could do this but Odysseus, who had returned disguised as a beggar. With the aid of the strung bow, Odysseus slaughtered the suitors and then revealed himself to Penelope. In another legend, however, Penelope was not faithful to her husband, but slept with one or all of the suitors and was banished by Odysseus on his return.

Penetanguishene (pĕn"ətăng"gəshēn', -gwəshēn'), town (1971 pop. 5,497), S Ont., Canada, on Georgian Bay. The name is an Indian word for "white rolling sands." Settled under the French regime, it has many French-speaking inhabitants. The town is a port with extensive lumber industries. It became a naval post in 1793 and had a role in the War of 1812. The hulls of the captured American vessels *Tecumseh* and *Tigris* are in the museum.

Peneus, river: see PINIÓS, river, Greece.

P'eng Teh-huai (pŭng' dŭ hwī), 1899–, Communist Chinese general and political leader. He held various command positions in the Red Army, and in 1934–35 he joined with Mao Tse-tung and Chu Teh in the long march. He became well known as the originator, with Mao, of the tactics of guerrilla warfare. In the Korean war P'eng commanded the Chinese Communist troops. He was minister of defense from 1954 to 1959, when, after a power struggle with Mao, he was replaced by Lin Piao. He served (1959–65) as vice premier. P'eng's rivalry with Mao Tse-tung made him an early target of the cultural revolution, and in 1967 he disappeared from public view after being arrested and losing his governmental posts.

penguin, originally the common name for the now extinct great AUK of the N Atlantic and now used, starting in the 19th cent., for the unrelated antarctic diving birds. Penguins are the most highly specialized of all birds for marine life. They swim entirely by means of their flipperlike wings, using their webbed feet as rudders. Their stiff feathers serve as insulation, and are waterproof when oiled. Underwater they can swim up to 25 mi (40.3 km) per hr as they pursue the fish, squid, and shrimp that form their diet. Their chief enemies are the leopard seal, killer whale, and skua gull. Since their legs are set far back on their bodies, they waddle awkwardly on land, and often travel by tobogganing on their bellies over the ice as they migrate—sometimes great distances—each fall to their nesting sites. They do not eat while on land, subsisting on a layer of fat under the skin; this results in weight losses of up to 75 lb (33.8 kg) during the two-month incubation period. The largest penguins, the emperor and the king (3–4 ft/91.5–122 cm in height), incubate their eggs between their feet in a fold of skin. The smaller jackass penguins, *Spheniscus demersus,* are named for their braying cry, and crested penguins are distinguished by yellow plumes on either side of the head. Smallest of all is the little blue penguin, *Eudyptula minor,* of New Zealand and Australia. Penguins are highly gregarious, and a population density of half a million birds in 500 acres has been counted at a colony in Antarctica. Penguins are classified in the phylum CHORDATA, subphylum Vertebrata, class Aves, order Sphenisciformes, family Spheniscidae.

penicillin, any of a group of chemically similar substances obtained from molds of the genera *Aspergillus* and *Penicillium* that were the first ANTIBIOTIC agents to be used successfully in the treatment of bacterial infections in man. The antagonistic effect of penicillin on bacteria was first observed by the Scottish biologist Sir Alexander Fleming in 1928. Although he recognized the therapeutic potential of penicillin, it was not until 1941 that a group of biologists working in England, including Sir H. W. Florey and the German E. B. Chain, purified the substance and established its effectiveness against infectious organisms and its lack of toxicity to humans. Despite the development of hundreds of different antibiotics in recent decades, penicillin remains important in antibiotic therapy. Small amounts of the antibiotic were first obtained from strains of the mold species *P. notatum* grown in fermentation bottles. During World War II need for the drug spurred development of better production methods; in the current method highly productive strains of *Penicillium* are grown in a cornsteep liquor medium in fermentation vats. The main form of penicillin produced by this method is benzylpenicillin, which, like all penicillins, is a derivative of 6-aminopenicillanic acid. Phenoxymethyl penicillin, which can be given orally because it is resistant to degradation by stomach acid, is produced by the species *P. chrysogenum.* Penicillin is effective against many gram-positive bacteria (see GRAM'S STAIN) including those causing syphilis, meningococcal meningitis, gas gangrene, pneumococcal pneumonia, and some staphylococcal and streptococcal infections. Most gram-negative bacteria are resistant to the antibiotic, but some, such as the bacteria causing gonorrhea, are susceptible and others are responsive to high penicillin concentrations. Tuberculosis bacteria, protozoans, most fungi, and true viruses are not affected by penicillin. AMPICILLIN, a synthetic penicillin, is active against both gram-positive and gram-negative bacteria. In susceptible microorganisms, penicillin interferes with synthesis of the cell wall. Use of the antibiotic is limited by the fact that, although it causes fewer side effects than many other antibiotics, it is quite allergenic, i.e., it causes allergic sensitivity in many individuals, including skin reactions and allergic shock. In addition, many microorganisms have developed resistance to the penicillins, and serious hospital epidemics involving infants and surgical patients have been caused by penicillin-resistant staphylococci (see DRUG RESISTANCE). Some organisms are resistant because they produce an enzyme, penicillinase, that destroys the antibiotic. Synthetically produced penicillins such as methicillin and oxacillin have been developed that are not degraded by the penicillinase enzyme, but these new penicillins have no effect on bacteria that have developed resistance by other means, e.g., by altered cell wall structure. Other antibiotics such as ERYTHROMYCIN have become important in treating infections by microorganisms resistant to penicillin.

Peniel (pēnī'əl), variant of PENUEL **1.**

Peninnah (pēnĭn'ə), wife of Elkanah. 1 Sam. 1.2.

Peninsular campaign, in the American Civil War, the unsuccessful Union attempt (April–July, 1862) to capture Richmond, Va., by way of the peninsula between the York and James rivers. Early in 1862, Gen. George B. MCCLELLAN, who had kept the Army of the Potomac inactive through the winter, proposed a plan for transporting his troops by sea to Urbana, near the mouth of the Rappahannock River, and from there advancing on Richmond. This plan was soon rendered unfeasible by the advance of the Confederate army under Joseph E. JOHNSTON to the Rappahannock, so McClellan chose Fort Monroe (at the tip of the peninsula between the York and James rivers) as the debarkation point for his offensive. President Lincoln, who preferred an overland advance, reluctantly agreed to McClellan's plan, provided that a force was left behind to protect Washington. The 1st Corps, under Irvin MCDOWELL, was detached from the Army of the Potomac for that purpose. Early in April, 1862, McClellan had about 100,000 men at Fort Monroe. Instead of trying to break through the Confederate line across the peninsula, he prepared to besiege Yorktown, the strongest point in the line. General Johnston evacuated Yorktown (May 3) just as McClellan had completed his preparations. An indecisive, though severely contested, rear-guard action was fought at Williamsburg (May 5) as the Confederates retired toward Richmond. The evacuation of Yorktown opened up the York River to the Union fleet, and on May 16, McClellan established his base at White House Landing (c.20 mi/32 km east of Richmond) on the Pamunkey River. Meanwhile, the Union advance into the interior forced the Confederates to abandon Norfolk (May 10) and to scuttle their formidable ironclad, the *Virginia* (see MONITOR and MERRIMACK), thus opening up the James as far as Drewry's Bluff (9 m/14 km south of Richmond), where Confederate batteries repulsed them on May 15. McClellan soon had his army encamped on both sides of the Chickahominy River near Richmond: the 3d and 4th corps were on the south side; the 2d, 5th, and 6th on the north. Irvin McDowell's corps (now called the Army of the Rappahannock) was to march south from its position near Fredericksburg and unite with the right wing north of the Chickahominy. McClellan would then move against the inferior forces of Johnston. However, the brilliant campaign of Thomas (Stonewall) JACKSON in the Shenandoah Valley caused the diversion of McDowell's corps from the army threatening Richmond. Late in May heavy rains swelled the Chickahominy so that communication between the two wings of McClellan's army became precarious. On May 31, Johnston moved against the left wing (on the south side of the river), where the lines extended to Fair Oaks, a railroad station c.6 mi (9 km) east of Richmond. In the ensuing battle of Fair Oaks, or Seven Pines (May 31–June 1, 1862), the Confederate attack, led by James Longstreet, was badly executed. With the help of some divisions of the 2d corps, which managed to cross the river, the Union left wing held its ground. Johnston, severely wounded on May 31, was succeeded on June 1 by Gen. Robert E. Lee, who withdrew the Army of Northern Virginia to Richmond. Lee's subsequent counteroffensive in the SEVEN DAYS BATTLES led to McClellan's withdrawal and the close of the campaign. Union forces did not again come so close to Richmond until 1864. See study by J. P. Cullen (1973).

Peninsular War, 1808–14, fought by France against Great Britain, Portugal, and Spanish guerrillas in the Iberian Peninsula. The conflict was precipitated when Portugal refused to comply with Napoleon's CONTINENTAL SYSTEM. By a secret convention reached at Fontainebleau (Oct., 1807), Spain agreed to support France against Portugal. A French army under Andoche JUNOT occupied (Nov., 1807) Portugal, and King JOHN VI and his family fled to Brazil without resisting. Napoleon then began a series of backhanded maneuvers to secure Spain for France. On the pretext that they were reinforcements for Junot, large numbers of French troops entered Spain and seized Pamplona and Barcelona (Feb., 1808). On March 23, French marshal Joachim MURAT entered Madrid. Meanwhile, a palace revolution (March 19) had deposed King CHARLES IV and his favorite, GODOY, and had placed FERDINAND VII on the throne. However, Charles and Ferdinand were lured into French territory and forced to abdicate (May 5–6). A bloody uprising in Madrid (May 2) was put down by Murat, and on June 15, Napoleon's brother Joseph BONAPARTE was proclaimed king of Spain. The Spanish rose in revolt throughout the country. When the insurrectionists captured (July 23) a French force dispatched to seize Seville, King Joseph evacuated Madrid (Aug. 1) and withdrew beyond the Ebro. Another French force was repulsed by José de PALAFOX in his heroic defense of Saragossa (June-August). In Portugal, where revolt had also broken out, a British expeditionary force under Arthur Wellesley (later duke of WELLINGTON) landed in Aug., 1808, and defeated Junot at Vimeiro (Aug. 21). Cut off from Joseph's army, Junot negotiated a convention at Cintra (Aug. 30), surrendering Lisbon in return for repatriation of his troops by British ships. With Sir John MOORE as commander in chief, the British invaded Spain, thus beginning a long series of seesaw campaigns. Napoleon hastened to Spain, stormed Madrid (Dec. 3, 1808), had Marshal Lannes lay siege to Saragossa, and ordered Marshal Soult to pursue Moore, who had retreated into Galicia. Soult was repulsed long enough at Coruña (Jan. 16, 1809) to permit the British to embark. Saragossa, which Palafox had held for two months at a huge cost in lives, fell in Feb., 1809. In April, Wellesley arrived in Lisbon to take charge of the British and Portuguese forces there. He drove the French out of Portugal, invaded Spain, and with the help of a Spanish army defeated the French under Joseph at Talavera (July 27-28). Driven back into Portugal by André MASSÉNA, whom he repulsed at Bussaco (Sept., 1810), Wellesley retired behind a strong fortified line centered at Torres Vedras. Lacking supplies, Masséna again retreated into Spain (March-April, 1811); meanwhile Soult had marched N from Cádiz to join Masséna, but their junction was prevented by Wellesley and William Carr BERESFORD at Fuentes de Oñoro and at Albuera (May, 1811). Early in 1812 Wellesley attacked once more, and on July 22 he defeated the French under MARMONT at Salamanca. He briefly occupied Madrid (Aug.-Oct., 1812), but retreated to Ciudad Rodrigo when the French, who had had time to consolidate their armies, counterattacked from three directions. Placed in command of all the allied forces in the peninsula, Wellesley took the offensive in May, 1813, routed the French under Joseph Bonaparte and Marshal Jourdan at Vitoria (June 21), and pushed them back into France. In October, Wellesley invaded France. He laid siege to Bayonne, heroically defended by Soult, and had reached Toulouse when, on April 12, 1814, news of Napoleon's abdication arrived; the Peninsular War was ended. It had immeasurably raised Britain's military prestige and had contributed heavily to Napoleon's downfall. The war marked the lowest point of the Spanish Bourbon dynasty, but the spirit of the Spanish people asserted itself in fearless guerrilla warfare against the French. In Latin America, the war served as detonator for the independence revolutions of the Spanish colonies. The brutal impact of the war on the common people of Spain was the theme of a celebrated series of etchings by Francisco de GOYA. There are histories of the Peninsular War by Robert Southey (3 vol., 1823-32), W. F. P. Napier (rev. ed. 1856, repr. 1970), H. R. Clinton (3d ed. 1890), C. W. C. Oman (7 vol., 1902-30), Michael Glover (1974), and Richard Humble (1974).

Penitentes (pĕnĭtĕn'tēz), secret lay order in the U.S. Southwest, particularly New Mexico, noted for flagellating rites during Holy Week. It arose from the third order of the Franciscans and is sometimes called Los Hermanos Penitentes del Tercer Orden de Franciscanos. Although condemned in 1889 by the Roman Catholic archbishop of Santa Fe, Penitente customs have persisted in modified form in many of the small villages of New Mexico. Until recently, the annual ceremony involved the carrying of heavy wooden crosses by penitents, who were beaten by heavy cord. On Good Friday the rites culminated with a crucifixion. The rites have been observed by very few outsiders.

penitential psalms: see PSALMS.

penitentiary: see PRISON.

Penitent Thief: see GOOD THIEF.

Penki: see PEN-CH'I, China.

Penn, John, 1729-95, lieutenant governor of Pennsylvania, b. London. A grandson of William Penn, he was the last proprietary official of the colony. He was under the domination of the Penn family in his two administrations (1763-71, 1773-76). During that time Pennsylvania was torn by a bitter struggle between those who favored proprietary government and those who sought to end it. Penn lost power when the proprietary government was displaced (1776) during the American Revolution. He yielded to the course of events, however, and remained in Philadelphia until his death.

Penn, John, 1740?-1788, political leader in the American Revolution, signer of the Declaration of Independence, b. Caroline co., Va. A lawyer, Penn moved (1774) to North Carolina and was (1775-77, 1778-80) a delegate to the Continental Congress.

Penn, Thomas, 1702-75, colonial proprietor of Pennsylvania, b. Bristol, England; son of William Penn. Coming to Philadelphia, he managed (1732-41) the proprietary rights he inherited with his brothers and thereafter remained in charge of the colony's business in England. His letters to his governors are of historical significance.

Penn, Sir William, 1621-70, British admiral. In the English civil war he served in Parliament's naval forces, and he joined the pursuit (1651-52) of Prince Rupert in the Mediterranean. He served in the first Dutch War and in 1654 was made commander of the fleet that sailed for the West Indies and captured Jamaica (1655). He was arrested shortly after his return to England and imprisoned briefly before being allowed to retire to his Irish estates. The reason for his disgrace has never been definitely established. It probably had nothing to do with his secret negotiations with the exiled Charles II, who, when restored to the throne, knighted Penn (1660) and made him a commissioner of the navy. In the second Dutch War Penn was second in command to the duke of York (later James II) in the action of the fleet in 1665 and retired to shore duty when the duke was relieved of command. Penn's son was William Penn, founder of Pennsylvania. See Granville Penn, *Memorials . . . of Sir William Penn* (1833).

Penn, William, 1644-1718, English Quaker, founder of PENNSYLVANIA, b. London, England; son of Sir William Penn. He was expelled (1662) from Oxford for his religious nonconformity and was then sent by his father to the Continent to overcome his leanings toward Puritanism. He continued his religious studies, however, and in Ireland, where he had been sent (1666) to oversee the family estates, he became a staunch member of the Society of Friends. He was imprisoned (1668) for writing a tract (*The Sandy Foundation Shaken*) against the doctrine of the Trinity, but, undaunted, he wrote *No Cross, No Crown* and *Innocency with Her Open Face* while in the Tower of London. After his release (1669), Penn continued his writing, his many tracts including *The Great Case of Liberty of Conscience* (1670), in which he argued for religious toleration. He also went on preaching missions through England, the Netherlands, and Germany. Penn became involved in the affairs of the American colonies when in 1675 he was appointed a trustee for Edward Byllynge, one of the two Quaker proprietors of West Jersey. He helped draw up Concessions and Agreements, a liberal charter of government for the Quakers settling there. In 1681, Penn and 11 others purchased East Jersey (see NEW JERSEY). In the same year, in payment of a debt owed his father, Penn obtained from King Charles II a charter for Pennsylvania (named by the king for Penn's father) for the establishment of his "holy experiment," a colony where religious and political freedom could flourish. Shortly afterward he received a grant of the Three Lower Counties-on-the-Delaware (present Delaware) from the duke of York (later James II). In 1682, Penn went to his province, where the earliest settlers were already laying out the city of Philadelphia in accordance with his plans. He drew up a liberal Frame of Government for the colony. He also established the friendly relations with the Indians that were to distinguish the early history of Pennsylvania. Returning to England (1684), he asserted his boundary claims against Charles CALVERT, 3d Lord Baltimore. Penn's friendship with James II led to his being accused of treason after that king's deposition (1688), and his colony was briefly (1692-94) annexed to New York. Penn continued writing religious and political tracts and preached extensively. Difficulties in Pennsylvania caused his return there for a short time (1699-1701), and he issued a new constitution, the Charter of Privileges (1701), granting more power to the provincial assembly. His last years were troubled ones. His own steward swindled him to such an extent that he was imprisoned (1707-8) for debt, and the continued difficulties of his colony and troubles concerning his eldest son caused him much grief. A stroke in 1712 removed him from active life. See biographies by W. I. Hull (1937) and M. M. Dunn (1967); Arthur Pound, *The Penns of Pennsylvania and England* (1932); E. C. O. Beatty, *William Penn as Social Philosopher* (1939, repr. 1974); Vincent Buranelli, *The King & the Quaker* (1962); M.B. Endy, Jr., *William Penn and Early Quakerism* (1973).

Pennacook Indians (pĕn'əko͝ok), group of North American Indians of the Algonquian branch of the Algonquian-Wakashan linguistic stock (see AMERICAN INDIAN LANGUAGES). Although of the Eastern Woodlands culture area, they depended to a large extent on seafood. In the early 17th cent. they occupied NE Massachusetts, SW New Hampshire, and SW Maine. They then numbered some 2,000, but by 1674 smallpox and wars had reduced them to some 1,250. Most of the Pennacook remained neutral in King Philip's war (1675), but when 200 of them were treacherously seized (1676), the remainder fled to Canada and to the West; the survivors of the western group settled with the Mahican. The Pennacook in Canada first settled near Quebec, but in 1700 this group moved to St. Francis, where they joined the exiled Abnaki. The two tribes became bitter enemies of the British.

Pennamite Wars: see WYOMING VALLEY.

Penn Central Company, U.S. transportation company, formed in 1968 by the merger of the NEW YORK CENTRAL RR and the PENNSYLVANIA RR.

Pennell, Joseph (pĕn'əl), 1857-1926, American illustrator, etcher, lithographer, and author, b. Philadelphia, studied at the Pennsylvania Academy of the Fine Arts. Much of his time was spent in Europe, particularly in London, where he was greatly influenced by Whistler. His subjects are chiefly landscapes and architectural views, and his art is distinguished for its simplicity, technical perfection, and illustrative quality. He is represented by etchings, drawings, and lithographs in the Library of Congress, Washington, D.C.; Pennsylvania Academy of the Fine Arts; Carnegie Institute, Pittsburgh; and Brooklyn Museum, N.Y. Pennell was a member (1909) of the National Academy of Design and of numerous European societies and was a lecturer on illustration at the Slade School of Art, London, and the Royal College of Art, South Kensington. His publications include *Pen Drawings and Pen Draughtsmen* (1889), *Modern Illustration* (1895), *Lithographs of New York* (1905), *Etchers and Etching* (1919), *Adventures of an Illustrator* (1925), and, with Elizabeth R. Pennell, his wife, a biography of James McNeill Whistler (1908). See *The Life and Letters of Joseph Pennell* (1929) by his wife.

Penner (pĕn'ər), river, 350 mi (563 km) long, rising in the Eastern Ghats, Karnataka state, S India, and flowing N into Andhra Pradesh state, then E to the Bay of Bengal, near Nellore. The river is used for irrigation.

Pennines (pĕn'īnz) or **Pennine Chain,** mountain range, sometimes called the "backbone of England," extending c.160 mi (260 km) from the Cheviot Hills on the Scottish border to the Peak District in Derbyshire. The range consists of a series of upland blocks, separated by transverse valleys (Tees, Aire, Wensleydale, and Wharfdale). There are caverns, and several chasms are more than 300 ft (91 m) in depth. Cross Fell (2,930 ft/893 m) is the highest peak. The range is sparsely populated; sheep raising, quarrying, and tourism are important economic activities there. Reservoirs in the Pennines store water for the cities of N England.

Pennsylvania (pĕnsəlvā'nyə), state (1970 pop. 11,793,909), 45,333 sq mi (117,412 sq km), E United States, one of the Middle Atlantic states and one of the Thirteen Colonies. It is bounded on the N by Lake Erie and New York; on the E by the winding Delaware River, which separates it from New York and New Jersey; on the S by Delaware, Maryland, and West Virginia; and on the W by West Virginia and Ohio. HARRISBURG, midway between the metropolitan areas of PHILADELPHIA and PITTSBURGH, is the capital. Except for coastal plains in the northwestern and southeastern parts of the state, Pennsylvania is a succession of mountains and rolling hills with narrow valleys. Mountain ridges rise from the Delaware River into the Piedmont, with the parallel ranges of the Blue Mts. and Allegheny Mts. occupying the central portion of the state. Uplands of the plateau extend to the western border. In the east Pennsylvania is drained by the Delaware and the Susquehanna river systems; in the west by the Allegheny and the Monongahela rivers, which join at Pittsburgh to form the Ohio River; and in the central part by the West Branch, which crosses the state and empties into the Chesapeake Bay. These turbulent streams and rivers have cut spectacularly beautiful water gaps, natural passageways for roads and rail lines. The great forests and lush vegetation that once covered the entire state were transformed during the Carboniferous period into tremendous deposits of anthracite coal in the east and extensive bituminous beds in the west. Large areas of woodland remain and, in some isolated sections, have retained an almost primitive wildness. In general, the vast resources of the state have been tapped and disciplined to yield abundantly. The valleys have become rural centers, the mountainsides have been slashed with quarries and mine shafts, and at strategic spots great metropolitan centers have developed. Iron smelting became important in the 18th cent., made possible by abundant supplies of ore and hardwoods for the furnaces. In the 19th cent., after the Bessemer process made the use of its great anthracite deposits economical, Pennsylvania quickly emerged as the nation's leading steel producer, and its giant mills now account for about one fourth of the total U.S. output. The state is also one of the leaders in nickel production and actively exploits a wide variety of other mineral resources, especially sand, gravel, and stone. Heavily industrialized as well, the state has factories that manufacture metal products, foodstuffs, machinery, chemicals, and wearing apparel; oil is also refined, but has less importance in the economy than during the 19th cent. Pittsburgh and Philadelphia, situated at opposite ends of the state and dominating the commercial and industrial life of their regions, present startling contrasts in production and culture. Other leading cities are ALLENTOWN, BETHLEHEM, ERIE, READING, SCRANTON, CHESTER, and WILKES-BARRE. Agriculture is concentrated in the fertile counties of the southeast, the principal crops being hay, corn, wheat, oats, tobacco, barley, rye, potatoes, and fruit. One of the prize farmlands of the nation is the Great Valley, a wide trough between the Piedmont and the mountains, rich with limestone soils; there the PENNSYLVANIA DUTCH farmer built a culture that is identified with the bountiful agrarian life. Transportation facilities have kept pace with the state's rapid development. The accessible and landlocked harbor of Philadelphia has been supplemented by the Great Lakes port of Erie (increasing in importance since the opening of the SAINT LAWRENCE SEAWAY in 1959) and access to the South and Midwest by Pittsburgh and the Ohio River. Over a fine system of highways and a complex network of railroads, the products of farms, factories, and mines are taken to port cities to be sent out to the rest of the world. Into the building of this rich and complex commonwealth has entered the work of many racial and economic groups, contributing not only to the advantages of diversity, but also to the pressures of conflicting interests. In the early 1600s the English, Dutch, and Swedes disputed right to the region. Explorations were confined to the Delaware River vicinity, and fur trading with the Indians was carried on. The original permanent settlement was made at TINICUM ISLAND in the Schuylkill River (1643) by Johan PRINTZ, governor of NEW SWEDEN, and was followed in the succeeding years by the neighboring colony of Uppland. Swedish jurisdiction was shortlived as the Dutch, operating from their stronghold in New Amsterdam, succeeded in gaining control of the mideastern region in 1655. In turn the Dutch were overpowered by the British forces of Col. Richard Nicolls, acting for the duke of York (later James II), and in 1664 the British took over the Delaware area. The duke of York remained in control until 1681, when, in payment of a royal debt, William PENN was granted proprietary rights to almost the whole of what is now Pennsylvania, and, in addition, leased the three Lower Counties (see DELAWARE). A devout Quaker who had suffered for his beliefs, Penn viewed his colony as a holy experiment, designed as an asylum for the persecuted under conditions of equality and freedom. In 1681 he sent William Markham as deputy to establish a government at Uppland and sent instructed commissioners to plot the City of Brotherly Love (Philadelphia), which was laid out at the forks of the Delaware and the Schuylkill rivers. Penn carefully constructed a constitution, known as the Frame of Government, that gave Pennsylvania the most liberal government in the colonies. Religious freedom was guaranteed to all who believed in God, a humane penal code was adopted, and the emancipation of slaves was encouraged. However, under the representative system that it established, the popular assembly was left in an inferior position in relation to the executive branches controlled by the proprietors. In 1682 Penn arrived at Uppland (renamed Chester). Shortly thereafter he met with the chiefs of the Delaware tribes at Shakamaxon (now part of Philadelphia), and a famous treaty was signed, which promoted long-lasting good will between the Indians and the white settlers. After William and Mary ascended (1689) the throne of England, Penn's friendship with the deposed James II

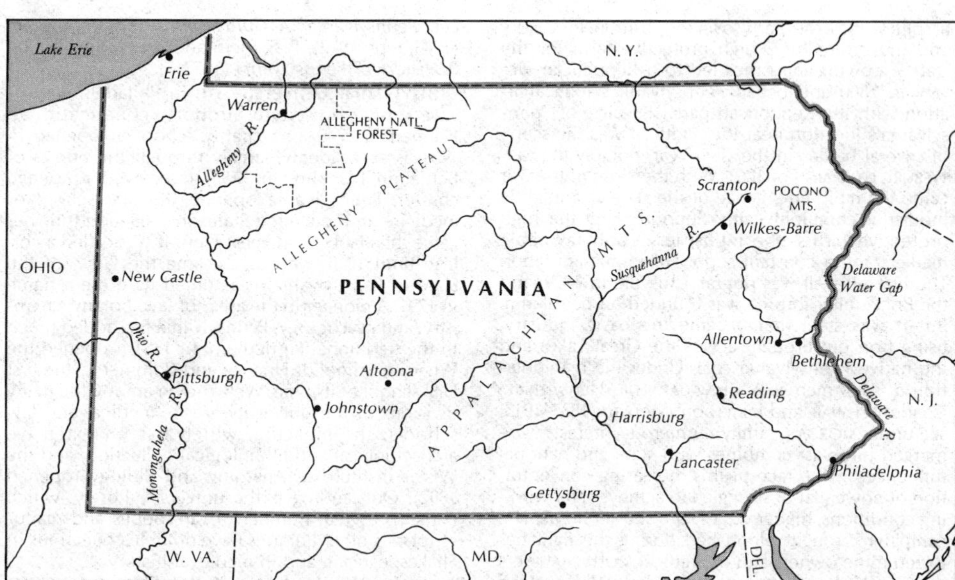

opened him to accusations of treason, and in 1692 the province was taken away from him and placed under the administration of Benjamin Fletcher, governor of New York, with William Markham as deputy. In 1694 full proprietary rights were restored, and in 1699 Penn returned to his colony, accompanied by James LOGAN, who was to become the leader of the dominant proprietary party. The colonists sought greater power than the liberal Frame of Government permitted, and political dissension persisted for many years, complicated by Penn's prolonged absences from the province and by the desire of the Anglicans to have Pennsylvania made into a royal colony. Under the leadership of David LLOYD, the provincial assembly attempted to gain more political power by refusing to give the necessary support to the executive branch. The controversy between the assembly and the proprietors ultimately led to Penn's formulating a new constitution, the Charter of Privileges, which increased the power of the assembly and provided for the voluntary withdrawal of the Delaware counties (accomplished in 1703). After Penn's death in 1718 proprietary rights were held by his heirs. By this time Pennsylvania had developed into a dynamic and growing colony, enriched by the continuous immigration of numerous different peoples. The Quakers, English, and Welsh were concentrated in Philadelphia and the eastern counties, where they acquired great commercial and financial power through foreign trade and where they achieved a political dominance which they held until the time of the American Revolution. Philadelphia had by then become the finest city in the nation, a leader in the arts and the professions. The Germans (Pennsylvania Dutch)—largely of the persecuted religious sects of Mennonites, Moravians, Lutherans, and Reformed—settled in the farming areas of SE Pennsylvania, where they retained their cohesion and to a considerable extent their language, customs, architecture, and superstitions. After 1718 the Scotch-Irish began colonizing in the Cumberland Valley and gradually pushed the frontiers toward W Pennsylvania. Their rugged independence and the peculiarities of their frontier problems made them rebellious against the established order. Throughout the province agriculture was the chief occupation, although industry was spurred by abundant water power and resources. In the west settlement was hindered by a growing unrest among the Indians. Penn's heirs lacked both the good sense and the ethical values that prompted Penn's fair and considerate treatment. Resentful of encroachment on their lands and of the land purchase made by the ALBANY CONGRESS (1754), the Indians allied themselves with the French, who were then fortifying positions in the Ohio valley (see FRENCH AND INDIAN WARS). The frontier settlements were severely ravaged until, after several initial reverses, the French abandoned (1758) FORT DUQUESNE to British and American forces under Gen. John Forbes. The power of the Indians was not completely broken until the suppression of the uprising of 1763 (see PONTIAC'S REBELLION). The inept defenses provided by the Quaker-controlled assembly during the Indian crisis aroused bitter resentment and intensified efforts to overturn proprietary rule. The struggle between proprietary and antiproprietary parties was soon overshadowed, however, by the opposition to British imperial policy that culminated in the American Revolution. Important Pennsylvanians of both parties emerged as leaders of the Revolutionary movement—Benjamin FRANKLIN, Benjamin RUSH, Joseph REED, Thomas MIFFLIN, John DICKINSON, Robert MORRIS, and Haym SALOMON. In 1776 a provincial convention dominated by radical patriots created the Commonwealth of Pennsylvania under one of the most democratic of the new state constitutions. The state was invaded by British troops, and notable engagements were fought in 1777 on the Brandywine (see BRANDYWINE, BATTLE OF) and at GERMANTOWN. Philadelphia was occupied by the British, while VALLEY FORGE witnessed the heroic endurance of Washington's troops in the winter of 1777-78, making the site a shrine of patriotism. Difficulties were increased by the renewal of Indian depredations, the worst being the WYOMING VALLEY massacre of 1778. In the postwar period, Pennsylvania's role as the geographical keystone of the new nation was strengthened by the resolution of boundary disputes that had persisted throughout the colonial period: agreement was reached with Maryland in 1784 by acceptance of the Mason-Dixon line; with Virginia and New York in 1786; with the United States and the Iroquois Confederacy in 1789; and with Connecticut in 1799 after bitter dissension in the Wyoming Valley. Philadelphia, host to the First and Second Continental Congresses (1774, 1775-81) and scene of the signing of the Declaration of Independence, was for many years the nation's leading city. It was the site of the Constitutional Convention of 1787, served as the seat of the new Federal government from 1790 to 1800, and became a financial center through the organization of the First Bank of the United States (1791) and the U.S. Mint (1792). In 1790 it was also the site of a convention that replaced the radical state constitution of 1776 with a more conservative one patterned after the Federal Constitution, though upholding such liberal achievements as the act (1780) providing for the gradual abolition of slavery. Philadelphia was not, however, typical of the state as a whole. Opposition to Federal taxation in rural Pennsylvania led to violence in the WHISKEY REBELLION of 1794 and the Fries Rebellion of 1798 (see FRIES, John), while anti-eastern sentiment forced removal of the state capital to LANCASTER in 1799, then to Harrisburg in 1812. Western influence in state affairs increased as the rapid movement of settlers into the Ohio country created new markets, stimulated the growth of new industries, and assured the importance of Pittsburgh and Erie as commercial centers. The economic and social development of W Pennsylvania also encouraged programs of internal improvements. The turnpike era, initiated by the incorporation of the Lancaster Turnpike in 1792, was followed by an extensive canal-building program in the 1820s and 1830s and, after the introduction of steam, by an era of railroad construction. Adequate provisions for free public education, championed by Gov. George Wolf and Thaddeus STEVENS, emerged in the Free School Act of 1834, which was implemented in 1849 by legislation requiring compulsory attendance. Much of the early education was denominational, and many schools remained church-affiliated. In political life the Democratic party was generally dominant, and in 1857 Pennsylvania gave the nation a Democratic President in James Buchanan. However, a split within the party over opposition to slavery and the desire for a high protective tariff for the state's growing industries led to a Republican victory in 1860 and began Pennsylvania's long affiliation with the Republican party. Because of Pennsylvania's location near the South, it was the scene of several battles in the Civil War, notably the GETTYSBURG CAMPAIGN of 1863. With the close of the war came the rapid emergence of the state as a mightly industrial commonwealth. Supported by the high protective tariffs, the industries found favorable markets and a constant supply of immigrant labor. The first oil well was dug at Titusville in 1859, and the Rockefeller fortune was founded on petroleum. But it was steel that became the basic industry, using iron ore brought across the Great Lakes and the native Pennsylvania coal. Under the manipulation of such men as Andrew CARNEGIE, Henry FRICK, Charles SCHWAB, and J. Pierpont Morgan (1837–1913; see under MORGAN, family) numerous interests were merged into vast combines with state and national influence. In the face of this increasing concentration of power, labor struggled to achieve safer working conditions, higher wages, and shorter hours. The campaign brought bloodshed during the fight between mine owners and the radical MOLLY MAGUIRES and reached a climax in the strike at Homestead (see HOMESTEAD STRIKE) in 1892. The miners, under the leadership of John MITCHELL and aided by the intervention of Theodore Roosevelt, achieved a qualified victory in the anthracite strike of 1902, but the great steel strike of 1919 was broken. During the 1930s the Congress of Industrial Organizations (CIO) successfully promoted unionization in many new areas and somewhat weakened the strength of the American Federation of Labor. By 1941 the CIO had succeeded in organizing the steel industry, while the United Mine Workers acquired increasing strength in the coal fields. The powerful and corrupt political machine that had been built by Simon Cameron continued into the 20th cent. under the leadership of such bosses as Boies Penrose. Gifford Pinchot, a Progressive Republican and a vigorous "dry," was governor for two terms (1923–27, 1931–35) and did much to repair government through a new administrative code, an improved budget system, and pioneer work in conservation. Pennsylvania is governed under the constitution adopted in 1873 and amended extensively since then, the last time in 1968. The governor serves a four-year term and may succeed himself for one additional term. Milton J. Shapp, a Democrat, was elected in 1970 and was relected in 1974. The state legislature, called the general assembly, consists of a senate of 50 members and a house of representatives of 203 members. Pennsylvania sends 2 Senators and 25 Representatives to the U.S. Congress and has 27 electoral votes. Visitors to Pennsylvania today are both intrigued and dismayed by the startling contrasts still existing within the state—between befogged mill and mine towns and the quiet charm of rural Lancaster and between the slums of Philadelphia and the suburban delights of the "Main Line." Of the many historic sites and parks which have been preserved, those under Federal ownership include Fort Necessity National Battlefield, Gettysburg National Military Park, and Independence National Historical Park (see NATIONAL PARKS AND MONUMENTS, table). The state enjoys a rich and varied cultural heritage beginning with the remarkable accomplishments of Benjamin Franklin and the eminent physician Benjamin Rush. The Pittsburgh Symphony Orchestra and the Philadelphia Orchestra have achieved nationwide recognition. Among the state's many institutions of higher education are Bryn Mawr College, at Bryn Mawr; Bucknell Univ., at Lewisburg; Carnegie-Mellon Univ., the Univ. of Pittsburgh, and Duquesne Univ., at Pittsburgh; Dickinson College, at Carlisle; Drexel Univ., Temple Univ., the Univ. of Pennsylvania, and La Salle College, at Philadelphia; Haverford College, at Haverford; Lehigh Univ., at Bethlehem; Pennsylvania State Univ., at University Park; Swarthmore College, at Swarthmore; Villanova Univ., at Villanova; and Lafayette College, at Easton. See F. A. Godcharles, *Pennsylvania: Political, Governmental, Military, and Civil* (5 vol., 1934); S. K. Stevens et al., *Exploring Pennsylvania* (3d ed. 1968); S. G. Fisher, *The Making of Pennsylvania* (2d ed. 1969); A. S. Bolles, *Pennsylvania, Province and State: A History from 1609 to 1790* (2 vol., 1970); P. H. Gibbons, *Pennsylvania Dutch* (3d ed. 1971); A. B. Hulbert, *Pioneer Roads and Experiences of Travelers* (2 vol., 1904; repr. 1971); W. H. Egle, *Pennsylvania Women in the American Revolution* (1898, repr. 1972); C. A. Hanna, *The Wilderness Trail* (2 vol., 1911; repr. 1972); Federal Writers' Project, *Pennsylvania: A Guide to the Keystone State* (1940, repr. 1972); P. S. Klein and Ari Hoogenboom, *A History of Pennsylvania* (1973).

Pennsylvania, University of, in Philadelphia; private with some state support; coeducational. Planned in 1740 as a charity school, it opened in 1751 as an academy, largely through the efforts of Benjamin Franklin. In 1755 it received a college charter. Pennsylvania opened the first school of medicine in the United States in 1765, and thus became the first U.S. university, but it was called a college until 1779, when it became the Univ. of the State of Pennsylvania. It assumed its present name in 1791. A pioneer in the areas of law, botany, chemistry, and psychology, Pennsylvania has added much to the traditional curriculum. In 1881 it opened the Wharton School of Finance and Commerce, the first U.S. school of its type. Well known among the many divisions of the university are its medical and law schools; the museum, which has an extensive archaeological and ethnological collection; and the Wistar Institute of Anatomy and Biology (opened 1892). Outstanding is the university library, which contains a great number of rare books and manuscripts; its other libraries have notable collections in Shakespeareana and in medieval history.

Pennsylvania Academy of the Fine Arts, Philadelphia, established in 1805, incorporated in 1806. It is supported by private endowment. The academy grew out of a proposal by Charles Willson Peale for an art institution; this led to the founding of the Columbianum, which mounted in 1795 the first art exhibition in the United States. The academy was formed to supersede it, sponsored by 71 public-spirited Philadelphia citizens, among them Peale, Charles Biddle, William Rush, and George Clymer. The present building was constructed in 1876 to house the academy's art collection, which includes the Temple Collection of modern American paintings, the Gibson Collection of 19th-century European paintings, and the John Frederick Lewis Collection of early American paintings. The academy, affiliated with the oldest American art school, owns more than 2,000 works by American artists, one of the richest collections in the field.

Pennsylvania Avenue National Historic Site: see NATIONAL PARKS AND MONUMENTS (table).

Pennsylvania Dutch [from Ger. *Deutsch*=German], people of E Pennsylvania of German descent who migrated to the area in the 18th cent., particularly those in the present counties of Northampton, Berks, Lancaster, Lehigh, Lebanon, York, and adjacent counties. The colony of Pennsylvania, established by William Penn as a refuge for Quakers, offered other groups the prospect of religious freedom. In 1683 the village of Germantown was established by a group of Mennonites led by Francis Daniel Pastorius, and in succeeding years other groups, such as the Dunkards and the Moravians, settled in Pennsylvania. However, the bulk of immigration occurred after 1710, when the Germans from the Palatinate first arrived. Many of these people had sought economic and religious freedom in England; from there a number were sent to the Hudson valley to engage in the production of naval stores, but with the failure of that project many Palatines moved to Pennsylvania. Enthusiastic reports brought other settlers from Germany, until by the time of the American Revolution the population of Pennsylvania, according to Benjamin Franklin, was one-third German. At first the large influx of German settlers antagonized the English, but they were gradually accepted, and during the Revolution they provided valuable assistance. Most of the settlers engaged in farming, at which they were extremely successful. For the most part they maintained their own language and customs; the family became the principal economic and social unit and the church was next in importance. The aim of the various religious sects was to establish a Christian, democratic society; for many years they opposed public schooling, preferring to retain their own standards and manners, and they strongly resisted signs of progress and worldly living. Several of the sects are completely pacifistic, such as the Amish and the Mennonites. The Amish are particularly strict in the matter of dress, maintaining a simple, but distinctive garb, and also have a strong aversion to automobiles, electric lights, and telephones. The Amish have continued to oppose public schooling and the U.S. Supreme Court ruled in 1972 that the Amish were exempt from state compulsory education laws. The Church of the Brethren, incorrectly but popularly known as the Dunkards or Dunkers from their manner of baptism, and the Schwenkfelders are two other sects. The Pennsylvania Dutch, or Pennsylvania German, language is a blend of several dialects, essentially Palatinate, with some admixture of standard German and English. A substantial Pennsylvania German literature, art, and architecture exists. Many written records were adorned with illuminated writing, and such articles as pottery, furniture, needlework, and barns made use of decorative motifs, often of a highly artistic nature. Their buildings are usually of heavy stone and timber construction, with steep roofs and small, irregular windows. Pennsylvania Germans have contributed much to the culture of Pennsylvania. The Pennsylvania-German Society, organized in 1891, has published much material relative to the history and folklore of the Pennsylvania Dutch. See J. F. Sachse, *The German Sectarians of Pennsylvania, 1708–1800* (2 vol., 1889; repr. 1971); William Beidelman, *The Story of the Pennsylvania Germans* (1898, repr. 1969), L. O. Kuhns, *The German and Swiss Settlements of Colonial Pennsylvania* (1901, repr. 1971); H. T. Rosenberger, *The Pennsylvania Germans, 1891–1965* (1966); Amos Long, *The Pennsylvania German Family Farm* (1972); J. J. Stoudt, *Pennsylvania German Folk Art* (rev. ed. 1966) and *Sunbonnets and Shoofly Pies: Pennsylvania Dutch Cultural History* (1973).

Pennsylvania Museum of Art: see PHILADELPHIA MUSEUM OF ART.

Pennsylvanian period: see CARBONIFEROUS PERIOD.

Pennsylvania Railroad, U.S. transportation company; inc. 1846 by the Pennsylvania legislature. It opened in 1854 as a single-track line between Philadelphia and Pittsburgh. Beginning in 1857, the company purchased many railroads, most notably the Allegheny Portage RR, that were owned and operated by the state of Pennsylvania. During the Civil War the Pennsylvania RR played an important role in the Union war effort. In the last decades of the 1800s, especially under the presidency of Thomas A. Scott (1874–80), the railroad rapidly extended its operations between the East coast and the Mississippi River and between the Great Lakes and the Ohio and Potomac rivers. In 1910 a tunnel under the Hudson River allowed the railroad to reach its new terminal in New York City, known in the mid-1900s as the world's busiest rail station. The Pennsylvania RR introduced many innovations to railroading, including air conditioning, electrification, and the practice of loading truck-trailers on flat cars. In 1968, after a long legal battle that reached the U.S. Supreme Court, the Pennsylvania RR merged with the New York Central RR to form the Penn Central Company. By the early 1970s the railroad was bankrupt and was able to continue operations only with the aid of Federal subsidies.

Pennsylvania State University, at University Park; land-grant and state supported; coeducational; chartered 1855, opened 1859 as Farmers' High School. It was named the Agricultural College of Pennsylvania in 1862, renamed Pennsylvania State College in 1874, and became a university in 1953. It has branch junior colleges in 18 cities throughout the state in addition to forestry camps and engineering test stations. Among the university's extensive laboratory facilities are a nuclear reactor, a seismograph, and one of the world's largest water tunnels (at the Ordnance Research Laboratory). A medical school at Hershey was opened in 1965.

pennyroyal, name for two similar plants of the family Labiatae (MINT family), usually distinguished as true, or European, pennyroyal (*Mentha pulegium*) and American, or mock, pennyroyal (*Hedeoma pulegioides*). Both have small bluish or purplish flowers in the leaf axils. The European pennyroyal is perennial and prostrate; the American is annual with numerous erect branches. Both contain a pungent oil said to be repellent to insects, especially fleas. The oil, obtained chiefly from the American pennyroyal, is used medicinally. Pennyroyal tea was an old domestic remedy. Other species of *Hedeoma* are sometimes called pennyroyal, but the false and bastard pennyroyals are different plants. Pennyroyals are classified in the division MAGNOLIOPHYTA, class Magnoliopsida, order Lamiales, family Labiatae.

pennyweight: see ENGLISH UNITS OF MEASUREMENT.

Penobscot (pənŏb'skŏt), river, 350 mi (563 km) long, rising in numerous lakes in central Maine and flowing generally east in four branches, uniting, then flowing S into Penobscot Bay; longest river in Maine. The river, navigable to Bangor, is an important source of power for pulpwood and paper mills; logs are floated down the river. The Penobscot's upper course is in a wooded region famous for hunting, fishing, and canoeing. Pulpwood and petroleum products are the principal freight on the river. The Penobscot was first explored by the English voyager Martin Pring in 1603; in 1604 the French explorer Samuel de Champlain sailed up the river to the site of present-day Bangor.

Penobscot Bay, inlet of the Atlantic Ocean, 35 mi (56 km) long and 27 mi (43 km) wide, S Maine. The bay was entered by the English explorer Martin Pring in 1603; the French explorer Samuel de Champlain claimed the area for France in 1604. Trading posts and missions were established, and for many years the possession of the area was disputed among the French, English, and Americans. An important shipbuilding center in the 19th cent., the bay is now a fishing and resort center and the site of a U.S. naval trial course.

Penobscot Indians, North American Indians whose language belongs to the Algonquian branch of the Algonquian-Wakashan linguistic stock (see AMERICAN INDIAN LANGUAGES). They were the largest group of the Abnaki Confederacy and resembled the other members culturally. In the early 17th cent. they inhabited the region around Penobscot Bay and the Penobscot River in Maine. A French mission was established among them in 1688 on the site of the present city of Bangor. The Penobscot were active in all the New England frontier wars, generally supporting the French, until 1749, when a peace treaty with the English put an end to their hostilities. The treaty created ill feeling with other Abnaki peoples, who remained firm supporters of the French. In 1750 the Penobscot numbered some 700. The assistance that the Penobscot gave the colonists in the American Revolution gained for them a reservation at Old Town, Maine, where today they number some 400. See F. G. Speck, *Penobscot Man* (1940, repr. 1970) and *Penobscot Shamanism* (1919, repr. 1974); Peter Anastas, *Glooskap's Children; Encounters with the Penobscot Indians of Maine* (1973).

Penrhyn: see COOK ISLANDS.

Penrose, Boies (boiz), 1860–1921, American political leader, b. Philadelphia. A lawyer, he was (1884–97) a member of the Pennsylvania legislature and coauthored a scholarly work, *The City Government of Philadelphia* (1887). His talent for political organization was soon employed for the state Republican party machine; he became the henchman of Matthew S. QUAY, the state boss. He was elected (1896) to the U.S. Senate, and after Quay's death (1904) Penrose became the Republican leader of Pennsylvania. He served until his death in 1921 in the Senate and there dominated the finance committee; he consistently supported a high protective tariff. He played a leading role in Republican national politics and, after the retirement of Nelson W. Aldrich, became Republican leader of the Senate, where his service was not notable. See biography by R. D. Bowden (1937, repr. 1971).

Penry, John, 1559–93, British Puritan author, an instigator of the MARPRELATE CONTROVERSY, b. Wales, grad. Cambridge and Oxford. While at college he became an ardent Puritan. In 1587 his pamphlet assailing the spiritual destitution of the Welsh clergy was seized and burned, and he was briefly imprisoned. Puritans were aroused, and Penry and several associates were helped to set up a hidden printing press from which emerged (1588–89) seven pamphlets attacking alleged evils of the Church of England and its clergy. They appeared under the pseudonym Martin Marprelate; Penry was perhaps the chief author. When his associate John Udall was arrested (1590), Penry fled to Scotland; he returned secretly in 1592. He was arrested, tried on the doubtful charge of writing with intent to excite rebellion, and hanged. See his *Notebook* (ed. by Albert Peel, 1944); biography by William Pierce (1923); D. J. McGinn, *John Penry and the Marprelate Controversy* (1966).

Pensacola (pĕnsəkō'lə), city (1970 pop. 59,507), seat of Escambia co., extreme NW Fla., on Pensacola Bay; inc. 1822. It is a port of entry with a good natural harbor and shipping and fishing industries. A major manufacturing center of W Florida, the city has industries that produce synthetic fibers, paper products, chemicals, naval stores, and nuclear-reactor parts. The Spanish established a short-lived settlement (1559–61) there. In 1698 a new Spanish colony was founded. Between 1719 and 1723 possession of Pensacola shifted between the Spanish and the French. The Spanish then held it until 1763, when it passed to the British. It again became Spanish in 1783, after its capture (1781) by Bernardo de Gálvez. It was the capital of West Florida until 1822. Although still Spanish, Pensacola was a British base in the War of 1812 until it was captured (1814) by Andrew Jackson. Relinquished by the United States, it was again seized (1818) by Jackson, and the United States took formal possession in 1821 after the purchase of Florida. During the Civil War, the city was abandoned (1862) to Union forces, but Fort Pickens had remained in Federal hands from the beginning. Much of the life of the city is related to the U.S. naval air station, established there in 1914. Eglin Air Force Base is in nearby Valparaiso. The Univ. of West Florida and a junior college are in Pensacola. Of interest are several historical museums and the naval-aviation museum at the air station. The ruins of old Fort Barrancas and of forts San Carlos (built in the 1780s), Pickens, and McRae (built in the 1830s) are on the shores of Pensacola Bay. The eastern section of Gulf Islands National Seashore is there.

Pensacola Bay, inlet of the Gulf of Mexico, 13 mi (21 km) long and c.2.5 mi (4 km) wide, NW Fla.; entered through a narrow channel between Santa Rosa Island and the mainland. The Escambia River flows into the bay from the north, near the city of Pensacola. The INTRACOASTAL WATERWAY passes through the bay, parts of which are included in Gulf Islands National Seashore (see NATIONAL PARKS AND MONUMENTS, table).

Pensacola Dam, 145 ft (44 m) high and 6,500 ft (1,980 m) long, on the Grand River (local name of the Neosho), NE Okla., NE of Tulsa; built 1938–41 by the state of Oklahoma. The dam impounds Lake of the Cherokees, one of the largest reservoirs in the United States; it is a major recreation area.

pension, periodic payments to one who has retired from work because of age or disability. Pensions, originally thought of as charity, are now viewed as an essential part of the social responsibility of employers or of the state. In the Roman Empire there was a well-established pension system to care for soldiers who were disabled or had grown old. The French government early in the 19th cent. and then the British (1834) made provision for superannuated public servants. In the United States pensions in various forms have been given veterans of all wars since the Revolution; military pensions are now covered by the Servicemen's and Veterans' Survivor Benefits Act passed in 1957. Retired servicemen and servicewomen receive, after 20 years' service, 50% of their base pay at time of retirement, with automatic increases as indicated by the consumer price index. Civil-service pensions were developed later in the United States than in Western Europe. Old-age pension plans were drawn up by cities for certain groups of public employees—firemen, policemen, and teachers—which provided for compulsory contributions from the employee. Pensions to Federal employees were authorized in 1920. The idea of extending such protection to all citizens also appeared earlier in Europe (notably in Germany) than in the United States, where it was a 20th-century development (see SOCIAL SECURITY). Many corporations and groups (such as labor unions, professional associations, and colleges) had made provision for pensions before the social security legislation was passed in 1935, and many groups now have pension plans that supplement social security. Until the 1940s, pension plans in private industry were set up primarily on the initiative of the employer. As workers gained the right to submit pension plans to collective bargaining, a growing number of plans were established; there are over 150,000 plans in the United States at present, with banks and insurance companies handling the majority of them. In the early 1970s legislative efforts at the Federal level were directed at protecting workers whose pension plans failed, e.g., in cases where a company declared bankruptcy, and at establishing Federal standards for private pension plans. See P. O. Dietz, *Pension Funds* (1966); D. M. Holland, *Private Pension Funds* (1966); Frank Kleiler, *European Regulation of Pension Plans* (1971; Joseph Melone, *Pension Planning* (1972).

Pentagon, the, building accommodating the U.S. Dept. of Defense. Located in Arlington, Va., across the Potomac River from Washington, D.C., the Pentagon comprises five concentric buildings, connected by corridors, covering an area of 34 acres (13.8 hectares). Completed in 1943, it is the largest office building in the world.

Pentagon Papers, government study of U.S. involvement in Southeast Asia. Commissioned by Secretary of Defense Robert S. McNamara in June, 1967, the 47-volume, top secret study covered the period from World War II to May, 1968. It was written by a team of analysts who had access to classified documents, and was completed in Jan., 1969. The study revealed a considerable degree of miscalculation, bureaucratic arrogance, and deception on the part of U.S. policymakers. In particular, it found that the U.S. government had continually resisted full disclosure of increasing military involvement in Southeast Asia—air strikes over Laos, raids along the coast of North Vietnam, and offensive actions by U.S. marines had taken place long before the American public was informed. On June 13, 1971, the New York *Times* began publishing a series of articles based on the study. The Justice Dept. obtained a court injunction against further publication on national security grounds, but the Supreme Court ruled (June 30) that constitutional guarantees of a free press overrode other considerations, and allowed further publication. The government indicted (1971) Daniel Ellsberg, a former government employee who made the Pentagon Papers available to the New York *Times,* and Anthony J. Russo on charges of espionage, theft, and conspiracy. On May 11, 1973, a Federal court judge dismissed all charges against them because of improper government conduct. See the New York *Times* ed., *The Pentagon Papers* (1971); S. J. Ungar, *The Papers and the Papers* (1972).

pentameter (pĕntăm'ətər) [Gr.,=measure of five], in prosody, a line to be scanned in five feet (see VERSIFICATION). The third line of Thomas Nashe's "Spring" is in pentameter: "Cold doth / not sting, / the pret / ty birds / do sing." Iambic pentameter, in which each foot contains an unaccented syllable and an accented syllable, is the most common English meter. Chaucer first used it in what was later called rhyme royal, seven iambic pentameters rhyming *ababbcc;* as Chaucer pronounced a final short *e,* his pentameters often end in an 11th, unstressed syllable. In his *Canterbury Tales* the pentameters are disposed in rhyming pairs. The pentameter couplet was used also by his imitators in Scotland, with the important difference that when the final *e* disappeared from speech the couplet became one of strict pentameters. This, known as the heroic couplet, became important in the 17th and 18th cent., notably in the hands of Dryden and Pope. Example:

True wit is Nature to advantage dress'd,
What oft was thought, but ne'er so well
express'd.
Pope, "Essay on Criticism"

Blank verse, a succession of unrhymed iambic pentameters, is primarily an English form and has been used in the loftiest epic and dramatic verse from Shakespeare and Milton to the present. Example:

And, like the baseless fabric of this vision,
The cloud-capp'd towers, the gorgeous palaces,
The solemn temples, the great globe itself,
Yea, all which it inherit, shall dissolve
And, like this insubstantial pageant faded,
Leave not a rack behind. We are such stuff
As dreams are made on, and our little life
Is rounded with a sleep.
Shakespeare, *The Tempest,* iv:1

The SONNET is one of the most familiar and successful uses of iambic pentameter in English poetry.

Pentastoma (pĕn'tăstō"mə), small phylum of fewer than 100 species of parasites living in the upper respiratory passages of reptiles, and occasionally of birds and mammals. The wormlike body, varying in length from ½ in. to 5 in. (1.3–13 cm), is unsegmented. The front of the body bears five short appendages; four of these are leglike, and the mouth is often located on the fifth prominence. Internal organs are much reduced, except the reproductive organs, which occupy most of the internal space. Eggs are released by the mature pentastomids and hatch when eaten by a suitable intermediate host. When the intermediate host, in turn, is eaten, the larvae migrate to the respiratory passages of the final host, where they take up permanent residence and mature.

Pentateuch (pĕn'tətyo͞ok) [Gr.,=five books], first five books of the OLD TESTAMENT.

pentathlon (pĕntăth'lən), composite athletic event. In ancient Greece it comprised leaping, foot racing, wrestling, discus throwing, and casting the javelin. The modern pentathlon, an OLYMPIC GAMES event since 1912, comprises a cross-country horseback ride, a cross-country run, a swimming race, foil fencing, and pistol shooting.

Pentecost (pĕn'təkôst) [Gr.,=fiftieth], important Jewish and Christian feasts, held in the spring. The Jewish feast of Pentecost, in Hebrew SHAVUOT, is the Palestinian celebration of the closing of the spring grain harvest, which began formally in Passover. On the Pentecost after the resurrection of Jesus (i.e., 50 days from the Passover, in which He was crucified), the Holy Ghost, according to Acts 2, descended on the disciples in the form of tongues of fire accompanied by the sound of a rush of wind, and gave them the power of speaking in such a way that people of different languages could understand them. The Christian feast of Pentecost is an annual commemoration of this event, and it is solemnly observed as the birthday of the church and the feast of the Holy Ghost. In ecclesiastical calendars Pentecost is the seventh Sunday after Easter and closes Eastertide. In the Western Church there are special observances, e.g., a penitential vigil, and in ancient times neophytes were baptized at this time. From the white garments of these converts comes Whitsunday, an English name for Pentecost. The Monday after is in many places a holiday, as in England, where it is called Whitmonday, or Whitsun Monday. The great Latin hymns VENI CREATOR SPIRITUS (sung in the divine office) and *Veni Sancte Spiritus* (the sequence of Mass) were composed for Pentecost. The Sunday after Pentecost is Trinity Sunday; until Advent the weeks are counted from Pentecost or Trinity.

Pentecostalism, fundamentalist Protestant religious movement that grew out of the holiness movement in the United States. It developed in the early 20th cent. Among the practices and beliefs of the Pentecostalists are baptism with the Holy Ghost, religious excitement accompanied by "speaking in tongues" (GLOSSOLALIA), faith healing, and the impending second coming of Christ. There are many Pentecostalist churches in the United States, the largest being the ASSEMBLIES OF GOD.

Pentelicus or **Pentelikon:** see PENDELIKÓN, Greece.

Penthesilea (pĕn"thĕsəlē'ə), in Greek mythology, an Amazon queen. In the Trojan War, she led a troop of Amazons against the Greeks. She was killed by Achilles, who then fell in love with her dead body.

Pentheus (pĕn'thēəs), in Greek mythology, king of Thebes, son of Cadmus' daughter Agave. When Dionysus came to Thebes, Pentheus denied his divinity and tried to prevent his ecstatic rites. The women of Thebes, led by Agave, were driven mad by the offended god and tore Pentheus to pieces. The story is the subject of Euripides' *Bacchae.*

Penticton, city (1971 pop. 18,146), S British Columbia, Canada, located where the Okanagan River flows into Okanagan Lake. It is a service and trade center for the Okanagan valley, a resort and fruit-growing area. There are canning plants and factories making wood and metal products.

pentimento (pĕn"təmĕn'tō), painter's term for the evidence in a work that the original composition has been changed. Often the opaque pigment with which the artist covered a mistake or unwanted beginning will, with time or injudicious cleaning, become transparent, and a disturbing revelation of original intentions will become visible through the finished composition. A celebrated example is El Greco's *Laocoön* (National Gall., Washington, D.C.), in which a bodyless head that had been painted out and repainted as a full-length figure further to the left was uncovered in the cleaning of the work.

Pentland Firth (pĕnt'lənd fûrth), channel, 6 to 8 mi (9.7–12.9 km) wide and c.14 mi (23 km) long, N Scotland. Connecting the North Sea with the Atlantic Ocean, it separates Caithness on the Scottish mainland from the Orkney Islands. The waters are rough and dangerous to small boats. There are small islands in the firth.

pentlandite (pĕnt'ləndīt), yellowish-bronze, opaque mineral, a sulfide of iron and nickel, $(Fe,Ni)_9S_8$. It is found in masses nearly always associated with the iron sulfide pyrrhotite. The largest deposit of this important ore of nickel is at Sudbury, Ont. Important deposits are mined in Manitoba, the USSR, and W Australia.

pentode: see GRID.

pentstemon (pĕnt"stē'mən): see FIGWORT.

Penuel (pənyo͞o'əl). **1** Unidentified place, E of the Jordan, in Gilead, by the river Jabbok where Jacob wrestled with the angel. It was destroyed by Gideon and later rebuilt by Jeroboam. Gen. 32.31; Judges 8.8; 1 Kings 12.25. Peniel: Gen. 32.30. **2** Founder of Gedor. 1 Chron. 4.4. **3** Benjamite chief. 1 Chron. 8.25.

penumbra (pĭnŭm'brə): see ECLIPSE.

penumbra rights, in U.S. law, those rights derived from specific guarantees in the Bill of Rights in the U.S. Constitution. For example, the First Amendment to the Constitution guarantees freedom of speech and press; this has been interpreted to include not only the rights to utter and print, but also the rights to distribute, receive, and read material. A right of privacy has been established from the right of association in the First Amendment, the freedom from unreasonable searches and seizures in the Fourth Amendment, and the right to refuse to incriminate oneself in the Fifth Amendment. The right of privacy was first developed in 1965 by Supreme Court Justice William O. Douglas in *Griswold* vs. *Connecticut*, when the court struck down a state statute forbidding the use of contraceptives. It was also one of the bases of the 1973 decisions recognizing the right of women to have abortions in the early term of pregnancy.

Penutian (pəno͞o'shən), linguistic family, or stock, of Indians of North and Central America. See AMERICAN INDIAN LANGUAGES.

Penza (pyĕn'zə), city (1970 pop. 374,000), capital of Penza oblast, S central European USSR, on the Sura River. It is a large railroad junction and the center of an extensive and fertile black earth district. There are machine, paper, and food-processing industries. Founded in 1666 as a fortress, Penza was occupied by Stenka Razin in 1670 and by Pugachev in 1774. Before the Bolshevik revolution, Penza was a major agricultural trading center.

Penzance (pĕnzăns'), municipal borough (1971 pop. 19,352), Cornwall, SW England, at the head of Mounts Bay. Penzance is the westernmost borough in England. It is a resort and a port for the Scilly Islands and has flour mills. Penzance Library has a notable Cornish collection. Penzance was sacked by the Spanish in 1595 and until the 18th cent. was subject to raids by Mediterranean pirates. Sir Humphry Davy was born there.

peonage (pē'ənĭj), system of involuntary servitude based on the indebtedness of the laborer (the peon) to his creditor. It was prevalent in Spanish America, especially in Mexico, Guatemala, Ecuador, and Peru. The system arose because labor was needed to support the agricultural, industrial, mining, and public works activities of conqueror and settler in the Americas. With the Spanish Conquest of the West Indies, the ENCOMIENDA, establishing proprietary rights over the Indians, was instituted. In 1542 the New Laws of Bartolemé de Las Casas were promulgated, defining Indians as free subjects of the king and prohibiting forced labor. Negro slave labor and wage labor were substituted. Since the Indians had no wage tradition and the amount paid was in any event pitifully small, the New Laws were largely ignored. To find a way out, the system of the *repartimiento* [assessment] and the *mita* was adopted; it gave the state the right to force its citizens, upon payment of a wage, to perform work necessary for the state. In practice, this meant that the Indian spent about one fourth of a year in public employment, but the remaining three fourths he was free to cultivate his own fields and provide for his own needs. Abuses under the system were frequent and severe, but the *repartimiento* was far less harsh and coercive than the slavery of debt peonage that followed independence from Spain in 1821. Forced labor had not yet included the working of plantation crops—sugar, cacao, cochineal, and indigo; their increasing value brought greater demand for labor control, and in the 19th cent. the cultivation of other crops on a large scale required a continuous and cheap labor supply. Through advances on wages, through requiring purchase of necessities from company-owned stores, and through loss of land that the Spanish government had set aside for his subsistence, the Indian found himself reduced to peonage, caught in a system from which there was little chance of escape. He could not change his employment until his debts were paid, and prices were so adjusted that he could not meet the obligations, while at the same time he inherited all the accumulated debts of deceased forebears. He became virtually a serf, but without the serf's customary rights. In Mexico a decree against peonage was issued in 1915, but the practice persisted. Partly to alleviate it, Lázaro Cárdenas instituted the EJIDO in 1936. In that year, too, debt peonage was abolished in Guatemala. In the United States after the Civil War, peonage existed in most Southern states as it had in the Southwest after its acquisition from Mexico. Not only Negroes and Mexicans but whites as well found themselves enmeshed. By the 20th cent., however, only a modified form of peonage called sharecropping persisted in the Southern states.

peony (pē'ənē), any plant of the genus *Paeonia* of the family Ranunculaceae (BUTTERCUP family), mostly Eurasian species popular as garden and florists' flowers. Herbaceous peonies (most varieties of *P. lactiflora*)—formerly and still sometimes called piney—are hardy, bushy perennials that die back each year. The large, usually spring-blooming, single or double flowers commonly range in shades from red to white. Tree peonies (*P. suffroticosa*) have a somewhat woody, persistent base and are usually taller than the herbaceous, with more abundant and larger blossoms; they often are very long lived but are less common in cultivation. Both kinds of peony have long been venerated in their native China and Japan. The peony was formerly regarded as both ornamental and medicinal—the roots were used to prevent convulsions. *P. brownii* is a species of small peony, not horticulturally important, that is native to the West Coast of North America. Peony is classified in the division MAGNOLIOPHYTA, class Magnoliopsida, order Ranunculales, family Ranunculaceae.

People's Charter: see CHARTISM.

People's party: see POPULIST PARTY.

Peor (pē'ôr) [Heb.,=opening], mountain, E of Jordan, to which Balak took Balaam to deliver his curses (Num. 23.28). In ancient times it was said to be near Heshbon. See BAAL-PEOR.

Peoria (pēôr'ēə), city (1970 pop. 126,963), seat of Peoria co., central Ill., on Lake Peoria and the Illinois River; inc. as a city 1845. A busy port of entry, it is the state's third most populous city and a regional trade and transportation point; grain, livestock, and coal from the area are marketed, processed, and shipped in Peoria. It has large distilleries, a brewery, and factories producing numerous heavy and light industrial goods. Although it is an industrial city, Peoria is known for its scenic beauty. La Salle established Fort Creve Coeur in the region in 1680, and the spot later became a French trading post. It was twice visited by military expeditions in the Revolutionary War. During the War of 1812 it was the scene of Indian depredations, and Fort Clark was built there in 1813. The first permanent American settlement was established in 1819. Bradley Univ. and a U.S. Dept. of Agriculture research laboratory are in the city. Nearby are a state park and Metamora courthouse (1845; now a state memorial).

Pepi I (pä'pē), fl. c.2325 B.C., king of ancient Egypt, of the VI dynasty. He was responsible for the rise of the official UNI. The reign of his son **Pepi II** (c.2275–c.2185 B.C.) is the longest recorded in history. It was successful because the powerful southern lords at Elephantine organized the Egyptian caravan trade route, which enabled expeditions to penetrate well into Nubia and carry on a prosperous trade with the Sudan and Punt as well as with Byblos in Phoenicia.

Pepin I (pĕp'ĭn), d. 838, king of Aquitaine (817–38), son of LOUIS I, emperor of the West. He joined in the uprisings of 830 and 833 against Louis, but each time helped to restore him shortly afterwards.

Pepin, Lake (pĕp'ĭn, pĭp'–), a widening of the Mississippi River, 21 mi (34 km) long and c.3 mi (5 km) wide, SE Minn., between Wabasha and Red Wing; formed by a natural dam of silt dropped by the Chippewa River. It is a popular recreation area.

Pepin of Heristal (Pepin II) (hĕr'ĭstəl), d. 714, mayor of the palace (680–714) of the Frankish kingdom of AUSTRASIA; grandson of PEPIN OF LANDEN and father of CHARLES MARTEL. After defeating the nobles of Neustria at the battle of Tertry (687), Pepin made himself ruler of all the Frankish kingdoms except Aquitaine, with the Merovingian dynasty retaining the nominal kingship. He defeated the Frisians, the Alemanni, and the Bavarians and established a strong government, thus laying the foundation for the empire of his descendants, the Carolingian mayors and kings.

Pepin of Landen (Pepin I), d. 639?, mayor of the palace of the Frankish kingdom of AUSTRASIA. With Arnulf, bishop of Metz, he called in King CLOTAIRE II of Neustria to overthrow (613) Queen BRUNHILDA of Austrasia. Clotaire II became king of Austrasia as well as Neustria but was forced to concede much of his authority to Pepin and Arnulf. From 623 they ruled Austrasia in the name of Clotaire's son DAGOBERT I, whom he had designated king. After Dagobert succeeded his father (629), Pepin lost his influence and withdrew into Aquitaine. By the marriage of Pepin's daughter with Arnulf's son, Pepin and Arnulf founded the CAROLINGIAN dynasty.

Pepin the Short (Pepin III), c.714–768, first Carolingian king of the FRANKS (751–68), son of CHARLES MARTEL and father of CHARLEMAGNE. Succeeding his father as mayor of the palace (741), he ruled Neustria, Burgundy, and Provence, while his brother CARLOMAN (d. 754) received Austrasia and what came to be Thuringia. In 743 the brothers chose Childeric III, a Merovingian, as nominal king of all the Franks. With their help St. Boniface effected far-reaching reforms that halted the decay of the Frankish church and advanced the conversion of the Saxons. After Carloman had retired (747) to religious life, Pepin, with the consent of the pope, St. Zacharias, forced Childeric into a monastery and had himself proclaimed king (751). In return for recognition by the pope, Pepin defended Rome against the Lombards (754, 756), from whom he wrested the exarchate of RAVENNA and other cities. These he ceded to the pope, thus laying the foundation of the PAPAL STATES.

Pepin also extended his territories and subdued AQUITAINE.

Pepper, Claude Denson, 1900–, U.S. Senator (1936–51) and Representative (1963–), b. Dudleyville, Ala. He was admitted (1928) to the bar, practiced law in Florida, and held many state offices. Elected to the Senate as a Democrat, Pepper proved himself an ardent supporter of social reform measures and a strong advocate of international cooperation. He was defeated in the 1950 Democratic primary for nomination to the U.S. Senate. He was elected to the House of Representatives in 1962.

Pepper, George Wharton, 1867–1961, American jurist, b. Philadelphia. Admitted (1889) to the bar, he practiced law in Philadelphia and was (1893–1910) professor of law at the Univ. of Pennsylvania. He lectured (1915) at Yale and was (1920–21) a member of the commission for revising the Pennsylvania constitution. Pepper was appointed in 1922 to the U.S. Senate to fill the vacancy caused by the death of Boies Penrose, and, elected on the Republican ticket later the same year, he served in the Senate until 1927. He wrote many books on law and was also the author of *In the Senate* (1930) and *Family Quarrels* (1931). See his autobiography, *Philadelphia Lawyer* (1944).

pepper, name for the fruits of several plants used as condiments or in medicine. **Black pepper** (*Piper nigrum*), the true pepper, is economically the most important species of the pantropical pepper family (Piperaceae). It is native to Java, whence it was introduced into other tropical countries, especially in the Orient, where it is now cultivated. A perennial climbing shrub, it bears pea-sized berries, the "peppercorns" of commerce. Black pepper, sold whole or ground, is the whole fruit; white pepper, made by removing the dark, outer hull, has a milder and less biting flavor. Pepper owes its pungency to a derivative of PYRIDINE. In the earliest days of commerce, black pepper was a great luxury and a staple article of trade between India and Europe. So high was its price that a few pounds made a royal gift, and the great demand was one of the causes of the search for a sea route to the East. Pepper was known to Hippocrates for its medicinal properties; it is a heart and kidney stimulant and is used as a powder or tincture, as a local irritant or liniment, or as a gargle. Other species of *Piper* are of value, particularly in the East Indies and the Pacific islands where they are indigenous. The leaves of the betel pepper (*P. betle*) are a principal ingredient of the masticatory BETEL. **Cubeb** is the name for the berry and for the oil obtained from the unripe berry of the East Indian climbing shrub *P. cubeba*. The dried fruits are sometimes used as a condiment or are ground and smoked in cigarette form as a catarrh remedy. The oil is used medicinally and also in soap manufacture. The masticated roots of *P. methysticum*, widely grown in its native Pacific islands, are made into a beverage called kavakava, which contains soporific alkaloids. It is an integral part of religious and social life there. The **red peppers,** native to warm temperate and tropical regions of America and widely cultivated elsewhere, are various species of *Capsicum* (of the NIGHTSHADE family), especially the numerous varieties of *C. frutescens*. These bushy, woody-stemmed plants were cultivated in South America prior to the time of Columbus, who is said to have taken specimens back to Europe. The "hot" varieties include **cayenne** pepper, whose dried, ground fruit is sold as a spice, and the **chili pepper**, sold similarly as a powder or in chili sauce (known in the United States by the trade name Tabasco). The chili pepper is much used in cooking in Mexico, where some 200 varieties are known. **Paprika** (the Hungarian name for red pepper) is a ground spice from a less pungent variety widely cultivated in Central Europe. The **pimiento,** or Spanish pepper, with a small fruit used as a condiment and for stuffing olives, and the sweet **red and green peppers,** with larger fruits used as table vegetables and in salads, are mild types. (The pimiento should not be confused with the PIMENTO or allspice, of the myrtle family.) A variety of *C. frutescens* with delicate leaves and cherrylike fruit is grown as an ornamental and house plant. True pepper is classified in the division MAGNOLIOPHYTA, class Magnoliopsida, family Piperaceae.

peppergrass, any species of the genus *Lepidium*, widely distributed peppery-tasting herbs of the family Cruciferae (MUSTARD family). They commonly have toothed leaves, clusters of small usually white flowers, and little flat, roundish pods that are often fed to tame birds, whence the name canary grass. Most species are weedy, but one—the garden cress (*Lepidium sativum*)—is sometimes cultivated as an annual salad plant. Shepherd's-purse (genus *Capsella*), often confused with peppergrass, has triangular pods. Peppergrass is classified in the division MAGNOLIOPHYTA, class Magnoliopsida, order Capparales, family Cruciferae.

pepperidge: see BLACK GUM.

peppermint: see MINT.

Pepperrell, Sir William, 1696–1759, American colonial military commander, b. Kittery Point, Maine (then part of Massachusetts). A wealthy merchant, landowner, and businessman, he became a colonel in the colonial militia, was a delegate to the Massachusetts General Court and a member of the governor's council, and was appointed chief justice in 1730. In 1745, in King George's War (see FRENCH AND INDIAN WARS), he commanded the land forces that, with a British fleet under Sir Peter Warren, captured the French fortress LOUISBURG, on Cape Breton, Canada. In recognition of this service, he was the first native American to be created baronet (1746). Sir William also commanded a regiment in the last of the French and Indian Wars, and as president of the council he briefly governed (1756–57) Massachusetts. His journal of the Louisburg expedition was published by the American Antiquarian Society in its *Proceedings*, Vol. XX (1911). See J. F. Sprague, *Three Men from Maine* (1924); study by Byron Fairchild (1954).

pepper tree: see SUMAC.

pepper-vine: see AMPELOPSIS.

pepperwood, name for several trees, among them the California LAUREL.

pepsin, enzyme produced in the mucosal lining of the stomach that acts to degrade protein. Pepsin is one of three principal protein-degrading, or proteolytic, enzymes in the DIGESTIVE SYSTEM, the other two being CHYMOTRYPSIN and TRYPSIN. The three enzymes were among the first to be isolated in crystalline form. During the process of digestion, pepsin breaks down dietary proteins to their components, i.e., PEPTIDES and AMINO ACIDS, which can be readily absorbed by the intestinal lining. In laboratory studies pepsin is most efficient in cleaving bonds involving the aromatic amino acids, phenylalanine, tryptophan, and tyrosine; however, pepsin attacks bonds between a variety of amino acids in whole proteins, which suggests that the enzyme is not specific in the natural state. Pepsin is synthesized in an inactive form by the stomach lining; hydrochloric acid, also produced by the gastric mucosa, is necessary to convert the inactive enzyme to its active form and to maintain the optimum acidity (*p*H 1–3) for pepsin function. Pepsin and other proteolytic enzymes are used in the laboratory analysis of various proteins; pepsin is also used industrially in the preparation of cheese and other protein-containing foods.

peptic ulcer: see ULCER.

peptide, organic compound composed of AMINO ACIDS linked together chemically by peptide bonds. The peptide bond always involves a single covalent bond between the oxygen-binding (carboxyl) carbon of one amino acid and the α-amino nitrogen of a second amino acid. In the formation of a peptide bond from two amino acids, a molecule of water is eliminated. Small peptides with fewer than about ten constituent amino acids are called oligopeptides, and peptides with more than ten amino acids are termed polypeptides. Compounds with molecular weights of more than 10,000 are usually termed proteins. Nearly all living tissues contain appreciable quantities of low-molecular-weight peptides that are neither derived from proteins nor utilized in protein structure. These molecules are of particular biochemical interest because they often incorporate many amino acids not found in proteins, including amino acids of the D-configuration. Among the biological peptides are many with physiological or antibacterial activity, such as the peptide hormones OXYTOCIN and vasopressin; ADRENOCORTICOTROPIC HORMONE (ACTH), secreted by the pituitary gland; and several cyclic peptides, in which the amino acid sequence forms a ring structure rather than a straight chain, such as the antibiotics tyrocidin and GRAMICIDIN. Laboratory synthesis of peptides has risen to the level of a well-defined art in recent years. Synthetic peptides, composed of as many as a hundred amino acids in specified sequence, have been prepared in the laboratory with good purity and high yields.

Pepusch, John Christopher (pā'po͞osh), 1667–1752, German musician, who lived in London from 1700 until his death. As a theorist he became expert in Greek music and helped found (1710) the Academy of Ancient Music. He was the predecessor of Handel as composer to the duke of Chandos. While director of Lincoln's Inn Theatre he wrote music, notably for John Gay's *The Beggar's Opera* (1728).

Pepys, Samuel (pēps), 1633–1703, English public official, author of the greatest diary in the English language, b. London, grad. Magdalene College, Cambridge, 1653. In 1656 he entered the service of a relative, Sir Edward Montagu (later earl of Sandwich), whose secretary he became in 1660. That same year he started as a clerk in the navy office and by 1668 he was an important naval official and owned a considerable estate. In 1672 he was made secretary to the admiralty. He sat in the Parliament of 1679, but he was charged with betraying naval secrets to the French in the same year. He was briefly imprisoned in the Tower but was vindicated and freed in 1680. In 1684 Pepys was reappointed secretary to the admiralty and was made president of the ROYAL SOCIETY. The accession of William III forced him into retirement, where he wrote his *Memoirs . . . of the Royal Navy* (1690). Pepys left his valuable library, including his diary in cipher, to his nephew John Jackson and in turn to Magdalene College, Cambridge. The diary was partially deciphered and in 1825 was first published; an almost complete text was edited by H. B. Wheatley (10 vol., 1893–99). An intimate record of the daily life and reflections of an ambitious, observing, and fun-loving young man, Pepys's diary extends from Jan. 1, 1660, to May 31, 1669, when failing eyesight forced him to stop writing. The diary gives a graphic picture of social life and conditions of the early Restoration period. See the diary (new ed., 9 vol., 1970–75) abridgment of the diary (ed. by O. F. Morshead, 1960); Pepys's letters (ed. by H. T. Heath, 1955); studies by P. Hunt (1958), C. Emden (1963), O. A. Mendelsohn (1963), M. H. Nicolson (1965), I. E. Taylor (1967), and R. Barber (1972).

Pequot Indians (pē'kwŏt), North American Indians whose language belongs to the Algonquian branch of the Algonquian-Wakashan linguistic stock (see AMERICAN INDIAN LANGUAGES). The Pequot were of the Eastern Woodlands cultural area. Originally they were united with the MOHEGAN INDIANS, but when UNCAS revolted, the Pequot moved southward to invade and drive off the Niantic. The warlike Pequot, under their chief, Sassacus, had by 1630 extended their territory W to the Connecticut River. Numerous quarrels between settlers in the Connecticut valley and the Pequot led to the Pequot War (1637). The precipitating cause was the murder of John OLDHAM, an English trader, by the Pequot. The English under John MASON and John UNDERHILL attacked the Pequot stronghold on the Pequot River and killed some 500 Indians. The remaining Pequot fled in small groups. One party went to Long Island, and a second escaped into the interior. A third, led by Sassacus, was intercepted near Fairfield, Conn.; here almost the entire party was killed or captured. The captives were forced into slavery under the colonists or were sold into the West Indies. A few Pequot, including Sassacus, who managed to escape were put to death by the Mohawk. A remnant of the Pequot were scattered among the S New England tribes; the colonial government later settled them in Connecticut. Some 35 Pequot lived on the Pequot Reservation in Connecticut in the early 1970s. See J. W. De Forest, *History of the Indians of Connecticut* (1851, repr. 1964).

Peraea (pērē'ə), in Roman times, the area E of the Jordan River, between the Sea of Galilee and the Dead Sea, and S of the DECAPOLIS.

Perak (pä'răk), state (1971 pop. 1,562,566), 8,030 sq mi (20,798 sq km), Malaysia, central Malay Peninsula, on the Strait of Malacca. Perak is bordered on the N by Thailand. The capital is IPOH; TAIPING is also important. The state is drained by the Perak River (c.200 mi/320 km long), which empties into the Strait of Malacca. In Perak, one of the most populous states of the federation, is the Kinta valley, an important tin-mining district. Chinese, mainly employed in the mines, constitute nearly half the population of the state; Malays, including the aboriginal Sakai, and Indians constitute the remainder. Rubber, coconut, and rice are the chief products. Fishing is a major industry. Before the 16th cent., Perak was the vassal state of the powers that in turn dominated the Malay Peninsula. After the fall of Malacca (1511), it was for a time dominated by the sultan of Acheh in Sumatra; in the 19th cent. it was invaded by Kedah at Siam's instigation. Civil war, augmented by disorders among the Chinese tin miners, plunged Perak in the 19th cent. into anarchy, and it became a British protectorate (1874). In 1896, Perak became one of the Federated Malay States, and in 1948 it became part of the Federation of Malaya. See MALAYSIA, FEDERATION OF. See J. F. McNair, *Perak and the Malays* (1878, repr. 1973).

Peralta Barnuevo, Pedro de (pā'thrō thā pārāl'tä bärnwä'vō), 1664–1743, Peruvian writer. Although his major literary interests were drama and poetry, he also wrote on astronomy, mathematics, and history. His play *La rodoguna* (1710) shows the influence of CORNEILLE. Other works are *Triunfos de amor y poder* [triumphs of love and power] (1711), a play in the Baroque tradition; and *Lima fundada o conquista del Perú* [the founding of Lima or conquest of Peru] (1732).

Perazim (pĕr'əzĭm): see BAAL-PERAZIM.

perception, in psychology, mental organization and interpretation of sensory information. One of the main concerns in psychology is the relation between variations in stimulus and response. Perceptual response is influenced by a variety of factors, including properties of the stimulus such as intensity and physical dimensions; activities of the sense organs, such as effects of preceding stimulation; the subject's experience, such as past learning; attention factors such as readiness to respond to a stimulus; and motivation and emotional states of the subject. Perception involves integration of information into mental structures, i.e., perceiving relations among objects. The organization of visual elements has been studied in GESTALT psychology. In visual organization the stimulus elements form perceived patterns according to their nearness to each other; their similarity; the tendency for one element to lead into another; the tendency for the subject to perceive complete figures in stimulus elements; and the ability to differentiate figures from a background. Constancy is the tendency of a subject to interpret an object in the same way regardless of visual variations. Three-dimensional, or depth, perception is produced by a variety of visual cues indicating perspective and, within the eyes, by a slight disparity in the images of an object on the two retinas. Perception in the other senses also involves patterning and cues. Threshold is the minimal amount of change in a stimulus that can be consciously detected by the subject. Subliminal perception is unconscious perception of stimuli below the threshold level. Extrasensory perception is perception of stimuli through no known sensory process (see PARAPSYCHOLOGY).

Percé Rock (pĕrsā'), E Que., Canada, just off the tip of the Gaspé Peninsula. It is a massive rock (1,420 ft/433 m long; c.300 ft/90 m wide; and 290 ft/88 m at the highest point), rising sheer from the Atlantic. It takes its name from an arch 50 ft (15 m) high near its seaward end. With nearby Bonaventure Island, it is a well-known tourist attraction.

Perceval, Spencer, 1762–1812, British statesman. He had a profitable law practice before he entered the House of Commons as a Tory in 1796. He was solicitor general (1801–2), attorney general (1802–6), and, under the duke of Portland, chancellor of the exchequer (1807–9) before becoming prime minister in 1809. Although he opposed (1811) the regency of the prince of Wales (later George IV), he continued in office under the prince. Despite conflicts with the duke of Wellington over the financing of the Peninsular War and despite a lack of solid parliamentary support, Perceval tenaciously and effectively carried on the war against Napoleonic France. He was assassinated in the House of Commons by a bankrupt madman. See biography by Dennis Gray (1963).

perch, common name for some members of the family Percidae, symmetrical freshwater fishes of N Europe, Asia, and North America. The perch belongs to the large order Perciformes (spiny-finned fishes) and is related to the sunfishes and the sea basses. Best known is the yellow (also called red) perch (*Perca flavescens*), a popular game and food fish abundant in lakes and large streams, where it feeds on insects, crayfish, and small fish and grows to an average length of 1 ft (30 cm) and weight of 1 lb (.5 kg). The voracious walleye, or walleyed pike (*Stizostedion vitreum*), another member of the family, is darker and larger (up to 10 lb/4.5 kg). Very similar to the walleye but slenderer and smaller is the Eastern sauger, or sand pike (*S. canadense*). The native American darters (2–3 in/5–8 cm), found E of the Rockies, are a subfamily containing many species, most of them brilliantly colored. Of separate families are the pirate perch, a chubby little fish of sluggish streams and bayous (family Aphredoderidae), and the trout perch, or sand roller, a small fish abundant in the Great Lakes (family Mugiloididae). Perches are classified in the phylum CHORDATA, subphylum Vertebrata, class Osteichthyes, order Perciformes, family Percidae.

Perche (pĕrsh), region and former county, NW France, in portions of Orne, Eure-et-Loir, and Eure depts. ALENÇON, an important town of the region, is world famous for its lace. Horse breeding is a significant industry, and Perche has given its name to the PERCHERON HORSE. Much of the region is forested, and there are many apple orchards and grasslands. Perche was attached to the French crown in 1525.

Percheron horse (pûr'chərŏn''), breed of DRAFT HORSE developed in NW France, originally of Flemish origin, but also containing some Arabian blood (see ARABIAN HORSE). For a heavy horse, it has considerable stamina and is a good trotter. It was used by armored knights during the Middle Ages and also later for extensive general freight work. Once the most popular draft horse in America, the breed is known for its beauty and is still popular as a circus horse. It averages over 16 hands (64 in./160 cm) high, weighs at least 2,000 lb (900 kg), and is usually black or gray in color.

perchlorate: see CHLORATE.

Percier, Charles (shärl pĕrsyā'), 1764–1838, French architect. He won (1786) the Grand Prix de Rome, and in 1794 he became associated with P. F. L. Fontaine. Napoleon appointed them as government architects, and this post lasted until the emperor's fall. In the development of the Empire style under Napoleon's official sponsorship, Percier and Fontaine became its official interpreters, not only for Paris but also in Antwerp, Brussels, and Rome, where they designed many residences. They worked (1802–12) on the palaces of the Louvre and the Tuileries, designed the Arc de Triomphe du Carrousel, and did alterations and decorations for the imperial châteaux of Versailles, Malmaison, Compiègne, and Saint-Cloud. As interior decorators they designed every detail of furniture, fabric, hardware, and wallpaper in conformity with Empire motives. The partnership dissolved in 1814, and Percier thereafter conducted a student atelier. With Fontaine he published several books on architecture in Rome and interior decoration.

Percivale, Sir: see ARTHURIAN LEGEND and PARSIFAL.

percussion instrument, any instrument that produces musical sound when its surface is struck with an implement (such as a mallet, a stick, or a disk) or with the hand. Perhaps the most universally familiar percussion instrument is the DRUM, common to the most primitive as well as the most sophisticated musical arts. Sticks clicked against each other are another simple form of percussion. These are related to CASTANETS, CYMBALS, and the TRIANGLE. Among the percussion instruments used in the West are the BELL, the CELESTA, the GLOCKENSPIEL, and the XYLOPHONE (marimba). In general, percussion instruments are not tuned by construction; pitch, tone, and volume depend on the skill of the performer. See GONG, KETTLEDRUM, SNARE DRUM, TAMBOURINE, and TOM-TOM.

Percy, family name of dukes and earls of NORTHUMBERLAND.

Percy, George, 1580–1631?, English colonial official in Virginia. He sailed to Virginia with the expedition of 1606–7 and was deputy governor (1609–10) after John Smith's return to England and, later, in the absence (1611) of Sir Thomas Gates. In 1612, Percy himself returned to England. He wrote *A True Relation of . . . Virginia* (c.1622) in self-defense after another writer (presumably John Smith) had criticized Percy's leadership in the "starving time." He also wrote a *Discourse of the Plantation of . . . Virginia.*

Percy, Sir Henry, 1366–1403, English nobleman, called Hotspur or Henry Hotspur; son of Henry Percy, 1st earl of NORTHUMBERLAND. Knighted in 1377, he aided his father in the Scottish Marches. In 1388 he participated in the famous battle of Otterburn, or Chevy Chase, against the Scots; he was captured but later ransomed, and he returned to his post of warden of Carlisle and the West Marches. He went to Calais in 1391 and served (c.1393–1395) as governor of Bordeaux, but by 1398 he was back on the Scottish border. He and his father joined the cause of Henry of Lancaster. After Henry's accession as HENRY IV, Hotspur was called upon to take command of the Welsh border. Sent once again to the defense of the Scottish border, he helped to win (1402) a notable victory over the Scots at Homildon Hill, capturing the Scottish leader, Archibald DOUGLAS, 4th earl of Douglas. A bitter quarrel between Hotspur and Henry IV ensued when Hotspur refused to turn Douglas over to the king except in exchange for the ransom of Sir Edmund de MORTIMER, Hotspur's brother-in-law. In 1403, Hotspur and his father planned with Thomas Percy, earl of WORCESTER, OWEN GLENDOWER, and Sir Edmund de Mortimer to dethrone Henry and crown Edmund MORTIMER, 5th earl of March, the nephew of Hotspur's wife. Henry anticipated the move, and in a battle near Shrewsbury (1403) the king was victorious and Hotspur was slain.

Percy, Thomas, 1729–1811, English antiquary and churchman, b. Shropshire. In 1782 he became Protestant bishop of Dromore (Ireland). He achieved literary fame as the editor of the *Reliques of Ancient English Poetry* (3 vol., 1765), a collection of 176 English and Scottish ballads. Its publication initiated a general interest in earlier literary forms and exercised a great influence on the romantic poets in Germany as well as England. See his letters (ed. by C. Brooks and D. N. Smith, 6 vol., 1944–61).

Percy, Walker, 1916–, American novelist, b. Birmingham, Ala. Trained as a physician, Percy turned to writing after he contracted tuberculosis and was forced to retire from practice. His novels *The Movie Goer* (1961) and *The Last Gentlemen* (1966) concern Southern Christian gentlemen who are feeling the impact of changing times. *Love in the Ruins: The Adventures of a Bad Catholic At A Time near the End of the World* (1971) is a science fiction satire written in characteristically cultivated prose.

Perdiccas (pərdĭk'əs), d. 321 B.C., Macedonian general under Alexander the Great. After the death of Alexander (323) he ruled as regent from Babylon. He strove in vain to hold the empire together, but was opposed by others of the DIADOCHI. He was defeated by Ptolemy I in Egypt and was killed in a mutiny of his troops.

Perdido, Monte (mōn'tā pārthē'thō), Fr. *Mont Perdu,* peak, 11,007 ft (3,355 m) high, NE Spain, near the French border. It is one of the highest peaks of the Pyrenees.

Perdu, Mont: see PERDIDO, MONTE.

Pereda, José María de (hōsā' märē'ä dā pārā'thä), 1833–1906, Spanish novelist. His stories are laid chiefly in his native Santander. An aristocrat by birth, he wrote sympathetically of the peasants but satirically of the bourgeoisie. His colorful descriptions of local landscape are preeminent in his *Escenas montañesas* [mountain scenes] (1864), a collection of stories and episodes, and *El sabor de la tierruca* [the taste of the earth] (1881). *Sotileza* (1884) and *Peñas arriba* (1894), among his best-known novels, are vivid regional works.

Père David's deer (pĕr dävēdz'), Asian deer, *Elaphurus davidianus,* known only in a semidomesticated state. It has a bulky, donkeylike body, reaching a shoulder height of nearly 4 ft (120 cm), with a tufted tail longer than that of any other deer. It is tawny red with white underparts and a white ring around each eye. Its hooves are very broad. It has curious antlers, with irregularly branching front prongs and usually straight posterior prongs. The antlers may reach 3 ft (90 cm) in length. *E. davidianus* came to the attention of Westerners in 1865, when it was observed by the missionary Père Armand David in the gardens of the Chinese emperor, near Peking. Several specimens were sent to Europe, where they flourished in captivity; those remaining in China all perished during the Boxer Rebellion. After World War II, breeding stock from England was distributed to the world's zoos, and in 1960 the species was reestablished in China. The natural habitat of this deer is unknown, but it is believed to have inhabited the swampy plains of China until it was displaced by agriculture. It is classified in the phylum CHORDATA, subphylum Vertebrata, class Mammalia, order Artiodactyla, family Cervidae.

peregrine falcon: see FALCON.

Peregrinus, Petrus (Peter the Pilgrim) (pē'trəs pĕrəgrī'nəs), c.1220–?, medieval scholar and soldier. The tutor of Roger Bacon, he wrote the first important study of magnetism, *Epistola de Magnete,* in which he described simple magnetic attraction and repulsion. He improved the compass by placing the lodestone on a pivot and surrounding it with a graduated directional scale. His ideas were further elaborated in the 16th cent. by William Gilbert.

Pereira, I. Rice (Irene Rice Pereira) (pərā'rə), 1907–71, American painter, b. Chelsea, Mass. In 1935, Pereira helped found the Federal Art Project design laboratory and taught there for several years. Her mature painting style is characterized by the play of light and space through open, framelike forms juxtaposed against bands or lines in mazelike patterns. These suspended forms and ambiguous spaces are conscious efforts to express in abstract art the idea of fourth-dimensional space. Pereira experimented with glass, parchment, plastics, and other materials.

A representative work is *Oblique Progression* (Whitney Mus., New York City). She was the author of several books including *The Nature of Space* (1956) and *The Transcendental Formal Logic of the Infinite* (1966). See John Baur, *Loren MacIver, I. Rice Pereira* (1953).

Pereira, Nun'Álvares (no͞on″äl′vərĭsh pərā′rə), 1360–1431, Portuguese hero, called the Great Constable. He was the friend, counselor, and general of JOHN I of Portugal. As a leader of the popular revolt against Castilian domination, he helped John to gain the throne and was the hero of the decisive Portuguese victory (1385) at Aljubarrota. In 1415 he took part in the conquest of Ceuta in N Africa. An astute statesman and able strategist, Nun'Álvares was also noted for his religious devotion and for his personal virtue. He ended his years as a monk in a Carmelite monastery that he founded in Lisbon and was beatified by Pope Benedict XV in 1918; his feast is Nov. 6. His daughter Beatriz married Alfonso, an illegitimate son of John I; from this union came the house of Braganza. See biography by Eliseo Battaglia (tr. 1962).

Pereira (pārā′rä), city (1968 est. pop. 216,200), capital of Risaralda dept., W central Colombia, in the upper Cauca valley. It is a major distribution center for coffee and cattle and for the mineral resources (gold and silver) of the region.

Perekop, Isthmus of (pĕrĭkôp′), c.19 mi (30 km) long and from 5 to 14 mi (8–23 km) wide, SW European USSR, in the Ukraine, connecting the Crimea with the Ukrainian mainland. It separates the Gulf of Perekop (an arm of the Black Sea) in the west from the Sivash Sea (an inlet of the Sea of Azov) in the east. Because of its strategic position and economic importance (salt extraction from the lakes in the southern part), the Greeks and Tatars fortified the isthmus with moats and ramparts and the Tatars built a fortress on the site of the village of Perekop and called it Or-Kapi; there are ruins of the Greek and Tatar fortifications. The Greeks and Byzantines called the isthmus Taphros. Before the 15th cent. there was a Genoese colony there. The isthmus passed to Russia in 1783. There the Red Army decisively defeated (1920) Wrangel in the Russian civil war. In 1944 the Germans were routed out of the Crimea north of the isthmus. The isthmus was transferred with the Crimea to the Ukrainian SSR in 1954.

Père-Lachaise: see CEMETERY; LA CHAISE, FRANÇOIS D'AIX DE.

Peremyshl: see PRZEMYŚL, Poland.

perennial, any plant that under natural conditions lives for several to many growing seasons, as contrasted to an annual or a biennial. Botanically, the term *perennial* applies to both woody and herbaceous plants (see STEM) and thus includes innumerable members of the kingdom. In horticulture, however, the term is usually restricted to hardy herbaceous perennials, particularly border plants such as alyssum, chrysanthemum, iris, peony, phlox, pink, and tulip, all of which characteristically die down to the ground each year and survive the winter on food stored in specialized underground stems (corms, rhizomes, and tubers; bulbous plants are not considered perennials). Perennials form seeds each year after reaching maturity, but since plants grown from seed do not normally bloom until the second season (unless forced), most garden perennials are propagated by dividing the rootstocks (see PROPAGATION OF PLANTS). In fact, division every few years—as well as judicious pruning—is usually necessary to prevent the plant's becoming straggly and weak. Perennials, including the woody perennials, may have a rest period of some duration during their life cycle. In the seed this period, called dormancy, precedes germination; in the plant different parts rest at different times and resume growth independently, e.g., the buds of deciduous plants, which form in late summer and remain dormant until spring. Even in tropical areas where plants appear to bloom and to retain their leaves the year round, some plants lose all their leaves for a brief period and others grow new and drop old leaves on a continuing basis, as do most conifers. See R. W. Cumming and R. E. Lee, *Contemporary Perennials* (1960); J. U. Crockett, *Perennials* (1972).

Peresh (pē′rĕsh), son of Machir the Manassite. 1 Chron. 7.16.

Pereslavl-Zalesski (pĕrĕəslä′vəl-zəlyĕs′kē), city (1970 est. pop. 30,000), central European USSR. It has industries that produce textiles, film, and food products. The city was founded in 1152, was included in the Suzdal principality, and from 1175 to 1302 was the capital of an independent principality; it passed to Moscow in 1302. The city is on Lake Pleshcheyevo (19 sq mi/49 sq km), where Peter I built the first ships of the Russian navy. Remains of the flotilla are in a nearby museum. Architectural remains include the earthen rampart of a fortress (founded 1152), the white stone Spaso-Preobrazhenski Cathedral (1152–57), the largest preserved monument of the 12th cent. in the area, and the Nikitski Cathedral (1561–64). The city was formerly called Pereyaslavl-Zalesski, and the lake was known as Lake Pereyaslavl.

Peretz or **Perez, Isaac Loeb** (both: pĕr′ĕts; lōb′), 1852–1915, Jewish poet, novelist, playwright, and lawyer, b. Zamosc, Poland. A voice of the Haskalah, or Jewish Enlightenment, Peretz was often accused of radicalism and once imprisoned for his socialist activities. In his first writings he described the material poverty and spiritual riches of European Jews. His early work was written in Hebrew and most of his later work in Yiddish. All of his writings are imbued with a warm understanding of Jewish life. His finest work is contained in his highly imaginative and sympathetic Hasidic sketches, such as *Stories and Pictures* (1900–1901, tr. 1906). Selections from his works were published (1947) in Yiddish and English. See A. Roback, *I. L. Peretz, Psychologist of Literature* (1935); Maurice Samuel, *Prince of the Ghetto* (1948); Moshe Spiegel, *In this World and the Next* (1958).

Pereyaslav-Khmelnitski (pĕrĕəsläv′-khmĭlnyĭt′skē), town, W central European USSR, in the Ukraine, on the Trubezh River. It was known in 907 and served as the fortified capital of the duchy of Pereyaslavl (11th–13th cent.). By 1239 the city was in ruins after Tatar attacks. In the second half of the 16th cent. it began to grow as a center of the Ukrainian Cossacks. In 1654, Bohdan CHMIELNICKI and his Cossacks met at Pereyaslavl to agree that Ukraine, for protection against Poland, become a protectorate of Russia. This alliance, however, led to the complete domination of the Ukraine by Russia in spite of guarantees to the people of the Ukraine of their rights and liberties. It is on this agreement that all later Ukrainian claims to autonomy were based (see UKRAINE). The city was called Pereyaslavl until 1943, when it was renamed in honor of Chmielnicki. Besides a historical museum, it has remains of the Cathedral of St. Michael (founded 1089), the monastery of St. Michael (17th–18th cent.), and the Cathedral of the Ascension (1695–1700).

Pereyaslavl-Zalesski: see PERESLAVL-ZALESSKI, USSR.

Perez (pē′rĕz), variant of PHARES.

Pérez, Antonio (äntô′nyō pā′rĕth), b. 1534 or 1539, d. 1611, Spanish politician. Ambitious and unscrupulous, he became secretary to King Philip II and was, with the princesa de EBOLI, a center of court intrigues. In 1578, Juan de ESCOBEDO, secretary to Don John of Austria, then governor of the Netherlands, was assassinated, and the following year Pérez was arrested for the murder. What actually happened is a matter of historical speculation, but the most probable train of events is that Perez instigated the murder after Escobedo threatened to reveal Pérez's political intrigues (possibly the fact that he was negotiating with the Dutch rebels) to the king. The suspicious Philip was probably told by Pérez that Escobedo was plotting treason, and the king almost certainly approved the murder. Pérez was prosecuted on various charges until in 1590 he fled to Saragossa, where he placed himself in the hands of the authorities of his native Aragón. He then openly accused Philip of having ordered Escobedo's murder. The king contested the procedure and ordered the Inquisition to claim jurisdiction, accusing Pérez of heresy. The case became a struggle between Philip and the people of Aragón, who, jealous of their privileges, sided with Pérez and revolted; the rising was ruthlessly suppressed (1591). Pérez fled (1591) to France and later England. See biography by Gregorio Marañón (tr. 1955).

Pérez, Carlos Andrés (kär′lōs ändrās′ pä′rās), 1922–, president of Venezuela (1974–). An aide to President Rómulo Betancourt, he was secretary of the interior in Betancourt's second administration (1959–64). He became secretary of the Democratic Action party in 1967. Elected president in Dec., 1973, he instituted a sweeping economic policy, aimed at the nationalization of the oil and the iron and steel industries and eventual Venezuelan control of other foreign enterprises.

Perez, Isaac Loeb: see PERETZ, ISAAC LOEB.

Pérez, Juan (hwän pā′räth), d. 1774, Spanish colonial naval officer, explorer on the coast of the Pacific Northwest. He commanded a vessel in an expedition to San Diego under general command of Gaspar de Portolá, and in 1774 he was in command of a fleet sent by the Spanish viceroy to investigate Russian advances down the northern coast, to visit the coast to lat. 60°N, and to take formal possession for Spain. He sailed from Monterey northward, but was prevented from landing by bad weather and turned back at lat. 55°N. He encountered the natives of Queen Charlotte Island, sighted Vancouver Island, and on Aug. 8, 1774, discovered Nootka Sound, which he called the harbor of San Lorenzo. He reached Monterey late in August and died at sea while bound for San Blas. The diary of one of the chaplains, Juan Crespi, gives a fine narrative of the voyage.

Pérez de Ayala, Ramón (rämōn′ pā′räth dā äyä′lä), 1880?–1962, Spanish writer. He was educated at Jesuit schools, which he satirized in the novel *A.M.D.G.* (1910). His early realistic novels, among them *The Fox's Paw* (1912, tr. 1924), reveal ties with the GENERATION OF '98. After 1916 his novels became increasingly mature and lyrical; his characters became symbolic representatives of general human problems. To this period belongs his masterpiece, *Belarmino y Apolonio* (1921), a droll and profound story of two Oviedo cobblers. *La paz del sendero* [the peace of the path] (1903), *El sendero innumerable* (1916), and *El sendero andante* (1921), his major poetic works, show the influence of French symbolism. He also wrote satiric essays and dramatic criticism. Pérez de Ayala was an early supporter of the Spanish republic, serving as its ambassador to London (1931–36). He resigned the post in 1936 as his sympathies moved to the right.

Pérez de Montalván, Juan (hwän pā′räth dā mōntälvän′), 1602–38, Spanish dramatic poet and novelist. Pérez de Montalván was the close friend and biographer of Lope de Vega. He wrote 48 plays; among the most successful of them was *Los amantes de Teruel* [the lovers of Teruel]. His eight novels enjoyed great popularity as well.

Pérez Galdós, Benito (bānē′tō pā′rĕth gäldōs′), 1843–1920, Spanish novelist and dramatist, b. Canary Islands. At 20 he went to Madrid, where he spent most of his adult life. For his masterly treatment of the vast panorama of Spanish society, he has been called the greatest Spanish novelist since Cervantes. His many works include a cycle of 46 historical novels, *Episodios nacionales*, which relates episodes in Spanish history from 1805 to the end of the century. *Doña Perfecta* (1876, tr. 1880) and *La familia de Léon Roch* (1878, tr. 1886) are among his better-known didactic novels. *La desheredada* [the disinherited] (1881) introduced a series of 21 novels on contemporary society, in which he sought to discover the cause of Spanish social decay. His plays were less successful than his novels. In 1897 he was elected to the Royal Academy, and in 1907 he became deputy of the republican party in Madrid. He went blind in 1912 but continued to dictate his books until his death. Among his works in English translation are *Tristana* (tr. 1961) and *Compassion* (tr. 1962). See study ed. by J. E. Varey (1970); bibliography by T. A. Sackett (1968).

Pérez Jiménez, Marcos (mär′kōs pā′rās hēmā′nās), 1914–, president of Venezuela (1952–58). An army colonel, he was a member of the three-man junta that overthrew President Rómulo Gallegos in 1948. After one of the junta members was mysteriously killed, he emerged (1952) as self-appointed president. He imposed a harsh dictatorship and spent money lavishly on highways and tourist attractions, especially in Caracas. He was ousted by a popular revolt in Jan., 1958. He lived in exile in Miami, Fla., until 1963, when he was extradited to Venezuela on charges of embezzling some $13 million during his presidential tenure. He was imprisoned (1963–68) and after his release was exiled to Madrid.

Perez-uzza or **Perez-uzzah** (both: pē′rĕz-ŭz′ə), threshing floor where Uzzah touched the Ark and died. It had previously been called Chidon or Nachon. Its exact location is unknown but it was probably somewhere W of Jerusalem. 2 Sam. 6.6–8; 1 Chron. 13.9–11.

perfect: see TENSE.

Perfectionists: see NOYES, JOHN HUMPHREY.

perfume, aroma produced by the essential oils of plants and by synthetic aromatics. The burning of INCENSE that accompanied the religious rites of ancient China, Palestine, and Egypt led gradually to the personal use of perfume. In Greece, where flower scents were first developed, the use of perfume became widespread. In Rome perfume was used extravagantly. During the Middle Ages the Crusaders brought the knowledge of perfumery back to Europe from the East. It was at this time that animal substances were first added as fixatives—MUSK, AMBERGRIS, CIVET, and castor (from the beaver). Italian perfumers settled in Paris (after 1500), and thereafter France became the leader of the industry. After 1500 scents became fashionable; both men and women wore an ornamental pomander or pouncet-box (dry-scent box), which hung from the waist. Each wealthy household had a "still room" where perfume was prepared by the women. Since the early 19th cent., chemists have analyzed many essential oils and have produced thousands of synthetics, some imitating natural products and others yielding new scents. Most perfumes today are blends of natural and synthetic scents and of fixatives that equalize vaporization of the blends and add pungency. The ingredients are usually combined with alcohol for liquid scents and with fatty bases for many cosmetics. Leading producers of perfume oils are the East Indies, Réunion island, and the South of France. Bulgaria and Turkey are noted for ATTAR OF ROSES, Algeria for geranium oils, Italy for citrus oils, and England for lavender and mint. The great fashion houses of Paris are renowned for perfumes that carry their names. See EAU DE COLOGNE. See Edward Sagarin, *The Science and Art of Perfumery* (2d ed. 1955); Roy Genders, *Perfume through the Ages* (1972).

Perga (pûr'gə), ancient city of Pamphylia, S Asia Minor, 10 mi (16 km) NE of the modern Antalya, Turkey. It was the seat of an Asiatic nature goddess. St. Paul came here on his first journey (Acts 14.25). The ruins of Perga include a theater and a stadium.

Pergamum (pûr'gəməm), ancient city of NW Asia Minor, in Mysia (modern Turkey), in the fertile valley of the Caicus. It became important c.300 B.C., after the breakup of the Macedonian empire, when a Greek family (the Attalids) established a brilliant center of Hellenistic civilization. The kingdom achieved major importance under Attalus I (d. 197 B.C.), Eumenes II (d. 160 or 159), and Attalus II (d. 138). These kings followed a pro-Roman policy through fear of the imperialism of Philip V of Macedon and of Antiochus III of Syria. The independence of Pergamum ended dramatically when Attalus III (d.133) bequeathed the kingdom to the Roman people. The chief glory of Pergamum was its sculpture, at two periods. The first Pergamene school (c.250–200) celebrated the decisive victory (c.230) of Attalus I over the Galatians; the Dying Gaul is an example of the realism of the art. The later period (200–150) produced a frieze for a great altar of Zeus, glorifying especially the defeat (190) of Antiochus III of Syria at MAGNESIA. Pergamum was the birthplace of GALEN. The cultured Pergamene rulers also built up a library second only to the one at Alexandria. One of the library's specialties was the use of PARCHMENT, which takes its name from the city. Eventually the library was given by Antony to Cleopatra. Under Rome, Pergamum was reconstituted as the province of Asia, and Ephesus rapidly eclipsed Pergamum as the chief city of Asia Minor. Pergamum accepted Christianity early; it was one of the Seven Churches of Asia (Rev.1.11; 2.12). Various forms of the name are Pergamus, Pergamon, and Pergamos. See E. V. Hansen, *The Attalids of Pergamon* (1947); R. B. McShane, *Foreign Policy of the Attalids of Pergamum (1964)*.

Pergolesi, Giovanni Battista (jōvän'nē bät-tēs'tä pārgōlā'zē), 1710–36, Italian composer of the Neapolitan school. Although he died at the age of 26, he is credited with masterpieces in two fields of music: *La serva padrona* (*The Maid as Mistress,* 1733), an intermezzo, or short comic opera; and a setting of the *Stabat Mater* for treble voices and strings. His fame rests chiefly on the popularity of *La serva padrona,* although much of his best music is contained in two serious operas, *Salustia* (1731) and *L'Olimpiade* (1735).

Peri, Jacopo (yä'kōpō pē'rē), 1561–c.1633, Italian composer and singer. *Dafne* (c.1597), perhaps the first opera, was composed by both Peri and Jacopo Corsi. The librettist, Ottavio Rinuccini, also wrote *Euridice,* which Peri and Caccini set to music (1600). The music for this opera was performed at the wedding of Henry IV of France to Marie de' Medici.

peri (pēr'ē), in Persian mythology, supernatural being. Peris were said to be fallen angels who were denied paradise until they did penance. Originally agents of evil, in later mythology they were identified as benevolent spirits.

Periander (pěr'ēăn"dər), d. 585 B.C., one of the SEVEN WISE MEN OF GREECE, tyrant of Corinth. His rule raised his city to a high state of prosperity, and he established friendly relations with other rulers. He established colonies at Potidaea (now Néa Potídhaia) and probably at Apollonia near the Adriatic coast, and he fought successfully against Epidaurus and Corcyra (now Kérkira). During his reign the arts flourished, as is evidenced by the ruins of the Apollo temple and the Peirene fountain at Corinth and the Gorgon pediment at Corcyra.

periastron (pěr"ēăs'trən): see APSIS.

Peribonca (pěrĭbŏng'kə), river, c.280 mi (450 km) long, rising in the Otish Mts., central Que., Canada, and flowing S through Peribonca Lake to Lake St. John. It is an important source of hydroelectric power.

pericardium: see HEART.

Pericles (pěr'ĭklēz), c.495–429 B.C., Athenian statesman. He was a member of the ALCMAEONIDAE family through his mother, a niece of Cleisthenes. He first came to prominence as an opponent of the AREOPAGUS (462) and as one of the prosecutors of CIMON, whom he replaced in influence. From then on he was the popular leader in Athens. As strategos, or military commander, c.454 he campaigned unsuccessfully against Sicyon and Oeniadae, and his plans to bring these Peloponnesian regions under Athenian control failed. While in Athens between campaigns, Pericles carried through a number of reforms that advanced democracy. As a result, all officials in Athens were paid salaries by the state and every office was opened to most citizens. In 451–450 he limited citizenship to those of Athenian parentage on both sides. He made an attempt, probably in 448, to call a Panhellenic conference, but Spartan opposition defeated his effort. Under Pericles the DELIAN LEAGUE reached its maximum efficiency as an instrument of Athenian imperialism; in 446 Pericles destroyed Euboea (now Évvoia), which had revolted against the league. A 30-year truce was arranged in 445 between Athens and Sparta. The 14 years of peace that followed gave Pericles a chance to develop the splendor of Athens. He became a great patron of the arts and encouraged drama and music. Under his direction Ictinus and Callicrates, Phidias and others produced such monuments as the Parthenon and the Propylaea on the Acropolis. Pericles established colonies at Thurii in Italy and at Amphipolis. He was one of the participants in the events that led to the PELOPONNESIAN WAR. The war, which began in 431, brought on the ruination of Athens. The celebrated funeral oration that Pericles made at the end of the first year of war (as told by Thucydides) was a strong appeal to the pride and patriotism of the citizens. However, Pericles was driven from office by his enemies, only to be reelected strategos in 429. He died six months later. See Victor Ehrenberg, *Sophocles and Pericles* (1954); A. R. Burn, *Pericles and Athens* (1966); C. M. Bowra, *Periclean Athens* (1971).

Perida (pērī'də), family that returned from the Exile. Neh. 7.57. Peruda: Ezra 2.55.

peridotite (pěr'ēdō'tīt): see OLIVINE.

Périer, Casimir Pierre (käzēmēr' pyěr pěryā'), 1777–1832, French statesman. He was a member of a wealthy bourgeois family. His father, Claude Périer, a manufacturer and financier of Grenoble, had been an important figure in the Bank of France. In 1801, Casimir Périer founded a bank at Paris with his brother Scipion. After the Bourbon restoration he, like many other bourgeois, opposed the reactionary policies of the government. He entered (1817) the chamber of deputies and bitterly fought the comte de Villèle and the prince de Polignac. Under King Louis Philippe he served (1830) as minister without portfolio. When the ministry of Jacques Laffitte fell, Périer became (1831) premier. His ministry was strong and conservative; he repressed republican sentiment and tried to check royal influence and maintain a constitutional monarchy. He quelled uprisings in Grenoble and Lyons and refused to aid the Polish and Italian revolutions but sent (1831) troops to Belgium to protect the new monarchy there from the Dutch invasion. Périer's exertions in the cholera epidemic of 1832 led to his death. The family remained prominent, taking the name CASIMIR-PERIER.

perigee (pěr'ĭjē), point nearest the earth in the orbit of a body about the earth. See APSIS.

Périgord (pārēgôr'), region of SW France, now included in Dordogne and parts of Lot-et-Garonne depts. PÉRIGUEUX (the capital) and BERGERAC are the chief cities. The region consists of low, arid limestone plateaus, the deep and fertile valleys of the Lot and Dordogne rivers, and extensive oak forests. Périgord is noted for its TRUFFLES and goose livers, which are its major exports. The agriculture of the region consists of the raising of wheat, corn, and tobacco, and the breeding of animals. The traditional metallurgical industry is concentrated at Fumel. Near Madeleine and Moustier are numerous cave dwellings from the PALEOLITHIC PERIOD. Occupied during Gallic and Roman eras by the Petrocorii, Périgord became a county under the MEROVINGIANS (9th cent). First enfeoffed to the dukes of AQUITAINE, it later passed to England, was returned to France c.1370 as a fief of the French crown, and passed eventually, through a complicated succession, to the house of Bourbon (1574). It was inherited by Henry of Navarre, and after he became king of France as Henry IV (1589), Périgord was incorporated (1607) into the royal domain as part of the province of Guienne.

Périgueux (pārēgö'), city (1968 pop. 40,091), capital of Dordogne dept., SW France, on the Isle River. A commercial center, it is famous for the pâtés (notably goose livers and truffles) that are its chief exports. The city's major manufactures are tobacco products, chemicals, and leather goods. Périgueux was the ancient Vesumna or Vésona of Gallic Petrocorii (see GAUL) and became the capital of Périgord in the 9th cent. It passed to Philip II of France in 1204, was taken by the English in 1356, was regained by France in 1454, and became (16th cent.) a Protestant stronghold. Remains from Roman times include large arenas, the Vésona tower, and an amphitheater. The Byzantine Cathedral of St. Front and the Basilica of St. Étienne date from the 12th cent.

perihelion (pěr"əhē'lēən), point nearest the sun in the orbit of a body about the sun. See APSIS.

Perim (pārēm', pěr'ĭm), Arab. *Barim,* island, c.5 sq mi (13 sq km), off SW Arabian Peninsula in the Bab el Mandeb strait; it is part of Southern Yemen. A rocky and barren island rising to c.215 ft (65 m), it is strategically located at the southern entrance to the Red Sea. Perim was occupied by France in the 18th cent., and then briefly by Britain in 1799. It was reoccupied by the British in 1857 and later connected administratively with Aden. Perim flourished between 1883 and 1936 as a coaling station but declined after 1936 when oil became more widely used by ships. In 1967 Perim's small population voted to become part of Southern Yemen.

Perino del Vaga (pārē'nō dĕl vä'gä) or **Pierino del Vaga** (pyärē'nō), 1500–1547, Italian mannerist painter, whose real name was Perino or Pierino Buonaccorsi. He worked chiefly in Rome and Genoa. He worked for Raphael in the loggia of the Vatican and painted the figures of the planets in the Appartamenti Borgi. After the sack of Rome (1527) he fled to Genoa, where his chief paintings were the very fine historical and mythological frescoes of the Doria Palace (partially destroyed), including *War of the Gods and Giants.* Shortly after 1536 he returned to Rome, under the patronage of Pope Paul III, and worked on the decorations of the Sala della Segnatura in the Vatican and the Sala Regia.

period: see PUNCTUATION.

period, in physics: see HARMONIC MOTION; WAVE.

period, unit of geologic time. It is characterized by more or less continous sedimentary deposition during a time of relative quiescence in tectonic activity, which causes deformations in the earth's crust. Periods are of variable length, generally lasting tens of millions of years, and characteristic fossils are found preserved in the sediments deposited during the period. See GEOLOGIC ERAS (table).

periodical, publication issued regularly. It is distinguished from the NEWSPAPER in format in that its pages are smaller and are usually bound, and it is published at weekly, monthly, quarterly, or other intervals, rather than daily. Periodicals range from technical and scholarly journals to illustrated magazines for mass circulation. The French *Journal des scavans* (1665–1792), edited by "Sieur de Hedouville" (Denis de Sallo), is considered the first periodical. A literary, scientific, and art weekly, it was widely imitated in Europe. German periodicals began late in the 18th cent. as information magazines in dialogue form, later evolving into literary and scientific journals. Under Hitler periodicals were primarily vehicles of Nazi propaganda, and the traditional magazines were suppressed or destroyed. Toward the end of the 17th cent. periodicals patterned after the *Journal des scavans* began to appear in England. The success of Sir Richard Steele's *Tatler* (1709–11) and its successor, the *Spectator* (1711–12), written almost entirely by Steele and by Joseph Addison, ushered in the great 18th-century English periodical literature. The *Rambler* (1750–52) virtually made Samuel Johnson's reputation; he contributed to all but five of its 208 issues. Tobias Smollett and Dr. Johnson wrote for the Tory *Critical Review* (1756–1817). The monthly *Gentleman's Magazine* (1731–1868) was the first to use the word *magazine* in the sense of a periodical for entertainment. During the 18th cent. periodicals intended for special-interest groups were developed: Magazines for lawyers, musicians, artisans, and for women appeared. Among the foremost English periodicals of the 19th cent. were the *Edinburgh Review* (1802–1929), which numbered among its contributors Sir Walter Scott, Thomas Macaulay, Thomas Carlyle, Matthew Arnold, and William Hazlitt; *Blackwood's Edinburgh Magazine* (now called *Blackwood's Magazine*) (1817–), noted for satire; and the *Westminster Review* (1824–1914), an organ of Benthamite reform. Nineteenth-century English novels often appeared first as magazine serials. Charles Dickens edited *Household Words* (1850–59) and *All the Year Round* (1859–95), and many of his novels appeared in them. The *Cornhill Magazine* (1860–), first edited by W. M. Thackeray, published his last two novels and some by Mrs. Gaskell and by Anthony Trollope. The *Yellow Book* (1894–97), edited by Aubrey Beardsley and Henry Harland was notable for literature, humor, and illustrations. The humorous weekly *Punch*, founded in 1841, is the most famous of its kind. In America, periodicals arose chiefly out of a desire to impress England with life in the colonies. At first publication was hampered by difficulties of distribution. Postage was practically prohibitive; since postmasters could frank (mail without charge) what they sent out, they frequently became publishers. Before the American Revolution only about 15 periodicals, with an average life of 10 months, were published. Andrew Bradford's *American Magazine; or, A Monthly View of the Political State of the British Colonies* (Philadelphia, 1741), Benjamin Franklin's *General Magazine and Historical Chronicle* (Philadelphia, 1741), and William Bradford's *American Magazine and Monthly Chronicle* (Philadelphia, 1757–58) were the most notable. During the Revolution outstanding periodicals included the *Pennsylvania Magazine* (Philadelphia, 1775–76), edited by Thomas Paine, and the *United States Magazine* (Philadelphia, 1779). After the war periodicals appeared in large numbers. Of more than 70 established before 1800 the most notable were the *Columbian Magazine* (1786–92); the *Massachusetts Magazine* (1789–96); and the *New York Magazine* (1790–97). One of the best-known American magazines of the early 19th cent. was the *Port Folio* (Philadelphia, 1801–27). The most important review in America was the *North American Review* (1815–1940). Among its editors were Jared Sparks, Edward Everett, E. T. Channing, James Russell Lowell, and Henry Adams. The *New-York Mirror* (1823–57) attained eminence for literary reviews and superior typography and illustration. Edgar Allan Poe contributed critical essays. The period from 1830 to 1850 saw the rise of nationally circulated monthlies. Advertising, a minor factor since its introduction in 1741 in the *General Magazine and Historical Chronicle*, became a mainstay of publishing. *Godey's Lady's Book* (Philadelphia, 1830–92; New York, 1892–98), edited from 1837 to 1877 by Sarah Josepha Hale, was among the most famous periodicals for women; its colored fashion plates are valued today by collectors. Among the notable American periodicals with long histories are the *Atlantic Monthly* (Boston, 1857–), edited for 10 years (1871–81) by William Dean Howells; *Harper's Magazine* (New York, 1850–), which, fully illustrated with woodcuts and carrying serial installments of English novels, achieved new heights of popularity; and the weekly *Saturday Evening Post* (Philadelphia, 1821–). *Scribner's Monthly* was renamed the *Century Illustrated Magazine* (1881) and the *Century Monthly* (1925) and united (1929) with the *Forum* to form the *Forum and Century* (1930–40). Noted American weeklies included Harper's *Weekly* (New York, 1857–1916), for which George W. Curtis wrote famous editorials and Thomas Nast drew cartoons; and the *Independent* (New York and Boston, 1848–1928), at first Congregationalist under Henry Ward Beecher (1861–63) and Theodore Tilton (1863–70) but later a nonsectarian, crusading publication. The *Overland Monthly* (San Francisco, 1868–1935) had many distinguished contributors and was edited (1868–70) by Bret Harte. The sensational exposés by the MUCKRAKERS of political, social and economic injustices brought fame to *McClure's* (New York, 1893–1928); *Hampton's Magazine* (New York, 1898–1912); *Cosmopolitan* (New York, 1886–1925, later revived and greatly altered); *Collier's* (New York, 1880–1957); and others. The new social critics joined literary innovators to create a number of specialized periodicals. The minority appeal of these journals limited their circulation and dictated modest formats; hence they were dubbed the LITTLE MAGAZINES. Many were short-lived; others survived because contributions of readers or philanthropists met their deficits. Yet because their readership comprised intellectuals and public figures, their influence far exceeded their circulation. The *Nation* (1865–), was a forerunner of this movement. Another liberal journal, the *New Republic* (1909–), has had among its editors Walter Lippmann (1914–17) and Henry A. Wallace (1946–48). *The Masses* (1911–1917), a radical organ, was later called the *Liberator* (1918–1924) but revived (1926) as *The New Masses.* A Communist periodical, it was merged with *Mainstream* in 1948. The *American Mercury* (1924–) was founded by H. L. Mencken, its editor until 1933; it opposed orthodoxy in general. The *Partisan Review* (1933–), a liberal quarterly, became celebrated for its literary and political articles, as did the *New Leader* (1924–). Conservative magazines, arising in response to the liberal ones, include *Common Sense* (1932–46) and the *National Review* (1955–), edited by William F. Buckley, Jr. Other notable "little magazines" were *Poetry* (1912–), established by Harriet Monroe with Ezra Pound as foreign editor; the *Little Review* (1914–29), edited by Margaret Anderson; the *Fugitive* (Nashville, Tenn., 1922–25); and the *Double Dealer* (New Orleans, 1921–26). By 1900 the number of American monthlies had expanded to about 1,800, reaching nearly 1 million families. Magazines for women came to dominate magazine circulation. The most important of these were the *Ladies' Home Journal* (1883–), the *Woman's Home Companion* (1873–1955), *McCall's Magazine* (1870–) and *Vogue* (1892–). *Vanity Fair* (1913–36), devoted to literature and the arts, was superbly edited (by Frank Crowninshield) and designed. The *Saturday Review/World* (New York, 1924–; formerly the *Saturday Review of Literature*) has remained a significant journal of literary and art criticism. The *New Yorker* (1935–) is known for urbane humor and high literary standards. *The Reader's Digest* (1922–), a small-format monthly, first offered condensations of books and magazine articles, and now prints original reports as well. It has built a vast circulation (nearly 20 million) and issues many foreign-language editions. News is summarized, analyzed, and categorized according to topics each week in *Time* (New York, 1923–) and *Newsweek* (Dayton, Ohio, and New York, 1933–). The great picture weeklies *Life* (1936) and *Look* (1937) despite their enormous circulations, succumbed in the late 1960s and early 70s to the pressure of rising production costs that has profoundly injured all but special-interest magazine publishing. Specialized periodicals serve most professions, industries, and organizations. The oldest American scientific periodicals include the *American Journal of Science* (New Haven, 1818–), the *Franklin Journal* (Philadelphia, 1826–), and the *Scientific American* (1845–). *National Geographic Magazine* (1888–), devoted to natural history, travel, and anthropological subjects, was one of the first periodicals to use color photographs. Other specialized magazines of interest include *Ms.* (1970–), a forum for the women's liberation movement; *Publishers Weekly*, a trade journal of book publishing; *Sports Illustrated* (1954–); *Ebony* (1946–), a picture weekly directed toward Negro readership; and the zany, satirical *National Lampoon* (1970–). In addition, a tremendous circulation exists for the cruder magazine forms: comic books (cheaply produced color pamphlets of cartoon sequences, selling some 90 million copies per month); fan magazines of the entertainment media; true romance, confession, and police magazines; and the various periodicals devoted to sex, including *Playboy* (1953–), *Cosmopolitan* (edited by Helen Gurley Brown since 1965), and *Penthouse* (first U.S. publication, 1969). Magazines of this last group constitute a publishing phenomenon and are widely imitated. For indexes to periodicals, see INDEX. See G. S. Marr, *Periodical Essayists of the Eighteenth Century* (1924); Walter Graham, *English Literary Periodicals* (1930); R. P. Bond, *Studies in the Early English Periodical* (1957). For periodicals in the United States, see F. J. Hoffmann, Charles Allen, and C. F. Ulrich, *The Little Magazine* (1947); Arthur and Lila Weinberg, ed., *The Muckrakers* (1961); T. B. Peterson, *Magazines in the Twentieth Century* (2d ed. 1964); F. L. Mott, *A History of American Magazines* (5 vol., 1957–1968); John Tebbel, *The American Magazine* (1969); N. W. Ayer & Son, *Directory of Newspapers and Periodicals* (pub. yearly).

periodic law, statement of a periodic recurrence of chemical and physical properties of the ELEMENTS when the elements are arranged in order of increasing ATOMIC NUMBER. The atomic number is the number of positive charges, or protons, contained in the atomic nucleus (see ATOM) or, equivalently, the number of negative charges, or electrons, outside the nucleus in a neutral atom. Such an arrangement in the form of a table in which the groupings of elements having similar properties are easily identified is called the periodic system or the PERIODIC TABLE. The periodic law can be explained on the basis of the electronic structure of the atom, which is believed to be the main factor underlying the chemical properties and many of the physical properties of the elements. In turn, the electronic structures of atoms have been successfully accounted for by the QUANTUM THEORY. D. I. Mendeleev was the first to state the periodic law close to its present form. He proposed in 1869 that the properties of elements are periodic functions of the ATOMIC WEIGHT and grouped the elements accordingly in a periodic system. Before the work of Mendeleev, however, a number of chemists had noticed certain relationships between the properties of elements and their atomic weight. In 1829 J. W. Döbereiner stated that there existed some three-element groups, or triads, in which the atomic weight of the middle element was the average of the other two and the properties of this element lay between those of the other two. For example, calcium, strontium, and barium form a triad; lithium, sodium, and potassium, another. The English chemist J. A. Newlands found (1863–65) that if the elements are listed according to atomic weight starting with the second, the 8th element following any given element has similar chemical properties, and so does the 16th. This became known as the law of octaves. About the same time, A. E. de Chancourtois arranged the elements according to increasing atomic weight in the form of a vertical helix with eight elements in a turn, so that elements having similar properties fell along vertical lines. Mendeleev's system came a few years later. Working independently and not aware of Mendeleev's work, Lothar Meyer arrived at a similar system, publishing his results about a year after Mendeleev's. When Mendeleev devised his periodic table a number of positions could not be fitted by any of the then known elements. Mendeleev suggested that these empty spaces represented undiscovered elements and by means of his system accurately predicted their general properties and atomic weights. In spite of its great success, his system had some discrepancies. Arranged strictly according to atomic weight, not all elements fell into their proper groups. Better arrangement could be made if the positions of certain neighboring couples were interchanged. For example, to suit the chemical order of the table, the inert gas argon (at. wt. 39.944) should come before the chemically active metal potassium (at. wt. 39.096). The work (1913–14) of H. G. Moseley on the X-ray spectra of elements (see X RAY) led to the present form of the periodic law. He found that the wavelength of the X-radiation of elements decreased with increasing atomic weight. However, the relationship was not a strict one. He assigned a new set of numbers, called atomic numbers, to the elements he had studied, so that there was a relation between the wavelength and the atomic number. It was found that although the atomic number of an element is roughly half its atomic weight, the atomic weight does not always increase with increasing atomic number. The discrepancies occur just for those elements where Mendeleev's law failed. Based on atomic number, the periodic law now has no exceptions. Although all the missing elements in the periodic table have been found (with the aid of the periodic table itself), the table retains its usefulness to the chemist as a reliable check for disputed or uncertain data concerning some of the known elements.

periodic table, chart of the elements arranged according to the PERIODIC LAW discovered by D. I. Mendeleev and revised by H. G. J. Moseley. In the accompanying periodic table the elements are arranged in columns and rows according to increasing ATOMIC NUMBER. The vertical columns, or groups, are numbered from I to VIII, with a final column numbered 0. Each group is divided into two categories, or families: one called the a series (the representative, or main group, elements); the other, the b series (the transition, or subgroup, elements). All the elements in a group have the same number of VALENCE electrons and hence similar chemical properties. The horizontal rows of the table are called periods. The elements of a period are characterized by the fact that they have the same number of electron shells; the number of electrons in these shells, which equals the element's atomic number, increases from left to right within each period. In each period the lighter metals appear on the left, the heavier metals in the center, and the nonmetals on

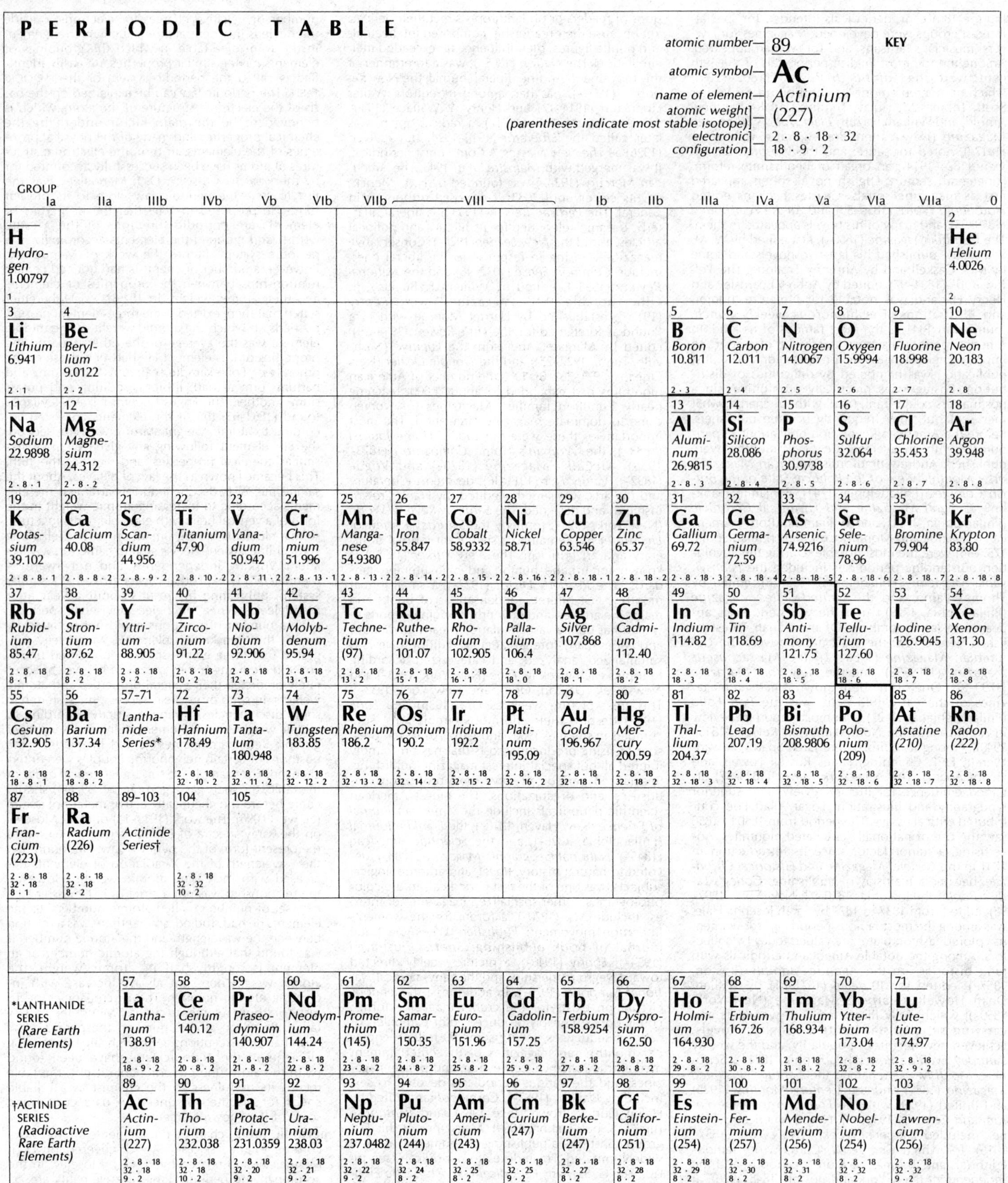

PERIODIC TABLE

KEY

atomic number	89
atomic symbol	**Ac**
name of element	*Actinium*
atomic weight (parentheses indicate most stable isotope)	(227)
electronic configuration	2 · 8 · 18 · 32 · 18 · 9 · 2

GROUP Ia	IIa	IIIb	IVb	Vb	VIb	VIIb	VIII	VIII	VIII	Ib	IIb	IIIa	IVa	Va	VIa	VIIa	0
1 **H** *Hydrogen* 1.00797 1																	2 **He** *Helium* 4.0026 2
3 **Li** *Lithium* 6.941 2 · 1	4 **Be** *Beryllium* 9.0122 2 · 2											5 **B** *Boron* 10.811 2 · 3	6 **C** *Carbon* 12.011 2 · 4	7 **N** *Nitrogen* 14.0067 2 · 5	8 **O** *Oxygen* 15.9994 2 · 6	9 **F** *Fluorine* 18.998 2 · 7	10 **Ne** *Neon* 20.183 2 · 8
11 **Na** *Sodium* 22.9898 2 · 8 · 1	12 **Mg** *Magnesium* 24.312 2 · 8 · 2											13 **Al** *Aluminum* 26.9815 2 · 8 · 3	14 **Si** *Silicon* 28.086 2 · 8 · 4	15 **P** *Phosphorus* 30.9738 2 · 8 · 5	16 **S** *Sulfur* 32.064 2 · 8 · 6	17 **Cl** *Chlorine* 35.453 2 · 8 · 7	18 **Ar** *Argon* 39.948 2 · 8 · 8
19 **K** *Potassium* 39.102 2 · 8 · 8 · 1	20 **Ca** *Calcium* 40.08 2 · 8 · 8 · 2	21 **Sc** *Scandium* 44.956 2 · 8 · 9 · 2	22 **Ti** *Titanium* 47.90 2 · 8 · 10 · 2	23 **V** *Vanadium* 50.942 2 · 8 · 11 · 2	24 **Cr** *Chromium* 51.996 2 · 8 · 13 · 1	25 **Mn** *Manganese* 54.9380 2 · 8 · 13 · 2	26 **Fe** *Iron* 55.847 2 · 8 · 14 · 2	27 **Co** *Cobalt* 58.9332 2 · 8 · 15 · 2	28 **Ni** *Nickel* 58.71 2 · 8 · 16 · 2	29 **Cu** *Copper* 63.546 2 · 8 · 18 · 1	30 **Zn** *Zinc* 65.37 2 · 8 · 18 · 2	31 **Ga** *Gallium* 69.72 2 · 8 · 18 · 3	32 **Ge** *Germanium* 72.59 2 · 8 · 18 · 4	33 **As** *Arsenic* 74.9216 2 · 8 · 18 · 5	34 **Se** *Selenium* 78.96 2 · 8 · 18 · 6	35 **Br** *Bromine* 79.904 2 · 8 · 18 · 7	36 **Kr** *Krypton* 83.80 2 · 8 · 18 · 8
37 **Rb** *Rubidium* 85.47 2 · 8 · 18 · 8 · 1	38 **Sr** *Strontium* 87.62 2 · 8 · 18 · 8 · 2	39 **Y** *Yttrium* 88.905 2 · 8 · 18 · 9 · 2	40 **Zr** *Zirconium* 91.22 2 · 8 · 18 · 10 · 2	41 **Nb** *Niobium* 92.906 2 · 8 · 18 · 12 · 1	42 **Mo** *Molybdenum* 95.94 2 · 8 · 18 · 13 · 1	43 **Tc** *Technetium* (97) 2 · 8 · 18 · 13 · 2	44 **Ru** *Ruthenium* 101.07 2 · 8 · 18 · 15 · 1	45 **Rh** *Rhodium* 102.905 2 · 8 · 18 · 16 · 1	46 **Pd** *Palladium* 106.4 2 · 8 · 18 · 18 · 0	47 **Ag** *Silver* 107.868 2 · 8 · 18 · 18 · 1	48 **Cd** *Cadmium* 112.40 2 · 8 · 18 · 18 · 2	49 **In** *Indium* 114.82 2 · 8 · 18 · 18 · 3	50 **Sn** *Tin* 118.69 2 · 8 · 18 · 18 · 4	51 **Sb** *Antimony* 121.75 2 · 8 · 18 · 18 · 5	52 **Te** *Tellurium* 127.60 2 · 8 · 18 · 18 · 6	53 **I** *Iodine* 126.9045 2 · 8 · 18 · 18 · 7	54 **Xe** *Xenon* 131.30 2 · 8 · 18 · 18 · 8
55 **Cs** *Cesium* 132.905 2 · 8 · 18 · 18 · 8 · 1	56 **Ba** *Barium* 137.34 2 · 8 · 18 · 18 · 8 · 2	57–71 *Lanthanide Series**	72 **Hf** *Hafnium* 178.49 2 · 8 · 18 · 32 · 10 · 2	73 **Ta** *Tantalum* 180.948 2 · 8 · 18 · 32 · 11 · 2	74 **W** *Tungsten* 183.85 2 · 8 · 18 · 32 · 12 · 2	75 **Re** *Rhenium* 186.2 2 · 8 · 18 · 32 · 13 · 2	76 **Os** *Osmium* 190.2 2 · 8 · 18 · 32 · 14 · 2	77 **Ir** *Iridium* 192.2 2 · 8 · 18 · 32 · 15 · 2	78 **Pt** *Platinum* 195.09 2 · 8 · 18 · 32 · 16 · 2	79 **Au** *Gold* 196.967 2 · 8 · 18 · 32 · 18 · 1	80 **Hg** *Mercury* 200.59 2 · 8 · 18 · 32 · 18 · 2	81 **Tl** *Thallium* 204.37 2 · 8 · 18 · 32 · 18 · 3	82 **Pb** *Lead* 207.19 2 · 8 · 18 · 32 · 18 · 4	83 **Bi** *Bismuth* 208.9806 2 · 8 · 18 · 32 · 18 · 5	84 **Po** *Polonium* (209) 2 · 8 · 18 · 32 · 18 · 6	85 **At** *Astatine* *(210)* 2 · 8 · 18 · 32 · 18 · 7	86 **Rn** *Radon* *(222)* 2 · 8 · 18 · 32 · 18 · 8
87 **Fr** *Francium* (223) 2 · 8 · 18 · 32 · 18 · 8 · 1	88 **Ra** *Radium* (226) 2 · 8 · 18 · 32 · 18 · 8 · 2	89–103 *Actinide Series†*	104 2 · 8 · 18 · 32 · 32 · 10 · 2	105													

	57	58	59	60	61	62	63	64	65	66	67	68	69	70	71
*LANTHANIDE SERIES *(Rare Earth Elements)*	**La** *Lanthanum* 138.91 2 · 8 · 18 · 18 · 9 · 2	**Ce** *Cerium* 140.12 2 · 8 · 18 · 20 · 8 · 2	**Pr** *Praseodymium* 140.907 2 · 8 · 18 · 21 · 8 · 2	**Nd** *Neodymium* 144.24 2 · 8 · 18 · 22 · 8 · 2	**Pm** *Promethium* (145) 2 · 8 · 18 · 23 · 8 · 2	**Sm** *Samarium* 150.35 2 · 8 · 18 · 24 · 8 · 2	**Eu** *Europium* 151.96 2 · 8 · 18 · 25 · 8 · 2	**Gd** *Gadolinium* 157.25 2 · 8 · 18 · 25 · 9 · 2	**Tb** *Terbium* 158.9254 2 · 8 · 18 · 27 · 8 · 2	**Dy** *Dysprosium* 162.50 2 · 8 · 18 · 28 · 8 · 2	**Ho** *Holmium* 164.930 2 · 8 · 18 · 29 · 8 · 2	**Er** *Erbium* 167.26 2 · 8 · 18 · 30 · 8 · 2	**Tm** *Thulium* 168.934 2 · 8 · 18 · 31 · 8 · 2	**Yb** *Ytterbium* 173.04 2 · 8 · 18 · 32 · 8 · 2	**Lu** *Lutetium* 174.97 2 · 8 · 18 · 32 · 9 · 2

	89	90	91	92	93	94	95	96	97	98	99	100	101	102	103
†ACTINIDE SERIES *(Radioactive Rare Earth Elements)*	**Ac** *Actinium* (227) 2 · 8 · 18 · 32 · 18 · 9 · 2	**Th** *Thorium* 232.038 2 · 8 · 18 · 32 · 18 · 10 · 2	**Pa** *Protactinium* 231.0359 2 · 8 · 18 · 32 · 20 · 9 · 2	**U** *Uranium* 238.03 2 · 8 · 18 · 32 · 21 · 9 · 2	**Np** *Neptunium* 237.0482 2 · 8 · 18 · 32 · 22 · 9 · 2	**Pu** *Plutonium* (244) 2 · 8 · 18 · 32 · 24 · 8 · 2	**Am** *Americium* (243) 2 · 8 · 18 · 32 · 25 · 8 · 2	**Cm** *Curium* (247) 2 · 8 · 18 · 32 · 25 · 9 · 2	**Bk** *Berkelium* (247) 2 · 8 · 18 · 32 · 27 · 8 · 2	**Cf** *Californium* (251) 2 · 8 · 18 · 32 · 28 · 8 · 2	**Es** *Einsteinium* (254) 2 · 8 · 18 · 32 · 29 · 8 · 2	**Fm** *Fermium* (257) 2 · 8 · 18 · 32 · 30 · 8 · 2	**Md** *Mendelevium* (256) 2 · 8 · 18 · 32 · 31 · 8 · 2	**No** *Nobelium* (254) 2 · 8 · 18 · 32 · 32 · 8 · 2	**Lr** *Lawrencium* (256) 2 · 8 · 18 · 32 · 32 · 9 · 2

the right. Elements on the borderline between metals and nonmetals are called metalloids. Group Ia (with one valence electron) and group IIa (with two valence electrons) are called the ALKALI METALS and the ALKALINE EARTH METALS, respectively. Two series of elements branch off from group IIIb, which contains the transition metals; elements 57 to 71 are called the lanthanide series, or rare earths, and elements 89 to 103 are called the actinide series, or radioactive rare earths. The nonmetals in group VIIa (with seven valence electrons) are called the HALOGENS. The elements grouped in the final column have no valence electrons and are called the INERT GASES, or noble gases, because they react chemically only with extreme difficulty. In the accompanying table, which is a relatively simple type of periodic table, each position gives the name and chemical symbol for the element assigned to that position; its atomic number; its ATOMIC WEIGHT (the weighted average of the masses of its stable isotopes, based on a scale in which carbon-12 has a mass of 12); and its electronic configuration, i.e., the distribution of its electrons by shells. The only exceptions are the positions of elements 103, 104, and 105; complete information on these elements has not been compiled. Larger and more complicated periodic tables may also include the following information for each element: atomic diameter or radius; common valence numbers or oxidation states; melting point; boiling point; density; specific heat; Young's modulus; the quantum states of its valence electrons; type of crystal form; stable and radioactive isotopes; and type of magnetism exhibited by the element (paramagnetism or diamagnetism).

periodontics: see DENTISTRY.

Peripatetics (pĕr″əpətĕt′ĭks) [from Gr.,=walking about; from Aristotle's manner in teaching], the followers of Aristotle. THEOPHRASTUS, friend of Aristotle and cofounder with him of the Peripatetic school of philosophy, succeeded him as its head (323 B.C.) and did much to bring it into favor. Strato of Lampsacus was the next leader of the school. Later Peripatetics were largely occupied in preparing paraphrases, commentaries, and interpretations of the teachings of Aristotle. The first complete edition (c.70 B.C.) in ancient times was arranged by Andronicus of Rhodes. The devotees of the school defended its essential doctrines against the Stoics and others, but some adopted variations, particularly concerning the explanation of nature.

peripheral nervous system: see NERVOUS SYSTEM.

periscope (pĕr'ĭskōp) [Gr.,=view around], instrument to enable a person to see objects not in his direct line of vision or concealed by some intervening body. Its essential parts are a tube, prisms, lenses, mirrors, and an eyepiece. The image is received in one mirror and reflected through the tube with its lenses to a mirror visible to the viewer. Periscopes used in submarines are so arranged that they can be turned to permit a view of the entire horizon. Such periscopes are of noncorrosive metal, have tubes up to 30 ft (9.1 m) long and about 6 in. (1.5 cm) in diameter (only a small section projects above the water), and may be withdrawn into the submarine. There are many smaller types of periscopes that are used in trenches and tanks.

peristalsis: see DIGESTIVE SYSTEM.

peritoneum (pĕrətənē'əm), multilayered membrane that lines the abdominal cavity and supports and covers the organs within it. The part of the membrane that lines the abdominal cavity is called the parietal peritoneum. The portion that covers the internal organs, or viscera, is known as the visceral peritoneum and forms the outer layer (serosa) of most of the intestinal tract. The supportive peritoneum forms sheets of greatly modified membranes called mesenteries. These tissues hold the organs of the digestive tract in position and convey nerves, blood vessels, and lymphatic ducts to the viscera. The space between the visceral and parietal membranes contains a watery fluid that permits the abdominal organs to slide freely against the abdominal wall.

peritonitis (pĕr"ĭtənī'tĭs), acute or chronic inflammation of the PERITONEUM, the membrane that lines the abdominal cavity and surrounds the internal organs. It is caused by invasion of bacterial agents or irritant foreign matter during rupture of an internal organ, by spreading infection from the female genital tract, by penetrating injuries of the abdominal wall, by dissemination of infections through the blood and lymphatic channels, or by accidental pollution during surgery. Typically, peritonitis is a serious complication of another abdominal disorder, such as appendicitis, ulcers, colitis, or rupture of the gall bladder. Severe abdominal pain, vomiting, prostration, and high fever are predominant symptoms. Treatment includes antibiotic therapy and the identification and elimination of the cause of the infection.

periwinkle, in botany: see DOGBANE.

periwinkle, any of a group of marine GASTROPOD mollusks having conical, spiral shells and considered to be a variety of snails. Periwinkles feed on algae and seaweed. They are found at the water's edge; out of water, they resist drying by closing themselves into the shell with a horny plate. The edible European species, called the common periwinkle, has become well established on the Atlantic coast of North America. About 12 other species are found on rocky beaches of both the Atlantic and the Pacific coasts. Periwinkles are classified in the phylum MOLLUSCA, class Gastropoda, order Mesogastropoda, family Littorinidae, genus *Littorina.*

Perizzite (pĕr'ĭzīt, pĕrĭz'-), aboriginal people of Palestine. Gen. 13.7; 15.20; 34.30; Ex. 3.8; Joshua 9.1; 11.3; 17.15; Judges 1.4; 3.5; 1 Kings 9.20; Ezra 9.1.

perjury (pûr'jərē), in criminal law, the act of willfully and knowingly stating a falsehood under oath or under affirmation in judicial or administrative proceedings. If the person accused of perjury had any probable cause for his belief that the statement he made was true, then he is not guilty of perjury. In U.S. Federal law, and in most states, a false statement must be material to a point of inquiry in order to constitute perjury. Perjury is a crime and may be punished by fine or imprisonment. The crime of inducing another person to commit perjury is called subornation of perjury.

Perkin, Sir William Henry, 1838–1907, English chemist. In 1856 he discovered the first aniline dye (aniline purple, known as mauve and mauveine); by founding a factory to make it, Perkin established the aniline dye industry in England. He was knighted in 1906. His son, **William Henry Perkin, Jr.** (1860–1927), also a chemist, synthesized numerous organic compounds, including camphor and several alkaloids.

Perkins, Frances, 1882–1965, U.S. Secretary of Labor (1933–45), b. Boston. She worked at Hull House, was executive secretary of the New York Consumers' League (1910–12) and of the New York Committee on Safety (1912–17), and directed (1912–13) investigations for the New York state factory commission. She became an authority on industrial hazards and hygiene and began lobbying in Albany for more comprehensive factory laws and for maximum-hour laws for women. Gov. Alfred E. Smith appointed (1923) her to the New York State Industrial Board, and later she served (1926–29) as its chairman. Gov. Franklin Delano Roosevelt named her (1929) industrial commissioner of New York state to direct the enforcement of factory and labor laws. As President, Roosevelt appointed her U.S. Secretary of Labor—the first appointment of a woman to the U.S. cabinet. Her appointment was bitterly criticized by business, labor, and political leaders. As Secretary of Labor, she promoted adoption of the Social Security Act, advocated higher wages, urged legislation to alleviate industrial strife, and helped standardize state industrial legislation. After she resigned, she served (1946–52) as a member of the U.S. Civil Service Commission. Besides books on labor problems, she wrote *The Roosevelt I Knew* (1946).

Perkins School for the Blind, at Watertown, Mass.; chartered 1829, opened 1832 in South Boston with Samuel G. Howe as its director; moved 1912. From 1877 to 1955 it was called Perkins Institution and Massachusetts School for the Blind. It was the first chartered school for blind children in the United States. Among the school's pupils were Laura Bridgman and Anne Sullivan Macy.

Perley, Sir George Halsey, 1857–1938, Canadian statesman, b. Lebanon, N.H. As a child, he moved with his parents to Ottawa. In 1904 he was elected to the Canadian House of Commons as a Conservative, serving there almost continuously until his death. In 1911 he was made minister without portfolio in the cabinet of Robert Borden; from 1914 to 1922 he was high commissioner for Canada in London. In the second brief government of Arthur Meighen (1926) he was secretary of state, and in Richard B. Bennett's administration (1930–35) he was minister without portfolio and, on occasion, acting prime minister. Out of his personal fortune derived from business, Perley contributed to philanthropic causes. He was knighted in 1915.

Perlis (pûr'lĭs), state (1971 pop. 121,062), 310 sq mi (803 sq km), Malaysia, central Malay Peninsula, on the Andaman Sea. The smallest of the states of Malaysia, it is bordered on the N and E by Thailand and on the SE by Kedah, of which it formed a part till 1842. KANGAR, its capital, is in the center of one of the richest rice-growing areas of Malaysia. Small quantities of tin are produced. The population is mostly Malay. In 1909 Siam transferred its suzerainty over Perlis to Great Britain. Perlis was one of the Unfederated Malay States before the creation (1948) of the Federation of Malaya. See MALAYSIA, FEDERATION OF.

Perm (pyĕrm), city (1970 pop. 850,000), capital of Perm oblast, NE European USSR, on the Kama River. It is a transfer center for rail and river traffic and a major producer of machinery in the Urals industrial region. Perm also has chemical plants and oil refineries. It was founded in 1780 and underwent rapid industrial growth in the 19th cent. Perm was called Molotov from 1940 to 1958. It is the seat of Gorky Univ. (founded 1916). Perm oblast is a major mining region.

permafrost, permanently frozen soil, subsoil, or other deposit, characteristic of arctic and some subarctic regions. In 1962 measurements in a borehole drilled on Melville Island, Northwest Territories, Canada, showed that the ground was frozen to a depth of at least 1,475 ft (450 m); comparable thicknesses have been found in other far north regions. TUNDRAS, though underlaid by permafrost, today support centers of population in Alaska, Canada, and Siberia. Permafrost is a very fragile system that may easily be damaged or destroyed by the presence of man-made heat. A controversy developed in the late 1960s and early 70s over the construction of an oil pipeline from the Alaska North Slope to the southern part of the state. Critics of the project argued that if the pipeline containing hot oil ever came into contact with the permafrost, it would melt the permafrost; the pipeline would then sink and eventually break. The oil spilled during the breakage would result in a major ecological disaster. It was decided to build the pipeline with insulated pipe raised above the permafrost or on gravel beds in order to prevent melting and thus preserve both the pipeline and the ecosystem.

Permanent Court of Arbitration: see HAGUE TRIBUNAL.

Permanent Court of International Justice: see WORLD COURT.

permeability, magnetic: see MAGNETISM; FLUX, MAGNETIC.

Permian period (pûr'mēən) [from the Perm region, USSR], sixth and last period of the PALEOZOIC ERA (see GEOLOGIC ERAS, table). During the Permian period changes in the earth's surface that had begun in the preceding CARBONIFEROUS PERIOD reached a climax. At the close of the Carboniferous, large areas of E North America were dry land. In the Lower Permian, sandy shales, sandstones, and thin limestones of the Dunkard formation (formerly called the Upper Barren measures) were deposited in the remaining submerged areas of West Virginia, Pennsylvania, and Ohio, but the continued rising of the land soon put an end to deposition. The Dunkard is the last Paleozoic formation of the E United States. More extensive deposits were formed in the West. Parts of Texas, Oklahoma, Kansas, and Nebraska were covered by an arm of the sea or possibly by one or more salt lakes or lagoons, now represented by masses of salt or gypsum in layers separated and overlaid by red beds. There are important Permian salt mines at Hutchinson and Lyons in Kansas and gypsum mines in Oklahoma, Texas, and Kansas. The longest marine submergence of the Lower Permian in North America was in W Texas and SE New Mexico, where there is a system of marine limestones and sandstones 4,000 to 6,000 ft (1,200–1,800 m) thick. The Cordilleran region was also submerged; here marine beds are more common toward the west, and land sediments, especially red beds, toward the east. The red beds are generally considered to be indicative of increasingly arid conditions in Permian times. In the Upper Permian practically all of North America was above sea level, and the continent was larger than at present. Toward the close of the Upper Permian the greatest earth disturbance of the Paleozoic era thrust up the Appalachian Mts. The Lower Permian, or Rotliegendes [red layers], of Europe was marked principally by erosion from the Paleozoic Alps of the Carboniferous into the low-lying land to the north; the formations are chiefly shale and sandstone, with some conglomerate and breccia. Red is a prominent color for the beds. The Upper Permian was a period of more extensive marine invasion; the Zechstein formation is predominantly limestone, though it includes rich deposits of copper, salt, gypsum, and potash. The Upper Permian beds of Germany were long the chief source of the world's potash. The Permian and late Carboniferous of the Southern Hemisphere were radically different from those of the Northern Hemisphere. Australia, S Africa, and South America experienced a series of glacial periods, as is shown by the presence of tillite and of conspicuous striations of the underlying rock formations. This condition prevailed also in India. Paleozoic glaciation in North America is suggested by the Squantum tillite near Boston, Mass. This glaciation and the aridity of which the red beds seem to be the result are the two most strongly marked characteristics of the Permian period. The life of the Permian was in general transitional between that of the Paleozoic and that of the succeeding MESOZOIC ERA. Some marine animals became extinct, but there was at the same time an evolution to more modern types, a marked change in the insects, and a notable increase in numbers and varieties of reptiles. The aridity of the Northern Hemisphere led to the dwarfing and gradual extinction of some of the Carboniferous types. Among plants, Lepidodendron and Sigillaria became rare, but ferns and conifers persisted. The "seed fern," *Glossopteris,* which spread over the Southern Hemisphere and part of the Northern and was apparently successful in resisting glacial conditions, was the most conspicuous development in the Permian flora. The wide distribution of *Glossopteris* in South America, Antarctica, Australia, and S Africa is a strong argument favoring the interconnection of these land masses in a large supercontinent during Permian time, since even a narrow strait of water would have stopped its spread.

permutations and combinations: see PROBABILITY.

Pernambuco (pərnəmbo͞o'ko͞o), state (1970 pop. 5,166,554), 37,946 sq mi (98,280 sq km), NE Brazil, on the Atlantic Ocean. The capital is RECIFE (also called Pernambuco).

Pernau: see PARNU, USSR.

pernicious anemia: see ANEMIA.

Pernik (pĕr'nĭk), city (1968 est. pop. 79,300), W Bulgaria, on the Struma River. The industrial center of a coal-mining region, it has iron smelters, glassworks, and power plants. Pernik is linked by rail with Sofia and Greece.

Perón, Eva Duarte de (ā'vä do͞oär'tā thā pĕrōn'), 1919–52, Argentine political leader. The wife of Juan Perón, whom she married in 1945, she virtually co-governed the country during his first six years as president. A minor actress before she met Perón, Evita, as she was known, became active in politics and helped organize the mass demonstration of workers that secured his release (Oct., 1945) from prison. After Perón became president, she in effect ran the ministries of health and labor. She formed the Eva Perón Social Aid Foundation, which doled out money to the needy; and she militantly championed the causes of women, labor, and the poor. A fiery orator, she commanded an enormous political following. She was, however, opposed by the army, which blocked her vice presidential bid in 1951. After her death from cancer at the age of 33, the Perón regime declined. See Eva Perón, *My Mission in Life* (tr. 1953); Mary Main, *The Woman with the Whip: Eva Perón* (1952).

Perón, Juan Domingo (hwän dōmĕng'gō pĕrōn'), 1895–1974, president of Argentina (1946–55; 1973–74). An army officer, he rose to prominence after the overthrow of the government of Ramón Castillo in 1943. He was the chief member of a clique of colonels who advocated Argentine hegemony in South America and favored the Fascist movements in Germany and Italy. First as secretary of labor and social welfare and later as minister of war and vice president, Perón was the real power behind the administration of Edelmiro Farrell. By backing the demands of labor unions and decreeing extensive welfare legislation, he won the allegiance of Argentine workers, who became the backbone of his support. Imprisoned in 1945 after a coup, he was released following mass demonstrations of workers. His prestige grew. Aided by an anti-Perón "blue book" issued by the U.S. Dept. of State during the 1946 elections, which produced violent Argentine reaction, Perón was elected president by a huge majority. He immediately instituted a program of revolutionary measures—collectively termed *peronismo*—which profoundly affected the country's economic and political structure. Strongly nationalistic, the program called for a rapid economic build-up leading to complete self-sufficiency. The totalitarian character of the regime became gradually more pronounced: political opponents were jailed, the press was muzzled or shut down (e.g., *La Prensa*), and education was strictly controlled. With the aid of his popular wife, Eva Duarte de Perón (see separate article), the dictator converted the trade unions into a militant organization, the *descamisados* [shirtless ones], along fascist lines. The course of *peronismo*, however, became unsteady by the late 1940s and early 1950s as sales of wheat and beef declined and the economy deteriorated. Perón's hold was further weakened in 1952 by the death of his wife, Eva, who had commanded an enormous political following. The unusual coalition of labor, reactionaries, nationalists, churchmen, and military leaders that had supported Perón began to disintegrate. An anticlerical campaign launched by Perón led to his excommunication in June, 1955, and heralded his downfall. He was unseated by a military coup the following September and fled, first to Paraguay and ultimately (1960) to Spain. *Peronismo* nevertheless remained a powerful political force in Argentina, contributing to considerable governmental chaos. In 1971, President Lanusse, convinced that political order could not be attained without Peronist cooperation, removed the obstacles that had prevented Perón's return to Argentina. Perón was forbidden to run in the March, 1973 presidential election, but his designated candidate, Hector Cámpora, won. Cámpora resigned in July, and the following September Perón was elected president by 62% of the vote; his wife, María Estela (Isabel) Martínez de Perón, whom he had married in 1961, was elected vice president. She succeeded to the presidency when he died of a heart attack, July 1, 1974. See G. I. Blanksten, *Perón's Argentina* (1953, repr. 1967); R. J. Alexander, *The Perón Era* (1951, repr. 1965); J. R. Barager, ed., *Why Perón Came to Power: The Background to Peronism in Argentina* (1968).

Péronne (pārôn'), town (1968 pop. 7,701), Somme dept., N France, in Picardy, on the Somme River. It is a farm trade center, and its manufactures include wool, bricks, furniture, and plastics. It was a residence (10th cent.) of the Frankish kings and was united to the French crown in 1477. It was there that Charles the Bold of Burgundy forced on Louis XI of France a humiliating treaty in 1468. In World War I the town was almost entirely destroyed during the five months of bloody fighting (1916) along the Somme. St. Jean Church (16th cent.) has been restored.

Pérouse, Jean François de Galaup, comte de La: see LA PÉROUSE.

Perov, Vasily Grigoryevich (vəsē'lyē grĭgôr'yəvĭch pyĭrôf'), 1833–82, Russian historical, genre, and portrait painter. He was the leader of the realist school in Russia. His early work was satirical, but he is best known for his sympathetic treatment of scenes of peasant life. Among his outstanding works are *A Village Funeral* and *The Arrival of the Governess.* His best-known portraits include those of Turgenev and Dostoyevsky.

peroxide (pərŏk'sīd), chemical compound containing two oxygen atoms, each of which is bonded to the other and to a radical or some element other than oxygen; e.g., in HYDROGEN PEROXIDE, H_2O_2, the atoms are joined together in the chainlike structure H—O—O—H. Peroxides are powerful oxidizing agents. They are unstable, releasing oxygen when heated. Peroxides may be formed directly by reaction of an element or compound with oxygen. In dry, carbon-dioxide-free air, sodium or barium metal reacts to form its peroxide. In moist air, zinc metal is oxidized and hydrogen peroxide is formed. When a metal peroxide is treated with a dilute acid, a solution of hydrogen peroxide and a metal salt is formed. ETHERS can react with oxygen from the air to form peroxides. This creates a special hazard, since the peroxides are often so unstable that they decompose explosively if heated.

Perpendicular style, term given the final period of English Gothic architecture (late 14th–middle 16th cent.) because of the predominating vertical lines of its tracery and paneling. It is also called rectilinear for the prevailing angularity of the designs. The work produced after 1485 is sometimes classified as TUDOR STYLE. The use at the Gloucester Cathedral, about the middle of the 14th cent., of numerous vertical panels of tracery for both windows and walls led to a rapid spread of the style. Its climax was reached in Henry VII's chapel, Westminster (c.1500–1525), where panelings cover both exterior and interior surfaces. At Winchester they cover the whole west front. In some cases church windows were of great size, making the west end practically a wall of glass with mullions running vertically for the entire height. Elaborate traceried fan vaulting was one of the distinctive creations of the style, and roofs of complex open-timber construction were numerous. A number of elaborate chapels were built in this period, especially at Oxford and at Cambridge (where King's College Chapel is a notable example), as well as various academic buildings, such as the divinity school at Oxford (completed 1480).

perpetual-motion machine, device that would be able to operate continuously and supply useful work, in violation of the laws of THERMODYNAMICS. A machine that would produce more ENERGY in the form of WORK than is supplied to it in the form of HEAT would violate the first law of thermodynamics, which is a special case of the law of conservation of energy (see CONSERVATION LAWS, in physics), and is known as a perpetual-motion machine of the first kind. A machine that would continuously supply work without a flow of heat from a warmer body to a cooler body would violate the second law of thermodynamics, which is concerned with ENTROPY changes, and is known as a perpetual-motion machine of the second kind. There were a number of early attempts to design and construct various types of perpetual-motion machines; however, since the 19th cent., when the laws of thermodynamics became understood, most such attempts have been abandoned.

Perpignan (pĕrpēnyäN'), city (1968 pop. 104,095), capital of Pyrénées-Orientales dept., S France, near the Spanish border and the Mediterranean. It is a farm trade center, handling wine, fruits, and vegetables. It has distilleries, canneries, and factories making chocolate, clothing, paper, and toys. Tourism is also important; there is a nearby international airport, and the city is a thoroughfare for motorists going to Spain. Founded c.10th cent., Perpignan was the fortified capital of the Spanish kingdom of ROUSSILLON. Its architecture shows much Spanish influence. Among its notable buildings are the Loge (14th cent.), built to house the merchants' exchange; the Gothic Cathedral of St. Jean (14th–15th cent.); and the castle of the kings of Majorca (13th–15th cent.); which forms part of the old citadel dominating the city.

Perrault, Charles (shärl pĕrō'), 1628–1703, French poet. His collections of eight fairy tales, *Histoires ou contes du temps passé* [stories or tales of olden times] (1697) gave classic form to the traditional stories of Bluebeard, Sleeping Beauty, Cinderella, Puss in Boots, Little Red Ridinghood, and Hop-o'-My-Thumb. In the frontispiece of the collection appears the expression "Contes de ma mère Loye" [tales of Mother Goose]. Perrault also published three tales in verse (1694). He is famous for the stormy literary quarrel that he aroused with a poem (1687) comparing ancient authors unfavorably with modern writers. Boileau, the chief defender of the ancients, bandied insults with Perrault until 1694. This "quarrel of the ancients and the moderns" is considered a harbinger of the 18th-century Enlightenment.

Perrault, Claude (klōd), 1613–88, French architect, scientist, and physician. One of the most eminent French scholars of his time, he advanced the study of anatomy and made other scientific contributions. His greatest architectural achievement is his work on the east facade of the Louvre, known as the Colonnade. In this project (1667–70) he collaborated with Le Vau and Le Brun. Perrault did much to establish the qualities of classical balance and order in French Renaissance architecture. He also built portions of the south facade of the Louvre and the Paris Observatory (1667–72), which, with adaptations to modern scientific requirements, is still in use. At the request of Colbert, he translated (1673) and added notes to the monumental work of VITRUVIUS. He also wrote (1683) a treatise on the five orders of columns in architecture. Charles Perrault was his brother. See study by Wolfgang Hermann (1974).

Perrers, Alice (pĕr'ərz), d. 1400, mistress of EDWARD III of England. She entered the service of Edward's queen, Philippa of Hainaut, and married a courtier, Sir William de Windsor. Becoming the king's mistress possibly as early as 1366, she wielded great influence over him. Her interference in the promotion of lawsuits in the courts led to her banishment from the royal household by the Good Parliament of 1376. She returned in 1377 and later gained, despite another sentence of banishment, some favor and much wealth at the court of Richard II.

Perret, Auguste (ōgüst' pĕrā'), 1874–1954, French architect. He left the Académie des Beaux-Arts in Paris to join the family construction firm with his brother Gustave, and began to experiment with the new building material, reinforced concrete. Early works in Paris, such as the house on the rue Franklin (1902–3), the Garage Ponthieu (1905–6), and the Théâtre des Champs-Élysées (1910–11), show the use of reinforced concrete in a classicizing framework of posts and beams. In the latter two buildings the concrete frame is itself exposed in some areas. Perret's famous church at Le Raincy, near Paris (1922–23), is perhaps the first architecturally satisfactory building in the new material. Tall, lithe columns support low-arching vaults, and the structure is surrounded by a continuous wall of glass supported by prefabricated concrete units. In warehouses and factories Perret also made use of concrete vaulting. After World War II he contributed plans for the rebuilding of parts of Le Havre, Amiens, and Marseilles. He is considered one of the most important French architects of his generation. See Peter Collins, *Concrete: The Vision of a New Architecture* (1959).

Perrin, Jean Baptiste (zhäN bätēst' pĕrăN'), 1870–1942, French physicist. From 1910 to 1940 he was professor at the Univ. of Paris, and in 1941 he came to the United States. Perrin specialized in the Brownian movement of particles. For his work on the discontinuous structure of matter and for his discovery of the equilibrium of sedimentation (which permitted an accurate calculation of the size of atoms), he received the 1926 Nobel Prize in Physics. He is noted also for his work on X rays and cathode rays. His works include *Atoms* (1903, tr. 1923). His son, **Francis Henri Perrin,** 1901–, became a director of the French atomic energy commission when it was founded in 1946. In 1951, Perrin took over as the organization's high commissioner of atomic energy, following Frédéric Joliet-Curie's dismissal.

Perrine, Charles Dillon (pərīn'), 1867–1951, American astronomer, b. Steubenville, Ohio. He was on the staff of Lick Observatory (1893–1909) and was (1909–36) director of the Argentine National Observatory in South America. He was the first to observe (1901) the extraordinary motion in the nebulosity about the nova in Perseus, and in 1905 he discovered the sixth and seventh satellites of Jupiter. Perrine also made special studies of comets, discovering several. Between 1900 and 1908 he accompanied four eclipse expeditions and was in charge of the one sent from Lick Observatory to Sumatra in 1901.

Perrine (pərīn'), uninc. town (1970 pop. 10,257), Dade co., SE Fla., a residential suburb of Miami, in a vegetable-growing and vegetable-packing area.

Perrot, Georges (zhôrzh pĕrō'), 1832–1914, French archaeologist. He was professor at the Sorbonne from 1875, director of the École normale supérieure, Paris, from 1888 to 1902, and permanent secretary of the Academy of Inscriptions. While a member of an archaeological expedition (1861) to Asia Minor, he reconstructed the text of a bilingual record of the reign of Augustus on the walls of a temple at Ancyra and published his results in *Exploration archéologique de la Galatia et de la Bithynie* (1862–72). Perrot edited and contributed to the *Revue archéologique*. His works include *Histoire de l'art dans l'antiquité* (with Charles Chipiez, 10 vol., 1882–1914).

Perrot, Jules (zhül), 1810–1892, French dancer and choreographer, b. Lyons. Perrot studied with Auguste Vestris and Salvatore Vigano. He gained fame as a dancer before turning to choreography. From 1848 to 1859 he worked at the Imperial Theatre in St. Petersburg. His ballets included *Esmeralda, Ondine, Le Corsaire,* and part of the original *Giselle* (1841).

Perrot, Nicolas (nĕkôlä'), 1644–c.1718, French explorer in Canada and the Old Northwest. He came to New France as a child and, in service of the Jesuit missionaries, became acquainted with the Indians and Indian languages. Later, as a fur trader around Green Bay, he acquired considerable influence over the Indians of Wisconsin and in 1670 was sent to the West by Frontenac to take formal possession for France. In 1684, with Duluth, he helped bring the Western Indians into the French campaign against the Iroquois, and in 1690 he visited Mackinac to prevent an Iroquois alliance. Perrot was made (1685) commandant of the territory around Green Bay and opened trade with the Sioux as well as with other Indians and in 1689 formally claimed possession of the upper Mississippi region for New France. Probably in 1690 he discovered the lead mines of SW Wisconsin. When all trading licenses were revoked, he returned to Lower Canada and was employed as Indian interpreter in 1701. He is best remembered for his *Mémoire sur les mœurs, coustumes et relligion des sauvages de l'Amérique Septentrionale* (1864), the one memoir to survive out of his many writings.

Perry, Antoinette, 1888–1946, American actress, manager, producer, b. Denver, Colo. Perry began her career as an actress. She later produced several successful plays with Brock Pemberton, including *Strictly Dishonorable, Personal Appearance,* and *Kiss the Boys Goodbye.* Perry was a founder of the American Theater Wing; she was noted for helping young people who were attempting careers in theater. The annual Antoinette Perry (Tony) Awards are presented in her honor for outstanding performances on the stage.

Perry, Matthew Calbraith, 1794–1858, American naval officer, b. South Kingstown, R.I.; brother of Oliver Hazard Perry. Appointed a midshipman in 1809, he first served under his brother on the *Revenge* and then was aide to Commodore John Rodgers on the *President,* which defeated the British ship *Little Belt* before the War of 1812 had been formally declared. Perry saw little action in that war because he was assigned to the *United States,* which the British bottled up at New London. He received his first command in 1821. From 1833 to 1843 he was assigned to the New York (later Brooklyn) navy yard, where he pioneered in the application of steam power to warships, commanding (1837) the *Fulton,* first steam vessel in the U.S. navy, and encouraged the broadening of naval education. Promoted to captain in 1837, Perry received the title of commodore in 1841 and in the same year became commandant of the New York navy yard. In 1843–44 he commanded the African squadron, which was engaged in suppressing the slave trade. In the Mexican War, as commander of the Gulf Fleet, he supported Gen. Winfield Scott in taking Veracruz. Perry was ordered (March, 1852) to command the East India squadron and charged with the delicate task of penetrating isolationist Japan. On July 8, 1853, he anchored his four ships, including the powerful steam frigates *Mississippi* and *Susquehanna,* in lower Tokyo (then Yedo) Bay. The Japanese ordered him to go to Nagasaki, the only port open to foreigners, where the Dutch operated a limited trading concession under humiliating conditions, but Perry firmly declined. On July 14 he presented his papers, including a letter from President Millard Fillmore to the Japanese emperor, requesting protection for shipwrecked American seamen, the right to buy coal, and the opening of one or more ports to trade. The expedition then retired to the China coast, returning, with an increased fleet, in Feb., 1854. Perry's show of pomp (at which he was expert) and power obviously impressed the insecure Tokugawa shogunate, and on March 31, 1854, near Yokohama a treaty was concluded that acceded to American requests, opening the ports of Shimoda and Hakodate to U.S. trade. For his successful expedition Perry was awarded $20,000 by Congress, which also paid for publication of the official *Narrative of the Expedition of an American Squadron to the China Seas and Japan* (3 vol., 1856), compiled under Perry's supervision. See E. M. Barrows, *The Great Commodore* (1935); Arthur Walworth, *Black Ships off Japan* (1946, repr. 1966); *Bluejackets with Perry in Japan* (ed. by H. F. Graff, 1952); S. E. Morison, *"Old Bruin"* (1967).

Perry, Oliver Hazard, 1785–1819, American naval officer, b. South Kingstown, R.I.; brother of Matthew Calbraith Perry. Appointed a midshipman in 1799, he served in the Tripolitan War, was promoted to lieutenant (1807), and from 1807 to 1809 was engaged in building gunboats. In the War of 1812 he was commissioned to build, equip, and man a fleet at Erie, Pa. On Sept. 10, 1813, Perry's fleet left Put-in-Bay, Ohio, and met a slightly inferior British force. In the subsequent battle, the battle of Lake Erie, Perry's flagship, the *Lawrence,* was reduced to ruins, but he transferred his flag to the *Niagara* and shortly forced the British to surrender. His report of the battle sent to Gen. William H. Harrison—"We have met the enemy and they are ours"—has become famous. The victory, which made Perry a national hero, gave the United States control of Lake Erie and helped pave the way for Harrison's victory in the battle of the Thames River, in which Perry participated. After the war he served as a captain in the Mediterranean. Later, on a mission to Venezuela, he contracted yellow fever, died, and was buried in Trinidad. His body was later brought to Newport, R.I., where a monument was erected to him. A memorial to Perry at Put-in-Bay, built 1912–15, was made a national monument in 1936. See biography by C. J. Dutton (1935); C. O. Paullin, ed., *The Battle of Lake Erie* (1918); C. S. Forester, *The Age of Fighting Sail* (1956).

Perry, Ralph Barton, 1876–1957, American realist philosopher, b. Poultney, Vt., grad. Princeton (B.A., 1896) and Harvard (Ph.D., 1899). He taught at Harvard from 1902, becoming professor of philosophy in 1913 and professor emeritus in 1946. He revised (1925) Alfred Weber's *History of Philosophy.* Editor of the works of William James, he won the 1936 Pulitzer Prize in biography for *The Thought and Character of William James* (1935). His other writings include *The New Realism* (1912), *General Theory of Value* (1926), *Puritanism and Democracy* (1944), *The Realms of Value* (1954), and *The Humanity of Man* (1956). See study by I. S. Steinberg (1970).

Perry's Victory and International Peace Memorial National Memorial: see NATIONAL PARKS AND MONUMENTS (table).

Perse, St.-John, pseud. of **Alexis Saint-Léger Léger,** 1887–, French poet and diplomat, b. West Indies. Léger, an opponent of appeasement of the Nazis, was enormously influential in France's foreign office and became known as one of Europe's foremost diplomats. His reputation as a poet of great lyric power grew after his self-imposed exile to the United States in 1940. Encouraged by Gide, he published his first poem, "Images à Crusoe," in 1909. His symbolic *Éloges* (tr. 1944) followed in 1911. For *Amitié du Prince* (1921) Léger drew upon ancient sacerdotal sources. *Anabase* (1924, tr. by T. S. Eliot, 1930), a symbolic history of mankind, brought him wide critical attention. Among his later works are *Exil* (1944, tr. 1949), *Vents* (1946, tr. *Winds,* 1953), *Amers* (1957, tr. *Seamarks,* 1958), *Chroniques* (1960, tr. 1961), and *Oiseaux* (1963, tr. 1966). His writings were published as *Oeuvres complètes* in 1972. His work has been translated by Auden, Eliot, and MacLeish. Léger was awarded the 1960 Nobel Prize in Literature. See studies by Arthur Knödel (1966), Pierre Emmanuel (1971), and René M. Galand (1972).

Perseids (pûr'sēĭdz''): see METEOR SHOWER.

Persephone (pərsĕf'ənē) or **Proserpine** (prōsûr'pənē), in Greek and Roman religion, goddess of fertility and queen of the underworld. She was the daughter of Zeus and Demeter. When she was still a beautiful maiden, Pluto seized her and held her captive in his underworld. Though Demeter eventually persuaded the gods to let her daughter return to her, Persephone was required to remain in the underworld for four months because Pluto had tricked her into eating a pomegranate (food of the dead) there. When Persephone left the earth, the flowers withered and the grain died, but when she returned, life blossomed anew. This story, which symbolizes the annual vegetation cycle, was celebrated in the ELEUSINIAN MYSTERIES, in which Persephone appeared under the name Kore.

Persepolis (pərsĕp'əlĭs) [Gr.,=city of Persia], ancient city of Persia, ceremonial capital of the Achaemenid empire under Darius I and his successors. The administrative capitals were elsewhere, notably at Susa and Babylon. The ruins of Persepolis lie 30 mi (48 km) NE of Shiraz in a fertile plain of the Pulvar River, with strong natural mountain defenses. There are ruins of the palaces of Darius I, Xerxes, and later kings as well as the citadel that contained the treasury looted by Alexander; the ruins lie on a huge platform constructed of limestone from the adjacent mountain. A few miles distant are the rock-hewn tombs of Achaemenid kings and monuments of the Sassanids on a mountainside called by the natives Naksh-i-Rustam [pictures of Rustam] for the legendary Persian hero Rustam. In the same place there is a 3,000-year-old inscription of Shutruk-Nakhkhunte, a famous Elamite king (c.1207–1171 B.C.). Scattered over the plain, a short distance from the platform of Persepolis, are the ruins of Stakhr or Estakhr, the official capital of the Sassanids, whose administrative capital was Ctesiphon. Excavations have disclosed, 2 mi (3 km) away, a village of the Neolithic period, with mural decorations in red ocher that date back to about 4000 B.C. The Iranian Room in the Oriental Institute of the Univ. of Chicago contains many pieces from Persepolis, products of the research from 1931 to 1941. See E. F. Schmidt, *Persepolis* (3 vol., 1953–70); Mortimer Wheeler, *Flames over Persepolis* (1968); D. N. Wilbur, *Persepolis, the Archaeology of Parsa* (1969).

Perseus (pûr'sēəs, -sōōs), in Greek mythology, son of Zeus and Danaë. His grandfather, Acrisius, had been warned by an oracle that his grandson would kill him and therefore put Perseus and his mother in a chest and threw it into the sea. It drifted to Seriphus, where King Polydectes befriended the two. After a time Polydectes fell in love with Danaë but was embarrassed by the presence of her full-grown son. He sent Perseus to fetch the head of the Gorgon Medusa, thinking that Perseus would die in the attempt. The gods, however, loved Perseus. Hermes gave him a curved sword and winged sandals, Athena a mirrorlike shield, and Hades a helmet that made Perseus invisible. Thus armed, Perseus slew Medusa. While fleeing the other Gorgons, Medusa's sisters, Perseus asked Atlas for help. Atlas refused, and Perseus, by means of the Medusa head, promptly turned him into a mountain of stone. On his way home Perseus rescued Andromeda from a sea monster and married her. When he arrived in Seriphus, he killed Polydectes and his followers. He then gave the Medusa head to Athena. He went with his mother and his wife to Argos. There, while competing in a discus contest, Perseus accidentally killed his grandfather. Thus the prophecy was fulfilled. Perseus was the father of Electryon, who was the grandfather of Hercules. The famous figure of Perseus by Benvenuto Cellini stands in the Loggia dei Lanzi in Florence.

Perseus, c.212–166 B.C., last king of Macedon (179–168 B.C.), son and successor of Philip V. He intrigued against his younger brother, Demetrius, eventually bringing about the latter's execution by Philip V. As king, his involvement in Greek politics excited the fears of Eumenes II of PERGAMUM, who, thinking that Pergamum's position was being endangered, went to Rome to provoke war against Perseus by pointing to alignments of Macedon with anti-Roman factions in Greece. The resultant Third Macedonian War (171–168) began with a Macedonian cavalry victory and then dragged on indecisively. Finally Aemilius PAULLUS took command of the Roman forces and soundly defeated (168) Perseus at Pydna on the Gulf of Thessaloníki. Perseus died in captivity.

Perseus, in astronomy, northern CONSTELLATION lying E of Cassiopeia and N of Taurus. It contains the bright star Mirfak (Alpha Persei) and ALGOL (Beta Persei), a visible VARIABLE STAR of the type known as an eclipsing variable. Perseus contains two STAR CLUSTERS (NGC 869 and NGC 884) that are visible to the naked eye, as well as an open cluster (M34) that is barely visible. A METEOR SHOWER known as the Perseids appears to radiate from a star in Perseus; this shower can be seen every year for several nights beginning Aug. 10, after midnight. In 1901 a brilliant nova was observed in the constellation. Perseus reaches its highest point in the evening sky in late December.

Pershing, John Joseph (pûr′shĭng), 1860–1948, American army officer and commander in chief of the American Expeditionary Force in World War I, b. Linn co., Mo. After graduating (1886) from West Point he served as a cavalry officer in campaigns against the Indian chief Geronimo (1886) and against the Sioux (1890–91). He was (1891–95) an instructor in military tactics at the Univ. of Nebraska, where he earned (1893) a law degree. He later taught (1897–98) at West Point. After fighting (1898) in the Spanish-American War, Pershing achieved national notice when he served (1899–1903) in the Philippines, commanding in the campaign against the hostile Moros (Muslim Filipinos) on Mindanao island. He was (1905) an American military attaché in the Russo-Japanese War and was promoted (1906) from captain to brigadier general. Again serving in the Philippines from 1906 he completely defeated the Moros in 1913. Pershing led the much-publicized but unsuccessful punitive expedition (1916–17) against Francisco ("Pancho") VILLA in Mexico. After U.S. entry into World War I, Pershing was appointed (1917) to head the American Expeditionary Force in France. His talent for organization was largely responsible for the molding of hastily trained American troops into well-integrated combat units. The Allied military leaders had hoped to use U.S. troops as replacements for the heavy French and British losses, but Pershing insisted that the Americans operate as a separate force under his command. His two books *Final Report* (1919) and *My Experiences in the World War* (1931) recount his war years. After the war he was promoted (1919) to permanent general of the armies of the United States. He was (1921–24) chief of staff before retiring from the army in 1924. He later served (1925) on the plebiscite commission in the TACNA-ARICA controversy. See biographies by Harold McCracken (1931), Frederick Palmer (1948, repr. 1970), Richard O'Connor (1961), F. E. Vandiver (1967), and Donald Smythe (1973); *The Yanks Are Coming* (ed. by *Army Times,* 1960).

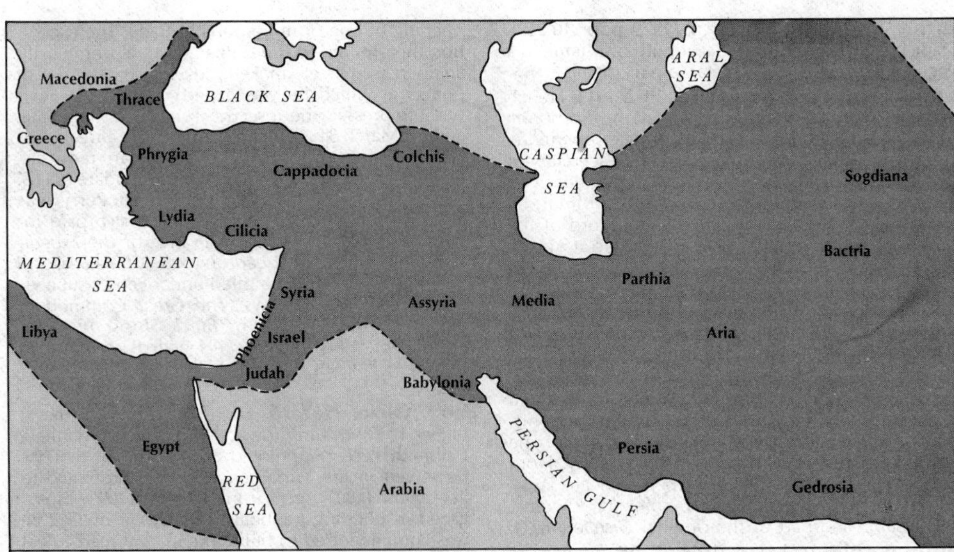

Persian Empire (c.500 B.C.)

Persia (pûr′zhə, -shə), old alternate name for the Asian country Iran. The article IRAN contains a description of the geography and economy of the modern country and a short account of its history since the Arab invasion of the 7th cent. The present article is a brief sketch of the history of the ancient Persian Empire, in which the present-day Iran has its roots. The speakers of Iranian languages may have migrated into that part of Asia as early as 1500 B.C. Presumably they were originally a nomadic tribe who filtered down through the Caucasus to the Iranian plateau. They apparently subjugated peoples already there and mingled with them, but their dominance of particular areas is recorded in the place names Parsua and Parsumash. The Assyrian rulers were by the 9th cent. B.C. sending expeditions against them, and the recurrence of those campaigns is evidence of the strength of the early Persians. By the 6th cent. B.C. they were established in the present-day region of Fars and were benefiting from the decline of Elam. Fars (or Persis to the Greeks) was a recognizable district of the Assyrian Empire like the neighboring but greater Media. The Persian rulers, claiming descent from one Achaemenes (or Hakhamanesh), were associated with the Medes, who created a strong state in the 7th cent. Cyaxares, son of Phraortes, founder of Median power, was one of the kings who brought about the fall of Nineveh (612 B.C.) and broke the hegemony of the Assyrians. The Persian ruler of about the same time, Cambyses I, was vassal to Cyaxares. According to Herodotus he married the daughter of the Median ruler Astyages (Cyaxares' son), and his son Cyrus was thus also grandson of Cyaxares; this account has been branded by some scholars as a pious attempt to falsify genealogy. At any rate, after the Persians had aided the Medes in establishing the power of the Medes, Cyrus, who later became known as CYRUS THE GREAT, took over the rule of Media from Astyages in the middle of the 6th cent. B.C. In an amazingly short time Cyrus had extended his conquests from Elam and Media west and north. He pushed into Asia Minor, where Croesus, the king of Lydia, vainly sought by an alliance with Nabonidus of Babylonia and Amasis II of Egypt to withstand the conqueror. Cyrus crushed the coalition, and by 546 B.C. the greatness of the Persian Empire was established. It was to endure long under his successors, the Achaemenids. From the beginning the Persians built on the foundations of the earlier states. The organization of the Assyrians was taken over and improved, and Cyrus himself imported artists and artisans from Babylonia and Egypt to create his palace and tomb at Pasargadae. The dynamic new state was, however, troubled almost from the start by dynastic troubles. Cambyses II, son of Cyrus, did away with Smerdis, another son of Cyrus, in order to have unchallenged power, but when Cambyses was absent on a successful raid into Egypt, an imposter claiming to be Smerdis appeared, and usurped the throne. A civil war ensued, and after Cambyses died, a new claimant, Darius I, appeared against the false Smerdis. He made his claims good, and after putting down disorders, he molded the administration of the empire into the centralized system that was remarkable for its efficiency. Satraps, or governors, were set up to rule firmly and arbitrarily over the various regions, but to keep check on the satraps, who were potential aspirants to central power, each was accompanied by a secretary and a military commander who were responsible to the great king alone. This centralized system was supported by an intricate and excellent system of communication, for the Persians were the first important ancient people to use the horse efficiently for communication and transport. Darius also continued and broadened Cyrus' policy of encouraging the local cultures within the empire, allowing the people to worship their own gods and to follow their own customs so long as their practices did not conflict with the necessities of Persian administration. Despite this tolerance there were rebellions by the Egyptians, Lydians, and Babylonians, all of which Darius ruthlessly suppressed. The religion of Persia itself was Zoroastrianism, and the unity of Persia may be attributed in part to the unifying effect of that broadly established faith. Darius was also a patron of the arts, and magnificent palaces standing on high terraces beautified the capitals of Susa and Persepolis (see PERSIAN ART AND ARCHITECTURE). He was also a conqueror. Persian rule was pushed far eastward past the Arius (Hari Rud) River into modern Afghanistan and Pakistan. Egypt had already been attacked by Cambyses, and although it was to prove recalcitrant and rebellious, succeeding Persian kings were to maintain hegemony there. Darius pushed as far north as the Danube in his exploits, but the fighting against the Scythians was obscure and certainly unfruitful. Even more unprofitable for Persia was its embroilment with the Greeks. The Persians in taking over Lydia had come into contact with the Greek colonies in Asia Minor (Ionia). There were Greeks (notably the exiled Athenian tyrant Hippias) at the court of Darius, and the Persians immediately began to borrow from Greek art and thought, as they did from all advanced cultures to the enrichment of Persia. At the beginning of the 5th cent. B.C., however, the Ionian cities were involved in trouble with the great king. Darius put down the rebellion, then organized an expedition to punish the city-states in Greece proper that had lent aid to the rebellious cities. This expedition began the PERSIAN WARS. Ultimately Darius' army was defeated at Marathon, and his son Xerxes I, who succeeded to the throne in 486 B.C., fared no better at Salamis. The Greeks had successfully defied the power of the great king. The effects of the Greek victory were, however, confined to Greece itself and had no consequences in Persia. Nor did the Greek triumph exclude Persia from taking part in the affairs of the Greek world. Persian influence was strong, and Persian gold was poured out to aid one Greek city-state or another in the interminable struggle for power. It is noteworthy that when Themistocles, the victor of Salamis, was exiled from Athens, he took refuge at the court of Artaxerxes I, who had succeeded Xerxes I in 464 B.C. In the time of Artaxerxes the difficulties of maintaining so wide an empire had begun to appear. Some of the satraps showed ambitions to rule, and the Egyptians, helped by the Athenians, undertook a long rebellion. Violence against the great king himself was a disturbing factor. Xerxes I had been murdered, and Xerxes II, son of Artaxerxes, was killed after a reign of 45 days by a half brother, who was in turn overthrown by another half brother, Darius II. In the reign of the second Darius the power of the satraps was shown in the careers of PHARNABAZUS and TISSAPHERNES, who interfered with some effect in the affairs of Greece. When Darius II died, the most celebrated of the dynastic troubles occurred in the rebellion of CYRUS THE YOUNGER against ARTAXERXES II, which came to an end with the death of Cyrus in the battle of Cunaxa (401 B.C.). Cyrus' defeat was recorded in Xenophon's *Anabasis,* and although the importance of Cyrus' revolt may be exaggerated it cannot be denied that there were signs of decay in the empire. Although Evagoras of Cyprus was brought to heel after the Peace of ANTALCIDAS (386 B.C.) was dictated to Greece by the great king, Egypt, which had become independent again in 405 B.C., continued to revolt and the efforts of the armies of Artaxerxes II to reassert control were fruitless. Artaxerxes III, who gained the throne by massacring his brother's family, was more successful in Egypt, but his triumph was brief. He was himself killed by his counselor, the eunuch Bagoas. Darius III in turn murdered Bagoas and ruled with considerable splendor after 336, but only for a short period. In 334, ALEXANDER THE GREAT and his Macedonian army crossed the Hellespont and routed the Persians on the Granicus. The battle of Issus followed in 333, and in 331 the battle of Gaugamela brought an end to the Achaemenid empire. Darius, last of the great kings, fled east before the conqueror to the remote province of Bactria, where he was assassinated by his own cousin, Bessus. Alexander also came east and, defeating Bessus, had the whole empire in his grasp. Alexander went on to India and created the greatest empire the world had yet seen. It lasted, however, only for the brief period of his life and then was torn apart by the quarrels of his successors (the DIADOCHI). Persia fell for the most part to Seleucus I and his successors (the Seleucids), but their grasp on the vast territories was weak administratively, although they did introduce a vital Hellenistic culture, mingling Greek with Persian elements. Media Atropatene (Azerbaijan) was never really under Seleucid rule. The rulers of Bactria from the beginning were at least quasi-independent and in the middle of the 3d cent. revolted and established absolute independence. At the same time Parthia under the leadership of the Arsacids (see under ARSACES) cast off Seleucid rule and established a Parthian empire as a sort of successor to the old Persian Empire. Although even under the greatest of the Parthians (Tiridates, Mithradates I, and Mithradates II) the realm did not have the old extent, it was formidable and was a rival to Rome. The Romans in almost continuous warfare failed to halt the Parthian drives to the west, which were often supported by local ambitious or frightened rulers under Rome. Only in the 2d cent. A.D. did the Parthian rule begin to wane. The Parthians were replaced (A.D. c. 226) by the more vigorous SASSANID dynasty, when ARDASHIR I (whose name is another form of Artaxerxes) ousted and killed the last Parthian ruler and built a new empire out of the ruins of Parthian and Seleucid power. The Sassanids were the true heirs of the Achaemenids. Ardashir I, Shapur I, and Shapur II all were strong kings, able and successful opponents of the Romans. Ctesiphon became the center of a magnificent state that persisted while the Roman Empire was whittled away. The Byzantines were unable to match them. Khosru I in the 6th cent. invaded Syria, and under Khosru II (whose affairs were linked with those of the Byzantines) the Sassanid court was legendary in its splendor. Ctesiphon and Firuzabad were magnificent cities, the administration of the empire was efficient, the productivity of the cities was remarkable, and the art in metalwork, in architecture, in sculpture, and in textiles was superb. Persia developed as a strong centralized state, based on a revived Zoroastrian religion and a class society. Shortly after the death of Khosru II, however, the old Sassanid power toppled. Invading Arabs succeeded in taking Ctesiphon in 637. Islam replaced Zoroastrianism, and the caliphate made Persia a part of a larger pattern, from which later was to emerge modern Iran. See E. E. Herzfeld, *Archaeological History of Persia* (1935); G. G. Cameron, *History of Early Iran* (1936, repr. 1969); P. S. R. Payne, *The Splendor of Persia* (1957); Sir Percy Sykes, *History of Persia* (3d ed. 1958, repr. 1969); A. T. Olmstead, *History of the Persian Empire* (2d ed. 1969); Roman Girshman et al., *Persia, the Immortal Kingdom* (1971).

Persian art and architecture. The high plateau of Iran, bounded by fierce mountains and deserts, has seen the flow of many migrations and the development of many cultures. Although earlier civilizations are known, the first finds of artistic importance are the superb ceramics from Susa and Persepolis (c.3500 B.C.). On tall goblets and large bowls are symmetrical designs that cover the surfaces with stylized abstractions of animals, particularly water birds and ibex. The choice of subjects from nature, simplified into almost unrecognizable patterns, may be called the formative principle of Persian art. Much of 4th-millennium Iranian art is strongly influenced by that of Mesopotamia. The 3d-millennium art of Elam, found at Sialk and Susa, also follows Mesopotamian styles, and this trend is continued in the less well-known Elam and Urartu art of the 2d millennium. From mountainous Luristan comes an art that has aroused much controversy. Probably dated 1200–700 B.C., the many small bronze objects are thought to be mostly weapons and horse trappings—bits, bridle ornaments, rein rings, and pole tops. The treasure of Ziwiye (Sakiz), a hoard containing gold, silver, and ivory objects, included a few Luristan pieces. These provide a definite link with the art of the Scythians known as the animal style. The Ziwiye Treasure is roughly divided into four styles: Assyrian, Scythian, proto-Achaemenid (with strong Greek influences), and native, or provincial. Dated c.700 B.C., this remarkable collection of objects illustrates the heterogeneity of types and sources in early Iranian art. A unified style emerges in the Achaemenid period (c.550–330 B.C.). Influenced by the Greeks, the Egyptians, and those from other provinces of the Persian Empire, the Achaemenids evolved a monumental style in which relief sculpture is used as an adjunct to massive architectural complexes. Foundations of the palace of Cyrus at Pasargadae, of Artaxerxes I at Susa, and above all extensive remains of the magnificent palace complex of Darius I and Xerxes I at Persepolis reveal plans that characteristically show great columned audience halls; in front of the halls were colonnaded porticoes, flanked by square towers and set on high terraces. The palaces were approached by double flights of steps converging at the top. Although there are marked analogies to Egyptian, Greek, and Assyrian architecture, the style as a whole and the feeling for space and scale are distinctive. The Persepolitan columns were slenderer and more closely fluted than those of Greece. The bases were high, often bell shaped. The capitals were composed of the foreparts of two bulls set back to back or of other animals above volutes with rosette ornament. In the sculpture, of an ordered clarity and simplicity, heraldic stylization is subtly combined with effects of realism. Typical are the low stone reliefs of a procession of tribute bearers that adorn the great double staircase approaching the audience hall of Xerxes I (Persepolis) and the famous *Frieze of Archers* (Louvre, from the palace of Darius I at Susa), executed in molded and enameled brick, a technique of Babylonian-Assyrian origin. The great care lavished on every stone detail is found in the fine gold and silver rhytons (drinking horns), bowls, jewelry, and other objects. After the death of Alexander the Great (323 B.C.), there was turmoil in Iran until the rise of the Parthians (c.250 B.C.). Theirs is essentially a crude art, synthesizing Hellenistic motifs with Iranian forms. Buildings of dressed stone and rubble and brick were decorated with sculpted heads and mural paintings. The larger-than-life-size bronze statue from Shami of a ruler is the most outstanding remaining Parthian monument. Of far greater artistic importance is the contribution of the Sassanids, who ruled Iran from A.D. 226 to the middle of the 7th cent. Adapting and expanding previous styles and techniques, they rebuilt the Parthian capital at Ctesiphon. There a great palace with a huge barrel vault (*ivan*) was constructed of rubble and brick. Sassanid architecture is decorated with carved stone or stucco reliefs and makes use of colorful stone mosaics. Beautiful gold and silver dishes, bowls, and ewers, often decorated with hunting scenes or animals in high relief, and textiles with symmetrical, heraldic designs also remain. The Sassanids recorded their triumphs on immense outdoor rock reliefs scattered throughout Iran, often using the same sites that the Achaemenids had covered with reliefs and inscriptions. In Afghanistan at BAMIAN are ruins that show the great impact of Iranian art forms on works from the 4th to the 8th centuries. Frescoes and colossal Buddhas adorn Bamian's monasteries, revealing a fusion of Greco-Buddhist and Sassano-Iranian elements. Little remains from the early centuries of Islam in Iran, but the influence of Persia on ISLAMIC ART AND ARCHITECTURE in Syria and Palestine is very strong. A significant innovation by the Persians is the raising of a dome over a square hall by means of SQUINCHES. Also influential was their use of cut-stucco decoration, various intricate motifs, and ever-apparent symmetry. The earliest important Islamic monument extant in Iran is the mausoleum of Ismail the Samanid at Bukhara. Dated 907, it is a solid, square building in cut-brick style, covered by a dome. During this early period, ceramics were raised to a major art form. The finest were the "calligraphy wares" of Nishapur and Samarkand. The star-shaped tomb tower of Qabus (1006) presents a form with far-reaching influence. Both pottery and metalwork were further developed under the Seljuk Turks in the 11th and 12th cent. Luster and "minai" ceramics—using overglaze enamel colors including leaf gilding—both with intricate scenes of court life, were produced at Rayy, Kashan, and elsewhere. The Mongol invasions of the first half of the 13th cent. destroyed many towns and much art. We know little of Persian painting until the so-called Mongol school of the 14th cent. The most famous work of this period is the magnificent Demotte *Shah Namah* (The History of Kings). The book has been divided up, and many leaves are in American collections. The pictures are large, somber in color, and free and lively in execution, with landscape playing an important role. Small *Shah Namahs* have simple illustrations in yellow, red, blue, and gold. Timurid painting of the 15th cent. employs smaller figures and more static compositions. Chinese influences have been integrated and patterned symmetry re-emerges. Bihzad, the greatest painter in this style, is renowned for his fine, firm line and exquisite delicacy. The Blue Mosque at Tabriz, named for its brilliant faïence casing, is contemporary. Mosaic faience-covered architecture reached its height in 16th-century Esfahan in the great building complex Maidan-i Shah. Under the Safavid dynasty palaces were decorated with mural paintings, which have been heavily restored. Single-figure portraits and ink drawings were also made for the Safavids. In book illustrations, figures become sinuous, color and pattern run riot, and, at best, the effect is that of ornate jewelry. A masterpiece of Safavid illumination is the *Shah Namah* of Shah Tamasp, which incorporates the greatest developments in painting of the early 1520s to the mid-1530s (published in facsimile as *The King's Book of Kings,* 1972). In the 17th-century, art fell under European and Indian influences and rapidly degenerated. Under the Qajar dynasty a distinctive, theatrical style is developed in architecture, painting, and the decorative arts. The so-called Neo-Achaemenid style, which characterizes the public buildings of modern Tehran, points to a conscious effort at reviving and integrating the ancient heritage in modern Iran. There are excellent collections of Persian art in Tehran; the Metropolitan Museum; the Museum of Fine Arts, Boston; and the Victoria and Albert Museum. See A. U. Pope, ed., *A Survey of Persian Art* (14 vol., 1965–67).

Persian cat: see CAT.

Persian Gulf, arm of the Arabian Sea, 90,000 sq mi (233,100 sq km), between Arabia and Iran, extending c.600 mi (970 km) from the Shatt al Arab delta to the Strait of Hormuz, which links it with the Gulf of Oman. The Persian Gulf, called the Arabian Gulf by the Arabs, is very shallow and has many islands, of which Bahrain is the largest. It was generally thought that the gulf extended farther north and that sediment dropped by the Tigris, Euphrates, Karun, and Karkheh rivers filled the northern part of the gulf to create a great delta; but geologic investigations now indicate that the coastline has not moved and that the marshlands of the delta represent a sinking of the earth's crust. The Persian Gulf was an important transportation route in antiquity but declined with the fall of Mesopotamia. In succeeding centuries control of the region was contested by Arabs, Persians, Turks, Russians, and Western Europeans. In 1853, Britain and the Arab sheikhdoms of the Persian Gulf signed the Perpetual Maritime Truce, formalizing the temporary truces of 1820 and 1835; the sheikhs agreed to stop harassing British shipping in the Arabian Sea and to recognize Britain as the dominant power in the gulf. These sheikhdoms thus became known as the Trucial States. An international agreement among the major powers in 1907 placed the gulf in the British sphere of influence. Although oil was discovered in the gulf in 1908, it was not until the 1930s, when major finds were made, that keen international interest in the region revived. Since World War II the Persian Gulf oil fields, among the most productive in the world, have been extensively developed, and modern port facilities have been constructed. In the late 1960s, following British military withdrawal from the area, the United States and the USSR sought to fill the vacuum. In 1971 the first U.S. military installation in the gulf was established at Bahrain. The long-standing Arab-Persian conflict in the gulf, combined with the desire of all the states for control of large oil reserves, has led to international boundary disputes. Iraq and Iran argued over navigation rights on the Shatt al Arab, through which Iran's main ports and most productive oil fields are reached. Iran and the sheikhdom of Ras al Khaima contested ownership of the oil-rich islands of Abu Musa and Greater and Lesser Tunb at the entrance to the gulf. Iranian forces occupied these islands in Dec., 1971.

Persian language, member of the Iranian group of the Indo-Iranian subfamily of the Indo-European family of languages (see INDO-IRANIAN LANGUAGES). The official language of Iran, it has about 15 million speakers, of whom 12 million live in Iran and 3 million in Afghanistan. Historically the Persian language falls into three periods: Old, Middle, and Modern. Old Persian is known chiefly from cuneiform inscriptions dating from the time of the Achaemenid kings of ancient Persia (6th–4th cent. B.C.). Old Persian was highly inflected, as was Avestan, which is regarded by some as a form of Old Persian and by others as a separate tongue. Avestan was the language of the sacred texts of ZOROASTRIANISM that are known as the Avesta (probably composed c.7th–5th cent. B.C.). Middle Persian derives directly from Old Persian. Also called Pahlavi, Middle Persian prevailed under the Sassanid, or Sassanian, rulers of Persia (3d–7th cent. A.D.). Grammatically, much simplification of inflection took place in Middle Persian, which was recorded both in an Aramaic alphabet and in a script called Pahlavi. Middle Persian also had a noteworthy literature of Manichaean and Zoroastrian texts. The modern form of Persian evolved directly from Middle Persian and may be said to have begun in the 9th or 10th cent. A.D. It has not changed much since that date. The grammar of Modern Persian is comparatively simple. The inflection of nouns and verbs has been greatly reduced since the ancient stage of the language. A number of Arabic words were added to the vocabulary as the result of the conquest of the Persians by the Muslim Arabs in the 7th cent. A.D. Modern Persian is the medium of an old and great literature and is written in a modification of the Arabic alphabet. See Roland G. Kent, *Old Persian* (1950); A. K. S. Lambton, *Persian Grammar* (1971).

Persian literature. The oldest extant writings of the Persians are found in ancient inscriptions, but these are of historical and not literary value. The first major literary works are religious, particularly the scriptures of the *Avesta* and the later Pahlavi writing of the Sassanian period (see ZOROASTRIANISM). After the Sassanids were overthrown by the invasion of the Arabs (7th cent. A.D.), the new religion of Islam became the dominant theme, and Arabic became the literary language for a time. Many notable works in

Arabic are, therefore, of Persian authorship (see ARABIC LITERATURE). In the 9th cent., however, Persian emerged again as the literary language, now garnished with many Arabic words. Despite a succession of political disasters, literature flourished in the 10th cent. and in the ages that followed. The national epic, the *Shah Namah,* was written by FIRDAUSI, and a century later the mathematician OMAR KHAYYAM wrote the verses that are, through Edward FitzGerald's superb adaptation, better known to the English-speaking world than any other Persian work. FARID AD DIN ATTAR (d. c.1229) was converted to SUFISM and produced mystical poetry of the highest order. Jalal ed-Din RUMI and SADI continued and expanded the mystic poetry of Sufism in the 13th cent., and the exquisite lyrics of the 14th-century HAFIZ are interpreted by Muslim scholars as religious allegories. The form of this mystic poetry and its subtle symbolism make it one of the greatest of all contributions to world literature. Its influence in the Muslim world was incalculably great. The prose literature too—tales, fables, allegories, and philosophical and scientific works—also had tremendous influence. Many of the stories that later had great popularity in the West are to be found in the earlier Persian collections. Persia also produced historical writings, and several of its historians surpassed their Arab models. Gardizi, who flourished in the 11th cent., dealt with Persian history from ancient times, while Baihaqi (d. 1077) chronicled the Ghaznivid period, Ali ar-Ravandi (d. 1203) wrote about the Seljuks, Rashid ad-Din (d. 1318) recorded the Mongol period, and Ali Yazdi (d. 1424) wrote of the Timurids. After the 15th cent. there was a decline in Persian literature. The revival of religious thought in the 19th cent., especially in BABISM and BAHAISM, gave rise to a new literature. The influence of Western ideas as well as the struggle for political independence and social justice occasioned many changes in the literature of the 20th cent. Political and social themes became paramount, and the language of literature forsook classical modes, becoming simple and direct. Among the major modern poets are Iradj, Abid e-Pishawari, Parwin, and Nima. The 1920s produced Persian experiments in fiction. Two celebrated modern novelists are S. Hedayet and M. M. Hejazi. See A. J. Arberry, *Classical Persian Literature* (1958); E. G. Browne, *A Literary History of Persia* (4 vol., 1928-30; repr. 1956-59); Reuben Levy, *The Epic of the Kings* (1967) and *An Introduction to Persian Literature* (1969).

Persian lynx: see CARACAL.

Persian Wars, 500 B.C.–449 B.C., series of conflicts fought between Greek states and the Persian Empire. The writings of Herodotus, who was born c.484 B.C., are the great source of knowledge of the history of the wars. At their beginning the Persian Empire of Darius I included all of W Asia as well as Egypt. On the coast of Asia Minor were a few Greek city-states, and these revolted (c.500) against Darius' despotic rule. Athens and Eretria in Euboea (now Évvoia) gave the Ionian cities some help but not enough, and they were subdued (494) by the Persians. Darius decided to punish Athens and Eretria and to add Greece to his vast empire. In 492 a Persian expedition commanded by Mardonius conquered Thrace and Macedon, but its fleet was crippled by a storm. A second expedition, commanded by Artaphernes and Datis, destroyed (490) Eretria and then proceeded against Athens. The Persians encamped 20 mi (32 km) from the city, on the coast plain of Marathon. Here they were attacked and decisively defeated (Sept.) by the Athenian army of 10,000 men aided by 1,000 men from Plataea. The Athenians were heavily outnumbered, but fought bravely under MILTIADES, whose strategy won the battle. They had sought the help of Sparta, by way of the Athenian courier Pheidippides, who covered the distance (c.150 mi; 241 km) from Athens to Sparta within two days. The Spartan forces, however, failed to reach Marathon until the day after the battle. The Persians did not continue the war. Darius at once began preparations for a third expedition, so powerful that the overwhelming of Greece would be certain. He died (486) before his preparations were completed, but they were continued by Xerxes I, his son and successor. The Athenians were persuaded by their leader THEMISTOCLES to strengthen their navy. In 480, Xerxes reached Greece with a tremendous army and navy. The route of the Persian land forces lay through the narrow pass of THERMOPYLAE. The pass was defended by the Spartan LEONIDAS; his small army held back the Persians but was eventually trapped by a Persian detachment; the Spartan contingent chose to die fighting in the pass rather than flee. The Athenians put their trust in their navy and made little effort to defend their city, which was taken (480) by the Persians. Shortly afterward the Persian fleet was crushed in the straits off the island of SALAMIS by a Greek force. The Greek victory was aided by the strategy of Themistocles. Xerxes returned to Persia but left a military force in Greece under his general, Mardonius. The defeat of this army in 479 at Plataea near Thebes (now Thívai) by a Greek army under the Spartan PAUSANIAS (with ARISTIDES commanding the Athenians) and a Greek naval victory at Mycale on the coast of Asia Minor ended all danger from Persian invasions of Europe. During the remaining period of the Persian Wars the Greeks in the Aegean islands and Asia Minor, under Athenian leadership (see DELIAN LEAGUE) strengthened their position without seeking conquest.

Persian wild ass: see ONAGER.

Persichetti, Vincent, 1915–, American composer, b. Philadelphia. Persichetti has taught at the Philadelphia Conservatory and at the Juilliard School of Music in New York City. His music is notable for polytonal combinations, contrapuntal density, and incisive rhythm. He has written four symphonies, numerous ballet and chamber works, and choral compositions. Persichetti is the author of *Twentieth-Century Harmony* (1961).

persimmon: see EBONY.

Persis (pûr'sĭs), Christian at Rome. Rom. 16.12.

Persius or **Aulus Persius Flaccus** (pûr'shēəs; ôl'əs, flăk'əs), A.D. 34–A.D. 62, Roman satirical poet, b. Etruria. A member of a distinguished family, he went to Rome in boyhood, was educated there, and came under the influence of the Stoic philosopher Lucius Annaeus Cornutus, to whom he became attached in lasting friendship. Gentle and modest by nature, Persius had high moral standards. His writings (only six short satires), influenced in manner by HORACE and LUCILIUS, preach Stoic moral doctrine. He exposed to censure the corruption and folly of contemporary Roman life, contrasting it with the ideals of the Stoics and of earlier Rome. Persius' writing is harsh, obscure, and difficult to translate.

personality, in psychology, the total of the distinctive characteristics of an individual, the stable and shifting patterns of relationships between these characteristics, their origins, and the ways they interact to help or hinder the adjustment of a person to other people and situations. Personality structure includes emotions and moods, or temperament, and the individual's outlook and attitudes. In understanding personality, psychologists make use of the terms *trait,* which denotes a personal characteristic that remains reasonably constant in different situations, such as sensitivity, and *type,* which denotes a fixed pattern of traits. Many comprehensive groupings of types, or typologies, have been devised. Thus there are generalized groupings based on ways in which individuals perceive images and groupings based on ways in which individuals look at value systems; Jung's classification of individuals as extroverts or introverts is also a typology (see EXTROVERSION and INTROVERSION). Typologies have also been devised based on empirical examination of personality traits in samplings of large numbers of individuals. G. W. Allport and other psychologists believe that, in general, typologies do not lead to a complete understanding of personality since individuals cannot be grouped together in a few discrete classes. Behavioral psychology emphasizes the role of learning (habits) in personality development and considers learning to be the main component of behavior (see BEHAVIORISM). In psychoanalytic theory, personality is seen to develop out of three components, the id, ego, and superego. PSYCHOANALYSIS and other schools of psychiatry emphasize unconscious levels of motivation and stress the importance of early childhood experiences in determining mature personality. Many psychiatrists accept the importance of childhood determinants but emphasize that personality changes occur throughout life as a result of changing social experiences (see PSYCHIATRY). Physical determinants of personality are emphasized in the constitutional theory of the American psychologist W. H. Sheldon, which relates physical body type with personality type. PSYCHOLOGICAL TESTS have been devised to measure personality variants.

personal property: see PROPERTY.

personification, figure of speech in which inanimate objects or abstract ideas are endowed with human qualities, e.g., allegorical morality plays where characters include Good Deeds, Beauty, and Death. John Ruskin termed sentimentalized, exaggerated personification the "pathetic fallacy." See also ALLEGORY; APOSTROPHE; and METONYMY.

personnel management: see INDUSTRIAL MANAGEMENT.

Persons or **Parsons, Robert** (both: pär'sənz), 1546–1610, English Jesuit missionary. He left a fellowship at Balliol College, Oxford, and went to the Continent to be received (1575) into the Roman Catholic Church, then entered the Society of Jesus and was ordained (1578). Active in the English College at Rome, Persons probably suggested the secret Jesuit mission that was sent to England. That mission (1580-81) to reestablish Roman Catholicism in England, which he undertook with Saint Edmund CAMPION, was the most notable event in Persons's career. When Campion was caught, Persons fled to the Continent, where he remained the rest of his life, trying to promote Catholicism in England by political schemes and by building up in France and Spain seminaries and monasteries for English Catholics. The school he founded at Eu was later transferred to Saint-Omer, and in 1794 it moved to Lancashire, England, where it became Stonyhurst College. Persons was rector of the English College from 1597 to 1610. Of his many works the best remembered is the devotional *Book of Resolution; or, The Christian Directory* (1582).

perspective, in art, any method employed to represent three-dimensional space on a flat surface or in relief sculpture. Although many periods in art showed some progressive diminution of objects seen in depth, linear perspective, in the modern sense, was probably first formulated in 15th-century Florence by the architects Brunelleschi and Alberti. Brunelleschi designed (c.1420) two panels depicting architectural views of Florence, in which he constructed a mathematically proportioned system of perspective. Alberti, in his *De pittura* (1435), harnessed the technique of perspective to the theory that painting is an imitation of reality. He viewed the picture plane as a window through which one looks at the visible world. Objects in the picture were to be systematically foreshortened as they receded into the distance. Orthogonal lines converged to a single vanishing point, which was to correspond to the fixed viewpoint of the spectator. Reflecting the growth of humanism, the spectator played a new role in art, as man was to determine the measurement of all things. The Italian artists who experimented with perspective, including Donatello, Masaccio, Uccello, and Piero della Francesca, sometimes diverged from the rules for a greater artistic effect. In general, however, the 15th-century Italian artists tended to work within a geometrical system, whereas the contemporary Flemish painters used more empirical means to achieve a convincing delineation of space. The technique of linear perspective had an immense influence on the development of Western art. In the 20th cent., however, its use has considerably declined, since many artists have rebelled against the conception of art as a mirror image of reality. Aerial or atmospheric perspective was developed primarily by Leonardo da Vinci. In general, it is based on the perception that contrasts of color and of light and dark appear greater, and contours more defined, in near objects than in far. Aerial perspective takes note of the recessive character of cool colors and the prominence of warm colors. In Far Eastern art, perspective effects were achieved by the atmospheric method, often incorporating zones of mist to separate near and far space. See studies by John White (2d ed., 1967) and R. V. Cole (1970).

perspiration: see SWEAT.

Perth, James Eric Drummond, 16th **earl of,** 1876–1951, British diplomat. He was the first secretary general of the League of Nations (1919-33) and ambassador to Rome (1933-39) and served (1939-40) as chief adviser on foreign publicity with the ministry of information. He succeeded to his earldom in 1937. From 1947 until his death he was deputy leader of the Liberal party.

Perth, city (1971 pop. 97,242; urban agglomeration pop. 639,622), capital of Western Australia, SW Australia, on the estuary of the Swan River. Fremantle is Perth's port. Perth is a communications and transportation center and the financial, commercial, and cultural hub of the state. The suburbs of Fremantle, Kwinana, and Welshpool have heavy industries. Perth was founded in 1829 but did not gain importance until the Coolgardie gold rush (1890s), the development of the port at Fremantle, and the construction of rail lines to the east (early 20th cent.). The Univ. of Western Australia and Murdoch Univ. are in Perth. It is also the seat of Roman Catholic and Anglican archbishops. Perth is a very isolated city; Adelaide, its closest large neighbor, is nearly 2,000 mi (3,219 km) away.

Perth, burgh (1971 pop. 43,051), county town of Perthshire, central Scotland, on the Tay River. It was called St. Johnstoun until the 17th cent. Perth is famous for dye works and cattle markets and has linen and wool factories. Strategically located between the Highlands and the Lowlands, Perth was long an important military fortress. It was the capital of Scotland from the 11th to the mid-15th cent. James I of Scotland was murdered there in 1437. John Knox preached his famous sermon against idolatry in the Church of St. John in 1559; the resulting iconoclasm leveled the city's four monasteries. Gowrie House (no longer standing) was the scene (1600) of a plot to seize James VI (James I of England; see RUTHVEN, family). James I in 1618 issued the Five Articles of Perth, which opened the battle between crown and church. The earl of Montrose took the city after the battle of Tippermuir in 1644; Oliver Cromwell seized it again in 1651. It was held by Jacobites in 1689, 1715, and 1745. Points of interest are Tay St., beside the river, and the Inches, parks that were formerly islands in the Tay. A prison built in 1812 for French prisoners of war is in Perth. In 1975, Perth became part of the Tayside region.

Perth Amboy (ăm'boi), city (1970 pop. 38,798), Middlesex co., NE N.J., with a harbor on Arthur Kill at the mouth of the Raritan River, which is crossed there to Staten Island by the Outerbridge Crossing (1928); settled 1683, inc. as a city 1718. A port of entry, Perth Amboy is a shipping center with industries that include the smelting and refining of lead, copper, and silver; oil refining; printing; and the manufacture of chemicals. The city's name combines the old Indian name *Amboy* with that of the Earl of Perth. It was the capital of East Jersey from 1684 until the union of East and West Jersey in 1702 and was alternate capital with Burlington until 1790. Perth Amboy grew after connections with the interior were established, particularly after it became the tidewater terminal of the Lehigh Valley RR in 1876 and a coal-shipping point. Of interest are the former mansion of Gov. William Franklin, which Gen. William Howe used as his headquarters in the Revolution, and St. Peter's Church (1722; Episcopal). The Grimké sisters, noted abolitionists, lived in Perth Amboy.

Perthshire, county (1971 pop. 127,138), 2,493 sq mi (6,457 sq km), central Scotland. The county town is PERTH. It is largely a mountainous region; the heights of the Ochils, the Sidlaws, and the Grampians are within its borders. Lochs Tay, Earn, Rannoch, Ericht, and Katrine are among the largest of its many lakes. The Forth and the Tay, with their tributaries, are the principal rivers. Wild forests and rolling moor cover much of the area, which is noted for its fine scenery. Agriculture is the leading occupation; both arable and pastoral farming are important. Strathearn and the Carse of Gowrie are especially fertile districts. Major hydroelectric projects have been built; all the power stations in the Highlands are controlled from Pitlochry. Fishing, tourism, textiles, and distilling are other industries. Kings of Scotland were long crowned at SCONE. In 1975, Perthshire was divided between the Tayside and Central regions.

Pertinax (Publius Helvius Pertinax) (pûr'tĭnăks), 126–193, Roman emperor (193), b. Liguria. Formerly a general, he reluctantly succeeded COMMODUS on the throne. Attempting to curb license in the Praetorian Guard, he was slain by a soldier, thus ending his brief reign of three months. DIDIUS JULIANUS succeeded him.

perturbation (pŭr"tərbā'shən), in astronomy and physics, small FORCE or other influence that modifies the otherwise simple motion of some object. The term is also used for the effect produced by the perturbation, e.g., a change in the object's ENERGY or path of motion. In the solar system the dominant force is the gravitational force exerted by the sun on each planet; assuming that this is the only force, the simple elliptical orbits described by KEPLER'S LAWS are derived. However, the perturbations caused by the gravitational interaction of the planets among themselves changes and complicates the curve of these orbits. The study of perturbations has led to important discoveries in astronomy. The existence and position of Neptune was predicted because of the deviations of Uranus from its computed path. Likewise, Pluto was discovered by its effect on Neptune. One important effect of perturbations is the advance, or precession, of the PERIHELION of a planet, which can be described as a slow rotation of the entire planetary orbit. A residual advance in the perihelion of Mercury provided a valuable test of Einstein's general theory of relativity. In the atom the dominant force is the electrical force between the nucleus and the electrons; this force determines the characteristic structure, or energy levels, of the atom. The forces exerted by the electrons among themselves are perturbations that slightly modify this structure.

pertussis: see WHOOPING COUGH.

Peru (pərōō'), Span. *Perú* (pārōō'), republic (1973 est. pop. 14,640,000), 496,220 sq mi (1,285,210 km), W South America, bordering on the Pacific Ocean in the west, on Ecuador and Colombia in the north, on Brazil and Bolivia in the east, and on Chile in the south. LIMA is the capital and largest city of the country, which is divided into 23 departments and one constitutional province with the status of a department. Peru, which varies greatly in climate and topography, falls into three main geographical regions—a narrow strip of desert along the coast, a region of high mountains in the center, and a large area of forested mountains and lowlands in the east. The desert region stretches the entire length (1,410 mi/2,269 km) of Peru's Pacific coastline and is somewhat wider in the north. It is extremely arid because of the effects of the cold Humboldt, or Peru, Current in the Pacific, which acts as a barrier to the moist air over the Pacific. When a warm current appears off the coast, as it does every five or so years, there are torrential and damaging rainstorms. The coast and also the mountains are in addition more frequently shaken by severe earthquakes. Within the desert are about 40 oases (irrigated by streams flowing from the mountains) where Peru's main commercial crops (sugarcane and cotton) are grown; the principal oases are near Lima, CHICLAYO, and TRUJILLO. CALLAO (near Lima) and Matarani, Peru's leading ports, are also in the desert region. Near PISCO and ICA are large vineyards. Off the coast are small islands, notably the Lobos and Chincha islands, where guano (used as fertilizer) is harvested. The central region (c.200 mi/320 km wide) is made up mostly of three ranges of the Andes Mts., the Cordillera Occidental in the west and the Cordillera Central and its continuation, the Cordillera Real, in the east. The Cordillera Occidental includes the loftiest peaks, notably Huascarán (22,205 ft/6,768 m, Peru's highest point) and El Misti (19,150 ft/5,837 m). The rugged eastern ranges receive considerable rainfall and are drained by numerous rivers, which have cut deep canyons. Subsistence agriculture is practiced in the upper parts of the valleys. Between the eastern and western ranges of the Andes in the south, and extending into Bolivia, is the Altiplano Plateau, which includes small, scattered basins of cultivable soil and pastureland and also part of Lake Titicaca. The central region includes about 60% of Peru's population; its main cities are AREQUIPA and CUZCO, an old Inca center. The eastern region, called La Montaña, includes more than half of the country's land area. It is made up of the highly forested Cordillera Oriental of the Andes and low-lying tropical plains, covered by rain forests and drained by the Amazon River and its tributaries, the Ucayali, Marañón, Huallaga, Pastaza, Tigre, and Napo rivers. The region is generally inaccessible and sparsely inhabited, but contains much fertile soil that has not yet been cleared and cultivated. IQUITOS is the chief city of the eastern region. Peru's population is made up of three main groups: Indians (about 50% of the population), whites (13%), and mestizos (mixed white and Indian, 37%), plus small numbers of persons of Japanese, Chinese, and black African descent. Most of the Indians speak Quechua or Aymara as their first language; they live in the Andes and have retained much of their traditional way of life. In addition, there are about 100,000 Indians, divided into about 100 groups, who live in the isolated rain forest of E Peru and speak other Indian languages. The whites and mestizos are westernized, speak Spanish (the official language) as their first language, and are Roman Catholic. Power and wealth in the country is generally monopolized by the whites and a small number of the mestizos; the bulk of the mestizos and virtually all of the Indians are laborers or subsistence farmers. Farming provides the livelihood for the majority of Peruvians, many of whom (mostly Indians) remain outside the money economy. However, industry was being developed at a high rate in the 1960s and early 1970s. Within the money economy in 1970, it was estimated that manufacturing contributed 20% of the national product, and agriculture 15%. The chief farm commodities produced are cotton, sugarcane, coffee, cacao, wheat, rice, maize, and barley. Large numbers of poultry, sheep, cattle, llamas, alpacas, and hogs are raised. Peru is one of the world's foremost fishing countries in terms of the value and weight of the annual catch. The fish, mostly anchovetas (small anchovies), are

caught in the Pacific and are processed into fish meal, which is used as animal feed. Most of the fish meal is exported, and it is usually Peru's chief source of foreign exchange. A warm current that remained unusually long off the coast and drove away the anchovies virtually eliminated the catch in 1973. Peru has a large mining industry, and the most valuable minerals produced are copper and silver; other minerals extracted include gold, iron ore, mercury, phosphate rock, salt, tin ore, and zinc. Most of these minerals are found in the mountains. Petroleum is produced along the northern coast and in the Amazon basin, and there is a large refinery at Talara. Peru's principal manufactures include iron and steel, processed food, cement, refined minerals (especially copper, zinc, and lead), textiles, consumer goods (including clothing, footwear, and household appliances), and processed fish (mainly fish meal and fertilizer). There is a substantial tourist industry. Economic development has been hindered by the country's very poor transportation network, which has left large blocks of Peru isolated. In the late 1960s and early 70s the annual value of exports was considerably higher than the value of imports; this was due mainly to the large sales abroad of fish meal and copper. Other major exports are sugar, iron ore, silver, cotton, and zinc. The main imports are machinery, food, metals, chemicals, and motor vehicles. The chief trade partners are the United States, West Germany, Japan, and Argentina. Peru is a charter member of the Latin American Free Trade Area (founded 1961) and of the Andean Development Corporation (founded 1967), which also includes Chile, Colombia, Ecuador, and Venezuela and is designed to foster freer trade and economic cooperation among the five nations. Although primary and secondary education are free, there are not sufficient numbers of schools to serve the entire population. As a result, in the early 1970s almost 40% of the population over 15 years of age was illiterate. There are numerous universities, most of which were founded in the 1960s. The leading universities are at Lima, Arequipa, Trujillo, and Ica.

The Spanish Conquest. Peru has been inhabited by man since at least the 9th millennium B.C. It was later the center of several developed Indian cultures, including the Chavín (see CHAVÍN DE HUÁNTAR), the CHIMU, the NAZCA, and the AYMARA. In the 12th cent. A.D., the Quechua-speaking INCA Indians settled around Cuzco, and in the mid-15th cent. they established by conquest a large, well-organized empire that included most of present-day Peru and Ecuador and parts of Bolivia, Chile, Argentina, and Colombia. Around 1530 the empire was weakened by civil war initiated by ATAHUALPA and HUASCAR, who had been designated as dual heirs by their father, HUAYNA CAPAC, but who each wanted to control the whole empire. Atahualpa had emerged victorious by

1532, when Francisco PIZARRO, a Spaniard, arrived on the coast of Peru with a small band of adventurers. Sensing no danger to his empire, Atahualpa agreed to meet Pizarro at CAJAMARCA. However, Pizarro, whose horses and firearms (both unknown to the Incas) gave him an overriding advantage, imprisoned Atahualpa after he had refused to accept Spanish suzerainty and Christianity. The emperor's followers collected a huge ransom in gold and silver for his release; nevertheless, the Spaniards executed him in mid-1533. By late 1533, Pizarro had captured Cuzco, the Inca capital, and the empire had disintegrated. In 1535, Pizarro founded Lima, which in 1542 became the center of Spanish rule in South America. From 1536 to 1544, MANCO CAPAC, who had succeeded Atahualpa as emperor, led several unsuccessful uprisings against the Spaniards. At the same time, Pizarro and his brothers and companions (including Sebastián de BENALCÁZAR) were unsuccessfully challenged by Pedro de ALVARADO and then by Diego de ALMAGRO (who had earlier conquered part of Chile for Pizarro) and his son, who was defeated (1542) by VACA DE CASTRO, a representative of the Spanish crown sent to restore order. Pizarro forced the Indians to work in the mines, on the lands held in ENCOMIENDA from Spanish landlords, and in the small textile mills (*obrajes*). The New Laws of Bartolomé de LAS CASAS, which would have ended the abuses of the encomienda system, caused Gonzalo Pizarro to revolt (1544). He defeated the viceroy, Blasco NÚÑEZ VELA, but was in turn defeated (and executed) by Pedro de la GASCA in 1548. However, the New Laws were never administered for the benefit of the Indians. Francisco de TOLEDO, who was viceroy from 1569 to 1581, improved administration, defeated an Indian revolt under TUPAC AMARU, and systematized the use of Indian labor. Also, the viceroyalty of Peru was expanded to include all of Spanish-ruled South America except Venezuela, and the mining of silver and gold increased. Lima was the administrative, religious, economic, and cultural center of the viceroyalty. In the 18th cent. Peru was drastically reduced in size by the creation of the viceroyalty of NEW GRANADA and a viceroyalty centered at Buenos Aires (see ARGENTINA); as a result, Lima lost control over considerable trade and mineral wealth. At the same time, government in Peru was reformed. However, Spaniards retained almost complete control in the viceroyalty, and the Indians and creoles (persons of Spanish descent born in Peru) remained powerless and poor, working mostly as laborers or subsistence farmers. Led by a man with Inca ancestry who called himself TUPAC AMARU II, the Indians began a revolt in 1780, but it was fully defeated by 1783. There were a few minor uprisings by Indians and creoles in the early 19th cent.

Independence. The ideas of the French Revolution and Napoleon I's conquest (1808) of Spain led to strong independence movements in each of Spain's Latin American holdings except Peru. Peru's loyalty to Spain was due to the relatively large number of Spaniards who resided there, to the concentration of Spanish power at Lima, and to the efficiency of the government in the viceroyalty. As a result, Peru achieved independence (1821) largely because of the efforts of outsiders, notably José de SAN MARTÍN and Simón BOLÍVAR. After he had ended Spanish rule in Chile in 1818, San Martín captured the Peruvian port of Pisco in 1820. Shortly thereafter the viceroy evacuated Lima, and on July 28, 1821, José de la SERNA proclaimed the independence of Peru. However, Spanish forces remained in the interior. Bolívar took over the leadership of the liberation movement from the self-effacing San Martín after a mysterious conference (July, 1822) between the two at Guayaquil. In 1824, Bolívar and his lieutenant Antonio José de SUCRE assured Peru's independence by defeating Spain at the battles of JUNÍN and AYACUCHO. Santa Cruz left Peru to govern Bolivia in 1828, and government in Peru became confused as several military leaders vied for power. Taking advantage of the disorder, Santa Cruz joined Bolivia and Peru in a confederation in 1836. Fearing the power of the new state, Chile intervened militarily and the confederation was terminated (1839) after the battle of Yungay. Peru continued to be torn by civil strife until the emergence of Gen. Ramón CASTILLA, who was president from 1844 to 1850 and from 1855 to 1862. Under Castilla, Peru enjoyed stability and economic development. He supervised the exploitation of guano and nitrate deposits, improved the country's transportation system, and encouraged the immigration of foreigners. Although he bettered somewhat the lot of the Indians and blacks, Peruvian society remained sharply divided between the wealthy oligarchy (made up mostly of creoles) and the great majority of inhabitants (mostly Indians) who remained poor. A republican constitution was promulgated in 1860 and remained in effect until 1920. After Castilla, Peruvian politics again were in turmoil because of corruption, growing foreign indebtedness, and an attempt by Spain to regain Peru. Claiming that Peru had not met its financial obligations, Spain seized the guano-rich Chincha Islands in 1863. Aided by Chile, Bolivia, and Ecuador, Peru defeated the Spaniards at Callao in 1866; a truce was signed in 1871 and in 1879 Spain formally recognized Peru's independence. Meanwhile, under President José BALTA (1868-72), who undertook a costly program of public works, Peru's foreign debt rose dramatically. Peru's first railroad, between Mollendo and Arequipa, was built from 1868 to 1871 under the direction of Henry Meiggs. The first civilian president of Peru, Manuel PARDO (1872-76), tried to better the country's financial position, but was seriously hampered by the declining international price of guano, one of Peru's major resources. In 1873, Peru signed a secret defensive alliance with Bolivia, whose valuable coastal nitrate deposits (especially in Atacama) were worked by Chileans. When disagreements over the mining led to war between Bolivia and Chile, Peru tried to mediate but refused to declare its neutrality. Therefore, Chile declared war (1879) on Peru (see PACIFIC, WAR OF THE). Chile badly defeated the allies and by the Treaty of Ancón (1883) Peru had to yield the nitrate-rich province of Tarapacá and also to surrender the other southern coastal provinces of Tacna and Arica to Chilean administration until a plebiscite would be held 10 years later. The plebiscite was never carried out, and there ensued the TACNA-ARICA CONTROVERSY, which was not resolved until 1929. Peru emerged nearly bankrupt from the War of the Pacific. President A. A. CÁCERES (1886-90) created a syndicate of foreign capitalists to manage the guano deposits and the railroads, and thus foreign influence and holdings in Peru grew stronger.

Twentieth-Century Peru. The first third of the century was dominated by President Augusto B. LEGUÍA (1908-12, 1919-30), who for much of his tenure in office governed as a virtual dictator and successfully promoted economic development in the interest of the country's dominant oligarchy. Peru benefited, in turn, from a rubber boom in the Putumayo River region, from the opening (1914) of the Panama Canal, and from a large increase in its exports that began during World War I. In 1924 a new political party, the Alianza Popular Revolucionaria Americana (APRA), was founded; it was headed by Víctor Raúl HAYA DE LA TORRE and called for radical reform, especially of the condition of the Indians. The party was banned by Leguía and was again outlawed after Sánchez Cerro overthrew Leguía in 1930. The 1930s were marked by a bitter rivalry between leftists and rightists, with the latter dominating politics under presidents Cerro (1931-33) and Óscar R. Benavides (1933-39). A more moderate course was followed by President Manuel Prado y Ugarteche (1939-45). Peru was involved in a serious boundary dispute with Ecuador in 1941 and sided with the Allies in World War II. APRA was allowed to take part in the 1945 elections and backed the victorious moderate, José Luís Bustamante y Rivero. However, APRA split with Bustamante in 1947, and the resulting disputes led to a military coup by Manuel ODRÍA in 1948. Odría, a conservative, was president until 1956, when Prado was again elected president, this time with APRA support. Under Odría and Prado (who was in office until 1962), Peru's economic situation improved because of increased sales and U.S. loans. However, under Prado the rate of inflation increased, and as a result there was much labor unrest. In the 1962 presidential elections Haya de la Torre won by a small plurality, but did not receive the required one third of the total vote. Fearing that he would win decisively in new elections, the military seized power and conducted elections in 1963 that were won by Fernando Belaúnde Terry, a moderate reformer. Belaúnde's regime was plagued by budgetary deficits, reduced sales abroad, spiraling inflation, and poor relations with foreign companies active in Peru. In 1968 he was deposed by a military junta, which installed General Juan Velasco Alvarado as president at the head of a revolutionary government. Velasco suspended the constitution and assumed dictatorial powers. His declared intention was to democratize Peruvian society and to give the masses a greater voice in government, but few steps were taken toward fulfilling these goals. He also sought (and with more concrete results) to diversify the country's economy by exploiting systematically its natural resources (especially petroleum) with foreign help but without foreign control. In 1970 a severe earthquake in N Peru killed about 50,000 people.

Government. Under the 1933 constitution as amended, Peru's chief executive and head of state is the president, who is directly elected to a six-year term. The president is assisted by a cabinet led by a prime minister. Legislative power is vested in a bicameral parliament, consisting of the 45-member senate and the 140-member chamber of deputies. Members of both are directly elected to six-year terms. The constitution was suspended in 1968 and the parliament dissolved. A classic narrative of the Spanish conquest is that of W. H. PRESCOTT. See H. D. Disselhoff, *Daily Life in Ancient Peru* (tr. 1967); Jean Descola, *Daily Life in Colonial Peru, 1710-1820* (tr. 1968); E. P. Lanning, *Peru before the Incas* (1968); J. M. Lockhart, *Spanish Peru, 1532-1560* (1968) and *The Men of Cajamarca: A Social and Biographical Study of the First Conquerors of Peru* (1972); R. H. Marett, *Peru* (1969); François Bourricaud, *Power and Society in Contemporary Peru* (tr. 1970); F. L. Tullis, *Lord and Peasant in Peru* (1970); Grant Hilliker, *The Politics of Reform in Peru* (1971); T. E. Weil et al., *Area Handbook for Peru* (1972).

Peru (pərōō'). **1** City (1970 pop. 11,772), La Salle co., N Ill., on the Illinois River; inc. 1835. Clocks, watches, and metal products are made there. **2** City (1970 pop. 14,139), seat of Miami co., N Ind., on the Wabash River; inc. 1847. It is a processing and rail center for a fertile farm area. Among its products are furniture, plastic items, and electrical equipment. An annual summer circus festival commemorates the seven circuses that once wintered there. Peru is the birthplace of Cole Porter. Grisson Air Force Base is to the south.

Peruda (pĕryōō'də), variant of PERIDA.

Perugia (pārōō'jä), city (1971 pop. 128,542), capital of Umbria and of Perugia prov., central Italy, situated on a hill overlooking the valley of the Tiber River. It is a commercial and industrial center. Manufactures include chocolate and textiles. Perugia was inhabited by the Umbrians and the Etruscans before it came under the control of Rome (c.310 B.C.). It became a Lombard duchy in the late 6th cent. A.D. In the 12th cent. it attained the status of a free commune and gradually gained hegemony over other Umbrian cities. Although nominally under papal control, it was in fact ruled by strong tyrants until 1540, when it was conquered by Pope Paul III. To help control the city Pope Paul built an imposing citadel (designed by Antonio da San Gallo and dismantled in 1860). Perugia was the artistic center of Umbria. The Umbrian school of painting (13th-16th cent.) reached its greatest splendor with Perugino (1445-1523), the teacher of Raphael, and with Pinturicchio (1454-1518). Points of interest in the city include the imposing Palazzo dei Priori (13th-15th cent.), which houses the National Gallery of Umbria; the marble Great Fountain (13th cent.), with sculptures by Nicolò Pisano and his son Giovanni; the Collegio del Cambio [exchange hall], with fine frescoes by Perugino and his followers; the Gothic cathedral (14th-15th cent., with later baroque additions); a large Etruscan arch (with Roman and 16th-century additions); the Church of San Pietro; the Gothic Church of San Domenico, which houses an archaeological museum; the Renaissance-style Oratory of San Bernardino; and well-preserved medieval quarters. Perugia is the seat of a university founded in 1308. Nearby is an Etruscan cemetery comprising ten chambers carved out of rock.

Perugino (pārōōjē'nō), c.1445-1523?, Umbrian painter, b. near Perugia. His real name was Pietro di Cristoforo Vannucci. Perugino is, after Raphael, the greatest painter of the Umbrian school. However, his tenderness of color and simplicity of style evolved into a sentimental expression in his later years. He studied under Fiorenzo di Lorenzo, assisted Piero della Francesco at Arezzo, and was a fellow pupil of Leonardo da Vinci and Lorenzo di Credi in Verrocchio's studio in Florence. In 1479 Perugino was summoned to Rome by Pope Sixtus IV to help decorate the Sistine Chapel. Some of his work there was destroyed to make room for Michelangelo's *Last Judgment.* The remaining fresco, *Christ Giving the Keys to St. Peter,* is famous. From 1486 to 1491 Perugino worked mainly in Florence. Important works of that period are the *Madonna with Saints and Angels* (Louvre); *Pietà* (Pitti Palace, Florence); *The Crucifixion,* fresco (Santa Maria Maddalena dei Pazzi, Florence); *Madonna Enthroned with Saints* (Vatican); and *The Crucifixion* (National Gall. of Art, Washington, D.C.). His last period, centering mainly about Perugia, was one of great productivity. He had many pupils and assistants, among them the youthful Raphael. From 1496 to 1498 Perugino worked on the great altarpiece, *The Ascension,* for San Pietro of Perugia. He also undertook the decoration of the audience hall of the Cambio in Perugia, consisting of allegorical figures and two sacred subjects, *Nativity* and *Transfiguration.* In 1500 he painted the altarpiece, *Madonna and Saints,* for the Certosa of Pavia. Other works of the last period are *Triumph of Chastity* (Louvre), a panel painted for the study of Isabella d'Este at Mantua; *Virgin between St. Jerome and St. Francis* and *The Adoration of the Shepherds,* his last work (both: National Gall., London); and *Annunciation* (National Gall. of Art, Washington, D.C.). See Bernard Berenson, *Italian Painters of the Renaissance* (Vol. II, 1897, repr. 1968); biography by Edward Hutton (1907).

Peruvian bark: see CINCHONA.

Peruzzi, Baldassare (bäldäs-sä'rā pārōōt'tsē), 1481–1536, Italian architect and painter of the High Renaissance and mannerist periods. His outstanding architectural works are the Villa Farnesina (c.1505–c.1511) and the Palazzo Massimi (c.1535) in Rome. He also did architectural and painting projects for the Vatican and succeeded Raphael in 1520 as architect of St. Peter's. In painting, his use of perspective illusionism and classical figures may be seen at the Villa Farnesina, while a turn toward mannerist composition and spatial arrangement is visible in *Presentation of the Virgin* (c.1518; Santa Maria della Pace, Rome). In both architecture and painting Peruzzi adapted forms derived from ancient art to his own elegant and sophisticated style.

Pesaro (pā'zärō), city (1971 pop. 84,373), capital of Pesaro e Urbino prov., in the Marche region, central Italy, on the Adriatic Sea at the mouth of the Foglia River. It is an agricultural and industrial center and a seaside resort. Manufactures include musical instruments, motor vehicles, and ceramics. A Roman colony, Pesaro was later one of the cities of the Pentapolis (5th–11th cent.). The house of Malatesta gained power there in the 13th cent.; it was succeeded by the Sforza (15th–16th cent.) and by the dukes of Urbino (16th–17th cent.) In 1631 the city passed directly under the Holy See. Of note in Pesaro are the ducal palace (15th cent.); the municipal museum containing paintings and a fine collection of ceramics; the Rocca Constanza, a fortress of the Sforza; and the Villa Imperiale, which has 16th-century frescoes. The city was the birthplace (1794) of the composer Rossini and has a conservatory of music.

Pescadores (pĕskədôr'əz, -rəs), Mandarin *P'eng-hu,* group of 64 small islands, area c.50 sq mi (130 sq km), in Formosa (Taiwan) Strait, c.25 to 30 mi (40–50 km) off the west coast of Taiwan. They comprise a county of Taiwan. The largest islands are P'eng-hu, Yu-weng, and Pai-sha; Ma Kung, on P'eng-hu island, is the chief population center. Fishing is the main occupation, and peanuts and sweet potatoes are grown; coral is an important product. The group was named the Pescadores, or fishermen's islands, by the Portuguese in the 16th cent. China ceded them (1895) to Japan after the First Sino-Japanese War, and they were returned to China after World War II. A bridge (completed 1970) linking Pai-sha and Hsiyu islands has 76 spans and is the longest interisland bridge in the Far East. The Pescadores are subject to frequent typhoons.

Pescara, Ferdinando Francesco d'Avalos, marchese di (fārdēnän'dō fränchās'kō dävä'lōs märkā'zā ~~thē~~ pāskä'rä), 1490?–1525, Spanish-Neapolitan general in the Italian Wars. He served Charles V, Holy Roman emperor and king of Spain, and was chiefly responsible for the brilliant Spanish victory over Francis I of France at Pavia (1525). A partisan of the dispossessed Sforza dukes of Milan tried to induce the general to join in promoting an Italian national alliance against Charles, but Pescara revealed the plot to the emperor. His wife was Vittoria COLONNA.

Pescara, city (1971 pop. 122,195), capital of Pascara prov., in Abruzzi, central Italy, on the Adriatic Sea at the mouth of the Pescara River. It is a fishing port and a seaside resort. Cement and textiles are produced there.

Pesellino, Il (ēl pāzāl-lē'nō), 1422–57, Italian painter of the Florentine school, whose real name was Francesco di Stefano. He was a grandson and pupil of Giuliano Giuochi, called Pesello. Also influenced by Fra Filippo Lippi, he painted with delicacy and charm. Pesellino specialized in executing small *cassone* pictures (decorative panels for chests), such as the *Judgment Scene* and the *Story of Griselda* (Bergamo) and the *Triumphs of Petrarch* (Gardner Mus., Boston). Among the larger paintings are *Madonna* (Chantilly); *Madonna and Saints* and *Crucifixion* (Metropolitan Mus.); *Crucifixion* and *Madonna and Child* (National Gall. of Art, Washington, D.C.).

Peshawar (pəshä'wär, pəshô'ər), city (1972 metropolitan area est. pop. 331,000), capital of the North-West Frontier Province, NW Pakistan. A road and rail center near the famed Khyber Pass, Peshawar is an important military and communications center and the major depot for trade with Afghanistan. Local handicrafts and farm produce from the surrounding fertile agricultural valley are sold at colorful bazaars in the city. Industries include food processing, and the manufacture of steel, cigarettes, firearms, textiles, pharmaceuticals, furniture, and paper and board. The city, once called Purushapura, was the capital of the ancient Greco-Buddhist center of GANDHARA. It was named Peshawar [frontier town] by the Mogul emperor Akbar. The Kushan leader KANISHKA (2d cent. A.D.) made it his capital. For centuries, it was the target of successive Afghan, Persian, and Mongol invaders. A favorite residence (18th cent.) of the Afghan Durrani rulers, it was taken by the Sikhs (early 19th cent.), from whom the British captured it in 1848. It became an important outpost of British India and was a base for British military operations against rebellious PATHAN tribes. Peshawar has a museum containing Buddhist relics and Gandhara sculpture, a 2d-century Buddhist stupa bearing an inscription by Kanishka, and a university (1950) with several affiliated colleges.

Peshkov, Aleksey Maximovich: see GORKY, MAKSIM.

pessimism, philosophical opinion or doctrine that evil predominates over good; the opposite of optimism. Systematic forms of pessimism may be found in philosophy and religion. In religion Buddhism and Hinduism pessimistically appraise the world, while Christianity's pessimism is more restricted. Numerous philosophers have been pessimistic, notably Arthur SCHOPENHAUER in the 19th cent. and Martin HEIDEGGER in the 20th cent.

Pest: see BUDAPEST, Hungary.

Pestalozzi, Johann Heinrich (yō'hän hīn'rĭkh pĕ"stälôt'sē), 1746–1827, Swiss educational reformer, b. Zurich. His theories laid the foundation of modern elementary education. He studied theology at the Univ. of Zurich but was forced to abandon his career because of his political activity on behalf of the Helvetic Society, a reformist Swiss political organization. From 1769 to 1798 he lived at his farm "Neuhof" near Zurich, where he conducted a school for poor children. He then directed a school at Burgdorf (1799–1804), and from 1805 until his retirement (1825) to "Neuhof" he was director of the experimental institute at Yverdon, which was established on Pestalozzian principles. Pestalozzi's theory of education is based on the importance of a pedagogical method that corresponds to the natural order of individual development and of concrete experiences. To Pestalozzi the individuality of each child is paramount; it is something that has to be cultivated actively through education. He opposed the prevailing system of memorization learning and strict discipline and sought to replace it with a system based on love and an understanding of the child's world. His belief that education should be based on concrete experience led him to pioneer in the use of tactile objects, such as plants and mineral specimens, in the teaching of natural science to youngsters. Running through much of Pestalozzi's writing is the idea that education should be moral as well as intellectual. Never losing his commitment to social reform, Pestalozzi often reiterated the belief that society could be changed by education. His theories also influenced the development of teacher-training methods. Although he respected the individuality of the teacher, Pestalozzi nevertheless felt that there was a unified science of education that could be learned and practiced. His belief that teacher training should consist of a broad liberal education followed by a period of research and professional training has been widely adopted throughout Europe and the United States. Pestalozzi's writings in English translation include *The Hours of a Hermit* (1780, tr. 1912), *Leonard and Gertrude* (4 parts, 1781–87; rev. ed. 1790–92, 1819–20; tr. 1801, 1894), and *How Gertrude Teaches Her Children* (1801, tr. 1915). See W. S. Monroe, *History of the Pestalozzian Movement in the United States* (1907, repr. 1969); John A. Green, *The Life and Work of Pestalozzi* (1912) and *The Educational Ideas of Pestalozzi* (1914, repr. 1969); M. R. Heafford, *Pestalozzi: His Thought and Its Relevance Today* (1967); Kate Silber, *Pestalozzi: The Man and His Work* (2d ed. 1974).

pesticide, biological, physical, or chemical agent used to kill plants or animals that are harmful to man; in practice, the term pesticide is often applied only to chemical agents. Various pesticides are known as INSECTICIDES, nematicides, FUNGICIDES, HERBICIDES, and rodenticides, i.e., agents primarily effective against insects, nematodes, or roundworms, fungi, weeds, and rodents, respectively. Biological pesticidal agents such as parasites, predators, or disease producers usually cause physical injury by feeding on the pests. Physical pesticidal agents operate by crushing, wounding, smothering, or otherwise injuring them physically. Chemical pesticides act primarily as contact, stomach, or fumigant poisons. The term "contact poison" applies to any material that is capable of poisoning after it has made physical contact with a pest; such poisoning can be immediate or delayed. DDT is an example of a contact insecticide that acts as a stomach poison as well. Fumigants, which may initially have the form of a solid, liquid, or gas, kill pests while in a gaseous state. For example, paradichlorobenzene, which is used against moths, can be purchased in the form of a solid cake that vaporizes when exposed to the atmosphere. Some insecticides and fungicides are systemic, i.e., they are translocated by a plant from the area of application to other plant parts; systemics therefore affect only pests which feed on the crop, not affecting beneficial insects or natural predators. Two rodenticides that are relatively selective and reasonably safe are red squill and warfarin. Other rodenticides include arsenic compounds, strychnine, and ANTU. The most important nematicides presently in use are 1,3-dichloropropene and 1,2-dibromoethane. Pesticides are applied in various forms: wet sprays, dusts, atomizable fluids, low pressure aerosols, smokes, and seed dressings. Because of concern about the harmful effects of their residues on food destined for human consumption and their direct and indirect ecological effects, pesticides undergo exhaustive and expensive trials prior to their registration, release, and usage recommendations. See Rachael Carson, *Silent Spring* (1962); D. E. H. Frear et al., ed., *Pesticide Handbook* (1969); G. S. Hartley and T. F. West, *Chemicals for Pest Control* (1969).

Pestszenterzsébet: see BUDAPEST, Hungary.

Pestszentlőrinc: see BUDAPEST, Hungary.

Petah Tiqwa (pĕtä' tēk'vä), town (1972 pop. 92,400), W central Israel. Its industries produce textiles, plastics, processed foods, tires and other rubber products, and soap. There are extensive citrus groves on the outskirts, and building stone is quarried nearby. Petah Tiqwa was founded in 1878 as the first modern Jewish agricultural settlement in Palestine.

Pétain, Henri Philippe (äNrē' fēlēp' pātăN'), 1856–1951, French army officer, head of state of the VICHY GOVERNMENT. In World War I he halted the Germans at VERDUN (1916) and became a military hero. In 1917 he was appointed French commander in chief and in 1918 was made a marshal. He later went to Morocco, where he brought the joint French and Spanish campaign against ABD-EL-KRIM to a successful conclusion (1926). He was briefly (1934) war minister in the cabinet of Gaston Doumergue. In 1939, Pétain was named ambassador to Spain after France had recognized the new regime under Francisco Franco, who had served under Pétain in Morocco. In World War II, when France was on the brink of collapse, Premier Paul REYNAUD recalled (May, 1940) Pétain from Spain and made him vice premier in an effort to bolster French morale with the name of the hero of Verdun. Pétain urged that France sue for an armistice, and on June 16 he succeeded Reynaud as premier. The armistice went into effect on June 25, and more than half of France was occupied by the Germans. On July 10, 1940, a rump parliament suspended the constitution of the Third Republic, and Pétain took office as "chief of state" at Vichy, in unoccupied France. The Vichy government was fascistic and authoritarian. Pétain sought to improve the lot of France and of French prisoners of war by collaborating "honorably" with Germany, but his popularity decreased as he yielded to harsh German demands and obtained little in return. In April, 1942, Pierre LAVAL took power, and thereafter the marshal was chiefly a figurehead. After the Allied invasion of France (June 6, 1944) Pétain was taken, allegedly against his will, to Germany. In 1945 he voluntarily returned to France to face treason charges. His trial (July–Aug., 1945), at which much contradictory evidence was heard, ended with conviction, a sentence of death, degradation, and loss of property. General de Gaulle, then provisional head of the French government, commuted the sentence to life imprisonment in a military fortress; detained at first in the Pyrenees, Pétain was later transferred to the island of Yeu, where he died. See biography by R. M. Griffiths (1970); Jules Roy, *The Trial of Marshal Pétain* (tr. 1968).

petal, one of the four basic parts of a FLOWER, next innermost organ from the sepal. The whorl of petals is known collectively as the corolla [Lat.,=little crown]. The number of petals is usually constant within groups (e.g., five in the rose family), as are the numbers of the other organs. Identification by number is, however, complicated by various factors; the petals may be fused, inconspicuous, or entirely absent, in which case their role as the showy part of the flower is sometimes supplanted by modified leaves, the bracts, as in the dogwood and poinsettia, or by modified stamens, as in the canna and the lady's-slipper. Selective breeding can produce petal-like stamens (e.g., in cultivated roses and geraniums) and so-called double flowers, i.e., varieties with more than the normal number of petals. Petals are usually brightly colored and often secrete perfume and nectar (in nectaries at the base of the petal) that attract insects and birds needed for cross-pollination. When fertilization has taken place the petals usually drop off; however, in some flowers they persist (see EVERLASTING). In general there are fewer petals and their fusion is greater as the evolutionary development increases. Radially symmetrical arrangement also gives way to bilateral symmetry or even asymmetry.

Petaluma (pĕtəlōō'mə), city (1970 pop. 24,870), Sonoma co., W Calif.; inc. 1858. It is a large poultry and dairy center. Cheese, twine, fishlines, canvas goods, and fabricated metal are also made. A U.S. coast guard training center is there.

Petavius, Dionysius (dīōnĭsh'ēəs pētā'vēəs), Fr. *Denys Pétau,* 1583–1652, French Jesuit theologian and philologist. His editions of late Greek theological works are still important. His chief work (incomplete), on Christian doctrine, was bold in imputing slight unorthodoxy to certain Fathers of the Church and a Jansenist tinge to St. Augustine.

Petchenegs: see PECHENEGS.

Petén (pātān'), region, c.15,000 sq mi (38,850 sq km), N Guatemala. A humid expanse of dense, tropical hardwood forests interrupted by savannas and crisscrossed by ranges of hills, it is related geographically to SE Mexico and Belize (British Honduras) rather than to the rest of Guatemala. The Usumacinta River system drains most of the region. Rainfall is very heavy. There are large, permanent lakes, notably Lake Petén Itzá. The region is relatively inaccessible and has been only partly developed. It produces lumber, chicle, and some rubber and cacao. The sparse population is mostly Indian. Flores is the chief town. Once Petén was a center of the Old Empire of the MAYA and had a dense agriculture-oriented population. It is noted chiefly today as the scene of large-scale excavations of great archaeological ruins, notably TIKAL and Uaxactún. Although the Spanish nominally conquered the area and Cortés passed through it on his march to Honduras (1524–25), efforts at subjugation were sporadic until the Itzá tribe was driven out (1697) from their stronghold at Lake Petén Itzá.

Peter, Saint, d. A.D. 64?, most prominent of the Twelve Disciples, listed first in the Gospels, and traditionally the first bishop of Rome. His original name was Simon, but Jesus gave him the nickname Cephas [Aramaic,=rock], which was translated into Greek as Petros [Gr. *petra*=rock]. Peter was a native of Bethsaida and the brother of St. Andrew; he was married. He and Andrew, both fishermen, were called by Jesus to be disciples at the same time as James and John, the sons of Zebedee (Mark 1.16–20, 29–31; 3.14–16; Luke 5.1–11; John 1.40–44). Peter appears throughout the Gospels as leader and spokesman of the disciples, and Jesus most often addressed him when speaking to them (Mat. 10.2; 14.28; 15.15; 17.24; 19.27; Luke 8.51; 12.41). His honored position comes out most clearly in two high points of Jesus' ministry—when Peter confessed Jesus to be the Christ and was told "upon this rock I will build my church"; and when he, together with James and John, was chosen to see the Transfiguration (Mat. 16.13–20; 17.1–13). After the Last Supper he, again with James and John, witnessed Jesus' agony in Gethsemane. When Jesus was betrayed, Peter drew his sword to defend him, but denied him later in the same night, as Jesus had predicted he would (John 13; Mat. 26.26–46,57–75). After the Resurrection, Jesus appeared by the Sea of Galilee and charged Peter to "feed my sheep" (John 20.1–10; 21). The first chapters of the Acts of the Apostles describe Peter's role as leader of the Twelve in the election of a replacement for Judas and in the public declaration at Pentecost (Acts 1.15–26; 2.14–40). Much attention is given to Peter's miracles and to his defense of Christianity; his deliverance from prison by an angel is a celebrated incident (Acts 3; 4; 5.1–11,29–32; 8.14–25; 9.32–43; 10; 11.1–18; 12.1–19). He was a leader at the council of Jerusalem that was called to discuss the integration of non-Jews into the Christian organization; his hesitation to accept them freely was rebuked by St. Paul (Acts 15; Gal. 2). A few facts of St. Peter's life are known from 2d-century sources. He apparently left Antioch for Rome A.D. c.55; there he died as head of the local church, a martyr under Nero. According to traditional accounts he was crucified with his head downward. From earliest times the Vatican hill has been pointed out as the place of his martyrdom. Constantine erected a church over the supposed burial place of Peter; when it had fallen into disrepair, the huge St. Peter's Church was built on the same location. It is the principal shrine of Europe. Excavation has yielded remains of human bones at the site, but they cannot be positively identified as those of St. Peter. There is a very ancient tradition, accepted by many scholars, that the Gospel of Mark was written with St. Peter's help and that it consists essentially of his memoirs. The epistles of Peter (see PETER, epistles) are regarded by most critics as mistakenly attributed. From earliest times Christians looked for leadership to the successors of Peter as the bishop of Rome. However, whether this primacy should be one of honor only (as held by the Orthodox Eastern Church) or of actual rulership of the whole church (as claimed by Roman Catholics; see PAPACY) is one of the dividing questions of Christian history. The biblical passages cited to support Petrine supremacy are Mat. 16.13–20 and John 21.15–25. From the first passage comes the familiar image of the keys, which are seen to represent papal power, as well as that of St. Peter as the gatekeeper of heaven. There are several feasts of St. Peter in the West: St. Peter and St. Paul, June 29; the Chair of St. Peter, Apostle, Feb. 22; and St. Peter in Chains, Aug. 1. A second feast commemorating the Chair of St. Peter (i.e., his episcopal throne) was celebrated on Jan. 18 until abolished in 1960. See W. T. Walsh, *St. Peter the Apostle* (1948; Roman Catholic); Oscar Cullmann, *Peter: Disciple, Apostle, Martyr* (tr. 1953; Protestant); D. W. O'Connor, *Peter in Rome* (2 vol., 1960); R. E. Brown et al., *Peter in the New Testament* (1973). bibliography by A. A. DeMarco, *The Tomb of Saint Peter* (1964).

Peter I or **Peter the Great,** 1672–1725, czar of Russia (1682–1725), major figure in the development of imperial Russia. He was the youngest child of Czar Alexis, by Alexis's second wife, Natalya Naryshkin. From Alexis's first marriage (with Maria Miloslavsky) were born Feodor III, Sophia Alekseyevna, and the semi-imbecile Ivan. On Feodor III's death (1682), a struggle broke out for the succession between the Naryshkin and Miloslavsky factions. The Naryshkins at first succeeded in setting Ivan aside in favor of 10-year-old Peter. Shortly afterward, however, the Miloslavsky party incited the *streltsi* (semi-military formations in Moscow) to rebellion. In the bloody disorder that followed, Peter witnessed the murders of many of his supporters. As a result of the rebellion Ivan, as IVAN V, was made (1682) joint czar with Peter, under the regency of SOPHIA ALEKSEYEVNA. A virtual exile, Peter spent most of his childhood in a suburb of Moscow, surrounded by playmates drawn both from the nobility and from the roughest social elements. His talent for leadership soon became apparent when he organized military games that became regular maneuvers in siegecraft. In addition, Peter began to experiment with shipbuilding on Lake Pereyaslavl (now Lake Pleshcheyevo). Peter learned the rudiments of Western military science from the European soldiers and adventurers who lived in a foreign settlement near Moscow. His most influential foreign friends, Patrick GORDON of Scotland, François LEFORT of Geneva, and Franz Timmermann of Holland, came from this colony. In 1689, Sophia Alekseyevna attempted a coup d'etat against Peter; this time, however, aided by the loyal part of the *streltsi*, he overthrew the regent. For several years, until Peter assumed personal rule, the Naryshkins ran the government. Ivan V, whose death in 1696 left Peter sole czar, took no part in the government.

Foreign Policy. Russia was almost continuously at war during Peter's reign. In the 16th and early 17th cent. the country had fought periodically in the northwest against Sweden, in an attempt to gain access to the Baltic Sea, and in the south against Turkey. While continuing the policy of his predecessors, Peter drew Russia into European affairs and helped to make it a great power. His earliest venture was the conquest of Azov from the Turks in 1696, after an unsuccessful attempt in 1695. Peter then embarked on a European tour (1697–98), traveling partly incognito, to form a grand alliance against Turkey and to acquire the Western techniques necessary to modernize Russia's armed forces. He failed to form an anti-Turkish alliance, but his conversations with the Polish king and others led eventually (1699) to a coalition against Sweden. Peter also gained considerable knowledge of European industrial techniques (he even spent some time working as a ship's carpenter in Holland) and hired many European craftsmen for service in Russia. In 1698 he returned to Russia, began to modernize the armed forces, and launched domestic reforms. After concluding (1700) peace with Turkey, Peter, in alliance with Denmark and the combined Saxony-Poland, began the NORTHERN WAR (1700–1721) against CHARLES XII of Sweden. Although disastrously defeated at first, he routed Charles at Poltava in 1709 and by the Treaty of Nystad (1721) retained his conquests of Ingermanland, Karelia, and Livonia. Peter's conquests in the south were less permanent. Azov was restored to Turkey in 1711; Derbent, Baku, and the southern coast of the Caspian Sea, conquered in a war (1722–23) with Persia, were soon lost again. In the east, Russia extended its control over part of Siberia but failed to subjugate either Khiva or Bokhara. Peter's first diplomatic missions to China were unsuccessful but his efforts led to the Treaty of Kyakhta (1727), which fixed the Russo-Chinese border and established commercial relations. Peter's interest in imperial expansion led to the financing of the first voyage of Vitus BERING.

Domestic Policy. Peter had returned to Russia in 1698 at the news of a military revolt allegedly instigated by Sophia Alekseyevna. He took drastic vengeance on his opponents and forced Sophia into a nunnery. On the day after his return, Peter personally cut off the beards of his nobles and shortly thereafter ordered them to replace their long robes and conical hats with Western dress. This attack on the symbols of old Muscovy marked the beginning of Peter's attempt to force Russia to adopt European appearance and other features of Western culture. Most of Peter's reforms followed his predecessors' tentative steps, but his demonic pace and brutal methods created an impression of revolutionary change. The reforms were sporadic and uncoordinated; many of them grew out of the needs of Peter's almost continuous warfare. He introduced conscription on a territorial basis, enlarged and modernized the army, founded and expanded the navy, and established technical schools to train men for military service. To finance this huge military establishment, he created state monopolies, introduced the first poll tax, and placed levies on every conceivable item. Peter encouraged and subsidized private industry and established state mines and factories to provide adequate supplies of war materials. Peter reformed the administrative machinery of the state. He introduced a supervisory senate and a new system of central administration and tried to reform provincial and local government. He also attempted to subordinate all classes of Russian society to the needs of the state. He enlarged the service nobility (the body of nobles who owed service to the state), imposed further duties on it, and forced the sons of nobles to attend technical schools. To control the nobles he introduced the Table of Ranks, which established a bureaucratic hierarchy in which promotion was based on merit rather than on birth. The nobility's economic position was strengthened by changes in the laws of land tenure. The serfs (who paid the bulk of taxes and made up most of the soldiery) were bound more securely to their masters and to the land. Peter subordinated the church to the state by replacing the patriarchate with a holy synod, headed by a lay procurator appointed by the czar. Peter introduced changes in manners and mores. The ban on beards and Muscovite dress was extended to the male population, women were released from their servile position, and attempts were made to improve the manners of the court and administration. Peter sent many Russians to be schooled in the West and was responsible for the foundation (1725) of the Academy of Sciences. He reformed the calendar and simplified the alphabet. The transfer of the capital from Moscow to St. Petersburg (see LENINGRAD), built on the swamps of Ingermanland at tremendous human cost, was a dramatic symbol of Peter's reforms. Although Peter sought to enforce all his reforms with equal severity, he was unable to eradicate the traditional corruption of officials or to impose Western ways on the peasantry. His reforms were often considered whimsical and sacrilegious and met widespread opposition. The conservatives among the clergy accused him of being antichrist. The discontented looked to Peter's son, ALEXIS, who was eventually tried for treason on flimsy evidence and was tortured to death (1718). In 1721, Peter had himself proclaimed "emperor of all Russia." In 1722 he declared the choice of a successor to be dependent on the sovereign's will; this decree (valid until the reign of Paul I) preceded the coronation (1724) of his second wife as Empress Catherine I. She was a Livonian peasant girl whom Peter had made his mistress, then his wife (1712) after repudiating his first consort. Her accession on Peter's death was largely engineered by Peter's chief lieutenant and favorite, A. D. MENSHIKOV. Although many of Peter's innovations were too hasty and arbitrary to be successful, his reign was decisive in the long process of transforming medieval Muscovy into modern Russia. Peter's personal traits ranged from bestial cruelty and vice to the most selfless devotion to Russia; his order to his troops at Poltava read, "Remember that you are fighting not for Peter but for the state." Despite the convulsive fits that plagued him, he had a bearlike constitution, was of gigantic stature, and possessed herculean physical prowess. He drank himself into stupors and indulged in all conceivable vices but could rouse himself at a moment's notice, and he was willing to undergo all the physical exertions and privations that he exacted from his subjects. Peter subordinated the lives and liberties of his subjects to his own conception of the welfare of the state. Like many of his successors, he concluded that ruthless reform was necessary to overcome Russia's backwardness. Peter remains one of the most controversial figures in Russian history. Those who regard Russia as essentially European praise him for his policy of Westernization, and others who consider Russia a unique civilization attack him for turning Russia from its special path of development. Those impressed by imperial expansion and state and social reforms tend to regard Peter's arbitrary and brutal methods as necessary, while others appalled by his disregard of human life conclude that the cost outweighed any gains. The first biographer of Peter the Great was Voltaire. Later biographies include those by Eugene Schuyler (1884, repr. 1967), Kazimierz Waliszewski (1897, repr. 1968), V. O. Kliuchevskii (tr. by Liliana Archibald, 1958), Ian Grey (1960), and L. J. Oliva (1970). See B. H. Sumner, *Peter the Great and the Emergence of Russia* (1951, repr. 1968).

Peter II, 1715–30, czar of Russia (1727–30). A grandson of Peter I and the son of the czarevich Alexis, he succeeded on the death of Catherine I. He was too young to rule, but he willingly lent himself to a court intrigue, led by the Gallitzin and Dolgoruki families, which resulted in the fall of the all-powerful minister, A. D. Menshikov. Peter was betrothed to Catherine Dolgoruki, but died of smallpox on his wedding day. He was succeeded by his cousin ANNA (Anna Ivanovna).

Peter III, 1728–62, czar of Russia (1762), son of Charles Frederick, dispossessed duke of Holstein-Gottorp, and of Anna Petrovna, daughter of Peter the Great. He succeeded to the throne on the death of his aunt, Czarina Elizabeth. One of his first acts was to take Russia out of the Seven Years War and to conclude an alliance with Frederick II of Prussia, whom he passionately admired. He thus saved Prussia from almost certain defeat and sacrificed all the advantages Russian arms had gained in the conflict. In 1744, Peter had married Sophie of Anhalt-Zerbst, who was to become Czarina CATHERINE II. Although he was dissolute and, it is alleged, mentally unbalanced, Peter's domestic policy was in some respects liberal. He abolished the secret police and granted greater religious freedom, and he virtually ended the nobles' obligation to give service to the state. He aroused hostility, however, by his contempt for the Orthodox Church and by his concern with gaining Holstein. In the summer of 1762 a conspiracy against Peter, headed by Catherine's lover Grigori ORLOV and his brother Aleksey, was set in motion. Catherine was proclaimed sole ruler, and the imperial guards, led by Catherine in person (who had donned the guards' uniform), set out for Peterhof, where they forced Peter to sign his abdication. A few days later he was assassinated by his guards, probably led by Aleksey Orlov. Catherine's role in this is uncertain. Peter's claim to ducal Holstein passed to his son Paul (later Czar Paul I), in whose name Catherine ceded it to Denmark in exchange for Oldenburg in 1773. See biography by R. N. Bain (1902).

Peter I, d. 1104, king of Aragón and Navarre (1094–1104), son and successor of Sancho I. He continued the fight against the Moors, taking (1096) Huesca and recapturing (1100) Barbastro. His brother Alfonso I succeeded him.

Peter II, 1174–1213, king of Aragón (1196–1213) and count of Barcelona, son and successor of Alfonso II. He had himself crowned (1204) at Rome by Pope Innocent III, whom he accepted as overlord of Aragón and Catalonia. In 1212 he helped Alfonso VIII of Castile defeat the Moors at Las Navas de Tolosa. In 1213, Peter went to the assistance of his brother-in-law Raymond VI of Toulouse and his own vassals in France against Simon de Montfort, leader of the Albigensian Crusade. He was slain in the battle of Muret, which marked the end of Aragonese hegemony in S France. His son James I succeeded him.

Peter III (Peter the Great), 1239?–1285, king of Aragón and count of Barcelona (1276–85) and king of Sicily (1282–85); son and successor of James I. In 1280 he established Aragonese influence on the northern shores of Africa. From his marriage (1262) to Constance, daughter and heir of MANFRED of Sicily, were derived the claims of the house of Aragón to Sicily and S Italy. After the insurrection of the SICILIAN VESPERS against CHARLES I of Anjou, Peter was offered the crown of Sicily and took possession of the island (1282). Pope Martin IV excommunicated him and declared him deprived of his states on the basis of Peter II's declaration of vassalage to the Holy See. A crusade against Aragón was organized by the pope and the French, who invaded Catalonia but were repulsed by Peter and defeated at sea by ROGER OF LORIA. Peter's Sicilian venture was unpopular with the Aragonese nobility and towns, and he was compelled to grant them wide privileges to quell their opposition. He founded the first university in Aragón at Huesca. Peter was succeeded in Aragón by his eldest son, Alfonso III, and in Sicily by his second son, James (later James II of Aragón).

Peter IV (Peter the Ceremonious), 1319?–1387, king of Aragón and count of Barcelona (1336–87); son and successor of Alfonso IV. He supported ALFONSO XI of Castile at the battle of Tarifa (1340), recovered (1343–44) the kingdom of Majorca, and engaged in an indecisive naval war with Genoa and Pisa over possession of Sardinia. Though forced to confirm the privileges granted to the nobles by Alfonso III, Peter later (1348) defeated the troops of the nobles and withdrew their charter. In 1381 he assumed suzerainty over the duchy of Athens. His son, John I, succeeded him.

Peter I, 1320–67, king of Portugal (1357–67), son and successor of Alfonso IV. He married (1336) Constance Manuel, a Castilian noblewoman, but subsequently fell in love with one of her ladies in waiting, Inés de CASTRO. Their tragic love affair has been a favorite theme in Portuguese literature. When Alfonso IV allowed Inés, whom Peter later claimed to have married, to be murdered (1355), the prince led a rebellion against his father. Peace was restored, and the prince formally pardoned the murderers. Nevertheless, when Peter became king, he had two of them executed by having their hearts drawn out. This act, and his concern for legal reform, earned him the names Peter the Severe, or the Cruel, and Peter the Justiciar. He was succeeded by his son, Ferdinand I.

Peter II, 1648–1706, king of Portugal (1683–1706), younger son of John IV; brother and successor of ALFONSO VI. In 1667, he seized power from his incompetent brother and ruled the country as prince regent until Alfonso's death. The marriage of Marie Françoise to Alfonso was annulled (1667), and she married Peter. The reign was one of prosperity and peace until its final years. Portugal became subservient to English foreign policy and, having signed the Treaty of Methuen (1703) with England, was reluctantly drawn into the War of the Spanish Succession. The allies were campaigning in Spain when Peter died. He was succeeded by his son, John V.

Peter III, 1717–86, king of Portugal, younger brother of Joseph. He married his niece MARIA I and was joint ruler with her.

Peter IV, king of Portugal: see see PEDRO I, emperor of Brazil.

Peter V, 1837–61, king of Portugal (1853–61), eldest son and successor of Maria II. Ascending the throne upon the death of his mother, he ruled under the regency of his father, FERDINAND II, until 1855. Well-traveled, cultured, and intelligent, he dedicated himself to his country's progress, promoting railroad and telegraph communications, abolishing slavery, and improving health and educational facilities. He married (1858) Stephanie of Hohenzollern-Sigmaringen, but she died a year later. Peter died childless and was succeeded by his brother Louis I.

Peter I, 1844–1921, king of Serbia (1903–18) and king of the Serbs, Croats, and Slovenes (1918–21), son of Prince ALEXANDER of Serbia (Alexander Karadjordjević). He was brought up in exile in Geneva and Paris while the Obrenović line ruled Serbia, and he fought in the French army in the Franco-Prussian War (1870–71). In 1875, he joined the Bosnian insurrection against the Turks. The assassination (1903) of King ALEXANDER of Serbia brought Peter to the throne. Peter proved an able and conscientious ruler and restored dignity to the court of Belgrade. He reformed the constitution, the army, and the school system and fostered improved methods of agriculture. The outstanding figure of his reign was Nikola Pašić, who directed Serbian policy in the BALKAN WARS (1912–13) and in World War I. Early in 1914 Peter, who was in ill health, retired from active rule and his son, later King Alexander of Yugoslavia, became regent. Peter took part in the retreat (1915–16) of the Serbian troops through Albania to Corfu. In 1918 he was chosen to rule the kingdom of the Serbs, Croats, and Slovenes (later known as Yugoslavia), while his son and successor remained regent.

Peter II, 1923–70, king of Yugoslavia (1934–45). He succeeded under the regency of his cousin, Prince Paul, when his father, King Alexander, was assassinated in Marseilles. In World War II, when Paul's government signed (March, 1941) an agreement with the Axis Powers, the army and people of Yugoslavia overthrew the regent. Peter's personal rule began with the German invasion (April, 1941) of Yugoslavia. His troops were soon defeated and Peter fled to England, where he headed a government in exile. After the war the newly elected Yugoslav assembly abolished (Nov., 1945) the monarchy and proclaimed a republic headed by Marshal Tito. Peter protested the action and remained in exile. He lived in the United States, where he died. He wrote *A King's Heritage* (1954).

Peter I (Pierre Mauclerc), d. 1250, duke or count of Brittany (1213–37). The son of Robert II, count of Dreux, he married Alix, half sister and heiress of ARTHUR I duke of Brittany. His surname, meaning "bad cleric," probably derived from the fact that he studied for the priesthood but abandoned it. Making peace with the church, he took part in the crusade against the Albigenses. Peter was a leader in the rebellions of the nobles against the regency of BLANCHE OF CASTILE. Upon his son's majority (1237) Peter ceded Brittany to him. Peter joined the Crusade of 1239 and later accompanied Louis IX on the Crusade to Egypt in 1248. He died on the return voyage. He is also known as Peter of Dreux. See Sidney Painter, *The Scourge of the Clergy* (1937, repr. 1969).

Peter or **Peters, Hugh,** 1598–1660, British Puritan clergyman, educated at Cambridge. He became a priest of the Established Church, but his Puritan doctrines forced him to leave England for Holland c.1629. In 1635 he went to the Massachusetts Bay colony, became pastor of the church at Salem, and was active in the colony's ecclesiastical and political affairs. He returned to England in 1641 as an agent for the colony; served (1642–49) in the civil war as chaplain with various Puritan forces, including Oliver Cromwell's; and was executed at the Restoration. See. R. P. Stearns, *The Strenuous Puritan* (1954).

Peter, two epistles of the New Testament, the 21st and 22d books in the usual order. They are classified among the Catholic (or General) Epistles. Each opens with a statement of authorship by the apostle St. Peter. First Peter, the longer book, is addressed from Rome to the Christians of Asia Minor. It opens with a reminder of the hope of redemption and an exhortation to holiness (1.1–2.10), then passes to duties of Christians—obedience to the state (2.11–17) and the obligations of slaves to their masters (2.18–25), of wives to their husbands (3.1–7), of all to each other (2.18–25). This leads to a section of consolation and encouragement under persecution (3.13–4.19). The conclusion is also exhortatory (5). This epistle contains many beautiful passages, often quoted. The ascription to St. Peter is questioned by many scholars, who then date the letter near A.D. 100. The book was accepted as canonical in the earliest times (see NEW TESTAMENT). This was not true of Second Peter, which is dated by many scholars as late as A.D. 150; it was one of the last New Testament books to be admitted to the canon. This epistle is an exhortation to virtue (1), followed by a passage (2) warning against false teachers, whose heresy leads to licentiousness; the book concludes with a reminder of the Second Coming (3). Various passages in the book appear to have been taken from the epistle of JUDE. See R. C. Kelcy, *The Letters of Peter and Jude* (1972).

Peter, Apocalypse of: see PSEUDEPIGRAPHA.

Peterborough, Charles Mordaunt, 3d earl of, 1658–1735, English general and diplomat. He supported the Glorious Revolution of 1688, and William III made him a privy councillor, first lord of the treasury, and earl of Monmouth. He lost favor with the king, however, and was briefly imprisoned (1696) in connection with the plot of Sir John FENWICK. He succeeded to the earldom of Peterborough in 1697 and returned to favor at the accession (1702) of Queen Anne. During the War of the Spanish Succession he went to Spain (1705) in command of a fleet and land force. In that year he led the successful assault on Barcelona, after which Archduke Charles (later Holy Roman Emperor Charles VI) was proclaimed king. Peterborough then moved on to Valencia, making no effort to return to help Barcelona against French siege, and he became involved in unauthorized negotiations with Victor Amadeus II of Savoy. He was recalled (1707) to England, charged with incompetence and exceeding his authority, and his actions became the subject of partisan controversy between the Tories, who supported him, and the Whigs, who did not. Vindicated in 1711, he served on various diplomatic missions, but he lost favor completely on the accession (1714) of George I. See biographies by William Stebbing (1890) and C. R. Ballard (1929).

Peterborough, city (1971 pop. 58,111), SE Ont., Canada, NE of Toronto. It is at the falls of the Otonabee River, which connects, through the Trent Canal, with lakes Ontario and Huron. Settled early in the 19th cent. as a lumber town, it has become a railroad and industrial center and is the headquarters of the Canadian General Electric Company. Peterborough is also a resort for the Kawartha Lakes region. It is the seat of Trent Univ. Archaeologically valuable Indian sites are nearby.

Peterborough, municipal borough (1971 pop. 70,021), Huntingdon and Peterborough, E central England, on the Nene River. The city was formerly the administrative center of the Soke of Peterborough, an administrative county originating from the soke (jurisdiction) of the Peterborough abbey. The Soke was abolished in 1965. Peterborough is a rail, engineering, and farm trade center; products include diesel engines, farm machinery, and processed foods. The nearby suburb of Old Fletton is noted for brickmaking. The great Benedictine abbey was founded c.655. In 870 it was destroyed by the Danes, in the 10th cent. it was restored, in the 11th plundered, and in 1116 burned. The impressive cathedral, formerly the abbey church, has three great arches in the west front. It was damaged by Cromwell's men in 1643. The bishop's palace and remains of the old abbey buildings and ancient gates are noteworthy. The original name of the town was Medeshamstede. Queen Katharine of Aragón is buried there. In 1974, Peterborough became part of the new nonmetropolitan county of Cambridgeshire.

Peter Canisius, Saint (kənĭsh'ēəs), 1521–97, Dutch Jesuit, Doctor of the Church, b. Nijmegen. He spent his life traveling widely strengthening wavering Roman Catholics, preaching, and instructing. He was one of the most vigorous of the Catholic preachers in the regions affected by Lutheranism, above all in W and S Germany. St. Peter wrote much; his catechism was especially important and was one of the earliest popular expositions of the faith. Feast: April 27.

Peter Claver, Saint (klā'vər), 1581–1654, Spanish Jesuit missionary, called the Apostle of the Negroes. He was sent to what is now Colombia in 1610 and began at once his life work of ministering to the bodies and souls of the West African slaves, then being imported in large numbers. He worked indefatigably under the most loathsome conditions and was generally unappreciated by Spanish officialdom and even by his colleagues. Feast: Sept. 9. See Arnold Lunn, *A Saint in the Slave Trade: Peter Claver* (1935).

Peter Damian, Saint (dā'mēən), Ital. *Pietro Damiani,* 1007?–1072, Italian reformer, Doctor of the Church, b. Ravenna. He became a Camaldolese monk at Fonte-Avellino (near Gubbio) and because of his rigor and asceticism was made prior. He was strong in the reforming party of Hildebrand (later Gregory VII) and c.1050 wrote a scathing denunciation of the clergy, called *Gomorrhianus;* this created a sensation. In 1057 Stephen X made him a cardinal against his will. Nicholas II sent him as legate to reform Milan, notorious for simony and clerical concubinage; the mission was successful. In 1069 he was sent as papal legate to settle the quarrel between Holy Roman Emperor Henry IV and the empress. In the dispute with Berengar of Tours, St. Peter deprecated the application of reason in theology. Feast: Feb. 23.

Peter Gonzalez, Saint (gŏnzä'lĭs), 1190–1246, Spanish Dominican priest. He worked first among the Moors, then among the mariners of NW Spain. As a patron of sailors he acquired the name St. Elmo, perhaps in confusion with an earlier mariners' saint of that name, a 4th-century martyr. SAINT ELMO'S FIRE was regarded as a mark of his protection. Feast: April 14.

Peterhead (pētərhĕd'), burgh (1971 pop. 14,164), Aberdeenshire, NE Scotland, on a peninsula on the North Sea. It is the easternmost burgh of Scotland and it has a good harbor. Chiefly a center of herring fisheries, Peterhead has fish canneries, distilleries, and woolen mills. The town was founded in 1593 by George Keith, 5th earl marischal of Scotland. James Francis Stuart, the Old Pretender, landed secretly at Peterhead in 1715. In 1975, Peterhead became part of the Grampian region.

Peterhof: see PETRODVORETS, USSR.

Peter Lombard, Lat. *Petrus Lombardus,* c.1100–c.1160, Italian theologian, often called Magister Sententiarum. He studied at Bologna, Rheims, and Paris, where he is said to have been a student of Abelard. He acquired some fame as a teacher and was given high offices, serving for a time as archbishop of Paris. His *Sentences,* one of the most celebrated of all theological works, is a compilation of opinions of earlier theologians, often in conflict and not always reconciled. It was particularly important because its doctrine on sacraments (that a SACRAMENT is both a symbol and a means of grace and that seven fulfill the required conditions) was adopted as the official doctrine of the Roman Catholic Church at the Council of Trent (see TRENT, COUNCIL OF). By the 13th cent., the *Sentences* had become the principal theological text in the universities, and many of the greatest scholastics wrote commentaries on it.

Peterloo massacre, public disturbance in St. Peter's Field, Manchester, England, Aug. 16, 1819, also called the Manchester massacre. A crowd of some 60,000 men, women, and children were peaceably gathered under the leadership of Henry HUNT to petition Parliament for the repeal of the corn laws and for parliamentary reform. The magistrates ordered the meeting to disband. A cavalry charge to aid the untrained Manchester yeomanry resulted in 11 deaths and injuries estimated at over 400. The government's endorsement of the magistrates' action created widespread indignation, which considerably aided the reform movement. The name Peterloo, later given the incident, was suggested by the name Waterloo. See F. A. Bruton, *Three Accounts of Peterloo* (1921); studies by G. R. Kestevan (1967) and Joyce Marlow (1969).

Petermann, August Heinrich (ou'gŏost hīn'rĭkh pä'tərmän), 1822–78, German geographer, an authority on the geography of Africa and the Arctic. He had (1847–54) a cartographical establishment in London and in 1854 became director of the Perthes Geographical Institution, Gotha. In 1855 he founded *Petermanns Geographische Mitteilungen,* a geographical journal now published quarterly.

Peter Martyr: see PETER OF VERONA, SAINT; VERMIGLI, PIETRO MARTIRE.

Peter of Blois (blwä), 1135?–1203?, French writer. He was educated in law and theology. From 1167 to 1169 he was tutor to King William II of Sicily. He went (c.1173) to England, where he served Henry II and the archbishop of Canterbury in secretarial and diplomatic capacities. He was later secretary to Henry II's widow, Eleanor of Aquitaine. Much of his historically invaluable correspondence survives.

Peter of Dreux: see PETER I, duke or count of Brittany.

Peter of Verona, Saint, 1206?–1252, Italian preacher, a Dominican. He traveled all over Italy on preaching tours and was especially known for his opposition to the CATHARI. He was murdered by some of that sect and canonized the next year as a martyr. He is called St. Peter Martyr. Feast: April 29.

Peters, Hugh: see PETER, HUGH.

Peters, Richard, 1744–1828, American jurist, b. Philadelphia. After serving as secretary of the board of war (1776–81), he was briefly in the Continental Congress (1782–83) and then in the state legislature (1787–91). After 1792 he was a judge of the U.S. District Court for Pennsylvania and handed down decisions in many admiralty cases. He was very interested in the improvement of agriculture.

Peters, Samuel, 1735–1826, American clergyman and historian, b. Hebron, Conn. Because of his Loyalist sympathies, he fled to England in 1774. There he wrote for English periodicals and published *A General History of Connecticut by a Gentleman of the Province* (1781). An unflattering and inaccurate description of the colony, it is particularly noted for its misrepresentation of the Connecticut blue laws.

Petersburg, city (1970 pop. 36,103), politically independent and in no county, SE Va., on the Appomattox River; inc. 1850. A port of entry and an important tobacco market, it has industries producing cigarettes, luggage, and optical parts. The city is best known for its historical past. Fort Henry was built there in 1646 on the site of an Indian village. A trading post was then established, and in 1784 three villages—Petersburg, Blandford (both laid out 1748), and Pocahontas (1752)—were combined as Petersburg town. In the American Revolution the area was taken (1781) by the British; from Petersburg Cornwallis began the campaign which ended at Yorktown. In the Civil War, Petersburg, which guarded the southern approaches to Richmond, was under siege from June 15, 1864, to April 3, 1865. After failing to destroy Lee's army in the WILDERNESS CAMPAIGN, Grant slipped unnoticed from Confederate lines at Cold Harbor and moved on the city. A small force under Gen. P. G. T. Beauregard repulsed Grant's first attacks, successfully holding until the arrival of Lee's army. Lee, forced to defend Petersburg at all costs in order to protect Richmond, entrenched his troops. Months of trench warfare followed, punctuated by desperate attempts by each side to break the other's lines. On July 30, 1864, Union forces exploded a large mine under part of the Confederate works. Union troops from Burnside's corps poured into "The Crater," but were driven out with heavy losses. Rifle, artillery, and mortar fire were exchanged throughout the winter, with Grant tightening his lines and Lee's troops suffering increasingly from cold and starvation. Grant gradually extended his left flank SW of Petersburg in order to cut off Lee's supplies from the lower South. Lee, forced to spread his smaller army thinly over many miles of entrenchments, contested Grant's move in many hard-fought actions. But Sheridan's victory at FIVE FORKS on April 1, 1865, followed by a general assault on the Petersburg lines, finally broke Lee's resistance. Petersburg fell on April 3, 1865. Union forces entered Richmond on the same day, and Lee surrendered the remnants of his army at Appomattox Courthouse one week later. Petersburg National Battlefield (est. 1926) encompasses much of the battle scene; many old earthworks and tunnels are preserved, including "The Crater." Other points of interest include Blandford Cemetery, with 30,000 Confederate dead; Blandford Church (1735–37); Center Hill Mansion (1823; now a museum); and Gen. William Mahone's home, now part of the public library. Virginia State College and a junior college are there. To the east is Fort Lee, a U.S. army quartermaster center, with a training school and a notable Quartermaster Museum.

Petersburg National Battlefield: see NATIONAL PARKS AND MONUMENTS (table).

Peterson, Martha, 1916–, American educator, b. Jamestown, Kansas, grad. Univ. of Kansas (A.B., 1937; Ph.D., 1959). She served as instructor in mathematics, assistant dean of women, and dean of women at the Univ. of Kansas. In 1956 she became dean of women at the Univ. of Wisconsin at Madison and later special assistant to the president of that university. She was named university dean for student affairs in 1963. In 1967 she became president of Barnard.

Peter's pence, in the Roman Catholic Church, the annual voluntary laymen's contribution to the support of the pope. Formerly Peter's pence was a yearly tax of a penny levied by the Holy See on every household in England and elsewhere. The name derives from the fact that the Holy See is called the see of Peter.

Peter the Cruel, 1334–69, Spanish king of Castile and León (1350–69), son and successor of Alfonso XI. His desertion of his wife, Blanche of Bourbon, for María Padilla and his favors to the Padilla family aroused the opposition of the nobles and led to several rebellions fomented by Peter's illegitimate half brother, Henry of Trastámara (later HENRY II). Peter ruthlessly suppressed the rebellions, but Henry later obtained the help of Aragón, which was already at war with Castile, and France, and in 1366 he invaded Castile with French mercenaries under DU GUESCLIN.

Peter fled, and Henry was crowned king at Burgos in 1366. Peter, however, had allied (1362) himself with England and with the help of EDWARD THE BLACK PRINCE, he defeated Henry and Du Guesclin at Nájera (1367). Henry raised a new army with Du Guesclin, defeated Peter at Montiel (1369), and killed him in a duel after the battle. Despite his reputation for cruelty, Peter has many apologists, who see him as a defender of the rights of the commoners and the throne against the turbulent nobles. Peter's daughter Constance married John of Gaunt, who contested Henry II's succession to Castile.

Peter the Great: see PETER I.

Peter the Hermit, c.1050-1115, French religious leader. In 1095 he was a very successful preacher of the First Crusade (see CRUSADES), and he led one of its bands. In 1096 he reached Constantinople with his undisciplined followers; when they arrived in Asia Minor, Peter went back to get help from the Byzantine emperor Alexius I. In 1098 at Antioch he tried to run away; however, he was trusted later with a mission to the Muslim ruler of Mosul. He went home after the taking of Jerusalem and founded the monastery of Neufmoutier at Liège, where he settled. His place in the Crusade was greatly exaggerated, for he seems to have been only one of many preachers and leaders, although a very early one.

Pethahiah (pĕth"əhī'ə). **1** Priest of David. 1 Chron. 24.16 **2** One who married a foreigner. Ezra 10.23. **3** Royal counselor. Neh. 11.24.

Pethor (pē'thôr), unlocated town. It was the home of Balaam. Num. 22.5; Deut. 23.4.

Pethuel (pĕthyōō'əl), father of Joel. Joel 1.1.

Pétion, Alexandre (älĕksäN'drə pātyôN'), 1770-1818, Haitian revolutionist. After taking part in the expulsion (1798) of the English from Haiti, he joined (1799) André RIGAUD against TOUSSAINT L'OUVERTURE and commanded the heroic but tragic defense of Jacmel, a southern port. Exiled, he returned with the French army under Leclerc in 1802. Rejoining the patriots because he feared the reestablishment of slavery, Pétion, after the death of DESSALINES, engaged in a fierce but inconclusive struggle with Henri CHRISTOPHE for control of Haiti. In 1807 he was chosen president for life of the republic in S Haiti. He confiscated the great French plantations, divided the land among the peasants, and gave his people unprecedented freedom. In 1816 he welcomed the exiled Spanish American revolutionist Simón Bolívar and provided him with military assistance. Nevertheless, his administration was tainted with waste and corruption. Pétion was succeeded by Jean Pierre Boyer.

Pétion de Villeneuve, Jérôme (zhārōm' pātyôN' də vēlnöv'), 1756-94, French revolutionary. A leader of the Jacobins, Pétion sat in the Constituent Assembly, was elected (Nov., 1791) mayor of Paris over the marquis de Lafayette, and by inaction aided the insurrection of June 20, 1792. Elected to the Convention, he clashed with Maximilien Robespierre and allied himself with the GIRONDISTS. Early in June his arrest was ordered but he escaped; he died probably by suicide while in hiding near Bordeaux.

Petipa, Marius (märyüs' pĕtēpä'), 1822-1910, French dancer and choreographer, b. Marseilles. Petipa rose to prominence at the Imperial Theatre in St. Petersburg. He was the principal creator of the modern classical ballet. Bringing French and Italian traditions to Russia, he gave increasing importance to pure dance over pantomime and greatly expanded the roles of male dancers. His major works include *Don Quixote* (1869), *La Bayadère* (1875), *The Sleeping Beauty* (1890), *The Nutcracker* (1892), *Swan Lake*, Acts One and Three (1893), and *Raymonda* (1898). See his memoirs (tr. 1958).

Petit, Roland, 1924-, French dancer and choreographer. Petit joined the Paris Opéra company at 15 and in 1948 founded Les Ballets de Paris de Roland Petit. His best-known work, *Carmen* (1949), set to music from Georges Bizet's opera, was created for his company, with Renée (Zizi) Jeanmaire, who later became his wife, in the title role. Petit later turned to less classical forms, e.g., the music-hall revue, but he returned to ballet in the 1960s when commissioned to present the Festivals populaires de ballet at the Chaillot theater in France.

Petition of Right, 1628, a statement of civil liberties sent by the English Parliament to CHARLES I. Refusal by Parliament to finance the king's unpopular foreign policy had caused his government to exact forced loans and to quarter troops in subjects' houses as an economy measure. Arbitrary arrest and imprisonment for opposing these policies had produced in Parliament a violent hostility to Charles and George Villiers, 1st duke of Buckingham. The Petition of Right, initiated by Sir Edward COKE, was based upon earlier statutes and charters and asserted four principles: no taxes may be levied without consent of Parliament; no subject may be imprisoned without cause shown (reaffirmation of the right of habeas corpus); no soldiers may be quartered upon the citizenry; martial law may not be used in time of peace. In return for his acceptance (June, 1628), Charles was granted subsidies. Although the petition is of immense importance as a safeguard of civil liberties, its spirit was immediately violated by Charles, who continued to collect tonnage and poundage duties without Parliament's authorization and to prosecute citizens in an arbitrary manner.

Petit Nord Peninsula: see GREAT NORTHERN PENINSULA, Canada.

Petitot, Jean (zhäN pətētō'), 1607-91, French painter in enamel, b. Switzerland. He was apprentice and later partner to a goldsmith, Pierre Bordier, whom he accompanied to England where he served Charles I until the monarch's execution. Returning to Paris, he enjoyed the patronage of Louis XIV and that of many celebrities of the court. On the revocation of the Edict of Nantes, Petitot was imprisoned as a Protestant, but escaped to Switzerland. He perfected the art of portrait painting in enamel, and his works are of great value. Examples are to be found in Amsterdam, in Geneva, and in the Louvre. His son and successor, **Jean Louis Petitot** (lwē'), 1653-c.1730, was in the service of Charles II of England. Specimens of his work are preserved in the Victoria and Albert Museum.

Petlyura, Simon (sĭmyōn' pyətlyōō'rə), 1879-1926, Ukrainian nationalist politician. In Jan., 1919, he became leader of an independent Ukrainian republic, which emerged after the collapse of the Russian empire and the defeat of Germany and Austria-Hungary in World War I. His power was challenged from the north by the Red Army, from the south by the anti-Soviet Russian forces of General Denikin. In 1920, Petlyura allied himself with Poland under Joseph Piłsudski, but the 1921 peace of Riga between Poland and Soviet Russia recognized Soviet control over the Ukraine. Exiled to Paris, Petlyura was assassinated by a Communist agent.

Peto, John F. (pē'tō), 1854-1907, American painter, b. Philadelphia. Largely self-taught, Peto worked in the exacting style of trompe l'oeil ILLUSIONISM perfected by William HARNETT. He sought to put down precisely what he saw without embellishment, choosing still-life subjects from 19th-century American life. These included weathered wood panels, lanterns, and scraps of paper. His *Old Cremona* (Metropolitan Mus.) is a characteristic work.

Petöfi, Sándor (shän'dôr pĕ'töfē), 1822-49, Hungarian poet and patriot. A failure as an actor, Petöfi became the author of exquisite lyrics. He composed the national poem "Talpra Magyar" (1848), and several epics, including *Janos Vitez* (tr. 1866). His poetry served as inspiration to the patriots of the Hungarian revolution, in which he was killed.

Petra (pē'trə), ancient rock city, in present-day Jordan, known to the Arabs as Wadi Musa for the stream that flows through it. It was early occupied by the Edomites (descendants of Esau) and by the Nabataeans (an Arab tribe), who had their capital there from the 4th cent. B.C. until the Roman occupation in A.D. 106. It was for many centuries the focal point of a vast caravan trade but declined with the rise of Palmyra; however, it remained a religious center of Arabia. Under the Romans in the 2d and 3d cent. it was included in the province of Arabia Petraea. An early seat of Christianity, it was conquered by the Muslims in the 7th cent. and in the 12th cent. was captured by the Crusaders, who built a citadel there. Petra was unknown to the Western world until its ruins were visited by Johann Burckhardt in 1812. A narrow, winding pass between towering walls leads to the open plain upon which stood the ancient city. The plain is surrounded by hills in which tombs have been carved in the pink rock. The city is referred to as Sela in the Bible (2 Kings 14.7). See M. I. Rostovtsev, *Caravan Cities* (1932, repr. 1971); Iain Browning, *Petra* (1974).

Petrarch (pē'trärk) or **Francesco Petrarca** (fränchĕs'kō pāträr'kä), 1304-74, Italian poet and humanist, one of the great figures of Italian literature. He spent his youth in Tuscany and Avignon and at Bologna. He returned to Avignon in 1326, may have taken lesser ecclesiastic orders, and entered the service of Cardinal Colonna, traveling widely but finding time to write numerous lyrics, sonnets, and canzoni. At Avignon in 1327 Petrarch first saw Laura, who was to inspire his great vernacular love lyrics. His verse won growing fame, and in 1341 he was crowned laureate at Rome. Petrarch's friendship with the republican Cola di Rienzi inspired the famous ode *Italia mia*. In 1348 both Laura and Colonna died of the plague, and in the next years Petrarch devoted himself to the cause of Italian unification, pleaded for the return of the papacy to Rome, and served the Visconti of Milan. In his last years Petrarch enjoyed great fame, and even after his death and ceremonial burial at Arquà his influence continued to spread. One of the greatest humanists, he was among the first to realize that Platonic thought and Greek studies provided a new cultural framework, and he helped to spread this Renaissance point of view through his criticism of scholasticism and through his wide correspondence and personal influence. His discovery of Latin manuscripts also furthered the new learning. In his *Secretum*, a dialogue, Petrarch revealed the conflict he felt between medieval asceticism and individual expression and glory. Yet in his poetry he ignored medieval courtly conventions and defined true emotions. In his portrait of Laura he surpassed the medieval picture of woman as a spiritual symbol and created the image of a real woman. He also perfected the sonnet form and is considered by many to be the first modern poet. He influenced contemporary historiography through his epic *Africa*, which brought attention to the virtues of the Roman republic. Petrarch had less pride in the "vulgar tongue" than in Latin, which he had mastered as a living language. Consequently he considered his *Trionfi* [triumphs] and the well-known lyrics of the *Canzoniere* [song book] less important than his Latin works, which include, besides *Africa, Metrical Epistles, On Contempt for the Worldly Life, On Solitude, Ecologues*, and the *Letters*. However, he reached poetic heights in both tongues, and his delicate, melodious, and dignified style became an important model for Italian literature for three centuries. Early translators of Petrarch's sonnets and songs include Chaucer, Spenser, Surrey, and Wyatt. See his letters tr. by M. Bishop (1966); E. H. Wilkins, *Life of Petrarch* (1961) and *Petrarch and the Renascence* (1965). See also study by A. S. Bernardo (1962).

Petre, Sir Edward (pē'tər), 1631-99, English Jesuit, confessor of James II of England. He attended the Jesuit seminary of Saint-Omer. He was imprisoned (1679-80) in connection with the Popish Plot (see OATES, TITUS) and again (1680-83) because of his appointment as Roman Catholic rector of the London district and vice provincial of the Jesuits in England. He succeeded to his family title and estates in 1679. At the accession (1685) of James II, Petre became his confessor and was one of the most influential members of the king's secret council of Roman Catholic advisers. Pope Innocent XI refused James's request (1686) for Petre's preferment in the church, but in 1687 Petre was made a privy councilor. Extremely unpopular with the people, he fled at the Glorious Revolution of 1688. He later was rector of the seminary of Saint-Omer.

petrel (pĕ'trəl), common name given various oceanic birds belonging, like the albatross and the shearwater, to the order known commonly as tube-nosed swimmers. There are two families of petrels: the storm petrels (Hydrobatidae) and the diving petrels (Pelecanoididae). Many skim the waves so closely that they give the appearance of walking on the water. They are tireless fliers by day and at night rest on the water; many return to land only to breed. Two species that frequent the Atlantic coast off North America are Wilson's petrel, *Oceanites oceanicus* (also called Mother Carey's chicken), a surface skimmer and habitual boat follower, and Leach's petrel, *Oceanodroma leucorhoa*, which has a bounding, erratic flight and breeds on islands off the New England coast. The giant petrel, or giant fulmar (the size of an albatross), and the auklike diving petrel, *Pelecanoides urinatrix*, are both found in the Southern Hemisphere; the fulmar (*Fulmarus glacialis*), or fulmar petrel, inhabits the North Atlantic. The giant petrel is actually a member of the family Procellariidae (SHEARWATER family). Petrels are classified in the phylum CHORDATA, subphylum Vertebrata, class Aves, order Procellariiformes, families Hydrobatidae and Pelecanoididae.

Petrie, Sir William Matthew Flinders (pē'trē), 1853-1942, English archaeologist, a noted Egyptologist. He excavated ancient remains in Britain (1875-80), Egypt (1880-1924), and Palestine (1927-38) and was (1892-1933) professor of Egyptology at University College, London. In 1894 he founded the Egyptian Research Account, which became (1905) the British School of Archaeology in Egypt. His most important excavations were at Memphis, but he made many other outstanding discoveries. Among these are the sites of Greek settlements at Naucratis (1885) and Daphnae (1886); tombs of the first dynasty at Abydos (1899); the stele of Merneptah at Thebes (1896), inscribed with the earliest known Egyptian reference to Israel; and ruins of 10 cities at Tel-el-Hesy (S of Jerusalem). His writings include many works on ancient Egypt, *Methods and Aims in Archaeology* (1904), and *Seventy Years in Archaeology* (1931). He edited *A History of Egypt* (rev. ed., 6 vol., 1923-27), of which he wrote the first three volumes.

petrifaction: see FOSSIL.

Petrified Forest National Park, 94,189 acres (38,118 hectares), E Ariz.; est. as a national monument 1906, as a national park 1962. A part of the Painted Desert, it contains the largest known display of petrified wood in the world. There are six separate "forests," with great logs of jasper and agate lying on the ground surrounded by the varied colors of endless fragments and small chips. Dating from the Triassic period, these "stone trees" were killed by natural processes, such as fire, insect attacks, and fungus (or rot). The trees were deeply buried in mud and sand that contained silica-rich volcanic ash. The logs became petrified as the mineral, carried into the wood by ground water, replaced the wood cells. As the surrounding material was eroded away, the petrified trees were exposed on the surface. Prehistoric Indians lived among the stone trees; ruins of their dwellings and their petroglyphs (ancient rock art) are present. Although the first known report of the petrified forests was made by Lt. Lorenzo Sitgreaves, an army officer who explored the area in 1851, it was virtually unknown until the late 1870s.

Petrikau: see PIOTRKÓW TRYBUNALSKI, Poland.

Petrillo, James Caesar (pĕtrĭl'ō, pĭ-), 1892–, American labor leader, president of the American Federation of Musicians (1940–58), b. Chicago. In 1915 he became president of the American Musicians' Union. However, three years later he joined the American Federation of Musicians (AFM) and in 1922 was elected the local's president. He built his local into a highly disciplined organization and became a force in municipal politics. As national president of the American Federation of Musicians, he called several strikes against radio, television, and recording companies in order to strengthen the AFM and to combat the increased use of technological devices that lessened employment for musicians. Petrillo continued to serve (until 1963) as president of the Chicago branch of the AFM after his resignation as national president. See R. D. Leiter, *The Musicians and Petrillo* (1953).

petrochemical, any one of a large group of chemicals derived from a component of petroleum or natural gas. The cracking processes for manufacturing gasoline produce vast quantities of gaseous hydrocarbons. Originally considered waste products suitable only for use as illuminants and fuels, the gases today are manufactured into petrochemical substances widely employed in industry. Important petrochemical compounds are alcohols and aldehydes, butylene, butadiene, ethylene, propylene, toluene, styrene, acetylene, benzene, ethylene oxide, ethylene glycol acrylonitrile, acetone, acetic acid, acetic anhydride, and ammonia. Materials made from the gases include carbon black, synthetic rubber, polystyrene, polypropylene, and polyethylene. Petrochemicals are widely used in agriculture, in the manufacture of plastics, synthetic fibers, and explosives, and in the aircraft and automobile industries.

Petrodvorets (pyĕ"trədvəryĕts'), formerly **Peterhof** (pĕtyĭrgôf'), city, NW European USSR, on Neva Bay of the Gulf of Finland. Administratively part of Leningrad, Petrodvorets is a port, a rail terminus, and a resort center. The city grew up around the palaces and gardens built for Peter I, who founded it in 1711. Peterhof, which became the most lavish of the czar's summer residences, contained several palaces surrounded by vast parks that rivaled Versailles and were famous for their fountains and cascades. Under the Soviet government, the palaces were converted to museums. Largely destroyed during World War II, Peterhof has since been restored.

Petrograd: see LENINGRAD, USSR.

Petrokov: see PIOTRKÓW TRYBUNALSKI, Poland.

Petrokrepost (pyĕ"trəkryĕ'pəstyə), formerly **Schlüsselburg** (shlü'səlbo͝orkh), town and fortress, NW European USSR, E of Leningrad. The town, the terminus of a railroad and of the lateral canals on Lake Ladoga, has shipbuilding and repair yards. Opposite the town, on an island in Lake Ladoga, stands the fortress, which dominates the lake's access from the Neva River. Built in 1323 by the republic of Novgorod and at first called Oreshek, the fortress fell to Sweden in 1611 and was renamed Noteborg. Peter I captured it from the Swedes in 1702, during the Northern War, and named it Schlüsselburg [Ger.,= key fortress], envisioning it as the major link in Russia's line of defense to the Baltic Sea. The following year he founded St. Petersburg (now Leningrad) on the Baltic. The fortress soon lost its military significance and was used until the 1917 Bolshevik Revolution as a prison for high-ranking persons (including several members of the imperial family) and for political prisoners. In 1928 it was converted into a museum. Schlüsselburg fell (1941) to the Germans during World War II; its recapture (1943) by Russian forces opened the land route to besieged Leningrad. The name Petrokrepost [Rus.,= Peter's fortress] was adopted in 1944.

petrolatum (pĕtrəlā'təm), colorless to yellowish-white hydrocarbon mixture obtained by fractional distillation of petroleum. In its jellylike semisolid form (known as petroleum jelly and also by several trade names) it is used in preparing medicinal ointments and for lubrication. As a nearly colorless, highly refined liquid known as liquid petrolatum, liquid paraffin, or mineral oil, it is used as a lubricant, as a laxative, and as a base for nasal sprays.

petroleum, oily, flammable liquid that occurs naturally in deposits, usually beneath the surface of the earth; it is also called crude oil. It consists principally of a mixture of hydrocarbons, with traces of various nitrogenous and sulfurous compounds. The physical properties and exact chemical composition of crude oil varies from one locality to another. One of the many types of crude oil is a light substance with little color that is rich in GASOLINE. Another is a black tarry substance that is rich in ASPHALT. During the past 600 million years incompletely decayed plants and animals have become buried under thick layers of rock. It is believed that petroleum consists of the remains of these organisms. Because of the subterranean origin of petroleum it must be extracted by means of WELLS. Until an exploratory well, or wildcat, has been dug, there is no sure way of knowing whether or not petroleum lies under a particular site. In order to reduce the number of exploratory wells drilled, scientific methods are used to pick the most promising sites. For example, geologists look for outcroppings of certain rocks, such as sandstone, below which petroleum has frequently been found. Sensitive instruments, e.g., the gravimeter, the magnetometer, and the seismograph, may be used to find subsurface rock formations that can hold crude oil. Most modern wells are bored by a rotary process in which a drilling bit is made to turn at the lowest point of the hole while mud is pumped from the surface to lubricate the cutting action and flush away the rock fragments produced by the action of the bit. The mud also creates pressure inside the well, thus supporting the sides until a casing can be inserted. Drilling is a fairly complex and often risky process. Some wells must be dug several miles deep before petroleum deposits are reached. Many are now drilled offshore from platforms standing in the ocean bed. Usually the petroleum from a new well will come to the surface under its own pressure. Later the crude oil must be pumped out or forced to the surface by injecting water, gas, or air into the deposits. By using these techniques a very high percentage of the petroleum contained in a deposit can be extracted. The crude oil is usually sent from a well to a refinery in pipelines (see under PIPE) or tanker ships. The different hydrocarbon components of petroleum vaporize at different temperatures. The portions of the crude oil that vaporize between defined limits of temperature are referred to as fractions. Generally the fractions vaporize in the following order: dissolved NATURAL GAS, gasoline, BENZINE, NAPHTHA, KEROSINE, diesel FUEL and light heating oils, heavy heating oils, and finally tars of various weights (see TAR AND PITCH). In order to be used efficiently the different fractions are separated from each other by some refining process. In a process called fractional DISTILLATION petroleum is heated and sent into a tower. The vapors of the different fractions condense on collectors at different heights in the tower. The separated fractions are then drawn from the collectors and further processed into various petroleum products. As the lighter fractions, especially gasoline, are in the greatest demand, cracking processes have been developed in which heat, pressure, and certain catalysts are used to break up the large molecules of heavy hydrocarbons into small molecules of light hydrocarbons. Some of the heavier fractions find eventual use as lubricating oils, paraffins, and highly refined medicinal substances such as PETROLATUM. Petroleum has been known throughout historical time. It is described by Herodotus and other ancient writers. It was used in mortar, for coating walls and boat hulls, and as a fire weapon in defensive warfare. Rarely it was burned in lamps. North American Indians used it in magic and medicine and in making paints. White pioneers bought it from the Indians for medicinal use and called it Seneca oil and Genesee oil. In Europe it was scooped from the tops of streams or dipped from holes in the ground, and in the early 19th cent. small quantities were made from shale. In 1815 several streets in Prague were lighted with petroleum lamps. The modern petroleum industry began in 1859, when the American oil pioneer E. L. Drake drilled a producing well on Oil Creek in Pennsylvania at a place that later became Titusville. Many wells were drilled in the region. Kerosine was the chief finished product, and kerosine lamps soon replaced whale oil lamps and candles in general use. Little use other than as lamp fuel was made of petroleum until the development of the gasoline engine and its application to automobiles, trucks, tractors, and airplanes. Today Western civilization is heavily dependent on petroleum for motive power, lubrication, fuel, dyes, drugs, and many synthetics. Among the leading producers of petroleum are the United States (chiefly Texas, California, Louisiana, Oklahoma, and Kansas), the USSR, Venezuela, Iran, Kuwait, Libya, Iraq, Saudi Arabia, Indonesia, and Rumania. The largest known reserves are in the Middle East. Estimates of the petroleum resources of the earth range from 1,350 billion to 2,100 billion barrels. However, the demand for petroleum, especially as a fuel, is so great that oil companies have been unable to recover and refine sufficient quantities to meet all needs. In the United States there are huge amounts of petroleum contained in shale rock deposits. In the past it has been much cheaper to obtain oil by extracting it from wells than by crushing and heating shale. However, shortages have driven up the price of oil from wells so that shale oil may no longer be more expensive. The widespread use of petroleum has created serious environmental problems. The great quantities that are burned as fuels generate most of the air POLLUTION in industrialized countries, and oil spilled from tankers and offshore wells has polluted oceans and coastlines. The opposition of conservationists has prevented or delayed the development of many oil deposits, e.g., those on the Alaska North Slope and in certain U.S. coastal waters. However, since the need for oil is so great, it may not prove feasible to hold up the exploitation of these resources until an environmentally safe technology is developed. See ENERGY, SOURCES OF; PETROCHEMICALS. See K. K. Landes, *Petroleum Geology* (2d ed. 1959) and *Petroleum Geology of the United States* (1970); Stewart Schackne and N. D. Drake, *Oil for the World* (2d ed. 1960); Leonard Mosley, *Power Play: Oil in the Middle East* (1973).

petrology, branch of geology specifically concerned with the origin, composition, structure, and properties of ROCKS. It comprises petrography, the systematic description of rocks, and petrogenesis, which deals with the origin of the various kinds of rock. Petrology is also concerned with the laboratory simulation of rock-forming processes and the application of principles of physical chemistry to natural environments. Petrologic analyses of lunar rocks returned by Apollo astronauts provided a wealth of information on the makeup and origin of the moon.

Petronius (pĭtrō'nēəs), d. A.D. c.66, Roman satirist, known as Petronius Arbiter because of his now generally accepted identity with Caius Petronius, to whom Tacitus refers as *arbiter elegantiae* in the court of Nero. According to Tacitus, Petronius served first as proconsul, then as consul of Bithynia. He is remembered chiefly, however, as an indolent and profligate lover of luxury, so accomplished in elegance as to be made its arbiter, directing the emperor's entertainments. When Tigellinus, a jealous rival for the favor of Nero, planned the downfall and caused the arrest of Petronius, the latter ended his own life, at Cumae, by slashing his veins. He made dying a leisurely procedure, attended by festivity among his associates. To him is accredited the authorship of a satirical work, *Petronii arbitri satyricon*, a romance with skillful delineation of characters, written in prose interspersed with verse. Parts of the 15th and 16th books have been preserved. Among the surviving fragments the most complete and valuable bit is the *Cena Trimalchionis* (*Trimalchio's Dinner*), presenting a humorous episode of vulgar display on the part of a freedman whose great wealth is newly acquired. These satires are unique in furnishing a vivid study of the life and manners of the time and in giving a sustained, connected example of the colloquial language. The Latin style of Petronius is among the best of its period.

Petropavlovsk (pyĕtrəpäv'ləfsk), city (1970 pop. 173,000), capital of North Kazakhstan oblast, Central Asian USSR, in Kazakhstan, on the Ishim River and at the junction of the Trans-Kazakhstan and Trans-Siberian railroads. Small motors, agricultural machinery, leather, felt, and foodstuffs are produced in the city. On the caravan route between Turkistan and W China, Petropavlovsk was founded as a fort in 1752 and became a center for trade between Russia and the central Asian kingdoms. Its industrial development began in the late 19th cent. and intensified after World War II.

Petropavlovsk or **Petropavlovsk-Kamchatski** (kəmchät'skē), city (1970 pop. 154,000), capital of Kamchatka oblast, Far Eastern USSR. It is a major port and naval base on the Northern Sea Route, and there are shipyards and lumber mills. Free of ice seven months of the year, it is the base for a large fishing and whaling fleet. Bering founded the port in 1740. During the Crimean War, there were attacks on the port by French and British naval units.

Petrópolis (pətrô'po͞olēs), city (1970 pop. 189,118), Rio de Janeiro state, SE Brazil, picturesquely situated in hills just N of Rio de Janeiro. It is a fashionable resort, with a healthful climate, beautiful wooded estates, flower gardens, and tree-lined avenues. There are also industries producing textiles, coffee, and cereals. It was colonized by German immigrants in 1845 and soon afterward became the summer residence of the emperor Dom Pedro II, for whom the city is named. Successive presidents made it the unofficial summer capital of Brazil. Among its many fine buildings are a Gothic cathedral and the old imperial palace, which is now a museum containing possessions of Portuguese and Brazilian royalty.

Petrosian, Tigran, 1929–, Soviet chess player. He won a number of Soviet chess championships and in 1952 became a grand master and then an international grand master. In 1963 he defeated Mikhail Botvinnik, the world champion. He held the title until 1966, when he lost it to Boris Spassky.

Petrov, Yevgeny Petrovich (yĭvgā'nyē pĕtrô'vĭch pētrôf'), 1903–42, Russian writer and journalist; brother of the dramatist Valentin P. Katayev. His original name was Yevgeny Petrovich Katayev. Petrov collaborated with Ilya Arnoldovich ILF on various satirical novels, including *The Little Golden Calf* (tr. 1933). After Ilf's death in 1937, Petrov became a journalist and later a war correspondent. He was killed during World War II in the siege of Sevastopol.

Petrovgrad: see ZRENJANIN, Yugoslavia.

Petrozavodsk (pyĕt''rəzəvôtsk'), city (1970 pop. 184,000), capital of Karelian Autonomous Republic, NW European USSR, a port on Lake Onega. It produces lumbering equipment and has shipyards, fish canneries, sawmills, and wood plants. Novgorodians worked the nearby iron deposits in the Middle Ages. Peter I founded a metal factory in 1703 at Petrozavodsk, whose name translates as "Peter's plant." The city has a university that was founded in 1940.

Petrucci, Ottaviano dei (ōt''tävyä'nō dā'ē pätro͞ot'chē), 1466–1539, Venetian printer. Petrucci was the inventor of printing music by movable metal type. His patent for the process was issued by the Venetian Republic in 1498, but expensive experiments with other techniques forced him to sell his rights. The music printed by his double process (first the staff, then the notes carefully laid on) is precise and fine. Examples are in the British Museum collection.

Petsamo: see PECHENGA, USSR.

Pettenkofer, Max von (mäks fən pĕt'ənkō''fər), 1818–1901, German chemist and hygienist. He studied medicine at Munich. Pettenkofer is considered a founder of epidemiology and is known for his researches in the ventilation of dwellings, sewage disposal, and the spread of cholera. He developed a reaction for the detection of bile acids and a method for the quantitative determination of carbon dioxide.

Petty, Sir William, 1623–87, English statistician and physician. He was a founder of the Royal Society and was physician general to the army of Ireland in 1652. Petty's survey of the Irish estates appropriated by Oliver Cromwell, begun in 1654 and carried out in 13 months, was the first attempt at scientific surveying on a large scale. He won favor with Charles II, was knighted (1662), and became surveyor general of Ireland. In 1673, Petty's detailed map of Ireland was completed. It is as a political economist, however, that Petty is remembered. He disapproved of the ban on bullion export, favored an Irish-British union, and contended that labor determines price. His important writings include *A Treatise on Taxes and Contributions* (1662) and *The Political Anatomy of Ireland* (1691). See biography by E. Fitzmaurice (1895, repr. 1973).

petunia, any plant of the genus *Petunia,* South American herbs of the family Solanaceae (NIGHTSHADE family). The common garden petunias, planted also in window boxes, are all considered hybrids of white-flowered and violet-flowered species from Argentina. The plants are of a straggling habit and produce an abundance of large, funnel-shaped, fragrant blossoms. Petunias are classified in the division MAGNOLIOPHYTA, class Magnoliopsida, order Polemoniales, family Solanaceae.

Peulthai (pēŭl'thā, –thī), son of Obed-edom. 1 Chron. 26.5.

Peutinger, Konrad (kôn'rät poi'tĭng-ər), 1465–1547, German antiquarian, diplomat, politician, and economist. One of the earliest writers in Germany on Roman inscriptions, he introduced the Italian Renaissance spirit into his native land. He is known chiefly as the owner of the *Tabula Peutingeriana,* or *Peutinger Table,* an ancient plan of military roads of the Roman Empire, now in the National Library, Vienna.

Pevensey (pĕv'ənzē), village, East Sussex, S England, on the English Channel. Modern Pevensey, called Pevensey Bay, is a shore resort. In the old town, the site of the Roman fort Anderida, are remains of Roman walls and a Norman castle. The town, the landing place of William the Conqueror, was a member of the CINQUE PORTS. It declined after the recession of the sea. The church is partly Early English.

Pevsner, Antoine (äNtwän' pyĕvz'nər), 1886–1962, Russian sculptor and painter. He was influenced by cubism while in Paris in 1911 and 1913. During World War I he was in Norway with his brother Naum GABO. They returned to Moscow after the Russian Revolution. Pevsner taught at the Moscow academy and associated with avant-garde artists such as Malevich and Tatlin. He and Gabo worked together in 1920 on the manifesto of CONSTRUCTIVISM. In sculpture Pevsner created constructivist works in bronze and other materials, such as his portrait of Marcel Duchamp (1926; Yale Univ.). His rhythmic, abstract designs intended a new synthesis of the plastic arts. Impending conflict with the regime caused Pevsner to leave the Soviet Union in 1922. The next year he settled in France. Several of his constructions are in the Museum of Modern Art, New York City. See biography by his brother, Alexi Pevsner (1964).

Pevsner, Nikolaus (pĕvz'nər), 1902–, English historian of architecture, b. Germany. Influenced by Heinrich WÖLFFLIN, Pevsner contends in his many works that art must be considered within its context. He asserts that the direction of the creative impulse is often determined by national and regional styles. Since 1949 he has been art editor of Penguin Books. His major works include *An Outline of European Architecture* (1942), *Mannerism to Romanticism* (2 vol., 1968), and *The Buildings of England,* a series of studies of regional English architecture (1951–74).

pewee: see FLYCATCHER.

Pew Memorial Trust, philanthropic foundation established (1948) by Joseph N. Pew (1886–1963) and other members of the Pew family of Philadelphia to provide funds for "general religious, charitable, scientific, literary, and educational purposes." The trust has generally supported politically conservative and evangelistic projects. Important recipients of its funds are the Billy Graham Evangelistic Association and the Christian Anti-Communism Crusade, an organization that conducts seminars on anti-Communism and distributes anti-Communist literature. The trust also helps to support hospitals and medical research, cultural enrichment programs, and theological seminaries and other institutions of higher education. In 1972 its assets were over $400 million.

pewter, any of a number of ductile, silver-white alloys consisting principally of tin. The properties vary with the percentage of tin and the nature of the added materials. Lead, when added, imparts a bluish tinge and increased malleability and tends to escape from the alloy in poisonous quantities if the percentage used is too large; antimony adds whiteness and hardness. Other metals including copper, bismuth, and zinc can also be added. Pewter is shaped by casting, hammering, or lathe spinning on a mold and is usually simply ornamented with rims, moldings, or engraving, although some Continental display ware, especially of the Renaissance period in France and Germany, shows intricate ornamentation. Pewter was early used in the Far East, and Roman pieces are extant. England was a pewter center from the Middle Ages; pewter was the chief tableware until it was superseded by china. America imported much English pewter in colonial times and from c.1700 made large quantities. The craft had virtually disappeared by 1850 but was revived in the 20th cent. in reproductions and in pieces of modern design. The collection and study of pewter are increasingly popular, although relatively little old pewter has been preserved because of its small intrinsic value and of the ease with which it may be melted and reused. Pieces made of BRITANNIA METAL are similar in appearance to pewter ware. See B. N. Osburn and G. O. Wilber, *Pewter, Spun, Wrought, and Cast* (1938); H. H. Cotterell, *Old Pewter* (1963); L. L. Laughlin, *Pewter in America* (1969); and H. J. Kauffman, *The American Pewterer* (1970); C. F. Montgomery, *A History of American Pewter* (1973).

peyote (pāō'tē), spineless cactus (*Lophophora williamsii*), producing a drug, also called peyote, that is used by Indians in Mexico and the United States. The plant is indigenous to the SW United States and Mexico, where it grows in dry soil. The plant is light blue, bears small pink flowers, and has a carrot-shaped root. The mushroomlike crown, called a peyote, or mescal button (but unrelated to MESCAL), is cut off, chewed until soft, and brewed into a concoction for drinking or rolled into pellets to be swallowed for its narcotic effect. The active substance in peyote is mescaline, one of several naturally occurring PSYCHOTOMIMETIC DRUGS. An alkaloid, mescaline tastes bitter, causes an initial feeling of nausea, then produces visions and changes in perception, time sense, and mood. There are no uncomfortable aftereffects, and the drug is not physiologically habit forming. Peyote has been used since pre-Columbian times and is regarded by the Indians as a panacea. It became the basis for the formation of a religion, the Native American Church, which fused Christian doctrine with peyote-eating tribal ritual. See Weston La Barre, *The Peyote Cult* (rev. ed., 1969).

peyotism, religion of some North American Indians in which the hallucinogenic cactus peyote is used as the sacramental food. It is the most widespread indigenous contemporary Indian religion. Peyotism teaches an ethical doctrine much like those of the monotheistic religions. However, it eschews specific Christian theology, its exponents often stating that while Christ came to the whites, peyote came to the Indians. The peyote rite lasts from sunset to sunrise and is usually held in a Plains-type tepee. The rite has four major elements: prayer, singing, eating the sacramental peyote, and contemplation. The religion probably originated among the Kiowa in Oklahoma about 1890. In 1918 many peyotists were brought together as the NATIVE AMERICAN CHURCH.

Pezuela, Joaquín de la (hwäkēn' dā lä pāswā'lä), d. 1830, Spanish general, viceroy of Peru (1816–21). During the South American wars of independence from Spain he fought against the insurgent armies but was forced to resign because of his vacillation in meeting the forces of José de San Martín. He was succeeded by José de la SERNA.

Pfalz: see PALATINATE.

Pfeffer, Wilhelm (vĭl'hĕlm pfĕ'fər), 1845–1920, German plant physiologist. He was professor of botany successively at the universities of Bonn, Basel, Tübingen, and Leipzig (from 1887). With Julius von Sachs, he was a leader in systematizing the fundamentals of plant physiology. Pfeffer's experiments in osmotic pressure were fundamental to modern physical chemistry. He wrote a standard work, *Physiology of Plants* (1881, tr. 1900–1906).

Pfister, Albrecht (äl'brĕkht pfĭs'tər), c.1420–c.1470, printer, of Bamberg, Bavaria. He is believed to have been the first to print illustrated books (c.1460) and to have been the printer of the Latin Bible called Pfister's Bible or the Bamberg Bible, in double-column pages of 36 lines. His type indicates that his work is related to that of Gutenberg. The illustrations he used are woodcuts.

Pfitzner, Hans (häns pfĭts'nər), 1869–1949, German conductor and composer, b. Moscow. Pfitzner studied music at Hoch's Conservatory in Frankfurt/Main. His music, conservative in idiom (Pfitzner wrote articles attacking modernism in music), was popular in Germany in the early part of the 20th cent. After World War II his work was largely forgotten, and he spent his last years in homes for the aged. In 1948, Pfitzner was tried for having been actively pro-Nazi, but was acquitted of the charge.

Among his compositions are the opera *Palestrina* (1917); the cantata *Von deutscher Seele* (1921) [from the German soul]; two symphonies; concertos for piano, violin, and cello; and songs. See biography by J. M. Müller-Blattau (1969).

Pforzheim (pfôrts'hīm), city (1970 pop. 90,338), Baden-Württemberg, SW West Germany, on the Enz River, at the northern end of the Black Forest. It is a major center of the West German jewelry and watchmaking industry. Other manufactures include machinery, hosiery, and paper. An important medieval trade center, Pforzheim often changed hands until it passed to the margraves of Baden in the 13th cent.; the city served as their residence until 1565. Pforzheim was damaged in the Thirty Years War (1618–48) and was devastated (1689) by the French in the War of the Grand Alliance; later, more than three quarters of the city was destroyed in World War II. Noteworthy buildings include an 11th-century church (the only remains of the former margravial residence) and the Romanesque Church of St. Martin. Johann Reuchlin, the German humanist, was born there (1455).

***p*H,** range of numbers expressing the relative acidity or alkalinity of a solution. In general, *p*H values range from 0 to 14. The *p*H of a neutral solution, i.e., one which is neither acidic nor alkaline, is 7. Acidic solutions have *p*H values below 7; alkaline, or basic, solutions have *p*H values above 7. A *p*H value provides a measure of the hydrogen ion concentration of a solution. In pure water the concentration of hydrogen ions is equal to 0.0000001, or 10^{-7}, moles per liter. (A mole is the amount of a substance, expressed in grams, that is equal to the molecular weight, or formula weight, of the substance.) When an acid is added to pure water, the hydrogen ion concentration increases above this level. When an alkaline substance, or base, is added to pure water, the hydrogen ion concentration decreases below this level. Once the concentration is determined, the *p*H value is found by taking the exponent used in expressing this concentration and reversing its sign. For example, if the hydrogen ion concentration of a solution is 10^{-4}, or 0.0001, moles per liter, the *p*H is 4. See INDICATORS, ACID-BASE.

Phaeacia (fēā'shə), in Greek mythology, island of Scheria (location unknown). It was inhabited by a seafaring people who were hospitable to sailors and fond of joyous, luxurious living. When Odysseus was shipwrecked in their coast, their king, Alcinoüs, and his daughter, Nausicaä, entertained him.

Phaedra (fē'drə), in Greek mythology, daughter of Minos and Pasiphaë. She was the wife of Theseus. When her stepson, HIPPOLYTUS, rejected her love, she accused him of raping her and hanged herself.

Phaedrus (fē'drəs), fl. 1st cent. A.D., Latin writer, a Macedonian, possibly a freedman of Augustus. He wrote fables in verse based largely on those of AESOP. The prose collections of fables that were popular throughout Western Europe in the Middle Ages were probably derived from Phaedrus.

Phaeophyta (fēŏf'ətə), division of the plant kingdom consisting of those organisms commonly called brown algae. Brown algae derive their color from the presence, in the cell chloroplasts, of several brownish xanthophyll pigments, in addition to the photosynthetic pigments chlorophyll *a* and *c*. With only a few exceptions, brown algae are marine, growing in the colder oceans of the world, many in the tidal zone, where they are subjected to great stress from wave action; others grow in deep water. Among the brown algae are the largest of all algae, the giant kelps, which may reach a length of over 100 ft (30 m). The cell wall consists of a cellulose differing chemically from that of most plants except the red algae. The outside of the plants is covered with a series of gelatinous pectic compounds, generically called algin; the substance, for which the large brown algae, or kelps, of the Pacific coast are harvested commercially, is used industrially as a stabilizer in emulsions, and for other purposes. The normal food reserve of the brown algal cell is a soluble polysaccharide called laminarin; mannitol and oil also occur as storage products. The plant body, or thallus, of the larger brown algae may contain tissues differentiated for different functions, with stemlike, rootlike, and leaflike organs, the most complex structures of all algae. Some groups of brown algae have evolved an alternation of generations, in which physiologically independent haploid gametophyte plants produce gametes, the fusion of which initiates the diploid sporophyte generation. The mature sporophyte plant produces, through MEIOSIS, haploid spores, which develop into new gametophytes. The two generations, or phases, may be indistinguishable in size and form, or they may differ greatly. The genus *Ectocarpus*, for example, is a common brown alga found growing attached to larger algae. It has similar-looking gametophyte and sporophyte plants. In the kelps, however, the gametophyte is only a microscopic filament, in contrast to the occasionally tree-sized sporophyte.

Phaëthon (fā'əthən, -tən) or **Phaëton** (fā'ətən), in Greek mythology, son of Helios and the nymph Clymene. He tried to drive his father's golden chariot, but he could not control its great steeds. As the chariot plunged to earth it burned Mt. Oeta and dried the Libyan Desert. The universe would have been destroyed by fire if Zeus had not killed Phaëthon with a thunderbolt.

phage: see BACTERIOPHAGE.

phagocyte (făg'əsīt"): see BLOOD.

phagocytosis (făg"əsītō'səs), process by which single cells engulf particles, carry them into the cell cytoplasm, and digest them. Single-celled organisms such as amebas phagocytize food particles, and human white blood cells and macrophages phagocytize foreign particles and invading microorganisms as part of the body's defense system (see BLOOD; IMMUNITY). The various phagocytic cells in higher animals are derived from relatively unspecialized cells called stem cells that are either fixed within a network of supporting (reticular) cells and fibers of the spleen, thymus, and bone marrow, or that wander freely throughout body tissues. Many phagocytic cells respond chemically to substances produced by foreign bodies or by degenerating tissue by moving toward the substances, a mechanism known as chemotaxis. When a particle of the proper charge or chemical composition adheres to the cell surface, the cell cytoplasm moves so that it finally surrounds the particle and traps it within a cytoplasmic vacuole. Various enzymes are then secreted into the vacuole to digest the foreign substance. In higher animals each phagocyte can ingest about 5 to 25 invading bacterial cells. Phagocytosis often precedes production of ANTIBODIES by the body, but some species of bacteria cannot be phagocytized unless specific antibody is already present. Although phagocytosis is an effective response to infection, some organisms, such as the bacteria causing brucellosis and tuberculosis, can survive for years within the descendant cells of the phagocytes that ingested them. The process of phagocytosis was first described in the late 19th cent. by the Russian zoologist Élie Metchnikoff. See MEMBRANE.

phalanger (fəlăn'jər), any of the numerous and varied MARSUPIALS, or pouched mammals, of the family Phalangeridae, found in Australia, New Guinea, and adjacent islands. Many are somewhat like squirrels in appearance. They are also called Australian opossums, although true opossums belong to a different marsupial family and are found in the Americas. The KOALA is a well-known but atypical phalanger. Typical phalangers are nocturnal, arboreal animals with woolly fur, long, often prehensile tails, dexterous forepaws, large claws, opposable first hind toes, and joined second and third hind toes. They feed on fruits, leaves, and insects. Commonest is the brush-tailed phalanger, or possum (*Trichosurus vulpecula*), with a thickly furred tail, heavy hindquarters, a pointed face, and large pointed ears. It is found throughout Australia and adjacent areas, especially in woods, but also in towns; it has adapted well to human settlement and clearing. Cuscus is a name applied to several species of slow-moving phalangers about the size of house cats. Cuscuses have rounded bodies and heads, inconspicuous ears, and large round eyes. They display a wide range of colors. The honey phalanger is a mouse-sized, shrub-dwelling animal of SW Australia, with a very long tongue used to gather nectar, pollen, and insects from flowers. Several types of phalanger have evolved a gliding mechanism consisting of a parachutelike fold of furry skin between the front and hind legs. These animals are called gliders, or flying squirrels, although they are not related to the true flying squirrels. Phalangers are classified in several genera of the phylum CHORDATA, subphylum Vertebrata, class Mammalia, order Marsupialia, family Phalangeridae.

phalanstère or **phalanstery:** see FOURIER, CHARLES.

phalanx, ancient Greek formation of infantry. The soldiers were arrayed in rows (8 or 16), with arms at the ready, making a solid block that could sweep bristling through the more dispersed ranks of the enemy. Originally employed by the Spartans, it was developed by Epaminondas of Thebes (d. 362 B.C.). Use of the phalanx reached its apex when Philip II and Alexander the Great used the great Macedonian phalanx (16 deep and armed with the *sarissa*, a spear c.13 ft/4 m long) to conquer all Greece and the Middle East. Later, the Macedonian phalanx deteriorated and had few Macedonians in it; it was defeated in several battles with the Romans who conquered (168 B.C.) the Macedonians at Pydna. Thereafter the phalanx was obsolete.

Phalaris (făl'ərĭs), c.570–c.554 B.C., tyrant of Agrigentum, Sicily, notorious for his cruelties. He burned his victims alive in a brazen bull (making his first experiment upon Perillus, its inventor), the cries representing the bellowing of the bull. Richard BENTLEY proved the forgery of 148 Greek letters signed by Phalaris that represented him as a gentle ruler and a patron of the arts.

phalarope (făl'ərōp"), common name for members of the family Phalaropodidae, shore birds, called "little swimming sandpipers." Phalaropes, small, dainty birds with webbed toes, are the most aquatic of the SHORE BIRD group. They are unusual in that the female is larger and more brightly colored than the male and is the aggressor in courtship, while the male builds the cup-shaped nest on open tundra, and incubates the eggs, which number three to five per clutch. Their plumage is thick and ducklike; they float buoyantly and swim expertly, dipping their slender bills into the water for food. The Wilson's phalarope, *Steganopus tricolor*, is the only member of the family that nests in the United States, breeding in marshes of the Great Plains. The northern and red phalaropes, *Phalaropus lobatus* and *P. julicarus*, respectively, breed in the Arctic and winter in the S Atlantic. Phalaropes are classfied in the phylum CHORDATA, subphylum Vertebrata, class Aves, order Charadriiformes, family Phalaropodidae.

Phalec (fā'lĕk), variant of PELEG.

phallic worship (făl'ĭk), worship of the reproductive powers of nature as symbolized by the male generative organ. Phallic worship is one of the oldest and most universal religious practices in the world. Phallic symbols have been found by archaeological expeditions all over the world, and they are usually interpreted as an expression of the human desire for regeneration. Phallic worship in ancient Greece centered around Priapus (the son of Aphrodite) and the Orphic and Dionysiac cults. In Rome, the most important form of phallic worship was that of the cult of Cybele and Attis; prominent during the empire, this cult was notorious for its festive excesses and its yearly "Day of Blood," during which the frenzied participants wounded themselves with knives; self-inflicted castration, a prerequisite for admittance into the priest caste of this phallic cult, took place during the festival. In India, the deity Shiva was often represented by and worshipped as a phallic symbol called the lingam. Phallic worship has also been practiced among the Egyptians in the worship of Osiris; among the Japanese, who incorporated it into Shinto; and among the American Indians, such as the Mandan, who had a phallic buffalo dance. See also FERTILITY RITES. See C. G. Berger, *Our Phallic Heritage* (1966); Thorkil Vanggaard, *Phallos* (1972).

Phallu (făl'yōō), variant of PALLU.

Phalti (făl'tī) or **Phaltiel** (făl'tīəl), husband of Michal, previously David's wife. 1 Sam. 25.44; 2 Sam. 3.15,16.

Pham Van Dong: see DONG, PHAM VAN.

Phanar or **Fanar** (both: făn'ər, fənär'), Greek quarter of Constantinople (now İSTANBUL). Under the Ottoman Empire, Phanar was the residence of the privileged Greek families, called **Phanariots.** They came into prominence in the late 17th cent. and held influential positions until the Greek war of independence began in 1821. The high clergy of the Greek Orthodox Church, the hospodars (governors) of Moldavia and Walachia, and the chief dragoman of the empire (equivalent to minister of foreign affairs) were ordinarily chosen from the Phanariots. These offices (except, in theory, the clerical dignities) were obtainable only by purchase, and the Phanariot officials recovered their expenses by accepting bribes and extorting excessive taxes. They often dominated commercial life. Their greed and arrogance earned them the hatred of the Christian subjects, including other Greeks, whose affairs they administered. The hold of the Phanariots over Ottoman diplomacy was due in part to their knowledge of foreign languages, which the Muslims spurned to acquire. Many Phanariots joined the cause of Greek independence in the 1820s. Being wealthier and better educated than most other Greeks, they played an important part in Greek politics in the 19th cent.

phanerogam: see CRYPTOGAM.

Phanuel (fănyo͞o'ĕl, făn'yo͞oĕl), father of Anna the prophetess. Luke 2.36.

pharaoh (fâr'ō) [Heb., from Egyptian,=the great house], title of the kings of ancient Egypt. Of the pharaohs in the Bible, Shishak is SHESHONK, Neco or Necoh is NECHO, and Hophra is APRIES. Many scholars believe that the pharaoh who oppressed the Jews (Ex. 1-14) was Seti I and that his son Ramses II was the pharaoh of the Exodus.

Phares (fā'rĕs) or **Pharez** (-rĕz) [Heb.,=breach], ancestor of David. Gen. 38.29; Mat. 1.3. Perez: 1 Chron. 27.3.

Pharisees (fâr'ĭsēz), one of the two great Jewish religious and political parties of the second commonwealth. Their opponents were the SADDUCEES. The important activity of the Pharisees began after the family of the MACCABEES succeeded in delivering the Jewish people from Syrian oppression and when John Hyrcanus I, who was high priest (135-105 B.C.), had established the secular principate. The strong nationalists who had supported the liberators and had cherished the sacred religious beliefs and customs of their ancestors were the HASIDIM. Their aim was to keep all that was Jewish set apart from all that was not Jewish and therefore would defile. Those who were extreme in this attitude and effort came to be known as Pharisees. Basing all upon the Law, without which there could be no authorization for religious customs, the Pharisees insisted on the strictest observance of the ordinances and dues of the Jewish religion. In addition to the Torah, the Written Law, the Pharisees laid great importance on the traditional, or Oral Law, which they as far as possible adjusted to the Written Law—thus upholding and advancing customs and practices that had grown out of popular usage. Pharisaism was democratic in its nature and influence and deeply affected the lives of the people. Great emphasis was placed upon exegesis of the Scriptures, that they might be the familiar possession of the people. All life was drawn more and more closely under the regulations of religious observance. Precepts and rules were magnified as well as multiplied. At the same time an ethical goal was pursued by developing the theological foundations of Jewish life. Despite such professed high ethical goals, the leaders were aware that there were Pharisees who failed to live up to those expectations and referred to them as "sore spots" or "plagues of the Pharisaic party." However, it is inaccurate to label all Pharisees as "hypocrites" or "offspring of the vipers" as the New Testament authors appear to do. St. Paul was himself a Pharisee and a student of Gamaliel, the grandson of HILLEL, and much of Christianity has its roots in Pharisaic ideas such as monotheism, messianism, apocalypticism, life after death, the resurrection of the dead, and the Day of Judgment. After the fall of the Temple (A.D. 70), the Pharisees became the dominant party, having survived the destruction because of their abhorrence of violence and their belief that God, the ruler of history, would ultimately vindicate them if they lived by his Torah. The active period of Pharisaism extended to A.D. c.135. It counted largely in the development of later Orthodox Judaism. See R. T. Herford, *Pharisaism: Its Aim and Its Method* (1912), and *The Pharisees* (1962); Leo Baeck, *Pharisees* (1947, repr. 1966); Louis Finkelstein, *The Pharisees: The Sociological Background of Their Faith* (3d ed., 2 vol., 1963); Asher Finkel, *The Pharisees and the Teacher of Nazareth* (1964); Jacob Neusner, *From Politics to Piety* (1973).

pharmacology, study of the changes produced in living animals by chemical substances, especially the actions of DRUGS, substances used to treat disease. Systematic investigation of the effects of drugs based on animal experimentation and the use of isolated and purified active substances developed in the mid-19th cent. Pharmacologists, emphasizing the mechanisms by which drugs act, draw on the disciplines of physiology, pathology, biochemistry, and bacteriology. Pharmacology embraces a number of sciences, including pharmacodynamics (the study of the action of drugs on a living body), therapeutics (use of drugs and method of administration in treatment for disease), materia medica (study of the source, composition, characteristics, and preparation of drugs), toxicology (the study of POISONS and their action and of methods of treating poisoning), pharmaceutical chemistry (chemistry in relation to drugs), and PHARMACY (the preparation and dispensing of drugs for medical use).

pharmacopoeia (fär"məkəpē'ə), authoritative publication designating the properties, action, use, dosage, and standards of strength and purity of drugs. It is compiled under the supervision of professional, usually governmental, authority, and all manufacture and dispensation of drugs and medications is required to conform to it. The first work of this kind, the *Nuremburg Pharmacopoeia,* was published in Germany in 1546. Similar volumes appeared from time to time in other cities, but there was a wide variation and the need became apparent to standardize such publications under national direction. The first pharmacopoeia published in the United States was compiled for army use and appeared in Philadelphia in 1778. The United States Pharmacopoeia (USP) was first published in 1820 following a convention of medical societies in Washington, D.C. This compendium became the legal standard in 1906 by enactment of the Food and Drug Act. The USP is brought up to date periodically by a committee of the U.S. Pharmacopoeial Convention; supplements are published as needed. Other nations have similar standardized pharmacopoeias.

pharmacy, art of compounding and dispensing drugs and medication. The term is also applied to an establishment used for such purposes. Until modern times medication was prepared and dispensed by the physician himself. In the 18th cent. the practice of pharmacy began to be separated from that of medicine. The Philadelphia College of Pharmacy and Science was founded in 1821, the first school of its kind in the United States. The American Pharmaceutical Association was formed in 1851. The progress of medicine, and therefore the expansion of pharmacy, has necessitated more stringent requirements in the training of pharmacists; it is of vital interest that medications be formulated accurately according to the physician's prescription. Schools of pharmacy are now associated with universities, and a degree in pharmacy follows a four-year course of instruction. Examination and licensing by the state is mandatory.

Pharnabazus (färnəbā'zəs), d. after 374 B.C., Persian governor. He had an important satrapy in Asia Minor under Darius II and Artaxerxes II. He was responsible for the assassination (404 B.C.) of Alcibiades, and in the same year he supported Artaxerxes in the rebellion of Cyrus the Younger. Pharnabazus and his fellow satrap TISSAPHERNES encouraged the revival of Persian power in the Greek world by alternately supporting Sparta and Athens in the Peloponnesian War and later. Pharnabazus collaborated (394) with Conon in the restoration of the Athenian fleet. He was in command of two unsuccessful Persian invasions of Egypt (385, 374).

Pharnaces II (fär'nəsēz), d. 47 B.C., king of Pontus, son of MITHRADATES VI. In the Roman civil war he overran Colchis and central Asia Minor. Julius Caesar came from Egypt and defeated (47 B.C.) him at Zela—with such ease that Caesar informed the senate with the words "Veni, vidi, vici" [I came, I saw, I conquered]. Pharnaces was killed soon afterward in a revolt.

Pharos (fâr'ŏs), peninsula, extending into the Mediterranean Sea, N Egypt, NE Africa, forming two harbors at Alexandria. Originally an island, it was joined to the mainland by a mole, constructed by order of Alexander the Great. On Pharos stood the celebrated lighthouse completed (c.280 B.C.) by Ptolemy II, which is usually included among the Seven Wonders of the Ancient World. No precise description of it has survived, and modern estimates of its height vary between 200 and 600 ft (60-180 m). It was destroyed by an earthquake in the 14th cent.

Pharosh (fā'rŏsh), variant of PAROSH.

Pharpar (fär'pər), river of Damascus. 2 Kings 5.12. Its identity with the Awaj, a river flowing easterly south of the city, is doubtful. The other river of Damascus was the ABANA.

Pharr (fär), city (1970 pop. 15,829), Hidalgo co., extreme S Texas; inc. 1916. It is located in the irrigated region of the lower Rio Grande valley. Its industries include the packing and canning of fruit and vegetables and the shipping of cotton. There are natural-gas wells in the city, and a recycling plant manufactures propane, diesel fuel, and kerosene from the natural gas.

Pharsala (fär'sälä) or **Pharsalus** (färsā'ləs), ancient city, Thessaly, Greece. Near there in 48 B.C., Julius Caesar routed Pompey. The battle, also called Pharsalia, was a brilliant tactical accomplishment. Lucan's *Bellum Civile* (often called *Pharsalia*) is an epic of the civil war.

pharynx (fâr'ĭngks), area of the gastrointestinal tract between the mouth and the esophagus. In humans, the pharynx is a cone-shaped tube about 4½ in. (11.43 cm) long. At its upper end it is continuous with the mouth and nasal passages, and connects with the ears via the Eustachian tubes. The lower end of the pharynx is continuous with the esophagus (see DIGESTIVE SYSTEM). It is also connected to the larynx by an opening that is covered by the epiglottis during swallowing, thus preventing food from entering the trachea. The pharyngeal area is the embryological source of several important structures in vertebrates. For example, the breathing apparatus (gill pouches of fish and lungs of land animals) arises in this area (see RESPIRATION).

phase, in astronomy, the measure of how much of the illuminated surface of a planet or satellite can be seen from a point at a distance from that body; the term is most often used to describe the moon as seen from the earth. The sun always illuminates half the surface of a planet or satellite, and only half the surface at most can be seen from the earth or another distant point; the phase depends on the overlap of the half we see with the half that is illuminated. When the moon is between the earth and the sun, we cannot see the lighted half at all, and the moon is said to be new. For a few days before and

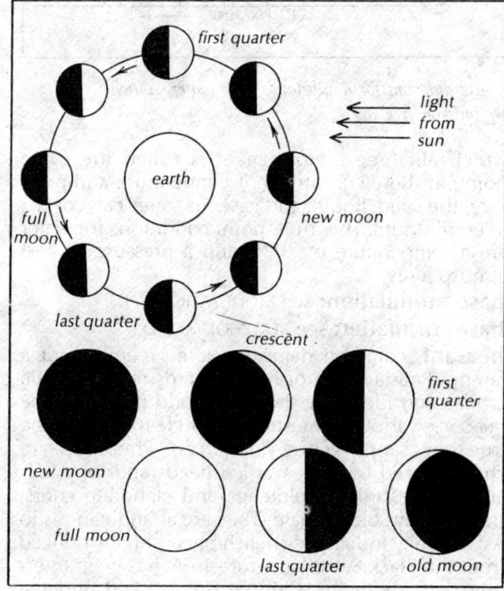

Phases of the moon

after the new moon we can see a small part of the lighted half, which appears as a crescent with the horns, or cusps, pointing away from the sun. When the moon has completed half its orbit from new moon to new moon, it is on the opposite side of the earth from the sun and we see the entire lighted half; this phase is called the full moon. When the moon is at QUADRATURE with the sun, having completed either one quarter or three quarters of its orbit from new moon to new moon, half the lighted side is visible; this phase is called the half-moon. The half-moon between the new moon and the full moon is known as the first quarter and that between the full moon and new moon is known as the last quarter. Between the first quarter and the full moon and between the full moon and the last quarter we see more than half the lighted side; this phase is called gibbous. Of the planets, only Mercury and Venus, whose orbits pass between the earth and sun, show all the phases that the moon shows; the other planets are always either gibbous or full. For an astronaut on the moon, the earth passes through phases like those of the moon but differing by half a month, being full when the moon is new and new when the moon is full.

phase, in physics: see WAVE.

Phaseah (fəsē'ə), variant of PASEAH **2.**

phase-contrast microscope: see MICROSCOPE.

phase diagram, graph that shows the relation between the solid, liquid, and gaseous states of a substance (see STATES OF MATTER) as a function of the temperature and pressure. The graph is divided into three regions, one for each of the physical states, and it specifies the range of temperatures at which the substance exists in each state for any value of the pressure. For example, a phase diagram for water shows that at a pressure of 1 atmosphere water is a solid up to a temperature of 0°C, a liquid from 0°C to 100°C, and a gas above 100°C. At a pressure of 0.5 atmospheres, the graph shows that although the melting point of ice remains 0°C, the boiling point of water is lowered to 82°C. Each substance has its own phase diagram, which must be determined experimentally. The border between two regions on the graph represents an equilibrium state, such as a melting point or boiling point, at which two states can coexist (see CHEMICAL EQUILIBRIUM). The point at

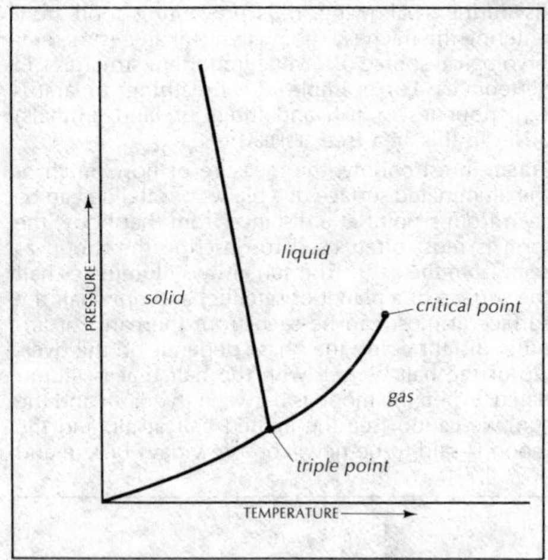

Phase diagram for a substance, like water, which expands on freezing

which all three regions meet is called the triple point; at these conditions of temperature and pressure, the solid, liquid, and gaseous states can coexist in equilibrium. The triple-point conditions for water are a temperature of .01°C and a pressure of .006 atmospheres.

phase modulation: see MODULATION.

phases of matter: see STATES OF MATTER.

pheasant, common name for some members of a family (Phasianidae) of henlike birds related to the grouse and including the Old World partridge, the peacock, various domestic and jungle fowls, and the true pheasants (genus *Phasianus*). Pheasants are characterized by their wattled heads and long tails and by the brilliant plumage and elaborate courtship displays of the male. They are all indigenous to Asia, chiefly India. The English pheasant, introduced from the Black Sea area before 1056, has been interbred with both the Chinese ring-necked and the Japanese pheasants, and the hybrid ring-necked pheasant, *Phasianus colchicus*, is established as a common game bird in the N United States. It eats berries, seeds, young shoots, and insects and prefers open country with brush cover. The body of the male ring-necked pheasant is mostly reddish brown, the head and neck an iridescent dark green, the face red, and the neck ringed with white. The protectively colored hen is distinguished from the grouse by her long tail. The closely related ruffed grouse is called pheasant in the central and S United States. Asian pheasants of great beauty are the argus (*Argusianus argus*), the golden (*Chrysolophus pictus*), the silver (*Gennaeus nycthemerus*), and the Lady Amherst (*C. amherstiae*), all of which inhabit the Himalayas—as do the Reeves pheasant (*Syrmaticus reevesii*), with an 8-ft (2.4-m) tail, the unique tree-dwelling Impeyan pheasant (*Tophophorus impejanus*), and the tragopan, or horned, pheasant (*Tragopan temmincki*). Pheasants are classified in the phylum CHORDATA, subphylum Vertebrata, class Aves, order Galliformes, family Phasianidae.

Phebe or **Phoebe** (both: fē'bē), deaconess at Cenchrea. Rom. 16.1.

Pheidias: see PHIDIAS.

Pheidippides (fīdĭp'ĭdēz), fl. 490 B.C., Athenian courier sent to Sparta to request help when the Persians landed at Marathon. He made four trips but dropped dead after running the 22 mi (35 km) back to Athens to inform the people of their victory.

Phelps, Edward John, 1822–1900, American lawyer and diplomat, b. Middlebury, Vt. He attended (1841–42) Yale law school, was admitted (1843) to the bar, and practiced law in Vermont and later in New York City. He was second comptroller of the U.S. Treasury (1851–53), U.S. minister to Great Britain (1885–89), and senior counsel (1893) for the United States in the arbitration of the BERING SEA Fur-Seal Controversy with Great Britain. He was a founder and president (1880) of the American Bar Association and taught law at Yale after 1881. His *Orations and Essays* appeared in 1901.

Phelps, Samuel, 1804–78, English actor-manager. After appearing in the provinces for some years he became known in London, in about 1837, for his portrayals of Shakespearean characters. His contribution to 19th-century theater was in opening (1844) and managing Sadler's Wells, London. There, where melodrama had reigned, he staged Shakespeare's works with imagination and taste; his productions were noted for their scenic beauty. He left Sadler's Wells in 1862 but continued acting.

phenacetin (fənăs'ĭtĭn), drug derived from coal tar and used to reduce fever and to relieve headache and other aches and pains. See ANALGESIC.

phenformin (fĕn"fôr'mĭn), drug used to treat certain types of DIABETES. It replaces or supplements INSULIN or sulfonylurea drugs such as ORINASE. Phenformin probably acts to limit the blood sugar level by inhibiting the formation of glucose from protein.

Phenice (fēnī'sē), in the Bible. **1** Same as Phoenicia. Acts. 11.19. **2** Harbor, SW Crete. It was also called Phoenix. Acts 27.12.

Phenicia: see PHOENICIA.

Phenix City (fē'nĭks), city (1970 pop. 25,281), a seat of Russell co., E Ala., on the Chattahoochee River opposite Columbus, Ga., in a cotton area; inc. 1883. Textiles are manufactured. In 1954 the state governor placed Phenix City under martial law for about five months—a result of the corruption that had long prevailed in the city. Nearby is the site of U.S. Fort Mitchell (1811–37).

phenol (fē'nōl), C_6H_5OH, a colorless, crystalline solid that melts at about 41°C, boils at 182°C, and is soluble in ethanol and ether and somewhat soluble in water. An aromatic ALCOHOL, it exhibits weak acidic properties and is corrosive and poisonous. Phenol is sometimes called carbolic acid, especially when in water solution. It reacts with strong bases to form salts called phenolates. Phenol is important in industry in the production of certain artificial resins, e.g., BAKELITE, and in the synthesis of many drugs, dyes, weed killers, insecticides, and explosives (e.g., PICRIC ACID). It is the simplest member of a class of hydroxy benzene derivatives, all of which contain a HYDROXYL GROUP attached to a BENZENE ring; these compounds may be thought of as derivatives of phenol and generically are called phenols.

phenol, 2,4,6-trinitro-, IUPAC name for PICRIC ACID.

phenolphthalein (fē'nôlthăl'ēən), or 2,2-Bis(*p*-hydroxyphenyl) phthalide, $C_{20}H_{14}O_4$, crystalline organic compound. It is used medicinally as a laxative and is widely employed in the laboratory as an INDICATOR of the acidity or basicity of solutions. In pure water it is insoluble, but it is soluble in basic solutions or in ethanol or acetone. In a solution with *p*H greater than 8 (*p*H 8 is mildly basic) phenolphthalein is pink to red in color, but at *p*H less than 8 it is colorless. Phenolphthalein is a phenol derivative of phthalic anhydride.

phenomenology, modern school of philosophy founded by Edmund HUSSERL. Its influence extended throughout Europe and was particularly important to the early development of existentialism. Husserl attempted to develop a universal philosophic method, devoid of presuppositions, by focusing purely on phenomena and describing them; anything that could not be seen, and thus was not immediately given to the consciousness, was excluded. The concern was with what is known, not how it is known. The phenomenological method is thus neither the deductive method of logic nor the empirical method of the natural sciences; instead it consists in realizing the presence of an object and elucidating its meaning through intuition. Husserl considered the object of the phenomenological method to be the immediate seizure, in an act of vision, of the ideal intelligible content of the phenomenon. Notable members of the school have been Roman Ingarden, Max Scheler, Emmanuel Levinas, and Marvin Farber. See Edmund Husserl, *Ideas: General Introduction to Pure Phenomenology* (tr. 1931, repr. 1962) and *Cartesian Meditations* (tr. 1960, repr. 1970); Marvin Farber, *The Foundation of Phenomenology* (1943, repr. 1967); R. M. Chisholm, ed., *Realism and the Background of Phenomenology* (1961); Pierre Thevanaz, *What is Phenomenology?* (1962); Richard Zanes, *Way of Phenomenology* (1970); M. A. Natanson, ed., *Phenomenology and the Social Sciences* (2 vol., 1973).

phenomenon, an observable fact or event; in philosophy the definitions and uses of the term have varied. In the philosophy of ARISTOTLE phenomena were the objects of the senses (e.g., sights and sounds), as opposed to the real objects understood by the mind. Later, phenomena were considered the observed facts and were contrasted with the theories used to explain them. Modern philosophers have used "phenomenon" to designate what is apprehended before judgment is applied. For Immanuel KANT a phenomenon was the object of experience and was the opposite of a NOUMENON, the thing-in-itself, to which Kant's categories did not apply.

phenothiazine (fē"nəthī'əzīn), any one of a class of drugs used to control mental disorders. Phenothiazines, along with other antipsychotic, or neuroleptic, drugs are used for such disorders as schizophrenia, paranoia, mania, psychosis resulting from mental deficiency, some forms of senility, hyperactivity in children, and even severe ANXIETY. Phenothiazines reduce psychiatric disorders without causing addiction or euphoria; sedation usually only occurs in the early stages of drug therapy. The most widely used phenothiazine, CHLORPROMAZINE (Thorazine), is prescribed for overactive schizophrenics; trifluoperazine (Stelazine) is used for inhibited and withdrawn schizophrenics. Typically, when a phenothiazine is taken over long periods of time, the frequency of recurring schizophrenic episodes decreases. Other phenothiazines are used in anesthesia and to control itching. Although many patients on phenothiazines and other neuroleptics show marked improvement, these drugs, when used over long periods of time, are fairly toxic. PARKINSONISM is a well known side effect. Some patients experience severe reduction of motor activity, abnormal skin pigmentation, and visual impairment. Chlorpromazine therapy is associated with JAUNDICE. Because many phenothiazines are potent anti-emetics, i.e., they control VOMITING, they may mask symptoms of toxic drug overdosage or of pathological disorders such as brain tumors. Phenothiazines also cause a disorder called tardive dyskinesia, which consists of bizarre muscular movements such as lip smacking and abnormal postures. It occurs in patients who have been given the drug for long periods of time. See also PSYCHOPHARMACOLOGY.

phenotype (fē'nətīp"): see GENETICS.

phenyl (fĕn'əl), C_6H_5, organic FREE RADICAL or ALKYL GROUP derived from BENZENE by removing one hydrogen atom.

phenylalanine (fĕn"əlăl'ənēn"), organic compound, one of the 22 α-AMINO ACIDS commonly found in animal proteins. Only the L-stereoisomer appears in mammalian protein. It is one of several essential amino acids needed in the diet; human beings cannot synthesize it from simpler metabolites. Young adults need about 31 mg of this amino acid per day per kg (14 mg per lb) of body weight. Phenylalanine can be degraded into simpler compounds by the enzymes of the body and is readily converted

CH_2 — H_2N—C—C(=O)OH, H

phenylalanine

to the amino acid TYROSINE. PHENYLKETONURIA (PKU), an inherited disease that, if left untreated, results in retarded mental development in children, has been shown to be associated with a complete lack of activity in the enzyme that converts phenylalanine to tyrosine. This results in the buildup of phenylalanine in the blood, an event leading to several pathological consequences. The incidence of this disease, about one in every 10,000 births, is high enough to have prompted several states to institute regular screening procedures for the detection of the disease in newborns. If diagnosed early the disease can be controlled to a great extent by administering a diet very low in phenylalanine. Phenylalanine contributes to the structure of proteins into which it has been incorporated by the tendency of its side chain to participate in hydrophobic interactions (see ISOLEUCINE). This amino acid was first isolated from a natural source (lupine sprouts) in 1879; it was first chemically synthesized in 1882.

phenylbutazone (fĕn"əlbyōōt'əzōn): see ANALGESIC.

phenylketonuria (fĕn"əlkēt"ənōōr'ēə) (PKU), inherited metabolic disorder caused by the absence of a specific enzyme (phenylalanine hydroxylase). The absence of this enzyme, a recessive trait, prevents the body from making use of phenylalanine, one of the amino acids in most protein-rich foods, and almost always leads to mental retardation and schizoid changes; convulsions also commonly occur. Early diagnosis and treatment, which includes a carefully regulated low-phenylalanine diet begun during the first few weeks of life, may prevent serious mental deficiency. Positive improvement has been seen even when therapy is started in well-established cases. Many states have made the PKU blood or urine test mandatory for all newborn infants.

phenyl salicylate (səlĭs'əlāt''), phenyl ester of SALICYLIC ACID.

Pherecrates (fərĕk'rətēz), fl. c.437 B.C., inventive and highly esteemed Greek poet of the Old Comedy. Fragments and titles of 15 of his plays are extant.

pheromones, any of a variety of substances, secreted by many animal species, that alter the behavior of individuals of the same species. Sex attractant pheromones, secreted by a male or female to attract the opposite sex, are widespread among insects. The pheromones produced by males include a substance produced by cockroaches that attracts females and orients them in the correct mating positions and a substance elaborated by the desert locust that accelerates sexual maturation in adults of both sexes. Male-attracting pheromones have been discovered in the females of many species of beetles, bees, and moths. The polyphemus moth will not mate unless red oak leaves are present; it has been found that the leaves give off a volatile aldehyde that stimulates the female to release a male-attracting pheromone. Attempts are being made to use pheromones in insect control, e.g., as bait to attract males to field traps or, in very high concentrations, to disorient insects and prevent mating.

Phi Beta Kappa: see FRATERNITY.

Phichol (fī'kŏl), chief captain of Abimelech's army. Gen. 21.22,32; 26.26.

Phidias or **Pheidias** (both: fĭd'ēəs), c.500–c.432 B.C., Greek sculptor, one of the greatest sculptors of ancient Greece. No original in existence can be attributed to him with certainty, although numerous Roman copies in varying degrees of supposed fidelity exist. However, the estimates of ancient writers, their descriptions of his statues, and his influence on all later sculpture have secured his fame. His greatest achievements were the *Athena Parthenos* at Athens and the *Zeus* in the temple of Olympia, both colossal figures of chryselephantine workmanship (draperies of beaten gold, flesh parts incrusted with ivory). The *Athena* (dedicated in the Parthenon c.447–439 B.C.) was the chief treasure of Athens. It was destroyed in antiquity, but several copies are preserved (National Mus. of Antiquities, Athens). It was also represented on coins and gems. The *Zeus* (c.435 B.C.), counted as one of the Seven Wonders of the World, was a majestic bearded figure seated upon a magnificently ornamented throne and wearing a mantle strewn with sculptured decorations. Terra-cotta moulds, found in 1955–56 at Olympia on the site identified as Phidias' workshop, showed that the gold for the drapery had been hammered into the moulds and then further decorated with glass inlays. Works of the master's younger years include a colossal bronze Athena (called the *Promachos*), the *Athena Lemnia* for the Acropolis, and a chryselephantine Athena for Pellene. Phidias has traditionally been credited with having been in charge of the Parthenon sculptures and other great works on the Acropolis, done for Pericles; but it is probable that they were made by pupils and assistants. Part of the frieze is now in the British Museum (see ELGIN MARBLES). See study by Charles Walston (1885, repr. 1971).

Phigalia (fĭgā'lēə), ancient city of Greece, in SW Arcadia (now Arkadhía). It gives its name to the **Phigalian Marbles,** a frieze c.100 ft (30 m) long and 2 ft (61 cm) high, in high relief, representing battles between the Lapithae, a legendary people from Thessaly, and the Centaurs and between the Amazons and the Greeks. The frieze, dating from c.420 B.C., was originally on the walls of a temple of Apollo at Bassae, near Phigalia. Since 1814 it has been in the British Museum. The geographer Pausanius names Ictinus as the architect of the temple.

Philadelphia, name of several ancient cities. One was in Lydia, W Asia Minor (now W Turkey). At the foot of Mt. Tmolus and near the location of modern ALASEHIR, it was founded in the 2d cent. B.C. by Attalus II Philadelphus of Pergamum. One of the Seven Churches in Asia was there (Rev. 3.7). The city was damaged several times by earthquakes. AMMAN was also renamed Philadelphia by Ptolemy II.

Philadelphia, city (1970 pop. 1,950,098), coextensive with Philadelphia co., SE Pa., on the Delaware River c.100 mi (160 km) upstream at the influx of the Schuylkill River; chartered 1701. It is the fourth largest city and port in the United States, and one of the largest freshwater ports in the world. An important trading and manufacturing hub even before the Revolution, it ranks high in the production of textiles, clothing, chemicals, electronic equipment, metal products (especially machinery), and a diversity of other manufactures. Its printing and publishing industry is important, and there are major oil refineries. Philadelphia is also an insurance and banking center. The site was first occupied by Indians, and in the 17th cent. there was a Swedish settlement. In 1681, Philadelphia, the "City of Brotherly Love," was founded as a Quaker colony by William Penn—hence the nickname Quaker City. Its commercial, industrial, and cultural growth was rapid, and by 1774 it was second only to London as the largest English-speaking city. It was the seat of the CONTINENTAL CONGRESS and served as the American capital from 1777 to 1788, except during the British occupation (Oct., 1777–June, 1778) after the battle of Brandywine. It was the capital of the new republic from 1790 to 1800, as well as the state capital (to 1799). The two Banks of the United States (1791–1811; 1816–36) were there (see BANK OF THE UNITED STATES). The bank buildings are examples of Greek revival architecture. A nucleus of American culture in colonial times (among its prominent citizens at that time was the scientist and statesman Benjamin Franklin), Philadelphia is still the seat of many philosophical, artistic, dramatic, musical, and scientific societies. Among these are the Pennsylvania Academy of the Fine Arts (1805); the Academy of Natural Sciences; the American Philosophical Society (1743); and the Science Museum of the Franklin Institute (1824), which now includes the Benjamin Franklin Memorial (1933), an important unit of which is the Fels Planetarium. Musical activities flourish in the city, which has an outstanding symphony orchestra. In Fairmount Park, the largest in the city, are the Philadelphia Museum of Art, zoological gardens, and many historic monuments and shrines. Many early historic shrines are also in Independence National Historical Park (est. 1956). Among them are INDEPENDENCE HALL, where the Declaration of Independence was signed and the LIBERTY BELL is kept; the neighboring Congress Hall, where Congress met from 1790 to 1800 and where Washington gave his farewell address; and Carpenters' Hall, where the First Continental Congress met. The large city hall, a conspicuous building with a tower surmounted by a statue of William Penn, contains numerous art objects. Also of interest are the Rodin Museum; the Gloria Dei (Old Swedes') Church; and Christ Church (begun in 1727), a representative example of Colonial architecture. Near Elfreth's Alley, a narrow street that has retained its colonial air, is the Betsy Ross House, where, according to one story, the first American flag was made. Edgar Allan Poe's house has also been preserved. The historic 18th century houses in the Society Hill section and on Germantown Ave. are additional tourist attractions. The U.S.S. *Olympia,* flagship in the battle of Manila Bay (1898), is docked in the harbor, and the Revolutionary War Fort Mifflin has been restored. Philadelphia has over 30 educational institutions, including the Univ. of Pennsylvania, Temple Univ., Drexel Univ., Dropsie Univ., La Salle College, Chestnut Hill College, St. Joseph's College, Curtis Institute of Music, Hahnemann Medical College and Hospital, Thomas Jefferson Univ., the Philadelphia College of Art, and the Philadelphia College of Textiles and Science. The mammoth John F. Kennedy Stadium is the site of major athletic events, including the annual Army-Navy football game, and the city fields major league teams in all professional sports. In the 1950s an ambitious urban redevelopment program was instituted, and today Philadelphia has one of the nation's largest industrial parks. The city is well served by railroads and has an international airport, an excellent harbor, and a complex network of modern highways. A U.S. mint is in the city, as is the Philadelphia Naval Shipyard, with "mothball facilities" and an adjoining naval factory and testing plants. Established in the early 1800s on Federal Street, the shipyard was moved to its present location at the foot of Broad Street (then League Island in the Delaware River) in 1867. Philadelphia will be a center of the national bicentennial celebration in 1976. See Federal Writers' Project, *Philadelphia* (1937); R. S. Wurman and J. A. Gallery, *Man-Made Philadelphia* (1972).

Philadelphia Museum of Art, established in 1875, chartered in 1876. When the city of Philadelphia planned to erect a building to house the Centennial Exposition of 1876, provision was made to keep the building permanently occupied; the Pennsylvania Museum and School of Industrial Art was privately established for that purpose. Its name was changed in 1929 to the Pennsylvania Museum of Art, and the present name was adopted in 1938. Its present building, modeled after a Greek temple, was opened in 1928. It is owned by the city. The museum has many fine collections, the outstanding one being the John G. Johnson Collection of European old masters. The other major bequests of European art in the museum are the Wilstach, Elkins, and McFadden collections. The Gallatin, Arensberg, and Stieglitz collections of modern art, and the Crozier Collection of Persian and Chinese art are outstanding. The museum houses more than 60 paintings by Thomas Eakins. The museum owns representative selections of Pennsylvania Dutch folk art; many period rooms, including a French Romanesque cloister and a Gothic chapel; and a collection of textiles and costumes. The museum complex includes the Museum College of Art; the Rodin Museum; and three colonial houses.

Philadelphia Orchestra, founded 1900 by Fritz Scheel, who was its conductor until 1907. Scheel was followed by Karl Pohlig (1907–12). Under the leadership (1912–38) of Leopold Stokowski, the orchestra became one of the world's finest ensembles. In 1936, Eugene Ormandy was appointed coconductor with Stokowski, and in 1938 he became music director. The orchestra has toured extensively in the United States and abroad; in 1973 it became the first American orchestra to play in mainland China. It has played summer seasons at the Robin Hood Dell amphitheater in Philadelphia and the Performing Arts Center in Saratoga Springs, N.Y. See study by Herbert Kupferberg (1969).

Philae (fī'lē), former island, SE Egypt, NE Africa, in the Nile River above Aswan High Dam. Of its temples, all dating from late Egyptian and classical times (600 B.C.–A.D. 600), the most famous was the temple to Isis, built by the early Ptolemies and not closed to pagan worship until the reign of Justinian. The island is now covered by the waters of Lake Nasser. An international fund (organized 1960) aided the removal of most of the monuments before the island was submerged.

philanthropy, the spirit of active good will toward others as demonstrated in efforts to promote their welfare. The term is often used interchangeably with *charity.* Every year vast sums of money are collected for an infinite number of philanthropic purposes, and an increasing number of people participate in the work of collecting money through highly organized campaigns the purpose of which is FUND RAISING. In many countries philanthropy has been incorporated in government policy in the form of tax exemptions for contributions to charitable agencies. It has become such an accepted form of behavior that few now escape the demands of giving, and many important institutions are partly or wholly dependent on it. In early times, charity was usually prompted by religious faith and helped to assure a reward in an afterlife, a notion found in Egypt many centuries before the Christian era. Throughout history, active participation in philanthropy has been a particular characteristic of Western societies. A traditional philanthropic ideal of Christianity is that of the tithe, which holds that one-tenth of a person's income should go to charity. At the end of the 19th cent. it was recognized that corporations could play a part in financing voluntary agencies when the Young Men's Christian Association set a new pattern for raising money: intensive drives over a short period of time, the use of sophisticated techniques to raise money, and an emphasis on corporation donations. Other voluntary agencies soon copied this pattern, and it is still the typical practice for large-scale fund-raising. During World War I, coordination of effort was established as a trend in philanthropic activity. In the U.S., this coordination took the form of Community Chests, which combined a number of charities under one appeal, and United Appeals. Today the organization and coordination of philanthropy has eliminated much of the spontaneity of giving. They have also brought about a more rational assessment of ability to give as well as the introduction of scientific methods of ascertaining community and national needs and of raising money. The focus has also shifted from the relief of immediate need to long-term planning that will prevent future need.

Philaret or **Filaret, Vasily Drosdov** ((both: vəsē'lyē drəsdôf' fēlərĕt'), 1782?-1867, Russian prelate, author, and preacher. He became archbishop of Tver and a member of the holy synod in 1819 and metropolitan of Moscow in 1826. He long urged the abolition of serfdom and is generally considered the author of the Edict of Emancipation promulgated by ALEXANDER II in 1861. Philaret also wrote a standard catechism of the Russian Orthodox Church.

philately (fĭlăt'əlē), collection and study of postage stamps and of materials relating to their history and use. Collecting stamps began soon after the first postage stamp was issued in 1840; the first printed catalog was issued in 1861, the first album in 1862. Scholarly study of the history of stamp issues and of details including watermarks, perforations, gum, and cancellations dates from the 1860s. Collectors usually concentrate on issues of definite areas (e.g., the Scandinavian countries) or on such specialties as air-mail or commemorative stamps, stamps depicting subjects such as bridges, trades, or animals, or covers with special markings. The value of stamps depends on demand, rarity, and condition. Queen Elizabeth II of Great Britain owns the most valuable private collection in Europe, and some of the most important public collections are at the British Museum and the Smithsonian Institution in Washington, D.C. See annual catalogs issued by the Scott Publishing Company. See *Scott's New Handbook for Philatelists* (1967); R. J. Sutton, ed., *The Stamp Collector's Encyclopedia (6th ed. 1966).*

Philby, Harry St. John Bridger, 1885-1960, British explorer, official, and author. He joined (1917) the British foreign service, was sent on a special mission to Arabia, and became the first European to visit the southern provinces of the Nejd. For some 30 years he was an adviser to King Ibn Saud of Saudi Arabia. Dissatisfied with British policy in the Middle East, he resigned (1930) from the foreign service, became a Muslim, and took the name of Hajj Abdullah. See his *Heart of Arabia* (1923), *Sa'udi Arabia* (1955), and *Forty Years in the Wilderness* (1957). His son, **Harold Adrian Russell Philby,** b. 1912, better known as Kim Philby, worked for many years as a Soviet spy within the British intelligence service. He came under suspicion when two of his associates, Donald Maclean and Guy Burgess, defected to the USSR in 1951, but his activities were not fully exposed until he himself defected in 1963. The case later received wide publicity.

Philemon (fīlē'mən), 361-262 B.C., Greek poet of the New Comedy. He was in ancient times considered second only to MENANDER. Fragments of his plays, originally numbering 97, survive.

Philemon (fīlē'mən), epistle of the New Testament, the 18th book in the usual order. It was written to a Colossian named Philemon by St. PAUL, probably when the latter was a prisoner in Rome (A.D. c.60). Onesimus, Philemon's fugitive slave, had fallen in with Paul, who sent him back to his master with a personal note adjuring the Christian master to forgive his slave, who was liable to crucifixion for escaping. Philemon, the shortest of the Pauline Epistles, is thought to have been written at the same time as COLOSSIANS and EPHESIANS.

Philemon and Baucis, in Greek mythology, Phrygian husband and wife. When Zeus and Hermes visited earth as men, only Philemon and Baucis offered them hospitality. As a reward they were saved from a punitive flood and were made priest and priestess to the gods. They died together and were turned into trees whose branches intertwined.

Philetus (fīlē'təs), Christian denounced by Paul. 2 Tim. 2.17.

Philidor (fĭl'ĭdôr, fēlēdôr'), assumed name of the Danican family of French musicians. The outstanding member of the family was **François André Danican Philidor,** 1726-95, chess player and composer. He earned nis living playing chess from the age of 18, touring Europe with great success. He wrote *Analyse du jeu des échecs* (1749) and gave exhibitions of simultaneous blindfold play that were remarkable in his time. From 1756 his many operas, among them *Le Maréchal ferrant* (1761), *Tom Jones* (1765), and *Ernelinde* (1767), were immensely popular.

Philip, Saint, one of the Twelve Disciples. Like Peter and Andrew, he came from Bethsaida in Galilee. He is mentioned several times in the New Testament (Mat. 10.3; John 1.43-51; 6.5,7; 12.21,22; 14.8,9; Acts 1.13). Philip is said to have been martyred at Hierapolis of Phrygia. He is sometimes confused with St. Philip the Evangelist. Feast (with St. James the Less): May 1.

Philip, Saint, one of the seven deacons chosen by the Twelve Disciples. He is also called St. Philip the Evangelist and St. Philip the Deacon. He evangelized Samaria and later converted an important eunuch of Queen Candace of Ethiopia (Acts 8.25-40). As a forerunner of St. Paul, he did much to bring the Gospel to the Gentiles (Acts. 6.5; 21.8-10). Feast: June 6.

Philip or **Philip the Arabian** (Marcus Julius Philippus), 204?-249, Roman emperor (244-49). He served under Gordian III against the Persians, instigated the assassination of the emperor, and concluded a peace with Persia. The millennium of Rome was celebrated by him with the splendor of secular games in the Circus Maximus. Philip sent Decius to the Danube to quell a mutiny, but when the troops hailed Decius as emperor, he marched at their head upon Italy. Philip met them near Verona and was slain. Philip had tolerated the Christians but probably did not become one.

Philip I, 1052-1108, king of France (1060-1108), son and successor of Henry I. He enlarged, by arms and by diplomacy, his small royal domain. In order to prevent the union of England and Normandy under a single ruler, he consistently supported ROBERT II of Normandy (Robert Curthose). In spite of his efforts, royal power remained weak. Philip's practice of simony and his consequent opposition to the reforms of Pope Gregory VII brought him into conflict with the Holy See. That conflict was intensified by Philip's scandalous private life. Philip repudiated his first wife, Bertha, daughter of the count of Holland, and married, over the opposition of the Roman Catholic Church, Bertrada of Montfort, wife of Count Fulk of Anjou, while both Bertha and Fulk were still living. Philip, excommunicated by popes Urban II and Paschal II, remained defiant until 1104. In his last years his son, Louis VI, ruled for him.

Philip II or **Philip Augustus,** 1165-1223, king of France (1180-1223), son of Louis VII. During his reign the royal domains were more than doubled, and the royal power was consolidated at the expense of the feudal lords. Philip defeated a coalition of Flanders, Burgundy, and Champagne (1181-86), securing Amiens, Artois, and part of Vermandois from the count of Flanders. He then attacked (1187) the English territories in France. Allied (Nov., 1188) with Richard, the rebellious son of King HENRY II of England, Philip compelled Henry to cede several territories to him. After Henry's death (1189), Philip and Richard, now king of England (see RICHARD I), left (1190) on the Third Crusade (see CRUSADES). They soon quarreled, and after the capture of ACRE Philip returned (1191) to France. Richard also left the crusade but was captured on his way home by Leopold V of Austria. During Richard's captivity (1192-94), Philip conspired against him with Richard's brother JOHN. After his release Richard made war (1194-99) on Philip, compelling him to surrender most of his annexations. When John acceded to the English throne on Richard's death (1199), Philip espoused the cause of ARTHUR I of Brittany and invaded John's French domains, forcing him to surrender (1204) Normandy, Brittany, Anjou, Maine, and Touraine. Philip later conquered Poitou. In 1214, at Bouvines, the French defeated the allied forces of John, Holy Roman Emperor Otto IV, and the count of Flanders; it was a victory that established France as a leading European power. When the English barons revolted against John (1215), they invited Philip's son Louis (later Louis VIII of France) to invade England and take the English throne; the venture failed. During Philip's reign the pope proclaimed the Crusade against the ALBIGENSES. Although Philip did not participate directly in the crusade, he allowed his vassals to do so. Their victories prepared the ground for the annexation of S France by King Louis IX. In internal affairs Philip's most important reform was the creation of a class of salaried administrative officers, the *baillis* [bailiffs], to supervise local administration of the domain. Philip also systematized the collection of customs, tolls, fines, and fees due to the crown. He supported the towns of France against the royal barons, thereby increasing their power and prosperity. In Paris, he continued the construction of NOTRE-DAME DE PARIS, built the first LOUVRE, paved the main streets, and walled the city. See biography by W. H. Hutton (1896, repr. 1970); Achille Luchaire, *Social France at the Time of Philip Augustus* (tr. 1912, repr. 1967).

Philip III (Philip the Bold), 1245-85, king of France (1270-85), son and successor of King Louis IX. He secured peaceful possession of Poitou, Auvergne, and Toulouse by a small cession (1279) to England. The marriage (1284) of his son (later Philip IV) to Joan of Navarre and Champagne brought the first union of France with these territories. To gain a throne for another son, he invaded (1285) the kingdom of Aragón but was forced to retreat and died on the march. Philip's reign was dominated by his father's officials and policies.

Philip IV (Philip the Fair), 1268-1314, king of France (1285-1314), son and successor of Philip III. The policies of his reign greatly strengthened the French monarchy and increased the royal revenues. Philip asserted his right to tax the clergy for the defense of the realm, thus making permanent a special tax permitted by the popes for support of crusades. Pope BONIFACE VIII opposed this measure by the bull *Clericis laicos* (1296), but when threatened with loss of revenues from France he capitulated (1297). The conflict was revived by the arrest and condemnation by the king's court (1301) of Bishop Bernard SAISSET. Boniface demanded that Saisset be sent to Rome for trial, issued two bulls denouncing Philip, and called for a council at Rome in Nov., 1302. Philip, in retaliation, convoked the nobility, clergy, and commons in the first French STATES-GENERAL (1302-3) to hear a justification of his course of action; and Boniface issued (1302) the bull *Unam sanctam*, an extreme statement of his right to intervene in temporal and religious matters. Threatened by excommunication, Philip had Boniface seized at Anagni. Although freed, Boniface soon died (1303). After the brief pontificate of Benedict XI, Philip secured the election as pope of CLEMENT V, who annulled Boniface's bulls, and in 1309 transferred the papal residence to Avignon, thus beginning the "Babylonian captivity" of the PAPACY. Clement cooperated with Philip in his persecution of the KNIGHTS TEMPLARS, whose wealth the king appropriated to finance his wars. Other wealthy groups persecuted by Philip were the Jews and the Lombards (Italian bankers). Philip also debased the coinage. Between 1294 and 1296, Philip overran Guienne, the duchy of King Edward I of England; in 1297 Edward came to the defense of his lands. A truce (1297) became (1303) a permanent peace, conceding Guienne to Edward. After the withdrawal of Edward, Philip turned his attention toward Flanders. He aided the Flemish towns against the count of Flanders, Guy of Dampierre, and after Guy's defeat (1300), he imposed French rule on the Flemish. They rebelled and defeated (1302) the French at the disastrous battle of Courtrai. Although Philip was victorious over the Flemish in 1304, he was forced, in subsequent treaties, to reduce his demands on them. Philip was more successful in his attempts to expand at the expense of the Holy Roman Empire; Lyons and Viviers were incorporated into France during his reign. Philip summoned the States-General twice more (1308, 1314), chiefly to obtain support for his warfare. His son, Louis X, succeeded him. See study by C. T. Wood (2d ed. 1971).

Philip V (Philip the Tall), c.1294-1322, king of France (1317-22), son of King Philip IV. He became regent in 1316 on the death of his brother Louis X, who was survived by his pregnant wife and infant daughter. On the death of JOHN I (1316), the posthumous son of Louis, Philip took the crown for himself in the absence of a direct male heir and was crowned (1317) king. This helped to establish the SALIC LAW in France, which excluded females from the royal succession. Philip's reign was notable for his frequent consultations of national assemblies and for his administrative, judiciary, and military reforms. He was succeeded by his brother, Charles IV.

Philip VI, 1293-1350, king of France (1328-50), son of CHARLES OF VALOIS and grandson of King Philip III. He succeeded his cousin Charles IV, invoking the SALIC LAW to set aside both Charles's daughter and King Edward III of England, the son of Charles's sister. He was the first French king of the house of VALOIS. By the victory of Cassel, Philip reinstated the count of Flanders, whom he supported against the rebellious Flemings. After 1337, Philip's reign was dominated by the opening phases of the Hundred Years War with England. In 1340 the French fleet was destroyed at Sluis. The following year Philip intervened in the succession conflict in Brittany (see BRETON SUCCESSION, WAR OF THE) on behalf of his nephew Charles of Blois; Edward III landed in Britanny to aid Charles's rival John of Montfort. Philip and Edward signed a three-year truce in 1343, but it lasted only two years. Edward invaded Normandy and defeated (1346) Philip at CRÉCY. In 1347 the English captured Calais, which they held for nearly two centuries. To finance the war Philip resorted to extraordinary sources of revenue, including the sale of privileges to provincial assemblies, a general salt tax (*gabelle*), loans, and the debasement of the coinage. Late in his reign France was ravaged by the Black Death (see PLAGUE). Philip added Montpellier and the Dauphiné to the royal domain. His son, John II, succeeded him.

Philip II, 382-336 B.C., king of Macedon (359-336 B.C.), son of Amyntas II. While a hostage in Thebes (367-364), he gained much knowledge of Greece and its people. He was appointed regent for Amyntas, young son of his brother Perdiccas III, but seized the throne for himself, ruthlessly suppressing foreign and Macedonian opposition. Reorganizing his army and training it in the effective Theban phalanx formation, he entered upon an ambitious career of expansion by conquest and diplomacy. In the first two years he moved eastward, taking over Amphipolis (357) and the gold mines of Thrace (356), in the same region where he had founded Philippi. In 351, DEMOSTHENES, fearing Philip's encroachments, delivered in Athens the first of the denunciatory *Philippics*. By 348 Philip had annexed the Chalcidice (now Khalkidhikí), including Olynthus, and was involved in a war over Delphi between PHOCIS and its neighbors. In the settlement (346) Philip became a member of the Delphic council, with a recognized position in Greece. But Demosthenes continued to agitate, and when Philip moved to absorb the European side of the straits and the Dardanelles (340), Athens and Thebes went to war with him. Philip crushed them at Chaeronea (338). Now master of Greece, he established a federal system of Greek states. He was preparing an attack on Persia when he was killed. His wife, OLYMPIAS, was accused (probably falsely) of the murder. Philip's consolidation of his kingdom and his reduction of Greece to relative peace made possible the campaigns of his son, Alexander the Great. Philip was the true founder of Alexander's army and trained some of his best generals, e.g., Antigonus Cyclops, Antipater, Nearchus, Parmenion, and Perdiccas. See D. G. Hogarth, *Philip and Alexander of Macedon* (1897); Samuel Perlman, ed., *Philip and Athens* (1973).

Philip V, 238-179 B.C., king of Macedon (221-179), son of Demetrius II, successor of Antigonus III. He won fame in a war in Greece (220-217), in which he sided with the Achaean League against the Spartans and the AETOLIAN LEAGUE. When Italy was weakened by Hannibal's invasion, Philip tried to take the Roman holdings in Illyria, and he made (215) a treaty with Hannibal. This began the First Macedonian War with Rome (215-205), which ended favorably for Macedon. Philip collaborated (202) with ANTIOCHUS III to expand in the Aegean by plundering the territorial possessions of PTOLEMY V. However, the frightened states of Rhodes and Pergamum coaxed Rome into entering the Second Macedonian War (200). This ended when Titus Quinctius Flamininus decisively defeated (197) Philip at Cynoscephalae (now Khalkodhónion, hills). From then on Philip collaborated with the Romans. He faced constant Roman interference, however, because of accusations against him from his neighbors. Philip extended his influence in the Balkans by three attacks on that region in 184, 183, and 181. His main efforts during this period were directed at rebuilding his kingdom. He was succeeded by his son Perseus. See biography by F. W. Walbank (1940, repr. 1967).

Philip I (Philip the Handsome), 1478-1506, Spanish king of Castile (1506), archduke of Austria, titular duke of Burgundy, son of Holy Roman Emperor MAXIMILIAN I and MARY OF BURGUNDY. Heir to his mother's Burgundian dominions (which included the Low Countries), he was held prisoner after her death (1482) by the city of Ghent, which objected to Maximilian's claim to be regent for Philip. Maximilian secured his son's release in 1485, but not until 1493 did he establish control over the Low Countries in Philip's name. In 1496, Philip married JOANNA, daughter of FERDINAND II (of Aragón) and Isabella I. When Joanna became (1504) queen of Castile under her father's regency, Philip contested Ferdinand's rights and in 1506 became joint ruler of Castile with his wife. His death in the same year acutely aggravated Joanna's insanity. Ferdinand again became joint ruler of Castile with Joanna, while Philip's dominions in the Low Countries passed to his son (later Holy Roman Emperor Charles V).

Philip II, 1527-98, king of Spain (1556-98), king of Naples and Sicily (1554-98), and, as Philip I, king of Portugal (1580-98). He ascended the Spanish throne on the abdication of his father, Holy Roman Emperor CHARLES V, who had previously made over to him Naples and Sicily, the Low Countries, Franche-Comté, and the duchy of Milan. His first wife, Maria of Portugal, died giving birth to the unfortunate Don CARLOS (1545-68), and in 1554 Philip married Queen MARY I of England. Continuing his father's war with France, he drew England into the conflict in 1557. In the same year Spain won the major victory of St.-Quentin, but in 1558 England lost Calais to France. After Mary's death (1558), Philip offered his hand to her sister ELIZABETH I of England, but he was refused. In 1559 the war with France was brought to an end by the Treaty of CATEAU-CAMBRÉSIS, which was sealed by Philip's marriage to ELIZABETH OF VALOIS. Although Philip was a devout Roman Catholic who sought to repress heresy wherever feasible, he subordinated religious questions to his political aims. His relations with the papacy were generally bad because most of the popes feared Spanish power in Italy. Religious persecution and the Spanish Inquisition were used to eliminate resistance to Philip's policy of centralizing power under an absolute monarchy. The repression of the MORISCOS, especially after the revolt from 1568 to 1571, assured Spanish religious unity; its main purpose, however, was to prevent the Moriscos from helping the Turks to invade Spain. Philip's half brother, JOHN OF AUSTRIA (1545-78), defeated the Turks at the battle of LEPANTO (1571), and Tunis was captured and held briefly (1573-74). The second half of Philip's reign was dominated by the revolt of the NETHERLANDS (see also NETHERLANDS, AUSTRIAN AND SPANISH). Philip appointed (1567) the duque de ALBA to replace his half sister, MARGARET OF PARMA, as governor, but when Alba's harsh methods failed to quell the revolt, Philip supported the more conciliatory tactics of Alba's successors—Luis de Zúñiga y REQUESENS, John of Austria, and Alessandro FARNESE, duke of Parma—who managed to reconquer the S Netherlands (approximately present-day Belgium). English support of the Dutch rebels and their persistent attacks on Spanish shipping led Philip to plan the invasion of England in 1588. However, the Invincible Armada (see ARMADA, SPANISH) was ignominiously defeated. The Dutch also received support from the French Protestants, and Philip intervened (1590) in the French Wars of Religion to aid the Catholic LEAGUE against the Protestant Henry IV. He claimed the French throne for his daughter Isabella but was finally forced (1598) to recognize Henry. The only major military success of Philip's later reign was the conquest of Portugal, to which he had a claim as the son of Isabella of Portugal, daughter of Manuel I. When King Henry of Portugal died (1580) without issue, Alba overran the country, and Philip was recognized as king by the Portuguese Cortes. The main stage of Spanish colonial expansion was completed before Philip's accession; during his reign, however, the Spanish established colonies and garrisons in the present S United States and conquered the Philippine Islands (named for the king). The debilitating effects of depopulation, of colonial overexpansion, and of the influx of gold began to make themselves strongly felt in Philip's Spain. American gold and the proceeds of an increasingly burdensome taxation were not enough to finance Philip's foreign wars and interventions and had to be supplemented with loans. The king repudiated his debts four times during his reign. Philip was not the bloodthirsty tyrant portrayed by his enemies and by later writers. The embodiment of the hard-working civil servant and bureaucrat, he sought to direct the destinies of a world empire from the seclusion of his cabinet, devoting infinite time and pains to the minutest administrative details, which he was unwilling to delegate. He did not trust even his ablest and most loyal servants, and partly as a result his court was riddled with faction. Philip's administration was generally just, but his bureaucratic absolutism, with its disregard for local conditions and privileges, inevitably caused discontent. This was true not only of the Netherlands but of Aragón, which rose in revolt (1591) over the affair of Antonio PÉREZ. Isolated from reality, Philip lived and died in his strange court at the ESCORIAL. He was succeeded by Philip III, his son by his fourth wife, Anne of Austria. See study by W. H. Prescott (3 vol., 1855-58); M. A. S. Hume, *Philip II of Spain* (1897, repr. 1970); R. B. Merriman, *The Rise of the Spanish Empire in the Old World and the New*, Vol. IV (1934, repr. 1962); Fernand Brandel, *The Mediterranean and the Mediterranean World in the Age of Philip II* (1949, tr. 1972); R. T. Davies, *The Golden Century of Spain, 1501-1621* (rev. ed. 1954, repr. 1965); J. H. Elliot, *Imperial Spain, 1469-1716* (1963, repr. 1966).

Philip III, 1578-1621, king of Spain, Naples, and Sicily (1598-1621) and, as Philip II, king of Portugal (1598-1621); son and successor of Philip II of Spain. He was as pious as his father, but lacked his intelligence and capacity for work. Preferring to pursue his own pleasure, Philip left the actual government to his favorite, the duque de LERMA. Peace had been made with France by the Treaty of Vervins (1598) shortly before Philip III's accession. Peace with England followed in 1604, and in 1609 a 12-year truce was made with the United Provinces of the Netherlands. In Italy, however, Spain was involved in war (1615-17) with Savoy over MONTFERRAT and in clashes with Venice. In 1620, Spain entered the THIRTY YEARS WAR by sending troops into the Palatinate. The Spanish occupation of the VALTELLINA in the same year also led (1622) to war with France. Philip's reign saw an increasing decline in Spain's economy, partly as a result of the expulsion (1609-14) of the MORISCOS, while the grandees accumulated huge estates and the church prospered. Yet Spanish culture was in the midst of a glorious period which gave the world Cervantes, Lope de Vega, El Greco, and Zurbarán. Philip III was succeeded by his son, Philip IV. His daughter, Anne of Austria, married Louis XIII of France.

Philip IV, 1605-65, king of Spain, Naples, and Sicily (1621-65) and, as Philip III, king of Portugal (1621-40); son and successor of Philip III of Spain. Philip IV was intelligent but lacked energy, and the affairs of state were handled (until 1643) by the conde de OLIVARES. During his reign, Spain continued to decline politically and economically. Spanish involvement in the THIRTY YEARS WAR increased as war was resumed (1621) in the Netherlands and fighting started (1622) with France over the VALTELLINA question. The war with France continued after the Peace of Westphalia (1648), became complicated by Spanish intervention in the French FRONDE, and ended (1659) with the humiliation of Spain (see PYRENEES, PEACE OF THE). The war gave Portugal the opportunity to revolt (1640) and to choose John IV as king. Catalonia also rose and was long occupied by the French. Spain had to recognize the independence of the United Provinces of the Netherlands at the Peace of Westphalia and lost Roussillon and part of the Spanish Netherlands to France at the Peace of the Pyrenees. Philip's daughter, Marie Thérèse, was married to Louis XIV of France. Thanks to the presence of Velázquez at his court, Philip was probably one of the most frequently portrayed monarchs in history. He was also a patron of Rubens and Cano. Calderón de la Barca and Tirso de Molina continued the great tradition of Spanish drama during his reign. Philip was succeeded by his son, Charles II.

Philip V, 1683-1746, king of Spain (1700-1746), first Bourbon on the Spanish throne. A grandson of Louis XIV of France, he was titular duke of Anjou before CHARLES II of Spain designated him as his successor. Louis XIV accepted the Spanish throne for his grandson and thus precipitated the War of the SPANISH SUCCESSION (1701-14), which severely reduced Spanish power. The peace treaties (see UTRECHT, PEACE OF) left Spain its colonial empire, but forced it to cede the Spanish Netherlands, Sardinia, Milan, and Naples to Austria and Sicily to Savoy. Philip kept the Spanish throne but was obliged to introduce the Salic law of succession in order to preclude the possibility of a personal union with France. For having sided with Philip's chief rival in the war, Archduke Charles (later Holy Roman Emperor Charles VI), Philip deprived Catalonia, Aragón, and Valencia of most of their autonomous privileges. Of indolent and melancholy disposition, Philip was dominated by women. At first the princesse des URSINS, lady in waiting to Philip's first consort, Maria Luisa of Savoy, dominated his court and made French influence paramount. In 1714, Philip married ELIZABETH FARNESE, who took complete control of her husband's policies and who was in turn dominated by the chief minister, Cardinal ALBERONI. The attempt by the queen and Alberoni to reconquer the former Spanish territories in Italy led to the formation of the QUADRUPLE ALLIANCE of 1718, to which Spain had to submit in 1720. In 1724, Philip abdicated in favor of his son, Louis I, possibly so that he might secure the French throne. However, on the death of Louis within the same year, Philip resumed his reign. Spain's foreign policy continued to be governed to a large extent by dynastic ambition and was successful so far as the house of BOURBON was concerned. In the War of the POLISH SUCCESSION (1733-35) Naples and Sicily passed to Don Carlos (later Charles III of Spain), son of Philip and Elizabeth; in the War of the AUSTRIAN SUCCESSION (1740-48) Parma and Piacenza passed to Charles's younger brother Philip. Spain's entry into the War of the Austrian Succession was preceded (1739) by the outbreak of the War of JENKINS'S EAR with Great Britain. In 1733 the first Franco-Spanish FAMILY COMPACT was concluded. Under Philip, Spain began to recover from the economic stagnation of the 17th cent., especially after the rise (1743) of the reforming minister ENSENADA. Philip was succeeded by Ferdinand VI, his son by Maria Luisa.

Philip, half brother of Herod Antipas, called Philip Herod. See HEROD, dynasty.

Philip, d. A.D. 34, tetrarch of Ituraea, son of Herod the Great. He was perhaps the ablest of the HEROD dynasty. Luke 3.1.

Philip (King Philip), chief of the Wampanoag Indians: see KING PHILIP'S WAR.

Philip Augustus: see PHILIP II, king of France.

Philip Neri, Saint (nā'rē), 1515–95, Italian reformer. His original name was Filippo Romolo de' Neri. From boyhood he was religious, and in 1533 he went to Rome to study. In about 1537 he sold his books and gave the money to the poor. He was supported by a Florentine whose sons he tutored. He then devoted his time to working among the people of Rome, visiting the sick, and frequenting crowded places to talk to people about the need of religion. In 1548, with his confessor, he founded the Confraternity of the Most Holy Trinity to care for pilgrims and convalescents. He preached (although still a layman) with great success at the exercises of the society. In 1551 he was ordained. He went to the Church of San Girolamo, where the priests conducted city missionary work. St. Philip's confessional was constantly frequented, and his informal meetings for men and boys wrought a religious awakening in Rome. So great was his personal effect on individuals of every class that he is called the Apostle of Rome. He built an oratory over the church and conducted exercises with vernacular prayers and hymns for the people. Concerts of sacred music were also included, and from those the oratorio derives its name. He accepted besides his place at San Girolamo the rectorship of the Florentine Church of San Giovanni and founded an oratory there. His community of secular priests was canonically established in 1575; this was the beginning of the Congregation of the ORATORY. In 1593 he resigned his position as superior of his community. Besides the extraordinary revivification of the faith, he is credited with extension of vernacular services and of the exposition of the Sacrament. Feast: May 26. See Louis Bouyer, *The Roman Socrates* (tr. 1958).

Philip of Hesse (hĕs), 1504–67, German nobleman, landgrave of Hesse (1509–67), champion of the Reformation. He is also called Philip the Magnanimous. Declared of age in 1518, he helped suppress the PEASANTS' WAR. Having embraced Protestantism in 1524 he vainly tried to reconcile Martin LUTHER and Ulrich ZWINGLI, but finally signed the Lutheran Augsburg Confession (see CREED). With John Frederick I of Saxony and others, Philip formed (1531) the SCHMALKALDIC LEAGUE to uphold Protestantism against the opposition of Holy Roman Emperor Charles V. Philip founded the first Protestant university (Marburg, 1527), helped Ulrich, the deposed Protestant duke of Württemberg, to recover his duchy, and otherwise did much to advance Lutheranism. However, the scandal following his bigamous marriage (1540), which had been reluctantly sanctioned by Luther and Philip MELANCTHON, led him to make peace with Charles in 1541. The peace was only temporary, and after Charles V had won MAURICE of Saxony from Philip's camp, the emperor crushed (1547) the Schmalkaldic League at Mühlberg. Philip, believing that he would be well treated, surrendered. He emerged (1552) from prison a broken man. In 1567 he divided his lands among his four sons (see HESSE).

Philip of Swabia (swā'bēə), 1176?–1208, German king (1198–1208), son of Holy Roman Emperor FREDERICK I. After the death (1197) of his brother, German King and Holy Roman Emperor HENRY VI, he unsuccessfully attempted to secure the succession in Germany of his infant nephew, the later Holy Roman Emperor FREDERICK II; for the sake of the house of HOHENSTAUFEN, he finally consented to his own election as German king. A small, anti-Hohenstaufen group led by the archbishop of Cologne elected (1198) OTTO IV antiking. In the ensuing war Philip was supported by Philip II of France, while Otto had the support of his uncle Richard I of England. Though successful at first, Philip's cause was weakened when Pope INNOCENT III declared (1201) for Otto. However, the year 1204 marked a turn in Philip's favor; with his capture (1206) of Cologne, the war was virtually ended. Negotiations with the pope had resulted in a satisfactory settlement when Philip was murdered by a personal enemy. Otto IV was elected his successor as German king. Philip became involved in the Fourth Crusade (1202–4; see CRUSADES) partly through his marriage to the Byzantine princess Irene, daughter of Emperor ISAAC II. The extent of Philip's influence in diverting the crusade to Constantinople is still debated.

Philippe Égalité: see ORLÉANS, LOUIS PHILIPPE JOSEPH, DUC D'.

Philippeville: see SKIKDA, Algeria.

Philippi (fĭlĭp'ī), ancient city, E Macedonia. Inhabited by Thracians and then Thasians, it was renamed (probably 356 B.C.) by Philip II of Macedon, who developed and fortified it. Near the city was fought the decisive battle in which Octavian (Augustus) and Antony defeated (42 B.C.) Brutus and Cassius. It was the scene of St. Paul's first preaching in Europe; the epistle to the Philippians was addressed to the Christians there (Acts 16.12; 20.6; 1 Thess. 2.2).

Philippians (fəlĭp'ēənz), epistle of the New Testament, the 11th book in the usual order. It was written by St. PAUL from captivity probably in Rome (A.D. c.60) to the Christians of Philippi (Macedonia), the first European city that he evangelized. The letter thanks them for gifts they had sent him, tells of his own situation, and gives advice and encouragement. It is more like an ordinary letter than any other epistle because of its careless arrangement and its intimate tone. Some of the most eloquent of St. Paul's lines are here, e.g., on his motives (1.21–26), on humility (2.1–11), on the Christian's joy and fear (2.12–18), on renunciation for Christ (3.7–16). See Karl Barth, *The Epistle to the Philippians* (tr. 1962); J. M. Boice, *Philippians* (1971).

Philippics (fĭlĭp'ĭks), series of three denunciations of PHILIP II of Macedon by DEMOSTHENES. The scathing polemics of CICERO against Marc ANTONY are also called Philippics.

Philippine Independent Church, religious body that separated from the Roman Catholic Church in 1902 and rejected the spiritual authority of the pope. It is known popularly as the Aglipayan Church, after its founder Gregorio Aglipay. Initially it drew large numbers as a result of nationalist feelings, but later its membership dwindled to about 5% of the population (1970). Doctrinal disputes and strong factionalism developed. One group allied with American Unitarians and split into various parties. Another, a trinitarian group, moved toward the Protestant Episcopal Church, by which their ministers were ordained after 1948 and with which they were formally united in 1961. In 1965 the Philippine Independent Church joined the Old Catholic Union of Utrecht. See P. S. de Achutegui and M. A. Bernad, *Religious Revolution in the Philippines* (2 vol. 1960–66).

Philippines, Republic of the (fĭl'əpēnz"), republic (1973 est. pop. 40,120,000), 115,830 sq mi (300,000 sq km), SW Pacific, in Malay Archipelago off the SE Asia mainland. It comprises over 7,000 islands and rocks, of which only c.400 are permanently inhabited. The 11 largest islands—LUZON, MINDANAO, SAMAR, NEGROS, PALAWAN, PANAY, MINDORO, LEYTE, CEBU, BOHOL, and MASBATE—contain about 95% of the total land area. QUEZON CITY, on Luzon, is the capital and the second largest city; nearby MANILA is the largest city and the heart of the country. Other important centers are Cebu, on Cebu Island; ILOILO, on Panay; DAVAO and ZAMBOANGA, on Mindanao; and Jolo, on Jolo Island in the Sulu Archipelago. The northernmost point of land, the islet of Y'Ami in the Batan Islands, is separated from Formosa by the Bashi Channel (c.50 mi/80 km wide). The Philippines extend 1,152 mi (1,855 km) from north to south, between Formosa and Borneo, and 688 mi (1,108 km) from east to west, and are bounded by the Philippine Sea on the east, the Celebes Sea on the south, and the South China Sea on the west. They comprise three natural divisions—the northern, which includes Luzon and attendant islands; the central, occupied by the Visayan Islands and Palawan and Mindoro; and the southern, containing Mindanao and the Sulu Archipelago. Administratively, the republic is divided into 68 provinces. The Philippines are chiefly of volcanic origin. Most of the larger islands are traversed by mountain ranges, with Mt. Apo (9,690 ft/2,954 m), on Mindanao, the highest peak. Narrow coastal plains, wide valleys, volcanoes, dense forests, and mineral and hot springs further characterize the larger islands. Earthquakes are common. Of the many navigable rivers, Cagayan, on Luzon, is the largest; there are also large lakes on Luzon and Mindanao. The Philippines are entirely within the tropical zone. Manila, with a mean daily temperature of 79.5°F (26. 4°C), is typical of the climate of the lowland areas—hot, humid, and enervating. The highlands, however, have a bracing climate; e.g., BAGUIO, the summer capital, on Luzon, has a mean annual temperature of 64°F (17.8°C). With their tropical climate, heavy rainfall, and naturally fertile volcanic soil, the Philippines are predominantly agricultural. Rice, corn, and coconut take up about 80% of all cropland. Sugarcane, sweet potatoes, manioc, bananas, hemp, tobacco, and coffee are also important crops. Chief agricultural exports are coconut products, lumber and plywood, sugar, and hemp (the Philippines lead the world in its production). Carabao (water buffalo), pigs, chickens, goats, and ducks are widely raised, and there is dairy farming near the large cities. Fishing is a common occupation; the Sulu Archipelago is noted for its pearls and mother-of-pearl shell. The islands have one of the world's greatest stands of commercial timber, and they also abound in mineral resources, with copper, gold, iron, and chromite (the Philippines are fifth in its production) the most valuable. Manganese, mercury, lead, silver, zinc, and molybdenum are also produced. Nonmetallic minerals include rock asphalt, gypsum, asbestos, sulfur, and coal. Limestone, adobe, and marble are quarried. Manufacturing is concentrated in metropolitan Manila, near the nation's prime port, but there has been considerable industrial growth on Cebu, Negros, and Mindanao in recent years. Chief products are processed foods, cement, chemicals, metalware, textiles, beverages, tobacco products, wood and cork materials, wearing apparel, and electrical machinery. The production and repair of motor vehicles is also an important industry. Major exports are foods, lumber, and minerals, and the major imports are machinery, transportation equipment, fuels and lubricants, and base metals. The great majority of the people of the Philippines belong to the Malay group and are known as Filipinos. The only markedly non-Malayan inhabitants are the Negritos (negroid pygmies) and the Dumagats (similar to the Papuans of New Guinea). The Filipinos live mostly in the lowlands and constitute the largest Christian group in that part of the world. Roman Catholicism, a heritage from their Spanish conquerors, is professed by 84% of the population; 5% are Aglipayans, members of the Philippine Independent Church, a nationalistic offshoot of Catholicism (see AGLIPAY, GREGORIO); 5% are Muslims (concentrated on Mindanao and the Sulu Archipelago; see MOROS); 3% are Protestants; and 3% are pagans and persons not belonging to any organized religious group. The Christian Filipinos of all sects are divided into eight groups differing from each other in habitat, speech, and other cultural elements. Largest of these groups are the Visayan, in the Visayan Islands; the Tagalog, native to the provinces adjoining Manila; and the Ilocano, of NW Luzon. Some 70 native languages are spoken in the Philippines, and much has been made of the language barrier as an obstacle to national unity; however, the nine most important languages are of the Malayo-Polynesian linguistic group and

bear similarities that enable Filipinos to learn easily the speech of groups other than their own. The government's solution to the problem was to adopt (1946) Tagalog as the basis of the new national language, now known as Pilipino. A considerable number of Filipinos speak English, the nation's second language; Spanish is spoken by a very small percentage of the population. The Negritos are believed to have migrated some 30,000 years ago across land bridges then existing from Borneo, Sumatra, and Malaya. The Malayans followed in successive waves, the earliest by land bridges. These people belonged to a primitive epoch of Malayan culture, which has apparently survived to this day among certain groups such as the Igorots. The Malayan tribes that came later had more highly developed material cultures. In the 14th cent. Arab traders from Malay and Borneo introduced Islam into the southern islands and extended their influence as far north as Luzon.

Arrival of the Spanish. The first Europeans to visit (1521) the Philippines were those in the Spanish expedition around the world led by the Portguese explorer Ferdinand Magellan. Other Spanish expeditions followed, including one from New Spain (Mexico) under López de Villalobos, who in 1542 named the islands for the infante Philip, later Philip II. Spanish conquest of the Filipinos did not begin in earnest until 1564, when another expedition from New Spain, commanded by Miguel LÓPEZ DE LEGASPI, arrived. He was a pacifier as well as a conqueror, and Spanish leadership was soon established over many small independent communities that previously had known no central rule. By 1571, when López de Legaspi established the Spanish city of Manila on the site of a Moro town he had conquered the year before, the Spanish foothold in the Philippines was secure, despite the opposition of the Portuguese, who were eager to maintain their monopoly on the trade of the Orient. Manila repulsed the attack of the Chinese pirate Limahong in 1574. For centuries before the Spanish arrived the Chinese had traded with the Filipinos, but evidently none had settled permanently in the islands until after the conquest. Chinese trade and labor were of great importance in the early development of the Spanish colony, but the Chinese came to be feared and hated because of their increasing numbers, and in 1603 the Spanish murdered thousands of them (later, there were lesser massacres of the Chinese). The Spanish governor, made a viceroy in 1589, ruled with the advice of the powerful royal audiencia. There were frequent uprisings by the Filipinos, who resented the ENCOMIENDA system. By the end of the 16th cent. Manila had become a leading commercial center of the Far East, carrying on a flourishing trade with China, India, and the East Indies. The Philippines supplied some wealth (including gold) to Spain, and the richly laden galleons plying between the islands and New Spain were often attacked by English freebooters. There was also trouble from other quarters, and the period from 1600 to 1663 was marked by continual wars with the Dutch, who were laying the foundations of their rich empire in the East Indies, and with Moro pirates. One of the most difficult problems the Spanish faced was the subjugation of the warlike Moros, who continued to harass the rest of the population. Intermittent campaigns were conducted against them but without conclusive results until the middle of the 19th cent. As the power of the Spanish Empire waned, the Jesuit orders became more influential in the Philippines and acquired great amounts of property. It was the opposition to the power of the clergy that in large measure brought about the rising sentiment for independence. Spanish injustices, bigotry, and economic oppressions fed the movement, which was greatly inspired by the brilliant writings of José RIZAL. In 1896 revolution began in the province of Cavite, and after the execution of Rizal that December, it spread throughout the major islands. The Filipino leader, Emilio AGUINALDO, achieved considerable success before a peace was patched up with Spain. The peace was short-lived, however, for neither side honored its agreements, and a new revolution was brewing when the Spanish-American War broke out in 1898. After the U.S. naval victory in Manila Bay on May 1, 1898, Commodore George Dewey supplied Aguinaldo with arms and urged him to rally the Filipinos against the Spanish. By the time U.S. land forces had arrived, the Filipinos had taken the entire island of Luzon, except for the old walled city of Manila, which they were besieging. They had also declared their independence and established a republic under the first democratic constitution ever known in Asia. Their dreams of independence were crushed when the Philippines were transferred from Spain to the United States in the Treaty of Paris (1898), which closed the Spanish-American War; in Feb., 1899, Aguinaldo led a new revolt, this time against U.S. rule. Defeated on the battlefield, the Filipinos turned to guerrilla warfare, and their subjugation became a mammoth project for the United States—one that cost far more money and took far more lives than the Spanish-American War. It also bitterly divided the American people, with sentiment polarizing along political lines. Democrats generally opposed the war and favored independence for the Filipinos, while the Republicans believed that the insurrection should be crushed and that the islands should remain under U.S. rule. The insurrection was effectively ended with the capture (1901) of Aguinaldo by Gen. Frederick Funston, but the question of Philippine independence remained a burning issue in the politics of both the United States and the islands. The matter was complicated by growing economic ties between the two countries. Although comparatively little American capital was invested in island industries, U.S. trade bulked larger and larger until the Philippines became almost entirely dependent upon the American market. Free trade, established by an act of 1909, was expanded in 1913. When the Democrats came into power in 1913, steps were taken to prepare the Filipino people for self-rule. Francis B. Harrison, who was appointed governor general, worked toward replacing many Americans in key positions of government with Filipinos. The Philippine assembly already had a popularly elected lower house, and the Jones Act, passed by the U.S. Congress in 1916, provided for a popularly elected upper house as well, with power to approve all appointments made by the governor general. It also gave the islands their first definite pledge of independence, although no specific date was set (an amendment proposing independence in two to four years was struck from the bill). Investigating commissions sent to the Philippines reported unfavorably on the islands' readiness for self-government, and when the Republicans regained power in 1921, the trend toward bringing Filipinos into the government was reversed. Gen. Leonard Wood, who was appointed governor general, largely supplanted Filipino activities with a semimilitary rule. After Wood's death, Governor General Henry L. Stimson, who served from 1927 to 1929, somewhat allayed the turmoil raised among the Filipinos by Wood's administration. The advent of the Great Depression in the United States in the 1930s and the first aggressive moves by Japan in Asia (1931) shifted U.S. sentiment sharply toward the granting of immediate independence to the Philippines. Americans, deeply involved with their own troubles, wanted no additional responsibilities abroad. The Hare-Hawes-Cutting Act, passed by Congress in 1932, provided for complete independence of the islands in 1945 after 10 years of self-government under U.S. tutelage. President Herbert Hoover maintained that the bill left the United States with responsibility but no power and vetoed it; however, Congress passed the bill over his veto (1933). It had been drawn up with the aid of a commission from the Philippines, but Manuel L. QUEZON, the leader of the dominant Nationalist party, opposed it, partially because of its threat of American tariffs against Philippine products but principally because of the provisions leaving naval bases in U.S hands. Under his influence, the Philippine legislature rejected the bill. The Tydings-McDuffie Independence Act (1934) closely resembled the Hare-Howes-Cutting-Act, but struck the provisions for American bases and carried a promise of further study to correct "imperfections or inequalities." The Philippine legislature ratified the bill; a constitution, approved by President Roosevelt (March, 1935) was accepted by the Philippine people in a plebiscite (May); and Quezon was elected the first president (September). When Quezon was inaugurated on Nov. 15, 1935, the Commonwealth of the Philippines was formally established. Quezon was reelected in Nov., 1941. To develop defensive forces against possible aggression, Gen. Douglas MacArthur was brought to the islands as military adviser in 1935, and the following year he became field marshal of the Commonwealth army. War came suddenly to the Philippines on Dec. 8 (Dec. 7, U.S. time), 1941, when Japan attacked without warning. Japanese troops invaded the islands in many places and launched a pincer drive on Manila. MacArthur's scattered defending forces (about 80,000 troops, four fifths of them Filipinos) were forced to withdraw to Bataan Peninsula and Corregidor Island, where they entrenched and tried to hold until the arrival of reinforcements, meanwhile guarding the entrance to Manila Bay and denying that important harbor to the Japanese. But no reinforcements were forthcoming. The Japanese occupied Manila on Jan. 2, 1942. MacArthur was ordered out by President Roosevelt and left for Australia on March 11; Lt. Gen. Jonathan Wainwright assumed command. The besieged U.S.-Filipino army on Bataan was directed to gain time by holding as long as possible. Lacking sea and air support and crippled from starvation and disease, it finally crumbled on April 9, 1942. Wainwright gallantly fought on from Corregidor with a garrison of about 11,000 men; he was overwhelmed on May 6, 1942. After his capitulation, the Japanese forced the surrender of all remaining defending units in the islands by threatening to use the captured Bataan and Corregidor troops as hostages. Many individual soldiers refused to surrender, however, and guerrilla resistance, organized and coordinated by U.S and Philippine army officers, continued throughout the Japanese occupation. Japan's efforts to win native loyalty found expression in the establishment (Oct. 14, 1943) of a "Philippine Republic," with José P. Laurel, former supreme court justice, as president. But the people suffered greatly from Japanese brutality, and the puppet government gained little support. Meanwhile, President Quezon, who had escaped with other high officials before the country fell, set up a government-in-exile in Washington. When he died (Aug., 1944), Vice President Sergio OSMEÑA became president. Osmeña returned to the Philippines with the first liberation forces, which surprised the Japanese by landing (Oct. 20, 1944) at Leyte, in the heart of the islands, after months of U.S. air strikes against Mindanao. The Philippine government was established at Tacloban, Leyte, on Oct. 23. The landing was followed (Oct. 23–26) by the greatest naval engagement in history, called variously the battle of Leyte Gulf and the second battle of the Philippine Sea. A great U.S. victory, it effectively destroyed the Japanese fleet and opened the way for the recovery of all the islands. Luzon was invaded (Jan., 1945), and Manila was taken in February. On July 5, 1945, MacArthur announced "All the Philippines are now liberated." The Japanese had suffered over 425,000 dead in the Philippines. The Philippine congress met on June 9, 1945, for the first time since its election in 1941. It faced enormous problems. The land was devastated by war, the economy destroyed, the country torn by political warfare and guerrilla violence. Osmeña's leadership was challenged (Jan., 1946) when one wing (now the Liberal party) of the Nationalist party nominated for president Manuel ROXAS, who defeated Osmeña in April.

The Republic of the Philippines. Roxas became the first president of the Republic of the Philippines when independence was granted, as scheduled, on July 4, 1946. The new republic was inaugurated with impressive ceremonies at Manila. Filipino ties with the United States were hardly severed, however. An act passed by the U.S. Congress provided for free trade between the two countries for a period of eight years after independence, and a Philippine plebiscite in March, 1947, approved granting the United States equal trading rights until 1974 in return for enormous rehabilitation funds. These moneys were supplemented throughout the years by continuing American aid, loans, and grants. In March, 1947, the two countries signed a military assistance pact (since renewed) and the Philippines gave the United States a 99-year lease on designated military, naval, and air bases (a later agreement reduced the period to 25 years beginning 1967). The sudden death of President Roxas in April, 1948, elevated the vice president, Elpidio QUIRINO, to the presidency, and in a bitterly contested election in Nov., 1949, Quirino defeated José Laurel to win a four-year term of his own. The enormous task of reconstructing the war-torn country was complicated by the activities in central Luzon of the Communist-dominated Hukbalahap guerrillas (Huks), who resorted to terror and violence in their efforts to achieve land reform and gain political power. They were finally brought under control after a vigorous attack launched by the minister of national defense, Ramón MAGSAYSAY. Magsaysay combined strong military pressure with a conciliatory approach, offering homesteads on Mindanao to Huks who surrendered. When the Huk leader, Luis Taruk, voluntarily surrendered in 1954, a relative peace was ensured. By that time Magsaysay was president of the country, having defeated Quirino in Nov., 1953. He had promised sweeping economic changes, and he did make progress in land reform, opening new settlements outside crowded Luzon island. His death in an airplane crash in March, 1957, was a serious blow to national morale. Vice President Carlos P. García succeeded him and won a full term as president in the elections of Nov., 1957. In foreign affairs, the Philippines maintained a firm anti-Communist policy; the Philippines joined the Southeast Asia Treaty Organization in 1954. There were difficulties with the United States over American military installations in the islands, and, despite formal recognition (1956) of full Philipppine sovereignty over these bases, tensions increased until some of the bases were dismantled (1959) and the 99-year lease period was reduced. The United States rejected Philippine financial claims and proposed trade revisions. Philippine opposition to García on issues of government corruption and anti-Americanism led, in June, 1959, to the union of the Liberal and Progressive parties, led by Vice President Diosdad MACAPAGAL, the Liberal party leader, who succeeded García as president in the 1961 elections. Macapagal's administration was marked by efforts to combat the mounting inflation that had plagued the republic since its birth; by attempted alliances with neighboring countries; and by a territorial dispute with Britain over North Borneo (later Sabah), which Macapagal claimed had been leased and not sold to the British North Borneo Company in 1878. Ferdinand E. MARCOS, who succeeded to the presidency after defeating Macapagal in the 1965 elections, inherited this dispute; in Sept., 1968, he approved a congressional bill annexing Sabah to the Philippines. Malaysia suspended diplomatic relations, and the matter was referred to the UN. The continuing need for land reform fostered a new Huk uprising in central Luzon, accompanied by mounting assassinations and acts of terror, and in Aug., 1969, President Marcos began a major military campaign to subdue them. Civil war also threatened on Mindanao, where bands of Moros were attacking Christian settlers. In Nov., 1969, Marcos won an unprecedented reelection, easily defeating Sergio Osmeña, Jr., but the election was accompanied by violence and charges of fraud, and Marcos's second term began with increasing civil disorder. In Jan., 1970, some 2,000 demonstrators tried to storm Malacanan Palace, the presidential residence; riots erupted against the U.S. embassy. When Pope Paul VI visited Manila in Nov., 1970, an attempt was made on his life. In Aug., 1971, at a Liberal party rally, hand grenades were thrown at the speakers' platform, and several people were killed. President Marcos declared martial law in Sept., 1972, charging that a Communist rebellion threatened. The next month the government announced that it had uncovered a plot to kill the president. In December, the president's wife, Imelda Marcos, was attacked and injured at a public ceremony. Meanwhile the fighting on Mindanao had spread to the Sulu Archipelago. Attempts to restore order with national troops had only spread the trouble. By Jan., 1973, some 3,000 people had been killed and hundreds of villages burned. President Marcos recalled the troops and tried a more diplomatic approach with Muslim leaders, offering economic aid and conceding that "some injustice" had been done to their people. In June, 1974, he offered amnesty to those Muslims who were willing to lay down their arms and negotiate. The 1935 constitution was replaced (1973) by a new one that provided the president with direct powers. A plebiscite (July, 1973) gave Marcos the right to remain in office beyond the expiration (Dec., 1973) of his term. See E. H. Blair and J. A. Robertson, ed., *The Philippine Islands, 1493–1888* (55 vol., 1903–9; Vol. LIII, *Bibliography);* W. C. Forbes, *The Philippine Islands* (1945; rev. and abr. from the 2-vol. ed. of 1928); David Bernstein, *The Philippine Story* (1947); J. E. Spencer, *Land and People in the Philippines* (1952); Louis Morton, *The Fall of the Philippines* (1953); Leon Wolff, *Little Brown Brother* (1961); Theodore Friend, *Between Two Empires; The Ordeal of the Philippines, 1929–1946* (1965); J. R. Hayden, *The Philippines: A Study a in National Development* (1942, repr. 1972); E. G. Maring and J. M. Maring, *Historical and Cultural Dictionary of the Philippines* (1973); Geoffrey Bocca, *The Philippines: America's Forgotten Friends* (1974); P. W. Stanley, *A Nation in the Making* (1974).

Philippines, University of the, at Quezon City, the Philippines; English language; founded 1908. It has colleges of agriculture, forestry, fisheries, veterinary medicine, business administration, public administration, education, home economics, architecture, fine arts, law, engineering, arts and sciences, medicine, nursing, pharmacy, dentistry, and music; schools of economics, allied medical professions, and graduate studies; as well as institutes of public health, library science, mass communication, planning, population studies, and social work and community development.

Philippopolis: see PLOVDIV, Bulgaria.

Philips, Ambrose, 1674–1749, English author. After resigning his fellowship from Cambridge in 1708, he moved to London and became known in the literary Whig coterie of Addison. He is principally remembered for his quarrel with Pope about the relative merits of their pastorals that appeared in the 1709 edition of Jacob Tonson's miscellany. He wrote three verse tragedies, of which only *The Distrest Mother* (1712), adapted from Racine's *Andromaque,* had any success. In 1718 he began the *Freethinker,* a periodical in imitation of the *Spectator.* His nickname "Namby-Pamby" was given to him by Henry Carey because of the cloying sentimentality of his poems in praise of childhood.

Philips, John, 1676–1709, English poet. He was one of the few to write in blank verse in an age when the heroic couplet was the standard form. His *Splendid Shilling* (1701, 1705) is a parody of Milton. *Cyder* (1708), a utilitarian poem describing the cultivation of apples and the pressing of cider, is modeled after Vergil's *Georgics.* See his poems (ed. by M. G. L. Thomas, 1927).

Philips, Katherine (Fowler), 1631–64, English poet. Conductor of several literary salons in London, she began the Society of Friendship under the pseudonym "Matchless Orinda." The first collected edition of her poems appeared in 1667.

Philipse, Frederick (fĭl'ĭps), 1626–1702, merchant and landowner in colonial America, b. Holland. He went (1647) with his family to New Amsterdam, where he became wealthy as a merchant. He bought (1672) a large estate, PHILIPSE MANOR, and later erected a church and also Philipsburg Manor at Upper Mills, North Tarrytown, N.Y. His town house in New York City was confiscated by the New York state government in the American Revolution (see MORRIS, ROGER).

Philipse Manor, colonial estate of Frederick PHILIPSE, confirmed by a royal charter (1693), extending from the present North Tarrytown, N.Y., to the present Bronx, with the Hudson River on the west and the Bronx River on the east. Its area was 90,000 acres (36,400 hectares). At Yonkers, Philipse built a mill and a manor hall (c.1682), the permanent family seat. The estate passed into British and then American hands in the Revolution, and its administration as a single unit was never restored. Soon after the Revolution a New York merchant bought the Yonkers manor house, and in 1868 the city of Yonkers purchased it for use as the city hall. The state now owns the surrounding ground and the manor house, where historical collections are displayed. Frederick Philipse also built (c.1683) a mill and a manor hall, **Philipsburg Manor,** the northern family seat, at Upper Mills, North Tarrytown, on the Pocantico River. After the Revolution it went through several hands and numerous changes. It was partially restored in 1943, and the manor hall was reopened as a museum of Dutch colonial life. A second restoration was begun in 1958 by Sleepy Hollow Restorations, Inc., with extensive archaeological exploration. The original manor house was restored, and a reconstructed mill, barn, slave quarters, and dam were opened to the public in 1969.

Philip the Arabian: see PHILIP, Roman emperor.

Philip the Bold: see PHILIP III, king of France.

Philip the Bold, 1342–1404, duke of Burgundy (1363–1404); a younger son of King JOHN II of France. He fought (1356) at Poitiers and shared his father's captivity in England. He was first made duke of Touraine (1360) and then duke of Burgundy. In 1369, Philip married Margaret, heiress of Flanders. With his brothers he was appointed by King Charles V as regent for the future CHARLES VI, and soon after the young king's accession (1380) Philip became the virtual ruler of France. He used his position to further his own dynastic ambition. In 1382 he led an expedition in support of his father-in-law, the count of Flanders, against the Flemish rebels under Philip van ARTEVELDE and defeated them at Roosebeke. In 1384 he inherited Flanders, in addition to Franche-Comté, Artois, Nevers, and Rethel, from his father-in-law. Through marriages of his children to the WITTELSBACH dynasty, Holland, Hainaut, and Zeeland eventually came to Burgundy. Philip retired (1388) to his duchy at the beginning of the personal rule of Charles VI, but he returned to prominence when the king became insane (1392). Philip was the chief rival for power of the king's brother Louis d'ORLÉANS; his son, JOHN THE FEARLESS, carried on the quarrel. See J. L. A. Calmette, *The Golden Age of Burgundy* (1949, tr. 1962); Richard Vaughan, *Philip the Bold: The Formation of the Burgundian State* (1962).

Philip the Fair: see PHILIP IV, king of France.

Philip the Good, 1396–1467, duke of Burgundy (1419–67); son of Duke John the Fearless. After his father was murdered (1419) at a meeting with the dauphin (later King CHARLES VII of France), Philip formed an alliance with King Henry V of England. Under the Treaty of Troyes (1420; see TROYES, TREATY OF) Philip recognized Henry V as heir to the French throne; the dauphin was disinherited. Philip aided the efforts of Henry and his successor to establish English rule in France. Finally, in return for important concessions, Philip ended the English alliance and made peace with Charles VII in the Treaty of Arras (1435; see ARRAS, TREATY OF). Despite the truce, Philip's relations with Charles were not always amicable. He temporarily supported (1440) the rebellious nobles in the PRAGUERIE and gave asylum to the dauphin (later King Louis XI), who was constantly in revolt against his father. During Philip's reign the territory of his duchy was more than doubled. Through inheritance, treaty, conquest, and purchase he acquired Hainaut, Holland, Zeeland, Friesland, Brabant, Limburg, Namur, Luxembourg, Liège, Cambrai, and numerous other cities and feudal dependencies. Uprisings in Bruges (1436) and in Ghent (1450–53) were suppressed. In 1463, Philip was forced to return some of his holdings to Louis XI. His vow (1454) to go on crusade was never fulfilled. Philip's court was the most splendid in the Western Europe of his time. He was succeeded by his ambitious son, CHARLES THE BOLD, who took control of the government from Philip in 1465. See biography by Richard Vaughan (1970); J. L. A. Calmette, *The Golden Age of Burgundy* (1949, tr. 1962).

Philip the Tall: see PHILIP V, king of France.

Philistia (fĭlĭs'tyə), ancient region of SW Palestine, comprising a coastal strip along the Mediterranean and a portion of S Canaan. The chief cities of Philistia were Gaza, Ashqelon, Ashdod, Ekron, and Gath; strategically located on the great commercial route from Egypt to Syria, they formed a confederacy. In the Bible the great Hebrew antagonists of the Philistines are SAMSON, SAUL, and DAVID. They were independent at the time of AMOS, and the Jews never really conquered them. Philistia was laid under tribute by Assyria, and the invasion of Palestine by SENNACHERIB was brought on by Hezekiah's imprisonment of the Assyrian tributary, the king of Ekron. See A. R. Burn, *Minoans, Philistines, and Greeks* (1930, repr. 1968); Robert Macalister, *The Philistines* (1965).

Philistines (fĭl'ĭstēnz, fĭlĭs'-), inhabitants of Philistia, a non-Semitic people who came to Palestine from the Aegean (probably Crete), in the 12th cent. B.C. Their control of iron supplies and their tight political organization of cities made them a rival of the people of Israel for centuries. *Philistine* has come to mean an uncultured, materialistic person.

Phillips, David Graham, 1867–1911, American writer, b. Madison, Ind., grad. College of New Jersey (now Princeton), 1887. He worked as a newspaper reporter in Cincinnati and New York City, rising to editorial rank on the New York *World,* for which he wrote until 1902. Phillips became noted as a MUCKRAKER and was famous as the author of a series of sensational articles exposing corruption in the U.S. Senate that appeared in *Cosmopolitan* magazine (1906). He also wrote articles for the *Saturday Evening Post* and other journals of the period. Phillips's novels, powerful although often crude, deal with corruptive influences in society and general social problems, such as the status of women. Among them are *The Great God Success* (1901), *The Conflict* (1911), and *Susan Lenox; Her Fall and Rise* (1917). Phillips was murdered by a young musician who accused him of having cast literary slurs on his family. See study by A. C. Ravitz (1966); I. F. Marcosson, *David Graham Phillips and His Times* (1932).

Phillips, Samuel, 1752–1802, American educator and politician, b. North Andover, Mass., grad. Harvard, 1771. A member of the Massachusetts provincial congress (1775–80) and a delegate to the state constitutional convention (1779–80), he served in the state senate (1780–1801), except for one year. He is best known, however, as the founder of PHILLIPS ACADEMY at Andover (opened 1778), a leading preparatory school for boys. His uncle, John Phillips (1719–95), the founder of PHILLIPS EXETER ACADEMY, provided financial backing. Samuel Phillips died shortly after his inauguration (1801) as lieutenant governor of Massachusetts. See C. M. Fuess, *An Old New England School* (1917).

Phillips, Ulrich Bonnell, 1877–1934, American historian, an authority on the antebellum South, b. La Grange, Ga. After teaching at the Univ. of Wisconsin (1902–8), he was professor of history and political science at Tulane Univ. (1908–11) and then professor of American history at the Univ. of Michigan (1911–29) and at Yale (1929–34). His doctoral dissertation, *Georgia and State Rights* (1902), received the Justin Winsor Prize from the American Historical Association. Phillips's works are distinguished by vast research and also by a fine literary style. *American Negro Slavery* (1918), which was long the standard work on the subject, is generally sympathetic to the slaveholders. *Life and Labor in the Old South* (1929) remains the classic account of the antebellum society and economy. Phillips edited *Plantation and Frontier Documents, 1649–1863* (1909) and *The Correspondence of Robert Toombs, Alexander H. Stephens, and Howell Cobb* (1913). See W. H. Stephenson, *The South Lives in History* (1955, repr. 1969).

Phillips, Wendell, 1811–84, American reformer and orator, b. Boston, grad. Harvard (B.A., 1831; LL.B., 1834). He was admitted to the bar in 1834 but, having sufficient income of his own, he abandoned his law practice to devote his life to fighting for sound causes, chiefly the abolition of slavery. Revolted by the mobbing (1835) in Boston of abolitionist William Lloyd GARRISON and prodded by his brilliant young wife, the former Ann Terry Greene, he entered wholeheartedly into the abolitionist crusade. His eloquent protest (1837) in Faneuil Hall on the assassination of the abolitionist editor Elijah P. LOVEJOY marked the beginning of his long and distinguished career as a lecturer. Phillips frequently contributed to the *Liberator* and, like its publisher, Garrison, refused to identify his abolitionism with any political party. He also followed Garrison in other causes, notably woman's rights. He was a delegate to the World Anti-Slavery Convention in London (1840), opposed the Mexican War and the annexation of Texas, came to advocate the dissolution of the Union, and aroused considerable hostility by his vehement denunciations of slaveholding. In the Civil War he attacked Lincoln for his moderate stand on emancipation of the slaves and opposed Lincoln's renomination. Phillips held that the government owed the Negro not merely his freedom, but land, education, and full civil rights as well. This led to a break between him and Garrison in 1865 when Garrison proposed to dissolve the American Anti-Slavery Society on the grounds that its purpose had been fulfilled. Phillips became the society's president and kept it active until the adoption of the Fifteenth Amendment enfranchised the Negroes. While most of the victorious crusaders for abolition were content to rest on their laurels, Phillips continued his agitation for social reform, speaking for many unpopular causes—prohibition, woman's suffrage, the abolition of capital punishment, currency reform (see GREENBACK), and the rights of labor. He was the unsuccessful candidate of the Labor and Prohibition parties for the governorship of Massachusetts in 1870. Phillips's advanced doctrines became indistinguishable from those of Marxian socialism, and he defended the Commune of Paris of 1871 and Russian nihilism. As an orator he was rated with Edward Everett and Daniel Webster; his style, however, was easy and colloquial. See his *Speeches, Lectures, and Letters* (1st series, 1863; 2d series, 1891); biographies by J. A. Green (1943, repr. 1964), Oscar Sherwin (1958), and Irving Bartlett (1961, repr. 1973).

Phillips Academy, at Andover, Mass.; college preparatory boarding and day school; opened 1778, chartered 1780 by Samuel PHILLIPS. Founded for boys, it is the oldest incorporated academy in the United States and has served as the model for many later schools. In 1972 the academy became coeducational when Abbot Academy, a neighboring girls' school, was incorporated. The school is often called Andover or Phillips Andover. Andover Theological Seminary (now part of Andover Newton Theological School at Newton Centre, Mass.) was affiliated from 1808 to 1908. The Addison Gallery of American Art houses well-known collections.

Phillipsburg, town (1970 pop. 17,849), Warren co., NW N.J., on the Delaware River opposite Easton, Pa.; settled 1739, inc. 1861. It is an important railroad and industrial center in a farm area. The city's industrial growth began after the arrival of the railroad and the establishment of iron and steel works there in the mid-1800s.

Phillips Exeter Academy (ĕk'sətər), at Exeter, N.H.; coeducational; chartered 1781, opened 1783 by John Phillips. It has been an influential preparatory school and has a notable school library. Heavily endowed (1931) by Edward S. Harkness, the school has a large campus and many fine buildings. Founded as a school for boys, it became coeducational in 1970. Its student body numbers about 1,000. See M. R. Williams, *Story of Phillips Exeter* (1957).

Philo (fī'lō) or **Philo Judaeus** (jo͞odē'əs) [Lat.,=Philo the Jew], c.20 B.C.–A.D. c.50, Alexandrian Jewish philosopher. His writings have had an enormous influence on both Jewish and Christian thought, and particularly upon the Alexandrian theologians Clement and Origen. All that is known of his life is that he was sent to Rome A.D. c.40 to represent the Jews of Alexandria in seeking the restoration of privileges lost because they had refused to obey an imperial edict to worship Caligula. Philo occupies a preeminent place among Hellenistic religious thinkers because he was the first to attempt to reconcile Biblical religion with Greek philosophy. In so doing he developed an allegorical interpretation of Scripture, which enabled him to find many of the doctrines of Greek philosophy in the Pentateuch. An eclectic and a mystic, Philo emphasized the total transcendence and perfection of God, and, in order to account for creation and the relation between the infinite God and the finite world, he introduced the concept of the Logos. Logos is the intermediary through which God's will acts and is thus the creative power that orders the world. Along with the Logos, Philo posited a whole realm of beings or potencies that bridge the gap between the Creator and his creation. Philo's doctrine of intermediary beings and the Logos has antecedents in Plato's Ideas and parallels certain New Testament writings. Only fragments of Philo's works remain, but numerous and ample quotations from his writings are found in early Christian literature. See his works (tr. by F. H. Colson and G. H. Whitaker, 10 vol., 1929–42, Loeb Classical Library); H. A. Wolfson, *Philo* (1947); E. R. Goodenough, *Introduction to Philo Judaeus* (2d ed. 1963).

Philochorus (fĭlŏk'ōrəs), fl. 3d cent. B.C., Greek historian. He wrote extensively on Greek religious customs. Philochorus is probably the best known of the many chroniclers of events in Athens and surrounding Attica. His *Atthis* is a 17-volume history of the region from mythological times to 260 B.C. In 250 B.C., Philochorus was murdered by political enemies.

Philoctetes (fĭlŏktē'tēz), in Greek mythology, son of Poias. He acquired, by gift, the bow and arrow of Hercules by lighting the pyre on which the hero was consumed alive. On his way to the Trojan War, Philoctetes was bitten by a snake. Because the smell of his wound and his cries made him offensive, his companions left him on the desolate island of Lemnos. When an oracle declared that Troy could not be taken without the weapons of Hercules, Philoctetes was brought to Troy by Neoptolemus (or Diomedes) and Odysseus. He was healed of his wound and helped conquer Troy by killing Paris. Sophocles' drama *Philoctetes* is based on the efforts of Neoptolemus and Odysseus to bring Philoctetes to Troy.

philodendron: see ARUM.

Philologus (fĭlŏl'ōgəs), Roman Christian. Rom. 16.15.

Philomela and Procne (fĭlōmē'lə, prŏk'nē), in Greek mythology, daughters of King Pandion of Attica. Procne married Tereus, king of Thrace, and bore him a son, Itys (or Itylus). Tereus later seduced Philomela and cut out her tongue to silence her. Philomela embroidered the story into some cloth, which she sent to her sister. In revenge, Procne murdered Itys and served up his flesh to her husband. Tereus pursued and tried to kill the sisters, but the gods changed them all into birds. Philomela became a swallow, Procne a nightingale, and Tereus a hoopoe. Itys was revived and became a goldfinch.

Philopoemen (fĭləpē'mən), c.252–183 B.C., Greek statesman and general, b. Megalopolis. For years he fought as a mercenary in Crete. In 209 he became commander of the Achaean cavalry, with which he defeated the Aetolians and Eleans. He next became (208) general of the ACHAEAN LEAGUE. He defeated Machanidas, tyrant of Sparta, at Mantinea. Nabis, successor of Machanidas, was driven out of Messene and was defeated (201–200) in Laconia by Philopoemen. When Nabis was assassinated, the Spartans were incorporated (192) into the Achaean League, but revolted and were again conquered (188) by Philopoemen. He was captured and poisoned by Messenian rebels. Philopoemen was glorified by his compatriot, the historian POLYBIUS.

philosopher's stone: see ALCHEMY.

philosophy [Gr.,=love of wisdom], study of the ultimate reality, causes, and principles underlying being and thinking. It has many aspects and different manifestations according to the problems involved and the method of approach and emphasis used by the individual philosopher. This search for truth began, in the Western world, when the Greeks first established (c.600 B.C.) inquiry independent of theological creeds. Philosophy is distinguished from theology in that philosophy ignores dogma and deals with speculation rather than faith. Philosophy differs from science in that both the natural and the social sciences base their theories wholly on established fact, whereas philosophy covers the area of inquiry where no facts as such are available; originally, science as such did not exist and philosophy covered the entire field, but as facts became available and tentative certainties emerged, sciences broke away from metaphysical speculation to pursue their different aims. Thus physics was once in the realm of philosophy, and it was only in the early 20th cent. that psychology was established as a science apart from philosophy. However, many of the greatest philosophers were also scientists, and philosophy still considers the methods (as opposed to the materials) of science as its province. Philosophy is traditionally divided into several branches: METAPHYSICS inquires into the nature and ultimate significance of the universe; LOGIC is concerned with the laws of valid reasoning; EPISTEMOLOGY investigates the nature of knowledge and the process of knowing; ETHICS deals with problems of right conduct; and AESTHETICS attempts to determine the nature of beauty and the criteria of artistic judgment. Within metaphysics a division is made according to fundamental principles. The three major positions are idealism, which maintains that what is real is in the form of thought rather than matter; materialism, which considers matter and the motion of matter as the universal reality; and dualism, which gives thought and matter equal status. Naturalism and positivism are forms of materialism. Historically, philosophy falls into three large periods: classical (Greek and Roman) philosophy, which was concerned with the ultimate nature of reality and the problem of virtue in a political context; medieval philosophy, which in the West is virtually inseparable from early Christian thought; and, beginning with the Renaissance, modern philosophy, whose main direction has been epistemology. The first Greek philosophers, the Milesian school in the early 6th cent. B.C., consisting of Thales, Anaximander, and Anaximenes, were concerned with finding the one natural element underlying all nature and being. They were followed by Heraclitus, Pythagoras, Parmenides, Leucippus, Empedocles, Anaxagoras, and Democritus, who took divergent paths in exploring the same problem. Socrates was the first to inquire also into social and political problems and was the first to use the dialectical method. His speculations were carried on by his pupil Plato, and by Plato's pupil Aristotle, at the Academy in Athens. Roman philosophy was based mainly on the later schools of Greek philosophy, such as Sophism, Stoicism, Cynicism, and Epicureanism. In late antiquity, Neoplatonism, chiefly represented by Plotinus, became the leading philosophical movement and profoundly affected the early development of Christian theology. Arab thinkers, notably Avicenna and Averroës, preserved Greek philosophy, especially Aristotelianism, during the period when these teachings were forgotten in Europe. Scholasticism, the high achievement of medieval philosophy, was again based on Aristotelian principles. St. Thomas Aquinas was the foremost of the schoolmen, just as St. Augustine was the earlier spokesman for the church of pure belief. The Renaissance, with its new physics, astronomy, and humanism, revolutionized philosophic thought. René Descartes is considered the founder of modern philosophy because of his attempt to give the new science a philosophic basis. The other great rationalist systems of the 17th cent., especially those of Baruch Spinoza and G. W. von Leibniz, were developed in response to problems raised by Cartesian philosophy and the new science. In England empiricism prevailed in the work of Thomas Hobbes, John Locke, and David Hume, as well as that of George Berkeley, who was the outstanding idealist. The philosophy of Immanuel Kant achieved a synthesis of the rationalist and empiricist traditions and was in turn developed in the direction of idealism by J. G. Fichte, F. W. J. von Schelling, and G. W. F. Hegel. The romantic movement of the 18th cent. had its beginnings in the philosophy of J. J. Rousseau; its adherents of the 19th cent. included Arthur Schopenhauer and Friedrich Nietzsche, as well as the American transcendentalists represented by Ralph Waldo Emerson. Opposed to the romanticists was the dialectical materialism of Karl Marx. The evolutionary theories of Charles Darwin profoundly affected mid-19th century thought. Ethical philosophy culminated in England in the utilitarianism of John Stuart Mill and in France in the positivism of Auguste Comte. The transition to the 20th cent. came with Henri Bergson. Pragmatism, the only essentially American philosophical movement, was founded at the end of the 19th cent. by C. S. Peirce and was later elaborated by William James and John Dewey. It was in the late 19th cent. also that philosophy was utterly separated from religious thinking. In contemporary philosophy there is a great gulf in orientation between the European and Anglo-American thinkers. In France and Germany the main philosophical tendencies are the phenomenology of Edmund Husserl and the existentialism of Martin Heidegger, Karl Jaspers, and Jean-Paul Sartre. In Britain and the United States the chief concerns are with the problems of formal logic, the philosophy of science, and epistemology, and the chief methods are the various forms of linguistic analysis. The leading early figures of this movement were G. E. Moore, Bertrand Russell, and Ludwig Wittgenstein; it is now represented by logical positivism. The idealism of George Santayana and the investigation of symbolic modes by Alfred North Whitehead and Ernst Cassirer were also influential. Eastern philosophy, while founded in religion, contains rigorously developed systems—see BUDDHISM; CONFUCIANISM; HINDUISM; ISLAM; JAINISM; SHINTO; TAOISM; VEDANTA. See Wilhelm Windelband, *A History of Philosophy* (2d ed. 1901, repr. 1968); B. A. Fuller, *A History of Philosophy* (3d ed., rev. by S. M. McMurrin, 1957); Bertrand Russell, *A History of Western Philosophy* (rev. ed. 1961); W. K. C. Guthrie, *A History of Greek Philosophy* (3 vol., 1962–69); H. W. Schneider, *A History of American Philosophy* (2d ed. 1963); A. H. Armstrong, ed., *The Cambridge History of Later Greek and Early Medieval Philosophy* (1966); John Passmore, *A Hundred Years of Philosophy* (2d ed. 1966); Anthony Flew, *Introduction to Western Philosophy* (1971); Charles Frankel, *The Pleasures of Philosophy* (1972).

Philostratus (Flavius Philostratus) (fĭlŏs'trətəs; flā'vēəs), fl. c.217, Greek Sophist. From a famous literary family in Lemnos, he settled in Athens in later life. His works include *Life of Apollonius of Tyana* (a philosopher) and *Lives of the Sophists.*

Philoxenus (fĭlŏk'sənəs), c.436–c.380 B.C., Greek dithyrambic poet, b. Cythera. Having fallen out of grace with the emperor Dionysius, he was imprisoned in Syracuse. There he wrote his *Cyclops,* mocking Dionysius. In *Cyclops* (fragments of which remain), the central character sang a solo to the lyre—an innovation in the dithyramb.

Phinees (fĭn'ēəs), variant of PHINEHAS.

Phinehas or **Phinees** (both: fĭn'ēəs). **1** Grandson of Aaron. His prompt punishment of two flagrant sinners made his name a symbol of holy, zealous indignation. Ex. 6.25; Num. 25; 31.6; Joshua 22.13; 24.33; Judges 20.28; 1 Chron. 6.4,50; 9.20; Ezra 7.5; Ps. 106.30; Ecclus. 45.23; 1 Mac. 2.26,54. **2** One of Eli's sacrilegious sons: see HOPHNI. **3** Father of a priest. Ezra 8.33.

Phips, Sir William, 1651–95, American colonial governor. Born in what is today Maine, he was a carpenter and shipbuilder in Boston and became interested in sunken treasure. On his second hunt for treasure, which was financed by the 2d duke of Albemarle, he recovered (1687) some £300,000 worth of Spanish gold off Haiti. His fortune made, he was knighted and became provost marshal general at Boston. He supported Increase MATHER in the fight against Sir Edmund Andros for restoration of charter government in Massachusetts, which ended with the overthrow (1689) of Andros. In King William's War (see FRENCH AND INDIAN WARS) Phips led (1690) the expedition that took Port Royal (now Annapolis Royal) but failed to take Quebec, and he was also involved in the unsuccessful expedition against Montreal. He was made first royal governor of Massachusetts through the influence of Increase Mather and took office in 1692. In the great witchcraft mania, he appointed a commission to try those accused of witchcraft. However, when his own wife was accused of witchcraft, he ordered an end to the trials. Many disputes won him enemies, and in 1694 he was called to London to answer charges, but he died before hearings began. The name is also spelled Phipps. The biography by Cotton Mather (ed. by Carl Van Doren, 1929) is, naturally, biased. See biography by Alice Lounsberry (1941); C. H. Karraker, *The Hispaniola Treasure* (1924).

Phiz: see BROWNE, HABLOT KNIGHT.

phlebitis (fləbī'tĭs), inflammation of a vein. Phlebitis is almost always accompanied by a blood clot, or thrombus, in the affected vein, a condition known as thrombophlebitis (see THROMBOSIS). Blood clot formation may follow injury or be associated with infections. Thrombophlebitis of deep veins, usually in the legs or pelvis, may occur in patients recovering from childbirth, surgery, or other conditions requiring prolonged bedrest; the clotting mechanism is thought to be impaired when the legs are immobilized. Pregnancy or the use of oral contraceptives predisposes some women to thrombophlebitis. The major danger is that a clot originating in the leg vein may dislodge and travel to the lung, a condition known as pulmonary embolism (see EMBOLUS). To avoid the risk of embolism, thrombophlebitis is usually treated with ANTICOAGULANTS.

Phlegethon (flĕg'əthŏn): see HADES.

Phlegon (flē'gən), Christian at Rome. Rom. 16.14.

Phlegraean Fields (flĭgrē'ən), Ital. *Campi Flegrei,* fertile volcanic region, Campania, S Italy, along the Tyrrhenian Sea between Pozzuoli and Naples. It is named for ancient *Phlegra,* in Macedonia, where in mythology the battle between the giants and the gods took place. In Roman times, the cities of Cumae, Baiae, and Puteoli (Pozzuoli) were fashionable watering places. Some of the region's approximately 30 craters still emit sulfurous vapors and mineral waters.

phloem (flō'ĕm): see BARK; STEM.

phlogiston theory (flōjĭs'tŏn), hypothesis regarding combustion. The theory, advanced by J. J. Becher late in the 17th cent. and extended and popularized by G. E. Stahl, postulates that in all flammable materials there is present phlogiston, a substance without color, odor, taste, or weight that is given off in burning. "Phlogisticated" substances are those that contain phlogiston and, on being burned, are "dephlogisticated." The ash of the burned material is held to be the true material. The theory received strong and wide support throughout a large part of the 18th cent. until it was refuted by the work of A. L. Lavoisier, who revealed the true nature of combustion. Joseph Priestley, however, defended the theory throughout his lifetime. Henry Cavendish remained doubtful, but most other chemists of the period, including C. L. Berthollet, rejected it.

Phlorina, Greece: see FLÓRINA.

phlox, common name for plants of the genus *Phlox* and for members of the Polemoniaceae, a family of herbs (and some shrubs and vines) found chiefly in the W United States. The family includes many popular wild and garden flowers, especially the genera *Phlox, Polemonium* (called Jacob's ladder), and *Gilia,* a plant common in desert and mountain areas. Although most phloxes are perennial, the common garden phloxes are annual hybrids of the Texas species *Phlox drummondii.* The moss pink (*Phlox subulata*) is a creeping evergreen plant native to the E United States and often cultivated in rock gardens. A few species of phlox and polemonium are found in E Asia. The phlox family is classified in the division MAGNOLIOPHYTA, class Magnoliopsida, order Polemoniales.

Phnom Penh (nŏm pĕn, pənŏm') or **Phnum Penh** (pənoom'), city (1970 est. pop. 470,000), capital of Cambodia, SW Cambodia, at the confluence of the Mekong and Tônlé Sap rivers. Situated 173 mi (278 km) from the sea, it is a busy river port accommodating vessels up to 2,500 tons. Phnom Penh is the commercial center of Cambodia, serving as the receiving, distribution, and collection point for the country's exports and imports. The city has large markets, cold storage facilities, slaughter houses, an automobile assembly plant, oil storage tanks, factories producing a variety of consumer goods, and numerous rice mills and other establishments processing the agricultural products of the country. The transportation center of Cambodia, Phnom Penh is the focus of seven highways radiating out to the provinces and the terminus of the country's only two railroads—one extending to the Thai border and another to the deepwater port of Kompong Som on the Gulf of Siam. There is an international airport. The city was founded in the 14th cent. and was made the Khmer capital after the abandonment (c.1432) of ANGKOR. It became the capital of Cambodia in 1867. The city was occupied by the Japanese in World War II. After the onset (1970) of civil war in Cambodia, the population of Phnom Penh tripled as refugees poured in from the war-torn countryside. Phnom Penh, as the seat of government and the stronghold of loyalist forces, was repeatedly under siege; throughout most of 1972 insurgents held six of the seven highways linking Phnom Penh with the provinces. Insurgents also on occasion held both banks of the Mekong River, the city's most important supply route. Despite daily airlifts of rice by U.S. planes, serious food shortages resulted; in Sept., 1972, food shortages sparked two days of rioting and large-scale looting, in which government troops participated. In 1974 the city was subjected to massive rocket attacks and by Jan., 1975, it was almost completely isolated. Phnom Penh has a modern European quarter, near the Phnom Penh hill (from which the city takes its name), and a Chinese quarter. The cultural and educational center of the country, Phnom Penh has numerous libraries and museums and is the seat of the National Univ. of Phnom Penh, a university of fine arts, a technical university, a Buddhist university, and the national military academy.

phobia: see PSYCHONEUROSIS.

Phobos (fō'bŏs), in astronomy, innermost moon, or natural satellite, of MARS.

Phocaea (fōsē'ə), ancient city, W Asia Minor, N of Smyrna (İzmir), in present Turkey. It was northernmost of the Greek Ionian cities. In the 7th cent. B.C. it grew into a maritime state; its chief colony was Massilia (now Marseilles). In 540 B.C., after a siege by the Persians, most of the inhabitants left, going mainly to Elea in Italy. The city never recovered from the loss. The modern Foça is on the site.

Phocion (fō'shən), c.402–318 B.C., Athenian general. He served successfully against the forces of Philip of Macedon—in Euboea (now Évvoia; 348 B.C.) and at Byzantium (339), when he forced Philip to abandon his siege of that city. In Athens, Phocion was a leader of the party that urged conciliation with the Macedonians; he was opposed by Demosthenes. When the Athenians refused to comply with Alexander's demand for the surrender of Demosthenes, Phocion led a successful embassy of conciliation to Alexander. In the turmoil following the death of ANTIPATER (319), Phocion intrigued with CASSANDER. Later, when the Athenian democracy, which had been curtailed by Antipater, was restored, the democrats forced Phocion to drink hemlock; shortly after his death, however, they raised a statue in his honor.

Phocis (fō'sĭs), ancient region of central Greece. It included Delphi, Mt. Parnassus, and Elatea; Boeotia (now Voiotía) was on the east, and the Gulf of Corinth was on the south. After the First Sacred War of c.590 B.C. ("sacred" because it involved the oracle of Delphi), Phocis lost control of Delphi to a council of states. With Athenian help Phocis regained (457 B.C.) hold of Delphi, thus precipitating the Second Sacred War. Early in the next century Phocis passed under Theban control. The Third Sacred War (355–346 B.C.) began with Phocis trying to reestablish itself and ended with the victory of PHILIP II of Macedon, who thereby became arbiter of Greece.

Phocylides (fəsĭl'ĭdēz), fl. 6th cent. B.C., Greek poet, b. Miletus. His gnomic (aphoristic) verses exist in fragments.

Phoebe, in the Bible: see PHEBE.

phoebe: see FLYCATCHER.

Phoebe (fē'bē), in astronomy, one of the 10 known moons, or natural satellites, of SATURN.

Phoebe, in Greek religion, a Titan. She was the mother of Leto and Asteria and the grandmother of Artemis. In some legends she was identified with Artemis as the goddess of the moon.

Phoebus (fē'bəs) or **Phoebus Apollo:** see APOLLO.

Phoenicia (fĭnē'shə), ancient territory occupied by Phoenicians. These people were Canaanites, and in the 9th cent. B.C. the Greeks gave the new appellation Phoenicians to those Canaanites who lived on the seacoast and traded with the Greeks. The geographic boundaries of the territory are vague, and the name Phoenicia may be applied to all those places on the shores of the E Mediterranean where the Phoenicians established colonies. More often it refers to the heart of the territory where the great Phoenician cities, notably Tyre and Sidon, stood (corresponding roughly to the coast of present-day Lebanon). At the dawn of history in the Middle East, a people speaking a Semitic language moved westward and occupied a very narrow coastal strip of the E Mediterranean. Recent excavations of the Phoenician city of Byblos have somewhat clarified the date of settlement by revealing that trade existed between Egypt and Byblos c.2800 B.C. and also that other important Phoenician centers existed at this time at Jerusalem, Jericho, Ai, and Megiddo. In the 2d millennium the Phoenicians were pushed by the Jews further westward along the Mediterranean. By 1250 B.C. they were well established as the navigators and traders of the Mediterranean world, enjoying the commerce that had once been in the hands of the Aegeans. The Phoenicians were organized into city-states; the greatest of these were Tyre and Sidon; others were Tripoli, Aradus, and Byblos. These were the home cities, but wherever the Phoenicians ranged across the Mediterrean they founded posts and colonies that later became independent states. Of these the most important were Utica and Carthage (founded in the 9th cent. B.C.). The Phoenicians had a language and culture like those of other Semitic peoples in the general area and may be said to have been identical with the Canaanites of N Palestine except for the development of their seagoing culture. They worshiped fertility gods and goddesses generally designated by the names *Baal* and *Baalat;* sacrifice of the first-born, both of humans and of animals, was practiced. Astarte and Adonis were also known. The Phoenicians were more or less under the intermittent influence and control of the Egyptians, but with the weakening of Egyptian power in the 12th cent., Phoenician seamen came to dominate the Mediterranean. They went to the edges of the known world, trading from the Iberian Peninsula to the Dardanelles. Some authorities believe they went as far as Cornwall, seeking tin. There is evidence that in Egyptian service they may have sailed down the western coast of Africa, and possibly their ships even rounded Africa and reached the East Indies. Their carrying trade was enormous, and their wares were varied. They had a monopoly on the great cedars of Lebanon from their homeland, and they made metal articles. They also colored cloth the famous Tyrian purple (*Phoenicia* is the Greek work for "purple") with dye obtained from shellfish and were famous for their finely carved ivories. Skilled architects, Phoenician artisans were imported by the Egyptians, and Hiram, king of Tyre, lent assistance to Solomon in building. Their greatest contribution to Western civilization was, however, the invention of an alphabet, an idea later taken over by the Greeks; the use of symbols for sounds in place of clumsier cuneiform and hieroglyphic was a tremendous advance. The great Phoenician cities were so well defended that they were able to withstand most of the attacks of the Assyrian kings. In the 6th cent. B.C., however, they submitted to the tolerant empire of the Persians, keeping their own autonomy but gradually being more and more absorbed into the Persian pattern. Phoenician sailors, architects, and craftsmen were all prominent in Persian service. They also served elsewhere, and Phoenician ships were in the Greek navy that defeated Xerxes I at Salamis. The individuality of the Phoenicians was dwindling, and with the rise of Greek naval and maritime power the importance of the Phoenicians disappeared. They were, however, able in the 4th cent. to offer serious resistance to Alexander the Great, who took Tyre only after a long and hard siege (333-332 B.C.). In Roman times the cities continued to exist, but Hellenistic culture had absorbed the last traces of Phoenician civilization. The name Phoenicia also appears as Phenice and Phenicia. See George Rawlinson, *Phoenicia* (1889, repr. 1972); Sabatino Moscati, *The World of the Phoenicians* (tr. 1968).

Phoenician art. The Phoenician region developed as a major trade center of the ancient world; consequently Phoenician art clearly reflects the influences of Egypt, Syria, and Greece. Phoenician deities were represented in Egyptian and Syrian attire and were surrounded with foreign symbolism adopted by Phoenician artists and used to illustrate indigenous beliefs. The Phoenicians excelled at metalcraft and carving. Their ivories and metal reliefs were copied in many neighboring regions, especially in Palestine, Greece, and Etruria. Their craftsmen settled in Egypt and Greece and imported Syrian work as well as their own, increasing the amalgamation of styles. The principal Phoenician excavations are at BYBLOS, but Phoenician works in jewelry, glass, clay, alabaster, ivory, many metals, faience, and wood are found in all Mediterranean countries and neighboring areas of Asia Minor. Their textiles too, particularly the famous blue and purple cloth, were widely exported. Among the most famous examples of Phoenician carving is a gem- and glass-inlaid ivory found at Nimrud depicting a Nubian man being attacked by a lion (British Mus.).

Phoenix (fē'nĭks), Crete: see PHENICE **2.**

Phoenix, city (1970 pop. 581,562), state capital and seat of Maricopa co., S Ariz., on the Salt River; inc. 1881. It is the largest city in Arizona, the hub of the rich Salt River valley, and an important center of data processing and electronics research and production. Aircraft, fabricated metals, machinery, food products, textiles, and apparel are also among its many manufactures. The sunny, dry climate, although hot in summer, has made Phoenix a winter retreat and a noted health resort. The city was founded (c.1868) on the site of ancient Indian canals; hence its name, signifying a new town which had risen from the ruins of an old civilization. A ditch was dug to divert water from the Salt River, and farming began, supplemented by mining and ranching in the surrounding desert and mountains. The completion (1911) of the Roosevelt Dam on the Salt River brought power and abundant water to the community and opened a new era of farming in the valley. Phoenix grew as an important trade and distribution center. It boomed during World War II, when three airfields were opened, bringing thousands of servicemen into the area. The phenomenal growth continued after the war; veterans who had been stationed in Phoenix returned to make it their home, and manufacturing concerns moved there to utilize the large labor supply. Today two air force bases, Luke and Williams, are still operating in the area. Among the city's many outstanding parks are the Desert Botanical Gardens, Japanese Flower Gardens, Southwestern Arboretum, Camelback Mountain, and the nearby 15,000-acre (6,070-hectare) South Mountain Park, which has an active gold mine. Among its museums are Arizona Museum, with pioneer relics; Heard Museum, with Indian exhibitions; the Phoenix Art Museum; the Pueblo Grande Museum, containing the excavations of Indian ruins c.800 years old; and the State Dept. of Archives Museum. Other attractions are the Phoenix Zoo, a U.S. Indian school, and the Mystery Castle, built of native rock. Phoenix is the seat of Grand Canyon College and a junior college. The city has a symphony orchestra and many sports and recreational facilities, including a coliseum. The Phoenix Suns play in the National Basketball Association. In the area are a number of Indian communities and reservations, national monuments, and many state parks.

phoenix, fabulous bird that periodically regenerated itself, used in literature as a symbol of death and resurrection. According to legend, the phoenix lived in Arabia; when it reached the end of its life (500 years), it burned itself on a pyre of flames, and from the ashes a new phoenix arose. As a sacred symbol in Egyptian religion, the phoenix represented the sun, which dies each night and rises again each morning. According to Herodotus the bird was red and golden and resembled an eagle.

Phoenix Islands, group of eight islands (1967 est. pop. 130), 11 sq mi (28 sq km), central Pacific, N of Samoa. The two most important are CANTON ISLAND and Enderbury Island; both are jointly administered by the United States and Great Britain. The other islands—Phoenix, Sydney, Birnie, McKean, Gardner, and Hull—are part of the British GILBERT AND ELLICE ISLANDS colony. The Phoenix Islands were discovered between 1823 and 1840 by British and American explorers, but most of them were annexed by Great Britain in the late 19th cent. After the United States took over Howland and Baker islands in 1935, Britain included (1937) the Phoenix group in the Gilbert and Ellice Islands colony. In 1938 the United States claimed sovereignty over Canton and Enderbury, and in 1939 Britain and the United States agreed to exercise joint control over the two islands for a period of 50 years. Previously uninhabited, Hull, Sydney, and Gardner islands (also called by their native names of Orona, Manra, and Nikumaroro, respectively) were colonized with people from the overcrowded Gilbert Islands between 1938 and 1940. By 1963, however, the three settlements had failed and the entire population was moved to the Solomon Islands. In the early 1970s the islands were uninhabited.

Phoenix Park murders, name given to the assassination on May 6, 1882, of Lord Frederick Cavendish, British secretary for Ireland, and Thomas Henry Burke, his undersecretary, in Phoenix Park, Dublin. They were stabbed to death by members of the "Invincibles," a terrorist splinter group of the FENIAN MOVEMENT. Two of those arrested turned state's evidence, five were hanged, and three were sentenced to penal servitude. Charles Stewart PARNELL was alleged (1887) by his political enemies to have been personally involved in the plot. A parliamentary commission appointed to investigate the charges exonerated him (1890).

Phoenixville (fē'nĭksvĭl), industrial borough (1970 pop. 14,823), Chester co., SE Pa., on the Schuylkill River; settled 1720, inc. 1849. Iron deposits in the region led to the early development of an iron industry and later (1886) to the manufacture of steel. Automotive parts, cotton yarn, apparel, rubber and metal closures, and lamps are among the other products. Phoenixville was the westernmost point in the state reached (1777) by the British during the Revolutionary War. Several 18th-century stone houses are there. Valley Forge is to the southeast.

phonetics (fōnĕt'ĭks, fə-) and **phonemics** (fōnē'mĭks, fə-), system of sounds of language, studied from two basic points of view. Phonetics is the study of the sounds of language according to their production in the vocal organs (articulatory phonetics) or their effect on the ear (acoustic phonetics). All phonetics are interrelated because human articulatory and auditory mechanisms are uniform. Systems of phonetic writing are aimed at transcribing accurately any sequence of speech sounds; the best known is the International Phonetic Alphabet. Each language uses a limited number of the possible sounds called phonemes, and the hearer-speaker is trained from childhood to classify them into groups of like sounds, rejecting as nonsignificant all sorts of features actually phonetically present. So the English speaker does not know that he always makes a puff of air when he pronounces the *p* of *pin* and never makes the puff with the *p* of *spin;* for him they are the same sound. Yet in some languages (as in Sanskrit) just the presence or absence of that puff in both words would make the sounds different, and two words might differ in meaning because of the puff. In English there is no phonemic difference between the two sounds, which belong to one group of like sounds, the phoneme *p.* In the other situation aspirated *p* (*p* with a puff) and unaspirated *p* are separate phonemes. Phonemes include all significant differences of sound, including features of voicing, place and manner of articulation, ACCENT, and secondary features of nasalization, glottalization, labialization, and the like. The study of the phonemes and their arrangement is the phonemics of a language. In transformational-generative grammars, phonological rules produce phonetic rather than phonemic representations, or symbols, to specify sound. Systematic sound change through time is treated by comparative and historical LINGUISTICS. See GRAMMAR; LANGUAGE; WRITING. See Daniel Jones, *An Outline of English Phonetics* (1940); Kenneth Pike, *Phonemics* (1947); Noam Chomsky and Morris Halle, *The Sound Pattern of English* (1968); Robert T. Harms, *Introduction to Phonological Theory* (1968); L. F. Brosnahan and Bertil Malmberg, *Introduction to Phonetics* (1970).

phonograph: see RECORD PLAYER.

phonon (fō'nŏn), quantum of vibrational energy. The atoms of any crystal are in a state of vibration, their average kinetic energy being measured by the absolute TEMPERATURE of the crystal. In certain phenomena it becomes evident that this energy is divided into discrete bundles (see QUANTUM THEORY); the energy bundles behave like particles in some respects and are termed phonons. These effects are most apparent at low temperatures where only a few phonons are present. For example, interactions between phonons and electrons are thought to be responsible for such phenomena as SUPERCONDUCTIVITY.

Phorcus (fôr'kəs), in Greek mythology, sea god, son of Pontus and Gaea. He married his sister Ceto, who bore him a brood of monsters, including the Gorgons, the Graeae, Scylla, and the Sirens.

Phoronida (fərŏn'ədə), small phylum of slender, wormlike marine tube-dwellers, typically found in temperate, shallow seas. About 15 species are known. Phoronids live permanently in their tubes, which are made of the tough horny substance CHITIN. Although the body is free in the tube, the organisms extend only a crown of ciliated tentacles (the lophophore) to capture food. Water currents generated by the lophophore cilia sweep food particles against mucus secreted at the base of the tentacles and ciliated grooves propel the food to the mouth. Phoronids have a U-shaped digestive tract, a blood-vascular system containing hemoglobin, and excretory organs called metanephridia. The coelom, or body cavity, is divided into compartments resembling those seen in the Ectoprocta and the Brachiopoda, which are phyla related to the Phoronida; the compartments also resemble those of the Echinodermata. Phoronids are ancient; tubes seen in early paleozoic sandstones appear to be identical with modern phoronid tubes, but little is known of their history.

phosgene (fŏs'jēn), colorless POISON GAS, first used during World War I by the Germans (1915). When dispersed in air, the gas has the odor of new-mowed hay. The gas is highly toxic; when inhaled it reacts with water in the lungs to form hydrochloric acid and carbon monoxide. Because the upper respiratory tract is little affected, warning signs of exposure are slight, and symptoms may fail to appear for from 2 to 24 hours after exposure. However, the release of hydrochloric acid in the lungs causes pulmonary edema and may also cause bronchial pneumonia and lung abscesses; in severe cases death may result within 36 hours. Phosgene is now used in chemical synthesis. It may be prepared by the reaction of carbon monoxide with chlorine in the presence of a catalyst or by the oxidation of chloroform or carbon tetrachloride. Phosgene has the formula $COCl_2$.

phosphate, salt or ester of PHOSPHORIC ACID, H_3PO_4. Because phosphoric acid is tribasic (having three replaceable hydrogen atoms), it forms monophosphate, diphosphate, and triphosphate salts in which one, two, or three of the hydrogens of the acid are replaced, respectively. Because replaceable hydrogens remain in monophosphates and diphosphates, they are sometimes called acid phosphates. The most important inorganic phosphate is calcium phosphate, $Ca_3(PO_4)_2$. It makes up the larger part of phosphate rock, a mineral that is abundantly distributed throughout the world. Since calcium phosphate is only slightly soluble in water, it is not very suitable as a source of the phosphorus necessary for plant life; however, by treating it with sulfuric acid the soluble calcium acid phosphate known as SUPERPHOSPHATE of lime is formed. Other important inorganic phosphates include ammonium phosphate, important as a fertilizer; trisodium phosphate, used in detergents and for softening water; and disodium phosphate, used to some extent in medicine and in preparing baking powders. Various acid phosphates, e.g., those of calcium, magnesium, and sodium, are sometimes present in carbonated beverages. Microcosmic salt, used in certain bead tests in chemical analysis, is sodium ammonium phosphate. Organic phosphates play an important role in metabolism. For example, in the metabolism of sugars (which have hydroxyl groups, —OH, in their molecules), phosphate esters are often formed as an intermediate compound. Formation of these esters is called phosphorylation. Nucleotides are phosphate esters that play an important role in the conservation and use of the energy released in the metabolism of foods in the body; ADENOSINE TRIPHOSPHATE is an important nucleotide. DNA and RNA (see NUCLEIC ACID) are complex polymeric organic phosphates.

phosphatidic acid: see PHOSPHOLIPID.

phospholipid (fŏs″fōlĭp′ĭd), LIPID that in its simplest form is composed of glycerol bonded to two FATTY ACIDS and phosphoric acid. Such a compound is called phosphatidic acid. In most phospholipids, however, the phosphoric acid is bonded to yet another chemical group. For example, it may be connected with choline (see VITAMIN); in such cases the resultant phospholipid is called phosphatidylcholine, or lecithin. Other phospholipids include phosphatidylglycerol, phosphatidylinositol, phosphatidylserine, and phosphatidylethanolamine. Phosphatidic acid joined with phosphatidylglycerol is known as diphosphatidylglycerol, or cardiolipin. Phospholipids are important in the metabolism of cells because they provide a substantial fraction of the lipid content of biological membranes. Phospholipids are also called phosphatides and phosphoglycerides.

phosphorescence (fŏs″fərĕs′əns), LUMINESCENCE produced by certain substances after absorbing radiant energy or other types of energy. Phosphorescence is distinguished from FLUORESCENCE in that it continues even after the radiation causing it has ceased. Phosphorescence was first observed in the 17th cent. but was not studied scientifically until the 19th cent. According to the theory first advanced by Philipp Lenard, energy is absorbed by a phosphorescent substance, causing some of the electrons of the crystal to be displaced. These electrons become trapped in potential troughs from which they are eventually freed by temperature-related energy fluctuations within the crystal. As they fall back to their original energy levels, they release their excess energy in the form of light. Impurities in the crystal can play an important role, some serving as activators or coactivators, others as sensitizers, and still others as inhibitors, of phosphorescence. Organophosphors are organic dyes that fluoresce in liquid solution and phosphoresce in solid solution or when adsorbed on gels. Their phosphorescence, however, is not temperature-related, as ordinary phosphorescence is, and some consider it instead to be a type of fluorescence that dies out very slowy.

phosphoric acid, any one of three chemical compounds made up of PHOSPHORUS, oxygen, and hydrogen (see ACIDS AND BASES). The most common, orthophosphoric acid, H_3PO_4, is usually simply called phosphoric acid. Two molecules of it are formed by adding three molecules of water, H_2O, to one molecule of phosphorus pentoxide (phosphoric anhydride, P_2O_5). It occurs as rhombic crystals or as a viscous liquid; both are deliquescent. The crystals melt at about 42°C. It has specific gravity 1.834 at 18°C, is soluble in alcohol, and is very soluble in water. It is a tribasic acid and forms orthophosphate salts with either one, two, or all three of the hydrogens replaced by some other positive ion. When it is heated to about 225°C, it dehydrates to form pyrophosphoric acid, $H_4P_2O_7$; at still higher temperatures metaphosphoric acid, HPO_3, is formed. Salts of pyrophosphoric acid are pyrophosphates; salts of metaphosphoric acid are metaphosphates. Phosphoric acid is prepared commercially by heating calcium phosphate rock with sulfuric acid; purer grades may be prepared by treating red phosphorus with nitric acid. It is used in pickling and rust-proofing metals, in acidifying jellies and beverages, and in preparing phosphate salts.

phosphorus (fŏs′fərəs) [Gr.,=light-bearing], nonmetallic chemical element; symbol P; at. no. 15; at. wt. 30.9738; m.p. 44.1°C; b.p. about 280°C; sp. gr. 1.82 at 20°C; valence −3, +3, or +5. Solid phosphorus has a tetratomic molecule (P_4) with molecular weight 123.8952 atomic mass units (amu). It exhibits ALLOTROPY; the physical constants given above are for the common white phosphorus. It is an extremely poisonous, yellow to white, waxy, solid substance, nearly insoluble in water but very soluble in carbon disulfide. When exposed to air it ignites spontaneously, burning to form white fumes of phosphorus pentoxide, P_2O_5. Because of its toxicity and pyrophoric nature, phosphorus is stored underwater. Contact with the skin may cause burns. White phosphorus is phosphorescent. When white phosphorus is heated to about 250°C in the absence of air, it changes into the more stable red phosphorus. This form appears as dull, reddish-brown cubic crystals or amorphous powder. Its specific gravity is 2.34. The red form is less dangerous than the white form, but should be handled with caution. It is insoluble in carbon disulfide and most other solvents. It does not ignite unless heated to about 200°C, does not phosphoresce, and is not poisonous. Another form of phosphorus is black phosphorus, a crystalline electrically conductive material similar to graphite in appearance. It was first prepared by P. W. Bridgman by heating white phosphorus to 200°C under a pressure of 12,000 atmospheres. Its specific gravity is 2.70. Because of its chemical activity phosphorus does not occur uncombined in nature but is widely distributed in many minerals. A major source is APATITE, an impure calcium phosphate mineral found in phosphate rocks. In the United States major deposits are found in Florida, Tennessee, Montana, and Idaho. White phosphorus is prepared commercially from phosphate rock in an electric furnace or blast furnace. It is used as a deoxidizing agent in the preparation of steel and phosphor bronze. It is also used in rat poisons and to make smoke screens (by burning) for warfare. Red phosphorus is used in making matches. However, the principal use of phosphorus is in compounds; for this reason, most of the phosphorus produced in furnaces is burned to make phosphorus pentoxide, a white powdery substance. While the pentoxide is used as a drying agent and chemical reagent, it is chiefly converted to PHOSPHORIC ACID, H_3PO_4, also called orthophosphoric acid, by reaction with water. Another important source of phosphoric acid is from phosphate rocks by treatment with sulfuric acid; this is the so-called wet-acid process. Phosphoric acid is primarily used in the production of PHOSPHATE compounds. It is also used in pickling metals, in sugar refining, and in soft drinks. Phosphorus forms a number of compounds with the halogens, e.g., the trichloride, PCl_3, and the pentachloride, PCl_5, both used as reagents. It also forms an oxychloride, $POCl_3$. It reacts with sulfur to form a pentasulfide, P_2S_5, and a thiochloride, $PSCl_3$, used in insecticides and oil additives. Phosphine, PH_3, is a poisonous gas. Besides the pentoxide, phosphorus forms several other oxides; there are several acids other than the orthophosphoric acid noted above. Phosphorus also combines with various other non-metals and with some metals. Phosphorus is present in plants and animals. There is over 1 lb (454 grams) of phosphorus in the human body. It is a component of ADENOSINE TRIPHOSPHATE (ATP), a fundamental energy source in living things. It is found in complex organic compounds in the blood, muscles, and nerves, and in calcium phosphate, the principal material in bones and teeth. Phosphorus compounds are essential in the diet. Organic phosphates, ferric phosphate, and tricalcium phosphate are added to foods. Dicalcium phosphate is added to animal feeds. The major use of phosphorus compounds is in fertilizers, especially in a mixture called superphosphate, obtained from phosphate minerals by sulfuric acid treatment; and in nitrophosphates. Phosphorus compounds are also used commercially in detergents, water softeners, pharmaceuticals, dentifrices, and in many other less important uses. Toxic nerve gases such as sarin contain phosphorus. Phosphorus was discovered c.1674 by Hennig Brand of Hamburg, an alchemist, who prepared it from urine. Phosphoric acid was discovered in 1770 by K. W. Scheele and J. G. Gahn in BONE ASH; Scheele later isolated phosphorus from bone ash (1774) and produced phosphoric acid by the action of nitric acid on phosphorus (1777).

phosphorylation, chemical process in which a phosphate group is added to an organic molecule. In living cells phosphorylation is associated with RESPIRATION, which takes place in the cell's mitochondria, and photosynthesis, which takes place in the chloroplasts. The energy released during metabolic or photosynthetic processes is captured in the energy-rich phosphate bonds of certain molecules, most commonly in the high-energy bonds of ADENOSINE TRIPHOSPHATE (ATP). In the process of oxidative phosphorylation ATP formation is associated with respiratory uptake of oxygen. In this process a cell substance known as NADH (one of a variety of COENZYMES) donates hydride ions (one proton and two electrons) to the first of a series of enzymes in the so-called electron transport chain. As the hydride ion is passed from one enzyme to another in the chain, energy is made available to power the formation of ATP from adenosine diphosphate (ADP) and inorganic phosphate. At the end, or lowest energy level, of the electron transport chain, the hydride ion combines with oxygen and a proton (hydrogen ion) to form a water molecule. The phosphorylation process is linked to cell metabolism in that metabolic degradation of food, e.g., glucose, allows formation of the coenzyme NADH. The electron transport enzymes are complex aggregates of cytochromes, i.e., proteins with iron-containing heme groups, and various coenzymes. The precise mechanisms by which chemical energy is coupled to ATP synthesis are not yet understood. In photosynthetic phosphorylation, or photophosphorylation, substances such as the reduced coenzyme NADPH also donate hydride ions to an electron transport system so that ATP is synthesized from ADP and inorganic phosphate; in photophosphorylation, however, the coenzyme is produced from chemical reactions initiated by illuminated photosynthetic pigments instead of from metabolism of food molecules. The net result in phosphorylation of ADP is the formation of the high-energy molecule ATP, which the cell can use as a kind of universal energy currency to power many important cell processes, such as protein synthesis. Other phosphorylation reactions occur in cells, some without mediation by the electron transport chain, e.g., ATP is formed from ADP and inorganic phosphate in a reaction coupled to the oxidation of glyceraldehyde phosphate to phosphoglyceric acid.

Photius (fō′shəs), c.820–892?, Greek churchman and theologian, patriarch of Constantinople, b. Constantinople. He came of a noble Byzantine family. Photius was one of the most learned men of his time, a professor in the university at Constantinople and, under Byzantine Emperor MICHAEL III, president of the imperial chancellery. He was a leader of the orthodox faction that wished to treat the repentant iconoclasts indulgently; the head of the sterner orthodox faction was the patriarch, St. IGNATIUS OF CONSTANTINOPLE. In 858, Ignatius was forced from the patriarchate, and Photius, a layman, was chosen to fill his place. He was rushed through the orders necessary within a week, a procedure uncanonical but not without precedent. In 861 the legates of Pope St. NICHOLAS I approved the election of Photius, but the pope refused to recognize him. In 867, Photius retaliated by calling a synod that challenged the rights of the pope in Bulgaria, questioned certain Latin practices, particularly the proposed inclusion of the *Filioque* phrase in the creed (see CREED **1**), and, finally, challenged the pope's right to judge the canonicity of the election of the patriarch. Nicholas died without learning of the synod's work. When BASIL I became Byzantine emperor (867), Photius stepped down and St. Ignatius became patriarch again. Two years later Photius was condemned (see CONSTANTINOPLE, FOURTH COUNCIL OF). Later, Photius became reconciled with Basil and Ignatius, and on the death of Ignatius he again became patriarch (877). Pope John VIII recognized him as patriarch and sent legates to a synod, held in 879–80, which the ORTHODOX EASTERN CHURCH regards as an ecumenical council. This synod affirmed that Photius had been legally elected, nullified those synods that had condemned him, ruled against the elevation of laymen to the episcopacy, and agreed that Constantinople would relinquish authority in Bulgaria. The acts of this council were apparently approved by Pope John VIII, but without any retraction of his predecessors' condemnations. Photius continued as patriarch until the accession of Byzantine Emperor LEO VI in 886, when he was forced to resign under imperial pressure; he died in exile. Photius is a figure of controversy. In later years the deep cleavage between East and West was reckoned from the schism of Photius, even though the formal schism between East and West did not occur until the 11th cent. Certainly Photius encouraged the growing self-consciousness in the Greek church, not only through his exposition of the theological differences between the two churches, but also through his humanist and scholarly works. He is venerated as a saint in the Orthodox Eastern Church. Many of his letters, homilies, and dogmatic and polemical works are extant. His *Myriobyblion*, or *Bibliotheca*, contains many quotations from lost Greek writings. See J. H. Freese, *The Library of Photius* (1920); Francis Dvornik, *The Photian Schism* (1948).

photocell: see PHOTOELECTRIC CELL.

photochemistry, study of chemical processes that are accompanied by or catalyzed by the emission or absorption of visible LIGHT or ULTRAVIOLET RADIATION. A molecule in its ground (unexcited) state can absorb a quantum of light energy, or PHOTON, and go to a higher-energy state, or excited state (see QUANTUM THEORY). Such a molecule is then much more reactive than a ground-state molecule and can undergo entirely different reactions than the more stable molecule, following several different reaction pathways. One possibility is that it can simply emit the absorbed light and fall back to the ground state. This process, called chemiluminescence, is illustrated by various glow-in-the-dark objects. Another possibility is for the molecule to take part in a photo-induced chemical reaction; it may break apart (photodissociate), rearrange, isomerize, dimerize, eliminate or add small molecules, or even transfer its energy to another molecule. Photochromic compounds—compounds that change color reversibly in going from the dark to the light—are generally compounds that are capable of reversible isomerization, or rearrangement. In the absence of light, the compound exists in its most stable form, which exhibits a particular color; in the presence of light, the compound goes to a less stable form, which exhibits a different color. After removal of the light, the compound will revert back to its original state. The best known and most important photochemical reaction is PHOTOSYNTHESIS, the complex, chlorophyll-catalyzed synthesis of sugars from carbon dioxide and water in the presence of light. Other extremely important and complex photochemical reactions take place in the eye. Photochemistry is indispensible to industries involved with dyes, photography, television, and many other applications of light and color.

photocomposition machines: see PRINTING.

photocopying, process whereby written or printed matter is directly copied by photographic techniques. Generally, photocopying is practical when just a few copies of an original are needed. When many copies are required, PRINTING processes are more economical. However, when a printing process is used, the master or stencil required can sometimes be produced by photocopying. Principal photocopying processes include silver halide, transfer, plan, thermographic (see THERMOGRAPHY), and electrostatic, e.g., XEROGRAPHY. Two well-known silver halide processes, photostating (see PHOTOSTAT) and microfilming, use cameras to make photographic copies of an original. Microfilming generates copies that are from 1/12 to as little as 1/100 the size of the originals, allowing great economy in space and materials when long-term storage is necessary. Microfilms are read by either projecting them or photographically printing them as enlargements. In transfer processes the original is placed in contact with negative paper and exposed to light. In the diffusion transfer the negative is developed while in contact with the positive. During development the chemicals forming the image in the negative diffuse to the positive, producing an image there. In gelatin transfer the negative is developed and then pressed against positive paper. A dyed gelatin on the negative is picked up by the positive, producing an image on it. Transfer methods are less expensive than silver halide processes, but the image produced by the former deteriorates with time. Plan copying is used to copy materials such as architects' drawings and engineers' plans. In one variety of plan copying known as the whiteprint process, an original is made on translucent paper. The paper is placed over a sheet coated with a diazo compound and exposed to a source of ultraviolet light. The compound covering the area that is exposed to the light decomposes. The compound shielded from the ultraviolet rays by the dark areas of the original can be developed to form a positive image. The BLUEPRINT process, another method of plan copying, has been largely superseded by whiteprints, which are of better quality and cost approximately the same.

photoelectric cell or **photocell,** device whose electrical characteristics (e.g., current, voltage, or resistance) vary when light is incident upon it. The most common type consists of two electrodes separated by a light-sensitive SEMICONDUCTOR material. A battery or other voltage source connected to the electrodes sets up a current even in the absence of light; when light strikes the semiconductor section of the photocell, the current in the circuit increases by an amount proportional to the intensity of the light. In the phototube, an older type of photocell, two electrodes are enclosed in a glass tube—an anode and a light-sensitive cathode, i.e., a metal that emits electrons in accordance with the PHOTOELECTRIC EFFECT. Although the phototube itself is now obsolete, the principle survives in the photomultiplier tube, which can be used to detect and amplify faint amounts of light. In this tube, electrons ejected from a photosensitive cathode by light are attracted toward and strike a positive electrode, liberating showers of secondary electrons; these are drawn to a more positive electrode, producing yet more secondary electrons—and so on, through several stages, until a large pulse of current is produced. Besides its use in measuring light intensity, a photomultiplier can be built into a television camera tube, making it sensitive enough to pick up the visual image of a star too faint to be seen by the human eye. The photovoltaic type of photoelectric cell, when exposed to light, can generate and support an electric current without being attached to any external voltage source. Such a cell usually consists of a semiconductor crystal with two zones composed of dissimilar materials. When light shines on the crystal, a voltage is set up across the junction between the two zones. A phototransistor, which is a type of photovoltaic cell, can generate a small current that acts like the input current in a conventional TRANSISTOR and controls a larger current in the output circuit. Photovoltaic cells are also used to make solar batteries (see SOLAR CELL). Since the current from a photocell can easily be used to operate switches or relays, it is often used in light-actuated counters, automatic door openers, and intrusion alarms. Photocells in such devices are popularly known as electric eyes.

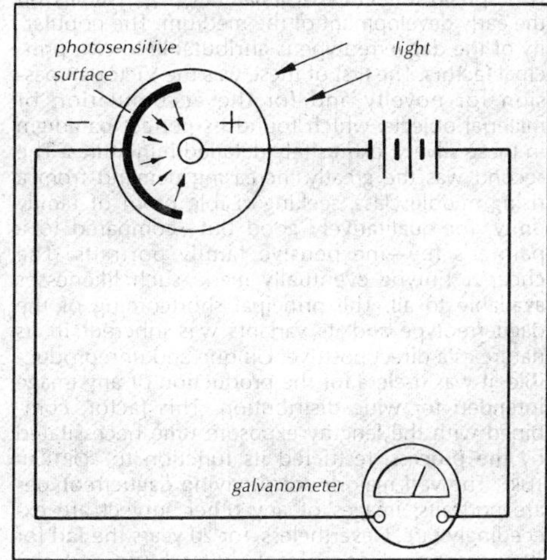

Photoelectric cell: Light causes a photosensitive surface to emit electrons, which flow as current to the positive terminal. A galvanometer measures the current and thus indicates light intensity.

photoelectric effect, emission of electrons by substances, especially metals, when light falls on their surfaces. The effect was discovered by H. R. Hertz in 1887. The failure of the classical theory of electromagnetic radiation to explain it helped lead to the development of the QUANTUM THEORY. According to classical theory, when light, thought to be composed of waves, strikes substances, the energy of the liberated electrons ought to be proportional to the intensity of light. Experiments showed that, although the electron current produced depends upon the intensity of the light, the maximum energy of the electrons was not dependent on the intensity. Moreover, classical theory predicted that the photoelectric current should not depend on the frequency of the light and that there should be a time lag between the reception of light on the surface and the emission of the electrons. Neither of these predictions was borne out by experiment. In 1905, Albert Einstein published a theory that successfully explained the photoelectric effect. It was closely related to Planck's theory of BLACK BODY radiation announced in 1900. According to Einstein's theory, the incident light is composed of discrete particles of energy, or quanta, called photons, the energy of each PHOTON being proportional to its frequency according to the equation $E = h\nu$, where E is the energy, ν is the frequency, and h is Planck's constant. The maximum kinetic energy, KE, that any photoelectron can possess is given by $KE = h\nu - W$, where W is the work function, i.e., the energy required to free an electron from the material, varying with the particular material. The effect has a number of practical applications, most based on the PHOTOELECTRIC CELL.

photoengraving, photomechanical process in the graphic arts, used principally for reproducing illustrations. The subject is photographed, and the image is recorded on a sensitized metal plate, which is then etched in an acid bath. In the case of line cuts (drawings in solid blacks and whites without gradations of color), the photoengraving is done on zinc, and the result is called a zinc etching. In the case of halftone cuts, the work is done on copper. The halftone effect is accomplished by photographing the subject through a wire or glass screen, which breaks the light rays so that the metal plate is sensitized in a dotted pattern; the larger dots create the darker areas, the smaller dots the high lights. The finer the screen, the greater the precision of detail in the printed product. Halftones made with a screen having 65 lines to the inch are considered coarse. Those having 150 lines to the inch are considered fine.

photogrammetry: see AERIAL PHOTOGRAPHY.

photographic magnitude: see MAGNITUDE.

photographic processing, set of procedures by which the latent, or invisible, image produced when a photographic film is exposed to light is made into a permanent visible image. An emulsion holding grains of photosensitive chemical compounds called silver halides is spread over a film or other material. Light coming through the camera lens from an object being photographed strikes certain areas of the film, rendering the silver halide grains in those areas unstable. This creates an invisible, or latent, image of the object on the film. The areas of the latent image that receive the most light contain the largest number of unstable grains. Upon development they become the darkest areas of the visible image. Conversely, areas that receive little light form the bright parts of the visible image. Because of this reversal of dark and bright areas, the visible image is often called a negative. The most common method of making the image visible is to bathe it in a chemical developer. This contains an agent that reduces the unstable silver halide grains to black metallic silver, which forms the image. In addition to the reducing agent, which is generally an organic compound such as a phenol or an amine, a chemical developer contains sodium sulfite, an alkali that causes development to go on at a desired rate, which prevents the reducing agent from being destroyed by the air, and compounds such as potassium bromide that keep unexposed silver halide from fogging the film. A developer is generally designed to be used with particular film emulsions and to produce certain desired effects, such as fineness of grain in the finished image. After development the negative must be stabilized, or fixed, so that it will no longer be sensitive to light. In fixing, the unexposed silver halide grains are removed by immersion in a water solution of sodium or aluminum thiosulfate. Between the developing and fixing processes the negative may be placed in an acid bath to neutralize excess alkali left by the developer. After fixing, the negative is washed and dried. Next the negative may be subjected either to intensification, a process in which additional silver is deposited in exposed areas to increase the contrast in the image, or to reduction, a process in which silver is removed to decrease the contrast. Toning is a process in which a photographic image is treated to change its color, as by changing the deposited silver to silver sulfide or causing a colored metal salt to form along with the silver. The negative may be used to produce a positive image, often called a print, or photograph, in which the light and dark areas of the object and the image correspond. The positive is produced by first projecting the negative onto a photosensitive paper. When this is done by direct contact, i.e., placing the negative and photosensitive paper together, the positive produced is the same size as the negative. When a system of lenses is interposed, the image may be enlarged or reduced. After this the latent image on the photosensitive paper is developed by a process similar to that used on the negative. In most color films there are three layers of emulsions, each sensitive to a different color of light and each capable of forming a different color dye when developed. There are many development processes in use. In one process the exposed film is made into a positive color transparency, in another a negative from which positive prints are produced. In both processes the finished product contains three layers, each one containing an image in a different color. The superposition of these images reproduces the colors of the photographed object. See D. H. O. Jolin, *Photographic Chemistry* (1963); L. F. A. Mason, *Photographic Processing Chemistry* (1966); K. S. Lialikov, *The Chemistry of Photographic Mechanisms* (1967); Andreas Feininger, *Darkroom Techniques* (1974).

photography, still, science and art of making permanent images on light-sensitive materials. Photography's basic principles, processes, and materials were discovered virtually simultaneously by a diverse group of individuals of different nationalities, working for the most part entirely independently of one another. The results of their experiments coalesced in the first half of the 19th cent., creating a tool for communication that was to become as powerful and significant as the printing press. The CAMERA itself is based on optical principles known at least since the age of Aristotle; indeed, a filmless version was in use in the mid-1500s as a sketching device for artists. Called the camera obscura (Lat., = dark chamber), it consisted of a small, light-proof box with a pinhole or lens on one side and a translucent screen on the opposite side. This screen registered, in a manner suitable for tracing, the inverted image transmitted through the lens. The human eye was the prototype for this device, which functioned as a primitive extension of seeing. Most experiments in photographic technology have been directed toward perfecting the medium as a surrogate, more sophisticated eye, but the necessary first breakthrough was in a different area—that of making permanent photographic images. Employing data from the researches of Johann Heinrich Schulze—who, in 1727, discovered that silver nitrate darkened upon exposure to light—Thomas Wedgwood and Sir Humphrey DAVY, early in the 19th cent., created what we now call photograms. These were made by placing assorted objects on paper soaked in silver nitrate and exposing them to sunlight. Those areas of the paper covered by the objects remained white; the rest blackened after exposure to the light. Davy and Wedgwood found no way of arresting the chemical action at this stage, however, and their images lasted only a short time before darkening entirely. Four men figure principally in the establishment of the rudiments of photographic science. A French physicist, Joseph Nicéphore Niepce, made the first negative, on paper, in 1816, and the first known photograph, on metal, in 1827. By the latter date he had directed his investigations away from paper surfaces and negatives (having invented, in the meantime, what is now called the photogravure process of mechanical reproduction) and toward sensitized metallic surfaces. In 1827, Niepce had also begun his association with Louis Jacques Mandé DAGUERRE, a French showman and painter who had been experimenting along parallel lines. A partnership was formed and they collaborated until Niepce's death in 1833, after which Daguerre continued their work for the next six years. In 1839, he announced the invention of a method for making a direct positive image on a silver plate, to which he had given his own name—the daguerreotype. Daguerre's announcement was a source of dismay to the English scientist William Henry Fox TALBOT, who had been experimenting independently along related lines for years. Talbot had evolved a method for making a paper negative from which an infinite number of paper positives could be created. He had also worked out an effective although imperfect technique for permanently "fixing" his images. Concerned that he might lose the rights to his own invention, the calotype process, Talbot wrote to the French Academy of Sciences, which had been charged with investigating Daguerre's claim, asserting the priority of his own invention. He then lost no time in presenting his researches to England's Royal Society, of which he was a distinguished member. All three pioneers, Niepce, Daguerre, and Talbot, along with Sir John HERSCHEL—who discovered in 1819 the suitability of hyposulfite of soda, or "hypo," as a fixing agent for sensitized paper images and who is generally credited with giving the new medium its name—deserve to share the title Inventor of Photography. Each made a vital and unique contribution to the invention of the photographic process. The process developed by Daguerre and Niepce was, in an unprecedented gesture, purchased from them by the French government and given, free of patent restrictions, to the world. Talbot patented his own process and then published a description of it, entitled *The Pencil of Nature* (1844-46). This book, containing 24 original prints, was the first ever illustrated with photographs. Daguerreotypy, however, spread most rapidly, except in England, where Daguerre had secretly patented his process before selling it to the French government. The legal problems attending the pursuit of photography as a profession account in part for the widespread influence of amateurs (e.g., Nadar) on the early development of the medium. The popularity of the daguerreotype is attributable to two principal factors. The first of these was the Victorian passion for novelty and for the accumulation of material objects, which found its perfect paradigm in these silvery, exquisitely detailed miniatures. The second was the greatly increasing demand from a rising middle class, seeking visible proof of family unity, for qualitatively good but—compared to a painter's fee—inexpensive family portraits. The cheaper tintype eventually made such likenesses available to all. The principal shortcoming of the daguerreotype and its variants was inherent in its nature as a direct positive. Unique and unreproducible, it was useless for the production of any image intended for wide distribution. This factor, combined with the lengthy exposure time necessitated by the process, restricted its function to PORTRAITURE. The vast majority of surviving daguerreotypes are portraits; images of any other subject are exceedingly rare. Nevertheless, for 20 years the fad for daguerreotypy completely overshadowed the greater utility of the calotype. In the United States, where it was equally popular, the daguerreotype was promoted by John W. DRAPER and Samuel F. B. MORSE. The calotype's paper negative made possible the virtually infinite reproduction of photographic images. The unavoidably coarse paper base for the negative, however, eliminated the delicate detail that made the daguerreotype so appealing. This lack of precision was understood and used to advantage by the Scottish painter David Octavius HILL and his assistant, Robert Adamson. From 1843 to 1848 they made an extensive series of calotype portraits of Scottish clergymen, intended to serve only as studies for a group portrait in oils, that stands today among the major bodies of work in the medium. Hill and Adamson composed their portraits in broad planes, juxtaposing bold masses of light and dark, creating works that are monumental in feeling despite their small size. The dilemma of detail versus reproducibility was resolved in 1851 by another Englishman, Frederick Scott Archer, who introduced the collodion process. This method, also known as the "wet plate" technique, involved coating a glass plate with silver iodide in suspension, exposing it while still wet, and developing it immediately. Once fixed and dried, the glass plate was covered with a thin, flexible film containing the negative image, the definition and detail of which approached that of the daguerreotype. As this process merged the advantages of both its predecessors, it was universally adopted within a very short time. With the advent of the collodion process came mass production and dissemination of photographic prints. The inception of these visual documents of personal and public history engendered vast changes in man's perception of history, of time, and of himself. The concept of privacy was greatly altered as cameras were used to record most areas of human life. The ubiquitous presence of photographic machinery eventually changed mankind's sense of what was suitable for observation. The photograph was considered incontestable proof of an event, experience, or state of being. It became a formidable tool for the political state and a source of comfort and support to the traveler. To fulfill the mounting and incessant demand for more images, photographers spread out to every corner of the world, recording all the natural and man-made phenomena they could find. By the last quarter of the 19th cent., most households could boast respectable photographic collections. These were in three main forms: the family album, which contained cabinet portraits and the smaller cartes-de-visite and tintypes; scrapbooks containing large prints of views from various parts of the world; and boxes of stereoscope cards, which in combination with the popular stereo viewer created an effective illusion of three-dimensionality. A number of photographers, including Timothy O'Sullivan, J. K. Hillers, and W. H. Jackson, accompanied exploratory expeditions to the new frontiers in the American West, while John Thomson returned from China and Maxime Du Camp from Egypt with records of vistas and peoples never before seen by Western eyes. Roger Fenton, who photographed the Crimean conflict, and Mathew Brady's photographic corps, who documented the American Civil War, provided graphic evidence of the hellishness of combat. E. J. Marey, the painter Thomas EAKINS, and Eadweard Muybridge all devised means for making stop-action photographs that demonstrated the gap between what the mind thinks it sees and what the eye actually perceives. Muybridge's major work, *Animal Locomotion* (1887), remains a basic source for artists and scientists alike. As accessory lenses were perfected, the camera's vision extended both telescopically and microscopically; the moon and the microcosm became accessible. The introduction of the halftone process (see PHOTOENGRAVING; PRINTING) in 1881 made possible the accurate reproduction of photographs in books and newspapers. In combination with new improvements in photographic technology, including dry plates and smaller cameras, which made photographing faster and less cumbersome, the halftone made immediate reportage feasible and paved the way for news photography. George EASTMAN's introduction in 1888 of roll film and the simple Kodak box camera provided everyone with the means of making photographs for themselves. Studies in sensitometry, the new science of light-sensitive materials, made exposure and processing more practicable as well. The fight to certify photography as a fine art has been among the medium's dominant philosophical preoccupations since its inception. Photography's legitimacy as an art form was challenged by artists and critics, who seized upon the mechanical and chemical aspects of the photographic process as proof that photography was, at best, a craft. Perhaps because so many painters came to rely so heavily on the photograph as a source of imagery, they insisted that photography could only be a handmaiden to the arts. To prove that photography was indeed an art, photographers at first imitated the painting of the time. Enormous popularity was achieved by such photographers as O. J. Rejlander and Henry Peach Robinson, who created sentimental GENRE scenes by printing from multiple negatives. Julia Margaret Cameron, an eccentric amateur, deliberately blurred her images to achieve a painterly softness of line, creating a series of remarkably powerful soft-focus portraits of her celebrated friends. In opposition to the painterly aesthetic in photography was P. H. Emerson, one of the earliest advocates of what has since become known as "straight" photography. According to this approach the photographic image should not be tampered with or subjected to handwork or other affectations, lest it lose its integrity. Emerson proposed this philosophy in his controversial and influential book, *Naturalistic Photography* (1889). Appropriately, Emerson was the first to recognize the importance of the work of Alfred Stieglitz, who battled for photography's place among the arts during the first part of the 20th cent. In revolt against the entrenched imitation of genre-painting known as "salon" photography, Stieglitz founded a movement which he called the Photo-Secession, related to the radical SECESSION movements in painting. He initiated publication of a magazine, *Camera Work* (1903-17), which was a forum for the Photo-Secession and for enlightened opinion and critical thought in all the arts. It remains the most sumptuously and meticulously produced photographic quarterly in the history of the medium. In New York City, Stieglitz opened three galleries, the first (1908–17) called "291" (from its address at 291 Fifth Ave.), then the Intimate Gallery (1925–30), and An American Place (1930–46), where photographic work was hung beside contemporary, often controversial, work in other media. Stieglitz's own photographs and those of several other Photo-Secessionists—Edward Steichen, one of his early protégés; Frederick Evans, the British architectural photographer; and the portraitist, Alvin L. Coburn—adhered with relative strictness to a "straight" aesthetic. The quality of their works, despite a pervasive self-consciousness, was consistently of the highest craftsmanship. Stieglitz's overriding concern with the concept "art for art's sake" kept him, and the audience he built for the medium, from an appreciation of an equally important branch of photography: the documentary. The power of the photograph as record was demonstrated in the 19th cent., as when William H. Jackson's photographs of the Yellowstone area persuaded the U.S. Congress to set that territory aside as a national park. In the early 20th cent. photographers and journalists were beginning to use the medium to inform the public on crucial issues in order to generate social change. Taking as their precedents the work of such men as Jackson and reporter Jacob Riis (whose photographs of New York City slums resulted in much-needed legislation), documentarians like Lewis Hine and James Van DerZee began to build a photographic tradition whose central concerns had little to do with the concept of art. The photojournalist sought to build, strengthen, or change public opinion by means of novel, often shocking images. The finished form of the documentary image was the inexpensive multiple, the magazine or newspaper reproduction. For a time, the two traditions, art photography and documentary photography, appeared to be merged within the work of one man, Paul Strand. Strand's works combined a documentary concern with a lean, modernist vision related to the avant-garde art of Europe. Seeking to determine the particular aesthetics of photography, the American Berenice Abbott and the Frenchmen Eugène Atget, André Kertész, and Henri Cartier-Bresson developed intensely personal styles. The exponents of SURREALISM in France and of FUTURISM in Italy, and the various German art movements that were focused in the BAUHAUS all explored the medium of photography. The international exhibition "Film und Foto," held in Stuttgart in 1929, helped to make formal a purely photographic aesthetic. The works exhibited combined elements of FUNCTIONALISM and abstraction. Photographic subject matter shifted from the past to the present—a present of new forms in machinery and architecture, new concern with the experience of the working classes, and a new interest in the timeless forms of nature. In California during the 1920s and 30s, Edward Weston and a handful of kindred spirits founded the *f*.64 group, taking their name from the smallest lens opening, that which provides the greatest precision of line and detail. This small and unofficial organization—which included Imogen Cunningham, Ansel Adams, and Willard Van Dyke—came to dominate photographic art, overshadowing the pictorial aesthetic. The *f*.64 group and its imitators eschewed all post-exposure handwork, and worked with 8x10-in. view cameras in order to obtain the largest possible negatives from which to make straightforward contact prints. They limited their subject matter to static things: the still life, the distant or closely viewed landscape, and the formal portrait. The influential teacher Minor White became known for his poetic, visionary work related in technique to this straight approach. The development of the 35-mm or "candid" camera by Oskar Barnack of the Ernst Leitz company, first marketed in 1925, made the documentarian infinitely more mobile and less conspicuous, while the manufacture of faster black and white film enabled him to work without flashbulbs in situations with a minimum of light. Color film for transparencies (slides) was introduced in 1935, and color negative film in 1942. Portable lighting equipment was perfected, and in 1947 the Polaroid Land camera, which could produce a positive print in seconds, was placed on the market. All of these technological advances granted the photojournalist enormous and unprecedented versatility. The advent of large-circulation picture magazines, such as *Life* (begun 1936) and *Look* (begun 1937), provided an outlet and a vast audience for documentary work. At the same time a steady stream of convulsive national and international events provided a wealth of material for the extended photo-essay, the documentarian's natural mode. One of these was the Great Depression of the 1930s, which proved to be the source of an important body of documentary work. Under the leadership of Roy Stryker, the photographic division of the Farm Security Administration (FSA) began to make an archive of images of America during this epoch of crisis. Walker Evans, Arthur Rothstein, Russell Lee, and Dorothea Lange of the FSA group photographed the cultural disintegration generated by the Depression and the concomitant disappearance of rural lifestyles. With the coming of World War II, photographers, including Margaret Bourke-White, Edward Steichen, W. Eugene Smith, and Robert Capa, documented the global conflict. The war was a stimulus to photography in other ways as well. From the stress analysis of metals to aerial surveillance, the medium was a crucial tool in many areas of the war effort, and, in the urgency of war, numerous technological discoveries and advances were made that ultimately benefited all photographers. After the war, museums and art schools opened their doors to photography, a trend that has continued to the present. Photographers began to break free of the oppressive strictures of the straight aesthetic and documentary modes of expression. As exemplified by Robert Frank in his highly influential book-length photo-essay, *The Americans* (1959), the new documentarians commenced probing what has been called the "social landscape," often mirroring in their images the anxiety and alienation of urban man. Such introspection naturally led to an increasingly personal form of documentary photography, as in the works of J. H. Lartigue and Diane Arbus. Many young photographers felt little inhibition against handwork, collage, multiple images, and other forms that were anathema to practitioners of the straight aesthetic. The practical applications of the photographic medium are legion; it is an important tool in education, medicine, commerce, and criminology, to name but four. Its scientific applications include telephoto work in astronomy; aerial mapping and surveying; geology; reconnaissance; meteorology; archaeology; and anthropology. New discoveries such as HOLOGRAPHY, a means of creating a true three-dimensional image, continue to expand the medium's technological and creative horizons. See articles on individual photographers, e.g., Eugène ATGET. See also PHOTOGRAPHIC PROCESSING; MOTION PICTURE PHOTOGRAPHY; MOTION PICTURES. See Helmut and Allison Gernsheim, *The History of Photography, 1685–1914* (1969); Arnold Gassan, *A Chronology of Photography* (new ed. 1972); Beaumont Newhall, *The History of Photography: 1839 to the Present Day* (1972); Nathan Lyons, ed., *Photographers on Photography* (1966); *The Focal Encyclopedia of Photography* (2 vol., rev. ed. 1965); *The Time-Life Library of Photography* (17 vol., 1970–72); Ansel Adams, *Basic Photo Series* (5 vol., 1950–59, repr. 1968–69); J. G. Lootens, *Lootens on Photographic Enlarging and Print Quality* (7th ed. 1967); Ralph M. Hattersley, *Beginner's Guide to Photography* (1974). Among the many outstanding volumes of collected photographs are Edward Steichen, ed., *The Family of Man* (1955) and *American Album* (1968; comp. by the editors of *American Heritage*).

photogravure: see PRINTING.

photometry (fōtŏm'ətrē), branch of physics dealing with the measurement of the intensity of a source of light, such as an electric lamp, and with the intensity of light such a source may cast on a surface area. Instruments used for such measurement, called photometers, make possible a comparison between an unknown intensity and a standard or known intensity. They are based on the inverse-square law, which states that as a light source is moved away from a surface it illuminates, the illumination decreases in an amount inversely proportional to the square of the distance. Thus the illumination of a surface by a source of light 2 ft away is ¼ of the illumination at 1 ft from the source. Conversely, for two light sources, one at 1 ft from a surface and the other at 2 ft, to give the same illumination to the surface, it would be necessary for the source at 2 ft to have an intensity 4 times that of the source at 1 ft. The Bunsen photometer (named for R. W. Bunsen) determines the light intensity of a source by comparison with a known, or standard, intensity. The two light sources (one of known, one of unknown intensity) are placed on opposite sides of the surface (a disk of paper) to be illuminated. In the center of this surface is a grease spot that, when illuminated equally from both sides, will appear neither lighter nor darker than the paper but will become almost invisible. Using the inverse-square law, the intensity of the unknown light source can be easily determined when the relative distances at which the two sources produce equal illumination are known. The Rumford photometer (named for Count Rumford), or shadow photometer, compares intensities of light sources by the density of the shadows produced. In the Lummer-Brodhun photometer, an opaque screen is placed between the two sources, and a comparison is made possible by an ingenious arrangement of prisms. A photometer thus measures relative rather than absolute intensity. The intensity of electric lights is commonly given as so many candlepower, i.e., so many times the intensity of a standard candle. Since an ordinary candle is not a sufficiently accurate standard, the unit of intensity has been defined in various ways. It was originally defined as the luminous intensity in a horizontal direction of a candle of specified size burning at a specified rate. Later the international candle was taken as a standard; not actually a candle, it is defined in terms of the luminous intensity of a specified array of carbon-filament lamps. In 1948 a new candle, about 1.9% smaller than the former unit, was adopted. It is defined as 1/60 of the intensity of one square centimeter of a BLACK BODY radiator at the temperature at which platinum solidifies (2046°K). This unit is sometimes called the new international candle; the official name given to it by the International Commission of Illumination (CIE) is candela. Other quantities of importance in photometry include luminous flux, surface brightness (for a diffuse rather than point source), and surface illumination. Luminous flux is the radiation given off in the visible range of wavelengths by a radiating source. It is measured in lumens, one lumen being equal to the luminous flux per unit solid angle (steradian) emitted by a unit candle. Surface brightness is measured in lamberts, one lambert being equal to an average intensity of $1/\pi$ candle per square centimeter of a radiating surface. The intensity of illumination, also called illuminance, is a measure of the degree to which a surface is illuminated and is thus distinguished from the intensity of the light source. Illumination is given in footcandles, i.e., so many times the illumination given by a standard candle at 1 ft. Another unit of illumination is the lux, one lux being equal to one lumen incident per square meter of illuminated surface. One lux equals 0.0929 footcandle.

photomultiplier: see PHOTOELECTRIC CELL.

photon (fō'tŏn), the particle composing light and other forms of ELECTROMAGNETIC RADIATION, sometimes called light quantum. About the beginning of the 20th cent., the classical theory that light is emitted and absorbed by matter in a continuous stream came under criticism because it led to incorrect predictions about several effects, notably the radiation of light by incandescent bodies (see BLACK BODY) and the PHOTOELECTRIC EFFECT. These effects can be explained only by assuming that the energy is transferred in discrete packets, or photons, the energy of each photon being equal to the frequency of the light multiplied by Planck's constant, h. Because the value of Planck's constant is extremely small (6.62×10^{-27} erg sec.), the discrete nature of light energy is not evident in most optical phenomena. The light imparts energy to a charged particle when one of the photons collides with it, as is demonstrated by the COMPTON EFFECT. See QUANTUM THEORY.

photosphere, luminous, apparently opaque layer of gases that forms the visible surface of the SUN. The photosphere lies between the dense interior gases and the more attenuated gases of the CHROMOSPHERE. The incandescent gases of the photosphere, estimated to be at temperatures near 6000°K, are so much brighter than the other layers of the sun that they seem to form a surface. These gases are in a constant state of agitation due to convection currents that reach down to 150,000 mi (241,000 km) below the photosphere. Differences in the density of the gases result in a grainy appearance of the photosphere; the small bright patches, or granules, are several hundred miles in diameter and are constantly shifting. Another feature of the photosphere, observed only near the sun's edge, is the appearance near sunspots of bright, veinlike regions known as faculae.

photostat (fō'təstăt"), reproduction of any printed or simple black-and-white material, such as drawings or manuscripts, made by the Photostat, a photographic camera. Widely used, the process is rapid and inexpensive.

photosynthesis (fō"tōsĭn'thəsĭs), process in which green plants utilize the energy of sunlight to manufacture carbohydrates from carbon dioxide and water in the presence of chlorophyll. Some of the plants that lack chlorophyll, e.g., the fungi and some others, secure their nutrients from organic material, as do animals, and a few bacteria manufacture their own carbohydrates with hydrogen and energy obtained from inorganic compounds (e.g., hydrogen sulfide) in a process called chemosynthesis. However, the vast majority of plants contain chlorophyll—concentrated, in the higher land plants, in the leaves. In these plants water is absorbed by the roots and carried to the leaves by the xylem, and carbon dioxide is obtained from air that enters the leaves through the stomata and diffuses to the cells containing chlorophyll. The green pigment CHLOROPHYLL is uniquely capable of converting the active energy of light into a latent form that can be stored (in food) and used when needed. The initial process in photosynthesis is the decomposition of water (H_2O) into oxygen, which is released, and hydrogen; direct light is required for this process. The hydrogen and the carbon and oxygen of carbon dioxide (CO_2) are then converted into a series of increasingly complex compounds that results finally in a stable organic compound, glucose ($C_6H_{12}O_6$), and water. This phase of photosynthesis utilizes stored energy and therefore can proceed in the dark. The simplified equation used to represent this overall process is $6CO_2+12H_2O+\text{energy}=C_6H_{12}O+6O_2+6H_2O$. In general, the results of this process are the reverse of those in respiration, in which carbohydrates are oxidized to release energy, with the production of carbon dioxide and water. The intermediary reactions before glucose is formed involve several enzymes, which react with the coenzyme ATP (see ADENOSINE TRIPHOSPHATE) to produce various molecules. Studies using radioactive carbon have indicated that among the intermediate products are three-carbon molecules from which acids and amino acids, as well as glucose, are derived. This suggests that fats and proteins are also direct products of photosynthesis. The main product, glucose, is the fundamental building block of carbohydrates (e.g., sugars, starches, and cellulose). The water-soluble sugars (e.g., sucrose and maltose) are used for immediate energy. The insoluble starches are stored as tiny granules in various parts of the plant—chiefly the leaves, roots, tubers, and fruits—and can be broken down again when energy is needed. Cellulose is used to build the rigid cell walls that are the principal supporting structure of plants. Animals and plants both synthesize fats and proteins from carbohydrates; thus glucose is a basic energy source for all living organisms. The oxygen released (with water vapor, in transpiration) as a photosynthetic by-product provides most of the atmospheric oxygen vital to respiration in plants and animals, and animals in turn produce carbon dioxide necessary to plants. Photosynthesis can therefore be considered the ultimate source of life for all plants and animals, by providing the source of energy that drives all their metabolic processes. See Isaac Asimov, *Photosynthesis* (1969); R. M. Devlin and A. V. Barker, *Photosynthesis* (1972).

photosynthetic phosphorylation: see PHOSPHORYLATION.

phototube, vacuum electron tube similar to a diode, except that the cathode, instead of being heated, is coated with a material that emits electrons when light (or other electromagnetic radiation) strikes it. Within certain limits the current through the tube is proportional to the amount of radiation striking the cathode. See PHOTOELECTRIC CELL.

Phou Bia (fo͞o byä), peak, 9,242 ft (2,817 m) high, in the Annamese Cordillera, N Laos. It is the highest point in Laos.

Phraates (frā-ā'tēz), kings of Parthia of the dynasty of ARSACES. **Phraates II,** fl. 130 B.C., decisively defeated (129 B.C.) Antiochus VII of Syria, permanently annexing E Mesopotamia to his kingdom. **Phraates IV,** d. 2 B.C., had an early success in driving (36 B.C.) Antony out of Parthia. After 31 B.C., Phraates had to cope with a stubborn rebellion by one of his generals, who briefly usurped the throne. Phraates subsequently acknowledged his dependency to Rome. He died in a palace intrigue.

phratry: see CLAN.

phrenology, study of the shape of the human skull in order to draw conclusions about particular character traits and mental faculties. The theory was developed about 1800 by the German physiologist Franz Joseph Gall and popularized in the United States by Orson Fowler and Lorenzo Fowler through their publication the *Phrenological Almanac* and other publications. Modern neurology and physical anthropology have refuted the theory and consider its use a form of quackery.

Phrixus (frĭk'səs): see GOLDEN FLEECE.

Phrygia (frĭ'jēə), ancient region, central Asia Minor (now central Turkey). The Phrygians, who settled here c.1200 B.C., came from the Balkans and apparently spoke an Indo-European language. A kingdom, associated in Greek legend with the names of MIDAS and GORDIUS, flourished from the 8th to the 6th cent. B.C., when it fell with the Cimmerian invasion (676–585 B.C.) and became dominated by Lydia. Phrygia was best known to the Greeks as a source of slaves and as a center of the cult of CYBELE. N Phrygia became part of Galatia with the invasion of the Gauls (3d cent. B.C.). The kings of Pergamum ruled much of Phrygia until it passed to the Romans. St. Paul visited Phrygia (Acts 16.6; 18.23). There has been much archaeological excavation in the area. See C. H. Haspels, *Highlands of Phrygia* (2 vol., 1971).

Phrynichus (frĭn'ĭkəs), c.512–476 B.C., Athenian tragedian, considered by some ancients (including Plato) to be the founder of tragedy. His historical play, *The Taking of Miletus,* which concerns the capture of Miletus by the Persians, had such a painful theme that it moved the Athenian audience to tears, and Phrynichus was fined. He is said to have been the first to use female characters and was famous for his choreography. Fragments of his dramas survive.

Phrynichus, fl. 430 B.C., Athenian comic poet. Fragments of his works, of the Old Comedy, survive.

Phuket (po͞o'kĭt), island, 206 sq mi (534 sq km), a province of Thailand, in the Andaman Sea, off the west coast of the Malay Peninsula. The town of Phuket is the capital. Flat, with isolated hills, the island is one of Thailand's chief tin-mining regions and also produces rubber, coconuts, and pepper. The population is mainly Chinese and Thai; the Chinese have mined tin there since ancient times. Phuket town was founded in the 1st cent. B.C. by colonists from India. European merchants began trading there in the 16th cent. The island, contested by the Siamese and the Burmese during their 18th-century wars, was finally incorporated into Thailand in the 19th cent. Phuket was known to the Malays as Ujong Salang (Cape Salang) and to early European voyagers as Junkceylon.

Phumiphon: see BHUMIBOL ADULYADEJ.

Phurah (fyo͞o'rə), servant of Gideon. Judges 7.10,11.

Phut (fŭt), son of Ham and eponym of an African people. It may also be a region, possibly Punt or Libya, and is perhaps the same as PUL **2.** Gen. 10.6; Ezek. 27.10. Put: Nahum 3.9.

Phuvah (fyo͞o'və), son of Issachar; the ancestor of the Punites. Gen. 46.13. Pua: Num. 26.23. Puah: 1 Chron. 7.1.

Phyfe, Duncan (fīf), c. 1768–1854, American cabinetmaker, b. Scotland. He emigrated to America c.1783, settling at Albany, N.Y., where he was apprenticed to a cabinetmaker. In the early 1790s he established a shop in New York City for the production of furniture; after several moves he finally settled in Partition St. (later changed to Fulton St.). He first spelled his name Fife but c.1793 adopted the form Phyfe. He made chairs, sofas or settees, tables, and sideboards, using in great part solid mahogany but also some mahogany veneer, satinwood and maple, and, in later years, rosewood. During his most productive period (until 1820) he was influenced by, and adapted the forms of, the Adam brothers, Hepplewhite, and Sheraton and characteristics of the French Directoire and Consulate styles. Later, his designs followed the Empire style, becoming in his final period heavy, overornamented, and to a great degree characterless. Phyfe employed in general the highest standards, applied under supervision to carefully selected woods. His first designs are characterized by excellent proportions, graceful curves often accentuated by parallel rows of reeding, simple ornaments well placed and carved with precision, and decorative motifs such as the lyre, the acanthus or oak leaf, and the drapery swag. Although much furniture termed Phyfe may not have been produced in his workshop, his designs were the nucleus of the Duncan Phyfe style.

Phygellus (fĭjĕl'əs), man who turned away from Paul. 2 Tim. 1.15.

phylacteries (fĭlăk'tərēz) [Gr.,=safeguard], two small leather boxes worn during morning prayers by Orthodox and Conservative Jews after the age of 13 years and one day. Each box contains strips of parchment inscribed with verses from the Scriptures: Ex. 13.1–10; 13.11–16; Deut. 6.4–9; 11.13–21. One box is fastened to the forehead and the other to the left arm; they are intended to serve as a reminder of the constant presence of God and of the need to keep Him uppermost in one's thoughts and deeds, thereby safeguarding the wearer against committing a sin. They are not worn on the Sabbath or holy days, since these days are in themselves a reminder of God. Phylacteries are also called tephillin [Aramaic,=attachment].

phylloxera (fĭlŏk'sīrə), small, sap-eating, greenish INSECT of the genus *Phylloxera,* closely related to the APHID. Phylloxeras feed on leaves and roots, and many species produce galls on deciduous trees. Their life cycle is complex; one species is known to pass through 21 different stages. Most notorious of the group is the grape phylloxera, *Phylloxera vitifoliae,* native to E North America. The species has winged and wingless generations, the former causing galls on grape leaves and the latter feeding on the roots, causing nodules and eventually killing the vine. The grape phylloxera came close to destroying the wine industry of France after its accidental introduction in about 1860; grafting of susceptible European vines onto resistant North American root stock saved the European vineyards. Phylloxeras are classified in the phylum ARTHROPODA, class Insecta, order Homoptera, family Phylloxeridae.

phylogeny: see BIOGENETIC LAW.

phylum, in taxonomy: see CLASSIFICATION.

physical chemistry, branch of SCIENCE that combines the principles and methods of physics and chemistry. It provides a fundamental theoretical and experimental basis for all of chemistry, including organic, inorganic, and analytical chemistry. In addition, it is the foundation of chemical engineering. Topics of interest are chemical equilibrium, reaction rates, solutions, molecular weights, molecular structure, and the properties of gases, liquids, crystals, and colloids. Among other factors, the influence of temperature, pressure, electricity, light, concentration, and turbulence are considered. There are three principal approaches in physical chemistry: THERMODYNAMICS, involving large numbers of molecules in equilibrium; kinetics, involving chemical changes with time; and molecular structure, involving the electronic and atomic arrangements that follow from the QUANTUM THEORY. The latter approach is primarily theoretical and provides an understanding of the CHEMICAL BONDS which are responsible for the structure of all materials. See W. J. Moore, *Physical Chemistry* (4th ed. 1972); G. M. Barrow, *Physical Chemistry* (3d ed. 1973).

physical education and training, organized instruction in motor activities that contribute to the physical growth, health, and body image of the individual. The historical roots of physical education go back as far as the ancient Chinese (c.2500 B.C.), who had a well-developed system of exercise and physical training. In ancient Greece the Athenians were concerned with both physical and mental development and consequently they accorded GYMNASTICS, sports, and rhythms an important educational role. During the period of the Roman Empire, and later during the Middle Ages, physical education was primarily used as a form of military training. Interest in physical education as a part of the total individual's development was revived during the Renaissance. It was not until the 19th cent., however, that systems of gymnastics were developed in several European countries, notably Germany, Sweden, and England. In the same century gymnastics spread to the United States. Interest in the new system led to a movement to have compulsory physical training in American public schools and to establish physical education in colleges and universities. The first department of physical education at an American college was established at Amherst (1860). Today physical education is a required part of most school curricula and a number of colleges and universities offer degrees in the field. Physical education classes generally include formal exercises, sports, and contests, although an increasing emphasis has been given to such Oriental techniques as yoga, karate, and judo. The American Association for Health, Physical Education, and Recreation (founded 1885 as the American Association for the Advancement of Physical Education) is a branch of the National Education Association concerned with increasing the public's knowledge and appreciation of physical education. See publications of the American Association for Health, Physical Education, and Recreation. See Jesse F. Williams, *Principles of Physical Education* (8th ed. 1964); Deobold Van Dalen, *A World History of Physical Education* (2d ed. 1971).

physical examination: see DIAGNOSIS.

physical fitness, combined good health and physical development. The object of any program of physical fitness is to maximize an individual's health, strength, endurance, and skill relative to age, sex, body build, and physiology. These ends can only be realized through conscientious regulation of exercise, rest, diet, and periodic medical and dental examinations. Exercise should be regular and vigorous, but begun slowly and only gradually increased in strenuousness. It is more important that periods of sleep be regular and restful than that they extend any fixed number of hours. Growing children may require more than the conventional eight hours of sleep, while many adults will need fewer than eight. A diet that is properly balanced in proteins, carbohydrates, vitamins, and minerals is essential. Excessive intake of any of these categories is as potentially harmful as their lack. Conscientious dental hygiene and periodic checkups are also strongly advised. Complete and regular physical examinations should be the basis of any program of physical development, and such a program is best planned with the consultation of a physician.

physical geography: see GEOGRAPHY.

physical therapy or **physiotherapy,** treatment of disorders of the muscles, bones, or joints, resulting from injury or disease of the muscles or nerves, by means of physical agents—heat, light, water, manual and electronic massage, and exercise. The type of treatment needed is prescribed by a physician and usually carried out by trained physiotherapists. The therapist attempts to prevent further damage and pain and may also train different muscles to compensate for those damaged by injury or disease. Whirlpool baths are a valuable means of treating injuries and chronic inflammatory conditions. Massage (a passive form of exercise) provides stimulation of nerves and prevents muscular atrophy in parts of the body disabled by paralysis or rheumatic disorders. Active exercises are also prescribed as treatment for various conditions. Physiotherapy is an important factor in sports, not only as part of the conditioning program for the participants but also in treating injuries incurred during participation.

physics, branch of SCIENCE traditionally defined as the study of MATTER, ENERGY, and the relation between them; it was called natural philosophy until the late 19th cent. and is still known by this name at a few universities. Physics is in some senses the oldest and most basic pure science; its discoveries find applications throughout the natural sciences, since matter and energy are the basic constituents of the natural world. The other sciences are generally more limited in their scope and may be considered branches that have split off from physics to become sciences in their own right.

Branches. Physics today may be divided loosely into classical physics and modern physics. Classical physics includes the traditional branches that were recognized and fairly well developed before the beginning of the 20th cent.—MECHANICS, SOUND, LIGHT, HEAT, and ELECTRICITY and MAGNETISM. Mechanics is concerned with bodies acted on by FORCES and bodies in MOTION and may be divided into STATICS (study of the forces on a body or bodies at rest), kinematics (study of motion without regard to its causes), and DYNAMICS (study of motion and the forces that affect it); mechanics may also be divided into solid mechanics and fluid mechanics, the latter including such branches as hydrostatics, hydrodynamics, aerodynamics, and pneumatics. ACOUSTICS, the study of sound, is often considered a branch of mechanics because sound is due to the motions of the particles of air or other medium through which sound waves can travel and thus can be explained in terms of the laws of mechanics. Among the important modern branches of acoustics is ULTRASONICS, the study of sound waves of very high frequency, beyond the range of human hearing. Optics, the study of light, is concerned not only with visible light but also with infrared and ultraviolet radiation, which exhibit all of the phenomena of visible light except visibility, e.g., REFLECTION, REFRACTION, INTERFERENCE, DIFFRACTION, DISPERSION, and POLARIZATION OF LIGHT. Heat is a form of energy, the internal energy possessed by the particles of which a substance is composed; THERMODYNAMICS deals with the relationships between heat and other forms of energy. Electricity and magnetism have been studied as a single branch of physics since the intimate connection between them was discovered in the early 19th cent.; an electric current gives rise to a magnetic field and a changing magnetic field induces an electric current. Electrostatics deals with electric charges at rest, electrodynamics with moving charges, and magnetostatics with magnetic poles at rest. Most of classical physics is concerned with matter and energy on the normal scale of observation. By contrast, much of modern physics is concerned with the behavior of matter and energy under extreme conditions or on the very large or very small scale. For example, atomic and nuclear physics studies matter on the smallest scale at which chemical elements can be identified. The physics of ELEMENTARY PARTICLES is on an even smaller scale, being concerned with the most basic units of matter; this branch of physics is also known as high-energy physics because of the extremely high energies necessary to produce many types of particles in large PARTICLE ACCELERATORS. On this scale, ordinary, commonsense notions of space, time, matter, and energy are no longer valid and the two chief theories of modern physics present a different picture of these concepts from that presented by classical physics. The QUANTUM THEORY is concerned with the discrete, rather than continuous, nature of many phenomena at the atomic and subatomic level, and with the complementary aspects of particles and waves in the description of such phenomena. The theory of RELATIVITY is concerned with the description of phenomena that take place in a frame of reference that is in motion with respect to an observer; the special theory of relativity is concerned with relative uniform motion in a straight line and the general theory of relativity with accelerated motion and its connection with gravitation. Both the quantum theory and the theory of relativity find applications in all areas of modern physics.

History. The earliest history of physics is interrelated with that of the other sciences. A number of contributions were made during the period of Greek civilization, dating from Thales and the early Ionian natural philosophers in the Greek colonies of Asia Minor (6th and 5th cent. B.C.). Democritus (c.460–370 B.C.) proposed an atomic theory of matter and extended it to other phenomena as well, but the dominant theories of matter held that it was formed of a few basic elements, usually earth, air, fire, and water. In the school founded by Pythagoras of Samos the principal concept was that of number; it was applied to all aspects of the universe, from planetary orbits to the lengths of strings used to sound musical notes. The most important philosophy of the Greek period was produced by two men at Athens, Plato (427–347 B.C.) and his student Aristotle (384–322 B.C.); Aristotle in particular had a critical influence on the development of science in general and physics in particular. The Greek approach to physics was largely geometrical and reached its peak with Archimedes (287–212 B.C.), who studied a wide range of problems and anticipated the methods of the calculus. Another important scientist of the early Hellenistic period, centered in Alexandria, Egypt, was the astronomer Aristarchus (c.310–220 B.C.), who proposed a heliocentric, or sun-centered, system of the universe. However, just as the earlier atomic theory had not become generally accepted, so too the astronomical system that eventually prevailed was the geocentric system proposed by Hipparchus (190–120 B.C.) and developed in detail by Ptolemy (85 A.D.–165 A.D.). With the passing of the Greek civilization and the Roman civilization that followed it, Greek learning passed into the hands of the Muslim world that spread its influence from the E Mediterranean eastward into Asia, where it picked up contributions from the Chinese (papermaking, gunpowder) and the Hindus (the place-value decimal number system with a zero), and westward as far as Spain, where important Islamic culture flourished in Córdoba, Toledo, and other cities. Little specific advance was made in physics during this period, but the preservation and study of Greek science by the Muslim world made possible the revival of learning in the West beginning in the 12th and 13th cent. The first areas of physics to receive close attention were mechanics and the study of planetary motions. Modern mechanics dates from the work of Galileo and Simon Stevin in the late 16th and early 17th cent. The great breakthrough in astronomy was made by Nicolaus Copernicus, who proposed (1543) the heliocentric model of the SOLAR SYSTEM that was later modified by Johannes Kepler, using observations by Tycho Brahe, into the description of planetary motions that is still accepted today. Galileo gave his support to this new system and applied his discoveries in mechanics to its explanation, but the full explanation of both celestial and terrestrial motions was not given until 1687, when Isaac Newton published his *Principia (Mathematical Principles of Natural Philosophy).* This work, the most important document of the Scientific Revolution of the 16th and 17th cent., contained Newton's famous three laws of motion and showed how the principle of universal GRAVITATION could be used to explain the behavior not only of falling bodies on the earth but also planets and other celestial bodies in the heavens. To arrive at his results Newton invented one form of an entirely new branch of mathematics, the CALCULUS (also invented independently by G. W. Leibniz), which was to become an essential tool in much of the later development in most branches of physics. Other branches of physics also received attention during this period. William Gilbert, court physician to Queen Elizabeth I, published (1600) an important work on magnetism, describing how the earth itself behaves like a giant magnet. Robert Boyle (1627–91) studied the behavior of gases enclosed in a chamber and formulated the GAS LAW named for him; he also contributed to physiology and to the founding of modern chemistry. Newton himself discovered the separation of white light into a SPECTRUM of colors and published an important work on optics, in which he proposed the theory that light is composed of tiny particles, or corpuscles. This corpuscular theory was related to the mechanistic philosophy presented early in the 17th cent. by René Descartes, according to which the universe functioned like a mechanical system describable in terms of mathematics. A rival theory of light, explaining its behavior in terms of WAVES, was presented in 1690 by Christian Huygens, but the belief in the mechanistic philosophy together with the great weight of Newton's reputation was such that the wave theory gained relatively little support until the 19th cent. Meanwhile, during the 18th cent. the mechanics founded by Newton was developed by several scientists and received brilliant exposition in the *Analytical Mechanics* (1788) of J. L. Lagrange and the *Celestial Mechanics* (1799–1825) of P. S. Laplace. Daniel Bernoulli made important mathematical studies (1738) of the behavior of gases, anticipating the kinetic theory of gases developed more than a century later, and has been referred to as the first mathematical physicist. The accepted theory of heat in the 18th cent. viewed heat as a kind of fluid, called caloric; although this theory was later shown to be erroneous, a number of scientists adhering to it nevertheless made important discoveries useful in developing the modern theory, including Joseph Black (1728–99) and Henry Cavendish (1731–1810). Opposed to this caloric theory, which had been developed mainly by the chemists, was the less accepted theory dating from Newton's time that heat is due to the motions of the particles of a substance. This mechanical theory gained support in 1798 from the cannon-boring experiments of Count Rumford (Benjamin Thompson), who found a direct relationship between heat and mechanical energy. In the 19th cent. this connection was established quantitatively by J. R. Mayer and J. P. Joule, who measured the mechanical equivalent of heat in the 1840s. This experimental work and the theoretical work of Sadi Carnot, published in 1824 but not widely known until later, together provided a basis for the formulation of the first two laws of thermodynamics in the 1850s by William Thomson (later Lord Kelvin) and R. J. E. Clausius. The first law is a form of the law of conservation of energy, stated earlier by J. R. von Mayer and Hermann Helmholtz on the basis of biological considerations; the second law describes the tendency of energy to be converted from more useful to less useful forms. The atomic theory of matter had been proposed again in the early 19th cent. by the chemist John Dalton and became one of the hypotheses of the KINETIC-MOLECULAR THEORY OF GASES developed by Clausius and James Clerk Maxwell to explain the laws of thermodynamics. The kinetic theory in turn led to the statistical mechanics of Ludwig Boltzmann and J. W. Gibbs. The study of electricity and magnetism also came into its own during this period. C. A. Coulomb had discovered the inverse-square laws of electrostatics and magnetostatics in the late 18th cent. and Alessandro Volta had invented the electric battery, so that electric currents could also be studied. In 1820, H. C. Oersted found that a current-carrying conductor gives rise to a magnetic force surrounding it, and in 1831 Michael Faraday (and independently Joseph Henry) discovered the reverse effect, the production of an electric potential or current through magnetism (see INDUCTION); these two discoveries are the basis of the electric motor and the electric generator, respectively. Faraday invented the concept of the FIELD of force to explain these phenomena and Maxwell, from c.1856, developed these ideas mathematically in his theory of ELECTROMAGNETIC RADIATION. He showed that electric and magnetic fields are propagated outward from their source at a speed equal to that of light and that light is one of several kinds of electromagnetic radiation, differing only in frequency and wavelength from the others. Experimental confirmation of Maxwell's theory was provided by Heinrich Hertz, who generated and detected electric waves in 1886 and verified their properties, at the same time foreshadowing their application in radio, television, and other devices. The wave theory of light had been revived in 1801 by Thomas Young and received strong experimental support from the work of A. J. Fresnel and others; the theory was widely accepted by the time of Maxwell's work on the electromagnetic field, and afterward the study of light and that of electricity and magnetism were closely related. Thus, by the late 19th cent. most of classical physics was complete, and optimistic physicists turned their attention to what they considered minor details in the complete elucidation of their subject. Several problems, however, provided the cracks that eventually led to the shattering of this optimism and the birth of modern physics. On the experimental side, the discoveries of X RAYS by Wilhelm Roentgen (1895), RADIOACTIVITY by A. H. Becquerel (1896), the ELECTRON by J. J. Thomson (1897), and new radioactive elements by Pierre and Marie Curie raised questions about the supposedly indestructible ATOM and the nature of matter. Ernest Rutherford identified and named two types of radioactivity and in 1911 interpreted experimental evidence as showing that the atom consists of a dense, positively charged NUCLEUS surrounded by negatively charged electrons. Classical theory, however, predicted that this structure should be unstable. Classical theory had also failed to explain successfully two other experimental results that appeared in the late 19th cent. One of these was the demonstration by A. A. Michelson and E. W. Morley that there did not seem to be a preferred frame of reference, at rest with respect to the hypothetical luminiferous ETHER, for describing electromagnetic phenomena. In 1905, Albert Einstein showed that this result could be interpreted by assuming the equivalence of all inertial (unaccelerated) frames of reference and the constancy of the speed of light in all frames; Einstein's special theory of relativity eliminated the need for the ether and implied, among other things, that mass and energy are equivalent and that the speed of light is the limiting speed for all bodies having mass. Hermann Minkowski provided (1908) a mathematical formulation of the theory in which space and time were united in a four-dimensional geometry of space-time. Einstein extended his theory to accelerated frames of reference in his general theory (1916), showing the connection between acceleration and gravitation. Newton's mechanics was interpreted as a special case of Einstein's, valid as an approximation for small speeds compared to that of light. A second theoretical problem was the explanation of the distribution of electromagnetic radiation emitted by a BLACK BODY; experiment showed that at shorter wavelengths, toward the ultraviolet end of the spectrum, the energy approached zero, but classical theory predicted it should become infinite. This glaring discrepancy, known as the ultraviolet catastrophe, was solved by Max Planck's quantum theory (1900). In 1905, Einstein used the quantum theory to explain the photoelectric effect, and in 1913 Niels Bohr again used it to explain the stability of Rutherford's nuclear atom. In the 1920s the theory was extensively developed by Louis de Broglie, Werner Heisenberg, Wolfgang Pauli, Erwin Schrödinger, P. A. M. Dirac, and others; the new quantum mechanics became an indispensable tool in the investigation and explanation of phenomena at the atomic level. Dirac's theory, which combined quantum mechanics with the theory of relativity, also predicted the existence of ANTIPARTICLES. During the 1930s the first antiparticles were discovered, as well as other particles. Among those contributing to this new area of physics were James Chadwick, C. D. Anderson, E. O. Lawrence, J. D. Cockcroft, E. T. S. Walton, Enrico Fermi, and Hideki Yukawa. The discovery of nuclear fission by Otto Hahn and Fritz Strassmann (1938) and its explanation by Lise Meitner and Otto Frisch provided a means for the large-scale conversion of mass into energy, in accordance with the theory of relativity, and triggered as well the massive governmental involvement in physics that is one of the fundamental facts of contemporary science. The growth of physics since the 1930s has been so great that it is impossible in a survey article to name even its most important individual contributors. Among the areas where fundamental discoveries have been made are SOLID-STATE PHYSICS, PLASMA physics, and cryogenics, or LOW-TEMPERATURE PHYSICS. Out of solid-state physics, for example, have come many of the developments in electronics (e.g., the TRANSISTOR and microcircuitry) that have revolutionized much of modern technology. Another development is the MASER and LASER (in principle the same device), with applications ranging from communication and controlled nuclear fusion experiments to atomic clocks and other measurement standards. See R. P. Feynman, *The Character of Physical Law* (1967); K. W. Ford, *Basic Physics* (1968); Isaac Asimov, *Understanding Physics* (3 vol. 1966, repr. separately 1969); L. N. Cooper, *An Introduction to the Meaning and Structure of Physics* (1970); V. F. Weisskopf, *Physics in the Twentieth Century* (1972); I. M. Freeman, *Physics* (2d ed. 1973); J. B. Marion, *Physics: the Foundation of Modern Science* (1973).

physiocrats (fĭz'ēəkrăts"), school of French thinkers in the 18th cent. who evolved the first complete system of economics. They were also referred to simply as "the economists" or "the sect." The founder and leader of physiocracy was François QUESNAY. His most ardent disciple, Victor de Mirabeau, was the author of the physiocratic tax doctrine; Pierre Samuel DU PONT DE NEMOURS and Mercier de la Rivière elaborated on Quesnay's and Mirabeau's ideas. Among the antecedents of physiocracy the single-tax schemes of the marquis de Vauban and the sieur de BOISGUILBERT and the free-trade ideas of Vincent de GOURNAY may be cited. However, Quesnay's original contribution, and the basis of the doctrine, was the axiom that all wealth originated with the land and that agriculture alone could increase and multiply wealth. Industry and commerce, according to the physiocrats, were basically sterile and could not add to the wealth created by the land. They did not advocate that industry and commerce be neglected in favor of agriculture, but they tried to prove that no economy could be healthy unless agriculture were given the fullest opportunity. Agricultural methods had to be scientifically improved, and—above all—fair prices had to be maintained for agricultural production; according to Quesnay's maxim, only abundance combined with high prices could create prosperity. This could be obtained only if the "economic law," which the physiocrats envisaged as being as immutable as the law of gravity, was allowed to act untrammeled. Absolute freedom of trade was necessary to stabilize prices at a fair level, and laissez faire was to restore the economic process to its natural course, from which all further benefits would flow. To tax anything but the land was futile because only the land produced wealth and because manufacturers and traders pass their tax burden on to the farmer; only taxation at the very source of wealth was reasonable and economical—an argument not without charm for industrialists. However, the experiments of Baron TURGOT and of Holy Roman Emperor JOSEPH II, both somewhat influenced by the physiocrats, were failures—in part because of the unfavorable conditions in which they were carried out. Although physiocracy, because of its dogmatism, has become dead doctrine, it profoundly influenced Adam SMITH (who even intended to dedicate his *Wealth of Nations* to Quesnay) and thus the entire classical school of economists. Henry GEORGE virtually repeated the single-tax argument of Mirabeau. The physiocrats made no contribution to purely political thought except the idea of "legal despotism," by which the king and his government were to enforce the "economic laws of nature." Their fanaticism in economic doctrine was much ridiculed by their contemporaries, notably by Voltaire and by the Abbé Galiani. See Henry Higgs, *The Physiocrats* (1897, repr. 1963); Max Beer, *An Inquiry into Physiocracy* (1939, repr. 1966); R. L. Meek, *The Economics of Physiocracy* (1962).

physiology (fĭzēŏl'əjē), study of the normal functioning of animals and plants during life and of the activities by which life is maintained and transmitted. It is based fundamentally on the activities of protoplasm. The study of function is usually undertaken along with a study of structure (see ANATOMY), the two being intimately related. Since the discovery of the cell structure of tissues, the science of physiology has undergone rapid development. It includes the study of vital activities in cells, tissues, and organs—of processes such as contractility of muscle tissue, coordination through the nervous system, feeding, digestion, excretion, respiration, circulation, reproduction, and secretion. Virtually every specialized field in the biological sciences (e.g., embryology, pathology, botany, zoology) involves a consideration of the physiological aspects of its subject. The study of human physiology was stimulated by the development of medicine, and it embraces many chemical and physical principles. Plant physiology includes also the study of photosynthesis and transpiration. A separate and specialized branch, plant physiology arose from attempts to apply the findings of animal physiology to plants and in its turn contributed to the development of general physiology, especially in the study of cells.

physiotherapy: see PHYSICAL THERAPY.

pi, in mathematics, the ratio of the circumference of a circle to its diameter. The symbol for pi is π. The ratio is the same for all circles and is approximately 3.1416. It is of great importance in mathematics not only in the measurement of the circle but also in more advanced mathematics in connection with such topics as continued fractions, logarithms of imaginary numbers, and periodic functions. Throughout the ages progressively more accurate values have been found for π; an early value was the Greek approximation $3\frac{1}{7}$, found by considering the circle as the limit of a series of regular polygons with an increasing number of sides inscribed in the circle. About the mid-19th cent. its value was figured to 707 decimal places and by the mid-20th cent. an electronic computer had calculated it to 100,000 digits. It would have taken a man working without error eight hours a day on a desk calculator 30,000 years to make this calculation; it took the computer eight hours. The exact value of π cannot be computed. It was shown by the German mathematician Johann Lambert in 1770 that π is irrational and by Ferdinand Lindemann in 1882 that π is transcendental; i.e., cannot be the root of any algebraic equation with rational coefficients. The important connection between π and e, the base of natural logarithms, was found by Leonhard Euler in the famous formula $e^{i\pi} = -1$, where $i = \sqrt{-1}$.

Piacenza (pyächān'tsä), city (1971 pop. 106,461), capital of Piacenza prov., in Emilia-Romagna, on the Po River. It is an agricultural, commercial, and industrial center. Manufactures include agricultural machinery, chemicals, and food products. The city was a Roman stronghold (called Colonia Placentia) against the Gauls and was later occupied by the Goths, the Lombards, and the Franks. A free commune by the 12th cent., Piacenza joined the Lombard League. In 1545 it formed, with PARMA and its territory, the duchy of Parma and Piacenza, ruled, until 1731, by the FARNESE family. Noteworthy buildings include the Lombard-Gothic Palazzo del Comune (1281); the cathedral (1122–1233), with frescoes by Guercino; and the churches of San Savino (12th cent.) and Madonna di Campagna (16th cent.).

Piaf, Edith (pēäf'), 1915–63, French cabaret singer, whose original name was Edith Giovanna Gassion. She began to sing at 15 in cafés and in the streets of Paris and was soon engaged to sing in a cabaret. Fame quickly followed her appearances in nightclubs all over Europe and America. She made numerous recordings and strenuous tours. Piaf appeared in several movies, starring in *Le Bel Indifférent* (1940), originally a play written for her by Jean Cocteau. Her highly emotional and powerful voice was enormously expressive. Her performance of the song *Milord* was especially cherished by international audiences. See biography by her half sister Simone Berteaut (1972).

Piaget, Jean (zhäN pyä'jā), 1896–, Swiss psychologist, D.Sc. Univ. of Neuchâtel, 1918. In 1929 he became professor of child psychology and of history and scientific thought at the Univ. of Geneva. From 1937 to 1954 he was professor of psychology at the Univ. of Lausanne. He is known for his unique contributions to child psychology, especially for his theory of the child's cognitive and intellectual development, according to which development proceeds in genetically determined stages that always follow the same sequential order. Piaget has shown that young children reason differently from adults, and are often incapable of understanding logical reasoning. Philosophically, his approach is phenomenological: What a child says he is thinking or doing is what he is thinking or doing. Influenced by the French anthropologist Claude Lévi-Strauss, Piaget has written on the applications of dialectics and structuralism in the behavioral sciences in *Structuralism* (1970). He has also attempted a synthesis of physics, biology, psychology, and epistemology, published as *Biology and Knowledge* (1971). Piaget's writings also include *The Child's Conception of the World* (tr. 1929), *The Moral Judgment of the Child* (tr. 1932), *The Language and Thought of the Child* (tr. of 3d ed. 1962), *Six Psychological Studies* (tr. 1968), *The Psychology of the Child* (with Bärbel Inhelder, tr. 1969), *The Child's Conception of Time* (tr. 1970), *The Child's Conception of Movement and Space* (tr. 1970), *Genetic Epistemology* (tr. 1970), and

Insights and Illusions of Philosophy (tr. 1971). See studies by H. G. Furth (1969) and M. A. S. Pulaski (1971); R. I. Evans, *Jean Piaget: The Man and His Ideas* (tr. 1973); Howard Gardner, *The Quest for Mind* (1973).

Piankhi (pēäng'kē, -ăng'-), king of ancient NUBIA (c.741–c.715 B.C.). After subduing Upper Egypt, he defeated (c.721 B.C.) Tefnakhte, lord of Saïs, who had just completed the conquest of Lower Egypt. Piankhi was also victorious at Memphis. He returned (c.718 B.C.) to his Nubian capital, Napata, and erected a granite stele on which he inscribed an account of his campaigns. Piankhi's rule in Egypt was too brief to achieve much; immediately after his withdrawal Tefnakhte reestablished his rule of Lower Egypt.

piano or **pianoforte,** musical instrument whose sound is produced by vibrating strings struck by felt hammers that are controlled from a keyboard. Its earliest predecessor was the DULCIMER. The first piano was made c.1709 by Bartolomeo Cristofori (1655–1731), a Florentine maker of harpsichords, who called his instrument *gravicembalo col piano e forte.* (One of the two existing Cristofori pianos is in the Metropolitan Mus. of Art.) It differed from the harpsichord in that by varying the touch one could vary the volume and length of duration of tone. This expressive quality was shared by the clavichord, but the latter was far more delicate in tone. During the 18th cent. changes in musical taste gradually favored the piano's greater volume and expressiveness, and the instrument largely supplanted both the harpsichord and clavichord by 1800. C. P. E. Bach, Mozart, Haydn, and Clementi were the first major composers to write for the piano. The main body of its enormous literature is from the 19th cent., particularly the works of Beethoven, Czerny, Schubert, Chopin, Schumann, Mendelssohn, Brahms, Franck, Tchaikovsky, and Liszt. Debussy and Ravel used the special effects peculiar to the piano in a highly original way. In the 20th cent. some composers, notably Bartók, have emphasized the piano's percussive qualities. The piano was originally built in the shape of a harpsichord, and this style, the grand piano, has always been the standard form. It was greatly improved by the 19th-century innovation of an iron framework, best applied by the Steinways of New York City. The square piano, with strings parallel to the keys, was the most popular domestic piano until the perfection, in Philadelphia, of the upright piano early in the 19th cent. The English piano maker John Broadwood (1732–1812) was the first to develop the present heavier, more sonorous instrument. In 1810 the double-action striking mechanism, which permits rapid repetition of a tone, was perfected. In the late 19th cent. a mechanical PLAYER PIANO was developed. A perforated paper roll was passed over a cylinder containing apertures connected to tubes that were in turn connected to the piano action. As often as a hole in the paper passed over an aperture a current of air passed through a tube and caused the corresponding hammer to strike the string. An electric piano has also been developed. See Ernest Hutcheson, *The Literature of the Piano* (3rd ed. 1964); Oscar Bie, *History of the Pianoforte* (2d ed. 1966); Herbert Westerby, *History of Pianoforte Music* (1924, repr. 1970); Alfred Dolge, *Pianos and their Makers* (1911, repr. 1972).

Piast (pyäst), 1st dynasty of Polish dukes and kings. Its name was derived from that of its legendary ancestor, a simple peasant. The first historic member, Duke MIESZKO I (reigned 962–92), began the unification of Poland and introduced Christianity. His son, BOLESLAUS I, was crowned king in 1025 with papal approval. However, some of his successors did not claim the royal crown. His successors were MIESZKO II (reigned 1025–34), CASIMIR I (reigned c.1040–1058), BOLESLAUS II (reigned 1058–79), LADISLAUS HERMAN (reigned 1079–1102), and BOLESLAUS III (reigned 1102–38). For his four sons Boleslaus III created four hereditary duchies—SILESIA, MASOVIA, Great Poland (with Gniezno and Poznan), and SANDOMIERZ. In addition, the royal throne at Kraków and the rest of the Polish territory was to be held by the oldest member of the dynasty; thus the supreme power would pass in rotation to the different branches. This law of succession caused the temporary disintegration of the kingdom. However, CASIMIR II (who, probably a posthumous child, was left out of Boleslaus's will) united Masovia and Sandomierz under his power, was made duke at Kraków in 1177, and secured (1180) for his descendants the hereditary right to the kingship. Nevertheless, dynastic struggles resumed after Casimir's death (1194) and continued until LADISLAUS I restored the royal authority in 1320. With the death (1370) of his son, CASIMIR III, the Piast dynasty ended in Poland; it was finally succeeded by the JAGIELLO dynasty. Another branch of the Piasts ruled as dukes of Masovia until 1526. In 1339, Casimir III had officially recognized John of Luxemburg, king of Bohemia, as suzerain over the Piast domains in Silesia, which in the meantime had broken up into many principalities. The Silesian Piasts, as vassals of Bohemia and mediate princes of the Holy Roman Empire, retained the ducal title and continued to hold the duchy of Oppeln until 1532 and the principalities of Brieg, Liegnitz, and Wohlau until their extinction in 1675.

Piatigorsky, Gregor (pyätĭgôr'skē), 1903–, Ukrainian-American cellist. Piatigorsky studied with his father and then at the Moscow Conservatory. In 1924 he became first cellist of the Berlin Philharmonic, leaving in 1928 to devote his time to solo work. He moved to the United States in 1929, where he has taught and performed with enormous success. Concertos have been written for him by several composers, including Hindemith and Prokofiev.

Piatra-Neamt (pyä'trä-nyämts), city (1970 est. pop. 54,000), NE Rumania, in the Bacău region. Oil refining, food processing, and the manufacture of chemicals are among the industries. Landmarks include the 15th-century church of St. Ion Domnescu and the St. Ion Tower.

Piauí (pyouē'), state (1970 pop. 1,680,954), 96,886 sq mi (250,935 sq km), NE Brazil, on the Atlantic Ocean. TERESINA is the capital.

Piave (pyä'vā), river, c.137 mi (220 km) long, rising in the Carnic Alps, Venetia, NE Italy, and flowing generally S, past Belluno, to the Gulf of Venice. The upper Piave basin is subject to severe seasonal flooding (see VAIONT DAM). Hydroelectric power is produced along the upper Piave; the lower river is used for irrigation. In World War I, after their defeat at Caporetto (1917), the Italians withdrew to the Piave. Despite fierce onslaughts by the Austrians, the line was held until Oct., 1918, when the Austrians were routed by a combined Allied attack.

Piazzetta, Giovanni Batista (jōvän'nē bätēs'tä pēätsĕt'tä), 1682–1754, Italian painter. An exponent of the Venetian school, Piazzetta combined soft colors with a dramatic, chiaroscuro technique reminiscent of CARAVAGGIO. His informal brushwork and shimmering figures foreshadowed ROCOCO style and influenced his pupil TIEPOLO. Among his major works are *Glory of St. Dominic* (1727; in the church of Santi Giovanni e Paolo, Venice), *The Fortune Teller* (c.1745; Accademia, Venice), and a series of charcoal studies of the nude. Engravings of his paintings by Pietro Monaco brought them international attention.

Piazzi, Giuseppe (jōōzĕp'pä pyät'tsē), 1746–1826, Italian astronomer, a Theatine priest from 1769. He became (1781) professor of mathematics at the Univ. of Palermo, supervised construction of a government observatory (opened 1791) at Palermo, and was its first director. He also established a government observatory at Naples (1817). He was the first to discover (Jan. 1, 1801) an asteroid and named it Ceres. In 1803 he published a catalog of the fixed stars, and in 1814 he enlarged it to include 7,646 stars. He wrote *Lezioni elementari di astronomia* (1817).

Pi-beseth (pī-bē'sĕth), biblical name of BUBASTIS.

Picabia, Francis (pĕkä'bēä), 1878–1953, French painter. After working in an impressionist style, Picabia was influenced by CUBISM and later was one of the original exponents of DADA in Europe and the United States. He contributed to avant-garde periodicals and became associated with the Paris surrealists. Picabia, possessed of an intensely individual temperament, influenced numerous artists of different schools without ever confining himself to one mode of artistic expression. His *Physical Culture* (1913) is at the Philadelphia Museum of Art.

Picard, Edmond (ĕdmôN' pēkär'), 1836–1924, Belgian jurist and author. A brilliant lawyer, he was at various times president of the Belgian bar association and a member of the supreme court. He wrote two works that explore the similarities between law and art: *Paradox sur l'avocat* (1881) and *Le Juré* (1887). Many of his novels are autobiographical, recounting his adventures as a sailor and explorer; notable among them is *L'Amiral* (1884). Picard also wrote seven plays.

Picard, Jean, 1620–82, French astronomer, noted for having made the first accurate measurement of a degree of the earth's meridian. The figures he established were of great value to Newton in his calculation of the force of gravitation. Picard, who had previously been the prior of Rillé, in Anjou, went to Paris to occupy the chair of astronomy in the Collège de France in 1655. He determined (1671) the latitude and longitude of Tycho Brahe's observatory at Ven (now Landskrona, Sweden) in order to be able to use Brahe's observations of the positions of heavenly bodies. To him is due in great part the establishment of the Paris Observatory and of the *Connaissance des temps,* the first five volumes (1679–83) of which he wrote.

Picardy (pĭk'ərdē), Fr. *Picardie,* region and former province, N France, on the English Channel. It includes the Somme, Oise, and Aisne depts. and has three main geographical regions: the plateau north of Paris, which is an important wheat and beet area; the Somme River valley, with manufacturing cities like Amiens, Abbeville, and Saint-Quentin; and the coast, with fishing and commercial seaports like Boulogne-sur-Mer and Calais and beach resorts such as Le Touquet and Le Crotoy. The name Picardy appeared about the 13th cent., designating the many small feudal holdings added to the crown by Philip II. During the Hundred Years War the area was contested by France and England. Louis XI occupied it in 1477, securing it for France. The word *Picard,* always vaguely used, also applies to the people of neighboring Artois.

Picasso, Pablo (Pablo Ruiz y Picasso) (pä'blō pēkä'sō; rōōēth' ē), 1881–1973, Spanish painter, sculptor, graphic artist, and ceramist, who worked in France. He was the leader of the SCHOOL OF PARIS and is generally considered in his technical virtuosity, enormous versatility, and incredible originality and prolificacy to have been the foremost figure in 20th-century art. A precocious draftsman, he was admitted to the advanced classes at the Royal Academy of Art in Barcelona at 15. After 1900 he spent much time in Paris, remaining there from 1904 to 1947, when he moved to the South of France. His power is revealed in his very early works, some of which were influenced by Toulouse-Lautrec (such as *Old Woman,* 1901; Philadelphia Mus. of Art). Picasso's artistic production is usually described in terms of a series of overlapping periods. In his "blue period" (1901–4) he depicted the world of the poor. Predominantly in tones of blue, these melancholy paintings (such as *The Old Guitarist,* 1903; Art Inst. of Chicago) are among the most popular art works of the century. Canvases from Picasso's "rose period" (1905–8) are characterized by a lighter palette and greater lyricism, with subject matter often drawn from circus life. Picasso's studio attracted the major figures of the avant-garde at this time, including Matisse, Braque, Apollinaire, and Gertrude Stein. He had already produced numerous engravings of great power and began his work in sculpture during these years. In 1907, Picasso painted *Les Demoiselles d'Avignon* (Mus. of Modern Art, New York City), a radical departure from the artistic ideas of the preceding ages and now considered the most significant work in the development toward CUBISM and modern abstraction (see MODERN ART). The influence of Cézanne and of African sculpture is apparent in its fragmented forms and unprecedented distortions. The painting heralded the first phase of cubism, called analytic cubism. This severe, intellectual style was conceived and developed by Picasso, Braque, and Gris c.1909–12. Picasso's *Female Nude* (1910–11; Philadelphia Mus. of Art) is a representative painting and his *Woman's Head* (1909; Mus. of Modern Art, New York City) a representative sculpture of this style. In the synthetic phase of cubism (after 1912) his forms became larger and more representational, and flat, bright decorative patterns replaced the earlier, more austere compositions. *The Three Musicians* (1921; Mus. of Modern Art, New York City) exemplifies this style. Picasso's cubist works established firmly that the work of art may exist as a significant object beyond any attempt to represent reality. As an offshoot of the experiments of this period, Picasso introduced several new techniques, including COLLAGE and papier collé. Picasso's enormous energy and fecundity was manifested by another development. In the 1920s he drew heavily on classical themes and produced magnificent monumental nudes and monsters that were reminiscent of antiquity and rendered with a certain anguished irony. These works appeared simultaneously with synthetic cubist paintings. Picasso was for a time saluted as a forerunner of SURREALISM, but his intellectual approach was basically antithetical to the irrational aesthetic of the surrealist painters. He sought to strengthen the emotional impact of his work and became preoccupied with the delineation of agony. In 1937 the bombing of the Spanish town of Guernica impelled him to produce his second landmark painting, *Guernica* (Mus. of Modern Art, New York City), an impassioned allegorical condemnation of facism and war. In his later years Picasso turned to creations of fantasy and comic invention. He worked consistently in sculpture, ceramics, and in the graphic arts, producing thousands of superb drawings, illustrations, and stage designs. With unabated vigor he painted brilliant variations on the works of other masters, including Delacroix and Velázquez, and continued to explore new aspects of his personal vision until his death at 91. By virtue of his vast energies and overwhelming power of invention Picasso remains outstanding among the masters of the ages. See biographical studies by Gertrude Stein (1938); Alfred Barr, Jr. (1946, rev. ed. 1966); Wilhelm Boeck (1955); A. F. Blunt and P. Pool (1962); Jean Leymarie (1972); Roland Penrose (rev. ed. 1973); Roland Penrose, *The Sculpture of Picasso* (1967); Pierre Daix and Georges Boudaille, *Picasso: The Blue and Rose Period* (tr. 1967); Douglas Cooper, *Picasso Theatre* (1968); Christopher Czwiklitzer, *Picasso's Posters* (tr. 1971); J. E. Cirlot, *Picasso: Birth of a Genius* (1972); Roland Penrose and John Golding, ed., *Picasso in Retrospect* (1973); Domenico Porzio and Marco Valsecchi, *Understanding Picasso* (1974).

Picayune (pĭkəyo͞on'), city (1970 pop. 10,467), Pearl River co., S Miss., near the Pearl River and the La. line; inc. 1904. It is the trade, processing, and shipping center for a tung tree, beef cattle, and dairy area. Tung oil and by-products, truck bodies, and blankets are among the city's varied products. The Earth Resources Research Center is on a former NASA rocket test site nearby.

Piccadilly (pĭk"ədĭl'ē), street of the City of Westminster borough, London, England. Starting at Piccadilly Circus (London's center of traffic and amusement), it runs to Hyde Park Corner. It is a street with shops, hotels, and clubs. The Albany, a club, was the residence of T. B. Macaulay, W. E. Gladstone, Edward Bulwer-Lytton, and George Canning.

Piccard, Auguste (ōgüst' pēkär'), 1884–1962, Belgian physicist, b. Basel, Switzerland. He became a professor of physics at the Polytechnic Institute of the Univ. of Brussels in 1922. He is known for his balloon ascents into the stratosphere; in May, 1931, he reached an altitude of 51,793 ft (15,787 m), and in Aug., 1932, he ascended to 55,500 ft (16,916 m). He was a close collaborator with Einstein in the development of instruments for measuring radioactivity. In 1946 he turned his attention to the ocean depths, making several notable dives with his son off the coast of Africa in a bathyscaphe of his own design. In 1953 he descended off the west coast of Italy to 10,330 ft (3,149 m). In 1960 his son, Jacques Piccard, descended to 35,800 ft (10,912 m) in the Marianas Trench.

Piccinni or **Piccini, Niccolò** (both: nēk-kōlô' pēchēn'nē, pēchē'nē), 1728–1800, Italian composer of more than 100 operas. His early works were very successful in Italy, and *La buona figliuola,* also known as *La Cecchina* (1760), an opera buffa, established his reputation throughout Europe. In 1776 he went to Paris, where the opponents of Gluck made him their unwilling champion in the quarrel over Italian operatic tradition versus Gluck's new realism. When the French Revolution began, Piccinni returned to Italy, but shortly before his death he was recalled to France to receive a position at the Paris Conservatory.

Piccirilli (pē"chērēl'lē), family of Italian-American marble cutters and sculptors. In 1888, the father and six sons, all sculptors, migrated from Italy and established a highly successful workshop in New York City. Specializing in cutting large works in stone from smaller models, they enlarged and cut figures for such leading American sculptors as MacMonnies, Saint-Gaudens, and D. C. French. French's figure of Lincoln in the Lincoln Memorial, Washington, D.C., is the most notable of these. Of the sons, Attilio and Furio achieved individual fame as sculptors. **Attilio Piccirilli,** 1866–1945, executed allegorical figures for the Maine monument in Columbus Circle, New York City, and for the north pediment of the Wisconsin state capitol building, Madison. Other works include numerous fauns and nymphs. See biography by J. V. Lombardo (1944). **Furio Piccirilli,** 1868–1949, is best known for his groups for the Court of the Seasons for the San Francisco Panama-Pacific Exposition, and for his execution of the entire sculptural decoration of the house of the provincial legislature in Winnipeg, Man., Canada.

piccolo, small transverse FLUTE pitched an octave higher than the standard flute. Its tone is bright and shrill, and it can produce the highest notes in the

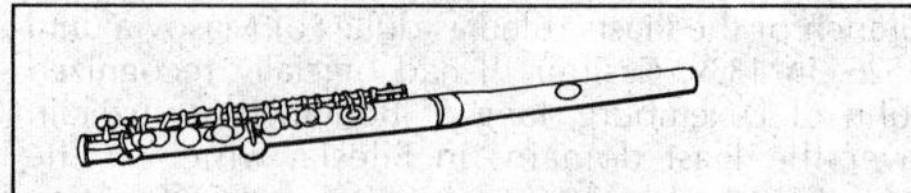

Piccolo

orchestral range. The piccolo is used in orchestras and especially in military bands. See FIFE.

Piccolomini, Enea Silvio de': see PIUS II.

Piccolomini, Ottavio (ōt-tä'vyō pēk-kōlô'mēnē), 1599–1656, Italian general in the service of the Holy Roman emperor during the Thirty Years War (1618–48). He came of a distinguished Sienese family. After fighting in Bohemia, Hungary, the Netherlands, and Italy, he served under General WALLENSTEIN (after 1627) and was a commander of Wallenstein's bodyguard. He was punished for extortion (1629) but was, nevertheless, among those who urged the reinstatement of Wallenstein, who had been dismissed from imperial service in 1630. Piccolomini distinguished himself (1632) at the battle of Lützen. He later supported the conspiracy that led to Wallenstein's deposition (1634) as imperial commander. He served (1636–39) in the Spanish army and was named duke of Amalfi (1639) for his services by Philip IV of Spain. Rejoining the imperial forces, he was defeated at Breitenfeld (1642), after which he again served the Spanish. Appointed (1648) lieutenant general in the imperial army, his service was terminated by the war's end. He was an imperial plenipotentiary in the negotiations for the execution of the Peace of Westphalia and in 1650 was created prince of Hagenau in the Holy Roman Empire.

Pic du Midi d'Ossau (dôsō'), double peak, 10,322 ft (3,146 m) high, SW France, in the Pyrenees, near the Spanish border. It is in a winter-sports area. The village of Gabas lies at its foot.

Pichegru, Charles (shärl pēshgrü'), 1761–1804, French general in the FRENCH REVOLUTIONARY WARS. Successful on the Rhine front (1793), he invaded (1794) the Netherlands, entered (1795) Amsterdam and captured the Dutch fleet, which had frozen in the ice. In the same year, however, he secretly negotiated with the Austrians in an attempt to restore the monarchy, to which his own fortune was tied. Pichegru deliberately allowed the Austrians to retake Mannheim. Recalled by the DIRECTORY, he was relieved of his command. A deputy to the Council of Five Hundred (1797), Pichegru was elected its president by the royalist majority. He was later arrested in the coup d'etat of 18 Fructidor (1797), but he escaped to England. He returned to France in 1803 to carry out a royalist conspiracy with Georges CADOUDAL. Pichegru was arrested but was found strangled in his cell before the trial.

pichiciago (pĭch"ĭsēä'gō): see ARMADILLO.

Pichincha (pēchēn'chä), volcano, 15,918 ft (4,852 m) high, N Ecuador, near Quito. It last erupted in 1881. On its lower slopes, in the decisive battle of Pichincha on May 24, 1822, patriot forces under Antonio José de Sucre routed the Spanish royalists and freed the territory that was to become Ecuador.

Pickel, Konrad: see CELTES, CONRADUS PROTUCIUS.

Pickens, Andrew, 1739–1817, American Revolutionary soldier, b. near Paxtang, Pa. He moved (1752) to South Carolina and took part (1761) in frontier warfare against the Cherokee Indians. During the American Revolution, Pickens rose in rank from captain of militia to brigadier general. He took part in the victories at Kettle Creek (1779) and at Cowpens, Augusta, and Eutaw Springs (all in 1781). Prominent in local politics, he served (1781–93, 1800–12) in the state legislature, was (1793–95) a U.S. Congressman, and frequently served as commissioner for Indian relations in the South. See A. N. Waring, *The Fighting Elder: Andrew Pickens* (1962).

Pickens, Francis Wilkinson, 1805–69, American politician, b. Colleton District, S.C.; grandson of Andrew Pickens. A lawyer, he served in the state house of representatives and was an ardent supporter of NULLIFICATION. Pickens was a Democrat in Congress (1834–43) and was minister to Russia (1858–60). Under his administration as governor of South Carolina (1860–62), the state seceded and demanded the surrender of the Federal forts in Charleston harbor.

Pickens, Fort: see FORT PICKENS.

picker: see HARVESTER.

pickerel: see PIKE.

pickerelweed, common name for the Pontederiaceae, a family of chiefly tropical perennial aquatic herbs found in fresh water. The pickerelweeds (genus *Pontederia*) range north into temperate regions, including most of the E United States and Canada. The water hyacinth (*Eichhornia crassipes*), a native of tropical America, has spread widely and is so prolific that it has clogged many waterways in the S United States and in other countries, including Java and Australia. It is sometimes cultivated in tanks and ponds for its ornamental foliage and blue-violet flowers. The pickerelweed family is classified in the division MAGNOLIOPHYTA, class Liliatae, order Liliales.

Pickering, Edward Charles, 1846–1919, American astronomer and physicist, b. Boston, grad. Harvard (B.S., 1865); brother of W. H. Pickering. He was professor of physics (1868–77) at the Massachusetts Institute of Technology and was the first in the United States to initiate general instruction in physics in a laboratory equipped with instruments and apparatus. The results of work in photographic photometry and spectroscopy done under his direction at the Harvard Observatory are recorded in more than a quarter of a million plates. Pickering devised several instruments, including the meridian photometer, used in the measurements. He set up a station in Arequipa, Peru, to observe the southern sky. In addition to editing 70 volumes (1855–1919) of the *Annals of Harvard Observatory,* he wrote *Elements of Physical Manipulations* (2 vol., 1873–76).

Pickering, Timothy, 1745–1829, American political leader and Revolutionary War army officer, b. Salem, Mass. He was admitted to the bar (1768) and played an active part in pre-Revolutionary activities against the British. In 1774 and 1775 he was connected with the Massachusetts committee of correspondence. A colonel in the Massachusetts militia, he joined George Washington's army in the American Revolution, served (1777) as Washington's adjutant-general, was a member of the board of war, and was (1780–85) quartermaster general. After the Revolution, he moved to Pennsylvania and was sent by the Pennsylvania government to the Wyoming valley region of Pennsylvania to organize the newly formed Luzerne co. and to represent the state in the dispute over land claims between Connecticut settlers and Pennsylvania. He was a member of the state constitutional convention (1789–90) and negotiated treaties with various Indian tribes for the Federal government. He was Postmaster General (1791–95), Secretary of War (1795), and Secretary of State (1795–1800). Pickering was dismissed after President John Adams learned that he had been scheming with the Alexander Hamilton branch of the Federalist party to steer the United States into war with France. Returning to Massachusetts, he became chief justice of the court of common pleas and was later a U.S. Senator (1803–11) and Representative (1813–17). A strong Federalist and an opponent of Adams, Pickering was a leading figure in the ESSEX JUNTO and an outspoken opponent of the War of 1812. He wrote *Political Essays* (1812). See biography by his son, Octavius Pickering, and C. W. Upham (4 vol., 1867–73); G. H. Clarfield, *Timothy Pickering and American Diplomacy, 1795–1800* (1969).

Pickering, William: see WHITTINGHAM, CHARLES.

Pickering, William Henry, 1858–1938, American astronomer, b. Boston, grad. Massachusetts Institute of Technology (B.S., 1879). He taught at the Massachusetts Institute of Technology (1880–87) and at Harvard Observatory. Between 1878 and 1901 he led five solar eclipse expeditions and established several observatories and astronomical stations. Pickering discovered (1899) the ninth satellite of Saturn, called Phoebe, and also announced (1905) the finding of a tenth satellite, which was not confirmed until 1967. In 1919 he predicted the existence and the location of a ninth planet, discovered later and named Pluto. His observations of the moon, including the study of lunar craters, is of lasting importance. He also accomplished important work in photographing the planets and measuring their brightness. His later researches were devoted to Mars. In addition to a number of papers in astronomical journals, his publications include *The Moon* (1903), *Lunar and Hawaiian Physical Features Compared* (1906), and *Mars* (1921).

picketing, act of patrolling a place of work affected by a strike in order to discourage its patronage, to make public the workers' grievances, and in some cases to prevent strikebreakers from taking the strikers' jobs. Picketing may be by individuals or by groups. It has also been used by political movements to influence legislation or to protest governmental policies. In the United States the use of pickets was for a long time held by the courts to be unlawful because of its intimidatory aspects and because it was considered harmful to the interests of the employer. Court decisions have in many cases set limits upon the number of pickets allowed, placed a firm ban on mass picketing, and also prohibited the use of vile and obscene language and of threatening gestures by the pickets. Some state laws have interdicted any picketing except when a majority of the pickets are employees of the firm involved and then only in issues directly relating to wages, hours, and working conditions.

Pickett, George Edward, 1825-75, Confederate general in the American Civil War, b. Richmond, Va. After distinguishing himself in the Mexican War (especially at Chapultepec), Pickett served on the Texas frontier (1849-55) and in Washington Territory (1856-61). He figured prominently in the SAN JUAN BOUNDARY DISPUTE as commander of the small U.S. force that occupied the island in 1859. On Virginia's secession Pickett resigned from the army, and in Feb., 1862, he became a Confederate brigadier general. He fought in the Peninsular campaign and was severely wounded at Gaines's Mill in the Seven Days battles. After his return to the army in Oct., 1862, he was promoted to major general and given a division in James Longstreet's corps. He is best remembered for his part in the GETTYSBURG CAMPAIGN. His assault, famous as "Pickett's charge," on the Union center on Cemetery Hill (July 3, 1863) resulted in the virtual annihilation of his division. Pickett later commanded in North Carolina and in 1864 was one of the defenders of Petersburg. See A. C. Inman, ed., *Soldier of the South: General Pickett's War Letters to his Wife* (1913, repr. 1971); study ed. by C. G. Laird (1965).

Pickett, Joseph, 1848-1918, American primitive painter, b. New Hope, Pa., where he lived all his life. He worked as a carpenter, canal-boat builder, and grocer. At about age 65, Pickett turned to painting. His best-known paintings exhibit a strong clarity of design and color; they are *Manchester Valley* (Mus. of Modern Art, New York City), *Washington Under the Council Tree* (Newark Mus., N.J.), and *Coryell's Ferry, 1776* and *Washington Taking Views* (Whitney Mus., New York City).

Pickford, Mary, 1893-, American movie actress, b. Toronto, Ont. As a child Pickford appeared in stock companies and later in two Belasco productions in New York. In 1909 she began working with D. W. Griffith and soon became known as "America's Sweetheart" in such films as *A Poor Little Rich Girl* (1917), *Pollyanna* (1919), *Tess of the Storm Country* (1922), and *Little Lord Fauntleroy* (1921). In 1919 she was a cofounder of United Artists with D. W. Griffith, Charlie Chaplin, and Douglas Fairbanks, her husband. She won an Academy Award for *Coquette* (1929). Pickford is married to the actor Buddy Rogers. See her autobiography (1955); biography by Robert Windeler (1974).

pickle, general term for fruits or vegetables preserved in vinegar or brine, usually with spices or sugar or both. Vegetables commonly pickled include the beet, cabbage, cauliflower, cucumber, olive, onion, pepper, and tomato. Mixed pickles include piccalilli, chowchow, mustard pickles, and chutney. Dill pickles are cucumbers matured in a brine of dill leaves and seed heads. Sweet pickles are made from various fruits or vegetables—e.g., tomatoes, cucumbers, peaches, or plums—with sugar added. Pickles have limited nutritional value and are often used as appetizers. Before the invention of refrigeration they served as a sort of winter substitute for salads. Cucumbers, the most commonly pickled of all vegetables, are placed underripe in 10% brine, allowed to undergo a lactic acid fermentation, soaked in hot water to remove excess salt, and then covered with vinegar and other ingredients. In a wider sense, a pickle is an acid or saline liquid, such as brine or saltpeter for meat, limewater or water glass for eggs, brandy for fruit, or alcohol for laboratory specimens.

Pickthall, Marjorie Lowry Christie (pĭk'thôl), 1883-1922, Canadian poet, b. England. Her poetry is notable for the freshness and intensity with which she treats nature. Among her volumes of poetry are *The Drift of Pinions* (1914) and *The Woodcarver's Wife and Other Poems* (1922). She also wrote a collection of short stories and two novels. Her complete poems appeared in 1937.

picnic, social gathering at which each participant generally brings food to be commonly shared. The Picnic Society was formed in London early in the 19th cent. by a group of fashionable people for purposes of social entertainment. Each member was expected to provide a share of the entertainment and of the refreshments, and this idea of mutual sharing or cooperation was fundamental to the original significance of the picnic. Later the word took on the additional meaning of an outdoor pleasure party. The word as now used includes almost every type of informal, outdoor meal or festivity, such as clambake, BARBECUE, or fish fry. The custom of cooperative dining is ancient; Greek men of letters are known to have held reunions where each guest contributed his quota of the food.

Pico (pē'kō) [Port., = peak], island (1960 pop. 21,626), 167 sq mi (433 sq km), in the N Atlantic, one of the central AZORES. It takes its name from the volcanic mountain, Pico Alto [high peak], which rises to 7,711 ft (2,350 m).

Pico della Mirandola, Giovanni, Conte (jōvän'nē kōn'tā pē'kō dĕl'lä mērän'dōlä), 1463-94, Italian philosopher and humanist. To many in the age of the Renaissance, Pico was the ideal man, whose physical beauty reflected his inner harmony. He appears in *Cortegiano* of Baldassare Castiglione. In 1484 he went to Florence where he soon became one of the most active members of Lorenzo de'Medici's Platonic Academy and the chief exponent of Italian Neoplatonism. His studies in Hebrew led to the composition of his celebrated 900 theses on a reconciliation of Christianity with Platonic philosophy. In 1487 he was forced to recant 13 propositions, and his clash with Pope Innocent VIII led to his arrest (1488) at Lyons. Although attacked by the church, Pico's theses were an important symbol of the Renaissance blending of Christian and Greek ideas. Lorenzo invited him back to Florence, where he remained until his death, becoming a follower of Girolamo Savonarola. His works include *Heptaplus,* a mystical account of the creation; *De ante et uno;* and an unfinished attack on astrology. Sir Thomas More's *Life of John Picus, Earl of Mirandula* is a translation of the biography by Pico's nephew, Giovanni Francesco, (1890). See selections of his works, tr. by C. F. Wallis, et al. (1965); Pearl Kibre, *The Library of Pico della Mirandola* (1936, repr. 1966).

Pico Rivera (pē'kō rĭvĕr'ə), city (1970 pop. 54,170), Los Angeles co., S Calif., on the San Gabriel and Rio Hondo rivers; inc. 1958 with the union of Pico and Rivera into one community. Among the city's many manufactures are automobiles, chemicals, furniture, and toys.

Picquart, Georges (zhôrzh pēkär'), 1854-1914, French general. As chief of the army intelligence section in 1896, he discovered that the memorandum that had been used to convict Captain Dreyfus (see DREYFUS AFFAIR) had probably been the work of Ferdinand Walsin ESTERHAZY. Higher officials warned Picquart to conceal his discovery; he persisted and was sent (Dec., 1896) to Tunis and demoted. After the trial of Émile ZOLA, Picquart was accused of forging the note that had convinced him of Esterhazy's guilt. He was dismissed from the service and arrested for forgery. The exoneration of Dreyfus in 1906 also served to absolve Picquart, who was promoted to general and entered Georges Clemenceau's cabinet as minister of war.

picquet: see PIQUET.

picric acid (pĭk'rĭk) or **2,4,6-trinitrophenol** (trī"-nī"trōfē'nōl), $C_6H_2(NO_2)_3OH$, a yellow crystalline solid that melts at 122°C and is soluble in most organic solvents. Picric acid is a PHENOL derivative with a highly acidic hydroxyl hydrogen; it reacts with active metals to form metal picrates, which are highly sensitive EXPLOSIVES. Picric acid is itself an explosive; like TNT (trinitrotoluene), it requires a detonator. It is the basic ingredient in the high explosives lyddite (British), melinite (French), and shimose (Japanese). Although picric acid can be synthesized by nitration of phenol, higher yields are obtained if chlorobenzene is used as a starting material; the latter method involves several steps and the formation of several intermediate products. In addition to its use in explosives, picric acid has been used as a yellow dye, as an antiseptic, and in the synthesis of chloropicrin, or nitrotrichloromethane, CCl_3NO_2, a powerful insecticide.

Pictor, Fabius: see under FABIUS.

Pictou (pĭk'tōō, pĭktōō'), town (1971 pop. 4,250), N N.S., Canada, on Pictou Harbour, an inlet of Northumberland Strait. It is a lobster-fishing port and the terminal of a ferry to Prince Edward Island. It has shipbuilding and repairing industries, and there are coal mines in the area. Pictou was settled (1763) by a group of colonists from Philadelphia and later received many settlers from the Scottish Highlands.

Picts, ancient inhabitants of central and N Scotland, of uncertain origin. First mentioned (A.D. 297) by the Roman writer Eumenius as northern invaders of Roman Britain, they were probably descendants of late Bronze Age and early Iron Age invaders of Britain. Their language is thought to have been a superimposition of Celtic on a pre-Celtic and non-Indo-European language, but there is no undisputed interpretation of it or their culture. By the early 7th cent. there was a unified Pictish kingdom north of a line from the Clyde to the Forth rivers. It apparently had a matrilinear system of succession and had probably adopted Celtic Christianity. To the south of the Picts, Scottish invaders from Ireland had established the kingdom of Dalriada in the 5th cent. Between 843 and 850 KENNETH I, king of Dalriada, established himself also as king of the Picts, although how and why is not clear. The kingdom of Alba thus formed became the kingdom of Scotland. See H. M. Chadwick, *Early Scotland* (1949); W. C. Dickinson, *Scotland from the Earliest Times to 1603* (rev. ed. 1965); Isabel Henderson, *Picts* (1967).

Pictured Rocks National Lakeshore: see NATIONAL PARKS AND MONUMENTS (table).

picturesque, term used in 18th-century England to refer to a landscape that looked as if it had come out of an academic painting. Used as derogatory criticism of such painting, the picturesque was considered pretty rather than beautiful.

piculet (pĭk'yələt), common name for a small bird of the family Picidae, which includes the WOODPECKER and the wryneck. Like the true woodpeckers, piculets are large-headed and have long, sticky tongues, but they lack the stiff, balancing tail feathers of the larger woodpeckers. Hence, while they can climb vertically, they are often found perched on horizontal branches. Their short, rounded bills also lack the power to drill into living trees and are used instead to probe for insects and larvae in rotted logs. Gray or olive green above with black-marked, white underparts, piculets are found throughout the tropical forests of both the Old and New Worlds. A common species is the Antillean piculet, *Nesoctites micromegas.* Solitary and vagrant birds, piculets lay from two to eight glossy white eggs per clutch in unlined tree-hole nests. Both mates share in incubation and in the care of the young, which are blind and featherless. Piculets are classified in the phylum CHORDATA, subphylum Vertebrata, class Aves, order Piciformes, family Picidae.

pidgin (pĭj'ən), a LINGUA FRANCA that is not the mother tongue of anyone using it and that has a simplified grammar and a restricted, often polyglot vocabulary. Pidgins that have developed from English and other tongues have been employed in different regions since the 17th cent. An example is the variety of pidgin English that resulted from contacts between English traders and the Chinese in Chinese ports. In fact, the word *pidgin* supposedly is a Chinese (Cantonese) corruption of the English word *business.* Another well-known form of pidgin English is the *Beach-la-Mar* (or *Bêche-de-Mer*) of the South Seas. The different kinds of pidgin English have preserved the basic grammatical features of English, at the same time incorporating a number of non-English syntactical characteristics. The great majority of words in pidgin English are of English origin, but there are also Malay, Chinese, and Portuguese elements. As a result of bringing to the Caribbean area large numbers of Negro slaves from West Africa who spoke different languages, other pidgins evolved in that region that were based on English, Portuguese, French, and Spanish. See Robert A. Hall, Jr., *Pidgin and Creole Languages* (1966); John J. Murphy, *The Book of Pidgin English* (rev. ed., 1966); Dell Hymes, ed., *Pidginization and Creolization of Languages* (1971).

pie, meat, fish, fowl, fruit, or vegetables baked with a crust of PASTRY, or pastry shells filled with custard or pudding. The pies of the Romans, especially at banquets in the days of the empire, were often elaborate concoctions, such as the showpieces in which were enclosed live birds. In England meat and fish pies had become common by the 14th cent., and fruit pies, often called tarts, by the 16th cent. The mince pie was an important feature of the Christmas festivities and was called superstitious pie by the Puritans in protest against what seemed to them a pagan manner of celebrating a holy feast. The mincemeat filling was a finely chopped, cooked mixture including raisins, currants, apples, suet, sugar, spice, and often meat, brandy or cider, candied peel, and other ingredients. The English settlers in North America retained their taste for pie and adapted it to their new conditions, creating the pumpkin and the cranberry pies. Pie has remained a popular dessert in the United States. In Italy, pie, or PIZZA, consists, in its most basic form, of a spread of dough covered with tomatoes and mozzarella cheese and baked in an oven.

piecework, work for which the laborer is paid on the basis of the amount of work done. The system is best adapted to standardized operations in which quantity is preferred to quality. Its advocates maintain that it pays the worker according to his ability. Its opponents argue that it tends to pay the best worker what he would receive on a time basis, while other workers receive less than they would by the hour and that it forces the pace of work. In the United States the 1949 amendment to the WAGES AND HOURS ACT in effect required that pieceworkers be paid at least the minimum wage.

Piedmont (pēd'mŏnt), Ital. *Piemonte,* region (1971 pop. 4,434,802), 9,807 sq mi (25,400 sq km), NW Italy, bordering on France in the west and on Switzerland in the north. TURIN is the capital of the region, which is divided into the provinces of Alessandria, Asti, Cuneo, Novara, Turin, and Vercelli (named for their capitals). The mostly mountainous and hilly region has the Alps in the north and west and the Apennines in the south. In the more elevated parts of Piedmont, forest products and fruit are produced and cattle are raised. In the fertile valley of the upper Po River wheat, maize, rice, grapes, honey, and chestnuts are grown. Piedmont has considerable industry, powered in part by well-developed hydroelectric facilities and aided by an extensive transportation network. Manufactures include motor vehicles (mainly at Turin), textiles, clothing, leather goods, aluminum, chemicals, wine, and office machines. There is a substantial tourist industry, notably at Lago Maggiore in the northeast. The area of Piedmont was incorporated by Rome in the 1st cent. B.C. It came to be known as Piedmont by the 13th cent., growing out of Turin and IVREA, western marches of the Lombard kingdom of Italy. Created in the 10th cent., the marches passed by marriage (11th cent.) to the Savoy dynasty. In the 12th cent. free communes were instituted in many cities, while others remained under feudal lords. Besides the counts (later dukes) of Savoy, the marquises of Saluzzo and MONTFERRAT were powerful nobles. By the 15th cent. Savoy emerged as the chief power. The French often entered Piedmont via the strategic Mont Cenis and Mont Genèvre passes through the Alps, either as allies or as enemies; they greatly influenced Piedmontese history and culture. Moreover, Piedmont was a major battlefield in the Italian Wars (15th-16th cent.), the wars of Louis XIV, and the French Revolutionary Wars. The dukes of Savoy, who in 1720 became kings of Sardinia, had acquired all of present-day Piedmont by 1748. From 1798 to 1814, Piedmont was held by France. After 1814, the region became the nucleus of Italian unification during the RISORGIMENTO, and Turin was the first capital (1861-64) of the new Italian kingdom. Valle d'AOSTA was part of Piedmont until 1945. There is a university at Turin.

Piedmont, city (1970 pop. 10,917), Alameda co., W Calif., within the confines of Oakland; inc. 1907. It is a hilly, residential city, with no industry. Many of its homes enjoy a spectacular view of the San Francisco Bay area.

piedmont, any area near the foot of a mountain, particularly the plateau (the Piedmont) extending from New York to Alabama E of the Appalachian Mts. and W of the Atlantic coastal plain. In Maryland, Virginia, and North Carolina it is E of the Blue Ridge Mts. The plateau is cut by numerous small rivers, whose fall line is along the eastern edge of the plateau.

Pied Piper of Hamelin, legendary figure of Hameln, Germany. He rid the town of its rats and mice by charming them away with his flute playing. When the citizens refused to pay him the price they had agreed upon, he charmed away their children out of revenge. Allegedly this occurred in 1284. Among those who immortalized this legend are Goethe, Robert Browning, and the brothers Grimm.

Piedras Negras (pyā'thräs nā'gräs) [Span.,=black stones], ruined city of the Classic era of the MAYA, NW Petén, Guatemala, in the Usumacinta valley. Reaching a peak of sculptural achievement (according to one dating system, between 731 and 795), Piedras Negras developed some of the finest pre-Columbian stonework.

Piedras Negras, city (1970 pop. 65,883), Coahuila state, N Mexico, on the Rio Grande opposite Eagle Pass, Texas. Founded in 1849, the city grew as an international shipping point. There is a large steel blast furnace. The surrounding valley is under cultivation, and coal is mined in the vicinity. In 1888, Piedras Negras was renamed Ciudad Porfirio Díaz in honor of the dictator, but the old name was restored after his overthrow.

Piegan Indians (pē'găn): see BLACKFOOT INDIANS.

Piekary Śląskie (pyĕkä'rĭ shlôN'skyĕ), town (1970 pop. 36,300), S Poland, in the Katowice mining and industrial region. Its manufactures include mining equipment, metals, and chemicals.

pieplant: see BUCKWHEAT.

pier, in engineering, term applied to a mass of reinforced concrete or masonry supporting a large structure, such as a bridge. When piers are built on ground of poor bearing value, it is often necessary to drive piles to obtain a firm base. Construction of piers built in riverbeds is facilitated by the use of cofferdams or caissons. Structures that extend out from the shore and over the water, serving as a place to land passengers and merchandise from vessels, are also known as piers. They are used in many harbors when there is ample width of stream; in New York harbor, for example, great economy of shore front is realized by building piers out at right angles to the shore. These piers are generally built on pile foundations. In architecture the term applies to the clustered Gothic pillar, to a wall between openings, and to a detached masonry mass serving as a gate post.

Pierce, Franklin, 1804-69, 14th President of the United States (1853-57), b. Hillsboro, N.H., grad. Bowdoin College, 1824. Admitted to the bar in 1827, he entered politics as a Jacksonian Democrat, like his father, Benjamin Pierce, who was twice elected governor of New Hampshire (1827, 1829). He served in the New Hampshire general court (1829-33), being speaker in 1831 and 1832, and had an undistinguished career in the U.S. House of Representatives (1833-37) and in the U.S. Senate (1837-42). On resigning from the Senate, he achieved success as a lawyer in Concord, N.H., and continued to be important in state politics. A strong nationalist, he vigorously supported and then served in the Mexican War, becoming a brigadier general of volunteers. In 1852 the Democratic party was split into hostile factions led by William L. MARCY, Stephen A. Douglas, James Buchanan, and Lewis Cass, none of whom could muster sufficient strength to secure the presidential nomination. Pierce, personally charming and politically unobjectionable to Southerners since he favored the COMPROMISE OF 1850, was made the "dark horse" candidate by his friends. He won the nomination (on the 49th ballot) and went on to defeat the Whig candidate, Gen. Winfield SCOTT, his commander in the Mexican War. His desire to smooth over the slavery quarrel and unite all factions of the Democratic party was reflected in the composition of his cabinet, for which he chose such outstanding sectional representatives as Marcy, Jefferson DAVIS, and Caleb CUSHING. A vigorous expansionist foreign policy was adopted, but it failed in most of its objectives. After the BLACK WARRIOR affair (1854), which brought the United States to the brink of war with Spain, Pierce authorized his European ministers, Pierre Soulé, John Y. Mason, and Buchanan, to confer on the means by which the United States might acquire Cuba. Their report, the so-called OSTEND MANIFESTO, was leaked to the press and caused such an uproar that the administration was forced to disavow it. Troubled relations with Great Britain were not improved by the U.S. naval bombardment (1854) of SAN JUAN DEL NORTE, British protectorate in Nicaragua; the filibustering activities of William WALKER further aggravated Central American affairs. Moves to annex Hawaii, acquire a naval base in Santo Domingo, and purchase Alaska ended fruitlessly. One achievement, the successful Japanese expedition of Commodore Matthew C. PERRY, had been initiated in Millard Fillmore's administration. On the domestic scene Pierce stood for development of the West (the GADSDEN PURCHASE was made during his administration), but plans for a transcontinental railroad fell through. The KANSAS-NEBRASKA ACT enraged many Northerners and precipitated virtual civil war between the pro- and antislavery forces in Kansas. Pierce, by that time very unpopular, was passed over by the Democrats for renomination, and Buchanan succeeded him. Pierce's opposition to the Civil War made him more than ever disliked in the North, where he died in obscurity. See biography by R. F. Nichols (rev. ed. 1958).

Pieria (pīēr'ēə), region of ancient Macedonia, W of the Thermaic Gulf (the modern Gulf of Thessaloníki). It included Mt. Pierus, an early seat of the worship of Orpheus and the Muses, and Mt. Olympus. The Muses were sometimes called the Pierides, a name given also to nine daughters of the legendary King Pierus of Macedonia. They contested with the Muses in song, were defeated, and were changed into magpies.

Pierino del Vaga: see PERINO DEL VAGA.

Pierné, Henri Constant Gabriel (äNrē' kôNstäN' găbrēĕl' pyĕrnā'), 1863-1937, French organist, conductor, and composer; pupil of Massenet and César Franck. His cantata *Edith* won the Prix de Rome in 1882. He succeeded Franck as organist at Ste Clotilde, 1890-98, and was chief conductor (1910-32) of the COLONNE Concerts. He was elected to the Académie des Beaux-Arts in 1924. His most popular works are the oratorio *La Croisade des Enfants* (1905) and the piano piece *Marche des petits soldats de plomb.* He also wrote eight operas, instrumental and orchestral music, and songs.

Piero della Francesca (pyĕ'rō dĕl'lä fränchās'kä), c.1420-1492, major Italian Renaissance painter, b. Borgo San Sepolcro. All his masterpieces were created in towns of central Italy, but early contact with the art of Florence proved decisive in Piero's development. In the *Baptism of Christ* (National Gall., London) he had already absorbed the Florentine theories of perspective and added his own acute perception of nature. He delighted in the play of mathematical ratios and painted *The Flagellation of Christ* (Urbino) in a perfect, geometric framework. His most famous cycle, *The Story of the True Cross* (1452-66; Church of San Francesco, Arezzo), depicts scenes from the *Golden Legend.* Particularly notable are the imposing portrayal of the *Queen of Sheba,* the stately array of battle scenes, and the stark night scene of the *Dream of Constantine.* He painted several court portraits, including one of *Sigismondo Malatesta before his Patron Saint,* a simplified geometric conception. This contrasts with the scrupulous detail he used in painting the profile portraits of the Duke and Duchess of Urbino (Uffizi). Piero also executed the awesome *Resurrection* (Borgo San Sepolcro) and several altarpieces, parts of which have been lost or scattered. One panel of a saint is in the Frick Collection, New York. He always painted slowly and deliberately, and toward the end of his life his activity slackened. *The Nativity* (National Gall., London) and *Virgin and Child with Saints* (Brera, Milan) are among the few pictures he produced in his later years. Devoting himself to works of a more theoretical nature, he wrote *Libellus de V Corporibus regularibus* (MS in Vatican Library) and *De Prospectiva pingendi* (MS in Ambrosian Library, Milan). See studies by Kenneth Clark (2d ed. 1970) and C. de Tolnay (1966).

Piero di Cosimo (dē kô'zēmō), 1462-1521, Florentine painter, whose name was Piero di Lorenzo. He adopted the name of his master, Cosimo Rosselli, whom he accompanied to Rome in 1482 and assisted in the decorating of the Sistine Chapel. His religious works have charm, but more important are his animated mythological scenes. Commissioned by the Florentine Francesco Pugliese, he painted many works depicting the life of primitive man. Among these pictures are the *Hunting Scene* and the *Return from the Hunt* (both: Metropolitan Mus.); *Discovery of Honey* (Worcester Mus.); *Discovery of Wine* (Fogg Mus., Cambridge); and *Vulcan and Aeolus* (National Art Gall. of Canada, Ottawa). Other well-known works by Piero are the *Death of Procris* (National Gall., London) and *Simonetta Vespucci* (Chantilly). The influence of Leonardo da Vinci is evident in some of his work, including the *Portrait of a Woman with a Rabbit* (Yale Univ.). See biography by R. L. Douglas (1946); S. J. Freedberg, *Painting of the High Renaissance* (1961).

Piérola, Nicolás de (nēkōläs' dā pyä'rōlä), 1839-1913, president of Peru (1879-81, 1895-99). Minister of finance under José Balta, he was accused of misappropriating funds and was exiled. From Chile he invaded Peru and unsuccessfully attempted to stir up revolution. Later he was allowed to return (1879) to take part in the war against Chile (see PACIFIC, WAR OF THE). When Mariano I. Prado abandoned Peru, Piérola took over the government, but continued failure in the war caused his own flight. He did not succeed in another attempt to seize the government in 1885. After ousting Andrés A. CÁCERES in 1894, he became president again and set about the reconstruction of devastated Peru by initiating fiscal, military, religious, and civil reforms.

Pierpont, Francis Harrison, 1814-99, Union leader in Virginia during the American Civil War, "Father of West Virginia," b. near Morgantown, Va. (now W.Va.). When Virginia seceded, he became a leader of the disaffected Unionist forces in the western part of Virginia and was elected head of the government set up by the Wheeling Convention of June, 1861. This government granted (1862) the approval, necessary under the Constitution, for the organization of the western counties into a new state, West

Virginia. Pierpont himself was never governor of West Virginia. After the admission (1863) of that state to the Union, he served as governor of "restored" Virginia (i.e., that part under Federal control but not incorporated in West Virginia). After the war he remained as governor until 1868. He himself seems to have spelled his name Pierpoint. See biography by C. H. Ambler (1937).

Pierpont Morgan Library, originally the private library of J. Pierpont Morgan, in 1924 made a public institution by his son J. P. Morgan as a memorial to his father. The library is privately supported; it is located at Madison Ave. and 36th St., New York City. It is especially rich in illuminated manuscripts and in authors' manuscripts (including works by Dickens, Scott, and Balzac); it has hundreds of Bibles in all languages, one of the largest collections of Aldine Press editions (see ALDUS MANUTIUS), and the only perfect copy of Malory's *Morte d'Arthur* printed by Caxton. In 1973 its holdings were estimated as 65,000 volumes. The publications of the library include monographs, catalogs of collections and exhibits, reprints, and fascimiles. It is open to scholars for research and to the general public for exhibitions and lectures.

Pierre (pēr), city (1970 pop. 9,699), state capital (since 1889) and seat of Hughes co., central S.Dak., on the east bank of the Missouri River, opposite Fort Pierre; inc. 1883. Its economy is centered around agriculture (chiefly grains and cattle) and the state government. Originally the fortified capital of the Aricara Indians, it served as the trade center of the middle Missouri River from 1822 to 1855. From 1876 to 1885 it was the steamboat head for the Black Hills gold trade. The city boomed with the arrival of the railroad (1880), becoming an important trading and shipping center for a farm and ranch area. A U.S. Indian school is there, and Oahe Dam, a major unit of the Missouri River basin project, is nearby.

Pierre de La Ramée: see RAMUS, PETRUS.

Pierrelatte (pyĕrlät'), town (1968 pop. 9,873), Drôme dept., SE France. The center of France's nuclear industry, Pierrelatte has a large uranium-producing complex. Other industries include jute weaving and the manufacture of wooden containers.

Pierrot (pē''ərō') [Fr.,=little Peter], character in French pantomime. A buffoon, he wore a loose white tunic with big buttons, balloon sleeves, and white pantaloons. His face was painted white. A creation of Giuseppe Giaratone or Geratoni (fl. 1639–97), Pierrot was introduced to early 19th-century France by DEBURAU.

Piers Plowman: see LANGLAND, WILLIAM.

Pietarsaari (pē'ĕtärsä''rē), Swed. *Jakobstad,* city (1970 pop. 18,725), Vaasa prov., W Finland, on the Gulf of Bothnia. It is an important port and industrial center. Most of the inhabitants speak Swedish. The city was founded in 1652. The Finnish national poet J. L. Runeberg was born (1804) there.

Pietermaritzburg (pē''tərmăr'ĭtsbûrg''), city (1970 pop. 112,666), capital of Natal, E South Africa, in the foothills of the Drakensberg Range. The city is an administrative and industrial center. Its products include wattle bark extract, furniture, footwear, chocolate, cloth, and diesel engines. Motor vehicles are assembled in the city, and iron ore is mined nearby. Pietermaritzburg was founded in 1838 and named for Piet Retief and Gert Maritz, Boer leaders of the Great Trek (see TREK). The Boers made it capital of the short-lived (1839–43) Voortrekker Republic of Natal.The city became capital of Natal when the province was annexed by Great Britain in 1843. In 1880 a railroad to Durban was opened. Pietermaritzburg is the seat of the Univ. of Natal (1909), a technical college, Natal Museum, and Tatham Art Gallery. Points of interest include the Church of the Vow (1839), built to commemorate the 1838 Boer victory over Zulu forces; Fort Napier, erected by the British in 1843; and the Provincial Council Buildings. Natal Lion Park is nearby. The city's name is sometimes shortened to Maritzburg

Pietersburg (pē'tərzbûrg''), city (1970 pop. 27,058), Transvaal, NE South Africa. It is primarily the commercial center for the surrounding agricultural area. Iron and other minerals are mined nearby. Pietersburg was founded in 1884 and named for Petrus (Piet) Joubert, a BOER general. In 1900 during the SOUTH AFRICAN WAR it was for a short time the capital of both the TRANSVAAL and the ORANGE FREE STATE. It was occupied by British troops in 1901. Nearby are Kruger National Park and the Univ. of the North (1959), which serves nearby black Africans.

Pietism (pī'ətĭzəm), a movement in the Lutheran Church, most influential between the latter part of the 17th cent. and the middle of the 18th. It was an effort to stir the church out of a settled attitude in which dogma and intellectual religion seemed to be supplanting the precepts of the Bible and religion of the heart. The first great leader was Philipp Jakob SPENER, who began (1670) to hold devotional meetings. His *Collegia Pietatis* were designed to bring Christians into helpful fellowship and increase Bible study. Spener's book, *Pia desideria* (1675), emphasized the need of earnest Bible study and the belief that the lay members of the church should have part in the spiritual control. Although Spener did not intend separation from the church, his repudiation of the importance of doctrine and his desire to limit church membership to those who had experienced personal regeneration tended to undermine orthodoxy, and Pietism was severely attacked. After Spener's death the work was carried on by August Hermann FRANCKE, but after his time Pietism declined. Its effect was strongest in N and central Germany, but reached into Switzerland, Scandinavia, and other parts of Europe. A number of foreign missions were begun. Through Count Zinzendorf the Moravian Church was influenced by it. Pietism earned a lasting place in the European intellectual tradition through its influence on such figures as Kant, Schleiermacher, and Kierkegaard. Although the movement bore resemblance to aspects of Puritanism, e.g., use of distinctive dress and the renunciation of worldly pleasures, the essential aim of the true Pietist was to place the spirit of Christian living above the letter of doctrine.

Pietro d'Abano: see ABANO, PIETRO D'.

piezoelectric effect (pīē''zōĭlĕk'trĭk), voltage produced between surfaces of a solid dielectric (nonconducting substance) when a mechanical stress is applied to it. A small current may be produced as well. The effect, discovered by Pierre Curie in 1883, is exhibited by certain crystals, e.g., quartz and Rochelle salt, and ceramic materials. When a voltage is applied across certain surfaces of a solid that exhibits the piezoelectric effect, the solid undergoes a mechanical distortion. Piezoelectric materials are used in TRANSDUCERS, e.g., phonograph cartridges, microphones, and strain gauges, which produce an electrical output from a mechanical input, and in earphones and ultrasonic radiators, which produce a mechanical output from an electrical input. Piezoelectric solids typically resonate within narrowly defined frequency ranges; when suitably mounted they can be used in electric circuits as components of highly selective filters or as frequency-control devices for very stable oscillators.

pig: see SWINE.

pigeon, common name for members of the large family Columbidae, land birds, cosmopolitan in temperate and tropical regions, characterized by stout bodies, short necks, small heads, and thick, heavy plumage. The names dove and pigeon are used interchangeably, though the former generally refers to smaller members of the family. The rock dove *Columba livia* of temperate Europe and W Asia is the wild progenitor of the common street and domestic pigeons. All pigeons have soft swellings (ceres) at the base of the nostrils, feed their young with "pigeon's milk" regurgitated from the crops of the parents, and have specialized bills through which they can suck up water steadily, unlike other birds. They eat chiefly fruits and seeds. The Australasian region has two thirds of the 289 species of pigeons, of which the fruit pigeons are the most colorful and the gouras, or crowned pigeons, the largest (to 33 in./84 cm). Many species are valued as game birds; their close relationship to the Gallinae (e.g., pheasants and turkeys) is illustrated by the sand grouse, an Old World pigeon named for its resemblance to the grouse. From the time of Noah pigeons—especially homing pigeons, which are also used as racing birds—have been used for carrying messages. Although electronics has largely replaced them as messengers, they are still of experimental importance. It is thought that they may navigate by the sun. Monogamous and amorous, pigeons are known for their soft cooing calls. The most common American wild pigeon is the small brown mourning dove *Zenaidura carolinensis* (sometimes called turtledove), similar to the once abundant passenger pigeon, which was slaughtered indiscriminately and became extinct in 1914. Other wild American species are the band-tailed, red-billed, and white-crowned pigeons, all of the genus *Columba,* and the gray ground dove *Chamaepelia passerina.* In Europe the turtledove, rock pigeon or dove, stock dove, and ringdove or wood pigeon are common. Domesticated varieties developed by selective breeding include the fantail, with numerous erectile tail feathers; the Jacobin, with a hoodlike ruff; the tumbler, which turns backward somersaults in flight; the pouter, with an enormous crop; and the quarrelsome carrier, with rosettelike eyes and nose wattles. In religion and art the dove symbolizes peace and gentleness, and in Greek mythology it was sacred to Aphrodite. The long-extinct dodo and solitaire were members of this order. Pigeons are classified in the phylum CHORDATA, subphylum Vertebrata, class Aves, order Columbiformes, family Columbidae.

pigeon English: see PIDGIN.

Piggott, Lester Keith, 1935–, British jockey. A major figure in British horse racing after 1955, Piggott rode over 100 winners a year in several racing seasons. He gained particular success in classic British races such as the Derby, which he won six times (1954, 1957, 1960, 1968, 1970, 1972) and in French races as well.

pig iron: see IRON.

pigment, substance that imparts color to other materials. In paint, the pigment is a powdered substance which, when mixed in the liquid vehicle, imparts color to a painted surface. The pigments used in paints are nearly all metallic compounds, but organic compounds are also used (see LAKE). Most black pigments are organic, e.g., bone black (animal black or charcoal) and lampblack. Some of the metallic pigments occur naturally. The brilliant and beautiful coloring of the rock and soil in some parts of the United States, especially in the Grand Canyon of the Colorado River, the Painted Desert of Arizona, and Bryce and Zion canyons of Utah, is largely produced by such compounds, chiefly oxides. Yellow ocher, sienna, and umber are oxides of iron. Litharge is a yellow oxide of lead. Red lead is also an oxide of this metal. Lead chromate, or chrome yellow, is an important yellow pigment. White lead, or basic lead carbonate, is a pigment long in use; it is rendered more durable by mixture with zinc oxide. Cadmium yellow is a sulfide of cadmium. Ultramarine is an important blue pigment, as is Prussian blue (ferric ferrocyanide). Green pigment is produced by mixing Prussian blue and chrome yellow. Vermilion (mercuric sulfide) is red. Pigments occur in plant and animal bodies. The bright colors of plants, for example, are the result of the presence of such substances as chlorophyll (green) and xanthophyll (yellow), both of which are also found in some animals. Among others are carotene, the yellow of carrots and certain other vegetables, and anthocyanin, which imparts blue, red, and purple to flowers. Blood receives its color from the hemoglobin in the red corpuscles. Coloration of human skin is caused by the presence of pigments (see PIGMENTATION).

pigmentation, name for the coloring matter found in certain plant and animal cells and for the color produced thereby. Pigmentation occurs in nearly all living organisms. Almost all plants synthesize their own pigments; animals either derive pigments from plant foods or synthesize them themselves. In plants the major pigments are the carotenes (reddish orange to yellow), the anthocyanins (red, blue, and violet), and the chlorophylls (green). The red and yellow colors of autumn foliage are due to the exposure of the anthocyanins after the green chlorophyll pigments, which usually mask them, have decomposed and faded. The major animal pigments are the hemes (red) of blood hemoglobin, the carotenes, the melanins (black and brown), and guanine (white and iridescent). The latter three produce the surface coloration of most animals. In humans the degree of darkness of the skin, hair, and iris of the eye depends primarily on the amount of melanin present. The presence of hemoglobin and carotene in the BLOOD contributes to skin color. Moles and freckles are caused by high local concentrations of melanin; albinism by a lack of melanin; and some birthmarks, e.g., "strawberry marks," by an unusual local proliferation of blood vessels (and hence of hemoglobin) near the skin surface. Tanning of human skin results from an increase of melanin production under the stimulation of ultraviolet light. The coloration of an organism may be caused by deposits of organic pigments in the tissues (as in human skin or in plant leaves), by optical effects of the refraction of light rays (as in mollusk shells and in some butterfly wings and bird feathers), or by a combination of both (see COLOR). The different modes are illustrated in the baboon and the mandrill: the predominantly brown coloring is due to melanin, but the red and blue markings are also caused by melanin, in the latter case by the refraction of light due to specific spatial arrangements of the pigment granules in the skin areas involved. The pigmentation of many animals is adapted to their environment and aids in their survival (see MIMICRY; PROTECTIVE COLORATION). In some animals the pigment is changeable; the flounder and the squid, for example, are capable of adapting themselves to the color of their background and thus often of escaping detection by their enemies. The exact mechanism of such changeability is not clearly understood, but in most cases it is due primarily to visual stimulation. In the squid the chromatophores (containing melanin granules) are controlled by muscles and can expand from an almost invisible pinpoint to 60 times their original size, giving the whole animal a dark appearance. Pigmentation changes are also at least partially controlled by hormones—as, in part, is pigmentation synthesis itself. Pigments not only provide external coloration but also function in some important physiological processes. In the retina of the eye the pigment cells (rods and cones) adjust or regulate the entering light (see VISION). Among its other functions, carotene operates in the synthesis of vitamins and of chlorophyll. Chlorophyll is essential for plant PHOTOSYNTHESIS. Hemoglobin in the blood carries oxygen for respiration. Chlorophyll and hemoglobin are structurally quite similar, both belonging to the pyrrole group of pigments.

Pigmy: see PYGMY.

pignolia: see PINE NUT.

pignut hickory: see HICKORY.

Pigou, Arthur Cecil (pĭ'gōō), 1877–1959, British economist, grad. King's College, Cambridge. He was a lecturer at University College, London, and at Cambridge. He was professor of political economy at Cambridge from 1908 to 1943. He served as a member of the committee on currency and foreign exchange (1918) and of the royal commission on income tax (1919). He was a leading exponent of the theory that economic waste due to unemployment, poor health, and poor housing is a responsibility of society, which should bear the costs. Among his many works are *Wealth and Welfare* (1912), *The Economics of Welfare* (1920), *The Political Economy of War* (1921; new ed., 1941), *The Theory of Unemployment* (1933), *Socialism versus Capitalism* (1937), and *Income: an Introduction to Economics* (1946).

pigweed, name for several weedy plants, particularly the common pigweed or lamb's-quarters of the family Chenopodiaceae (GOOSEFOOT family), the rough pigweed, or green AMARANTH, of the family Amaranthaceae (AMARANTH family), and the winged pigweed, a TUMBLEWEED. Pigweeds are classified in the division MAGNOLIOPHYTA, class Magnoliopsida, order Caryophyllales.

Pi-hahiroth (pī'-həhī'rəth), place in Egypt, between Migdol and Baal-zephron, where the Israelites encamped. Ex. 14.2,9; Num. 33.7.

pika (pī'kə), short-haired mammal related to RABBITS and HARES, also called mouse hare and rock rabbit. Pikas live above the timber line in the mountains of N Asia and W North America. The pika differs from the rabbit in that its body is smaller and the ears on its blunt head are shorter; also unlike the rabbit, the fore and hind limbs are about equal in length. The pika moves with a scampering gait. Its fur varies from red to gray and covers the soles of its feet. Pikas generally shelter in communities beneath rocks, although some Asian species burrow. Their diet consists primarily of green plants. Because food is difficult to obtain in winter in the harsh tundra environment, pikas cut, sun-dry, and store vegetation for winter use. Pikas are classified in the phylum CHORDATA, subphylum Vertebrata, class Mammalia, order Lagomorpha, family Ochotonidae.

Pike, Albert, 1809–91, American lawyer, Confederate general in the Civil War, b. Boston. He settled (1832) in Arkansas, where he became a newspaper editor and a lawyer. He was a captain in the Mexican War. In the Civil War, Pike secured for the Confederacy the loyalty of the tribes in the Indian Territory. Criticized for inept handling of his Indian brigade, especially at the battle of Pea Ridge (March, 1862), he resigned. After the war he practiced law in Memphis and Washington. His *Prose Sketches and Poems Written in the Western Country* (1834) resulted from a trip over the Santa Fe Trail. A prominent Freemason (he joined the order in 1850), his writings on the movement include *Morals and Dogma of the Ancient and Accepted Scottish Rite of Freemasonry* (1871). See biography by R. L. Duncan (1961).

Pike, James Albert, 1913–1969, American Protestant Episcopal bishop, b. Oklahoma City. He was admitted to the California bar in 1936 and began a successful career as a lawyer. While serving (1943–45) in the U.S. navy he decided to study for the Episcopal ministry, although he had been raised as a Roman Catholic. He was ordained a deacon in the Protestant Episcopal Church and served as chaplain at George Washington Univ. After being ordained a priest in 1946 he studied at Union Theological Seminary, from which he received a B.D. in 1951. He was rector of Christ Church in Poughkeepsie, N.Y., and Episcopal chaplain at Vassar (1947–49) and then became chaplain and head of the religion department at Columbia. From 1952 to 1958 he was dean of the Cathedral of St. John the Divine in New York City and also continued teaching at Columbia. From his post at St. John, Pike criticized McCarthyism and became an outspoken advocate of civil rights and planned parenthood. In 1958 he was appointed bishop of California, serving until 1966. He outlined misgivings about church doctrine, including that of the Virgin birth and the Trinity, in *A Time for Christian Candor* (1963). In 1966 he joined the Center for Democratic Institutions, and two years later he renounced the church to form the Foundation for Religious Transition. He died while on an expedition in the Judean desert. Among his many books are *Beyond Anxiety* (1953); *The Church, Politics, and Society* (with J. W. Pyle, 1955); *The Next Day* (1957); and *The Other Side* (1967). See *Search* by his wife, D. K. Pike (1970); William Stringfellow and Anthony Towne, *The Bishop Pike Affair* (1967).

Pike, Zebulon Montgomery, 1779–1813, American explorer, an army officer, b. Lamberton (now part of Trenton), N.J. He joined the army (c.1793) and was commissioned second lieutenant in 1799. In 1805 he led an exploring party to search for the source of the Mississippi River; although he mistakenly identified Red Cedar Lake (now Cass Lake) in Minnesota as the source, he was not far wrong. After his return he was sent on an expedition (1806–7) to explore the headwaters of the Arkansas and Red rivers and to reconnoiter Spanish settlements in New Mexico. Pike and his men went up the Arkansas River to the site of Pueblo, Colo., and explored much of the country, sighting the peak that is named after him, Pikes Peak. When he and a small party went to the Rio Grande, they were taken into custody by the Spanish who brought them to Santa Fe and then to Chihuahua and finally released them at the border of the Louisiana Territory. Upon his return, Pike was accused of complicity in the plot of Aaron BURR and James WILKINSON to detach Western territory from the United States, but he was exonerated by the Secretary of War. Pike was promoted to the rank of brigadier general during the War of 1812. He was killed while commanding his troops during the successful assault on York (now Toronto). See his journals (ed. by Donald Jackson, 2 vol., 1966) and biographies by W. E. Hollon (1949, repr. 1970) and John Terrell (1968).

pike, common name for the family Esocidae, freshwater game and food fishes of Europe, Asia, and North America. The pike, the muskellunge, and the pickerel form a small but well-known group of long, thin fishes with spineless dorsal fins, large anal fins, and long, narrow jaws with formidable teeth. There are five species in the single genus *Esox,* found in the lakes and streams of central and E North America. The muskellunge, named by the American Indians, is the largest of these, averaging from 2 to 7 ft (61–213.5 cm) in length and from 10 to 20 lb (4.5 to 9 kg) in weight, though some may reach 60 lb (27 kg). Carnivorous and solitary except at spawning time, muskellunges feed on fish, frogs, snakes, and even the young of aquatic mammals and waterfowl. The American, northern, or great northern pike, *Esox lucius,* called jackfish in Canada, is also voracious, lurking in weedy shallows to ambush its prey. This pike, believed to be the same species as the European pike, is said to consume one fifth of its own weight (10–35 lb or 4.5–16 kg) daily. The pickerels are smaller members of the family. The grass, or barred, pickerel rarely exceeds 1 ft (30 cm) in length and 1 lb (.45 kg) in weight; the larger Eastern pickerel is found in clear lakes and streams together with bass. Pikes are stubborn fighters and are valued as game fishes; their flesh, though bony, is delicious. The walleyed pike is really a PERCH. Pikes are classified in the phylum CHORDATA, subphylum Vertebrata, class Osteichthyes, order Clupeiformes, family Esocidae.

pike, in U.S. history: see TURNPIKE.

pike, weapon: see SPEAR.

Pikes Peak, 14,110 ft (4,301 m) high, central Colo., in the Front Range of the Rocky Mts.; discovered by U.S. explorer Zebulon Pike in 1806. There are many higher peaks in the Rockies, but this is the best known and most conspicuous because of its location on the edge of the Great Plains. At its eastern base is Colorado Springs; to the north is Denver. Its summit, generally snow covered, is reached by a cog railroad and a highway.

Pikesville, uninc. city (1970 pop. 25,395), Baltimore co., central Md., a residential suburb of Baltimore; settled in the late 18th cent.

Piła (pē'lä), Ger. *Schneidemühl,* town (1970 pop. 43,778), NW Poland. Once the capital of Grenzmark Posen-West Prussia, it is now chiefly a trade and industrial center. There are lignite mines nearby. The city was chartered in 1380.

pilaster (pĭlăs'tər), in architecture, upright supporting member, attached to and projecting slightly from the face of a wall and equipped with a base and capital like a column; also, a similar form used decoratively. The pilaster in general follows the rules and proportions of the classic orders; it may be fluted or not, but usually has no entasis or taper. It was used by the Romans. The Greek antae (projections of the wall at the corners only), although similar in function, differ in base and capital from the columns that stand between them. In the Renaissance, the pilaster, used as a purely decorative device, was often paneled and ornamented.

Pilate: see PONTIUS PILATE.

Pilatus (pēlä'tōōs), mountain, 6,800 ft (2,073 m) high, in the Alps of the Four Forest Cantons, central Switzerland. According to medieval legend, the corpse of Pontius Pilate was thrown into a small lake on the mountain.

Pilcomayo (pēlkōmä'yō), river c.700 mi (1,130 km) long, rising in the Bolivian Andes E of Lake Poopó and flowing SE in a marshy course across the Gran Chaco to the Paraguay River near Asunción. It forms part of the Argentina-Paraguay border.

Pildash (pĭl'dăsh), son of Nahor. Gen. 22.22.

pile, post of timber, steel, or concrete used to support a structure. Vertical piles, or bearing piles, the most common form, are generally needed for the foundations of bridges, docks, piers, and buildings. Slender tree trunks, roughly trimmed and about 10 in. (25.4 cm) thick at the butt, are used in foundations for houses. Wooden piles last a very long time underwater but are subject to decay when buried underground. They are shaped for driving and sometimes have a pointed iron shoe set on the sharp end, with the butt end encircled by an iron band to prevent brooming under the blows of the pile driver. Their length is usually 20 to 60 ft (6.1–18.3 m), and they are generally spaced 3 or 4 ft (.9 or 1.2 m) apart from center to center. Concrete piles are generally of two types, the precast and the cast-in-place. They are very strong and durable, do not deteriorate when wholly in the ground, and are immune to the attacks of boring insects. Precast piles are made of concrete reinforced with steel bars looped one to the other and are tipped and topped with protective steel when driven into the ground. The steel is not needed when the piles are set by the force of jets of water; in this method an iron pipe is set in the center of the pile, and water under pressure is sent down to wash away the sand, silt, or soft earth that it is to displace. Only in such subsurfaces can the water-jet system be employed. Cast-in-place piles are variously made. One method consists of driving a steel shell into the ground and filling it with concrete, after which the shell is withdrawn and the molded concrete is in place. Sheet piling consists of wooden boards or interlocking steel plates and is used largely as a cofferdam to keep water from structural work, piers, and buildings. Concrete sheet piling is also used. Pilings are driven into the ground by pile drivers using drop hammers, diesel hammers, steam hammers, or compressed-air hammers. More recently, high-powered ultrasonic vibrators have come into use for driving piles.

pile dwelling: see LAKE DWELLING.

Pileha (pĭl'ēhə), signer of the Covenant. Neh. 10.24.

piles: see HEMORRHOIDS.

pilgrim, one who travels to a shrine or other sacred place out of religious motives. Pilgrimages are a feature of many religions and cultures. Examples in ancient Greece were the pilgrimages to Eleusis and Delphi. Pilgrimages are well established in India (e.g., to Varanasi, or Benares, on the sacred Ganges River), in China (e.g., to Mt. Tai), and in Japan (e.g., to Uji-yamada and Taisha). The Temple at Jerusalem was the center of an annual pilgrimage of Jews at Passover. Every Muslim tries to make the pilgrimage to Mecca once in his life; this is the pilgrimage (Hajj) par excellence and has had a remarkable effect in unifying ISLAM. A favorite Shiite shrine is KARBALA. The Christian pilgrimage to the Holy Places of Jerusalem, Bethlehem, and Nazareth, already well established, received great impetus in the 4th cent.

from the supposed finding of the True Cross by St. Helena. The CRUSADES were launched to protect this pilgrimage. In Western Europe the principal shrine is Rome, sacred to St. Peter and St. Paul and the martyrs. Since 1300 the popes have set aside holy years (see JUBILEE) for special pilgrimages to Rome. Another historic shrine is SANTIAGO DE COMPOSTELA, NW Spain; one explanation of the origin of the *Chanson de Roland* connects it with songs sung to entertain the Compostela pilgrims. The chief shrine of medieval England was the tomb of St. Thomas à Becket at Canterbury—its pilgrimage was immortalized by Geoffrey Chaucer. Other English pilgrimages were to Walsingham and Glastonbury. Badges to show what pilgrimages one had made were a feature of medieval dress. Thus, a palm badge symbolized the visit to the Holy Land, and its wearer was called a palmer. Modern Roman Catholic centers of pilgrimage include Rome, the Holy Land, LORETO, Compostela, MONTSERRAT (Spain), FÁTIMA, LOURDES, Ste Anne d'Auray (see AURAY), EINSIEDELN, CZESTOCHOWA, SAINTE ANNE DE BEAUPRÉ (Quebec), and GUADALUPE HIDALGO (Mexico).

Pilgrimage church architecture: see ROMANESQUE ARCHITECTURE AND ART.

Pilgrimage of Grace, 1536, rising of Roman Catholics in N England. It was a protest against the government's action in abolishing papal supremacy (1534) and confiscating (1536) the smaller monastic properties, intensified by grievances against INCLOSURES and high rents and taxes. The Catholics protested their loyalty to Henry VIII, citing as their "great grudge" the position and influence of Thomas CROMWELL, who was largely responsible for the state policy. In Oct., 1536, several thousand men gathered at Louth, Lincolnshire, to protest the suppression of the monasteries. They occupied the city of Lincoln, but dispersed after receiving a sharp rebuke from the king, with the assurance, however, that Parliament had sanctioned the suppressions. Almost before this was over there was a great rally in Yorkshire for the restoration of papal supremacy and monasteries. The movement, which rapidly gathered strength in N England, was led by Robert Aske, a Yorkshire lawyer; its banner bore the device of the Five Wounds of Christ. Aske and his followers occupied York and forced the royal officers to obey them. They moved on to Doncaster, where the number of men reached at least 35,000; participants came from all walks of life, and included such noblemen as Baron DARCY. Thomas Howard, 3d duke of Norfolk, met them and promised from the king a general pardon and a Parliament to be held at York within a year. The men dispersed and went quietly home. Aske was invited to London and was well received by the king. In Jan., 1537, Sir Francis Bigod of Settrington, Yorkshire, led an uprising at Beverley. Although Aske and other leaders of the Pilgrimage of Grace tried to prevent this new disorder, they were arrested, tried in London, and executed in June, 1537. The northern counties were placed under martial law, and many people were hanged on mere suspicion of disaffection. The repression in N England after the Pilgrimage of Grace put an end to open opposition to the government's religious policy. See study by M. N. Dodds and R. Dodds (2 vol., 1915, repr. 1971).

Pilgrims, in American history, the group of separatists and other individuals who were the founders of PLYMOUTH COLONY. The nucleus of the group came into being in the meetings of a group of Puritans at Scrooby, a village in Nottinghamshire, England. Opposed to the episcopal jurisdiction and the rites and discipline of the Church of England, the group had formed as a separatist church by 1606, with John ROBINSON eventually becoming their minister. The congregation was composed mainly of farmers and artisans; men of little education or position, although William BREWSTER, one of their leaders, was a man of some importance in the town and had spent some time at Cambridge Univ. Although not actively persecuted, the group was subjected to ecclesiastical investigation and to the mockery, criticism, and disfavor of their neighbors. To avoid contamination of their strict beliefs and to escape the hated church from which they had separated, the sect decided to move to Holland, where other groups had found religious liberty, despite an English law that forbade emigration without royal permission. After several false starts, two of which were frustrated by the law, small groups made their way to the Netherlands in 1607, and by the middle of 1608 most of them had reached Amsterdam. They went from there to Leiden, where they established themselves as artisans and laborers. Life in Holland was not easy, however, and the immigrants found the presence of radical religious groups there objectionable. Dutch influence also seemed to be altering their English ways, and the prospect of renewed war between the Netherlands and Spain threatened. For these reasons they considered moving to the New World. In 1617, John CARVER and Robert Cushman went to London to make arrangements with the London Company, cautiously negotiating to make pledges that would satisfy company, king, and bishops and still keep the religion of the dissenters pure. In 1619 a charter was secured from the company in the name of one John Wincob, but it was never used. The matter lapsed until early in 1620, when Thomas Weston, speaking for a group of London merchants, offered them support and the use of a charter already obtained from the London Company. A joint-stock company for seven years was arranged. The congregation voted on the voyage, but only about half of the members decided to go. A small vessel, the *Speedwell,* was obtained to carry the Pilgrims to England, where that vessel joined the MAYFLOWER for the trip to America. Difficulties arose, however, over restrictive arrangements included by Weston in the agreement in order to guarantee more strongly the investment by the merchants, and the Pilgrims, unwilling to accept the revised agreement, sailed without reaching a settlement. The *Speedwell* proved unseaworthy and returned to port; many of the passengers and much of her cargo were crowded on the *Mayflower,* which set out alone. The Leiden group constituted only 35 of the 102 passengers on the *Mayflower;* many of the English group gathered for the trip were not even separatists (they were thus called "Strangers"). Nonetheless, the Leiden group (the "Saints") retained control and were the moving force behind the emigration. Before landing, an agreement providing for a government by the will of the majority was drawn up and called the MAYFLOWER COMPACT. In Dec., 1620, the *Mayflower* entered Plymouth harbor, where the settlers established dwellings. The name Pilgrim Fathers is given to those members who made the first crossing on the *Mayflower.* See William Bradford, *History of Plimouth Plantation* (1856; new ed. 1967); H. M. Dexter, *The England and Holland of the Pilgrims* (1905); R. G. Usher, *The Pilgrims and Their History* (1918); G. F. Willison, *Saints and Strangers* (1945, rev. ed. 1965) and *The Pilgrim Reader* (1953); S. E. Morison, *The Story of the Old Colony of New Plymouth* (1956).

Pilgrims' Way, ancient English road that ran from Hampshire to Kent, over the Sussex Downs. It is so called because it may have been used during the Middle Ages by pilgrims who came to Canterbury to the shrine of Thomas à Becket from the southwest, via Winchester.

Pilibhit (pēlēbēt'), city (1971 pop. 68,380), Uttar Pradesh state, N India. This trade center was the center of the Muslim Rohilla kingdom in the late 18th cent.

pillar, freestanding columnar supporting member. It is a general term, little used as an exact architectural definition except as applied to an upright support in the medieval styles, consisting of an assemblage of juxtaposed shafts and moldings; unlike the column, it does not adhere to the rules of the ORDERS OF ARCHITECTURE.

Pillars of Hercules, ancient mythological name for promontories flanking the east entrance to the Strait of Gibraltar. They are usually identified with Gibraltar in Europe and with Mt. Acha at Ceuta in Africa. The Jebel Musa (W of Ceuta) is also considered one of the pillars. They are also referred to as the Gates of Hercules.

pillbox, small, low fortification that houses machine guns and antitank weapons. Similar to a blockhouse, it is usually made of concrete, steel, logs, or filled sandbags. Pillboxes came into use during the early 20th cent. in the Belgian and French fortresses that were built before World War I. They were first used extensively by the Japanese in World War II. The Germans employed pillboxes in the defense of Normandy and the Siegfried Line and developed a portable steel pillbox that was used in Italy.

Pillnitz (pĭl'nĭts), district of Dresden, SE East Germany, on the Elbe River. It is the site of an 18th-century castle, formerly a royal residence, that today houses an art collection. In the castle in Aug., 1791, Emperor Leopold II and King Frederick William II of Prussia met to discuss the problems arising out of the French Revolution and issued a declaration stating that if all other European powers would join them (a condition that could not be fulfilled, owing to England's position at the time that French domestic affairs did not concern England), they were prepared to restore Louis XVI to his full authority as king of France, by force if necessary. French émigrés made much of the statement in order to provoke armed conflict, and the declaration could not help but stir the French Revolutionaries. It thus helped to bring on the FRENCH REVOLUTIONARY WARS.

Pillow, Gideon Johnson, 1806–78, American general, b. Williamson co., Tenn. In the Mexican War he was appointed brigadier general of Tennessee volunteers by his former law partner, President James K. Polk. He took part in the battles leading to the surrender of Mexico City and was made a major general (1847). He was charged with insubordination by Gen. Winfield Scott but acquitted by a court of inquiry. When the Civil War broke out he became a Confederate brigadier general. His conduct in escaping from FORT DONELSON before the Confederate surrender caused the suspension of his command.

Pillow, Fort: see FORT PILLOW.

Pillsbury, John Sargent, c.1828–1901, American miller and politician, b. Sutton, N.H. He went west in 1855 and settled at St. Anthony (now Minneapolis), Minn. He was a member of the milling firm of his nephew Charles A. Pillsbury and later of the Pillsbury-Washburn Company. He served several terms as state senator and was governor of Minnesota (1876–82). He was for 38 years a regent of the Univ. of Minnesota.

Pilnyak, Boris (bərēs' pĕlnyäk'), pseud. of **Boris Andreyevich Vogau** (əndrā'yəvĭch vô'gou), 1894–1937?, Russian novelist and short-story writer. Pilnyak first attracted wide attention with his novel *The Naked Year* (1922, tr. 1928), a loosely constructed work concerning the social chaos following the Revolution of 1917. He accepted the revolution itself, but did not embrace orthodox Communism. His short novel *Mahogany* (1927), denied publication in the USSR, was first published in Berlin in 1929. Later Pilnyak utilized some of its material in his novel about the Five-Year Plans, *The Volga Falls to the Caspian Sea* (1930, tr. 1931). Both were severely criticized by the Soviet regime as bourgeois. In 1931, Pilnyak visited the United States and attacked American industrialization in *OK* (1932). Some of his short stories have been translated in *Tales of the Wilderness* (1925) and *Mother Earth and Other Stories* (1968). He disappeared in 1937, and is thought to have been arrested and executed.

pilocarpine (pīlōkär'pēn), naturally occurring alkaloid obtained from plants of the genus *Pilocarpus* (family Rutaceae). By mimicking the effects of ACETYLCHOLINE, pilocarpine acts as a stimulant of the parasympathetic NERVOUS SYSTEM. It promotes the flow of saliva and urine and increases perspiration. Because it increases the outflow of fluid from the eye, reduces the pressure within the eye, and causes the pupil to contract, the drug is used to treat some types of glaucoma. It is also used for some tongue disorders.

Pilon, Germain (zhĕrmăN' pēlôN'), 1535–90, French sculptor. He was court sculptor under the later Valois sovereigns. He executed several sculptures on Henry II's mausoleum at Saint-Denis. In the Louvre are a number of his vigorously realistic works including *The Three Graces,* supporting an urn that once held the heart of Henry II; portrait busts of Henry II and Francis II; *The Virgin;* and, his masterpiece, the figure of Chancellor René de Birague. As controller of the mint under Charles IX he made the finest medallions, medals, and coins of his time.

pilot, person responsible for safe navigation of a ship or airplane. A ship's pilot is an individual possessing local knowledge of coastal waters. Usually licensed by public authority (in the United States, by the U.S. coast guard), he is taken on board to conduct a ship to or from port. The airplane pilot, in contrast to the ship's pilot, has overall command of the craft, which he operates, generally, with the assistance of a copilot. Before an airplane pilot can be licensed in the United States, he must clock a prescribed amount of solo flying experience and pass a flying test given by the U.S. Civil Aeronautics Board.

pilotage: see AIR NAVIGATION.

pilot balloon: see WEATHER BALLOON.

pilot fish: see POMPANO.

Piloty, Karl von (kärl fən pēlō'tē), 1826–86, German historical painter; son of Ferdinand Piloty (1786–1844), a noted German lithographer. Karl first won recognition for his genre paintings, such as *The Nurse* (1853). He soon specialized in historical paintings, which were famous in his day for realism and emphasis on color. As a popular professor at the Munich Academy he exercised a great influence on many German painters. Among his well-known works are *The Death of Caesar* and *Galileo in Prison.*

Pilsen: see PLZEŇ, Czechoslovakia.

Pilsudski, Joseph (pĭlsŏŏd'skē), Pol. *Józef Piłsudski* (yōō'zĕf pēl"sōōt'skē), 1867–1935, Polish general and politician. He was exiled (1887–92) to Siberia for an alleged attempt on the life of Czar Alexander III, who ruled a large section of Poland. On his return he joined the Polish Socialist party and began (1894) publication of the *Robotnik* [worker], a secret party organ. Again imprisoned in 1900, he soon escaped. Pilsudski, who subordinated social aims to national emancipation, struggled exclusively for Polish independence. To that end he organized various anti-Russian militant groups—notably, after the outbreak (1914) of World War I, the Polish Legions, which he commanded under Austrian sponsorship. When the Central Powers demanded extensive Polish mobilization in return for vague promises of independence, Pilsudski refused to give his support and was imprisoned (1917) at Magdeburg. Released in Nov., 1918, he returned to Warsaw, assumed command of the Polish armies, and proclaimed an independent Polish republic, which he headed. Meanwhile a more conservative Polish national committee, that had favored cooperation with the Allies in the war, had established itself at Paris and won Allied recognition. A compromise was reached in 1919, when PADEREWSKI became premier while Pilsudski continued as chief of state. Pilsudski used force to expand the eastern frontier of Poland, and the peace treaty with Russia (see RIGA, TREATY OF, 1921) incorporated several million Ukrainians and White Russians into Poland. In accordance with the Polish constitution of 1921, Pilsudski surrendered (1922) his powers and soon retired to private life. Disagreeing with the policies of the WITOS cabinet, he overthrew the government by a coup d'état in 1926. As war minister he exercised a virtual dictatorship until his death. He also was premier from 1926 to 1928 and in 1930. The constitution of 1935 made a pretense of parliamentary democracy. Pilsudski's authoritarian regime was a military dictatorship with slight fascistic overtones, although it never was formalized as in fascist countries. His succession was assumed by a group of military men, among them Rydz-Smigly. See Pilsudski's memoirs (tr. 1931, repr. 1972); biography by his wife, Alexandra Pilsudska (1941, repr. 1970); study by M. K. Dziewanowski (1969).

Piltai (pĭl'tā, pĭltā'ī), member of a priestly family. Neh. 12.17.

Piltdown man, name given to human remains found (1908) at Piltdown, Sussex. The find led to much speculation and argument. Since they were found with remains of mammals of the Lower Pleistocene epoch, they were supposed to belong to a "Piltdown man" who lived 200,000 to 1,000,000 years ago. Many scientists doubted the whole proposition. They were justified when fluorine tests showed in 1950 that the Piltdown fossil was no more than 50,000 years old. X-ray analysis proved that the jaw and canine tooth had been deliberately altered, and further tests demonstrated conclusively that they were of modern origin. See J. S. Weiner, *The Piltdown Forgery* (1955); R. W. Millar, *The Piltdown Men* (1972).

Pima Indians (pē'mə), North American Indian tribe of S Arizona. They speak the Pima language of the Uto-Aztecan branch of the Aztec-Tanoan linguistic family (see AMERICAN INDIAN LANGUAGES). There are two divisions, the Lower Pima and the Upper Pima. Before the mission period, the Pima and the PAPAGO, who spoke variations of the same language, called themselves the People—River People (Pima) and Desert People (Papago). Archaeological evidence shows their ancestors to have been the Hohokam Peoples who built a network of irrigation canals for farming. Many of the ruined pueblos in the Pima territory have been attributed to an ancient Pueblo tribe. Tradition further states that increased population caused the Pima to spread over a larger territory, but invading hostile tribes (probably Apache) forced them to consolidate. Thus in 1697, when visited by Father Eusebio KINO, the Pima were living on the Gila River in S central Arizona. Although the Pima were warlike toward the Apache, they were friendly to the Spanish and, later, to the pioneers from the E United States; the Pima villages were a stopping place for pioneers who took the southern route to California. The Pima were sedentary farmers of the Southwest area; they farmed corn, squash, beans, cotton, and wheat (introduced by the Spanish). They lived in domeshaped huts built of poles and covered with mud and brush. Marriage among the Pima was not binding. Women performed much of the labor including basketmaking; their baskets are noted for their beauty. The Pima were expert with the bow and arrow and had war clubs and rawhide shields. The Pima numbered some 2,500 in 1775, but their population was increased when the Maricopa joined them in the early 19th cent. The Pima now live, together with the Maricopa, on the Gila River and Salt River reservations in S Arizona, where together they number about 10,000. See P. H. Ezell, *The Hispanic Acculturation of the Gila River Pimas* (1961).

pimento or **allspice,** common names for a tree (*Pimenta officinalis* or *P. dioica*) of the family Myrtaceae (MYRTLE family) cultivated in the West Indies for its dried unripe berries, used medicinally and as a spice (also called pimento or allspice). The spice supposedly combines the flavors of several other spices; it is used chiefly in pickles and relishes. The leaves and berries yield an essential oil used for flavoring. In America the names *pimento* and *allspice* are also applied to plants of other families: *pimento* to the large, sweet Spanish pepper (Span. *pimento*) of the nightshade family, and *allspice* to several aromatic shrubs, e.g., the Carolina allspice (*Calycanthus floridus*), a cultivated ornamental, and the wild allspice, or spicebush (*Benzoin aestivale*), of the family Lauraceae (laurel family). Pimento is classified in the division MAGNOLIOPHYTA, class Magnoliopsida, order Myrtales, family Myrtaceae.

Pimería Alta (pēmārē'ä äl'tä), region in the U.S. Southwest and N Mexico, chiefly in present SW Arizona and NW Sonora. It was inhabited by the Pima Indians and was the scene of the missionary labors of Father Eusebio Kino in the late 17th and early 18th cent.

pimiento: see PEPPER.

pimpernel: see PRIMROSE.

pimple, small pointed elevation of the skin that may or may not contain pus. The formation of pimples is frequently associated with infection, irritation, or overactivity of the sebaceous and sweat glands. Repeated eruptions of pimples are often termed ACNE.

pin. One of the earliest artifacts of man, pins were at first made of thorns, bone, or wood and were used as clothing fasteners, hairpins, and meat skewers. These long, single-shaft pins were early imitated in metal and were often tipped with ornamental knobs. The fibulae, prototype of the safety pin and probably one of the earliest applications of the spring coil, was popular from early antiquity through medieval times. It was the forerunner of the modern brooch through the hinged pin, which was developed by the Romans. Bent-wire hairpins are believed to have originated in England in the 16th cent.; the modern bobby pin was introduced in the 20th cent. In the 14th and 15th cent. in England the costliness and scarcity of plain pins caused Parliament to limit their sale to the first two days of January, for which women saved money all year—hence the term "pin money." In the 19th cent., with the fashion for enormous hats came the development of ornate jeweled hatpins.

Pinang or **Penang** (both: pənăng'), state (1971 pop. 776,770), c.400 sq mi (1,040 sq km), Malaysia, on the Strait of Malacca. It consists of Pinang Island (108 sq mi/280 sq km), formerly known as Georgetown, and Province Wellesley (292 sq mi/756 sq km), a strip of territory on the Malay Peninsula adjacent to Pinang Island. The capital, on the island, is Pinang (also known as Pulau Pinang or Georgetown; 1971 est. pop. 270,000). The city of Pinang is also Malaysia's leading port. The island is largely agricultural, with some rubber production. Province Wellesley has tin-smelting works and large areas devoted to rice and rubber. Well over half the inhabitants of the state are Chinese. Indians are less numerous; less than a third are Malays. Pinang Island was the first British settlement on the Malay Peninsula. It was occupied in 1786 by Francis Light of the British East India Company with the permission of the sultan of KEDAH. After an unsuccessful attempt to retake the island (1791), the sultan agreed on a settlement from the British of an annual stipend, and in 1800 he also ceded Province Wellesley. Pinang, together with Province Wellesley, Malacca, and Singapore, became known as the STRAITS SETTLEMENTS. Under the British, Pinang grew rapidly in commercial importance, although it was surpassed by Singapore. Pinang joined the Federation of Malaya in 1948. See MALAYSIA, FEDERATION OF.

Pinar del Rio (pēnär' dĕl rē'ō), province (1970 pop. 542,423), W Cuba, the westernmost province of Cuba. PINAR DEL RIO is the capital. The province, occupying a narrow area, has an irregular and swampy coast; it is mostly level, with one important mountain range, the Cordillera de Guaniguanico. The chief river is the Cuyaguateje. The traditional industry of Pinar del Rio, Cuba's poorest province, is the growing of tobacco, which is cultivated in the Vuelta Abajo region and is among the world's best. Cattle raising is of limited importance; mines at Matahambre yield copper.

Pinar del Rio, city (1970 pop. 73,206), capital of Pinar del Rio prov., W Cuba. It is linked by rail and highway to Havana and is the center of a road network running through the province. The city, founded in 1699, is famous for the tobacco grown in the Vuelta Abajo district. Near the city is the picturesque valley of Viñales.

Pinchot, Gifford (pĭn'shō), 1865–1946, American forester and public official, b. Simsbury, Conn. He studied forestry in Europe and then undertook (1892) systematic work in forestry at the Vanderbilt estate in North Carolina. He became (1896) a member of the National Forest Commission and served (1898–1910) in the division of forestry, which in the period of his service became a bureau and then the Forest Service. He was dismissed (1910) by President Taft because he publicly criticized Secretary of Interior Richard A. BALLINGER'S administration of coal lands in Alaska. Pinchot's dismissal helped widen the rift in the Republican party and the estrangement between President Taft and Theodore Roosevelt. In 1912, Pinchot joined Roosevelt in forming the PROGRESSIVE PARTY. After he helped found the Yale school of forestry, Pinchot was (1903–36) professor there while serving on numerous conservation commissions. He was twice (1923–27, 1931–35) governor of Pennsylvania. In his first term Pinchot directed the reorganization of the state government. He wrote many books on forestry and timber; his autobiography, *Breaking New Ground* (1947), sums up many years of his study of conservation. See biographies by M. N. McGeary (1960) and M. L. Fausold (1961, repr. 1973); studies by J. L. Penick (1968) and H. T. Pinkett (1970).

Pinckney: see also PINKNEY.

Pinckney, Charles, 1757–1824, American statesman, governor of South Carolina (1789–92, 1796–98, 1806–8), b. Charleston, S.C.; cousin of Charles C. Pinckney and Thomas Pinckney. He fought in the American Revolution and was taken prisoner in the British capture of Charleston (1780). A delegate to the Federal Constitutional Convention of 1787, he submitted a plan for the Constitution. Although its exact provisions are not known, his plan had considerable influence on the final draft of the Constitution. In 1798 he became a U.S. Senator, and his services in forwarding Thomas Jefferson's presidential candidacy were rewarded by his appointment (1801) as minister to Spain. His principal assignment was to secure, with James Monroe's help, the cession of Florida to the United States. The attempt failed, and Pinckney returned home in 1805. From 1819 to 1821 he was a member of the House of Representatives, where he made a celebrated speech against the Missouri Compromise. See G. C. Rogers, *Charleston in the Age of the Pinckneys* (1969).

Pinckney, Charles Cotesworth, 1746–1825, American political leader and diplomat, b. Charleston, S.C.; brother of Thomas Pinckney and cousin of Charles Pinckney. After attending Oxford and the military academy at Caen, France, he returned to Charleston, where in 1769 he began to practice law. Subsequent to serving (1775) in the provincial congress, he joined the Continental Army in the American Revolution and was captured by the British at Charleston in 1780. A delegate to the Federal Constitutional Convention of 1787, he helped to secure South Carolina's ratification of the Constitution. In 1796 he was sent as minister to France but was not received by the French government. The next year he was joined by Elbridge Gerry and John Marshall in the mission that led to the notorious XYZ AFFAIR; Pinckney refused to bribe French officials as a prerequisite for opening negotiations with them. He was unsuccessful Federalist candidate for the vice presidency in 1800 and for the presidency in 1804 and 1808. See biography by M. R. Zahniser (1967).

Pinckney, Thomas, 1750–1828, American political leader and diplomat, b. Charleston, S.C.; brother of C. C. Pinckney and cousin of Charles Pinckney. At the outbreak of the American Revolution he joined the militia; he saw action in Florida, took part in the defense of Charleston (1780), and was wounded and captured at Camden in the Carolina campaign. After the war he served as governor (1787–89). While minister to England (1792–96), he was sent as envoy extraordinary to Spain (1794–95). His treaty with

Spain (1795) established commercial relations between the United States and Spain, provided for free navigation of the Mississippi by American citizens and Spanish subjects, granted the right of deposit at New Orleans, and set the boundaries of Louisiana and E and W Florida. As a member of Congress (1797–1801) he upheld Federalist measures but voted against the Sedition Act and expressed no eagerness for war with France. In the War of 1812 Pinckney was a major general. See biography by C. C. Pinckney (1895); S. F. Bemis, *Pinckney's Treaty* (1960, repr. 1973); J. L. Cross, *London Mission* (1968).

pincushion flower: see TEASEL.

Pindar (pĭn'dər), 518?–c.438 B.C., Greek poet, generally regarded as the greatest Greek lyric poet. A Boeotian of noble birth, he lived principally at Thebes. He traveled widely, staying for some time at Athens and in Sicily at the court of Hiero I at Syracuse and also at Acragas (modern Agrigento). His chief medium was the choral lyric, and he set the standard for the triumphal ode or epinicion. Of his complete works 45 odes survive; these make one of the greatest collections of poems by a single author in Greek. His fragments are exceptionally numerous and some of them widely famous. The epinicia celebrate victories in athletic games: there are 14 Olympian odes, 12 Pythian odes, 11 Nemean odes, and 8 Isthmian odes. Each was written to be sung in a procession for the victor, usually on his return to his home city. The outstanding feature of each ode is its narrative myth, which is always connected with the winner. The myth makes appropriate the elevated moral tone and religious flavor characteristic of Pindar's poems. His style loses a great deal in translation. It has a high-flown diction and an intricate word order, dependent partly upon the complexity of his metrical requirements. Pindar wrote on commissions, but he was quite independent of any meretriciousness, because of his lofty conception of the poet's vocation. See his works (tr. by L. R. Farnell, 1930–32); his odes (tr. by R. A. Swanson, 1974); study by Gilbert Norwood (1945). The term **Pindaric ode** refers to a verse form used primarily in England in the 17th and 18th cent. The form, based on a somewhat faulty understanding of the metrical pattern used by Pindar, originated with Abraham COWLEY in his *Pindarique Odes* (1656) and was later used by John DRYDEN, among others. It is characterized by irregularity in the rhyme scheme, length of the stanzas, and number of stresses in a line.

Pindar, Peter: see WOLCOT, JOHN.

Pindling, Lynden Oscar, 1930–, prime minister of the Bahamas (1967–). The son of a policeman, he received a law degree (1952) from London Univ. As leader of the Progressive Liberal party, he represented the large Negro majority in the Bahamas and became the country's first black prime minister when his party won a close, but surprising, victory (1967); in elections the next year his party won by a good majority, and its position in power was reaffirmed by elections in 1972. As prime minister, he emphasized public aid to education and the continued attraction of foreign investment and tourism. He led his country to independence within the Commonwealth of Nations in 1973.

Pindus (pĭn'dəs), Gr. *Píndhos,* chief mountain range of Greece, extending c.100 mi (160 km) S from the Albanian border through NW Greece. Mt. Smólikas (8,650 ft/2,637 m) is the highest peak. The Pindus are a continuation of the Dinaric Alps but have a lower limestone content than the Dinarics. The steep western slopes of the Pindus intercept moist westerly winds, causing a rain shadow on the gently sloping eastern side. The sparsely populated range is rich in timber and in wildlife.

pine, common name for members of the Pinaceae, a family of resinous woody trees with needlelike, usually evergreen leaves. The Pinaceae reproduce by means of cones (see CONE) rather than flowers and have winged seeds, suitable for wind distribution. They are found chiefly in north temperate regions, where they form vast forests. The family was apparently more abundant in the mid-Cenozoic era, but it has maintained its population better than other gymnosperms because the trees are more adaptable to cold, dry climates; the reduced leaf surface and deep-set stomata minimize loss of water by transpiration. The family is the largest and most important of the conifers, providing naval stores, paper pulp, and more lumber by far than any other family. As in other gymnosperm families (in contrast to the hardwood angiosperms), the Pinaceae are limited in the variety of genera and species, permitting economical lumbering of large numbers of a given type of tree; in some localities almost pure stands occur. Of the family's nine genera, four are widely dispersed throughout North America and the Old World. *Abies* (FIR) species are usually of more northern distribution and found at higher altitudes. Sap-filled "blisters" on the trunks of some species provide BALSAM. *Larix* (LARCH) and *Pseudolarix* (golden larch, of China) are the only two deciduous genera; all the others are evergreen. *Picea* (SPRUCE) is the world's most important source of paper. *Pinus* (the pines) is the largest and most widespread genus, characteristic of tropical mountain slopes and of most north temperate regions (except the plains), especially at lower altitudes. From the pines come the naval stores—pitch (see TAR AND PITCH), TURPENTINE, and ROSIN. *Tsuga* (HEMLOCK) and *Pseudotsuga* are native only to North America and E Asia. *Pseudotsuga menziesii* (the Douglas fir) of W North America, one of the tallest trees known (up to 385 ft/117 m) and the leading timber-producing tree of the continent, is carefully controlled by FORESTRY measures. Its wood, usually hard and strong, is of great commercial importance for construction. Named for David Douglas, the tree has many local names, e.g., Douglas spruce, Oregon pine, red fir, and yellow fir. *Cedrus* (CEDAR) ranges from the Mediterranean area to the Himalayas; *Keteleeria* is restricted to China. Members of all nine genera are represented in horticulture as introduced timber trees or ornamentals. Species of *Pinus,* the true pines, can often be identified by the leaf arrangement, one needle or clusters of from two to five (in all cases enclosed in a sheath at the base) being consistently produced by each type. Many of the pines are economically valuable. The ponderosa, or western yellow, pine (*P. ponderosa*), is a hard pine second only to the Douglas fir as a commercial timber tree in North America. The white pine (*P. strobus*) has straight-grained soft wood with little resin, used especially for interior trim and cabinetwork. It once grew densely from Newfoundland to Manitoba and over much of the E United States westward to Minnesota, but constant cutting and attacks of white-pine blister RUST have greatly depleted the stands, especially in the NE United States. The Norway, or red, pine (*P. resinosa*) has a similar range and has also suffered from overcutting. Its wood is somewhat heavier and suitable for general construction. The Norway pine is frequently used in reforestation programs. The jack pine (*P. banksiana*), the most northern of the American species, thrives on poor and sandy soils and is much used to colonize areas where more valuable species may later be introduced. Although the trunk is often gnarled, making it unsuitable for good lumber, it supplies much pulpwood and is used locally for rough lumber, fuel, and crating. The longleaf, or Southern yellow, pine (*P. palustris*) has highly resinous wood used for heavy construction and as a major source of naval stores and pulpwood. It and the faster growing slash pine (*P. caribea*) of the same region have gained importance as northern pine stands have been depleted. The Scotch pine (*P. sylvestris*), ranging from Scotland to Siberia, is one of the most valuable timber trees of Europe. The cluster pine (*P. pinaster*), widespread in S France and in Spain, is the chief European source of turpentine. The Monterey pine (*P. radiata*) of California has been widely planted in New Zealand and Chile for reforestation. Several Mediterranean and American species yield edible seeds (see PINE NUT). Drying and nondrying oils are made from the seeds of some pines. The so-called kauri pine, though pinelike in appearance, belongs to another family (see MONKEY-PUZZLE TREE). Pine is classified in the division PINOPHYTA, class Pinopsida, order Coniferales.

pineal body (pĭn'ēəl), small organ (about the size of a pea) situated in the BRAIN. The structure, which is also called the pineal gland and the epiphysis, is generally regarded as an endocrine gland, even though no pineal hormone has been isolated in humans. It has been speculated that the pineal body exerts some influence on sexual development by secreting a substance called melatonin. In humans the pineal tissue begins to retrogress and become fibrotic at about seven years of age. It is occasionally subject to tumor formation, especially in children, and such a development in males may be associated with precocious sexual development. The pineal gland is present in a rudimentary form in all lower vertebrates and is probably the vestige of a functional eye. In present-day fish, amphibians, and reptiles, it is generally buried below the skin and has only slight visual importance, i.e., it retains a sensitivity to light.

pineapple, common name for one member of and for the Bromeliaceae, a family of chiefly epiphytic herbs and small shrubs native to the American tropics and subtropics. The spiny leaves of various species of the genus *Ananas* yield a hard fiber called gravata in South America and piña, or pineapple cloth, in the Philippines. *A. sativa* is the cultivated pineapple. It produces a spiny, sweet and juicy fruit for which it is grown throughout warmer regions—especially in Hawaii, which supplies the major portion of the world's canned pineapple. Species of *Ananas, Tillsandia,* and other genera are sometimes cultivated as ornamentals. SPANISH MOSS (*T. usenoides*) is a member of this family. Many epiphytic bromeliads, growing in moist tropical American forests, have become highly modified for retaining water between rainfalls. The pineapple family is classified in the division MAGNOLIOPHYTA, class Liliatae, order Bromeliales.

Pine Barrens, coastal plain region, c.3,000 sq mi (7,770 sq km), S and SE N.J.; composed chiefly of sandy soils, swamp-edged streams, pine stands, and tracts of cranberries and blueberries. Originally a well-forested area of pine, cedar, and oak, its trees were indiscriminately cut for shipbuilding and charcoal-making until the 1860s, when they were nearly exhausted. A second growth of pine was of poor quality, and most of the region, except for scattered stands, remained bare. Several state forests and Fort Dix, a U.S. army base, are there. See J. A. McPhee, *The Pine Barrens* (1968).

Pine Bluff, city (1970 pop. 57,389), seat of Jefferson co., S central Ark., on the Arkansas River; inc. 1839. It is a port and trade center for an agricultural area and has industries producing electric transformers, wood and paper products, metal goods, and furniture. It is also a research center and the seat of the Univ. of Arkansas, Pine Bluff. Of economic importance to the city is the huge Pine Bluff Arsenal to the north; established during World War II, it is the center of U.S. army chemical, biological, and toxicological research. Pine Bluff has an arts and science center and a new civic complex designed by Edward Durell Stone.

Pinel, Philippe (fēlēp' pēnĕl'), 1745–1826, French physician, M.D. Univ. of Toulouse, 1773. After moving to Paris in 1778, he was appointed (1793) director of the Bicêtre hospital and shortly thereafter of the Salpêtrière. His *Traité médico-philosophique sur l'aliénation mentale* (2d ed. 1809), based on observations in both these hospitals, advocated humane treatment of mentally ill persons, then called the insane, and a more empirical study of mental disease. He further contributed to the development of psychiatry through his establishment of the practice of keeping well-documented psychiatric case histories for research.

Pinellas Park (pĭnĕl'əs), city (1970 pop. 22,287), Pinellas co., W Fla.; inc. 1915. Mainly residential, it has industries that manufacture electronic equipment, tools and dyes, and boats.

pine marten: see MARTEN.

pine nut or **piñon** (pĭn'yən, pē'nyōn), edible seed of various species of PINE trees of W North America and Mexico. Among the North American species that bear such edible seeds are the nut pines or piñons, *Pinus edulis* and *P. monophylla,* and the Digger pine, *P. sabiniana,* named after the Digger Indians of California. The nuts have a thin red-brown shell and range in size from about ¾ in. (1.91 cm) to about 1½ in. (3.75 cm). Pine nuts, or Indian nuts, were an important food for the early American Indians and are still harvested in quantity both for food and for trading. They are picked from the ground, taken from squirrel caches, or extracted by hand from the cones. Some pine stands are in danger of depletion because insufficient seeds are left for reproduction. Pignolia nuts are the seeds of *P. pinea* of S Europe, where they are much used for food. Quantities are exported to be used salted and in confectionery. Seeds of numerous other European and Asiatic pines are gathered under many local names. The name pignolia is often applied to all pine nuts.

Pinero, Sir Arthur Wing (pĭnēr'ō), 1855–1934, English dramatist. He achieved initial success with farces, such as *The Magistrate* (1885), and sentimental comedies, such as *Sweet Lavender* (1888). However, with *The Profligate* (1889), he launched his career as a serious social dramatist. In 1893 the production of *The Second Mrs. Tanqueray,* his best-known work, raised protest because of its sympathetic portrayal of a woman with a questionable past. His later dramas include *The Notorious Mrs. Ebbsmith* (1895) and *Mid-Channel* (1909). All Pinero's plays are noted for their superb craftsmanship. He was knighted in 1909. See his collected letters, ed. by J. P. Wearing (1974); biographies by W. D. Dunkel (1941) and Walter Lazenby (1972).

Pinerolo (pĕnärô'lō), Fr. *Pignerol,* city (1971 pop. 37,483), Piedmont, NW Italy, at the foot of the Alps. It is an agricultural and industrial center. Manufactures include paper, textiles, machinery, and processed food. First mentioned in the 10th cent., Pinerolo was a strongly fortified citadel that passed to the house of Savoy in the 13th cent. It was often in French hands from 1536 to 1814, and the fortress was made a French state prison. Nicholas FOUQUET, an official of Louis XIV, died in the citadel after 19 years of imprisonment (1680), and the Man with the Iron Mask was held there for some years after his seizure in 1679. The city has an 11th-century cathedral (frequently restored).

Pines, Isle of, Span. *Isla de Pinos,* island (1970 pop. 30,103), 1,180 sq mi (3,056 sq km), off SW Cuba, from which it is separated by the Batabanó Gulf. The island's capital is Nueva Gerona. Pine forests cover much of the island and there are numerous mineral springs. Marble is quarried from low ridges in the northern part; the southern quarter of the island is an elevated plain. The economy is based on fishing and agriculture (citrus fruits, vegetables). Until the break in U.S.-Cuban relations in the early 1960s, much of the land was owned by American citizens, and the mild, healthful climate and excellent fishing waters made the island an important resort. Bibijagua beach remains a popular attraction. Discovered by Columbus in 1494, the Isle of Pines was later used as a penal colony and was a rendezvous for buccaneers. During the colonial period it was a summer resort and a rest area for the Spanish military. The island was ceded to the United States after the Spanish-American War (1898), and because its name was omitted from the Platt Amendment, which defined Cuba's boundaries, it was claimed by the United States as well as by Cuba. Finally, in 1907, the U.S. Supreme Court declared that the island did not belong to the United States; a treaty was later signed (1925) confirming the island as Cuban. Near Nueva Gerona is a large prison, often used for political prisoners; during the regime of Fidel Castro, himself jailed there in 1953, the island was extensively beautified, but political prisoners were incarcerated in unprecedented numbers. The Isle of Pines has suffered frequent damage from hurricanes.

Pines, Isle of, or **Kunié** (kōō'nyā), island (1969 pop. 978), c.58 sq mi (150 sq km), South Pacific, a part of the French overseas territory of NEW CALEDONIA. The Isle of Pines, formerly a penal colony, is now a popular tourist resort.

P'ing-ch'üan or **Pingchüan** (both: pĭng-chüän), town, NE Hopeh prov., China. It is a trade center. Gold and silver are mined nearby. The town was formerly called Pakow.

P'ing-hsiang or **Pingsiang** (both: pĭng-shēäng), city, W Kiangsi prov., China. It is a major coal-mining center, producing quality coking coal for the Huang-shih iron and steel mills and coal fuel for the railroads of S China. The city also has food-processing, paper, and pottery industries.

Ping-Pong: see TABLE TENNIS.

Pingsiang: see P'ING-HSIANG, China.

P'ing-tung or **Pingtung** (both: pĭng-dōōng), town (1969 pop. 161,590), S Taiwan. It is a major sugar-refining center. Other industries produce metals, machinery, chemicals, and alcoholic beverages. A large military base is nearby.

Piniós (pēnēôs') or **Peneus** (pĭnē'əs), river, 134 mi (216 km) long, rising in the Pindus Mts., NW Greece, and flowing generally E past Tríkkala and Lárisa and through the Vale of Tempe into the Aegean Sea.

pink, common name for some members of the Caryophyllaceae, a family of small herbs found chiefly in north temperate zones (especially the Mediterranean area) but with several genera indigenous to south temperate zones and high altitudes of tropical mountains. Plants of this family typically have stems that are swollen at the nodes and notched, or "pinked," petals ranging in color from white to pink, red, and purple. The family includes several ornamentals and many wildflowers and weeds, many of them European species now widely naturalized elsewhere. Ornamental pinks include the spicily fragrant flowers of the large genus *Dianthus,* an Old World group including the carnation (*D. caryophyllus*), sweet William (*D. barbatus*), Deptford pink (*D. armeria*), and most other flowers called dianthus or pink (some of the latter belong to other genera of the family). In over 2,000 years of cultivation (the name *Dianthus* was mentioned by Theophrastus c.300 B.C.) the carnation has given rise to about 2,000 varieties, all derived from the single-flowered, flesh-colored clove pink, known in Elizabethan times as gillyflower. Formerly added to wine

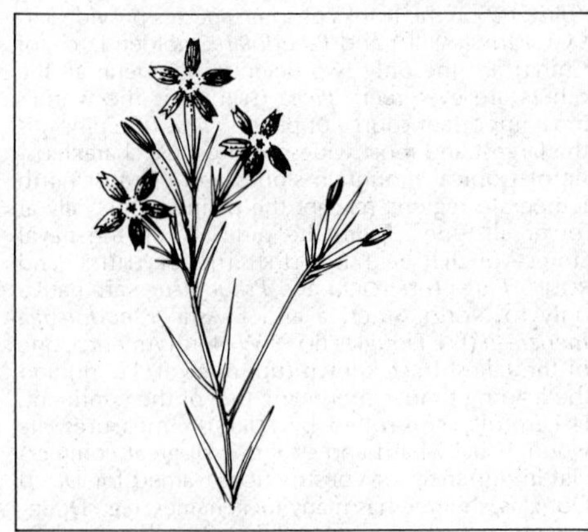

Deptford pink, Dianthus armeria

and beer as a flavoring, it is now used in perfumery. The sweet William bears its blossoms in dense clusters; wild sweet William, an American wildflower, is an unrelated species of the phlox family. The most popular ornamental pinks—the maiden pink (*D. deltoides*) and especially varieties of the garden, or grass, pink (*D. plumarius*)—have escaped from cultivation and now grow wild in the United States. This is true also of other ornamentals, e.g., the ragged robin, or cuckoo flower (*Lychnis flos-cuculi*), the bouncing Bet (*Saponaria officinalis*), and the baby's breath (*Gypsophila paniculata*). The ragged robin was once known as crowflower; it was probably the crowflower used by Ophelia in her garland (Shakespeare's *Hamlet*). The bouncing Bet, cultivated in colonial America, is the best known American SOAP PLANT; it is also called soapwort, as are other species of the genus. The baby's breath is an unusual member of the family in being a bushy plant; it is much used as a bouquet filler. Wildflowers of the family that have indigenous American species include the pearlworts (genus *Sagina*), sandworts (*Arenaria*), campions and catchflies (species of several genera, especially *Lychnis* and the widespread *Silene*), sand spurries (*Spergularia*), and chickweeds (species of several genera, e.g., *Stellaria* and *Cerastium*). Chickweed, relished by birds, is sometimes used for greens and for poultices; catchflies (e.g., *Silene virginica* of the E United States, also called fire pink) are named for the fringed teeth or claws of their deeply lobed petals. The common chickweed (*Stellaria media*), the moss campion (*Silene acaulis*), and the common spurry (*Spergula arvensis*) are now nearly cosmopolitan weeds, having spread from parts of the Old World. Spurry, cultivated in Europe as a pasture, hay, and cover crop, is sometimes planted to hold sand in place. Pinks are classified in the division MAGNOLIOPHYTA, class Magnoliopsida, order Caryophyllales, family Caryophyllaceae.

pink bollworm, destructive larva of a moth, *Pectinophora gossypiella.* Probably of Indian origin, it is a serious pest of cotton in the S United States, chiefly along the Mexican border. The larva feeds on the blossoms, lint, and seeds of cotton and may pupate in the buds. It causes a 20% to 50% crop loss in infested areas. The pink bollworm is classified in the phylum ARTHROPODA, class Insecta, order Lepidoptera, family Gelechiidae.

Pinkerton, Allan, 1819-84, American detective, founder of the Pinkerton National Detective Agency, b. Glasgow, Scotland. A cooper by trade, he emigrated to the United States in 1842 and opened in West Dundee, Ill., a cooper's shop, which became a station on the Underground Railroad. His discovery and capture of a band of counterfeiters led to his appointment (1846) as county sheriff and, in 1850, to an appointment as the first city detective on the Chicago police force. He established in the same year a private detective agency, which had considerable success in solving train- and express-company robberies. In 1861 he foiled a plot to assassinate Abraham Lincoln, and in the Civil War Pinkerton organized and directed an espionage system behind the Confederate lines. His agency secured (1869) evidence on which the MOLLY MAGUIRES were broken up. After Pinkerton's death, the agency was continued by his sons, Robert A. Pinkerton and William A. Pinkerton, and was active in breaking the Homestead strike of 1892. For its role in industrial disputes on behalf of management, particularly in its use of labor spies, the agency was denounced by organized labor. Pinkerton wrote of his own experiences in *Criminal Reminiscences and Detective Sketches* (1879) and other books. See biography by S. A. Lavine; R. W. Rowan, *The Pinkertons* (1931); J. D. Horan, *Desperate Men* (1949) and *The Pinkertons* (1967).

pinkeye: see CONJUNCTIVITIS.

Pinkie, battlefield, E of Edinburgh, Scotland. There the English under Edward Seymour, duke of Somerset, defeated a larger Scottish force on Sept. 10, 1547. Somerset's invasion of Scotland, to enforce a marriage treaty (arranged by Henry VIII) between the young Edward VI and Mary Queen of Scots, so angered the Scots that Mary was sent to France to avoid the marriage.

Pinkney: see also PINCKNEY.

Pinkney, William, 1764-1822, American political leader and diplomat, b. Annapolis, Md. Admitted to the bar in 1786, he soon became prominent in state politics. In 1796 he was sent to England as a commissioner to adjust maritime claims, remaining until 1804. Two years later he was sent with James Monroe on a special mission to England to deal with impressment and reparations for ship seizures. Pinkney remained as minister to England (1807-11), but was unsuccessful in settling difficulties between the two countries. He was U.S. Attorney General (1811-14) and fought in the War of 1812, being wounded at Bladensburg (1814). After serving as a U.S. Congressman (1815-16), he was minister to Russia (1816-18). After his return he practiced law, gaining a considerable reputation as a constitutional lawyer; he appeared before the U.S. Supreme Court as counsel for the Bank of the United States in MCCULLOUGH VS. MARYLAND. He also served (1819-22) in the U.S. Senate. See biography by his nephew, William Pinkney (1853, repr. 1969); H. H. Hagan, *Eight Great American Lawyers* (1923).

pinnacle (pĭn'ĭkəl), minor architectural motif of vertical tapering shape, usually crowning a pier, buttress, or gable. Although sometimes it appears in Renaissance design, as in the Certosa di Pavia, it is almost exclusively a medieval form, originating in the late Romanesque and becoming common in Gothic. Topping the piers of the flying buttresses of side aisles and choirs, pinnacles weighted the pier and thus counteracted the thrust of the flying arch, while furnishing also effective vertical adornments. At the summit of a square tower bearing an octagonal spire they filled the corner angles and created a graceful transition. With the advance of the Gothic, pinnacles appeared in all parts of the church. In France they multiplied and assumed the widest variety of forms, adorned with gables, tracery, colonnettes, and canopied niches and culminating in a richly crocketed finial. In some flamboyant churches they rise in a veritable forest from buttresses and chapel piers. In England they were far less important and remained relatively simple. Pinnacles also adorned tombs, choir screens, pulpits, and furniture, as well as numberless objects of medieval art.

Pinnacles National Monument: see NATIONAL PARKS AND MONUMENTS (table).

pinniped: see SEAL.

Pinocchio: see COLLODI, CARLO.

Pinochet Ugarte, Augusto (ougōōs'tō pēnōchā' ōōgär'tā), 1915-, president of Chile (1973-). An army general who served as chief of staff (1972-73) and commander of the army (1973), he led the coup that overthrew President Salvador Allende (Sept., 1973). As head of a four-man military junta, he launched a rightist regime that resorted to mass arrests and other abrogations of civil rights in order to remove Marxists and Socialists from positions of power. He returned many nationalized businesses to private owners and promised the restoration of most farm properties seized during the Allende regime.

pinochle (pē'nŭ"kəl), card game played by two, three, or four players, with a deck of 48 cards made up of two each of every suit from nine in all four suits. The cards rank ace, ten, king, queen, jack, nine. Auction pinochle, probably the most popular form of the game, is played by three persons at a time, although up to six may play in rotating units of three. Each of the three active players is dealt a hand of 15 cards, three at a time, and three are dealt face down in the center of the table, forming the widow. Bidding starts at 300 points (lower in some cases) and progresses in rotation by minimum 10-point advances. Once a player passes he may not bid again. Two passes end the auction, and the highest bidder wins. He exposes the widow, adds it to his hand, and then melds, i.e., displays combinations of cards ranging in scoring value from ace through ten in one suit (flush), worth 150 points, to nines of the same suit, worth 10 points each. He then buries, or discards, three cards (not used in his melds) to restore his hand to 15 cards. At this point the bidder may concede defeat if he feels he cannot equal or exceed his bid with a total of melded points and points won in play. The two opponents, who play in temporary partnership, may also concede if they agree they cannot prevent the bidder from filling his contract. In play each ace counts 11 points, tens 10 points, kings 4, queens 3, jacks 2, last trick 10. These values are sometimes simplified to 10 points each for aces and tens, 5 each for kings and queens. In either case the total points in play equal 240 for card values plus 10 for last trick. In play, the suit led must be followed. If a player has no cards in that suit, he must play trump. Highest card in suit or highest trump wins the trick. The first of identical cards wins. In two-handed pinochle 12 cards are dealt to each player, a card is turned up to determine trump suit, and players may meld after each trick won. Thus meld and play continue concurrently until the stock is used up—after which play continues until the last 12 cards in the hand are exhausted—and the highest combination score of meld and tricks wins. Four-hand, or partnership, pinochle may be played on an auction basis—in which case each member receives 12 cards and bids to meld and to name trump. After melding, the bidder joins forces with his partner in play against the other set of partners. Another form of partnership pinochle is played by opening the bottom card to determine trump. All four players meld before the opening trick is led. In all these forms of pinochle, an arbitrary point goal is often set, e.g., 1,000 points, instead of just playing for game. Pinochle, probably derived from BEZIQUE, was developed in the United States in the 19th cent. See study by Rufus Perry (1965).

pinocytosis, transport of water and dissolved substances across the cell membrane. In pinocytosis the cell membrane responds to protein molecules in the solution by adsorbing them; then the cell cytoplasm streams to surround the solution, forming a vacuole around it. It is thought that the cell secretes digestive enzymes into the vacuole, increasing the permeability of the surrounding membrane and allowing diffusion of molecules into the cell. Pinocytosis has been observed in amebas and many human and animal tissue cells, such as endothelial cells, muscle cells, and gland cells. In the manner in which cells engulf substances and transport them into the cytoplasm, the process resembles PHAGOCYTOSIS.

Pinole (pĭnōl′), city (1970 pop. 13,266), Contra Costa co., W Calif., on San Pablo Bay, in a farm and livestock area; inc. 1903. Primarily residential, it has a concrete plant.

Pinon (pī′nŏn), one of the dukes of Edom. Gen. 36.41; 1 Chron. 1.52.

piñon: see PINE NUT.

Pinophyta (pī″nŏf′ətə), division of the plant kingdom consisting of those organisms commonly called gymnosperms. The gymnosperms, a group that includes the pine, have stems, roots and leaves, and vascular, or conducting, tissue (xylem and phloem). In these plants the ovules, or young seeds, are exposed to the air at the time of pollination, hence the term gymnosperm, meaning naked seed. Pollination is always by wind. Because the seed-bearing structures of many gymnosperms are organized into a cone, or strobilus, these plants have been called CONIFERS; because the leaves of many species are perennial, they have also been called evergreens. The subdivision Cycadicae, or cycads, are only the small evolutionary vestige of a large and varied group of plants that flourished in late Paleozoic and Mesozoic times. The only order of living cycads, the Cycadales, is dioecious, i.e., male and female cones are borne on separate plants. Although cycads resemble the palms in form and usually have erect stems that reach 50 ft (15 m) in height, they have very little wood; rather, they are supported largely by a hard outer layer of the stem. They have large, fernlike leaves and produce seeds in terminal cones. In their reproduction, pollen grains, or microspores, are transported by wind to the female spore case, or megasporangium. Within the microspore wall, motile flagellated sperms are produced, unlike the nonmotile sperms of the higher gymnosperms. The subdivision Pinicae is characterized by generally small, always simple leaves and by the active secondary growth of stem and root. Many members of this group flourished from Lower Carboniferous times to the Permian age. Plants of the order Pinales (conifers) occur in the Northern Hemisphere; a few species occur within the tropics at sea level. Conifers are the most numerous of living gymnosperms and form large and relatively pure forests. Common examples of conifers are the pines, firs, spruces, redwoods, cedars, junipers, hemlocks, and larches. The wood of conifers is used extensively for construction of all kinds. It has no vessels and thus differs from the wood of angiosperm trees. Although conifers are called softwoods and angiosperm trees hardwoods, the wood of some pines is much harder than that of some angiosperms. Most conifers are monoecious, i.e., the male and female cones occur on the same tree. The mircrospores, or pollen grains, are produced in such vast abundance that clouds of pollen, carried on the wind, have settled on ships far at sea. In plants of the order Taxales (YEWS), the seeds, produced individually on short shoots, are surrounded by a conspicuous fleshy covering. The order Ginkgoales contains only the GINKGO, *Ginkgo biloba,* the last surviving species of a once large and flourishing group of gymnosperms. The subdivision Gneticae contains three genera in separate orders, all of great botanical and evolutionary interest. *Gnetum* is a tropical tree or shrub with broad leaves much like those of an angiosperm. *Ephedra* is a low shrub with scalelike leaves that grows in arid regions of western North America and in China; from it is produced the drug EPHEDRINE. *Welwitschia,* a desert plant of southwestern Africa, has only two large, leathery leaves that persist for the life of the plant, which can be as long as 100 years.

Pinos, Isla de: see PINES, ISLE OF, Cuba.

Pinsk (pĭnsk, Rus. pēnsk), city (1969 est. pop. 62,000), W European USSR, in Belorussia, in the Pripyat Marshes and at the confluence of the Pina and Pripyat rivers. A port on the Pina River (part of the Dnepr-Bug waterway), it has long been a noted water transport junction; timber is now the chief export. Pinsk is also a rail terminus. Industries include shipbuilding and repair and the manufacture of metal products, building materials, and clothing. Mentioned in the chronicles in 1097 as part of the Kievan state, the city became the capital of Pinsk duchy in the 13th cent. It passed to Lithuania in 1320 and to Poland in 1569. Pinsk was transferred to Russia in 1793 with the second partition of Poland; it reverted to Poland in 1921 but was ceded to the USSR in 1945. During the German occupation of World War II, the city's Jews (who had formed a majority of the population) were mostly exterminated.

Pinski, David (pĭn′skē), 1872–1959, Yiddish dramatist and novelist, b. Russia. He wrote stories and plays in Yiddish about the ghetto and assisted in editing a Yiddish periodical in Moscow. After studying medicine in Berlin for two years, he emigrated (1899) to the United States. In New York City he edited several labor and socialist papers. He was one of the most successful playwrights of the Yiddish Theatre, and his play *The Treasure* was produced in English by the Theatre Guild in 1920. He went to live in Israel in 1950. Among his works available in English are *Ten Plays* (tr. 1920); *King David and His Wives* (tr. 1923), a play; and *Arnold Levenberg* (1928), a novel.

Pinsk Marshes, USSR: see PRIPYAT.

pint: see ENGLISH UNITS OF MEASUREMENT.

Pinter, Harold, 1930–, English dramatist. Probably the most important English playwright of the 1960s, Pinter writes so-called "comedies of menace." Using apparently commonplace characters and settings, he invests his plays with an atmosphere of fear, horror, and mystery. The peculiar tension he creates frequently derives as much from the long silences between speeches as from the speeches, often curt and ambiguous, themselves. His plays often concern struggles for power in which the issues are obscure and the reasons for defeat and victory undefined. Pinter began his theatrical career as an actor, touring with provincial repertory companies. His first successful drama was *The Room* (1957), which was followed by such other plays as *The Dumbwaiter* (1957), *The Birthday Party* (1958), *A Slight Ache* (1959), *The Dwarfs* (1960), *The Caretaker* (1960), *The Collection* (1962), *The Homecoming* (1965), *Landscape* (1968), and *Old Times* (1970). Pinter has also written the screenplays for several highly acclaimed motion pictures, including *The Servant* (1963), *The Pumpkin Eater* (1964), *Accident* (1966), and *The Go-Between* (1971). He has also published *Mac—a Memoir* (1969) and *Poems* (1971). See studies by Walter Kerr (1967), A. F. Ganz, ed. (1972), Ronald Hayman (1973), and William Baker and S. E. Tabachnick (1974).

Pinto, Fernão Mendes (fĕrnouN′ mĕn′dĕsh pēn′to͞o), c.1509–1583, Portuguese traveler. For some 20 years he traveled in Africa and Asia, journeying to far places and experiencing great hardships, including years as a slave. His account, *Peregrinação* [wanderings] (1614), is one of the most colorful narratives of world travel literature. Its truthfulness has been questioned, but there is now general agreement that the story is merely exaggerated. See Maurice Collis, *The Grand Peregrination* (1949).

pinto horse, American LIGHT HORSE, characterized by large, irregular color markings—most commonly black (or dark) and white. Horses of this pattern, known regionally as "paints" [Span. *pinto*= painted] were favored by the buffalo hunters of the American Great Plains. Although the pinto coloring may occur in various horses, a pinto breed has been developed and was recognized in the United States in 1963. It is a popular general purpose riding horse.

Pinturicchio (pēnto͞orēk′kyō) or **Pintoricchio** (pēntō-) [Ital.,=little painter], c.1454–1513, Umbrian painter whose real name was Bernardino di Betto. A prolific and facile painter, he was influenced by Perugino, with whom he collaborated on the frescoes for the Sistine Chapel. Pinturicchio worked chiefly in Perugia, Rome, and Siena. He decorated the Borgia apartments in the Vatican and several churches in Rome. His most elaborate project was the decoration of the cathedral library in Siena. In the Metropolitan Museum are many panels of mythological scenes from the ceiling of the reception room in the Palazzo del Magnifico in Siena. The National Gallery of Art, Washington, D.C., has several of his religious works.

pinworm, roundworm, *Enterobius vermicularis,* worldwide in distribution and the most common source of worm infestation of humans in the United States. Children are more commonly infested than adults. Adult pinworms inhabit and mate in the cecum of the large intestine and adjacent areas. When mature females become gravid they migrate down the colon and out onto the skin around the anus where they lay about 10,000 eggs and then die. Such movements cause intense anal itching. The eggs are infective within a few hours and are easily spread by the hands to the mouth, most often through touching contaminated household objects or food supplies. If infective eggs are swallowed the young worms hatch in the duodenum and migrate to the cecum. Development from ingested egg to gravid female requires 2 months. The most prominent symptom of the disease resulting from pinworm infestation, called enterobiasis, is anal itching, particularly at night; restlessness and insomnia are common, and sometimes gastrointestinal symptoms such as abdominal pain, nausea, and diarrhea, are also present. Since reinfection is a major problem, enterobiasis is treated by the following of strict hygienic measures, including careful cleansing of hands, body, and bed linens. Often, all members of the household must be treated for the disease. Pinworms are classified in the phylum ASCHELMINTHES, class Nematoda, order Oxyuroidea, family Oxyuridae.

pinxter flower: see AZALEA.

Pinza, Ezio (āts′yō pēn′tsä), 1895–1957, Italian-American basso, b. Rome, studied at the Bologna Conservatory. After military service (1915–19), he resumed his operatic career in Rome, later singing at La Scala in Milan. In 1926 he was engaged by the Metropolitan Opera. There, in revivals of Mozart's *Don Giovanni* (1929) and *The Marriage of Figaro* (1939) and in Mussorgsky's *Boris Godunov* (1939), he achieved outstanding success. He also appeared on the New York stage in *South Pacific* (1949) and in motion pictures.

Pinzón, Martín Alonso (märtēn′ ālōn′sō pēnthōn′) d.1493, Spanish navigator. The commander of the *Pinta* on Columbus's first voyage to the New World in 1492, he was already an experienced seaman and an influential citizen of Palos de la Frontera. The support given to Columbus by Pinzón and his brothers is not definitely known, but it was important to the eventual success of the expedition. For reasons that are not clear, he abandoned Columbus in the Antilles for more than six weeks and upon rejoining him was censured for treasonable conduct. On the return voyage his ship was separated from that of Columbus in a storm, but both reached Palos the same day, March 15, 1493. He died soon afterwards. His younger brother, **Francisco Martín**

Pinzón, fl. 1492, was master of the *Pinta.* Another brother, **Vicente Yáñez Pinzón,** fl. 1492–1509, commanded the *Niña* on Columbus's expedition. When the *Santa María* was wrecked on the coast of Hispaniola, Vicente Pinzón took aboard Columbus, who finished the voyage in the *Niña.* In 1495, Pinzón received letters patent for an expedition, but it is unknown whether he made a voyage immediately. He commanded an expedition which sailed from Palos in Nov., 1499, reached the coast of Brazil (Jan., 1500), probably near its easternmost point, and discovered the mouth of the Amazon River. In 1505 he was made governor of Puerto Rico, with permission to colonize the island. He explored (1508–9) the coasts of Yucatán, Honduras, and Venezuela with Juan Díaz de SOLÍS.

Piombo, Sebastiano del: see SEBASTIANO DEL PIOMBO.

pion (pī'ŏn) or **pi meson,** lightest of the MESON family of ELEMENTARY PARTICLES. The existence of the pion was predicted in 1935 by Hideki Yukawa, who theorized that it was responsible for the strong nuclear FORCE holding the atomic NUCLEUS together. It was first detected in COSMIC RAYS by C. F. Powell in 1947. The pion is actually a multiplet of three particles. The neutral pion, π^0, has a mass about 264 times that of the electron. The charged pions, π^+ and π^-, each have a mass about 273 times that of the electron. The neutral pion is its own ANTIPARTICLE, while the negative pion is the antiparticle of the positive pion. Protons and neutrons are held together within the nucleus by the exchange of virtual pions (pions existing briefly in violation of the conservation of energy, as allowed by the UNCERTAINTY PRINCIPLE). Every proton is surrounded by a cloud of these pions, even those not bound in nuclei. Free pions are unstable. The charged pions decay with an average lifetime of 2.55×10^{-8} sec into a MUON of like charge and a NEUTRINO or antineutrino; the neutral pion decays in about 10^{-15} sec, usually into a pair of photons but occasionally into a positron-electron pair and a photon.

Piotrków Trybunalski (pyô'tərkoof trĭboonäl'skē), Rus. *Petrokov,* Ger. *Petrikau,* city (1970 pop. 59,683), central Poland. A textile center, it also manufactures mining equipment, agricultural machinery, glass, chemicals, bricks, and leather goods. There are silicate deposits in the vicinity. One of Poland's oldest cities, it was first mentioned in 1217 and became the seat of several Polish diets (1347–1578) and tribunals (1578–1792). The city passed (1815) to Russia and was (1867–1915) the capital of Petrokov province. It reverted to Poland in 1919. Piotrków Trybunalski has several old churches and the ruins of a castle built by Casimir the Great.

Piozzi, Mrs.: see THRALE, HESTER LYNCH.

pipal (pī'pəl): see BO TREE.

pipe, hollow structure, usually cylindrical, for conducting materials. It is used primarily to convey liquids, gases, or solids suspended in a liquid, e.g., a slurry. It is also used as a conduit for electric wires. The earliest pipes were probably those made of bamboo used by the Chinese to carry water c.5000 B.C. The Egyptians made the first metal pipe of copper c.3000 B.C. Until cast iron became relatively cheap in the 18th cent. most pipes were made of bored stone or wood, clay, lead, and, occasionally, copper or bronze. Modern materials include cast iron, wrought iron, steel, copper, brass, lead, concrete, wood, glass, and plastic. Welded steel pipe is made by bending strips of steel in the form of a tube and welding the longitudinal seam either by electric resistance, by fusion welding, or by heating the tube and pressing the edges together. If one edge is laid over the other, the pipe is lap welded. If the two edges are laid side by side, it is butt welded. Seamless pipe is made from a solid length of metal pierced lengthwise by a mandrel with a rounded nose. Steel pipe is widely used, especially for conducting substances at extremely high pressures and temperatures. Cast iron pipes resist corrosion better than steel pipes and are therefore frequently used underground. Clay and concrete pipes usually carry sewage, and concrete pipes are also used to carry irrigation water at low pressures; for moderate pressures, the concrete is reinforced with steel or mixed with asbestos. Seamless copper and brass pipes are used for plumbing and boilers. Because of its softness and resistance to corrosion, lead is used for flexible connections and for plumbing that does not carry drinking water. The chemical and food industries use glass pipes. During World War II manufacturers developed plastic pipe to replace metals that were in short supply. Plastic pipe is still sometimes used to carry water as well as certain corrosive liquids. A **pipeline** carries water, gas, petroleum, and many other fluids long distances. The first step in laying an oil pipeline is to clear and scrape the ground. Then a trench is dug deep enough to cover the pipe with about 20 in. (51 cm) of dirt. Commonly, 40-ft (12-m) sections of seamless steel pipe are electrically welded together while held over the trench. Before being lowered into place the pipe is coated with a protective paint and wrapped with a substance composed of treated asbestos felt and fiber glass. Pumping stations located usually from 50 to 75 mi (80–121 km) apart boost the dwindling pressure back up to as much as 1,500 lb per sq. in. A steady flow of oil moves through the 6- to 24-in (15-61-cm) pipe at about 3 to 6 mi (5–10 km) per hr. Water has been moved since ancient times in pipelines called AQUEDUCTS. The first natural gas and petroleum pipelines in the United States were built during the 19th cent. Today in many parts of the world pipelines are an extremely important means of transporting diverse fluids. Many pipelines are over 1,000 mi (1,609 km) long, e.g., the Trans-Arabian Pipeline, which carries oil from the Persian Gulf to the Mediterranean.

pipefish: see SEAHORSE.

pipe rolls, ancient records of the crown revenue and expenditures of England, so called, probably, because of the pipelike form of the rolled parchments on which these records were kept. The oldest extant pipe roll dates from the 31st year of the reign of Henry I (1130), and from 1156 they are almost completely intact. The earliest of these records have been published and are an invaluable source for social and administrative history. The pipe rolls were not completely abandoned for modern accounting methods until 1833.

pipe smoking. The habit of smoking various substances probably arose independently in different parts of the world. Herodotus in the 5th cent. B.C. describes the Scythians as inhaling the fumes of burning leaves until they were intoxicated. The leaves may have been MARIJUANA, which was smoked in Africa and Asia long before the diffusion of TOBACCO from America in the 16th cent. Among the Indians of the Americas, pipe smoking was practiced long before the arrival of Europeans. The peace pipe, or CALUMET, was smoked in ceremonies to signify a covenant between tribes. The use of tobacco and pipes spread around the world rapidly. In Asia, OPIUM, which up to that time had only been eaten, was first smoked in the 17th cent. The hookah of Persia and the nargile of India, both of which filter smoke through water, may have evolved independently from the marijuana-smoking practices among aboriginal groups of S Africa and of central Asia. Everywhere, pipes have acquired particular national characteristics and have blossomed into many shapes, fashioned from many materials, including brier, stone, clay, wood, porcelain, MEERSCHAUM, and corncobs. See A. Dunhill, *The Pipe Book* (1924).

Pipe Spring National Monument: see NATIONAL PARKS AND MONUMENTS (table).

pipestone, hard, dull red or mottled pink-and-white clay stone, carved by American Indians into pipes. Called calumets (see CALUMET) the pipes were used extensively in ceremonials. The Indians held pipestone sacred, and even in time of war the quarries were regarded as neutral ground. Pipestone is sometimes called catlinite, for the artist and author George Catlin, who lived among the Indians. It is found mainly in Minnesota, in the Dakotas, and in Canada. Pipestone, Minn., and the Pipestone River in Manitoba, Canada, are named after the stone.

Pipestone National Monument: see NATIONAL PARKS AND MONUMENTS (table).

pipe tree: see LILAC; SAXIFRAGE.

pipe vine: see BIRTHWORT.

pipistrelle: see BAT.

pipit, common name for a group of chiefly Eurasian and African birds that together with the wagtails constitute a subfamily of songbirds related to the Old World warblers and thrushes. Pipits are trim, slender birds with thin, pointed bills. They are chiefly terrestrial and walk or run rapidly, catching insects on or near the ground. The pipit's plumage is streaked and mottled brown; the wagtail's is more boldly patterned. Pipits resemble larks and are sometimes called field larks, or titlarks. The few American species include the water, or rock, pipit, *Anthus spinoletta,* which breeds in the Arctic and winters in the E United States, and the Sprague's pipit of the Great Plains, noted for the spectacular courtship flight and song of the male. The African longclaw has elongated hind toes suited to running over the veldt. The wagtails, members of the same family, are named for their habit of bobbing their tails, and are usually found near water in temperate Eurasia and Africa; the only New World species is the yellow wagtail of the northern tundra. Pipits and wagtails are classified in the phylum CHORDATA, subphylum Vertebrata, class Aves, order Passeriformes, family Motacillidae.

Pippi, Giulio: see GIULIO ROMANO.

Pippin. For Frankish rulers thus named, see PEPIN.

Pippin, Horace, 1888–1946, American primitive painter, b. West Chester, Pa. He worked as a porter and warehouseman. He was severely wounded in World War I. The naïve fervor and bold design of his painting brought him recognition in the 1930s. Among his works in public collections are *Self-Portrait* (Albright-Knox Art Gall., Buffalo, N.Y.); *Suppertime* (Barnes Foundation, Merion, Pa.); and *End of the War* (Philadelphia Mus. of Art). See studies by Selden Rodman (1947 and 1972).

pipsissewa (pĭpsĭs'əwä), any plant of the genus *Chimaphila,* perennial herbs of dry wooded regions in the Northern Hemisphere. The pipsissewas, closely related to the wintergreens, have thick, shiny leaves and pinkish or white flowers. *C. umbellata* is the common species of North America; its variety *cisatlantica* is the plant known as prince's pine in the Eastern states. Other varieties are found in the West and in Europe and Asia. Folia Chimaphilae, extracted from the leaves, is a tonic and diuretic used in the treatment of bladder stones. *C. maculata* is called spotted wintergreen. Pipsissewa is classified in the division MAGNOLIOPHYTA, class Magnoliopsida, family Pyrolaceae. See HEATH, in botany.

Piqua (pĭk'wä), city (1970 pop. 20,741), Miami co., W Ohio, on the Miami River; settled 1797, chartered 1929. It is an industrial city with a great diversity of manufactures, including airplane and automobile parts, steel and iron, paper, aluminum, wood, and metal products. Of special interest is a historical area just north of the city, the site of a number of old Indian villages and of battles during the French and Indian War.

piquet or **picquet** (both: pēkā'), card game played by two persons with a deck of 32 cards—7 (low) up to ace (high) in each suit. Each player receives 12 cards, and eight cards are left on the table face down. The nondealer (the minor) discards from one to five cards and picks up an equal number from the table. The dealer (the major) is entitled to exchange the remaining number of cards. Trumps are not named. After the draw from the table, the hands are compared and points are given for point (the most cards in a suit), sequence (longest sequence), and highest set of three or four of a kind. Carte blanche, a hand without a face card, also scores points. Play of cards from the hands follows with points scored for tricks won. One hundred points wins. There are variations for three or four hands. Piquet was established by the 16th cent., was popular in France, Spain, and Italy, and spread to England under the name cent (one hundred).

Piracicaba (pērəsēkä'bə), city (1970 pop. 152,626), São Paulo state, SE Brazil, on the Tietê River. It is the processing center of a rich agricultural region where sugarcane, cotton, rice, maize, coffee, and many other products are grown. The city houses a noted agricultural institute.

piracy, robbery committed or attempted on the high seas by force of arms. It is distinguished from PRIVATEERING in that the pirate holds no commission and receives the protection of no national flag, but, on the contrary, usually attacks vessels of all nations. A pirate, therefore, is a highwayman of the sea. Since piracy is a crime against mankind, not against any one nation, those practicing it may be tried in any competent court, regardless of nationality. Except in time of war, pirates may not be executed without trial. To the forms of piracy defined by international law, a nation may add offenses committed on board its own vessels or in its own territorial waters. Such crimes can be punished only by the nation that passes the law. Since the line between privateering and piracy is often hard to draw, opportunity exists for varied determinations as to what acts constitute piracy, and any act of doubtful legality committed on the high seas may be characterized as piracy. Thus the sinking of merchant vessels by the Germans in World War I was characterized by some as piracy, but the validity of this theory is questionable as the act was done on the authority of a national state. However, at the Washington Conference of 1921 a treaty was concluded that declared that improper visit and search (see SEARCH, RIGHT OF) by a person in the service of any power would constitute piracy. Because it is often the result of failure or laxity in patrolling sea routes, piracy flourished in times of unrest, or when navies ordinarily protecting commerce were engaged in war. Pirates found their most suitable base of operations in an archipelago that offered shelter together with proximity to trade routes. Pirates preyed upon Phoenician and Greek commerce and were so active in the 1st cent. B.C. that Rome itself was almost starved by their interception of the grain convoys. Pompey swept piracy from the Mediterranean, but with the decline of the Roman empire it revived there and was prevalent until modern times. Muslim pirates infested the W Mediterranean; the Venetians, who ostensibly policed the E Mediterranean, preyed upon the maritime trade of rival cities; and the Barbary states got much of their revenue from piracy. In the North, the Vikings harassed the commerce of the Baltic Sea and the English Channel. Emerging in the 13th cent., the Hanseatic League succeeded in curbing the piracy of its era. New trade routes opened during the Renaissance, e.g., the shipment of precious metals from the Spanish colonies, the rich trade with the East, and the development of the slave trade, that made piracy especially lucrative. At this period no great stigma was attached to piracy, because maritime law had not been systematized. This fact, together with the increasing colonial rivalry of the powers, led states to countenance those pirates who promoted the national cause by attacking the commerce of rival nations. With the tacit approval of the provincial authorities, the Antilles became a pirates' rendezvous, and the English buccaneers of the SPANISH MAIN in the 17th and 18th cent., who despoiled the Spanish treasure armadas and pillaged Spanish-American coast settlements, returned to England to divide their spoils with the crown and to receive the royal pardon. The development of national navies caused the decline of piracy. Beginning in 1803, the United States endeavored to crush the corsairs of Tripoli. In 1815 and 1816 the United States, the Netherlands, and Great Britain wiped out the Barbary pirates, who had exacted tribute under the threat of capturing ships and imprisoning their crews. In 1816, Great Britain and the United States began operations against pirates in the West Indies, particularly those on the Cuban coast, and in 1824 the United States sent David PORTER to complete the task. The power of the pirates along the Straits of Malacca and the China seas, the last existing stronghold of piracy, was broken after the Opium War in the late 19th cent. During the Spanish Civil War the major powers agreed (1937) at the Nyon Conference on an antipiracy pact after mysterious attacks on merchant ships in the Mediterranean. Famous names appearing in the long history of piracy include Sir Francis DRAKE and Sir John HAWKINS, the Elizabethan buccaneers, Edward MANSFIELD, Henry MORGAN, Jacques NAU, Jean LAFFITE, and Edward Teach (BLACKBEARD). There is some doubt as to whether the activities of Captain KIDD constitute piracy. The pirate is a frequent figure in literature, especially in books written for children. Perhaps the most famous fictional pirate is Long John Silver in R. L. Stevenson's *Treasure Island.* Sir Walter Scott and James Fenimore Cooper each wrote a novel entitled *The Pirate,* Charles Kingsley wrote of buccaneers in *Westward Ho!,* and Sir William Gilbert ridiculed pirate stories in his *Pirates of Penzance.* See H. A. Ormerod, *Piracy in the Ancient World* (1924); Philip Gosse, *The History of Piracy* (1932, repr. 1968); C. H. Karraker, *Piracy Was a Business* (1953); A. L. Hayward, *The Book of Pirates* (1956); Robert Carse, *The Age of Piracy* (1957, repr. 1965); Hamilton Cochran, *Freebooters of the Red Sea* (1965); A. G. Course, *Pirates of the Eastern Seas* (1966).

Piraeus, Greece: see PIRAIÉVS.

Piraiévs (pĕrāĕfs') or **Piraeus** (pīrē'əs), city (1971 pop. 187,458), E central Greece, in Attica, on the Saronic Gulf; part of Greater Athens. It is the port of Athens and the chief port in Greece. A commercial center, Piraiévs has shipyards and industries that manufacture chemicals, textiles, and machinery. The construction of Piraiévs was planned by Themistocles and executed (c.450 B.C.) by the architect Hippodamus of Miletus. It quickly replaced Phaleron as the port of Athens. The famed Long Walls, two parallel walls about 600 ft (183 m) apart, connected Athens with Piraiévs and enabled Athens to receive supplies from its port during the Peloponnesian War. The port, itself strongly fortified, consisted of three harbors—one for grain vessels, one for merchant ships in general, and one for warships. In 404 B.C. the Spartans destroyed the Long Walls to the accompaniment of flute music, but Conon rebuilt them in 393 B.C. The arsenal (built 347–323 B.C.) and fortifications were destroyed by the Roman general Sulla in 86 B.C., and few traces of the Long Walls remain. The modern development of Piraiévs began only after Greece achieved independence in the 19th cent. The city was heavily bombed by Germany in World War II.

Piram (pī'răm), Amorite king defeated and killed by Joshua. Joshua 10.3–27.

Pirandello, Luigi (lwē'jē pērändĕl'lō), 1867–1936, Italian author, b. Sicily. One of the great figures in 20th-century European theater, Pirandello was awarded the 1934 Nobel Prize in Literature. After an extensive education, he began in the 1890s to write poetry and short stories, many of which reflect his interest in Sicilian folklore. In 1897 he became professor of Italian literature at the Normal College for Women in Rome. Before achieving fame Pirandello had many difficult years. Lack of public recognition, the failure of his father's mining business, and the 14-year-long insanity of his wife may account in part for the pessimism of his work. Pirandello wrote seven novels, among them *Il fu Mattia Pascal* (1904, tr. *The Late Mattia Pascal,* 1923) and *I vecchi e i giovani* (1913, tr. *The Young and the Old,* 1928), as well as nearly 300 short stories. His fame rests primarily, however, on his intellectual and grotesquely humorous plays. He began writing for the theater during World War II and from that time until his death produced more than 40 dramas. By 1924 his plays were being performed in most of the great cities of the world. The best known include *Così è, se vi pare* (1917, tr. *Right You Are If You Think You Are,* 1922), *Il piacere dell' onestà* (1917, tr. *The Pleasure of Honesty,* 1923), *Sei personaggi in cerca d'autore* (1921, tr. *Six Characters in Search of an Author,* 1922), *Enrico IV* (1922, tr. *Henry IV,* 1922), and *Come tu mi vuoi* (1930, tr. *As You Desire Me,* 1931). The grim humor of his plays flows from their central theme—the shattering search to distinguish between reality and illusion. Reality he saw as an intangible, and what is taken for reality as a series of illusions. Since truth was not ascertainable, man was condemned to live in moral and cultural confusion, or even anarchy. These alienated beliefs may partly explain Pirandello's acceptance of Mussolini as a man of order. Pirandello's works are influential models for later existential drama. See studies by W. F. Starkie (3d ed. 1965); O. Büdel (2d ed. 1969), Renate Matthaei (tr. 1973), and Anne Paolucci (1974).

Piranesi, Giovanni Battista (jōvän'nē bät-tē'stä pĕrānā'zē), 1720–78, Italian engraver and architect. The greater part of his life was spent in Rome, where he made engravings of the buildings and monuments of the ancient and modern city. His architectural plates are notable for their accuracy and grandeur. He often digressed from documentary precision and created fanciful reconstructions of Roman monuments or romanticized architectural dreams, as in the *Carceri* plates. The one existing building that he designed is the Church of Santa Maria Priorato, Rome (1764–65). See studies by A. M. Hind (1922), A. H. Mayor (1952), Hylton Thomas (1954), and Peter Murray (1972).

piranha: see CHARACIN.

Pirate Coast: see UNITED ARAB EMIRATES.

Pirathon (pĭr'əthŏn), unidentified place, central Palestine, the native town of one of David's captains, Benaiah, and of one of the judges, Abdon. Judges 12.13, 15; 2 Sam. 23.30; 1 Chron. 27.14. It is probably identical with Pharathon. 1 Mac. 9.50.

Pire, Georges Henri (zhôrzh äNrē' pēr), 1910–69, Belgian priest. He entered a Dominican monastery at the age of 18 and was ordained in 1934. He taught moral philosophy and sociology and during World War II participated in the Belgian resistance movement. After the war he became deeply concerned with the plight of Europe's refugees and in 1949 established an organization, Aid to Displaced Persons, which did much to improve the living conditions and resettlement of refugees. Father Pire was awarded the 1958 Nobel Peace Prize.

Pirenne, Henri (äNrē' pērĕn'), 1862–1935, Belgian historian. He was for many years a professor of history at the Univ. of Ghent. A leader of Belgian passive resistance in World War I, he was held (1916–18) as a hostage by the Germans. In his *History of Belgium* (tr., 7 vol., 1899–1932), he showed how traditional and economic forces had drawn Flemings and Walloons together. In *Mohammed and Charlemagne* (tr. 1939) he attributed the collapse of western civilization to the spread of Islam; this thesis raised much controversy among historians. Pirenne emphasized the historical role of the capitalist middle class, and in *Medieval Cities* (tr. 1925) he revolutionized accepted views by attributing the origins of medieval cities to the revival of trade. Other works include *Belgian Democracy: Its Early History* (tr. 1915) and *Economic and Social History of Medieval Europe* (tr. 1936). See studies by A. F. Havighurst, ed. (rev. ed. 1969) and B. P. Lyon (1972).

Pírgos or **Pyrgos** (both: pēr'gôs), town (1971 pop. 20,599), capital of Ilía prefecture, SW Greece, in the Peloponnesus, near the mouth of the Alfiós River. It is a commercial center and has industries that manufacture cigarettes and alcoholic beverages. Pírgos was sacked by the Ottoman Turks in the Greek War of Independence.

Pirithoüs or **Peirithoüs** (both: pīrĭth'ōəs), in Greek mythology, king of the Lapithae. He and THESEUS swore an oath of eternal friendship. Together they went on the Calydonian hunt and invaded the land of the Amazons. In a later exploit they attempted to abduct Persephone from Hades, where they were tricked into sitting on a magic bench from which they were unable to rise. After four years of torture Hercules descended to Hades and pulled Theseus from the bench, but when he reached for Pirithoüs the ground trembled and Pirithoüs was left behind. In some accounts Pirithoüs also escaped.

Pirke Avot: see MISHNA.

Pirmasens (pĭrmäzĕns'), city (1970 pop. 55,692), Rhineland-Palatinate, SW West Germany, near the French border. It is the leading West German shoe and boot manufacturing center. Other products of the city include chemicals, plastics, and machines. Founded in the 8th cent., Pirmasens belonged to the counts of Hanau-Lichtenberg until 1736. It later passed to Hesse-Darmstadt and in 1816 to Bavaria. The city was heavily damaged in World War II.

Pirna (pĭr'nä), city (1970 pop. 47,468), Dresden district, SE East Germany, on the Elbe River. Manufactures of this industrial city include rayon, paper, steel, furniture, and ceramics. Nearby are sandstone quarries. Known in 1233, Pirna passed to Bohemia in 1298 and to Meissen in the early 15th cent. The Saxonians surrendered (1756) there to Prussia in the Seven Years War. Noteworthy buildings include a 16th-century Gothic church, the city hall (begun 1555), and Sonnenstein castle (16th cent.).

Pirogov, Nikolai Ivanovich (nyĭkəlī' ēvä'nəvĭch pĭrōgôf'), 1810–1881, Russian surgeon, b. Moscow. He entered the Univ. of Moscow at the age of 14 and completed the medical curriculum at 17. He then studied in Germany, receiving a doctor of philosophy degree at Dorpat, where he served as professor of surgery from 1836 to 1840. He first gained prominence in the United States for his anatomical studies on arteries and fascia. In 1840 he returned to Russia and became professor of hospital surgery at the Military Medical Academy at St. Petersburg. The opening of the Crimean War in 1854 found him in Sevastopol. Considered the founder of field surgery, he devised the plaster cast, first used successfully in the Sevastopol campaign, and the Pirogov amputation, a method of severing the foot so that part of the heel bone is left in the stump to give added support to the lower ends of the leg bones. He was one of the first to use ether as an anesthetic (1847) and was the author of many scientific treatises.

Pisa (pī'sə), in ancient Greece, region around Olympia, center of an area called Pisatis. The inhabitants long contended with Elis for control of the Olympic games until the early 6th cent. B.C., when they were defeated by the Eleans and the Spartans. There may have been a city Pisa, but all traces have been lost.

Pisa (pē'sä), city (1971 pop. 103,677), capital of Pisa prov., Tuscany, N central Italy, on the Arno River. It is now c.6 mi (9.7 km) from the Tyrrhenian Sea, which once reached the city. Pisa is a commercial and industrial center; manufactures include glass, textiles, pharmaceuticals, and processed food. Probably a Greek colony, later certainly an Etruscan town, it became a Roman colony (180 B.C.) and prospered. During the 9th to 11th cent. A.D. it developed into a powerful maritime republic, fighting the Arabs throughout the Mediterranean and rivaling Genoa and Venice. Pisa's political and commercial power increased upon acquisition of possessions and trading privileges in the eastern Mediterranean during the Crusades. While competing with Genoa for the possession of Corsica and Sardinia, Pisa was crushed by the Genoese in the naval battle of Meloria (1284). As a Ghibelline center in the 13th and 14th cent., the city was also chronically at war with Florence, to which it fell in 1406. At the same time, a school of sculpture founded by Nicola Pisano flourished in Pisa and gave the city some of its great art treasures. The Council of Pisa met there in 1409. The university (founded in the 14th cent.) enjoyed a great reputation during the Renaissance; Galileo, who was born in Pisa in 1564, was a student and later a teacher there. Pisa was badly damaged in World War II but was extensively reconstructed after 1945; the characteristic Pisan style, a variation of the Romanesque, was largely retained. The city's noteworthy structures include the Pisan Romanesque cathedral (1068–1118), which has a fine marble facade, bronze panels by Bonnano Pisano, and a pulpit by Giovanni Pisano (reconstructed after a fire in 1926); the marble baptistery (1153–1278); the marble Leaning Tower (180 ft/55 m high and 16 ft/4.9 m out of the perpendicular); the *Camp Santo* (cemetery), with frescoes of the 14th and 15th cent. (many badly damaged in World War II); and the churches of Santa Maria della Spina (early 14th cent.) and Santa Caterina. Nearby is the Carthusian Monastery of Pisa, with large classical cloisters.

Pisa, Council of, 1409, uncanonical council of the Roman Catholic Church. It was summoned to end the Great Schism (see SCHISM, GREAT) by members of the colleges of cardinals of the two rivals, Gregory XII (in Rome) and Benedict XIII (Pedro de LUNA, in Avignon). The plan was to depose both men claiming to be pope and elect a new one. The council was brilliant, having wide international attendance. It declared both popes to be heretical and schismatic and therefore not popes; the cardinals proceeded to elect Pietro Cardinal Philarghi as Alexander V. This move served to complicate the schism with a third claimant rather than to dissolve it. The council first gave quasi-official expression to the conciliar theory, i.e., that councils are supreme in the church, a notion that became prominent again at Constance and at Basel (see CONSTANCE, COUNCIL OF; BASEL, COUNCIL OF). The canonical illegality of the council rests on several features; e.g., most of the cardinals involved owed their creation to popes whom they declared to be holding office illegally.

Pisan, Christine de (krēstēn' də pēzäN'), 1364–c.1430, French poet, of Italian descent. She wrote many verse romances and works in prose, as well as the lyric poems for which she is most famous. Remarkable in character and learning, Christine sought to express the dignity of woman. Her writings include *Le Livre des fais d'armes et de chevalerie*, first translated and printed by Caxton as *The Book of Fayttes of Armes and of Chivalrye* (1489; new ed. 1932) and *Le Livre du duc des vrais amans* (tr. *The Book of the Duke of True Lovers,* 1908).

Pisanello (pēzänĕl'lō), c.1395–1455?, Italian medalist, painter and draftsman of the early Renaissance. He was also called Vittore Pisano, but his real name was Antonio Pisano. His art shows the influence of Gentile da Fabriano, whom he assisted in the ducal palace in Venice. Nothing remains of the Venetian frescoes or of those that he executed in the Lateran, Rome, or in Castello, Pavia. The only frescoes that have survived are those in Verona, the *Annunciation* in San Fermo, and *St. George and the Princess* in Sant' Anastasia. Pisanello was in great demand by the leading patrons of the time. He stayed at the courts of Mantua, Ferrara, Milan, Urbino, and Naples, working mainly on portraits. He is the first important Renaissance artist to use the medal form and to revive the antique style of portraiture. His medals are greatly valued for their historic as well as their artistic merit. Among them are portraits of Filippo Visconti, Lionello d'Este, Francesco Sforza, Alfonso V, and Sigismondo Malatesta (all: Victoria and Albert Mus., London). Pisanello was also a superb draftsman. The Vallardi Codex (Louvre) contains his studies for paintings, antique motifs, costumes, and animals, all depicted with keen perception. Among the rare panel paintings that have survived are the *Vision of St. Eustache* and *Saints Anthony and George* (National Gall., London); portraits of *Lionello d'Este* (Bergamo), *Ginevra d'Este* (Louvre), and the *Emperor Sigismondo* (Vienna). See studies by Enio Sindona (1964) and Giovanni Paccagnini (1973).

Pisano, Andrea (ändrĕ'ä pēzä'nō), c.1290–c.1348, Italian sculptor, also called Andrea da Pontedera. His most important work, the first bronze doors of the baptistery in Florence, was begun in 1330. In 28 panels he depicted scenes from the life of John the Baptist. Through Andrea, Italian sculpture came under the influence of the painter and architect GIOTTO, whom he succeeded as head of the work on the cathedral and the campanile in Florence. It is still debated whether the design for the campanile reliefs is to be credited to Giotto or to Andrea. Andrea spent his last year in Orvieto, directing work on the facade of the cathedral.

Pisano, Nicola (nēkō'lä), b. c.1220, d. between 1278 and 1287, major Italian sculptor, believed to have come from Apulia. He founded a new school of sculpture in Italy. His first great work was the marble pulpit for the baptistery in Pisa, completed in 1259. Its form was hexagonal, with panels in high relief consisting of scenes from the life of Christ. The pulpit is supported by elaborate columns, three of which rest on carved lions. The shape of the pulpit and the strong use of antique prototypes are thought to derive from an early training in S Italy. Imbued with the classic spirit, Nicola concentrated on the human figure, recreating a style of monumental dignity. From 1265 to 1268 he worked on a larger pulpit for the cathedral at Siena. Assisted by his son Giovanni and other pupils, he allowed them a greater part of the execution. The narrative scenes show more freedom of treatment and a tendency toward the more linear French Gothic form. His last great project was the fountain at Perugia. With Giovanni he designed 24 statues and twice as many reliefs, all finished (1278) within one year. Nicola Pisano was the earliest great Italian sculptor. See study by G. H. Crichton and E. R. Crichton (1938). His son, **Giovanni Pisano,** b. c.1250, d. after 1314, was a sculptor and architect. With his dramatic use of line and his taste for elaborate decoration, he is thought to have had a firsthand acquaintance with the Gothic art of France. Besides assisting his father in work on the pulpit for the cathedral at Siena and on the fountain at Perugia, he independently executed a pulpit (1298–1301) for Sant' Andrea, Pistoia, and a pulpit (1302–10) for the cathedral at Pisa. The last was reconstructed in 1926, though several fragments are dispersed (Metropolitan Mus.; Berlin). He carved several free-standing statues of the Madonna, which are in Pisa, Padua, and Prato. In 1312 he made the tomb of Margaret, wife of Emperor Henry VII. Fragments of it are still in Genoa. Giovanni also designed an ornate facade for the cathedral at Siena. See study by Michael Ayrton (1969).

Pisano, Vittore: see PISANELLO.

Piscataqua (pĭskăt'əkwə, –kwā), navigable river, 12 mi (19 km) long, formed by the junction of the Cocheco and the Salmon Falls rivers, SE N.H., and flowing SE to Portsmouth harbor, forming part of the N.H.-Maine border. The tidal harbor from Portsmouth to the Atlantic Ocean is one of the finest in the United States and is the site of Portsmouth Naval Shipyard (est. 1800).

Piscataway Park: see NATIONAL PARKS AND MONUMENTS (table).

Piscator, Erwin (pĭskä'tôr), 1893–1966, German theatrical director and producer who, with Bertolt BRECHT, was the foremost exponent of epic theater. He worked experimentally in Berlin after 1919. As director of the Volksbühne (1924–27), and later at his own theater (on Nollendorfplatz), he produced the social and political plays especially suited to his theories. He used constructivist sets, lectures, movies, and mechanical devices that appealed to his audiences. In 1927 he produced a notable adaptation of a Czech novel (tr. *The Good Soldier Schweik*). Piscator went to the United States in 1939 and became director of the Dramatic Workshop and the Studio Theater, which he founded in New York City. He returned to Germany c.1958; he was appointed manager and director of the Volksbühne in West Berlin and received honors from the West German government for his contribution to the arts. His influence on European and American production methods was extensive. See C. D. Innes, *Erwin Piscator's Political Theatre* (1974).

Pisces (pī'sēz) [Lat.,= the fishes], CONSTELLATION lying directly S of Andromeda and on the ECLIPTIC (the sun's apparent path through the heavens) between Aries and Aquarius; it is one of the constellations of the ZODIAC. Pisces is traditionally depicted as two fishes. Because of the PRECESSION OF THE EQUINOXES, the vernal equinox has moved westward from the constellation Aries (where it was located c.2,000 years ago) into Pisces. There are no exceptionally bright stars in Pisces, but a nova was observed there in 1925. Pisces reaches its highest point in the evening sky in November.

Pisco (pēs'kō), city (1969 est. pop. 26,700), capital of Ica dept., SW Peru, a port on the Pacific Ocean. The major industries are the production of the famous Pisco brandy and the cultivation and processing of cotton. On the adjacent PARACAS peninsula are some ruins from a pre-Inca civilization.

pisé de terre: see RAMMED EARTH.

Písek (pē'sĕk), city (1970 pop. 22,994), SW Czechoslovakia, in Bohemia, on the Otava River. It has woodworking, tobacco, and textile industries. Písek was founded in the 13th cent. and later suffered heavily in the Thirty Years War (1618–48). The city has a 13th-century palace, a 14th-century stone bridge (the oldest in Czechoslovakia), and several Gothic churches.

Pisemsky, Aleksey Feofilaktovich (əlyĭksyā' fä"əfēläk'təvĭch pē'syĭmskē), 1820–81, Russian novelist and playwright. In his realistic descriptions of country life he portrayed the peasant sympathetically. His novel *A Thousand Souls* (1858, tr. 1959) is the story of an ambitious man who marries the owner of a thousand "souls," or serfs. His best-known works include the play *A Bitter Fate* (1860, tr. 1933), a tragic story of the seduction of a peasant's wife by a landowner, and the novels *A Love Match* and *The Doormat.* See study by C. A. Moser (1969).

Pishpek: see FRUNZE, USSR.

Pisidia (pĭsĭd'ēə, pī–), ancient country of S Asia Minor, S of Phrygia and N of Pamphylia. It was a mountainous country, traversed by the Taurus range. Its warlike tribes maintained their independence until the country was incorporated into a Roman province in the early 1st cent. A.D.

Pisistratus (pĭsĭs'trətəs), 605?–527 B.C., Greek statesman, tyrant of Athens. His power was founded on the cohesion of the rural citizens, whom he consolidated with farseeing land laws. His coup d'etat (c.560 B.C.) was probably not unpopular. His rivals, the ALCMAEONIDAE and the aristocracy, managed to exile him twice, but in his last years he established himself sufficiently to leave Athens in the hands of his sons, HIPPIAS and HIPPARCHUS. He first won Salamis for Athens and established Attic hegemony in the Dardanelles. He did much to enhance Athenian cultural prestige, held great festivals like the Panathenaea, and beautified the city. His building efforts included fountains and temples, such as the great temple of Zeus at Athens. He had an official text of Homer written down, probably the first. His name also appears as Peisistratus.

Piso (pī'sō), distinguished family of the ancient Roman gens Calpurnia. One of the best-known members was **Lucius Calpurnius Piso Caesoninus,** d. after 43 B.C., father-in-law of Julius Caesar. As consul (58 B.C.), he aided in the banishment of Cicero; Macedonia was his proconsular province (57 B.C., 56 B.C.). Cicero, after he returned from exile in 57 B.C., attacked him in the senate for extortion, especially in the orations *De provinciis consularibus* and *In Pisonem.* In 50 B.C., Piso was censor. Although he fought with Pompey at the outbreak of the civil war (49 B.C.), he later was friendly with Caesar. **Caius Calpurnius Piso,** d. A.D. 65, was a prominent patron of literature. He led a conspiracy against Nero; it was discovered, and Piso killed himself.

Pison (pī'sən), unidentified river of Eden. Gen. 2.11.

Pispah (pĭs'pə), son of Jether. 1 Chron. 7.38.

Pissarro, Camille (kämē'yə pēsärō'), 1830–1903, French impressionist painter, b. St. Thomas, Virgin Islands. In Paris from 1855, he came under the influence of Corot and the Barbizon school. Later he allied himself with the impressionists, and was represented in all of the eight impressionist exhibitions (1874–1886). In 1884 he experimented with the theories of color devised by SEURAT. Abandoning divisionism in the 1890s, he reverted to a freer, more vital interpretation of nature. It was not until then that his works began to be popular. Pissarro's warmth and generosity made him an endearing figure to many French painters. He was especially beloved as teacher and friend to Gauguin, Cézanne, and Cassatt. His son Lucien was also his pupil. Pissarro's paintings are in many leading American collections, including *Le Fond de l'Hermitage* (Cleveland Mus. of Art) and *Bather in the Woods* (Metropolitan Mus.). See his works ed. by J. Rewald (1963); his *Letters to his Son Lucien* ed. by J. Rewald (1943); W. S. Meadmore, *Lucien Pissarro* (1963).

pistachio (pĭstăsh'ēō, pĭstä'shēō), tree or shrub (of the genus *Pistacia*) of the family Anacardiaceae (SUMAC family). The species that yields the pistachio nut of commerce is *P. vera,* native to Asia Minor, Syria, and Palestine. It is now cultivated on a small scale in parts of the SW United States and in many of the warmer parts of Europe and Asia; the trade supply comes largely from Iran, Syria, Afghanistan, Italy, and Sicily. The "nut," a greenish seed, is eaten salted and is used in making confections. In Syria and some other countries it is more widely used and is traditional at weddings and on other occasions. A flavoring oil is derived from the nuts. Related species include the TEREBINTH, or turpentine tree; the Chinese pistachio, *P. chinensis,* grown in Florida and California both for ornament and as grafting stock for *P. vera;* and the mastic (*P. lentiscus*). Pistachio is classified in the division MAGNOLIOPHYTA, class Magnoliopsida, order Sapindales, family Anacardiaceae.

pistil (pĭs'tĭl), one of the four basic parts of a FLOWER, the central structure around which are arranged the stamens, the petals, and the sepals. The pistil is usually called the female reproductive organ of a flowering plant, although the actual reproductive structures are microscopic. The pistil has a bulbous base (the ovary) containing the ovules, which develop into seeds after fertilization of eggs. A pistil is composed of one or more highly modified leaves (carpels), each containing one or more ovules. A flower may have one or more simple pistils, each a separate organ, or, in higher orders, a compound pistil, formed of several fused carpels. Usually, there is above the ovary a stalk (the style) bearing on its tip the stigma, where the pollen grains land and germinate (see POLLINATION). The style is usually long and slender, which improves the chances of cross-pollination, and the stigma is often sticky or hairy, to retain the pollen. The degree of evolutionary development is also indicated by the location of the ovary in relation to the other parts of the flower. If the stamens, petals, and sepals are attached beneath the ovary, the flower is hypogynous and the ovary is superior; if they are attached above, the ovary is inferior and the flower epigynous; if the ovary is located in a receptacle at the outer edges of which are attached the other flower parts, it is called superior or half-inferior and the flower perigynous. A flower that has one or more pistils but no stamens is called pistillate, or female, as distinguished from a staminate, or male, flower, which lacks pistils altogether.

Pistoia (pēstô'yä), city (1971 pop. 93,263), capital of Pistoia prov., Tuscany, central Italy, at the foot of the Apennines. It is an agricultural and industrial center. Manufactures include leather and metal goods, glass, textiles, canned foods, and footwear. Pistoia was under Roman rule from the 6th cent. B.C. In 62 B.C., Catiline, the Roman politician and conspirator, was killed in battle nearby. The city rose to prominence in the 12th and 13th cent., and its citizens made important contributions to architecture and sculpture. Hampered by wars and by internal strife between the Blacks and the Whites (these factions were transferred from Pistoia to Florence), it fell under the hegemony of Florence in the 14th cent. Noteworthy buildings include the Pisan-Romanesque cathedral (13th–14th cent.); the churches of Sant' Andrea (with a pulpit by Pisano) and San Pietro; a 14th-century baptistery; the Palazzo Pretorio (14th cent.); and the Ospedale del Ceppo (13th–16th cent.), with a fine terra-cotta frieze by Giovanni della Robbia.

pistol: see SMALL ARMS.

Piston, Walter, 1894–, American composer and teacher, b. Rockland, Maine. Piston studied at Harvard and with Nadia Boulanger in Paris; he joined the faculty of Harvard in 1926. He became a Guggenheim Fellow in 1934. As a composer Piston is a neoclassicist, using traditional forms with sure technique and intellectual style. His works often incorporate masterful counterpoint and employ complex jazz rhythms. Piston's compositions include symphonies, suites for orchestra, a concertino for piano and orchestra, a violin concerto, a viola concerto, a toccata and a concerto for orchestra, a ballet, and string quartets and other chamber music. He is the author of *Principles of Harmonic Analysis* (1933), *Harmony* (1941, rev. ed. 1948), *Counterpoint* (1947), and *Orchestration* (1955).

Pitcairn, John (pĭt'kârn), 1722–75, British royal marine officer in the American Revolution. Major Pitcairn commanded the advance guard of the British troops at Lexington (see LEXINGTON AND CONCORD, BATTLES OF) on April 19, 1775, but whether he ordered his men to fire on the colonial militia or was forced to return their fire is a historical problem. He was later killed in the battle of Bunker Hill. Pitcairn Island is named for his son Robert Pitcairn (c.1747–c.1770), who as a midshipman under Philip Carteret first sighted it on July 2, 1767.

Pitcairn Island, volcanic island (1971 pop. 91), 2.5 sq mi (6.5 sq km), South Pacific, SE of Tuamotu Archipelago. A British possession since 1839, the island is officially administered by the British High Commissioner to New Zealand. Local matters, however, are handled by a council of islanders. The Pitcairn Island district includes the uninhabited atolls of Henderson, Ducie, and Oeno islands. The only economic activity is the growth of oranges and pineapples for export. The island was discovered in 1767 by Philip Carteret, a British admiral, but was named after Robert Pitcairn, the midshipman who first sighted it. It was colonized in 1790 by mutineers from the BOUNTY and Tahitian women. Their descendants, who speak English, still inhabit the island. In 1856 overpopulation caused the removal of the inhabitants, at their request, to NORFOLK ISLAND, but some soon returned to Pitcairn. In 1957 the remains of the *Bounty* were discovered off the southern end of the island.

pitch, in aviation: see AIRPLANE; AIRFOIL.

pitch, in music, the position of a tone in the musical SCALE, today designated by a letter name and determined by the frequency of vibration of the source of the tone. Pitch is an attribute of every musical tone; the first HARMONIC of any tone is perceived as its pitch. The earliest successful attempt to standardize pitch was made in 1858, when a commission of musicians and scientists appointed by the French government settled upon an A of 435 cycles per second; this standard was adopted by an international conference at Vienna in 1889. In the United States, however, the prevailing standard is an A of 440 cycles per second. Before the middle of the 19th cent., pitch varied according to time, place, and medium of musical performance; since the classical period the trend has been gradually upward. The relative pitch of a tone, in contrast to ABSOLUTE PITCH, is an expression of its pitch in relation to the pitch of some other tone taken as a standard.

pitch: see TAR AND PITCH.

pitchblende (pĭch'blĕnd"), dark, lustrous, heavy mineral, a source of radium and uranium. Largely natural uranium oxide, UO_2 and UO_3, it usually contains some lead and variable amounts of thorium and rare-earth elements. It is massive in form, frequently with a botryoidal, or grape-cluster, appearance, and has a variable but high specific gravity. Pitchblende is greenish, brownish, or black in color, with a pitchy to submetallic luster. The uranium yield is from 50% to 80%. Uraninite, a closely related ore richer in uranium, commonly crystallizes in the cubic system. It yields 65% to 80% uranium and has a specific gravity somewhat higher than that of pitchblende. The color range is from deep black to brown. Both ores occur as primary constituents of quartz veins and with other metals. They supply radium and polonium in addition to uranium. Although the ores occur in small quantities throughout the world, the Great Lakes region of Canada, Zaïre, Czechoslovakia, the Colorado Plateau, Australia, and South Africa are the major sources.

Pitcher, Molly, 1744–1832, American Revolutionary heroine, whose real name was Mary Ludwig Hays or Heis, b. near Trenton, N.J. As the wife of John Hays or Heis, she carried water for her husband and other soldiers in the battle of Monmouth (1778) and earned her nickname. The legend that she manned her husband's gun is apocryphal and possibly rose from confusion with Margaret CORBIN. After her husband's death, she married George McCauley, and in 1822 she was pensioned by Pennsylvania. See W. S. Stryker, *The Battle of Monmouth* (1927).

pitcher plant, any of several insectivorous plants with leaves adapted for trapping insects. Each leaf forms a "pitcher," a somewhat trumpet-shaped enclosure, usually containing a liquid. An insect that enters, lured by nectar and sometimes by brilliant coloration, is prevented from retreating by deflexed bristles and ultimately is drowned in the fluid. The trapped insects are apparently digested by plant enzymes and perhaps by bacteria present in the collected rainwater solution. There are three families of pitcher plants. The American family (the Sarraceniaceae) comprises three genera of bog plants, *Sarracenia* of E North America, *Darlingtonia* of N California and adjacent Oregon (the single species is *D. californica*), and *Heliamphora* of N South America. The common pitcher plant, or side-saddle flower (*S. purpurea*), is found in bogs from Labrador to Florida and Iowa. It has been used medicinally by both Indians and white men. An Old World tropical family, ranging from China to Australia and found chiefly in Borneo, consists of the single genus *Nepenthes*. Many of its species and hybrids, sometimes also called monkey cups, are cultivated as novelties for their large and showy pendent pitchers. The Australian pitcher plant (*Cephalotus follicularis*) is the single species of its family. The bottom leaves of its low rosette are modified into brightly colored, slipper-shaped receptacles with lids and teeth. Other insectivorous plants include the BLADDERWORT, butterwort, VENUS'S-FLYTRAP, and sundew.

Pitch Lake, pool of pitch (asphalt), c.114 acres (46 hectares), SW Trinidad island, Trinidad and Tobago, near La Brea. The lake is believed to be formed and supplied by the seepage of natural pitch, a form of petroleum, from the surrounding oil-rich region. The pitch, hard around the edges of the pool, becomes more viscous towards the center. The seemingly inexhaustible supply has yielded millions of tons of pitch since the 16th cent. Fossils of prehistoric animals have been found in Pitch Lake, which has also become a tourist attraction.

pitch pine, common name for the species *Pinus rigida*, a small PINE of the northeastern coastal United States.

pitch pipe, in music, small pipe used to establish a certain PITCH and having either a constant note or a gauged slide. In 1946 an electronic device for producing constant pitch was developed in the United States. This device is now used frequently for orchestral tuning.

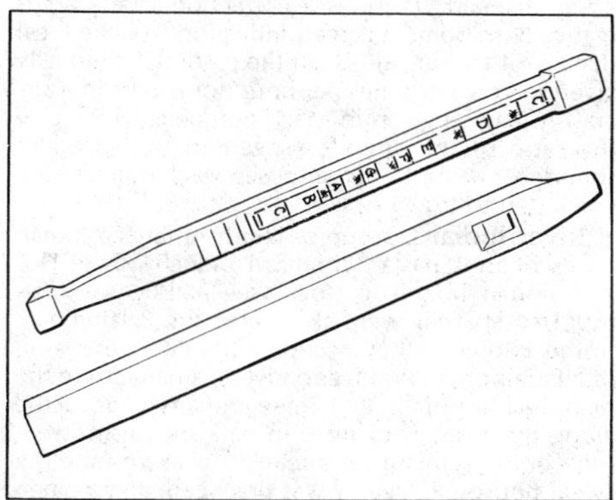

Pitch pipe

Pitești (pētĕsht'), city (1970 est. pop. 74,000), S central Rumania, in Walachia, on the Argesul River. It is the administrative and commercial center of the Argeș region and an important rail junction. Pitești is famous for its wines. The city has heavy and light industries, and there are several resorts nearby.

pith, in botany, core of the STEM of most plants. Pith is composed of large, loosely packed food-storage cells. As the stem grows older the pith usually dries out, and in some it disintegrates and the stem becomes hollow. In trees the pith becomes much reduced as the woody tissue (xylem) grows. In the Orient, rice paper is made from the pith of some shrubs. Candlewicks are made of the pith of certain rushes.

Pithecanthropus erectus: see HOMO ERECTUS.

Pithom (pī'thŏm), ancient treasure city of Egypt, in the eastern part of the Nile delta, built by the Israelites for the pharaoh. Ruins include walls of storage chambers. Ex. 1.11.

Pithon (pī'thŏn), descendant of Saul, one of the sons of Micah. 1 Chron. 8.35; 9.41.

Pitman, Sir Isaac, 1813–97, English inventor of phonographic shorthand. In *Stenographic Soundhand* (1837) he set forth a shorthand system based on phonetic rather than orthographic principles; adapted to more than a dozen languages, it became one of the most-used systems in the world. Through his own publishing house he published many manuals, journals, and books about shorthand. The Pitman system was introduced to the United States through Stephen P. Andrews and Sir Isaac's brother, **Benn Pitman,** 1822–1910, who emigrated to the United States in 1852 and created in Cincinnati the Phonographic Institute to teach and publish works on shorthand. He taught wood carving at the Cincinnati Art Academy, invented (1855) an electrochemical process of relief engraving, and wrote a biography of his brother (1902).

Pitman, residential borough (1970 pop. 10,257), Gloucester co., SW N.J.; settled 1871 as a place for Methodist camp meetings, inc. 1905. In an orchard and truck-farming area, it is now a resort.

Pitoëff, Georges (zhôrzh pē'tōĕf), 1887?–1939, Russian actor-manager. Although he had both an engineering and a law degree, Pitoëff was drawn to the theater and first appeared on stage in 1912 in St. Petersburg. After World War I he emigrated to Paris, where he and his wife, the actress Ludmilla, greatly influenced French theater through their productions of more than 200 plays. The Pitoëffs introduced the works of foreign playwrights and French innovators, including Ibsen, Cocteau, and Anouilh.

pitot static system (pētō'), device for measuring the rate at which a fluid flows. Among the principal applications of the device are an airspeed indicator for aircraft and a distance and speed indicator for ships. The device contains a short tube with one open end that faces directly toward the stream of air or other fluid. When no fluid is moving into the opening, a minimum pressure, called the static pressure, is exerted against it. When a stream is flowing into it, the pressure rises by an amount that depends on the velocity of the stream. Behind this tube is another tube with a number of small vents at right angles to the direction of the first tube. When a stream raises the pressure against the opening of the first tube, the pressure against the vents is still equal to the static pressure. A suitable gauge compares these pressures, using the static pressure as a reference, and gives a reading in units of velocity. For an aircraft this reading is called "indicated airspeed"; "true airspeed" requires a correction, made automatically by some airspeed indicators, for the local density of the air. Although the reading is normally given in knots or miles per hour, for supersonic aircraft it may be given in Mach numbers, which give the ratio of the aircraft's speed to the speed of sound. For navigational purposes Mach numbers are converted to true airspeed.

Pit River Indians, group of North American Indian tribes of the Shasta-Achumawi branch of the Hokan-Siouan linguistic stock (see AMERICAN INDIAN LANGUAGES). They were also called the Palaihnihan. In the 19th cent. they occupied the Pit River region in NE California. Pit River derived its name from the many game pitfalls that these Indians constructed along the river. They lived in bark or brush dwellings or in semisubterranean houses resembling sweat houses. Polygamy was practiced, and women held a low status. Religious ceremonies were not prominent, but the Pit River Indians had an elaborate creation myth. Today there are some 300 living on reservations in California.

Pitt, William (1708–78): see CHATHAM, WILLIAM PITT, 1ST EARL OF.

Pitt, William, 1759–1806, British statesman; 2d son of William Pitt, 1st earl of Chatham. Trained as a lawyer, he entered Parliament in 1781 and in 1782 at the age of 23 became chancellor of the exchequer under Lord Shelburne. At the fall (1783) of the coalition government of Lord North and Charles James FOX, who was to be Pitt's lifelong rival, Pitt was made prime minister by GEORGE III. He overcame strong opposition in Parliament, where the king's interference was sharply resented, and a long-postponed general election (1784) gave him a parliamentary majority. Pitt's policies included reduced expenditures, new taxes to decrease the national debt, and lower customs duties in accordance with the theories of Adam SMITH. He also advocated parliamentary reform but failed (1785) to secure Parliament's approval of it. His India Act (1784) strengthened the government's powers there, but left patronage in the hands of the East India Company. His Constitutional Act (1791) divided Canada into Upper and Lower Canada and sanctioned the institutions of the French Canadians in the latter province. Pitt's popularity increased steadily; when the king became temporarily insane (1788–89), the prime minister was able, despite the efforts of Fox, to prevent the establishment of an unlimited regency and remain in office. His liberal policies ended when Great Britain became involved in the FRENCH REVOLUTIONARY WARS, followed by the Napoleonic Wars (see NAPOLEON I). When the French Revolution began (1789), Pitt's desire was for peace and neutrality, and after France finally declared war (1793) on Britain, he failed to foresee either the length or the seriousness of the conflict. Within Great Britain he suspended (1794) habeas corpus and enacted other repressive legislation to halt radical agitation. His military coalitions against France (1793 and 1798) were unsuccessful on land, although the British navy won some overwhelming victories, and his financial support of Britain's allies brought on a monetary crisis. Rebellion in Ireland hampered the war effort and convinced Pitt that the solution to the Irish problem lay in the parliamentary union of Ireland with England, accompanied by CATHOLIC EMANCIPATION, so that Roman Catholics might hold office. The union was achieved (1800) by wholesale bribery, but the king then refused to approve Catholic Emancipation, and Pitt resigned (1801). He was recalled (1804) as prime minister to repel an expected invasion by Napoleon, which never materialized. He organized a third coalition against France, but Horatio Nelson's great naval victory at Trafalgar was soon followed by the defeat of Britain's allies at Austerlitz (1805). The latter news hastened Pitt's death. See biographies by P. H. Stanhope, 5th Earl Stanhope (4 vol., 3d ed. 1867, repr. 1970), Lord Rosebery (1891, repr. 1968), and John Ehrmann (1972); studies by J. H. Rose (1911, repr. 1971) and D. G. Barnes (1939, repr. 1965).

Pitt, Fort: see FORT DUQUESNE; PITTSBURGH.

pitta (pĭt'ə), name used to refer to a genus (*Pitta*) of small, plump, brightly-colored birds. The genus, including some twenty-three species, constitutes the whole of the family Pittidae. Known also as jewel thrushes, pittas are thrushlike only in their shy, retiring habits; they are not closely related to any other birds. They are characterized by unusually short, stubby tails, which are reduced to mere tufts in some species; long legs; and erectile crown feathers. Pittas are inhabitants of wet tropical forests and are distributed in Africa, SE Asia, India, China, Japan, the Solomon Islands and Australia. They seldom fly, except for migration. Normally, they progress by short, rapid hops. Pittas feed on grubs, insects, and land mollusks, scratched from among dead leaves and litter; they are thus sometimes called ground, or ant, thrushes. The "noisy pitta" of Australia choses a rock or stump within its territory and uses it exclusively for cracking open land snail shells. Its large, oval nest built from roots and leaves is usually placed among roots or on the ground, but may also be built in trees. The hard, glossy eggs usually number from two to seven per clutch, and are typically white or cream colored, with red or purple specklings and lilac or gray undermarkings. Both male and female share incubation duties. The 6½-in. (16.3-cm) garnet pitta (*P. granatina*) is found in Borneo. Steere's pitta (*P. steerii*), measuring 8 in. (20 cm), is common in the Philippines. Pittas are classified in the phylum CHORDATA, subphylum Vertebrata, class Aves, order Passeriformes, family Pittidae.

Pittacus (pĭt'əkəs), c.650–c.570 B.C., Greek statesman and military leader; one of the SEVEN WISE MEN OF GREECE. He helped to overthrow the tyrant of Mytilene in Lesbos and became the lawgiver there, ruling for 10 years. A moderate democrat, Pittacus prevented the nobles in exile (among them Alcaeus) from returning.

Pitt Island: see BUTARITARI.

Pittsburg (pĭts'bərg). **1** Industrial city (1970 pop. 20,651), Contra Costa co., W Calif., on the edge of the San Francisco Bay area, at the junction of the Sacramento and the San Joaquin rivers; laid out 1849, inc. 1903. Manufactures include steel, chemicals, roofing materials, and cans. Coal was discovered there in 1855 and was mined until 1902. The city's Camp Stoneman (now closed) was an important embarkation point during World War II and the Korean War. Pittsburg has a creative arts auditorium and a marina. **2** City (1970 pop. 20,171), Crawford co., SE Kansas, near the Mo. line; founded 1876 as a mining town and named for Pittsburgh, Pa., inc. 1880. It is a mining center near large coal deposits. Clay, limestone, zinc, lead, and oil are also found in the area. The city's manufactures include coal-mining equipment, aircraft, livestock food supplements, building supplies, and clay pipe. Kansas State College of Pittsburg is there, and a state quail farm is nearby.

Pittsburgh (pĭts'bərg), city (1970 pop. 520,117), seat of Allegheny co., SW Pa., at the confluence of the Allegheny and the Monongahela rivers, which there form the Ohio River; inc. 1816. A port of entry, it is among the nation's leading industrial centers, located at the junction of east-west transportation arteries, and has access to large reserves of raw material. Steel is the city's chief manufacture. However, in recent years the number of those employed in the steel industry has declined, and the economy of the city has shifted somewhat from manufacturing to commercial enterprises. Glass, machinery, mine-safety equipment, chemicals, petroleum products, paper goods, and electrical equipment are also produced. Printing and publishing are important, and extensive industrial research and testing are done. Pittsburgh was founded on the site of the Indian town of Shannopin, a late 17th-century fur-trading post with many canoe routes and trails. The area was contested by the French and the English. FORT DUQUESNE, built by the French in the middle of the 18th cent., later fell to the English and was renamed Fort Pitt. The village surrounding the fort was settled in 1760, prospering thereafter with the opening of the Northwest Territory. Today, the modern "Steel City," sprawled over a hilly area, is no longer the "Smoky City" of the past. An urban redevelopment program begun in the late 1940s included strict measures for smoke control. The business district has been refurbished. The downtown area is now known as the Golden Triangle, and the new Gateway Center is the headquarters for a number of large corporations. The broad 64-story U.S. Steel building, completed in 1970, is one of the largest office buildings in the country. Pittsburgh is the seat of the Carnegie-Melon Univ., the Univ. of Pittsburgh, Chatham College, Duquesne Univ., Carlow College, three junior colleges, and an experiment station of the U.S. Bureau of Mines. Two of the city's seminaries are Pittsburgh Theological and Reformed Presbyterian. The Pittsburgh Symphony Orchestra, the Heinz Hall for the Performing Arts, the Carnegie Museum, and the Carnegie Library (a pioneer in methods, with extensive collections) are well known. On the Univ. of Pittsburgh campus is a memorial hall dedicated to Stephen Foster, who was born in Pittsburgh. The city has a fine park system, of which Schenley Park is the principal unit. The blockhouse of old Fort Pitt is preserved in Point State Park. Two botanical conservatories, a planetarium, an observatory, a civic arena (with a retractable dome), an aviary, the Flag Plaza, the Three Rivers Stadium, and a zoo are among the city's other features. Pittsburgh has professional football, ice hockey, and baseball teams. In March, 1936, the city suffered the most disastrous flood of its history when the Allegheny and the Monongahela rivers rose 46 ft (14 m), inundating much of the business and industrial district, paralyzing the city, and taking 45 lives. See S. Lorant, *Pittsburgh: The Story of an American City* (1964).

Pittsburgh, University of, at Pittsburgh; private with some state support; coeducational; chartered and opened as an academy 1787, called Western Univ. of Pennsylvania 1819–1908. It operates two-year colleges at Johnstown, Bradford, Greensburg, and Titusville. Notable on the Pittsburgh campus are a 42-story skyscraper (the Cathedral of Learning) and the Stephen Collins Foster Memorial. The university's medical program is noted for polio research.

Pittsburgh Symphony Orchestra, founded in 1895, gave its first concert the following year under the direction of Frederic Archer. Victor Herbert was the chief conductor from 1898 to 1904; he was succeeded by Emil Pauer (1904–10). The orchestra was then disbanded. It was revived in 1926, and over the next decade it was led by Elias Breeskin (1927–30) and Antonio Modarelli (1930–37). The orchestra was reorganized by Otto Klemperer in 1937. Fritz Reiner was chief conductor from 1938 to 1948, followed by William Steinberg (1952–).

Pittsfield, city (1970 pop. 57,020), seat of Berkshire co., W Mass., between mountain ranges, on branches of the Housatonic River; inc. as a town 1761, as a city 1889. The city is the metropolis of the Berkshire resort area. Electrical products are produced. Oliver Wendell Holmes lived nearby, and "Arrowhead" was Herman Melville's home from 1850 to 1863.

Pittston, industrial city (1970 pop. 11,113), Luzerne co., NE Pa., on the Susquehanna; settled c.1770 by the Susquehanna Company of Connecticut, inc. as a city 1894. It is a mining center for anthracite coal.

pituitary gland, small oval endocrine gland that lies at the base of the BRAIN. It is sometimes called the master gland of the body because all the other endocrine glands are dependent on its secretions for stimulation (see ENDOCRINE SYSTEM). Physiologically the pituitary is divided into two distinct lobes that arise from different embryological sources. The anterior lobe, or adenohypophysis, grows upward from the pharyngeal tissue at the roof of the mouth. There is also an intermediate lobe that is pharyngeal in origin, but in humans it is greatly reduced in structure and function. The posterior lobe, or neurohypophysis, grows downward from neural tissue. It is structurally continuous with the HYPOTHALAMUS of the brain to which it remains attached by the hypophyseal, or pituitary, stalk. Almost all secretions of the pituitary are controlled by the hypothalamus. The posterior lobe is controlled by nerve fibers that originate in hypothalamic neurons and the anterior lobe by substances that are transported from the hypothalamus by tiny blood vessels. The tissues in the anterior lobe consist of extensive vascular areas interspersed among glandular cells that secrete at least six different hormones. It was formerly believed that a master molecule was stimulated by various enzymes to produce these hormones, but it has now been concluded that each is individually synthesized, probably by a specific type of glandular cell. Three such types of cells have been identified: acidophils, basophils, and chromophobes. The GROWTH HORMONE, thought to be synthesized by certain acidophils, stimulates all the tissues in the body to grow by effecting protein formation. The remaining five important hormones influence body functions by stimulating target organs. ADRENOCOR-

TICOTROPIC HORMONE (ACTH) controls the secretion of steroid hormones by the adrenal cortex, which affects glucose, protein, and fat metabolism; THYROTROPIC HORMONE controls the rate of thyroxine synthesis by the thyroid gland, which is the principal regulator of body metabolic rate; and three separate GONADOTROPIC HORMONES (follicle-stimulating hormone, luteinizing hormone, and luteotropic hormone) control the growth and reproductive activity of the gonads. The release of each of the hormones from the anterior lobe is controlled by a specific substance secreted by nerve cells in the hypothalamus. These substances, called releasing factors, are transmitted by nerve fibers to tiny capillaries in the hypophyseal stalk. They are then transmitted through blood vessels to the anterior lobe where each releasing factor is responsible for the release of a specific pituitary hormone. The two hormones that are produced by the posterior lobe are synthesized by nerve cells in the hypothalamus. They are transported by nerve fibers to nerve endings in the posterior lobe where they are released. The hormones are ANTIDIURETIC HORMONE, which alters the permeability of the kidney tubules, permitting more water to be retained by the body; and OXYTOCIN, which aids in the release of milk from mammary glands and causes uterine contractions. The only hormone that is synthesized by the intermediate lobe is the melanocyte-stimulating hormone, which appears to control skin pigmentation. Oversecretion of pituitary hormones can cause GIGANTISM if it occurs before growth of the long bones is complete or ACROMEGALY if it occurs during adulthood. Underactivity of the gland causes DWARFISM if it occurs during childhood, and decreased endocrine function accompanied by lethargy and loss of sexual capacity in the adult.

pit viper, poisonous SNAKE of the family Crotalidae, primarily a New World family. Like the Old World true VIPERS (family Viperidae), pit vipers have long, hollow, erectile fangs that are folded back against the roof of the mouth except when the snake is striking. In addition, the pit vipers have developed special organs of heat reception that help them to sense warm-blooded animals, an ability that is especially useful at night, when many of them hunt. These organs consist of pits, for which the group is named, located just behind the nostrils and covered with a temperature-sensitive membrane. The largest group of pit vipers is the RATTLESNAKE genus *Crotalus,* found in North, Central, and N South America. Other New World forms are the FER-DE-LANCE (genus *Bothrops*) and the BUSHMASTER (genus *Lachesis*). The genus *Ancistrodon* includes the COPPERHEAD and WATER MOCCASIN, as well as about a dozen Asian species. Pit vipers are classified in the phylum CHORDATA, subphylum Vertebrata, class Reptilia, family Crotalidae.

Pitzer College: see CLAREMONT COLLEGES.

Piura (pyo͞o'rä), city (1969 est. pop. 106,400), capital of Piura dept., NW Peru, in the irrigated Piura valley of the Peruvian coastal desert. It is the commercial center for the cotton, sugarcane, rice, and corn raised in the region and for cattle shipped from Ecuador. San Miguel de Piura, the first settlement in Peru, was founded on the coast by Francisco PIZARRO in 1532, but the site was unhealthful, and the settlement was moved to the present Piura. From there, in 1533, Sebastián de BENALCÁZAR set out on his conquest of Ecuador. Piura was severely damaged by an earthquake in 1912.

Pius II (pī'əs), 1405–64, pope (1458–64), an Italian (b. Corsigniano, renamed after him Pienza) named Enea Silvio de' Piccolomini (often in Latin, Aeneas Silvius); successor of Calixtus III. He attended the Council of Basel (1432; see BASEL, COUNCIL OF) as a layman and joined its secretariat. He was an opponent of Pope Eugene IV and in 1439 became secretary to Antipope Felix V (AMADEUS VIII of Savoy). Meanwhile he gained a European reputation as a humanist scholar. Holy Roman Emperor FREDERICK III made him court poet and in 1442 secretary to the chancery in Vienna. In 1445, Piccolomini abandoned his rather dissipated way of life and began a new career. He went to Rome to submit to the pope and became (1446) a priest. He was made bishop of Trieste (1447), bishop of Siena (1449), and a cardinal (1456). As pope, Pius issued (1460) a bull condemning as heretical the conciliar theory (the doctrine that ultimate authority in the church rested in the general council rather than the pope). He was in continual dispute with Louis XI of France, who repeatedly attempted to control ecclesiastical affairs. He also quarreled with the Bohemian king GEORGE OF PODEBRAD, rejecting (1462) the latter's petition that he confirm the Compactata (see HUSSITES). Such quarrels hampered him in achieving his aim of uniting the Christian rulers in a crusade against the Turks. He was about to set out on a crusade himself when he died. He was succeeded by Paul II. Pius did not patronize art or literature, despite his own literary interests and considerable literary talents. Of his works the most useful is his autobiography, the only one written by a pope. See L. C. Gabel, ed., *Pius II: Memoirs of a Renaissance Pope* (1959, repr. 1962); R. J. Mitchell, *The Laurels and the Tiara* (1962).

Pius IV, 1499–1565, pope (1559–65), a Milanese named Giovanni Angelo de' Medici; successor of Paul IV. He was probably not related to the great Medici family. His career in Rome began in 1527, and he held increasingly important offices under Clement VII, Paul III (who made him a cardinal), and Julius III. Cardinal Medici was one of the reform party, but he was no rigorist, hence he was out of favor with Paul IV. The great feature of his pontificate was the reconvening of the Council of Trent (see TRENT, COUNCIL OF) for its last and most important session (1562–63). By backing the council in everything, Pius made himself one of the great popes of the Catholic Reformation. He welcomed the final break with Protestantism, which the council brought about. His good political relations with Spain were in contrast with Paul IV's anti-Hapsburg policy. Pius's chief aid was his nephew, St. CHARLES BORROMEO. He was succeeded by St. Pius V.

Pius V, Saint, 1504–72, pope (1566–72), an Italian (b. near Alessandria) named Michele Ghislieri; successor of Pius IV. He was ordained in the Dominicans (1528) and became celebrated for his austerity. Paul IV made him cardinal (1557) and inquisitor general; under his direction the Roman Inquisition reached a new level of efficiency. On his election he set about putting the decrees of the Council of Trent (see TRENT, COUNCIL OF) into effect; he thus occupies a key position in the Catholic Reformation, for his activity in those years just after the council insured the permanence of its work. He governed the Papal States with severity. St. Pius was the first pope after the Reformation to put Catholicism on the political offensive. He excommunicated (1570) Queen Elizabeth I of England and forbade English Roman Catholics to give her their allegiance, a serious political mistake on his part since it had the effect of rallying the English to Elizabeth. He united Venice and Spain with him against the Turks, an alliance that helped to bring the victory of Austria over the Turks at Lepanto (see LEPANTO, BATTLE OF). He has been much attacked as a persecutor of heresy, but he was certainly not privy to the massacre of St. Bartholomew's Day in France. He was succeeded by Gregory XIII. Feast: May 6.

Pius VI, 1717–99, pope (1775–99), an Italian named G. Angelo Braschi, b. Cesena; successor of Clement XIV. He was created cardinal in 1774. Early in his reign he was faced with the attempts of Holy Roman Emperor JOSEPH II to "reform" the church by suppressing monasteries, assuming rights of appointment of clergy, and by other changes. Joseph's actions were imitated in Spain and Italy, and in 1786 a synod at Pistoia, Italy adopted antipapal resolutions. Joseph's attempts to make the state supreme in matters of conscience were not less extreme than the efforts in the FRENCH REVOLUTION to set up a state church by the Civil Constitution of the Clergy (1790). Pius eventually (April, 1791) condemned this new Gallican church and forbade the clergy to take the oaths. The French annexed the papal property at Avignon and Venaissin. The pope protested Louis XVI's execution and sided with the anti-French coalition, and Napoleon attacked the Papal States. In 1797 a treaty at Tolentino ceded Avignon, Venaissin, Ferrara, Bologna, and the Romagna to the French, along with a huge indemnity and many treasures. The pope was taken to Siena, thence to Florence; soon, though he was ill and feeble, the French took him to Turin and to Grenoble; he died at Valence. He was succeeded by Pius VII. In 1802 his body was taken to Rome.

Pius VII, 1740–1823, pope (1800–1823), an Italian (b. Cesena) named Barnaba Chiaramonti; successor of Pius VI, who had created him cardinal in 1785. He conducted himself ably during the period of the French Revolution, showing sympathy for the social aims of the Revolution. A protracted conclave in 1799–1800 ended with his election. His secretary, Ercole CONSALVI, was a guiding force throughout his pontificate. An early event was the CONCORDAT OF 1801 with Napoleon, to reestablish the church in France and set up a new hierarchy; much of it was vitiated by Napoleon's Organic Articles, which Pius would not accept. In 1804, Napoleon forced Pius to come to Paris to consecrate him as emperor, only to demean him at the last minute by taking the crown from the pope's hands and crowning himself. Napoleon found Pius intractable when not directly under his influence, and the French eventually took Rome (1808) and the Papal States (1809). Pius excommunicated the assailants of the Holy See, and Napoleon had him taken prisoner and removed to Fontainebleau. The pope was browbeaten into signing a new concordat, which he disavowed after the battle of Leipzig. In 1814, after Napoleon's downfall, Pius returned to Rome in triumph. One of his first acts was to restore the Society of Jesus. The rest of Pius's pontificate was devoted to reestablishing the church in Europe. The Papal States were restored at the Congress of Vienna and a series of concordats were signed with European powers. At the same time Pius VII's stolidity in the face of humiliation began a revival of personal popularity for the pope that has since characterized Catholicism. Napoleon had treated Pius VII with sneering brutality, yet the pope's treatment of the fallen emperor's family was a model of benevolence: he gave them haven at Rome and interceded with the British to lighten Napoleon's treatment. He was on better terms with Great Britain than any pope had been since the Reformation, and he was keenly interested in the United States and in the Roman Catholic Church there. His patronage of artists was munificent. Leo XII succeeded him. See E. E. Y. Hales, *The Emperor and the Pope* (1961).

Pius IX, 1792–1878, pope (1846–78), an Italian named Giovanni M. Mastai-Ferretti, b. Senigallia; successor of Gregory XVI. He was cardinal and bishop of Imola when elected pope. For two years he pursued a progressive policy in governing the Papal States and granted a constitution. However, in 1848 rioting drove him from Rome to Gaeta, and he returned (1850) to be supported in power only by the forces of Napoleon III. The Italian nationalists were eager for Rome and the Papal States, and in 1860 Victor Emmanuel II seized all but Rome and its neighborhood. In 1870, on the collapse of Napoleon III, the Italians entered Rome, and Pius retired to the Vatican, refusing to recognize the new kingdom and to accept the proffered indemnity. The anomalous situation, called the Roman Question, was settled eventually by the LATERAN TREATY. Pius's dealings with other nations were not fortunate, and he did not conduct his side of the KULTURKAMPF with the finesse of his successor. In 1854, Pius declared the dogma of the Immaculate Conception of the Virgin to be an article of faith. In 1864 he issued the encyclical *Quanta cura,* accompanied by a list (*Syllabus*) of erroneous modernistic statements. In 1869 he convoked the First VATICAN COUNCIL, the principal work of which was the enunciation of papal infallibility. Pius IX's pontificate—the longest in history—helped define the role of Roman Catholicism in the modern world. He was succeeded by Leo XIII.

Pius X, Saint, 1835–1914, pope (1903–14), an Italian named Giuseppe Sarto, b. near Treviso; successor of Leo XIII and predecessor of Benedict XV. Ordained in 1858, he became bishop of Mantua (1884), a cardinal (1893), and patriarch of Venice (1893). Soon after his accession to the Holy See he found himself in major conflict with the French government over the latter's regulation of church affairs. The government finally decreed (1905) the separation of church and state and sequestered church property. Pius was more conciliatory toward the Italian government, relaxing the church's strictures on participation by Roman Catholics in political life. In the decree *Lamentabili* (1907) and the encyclical *Pascendi* (1907), Pius condemned religious MODERNISM, and disciplinary measures were taken to stamp out what he called the "synthesis of all heresies." The pope set up a commission to recodify the canon law; he encouraged the use of plainsong; he set up the new Roman breviary as the norm for the whole church; he made the Roman congregations more efficient; he set up a commission to translate the Bible anew; and he regularized the position of the hierarchies in many countries. Known for his interest in the poor, he was widely venerated during his lifetime. He was canonized (1954) by Pius XII. Feast: Sept. 3. See *All Things in Christ: Encyclicals and Selected Documents of Saint Pius X* (ed. by V. A. Yzermans, 1954); biographies by M. G. Dal-Gal (tr. 1954), Leonard von Matt and Nello Vian (tr. 1955, repr. 1963), and J. O. Smit (tr. 1965).

Pius XI, 1857–1939, pope (1922–39), an Italian, b. Desio, near Milan, as Achille Ratti; successor of BENEDICT XV. His father was a silk manufacturer. He studied in Milan and at the Gregorian Univ., Rome, and was ordained in 1879. His excellence in philosophy brought him to the attention of Leo XIII. He taught in the Milan seminary, was appointed (1888) one of the college of doctors of the Ambrosian Library, Milan, and won a name for his studies in paleography. In 1907 he was made chief librarian. Called by Pius X to Rome, he was vice prefect of the Vatican Library. In 1918, Benedict XV entrusted him with the difficult legateship in Poland. There he put the church on good terms with the new government and helped, as much as possible, the Roman Catholics of Russia. In 1919 he was made nuncio to Poland. Two years later Benedict appointed him archbishop of Milan and created him cardinal. Cardinal Ratti was elected pope eight months later (Feb. 6, 1922). Pius's pontificate was marked by great diplomatic activity and by many important papers, often in the form of encyclicals. In diplomatic affairs Pius was aided at first by Pietro Gasparri and after 1930 by Eugenio Pacelli (who succeeded him as Pius XII). Cardinal Gasparri's masterpiece was the LATERAN TREATY (1929). Nevertheless, the Fascist government and the pope were in open disagreement over the restriction of youth activities; this culminated in a strong papal letter (*Non abbiamo bisogno,* 1931), showing the impossibility of being at once a Fascist and a Catholic. Relations between Mussolini and the Holy See were cool ever after. It fell to Cardinal Pacelli to negotiate a concordat for all Germany (1933). The Hitler government never pretended to observe the treaty. In 1937, after interference of every sort by the Nazis in Catholic life, the pope denounced the government and the Nationalist Socialist theory in a powerful encyclical, *Mit brennender Sorge.* A few days later he issued a definitive analysis of Communism from the Roman Catholic point of view in *On Atheistic Communism.* Pius also denounced persecutions in Russia, Mexico, and Spain. With England, the Netherlands, and France (where he condemned the royalist *Action française* movement in 1925) the pope was on unprecedentedly cordial terms. He spoke out continually against nationalism, racism, and totalitarianism and their menace to human dignity; hence the new feast of Christ the King, established to recall the rights of religion in the state, and hence, too, his denunciation of anti-Semitism. The pope, highly critical of laissez-faire capitalism, urged social reform especially in his encyclical *Quadragesimo anno* (1931), which renewed the plea made 40 years earlier by Leo XIII. Pius appealed directly to the laity for greater participation in all things religious—this he called Catholic Action. In the church's missionary activity he laid great stress on the necessity of integrating Christianity with native cultures rather than trying to make them European. This is seen in the Pontifical Work of St. Peter the Apostle for the Native Clergy, which he set up in 1929. To protect Catholics of Eastern rites from Latin influence he augmented the powers of their congregation and established a commission to study their canon law. He also called on Western Catholics to exhibit greater understanding of the Orthodox and other ancient churches of the East, notably in the encyclical *Rerum Orientalium* (1928). Pius took delight in new technological developments; he established a broadcasting station at the Vatican and advanced the modernization of the Vatican Library. To signalize his interest in the progress of science he reconstituted the Pontifical Academy of the Sciences (1936), with a large international membership. Many of Pius's papers have been published. See biographies by Philip Hughes (1938) and Zsolt Aradi (1958).

Pius XII, 1876–1958, pope (1939–58), an Italian (b. Rome) named Eugenio Pacelli; successor of Pius XI. Ordained a priest in 1899, he entered the Vatican's secretariat of state. He became (1912) undersecretary of state and, after becoming a bishop, was appointed (1917) nuncio to Bavaria. He stayed in Germany until 1929 and concluded concordats with Bavaria and Prussia. He was made cardinal in 1929 and papal secretary of state in 1930, succeeding his teacher, Cardinal Gasparri. He negotiated the concordat with Nazi Germany in 1933. Elevated to the papacy in 1939, Pius was the first papal secretary to be elected in centuries and the first Roman pope since 1730. In his first encyclical (*Summi pontificatus,* 1939) Pius made a general attack on totalitarianism. During World War II, however, he believed that the Vatican could best work to achieve peace by maintaining formal relations with all the belligerents. He was later much criticized for not speaking out against the Nazi persecution of the Jews and accused of not doing enough to protect them within Italy. After the war Pius was alarmed by the resurgence of Communism in Italy and fostered the growth of Catholic Action groups to strengthen the Christian Democratic party. In 1949 he excommunicated Italian Catholics who joined the Communist party. In retaliation for the political persecution of the church in Communist Eastern Europe, Pius excommunicated the political leaders of Yugoslavia, Hungary, Czechoslovakia, Rumania, and Poland. Pius issued his main directives in encyclical form; their subjects included the doctrine of the mystical body of Christ, i.e., the church (*Mystici Corporis Christi,* 1943); biblical studies (*Divino afflante spiritu,* 1943); the 14th centenary of St. Benedict (1947) and the liturgy and practices surrounding it (*Mediator Dei,* 1947); and the future of Africa (*Fidei donum,* 1957). He continued Pius XI's educational pontifical universities in South America (at Lima, Medellín, Rio de Janeiro, and Santiago de Chile), and he favored the appointment of native hierarchies in overseas dioceses. In 1950, in the papal bull *Munificentissimus Deus,* the pope defined the dogma of the Assumption of the Virgin Mary. He reformed (1956) the Holy Week liturgy, relaxed the rules for fasting, and increased the hours during which Mass may be said. Pius had only one secretary of state, Cardinal Luigi Maglione; after his death (1944) the pope acted as his own secretary of state. He was succeeded by John XXIII. Pope Pius was widely venerated during his lifetime, and proceedings for his beatification were begun in 1965. See his *Guide for Living,* ed. by Maurice Guinlan (1960); biographies by K. K. Burton (1958), T. J. Kierman (1958), and J. H. L. Smyth (1958); Carlo Falconi, *The Silence of Pius XII* (tr. 1970).

Piute Indians: see PAIUTE INDIANS.

pixie, in English folklore, spirit or fairy. The pixie is commonly represented as a mischievous imp who delights in flustering young maidens and leading travelers astray.

Pi y Margall, Francisco (fränthēs'kō pē ē märgäl'), 1824–1901, Spanish statesman and writer. A liberal journalist, he fled to France after the unsuccessful uprising of 1866 against Gen. Leopoldo O'Donnell. After the overthrow of Isabella II in 1868 he was elected (1869) to the Cortes. He was briefly president (1873) of the short-lived first Spanish republic, and he continued as deputy in the Cortes after the restoration of the monarchy (1875). He defended the principle of federalism against centralism, thus gaining wide popularity in Catalonia. He also favored autonomy for Cuba. His uprightness and intelligence won him the respect even of the hostile right.

Pizarro, Francisco (pĭzä'rō, Span. fränthēs'kō pēthär'rō), c.1476–1541, Spanish conquistador, conqueror of Peru. Born in Trujillo, he was an illegitimate son of a Spanish gentleman. As a child he was an illiterate swineherd. Pizzaro accompanied Ojeda to Colombia in 1510 and was with Balboa when he discovered the Pacific. Hearing of the fabled wealth of the Incas, he formed (1524) a partnership with Diego de ALMAGRO and Fernando de Luque (a priest who secured funds). The first expedition reached the San Juan River, part of the present boundary between Ecuador and Colombia, and on the second (1526–28), Pizarro explored the swampy coast farther south while his pilot, Bartolomé Ruiz, crossed the equator and then returned to bring definite news of the southern realms. Ruiz and Almagro went back to Panama for supplies; Pizarro and a few followers remained behind and endured severe hardships. When supplies finally came, Pizarro sailed S along the Peruvian coast before returning to Panama. In 1528 his partners sent him to Spain to secure aid from Emperor Charles V; he achieved this and gained for himself most of the future profits. Pizarro managed to soothe the disgruntled Almagro. Sailing south, Pizarro landed at Tumbes (1532) and ascended the Andes to Cajamarca, where the Inca, ATAHUALPA, awaited him. Professing friendship, he enticed Atahualpa into the power of the Spanish, seized him, exacted a stupendous ransom, and then treacherously had him executed. The conquest of Peru was virtually completed by the capture of CUZCO, which was later defended against Inca forces led by Manco Capac. Pizarro set about consolidating his conquest by founding new settlements, notably the present capital of Peru, Lima, and allotting land and Indians in encomienda to his followers. An attempt by Pedro de ALVARADO to claim Quito was forestalled by Sebastián de BENALCÁZAR and Almagro. Pizarro now made a pact with Almagro, whom he had cheated several times in the division of spoils, granting him the conquest of Chile. When he failed to receive the territory promised him, Almagro attempted to redress the injustice by seizing Cuzco. Pizarro sent his half brother, Hernando Pizarro, to Cuzco, and Almagro was defeated and put to death. In 1539, Francisco appointed his brother Gonzalo Pizarro governor of Quito. Francisco's greed and ambition, extreme even in a conquistador, had, however, offset his resourcefulness, courage, and cunning. By alienating the Almagro faction he paved the way for conspiracy. A band of assassins surprised him at dinner, and although he fought desperately, he was overpowered and slain. The account by W. H. Prescott, *History of the Conquest of Peru* (1847), is classic. An early account is Pedro Pizarro, *Relation of the Discovery and Conquest of the Kingdoms of Peru* (tr. 1921). See biographies by F. A. Ober (1906) and Felix Shay (1932); Hoffman Birney, *Brothers of Doom* (1942).

Pizarro, Gonzalo (gônthä'lō), c.1506–1548, Spanish conquistador, brother of Francisco Pizarro. A lieutenant of his brother in the conquest of Peru, Gonzalo aided in the defense of Cuzco (1536–37) against the Inca MANCO CAPAC, subdued Charcas (present Bolivia), and fought against Diego de ALMAGRO (1537–38). Appointed (1539) governor of Quito, in 1540 he commanded a disastrous expedition down the Napo River to the Amazon River in search of EL DORADO. After extreme hardships, augmented by the disaffection of ORELLANA, he and his few remaining men staggered back two years later. Gonzalo then learned of the assassination of Francisco and offered to help the crown's representative, VACA DE CASTRO, but was refused. When the newly arrived viceroy, Blasco NÚÑEZ VELA, peremptorily enforced the New Laws, framed by Bartolomé de LAS CASAS and promulgated in 1542 to protect the Indians, popular indignation broke out, and Gonzalo was chosen to lead the revolt. In 1546, aided by Francisco de CARVAJAL, he defeated Núñez. His support evaporated, however, when the king's new representative, Pedro de la GASCA, arrived and offered pardon as well as repeal of the New Laws. Most of his army deserted just before the crucial battle. Their commander surrendered and was beheaded. See Pedro de Cieza de León, *The War of Quito* (tr. 1967).

Pizarro, Hernando (ĕrnän'dō), fl. 1530–60, Spanish conquistador, half brother of Francisco Pizarro. Much older than his half brothers, Francisco, Juan, and Gonzalo, and, unlike them, legitimate by birth and educated, Hernando accompanied Francisco from Spain in 1530. After the conquest he returned (1533) to advance the fortunes of the family at court at the expense of Diego de ALMAGRO, Francisco's partner. In 1536, back in Peru, he defended (1536–37) Cuzco against the Inca MANCO CAPAC. Hernando then fought against Diego de Almagro, was captured (1537), released, and returned (1538) to defeat and execute Almagro. Because of his standing at court, he was sent (1539) to Spain to argue the cause of the Pizarros in the recent civil war, but bribery was not enough. Hernando suffered mild imprisonment for 20 years. Released in 1560, he died some time later, according to one chronicler at the age of 100.

Pizarro, Juan (hwän), d. 1536, Spanish conquistador, brother of Francisco Pizarro. He aided Francisco in the conquest of Peru. With his other brothers, Gonzalo and Hernando, he fought valiantly against the Inca MANCO CAPAC during the siege of Cuzco in 1536. He was killed leading an attack on the Indian fortress Sacsahuamán.

pizza, [Ital.,=pie], pie consisting in its most basic form of yeast dough covered with a layer of tomatoes and mozzarella cheese and baked in an oven. There are many varieties of pizza: the Ligurian pizza has anchovies, ripe olives, and onions; the Neapolitan pizza, perhaps the most famous, is thicker than other types; and the Roman pizza has few tomatoes but plenty of onions. It is one of the most commonly sold foods of European origin in the United States.

Pizzetti, Ildebrando (ēldābrän'dō pēt-tsĕt'tē), 1880–1968, Italian composer. In 1909 he joined the faculty of the Instituto Musicale, Florence, becoming director in 1917. He was director (1924–36) of the Conservatorio G. Verdi, Milan, and at the Academy of St. Cecilia in Rome, later serving as its president (1948–51). Primarily an opera composer, he was chiefly concerned with dramatic projection. Among his outstanding operas are *Fedra* (Milan, 1915; libretto by D'Annunzio) and *Debora e Jaele* (Milan, 1922). Pizzetti often employed polyphonic choruses in his operas and wrote numerous independent choral works.

pizzicato (pĭt"səkä'tō), in music, the technique of plucking the strings of an instrument that is usually bowed. Directions for playing pizzicato are found in early 17th-century music. Paganini introduced left-hand pizzicato, making it possible to play bowed tones and pizzicato tones simultaneously or in alternation.

PKU: see PHENYLKETONURIA.

Place, Francis, 1771–1854, English radical reformer. A tailor for many years, he educated himself and made his shop a meeting center for radicals and reformers. He was especially active in the trade-union movement; through his efforts the antiunion Combination Acts of 1799–1800 were repealed (1824). He was also an early leader of the Chartists (see CHARTISM), helping to draft the "People's Charter." His pamphlets on social questions include *Illustrations and Proofs of the Principle of Population* (1822), one of the earliest tracts on birth control. See his autobiography, ed. by Mary Thale (1972); biography by Graham Wallas (4th ed. 1925, repr. 1951).

placebo (pləsē'bō), inert substance given instead of a potent DRUG. Placebo medications are sometimes prescribed when no drug is really needed because they make patients feel well taken care of. Placebos are also used as controls in scientific studies on the effectiveness of drugs. So-called double blind experiments, where neither the doctor nor the patient knows whether the given medication is the experimental drug or the placebo, are often done to assure unbiased, statistically reliable results.

placenta (pləsĕn'tə) or **afterbirth,** organ that develops in the uterus during pregnancy. It is a unique characteristic of the higher (or placental) mammals. In humans it is a thick mass, about 7 in. (18 cm) in diameter, liberally supplied with blood vessels. The placenta is attached to the uterus, and the fetus is connected to the placenta by the umbilical cord. The placenta draws nourishment and oxygen, which it supplies to the fetus, from the maternal circulation. In turn, the placenta receives the wastes of fetal metabolism and discharges them into the maternal circulation for disposal. It also acts as an endocrine gland, producing estrogen, progesterone, and gonadotrophin. Shortly after delivery of the fetus the placenta is forced out by contractions of the uterus. Severe hemorrhage may occur if the placenta does not emerge in its entirety or if the uterus fails to contract properly.

Placentia (pləsĕn'shə), town (1971 pop. 2,211), SE N.F., Canada, on Placentia Bay. It is mainly a residential area for personnel of the U.S. naval base on Argentia. The town was founded by the French in 1662 as Plaisance and was the French headquarters on Newfoundland until 1713.

Placentia, city (1970 pop. 21,948), Orange co., S Calif.; inc. 1926. Once a rural farming community, it became a residential city with shopping centers and light manufacturing industries. There are many orange trees throughout the city. Many residents work in nearby aerospace industries.

Placentia Bay, c.100 mi (160 km) long and up to 80 mi (129 km) wide, SE N.F., Canada. There are many fishing settlements and canneries along the shore. Placentia, site of a naval base since 1622, is the largest town on the bay.

placer mining: see MINING.

Placetas (pläsä'täs), city (1970 pop. 32,261), Las Villas prov., central Cuba. Tobacco processing is the city's chief industry. Placetas is located on a major highway and serves as a railroad center. The city was founded in 1867.

Placid, Lake, 4 mi (6 km) long and c.1.5 mi (2.4 km) wide, NE N.Y., in the Adirondack Mts., near Mt. Marcy. The lake, with LAKE PLACID village at the southern end, is a noted winter-sports center.

Placidia, Roman empress: see GALLA PLACIDIA.

plage (pläzh): see CHROMOSPHERE.

plagioclase feldspar (plā'jēəklās"): see FELDSPAR.

plague, any contagious, malignant, epidemic disease, in particular the bubonic plague and the black plague (or Black Death), both forms of the same infection. This acute febrile disease is caused by *Pasteurella pestis* (discovered independently by Shibasaburo Kitasato and Alexandre Yersin in 1894), a bacterium that is transmitted to man by fleas from infected rats, in whom epidemic waves of infection always precede great epidemics. Sylvatic plague, still another form, is carried by other rodents, e.g., squirrels, rabbits, chipmunks, in rural or wooded areas where they are prevalent. Bubonic plague, the most common form, is characterized by very high fever, chills, prostration, delirium, and enlarged, painful lymph nodes (buboes), which suppurate and may discharge. Invasion of the lungs by the organism (pneumonic plague) may occur as a complication of the bubonic form or as a primary infection. This type is rapidly fatal and is the only type that can be spread from man to man (by droplet spray) without intermediary transmission by flea. In the black form of plague, hemorrhages turn black, giving the term "Black Death" to the disease. An overwhelming infection of the blood may cause death in 3 or 4 days, even before other symptoms appear. The earliest known visitation of the plague to Europe occurred in Athens in 430 B.C. A disastrous epidemic occurred in Rome in the 3d cent., in which 5,000 persons are reported to have succumbed daily. The most widespread epidemic began in Constantinople in 1334, spread throughout Europe (returning Crusaders were a factor in this respect), and in less than 20 years is estimated to have killed as much as three quarters of the population of Europe and Asia. The great plague of London in 1665 is recorded in many works of literature. Quarantine measures helped to contain the disease somewhat, but serious epidemics continued to occur even in the 19th cent. The disease is still prevalent in many parts of Asia. In untreated cases of plague the mortality rate is as high as 90%. Streptomycin has reduced this to 5%, and the drug is life-saving even in primary pneumonic plague. Vaccine is available for preventive purposes. Rodent control is important in areas of known infection. See Philip Ziegler, *The Black Death* (1969).

plagues of Egypt, in the Bible, the plagues and other troubles brought on Egypt by God through the hands of Moses, because Pharaoh would not let the people of Israel go out of Egypt. The account, in Exodus, tells how Pharaoh relented each time until the plague was removed, then hardened his heart; in the end he let the children of Israel go, only to pursue them into the Red Sea. The plagues were 10 in number: plague of blood by which the waters of Egypt were turned to blood, Ex. 7.19–25; plague of frogs, 8.1–15; plague of lice, 8.16–19; plague of flies, 8.20–32; plague of murrain, by which all the cattle of Egypt and none of the Israelites' cattle were killed, 9.1–7; plague of boils, 9.8–12; plague of hail, 9.13–35; plague of locusts, 10.1–20; plague of darkness, by which for three days darkness covered Egypt, 10.21–29; plague of the first-born, by which all the first-born of Egypt were killed, 11; 12.1–36. By tradition the first Passover was observed the night of the 10th plague. After it the Israelites left Egypt.

plaice: see FLATFISH.

plaid, a long shawl or blanketlike outer wrap of woolen cloth, usually patterned in checks or tartan figures. Now a distinctive feature of the Highland costume, it was formerly worn in all parts of Scotland and in N England by both men and women. The early Celtic people excelled in dyeing and in Roman times wore gay, many-colored, checkered plaids, woven or sewed together in squares of different colors. Through the Middle Ages and until the 18th cent. the people of North Britain belted their plaids about them, the lower part forming the kilt, the upper part the cloak. A shepherd's plaid is of black-and-white check. A tartan plaid has crossbars of three or more colors combined in designs distinctive of the different Highland clans and serving a heraldic purpose. In modern usage *plaid* may signify merely pattern, as a plaid gingham. See Christian Hesketh, *Tartans* (1961); Thomas Innes, *The Tartans of the Clans and Families of Scotland* (8th ed. 1971).

Plain, the, in French history, term designating the independent members of the National Convention during the FRENCH REVOLUTION. The name was applied to them because, in contrast to the radical MOUNTAIN, they occupied the lower benches of the chamber. The Plain was a leaderless mass and a pliable instrument, but it was numerically in the majority and consequently determined many votes. It played an important role in bringing about the overthrow (9 Thermidor; July 27, 1794) of Maximilien ROBESPIERRE, but after this effort it again lost its cohesion.

plain, large area of level or nearly level land. Elevated plains are called PLATEAUS, or tablelands, and very low, wet plains are called SWAMPS. Plains have different names in different climates and countries. They include the TUNDRAS, STEPPE, PRAIRIES, PAMPAS, SAVANNA, LLANOS, flood plains of rivers, coastal plains, loess plains, arid plains (see DESERT), and lacustrine plains. The erosive action of water, glaciation, the draining of a lake, deposition of sediment, and the uplift of a continental shelf are some of the causes of the formation of plains. The extensive area comprising the western part of the Mississippi watershed, very gradually rising to the foothills of the Rockies, and having, largely, a steppe climate, is called the Great Plains region of the United States. The coastal plains region of the United States along the Gulf Coast and the Atlantic seaboard is widest in the south and southeast.

plainchant: see PLAINSONG.

Plaine des Jarres (plĕn dā zhär) or **Plain of Jars,** region, N Laos, at the northern end of the Annamese Cordillera.

Plainedge, uninc. area (1970 pop. 10,759), Nassau co., SE N.Y., on S Long Island. Chiefly residential, it is one of more than 30 communities that constitute the town of Oyster Bay.

Plainfield. 1 Town (1970 pop. 11,957), Windham co., E Conn., on the Quinebaug River; settled 1689, inc. 1699. Textiles have been made there since the early 19th cent. **2** City (1970 pop. 46,862), Union co., NE N.J.; settled 1684 by Friends, inc. as a city 1869. Formerly a residential city in the New York metropolitan area, it has become the urban center of 10 closely allied municipalities, with diversified industries, including printing, construction, and the manufacture of packaging machinery, starch and chemicals, processed metals, housewares, and tools and gauges. Among the several 18th-century buildings remaining are a Friends' meetinghouse (1788), the Martine house (1717), and the Nathaniel Drake House (1746), known as Washington's Headquarters. Nearby Washington Rock, overlooking the Hudson River, is reputed to be the vantage point from which George Washington watched British troop movements.

Plain of Jars: see PLAINE DES JARRES, region, Laos.

Plains of Abraham: see ABRAHAM, PLAINS OF.

plainsong or **plainchant,** all early unharmonized melody in free rhythm, but usually synonymous with Gregorian chant, the liturgical music of the Roman Catholic Church. In the Western church there developed four main dialects of plainsong—Ambrosian, Roman, Mozarabic and Gallican—that seem to have been derived from similar sources. Mozarabic chant and Gallican chant are no longer used, but Ambrosian chant, the plainsong introduced by St. AMBROSE into the cathedral of Milan, is still in use in that diocese. It is less strictly systematized and melodically more ornate than Gregorian chant, which is used throughout the rest of the Catholic Church. Gregorian chant is named for Pope Gregory I, who established or reorganized the Schola Cantorum at Rome during his reign (590–604) and whose name is connected with a great codification of the official music of the church at that time. The origins of the chant go back to early Christian times, and it seems to have derived from Jewish and Greek music. How much it owes to each is a subject of controversy, but the strongest links are considered to be Gregorian theory to Greek theory (rather than actual Greek music) and Gregorian melody to Hebrew melodic practice. During the late Middle Ages the chant melodies were used as the basis for polyphonic composition that caused the traditional Gregorian method of performance to be forgotten, and in succeeding centuries various reforms abused and mutilated Gregorian chant still further. In the 19th cent. the Benedictine monks of Solesmes undertook many years of research to restore the Gregorian chant to its original form and to establish its proper rhythm. They began to publish the results of their labors in 1889, and in 1903 Pope Pius X decreed the use of the chant in the Solesmes version as the official music of the Catholic Church. The texts of plainsong are the words of the Mass, the Psalms, canticles, and certain verse hymns. The tonality of Gregorian chant is based on the system of eight modes (see MODE). Since most of the melodies existed prior to the adoption of modal theory in the 9th and 10th cent., there are some exceptions and deviations from the theory in the actual music. The notation of the chant evolved into systems of neumes (see MUSICAL NOTATION) that are still used in preference to modern mensural notation for plainsong. There are various solutions to the problems of Gregorian rhythm, but it is apparent that the speech rhythm inherent in the text, whether prose or verse, is the most important governing factor. Three styles have been traced in Gregorian chant—syllabic, or one note for each syllable; short groups of notes for most syllables; and long melismatic flourishes for most syllables. These styles are systematically applied according to the liturgical place and function of any given text. Most of the Gregorian melodies for the Mass and for the offices are contained in an ecclesiastical manual, *Liber usualis.* See Willi Apel, *Gregorian Chant* (1958); J. R. Bryden and D. G. Hughes, ed., *An Index of Gregorian Chant* (2 vol., 1969).

Plainview. 1 Uninc. city (1970 pop. 32,195), Nassau co., SE N.Y., on Long Island. It is chiefly residential. 2 City (1970 pop. 19,096), seat of Hale co., NW Texas, on the Llano Estacado; inc. 1907. The level plain, irrigated by shallow wells from a large underground water belt, yields wheat, grain sorghum, soybeans, castor beans, cotton, and vegetables. The city has large meat-packing and meat-processing industries. Manufactures include farm machinery, hybrid seeds, and irrigation equipment. Wayland Baptist College is there. Major archaeological finds of a late Ice Age civilization that hunted prehistoric giant bisons were made there in 1944–45.

Plainville, town (1970 pop. 16,733), Hartford co., central Conn., in the sandy headwaters of the Quinnipiac River; settled 1657, inc. 1869. Electrical products, ball bearings, tools, and other metal products are manufactured. The city park contains a restored portion of the New Haven-Northampton Canal, which operated there in the 1840s. During the American Civil War the town was a manufacturing center, and from the late 1890s through the 1920s it had a major railroad yard. Several 18th-century buildings survive.

planarian, common name for several genera of the free-living (turbellarian) flatworms belonging to the order Tricladida, a name that derives from their characteristic three-branched digestive cavities. Most species range from 1/8 in. to about 1 in. in length (.32–2.54 cm) although some giant tropical forms range up to 2 ft. (60 cm). The different species are white, gray, brown, or black; a few forms are transparent. Many are striped or streaked and some of the large terrestrial species are brightly colored. Although planarians can be found in marine or moist terrestrial habitats, most inhabit freshwater areas. They crawl about over a trail of mucus that is secreted by specialized epidermal cells; the smaller forms move about by means of cilia on their ventral, or lower, surface, and larger species utilize muscular contractions as well. Tactile and chemoreceptive cells, located in the epidermis, serve as general sense organs. In many species these cells are clumped in lobes at the sides of the head. Most planarians are also light-sensitive and in some, pigmented light-sensitive cells are clumped in two cups that serve as primitive eyes. Planarians are usually either carnivorous or scavengers. The mouth is located near the middle of the ventral surface. The tubelike pharynx can be everted from the mouth and inserted into the prey; food is partially digested externally before it is sucked into the gut. Planarians are hermaphroditic, each individual worm contains both male and female organs, and, most commonly, they reproduce sexually. However, species similar to the 1/2-in.-long (1.27-cm) *Dugesia tigrina,* the most common planarian in the United States, are much studied in classrooms and laboratories for their additional capacity to reproduce asexually by transverse rupture of the body: a rupture line develops behind the mouth, and while the back half of the worm is anchored, the front half moves forward until the worm snaps in half. Each half regenerates the missing parts. Such planarians can also regenerate parts that are cut from the body. Planarians are classified in the phylum PLATYHELMINTHES, class Turbellaria, order Tricladida.

Planck, Max (mäks plängk), 1858–1947, German physicist. Seeking to explain the experimental SPECTRUM (distribution of electromagnetic energy according to wavelength) of black body radiation (see BLACK BODY), he introduced the hypothesis (1900) that oscillating atoms absorb and emit energy only in discrete bundles (called quanta) instead of continuously, as assumed in classical physics. The success of his work and subsequent developments by Albert Einstein, Niels Bohr, Werner Heisenberg, Erwin Schrödinger, and others established the revolutionary QUANTUM THEORY of modern physics, of which Planck is justly regarded as the father. In 1918, Planck received the Nobel Prize in physics for his work on black body radiation. He was professor at the Univ. of Berlin (1889–1928) and president (1930–35) of the Kaiser Wilhelm Society for the Advancement of Science, Berlin, which after World War II was reconstituted as part of the Max Planck Institutes. He was an editor of the *Annalen der Physik* and member of the Royal Society (London) and the American Physical Society. His name is honored in PLANCK'S CONSTANT. English translations of his works include *A Survey of Physics* (1925, new ed. 1960), *Introduction to Theoretical Physics* (5 vol., 1932–33), *Treatise on Thermodynamics* (3d rev. ed. 1945), and *Scientific Autobiography and Other Papers* (1949).

Planck's constant (plängks), fundamental constant of the QUANTUM THEORY. It is represented by the letter h and has a value of 6.63×10^{-34} J-sec. The combination $h/2\pi$, denoted by $\hbar$, occurs frequently.

plane, in mathematics, flat surface of infinite extent but no thickness. An example of a plane, or more exactly of a bounded portion of a plane, is the surface forming one face, or side, of a cube. A plane is determined, or defined, by any of the following: (1) three points not in a straight line; (2) a straight line and a point not on the line; (3) two intersecting lines; or (4) two parallel lines. Two straight lines in space do not usually lie in the same plane. For a given plane in space, a line can either lie outside and parallel to it, intersect the plane in a single point, or lie entirely in the plane; if more than one point of a straight line lies in the plane, then the entire line must lie in the plane.

planet [Gr.,=wanderer], any of the nine solid, nonluminous bodies that revolve around the sun. The term is sometimes used to include the asteroids (minor planets), but excludes the other members of the SOLAR SYSTEM: comets and meteoroids. By extension, any similar body discovered revolving around another star would be called a planet. The ancient Greeks applied the term to the five major planets then known—MERCURY, VENUS, MARS, JUPITER, and SATURN—as well as to the sun and moon; all these bodies were observed to move back and forth against the background of the apparently fixed stars and to shine with a steady light. In the PTOLEMAIC SYSTEM, a geocentric, or earth-centered, model of the SOLAR SYSTEM proposed by Ptolemy (2d cent. A.D.), the earth was thought to lie at rest in the center of the universe while the planets moved about it in a complicated scheme of circles. The heliocentric, or sun-centered, Copernican system, introduced in the 16th cent., eliminated many of the complexities of the Ptolemaic system by viewing the planets, including the earth, as revolving about the sun; the moon was viewed as a natural SATELLITE of the earth. At the start of the 17th cent. Johannes Kepler refined the Copernican model by showing that the orbits of the planets around the sun were elliptical rather than circular. With the development of the telescope other members of the solar system became visible. URANUS, detected in 1781 by Sir William Herschel, was the first planet discovered in modern times. NEPTUNE was discovered in 1846 as the result of a mathematical analysis of the irregularities in the motion of Uranus, and PLUTO, whose existence was predicted from the perturbations of both Uranus and Neptune, was found in 1930. In addition to the major planets, the telescope has revealed thousands of minor planets, or ASTEROIDS, which orbit the sun in a bandlike cluster between Mars and Jupiter; the largest of these, CERES, was also the first discovered (1801). The major planets are classified either as inferior, with an orbit between the sun and the orbit of the earth (Mercury and Venus), or as superior, with an orbit beyond that of the earth (Mars, Jupiter, Saturn, Uranus, Neptune, and Pluto). On the basis of their physical properties the planets are further classified as terrestrial or Jovian. The terrestrial planets—Mercury, Venus, Earth, Mars, and Pluto—resemble the earth in size, chemical composition, and density. Their periods of rotation range from about 24 hr for Mars to 249 days for Venus. The Jovian planets—Jupiter, Saturn, Uranus, and Neptune—are much larger in size and have thick, gaseous atmospheres and low densities. Their periods of rotation range from about 10 hr for Jupiter to 15 hr for Neptune. This rapid rotation results in polar flattening of 2% to 10%, giving the planets an elliptical appearance. Outside the solar system one planet is known to exist, an unseen companion of Barnard's Star having a mass about 2.5 times that of Jupiter. The existence of this planet was established in 1963 from the apparent angular motion of the star; the immensity of the planet's computed mass suggests that it may be the total mass of two planets. It is reasonable to believe that many stars have developed planetary systems, but the remoteness of the stars and the nonluminous nature of planets make them nearly impossible to detect with present technology. See G. P. Kuiper and B. M. Middlehurst, ed., *Planets and Satellites* (1961); F. L. Whipple, *Earth, Moon, and Planets* (3d ed. 1968); P. A. Moore, *The New Guide to the Planets* (1972).

planetarium, optical device used to project a representation of the heavens onto a domed ceiling; the term also designates the building that houses such a device. A modern planetarium consists of as many as 150 motor-driven projectors mounted on an axis. As the axis moves, beams of light are emitted through lenses and travel in predetermined paths on the ceiling. The juxtaposition of lights reproduces a panorama of the sky at a particular time as it might be seen under optimum conditions. The motions of the celestial bodies are accurately represented, although they can be compressed into much shorter time periods, allowing spectators to see in minutes the motions that may actually take the celestial bodies days or years to complete. A typical planetarium projects the fixed stars, the sun, moon, and planets, and various nebulas. A larger planetarium can reproduce the Milky Way, comets, and more than 9,000 fixed stars. It may also project a set of coordinate lines for locating objects, in addition to pictures of animals and other forms associated with the constellations of the zodiac. Some projectors can take into account the apparent motions of the stars, thereby depicting the sky as it will look thousands of years in the future or as it looked thousands of years in the past. A recently developed planetarium is capable of showing the heavens as they would appear to space travelers viewing them from the moon and from other locations in space. The first of the modern planetariums was constructed in 1924 by the Carl Zeiss Optical Works in Jena, Germany. The Adler Planetarium (1930) in Chicago was the first in the United States; in 1934 the Fels Planetarium was added to the Franklin Institute in Philadelphia; and the Hayden Planetarium in New York City was established the following year. Planetariums are now in operation in most large cities of the world. A mechanical device known as an orrery (for Charles Boyle, earl of Orrery) was a forerunner of the planetarium. It is a framework supporting globes that represent the sun, planets, and natural satellites in their approximate sizes and spatial relations and in their revolutions and rotations. Several orreries were built in the 16th and 17th cent. to explain the Copernican (heliocentric) model of the solar system. Today the orrery finds considerable use as an aid in the teaching of celestial mechanics.

planetary nebula: see NEBULA.

planetesimal theory (plăn″ĭtĕs′əməl): see SOLAR SYSTEM.

planetoid: see ASTEROID.

plane tree, sycamore, or **buttonwood,** any species of the genus *Platanus,* deciduous trees indigenous to most temperate regions of the Northern Hemisphere, exclusive of Africa. The dry, seedlike fruits are densely packed into a hard brown ball—whence the name buttonwood—which separates when ripe into windborne tufts of down. The large American sycamore, or plane (*P. occidentalis*), supplies a hardwood popular for carpentry, furniture, and butchers' blocks. The Oriental plane (*P. orientalis*) of the Mediterranean area and W Asia is used for wood pulp. The London plane (*P. acerifolia*), sometimes miscalled Oriental plane, is much planted as an ornamental shade tree in cities; it is probably a hybrid of the American and Oriental planes. The names sycamore and buttonwood are most commonly applied to the North American species and plane to the Old World species. *Sycamore* is sometimes spelled *sycomore,* but should not be confused with the unrelated sycomore fig (*Ficus sycomorus*) of the family Moraceae. Plane trees are classified in the division MAGNOLIOPHYTA, class Magnoliopsida, order Hamamelidales, family Platanaceae.

plankton: see MARINE BIOLOGY.

Plano (plā′nō), city (1970 pop. 17,872), Collin co., N Texas; inc. 1873. It is in a farm and livestock area on the blackland prairie. There are cotton gins and feed and flour mills. Among the manufactures are brass fittings, cast-iron products, and boats and trailers.

plant, any organism of the plant kingdom, as opposed to one of the ANIMAL kingdom. A plant may be microscopic in size and simple in structure, as are certain one-celled algae, or a many-celled complex system, such as a tree. Plants have an extremely important role in the balance of nature and the life of man. Green plants, i.e., those possessing CHLOROPHYLL, manufacture their own food and give off oxygen in the process called PHOTOSYNTHESIS, in which water and carbon dioxide are combined by the energy of light. Plants, which provide the oxygen in the earth's atmosphere, are also the ultimate source of food and metabolic energy for all animals, which cannot manufacture their own food. Besides foods (e.g., grains, fruits, and vegetables), plant products vital to man include WOOD and wood products, fibers, drugs, oils, latex, pigments, and resins. Coal and petroleum are also of plant origin. Thus plants provide man not only sustenance but shelter, clothing, medicines, and the raw materials from which innumerable other products are made. Plants are generally distinguished from animals in that they possess chlorophyll, are fixed in one place, have no nervous system or sensory organs and hence respond slowly to stimuli, and have rigid supporting cell walls containing CELLULOSE. In addition, plants grow continually throughout life and have no maximum size or characteristic form in the adult, as do animals. No two seaweeds or oak trees are identical in the number, size, and shape of their parts nor do they exhibit the exact structural symmetry that starfish and humans do. Even one-celled plants grow continually, although they reproduce when they reach a certain size rather than expanding indefinitely. In higher plants the meristem tissues in the root and stem tips, in the buds, and in the cambium are areas of continual active growth. There are exceptions to these basic differences: Some plants, such as fungi, do not manufacture their own food; some unicellular plants (e.g., *Euglena*) and plant reproductive cells are motile; certain plants (e.g., *Mimosa pudica,* the sensitive plant) respond quickly to stimuli; and some lower plants do not have cellulose cell walls, while the animal tunicates (e.g., the sea squirt) do produce a celluloselike substance. Plants also differ from animals in the internal structure of the CELL and in certain details of the process of reproduction (see MITOSIS). The systems of CLASSIFICATION of the plant kingdom vary in naming and placing the larger categories (chiefly the divisions) because there is little fossil evidence, as there is in the case of animals, to establish the true evolutionary relationships of and distances between these groups. In some systems the lower plants are regarded as members of one or more separate kingdoms (see PROTISTA; MONERA). However, the general order of evolution and the demarcation of species is clear and agreed upon. Today the plant kingdom is commonly divided into two large groups, or subkingdoms, based chiefly on reproductive structure. These are the thallophytes (subkingdom Thallobionta), which do not form embryos, and the embryophytes (subkingdom Embryobionta), which do. All embryophytes and most thallophytes have a life cycle in which there are two alternating generations (see REPRODUCTION). The plant form of the thallophytes is an undifferentiated thallus lacking true roots, stems, and leaves. The subkingdom Thallobionta is composed of more than 10 divisions of ALGAE, FUNGI, and BACTERIA. The subkingdom Embryobionta is composed of two groups: the bryophytes (LIVERWORT and MOSS), division BRYOPHYTA, which have no vascular tissues, and a group consisting of seven divisions of plants that do have vascular tissues. The Bryophyta, like other nonvascular plants, are simple in structure and lack true roots, stems, and leaves; they therefore usually live in moist places or in water. The vascular plants have true roots, stems, and leaves and a well-developed vascular system composed of xylem and phloem for transporting water and food throughout the plant; they are therefore able to inhabit land. Three of the divisions of the vascular plants are currently represented by only a very few species. They are the PSILOTOPHYTA, with only three living species, of no importance to man; the LYCOPODIOPHYTA (club moss); and the EQUISETOPHYTA (horsetail). All the plants of a fourth subdivision, the RHYNIOPHYTA, are extinct. The remaining divisions include the dominant vegetation of the earth today: the ferns (see POLYPODIOPHYTA), the cone-bearing gymnosperms (see PINOPHYTA), and the angiosperms, or true flowering plants (see MAGNOLIOPHYTA). The latter two classes, because they both bear seeds, are often collectively called spermatophytes, or seed plants. The gymnosperms are all woody perennial plants and include several orders, of which most important are the CONIFER, the GINKGO, and the CYCAD. The angiosperms are separated into the monocotyledonous plants—with one cotyledon per SEED, scattered vascular bundles in the STEM, little or no CAMBIUM, and parallel veins in the LEAF—and the dicotyledonous plants, which have two cotyledons per seed, cylindrical vascular bundles in a regular pattern, a cambium, and net-veined leaves. There are some 40,000 species of monocotyledon, including the grasses (e.g., bamboo and such cereals as corn, rice, oats, and wheat), cattails, lilies, bananas, and orchids. The dicotyledons contain over 150,000 species of plant, from tiny herbs to great trees; this enormously varied group includes the bulk of all plants cultivated as ornamentals and for vegetables and FRUIT. One suggested scheme of plant evolution is that the green algae gave rise on the one hand to the mosses and liverworts and on the other hand to an extinct predecessor of the vascular plants. From this ancient form evolved the club mosses, horsetails, and ferns, and from some remote fern ancestor, in turn, arose the seed plants. The scientific study of plants is called BOTANY; the study of their relationship to their environment and of their distribution is plant ECOLOGY. The cultivation of plants for food and for decoration is HORTICULTURE. For specific approaches to the study of plants and animals, see BIOLOGY.

Plantagenet: see ANGEVIN.

plantain (plăn'tĭn), any plant of the genus *Plantago,* chiefly annual or perennial weeds of wide distribution. Many species are lawn pests and the pollen is often a hay fever irritant. *P. psyllium,* called psyllium, or fleawort, is cultivated in Spain and France for its mucilaginous seed-coatings, exported under the name psyllium seed for use as a laxative. In the United States wild plantains are occasionally utilized locally for forage. The name plantain is also used for a tropical plant related to the BANANA; the water plantain, *Alisma plantago-aquatica,* is another unrelated species. Plantains are classified in the division MAGNOLIOPHYTA, class Magnoliopsida, order Plantaginales, family Plantaginaceae.

plantain lily: see LILY.

Plantation, city (1970 pop. 23,523), Broward co., SE Fla., a residential suburb of Fort Lauderdale; inc. 1953.

plant breeding, science of altering the genetic pattern of plants in order to increase their economic value. Increased crop yield is the primary aim of most plant-breeding programs; advantages of the hybrids and new varieties developed include adaptation to new agricultural areas, greater resistance to disease and insects, and greater physiological efficiency. Other goals are adaptation of crops to modern production techniques such as mechanical harvesting and improvement in the market quality of the product. Plant breeders make genetic changes in crops by using various crossing and selection methods; attempts have also been made to introduce favorable mutations by the use of ultraviolet or gamma rays.

Plant City, city (1970 pop. 15,451), Hillsborough co., W central Fla.; inc. 1885. It is a processing, trade, and shipping center in a farm region. The city is known especially for its strawberries. It was settled on the site of an Indian village and developed with the coming of the railroad in 1884. A large state farmers' market is there.

planter, farm or garden implement that places propagating material such as seeds or seedlings into the ground, usually in rows. Broadcasting, i.e., scattering seed in all directions, by hand followed by harrowing (see HARROW) to cover the seed with soil was an early method of planting. Mechanical planters for small grains appeared in the United States around 1800; corn and cotton planters followed (1840–1880). Machines are currently available for almost every crop, including transplanting or plant-setting machines, which place live seedlings into the soil at spaced intervals, supply them with water and fertilizer, then close and pack the soil around them. See H. P. Smith, *Farm Machinery and Equipment* (5th ed. 1964); C. Culpin, *Farm Machinery* (8th ed. 1969).

Plantin, Christophe (krēstôf' pläNtăN'), 1514–89, printer. Plantin left his native France for Belgium because of religious persecution. In Antwerp his work, at first as a bookbinder, began in 1549. He began the production and publishing of books in 1555. His establishment continued to work until 1867 and is now preserved as the Plantin-Moretus Museum. Plantin was the leading printer of the second half of the 16th cent., and his books are admired for their accuracy and their typography. His equipment included types designed by Garamond and Granjon. The most famous work from his press is the Polyglot Bible (Bible regia) in eight volumes. In the center of his printer's mark is a pair of compasses.

plant louse: see APHID.

Planudes Maximus (plənōō'dēz măk'sĭməs) or **Maximus Planudes,** c.1260–c.1330, Byzantine scholar, an exceptionally learned monk. His edition of the GREEK ANTHOLOGY was long the standard. His prose collection of Aesop's *Fables* is outstanding.

plasma, in physics, fully ionized gas of low density, containing approximately equal numbers of positive ions and negative ions (see ELECTRON and ION). It is electrically conductive and is affected by magnetic fields. The study of plasma, called plasma physics, is especially important in research efforts to produce a controlled thermonuclear reaction (see NUCLEAR ENERGY). Such a reaction requires extremely high temperatures; it has been computed that a temperature of about 10 million degrees Celsius would be needed to initiate the reaction between deuterium and tritium. By passing a very high electric current through plasma great heat is produced and, simultaneously, an electromagnetic field is created causing the plasma to withdraw from the walls of its container. The contraction of the plasma, called the pinch effect, prevents the container from being destroyed, but the effect may become unstable too quickly for the fusion reaction. The properties of plasma are distinct from those of the ordinary STATES OF MATTER, and for this reason many scientists consider plasma a fourth state of matter. Interstellar gases are thought to be in the form of plasma, thus making plasma a common form of matter in the universe. At present, research is proceeding in the use of plasma for the propulsion of space vehicles.

plasma, biological: see BLOOD.

plasmodium, name for a stage in the life cycle of a SLIME MOLD. Also, *Plasmodium* is the name given to the genus of the protozoan parasite that causes MALARIA.

Plassey (plăs'ē), village, West Bengal state, NE India. In Plassey, Robert Clive decisively defeated (1757) the Nawab of Bengal, preparing the way for British dominion over NE India and earning him the title Baron Clive of Plassey.

plaster casting, as a sculpture process, is of three kinds. One employs a waste mold, another a piece mold (both plaster of paris), and the third a gelatin mold; all reproduce the original clay or wax model executed by the sculptor. The waste mold is chipped away (wasted) to free the hardened cast, which was poured in as liquid plaster. The gelatin mold, being pliable, may with care be sprung from the cast and removed intact and used for replicas. The piece mold also may be used again, being so divided as to be readily drawn away from the undercutting of the cast without damage to either. Plaster casts are used not only for the creation of new sculptures, but also for the numerous replicas of famous marble or stone statues. The ancient Egyptians used models of plaster taken directly from the human body. The Romans cast in plaster many thousands of copies of Greek statues. In another sense of the term, plaster casting refers to the surgical technique of encasing any part of the body in which bones are broken in a plaster-of-Paris cast, so that the bones may set smoothly without interference by motion, jarring, or physical shock.

plastering, house construction technique involving the application of plaster to walls and ceilings, exterior plasterwork being of a different composition and generally known as STUCCO. Plaster was used by the Egyptians (chiefly as a surface to receive color decorations) and by the Greeks. The Romans used it extensively, and there remain, especially at Pompeii, many ceilings and walls, with beautiful relief ornamentation, of a hard, fine plaster. Italian Renaissance artists imitated this Roman work, and relief ornament in plaster was employed in England for the rich ceilings and interiors of the reigns of Henry VIII, Elizabeth I, and James I and later in those designed by the architects Robert and James Adam. In the United States many fine ornamented plaster ceilings were executed in the 18th cent. Interior plastering is applied over a base that will furnish a proper grip—by means of interstices provided by wood lath or metal lath or by irregularities of surface such as in hollow tile. To secure best results three successive coats of plaster are requisite in most types of work. The first, or scratch, coat, composed of sand and lime mixed with abundant hair or fiber, must be thoroughly grounded into the lath and before it hardens is scratched to provide key, or adhesion, for the next coat. The second, called the brown coat in the United States and the floating coat in Great Britain, is composed of sand and lime, without hair, and is worked to a hard, compact texture, with its surface roughened to receive the final coat. The third, or white, finishing coat is composed of plaster of paris, slaked lime, and white sand, mixed with water to form a paste. It is troweled on the wall to form a hard, smooth surface, the process requiring a skilled worker. Moldings, cornices, and relief ornament are cast separately and then mounted into place. In former times ornamental details were molded in their location, from the damp plaster. Often substituted for plastered walls is plasterboard, a prefabricated material composed of paperboard and gypsum. See F. Van Den Branden and M. Knowles, *Plastering Skill and Practice* (1953, repr. 1971); J. R. Diehl, *Manual of Lathing and Plastering* (1960, repr. 1965).

plaster of Paris: see GYPSUM.

plastic, any organic material with the ability to flow into a desired shape when heat and pressure are applied to it and to retain the shape when they are withdrawn. There are two basic types of plastic: thermosetting, which cannot be resoftened after being subjected to heat and pressure; and thermoplastic, which can be repeatedly softened and remolded by heat and pressure. A plastic is made up principally of a binder together with plasticizers, fillers, pigments, and other additives. The binder gives a plastic its main characteristics and usually its name. Thus, *polyvinyl chloride* is both the name of a binder and the name of a plastic into which it is made. Binders may be natural materials, e.g., cellulose derivatives, casein, or milk protein, but are more commonly synthetic resins. In either case, the binder materials consist of very long chainlike molecules called POLYMERS. Cellulose derivatives are made from cellulose, a naturally occurring polymer; casein is also a naturally occurring polymer. Synthetic resins are polymerized, or built up, from small simple molecules called monomers. When heat and pressure are applied to a thermoplastic binder, these chainlike molecules slide past each other, giving the material "plasticity." However, when heat and pressure are initially applied to a thermosetting binder, the molecular chains become cross-linked, thus preventing any slippage if heat and pressure are reapplied. Plasticizers are added to a binder to increase flexibility and toughness. Fillers are added to improve particular properties, e.g., hardness or resistance to shock. Pigments are used to impart various colors. Virtually any desired color or shape and many combinations of the properties of hardness, durability, elasticity, and resistance to heat, cold, and acid can be obtained in a plastic. Plastics are available in the form of bars, tubes, sheets, coils, and blocks, and these can be fabricated to specification. However, plastic articles are commonly manufactured from plastic powders in which desired shapes are fashioned by compression, transfer, injection, or extrusion molding. In compression molding, materials are generally placed immediately in mold cavities, where the application of heat and pressure makes them first plastic, then hard. The transfer method, in which the compound is plasticized by outside heating and then poured into a mold to harden, is used for designs with intricate shapes and great variations in wall thickness. Injection-molding machinery dissolves the plastic powder in a heating chamber and by plunger action forces it into cold molds, where the product sets. The operations take place at rigidly controlled temperatures and intervals. Extrusion molding employs a heating cylinder, pressure, and an extrusion die through which the molten plastic is sent and from which it exits in continuous form to be cut in lengths or coiled. The first important plastic, CELLULOID, was discovered (c.1869) by the American inventor John W. Hyatt and manufactured by him in 1872; it is a mixture of cellulose nitrate, camphor, and alcohol and is thermoplastic. However, plastics did not come into modern industrial use until after the production (1909) of BAKELITE by the American chemist L. H. Baekeland. Bakelite, made by the polymerization of phenol and formaldehyde, is thermosetting. New uses for plastics are continually being discovered. Following World War II optical lenses, artificial eyes, and dentures of acrylic plastics, splints that X rays may pierce, nylon fibers, machine gears, fabric coatings, wall surfacing, and plastic lamination were developed. More recently a hydrophilic, or water-attracting, plastic suitable for use in non-irritating contact lenses has been developed. Among the trade names by which many plastic products are widely known are Plexiglas, Lucite, Polaroid, Cellophane, Vinylite, and Koroseal. Plastics reinforced with fiberglass are used for boats, automobile bodies, furniture, and building panels. Plastics are so durable that they will not rot or decay as do natural products such as those made of wood. As a result great amounts of discarded plastic products accumulate in the environment as waste. It has been suggested that plastics could be made to decompose slowly when exposed to sunlight by adding certain chemicals to them. Plastics present the additional problem of being difficult to burn. When placed in an incinerator, they tend to melt quickly and flow downward, clogging the incinerator's grate. They also emit harmful fumes; i.e., burning polyvinyl chloride gives off hydrogen chloride gas. See EPOXY RESINS; POLYPROPYLENE; POLYURETHANES; POLYOLEFINS; POLYETHYLENE; VINYL PLASTICS; POLYCARBONATES; POLYACRYLICS; TEFLON; POLYVINYL CHLORIDE; POLYSTYRENE. See J. A. Wordingham et al., *Dictionary of Plastics* (1964); L. K. Arnold, *Introduction to Plastics* (1968); J. A. Brydson, *Plastics Materials* (2d ed. 1969); J. H. DuBois, *Plastics History, U.S.A.* (1972).

plastic surgery, surgical repair of congenital or acquired deformities and the restoration of contour to improve the appearance and function of tissue defects. Development of this specialized branch of surgery received impetus from the need to repair gross deformities sustained in time of war. By the grafting of tissue or the use of artificial materials such as silicone, some remarkable restorations have become possible. Severe burns and the removal of fairly extensive skin cancers leave scars that must be covered by skin grafts. In addition to correcting the disfigurement, plastic surgery is often needed to restore vital movement and function of tissues that have been destroyed. It is also performed for purely cosmetic purposes, improving the shape of a nose, bringing outstanding ears closer to the head, or lifting the skin to erase wrinkles.

Plata, Río de la (rē'ō thā lä plä'tä), estuary, c.170 mi (270 km) long, SE South America, formed by the Paraná and Uruguay rivers. Between Argentina and Uruguay, the estuary is c.120 mi (190 km) wide at its mouth on the Atlantic Ocean and decreases to c.20 mi (30 km) near its head. Focal point of the second largest river system of the continent, the estuary receives a tremendous volume of water. Its northwestern end contains freshwater. Extensive sandbanks and shoals reduce the navigability, but dredged channels permit navigation by large vessels; Buenos Aires and Montevideo are the chief ports. Discovered (1516) by Juan Díaz de Solís, it was explored by Ferdinand Magellan in 1520 and by Sebastian Cabot from 1526 to 1529. The first settlement on its banks was made (1536) at Buenos Aires by Pedro de Mendoza, the Spanish conquistador. A principal channel into the interior of SE South America, it is very important commercially. In English it is sometimes called River Plate. The viceroyalty of Río de la Plata, more or less corresponding to the present Argentina, Bolivia, Uruguay, and Paraguay, was established in 1776.

Plataea (plətē'ə), ancient city of Greece, in S Boeotia (now Voiotía), on the slope of Mt. Cithaeron (Kithairón). Plataea had voluntarily passed from Theban to Athenian protection before the PERSIAN WARS and stood by Athens at Marathon (490 B.C.). In 479 B.C., Plataea was the scene of the decisive defeat of the Persians by the Greeks under Pausanias (with Aristides commanding the fleet). At the beginning of the Peloponnesian War, Thebes attacked (431) the city. It was besieged for two years (429–427), and then captured and sacked. It was subsequently rebuilt, razed (c.373) by the Thebans, and reconstructed by Alexander the Great.

plate, principal anode in an ELECTRON TUBE, i.e., the electrode through which electrons leave (or current enters) the tube. In tubes designed to handle large amounts of power, the plate must be cooled in order to compensate for the heat generated by electron impacts.

Plate, River: see PLATA, RÍO DE LA.

plateau, elevated, level or nearly level portion of the earth's surface, larger in summit area than a MOUNTAIN and bounded on at least one side by steep slopes. The origin of plateaus is assumed to be similar to that of mountains, the earth movements involved being distributed more uniformly over a wider area. Some plateaus, e.g., the Deccan of India and the Columbia Plateau of the NW United States, are basaltic and were formed as the result of a succession of lava flows covering hundreds of thousands of square miles that built up the land surface. Others are the result of upward folding; still others have been left elevated by the erosion of adjacent lands. Plateaus, like all elevated regions, are subject to dissection by erosion, which removes greater and greater amounts of the upland surface. Low plateaus are often agricultural regions, like the neighboring plains, while high plateaus are usually fit chiefly for stock grazing. Many of the world's high plateaus are deserts. Other notable plateaus are the Colorado Plateau of the W United States, the Bolivian plateau in South America, and the plateaus of Anatolia, Arabia, Iran, and Tibet.

platelet: see BLOOD CLOTTING.

Platen, August Graf von (ou'go͝ost gräf fən plä'tən), 1796–1835, German poet, whose original name was August Graf von Platen-Hallermünde. An opponent of romanticism, he satirized it in several works such as his travesty of the "fate tragedy," *Die verhängnissvolle Gabel* [the fatal fork] (1826). His best work was his cold but classic verse, including his fine *Sonnets on Venice* (1825, tr. 1914); odes; and verse on the Polish insurrection of 1830.

plateresque (plătərĕsk') [Span.,=silversmith], earliest phase of Spanish Renaissance architecture and decoration, in the early 16th cent. Its richness of effect was primarily based upon the work of the Italian Renaissance, mingled, however, with surviving Moorish and late Gothic design. In characteristic Spanish decorative spirit, structure received little emphasis, while doorways and other details displayed clusters of ornament against a foil of bare wall space. Columns in candelabrum form were among the favorite motifs, as were pilasters enriched with arabesque reliefs and topped with free Corinthianesque capitals; columns with bracketed capitals; heraldic escutcheons; and fancifully twisted scrolls. It was in the plateresque period that Spanish workers in wrought iron reached an unlimited technical skill, translating Renaissance motifs into terms of metalwork to form the superb rejas of the churches (see REJERÍA). Among the great plateresque buildings are the town hall at Seville; the university at Alcalá de Henares; and the cathedral at Granada by Diego de Siloe. From the latter half of the 16th cent. a much more classical and restrained form of Renaissance design supplanted the plateresque.

plate tectonics, modern CONTINENTAL DRIFT theory that has revolutionized geologists' understanding of continents, ocean basins, mountains, and earth history. Synthesized from findings in geology, oceanography, and geophysics, plate tectonics theory holds that the LITHOSPHERE, the hard outer layer of the earth, is divided into about 7 major plates and perhaps as many as 12 smaller plates, c.60 mi (100 km) thick, resting upon a lower soft layer called the ASTHENOSPHERE. The continents, which are c.25 mi (40 km) thick, are embedded in some of the plates, passively drifting as the plates move about on the earth's surface like boxes on conveyor belts. The mechanism moving the plates is at present unknown, but is probably related to the transfer of heat energy within the earth. The boundaries between plates are marked by lines of earthquake and volcanic activity. Zones from which the earth's crust

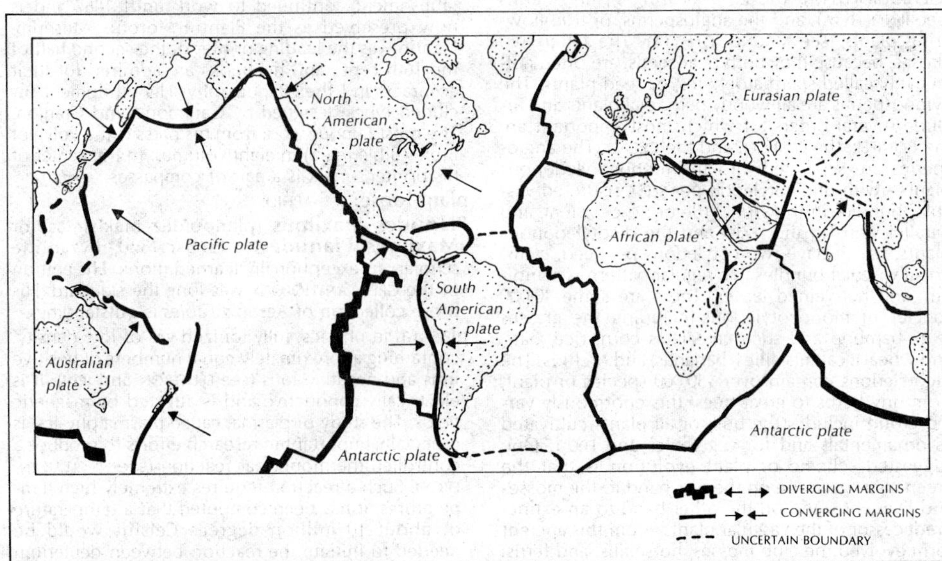

Map of the world showing major plates and plate boundaries

spreads mark one type of boundary where tensional forces open rifts, allowing new basaltic crustal material to upwell from the earth's mantle and become welded to the trailing edges of the plates. When a continental mass straddles such a rift, it is split apart, forming new ocean areas. This is happening today in the Red Sea and the Gulf of California. In oceans crustal spreading from rifts occurs along an underwater mountain range called the midocean ridge (see SEA-FLOOR SPREADING). In other parts of the crustal conveyor system, subduction zones along the leading edges of the shifting plates form a second type of boundary marked by ocean trenches where the edges of crustal plates dive steeply into the earth's mantle and are reabsorbed at depths of over 400 mi (640 km). A third type of boundary occurs where two plates slide past one another in a grinding, shearing manner along great FAULTS called transcurrent (strike-slip) faults. The San Andreas fault in the W United States and the Alpine fault of New Zealand are examples of such faults. Volcanoes are found along spreading centers of the midocean ridge, at isolated "hot spots" on the asthenosphere, such as the Hawaiian Islands, and in the subduction zones, where the descending plate partially melts, forming masses of magma. Earthquakes whose point of origin in the earth, or focus, is shallow are seen as the result of crustal plates shearing past one another. Earthquake foci also form steeply inclined planes along the subduction zones, extending to depths of about 440 mi (710 km). Mountain ranges are formed when two plates containing continental crust collide. For example the Himalayas were thrust up when the plates carrying India and Eurasia came together. Mountains are also formed when ocean crust is subducted along a continental margin, resulting in melting of rock, volcanic activity, and compressional deformation of the continent margin. This is currently happening with the Andes mts., and is believed to have occurred with the uplift of the Rockies and the Appalachians in the past. According to plate tectonics, the ocean basins are viewed as transient features that have periodically opened and closed, first rending and then suturing the continents, which are permanent features on the earth's surface. Geologists now believe that the continents were sutured together 200 million years ago at the beginning of the Mesozoic era to form a supercontinent named Pangaea. Initial rifting along the Tethys Sea formed a northern continental mass, Laurasia, and a southern continental mass, Gondwanaland. Then plate movements caused North American and Eurasian separation coincidently with the separation of South America, Africa, and India. Australia and Antarctica were the last to separate. These motions caused the opening of the Atlantic and Indian oceans at the expense of the Pacific, which has shrunk. The major plates are named after the dominant geographic feature on them and include the North American and South American plates, the Eurasian plate, the African plate, the Indian or Australian plate, the Pacific plate, and the Antarctic plate. See N. Calder, *The Restless Earth: A Report on the New Geology* (1972); A. Klein, *Oceans and Continents in Motion* (1972); A. Hallam, *A Revolution in the Earth Sciences* (1973); M. W. McElhinny, *Palaeomagnetism and Plate Tectonics* (1973).

Plath, Sylvia, 1932–63, American poet, b. Boston. Educated at Smith College and Cambridge, Plath published poems even as a child and won many academic and literary awards. Her first volume of poetry, *The Collosus* (1960), is at once highly disciplined, well crafted, and intensely personal; these qualities are present in all her work. *Ariel* (1968), considered her finest book of poetry, was written in the last months of her life and published posthumously, as were *Crossing the Water* (1971) and *Winter Trees* (1972). These late poems reveal an objective detachment from life and a growing fascination with death. They are rendered with impeccable and ruthless art, anatomizing the most extreme reaches of Plath's consciousness and passions. Her one novel, *The Bell Jar* (1971), originally published pseudonymously in England in 1962, is autobiographical, a fictionalized account of a nervous breakdown Plath had suffered when in college. Plath was married to the poet Ted HUGHES and was the mother of two children. She committed suicide in London in Feb., 1963. See *The Art of Sylvia Plath* (ed. by Charles Newman, 1971); study by E. M. Aird (1973).

plating, application of a plate, or coat, of metal to a surface for decoration, reflection of light, protection against corrosion, or increased wearing quality. The practice is of ancient origin: GILDING was developed early; the Romans soldered silver plates to articles of baser metals; and in the 5th cent. a process was described by which iron weapons were coated with copper by dipping in a copper solution. In the 18th cent. the plating of copper or brass with silver by fusion was originated in England (see SHEFFIELD PLATE). Plating by ELECTROLYSIS, or electroplating, is the most common method because it permits the control of the thickness of the plating. Cadmium, zinc, silver, gold, tin, copper, nickel, and chromium are the most frequently used plating metals. Any of the common metals and some nonmetals, e.g., plastics, with suitably prepared surfaces can be used as a base. In electroforming, a mold made of specially prepared wax is electroplated. The wax is then melted and the plating itself constitutes the finished product (see ELECTROTYPE). The part to be plated may be dipped in molten metal. For example, molten zinc is used in galvanizing; lead-tin alloy, in terneplating; and tin, in tinning. Without electricity, some metals can be precipitated from chemical solutions onto the surface of plastics or metals. A powdered, liquid, or gaseous plating metal can be made to diffuse into a heated base-metal surface. Sherardizing is the diffusion coating of zinc on steel; chromizing, chromium on steel; and calorizing, aluminum on steel. The application by welding or brazing of a sheet or plate to the base metal is called cladding. Decorative metal coatings are applied to plastic by vapor deposition. The metal, usually aluminum, and the plastic parts are put in a vacuum chamber. When the aluminum is vaporized by a surge of electricity, the particles settle on any exposed surface. Worn parts can be sprayed with molten metal to build them up to their original dimensions. Iron or steel is best protected from corrosion by a coating of cadmium or zinc, which oxidizes, creating a protective coat for the underlying material. Parts such as automobile bumpers usually have an undercoating of copper, a protective layer of nickel, and a thin, shiny surface layer of chromium for decoration. In the manufacture of phonograph records an original recording is made on a metal disk coated with lacquer, which is then plated. From the plated master a DIE is made to be used in a hydraulic press. The silvering of mirrors is a type of plating in which silver is precipitated chemically on glass.

platinite, alloy that is 46% nickel and 54% iron. It is used in the manufacture of electric light bulbs because its coefficient of expansion, i.e., the rate at which its volume increases with temperature, is the same as that of glass.

platinum (plăt'ənəm), metallic chemical element; symbol Pt; at. no. 78; at. wt. 195.09; m.p. 1772°C; b.p. about 3800°C; sp. gr. 21.45 at 20°C; valence +2 or +4. Pure platinum is a malleable, ductile, lustrous, silver-white metal with a face-centered cubic crystalline structure. Chemically inactive, it is unaffected by common acids but dissolves in aqua regia, forming chloroplatinic acid (H_2PtCl_6). It is attacked by the halogens, sulfur, or caustic alkalies. It does not combine with oxygen even at high temperatures. Like palladium, it absorbs large quantities of hydrogen, which it releases at red heat. Platinum is found in nature alloyed with the other metals of the so-called platinum group, found in group VIII of the PERIODIC TABLE; the other five metals in this group are iridium, osmium, palladium, rhodium, and ruthenium. These metals are found in alluvial deposits in the Soviet Union, South Africa, Colombia, and Alaska. Platinum and the related metals are recovered commercially as a by-product of the refining of nickel ores mined near Sudbury, Ont., Canada; from gold mines in South Africa; and from the alluvial deposits in the Soviet Union. There is no routine method for separating platinum from other metals; it is usually recovered by complex chemical methods. Platinum has many uses, especially in alloys. Most important of the alloys are those with iridium. Platinum and its alloys are used in surgical tools, laboratory utensils, electrical resistance wires, contact points, and standard masses. (The International Prototype Kilogram, kept at Sèvres, France, is a cylinder of platinum-iridium alloy.) Because its thermal coefficient of expansion is nearly equal to that of glass, platinum is used to make electrodes sealed in glass. It is used extensively in jewelry and in dentistry. A platinum-cobalt alloy is used to make very powerful magnets. Platinum is specially prepared for use as a CATALYST. Finely divided, the metal is platinum black, a powder. It also may be used as platinum sponge, formed when platinic ammonium chloride, $(NH_4)_2PtCl_6$, is ignited, or as platinized asbestos, prepared by heating asbestos after dipping it in chloroplatinic acid. Platinum catalysts are used in the contact process for producing sulfuric acid, in the Ostwald process for the production of nitric acid, and in petroleum cracking, as well as in a variety of other reactions. Although natural platinum alloys may have been used several centuries before Christ, modern knowledge of the metal dates from about 1736, when its existence in South America was reported by A. de Ulloa. Some of this "platina" was taken to England, and soon thereafter many leading chemists published reports on it. A process discovered about 1803 by W. H. Wollaston for making the metal malleable made possible its commercial use for laboratory apparatus and other purposes. Although platinum was used as an adulterant for gold over a century ago, it is now about four times as expensive as gold.

Plato (plā'tō), 427?–347 B.C., Greek philosopher. After pursuing the liberal studies of his day, he became in 407 B.C. a pupil and friend of Socrates. From about 388 B.C. he lived for a time at the court of Dionysius the Elder, tyrant of Syracuse. On his return to Athens, Plato founded a school, the ACADEMY, where he taught mathematics and philosophy until his death. His teaching was interrupted by two more visits to Syracuse (367 and 361 B.C.), which he made in the vain hope of realizing his political ideals in Sicily. Plato's extant work is in the form of dialogues and epistles. Some of the dialogues and many of the epistles attributed to him are known to be spurious, while others are doubtful. The dialogues are divided into three groups according to the probable order of composition. The earliest group, called Socratic, include chiefly the *Apology,* which presents the defense of Socrates; the *Meno,* which asks whether virtue can be taught; and the *Gorgias,* which concerns the absolute nature of right and wrong. These early dialogues present Socrates in conversations that illustrate his main ideas—the unity of virtue and knowledge and of virtue and happiness. Each dialogue treats a particular problem without necessarily resolving the issues raised. Plato was always concerned with the fundamental philosophical problem of working out a theory of the art of living and knowing. Like Socrates, Plato began with a conviction of the ultimately harmonious structure of the universe, but he went further in trying to construct a comprehensive philosophical scheme. His goal was to show the rational relationship between the soul, the state, and the cosmos. This is the general theme of the great dialogues of his middle years: the *Republic, Phaedo, Symposium, Phaedrus, Timaeus,* and *Philebus.* In the *Republic* he shows how the operation of justice within the individual can best be understood through the analogy of the operation of justice within the state, which Plato proceeds to set out in his conception of the ideal state. However, justice cannot be understood fully unless seen in relation to the Idea of the Good, which is the supreme principle of order and truth. It is in these dialogues that the famous Platonic Ideas are discussed. Plato argued for the independent reality of Ideas as the only guarantee of ethical standards and of objective scientific knowledge. In the *Republic* and the *Phaedo* he postulates his theory of Forms. Ideas or Forms are the immutable Archetypes of all temporal phenomena, and only these Ideas are completely real; the physical world possesses only relative reality. The Forms assure order and intelligence in a world that is in a state of constant flux. They provide the pattern from which the world of sense derives its meaning. The supreme Idea is the Idea of the Good, whose function and place in the world of Ideas is analogous to that of the sun in the physical world. Plato saw his task as that of leading men to a vision of the Forms and to some sense of the highest good. The principal path is suggested in the famous myth of the cave in the *Republic,* in which man in his uninstructed state is chained up in a world of shadows. However, man can move up toward the sun, or highest good, through the study of what Plato calls dialectic. The supreme science, dialectic, is a method of inquiry that proceeds by a constant questioning of assumptions, and by explaining a particular idea in terms of a more general one, until the ultimate ground of explanation is reached. The *Republic,* the first Utopia in literature, asserts that the philosopher is the only one capable of ruling the just state, since through his study of dialectic he understands the harmony of all parts of the universe in their relation to the Idea of the Good. Each social class happily performs the function for which it is suited; the philosopher rules, the warrior fights, and the worker enjoys the fruits of his labor. In the *Symposium,* perhaps the most poetic of the dialogues, the path to the highest good is described as the ascent by true lovers to eternal beauty, and in the *Phaedo* the path is viewed as the pilgrimage of the philosopher through death to the world of eternal truth. Many of the late dialogues are devoted to technical philosophic issues. The most important of these are the *Theaetetus;* the *Parmenides,* which deals with the relation between the one and the many; and the *Sophist,* which discusses the nature of nonbeing. Plato's longest work, the *Laws,* written during his middle and late periods, discusses in practical terms the nature of the state. Plato's teachings have been among the most influential in the history of Western civilization. In the various dialogues he touched upon almost every problem that has occupied subsequent philosophers. Plato was also a superb writer, and his works are part of the world's literature. See translation of the dialogues by Benjamin Jowett, ed. by D. J. Allan and H. E. Daley (4 vol., 4th ed., rev. 1953); A. E. Taylor, *Plato: The Man and His Work* (1927); R. S. Brumbaugh, *Plato for the Modern Age* (1962); Renford Bambrough, ed., *New Essays on Plato and Aristotle* (1965); G. C. Field, *Plato and His Contemporaries* (3d ed. 1967); J. H. Randall, *Plato: Dramatist of the Life of Reason* (1970); Gregory Vlastos, *Platonic Studies* (1973).

Platonic Solids: see POLYHEDRON.

Platt, Charles Adams, 1861-1933, American architect, landscape architect, painter, and etcher, b. New York City. He studied etching with Stephen Parrish and painting, in Paris, under Boulanger and Lefebvre. He won distinction in both fields before travels in Italy turned his interests toward architecture and garden design. His architectural designs are based upon Italian and Georgian traditions. Platt's works include numerous important city and country residences, the latter complete with their gardens; the Freer Gallery of Art at Washington, D.C. (1918); an addition to the Corcoran Gallery; a building for the *Leader News* in Cleveland; buildings for the Univ. of Illinois at Urbana, including its library; and a number of buildings (e.g., chapel, library) for Phillips Academy, Andover, Mass. He wrote *Italian Gardens* (1894).

Platt, Orville Hitchcock, 1827-1905, U.S. Senator (1879-1905), b. Washington, Litchfield co., Conn. Platt held many public offices in Connecticut before he served in the U.S. Senate. He helped frame the high protective tariff measures of 1883, 1890, and 1897 and opposed "cheap money" schemes and attempts to regulate big business. Platt was influential in the annexation of Hawaii and the occupation of the Philippines. He also sponsored the **Platt Amendment**—a rider attached to the Army Appropriations Bill of 1901. It stipulated the conditions for U.S. intervention in Cuban affairs and permitted the United States to lease lands for the establishment of a naval base in Cuba. The amendment, which virtually made Cuba a U.S. protectorate, was forced into the constitution of Cuba and was incorporated in a permanent treaty between the United States and Cuba; it set the terms under which the United States intervened in Cuban affairs in 1906, 1912, 1917, and 1920. Rising Cuban nationalism and widespread criticism led to its abrogation in 1934, although the United States retained its lease on Guantánamo Bay, where a naval base had been established.

Platt, Thomas Collier, 1833-1910, American legislator and political boss, b. Owego, N.Y. He was president of the Tioga County National Bank and had acquired considerable commercial interests by the time he served in the U.S. House of Representatives as a Republican (1873-77). In 1881 he became a U.S. Senator, but, following his mentor, Roscoe CONKLING, in a quarrel with President Garfield over patronage, resigned almost immediately, thereby winning the nickname "Me Too" Platt. With Conkling he sought vindication in a new election, but withdrew his name in the deadlock that followed in the state legislature. Platt remained prominent in New York politics, gaining new power and consolidating his control of patronage. Again from 1897 to 1909 he was a U.S. Senator. One of the most powerful of Republican politicians, he was largely responsible for the election (1898) of Theodore ROOSEVELT as governor of New York. Although Roosevelt often consulted with Platt, he was largely independent in political matters, and in 1900 Platt succeeded in shelving him (as he thought) into the vice presidency. Afterward Platt's power declined. See his autobiography (1910, repr. 1974); H. F. Gosnell, *Boss Platt and His New York Machine* (1924, repr. 1971).

Platt Amendment: see PLATT, ORVILLE HITCHCOCK.

Plattdeutsch: see GERMAN LANGUAGE.

Platte, river, c.310 mi (500 km) long, formed by the confluence of the North Platte (680 mi/1,090 km long) and South Platte (430 m/690 km) rivers at North Platte, Neb. It flows generally E across S Nebraska to join the Missouri River at Plattsmouth, Neb. The river is too flood-prone in spring and too shallow and braided the rest of the year for navigation. Much of its water and the water of its tributaries is diverted for irrigation, municipal uses, and hydroelectric power production. The Platte valley was an important route to the West in the 19th cent.; the Mormon Trail followed the north bank, and the Oregon Trail followed the south bank.

Platt National Park: see NATIONAL PARKS AND MONUMENTS (table).

Plattsburgh, city (1970 pop. 18,715), seat of Clinton co., NE N.Y., on Lake Champlain; settled 1767, inc. 1902. It is a trade and distribution point, with plants that make paper and plastics. A major source of employment is the adjoining Plattsburgh Air Force Base, a strategic air command installation. The city is also a summer-vacation center, attracting Canadians as well as Americans. During the War of 1812 a makeshift American fleet under Thomas Macdonough decisively defeated the British in a pitched battle on Lake Champlain near Plattsburgh, compelling an accompanying land-invasion force under Sir George Prevost to return to Canada. The State Univ. College at Plattsburgh and a junior college are in the city. Clinton state prison and a state hospital are at nearby Dannemora.

Platyhelminthes (plăt″ēhĕlmĭn′thēz), phylum of soft-bodied, bilaterally symmetrical, invertebrate animals, commonly called flatworms. There are three classes, containing more than 9,000 known species: The free-living, primarily aquatic class, Turbellaria, may be used to illustrate most of the typical features of the phylum, since the two remaining classes, Trematoda and Cestoda, are considerably modified for their exclusively parasitic existence. Flatworms, considered the most primitive bilaterally symmetrical animals, are dorso-ventrally flattened. The epidermis is generally ciliated in the turbellarians, while trematodes and cestodes are covered with a cuticle. Beneath the outer covering are two layers of muscle, an outer circular layer, and an inner longitudinal layer; this arrangement permits an undulating form of locomotion that can be observed in the larger turbellarian species. A saclike digestive cavity, with a single opening to the outside that serves as both mouth and anus, is sometimes present; in the simpler forms it is absent or unbranched, but in higher forms it branches to all parts of the body. The major sense organs, when present, are concentrated in the head, or front end. Although a primitive nerve net is present in some of the simpler forms, others have several nerve cords extending from a brain along the length of the body. The latter pattern of organization is retained in the nervous systems of higher invertebrates, specifically annelids and arthropods. The reproductive system of flatworms is characteristically hermaphroditic (i.e., each individual produces both eggs and sperm), and cross-fertilization between individuals is typical. While trematodes and cestodes shed eggs almost continuously, turbellarians exhibit seasonal reproductive activity and, in addition, display asexual reproduction and the ability to regenerate severed parts of the body. All except the simplest flatworms have nephridial tubules, called protonephridia, usually distributed throughout the body. Such structures consist of an external opening and a tubule that branches internally, terminating in a number of blind, bulb-shaped structures called flame bulbs, which bear tufts of cilia. Opinion differs as to what extent the protonephridia actually function as excretory organs.

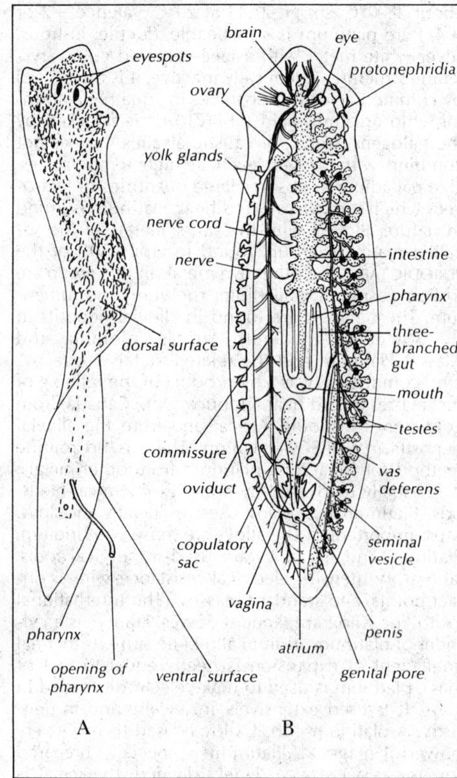

A. Planaria, *representative of the phylum Platyhelminthes*

B. *Internal anatomy of* Planaria

Class Turbellaria. The mostly free-living, primarily carnivorous, flatworms of class Turbellaria are characterized by a soft epidermis that is ciliated, at least on the ventral surface. The movement of the cilia propels the smaller forms. Larger species glide along by muscular waves, usually over mucous beds secreted by special cells. Turbellarians are generally divided into five groups (considered by some to be five orders), based primarily on differences in the form of the digestive cavity, a structure that is readily observable through the transparent body wall. The most primitive turbellarians, the acoels, have no digestive cavity. The ventral mouth, and sometimes a simple pharynx, leads to an inner mass of nutritive cells. Most species measure less than 1/8 in. (3 mm) in length. The rhabdocoels have straight, unbranched digestive cavities. Some authorities believe that the rhabdocoels gave rise to both the trematodes and cestodes because several rhabdocoel species exhibit commensal relationships, which presumably could have given rise to parasitism. The allocoels were formerly classified together with the rhabdocoels; the gut can be either saclike or branched. The triclads, also known as PLANARIANS, are relatively large flatworms named for their three-branched gut. Most species range from 1/8 in. (3 mm) to about 1 in. (2.5 cm) in length. Planarians have more sense organs and a more complex brain than the other turbellarians. The freshwater species *Dugesia tigrina* has primitive eyes and tactile lobes, or auricles, on the sides of the head. The muscular pharynx can be extruded for food capture. *Dugesia,* and many other planarians, can regenerate entirely new individuals from small pieces cut from the body. The group of turbellarians known as polyclads tend to be larger (1-2 in./2.5-5 cm) and more oval in shape than the triclads. Their bodies are extremely flat and leaflike, and the gut is subdivided into numerous branches. Many are brightly colored, and some have ruffled edges. Some species have numerous eyes scattered over the front end of the body.

Class Trematoda. The parasitic flatworms of class Trematoda, also called FLUKES, have oral suckers, sometimes supplemented by hooks, with which they attach to their vertebrate hosts. Trematodes have retained the same body form and digestive cavity as the turbellarians. However, practically the entire interior is occupied by the reproductive system; the organism is capable of producing huge numbers of offspring. Trematodes of the order Digenea have complex life cycles involving two or more hosts. The larval worms occupy small animals, typically snails and fish, and the adult worms are internal parasites of vertebrates. Many species, such as the liver fluke *Clonorchis sinensis* and the blood fluke (*Schistosoma*), cause serious diseases in humans. Members of the second order of trematodes, *Monogenea,* spend their entire life cycle on a single host, often on the gills and skin of fish.

Class Cestoda. The body of the cestodes, also known as TAPEWORMS, has lost the typical turbellarian form. Although there are a few unsegmented species, the bulk of a typical cestode body consists of a series of linearly arranged reproductive segments called proglottids. There is no mouth or digestive system; food is absorbed through the cuticle. Adults live in the digestive tract of vertebrates, and larval forms encyst in the flesh of various vertebrates and invertebrates. The body of an adult tapeworm is virtually a reproductive factory. Behind a small securing knob, called a scolex, which bears a circle of hooks or other attachment organs, the proglottids constantly bud off and gradually enlarge. As they mature they become filled with male and female reproductive organs. Cross-fertilization takes place with adjacent worms or neighboring proglottids; in some cases self-fertilization occurs. In some species the ripe proglottids, filled with eggs, are shed. In others the fertilized eggs leave the adult host in the feces. If the eggs are consumed by the intermediate host, the life cycle continues. Tapeworm species that infest human intestines as adults include *Taenia saginata, T. solium,* the dwarf tapeworm, *Hymenolepsis nana,* and the fish tapeworm, *Diphyllobothrium latum,* which can reach lengths of up to 50 ft (15 m). For some species man serves as the intermediate host.

platypus (plăt'əpəs), semiaquatic egg-laying mammal, *Ornithorhynchus anatinus,* of Tasmania and E Australia. Also called duckbill, or duckbilled platypus, it belongs to the order Monotremata (see MONOTREME), the most primitive group of living mammals. The only other member of this group is the ECHIDNA, or spiny anteater. The head, trunk, and tail of the platypus are broad and flattened and covered with thick dark brown fur. The muzzle is shaped like a duck's bill and is soft and rubbery. It contains ridges used for crushing food; the animal has no teeth. The eyes are small and there are no external ears. The five-toed feet are webbed. The heel of the male bears a hollow spur connected to a poison-secreting gland; this spur is probably used as a weapon. The adult male platypus is about 2 ft (60 cm) long, including the 5 or 6 in. (13–15 cm) tail; it weighs about 4 lb. The female is slightly smaller. The platypus is found from tropical swamps at sea level to cold lakes at altitudes of 6,000 ft (1,830 m). Its diet consists entirely of small freshwater animals dredged from muddy bottoms. Prey captured underwater are stored in cheek pouches and eaten at the surface or on land. Platypuses live in pairs in simple burrows in stream banks, except during the breeding season, when the female makes a separate and more elaborate burrow containing a nesting chamber approached by a long tunnel. One, two, or three eggs are laid at a time and are incubated, in birdlike fashion, by the female. The female lacks nipples, and the young lick milk from the fur around the many small abdominal openings of the mammary glands. The platypus is classified in the phylum CHORDATA, subphylum Vertebrata, class Mammalia, order Monotremata, family Ornithorhynchidae.

Plauen (plou'ən), city (1970 pop. 81,907), Karl-Marx-Stadt district, S East Germany, on the White Elster River and at the northwestern foot of the Erzgebirge. It has been a textile-milling center since the 15th cent. Other manufactures include machinery, machine tools, electrical equipment, and motor vehicles. Originally founded by the Slavs, Plauen became (c.1224) the seat of a branch of the Teutonic Knights. It passed to Bohemia in 1327 and to Saxony in 1466. It was severely damaged in World War II. Noteworthy buildings include a 12th-century church, a castle (early 13th cent.), and the city hall (16th cent.).

Plautus (Titus Maccius Plautus) (plô'təs), c.254–184 B.C., Roman comic poet, b. Umbria. His plays, adapted from those of Greek New Comedy, are popular and vigorous representations of middle-class and lower-class life. Written with a mastery of idiomatic spoken Latin and governed by a genius for situation and coarse humor, Plautus' comedies achieved a great reputation. Characteristic of his plays are the stock comic figures—the knavish, resourceful slave, the young lover and his mistress, the courtesan, the parasite, and the braggart soldier. His plots and characters have had great influence upon later literature, with adaptations and imitations by many writers, e.g., Molière, Corneille, Jonson, and Shakespeare. The chronological order for Plautus' plays is unknown; 21, more or less complete, survive: *Amphitruo (Amphitryon), Asinaria, Aulularia, Bacchides, Captivi, Casina, Cistellaria, Curculio, Epidicus, Menaechmi, Mercator, Miles gloriosus, Mostellaria, Persa, Poenulus, Pseudolus, Rudens, Stichus, Trinummus, Truculentus,* and *Vidularia* (in fragments). See G. E. Duckworth, *The Complete Roman Drama* (1942) and other translations by Paul Nixon (5 vol., 1950–57), Moses Hadas (1965), and Smith Palmer Bovie (1970); studies by P. W. Harsh (1949) and Erich Segal (1968).

player piano, an upright piano incorporating a mechanical system that automatically plays the encoded contents of a paper strip. This strip, perforated with holes whose position and length determine pitch and duration, is drawn over a pneumatic device that shoots streams of air through the holes. The air is guided through a tube to the corresponding hammer, which strikes the string. The pieces used in player pianos often reproduced performances by famous pianists. Although popular during the late 19th and early 20th cent., the player piano was eclipsed by phonographs and radios.

Player piano

Playfair, John, 1748–1819, Scottish mathematician, physicist, and geologist. He was educated at St. Andrews and Edinburgh and taught first mathematics and then physics and astronomy at the latter university. His *Illustrations of the Huttonian Theory of the Earth* (1802) elucidated the methods and principles of his friend James Hutton and established uniformitarianism as the foundation of the new science of geology. He also published texts on geometry, physics, and astronomy.

Playfair, Sir Nigel (nī'jəl plā'fâr), 1874–1934, English actor-manager. He made his acting debut in 1902 and later appeared in major London productions of Shaw and Shakespeare. He took on the management of the Lyric Theatre from 1919 to 1932. There Playfair's greatest achievements were his revival (1920) of John Gay's *Beggar's Opera,* which ran for more than three years, and a stylized production of *The Importance of Being Earnest.* Playfair was knighted in 1928. See his two volumes of memoirs of the Lyric Theatre (1925 and 1930).

playground: see RECREATION.

playing cards, parts of a set or deck, used in playing various games of chance or skill. The origin of playing cards is unknown, and almost as many theories exist as there are historians of the subject. Playing cards were used hundreds of years ago in Europe and probably long before that in the Orient. In the British Museum there is a 14th-century manuscript depicting a card game played by a king and two courtiers; the arrangement of the pips on the cards is similar to that of the present day. Playing cards are referred to in the household expense accounts of Charles VI of France for 1392. In 1397 the provost of Paris issued an edict prohibiting the people from playing certain games on working days, and among these, cards are mentioned. The manufacture of playing cards in Germany dates from the beginning of the 15th cent., and in Italy they were made in 1425. Playing cards appeared in England in 1463, and the earliest designs produced there were painted by hand. There were usually four suits; in Germany these were called hearts, bells, leaves, and acorns, while in Italy they were known as swords, batons, cups, and money. The present-day variety of hearts, diamonds, clubs, and spades was adopted in France in the 16th cent. In addition to these cards, called numeral cards, there were also cards known as TAROTS, or *triomphes* (trumps), because when played in combination with numeral cards the tarots had a higher value. A full pack consisted of 78 cards, the 22 tarots and 56 others that were divided into four suits of 14 cards each. Out of this pack developed the modern standard deck, consisting of 52 cards, divided into four suits (spades and clubs, black; hearts and diamonds, red). In each suit there are king, queen, knave (or jack), and 10 cards bearing pips from 1 (the ace, the highest card in most games) to 10. In gambling games such as poker, an extra card called the joker is often used. See Roger Tilley, *A History of Playing Cards* (1973); Detleff Hoffman, *The Playing Card: An Illustrated History* (1974).

Plaza Lasso, Galo (gä'lō plä' sä lä'sō), 1906–, president of Ecuador (1948–52) and secretary general of the Organization of American States (OAS) (1968–), b. New York City. He served (1944–46) as Ecuadorian ambassador to the United States and was a signer of the Charter of the United Nations. A liberal democrat and an expert in mechanized agriculture, as president he forwarded the agricultural development of Ecuador. Bananas, coffee, and cacao exports reached record heights. In spite of chronic political turbulence, Plaza brought a measure of economic prosperity to the country; he was the first constitutionally elected president in 28 years to complete his term. He later served as a UN mediator in Lebanon (1958), the Congo (1960), and Cyprus (1964–65). As secretary general of the OAS, he earned a reputation for vigorous leadership.

pleadings: see PROCEDURE.

Pleasant Hill, residential city (1970 pop. 24,610), Contra Costa co., W Calif.; inc. 1961. First settled in 1844, the area remained rural until the housing boom of World War II. A junior college is there.

Pleasant Hills, borough (1970 pop. 10,409), Allegheny co., SW Pa., a residential suburb of Pittsburgh; inc. 1947.

Pleasanton, city (1970 pop. 18,328), Alameda co., W Calif., a suburb of the San Francisco-Oakland area, in a vineyard and dairy region; inc. 1894. Wine and cheese are produced, and there are also publishing and research enterprises.

Pleasantville, residential and resort city (1970 pop. 13,778), Atlantic co., SE N.J., just W of Atlantic City; settled 1702, inc. 1888. It is the trade center of an area known as "the Mainland." Tourism, shellfishing, deep-sea fishing, and boatbuilding are important activities.

Pleasonton, Alfred, 1824–97, Union general in the American Civil War, b. Washington, D.C. He served in the Mexican War and in the Indian wars on the frontier. In the Civil War, he distinguished himself in the Peninsular campaign (1862) and was made brigadier general of volunteers. He fought at Antietam and Fredericksburg, and his stand against Stonewall Jackson at Chancellorsville averted a total Union defeat. He commanded the Union cavalry at BRANDY STATION and in the ensuing Gettysburg campaign, as well as later engagements. Transferred to Missouri, Pleasonton defeated Gen. Sterling Price at Westport and Marais des Cygnes (1864), ending the last Confederate threat in the West.

Pleasure Ridge Park, uninc. town (1970 pop. 28,566), Jefferson co., N Ky., a residential suburb of Louisville.

plebeians: see PLEBS.

plebiscite (plĕb'ĭsīt) [Lat.,=popular decree], vote of the people on a question submitted to them, as in a REFERENDUM. The term, however, has acquired the more specific meaning of a popular vote concerning changes of sovereignty, as compared to a regularized system of popular voting upon laws and constitutional amendments. This more modern use of the plebiscite arose out of the French Revolution and the French Republic's policy of holding popular votes on the question of French annexation of a territory it had occupied. Many, although not all, of these plebiscites and those held in the following century were manipulated by the occupying power to legitimate an outcome already achieved through military or diplomatic means. The use of the plebiscite reached a high point following World War I, when it was employed extensively in Central and Eastern Europe to determine the boundaries of newly created nation states. Since then, it has been used in settling the status of disputed or border territories, e.g., SAARLAND (1935), and, most recently, in the process of the decolonization of Africa and Asia, e.g., West New Guinea (1969; see IRIAN BARAT). See Sarah Wambaugh, *Plebiscites since the World War* (1933).

plebs (plĕbz) or **plebeians** (plĭbē'ənz) [Lat. *plebs*=people], general body of Roman citizens, as distinct from the PATRICIAN class. They lacked, at first, most of the patrician rights, but with the establishment of the tribune of the people from 500 to 450 B.C., they gradually achieved political equality with the patricians. Marriage of plebians with patricians was validated (445 B.C.), and plebeians were admitted to the quaestorship (421), to the consulate (367), to the dictatorship (365), to the censorship (351), and to the praetorship (337); they finally obtained the important priestly offices of the pontificate and augurship in 300. The gulf between plebs and patricians was bridged, under the emperors, by the nobiles, a new aristocracy of office, and from this time the name plebs passed to the lower ranks of the people as contrasted with the nobler class. See Z. Yavetz, *Plebs and Princeps* (1969).

Plehve, Vyacheslav Konstantinovich (vyĕ″chĭsläf′ kənstəntyē′nəvĭch plyĕ′vyĭ), 1846-1904, Russian public official. As director of the police (1881-84), vice minister of the interior (1884-99), secretary of state for Finnish affairs (1899-1902), and minister of the interior (1902-4), he consistently pursued an ultrareactionary policy. He subjected minorities to forced Russification, secretly organized Jewish pogroms, and allegedly helped precipitate the Russo-Japanese War in order to forestall revolution and win support for the autocracy. He was killed by a member of the Socialist Revolutionary party.

Pleiad (plē′ăd) [from Pleiades], group of seven tragic poets of Alexandria who flourished c.280 B.C. under Ptolemy II Philadelphus. Of the works of the men usually given in lists of the Pleiad only those of LYCOPHRON survive. A group of enthusiastic French poets took c.1553 the name **Pléiade** from the Alexandrian Pleiad. The conventional seven of this group are RONSARD (the leader), Joachim DU BELLAY, BELLEAU, JODELLE, TYARD, BAÏF, and DAURAT. Their avowed purpose was to encourage the writing of French as against Latin, in order to enrich the French language and to establish a modern literature equal to other literatures. They cultivated the use of classical and Italian forms, especially of the sonnet. See George Wyndham, *Ronsard and the Pléiade* (1906); Grahame Castor, *Pléiade Poetics* (1964); R. J. Clements, *Critical Theory and Practice of the Pléiade* (1942, repr. 1970).

Pleiades, (plē′ədēz, plī′-), in astronomy, famous open STAR CLUSTER in the constellation Taurus; cataloged as M45. The cluster probably consists of several hundred stars and is more than 400 light-years distant from the earth. Six stars are easily visible to the naked eye—Alcyone (the brightest), Electra, Celaeno, Sterope, Maia, and Taygete. Known as the Seven Sisters, this group was named by the Greeks for the seven daughters of Atlas and Pleione; the seventh Pleiad was, according to legend, lost or in hiding. A faint star associated with the other six is visible with the telescope; it is believed that in very early times this star may have been much brighter and visible to the naked eye, thus accounting for the many early references to seven stars. A line drawn from Betelgeuse in Orion NW through Aldebaran in Taurus and extended almost an equal distance past Aldebaran will terminate slightly S of the Pleiades.

Pleiades, in Greek mythology, seven daughters of Atlas and the nymph Pleione. According to one legend they were the attendants of Artemis and were changed into stars by the gods when they were pursued by the amorous hunter Orion. Their names were Maia, Merope, Electra, Celaeno, Taygete, Sterope (or Asterope), and Alcyone. The lost Pleiad was either ELECTRA **2** or MEROPE.

Pleiku (plākōō′), town, N central South Vietnam. A highway junction for roads going east (to Qui Nhon), west (to Cambodia), north (to Da Nang), and south (to Saigon), it was a large U.S. base in the Vietnam War. The town has a commercial airport.

plein-air (plān-âr′, Fr. plĕn-ĕr′) [Fr.,=open-air], term used for paintings or drawings made directly from nature and infused with a feeling of the open air. Painting outdoors is a relatively recent practice; the impressionists and the painters of the BARBIZON SCHOOL made plein-air painting an important dimension of their landscape work.

Pleistocene epoch (plī′stəsēn), 6th epoch of the CENOZOIC ERA of geologic time (see GEOLOGIC ERAS, table). According to a classification that considered its deposits to have been formed by the biblical great flood, the epoch was originally called the Quaternary. The Pleistocene is the best-known glacial period (Ice Age) of the earth's history. Its ice sheets at one time covered all of Antarctica, large parts of Europe, North America, and South America, and small areas in Asia. In North America they stretched over Greenland and Canada and over the United States as far south as a line drawn westward from Cape Cod through Long Island, New Jersey, and Pennsylvania, along the line of the Ohio and Missouri rivers to North Dakota, and through N Montana, Idaho, and Washington to the Pacific. In Europe ice sheets covered Scandinavia, Finland, NW USSR, N Germany, and the British Isles. Glaciers distinct from the main sheets were formed in the Rockies and the Alps. In South America, Patagonia and the S Andes lay under an extension of the antarctic sheet, while in Asia the Caucasus, the Himalayas, and other mountain regions were glaciated. In North America two major centers of ice accumulation have been recognized—the Laurentide, centered on the Hudson Bay region, and the Cordilleran glacier complex, occupying the mountains of W Canada. Accumulating probably in E Labrador, the Laurentide ice sheet expanded to cover most of Canada and the Great Lakes region, extending eastward into the Atlantic Ocean and possibly joining the Greenland ice sheet in the north. Of much lesser extent, the Cordilleran probably spread into the Pacific Ocean and the NW United States. The ice sheets of Europe radiated from Scandinavia. The glaciation of the Pleistocene was not continuous but consisted of several glacial advances interrupted by interglacial stages, during which the ice retreated and a comparatively mild climate prevailed. In the Mississippi valley of North America the Nebraskan glacial stage was succeeded by the Aftonian interglacial stage; there followed the Kansan (glacial), Yarmouth (interglacial), Illinoian (glacial), Sangamon (interglacial), Iowan (glacial), Bradyan (interglacial), and Wisconsin (glacial) stages—as named, five glacial and four interglacial stages. In all probability there were actually only four glacial stages, the Iowan and Bradyan being included in the Wisconsin as one complex stage. In the Alps, the other region in which Pleistocene glaciation has been extensively studied, four glacial stages are recognized and are known as Günz, Mindel, Riss, and Würm. Carbon-14 analysis of its fossils shows that the last glacial period ended about 11,000 years ago. The characteristic formation laid down in the glacial stages of the Pleistocene, as in all glacial periods, is the DRIFT. The interglacial stages were marked by the weathering of the till of the drift to form a sticky, heavy soil called the gumbotil and by the deposition of peat and loess. Peat is plentiful in the Aftonian, Yarmouth, and Sangamon of North America. The Pleistocene glaciers made important alterations in the topography of the glaciated regions, leveling hilly sections to low, rolling plains, both by erosion and by deposition of drift, eroding hollows that later became lakes, and forcing rivers to cut new channels by filling their former beds. Among the characteristic surface features formed in the Pleistocene are the DRUMLIN, KAME, ESKER, and MORAINE. The retreat of the ice after the Wisconsin glacial stage was followed by the formation, at the edge of the melting glaciers, of lakes, such as the extinct Lake AGASSIZ and the Great Lakes. The further retreat of the ice led to the flooding by the Atlantic of the NE United States and SE Canada, which had been depressed below sea level by the weight of the ice. The valley of the St. Lawrence to Lake Ontario, the valley of the Ottawa River, and Lake Champlain were covered by a shallow sea connected with the Atlantic to the south by a strait over the site of the Hudson, but a rise of the land caused this area to assume its present topography. In the areas of North America not covered by ice, the Pleistocene was marked chiefly by erosion, with only very slight marine transgressions over the coast. On the Atlantic coast S of New Jersey the Columbia sediments (sand, gravel, and clay) were laid down as a result of erosion, while in Florida the sea deposited limestone. During the various glacial stages many areas not covered with ice, including the arid and semiarid parts of the W United States, had periods of increased rainfall and lessened evaporation. Called pluvial periods, they were characterized by the spread of vegetation and the formation of many lakes. Heavy precipitation in the West was responsible for two great lakes—Lake Lahontan of Nevada and Lake Bonneville of Utah (which today forms the Great Salt and Utah lakes). During the Pleistocene, volcanic activity and warping of the earth's surface occurred on the Pacific coast. The cutting of the Grand Canyon took place chiefly in Pleistocene time. The interglacial periods of the Pleistocene were of longer duration than the time elapsed since the retreat of the Wisconsin ice. Based on this fact it is sometimes suggested that the Holocene, or Recent, epoch, which is occurring now, may be merely another such interglacial stage and that the glaciers may return at some future time. Among the characteristic Pleistocene mammals of North America were at least four species of elephants, including the mastodon and the mammoth, true horses, of the same genus as the domestic horse though not of the same species, saber-tooth carnivores, large wolves, giant armadillos and ground sloths, bisons, camels, and wild pigs. Among the arctic mammals that ranged far south in the glacial stages were the musk ox in North America and the woolly mammoth in Europe. The Pleistocene saw the beginning of the trend toward the extinction of the mammals, which continued into historic times. The Pleistocene is noted also for the first appearance of modern man approximately 500,000 years ago and the migration of man to the American continents. About 1966, analyses of the magnetic polarity in deep sea sediment cores indicated that the Pleistocene began more than 1.8 million years ago—much earlier than had previously been suspected.

Plekhanov, Georgi Valentinovich (gēôr′gē vəlyĭntyē′nəvĭch plyĭkhä′nəf), 1857-1918, Russian revolutionary and social philosopher. He was a leader in introducing Marxist theory to Russia and is often called the "Father of Russian Marxism." As a youth he joined the Populist organization Land and Freedom (see NARODNIKI), but he broke (1879) with it because of his opposition to political terror. He left Russia in 1880 as a political refugee and spent most of his exile in Geneva, Switzerland. Turning to Marxist socialism, he became one of the chief founders of the League for the Emancipation of Labor (1883), the nucleus of the Russian Social Democratic Labor party, and in 1900 with V. I. LENIN began to publish the Socialist newspaper *Iskra* [spark]. In his writings Plekhanov took the view that conditions in Russia would not be ripe for socialism until capitalism and industrialization had progressed sufficiently. This opinion was the basis of Menshevik thought after the split (1903) of the Social Democratic Labor party into BOLSHEVISM AND MENSHEVISM. Although Plekhanov still supported Lenin at the fateful party congress of 1903, he thereafter generally opposed Bolshevism. From this time until the outbreak of World War I, he occupied a largely independent position and attempted to reunite the two factions. Plekhanov supported Russia's participation in the war. After the outbreak of the February Revolution of 1917, he returned from exile and concentrated on rousing support for continuing the war and fighting the growing influence of the Bolsheviks. Following the October Revolution of 1917 and the triumph of Lenin, he retired from public life. Among his translated works are *Socialism and Anarchism* (tr. 1895) and *Fundamental Problems of Marxism* (tr. 1929). See Samuel Baron, *Plekhanov* (1963).

Pleshcheyevo, Lake, USSR: see PERESLAVL-ZALESSKI.

Plesianthropus (plē″sēăn′thrəpəs): see AUSTRALOPITHECUS.

plesiosaurus (plē″sēəsôr′əs), extinct predatory marine reptile, belonging to the genus *Plesiosaurus*, that arose in the Triassic period of geologic time and continued into the Jurassic and Cretaceous periods. They became extinct at the close of the Mesozoic era. Fossilized skeletons of them have been found in North America, Europe, and Australia. The plesiosaurus had a small, short head, a long, snakelike neck, a broad, solid body, and a short tail. Its sharp interlocking teeth were well equipped for catching fish and its four paddlelike legs were similar to those of a marine turtle. In total length the plesiosaurus ranged from 10 to 60 ft (3–18 m). The term plesiosaur is sometimes applied more generally to all forms in the order Sauropterygia, which produced two lines of marine reptiles. The plesiosaurus is an example of one trend. The other group evolved into forms possessing short necks and gigantic skulls; the most extreme example, that of the *Kronosaurus*, is the largest known reptile skull ever found, reaching 9 ft (2.7 m) in length. Plesiosaurs are classified in the phylum CHORDATA, subphylum Vertebrata, class Reptilia, order Sauropterygia.

Plessy vs. Ferguson, case decided by the U.S. Supreme Court in 1896. The court upheld an 1890 Louisiana statute mandating racially segregated but equal railroad carriages. The court ruled that the equal protection clause of the Fourteenth amendment to the U.S. Constitution dealt with political and not social equality. Justice John Harlan (1833-1911) dissented, arguing that the U.S. Constitution was color-blind. The decision led to the adoption throughout the South of a comprehensive series of JIM CROW LAWS, which were maintained until overruled in 1954 by BROWN VS. BOARD OF EDUCATION OF TOPEKA, KANSAS.

Plethon, Georgius: see GEMISTUS PLETHO, GEORGIUS.

pleura (plōō′rə), membranous lining of the upper body cavity and covering for the LUNGS. The pleura is a two-layered structure: the parietal pleura lines the walls of the chest cage and covers the upper surface of the diaphragm, and the pulmonary pleura tightly covers the surface of the lungs. The two layers, which are in fact one continuous sheet of tissue, closely appose each other, with only a potential space, called the pleural cavity, between them. There is normally a slight amount of watery fluid within the pleural cavity that lubricates the pleural surfaces and allows the lungs to slide freely over the inner surface of the thoracic wall during breathing. In humans, the pleural cavity is separated into left and right sides by the heart and pericardial cavity.

pleurisy (plo͝or'ĭsē), inflammation of the pleura (the membrane that covers the lungs and lines the chest cavity). It is sometimes accompanied by pain and coughing. The inflammation may be dry or it may be accompanied by an effusion, or fluid, that fills the chest cavity; when the effusion is infected, the condition is known as emphysema. The dry type of pleurisy usually occurs in association with bacterial infections such as pneumonia or rheumatic fever, whereas pleurisy with effusion is often associated with such chronic lung conditions as tuberculosis or tumors. Epidemic pleurodynia, a pleurisy attributed to a virus, is a mild disease of short duration. Treatment of pleurisy is directed at the underlying condition as well as the symptoms.

pleurisy root: see MILKWEED.

Pleven, René (rənā' plĕväN'), 1901–, French political leader. He held various diplomatic and financial posts in the Free French government during World War II and served (1944–46) as minister of finance in the provisional French government. As premier (1950–51), Pleven worked for European political unity. His centrist coalition government fell in March, 1951, and he served as vice-premier until August when he again became premier until Jan., 1952. He held several other ministerial posts until 1958. Out of ministerial office during Charles De Gaulle's tenure, he maintained his seat in the national assembly. He was minister of justice from 1969 to 1973, when he lost his assembly seat.

Pleven (plĕ'vĕn) or **Plevna** (plĕv'nə), city (1968 est. pop. 89,800), N Bulgaria. A commercial center for a fertile agricultural region, it has food-processing industries and manufactures cotton textiles, ceramics, agricultural machinery, cement, and rubber goods. An old Thracian settlement, Pleven was later occupied by the Romans. It became a trade center under Turkish rule (15th–19th cent.). The city is famous for its defense by the Turks against Russian and Rumanian troops in the Russo-Turkish War of 1877–78. Its fall (1877) to the Russians after four months of fighting caused the Turks to demand an armistice.

Plevna: see PLEVEN, Bulgaria.

Plexiglas: see POLYACRYLICS.

Pliesetskaya, Maya (mä'yä plēsĕts'käyä), 1925–, Soviet dancer. Pliesetskaya became a soloist with the Bolshoi Theatre in Moscow on graduating from its school in 1943. She soon gained recognition as one of the world's foremost ballerinas, combining flawless technique with a sensitivity to emotional nuance. Her roles ranged from Odette-Odile in the romantic *Swan Lake* to the passionate title role in *Carmen*.

Plimer, Andrew, c.1763–1837, English miniature painter. He was an apprentice to Richard COSWAY. His fine portraits are to be seen in the Victoria and Albert Museum and in the Metropolitan Museum. His brother **Nathaniel Plimer,** c.1757–1822, was also an able miniaturist.

Plimsoll, Samuel (plĭm'səl), 1824–98, English reformer. Plimsoll was particularly interested in the welfare of sailors. As a member of Parliament (1868–80) he secured legislation limiting the loading of ships. It required that a line be painted on the sides of all British merchant vessels to show the limit of submergence allowed by law. This line has come to be known as Plimsoll's mark. He wrote *Our Seamen* (1872). See David Masters, *The Plimsoll Mark* (1955).

Plinlimon: see PLYNLIMON, mountain, Wales.

Pliny the Elder (Caius Plinius Secundus) (plĭ'nē), A.D. c.23–A.D. 79, Roman naturalist, b. Cisalpine Gaul. He was a friend and fellow soldier of Vespasian, and he dedicated his great work to Titus. He died of asphyxiation in the neighborhood of Vesuvius, having gone to investigate the eruption. His one surviving work is an encyclopedia of natural science (*Historia naturalis*). It is divided into 37 books and, after a preface, deals with the nature of the physical universe; geography; anthropology; zoology; botany, including the medicinal uses of plants; curatives derived from the animal world; and mineralogy, including an account of the uses of pigments and a history of the fine arts. Pliny's industry was immense and his knowledge of sources extensive, but his information is mostly secondhand and quite useless as science. See *Selections from the History of the World,* ed. by Paul Turner (1962). His nephew and ward, **Pliny the Younger** (Caius Plinius Caecilius Secundus), A.D. 62?–A.D. c.113, was an orator and a statesman. He was quaestor (A.D. 89), tribune (A.D. 91), and praetor (A.D. 93) and subsequently held treasury posts. He was consul (A.D. 100) and died in his proconsular province of Pontus-Bithynia. His fame rests on his letters, written probably for publication, which are an excellent mirror of Roman life. See his *Letters and Panegyricus,* tr. by Betty Radice (2 vol., 1969); studies by S. E. Stout (1954) and A. N. Sherwin-White (1966).

Pliocene epoch (plī'əsēn), fifth epoch of the CENOZOIC ERA of geologic time. If the Paleocene is not considered a separate epoch preceding the Eocene, the Pliocene is the fourth Cenozoic era (see GEOLOGIC ERAS, table). By the beginning of the Pliocene, the outlines of North America were almost the same as in recent time. Encroachments by the sea were limited to a narrow strip along the coasts of the Carolinas, Georgia, Florida, and the Gulf Coast states and an embayment, smaller than that of the preceding MIOCENE EPOCH, in California. The Pliocene formations on the Atlantic coast are chiefly marine marls; on the Gulf they are nonmarine sediments resulting from erosion. In California they contain much volcanic ash and some are oil-bearing. The Pliocene formations of the western interior are small and scattered. In western interior North America and on the west coast, volcanic activity continued into the Pliocene from the Miocene. The close of the Pliocene was marked in North America by the Cascadian revolution, in the course of which the Sierra Nevada was elevated and tilted to the west. The Cascades, Rockies, Appalachians, and the Colorado plateau were uplifted, and there was activity in the mountains of Alaska and in the Great Basin ranges of Nevada and Utah. In Europe the Pliocene sea covered small parts of the northwest of the continent and a large area around the present Mediterranean; a number of volcanoes were active, among them Vesuvius and Etna. There was considerable mountain building, including the folding and thrusting of the Alps. The climate of the Pliocene was markedly cooler and drier than that of the Miocene and foreshadowed the glacial climates of the PLEISTOCENE EPOCH. The life of the Pliocene was notable for its modern appearance; the Pliocene marked the climax, and perhaps the initial decline, of the supremacy of the mammals.

Płock (plôtsk), city (1970 pop. 71,727), E central Poland, a port on the Vistula River. Located on a pipeline from the USSR to Poland, Płock is a major oil-refining and petrochemical center. Other industries include metalworking, sawmilling, and the manufacture of farm machinery and barges. Known in the 10th cent., it became a bishopric in 1075 and was the capital of the duchy of Masovia from 1138 to 1351. The city passed in 1793 to Prussia and in 1815 to Russia. It reverted to Poland in 1921. Płock's 12th-century cathedral, containing tombs of Polish kings and dukes, was badly damaged during World War II.

Ploieşti (ployĕsht'), city (1970 est. pop. 163,000), S central Rumania, in Walachia. It is the chief center of the Rumanian petroleum industry and of the Ploieşti oil region. The city is a railroad hub and is linked by oil pipelines with Bucharest and with the ports of Giurgiu on the Danube River and Constanţa on the Black Sea. It has large refineries and oil storage installations and is an industrial center with varied manufactures. Founded in 1596 by Prince Michael the Brave of Walachia, Ploieşti grew in the 19th cent. into the largest oil-producing center of SE Europe. After Rumania signed (1940) a mutual cooperation pact with the Axis powers that provided substantial Rumanian oil to Germany, the Allies heavily bombed the city. An earthquake in 1940 also inflicted severe damage. After World War II, Rumania nationalized the Ploieşti oil industry, which until then had been owned largely by foreign interests.

Plombières (plôNbyĕr') or **Plombières-les-Bains** (-lā-băN), village (1968 pop. 1,183), Vosges dept., NE France, in the Vosges mts. It is a fashionable spa, with radioactive springs used since Roman times for medicinal purposes. Housewares and embroidered goods are also made there. Plombières was the scene of a meeting (1858) between Napoleon III and Cavour, which resulted in the cession of Savoy and Nice to France.

Plotinus (plōtī'nəs), 205–270, Neoplatonist philosopher. A native of Egypt, perhaps of Roman descent, he went to Alexandria c.232 to devote himself to philosophy. For 10 years he was a dedicated disciple of Ammonius Saccas. To study the philosophies of India and Persia, Plotinus in 242 traveled in the Eastern expedition of Gordian III, the Roman emperor. From 244 he lived in Rome, where his school attracted wide attention. Many followed his advice and example; they gave their wealth to those in need and turned to contemplative thought. However, Plotinus never taught or practiced extreme asceticism. His pupil PORPHYRY wrote a biography of him and was responsible for the arrangement of his works, which were written after 253, into six Enneads, or groups of nine treatises. The theories of Plotinus were fundamentally those of Plato but included elements of other Greek philosophies as well, all drawn together into an original system that rapidly won followers and in time had considerable influence on the thinkers of the Christian Church, although Plotinus himself opposed Christianity. His development of the idea of EMANATION was fuller than that found in the teachings of the Stoics and of Philo. This cosmological conception is the chief point of NEOPLATONISM, which received its form from Plotinus. All else, even his ethics, depends upon this view of the world. Among the virtues set forth by Plotinus are political or social virtues, concerning man's relations to his fellowmen; the higher purifying virtues, needed to help the soul become like God by removing from it as much as possible that which is of the senses; and the still higher deifying or enlightening virtues, through the exercise of which man may attain to the fulfillment of his true nature. But unification with the highest, with God, is not possible through thought. It is attained only when the soul, in an ecstatic state, loses the restraint of the body and has for a time an immediate knowledge of God (see MYSTICISM). See *The Essence of Plotinus* (extracts from the six *Enneads* and Porphyry's life of Plotinus, comp. by G. H. Turnbull, 1934); Émile Bréhier, *The Philosophy of Plotinus* (tr. 1958); J. M. Rist, *Plotinus* (1967); G. J. O'Daly, *Plotinus' Philosophy of the Self* (1972).

plough: see PLOW.

Plovdiv (plôv'dĭf), anc. *Philippopolis,* city (1968 est. pop. 236,600), S central Bulgaria, on the Maritsa River. It is the second largest city of Bulgaria, a transportation hub, and the chief market for a fertile area. Plovdiv's major industries are food processing, lead and zinc smelting, brewing, and the manufacture of textiles, metal products, and shoes. There are also motor repair works in the city. Originally built by the Thracians, the city was captured in 341 B.C. by Philip II of Macedon, who named it Philippopolis and established a military post there. Known under Roman rule as Trimontium, it was the capital of Thracia. It was razed by the Goths but recovered after Byzantine Emperor Constantine V settled the Armenian PAULICIANS there. Destroyed (early 13th cent.) by the Bulgarians, Plovdiv later became the center of the BOGOMILS. It was retaken by the Greeks in 1262 and was captured by the Turks c.1360. The city passed to Russia in 1877 and became the capital of Eastern RUMELIA (1878–85); it was united with Bulgaria in 1885. Plovdiv is the seat of a Bulgarian Orthodox eparch and has several Orthodox churches and Turkish mosques, as well as a university and other higher educational institutions. The ancient town walls and gate still stand.

plover (plŭv'ər), common name for some members of the large family Charadriidae, shore birds, small to medium in size, found in ice-free lands all over the world. Plovers are plumpish wading birds with pigeonlike bills and strong markings of black or brown above with white below. In flocks they frequent ocean beaches and sand and mud flats, following the backwash of waves in search of the small marine invertebrates that form their diet. The best-known plovers in America are the noisy killdeer (*Charadrius vociferus*), found in pasturelands; the larger (11 in./27.5 cm) black-bellied (*Squatarola squatarola*) and golden (*Pluvialis dominica*) plovers, which migrate as far as 2,000 mi (3,220 km) annually; and the ruddy turnstone (*Arenaria interpres*). The Old World dotterel and the European LAPWING are members of the family, as are the crocodile birds of Africa, insectivorous plovers described by Herodotus as picking the teeth of crocodiles. Lapwings are slightly larger than plovers, and are found in most tropical and temperate countries, with the notable exception of North America, where they have been extinct since the Pleistocene era. Both lapwings and plovers nest on open ground and dig shallow hollows lined with pebbles or plant debris where their clutch of eggs (usually four) are deposited. Both male and female share the duties of rearing the young. The crab plover (*Dromas ardeola*) of India, Arabia, and E Africa, with its heronlike bill and webbed toes, is so distinct that it is placed in a family by itself, the Dromadidae. It derives its name from its habit of pounding crabs and mollusks to pieces with its heavy bill. Crab plovers lay only one egg per clutch in a deep nest dug into a sand bank. They are easily approached and flock in large groups on coastal mud flats and beaches. Plovers are classified in the phylum CHORDATA, subphylum Vertebrata, class Aves, order Charadriiformes, family Charadriidae. Crab plovers belong to the same order.

plow or **plough,** agricultural implement used to cut furrows in and turn up the soil, thus preparing it for sowing and planting. The plow is generally considered the most important tillage tool. In the Bronze Age the plow saw its beginnings, which are associated with the domestication of draft animals and the need for food supplies presented by the rise of cities. The plow is depicted on Egyptian monuments, mentioned in the Old Testament, and described by Hesiod and Vergil. Early plows consisted simply of a wooden wedge tipped with iron and fastened to a single handle and a beam, which was pulled by men or oxen. Such implements were capable of breaking but not of inverting the soil. The evolution of the plow was gradual until c.1600, when British landlords attempted greater improvements. The first half of the 18th cent. saw the introduction into England of the moldboard, a curved board that turns over the slice of earth cut by the share. Important improvements in design and materials were made in the early part of the 19th cent. They included streamlined moldboards, replaceable shares, and steel plows with self-scouring moldboards. Standardized by 1870, the modern moldboard plow has been improved by various attachments, e.g., the colter, a sharp blade or disk that cuts the ground in advance of the share. In 19th-century America horses largely replaced oxen for drawing plows. Tractors now supply this power in most developed parts of the world. With more powerful tractors, larger plows have come into use. Among the various types of plows in use today are the reversible two-way plow for contour plowing; listers and middlebusters, which prepare shallow beds; the DISK PLOW, whose revolving concave disks are useful in working hard or dry soil; and the rotary plow, with an assembly of knives on the shaft that mix the surface growth with the soil. The plow often symbolizes agriculture, as in the great seals of New Jersey, Pennsylvania, Tennessee, and other states. See H. P. Smith, *Farm Machinery and Equipment* (5th ed. 1964); publications of the U.S. Dept. of Agriculture; C. Culpin, *Farm Machinery* (8th ed. 1969); M. Partridge, *Farm Tools through the Ages* (1973).

Plücker, Julius (yo͞o'lyo͝os plü'kər), 1801–68, German mathematician and physicist. He became professor of mathematics (1836) and of physics (1847) at the Univ. of Bonn. He is known for his work in analytical geometry, in magnetic and electrical properties (he discovered the fluorescence of cathode rays), and in spectroscopy (he first suggested that the lines in the spectrum of an element were peculiar to that element). Plücker originated line geometry, which substitutes the straight line for the point as the unit in space.

Plum, borough (1970 pop. 21,922), Allegheny co., SW Pa., a residential suburb of Pittsburgh, on the Allegheny River, in a bituminous coal area; founded 1788, inc. 1956.

plum, common name for a tree of any of many species of the genus *Prunus* of the family Rosaceae (ROSE family) and for its fruit, a drupe. The plum is generally cultivated in the temperate zones, though among the numerous varieties and hybrids are types suitable for almost any soil and site. Of the plum's more than 100 species 30 are native to North America. It has been cultivated since prehistoric times, longer perhaps than any other fruit except the apple. Alexander the Great is said to have introduced it into Greece from Syria or Persia, where the damson plum had long been grown. The name damson is now applied to several varieties of *Prunus domestica,* the common garden plum of European or Asiatic origin, e.g., *P. domestica insititia* and others having small leaves and small, oval fruits usually borne in clusters. The fruits are generally tart and are favored for preserves. The greengages and PRUNE plums are also varieties of *P. domestica.* Plum trees that grow in the wild usually revert to the damson type. In the United States the wild red plum (*P. americana*) is found along streams and in thickets from New York to the Rocky Mts. Its small, sweet fruit has a purple bloom. This plum was utilized by the Indians, who ate it raw, cooked, and dried; when dried it was a staple article of diet. Plum butter is made from it. Another American variety is the beach plum or shore plum (*P. maritima*), a low-growing shrub common along the eastern coast, especially on Cape Cod, where the gathering of fruit for jelly and preserves has become a commercial project. Most of the cultivated plums in the United States are derived from European and Japanese varieties (e.g., *P. salicina,* introduced by Burbank into the United States from Japan in 1870), although some good ones have come from native species and are valuable in that they thrive in the extreme north and south. The myrobalan or cherry plum (*P. cerasifera*) is often used as an understock in plum cultivation. The European plum may be an ancient natural hybrid of this and another Near Eastern species. The typical plum tree is low and wide-spreading and is one of the earliest fruit trees to bloom. In Japan, where there are many famous plum gardens, the feathery blossoms are much used in decoration. The plum is also of ornamental value in the United States, many of the varieties so used having red or purple foliage and double white, pink, or lilac flowers. The plum is closely related to the almond, cherry, peach, and other species of the genus *Prunus.* Plums are classified in the division MAGNOLIOPHYTA, class Magnoliopsida, order Rosales, family Rosaceae.

plumage, of birds: see FEATHERS.

Plumb, John Harold, 1911–, British historian. Educated at the universities of London (B.A., 1933) and at Cambridge (Ph.D., 1936), he remained at Cambridge as a research fellow (1938–46), a fellow, and a member of the university faculty, (1946–). He became professor of modern English history there in 1966 and was a visiting professor at Columbia (1960) and New York Univ. (1971–72). Among his most important works are *England in the Eighteenth Century* (1950), *The First Four Georges* (1956), and biographies of Sir Robert Walpole (2 vol., 1956–60) and the earl of Chatham (2d ed. 1965). He has edited several multivolume works and is a prolific writer of articles and book reviews.

plumbago (plŭm"bā'gō): see GRAPHITE.

plumbing, piping systems inside buildings for water supply and sewage. The Romans had a considerably developed plumbing system; water was brought to Rome by aqueducts and distributed to homes in lead pipes—hence the name plumbing from the Latin word *plumbum* for lead. However, during the Middle Ages plumbing became almost nonexistent. In fact, London's first water system after the Middle Ages (c.1515) consisted partly of the rehabilitated Roman system; the rest was patterned after it. Modern plumbing began in the early 1800s when the new steam engine was used to supply water under pressure and cheap cast iron pipes were employed to carry it. The common materials used today in water supply pipes are steel, copper, brass, plastic, and lead. Plumbing for sewage is made of cast iron, steel, asbestos cement, and copper. If municipal water pressure is insufficient or intermittent, tall buildings require storage tanks on the roof into which a pump lifts water. The water then flows through the piping system of the building by gravity. Smaller buildings may have a pneumatic tank for the same purpose. The tank is partly filled with air, which is compressed when water is pumped in so that it will force water through the pipes. Sewage and drain systems should have a trap, often a loop-shaped section of pipe, to seal off vapors in the pipes from the rest of the building. At the same time, vent pipes lead the vapors to the outside of the building; they also break the suction in the piping and thus prevent the siphoning of water from traps when a nearby fixture discharges.

Plunket, Oliver, 1629–81, Irish Roman Catholic churchman and martyr, b. Co. Meath. He was educated at Rome and named Roman Catholic archbishop of Armagh and primate of all Ireland in 1669. He was on good terms with local Protestants and worked with much success. After the Test Act (1673) he kept mainly in hiding. In his fabrication of tales about the Popish Plot, Titus Oates accused him of planning a foreign invasion of Ireland. Plunket was tried and acquitted in Ireland; he was then taken to London, tried again, convicted, and hanged, drawn, and quartered. The accusations and the witnesses' testimony against him were manifestly false from beginning to end. Plunket was the last Roman Catholic to be executed at Tyburn on politico-religious grounds. He was beatified as a martyr in 1920. Feast: July 11. See Alice Curtayne, *The Trial of Oliver Plunkett* (1953).

Plunkett, Sir Horace Curzon, 1854–1932, Irish statesman and agricultural reformer. Educated in England, Plunkett spent 10 years (1879–89) in Wyoming as a cattle rancher. Returning to Ireland, he became an ardent exponent of farming cooperatives. His work was highly important in face of the serious agrarian problems of Ireland (see IRISH LAND QUESTION). He founded (1894) the Irish Agricultural Organization Society and as a member of Parliament (1892–1900) drafted legislation for Irish agricultural needs. From 1900 to 1907 he was vice president of the new department of agriculture for Ireland. He was a prominent mediator in the Irish uprisings prior to and during World War I, serving (1917–18) as chairman of the Irish convention founded to effect a peaceful settlement of the outbreaks. He wrote *Ireland in the New Century* (1904), *The Rural Life Problem in the United States* (1910), and numerous pamphlets. See study by R. A. Anderson (1935); biography by Margaret Digby (1949).

pluralism, in philosophy, theory that considers the universe explicable in terms of many principles or composed of many ultimate substances. It describes no particular system and may be embodied in such opposed philosophical concepts as materialism and idealism. Empedocles, G. W. von Leibniz, William James, and Bertrand Russell are among the philosophers generally considered as pluralistic.

Plutarch (plo͞o'tärk), A.D. 46?–A.D. c.120, Greek essayist and biographer, b. Chaeronea, Boeotia. He traveled in Egypt and Italy, visited Rome (where he lectured on philosophy) and Athens, and finally returned to his native Boeotia, where he became a priest of the temple of Delphi. His great work is *The Parallel Lives* comprising 46 surviving biographies arranged in pairs (one Greek life with one comparable Roman) and four single biographies; some 19 short comparisons affixed to the lives are of doubtful authenticity. The English translation by Sir Thomas NORTH had a profound effect upon English literature; it supplied, for example, the material for Shakespeare's *Coriolanus, Julius Caesar, Antony and Cleopatra,* and *Timon of Athens.* A translation by John Dryden was revised by A. H. Clough in 1957. Although Plutarch displays evident pride in the culture and greatness of the men of Greece, he is nevertheless fair and honest in his treatment of the Romans. As a biographer Plutarch is almost peerless, although his facts are not always accurate. Since his purpose was to portray character and reveal its moral implications, his technique therefore included the use of much anecdotal material. Less known, but also of great charm and interest, are Plutarch's *Moralia* (tr. by F. C. Babbitt et al., 14 vol., 1927–59). They consist of dialogues and essays on ethical, literary, and historical subjects, such as *The Late Vengeance of the Deity, On Superstition, The Right Way of Hearing Poetry,* and *Advice to Married Couples.* Plutarch's quotations (frequent and long) from the old dramatists are often our only record of such writings. See biography by R. H. Barrow (1967); studies by C. J. Gianakaris (1970), C. P. Jones (1971), D. A. Russell (1973), and Alan Wardman (1974).

Pluto, in astronomy, 9th and most distant known planet from the sun, with an orbit lying beyond that of Neptune; its mean distance from the sun is 3.66 billion mi (5.89 billion km) and its period of revolution is about 248 years. Pluto has the most elliptical and tilted orbit of any planet (eccentricity .250, inclination 17°); at its closest points to the sun it passes inside the orbit of Neptune, but because of its large inclination the two planets get no closer than c.238 million mi (383 million km) of each other. The existence of Pluto was first proposed by Percival Lowell on the basis of observed perturbations of Neptune. He began searching for the planet in 1905, although he did not publish his calculations of its predicted position until 1914. Independent calculations were published by W. H. Pickering in 1919, but Pluto was not detected until 1930, when C. W. Tombaugh confirmed its existence by means of a BLINK MICROSCOPE. Pluto differs from the other distant planets in that it appears to have a small mass and a high density. These terrestrial characteristics, plus its highly eccentric orbit, suggest it may have been a satellite of Neptune that escaped and went into orbit about the sun. Because of its great distance, accurate measurements of Pluto's size and mass are difficult to make. G. P. Kuiper has calculated its diameter to be c.3,600 mi (5,800 km), and estimates of its mass range from 10% to 80% of the earth's mass. Its surface temperature is estimated to be about −360°F (−218°C), a temperature at which most gases would exist in the frozen state. Variations in light reflected from the surface indicate a period of rotation of about 6.39 days.

Pluto, in Greek religion, god of the underworld, son of Cronus and Rhea; also called Hades. After the fall of the TITANS, Pluto and his brothers Zeus and Poseidon divided the universe, and Pluto was awarded everything underground. There, with Persephone as his queen, he ruled over Hades. Not only a god of the dead, he is identified as a god of the earth's fertility. The Romans derived their god of the dead—Orcus, Dis, or Dis Pater—from Pluto.

plutonium (plōōtō'nēəm), artificially produced radioactive chemical element; symbol Pu; at. no. 94; mass no. of most stable isotope 244; m.p. about 640°C; b.p. about 3235°C; sp. gr. 19.84 at 20°C; valence +3, +4, +5, or +6. Plutonium is a silver-gray radioactive metal that has several allotropic forms (see ALLOTROPY). It is a member of the ACTINIDE SERIES in group IIIb of the PERIODIC TABLE. It is chemically reactive. It tarnishes in air, taking on a yellow cast when oxidized. It dissolves in acids and reacts with the halogens, carbon, nitrogen, and silicon. Plutonium, the second TRANSURANIUM ELEMENT, is named for Pluto, the second planet beyond Uranus. It was first produced in 1940 at the Univ. of California at Berkeley by G. T. SEABORG, E. M. McMillan, J. W. Kennedy, and A. C. Wahl; by cyclotron bombardment of uranium oxide with deuterons, they produced plutonium-238 (half-life about 85 years). Fifteen additional isotopes of plutonium are known. The most stable is plutonium-244 (half-life about 80 million years). By far the most important is plutonium-239 (half-life about 25,000 years), a nuclear fission fuel. This isotope is found to a very limited extent in naturally occurring uranium ores. It is produced in large quantities in nuclear reactors from uranium-238, an abundant but nonfissionable isotope. Uranium-238 absorbs neutrons emitted by the fission of uranium-235; uranium-239 is formed, which emits a beta particle and decays to neptunium-239; the neptunium-239 emits another beta particle, becoming plutonium-239. Once begun, the reaction proceeds spontaneously until the uranium fuel rods in the reactor are converted to a certain uranium-plutonium mixture. The rods are dissolved in acid and the plutonium separated by chemical means, especially by solvent extraction. Pure plutonium metal may be prepared by reduction of the trifluoride, PuF_3, with calcium metal. Plutonium is important for its use in nuclear weapons and nuclear reactors. Plutonium-238 has been used to power scientific equipment in lunar exploration. Plutonium is an extremely dangerous poison; it collects in the bones and interferes with the production of white blood cells.

Plymouth, county borough (1971 pop. 239,314), Devonshire, SW England, on Plymouth Sound. The Three Towns that Plymouth has comprised since 1914 are Plymouth, Stonehouse, and Devonport. Modern Plymouth is well situated on a peninsula between the estuaries of the Plym and Tamar rivers. The southern waterfront and adjacent promenade are called the Hoe. Plymouth is an important port and naval base. Foodstuffs and raw materials are imported and manufactures of many kinds exported. Other items traded are granite, marble, kaolin, and fish. In Stonehouse is a Royal Naval Hospital (1762). The Royal Marine Barracks and Naval Dockyard (1691) are in Devonport. In 1588 the port was the rendezvous of the anti-Armada fleet. From there Drake, Hawkins, Raleigh, and several later explorers set forth. It was the last port touched by the *Mayflower* before its American voyage. Plymouth was held by the parliamentarians for four years during the civil war, when the rest of Devonshire and Cornwall were royalist. The first English factory to make Chinese porcelain was established in Plymouth in 1768. A tablet commemorates the arrival in 1919 of the first transatlantic airplane. Among the principal points of interest on the Hoe are the old Royal Citadel (17th cent.), the upper part of Smeaton's lighthouse brought from EDDYSTONE, an Armada memorial, a statue of Sir Francis Drake, and a naval war memorial. Noteworthy also are the marine-biological laboratories, the aquarium, the City Museum and Art Gallery, the Gothic guildhall, several 15th-, 16th-, and 17th-century churches, and the Roman Catholic cathedral. The Royal Naval Engineering College is in Devonport. There are also technical and teacher-training schools.

Plymouth. 1 Town (1970 pop. 10,321), Litchfield co., W Conn.; settled 1725, inc. 1795. Locks, tools and dies, and other metal products are manufactured. **2** Uninc. town (1970 pop. 18,606), seat of Plymouth co., SE Mass., on Plymouth Bay; founded 1620. Rope and twine, wire, metal products, and textiles are manufactured. The town, with summer resort facilities and major historic attractions, has a large tourist industry. Its harbor, now used by fishing boats and pleasure craft, was the scene of the famous landing by the Pilgrims in 1620, and the town was the first permanent white settlement in New England (see PILGRIMS; PLYMOUTH COLONY). Most famous of its many monuments is Plymouth Rock, returned to its original site in 1880; according to legend, the Pilgrims stepped on this boulder when disembarking from the *Mayflower.* The *Mayflower II,* a replica of the original ship, is moored there. The sites of the first houses are marked by tablets on Leyden St., the first street laid out by the Pilgrims. A number of 17th-century houses on nearby streets are maintained as museums. Cole's Hill and Burial Hill contain graves of many of the first settlers, and Pilgrim Hall has numerous valuable relics. Near the site of the original village is the 80-ft (24-m) granite *National Monument to the Forefathers* (1889). Of great interest is nearby Pilgrim Village, a re-creation of the early settlement. The town also has a wax museum and a marine museum and aquarium. Myles Standish State Forest is to the south. **3** Industrial city (1970 pop. 11,758), Wayne co., SE Mich.; inc. 1867. Telephones, automotive parts, business machines, heating equipment, paper products, steel tanks, and packaging materials are made. **4** Village (1970 pop. 18,077), Hennepin co., SE Minn., a suburb of Minneapolis-St. Paul; inc. 1955. Computer systems, heating units, games, and aluminum and steel products are manufactured.

Plymouth Brethren, sect of Christian believers originating in the early 19th cent. in Ireland and spreading from there to the Continent (especially Switzerland), the British dominions, and the United States. One of their notable leaders was John Nelson DARBY; the members are sometimes known as Darbyites. They refer to themselves as Brethren, Christians, or Believers. In a reaction against the formality of prescribed ritual, the requirements of ministerial ordination, and other established conditions in the churches of the times, groups of believers began to meet independently in Dublin and elsewhere for spiritual communion. Associations were formed c.1828 in Dublin and c.1830 at Plymouth, England, whence the popular name Plymouth Brethren. Brethren hold differing opinions concerning baptism, and expect the personal premillennial second coming of Christ. The Lord's Supper, as a commemorative act of worship, is observed once a week. Followers of different leaders withdrew from time to time from the main body to form new congregations. This tendency to divide was carried over into the United States and Canada by emigrants, who established new meetings of the Brethren there. In the United States there are eight separate divisions, some of the exclusive type, stressing congregational interdependency, and some of the open type, stressing the independence of congregations. Basically fundamentalist, the Brethren consider the Scriptures the only true guide. No officers are chosen to preside over the congregations; the privileges and duties of the ministry depend upon the personal gift of the individual member. Membership in the United States is c 33,000. See studies by W. B. Neatby (1901); D. J. Beattie (1939); H. A. Ironside (1942); F. R. Coad (1968).

Plymouth Colony, settlement made by the PILGRIMS on the coast of Massachusetts in 1620. Previous attempts at colonization in America (1606, 1607-8) by the Plymouth Company, chartered in 1606 along with the London Company (see VIRGINIA COMPANY), were unsuccessful and resulted in the company's inactivation for a number of years. In 1620 the Plymouth Company, reorganized as the Council for New England, secured a new charter from King James I, granting it all the territory from lat. 40° N to lat. 48° N and from sea to sea. Also in 1620 the Pilgrims, having secured a patent granting them colonization privileges in the territory of the London Company, left Leiden and proceeded to Southampton, where the MAYFLOWER was fitting out for Virginia. The *Mayflower* sailed from Plymouth, England, and in Nov., 1620, sighted the coast of Cape Cod instead of Virginia. In December, after five weeks spent in exploring the coast, the ship finally anchored in Plymouth harbor, and the Pilgrims established a settlement. As the patent from the London Company was invalid in New England, the Pilgrims drew up an agreement called the MAYFLOWER COMPACT, which pledged allegiance to the English king but established a form of government by the will of the majority. Patents were obtained from the Council for New England in 1621 and in 1630, but the Mayflower Compact remained the basis of the colony's government until union with Massachusetts Bay colony in 1691. During the first winter of the colony, about half of the settlers died from scurvy and exposure, but none of the survivors chose to return with the Mayflower to England. A little corn was raised in 1621, and in October of that year the settlers celebrated the first THANKSGIVING DAY. However, the arrival of more colonists necessitated half rations, and it was several years before the threat of famine passed. John CARVER, the first governor, died in 1621. William BRADFORD then assumed the post and served, except for the five years he refused the position, until his death in 1657. A treaty made in 1621 with MASSASOIT, chief of the Wampanoag Indians, resulted in 50 years of peace with that tribe. The Narragansett tribe farther west were hostile, but Bradford averted trouble from that quarter. In 1623, Capt. Miles STANDISH marched against the Indians to the northwest, who were accused of plotting to exterminate the colonists settled at Weymouth by Thomas Weston. The Indians were gradually pushed back and deprived of their lands. A communistic system of labor, adopted for seven years, was abandoned in 1623 by Bradford because it was retarding agriculture, and land was parceled out to each family. A well-managed fur trade enabled the colony to liquidate (1627) its debt to the London merchants who had backed the venture. The colony, which developed into a quasi-theocracy, expanded slowly due to the infertility of the land and the lack of a staple money-making crop. After several years the colonists could no longer be restrained from settling on the more productive land to the north, and settlements such as Duxbury and Scituate were founded. With the growth of additional towns, a representative system was introduced in 1638, using the town as a unit of government and establishing the General Court, along with the governor and his council, as the lawmaking body. By the time the colony joined the NEW ENGLAND CONFEDERATION in 1643, 10 towns had been established. Plymouth suffered severely in King Philip's War (1675–76), and but for aid from the confederation might have been destroyed. The colony became part of the Dominion of New England under the governorship of Sir Edmund ANDROS. After the Glorious Revolution of 1688-89 in England, the territory that had been under Andros's authority was reorganized, and Massachusetts Bay, Plymouth, and Maine were joined (1691) in the royal colony of Massachusetts. See N. B. Shurtleff and David Pulsifer, ed., *Records of the Colony of New Plymouth in New England* (12 vol., 1855–61, repr. 1968); J. G. Palfrey, *History of New England* (5 vol., 1858-90, repr. 1966); L. G. Tyler, *England in America, 1580-1652* (1904, repr. 1968); H. L. Osgood, *The American Colonies in the Seventeenth Century* (3 vol., 1904–7, repr. 1957); Arthur Lord, *Plymouth and the Pilgrims* (1920); J. T. Adams, *The Founding of New England* (1921, repr. 1963); C. M. Andrews, *The Colonial Period of American History,* Vol. I (1934, repr. 1964); G. F. Willison, *Saints and Strangers* (1945, rev. ed. 1965) and *The Pilgrim Reader* (1953); S. E. Morison, *The Story of the Old Colony of New Plymouth* (1956).

Plymouth Rock chicken, one of the most popular early breeds of poultry. The Barred Plymouth Rock was a favorite farm chicken since it was both a good egg producer and also developed a large quantity of meat. As the demand for white eggs increased, the breed lost popularity. It is still retained for breeding purposes, a popular cross being that of a Barred Plymouth Rock female and a RHODE ISLAND RED male. See RED ROCK CHICKEN.

Plymouth Sound, deep inlet of the English Channel, Devonshire and Cornwall, SW England. It is a famous roadstead and forms a bay c.3 mi (5 km) wide. It receives the Tamar River through the Hamoaze estuary and the Plym River through the Cattewater estuary. A breakwater, c.2 mi (3 km) long, protects the harbor. The inlet has been protected by forts for centuries. Plymouth, long a major port, is located at its head.

Plynlimon or **Plinlimon** (both: plĭnlĭm'ən), mountain, 2,468 ft (752 m) high, W Wales, on the Montgomeryshire-Cardiganshire border W of Llanidloes. It has three summits and is the source of the Wye, Severn, and other streams.

plywood, manufactured board composed of an odd number of thin sheets of wood glued together under pressure with grains of the successive layers at right angles. Laminated wood differs from plywood in that the grains of its sheets are parallel. Plywood is noted for its strength, durability, lightness, rigidity, and resistance to splitting and warping. It can be molded into curved or irregular forms for use in truck, airplane, and boat bodies, luggage, furniture, and tubing, or it can be made into large panels suitable for structural use. Plywood was made in ancient Egypt and China, and it was first introduced in the United States in 1865. The two types commonly in use today are those made of softwood (fir) or hardwood (birch, mahogany, walnut, or white ash). The layers in inexpensive plywood are glued together with starch pastes, animal glues, or casein, but those of the strongest plywood are glued with waterproof synthetic resins. Other material, such as metal or fabric, may be substituted for the usual wood core.

Plzeň (pŭl'zĕnyə), Ger. *Pilsen,* city (1970 pop. 148,032), W Czechoslovakia, in Bohemia, at the confluence of several rivers. One of Czechoslovakia's largest cities, it lies near a belt of coalfields in an area where sugar beets and hops are raised. Plzeň is internationally famous for its beer (Pilsner), exported worldwide, and for the huge Skoda works (nationalized and renamed Lenin Works), which produce heavy machinery, machine tools, locomotives, automobiles, and armaments. Other industries in the city include distilling, sugar refining, papermaking, and the production of cement and pottery. Founded in 1290 by King Wenceslaus II of Bohemia, the city was an important Bohemian trade center. It remained a stronghold of Catholicism in the HUSSITE WARS (15th cent.) and served briefly (1633–34) as the headquarters of the German imperial general Wallenstein during the THIRTY YEARS WAR. One of the earliest printing presses was established in Plzeň in 1468. Rapid industrialization dates from the late 19th cent., when the Skoda works grew quickly. Plzeň was part of the Austro-Hungarian monarchy until 1918, when it was included in newly independent Czechoslovakia. It was taken by German forces in 1939 and became a leading producer of German armaments during World War II; Allied bombing heavily damaged the munitions factories. In 1945 the city was liberated and returned to Czechoslovakia. Plzeň's historic buildings include the 13th-century Gothic Church of St. Bartholomew and a 16th-century Renaissance town hall. Among the city's educational and cultural facilities are a medical school, a technical university, and museums and theaters.

Pm, chemical symbol of the element PROMETHIUM.

pneumatic tool (no͝omăt'ĭk), instrument activated by air pressure. Pneumatic tools are designed around three basic devices: the air cylinder, the vane motor, and the sprayer. The air cylinder contains a piston that is pushed the length of the cylinder by compressed air and returned by air or by a spring. In a common type of pneumatic hammer, called a hammer drill, the piston is not connected to anything but runs freely in the cylinder. At one end of the power stroke the piston hits the top of the drill; an additional mechanism in the hammer drill turns the bit slightly after each blow. Light handheld pneumatic hammers are used for chipping paint from metal, carving rock, and riveting. Much larger hammers are used in mining and quarrying; some of them are mounted on mechanically propelled vehicles. Hammers designed to clamp onto the side of a vat or other container are used to pack sand or concrete, the vibration causing the contents to settle. The vane motor is better adapted to rotary motion, and it can run at high speeds. In this motor, sliding vanes radiate from the end of a shaft extending into a cylinder. The center of the shaft is not at the center of the cylinder; consequently the pockets formed by the vanes and the cylinder wall are unequal in size. Air admitted through an opening in the cylinder wall at a point where the pockets are small tends to push the vanes around to the point where the pockets are large. There the air escapes through a second opening in the cylinder wall. The shaft is connected without gearing to wire brushes, drills, screwdrivers, and grinders, where high speeds are required; speeds of 10,000 to 20,000 rpm are common. With gearing, lower speeds and greater torque, or twisting force, are achieved for screw-thread tappers and for other heavy-duty applications. With suitable gearing the vane motor can drive a type of hoist to wind a cable or chain around a drum. The pneumatic sprayer applies not only paint but many other materials, such as cement and plaster in construction work. Insecticides, molten metal, and plastic fibers are also sprayed. Paint sprayers, also called air brushes, do faster work, spread a more even coat, and penetrate cracks better than do brushes wielded by hand. In a pneumatic sprayer, paint is drawn from its container by the reduced pressure created by a stream of air passing through a pipe connected with the container. The stream then entrains the paint and sprays it.

pneumoconiosis (no͞o"məkō"nēō'sĭs), chronic disease of the lungs. Primarily an occupational disease of miners, sandblasters, and metal grinders, it is a result of repeated inhalation of dusts, including iron oxides (e.g., rust and filings), silicates (e.g., talc, asbestos, and rock dust), and carbonates (especially coal dust). Particles collect in the lungs and become sites for the formation of fibrous nodules. As the disease progresses, fibrous tissue continually replaces elastic lung tissue. Loss of lung function is signaled by shortness of breath, wheezing, coughing, and difficulty in expectorating. Heart failure may result and a high incidence of lung cancer has been noted, especially among asbestos workers. Sufferers are particularly vulnerable to infectious lung diseases such as tuberculosis. Pneumoconiosis is incurable and treatment is purely symptomatic. Because the inhaled dusts cause darkening of the lung tissue, the disease is also known as black lung. Silicosis, the form of the disease prevalent among miners, is commonly called miner's lung.

pneumonia (no͝omōn'yə), acute infection of one or both lungs that can be caused by a bacterium or virus but is most frequently due to the pneumococcus bacterium. When one or more entire lobes of the lung are involved, the infection is considered a lobar pneumonia. When the disease is confined to the air spaces adjacent to the bronchi, it is known as bronchopneumonia. The pneumococci reach the lungs through the respiratory passages. Usually an upper respiratory infection precedes the disease. Chronic alcoholism, malnutrition, debility, inhalation of noxious gases, or long confinement to bed are predisposing factors. The symptoms are high fever, chill, pain in the chest, difficulty in breathing, cough, and a sputum that is pinkish at first and becomes rust-colored as the infection progresses. The skin may turn bluish because the lungs are not sufficiently oxygenating the blood. Complete bed rest and good supportive care are important. Oxygen helps to relieve severe respiratory difficulty. Penicillin is the most effective antibiotic in the treatment of pneumonia caused by bacteria and, with the other antibiotic and sulfa drugs, is responsible for the marked decline in the mortality figures for this disorder; viral pneumonia is generally milder than the bacterial form. Nevertheless, pneumonia is still a serious disease, especially in elderly persons or when complicated by bacterial invasion of the blood stream, or membranes of the heart, or of the central nervous system.

pneumothorax (no͝omōthôr'ăks), collapse of a lung with escape of air into the pleural cavity between the lung and the chest wall. The cause may be traumatic (e.g., gunshot or stab wound), spontaneous (rupture due to disease or localized weakness of the lung lining), or environmental (extreme change in atmospheric pressure). The only symptom may be a sudden pain in the chest. Physical and radiological examination reveal characteristic signs of lung collapse. Simple pneumothorax of only one lung generally requires only rest; the break in the pleura usually heals quickly after collapse of the lung has taken place. In tension pneumothorax (where there is high intrapleural pressure), or if both lungs are collapsed, it is advisable to remove the air from the pleural cavity immediately. An artificial pneumothorax is one deliberately induced, as in the treatment of tuberculosis of the lung before modern drugs became available, or in the diagnosis of lung disease.

Po (pō, It. pô), Latin *Padus,* longest river of Italy, c.405 mi (650 km) long, rising in the Cottian Alps of Piedmont, NW Italy. It winds generally east in a wide valley, past Turin, Pavia, Piacenza, Cremona, and Ferrara, to enter the Adriatic Sea through several mouths. Its marshy delta is constantly expanding eastward. The Dora Baltea, Tanaro, Ticino, Adda, and Oglio rivers are its chief tributaries; hydroelectricity is produced there. The Po River is navigable for small craft c.300 mi (480 km) upstream, but seasonal variations in flow hamper navigation. It is extensively used for irrigation. The Po valley is densely populated and is the most important industrial and agricultural region of Italy. Grains, sugar beets, livestock, and fruits are raised. Turin, Asti, Milan, Brescia, and Verona are the chief cities of the Po valley.

Po, chemical symbol of the element POLONIUM.

Pobeda Peak, USSR-China: see TIEN SHAN.

Pobyedonostzev, Konstantin Petrovich (kənstəntyĕn' pĕtrô'vĭch pəbyĕdənôs'tsyĭf), 1827–1907, Russian public official and jurist. He was professor of civil law at Moscow when he attracted the attention of Czar Alexander II and was appointed (1865) tutor to the future Alexander III. As procurator of the holy synod (1880–1905), he became the champion of autocracy, orthodoxy, and Russian nationalism. He had great power and under his influence Alexander III opposed any limitation of autocratic powers, tightened censorship, attempted to suppress opposition opinion, persecuted religious nonconformists, and adopted a policy of Russification of all national minorities. Pobyedonostzev also supported Pan-Slavism and in his writings strongly attacked Western rationalism and liberalism. He tutored Nicholas II and was one of his most influential advisers until the Revolution of 1905. He wrote a three-volume work on Russian civil law. See his *Reflections of a Russian Statesman* (tr. 1898); study by R. F. Byrnes (1968).

Pocahontas (pōkəhŏn'təs), c.1595–1617, North American Indian woman, daughter of Chief POWHATAN. Pocahontas, meaning "playful one" (her real name was said to be Matoaka), used to visit the English in Virginia at Jamestown. According to the famous story, she saved the life of the captured Capt. John SMITH, just as he was about to have his head smashed at the direction of Powhatan. Although the story's authenticity is still disputed among historians, it probably happened. In 1613, Pocahontas was captured by Capt. Samuel Argall, taken to Jamestown, and held as a hostage for English prisoners then in the hands of her father. At Jamestown she was converted to Christianity and baptized as Rebecca. John ROLFE, a settler, gained the permission of Powhatan and the governor, Sir Thomas Dale, and married her in April, 1614. The union brought peace with the Indians for eight years. With her husband and several other Indians, Pocahontas went to England in 1616. There she was received as a princess and presented to the king and queen. She started back to America in 1617 but was taken ill and died at Gravesend, where she was buried. Pocahontas bore one son, Thomas Rolfe, who was educated in England, went (1640) to Virginia, and gained considerable wealth. See P. L. Barbour, *Pocahontas and Her World* (1969); G. S. Woodward, *Pocahontas* (1969).

Pocatello (pōkətĕl'ō), city (1970 pop. 40,036), seat of Bannock co., SE Idaho, between mountains on the Portneuf River near its junction with the Snake (there dammed to form the American Falls Reservoir); inc. 1889. A railroad center since 1882, Pocatello is a major shipping and processing point for a livestock and farm area. It has an important mining industry (large phosphate deposits are nearby), canneries, and plants making prefabricated homes, electronic equipment, and steel fabricators. Tourism is significant; excellent skiing and water sport facilities are in the area. Pocatello is the seat of Idaho State Univ. and the headquarters for Caribou National Forest. Fort Hall Indian Reservation with its irrigation project is to the northwest; the site of Fort Hall (1834) is on the Snake River nearby.

Pochereth (pŏk'ərĕth), family that returned from Exile. Ezra 2.57; Neh. 7.59.

Po Chü-i (bô jü-ē), 772–846, Chinese poet. Po Chü-i occupied several important government posts, rising to the presidency of the imperial board of war in 841. He wrote over 3,000 poems, brief, topical verses expressed in very simple, clear language. Perhaps his most noted poem is *The Everlasting Wrong* (806), which recounts the sufferings of Emperor Ming Huang (685–762) on the murder of his concubine by rebels. Po Chü-i continued to write despite partial paralysis and arthritis, and he had the satisfaction of enjoying great fame during his lifetime. See Arthur Waley, *The Life and Times of Po Chü-i* (1949); Eugene Feifel, *Po Chü-i as a Censor* (1961).

pocket gopher: see GOPHER.

pocket mouse, small jumping rodent of W North America and as far south as N South America. More closely related to the squirrel than the true mouse, the pocket mouse gets its name from the fur-lined cheek pouches in which it carries its food. It varies in length from 3 to 12 in. (7.6–30.5 cm) according to the species and has hind legs elongated for jumping. Species of the genus *Perognathus* are soft furred; species of the genera *Liomys* and *Heteromys* have stiff, flattened spines mixed in with the fur. The pocket mouse is a solitary, nocturnal animal, living in grass-lined burrows in desert and semidesert regions; one *Heteromys* species lives in humid forests. The rodent feeds on seeds and other vegetable matter. It can live for long periods without free water by utilizing the moisture available from food and its own digestive processes and by secreting concentrated urine. Females give birth to several litters a year, each litter containing from one to eight young. Gestation takes from 24 to 33 days. Pocket mice have many natural enemies but in captivity have lived as long as five years. They are classified in the phylum CHORDATA, subphylum Vertebrata, class Mammalia, order Rodentia, family Heteromyidae.

Pococke, Edward (pō'kŏk), 1604–91, English Orientalist, b. Oxford. Ordained a priest in 1629, he resided at Aleppo in Syria as a chaplain, where he collected valuable manuscripts and studied Arabic, Hebrew, Syriac, Samaritan, and Ethiopic. Living in

England from 1636, he wrote a series of essays on Arabic history, *Specimen historiae Arabum* (1636), the first book printed in Arabic type. In 1663 he published the Arabic text and his Latin translation of the history by Bar-Hebraeus that had inspired his essays. This important work of scholarship was entitled *Historia compendiosa dynastiarum*. Pococke also wrote commentaries on Hosea, Joel, Micah, and Malachi, and made his superb collection and his vast knowledge available to other scholars. His library is now part of the Bodleian Library at Oxford. His name appears also as Pocock.

Pocono Mountains (pō'kənō), range of the Appalachian system, c.2,000 ft (610 m) high, NE Pa. Forested and having many lakes and streams, the Poconos are a major year-round resort area.

pod, in aviation: see AIRPLANE.

pod or **legume,** dehiscent FRUIT of a member of the family Leguminosae (PULSE family). At maturity the pod splits along its two seams and releases the enclosed seeds.

Podgorica: see TITOGRAD, Yugoslavia.

Podgorny, Nikolai Viktorovich (nēkôlyī' vēktô'rəvĭch pōdgôr'nyē), 1903–, Soviet Communist leader, b. the Ukraine. An engineer, trained at the Technological Institute of the Food Industry in Kiev, he became deputy commissar of the Ukraine food industry before entering (1950) the official ranks of the Communist party. He was elected a member of the central committee of the party (1956) and of the presidium (1960, now the politburo). In 1965 he became president of the presidium, or chief of state, succeeding Anastas Mikoyan. He traveled widely and enhanced the position of president of the USSR.

podiatry (pōdī'ətrē, pə–), science concerned with disorders, diseases, and deformities of the feet, also called chiropody. Podiatrists treat such common conditions as bunions, corns and calluses, and ingrown toenails. They may also perform minor surgery and prescribe medicines or orthopedic devices. In the United States a practitioner must hold a degree from an accredited college of podiatry and pass a licensing examination; some states require a period of internship as well. Training is similar in most respects to that of medical students with the exception that it is largely limited to a single area of the body. The National Association of Chiropodists was founded in 1912. In 1958 its name was changed to the American Podiatry Association. It maintains local societies and licensing boards in each of the fifty states, Puerto Rico, and the District of Columbia.

Podillya: see PODOLIA, USSR.

Podmokly: see DĚČÍN, Czechoslovakia.

Podolia (pōdō'lyə), region, W central European USSR, in Ukraine, separated in the south from the Moldavian SSR by the Dnestr and in the west from W Galicia by the Southern Bug. It borders on Volhynia in the north. KAMENETS-PODOLSKI (its historic capital), MOGILEV-PODOLSKI, VINNITSA, and KHMELNITSKY are the chief cities. The population is predominantly Ukrainian; the large Jewish minority that settled in Podolia in the Middle Ages was virtually exterminated by German occupation forces in World War II. A fertile hilly plain drained by the Dnestr and the Southern Bug, Podolia is one of the richest and most densely populated agricultural regions of the Ukraine. The principal crops are sugar beets, wheat, tobacco, and sunflowers. Dairy farming and beekeeping are also important, and phosphate is mined. Food processing, especially sugar milling, is the major industry. One of the Ukraine's oldest regions, Podolia was part of Kievan Russia from the 10th cent. and later belonged to the Galich and Volhynia principalities. In the 14th cent. Polish colonists began to convert the region of Podolia from steppe into arable farmland. W Podolia was annexed to Poland in 1430; the eastern section was part of Lithuania until the latter's union with Poland in 1569. Occupied by Turkey in 1672, Podolia was returned to Poland by the Treaty of Karlowitz in 1699. E Podolia passed to Russia in 1793. The western portion was transferred to Austria in 1772, belonged to Poland from 1918 to 1939, and was then annexed by the USSR.

Podolsk (pədôl'yəsk), city (1970 pop. 169,000), central European USSR, on the Pakhra River, a tributary of the Moskva. The center of a fertile agricultural region, Podolsk is a rail terminus and lies on the main highway from Moscow to the Crimea. There are electrotechnical industries and factories that produce heavy machinery, oil-refining equipment, and cables. The medieval village of Podolsk was a fief of the Danilov monastery in Moscow until 1764 and received a city charter in 1781. Prior to the 1917 Bolshevik Revolution, Podolsk was a frequent meeting place for Lenin and other revolutionaries. The city has a Lenin museum and numerous educational establishments.

podzol (pŏd'sŏl), or **podzolic soil,** member of a group of soils that are gray in color, have an ashy appearance, and extend immediately south of the tundra regions of the Northern Hemisphere. Although characteristically capped with an abundant surface accumulation of organic matter, these soils are often severely leached and highly acid. They are thus generally low in agricultural value, forests being their most common and practical coverage. South of the podzolic soils, prairie soils are sometimes found. These dark semipodzolic soils have unusual fertility owing primarily to a vegetative cover of grass rather than forest. They are generally leached free of carbonate but retain mineral fertility.

Poe, Edgar Allan, 1809–49, American poet, short-story writer, and critic, b. Boston. He is acknowledged today as one of the most brilliant and original writers in American literature. His skillfully wrought tales and poems convey with passionate intensity the mysterious, dreamlike, and often macabre forces that pervaded his sensibility. He is also considered the father of the modern detective story. After the death of his parents, both of whom were actors, by the time he was three years old, Poe was taken into the home of his godfather, John Allan, a wealthy Richmond merchant. The Allans took him to Europe, where he began his education in schools in England and Scotland. Returning to the United States in 1820, he continued his schooling in Richmond and in 1826 entered the Univ. of Virginia. He showed remarkable scholastic ability in classical and romance languages but was forced to leave the university after only eight months because of quarrels with Allan over his gambling debts. Poverty soon forced him to enlist in the army. Because of the deathbed plea of his foster mother, he achieved an unenthusiastic reconciliation with Allan, which resulted in an honorable discharge from the army and an appointment to West Point in 1830. However, when Allan remarried the following year Poe lost all hope of further assistance from him and was expelled from the Academy for infraction of numerous minor rules. His first book, *Tamerlane and Other Poems,* was published in 1827. It was followed by two more volumes of verse in 1829 and 1831. None of these early collections attracted critical or popular recognition. Poe went to Baltimore to live with his aunt, Mrs. Maria Clemm, and her daughter Virginia. In 1835, J. P. Kennedy helped him become an editor of the *Southern Literary Messenger* in Richmond. He contributed stories, poems, and astute literary criticism, but his drinking lost him the editorship. In 1836 he married Virginia Clemm, then only 13, and in 1837 they went to New York City, where he published *The Narrative of Arthur Gordon Pym* (1838). From 1838 to 1844, Poe lived in Philadelphia, where he edited *Burton's Gentleman's Magazine* (1839–40) and *Graham's Magazine* (1841–42). His criticism, which appeared in these magazines and in the *Messenger,* was direct and incisive and made him a respected and feared critic. Some of his magazine stories were collected as *Tales of the Grotesque and Arabesque* (1840). At that time he also began writing mystery stories. In 1844, Poe moved back to New York, where he worked on the *Evening Mirror* and later edited and owned the *Broadway Journal. The Raven and Other Poems* (1845) won him fame as a poet both at home and abroad. In 1846 he moved to the Fordham cottage (now a museum) and there wrote "The Literati of New York City" for *Godey's Lady's Book.* His wife died in 1847, and by the following year Poe was courting the poet Sarah Helen WHITMAN. However, in 1849 he returned to Richmond and became engaged to Elmira Royster, a childhood sweetheart who was by then the widowed Mrs. Shelton. On his way north to bring Mrs. Clemm to the wedding, he became involved in a drinking debauch in Baltimore. This indulgence proved fatal, for he died a few days later. Poe's literary executor, R. W. GRISWOLD, overemphasized Poe's personal faults and distorted his letters. Poe was a complex person, tormented and alcoholic yet also considerate and humorous, a good friend, and an affectionate husband. Indeed, his painful life, his neurotic attraction to intense beauty, violent horror, and death, and his sense of the world of dreams contributed to his greatness as a writer. Such compelling stories as "The Masque of the Red Death" and "The Fall of the House of Usher" involve the reader in a universe that is at once beautiful and grotesque, real and fantastic. His poems (including "To Helen," "The Raven," "The City in the Sea," and "Annabel Lee") are rich with musical phrases and sensuous, at times frightening images. Poe was also an intelligent and witty critic who often theorized about the art of writing. The analytical mind he brought to criticism is evident also in his famous stories of ratiocination, notably "The Murders in the Rue Morgue" and "The Purloined Letter." Poe influenced such diverse authors as Swinburne, Tennyson, Dostoyevsky, Conan Doyle, and the French symbolists. See his complete poems and stories, ed. by A. H. Quinn and E. H. O'Neill (1947); his letters, ed. by J. W. Ostrom (2 vol., 1966); biographies by W. R. Bittner (1962) and A. H. Quinn (1941, repr. 1970); studies by Daniel Hoffman (1972) and G. R. Thompson (1973); bibliography by J. W. Robertson (1934, repr. 1969).

poet laureate (lô'rēĭt), title conferred in England by the monarch on a poet whose duty it is to write commemorative odes and verse. It is an outgrowth of the medieval custom of having versifiers and minstrels in the king's retinue, and of the later royal patronage of poets, such as Chaucer and Spenser. Ben Jonson seems to have had what amounted to the laureateship from Charles I in 1617, but the title of laureate, adopted from the Greek and Roman custom of crowning with a wreath of laurel, was first given to John Dryden in 1670. His successors have been Thomas Shadwell (1688–92), Nahum Tate (1692–1715), Nicholas Rowe (1715–18), Laurence Eusden (1718–30), Colley Cibber (1730–57), William Whitehead (1757–85), Thomas Warton (1785–90), Henry Pye (1790–1813), Robert Southey (1813–43), William Wordsworth (1843–50), Alfred, Lord Tennyson (1850–92), Alfred Austin (1892–1913), Robert Bridges (1913–30), John Masefield (1930–67), Cecil Day Lewis (1968–72), and John Betjeman (1972). See Kenneth Hopkins, *The Poets Laureate* (1954, repr. 1966).

poetry. For lyric poetry, see BALLAD; ELEGY; HYMN; LYRIC; ODE; PASTORAL; SONNET. For narrative poetry, see CHANSONS DE GESTE; EPIC; IDYL; ROMANCE. Dramatic poetry is incidentally treated in the articles DRAMA, WESTERN; and TRAGEDY. See also articles on individual poets and on various national literatures. For technical discussions of poetry, see FREE VERSE; PENTAMETER; RHYME; VERSIFICATION.

Pogány, Willy (vĭl'ē pō'gänyə), 1882–1955, American artist, b. Hungary, studied in Budapest, Munich, and Paris. Arriving in New York City in 1914 from England, he soon achieved renown as a designer of stage sets for the Metropolitan Opera and for Broadway productions. His subsequent achievements included murals for theaters, hotels, and business and institutional buildings; book illustration; art direction for Hollywood motion pictures; architectural designs; sculpture; and portraiture. Among the more than 150 books, chiefly for children, that he illustrated were *Arabian Nights, Bhagavad Gita, The Rubaiyat* (1916), and *Willy Pogány's Mother Goose.* His films included *Devil Dancer* (1926) and *Modern Times* (1936), and among his murals are those in the Children's Theater of the Heckscher Foundation and the building of the Niagara Falls (N.Y.) Power Company. Portraiture occupied much of his last few years; two of his better-known subjects were John Barrymore and Carole Lombard.

Poggendorff, Johann Christian (yō'hän krĭs'tyän pôg'əndôrf''), 1796–1877, German physicist and chemist. He founded (1824) and edited the important *Annalen der Physik und Chemie* and edited the first two volumes (1863) of *Biographisch-literarisches Handwörterbuch.* Professor of chemistry at the Univ. of Berlin from 1834, he investigated problems in electricity and magnetism.

Poggio Bracciolini, Gian Francesco (jän fränchäs'kō pôd'jō brät''chōlē'nē), 1380–1459, Italian humanist. A secretary in the Roman curia, he later became chancellor and historiographer of the republic of Florence. A prodigious copyist, he rediscovered many lost classical works, including Lucretius' *De natura rerum* and Quintilian's *Institutio oratorica.* His *Facetiae* (1474), a collection of earthy fables and anticlerical satires, was printed in England by William Caxton in 1484.

Pogodin, Mikhail Petrovich (mēkhəyēl' pĕtrō'vĭch pəgô'dyĭn), 1800–1875, Russian historian and publisher. His conservative journal *The Muscovite* (1841–56) defended the policies of Nicholas I. He was professor of Russian history at Moscow Univ. (1835–44) and wrote a history of Russia (7 vol., 1846–57) and a study of the origins of Russia (3 vol., 1871).

Pogodin, Nikolai (nyĭkəlī'), pseud. of **Nikolai Feodorovich Stukalov** (fyô'dərəvĭch stōōkä'lôf), 1900–1962, Russian dramatist. Pogodin wrote many colorful, optimistic, and popular plays generally dealing with the theme of man's conquest of the machine. In *Tempo* (1930, tr. 1936), a play concerning the Five-Year-Plan period, an American engineer helps speed up tractor production. In *The Aristocrats* (1935, tr. 1937) Pogodin depicts the rehabilitation of criminals in a labor camp. All of his plays are noted for their hearty good humor and reverence for the common man.

pogonia: see ORCHID.

pogrom (pō'grəm, pōgrŏm'), Russian term, originally meaning "riot," that came to be applied to a series of violent attacks on Jews in Russia in the late 19th and early 20th cent. Pogroms were few before the assassination of Alexander II in 1881; after that, with the connivance of, or at least without hindrance from, the government, there were many pogroms throughout Russia. Soldiers and police often looked on without interfering. These pogroms encouraged the first emigration of Russian Jews to the United States. After 1882 there were few pogroms until 1903, when there was an extremely violent three-day pogrom at Kishinev resulting in the death of 45 Jews. Although it has not been conclusively proved that the czarist government organized pogroms, the government's anti-Semitic policies certainly encouraged them. After the abortive revolution of 1905, pogroms increased in number and violence. With the success of the Bolshevik Revolution, pogroms ceased in the Soviet Union; they were revived in Germany and Poland after Adolf Hitler attained power.

Po Hai or **P'o-hai** (both: pō hī), arm of the Yellow Sea, indenting the coast of N China; bordered by Shantung, Hopeh, and Liaoning provs. and Tientsin Municipality; the Liaotung Gulf is its northeast extension. The Huang Ho (Yellow River) empties into the Po Hai. Lü-shun (Port Arthur), Ying-k'ou, and Tientsin are major ports. Po Hai was formerly called the Gulf of Chihli.

Pohang (pô'häng'), city (1970 est. pop. 79,000), SE South Korea, on Yongil Bay of the Sea of Japan. The chief economic activities are fish canning and the production of iron and steel.

poi, slightly fermented, sticky food paste eaten in the Pacific islands, usually accompanied with meat, fish, or vegetables. It is made by grinding or pounding the roasted, peeled roots of the taro.

Poincaré, Jules Henri (zhül äNrē' pwăNkärā'), 1854–1912, French mathematician, physicist, and author. He was from 1881 connected with the faculty of sciences at the Univ. of Paris. One of the greatest mathematicians of his age, Poincaré, by research in the theory of functions, especially the automorphic, Fuchsian, and Abelian functions, enlarged the field of mathematical physics. He did notable work also in differential equations and celestial mechanics, particularly the problem of three or more bodies moving under their mutual gravitational attractions. Poincaré not only made important contributions across the full range of mathematics, both pure and applied, but also wrote extensively on the philosophy of science. He was elected to the Academy of Sciences in 1887, became its president in 1906, and was elected to the Academie Française in 1909. His works include *Les Méthodes nouvelles de la mécanique céleste* (3 vol., 1892–99; tr., 3 vol., 1967) and three works (1902, 1904, 1908) published in English as *The Foundations of Science* (1913, repr. 1946). See Tobias Dantzig, *Henri Poincaré, Critic of Crisis: Reflections on His Universe of Discourse* (1954).

Poincaré, Raymond (rāmôN'), 1860–1934, French statesman, president of France (1913–20); cousin of Jules Henri Poincaré. A member of the chamber of deputies from 1887, he held numerous cabinet posts from 1893 to 1906. In 1912 he became premier and foreign minister, and in 1913 he was elected to succeed Armand Fallières as president. A conservative and a nationalist, he proceeded to strengthen France to face possible hostilities. A bill increasing military service to three years was passed, and French alliances with Great Britain and Russia were tightened. During World War I, Poincaré called on (1917) Georges CLEMENCEAU to form a new cabinet, despite his personal hatred of the man. After the war Poincaré called for harsh punishment of Germany and for adequate guarantees of French security. He regarded the Treaty of Versailles as too lenient. On completing his presidential term, Poincaré returned to the senate, which he had entered first in 1903, and became a leader of the *bloc national,* a coalition of conservative parties. This brought him again to the premiership and the ministry of foreign affairs in 1922. In the face of Germany's failure to pay the heavy reparations assigned by the peace treaty, Poincaré sent French troops to occupy the RUHR in 1923. He failed, however, to coerce Germany into paying its reparations, and in May, 1924, he was forced to resign following the conservatives' defeat in the general elections. Financial crisis returned him to office in 1926. He retained Aristide Briand, who supported cooperation with Germany, as his foreign minister. To deal with the financial situation, Poincaré pursued an extreme deflationary policy, balancing the budget and securing (1928) the stabilization of the franc at one fifth of its former value. He retired from office in 1929 but continued to preach the need for security and to proclaim his opposition to treaty revision. Among Poincaré's writings are *How France Is Governed* (tr. 1919) and his memoirs (tr. 1926). See Sisley Huddleston, *Poincaré* (1924); Gordon Wright, *Poincaré and the French Presidency* (1942, repr. 1967).

poinciana (poinsēă'nə, -ä'nə), any shrub or tree of the tropical and subtropical genus *Poinciana* of the family Leguminosae (PULSE family). Poincianas are popular ornamentals for their showy orange or scarlet blossoms. The royal poinciana or peacock flower (*P. regia*), native to Madagascar, is one of the most striking of tropical trees. It is widely cultivated elsewhere, e.g., the West Indies, the S United States, and Bermuda. Poincianas are classified in the division MAGNOLIOPHYTA, class Magnoliopsida, order Rosales, family Leguminosae.

Poindexter, George (poin'dĕk"stər), 1779–1853, American political leader, b. Louisa co., Va. After practicing law in Virginia, he moved (1802) to Mississippi. As attorney general of Mississippi he took part in the efforts to bring Aaron Burr to trial. He served (1807–13) in the U.S. Congress and later was (1813–17) U.S. district judge. He was influential in framing (1817) the Mississippi constitution and was chiefly responsible for the revised state law code (1824). Poindexter again served (1817–19) in Congress and was later (1820–21) governor of Mississippi. As U.S. Senator (1830–35) he broke with President Jackson, with whom he had served in the War of 1812.

Poinsett, Joel Roberts (poin'sĕt), 1779–1851, American diplomat and politician, b. Charleston, S.C. In 1810 he was sent as a special commissioner to South America to investigate political conditions of the countries struggling for independence. He served in the South Carolina legislature, was a member of the U.S. House of Representatives (1821–25), and later was minister (1825–29) to Mexico. A strong opponent of NULLIFICATION, he was Secretary of War (1837–41) under Martin Van Buren. He introduced the flowering plant called the poinsettia (named after him) into the United States. See biography by J. F. Rippy (1935, repr. 1972).

poinsettia: see SPURGE.

Point Barrow, northernmost point of Alaska, on the Arctic Ocean, at lat. 71°23'N and long. 156°30'W. Discovered in 1826 by Frederick W. Beechey, a British explorer, and named by him for the British geographer Sir John Barrow, it has since been visited by many expeditions and has figured prominently in arctic aviation. Navigation is open for only two or three months a year. To the southwest is the village of Barrow. Farther south is a monument to Will Rogers and Wiley Post, who lost their lives there in an airplane crash in 1935.

Pointe-à-Pitre (pwăNtäpē'trə), city (1967 pop. 29,757), Guadeloupe dept., French West Indies. It is on Grande-Terre island at the southern entrance of the Rivière Salée, the narrow, shallow ocean channel that separates Guadeloupe proper from Grande-Terre. Pointe-à-Pitre is the largest city and leading port in the department. Its chief exports are sugar, rum, coffee, and bananas.

Pointe-Noire (pwăNt-nwär), city (1970 pop. 135,000), SW Congo Republic, Africa, a port on the Atlantic Ocean. It exports tropical timber, cotton, palm products, peanuts, and coffee. Plywood, aluminum ware, and soap are manufactured, and the city has shipbuilding and food-processing industries. It is also a noted center for sport fishing. Founded in 1883, it acquired importance only after the completion (1948) of the railroad to Brazzaville and the construction (1934–39) of an artificial harbor. From 1950 until 1958 the city was the capital of the French Congo.

pointer, breed of large SPORTING DOG developed in England more than three hundred years ago. It stands between 23 and 26 in. (58.4–66.4 cm) high at the shoulder and weighs between 50 and 60 lb (22.7–27.2 kg). Its short, dense, shiny coat may be solid liver, black, yellow, or orange, or, more frequently, white with any of these colors as markings. The pointer is a scent hunter used for upland game birds. Having located its quarry, it stands rigidly poised with its body and nose facing the game, thus directing the hunter to it. Bred from crosses of foxhound, greyhound, and bloodhound with an early "setting" spaniel, the pointer was originally used to find and point hares, which were then chased and killed by greyhounds. With the rise in popularity of wing-shooting in the early 1700s, the pointer quickly became regarded as an expert gundog, a reputation it continues to enjoy today. The term *pointer* is also widely used to designate a dog of any breed that characteristically points its quarry. See DOG.

Point Four program, U.S. foreign aid project aimed at providing technological skills, knowledge, and equipment to poor nations throughout the world. The program also encouraged the flow of private investment capital to these nations. The project received its name from the fourth point of a program set forth in President Truman's 1949 inaugural address. In the COLD WAR the U.S. government used Point Four to win support from uncommitted nations. From 1950 until 1953, Point Four aid was administered by the Technical Cooperation Administration, a separate unit within the Dept. of State. During the administration of President Eisenhower it was integrated into the overall foreign aid program. See J. B. Bingham, *Shirt-sleeve Diplomacy: Point 4 in Action* (1954).

Point Grey, suburb of Vancouver, SW British Columbia, Canada. It is the site of the Univ. of British Columbia.

pointillism (pwăn'təlĭz"əm): see POSTIMPRESSIONISM.

Point Judith, promontory extending into Block Island Sound, S R.I., in the town of Narragansett. A U.S. coast guard station and a lighthouse are there. The village of Point Judith is a resort.

Point Pelee (pē'lē), peninsula, c.10 mi (16 km) long, extending into W Lake Erie, S Ont., Canada, near Leamington. It is the southernmost part of the Canadian mainland. **Point Pelee National Park** (6 sq mi/15.5 sq km; est. 1918) is there. The park is a wildlife sanctuary (especially for migratory birds) and is noted for its cattail marsh, woodland, and sandy beaches.

Point Pleasant, residential and resort borough (1970 pop. 15,968), Ocean co., E N.J., near the Manasquan Inlet; settled 1850, inc. 1920.

Point Reyes National Seashore (rā'ĭs), 64,546 acres (26,122 hectares), W Calif.; est. 1962. Included in the area are steep bluffs overlooking the Pacific Ocean, lagoons, and esteros enclosed by sand dunes, rolling hills, and forests. On offshore rocks are bird rookeries and sea-lion herds. The SAN ANDREAS FAULT passes through the park; there is a 15 to 20 ft (4.6–6.1 m) horizontal displacement of rock (a result of the 1906 earthquake). Sir Francis Drake probably stopped there (1579) to repair his ship, the *Golden Hinde,* before crossing the Pacific Ocean.

Poiret, Paul: see under FASHION.

poison, any agent that may produce chemically an injurious or deadly effect when introduced into the body in sufficient quantity. Some poisons can be deadly in minute quantities, others only if relatively large amounts are involved. Factors of importance in determining the severity of a poison include the nature of the poison itself, the concentration and amount, the route of administration, the length of exposure, and the age, size, and physical health of the individual. If poisoning is suspected a physician or poison control center should be called immediately. The remainder of the poison and its container should be saved; the label may list ingredients, first aid measures, or antidotes. For most ingested poisons emptying the stomach is the most important treatment; vomiting is best accomplished in the conscious individual by administering syrup of ipecac with large quantities of water. The major exceptions to this treatment are in cases of ingestion of corrosives, such as lye, and certain hydrocarbons, such as kerosine. In corrosive ingestions a small amount of milk may be given, but vomiting should not be induced since the damage that may have already been sustained by the mucous membranes of the esophagus and stomach may advance to perforation; the patient should be seen by a physician as soon as possible. Hydrocarbons are extremely volatile, and the dangers of their being aspirated into the lungs when vomiting is induced are greater than their toxicity if absorbed into the body. In gas or vapor poisoning the patient should be carried to a nonpolluted atmosphere; ARTIFICIAL RESPIRATION should be employed if necessary. If any poison has been absorbed through the skin, all contaminated garments should be removed immediately and the skin washed with soap and water. Poisoning is a significant cause of accidental death in children and is best treated by prevention; potential poisons in the home should be stored in locked cabinets. In chemistry, poison refers to a substance that inhibits or slows a chemical reaction. See separate articles on BOTULISM; CARBON MONOXIDE; FOOD POISONING; LEAD POISONING; MERCURY POISONING; POISON GAS; POISON IVY; SNAKEBITE; TOXIN.

Poison Affair, in French history, scandal implicating a number of prominent persons at the court of King Louis XIV. It began with the trial of Marie Madeleine d'Aubray, marquise de Brinvilliers (c.1630–76). She conspired with her lover, Godin de Sainte-Croix, an army captain, to poison her father and two brothers in order to secure the family fortune and to end interference in her adulterous relationship. Her husband escaped the same fate by his complaisance. An investigation was made, and the marquise fled abroad, but in 1676 she was arrested at Liège. The affair greatly worked on the popular imagination, and there were rumors that she had tried out her poisons on hospital patients. She was beheaded and then burned. The Brinvilliers trial attracted attention to other mysterious deaths. Parisian society had been seized by a fad for spiritualist séances, fortune-telling, and the use of love potions. Some of the quack practitioners undoubtedly also sold poison (called "inheritance powders" at the time); after their arrest they furnished the police with lists of their clients, who often were guilty merely of having their palms read or of buying an aphrodisiac, and accused them of complicity in their crimes. The most celebrated case was that of La Voisin, a midwife and fortune-teller whose real name was Catherine Deshayes Monvoisin and whose clientele included the marquise de MONTESPAN, Olympe Mancini (niece of Cardinal Mazarin and mother of Prince Eugene of Savoy), her sister Marie Anne Mancini, and Marshal Luxembourg (duke and peer of France and one of the military heroes of the time). No formal charges were made against any of these, and there is no evidence that they were seriously implicated, yet a permanent stain was left on their names. La Voisin was burned as a poisoner and a sorceress in 1680. A special court, the *chambre ardente* [burning court], was instituted to judge cases of poisoning and witchcraft, and the poison epidemic came to an end in France. The affair was symptomatic of the witchcraft trials of the period throughout Europe and in New England; however, the judicial investigation was conducted generally with far more regularity and far less hysteria than elsewhere.

poison gas, any of various gases sometimes used in warfare or riot control because of their poisonous or corrosive nature. These gases may be roughly grouped according to the portal of entry into the body and their physiological effects. Vesicants (blister gases) produce blisters on all body surfaces (see LEWISITE; MUSTARD GAS); lacrimators (TEAR GAS) produce severe eye irritation; sternutators (vomiting gases) cause nausea; NERVE GASES inhibit proper nerve function; and lung irritants attack the respiratory tract, causing pulmonary edema. By the middle of the 19th cent. the possibility of the use of poison gas as a weapon was already envisaged and was viewed by most men with a peculiar horror—a feeling that has persisted. The first effective use of poison gas came in World War I, when the Germans released (1915) chlorine gas against the Allies in the Ypres sector of the Western Front. The success was immediate, but the attackers, uncertain as to the effect, failed to pursue the retreating French. Shortly afterwards protective measures (see GAS MASK) were introduced as both sides used gas more extensively. The gas shell (much more suitable than wind-blown gas) was introduced by the French. Gas did not have any dominant influence on the course of the war, but it did seem to point toward wide-scale use in the future. However, except for the use of poison gas by the Italians in the war against Ethiopia (1935–36) and by the Japanese against Chinese guerrillas (1937–42), poison gas was not employed in warfare after World War I out of fear of retribution, even though the military powers of the world continued to develop new gases.

poison glands: see VENOM.

poison hemlock, lethally poisonous herbaceous plant (*Conium maculatum*) of the family Umbelliferae (CARROT family). It has rank, finely divided foliage, flat-topped clusters of small white flowers, and a hollow, purple-mottled stem. Although native to the Old World, it is now naturalized and common in parts of the United States. The poisonous principle (the alkaloid coniine) causes paralysis, convulsions, and eventual death. Poison hemlock was used in ancient Greece to execute criminals; a famous example was the philosopher Socrates. Today coniine is extracted for medicinal purposes; in prescribed quantities it serves as a sedative, anodyne, and antispasmodic. The related water hemlock (any species of *Cicuta*) is similar in appearance and as poisonous. *C. maculata*, called also musquash-root, spotted cowbane, and beaver poison, is the common species of E North America. The evergreen trees called HEMLOCK are unrelated. Poison hemlock is classified in the division MAGNOLIOPHYTA, class Magnoliopsida, order Umbellales, family Umbelliferae.

poison ivy, poison oak, and **poison sumac,** woody vines and trailing or erect shrubs of the family Anacardiaceae (SUMAC family), native to North America. They are sometimes considered as several species of *Rhus*, the sumac genus, but are usually distinguished as *Toxicodendron radicans* (poison ivy and poison oak) and the larger *T. vernix* (poison sumac). The whitish berrylike fruits often persist through winter. The leaves of *T. radicans* are composed of three smooth leaflets. Both species have vivid red autumn foliage. Poison oak is a name generally used in the South and West for the bushy kinds. The irritant principle, urushiol, is present in almost all parts of the plant. Direct or indirect contact (clothing, tools, or animals that have touched the plant, or smoke from burning the plants) sets off a skin eruption that may vary from simple itching inflammation to watery blisters, depending upon the sensitivity of the individual. The eruption appears within a day or two in highly sensitive individuals, and as much as two weeks later in those less sensitive. It begins on the portion of the body that has come in contact with the plant, usually the hands, which then can spread it to the face and other parts of the body. It is important therefore that contaminated hands be kept from contact with other portions of the skin. If the exposed parts of the body are washed immediately with water and a strongly alkaline soap, subsequent skin irritation may be avoided. Treatment with cortisone ointments and antihistamines measurably reduces the course of the eruption. Poison ivy vaccine is effective only if administered before exposure. Highly sensitive persons with recurrent involvement should have desensitization therapy during the winter months. Clothing that has been in contact with poison ivy must be dry-cleaned; soap-and-water cleansing alone is not always effective. These plants are classified in the division MAGNOLIOPHYTA, class Magnoliopsida, order Sapindales, family Anacardiaceae.

poison oak: see POISON IVY.

poisonous plant, any plant possessing a property injurious to man or animal. Plants may be poisonous to the touch (e.g., poison ivy, poison sumac), orally toxic (e.g., poison hemlock, deadly amanita), or poisonous because of the physical injury inflicted (chiefly to grazing animals, e.g., cocklebur, needlegrass, and thistle). Many poisonous plants are of great value medicinally, e.g., digitalis, belladonna, and aconite. Numerous plants have long been known and gathered (some from prehistoric times) for specific medicinal uses in controlled dosage. Some have been used for hunting poisons (e.g., strychnine) and for insecticides (e.g., pyrethrum). Some plants are poisonous in part and harmless otherwise (the leaf blades, not the stalks, of rhubarb are poisonous) or poisonous at one season and not at another (the very young poke, or pokeweed, shoot is sometimes cultivated as a green vegetable but the older plant is poisonous). Some plants contain properties that are poisonous only under certain conditions, such as those causing photosensitivity. White animals that feed on these plants (buckwheat and others) and are subsequently exposed to sunlight develop a serious skin disorder called photosensitization. A poisonous property (selenium) of some soils, particularly in parts of the West, is absorbed by some of the growing plants, not always in themselves poisonous, and transmitted to animals and sometimes to man. Since this poison is returned to the soil by the death of the plants and animals that have absorbed it, it is again available to other plants and may even be absorbed by crop plants. Locoweed is an example of a selenium-poisonous plant. Many of our ornamental plants are poisonous—larkspur, oleander, English ivy, and lily of the valley. Poisoning by ingestion of plants by human beings is usually a matter of mistaken identity, particularly with mushrooms. Poisonous plants are avoided by animals unless the pasture is overgrazed. Poisonous principles may be found throughout the plant kingdom from bacteria and fungi to ferns and flowering plants. See W. C. Muenscher, *Poisonous Plants of the United States* (rev. ed. 1951); J. M. Kingsbury, *Deadly Harvest: A Guide to Common Poisonous Plants* (1965).

poison sumac: see POISON IVY.

Poisson, Siméon Denis (sēmāôN' dənē' pwäsôN'), 1781–1840, French mathematician and physicist. From 1802 he taught at the École polytechnique, Paris, and was also on the faculty of sciences at the Univ. of Paris from 1809. His chief interest lay in the application of mathematics to physics, especially in electrostatics and magnetism. He developed a two-fluid theory of electricity and provided theoretical support for the experimental results of others, notably C. A. de Coulomb. Poisson also made important contributions to mechanics, especially the theory of elasticity; to optics; to the calculus, especially definite integrals; to differential geometry; and to probability theory. Other studies were concerned with heat and the motions of the moon. In all he wrote more than 300 papers on mathematics, physics, and astronomy, and his *Traité de mécanique* (1811) was long a standard work.

Poissy, Colloquy of (pwäsē'), 1561, conference of Roman Catholic prelates and Protestant ministers, initiated by Catherine de' Medici and Michel de L'Hôpital in the hope of bringing about a peaceful reunion of the two communions. The conference was unsuccessful as a result of the opposition of both parties to compromise on essential points. Those present included Theodore Beza, Pietro Martire Vermigli, Diego Lainez, and Charles de Guise, Cardinal de Lorraine.

Poitiers, Diane de: see DIANE DE POITIERS.

Poitiers (pwätyā'), city (1968 pop. 74,852), capital of Vienne dept., W central France, on the Clain River. The ancient capital of POITOU, it is now an industrial, agricultural, and communications center. Poitiers's industries include metallurgy, machine building, printing, and the manufacture of chemicals and electrical equipment. The city was the capital of the Pictons, a Gallic people, and under the Romans was called Limonum. Christianized early in Roman times, it was a stronghold of orthodoxy under its first bishop, St. Hilary of Poitiers (4th cent.), and, because of its important monasteries, was a great religious center of Gaul. A residence of VISIGOTH kings, the city was captured (507) by the Franks under Clovis I. In 1732, Charles Martel turned the Muslim tide by defeating the Saracens between Poitiers and Tours. Poitiers was often sacked by the Normans in the 9th cent. It was twice under English rule (1152–1204, 1360–72) and was the location of the brilliant court of Eleanor of Aquitaine. At Poitiers in 1356, Edward the Black Prince defeated and captured John II of France and his son, Philip the Bold of Burgundy. Charles VII had his court in Poitiers from 1423 to 1436 and founded a university there in 1432. In the Wars of Religion (1562–98) the city was unsuccessfully besieged (1568) by the HUGUENOTS; in 1577 the Peace of Bergerac (also known as the Edict of Poitiers) was signed there granting religious freedom (see RELIGION, WARS OF). Architecturally, Poitiers is one of the most interesting cities in Europe. There are Roman amphitheaters and baths, the baptistery of St. John (4th–12th cent.), the Cathedral of St. Pierre (12th–14th cent.), the courthouse (12th–15th cent., formerly a royal residence), as well as numerous other churches and late medieval and Renaissance residences.

Poitou (pwätōō'), region and former province, W France, stretching from the Atlantic coast eastward beyond the Vienne River. It now includes three departments—Vendée in the west, Deux-Sèvres in the center, and Vienne in the east, as well as small areas of several other departments. POITIERS, the historic capital, is the chief industrial center. Other industrial towns are Châtellerault, Niort, La Roche-sur-Yon, and Les Sables-d'Olonne. The Vendée region, or Lower Poitou, extends beyond the departmental boundary of Vendée; it is mostly a pastoral hedgerow country (the *bocages*), with swamps in the west and in the south. A narrow strip, the Vendean plain, is an intensive wheat-growing region. Upper Poitou is a rich agricultural area; it also has a large dairy industry. A part of the Roman province of Aquitaine, Poitou (known as "the city of the Pictons") fell to the Visigoths (5th cent.) and to the Franks (507). The counts of Poitiers, who originated in the 9th cent., assumed the title duke of AQUITAINE. The area was frequently contested by England and France, passing back and forth in possession until the end of the Hundred Years War, when Charles VII definitively incorporated it in the French crown lands.

Pokanoket Indians: see WAMPANOAG INDIANS.

poker, card game, believed to have originated in the Orient and first played in the United States in the 19th cent. A traditional cutthroat gambling game at first, it is now an internationally popular social game. It remains basically a gambling game and is played either for money or for chips purchased from the game's banker. In all of the many variations there are betting intervals during which each player in the game must drop (leave the game), call (equal the bet made), or raise (increase the bet made). All bets are placed together to form a pot. The object of all poker games is to win the pot either by holding the best hand or by inducing (bluffing) the others to drop. The two basic forms are draw poker and stud poker, in both of which a deck of 52 cards is used and sometimes a joker added. Five players are said to make the best game, although from 2 to 10 are able to play at once. All suits are equal, and cards rank from the ace as high (it is also low) down through the two, or deuce—which often upon unanimous agreement is designated "wild," thereby counting optionally for any other card. There are 2,598,960 possible poker hands with 52 cards. In both draw and stud poker the player who holds in his hand the best combination of cards wins the game. The principal combinations rank as follows: straight flush (a five-card sequence in one suit, e.g., the ace, king, queen, jack and ten, also called a royal flush, the highest possible combination in the game), four of a kind (e.g., four aces), full house (three of a kind plus a pair), flush (five of one suit), straight (a five-card sequence regardless of suit), three of a kind, two pairs, and one pair. Below this, pots are won by the hand holding the highest cards. In draw poker five cards are dealt singly, face down and in rotation, to each player, who pays an ante to the pot before play begins. Betting proceeds in clockwise fashion from the player at the dealer's left, who may either put up an opening wager or check (defer to the next player). Once a player has opened, the others must call his bet to stay in the game. In jackpots, perhaps the commonest variety of draw poker, a player must have at least a pair of jacks to open. A player may now stand pat (hold his five original cards) or draw from one to four cards (i.e., discard from his hand and have new cards dealt to him). A betting interval follows, beginning with the opener. If a bet is not met, the winner is not required to show his hand. When a bet is called, all hands are shown and the best hand wins. In stud poker, sometimes called open poker, each player is dealt singly one card down (hole card) and one card face up. Each player looks at the card he has in the hole, but lets it remain face down. The player with the highest card showing starts a betting interval, and when all players have completed their betting another card is dealt. This goes on until each player has four cards showing and one face down. After the final betting interval, the hole cards are exposed and the best hand wins. The many variations of poker include high-low poker, seven-card stud poker, and spit in the ocean. See A. H. Morehead, *The Complete Guide to Winning Poker* (1967); A. N. Darling, *The Great American Pastime* (1970).

pokeweed or **pokeberry,** tall, bushy perennial herb (*Phytolacca americana*) native to North America but cultivated and naturalized in Europe. The long clusters of white flowers are followed by purplish black flattened berries, whose crimson juice has been used as ink and to color wines but is considered poisonous. The dried roots are sometimes used as an emetic or purgative; the young shoots are used for greens or eaten like asparagus. The plant is also called poke, inkberry, and garget. Pokeweed is classified in the division MAGNOLIOPHYTA, class Magnoliopsida, order Chenopodiales, family Phytolaccaceae.

Pokrovsk: see ENGELS, USSR.

Poland, Pol. *Polska,* republic (1970 pop. 32,589,209), 120,725 sq mi (312,677 sq km), central Europe, bordering on East Germany in the west, on the Baltic Sea in the north, on the USSR in the east, and on Czechoslovakia in the south. The country's major cities include WARSAW (the capital), BIAŁYSTOK, BYDGOSZCZ, BYTOM, CZĘSTOCHOWA, GDAŃSK, GDYNIA, GLIWICE, KATOWICE, KRAKÓW, ŁÓDŹ, LUBLIN, POZNAŃ, RADOM, SZCZECIN, TARNOWSKIE GÓRY, and WROCŁAW. Poland is divided into 22 provinces (including 5 city provinces). The country is largely low-lying, except in the south, which includes the Carpathians, the Sudeten Mts., and the Małopolska Hills. The highest point is Rysy Mt. (c.8,200 ft/2,500 m), located in the High Tatra Mts. near the Czechoslovak border. Poland's main rivers (including the Vistula, the Oder, the Warta, and the Western Bug) are connected to the Baltic Sea and are important traffic lanes. The

country has three important Baltic ports (Gdańsk, Gdynia, and Szczecin) and a dense rail network. There are many lakes, especially in the north. About 50% of Poland's land area is arable (with the best soil in the south) and about 25% is forested. Poland has traditionally been an agricultural country, but since World War II there has been a rapid expansion of industry, so that by the 1970s industry contributed a little more than half the national product. Industry is largely controlled and planned by the state, but farming is mainly privately run (mostly on small farms of 5 to 25 acres/2 to 10.1 hectares). The main agricultural products are potatoes, sugar beets, rye, wheat, and barley. The country's leading manufactures include iron and steel, machinery, electronic equipment, cement, chemicals, textiles, forest products, and processed food. The chief minerals produced are coal, iron ore, zinc-lead ores, sulfur, and petroleum. Much natural gas is also produced. Poland's leading exports are coal, processed meat, ships, railroad freight cars, and metal products; the main imports are iron ore, petroleum, metal products, fertilizer, and cotton. The chief trade partners are the USSR, East Germany, and Czechoslovakia. As a result of World War II, of the 1945 boundary treaty with the USSR, and of the emigration of most of the German-speaking population, the country has considerable ethnic homogeneity. Nearly the entire population is Polish-speaking and the vast majority of those affiliated with any creed are Roman Catholic. There are universities at Gdańsk, Katowice, Kraków, Łódź, Lublin, Poznań, Toruń, Warsaw, and Wrocław.

Beginnings through the Age of Greatness. The territorial dimensions of Poland have varied considerably during its history. In the 9th and 10th cent., the Polians [dwellers in the field] gained hegemony over the other Slavic groups that occupied what is roughly present-day Poland. Under Duke MIESZKO I (reigned 960-92) of the PIAST dynasty began (966) the conversion of Poland to Christianity. Gniezno was the first capital of Poland and Poznań the first episcopal see. The Piasts expanded their domains in wars against the German emperors, Hungary, Bohemia, Pomerania, Denmark, and Kiev, and in 1025 BOLESLAUS I (reigned 992-1025) took the title of king. At the death (1138) of BOLESLAUS III the kingdom was broken up; its reunification was begun by LADISLAUS I, who was king from 1320 to 1333. During the period of disunity, the TEUTONIC KNIGHTS gained a foothold in the then pagan N Poland. Their power was only broken by their defeat at the hands of Polish-Lithuanian forces at TANNENBERG (1410); by the second treaty of Toruń (1466) they became vassals of the Polish kings. The main line of the Piast dynasty ended with the death (1370) of CASIMIR III, whose enlightened economic, administrative, and social policies included the protection of the Jews. He also completed the reunification of the kingdom. After Casimir, the crown passed to his nephew, LOUIS I of Hungary (reigned 1370-82) and then to Louis' daughter, JADWIGA (reigned 1384-99). Jadwiga married Ladislaus Jagiello, grand duke of Lithuania, who became king of Poland as LADISLAUS II (reigned 1386-1434). The Jagiello dynasty ruled Poland until 1572; this period—especially the 16th cent.—is considered the golden age of Poland. Although involved in frequent wars with Hungary, Moscow, Moldavia, the Tatars, and the Ottoman Turks, the closely allied Polish and Lithuanian states maintained an empire that reached from the Baltic to the Black Sea. LADISLAUS III (reigned 1434-44; after 1440 also king of Hungary), although routed and killed by the Ottoman Turks at the battle of Varna (1444), gave Poland the prestige of championing the Christian cause against the Muslim invaders. Casimir V (1447-92) placed Poland and Lithuania on equal terms and decisively defeated (1462) the Teutonic Knights. Under SIGISMUND I (reigned 1506-48) internal power was consolidated, the economy developed, and the culture of the Renaissance was introduced. During the reign of SIGISMUND II (reigned 1548-72) a unified Polish-Lithuanian state was created by the Union of Lublin (1569). The arts and sciences flourished under Jagiello rule; a towering figure of the age was the astronomer COPERNICUS. At the same time, however, the Jagiellos were forced to contend with the growing power of the gentry, who by the 15th cent. began to acquire considerable political influence. In 1505 the gentry forced King Alexander (reigned 1501-6) to recognize the legislative power of the Sejm, or diet, which comprised a senate (made up of representatives of the landed magnates and of the high clergy) and a chamber (consisting of the deputies of the nobility and of the gentry). The *liberum veto,* which allowed any representative to dissolve the Sejm and even to annul its previous decisions, was applied with growing recklessness in the 17th and 18th cent. The Polish kings had always been elective in theory, but in practice the choice had usually fallen on the incumbant representatives of the ruling dynasty. After the death (1572) of Sigismund II, last of the Jagiellos, the theory that the entire nobility could take part in the royal elections was newly guaranteed. In practice, this meant that internal factional rivalry prevented the establishment of any great Polish dynasty; contested elections and insurrections by the gentry were frequent. Although the state was weakened, the constitution of the royal republic created a certain democratic egalitarianism among the gentry and noble classes. The peasantry, however, had been reduced to serfdom, and its condition tended to worsen rather than improve. The middle class was largely Jewish or German. There was considerable religious toleration in 16th-century Poland and the progress of Protestantism was arrested without coercion by the Jesuits, who introduced the Catholic Reformation in 1565. Relations between the Roman Catholic ruling class and the followers of the Greek Orthodox Church in Belorussia and the Ukraine (then parts of Lithuania) were less harmonious and helped to involve Poland in several wars with Russia. Much of the reigns of STEPHEN BÁTHORY (1575-86) and SIGISMUND III (1587-1632) was occupied by attempts to conquer Russia. The outstanding figure of their reigns was Jan ZAMOJSKI (1542-1605). Sigismund III, a prince of the Swedish ruling house of VASA, also became king of Sweden; after his deposition (1598) by his Swedish subjects he continued to advance his claims and started a long series of Polish-Swedish wars. In addition, Sigismund defeated an armed revolt (1606-7) by the gentry and fought the Ottoman Turks. He was succeeded by his sons LADISLAUS IV (1632-48) and JOHN II (1648-68). John's reign came to be known in Polish history as the "Deluge." During his rule discontent in the Ukraine flared in the rebellion of the Cossacks under Bohdan CHMIELNICKI. In 1655, CHARLES X of Sweden overran Poland, while Czar ALEXIS of Russia attacked from the east. Inspired by their heroic defense of the monastery at CZĘSTOCHOWA, the Poles managed to regroup and to save the country from complete dismemberment. The Peace of OLIVA (1660) cost Poland considerable territory (including N Livonia), and by the Treaty of ANDRUSOV (1667) the E Ukraine passed to Russia. The Vasa dynasty ended with the death of John II. John III (John Sobieski; reigned 1674-96), who defended (1683) Vienna from the Ottoman Turk invaders, temporarily restored the prestige of Poland, but with his death Poland virtually ceased to be an independent country.

Division and Regeneration. After John III, the fate of Poland was determined with increasing cynicism by its three powerful neighbors—Russia, Prussia, and Austria. In 1697 the elector of Saxony was chosen king of Poland as AUGUSTUS II by a minority faction supported by Czar Peter I. Augustus allied himself with Russia and Denmark against Charles XII of Sweden. In the ensuing NORTHERN WAR (1700-21), during which Poland was plundered several times, Charles XII maintained STANISLAUS I (Stanislaus Leszczynski) as Polish king from 1704 to 1709. The War of the POLISH SUCCESSION (1733-35), precipitated by Augustus's death, resulted in the final abdication of Stanislaus and the accession of Augustus III (1734-

63). Under Augustus III, the Polish economy (still largely agricultural) declined and orderly politics was undermined by feuding among the great landed families, which was evident in the frequent use of the *liberum veto.* As a result of the support of Catherine II of Russia and Frederick II of Prussia, STANISLAUS II (Stanislaus Poniatowski; reigned 1764–95), a member of the powerful CZARTORYSKI family, was elected king of Poland. Prince Nikolai Repnin, the Russian minister at Warsaw, gained much influence in Polish internal affairs. Opposition to Russian domination led to the formation (with French help) in 1768 of the Confederation of the BAR, which, however, was suppressed militarily by Russia in 1772. Fearing that all Poland might fall into Russian hands, Frederick II proposed (1772) a partition plan to Catherine II, which later in the same year was modified to include Austria. Three successive partitions (1772, 1793, 1795) resulted in the disappearance (1795) of Poland from the map of Europe. Russia gained the largest share. Despite the severe losses that the country suffered, there was a renewed spirit of national revival after 1772. It manifested itself in the thorough reform (including the abolition of the *liberum veto*) embodied in the May Constitution (1791) for the remaining independent part of Poland and in the heroic revolt (1794) led by KOSCIUSKO. By the Treaty of Tilsit (1807), Napoleon I created a Polish buffer state, the grand duchy of Warsaw, under King Frederick Augustus I of Saxony. After Napoleon's defeat, the Congress of Vienna (1814–15) established a nominally independent Polish kingdom ("Congress Poland"), in personal union with the czar of Russia. The western provinces of Poland were awarded to Prussia; GALICIA was given to Austria; and Kraków and its environs were made a separate republic. A Polish nationalist revival led to a general insurrection in 1830 (known as the November Revolution) in Russian Poland. The Poles were at first successful, but their army was defeated (1831) at Ostroleka, and the Russians reentered Warsaw. The Polish constitution was suspended, and the kingdom became virtually an integral part of Russia. Thousands of Poles emigrated, notably to Paris, which became the center of Polish nationalist activities. In 1846 an insurrection in Galicia by the peasantry against the gentry led to the annexation of Kraków by Austria. Rebellions broke out in 1848 in Prussian and Austrian Poland, and in 1863 the Poles in Russian Poland rose in the so-called January Revolution. After crushing the revolt, the Russians began an intensive program of russification. At the same time industry (especially the manufacture of textiles and iron goods) was developed and large estates were divided and given in freehold to peasants. A similar policy of germanization in Prussian Poland was linked with Bismarck's Kulturkampf (see ŁEDÓCHOWSKI, COUNT MIECZISŁAW). Only in Austrian Galicia did the Poles enjoy a considerable degree of autonomy, but there the economy was very weak.

The Restoration. In World War I the early efforts of the Polish nationalists were directed against Russia. Polish legions, led by Joseph PILSUDSKI, fought for two years alongside Germany and Austria. In Nov., 1916, Germany and Austria proclaimed Poland an independent kingdom, but Germany, which occupied the country, retained control over the Polish government. Pilsudski resigned and was imprisoned (July, 1917), and the independence movement from then on was centered at Paris. The defeat of the partitioning powers allowed Poland to regain its independence, which was proclaimed on Nov. 9, 1918. Pilsudski returned on Nov. 10 and was declared chief of state. The Treaty of Versailles (1919) gave Poland access to the Baltic Sea via the POLISH CORRIDOR and forced Germany to return Prussian Poland to Poland. Gdańsk became a free city and parts of Silesia were awarded to Poland as a result of plebiscites. The Polish-Russian border proposed at the Paris Peace Conference (and later named after Lord CURZON of Great Britain) would have awarded to Russia large parts of the former eastern provinces of Poland, inhabited mainly by Belorussians and Ukrainians. However, Poland insisted on its 1772 borders. War broke out between Poland and Russia, and in 1920 the Poles drove the Russians back from Warsaw. In the Treaty of Riga (1921), Poland secured parts of its claims. Poland also became involved in protracted disputes over VILNA with Lithuania and over TESCHEN with Czechoslovakia. About one third of newly created Poland was made up of ethnic Germans, Ukrainians, Belorussians, Jews, and Lithuanians, and these minorities were generally treated inequitably. A republican constitution was adopted in 1921. Financial and agrarian reforms were undertaken and industrialization progressed, but the condition of the peasantry remained generally poor, and the the landowning aristocracy retained most of its wealth. In 1926 a parliamentary government was suspended by a military coup d'etat that made Pilsudski virtual dictator. After his death (1935), Marshall Edward RYDZ-ŚMIGŁY assumed control, and under a new constitution (1935) parliament became a tool of the governing clique ("the colonels"). Foreign policy in the 1920s was based on alliances with France and Rumania; in the 1930s, under the guidance of Col. Josef Beck, Poland attempted to steer a course among the powers of Europe (especially Germany and the USSR) by following a pragmatic policy of balance. In the economic depression of the 1930s unemployment was widespread; also, anti-Semitism became increasingly virulent. In early 1939, after having secured guarantees against aggression from England and France, Poland rejected Germany's demand for Gdańsk. In Aug., 1939, the negotiations of England and France with the USSR for a military agreement fell through, partly because Poland would not agree to allow Soviet troops to march across Poland in case of a conflict with Germany. On Aug. 23, 1939, Germany and the USSR signed a nonaggression treaty, which included secret clauses providing for the partition of Poland between them. On Aug. 25, 1939, a treaty of alliance between Poland and England was concluded. On Sept. 1, 1939, Germany, having refused further negotiations, invaded Poland and thus precipitated World War II. German columns advanced with spectacular speed. On Sept. 17, Soviet troops invaded Poland from the east. Polish resistance was crushed, and the country was partitioned between Germany and the USSR, except for a central portion that was annexed by neither power but was placed under German rule. After the German attack (1941) on the USSR, all Poland passed under German rule.

World War II and the Communist Regime. Poland suffered tremendous losses in life and property in the war. The Nazi authorities eliminated a large part of the population by massacres and starvation and in extermination camps such as the one at OŚWIĘCIM (Auschwitz). About 6 million Poles were killed and 2.5 million were deported to Germany for forced labor. Polish Jews suffered the worst fate; all but about 100,000 of the prewar Jewish population of some 3,113,900 were exterminated. Despite German oppression, the Poles did not cease to fight for their independence. An underground resistance movement was organized, and a government in exile (led initially by General Władysław SIKORSKI and later by Stanislaus MIKOŁAJCZYK) was established first in France and then in London. Polish prisoners of war in the USSR were allowed to form a corps under Wladislaw Anders and fought with distinction with the Allies; other Polish units were organized in Great Britain and Canada. The German announcement (1943) that a mass grave of some 10,000 Polish officers, allegedly executed by the Soviets, had been discovered in the KATYN forest led to a break between the Polish government in exile and the Soviet Union. The rift was widened by Soviet demands for the Curzon line as the new Polish-Soviet border. When Soviet troops entered Poland, a provisional Polish government was established (July, 1944) under Soviet auspices at Lublin. A Polish uprising (Aug.-Oct., 1944) at Warsaw, organized by the resistance movement and controlled by the Polish government in exile in London, was crushed by the Germans while Soviet forces remained inactive outside Warsaw. The last German troops were expelled from Poland in early 1945. By an agreement at the Yalta Conference (Feb., 1945), Mikołajczyk joined the Lublin government, and this new government was subsequently recognized by Great Britain and the United States. The Polish-Soviet border was fixed by treaty slightly east of the Curzon line, and 15% of German reparation payments to the USSR was allotted to Poland. At the Potsdam Conference (July-Aug., 1945), the sections of Prussia east of the Oder and Neisse rivers, including Gdańsk and the southern part of East Prussia (altogether c.39,000 sq mi/101,010 sq km) were placed under Polish administration pending a general peace treaty. The expulsion of the German population from these territories was sanctioned. A unicameral parliament was established (1946) after a referendum. Legal opposition was limited almost entirely to Mikołajczyk's Peasant party, but nationalists, rightists, and some other opponents operated as underground forces. The government-controlled elections of 1947 gave the government bloc an overwhelming majority; Mikołajczyk resigned and fled abroad. Bolesław Beirut, a Pole who was a Communist and a citizen of the USSR, was elected president of Poland by the parliament. The sovietization of Poland was accelerated; in 1949, Soviet Marshall Konstantin ROKOSSOVSKY was made minister of defense and commander in chief of the Polish army. The constitution of 1952 made Poland a people's republic on the Soviet model. In 1949, Poland joined the Council for Mutual Economic Assistance (COMECON), and in 1955 it became a charter member of the WARSAW TREATY ORGANIZATION. Polish foreign policy became identical with that of the USSR. Relations with the Vatican were severed; the church became a chief target of government persecution, which included the arrest (1953) of the primate of Poland, Cardinal Wyszynski. Partly as a result of the more relaxed atmosphere following Stalin's death (1953), workers and students in Poznań rioted (late June, 1956) in a mass demonstration against Communist and Soviet control of Poland. Discontent soon became widespread, and the government was forced to reconsider its policies. In Oct., 1956, Władysław Gomułka, purged in 1949 from the Polish Communist party as a "rightist deviationist" and imprisoned from 1951 to early 1956, was elected leader of the Polish United Workers (Communist) Party (PZPR) and became the symbol of revolt against Moscow. Gomułka denounced the terror of the Stalinist period, ousted many Stalinists from the government and the party, relieved Rokossovsky of his posts, and freed Cardinal Wyszynski from detention. Collectivization of agriculture was halted, and the Poles were given far more freedom than under the previous regime. Relations with the church improved, and economic and cultural ties with the West were broadened. However, Poland retained close ties with the USSR. By the early 1960s Gomułka was tightening the party's hold on Poland; intellectual freedom was curbed, the church again was target of government polemics, and renewed attempts were made to have peasants join state groups. In Aug., 1968, Poland joined other East European countries and the USSR in invading Czechoslovakia. In early Dec., 1970, Poland and West Germany signed a treaty (ratified in 1972) that recognized the Oder-Neisse line as Poland's western boundary (recognized in 1950 by East Germany) and provided for normal diplomatic relations. Later in the same month, rapidly increasing food prices led to riots by workers in the Baltic ports of Gdańsk, Gdynia, and Szczecin. Gomułka was ousted and replaced by Edward Gierek, who sought, with some success, to ease the living conditions of the average citizen. Gierek also made cultural life freer and ended the anti-Semitic campaign begun by Gomułka in 1968. By the mid-1970s wages had been raised significantly and the standard of living was on the rise.

Government. The 1952 constitution vests legislative power in the unicameral Sejm, or parliament, whose members are elected to four-year terms. The Sejm appoints the council of ministers, which is the state's main executive and administrative body, and the council of state, which nominates high officials, passes on international agreements, and has judicial functions. In practice, power is controlled by the politburo of the Polish United Workers' Party, whose first secretary is the most powerful individual in the country. The politburo controls elections to the Sejm and decides on appointments of officials.

See Hans Roos, *A History of Modern Poland* (1966); Stefan Kieniewicz, *The Emancipation of the Polish Peasantry* (1970); Lucjan Blit, *The Origins of Polish Socialism* (1971); *The Cambridge History of Poland,* ed. by W. F. Reddaway and others (2 vol., 1941–50, repr. 1971); Norman Davies, *White Eagle, Red Star: The Polish-Soviet War, 1919–20* (1972); A. J. Groth, *People's Poland: Government and Politics* (1972); H. H. Kaplan, *The First Partition of Poland* (1962, repr. 1972); P. W. Knoll, *The Rise of the Polish Monarchy* (1972); Antony Polonsky, *Politics in Independent Poland, 1921–29* (1972); D. S. Lane and George Kolankiewicz, eds., *Social Groups in Polish Society* (1973); Adam Bromke and J. W. Strong, ed., *Gierek's Poland* (1973).

Poland, Partitions of. The basic causes leading to the three successive partitions (1772, 1793, 1795) that eliminated Poland from the map were the decay and the internal disunity of Poland and the emergence of its neighbors, Russia and Prussia, as leading European powers. The first partition was proposed when Frederick II of Prussia feared that Russia was about to take the Danubian principalities from Turkey and thus provoke an Austro-Russian war. Frederick proposed that Russia annex part of Poland in return for renouncing the Danubian principalities and that Prussia and Austria take parts of Poland to balance Russia's gain. This arrangement satisfied Catherine II of Russia, who had long contemplated such a partition. Maria Theresa of Austria, though opposing the scheme both on moral and political grounds, nevertheless partook in the spoils, which otherwise would have fallen entirely to Russia and Prussia. King STANISLAUS II of Poland was unable to resist his three neighbors. The partition of 1772 gave Pomerelia and Ermeland to Prussia, Latgale and Byelorussia E of the Dvina and Dnepr rivers to Russia, and Galicia to Austria. When in 1791 the remainder of Poland showed signs of regeneration, particularly in the adoption of a new constitution, a Russian army invaded Poland (1792). Prussia invaded the country in turn, and in 1793 a second partition—this time without Austrian participation—was arrived at. Only the central section of Poland was left independent, and that under Russian control. The national uprising under Thaddeus KOSCIUSKO (1794) and the conservative rulers' reaction to the French Revolution led to the final partition of 1795; all of Poland was divided among Russia, Prussia, and Austria. Russia, which also formally annexed COURLAND, received the major share of territory, but the capital, Warsaw, went to Prussia. At the Congress of Vienna (1814-15) Poland remained partitioned, although the boundaries were radically changed in favor of Russia. (For the provisions made at Vienna and for the Polish partition of 1939, see POLAND). See H. H. Kaplan, *The First Partition of Poland* (1962, repr. 1973); R. H. Lord, *The Second Partition of Poland* (1915, repr. 1969); G. J. Eversley, *The Partitions of Poland* (1915, repr. 1973).

Poland China swine, oldest breed of swine to have originated in the United States and one of the most popular. A number of strains have contributed to the development of this breed, notably the Irish Grazier and the Berkshire. Poland Chinas, among the largest of swine, are usually black; some have white spots on different parts of the body, particularly on the feet, nose, and tail.

polar bear, large white BEAR, *Thalarctos maritimus,* of the coasts of arctic North America. Polar bears usually live on drifting pack ice, but sometimes wander long distances inland. They are powerful swimmers and may cross 20 to 30 mi of water at a time. The polar bear's body is long and streamlined, with a long neck and small head. Adult males are 7 to 9½ ft (210-290 cm) long, stand 4 to 4½ ft (122-137 cm) at the shoulder, and weigh 700 to 1600 lbs (320-730 kg). Females are somewhat smaller. The extremely dense fur is yellowish white all over. Unlike other bears, polar bears have hairy soles, which help them grip the ice. They may attain a running speed of 25 mi (40 km) per hr on ice. Polar bears are omnivorous, but feed chiefly on marine animals such as seals and young walruses. Quite fearless, they will stalk any animal, including man. They take advantage of carcasses left by hunters, and in summer eat vegetation on the shore. Except for a brief courtship in summer, polar bears are solitary. Males and nonpregnant females are thought to wander all winter. A pregnant female makes a winter den in the snow; two tiny, helpless cubs are born in January and nursed in the den until March. They usually remain with the mother for about a year and a half, while learning to hunt. Polar bears have been extensively hunted, especially by Eskimos, for fur, flesh, and ivory, and they have declined greatly in numbers. Although extremely dangerous to humans, they do well in captivity. They are classified in the phylum CHORDATA, subphylum Vertebrata, class Mammalia, order Carnivora, family Ursidae.

polar exploration: see ANTARCTICA; ARCTIC REGIONS.

polar front, zone of transition between polar and tropical AIR MASSES. Its average position during the winter is at about 30° lat. and during the summer at about 60° lat. In the N Atlantic Ocean, for example, the polar front can often be traced as a continuous line extending over thousands of miles, usually toward the northeast from a point just off the coast of the United States at about 30°N. Most CYCLONES outside the tropics develop along the polar front from waves caused by the juxtaposition of cold air moving toward the equator and hot air moving toward the poles; the earth's rotation gives this air its cyclonic twist. See FRONT.

polarimeter: see POLARIZATION OF LIGHT.

Polaris (pōlâr'ĭs) or **North Star,** star nearest the north celestial pole (see EQUATORIAL COORDINATE SYSTEM). It is in the constellation URSA MINOR (Bayer designation Alpha Ursae Minoris) and marks the end of the handle of the Little Dipper. Polaris's location less than 1° from the pole (1975 position R.A. 2^h03^m, Dec. +89°07′) makes it a very important navigational star even though it is only of second magnitude; it always marks due north from an observer. Polaris can be located by following the line upward from the two stars (the Pointers) at the right end of the bowl of the Big Dipper or, if the Big Dipper is not visible, by following the line through the left side of the square in Pegasus through the end star in Cassiopeia. Because of the PRECESSION OF THE EQUINOXES, Polaris will not remain the polestar indefinitely; in 2300 B.C. the polestar was in the constellation Draco, and by A.D. 12,000 the star VEGA in the constellation Lyra will be the polestar.

polariscope: see POLARIZATION OF LIGHT.

polarization of light. Polarization is a phenomenon peculiar to transverse waves, i.e., waves that vibrate in a direction perpendicular to their direction of propagation. Light is a transverse electromagnetic wave (see ELECTROMAGNETIC RADIATION). Thus a light wave traveling forward can vibrate up and down (in the vertical plane), from side to side (in the horizontal plane), or in an intermediate direction. Ordinarily a ray of light consists of a mixture of waves vibrating in all the directions perpendicular to its line of propagation. If for some reason the vibration remains constant in direction, the light is said to be polarized. It is found, for example, that reflected light is always polarized to some extent. Light can also be polarized by double REFRACTION. Any transparent substance has the property of refracting or bending a ray of light that enters it from outside. Certain crystals, however, such as calcite (Iceland spar), have the property of refracting unpolarized incident light in two different directions, thus splitting an incident ray into two rays. It is found that the two refracted rays (the ordinary ray and the extraordinary ray) are both polarized and that their directions of polarization are perpendicular to each other. This occurs because the speed of the light in the crystal—hence the angle at which the light is refracted—varies with the direction of polarization. Unpolarized incident light can be regarded as a mixture of two different polarization states separated into two components by the crystal. (In most substances the speed of light is the same for all directions of polarization, and no separation occurs.) Unpolarized light can be converted into a single polarized beam by means of the NICOL PRISM, a device that separates incident light into two rays by double refraction; the unwanted ray is removed from the beam by reflection. Polarized light can also be produced by using a tourmaline crystal. Tourmaline (a double-refracting substance) removes one of the polarized rays by absorption. Another commonly used polarizer consists of a sheet of transparent material in which are embedded many tiny polarizing crystals. Any system by which light is polarized in a particular direction is transparent only to light polarized in that direction. Thus, when originally unpolarized light passes successively through two polarizers whose directions of polarization are mutually perpendicular the light is completely blocked; light transmitted by the first polarizer is polarized and is stopped by the second. If the second polarizer is rotated so that the directions of polarization are no longer perpendicular, the amount of light transmitted gradually increases, becoming brightest when the polarizers are exactly aligned. This property is used in various light filter combinations. A number of substances can polarize light in other ways than in one plane, causing what are called circular polarization or elliptical polarization, for example. Organic substances that affect polarized light that passes through their solution are called optically active. In certain acids and other solutions the plane of polarized light is rotated to either the right or the left; their activity is usually indicated by the prefix *dextro-* or *d-* if the rotation is to the right and by *levo-*, *laevo-*, or *l-* if the rotation is to the left. The instrument used to determine in which direction this optical rotation occurs is called a polariscope. A very simple form consists essentially of two crystals of some polarizing substance such as tourmaline. The solution to be tested is placed between them. Light is then directed through the first crystal, or polarizer, and is plane-polarized. After passing through the solution its plane is rotated; the direction and the degree of rotation are indicated by the position in which the second crystal must be placed to permit passage of the light that has gone through the solution. The polarimeter is a polariscope that measures the amount of rotation; when used for sugar solutions it is commonly called a saccharimeter.

polarography (pō″lərŏg'rəfē), in chemistry, method for analyzing the composition of a dilute electrolytic SOLUTION (see ELECTROLYTE). Two electrodes are placed in the solution: One has a fixed potential (voltage) and is called the reference electrode, and the other has a variable potential and is called the polarizable electrode. As voltage is applied to the polarizable electrode, the resulting change in the current through the solution is monitored. By plotting the pairs of values for voltage and current, a series of current-voltage curves (polarograms) can be generated. The general name for this method is *voltametry*; the term *polarography* was formerly restricted to those cases where the polarizable electrode is a dropping mercury electrode, though now this distinction is often disregarded. Current-voltage curves, which look like a series of steps called polarographic waves, can be used to determine the reduction potentials of any reducible species present in the solution, e.g., inorganic ions or complex organic intermediates (see OXIDATION AND REDUCTION; ELECTROMOTIVE SERIES). Conversely, unknown substances can be identified by their characteristic reduction potentials. Quantitative TITRATIONS of an oxidizing agent by a reducing agent can be performed using a polarographic cell to determine the equivalence point by monitoring changes in the current.

Polaroid: see LAND PROCESS.

polar regions: see ARCTIC REGIONS; ANTARCTICA.

Poldhu (pôldyōō', pŏl'dyōō), village, Cornwall, SW England. Guglielmo Marconi sent the first transatlantic radio transmission (1901) from Poldhu to Newfoundland.

Pole, English noble family. The first member of importance was **William de la Pole,** d. 1366, a rich merchant who became the first mayor of Hull (1332) and a baron of the exchequer (1339). His oldest son, **Michael de la Pole,** 1st **earl of Suffolk,** 1330?-1389, fought in France in the Hundred Years War under Edward the Black Prince. He became the trusted adviser of RICHARD II, who made him chancellor (1383) and earl of Suffolk (1385). In the Parliament of 1386 his enemies forced his dismissal, and he was impeached and imprisoned. Richard soon released and reinstated him, but when the baronial opposition again demanded his arrest, De la Pole fled (1387) to France. "Appealed" of treason and sentenced to death in the Merciless Parliament of 1388, he died in exile. His grandson, **William de la Pole,** 4th **earl** and 1st **duke of Suffolk,** 1396-1450, played an active role in the later stages of the Hundred Years War and for a time held the chief command. He arranged the marriage (1445) of MARGARET OF ANJOU to HENRY VI and rose to a position of great political authority, reaching the peak of his power in 1448 when he was made duke. His persistent efforts to gain peace with France enabled his enemies to accuse him of treason, especially after disastrous losses in Normandy. His long record of service, his eloquent appeal to Parliament, and even the favor of the king could not save him from impeachment. When setting out for a five-year exile he was abducted from his ship and beheaded in a boat off Dover. His wife was the granddaughter of Geoffrey Chaucer. His son, **John de la Pole,** 2d **duke of Suffolk,** 1443-91, married Edward IV's sister Elizabeth and held offices under that king. He later supported Richard III, yet was favored by Henry VII. Of his sons, the eldest was **John de la Pole, earl of Lincoln,** 1464-87, who was recognized by Richard III as his heir presumptive. At first he appeared to accept Henry VII, but he soon joined the rebellion in favor of Lambert SIMNEL. He led an invading army from Ireland and was killed at the battle of Stoke. The second son, **Edmund de la Pole, earl of Suffolk,** 1472?-1513, agreed to the wish of Henry VII that he forego the ducal title in return for some of the property forfeited as a result of his brother's treason. Later he declared his ambition for the throne and tried to get help on the Continent. He was eventually delivered (1506) as a prisoner to Henry VII by the Burgundians. He was imprisoned for years and finally executed by Henry VIII. The fifth son, **Richard de la Pole,** d. 1525, took over Edmund's claim to the throne and received intermittent support from the French. He was killed in the battle of Pavia fighting for Francis I of France. He was the last of his line.

Pole, Reginald, 1500-1558, English churchman, archbishop of Canterbury (1556-58), cardinal of the Roman Catholic Church. He was a cousin of the Tudors, being the son of Sir Richard Pole and of Margaret, countess of Salisbury, who was the daughter of George, duke of Clarence, and the niece of kings Edward IV and Richard III. Although he did not take priestly orders until late in life, he was devout from the first and received many church benefices from Henry VIII. When his benefactor broke with the pope, Pole went abroad. In 1536 he made a formal statement of his views on the king's divorce, attacking the doctrine of royal supremacy. In the same year he accepted Pope Paul III's summons to sit on the commission to reform the pontifical administration and was created cardinal. In 1537 and again in 1538-39, Pole was active in trying to organize a league against Henry, who now was setting out to destroy the Pole family. However, Pole was unsuccessful in this endeavor, and he returned to Rome and received the legatine governorship of Viterbo. He was one of the legates appointed to open the Council of Trent (1545). In 1553, on Edward VI's death, Pope Julius III made him legate to England, and he and MARY I set about restoring the Roman Catholic Church. However, he ran afoul of Mary's husband, Philip II of Spain, and then of Pope Paul IV, and his difficulties were multiplied. He was always a mild man and would have nothing to do with the burning of heretics. In 1556 he was ordained priest and consecrated archbishop of Canterbury. He died the same day as Mary. See biography by Wilhelm Schenk (1950).

Pole, Richard de la: see POLE, family.

Pole, William de la: see POLE, family.

pole, in electricity and magnetism, point where electric or magnetic force appears to be concentrated. A single electric CHARGE located at a point is sometimes referred to as an electric monopole. An electric dipole consists of two equal and opposite charges separated by a distance. Some molecules, although electrically neutral as a whole, do not have their charges distributed symmetrically, so that the separation of the centers of positive and negative charge constitutes an electric dipole; such molecules are called polar molecules. In calculating the electric POTENTIAL at a distance *r* from an electric dipole, it is found that it varies principally as $1/r^2$, while the potential around a single charge varies as $1/r$. More complex arrangements of charges may have potentials whose principal term contains a higher power of the distance *r*. A charge configuration for which the principal term of the potential varies as $1/r^3$ is called an electric quadrupole; similarly, an octupole is characterized by a potential varying as $1/r^4$, a 16-pole by $1/r^5$, and so forth. In MAGNETISM, poles may be defined in an analogous way, so that an ordinary bar magnet with a north pole at one end and a south pole at the other constitutes a magnetic dipole. The potential energy associated with a given arrangement of magnets may be analyzed similarly to that of an array of charges. The analogy is not complete, however, since most authorities agree that magnetism is ultimately due to the motions of electric charges; this explains why no magnetic monopoles have yet been found in nature, although some scientists believe their existence possible.

pole, magnetic: see MAGNETIC POLE.

polecat, carnivorous mammal of the WEASEL family. The name refers especially to the common Old World polecat, *Mustela putorius*, found in wooded areas of N Eurasia and N Africa. Similar to weasels, but larger and with longer fur, polecats grow to nearly 2 ft (60 cm) long, including the 6-in. (15-cm) tail. The fur, sold under the name fitch and much used in the early 19th cent., is dark brown above, with yellow patches on the ears and face. The belly, feet, and tail are nearly black. Like other members of its family, polecats have a scent gland under the tail which emits a fetid secretion used for territorial marking; the gland is most active when the animals are alarmed. Solitary, nocturnal animals, they spend the day in dens. They feed on small animals and eggs and are quite destructive to poultry and small game. Farmers have exterminated polecats in many areas, but they still survive in wilder places over most of their former range. Domesticated strains of polecat have been developed for hunting; these are called FERRET, a name also applied to a wild polecat species of North America. The marbled polecat and striped polecat (see ZORILLA) are related animals of Africa and W Asia. The SKUNK, a New World member of the weasel family, is called polecat in some regions. Polecats are classified in the phylum CHORDATA, subphylum Vertebrata, class Mammalia, order Carnivora, family Mustelidae.

polemonium: see PHLOX.

Polestar: see POLARIS.

Polesye, lowland, USSR: see PRIPYAT.

pole vaulting: see TRACK AND FIELD ATHLETICS.

Polhem, Christopher (po͝ol'hĕm), 1661-1751, Swedish inventor and industrialist. After studying engineering techniques used in Germany, the Netherlands, France, and England, Polhem set up a mechanical laboratory that gave considerable impetus to Swedish technology. He constructed water-powered machines such as rollers and shearing machines employed in the fabrication of metal products. In gratitude for his services the Swedish government ennobled him in 1716.

police, public and private agents concerned with the enforcement of law, order, and public protection. In modern cities their duties cover a wide range of activities, from criminal investigation and apprehension to crime prevention, traffic regulation, and maintenance of records. In many countries they also have a political function (see SECRET POLICE). The foundations of the present English metropolitan police system were formulated in 1829 by Sir Robert PEEL. In that year also SCOTLAND YARD was reorganized. On the North American frontier, before the government was well organized, vigilance committees (see VIGILANTES) functioned as volunteer police. The TEXAS RANGERS and the ROYAL CANADIAN MOUNTED POLICE are examples of organizations that function especially in large, sparsely populated areas. The colonies maintained constables, and this office survives in the rural sheriff. Regular police forces appeared in many states after the establishment (1844) of the New York City organization. Administration of the police system varies in different countries. In Europe, especially on the Continent, it tends to be centralized. In the United States there is decentralization: Metropolitan police have the widest functions, and state police are chiefly concerned with traffic control and rural protection. Police agents of the Federal government include members of the Federal Bureau of Investigation, agents of the Treasury Dept. (including the members of the Secret Service, who guard the President and certain other public figures), and agents of the Justice Dept. The fight against crime on the international level is coordinated by the International Criminal Police Commission. See Bruce Smith, *Police Systems of the United States* (1960); James Cramer, *The World's Police* (1964); D. J. Bordue, ed., *The Police* (1967); Harlan Hahn, ed., *Police in Urban Society* (1971); H. K. Becker, *Police Systems of Europe* (1973).

police court, court with jurisdiction limited to minor offenses, chiefly the least grave MISDEMEANORS and breaches of municipal ordinances. In practice the trial is usually held before a judge sitting without a jury. A police court may also examine persons accused of FELONY and commit them to jail pending INDICTMENT and trial or release them on reasonable BAIL. Magistrate's court, justice's court, and municipal court are other names for the police court.

police dog: see GERMAN SHEPHERD.

police power, in law, right of a government to make laws necessary for the health, morals, and welfare of the populace. The term has greatest currency in the United States, where it has been defined by the Supreme Court as the power of the states to enact laws of that type even though they may contravene the literal terms of the Constitution. The doctrine was first stated by Chief Justice John Marshall, who ruled that the power of Congress over interstate commerce (Article 1, Section 8) could not prevent the states from controlling goods shipped from another state after they had been broken out of the original package. The concept of police power became very important after the passage (1868) of the FOURTEENTH AMENDMENT; on the one hand, the states had to be restrained from taking liberty or property without due process of law; on the other hand, the states could not be made helpless in dealing with grave problems of an economic and social nature. Gradually the court moved away from its initial strict interpretation of the Fourteenth Amendment, during which time it had struck down economic regulations such as minimum wages and maximum hours as a violation of the amendment's due process clause. Since the late 1930s, however, the court has upheld almost all state economic regulation as falling within the police power.

Polignac, Jules Armand, prince de (zhül ärmäN' prăNs də pôlēnyäk'), 1780-1847, French statesman. Belonging to one of the oldest families of France, he emigrated with them during the French Revolution. Under Napoleon I he was imprisoned (1804-14) for his part in the conspiracy of Georges CADOUDAL. In 1815, Louis XVIII named him a peer of France. He served as ambassador to England from 1823 to 1829. A champion and leader of the ultraroyalists in the reigns of LOUIS XVIII and CHARLES X, Polignac was strongly clerical, even refusing to take the oath to the constitutional charter on religious grounds. He became minister of foreign affairs and premier in Aug., 1829, and by his reactionary measures precipitated the JULY REVOLUTION of 1830. In March, 1830, a majority of the chamber of deputies demanded the dismissal of the Polignac ministry. Instead, the chamber was dissolved, and when the new elections again resulted in a liberal majority, Polignac issued (July 26, 1830) the July Ordinances, which dissolved the new chamber even before it met, established a new electoral law, and ended the freedom of the press. The revolution broke out immediately. Polignac was arrested and condemned by the chamber of peers to life imprisonment. Amnestied in 1836, he was banished and went to England. He returned in 1845. He wrote *Considérations politiques* (1832, tr. 1832), *Études historiques, politiques et morales* (1845), and *Réponse à mes adversaires* (1845).

Polignac, Melchior de (mĕlkyôr'), 1661-1742, French diplomat, churchman, and author, cardinal of the Roman Catholic Church. As ambassador to Poland he directed (1697) the unsuccessful candidacy of François Louis de Conti for the Polish crown. He was one of the negotiators of the Peace of Utrecht (1713-14). After being in disgrace during the regency of Philippe II d'Orléans, he served as ambassador to the Holy See. His *Anti-Lucretius* (1745, in Latin; tr. 1757) is a philosophical poem attacking materialism from the Cartesian viewpoint.

Polignac, Yolande Martine Gabrielle de Polastron, duchesse de (yôläNd' märtēn' gäbrēĕl' də pôlästôN' düshĕs' də), c.1749-1793, favorite of Queen Marie Antoinette of France. Her husband, Jules, comte de Polignac, was created duke and acquired a huge fortune through her favor with the queen. Fearing the hatred of the revolutionaries, she emigrated in 1789 and died in Vienna. She was the mother of Jules Armand de Polignac.

Poling, Daniel Alfred (pō'lĭng), 1884-1968, American clergyman, editor, author, and political figure, b. Portland, Oregon. He was pastor of the Marble Collegiate Church, New York City (1923-29), and of the Baptist Temple, Philadelphia (1936-48). In 1948 he assumed direction of the Chapel of the Four Chaplains in Philadelphia, a memorial to the four chaplains, one of whom was Poling's son, who died on the torpedoed transport ship *Dorchester* in 1943. He was twice defeated as a political candidate: for governor of Ohio on the Prohibition party ticket in 1912 and for the mayoralty of Philadelphia in 1951. As editor of the *Christian Herald* and *Christian Endeavor World* from 1925 to 1965, Poling stated his support of religious orthodoxy and opposition to Communism and pacifism. He edited *A Treasury of Best-loved Hymns* (1942) and *A Treasury of Great Sermons* (1944). Among his most notable writings are *Learn to Live* (1923), *The Heretic* (1928), *Youth and Life* (1929), *A Preacher Looks at War* (1943), *Jesus Says to You* (1961), and *He Came from Galilee* (rev. ed. 1965). See his autobiography, *Mine Eyes Have Seen* (1959).

poliomyelitis (pō"lēōmī"əlī'tĭs) or **infantile paralysis,** acute viral infection, mainly of children but also affecting older persons. There are three immunologic types of poliomyelitis virus; exposure to one type produces immunity only to that type, so that infection with the other types is still possible. Poliomyelitis is both endemic and epidemic in all parts of the world. Spread of the infection is primarily by contact with an infected person. Most people who contract polio either exhibit no symptoms or experience only minor illness; however, such individuals can harbor the virus and spread it to others. The virus enters the body by way of the mouth, invades the bloodstream, and may be carried to the central nervous system, where it causes lesions of the gray matter of the spinal cord and brain. The illness begins with fever, headache, stiff neck and back, and muscle pain and tenderness. If there is involvement of the central nervous system, paralysis ensues. Of those patients who develop paralytic poliomyelitis, about 25 percent sustain severe permanent disability, another 25 percent have mild disabilities, and 50 percent recover with no residual paralysis. The disease is usually fatal if the nerve cells in the brain are attacked (called bulbar poliomyelitis), causing paralysis of essential muscles, such as those controlling swallowing, heartbeat, and respiration. There is no specific drug for treatment. The incidence of poliomyelitis began to decline radically in the United States when a mass immunization program with the Salk vaccine was begun in 1955. By 1961 the Sabin vaccine, a preparation made from living organisms (one for each of the three polio viruses) and taken orally, was released for use in the United States.

Polish Corridor, strip of German territory awarded to newly independent Poland by the Treaty of Versailles in 1919. The strip, 20 to 70 mi (32-112 km) wide, gave Poland access to the Baltic Sea. It contained the lower course of the Vistula, except the area constituting the Free City of Danzig (see

GDANSK) and the towns of Toruń, Grudziąz, and Bydogoszcz. Gdynia was developed as Poland's chief port and came to rival the port of Danzig. Free German transit was permitted across the corridor, which separated East Prussia from the rest of Germany. Although the territory had once formed part of Polish POMERANIA, a large minority of the population was German-speaking. The arrangement caused chronic friction between Poland and Germany. In March, 1939, Germany demanded the cession of Danzig and the creation of an extraterritorial German corridor across the Polish Corridor. Poland rejected these demands and obtained a French and British guarantee against aggression. On Sept. 1, 1939, the Polish-German crisis culminated in the German invasion of Poland and World War II.

polishes, substances applied to surfaces to produce smoothness and gloss. Smoothness is achieved by using an ABRASIVE to wear away irregularities on a surface or by applying a coat of some substance to fill scratches and irregularities. Among the abrasives most commonly employed are natural and synthetic materials, including emery, sandpaper, steel wool, pumice, diatomaceous earth, alumina, powdered feldspar, the carbides of tungsten and boron, and rottenstone. Diamond, the hardest substance known, can be polished only by using diamond dust suspended in oil. Various chemical compounds that may contain relatively soft abrasives are prepared as polishes for such soft metals as silver, copper, and brass. Metal and glass surfaces requiring a high polish are often rubbed with jeweler's rouge (finely divided iron oxide); cerium oxide is used in polishing optical mirrors and lenses. Finished surfaces cannot be treated with abrasives since these will scratch and eventually remove the paint, enamel, varnish, or other material. Polishes for finished surfaces and leathers fill in irregularities of the surface and leave a level film of wax over it which can be made smooth and lustrous by rubbing.

Polish language, member of the West Slavic group of the Slavic subfamily of the Indo-European family of languages (see SLAVIC LANGUAGES). Polish is spoken as a first language by about 33 million people in Poland, where it is the official language; by more than 3 million in the United States; and by more than 1 million elsewhere. The Polish language is written in the Roman alphabet augmented by the use of diacritical marks. It is extremely rich phonetically, having 10 vowels and 35 consonants. In pronunciation the stress is normally placed on the penultimate syllable of a word. A distinctive feature is the preservation in spoken Polish of the nasal vowels ą and ę, which are no longer found in the other modern Slavic tongues. As in Czech, the nouns, pronouns, and adjectives have seven cases (nominative, genitive, dative, accusative, vocative, instrumental, and locative). The verb is inflected to indicate gender as well as person and number, and can do so without the use of the personal pronoun. There are three genders (masculine, feminine, and neuter) and two numbers (singular and plural). A large number of diminutive and augmentative forms is also characteristic. The vocabulary of Polish is basically Slavic, but it has been enriched by borrowings from German in the Middle Ages, from Italian during the Renaissance, from French in the 17th and 18th cent., and also from English, White Russian, and Ukrainian. The earliest surviving manuscripts containing Polish words are some 12th-century Latin texts containing Polish proper names; there are no extant Polish writings of substantial length from before the 14th cent. Modern Polish came into use in the 16th cent., developing as the sophisticated and expressive language of a great literature (see POLISH LITERATURE). See A. M. Schenker, *Beginning Polish* (2 vol., 1966–67); S. S. Birkenmayer, *Introduction to the Polish Language* (2d ed. 1967).

Polish literature. Poland has had an exceptionally rich literary heritage. The early literature of Poland was written in Latin; its chief figures included the historians Martin Gallus (12th cent.) and Jan Dlugosz (1415–80), the astronomer COPERNICUS, and the poet Klemens Janitius (1516–43). The first book printed in Poland was issued in Wrocław in 1475. The 16th cent., under the impact of humanism, religious reform, and the increasing sophistication of the gentry, became the golden age of Polish literature. In this era were produced the works of Mikolaj Rej (1505–69), considered the father of Polish literature; the great poet Jan KOCHANOWSKI; the humanitarian Andrzej Frycz Modrzewski (1503–72); and Piotr Skarga (1536–1612), a spokesman for the Catholic Reformation. Other major writers of the period were the historian Martin BIELSKI and the political writer Stanislaus Orzechowski (1513–66). Political and cultural life was static in the 17th cent., but from the mid-18th cent. there was a revival of classicism and a new flowering of the arts. Influenced by the French Enlightenment, Ignacy KRASICKI wrote satire and fables, modern Polish journalism was born, and light drama flourished under the playwrights Wojciech Bogusławski (1757–1829) and Franciszek Zablocki (1754–1821). A versatile disciple of Voltaire, Julian NIEMCEWICZ, bridged the classical and romantic periods in Polish literature. Contiguous with revolutionary and reform movements, the romantic era was one of extraordinary productivity. Themes of nationalism and freedom predominated, developed by the patriot poets Adam MICKIEWICZ, Juliusz SŁOWACKI, and Zygmunt KRASIŃSKI. Romantic novelists of note were Jozef Korzeniowski (1797–1863) and Henryk Rzewuski (1791–1866), and the major dramatist was Alexander FREDRO (1793–1876). In the 19th cent. much Polish literature was written by emigrés in Paris and other European centers; these included the poet Cyprjan Norwid (1821–83). Positivism, stimulated by the revolutionary fiasco of 1863, became a major movement to gain national strength through literary attacks on ignorance and reaction. A notable representative of this school was Bolesław PRUS. The colorful historical novels of the Nobel laureate Henryk SIENKIEWICZ gained international popularity at this time. The last decade of the 19th cent. saw the appearance of the neoromantic school of Young Poland, influenced by French poetry and by Nietzsche. The poet and dramatist Stanisław WYSPIAŃSKI, the novelists and dramatists Stefan ŻEROMSKI and Stanisław PRZYBYSZEWSKI, and the novelist Władisław Stanisław REYMONT were the outstanding writers of this period. The regaining of Polish independence in 1919 after generations of partition inspired new literary activity. The Skamander group of urban poets set the tone; they called for an end to nationalist preoccupation and for experimental freedom. The group included Julian Tuwim and Kazimierz WIERZYŃSKI. Novelists of the new school included Marja DĄBROWSKA and Zofia Nalkowska (1885–1954); leading dramatists were Karol Hubert Rostworoski (1877–1938) and Jerzy Szaniawski. The German occupation in 1939 crushed Polish cultural life. Writers of note who wrote during the postwar years of the anguish of the period include Tadeusz Borowski (1922–51), Jerzy Putrament, and Leon Kruczkowski (1900–1962). The advent of the Communist regime brought themes of SOCIALIST REALISM to dominate Polish literature. Communist writers include the poet Constantine Galcyzynski (1906–53) and the novelists Aleksander Ścibor-Rylski and Kazimierz Brandys. In 1956 writers joined in the popular uprising against the Moscow-dominated regime, and subsequently some relaxation of literary strictures was felt. The thaw resulted in renewed contact with Western developments and a burgeoning of literary experimentation. Many novelists continued to explore themes related to the war experience and its aftermath; others wrote works of psychological and political realism, reflecting current European trends. Among the foremost postwar novelists are Wilhelm Mach, Leopold Buczkowski, Roman Bratny, Bohdan Czeszko, Julian Stryjkowski, Stanisław Dygat, Stanisław Lem, and Sławomir Mrożek, also well known for his plays and short stories. Postwar poetry in Poland deals principally with philosophical concerns. The chief poets of the era include Stanisław Jerzy Lec, Zbigniew Herbert, Tadeusz Różewicz, and Wislawa Szymborska. The works of Miron Białoszewsky, Jerzy Harasymowicz, and Stanisław Grochowiak are in a more lyrical vein. Principal essayists and critics include Tadeusz Breza, Artur Sandauer, Jan Kott, and Jan Błoński. See histories by Manfred Kridl (tr. 1967) and Czesław Miłosz (1969).

Polish Succession, War of the, 1733–35. On the death (1733) of Augustus II of Poland, STANISLAUS I sought to reascend the Polish throne. He was supported by his son-in-law, Louis XV of France. The rival candidate for the throne was the son of Augustus II, the elector of Saxony, who was supported by Holy Roman Emperor Charles VI and by Anna of Russia. Stanislaus was elected by a majority of the Polish nobles, but a minority proclaimed the elector of Saxony king of Poland as AUGUSTUS III. Stanislaus, being without troops, could not resist the Russian forces that intervened in his rival's behalf; after the fall (1734) of Danzig, he fled to France. The war continued to be fought along the Rhine and in Italy, with Spain and Sardinia joining France against the emperor. Spain sought to recover Naples and Sicily, which it had ceded to Austria at the Peace of Utrecht, and Sardinia sought to dislodge the Austrians from Lombardy. The allies were successful in Italy, where Spanish troops seized Sicily and Naples. The territories of the duke of Lorraine (the son-in-law of Charles VI, later Emperor FRANCIS I) were in the meantime occupied by the French. In 1735, by the preliminary Treaty of Vienna, peace was obtained through a general dynastic reshuffle. Stanislaus I renounced Poland, though he retained his royal title, and was compensated with the duchies of Lorraine and Bar, which were to pass to the French crown at his death. The dispossessed duke of Lorraine was promised the succession to the grand duchy of Tuscany after the death of its last Medici ruler (which occurred in 1737). Spain received Naples and Sicily and in exchange ceded to Austria its claims to the duchy of Parma. Austria retained Lombardy; in addition, the emperor received from France a guarantee of the Pragmatic Sanction. Sardinia neither gained nor lost anything. A final peace treaty was signed after lengthy negotiations in 1738.

politburo, the central policy-making and governing body of the Communist party of the Soviet Union and, with minor variations, of other Communist parties. It was first created on the eve of the Bolshevik revolution in Russia in 1917. Nominally elected by the central committee to direct the party between the committee's plenary sessions, the politburo, in reality, governs the country. Although the size of the politburo in the Soviet Union has varied, it has usually consisted of 11 to 12 full members and 6 to 9 alternate members. From 1952 until 1966 it was called the presidium.

Politian: see POLIZIANO, ANGELO.

political science, the study of GOVERNMENT and political processes, institutions, and behavior. Government and politics have been studied and commented on since the time of the ancient Greeks. However, it is only with the general systematization of the social sciences in the last 100 years that political science has emerged as a separate definable area of study. Political science is commonly divided into a number of subfields, the most prominent being political theory, national government, comparative government, international relations, and special areas shared with other social sciences such as sociology, psychology, and economics. In practice, these subfields overlap. Political theory encompasses the following related areas: the study of the history of political thought; the examination of questions of justice and morality in the context of the relationships between individuals, society, and government; and the formulation of conceptual approaches and models in order to understand more fully political and governmental processes. The study of national government focuses on the political system of the researcher's particular country, including the legal and constitutional arrangements and institutions; the interaction of various levels of government, other social and political groups, and the individual; and proposals for improving governmental structure and policy. Comparative government covers many of the same subjects but from the perspective of parallel political behavior in several countries, regions, or time periods. International relations deals both with the more traditional areas of study, such as international law, diplomacy, international organizations, and other forms of contact between nation states, and with the development of general, scientific models of international political systems. None of the political science subfields can be clearly separated. All of them, for example, deal with questions closely associated with political theory. Valuable and sophisticated discussions of almost all the areas of political science, including the areas now generally classified under such titles as political sociology, can be found throughout intellectual history as far back as Plato and Aristotle. Through the centuries, the questions of political science have been discussed in contexts varying with the changing perspectives of the time. During the Middle Ages, for example, the major concerns revolved around the problem of where the state stood in relation to man and his God. Karl Marx, on the other hand, viewed political questions in the context of society's economic structure. Modern political science stresses the importance of using political concepts and models that are subject to empirical validation and that may be employed in solving practical political problems. See G. H. Sabine, *A History of Political Theory* (3d ed. 1961); V. O. Key, *Politics, Parties, and Pressure Groups* (5th ed. 1964); David Easton, *A Systems Analysis of Political Life* (1965); Gabriel Almond and G. B. Powell, *Comparative Politics: A Developmental Approach* (1966); and John Rawls, *A Theory of Justice* (1971).

Poliziano, Angelo (än'jālō pōlētsēä'nō) or **Politian** (pōlĭsh'ən), 1454–94, Italian poet, philologist, and humanist. Of middle-class origin, he was given a classical education, completed under the patronage of Lorenzo de' Medici. He became Lorenzo's companion and was tutor to the young Medici. For Lorenzo he translated much of the *Iliad* into Latin, and he later taught classics at Lorenzo's school. A fine classical scholar, he was a leader, with Lorenzo, in the use of the Tuscan vernacular in poetry. His ideas had substantial influence on the major Florentine artists of his time, including Botticelli and Michelangelo. His verse, tranquil and beautiful, shows the growing emphasis on style and form. Among his poetic works are the charming *Stanze per la giostra,* which is classical in tone, celebrating the jousting prowess of Lorenzo's brother Giuliano, and *Orfeo* (1475, tr. 1929, 1931), one of the earliest plays in the Italian language. He also wrote many lyrics in both Latin and Italian.

Polk, James Knox (pōk), 1795–1849, 11th President of the United States (1845–49), b. Mecklenburg co., N.C. His family moved (1806) to the Duck River valley in Tennessee and there, after graduating from the Univ. of North Carolina (1818) and studying law under Felix Grundy, he began (1820) to practice law in Columbia. Polk served in the state legislature (1823–25) and in the U.S. House of Representatives (1825–39), where he was speaker for the years 1835–39. He was a leading Jacksonian Democrat. In 1839 he was elected governor of Tennessee, but he was defeated for reelection by the Whig candidate in 1841 and 1843. Polk had vice presidential ambitions, but Andrew Jackson, convinced that Martin Van Buren had committed political suicide by announcing his opposition to the annexation of Texas, urged Polk to consider the presidency. With the Van Buren and Lewis Cass factions deadlocked at the Democratic convention at Baltimore in 1844, George BANCROFT advanced Polk as a candidate behind whom both sections could unite, and the "dark horse" won the nomination. Polk campaigned on an expansionist platform and narrowly defeated Henry CLAY by carrying New York state, where the presidential candidacy of James G. Birney of the LIBERTY PARTY cut into Clay's vote. To the surprise of many, the new President proved to be his own man; he even ignored Jackson's wishes on several matters. Renouncing a second term for himself, he required the members of his cabinet, which included James BUCHANAN, Robert J. WALKER, William L. MARCY, and Bancroft, to devote all their energies to their offices, not to campaigning to succeed him. Polk announced that his administration would achieve "four great measures": reduction of the tariff; reestablishment of the independent treasury; settlement of the Oregon boundary dispute; and the acquisition of California. All were accomplished. The Walker Tariff, one of the lowest in U.S. history, was enacted in 1846, as was the bill restoring the INDEPENDENT TREASURY SYSTEM. Despite the aggressive Democratic slogan "54°40' or fight," the dispute with Great Britain over Oregon was peaceably resolved with the adoption of lat. 49°N (the 49th parallel) as Oregon's northern boundary. Relations with Mexico, on the other hand, reached a breaking point after the annexation of Texas. Polk had hoped to purchase California and to settle other difficulties with Mexico by negotiation. However, after the failure of the mission of John SLIDELL to Mexico, the President ordered the American advance to the Rio Grande that precipitated the MEXICAN WAR. As a result of the war, the United States acquired not only California but the entire Southwest. Few presidents have worked harder, and few have equaled Polk's record of attaining specific, stated aims. He labored so strenuously in fact that his health gave way, and he died a few months after leaving office. See *The Diary of James K. Polk* (ed. by M. M. Quaife, 4 vol., 1910; abr. in 1 vol. by Allan Nevins, 1952); his correspondence, ed. by Herbert Weaver and P. H. Bergeron (2 vol. 1969–72); biographies by C. G. Sellers, Jr. (2 vol., 1957–66) and C. A. McCoy (1960, repr. 1973).

Polk, Leonidas, 1806–64, American Protestant Episcopal bishop and Confederate general in the Civil War, b. Raleigh, N.C. He left the army to study for the ministry and was ordained in 1831. He served as missionary bishop of the Southwest (1838–41) and bishop of Louisiana (1841–61) and was the principal founder of the Univ. of the South, Sewanee, Tenn. (1857). In the Civil War he became a major general (June, 1861) in the Confederate army and was at first engaged in the defense of the Mississippi River. He commanded a corps at Shiloh (April, 1862), was promoted to lieutenant general shortly after fighting at Perryville (Oct.), and commanded the Confederate right at Murfreesboro (Dec., 1862–Jan., 1863). In the Chattanooga campaign Braxton Bragg accused him of dilatoriness at Chickamauga (Sept.) and had him relieved. Polk assumed command of the Army of Mississippi (Dec.) and fought in the Atlanta campaign until he was killed (June, 1864) at Pine Mountain, Ga. See biography by J. H. Parks (1962); Kathleen Elgin, *The Episcopalians* (1970).

Polk, Leonidas Lafayette, 1837–92, American agrarian leader, b. Anson co., N.C. After studying agriculture at Davidson College, he managed a plantation in North Carolina, served with the Confederate army in the Civil War, and then returned to farming. He led in the North Carolina Granger movement after 1872 and helped bring about many state reforms, including the creation (1877) of the North Carolina department of agriculture and the founding (1887) of what today is the North Carolina Agricultural and Technical State Univ. He became (1887) president of the National Farmers Alliance and played an important role in the formation (1891) of the Populist party. See biography by Stuart Noblin (1950).

polka, ballroom dance for couples in 2/4 time. Originated by Bohemian peasants about 1830 from steps of the schottische and other dances, the polka by 1835 reached the drawing rooms of Prague, from which it spread to the capitals of Europe. The modern polka is a mere remnant of a much livelier, more complicated dance based on five to ten intricate figures in which the partners tossed their feet in the air while executing turns in close embrace, toe-heel steps, and other movements. Related dances include the galop and the mazurka.

poll, technique for ascertaining the attitudes or opinions of the total, or some segment of the total, population on given questions, usually on political, economic, and social conditions. The history of polling in the United States goes back to 1824, when two newspapers, the Harrisburg *Pennsylvanian* and the Raleigh *Star,* organized "show votes" to determine the political preferences of voters prior to the presidential election of that year. In 1883 the Boston *Globe* attempted to speed up its reporting of election returns by sending reporters to poll various precincts. By the turn of the century many newspapers were conducting polls to determine political preferences. Later polls were conducted by magazines; the first among them were the *Farm Journal* (1912) and the *Literary Digest* (1916). Those early polls were generally local or regional rather than national and were confined to obtaining election preferences rather than opinions on political issues. During World War I, however, a poll as to whether or not the United States should enter the war was conducted. The methods used in the early polls made no claim to being scientific; polling was usually done by canvassers hired to go out and question people or by "straw ballots" in the newspapers, which readers were asked to fill out and mail in. A more scientific method of polling called sampling was developed in the mid-1930s. This method enables the polltaker to question a small percentage of the group whose opinions he wishes to ascertain and to analyze from their responses the opinions of the whole group. The superiority of this method over the old straw-ballot system was demonstrated in the 1936 presidential election when the *Literary Digest* poll, which based its predictions on the older technique, produced a staggeringly inaccurate forecast, while the poll of a newer group organized by George GALLUP predicted the result of the election correctly. By the 1940s the polls were concerned with social and economic questions as well as with political issues. An unusual failure of polling took place in 1948 when the polling organizations predicted the defeat of Harry S. Truman, who won. Sampling techniques have become increasingly sophisticated and include various types, which may be random, stratified, or purposive, or a combination of any of these. The information may be elicited by personal interview, telephone interview, or mail questionnaire, and the polling is completed only after the data has been tabulated and evaluated. Polling has been much used by politicians to determine the opinions of voters on significant issues. It has also been used to forecast patterns of voting. Besides playing an increasingly important role in national and local political campaigns, the technique of modern polling has developed into one of the more important tools in the methodology of contemporary social science, particularly in sociology. Commercial polltakers claim that they not only provide valuable information in such fields as market research and advertising but that they also aid the process of democratic government by making known the views of the people. Critics of polling question the validity of the claim that it provides a true picture of public opinion, and it has been suggested that the polls themselves may influence public opinion by creating a "bandwagon effect." Some of the pioneer commercial polling organizations were the *Fortune* survey (1936) conducted by Elmo Roper; the Crossley Poll (1936); and the Gallup Poll (1935). The Harris Survey, begun in 1956, together with the Gallup Poll, are the best known polling organizations. Nonprofit polling organizations include the Princeton Office of Public Opinion Research (1940), the National Opinion Research Center (1941), and the National Council of Public Polls (1968). Many other countries have polling organizations, and a number of international societies (e.g., The European Society for Public Opinion and Market Research) facilitate exchanges of information. See G. H. Gallup and S. F. Rae, *The Pulse of Democracy* (1940, repr. 1968); Leo Bogart, *Silent Politics* (1972); C. W. Roll, Jr., and A. H. Cantril, *Polls* (1972).

pollack: see COD.

Pollaiuolo (pōl-läyōō-ô'lō), family of Florentine artists. **Jacopo Pollaiuolo** was a noted 15th-century goldsmith. His son and pupil **Antonio Pollaiuolo,** 1429?–1498, goldsmith, sculptor, painter, and engraver, became head of one of the foremost Florentine workshops, with many pupils and assistants. He was a great draftsman and is said to have been the first artist to study anatomy by dissection. Many of Antonio's paintings were executed in collaboration with his brother Piero. Although greatly influenced by Castagno and Donatello, Antonio developed his own highly dynamic style. He displayed considerable skill in his delineation of anatomy and attained a mastery of figures in action by his energetic use of line. Highly regarded by the Medici, Antonio and his brother painted for them three canvases depicting the *Labors of Hercules* (lost). Small versions exist of *Hercules and the Hydra* (Uffizi); a painting and a bronze statuette of *Hercules and Antaeus* (both: Uffizi); and *Hercules and Deianira* (Yale Univ.). Other famous canvases are *Apollo and Daphne* and *The Martyrdom of St. Sebastian* (National Gall., London); the lively *Dancing Nudes* (Arcetri); and *Tobias and the Angel* (Turin). One of Antonio's rare signed engravings, *Ten Fighting Nudes,* is in the Uffizi. In 1484 he was summoned with his brother to Rome by Pope Innocent VIII and there executed the bronze tomb of Sixtus IV and the monument to Innocent VIII in St. Peter's. See study on Antonio Pollaiuolo by Maud Crutwell (1907); Charles Seymour, *Sculpture in Italy, 1400 to 1500* (1966). **Piero Pollaiuolo,** 1443–96, a painter, was associated with his brother. He is generally considered to be an inferior artist, judging by his independent works. They include the *Virtues* (Uffizi) and *Coronation of the Virgin* in the Church of Sant' Agostino in San Gimignano. Their nephew, **Simone del Pollaiuolo,** 1457–1508, Italian architect, worked chiefly in Florence. After a visit to Rome to study the remains of antiquity, he was nicknamed Il Cronaca [Ital.,=chronicle] because of the endless tales he told. His chief monument is the noble Strozzi Palace, which he finished after the death of Benedetto da Majano; Cronaca is responsible for the beautiful cornice and the interior courtyard. He also worked on the Great Hall of the Palazzo Vecchio (1495) and the Church of San Salvatore al Monte (1504), admired for its purity of design. He may have worked on the sacristy of Santo Spirito and the Palazzo Guadagni.

Pollard, Albert Frederick (pŏl'ərd), 1869–1948, English historian, educated at Oxford. He served (1893–1901) as one of the editors of the *Dictionary of National Biography.* He was professor at the Univ. of London from 1903 to 1931 and founder and director (1920–39) of the Institute of Historical Research. Pollard's historical contributions were largely in the field of Tudor constitutional history. His *Evolution of Parliament* (2d ed. 1926) traces the development of Parliament from a high court. In *Henry VIII* (new ed. 1951) and other works, he sought to show Henry's parliaments as largely free rather than manipulated and thus modify views of Henry as a heavy-handed despot. His other major works include studies of Thomas Cranmer (new ed. 1926) and Cardinal Wolsey (new ed. 1953).

Polled Shorthorn cattle: see SHORTHORN CATTLE.

pollen, minute grains, usually yellow in color but occasionally white, brown, red, or purple, borne in the anther sac at the tip of the slender filament of the stamen of a flowering plant or in the male (staminate) cone of a conifer. The pollen grain is actually the male GAMETOPHYTE generation of seed plants (see REPRODUCTION). Inside the anther, pollen mother cells divide by MEIOSIS to form pollen grains whose nuclei contain half the number of chromosomes characteristic of the parent plant. Each pollen grain contains two sperm nuclei and one tube nucleus. After successful POLLINATION, the pollen germinates on the surface of the stigma of the pistil and produces a tube that grows down through the style to an ovule inside the ovary at the base of the pistil. The sperm nuclei are then discharged into the ovule; one fuses with the egg nucleus (see FERTILIZATION) and the other fuses with the polar nuclei to form endosperm (food-storage tissue) that will nourish the developing embryo in the seed. This process is basically similar in the conifers, except that in conifers there is no double fertilization and there may be a season's lapse between pollination and fertilization (see CONE). Pollen grains, like sperms, are always produced in much greater quantities than are actually used, particularly by those plants that rely on the wind for pollination (e.g., grasses and conifers). Often clouds of dustlike pollen can be seen floating from wind-pollinated trees. Plants pollinated by insects and birds usually have sticky pollen and conspicuous flowers with colorful petals that often secrete perfume or nectar or both to attract the agents. Although pollen grains are microscopic in size and are thus visible to the human eye only in quantity, they are so diversified in appearance that plants are identifiable by their pollen alone, e.g., by pollen analysis. The waxy outer covering (which contains proteins and sugar—an additional attraction to pollen-gathering insects) is marked by characteristic patterns of ridges, spines, and knobs and is capable of expanding and contracting in the presence of moisture or dryness. Pollen grains are also remarkable for the length of the tubes some must produce: corn pollen tubes may grow 8 or 10 in. (20.3-25.4 cm) from the stigmas through the filamentous styles (commonly called "silk") to the ovaries. The life span of pollen may be less than two hours; its ability to produce the allergic reaction of HAY FEVER continues indefinitely.

pollination, transfer of POLLEN from the male reproductive organ (stamen or staminate cone) to the female reproductive organ (pistil or pistillate cone) of the same or of another flower or cone. Pollination is not to be confused with fertilization, which it may precede by some time—a full season in many conifers. The most common agents of pollination are flying insects (as in most flowering plants) and the wind (as in most trees and all grasses and conifers), but crawling and hopping insects, snails, bats, and hummingbirds may also serve. The devices that operate to ensure cross-pollination and prevent self-pollination (see SEX) are endlessly varied and sometimes extremely intricate. Among them are different maturation times for the pollen and eggs of the same flower or plant, separate staminate and pistillate flowers on the same or on different plants, chemical properties that make the pollen and eggs of the same plant sterile to each other, and specialized mechanisms or structural arrangements that prevent the pollinating agent from transferring the pollen of a flower to its own stigma. In the lady's-slipper the bee enters the nectar-filled pouch by one opening and must leave by another; in so doing it brushes first past the stigma, which scrapes pollen off its back, and then past the stamens, which deposit another load of pollen. The stamens of the mountain laurel are bent back and held like springs by notches in the petals; when the bee alights it contacts the tall pistil and then, in probing deeper for nectar, triggers the stamens. Pollen is catapulted onto the insect's underside, ready for contact with the next pistil. Other examples of floral adaptations to their pollinating agents are the FIG and its wasp and the YUCCA and its moth. Wind pollination, depending as it does on statistical chance for successful pollination, requires (and gets) vast quantities of pollen, which may be forcefully ejected by the anther sac (as in grasses and ragweed) or may be exposed (as in cones and catkins) to the slightest breeze. See BREEDING.

Pollio, Caius Asinius (kā'əs ăsĭn'ēəs pŏl'ēō, kī'əs), c.76 B.C.–A.D. c.5, Roman historian. He was a partisan of Julius Caesar and of Marc Antony, but his account (now lost) of the civil war was renowned for its impartiality and its scientific handling of evidence. He was a friend of Vergil and also wrote poetry and drama.

polliwog: see TADPOLE.

Pollock, Sir Frederick (pŏl'ək), 1845–1937, English jurist, b. London. He was educated at Eton and Cambridge and was admitted to the bar in 1871. He succeeded to his baronetcy in 1888. Pollock was (1883-1903) professor of jurisprudence at Oxford. He devoted himself to legal study and writing; after 1914, however, he was judge of the admiralty court of the Cinque Ports. Some of his books, including *The Principles of Contract* (1876) and the *Law of Torts* (1887), have been frequently republished. Pollock was editor (1885-1919) of the *Law Quarterly Review*, a major British legal periodical, and editor in chief (1895-1935) of the *Law Reports*, the chief medium for publishing decisions of the British courts. He collaborated with F. W. Maitland on *The History of English Law* (1895), contributing the material on Anglo-Saxon law. He wrote monographs on Spinoza (1880, 1935); *Leading Cases Done into English* (1876), a parody of legal style; and his reminiscences, *For My Grandson* (1933). His correspondence with Oliver Wendell Holmes was published as *The Holmes-Pollock Letters* (1941). See studies by H. D. Hazeltine (1953) and C. H. Fifoot (1971).

Pollock, Jackson, 1912–56, American painter, b. Cody, Wyo. He studied (1929–31) in New York City, mainly under Thomas Hart Benton, but he was more strongly influenced by A. P. Ryder and by the Mexican muralists, especially Siqueiros. From 1938 to 1942, Pollock worked on the Federal Art Project in New York City. Affected by surrealism and also by Picasso, he moved toward a highly abstract art in order to express, rather than illustrate, feeling. His experimentations led to the development of his famous "drip" technique, in which he energetically drew or "dripped" complicated linear rhythms onto enormous canvases. He sometimes applied paint directly from the tube, and he also used aluminum paint to achieve a glittery effect. His vigorous attack on the canvas and his devotion to the very act of painting led to the term "action painting." Pollock had become a symbol of the new artistic revolt, ABSTRACT EXPRESSIONISM, when he was killed in an automobile accident. His paintings are in many public and private collections, including museums in New York City, San Francisco, Dallas, and Chicago. See biography by B. H. Friedman (1972); studies by Frank O'Hara (1959), Bryan Robertson (1966), and F. V. O'Connor (1967).

Pollock, Oliver, 1737–1823, American merchant, b. Ireland. He arrived in America at the age of 23 and became a successful merchant. After moving to New Orleans, Pollock speculated advantageously in land and in the slave trade and gained the confidence of the Spanish government. He contributed generously to the cause of the colonies in the American Revolution, obtained supplies from the Spanish, and helped finance George Rogers Clark's conquest of the Northwest. After the war the American government met its debts to him, but repayment was tardy and incomplete. See biography by J. A. James (1937, repr. 1970).

Pollonarrua or **Polonnaruwa** (both: pŏl"ənəro͞o'ə), ruined ancient city, NE Sri Lanka. Pollonarrua, beautifully situated on a lake, was once the most splendid city of Sri Lanka, or Ceylon. It became a royal residence in the mid-4th cent. and the capital of Ceylon after the fall (late 8th cent.) of ANURADHAPURA. The city reached its height under the rule of king Parakrama Bahu I (1164–97), the last notable monarch of the Singhalese dynasty. He embellished the capital with temples, stupas, and huge stone images of Buddha; among these is a famous colossal statue of the recumbent Buddha. Pollonarrua fell to the Hindu Tamils in the 13th cent. The name is also spelled Pollanarrua.

poll tax, a capital tax levied equally on every adult in the community. This practice can be traced back to the most ancient tax systems. Although no longer a significant source of revenue for any major country, the poll tax did provide large sums for many governments until well into the 1800s. The tax has long been attacked as being an unfair burden upon those less able to pay. The poll tax has a special history in the United States due to its connection, especially in various Southern states, with the right to vote. Poll taxes enacted in these states between 1889 and 1910 had the effect and, largely, the purpose of disenfranchising many blacks as well as poor whites, because payment of the tax was a prerequisite for voting. By the 1940s some of these taxes had been abolished, and in 1964 the 24th Amendment to the U.S. Constitution disallowed the poll tax as a prerequisite for voting in Federal elections. In 1966 this prohibition was extended to all elections by the Supreme Court, which ruled that such a tax violated the "equal protection" clause of the 14th Amendment to the Constitution. See F. D. Ogden, *The Poll Tax in the South* (1958).

pollution, contamination of the environment as a result of the activities of man. The term *pollution* refers primarily to the fouling of air, water, and land by wastes (see AIR POLLUTION; WATER POLLUTION; SOLID WASTE). In recent years it has come to signify a wider range of disruptions to environmental quality. Thus litter, billboards, and auto junkyards are said to constitute visual pollution; noise excessive enough to cause psychological or physical damage is considered NOISE POLLUTION; and waste heat that alters local climate or affects fish populations in rivers is designated thermal pollution. The 20th cent. has seen pollution approach crisis proportions in parts of the United States, Great Britain, continental Europe, the USSR, Japan, and other land areas. The Mediterranean, the Baltic, the North Sea, the Great Lakes, Lake Baykal, and various coastal waters and stretches of ocean are similarly threatened. At issue is the capacity of the BIOSPHERE to disperse, degrade, and assimilate man's wastes (see ECOLOGY). The biosphere is a closed ecological system with finite resources and is maintained in equilibrium by grand-scale recycling. Under natural conditions organic and certain inorganic materials in the biosphere are continually recycled by processes including PHOTOSYNTHESIS and RESPIRATION, nitrogen fixation and denitrification (see NITROGEN CYCLE), evaporation and precipitation, and diffusion by wind and water action. But the introduction of massive quantities of waste matter at any point in the biosystem may "overload" it, disrupting the natural recycling mechanisms. Early indications that the environment could not absorb limitless amounts of waste came with the Industrial Revolution. By the latter part of the 19th cent. many industrial areas were experiencing severe air pollution caused by the burning of coal to run mills and machinery. The quantities of fly ash, smoke, carbon and sulfur gases, and other wastes had become too great for local environments—like those of London and Pittsburgh—to disperse rapidly. Similarly, industrial effluents and sewage were polluting river systems. Not until after World War II, however, was pollution generally viewed as more than a nuisance that blackened buildings and sullied streams, i.e., as a pervasive threat to human health. By the 1960s the threat had become great enough, many believed, to challenge the integrity of the ecosystem and the survival of numerous organisms including man. Population explosion, industrial expansion, burgeoning truck and automobile use—these were producing wastes in such gigantic quantities that natural dispersing and recycling processes could not keep pace. Exacerbating the problem was the appearance of new substances that degraded with extreme slowness or not at all: plastics, synthetic fibers, detergents, synthetic fertilizers, synthetic organic pesticides such as DDT, synthetic industrial chemicals such as the polychlorinated biphenyls (PCB's), and the wastes from their manufacture. Thus waterways and dumps festered with disease-breeding garbage. Industrial wastes created corrosive smogs and, with municipal wastes, polluted inland and marine waters, including drinking supplies. Automobile emissions choked urban and suburban communities. Pesticides and PCB's poisoned fish and birds. These conditions, persisting into the 1970s as year by year waste output increased, evoked demand in many nations, and on the part of the United Nations, for worldwide pollution abatement. In the United States, under pressure from private citizens, environmental organizations, leaders in science and technology, and concerned public officials, Congress passed legislation aimed at restricting automobile emissions. A Federal Council on Environmental Quality and an Environmental Protection Agency were created. A "Clean Water Act" and a "Clean Air Act" were adopted to diminish industrial and municipal pollution. All citizens were given the right to sue any individual, corporation, or governmental agency to achieve compliance with abatement laws. State and local governments adopted various abatement statutes and procedures. However, the cost of substantially reducing industrial pollution is high; how to finance it without undue economic burden remains a question. Some experts hold that since population growth automatically increases waste production, pollution can best be combated by population control. Another view is that worldwide proliferation of industry and technology is the chief culprit, and therefore must be sharply curtailed if pollution is to be conquered. There is considerable agreement, nonetheless, on the need for revised technology to diminish industrial and automotive emissions, to produce degradable rather than nondegradable wastes, and to dispose of all wastes in ways less damaging to the environment—for example by returning sewage to the farm as fertilizer and by recycling glass and metal materials. Finally, improvement is required in techniques for preventing pollution by especially hazardous wastes. These include (1) nerve gas and biological weapons discarded by the military, (2) lead, mercury, beryllium, asbestos, and other metallic poisons released by industrial processes, and (3) radioactive wastes associated with the production of NUCLEAR ENERGY. See ENVIRONMENTALISM; LAND USE. See Henry Still, *The Dirty Animal* (1967); G. R. Stewart, *Not So Rich As You Think* (1968); Wesley Marx, *Man and his Environment: Waste* (1971); Barry Commoner, *Science and Survival* (1966) and *The Closing Circle* (1971); Laurent Hodges, *Environmental Pollution* (1973).

Pollux, Greek hero: see CASTOR AND POLLUX.

Pollux, Julius (pŏl'əks), fl. 170, Egyptian Greek lexicographer, b. Naucratis. He compiled a Greek lexicon for Emperor Commodus.

Pollux, brightest star in the constellation GEMINI; Bayer designation Beta Geminorum; 1970 position R.A. $7^h43.5^m$, Dec. +28°06′. An orange giant of SPECTRAL CLASS K0 III, it is the nearest giant star, lying at a distance of 35 light-years. Its apparent MAGNITUDE of 1.13 makes it one of the 20 brightest stars in the sky. Pollux is the brighter of the Twins, CASTOR being slightly dimmer.

pollyfish: see PARROTFISH.

Polo, Marco (mär'kō pō'lō), 1254?–1324?, Venetian traveler in China. His father, Niccolo Polo, and his uncle, Maffeo Polo, had made (1253–60) a trading expedition to Constantinople. A war blocked their return, and they journeyed eastward to reach Kublai Khan's eastern capital at Kaifeng in 1266. They returned to Venice in 1269, and in 1271 they left with Marco and two Roman Catholic missionaries for Kublai's court. The missionaries soon abandoned the party, which reached Cambuluc (modern Peking) in 1275. Marco Polo became a favorite of the khan, who employed him on business in central and N China and in the states of SE Asia, including India. For three years he apparently ruled a Chinese city (Yangchow). In 1292 the travelers, acting as escort for a wife of the khan of Persia, left Kublai's realm and were back in Venice in 1295. Marco Polo soon joined the Venetian forces fighting Genoa and was taken prisoner (1296). During his two-year captivity he dictated an account of his travels. The prologue of the work tells of Polo's life. The remainder of the book describes places he had visited and heard of and recounts the customs of the inhabitants. Polo made reference to much of Asia, including the Arab world, Persia, Japan, Sumatra, and the Andaman Islands, and to E Africa as far south as Zanzibar. He told of paper currency, asbestos, coal, and other phenomena virtually unknown in Europe. Polo was wonder-struck at Oriental splendors and was sometimes credulous of exaggerated accounts, but the book seems to be factual and has been of great value to historians. During the Renaissance it was the chief—almost the sole—Western source of information on the East, and until the late 19th cent. there was no other European material on many parts of central Asia. Of the annotated translations of his book the most useful is that by Sir Henry Yule (3d ed. 1903). See studies by M. S. Collis (1960), H. H. Hart (1967), and C. A. Burland (1970).

polo, indoor or outdoor ball and goal game played on horseback. Outdoor polo is played by two teams of four on a level grass field that measures 200 by 300 yd (182.88 by 274.32 m). Safety zones surround the playing field, and at either end goal posts stand 10 ft (3.05 m) high and 24 ft (7.32 m) apart. The outdoor ball, weighing about 4½ oz (.13 kg) and measuring not more than 3¼ in. (8.26 cm) in diameter, is made of wood, often willow root. The indoor field, usually composed of a tanbark surface and surrounded by embankments, is not standardized in dimensions, and sometimes the goal posts—10 ft (3.05 m) high and 8 ft (2.44 m) apart—are represented by stripes painted on the wall. Teams of three men play the indoor game, and the ball, measuring about 4½ in. (11.43 cm) in diameter and weighing about 6¼ oz (.18 kg), is made of inflated rubber. Whereas an outdoor match is made up of eight periods (called chukkers) of 7½ min each, the indoor match comprises four chukkers. Standard polo equipment includes a specially made brimmed helmet, a long, flexible-stemmed mallet some 4 ft (1.22 m) long, and the usual equestrian equipment. Play is directed toward hitting the ball through the opponents' goal. Substitution of players is permitted only in case of injury. Penalties—e.g., automatic goals, free shots on goal, and disqualification—are meted out by an umpire, also on horseback, for dangerous riding, carrying the ball, or illegal use of the mallet. The umpire starts each period and begins play after each goal by throwing the ball into a marked-off center court between the two lines of opposing players. Polo ponies, actually standard-size horses of no particular breed, are required to undergo a long, rigorous period of training in order to meet the bruising requirements of the game. Because a typical polo match involves so many high-speed collisions among the horses, each player must maintain a "string" of expensive ponies in order to change mounts several times during the course of a game. Thus, polo is by and large a rich man's sport. Some historians claim that polo originated in Persia, whence it spread to Turkey, India, and Tibet and, with some modifications, to China and Japan. According to this view, it was revived in India during the 19th cent., where it became popular with British army officers stationed there, and spread to other countries. Others contend that polo was first created (1862) by the British officers themselves who, after seeing Manipur tribesmen stage a horsemanship exhibition, decided to imitate the latter's feat of hitting a ball with a stick while galloping at full speed. Borrowing from their experience with soccer, the officers soon decided to choose teams and aim their shots at a goal, thus creating a crude form of polo. At any rate, the sport was introduced into England in 1869, and seven years later it was brought to America. After 1886, tournaments for the International Polo Challenge Cups were played from time to time between English and American teams. Other international matches are played between Argentinian and American and between Mexican and American teams. Polo players are ranked according to their playing ability on a scale from 1 to 10, depending on how many goals they are expected to score in a regular game. See R. K. McMaster, *Polo* (1954); John Board, *Polo* (1957).

polonaise (pŏl″ənāz', pō″-), Polish national dance, in moderate 3–4 time and of slow, stately movements. It evolved from peasant and court processions and ceremonies of the late 16th cent. and was later used by J. S. and W. F. Bach, Handel, Mozart, Beethoven, Schubert, and Liszt. Chopin, exiled from Poland, expressed his patriotic fervor in 13 polonaises.

polonium (pəlō'nēəm), radioactive chemical element; symbol Po; at. no. 84; mass no. of most stable isotope 209; m.p. 254°C; b.p. 962°C; sp. gr. about 9.4; valence +2 or +4. Polonium is an extremely rare element found in uranium ores (about 0.1 gram per ton). A product of radium decay, it is sometimes called radium F. In its physical and chemical properties it resembles tellurium (the element above it in group VIa of the PERIODIC TABLE) and bismuth. Polonium has 34 isotopes, more than any other element. All of these isotopes are radioactive. The most stable, polonium-209, has a half-life of about 103 years. Polonium-208 (half-life about 3 years) is the only other polonium isotope with a half-life over one year. Although these two isotopes can be prepared in small quantities in a particle accelerator, they are very expensive to produce. All other polonium isotopes are short-lived except polonium-210 (half-life about 138 days), which is the most commonly used isotope. It is prepared by bombarding bismuth with neutrons in a nuclear reactor. It is a highly radioactive material. A milligram of polonium-210 emits as much alpha radiation as about 5 grams of radium, and enough gamma radiation to cause a blue glow in the air around it. It can be used as a heat source, since most of the energy of the alpha radiation is absorbed as heat within the polonium and its container. Polonium has found use in small portable radiation sources and in the control of static electricity. However, it is an extremely toxic substance and must be handled with great care. Polonium was the first element to be discovered because of its radioactivity; it was discovered in pitchblende in 1898 by Marie CURIE and named for her native country, Poland.

Polonnaruwa: see POLLONARRUA.

Polotsk (pô'lətsk), city (1969 est. pop. 64,000), W European USSR, on the Western Dvina River at its confluence with the Polota. It is a large rail junction and agricultural trade center and has lumber mills, plants for processing food and flax, motor vehicle repair shops, and oil refineries. Manufactures include building materials, farm implements, metal goods, and glass filaments. One of Russia's oldest cities, Polotsk was the capital of a principality of the same name from the 10th to 13th cent., when it passed to Lithuania. Polotsk became self-governing in 1498. A flourishing center for trade, first with Scandinavia, Novgorod, and Pskov and then (13th-16th cent.) with Riga, Polotsk was transferred to Russia in 1772. The city retains the Cathedral of Sofia (1044-66) and the Cathedral of the Spaso-Evfrosina monastery (12th cent.).

Polovtsi: see CUMANS.

Poltava (pəltä'və), city (1970 pop. 220,000), capital of Poltava oblast, S European USSR, in the Ukraine, on the Kiev-Kharkov highway and on the Vorskla River, a tributary of the Dnepr. It is an industrial center and important rail junction in the rich black-earth agricultural region. The city has railroad shops, food-and tobacco-processing plants, and factories that produce machinery, railroad equipment, automobiles, tractors, building materials, footwear, leather goods, textiles, and wood products. One of the oldest Ukrainian cities, Poltava was the site of a Slavic settlement in the 8th and 9th cent. It became part of Lithuania in 1430. In the 17th cent., under Bohdan CHMIELNICKI, it was the chief town of a Ukrainian Cossack regiment. Poltava was a flourishing commercial center in the 18th and 19th cent., a principal focus of the Ukrainian literary and national movement, and, under Czar Nicholas I, a place of exile. Nearby lies the battlefield where Czar Peter I defeated Charles XII of Sweden and the hetman Mazeppa of Ukraine in 1709 (see NORTHERN WAR) during a battle that marked Russia's emergence as a major European power. Poltava was the home of the writer Nikolai Gogol, many of whose stories are set in the nearby village of Dikanka. The city is the location of the gravitational observatory of the Ukrainian Academy of Sciences.

poltergeist (pōl'tərgīst) [Ger., = knocking ghost], in SPIRITISM, certain phenomena, such as rapping, movement of furniture, and breaking of crockery, for which there is no apparent scientific explanation. Believers in spiritism interpret these phenomena, particularly common during séances, as evidence of the presence of supernatural spirits.

polyacrylics (pŏl″ēəkrĭl'ĭks), group of thermoplastics that are transparent and highly decorative (see PLASTIC). Polyacrylics, or acrylic plastics, are POLYMERS (and copolymers) of derivatives of acrylic acid, $H_2C{=}CH{-}COOH$. The best known acrylic plastic, sold under the trade names Plexiglas and Lucite, is polymethyl methacrylate. It takes a high polish, is clear and colorless, and is transparent to visible and ultraviolet light. Since it is a thermoplastic, it can be shaped while hot to form a number of objects, such as windshields for airplanes and transparent ornamental objects. Other esters of acrylic acid and methylacrylic acid similarly polymerize and copolymerize to transparent thermoplastics differing somewhat in hardness and in softening temperatures.

Polyaenus (pŏl″ē-ē'nəs), fl. c.153, Macedonian Greek writer. His *Stratagems*, anecdotes on the ruses of war, takes much from various ancient sources now lost.

polyandry: see MARRIAGE.

Polybius (pōlĭ'bēəs), 203? B.C.–c.120 B.C., Greek historian, b. Megalopolis. As one of the leaders of the ACHAEAN LEAGUE and a friend of PHILOPOEMEN, he was influential in Greek politics. Having advocated the neutral stand of the League in the war between Rome and Macedon, he was deported (167 B.C.) with a large number of Achaeans to Rome after the Roman victory over Macedon. He obtained the protection of Aemilius Paullus and of the SCIPIO family, and under their patronage he undertook several voyages, notably one to Achaea, where he sought to win favor for the Roman government. It was also under the Scipios' patronage that Polybius undertook his universal history, one of the great historical works of all time (see tr. by W. R. Paton in the Loeb Classical Library, 6 vol., 1954). Of the 40 books only the first five survive intact; of the rest there are generous fragments. It was Polybius' chief aim to trace for his contemporaries the causes of the sudden rise of Rome; his history covered the Mediterranean world from before 220 B.C. to 146 B.C. A historian of the school of Thucydides, Polybius spared no efforts in his research for detail, accuracy, and unbiased truth; he could not, however, avoid a measure of partiality. Although his style has been criticized for its superabundance of tedious details and its moralizing tone, his presentatation is nevertheless soberly analytical and devoid of rhetoric. Not content with setting forth the facts, Polybius stopped his narrative to insert general discussions on the purpose of history writing (which he considered, like Thucydides, a guide to political conduct), on the principles of the Roman state, and on other broad subjects. See studies by Kurt Von Fritz (1954)and F. W. Walbank (1973); F. W. Walbank, *A Historical Commentary on Polybius* (Vol. I, 1957; Vol. II, 1967).

polycarbonates, group of clear, thermoplastic POLYMERS used mainly as molding compounds (see PLASTIC). Polycarbonates are prepared by the reaction of an aromatic difunctional phenol with either phosgene or an aromatic or aliphatic carbonate. The commercially important polycarbonates use 2,2-bis(4-hydroxyphenol)-propane (bisphenol A) and diphenyl carbonate. Marketed under the trade name Lexan, this polymer is a clear plastic with a slight yellow discoloration. It has excellent electrical properties and a high impact strength.

Polycarp, Saint (pŏl'ĭkärp), A.D. c.70–A.D.156?, Greek bishop of Smyrna, Father of the Church. He was a disciple of St. John, who appointed him bishop. Thus he linked the apostles and such 2d-century Christian expositors as St. IRENAEUS. St. Polycarp was a close friend of St. IGNATIUS OF ANTIOCH. As a very old man, Polycarp went to Rome to discuss the problem of dating Easter; he died a martyr there. His one surviving work, the *Epistle to the Philippians*, has been the subject of controversy. Some scholars have maintained that the letter is really two—one written c.115, enclosing St. Ignatius' epistles, and the other written c.135 to warn the Philippians against the teachings of Marcion. He was in his time the mainstay of Christianity in Asia Minor. Feast: Jan. 26. See P. N. Harrison, *Polycarp's Two Epistles to the Philippians* (1936).

polychlorinated biphenyl or **PCB,** any of a group of organic compounds originally widely used in industrial processes but later found to be dangerous environmental pollutants. Polychlorinated biphenyl is a fat-soluble, water-insoluble hydrocarbon containing chlorine. It is extremely stable, withstanding temperatures of up to 1600°F (870°C), is fire-resistant, and has been used as a heat-transfer and insulating fluid in cooling systems and electrical equipment; it has also been used in sealants, rubber, paints, plastics, printing ink, and insecticides. The chemical has entered the environment largely as a pollutant from equipment leaks, the weathering of many materials that contain PCB, and through interaction with food products. In 1971 a leak in a cooling system at a chicken-feed plant resulted in PCB-contaminated eggs reaching the Washington, D.C., market. In another case it was found that cardboard food containers made from recycled paper contained the pollutant; the PCB was traced to printer's ink on the original paper. Research indicates that the chemical is toxic to a wide variety of animals, especially fish, and may also affect animal reproduction. As the result of a PCB leak in Japan in 1968 that contaminated rice oil, 1,000 people developed a skin disease, and babies showed signs of poisoning. In the 1970s the single U.S. manufacturer of PCB discontinued sales of the compound except where no other industrial substitutes were available, e.g., in electrical equipment.

Polycletus: see POLYKLEITOS.

Polyclitus: see POLYKLEITOS.

polyconic map projection: see MAP PROJECTION.

Polycrates (pōlĭk'rətēz), d. c.522 B.C., tyrant of Samos. By piratic raids and indiscriminate warfare he dominated the E Aegean, capturing the island of Rhenea (now Rinía) and defeating the Lesbians, who had gone to the aid of Miletus. His tyranny drove the philosopher Pythagoras from Samos. He sent (c.525) 40 ships manned by malcontents from Samos to aid the Persian king Cambyses against the Egyptians, but the crews revolted and, with Spartan aid, unsuccessfully warred against Polycrates. Oroetes, Persian satrap of Sardes, lured him to the mainland and crucified him. He did much to aid industry and art in Samos.

polycythemia (pŏl"ēsīthē'mēə), condition characterized by an increase in the production of red blood cells, or erythrocytes, in the blood. Primary polycythemia, also called erythremia, or polycythemia vera, is a chronic, progressive disease, most common in middle-aged men. It is characterized by overgrowth of the bone marrow, abnormally increased red blood cell production, and an enlarged spleen. Symptoms, which result from an increase in both blood viscosity and metabolic rate, include headache, inability to concentrate, and pain in the fingers and toes. There is a danger of blood clotting or hemorrhage (see THROMBOSIS). Primary polycythemia is treated by radiation, periodic removal of some blood, or chemotherapy with antimetabolite drugs, e.g., CYTOXAN. In secondary polycythemia, or erythrocytosis, the proliferation of red blood cells results from the body's attempt to compensate for other conditions, such as prolonged lack of oxygen at high altitudes or chronic lung or heart insufficiency. Certain tumors are also associated with increased red blood cell production. In secondary polycythemia the treatment is directed toward the underlying cause.

Polydeuces (pŏl"ĭdo͞o'sēz): see CASTOR AND POLLUX.

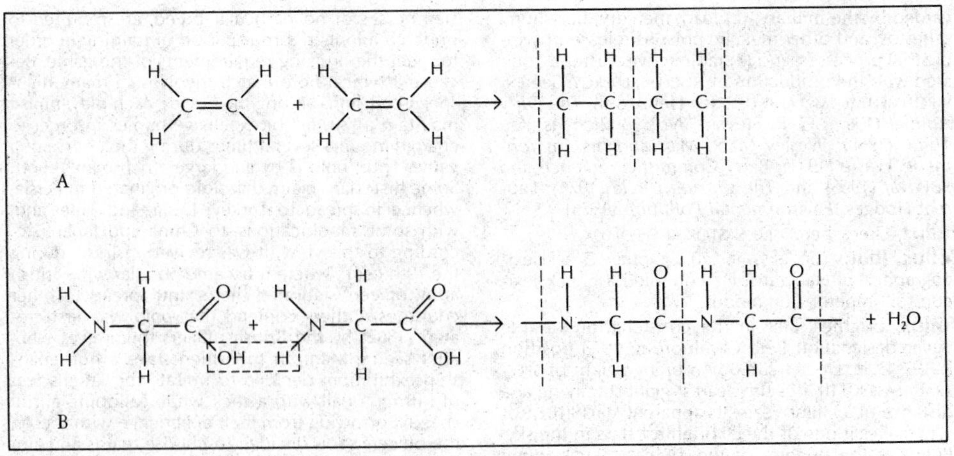

A. *Addition polymerization: Two ethylene molecules,* C_2H_4*, combine to form two links in the polyethylene chain molecule,* $(C_2H_4)_n$.
B. *Condensation polymerization: Two glycine molecules,* NH_2CH_2COOH*, combine to form two links in a polypeptide chain molecule,* $(NHCH_2CO)_n$*, with water being eliminated in the process.*

See POLYMER article, page 2185.

Polydorus, Greek sculptor: see LAOCOON.

Polydorus, in Greek legend: see HECUBA.

polyester, man-made fiber, produced by the polymerization of the product formed when an alcohol and organic acid react. The outstanding characteristic of polyesters is their ability to resist wrinkling and to spring back into shape when creased. In addition, polyesters have good dimensional stability, wash and dry easily and quickly, and have excellent wash-and-wear or minimum-care characteristics; one of their principal uses is in apparel fabrics of this kind. Polyesters are also used in casement curtains, throw rugs, and as a cushioning or insulating material.

polyethylene (pŏl"ēĕth'əlēn), widely used PLASTIC. It is a POLYMER of ETHYLENE, $CH_2{=}CH_2$, having the formula $(-CH_2-CH_2-)_n$, and is produced at high pressures and temperatures in the presence of any one of several CATALYSTS, depending on the desired properties for the finished product. Polyethylene is resistant to water, acids, alkalies, and most solvents. Its many applications include films or sheets for packaging, shower curtains, unbreakable bottles, pipes, pails, drinking glasses, and insulation for wire and cable.

polygamy: see MARRIAGE.

Polyglot Bible (pŏl'ēglŏt), Bible in which different versions, often in different languages, are given in parallel columns. They serve mainly as textual criticism. Origen's Hexapla was the most famous ancient example. Modern Polyglot Bibles include the Complutensian Polyglot, which contained the first printed Greek New Testament (prepared at Alcalá, Spain, 1514–17, under Cardinal Jiménez); the Antwerp Polyglot (1572); the Paris Polyglot (1645); and the London, or Walton's, Polyglot (1657), the most elaborate, containing, besides the usual Hebrew and Greek, the Samaritan Pentateuch and Syriac, Ethiopic, Arabic, and Persian versions of the New Testament.

Polygnotus (pŏl"ĭgnō'təs), fl. c.460 B.C.–447 B.C., Greek painter, b. Thasos. He later became an Athenian citizen. He painted the *Capture of Troy* and *Descent of Odysseus to Hades* in the Cnidian Lesche or clubhouse at Delphi and the *Fall of Troy* in the Painted Porch, Athens. He is credited with having developed a series of physical attitudes to express emotion that may be reflected in vase painting of the late 5th cent. None of his works have survived.

polygon, closed plane figure bounded by straight line segments as sides. A polygon is convex if any two points inside the polygon can be connected by a line segment that does not intersect any side. If a side is intersected, the polygon is called concave. In a regular polygon the sides are of equal length and meet at equal angles; all other polygons are not regular, although either their sides or their angles may be equal, as in the cases of the rhombus and the rectangle. The simplest regular polygons are the equilateral TRIANGLE, the SQUARE, the regular pentagon (of 5 sides), and the regular hexagon (of 6 sides). Although the Greeks had developed methods of constructing these four polygons using only a straightedge and compass, they were unable to do the same for the regular heptagon (of 7 sides). In the 19th cent. C. F. Gauss showed that a regular heptagon was impossible to construct in this way. He proved that a regular polygon is constructible with a straightedge and compass only when the number of sides p is a prime number (see NUMBER THEORY) of the form $p = 2^{2^n} + 1$ or a product of such primes. The first five regular polygons with a prime number of sides that can be constructed using a straightedge and compass have 3, 5, 17, 257, and 65,537 sides.

polyhedron (pŏl"ēhē'drən), closed solid bounded by plane faces; each face of a polyhedron is a POLYGON. A cube is a polyhedron bounded by six polygons (in this case squares) meeting at right angles. Although regular polygons are possible for any number of sides, there are only five possible regular polyhedrons, having congruent faces, each a regular polygon and meeting at equal angles. The five regular polyhedrons are also known as the Platonic solids, although they were known to the Greeks before the time of Plato. They are the tetrahedron, bounded by four equilateral triangles; the hexahedron, or CUBE, bounded by six squares; the octahedron, bounded by eight equilateral triangles; the dodecahedron, bounded by twelve regular pentagons; and the icosahedron, bounded by twenty equilateral triangles. The 18th-century Swiss mathematician Leonhard Euler showed that for any polyhedron the sum of the number of vertices V and the number of faces F is equal to the number of edges E plus 2, or $V+F=E+2$.

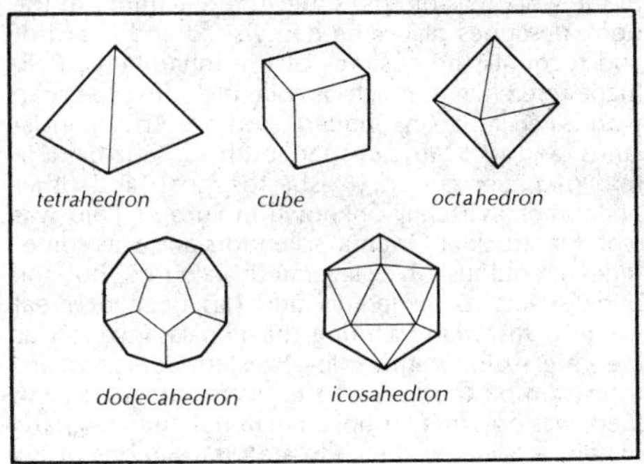

Polyhedrons

Polyhymnia (pŏl"ĭhĭm'nēə): see MUSES.

Polykleitos, Polycletus, or **Polyclitus** (pŏlĭklī'təs, -klē'-, -klī-), two Greek sculptors of the school of Argos. **Polykleitos,** the elder, fl. c.450–c.420 B.C., was a contemporary of Phidias. Born either in Sicyon or Argos, he became head of the Argive school. He worked principally in bronze and made a number of statues of athletes. His most famous statue embodied his ideal of physical perfection. This "canon of Polykleitos," which emphasized a counterbalance of tension and relaxation through shoulders and hips, known as chiastic balance, became the standard of proportions for sculptors. It is best known through a copy, the *Doryphorus* or *Spear-Bearer* (Naples). Other sculptures representing his athletic, muscular, square-headed type, preserved through copies, are the *Diadumenus* (National Mus., Athens), a man binding a fillet about his head, and an *Amazon.* Another of his works praised by ancient writers was a gold and ivory Hera for a temple at Argos; now known only from Pausanias' description and from representations on Roman coins. No recognized originals by Polykleitos exist today. **Polykleitos,** the younger, worked in the 4th cent. B.C. Although he was also a sculptor of athletes, his greatest fame was won as an architect. He designed the great theater at Epidaurus.

polymer (pŏl'əmər), chemical compound with high molecular weight consisting of a number of structural units linked together by covalent bonds (see CHEMICAL BOND). The simple molecules that may become structural units are themselves called monomers; two monomers combine to form a dimer, and three monomers, a trimer. A structural unit is a group having two or more bonding sites. A bonding site may be created by the loss of an atom or group, such as H or OH, or by the breaking up of a double or triple bond, as when ethylene, $H_2C{=}CH_2$, is converted into a structural unit for POLYETHYLENE, $—H_2C—CH_2—$. In a linear polymer, the structural units are connected in a chain arrangement and thus need only be bifunctional, i.e., have two bonding sites. When the structural unit is trifunctional (has three bonding sites), a nonlinear, or branched, polymer results. Ethylene, styrene, and ethylene glycol are examples of bifunctional monomers, while glycerin and divinyl benzene are both polyfunctional. Polymers containing a single repeating unit, such as polyethylene, are called homopolymers. Polymers containing two or more different structural units, such as phenol-formaldehyde, are called copolymers. All polymers can be classified as either addition polymers or condensation polymers. An addition polymer is one in which the molecular formula of the repeating structural unit is identical to that of the monomer, e.g., polyethylene and POLYSTYRENE. A condensation polymer is one in which the repeating structural unit contains fewer atoms than that of the monomer or monomers because of the splitting off of water or some other substance, e.g., polyesters and POLYCARBONATES. (See illustration, p. 2184.) Many polymers occur in nature, such as silk, CELLULOSE, natural RUBBER, and PROTEINS. In addition, a large number of polymers have been synthesized in the laboratory, leading to such commercially important products as plastics, synthetic fibers, and synthetic rubber. Polymerization, the chemical process of forming polymers from their component monomers, is often a complex process that may be initiated or sustained by heat, pressure, or the presence of one or more catalysts.

polymorphism, of minerals, property of crystallizing in two or more distinct forms. Calcium carbonate is dimorphous (two forms), crystallizing as calcite or aragonite. Titanium dioxide is trimorphous; its three forms are brookite, anatase (or octahedrite), and rutile. Polymorphism of an element is called ALLOTROPY. The process was discovered (1821) by Eilhard Mitscherlich. See ISOMORPHISM; MINERAL; CRYSTAL.

Polynesia (pŏlĭnē'zhə, -shə) [Gr.,=many islands], one of the three main divisions of Oceania, in the central and S Pacific Ocean. The larger islands are volcanic; the smaller ones are generally coral formations. The principal groups are the Hawaiian Islands, Samoa, Tonga, and the islands of French Polynesia. Ethnologically though not geographically, Polynesia embraces New Zealand. The languages of the area are Malayo-Polynesian. See Terence Barrow, *Art and Life in Polynesia* (1972).

Polynesian languages: see MALAYO-POLYNESIAN LANGUAGES.

Polynices (pŏl"ənī'sēz): see SEVEN AGAINST THEBES.

polynomial, mathematical expression containing terms of one or more variables that are connected by the operation of addition or its inverse, subtraction. No variable can appear as a divisor or have fractional exponents. In one unknown the general form of a polynomial is $a_0x^n+a_1x^{n-1}+a_2x^{n-2}+\ldots+a_{n-1}x+a_n$ where n is a positive integer and $a_0, a_1, a_2, \ldots, a_n$ are any numbers. An example of a polynomial in one variable is $11x^4-3x^3+7x^2+x-8$. The degree of a polynomial in one variable is the highest power of the variable; in the example given above, the degree is 4.

polyolefins (pŏl"ēōl'əfən), group of PLASTICS that are POLYMERS of various ALKENES, or olefins. The most important are POLYETHYLENE and POLYPROPYLENE.

polyp, in medicine, a benign tumor occurring in areas lined with mucous membrane such as the nose, gastrointestinal tract (especially the colon), and the uterus. Some polyps are pedunculated tumors, i.e., they grow on stems; others, attached by a broad base, are called sessile. Nasal polyps are usually associated with an allergic condition; since they interfere with breathing, it is advisable that they be removed. Uterine and gastrointestinal polyps are likely to cause bleeding, but, more important, they may undergo malignant degeneration and for this reason are also usually removed.

polyp and medusa, names for the two body forms, one nonmotile and one typically free swimming, found in the aquatic invertebrate phylum CNIDARIA (the coelenterates). Some animals of this group are always polyps, some are always medusae, and some exhibit both a polyp and a medusa stage in their life cycles. The polyp is a sessile, or nonmotile, organism; well-known solitary polyps are the SEA ANEMONE and the freshwater HYDRA. The medusa, when free swimming, is popularly known as a JELLYFISH. The two forms are similar in construction; both consist of a cylindrical body surrounding a digestive cavity, with a single opening, the mouth, at one end. The mouth is surrounded by tentacles, which are used to capture food and convey it to the mouth; these tentacles are armed with stinging cells which paralyze the prey. The body wall is composed of three layers of tissue. Thin layers called endoderm and ectoderm line the outside and inside, respectively; between these is a layer of jellylike material, called mesoglea, of varying thickness. The polyp, also called the hydroid, tends to be elongated, with a thin body wall; it is attached to the ocean bottom or other surface by the end opposite the mouth, its tentacles pointing upward. The medusa tends to be rounded, with a thick body wall containing much mesoglea; it swims or is carried in the current with the mouth side down and the tentacles dangling. In organisms which exhibit both forms, such as members of the cosmopolitan genus *Obelia,* the polyp is the asexual stage and the medusa the sexual stage. In such organisms the polyp, by budding, gives rise to medusae, which either detach themselves and swim away or remain permanently attached to the polyp. The medusae then produce new polyps by sexual reproduction. A medusa produces eggs or sperm, which are usually shed into the water; when an egg is fertilized, it develops into a swimming larva, which eventually settles and grows into a polyp. In addition to this elaborate means of reproduction, the polyp can form new polyps by budding. In some groups of coelenterates either the polyp or the medusa has become highly developed, with the reduction or complete loss of the other form. Where only the medusa occurs, as in many jellyfish, the larva never settles, and grows directly into a medusa. Where only the polyp exists, as in the hydra and the sea anemone, the organism has the ability to produce new polyps sexually, as well as by budding. In many species the polyp, or hydroid, stage is colonial: as new polyps are created by budding, they remain attached to a branching common stalk, often hardened with nonliving material, forming a plantlike structure called a hydroid colony. The branching, hydroid colonies of *Obelia* are commonly found on North American seashores; the individual polyps are microscopic, but the feathery white or yellow colony grows up to 12 in. (30 cm) tall. Individual polyps project from the branches of such a colony; they produce the tiny, free-swimming *Obelia* medusae, barely visible to the naked eye. Other hydroid colonies are colonial CORAL and the SEA PENS; these have no medusa stage. All hydroid colonies have at least two types of individual polyps, specialized for feeding and reproduction respectively; some have additional specialized types. The purple sail, genus *Vellela,* and the Portuguese man-of-war, genus *Physalia,* are elaborate floating colonies composed of many types of specialized individuals, both polyplike and medusalike in structure; the entire colony is equipped with a float.

polypeptide: see PEPTIDE.

Polyphemus (pŏlĭfē'məs), in Greek mythology, a Cyclops. He was a shepherd and the son of Poseidon. In the *Odyssey,* Polyphemus imprisoned Odysseus and his men in his cave. They gave him wine and then, when he was drunk, they blinded him and escaped, hiding under Polyphemus' sheep as they left the cave. A later legend tells of the giant's futile love for the nymph GALATEA.

polyphony (pəlĭf'ənē), music whose texture is formed by the interweaving of several melodic lines. The lines are independent but sound together harmonically. Contrasting terms are homophony, wherein one part dominates while the others form a basically chordal accompaniment, and monophony, wherein there is but a single melodic line (e.g., PLAINSONG). Polyphony grew out of the practice of organum, in which a plainsong melody is paralleled by another melody at the interval of a fourth or a fifth. This practice, first described in the *Musica enchiriadis* (late 9th cent.), developed into freer forms of countermelody, culminating in the great age of polyphony in the 15th and 16th cent. In the music of this period, harmonies seem to be generated by the melodic lines sung simultaneously. The gradual ascendancy of harmonic relationships over melodic considerations and the resultant development of major and minor tonalities led in the baroque era to a polyphony controlled by harmony. The fugues and chorale settings of J. S. Bach are the epitome of this type. Homophonic texture is more characteristic of the music of the classical and romantic eras, but in the 20th cent. there has been renewed interest in polyphonic aspects of musical texture and structure. See COUNTERPOINT. See Gustave Reese, *Music in the Middle Ages* (1940); Willi Apel, *Notation of Polyphonic Music* (5th ed. 1961).

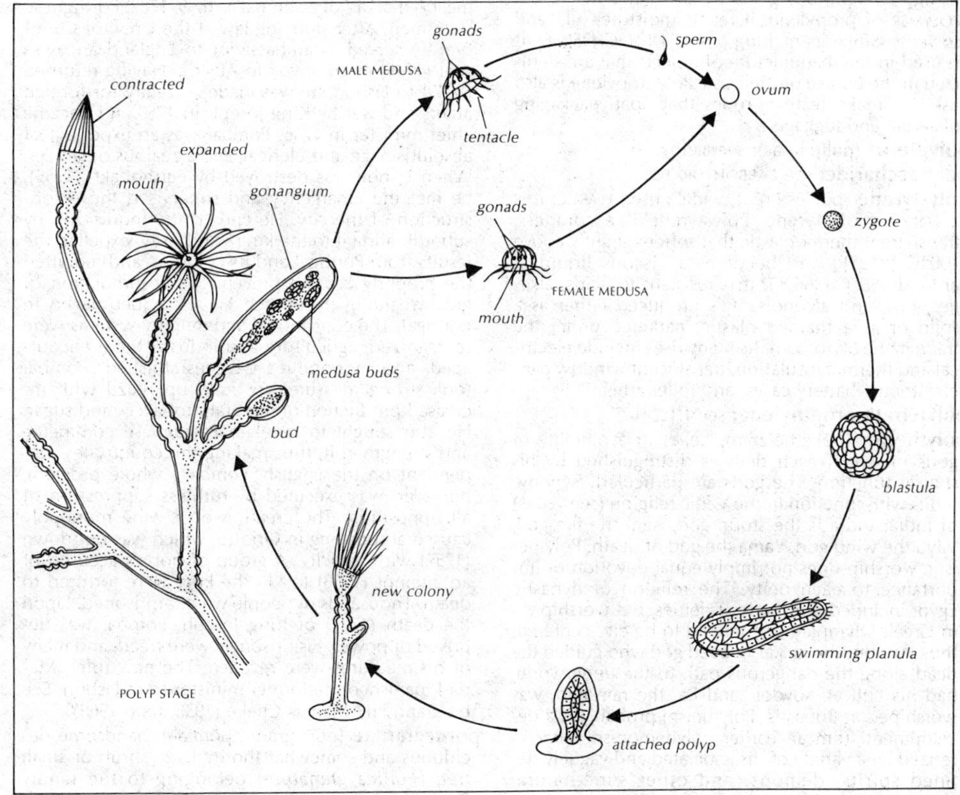

Polyp and medusa stages in the life cycle of Obelia, *representative of the phylum Cnidaria*

Polypodiophyta (pŏl″ēpō″dēŏf′ətə), division of the plant kingdom consisting of the plants commonly called FERNS. The ferns are vascular plants with stems, roots, and leaves, in which the small and inconspicuous GAMETOPHYTE and the large spore-producing fern plant are quite independent of each other. The sporophyte plant, which is the plant form popularly recognized as a fern, may have an erect stem of more than 50 ft (150 m) in height, or a prostrate stem lying in or on the ground. The anatomy of fern stems, especially in the arrangement of the vascular bundles, differs greatly from group to group and is used as a means of interpreting the evolutionary levels of the various groups. Typically, the leaf, or frond, is large and much divided, although many ferns have simple leaves, i.e., leaves with the blade all in one piece. Fern leaves generally unroll as they develop from a coiled early bud stage called the fiddlehead. Sporangia, the spore-producing structures, are generally found on the back of the leaf, but occasionally occur on special structures, which are probably evolutionarily modified leaves. In the great majority of ferns, the spore cases, or sporangia, are produced in groups, with each group called a sorus. These sori can often be seen on the back of the leaves. The sporangia in the sorus are usually protected in some manner, sometimes by an umbrellalike structure, the indusium, and sometimes by the inrolling of the leaf edge. The sporangium consists of a jacket of thin cells, partly surrounded at one side by a row of very thick-walled cells, the annulus. When the spores are mature, a springlike mechanism in the annulus serves to tear open the sporangium and eject the spores. Germinating spores produce a green, thin, sometimes heart-shaped, gametophyte, or prothallus, on the lower side of which are produced the sex organs, the sperm-producing antheridia and the egg-producing archegonia. The gametophytes are thin and delicate and thrive only in moist places; the lower side usually has a film of water, which facilitates the swimming of the motile, flagellated sperm from the antheridium to the neck of the archegonium and to the egg within it. The resulting diploid zygote develops slowly into a mature sporophyte with stem, root, and leaves. Ferns were abundant in Carboniferous times, and many are known only from fossil records. Of the 10,000 known species of living ferns, almost all belong to the order Filicales (true ferns). The grape ferns and the adder's-tongue ferns, of the order Ophioglossales, are very few in number. The genus *Marsilea,* of the order Marsileales, and the genera *Salvinia* and *Azolla,* both of the order Salviniales, have complex life histories. *Marsilea* grows in wet places, and *Salvinia* and *Azolla* float on the surfaces of ponds and lakes.

polypropylene (pŏl″ēprō′pəlēn), PLASTIC noted for its light weight, being less dense than water; it is a POLYMER of propylene. It resists moisture, oils, and solvents. Since its melting point is 121°C (250°F), it is used in the manufacture of objects that are sterilized in the course of their use. Polypropylene is also used to make textiles, ropes that float, packaging material, and luggage.

polypterus (pəlĭp′tərəs): see BICHIR.

polysaccharide: see CARBOHYDRATE.

polystyrene (pŏl″ēstī′rēn), widely used PLASTIC; it is a POLYMER of styrene. Polystyrene is a colorless, transparent thermoplastic that softens slightly above 100°C (212°F) and becomes a viscous liquid at around 185°C (365°F). It is resistant to acids, alkalies, oils, and alcohols. It is produced either as a solid or as a foamed plastic marketed under the trade name Styrofoam. Its many uses include electrical and thermal insulation, translucent window panels, storage-battery cases, and toilet articles.

polytetrafluoroethylene: see TEFLON.

polytheism (pŏl′ēthēĭzəm), belief in a plurality of gods in which each deity is distinguished by his special function. The gods are particularly synonymous with function in the Vedic religion (see VEDAS) of India: Indra is the storm god, Agni the fire god, Vayu the wind god, Yama the god of death. Polytheistic worship does not imply equal devotion or importance to each deity. The religion of dynastic Egypt included hundreds of deities, but worship (as in Greek Olympianism) tended to be city-centered; thus, Anubis, the jackal-headed god who guided the dead along the dangerous path to the underworld, had his cult at Abydos, and Ba, the ram-god, was worshiped at Bubastis. Polytheism probably is a development from an earlier polydemonism, characterized by a variety of disassociated and vaguely defined spirits, demons, and other supernatural powers. It is also related to ANIMISM, ANCESTOR WORSHIP, and totemism. All of these forms of belief are based on man's propensity to worship all objects on earth and in heaven, all that is unusual or useful, strange or monstrous. Unlike the supernatural forces in polydemonism, however, those of polytheism are personified (see ANTHROPOMORPHISM) and organized into a cosmic family. This family becomes the nucleus of legends and myths and, eventually, of a cosmology that seeks to explain natural phenomena and to establish man's relation to his universe. As polytheistic religions evolve, lesser deities diminish in stature or vanish completely, their attributes being assigned to preferred gods, until the religion begins to exhibit monotheistic tendencies—thus the Olympian Zeus, originally a sky god, became the titular head and most powerful of all Olympian deities; the Egyptian Ra was the original, self-generating and supreme deity; and the Vedic gods of India, once numbering several thousand, were gradually displaced by the trinity of Vishnu, Siva, and Brahma. Significantly, both the Greeks and Indians subordinated their supreme deities to a more profound principle of Oneness or Supreme Fate, which the Greeks called Moira and the Vedic Indians named Rita.

polyurethanes (pŏl″ēyŏŏr′əthănz), group of PLASTICS that may be either thermosetting or thermoplastic. Polyurethane can be made into both flexible and rigid foams. The flexible foam is often used in furniture and automobile cushions, in mattresses, and for carpet backings. The rigid foam is used for the thermal insulation of refrigerators, trucks, and buildings. In the furniture industry the rigid foam is molded into mirror frames, chair shells, and other parts that were formerly made from wood. Some polyurethanes are highly elastic materials that are resistant to chemical attack and to abrasion. They are used in such things as solid rubber tires and shoe heels. Lycra, a fiber used in stretch clothing, is a polyurethane. Polyurethanes are also used as decorative and protective coatings, exhibiting high gloss, hardness, and toughness.

polyvinyl chloride (PVC), thermoplastic that is a POLYMER of vinyl chloride. Resins of polyvinyl chloride are hard, but with the addition of plasticizers a flexible, elastic PLASTIC can be made. This plastic has found extensive use as an electrical insulator for wires and cables. Cloth and paper can be coated with this plastic to produce fabrics that may be used for upholstery materials and raincoats.

Polyxena (pōlĭk′sĭnə), in Greek mythology, daughter of Priam and Hecuba. After the death of Achilles, she was claimed by his ghost and was sacrificed at his tomb. According to later legends Achilles loved her and was treacherously killed while meeting with her; therefore he demanded her sacrifice.

Pombal, Sebastião José de Carvalho e Melo, marquês de (səbəstyouN′ zhŏŏzĕ′ dĭ kərvä′lyŏ ē mĕ′lŏŏ märkās′ dĭ pŏŏmbäl′), 1699–1782, Portuguese statesman. After studying law at the Univ. of Coimbra, he served as ambassador to England and was sent (1745) as an envoy to Austria. Having returned (1749) to Lisbon, he was made secretary for foreign affairs and war by King Joseph in 1750 and became chief minister in 1756. Pombal was an exponent of absolutism, an anti-clerical, and a zealous organizer. When Lisbon was destroyed by earthquake (1755), he met the emergency and supervised the reconstruction of the city. He curbed the Inquisition by subordinating it to the king's authority, expelled the Jesuits from Portugal and its colonies, and redrafted the property laws to prevent the accumulation of great wealth by the church. He also ended slavery in Portugal. The educational and military systems were reorganized, agriculture and industry were encouraged, and monopolies were established. Pombal took strong measures to build up Brazil with increased production of minerals, tobacco, and sugar. He also sought to regulate Portuguese commerce and strengthen it, thus making the country less dependent on the English. Pombal's whole program, however, was executed by ruthless suppression of all opposition. The creation of a wine monopoly caused an uprising in Oporto, which was put down (1757) with ferocity. A group of nobles accused of an attempt (1758) to kill the king were tortured to death. Thousands of people were imprisoned. Upon the death (1777) of King Joseph, Pombal was deprived of power, his prisoners were freed, and many of his measures were revoked. The new ruler, Maria I, banished the former minister from Lisbon. See biography by Marcus Cheke (1938, repr. 1969).

pomegranate (pŏm′grănĭt, pŏm′ə-), handsome deciduous and somewhat thorny large shrub or small tree (*Punica granatum*) belonging to the family Punicaceae, native to semitropical Asia and naturalized in the Mediterranean region in very early times. It has long been cultivated as an ornamental and for its edible fruit. The fruit, about the size of an apple, bears many seeds, each within a fleshy crimson seed coating, enclosed in a tough yellowish to deep red rind. Pomegranates are either eaten fresh or used for grenadine syrup, in which the juice of the acid fruit pulp is the chief ingredient. Grenadine syrup, sometimes made from red currants, is a flavoring for wines, cocktails, carbonated beverages, preserves, and confectionery. The astringent properties of the rind and bark have been valued medicinally for several thousand years, especially as a vermifuge. The pomegranate is now cultivated in most warm climates, to a greater extent in the Old World than in America; in North America it is grown commercially chiefly from California and Arizona south into the tropics. The fruit has long been a religious and artistic symbol. It is described in the most ancient of Oriental literature. In the Old Testament, Solomon sang of an "orchard of pomegranates." Because of its role in the Greek legend of PERSEPHONE, the pomegranate came to symbolize fertility, death, and eternity and was an emblem of the Eleusinian Mysteries. In Christian art, it is a symbol of hope. Pomegranates are classified in the division MAGNOLIOPHYTA, class Magnoliopsida, order Myrtales, family Punicaceae.

pomelo (pŏm′əlō″): see GRAPEFRUIT.

Pomerania (pŏm″ərā′nēə), region of N central Europe, extending along the Baltic Sea from a line W of Stralsund, East Germany, to the Vistula River in Poland. From 1919 to 1939, Pomerania was divided among Germany, Poland, and the Free City of Danzig (Gdańsk). The German part constituted the Prussian province of Pomerania (Ger. *Pommern;* 14,830 sq mi/38,410 sq km), with Stettin (SZCZECIN) as its capital. The Polish part formed the province of Pomerelia (Ger. *Pommerellen,* Pol. *Pomorze*; 6,335 sq mi/16,408 sq km), with BYDGOSZCZ as its capital. After the POTSDAM CONFERENCE in 1945, all that part (c.2,800 sq mi/7,250 sq km) of former Prussian Pomerania W of the Oder (but excluding Stettin) was incorporated into the Soviet-occupied German state of MECKLENBURG; the remaining and much larger part was transferred to Polish administration and organized ultimately into the provinces of Koszalin, Szczecin, and Gdańsk. A part of the North European plain, Pomerania is a primarily agricultural lowland, with generally poor, often sandy or marshy soil. It is dotted with numerous lakes and forests and is drained by many rivers, including the Oder, Ina, and Rega. Cereals, sugar beets, and potatoes are the main crops; livestock raising and forestry are important occupations. Industrial products include ships, metal products, refined sugar, and paper. Along the Baltic coast are numerous seaside resorts and fishing villages. Rügen, Wolin, and Usedom are the chief offshore islands. The history of Pomerania is extremely complex. By the 10th cent. A.D., when its recorded history began, Pomerania was inhabited by Slavic tribes. It was conquered by Boleslaus I (992–1025) of Poland but became an independent duchy early in the 11th cent. Poland regained control in the 12th cent. and introduced Christianity. The country was split into two principalities, and in 1181 the duke of W Pomerania paid allegiance to Emperor Frederick I, thus becoming a prince of the Holy Roman Empire and severing his ties with Poland. Pomerelia, as E Pomerania came to be known, became independent in 1227, was annexed to Poland in 1294, and was taken in 1308–9 by the TEUTONIC KNIGHTS, who incorporated it into their domain in East Prussia. The histories of Pomerania and Pomerelia after 1308 must be traced separately. Pomerelia, including Danzig, was formally restored by the Teutonic Knights to Poland at the Treaty of Torun of 1466. Although frequently overrun in the wars of the following three centuries, it remained an integral part of Poland until the first Polish partition (1772), when it passed to Prussia and was constituted into the province of WEST PRUSSIA. In 1919 part of West Prussia was given to Poland (see POLISH CORRIDOR), where it constituted Pomorze prov.; Danzig became independent; and a small part of West Prussia, including Marienwerder (Kwidzyń) and Elbing (Elbląg), was incorporated into neighboring East Prussia. After the outbreak (1939) of World War II, Danzig and Pomorze were reannexed to Germany, which lost them again to Poland in 1945. In the meantime, Pomerania, which gained the island of Rügen in 1325, continued as a duchy of the Holy Roman Empire until the death (1637) of Bogislav XIV. The dukes accepted the Reformation in the 16th cent. In the Thirty Years War, Wallenstein, the imperial general, undertook the occupation of Pomerania in 1628, with the consent of Duke Bogislav;

the city of STRALSUND, however, resisted, and its defense, supported by Denmark, helped to precipitate the intervention (1630) of GUSTAVUS II of Sweden. The Peace of Westphalia (1648) gave Hither Pomerania (*Vorpommern*)—i.e., the western part, with Stettin, Stralsund, and the island of Rügen—to Sweden, while Farther Pomerania (*Hinterpommern*)—i.e., the eastern part, with Stargard—went to the electorate of Brandenburg (after 1701, the kingdom of Prussia). In the third of the Dutch Wars, Charles XI of Sweden lost most of Hither Pomerania to Elector Frederick William of Brandenburg, but by virtue of French influence he recovered all but a strip E of the Oder at the Treaty of Saint-Germain (1679). In 1720, as a result of the NORTHERN WAR, Sweden lost about half of its part of Pomerania (including Stettin but not Stralsund) to Prussia. In the rest of Swedish Pomerania, the kings of Sweden remained princes of the Holy Roman Empire until the dissolution of the empire in 1806. NAPOLEON I overran Swedish Pomerania in the War of the Third Coalition but restored it on making peace with Sweden in 1809. In the Treaty of Kiel (1814), Sweden exchanged Pomerania with Denmark in return for Norway, but at the Congress of Vienna (1815) Denmark ceded its share of Pomerania to Prussia, receiving the duchy of Lauenburg in return. Thus, from 1815 to 1919, all Pomerania and all Pomerelia were in Prussian hands. Pomerania had by then been thoroughly Germanized; Pomerelia, like the rest of Prussian Poland, was subjected to intense Germanization. However, the majority of the population in what became (1919) the Pomorze prov. of Poland remained Polish-speaking. Pomerelia, moreover, was predominantly Catholic, while Pomerania was Protestant. After the transfer in 1945 of the larger part of Pomerania to Polish administration, the German-speaking population was largely expelled. Its fate was shared by the German population of S East Prussia, which contained the section of West Prussia that had remained German after 1919. The history of the principal cities of Pomerania and Pomerelia differs somewhat from the history of the territories in which they are located. The most important of these cities—Danzig, Stralsund, Stettin, Stargard, Toruń, Chetmno, and Marienburg (Malbork)—were, for a long time, flourishing members of the HANSEATIC LEAGUE; by the 17th cent., however, they had lost the virtual independence they had enjoyed during the greatness of the League.

Pomeranian (pŏm″ərā′nēən), breed of small, sturdy TOY DOG descended from the sledge dogs of Iceland and Lapland. It stands about 6 in. (15.3 cm) high at the shoulder and weighs from 3 to 7 lb (1.4–3.2 kg). Its double coat consists of a short, fluffy underlayer and an abundant, long, straight topcoat that forms a ruff of stand-off hair on the neck and a fringe of feathery hair on the hindquarters. Many colors are acceptable, e.g., red, cream, black, brown, sable, blue, white, and parti-color. The immediate ancestor of the Pomeranian was a heavier dog, sometimes weighing as much as 30 lb (13.6 kg). It was used in Europe as a sheepherder and became popular in England when a small specimen was brought from Italy by Queen Victoria in the late 19th cent. Today it is raised as a pet and watchdog. See DOG.

Pomeranus: see BUGENHAGEN, JOHANN.

Pomerelia: see POMERANIA.

Pomfret, John, 1667–1702, English poet and cleric. He is known solely for *The Choice* (1700), a genteel poem celebrating moderation and temperance.

Pommerellen: see POMERANIA; WEST PRUSSIA.

Pommern: see POMERANIA.

Pomo Indians, Indians of N California, belonging to the Hokan language group (see AMERICAN INDIAN LANGUAGES). The Pomo were the most southerly Indians on the California coast not brought under the mission influence of the Franciscans in the early 18th and 19th cent. The Pomo are especially noted for their basketry arts, and many of their works are now valued art objects in museums and private collections. Of these arts, the Pomo have developed feather-covering, lattice-twining, checker-work, single-rod coiling, the mortar hopper, and several other specializations. There are some 900 Pomo living in California.

Pomona (pəmō′nə), city (1970 pop. 87,384), Los Angeles co., S Calif., a residential and industrial suburb of Los Angeles; inc. 1888. Citrus fruits and vegetables are canned and shipped. Pomona is the seat of California State Polytechnic Univ. and is the site of the Los Angeles County Fair.

Pomona, Scotland: see MAINLAND.

Pomona College: see CLAREMONT COLLEGES.

Pomorze: see BYDGOSZCZ; POMERANIA; WEST PRUSSIA.

Pompadour, Jeanne Antoinette Poisson Le Normant d'Étioles, marquise de (pŏm′pədôr, Fr. zhän äNtwänĕt′ pwäsôN′ lə nôrmäN′ dātyôl′ märkēz′ də pôNpädo͞or′), 1721–64, mistress of King Louis XV of France. She was the king's mistress for about 5 years after 1745 and remained his confidante until her death. Of middle-class origin, she owed her success mainly to her intelligence and capabilities. She urged the appointment of the duc de Choiseul and other ministers and encouraged the French alliance with Austria, which involved France in the Seven Years War. The extent of her influence over state policy has, however, been exaggerated. She favored Voltaire and other writers of the *Encyclopédie*. She employed many artists to decorate her residences, and she encouraged the manufacture of SÈVRES WARE. See biographies by Jacques Levron (tr. 1963) and Nancy Mitford (2d ed. 1968).

pompano, common name for fishes of the genus *Trachinotus*, and for *Palometus simillimus*, members of a large and important family of mackerellike fishes, abundant in warm seas around the world. They have deeply forked tails set on thin stalks and swim swiftly, often with the dorsal fin above the water surface. Most of the 200 species are valuable food fishes. Of the 30 genera that constitute the family, the 6 most important are the leather jacks, the amberfishes, the cavallas or jacks, the moonfishes, the casabes, and the pompanos. Best known of the leather jacks is the pilot fish, a slender variety rarely over 2 ft (61 cm) long. Pilot fish, *Naucrates ductor*, often follow ships and sharks, feeding on the scraps left behind. Another species also called pilot fish belongs to the amberfish genus *Seriola* (also called amberjacks and coronados). They are moderate to large size and often beautifully colored. The genus includes the streamlined California yellowtail, a popular game and food fish, weighing up to 40 lb (18 kg). Amberjacks are common off the Florida coast. They are grayish purple on the back and golden on the sides, and average 12 lb (5.4 kg) in weight, though specimens may reach 100 lb (45 kg). They prefer deeper water and feed on smaller fishes, as does the rainbow runner, strikingly colored in blue, yellow, and silver. Others of this group are the mackerel scad and the saurel, 2-ft (61 cm) food fish of commercial importance in San Francisco. Most abundant and valuable of the cavallas (genus *Caranx*) is the crevalle, or common jack, *C. hippos*, found in dense schools on both coasts of tropical America as far north as Cape Cod and the Gulf of California. Crevalles have olive backs, silvery and yellow sides, and reach 2 ft (61 cm) in length and 40 lb (18 kg) in weight. The kingfish, or king cero, is an important food and game cavalla of tropical Atlantic waters. The blue runner, or hard-tailed jack, 1 ft (30 cm) long and 1 lb (.45 kg) in weight and found from Brazil to Cape Cod, is an important food fish in the West Indies. The horse-eye jack is found in both the Atlantic and the Pacific. It is most abundant in the tropics, where its flesh is reputed to be poisonous. The Cuban jack, or African pompano, averaging 2 ft (61 cm) in length and 12 lb (5.4 kg) in weight, is a beautiful fish with an iridescent silvery sheen, similar in coloration and in its compressed, angular body to the moonfishes, silvery marine fishes of the genus *Vomer*. Two moonfishes are the lookdown and the silvery moonfish. Both average from 7 to 9 in. (17.5–22.5 cm) in length and ½ lb (.27 kg) in weight and are important food fishes. They frequent sandy bottoms, feeding on small fish, crustaceans, and marine worms. The lookdown differs from the moonfish in its elongated dorsal and anal fins and in its rainbow iridescence. The casabe, or bumper, a smaller fish (up to 1 ft/30 cm) found from Brazil to Cape Cod, is of little value as food. Commercially the most important of the family are the pompanos, species of which are among the most delicious of all food fishes. *Pompano en papillote* is a delight of epicurean tables. Prized as a food and game fish, the common pompano reaches a maximum length of 18 in. (45 cm) and weight of 8 lb (3.6 kg). It is most common from the Carolinas to Texas. It prefers sandy bottoms and feeds on small crustaceans, especially shrimps and sand fleas. A warm-water fish, it migrates to avoid cold, and an unseasonal cold spell will kill it. Of similar habits and distribution are the round pompano, named for its shape, and the gaff-topsail pompano, or palometa, a beautiful fish with a cerulean blue back and silvery yellow sides. Its counterpart in Pacific waters is the pompanito. The permit, or great pompano, of the Florida reefs is the largest of the family, weighing up to 30 lb (13.5 kg) and reaching a length of 3 ft (91 cm). Pompanos are classified in the phylum CHORDATA, subphylum Vertebrata, class Osteichthyes, order Perciformes, family Carangidae.

Pompano Beach (pŏm′pənō), city (1970 pop. 38,544), Broward co., SE Fla., on the Atlantic coast and the Intracoastal Waterway; inc. 1908. It is a resort city with ocean beaches, excellent fishing, and a harness-racing track. Among the city's manufactures are pleasure boats, plastic and metal products, and electronic equipment. The raising of winter vegetables has long been an important industry and a huge state farmers' market has been operating there since 1939. The city has many miles of small canals that are lined with homes. A junior college and a U.S. coast guard station are there. Also of interest are a lighthouse, built in 1906, and an Indian mound park.

Pompeia (pŏmpē′yə), fl. 61 B.C., Roman matron, wife of Julius Caesar, daughter of Quintus Pompeius Rufus and granddaughter of Sulla. She married Caesar in 67 B.C. and was divorced in 61 B.C., because of an intrigue with CLODIUS while celebrating the mysteries of Bona Dea.

Pompeii (pŏmpā′, Ital. pōmpĕ′ē), ancient city of S Italy, a port near Naples and at the foot of Mt. Vesuvius. Possibly an old Oscan settlement, it was a Samnite city for centuries before it passed under Roman rule at the time of Lucius Cornelius Sulla (1st cent. B.C.). Pompeii was not only a flourishing port but a prosperous resort with many villas. An earthquake in A.D. 63 did much damage, and an eruption of Mt. Vesuvius in A.D. 79 (which was described by Pliny the Younger) buried Pompeii, along with HERCULANEUM and Stabiae, under cinders and ashes that preserved the ruins of the city with magnificent completeness—down to the fresh colors of the wall paintings. The long-forgotten site of the city was rediscovered in 1748 and has been sporadically excavated since that time. The habits and manners of life in Roman times have been revealed in great detail at Pompeii by the plan of the streets and footpaths, the statue-decorated public buildings, and the simple shops and homes of the artisans. The houses and villas have yielded rare and beautiful examples of Roman art. Among the most famous are the house of the Vetti, the villa of the Mysteries, and, in the suburbs of Pompeii, the villa of the Boscoreale. See A. W. Van Buren, *A Companion to the Study of Pompeii and Herculaneum* (1933); Marcel Brion, *Pompeii and Herculaneum* (tr. 1960); Amedeo Maiuri, *Pompeian Wall Paintings* (1960); Duncan Taylor, *Pompeii and Vesuvius* (1969); Michael Grant, *Cities of Vesuvius* (1971).

Pompeius, Sextus (sĕk′stəs pŏmpā′əs), d. 35 B.C., Roman commander; one of the sons of Pompey the Great. He fought for his father at Pharsala, then went to Egypt and, after the battle of Thapsus, to Spain, where he continued warring against Caesar's followers after the death of his elder brother in 45 B.C. In 44 B.C., Lepidus (d. 13 B.C.) made a settlement with Sextus, and he was given command of a Roman fleet in 43 B.C. Later outlawed by the Romans, he seized Sicily and prevented grain ships from reaching Rome. He supported Antony, but in 40 B.C. came to a settlement with Octavian (later Augustus). Two years later Octavian accused Sextus of breaking their agreement and attacked him. Sextus defeated Octavian in 38 B.C. and again in 36 B.C. Later that year Sextus was crushed at Mylae and then at Naulochus. He fled to Asia Minor, where he was captured and killed. See biography by Moses Hadas (1930).

Pompeius Magnus: see POMPEY.

Pompey (Cneius Pompeius Magnus) (pŏm′pē), 106 B.C.–48 B.C., Roman general, the rival of Julius CAESAR. Sometimes called Pompey the Great, he was the son of Cneius Pompeius Strabo (consul in 89 B.C.), a commander of equivocal reputation. The young Pompey fought for SULLA in Picenum, in Sicily, and in Africa so successfully that Sulla allowed him to enter Rome in triumph and receive (81 B.C.) the title Magnus. He helped drive (77 B.C.) LEPIDUS from Italy and went (76 B.C.) to Spain to fight the remnants of the Marius party led by SERTORIUS. After this he returned (72 B.C.) to Italy and helped to end the slave revolt of SPARTACUS. Although he was not legally eligible, he was elected consul in 70 B.C.; he supported laws restoring the powers of the tribunes and forcing the senate to share some of the magistracies with the knights. Pompey's main career as a general began in 67 B.C., when he was commissioned by the law proposed by Aulus Gabinius to destroy the pirates infesting the Mediterranean. From this success he went on to vanquish MITHRADATES VI and Tigranes, king of Armenia. He next annexed Syria and Palestine and began the Roman organization of the East. In 62 B.C. he returned to Rome. The senate, jealous and ungrateful, had been influenced by the METELLUS faction of senatorial extremists, who eventually drove Pompey into alliance with their deadly enemy, Caesar. The First Triumvirate was established in 60 B.C., and Caesar, Crassus, and Pompey became rulers of Rome. Pompey profited least from the combination. He was never popular, and his residence in Rome, while Caesar was away, diminished his hold on the people. At the same time the irresponsible behavior of CLODIUS and Pompey's own inclinations made him more and more sympathetic to the senate. The relations of Pompey and Caesar, however strained, were always amicable while Pompey's wife Julia, Caesar's daughter, was alive, but after her death (54 B.C.) Pompey became Caesar's jealous enemy. Finally, after the disorders of the gangs organized by Clodius and MILO, in 52 B.C., Pompey received the sole consulship as the leader of the senatorial party. He made Quintus Caecilius Metellus Pius Scipio his colleague. Caesar broke with the senate and crossed (49 B.C.) the Rubicon, and the civil war began. Pompey was defeated at Pharsala (48 B.C.) and fled to Egypt, where he was assassinated. Although a good soldier, Pompey was scarcely a great general, and as a statesman he showed himself weak and irresolute. See studies by W. S. Anderson (1963) and V. L. Holliday (1969).

Pompidou, Georges (zhôrzh pôNpēdo͞o'), 1911-74. French political leader, president of France (1969-74). Georges Jean Raymond Pompidou taught school and then served in World War II until the fall (1940) of France, when he returned to teaching. In 1944 he served on the staff of General De Gaulle and later became a trusted aide. Joining the Rothschild banking firm in 1954, he soon became its director general. He remained an important adviser to De Gaulle, and in 1962 President De Gaulle named him premier. During the 1968 strikes and riots in France, Pompidou emerged as a strong figure. Not long afterward, however, he was dismissed as premier by De Gaulle. After De Gaulle's resignation in 1969, Pompidou was elected president with the solid support of the Gaullist party. He immediately began to deal with France's economic problems, devaluing the franc and instituting a price freeze. In foreign affairs, he attempted to improve French relations with other countries and rejected De Gaulle's policy of opposition to Great Britain's entry into the European Common Market. Despite rumors that he was gravely ill Pompidou remained in office; he died of cancer.

Pomponazzi, Pietro (pyĕ'trō pōmpōnät'tsē), 1462-1525, Italian philosopher, b. Mantua. He was a professor at Padua, Ferrara, and Bologna. Pomponazzi aroused great interest in intellectual circles when he questioned St. Thomas Aquinas's interpretation of Aristotle. In his *De immortalitate animae* (1516), Pomponazzi argued that evidence suggests that the soul is mortal; its immortality, therefore, must be accepted as an article of faith. His naturalist position is developed in *De incantationibus* (1520), in which he stressed the evolution of man and of nature. He sought to reconcile this position with the dogmas of the church by distinguishing between faith and knowledge and by asserting that what is true in theology may not be true in philosophy.

Pomponius Laetus, Julius (pŏmpō'nēəs lē'təs), 1425-1498?, Italian humanist, also called Giulio Pomponio Leto. His knowledge of ancient Rome was immense and his works numerous; they included a historical compendium of Roman and Byzantine emperors and a commentary on Vergil. As a tutor he exerted great influence on Alessandro Farnese, who became Pope Paul III.

Pomponius Mela (mē'lə), fl. A.D. c.50, Roman geographer, b. Spain. His *De situ orbis,* a description of the then known world, was published in Latin in 1471 and translated into English by Arthur Golding as *The Cosmographer* (1585).

Pompton Lakes, borough (1970 pop. 11,397), Passaic co., NE N.J.; settled 1682 by the Dutch, inc. 1895. It is chiefly residential, but textiles and explosives are made. Several pre-Revolutionary houses remain.

Ponape (pō'näpä), volcanic island (129 sq mi/334 sq km), W Pacific, in the E CAROLINE ISLANDS (see also PACIFIC ISLANDS, TRUST TERRITORY OF THE). With eleven smaller islands, it makes up the Ponape district, one of six administrative districts of the trust territory. The population of the district (1970) is 18,536. Ponape island is a flat dome of black basaltic rock, rising to c.2,100 ft (640 m), with a rim of fertile coastal land. There are deposits of bauxite, iron, and iron sulfate; copra, dried bonito, and handicrafts are the chief products. Ruins of ancient stone walls, dikes, and basaltic columns dot the island. Ponape was formerly called Ascension Island.

Ponca City, city (1970 pop. 25,940), Kay co., N Okla., on the Arkansas River; founded 1893 with the opening of the Cherokee Strip, inc. 1899. It is a trade, processing, and shipping hub in a grain, livestock, and oil area. There are oil refineries and plants that make oil well equipment. The city has many parks, a pioneer museum, and an Indian museum. Nearby are several Indian reservations.

Ponca Indians, North American Indians whose language belongs to the Siouan branch of the Hokan-Siouan linguistic stock (see AMERICAN INDIAN LANGUAGES). According to tradition the group lived in the Ohio valley, but migrated to the mouth of the Osage River. There the Ponca and the Omaha separated from the main group and went to SW Minnesota. War with the Sioux forced the Ponca to flee to the Black Hills, in South Dakota. The Ponca subsequently rejoined their allies and moved to the mouth of the Niobrara River, in Nebraska. The Ponca remained there, but the other Indians moved on. Lewis and Clark met them in 1804 when the Ponca, recovering from a smallpox epidemic, numbered only some 200. The Ponca's culture was of the Plains area; they farmed corn and hunted buffalo. Raids by the Sioux forced the Ponca to migrate to Oklahoma in 1877. A commission appointed (1880) by President Rutherford B. Hayes studied the land claims of the Ponca; as a result most of them remained in Oklahoma, while a group numbering some 225 returned to their former home in Nebraska. Today the Ponca living on a reservation in Oklahoma number some 1,000. See J. H. Howard, *The Ponca Tribe* (1965); Joseph Jablow, *Ethnohistory of the Ponca* (1974).

Ponce (pōn'sā), city (1970 pop. 128,233), S Puerto Rico. One of Puerto Rico's largest cities, it is the island's chief Caribbean port. The city is also an agricultural trade and distribution center. Industries include tourism, the processing of agricultural products, rum distilling, and varied manufacturing. Founded in the early 16th cent., Ponce is one of the oldest cities in the Americas. It is the seat of the Catholic Univ. of Puerto Rico (est. 1948). Landmarks include a cathedral and an 18th-century fort.

Ponce de León, Juan (pŏns də lē'ŏn, Span. hwän pōn'thā dā lāōn'), c.1460-1521, Spanish explorer, discoverer of Florida. He served against the Moors of Granada, and in 1493 he accompanied Columbus on his second voyage to America. From 1502 to 1504 he assisted in the conquest of Higuey (the eastern part of Hispaniola, now the Dominican Republic) and was made governor of that province. After finding gold on Boriquén (Puerto Rico) in 1508, he conquered the island and, as governor (1509-12), made a fortune in gold, slaves, and land. Hearing tales from the Carib Indians of a wonderfully rich island called Bimini, said to be N of Cuba, Ponce de León secured a commission (1512) to discover, conquer, and colonize that land. There is a legend that he was seeking a spring with waters having the power of restoring youth. From Puerto Rico on March 3, 1513, with three vessels, he sailed NE through the Bahamas, sighting the Florida peninsula (which he took to be an island) late in March and landing near the site of St. Augustine early in April. Probably because the discovery occurred at the time of the Easter feast (*Pascua Florida*), Ponce de León named the land (which he claimed for Spain) La Florida. He turned south, exploring the coast to Key West, and proceeded up the west coast as far as Cape Romano. Then, retracing his route, he sailed to Miami Bay via Cuba and from there returned to Puerto Rico, arriving Sept. 21, 1513. After partly pacifying Puerto Rico, which had been in revolt, he sailed to Spain, where the king commissioned him (Sept., 1514) to subdue the Carib Indians of Guadeloupe and to conquer and colonize the "isle of Florida." In 1515 he led an unsuccessful expedition against the Caribs and returned to Puerto Rico, where he resided until 1521. With two vessels, 200 men, 50 horses and other domestic animals, and farm implements, he sailed for Florida in 1521. Upon landing on the west coast, probably in the vicinity of Charlotte Harbor or Tampa Bay, his party was fiercely attacked by Indians, and he was severely wounded by an arrow. The expedition sailed immediately for Cuba, where Ponce de León soon died. See biography by F. A. Ober (1908); studies by W. B. Fraser (1956) and E. M. King (1963).

Poncelet, Jean Victor (zhäN' vĕktôr' pôNslā'), 1788-1867, French mathematician and army engineer. He taught at the school of mechanics at Metz and at the Faculté des Sciences and the École Polytechnique, both in Paris. While a prisoner of war (1813-14) in Russia during Napoleon I's campaign, he evolved the foundations of the modern form of PROJECTIVE GEOMETRY and incorporated his results in *Traité des propriétés projectives des figures* (1822; 2d ed., 2 vol., 1865-66).

Poncha Pass (pŏn'chə), 9,012 ft (2,747 m) high, central Colo., in the northern tip of the Sangre de Cristo Mts. One of the lowest mountain passes in Colorado, it was much used in the 19th cent. by Indians, overland immigrants, and mountain men. Now it is crossed by a highway.

Ponchielli, Amilcare (ämēlkä'rā pōngkyĕl'lē), 1834-86, Italian composer of several very successful operas. Only *La Gioconda* (1876), with libretto by Boito after Hugo's *Angelo,* is still performed.

Pond, Peter, 1740-1807, American fur trader and explorer of the Old Northwest, b. Milford, Conn. He served in the French and Indian War and in 1765 became a western trader from Detroit. He later removed to Mackinac and made journeys (1773-75) to the upper Mississippi River country and to Wisconsin. He then went by way of Lake Superior N to the Saskatchewan River. In 1778 he went to the Athabaska district with stock pooled from several traders and established the first post in the region on the Athabaska River. Accused of the murder of a rival trader in 1782, Pond was acquitted when tried. He was included in the organization (1783-84) of the North West Company, but in 1788 withdrew in anger. Pond is best known for his maps of the country covered in his voyages, which he presented to Congress. The accusations that Pond was guilty of violence, dishonesty, and lawlessness appear at least partly unjust. His narratives appear in *Five Fur Traders of the Northwest* (ed. by C. M. Gates, 1933). See biographies by H. A. Innis (1930) and H. R. Wagner (1955).

Pondicherry (pŏndĭchĕ'rē, -shĕ'rē) or **Pondichéry** (pôNdēshārē'), union territory (1971 pop. 471,347), 183 sq mi (474 sq km) of India. It comprises the noncontiguous enclaves of former FRENCH INDIA: Pondicherry (or Pondichéry) and Karikal on the Coromandel Coast in Tamil Nadu state, Yanaon (or Yanam) in Andhra Pradesh state, and Mahé on the Malabar Coast of Kerala state. The capital of the territory is Pondicherry town (1971 pop. 90,639) in the Pondicherry enclave. The four enclaves and Chandernagor, an island town near Calcutta, were remnants of French imperial ambition in India in the 17th and 18th cent. In 1949, Chandernagor was incorporated into West Bengal state. Under an agreement with France, India took over administration of the four enclaves on Nov. 1, 1954; a treaty ceding the settlements to India was signed in May, 1956, but it was not until Aug., 1962, that the formal transfer occurred. Despite some agitation to merge the enclaves with the states surrounding them, the territory remains under the administration of the central government of India.

Pond Inlet, trading post, N Baffin Island, Franklin dist., Northwest Territories, Canada, opposite Bylot Island. A government radio station, a post of the Royal Canadian Mounted Police, and Anglican and Roman Catholic missions are located there.

pond lily: see WATER LILY.

pond scum, accumulation of floating green filamentous ALGAE on the surface of stagnant or slowly moving waters, such as ponds and reservoirs. One of the commonest forms is *Spirogyra.* Pond scums can be destroyed by adding adequate copper sulfate (blue vitriol or bluestone) to the water.

pondweed, common name for the family Potamogetonaceae, and for weedy aquatic herbs of the genus *Potamogeton,* of which about 50 known species inhabit North American ponds and slow streams. They have slender stems and small spikes of inconspicuous flowers appearing above the water. A few species are cultivated—some as waterfowl food and for fish protection in conservation projects. The saltwater eelgrass (genus *Zostera*) of gently sloping shores is closely related. Pondweeds are classified in the division MAGNOLIOPHYTA, class Liliatae, order Najadales.

Ponge, Francis (fräNsēs' pôNzh), 1899-, French essayist and poet. A controversial figure, he is opposed to emotional and symbolic poetic methods. His method is to observe things meticulously and describe them in rational, yet lyric terms. His works include *Le Parti-pris des choses* (1942; tr. *The Voice of Things,* 1972), and *La Rage de l'expression* (1952).

Poniatowski, Józef Anton, Prince (yo͞o'zĕf än'tôn pônyätôf'skē), 1763-1813, Polish general and marshal of France; nephew of Stanislaus II. He fought (1792) the Russians in the campaign preceding the second Polish partition and in the insurrection led (1794) by Thaddeus Kosciusko. He became minister of war of the grand duchy of Warsaw set up by

Napoleon I and in 1809 led the Polish troops in Napoleon's campaign against Austria. He again commanded under Napoleon in the Russian campaign of 1812. In the battle of Leipzig he covered the withdrawal of the French troops; then, cut off from aid, he plunged his mount into a river and was drowned.

Poniatowski, Stanislaus Augustus: see STANISLAUS II.

Pons, Lily (pänz, Fr. pôNs), 1904–, French-American coloratura soprano. Pons studied piano at the Paris Conservatory. She made her debut in Delibes's *Lakmé* at Mulhouse, Alsace, in 1927. She first appeared at the Metropolitan Opera in 1931, and the company revived *Lakmé*, Vincenzo Bellini's *La Sonnambula*, and Donizetti's *La Fille du regiment* especially for her. Pons appeared in three motion pictures. In 1938 she married the conductor André Kostelanetz.

pons: see BRAINSTEM.

Ponselle, Rosa (pŏnzĕl'), 1897–, American operatic soprano, b. Meriden, Conn. After appearing on the vaudeville stage, she made her debut (1918) at the Metropolitan Opera in Verdi's *La forza del destino*, opposite Caruso. She was an outstanding member of that company until her retirement in 1937. Ponselle was noted for her powerful, expressive voice and her handling of low tones. Her fame has endured as a result of several important recordings. Her sister, **Carmela Ponselle,** 1892–, mezzo-soprano, b. Schenectady, N.Y., also sang with the Metropolitan Opera company (1925–28, 1930–35), and thereafter taught.

Ponta Delgada (pôn'tə dĕlgä'də), city (1970 pop. 69,930), capital of Ponta Delgada dist., in the AZORES, Portugal. An important port on São Miguel island, it is the largest city and chief commercial center of the Azores. It is also a winter resort.

Pontano, Giovanni (jōvän'nē pōntä'nō), 1426–1503, Italian poet, historian, and statesman, who used also the Latin form Jovianus Pontanus. He was protected by Alfonso of Aragón, who made him his chancellor of Naples (1447) and later his secretary. Pontano personally surrendered Naples to the French invaders. A noted humanist, he discovered Donatus' commentary on Vergil. His verse, in Latin, is notable for its grace, harmony, variety of subject matter, and natural expression of sentiment. He is thought to have greatly influenced Erasmus.

Pontchartrain, Lake (pŏn'chərtrān), shallow lake, c.630 sq mi (1,630 sq km), 41 mi (66 km) long and 25 mi (40 km) wide, SE La., N of New Orleans. It is linked with Lake Maurepas at its western end and with the Gulf of Mexico at its eastern end through Lake Borgne. The lake is tidal and has brackish water. The Bonnet Carre Spillway diverts part of the floodwaters of the Mississippi River into the lake. Two causeways, each c.24 mi (40 km) long, connect New Orleans with Covington, La.; Pontchartrain Causeway II (opened 1969) is the longest multispan bridge in the world. The lake is a popular resort and recreational region.

Pont du Gard (pôN dü gär), Roman aqueduct across the Gard River, Gard dept., S France. Built 19 B.C. to supply NÎMES with water, it consists of three tiers of arches and is c.900 ft (270 m) long and c.160 ft (50 m) high. This famous construction is admired for its architectural proportions. The lowest tier is now used as a road bridge.

Pontefract (pŏn'tĭfrăkt, pŭm'frĭt), municipal borough (1971 pop. 31,335), West Riding of Yorkshire, N England. It is an industrial city; furniture, iron products, and textiles are made. Pomfret cakes are licorice lozenges made there. Situated on the edge of coal fields, Pontefract grew around a great castle built in the 11th cent. on the site of a Saxon fort. It was the scene of the death of Richard II, was taken in the PILGRIMAGE OF GRACE in 1536, and was besieged four times in the civil wars. West of Pontefract is a racecourse. In 1974, Pontefract became part of the new metropolitan county of West Yorkshire.

Pontevedra (pōntāvā'thrä), city (1970 pop. 52,452), capital of Pontevedra prov., NW Spain, in Galicia, on the Atlantic Ocean at the mouth of the Lérez River. It is a fishing port. Clothing, leather goods, and fertilizers are made, and farm products are traded. Among its many old structures are the Gothic Church of Santa María, the picturesque ruins of a 14th-century convent, and a Roman bridge. The city may have been Columbus's birthplace. His ship, the *Santa Maria*, was built there.

Ponthierville, Zaïre: see UBUNDI.

Pontiac, fl. 1760–66, Ottawa Indian chief. He may have been the chief met by Robert Rogers in 1760 when Rogers was on his way to take possession of the Western forts for the English. Although the Indian uprising against the English colonists just after the French and Indian Wars is known as PONTIAC'S REBELLION or Pontiac's Conspiracy, Pontiac's role is uncertain. He definitely was present at the siege of Detroit, and encouraged other tribes to fight the British, but most of the actual fighting and strategy was probably planned independently by other Indian leaders. After the rebellion had failed and a treaty had been concluded (1766), Pontiac is supposed to have gone west and to have been murdered by Illinois Indians at Cahokia. This story is, however, accepted by few authorities. See bibliography under PONTIAC'S REBELLION.

Pontiac, industrial city (1970 pop. 85,279), seat of Oakland co., SE Mich., on the Clinton River; founded 1818 by promoters from Detroit, inc. as a city 1861. Industries developed early and expanded after the railroad came. Carriage making, important in the 1880s, gave way to the automobile industry, and today Pontiac is a noted auto-manufacturing center. It was named for the Ottawa chief Pontiac, who is said to be buried nearby. A junior college is in the city. Eleven state parks and several hundred lakes are in the area.

Pontiac's Rebellion or **Pontiac's Conspiracy,** 1763–66, Indian uprising against the British just after the close of the French and Indian Wars, so called after one of its leaders, PONTIAC. The French attitude toward the Indians had always been more conciliatory than that of the English. French Jesuit priests and French traders had maintained friendly and generous dealings with their Indian neighbors. After conquering New France (Old Canada), the English aroused the resentment of the Western tribes by treating them arrogantly, refusing to supply them with free ammunition (as the French had done), building forts, and permitting white settlement on Indian-owned lands. In April, 1763, a council was held by the Indians on the banks of the Ecorse River near Detroit; there an attack on the fort at Detroit was planned. Pontiac's scheme was to gain admission to the garrison for himself and some of his chiefs by asking for a council with the commandant, but the Indians, who would be carrying weapons, were then to open a surprise attack. Major Henry Gladwin, the commandant, was warned of the plot and foiled it. However, Pontiac and his Ottawa Indians, reinforced by Wyandot, Potawatomi, and Ojibwa, stormed the fort on May 10. The garrison was relieved by reinforcements and supplies from Niagara in the summer, but Pontiac continued to besiege it until November, when, disappointed at finding he could expect no help from the French, he retired to the Maumee River. Fort Pitt in Pennsylvania had been warned of the uprising by a messenger from Gladwin and withstood attack until relieved by Col. Henry BOUQUET. Bouquet and his forces on their way to Fort Pitt in Aug., 1763, had been victorious in a severe engagement at Bushy Run. Meanwhile, Pontiac's allies, the Delaware, Seneca and Shawnee tribes, captured and destroyed many British outposts, among them Sandusky, Michilimackinac (see MACKINAC), and Presque Isle. In an attempt by the British to surprise Pontiac's camp, the battle of Bloody Run was fought on July 31, 1763, with great loss to the British. The borders of Pennsylvania, Maryland, and Virginia were kept in a state of terror. In the spring of 1764 an offensive campaign was planned by the English, and two armies were sent out, one into Ohio under Colonel Bouquet, and the other to the Great Lakes under Col. John Bradstreet. Bradstreet's attempts at treaties were condemned by Gen. Thomas Gage, who had succeeded Sir Jeffrey Amherst as commander in chief, and Colonel Bradstreet returned home with little achievement. Bouquet, by his campaign in Pennsylvania, brought the Delaware and the Shawnee to sue for peace, and a treaty was concluded with them by Sir William Johnson. After failing to persuade some of the tribes farther west and south to join him in rebellion, Pontiac finally completed in 1766 a treaty with Johnson and was pardoned by the English. Francis Parkman's *History of the Conspiracy of Pontiac* (1851, 10th rev. ed. 1913), although it contains certain inaccuracies, is the classic work. See H. H. Peckham, *Pontiac and the Indian Uprising* (1947).

Pontianak (pôntēä'näk), city (1961 pop. 150,220), capital of West Kalimantan prov., W Borneo, Indonesia, at the mouth of a small stream in the Kapuas delta near the west coast. The chief city of W Borneo and an important port, it serves an area producing rubber, palm oil, sugar, coconuts, pepper, rice, tobacco, and gold. Industries include shipbuilding and the processing of the region's products. In the city are the Univ. of East Kalimantan and a private university.

Pontics, mountain system, N Turkey, extending c.700 mi (1,100 km) along the southern coast of the Black Sea. The Pontics generally increase in height from west to east, culminating in Kaçkar Dağı (12,917 ft/3,937 m high) in the Rize Mts., NE Turkey. The Pontics, which generally lack porous rock, have been greatly dissected by the large amount of surface drainage. The Sakarya, Kızıl Irmak, and the Yeşil Irmak are the largest rivers flowing through the Pontics. The northern slopes of the mountains receive an average annual precipitation of c.95 in. (241 cm) and have lush vegetation. The southern slopes are much drier. Population centers are located on fertile river plains. Coal, antimony and copper are mined in the mountains; lumbering is important.

Ponticus, Aquila: see AQUILA PONTICUS.

pontifex maximus (pŏn'tĭfĕks măk'sĭməs), highest priest of Roman religion and official head of the college of pontifices. As the chief administrator of religious affairs he regulated the conduct of religious ceremonies, consecrated temples and other holy places, and controlled the calendar. During the time of the empire, and until Christianity became firmly established, the emperor was designated pontifex maximus. After the supremacy of Christianity, the popes assumed the title.

Pontine Marshes (pŏn'tēn, -tīn), Ital. *Pontina*, low-lying region, c.300 sq mi (780 sq km), in S Latium, central Italy, between the Tyrrhenian Sea and the Apennine foothills; it is crossed by drainage canals. The Appian Way, a Roman-built road, passes through the region. In pre-Roman and early Roman times the area was populated and fertile, but it was later abandoned because of the malaria in its unhealthful marshlands. The Roman emperors Trajan and Theodoric and several popes started reclamation works, but a drainage system was not completed until the 1930s under Mussolini. The large estates in the area were then broken into lots, and farmers from N Italy settled there permanently. The first rural town, Littoria (now Latina), was inaugurated in 1932. Sabaudia, Pontinia, Aprilia, and Pomezia were founded in the following years. During World War II the drainage works were damaged and the region was flooded. Wheat and cotton are now produced, and livestock is raised.

Pontius Pilate (pŏn'shəs pī'lət), fl. A.D. 26, Roman procurator of Judaea. He was supposedly a ruthless governor, and he was removed at the complaint of Samaritans among whom (along with Galileans) he engineered a massacre. Luke 13.1. His attempt to evade responsibility in the trial of Jesus was caused by his fear of the high priests' power and his difficult responsibility for the peace of Palestine. According to tradition he committed suicide at Rome. Mat. 27; John 18.29–38; 19.1–38. The Acts of Pilate, one of the PSEUDEPIGRAPHA (part of the Gospel of Nicodemus) tell of him as a Christian. Legend connects him with Mt. PILATUS.

Pontoise (pôNtwäz'), city (1968 pop. 19,435), capital of Val-d'Oise dept., N central France. It is the site of a technical school.

pontoon, one of a number of floats used chiefly to support a bridge, to raise a sunken ship, or to float a hydroplane or a floating dock. Pontoons have been built of wood, of hides stretched over wicker frames, of copper or tin sheet metal sheathed over wooden frames, of aluminum, and of steel. The original and widespread use was to support temporary military bridges. Cyrus the Great built (536 B.C.) the earliest pontoon bridge in history, using skin-covered pontoons. However, Homer mentions pontoon bridges as early as c.800 B.C. The U.S. army began experimenting with rubber pontoons in 1846 and in 1941 adopted collapsible floats of rubber fabric with steel-tread roadways. At the same time the navy developed box pontoons of light welded steel for ship-to-shore bridges during landing operations. These box pontoons could be assembled into bridges, docks, causeways and, by adding a motor, into self-propelling barges. Permanent civilian pontoon bridges have been built where the water is deep and the water level fairly constant or controllable, often also where the crossing is narrow or where the bottom makes it difficult to sink piers. The modern permanent pontoon is composed of many compartments, so that if a leak occurs in one compartment, the pontoon will not sink. Permanent pontoons are fastened together and several anchors are dropped from each. Often a section of a bridge built on them can swing aside to let a ship pass. Several pontoon bridges have been built across the Mississippi River. Pontoons for raising sunken ships are watertight cylinders that are filled with water, sunk, and fastened to the submerged ship; when emptied by compressed air, they float the ship to the surface. A pontoon lifeboat consists of a raft supported by watertight cylinders.

Pontoppidan, Henrik (hăn'rĕk pôntô'pĭdän), 1857–1943, Danish novelist. He shared the 1917 Nobel Prize in Literature with Gjellerup. Pontoppidan devoted himself to engineering, journalism, and travel before the appearance of his first major work, *The Promised Land* (tr. 1896), originally published as a trilogy (1891–95). His outstanding novel, *Lucky Peter* (5 vol., 1898–1904), depicts, in philosophical terms, revolt against the bourgeois life in Copenhagen. In his pessimistic *Kingdom of the Dead* (5 vol., 1912–16) he explores the problem of human weakness.

Pontormo, Jacopo da (yä'kōpō dä pōntôr'mō), 1494–1556, Florentine painter, one of the creators of mannerism. His real name was Jacopo Carrucci. In his youth he assisted Andrea del Sarto, who at first influenced him greatly. In later years, however, Pontormo's style became more nervous and contorted. His works include the *Visitation* (the Annunziata, Florence); the light mythological frescoes for the Medici Villa at Poggio a Caiano; and the intensely spiritual *Descent from the Cross* (Santa Felicità, Florence). Pontormo was also an excellent portraitist, depicting Cosimo the Elder (Uffizi) and many others. Examples of his art are in the National Gallery of Art, Washington, D.C.; the Fogg Museum, Cambridge; and the Yale Univ. Art Gallery. Pontormo left an interesting diary. See Walter Friedlander, *Mannerism and Anti-Mannerism in Italian Painting* (1957).

Pontresina (pōntrāzē'nä), village, Grisons canton, SE Switzerland, at the foot of the Bernina Alps. It is a summer and winter resort and sports center.

Pontus (pŏn'təs), in Greek religion, sea god. He was the son of Gaea and by her the father of Ceto, Nereus, Thaumus, Phorcus, and Eurybia.

Pontus, ancient country, NE Asia Minor (now Turkey), on the Black Sea coast. On its inland side were Cappadocia and W Armenia. It was not significantly penetrated by Persian or Hellenic civilization. In the 4th cent. B.C., Pontus was taken over by a Persian family, profiting by the breakup of the empire of Alexander the Great, and by 281 B.C. the ruler (Mithradates II) called himself king. A century later Pharnaces I was able to annex Sinope, and Mithradates V (d. 120 B.C.) gained Phrygia by a profitable alliance with Rome. The greatest Pontic ruler was MITHRADATES VI, who conquered Asia Minor, gained control of the Crimea, and threatened Rome in Greece. But the Pontic "empire" had neither economic nor political stability, and Mithradates prospered only because Rome was preoccupied elsewhere. Pompey defeated him (65 B.C.), and when PHARNACES II tried to take advantage of the Roman civil war, Julius Caesar easily removed (47 B.C.) the threat at Zela. The Romans joined Pontus to the province of Galatia-Cappadocia. The principal Pontic cities were Amasia, Neocaesarea, and Zela. Pontus is mentioned three times in the New Testament (Acts 2.9; 18.2; 1 Peter 1.1).

Pontus Euxinus: see BLACK SEA.

Pontypool (pŏntēpo͞ol'), urban district (1971 pop. 37,014), Monmouthshire, SE Wales. There are coal-mining, steel, nylon, glass, and toy industries. Pontypool absorbed nearby Abersychan in 1935. In 1974, Pontypool became part of the new nonmetropolitan county of Gwent.

Pontypridd (pŏntəprēth'), urban district (1971 pop. 34,465), Glamorganshire, S Wales. It is a railroad junction and port for coal from the Rhondda and Taff valleys. Electrical equipment, cables, and chains are made. The famous stone single-span bridge over the Taff was built in 1756. In 1974, Pontypridd became part of the new nonmetropolitan county of Mid Glamorgan.

pony, small horse, officially any HORSE under 14.2 hands (58 in./145 cm) high. Most ponies are of Celtic origin. They are noted for their extreme hardiness and gentle natures. Some ponies are only 26 in. (65 cm) high. See SHETLAND PONY; WELSH PONY.

pony express, in U.S. history, relay mail service. At its inception in April, 1860, the pony express operated between St. Joseph, Mo., the western end of a telegraph line, and Sacramento, Calif. Riders carried the mail a distance of nearly 2,000 mi (3,200 km) in about eight days, often traveling through hostile Indian territory. Stations where the riders changed horses were roughly 10 to 15 mi (16–24.1 km) apart. After a rider had covered a certain distance, the mail was turned over to another rider; this continued until the destination was reached. The pony express was operated by the freighting firm of Russell, Majors, and Waddell. As a business venture, it was unsuccessful. Before the pony express, letters to and from California had been carried by ships, wagon trains, and stagecoaches and had required much more time for the journey. The first telegram to San Francisco was transmitted Oct. 24, 1861, and the pony express was then gradually discontinued. Its existence was brief but picturesque, and the pony express lives in legend as well as in history. See L. R. Hafen, *The Overland Mail* (1926); Arthur Chapman, *The Pony Express* (1932, repr. 1971); S. A. Adams, *The Pony Express* (1950); R. W. Settle and M. A. L. Settle, *Saddles and Spurs* (1955, repr. 1972); G. D. Bradley, *Story of the Pony Express* (2d ed. 1960).

poodle, popular breed of dog probably originating in Germany but generally associated with France, where it has been raised for centuries. There are three varieties, differing in size only. The standard poodle, classified in the nonsporting-dog group (see NONSPORTING DOG), stands over 15 in. (38.1 cm) high at the shoulder and weighs from 40 to 55 lb (18.1–24.9 kg). The miniature, also listed in the nonsporting-dog group, stands from 10 to 15 in. (25.4–38.1 cm) high at the withers and weighs from 14 to 16 lb (6.4–7.3 kg). The toy poodle, which is classified as a TOY DOG, stands up to 10 in. (25.4 cm) high at the shoulder and weighs about 6 lb (2.7 kg). The profuse coat is dense and hard-textured and may be any solid color. If left untended, the coat will grow out in matted, ropelike cords. The poodle is clipped in a variety of styles (e.g., the puppy trim, the continental clip, and the English-saddle clip), a practice now carried out largely for show or aesthetic purposes but originally of utilitarian value. The poodle was widely used in France as a waterfowl retriever, but its heavy coat required clipping so as not to hinder the dog's progress through water. The poodle has also been raised as a circus and vaudeville performer and as a hunter of truffles. Today it is usually kept as a companion and pet. See DOG.

pool, game: see BILLIARDS.

Poole, Ernest (po͞ol), 1880–1950, American writer, b. Chicago, grad. Princeton, 1902. He was a magazine correspondent in Russia, France, and Germany before and during World War I. His best-known novel is *The Harbor* (1915), a story about changing industry on the Brooklyn waterfront. *His Family* (1917; Pulitzer Prize) is a portrait of a New York family. Among his other works are *The Little Dark Man and Other Russian Sketches* (1925); *Giants Gone: Men Who Made Chicago* (1943); and *Great White Hills of New Hampshire* (1946). See his autobiography, *The Bridge* (1940).

Poole, William Frederick, 1821–94, American librarian, bibliographer, and historian, b. Essex co., Mass. Poole was librarian of the Boston Athenaeum (1856–69), of the public libraries of Cincinnati (1871–73) and Chicago (1874–87), and of the NEWBERRY LIBRARY (1887–94). A pioneer in theories of library administration, he assisted in organizing many libraries, including the Chicago Public Library, the Newberry Library, and the library of the U.S. Naval Academy. A founder of the American Library Association (1876), he was later its president. He compiled the first general index to U.S. periodicals, *Poole's Index to Periodical Literature* (1848), and edited two other editions (1853, 1882). Later editions were edited by W. J. Fletcher; the last appeared in 1907. This index was replaced by the *Readers' Guide to Periodical Literature.* Among Poole's numerous writings are monographs on American history, including *Cotton Mather and Salem Witchcraft* (1869) and *Anti-Slavery Opinions before 1800* (1873).

Poole, municipal borough (1971 pop. 106,697), Dorset, S England, on the north side of Poole Harbour. Poole has shipbuilding, pottery-making, and other industries. It is a naval supply station and a seaplane base and has a considerable coastal trade. There is a technical college. Within Poole Harbour is Brownsea Island.

Poona (po͞o'nə), city (1971 pop. 853,226), Maharashtra state, W central India. It is a district administrative and commercial center with metalworks. There are several palaces and temples from the 17th and 18th cent., when Poona was the capital of the Mahrattas. Under British rule it was an important military center. Poona Univ., a meteorological observatory, a national chemical laboratory, and a national-defense academy are in the city.

Poopó (pō''ōpō'), salt lake, 965 sq mi (2,499 sq km), on the high plateau of W Bolivia. It is more than 11,000 ft (3,353 m) above sea level and averages only 10 ft (3 m) in depth. Fed by the Desaguadero River, it has no outlet except in time of flood, when it drains W to the Salar de Coipasa, a salt flat.

Poor, Henry Varnum, 1888–1970, American painter, b. Chapman, Kansas. Poor's lyrical still lifes, portraits, and landscapes are simply painted in many media. He painted murals in fresco for the Dept. of Justice and Dept. of Interior buildings, Washington D.C., and for Pennsylvania State College. Poor taught art at Columbia and in Maine. His work is represented in many American museums, including the Whitney Museum and the Metropolitan Museum, in New York City. He was also famed for his work in ceramics. Poor wrote *Artist Sees Alaska* (1945) and *A Book of Pottery* (1958).

Poor Clares: see CLARE, SAINT.

poor law, legislation relating to public assistance for the poor. Early measures to relieve pauperism were usually designed to suppress vagrancy and begging. In 1601, England passed the Elizabethan poor-relief act, which recognized the state's obligation to the needy; it provided for compulsory local levies to be administered by the parish, and it required work for the able-bodied poor and apprenticeships for needy children. Local reluctance to support the poor from other areas led to settlement laws limiting migration. Institutional relief was provided by poorhouses, where the aged, sick, or insane were grouped together. From c.1700 workhouses were established where the poor were expected to support themselves by work. However, because of widespread unemployment and low wages, it became customary in the late 18th cent. to give home relief. Poor-law amendments of 1834 sought to establish uniform assistance by placing relief under national supervision; they curtailed home relief and modified the settlement laws. Those amendments assumed that pauperism stemmed partly from unwillingness to work rather than from inadequate employment opportunities. As a result poor relief was maintained at a level below that of the poorest laborer. The Local Government Act of 1929 established the basis for a more far-reaching and humane approach to the conditions of the poor. In many European countries the churches retained control of poor relief until the 19th cent., when measures to provide public relief increased. A system geared to individual needs was developed in Elberfeld, Germany, and became the pattern for many communities. This system provided for thorough examination of each case, guardianship during the period of dependence, and constant assistance until economic self-reliance could be regained. In the United States most states have retained poor laws based on the English poor law introduced by the colonists; there has been little uniformity in the different states or even in communities within a state. The 20th cent. has brought recognition of an obligation for uniform relief on a national scale. In the United States special categories of relief, notably for children, the blind, the aged, veterans, and Indians, have been placed under national supervision. Palliative measures have been supplemented by preventive measures, such as unemployment compensation and old-age pensions. See also SOCIAL SECURITY. See Sidney Webb and Beatrice Webb, *English Poor Law History* (1927–29, repr. 1963); J. R. Poynter, *Society and Pauperism* (1969); M. E. Rose, *English Poor Law, 1780–1930* (1971).

poor-man's-orchid: see BUTTERFLY FLOWER.

pop art, a movement that emerged at the end of the 1950s as a reaction against the seriousness of ABSTRACT EXPRESSIONISM. Pop artists employed a common imagery found in comic strips, soup cans, ice bags, and Coke bottles to express formal abstract relationships. By this means they provided a meeting ground where artist and layman could come to terms with art. Incorporating techniques of sign painting and commercial art into their work, as well as commercial literary imagery, pop artists such as Roy LICHTENSTEIN and Andy WARHOL attempted to fuse elements of popular and high culture to erase the boundaries between the two. See John Russell and Suzi Gablik, *Pop Art Redefined* (1969); Harold Rosenberg, *The De-Definition of Art* (1972); Lawrence Alloway, *American Pop Art* (1974).

Popayán (pōpäyän'), city (1968 est. pop. 65,500), alt. 5,500 ft (1,676 m), capital of Cauca dept., SW Colombia, on a volcanic terrace high above the Cauca River. There is some mining in the surrounding region, but coffee growing is the chief commercial activity. Textiles and foodstuffs are produced in the city. Popayán was founded in 1536 by Sebastián de BENALCÁZAR and during colonial times was a wealthy and aristocratic trade center. After Colombia gained independence in the 19th cent., the city lost much of its commercial preeminence but remained a major cultural center. Points of interest include many fine examples of Spanish colonial architecture and a university founded in 1640.

popcorn, variety of Indian CORN (*Zea mays everta*), characterized by small ears, small pointed or rounded kernels, usually white but sometimes yellow or red, and a larger proportion of hard food material stored about the germ. Steam is formed when heat is applied, and the grain, enlarging six to eight times in bulk, explodes and exposes the pure white pulp. Freshly popped corn, seasoned with salt and butter or formed into balls with molasses taffy, is especially popular in the United States. Popcorn was introduced to white men by the American Indians, who had long cultivated it. Popcorn has been found in graves of pre-Columbian Indians. Corn, including popcorn, is classified in the division MAGNOLIOPHYTA, class Liliatae, order Cyperales, family Gramineae.

Popé (pōpā'), d. c.1690, medicine man of the PUEBLO INDIANS. In defiance of the Spanish conquerors, he practiced his traditional religion and preached the doctrine of independence from Spanish rule and the restoration of the old Pueblo life. In August, 1680, he organized the revolt of the Pueblo Indians against their Spanish oppressors. The Indians attacked Santa Fe, the capital city, killing some 400 colonists and missionaries and forcing the survivors to retreat down the Rio Grande to El Paso. For the first time in 82 years the Pueblo Indians were free of Spanish rule. Popé, assuming a despotic role, then began a campaign to wipe out all traces of the Spanish conquerors—prohibiting the Spanish language, destroying Christian churches, and even washing clean those who had been baptized. Internal dissension and Apache raids soon weakened the unity of the Pueblo Indians, and in 1692, shortly after Popé's death, they were reconquered by the Spaniards.

Pope, Alexander, 1688–1744, English poet. He was born in London of Roman Catholic parents and moved to Binfield in 1700. During his later childhood he was afflicted by a tubercular condition known as Pott's disease that ruined his health and produced a pronounced spinal curvature. He never grew taller than 4 ft 6 in. (1.4 m). His religion debarred him from a Protestant education and from the age of 12 he was almost entirely self-taught. Although he is known for his literary quarrels, he never lacked close friends. In his early years he won the attention of William Wycherly and the poet-critic William Walsh, among others. Before he was 17 he was admitted to London society and encouraged as a prodigy. The shortest lived of his friendships was with Joseph Addison and his coterie, who eventually insidiously attacked Pope's Tory leanings. His attachment to the Tory party was strengthened by his warm friendship with Swift and his involvement with the SCRIBLERUS CLUB. Pope's poetry basically falls into three periods. The first includes the early descriptive poetry; the *Pastorals* (1709); *Windsor Forest* (1713); the *Essay on Criticism* (1711), a poem written in heroic couplets outlining critical tastes and standards; *The Rape of the Lock* (1714), a mock-heroic poem ridiculing the fashionable world of his day; contributions to the *Guardian*; and "Elegy to the Memory of an Unfortunate Lady" and "Eloise to Abelard," the only pieces he ever wrote dealing with love. In about 1717 Pope formed attachments to Martha Blount, a relationship that lasted his entire life, and to Lady Mary Wortley Montagu, with whom he later quarreled bitterly. Pope's second period includes his magnificent, if somewhat inaccurate, translations of Homer, written in heroic couplets; the completed edition of the *Iliad* (1720); and the *Odyssey* (1725–26), written with William Broome and Elijah Fenton. These translations, along with Pope's unsatisfactory edition of Shakespeare (1725), amassed him a large fortune. In 1719 he bought a lease on a house in Twickenham where he and his mother lived for the rest of their lives. In the last period of his career Pope turned to writing moral poems and satires, including *The Dunciad* (1728–43), a scathing satire on dunces and literary hacks in which Pope viciously attacked his enemies including Lewis Theobald, the critic who had ridiculed Pope's edition of Shakespeare, and the playwright Colley Cibber; *Imitations of Horace* (1733–38), satirizing social follies and political corruption; *An Essay on Man* (1734), a poetic summary of current philosophical speculation, his most ambitious work; *Moral Essays* (1731–35); and the "Epistle to Arbuthnot" (1735), a defense in poetry of his life and his work. Although his literary reputation declined somewhat during the 19th cent., he is now recognized as the greatest poet of the 18th cent. and the greatest verse satirist in English. See the Twickenham edition of his poems (7 vol., 1951–61); his prose works ed. by Norman Ault (1936, repr. 1968); his letters ed. by George Sherburn (5 vol., 1956); biographies by George Sherburn (1934, repr. 1963), Norman Ault (1949, repr. 1967), and Peter Quennell (1968); studies by Geoffrey Tillotson (1946; 2d ed. 1950; and 1958), F. W. Bateson and N. A. Joukovsky, ed. (1972), J. P. Russo (1972), Peter Dixon, ed. (1973), and F. M. Keener (1974).

Pope, John, 1822–92, Union general in the American Civil War, b. Louisville, Ky. He fought with distinction at Monterrey and Buena Vista in the Mexican War and later served with the topographical engineers in the West. At the outbreak of the Civil War, Pope was made a brigadier general of volunteers. He served in Missouri under John C. Frémont and then under Henry W. Halleck. He was promoted to major general in March, 1862. As commander of the Army of the Mississippi, Pope captured New Madrid and ISLAND NO. 10 and took part in Halleck's move on Corinth. These successes brought him the command of the newly organized Army of Virginia (June, 1862) and a brigadier generalcy in the regular army. He attributed his bad defeat at the second battle of BULL RUN to alleged disobedience on the part of Fitz-John PORTER. Removed from command, Pope later campaigned against the Sioux Indians. He commanded (1870–83) the Dept. of the Missouri. See study by R. N. Ellis (1970).

Pope, John Russell, 1874–1937, American architect, b. New York City, studied at the College of the City of New York and the School of Mines, Columbia (Ph.B., 1894). He won a fellowship (1895) to the American Academy in Rome. Pope's firm, established in New York City in 1900, consistently produced dignified architecture of classical inspiration. His designs include a long list of town and country residences. His public works at Washington, D.C., include the Scottish Rite Temple, the National Archives Building, Constitution Hall for the Daughters of the American Revolution, and the National Gallery of Art. He also designed the Lincoln Memorial, Hodgenville, Ky.; the Baltimore Museum of Art; and a war memorial at Montfaucon, France.

pope: see PAPACY; ROMAN CATHOLIC CHURCH.

Popham, George (pŏp'əm), c.1550–1608, early colonist in Maine, b. England. He was named in the patent granted to the Plymouth Company in 1606. In consequence of the colonization project of his uncle, Sir John Popham, and Sir Ferdinando GORGES, George Popham, in the *Gift of God,* with Ralegh Gilbert in the *Mary and John,* set out in 1607 from Plymouth, England, to plant a colony in North America. They explored the Maine coast and settled at the mouth of the Kennebec (then called the Sagadahoc) River on the present site of Phippsburg. A fort was erected, called Fort St. George, and Popham became president of the colony. He died that winter, and the colony was abandoned in the following summer.

Popham, Sir Home Riggs, 1762–1820, British admiral. He served in the French Revolutionary and Napoleonic Wars and was naval commander at the recapture (1806) of Cape Town. He sailed from there to South America with William Carr Beresford (later Viscount BERESFORD) and captured Buenos Aires, which was held for only six weeks. Recalled (1807) to England, Popham was reprimanded by a court-martial for withdrawing from the Cape Colony without orders. He commanded the Jamaica station from 1817 to 1820.

Popish Plot: see OATES, TITUS.

Poplar, former metropolitan borough, SE England. See TOWER HAMLETS.

poplar: see WILLOW.

Poplar Bluff, city (1970 pop. 16,653), seat of Butler co., SE Mo., in the Ozark foothills, on the low bluffs of the Black River near the Ark. line; inc. 1870. It is a trade, shipping, and medical center in a rich farming area. Plastics, wood and paper products, electric transformers, shoes, and concrete items are among its manufactures. A junior college and a veterans hospital are there. Nearby are Clark National Forest, Wappapello Dam, a wildlife refuge, and several state parks.

Popocatépetl (pōpəkăt'əpĕtəl, pōpō"kätā'pətəl) [Aztec, =smoking mountain], volcano, 17,887 ft (5,452 m) high, in the Cordillera de Anáhuac, central Mexico, on the Puebla-Mexico state border; the second-highest peak in Mexico. The perpetually snow-capped cone is symmetrical, and the large crater has practically pure sulfur deposits only partially exploited. The ascent, which is fairly easy, was probably first made by Europeans in 1519 by one of Cortés's men. Active during the first two centuries of Spanish colonial times, the volcano has been dormant since 1702. Occasionally it emits vast clouds of smoke.

Popol Vuh (pōpōl' vōō') [Quiché, =collection of the council], sacred book of the QUICHÉ Indians. The most important document of the cosmogony, religion, mythology, migratory traditions, and history of the Quiché, the original Popol Vuh was destroyed by the Spanish conquistador Pedro de Alvarado, but it was rewritten in Spanish by a converted Quiché shortly after the Spanish conquest. The language and literary style, the philosophy, and the life it reveals show the Quiché had reached a high degree of learning. A similar document, more historical in content and treating of the neighboring Cakchiquel, is the *Annals of the Cakchiquel.* See the English version of the Popol Vuh by Delia Goetz and S. C. Morley (1950); study by Lewis Spence (1908, repr. 1972).

Popović, Koča (kō'chä pō'pōvĭ'tyə), 1908–, Yugoslav soldier and political leader. He early joined (1933) the Yugoslav Communist party and fought (1937–39) in the Spanish Civil War. During World War II he was one of the chief organizers of Serbian resistance. After the war, Popović served as chief of the general staff of the Yugoslav army (1945–53), minister of foreign affairs (1953–65), and Yugoslav vice president (1966–67). He also headed numerous Yugoslav delegations to the United Nations. In 1971 he was chosen one of 22 members of Yugoslavia's newly established collective presidency, but resigned (Nov., 1972) in disagreement over policies aimed at restricting the autonomy of the federal republics.

Popović, Milentije (mēlĕn'tēyə), 1913–71, Yugoslav politician. Active in the Communist student movement, he became a member of the Yugoslav Communist party in 1939. He joined the partisans of Josip Broz Tito in Oct., 1941. After Yugoslavia's liberation, Popović held various ministerial positions. In 1953 he became a member of the federal executive council and from 1958 he was chairman of the federal council of education. A member of the presidium of the Yugoslav Communist party, Popović served as chairman of the federal parliament from 1967 until his death.

Poppaea Sabina (pŏpē'ə səbī'nə), d. A.D. 65, Roman empress, wife of NERO. While married to OTHO, her second husband, she became mistress of Nero, whom she finally married in A.D. 62. She had great influence over Nero, inducing him to have his mother (Agrippina II), his former wife (Octavia), and the philosopher Seneca killed. One story has it that in a fit of temper Nero kicked her to death.

Popper, Sir Karl Raimund, 1902–, Anglo-Austrian philosopher, b. Vienna. He became familiar with the Vienna circle of logical positivists while a student at the Univ. of Vienna (Ph.D., 1928). He taught at Canterbury Univ., New Zealand (1937–45), and then at the London School of Economics. Popper's thought develops from his view of knowing as an individual, unpredictable act of genius, not acquired merely by induction, as empiricists hold, nor limited to verifiable statements, as the logical positivists hold. Like the logical positivists, Popper worked with the distinction between scientific knowledge and pseudoscience, but he understood the two to be related as well as distinct: pseudoscience or "myth," as he sometimes termed it, can inspire or grow into science, or overlap with it (as in the case of psychology). Popper rejected the certainty of knowledge, whether secured on empiricist or rationalist ground. He also questioned historicism (the doctrine that there are general laws of history) because history, as he saw it, is influenced by the growth of knowledge, and, since knowing is a matter of unpredictable insight, neither the growth of knowledge nor its historical consequences can be systematized. Popper was knighted in 1964. His works include *The Logic of Scientific Discovery* (1935), *The Open Society and Its Enemies* (5th rev. ed. 1966), *The Poverty of Historicism* (1961), and *Objective Knowledge: An Evolutionary Approach* (1972). See studies by I. C. Jarvie (1972) and Brian Magee (1973).

Popper-Lynkeus, Josef (yō'zĕf pôp'ər-lün'kōōs), 1838–1921, Austrian philosopher, social reformer, and inventor. His unpopular views kept him from any academic position, so he worked at various jobs until his inventions (the most notable being a device that improved the working capacity of engine boilers) gave him financial security. Popper-Lynkeus placed his highest value on the life of the individual and defended its worth against such abstractions as the good of the state or church—religion he considered a social bane—or the advancement of art or science; he held that society had a duty to secure each individual against want, regardless of his talents or qualifications. He was the first to suggest the possibility of transmitting electric power, and he also anticipated several of Sigmund Freud's insights about dreams, although he claimed never to have understood Freud's work. His books, which were rarely translated or read later, were widely popular early in the 20th cent. He himself was respected highly by such men as Ernst Mach, Albert Einstein, and Freud. See study by H. I. Wachtel (1955, introd. by Einstein).

poppy, common name for some members of the Papaveraceae, a family composed chiefly of herbs of the Northern Hemisphere having a characteristic milky or colored sap. Most species are native to the Old World; many are cultivated in gardens for their brilliantly colored but short-lived blossoms. Many of the species have several varieties and show a wide range of colors, especially in red, yellow, and white shades. The "true" poppy genus is *Papaver,* but many flowers of related genera are also called poppies. The most frequently cultivated are the Oriental poppy (*P. orientale*), usually bearing a large scarlet flower with a purplish black base, and the corn poppy (*P. rhoeas*) and its variety, the Shirley poppy. Other well-known species include the arctic Iceland poppy (*P. nudicaule*), the celandine poppy

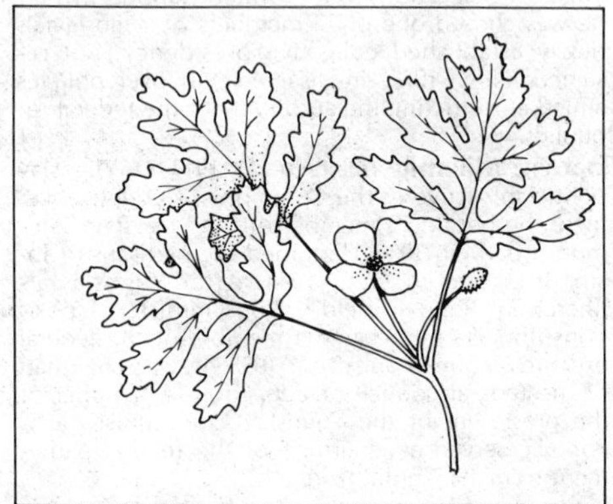

Greater celandine poppy, Chelidonium majus

(*Stylophorum diphyllum*) of North America, and the cream cups (*Platystemon californica*) and California poppy, or eschscholtzia (*Eschscholtzia californica*), of the W United States (the latter is the state flower of California). The Old World greater celandine (*Chelidonium majus*), also called swallowwart or wartweed, was formerly believed efficacious in removing warts and in restoring failing eyesight. (The lesser celandine is an unrelated plant of the buttercup family.) The orange-red sap of the bloodroot (*Sanguinaria canadensis*), an early spring wildflower of E North America, was used by the Indians as a dye and skin stain. This and many other members of the family are employed for various medicinal purposes. Economically, the most important plant in the family is the opium poppy (*P. somniferum*), now widely cultivated from Europe to the Far East. The milky sap of its unripe seed pods is the source of OPIUM and several other similar drugs, e.g., MORPHINE, CODEINE, and HEROIN. Poppyseed, also called maw seed, is not narcotic; used as birdseed and for flavoring in baking, it is also ground for flour. Poppy oil, derived from the seeds, is employed in cooking and illumination and in paints, varnishes, and soaps. The poppy has been the symbol of the dead and of sleep since antiquity. The poppies of "Flanders fields" are celebrated in a poem by John McCrae and are the Memorial Day emblem of World War veterans. Poppies are classified in the division MAGNOLIOPHYTA, class Magnoliopsida, order Papaverales, family Papaveraceae.

popular music: see COUNTRY AND WESTERN MUSIC; FOLK SONG; GOSPEL MUSIC; JAZZ; ROCK MUSIC.

popular sovereignty, in U.S. history, doctrine under which the status of slavery in the territories was to be determined by the settlers themselves. Although the doctrine won wide support as a means of avoiding sectional conflict over the slavery issue, its meaning remained ambiguous, since proponents disagreed as to the stage of territorial development at which the decision should be made. Stephen A. DOUGLAS, principal promoter of the doctrine, wanted the choice made at an early stage of settlement; others felt that it should be made just before each territory achieved statehood. First proposed in 1847 by Vice President George Dallas and popularized by Lewis Cass in his 1848 presidential campaign, the doctrine was incorporated in the COMPROMISE OF 1850 and four years later was an important feature of the KANSAS-NEBRASKA ACT. Douglas called it "popular sovereignty," but proslavery Southerners, who wanted slavery extended into the territories, contemptuously called it "squatter sovereignty."

population. The world's population was about 3.8 billion in the mid-1970s. From the time of the Roman Empire to the colonization of America, the world population grew from about a quarter billion to a half billion persons. By the mid-19th cent., however, it had grown to about one billion, and by 1930 it had risen to 2 billion; it is expected to double again by 1980. In world terms, a birth rate of 35 to 40 persons per 1,000 population per year combined with a death rate of 15 to 20 is producing a 2% annual increase (compared with 0.1% in ancient times). Although a 2% growth rate may appear small, it annually adds, for example, 9 million persons to India's population and almost 4 million to that of the United States. General population increase in the world was negligible until the Industrial Revolution, when there was a great surge in the population growth of Europe, especially in the British Isles. During that period advancements in sanitation, technology, and the means of food distribution made possible a drop in the death rate so significant that between 1650 and 1900 the population of Europe almost quadrupled (from about 100 million to about 400 million) in spite of considerable emigration. As the rate of population growth increased, so did concern that the earth might not be able to sustain future populations. The phenomenal increase in numbers led Thomas Robert MALTHUS to predict that the population would eventually outstrip the food supply. Karl Marx emphatically rejected this view and argued that the problem was not one of overpopulation but of unequal distribution of goods, a problem that even a declining population would not solve. A major population difference lies in the comparative growth rates of the industrialized and nonindustrialized nations. At current rates of increase, many of the latter countries will double their populations in 25 years or less, compared to 50 years or more for the former. Great Britain, for example, has a present doubling rate of 140 years, while Costa Rica has one of 19 years. Great Britain has accomplished what is known as demographic transition, i.e., it has moved from a condition of high birthrate and high death rate (before the Industrial Revolution), to one of high birthrate and low death rate (during industrialization), and finally to one of low birthrate and low death rate (as a postindustrial society). Most of the countries in the underdeveloped regions of the world are in a condition of high birthrate and declining death rate, thus, contributing most to what is known as the population explosion. A declining birthrate depends to a large extent upon the availability and use of BIRTH CONTROL information. Family planning, as it is now called, is national policy in almost all industrial countries, e.g., Japan, the United States, the Soviet Union, and most of Europe. As a result, in most cases the birthrate has declined, most dramatically in Japan. Many underdeveloped countries have followed the lead of India (which has since 1952 conducted an extensive, but not totally successful, birth control program) in trying to promote family planning as national policy, e.g., the People's Republic of China, Pakistan, Taiwan, Turkey, Egypt, Chile, and others. A number of nongovernmental organizations concerned with population growth have also appeared. Zero Population Growth, an educational group founded in 1970, aims to stop population growth, first in the United States and then in other countries. On the international level, besides the International Planned Parenthood Federation, the United Nations Economic and Social Council provides birth control aid to underdeveloped nations. See Gunnar Myrdal, *Population: A Problem for Democracy* (1962); American Assembly, *The Population Dilemma* (2d ed. 1969); W. D. Borrie, *The Growth and Control of World Population* (1970); N. W. Chamberlain, *Beyond Malthus* (1970); P. R. Ehrlich, *The Population Bomb* (rev. ed. 1971); Dean Fraser, *The People Problem* (1971).

population I and II, in astronomy: see STELLAR POPULATIONS.

Populist party, in U.S. history, political party formed primarily to express the agrarian protest of the late 19th cent. During the Panic of 1873 agricultural prices in the United States began to decline. The economic welfare of farmers suffered badly; many believed that the management of currency was at fault and that the government's currency policy was determined by Eastern bankers and industrialists. After attempts at independent political action failed (see GREENBACK PARTY), loosely knit confederations called Farmers' Alliances were formed during the 1880s. Separate organizations were founded in the North and South, and Southern blacks organized their own alliances. The Farmers' Alliances agitated for railroad regulation, tax reform, and unlimited coinage of silver and attempted to influence the established political parties. Growth was so rapid, however, that interest in a third party began to increase; in 1891 delegates from farm and labor organizations met in Cincinnati. No decision was made to form a political party, but when the Republican and Democratic parties both straddled the currency question at the 1892 presidential conventions, a convention was held at Omaha, and the Populist party was formed (1892). The party adopted a platform calling for free coinage of silver, abolition of national banks, a subtreasury scheme or some similar system, a graduated income tax, plenty of paper money, government ownership of all forms of transportation and communication, election of Senators by direct vote of the people, nonownership of land by foreigners, civil service reform, a working day of eight hours, postal banks, pensions, revision of the law of contracts, and reform of immigration regulations. The goal of the Populists in 1892 was no less than that of replacing the Democrats as the nation's second party by forming an alliance of the farmers of the West and South with the industrial workers of the East. James B. WEAVER was the Populist candidate for President that year, and he polled over 1,041,000 votes. The Populist votes in the 1894 congressional elections increased to 1,471,000 as the party gained momentum. In 1896, while the Republican party adhered to the "sound money" platform, the Populists kept intact their platform of 1892; the Democratic party, however, adopted the plank of free coinage of silver and nominated William Jennings BRYAN for President. Although the Populists tried to retain their independence by repudiating the Democratic vice presidential candidate, the Democratic party, helped by the eloquence of Bryan, captured the bulk of the Populist votes in 1896. The 1896 election undermined agrarian insurgency, and a period of rapidly rising farm prices helped to bring about the dissolution of the Populist party. Another important factor in the failure of the party was its inability to effect a genuine urban-rural coalition; its program had little appeal for wage earners of the industrial East. In some states the party was known as the People's party. See F. L. McVey, *The Populist Movement* (1896); J. D. Hicks, *The Populist Revolt* (1931, repr. 1961); Richard Hofstadter, *The Age of Reform* (1955, repr. 1963); R. F. Durden, *The Climax of Populism: The Election of 1896* (1965); Norman Pollack, ed., *The Populist Mind* (1967); Carleton Beals, *The Great Revolt and Its Leaders* (1968).

populists, in Russian history: see NARODNIKI.

Poratha (pŏr'əthə), one of the 10 sons of Haman. Esther 9.8.

Porbander (pōr'bəndər), town (1971 pop. 96,756), Gujurat state, W central India, on the Arabian Sea. Porbander trades with Persian Gulf and East African ports and is the terminus of a rail line. Fishing is an important industry. Noted for its high-quality ghee, Porbander also produces textiles, vegetable oil, salt, cement, and chemicals.

porbeagle: see MAKO.

porcelain [Ital. *porcellana*], white, hard, permanent, nonporous pottery having translucence. Porcelain was first made by the Chinese to withstand the great heat generated in certain parts of their kilns. The two natural substances used were kaolin, a white clay that melts only at very high temperature, and a feldspar mineral called petuntse that forms a glassy cement, binding the vessel permanently. Porcelain was manufactured during the T'ang period (A.D. 618–906) and was exported to the Islamic world where it was highly prized. The ware was refined during the Sung period (960–1279). During the Yuan period (1280–1368), blue and white ware was produced by utilizing cobalt blue from the Middle East. The Ming period (1368–1644) developed this blue and white ware but used other colors as well. The Ch'ing period (1644–1912) designed porcelain especially for export often utilizing Western designs. In Europe porcelain was first commercially produced (1710) in Meissen, Germany. Most of the European porcelain is soft paste (made from clay and an artificial compound such as ground glass) and is not as strong as the Chinese hard-paste porcelain. The porcelain makers at Bow, in London, began adding bone ash to their porcelain formula (c.1750) to strengthen the piece during firing. Important European centers for porcelain are Bow, Chelsea, Worcester, Staffordshire, Vienna, Meissen, Sèvres,

Limoges, and Rouen. See George Savage, *Porcelain through the Ages* (1955, repr. 1963); F. Litchfield, *Pottery and Porcelain* (6th ed. 1953, repr. 1967).

Porcius Festus: see FESTUS, PORCIUS.

Porcupine (pôr'kyəpīn''), river, 448 mi (721 km) long, rising in the Ogilvie Mts., NW Yukon Territory, Canada. It flows in a great arc NE through the Eagle Plain, then W into Alaska and to the Yukon River (of which it is a main tributary) at Fort Yukon. The river was discovered (1842) by John Bell, a chief trader for the Hudson's Bay Company.

porcupine, member of either of two RODENT families, characterized by having some of its hairs modified as bristles, spines, or quills. The quills are loosely attached to the porcupines' skin and pull out easily, remaining imbedded in any predator that comes in contact with them. The New World, or tree, porcupines (family Erethizontidae) are slow-moving, more or less arboreal animals. The ends of their quills bear minute overlapping barbs; when imbedded they are very difficult to pull out and tend to work inward, piercing internal organs. The North American, or Canadian, tree porcupine, *Erethizon dorsatum,* is found in wooded areas over most of North America, excluding the SE United States. This animal has a coat of long, shaggy, brown or black hair mixed with shorter quills. When threatened it erects its quills and backs toward its enemy, delivering a blow with its tail. Even if no contact is made quills may fly out; this has given rise to the erroneous belief that porcupines can shoot their quills. North American porcupines spend the day, singly or in groups, in rock cavities, hollow logs, or burrows. At night they forage in trees, feeding on leaves, buds and bark. They subsist in winter entirely on bark stripped from evergreens. The damage they do to trees is conspicuous, but seldom fatal. The Central and South American tree porcupines, species of the genus *Coendou,* have naked-tipped, prehensile tails, with which they hang from branches. Also called coendous, they are up to 20 in. (50 cm) long, including the tail, which is as long as the body. The Old World porcupines (family Hystricidae) have no barbs on their spines. The larger species belong to the genus *Hystrix,* and are found in scrubby areas in Asia, Africa, and SE Europe. These animals are unable to climb trees. They have extremely long black-and-white-striped quills on the hind part of the back and on the tail; some species also have crests of long bristles on their heads. The rest of the coat is a mixture of bristles or spines and short hair. The tail quills are hollow and are used to make noise; when the animal is alarmed it erects its quills and rattles its tail. If attacked it runs backwards into its enemy, leaving the attacker full of quills. It forages at night for roots and other plant foods, scuffling and grunting as it moves about. Old World porcupines dig deep burrow systems, where a number of them may live in adjoining burrows. Members of most species weigh 50 to 60 lb (23–27 kg); despite their large size they can move swiftly when alarmed. Species of several other genera, smaller and possessing spines or bristles, but no quills, are found in Africa and SE Asia; these are good tree climbers. Porcupines are classified in the phylum CHORDATA, subphylum Vertebrata, class Mammalia, order Rodentia, families Erethizontidae and Hystricidae. See study by D. F. Costello (1966).

Pordenone, Giovanni Antonio de (jōvän'nē äntō'nyō dā pōrdānō'nā), c.1484–1539, Venetian painter. His real name was Giovanni Antonio de Sacchis. He studied in Venice and probably in Rome c.1515. Strong elements of Raphael and Michelangelo are present in his works at the churches of Treviso, Cortemaggiore, Piacenza, and Terlizzi. In Venice his services were in great demand for the decorating of Venetian palaces. Most of his Venetian frescoes have perished. Some of his paintings are in the National Gallery, London; the Brera, Milan; the Philadelphia Museum; and in Vienna.

porgy (pôr'gē), common name for members of the Sparidae, a family of small-mouthed fishes with strong teeth adapted for crushing their food of shellfish and crustaceans. Porgies are found in warm and tropical coastal areas and are especially abundant in the Mediterranean and Red seas and in the West Indies. Best known of the North American species is the migratory porgy, *Pagrus pagrus,* found from the Carolinas to Cape Cod and called scup in New England, porgy in New York, and fair maid in the South. It is an excellent food fish. Common S of Chesapeake Bay is the sheepshead porgy. The jolthead porgy, named for its habit of butting shellfish loose from rocks and pilings, is the largest (up to 10 lb/4.5 kg) of the family. Of commercial importance in the area of the Gulf of Mexico is the pinfish (6–10 in./15–25 cm). In Europe the name porgy generally refers to the red porgy or sea bream, a red fish with blue spots common in Mediterranean and European Atlantic waters. Porgies are classified in the phylum CHORDATA, subphylum Vertebrata, class Osteichthyes, order Perciformes, family Sparidae.

Pori (pô'rē), Swed. *Björneborg,* city (1970 pop. 72,938), capital of Turku-and-Pori prov., SW Finland, near the mouth of the Kokemaënjoki River. Timber and metals are exported, and wood products are manufactured. Pori was chartered in 1564 and was initially dominated by the HANSEATIC LEAGUE. By 1840 the city had the largest commercial fleet in Finland.

Porifera (pōrĭf'ərə) [Lat.,=pore bearer], animal phylum consisting of the organisms commonly called SPONGES. It is the least evolutionarily advanced group of the subkingdom METAZOA (multicellular animals) and is sometimes separated into the subkingdom Parazoa to distinguish it from the more advanced animals, as well as from the Protozoa, or single-celled animals. All adult sponges are sessile (nonmotile), and nearly all are marine. There is one family of freshwater sponges. Although sponges lack true organs, they are organized into primitive tissues in which the cells exhibit considerable independence. The sponge is basically a three-layered sac. The outer (epidermal) layer consists of flattened polygonal cells called pinacocytes. The middle (mesenchymal) layer consists of gelatinous protein material, motile cells called amoebocytes, and a skeleton of calcareous or siliceous spicules, or of elastic fibers of a protein called spongin. The inner layer consists of flagellum-bearing cells called collar cells, or choanocytes. The body wall is permeated by numerous pores called ostia that open into the inner cavity, the spongocoel; there is also a single large opening, the osculum. The spongocoel is lined with choanocytes; the concerted whipping action of their flagella creates a current of water that flows into the spongocoel through the ostia and out through the osculum. The choanocytes filter plankton and small bits of organic detritus from the water and absorb oxygen. Food is digested either in the choanocytes or in amoebocytes. Waste products are carried out through the osculum. Different types of amoebocytes are also responsible for secreting the skeletal material, controlling the size of the osculum opening, and giving rise to egg and sperm cells and to other cells as needed. The body of most sponges is irregular in form, although radial symmetry is displayed by the more primitive members. Three types of sponge structure are recognized: the asconoid, the most primitive, is regular, urn-shaped, and radially symmetrical; the syconoid is a more irregular structure that displays some degree of folding of the body wall while still maintaining a basic radial symmetry; the leuconoid is highly irregular, displays the greatest degree of folding of the body wall, and has lost radial symmetry. In the leuconoid sponges choanocytes line the pockets formed by the convoluted body wall. Sponges are limited in size by the rate at which water can flow in and out of the spongocoel, bringing in water and oxygen and removing waste products. Because the asconoid type has the smallest surface area, sponges of this structure are among the smallest in the phylum; leuconoid sponges, with a large amount of surface area, represent some of the largest members of the phylum. Pieces of sponge are able to regenerate into whole new sponges. Asexual reproduction occurs by budding or by fragmentation. The buds may remain attached to the parent or separate from it, and each bud develops into a new individual. Freshwater sponges, as well as several marine species, form resistant structures called gemmules that can withstand adverse conditions such as drying or cold and later develop into new individuals. Gemmules are aggregates of sponge tissue and food, covered by a hard coating containing spicules or spongin fibers. Sexual reproduction also occurs. Most sponges are hermaphroditic, the same individual producing eggs and sperm, but in some species the sexes are separate. The larvae are flagellated and swim about freely for a short time. After settling and attaching to a suitable substrate, the larvae develop into young sponges. Sponges are subdivided into three classes according to the type of skeleton secreted by the cells of the mesenchyme.

Class Calcarea (calcareous sponges). Sponges in this class are typified by skeletal spicules composed of calcium carbonate. The spicules often protrude through the epidermal covering of the body wall, giving the organism a rough texture. Calcareous sponges are small, usually only a few inches high, and are generally dull in appearance, although several species are brightly colored. The members of this class are the simplest sponges, and all three morphological types—asconoid, syconoid, and leuconoid—are represented. There are approximately 150 known species, exclusively marine and shallow-water dwellers.

Class Hexactinellida (glass sponges). These are deep-sea sponges. They lack an epidermal covering and their skeletons are composed of spicules of silica. The spicules, which often form a latticework, have six points or some multiple thereof. Glass sponges are pale in color and are cup- or basket-shaped. The spongocoel is large, and the osculum is covered by a grillwork of fused spicules. When the living tissue is removed, the cylindrical skeletons often have the appearance of spun glass. The glass sponge known as Venus's-flower-basket (*Euplectella*) supplies a home for certain shrimps that become trapped by the lattice of spicules. The body plan of Hexactinellida is between syconoid and leuconoid.

Class Demospongiae (siliceous sponges). Most sponges belong in this class. It includes sponges with a skeleton made up of silicon-containing spicules or spongin fibers or both. In the latter case, the spongin provides a matrix in which the spicules are embedded. The Demospongiae vary in size from small, encrusting forms to very large, irregular masses. All are leuconoid; many are brightly colored. The freshwater sponges (family Spongillidae) belong to this class; they are frequently green because of symbiotic algae that live in the amoebocytes. The horny sponges (family Spongidae) also belong to this class; they include the common bath sponge, *Hippospongia elastica,* and most of the other sponges used commercially. The boring sponges (family Clionidae) are extremely interesting because of their ability to bore into calcareous rocks and

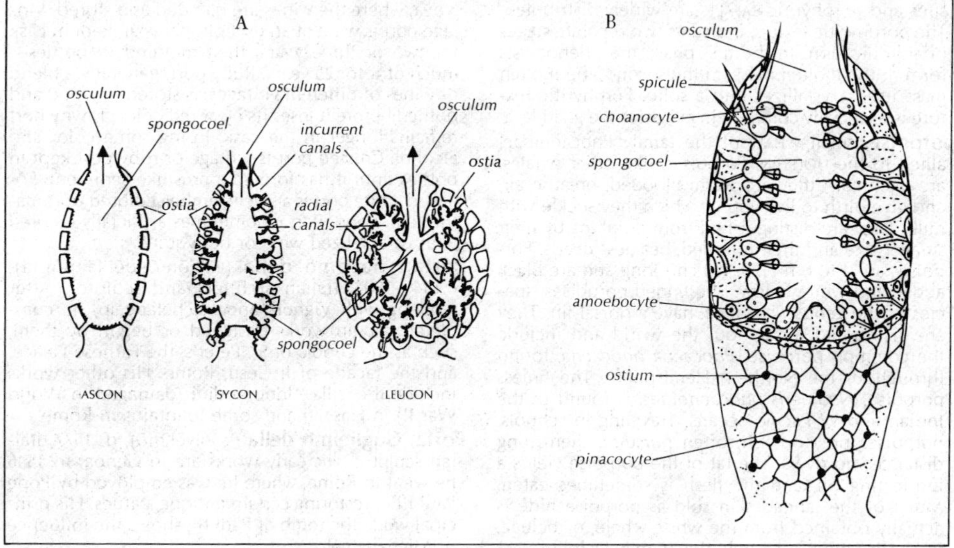

A. *Canal systems of the three morphological types of sponges*
B. *Internal anatomy of an asconoid sponge, representative of the phylum Porifera*

mollusk shells. They begin their boring as larvae and spend their lives in the tunnels they form. Sulfur sponges (*Cliona* species) are bright yellow boring forms inhabiting shallow waters on the east and west coasts of the United States.

Porjus, town: see LULEÄLV, river, Sweden.

pork, flesh of swine prepared as food, one of the principal commodities of the MEAT-PACKING industry. Pork has long been a staple food in most of the world, although religious taboos have limited its use, especially among Jews and Muslims. It is sold either as fresh meat or as HAM, BACON, SAUSAGE, LARD or a variety of other products. The fresh pork and the choicest cured products are taken from smooth carcasses weighing from 240 to 400 lb (110–180 kg). Fresh pork is sold either chilled or frozen. Pork may be cured either by injecting it with a brine or by rubbing it with a mixture of salt, sugar, and other chemicals (the dry method). The skin and fat of fresh pork should be white, and the flesh should be clear, pink, and fine-grained. The principal fresh cuts are hams, loins, spareribs, shoulders, butts, and feet. The brains, snout, ears, jowls, tail, and tongue are ground up and often used in combination with other meat products.

Porkkala (pôrk'kälä), small strategic peninsula, Uusimaa prov., in the Gulf of Finland, near Helsinki. According to the Soviet-Finnish armistice of 1944, Finland leased this area to the USSR for 50 years, for use as a naval base. The USSR returned it to Finland in 1956.

pororoca, tidal bore: see AMAZON, river, Brazil.

Póros (pô'rôs), anc. Greek *Calauria,* island (1971 pop. 4,051), c.8 sq mi (20 sq km), SE Greece, in the Aegean Sea near the Argolis peninsula of the Peloponnesus. It is famous for its fine marble. There are remains of a temple of Poseidon where Demosthenes took poison and died in 322 B.C. Representatives of Britain, France, and Russia met on Póros in 1828 to discuss the future of the new Greek state.

Porphyry (pôr'fĭrē), c.232–c.304, Greek scholar and Neoplatonic philosopher. He studied rhetoric under Cassius Longinus and philosophy under PLOTINUS. He later lectured in Rome on the philosophy of Plotinus and was the teacher of the Neoplatonist IAMBLICHUS. He wrote lives of Pythagoras and of Plotinus and edited the *Enneads* of Plotinus. He wrote extensively against Christianity and on rhetorical and literary themes. His most influential work is the *Isagoge,* an introduction to the logic of Aristotle, which became a standard medieval text.

porphyry (pôr'fərē), igneous rock composed of large, conspicuous crystals (phenocrysts) and a groundmass in which the phenocrysts are embedded. Some authorities consider the expression "porphyritic rock" better usage than porphyry, since the term refers only to the texture of the rock—not its chemical, physical, or mineralogical composition or color. The texture is important in the determination of the circumstances under which the rock formed. The phenocrysts vary in size; the groundmass may be either glassy or made up of coarse or fine granules or crystals. The varieties of porphyry are many, the specimens being named by the character of the phenocrysts in the groundmass. They are found in main classes of igneous rocks, e.g., in granite, syenite, diorite, gabbro, and peridotite. Porphyritic felsites and porphyritic BASALTS are widely distributed. The porphyritic texture indicates two separate stages of solidification. In the first phase the phenocrysts form in the molten mass; in the second, the molten mass itself crystallizes into a solid. Porphyritic texture is especially common in extrusions, e.g., in lava.

porpoise, small WHALE of the family Phocaenidae, allied to the DOLPHIN. Porpoises, like other whales, are mammals; they are warm-blooded, breathe air, and give birth to live young, which they suckle with milk. They are distinguished from dolphins by their smaller size and their rounded, beakless heads. Porpoises are 4 to 6 ft (120–180 cm) long and are black above and white below. The finned porpoises, species of the genus *Phocaena,* have a dorsal fin. They are distributed throughout the world and include the common porpoise, *Phocaena phocaena,* found throughout the Northern Hemisphere. The finless porpoise, *Neomeris phocaenoides,* is found in the Indian and W Pacific oceans. Traveling in schools, porpoises prey on fish, often pursuing them long distances up rivers. The fat of the porpoise yields a lubricating oil, and the flesh is sometimes eaten. Much of the tanned skin sold as porpoise hide is actually obtained from the white whale, or beluga. In North America the dolphins (family Delphinidae) are sometimes called porpoises and the bottlenosed dolphin is sometimes called the common porpoise. True porpoises are classified in the phylum CHORDATA, subphylum Vertebrata, class Mammalia, order Cetacea, family Phocaenidae. See K. S. Norris, *The Porpoise Watcher* (1974).

Porpora, Niccolò Antonio (nēk-kōlô' äntô'nyō pôr'pōrä), 1686–1766, Italian composer and one of the greatest singing teachers. As an opera composer he was employed to be Handel's rival in London, but he is remembered for his vocal teaching. Metastasio and Haydn were among his pupils, as were many of the major singers of the 18th cent., including Farinelli.

Porrentruy (pôräNtrüē'), Ger. *Pruntrut,* town (1970 pop. 7,827), Bern canton, NW Switzerland, in the Bernese Jura mts. It is an old watchmaking center; knitted goods and shoes are also made. It was the residence (1528–1792) of the prince-bishops of Basel.

Porres, Saint Martin de (märtĕn' dā pôr'rās), 1579–1639, Peruvian Dominican lay brother, b. Lima. He was the son of a Spanish soldier and a Negro freedwoman from Panama. Apprenticed to a barber-surgeon, he later joined a monastery as a tertiary, or lay brother, in Lima and devoted himself wholly to the sick and unfortunate. He built an orphanage, founded several nurseries, and lived an extraordinarily ascetic life. He was canonized in 1962. Feast: Nov. 5.

porridge, food made of the meal or flour of wheat, oats, or other grain or of peas or beans, stirred into milk or water and cooked until thick. The early porridge seems to have been a thick stew of vegetables or a combination of foods.

Porsena, Lars: see LARS PORSENA.

Porsgrunn (pôrs'grōōn"), town (1970 pop. 31,566), Telemark co., SE Norway, a port on the Frierfjord (an arm of the Skagerrak); chartered 1842. Manufactures include chemicals (including fertilizers), metal goods, and electrical appliances. The town is noted for the porcelain made there.

Porson, Richard, 1759–1808, English classical scholar, b. Norfolk. A poor boy, he showed such astonishing powers of memory that patrons sent him through Eton and Cambridge. He was appointed regius professor of Greek at Cambridge in 1792, and lived in London, where he edited several plays of Euripides. A scrupulous scholar, Porson was a textual critic of the highest order and changed existing ideas of Greek meter. His treatises and criticism were edited by Thomas Kidd (1815) and his correspondence by H. R. Luard (1851). See biography by M. L. Clarke (1937).

port, a harbor and its terminal facilities for the transfer of goods and passengers to or from waterborne means of transport. Port cities are located on oceans, lakes, rivers, and canals in places where access to the hinterland provides a large volume of commerce. The importance of a port depends on the availability of transportation and on the extent of terminal facilities such as wharfs, storage space, and machinery. See also FREE PORT.

port [from Oporto], fortified wine made in Portugal from grapes grown in the Douro valley; Portuguese law allows only this wine to be called port. Various grapes are blended by the growers, and brandy is added before fermentation is complete. In the spring the casks are brought to Oporto and Villa Nova, where the wines are blended and stored. Vintage port is wine of an exceptional year, kept in cask for two or three years, then matured in bottles—much of it for 25 years. Ruby port, generally a blend of wines of different vintages, is stored in wood and bottled before it loses its clear red color. Tawny port remains longer in the cask, losing some color and alcohol. Crusted port is vintage or ruby port kept in bottles until it has formed a crustlike sediment. So-called white port is a sweet, amber-colored port matured in wood. Port is sometimes artificially colored with caramelized wine or berry juice.

Porta, Giacomo della (jä'kōmō dĕl'lä pôr'tä), c.1540–1602, Italian architect and sculptor. After working with Vignola and Michelangelo, he completed certain works designed or begun by them, such as the cupola of St. Peter's, the Farnese Palace, and the facade of Il Gesù, Rome. His other works include the Villa Aldobrandini (damaged in World War II) in Frascati and some fountains in Rome.

Porta, Guglielmo della (gōōlyĕl'mō), d. 1577, Italian sculptor. His early works are in Genoa. In 1546 he went to Rome, where he was employed by Pope Paul III in restoring certain antique statues. His principal work, the tomb of Paul III, shows the influence of Michelangelo.

Port Adelaide, city (1971 pop. 39,039), South Australia, S Australia, a suburb of Adelaide, on an inlet of Gulf St. Vincent. It is the principal port and wool-trading center of the state. The chief exports are wheat, flour, and wool. Sulfuric acid, processed foods, and automobile parts are made.

Portadown (pôrtədoun'), municipal borough (1971 pop. 21,906), Co. Armagh, central Northern Ireland, on the Bann River. It is an important railroad and industrial center. Roses from Portadown nurseries are famous.

Portage (1, 2 pôr'təj; **3** pôr'tĭj). **1** Town (1970 pop. 19,127), Porter co., NW Ind., a suburb of Gary, on Lake Michigan; inc. 1959. A new port, accommodating ocean vessels, began operating there in the early 1970s. The town, located in a highly industrialized portion of the state, has a steel industry. **2** City (1970 pop. 33,590), Kalamazoo co., SW Mich.; inc. 1963. Its manufactures include pharmaceuticals, industrial and medical gases, machinery, and paper and plastic products. **3** City (1970 pop. 7,821), seat of Columbia co., central Wis.; inc. 1854. It is on the Wisconsin at the point where that river is close enough to the Fox to make canoe portage feasible. In 1673, Louis Jolliet and Father Marquette were the first white men to use this important portage link in the water route from the Great Lakes to the Mississippi. The path is now a ship canal, and the present city is a farm trade center with some light manufacturing industry. The site of Fort Winnebago (1828) and the restored Indian Agency house (1832) are there. Zona Gale and Frederick Jackson Turner were born in Portage.

Portage Lake, inlet of Keweenaw Bay, c.20 mi (32 km) long and 2 mi (3.2 km) wide, N Mich., indenting the southeast shore of Keweenaw peninsula. An old portage route connected it with Lake Superior, and now a short ship canal, the Keweenaw Waterway, links the two lakes.

Portage la Prairie (pôr"tĭj lə prâr'ē), city (1971 pop. 12,950), S Man., Canada. It is the center of a mixed-farming region and has diversified industries. The city is near the site of Fort La Reine, an important fur-trading post built (1738) by Vérendrye as a carrying point between the Assiniboine River and Lake Manitoba.

Port Alberni (ălbûr'nē), city (1971 pop. 20,063), SW British Columbia, Canada, on Vancouver Island, at the head of Alberni Canal and Barkley sound. It is a fishing port with boat-building and wood-products industries.

Portales, Diego (dyā'gō pôrtä'lās), 1793–1837, Chilean statesman. Founder of constitutional order and of the conservative regime in Chile, he was general minister (1830–31) and minister of war and marine (1831–32, 1835–37). The brilliantly conceived, highly centralistic constitution of 1833 was largely his work. Refusing the presidency, but ruling in fact, he reorganized the army, the treasury, the internal administration, commerce, and industry. His one aim was to bring order out of the bloody chaos that followed independence, but the parliamentarian became the autocrat; his strict measures aroused bitter opposition and he was assassinated by mutinous soldiers.

Portales (pôrtăl'ĭs), city (1970 pop. 10,554), seat of Roosevelt co., E N.Mex., near the Texas line; inc. 1910. It is the trade center of an agricultural and livestock area. There are oil wells in the vicinity. Eastern New Mexico Univ. is there. Cannon Air Force Base is nearby.

Portalis, Jean Étienne Marie (zhäN ātyĕn' märē' pôrtälēs'), 1746–1807, French statesman and lawyer. A moderate, he was suspected of royalist sympathies during the French Revolution but was made a councilor of state and director of ecclesiastic affairs by Napoleon Bonaparte (later French Emperor Napoleon I). Portalis had an important part in making the Concordat of 1801 and in drawing up the Code Napoléon.

Port Angeles (ăn'jələs), city (1970 pop. 16,367), seat of Clallam co., NW Wash., on Juan de Fuca Strait opposite Victoria, British Columbia; inc. 1890. A port of entry with a fine harbor, Port Angeles is a boating and fishing center and has pulp and paper mills. The city is also a resort and the headquarters for Olympic National Park (see NATIONAL PARKS AND MONUMENTS, table). A junior college and a U.S. coast guard air rescue station are there.

Port Apra, Guam: see APRA HARBOR.

Port Arthur: see THUNDER BAY, Ont., Canada.

Port Arthur: see LÜ-SHUN, China.

Port Arthur, city (1970 pop. 57,371), Jefferson co., SE Texas, on Sabine Lake; inc. 1898. A deepwater port of entry on the Sabine-Neches Canal, it is a giant oil port, with many large refineries, tank farms, chemical plants, and shipyards. Oil-drilling equipment and metal, steel, and aluminum products are also manufactured. The Sabine region had been visited, settlements had been made, and livestock and rice had been raised before Arthur E. Stilwell decided (1894) to found a railroad terminus there. John Warne Gates (Bet-a-Million Gates) also contributed to the early growth of the city. A ship channel was completed in 1899. Port Arthur boomed after the discovery (1901) of oil at Spindletop. Points of interest include the pleasure pier on reclaimed land in Sabine Lake and the extremely high bridge (1938) over the Neches River on the road to Orange.

Port Augusta, city (1971 pop. 12,095), South Australia, S Australia, at the head of Spencer Gulf. It is a port and railroad center.

Port-au-Prince (pôrt-ə-prĭns', Fr. pôrtōprăNs'), city (1971 pop. 493,932), capital of Haiti, SW Haiti, on a bay at the end of the Gulf of Gonaïves. The country's chief seaport, it exports mainly coffee and sugar. The city has food- and tobacco-processing plants, rum distilleries, and textile and cement industries. It was founded in 1749 by French sugar planters. In 1770 it replaced Cap-Haïtien as capital of the French colony of Saint-Domingue (as Haiti was then known), and in 1804 it became the capital of newly independent Haiti. Port-au-Prince has remained unsanitary and economically backward, however, and has suffered frequently from earthquakes, fires, and civil warfare. The city is laid out like an amphitheater, with business and commercial quarters along the water and residences on the hills above. Landmarks include the French-built quay (1780), the Univ. of Haiti (est. 1944), the National Palace, the National Museum, and the Basilica of Notre Dame.

Port Authority of New York and New Jersey, self-sustaining public corporation established in 1921 by the states of New York and New Jersey to administer the activities of the New York–New Jersey port area, which has a waterfront of c.900 mi (1,448 km) lying in both states. Originally called the Port of New York Authority, the name was changed in 1972 to reflect the joint administration of the port. In 1917 an attempt was made to solve the many disputes between the states concerning such matters as boundaries, marine police jurisdiction, and freight rates; the governors of New York and New Jersey appointed a bistate commission to study the problem of coordinating port and harbor development for the two states as a whole. Out of this group's recommendations grew the idea for the authority, and in 1921 a compact was signed (the Port Compact) that defined a single Port District and provided for its administration by a Port Authority that was to coordinate terminal, transportation, and other facilities of commerce. The authority consists of 12 unsalaried commissioners, 6 appointed by the governor of each state. Since the commissioners constitute agents of the state, their instructions take the form of legislative mandates. The work of the commissioners, in addition to administration, includes development, construction, operation, and protection of the Port District. The authority finances its activities from income such as tolls and charges, and by selling revenue bonds in the public market. The authority has been so successful that it has set a pattern in administration. It has given to the inhabitants of the Port District a modern and efficient network of bridges, tunnels, and terminal facilities without adding to the burden of the New York or New Jersey taxpayers. Among its projects have been the refinancing of the Holland Tunnel and the construction of the George Washington Bridge, the Lincoln Tunnel, the Port Authority Bus Terminal in New York City, marine terminals in Newark and Elizabeth, and the Port Authority Trans-Hudson RR, known as PATH. The agency also administers numerous facilities, including the New York City airports and Newark International Airport. See study by E. W. Bard (1939, repr. 1968).

Port Blair, India: see ANDAMAN AND NICOBAR ISLANDS.

Port Charlotte, uninc. town (1970 pop. 10,769), Charlotte co., SW Fla., on Charlotte Harbor (an inlet of the Gulf of Mexico) and the Peace and Myakka rivers. It is a planned residential community—one of several on a peninsula once owned by the Vanderbilt family. The area, formerly cattle pasture land, has been rapidly developed since the 1950s. Port Charlotte has 145 mi (233 km) of man-made waterways, many with access to the Gulf of Mexico; 38 mi (61 km) of natural shoreline; and 42 bridges. Its cultural center is the focus for the county's educational, cultural, recreational, and social activities.

Port Chester, village (1970 pop. 25,803), Westchester co., SE N.Y., an industrial suburb of New York City, on Long Island Sound at the mouth of the Byram River, and on the Conn. border; settled after 1660, inc. 1868. Candy, nuts and bolts, brushes, toys, and lamps are among its many manufactures. Gen. Israel Putnam had his headquarters there in 1777–78. Several colonial homes remain.

Port Colborne (kōl'bərn), town (1971 pop. 21,420), S Ont., Canada, on Lake Erie, at the south end of the Welland Ship Canal. It is an important transshipment center between Montreal and points to the west. It has a nickel refinery, grain elevators, and a cement plant.

portcullis (pôrtkŭl'ĭs), grating or framework of strong bars of wood or iron, sharp-pointed at their lower ends, sliding vertically in the grooved jambs of a fortified portal as a protection in case of assault. First used in Roman times against Hannibal, the portcullis reached its highest development in the 12th cent. as a characteristic feature of the defensive system of a castle or fortified town. It could be dropped suddenly in a surprise attack. Through its grating the defenders could keep up a fire of arrows and other missiles. In the 14th cent., with the development of gunpowder, its tactical value was reduced.

Port Darwin: see DARWIN, Australia.

Port Elizabeth, city (1970 pop. 386,577), Cape Prov., SE South Africa, on Algoa Bay, an arm of the Indian Ocean. It is a tourist center and a major seaport that ships diamonds, wool, fruit, and other items. Automobile assembly is the chief industry; shoe manufacturing, metal and timber processing, and electrical engineering are also important. There is some food processing, tanning, and chemical production. Port Elizabeth was founded by British settlers in 1820 near Fort Frederick (1799; now a monument). The city grew rapidly after 1873, when a railroad to Kimberley began. The Univ. of Port Elizabeth (1964) and a technical college (1925) are in the city. A snake park is maintained.

Porteous, John (pôr'tēəs), d. 1736, British soldier. He was captain of the Edinburgh town guard at the execution (1736) of Andrew Wilson, a smuggler. When the crowd, which was sympathetic to Wilson, rioted, the guard fired into it, killing eight or nine persons. Porteous was tried and sentenced to death, but his execution was postponed. On Sept. 7, 1736, an indignant mob took him from prison and hanged him, a crime for which no one was brought to justice despite the efforts of the government. Incidents of the Porteous riot are used by Sir Walter Scott in *The Heart of Midlothian.*

Porter, Anna Maria: see PORTER, JANE.

Porter, Arthur Kingsley, 1883–1933, American art historian. Interested primarily in medieval and ancient art, Porter revolutionized the understanding of the chronology and diffusion of Romanesque sculpture. His works include *Lombard Architecture* (4 vol., 1915–17), *Romanesque Sculpture of the Pilgrimage Roads* (10 vol., 1923), and *Spanish Romanesque Sculpture* (2 vol., 1928).

Porter, Cole, 1893–1964, American composer and lyricist, b. Peru, Ind., grad. Yale, 1913. Porter's witty, sophisticated lyrics and his affecting melodies place him high in the ranks of American composers of popular music. He was an elegant and debonair man, in spite of a riding accident (1937) that left him crippled. He studied music at Harvard and with D'Indy at the Schola Cantorum in Paris. After one early failure, most of his musicals were vastly successful. They include *Greenwich Village Follies* (1924); *Gay Divorce* (1932); *Anything Goes* (1934); *Jubilee* (1935); *Red, Hot and Blue* (1936); *Du Barry Was a Lady* (1939); *Panama Hattie* (1940); *Something for the Boys* (1943); *Kiss Me, Kate* (1948); *Can-Can* (1953); and *Silk Stockings* (1955). Among Porter's film scores are *Born to Dance* (1936) and *High Society* (1956). His most popular songs include "Night and Day," "Begin the Beguine," "Let's Do It," and "In the Still of the Night." See *The Cole Porter Song Book* (1959); *Cole,* ed. by Robert Kimball (1971).

Porter, David, 1780–1843, American naval officer, b. Boston. Appointed a midshipman in 1798, he served in the West Indies and in the war with Tripoli. In 1803 his ship, the *Philadelphia,* was captured off the coast of Tripoli, and Porter was a prisoner until peace was declared in 1805. He achieved his greatest success as commander of the *Essex* in the War of 1812. In that year he captured several British ships carrying troops to Halifax and the British war vessel *Alert.* Then, accompanied by young David FARRAGUT, he sailed the *Essex* around the Horn and cruised in the Pacific, warring on British commercial vessels. He took formal possession of Nuku Hiva, one of the MARQUESAS ISLANDS, in Nov., 1813, but this act was not recognized by the U.S. government. In 1814 the *Essex* was blockaded by British ships in the harbor of Valparaiso, Chile. Porter escaped to sea, but a squall disabled his ship, forcing him back to the coast. He was attacked by two British warships and after a hard-fought battle was forced to surrender. While in the West Indies in 1824 on an expedition for suppressing piracy, Porter forced the officials of the town of Foxardo (Fajardo), Puerto Rico, to apologize for jailing an officer from his fleet. The government did not sanction Porter's act, and he was court-martialed and suspended for six months. Porter resigned and in 1826 entered the Mexican navy as its head. Disgusted with the jealous intrigues of the Mexican officers, he resigned in 1829. After his return to the United States, he became (1831) chargé d'affaires and later (1839) minister at Constantinople and held this post until his death. See biographies by his son, David Dixon Porter (1875), and D. F. Long (1970); Richard Wheeler, *In Pirate Waters* (1969).

Porter, David Dixon, 1813–91, American admiral, b. Chester, Pa.; son of David Porter. He served under his father in the Mexican navy before he was appointed (1829) midshipman in the U.S. navy. He held his first command, the *Spitfire,* in the Mexican War. From 1850 to 1854, Porter, on leave, commanded passenger and mail ships. In the Civil War he led the mortar flotilla of the Union fleet commanded by David FARRAGUT in the successful assault on New Orleans (1862) and contributed to Ulysses S. Grant's success in the VICKSBURG CAMPAIGN (1863). For these services on the Mississippi River he was made rear admiral. He cooperated (1864) with Gen. Nathaniel P. BANKS in the Red River expedition and later was given command of the North Atlantic Blockading Squadron. In the joint land-sea expedition against FORT FISHER (1864–65), the naval forces were under his direction. Next to Farragut, Porter was the outstanding Union naval commander. As superintendent (1865–69) of the U.S. Naval Academy he proved himself an able organizer and administrator. Porter was promoted to vice admiral in 1866; in 1870, on Farragut's death, he became full admiral. See biography by N. B. Gerson (1968).

Porter, Fitz-John, 1822–1901, Union general in the American Civil War, b. Portsmouth, N.H.; nephew of David Porter. He saw service in the Mexican War and was an instructor at West Point (1849–55). At the outbreak of the Civil War, Porter was made a brigadier general of volunteers. In 1862 he distinguished himself as a corps commander in the Peninsular campaign, especially in the SEVEN DAYS BATTLES. Later that year, however, John Pope alleged that the Union defeat in the second battle of BULL RUN was due to Porter's disobedience. At his court-martial Porter declared that it was impossible to carry out Pope's orders, but he was, nevertheless, cashiered. A review of the case in 1879 vindicated him. In 1886 he was reappointed colonel of infantry and retired. See study by Otto Eisenschiml (1950).

Porter, Horace, 1837–1921, American soldier and diplomat, b. Huntingdon, Pa. In the Civil War he saw varied service, mostly as an ordnance officer, before becoming (1864) aide-de-camp to Gen. U. S. Grant. After the war, Porter was briefly Assistant Secretary of War when Grant was Secretary of War. During Grant's presidency Porter served as one of his executive secretaries until 1872. He was ambassador to France (1897–1905), where, at his own personal expense, he recovered the body of John Paul Jones for reburial in the United States. As delegate to the Hague Conference of 1907, he amended the DRAGO DOCTRINE with his Porter Proposition, which provided that strong nations whose nationals had contract-debt claims against weaker nations should submit the claims to arbitration before trying to collect them by force. He wrote *West Point Life* (1866; verse) and *Campaigning with Grant* (1897). See biography by his daughter, E. P. Mende, and H. G. Pearson (1927).

Porter, Jane, 1776–1850, Scottish novelist. Her historical novels, particularly *Thaddeus of Warsaw* (4 vol., 1803) and *Scottish Chiefs* (5 vol., 1810), were exceptionally popular in their day. **Anna Maria Porter,** 1780–1832, her sister, wrote *The Hungarian Brothers* (3 vol., 1807) and other novels.

Porter, Katherine Anne, 1890–, American author, b. Indian Creek, Texas. Although the amount of her published work is small, she is regarded as one of the masters of the short story. Her first book of stories, *Flowering Judas* (1930), won her immediate recognition and critical acclaim. It was followed by *Pale Horse, Pale Rider* (1939) and *The Leaning Tower* (1944). Her stories have been praised particularly for their technical accomplishments in matters of style, form, and language. A collection of her essays and occasional pieces appeared as *The Days Before* (1952). *Ship of Fools,* her first long novel, was published in 1962. Set aboard a German ship shortly before Hitler's accession to power, the novel is a moral allegory that attempts to recreate the atmosphere of a world on the brink of disaster. See her *Collected Stories* (1965).

Porter, Noah, 1811-92, American educator and philosopher, b. Farmington, Conn., grad. Yale, 1831. He entered the ministry in 1836. In 1846 he became professor of moral philosophy and metaphysics at Yale and from 1871 to 1886 was 12th president of the university. As president he steadfastly opposed modern tendencies in education, urging the retention of Greek and Latin as the basis for the liberal arts course, the subordination of science to the humanities, and a prescribed curriculum rather than an elective system. He edited (1864, 1890) revised editions of Noah Webster's dictionary and wrote a number of educational and philosophical works, the most popular of which was *The Human Intellect* (1868). See biography by Timothy Dwight (1892).

Porter, William Sydney: see O. HENRY, pseud. of William Sydney Porter.

porter: see BEER.

Porterville, city (1970 pop. 12,602), Tulare co., S central Calif., on the Tule River; founded 1859 on the old Los Angeles-San Francisco stage route, inc. 1902. The city is chiefly residential, with some agriculture and light manufacturing. It is the headquarters for Sequoia National Forest. A junior college and a state hospital are there.

Port-Gentil (pôr-zhäNtēl'), city (1970 est. pop. 48,000), W Gabon, a seaport on Cape Lopez Bay (an arm of the Atlantic Ocean). Timber and locally manufactured plywood are exported. Petroleum is produced nearby.

Port Glasgow, burgh (1971 pop. 22,399), Renfrewshire, W Scotland, on the Firth of Clyde. Its dry dock, built in 1762, was one of the first of its kind in Scotland. There are shipbuilding plants and textile, rope, and canvas factories. It was founded in 1668 as a port for Glasgow, before that city had been made accessible to large ships; it became a burgh in 1775. For a time Port Glasgow held a leading place in Clyde traffic. The ruins of 16th-century Newark Castle are preserved among the Clydeside docks. In 1975, Port Glasgow became part of the Strathclyde region.

Port Harcourt (här'kərt, -kôrt), city (1969 est. pop. 208,000), SE Nigeria, a deepwater port on the Bonny River in the Niger delta. It is an industrial and commercial center where steel and aluminum products, pressed concrete, glass, tires, paint, footwear, furniture, and cigarettes are manufactured and bicycles and motor vehicles are assembled. Port Harcourt, the operational headquarters of the Nigerian petroleum industry, refines oil and pipes it mostly to BONNY for export. Palm oil and kernels, cacao, coal, tin, and groundnuts are Port Harcourt's chief exports. The city is also a rail terminus and has an airport. Port Harcourt was founded by the British in 1912 and named for Viscount Lewis Harcourt, secretary of state for the colonies (1910-15).

Port Hope, town (1971 pop. 8,872), SE Ont., Canada, on Lake Ontario, E of Toronto. It has a large plant for refining radioactive ores and is a summer resort.

Port Hueneme (wī''nē'mē), city (1970 pop. 14,295), Ventura co., S Calif., on the Pacific coast; founded 1870, inc. 1948. It has a deep-sea harbor and is the site of a huge naval construction-battalion (Seabee) center. Fruits and vegetables are also processed, and there are fine sportsfishing facilities. A notable Seabee museum is there. Nearby are a state park and a navy missile range.

Port Huron (hyo͝or'ən), city (1970 pop. 35,794), seat of St. Clair co., S Mich., a port of entry at the junction of the St. Clair River with Lake Huron; inc. 1857. It is a shipping center with railroad shops and plants making automobile wires and cables, and copper, brass, and paper products. The earliest settlement there began (1686) with the French fort, St. Joseph. The town grew after the building (1826) of Fort Gratiot Turnpike (between Port Huron and Detroit), ushering in a lumbering era. After the lumber industry declined (in the 1880s), local deposits of salt, oil, and natural gas were developed, and sawmilling, boatbuilding, and papermaking became important. Port Huron is connected by a railway tunnel and an international bridge with Sarnia, Ont. It has a junior college. The Fort Gratiot lighthouse, which marks the St. Clair straits off Port Huron, is the oldest on the Great Lakes. Thomas Edison grew up there.

portico (pôr'tĭkō), roofed space using columns or posts, generally included between a wall and a row of columns or between two rows of columns. In Greece the STOA was a portico of the first type; in Greek temples porticoes terminated the front and rear ends of the NAOS—called pronaos and opisthodome, respectively—and were included in the colonnade surrounding the building. Roman temples, rarely peripteral (surrounded by columns), had a portico at the front end only. Such temples were called prostyle temples; those having porticoes at both front and rear were termed amphiprostyle. The projection of Roman porticoes was generally three columns deep. In recessed porticoes the front colonnade is flanked by the extended side walls of the building, as in most Greek examples. Roman public squares provided sheltered walks or passages between two rows of columns.

Porţile de Fier: see IRON GATE, gorge, Rumania and Yugoslavia.

Portinari, Cândido (kän'dētho͞o pôrtēnä'rē), 1903-62, Brazilian painter. He studied at the National School of Fine Arts in Rio de Janeiro. In 1928 a European fellowship enabled him to visit France, Italy, Spain, and England. Upon his return he broke with his earlier somewhat academic style to paint scenes of Brazilian life, characteristically soft brown in tonality with small figures schematically represented by flecks of color and play of light. His painting *Coffee* (1935; National Museum of Fine Arts, Rio de Janeiro) revealed an interest in the expression of plastic form that became a dominant factor in his subsequent works. Portinari turned (c.1940) to a more fluid and expressionistic style, touched with surrealism, as in the series of frescoes in the Hispanic Foundation, and the Library of Congress and in paintings such as the *Scarecrow* (Mus. of Modern Art, New York City). In 1955 he executed two large murals of *War* and *Peace* for the United Nations General Assembly Building, New York City.

Port Jackson: see JACKSON, PORT.

Port Kembla, Australia: see WOLLONGONG.

Portland, William Bentinck, 1st earl of, 1649-1709, Dutch statesman in England. He was William III's most trusted personal adviser. In 1677 he engaged in negotiating the marriage of William (then prince of Orange) and Mary, daughter of James, duke of York (later James II). With the Glorious Revolution (1688) he went to England with William, was made earl of Portland, and was given extensive estates and honors. Portland fought for William at the battle of the Boyne (1690) and in the War of the Grand Alliance and negotiated the Peace of Ryswick (1697) with France. For negotiating and signing the unpopular Partition Treaties (see SPANISH SUCCESSION, WAR OF THE), he was impeached (1701), but the proceedings were soon dropped. See M. E. Grew, *William Bentinck and William III* (1924, repr. 1971).

Portland, William Henry Cavendish Bentinck, 3d duke of, 1738-1809, British statesman; great-grandson of the 1st earl of Portland. He was lord lieutenant of Ireland (1782) and nominal head of the coalition ministry (1783) dominated by Charles James Fox and Lord North. When the French Revolution shocked the British into passing severe laws against agitators, Portland, as home secretary (1794-1801) under William Pitt, administered them with prudence, mercy, and wisdom. He promoted the parliamentary union (1800) of Ireland with England and was again—and uneventfully—prime minister from 1807 to 1809.

Portland, urban district (1971 pop. 12,306), Dorset, S England. It is on the Isle of Portland, a small rocky peninsula. Portland stone has been used in St. Paul's Cathedral and other important London buildings. Lobsters and crabs are harvested. There is a naval base in Portland harbor.

Portland. 1 City (1970 pop. 65,116), seat of Cumberland co., SW Maine, situated on a small peninsula and adjacent land, with a large, deepwater harbor on Casco Bay; settled c.1632, set off from Falmouth and inc. 1786. The largest city in Maine, it is a port of entry, the commercial center of the state, and the rail, highway, shipping, and processing center for a vast farming, lumbering, and resort area. It is the eastern terminus of the Portland-Montreal oil pipeline and a major receiving port for goods destined for Montreal. Portland has shipyards, canneries (especially for fish), printing and publishing firms, foundries, and important lumbering, paper-milling, fishing, chemical, and textile industries. George Cleeve settled there to trade c.1632. His post grew in importance, and the settlement known as Falmouth developed and, in spite of Indian raids in the late 17th cent., became a commercial center. It was almost completely destroyed by the British in 1775 but was rebuilt shortly afterward. Portland served as state capital from 1820 to 1832. Maine's first newspaper, the Falmouth *Gazette,* was issued there in 1785. In 1866 a great fire destroyed much of the city. The Univ. of Maine at Portland, the Univ. of Maine School of Law in Portland, and a junior college are in the city. Longfellow, whose house is now a memorial, and Robert E. Peary lived in Portland. Many beaches and resort islands are nearby. The lighthouse, established in 1791, is still in use. **2** City (1970 pop. 380,555), seat of Multnomah co., NW Oregon, on the Willamette River near its junction with the Columbia; inc. 1851. The largest city in the state, it is a port of entry, a leading financial and industrial center, and an important deepwater port, with shipyards and a busy foreign trade. Manufactures include lumber, wood products, paper, metals, machinery, foodstuffs, woolen textiles, clothing, and furniture. The city was founded in 1845 and named for Portland, Maine. Its growth was rapid after 1850, when it served as a supply point for the California gold fields, and continued with the coming of the railroad (1883), the Alaska gold rush (1897-1900), and the Lewis and Clark Centennial Exposition (1905). An educational center, Portland is the seat of the Univ. of Portland, Concordia College, Lewis and Clark College, Reed College, Warner Pacific College, two junior colleges, several theological schools, the Oregon Graduate Center, the Univ. of Oregon medical, nursing, and dental schools, and the Museum Art School. Portland has an art museum, a museum of science and industry, a planetarium, a forestry center, a zoo, a Japanese garden, and a symphony orchestra. The state historical society is there. The *Oregon Journal,* once owned by C. S. Jackson (who influenced the adoption of many political reform measures), is published there. Important annual events are the rose festival, Oregon Products Week, and the Pacific International Livestock Exposition and Rodeo. Near the city are an international airport and a U.S. air force base. The area is noted for its beautiful scenery. The Columbia River Gorge and Mt. Hood are easily accessible.

Portland vase, a Roman glass vase, known also as the Barberini vase. It is an unusually fine work of the late Augustan era (early 1st cent. B.C.). About 10 in. (25 cm) high and 22 in. (56 cm) in circumference, it is made of a deep violet-blue glass overlaid with opaque white glass into which figures are cut in cameo relief. The mythological scene probably represents Peleus and Thetis accompanied by Poseidon on one side and Aphrodite on the other; on the bottom there is a bust of a young man in a Phrygian cap, possibly Paris. The vase, found in an ancient marble sarcophagus excavated at Monte del Grano near Rome in the pontificate of Urban VIII (1623-44), was placed in the palace of the Barberini family. Sold c.1782, it passed through several hands until acquired by the Duke of Portland, who lent (1810) it to the British Museum. While on loan it was vandalized and completely shattered (1845) but was so skillfully reconstructed that little trace of the destruction remains. In 1945 it was bought by the British Museum. The vase has been widely reproduced and copied; the most famous replicas were made (c.1789) in jasper ware by Josiah Wedgwood. See Wolf Mankowitz, *The Portland Vase and the Wedgwood Copies* (1954).

Port Lavaca (ləvăk'ə), city (1970 pop. 10,491), seat of Calhoun co., S Texas, on Lavaca Bay; inc. 1907. It is a port of entry and a resort city with fishing. There are shrimp- and oyster-processing industries, and it is a shipping point for an area that produces grain, cotton, rice, and cattle. Aluminum, plastic, cement, and fertilizer are manufactured in the city. Port Lavaca was founded on the site of Linnville, which had been destroyed by the Comanches in 1840. A deepwater port of some prominence until late in the 19th cent., Port Lavaca declined but later revived when oil was discovered. Nearby are a state park and Matagorda Air Force Base.

Port Louis, city (1969 est. pop. 138,000), capital of Mauritius, NW Mauritius, a port on the Indian Ocean. It is the nation's largest city and its economic and administrative center. The city's economy is dominated by its well-sheltered port, which handles Mauritius's international trade; there are extensive facilities for processing and storing sugar, the main export. Port Louis is connected with the interior of the country by railroads and roads and has an international airport. Manufactures include cigarettes, rum and wine, food products, and aloe fiber. Port Louis was founded in 1735 by Bertrand François Mahé de La Bourdonnais, governor of the French colony on Mauritius (then called Île de

France). The population of Port Louis is now largely made up of the descendants of laborers who immigrated from India in the 19th cent. The hill-top Citadel (1838) dominates the city, which is laid out in a rectangular pattern. The Mauritius Institute (1880), which studies the island's flora and fauna and operates a natural history and an art museum, is located in Port Louis.

Port Lyautey: see KENITRA, Morocco.

Port Moresby (môrz'bē), town (1970 est. pop. 56,200), capital of Papua New Guinea, on New Guinea island and on the Gulf of Papua. Rubber, gold, and copra are exported. Port Moresby was founded by Capt. John Moresby, who landed there in 1873. The British occupied it in 1883. During World War II the chief Allied base on New Guinea was there.

Port Neches (nĕch'ĭz), city (1970 pop. 10,894), Jefferson co., SE Texas, on the Neches River; inc. 1927. It is an oil-shipping port on the deepwater Sabine-Neches Canal.

Porto: see OPORTO, Portugal.

Pôrto Alegre (pōr'to͝o əlĕ'grə), city (1970 pop. 885,564), capital of Rio Grande do Sul state, SE Brazil, on the Guaíba River. One of the chief industrial and commercial centers of Brazil, it is also the nation's major river port, exporting the products of the rich agricultural and pastoral hinterland. It has a modern shipyard, meat-packing plants, foundries, and varied processing industries. The city was founded (c.1742) by immigrants from the Azores. Since the 19th cent. its development has been aided by numerous German and Italian settlers. A modern city with handsome business and government buildings, Pôrto Alegre has also preserved many old, narrow streets and colonial buildings. It is the seat of two large universities and is an important cultural and literary center.

Porto Bello: see PORTOBELO, Panama.

Portobelo, Porto Bello (both: pôr"tōbĕl'ō), or **Puerto Bello** (pwār'tō bā'yō), town (1970 pop. 551), central Panama, on the Caribbean Sea. The site, an excellent harbor, was visited by Columbus. The town was founded in 1597. A thriving colonial city, it was connected by a stone highway with Panama city; both ports were the points of transshipment for riches from the Spanish Pacific domains. Believed impregnable—Sir Francis Drake, before he could capture it, died of fever and was secretly buried in the bay—Portobelo was, nevertheless, sacked by English buccaneers (William Parker in 1601, Sir Henry Morgan in 1688, and Edward Vernon in 1739). With the building of the trans-Panama railroad (1848–55) and finally the digging of the Panama Canal, Portobelo declined.

Portocarrero, Luis Manuel Fernández de (lwēs mänwĕl' fĕrnän'dāth dā pôr'tōkärā'rō), 1635–1709, Spanish statesman, cardinal of the Roman Catholic Church. Created cardinal in 1669, he served temporarily as viceroy of Sicily (1677–78) and in 1678 became archbishop of Toledo. His influence was crucial in persuading Charles II to name Louis XIV's grandson (later Philip V) heir to the Spanish throne in 1701—an act that led to the War of the Spanish Succession (see SPANISH SUCCESSION, WAR OF THE). Under Philip, Portocarrero, one of a ruling triumvirate, put through important but unpopular financial reforms. In 1703 he fell into disgrace at court because of political intrigues by the princesse des Ursins, was reinstated by Louis XIV, but resigned anyway. Portocarrero later supported the cause of Archduke Charles, the Austrian contender for the Spanish throne, until Charles's defeat by Philip in 1706.

Portoferraio (pôr'tōfār-rä'yō), town (1971 pop. 10,615), Tuscany, Italy, on the north coast of Elba Island. The principal port of Elba, it handles most of the iron shipped from the island. It is also a seaside resort. The town was strongly fortified (16th–18th cent.) by the Medici. Napoleon I resided there (1814–15) as sovereign of the island during his exile from France. His house, the Villa dei Mulini, is preserved as a museum.

Port of Spain, city (1970 pop. 67,867), capital of Trinidad and Tobago, on the Gulf of Paria. It is the industrial and commercial center of the country. From 1958 to 1962, Port of Spain was the capital of the now dissolved Federation of the West Indies. It is one of the major shipping hubs of the Caribbean, with exports of agricultural products and asphalt. Bauxite from the Guianas and iron ore from Venezuela are transferred there for overseas shipment. The city has attractive public buildings and botanical gardens, and it is a focal point of the tourist trade.

Portolá, Gaspar de (gäspär' dā pôrtōlä'), fl. 1734–84, Spanish explorer in the Far West. After serving in Italy and Portugal, he was sent (1767) to America as governor of the Californias to expel the Jesuits and to save Franciscan missions. In 1769, Portolá commanded an expedition sent out from Mexico to extend Spain's control up the Pacific coast by establishing a colony at Monterey Bay, which had been discovered and described by earlier explorers. Portolá's expedition, composed of two ships and two land parties, left Velicatá and met at San Diego Bay, where Portolá established a small colony. From there he continued with a small land party to Monterey Bay, which he failed to recognize. After exploring the region, he returned (1770) to San Diego. Convinced by one of his captains that he had actually seen Monterey Bay, Portolá again marched north. Recognizing at last the bay described by earlier explorers and the site chosen for Spanish occupation of Upper California, he established the mission and presidio of San Carlos. Portolá became governor of Puebla, Mexico, in 1776 and in 1784 returned to Spain. See H. H. Bancroft, *History of California* (1890); Z. S. Eldredge, *The March of Portolá* (1909); H. E. Bolton, *Fray Juan Crespi* (1927, repr. 1971), and his edition of Francisco Palóu's *Historical Memoirs of New California* (4 vol., 1926, repr. 1966).

Porto-Novo (pôr'tō nō'vō), city (1972 est. pop. 84,000), capital of Dahomey and its Ouémé dept., S Dahomey, a port on Porto-Novo lagoon, an arm of the Gulf of Guinea. It is Dahomey's second largest city and an administrative and shipping center. However, it is less important commercially and industrially than COTONOU, to which it is connected by rail. Porto-Novo is the trade center for an agricultural region whose chief product is palm oil; the city's exports include palm oil, cotton, and kapok. Probably founded in the late 16th cent. as the capital of a small kingdom, Porto-Novo [new port] got its name from the Portuguese, who built a trading post there in the 17th cent. Africans were shipped as slaves from Porto-Novo to the Americas. The Porto-Novo kingdom accepted French protection in 1863 as a means of fending off Great Britain, which was active in nearby S Nigeria. However, the inland Dahomean kingdom of Abomey resented the French presence, and fighting eventually broke out. In 1883 the French navy landed at Porto-Novo and Cotonou. Porto-Novo was incorporated into Dahomey colony and in 1900 was made its capital. The Institute of Higher Studies of Bénin, which attained university status in 1970, is in the city.

Porto Rico: see PUERTO RICO.

Pôrto Velho (pōr'to͝o vĕ'lyo͝o), city (1970 pop. 86,246), capital of Rondônia federal territory, NW Brazil, on the Madeira River. It is a rail terminus and the last point of navigation on the river. The city's economy is based on the exploitation and shipment of the rubber and Brazil nuts found in surrounding forests.

Port Phillip Bay, large deepwater inlet of Bass Strait, 30 mi (48 km) long and 25 mi (40 km) wide, Victoria, SE Australia. Port Melbourne and Williamstown are on Hobson's Bay, its northern arm.

Port Pirie (pĭr'ē), city (1971 pop. 13,269), South Australia, S Australia, on an inlet of Spencer Gulf. It is a railroad center and has uranium refineries and smelting works for the silver-lead mines at Broken Hill. Silver-lead ore and refined lead are exported.

Port Radium, mining village, N central Northwest Territories, Canada, on Great Bear Lake. The mines were discovered in 1930 and yielded deposits of pitchblende, from which much radium was produced. During World War II the mines were expropriated by the Canadian government when scientists found that these ores contained a rich store of uranium oxide, a source of atomic energy. They were exhausted and closed in 1960.

portraiture, art of representing the physical or psychological likeness of a real or imaginary individual. The principal portrait media are painting, drawing, sculpture, and photography. From earliest times the portrait has been considered a means to immortality. Many cultures have attributed magical properties to the portrait: symbolization of the majesty or authority of the subject, substitution for a deceased individual's living presence, theft of the soul of the living subject. Two conflicting objectives characterize portrait art in all cultures: the desire to represent the subject accurately and the desire to transform or idealize the subject. The conflict is particularly manifest in the self-portrait, the genre that gives the artist his greatest freedom from external constraints. Because the artist is his or her own cheapest and most available model, the self-portrait is the finest opportunity to make the most flattering statement or the most penetrating revelation of character of which he is capable. More deeply acquainted with this subject than with any other, the artist is nevertheless forced to view himself as a mirror-image and, as with his less immediate subjects, through the distorting glass of his understanding. Since the 6th cent. B.C. artists have often portrayed themselves with the identifying attributes of their profession: palette, brush, and easel. During the Renaissance pictorial signatures abounded in which the artist worked himself into a crowd scene or somewhere else within his composition. Striking examples are Botticelli's confrontation of the viewer in his *Adoration of the Magi* (Uffizi); Ghiberti's two busts, youthful and aged, on the Doors of Paradise of the Florence cathedral baptistry; and Michelangelo's Nicodemus figure in the late *Pietà* (Cathedral, Florence). A modern example is James Ensor's strange *Self-Portrait* (Uffizi) in which the artist appears as the only real being among a host of grotesques. Dürer was among the first masters to reveal a psychological self-awareness by means of the self-portrait. Later artists, notably Jordaens, Rigaud, Ingres, and Reynolds, asserted their social and material success in their images of themselves. The classic of self-aggrandizement is Courbet's *Painter's Studio* (1855; Louvre). Portrait art has taken many forms; variation in styles and tastes has contributed as much to portrait art as to other modes of artistic expression. The Egyptians made sculptured monuments that were idealized portraits of their monarchs intended to grant them immortality. Such ideal likenesses were painted onto sarcophagi of lesser persons as well. In the Orient this religious use of the portrait was widespread until the 15th cent., when realistic Western portraiture began to influence Eastern art. In Europe the principal medieval portraitists known by name were the French court painters Fouquet and Limousin. Limousin's enamel portraits of Francis I are among the masterpieces of enamel work. The profile medals and coins of rulers, common in the early Renaissance, were greatly simplified likenesses, as were the profile portraits of donors within devotional compositions. Masters such as Pollaiuolo and Piero della Francesca excelled at the profile view. The Flemish and German masters developed the three-quarter and frontal portrait types, which allowed greatly increased contact between subject and viewer and enhanced the illusion of vitality. These conventions were soon adopted generally. The powerful equestrian portrait was developed in Italy. Verrocchio's sculpture of Bartolomeo Colleoni is an outstanding example of this genre, whose major practitioners also included Donatello, Titian, Uccello, Velázquez, and Bernini. The portrait subject was eventually revealed at full length by such masters as Holbein, Titian, Tintoretto, and Veronese, thereby increasing enormously the compositional possibilities. The Italian mannerists Bronzino, Pontormo, and Parmigiano expressed a cold splendor in their studies of the aristocracy. The Elizabethans favored the MINIATURE, worn in a locket or set in an elaborate frame on a tiny stand. The foremost masters of this intimate and delicate form were Hilliard, Holbein, and Oliver. The giant among all makers of portraits was Rembrandt Harmenszoon van Rijn. In nearly 80 self-portraits he created a detailed psychological autobiography, from his joyous and exalted youth to his agonized old age. This series forms an introspective monument unique in art history. Rembrandt's portraits of others are equally penetrating. The principal baroque portraitists other than Rembrandt include Bernini, Hals, Rubens, and Van Dyck. They were followed by the French neoclassical masters David and Ingres; the Italian sculptor Canova; the English painters Hogarth, Raeburn, Lawrence, Romney, and, most notably, Gainsborough and Reynolds; the brilliant Spanish delineator of character, Goya; and the German Kneller. The 18th-century English conversation piece was a small portrait group in a domestic or landscape setting, representing people in conversation. Hogarth, Zoffany, and Gainsborough excelled at this genre. The Dutch painters of the 17th cent. had made popular group portraits of members of the rising burgher class, military companies, professional groups, and the like, and as the popularity of portraits spread throughout the social classes, portraits of couples, families, and other groups became common. Of modern masters Renoir, Degas, and Sargent were noted for their family groups. The portrait had been a major source of income to the painter since the Renaissance, and many modern European masters became, perforce, adept at the art. The French impressionists, Manet, Modigliani, Van Gogh, Gauguin, Soutine, Klee, Kokoschka, Matisse, and Picasso are all known for their portraits, although for none of them was portraiture the principal subject matter. In the United States during the 18th cent. the painters John Singleton Copley, Benjamin West, Charles Willson Peale, and Gilbert Stuart modeled their styles on the prevailing English fashion. Copley, however, brought an illuminating understanding to the depiction of his sitters that clearly owed nothing to English influence. By the 19th cent. portraiture had become the specialty of numerous American artists including John Trumbull, Thomas Sully, and the sculptors Horace Greenough, Thomas Crawford, and Hiram Powers. Later celebrated portraitists included Frank Duveneck and the expatriates Whistler, Sargent, and Cassatt. But it was Thomas Eakins who regained for the 19th cent. Copley's sensitivity, revealed in both his paintings and his photographs. American 20th-century masters of portraiture include Robert Henri and Andrew Wyeth, who continues the Copley-Eakins tradition. The miniature portrait had retained its popularity with all social classes until the middle of the 19th cent., when it was replaced by the more intimate and more simply executed technique of photography. The earliest protrait photographers were thoroughly painterly in their approach, since they faced fierce competition from painters. Outstanding from the common run of the early portrait photographers were Matthew Brady, the team of Hill and Adamson, Julia Margaret Cameron, and Thomas Eakins. The American pioneers of the aesthetic movement in photography in the early 20th cent. were Alfred Stieglitz and Edward Steichen, both noted for their luminous portrait studies. In Germany during the same period August Sander produced photographs that characterized the entire range of the German social classes. A number of American photographers working during the Great Depression produced a moving composite portrait of poverty-stricken rural America. These included, among others, Dorothea Lange, Walker Evans, Margaret Bourke-White, Russel Lee, Carl Mydans, Arthur Rothstein, John Vachon, and Ben Shahn. Other outstanding American portrait photographers of the 20th cent. include Edward Weston, Berenice Abbott, Immogen Cunningham, and Evelyn Hofer, whose work is reminiscent of August Sander's. In 1955 the Museum of Modern Art, New York City, mounted a vast exhibition of photographs entitled "The Family of Man." Selected by Steichen from hundreds of thousands of entries from all over the world, it presented a composite visual record, a profound portrait of the human family. Since then photographic portraiture has taken several new directions in the second half of the 20th cent. Nude portraits and multimedia works have proliferated, and the confrontation with the grotesque in human nature and physiognomy, masterfully explored by Diane Arbus, has spawned a number of imitators. See also PHOTOGRAPHY, STILL; LIMNER; SILHOUETTE. See J. D. Breckenridge, *Likeness: A Conceptual History of Ancient Portraiture* (1968); Georges Schreiber, *Portraits and Self-Portraits* (1968); *The Human Face* (*Man through His Art*, Vol. VI, 1969); L. E. Marrits, *Modeled Portrait Sculpture* (1970); *Frank Covino, The Fine Art of Portraiture* (1971); E. R. Kinstler, *Painting Portraits* (1971).

Port Republic, village, NW Va., on the South Fork of the Shenandoah River. During the Civil War, on June 8–9, 1862, the last battle of Confederate Gen. Stonewall Jackson's successful SHENANDOAH VALLEY campaign was fought nearby.

Port Royal: see ANNAPOLIS ROYAL, N.S., Canada.

Port-Royal (Fr. pôr-rwäyäl'), former abbey of women, c.17 mi (27 km) W of Paris, founded in 1204. It was at first Benedictine, later Cistercian. In 1608 the abbess, Angélique Arnauld (see ARNAULD, family), undertook a reform with the counsel of St. Francis of Sales. The nuns became renowned for piety, and their help was sought all over France for the reform of conventual discipline. In 1626 the abbey was moved to Paris because of the unsalubrious climate; the old buildings were now called Port-Royal-des-Champs [in the country], the new foundation Port-Royal-de-Paris. Under the influence of Jean Duvergier de Hauranne, the abbey soon became the prime center of Jansenism (see under JANSEN, CORNELIS). Port-Royal-des-Champs became a retreat for men, some of whom opened classes there for boys (1638). These, "the little schools," were successful from the start, and many celebrated Frenchmen were educated there. The pedagogy was novel in emphasizing knowledge as a means rather than an end, in using "natural" methods, and in distrusting corporal punishment. The textbooks became famous. The religious tone of the teaching did much to create the Jansenist and antipapal tendencies of 18th-century Roman Catholicism in France. Port-Royal fared as Jansenism did, and persecution became severe toward the end of the 17th cent. Port-Royal-des-Champs was suppressed by papal bull in 1704, and the buildings were razed in 1710. The nuns were expelled from Port-Royal-de-Paris.

Port Royal Island: see SEA ISLANDS.

Port Royal Sound, arm of the Atlantic Ocean, between St. Helena and Parris islands to the north and Hilton Head Island to the south, in S S.C.; it receives the Broad River. The sound was named in 1562 by French explorer Jean Ribaut, founder of a short-lived Huguenot settlement on Parris Island. In Nov., 1861, during the Civil War, Union Comdr. Samuel F. Du Pont reduced the forts guarding the sound, and the area remained in Union hands for the rest of the war, becoming a major naval base.

Port Said (sīd, säd, säēd') or **Bur Said** (bo͝or-), city (1970 est. pop. 313,000), NE Egypt, a port on the Mediterranean Sea at the entrance to the Suez Canal. It is a fueling point for ships using the canal and is the site of the main workshops of the canal administration. Salt is produced in Port Said by evaporating sea water, and there is a fishing industry. The city is a principal port for steamer service on the Nile. Situated on a narrow peninsula between Lake Manzala and the sea, Port Said was founded in 1859 by the builders of the Suez Canal and named for Said Pasha, then khedive of Egypt. In 1904 a railroad to Cairo was completed. In 1956, French and British paratroops landed at Port Said during the Suez campaign. Port Said came under Israeli attack during the 1967 and 1973 Arab-Israeli Wars. Its harbor was closed to shipping from 1967 to 1974.

Portsmouth, Louise Renée de Kéroualle, duchess of (lwēz rənā' də kāro͞oäl'), 1649–1734, French mistress of Charles II of England. She exerted a powerful influence over the king in favor of France—and to her own advantage—from 1671 until his death in 1685. She was made duchess of Portsmouth in 1673 and was the mother by the king of Charles Lennox, duke of Richmond. Hated by the English people, she lived mostly in France after 1685. See Jeanine Delpech, *The Life and Times of the Duchess of Portsmouth* (tr. by Ann Lindsay, 1953).

Portsmouth, county borough (1971 pop. 196,973), Hampshire, S England, on Spithead Channel. It includes Portsea (naval station), Southsea (residential district and resort), and the old town of Portsmouth proper. Since Henry VII built stone fortifications and docks there, Portsmouth has almost continuously been the foremost naval base of Great Britain. There are also aircraft-engineering and other industries. The Cathedral of St. Thomas of Canterbury dates partly from the 12th cent. Southsea Castle was built by Henry VIII. The 1st duke of Buckingham was assassinated in Buckingham House (then the Spotted Dog Inn) in Portsmouth in 1628. The house in which Charles Dickens was born has been converted into a museum, as has H.M.S. *Victory*, Nelson's flagship at Trafalgar in 1805. Charles II married Catherine of Braganza in Portsmouth, and George Meredith and Walter Besant were born there. An 18th-century boys' school and a teacher-training college are in Portsmouth.

Portsmouth. 1 City (1970 pop. 25,717), Rockingham co., SE N.H., a port of entry with a good harbor and a state-owned port terminal at the mouth of the Piscataqua River opposite Kittery, Maine; inc. 1653. A regional trade center, it has a fishing industry and plants making shoes, wire and cable, and electric products. Tourism is also important; the city's population doubles in the summer. Part of a grant to Sir Ferdinando Gorges and John Mason, Portsmouth is the oldest community in New Hampshire (settled c.1623). It was a point for exporting lumber and fish and served as colonial capital until the Revolution. Shipbuilding was an early industry; men-of-war and privateers were made there during the Revolution and the War of 1812. The city gives its name to the great Portsmouth Naval Shipyard (est. 1800), which is located on two islands (now joined together) in the Piscataqua River; geographically it is in the town of Kittery but owned by the U.S. government. It is an important submarine base and repair yard. The Treaty of Portsmouth, ending the Russo-Japanese War, was signed (1905) at the base. Portsmouth is the site of the U.S. Naval Disciplinary Command, a naval hospital, and Pease Air Force Base, a large strategic air command installation. A state vocational technical college is there. Many fine old houses are in "Strawberry Banke," a restored colonial community on the original seaport; they include the Richard Jackson house (1664), the Warner house (1716), and the John Paul Jones house (1758), where the naval hero once lived. The first newspaper in the state, the *New Hampshire Gazette*, was published there. **2** City (1970 pop. 27,633), seat of Scioto co., S Ohio, in a hilly area on the Ohio River at the mouth of the Scioto, across from South Portsmouth, Ky.; inc. 1814. It is an important industrial and rail center with repair shops. Completion of the Ohio Canal (1832), linking Portsmouth with Cleveland, and the discovery of iron ore in the area started the city's industrial growth. Of interest are the 1810 house; Mound Park, with ancient Indian burial grounds (now in the heart of the city); a civic center; and traces of the old Ohio River Canal. A branch of Ohio Univ. and a state prison are there. Nearby are an Atomic Energy Commission plant producing fissionable material; Shawnee State Forest; Wayne National Forest; and Portsmouth State Park. **3** Town (1971 pop. 12,521), Newport co., SE R.I., on Rhode Island; founded by William Coddington, John Clarke, Anne Hutchinson, and others 1638, inc. 1644. It is a summer resort and farming center. The Indians called this area Pocasset. The second white settlement in the state, it was an early fishing, shipping, and shipbuilding center, with some farming. The first general assembly of the new colony met at Portsmouth in 1647. The British general Richard Prescott was captured (1777) at his own headquarters in the town by American raiders, and the battle of Rhode Island was fought there (1778). Coal mining was important in the 19th cent. The Mt. Hope Bridge (1929) and the Sakonnet Bridge (1956) connect the town to Bristol and Tiverton respectively. **4** City (1970 pop. 110,963), SE Va., on the Elizabeth River and Hampton Roads, adjacent to and opposite Norfolk, with which it is connected by two bridges and two tunnels; founded 1752 on the site of an Indian village, inc. 1858. The city, one of the ports of HAMPTON ROADS, forms with Norfolk the largest operating naval installation in the world. In Portsmouth itself are one of the world's largest shipyards, with more drydocks than any other yard in the nation; a huge naval hospital; a naval ammunitions dump; and the headquarters of the Fifth U.S. Coast Guard district. Portsmouth is also a busy commercial seaport and a rail center, with railroad shops and terminals. A private shipyard was built there in 1767; it served as a British base in the Revolutionary War, after which it became a U.S. base (the U.S.S. *Chesapeake* was built there). In the Civil War the navy yard was burned and evacuated by the Federals in 1861 and then retaken in 1862. During the brief Confederate occupation, the steamship *Merrimack* was converted into the world's first ironclad (see MONITOR AND MERRIMACK). The nation's first battleship (*Texas*) was built there in 1892 and the first aircraft carrier (*Langley*) in 1922. Of interest in the city are Trinity Church (1762); the Shipyard Museum, with a model of the *Merrimack;* and the Old Towne Historic District, with many old homes. A junior college is there. A recently completed floodwall also serves as a pedestrian promenade along the waterfront.

Portsmouth, Treaty of, 1905, treaty ending the Russo-Japanese War. It was signed at the Portsmouth Naval Base, New Hampshire, on Sept. 5, 1905. Negotiations leading up to the treaty began in the spring of 1905 when Russia had suffered severe defeats and Japan was in financial difficulties. Therefore, both nations indicated a desire for peace. Germany, the United States, and Great Britain were instrumental in forcing conciliation between the belligerents. However, the United States and Britain exacted certain concessions from Japan before smoothing the way for the treaty. President Theodore ROOSEVELT demanded that Japan follow the OPEN DOOR policy in Manchuria and return the region to Chinese administration. In the Taft-Katsure agreement of July, 1905, Roosevelt agreed to Japanese dominance in Korea in return for American freedom of action in the Philippines. Great Britain had the Anglo-Japanese treaty extended to cover all of E Asia and in return also gave Japan a free hand in Korea. Under the terms of the Portsmouth agreement, Russia was compelled to recognize Korea's independence and the "paramount political, military, and economic interests" of Japan in Korea. Russia also agreed to place Manchuria again under the sovereignty of China, and all foreign troops were to be removed. The railway lines in S Manchuria, constructed by Russia, were ceded to Japan without payment. The disputed Liaotung peninsula (see LIAONING), containing the ports of Talien and PORT ARTHUR, was turned over to Japan, as was the southern part of the island of SAKHALIN. Japan also obtained fishing rights in the waters adjacent to the Russian Far East. The Treaty of Portsmouth marked the temporary decline of Russian power in the Far East and the emergence of Japan as the strongest power in the area.

Port Sudan (so͞odăn'), city (1969 est. pop. 101,000), NE Sudan, on the Red Sea. The country's major seaport, it handles the bulk of Sudan's foreign trade. The city is also a rail terminus that serves a rich cotton-growing area of the Nile Valley. Construction of a railroad linking the Nile and the Red Sea coast in 1905 led to the founding of Port Sudan as a harbor for the region.

Port Talbot (tôl'bət), municipal borough (1971 pop. 50,658), Glamorganshire, S Wales, at the mouth of the Avon (Afon) River on Swansea Bay. It includes the town of Aberavon and the urban district of Margam, united in 1921 as Port Talbot. The borough has large steelworks. Iron and tin plate are also made in the area. Port Talbot is an export point for the coal and mineral industries of the Avon valley. Large amounts of iron ore are imported. In 1974, Port Talbot became part of the new nonmetropolitan county of West Glamorgan.

Portugal (pôr'chəgəl), republic (1970 pop. 8,668,267), 35,553 sq mi (92,082 sq km), SW Europe, on the western side of the Iberian Peninsula and including the MADEIRA ISLANDS and the AZORES in the Atlantic Ocean. The capital is LISBON. Other notable cities are OPORTO, COIMBRA, SETÚBAL, BRAGA, ÉVORA, and FARO. The republic, including the island groups, is divided into 18 administrative districts, although the names of the six historic provinces are still used. Portuguese overseas territories are, in Africa, ANGOLA, MOZAMBIQUE (scheduled for independence in 1975), the CAPE VERDE ISLANDS, and SÃO TOMÉ AND PRINCIPE; in Asia, MACAO; and in Oceania, part of TIMOR. Portuguese Guinea, in W Africa, became independent as GUINEA-BISSAU in 1974. Portugal is bordered by Spain on the east and north and by the Atlantic Ocean on the west and south. The country is crossed by rivers rising in Spain and flowing to the Atlantic; among them are the Douro, the Tagus, the Sado, and the Guadiana. The river valleys support agriculture, and in the Douro and Tagus valleys extensive vineyards are maintained. On the lower hillslopes there are olive groves; on the flatter uplands as well as on the plains near the coast grains are grown and livestock are raised. There are great variations in terrain and climate among the historic provinces. TRÁS-OS-MONTES in the extreme northeast has a rigorous mountain climate, as have parts of Entre-Minho-e-Douro (officially Douro). BEIRA has the highest mountains of the country, the scenic Serra de Estrela, dotted with resorts. ESTREMADURA, in W Portugal, has broad alluvial plains, rising to cool and rocky uplands; along the Atlantic coast is a celebrated resort region, reaching to the town of CINTRA, near Lisbon. Most of ALENTEJO has a continental climate; although much of its soil is poor, together with Estremadura it is the granary of Portugal. A large irrigation project has been begun in Alentejo. The southernmost of the old provinces, ALGARVE, resembles the northern shores of Africa; mountains curve across the north of the province down to Cape St. Vincent, the southwestern tip of Europe; citrus crops thrive in the mild Mediterranean climate, and there are acres of almond trees. Portuguese agriculture is backward and inefficient; cereals must be imported. The country's fishing fleets bring in vital cargoes of sardine and tuna; fishing ports extend all the way from Cape St. Vincent in the south to the mouth of the Minho River on the Spanish border. Slightly more than half of the labor force is employed in various industries, of which food processing and the manufacture of textiles and chemicals are the largest; there is also a sizable cement industry, and low-grade coal, copper pyrites, iron ore, wolfram, and other minerals are mined. Most of the mines are in the northern mountains and in Beira. Portugal's forests provide a major portion of the world's supply of cork. The country trades heavily with West Germany, Great Britain, France, the United States, and Italy. Machinery and motor vehicles, textile fibers, petroleum, and cereals are major imports, and cotton textiles and wine as well as cork and other wood products are major exports. Portugal is one of the charter members of the European Free Trade Association (EFTA). Portugal is governed under a 1933 constitution that established a CORPORATIVE STATE. A corporative chamber, representing societal institutions, industries, and professions, operates alongside the national assembly, which is elected for four years by direct suffrage. The president, elected for seven years by an electoral college of members of the chamber and assembly, appoints the cabinet and is assisted by a state council. The majority of the Portuguese people are Roman Catholic. There are universities at Coimbra, Oporto, and Lisbon.

Growth of the State. There is little direct filiation between the Portuguese of today and the early tribes who inhabited this region, although the Portuguese long considered themselves descendants of the Lusitanians, a Celtic people who came to the area after 1,000 B.C. The Lusitanians had their stronghold in the Serra da Estrela. Under VIRIATUS (2d cent. B.C.) and under SERTORIUS (1st cent. B.C.), they stoutly resisted the Romans (see LUSITANIA). Other tribes, such as the Conii in Algarve, submitted more readily. Julius Caesar and Augustus completed the Roman conquest of the area, and the province of Lusitania thrived. Roman ways were adopted, and it is from Latin that the Portuguese language is derived. At the beginning of the 5th cent. A.D., the whole Iberian Peninsula was overrun by Germanic invaders; the VISIGOTHS eventually established their rule, but in the north the Suebi established a kingdom that endured until late in the 6th cent., when they were absorbed by the Visigoths. Present-day Algarve was part of the Byzantine Empire during the 6th and 7th cent. In 711 the Visigoths were defeated by the MOORS, who conquered the whole peninsula except for Asturias and the Basque country. Muslim culture and science had a great impact, especially in the south. Religious toleration was practiced, but a large minority converted to Islam. It was during the long period of the Christian reconquest that the Portuguese nation was created. The kings of Asturias drove the Moors out of Galicia in the 8th cent. Ferdinand I of Castile entered Beira and took the fortress of Viseu and the city of Coimbra in 1064. Alfonso VI of Castile obtained French aid in his wars against the Moors. HENRY OF BURGUNDY married an illegitimate daughter of Alfonso VI and became (1095?) count of Coimbra and later count of Portucalense. Henry's son Alfonso Henriques, wrested power (1128) from his mother and maintained the independence of his lands. After a victory over the Moors in 1139, he began to style himself ALFONSO I, king of Portugal. Spain recognized Portugal s independence in 1143 and the Pope did so in 1179. Alfonso's successors were faced with the tasks of recapturing Alentejo and Algarve from the Moors and of rebuilding the areas devastated by the long wars. There was conflict with other Portuguese claimants and between the kings and powerful nobles, and there was continual strife between the crown and the church over land and power. Until the late 13th cent. the church was victorious, winning inviolability for ecclesiastic law as well as exemption from general taxation. SANCHO I (reigned 1185-1211) captured the Moorish capital of Silves but could not hold it. Alfonso II (reigned 1211-23) summoned the first Cortes (council to advise the king). After Sancho II (reigned 1223-48) was deposed, ALFONSO III (reigned 1248-79) took (1249) Algarve and thus consolidated Portugal. In Alfonso's reign the town gained representation in the Cortes.

Glory and Decline. The reconquest and resettlement aided local liberties, since *forais* (charters) guaranteeing municipal rights were granted in order to encourage settlement. As former serfs became settlers, serfdom declined (13th cent.), but in practice many servile obligations remained. Alfonso's son DINIZ (reigned 1279-1325) attempted to improve land conditions. He also established a brilliant court and founded the university that became the Univ. of Coimbra. The reign of his son, ALFONSO IV, is remembered chiefly because of the tragic romance of Inés de CASTRO, the mistress of Alfonso's son, Peter (later PETER I; reigned 1357-67); to avenge her fate, Peter, on his succession, had two of her murderers executed. FERDINAND I (reigned 1367-83) indulged in long Castilian wars. Ferdinand's heiress was married to a Castilian prince, John I of Castile; after the death of Ferdinand, John claimed the throne. The Portuguese, largely due to the efforts of Nun'Álvares PEREIRA, defeated the Castilians in the battle of Aljubarrota (1385) and established JOHN I, a bastard son of Peter, as king. At this time began the long alliance of Portugal with England. John's reign (1385-1433) commenced the most glorious period of Portuguese history. Portugal entered an era of colonial and maritime expansion. The war against the Moors was extended to Africa, and CEUTA was taken. Under the aegis of Prince HENRY THE NAVIGATOR, Portuguese ships sailed out along the coast of Africa. The Madeira Islands and the Azores were colonized. DUARTE (reigned 1433-38) failed to take Tangier, but his son ALFONSO V (reigned 1438-81) succeeded (1471) in doing so. Alfonso's attempt to gain the Castilian throne ended in defeat. Under his son JOHN II (reigned 1481-95) voyages of exploration were resumed. Bartholomew Diaz rounded (1488) the Cape of Good Hope. By the Treaty of Tordesillas (1494), Spain and Portugal divided the non-Christian world between them. During the glittering reign of MANUEL I (reigned 1495-1521), Vasco da Gama sailed (1497-98) to India, Pedro Alvarez Cabral claimed (1500) Brazil, and Afonso de Albuquerque captured Goa (1510), Melaka (1511), and Hormoz (1515). The Portuguese Empire extended across the world, to Asia, Africa, and America. Manuel's reign and that of JOHN III (reigned 1521-57) marked the climax of Portuguese expansion. The slender resources of Portugal itself were steadily weakened by depletion of manpower and the neglect of domestic agriculture and industry. Government policy and popular ambition concentrated on the rapid acquisition of riches through trade with the Orient, but foreign competition and piracy steadily decreased profits from this trade. Lisbon was for a time the center of the European spice trade, but, for geographical considerations and because of limited banking and commercial facilities, the center of the trade gradually shifted to N Europe. The reign (1557-78) of SEBASTIAN proved disastrous. His rash Moroccan campaign was a national catastrophe, and he was killed at ALCAZARQUIVIR (1578); but the lack of news of his death led to a legend that he would return, and Sebastianism (a messianic faith) persisted into the 19th cent. The house of Aviz, founded by John I, disappeared with the death of Henry, the cardinal-king, in 1580. Philip II of Spain, nephew of John III, validated his claims to the Portuguese throne (as Philip I) by force of arms, and the long "Spanish captivity" (1580-1640) began. Spain's wars against the English and the Dutch cut off Portuguese trade with these nations; moreover, the Dutch attacked Portugal's overseas territories in order to obtain for themselves direct access to the sources of trade. Eventually the Dutch were driven from Brazil, but most of the Asian empire was permanently lost. Portugal was never again a great power.

Absolutism and Reform. Portugal was compelled to pay for Spain's wars against the Dutch and for the Thirty Years War. Finally in 1640 the Portuguese took advantage of the preoccupation of Philip IV with a rebellion in Catalonia to revolt and throw off the Spanish yoke. John of Braganza was made king as John IV (reigned 1640-56). Portugal, however, continued to be threatened by its larger neighbor. ALFONSO VI (reigned 1656-67), weak in mind and body, signed the crown away to his brother PETER II (reigned 1667-1706), who was first regent and then king. The alliance with England was revived by the Treaty of Methuen (1703), which gave mutual trade advantages to Portuguese wines and English woolens, and Portugal reluctantly entered the War of the Spanish Succession against Louis XIV. Gold from Brazil helped to recreate financial stability by 1730, but it also freed JOHN V (reigned 1706-50) from dependence on the Cortes (last called in 1677). Absolutism reached its height under John V and under Joseph (reigned 1750-77), when the marquês de

POMBAL was the de facto ruler of the land. Pombal attempted to introduce aspects of the Enlightenment in education, to achieve monarchical centralization, and to revitalize agriculture and commerce through the policies of mercantilism. His policies disturbed entrenched interests, and his new wine monopoly led to the Oporto "tippler's rebellion," which Pombal put down harshly. He also won a long contest with the Jesuits, expelling them from the land. After the terrible earthquake of 1755, Pombal began the rebuilding of Lisbon on well-planned lines. Finances again became disorganized as Brazilian treasure dwindled. Most of Pombal's reforms were rescinded in the reign of MARIA I (1777–1816) and her husband, PETER III. Under the regency of Maria's son (later JOHN VI; reigned 1816–26) Portugal's alliance with Britain led to difficulties with France; in 1807 the forces of Napoleon I marched on Portugal. The royal family fled (1807) to Brazil, and Portugal was rent by the PENINSULAR WAR. The French were driven out in 1811, but John VI returned only after a liberal revolution against the regency in 1820. He accepted a liberal constitution in 1822, and forces supporting him put down an absolutist movement under his son Dom MIGUEL. Brazil declared its independence, with Pedro I (John's elder son) as emperor. After John's death (1826) Pedro also became king of Portugal but abdicated in favor of his daughter, MARIA II (reigned 1826–53), on condition that she accept a new charter limiting royal authority and marry Dom Miguel. Miguel instead seized the throne and defeated the liberals, but Pedro abdicated the Brazilian crown, came (1832) to Portugal and led the liberals in the Miguelist Wars. Maria was restored to the throne. Although her reign was marred by coups and dictatorship, the activities of moderates and liberals laid a groundwork for the reforms—penal laws, a civil code (1867), and commercial regulations—of the reigns of Peter V (1853–61; begun under the regency of Maria's husband FERDINAND II) and of LOUIS I (reigned 1861–89). Portuguese explorations in Africa strengthened Portugal's hold on Angola and Mozambique; conflicting claims with Britain in E Africa were settled in 1891. To prevent republicans from coming to power, CHARLES I (reigned 1889–1908) established (1906) a dictatorship under the conservative João Franco, but, in 1908, Charles and the heir apparent were assassinated. Manuel II succeeded to the throne, but in 1910 a republican revolution forced his abdication.

Modern Portugal. The republic was established in 1910 with Teófilo BRAGA as president. The change of rule did not cure Portugal's chronic economic problems. Anticlerical measures aroused the hostility of the Roman Catholic Church. In World War I, Portugal was at first neutral, then joined (1916) the Allies. The economy deteriorated, and insurrections of both the right and the left made conditions worse. In 1926 a military coup overthrew the government, and General (later Marshal) CARMONA became president. António de Oliviera SALAZAR, the new finance minister, successfully reorganized the national accounts. Salazar became prime minister in 1932; he was largely responsible for the corporative constitution of 1933 and dominated the government until he suffered a stroke in 1968. Portugal was neutral in World War II but allowed the Allies to establish naval and air bases. It became a member of the North Atlantic Treaty Organization in 1949 but was not admitted to the United Nations until 1955. Portugal's possessions Goa, Daman, and Diu were seized by India in 1961. In Africa, armed resistance to Portuguese rule developed in Angola, Mozambique, and Portuguese Guinea in the early 1960s; Angola and Mozambique were granted increased autonomy in dealing with internal affairs in 1972. Domestically, little opposition to the government was permitted. All seats in the assembly were held by progovernment delegates. In the presidential election of 1958 the antigovernment candidate, Gen. Humbert Delgado, received almost a quarter of the vote. Consequently, a constitutional amendment the following year changed the method of electing the president. Previously chosen by popular vote, an electoral college of members of the national assembly and corporative chamber was now created to elect him. Delgado went into exile, and in 1965 he was found dead near the Portuguese border. Censorship of the press and of cultural activities grew especially severe in the mid-1960s, and student demonstrations were sternly repressed. In 1968, Salazar was replaced by Marcello Caetano as prime minister. Under Caetano repression was somewhat eased and the period before the 1973 national assembly elections saw a liberalization of the government's political policies. However, just before the election, many of the opposition candidates withdrew from the race on the grounds that they could not campaign freely; progovernment candidates won all the contested seats. Under the Caetano government development programs were started in Portugal and in the overseas territories. However, the continuing armed conflicts with guerrillas in the African territories, requiring about 40% of Portugal's annual budget to be devoted to military spending, drained the country's resources. By early 1974 dissatisfaction with the debilitating and seemingly endless war in Africa, and with the four-year compulsory military service, together with political suppression and a deteriorating economy, resulted in growing unrest and increased urban guerrilla activity within Portugal. The general unrest was exacerbated in Feb., 1974, with the publication of a book, *Portugal and the Future,* by Gen. António de Spínola, a popular army officer, critical of the government and attacking its policy toward the African territories. The book's immediate and widespread popularity lead to the dismissal from the army of Spínola as well as of the army chief of staff, Gen. Francisco da Costa Gomes, who had sympathized with Spínola's views. Inspired by the book, a group of young army officers staged (March) an unsuccessful coup. However, on April 25, a better organized group of officers toppled the government, encountering a minimum of resistance from loyal forces and widespread acceptance from the people. Spínola, who did not play an active role in the coup, was appointed head of the ruling military junta. Following the coup, the secret police force was abolished; all political prisoners, including those in the African territories, were released; full civil liberties, including freedom of the press and the open operation of all political parties, were restored; and overtures were made to the guerrilla groups in the African territories for a peaceful settlement of the conflict. The return to a popularly elected government was also promised. On May 15 a provisional coalition government was sworn in with Spínola as president and Adelino da Palma Carlos as premier. Spínola implemented the policy of decolonialization and recognized the rights of the territories to independence. Talks with the rebel groups in Portuguese Guinea led to the independence of that country. Within the Portuguese government, however, conflicts developed between rightist and leftist factions. Following the rejection by the council of states of the request to increase the powers of the president and the premier, Palma Carlos resigned. Spínola appointed (July) Vasco dos Santos Gonçalves, a leftist army officer, premier who then formed a cabinet. The continued strife precipitated the resignation of Spínola on Sept. 30. He was succeeded by Gen. Costa Gomes. By late 1974 the government was dominated by leftists. In Jan., 1975, Portugal agreed to grant independence in 1975 to Angola, Mozambique, São Tomé and Principe, and the Cape Verde Islands. An excellent short history of Portugal is that by H. V. Livermore (1966, repr. 1969). Earlier short histories are those of H. M. Stephens (4th ed. 1908) and Sir George Young (1917). See also Ruth Way and Margaret Simmons, *A Geography of Spain and Portugal* (1962); C. R. Boxer, *The Portuguese Seaborn Empire, 1414–1825* (1969); John Dos Passos, *The Portugal Story* (1969); Dan Stanislawski, *The Individuality of Portugal* (1959, repr. 1969); Hugh Kay, *Salazar and Modern Portugal* (1970); A. H. Marques, *Daily Life in Portugal in the Late Middle Ages* (tr. 1971) and *History of Portugal* (2 vol., 1972); George Kubler, *Portuguese Plain Architecture* (1972); C. H. Nowell, *Portugal* (1973).

Portuguese East Africa: see MOZAMBIQUE.

Portuguese Guinea: see GUINEA-BISSAU.

Portuguese India, the former Portuguese possessions on the Indian subcontinent. It comprised the colonies of GOA, DAMAN, AND DIU (with the capital at Pangim), all of which were annexed by India in Dec., 1961.

Portuguese language, member of the Romance group of the Italic subfamily of the Indo-European family of languages (see ROMANCE LANGUAGES). It is the mother tongue of about 85 million people, chiefly in Portugal and the Portuguese islands in the Atlantic (9 million speakers); in Brazil (72 million speakers); and in Portugal's overseas provinces in Africa and Asia (more than 3 million speakers). Although the Portuguese spoken in Portugal differs to some extent from the Portuguese current in Brazil, with reference to pronunciation, grammar, and vocabulary, the differences are not major. A distinctive phonetic feature of Portuguese is the nasalization of certain vowels and diphthongs, which can be indicated by a *tilde* (˜) placed above the appropriate vowel. The acute (´) and circumflex (ˆ) accents serve to make clear both stress and pronunciation and also to distinguish homonyms (for example, *e* "and," but *é* "is"). The grave accent (`) is a guide to pronunciation. It can also indicate a contraction, as in *às,* which is a combination of *a* "to" and *as* "the" (feminine plural). A *c* with a cedilla (*ç*) is pronounced like *c* in English *place* when used before the vowels *a, o,* and *u.* As in Spanish, there are two forms of the verb "to be": *ser,* which denotes a comparatively permanent state and which also precedes a predicate noun, and *estar,* which denotes a comparatively temporary condition. Again like Spanish, Portuguese tends to use reflexive verbs instead of the passive voice. Historically, Portuguese, which developed from the Vulgar Latin (see LATIN LANGUAGE) brought to the Iberian Peninsula by its Roman conquerors, could be distinguished from the parent tongue before the 11th cent. The Portuguese spoken in Lisbon and Coimbra gave rise to the Standard Portuguese of today. Although the greater part of the Portuguese vocabulary comes from Latin, a number of words have also been absorbed from Arabic, French, and Italian, and also from some of the South American Indian and African Negro languages. The close relationship of Portuguese to other Romance tongues and to Latin, the parent language of all of them, is demonstrated by the examples in the accompanying table. See W. J. Entwistle, *The Spanish Language, Together with Portuguese, Catalan and Basque* (2d ed. 1962); E. B. Williams, *From Latin to Portuguese* (2d ed. 1962); M. E. de Alvelos Naar, *Colloquial Portuguese* (1968); J. M. Câmara, *The Portuguese Language* (tr. 1972).

English	*Latin*	*Portuguese*	*Italian*	*Rumanian*
black	niger	negro	nero	negru
do	facere	fazer	fare	face
green	viridis	verde	verde	verde
horse	caballus	cavalo	cavallo	cal
iron	ferrum	ferro	ferro	fier
three	tres	três	tre	trei

Portuguese literature. Literature in the Portuguese language first emerged in lyric poetry, the courtly love poems collected in *cancioneiros* [song books]. The earliest of these, three in number, are the *Cancioneiro da Ajuda, da Vaticana,* and *Colocci-Brancuti,* written in the 13th cent. In the early 20th cent., the scholarly work of Carolina Micaëlis de Vasconcelos on the *Cancioneiro da Ajuda* opened large vistas into the past of Portuguese literature. The early poems were greatly influenced by the Provençal language and literature, but they had the individual flavor and meter of Portuguese and Galician, then a dialect of Portuguese (see PROVENÇAL LITERATURE). King Diniz, who ruled Portugal in the late 13th and early 14 cent., was an accomplished poet and, like his father, Alfonso III, followed the Provençal custom of encouraging poetic activity in his court. Significant also were the early *romanceiros,* collections of ballad poetry that dealt with themes of adventure, war, chivalry, and love. These romances can probably be dated no earlier than the 15th cent. Prose writing took longer to develop. Religious and historical writings ultimately led to the romances of chivalry, the progenitor of which, AMADIS OF GAUL, most likely originated in Portugal. Among the greatest achievements of medieval Portuguese prose are the vivid and well-documented chronicles written by Fernão Lopes (c.1380–c.1460) and Gomes Eanes de Zurara (c.1420–c.1474). Portuguese poetry in the 15th cent. was marked by the influence of Spain, which can be seen in Garcia de Resende's collection, *Cancioneiro geral* (1516). The impact of the Renaissance in Portugal was particularly strong in poetry and drama. The plays of Gil Vicente, who wrote both in Portuguese and Spanish, are infused with the Renaissance spirit, particularly the ideals of humanism. The Italianate school strongly influenced 16th-century Portuguese poetry. The humanist Francisco de Sá de Miranda introduced new poetic forms upon his return from Italy. He, Diogo Bernardes, and others mastered the new forms of lyric poetry, which reached their highest point in the works of Luís de Camões. Camões, known for his national epic *Os Lusíadas* [the Portuguese] (1572), was also the author of a superb body of lyric poems. Sá de Miranda and his followers also introduced the prose comedy and tragedy into Portugal. The Renaissance saw a spate of writing by historians who wrote of the discoveries and conquests in Africa, Asia, and America. João de Barros ranks among the best of these. The Portuguese Bernardim Ribeiro's pastoral novel *Menina e Moça* [the book of the young girl]

(1554) was certainly the inspiration in part for the Spaniard Jorge de Montemôr's *Diana* (1559), one of the most important novels in Spanish literature. The leading figures of the 17th cent. were the poet Francesco Rodrigues Lobo (1580–1622) and the prose writer Francesco Manuel de Melo (1608–66), whose writings stand out in a century marked by subservience to Spanish form and style, especially Gongorism. The 18th cent. developed gradually into the literary revolution that was the romantic movement (see ROMANTICISM). Liberal ideas from abroad invaded every branch of letters and learning. Various academies dedicated to scholarly research in language, literature, history, and science were established. João B. de Almeida Garrett, the chief exponent of French-inspired romanticism, exercised great influence over a generation of poets, playwrights, and novelists. A group of dissident poets, including Antero de Quental, Téofilo Braga, and Abílio Manuel Guerra Junqueiro, revolted against romanticism and laced their works with philosophical and social ideas. José Maria Eça de Queirós introduced realism into the novel and set the tone for the next half century. Author of the powerful *O Crime do Padre Amaro* [the sin of Father Amaro] (1880), he wrote realistic regional novels with great sensitivity and imagination. Other novelists of the late 19th cent. were Lourenço Pinto, Luís de Magalhães, and Francisco Teixeira de Queirós. Historiography, of a more narrative than scientific sort, flourished at the same time. Joaquim P. de Oliveira Martins was one of the more popular writers of this genre. The modern period in Portuguese letters dates from the establishment of the republic in 1910. Various writers fostered a cult of nostalgic regret for the past. Later writing became more sensitive to developments in other countries. Fernando Pessoa distinguished himself as a poet, and José Régio as a poet and playwright. The novel was cultivated by Aquilino Ribeiro, J. M. Ferreira de Castro, J. Paço de Arcos, Agustina Bessa Luís, and others. Literary criticism reached a new level in the work of Fidelino de Figueiredo. In the early 1970s Portuguese literary circles were shaken by the publication of a volume of collected notes, stories, letters, and poems by three young women, Maria Isabel Barreno, Maria Teresa Horta, and Maria Velho da Costa. Because of its erotic and feminist nature, the book was banned and its authors tried for abusing freedom of the press and outraging public decency. Their trial was still in progress when the Portuguese government fell in April, 1974; the new revolutionary government pardoned the "three Marias" and declared their book "literature." In the United States the book was published in 1975 as *The Three Marias: New Portuguese Letters.* See articles on individual writers, e.g., Luís de CAMÕES. See B. Vidigal, ed. *Oxford Book of Portuguese Verse* (2d ed. 1952); A. F. G. Bell, *Portuguese Literature* (rev. ed. 1970).

Portuguese man-of-war: see JELLYFISH; POLYP AND MEDUSA.

Portuguese West Africa: see ANGOLA.

portulaca (pôr″chəlăk′ə): see PURSLANE.

Port Washington, uninc. town (1970 pop. 15,923), Nassau co., SE N.Y., a suburb of New York City, on the north shore of Long Island and Manhasset Bay. It is a resort and yachting center.

Porvoo, Finland: see BORGÅ.

Porz am Rhein (pôrts äm rīn), city (1970 pop. 74,915), North Rhine-Westphalia, W West Germany, on the Rhine River; chartered 1951. Manufactures of this industrial city include glass and electrical goods. Motor vehicles are assembled there.

Posada, José Guadalupe (hōsā′ gwä″thälo͞o′pā pōsä′thä), 1852–1913, Mexican artist. Of peasant stock, he became one of the greatest popular artists of the Americas and influenced the generation of Orozco and Rivera. An imagery of violence was characteristic of him, and he used distortion, caricature, and vigorous lines and contrasts. Working mainly in lithography, woodcuts and metalcuts, and relief etching, he produced thousands of prints that were sold cheaply to the masses; prints are often called Posadas after him. He attacked the Porfirio Díaz dictatorship and was sympathetic to the workers and peasants who became revolutionaries in 1910. Posada also illustrated popular ballads and festivals and did a series on the dance of death and on crimes and executions. See study by Fernando Gamboa (1944).

Posadas (pōsä′thäs), city (1970 pop. 104,091), capital of Misiones prov., NE Argentina, a port on the upper Paraná River. Posadas is a center of the maté industry; tobacco and cereals are also grown. It is a point of departure for visits to Iguaçu Falls and to the nearby ruins of 17th-century Jesuit missions. The city was settled in 1849.

Poseidon (pōsī′dən), in Greek religion, god of the sea, protector of all waters. After the fall of the TITANS, Poseidon was allotted the sea. He was worshiped especially in connection with navigation; but as the god of fresh waters he also was worshiped as a fertility god. In Thessaly and other areas he was important as Hippios, god of horses, and was the father of Pegasus. Poseidon was represented as extremely powerful, with a violent and vengeful disposition. He carried the TRIDENT, with which he could split boulders and cause earthquakes. When LAOMEDON failed to pay him for building the walls of Troy, Poseidon sent a sea monster to ravage the Troad and years later vengefully assisted the Greeks in the Trojan War. His grudge against Odysseus is one of the themes of the *Odyssey.* He was the husband of Amphitrite, who bore him Triton, and by others he fathered many more sons, who usually turned out to be strong, brutal men (like Orion) or monsters (like Polyphemus). The Romans identified him with Neptune.

Posen: see POZNAŃ, Poland.

Posidonius (pōsĕdō′nēəs), c.135–c.51 B.C., Greek Stoic philosopher, b. Apamea, Syria. He settled in Rhodes after extensive travels. Noted for his learning, Posidonius gave new life to Stoicism by fortifying it with contemporary learning. Although his writings have been lost, it is known that they were copious. He made contributions to Stoic physics and ethics—notably the theory that a vital force emanating from the sun permeated the world and his doctrine of cosmic sympathy, through which man and all things in the universe are united. Other writings dealt with the natural sciences, mathematics, and military tactics. He had strong influence on the Romans.

Posillipo (pōzēl′lēpō), volcanic ridge, in Campania, S Italy, projecting into the northern part of the Bay of Naples. The town of Posillipo, a picturesque suburb of Naples, has interesting ruins of Roman villas.

positive: see PHOTOGRAPHIC PROCESSING.

positivism (pŏ′zĭtĭvĭzəm), philosophical system of thought that denies any validity to speculation or metaphysics. It maintains that the goal of knowledge is not to explain but simply to describe the phenomena experienced. The basic tenets of positivism are contained in an implicit form in the works of Francis BACON, George Berkeley, and David Hume, but the term is specifically applied to the system of Auguste COMTE, who coined the name and developed the coherent doctrine. In addition to being a dominant theme of 19th-century philosophy, positivism has greatly influenced various trends of contemporary thought. LOGICAL POSITIVISM is often considered a direct outgrowth of 19th-century positivism. See W. M. Simon, *European Positivism of the Nineteenth Century* (1963); Leszek Kolakowski, *The Alienation of Reason* (tr. 1968) and *Positivist Philosophy* (tr. 1972).

positron: see ANTIPARTICLE.

Post, Emily (Price), 1873–1960, American authority on etiquette, b. Baltimore. Born into a wealthy family, Post began her literary career as a novelist. Her best-known book, however, is *Etiquette* (1922), a practical guide to proper social behavior, written in a lively style. *Etiquette* gained wide popularity and sold over a million copies; the 12th revised edition (1969) was edited by Post's granddaughter-in-law, Elizabeth L. Post. Emily Post broadcast on the radio after 1931 and produced a daily column on good taste that was syndicated in more than 200 newspapers. Also an authority on interior decoration, she wrote *The Personality of a House* (1930).

Post, George Browne, 1837–1913, American architect, b. New York City, grad. New York Univ., 1858, in civil engineering, and studied architecture with R. M. Hunt. He was one of the leaders in a notable group that helped regenerate American architecture in the period from 1875 to 1890. A member of the National Commission of Fine Arts, he was a medalist and president (1876–99) of the American Institute of Architects. He designed, among other buildings, the Produce Exchange, the Stock Exchange, the buildings of the College of the City of New York, and the *World* building, all in New York City, and the Wisconsin state capitol.

Post, Wiley, 1899–1935, American aviator, b. Grand Plain, Texas. He won fame in 1931 when he and Harold Gatty flew around the northern part of the earth in 8 days 15 hr 51 min. In 1933 he made a second flight alone. Post was killed in an airplane crash near Point Barrow, Alaska, while on a flight with Will Rogers.

postage stamp, government stamp affixed to mail to indicate payment of postage. The term includes stamps printed or embossed on postcards and envelopes as well as the adhesive labels. The use of adhesive postage stamps was advocated by Sir Rowland HILL; it was adopted in Great Britain in 1839. Zurich (Switzerland) and Brazil issued stamps in 1843, and by 1850 the custom had spread throughout the world. Although the postmasters of several cities had previously issued provisional stamps, the first U.S. official issue was in 1847. Stamps are usually printed from engraved steel plates or cylinders or by typographic or lithographic means. Besides regular stamps, which date from 1847, the U.S. government also issues commemorative stamps, which celebrate events or persons; memorial stamps in honor of officials who die in office; airmail stamps; and special stamps, e.g., special delivery, postage due, and revenue stamps. The popularity of PHILATELY has led some governments to issue a great many stamps, usually commemoratives. Some small countries, like San Marino, receive much of their revenue by issuing stamps attractive to collectors. See John Easton, *De La Rue History of British and Foreign Postage Stamps* (1958); Gustav Schenk, *The Romance of the Postage Stamp* (1962); A. S. B. New, *The Observer's Book of Postage Stamps* (1967).

postal service, arrangements made by a government for the transmission of letters, packages, and periodicals, and for related services. Early courier systems for government use were organized in the Persian Empire under Cyrus, in the Roman Empire, and in medieval Europe. Private systems operated sporadically but were gradually abandoned or incorporated into government services. The English postal service, an outgrowth of royal courier routes, was established in 1657. Reforms proposed by Sir Rowland HILL were adopted in 1839; they provided for universal penny postage prepaid by an adhesive POSTAGE STAMP or an official envelope. The first organized system of post offices in America was created by the British Parliament in 1711, but as early as 1639 there was a post office in Boston. The mails were carried over a system of post roads; the New York City–Boston service was established in 1672. Postage stamps were first used in the United States in 1847; other developments were the registering of mail (1855), city delivery (1863), money orders (1864), and penny post cards (1873). Special-delivery service started in 1885, rural delivery in 1896, the postal savings system in 1911 (discontinued 1966), and parcel post in 1913. Mail was transmitted to the West Coast by the PONY EXPRESS of 1860–61. Mail service by railroad was instituted in 1862, and AIRMAIL in 1918. In the United States, postal service is under the direction of the U.S. Postal Service, having been reorganized in 1970 from the old Post Office Department. It is governed by an 11-member board, headed by the Postmaster General, who is no longer a member of the cabinet. A separate 5-member commission is charged with proposing rate changes. The U.S. Postal Service operates as an independent agency within the government, with the goal of becoming self-supporting by 1984; it has operated at a deficit for many years. Just as the department is empowered to ban what it considers seditious or obscene materials from the mails, it has also at times acted as censor of political and literary works. The UNIVERSAL POSTAL UNION, which facilitates the exchange of mail among nations, was established after the International Postal Convention of 1874, for which Heinrich von Stephan was largely responsible. It is now an agency of the United Nations. Many governmental postal services have special divisions for serving stamp collectors (see PHILATELY). In the United States in the early 1970s, several private postal services were created for the purpose of delivering third-class (advertising) mail. See F. G. Kay, *Royal Mail* (1951); Frank Staff, *The Transatlantic Mail* (1957); C. H. Scheele, *A Short History of the Mail Service* (1970); W. E. Fuller, *The American Mail* (1972); Gerald Cullinan, *The United States Postal Service* (rev. ed. 1973).

poster, placard designed to be posted in some public place for purposes of commercial announcement or propaganda. Advertising makes wide use of posters, as do charitable and political organizations. In ancient civilizations a simple form of written public announcement was used. The invention of printing and particularly the development of the lithographic process were of paramount importance to poster art. The advertising poster originated in the 1870s. The art of poster design requires, above all, a very clear expression of the idea or product being advanced. It must be visible at a distance and comprehended in one glance, so that lines are generally simple and colors few and bold. Lettering is kept at a minimum. In the 19th and 20th cent. numerous artists designed posters as a sideline to their other work. These include Daumier, Manet, Picasso, Ben Shahn, and Norman Rockwell. Other artists' reputations were based on their poster work. Jules Chéret, Alexandre Steinlen, Alphonse Mucha, and Henri de Toulouse-Lautrec made striking posters advertising entertainments and restaurants. In England outstanding poster designers included Fred Walker, Aubrey Beardsley, William Nicholson and James Pryde (the latter two collaborating under the name "the Beggarstaff Brothers"), Will Owen, and Dudley Hardy. These English artists created highly decorative posters in which the elements of picture and typography remained unified, revealing the influence of Far Eastern prints. Other leaders in the medium included Ludwig Hohlwein and Paul Scheurich in Germany; the Belgian Hendrik Cassiers; Lev Bakst in Russia; Toyokuni in Japan; and Ramón Casas in Spain. The American poster can be said to have originated with Matt Morgan's circus advertisements (c.1890) and was developed by Edward Penfield, Will H. Bradley, Maxfield Parrish, Howard Chandler Christie, James Montgomery Flagg, Charles Dana Gibson, and Harrison Fisher. The two World War periods produced enormous numbers of political posters; memorable among these were the works of Abram Games in England, Paul Colin in France, and Joseph Binder in the United States. Outstanding poster designers of the 20th cent. are Frank Pick, Gregory Brown, and Clive Gardiner in England; the Americans E. McKnight Kauffer, Paul Rand, Austin Cooper, Pat Keely, Robert Gage, and Peter Max; in France, A. M. Cassandre, Jean Carlu, and Charles Loupot. In Latin America and India posters are widely used in education. There has been an enormous resurgence of interest in posters used for interior decoration in the United States. Among the most popular are reprints of World War I posters; movie advertisements; works by Toulouse-Lautrec, Mucha, and Picasso; and photographs of celebrities and animals. See H. F. Hutchinson, *The Poster: An Illustrated History from 1860* (1968); Norman Laliberté, *The Book of Posters* (1970); Maurice Rickards, *The Rise and Fall of the Poster* (1971); John Barnicoat, *A Concise History of Posters: 1870–1970* (1972).

postimpressionism, term coined by Roger Fry to refer to the work of a number of French painters active at the end of the 19th cent. who, although they developed their varied styles quite independently, were united in their rejection of IMPRESSIONISM. The foremost of these were CÉZANNE, VAN GOGH, GAUGUIN, MATISSE, PICASSO, and BRAQUE. The first major exhibitions of their works were held in London in 1910–11 and in 1912. The term embraces a far wider school of thought than the neo-impressionism of SEURAT and SIGNAC. In this more systematic and precise approach, also called divisionism or pointillism, small dabs of pure color on the canvas were meant to be mixed by the eye of the viewer to produce intense color effects. See studies by J. Rewald (1962) and L. Nochlin (1966).

post-mortem examination or **autopsy,** systematic examination of a cadaver for study or for determining the cause of death. Post-mortems may be performed at the request of the authorities in cases of unexplained and suspicious death or where death was not attended by a physician. In other circumstances post-mortem examination may be performed only with the consent of the deceased's family or with permission granted by the person himself before death. It may be necessary to dissect the organs for microscopic study and to submit certain fluids and tissues to chemical analysis before the cause of death can be ascertained.

Postojna (pô'stoinä), Ger. *Adelsberg,* Ital. *Postumia,* town (1971 pop. 18,835), NW Yugoslavia, in Slovenia, on the Karst Plateau. A summer resort, it is famous as the site of Europe's largest stalactite caverns, which are traversed by a subterranean river. Formerly Austrian, the town passed to Italy in 1919 and to Yugoslavia in 1947.

Poston, Charles Debrill (pōs'tən), 1825–1902, American explorer and author, b. Hardin co., Ky. After practicing law in Tennessee, he moved to California in 1850 and from there led a party to explore the east coast of the Gulf of California for harbors and S Arizona for minerals. A subsequent mining enterprise undertaken by Poston in Arizona was abandoned (1861) after five years because of Apache wars. An advocate of territorial organization for Arizona, he was appointed (1863) superintendent of Indian affairs and served (1864–65) as the first delegate to Congress from the new territory. In 1868 he received a commission to study irrigation and immigration in Asia. Later he served in the Southwest in various government posts. In 1925 a monument was erected to his memory on Poston's Butte near Florence, Ariz. Among his writings are *Europe in the Summer-Time* (1868), *The Sun Worshipers of Asia* (1877), and *Apache Land* (1878). See biography by A. W. Gressinger (1961).

post-painterly abstraction, phrase first used by the critic Clement GREENBERG to distinguish the abstract painting of the 1960s from works associated with the abstract expressionist movement of the 1950s (see ABSTRACT EXPRESSIONISM). The production of the abstract expressionists involved a strong personal emotionalism, a painterly quality, and occasionally, as in the works of Willem DE KOONING, elements of CUBISM. The artists working in the various styles of post-painterly abstraction moved toward a more impersonal and austerely intellectual aesthetic. In their works they dealt with what they considered to be the fundamental formal elements of abstract painting: pure, unmodulated areas of color; flat, two-dimensional space; monumental scale; and the varying shape of the canvas itself. Among the specific trends encompassed by the term "post-painterly abstraction" are minimalism and color-field painting. Painters associated with the movement include Ellsworth KELLY, Jules OLITSKY, Kenneth NOLAND, Frank STELLA, and Morris LOUIS.

postulate: see AXIOM.

Postumus (Marcus Cassianius Latinius Postumus)(pŏs'tyo͞oməs), d. 269?, Roman commander. Governor of Gaul under Gallienus, he revolted (257) and established an independent empire there. Although defeated (263) by Gallienus, Postumus escaped and continued to maintain his state until murdered by his own men. Postumus' measures weakened the authority of Rome, but in a sense he saved the West by creating a strong state that was able to check the barbarians.

Potala: see LHASA.

potash: see POTASSIUM CARBONATE.

potassium (pətăs'ēəm), a metallic chemical element; symbol K [Lat. *kalium*=alkali]; at. no. 19; at. wt. 39.102; m.p. 63.65°C; b.p. about 770°C; sp. gr. .862 at 20°C; valence +1. Potassium is a soft, silver-white metal. Physically and chemically it resembles the other ALKALI METALS in group Ia of the PERIODIC TABLE. It is extremely reactive, more so than sodium. It combines so readily with oxygen that it is usually stored submerged in kerosene or some other hydrocarbon, out of contact with air. It reacts violently with water to form potassium hydroxide, KOH, releasing hydrogen, which usually ignites. It combines directly with the halogens, sulfur, and other nonmetallic elements (except nitrogen). It reacts with many organic compounds. The metal has limited use since it so closely resembles sodium, which is readily available at lower cost; however, postassium compounds are widely used in industry, although they are usually more expensive than the similar sodium compound. POTASSIUM CARBONATE, or potash, K_2CO_3, is used principally in soap and glass manufacture. The chloride, KCl, is used in fertilizers and in the production of other potassium compounds. The chlorate, $KClO_3$, and perchlorate, $KClO_4$, are used in explosives and fireworks. The hydroxide, or caustic potash, KOH, is used in soaps. The nitrate, saltpeter (or niter), KNO_3, is used in matches and explosives. Other commercially useful compounds include the bromide, KBr, the cyanide, KCN, the chromate, K_2CrO_4, the dichromate, $K_2Cr_2O_7$, and the iodide, KI. JAVELLE WATER contains potassium hypochlorite, KClO, a compound found only in solution. The *meta*silicate, K_2SiO_3, is used in WATER GLASS. Potassium has several useful tartaric acid salts, e.g., ROCHELLE SALT (sodium potassium tartrate), TARTAR (argol) and CREAM OF TARTAR (potassium hydrogen tartrate), and TARTAR EMETIC (potassium antimony tartrate). Potassium aluminum sulfate, $KAl(SO_4)_2 \cdot 12H_2O$, is a compound used in tanning, in water purification, and in baking powder; usually called ALUM, it is also called potash alum to distinguish it from other alkali aluminum sulfates. Potassium permanganate, $KMnO_4$, a purple-black crystalline compound that forms deep purple aqueous solutions, is used in the chemical laboratory as a powerful oxidizing agent and in medicine as an antiseptic and disinfectant. With sodium the metal forms alloys that are liquid at room temperature; these alloys are sometimes used in chemical reactions. Substances containing potassium impart a purple color to a flame. Potassium does not occur uncombined in nature but is found widely distributed in sylvite (KCl), carnallite ($MgCl_2 \cdot KCl$), feldspar, mica, and other minerals. It is the seventh most abundant element in the earth's crust and the sixth most abundant of the elements in solution in the oceans. It is found in mineral waters, brines, and salt deposits. Potassium is an essential nutrient for plants and animals. Potassium metal is produced commercially by a thermochemical process in which molten potassium chloride is reacted with sodium vapor; this method is also used to produce liquid sodium-potassium alloys. The metal may be produced electrolytically from fused potassium hydroxide, but, unlike sodium and lithium, it reacts with carbon electrodes and may form explosive compounds. Potassium was discovered in 1807 by Humphry DAVY, who decomposed potash with an electric current. Potassium was the first metal so discovered; Davy discovered sodium a few days later by a similar experiment.

potassium carbonate, chemical compound, K_2CO_3, white crystalline deliquescent substance that forms a strongly alkaline water solution. It is available commercially as a white, granular powder commonly called potash, or pearl ash. It was originally obtained from wood ashes or from the residue left in pots after certain plants, e.g., kelp, were burned in them. It is prepared commercially chiefly by electrolysis of potassium chloride to form potassium hydroxide, which is then carbonated (e.g., by adding carbon dioxide gas). It is used in the manufacture of soft soaps and glass, for washing wool, and in the production of other potassium compounds.

potassium chloride, chemical compound, KCl, a colorless or white cubic crystalline compound that closely resembles common salt (sodium chloride). It is soluble in water, alcohol, and alkalies. Potassium chloride occurs pure in nature as the mineral sylvite and is found combined in many minerals and in brines and ocean water. It is recovered (with other compounds) from the brine of Searles Lake in California. It is produced from sylvinite, a sodium chloride–potassium chloride mineral that is mined extensively near Carlsbad, N. Mex., and it is refined by fractional crystallization and by a flotation process. It is also recovered from lake brines in Utah and from ores in Saskatchewan, Canada. The chief use of potassium chloride is in the production of FERTILIZERS; it is also used in chemical manufacture. For agricultural use it is often called muriate of potash; the concentration of potassium chloride in muriate of potash is expressed as a corresponding concentration of potassium oxide (K_2O), i.e., the concentration of potassium oxide that there would be if the potassium were present as its oxide instead of as its chloride. Thus, muriate of potash that contains (typically) 80% or 97% KCl by weight is said to contain 50% or 60% K_2O, respectively. Manure salts contain some potassium chloride.

potassium hydrogen tartrate: see CREAM OF TARTAR.

potassium hydroxide, chemical compound with formula KOH. Pure potassium hydroxide forms white deliquescent crystals. For commercial and laboratory use it is usually in the form of white pellets. A strong base, it dissolves readily in water, giving off much heat and forming a strongly alkaline, caustic solution (see ACIDS AND BASES). It is commonly called caustic potash. It closely resembles sodium hydroxide in its chemical properties and has similar uses, e.g., in making soap, in bleaching, and in manufacturing chemicals, but is less widely used because of its higher cost. It is prepared chiefly by electrolysis of potassium chloride; commercial grades of it sometimes contain the chloride as well as other impurities.

potassium nitrate, chemical compound, KNO_3, occurring as colorless prismatic crystals or as a white powder; it is found pure in nature as the mineral saltpeter (or niter). It is slightly soluble in cold water and very soluble in hot water. When it decomposes (on heating) it releases oxygen. Potassium nitrate is prepared commercially by the reaction of potassium chloride with SODIUM NITRATE. It has been used extensively in the manufacture of gunpowder since about the 12th cent.; it is also used in explosives, fireworks, matches, and fertilizers, and as a preservative in foods (especially meats). It is sometimes used in medicine as a diuretic; it has a sharp, saline taste.

potato or **white potato,** common name for a perennial plant (*Solanum tuberosum*) of the family Solanaceae (NIGHTSHADE family) and for its swollen underground stem, a tuber, which is one of the most widely used vegetables in Western temperate climates. The plant is probably native to the Andes, where it was cultivated by the Incas. In pre-Columbian times its culture spread widely among Indians, for whom it was a staple food. Its history is difficult to trace, partly because the name *potato* was also used by early writers for the SWEET POTATO and for other unrelated plants. Spanish explorers are believed to have brought it in the 16th cent. from Peru to Spain, whence it spread N and W throughout Europe. It was brought to North America by European settlers probably c.1600; thus, like the closely related tomato, it is a reintroduced food plant in the New World. The potato was first accepted as a large-scale crop in the British Isles. It became the major food in Ireland during the 18th cent. and is hence often called Irish potato to distinguish it from the sweet potato. Ireland was so dependent on the potato that the failure (resulting from blight) of the 1845–46 crop caused a famine resulting in widespread disease, death, and emigration. The potato was also important to the course of history in the 20th cent. in Europe, especially in Germany, where it kept the country alive during two world wars. With its high carbohydrate content, the potato is today a primary food of Western peoples, as well as a source of starch, flour, alcohol, dextrin, and fodder (chiefly in Europe, where more is used for this purpose than for human consumption). It grows best in a cool, moist climate; in the United States mostly in Maine and Idaho. Germany, the Soviet Union, and Poland are the greatest potato-producing countries of Europe. Potatoes are usually propagated by planting pieces of the tubers that bear two or three "eyes," the buds of the underground stems. The plant is sensitive to frost, is subject to certain fungus and virus diseases (e.g., mosaic, wilt, and blight), and is attacked by several insect pests, especially the POTATO BEETLE. Chemical analysis of the potato shows it to be a good source of potassium, phosphorus, and iron. Most of the minerals and protein are concentrated in a thin layer beneath the skin; health authorities therefore recommend cooking and eating it unpeeled. Potatoes are classified in the division MAGNOLIOPHYTA, class Magnoliopsida, order Polemoniales, family Solanaceae.

potato beetle, name for two BEETLES of the leaf beetle family and for two of the BLISTER BEETLE family, all destructive to the potato plant and its relatives. Most notorious is the Colorado potato beetle, or potato bug (*Leptinotarsa decemlineata*), a black-and-yellow striped member of the leaf beetle family. It was once confined to the Rocky Mts., where it lived on wild members of the nightshade, or potato, family. When settlers introduced the Irish, or white, potato (c.1855), the insect spread through most of the United States and then to Europe. Its orange-yellow eggs are laid in clusters on the undersides of the leaves, on which the reddish, black-spotted larvae feed. Pupation (see INSECT) takes place on the ground, and the adults emerge to feed on the potato plants; they hibernate underground during the winter. The destruction caused by the Colorado potato beetle has been one of the chief reasons for the development of insecticides; Paris green and other arsenic compounds have been used extensively, as well as DDT. A member of the same family is the three-lined potato beetle (*Lema trilineata*) of the E United States, sometimes called old-fashioned potato beetle. The adults are yellow-orange with black stripes and lay their eggs scattered randomly over potato leaves. Two blister beetles of the genus *Epicauta* are also known as old-fashioned potato beetles. They are slender insects with complex life histories, passing through several larval stages before pupating. They feed on potatoes, tomatoes, and other members of the nightshade family. One (*Epicauta vittata*) has orange and black stripes and is also called striped potato beetle, or striped blister beetle; the other (*E. marginata*) is black with gray margins. The various potato beetles termed "old fashioned" were considered major pests before the spread of the more destructive Colorado potato beetle. Potato beetles are classified in the phylum ARTHROPODA, class Insecta, order Coleoptera. The Colorado potato beetle and the three-lined potato beetle are classified in the family Chrysomelidae and the old-fashioned potato beetles (*Epicauta*) in the family Meloidae.

Potawatomi Indians (pŏt″əwŏt′əmē), North American Indians whose language belongs to the Algonquian branch of the Algonquian-Wakashan linguistic stock (see AMERICAN INDIAN LANGUAGES). They are closely related to the Ojibwa and Ottawa; their traditions state that all three were originally one people. The Potawatomi were of the Eastern Woodlands area. In the early 17th cent., when first encountered by the whites, the Potawatomi lived near the mouth of Green Bay in Wisconsin. By the end of the century, however, they had been driven (probably by the Sioux) S along Lake Michigan and were settled on both sides of the southern end of the lake. After the Illinois were conquered (c.1765), they advanced into NE Illinois, S Michigan, and, later, NW Indiana. They were friendly to the French and aided them against the English. The Potawatomi supported PONTIAC'S REBELLION, fought against the United States in the battles headed by Little Turtle, took part in the battle of Fallen Timbers, and signed the Treaty of Greenville (1795). They sided with the British in the War of 1812. With the advancing frontier, the Potawatomi retreated westward to Iowa and Kansas, although a portion went to Walpole Island in Canada. From the reservation in Kansas where they had gathered, a large group moved (1868) to Oklahoma Indian Territory; this group, which held lands in severalty, became known as Citizen Potawatomi. Today those still living on reservations in Kansas, Michigan, Oklahoma, and Wisconsin number some 1,300. Their name is also spelled Potawatami, Pottawatami, and Pottawatomi. See Ruth Landes, *The Prairie Potawatomi* (1970).

Potchefstroom (pŏch′əfstrŏm, -strōōm), town (1970 pop. 55,296), Transvaal, NE South Africa. Located in a fertile farming region, Potchefstroom is the center of one of the world's richest gold-mining districts. Uranium is also mined. The town has malt factories and timber and metal industries. The oldest town in the Transvaal, Potchefstroom was founded in 1838 and served as capital of the Transvaal until 1860. The fort where British forces were defeated during the Transvaal rebellion of 1880–81 is now a national monument. The British captured Potchefstroom during the SOUTH AFRICAN WAR of 1899 to 1902. The town's main growth dates from 1933, when gold was discovered nearby. Potchefstroom Univ. for Christian Higher Education, an agricultural college, and a theological seminary are in the town.

Potemkin, Grigori Aleksandrovich (pōtĕm′kĭn, Rus. grĭgō′rē əlyĭksän′drəvĭch pŭtyôm′kĭn), 1739–91, Russian field marshal and favorite of CATHERINE II. He studied at the Univ. of Moscow and then entered the army. His part in the coup d'etat (1762) that made Catherine czarina brought him to her notice. Having distinguished himself in Catherine's first war with Turkey (1768–74), he was created count (1774). About the same time he became Catherine's lover. Even after others had taken his place, he remained one of Catherine's chief advisers, particularly with regard to her foreign policy, and he retained great influence at her court. He encouraged Catherine in the so-called Greek project, which aimed at breaking up the Ottoman Empire and reestablishing a Christian empire in the conquered area. Catherine's grandson Constantine was to be emperor and Potemkin ruler of an independent kingdom comprising Moldavia, Walachia, and Bessarabia. The scheme did not succeed. Potemkin played an important part in the annexation (1783) of the Crimea, for which he was created prince. As governor of the new province, he organized Catherine's fabulous Crimean tour of 1787. The allegation that he had sham villages ("Potemkin villages") built along her route is, at best, an extreme exaggeration, for Potemkin was in fact an able administrator, and he did much to develop the Crimea. Personally, Potemkin was one of the most eccentric figures of an age that abounded in eccentrics. See biography by George Soloveytchik (1947).

potential, electric, work per unit of electric charge expended in moving a charged body from a reference point to any given point in an electric FIELD (see ELECTROSTATICS). The potential at the reference point is considered to be zero, and the reference point itself is usually chosen to be at infinity. It can be shown that the potential associated with a charged body at a given point in an electric field is independent of the path along which the body has traveled in passing from infinity to the given point. Potential is measured in VOLTS and is sometimes called voltage.

potentiometer. **1** Manually adjustable variable electrical resistor. It has a resistance element that is attached to the circuit by three contacts, or terminals. The ends of the resistance element are attached to two input voltage conductors of the circuit, and the third contact, attached to the output of the circuit, is usually a movable terminal that slides across the resistance element, effectively dividing it into two resistors. Since the position of the movable terminal determines what percentage of the input voltage will actually be applied to the circuit, the potentiometer can be used to vary the magnitude of the voltage; for this reason it is sometimes called a voltage divider. Typical uses of potentiometers are in radio volume controls and television brightness controls. **2** Device used to make a precise determination of the ELECTROMOTIVE FORCE, or maximum output voltage, of a cell or generator by comparing it with a known voltage.

Potenza (pōtăn′tsä), city (1971 pop. 56,658), capital of Basilicata and of Potenza prov., S Italy, in the Apennines. It is an agricultural, commercial, and industrial center. Manufactures include machinery, chemicals, and processed food. Founded in the 2d cent. B.C. by the Romans, Potenza was later incorporated (847) into the principality of Salerno. Of note in the city is the Church of San Francesco (begun 1274).

Potgieter, Everhardus Johannes (āvərhär′dəs yōhän′əs pôt′gētər), 1808–75, Dutch critic, essayist, and poet. He was the first editor (1837–65) of and a major contributor to *De Gids*, the most influential Dutch literary periodical of its era. In opposition to romanticism and to contemporary pedestrianism, he wrote the brilliant prose work *Het Rijksmuseum te Amsterdam* (1844), which set up for emulation the 17th-century Golden Age of Dutch literature. *Florence* (1868) was a poetic masterpiece on medieval Italy. The most complete edition of his work was published in 19 volumes (1885–90).

pothole, cylindrical pit formed in the rocky channel of a turbulent stream. It is formed and enlarged by the abrading action of pebbles and cobbles that are carried by eddies, or circular water currents that move against the main current of a stream. Potholes are most commonly found at the bottoms of eddies in rivers and in plunge pools below cataracts; sometimes potholes in a rock outcrop indicate the former site of a rapid or cataract. Potholes are also found in formerly glaciated regions where whirling columns of glacial meltwater sank well-like holes, or moulins, through the ice. Notable potholes are found in Ausable Chasm, N.Y., and Shelburne Falls, Mass.

Poti (pô′tyē), city (1970 pop. 46,000), SE European USSR, in Georgia, on the Black Sea at the mouth of the Rion River. It is a port that ships manganese (from Chiatura), corn, lumber, and wine. The region around Poti is the swampy Colchis lowland. The city was known as Phasis in the 5th cent. B.C., when it was a Greek colony. It later became a Turkish fortress and was taken by the Russians in 1828.

Potidaea (pŏtĭdē′ə), ancient city, NE Greece, at the narrowest point of the Pallene (now Kassándra) peninsula in Chalcidice (now Khalkidhikí). It was a Corinthian colony (c.600 B.C.) but joined the Athenian-dominated Delian League. Potidaea revolted (432) against Athens with Corinthian help, providing one of the incitements to the PELOPONNESIAN WAR. Athens recaptured (430 or 429) the city. PHILIP II of Macedon took (356) Potidaea and may have destroyed it in the ensuing war. Rebuilt by Cassander, the city was named Cassandreia.

Potiphar (pŏt′ĭfər), chief official of Pharaoh who bought Joseph and gave him a high position in his house. Later when his wife falsely accused Joseph, Potiphar put Joseph into prison. Gen. 39.

Poti-pherah (pŏtĭf′ərə, pŏt″ĭfē′rə), priest of On and father of Joseph's wife Asenath. Gen. 41.45,50; 46.20.

potlatch (pŏt′lăch″), ceremonial feast of the Indians of the NW coast of North America entailing the public distribution of property. The host, along with his relatives, lavishly distributed gifts to the people invited to the potlatch; guests were expected to accept any gifts offered, with the understanding that at a future time they would give the host an even larger gift. The gifts were usually copper plates and goat's hair blankets. In a society based on the public disposal of wealth, the giver of gifts reaped an abundant harvest in the respect his neighbors showed him. Since custom demanded that a larger gift be given in return, the potlatch was sometimes used to impoverish a disliked person. The ceremony involved dancing, feasting, and boasting. Potlatches are seldom practiced today. See Philip Drucker, *To Make My Name Good* (1967); Abraham Rosman, *Feasting with Mine Enemy* (1971).

pot liquor, liquid remaining in a kettle after meat has been boiled with a vegetable such as beans, greens, or peas. Traditionally served in the S United States, it is usually accompanied by crisp corn bread.

pot marigold: see CALENDULA.

Potomac (pətō′mək), river, 285 mi (459 km) long, formed SE of Cumberland, Md., by the confluence of its North and South branches and flowing generally SE to Chesapeake Bay. It forms part of the boundary between Maryland and West Virginia and then separates Virginia from both Maryland and the District of Columbia. The upper course of the Potomac has cut several gaps across the parallel ridges of the Appalachian Mts.; the water gap at Harpers Ferry, W.Va., is the largest. The river passes over the

Great Falls above Washington, D.C., where it is crossed by Arlington Memorial Bridge and others, and enters a tidal estuary below the city. It is navigable for large ships to Washington, D.C., and formerly many smaller boats went to Cumberland, Md., via the CHESAPEAKE AND OHIO CANAL. Its principal tributary is the Shenandoah River, which it receives at Harpers Ferry. The river is noted for both its beauty and its historical associations. Mt. Vernon is on the Virginia shore below Washington, D.C.

Potosí (pōtōsē'), city (1969 est. pop. 63,600), capital of Potosí dept., S Bolivia, at the foot of one of the world's richest ore mountains. In the cold, bleak high Andes at an altitude of c.13,780 ft (4,200 m), Potosí is one of the highest cities in the world. There is no agriculture in the region and scarcely any fuel. Potosí was founded in 1545 and during its first 50 years was the most fabulous source of silver the world had ever known. Because of isolation, living discomfort, and a series of disasters, such as the flood of 1626, the mines proved unable to compete with those of Peru and Mexico. Improved technology and communications, however, have made possible the exploitation of silver, as well as tin, wolfram, and copper, and the revival of commercial life. Furniture, shoes, and appliances are manufactured. The city's colonial landmarks include the Mint House, a replica of Spain's Escorial. Potosí's university was founded in 1571.

Potsdam (pŏts'dăm), city (1970 pop. 111,288), capital of Potsdam district, central East Germany, on the Havel River, near Berlin. It is an industrial center and rail junction. Manufactures include processed food, textiles, pharmaceuticals, electrical equipment, and locomotives. The suburb of Babelsberg (incorporated into Potsdam after 1940) is the main center of the East German motion-picture industry. First mentioned in the late 10th cent. and chartered in the 14th cent., Potsdam was insignificant until Elector Frederick William of Brandenburg made it a residence (1660). The city's chief development came under Frederick II of Prussia (ruled 1740-86), who made Potsdam his chief residence and who built the palace and park of SANS SOUCI (1745-47) and the New Palace (1763-69). Also, the Town Palace was rebuilt (c.1745; destroyed in World War II) during his reign. The royal family of Prussia (later also the imperial family of Germany) continued to favor Potsdam as a residence, and numerous palaces were added by them. Ever since the reign (1713-40) of Frederick William I, Potsdam has stood as the symbol of Prussian militarism. Its immense parade grounds and the somewhat ponderous architecture of some of its palaces contribute to the impression, but the graceful palace and park of Sans Souci are notable exceptions. They evoke the memory of Frederick II the philosopher-king and of his cultured circle rather than that of his military achievements. During World War II, Potsdam was severely damaged, and in 1945 it was the scene of the Potsdam Conference (see separate article). In addition to the numerous palaces, the city's notable structures include the Garrison Church (1731-35), where Frederick William I and Frederick II were buried until 1945, when their remains were transferred to Marburg, West Germany. Potsdam is the site of the observatory of the Humboldt Univ. of East Berlin; the Einstein Tower, an astrophysical observatory; and part of the state archives of the German Empire.

Potsdam Conference, meeting (July 17-Aug. 2, 1945) of the principal Allies in World War II (the United States, the USSR, and Great Britain) to clarify and implement agreements previously reached at the YALTA CONFERENCE. The chief representatives were President Truman, Premier Stalin, Prime Minister Churchill, and, after Churchill's defeat in the British elections, Prime Minister Attlee. The foreign ministers of the three nations were also present. The so-called Potsdam Agreement transferred the chief authority in Germany to the American, Russian, British, and French military commanders in their respective zones of occupation and to a four-power Allied Control Council for matters regarding the whole of Germany. The Allies set up a new system of rule for Germany, aimed at outlawing National Socialism and abolishing Nazi ideology, at disarming Germany and preventing its again becoming a military power, and at fostering democratic ideals and introducing representative and elective principles of government. The German economy was to be decentralized, and monopolies were to be broken up; the development of agriculture was to be emphasized in reorganizing the German economy. All former German territory E of the Oder and Neisse rivers was transferred to Polish and Soviet administration, pending a final peace treaty. The German population in these territories and in other parts of Eastern Europe was to be transferred to Germany. A mode for German REPARATIONS payments was outlined. A Council of FOREIGN MINISTERS was established to consider peace settlements. The so-called Potsdam Declaration issued (July 26) by the conference presented an ultimatum to Japan, offering that nation the choice between unconditional surrender and total destruction. (The atom bomb was not actually mentioned.) Rarely was any agreement so consistently breached as was the Potsdam Agreement. The work of the Allied Control Council for Germany was at first blocked by France, which did not feel bound by an agreement to which it had not been party; the council had not even begun to function when the rift caused by the COLD WAR broke it up. The vague wording and tentative provisions of the Potsdam Agreement, allowing a wide range of interpretation, have been blamed for its failure.

Pott, Percivall, 1714-88, English surgeon at St. Bartholomew's Hospital. He described a fracture of the ankle subsequently known by his name and a deformity of the spine (Pott's disease) caused by tuberculosis. He wrote various treatises on rupture and other conditions.

Pottawatami Indians or **Pottawatomi Indians:** see POTAWATOMI INDIANS.

Potter, Alonzo, 1800-1865, American Episcopal bishop, b. near Poughkeepsie, N.Y. Ordained a priest in 1824, he served (1826-31) as rector of St. Paul's Church in Boston. In 1831 he became professor of philosophy and political economy at Union College; he was its vice president from 1838 to 1845. As bishop of Pennsylvania (1845-65), he founded in Philadelphia an Episcopal hospital (1860) and a divinity school (1863). His notable Lowell Lectures, delivered in Boston, appeared posthumously as *Religious Philosophy* (1872). See biography by M. A. De Wolfe Howe (1871).

Potter, Beatrix, 1866-1943, English author and illustrator. She published her first animal stories, *The Tale of Peter Rabbit* (1902) and *The Tailor of Gloucester* (1903), at her own expense before she found a publisher, Frederick Warne & Company. Over a period of 30 years, Warne published 23 of her books. Potter's stories, although fantasy, depict animals in an intelligent, unsentimental, and humorous manner. The books are enhanced by her delicate drawings and watercolor paintings. Now considered classics, Potter's stories are still popular and have been translated into several languages. See biography by Margaret Lane (rev. ed. 1968); Leslie Linder, *A History of the Writings of Beatrix Potter* (1971).

Potter, Henry Codman, 1835-1908, American Episcopal bishop, b. Schenectady, N.Y., son of Alonzo Potter. He was ordained a priest in 1858 and served in churches in Troy, N.Y., and Boston before he became (1868) rector of Grace Church in New York City. In 1883 he was consecrated bishop coadjutor of New York, assisting his uncle, Bishop Horatio Potter, whom he succeeded in 1887. The first stages in the building of the Cathedral of St. John the Divine in New York City were initiated by Bishop Potter. He was actively interested in social improvement and civic reform; among his writings are *The Citizen in Relation to the Industrial Situation* (1902) and *The Drink Problem in Modern Life* (1905). See H. A. Keyser, *Bishop Potter, the People's Friend* (1910).

Potter, Paul or **Paulus,** 1625-54, Dutch animal and landscape painter and etcher. In The Hague he enjoyed the patronage of the prince of Nassau, for whom he painted the celebrated life-sized *Young Bull* (1647; Mauritshuis, The Hague). He moved to Amsterdam in 1652. In his brief life Potter painted over 175 pictures, considered the finest animal paintings of the Dutch school. He was also able to render landscape with a sensitive feeling for atmosphere. His works are to be seen in many important European collections. Well-known examples are *Bear Hunt* and *Shepherds with Their Flocks* (Rijks Mus.), *Landscape with Cattle* (National Gall., London), and *Meadow with Oxen* (Louvre). His etchings of animals are characterized by the same simplicity and naturalism as his paintings.

Potteries, the, district, c.9 mi (15 km) long and 3 mi (4.8 km) wide, Staffordshire, W central England, extending northwest-southeast in the upper Trent valley. The area includes STOKE-ON-TRENT and part of NEWCASTLE-UNDER-LYME. The Potteries is very densely populated and has been a center for the manufacture of china and earthenware since the 16th cent.; Josiah Wedgwood, Josiah Spode, and Thomas and Herbert Minton are among the famous men who worked there. Most of the raw materials are now brought in from other districts, the clay (since the 18th cent.) largely from Cornwall and Dorset. The coal kilns of the area have been mostly replaced by electric or gas kilns. This region is the "Five Towns" of Arnold Bennett's novels.

Potter's Bar, urban district (1971 pop. 24,583), Hertfordshire, central England, in the Midlands. Potter's Bar is a residential district, most of which is within the Green Belt Zone barred to industrial development. There is an aircraft museum in the 17th-century Salisbury House.

potter's field: see ACELDAMA.

pottery, the baked-clay wares of the entire ceramics field. It usually falls into three main classes—porous-bodied pottery, STONEWARE, and PORCELAIN. Raw clay is transformed into a porous pottery when it is heated to a temperature of about 500°C. This pottery, unlike sun-dried clay, retains a permanent shape and does not disintegrate in water. Stoneware is produced by raising the temperature, and porcelain is baked at still greater heat. In this process part of the clay becomes vitrified, or glassy, and the strength of the pottery is increased. Pottery is formed while clay is in its plastic form. Either a long piece of clay is coiled and then smoothed, or the clay is centered upon a potter's wheel (used in Egypt before 4000 B.C.) that spins the clay while it is being shaped by the hand, or thrown. Decoration may be incised, and the piece is allowed to dry to a state of leather hardness before firing it in a KILN. The type of finish, depending on the kind or number of glazes, dictates the total number of firings. When slip and GRAFFITO are used, they are applied before the first firing. There are two types of fires—reducing and oxidizing. The former removes oxygen while the latter, a smokeless fire, adds it. Reduction and oxidation change the color of the fired clay and gave the early potter his palette of red, buff, and black. Pottery is one of the most enduring materials known to man. In most places it is the oldest and most widespread art; primitive peoples the world over have fashioned pots and bowls of baked clay for their daily use. Prehistoric (sometimes Neolithic) remains of pottery, e.g., in Scandinavia, England, France, Italy, Greece, and North and South America, have proved of great importance in archaeology and have often supplied a means of dating and establishing an early chronology. Pottery has also been of value as historical and literary records; ancient Assyrian and Babylonian writings have been inscribed upon clay tablets. Simple geometric patterns in monochrome, polychrome, or incised work are common to pottery of prehistoric and primitive cultures. By 1500 B.C. the use of glazes, such as the famous greens and blues, was known in Egypt. Especially noteworthy is the early Aegean pottery of the Minoan and Mycenaean periods with its curvilinear, painted decoration. In Assyria and Neo-Babylonia, painted and glazed bricks were in common use. The Ishtar gate in Babylon, with its ceramic reliefs, is an early example of the MAJOLICA technique. The Greek vases (800-300 B.C.), famous for symmetry of form and beauty of decoration, include red, black, and varicolored examples. The last were for tombs only, as the colors were painted, unfired, and easily marred. The red ware is decorated with black figures, or the ground is black and the figures shown red. Water, oil, and wine jars were numerous. Of the Greco-Roman wares, the Arretine or Samian, also a red ware, was molded after first being turned on the wheel to the size of the mold, which carried the decoration in intaglio. Painted pottery of the Neolithic period has been found in China. By the 2d cent. B.C. the Early Han period had developed a green glaze which may have come from the Middle East. In the Sui period (A.D. 581-618) and the T'ang period (618-906), porcelain and porcelanneous ware (the envy of the Western world) began to be made and exported to Korea and Japan and to the Islamic world. Technical knowledge, however, was not exchanged, and Islam made no true porcelain. Islamic pottery making was centered at Baghdad in the 10th cent. Blue and green clear glazes were used, and LUSTERWARE was first employed as an overglaze. Lusterware was highly developed under the Fatimites in Egypt (969-1171), and the technique continued in use at major pottery centers over the centuries that followed. During the 13th cent. Mongol domination of Persia brought renewed Chinese influence to Islamic pottery making. Fine examples of Hispano-Moorish pottery date from the 14th cent. Islamic architecture in the 15th cent. utilized ceramic tile in immense quantities, as on the Blue Mosque at Tabriz. In Europe there was little pottery of great aesthetic importance before the 15th cent., except perhaps some German stonewares. Majolica was mainly developed in Italy and from there spread to Spain, France (where it was called faïence), and to Holland (where it came to be known as DELFTWARE). Majolica and stoneware were the main pottery forms in Europe until the advent (18th cent.) of porcelain. Prehistoric pottery found in Peru, Mexico, and the SW United States reveals a high degree of skill in color, form, and decorative motifs. Baked-clay work by colonists in North America began in 1612 with the making of bricks and tiles in Virginia and Pennsylvania. In these states and among the Dutch settlers of New York, potteries were soon established. The first whiteware was made in 1684. A stoneware factory was opened in New York in 1735, and c.1750 the Jugtown pottery of North Carolina was first produced. Terra-cotta works were operating in Massachusetts and Pennsylvania after the middle of the 18th cent. Palatinate refugees produced slip-decorated and graffito earthenware, and their product formed the foundation of Shenandoah pottery. In Philadelphia fine china was made (1769) for the first time in America. The potteries of Bennington, Vt., which opened in 1793, were known especially for their jugs. East Liverpool, Ohio, since 1839 one of the foremost centers of the industry, produced the first American Rockingham ware. Another center, begun in 1852 at Trenton, N.J., made fine Belleek or eggshell china. The Centennial Exposition of 1876 in Philadelphia and the World's Columbian Exposition of 1893 in Chicago did much to awaken native consciousness of pottery as a form of art. In spite of the development of mass-production techniques and synthetic materials, the demand for hand-crafted ware of fine quality has not diminished. Many of the major artists of the 20th cent. have created exquisite ceramic works. Especially notable are those by Picasso, Matisse, and Miró. For a description of the nature of the material, see CLAY. See R. J. Charlston, ed., *World Ceramics: An Illustrated History* (1968); L. A. Boger, *The Dictionary of World Pottery and Porcelain* (1970); W. E. Cox, *Book of Pottery and Porcelain* (2 vol., rev. ed. 1970); Emmanuel Cooper, *A History of Pottery* (1973); George Savage and Harold Newman, *An Illustrated Dictionary of Ceramics* (1974).

potto: see LORIS.

Pottstown, borough (1970 pop. 25,355), Montgomery co., SE Pa., on the Schuylkill River; settled c.1700, inc. 1815. The borough's manufactures include rubber tires and tubes, fabricated steel, aluminum castings, motor vehicle parts, and baked goods. The state's first ironworks were established there in 1715. The Hill School, a preparatory school, is in Pottstown. Other points of interest are an antique-automobile museum and the home of John Potts (1754), colonial ironmaster and the community's planner.

Pottsville, industrial city (1970 pop. 19,715), seat of Schuylkill co., E Pa., on the Schuylkill River; inc. 1847. Once an anthracite coal mining center, it now manufactures many varied products, including textiles, extrusions, trailers, and plastics. Pottsville was a rallying place for the MOLLY MAGUIRES, who were tried there in 1877.

Poughkeepsie (pəkĭp'sē), city (1970 pop. 32,029), seat of Dutchess co., SE N.Y., on the Hudson River; settled 1687 by the Dutch, inc. as a city 1854. It is a trade center with a great variety of industries, including printing, electronics research, and the manufacture of business and milking machines, precision instruments, elevators, and hardware items. It became the temporary state capital in 1777, and the U.S. Constitution was ratified (1788) there. Poughkeepsie is the seat of Vassar College, Marist College, a junior college, and a state mental hospital. An annual intercollegiate regatta is held on the river there in June. Several historic 18th-century buildings remain. The Mid-Hudson Bridge crosses the river at Poughkeepsie. Hyde Park and two state parks are nearby.

Poulenc, Francis (fräNsēs' po͞oläNk'), 1899-1963, French composer and pianist. He was one of Les Six, a group of French composers who subscribed to the aesthetic ideals of Erik SATIE. The spontaneity and lyricism of Poulenc's style are best adapted to small forms—piano pieces such as *Mouvements perpetuels* (1918) and songs. Also outstanding are the ballet *Les Biches* (1924); *Concert Champêtre* (1929), for harpsichord and orchestra; the Mass in G (1937), for chorus and organ; *Litanies à la Vierge noire* (1936), for women's choir and organ; the Intermezzo in A Flat Major (1944), for piano; and the Concerto in G Minor for organ, strings, and percussion (1938). His operas are *Les Mamelles de Tirésias* (1947) and *Dialogue des Carmélites* (1957).

Poulsen, Valdemar (väl'dəmär poul'sən), 1869-1942, Danish electrical engineer. He invented the telegraphone (an apparatus for recording telephone conversations electromagnetically) and the high-frequency Poulsen arc used in wireless telegraphy and radio.

poultry, domestic birds raised for food, feathers, and to a limited extent as ornamental birds or pets. The group comprises three main divisions: the Galliformes, or comb bearers, e.g., the chicken, TURKEY, GUINEA FOWL, PHEASANT, and PEACOCK; the natatorial type, or swimmers, e.g., the DUCK, GOOSE, and SWAN; and the doves, represented domestically by the PIGEON. Several poultry birds, including the chicken and the goose, were domesticated over 3,000 years ago. The chief poultry bird is the chicken, which probably originated as a jungle fowl in SW Asia. Until recently, chickens were raised on almost all of the farms in the United States. Large-scale commercial operations currently monopolize poultry production, however, and relatively few farms still raise chickens to any significant extent. Commercial growers raise their birds in highly mechanized indoor chambers in which temperature, humidity, and diet are carefully controlled. Baby chicks are artificially hatched in an INCUBATOR. Chickens are usually classified according to the uses to which they are adapted. These include meat, egg, dual-purpose, and ornamental classes. Each class has included a variety of popular breeds over the years, each of which possessed one of an equal variety of desirable characteristics. Today, however, these original breeds are retained only for their genetic input into breeding programs, which have resulted in essentially one or two extremely efficient modern strains. The meat class is currently dominated by a bird that resulted from a cross between the fast-growing Plymouth Rock Chicken, and the deep-breasted Cornish chicken (see CORNISH HEN). The predominant egg type in the United States today is the LEGHORN CHICKEN. Dual-purpose breeds have all but disappeared, although the RED ROCK CHICKEN, which is a cross between two earlier dual-purpose types, is still popular in New England. Those few breeds of chickens which are raised chiefly for their ornamental appearance or as pets include the Polish varieties, characterized by their large showy headcrests; the fighting, or game, varieties, formerly raised for fighting and still bred for this purpose in countries where cockfighting is permitted; and the Bantams, which are primarily miniature counterparts of standard breeds. See M. O. North, *Commercial Chicken Production Manual* (1972); L. E. Card and M. C. Nesheim, *Poultry Production* (11th ed. 1972).

Pound, Ezra Loomis, 1885-1972, American poet, critic, and translator, b. Hailey, Idaho, grad. Hamilton College, 1905, M.A. Univ. of Pennsylvania, 1906. An extremely important influence in the shaping of 20th-century poetry, he was one of the most famous and controversial literary figures of this century—praised as a subtle and complex modern poet, dismissed as a naïve egotist and pedant, condemned as a traitor and reactionary. In 1907 he left the United States to travel in Europe, eventually settling in England. There he published a series of small books of poetry—including *Personae* (1909), *Exultations* (1909), *Canzoni* (1911), and *Ripostes* (1912)—which attracted attention for their originality and erudition. In England he came to dominate the avant-garde movements of the time—first leading the IMAGISTS and later championing VORTICISM. Both these movements sought to free post-Victorian verse from its staleness and conventionality. Pound encouraged many young writers, notably T. S. Eliot and James Joyce. In the early 1920s he moved to Paris, where he became associated with Gertrude Stein and Ernest Hemingway. By 1925 he was settled in Italy; there his literary ideas began to take a political and economic turn, and, discouraged by the faults and failings of English and American democracy, he began to develop many of the theories that were to make him unpopular in Great Britain and the United States. During World War II he broadcast Fascist propaganda to the United States for the Italians and was indicted for treason. He was brought to the United States for trial and from 1946 to 1958 was confined to a hospital in Washington after being ruled mentally unfit to answer the charges. On his release he returned to Italy, where he remained until his death at the age of 87. Pound's major works are "Homage to Sextus Propertius" (1918), *Hugh Selwyn Mauberley* (1920), and the *Cantos* (1925-60), a brilliant, though sometimes obscure, epic work. Weaving together such diversified threads as myth and legend (particularly the story of Odysseus), Oriental poetry, troubadour ballads, political and economic theory, and modern jargon, the *Cantos* attempt to reconstruct the history of civilization. Pound's translations, noted more for tone and feeling than for scholarly accuracy, include the Anglo-Saxon *Seafarer*, poems from the Chinese, the Confucian books, Japanese No drama, Egyptian love poetry, and Sophocles' *Women of Trachis*. See his letters to James Joyce, ed. by Forrest Read (1968); the memoirs of his daughter, Mary de Rachewiltz (1971); biography by Noel Stock (1970); studies by Michael Reck (1967), Hugh Kenner (1972), S. Y. McDougal (1973), and M. B. Quinn (1973); Eric Homberger, ed., *Ezra Pound: The Critical Heritage* (1973).

Pound, Roscoe, 1870-1964, American jurist, b. Lincoln, Nebr. He studied (1889-90) at Harvard law school, but never received a law degree. Already prominent as a botanist, Pound was (1910-17) professor of law at Harvard and dean (1916-36) of the law school, where he introduced many reforms. He advanced the "theory of social interests" in law, asserting that law must recognize the needs of humanity. His books on jurisprudence include *The Spirit of the Common Law* (1921, rev. ed. 1954), *Introduction to the Philosophy of Law* (1922), *Contemporary Juristic Theory* (1940), *Social Control through Law* (1942), and *The Task of Law* (1944). See studies by Sheldon Glueck, ed. (1965) and David Wigdor (1974).

pound, abbr. lb, unit of either MASS or FORCE in the customary system of ENGLISH UNITS OF MEASUREMENT. Two different pounds of mass are defined, one in the avoirdupois system of units and one in the Troy system. The avoirdupois pound (lb avdp) is now defined in terms of the KILOGRAM, the metric unit of mass; 1 lb avdp is equal to 0.45359237 kg. The Troy pound is used only for the measurement of precious metals and is defined as 5760/7000 of the avoirdupois pound. The apothecaries' pound is identical to the Troy pound. As a unit of force, or weight, the pound is the weight that a mass of 1 lb avdp has when the acceleration of gravity has its standard value (9.80665 meters per second per second). In ordinary usage, the term *pound* is often used without specifying whether force or mass is meant, but for scientific purposes it is important to make this distinction.

pound-foot: see FOOT-POUND.

Pourbus (po͝or'bəs, -büs), family of Flemish painters. **Pieter Pourbus,** 1510-84, painted portraits and religious subjects. His *Last Judgment* is in the Bruges Museum; the Metropolitan Museum has his *Portrait of a Young Woman*. His son, **Frans Pourbus,** 1545-81, was a pupil and follower of Frans Floris. In Ghent there is an altarpiece executed by him. He is also known for his fine portraits. His son, **Frans Pourbus,** c.1569-1622, was a favorite portrait painter in the Brussels and Gonzaga courts and, from 1609 until his death, in the court of Marie de' Medici. His portrait of her (Louvre) is one of his best-known works. A leading mannerist, he vied with Rubens for commissions.

Pourri, Mont (môN po͞orē'), Alpine peak, 12,428 ft (3,788 m) high, Savoie dept., SE France, near the Italian border.

Pousseur, Henri (äNrē' po͞osör'), 1929-, Belgian composer, b. Malmédy. Pousseur is considered the leader of the Belgian avant-garde. He studied composition with André Souris and Pierre Boulez and worked with Karl Heinz Stockhausen, Luciano Berio, and Bruno Maderna in ELECTRONIC MUSIC. He has been strongly influenced by Anton von Webern. Pousseur has composed for both traditional and electronic instruments. Among his works are *Seismogrammes* (1953) for magnetic tape and *Mobile* (1958) for two pianos.

Poussin, Gaspard (gäspär' po͞osăN'), 1615-75, French landscape painter, b. Rome. The son of a Frenchman named Dughet, he adopted the name of his brother-in-law, Nicolas POUSSIN, in whose studio he worked and whose influence is visible in his interpretations of the Italian countryside. Gaspard is particularly noted for his storm effects. He is best represented in the Colonna Palace and the Doria Palace, both in Rome.

Poussin, Nicolas (nēkôlä'), 1594-1665, French painter. Poussin was considered the greatest of living painters by his contemporaries. Although he spent most of his life in Italy, his painting became the standard for French classical art. He studied painting in the mannerist style in France until 1624, when he traveled to Rome via Venice. His early work in Rome (1624-33) manifests diversified tendencies. He executed many drawings of antique monuments for the great patron of the arts Cassiano del Pozzo. He experimented also with the baroque style of Pietro da Cortona and Lanfranco in works such as the *Martyrdom of St. Erasmus* (1629; Vatican). The paintings of Titian and Veronese influenced his choice of mythological and elegiac subjects. Poussin's growing preoccupation with the works of antiquity and of Raphael resulted in a new clarity of composition in such paintings as the *Adoration of the Magi* (1633; Dresden) and *The Golden Calf* (c.1635; National Gall., London). His figures began to exhibit greater linear precision and sculptural solidity. Poussin became especially concerned with the didactic and philosophical possibilities of painting. He formulated the doctrines that became the basis of French classical and academic art, whereby a work was intended to arouse rational and intellectual, rather than visual, response in the viewer. His approach to and successful justification of this intellectualization profoundly influenced painting far into the 19th cent. In 1640, Poussin was called to Paris by Louis XIII to displace Vouet as first painter to the king. Both the intrigues of Vouet and the task of administering the large-scale decoration of the Grand Gallery of the Louvre were distasteful to Poussin. A cold austerity characterizes his few works that remain from this period, e.g., *Truth Rescuing Time* (Louvre). By 1643, Poussin had returned to Rome. He then produced works that are considered the purest embodiments of French classicism. A comparison of his early and late versions of *Shepherds of Arcadia* (c.1629, Chatsworth Coll., England; and c.1650, Louvre) shows the fundamental change in his outlook. The poetic, dynamic emphasis of the early work was abandoned for the contemplative aspects of the subject in the later work. In his two series of the *Seven Sacraments* (1640s), he concentrated upon the symbolic meaning of each sacrament, stressing monumental solemnity and dignity. During the late 1640s he turned to landscape painting. In such works as the *Death of Phocion* (1648) he constructed a classical landscape, ordered with mathematical precision through the use of architecture. A renewed interest in mythology led him to favor esoteric themes, as in the *Landscape with Orion* (1658; Metropolitan Mus.). In his late work he developed a freer conception of nature, while his figures were considerably reduced in size and importance. Of his last works, the paintings in the series known as the *Four Seasons* (1660-64; Louvre) are among his most imposing. See his drawings ed. by W. F. Friedlander (4 vol., 1939-63); his paintings ed. by A. Blunt (1966); studies by W. F. Friedlander (1966) and A. Blunt (1967).

powder, any mass of fine particles or dust prepared by various mechanical means, e.g., grinding of solid substances, or by chemical means, e.g., precipitation from solutions. In a special sense, the word is applied to powdered propellant explosives, e.g., gunpowder, and to powdered substances that produce a bright light when ignited. See EXPLOSIVE.

Powderly, Terence Vincent, 1849-1924, American labor leader, b. Carbondale, Pa. Apprenticed in a machine shop, he joined (1871) the Machinists and Blacksmiths National Union, becoming its president in 1872. He joined the Knights of Labor in 1874 and served as grand master workman from 1879 to 1893, when he resigned because of disagreement with the officers on policy. He was elected mayor of Scranton, Pa., three times (1878, 1880, 1882). In 1894 he was admitted to the bar in Lackawanna co., Pa. He served (1897-1902) as U.S. commissioner general of immigration and was (1907-21) chief of the division of information in the U.S. Bureau of Immigration. See his *Thirty Years of Labor, 1859 to 1889* (1890, repr. 1967) and his autobiography, *The Path I Trod* (1940, repr. 1967).

Powell, Adam Clayton, Jr., 1908-72, American politician and clergyman, b. New Haven, Conn. In 1937 he became pastor of the Abyssinian Baptist Church in New York City, and he soon became known as a militant Negro leader. He was elected to the city council of New York in 1941, and was elected for the first time to the U.S. Congress in 1945. Although a Democrat, he campaigned for President Eisenhower in 1956. As chairman of the House Committee on Education and Labor after 1960, he acquired a reputation for flamboyance and disregard of convention. In March, 1967, he was excluded by the House of Representatives, which had accused him of misuse of House funds, contempt of New York court orders concerning a 1963 libel judgment against him, and conduct unbecoming a member. He was overwhelmingly reelected in a special election in 1967 and again in 1968. He was seated in the 1969 Congress but fined $25,000 and deprived of his seniority. In June, 1969, the U.S. Supreme Court ruled that his expulsion from the House had been unconstitutional. Powell was defeated for reelection in 1970. See his autobiography (1971); study by Andy Jacobs (1973).

Powell, Anthony, 1905-, English novelist. A distinguished writer of social comedy, he is best known for the series of novels, as yet unfinished, entitled *The Music of Time*. The series is a detailed yet panoramic study of the changes in the snobbish, insular world of the English upper and middle classes during the decades after World War I. Novels in the series include *A Question of Upbringing* (1951), *The Acceptance World* (1955), *Casanova's Chinese Restaurant* (1960), *The Valley of Bones* (1964), *The Military Philosophers* (1969), and *Books Do Furnish a Room* (1971). Among Powell's early novels are *Afternoon Men* (1931) and *From a View to a Death* (1933). He is also the author of *John Aubrey and His Friends* (1948) and *Two Plays* (1972). See studies by R. K. Morris (1968), Bernard Bergonzi (rev. ed. 1971), and Neil Brennen (1974).

Powell, Enoch, 1912-, British politician. Educated at Trinity College, Cambridge, he was a fellow there (1934-38) and professor of Greek at the Univ. of Sydney, Australia (1937-39). He entered the British Parliament in 1950 as a Conservative and served as minister of health from 1960 to 1963. When Sir Alec Douglas-Home succeeded Harold Macmillan as prime minister in 1963, Powell resigned from the government. After the Conservatives lost power he became (1965) shadow minister of defense, but he was ousted from that position in 1968 when he stirred widespread controversy by calling for an end to nonwhite immigration into Britain. Later he emerged as the leading Conservative opponent to Britain's entry into the European Common Market. Powell declined to seek reelection in the election of Feb., 1974, but he was returned to Parliament from a Northern Ireland constituency in Oct., 1974.

Powell, John, 1882-1963, American pianist and composer, b. Richmond, Va., grad. Univ. of Virginian, 1901. In Vienna he studied piano and composition and in 1908 made his debut as a pianist in Berlin. His compositions employ much material from folk song. His outstanding works are *Rhapsodie nègre* (1919); the Virginia country dances *Natchez on the Hill* (1932); a folk carol, *The Babe of Bethlehem* (1934); his Symphony in A (1937); a symphony on Virginian folk themes (1945); and concertos, songs, and chamber music. See J. T. Howard, *Our American Music* (rev. ed. 1946).

Powell, John Wesley, 1834-1902, American geologist and ethnologist, b. Mt. Morris (now part of New York City). The family moved to Illinois, where Powell joined the Natural History Society, making collections and serving as secretary of the society. After the Civil War, in which he lost an arm at Shiloh, he was appointed professor of geology at the Illinois Wesleyan College, Bloomington. He led geological expeditions into Colorado and Utah in 1867 and 1868 and in May, 1869, began, under the direction of the Smithsonian Institution, a geographical and geological survey of the Colorado River. In the course of this expedition his party passed by boat through the Grand Canyon, a hazardous feat first described in his *Explorations of the Colorado River of the West* (1875) and later in his *Canyons of the Colorado* (1895). He was later engaged in geological and ethnological explorations in Arizona and Utah. His efforts toward the reorganization of rival surveys in the West were a factor in bringing about the establishment (1879) of the U.S. Geological Survey, of which he served as director from 1881 to 1894. In 1879 he became director of the Bureau of American Ethnology, and many of his contributions to ethnology appeared in its *Reports*. See biographies by W. C. Darrah (1951, repr. 1969) and J. U. Terrell (1969); W. E. Stegner, *Beyond the Hundredth Meridian* (1954, repr. 1962).

Powell, Lewis Franklin, Jr., 1907-, American lawyer, Associate Justice of the U.S. Supreme Court (1971-), b. Suffolk, Va. He studied law at Washington and Lee Univ. and was admitted to the Virginia bar in 1931. He had a successful law practice in Richmond and held several local offices, including chairman of the Richmond school board (1952-61). Powell was a president of the American Bar Association. He was appointed to the Supreme Court by President Nixon and is generally regarded as a conservative.

Powell, William, 1892-, American movie actor, b. Pittsburgh. Powell made his stage debut in 1912. Thereafter he played blackguards in many silent movies, including *Sherlock Holmes* (1921), *Romola* (1924), and *Beau Geste* (1926). In sound films he was first cast as an elegant sleuth in *The Canary Murder Case* (1929). Teamed with Myrna Loy, he developed the sleuth character to cynical perfection in the witty *Thin Man* series (five films, 1934-47). Powell's other notable films include *The Great Ziegfeld* (1936), *My Man Godfrey* (1936), *Life with Father* (1947), and *Mister Roberts* (1955).

power, in mathematics: see EXPONENT.

power, in physics, time rate of doing WORK or of producing or expending ENERGY. The unit of power based on the English units of measurement is the HORSEPOWER, devised for describing mechanical power by James Watt, who estimated that a horse can do 550 ft-lb of work per sec; a foot-pound is the work done when a weight (force) of 1 lb is moved through a distance of 1 ft. The unit of power in the metric system is the WATT, named in honor of James Watt and equal to 1 JOULE per sec; the watt is used for measuring electric power in most countries, even those still using English units for other quantities. In common usage, the terms *power* and *energy* have become synonymous; for example, electrical energy is usually referred to as electric power (see POWER, ELECTRIC). See also ENERGY, SOURCES OF.

power, electric, rate at which electricity is consumed in an electric apparatus. Electric POWER is often referred to as electric ENERGY, a more basic concept. The electric energy supplied by a current to an appliance enables it to do work or provide some other form of energy such as light or heat. The rate at which electric energy is consumed by an appliance per unit of time is called electric power. For example, a definite amount of electric energy is required by an electric motor to lift a weight through a distance. The faster the motor lifts the weight, the more power it is using, i.e., the more energy it is consuming per unit of time. Electric power is usually measured in WATTS and kilowatts (1,000 watts). The amount of electric energy used by an appliance is found by multiplying its power rating by the length of time of operation. The units of electric energy are usually watt-seconds (joules), watt-hours, or kilowatt-hours. For commercial purposes the kilowatt-hour is the unit of choice. Electric energy occurs naturally, but seldom in forms that can be used. For example, although the energy dissipated as lightning exceeds the world's demand for electricity by a large factor, lightning has not been put to practical use because of its unpredictability and other problems. Generally, practical electric-power-generating systems convert the mechanical energy of moving parts into electric energy (see GENERATOR). While systems that operate without a mechanical step do exist, they are at present either excessively inefficient or dependent on elaborate technology. While some electric plants derive mechanical energy from moving water (hydroelectric power), the vast majority derive it from heat engines in which the working substance is steam. The steam is generated with heat from combustion of fossil FUELS or from nuclear reactions (see NUCLEAR ENERGY; NUCLEAR REACTOR). While the conversion of mechanical energy to electric energy can be accomplished with an efficiency approaching 100%, the conversion of heat to mechanical energy cannot. The efficiency of this process, which is limited by the need to operate at a safe temperature, is about 41% for a fossil-fuel plant and about 30% for a nuclear plant, in which the maximum operating temperature is lower. The heat that is not ultimately converted into electric energy is called waste heat. It is anticipated that in the year 2000 an amount of energy equal to half of all the energy now consumed annually in the United States will be dissipated as waste heat from power plants. The environmental impact of this waste is potentially catastrophic, especially when, as is often the case, the heat is absorbed by streams or other bodies of water. Methods are available for disposing of waste heat in the atmosphere, but the higher cost associated with these methods tends to limit their adoption by industry. Waste heat disposal and fuel shortages may be the factors that limit the amount of electricity that can be produced in a country. In 1970 world production of electricity approached 5 trillion kilowatt-hours. Of this total the United States produced some 1.6 trillion kilowatt-hours. The electric energy demand in the United States has been doubling every ten years. If this rate were to continue for a period of 100 years, the demand per year at the end of that time would be roughly equal to the annual radiant energy received from the sun. Although it seems unlikely that the demand for electrical energy could continue to increase at this rate for so long, the projected demand for the year 2000 already poses enormous problems. Associated with nuclear plants, in addition to the problem of waste heat, are difficulties attending the disposal and confinement of reaction products that remain dangerously radioactive for many thousands of years and the adjustment of such plants to variable demands for power. It is thought that by the use of MAGNETOHYDRODYNAMIC generators the efficiency of conventional plants can be raised somewhat. These devices operate by using directly the kinetic energy of gases produced by combustion. A generator of this type would have an efficiency of about 50%. FUEL CELLS develop electricity by direct conversion of hydrogen, hydrocarbons, alcohol, or other fuels, with an efficiency of 50% to 60%, but their high cost has restricted their use to space programs. Controlled nuclear fusion could provide a virtually unlimited source of heat energy to produce steam in generating plants; however, many problems surround its development, and no appreciable contribution is expected from this source in the near future. Solar energy has been recognized as a feasible alternative. It has been suggested that efficient collection of the solar energy incident on 14% of the western desert areas of the United States would provide enough electricity to satisfy additional demand until about 1990. By the use of special coatings that absorb sunlight readily and emit infrared radiation slowly, it would be possible to heat fluids to 1,000°F (540°C) by solar radiation. The heat in turn can be converted to electricity. Some of this heat would be stored to allow operation at night and during periods of heavy cloud cover. The projected efficiency of such a plant would be about 30%, but this fairly low efficiency must be balanced against the facts that energy from the sun costs nothing and that the waste heat from such a plant places virtually no additional burden on the environment. The principal problem with this and other exotic systems for generating electricity is that the time needed for their implementation may be considerable. Electric energy is of little use unless it can be made available at the place where it is to be used. To minimize energy losses from heating of conductors and to economize on the material needed for conductors, electricity is usually transmitted at the highest voltages possible. As modern TRANSFORMERS are virtually loss free, the necessary steps upward or downward in voltage are easily accomplished. Transmission lines for alternating current using voltages as high as 230,000 volts are not uncommon. For voltages higher than this it is advantageous to transmit direct current rather than alternating current. Recent advances in rectifiers, which turn alternating current into direct current, and inverters, which convert direct into alternating, have made possible transmission lines that operate at 700,000 volts and above. Electric utilities are tied together by transmission lines into large systems called power grids. They are thus able to exchange power so that a utility with a low demand can assist another with a high demand to help prevent a blackout, which involves the partial or total shutdown of a utility. Under such a system a utility experiencing too great a load, as when peak demand coincides with equipment failure, must remove itself from the grid or endanger other utilities. During periods in which demand exceeds supply a utility can reduce the power drawn from it by lowering its voltage. These voltage reductions, which are normally of 3%, 5%, or 8%, result in power reductions, or brownouts, of about 6%, 10%, or 15%, causing inefficient operation of some electric devices. See ENERGY, SOURCES OF.

power brake: see BRAKE.

Powers, Hiram, 1805–73, American sculptor, b. Woodstock, Vt. Having moved to Ohio, he made wax models for a Cincinnati museum. In 1835 he began his career as a sculptor, spending some time in Washington, D.C., where he modeled several portrait busts, including one of President Jackson (Metropolitan Mus.). In 1837 he went to Florence to study classical art. There he flourished to the end of his life. His *Greek Slave* (1843) became the most popular statue of the period in Europe and the United States. The second of several copies is in the Corcoran Gallery. His sculptures of Franklin and Jefferson are in the Capitol, Washington, D.C. See S. E. Crane, *White Silence* (1972).

Powhatan (pou"ətăn'), d. 1618, North American Indian chief of the Powhatan tribe in Virginia, whose personal name was Wahunsonacock. He greatly extended the dominion of the POWHATAN CONFEDERACY and after the marriage (1614) of his daughter POCAHONTAS to John Rolfe kept peace with the English colonists.

Powhatan Confederacy, group of North American Indians, belonging to the Algonquian branch of the Algonquian-Wakashan linguistic stock (see AMERICAN INDIAN LANGUAGES). Their area embraced most of tidewater Virginia and the eastern shore of Chesapeake Bay. Wahunsonacock, or Powhatan, as the English called him, was the leader of the confederacy when Jamestown was settled in 1607. The Powhatan are said to have been driven N to Virginia by the Spanish, where their chief, Powhatan's father, subjugated five other Virginia tribes. With Powhatan's own conquests, the empire included, among some 30 peoples, the Pamunkey, Mattapony, Chickahominy, and others likewise commemorated in the names of the streams and rivers of E Virginia. They were sedentary Indians, with some 200 settlements, many of them protected by palisades when the English arrived. They cultivated corn, fished, and hunted. Of his many capitals, Powhatan favored Werowocomoco, on the left bank of the York River, where Capt. John Smith first met him in 1608. The English soon seized the best lands, and Powhatan quickly retaliated. To appease him, he was given a crown, and a coronation ceremony was formally performed by Christopher Newport in 1609. Peace with Powhatan was secured when his daughter Pocahontas married (1614) John Rolfe. On Powhatan's death in 1618, Opechancanough, chief of the Pamunkey, became the central power in the confederacy, and he organized the general attack (1622) in which some 350 settlers were killed. English reprisals were equally violent, but there was no further fighting on a large scale until 1644, when Opechancanough led the last uprising, in which he was captured and murdered at Jamestown. In 1646 the confederacy yielded much of its territory, and beginning in 1665 its chiefs were appointed by the governor of Virginia. After the Iroquois, traditional enemies of the confederacy, agreed to cease their attacks in the Treaty of Albany (1722), the tribes scattered, mixed with the settlers, and all semblance of the confederacy disappeared. By the early 1970s some 3,000 Powhatan lived in the eastern part of Virginia. See F. G. Speck, *Chapters on the Ethnology of the Powhatan Tribes of Virginia* (1928).

Pownall, Thomas (pou'nəl), 1722–1805, English colonial governor in North America. In 1753 he went to New York as secretary to Sir Danvers Osborn, newly appointed governor. Following Osborn's suicide after their arrival, Pownall aided the English in their attempt to expel the French from North America, entered into a study of colonial administration and defense, and was lieutenant governor of New Jersey. He was appointed (1757) governor of Massachusetts, where he vigorously pressed the last of the French and Indian Wars, but was transferred (1759) to the governorship of South Carolina. Upon return to England in 1760, however, he resigned that post and became director of supply for the English forces in Germany (1761–63). In 1764 he published *The Administration of the Colonies,* in which he proposed the unification of the American colonies into one dominion and urged a stronger union of the colonies with the mother country. From 1767 to 1780 he was a member of Parliament. He opposed Edmund Burke's bill for conciliation with the colonies in 1775; but, protesting the hopelessness of the English cause, he introduced a peace bill in 1780. He spent the latter part of his life in travel and in writing. See biography by J. A. Schutz (1951).

Powys, John Cowper (pō'ĭs), 1872–1963, English author and lecturer. Best known of his novels is *Wolf Solent* (1929); he also wrote poetry and lectured on literature. Among his essays and criticisms, noted for their acute observations, are *The Meaning of Culture* (1929) and *A Philosophy of Solitude* (1933). See his autobiography (1934); studies by H. P. Collins (1966) and Glen Cavaliero (1973). His brother **Theodore Francis Powys,** 1875–1953, was a novelist. His original, realistic novels are concerned with the Dorsetshire village where he lived; they include *Black Bryony* (1923) and *Mr. Weston's Good Wine* (1927). He also wrote a number of short stories. See study by Henry Coombes (1960). Another brother, **Llewelyn Powys,** 1884–1939, was also an author. His rational yet poetic outlook is reflected in his writings, which include *Black Laughter* (1924) and *Earth Memories* (1938). See his autobiographical *The Verdict of Bridlegoose* (1926) and *Love and Death: An Imaginary Autobiography* (1939).

Powys, nonmetropolitan county (1972 est. pop. 100,000), central Wales, created under the Local Government Act of 1972 (effective 1974). It comprises the former counties of MONTGOMERYSHIRE and RADNORSHIRE and portions of the former county of BRECONSHIRE.

P'o-yang or **Poyang** (both: pō-yăng), shallow lake, c.1,000 sq mi (2,590 sq km), N Kiangsi prov., SE China; one of China's largest lakes. It serves as a natural overflow reservoir for the Yangtze River, with which it is connected by canal. It receives the Kan River and several smaller rivers. The lake basin is one of China's richest rice-producing regions.

Poynings, Sir Edward, 1459–1521, English statesman. After taking part in an insurrection (1483) against Richard III, he fled to the Continent, where he joined the followers of Henry Tudor, earl of Richmond, who in 1485 ascended the English throne as Henry VII. Poynings served Henry on the Continent and was sent (1494) to Ireland as lord deputy. He put down the numerous supporters of the Yorkist party and set about subjugating Ireland completely. He summoned to Drogheda a Parliament that enacted statutes for the further anglicization of the Irish government. After his return (1496) to England, he had military and diplomatic posts and was warden of the Cinque Ports. **Poyning's Law** is the name given to the Drogheda statutes (1494) that provided that the English privy council must give previous assent to the summoning of an Irish Parliament and to the introduction of any specific legislation in the Irish Parliament, and that all laws passed in England should apply to Ireland. Its effect was to render a free Irish Parliament impossible. Henry GRATTAN procured its repeal in 1782.

Poynting, John Henry, 1852–1914, British physicist. He was educated at Liverpool and Cambridge and was professor of physics at the Univ. of Birmingham for most of his life. He is best known for the Poynting vector, which gives the direction and magnitude of the propagation of electromagnetic radiation in space, and for his determination of the gravitational constant by use of an ordinary balance. He also did research in experimental physics and in various areas of physical chemistry (e.g., on phase changes and osmotic pressure).

Požarevac: see PASSAROWITZ, TREATY OF.

Pozharski, Dmitri Mikhailovich, Prince (dəmē'trē mēkhī'ləvĭch, pəzhär'skē), 1578–1642, Russian hero. During the "Time of Troubles" (1598–1613), when various pretenders vied for the Russian throne, he fought against the Poles, who invaded Russia, taking advantage of unstable political conditions. In 1611 he took command of a national militia formed on the initiative of the merchant Kuzma Minin of Nizhni Novgorod. With his improvised army he marched on Moscow in 1612 and drove out the Poles, ending the effort of King Sigismund III of Poland to subjugate Russia. Pozharski summoned a representative assembly, which in 1613 elected Michael Romanov czar.

Poznań (pôz'nänyə), Ger. *Posen* (pō'zən), city (1970 pop. 469,085), W central Poland, port on the Warta River. It is an important industrial and railway center. Manufactures include machinery (chiefly engines, freight cars, and machine tools), metals, and chemicals. Founded before the advent of Christianity in Poland, it became (968) the first Polish episcopal see and a nucleus of the Polish state. It remained in Poland until the second partition (1793), when it passed to Prussia. Poznań was included in the grand duchy of Warsaw in 1807, again passed to Prussia in 1815, and reverted to Poland in 1919. In World War II it was annexed to Germany, and thousands of Poles were expelled. The city is the see (created 1821) of the archbishop of Poznań and Gniezno and has a university (founded 1919). Since 1922 it has been the site of an annual international spring fair. In 1956 a workers' strike at a metallurgical plant in Poznań spread to other cities and led to changes in the high-ranking leadership of the Polish Communist party. The city has many old churches and museums with important art objects. Its most notable buildings are a Gothic cathedral (badly damaged in World War II) and a 16th-century city hall. A city-province, it is also the capital of Poznań prov.

Pozsony: see BRATISLAVA, Czechoslovakia.

Pozzo, Andrea dal (ändrĕ'ä däl pŏt'tsō), 1647–1709, Italian painter. Pozzo was a Jesuit priest and leading exponent of the BAROQUE style. He was celebrated for his bold foreshortening and quadratura PERSPECTIVE, in which the lines of focus begin at the corners of the work and converge at a central vanishing point. Pozzo painted church ceilings (e.g., Sant' Ignazio in Rome, 1688) with seemingly endless heavenly vistas. His ILLUSIONISM influenced Solimena and Tiepolo and his treatise on perspective (1692–97) spread understanding of his techniques throughout Europe.

Pozzo di Borgo, Carlo Andrea (kär'lō ändrĕ'ä pôt'tsō dē bôr'gō), 1764–1842. Corsican politician and diplomat in Russian service, b. Corsica. In the French Revolution, he allied with Pasquale PAOLI against the Jacobins on Corsica and supported the British occupation of the island in 1794. He became head of the British-backed civil government, superseding Paoli. After the French reconquest of Corsica (1796), Pozzo di Borgo left the island. He entered the Russian diplomatic service in 1804. An irreconcilable enemy of the Bonapartes (largely because of the role they had played in Corsican events), he helped to promote the Russo-Austrian alliance of 1805 against Napoleon I. The treaty of Tilsit (1807) between Czar Alexander I and Napoleon (1807) caused him to retire from the Russian service. Alexander recalled him in 1812, when hostilities with France reopened. In 1814, after Napoleon's first abdication, he was appointed Russian ambassador in Paris. Strongly sympathetic to the restored Bourbon regime, he strove to lighten the burdens laid on it by the allies. His pro-French attitude eventually caused his transfer to London, where he served (1835–39) as ambassador. See study by Egon Lehrburger (1968).

Pozzuoli (pōt-tswô'lē), Latin *Puteoli,* city (1971 pop. 58,990), Campania, S Italy, on the Bay of Naples. It is a port and an industrial and tourist center. Manufactures include iron and steel, machinery, and textiles. Pozzuoli was founded (6th cent. B.C.) by Greek exiles from Sámos island and was later a wealthy Roman seaport. Among the Roman remains are a large amphitheater and the ruins of the temple of Serapis (now partly under water), which once was a marketplace. Nearby is the Solfatara, a crater emitting sulfuric waters and thermal mud.

Pr, chemical symbol of the element PRASEODYMIUM.

Prado, Mariano Ignacio (märyä'nō ēgnä'syō prä'thō), 1826–1901, president of Peru (1865–67, 1878–79). He aided Ramón CASTILLA in the revolution of 1854. Indignant at the treaty that compensated Spain for losses during the revolution—a treaty he considered humiliating to Peru—Prado led a revolution. He became dictator and severed diplomatic relations with Spain. The war that followed was limited to small naval engagements, but before its conclusion Prado was deposed. He was forced to leave the country, but he later returned and was reelected. The war with Chile (see PACIFIC, WAR OF THE) broke out in 1879. After some months of dismal failure and defeat, Prado left for Europe and did not return for many years.

Prado (prä'dō, Span. prä'thō), national Spanish museum of painting and sculpture, Madrid, one of the finest in Europe. Situated on the Paseo del Prado, it was begun by Juan de Villanueva in 1785 for Charles III, as a museum of natural history, and finished under Ferdinand VII; the inaugural ceremony took place in 1819, when the collection consisted entirely of Spanish paintings. It was maintained by the royal family and called the Royal Museum until 1868, when it became national property. The Spanish, Flemish, and Venetian schools are particularly well represented in the Prado. There are outstanding masterpieces of Titian, Tintoretto, Veronese, Rubens, Van Dyke, Dürer, Brueghel, and Hieronymus Bosch, and Velázquez, El Greco, Ribera, and Goya, nowhere else to be seen to such advantage. The Prado collection also includes jewelry, furniture, and tapestries. In 1894 contemporary paintings in the museum were transferred to a separate building, which became the Museum of Modern Art. See Harry B. Wehle, *Great Paintings from the Prado Museum,* with a foreword by F. J. Sánchez Cantón (1963), and C. L. Riagghiangi, *Prado, Madrid* (1968).

Prados, Emilio (āmē'lyō prä'thōs), 1899–1962, Spanish poet, b. Málaga. After 1939 he lived in Mexico, and his post-civil war lyrics decry the anguish, death, and injustice of that upheaval. A literary associate of Manuel ALTOAGUIRRE, he cofounded the journal *Litoral.* His poetry is marked by the musicality and grace of the Andalusian school. Among his works are *Romancero general de la guerra España* [ballads of the war of Spain] (1937), *Jardín cerrado* [closed garden] (1946), and *La piedra escrita* [written stone] (1961).

Praed, Winthrop Mackworth (prād), 1802–39, English poet and essayist. A Conservative member of Parliament (1830–32, 1834–39) and an accomplished political satirist, he is best remembered for his graceful light verse—"Letter of Advice," "Molly Mog"—and his serious poems, such as "Arminius" and "Time's Song." See Derek Hudson, *A Poet in Parliament* (1939).

praefect: see PREFECT.

Praeneste: see PALESTRINA, Italy.

Praenestine Way: see ROMAN ROADS.

Praesepe (prēsē'pē) [Lat.,=manger], open STAR CLUSTER in the constellation Cancer; cataloged as M44 or NGC 2632. It was first recorded by Hipparchus (c.150 B.C.). The cluster is often called the Beehive because of its shape. It contains several hundred stars, many of which are doubles. It is faintly visible to the naked eye and an excellent object for a low-power telescope.

praetor or **pretor** (both: prē'tər), in ancient Rome, originally a consul, and later a magistrate (from c.366 B.C.). In 242 B.C. two praetors were appointed, the urban praetor (*praetor urbanus*), deciding cases to which citizens were parties, and the peregrine praetor (*praetor peregrinus*) deciding cases between foreigners. The urban praetor exercised the functions of the consuls in their absence and of the peregrine praetor when he was holding a military command. Two additional praetors were appointed (227) to administer Sicily and Sardinia, and two more (197) to administer Spain. A principal duty of praetors was the production of the public games. Under the empire the functions of the praetor were gradually taken over by other magistrates.

Praetorians (prētôr'ēənz), bodyguard of the ancient Roman emperors. Growing out of an early troop that served as bodyguard to the general commanding in Rome, they were formally organized in the time of Augustus. The number of cohorts (from 500 to 1,000 men each) forming the guard varied, but in the days of the later empire it was 10. The Praetorians under a PREFECT attended the emperor wherever he went. They had special privileges and, in the period when the empire declined, held almost unchallenged authority. Constantine I disbanded them in 312.

Praetorius, Michael (prētôr'ēəs), 1571–1621, German composer and musicographer, whose name originally was Schultheiss. He was a prolific composer, his *Musae Sioniae* (9 vol., 1605–11) alone containing 1,244 choral works. Now he is remembered chiefly for his *Syntagma musicum* (3 vol., 1615–19), which minutely describes the musical practices and the instruments of his day.

pragmatic sanction, decision of state dealing with a matter of great importance to a community or a whole state and having the force of fundamental law. The term originated in Roman law and was used on the continent of Europe until modern times. The **Pragmatic Sanction of Bourges,** issued by Charles VII of France in 1438, sharply limited the papal authority over the church in France and established the liberty of the Gallican Church (see GALLICANISM). It was revoked in 1461 by Louis XI, who sought to improve relations with the Holy See, but relations between church and state remained dubious until Francis I concluded the Concordat of 1516 (see CONCORDAT). There have been many other pragmatic sanctions, but the term, if unqualified, always refers to the **Pragmatic Sanction** of 1713, issued by Holy Roman Emperor CHARLES VI to alter the law of succession of the HAPSBURG family. Soon after Charles succeeded (1711) his elder brother Joseph I as emperor, he undertook to change the law so that, in the event of no male heir, the Hapsburg lands would be inherited through his own daughters rather than through Joseph's daughters. As it became apparent that there would be no male heir, the law took on great importance. By its terms, the succession to all Hapsburg dominions (but not to the imperial dignity, which was elective) was reserved for Charles's daughter MARIA THERESA. The principal aim of the law was to guarantee the continued integrity of the Hapsburg territories and to prevent a struggle for the succession. Charles labored throughout his reign to obtain the adherence to the Pragmatic Sanction of the European sovereigns and of the diets and estates of the various Hapsburg lands. France gave it its support in 1738, and at the time of Charles's death (1740) most other powers and all the diets and estates of the Hapsburg domains (including those of the Austrian Netherlands, Bohemia, and Hungary) had endorsed it; the diet of the Holy Roman Empire had guaranteed it in 1732. A notable exception was that of Elector Charles Albert of Bavaria (later Holy Roman Emperor CHARLES VII), who was married to Maria Amelia, one of the daughters of Joseph I who had been displaced by the Pragmatic Sanction. The other daughter, Maria Josepha, had been married to Elector Frederick Augustus II of Saxony (Augustus III of Poland), who had ratified the Pragmatic Sanction in 1733 in exchange for Austrian support in his struggle for the Polish throne. When Maria Theresa acceded to the Hapsburg succession in 1740, she had to defend her right in a long and bitter struggle, the War of the AUSTRIAN SUCCESSION (1740–48), in spite of all the guarantees her father had obtained. The Treaty of Aix-la-Chapelle of 1748 confirmed the Pragmatic Sanction.

pragmatism (prăg'mətĭzəm), method of philosophy in which the truth of a proposition is measured by its correspondence with experimental results and by its practical outcome. Thought is considered as simply an instrument for supporting the life aims of the human organism and has no real metaphysical significance. Pragmatism stands opposed to doctrines that hold that truth can be reached through deductive reasoning from a priori grounds and insists on the need for inductive investigation and constant empirical verification of hypotheses. There is constant protest against speculation concerning questions that have no application and no verifiable answers. Pragmatism holds that truth is modified as discoveries are made and is relative to the time and place and purpose of inquiry. In its ethical aspect pragmatism holds that knowledge that contributes to human values is real and that values inhere in the means as vitally as they do in the end itself. The principles of pragmatic theory were developed as formal doctrine by C. S. PEIRCE (c.1878). He was followed by William JAMES, who held that in vital matters of faith the criterion for acceptance was the will to believe, a theory reminiscent of the Kantian ethic. John DEWEY in his works developed the instrumentalist aspects of the doctrine. In Europe, F. C. S. Schiller, Hans Vaihinger, Henri Bergson, and others took up the theory. The similarity between pragmatism and the ideas of the Greek SOPHISTS has often been noted. See William James, *Pragmatism and Other Essays* (ed. by R. B. Perry, 1965); E. C. Moore, *American Pragmatism* (1961); Kenneth Winetrout, *F. C. S. Schiller and the Dimensions of Pragmatism* (1967); A. J. Ayer, *The Origins of Pragmatism* (1968); H. S. Thayer, *Meaning and Action: A Critical History of Pragmatism* (1968); Charles Morris, *The Pragmatic Movement in American Philosophy* (1970).

Prague (präg, prāg), Czech *Praha,* Ger. *Prag,* city (1970 pop. 1,078,096), capital and largest city of Czechoslovakia, on both banks of the Vltava (Ger. *Moldau*) River. A road, rail, and air transportation hub, the city also has an inland harbor that is the terminus of shipping on the Vltava and Elbe rivers. Prague is a leading European commercial and industrial center and is Czechoslovakia's most important industrial city. There are large engineering plants, machine-building and machine tool enterprises, printing and publishing houses, and factories producing automobiles, rolling stock, airplanes, iron and steel, construction materials, chemicals, and a wide variety of consumer goods. Prague is also the see of a Roman Catholic archbishop, an Eastern Orthodox archbishop, and the archbishop of the Czechoslovak church. Educational and cultural facilities in the city include Charles Univ. (founded 1348), one of the oldest and most famous in Europe; a technical university (1707); the Czechoslovak Academy of Sciences; the National Gallery; the National Museum; and many other museums and theaters. The earliest settlements, dating from at least the 9th cent., began around the castles standing on top of the Hradčany and Vysehrad hills (on the left and right bank, respectively, of the Vltava) that still dominate Prague's skyline. Already an important trading center by the 10th cent., Prague achieved real prominence after King Wenceslaus I of Bohemia established (1232) a German settlement there. It grew rapidly in size and prosperity as Bohemia's capital and became under Emperor Charles IV (14th cent.) one of the most splendid cities of Europe. The city's location at the intersection of vital trade routes stimulated its economy, while scholars and students from all over Europe came to its university. From the 14th to the early 17th cent., the emperors of the Holy Roman Empire resided at Prague as well as at Vienna. Rivalry between the Czech and German elements in the city was a major factor in the popular religious reform movement led by John Huss, a professor at the university. Huss, who also condemned the secular power of the Roman Catholic Church, was burned at the stake in 1415; his martyrdom sparked the HUSSITE WARS. Prague's attempt to follow a moderate course in the wars was frustrated (1424) by an army led by John Žižka. Hapsburg rule of Prague began in 1526, when the Ottoman Turks were casting their shadow over Europe. In the late 16th and early 17th cent., under Emperor Rudolf II, Prague shone as a center of science where the astronomers Tycho Brahe and Johannes Kepler worked. When in 1618 the Protestant Czech nobles felt the liberties of Bohemia threatened by Emperor Matthias, they vented their dissatisfaction by throwing two royal councilors and the secretary of the royal council of Bohemia out of the windows of Hradčany Castle (May 23, 1618). Although none of the victims of the so-called Defenestration of Prague were hurt, the event opened the THIRTY YEARS WAR. The battle of the WHITE MOUNTAIN (1620), fought near Prague, resulted in Bohemia's total subjugation to Austrian rule. Until 1860, German was the only official language in Prague. The Peace of Prague (1635) failed to end the Thirty Years War, in the last year of which (1648) a section of the city was occupied by the Swedes. In the War of the Austrian Succession, Prague was occupied by the French (1742) and the Prussians (1744); and in the Seven Years War it was (1757) the scene of a major victory of Frederick II of Prussia. Although it had lost much of its former importance, Prague in the 18th cent. remained a brilliant cultural center. The building activities of Empress Maria Theresa and the great Bohemian nobles gave the city a predominantly baroque and rococo character. The center of the Czech national revival in the 19th cent., Prague played an important part in the Revolution of 1848 until its bombardment and capture by the Austrian field marshal WINDISCHGRÄTZ. In 1918, Prague became the capital of the newly created Czechoslovak republic. Occupied (1939–45) by the Germans, the city suffered great hardship in World War II. Prague was liberated in May, 1945, by Soviet troops after a Czech rebellion (May 5) against the Germans. Until the war Prague was characterized by the generally peaceful coexistence of Czech, German, and German-Jewish cultures. It was the city of Rilke and Kafka as well as of Smetana, Dvořák, and Čapek. The city's literary, artistic, and musical life, which has a long and distinguished tradition, was very active between the two World Wars. The old section of Prague, which occupies the center of the city, is an architectural treasure enhanced by the beauty of its location on the hilly banks of the Vltava. Hradčany Castle dominates the city; the seat of the presidents of Czechoslovakia and the former royal residence, it is an imposing and many-winged structure, dating mostly from the reign of Charles IV. Next to it stands the largely Gothic Cathedral of St. Vitus, first built in the 10th cent., rebuilt under Charles IV, and completed only in 1929; it contains the tombs of St. Wenceslaus, St. John of Nepomuk, and many kings and emperors. Contiguous to the castle is the elegant 18th-century archiepiscopal palace. The Hradčany quarter also contains many other fine churches and palaces, notably the Romanesque basilica of St. George; the baroque churches of Our Lady of Victory (with the miraculous statuette of the Infant Jesus or Holy Child of Prague), of St. Nicholas, and of Loretto; the magnificent Waldstein Palace, built for the imperial general Wallenstein; and the Czernin Palace. On the slope extending from the castle to the Vltava is the quaint Mala Strana [lesser town] quarter, the best-preserved part of old Prague. Mala Strana is connected with the Old Town (Czech *Staré Město*), on the eastern bank of the river, by the 14th-century Charles Bridge, the most beautiful of Prague's 13 bridges. The Old Town contains the Carolinum, the oldest part of the university; the adjacent Stavovske Theater, where Mozart's *Don Giovanni* had its first performance; the vast Clementinum Library; the Gothic Old Town Hall (13th cent.; burned in May, 1945); the ancient clock of the seasons; the Gothic Tyn Cathedral (14th cent., formerly the main Hussite church, with the tomb of Tycho Brahe); and the Powder Tower (15th cent., last of the city gates). Situated in the adjacent former Jewish quarter is the Old Synagogue (13th cent.). In the heart of modern Prague is Wenceslaus Square, with its statue of St. Wenceslaus, which was the center of Czech resistance to the 1968 Soviet invasion of the country.

Prague, Peace of, 1635: see THIRTY YEARS WAR.

Prague, Treaty of, 1866: see AUSTRO-PRUSSIAN WAR.

Prague, University of: see CHARLES UNIV.

Praguerie (prägərē'), 1440, revolt against King Charles VII of France, so called in allusion to the Hussite uprising in Prague. It was led by several great feudal lords, including the comte de Dunois, who resented the diminution of their influence over the royal government. They were joined by the dauphin (later Louis XI) and were supported by Philip the Good of Burgundy. The revolt was quickly suppressed, and the rebels were treated leniently by the king.

Praha: see PRAGUE, Czechoslovakia.

Praia: see CAPE VERDE ISLANDS.

prairie chicken: see GROUSE.

prairie dog, short-tailed, ground-living rodent, genus *Cynomys,* of the SQUIRREL family, closely related to the ground squirrels, chipmunks, and marmots. There are several species, found in the W United States and N Mexico. Prairie dogs, named for their barking cries, are 12 to 15 in. (30 to 36 cm) long, including the 1- to 4-in. (2.5 to 10 cm) tail, and have short, coarse, buff-colored fur. The black-tailed prairie dog, *Cynomys ludovicianus,* is found on the Great Plains. Members of this species live in connecting burrows, forming colonies, or "towns," which may extend many miles and include thousands of individuals. The entrances of the burrows are surrounded by cone-shaped mounds, which serve to keep out rainwater; the entrance shafts drop straight down for several feet. Prairie dogs spend much time maintaining the mounds by tamping down damp earth. They often sit upright on their haunches in rows, one animal on each mound; this behavior has given them the name "picket pins" in some regions. At any sign of danger the animals give a warning cry and duck down into the burrows. Rattlesnakes and burrowing owls sometimes live in the burrows and prey on young prairie dogs. Three species of white-tailed prairie dogs inhabit open or brushy valleys of the Rocky Mts; their burrows are usually less extensive than those of the black-tailed species. Prairie dogs feed mainly on grasses, but also eat insects; they hibernate in winter. Prairie dog towns were formerly much more common and extensive than now; some towns on the plains encompassed millions of individuals. Ranchers regard the animals as competitors for grazing lands and have destroyed them in large numbers. Prairie dogs are classified in the phylum CHORDATA, subphylum Vertebrata, class Mammalia, order Rodentia, family Sciuridae.

Prairie Provinces, Canada: see MANITOBA; SASKATCHEWAN; ALBERTA.

prairies, generally level, originally grass-covered and treeless plains of North America, stretching from W Ohio through Indiana, Illinois, and Iowa to the Great Plains region. The prairie belt also extends into N Missouri, S Michigan, Wisconsin, Minnesota, E North and South Dakota, and S Canada. Many of the prairies of the world were formerly used for grazing purposes, but more and more are now coming under cultivation; hence they are often referred to today as the "vanishing grasslands." The soil of the prairies is basically a black CHERNOZEM, which is extremely fertile. The prairies correspond to the PAMPA of Argentina, the LLANOS in northern South America, the STEPPE of Eurasia, and the high veld of South Africa. Because they have the favorable climate and soil fertility characteristic of prairies, the wheat belts in the United States, the Ukraine, and the Pampa of Argentina are among the world's most productive agricultural regions.

prairie schooner, wagon covered with white canvas, made famous by its almost universal use in the migration across the Western prairies and plains, and so called in allusion to the white-topped schooners of the sea. It was a descendant of the CONESTOGA WAGON. Whereas the latter usually required a six-horse team even on good roads, the prairie schooner was much lighter and rarely needed more than four horses, and sometimes only two, even on virgin prairie trails. Oxen were frequently used instead of horses. The average prairie schooner was an ordinary farm wagon fitted with a top, drawn in at both ends, with only an oval opening to admit air and light to the interior, where women and children usually slept and rode. In crossing the Great Plains groups of prairie schooners customarily traveled together for protection (see WAGON TRAIN).

prairie smoke: see PASQUEFLOWER.

prairie soil: see PODZOL.

Prairie View Agricultural and Mechanical College, at Prairie View, Texas; land-grant, state supported; coeducational; chartered and opened 1876 to provide higher education for Negro students. Although it focuses on teacher training, the college also offers a basic liberal arts curriculum as well as programs in agriculture, home economics, and engineering. The college is a member of the Texas Agricultural and Mechanical University system.

Prairie Village, city (1970 pop. 28,138), Johnson co., NE Kansas, a residential suburb in the greater Kansas City area; inc. 1951.

prairie wolf: see COYOTE.

Prajadhipok (prəchä'tĭpôk), 1893–1941, king of Siam (1925–35). He was educated in England and France. He succeeded his brother Rama VI, and in 1932 a coup d'etat forced him to grant a constitution, which allowed for national suffrage and a representative parliament. In 1933 he dismissed the cabinet as too radical. A second rebellion further weakened his already faltering position. Differences over the limits subsequently placed on the royal prerogative led to his abdication in 1935. He moved to England, where he died. He was succeeded by his nephew, Ananda.

Prakrit (prä'krĭt), any of a number of languages belonging to the Indic group of the Indo-Iranian subfamily of the Indo-European family of languages (see INDO-IRANIAN LANGUAGES). The Prakrits are usually classified as Middle Indic languages that followed the Old Indic stage of Sanskrit and Vedic but preceded the Modern Indic period. Some scholars, however, use the term *Prakrit* to include the Modern Indic vernaculars as well as those of the Middle Indic period—in short, to designate all Indic languages other than Sanskrit and Vedic. Other authorities say that the Modern Indic languages, which began to take form between 1000 and 1200, developed from the various medieval Prakrits. The oldest written records of the Prakrits are inscriptions of the 3d cent. B.C., but the languages were in use as vernaculars by the 6th cent. B.C. The Prakrits have been described as regional or vernacular dialects of classical SANSKRIT. They were popular forms of speech, but a few of them developed into literary languages. Some estimates put the number of Prakrits at 38. In the ancient Indian drama, upper-class male (and sometimes female) characters use Sanskrit, while the characters (both male and female) of the lower classes speak various Prakrits. It can therefore be inferred that in this early period the Prakrits as popular forms of speech were used side by side with Sanskrit, the language of the priests and the nobility. PALI, a Middle Indic language that became the language of the Buddhists and their sacred literature, is considered a Prakrit by some scholars, though not by all. There are important phonetic and grammatical differences between the Old Indic and Middle Indic languages. For example, the Prakrits were much simpler grammatically than classical Sanskrit, having discarded the dual number for noun and verb, reduced the eight-case system of Sanskrit for the noun, and generally simplified the verb. On the whole, the vocabulary of Prakrit is of Old Indic origin. See Alfred C. Woolner, *Introduction to Prakrit* (2d ed. 1928); Richard Pischel, *Comparative Grammar of the Prakrit Languages* (2d ed., tr. by Subhadra Jhā, 1965).

Prakrit literature. By the 6th cent. B.C. the people of India were speaking and writing languages that were much simpler than classical Sanskrit. These vernacular forms, of which there were several, are called the Prakrits [Skt.,=natural]. One very important and early Prakrit was Pali (see PALI LITERATURE), which became the language of the Buddhists. However, most of the literature generally called Prakrit is devoted to JAINISM. The sacred texts (*Siddhanta* or *Agama*) of the two main sects of the Jains employed three types of Prakrit. The oldest sutras of the Svetambara sect are written in Ardha-Magadhi, while later books are in Maharastri. The Svetambara canon, written in verse and prose, received its final form in A.D. 454. The sacred books of the Digambara sect are written in Savraseni. An important source of knowledge of Prakrit is the Sanskrit drama. KALIDASA is included among many dramatists, who, in order to obtain a realistic effect, had the common people in their plays speak in Prakrit. See SANSKRIT LITERATURE. See Moriz Winternitz, *A History of Indian Literature* (2 vol., tr. 1927–33, repr. 1971).

Prasad, Rajendra (rəjĕn'drə prəsäd'), 1884–1963, first president of India. Before entering politics, he taught English literature, history, economics, and law. In 1917 he began working with Mohandas K. Gandhi, and in 1920 he joined the Indian National Congress and was several times (1934, 1939, 1947–48) its president. He was imprisoned (1942–45) for supporting the Congress opposition to the British war effort in World War II. Prasad became president of India in 1950, when the republic of India was proclaimed, and held that office until 1962. His many writings include his autobiography (tr. 1958) and *At the Feet of Mahatma Gandhi* (1961). See biography by K. L. Panjabi (1960).

praseodymium (prā"zēōdĭm'ēəm,-sēō-) [Gr.,=green twin], metallic chemical element; symbol Pr; at. no. 59; at. wt. 140.907; m.p. about 930°C; b.p. about 3120°C; sp. gr. about 6.8; valence +3 or +4. Praseodymium is a soft, malleable, ductile, silver-yellow metal. It exhibits ALLOTROPY; the α-form (hexagonal crystalline structure) has the density given above, but the β-form (above 800°C, body-centered cubic crystalline structure) is less dense. Praseodymium is a RARE-EARTH METAL of the LANTHANIDE SERIES in group IIIb of the PERIODIC TABLE. When exposed to air it forms a green oxide that does not protect it from further oxidation. Although the pure metal may be prepared by reduction of the chloride, it has few commercial uses. A major use of the metal is in a pyrophoric alloy used in cigarette lighter flints, but it need not be purified for this application. Praseodymium compounds have many uses. The oxide is used in carbon electrodes for arc lighting. The salts are used to color enamels and glass. Didymium glass used in glassblower's goggles contains praseodymium; this glass absorbs the yellow sodium glare of light from the torch flame. The major commercial source of praseodymium is the rare-earth minerals MONAZITE and bastnasite. Praseodymium was discovered in 1885 by C. A. Von WELSBACH, who separated Mosander's "didymium" into two components, the earths neodymia and praseodymia.

Pratas Island (prä'täs), Chinese *Tungsha,* in the South China Sea, administered by Kwangtung prov., SE China. The island has guano deposits. Occupied by the Japanese in 1907–9 and again in 1939–45, Pratas Island passed to the Chinese government in 1950.

Pratinas (prăt'ĭnəs), fl. c.500 B.C., Greek dithyrambic poet of Phlius, said to have introduced the satyr play into Athens.

pratincole (prăt'ənkōl"), common name for a large-winged shore bird including seven species in the subfamily *Glareolinae* of the family Glareolidae. Swift and graceful flyers, their sharply pointed, decurved bills are broad-based and open wide as adaptations for feeding on the wing. They have long wings and long, forked tails. Their diet consists primarily of grasshoppers and dragonflies. With their small, partially webbed feet, pratincoles wade rather than swim. Both sexes are similar in appearance, being 7 to 9 in. (18–23 cm) in length and generally dull brown with a white rump and tail. They are active chiefly at dusk. Three species in the genus *Glareola* and three in the genus *Galachrysia* are found from S Europe through Africa and S Asia. *Stiltia isabella* is the sole Australian species. Most pratincoles nest on the ground in shallow depressions or unlined scrapes. They lay from two to four smooth, oval-shaped eggs per clutch; these are dullish and colored, blending with varying soil backgrounds. Pratincoles are classified in the phylum CHORDATA, subphylum Vertebrata, class Aves, order Charadriiformes, family Glareolidae.

Prato (prä'tō) or **Prato in Toscana** (ēn tōskä'nä), city (1971 pop. 143,595), Tuscany, central Italy. It is a major textile-making center, known for its wool industry since the 13th cent. Weaving machinery and leather goods are also manufactured. Prato was an Etruscan settlement. It came under Florence in the 14th cent. Among the city's noteworthy structures are the cathedral (12th–15th cent.), which has frescoes by Filippo Lippi and works by Donatello, Giovanni Pisano, and Andrea della Robbia; the Church of Santa Maria delle Carceri, designed by Giuliano da Sangallo; and a 13th-century town hall and fortress.

Pratt, Charles, 1st **Earl Camden,** 1714–94, British jurist. Appointed (1761) chief justice of the Court of Common Pleas, he earned wide popularity by pronouncing (1763) against the legality of the general warrant under which John WILKES was prosecuted. He became lord chancellor in 1766, but his constant denunciation of the government's policy toward the American colonists and opposition to the taxes imposed on the colonists resulted in his dismissal in 1770. He served as president of the council under the marquess of Rockingham (1782–83) and under William Pitt (1784–94). In 1786 he was created Earl Camden. His lifelong fight against the existing definition of libel culminated in the passage of Fox's Libel Act of 1792 (see PRESS, FREEDOM OF THE). Camden's son, **John Jeffreys Pratt,** 2d **Earl** and 1st **Marquess Camden,** 1759–1840, was lord lieutenant of Ireland from 1794 to 1798. His repressive policies there were a major factor in the outbreak of the 1798 revolution. He later served as secretary of war (1804–5) and president of the council (1805–6 and 1807–12). He was created marquess in 1812.

Pratt, Daniel, 1799–1873, American industrialist, b. Temple, N.H. He moved to Georgia at the age of 20, and after he had become a partner in a cotton gin he went (1833) to Alabama, where he founded (1835) Prattville, 12 mi (17 km) NW of Montgomery. Here he built up numerous industries, promoted business, and became one of the first important industrialists of Alabama. He became interested in coal and iron industries in Birmingham. As a representative in the Alabama legislature during the Civil War, he at first opposed secession but later ardently supported the Confederacy. See biography by S. F. H. Tarrant (1904).

Pratt, Edwin John, 1883–1964, Canadian poet, b. Newfoundland. He broke away from the old romantic tradition of Canadian poetry to write imaginative narratives of epic events. Among these are *Titans* (1926), *The Roosevelt and the Antinoe* (1930), *The Titanic* (1935), and *Dunkirk* (1941). His most ambitious work, *Brébeuf and His Brethren* (1940), records the heroism of martyred Jesuit missionaries. See his *Collected Poems* (1944).

Pratt, Matthew, 1734–1805, American portrait painter, b. Philadelphia. After he was an apprentice to his uncle, a painter in Philadelphia, he practiced portrait painting and then studied under Benjamin West in London (1764–66). His most famous paintings are *The American School* (Metropolitan Mus.) and portraits of Benjamin Franklin, Benjamin West, and Cadwallader Colden. See study by William Sawitzky (1942).

Pratt, Orson, 1811–81, Mormon apostle, b. Hartford, N.Y.; brother of Parley Parker Pratt. He entered (1830) the Mormon Church and became (1835) an apostle. An eloquent speaker, he was a successful missionary in England and elsewhere; in Utah, where he was (1847) one of the first immigrants, he was long an influential member of the assembly. Pratt also taught at the Univ. of Deseret (now the Univ. of Utah). He wrote books on mathematics as well as on the Mormon Church.

Pratt, Parley Parker, 1807–57, Mormon apostle, b. Otsego co., N.Y.; brother of Orson Pratt. He joined (1830) the Mormon Church and was made an apostle in 1835. In 1838, Pratt was imprisoned in Missouri during the persecution of the Mormons there. On the first of his missionary visits to England he founded (1840) the *Millennial Star* in Manchester. In Utah, where he went in 1847, he aided in framing the constitution of the State of Deseret (which later became the Utah Territory) and devised a Mormon alphabet. See his autobiography (ed. by his son, 1874; 3d ed. 1938); biography by Reva Stanley (1937).

Pratt, Richard Henry, 1840–1924, American soldier and educator, b. Rushford, N.Y. He served in the Union army during the Civil War and then in the Indian wars in the West, where he became interested in the cultural problems of the Indians. He experimented in educating Indians, believing that they must be taught to reject tribal culture and adapt to white society. In 1879, he founded at Carlisle, Pa., a nonreservation school for Indians. He retired from the U.S. army in 1903 but supervised the CARLISLE INDIAN SCHOOL, maintained by the U.S. government and housed in an army barracks, until 1904. See E. G. Eastman, *The Red Man's Moses* (1935).

Pratt Institute, at Brooklyn, N.Y.; coeducational; chartered and opened 1887. Founded by Charles Pratt as a school for practical training, it now offers general and professional studies, including programs in industrial design, interior design, architecture, and engineering. It operates the Pratt Graphics Center (est. 1956 as an extension of the School of Art and Design) in Manhattan. The institute's library opened in 1896 as the first general public library in Brooklyn but was closed to the public in 1940.

Prattville, city (1970 pop. 13,116), seat of Autauga co., central Ala.; inc. 1872. It has textile and related industries and a paper mill. Cotton gins have been manufactured there since 1838. A state game farm is in the city.

Pravdinsk (präv'dyĭnsk), formerly **Friedland** (frēt'-länt), town, NW European USSR, formerly in East Prussia. In 1807 the city was the scene of a battle in which Napoleon I defeated the Russians, thus precipitating the fall of Königsberg and the Treaty of Tilsit.

prawn: see SHRIMP.

Praxiteles (prăksĭt'əlēz), fl. c.370–c.330 B.C., famous Attic sculptor, probably the son of CEPHISODOTUS. His *Hermes with the Infant Dionysus,* found in the Heraeum, Olympia, in 1877, is the only example of an undisputed extant original by any of the greatest ancient masters. It was found in the same place where Pausanias had seen it 17 centuries earlier. The workmanship of the sculptor can be judged directly from it—the delicate and perfect modeling, as well as the strength and grace of conception, are characteristic of his figures. His most renowned statues are lost entirely or known only through Roman imitations. Out of some 50 works mentioned as his in ancient writings, the one chosen as finest of all was the *Aphrodite of Cnidus.* There is a copy in the Vatican. Of the *Eros of Thespiae,* only the fame remains. Praxiteles made several statues of young satyrs; the one in the Capitoline Museum (Rome) is celebrated in Hawthorne's *Marble Faun.* Other copies of the sculptor's works are *Apollo Sauroctonus* (Vatican); *Apollino* (Florence); and *Silenus and Dionysus* (Louvre). All of these illustrate his choice of youthful gods and other beings in which joy of life finds expression. Praxiteles' modeling of face and hair and his treatment of the surface of the marble are unsurpassed.

Prayer, Book of Common: see BOOK OF COMMON PRAYER.

praying Indians, name for North American Indians who accepted Christianity. Although many different groups are called by this name, e.g., the Roman Catholic Iroquois of St. Regis, it was more commonly applied to those Indians of E Massachusetts who were organized into villages by the Puritan missionary John ELIOT. In 1674 there were seven principal praying towns—Hassanamesit, Magunkaquog, Nashobah, Natick, Okommakamesit, Punkapog, and Wamesit. Natick, founded in 1651, was the oldest. In King Philip's War (1675) the praying Indians were practically destroyed by the other Indians, who viewed them as traitors, and by the English, who thought they were secret allies of King Philip. From a population of 1,100 in 1674, they were reduced to 300 by 1680.

praying mantis: see MANTID.

Preachers, Order of: see DOMINICANS.

Preble, Edward (prĕb'əl), 1761–1807, American naval officer, b. Falmouth (now Portland), Maine. In the American Revolution he ran away from home to serve on a privateer, entered (1779) the Massachusetts state marine as a midshipman, and saw service aboard the *Protector,* which was captured in 1781. After his release he joined the *Winthrop* and, when the Revolution was over, was engaged in the merchant service. Commissioned lieutenant in the U.S. navy in 1798, he was promoted (1799) to captain and given command of the *Essex,* which sailed to China and convoyed 14 merchant vessels to New York. In 1803, Preble was transferred to the *Constitution* and set out in command of a squadron for the Mediterranean, where he took a leading part in the TRIPOLITAN WAR. After the *Philadelphia* of his squadron had been captured and held in the harbor of Tripoli, Preble blockaded that port and made a number of attacks, but he failed to capture the strongly fortified town. He was relieved of his command on the arrival of Commodore Samuel Barron. Many of those who served under Preble, such as David Porter and Stephen Decatur, rendered distinguished service in the War of 1812. See biography by Christopher McKee (1972).

Precambrian era, name for the first two major divisions of geologic time (see GEOLOGIC ERAS, table): the Early Precambrian, or Archeozoic, era and the Late Precambrian, or Proterozoic, era. The oldest ROCKS found in the earth's crust were formed during the Early Precambrian era. They are mostly covered by rock systems of more recent origin, but where visible they commonly display evidence of having been altered by intense METAMORPHISM. Precambrian rocks often occur in shields, which are large areas of relatively low elevation that form parts of continental masses. One of the largest exposed areas of Early Precambrian rocks is the Canadian Shield, where geologist Sir William Logan did his pioneer work. It covers most of Greenland, extends over more than half of Canada, and reaches into the United States as the Superior Highlands and the Adirondack Mts. The rocks of this region, and of the Early Precambrian as a whole, are generally GRANITE, SCHIST, or GNEISS. The most notable formations are the Keewatin and Coutchiching of Minnesota and the adjoining part of Canada; the Grenville of Ontario, which, however, may be Late Precambrian; and the widely distributed Laurentian. The Keewatin series of rocks is composed chiefly of metamorphosed lava, with some sediments; the Coutchiching series is chiefly of sedimentary gneisses and schists. The Grenville limestone, marble, gneiss, and quartzite are predominantly metamorphosed sediments; the Laurentian gneiss and granite are probably younger than the other series, having been forced up through the Grenville as igneous rock in some great earth movement. After the appearance of the Laurentian the Temiskaming, or Sudburian, sediments were deposited, and a second series of gneisses and granites, the Algoman, was formed. Elsewhere in North America, Early Precambrian rocks are exposed in the Grand Canyon of Arizona and in the Teton Range of Wyoming. Among the other shield areas composed of Early Precambrian rocks are the Angara Shield in Siberia, the Australian Shield, the Baltic Shield in Europe, the Antarctic Shield, and the African Shield comprising most of the African continent. In South America, the Amazon River basin separates the shields into the Guiana and the Brazilian sections. Fossils have been reported from this era, but none have yet been found in strata universally acknowledged to be Early Precambrian. Indirect evidence, however, supports the belief that rudimentary life existed. In the formation of the Late Precambrian rocks sedimentation played a comparatively greater part than in the preceding Early Precambrian era. There was less igneous or volcanic activity; warping and metamorphism, however, continued to be important. Notable Late Precambrian formations occur in the mountains of Montana, in the Grand Canyon, in the Lake Superior region, and also in Scotland, Scandinavia, and Brazil. The life of the Late Precambrian is poorly represented by fossils, but a few invertebrates including creatures resembling jellyfish and worms have been discovered. The best evidence that there probably were numerous forms of life is the variety and complexity which suddenly appears in Cambrian fauna. Mineral deposits associated with Precambrian rocks have yielded most of the world's gold and nickel in addition to large quantities of copper, silver, radium, and uranium. Although the durations of the Early Precambrian and the Late Precambrian are uncertain, the length of the entire Precambrian era probably exceeded four billion years.

precentor (prēsĕn'tər) [Lat.,=one who sings first], the director of the music of a cathedral or a monastic church and also a CANTOR.

precession: see GYROSCOPE.

precession of the equinoxes, westward motion of the EQUINOXES along the ECLIPTIC. This motion was first noted by Hipparchus c.120 B.C. The precession is due to the gravitational attraction of the moon and sun on the equatorial bulge of the earth, which causes the earth's axis to describe a cone in somewhat the same fashion as a spinning top. As a result, the celestial equator (see EQUATORIAL COORDINATE SYSTEM), which lies in the plane of the earth's equator, moves on the CELESTIAL SPHERE, while the ecliptic, which lies in the plane of the earth's orbit around the sun, is not affected by this motion. The equinoxes, which lie at the intersections of the celestial equator and the ecliptic, thus move on the celestial sphere. Similarly, the celestial poles move in circles on the celestial sphere, so that there is a continual change in the star at or near one of these poles (see POLARIS). After a period of about 26,000 years the equinoxes and poles lie once again at nearly the same points on the celestial sphere. Because the gravitational effects of the sun and moon are not always the same, there is some wobble in the motion of the earth's axis; this wobble, called NUTATION, causes the celestial poles to move, not in perfect circles, but in a series of S-shaped curves with a period of 18.6 years. There is some further precession caused by the gravitational influences of the other planets; this precession affects the earth's orbit around the sun and thus causes a shift of the ecliptic on the celestial sphere. The precession of the earth's orbital plane is sometimes called planetary precession, and that of the earth's equatorial plane (caused by the sun and moon) is called luni-solar precession; the combined effect of the moon, the sun, and the planets is called general precession. Planetary precession is much less than luni-solar precession. The precession of the equinoxes was first explained by Isaac Newton in 1687.

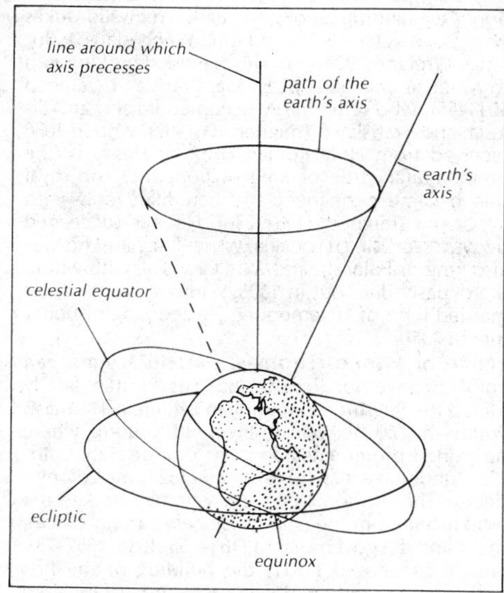

Precession of the equinoxes (the points at which the earth's celestial equator intersects its ecliptic) is due to the slow rotation of the earth's axis around a perpendicular to the ecliptic.

precious stone: see GEM.

precipitation, in chemistry, a process in which a solid is separated from a suspension, sol, or solution. In a suspension such as sand in water the solid spontaneously precipitates (settles out) on standing. In a sol the particles are precipitated by COAGULATION. A solute (dissolved substance) may be precipitated from a solution by several means. A solution of salt may be concentrated by evaporation until the salt crystallizes. When a saturated solution of sugar is cooled, sugar crystals form. The addition of a solution of silver nitrate to a solution containing chloride ions results in the formation of insoluble silver chloride: $AgNO_3 + Cl^- \rightarrow NO_3^- + AgCl\downarrow$. In each case the precipitate formed may settle out spontaneously or may be collected by filtration or centrifugation. It is often difficult to obtain a pure substance by a single precipitation, and a substance may be further purified by reprecipitation after it has been redissolved. The term *precipitation* is also applied to the separation of particles of a solid or liquid suspended in a gas.

precipitation, in meteorology, condensed moisture that falls to the surface of the earth in the form of RAIN, SLEET, SNOW, HAIL, FROST, or DEW.

pre-Columbian art and architecture. Long before the arrival of Europeans in the Western Hemisphere, the regions of Mexico and Guatemala and the Andean region of South America had been the cradle of Indian civilizations whose remains bear witness to an exceptional degree of artistic advancement. The MAYA occupied the general area of Yucatán and adjacent parts of Central America from very early times. Their roots were in the Archaic period (c.2000 B.C.), but it was only during the Late Formative (300 B.C.–A.D. 150) and the Proto-Classic (A.D. 150–300) periods that the traits associated with the Classic Maya were developed. Their greatest artistic achievements included their elaborate calendar, writing, palaces and temple pyramids with vaulted rooms made of limestone, polychrome pottery, stone stelae, and stylized wall paintings and bas-reliefs. The Classic Maya (A.D. 300–900) was the apex of Maya civilization and is described as that period when the Maya inscribed the "Long Count Calendar" on their monuments. The remains of BONAMPAK, with its famous murals, can be dated to shortly after 800. Maya cities were ceremonial centers, and some of the edifices may be more properly identified as sculptured monuments. Maya architectural styles are found in three main regions: the Petén district (Uaxactún and TIKAL); the cities of the river valleys, such as PIEDRAS NEGRAS and PALENQUE; and the cities of central and N Yucatán (UXMAL). The cause of the collapse of the Maya civilization is not precisely understood. The culture persisted over so long a period that it is easier to understand the rest of Mesoamerican art and culture from the framework of Maya chronology. The OLMEC civilization, to the west, in the area of Vera Cruz and Tabasco, Mexico, was developing in the Formative period; specifically, the period 800 B.C. to 400 B.C. marks the finest period of Olmec art as typified by the finds made at the site of La Venta. It is believed that the Olmec devised the Long Count Calendar and invented writing and that they may well be the source of these developments among the Maya. Noted for the excellence of their stone carving—ranging from small, finely detailed jade objects to colossal, often realistic basalt heads—the Olmec frequently used a motif combining human and jaguar features. TEOTIHUACÁN is much to the west of the Olmec and Maya areas and dates from the 1st cent. A.D. to A.D. 700, but the major part of the site and the height of its artistic expression belong to the periods Teotihuacán II and Teotihuacán III (c.300–700). Teotihuacán is an urban center, perhaps the greatest in Mexico; its monumental pyramids, temples, and royal processional roads are an extraordinary architectural achievement. In the latter part of Maya Early Classic (c.400–600) there is evidence of great influence from Teotihuacán, as exemplified at the site of Kaminaljuyú and in varying degrees at other sites, including Tikal and Uaxactún. Uaxactún and Tikal, erected on high land above the surrounding swamps, reveal their massive, richly decorated temples in the midst of tropical jungles. In the valley of the Motagua River to the south are COPÁN and QUIRIGUÁ, where sculpture flourished in the form of huge, elaborately carved stone stelae, whereas more delicate forms and a refined spatial sense are evident in the famous stucco sculpture of Palenque and the airiness and grace of its buildings. In the flat, dry country of N Yucatán, Maya architecture underwent changes in style. The erection of stone stelae was largely abandoned, and decoration, notably at Uxmal, became geometric. The site of Teotihuacán apparently was deliberately destroyed by invaders c.700 and thereafter ceased to be a factor in Maya civilization. After the fall of Teotihuacán, a period of nearly two centuries (700–900) seems to have ensued during which there was no single dominant force, but a number of warring factions. One of these, the TOLTEC, made their capital at TULA (c.900–1200), NW of Teotihuacán. The Toltec achieved power and dominated much of North and Central Mexico until they were vanquished in 1156 or 1168. They invaded Maya country, principally CHICHÉN ITZÁ (c.987), where they had a profound influence as revealed by the pyramids at Tula and Chichén Itzá with their deep colonnades, an unusual feature in Mesoamerican architecture, and their decorative bas-relief and sculptured structural elements, e.g., the 15-ft-tall (4.5 m) caryatids at Tula. Toltec occupation has also been identified at other sites in the Yucatán. Indications are that Chichén Itzá was abandoned by the Toltec around 1224. The final great native conquest in Mesoamerica was by the AZTEC, who rose to power following a period of anarchy after the destruction of the Toltec's Tula. By 1344 the Aztecs had founded their magnificent capital, TENOCHTITLÁN, at the site of present-day Mexico City in the Valley of Mexico, which became one of the architectural wonders of ancient America. Aztec art was eclectic, drawing on the traditions of conquered areas; but under the influence of the harsh Aztec religion, it developed a unique character. The importance of human sacrifice in the cult of the war god, Huitzilopochtli, permeated life and art, and representations of skulls, hearts, hands, and sacrificial scenes were common. Much of the stone sculpture was huge and elaborate, a remarkable example being the statue of the earth goddess Coatlicue. Masses of intertwined serpents dominate the statue, which bears a necklace of human hearts and hands. Less ominous subjects, such as the plumed serpent, Quetzalcoatl, and various animals, were often beautifully carved in a smooth, compact style. Featherwork, jade carving, goldwork, extraordinary ceremonial vases, and superb textiles were produced by the craftsmen of subjugated groups, especially the Mixtec. Aztec power over Central Mexico extended until the arrival of Cortés in 1519. The area of the MIXTEC and ZAPOTEC in OAXACA, Mexico, was not completely conquered by the Aztecs. The Zapotec originally occupied the site of MONTE ALBÁN from late Olmec times (c.600 B.C.) until about A.D. 900. Then a new seat of Zapotec civilization was founded at MITLA. Later, the Mixtec began to infiltrate, intermarry with, occupy, and absorb the Zapotec. Apart from architecture, the Mixtec also excelled at the minor arts: goldwork, jewelry, vessels fashioned with semiprecious stones, turquoise and feather mosaics, extremely fine polychrome pottery, and painted books known as codices. Many of the Mexican cultures produced ceramic figurines and pottery, often of superior artistic merit. The site of Tlatilco, in the Valley of Mexico, has yielded famous ceramics of remarkably early date, about 500 B.C. Delicacy of detail characterizes the figurines of Teotihuacán, and the finely decorated funerary urns of Monte Albán (c.400 B.C.) are particularly well wrought. In the western states of Nayarit, Jalisco, and Colima, early cultures produced an enormously varied array of fanciful and often grotesque terracotta figurines and pottery during the classic period, A.D. 300 to 900. The TARASCAN Indians of lake Pátzcuaro were one of these groups; they still produce excellent lacquerware. In the jungle states of Veracruz, Campeche, and Tabasco many sites, particularly REMOJADAS, have yielded fine examples of clay sculpture.

The Cultures of Ancient Peru. The first great art style of Peru was that of the civilization that flourished at CHAVÍN DE HUÁNTAR in the northern highlands c.900 to 200 B.C. A more or less contemporaneous culture of the north coast produced a style of pottery known as Cupisnique. The Paracas culture of the south coast, of the same era, left some of the most beautiful textiles of pre-Inca Peru as well as fine pottery decorated with resin paint. Excellent painted ceramics were also characteristic of the NAZCA civilization (c.200 B.C.–A.D. 600) to the south, but their contemporaries on the north coast, the MOCHICA, surpassed them in the art of painted pottery. Battle scenes, rituals, animals, and mythological beings were masterfully depicted. Their ceramic "portrait vessels" in the form of human heads are the high point of realism in pre-Columbian art. They were also master builders, the Mochica Pyramid of the Sun being the largest in South America. During the following period (c.600–800), the TIAHUANACO culture gained ascendancy. With the decline of Tiahuanaco the kingdom of the CHIMU flourished. Their capital, CHANCHAN, has long been considered one of the great centers of ancient Peru, surpassed only by the colossal achievements of the INCA, who conquered the Chimu in the latter part of the 15th cent. As engineers the Inca were unsurpassed in ancient America. Their agricultural terraces are still in use, and the extensive network of roads and bridges that spanned their empire would merit the envy of modern road builders; but their cities and fortresses remain their towering achievement. The great cities of CUZCO and MACHU PICCHU and the imposing fortresses of Sacsahuamán and Ollantaytambo are typical examples of their skill. The Inca also excelled at stone carving and metalwork, achieving in this latter art a degree of perfection comparable to that reached anywhere in the world. Their civilization fell to the Spanish invaders in 1538. See bibliography under individual cultures, e.g., AZTEC. For Indian art in North America, see NORTH AMERICAN INDIAN ART. See H. D. Disselhoff, *The Art of Ancient America* (tr. 1961); George Kubler, *The Art and Architecture of Ancient America* (1962); S. K. Lothrop, *Treasures of Ancient America* (1964); Frederick Dockstader, *Indian Art in Middle America* (1964) and *Indian Art in South America* (1967); Hasso von Winning, *Pre-Columbian Art of Mexico and Central America* (1968); Ferdinand Anton, *The Art of Ancient Peru* (tr. 1972).

predella (prĕdĕl'lä), Italian term for a painted panel, usually small, belonging to a series of panels at the bottom of an altarpiece. The form was used mainly in Italy from the 13th to the 16th cent. Often added as a "footnote" to the main theme of an altarpiece, predella panels generally consist of narrative scenes, e.g., the Passion of Christ or the lives of the saints. The artist had an opportunity to express himself with more inventiveness and vivacity in these episodes than in the main panel, where the image was conventionalized to a greater extent. Several beautiful panels from the *Maestà* by Duccio are in the National Gallery, Washington, D.C., which also has two scenes by Domenico Veneziano. See study by Roberto Salvini and Leone Traverso (tr. 1961).

predestination, in theology, doctrine that asserts that God predestines from eternity the salvation of certain souls. So-called double predestination, as in CALVINISM, is the added assertion that God also foreordains certain souls to damnation. Predestination is posited on the basis of God's omniscience and omnipotence and is closely related to the doctrines of divine providence and GRACE. A predestinarian doctrine is suggested in St. Paul, but it is not developed. Rom. 8.28–30. St. Augustine's interpretation of the doctrine has been the fountainhead for most subsequent versions, both Protestant and Roman Catholic. PELAGIANISM argued against St. Augustine that God wills the salvation of all souls equally, a view that became popular in liberal Protestant theology. The Roman Catholic view, as stated by St. Thomas Aquinas, maintains that God wills the salvation of all souls but that certain souls are granted special grace that in effect foreordains their salvation. The damned may be said to be reprobated to hell only in the sense that God foresees their resistance to the grace given them. The Roman Catholic Church teaches that predestination is consistent with free will since God moves the soul according to its nature. Calvinism, on the other hand, rejects the role of free will and teaches that grace is irresistible and that God by an absolute election saves the souls of some and abandons the souls of others. Jansenism (see under JANSEN, CORNELIS) was a corresponding predestinarian movement within the Roman Catholic Church. Traditional Jewish theology may be said to be predestinarian in the general sense that everything ultimately depends upon God. Islam teaches an absolute predestination, controlled by a God conceived of as absolute will. See ATONEMENT; SIN. See Loraine Boettner, *Reformed Doctrine of Predestination* (1932, repr. 1968); Réginald Garrgou-Lagrange, *Predestination* (tr. 1939); Pierre Maury, *Predestination* (1960).

Predis, Ambrogio de: see DE PREDIS, AMBROGIO.

prednisone (prĕd'nĭsōn): see CORTICOSTEROID DRUG.

Preemption Act, statute passed (1841) by the U.S. Congress in response to the demands of the Western states that squatters be allowed to preempt lands. Pioneers often settled on public lands before they could be surveyed and auctioned by the U.S. government. At first the squatter claims were not recognized, but in 1830 the first of a series of temporary preemption laws was passed by Congress. Opposition to preemption came from Eastern states, which saw any encouragement of western migration as a threat to their labor supply. A permanent preemption act was passed only after the Eastern states had been placated by the principle of distribution (i.e., the proceeds of the government land sales would be distributed among the states according to population). Distribution was discarded in 1842, but the preemption principle survived. The act of 1841 permitted settlers to stake a claim of 160 acres (65 hectares) and after about 14 months of residence to purchase it from the government for as little as $1.25 an acre before it was offered for public sale. After the passage (1862) of the HOMESTEAD ACT, the value of preemption for bona fide settlers declined, and the practice more and more became a tool for speculators. Congress repealed the Preemption Act in 1891.

prefabrication, in architectural construction, a technique whereby large units of a building are produced in factories to be assembled, ready-made, on the building site. The technique permits the speedy erection of very large structures. It has been applied to a moderate degree to urban housing for more than a century. Modern prefabrication, still largely in experimental stages, involves the production of whole sides of buildings and entire rooms. Major architects, including Walter GROPIUS, Konrad WACHSMANN, and Buckminster FULLER, have been involved significantly in the development of prefabrication, which requires the extensive cooperation of industry. See also MODULE.

prefect or **praefect** (both: prē'fĕkt), in ancient Rome, various military and civil officers. Under the empire some prefects were very important. The Praetorian prefects (first appointed 2 B.C.) usually numbered two; they commanded the powerful PRAETORIANS. From the 2d cent. A.D. they had juridical functions, and important legists (e.g., Papinian and Ulpian) held the post. The prefect of the city was at first a deputy for absent consuls; the office fell out of use but was revived by Julius Caesar. Under the empire this prefect had power over the summary court for the region within 100 mi (160 km) of Rome. The prefect of the watch had charge of the fire brigade set up by Augustus. Augustus also established a prefect of the grain supply. There were other officers called prefects, such as the Roman viceroy of Egypt and many other officials of Italian cities. See L. L. Howe, *The Praetorian Prefect from Commodus to Diocletian* (1942).

Pregl, Fritz (frĭts prā'gəl), 1869–1930, Austrian physiologist and chemist, M.D. Univ. of Graz, 1894. He taught at the universities of Innsbruck (1910–13) and Graz (from 1913). For his methods of quantitative organic microanalysis he received the 1923 Nobel Prize in Chemistry. His other contributions include several micromethods for measuring atomic groups and a sensitive microbalance.

pregnancy, period of time between fertilization of the ovum (conception) and birth, during which mammals carry the developing young in the uterus (see GESTATION). The duration of pregnancy in humans is about 280 days, equal to 9 calendar or 10 lunar months. After the fertilized egg is implanted in the uterus, rapid changes occur in the reproductive organs of the mother. The uterus becomes larger and more flexible, enlargement of the breasts begins, and alteration of renal function, blood volume, blood cell count, and chemical composition of the blood occur. Movement of the fetus can be felt at the end of the fourth month, and the fetal heart sounds can be detected from the outside at the end of the fifth month. A diagnosis of pregnancy can be made fairly soon after conception by observing physiological changes that occur in female test animals such as rabbits, mice, or frogs injected with urine from a pregnant woman; these changes result from the injected hormones of pregnancy. More recently, inexpensive clinical tests are being used in which certain hormones are injected into the patient; if menstruation does not occur in 7 to 10 days, the pregnancy test is positive.

prehistoric man: see MAN, PREHISTORIC.

prehistory, period of human evolution before writing was invented and records kept. The term was coined by Daniel Wilson in 1851. It is followed by protohistory, the period for which we have some records but must still rely largely on archaeological evidence to provide a coherent account. The study of prehistory is concerned with the activities of a society or culture, not of the individual, and is limited to the material evidence that has survived.

prejudice, unsubstantiated prejudgment of an individual or group, favorable or unfavorable in character, tending to action in a consonant direction. The hostility that prejudice can engender and the discrimination to which it may lead on the part of a dominant population toward an ETHNIC GROUP or minority have caused great human suffering throughout history. It is through learning, mainly unconscious, that a child acquires and incorporates the prejudices prevalent in a society. Contact between members of different ethnic communities has been effective in reducing prejudice under certain conditions: best results are obtained when contact occurs between persons of equal status, and when two groups work together toward the realization of a common goal, depending upon each other for its realization. Prejudice and discrimination each contribute to the origin and growth of the other. Prejudice can be reduced by removing discrimination, and a change in discriminatory institutions usually leads to a change in attitudes.

Preller, Friedrich (frē'drĭkh prĕl'ər), 1804–78, German painter and etcher, professor at the Weimar Academy. He is best known for his Odyssey landscapes, a series of 16 encaustic paintings. Also notable are his Thuringian landscapes in tempera and his Norwegian landscapes.

prelude (prā'lo͞od), musical composition of no universal style, usually for the keyboard. It was originally used to precede a ceremony and later a larger piece. Early preludes represent the first example of idiomatic keyboard music. During the baroque period the prelude formed the first movement of suites and fugues. The most widely known preludes, those written for the piano by Frédéric Chopin and Aleksandr Scriabin, are independent works with no introductory function.

premier: see PRIME MINISTER.

Přemysl (pərzhĕm'ĭsəl), earliest dynasty of BOHEMIA. Its semilegendary founder was the peasant Přemysl, whom the Bohemian Princess (sometimes called Queen) Libussa chose as her husband at some time in the 8th cent. Their successors united Bohemia into a single duchy and completed its Christianization. Outstanding among the early Přemyslid dukes were St. WENCESLAUS ("Good King Wenceslaus"); Boleslav I (reigned 929–67), who extended his kingdom to Moravia and parts of Silesia; Bratislav I (reigned 1034–55), who temporarily occupied Poland and Silesia; and Vratislav II (reigned 1061–92), who in 1086 received from Holy Roman Emperor Henry IV the nonhereditary title of king of Bohemia. The royal title became permanent and hereditary only with OTTOCAR I (reigned 1198–1230). He was succeeded by WENCESLAUS I, OTTOCAR II, WENCESLAUS II (who was also king of Poland), and WENCESLAUS III, with whom the dynasty died out in 1306. Wenceslaus III's sister married John of Luxembourg, elected king of Bohemia in 1310.

Prence or **Prince, Thomas,** 1600–1673, American colonial governor, b. England. His Puritan family joined the Pilgrim community in Leiden in Thomas's youth. In 1621 he went to Plymouth Colony, where he gained prominence and was one of eight colonial "undertakers" who assumed (1627) the colony's debt to the London merchants who had backed the establishment of the colony. He held various offices, including the governorship (1634–35, 1638, 1657–73). Prence supervised (1641) the building of the first bark constructed in the colony and established (1650) the Cape Cod fisheries. As governor he served with credit through a period of Indian wars and internal religious troubles and was noted for his successful effort to secure public revenues in support of schools.

Prendergast, Maurice Brazil, 1859–1924, American painter, b. St. John's, N.F., Canada, educated in Boston. In 1886 he worked his way to Europe on a cattle boat and studied in Paris at Julian's and at the Colarossi Academy. His brother, Charles Prendergast (1869–1948), an artist and frame maker, often assisted him financially. He again went abroad in the early 1890s, and during the rest of his life he gravitated between New York City and Europe, visiting various countries. In New York he joined the independent group of artists called the EIGHT. Prendergast evolved a style akin to postimpressionism. Much freer in his brush stroke, his landscapes and figure compositions evoked the quality of a gay tapestry. His *Promenade, Gloucester* (Whitney Mus., New York City) is characteristic. He is well represented in the Barnes Foundation, Merion, Pa., and in other leading collections throughout the United States. See catalog by R. J. Wattenmaker (1968); studies by Margaret Bruening (1931) and H. H. Rhys (1960).

preparatory school: see SCHOOL.

preposition, in English, the PART OF SPEECH embracing certain words used before nouns and pronouns to connect them to the preceding material, e.g., *of,* *in,* and *about.* Prepositions are a class that is typical of the structure of Indo-European languages, but similar classes are found in some other languages.

Preradović, Petar (pĕ'tär prĕrä'dôvĭch), 1818–72, Croatian soldier, poet, and Slavophile. His early works were in German. His later lyrics, written in Croatian under Kollár's inspiration, were imbued with Slavonic symbolism. Preradović's outstanding work was an epic poem, *The First Men* (1862). He is considered the finest lyricist of the Illyrian literary movement.

Pre-Raphaelites (prē"-răf'ēəlīts"), brotherhood of English painters and poets formed in 1848 in protest against the low standards of British art. The principal founders were D. G. ROSSETTI, W. Holman HUNT, and John MILLAIS. In poetry as well as painting, the Pre-Raphaelites turned away from the growing materialism of industrialized England. They sought refuge, through literary symbolism and imagery, in the beauty and comparative simplicity of the medieval world. In the works of the Italian painters prior to Raphael, they found a happy innocence of style that they tried to imitate. Influenced by the NAZARENES, a similar group of German painters founded in Rome in 1810, the Pre-Raphaelites declared themselves devotees of nature and truth. In the early 1850s their works were violently criticized, first by Charles Dickens, as being vulgar and ugly. They were defended by John Ruskin and attracted numerous followers, among whom were Edward BURNE-JONES, G. F. WATTS, and William MORRIS, but the group disbanded after 1853 and the movement died out before the end of the century. The paintings of the Pre-Raphaelites are characteristically nostalgic in tone and bright in color. Despite their predilection for simplicity, they were highly meticulous in detail and mannered in style. Eventually their painting became as artificial as the historical painting they had organized to protest. There is a fine collection of Pre-Raphaelite works at the Wilmington Society of the Fine Arts, Del. See J. D. Hunt, *The Pre-Raphaelite Imagination* (1969); John Nicoll, *The Pre-Raphaelites* (1970); Lionel Stevenson, *The Pre-Raphaelite Poets* (1972).

Přerov (pərzhĕ'rôf), Ger. *Prerau,* city (1970 pop. 39,858), central Czechoslovakia, in Moravia. A railway center, Přerov also has iron and machinery works and manufactures optical and precision instruments and electrical equipment. The 16th-century Žerotín Castle is now a museum.

Presbyterianism, form of Christian church organization based upon administration by a pyramidal hierarchy of courts composed of clerical and lay presbyters. It holds the position between episcopacy (government by bishops) and CONGREGATIONALISM, the other principal types of Protestant ecclesiastical polity. Presbyterianism was originally based upon a return to the early practice of appointing elders as described in the New Testament; most Presbyterians, however, do not hold the view that this system is the only biblically ordained form of church government. The basic spiritual order of the church is composed of the presbyters (or elders), all of equal status, divided according to function into teaching elders (ministers) and ruling elders. The minister's duties are to preach, to teach, and to administer the sacraments. The ruling elders, elected by the congregation from among its members, are associated with the minister in the conduct of the church; deacons and trustees may manage the temporal affairs. The court of the congregation is the session or consistory, the first in the hierarchy. It is composed of the minister, who presides, and the ruling elders. Since both the ruling elders and the minister are elected by the congregation, Presbyterian polity is ultimately determined by the people. Appeal from the session may be made to the presbytery or colloquy, the next highest court. The presbytery includes equal numbers of ministers and lay elders from each of the congregations in a prescribed area. The presbytery holds jurisdiction over church properties and ministers and confirms a church's call to a minister. Thus, although a minister must be first called by a congregation through election, his placement in office is an act of the presbytery. The synod, the next court in the hierarchy, consists of ministers and elders from a stated number of presbyteries; it exercises limited supervisory authority over both presbyteries and congregations. Finally, there is the general assembly, composed of lay and clerical representatives in equal numbers, which meets annually to supervise interests of the whole denomination. Its presiding officer, the moderator, is the official head of the church, elected yearly. A permanent officer, the stated clerk, is appointed by the general assembly to direct church boards and agencies. Spiritually, Presbyterianism embodies the principles of CALVINISM and forms the main branch of the Reformed churches. The Westminster Confession (see CREED) and the Larger and Shorter Catechism composed by the Westminster Assembly, convened (1643–49) by the British Parliament, provide the doctrinal and liturgical standards for Presbyterian churches. These documents assert the sovereignty of God and the prime authority of Scripture as guides to church doctrine. The Bible is held to be the rule of government and discipline, as well as faith. Presbyterians accept the sacraments of baptism and the Lord's Supper. They are opposed to state interference in ecclesiastical affairs. The Protestant churches first influenced by Calvin were those of Geneva and of the HUGUENOTS. In the Netherlands the Protestant church was Presbyterian in government but not independent of the state until the middle of the 19th cent. By the mid-16th cent. Presbyterian sentiment was strong in England and Scotland. The English Presbyterians were never numerous after Oliver Cromwell's time; in 1876 various branches among them united to form the Presbyterian Church of England; it now has about 70,000 members. The Church of Scotland, founded in 1557 under the leadership of John KNOX, is the only Presbyterian state church established by law; however, it maintains the traditional independence from the state; there are about 1.3 million members. (For the history of Presbyterianism in Scotland, see SCOTLAND, CHURCH OF, and SCOTLAND, FREE CHURCH OF.) Presbyterianism in Northern Ireland began early in the 17th cent. The Presbyterian Church of Ireland (organized 1840) is the principal body; it has a membership of about 150,000. The largest Protestant church of Wales, the Calvinistic Methodist Church, is a branch of Presbyterianism; it claims about 125,000 members.
Presbyterianism in America. Presbyterians were to be found in most of the English colonies of North America. Through the efforts of Francis Makemie, a missionary from Ireland to America (1683), the first presbytery in America was formed at Philadelphia in 1706; a synod was constituted in 1716. New England had its own synod from 1775 to 1782. In the 18th cent. American Presbyterians divided temporarily over the question of revivals and evangelism: The group known as the Old Side rejected them; the group known as the New Side encouraged them. Before the Revolution the Presbyterians established the College of New Jersey, now Princeton Univ. The General Assembly of 1789 in Philadelphia represented a united Presbyterian Church. A Plan of Union with the Congregational associations of New England that existed from 1792 until 1837 was disrupted when the Old School party of the Presbyterians, favoring separate denominational agencies for missionary and evangelistic work, prevailed. The Presbyterian Board of Foreign Missions was then established. The main body of Presbyterianism in North America is the United Presbyterian Church in the United States of America; it has over 3 million members. It was formed by the merger (1958) of the Presbyterian Church in the United States of America, descending from the Philadelphia presbytery of 1706, and the United Presbyterian Church of North America, which had been constituted (1858) by a union of two older churches. Next largest in membership is the Presbyterian Church in the United States, which originated shortly before the Civil War in a separation over the issue of slavery; it claims a membership of around one million. Sometimes referred to as the Southern Presbyterian Church, it took its present name in 1865. In 1810 the Cumberland Presbyterian Church was established by secession of revivalist groups in Kentucky; many of its congregations were reunited in 1906 with the main body. The ones who remained independent number about 90,000. The black members of this church were set apart in 1869 as the Colored Cumberland Presbyterian Church, now called the Cumberland Presbyterian Church in the United States and Africa; they now number about 20,000. The Associate Reformed Presbyterian Church (General Synod), formed in 1822, continued to maintain its own identity when the main body of that church merged in 1858 with the United Presbyterians. Other branches of Presbyterianism in the United States include the Orthodox Presbyterian Church (arising when in 1936 a group of believers in fundamentalism followed Gresham Machen, a minister, out of the main body), the Reformed Presbyterian Church of North America (Old School), and the Reformed Presbyterian Church of North America (General Synod). Presbyterians are the fourth largest Protestant denomination in the United States, after the Baptists, Methodists, and Lutherans. The Alliance of the Reformed Churches Throughout the World Holding the Presbyterian System (organized 1876, formerly called the Pan-Presbyterian Alliance, now called the World Presbyterian Alliance) meets quadrennially. The Presbyterian Church in Canada was formed in 1875; some Presbyterians joined in 1925 with the Methodist and Congregational churches to form the United Church of Canada. See James Moffat, *The Presbyterian Churches* (1928); P. J. Garrison, Jr., *Presbyterian Polity and Procedures* (1953); L. A. Loetscher, *The Broadening Church* (1954, repr. 1957) and *A Brief History of the Presbyterians* (rev. ed. 1958); W. L. Lingle, *Presbyterians: Their History and Beliefs* (rev. ed. 1960); A. M. Davies, *Presbyterian Heritage* (1965); Julius Melton, *Presbyterian Worship in America* (1967); G. M. Marsden, *The Evangelical Mind and the New School Presbyterian Experience* (1970).

presbytery (prĕz'bĭtĕr"ē, prĕs'–), in architecture, the space in the eastern end of a church reserved for the higher clergy. It was also known in the early Christian Church as the APSE, tribune, or exedra. The priests of the early church sat in a half-circle centered in the bishop's throne, and this primary arrangement is still preserved in the cathedral at Torcello near Venice. In the English medieval cathedrals the presbytery usually occupies a large space between the high altar and the choir stalls. The term is used in Presbyterian churches for the court composed of the ministers and representative elders (one from each congregation) of a district.

preschool education: see KINDERGARTEN; NURSERY SCHOOL.

Prescott, Samuel (prĕs'kət), 1751–c.1777, American Revolutionary figure, b. Concord, Mass. On the night of April 18, 1775, he, Paul REVERE, and William DAWES set out to warn the countryside of the British advance toward Concord. Revere was captured on the way, but Prescott got through with the news. He was later captured and died in prison.

Prescott, William, 1726–95, American Revolutionary officer, b. Groton, Mass. He saw service in the French and Indian Wars. In the American Revolution, he fortified (1775) Breed's Hill for the colonists and was prominent in the subsequent battle that was erroneously called the battle of Bunker Hill. Later he served around New York City (1776) and in the Saratoga campaign (1777). See S. A. Green, *Colonel William Prescott and Groton Soldiers in the Battle of Bunker Hill* (1909).

Prescott, William Hickling, 1796–1859, American historian, b. Salem, Mass. He entered his father's law office, but was compelled by a serious eye injury to abandon law. He received medical attention on a European trip and finally, resolving to devote himself to historical writing, began a thorough preparation for the task. His first important historical work, *The History of the Reign of Ferdinand and Isabella* (1837), achieved an immediate success. He wrote critical and historical essays while engaged in writing a *History of the Conquest of Mexico* (1843). *The Conquest of Peru* (1847), his next major effort, enjoyed a success comparable to his earlier efforts, and though his sight was practically gone he started a monumental work, *The History of Philip II* (unfinished; Vol. I and II, 1855; Vol. III, 1858). Though Prescott's work is now outdated because of subsequent research, it lives as literature. He is considered to be one of the greatest of American historians. His strength lay not in philosophical insight or deep analysis but in the excellent style and presentation of material that made his facts and his narrative alive, colorful, and vivid. His *Biographical and Critical Miscellanies* appeared in 1859. His works were edited by W. H. Munro (22 vol., 1904, repr. 1968). His correspondence was edited by Roger Wolcott (1925) and his literary memoranda by C. Harvey Gardiner (1961). A volume of *Representative Selections* (ed. by William Charvot and Michael Kraus) appeared in 1943. See *William Hickling Prescott: A Memorial* (ed. by H. F. Cline et al., 1959); biographies by H. T. Peck (1905, repr. 1969) and C. H. Gardiner (1969).

Prescott (prĕs'kət), town (1971 pop. 5,165), SE Ont., Canada, on the St. Lawrence River, opposite Ogdensburg, N.Y. Fort Wellington, built during the War of 1812, is now a military museum. At nearby Windmill Point the British repulsed an American attack in 1838.

Prescott, city (1970 pop. 13,283), alt. 5,389 ft (1,643 m), seat of Yavapai co., central Ariz.; inc. 1883. It is a mining and ranching center, as well as a health and summer resort. Lumber and wood products, motors, molds and dyes, electronic products, and clothing are manufactured. Gold was discovered in the county in 1863, and Prescott was built in 1864 near

Fort Whipple. It was twice territorial capital (1864–67, 1877–89). Annual events are a Frontier Days rodeo and a Smoki Indian ceremonial, featuring historic rituals and dances. The city is the seat of Prescott College and a junior college. A veterans hospital, a racetrack, and the county fairgrounds are there. Points of interest include the Smoki Indian museum and the old territorial capitol.

presentment: see INDICTMENT.

preserving: see CANNING.

president, in modern republics, the chief executive and, therefore, the highest officer in a government. Many nations of the world, including the United States, France, West Germany, India, and the majority of Latin American nations, have a president as the official head of state. However, the actual power of the presidency varies considerably from country to country. In West Germany the presidential power is relatively weak. True executive power rests with the chancellor, and all acts of the president must have his approval or the approval of one of his ministers. The presidential power in India is similarly subordinated to a cabinet of ministers and restricted primarily to ceremonial functions. By contrast, France (under the Fifth Republic), the United States, and some Latin American countries have given the office of the president considerable authority. In Latin America heads of state have not infrequently assumed dictatorial powers, while retaining the title president. The power of the French president is such that he may dissolve parliament at any time, although not more than once a year, and may veto parliamentary bills. He is commander in chief of the armed forces and possesses extraordinary emergency powers. In the United States, Article II of the Constitution provides for the office of the presidency, which is held for four-year terms and filled by election through the ELECTORAL COLLEGE. The President is given full responsibility for the execution of the laws and is therefore the head of all executive agencies. With the consent of Congress he appoints cabinet members and any other executive officials he sees fit. As commander in chief of armed forces the President has virtually unlimited control over the military. He is also responsible for the conduct of foreign affairs, though his treaties and appointments must be approved by the Senate and his expenditures by the House of Representatives. To be eligible for the presidency one must be a native-born citizen, over 35 years old, and at least 14 years resident in the United States. The Twenty-second Amendment (1951) limits a President to two four-year terms. For a list of U.S. Presidents, see UNITED STATES; for the presidential succession, see CABINET. See Marcus Cunliffe, *American Presidents and the Presidency* (1972); Louis Fisher, *President and Congress* (1972).

Presidential Range, group of the White Mts., N N.H., so called from the names of its peaks. Mt. Washington (6,288 ft/1,917 m) is the highest peak in New Hampshire; a hotel and meteorological station are at the summit. A year-round resort center, it was developed for tourists in the mid-1800s. Other peaks include Mt. Adams (5,798 ft/1,767 m), Mt. Jefferson (5,715 ft/1,742 m), Mt. Clay (5,532 ft/1,686 m), Mt. Monroe (5,385 ft/1,641 m), and Mt. Madison (5,363 ft/1,635 m).

Presley, Elvis, 1935–, American popular singer, b. Tupelo, Miss. Exposed to gospel music from childhood, Presley began playing guitar before his adolescence. He first recorded in 1953, became a national sensation by 1956, and dominated ROCK MUSIC until 1963. Presley sang successfully in three popular idioms: country and western, rock 'n' roll, and rhythm and blues. Although he had a pleasant baritone voice and a sincere delivery, it was his pelvic gyrations, considered wildly sexual by an entire generation of teenagers and their appalled parents, which skyrocketed Presley to fame. Among his most successful songs are "Heartbreak Hotel," "Love Me Tender," "Hound Dog," and "Don't Be Cruel." He has appeared in such motion pictures as *Love Me Tender* (1956) and *Follow That Dream* (1962). Presley remained a popular and influential performer through the 1960s and 70s. See biographies by Jerry Hopkins (1971) and Roger Tomlinson (1972).

Prespa, Lake (prĕs'pä), Albanian *Prespës*, Serbo-Croatian *Prespansko*, 112 sq mi (290 sq km), SW Yugoslavia, NW Greece, and E Albania; highest lake (alt. 2,798 ft/853 m) of the Balkans. It is connected with Lake Ohrid by underground channels. The smaller Mikrí Prespa Lake is nearby; it lies in Greece and Albania.

Presque Isle (prĕsk īl) [Fr.,=peninsula], city (1970 pop. 11,452), Aroostook co., NE Maine, inc. 1859. It is the trade, tourist, and shipping center of the Aroostook valley. During World War II an important air base there served as a ferry point for planes to Britain. Today the city is the seat of the Univ. of Maine at Presque Isle.

press, freedom of the, liberty to print without previous license or restraint. This freedom is subject to the consequences of law, and the publisher is legally responsible for any material he prints. In the United States freedom of the press is provided for by the First Amendment to the Constitution and is considered a right of the people. Freedom of the press is not universal, however, and exists in only the most advanced democratic nations. Historically, restriction of the press has occurred in two ways. The first may be either CENSORSHIP or mandatory licensing by the government in advance of publication; the second is punishment for printed material that is considered by the government to be seditious libel, i.e., material that may "excite disaffection" against constituted authority. Censorship of the press began not long after the invention of the printing press. Pope Alexander VI issued (1501) a bull requiring printers to submit copy to church authorities before publication in order to prevent heresy. Penalties for bypassing the censors included fines and excommunication. In England, where the struggle for press freedom first began, the appearance of unauthorized publications resulted in a royal proclamation (1534) requiring prepublication licensing. Stronger restrictive measures were later taken by the Tudor and Stuart monarchs when censorship came to be applied more to political criticism than religious heresy. John Milton, in his work *Areopagitica* (1644), attacked the licensing law and called on Parliament to suppress offensive publications after their appearance if necessary. Milton's objections to prior restraint eventually became a cornerstone of press freedom, but it was not until 1695 that the licensing and censorship laws were abolished. However, severe restrictions on the press continued in the form of seditious libel laws in which the government was able to arrest and punish any printer who published material in any way critical of the government. There was no clear definition of what constituted seditious libel, and in the 18th cent. the printing of parliamentary debates had to be disguised as debates between classical figures. At this time both true and false criticism of the government was considered libel. In fact, legal doctrine proclaimed that "the greater the truth the greater the libel." In the American colonies the famous John Peter ZENGER case (1734) established the precedent that criticism that was true was not libelous. In England, Charles James Fox's Libel Act of 1792 stated that juries in seditious libel cases should judge whether a publication was indeed libelous. By 1868 truth had become admissible as a defense in English libel cases. After the American Revolution several states provided for freedom of the press, and the First Amendment (1791) of the U.S. Constitution declared that "Congress shall make no law abridging the freedom . . . of the press." Implicit in this statement is the rejection of all forms of governmental pre-censorship and licensing or prosecution for seditious libel. The First Amendment was later applied to all the states by judicial interpretation of the Fourteenth Amendment (1868). Freedom of the press had become a national tradition in the United States long before 1860, but what was looked upon as irresponsible reporting during the Civil War led to attempts by civil and military authorities to impose restrictions upon the press. Appeals by the War Department for publishers to voluntarily suppress news that was strategic to the war were, however, largely ineffective. During World War I, near hysteria over the possibility of sabotage led Congress to pass the Espionage Acts (1917) and the Sedition Act (1918). These acts limited freedom of the press to such an extent that not only was censorship exercised against pro-German publications but also against German-language publications and those advocating socialism or pacifism. After 1919, however, the "clear and present danger" criterion applied by Justice Oliver Wendell Holmes—to determine whether published words would actually generate the substantive evils that Congress has a right to prevent—was often cited in Supreme Court cases. In World War II the Office of Censorship, under the direction of Byron Price, expanded upon techniques developed by George Creel's Censorship Board of World War I. The new office supervised (1941–45) the most comprehensive censorship in U.S. history. Compliance was voluntary, however, and was based on the office's suggestion to editors on topics to avoid. Because Price and his assistants were respected journalists themselves, newspapers and journals cooperated faithfully. Similar cooperation was accorded to the Office of War Information, which controlled the flow of news from government agencies. As a result the government rarely had to take punitive action. After the war many journalistic organizations undertook campaigns against secrecy in government, maintaining that the withholding of public records threatens freedom of the press. As world tensions heightened in the 1950s and 60s, defense officials often protested that the mere absence of war did not justify peacetime openness in the press. In the late 1960s and early 70s there were frequent charges and countercharges between newsmen and government officials concerning the withholding of information on the Vietnam War by the government. While the government claimed it kept secret only material that had a strategic bearing upon the war, many newsmen and citizens claimed the government classified as secret any information that was adverse to government policy or propaganda. In 1971, Daniel Ellsberg, a former government employee who believed that information that should be made public was being withheld by the government, released the controversial "Pentagon Papers," a collection of so-called secret government documents concerning the Vietnam War. The government attempted to stop publication of the papers, but its case for prior restraint was rejected by the Supreme Court. Today freedom of the press is rarely attacked in democracies by overt government censorship, but many feel that it is threatened by the government's power to withhold information. See Zachariah Chafee, Jr., *Free Speech in the United States* (1948); J. E. Gerald, *The Press and the Constitution* (1948); W. L. Chenery, *Freedom of the Press* (1955); Frank Thayer, *Legal Control of the Press* (rev. ed. 1956); Edwin Emery, *The Press and America* (3d ed. 1972).

Pressburg: see BRATISLAVA, Czechoslovakia.

Pressburg, Treaty of, 1805, peace treaty between Napoleon I and Holy Roman Emperor Francis II (also emperor of Austria), signed at Pressburg (now Bratislava, Czechoslovakia). Defeated at Austerlitz, Austria ceded Venetia, Istria, and Dalmatia to Italy; recognized Napoleon as king of Italy; acknowledged the elevation of the electors of Bavaria and Württemberg to be kings; ceded Tyrol, Vorarlberg, and Augsburg to Bavaria; and yielded the Hapsburg lands in Swabia to Württemberg and Baden. Austria was allowed to annex Salzburg, and France acquired Piedmont, Parma, and Piacenza.

pressure, in mechanics, ratio of the FORCE acting on a surface to the area of the surface; it is thus distinct from the total force acting on a surface. A force can be applied to and sustained by a single point on a solid. However, a force can only be sustained by the surface of an enclosed fluid, i.e., a liquid or a gas. Thus it is more convenient to describe the forces acting on and within fluids in terms of pressure. Units of pressure are frequently force units divided by area units, e.g., pounds per square inch, dynes per square centimeter, or newtons (N) per square meter. A fluid exerts a pressure on all bodies immersed in it. For a fluid at rest the difference in pressure between two points in it depends only upon the density of the fluid and the difference in depth between the two points. For example, a swimmer diving down in a lake can easily observe an increase in pressure with depth. For each meter (foot) increase in depth, the swimmer is subjected to an increase in pressure of 9,810 N per sq m (62.4 lb per sq ft), the density of water being 9,810 N per cu m (62.4 lb per cu ft). Since a liquid is nearly incompressible, its density does not change with increasing depth. Therefore, the increase in pressure is caused solely by the increase in depth. The variations in pressure of a gas are more complicated. For example, since air has such a low density compared to a liquid, a change in its pressure is only measurable between points that have a great height difference. The air pressure in a typical room is the same everywhere, but it is noticeably lower at the top of a mountain than at sea level. Because air is a gas, it is compressible. Its density decreases with increasing altitude. Thus changes in air pressure (or the pressure in any gas) depend upon both the variations in the density of air and changes in the altitude at which it is measured. These two factors combine to reduce the air pressure at an altitude of 5,500 m (18,000 ft) to one half its value at sea level. Atmospheric (air) pressure at sea level will support a column of mercury that is about 76 cm (30 in.) high. The exact height varies with the weather. A unit called a standard atmosphere exerts a pressure equivalent to a column of mercury 76 cm high at sea level when the temperature is 0°C; it is equal to 101,300 N per sq m (14.7 lb per sq in.). A body immersed in a fluid experiences a larger upward pressure on its lower surface than a downward pressure on its upper surface because of the difference in height or depth between the two surfaces; this difference in pressure results in a buoyant force that pushes the body upward (see ARCHIMEDES' PRINCIPLE). If the weight of the body is less than the buoyant force, the body will rise; if the weight is greater, the body will sink. The buoyant effect of this pressure may be noted in the rise of balloons or other objects filled with gases, such as hydrogen or helium, that are less dense than air. According to PASCAL'S LAW the pressure exerted on an enclosed fluid is transmitted undiminished throughout the fluid and acts equally in all directions. On the basis of this law, various hydraulic devices are used to multiply a force. For example, a force of 10 N exerted on a piston whose area is 1 sq m and which is inserted into an enclosed chamber filled with water or another fluid transmits a pressure of 10 N per sq m throughout the fluid. If a second piston, at another part of the chamber, has an area of 10 sq m, then this pressure results in a force of 10 N being exerted on each square meter of its area, or 100 N total force. BERNOULLI'S PRINCIPLE relates the effect of the velocity of a fluid on the pressure within the fluid. Different GAS LAWS relate the pressure of a gas to its volume, its temperature, or both. A rise in pressure affects both the MELTING POINT and the BOILING POINT of a substance, raising the melting and boiling points of most substances. In the case of water, however, an increase in pressure lowers its melting point so that the pressure of a skate blade on an ice surface causes the ice below it to be converted to the liquid state (see STATES OF MATTER; EXPANSION). The instrument for measuring atmospheric pressure, the BAROMETER, is calibrated to read zero when there is a complete vacuum; the pressure indicated by the instrument is therefore called absolute pressure. The term "pressure gauge" is commonly applied to the other instruments used for measuring pressure. They are manufactured in a great variety of sizes and types and are employed for recording pressures exerted by substances other than air—water, oil, various gases—registering pressures as low as 13.8×10^3 N per sq m (2 lb per sq in.) or as high as 13.8×10^7 N per sq m (10 tons per sq in.) and over (as in hydraulic presses). Some pressure gauges are made to carry out special operations, such as the one used on a portable air compressor. In this case, the gauge acts automatically to stop further operation when the pressure has reached a certain point and to start it up again when compression has fallen off to a certain limit. In general, a gauge consists of a metal tube or diaphragm that becomes distorted when pressure is applied and, by an arrangement of multiplying levers and gears, causes an indicator to register the pressure upon a graduated dial. The Bourdon gauge used to measure steam pressure and vacuum consists essentially of a hollow metal tube closed at one end and bent into a curve, generally elliptic in section. The open end is connected to the boiler. As the pressure inside the tube (from the boiler) increases, the tube tends to straighten out. The closed end is attached to an indicating needle, which registers the extent to which the tube straightens out. For pressure too small to be accurately measured by the Bourdon gauge, the manometer is used. The simplest type of manometer consists of a U tube partially filled with a liquid (i.e., mercury), leaving one end open to the atmosphere and the other end to the source of pressure. If the pressure being measured is greater or less than atmospheric pressure, the liquid in the tube moves accordingly. Pressures up to several million pounds per square inch have been produced in experiments to determine the effect of high pressure on various substances. For example, under high pressure rubber loses its elasticity.

pressure group, body, organized or unorganized, that actively seeks to promote its particular interests within a society by exerting pressure on public officials and agencies. Pressure groups direct their efforts toward influencing legislative and executive branches of government, political parties, and sometimes general public opinion. A major area of concentration for pressure groups in the United States is the Congress, which may draw up legislation affecting the interests of the group (see LOBBYING). Through promises of financial support or of votes by interest group members at the next election, the organization hopes to persuade certain legislators, especially appropriate committee chairmen, to endorse favorable legislation. A great deal of effort is also expended in influencing the decisions of the executive bureaucracy, which often possesses considerable discretion in implementing legislation. This is especially true of the independent regulatory agencies (e.g., the Federal Communications Commission, the Securities and Exchange Commission, and the Interstate Commerce Commission). Such agencies are especially open to the influence of those who are being regulated because of the continuing relationship between the agencies and the groups they oversee; they receive much more sporadic attention from the possible countervailing forces such as Congress or general public opinion. Political parties are also targets for pressure groups. However, because influencing public policy rather than electing a certain candidate is the aim of an interest group, most groups avoid heavy involvement with one party and generally remain at least formally nonpartisan. Some large pressure groups make a considerable effort to mold public opinion by means of mailing campaigns, advertising, and use of the communications media. On the other hand, there are other groups, especially the more powerful organizations representing very narrow interests, that prefer to have their activities and influence go unnoticed by the public at large. Because any particular pressure group reflects the interests of only a part of the population, it has been suggested that such organizations are contrary to the interests of the general public. However, it can also be argued that some interest groups supply legislators with much needed information, while many others, such as the labor unions, perform a broad representative function. The power of an interest group is usually dependent on the size of its membership, the socioeconomic status of its members, and its financial resources. There are a great many categories of interest groups, including economic, patriotic, racial, women's, occupational, and professional groups. The National Association of Manufacturers, the American Legion, and the American Farm Bureau Federation are examples of well-known pressure groups. See D. C. Blaisdell, *American Democracy under Pressure* (1957); American Academy of Political and Social Science, *Unofficial Government: Pressure Groups and Lobbies* (ed. by D. C. Blaisdell, 1958); V. O. Key, *Politics, Parties, and Pressure Groups* (5th ed. 1964); Grant McConnell, *Private Power and American Democracy* (1967); Michael Lipsky, *Protest in City Politics* (1969); David Truman, *Governmental Process* (2d ed. 1971).

Presteigne (prĕstēn'), urban district (1971 pop. 1,130), county town of Radnorshire, E Wales, on the Lugg River where it forms the border with England. Presteigne has an agricultural market, timber yards, an iron foundry, and die-casting works. It also receives tourists. In 1974, Presteigne became part of the new nonmetropolitan county of Powys.

Prester John, legendary Christian priest and monarch of a vast, wealthy empire in Asia or in Africa. The legend first appeared in the latter part of the 12th cent. and persisted for several centuries. At first the utopian realm of this Christian king was supposed to be in Asia, but later it was more generally placed in Africa. Letters supposed to have been written by him and about him were widely circulated in Western Europe. See studies by Vsevolod Slessarev (1959) and Robert Silverberg (1972).

Preston, John Smith, 1809–81, Confederate general in the American Civil War, b. near Abingdon, Va. He practiced law at Abingdon and Columbia, S.C., but made his fortune operating a Louisiana sugar plantation. Preston, an ardent advocate of states' rights in the South Carolina senate (1848–56), strongly supported secession. In the Civil War he first served as an aide to General Beauregard and later (1863–65) headed the bureau of conscription at Richmond, being promoted to brigadier general in 1864. He went to England after the war, and although he returned in 1868, he remained a defender of the Confederacy until the end. See A. B. Moore, *Conscription and Conflict in the Confederacy* (1924).

Preston, county borough (1971 pop. 97,365), Lancashire, N England, on the Ribble River. It has an active port. Preston is a center of cotton and rayon manufacturing; aircraft, motor vehicles, industrial machinery, and electrical appliances are also produced. A great guild-merchant festival has been held in Preston every 20 years for more than four centuries. One of the oldest boroughs in England, Preston has sent representatives to Parliament since the 13th cent. It was the scene of a Cromwellian victory in 1648 and of the surrender of the Jacobites after the rising of 1715. The Gothic town hall was completed in 1867 from designs of Sir George Gilbert Scott. The Harris Museum and Art Gallery is noted. Preston is the birthplace of Richard Arkwright and of Francis Thompson.

Prestwich, municipal borough (1971 pop. 32,838), Lancashire, N England. It is a residential suburb of Manchester and a cotton- and rayon-manufacturing center. In 1974, Prestwich became part of the new metropolitan county of Greater Manchester.

Prestwick, burgh (1971 pop. 13,441), Ayrshire, SW Scotland, on the Firth of Clyde. It is a seaside resort. There are aircraft manufacturing, coal mining, and other industries. Prestwick has an international airport. In 1975, Prestwick became part of the Strathclyde region.

Preti, Mattia (mät-tē'ä prĕ'tē), 1613–99, Italian baroque painter, called Il Calabrese for his birthplace. Preti went to Rome c.1630 and studied with Lanfranco. His most dramatic works were the Caravaggesque paintings of his period in Naples (1656–60). His frescoes in the Valmontone Palace in Rome (1661) show a change to the late baroque manner in the flickering, restless treatment of the figures. After 1661, Preti settled in Malta, where he decorated the vault of San Giovanni in Valletta.

pretor: see PRAETOR.

Pretoria (prĭtô'rēə), city (1970 pop. 543,950), administrative capital of the Republic of South Africa and capital of its TRANSVAAL prov. Although it is primarily an administrative center, there are important industries, especially iron and steel. The city has automobile assembly plants, railroad and machine shops, and flour mills. Pretoria is linked with the rest of South Africa by highways and railroads; an international airport is nearby. Founded in 1855, the city was named for Andries Pretorius, a BOER leader. Pretoria became the capital of the South African Republic (the Transvaal) in 1860. During the SOUTH AFRICAN WAR (1899–1902), Winston Churchill was imprisoned in Pretoria but escaped to Mozambique. The Peace of Vereeninging, which ended the war, was signed in Pretoria. When the Union of South Africa was founded in 1910, Pretoria became its administrative capital and CAPE TOWN its parliamentary capital. An educational and cultural center, Pretoria is the seat of the Univ. of South Africa (1873), the Univ. of Pretoria (founded 1908 as Transvaal Univ. College), and a technical college. The Transvaal Museum, the National Historical Cultural Museum, the National Zoological Gardens, and the home of S. J. P. Kruger, a former president of South Africa, are also in the city.

Pretorius, Andries Wilhelmus Jacobus (prĭtôr'ēəs, Du. än'drēs vĭlhĕl'məs yäkō'bəs prātôr'ēəs), 1799–1853, Boer leader. He was elected (1838) commandant general of the Boers of Natal and in that year defeated a large force of Zulus at Blood River. This victory made possible the organization of a Boer Republic of Natal. In 1848, Pretorius led a party of Boers across the Drakensberg and created there the nucleus of the South African Republic (the Transvaal). The city of Pretoria was named in his honor.

Pretorius, Martinus Wessel (märtē'nəs vĕs'əl), 1818?–1901, Boer statesman; son of Andries Pretorius. In 1857 he was elected the first president of the South African Republic (the Transvaal), and in 1859, while holding this position, he became the third president of the adjoining Orange Free State Republic. In 1863, after failing to effect a union of the two republics, he resigned the presidency of the Orange Free State in order to maintain his position in the Transvaal. As a result of public dissatisfaction at British encroachments Pretorius was forced (1871) from the presidency of the Transvaal. After Great Britain annexed the Transvaal in 1877, he served with Paul Kruger and Petrus Joubert in a government opposed to British rule.

Preussisch Eylau: see BAGRATIONOVSK, USSR.

preventive medicine, branch of MEDICINE dealing with the prevention of disease and the maintenance of good health practices. Until recently preventive medicine was largely the domain of the United States Public Health Service or state and local health departments, but it is becoming an important consideration of private practitioners and other concerned individuals. Preventive medicine encompasses such activities as research into the causes of contagious diseases; vaccination against those diseases for which the causes are known, e.g., poliomyelitis, smallpox, and measles; studies of environmental deterrents to good health; and instruction in public health and hygiene. See EUGENICS.

Prévert, Jacques (zhäk prāvĕr'), 1900–, French poet. One of the most popular of 20th-century French writers, Prévert produces poetry ranging from the humorous to the satiric to the melancholy. Many of his poems and songs were sung in nightclubs before being collected and published. His volumes of poetry include *Paroles* (1946), *Spectacle* (1951), and, in

English translation, *Selections from Paroles* (1958) and *To Paint the Portrait of a Bird* (tr. by Lawrence Ferlinghetti, 1970). Prévert has written many important screenplays, including those for Marcel Carné's *Le Jour se lève* (1939) and *Les Enfants du paradis* (1945).

Prevost, Sir George (prĕ'vō), 1767–1816, British soldier and governor in chief of Canada (1811–15). He held several administrative posts in the West Indies before becoming (1808) lieutenant governor of Nova Scotia. In 1811 he became governor in Canada and was conspicuous for his conciliation of the French Canadians. As commander in chief of the British forces in Canada in the War of 1812, he suffered public humiliation for the retreat at Sackets Harbor (1813) and the defeat at Plattsburg (1814). He was recalled to England but died before his court-martial started. He was created baronet in 1805.

Prévost, Marcel (märsĕl' prävō'), 1862–1941, French novelist. His novels deal chiefly with feminine questions, portraying severely what Prévost regarded as the moral frailty of modern woman. He won fame with *The Demi-Virgins* (1894, tr. 1895) in which he attacks feminism. His *Lettres à Françoise* (1902–12) presents his program for the ideal education of a girl. The combination of mysticism and eroticism in *Retraite ardente* (1927) aroused protests from the Roman Catholic clergy.

Prévost, Pierre, 1751–1839, Swiss philosopher and physicist. He was professor of philosophy (from 1784) and of physics (from 1810) at Geneva. Known for his studies of magnetism and heat, he formulated (1792) his theory of exchanges, in which he suggested that there is an exchange of radiant energy between bodies, hotter bodies radiating more energy than colder ones.

Prévost d'Exiles, Antoine François (äNtwän' fräNswä' prävō' dāgzēl'), known as **Abbé Prévost** (äbā' prävō'), 1697–1763, French novelist, journalist, and cleric. After a dissolute youth he entered (1720) the Benedictine abbey of Saint-Maur. He later had himself transferred to the abbey of Saint-Germain-des-Prés, in Paris, but in 1728 he grew weary of monastic discipline and fled to England. Even before leaving the order, he had begun to write the first of a long series of novels, *Mémoires et aventures d'un homme de qualité* (7 vol., 1728–32). He led an adventurous life in England, Holland, and Germany, but he later returned to France, was received back into the order, and was made head (1754) of a priory by the pope. Only one of Prévost's innumerable writings is still widely read, but that one book ranks among the masterpieces of world literature: The *Histoire du chevalier des Grieux et de Manon Lescaut*, popularly known as *Manon Lescaut* (Vol. VII of the *Mémoires*) is the moving account of the passion of a likeable but weak young man for an amoral woman whose frivolity leads him to crime and her to death as a deportee in America. The novel is admired for its lucid, realistic style and for its psychological insight into moral weakness. Two well-known operas, *Manon*, by Massenet (1884), and *Manon Lescaut*, by Puccini (1893), are based on the novel. Other works by Prévost include *Histoire de Monsieur Cleveland* (4 vol., 1731–32) and a literary journal, published at London and later at Paris, *Le Pour et le Contre*, which popularized English literature in France. See study by G. R. Havens (1921, repr. 1969).

Priam (prī'əm), in Greek mythology, king of Troy during the Trojan War, son of Laomedon. Priam had several wives and was the father of 50 sons and many daughters. His chief wife, Hecuba, bore him 19 children, including Hector, Paris, Polyxena, Helenus, Cassandra, Troilus, Creusa, Polydorus, and Deiphobus. When the Greeks sacked Troy, Priam was killed by Neoptolemus.

Priapus (prīā'pəs), in Greek religion, fertility god of gardens and herds; son of Aphrodite and Dionysus. He was represented as a grotesque little man with an enormous phallus. Priapus was obviously important in fertility rites.

Pribilof Islands (prĭb'ĭlôf"), group of four volcanic islands, off SW Alaska in the Bering Sea, c.230 mi (370 km) N of the Aleutian Islands; discovered and named in 1786 by Gerasim Pribilof, a Russian navigator. The larger islands, St. Paul and St. George, are famous as the breeding place of the Alaska fur seal. The islands, part of the 1867 U.S. purchase of Alaska, became a seal reservation in 1868; they are presently administered by the U.S. Bureau of Fisheries. Prior to 1911, competition and ruthless hunting methods threatened extinction of the seals. At that time, the United States, Great Britain, Japan, and Russia entered into the North Pacific Sealing Convention, giving the United States the right to enforce the provisions of the convention (see Bering Sea Fur-Seal Controversy under BERING SEA). Japan withdrew from the convention in 1941. Under protection, the seal herd has greatly increased. Blue and white foxes are native to the islands. The Aleuts, brought to the islands in the late 1700s by the Russians, make a living by processing the seal and fox furs.

Příbram (pərzhĭb'räm), town (1970 pop. 28,781), W Czechoslovakia, in Bohemia. It is one of the oldest gold- and silver-mining centers of Bohemia, with mine shafts more than 3,000 ft (914 m) deep.

Price, Leontyne (Mary Leontyne Price) (lā'əntēn), 1927–, American soprano, b. Laurel, Miss. She studied voice at the Juilliard School of Music with Florence Page Kimball. Subsequently she appeared as Bess in Gershwin's *Porgy and Bess* on Broadway (1952–54), repeating her performance in a highly successful international tour sponsored by the U.S. State Dept. She made her operatic debut on television in 1955, singing the title role in *Tosca*. In 1961 she made her debut at the Metropolitan Opera as Leonora in Verdi's *Il Trovatore*. Five years later, in 1966, she created the role of Cleopatra in Samuel Barber's *Antony and Cleopatra*, which opened the Metropolitan's new building at Lincoln Center. Price's voice is noted for its extraordinary range and power. She is particularly noted for her performances of the title roles in Verdi's *Aïda* and Puccini's *Madame Butterfly*.

Price, Richard, 1723–91, English nonconformist minister and philosopher. His philosophical importance rests on his ethical discussion, *Review of the Principal Questions and Difficulties in Morals* (1757), in which Price stresses the power of reason in making moral judgments, a position closely allied to that of Kant. He achieved fame with his sponsorship of the American colonists' cause in a pamphlet called *Observations on the Nature of Civil Liberty, the Principles of Government, and the Justice and Policy of the War with America* (1776). He also defended the French Revolution and was subsequently criticized by Edmund Burke in his *Reflections on the Revolution in France*. Price's writings on governmental finance were also well known. See studies by C. B. Cone (1952) and W. D. Hudson (1970).

Price, Sterling, 1809–67, Confederate general in the American Civil War, b. Prince Edward co., Va. After moving to Missouri, he practiced law and entered politics. He served in Congress (1844–46), resigning to lead a Missouri regiment in the Mexican War. Made military governor of New Mexico, he put down a rising of Indians and Mexicans. Price was governor of Missouri (1853–57) and president of the state convention of March, 1861, which opposed secession. However, his displeasure at the activities of the extreme Unionists led him to accept the command of the Missouri secessionist militia in May, 1861. At WILSON'S CREEK (Aug., 1861) he and Ben McCulloch defeated the Union forces. Price then took Lexington but was soon obliged to retreat into Arkansas. After the Union victory at Pea Ridge (March, 1862), Price accepted a regular Confederate commission. His campaign around Iuka and CORINTH, Miss. (Oct., 1862), was unsuccessful. He opposed Gen. Frederick Steele in Arkansas (1863–64). Price's raid through Missouri (Sept.–Oct., 1864), after initial successes, was finally turned back at Westport and was the last Confederate threat in the Far West. See studies by A. E. Castel (1968) and R. E. Shalhoyse (1971).

price, amount of money for which a unit of goods or services is exchanged. Price is equivalent to market value and may or may not measure the intrinsic value of the goods or services to the buyer or seller. Most economists hold that, in the long run, price in a competitive market will equal the cost of production. Such a long-term equilibrium price is called the normal price. In the short run, however, the market price will be determined by supply and demand without reference to cost. The price of an individual item changes with time as well as in its relation to the prices of other goods. In general, prices are closely related to the amount of currency in circulation. If money is plentiful compared with the supply of goods, prices are high and money is said to be "cheap"; when the opposite condition prevails, goods are cheap and money is "dear." The general price level may therefore be influenced by the action of government agencies (such as, in the United States, the Federal Reserve Board) that regulate the supply of currency. Because of the relation of the general price level to the business cycle, government action is usually designed to steer a middle course between the inflationary effects of a too plentiful currency and the deflationary effects of a glut of goods. Stabilization of prices, a goal of most economic systems, would ensure that the dollar used in repaying a loan would have the same value as the dollar borrowed. The price level is an average of prices of a number of commodities that are important in the economy. It is generally converted into an index, with a particular year designated as the norm and given a value of 100. By comparing the value of an index at different dates, it is possible to ascertain whether prices are rising or falling. Common indexes used by U.S. government economists include the consumer price index and the wholesale price index. Historically, prices have tended to move upward; the wholesale price index, for example, more than doubled between 1930 and 1970. For the history of prices, classic works are Thomas Tooke, *A History of Prices . . . . from 1793 to 1856* (6 vol., 1838–57; repr. 1928) and J. E. T. Rogers, *A History of Agriculture and Prices in England* (7 vol., 1866–1902; repr. 1963). See also P. C. Dooley, *Elementary Price Theory* (1967); W. D. Maxwell, *Price Theory and Applications in Business Administration* (1970).

Prichard (prĭch'ərd), city (1970 pop. 41,578), Mobile co., SW Ala., an industrial suburb of Mobile; settled 1900, inc. 1925. Meat and seafood are packed, cotton is processed, and chemicals, fertilizer, naval stores, lumber, and paper products are manufactured in Prichard.

prickly ash, name for two deciduous shrubs or small trees (*Zanthoxylum americanum* and *Z. clava-herculis*) of the family Rutaceae (RUE family). They are native to E North America and have prickly twigs and foliage similar to that of the unrelated ash tree. A pungent aromatic principle in the bark has been used as a home remedy for various ailments including rheumatism and toothache (hence the local name toothache tree). *Z. clava-herculis*, of more southerly distribution, is also known as Hercules'-club. Both Hercules'-club and prickly ash are names sometimes used for an unrelated plant of the family Araliaceae (GINSENG family). Prickly ash of the genus *Zanthoxylum* is classified in the division MAGNOLIOPHYTA, class Magnoliopsida, order Sapindales, family Rutaceae. The family Araliaceae belongs to the order Umbellales.

prickly heat (miliaria), inflammatory skin eruption due to obstruction of the sweat glands by keratin, the substance that forms the horny cells of the epidermis. It consists of blisterlike elevations with burning and itching, and is common in infants, obese persons, and those exposed to a hot, moist atmosphere for long periods of time. Relief may be obtained by applying soothing and drying lotions.

prickly pear: see CACTUS.

Pride, Thomas, d. 1658, English parliamentary soldier in the ENGLISH CIVIL WAR. In Dec., 1648, acting on the orders of the army council, he carried out **Pride's Purge,** expelling from Parliament 143 members (mostly Presbyterians) on the ground that they were royalist sympathizers. The remaining Rump Parliament, completely under army control, then arranged the trial of Charles I. Pride, as a member of the court that condemned him, signed the king's death warrant.

Priene (prīē'nē), ancient Ionian city of W Asia Minor, near the mouth of the Maeander (now Menderes) River. It was rebuilt in the 4th cent. B.C. and was the site of a temple of Athena Polias. Carefully planned, it is an extremely well-preserved Greek city of this period.

priest: see ORDERS, HOLY.

Priestley, J. B. (John Boynton Priestley), 1894–, English author. An extraordinarily prolific writer, Priestley has worked in a variety of genres. He first wrote literary criticism as a student at Cambridge and has since produced such celebrated volumes as *The English Novel* (1927) and *Literature and Western Man* (1960). Among his many novels are *The Good Companions* (1929), *Angel Pavement* (1930), *Bright Day* (1946), *It's an Old Country* (1967), and *The Image Men* (1969). He experimented with expressionist forms and psychological themes in some of his plays, including *Time and the Conways* (1937), whereas social criticism, especially of the middle class, was evident in dramas like *Dangerous Corner* (1932). Other plays include *An Inspector Calls* (1945) and *The Glass Cage* (1957). Priestley has also written numerous mystery stories and what he calls personal history, as well as social criticism— *English Journey* (1934), *Rain upon Gadshill* (1939), and *Thoughts in the Wilderness* (1957). His works of history include *The Edwardians* (1970) and *Victoria's Heyday* (1972). See his reminiscences, *Margin Released* (1962).

Priestley, Joseph, 1733–1804, English theologian and scientist. He prepared for the Presbyterian ministry and served several churches in England as pastor but gradually rejected orthodox Calvinism and adopted Unitarian views. His *Essay on Government* (1768) suggested the idea of "the greatest happiness of the greatest number" to Jeremy Bentham. In 1769 he founded the *Theological Repository* for critical discussion. In his *History of Electricity* (1767), he explained the rings (known as Priestley's rings) formed by a discharge upon a metallic surface. His improvements in the manipulation of gases enabled him to investigate the properties of gases and to discover new ones, including sulfur dioxide, ammonia, and what Priestly called "dephlogisticated air," the gas that LAVOISIER named oxygen and made the basis of experiments that were the foundation of modern chemistry. Priestley himself failed to realize the importance of his discovery of oxygen. His *Examination of Scottish Philosophy* appeared in 1774; his *History of the Corruptions of Christianity,* published in 1782, was officially burned in 1785; and his *History of Early Opinions concerning Jesus Christ* appeared in 1786. In 1790 he wrote two volumes of a *General History of the Christian Church to the Fall of the Western Empire,* and four volumes of the later history of the church appeared between 1802 and 1803. In the meantime he pursued his scientific and philosophical studies; opposed orthodox doctrines, the government's colonial policy, and slave trade; advocated the repeal of the Test Act and Corporation Act; and carried on a seven-year controversy (1783–90) with the Rev. Samuel Horsley. His sympathy with the aims of the French Revolution aroused popular prejudice against him, which led in 1791 to the wrecking of his house and the destroying of his library and scientific apparatus. Priestley emigrated to the United States in 1794 and lived at Northumberland, Pa., for the remainder of his life. He continued his chemical experimentation and engaged in a controversy on the phlogiston theory with leading American chemists. His *Theological and Miscellaneous Works,* in 25 volumes, edited by J. T. Rutt, were published between 1817 and 1832. See his letters, ed. by R. E. Schofield (1966); his memoirs (2 vol., 1806, repr. 1970); biography by Anne Holt (1931, repr. 1970); studies by K. S. Davis (1966) and F. W. Gibbs (1967); bibliography by R. E. Crook (1966).

Prilep (prē'lĕp), city (1971 pop. 96,521), S Yugoslavia, in Macedonia. It is the trade center of an agricultural region and a manufacturing city where tobacco, textiles, and leather products are produced. Prilep was a residence of Stephen Dušan as well as the birthplace of 14th-century Serbian hero Marko Kraljevič, parts of whose castle still stand. The city also has several medieval churches and monasteries.

Prim, Juan (hwän prēm), 1814–70, Spanish general and statesman. A Catalan officer, he fought for Isabella II against the Carlists and became one of the chief factional leaders in the fierce political rivalry of Isabella's reign. After contributing to the fall of ESPARTERO in 1843, he became a leader in the Cortes. He was briefly imprisoned and exiled for plotting against Gen. Ramón M. Narváez. Later pardoned, he became (1847) governor general of Puerto Rico, where he proved a stern administrator. As a commander (1859–60) in Morocco, he won the battle of Los Castillejos, for which he was made a grandee. He commanded the Spanish contingent in the international force sent against Mexico in 1861–62, but withdrew his troops when he realized that the French had ambitions to conquer Mexico. From 1863 to 1867, Prim made repeated attempts at military rebellion, and in 1868 he was finally successful, playing a large part in the overthrow of Isabella. As prime minister in the provisional government, he was a key figure in the choice of a new monarch. When the offer of the throne to a Hohenzollern prince fell through (indirectly bringing on the Franco-Prussian War), he secured the choice of AMADEUS. However, before that prince could arrive in Spain, Prim was assassinated by his political enemies.

primary, in the United States, a preliminary election in which the candidate of a party is nominated directly by the voters. The establishment of the primary system resulted from the demand to eliminate the abuses of nomination by party conventions, which were often open to manipulation by party bosses. The primary was first used in local elections—as early as 1842 in Crawford co., Pa. The Wisconsin legislature established the first primary for the nomination of statewide candidates in 1903. In 1917 all but four states had enacted primary laws, which varied widely from state to state in scope and detail of administration. Some states extend the primary principle to the presidential level, providing for an election in which voters register their preference among presidential candidates and select state delegates to nominating conventions of the national parties. A primary may be nonpartisan (usually in local and judicial elections), open, or closed, the last allowing only registered party members to vote for the party's slate of candidates. In one-party states and localities the primary, rather than the regular election, is crucial in the selection of officeholders. Critics of the primary system point to the great cost of primary campaigns and to the often unrepresentative nature of the comparatively few voters who thus select the party candidates.

primate, member of the mammalian order Primates, which includes man, APES, MONKEYS, and prosimians, or lower primates. The group as a whole is arboreal, although a few species are terrestrial; nearly all inhabit warm climates. All higher primates and some prosimians display some degree of social organization. Primates are very unspecialized anatomically, and the order is more easily described by the evolutionary trends within it, tending generally toward increased dexterity and intelligence, than by specific traits characteristic of all its members. Significant trends have been the enlargement of the braincase, elaboration of the brain and of the sensory pathways to it, flattening of the face and shifting of the eyes to a forward position, development of stereoscopic vision, and increased flexibility of the hands and feet. Nearly all primates have flat fingernails and opposable thumbs and big toes. The prosimians ("premonkeys") are small, arboreal, mostly nocturnal animals. The most primitive, the tree-shrews, strongly resemble the INSECTIVORES, a primitive, unspecialized group of mammals from which primates branched at an early stage of mammalian evolution. The prosimians also include the LEMURS and the AYE-AYE of Madagascar, the LORISES of Africa and Asia, and the TARSIERS of SE Asia. Monkeys are diurnal animals, generally with flatter, more expressive faces and better developed brains than the prosimians. Like prosimians, they retain the skeletal structure of quadrapedal animals and usually walk or run on four feet. The New World monkeys are anatomically distinct from Old World monkeys; most have prehensile tails, and all are arboreal. The Old World monkeys, which lack prehensile tails and include some terrestrial species, are more closely related to the hominids (apes and man). The apes (GIBBONS, ORANGUTANS, CHIMPANZEES, and GORILLAS) are characterized by modification of the upper skeleton for brachiation (arm swinging) and by high intelligence. Tool use and limited toolmaking are found among apes. Man, of which *Homo sapiens* is the only living species, has a pelvic structure adapted to upright posture and is characterized by the use of language and by a highly developed ability to manipulate the environment. See MAN, PREHISTORIC.

Primaticcio, Francesco (fränchäs'kō prēmätēt'chō), 1504–70, Italian painter, called Le Primatice by the French. He was influenced by Correggio and by Michelangelo. As assistant to Giulio Romano in the frescoing of the Palazzo del Tè in Mantua, he adapted the master's methods of illusionism and mannerist idiom. In 1532, Francis I invited Primaticcio to participate in the decoration of the château at Fontainebleau. Working with Il Rosso on the fresco and stucco ornamentation, he became director of the whole project in 1540 upon Rosso's death. Only a few of Primaticcio's works at Fontainebleau survive. The most important scenes from the *Odyssey* in the Gallery of Ulysses have been destroyed. Many drawings for the project still exist (Louvre; École des Beaux-Arts, Paris; Chantilly; and Vienna). He remained in the royal service under four successive monarchs, painting decorations for royal châteaus and other buildings, designing tomb monuments of Francis I and Henry II, and executing other architectural works. Primaticcio, although not a first-rate artist, did much to extend the influence of Italian art in France.

Prime, Samuel Irenaeus, 1812–85, American Presbyterian clergyman and editor, b. Ballston Spa, N.Y. After holding pastorates at Ballston Spa and Matteawan, N.Y., he became assistant editor (1840–49) of the *New-York Observer* and later editor (1851–85). In this religious periodical, which he helped to make among the best of its kind, his "Irenaeus" articles (later published in two series as *Irenaeus Letters,* 1882, 1885) were a noted feature. From 1853, Prime conducted the "Editor's Drawer" in *Harper's Magazine.* Among his many books are *The Power of Prayer* (1859) and *The Alhambra and the Kremlin* (1873).

prime meridian, MERIDIAN that is designated zero degree (0°) longitude, from which all other longitudes are measured. By international convention, it passes through the original site of the Royal Observatory in Greenwich, England; for this reason, it is sometimes called the Greenwich meridian. GREENWICH MEAN TIME, the standard basis for determining time throughout the world, is civil time measured at the prime meridian.

prime minister or **premier,** chief member of the CABINET in a parliamentary system of government. The prime minister is head of the government, in contrast with the head of state, who may be a constitutional monarch, as in Great Britain, or an elected official, as in the case of the president of India. Procedures governing the selection of the prime minister vary from country to country, but under the system that has evolved in Great Britain (which has provided the model for Commonwealth countries) he is usually the leader of the majority party in Parliament and must by convention be a member of the lower house. The prime minister appoints the other cabinet ministers, makes and coordinates the policy of the government, controls the administration, and dispenses patronage. In major policy areas he must have the support of the legislature; otherwise he and his cabinet are customarily expected either to resign or to dissolve the legislature and call new elections. An individual cabinet minister who is unable to support the prime minister is also expected to resign. In France (under the Fifth Republic) and in a few other countries with parliamentary governments, the powers of the prime minister are considerably less than those described above; most of the executive authority is exercised by the president, while the prime minister plays a comparatively minor role. In the United States the President combines the functions of head of government and head of state. See Byrum Carter, *The Office of Prime Minister* (1956); W. I. Jennings, *Cabinet Government* (3d ed. 1959); F. W. G. Benemy, *The Elected Monarch* (1965); S. E. Finer, *Comparative Government* (1971).

prime mover: see ENERGY, SOURCES OF.

prime number: see NUMBER THEORY.

primitivism, in art, the style of works of untrained artists who develop their talents in a fanciful and fresh manner, as in the paintings of Henri ROUSSEAU and Grandma MOSES. The term *primitive* has also been used to describe the style of early American naïve painters such as Edward HICKS and has been applied to the art the various Italian and Netherlandish schools produced prior to c.1450.

Primo de Rivera, Miguel (mēgĕl' prē'mō thā rēvä'rä), 1870–1930, Spanish general and dictator. After a rapid and brilliant military career in Cuba, the Philippines, and Morocco, he became governor of Cádiz (1915), then in turn captain general of Valencia, Madrid, and Catalonia. From Catalonia he staged a coup d'etat in Sept., 1923, dissolving the Cortes and then establishing, with the full approval of King Alfonso XIII, a military directory. The constitution of 1876 as well as civil liberties were suspended. The military dictatorship was replaced by a civil one (1925), but Primo de Rivera continued as the sole ruler and dictator of Spain. He ended the war in Morocco (1926) and launched an ambitious program of public works, but his rule aroused the opposition of anarcho-syndicalists, Catalan separatists, and all liberals. An uprising in 1929 by the liberals did not succeed, but the economic failures of the regime soon led to his resignation (Jan., 1930). He died in exile in Paris. His son José Antonio, founder of the FALANGE, was executed (Nov., 1936) by the Loyalists after the outbreak of the Spanish civil war. See study by D. F. Ratcliff (1957).

primogeniture, in law, the rule of inheritance whereby land descends to the oldest son. Under the feudal system of medieval Europe, primogeniture generally governed the inheritance of land held in military tenure (see KNIGHT). The effect of this rule was to keep the father's land for the support of the son who rendered the required military service. When feudalism declined and the payment of a tax was substituted for military service, the need for primogeniture disappeared. In England, consequently, there was enacted the Statute of Wills (1540), which permitted the oldest son to be entirely cut off from inheriting, and in the 17th cent. military tenure was abolished; primogeniture is, nevertheless, still customary in England. In the United States primogeniture never became widely established. For other traditional types of inheritance, see GAVELKIND; BOROUGH-ENGLISH.

Primorsky Kray (prēmôr'skē krī) or **Maritime Territory,** administrative division (1970 pop. 1,721,000), c.64,900 sq mi (168,100 sq km), Far Eastern USSR, between Manchuria in the west and the Sea of Japan in the east. VLADIVOSTOK is the capital. The population (constituting 50% of the people of the Soviet Far East) is predominantly Russian, Ukrainian, and Belorussian, with small Asian ethnic groups. The territory's coastal mountain range contains coal, iron ore, lead, zinc, lignite, tin, and silver. Fisheries (salmon and sardines) are located along the shore. An agricultural plain with millet and rice crops extends along the Manchurian border. The Trans-Siberian RR links Vladivostok with USSURIYSK, the territory's other major city. For history of the Primorsky Kray, see SOVIET FAR EAST.

Primrose, William, 1904–, Scottish-American violist. He studied violin (1919–25) at the Guildhall School of Music in London, where he made his debut in 1923. Next he studied with Eugène Ysaÿe, who encouraged him to change to the viola. He toured (1930–35) as violist of the London String Quartet and became first violist of the NBC Symphony Orchestra (1937–42). In 1938 he formed his own quartet. As a soloist he ranks among the world's outstanding violists, and several concertos have been written for him.

primrose, common name for the genus *Primula* of the Primulaceae, a family of low perennial herbs with species found on all continents, most frequently in north temperate regions. Among the better known members of the family are the primroses (genus *Primula*), cyclamens (genus *Cyclamen*), pimpernels (genus *Anagallis*), and loosestrifes (chiefly genus *Lysimachia*). Species of all these genera are cultivated as rock-garden, border, and pot plants. The primrose, a common and favored wildflower of England, has often been celebrated in poetry. Benjamin Disraeli's preference for it gave the name PRIMROSE LEAGUE to an English political organization. A common yellow species (*P. veris*) is called cowslip in England. Several primroses are indigenous to North America. The American cowslip, often called shooting star, is a separate genus (*Dodocatheon*); it is an Eastern wildflower. The EVENING PRIMROSE is not a true primrose. Tuberous-rooted cyclamens are native chiefly to the European Alps; *C. indicum* is a common florists' pot plant in the United States. The scarlet pimpernel, or poorman's-weatherglass (*A. arvensis*), is native to Eurasia but has been naturalized in North America; its flowers close on the approach of bad weather. Loosestrifes are easily cultivated flowers that thrive under moist conditions; some are creeping species, e.g., the moneywort, or creeping Jenny, of E North America. Several unrelated plants are also called LOOSESTRIFE. Primroses are classified in the division MAGNOLIOPHYTA, class Magnoliopsida, order Primulales.

Primula (prĭm'yələ): see PRIMROSE.

Prince, Harold, 1928–, American theatrical producer and director, b. New York City. After working as an assistant stage manager, Prince became at 26 the coproducer of *Pajama Game,* a major Broadway musical of 1954. He followed this with many more successful productions, including *Damn Yankees, West Side Story, Fiorello!,* and *Fiddler on the Roof.* Among the shows that he has both produced and directed are *Cabaret* and *Follies.*

Prince, Morton, 1854–1929, American physician, b. Boston, M.D. Harvard, 1879. He specialized in neurology and abnormal psychology as physician in Boston and as teacher at Tufts Medical School (1902–12) and Harvard (1926–28). Founder (1906) and editor until his death of the *Journal of Abnormal Psychology,* he was a leading investigator of the pathology of mental disorders. His most famous book is *The Dissociation of a Personality* (1906). See study by W. S. Taylor (1928).

Prince, Thomas, 1600–1673: see PRENCE, THOMAS.

Prince, Thomas, 1687–1758, American clergyman, scholar, and historian, b. Sandwich, Mass., grad. Harvard, 1709. From 1709 to 1717 he was abroad; he studied in London and preached at a Congregationalist chapel in Suffolk. Returning (1717) to Massachusetts, he became copastor (1718) of Old South Church in Boston, a position he held until his death. He bequeathed to his church his large and excellent library; during the British occupation of Boston, some of the volumes were destroyed, but the many books and manuscripts that were preserved are now in the Boston Public Library. Prince published a number of sermons, *A Vade Mecum for America: a Companion for Traders and Travelers* (1732), and *Psalms, Hymns & Spiritual Songs . . . the New England Psalm-Book Revised and Improved* (1758), but he is best remembered for his informative *Chronological History of New England* (Vol. I, 1736; Vol. II entitled *Annals of New England,* 1755). Designed by its author to cover the years 1602 to 1730, the annals are carried only to Aug. 5, 1633. An edition of his history published in 1852 has a memoir of Prince by S. G. Drake.

Prince Albert, city (1971 pop. 28,464), central Sask., Canada, on the North Saskatchewan River. Prince Albert is a commercial and distribution center for a lumbering, fur-trapping, and mixed-farming area. There are wood-products and meat-packing industries. It was founded in 1866 as a Presbyterian mission to the Cree Indians. It is the gateway to Prince Albert National Park, to the northwest. The city is the seat of Anglican and Roman Catholic cathedrals and headquarters of the Royal Canadian Mounted Police for central and N Saskatchewan, as well as the site of the provincial penitentiary.

Prince Albert National Park, 1,496 sq mi (3,875 sq km), central Sask., Canada, NW of Prince Albert, in a forested area; est. 1927. The numerous streams and lakes afford excellent fishing and canoeing. The park is a sanctuary for moose, elk, deer, caribou, bear, pelicans, and double-crested cormorants. Administration and tourist headquarters are at Waskesiu, on Lake Waskesiu.

Prince Edward Island, province (1971 pop. 111,641), 2,184 sq mi (5,657 sq km), E Canada, off N.B. and N.S. The capital is CHARLOTTETOWN. One of the MARITIME PROVINCES, it is separated on the S from Nova Scotia and New Brunswick by the Northumberland Strait. The generally low, level land is c.140 mi (225 km) long and 5 to 35 mi (8–56 km) wide. White sandy beaches line the deeply indented north shore, and much of this favorite resort spot is now Prince Edward Island National Park (est. 1937). Low, red sandstone cliffs rim the south shores. The tide reaches back into the headwaters of the island's short rivers. With fertile soil and an agreeable climate, the island is known as the Garden of the Gulf. Agriculture and fishing dominate the economy.

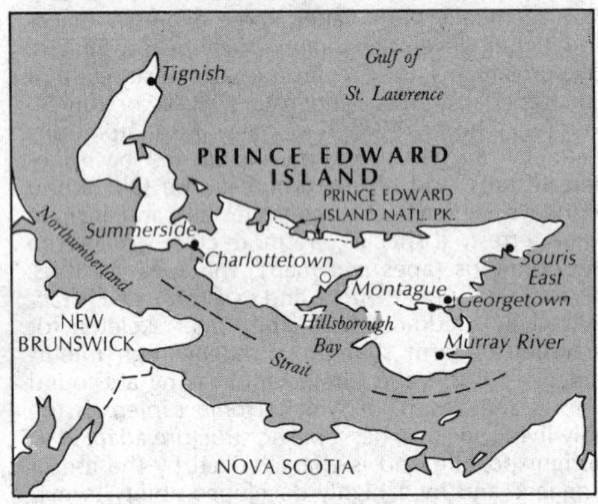

Since earliest settlement, fishing has been an important industry, yielding an abundance of lobsters, oysters, codfish, halibut, mackerel, and herring. Livestock, fruit, and vegetables are produced, and potatoes are exported. Because of the lack of raw materials and cheap sources of power, manufacturing is largely limited to food processing, such as the making of butter and cheese and the canning of pork and lobsters. Islanders held a monopoly in the breeding of silver foxes from the beginning of the industry, in 1887, until 1912. Micmac Indians lived on the island before white men arrived. Jacques Cartier wrote enthusiastically about the island after landing there in 1534. Samuel de Champlain named it Île St. Jean in 1603, and it was known by that name, or Isle St. John, until 1799, when it was renamed after Edward, duke of Kent, who became the father of Queen Victoria. The first permanent settlement was made by the French in 1719 near present-day Charlottetown. The British gained permanent control under the Treaty of Paris in 1763. Many of the French settlers were deported by the British (see ACADIA), but others remained and their descendants still live on the island. In 1803, Lord Selkirk's first colony of impoverished Scots settled there, and their descendants still constitute about one third of the present inhabitants. In 1763, Prince Edward Island was annexed to Nova Scotia, but it became a separate colony in 1769. Responsible, or cabinet, government was granted in 1851. In 1864 delegates from the Maritime Provinces met in Charlottetown to discuss union—the first step toward the Canadian confederation, achieved in 1867. However, Prince Edward Island did not join the confederation until 1873. See Frank Mackinnon, *The Government of Prince Edward Island* (1951); A. H. Clark, *Three Centuries and the Island* (1957); L. C. Calbeck, *The Cradle of Confederation* (1964); D. C. Harvey, *The French Regime in Prince Edward Island* (1926, repr. 1970).

Prince Edward Island National Park, 7 sq mi (18 sq km), NW P.E.I., Canada, on the Gulf of St. Lawrence; est. 1937. It extends 25 mi (40 km) along the coast and contains sand dunes, cliffs, salt marshes, and bathing beaches.

Prince George, city (1971 pop. 33,101), central British Columbia, Canada, at the confluence of the Fraser and Nechako rivers. It is a railroad division point and a distributing center for a lumber region. There are sawmills, pulp mills, chemical plants, and an oil refinery. In 1807, Simon Fraser of the North West Company established on the site the fur-trading post of Fort George, which was taken over (1821) by the Hudson's Bay Company. Settlement began c.1910 with the building of a railroad via Fort George to Prince Rupert, and in 1915 the city was incorporated and the name was changed.

Prince of Wales, Cape, at the tip of the Seward Peninsula, NW Alaska, on the Bering Strait; westernmost point of North America. Cape Dezhnev, Siberia, is only 55 mi (89 km) to the west.

Prince of Wales Island, c.12,800 sq mi (33,150 sq km), S central Franklin dist., Northwest Territories, Canada, between Victoria and Somerset islands. The low tundra-covered island has an irregular coastline and is deeply indented by Ommanney Bay and Browne Bay.

Prince of Wales Island, 2,231 sq mi (5,778 sq km), off SE Alaska; largest island of the Alexander Archipelago. The island is heavily forested. Lumbering, fishing, and canning are the main industries. Craig (1970 pop. 272), the largest town, is the supply center for the Alaska fishing fleets.

Prince Rupert, city (1971 pop. 15,747), W British Columbia, Canada, on Kaien Island, in Chatham Sound near the mouth of the Skeena River, S of the Alaska border. A railroad and highway terminus and an ice-free port, it serves the mining, lumber, and agricultural areas of central and W British Columbia. It is a major fish-processing center, and there are wood-processing plants. The city's growth dates from the arrival (1914) of the railroad. During World War II the city was a major supply base for U.S. forces in Alaska.

Princes Islands, Turkey: see KIZIL ADALAR.

prince's pine: see PIPSISSEWA.

Princeton, borough (1970 pop. 12,311), Mercer co., W N.J.; settled late 1600s, called Stony Brook until 1724, inc. 1813. It is the seat of Princeton University, the Institute for Advanced Study, Princeton Theological Seminary, Westminster Choir College, St. Joseph's College, and other institutions, including numerous corporate research centers. In the American Revolution, the British and later colonial troops occupied Nassau Hall (of Princeton Univ.) as barracks. Shortly after the battle of Trenton, Princeton was the scene of a battle (Jan. 3, 1777) in which Washington surprised and defeated a superior British force. Gen. Hugh Mercer was mortally wounded in the attack. A monument with sculptures by Frederick MacMonnies commemorates the battle. "Morven" (1701), home of Richard Stockton, was Cornwallis's headquarters and a center of social and political life during and after the Revolution; since 1954 it has been the state executive mansion. The Continental Congress met in Nassau Hall from June to Nov., 1783. In 1869 the first intercollegiate football game (between Rutgers and Princeton) took place. William Bainbridge's birthplace, later to become the public library, is now the headquarters of a historical society. Palmer Square, a civic center on Nassau St., has buildings designed in colonial style by Thomas Stapleton. Paul Robeson was born in Princeton, and Albert Einstein spent the last 20 years of his life there.

Princeton University, at Princeton, N.J.; coeducational; chartered 1746, opened 1747, rechartered 1748, called the College of New Jersey until 1896. Established by the "New Light" (evangelical) Presbyterians it was originally intended to train ministers, but this purpose disappeared as higher education gained hold. The college opened at Elizabeth, N.J., under the presidency of Jonathan DICKINSON. Its second president was Aaron Burr, the elder, father of Aaron BURR. In 1756 the college moved to Princeton. During the American Revolution, Princeton was occupied by both sides, and the college's buildings were heavily damaged. Under John WITHERSPOON the college was rebuilt. During the 19th cent. the college expanded, and in 1896 Princeton became a university. Under Woodrow WILSON, Princeton introduced the preceptorial system (1905), a change that led to a greater degree of individualized instruction. One of the nation's foremost universities, Princeton has in addition to its college and graduate school noted schools of architecture, engineering, and public and international affairs. Research is carried on in many areas, including plasma physics and jet propulsion. The university is affiliated with the Brookhaven National Laboratories. The Harvey S. Firestone library (opened 1948) and the art museum house many outstanding collections. The INSTITUTE FOR ADVANCED STUDY at Princeton, N.J., is not connected with the university. See T. J. Wertenbaker, *Princeton, 1749–1896* (1946); C. G. Osgood, *Lights in Nassau Hall* (1951); and Hardin Craig, *Woodrow Wilson at Princeton* (1960).

Prince William Forest Park: see NATIONAL PARKS AND MONUMENTS (table).

Prince William Sound, large, irregular, islanded inlet of the Gulf of Alaska, S Alaska. There are good harbors, and access to the interior is by highway and railroad. Extensive fishing and some mining are carried on in the area. Valdez (1970 pop. 1,005) and Cordova (1970 pop. 1,164) are the largest towns on the sound.

Princip, Gavrilo (gäv'rēlō prēn'tsēp), 1895–1918, Serbian political agitator, b. Bosnia. As a high school student and a member of the Serbian nationalist secret society Union or Death (known as the Black Hand), he assassinated Archduke FRANCIS FERDINAND and his wife at Sarajevo in 1914. His act precipitated World War I. Princip died of tuberculosis in an Austrian prison. He remains a Serbian hero.

Principe, island, Africa: see SÃO TOMÉ AND PRINCIPE.

principle of indeterminacy: see UNCERTAINTY PRINCIPLE.

Pringle-Pattison, Andrew Seth: see SETH, ANDREW.

Pringsheim, Nathanael (nätän'äēl prĭngs'hīm), 1823–94, German botanist, one of the founders of the scientific study of algae. He made important discoveries in the morphology and physiology of plants, especially in the fields of reproduction and evolution. He founded the German Botanical Society and the *Jahrbücher für wissenschaftliche Botanik.* His treatises are collected in *Gesammelte Abhandlungen* (4 vol., 1895–96).

printed circuit, electric circuit in which the metallic conducting paths connecting circuit components are affixed to a flat, insulating base board. The base is typically of plastic, glass, ceramic, or some other DIELECTRIC, and the conducting paths may be placed on it by a variety of methods. The etched circuit is the result of one common method. A metallic foil is bonded to the base, the circuit pattern is drawn on the foil with an acid-resistant wax, and the remainder of the foil is then etched away with acid, leaving the desired conducting pattern. Another method uses a heated die to stamp the circuit out of the foil, the heat causing the foil to stick to the base material while the rest of the foil can be removed. The conducting pattern can also be sprayed onto the base through a stencil or mask. The circuit components themselves—resistors, capacitors, and so on—are not usually produced by these processes but rather are mounted on the finished base afterwards, their leads being inserted through holes drilled through both the conducting pattern and the base and soldered to the conducting strips, usually in a single step in a bath of molten solder.

Printemps, Yvonne: see GUITRY, LUCIEN GERMAIN.

printing. The story of the invention of printing and of its early days on the continent of Europe is told in the article TYPE. In the 15th cent. the art spread, directly and indirectly, from Mainz to many parts of Europe. It was brought to England in 1476 by William Caxton; to the New World in 1539 by Juan Pablos, who set up his press in Mexico city; and in the region that is now the United States it first appeared at Cambridge, Mass. The first papermaking machine producing a continuous roll of paper and capable of delivering sheets in specific sizes—the Fourdrinier machine—was installed in London in 1803. Steam power was successfully applied to the printing press in 1810 by Friedrich Koenig, a German; in announcing its adoption of this invention in 1814, *The Times* of London called it "the greatest improvement connected with printing since the discovery of the art itself." The invention did not improve the quality of the product but greatly increased the output of the machine. In Koenig's press, the type bed remained flat as in hand presses, but the paper was pressed on the type by a cylinder. The Adams power press was invented by an American, Isaac Adams, in 1827. In 1846 and 1847, Richard March Hoe designed a rotary press in which STEREOTYPE plates were for the first time arranged in a true cylinder. In 1866 a press known later as the Walter press was patented in England; in this press the printing surfaces were not types but stereotype plates curved to form parts of cylinders. The leading newspapers now regularly use stereotype plates on their presses. The invention of ways of making paper in sheets of any desired length, so that paper may be fed to cylinder presses from rolls, assisted in increasing the speed of printing. Machines for folding newspapers were incorporated with the power cylinder press. Not until the late 19th cent. were typesetting machines invented. The Linotype machine, invented by Ottmar Mergenthaler in Baltimore in 1884, produces a metal slug corresponding to a single line of type as set by hand in printing. It was first put into operation at the New York *Tribune* in 1886. It is operated by a keyboard like that of a typewriter. The machine assembles brass matrices into a line, casts the line, and distributes the matrices. The Intertype machine, manufactured by the International Typesetting Machine Company (est. 1912), is similar in principle to the Linotype machine, and the matrices made by either machine may be used in the other. The other principal typesetting machine is the Monotype, patented by Tolbert Lanston in 1887 and first produced commercially in 1897. Unlike the Linotype and Intertype, the Monotype makes each character separately, assembling the characters as in hand composition, for which the Monotype characters can be used. The machine consists of two distinct units. The keyboard unit, resembling a typewriter, punches holes in a roll of paper. This roll, similar to that of a player piano, is taken to the casting unit of the machine, where the holes in the roll of paper govern the casting and assembling of the type. The machine is run by compressed air. Monotype has an advantage in setting certain kinds of copy, e.g., mathematical and scientific material, where special symbols or other problems may be involved. Printing surfaces were originally in relief, as in type, the stereotype, and the ELECTROTYPE. The generic term for all printing methods using plates where copy areas stand in relief is letterpress. Relief printing is still the most widely used form despite the development, by many inventions, of several additional kinds of printing surfaces. Flexographic printing is a form of rotary letterpress printing using flexible rubber plates and rapid-drying inks. In INTAGLIO printing, such as the ETCHING and the steel ENGRAVING, the design to be printed is lower than the surface of the plate, which is wiped clean before each impression, leaving the incised design filled with ink, which the paper receives. In gravure intaglio printing, tone is produced by varying the thickness of the ink of the printing surface through depressions of varying depth; minute points constitute the clean surface that keeps the paper from being pressed into the depressions. In photogravure the gravure plate is made by a photographic process. Rotogravure is photogravure adapted for printing by a rotary or cylinder press. The third kind of printing, known as planographic, is from a flat surface, as in LITHOGRAPHY, the original planographic process, devised by Aloys Senefelder. Flat stones were the first lithographic plates and are still used, though metal plates also are used. A drawing is made on the plate with greasy ink or crayon, and water is then applied to the plate. When the plate is inked for printing, the greasy parts accept the ink and the wet parts do not. Preparing a printing surface so that ink will adhere only to parts of it is basic in all planographic printing. Collotype, also called photogelatin, is a lithographic process using a gelatin-faced plate to achieve the tonal distribution obtained through screen dots in engraving. It is chiefly used in the reproduction of fine illustrations or of scientific subject matter requiring accuracy of detail. In the pantone process, mercury is used instead of water to coat the parts of the printing surface that are not to accept ink. Photolithography, offset, litho-offset, and offset lithography are synonymical in commercial printing with the most widely used form of planographic printing. It is based on a modification of the lithographic press featuring a rubber-covered cylinder between the printing cylinder and the impression cylinder. The plate cylinder transfers the image to the rubber blanket cylinder, which in turn offsets it on the paper carried by the impression cylinder. Offset and other forms of planographic printing, through many technical refinements, make possible increased production speeds, improved quality in the reproduction of fine tones, and a substantial reduction in the number of impressions required to reproduce full-color copy. In all three kinds of printing—relief, intaglio, and planographic—illustrations are often produced by the halftone process, in which a plate is made by photographing through glass marked with a network of fine lines (see also PHOTOENGRAVING). A usual form of color printing is by the Ben Day, or Benday, process, invented by New York printer Benjamin Day, which utilizes celluloid sheets to achieve proper shading and color. Printing in colors is sometimes done, as excellently in Japan, by applying inks of different colors by hand to the printing surface, but usually a separate printing surface is used for each ink. In full-color printing four standard colors are used—yellow, cyan (a hue between blue and green), magenta, and black—the first three being the complementary colors of blue, red, and green. Other colors are produced by printing one color over another, as green by printing cyan on yellow. Black is used to print the text accompanying the illustration, and it is often used as a fourth color in the illustration itself to add strength and detail. In recent years the use of photographic processes has expanded greatly, and the development of electronic devices, as well as other technological advances, has introduced a new era in the evolution of printing. The development of typewriters capable of delivering justified (properly spaced) copy has made possible the production of typewritten books and has met the demands for several special types of printing. Perhaps the most revolutionary innovation has been the introduction of photocomposition machines for setting type by photographic means. Two of these are analogous in principle to the Monotype and Intertype casting machines and have been produced by the respective companies under the trademarks of Monophoto and Intertype Fotosetter. The Linofilm is a phototypesetting machine developed by the Linotype Corporation. The Photon machine, invented by the Frenchmen René Higonnet and Louis Moyroud, using an electric typewriter connected with an electronic computer and a photographing unit, is probably the most noteworthy. Almost exclusively electronic, it can deliver justified type on film in a wide variety of styles at extraordinary speed. Today photocomposition has been widely adopted in lithography, gravure, and letterpress printing, and experts predict that its use, together with other electronic techniques, will revolutionize the printing industry (see OPTICAL SENSING). Many reproduction processes other than those cited above have been developed. Some of these, such as silk screen and XEROGRAPHY, have special applications in the printing industry. Silk screen printing is a form of stencil printing, i.e., printing where the ink is applied to the back of the image carrier and pushed through porous or open areas. The image is on a piece of silk stretched on a frame and backed by a rubber squeegee containing ink. The nonprinting areas on the silk screen are blocked out, and the ink is pushed through the porous areas corresponding to the design; the process is widely used for posters and for printing on glass, plastics, and textured surfaces. Mimeographing is the other major commercial application of stencil printing. Xerography has been widely adopted for duplicating purposes. It is an effective means of producing master plates for offset printing. One xerographic device is used for making full-size reprints of out-of-print books from microfilm. Other duplicating processes of commercial importance are the Multigraph, which operates on the letterpress principle; the Multilith, basically a small offset press; the Ditto, a duplicator using a special fluid to remove ink from the master plate and transfer it to the paper; and the well-known PHOTOSTAT process. A multitude of office copying machines using a wide variety of chemical and mechanical processes have been developed in recent years. For an account of type design, see TYPE; TYPOGRAPHY. See also BOOK; BOOKBINDING. An excellent selected bibliography is Hellmut Lehmann-Haupt, *One Hundred Books about Bookmaking* (1949). See Kenneth Day, *Book Typography* (1966); Warren Chappell, *A Short History of the Printed Word* (1970); James Moran, *Printing Presses* (1973).

Printz, Johan Björnsson (yo͞o'hän byörn'sōn prĭnts), 1592–1663, colonial governor of NEW SWEDEN, b. Bottnaryd, Sweden. After serving as a mercenary in the armies of various European princes, he obtained a post in the Swedish army (1625) and rose to the rank of lieutenant colonel. After his defeat (1640) at Chemnitz in the Thirty Years War, Printz was court-martialed but exonerated; subsequently he was made governor of New Sweden, for which he sailed in 1643. He landed near the present city of Wilmington, Del., explored his territory, built forts, assigned land to the settlers for farming, established trade relations with the Indians, the English, and the Dutch, and upheld the Swedish claims to the land. However, continued Swedish disinterest in the colony and the alleged harshness of his rule brought Printz's resignation and return to Sweden (1653). See biography by Amandus Johnson (1930, repr. 1969).

Prior, Matthew, 1664–1721, English poet and diplomat, b. Wimborne, Dorset. With his appointment as secretary to the embassy at The Hague during the negotiations leading to the Treaty of Ryswick (1697), Prior began a long diplomatic career. During Anne's reign he joined the Tories (1711) and helped, as special envoy, to conclude the Peace of Utrecht. With the accession of George I, Prior was ruined politically and was imprisoned by the Whigs for two years (1715–16). As a poet he is best remembered for his light verse and raillery. With Charles Montagu, he wrote a burlesque of Dryden's *The Hind and the Panther* called *The Country Mouse and the City Mouse* (1687). He is also known for two long satiric poems, *Alma* and *Solomon* (both 1718). He is buried in Westminster Abbey. See his complete works (ed. by H. B. Wright and M. K. Spears, 1959); biography by C. K. Eves (1939, repr. 1972).

Pripet: see PRIPYAT, USSR.

Pripyat (prē'pyətyə) or **Pripet** (prĭ'pĕt), Pol. *Prypeć*, river, c.440 mi (710 km) long, rising NW of Kovel, NW Ukraine, W USSR, near the Polish border, and flowing generally E through the Pripyat Marshes, S Belorussia, into the Dnepr River in NE Ukraine. Navigable below Pinsk, it is connected by canals with the Western Bug River (forming part of the Vistula-Dnepr waterway) and with the Neman River. The **Pripyat Marshes** are a forested, swampy area (c.38,000 sq mi/98,400 sq km) extending along the Pripyat River and its tributaries from Brest in the west to Mogilev in the northeast and Kiev in the southeast. With a dense network of rivers, lakes, and canals, the marshes are largely coextensive with the Polesye lowland. Drainage of the swamps was begun c.1870; the eastern part is now used for pasturage and cultivation (especially potatoes). The marshes are also called the Pinsk Marshes.

Prisca (prĭs'kə), wife of AQUILA.

Priscian (Priscianus Caesariensis) (prĭsh'ən), fl. 500, Latin grammarian, b. Caesarea in Mauretania. Priscian taught grammar at Constantinople. His *Commentarii grammatici*, in 18 books, was long a standard text, and it was the basis of the work of Rabanus Maurus in the Middle Ages. Other extant writings of Priscian are a textbook on 12 lines of the *Aeneid*, a treatise on accents, a study of the meters of Terence, a treatise on symbols of weights and measures, and a work on the declensions of nouns.

Priscilla (prĭsĭl'ə) [diminutive of Lat. *Prisca*=ancient], wife of AQUILA.

Priscillian (prĭsĭl'yən), d. 385?, Spanish churchman, bishop of Ávila. His appointment to the bishopric was protested by orthodox leaders, who had condemned his former activities as a lay preacher in S Spain, at the Synod of Saragossa (380). Although Priscillian's ideas were repeatedly denounced, it is not clear that they were heretical. He was suspected of Manichaean and Gnostic leanings because he stressed puristic ideals, sought perfection in asceticism, and dabbled in astrology. The church had been attacking his views for some time when Roman Emperor Maximus ordered that Priscillian be put to death for practicing magic. His execution was strongly protested by his former opponents in the church, St. Ambrose, St. Martin, and the pope. After his death Priscillian was venerated as martyr and saint, and his followers grew. Not until after a council held at Braga (563?) finally condemned Priscillianism did it disappear from Spain.

prism, in optics, a piece of translucent glass or crystal used to form a SPECTRUM of light separated according to colors. Its cross section is usually triangular. The light becomes separated because different wavelengths or frequencies are refracted (bent) by different amounts as they enter the prism obliquely and again as they leave it (see REFRACTION). The shorter wavelengths, toward the blue or violet end of the spectrum, are refracted by the greatest amount; the longer wavelengths, toward the red end, are refracted the least. The NICOL PRISM is a special type of prism made of calcite; it is used for POLARIZATION OF LIGHT.

prison, place of confinement for the punishment and rehabilitation of criminals. By the end of the 18th cent. imprisonment was widespread as the chief mode of punishment for all but capital crimes. At that time, largely as a result of the writings of Cesare BECCARIA in Italy and John HOWARD and others in England, there was a wave of penal reform and improvement in the inhumane conditions under which prisoners were forced to live. The earliest North American reform centered in Philadelphia (1790) and in Auburn, N.Y., where systems of solitary confinement and congregate labor were introduced. Reform efforts continued through the 19th cent., with two notable women (Elizabeth Fry and Dorothea Dix) among the reformers. British (especially Irish) influences led to the practice of parole. In the 20th cent. efforts were made in the United States to do away with unsanitary and demoralizing prison conditions. Reforms included the individualization of treatment, psychiatric assistance, constructive labor and vocational training (see CONVICT LABOR), professionalization of correctional officers, and the introduction of work release programs. There has been a growing tendency to regard the basic aim of imprisonment as rehabilitation of the criminal rather than as retributive punishment or protection of society. In some places, corporal punishment is still used as a method for disciplining, and such measures as the chain gang are notorious for their brutality. The chief types of prisons in the United States (with similar institutions in other countries) are the local jail, for pretrial detention and short sentences, and the state and Federal penitentiaries, for convicts with long sentences. Special penal institutions are provided for the sick and the criminally insane. Juvenile delinquents are usually sent to reformatories or other corrective institutions. In England the BORSTAL SYSTEM is used to correct young offenders. Among famous prisons in history are the Bastille in Paris and the Tower of London. In the United States, Sing Sing and Alcatraz (now closed) are the two best known. See N. K. Teeters, *World Penal Systems* (1945); D. R. Cressey, ed., *The Prison* (1961); David Dressler, ed., *Readings in Criminology and Penology* (1964); Daniel Glaser, *The Effectiveness of a Prison and Parole System* (1964); N. B. Johnston, ed., *The Sociology of Punishment and Correction* (2d ed. 1970); Jessica Mitford, *Kind and Usual Punishment* (1973).

prisoners of war, in international law, persons captured by a belligerent while fighting in the military. International law includes rules on the treatment of prisoners of war but extends protection only to combatants. This excludes civilians who engage in hostilities (by international law they are WAR CRIMINALS) and forces that do not observe conventional requirements for combatants (see WAR, LAWS OF). Attitudes towards prisoners of war have changed. Originally slaughtered, captives were later considered war booty. The captor still held life-and-death power, but it became more useful to make slaves of the prisoners. In feudal Europe the nobles were ransomed, and the Ottoman Empire and the Barbary States generally ransomed their Christian captives. The basis of the modern treatment of prisoners of war was stated by Montesquieu in *De l'esprit des lois* and by J. J. Rousseau in his *Social Contract;* both held that the right of the captor over the prisoner was limited to preventing him from taking up arms again and ceased altogether with the end of hostilities. Their view was elaborated by Emerich de VATTEL. During the American Civil War, Francis LIEBER drew up the first systematic, written regulations on the treatment of prisoners of war. The first international convention on prisoners of war was signed at the Hague Peace Conference of 1899. It was widened by the Hague Convention of 1907. These rules proved insufficient in World War I, and the International RED CROSS proposed a more complete code. In 1929 the Geneva Convention Relative to the Treatment of Prisoners of War was signed by 47 governments. Chief among the nations that did not adhere to the Geneva Convention of 1929 were Japan and the USSR. Japan, however, gave a qualified promise (1942) to abide by the Geneva rules, and the USSR announced (1941) that it would observe the terms of the Hague Convention of 1907, which did not provide (as does the Geneva Convention) for neutral inspection of prison camps, for the exchange of prisoners' names, and for correspondence with prisoners. According to the Geneva Convention no prisoner of war could be forced to disclose to his captor any information other than his identity (i.e., his name and rank, but not his military unit, home town, or address of relatives). Every prisoner of war was entitled to adequate food and medical care and had the right to exchange correspondence and receive parcels. He was required to observe ordinary military discipline and courtesy, but he could attempt to escape at his own risk. Once recaptured, he was not to be punished for his attempt. Officers were to receive pay either according to the pay scale of their own country or to that of their captor, whichever was less; they could not be required to work. Enlisted men might be required to work for pay, but the nature and location of their work were not to expose them to danger, and in no case could they be required to perform work directly related to military operations. Camps were to be open to inspection by authorized representatives of a neutral power. In World War II, Switzerland and Sweden acted as protecting powers. The International Red Cross at Geneva acted as clearing house for the exchange of all information regarding prisoners of war and had charge of transmitting correspondence and parcels. With minor and inevitable exceptions on the lower levels, the United States and Great Britain generally honored the Geneva Convention throughout the conflict. Japan at first committed such atrocities as the "death march of Bataan," but began to abide by the rules after a sufficient number of Japanese prisoners had fallen into Allied hands to make reprisals possible. Germany did not treat all its prisoners alike. Americans and British subjects received the best treatment, Polish prisoners the worst. The changed methods of World War II, the maltreatment of prisoners of war that constituted an important part of the WAR CRIMES indictments, and the retention of a great number of German prisoners of war by the USSR for several years after the war showed that the 1929 Convention required revision on many points. A new convention, reaffirming and supplementing the 1929 Convention, was signed at Geneva in 1949 and subsequently ratified by almost all nations. It broadened the categories of persons entitled to prisoner-of-war status, clearly redefined the conditions of captivity, and reaffirmed the principle of immediate release and repatriation at the end of hostilities. Although the North Koreans promised to respect the Geneva Convention in the Korean War, they refused to recognize the impartial status of the Red Cross and denied it access to the territory they controlled. The unprecedented refusal of prisoners to be repatriated, moreover, established a new principle of political asylum for prisoners of war. The governments of North and South Vietnam, parties to the 1949 Geneva Convention, were charged with violating it in the Vietnam War—the North by not permitting full reporting, correspondence, and neutral inspection, and the South by allegedly torturing captives and placing them in inhumane prisons.

Priština or **Prishtina** (both: prē'shtĭnä), city (1971 pop. 152,733), S Yugoslavia, in Serbia. The chief city of the Kossovo-Metohija region, Priština is a commercial center where jewelry and textile products are made. Magnesite and lignite are mined nearby. Priština was a capital of the Serbian empire in the 14th cent.

Prithvi Raj (prĭt'vē räj), d. 1192, ruler of the RAJPUTS in Rajputana, India. A great Hindu warrior, he later became the subject of many romantic epics, including the *Chand Raisa*, and he remains one of the most popular heroes of India. He was the Rajput leader who fiercely resisted the incursions of the Muslim Afghans led by Muhammad of Ghor. In 1191 he defeated the army of Ghor, but the following year at the second battle of Taraori his Hindu army was routed and he himself killed. After the defeat, the Delhi Sultanate was established, marking the beginning of Muslim dominance in India.

privateering, former usage of war permitting privately owned and operated war vessels (privateers) under commission of a belligerent government to capture enemy shipping. Private ownership distinguished the privateer from an ordinary warship; letters of marque and reprisal (commission issued by a government) distinguished it from a pirate craft. The primary object of privateering was to harass the enemy, but it was often practiced as a retaliatory measure. Licensed privateering dates back to the 13th cent., but the great era of privateering was the period from 1589 to 1815, when privateers became auxiliaries to or substitutes for regular navies, and when weaker naval powers used privateers as an effective method of injuring a more powerful maritime rival. Privateersmen, who kept all or a part of their booty, often gained great wealth. After the defeat (1692) of the French fleet by the Dutch and English, France commissioned privateers, who preyed upon English commerce. In the American War of Independence and in the War of 1812 American privateersmen captured hundreds of PRIZES. The Confederate States issued letters of marque to the last privateers in history, but the Federal blockade limited their effectiveness. In attempting to curb the abuses of privateering, nations required that captures be condemned in prize courts and that commissions (in restricted number) be granted only in the name of the sovereign. Privateersmen were free of naval discipline, and their desire for prize often led them to make no distinction between friendly and enemy shipping, to violate the rules of war, and to indulge in lawlessness after the conclusion of peace. These abuses led to the abolition of privateering by the Declaration of Paris (1856). This declaration does not prohibit the creation of voluntary navies consisting of private vessels under the control of a state, such as those used in World War II in the evacuation from Dunkirk. See E. S. Maclay, *History of American Privateers* (1924, repr. 1968); W. B. Johnson, *Wolves of the Channel* (1931); C. W. Kendall, *Private Men-of-War* (1932); J. P. Cranwell and W. B. Crane, *Men of Marque* (1940); David Woodward, *The Secret Raiders* (1955); D. B. Chidsey, *The American Privateers* (1962); C. L. Alderman, *The Privateersmen* (1965).

privet (prĭv'ĭt), any plant of the genus *Ligustrum*, Old World shrubs or small trees of the family Oleaceae (OLIVE family), some of which are common as hedge plants. Privet hedges are popular for their dark green leaves and their ease of cultivation even in adverse city conditions. Some are fairly hardy in the north but may be killed back to the ground by severe winters. The various species are evergreen, nearly evergreen, or deciduous, some producing small white flowers in profusion. They are usually propagated by cuttings. The common privet (*L. vulgare*) has become naturalized in the E United States; the California privet (*L. ovalifolium*) is a native of Japan. Privet is classified in the division MAGNOLIOPHYTA, class Magnoliopsida, order Scrophulariales.

Prix de Rome, Grand (gräN prē də rôm), prize awarded annually by the French government, through competitive examination, to students of the fine arts. It entitles them to four years' study at the Académie de France à Rome. The prize is open to all French painters, sculptors, architects, engravers, and musicians between the ages of 15 and 30 who have completed required work at the École des Beaux-Arts or elsewhere. It was instituted by Louis XIV in 1666 for the purpose of enabling talented artists to complete their education by study of classical art in Rome.

prize, in maritime law, the private property of an enemy that a belligerent captures at sea. For the capture of the vessel or cargo to be lawful it must be made outside neutral waters and by authority of the belligerent. A prize court, in the territory of the belligerent or in that of an allied power, must adjudicate that the property belonged to an enemy national. After the prize is captured, it is ordinarily placed in charge of a prize master and sent into port for judicial proceedings; however, if the enemy character of the ship is readily apparent, it may be destroyed at sea (after passengers, crew, and ship's papers have been removed), with the captor's government being liable for the losses of neutrals. If the prize is sold before being adjudicated, the proceeds must be delivered to the court for distribution. In the case of condemnation, the entire proceeds go to the belligerent government. In the United States, since 1899, the crew of the vessel effecting capture has had no right to share in the profits of the sale. A prize court renders a decision on the basis of the ship's papers, the testimony of those on board, and other relevant factors. If the ship is not condemned, it is released and damages are awarded where no justifiable reason for its capture has been shown. Prize law initially developed from the desire of governments to share in the profits made by ships engaged in PRIVATEERING. The governments also wished to minimize diplomatic claims for damages by establishing regular procedures for disposing of captures. Although they nominally apply international law, prize courts (in the United States, the Federal courts) in awarding judgment have been influenced, or even bound, by the national law. To avoid this, prize cases are sometimes referred to international tribunals. Efforts to establish an international prize court with appellate jurisdiction, however, have not succeeded. See J. W. Garner, *Prize Law during the World War* (1927); C. J. Colombos, *Treatise on the Law of Prize* (3d ed. 1949).

prize fighting: see BOXING.

Prizren (prē̆z'rĕn), city (1971 pop. 97,776), S Yugoslavia, in the Kossovo-Metohija region of Serbia. It is a commercial center with industries that produce filigree silver jewelry, carpets, and embroideries. Prizren is the seat of a Roman Catholic archbishop and of an Orthodox Eastern bishop. An important medieval trade center, the city reached its height as capital (1376-89) of Serbia under Stephen Dušan, who is buried in a nearby monastery. In Prizren are numerous ancient churches and monasteries, some in ruins.

probability, in mathematics, assignment of a number as a measure of the "chance" that a given event will occur. There are certain important restrictions on such a probability measure. In any experiment there are certain possible outcomes; the set of all possible outcomes is called the sample space of the experiment. To each element of the sample space (i.e., to each possible outcome) is assigned a probability measure between 0 and 1 inclusive (0 is sometimes described as corresponding to impossibility, 1 to certainty). Furthermore, the sum of the probability measures in the sample space must be 1. A simple illustration is given by the experiment of tossing a coin. The sample space consists of one of two outcomes—heads or tails. For a perfectly symmetrical coin, the likely assignment would be ½ for heads, ½ for tails. The probability measure of an event is sometimes defined as the ratio of the number of outcomes. Thus if weather records for July 1 over a period of 40 years show that the sun shone 32 out of 40 times on July 1, then one might assign a probability measure of 32/40 to the event that the sun shines on July 1. Probability computed in this way is the basis of insurance calculations. If, out of a certain group of 1,000 persons who were 25 years old in 1900, 150 of them lived to be 65, then the ratio 150/1,000 is assigned as the probability that a 25-year-old person will live to be 65 (the probability of such a person's not living to be 65 is 850/1,000, since the sum of these two measures must be 1). Such a probability statement is of course true only for a group of people very similar to the original group. However, by basing such life-expectation figures on very large groups of people and by constantly revising the figures as new data are obtained, values can be found that will be valid for most large groups of people and under most conditions of life. In addition to the probability of simple events, probabilities of compound events must be computed. If, for example, A and B represent two independent events, the probability that both A and B will occur is given by the product of their separate probabilities. The probability that either of the two events A and B will occur is given by the sum of their separate probabilities minus the probability that they will both occur. Thus if the probability that a certain man will live to be 70 is 0.5, and the probability that his wife will live to be 70 is 0.6, the probability that they will both live to be 70 is $0.5\times0.6=0.3$, and the probability that either the man or his wife will reach 70 is $0.5+0.6-0.3=0.8$.

Permutations and Combinations. In many probability problems, sophisticated counting techniques must be used; usually this involves determining the number of permutations or combinations. The number of permutations of a set is the number of different ways in which the elements of the set can be arranged (or ordered). A set of 5 books in a row can be arranged in 120 ways, or $5\times4\times3\times2\times1=5!=120$ (the symbol 5!, denoting the product of the integers from 1 to 5, is called factorial 5). If, from the five books, only three at a time are used, then the number of permutations is 60, or

$$P(5,3)=\frac{5!}{(5-3)!}=\frac{5\times4\times3\times2\times1}{2\times1}=60$$

In general the number of permutations of *n* things taken *r* at a time is given by

$$P(n,r)=\frac{n!}{(n-r)!}$$

On the other hand, the number of combinations of 3 books that can be selected from 5 books refers simply to the number of different selections without regard to order. The number in this case is 10:

$$10=\frac{5!}{2!3!}$$

In general, the number of combinations of *n* things taken *r* at a time is

$$C(n,r)=\frac{n!}{r!(n-r)!}$$

Statistical Inference. The application of probability is fundamental to the building of statistical forms out of data derived from samples (see STATISTICS). Such samples are chosen by predetermined and arbitrary selection of related variables and arbitrary selection of intervals for sampling; these establish the degree of freedom. Many courses are given in statistical method. Elementary probability considers only finite sample spaces; advanced probability by use of calculus studies infinite sample spaces. The theory of probability was first developed (c.1654) by Blaise Pascal, and its history since then involves the contributions of many of the world's great mathematicians. See Ernest Nagel, *Principles of the Theory of Probability* (1939); William Feller, *An Introduction to Probability Theory and Its Application* (3d ed. 1966-68); D. H. Mellor, *Matter of Chance* (1971); H. L. Alder and E. B. Roessler, *Introduction to Probability and Statistics* (5th ed. 1972); D. J. Koosis, *Probability* (1973); H. J. Malik and Kenneth Mullen, *A First Course in Probability and Statistics* (1973).

probate (prō'bāt), in law, the certification by a court that a WILL is valid. Probate, which is governed by various statutes in the several states of the United States, is required before the will can take effect. The procedure requires that notification of a hearing be given to all persons who may possibly inherit the deceased's property. Lost wills and oral wills may also be probated in some states if proof of due execution is furnished. If the will is certified, the court will issue letters testamentary authorizing EXECUTORS to carry out the will's provisions. The judge sitting on a probate court is ordinarily called a surrogate.

probation, method by which the punishment of a convicted offender is conditionally suspended. The offender must remain in the community and under the supervision of a probation officer, who is usually a court-appointed official. Probation is not a form of leniency but is intended for offenders whose rehabilitation can be better achieved by community care than by imprisonment. However, the offender's original sentence remains in force and can be invoked should he violate the provisions of the probation. Probation differs from PAROLE in that the latter requires the offender to have served a portion of his sentence in an institution. The first law in the United States that established the essentials of a modern probation system was enacted in Massachusetts in 1878.

Probus (Marcus Aurelius Probus) (prō'bəs), d. 282, Roman emperor (276–82), b. Pannonia. He was governor of the East under Marcus Claudius TACITUS, whom he succeeded as emperor. He defeated the barbarians in Gaul and in Illyria. He reformed the administration and embellished Rome with fine buildings. His troops mutinied, and he was killed. His successor was Marcus Aurelius CARUS.

procaine (prōkān'), anesthetic drug, commonly called novocaine, that gives prolonged relief from pain (see ANESTHESIA). It is used as a local anesthetic and in rectal and other SURGERY. It is marketed under the trade name Novocain.

procedure, in law, the rules that govern the obtaining of legal redress. This article deals only with civil procedure in Anglo-American law (for criminal prosecution, see CRIMINAL LAW). Except for EVIDENCE, procedure conventionally embraces all matters concerning legal actions that come to trial; thus, procedure is the means for enforcing the rights guaranteed by the substantive law. A legal action, in its simplest form, is a proceeding of a plaintiff against a defendant from whom he seeks redress. The plaintiff begins a lawsuit by filing a complaint, a written statement of his claim and the relief desired, with a court that has jurisdiction (authority to hear the case). The defendant is served a process (e.g., a summons) that notifies him of the suit; he usually responds with an answer, but, if he does not, the plaintiff is ordinarily entitled to a judgment by default. Today, liberal rules of pretrial discovery allow parties to a civil action to obtain information from other parties and their witnesses through depositions and other devices. Discovery (i.e., disclosure) is now used to ascertain the facts believed by the other side to exist, and to narrow the issues to be tried. At COMMON LAW, pleadings performed this function, and they were continued beyond the complaint and answer until an issue was agreed upon. The issue is one of law if the defendant denies that his alleged acts are a violation of substantive law entitling the plaintiff to relief; it is one of fact if the defendant denies committing any of the alleged acts. The judge rules on an issue of law, and if he upholds the defendant the suit is dismissed. An issue of fact is resolved by the presentation of evidence to the JURY, or, in cases tried without a jury, by the judge. After the jury has delivered a verdict on the factual issue, the judge renders his JUDGMENT, which in most (but by no means all) instances upholds the verdict. At this point the case is closed (unless the losing party prosecutes an APPEAL), and if the plaintiff has won, he proceeds to execution of the judgment. Current procedural law has had a long historical evolution. The early common law allowed an action to be brought only if it closely conformed to a WRIT. Rigorous enforcement of the rule, "no writ, no right," and the small number of available writs acted to deny relief even in meritorious cases and stimulated the growth of EQUITY, which, in its early days, gave redress generously. By the 19th cent., however, the technical intricacy of equity and law procedure and the tendency to make cases hinge on procedural details rather than on substantive rights made reform imperative. The way was led by the New York code of civil procedure of 1848 (largely the work of David Dudley FIELD), which abolished the distinction between law and equity (thereby effecting great simplification) and established the cause of action as the procedural cornerstone. A similar reform was accomplished in Great Britain by the Judicature Acts of 1875. Today the procedure of most American jurisdictions is based on codes (like that of New York) rather than on common law and equity, although the influence of these separate categories is still frequently discernible. See Jerome Michael, *The Elements of Legal Controversy* (1948); Paul Carrington, *Civil Procedure* (1969).

process, in law: see PROCEDURE.

Prochorus (prŏk'ərəs), one of the seven deacons. According to tradition he became bishop of Nicomedia. Acts 6.5.

Procida, John of: see JOHN OF PROCIDA.

Procida (prō'chēdä), narrow volcanic island, c.2 mi (3.2 km) long, Campania, S Italy, at the northwest entrance to the Bay of Naples. The chief town is Procida (1971 pop. 10,005). Wine, fruit, and fish are produced. The 13th-century conspirator JOHN OF PROCIDA was lord of the island.

Proclus (prō'kləs), 410?-485, Neoplatonic philosopher, b. Constantinople. He studied at Alexandria and at Athens, where he was a pupil of the Platonist Syrianus, whom he succeeded as a teacher. As a partisan of paganism he was forced to leave Athens, but he returned at the end of a year. A synthesizer of Neoplatonic doctrines, Proclus gave the philosophy its most systematic form. He kept the elements of Plotinus, but introduced a principle of triadic development in the series of emanations; the three stages are an original, an emergence from the original, and a return in a lower form to the original. Proclus differed from Plotinus in regard to the origin of matter, which he held to emerge from the first emanation rather than from the plastic forces. Among his writings are commentaries on several Platonic dialogues and two treatises, *On Plato's Theology* and *Institutes of Theology*. See NEOPLATONISM. See Thomas Whittaker, *The Neo-Platonists* (2d ed. 1928, repr. 1970).

Procne: see PHILOMELA AND PROCNE.

Proconsul, extinct group of apes, now considered a subgroup of *Dryopithecus. Proconsul* fossils have been discovered in E Africa. It is a probable ancestor of the chimpanzee and lived from 12 to 25 million years ago.

proconsul, in ancient Rome, governor of a province. The post was often conferred on a retiring consul or praetor. A proconsul usually held office for 12 months after reaching his post, or until his successor arrived. He was in sole charge of the army, of justice, and of administration in his province and could not be prosecuted for maladministration until his office expired. In modern times the title has sometimes been used for a colonial governor with far-reaching powers. See W. M. Jashemski, *The Origin and History of the Proconsular and the Propraetorian Imperium to 27 B.C.* (1950); W. T. Arnold, *The Roman System of Provincial Administration* (3d ed. 1914, repr. 1968).

Procopius (prōkō'pēəs), d. 565?, Byzantine historian, b. Caesarea in Palestine. He accompanied BELISARIUS on his campaigns as his secretary, and later he commanded the imperial navy and served (562) as prefect of Constantinople. His education, high connections, and public offices give his histories great value as firsthand accounts. His chief works are generally known as *Procopius' History of His Own Time*, dealing mainly with the wars against the Goths, Vandals, and Persians, and as the *Secret History of Procopius*, which is largely a scandalous and often scurrilous court chronicle. His authorship of the *Secret History* has been questioned, but most scholars now agree that it is an authentic work of Procopius. He also wrote *On Buildings*, a work in six books describing buildings erected by Justinian throughout the empire. In his polished style Procopius imitated the historians of the Greek classical period. His descriptions of social and religious customs among the barbarians are very valuable, but his histories are marred by his violent personal prejudices, e.g., in favor of Belisarius and against Empress Theodora. See study by J. A. S. Evans (1972).

Procopius the Great, Czech *Prokop Holý*, d. 1434, Czech Hussite leader. A priest, he joined the Hussite movement (see HUSSITES) and distinguished himself as a captain under John ZIZKA in the HUSSITE WARS. He succeeded Zizka as head of the radical Hussites or Taborites after Zizka's death (1424) and commanded in the great Hussite victory (1426) against the Saxon forces of the anti-Hussite Crusade at Usti-nad-Labem. In the subsequent four years Procopius led Hussite forces to victory in Hungary, Silesia, Saxony, and Thuringia and commanded the Czech forces against a new crusade launched by Holy Roman Emperor Sigismund in 1431. The crushing defeat that he inflicted (Aug., 1431) on the crusaders at Domazlice led to peace negotiations (1432) at Eger (Cheb) between the Hussites and representatives of the Council of Basel (see BASEL, COUNCIL OF). Procopius, however, continued to campaign in Lusatia, Silesia, and Brandenburg even after Hussite delegates had arrived (1433) at Basel to negotiate a religious compromise. He rejected the Compactata, arrived at by the council, which reconciled the Utraquists, the moderate wing of the Hussites, with the Roman Catholic Church. The Utraquists and Catholics of Bohemia then united against the Taborites, whom they crushed (1434) at Lipany; Procopius died in the battle. As a general, Procopius was a worthy successor of Zizka. His ally **Procopius the Little,** Czech *Prokupek*, d. 1434, was a leader of the Orphans (formerly the "Union," led by Zizka), a less radical group close to the Taborites. He commanded at the unsuccessful siege (1432-34) of Pilsen, a Catholic stronghold, and he too perished in the battle of Lipany.

Procris: see CEPHALUS.

Procrustes (prōkrŭs'tēz), in Greek mythology, cruel highwayman. He forced passersby to lie on a very long bed and then stretched them to fit it. Some said that he also had a very short bed; to make passersby fit this he sawed off their legs. Using Procrustes' own villainous methods, Theseus killed him.

Procter, Bryan Waller: see CORNWALL, BARRY.

Proctor, Redfield, 1831-1908, American industrialist and political leader, b. Proctorsville, Vt. He studied law, practiced in Boston, and served in the Union army in the Civil War. After he returned (1863) to Vermont he joined the Vermont Marble Company at Sutherland Falls (now Proctor) and made the company one of the largest of its kind in the country. He became its president in 1880. Proctor served in both houses of the state legislature and was lieutenant governor (1876-78) and governor (1878-80) before he became (1889) U.S. Secretary of War. He resigned (1891) this post to enter the U.S. Senate, where he served until his death. He visited Cuba in 1898, and the speech he made depicting conditions there was influential in bringing the United States into the Spanish-American War.

Procyon (prō'sēŏn"), brightest star in the constellation CANIS MINOR; Bayer designation α Canis Minoris; 1970 position R.A. $7^h37.7^m$, Dec. $+5°18'$. A yellow-white star of SPECTRAL CLASS F5 IV-V, it is one of the nearer bright stars, lying about 11.5 light-years away. Its name is from the Greek meaning "before the dog," i.e., before the Dog Star, SIRIUS, the brightest star in the sky. Procyon is a brilliant star in its own right, its apparent MAGNITUDE of 0.35 making it one of the 10 brightest stars in the sky. It is a visual BINARY STAR.

prodigal son, parable of Jesus about heaven and the sinner who repents. A young man leaves home and becomes a wastrel; repentant, he returns to be received with joyful welcome. Luke 15.11-32.

producer gas, fuel gas consisting chiefly of carbon monoxide and nitrogen. It is prepared in a furnace or generator in which air is forced upward through a burning fuel of coal or coke. Although the fuel is introduced through the top, no air is admitted there. The carbon of the fuel is oxidized by the oxygen of the air from below to form the carbon monoxide. The nitrogen of the air, being inert, passes through the fire without change. When steam is introduced with the air, the final gaseous product contains hydrogen also. Producer gas has a low heating value because it is about 60 percent inert nitrogen. It is widely used in industry because it can be made with cheap fuel. When producer gas contains hydrogen, it is also a source material for the manufacture of synthetic ammonia.

production, in economics, all those activities of mankind that have to do with the creation of wealth, i.e., with imparting to raw materials utility, or the ability to satisfy human wants. The farmer who manipulates the forces of nature to grow wheat, the miller who grinds the wheat into flour, and the baker who transforms flour into bread are examples of producers who, each in his own way, impart what is known as form utility to a natural material. Another class of producers, those engaged in transportation, add place utility to goods or commodities, and a third class, including those engaged in canning, storage, and refrigeration, add time utility. The creation of time and place utilities, thought of by businessmen as MARKETING, is regarded by economists as a part of production because, until goods are made available at the right time and place, they cannot satisfy human wants. For any kind of production in modern society, large amounts of capital in the form of machinery are required. Equally essential are land or nature, from which the raw materials are obtained, and labor, which, with the aid of capital, extracts and transforms the raw materials. To these three primary factors of production is sometimes added a fourth: the entrepreneur, or enterpriser, who organizes the forces of production and assumes the risks. Since under capitalism production is for a market, an important function of the entrepreneur is to anticipate as accurately as he can the economic demands for goods and to produce the kind and quantity of goods that will meet that demand. With the development of power and automatic machinery and with the many other practical applications of science, the production of goods to satisfy human wants ceased to be a major economic problem in most parts of the world. Goods can readily be produced in excess of financial ability to buy them. The problem of DISTRIBUTION has generally become more difficult than that of production. Overproduction is production in excess of effective economic demand, i.e., of ability to buy, not of ability or desire to consume. A surplus is what cannot be sold profitably, and not what cannot be used. The tendency is more and more to standardize goods and so produce them at low cost by extensive use of automatic machinery and minute division of labor, as exemplified by the assembly-line methods of automobile plants. Such mass production is necessarily accompanied by large-scale purchase of raw materials and mass distribution of the manufactured goods. Automation is a type of production in which self-acting and self-regulating machines, usually including computers, perform tasks previously done by human beings.

professional, in athletics: see AMATEUR.

profit, in economics, return on capital, also called earnings. Classical economics distinguishes between various kinds of profit: that of the entrepreneur, as remuneration for management and risk taking; that of the capitalist, in the form of interest; and that of the landlord, in the form of rent. In accounting, gross profit is the difference between the value of sales and the cost of the goods sold; net profit is gross profit minus all other expenses, including taxes. With the development of the CORPORATION, profits are divided between dividends to the holders of stock, and investment and depreciation funds in the control of hired managers. Profit is often considered to be the major incentive for production in a capitalist economy, although with the decline of the entrepreneur and the rise of a salaried managerial class, it has become less personal and more institutional in character. See PROFIT SHARING. See H. W. Stevenson and J. R. Nelson, ed., *Profits in the Modern Economy* (1967); H. J. Sherman, *Profits in the United States* (1968).

profit sharing, arrangement by which employees receive, in addition to their wages, a share of the net profits of a business. The purpose is to give them an incentive to increase their output through enhanced morale, less wasteful use of materials, better care of equipment, and the like. Profit sharing does not imply participation by the workers in management. The employer determines the rate at which profits are shared; since the rate is fixed beforehand, profit sharing differs from the BONUS system. Profit sharing plans have been in operation in France since 1842 but have not been widely adopted in the United States. The plan has been most successful in businesses where employees work without direct supervision or where it is limited to supervisory employees or lesser executives, e.g., branch managers and department managers in department stores.

progesterone (prōjĕs'tərōn"), female sex HORMONE that induces secretory changes in the lining of the UTERUS essential for successful implantation of a fertilized egg. A STEROID, progesterone is secreted chiefly by the corpus luteum, a group of cells formed in the OVARY after the follicle ruptures during the release of the egg cell. If fertilization does not take place, the secretion of progesterone decreases and menstruation occurs. If fertilization does occur, progesterone is secreted during pregnancy by the placenta and acts to prevent spontaneous abortion; the hormone also prepares the mammary glands for milk production. Progesterone is also synthesized from CHOLESTEROL in the cortex of the ADRENAL GLAND where it is a precursor for the synthesis of other steroids including TESTOSTERONE. Synthetic compounds with progesteronelike activity have been developed that, along with ESTROGEN, are used in oral contraceptives.

programmed instruction, method of presenting new subject matter to students in a graded sequence of controlled steps. The student works through the program by himself at his own speed and after each step tests his comprehension by answering an examination question or filling in a diagram to which he is immediately shown the correct answer. Teaching machines are often used to present the programmed material, although books may also be used. The first teaching machine was invented (1934) by Sydney L. Pressey, but it was not until the 1950s that practical methods of programming were developed. Programmed instruction was reintroduced (1954) by B. F. SKINNER of Harvard, and much of the system is based on his theory of the nature of learning. In the 1960s the technology of programming developed rapidly, and many types of teaching machines are now manufactured. Programs have been devised for the teaching of spelling, arithmetic, foreign languages, physics, psychology, and a number of other subjects. Although there has been considerable controversy regarding the merits of programmed instruction as the sole method of teaching, many educators agree that it can contribute to more efficient classroom procedure and supplement conventional teaching methods. Teaching machines enable students to work individually, calling for active participation of the learner. In industry programmed instruction is often used to train personnel. See Arthur A. Lumsdaine, *Teaching Machines and Programmed Learning* (2 vol., 1960-65); William A. Deterline, *An Introduction to Programmed Instruction* (1962); Harry Kay et al., *Teaching Machines and Programmed Instruction* (1968); Patricia Callender, *Programmed Learning* (1969).

programming: see COMPUTER.

program music is so called because a program is needed to explain its external associations. It endeavors to arouse mental pictures or ideas in the thoughts of the listener—to tell a story, depict a scene, or impel a mood. Berlioz's *Symphonie fantastique*, intended by the composer as program music, might be contrasted with a symphony of Brahms, which is considered as ABSOLUTE MUSIC.

progression, in mathematics, SEQUENCE of quantities, called terms, in which the relationship between consecutive terms is the same. An arithmetic progression is a sequence in which each term is derived from the preceding one by adding a given number, d, called the common difference. It has the general form $a, a+d, a+2d, \ldots, a+(n-1)d, \ldots$, where a is some number and $a+(n-1)d$ is the nth, or general, term; e.g., the progression 3, 7, 11, 15, . . . is arithmetic with $a=3$ and $d=4$. The value of the 20th term, i.e., when $n=20$, is found by using the general term: for $a=3$, $d=4$, and $n=20$, its value is $3+(20-1)4=79$. An arithmetic SERIES is the indicated sum of an arithmetic progression, and its sum of the first n terms is given by the formula $[2a+(n-1)d]n/2$; in the above example the arithmetic series is $3+7+11+15+\ldots$, and the sum of the first 5 terms, i.e., when $n=5$, is $[2\cdot 3+(5-1)4]\ 5/2=55$. A geometric progression is one in which each term is derived by multiplying the preceding term by a given number r, called the common ratio; it has the general form $a, ar, ar^2, \ldots, ar^{n-1}, \ldots$, where a and n have the same meanings as above; e.g., the progression 1, 2, 4, 8, . . . is geometric with $a=1$ and $r=2$. The value of the 10th term, i.e., when $n=10$, is given as $1\cdot 2^{10-1}=2^9=512$. The sum of the geometric progression is given by the formula $a(1-r^n)/(1-r)$ for the first n terms. A harmonic progression is one in which the terms are the reciprocals of the terms of an arithmetic progression; it therefore has the general form $1/a, 1/(a+d), \ldots, 1/[a+(n-1)d]$. This type of progression has no general formula to express its sum.

progressive education, movement in American education. Confined to a period between the late 19th and mid-20th cent., the term "progressive education" is generally used to refer only to those educational programs that grew out of the American reform effort known as the progressive movement. The sources of the movement, however, partly lie in the pedagogy of Jean Jacques Rousseau, Johann Pestalozzi, and Friedrich Froebel. Progressive education was a pluralistic phenomenon, embracing industrial training, agricultural education, and social education as well as the new techniques of instruction advanced by educational theorists. Postulates of the movement were that the child learns best in those experiences in which he has a vital interest and that modes of behavior are most easily learned by actual performance. The progressives insisted, therefore, that education must be a continuous reconstruction of living experience based on activity directed by the child. The recognition of individual differences were also considered crucial. Progressive education opposed formalized authoritarian procedure and fostered reorganization of classroom practice and curriculum as well as new attitudes toward the individual student. John DEWEY, an early proponent of progressive education, maintained that schools should reflect the life of the society. He suggested that the schools take on such responsibilities as the acculturation of immigrants in addition to merely teaching academic skills. Dewey also proposed a number of specific curricular changes that had strong impact on subsequent reformers. At his Laboratory School in Chicago, for example, Dewey developed (1896-1904) a method in which younger student groups worked on a central project related to their own interests. The division of more advanced work into units organized around some central theme was an attempt to adapt the method to the academic needs of older children. Other efforts to reorganize the schools included the Gary plan, developed (1908-15) in Gary, Ind. Devised to utilize the school plant more efficiently, to provide opportunity for more practical work, and to coordinate various levels of schooling, the plan divided the school building into classrooms and space for auditorium, playground, shops, and laboratories. Two schools ran simultaneously in this space so that every facility was in constant use. The school day was eight hours long, and schools were open six days a week. The Gary plan was widely adopted. The Dalton plan (1919), at Dalton, Mass., subdivided the work of the traditional curriculum into contract units, which the student undertook to accomplish in a specified amount of time. The Winnetka plan, established (1919) at Winnetka, Ill., separated the curriculum into the subjects handled by the Dalton technique and used the cooperative method of creative social activities developed by Dewey. A prominent experimental school was established by Francis Parker at the Cook County Normal School (Chicago, 1883). The Horace Mann School (New York City, 1887), the Lincoln School (1917) at Teachers College, Columbia Univ., and the experimental school (1915) at the State Univ. of Iowa were other notable progressive institutions. Activities programs were designed to supply certain aspects of progressive education to those schools in which more radical adjustments were not possible; the activities included clubs, student self-government, and school publications. The principles and practices of progressive education gained wide acceptance in American school systems during the first half of the 20th cent.; similar pedagogical innovations were instituted in many of the schools of Europe. From its inception, however, the movement elicited rather sharp criticism from a variety of different sources, particularly for its failure to emphasize systematic study of the academic disciplines. Opposition increased greatly in the years following World War II, and many hold that by the late 1950s the movement had collapsed. By that time, however, the progressive movement had effected a permanent transformation in the character of the American school, and many progressive schools across the country were firmly established. Other educational reform movements that have been affected by or are similar to progressive education are OPEN EDUCATION, the SUMMERHILL school, and the reforms of Maria MONTESSORI. See KINDERGARTEN; NURSERY SCHOOL; ADULT EDUCATION; GUIDANCE. See John Dewey, *The School and Society* (1899, rev. ed. 1943, repr. 1961), *Schools of To-morrow* (1915, repr. 1962), and *Democracy and Education* (1916, rev. ed. 1944, repr. 1966); Harold Rugg and Ann Shumaker, *The Child-Centered School* (1928, repr. 1969); William H. Kilpatrick, ed., *The Educational Frontier* (1933, repr. 1969); Adolph E. Meyer, *The Development of Education in the Twentieth Century* (2d ed. 1949); Lawrence A. Cremin, *The Transformation of the School* (1961, repr. 1964); P. A. Graham, *Progressive Education from Arcady to Academe* (1967).

Progressive party, in U.S. history, the name of three political organizations, active, respectively, in the presidential elections of 1912, 1924, and 1948.

Election of 1912. Republican insurgents dissatisfied with the conservative administration of President William Howard TAFT formed (Jan., 1911) the National Progressive Republican League. Senator Robert M. LA FOLLETTE was their choice for the Republican presidential nomination in 1912 until former President Theodore ROOSEVELT, at odds with his old friend Taft for various personal and political reasons, threw his "hat into the ring" (Feb. 24, 1912). The regular Republicans, however, controlled the national convention at Chicago (June) and renominated Taft, whereupon the Roosevelt supporters organized the new Progressive party (the Bull Moose party) and nominated, also at Chicago (August), Roosevelt for President and Hiram W. JOHNSON for Vice President. The Progressive platform called for the direct election of U.S. Senators, the initiative, referendum, and recall, woman suffrage, reduction of the tariff, and many social reforms. As a result of the split in Republican ranks, Woodrow Wilson, the Democratic candidate, won, but Roosevelt, who received 88 electoral votes and over 4 million popular votes, fared better than Taft. The party maintained its organization until 1916, when, after Roosevelt declined another nomination, most Progressives supported the Republican presidential candidate, Charles Evans Hughes. See B. P. De Witt, *The Progressive Movement* (1915, repr. 1968); G. E. Mowry, *Theodore Roosevelt and the Progressive Movement* (1946, repr. 1960); A. R. E. Pinchot, *History of the Progressive Party, 1912-1916,* ed. by H. M. Hooker (1958).

Election of 1924. The success of the Conference for Progressive Political Action, sponsored by the railroad brotherhoods, in the congressional elections of 1922 led to the nomination at Cleveland in 1924 of another Progressive party ticket, with La Follette for President and Burton K. WHEELER for Vice President. La Follette's program, supported by the American Federation of Labor, the Socialist and Farmer-Labor parties, and most other non-Communist left-wing groups, called for public control and conservation of natural resources, abolition of child labor, recognition of the right of labor to organize and bargain collectively, and the breakup of monopolies. In the Republican landslide that followed, La Follette won only the 13 electoral votes of Wisconsin, but polled nearly 5 million popular votes. Under La Follette's sons, Robert M., Jr., and Philip F., the Progressives continued strong in Wisconsin until 1938, when they were defeated by the Republicans. In 1946 the Wisconsin party dissolved itself and joined the Republicans. See K. C. MacKay, *The Progressive Movement of 1924* (1947, repr. 1966).

Election of 1948. At Philadelphia in July, 1948, a new third party, organized as a challenge to the Democratic party, adopted the name Progressive and nominated Henry A. WALLACE for President and Senator Glen H. Taylor for Vice President. Endorsed by the COMMUNIST PARTY, and by the AMERICAN LABOR PARTY of New York state, the Progressive party accused the Truman administration of failing to cooperate with the Soviet Union to end the cold war and advocated repeal of the Taft-Hartley Act and reestablishment of wartime price controls. Its candidates won no electoral votes and only slightly more than one million popular votes as Truman defeated Thomas E. Dewey, the Republican candidate, by a close margin. See K. M. Schmidt, *Henry A. Wallace: Quixotic Crusade, 1948* (1961); C. D. MacDougall, *Gideon's Army* (3 vol., 1965). See also bibliography under PROGRESSIVISM.

progressive school: see PROGRESSIVE EDUCATION.

progressivism, in U.S. history, a broadly based reform movement that reached its height early in the 20th cent. In the decades following the Civil War rapid industrialization transformed the United States. A national rail system was completed; agriculture was mechanized; the factory system spread; and cities grew rapidly in size and number. The progressive movement arose as a response to the vast changes brought by industrialization. It began in the cities, where the problems were most acute. Dedicated men and women of middle-class background moved into the slums and established settlement houses. Led by women such as Jane Addams in Chicago and Lillian Wald in New York City, they hoped to improve slum life through programs of self-help. Other reformers attacked corruption in municipal government; they formed nonpartisan leagues to defeat the entrenched bosses and their political machines. During the 1890s, reform mayors such as Hazen Pingree in Detroit, Samuel JONES in Toledo, and James Phelan in San Francisco were elected on platforms promising municipal ownership of public utilities, improved city services, and tenement housing codes. Urban reformers were often frustrated, however, because state legislatures, controlled by railroads and large corporations, obstructed the municipal struggle for home rule. Reformers turned to state politics, where progressivism reached its fullest expression. Robert LA FOLLETTE'S term as governor of Wisconsin (1901–6) was a model of progressive reform. He won from the legislature an antilobbying law directed at large corporations, a state banking control measure, and a direct primary law. Taxes on corporations were raised, a railroad commission was created to set rates, and a conservation commission was set up. In state after state, progressives advocated a wide range of political, economic, and social reforms. They urged adoption of the secret ballot, direct primaries, the initiative, the referendum, and direct election of senators. They struck at the excessive power of corporate wealth by regulating railroads and utilities, restricting lobbying, limiting monopoly, and raising corporate taxes. To correct the worst features of industrialization, progressives advocated workmen's compensation, child labor laws, minimum wage and maximum hours legislation (especially for women workers), and widows' pensions. As progressives gained strength on the state level, they turned to national politics. Little headway was made, however, since conservatives controlled the Senate. Some progress was made against the trusts during Theodore Roosevelt's administration, and Congress passed two bills regulating railroads, the Elkins Act (1903) and the Hepburn Act (1906). The exposés of business practices by the MUCKRAKERS aroused public opinion. The Pure Food and Drug Act and the Meat Inspection Act were passed (1906) to eliminate the worst practices of the food industry. While Roosevelt supported the progressive drive for regulation of corporations and for social welfare legislation, Congress remained adamant. Roosevelt's successor, William Howard Taft, was a determined opponent of progressive reform; in 1911 progressives, whose ranks had been swelled by middle-class professionals, small businessmen, and farmers, formed the National Progressive Republican League to prevent Taft's renomination. When this failed, progressives united in a third party (see PROGRESSIVE PARTY) and nominated (1912) Roosevelt for President. Although Roosevelt was defeated, the new President, Woodrow Wilson, sponsored many progressive measures. The Federal Reserve Act of 1913 reformed the currency system; the Clayton Antitrust Act and the Federal Trade Commission Act (1914) extended government regulation of big business; and the Keating-Owen Act (1916) restricted child labor. America's entry into World War I diverted the energy of reformers, and after the war progressivism virtually died. Its legacy endured, however, in the political reforms that it achieved and the acceptance that it won for the principle of government regulation of business. Most of the social welfare measures advocated by progressives had to await the New Deal years for passage. See G. E. Mowry, *The California Progressives* (1951, repr. 1963); A. S. Link, *Woodrow Wilson and the Progressive Era* (1954, repr. 1963); S. P. Hays, *The Response to Industrialism* (1957); R. B. Nye, *Midwestern Progressive Politics, 1870–1958* (1959, repr. 1965); Richard Hofstadter, *The Age of Reform* (1955, repr. 1963), and *The Progressive Movement, 1900–1915* (1963); Gabriel Kolko, *The Triumph of Conservatism* (1963, repr. 1967); D. A. Shannon, ed., *Progressivism and Postwar Disillusionment, 1898–1928* (1966); Allen Davis, *Spearheads for Reform* (1967); R. H. Wiebee, *The Search for Order* (1967); David Kennedy, ed., *Progressivism* (1971); B. M. Stave, ed., *Urban Bosses, Machines, and Progressive Reformers* (1971); J. D. Bunker, *Urban Liberals and Progressive Reform* (1973).

prohibition, legal prevention of the manufacture, transportation, and sale of alcoholic beverages, the extreme of the regulatory LIQUOR LAWS. The modern movement for prohibition had its main growth in the United States and developed largely as a result of the agitation of 19th-century TEMPERANCE MOVEMENTS. A number of states passed temperance laws in the early part of the century, but most of them were soon repealed. A new wave of state prohibition legislation followed the creation (1846–51) of a law in Maine, the first in the United States. Thus, emphasis shifted from advocacy of temperance to outright demand for government prohibition. Chief of the forces in this new and effective approach was the ANTI-SALOON LEAGUE. Prohibition had now become a national political issue, with a growing PROHIBITION PARTY and support from a number of rural, religious, and business groups. The drive was given impetus in World War I, when conservation policies limited liquor output. After the war national prohibition became the law, the Eighteenth Amendment to the Constitution forbidding the manufacture, sale, import, or export of intoxicating liquors. In spite of the strict VOLSTEAD Act (1919), law enforcement proved to be very difficult. Smuggling on a large scale (see BOOTLEGGING) could not be prevented, and the illicit manufacture of liquor sprang up with such rapidity that authorities were unable to suppress it. There followed a period of unparalleled illegal drinking (often of inferior and dangerous beverages) and lawbreaking. In 1933 the Twenty-first Amendment, repealing prohibition, was ratified. A number of states, counties, and other divisions maintained full or partial prohibition under the right of local option. By 1966 no statewide prohibition laws existed. Prohibition laws were passed in Finland, the Scandinavian countries, and most of Canada after World War I, but were repealed, partly because of serious consequences to the countries' commerce with wine-exporting nations. See *Report on the Enforcement of the Prohibition Laws* (1931) by the National Commission on Law Observance and Enforcement (Wickersham Commission); Clark Warburton, *The Economic Results of Prohibition* (1932, repr. 1969); Herbert Asbury, *The Great Illusion* (1950, repr. 1968); Andrew Sinclair, *Prohibition, the Era of Excess* (1962); J. H. Timberlake, Jr., *Prohibition and the Progressive Movement* (1963); Joseph Gusfield, *Symbolic Crusade* (1963); Harold Waters, *Smugglers of Spirits* (1971); John Kobler, *Ardent Spirits* (1973).

Prohibition party, in U.S. history, minor political party formed (1869) for the legislative prohibition of the manufacture, transportation, and sale of alcoholic beverages. The temperance movement was in existence as early as 1800, but it was not until 1867 that its leaders marshaled their forces to establish a separate political party to campaign for prohibition. The result was the organization (Sept., 1869) of the Prohibition party at a convention in Chicago attended by delegates from 20 states. The failure of the temperance cause to gain active support from the major political parties, the failure of public officials to enforce existing local prohibition laws in several states, and the nationwide founding of the United States Brewers' Association were factors contributing to the creation of the Prohibition party. Before entering a presidential race, the Prohibition party entered elections in nine states during the period from 1869 to 1871. The first three presidential candidates—James BLACK (1872), Green C. Smith (1876), and Neal DOW (1880)—each polled a very small number of votes. Although the central issue of the party was prohibition, typical party platforms included women's suffrage, free public education, prohibition of gambling, and prison reform. In 1882 the party made sizable gains in state elections, and in 1884 a vigorous presidential campaign by John P. SAINT JOHN resulted in the party's first large popular vote (150,626). Of these votes, 25,000 came from New York state, which the Democratic candidate Grover Cleveland carried by fewer than 1,200 votes. As most of St. John's support came from Republicans angered at the comtemptuous treatment accorded a temperance petition at their national convention, the Prohibitionists helped swing a key state to Cleveland. Four years later the temperance leader Clinton B. Fisk received almost 250,000 votes. But the peak of popular support was reached in 1892, when John Bidwell won almost 265,000 votes. The popularity of the temperance cause had been greatly furthered by the WOMAN'S CHRISTIAN TEMPERANCE UNION (1874), and later by the ANTI-SALOON LEAGUE (1893), despite the latter's nonpartisan political position. Although the Prohibition party never received a large percentage of the national vote, its influence on public policy far outweighed its electoral strength. This can be seen in state platform declarations of the major parties at this time and in the institution of PROHIBITION by the Eighteenth Amendment. Although the Prohibition party continues to run presidential candidates, the repeal of prohibition by the Twenty-first Amendment had a decidedly weakening effect on the party. See D. Leigh Colvin, *Prohibition in the United States* (1926); W. B. Hesseltine, *The Rise and Fall of Third Parties* (1948); Howard P. Nash, *Third Parties in American Politics* (1959); John Kobler, *Ardent Spirits* (1973).

projection, in psychology: see DEFENSE MECHANISM.

projection, map: see MAP PROJECTION.

projective geometry, branch of GEOMETRY concerned with those properties of geometric figures that remain invariant under projection. The basic elements are points, lines, and planes, and the following statements are usually taken as assumptions: (1) two points determine a line; (2) three points not on the same line determine a plane; (3) two lines determine a point; (4) two planes determine a line; (5) three planes not containing the same line determine a point. The basic elements retain their character under projection; e.g., the projection of a line is another line, and the point of intersection of two lines is projected into another point that is the intersection of the projections of the two original lines. However, lengths and ratios of lengths are not invariant under projection, nor are angles or the shapes of figures. The concept of parallelism does not appear at all in projective geometry; any pair of distinct lines intersects in a point, and if these lines are parallel in the sense of Euclidean geometry, then their point of intersection is at INFINITY. The plane that includes the ideal line, or line at infinity, consisting of all such ideal points, is called the projective plane. Two properties that are invariant under projection are the order of three or more points on a line and the harmonic relationship, or cross ratio, among four points, *A, B, C, D*, i.e., *AC*/*BC* : *AD*/*BD*. One important concept in projective geometry is that of duality. In the plane, the terms *point* and *line* are dual and can be interchanged in any valid statement to yield another valid statement, e.g., statements (1) and (3) above; in space, the terms *plane, line,* and *point* are interchanged with *point, line,* and *plane,* respectively, to yield dual statements (sometimes with slight changes in wording) as in statements (2) and (5) and statements (1) and (4) above. The origins of projective geometry are found in the work of Pappus, Gérard Desargues, and others. It first emerged as a discipline in its own right with the work of J. V. Poncelet (1822) and was placed on an axiomatic basis by K. G. C. von Staudt (1847), both these mathematicians adopting the pure, or synthetic, approach, in which algebraic and analytic methods are avoided and the treatment is purely geometric, in contrast to the approach of A. F. Möbius, Julius Plücker, and others. Projective geometry is more general than the familiar Euclidean geometry and includes the metric geometries (both Euclidean and non-Euclidean) as special cases.

Prokofiev, Sergei Sergeyevich (syĭrgā' syĭrgā'əvĭch prōkôf'ēĕf), 1891–1953, Russian composer, pianist, and conductor. Prokofiev achieved wide popularity with his lively music, in which he achieved a pungent mixture of modern and traditional elements. He was a pupil of Reinhold Glière and of Nicolai Rimsky-Korsakov at the St. Petersburg Conservatory. In 1918 he toured through Siberia and Japan to the United States, where he settled for a short time. He lived in Paris from 1922 to 1933, when he returned permanently to the USSR, although he visited Europe and the United States several times until 1938. Among his important works are seven symphonies, especially the First, the Classical Symphony (1916–17), and the Fifth (1944); two violin concertos; five piano concertos; nine sonatas and other piano music; and chamber music. His operas include *The Gambler* (1915–16; rev. 1927; Brussels, 1929), after Feodor Dostoyevsky; *The Love for Three Oranges* (1921), after Carlo Gozzi; *Betrothal in a Convent* (1940; 1946), based on Richard Sheridan's *Duenna;* and *War and Peace* (1946; rev. version, 1955), after Leo Tolstoy. Other works are the ballets *Chout (The Buffoon,* 1921), *Le Pas d'acier* (1927), and *Romeo and Juliet* (1935–36; 1940); the symphonic fairy tale *Peter and the Wolf* (1936); and suites from the scores for the films *Lieutenant Kije* (1934) and *Alexander Nevsky* (1939). Prokofiev's early works are often harsh and strident, deliberately avoiding emotionalism. Later he wrote in a more simplified, popular style, although he never lost his individuality. He used sharp and vigorous rhythms, and he was a master of orchestration. His own virtuosity at the piano is reflected in the brilliance of his piano music. See his autobiography (tr. 1959); biographies by Israel Nestyev (rev. ed., tr. 1960), Victor Seroff (1968), and Claude Samuel (tr. 1971).

Prokopovich, Feofan (fāəfän' prəkəpô'vĭch), 1681–1736, Russian churchman. He was appointed bishop by Czar Peter I to carry out his ecclesiastic reforms and wrote *Spiritual Regulation* (1721), which helped strengthen state control of the church. Made archbishop of Novgorod (1724), he implemented Peter's policy, working against scholasticism and clerical ignorance and expanding the rights of Protestants. Prokopovich, a highly cultured man, wrote theological works and fiction and founded the Greco-Slavonic Academy.

Prokopyevsk (prəkôp'yĭfsk), city (1970 est. pop. 274,000), E Siberian USSR. A major coal producer of the KUZNETSK BASIN, it also manufactures mining machinery, chemicals, and food products. It was founded after the Russian Revolution of 1917.

proletariat (prōlətâr'ēət), in Marxian theory, the class of exploited workers and wage earners who depend on the sale of their labor for their means of existence. In ancient Rome, the proletariat was the lowest class of citizens; its members had no property or assured income and were a source of discontent and political instability. According to Karl MARX, the breakup of feudalism and the development of capitalism created a new, propertyless class from the dispossessed peasants and retainers who were forced to sell their labor for wages in the new industrial centers. Marx believed that the seizure of power by the proletariat from the capitalist class was a necessary step to a classless society. Under Lenin and the Bolsheviks, this revolution was to be directed by the Communist party, as the vanguard of the proletariat. See L. P. Adams and R. L. Aronson, *The History of Workers and Industrial Change* (1957); Jurgen Kuczynski, *The Rise of the Working Classes* (tr. 1967); Shlomo Avineri, *The Social and Political Thought of Karl Marx* (1968).

proline (prō'lēn), organic compound, one of the 22 α-AMINO ACIDS commonly found in animal proteins. Only the L-stereoisomer appears in mammalian protein. It is not essential to the human diet, since it can be synthesized in the body from GLUTAMIC ACID. Proline is the only one of the 22 amino acids that has a secondary, rather than a primary, α-amino

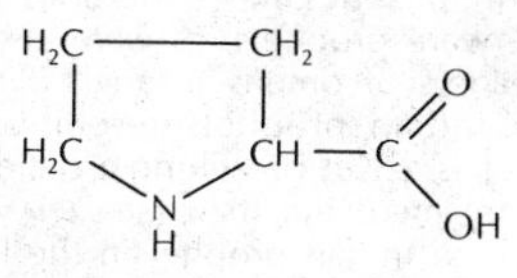

proline

group. This is significant when the amino acid is incorporated into protein; because of its peculiar structure it makes sharp bends, or kinks, in the peptide chain that makes up a protein, thus figuring prominently in the determination of the protein's shape. Proline and its derivative hydroxyproline, make up some 21% of the amino acid residues found in COLLAGEN, the fibrous protein of connective tissue. Its chemical synthesis was accomplished in 1900; in 1901 proline was isolated from casein, the milk protein, and its structure was shown to be the same as that of the synthetic compound.

Prome: see PYE, Burma.

Prometheus (prōmē'thēəs), in Greek mythology, great benefactor of mankind. He was the son of the Titan Iapetus and of Clymene or Themis. Because he foresaw the defeat of the TITANS by the Olympians he sided with Zeus and thus was spared the punishment of the other Titans. According to one legend Prometheus created mankind out of clay and water. When Zeus mistreated man, Prometheus stole fire from the gods, gave it to man, and taught him many useful arts and sciences. In another legend he saved the human race from extinction by warning his son, DEUCALION, of a great flood. This sympathy with mankind roused the anger of Zeus, who then plagued man with Pandora and her box of evils and chained Prometheus to a mountain peak in the Caucasus. In some myths he was released by Hercules; in others Zeus restored his freedom when Prometheus revealed the danger of Zeus' marrying Thetis, fated to bear a son who would be more powerful than his father. Prometheus is the subject of many literary works, of which the most famous are Aeschylus' *Prometheus Bound* and Shelley's *Prometheus Unbound.*

promethium (prōmē'thēəm), artificially produced radioactive chemical element; symbol Pm; at. no. 61; mass no. of most stable isotope 145; m.p. about 1080°C; b.p. about 2460°C; sp. gr. unknown; valence +3. Although the chemical and physical properties of promethium are not well defined, it is similar to neodymium and samarium, the RARE-EARTH METALS preceding and following it in the LANTHANIDE SERIES in group IIIb of the PERIODIC TABLE. All its isotopes are radioactive and fairly short-lived. Promethium-145, the most stable isotope, has a half-life of about 18 years. The most useful isotope is promethium-147 (half-life 2.64 years); it is produced in nuclear reactors. It is a beta emitter and has found use in making phosphorescent materials. When it is mixed with a phosphor, the light emitted can be used to power a photocell. It must be used with caution; although the beta rays it emits are relatively harmless, they may produce X rays when they interact with atoms of heavy elements. The existence of promethium was predicted at the beginning of the 20th cent. In 1926, B. S. Hopkins and his co-workers claimed to have discovered the element and proposed the name illinium. About the same time Luigi Rolla and his associates (in Italy) reported its discovery and suggested the name florentium. However, definite chemical identification of the element did not occur until 1945, although it may have been synthesized earlier. J. A. Marinsky, L. E. Glendenin, and C. D. Coryell identified the element by ion-exchange chromatography during the course of experiments at Oak Ridge National Laboratory, Tenn., involving the fission of uranium and subsequent neutron bombardment of neodymium. Since observable quantities of the element have never been found in nature, this identification is considered the first actual discovery of the element. The name *promethium* was suggested by these investigators and adopted in 1949 by the International Union of Pure and Applied Chemistry.

prominences: see CHROMOSPHERE.

promissory note, unconditional written promise to pay a certain sum of money at a definite time to bearer or to a specified person on his order. Promissory notes are generally used as evidences of debt. The holder of a note made payable to bearer may transfer his rights to another by delivery of the note. If the note is payable to order, it may be transferred by endorsement and delivery.

pronghorn or **prongbuck,** hoofed herbivorous mammal, *Antilocapra americana,* of the W United States and N Mexico. Although it is often called the American, or prong-horned, antelope, it does not belong to the true antelope family of Africa and Asia, but to a related family, the Antilocapridae, of which it is the only living member. The pronghorn is about the size of a goat, standing 3 ft (90 cm) high at the shoulder and weighing about 100 lb (45 kg). The coat is light brown with white underparts, two white throat stripes, and a white rump patch. The tail is short, and the ears are long and pointed. Both sexes have horns, which consist of a horny sheath and a bony core, like those of antelopes; unlike antelope horns, those of the pronghorn bear a single branch, or prong, and lose the outer sheath each year. Pronghorns live in small bands on open plains. Chiefly browsers, they feed largely on sagebrush and other shrubs, but also eat grasses. The swiftest of North American mammals, they attain speeds of 60 mi (96 km) per hr, but are poor jumpers. Their principal enemies, besides humans, are wolves and coyotes. Before the settlement of North America by Europeans pronghorns were comparable in numbers to buffalo; by the beginning of the 20th cent., however, they had been nearly exterminated by hunting. They are now protected on reservations, where they have made a good recovery. Pronghorns are classified in the phylum CHORDATA, subphylum Vertebrata, class Mammalia, order Artiodactyla, family Antilocapridae. See Joe van Wormer, *The World of the Pronghorn* (1968).

pronoun, in English, the PART OF SPEECH used as a substitute for an antecedent noun that is clearly understood, and with which it agrees in person, NUMBER, and GENDER. In English the pronouns are classified as personal (*I, we, you, thou, he, she, it, they*), demonstrative (*this, these, that, those*), relative (*who, which, that, as*), indefinite (e.g., *each, all, everyone, either, one, both, any, such, somebody*), interrogative (*who, which, what*), possessive, sometimes termed possessive adjectives (*my, your, his, her, our, their*), and reflexive (e.g., *myself, herself*). The CASE of the pronoun depends upon its function in the sentence structure.

Prontosil (prŏn'təsĭl"): see SULFA DRUG.

pronunciation: see PHONETICS.

proof, in law: see EVIDENCE.

proof, in mathematics, finite sequence of propositions each of which is either an AXIOM or follows from preceding propositions by one of the rules of logical inference (see SYMBOLIC LOGIC). Mathematical proofs are quite distinct from inductive, statistical, heuristic, analogical, and other types of reasoning or persuasion that are sometimes accepted as proofs in other fields of science or human affairs. Proof theory has developed into one of the important branches of modern mathematical logic. Some schools of mathematical logic reject certain methods in proofs, such as use of the law of excluded middle (either *p* is true or *p* is false) or of mathematical definitions involving properties that are not effectively verifiable.

proof, in printing, a trial impression for inspection. **Proofreading** is the inspection and marking of proof for correction of errors and imperfections. Proofreaders' marks are included in dictionaries. Directions for proofreading are given in several sources including *A Manual of Style,* published by the Univ. of Chicago Press (12th ed. 1970); *Words into Type,* by M. E. Skillin and R. M. Gay (3d ed. 1974); and *Proofreading and Copy-Preparation: A Textbook for the Graphic Arts Industry,* by Joseph Lasky (1954).

propaganda, systematic manipulation of public opinion, generally by the use of symbols such as flags, monuments, oratory, and publications. The term derives from the *Congregatio de Propaganda Fide* [Congregation for the Propagation of the Faith], the office of the Vatican that has directed Roman Catholic mission activities since 1622. Modern propaganda is distinguished from other forms of communication in that it is consciously and deliberately used to control group attitudes; all other functions are secondary. Thus, almost any attempt to influence public opinion, including lobbying, commercial advertising, and missionary work, can be broadly construed as propaganda. Generally, however, the term is restricted to the manipulation of political beliefs. Although allusions to propaganda can be found in ancient writings (e.g., Aristotle's *Rhetoric*), the organized use of propaganda did not develop until after the Industrial Revolution, when modern instruments of communication first enabled propagandists to easily reach mass audiences. The printing press, for example, made it possible for Thomas Paine's *Common Sense* to reach a large number of American colonists. Later, during the 20th cent., the advent of radio and television enabled propagandists to reach even greater numbers of people. In addition to the development of modern media, the rise of total warfare and of political movements has also contributed to the growing importance of propaganda in the 20th cent. In *What Is To Be Done?* (1902) V. I. Lenin emphasized the use of "agitprop," a combination of political agitation and propaganda designed to win the support of intellectuals and workers for the Communist revolution. Adolf Hitler and Benito Mussolini also used propaganda, especially in oratory, to develop and maintain the support of the masses. During World War II all the warring nations employed propaganda, often called psychological warfare, to boost civilian and military morale as well as to demoralize the enemy. The U.S. agency charged with disseminating wartime propaganda was the OFFICE OF WAR INFORMATION. In the postwar era propaganda activities continue to play a major role in world affairs. The United States Information Agency (USIA) was established in 1953 to facilitate the international dissemination of information about the United States. Radio Moscow, Radio Havana, and The Voice of America are just three of the large radio stations that provide information and propaganda throughout the world. In addition, certain refinements of the propaganda technique have developed, most notably brainwashing, the intensive indoctrination of political opponents against their will. See Jacques Ellul, *Propaganda* (1965, repr. 1973); T. C. Sorensen, *The Word War* (1967).

propagation of plants is effected in nature chiefly sexually by the SEED and the SPORE, less often by rhizomes and other methods (see REPRODUCTION). Vegetative means include CUTTING, LAYERING, GRAFTING, and division of the roots (see PERENNIAL) and of the tubers (see POTATO). Most farm and garden crops are propagated by seed, but some plants will not breed true from seed and must be propagated by various vegetative methods, depending on the type of plant. See H. T. Hartmann and D. E. Kester, *Plant Propagation* (2d ed. 1968).

propane, $CH_3CH_2CH_3$, colorless, gaseous ALKANE. It is readily liquefied by compression and cooling. It melts at -189.9°C and boils at -42.2°C. Propane occurs in nature in natural gas and (in dissolved form) in crude oil; it is also a by-product of petroleum refining. It is used chiefly as a fuel. For this purpose it is sold compressed in cylinders of various sizes, often mixed with other hydrocarbons, e.g., butane. Propane fuel is used in a type of cigarette lighter and in portable stoves and lamps.

propane, 2-methyl, IUPAC name for isobutane (see BUTANE).

propanetricarboxylic acid, 2-hydroxy-1,2,3-, IUPAC name for CITRIC ACID.

propanetriol, 1,2,3-, IUPAC name for GLYCEROL.

propanoic acid, 2-methyl-, IUPAC name for isobutyric acid (see BUTYRIC ACID).

propanol, 2-, IUPAC name for ISOPROPANOL.

propanone, 2-, IUPAC name for ACETONE.

propeller, device consisting of a hub with one or more blades that propels a craft to which it is attached by rotating its blades in a fluid such as air or water. In the latter part of the 1830s the Swedish-American engineer John Ericsson and the English inventor Sir Francis P. Smith independently patented screw propellers. Screw propellers have almost entirely replaced paddle wheels and a variety of other devices that were designed to propel waterborne vessels. In a single-screw ship the propeller is mounted on the end of a shaft immediately in front of the rudder; the shaft is connected to a transmission or directly to an engine, which turns it and the propeller. The thrust generated by the propeller is transmitted to the hull of the ship by a thrust bearing attached to the shaft. Twin-screw vessels were first introduced c.1860 in England. Located on either side of the rudder, the two propellers may be used to assist in steering; if one breaks down, the other can still propel the vessel. The introduction of steam turbines has brought about the use of four propellers on large ships. Screw propellers are made of cast iron, cast steel, or manganese bronze, the last being noted for its resistance to corrosion. Propellers on airplanes generally have from two to six blades. These are usually made of wood, aluminum alloy, or steel. At first, all were of fixed pitch, i.e., the angle of the blades was not variable. Later, advantages in speed and power brought variable-pitch propellers into general use; their blades are set into sockets in the hub with gear arrangements capable of altering the pitch in flight. The development of automatic equipment to alter the pitch as needed for maintaining a predetermined speed produced the constant-speed propeller. Variable-pitch propellers generally take the name of the pitch-controlling device; the principal types are hydraulic, mechanical, automatic, and electric. With modifications they can also act as air brakes. When the number of blades was increased from two to three, then from three to six, to achieve greater thrust or propulsion or to keep the blade size down, new stress problems arose. These were met by the development of contrarotating propellers, in which the blades were arranged as two separate three-bladed units rotating in opposite directions.

properdin (prō'pərdən), protein found in the blood serum of man and some of the higher animals that appears to participate in certain specific immune responses. It is associated with the engulfing of foreign particles and invading cells by phagocytes and with tissue inflammation (see BLOOD; IMMUNITY). Properdin has been isolated in highly purified form.

proper motion, in astronomy, apparent movement of a star on the CELESTIAL SPHERE, usually measured as seconds of arc per year; it is due both to the actual relative motions of the sun and the star through space. Proper motion reflects only transverse motion, i.e., the component of motion across the line of sight to the star; it does not include the component of motion toward or away from the sun. The most distant stars show the least proper motion. Barnard's Star, one of the closest stars, has the largest measured proper motion, 10.27 sec of arc per year. The average proper motion of the stars that can be seen with the naked eye is 0."1 per year.

Propertius, Sextus (sĕk'stəs prōpûr'shəs), c.50 B.C.–c.16 B.C., Roman elegiac poet, b. Umbria. He was a member of the circle of MAECENAS. A master of the Latin elegy, he wrote with vigor, passion, and sincerity. See translations by Constance Carrier (1963) and John Warden (1972); studies by Maurice Platnauer (1951) and D. R. S. Bailey (1956).

property, rights to the enjoyment of things of economic value, irrespective of whether the enjoyment is exclusive or shared, present or prospective. The rightful possession of such rights is called *ownership.* Ownership necessarily is supported by correlative rights to exclude others from enjoyment. Protection and content are given to ownership by custom or law. By extension of usage, the things in which one has property rights are called one's property; thus the person who holds title to a house, even though there is a MORTGAGE outstanding, calls it his "property." The type of property law in a society may be taken as an index of its social and economic system. For example, a primitive pastoral tribe that must be closely united to resist its enemies may hold pasture lands in common or rotate ownership, thereby avoiding disruptive quarrels. By contrast, in societies that enjoy an economic surplus and relative security, the institution of private property may be highly developed, with marked division of ownership and a competitive struggle for control. On the other hand, private property may be eliminated in certain societies, as in those envisioned by Karl Marx. Modern Anglo-American property law provides at least potentially for the ownership of nearly all things that have or may have value. The need for unobstructed intercourse between nations, of course, prohibits the assertion of ownership on the high seas; and special rules apply to territorial waters (see WATERS, TERRITORIAL) and to domestic NAVIGABLE WATER. Air space beyond that which can be used by airplanes is often considered not subject to ownership. In a sense, all land presently or ultimately belongs to the state, for whatever is not actually owned by the public authority may be transferred to it by condemnation proceedings under the power of eminent domain (see PUBLIC OWNERSHIP). In fact, most land in capitalist societies is in private hands, although ownership of subsoil mineral wealth or of buried objects (see TREASURE-TROVE) in some instances may be public. The terminology and much of the content of modern property law stem from its origins in FEUDALISM. The fundamental division is into realty (or real estate or real property) and personalty (or personal property). Realty is chiefly land and improvements built thereon. Sometimes it is comprehensively, but loosely, described as lands, tenements (holdings by another's authority), and hereditaments (that which is capable of being inherited). Formerly its chief characteristics in a legal sense were that it went by descent to the heir of the owner (who had no control over its disposition) and that ownership might be recovered by a lawsuit (a so-called real action). Also possessing such characteristics, and hence classified as real property, were titles of honor, heirlooms, and advowsons, i.e., the right to sell an ecclesiastical benefice. The manner in which realty is owned is said to be an estate; specifically, ownership is a fee of some sort, for example, an estate in fee simple (see TENURE). Personal property consists chiefly of movables, that is, portable objects. Typically (but by no means invariably) the owner can by WILL, GIFT, or sale determine its distribution (note the contrast with the term *descent*), and if it has been wrongly taken, a lawsuit (a so-called personal action) will give damages only but will not restore the object. Certain types of interests in land are also classified as personalty; examples are leases drawn for a period of years, mortgages, and liens. The distinction of realty and personalty served the purposes of early feudal society. The ownership and disposition of land, the basis of most wealth and the keystone of the social structure, was controlled to protect society, while the ownership of personalty, being of minor importance, was almost unfettered. As the economic system was altered during the late Middle Ages, however, personalty lost its subordinate position and grew to be the economic mainstay of the rising middle class of merchants and manufacturers. Personalty could be bought and sold in relative freedom without the hindrances that beset the disposal of land. By taking advantage of its economic freedom, the middle class was able to replace the landed aristocracy as society's dominant class. Concurrently, it also sought to relieve real property of its medieval fetters in order to use it, along with personalty, as revenue-producing capital. Gradually the law of realty tended in all important respects to be assimilated to that of personalty. In time land could be sold with almost perfect freedom and distributed by will; fundamentally it joined the list of other commodities. Only differences of detail in the law of realty and personalty still persist, especially in the transfer of realty, which is attended with great formality. There are also many distinctions of detail and some of substance in the property laws of various of the United States. For rules affecting marital property, see HUSBAND AND WIFE. For certain special types of property, see COPYRIGHT and PATENT.

prophet [Gr.,=foreteller], in the Bible, religious leader of Israel, especially in the period of the kingdoms and the Babylonian captivity. The Major Prophets are Isaiah, Jeremiah, Ezekiel, and Daniel. The Minor Prophets are Hosea, Joel, Amos, Obadiah, Jonah, Micah, Nahum, Habbakuk, Zephaniah, Haggai, Zechariah, and Malachi. In the Jewish tradition, the Prophets are classified as Former (historical books from Joshua through 2 Kings, excluding Ruth) and Latter (the Major Prophets, excluding Daniel, and the Twelve, i.e., the Minor, Prophets taken as one). The title is accorded to other men of varying importance, e.g., Abraham, Moses, Elijah, Elisha, Nathan, and Jehu (see JEHU **2**). In Israel the prophet was believed to have been inspired by God to guide the chosen people. The prophets, sure of their divine mission to purify Israel's religion, attacked the whole life of the people and came forward as the advocates of the poor and oppressed and as the leaders in social reform. According to them Israel could be reconciled with God only by complete purification in religion and in the state. In the writings of the Prophets are many of the most beautiful portions of the Old Testament; monotheism receives its most eloquent support, and Judaism makes its convincing universal appeal. From earliest times the Prophets were studied for revelations of the future, especially of the glories of Israel and the MESSIAH to come; they were imitated by prophetic PSEUDEPIGRAPHA. The Gospels give many examples of the interpretation of Old Testament passages as predictive, and it is part of traditional Christian belief that the Holy Ghost "spoke through the prophets" (Nicene Creed), who foretold the life and passion of Christ. Exegesis of the Prophets before the 19th cent. hardly touched any aspect but this. In the New Testament the term *prophecy* is used of enthusiastic, presumably inspired, utterance, and this was the principle of MONTANISM, an early Christian deviation (2d cent. A.D.). Such prophecy has had a somewhat dubious history in Christianity (e.g., in Joachim of Floris and Joanna Southcott), but there have been millennialists and miracle-working preachers among the unassailably orthodox (e.g., St. Vincent Ferrer). Some varieties of Protestantism have emphasized "inspired" utterance or behavior; the most spectacular were the Anabaptists (e.g., Thomas Münzer and John of Leiden). Prophecy is essential also in Quakerism. Emanuel Swedenborg and Joseph Smith are examples of self-proclaimed prophets who came out of Protestant backgrounds. Outside Christianity, Islam knows Muhammad as the last and greatest of prophets. In ancient Greece the priests attached to an ORACLE were prophets, as were also the official Roman readers of omens through divination. The American Indian prophets resembled the great prophets of Israel in preaching a definite message; the ordinary medicine man (see SHAMAN) had no such role. The Indian prophet in the late 18th and the 19th cent. normally foretold the regeneration of the red man and the recapture of the lands from the white man, provided all Indians accepted the idea of Indian brotherhood and followed prescribed religious practices. Frequently they were connected with Indian military leaders, more or less closely, as the DELAWARE PROPHET with Pontiac and the SHAWNEE PROPHET with his brother, Tecumseh. Two later prophets of renown were SMOHALLA and Wovoka (of the GHOST DANCE). The holy man (or woman) who interprets for a divine power is a commonplace in religion (e.g., in VOODOO), and his function varies according to the culture. The terms therefore can be defined only with respect to a given religion; usually *prophet* connotes inspired utterance of a spontaneous nature, while *priest* suggests established ritual duties. See A. C. Welch, *Kings and Prophets of Israel* (1952; Protestant); Joseph Dheilly, *The Prophets* (tr. 1960; Catholic); A. J. Heschel, *The Prophets* (1962; repr. 2 vol., 1969–1971; Jewish); E. G. Kraeling, *The Prophets* (1969; Jewish).

prophylaxis (prō″fĭlăk'sĭs), measures designed to prevent the occurrence of disease or its dissemination. Some examples of prophylaxis are immunization against serious diseases such as smallpox or diphtheria, QUARANTINE to confine communicable disease, public health measures to insure the safety of food, milk, and water, the care of teeth to offset decay, and restrictions put on persons with such disorders as diabetes or heart disease to prevent the aggravation of these conditions.

Propontis: see MARMARA, SEA OF.

proportion, in mathematics, the equality of two RATIOS. Two pairs of quantities a,b and c,d are in proportion if their ratios a/b and c/d are equal, i.e., if the equation $a/b=c/d$ is true. For example, the lengths of two sides of any triangle and the lengths of the corresponding two sides of any similar (same-shaped) triangle are in proportion, for the ratio of the two sides of the first can be proved to be the same as the ratio of the two sides of the second. The proportion $a/b=c/d$ was formerly written $a:b :: c:d$ and is read as "a is to b as c is to d." In this form it is customary to call b and c the means and a and d the extremes. These terms are used in the statement of the rule—the product of the means equals the product of the extremes. When the proportion is written in equation form, however, this rule is seen to be simply the result of a familiar algebraic operation. Similarly all the other rules stated for proportions become obvious when the proportion is written as an equation and the usual rules of algebra are applied. The special proportion $a/b=b/(a+b)$ is known as the Divine Proportion, or GOLDEN SECTION.

proportional representation: see REPRESENTATION.

propylaeum (prŏpĭlē'əm), in Greek architecture, a monumental entrance to a sacred enclosure, group of buildings, or citadel. A roofed passage terminated by a row of columns at each end formed the usual type. Known examples include those at Athens, Olympia, Eleusis, and Priene. The most splendid example is the **Propylaea** at Athens upon the west end of the Acropolis; its restored remains still stand. Of Pentelic marble, it was built (437–432 B.C.) at the command of Pericles by the architect MNESICLES.

prose [Lat. *prosa oratio*=straightforward, or direct, speech], meaningful and grammatical written or spoken language that does not utilize the metrical structure, word transposition, or rhyme characteristic of poetry or verse; it is, however, raised above the level of lifeless composition or commonplace conversation by the use of balance, rhythm, repetition, and antithesis. In literature, prose is the usual mode of expression in such forms as the novel, short story, essay, letter (epistle), history, biography, sermon, and oration. The earliest European prose extant is that of HERODOTUS (5th cent. B.C.).

Proserpine: see PERSEPHONE.

prosimian: see PRIMATE.

Proskurov: see KHMELNITSKY, city, Ukrainian SSR.

prosody: see VERSIFICATION.

prospecting, search for mineral deposits suitable for MINING. Modern prospecting has replaced earlier methods based on chance or superstition (e.g., use of the divining rod) with others based on a scientific knowledge of modern geology and mineralogy. Surface indications of deposits are confirmed by extensive sampling, e.g., by examination and analysis of material taken from holes drilled at regular intervals. Modern geophysical methods of prospecting use instruments that measure variations in the earth's magnetic or gravitational field, or in the direction, nature, and velocity of waves set up in the ground by underground explosions. Electrical methods employ instruments that indicate relative electrical conductivity between points in the earth's surface or electromotive forces generated by large ore bodies. Geochemical prospecting involves the chemical or spectrographic analysis of soil, plant, and water samples. Scintillometers or geiger counters are used to locate radioactive materials. A portable radioactive source is the basis of the berylometer, useful in locating beryl. Some minerals fluoresce in the presence of ultraviolet light; they are sought in the dark with portable ultraviolet lamps. Aerial photography and airborne instruments have proved useful for preliminary prospecting in unexplored territories.

Prospect Island: see WASHINGTON ISLAND.

Prossnitz: see PROSTĚJOV, Czechoslovakia.

prostaglandin (prŏs″təglăn′dən), any of a group of about a dozen compounds synthesized from fatty acids in mammals as well as in lower animals. Prostaglandins are highly potent substances that are not stored but are produced as needed by cell membranes in virtually every body tissue. Different prostaglandins have been found to raise or lower blood pressure and regulate smooth muscle activity and glandular secretion. One such substance, which stimulates contraction of the uterus, is used clinically to induce labor; another has been in experimental use as a birth control agent. Prostaglandins also control the substances involved in the transmission of nerve impulses, participate in the body's defenses against infection, and regulate the rate of metabolism in various tissues. Several prostaglandins have been shown to induce fever, possibly by participating in the temperature-regulating mechanisms in the hypothalamus; they also play a part in causing inflammation. The fact that aspirin has been shown to inhibit prostaglandin synthesis may account for its usefulness in reducing fever and inflammation. Researchers are looking for new drugs that, like aspirin, inhibit prostaglandin synthesis. Many naturally occurring prostaglandins as well as many artificial forms have been synthesized in the laboratory.

prostate gland, gland that is part of the male REPRODUCTIVE SYSTEM. It is an organ about the size of a chestnut, and consists of glandular and muscular tissue. It is situated below the neck of the bladder, encircling the urethra. The prostate produces a thin, milky, alkaline fluid that is secreted into the urethra at the time of emission of semen, providing an added medium for the life and motility of sperm. It is probable that prostatic fluid enhances fertility since the fluid flowing from the testes and seminal vesicles is acidic and sperm are not optimally mobile unless their medium is relatively alkaline. In men over 50 enlargement of the prostate is common. Sometimes the result is pressure on the urethra and bladder, which interferes with urination, precipitating urinary retention and kidney disease. The usual treatment for an enlarged prostate is surgical removal.

prostatitis (prŏs″tətī′tĭs), inflammation of the PROSTATE GLAND. Acute prostatitis is usually a result of infection in the urinary tract or infection carried by the blood. Symptoms include fever, low back pain, and difficulty or pain in urination; the gland is tender and swollen. Infection, caused by a variety of pathogenic bacteria and certain protozoans, is treated by an appropriate ANTIBIOTIC. Healing is usually complete, but the condition may become chronic if the infecting organism persists.

Prostějov (prô′styĕyôf), Ger. *Prossnitz,* city (1970 pop. 36,923), central Czechoslovakia, in Moravia. A railway junction and trade center of the fertile Haná agricultural region, Prostějov has breweries, distilleries, and industries manufacturing farm machinery, textiles, electrical equipment, clothing, and iron goods. A 16th-century castle dominates the city skyline; other landmarks include a 16th-century Renaissance town hall and a 14th-century church.

prosthesis (prŏs′thĭsĭs): see ARTIFICIAL LIMB.

prosthetic group, non-amino acid portion of a conjugated PROTEIN molecule, which is recovered as a discrete component of many proteins after decomposition into subunits. The prosthetic group may be either organic or inorganic in chemical composition, is more or less tightly associated with the parent protein molecule, and is usually required for biological activity, especially when the prosthetic group is complexed with an ENZYME.

prosthodontics: see DENTISTRY.

prostitution, act of granting sexual access for payment. Although the practice is most commonly conducted by females for males, it may be performed by females or males for either females or males. In ancient times and in some primitive societies, prostitution often had religious connotations—sexual intercourse with temple maidens was an act of worship to the temple deity. In Greece the *hetaerae* [Gr.,=companions or associates] were often women of high social status, but in Rome the *meretrices* were on a low social level and were forced to wear wigs and special garments signifying their trade. In the Middle Ages prostitution flourished, and licensed brothels were a source of revenue to municipalities. As a result of the epidemic of venereal disease in Europe in the 16th cent., serious efforts were begun to control prostitution. Brothels were closed throughout Western and Central Europe during parts of the 16th cent., and stricter punishment was meted out to those engaged in the trade. When these measures failed to stop prostitution and venereal disease continued to claim thousands of victims, many cities began to institute even stricter controls. Berlin required medical inspection in 1700; Paris began to register its prostitutes in 1785. In Great Britain legislation to control the spread of venereal disease was embodied in a series of Contagious Diseases Prevention Acts (1864, 1866, and 1869), requiring periodic medical examination of all prostitutes in military and naval districts and the detention of all those found to be infected. Having failed to control the disease, the acts were repealed in 1886. In 1898 the Vagrancy Act prohibited males from living on the earnings of prostitutes. During the latter part of the 19th cent. efforts were made to control the international traffic in women for the purpose of prostitution. Cooperation on an international scale to stamp out such traffic began in 1899 with a congress in London. This was followed by other conferences in Amsterdam (1901), London (1902), and Paris (1904), which resulted in an international agreement providing for a specific agency in each nation to cooperate in the suppression of the international traffic in women for the purpose of prostitution. In 1919 the League of Nations appointed an official body to gather all facts pertaining to the trafficking of prostitutes, and in 1921 a conference held at Geneva and attended by 34 countries established the Committee on the Traffic in Women and Children (the work of the committee was assumed by the United Nations in 1946). In 1949 a convention for the suppression of prostitution was adopted by the UN General Assembly. In the United States, where prostitution existed in almost every town, it was thought to be closely connected with other crimes. No major effort to stamp out prostitution appeared until about the end of the 19th cent. In 1910 the Mann Act, or White Slave Traffic Act, was passed through the efforts of James Robert MANN; it forbade under high penalty the interstate and international transportation of women for immoral purposes. By 1915 nearly all the states had passed laws regarding the keeping of brothels or profiting in other ways from the earnings of prostitutes. Nevertheless, during World War I there was a great increase in prostitution, accompanied by an increase in venereal disease. In 1941, Congress, spurred by reports of widespread prostitution near military bases and a rise in venereal disease, passed the May Act; the law made it a Federal offense to practice prostitution in areas designated by the Secretaries of the Army and the Navy. On a local basis all states except Nevada have legislation that makes it a crime to operate a house of prostitution. Most states have laws against all forms of prostitution, although they often exempt from prosecution the customers of prostitution. Current legislation both in the United States and elsewhere concerning prostitution has tended to concern itself less with the suppression of the practice of prostitution than with the removal of crimes thought to be connected with it. Outstanding in this field of legislation is a British parliamentary act of 1959 (based on the Wolfenden Report) that treats the entire problem of prostitution and other forms of sexual conduct between consenting adults. It forbids open solicitation by prostitutes, but it permits prostitutes to practice their trade in their own homes. For those wishing to give up prostitution, the teaching of commercial or technical skills at rehabilitation centers is provided. The act also removes voluntary sexual acts between adults from the category of a punishable crime. Other countries, e.g., the Netherlands and West Germany, have emphasized the hygienic aspect in their legislation by rigidly enforcing the periodic medical examination of prostitutes and by providing free compulsory hospitalization for those found infected. This emphasis on regulation rather than suppression has resulted in a marked decline in the incidence of venereal disease and has removed an important cause of the bribery of law enforcement officers. Prostitution in Asia has been a serious problem for many years, mainly due to economic factors (i.e., poverty and unemployment) and custom. In countries such as Burma, Sri Lanka (formerly Ceylon), and Indonesia, the problem is largely confined to urban areas. In India and Japan prostitution is fairly widespread in rural areas as well. In recent years most of these countries have made efforts to control prostitution by enacting legislative measures. Prostitution has been abolished in the People's Republic of China since 1949. Among the many agencies in the United States and elsewhere that have worked for the suppression of prostitution are the Society for the Prevention of Crime, organized in 1877; the Committee of Fourteen (1905); the National Vigilance Association; and the American Social Hygiene Association. See Fernando Henriques, *Prostitution and Society* (3 vol., 1962–68); Hermann Schreiber, *The Oldest Profession* (tr. 1968); G. R. Scott; *Ladies of Vice: A History of Prostitution from Antiquity to the Present Day* (rev. ed. 1968); Charles Winick, *The Lively Commerce* (1971).

protactinium (prō″tăktĭn′ēəm), radioactive chemical element; symbol Pa; at. no. 91; mass no. of most stable isotope 231; m.p. about 1200°C; b.p. unknown; sp. gr. 15.37 (calculated); valence +4 or +5. Protactinium is a shiny silver-gray radioactive metal. It does not tarnish rapidly in air. Known compounds include a chloride ($PaCl_4$), a fluoride (PaF_4), a dioxide (PaO_2), and a pentoxide (Pa_2O_5). Protactinium has 14 isotopes. The most stable is protactinium-231 (half-life about 32,500 years); it is also the most common, being found in nature in uranium ores in about the same abundance as radium. Protactinium has been called the "mother" of actinium, which is formed by the alpha decay of protactinium. The first discovery of protactinium was in 1913 by K. Fajans and O. Göhring, who found the isotope protactinium-234m (half-life 1.2 min), a decay product of uranium-238; they named it brevium for its short life. Protactinium-231 was first identified in 1918 by O. Hahn and L. Meitner and independently by F. Soddy and J. A. Cranston; the name protoactinium was adopted at this time. In 1927, A. V. Grosse prepared the pentoxide, and in 1934 isolated the metal from a purified sample of oxide. The name *protactinium* was adopted in 1949 by the International Union of Pure and Applied Chemistry.

Protagoras (prōtăg′ərəs), c.490–c.421 B.C., Greek philosopher of Abdera, one of the more distinguished SOPHISTS. He taught for a time in Athens, where he was a friend of Pericles and knew Socrates, but was forced to flee because of his professed agnosticism. Protagoras was the author of the famous saying, "Man is the measure of all things." He held that each man is the standard of what is true to himself, that all truth is relative to the individual who holds it and can have no validity beyond him. Thus he denied the possibility of objective knowledge and refused to differentiate between sense and reason. None of his works have survived, but one of Plato's most famous dialogues bears his name.

protection, practice of regulating imports and exports with the purpose of shielding domestic industries from foreign competition. To accomplish that end, certain imports may be excluded entirely, import quotas may be established, or bounties paid on certain exports. The usual method is to impose duties on imports (see TARIFF). Protective duties increase the price of the imported article, making it less attractive to the consumer than the cheaper, domestically produced article. Customs duties were first levied as a tax to create revenue, but statesmen of the 17th and 18th cent. found such duties effective in developing home industries and attracting gold into the nation (see MERCANTILISM). Great Britain became the first nation to abandon protective tariffs after it attained industrial and commercial preeminence in the 19th cent. (see FREE TRADE). In the 20th cent. Britain returned to a system of protection known as imperial preference and later as Commonwealth preference, designed to promote close economic relations between the mother country and former colonial dependencies. The United States, however, followed the policy of protecting "infant industries" from the very beginning of its national history. Since bounties on exports are forbidden in the Constitution, the protective tariff was the chief instrument of such policy. A brief attempt was made in 1913 to lower duties, but after World War I tariff rates were raised to the highest point in U.S. history. Many rates were not merely protective; some were prohibitive and discriminated against the products of certain countries. Although American industries had grown to a position of great strength, it was still held that they needed protection from the cheaper labor and lower costs of production of many foreign countries. To promote freer trade during the Great Depression, President Franklin Delano Roosevelt received authorization in 1934 to negotiate RECIPROCAL TRADE AGREEMENTS, reducing tariff rates on a far-reaching basis through the use of the MOST-FAVORED-NATION CLAUSE. After World War II, the United States played a leading role in the formation (1948) of the General Agreement on Tariffs and Trade (GATT) and in negotiating the Dillon (1962) and Kennedy (1967) Rounds of multilateral tariff reductions. Other important steps in the movement toward freer trade and away from protection have been the formation of the COMMON MARKET in 1957 and the European Free Trade Association in 1959. Although the United States is no longer a high-tariff nation, it still has a number of restrictive import quotas. Japan, one of the world's major industrial nations, also has many import quotas. See L. E. Lewis, *Tariffs: The Case for Protection* (1955); W. M. Corden, *The Theory of Protection* (1971).

protective coloration, coloration or color pattern of an animal that affords it protection from observation either by its predators or by its prey. The most widespread form of protective coloration is called cryptic resemblance, in which various effects that supplement the similarity of color between the animal and its surroundings enable the creature to blend into the background of its habitat. Disruptive coloration, or irregular patches of contrasting colors, serve to distract the observer's eye from the outline of the animal. Thus the stripes of the tiger and the zebra make detection among the jungle grasses more difficult, whereas the leopard's spots are more suited to the mottled light and shade of the low branches from which it drops onto its prey. Many other creatures (e.g., frogs, lizards, and snakes) are dappled, barred, speckled, mottled, or otherwise distinctively marked or colored so that they blend with sand, water, snow, or specific vegetation, depending on their natural habitat. The PIGMENTATION of some animals (e.g., the chameleon and the flounder) changes to resemble different backgrounds. In countershading, the upper surface of the animal is darker than the undersurface and produces the illusion of flatness. Countershading also aids many fish and birds by blending them with the sky or with the upper water surface when viewed from below and with the land or the sea bottom when viewed from above. Some animals undergo a seasonal variation in color: The stoat and the caribou turn from brown in summer to white in winter (when the stoat is known as ermine). A second type of protective coloration, in animals whose coloration or markings distinctly contrast with their habitat, serves as a warning device either to its predators (e.g., the skunk's stripe and the brilliant colors of many venomous snakes and distasteful insects) or to other members of their species in the vicinity (as the white tail patches of the pronghorn and the jack rabbit that are flashed on approaching danger). The adaptation of an organism's appearance to resemble that of another organism that is repugnant or dangerous to a potential predator is called MIMICRY. Coloration may thus be categorized as concealing, revealing, or deceiving. Although these devices are not invariably successful, they do increase the statistical chance for survival of the species. The most widely accepted explanation of the phenomenon of protective coloration is Darwin's theory of natural SELECTION. See H. B. Cott, *Adaptive Coloration in Animals* (rev. ed. 1957); R. A. Carr, *Protective Coloration and Mimicry* (1972).

Protectorate, in English history, name given to the English government from 1653 to 1659. Following the ENGLISH CIVIL WAR and the execution of Charles I, England was declared (1649) a COMMONWEALTH under the rule of the Rump Parliament. In 1653, however, Oliver CROMWELL dissolved the Rump, replacing it with the Nominated, or Barebone's, Parliament (see BAREBONE, PRAISE GOD), and when the latter proved ineffectual, he accepted (Dec., 1653) the constitutional document entitled the Instrument of Government, which had been drawn up by a group of army officers. By its terms, Cromwell assumed the title lord protector of the commonwealth of England, Scotland, and Ireland and agreed to share his power with a council of state and a Parliament of one house. However, although Parliament met regularly, Cromwell's protectorate was a virtual dictatorship resting on the power of the army. After a royalist uprising, he divided (1655) the country into 11 military districts, each under the administration of a major general who enforced the rigidly puritanical laws and collected taxes. Toleration was extended to Jews and all non-Anglican Protestants, but not to Roman Catholics. In 1654, the first of the DUTCH WARS was brought to a close and English sea power turned against Spain. In the Humble Petition and Advice of 1657, Parliament offered Cromwell the throne (which he refused), allowed him to name a successor, and set up an upper house to be chosen by him; but this attempt at constitutional revision had little practical effect on the government. Richard CROMWELL succeeded as lord protector on the death of his father in 1658, but he was unable to control the army and resigned in May, 1659. The Rump was recalled and the Commonwealth resumed, and after a period of chaos Gen. George MONCK recalled the Long Parliament and brought about the RESTORATION of Charles II. See S. R. Gardiner, *History of the Commonwealth and Protectorate* (4 vol., 1903, repr. 1965); Charles Firth, *The Last Years of the Protectorate* (2 vol., 1909; repr. 1964); Ivan Roots, *Commonwealth and Protectorate: The English Civil War and Its Aftermath* (1966).

protectorate, in international law, a relationship in which one state surrenders part of its SOVEREIGNTY to another. The subordinate state is called a protectorate. The term covers a great variety of relations, but typically the protected state gives up all or part of its control over foreign affairs while retaining a large measure of independence in internal matters. The relation may originate when the dominant power threatens or uses force or when the subordinate sees advantages (usually military protection) in the arrangement. A protectorate is distinguishable from the relation of home country and colony, for the protected state retains its sovereignty (though often only nominally), its territory remains distinct from that of the protector, and its citizens do not become nationals of the protecting state. Initially, in most cases, the extent to which the dominant state may interfere in local affairs is governed by treaty; but since a protected state usually has no access to diplomatic channels, it is in a poor position to resist attempts at increased control. Protectorates in connection with large empires probably have existed from earliest times, and there are known instances in Greek and Roman history. In World War I, Great Britain made Egypt a protectorate. Before the abrogation (1934) of the Platt Amendment, Cuba was essentially a protectorate of the United States. Today the number of protectorates has been reduced, although some British possessions such as the British Solomon Islands are classified as protectorates. Trust territories of the United Nations (see TRUSTEESHIP, TERRITORIAL) are distinguishable in that they are being prepared for ultimate independence and also that the control of the dominant state is subject to scrutiny by the Trusteeship Council of the United Nations.

protein, any of the group of highly complex organic compounds found in all living cells and comprising the most abundant class of all biological molecules. Protein comprises approximately 50% of cellular dry weight. Hundreds of protein molecules have been isolated in pure, homogeneous form; many have been crystallized. All contain carbon, hydrogen, and oxygen, and nearly all contain sulfur as well. Some proteins also incorporate molecules of phosphorous, iron, zinc, and copper. Proteins are large molecules with high molecular weights (from about 10,000 for the smallest compounds to more than 1,000,000 for certain multiple forms); they are composed of varying amounts of the same 22 α-AMINO ACIDS, which in the intact protein are united through covalent chemical linkages called PEPTIDE bonds. The large numbers of amino acids, linked together, form linear unbranched polymeric structures called polypeptide chains; such chains may contain hundreds of amino acid residues arranged in specific, invariant order. In no case is a protein a random polymer of varying length. A protein molecule that consists of but a single polypeptide chain is said to be monomeric; proteins made up of more than one polypeptide chain are called oligomeric. Based upon chemical composition, proteins are easily divided into two major classes: simple proteins, which are composed of only amino acids, and conjugated proteins, which are composed of amino acids and additional organic and inorganic groupings termed prosthetic groups. Conjugated proteins include GLYCOPROTEINS, which contain carbohydrates; LIPOPROTEINS, which contain lipids; and nucleoproteins, which contain NUCLEIC ACIDS. Classified by biological function, proteins include the ENZYMES, which are responsible for catalyzing the thousands of chemical reactions of the living cell; KERATIN, elastin, and COLLAGEN, which are important types of structural, or support, proteins; HEMOGLOBIN and other gas transport proteins; ovalbumin, CASEIN, and other nutrient molecules; ANTIBODIES, which are molecules of the immune system (see IMMUNITY); protein HORMONES, which regulate METABOLISM; and proteins that perform mechanical work, such as ACTIN and MYOSIN, the contractile muscle proteins. Every protein molecule has a characteristic three-dimensional shape, or conformation. Fibrous proteins, such as collagen and keratin, consist of polypeptide chains arranged in roughly parallel fashion along a single, linear axis, thus forming tough, usually water-insoluble, fibers or sheets. Globular proteins, e.g., all of the known enzymes, show a tightly folded structural geometry approximating the shape of an ellipsoid or sphere. Because the physiological activity of most proteins is closely linked to their three-dimensional architecture, specific terms are used to refer to different aspects of protein structure. The term primary structure denotes the precise linear sequence of amino acids that constitutes the polypeptide chain of the protein molecule. Automated techniques for amino acid sequencing has made possible the determination of the primary structure of hundreds of proteins. The physical interaction of sequential amino acid subunits results in a so-called secondary structure, which can either be a twisting of the polypeptide chain approximating a linear helix (α-configuration), or a zig-zag pattern (β-configuration). Most globular proteins also undergo extensive folding of the helical chain into a complex three-dimensional geometry designated as tertiary structure. Many protein molecules of this type are easily crystallized and have been examined by X-ray diffraction, a technique that allows the visualization of the precise three-dimensional positioning of atoms in relation to each other in a crystal. The tertiary structure of several protein molecules has been proposed from X-ray diffraction analysis. Two or more polypeptide chains that behave in many ways as a single structural and functional entity are said to exhibit quaternary structure. The separate chains are not linked through covalent chemical bonds, but by weak forces of association. The precise three-dimensional structure of a protein molecule is referred to as its native state and appears, in almost all cases, to be required for proper biological function (especially for the enzymes). If the tertiary or quaternary structure of a protein is altered, e.g., by such physical factors as extremes of temperature, changes in pH, or variations in salt concentration, the protein is said to be denatured; it usually exhibits reduction or loss of biological activity. The cell's ability to synthesize protein is, in essence, the expression of its genetic makeup. The process is best understood in bacteria; many of the events seem similar in higher animals. Protein synthesis is a complex set of chemical reactions that occur in four distinct stages, i.e., activation of the amino acids that ultimately will be joined together by peptide bonds; initiation of the polypeptide chain at a cell organelle known as the ribosome; elongation of the polypeptide by stepwise addition of single amino acids to the chain; and termination of amino acid additions and release of the completed protein from the ribosome. The information for the synthesis of specific amino acid sequences is carried by one type of nucleic acid molecule known as messenger RNA. (For information on protein synthesis, see the article on nucleic acid.) Elucidation of the major features of protein synthesis has provided considerable explanation for the mechanism of action of many widely used antibiotics, especially puromycin, STREPTOMYCIN, CHLORAMPHENICOL, cycloheximide, and TETRACYCLINE. All of these compounds are toxic to bacterial cells because of their ability to interfere with some stage of protein synthesis.

Proterozoic era: see PRECAMBRIAN ERA.

Protesilaus (prō″tĕsĭlā′əs), in Greek mythology, Thessalian prince who was killed in the Trojan War. A prophecy foretold that the first man who touched Trojan soil would be the first to die. When the Greek ships arrived at Troy, Protesilaus leaped ashore and was immediately killed. His wife, Laodamia, mourned his death so excessively that the gods allowed his image to visit her for three hours. When he returned to Hades, she was overcome with grief and took her own life.

Protestant Episcopal Church: see EPISCOPAL CHURCH, PROTESTANT.

Protestantism, form of Christian faith and practice that originated with the principles of the REFORMATION. The term is derived from the *Protestatio* delivered by a minority of delegates against the recess (1529) of the Diet of Speyer, which had forbidden further religious innovation. Since that time the term has been used in many different senses, but not as the official title of any church until it was assumed (1783) by the Protestant Episcopal Church in the United States, the American branch of the Anglican Communion. Protestantism as a general term is now used in contradistinction to the other major Christian faiths, Roman Catholicism and Eastern Orthodoxy. The chief characteristics of original Protestantism were the acceptance of the Bible as the only source of infallible revealed truth, the belief in the universal priesthood of all believers, and the doctrine that a Christian is justified in his relationship to God by faith alone, not by good works or dispensations of the church. There was a tendency to minimize liturgy and to stress preaching by the ministry and the reading of the Bible. Although Protestants rejected asceticism, an elevated standard of personal morality was advanced; in some sects, notably PURITANISM, a high degree of austerity was reached. Their ecclesiastical polity, principally in such forms as episcopacy (government by bishops), Congregationalism, or Presbyterianism, was looked upon by Protestants as a return to the early Christianity described in the New Testament. Two distinct branches of Protestantism grew out of the Reformation. The evangelical churches in Germany and Scandinavia were followers of Martin LUTHER, and the reformed churches in other countries were followers of John CALVIN and Huldreich ZWINGLI. A third major branch, episcopacy, developed in England. Particularly since the OXFORD MOVEMENT of the 19th cent., many Anglicans have rejected the word Protestant because they tend to agree with Roman Catholicism on most doctrinal points, rejecting, however, the primacy of the pope (see ENGLAND, CHURCH OF; EPISCOPAL CHURCH, PROTESTANT; IRELAND, CHURCH OF). In addition, there have been several groups commonly called Protestant but historically preceding the rise of Protestantism (see HUSSITES; LOLLARDRY; WALDENSES). Protestantism has largely been adopted by the peoples of NW Europe and their descendants, excepting the southern Germans, Irish, French, and Belgians; there have been important Protestant minorities in France, Bohemia, Hungary, and Poland. The doctrine that the individual conscience is the valid interpreter of Scripture led to a wide variety of Protestant sects; this fragmentation was further extended by doctrinal disputes within the sects notably over GRACE, predestination, and the sacraments. Certain movements have claimed new revelations of such a nature that they may be said to be Protestant only in name (see AGAPEMONE; MORMONS; NEW JERUSALEM, CHURCH OF THE). Of a fundamentally distinct nature is CHRISTIAN SCIENCE, which as an article of faith repudiates any medical treatment. After the mid-20th cent. a main thrust in Protestantism was toward reunification (see ECUMENICAL MOVEMENT); this was particularly strong in North America. Most Protestant and many Orthodox Eastern churches are allied in federated councils on the local, national, and international levels (see WORLD COUNCIL OF CHURCHES and NATIONAL COUNCIL OF THE CHURCHES OF CHRIST IN THE UNITED STATES OF AMERICA). In the realm of theology, Protestantism saw many developments, particularly after the 18th cent. Under the influence of ROMANTICISM, which stressed the subjective element in religion rather than the revelation of the Bible, the formal systems of early Protestant theology began to dissolve; this doctrine was best expressed by Friedrich SCHLEIERMACHER, who placed religious feeling at the center of Christian life. Along with this came the assertion that the fatherhood of God and the brotherhood of man were the basic themes of Christianity. Later there was a neoorthodox movement, which, under the leadership of Karl BARTH and Reinhold NIEBUHR, sought a return to a theology of revelation; a new school of Bible interpretation as expressed in the work of Rudolf BULTMANN; and a theology, derived in part from EXISTENTIALISM and developed by Paul TILLICH. In the United States, three broad doctrinal positions cut across denominational lines: FUNDAMENTALISM, which stems from the antitheological periods of revivalism in the 18th and 19th cent. (see GREAT AWAKENING) and adheres to a literal interpretation of the Bible and a pietistic morality (fundamentalist groups were relatively successful in the United States in the early 1970s, especially among some young people); liberalism, the heir to the SOCIAL GOSPEL movement, which encourages freer interpretation of theological doctrines and emphasizes church responsibility for social justice; and the neoorthodoxy of Niebuhr and Barth. For some of the major tendencies in Protestantism, see ADVENTISTS; ANABAPTISTS; BAPTISTS; CALVINISM; CONGREGATIONALISM; LUTHERANISM; METHODISM; PENTACOSTALISM; PRESBYTERIANISM; PURITANISM; SPIRITISM; UNITARIANISM. For individual churches in addition to those already mentioned, see BRETHREN; CHRISTIAN CATHOLIC CHURCH; CHRISTIAN REFORMED CHURCH; CHRISTIANS; CHURCHES OF CHRIST; CHURCHES OF GOD IN NORTH AMERICA; DISCIPLES OF CHRIST; PROTESTANT; EVANGELICAL AND REFORMED CHURCH; EVANGELICAL UNITED BRETHREN CHURCH; FRIENDS, RELIGIOUS SOCIETY OF; HUGUENOTS; MENNONITES; MORAVIAN CHURCH; RANTERS; REFORMED CHURCH IN AMERICA; SALVATION ARMY; SCOTLAND, CHURCH OF; SCOTLAND, FREE CHURCH OF; SEVENTH-DAY BAPTISTS; SHAKERS; UNITED CHURCH OF CANADA; UNIVERSALIST CHURCH OF AMERICA. See Paul Tillich, *The Protestant Era* (1948, repr. 1957); John Dillenberger and Claude Welch, *Protestant Christianity* (1954, repr. 1958); J. S. Whale, *The Protestant Tradition* (1955, repr. 1960); R. McA. Brown, *The Spirit of Protestantism* (1961); E. G. Léonard, *A History of Protestantism* (2 vol., tr. 1965–67); Wilhelm Pauck, *The Heritage of the Reformation* (rev. ed. 1968); Roger Mehl, *The Sociology of Protestantism* (tr. 1970); M. E. Marty, *Protestantism* (1972).

Protestant Union, in German history, an alliance of German Protestant leaders of cities and states, founded in 1608 for the avowed purpose of defending the lands, person, and rights of each individual member. Also known as the Evangelical League, it came into being after the Holy Roman emperor attempted (1607) to reestablish Roman Catholicism in DONAUWÖRTH and after a majority of the Reichstag, meeting in Augsburg, declared that renewal of the religious peace of 1555 (see AUGSBURG, PEACE OF) should be conditional on the restoration of all church lands appropriated by the Protestant princes after 1552. A Catholic League, headed by Duke MAXIMILIAN I of Bavaria, was formed shortly afterward. The Protestant Union was weakened from the start by the absence of such powerful Protestant princes as the elector of Saxony, and it never operated very effectively. In 1621, three years after the outbreak of the THIRTY YEARS WAR, the union went out of existence. In French history, the alliance (1573–74) of Huguenot cities, districts, and nobles in the Wars of Religion is also known as the Protestant Union.

Proteus (prō′tēəs, -tyōōs), in Greek mythology, prophetic old man of the sea who tended the seals of Poseidon. He could change himself into any shape he pleased, but if he were nevertheless seized and held, he would foretell the future. The word *protean* is derived from his name.

Protevangelium of James: see PSEUDEPIGRAPHA.

Prothero, Rowland Edmund: see ERNLE, ROWLAND EDMUND PROTHERO, 1ST BARON.

Protić or **Protich, Stojan** (both: stō′yän prō′tĭch), 1857–1923, Serbian politician. A leader of the Radical party, he edited a radical newspaper, served in parliament, and after 1903 held several important cabinet posts in Radical party governments. As minister of the interior at the outbreak (1914) of World War I, he worded the Serbian reply to the Austro-Hungarian ultimatum. He was influential in bringing about the creation (1918) of the kingdom of the Serbs, Croats, and Slovenes (later Yugoslavia). Protić served (1918–19) as first premier of the new state and adopted a conciliatory attitude toward Croatian and Slovene aspirations for autonomy.

Protich, Stojan: see PROTIĆ, STOJAN.

Protista, in some systems of biological CLASSIFICATION, a kingdom comprising the unicellular and simple multicellular organisms, some of which cannot be definitely regarded as plants or animals. The boundaries of this kingdom overlap those of the plant and animal kingdoms. Included in the Protista are the protozoans, algae, fungi, and bacteria. The bacteria and blue-green algae, which lack well-defined cell nuclei, are sometimes placed in a separate kingdom, the Monera.

protoactinium: see PROTACTINIUM.

protocol (prō′təkŏl), term referring to rules governing diplomatic conduct or to a variety of written instruments. Examples of the latter are authenticated minutes of international conferences; preliminary agreements, or statements of principle, which eventuate in a formal treaty; and agreements that do not require ratification. Sometimes the term *protocol* is applied to an agreement that in all essentials of form or content is similar to a treaty; an example of this was the Geneva Protocol approved by the Assembly of the League of Nations in 1924, which branded aggressive war an international crime. It provided that no signatory would engage in war with other signatories who observed their international obligations. Differences that might lead to war were to be referred in appropriate cases to the Council of the League of Nations, to the World Court, or to arbitration committees. Signatories were not to mobilize while awaiting settlement of disputes. Nations that refused arbitration or rejected arbitral awards and went to war were to be branded aggressors. The council might subject them to economic sanctions, and they should be made to bear the costs of the attacked country but not made to cede any of their territory. Finally, signatories were to participate in an international disarmament conference. The protocol was supported by most nations, but British refusal to support it in the League Council prevented it from coming into force. The LOCARNO PACT and the KELLOGG-BRIAND PACT were later agreements having the general tenor of the Geneva Protocol. Diplomatic protocol is the code of international courtesy governing the conduct of those in the DIPLOMATIC SERVICE or otherwise engaged in international relations. It is basically concerned with procedural matters and precedence among diplomats. Each office of foreign affairs (or equivalent body) has an official in charge of protocol. See J. T. Shotwell, *Plans and Protocols to End War* (1925); J. R. Wood, *Diplomatic Ceremonial and Protocol* (1970).

Protocols of the Elders of Zion, a fraudulent document that reported the alleged proceedings of a conference of Jews in the late 19th cent., at which they discussed plans to overthrow Christianity through subversion and sabotage and to control the world. The *Protocols* first appeared in their entirety in Russia in 1905. They were widely disseminated in the 1920s and became a classic defense for anti-Semitism. First published in the United States in 1920, the *Protocols* were championed by Henry Ford in his newspaper, the Dearborn *Independent,* and cited throughout the 1930s by some anti-Roosevelt and fascist groups. As early as 1921, the English journalist Philip Graves exposed the similarity between the *Protocols* and a political satire by Maurice Joly, *Dialogue aux enfers entre Machiavel et Montesquieu* (1864). Subsequent investigation showed the original document to be a forgery written by members of the Russian secret police. See Herman Bernstein, *The Truth About the "Protocols of the Elders of Zion"* (1935, repr. 1972); Norman Cohn, *Warrant for Genocide* (1967, repr. 1970).

Protogenes (prōtŏj′ənēz), fl. c.300 B.C., one of the most celebrated Greek painters of Rhodes and Athens. Apelles is said to have been the first to recognize the talents of Protogenes, then 50 years old and known only as a painter of decorations for ships. For 20 years he enjoyed a reputation second only to that of Apelles. Ancient writers, notably Pliny the Elder, record that his works were held in high esteem by the Rhodesians. His best-known work was the *Ialysus,* which was removed by Vespasian to Rome where it perished in the burning of the Temple of Peace.

proton, elementary particle having a single positive electrical charge and constituting the nucleus of the ordinary hydrogen atom. The positive charge of the nucleus of any atom is due to its protons. Every atomic nucleus contains one or more protons; the number of protons, called the atomic number, is different for every element (see PERIODIC TABLE). The mass of the proton is about 1,840 times the mass of the electron and slightly less than the mass of the NEUTRON. The total number of nucleons, as protons and neutrons are collectively called, in any nucleus is the mass number of the nucleus. The existence of the nucleus was postulated by Ernest Rutherford in 1911 to explain his experiments on the scattering of alpha particles; in 1919 he discovered the proton as a product of the disintegration of the atomic nucleus. The proton and the neutron are regarded as two aspects or states of a single entity, the nucleon. This theory was confirmed by Robert Hofstadter, whose experiments indicated also that the proton and neutron are surrounded by clouds of virtual PIONS whose continual exchange is responsible for the FORCE binding protons and neutrons together in a nucleus. Owing to the emission of pions, the proton spends part of its time as a neutron, and vice versa. The proton is the lightest of the BARYON class of ELEMENTARY PARTICLES. Its ANTIPARTICLE, the antiproton, was discovered in 1955; it has the same mass as the proton but a unit negative charge and opposite magnetic moment. Protons are frequently used in a PARTICLE ACCELERATOR as either the bombarding (accelerated) particle, the target nucleus, or both.

protonation (prō'tənā"shən), in chemistry, addition of a PROTON to an atom, molecule, or ion. The proton is the nucleus of the HYDROGEN atom; the positive hydrogen ion, H^+, consists of a single proton. An example of protonation is the formation of the AMMONIUM GROUP NH_4^+ from ammonia, NH_3. Protonation often occurs in the reaction of an acid with a base to form a salt (see ACIDS AND BASES; SALTS). Protonation differs from HYDROGENATION in that during protonation a change in charge of the protonated species occurs, whereas the charge is unaffected during hydrogenation.

proton-proton cycle: see NUCLEOSYNTHESIS.

protoplanet theory: see SOLAR SYSTEM.

protoplasm, fundamental material of which all living things are composed. It was studied by a number of early scientists, especially by Félix Dujardin, J. E. Purkinje, M. J. S. Schultze, and Hugo von Mohl (who is credited with introducing the name), all working in the 19th cent. Protoplasm exists in all plants and animals in the small units called CELLS, and it is always enclosed by a thin surface called a plasma membrane, actually a part of the protoplasm, that controls the passage of materials into and out of the cell. Under a microscope protoplasm has a granular appearance; the granules exhibit the irregular motion known as BROWNIAN MOVEMENT, typical of colloids. Protoplasm is an aqueous colloidal suspension of these visible granules and globules and of submicroscopic particles. It has the essential properties of fluidity, elasticity, and tensile strength. The chief component of protoplasm is water, which comprises from 85% to 90% by weight of the average cell. Inorganic salts (forming 1%–1.5% by weight of protoplasm) are dissolved in the water. The organic constituents of protoplasm include proteins (7%–10% by weight), fatty substances (1%–2%) and other organic substances (1%–1.5%) including carbohydrates. The corresponding molecular ratio is approximately 18,000 water molecules for every molecule of protein and every 100 molecules of inorganic substances. The four elements oxygen, hydrogen, carbon, and nitrogen make up about 99% of protoplasm; following these in importance as constituents of living material are the elements sulfur, phosphorus, potassium, iron, and magnesium. Although the proportion of the chemical elements in protoplasm is essentially the same in all forms of life, there are differences in the qualities and chemical characteristics of the protoplasm of different species and even of different cells in the same multicellular animal or plant. The protoplasm in both plant and animal cells is distinguishable as a dense portion forming the rounded or ovoid nucleus of the cell and a less dense portion, the cytoplasm. (A distinct nucleus is lacking in bacteria and in some other minute cells and also in mature red blood corpuscles in humans.) In most plant cells the cytoplasm forms a relatively thin layer between the vacuoles (saclike structures containing cell sap) and the cell wall, which is composed of a celluloselike rather than a protoplasmic substance; the cytoplasm also surrounds the nucleus and often extends through the cell in strands radiating from the region of the nucleus. In animal cells, in which vacuoles are much less common, the cytoplasm forms the bulk of the cell. Since protoplasm is living matter, it displays the general properties associated with life, i.e., it possesses irritability (the capacity to respond to stimuli) and the ability to perform the essential physiological functions. In some forms of life (e.g., protozoans) the protoplasm of the single cell is capable of performing all the life functions, e.g., locomotion, ingestion of food, digestion, absorption, circulation, excretion, and reproduction. In multicellular animals and plants, in which specialized cells are united to form tissues adapted to special functions, the protoplasm is particularly fitted for those functions, e.g., nerve-cell protoplasm for receiving and conveying stimuli, and muscle cells for contractility. See E. D. P. de Robertis et al., *General Cytology* (4th ed., 1969).

Protopopov, Aleksandr Dmitreyevich (əlyĭksän'-dər dəmē'trēyəvĭch prətəpô'pəf), 1866–1918, Russian public official. Long active in ZEMSTVO affairs, and a member of the Octobrist party, which favored a constitutional monarchy, he served in the third and fourth Dumas and was vice president of the Duma from 1914. His friendship with RASPUTIN, however, brought his appointment (Sept., 1916) as minister of the interior. Although Protopopov became nearly insane, the czarina blocked all efforts to have him removed. When the February Revolution of 1917 overthrew the government, he was arrested by the provisional government and was later shot.

Protozoa, large, diverse phylum of microscopic or near-microscopic animals that live as single cells or in simple colonies and that show no differentiation into tissues. Most are motile and most ingest food, as do other animals, rather than produce it themselves, as do plants. The 15,000 species are cosmopolitan in distribution; they are found in fresh water and at all depths in the ocean; some live in soil. Some are parasites in the bodies of humans or other animals, sometimes causing diseases. The various forms have in common a unicellular structure consisting of a mass of cytoplasm with one or more nuclei (see CELL). Like all cells, they are bounded by a thin cell membrane; in addition, most have a tough outer membrane called a pellicle, which maintains their form. Despite their small size and lack of organization into multicellular systems, protozoans carry on all the metabolic functions of higher animals. Organelles, or intracellular structures, carry out a variety of functions, such as digestion, excretion, respiration, and coordination of movement; some protozoans are much more complex in their internal structure than are the cells of multicellular animals. Some have complex digestive systems and feed on large food particles, such as other microorganisms. The food is digested by means of enzymes and the wastes transported to the cell surface or stored in vacuoles (bubblelike spaces in the cytoplasm). Others have no digestive system and absorb dissolved organic matter through the cell membrane. Respiration is accomplished by the diffusion of dissolved gases through the cell membrane. Oxygen diffuses into the cell, where it oxidizes food molecules, producing energy and the organic molecules used for the building and maintenance of the cell. Carbon dioxide and water, the waste products of this oxidation, diffuse out of the cell. Reproduction is usually asexual, occurring mostly by cell division, or binary fission; some forms reproduce asexually by budding or by the formation of spores (reproductive cells that give rise to a new organism without fertilization). In certain groups sexual reproduction sometimes also occurs. In these instances, cell division is preceded by the fusion of two individuals or, in ciliates, by conjugation and exchange of nuclear material. The phylum is commonly divided into four subphyla: flagellates, ameboid forms, spore formers, and ciliates. The flagellates (Mastigophora) have oval bodies with one or more flagella—whiplike extensions of the cell. They swim by means of lashing motions of the flagella. In colonial flagellates, such as the spherical *Volvox*, the component cells coordinate the movements of their flagella in swimming. The dinoflagellates float on the surface of the ocean, sometimes imparting a reddish cast to the water, a phenomenon known as the red tide; several species are luminescent. The phytoflagellates may be classified either as animals or as plants (simple ALGAE); they include many forms that are capable of photosynthesis (such as *Volvox*), as well as closely related forms that are not. The well-known phytoflagellate *Euglena* normally carries on photosynthesis but in the absence of light will absorb dissolved food from its surroundings. Parasitic flagellates include the TRYPANOSOMES, which cause African sleeping sickness and Chagas's disease. Certain harmless flagellates sometimes infest drinking water, imparting to it a fishy taste and odor. The ameboid protozoans (Sarcodina) are all solitary cells that move and capture food by means of pseudopods, flowing temporary extensions of the cytoplasm and body wall; Sarcodina include the naked forms called AMEBAS and forms with perforated shells through which pseudopods may be extended. Best known of the shelled forms are the FORAMINIFERANS, with calcium carbonate shells, and the radiolarians, with silica or strontium sulfate shells. The spore formers (Sporozoa) are exclusively parasitic protozoans, responsible for many human diseases. Their complex life cycles may include both sexual and asexual reproduction and usually involve more than one host. They are immotile in their adult forms. MALARIA is caused by the sporozoan *Plasmodium*, which alternates between humans and mosquitos. The ciliates (Ciliophora) are the largest and most complex protozoans. Each has two nuclei and a variety of organelles, including a mouth and a gullet. They swim by the coordinated beating of their cilia—short, hairlike projections that cover the cell surface. The ciliates include the slipper-shaped paramecium and the trumpet-shaped stentor. The suctorians are sessile ciliates that suck out the protoplasm of their prey through tentacles. Because the distinction between animals and plants is not sharp at the unicellular level of organization, the protozoans and the lower plants (algae and fungi) are sometimes classified together in a third kingdom, the PROTISTA. The Protozoa may therefore be regarded either as a phylum of unicellular animals (some of which display plantlike characteristics) or as a phylum of mostly animallike protists.

Proudhon, Pierre Joseph (pyĕr zhôzĕf' proo-dhôN'), 1809–65, French social theorist. Of a poor family, Proudhon won an education through scholarships. Much of his later life was spent in poverty. He achieved prominence through his pamphlet *What Is Property?* (1840, tr. 1876), in which he condemned the abuses of private property and embraced anarchism. He also edited radical journals. After the Revolution of 1848, he was elected a member of the constituent assembly; at that time he tried unsuccessfully to establish a national bank for reorganization of credit in the interest of the workers. As a replacement for the existing social and political order, Proudhon developed a theory of "mutualism," by which small, loosely federated groups would bargain with each other over economic and political matters within the framework of a consensus on fundamental principles. He hoped that man's ethical progress would eventually make government unnecessary and rejected the use of force to impose any system. Proudhon left a great mass of literature, which influenced the French syndicalist movement. Among the most important of his books are *System of Economic Contradictions; or The Philosophy of Poverty* (1846; tr. of Vol. I, 1888) and *De la justice dans la révolution et dans l'église* [of justice in the revolution and in the church] (3 vol., 1858). See his selected writings, ed. by Stewart Edwards (1970); biography by George Woodcock (1956, repr. 1969); Alan Ritter, *The Political Thought of Pierre-Joseph Proudhon* (1969); C. M. Hall, *The Sociology of Pierre-Joseph Proudhon* (1971); R. L. Hoffman, *Revolutionary Justice* (1972).

Proust, Joseph Louis (zhôzĕf' lwē proost), 1754–1826, French chemist. He was professor of chemistry at the artillery school in Segovia, Spain, and director of the laboratory of Charles IV at Madrid from 1789. He returned to France c.1806. He discovered grape sugar and established the law of definite proportions (sometimes known as Proust's law), which states that in any compound the elements are present in a fixed proportion by weight.

Proust, Marcel (märsĕl'), 1871–1922, French novelist, b. Paris. He is one of the great literary figures of the modern age. Born to wealthy bourgeois parents, he suffered delicate health as a child and was carefully ministered to by his mother. As a young man he ambitiously mingled in high Parisian society and wrote his unpromising first work, *Les Plaisirs et les jours* (1896, tr. *Pleasures and Regrets*, 1948). Troubled by asthma and by growing pessimism, as well as by the deaths of his parents, he increasingly withdrew from external life and after 1907 lived mainly in a cork-lined room, working at night on his monumental cyclic novel, *À la recherche du temps perdu* (16 vol., 1913–27, tr. *Remembrance of Things Past*, 1922–32). The first of the series, *Du côté de chez Swann* (1913, tr. *Swann's Way*, 1928) went unnoticed, but the second, *À l'ombre des jeunes filles en fleurs* (1919, tr. *Within a Budding Grove*, 1919), was awarded the Goncourt Prize. Proust's semiautobiographical novel cycle is superficially concerned with its hero's development through childhood and through youthful love affairs to the point of commitment to literary endeavor. It is less a story than an interior monologue. Discursive, but alive with brilliant metaphor and sense imagery, the work is rich in psychological, philosophical, and sociological understanding. A vital theme is the link between external and internal reality found in time and memory, to which Proust sees man's strivings subjugated—time mocks man's intelligence and his endeavors; memory synthesizes yet distorts past experience. Most experience causes inner pain, and the objects of man's desires are the chief causes of his suffering. In Proust's scheme man is isolated, society is false and ruled by snobbery, and artistic endeavor is raised to a religion and is superior to nature. Proust's ability to interpret man's innermost experience in terms of such eternal forces as time and death created a profound and protean world view. Much of his correspondence has been published, as has his draft of an early novel, *Jean Santeuil* (1952, tr. 1955), and *Contre Sainte-Beuve* (1954, tr. *On Art and Literature, 1896-1919,* 1958). See biographies by A. Maurois (1950), R. H. Barker (1958), L. Bersani (1965), G. Brée (1966), and G. D. Painter (Vol. I, 1959 and Vol. II, 1965); studies by M. Hindus (1954), S. Beckett (1957), W. A. Strauss (1957), W. S. Bell (1962), P. Quennell (1971), S. L. Wolitz (1971), and G. Deleuze (1972); M. Hindus, *Reader's Guide to Marcel Proust* (1962).

Prout, Father: see MAHONY, FRANCIS SYLVESTER.

Prout, William, 1785-1850, English chemist and physician. Prout's hypothesis, advanced in 1815-16, suggested that atomic weights of elements are multiples of that of hydrogen and that elements are formed by a condensation or grouping of hydrogen atoms. Later work on the determination of atomic weights showed that part of the hypothesis does, in general, apply. Prout won contemporary renown for his demonstration (1823) of the presence of free hydrochloric acid in the gastric juice of the stomach. He wrote many papers on the chemistry of the blood and urine.

Provençal (prôväNsäl'), member of the Romance group of the Italic subfamily of the Indo-European family of languages (see ROMANCE LANGUAGES). The language label *Provençal* is often restricted in its reference to the dialects of Provence, a region of SE France, but it can be extended to include other related dialects of S France. In its latter, broader sense, Provençal is spoken today, usually along with French, by some 9 or 10 million people in France; however, it has no official status in that country. In the Middle Ages, Provençal, also called *langue d'oc* (see LANGUE D'OC AND LANGUE D'OÏL), became important as the medium of the great literature of the TROUBADOURS, who developed it into a standard local Romance language. After the Albigensian Crusade (see under ALBIGENSES) weakened S France, Provençal culture declined and in time the Provençal language was wholly replaced by French as the standard language of France. In the 19th cent. an unsuccessful movement arose to bring back the former glory of Provençal by restoring it as the literary and regional tongue of S France. See Daniel C. Haskell, *Provençal Literature and Language* (1925).

Provençal literature, vernacular literature of S France. Provençal, or Occitan, as the language is now often called, appears to have been the first vernacular tongue used in French commerce and literature. Provençal literature, originating in Limousin, flourished (11th-12th cent.) in the whole area of S France, where LANGUE D'OC was spoken and medieval civilization flowered. Elements drawn from a Latin heritage, from the Arabic civilization to the south, and from Christian concepts were combined to create a new and striking lyric poetry. From Latin models came the bases for imagery, rhetoric, and metrics; from Arabic poetry may have been drawn ideas of service, secret love, and spiritualization of passion, and to the latter source Christian beliefs probably contributed. Idealization of love emerged in Provençal poetry as a concept of humble (and often unrewarded) service of a lady worshiped from afar; this was a new and important theme in Western literature. Also significant was the great mastery of form, which became increasingly complex in the 13th cent. Although texts are extant from 1000, the first known troubadour was William IX, Duke of Aquitaine (c.1080-1127). He and his descendants, Eleanor of Aquitaine and her son King Richard I of England, were famous patrons of poetry. Among the great Provençal poets of the 12th cent. were Bernard de Ventadour, BERTRAND DE BORN, Arnaud Daniel (admired by both Dante and Petrarch), Geraut de Borniel, and Jaufré Rudel. The outstanding work of the period is the epic *Girart de Roussillon.* Although Provençal poetry declined with the waning of the 13th cent., it exerted enormous influence on poets throughout Western Europe. The Albigensian Crusade (1209-29) and the introduction of the Inquisition resulted in the flight of many troubadours to Spain and Italy. But important works remain from the 13th cent., including *Jaufré,* an Arthurian romance; *Flamenca,* a masterly romance of manners; and biographies of the troubadours. An academy, established (1324) at Toulouse, published (c.1345) a book of rules for poetry. Provençal literature continued to live during the next centuries, with its most significant output in the popular genres: drama, carols, and burlesques. The 19th-century romantic interest in the Middle Ages and in national literatures inspired a revival, led by Joseph Roumanille (1818-91). An association of Provençal poets, the Félibrige, was formed (1854) to establish a common orthography for the various dialects and to purify and enrich the vocabulary. Frédéric MISTRAL won international acclaim for his national epic *Mirèio* (1859). Other fine works include those of Théodore Aubanel (1829-86). Literary activity in the language continues today at a lesser pace. See R. T. Hill and T. G. Burgin, *Anthology of the Provençal Troubadours* (2 vol., 2d rev. ed. 1973).

Provence (prôväNs'), region and former province, SE France. It now encompasses Var, Vaucluse, and Bouches-du-Rhône depts. and (in part) Alpes-de-Haute-Provence and Alpes-Maritimes depts. Nice, Marseilles, Toulon, Avignon, Arles, and Aix-en-Provence (the historic capital) are the chief cities. The fertile valley of the Rhône and the French Riviera produce fruits and vegetables (citrus fruits, olive oil, mulberry trees). Cattle are raised in the Camargue. The startling scenery has inspired such painters as Cézanne. There are many old towns and historic remains. The coastal strip was settled c.600 B.C. by Greeks; Phoenician merchants also settled there, and in the 2d cent. B.C. the Romans established colonies. A part of Narbonensis (see GAUL), Provence was the oldest of the Roman possessions beyond the Alps; it took its name from *Provincia,* meaning province. Christianity was implanted very early, and by the 4th cent. the area was a haven for monasteries. It was invaded by the Visigoths (5th cent.), the Franks (6th cent.), and the Arabs (8th cent.), who were repelled by Charles Martel. But Roman institutions continued to have a profound cultural influence. The Provençal language was the standard literary idiom throughout S France in the Middle Ages and is used by some Provençal writers today (see LANGUE D'OC AND LANGUE D'OÏL; PROVENÇAL LITERATURE). In 879 the count of Arles established the kingdom of Cisjurane Burgundy, or Provence, which in 933 was united with Transjurane Burgundy to form the Kingdom of Arles (see ARLES, KINGDOM OF). The major part of Provence, held by the house of ARAGÓN, passed (1246) to the ANGEVIN dynasty of Naples through marriage, and under the Angevins the towns became virtually independent republics. King René left Provence to his nephew, Charles of Maine, who left it to the French crown (1486). ORANGE was added in 1672; Avignon and the Comtat Venaissin in 1791; and Nice and Menton in 1860.

proverb, short statement of wisdom or advice that has passed into general use. More homely than aphorisms, proverbs generally refer to common experience and are often expressed in metaphor, alliteration, or rhyme, e.g., "A bird in the hand is worth two in the bush," "When the cat's away, the mice will play." Proverbs abound in the Old Testament, in early Greek and Roman literature, and in the gnomic verse of the Anglo-Saxons. In medieval literature proverbs serve in homilies and *exempla* to drive home moral lessons and, as in the works of Chaucer, to add a humorous note. To the traditional folk sayings the Renaissance writers added the more literary proverbs from the classics; the most famous collection was *Adagia* by Erasmus (1500). Proverbs were extremely popular among the Elizabethans, the most famous collections being those of John Heywood (1549?) and Florio (1578). Although the popularity of proverbs declined in the 18th cent., they have become a subject for research and classification in more modern times. There is a famous collection by William Hazlitt (1869). Noted 20th-century compilations include *The Book of Proverbs* (1965), ed. by Paul Rosenzweig, and *The Oxford Dictionary of English Proverbs* (1970), ed. by W. G. Smith and F. P. Wilson.

Proverbs, book of the Old Testament, in the 20th place in the Authorized Version. It is a collection of sayings, many of them moral maxims, in no special order. The teaching is of a practical nature; it is not nationalistic, but is individual and universal. There are eight divisions, some having traditional ascriptions: first, to Solomon, 1-9; second, also to Solomon, 10-22.16; third, 22.17-24.22; fourth, 24.23-34; fifth, to Solomon, copied by the men of King Hezekiah, 25-29; sixth, to Agur, unknown, 30; seventh, to King Lemuel, unknown, 31.1-9; eighth, an acrostic in praise of a virtuous woman, 31.10-31. The book is an early example of a type of literature popular among the Jews of postexilic times, wisdom literature (see WISDOM); the praise of abstract wisdom (1.20-33; 8) is typical of such writing. The dating of Proverbs is difficult. Although tradition attributes Proverbs to Solomon, the book is probably a collection of various origins, dating from the 9th-2d cent. B.C. See R. B. Y. Scott, *Proverbs* (1965).

Providence, city (1970 pop. 179,116), state capital and seat of Providence co., NE R.I., a port at the head of Providence Bay; founded by Roger Williams 1636, inc. as a city 1832. The largest city in the state and the second largest in New England, it is a port of entry and a major trading center. The bay receives the Seekonk and other rivers, opens into Narragansett Bay, and forms an excellent harbor from which oil and coal are shipped. Providence is widely known as a silverware- and jewelry-manufacturing center. Textiles, machinery, metal products, electronic equipment, rubber goods, and machine tools are also made, and there are printing and publishing enterprises. Roger Williams chose this site in 1636 after he was exiled from Massachusetts. He secured title to the land from Narragansett chiefs and named the place in gratitude for "God's merciful providence." The settlement grew as a refuge for religious dissenters. Many of its buildings were burned in King Philip's War (1675-76). Prosperity came in the 18th cent. with foreign commerce, especially trade in Negro slaves and rum, and after the Revolution industrial development was rapid. The Brown brothers, John, Nicholas, and Moses, played leading roles in the growth of the town, prospering in foreign trade and fostering the textile and other industries. In 1842, Thomas W. Dorr led a rebellion that collapsed after an abortive assault on the armory there. The city became sole capital of Rhode Island in 1900 (Newport had been joint capital until then). In 1901 the state legislature began to meet in the impressive marble-domed capitol designed by McKim, Mead, and White. Providence is the seat of the noted Rhode Island School of Design, some of whose work is related to the city's famous silverware and jewelry industry; and of Brown Univ., Catholic Teachers College, Johnson and Wales College, Providence College, Rhode Island College, and a junior college. It has several fine libraries, including the John Carter Brown Library of Brown Univ. and the Atheneum (1753), one of the oldest libraries in the United States. Among the city's many historic structures are the old statehouse (where the general assembly met 1762-1900; now a courthouse), the old market building (1773), Stephen Hopkins House (c.1755), John Brown House (1786), and the First Baptist Meetinghouse (1775; the congregation was organized in 1638). The city has monuments to Oliver Hazard Perry (1928) and Nathanael Greene (1931). On Prospect Terrace is Leo Friedlander's heroic statue of Roger Williams (1939). Another memorial to the founder is in Roger Williams Park, which contains a museum of natural history and a natural amphitheater. Providence suffered severely in hurricanes in 1938 and 1954. A hurricane barrier was completed in 1966. See J. H. Cady, *The Civic and Architectural Development of Providence, 1635-1950* (1957); G. F. Kimball, *Providence in Colonial Times* (1912, repr. 1972).

Provincetown, resort town (1970 pop. 2,911), Barnstable co., SE Mass., on the tip of Cape Cod, with a good harbor on Cape Cod Bay; inc. 1727. The principal industries are tourism and fishing. The Pilgrims landed there in 1620 and stayed about a month before moving on to Plymouth. Permanent settlement was not made until c.1700. Fishing was always the town's staple industry, but whaling, salt making, rum-running, and smuggling were also practiced. In the 20th cent. the town gained fame as a resort favored particularly by artists. Points of interest include the granite Pilgrim Monument and Museum (1910), on a hill overlooking the sea; the Cape Cod National Seashore's visitor center; and the Provincetown Playhouse. An air force radar station is in nearby North Truro. See M. M. H. Vorse, *Time and the Town* (1942).

Provincetown Players, American theatrical company that first introduced the plays of Eugene O'Neill. The company opened with his *Bound East for Cardiff* at the Wharf Theatre, Provincetown, on Cape Cod in 1916 and later worked in New York City in conjunction with the Greenwich Village Theatre under the auspices of Robert Edmond Jones, Kenneth Macgowan, and O'Neill. By producing plays that were generally considered noncommercial, the company gave unrecognized dramatists the opportunity to experiment with new ideas. The group disbanded in 1929 but through its efforts, together with those of the Washington Square Players, a native American theater was realized. Among the well-known writers to be associated with the Provincetown Players were Edna St. Vincent Millay and Djuna Barnes. See Helen Deutsch and Stella Hanau, *The Provincetown* (1931).

Province Wellesley: see PINANG, Malaysia.

Provins (prôvăN'), town (1968 pop. 11,869), Seine-et-Marne dept., N central France. It is a tourist and commercial center. Built by the Romans on a rocky height, it was (11th–13th cent.) a prosperous trade hub and the site of one of the great fairs of CHAMPAGNE. The picturesque upper town has preserved its ramparts dating from the 12th to the 14th cent. There is also a 12th-century castle keep (*tour de Cesar*) and the fine Church of St. Quiriace (begun 1160).

Provisions of Oxford, 1258, a scheme of governmental reform forced upon HENRY III of England by his barons. In 1258 a group of barons, angered by the king's Sicilian adventure and the expenditures it entailed, compelled Henry to accept the appointment of a committee of 24 nobles, half of whom were to be chosen by the king, for the purpose of drafting a scheme of constitutional reform. Under the leadership of Simon de MONTFORT, earl of Leicester, the plan was drawn up at Oxford in June, 1258. It provided for a council of 15 members to advise the king and to meet three times a year to consult with representatives of the realm. Committees were chosen by an involved electoral system to keep check upon the various branches of the government. Local administrative reforms were instituted and an effort made to limit the taxing power of the king. The committee of 24 completed their work the following year by drawing up an enlarged version of the Provisions of Oxford known as the Provisions of Westminster. The new document provided for additional inheritance and taxation reforms. Divisions among the barons themselves enabled Henry to repudiate the provisions, with papal sanction, in 1261. There followed a period of strife known as the BARONS' WAR (1263–67), which terminated in a victory for the king. The clauses of the provisions that limited monarchical authority were then annulled, but the legal clauses of the Provisions of Westminster were reaffirmed in the Statute of Marlborough (1267).

Provo (prō'vō), city (1970 pop. 53,131), seat of Utah co., N central Utah, on the Provo River near Utah Lake; inc. 1851. It is a distribution, processing, and manufacturing center in an extensive mining and irrigated farm and fruit area. A major source of employment is a large steel mill nearby. Provo was settled by Mormons in 1849 and successfully defended against Indians in a war from 1865 to 1868. Railroad connections from Salt Lake City (1873) and Scofield (1878) made it a shipping point for the region's mines. The seat of Brigham Young Univ., Provo also has a state mental hospital. Near the city are peaks of the Wasatch Range.

Provo, river, c.70 mi (110 km) long, rising in the Uinta Mts., NE Utah, and flowing SW past Provo to Utah Lake. It was early used for irrigation, but after Utah Lake was badly depleted in the 1930s, the Bureau of Reclamation rehabilitated the old irrigation installations and built new ones centering on the Provo River. The project also gets water from the Weber River by a canal (built 1929–30; enlarged 1941–47) and from the Duchesne River, a tributary of the Green River, by a tunnel (completed 1942) across the mountain divide. The water is used to irrigate the valley of Utah Lake and to supply the needs of the towns there; in addition, Salt Lake City is served by the 42-mi-long (68-km) Salt Lake Aqueduct (completed 1951). The Deer Creek Dam (completed 1941) is the chief dam on the Provo River; it impounds a large reservoir, and its power plant has a 4,950-kw capacity.

Provoost, Samuel (prō'vōst), 1742–1815, first Episcopal bishop of New York, b. New York City, grad. King's College (now Columbia Univ.), 1758. He studied at Cambridge and in 1766 was ordained. He was appointed assistant minister of Trinity parish in New York City. Because of his sympathy with the colonial cause, Provoost was forced (1771) to resign from Trinity but returned as rector in 1784. Created bishop of New York (1786), he was consecrated (1787) in England. He served as chaplain to the Continental Congress (1785) and to the U.S. Senate (1789). See J. G. Wilson, *Samuel Provoost* (1887).

Proxima Centauri: see ALPHA CENTAURI.

Proxmire, William (Edward William Proxmire), 1915–, U.S. Senator (1957–), b. Lake Forest, Ill. He worked in army counterintelligence during World War II and later entered politics, serving (1951–52) as a Democrat in the Wisconsin state assembly. After three unsuccessful attempts at the governorship, he was elected (1957) to the Senate to fill the vacancy created by the death of Joseph McCarthy. Considered a maverick by his Senate colleagues, Proxmire opposed wasteful government spending, especially by the military. He led (1970–71) the successful fight in Congress against financing the supersonic transport plane. Proxmire wrote *Report from Wasteland* (1970) and *Uncle Sam—the Last of the Bigtime Spenders* (1972). See biography by J. G. Sykes (1972).

Prudentius (Aurelius Clemens Prudentius) (proŏdĕn'shəs), b. 348, Christian Latin poet, b. Spain. He wrote a number of hymns, occasional Christian lyrics, and poems on saints. Although he held a high place at the Roman court, he eventually retired to devote himself to religion. See B. M. Peebles, *The Poet Prudentius* (1951).

Prudhoe Bay, inlet of the Arctic Ocean, N Alaska, in the Alaska North Slope region, east of the Colville River delta. In 1968 one of the largest oil reserves in North America was discovered there. Harsh climate and terrain make the extraction and shipment of the oil difficult.

Prud'hon, Pierre Paul (pyĕr pôl prüdôN'), 1758–1823, French painter; 13th child of a Cluny stonemason. He gained recognition in 1796 with his *Truth Descending from the Heavens Led by Wisdom* (Louvre). A favorite of two empresses, Josephine and Marie Louise, he received many commissions for the decoration of public and private buildings, including the Gallery of Laocoön of the Louvre. Prud'hon's private life was tragic. An unfortunate marriage embittered his earlier years, and his long and happy relationship with his pupil Constance Mayer ended with her suicide in 1821. Prud'hon is noted for his subtle use of light and shadow, derived in part from his admiration for the Italian masters, especially Correggio. His work reveals a tender and poetic quality, especially evident in his portrait of Empress Josephine (Louvre). Many of his canvases are badly deteriorated because of his experiments with bitumen pigments. He is represented in many galleries, including the Wallace Collection, London, the Metropolitan Museum, and the New-York Historical Society. See his selected writings ed. by S. Edwards (1969).

prune, popular name for any dried PLUM. Fruits of the many varieties of *Prunus domestica,* which are firm fleshed and dry easily without removal of the stone, are gathered after falling from the tree, dipped in lye solution to prevent fermentation, dried in the sun or in kilns, and then "glossed" with a steam, glycerin, or fruit-juice bath to produce a sterile, glossy skin. Most of the commercial product comes from the Pacific coast states. A type of prune was used by the American Indians as a staple item of diet. Prunes are classified in the division MAGNOLIOPHYTA, class Magnoliopsida, order Rosales, family Rosaceae.

pruning, the horticultural practice of cutting away an unwanted, unnecessary, or undesirable plant part, used most often on trees, shrubs, hedges, and woody vines. Natural pruning occurs when strong winds blow away decayed and dying branches and when the lower branches of forest trees wither and drop off for lack of sunlight. Man uses pruning to remove diseased or injured parts of the plant (see TREE SURGERY), to influence vertical or lateral growth for various reasons, and to increase flowering and fruit yield. Top pruning, or topping, induces lateral growth, and in fruit trees not only produces a more easily accessible shape but also diverts the expenditure of nourishment from the formation of useless wood to that of buds and fruit. In TRANSPLANTING, the aerial parts of the plant are pruned to balance the amount of root destruction, so that the transpiration area is reduced and the roots have a chance to concentrate their activity on taking a firm hold in the soil. Judicious pruning of garden perennials helps to maintain plant vigor and prolongs blooming. In TOPIARY WORK shrubs and trees are pruned to form decorative shapes. As in other horticultural practices, the type of pruning and its timing varies and must be adapted to the specific plant and the conditions of its environment. See E. P. Christopher, *The Pruning Manual* (1954); R. L. Hudson, *The Pruning Handbook* (1973).

Prus, Bolesław (bôlĕsläf' proōs), 1845?–1912, Polish writer, whose original name was Alexander Głowacki. Prus is considered a founder of the modern Polish novel. His articles and short stories exposed the prejudice and class pride in Poland and urged the creation of a sober, cooperative, and industrious society. Prus's realistic novels include *The Outpost* (1886), about the struggle of a Polish peasant to hold his lands, *The Emancipated Women* (4 vol., 1894), and *The Pharaoh* (1896). *The Doll* (1890), Prus's finest work, presents a broad picture of middle-class life in Warsaw.

Prusa: see BURSA.

Prussia (prŭsh'ə), Ger. *Preussen,* former state, the largest and most important of the German states. BERLIN was the capital. The chief member of the German Empire (1871–1918) and the Weimar Republic (1919–33), Prussia occupied more than half of all Germany and the major part of N Germany. It consisted of 13 provinces: Berlin, BRANDENBURG, EAST PRUSSIA (separated after 1919 from the rest of Prussia by the POLISH CORRIDOR), HANOVER, Hesse-Nassau (see HESSE), HOHENZOLLERN (a Prussian enclave between Württemberg and Baden in SW Germany), POMERANIA, RHINE PROVINCE, SAXONY, SCHLESWIG-HOLSTEIN, Upper Silesia and Lower Silesia, and WESTPHALIA. (Grenzmark Posen-West Prussia was sometimes considered a 14th province.) Prussia surrounded several smaller German states and stretched from the borders of the Netherlands, Belgium, and Luxembourg in the west to those of Lithuania and Poland in the east, and from the Baltic Sea, Denmark, and the North Sea in the north to the Main River, the Thuringian Forest, and the Sudetes mts. in the south. The region of Prussia mainly was made up of low-lying land, drained by several rivers, notably the Rhine; the Weser; the Oder; and the Elbe, which divided the state into roughly equal eastern and western parts. After Berlin, the largest cities of the area were Cologne, Breslau (Wrocław), Essen, Frankfurt, Düsseldorf, Hanover, Dortmund, Magdeburg, and Königsberg. The region also included the gigantic industrial RUHR district. Industrially and politically the most prominent state of Germany prior to World War II, Prussia was partitioned among the four Allied occupation zones after 1945. In 1947 the Allied Control Council for Germany formally abolished the state of Prussia. This action not only confirmed an accomplished fact; it was also intended as a blow against the spirit of German militarism and aggression, long held to be connected with Prussia. Most of the former Prussian provinces became part of the new states of the Federal Republic of Germany and of the German Democratic Republic (see GERMANY). The USSR annexed the northern part of East Prussia; Poland acquired the rest, as well as all Prussian territory E of the Oder and Neisse rivers.

Growth of Brandenburg-Prussia. Prussia in its modern meaning came into existence only in 1701, when the elector of Brandenburg assumed the title "king in Prussia." Before then Prussia meant only the flat, sandy region later known as East Prussia (excluding the bishopric of ERMELAND), separated from Brandenburg by a part of Poland (later known as West Prussia) and bordering on the Baltic Sea. The original inhabitants, the Borussi (or Prussians), were of Baltic stock. They were conquered and largely exterminated by the TEUTONIC KNIGHTS in the 13th cent. The Knights effected the germanization of Prussia. Through the secularization (1525) of the domain of the Teutonic Order by the grand master ALBERT OF BRANDENBURG, the domain became a hereditary duchy under Polish suzerainty, ruled by a branch of the Hohenzollern dynasty of Brandenburg. In 1618 the duchy of Prussia passed through inheritance to the elector of Brandenburg, and in 1660, by the treaty of OLIVA, full independence from Polish suzerainty was confirmed to FREDERICK WILLIAM, the Great Elector. In the course of the 17th cent. the electors of Brandenburg directed themselves westward, acquiring the duchy of CLEVES, together with the counties of Mark and Ravensberg (1614) and the bishoprics of Minden, Magdeburg, and Halberstadt (1648). In the east, Brandenburg gained (1648) Farther (i.e., eastern) Pomerania, which connected it with the Baltic Sea but not with Prussia.

Rise of the Prussian State. The electorate with its dependencies had become a major German state, a position that it owed largely to the secularization of church lands during the Reformation (the major part of its new acquisitions had been ecclesiastic territory) and to its successful diplomacy at the Peace of Westphalia (1648). In 1701, Elector Frederick III had himself crowned "king in Prussia" at Königsberg (Kaliningrad) and styled himself King FREDERICK I. He remained a prince of the Holy Roman Empire by virtue of his rank as margrave and elector of Brandenburg and his holdings within the empire, but not as king of Prussia, which lay outside the imperial boundaries. This technicality gave the kings of Prussia a measure of independence from the emperor not possessed by the other princes of the empire. As a result of the NORTHERN WAR, Prussia gained (1720) the eastern part of Swedish Pomerania (including Stettin). In the following 20 years, however, King FREDERICK WILLIAM I, the true creator of the Prussian state, avoided military ventures and used diplomacy in order to create a unified state. He fully developed the features that had distinguished Prussia since the time of the Great Elector. The army, necessary to defend Prussia's scattered lands, was also the chief force in unifying and shaping the state. In order to build a strong army in their relatively poor country, Prussia's rulers developed a government-controlled economy and an obedient central bureaucracy (the *Generaldirektorium*). The landed aristocrats, the Junkers, were brought into military and state service and in turn were left free to enserf their peasants. Frederick William's successor, FREDERICK II, or Frederick the Great (reigned 1740–86), used the efficient military instrument bequeathed him by his father to enter upon a period of conquest. On a slim pretext (see SILESIA) and without a declaration of war, he invaded (1740) Austrian territory, thus gaining the initiative in the War of the AUSTRIAN SUCCESSION (1740–48). Acting with utter disregard for its allies, Prussia got out of the war in 1742 by the Treaty of Berlin, reentered it in 1744, and quit again in 1745 at the Treaty of Dresden. In both treaties Maria Theresa of Austria was forced to cede nearly all of Silesia to Prussia. Although it gained no additional territory in the SEVEN YEARS WAR (1756–63), Prussia emerged from the war as the chief military power of the Continent. By the partition of Poland of 1772 (see POLAND, PARTITIONS OF) Prussia gained Pomerelia (except Danzig) and Ermeland. Pomerelia was organized into the province of WEST PRUSSIA, and the original Prussia became known as East Prussia. Frederick was succeeded (1786) by FREDERICK WILLIAM II, who further added to Prussia by the partitions of Poland of 1793 and 1795. However, under his rule and that of his successor, FREDERICK WILLIAM III (1797–1840), Prussia underwent a period of eclipse as a result of the FRENCH REVOLUTIONARY WARS and the wars of NAPOLEON I. Defeated by the French, Prussia withdrew from the antirevolutionary coalition in the Treaty of Basel (1795) and remained neutral until 1806. Its armies were crushed by Napoleon in the twin battles of Jena and Auerstedt, and in 1807 Prussia had to accept the harsh Treaty of Tilsit, by which it lost all lands W of the Elbe and most of its share of Poland and became a virtual dependency of France. Yet Prussia was fortunate to possess, at a low ebb in its history, such able and energetic reformers as Karl vom und zum STEIN, Karl August von HARDENBERG, and Wilhelm von HUMBOLDT. These men helped transform Prussia into a progressive state by abolishing serfdom and nobiliary privileges, introducing agrarian and other social and economic reforms, and laying the groundwork for an exemplary system of universal education. Gerhard von SCHARNHORST and August, Graf von GNEISENAU at the same time put the Prussian army on a modern basis. Prussia was forced to send auxiliary troops for Napoleon's 1812 campaign in Russia, but late in the year YORCK VON WARTENBURG concluded a separate truce with Russia, and in 1813 Prussia joined the coalition against France. Field Marshal Blücher played a major role in defeating Napoleon at Leipzig (1813) and at Waterloo (1815). At the Congress of Vienna, Prussia gained, in addition to its recovered territories, the entire Rhine prov. and Westphalia, the northern half of Saxony, the remainder of Swedish Pomerania, and a large part of W Poland, including Danzig (Gdańsk), Poznań, and Gniezno. However, Prussia disappointed the hopes of German liberals by following the lead of the Austrian chancellor, Metternich, in the HOLY ALLIANCE. A constitution promised in 1811 failed to materialize under the increasingly reactionary government of Frederick William III, and the half-hearted constitutional schemes of FREDERICK WILLIAM IV were impracticable. By 1834 Prussia had, however, taken the lead in the economic unification of Germany (see ZOLLVEREIN), which was a prerequisite to political union. The March Revolution of 1848 was put down by force, and in 1849 Frederick William IV refused the imperial crown of Germany offered by the FRANKFURT PARLIAMENT. His scheme for a German Union under Prussian leadership and excluding Austria was punctured in the Convention of OLOMOUC (1850), and Prussia returned to the restored GERMAN CONFEDERATION. In 1861, WILLIAM I (regent since 1858) became king, and in 1862 he appointed as premier Otto von BISMARCK, who directed the destiny of Prussia and (after 1871) of Germany until 1890.

Supremacy of Prussia. Bismarck effected the elimination of Austria from German affairs and the union of Germany under Prussian hegemony by means of three deliberately planned wars. The first war (1864) was fought in alliance with Austria against Denmark over Schleswig-Holstein. Its settlement furnished a pretext for the AUSTRO-PRUSSIAN WAR of 1866, in which Prussia quickly and thoroughly defeated Austria and its allies and gained additional territory by the annexation of Hanover, Electoral Hesse, Nassau, Schleswig-Holstein, and the free city of Frankfurt am Main. The German Confederation was dissolved, and the Prussian-led NORTH GERMAN CONFEDERATION took its place. Finally, in the FRANCO-PRUSSIAN WAR (1870–71), the North German Confederation overwhelmed France, and in 1871 William I of Prussia was proclaimed emperor of Germany. In its main features the subsequent history of Prussia was that of Germany. However, Bismarck's KULTURKAMPF against the Roman Catholic Church was largely confined to the kingdom of Prussia, which, like the other German states, continued as an individual member of the empire. The Prussian constitution adopted in 1850 and amended in the following years was far less liberal than the federal constitution of the empire. The government was not responsible to the Prussian Landtag (lower chamber), whose powers were small and whose members were elected by a suffrage system based on tax-paying ability. The house of lords was largely controlled by the conservative Junkers, who held immense tracts of generally poor land E of the Elbe (particularly in East Prussia). Endowed with little money and much pride, they had continued to form the officer corps of the army. The rising industrialists, notably the great Rhenish and Westphalian mine owners and steel magnates, although their interests were often opposed to those of the Junkers, exerted an equally reactionary influence on politics. The Prussian constitution was liberalized after Prussia became a republic in 1918, and the Junkers lost many of their estates through the cession of Prussian territory to Poland. However, both the Junkers and the Rhenish industrialists continued to exert much power behind the scenes, and when Franz von PAPEN became (1932) German chancellor and commissioner for Prussia, they came into their own. In July, 1932, Papen suspended the Prussian parliament and ousted the Social Democrat Otto Braun, who had been premier of Prussia (with brief interruptions) from 1920. Early in 1933, Adolf Hitler seized power and made Hermann Goering premier of Prussia; Hitler's rise had been aided by the Rhenish industrialists. By a decree of Hitler issued in Jan., 1934, the German states ceased to exist as political units, and it was no longer possible to differentiate clearly between Prussia and the rest of Germany. The classic histories of Prussia are those of RANKE, TREITSCHKE, and DROYSEN. See Sir John A. R. Marriott and C. G. Robertson, *The Evolution of Prussia* (1915, rev. ed. 1946); F. L. Carsten, *Origins of Prussia* (1954); S. B. Fay, *The Rise of Brandenburg-Prussia to 1786* (1937, rev. ed. 1964); G. A. Craig, *The Politics of the Prussian Army, 1640–1945* (1955, repr. 1964); E. J. Feuchtwanger, *Prussia: Myth and Reality* (1970); Herbert Tuttle, *History of Prussia* (4 vol., 1884–96, repr. 1971).

Prussian blue, PIGMENT widely used for laundry bluing, in dyeing compounds, and in the manufacture of inks and paints. Several varieties are known, one of which consists of the chemical compound ferric ferrocyanide.

prussic acid: see HYDROGEN CYANIDE.

Prut or **Pruth** (both: pro͞ot), river, c.530 mi (850 km) long, rising in the Carpathian Mts., W Ukraine, USSR, and flowing generally SE to the Danube River at Reni. It forms the border between Rumania and Moldavia, USSR. The Prut is navigable to Leovo. By the Peace of the Pruth (1711) Peter I of Russia restored Azov to the Turks (see RUSSO-TURKISH WARS).

Prutkov, Kozma: see TOLSTOY, ALEKSEY KONSTANTINOVICH.

Prynne, William (prĭn), 1600–69, English political figure and Puritan pamphleteer. Beginning his attacks on Arminian doctrine in 1627, he soon earned the enmity of William LAUD. When Prynne's strictures on the theater in his book, *Historiomastix* (1632), were interpreted as an attack on Charles I and his queen, he was fined, imprisoned (1633), pilloried (1634), and partly shorn of his ears. He continued his pamphleteering in jail and in 1637 was again fined, sentenced to life imprisonment, deprived of the remainder of his ears, and branded with the letters *S.L.* (for seditious libeler). He was released from prison by the Long Parliament in 1640 and was voted financial reparation. During the ENGLISH CIVIL WAR, Prynne strongly supported the parliamentary cause in his writings and took a vindictive part in prosecuting his old enemy, Laud. In defending his moderate theological position, however, he found himself opposing both Presbyterians and Independents. He also came into conflict with John Milton over Milton's advocacy of divorce. Prynne entered Parliament in 1648; but he opposed the demand of the army for the execution of Charles I and so was expelled in Pride's Purge. He wrote attacks against the Commonwealth, for which he was imprisoned (1650–53), and against the Protectorate, and later supported the Restoration of Charles II. In 1660 he became keeper of the records of the Tower of London. See biography by E. W. Kirby (1931, repr. 1972); W. M. Lamont, *Marginal Prynne, 1600–1669* (1963).

Prypeć: see PRIPYAT, USSR.

Przemyśl (pshĕ'mĭshəl), Ukr. *Peremyshl,* city (1970 pop. 53,228), extreme SE Poland, on the San River in the Carpathian foothills. It is a trade center and has metalworking, clothing, food-processing, electrical engineering, and timber-working industries. Oil and natural gas are also produced. The city was allegedly founded in the 8th cent. Between 981 and 1340 it was ruled by Kiev and Vladimir-Volynski. Przemyśl obtained municipal rights and passed to Poland in the late 14th cent. Austria took the city in 1772; it reverted to Poland after World War I. Przemyśl has several old churches and the remains of a 14th-century castle.

Przewalski's horse (pshəväl'skēz), wild HORSE of Asia, *Equus przewalski,* the only extant wild horse that, in the purebred state, is not descended from the domestic horse. Smaller than most domestic horses, it has a large head and bulging forehead. It is dun-colored, with an upright crest of dark hair on its head and neck, a dark stripe along the backbone, and a dark, plumed tail. Its former range probably extended from W Mongolia to N Sinkiang, China, but it survives now only on the semidesert plain of the Altai mts. in SW Mongolia, although the herds migrate seasonally into the Gobi Desert. The reduction of the species is largely due to competition with domestic livestock for grazing land and water. Surviving members have interbred with feral horses (wild descendants of domestic horses) to such an extent that it is not certain that there are any purebred herds left in the wild. Indeed, since interbreeding with Mongol horses may have begun centuries ago, it is possible that even the original specimens of Przewalski's horse to be described were actually of mixed descent. There are many specimens in zoos, where they breed well. Tarpan is the name for members of another race of the same species, *E. przewalski gmelini,* which formerly ranged over the steppes of E Europe and W Asia, but has been extinct since the last century. Wild horses are classified in the phylum CHORDATA, subphylum Vertebrata, class Mammalia, order Perissodactyla, family Equidae.

Przhevalsky, Nikolai Mikhailovich (nyĭkəlī' mĕkhī'ləvĭch pərzhĭväl'skē), 1839–88, Russian geographer and explorer in central Asia and the Far East. He made five major expeditions—one to the Ussuri area in the Russian Far East (1867–68) and four to Mongolia, Sinkiang, and Tibet (1870–85). Przhevalsky is credited with the discovery of Lop Nor (Lo-pu po) and the Altyn Tagh range on his trip in 1876–77. He studied the orography, climate, and flora and fauna (discovering the wild horse named after him) of these regions. He wrote *Mongolia, and the Tangut Country* (tr. 1876) and *From Kulja, Across the Tian Shan to Lob-Nor* (tr. 1879).

Przybyszewski, Stanisław (stänēs'läf pshĭbĭshĕf'skē), 1868–1927, Polish novelist, essayist, and dramatist. He studied in Berlin, where his friendship with a socialist led him to prison. Under Scandinavian influence he developed his neoromantic philosophy of medievalism, which repudiates reason and upholds intuition. His works describe the clash of intellect and sexuality. They were more important for the furor their content roused than for literary merit. His best-known works are the dramas *For Happiness* (1912, tr. 1912) and *Snow* (1903, tr. 1920), and the novel *Homo Sapiens* (1898, tr. 1915).

Psalmanazar, George (săl″mənā′zər), 1679?–1763, English literary imposter. His real name is not known. Born and educated in France, he developed a marked ability in learning languages. He traveled through Europe posing as a Japanese convert to Christianity. In Holland (1702) he was examined by William Innes, an English army chaplain who, though he penetrated Psalmanazar's pose, sent him to England as a Formosan convert in order to gain credit for the conversion. Psalmanazar was able without detection to publish *An Historical and Geographical Description of Formosa* (1704), to invent a complete "Formosan" language, and to instruct Oxford students in the use of it. However, suspicions arose, and after 1706 he was forced to repudiate his claims. He scraped a meager living by literary hack work, became intensely religious, and wrote the story of his life and impostures, *Memoirs of —— Commonly Known by the Name George Psalmanazar* (1764).

Psalms (sämz) or **Psalter** (sôl′tər), book of the Old Testament, in the 19th place in the Authorized Version (AV), a collection of 150 poetic pieces. This has been since the last centuries B.C. the chief hymnal of the Jews and subsequently of Christians. The poems are of varying date and authorship, but many are ascribed to David (cf. Ecclus. 47.8) and some to ASAPH **1**, Solomon, Moses, and the sons of Korah. The tradition of David's authorship was rejected until recently; many scholars now believe that some of the Psalms originated in David's time and some even earlier. Most of them took their present form between c.537 B.C. and c.100 B.C. The versions vary extensively in dividing individual psalms, and therefore citation of number and verse is confusing. The Hebrew and AV and most other Protestant versions use one numbering, while the Greek and Latin versions have another, which is followed in Douay. Thus, AV Pss. 1–8 = Douay Pss. 1–8; AV 9–10 = Douay 9; AV 11–113 = Douay 10–112; AV 114–115 = Douay 113; AV 116 = Douay 114–115; AV 117–146 = Douay 116–145; AV 147 = Douay 146–147; AV 148–150 = Douay 148–150. According to the text the Psalms are divided into five books (citations are in AV numbers): Pss. 1–41; 42–72; 73–89; 90–106; 107–150. The poems vary in tone and subject. Thus, some express contrition and are called the penitential psalms, e.g., 6, 32, 38, 51 (called, from the opening word in Latin, Miserere), 102, 130 (De profundis), 143; some are imprecatory, e.g., 52, 54–59, 64, 68, 109, 137; some emphasize the history of Israel, e.g., 78, 105–107, 114–115 (In exitu Israel), 135, 136; some are didactic, e.g., 37, 49, 50, 73; some seem to have been especially adapted to public worship, e.g., 47, 95 (Venite), 105, 134–136, 148–150; some have been regarded as messianic, e.g., 2, 8, 16, 22, 45, 89, 110 (Dixit Dominus), 132; cf. Luke 20.40–44; John 19.36, 37. Eight are acrostics: 10, 25, 34, 37, 111, 112, 119, 145. There are psalms elsewhere in the Old Testament, e.g., 1 Sam. 2.1–10; 2 Sam. 22 (cf. Ps. 18); 1 Chron. 16; Isa. 38.10–20; Hab. 3. Many psalms have "titles" or musical and other directions. Most of these are obscure. The history of translations of the Psalms is more extensive than that of any other part of the Old Testament. Earlier English versions include those of St. Aldhelm and of Richard ROLLE; the Psalms have been translated into English metrical verse a number of times, e.g., the BAY PSALM BOOK and versions by Nahum TATE and Nicholas Brady and by Isaac WATTS. In the Book of Common Prayer the Psalms are in the version of the Great Bible of 1539 (by Miles Coverdale from the Vulgate); the use of this version instead of AV was continued because of its popularity, just as St. Jerome had incorporated a corrected Old Latin version (called the Gallican Psalter) into the VULGATE, not using his own (superior) translation from Hebrew. See (besides books listed under OLD TESTAMENT) W. A. Wright, ed., *The Hexaplar Psalter; or, The Psalms in Six English Versions* (1911); W. O. E. Oesterley, *The Psalms* (1939); Ronald Knox, *The Psalms: a New Translation* (1947); S. L. Terrien, *The Psalms and Their Meaning for Today* (1952); Mary Ellen Chase, *The Psalms for the Common Reader* (rev. ed. 1962); C. F. Barth, *Introductions to the Psalms* (tr. 1966).

Psalms of Solomon: see PSEUDEPIGRAPHA.

Psalter: see PSALMS.

psaltery (sôl′tərē, -trē), stringed musical instrument. It has a flat soundboard over which a variable number of strings are stretched. Its origin was in the Middle East, and it is referred to in the Bible. It appeared in Europe in the 12th cent. and flourished until the late Middle Ages. The term *psaltery* is sometimes used as a generic term for all plucked zithers having flat bodies. The instrument is similar to a DULCIMER but is plucked instead of hammered. See illustrations accompanying dulcimer and ZITHER entries.

Psamtik (säm′tĭk, săm′-), Lat. *Psammetichus*, d. 609 B.C., king of ancient Egypt, founder of the XXVI dynasty. When his father, NECHO, lord of Saïs under the Assyrians, was defeated and killed (663 B.C.), by the Nubian Tanutamon, Psamtik fled to his overlord, ASSURBANIPAL, who reinstated (661) him at Saïs as viceroy of Lower Egypt. While Assurbanipal was busy in Babylonia and other regions, Psamtik shook off his Assyrian allegiance and became master of all Egypt. During his long and eminently prosperous reign, he encouraged the settlement (especially at Naucratis) of Greek soldiers and traders, who for the first time became important in Egypt. His incursion into Palestine was stopped by the Scythians. His son was the pharaoh NECHO.

pseudepigrapha (sū″dĭpĭ′grəfə) [Gr., = things falsely ascribed], uncanonical writings of a biblical type, usually of spurious date and authorship. Three of the best-known pseudepigrapha are placed in the APOCRYPHA in the Authorized Version of the Bible: Third and Fourth (also called First and Second) ESDRAS and the Prayer of Manasses (see MANASSEH **2**); the rest of the books of the Apocrypha are not pseudepigraphic but deuterocanonical. The pseudepigrapha are both Jewish, composed 200 B.C.–A.D. 200, and Christian, A.D. 50–A.D. 400. The writings so classified were originally composed in Hebrew, Aramaic, and Greek. Many of them were preserved in various Eastern churches and have been transmitted in such languages as Syriac, Ethiopic, Coptic, Georgian, Armenian, and Slavonic. Fragments of known and unknown pseudepigraphic works in Hebrew and Aramaic have been found among the DEAD SEA SCROLLS. Such Jewish writings were composed either in Palestine or by Jewish-Hellenistic groups. The greater number are apocalyptic (see APOCALYPSE). Jewish apocalyptic pseudepigrapha include the Ethiopic Book of Enoch (150 B.C.–100 B.C.), of composite authorship, accepting the resurrection and judgment; the Secrets of Enoch (A.D. c.50), by a Hellenistic Jew under strong non-Jewish influence; the Testaments of the Twelve Patriarchs (c.100 B.C.), by an idealistic Pharisee, which were probably popular with early Christians; the Assumption of Moses (A.D. c.1), by a Pharisee opposed to the politicians of his sect; the Sibylline Oracles, an accumulation (200 B.C.–A.D. 200) of Messianic prophecies; and the Apocalypse of Baruch (1st cent. A.D.), similar in hope to Fourth (or Second) Esdras. Biblical stories romantically elaborated include the books of Adam and Eve, Joseph and Asenath (see Gen. 41.45), and JANNES AND JAMBRES. The Psalms of Solomon (c.50 B.C.), by Pharisees, denounce the later Maccabees. Remnants of the Psalms of Joshua, other psalms of this period, were found among the Dead Sea Scrolls. Two histories of the world—the Book of Jubilees, or Little Genesis (c.100 B.C.), which ends with the giving of the Law on Mt. Sinai, and the Book of Biblical Antiquities (A.D. c.100), ascribed to Philo, which ends with the accession of David—are intended to bear the same relation to the canonical books covering their material as the two books of CHRONICLES do to Second Samuel and the two books of Kings. Supposedly historical, Third Maccabees tells how the Egyptian Jews escaped a massacre in the 3d cent. B.C.; Fourth Maccabees is an essay on the Law with Greek philosophical elaborations; Fifth Maccabees is an imitation of First Maccabees and the material of Josephus on that family. From Christian authors there are apocalypses attributed to most apostles and Jewish heroes, often simply revisions of Jewish works. They include the Apocalypse of Peter (A.D. c.150), the Shepherd of Hermas (see HERMAS, SHEPHERD OF), and the Ascension of Isaiah, which is composed of Jewish legends on Isaiah's death and an apocalypse offering information on Christian trends. The canonical books of the New Testament became models for many pseudepigrapha, the majority of which were written in an attempt to give legitimacy to beliefs challenged as heretical. The fragmentary Gospel according to the Hebrews (c.100) was apparently similar to the Gospel according to St. Matthew. The Gospel of Nicodemus (300–500) was influential in the Middle Ages; it contains the Acts of Pilate (Pilate's report on the crucifixion of Jesus) and the HARROWING OF HELL. GNOSTICISM is apparent in many gospels, e.g., the Protoevangelium of James and the Gospel of Thomas (both probably 2d cent.); these are full of legends on Mary and Jesus. Elaborations of these gospels were popular, e.g., the Arabic Gospel of the Infancy of Jesus. Fragmentary heretical gospels include the Gospels of the Twelve and of the Egyptians. There are books of Acts named for most apostles, mainly heretical. The Acts of Thomas, or Judas Thomas, is informative on Christianity in Mesopotamia. The DIDACHE and the Apostolic Constitutions (see CONSTITUTIONS, APOSTOLIC) are ancient, probably genuine, compilations. Undoubtedly genuine are certain epistles, one of St. CLEMENT I, seven of St. IGNATIUS OF ANTIOCH, one of St. POLYCARP, and one of the church of Smyrna on Polycarp's martyrdom. An epistle of the 1st cent. denouncing the reaction toward Judaism in Christian circles is ascribed traditionally to St. Barnabas. The Epistles of Abgar (c.200) were popular for their pretended authorship by Jesus and a sick king of Edessa. The spurious epistles of Paul, Clement, Ignatius, and others throw light on the Christian tendencies of the first four centuries. See AGRAPHA OF JESUS. See R. H. Charles, ed., *The Apocrypha and Pseudepigrapha of the Old Testament* (1913, repr. 1964); C. C. Torrey, *The Apocryphal Literature* (1945, repr. 1963); R. H. Pfeiffer, *History of New Testament Times* (1949, repr. 1972). See also bibliography under APOCRYPHA.

pseudocyesis (sōō″dōsīē′sĭs), imaginary pregnancy in women usually resulting from a strong desire or need for motherhood. In the absence of conception, the menstrual periods nevertheless cease, the abdomen becomes enlarged and the breasts swell and even secrete milk, mimicking genuine pregnancy. The uterus and cervix may show signs of pregnancy, urine tests may be falsely positive, and the woman may report sensations of fetal movements. A woman may believe in her pregnancy to the point of DELUSION and show acute DEPRESSION when no baby is born. It has been suggested that depression can sometimes alter the activity of the PITUITARY GLAND so as to cause hormone level changes that mimic the hormone changes of real pregnancy.

Pseudo-Dionysius: see DIONYSIUS THE AREOPAGITE, SAINT.

pseudonym (sōō′dənĭm) [Gr., = false name], name assumed, particularly by writers, to conceal identity. A writer's pseudonym is also referred to as a nom de plume (pen name). Famous examples in literature are George Eliot (Mary Ann Evans), Mark Twain (Samuel Clemens), Lewis Carroll (Charles Lutwidge Dodgson), O. Henry (William Sydney Porter), Stendhal (Marie Henri Beyle), and George Sand (Mme Amandine Aurore Lucie Dupin, baronne Dudevant). Perhaps because the genre is not considered a serious one, detective story writers often use pseudonyms, especially if they are noted in other fields; for example, the poet C. Day Lewis wrote mysteries under the name Nicholas Blake. See Samuel Halkett and John Laing, *Dictionary of Anonymous and Pseudonymous English Literature* (7 vol., rev. ed. 1926–34; repr. 1971).

psilocybin (sĭl″əsī′bən), perception-altering substance found in some species of mushroom. See PSYCHOTOMIMETIC DRUG.

Psilotophyta (sīlō″tŏf′ətə), division of vascular plants consisting of only two genera, *Psilotum* and *Tmesipteris*, with very few species. These plants are characterized by the lack of roots, and, in one species, leaves are lacking also. The green, photosynthetic stem is well-developed. Like higher plants, e.g., the angiosperms (MAGNOLIOPHYTA), Psilophyta has specialized conducting, or vascular, tissue (xylem and phloem). *Psilotum*, with only two species, is widespread in tropical and subtropical areas, whereas the single *Tmesipteris* species is restricted to Australia and neighboring islands. The spore-producing structures are produced in clusters in the axil of a leaf at the end of a short lateral branch. The GAMETOPHYTE plant, arising from germination of a spore, is small and colorless, and derives its nutrition through a specialized association with a fungus. Sexual structures on the gametophyte produce eggs and sperms. The motile sperms, with numerous flagella, are able to swim through a film of water to the egg. The fertilized egg, or zygote, first absorbs nourishment from the gametophyte, and later becomes photosynthetic and self-sustaining. The life cycle is very much like that of FERNS.

psittacosis (sĭtəkō′sĭs) or **parrot fever,** infectious disease caused by a virus and transmitted to man by birds. Parrots, parakeets, and lovebirds are the principal carriers, but poultry, pigeons, and canaries are also implicated. In birds the disease takes the form of an intestinal infection, but in man the illness runs the course of a virus pneumonia; infection follows inhalation of dust from feathers or cage contents or the bite of an infected bird. Human psittacosis, which can be transmitted to others by cough droplets and sputum, should have much the same treatment as pneumonia. The mortality rate may run as high as 20%. Restrictions on bird importation and attention to infected flocks of pigeons have been used in control of the disease.

Pskov (pəskôf'), city (1970 pop. 127,000), capital of Pskov oblast, NW European USSR, on the Velikaya River. It is an important rail junction in the heart of a flax-growing area. Industries include food processing and the manufacture of metals, machinery, building materials, and linen. Known in antiquity as Pleskov, it became (903) an outpost of Novgorod. Its large-scale stone construction, almost equal in extent to that of Novgorod, shows that it was already a rich town in the 12th cent. Pskov became (1347) an independent, democratic city-state and a flourishing commercial center that traded with the Hanseatic League. It was capital of Pskov Republic from 1348 to 1510 and had a form of government similar to that of Novgorod. With its annexation (1510) by Moscow, Pskov lost its democratic institutions. Its importance, except as a strategic fortress, soon declined. The railroad station at Pskov was the scene (1917) of the abdication of Nicholas II. The historic core of Pskov is the inner walled city, containing a kremlin (12th–16th cent.), with towers in the Byzantine style, a cathedral, and numerous medieval churches and monasteries. The country around Pskov is rich in architectural monuments from the 14th to the 18th cent.

psoriasis (sôrī'əsĭs), occasionally acute but usually chronic and recurrent disorder of the skin. The exact cause of psoriasis is unknown, and no cure has been found. Psoriasis may occur at any age but is uncommon in children. The characteristic lesion is a scaly "mother-of-pearl" patch, appearing anywhere on the body. Involvement may range from a single plaque to numerous patches that cover most of the skin. Treatment is directed at the symptoms and may include the application of ointments, exposure to sunlight and ultraviolet light, and X-ray therapy.

Psyche (sī'kē), in Greek mythology, personification of the human soul. She was so lovely that Eros (Cupid), the god of love, fell in love with her. He swept her off to a beautiful, isolated castle but forbade her to look at him since he was a god. When she disobeyed, he abandoned her, but she ceaselessly searched for him, performing difficult and dangerous tasks, until at last she was reunited with him forever and made immortal.

psychedelic drug (sī"kədĕl'ĭk): see PSYCHOTOMIMETIC DRUG.

psychiatry (səkī'ətrē, sī-), diagnosis and treatment of mental disorders such as DEPRESSION, ANXIETY, HYSTERIA and other forms of PSYCHONEUROSIS, and various forms of PSYCHOSIS. Although the Greeks recognized the significance of emotions in mental disorders, medieval thought emphasized demoniac influence. From the Middles Ages until the time of the French physician Philippe Pinel (1745–1826), who instituted humanitarian reforms in the care of the mentally ill, there was no organized attempt to study or treat mental abnormalities or to provide decent institutional conditions for the insane. Throughout the 19th cent. reformers such as Dorothea L. DIX, whose efforts were primarily humanitarian, fought for legislation and improved conditions. The early 20th cent. saw the organization of the MENTAL HYGIENE movement, dedicated to the prevention of mental disease through guidance clinics and education. During this period scientists were seeking the underlying cause of mental and nervous disorders. The German psychiatrist Emil KRAEPELIN, on the basis of prognostic considerations, was the first to divide psychosis into the two general classifications of MANIC-DEPRESSIVE PSYCHOSIS and SCHIZOPHRENIA. Gradually, some psychiatrists, led by Sigmund FREUD, turned to the behavior and emotional history of the patient as a clue to the nature of psychoneurosis and psychosis. PSYCHOTHERAPY, GROUP PSYCHOTHERAPY, and PSYCHOANALYSIS are now in general use and are being applied with some success even to disorders whose symptoms appear to be essentially physical (see PSYCHOSOMATIC MEDICINE). In recent years the pharmacological approach to mental illness has achieved significant developments and has produced substantial changes in the basic management of psychiatric patients (see PSYCHOPHARMACOLOGY). See also SHOCK THERAPY. See Gregory Zilboorg, *A History of Medical Psychology* (1941, repr. 1967); S. A. Arieti, ed., *American Handbook of Psychiatry* (3 vol., 1959–66); M. D. Altschule, *Roots of Modern Psychiatry* (2d ed. 1965); F. G. Alexander and S. T. Selesnick, *The History of Psychiatry* (1966); C. E. Goshen, *Documentary History of Psychiatry* (1967); E. H. Ackernecht, *A Short History of Psychiatry* (rev. ed. 1968); A. P. Noyes and L. C. Kolb, *Modern Clinical Psychiatry* (7th ed. 1968).

psychical research: see PARAPSYCHOLOGY.

psychoanalysis, name given by Sigmund Freud both to a system of psychopathology and to a therapeutic procedure designed primarily for the treatment of PSYCHONEUROSIS. It is one type of psychotherapy used in PSYCHIATRY. Psychoanalysis began after Freud studied (1885–86) with the French neurologist J. M. Charcot in Paris and became convinced that HYSTERIA was caused not by organic changes in the nervous system but by emotional disorders. Later, in collaboration with, and influenced by, the Viennese physician Josef Breuer, he wrote two papers on hysteria (1893, 1895) that were to be the precursors of the vast body of psychoanalytic theory. The basic postulate of psychoanalysis, the concept of a dynamic UNCONSCIOUS, grew out of Freud's observation that the physical symptoms of hysterical patients tended to disappear after apparently forgotten material was made conscious. He saw the unconscious as an area of great psychic activity, which influenced every action but operated with material not subject to recall by normal processes. The mechanism inducing this so-called forgetfulness he called repression, and the one preventing repressed material from being brought to the surface he called resistance. Observing the relationship between psychoneurosis and repressed memories, Freud made conscious recognition of these forgotten experiences the keystone of psychoanalytic therapy. Hypnosis was the earliest method used to probe the unconscious, but due to its limited effectiveness it was soon discarded in favor of free ASSOCIATION (see also HYPNOTISM). DREAMS, which Freud interpreted as symbolic wish fulfillments, were another key to the unconscious. A further factor in the analytic situation was what Freud called transference, the heightened emotional reaction of the patient to the analyst, which was believed to be a reactivation of the patient's infantile feelings for important figures of his early life, such as parents and siblings. To clarify the operation of the human psyche Freud and his followers introduced a vast body of theory. On the basis of observation and speculation, Freud conceived of the presence of two oppositional instincts or, more precisely, drives toward a particular type of behavior. One of these, the death instinct, impels the individual toward aggressive, hostile, and destructive behavior; the other, the sexual instinct, moves in the direction of erotic, constructive, and affectionate behavior. Freud believed that under ideal circumstances of adjustment the two drives would interact in such a way as to neutralize the overt primitive expressions of each other. It is basic psychoanalytic theory that damming up the energy of instinctual drives is crucial in producing psychoneurosis. Freud's theory of psychosexuality developed from the theory of infantile sexuality, in which he saw the libido, or sexual energy, of the infant progressively seeking outlet through different body zones (oral, anal, urethral, phallic, and genital) during the first five years of life. In addition to the changes in bodily localization, the libido is also believed to undergo development with respect to the object toward which it is directed. The first object is the child's own body, the stage of NARCISSISM; later it is directed toward the parents, at which time the OEDIPUS COMPLEX develops; finally, if mature, it transfers to objects in the outer world, the so-called genital stage. These impulses, however, may be arrested, or fixated, at some point in the process of libidinal development; or the libido of the adult, because of prolonged frustration, can be diverted from its normal genital outlet by means of regression, a return to objects or satisfactions associated with infantile life. Diversion of libidinal energy from its proper channel is thought to prevent a mature response to the complexities of adulthood. However, Freud believed that in the emotionally mature person a good part of the libidinal energy could be deflected by the process of sublimation from its unconscious sexual aim to nonsexual, socially useful goals. In considering the human personality as a whole Freud divided it into three functional parts: id, ego, and superego. He saw the id as the reservoir of the instinctual drives, imbedded in the deepest level of the unconscious and dominated by the pleasure principle, an automatic aspect of mental activity, with its object the immediate gratification of drives. The superego, originating in the child through identification with parents and others and in response to social pressures, functions as an internal censor, embracing both a conscious and an unconscious conscience. Freud considered the ego that part of the id modified by contact with the external world. Although only partly conscious, it makes up the bulk of what is commonly referred to as CONSCIOUSNESS. It is seen as the mental agent mediating between three contending forces: the outside demands of social pressure or reality, the libidinal demands for immediate satisfaction arising from the id, and the claims of the superego. In reconciling these forces that converge upon it, the mature ego conforms to the reality principle, the acceptance of temporary denial of immediate pleasure in order to avoid painful consequences or to make gratification possible at a later date. Furthermore psychoanalysts believe that the ego has available, besides repression and sublimation, several other means that it utilizes in protecting itself against demands of the id (see DEFENSE MECHANISM). Psychoanalysis, from its inception until 1906, was for all intents and purposes the private preserve of Freud. After that date he was joined by an increasing number of students and physicians, among whom were C. G. Jung and Alfred Adler. Both made significant contributions, but by 1913 ceased to be identified with the main body of psychoanalysts because of theoretical disagreements in relation to Freud's strong emphasis on sexual motivation. Orthodox Freudian psychoanalysis was challenged in the 1920s by Otto Rank, Sandor Ferenczi, and Wilhelm Reich; later, in the 1930s, by Karen Horney, Erich Fromm, and Harry Stack Sullivan. This latter group emphasized social and cultural factors in psychoneurosis and, in therapy, stressed the interpersonal aspect of the analyst-patient relationship (see TRANSFERENCE). Psychoanalysis has had a great influence on child rearing, education, the cultural and social sciences, medicine, and the arts. Existential psychoanalysis, a psychotherapy strongly influenced by existential philosophy, particularly that of Martin Heidegger, was furthered in the United States by the work of the German-American theologian Paul Tillich and the American psychologist Rollo May. The client-centered therapy of the American psychologist Carl Rogers is based on similar views. See GROUP PSYCHOTHERAPY. See the works of Freud; C. G. Jung, *The Theory of Psychoanalysis* (1915); Karen Horney, *New Ways in Psychoanalysis* (1939); Franz Alexander, *Fundamentals of Psychoanalysis* (2d ed. 1963); Rollo May et al., *Existence* (1958, repr. 1967); K. A. Menninger and P. S. Holzman, *Theory of Psychoanalytic Technique* (2d ed. 1973); Dieter Wyss, *Psychoanalytic Schools from the Beginning to the Present* (tr. 1973).

psychoanalytic group therapy: see GROUP PSYCHOTHERAPY.

psychodrama: see GROUP PSYCHOTHERAPY.

psychological tests, standardized tests for measuring psychological traits and behavior or for studying some specialized aspect of ability. Achievement tests measure attainments in a variety of fields, e.g., academic subjects. Tests of abilities include IQ tests (see INTELLIGENCE), spatial-perceptual tests, and motor skills tests. The Strong Vocational Interest Blank, which matches up an individual's interests against the empirically determined interests of individuals in various occupations, is used in vocational counseling. Schools use educational aptitude and achievement tests to compare ability with actual accomplishment, while administrators in business use tests to learn the potential special talents, interests, motor skills, and other such capacities of a prospective employee. Sensory functions, e.g., visual acuity and hearing, are also measured, and tests have also been devised for special aptitudes, e.g., memory and creativity. A number of so-called projective tests have come into extensive use. They are based on the theory that individuals tend to project their own unconscious attitudes into ambiguous situations. The most widely used of these tests is that of the Swiss psychiatrist, Hermann Rorschach, who used 10 standardized inkblots and had the patient tell what he saw. The interpretation is based on whether the whole blot or details are described, the reaction to color, how much movement is seen, and a great many other factors. The thematic apperception test, or TAT, developed by the American psychologist H. A. Murray, uses a standard series of pictures about which short stories must be told. Each story is carefully analyzed to uncover underlying needs, attitudes, and patterns of reaction. A Hungarian psychiatrist, Lipot Szondi, introduced a test designed to bring forth the hidden dynamic processes in the human personality, using photographs of mentally disturbed or sexually deviant people from which a given number of those liked and those disliked must be chosen. Another commonly used projective test is the word-association test, made famous by C. G. Jung, used to uncover COMPLEXES. See Anne Anastasi, *Psychological Testing* (3d ed., 1968); R. L. Thorndike and Elizabeth Hagen, *Measurement and Evaluation in Psychology and Education* (3d ed. 1969).

psychology, science or study of the activities of living things and their interaction with the environment. Psychologists study processes of sense PERCEPTION, responses to stimuli, thinking, LEARNING, remembering and problem solving, emotions and MOTIVATIONS, PERSONALITY, mental disorders, and the interaction of the individual and the group. The field is closely allied with anthropology in its concerns with human behavior, with physics in its treatment of vision, hearing, and touch, and with biology in the study of the physiological basis of behavior. In its earliest speculative period psychological study was chiefly embodied in philosophical and theological discussions of the soul. The *De anima* of Aristotle is considered the first monument of psychology as such, while the foundations of modern psychology were laid by Hobbes in the 17th cent. The three body-mind theories that dominated later psychological thought were outlined in the 17th cent.—interactionism by Descartes, monism by Spinoza, and parallelism by Leibniz. The Leibniz theory of monads contributed also to the founding of faculty psychology by Christian von Wolff. The school was so called because it attributed separate faculties to the soul or mind. In England empirical psychology originated in the work of Locke, Berkeley, Reid, and Hume. It was followed by the associational psychology of David Hartley, James Mill, John Stuart Mill, and Alexander Bain, who stressed the relation of physiology to psychology, thus giving rise to physiological psychology. There were important contributions made in this field by the French philosopher Condillac, F. J. Gall, the German founder of phrenology, and the French surgeon Paul Broca, who localized speech centers in the brain. Two factors dominating the beginnings of scientific psychology in the 19th cent. were the experimental method and the principle of evolution. The former was represented by the great laboratory work of the Germans E. H. Weber, G. T. Fechner, Wilhelm Wundt, and H. L. F. von Helmholtz and the Englishman E. B. Titchener. The principle of evolution, stemming from Charles Darwin, gave rise to what was later called dynamic psychology, an approach presented by the American William James in his *Principles of Psychology* (1890). Out of the new orientation in psychology grew the clinical experiments in HYSTERIA and HYPNOTISM carried on by J. M. Charcot and Pierre Janet in France. Sigmund Freud, in his elaborate theory of the unconscious, gave a new direction to psychology and laid the groundwork for PSYCHOANALYSIS. Freudian theory took psychology into such fields as education, anthropology, and medicine. The BEHAVIORISM of the American J. B. Watson played a highly influential part in American thought in the 1920s and '30s. Educational psychology derives from Froebel and Pestalozzi and their follower Herbart, and in later times it was developed by G. Stanley Hall and by E. L. Thorndike. Social psychology was developed by such men as the British psychologists William McDougall and Havelock Ellis. Other branches of the field include child psychology, individual psychology, and religious psychology. Animal psychology, or the study of animal behavior, has become especially prominent in the 20th cent., and much research has been done on the sense perceptions of animals (vision and hearing) and their learning ability and intelligence, with great impetus given by the work of German-American psychologist Wolfgang Köhler on the chimpanzee (see ETHOLOGY). Köhler also helped develop the school of GESTALT psychology. In so-called applied psychology, psychological principles are adapted to industry and commerce. See Gardner Murphy, *Historical Introduction to Modern Psychology* (rev. ed. 1949); J. P. Chaplin, *Systems and Theories of Psychology* (1960); R. S. Woodworth and M. R. Sheehan, *Contemporary Schools of Psychology* (3d ed. 1964); J. P. Chaplin and T. S. Krawiec, *Systems and Theories of Psychology* (2d ed. 1968); Gardner Murphy and J. K. Kovach, *Historical Introduction to Modern Psychology* (3d ed. 1972); Gardner Lindzey et al., *Psychology* (1975).

psychoneurosis, mild form of mental disorder with no apparent organic cause. Psychoneurosis, or neurosis, arises from inner conflicts and may produce a variety of mental disorders, including ANXIETY, DEPRESSION, and HYSTERIA. Psychoneurosis is typified by a variety of reactions to fear and anxiety including phobias, or intense fears of various things or situations; obsessive-compulsive behavior, in which an individual compulsively pursues the completion of a thought or action in order to relieve anxiety; and dissociative reactions, in which some personality traits and memories seem to be dissociated from each other. Common physical symptoms of psychoneurosis include tenseness, fatigue, and psychosomatic disorders (see PSYCHOSOMATIC MEDICINE). Psychoneurosis is usually accompanied by a variety of DEFENSE MECHANISMS, which are employed in an attempt to overcome anxiety. Even in persons relatively free from external anxiety, neurotic reactions can be traced back to anxiety and the mechanisms for avoiding it. It is differentiated from PSYCHOSIS in that it involves no appreciable loss of reality sense, primary mood disturbance, or deterioration in intellectual functions. Freud, who originated the term *psychoneurosis*, believed that the causal factors could be found roughly in the first six years of life, when the personality, or ego, is weak and afraid of censure; he attributed psychoneurosis to the frustration of infantile sexual drives, as when severe eating and toilet habits and other restrictions are parentally imposed (see OEDIPUS COMPLEX). These infantile conflicts, remaining unresolved, appear in adulthood under conditions of stress as neurotic symptoms (see PSYCHOANALYSIS). Other authorities emphasize consitutional and organic factors. Among the psychoanalysts, Alfred Adler and H. S. Sullivan stressed social determinants of personal adjustment, and Karen Horney emphasized insecurity in childhood as causes of psychoneurosis. Theoretical distinctions between normality, psychoneurosis, and psychosis are no longer regarded as distinct and clearly differentiated and in practice it is often difficult to distinguish between them. The rising incidence of psychoneurosis in the population is believed to be in part attributable to the complexity of industrialized society. Social anthropologists such as the Americans Ruth Benedict and Margaret Mead have shown that behavior patterns considered neurotic in one culture may be considered normal in another. Treatment of psychoneurosis includes behavior therapy to condition an individual to change neurotic habits, PSYCHOTHERAPY, and GROUP PSYCHOTHERAPY. Various drugs are available to alleviate symptoms (see PSYCHOPHARMACOLOGY). See Otto Fenichel, *Psychoanalytic Theory of Neurosis* (1945); Andras Argyal, *Neurosis and Treatment* (1965); H. J. Eysenck, *The Causes and Cures of Neurosis* (1965); Sigmund Freud, *Outline of Psychoanalysis* (tr. 1940, repr. 1969); Karen Horney, *The Neurotic Personality of Our Time* (1937, repr. 1964) and *Neurosis and Human Growth* (1950, repr. 1970); Alfred Adler, *The Neurotic Constitution* (tr. 1926, repr. 1972).

psychopathy, term for a variety of mental disorders characterized by antisocial and amoral behavior and social maladjustment. The antisocial, or psychopathic, personality is an individual who appears never to have developed a conscience or internalized social behavior standards during development. Psychoanalytic theory attributes such behavior to incomplete development of the superego (see PSYCHOANALYSIS). Such individuals are impulsive, insensitive to others' needs, and unable to anticipate the consequences of their behavior, to follow long-term goals, or to tolerate frustration. The psychopathic individual is characterized by absence of the guilt feelings and anxiety that normally accompany an antisocial act. The psychopathic pattern usually begins in childhood; by adulthood these antisocial impulses may result in unhappy marriage, sexual deviations, criminal activities, or feelings of bitterness and resentment, alcoholism, and drug addiction. Psychopaths, unlike individuals suffering from various PSYCHOSES or PSYCHONEUROSES, do not usually benefit from psychotherapy or other forms of treatment, although behavior therapy has been used with moderate success.

psychopharmacology (sī″kōfär″məkŏl′əjē), in its broadest sense, the study of all pharmacological agents that affect mental and emotional functions. However, the term is usually applied specifically to the study and synthesis of drugs used in the treatment of psychiatric illnesses, namely the antipsychotic, anti-anxiety, and antidepressant medications. Antipsychotic drugs, or major tranquilizers, can ameliorate psychotic states characterized by severe, disorganizing ANXIETY. The first of this group was RESERPINE, whose use dates from ancient Hindu medicine but whose reintroduction as an antipsychotic agent in 1954 marked the beginning of the large-scale use of tranquilizers. Because of side effects, including depression, reserpine has been supplanted by the phenothiazine tranquilizers (see PHENOTHIAZINE). Tranquilizing drugs, despite their name, calm patients without causing drowsiness, disequilibrium, or dulling of speech and thought as did older remedies such as the bromides and BARBITURATES. The phenothiazine CHLORPROMAZINE (Thorazine), used originally to increase the effectiveness of anesthetics, was the first to be widely applied to mental disorders and remains the standard drug. Drugs of the phenothiazine family are useful in the treatment of severe anxiety, agitation, and delusions, in schizophrenia, mania, and organic brain conditions. They are thought to act in part by rendering the membranes of neurons at the synapse less permeable to transmitter amines; in contrast, reserpine probably depletes stores of these amines. The phenothiazines have been credited with a revolutionary transformation of mental health care, enabling increasing numbers of psychotic persons to function out of the hospital. Anti-anxiety drugs, or minor tranquilizers, including MEPROBAMATE (Miltown), chlordiazepoxide (Librium), and the barbiturates, have found wide and often controversial applications. Although they form a chemically diverse group, the physiological effects of each are similar; in small doses they relieve anxiety, and in larger doses produce sedation, sleep, and anesthesia (see DEPRESSANT). These tranquilizers are the most frequently prescribed drugs in the United States. Antidepressant drugs appeared in the late 1950s with iproniazid, whose stimulating effects were discovered during treatment of tuberculosis patients by a related drug. Iproniazid and structurally similar substances are thought to work by inhibiting monoamine oxidase, an enzyme that breaks down transmitter amines in the brain. These drugs have the effect of increasing the concentration in the nervous system of CATECHOLAMINES such as EPINEPHRINE. The toxic effects of the monoamine oxidase inhibitors, including iproniazid, have resulted in their removal from therapeutic use; they have been supplanted by compounds such as imipramine (Tofranil) that are chemically similar to phenothiazines, but that activate rather than tranquilize (see STIMULANT). Imipramine and chemically similar stimulant compounds are not monoamine oxidase inhibitors and do not act primarily on the central nervous system; their mode of action is not known. The element LITHIUM, in the form lithium carbonate, has been used in cases of manic-depressive psychosis, particularly to control manic episodes. Lithium alters the transport of sodium ions in nerve and muscle cells and affects the metabolism of catecholamines; the exact mechanism of action is unknown. The psychotomimetic, or hallucinogenic, drugs, such as mescaline and LYSERGIC ACID DIETHYLAMIDE, have been of research interest because they often mimic natural psychotic states (see PSYCHOTOMIMETIC DRUGS).

psychosis (sīkō′sĭs), in PSYCHIATRY, mental disorder involving emotional disturbances that render the individual incapable of adjusting realistically to his environment. The symptoms may include, either separately or in combination, disturbance of reality appreciation (hallucinations and delusions); severe deviation of mood (depression and mania); lack of, or inappropriateness of, apparent emotional response; and severe distortion of judgment. In legal usage the term INSANITY, not used in psychiatry, is applied to those psychoses in which the moral judgment of the individual is considered impaired. Among the more common of the organic psychoses, so called because of the structural damage of the brain, are those associated with advanced syphilis, senile DEMENTIA, and certain late and neglected stages of genuine epilepsy. Functional psychoses, i.e., those in which no organic damage is apparent, include SCHIZOPHRENIA, PARANOIA, MANIC-DEPRESSIVE PSYCHOSIS, and INVOLUTIONAL PSYCHOTIC REACTIONS. PSYCHOTHERAPY, SHOCK THERAPY, and pharmacological therapy have proved valuable in the treatment of certain psychoses. See PSYCHOPHARMACOLOGY.

psychosomatic medicine (sī″kōsōmăt′ĭk), study and treatment of those emotional disturbances that are manifested as physical disorders. The term *psychosomatic* emphasizes essential unity of the psyche and the soma, a combination rooted in ancient Greek medicine. Common disorders caused at least partly by psychological factors include childhood ASTHMA, ULCERS and other gastrointestinal problems, hypertension, endocrine disturbances, and possibly even heart disease. In most psychosomatic conditions there is usually some interaction between psychological factors and a physiological predisposition to the illness; for example, an ulcer is often caused by a combination of external stress, ANXIETY, and a constitutional susceptibility to ulcers. The treatment of psychosomatic ailments ordinarily involves a medical regimen as well as some form of PSYCHOTHERAPY for the patient. In recent years the term *psychosomatic medicine* has taken on the broader meaning of psychotherapeutic medicine.

Sigmund Freud, at the end of the 19th cent., laid the scientific groundwork for psychosomatic study with his theoretical formulations based on new methods of treating HYSTERIA. His methods were reinforced by the psychobiology of the American psychiatrist Adolf Meyer and the research of the American physiologist W. B. Cannon on the physiological effects of acute emotion. Psychosomatic complaints, which usually involve organs under control of the involuntary (autonomic) NERVOUS SYSTEM, are distinguished from hysteria, which typically involves parts under voluntary control, eg., a limb. See Edward Weiss and O. S. English, *Psychosomatic Medicine* (3d ed. 1957); H. R. and M. F. Lewis, *Psychosomatics* (1972).

psychotherapy, treatment of mental disorders by psychological methods. Although this type of treatment has been used in one form or another through the ages in many societies, it was not until the late 19th cent. that it received scientific impetus, primarily under the leadership of Sigmund Freud. His use of hypnosis in the treatment of HYSTERIA led to the development of PSYCHOANALYSIS, now a specialized field. Most psychotherapists agree that mental disorders are largely a result of ANXIETY and are an expression of unresolved inner conflicts. Treatment involves an interpersonal relationship between therapist and patient and relief of the patient's symptoms in order to initiate therapy, and requires some commitment on the part of the patient. In addition to psychoanalysis, which requires an understanding of psychoanalytic theory, other forms of therapy stress helping the patient to examine his own ideas about himself and his life. Behavior therapy aims to help the patient learn to eliminate undesirable habits by principles of conditioning. In recent years the group treatment of mental disorders has gained added acceptance (see GROUP PSYCHOTHERAPY). See Walter Bromberg, *Man above Humanity: A History of Psychotherapy* (1954); B. G. Berenson and R. R. Carkhuff, eds., *Sources of Gain in Counseling and Psychotherapy* (1967); Allen Bergin et al., eds., *Psychotherapy* (1972); C. H. Patterson, *Theories of Counseling and Psychotherapy* (1973).

psychotomimetic drug (sīkŏt″ōmĕmĕt′ĭk), any of several chemically similar alkaloid substances that alter consciousness. The term psychotomimetic refers to the fact that the effects of these drugs sometimes mimic the manifestations of PSYCHOSIS; thus they are also popularly called mind-expanding, hallucinogenic, or psychedelic. The group includes mescaline, or PEYOTE, which comes from the cactus *Lophophora williamsii*; psilocin and psilocybin, from the mushrooms *Psilocybe mexicana* and *Stropharia cubensis*; and LYSERGIC ACID DIETHYLAMIDE (LSD), synthesized from lysergic acid, found in the fungus *Claviceps purpurea* (see ERGOT). These alkaloids have also been produced synthetically. MARIJUANA has hallucinogenic properties but is pharmacologically distinct. Many psychotomimetic drugs share a basic chemical structural unit, the indole ring, which is also found in the nervous system substance SEROTONIN; mescaline has chemical similarities to both the indole ring and the adrenal hormone EPINEPHRINE. Psychotomimetic drugs have been used for centuries by certain peoples, e.g., the Hindus and the Aztec Indians, to facilitate meditation, cure illness, and enhance mystical powers. Many North American tribal Indians still use the mushroom and the cactus in tribal rituals. The psychotomimetic drugs produce a wide range of effects, depending on the properties, dosage, and potency of the drug, the personality and mood of the drug taker, and the immediate environment. Visually, perception of light and space is altered, and colors and detail take on increased significance. If the eyes are closed the drug taker often sees intense visions of different kinds. Nonexistent conversations, music, odors, tastes, and other sensations are also perceived. The sensations are often either very pleasant or very distasteful and disturbing. The drugs frequently alter the sense of time and cause feelings of emptiness. For many individuals the separation between self and environment disappears, leading to a sense of oneness or holiness. Physiologically the drugs act as mild stimulants of the sympathetic nervous system, causing dilation of the pupils, constriction of some arteries, a rise in blood pressure, and increased excitability of certain spinal reflexes. Although the drugs are not physiologically habit-forming, individuals taking mescaline, lysergic acid diethylamide, or psilocybin can develop physiological tolerance for them and need to take increased quantities to reproduce the original effect.

psychrometer (sīkrŏm′ĭtər), instrument used for measuring the water vapor content or relative humidity of the atmosphere. It consists of two identical liquid-in-glass thermometers—one is called the wet-bulb thermometer because its bulb is covered with a jacket of tight-fitting muslin cloth that can be saturated with distilled water; the other is called the dry-bulb thermometer. When the cloth is soaked and the thermometers are properly ventilated, the wet-bulb temperature will be lower than the dry-bulb temperature (actual air temperature) because of cooling due to the evaporation of water from the cloth. The drier the air is, the greater the evaporation and thus the more the wet-bulb temperature is depressed. Psychrometric tables list various humidity variables, such as relative humidity, according to dry-bulb temperature and wet-bulb depression at equilibrium. Ventilation is provided by whirling the thermometers at the end of a chain (sling psychrometer) or by a suction fan (aspiration psychrometer). See HYGROMETER.

psyllium seed (sĭl′ēəm): see PLANTAIN.

Pt, chemical symbol of the element PLATINUM.

Ptah (ptä), in Egyptian religion, great god of Memphis. He was one of the important gods of ancient Egypt and, according to Memphite theology, created the universe through the thought of his heart and the utterance of his tongue. As master craftsman, he was a patron of metalworkers and artisans. The Greeks identified him with Hephaestus.

ptarmigan (tär′məgən): see GROUSE.

pterodactyl (tĕrədăk′tĭl), extinct flying reptile of the order Pterosauria, common in the Mesozoic era. The flying apparatus of the pterodactyl comprised a membranous wing stretched between the fourth finger of the hand and the side of the body. There is no fossil evidence of either scales or feathers. The fifth finger was degenerate, and the first three were free of the wing. The earlier varieties had fully toothed jaws and long tails, while in the later forms the tail was a stump, the teeth were lacking, and the jaws were modified into a beak. About 29 kinds of pterosaurs have been found, sizes ranging from that of a sparrow to that of a dragonlike creature with a wingspread of more than 20 ft (6.1 m). The pterodactyl, unlike the ARCHAEOPTERYX, was not ancestral to the birds, but represented a wholly separate line of development. The pterodactyl is classified in the phylum CHORDATA, subphylum Vertebrata, class Reptilia.

pteroylglutamic acid (tĕrō″ĭlglōōtăm′ĭk): see VITAMIN.

Ptolemaic system (tŏl″əmā′ĭk), historically the most influential of the geocentric cosmological theories, i.e., theories that placed the earth motionless at the center of the universe with all celestial bodies revolving around it (see COSMOLOGY). The system is named for the astronomer Ptolemy (fl. 2d cent. A.D.); it dominated astronomy until the advent of the heliocentric COPERNICAN SYSTEM in the 16th cent. The ancient philosophers imagined the universe to resemble a complex clockwork consisting of concentric crystalline spheres, nested inside one another, which carried the sun, moon, and planets in their motions and made the "music of the spheres" as they revolved. Professional astronomers did not claim that such a mechanism physically existed; rather, they treated it as the hypothetical basis for constructing geometrical schemes that would allow them to make accurate predictions of the motions and future positions of celestial bodies. Partly on aesthetic grounds and partly because no other hypothesis suggested itself, Ptolemy generally retained the semimystical Pythagorean belief that nothing but motion at constant speed in a perfect circle is worthy of a celestial body. He combined simple circular motions to explain the complicated wanderings of the planets against the background of the fixed stars. The motions of the planets against the stars are not uniform and circular but exhibit a host of irregularities. For a superior planet (Mars and those farther from the sun), the most important of these is the planet's RETROGRADE MOTION at the time of opposition. The planet seems to halt and then reverse its motion for a few months, so that its complete circuit of the ECLIPTIC is attended by a series of yearly loops or switchbacks. Ptolemy explained retrograde motion by assuming that each planet moved in a circle called an epicycle, whose center was in turn carried around the earth in a circular orbit called a deferent. Thus, the motion of all the planets around the earth in the Ptolemaic system was somewhat similar to the motion that modern astronomy ascribes to the moon as it revolves around the earth while the earth itself is revolving around the sun. The fact that the inferior planets (Venus and Mercury) never stray far from the sun was explained by the provision that the centers of their epicycles always had to lie on the line connecting the earth and sun. In the final version of his system, Ptolemy modified the postulate of uniform motion in order to explain the variations in the apparent speeds of the planets. He found that these variations could be reproduced most conveniently by displacing the earth from the center of the deferent to a point called the eccentric. He then assumed that the motion of the center of the epicycle along the deferent appeared uniform, not from the center of the deferent or from the eccentric, but from a third point symmetrically displaced from the eccentric, called the equant. This modification was tantamount to abandoning the postulate of uniform motion. Ptolemy considered it more important to achieve a closer agreement with the observed astronomical data than to adhere to any preconceived first principles. His work thus anticipates the positivist spirit of modern empirical science, which makes no ontological claim for its constructs but merely asserts that nature behaves "as if" these constructs lay behind appearances.

Ptolemaïs (tŏləmā′ĭs), ancient name given to several cities to honor members of the dynasty of the Ptolemies. One of these later became known as AKKO, in modern Israel. Another was one of the great Hellenistic cities of Upper Egypt, on the Nile and N of Abydos. A third, in Cyrenaica, was one of the cities of the Libyan Pentapolis. A fourth was a small town, sometimes called Ptolemaïs Theron, on the western coast of the Red Sea.

Ptolemaïs (ptôlĭmĭs′), town (1971 pop. 16,588), N Greece, in Macedonia. It was a small market town until 1958, when it began to be developed as an industrial center. Lignite, mined there in vast quantities, is used to power thermoelectric plants, which produce electricity for iron and steel mills, aluminum factories, and chemical plants.

Ptolemy I (Ptolemy Soter) (tŏl′əmē sō′tər), d. 284 B.C., king of ancient Egypt, the first ruler of the Macedonian dynasty (or Lagid dynasty), son of a Macedonian named Lagus. He was one of the leading generals of Alexander the Great, and after Alexander's death (323 B.C.) he joined the other DIADOCHI in dividing and quarreling over the empire. Ptolemy received Egypt and managed to keep control of it in the midst of incessant warfare. To strengthen his position he married Eurydice, daughter of ANTIPATER (though he soon shifted his affection to her niece and his own half sister, BERENICE). He defeated (321) PERDICCAS, and he at first supported ANTIGONUS I in the confused struggle for imperial power. He defeated EUMENES, then fearing Antigonus' efforts to remake the empire, allied himself with CASSANDER and LYSIMACHUS. Ptolemy defeated the troops of Antigonus in 312 but he was defeated at Salamis in 306, and the ultimate defeat and death of Antigonus at Ipsus in 301 resolved the situation. Ptolemy had already declared himself king in 305. Subsequently he laid the outline for Ptolemaic administration in Egypt and did much to make Alexandria a fountainhead of culture and art by founding the library there. Through Arrian, we know that he wrote a history of Alexander. See J. P. Mahaffy, *The Empire of the Ptolemies* (1895); E. R. Bevan, *A History of Egypt under the Ptolemaic Dynasty* (1927).

Ptolemy II (Ptolemy Philadelphus) (fĭlədĕl′fəs), c.308–246 B.C., king of ancient Egypt (285–246 B.C.), of the Macedonian dynasty, son of Ptolemy I and BERENICE (c.340–281 B.C.). He continued his father's efforts to make Alexandria the cultural center of the Greek world. He completed the Pharos and encouraged the translation of the PENTATEUCH into the Greek SEPTUAGINT. Finances were reformed, and a canal was built from the Nile to the Red Sea. He warred against Syria until he married his daughter Berenice to the Syrian Antiochus II. By supporting Rome in the First Punic War, he increased his prestige. Ptolemy repudiated his wife Arsinoë to marry his sister, also named Arsinoë. Manetho, the Egyptian historian, compiled his history.

Ptolemy III (Ptolemy Euergetes) (yōōûr′jĭtēz), d. 221 B.C., king of ancient Egypt (246–221 B.C.), of the Macedonian dynasty, son of Ptolemy II and the first Arsinoë. He plunged immediately into a war with Syria, where his sister, Berenice, was trying to secure the throne for her son. Berenice and her son seem to have been murdered before Ptolemy could arrive, and Seleucus II held the throne, though the Egyptian king won a brilliant if impermanent victory. Egyptian fleets controlled most of the coasts of Asia Minor and E Greece, and the kingdom was enlarged by Ptolemy's marriage to Berenice, daughter and heiress of the king of Cyrene.

Ptolemy IV (Ptolemy Philopator) (fĭlŏp′ətər), king of ancient Egypt (221–205 B.C.), of the Macedonian dynasty, son of Ptolemy III and Berenice of Cyrene. He had his mother, his brother, his uncle, and possibly his wife (who was his sister Arsinoë) killed. ANTIOCHUS III invaded the Egyptian lands in Palestine, and Ptolemy managed to defeat him at Raphia in 217 (an event mentioned in 3 Maccabees), but administration disintegrated in Egypt. Ptolemy's main interest was building remarkable ships, each equipped with 4,000 oars.

Ptolemy V (Ptolemy Epiphanes) (ĭpĭf′ənēz), d. 180 B.C., king of ancient Egypt (205–180 B.C.), of the Macedonian dynasty, son of Ptolemy IV. He succeeded to the throne as a small boy, and his reign began with disastrous civil wars. Invasions by Antiochus III of Syria and Philip V of Macedon cost Egypt all of Palestine and the Egyptian possessions in Asia Minor. Antiochus defeated Ptolemy decisively at the Battle of Paneas in 198 B.C. Peace was confirmed by the marriage of Ptolemy to Cleopatra, daughter of Antiochus. Egypt was much weakened when his reign ended. The ROSETTA STONE inscriptions concern Ptolemy's ascension to the throne.

Ptolemy VI (Ptolemy Philometor) (fĭləmē′tər), d. 145 B.C., king of ancient Egypt (180–145 B.C.), of the Macedonian dynasty, son of Ptolemy V. He became king when an infant, and his mother, Cleopatra, was regent. After her death, Antiochus IV of Syria invaded Egypt, and Ptolemy was captured (170 B.C.) at Pelusium. He was forced to share the rule with his wife (also his sister), Cleopatra, and his brother, Ptolemy Physcon (later PTOLEMY VII). Ptolemy Physcon ruled over Cyrene, Ptolemy Philometor over Egypt; trouble between the brothers ultimately caused the intervention of Rome. Ptolemy VI aided Demetrius II to gain the throne of Syria and was killed in battle with the rival claimant, Alexander Balas. His young son in theory succeeded to the throne and is sometimes called Ptolemy VII, but he was put to death as soon as Ptolemy Physcon (who is sometimes counted as Ptolemy VIII) could reach Egypt.

Ptolemy VII (Ptolemy Physcon) (fĭs′kən), d. 116 B.C., king of ancient Egypt (145–116 B.C.), of the Macedonian dynasty, brother of PTOLEMY VI. He is also called Ptolemy Euergetes II. He was coruler with his brother and his brother's wife from 170–164 B.C. Trouble resulted in a settlement by which Ptolemy Physcon ruled Cyrene. On his brother's death he returned to Egypt, had his nephew put to death, and married Cleopatra, his brother's widow. He soon repudiated her and married her daughter, also named Cleopatra. The elder Cleopatra led a revolt and drove him (130 B.C.) out of Egypt. He returned in 127 B.C. and later ruled peacefully though despotically. Both queens survived him. His reign was one of great cruelty; he drove the scholars from Alexandria and thus precipitated the spread of Alexandrian culture.

Ptolemy VIII (Ptolemy Lathyrus) (ləthī′rəs), d. 81 B.C., king of ancient Egypt (116–107 B.C., 88–81 B.C.) of the Macedonian dynasty, son of Ptolemy VII and the younger Cleopatra. He is also called Ptolemy Soter II. His mother ruled jointly with him and held the actual power. She forced him to accept (110 B.C.) as coruler his brother, Ptolemy Alexander (Ptolemy IX), who drove him from the throne in 107 B.C. Ptolemy VIII went to Cyprus and then to Syria. He returned to conquer Cyprus, and in 88 B.C. he reconquered Egypt.

Ptolemy IX (Ptolemy Alexander), d. 88 B.C., king of ancient Egypt (107 B.C.–88 B.C.), of the Macedonian dynasty, brother of Ptolemy VIII. He was governor in Cyprus when called (110 B.C.) by his mother to be coruler with his brother. He became sole king in 107 B.C. He was ousted by a revolt in Alexandria and died when trying to recover the kingdom.

Ptolemy X (Ptolemy Alexander), d. 80 B.C., king of ancient Egypt (80 B.C.), of the Macedonian dynasty, son of Ptolemy IX. His stepmother, Cleopatra Berenice, was joint ruler with her father, Ptolemy VIII, and sole ruler after his death until the Romans under Sulla brought about her marriage to Ptolemy X, who became joint ruler. A few days later he murdered her, and the Alexandrians rose up and killed him.

Ptolemy XI (Ptolemy Auletes) (ôlē′tēz), d. 51 B.C., king of ancient Egypt (80–58 B.C., 55–51 B.C.), of the Macedonian dynasty, illegitimate son of Ptolemy VIII. He is also called Ptolemy Neos Dionysus. He succeeded Ptolemy X to the throne, but his violent misrule and reprehensible life caused the Alexandrians finally to rebel and unseat him in 58 B.C. He sought Roman aid and with the help of Pompey paid Aulus Gabinius, proconsul of Syria, a huge sum to put him back on the throne. He made the Roman senate executor of his will and Pompey the guardian of his son Ptolemy XII.

Ptolemy XII, 61?–47 B.C., king of ancient Egypt (51–47 B.C.), of the Macedonian dynasty; son of Ptolemy XI. On the death of his father he was under the guardianship of Pompey. He was completely overshadowed from the start by his brilliant and celebrated sister, CLEOPATRA, who became his wife and ruled with him. She disagreed with his advisers, notably the eunuch Pothinus, and fled to Syria. She came back (48 B.C.) with an invading army. At this juncture the defeated Pompey arrived seeking refuge and was put to death by Pothinus. Julius CAESAR followed immediately. He fell under the influence of Cleopatra, forced Ptolemy XII to share the throne with her again, and put down a rebellion raised by Pothinus. Ptolemy was thus defeated. He drowned accidentally in the Nile.

Ptolemy XIII, d. 44 B.C., king of ancient Egypt (47–44 B.C.), the last of the Macedonian dynasty, but for his sister, CLEOPATRA. He was a child when his brother Ptolemy XII drowned. Julius Caesar married him to Cleopatra in 47 B.C. and made him joint ruler with her; she later had him murdered.

Ptolemy XIV (Ptolemy Caesarion), 47–30 B.C., son of CLEOPATRA and (almost certainly) Julius Caesar. He became joint ruler with his mother, but played no role in the great and tragic events that brought Egypt and Cleopatra to their doom. Fearing that he might gain popular support, Octavian (later Emperor Augustus) had him put to death.

Ptolemy (Claudius Ptolemaeus), fl. 2d cent. A.D., celebrated Greco-Egyptian mathematician, astronomer, and geographer. He made his observations in Alexandria and was the last great astronomer of ancient times. Although he discovered the irregularity in the moon's motion, known as evection, and made original observations regarding the motions of the planets, his place in the history of science is that of collator and expounder. He systematized and recorded the data and doctrines that were known to Alexandrian men of science. His works on astronomy and geography were the standard textbooks until the teachings of COPERNICUS came to be accepted. The mathematical and astronomical systems developed by the Greeks are contained in his 13-volume work, *Almagest*. With credit to HIPPARCHUS as his chief authority, he presented in his famous book problems and explanations dealing with the known heavenly bodies and their relations to the earth. The PTOLEMAIC SYSTEM thus evolved represented the earth (a globe in form) as stationary in the center of the universe, with sun, moon, and stars revolving about it in circular orbits and at a uniform rate. From the center outward the elements were earth, water, air, fire, and ether. Beyond lay zones, or heavens, each an immense sphere. The planets were assumed to revolve in small circles, called epicycles, whose centers revolved around the earth in the vast circles, or deferents, of the spheres. (To account for the precession of the equinoxes and other phenomena, later astronomers found it necessary to add more epicycles and to make both epicycles and deferents eccentric.) The *Almagest* also contains other astronomical information, including a catalog of more than 1020 stars (giving their latitudes, longitudes, and magnitudes), as well as mathematical information, including a table of chords. Ptolemy's system of geography is founded upon the works of Marinus of Tyre; many errors stem from his underestimation of the earth's circumference. However, his system was in use until the 16th cent. His mathematical theories, most valuable in the field of trigonometry, are preserved in his *Analemma* and *Planisphaerium*. His writings, circulated in the original Greek and in Arabic and Latin translations, include also the *Tetrabiblos*, a study of astrology. See tr. of his *Geography* by E. L. Stevenson (1932) and of his *Almagest* by R. C. Taliaferro (1952).

ptomaine poisoning (tō′mān, tōmān′): see FOOD POISONING.

ptyalin (tī′əlĭn): see AMYLASE.

Pu, chemical symbol of the element PLUTONIUM.

Pua (pyōō′ə), variant of PHUVAH.

Puah (pyōō′ə). **1** Midwife ordered by Pharaoh to kill Jewish boys at birth. Ex. 1.15,16. **2** Father of the judge Tola. Judges 10.1. **3** See PHUVAH.

puberty (pyōō′bərtē), period during which the onset of sexual maturity occurs. It takes place in females between the ages of 11 and 14 and in males between 12 and 16. The pituitary gland secretes hormones that stimulate the enlargement and development of the sex organs, which thus become capable of reproduction. The appearance of secondary sex characteristics also occurs during puberty. In females the reproductive cycle of ovulation and menstruation begins, pubic hair appears, and the development of the breasts and other body contours takes place. Physical changes in males include the production and discharge of semen, the appearance of facial and body hair, and deepening of the voice. Skin difficulties, such as the development of acne, may affect both sexes. Puberty, a transition period coinciding with ADOLESCENCE, involves both physiological and psychological adjustment. It is often marked by emotional stress arising as the adolescent relinquishes the behavior patterns of childhood and adopts those of an adult.

publican [Lat.,=state employee], in ancient Rome, man who was employed by the state government under contract. As early as c.200 B.C. there was a class of men in Rome accustomed to undertaking contracts involving public works and tax collecting; the tax collectors made the most profit. The publicans were usually EQUITES, or capitalists. In the Gospels—which showed the general detestation, particularly in Asia Minor, Syria, and Palestine, in which the publicans were held—the publicans mentioned were tax collectors. From the 1st cent. A.D. the abuses of the publicans began to be corrected, and by the end of the 2d cent. the publicans as a group had disappeared.

public broadcasting: see BROADCASTING.

public defender, governmental official who represents indigent persons accused of crime. Recent U.S. Supreme Court decisions expanding the right to counsel to pretrial proceedings and holding that a person cannot be sentenced to even one day in jail unless a lawyer was provided have created a need for more lawyers to represent the indigent. Proponents of the public defender office claim that it is the most efficient and effective method of protecting the indigent. Other systems include court-appointed counsel from the local bar, clinics operated by law schools, and legal aid societies. The societies are privately funded and offer civil and criminal representation.

public domain, in law, legal availability for public use, free of charge, of materials, processes, devices, skills, and plans that are not protected by copyright or patent, including those on which copyright or patent has lapsed. Historically in the United States, the term has been important in reference to PUBLIC LAND under the administration of national or local authorities.

public health, field of medicine and hygiene dealing with the prevention of disease and the promotion of health by government agencies. In the United States, public health authorities are engaged in many activities, including inspection of persons and goods entering the country to determine that they are free of contagious disease. They are empowered to isolate persons with certain diseases and to quarantine such individuals, if necessary, for the public good. Public health officials are responsible for supervising the purity of the water, milk, and food supply as well as the persons who handle these items and the public eating places that dispense them. They are responsible for the good health of animals that supply food and for the extermination of wildlife and insects that contribute to disease. The inoculation of household pets against rabies and the importation of birds that harbor psittacosis are under public health jurisdiction. The authorities are also concerned with the pollution levels in air and water, and must assure the safety of waters used for swimming and as sources of sea food. Health authorities also license persons who dispense health services—doctors, dentists, nurses, masseurs, technicians. In addition, they collect vital statistics on death rates, birth rates, communicable and chronic diseases, and other indicators of the state of public health. The duties of carrying out the many services required to keep the population healthy and to prevent serious outbreaks of disease are divided among local, state, and Federal government agencies. Each city or county has its own department of health and its own hospitals and clinics. Local government also supervises the voluntary and private hospitals in the community. It provides health officers and nurses for the schools and visiting nurses for the home. It oversees the water supply, the disposal of sewage, the production and distribution of milk, and the proper handling of food in restaurants. State government is concerned with the licensing of professional personnel and the maintenance of institutions for chronic diseases, notably hospitals for mental disease and tuberculosis. It may impose standards of public health on local communities where these are not being met. It gives financial and technical assistance to local communities in time of crisis, such as that caused by an epidemic. The principal Federal health agency is the Public Health Service, established in 1870 and made a constituent of the Dept. of Health, Education, and Welfare in 1953. Federal public health authorities have jurisdiction over all persons, animals, and goods entering the country from abroad. They set standards for the handling and production of food involved in interstate commerce as well as for the manufacture of drugs, serums, vaccines, and cosmetics. They come to the aid of localities and states whenever there is a widespread epidemic. In addition, the Federal government supports medical research in its own laboratories, as well as in universities and other organizations. To carry out all these activities the public health services employ large numbers of physicians, dentists, veterinarians, laboratory technicians, nurses, sanitary engineers, health educators, psychologists, and social workers.

public land, in U.S. history, land owned by the Federal government but not reserved for any special purpose, e.g., for a park or a military reservation. Public land is also called land in the public domain. Except in Texas, which made retention of its public lands one of the conditions for joining the Union, there are no state public lands. Seven of the original states ceded their western lands to the Federal government when they entered the Union. Additional public land was acquired with the Louisiana Purchase (1803), Florida (1819), Oregon (1846), the Mexican Cession (1848), the Gadsden Purchase (1853), and Alaska (1867). Almost as soon as public land was acquired the Federal government began to dispose of it through grants to states, railroad companies, settlers (see HOMESTEAD ACT, 1862), colleges (see LAND-GRANT COLLEGES AND UNIVERSITIES), and cash sales. It was charged that large companies frequently acquired extensive holdings by dishonest means, and many of the new owners obtained considerable revenue by selling the land. A reaction to this easy policy set in toward the end of the 19th cent., and steps were taken to insure the CONSERVATION OF NATURAL RESOURCES by withdrawing public lands from sale. Thereafter the government leased such land for grazing, lumbering, mining, the harnessing of water power, and other purposes, while maintaining regulatory control. By the 1970s there was considerable controversy over the need to make the best use of the public land's valuable resources while still preserving the land for future use and expanded recreational activities. Most of the nation's remaining public land is in the western part of the country, about half of it in Alaska. See E. L. Peffer, *The Closing of the Public Domain* (1951, repr. 1972); W. C. Calef, *Private Grazing and Public Lands* (1960); Vernon Carstensen, ed., *The Public Lands* (1962); Paul Gates, *History of Public Land Law Development* (1968); M. J. Rohrbough, *The Land Office Business* (1968).

public opinion poll: see POLL.

public ownership, government ownership of lands, streets, public buildings, utilities, and other business enterprises. The theory that all land and its resources belong ultimately to the people and therefore to the government is very ancient. From it comes the doctrine of eminent domain, asserting that the state has ultimate control over lands and buildings within its borders. Until the policy of laissez faire in the 18th cent. emphasized capitalistic activity, public ownership was unquestioned. In ancient times governments owned and conducted many enterprises, such as water systems, theaters, and baths. In the United States, governmental units own and manage the public school system, public highways and bridges, dams for the reclamation of land and for power (and the management and sale of power), and many other enterprises. The Tennessee Valley Authority is an example of public ownership. The importance of public utilities to the life of the community has frequently led to municipal ownership of water, sewerage, electric light, power, gas, and transportation systems. In Europe, where public ownership is more extensive and of longer standing than in the United States, it has been extended to include railroads, telephone and telegraph lines, radio and television, coal mining and other power resources, and banking. Since World War II many Western nations have practiced public ownership of business enterprises through public corporations. AMTRAK is such a corporation. Public ownership is practiced most extensively in Soviet Russia and other Communist countries, where government owns almost all land and all natural resources, and where utilities, banking, transportation, and nearly all industries are carried on by state corporations or trusts. Many developing countries also have large-scale public ownership, especially of vital industries and resources. Public ownership is to be distinguished from government control of private enterprises in utilities, business, and agriculture. In the United States such control has been increased through loans, direct financing, and laws providing for the government's regulation of corporate activities. See NATIONALIZATION.

public relations, activities and policies used to create public interest in a person, idea, product, institution, or business establishment. By its nature, public relations is devoted to serving particular interests by presenting them to the public in the most favorable light. Thus, the goal of the public relations consultant is to create, through the organization of news and advertising, an advantageous image for his client, be it a business corporation, cultural institution, or private or public individual; toward this end—the making of favorable public opinion—many research techniques and communications media are used. Although many of the same methods are employed, public relations differs from PROPAGANDA, which is generally government supported, international in scope, and political in nature. The earliest form of public relations and still the most widely practiced is publicity. The principal instrument of publicity is the press release, which provides the mass media with the raw material and background for a news story. The growth of modern public relations is generally attributed to the development of the mass media, which accelerated the spread of ideas and increased the importance of public opinion by giving more people access to current events. Public relations as a field can be traced to the early 20th cent., when American businessmen found it necessary to respond to attacks by social reformers. A milestone in the industry was the opening (1904) of Ivy Lee's publicity office in New York City. Soon there were other firms in the field, and by World War I the concept of public relations had gained general acceptance. Public relations techniques have been widely used in politics and political campaigns. By the 1960s the public relations agency had become a fact in American life, numbering among its clients branches of national, state, and local government, industry, labor, professional and religious groups, and some foreign countries. See B. R. Canfield, *Public Relations* (5th ed. 1968); E. L. Bernays, *The Engineering of Consent* (3d ed. 1969) and *Public Relations* (1970); S. M. Cutlip and A. H. Center, *Effective Public Relations* (4th ed. 1971); L. R. Blumenthal, *The Practice of Public Relations* (1972).

public school, in the United States, a tax-supported elementary or high school open to anyone. In England the term was originally applied to grammar schools endowed for the use of the lay public; however, it has come to be used for the famous endowed preparatory schools that now charge tuition. The English public schools include Charterhouse, Cheltenham, Clifton, Eton, Harrow, Rugby, Westminster, and Winchester. See SCHOOL. See also Vivian Ogilvie, *The English Public School* (1957).

public utility: see UTILITY, PUBLIC.

Public Works Administration (PWA), in U.S. history, New Deal government agency established (1933) by the Congress as the Federal Administration of Public Works, pursuant to the National Industrial Recovery Act. In the hope of promoting and stabilizing employment and purchasing power, President Franklin Delano Roosevelt brought about the creation of this agency to administer the construction of various public works, such as public buildings, bridges, dams, and housing developments, and to make loans to states and municipalities for similar projects. Subsequent legislation continued its operation; under the administration (1933–39) of Harold L. ICKES, the PWA completed a great many public projects. President Roosevelt's reorganization plan of 1939 made the PWA a division of the Federal Works Agency. The PWA was liquidated in the 1940s.

publishing: see BOOK PUBLISHING.

Publius (pŭb'lēəs), Paul's host at Malta. Acts 28.7–10.

Pucci, Emilio: see under FASHION.

Puccini, Giacomo (jä'kōmō po͞ot-chē'nē), 1858–1924, Italian composer of operas. He composed some of the most popular works of the opera repertory. A descendant of a long line of musicians, he studied the piano and the organ at Lucca and in 1880 entered the Milan Conservatory. He first gained recognition with a one-act opera, *Le Villi* (1884). His finest operas, *Manon Lescaut* (1893), *La Bohème* (1896), *La Tosca* (1900), *Madama Butterfly* (1904), and *Turandot* (produced posthumously in 1926), display his characteristically lyric style and masterful orchestration, evoking strongly dramatic and emotional effects. Although the characters in his operas are rather generalized, romantic figures, they are made to come alive through expressive melody. A penchant for exotic settings produced some incongruities in his music, as in *La Fanciulla del West* (*The Girl of the Golden West*, 1910), and some of his works have been criticized for their excessive sentimentality. However, wit and dramatic vivacity are shown in his comic opera *Gianni Schicchi* (1918), and Puccini has remained, along with Verdi, a preeminent master of the Italian operatic stage. See his letters, ed. by Giuseppi Adami (tr. 1931, repr. 1973); biographies by Vincent Seligman (1938), Mosco Carner (1959), and Richard Specht (tr. 1933, repr. 1970); study by William Ashbrook (1968).

Pucelle, Jean (zhäN püsĕl'), c.1300–1355, French manuscript illuminator. Master of a celebrated workshop in Paris during the 1320s, Pucelle produced a masterpiece of ILLUMINATION and a stylistic landmark in his *Hours of Jeanne d'Évreux* (c.1325; Cloisters, New York City). This tiny BOOK OF HOURS, commissioned for the Queen of France, was filled with exquisite, restrained drawings, many concerning the life of Louis IX (Saint Louis). Other works with MINIATURE PAINTINGS by Pucelle include the *Belleville Breviary* (Bibliothèque nationale).

puck (pŭk), in Germanic folklore, generic name for various malevolent spirits. The medieval English *pouke* was often identified with the devil. However, the Puck of Shakespeare's *A Midsummer Night's Dream* is a mischievous but friendly fairy.

pudding. Early writers on cookery class puddings and dumplings together. The earliest puddings were boiled in a bag or cloth. Later they were placed in a buttered bowl, covered with a cloth, and steamed. The baked or chilled puddings evolved even later. Puddings are classed as those served with meat, such as Yorkshire pudding (batter baked under the meat or in the drippings), or which form the meat course, such as Sussex pudding (a large dumpling filled with meat instead of fruit), and those served as a sweet or dessert, such as almond, cabinet, and suet puddings, plum or Christmas pudding, and Indian pudding, as well as puddings made with milk, eggs, rice, sago, tapioca, arrowroot, cornstarch, bread crumbs, and fruit. Custards are included by some writers, and jellied fruits by others. An early use of the word, as in black pudding or white pudding, referred to forms of SAUSAGE.

Pudens (pyo͞o'dĕnz), Christian of Rome. 2 Tim. 4.21.

Pudovkin, Vsevolod Ilarionovich (fsyĕ'vələt ēləryôn'əvĭch po͞odôf'kĭn), 1893–1953, Russian film director. His best film, *Mother* (1925), was followed by *The End of St. Petersburg* and *Storm over Asia*, the two films that made him famous. Known for his innovations in technique, he wrote *Film Technique* (tr., enl. ed., 1933) and *Film Acting* (tr. 1935), which have become standard reference works.

Pudsey (pŭd'sē, -zē), municipal borough (1971 pop. 36,187), West Riding of Yorkshire, N England. It is a center of woolen- and worsted-textiles industries. A Moravian school and settlement were established nearby at Fulneck in the 18th cent. In 1974, Pudsey became part of the new metropolitan county of West Yorkshire.

Puebla (pwä'blä), state (1970 pop. 2,483,770), 13,126 sq mi (33,996 sq km), E central Mexico. The city of Puebla is the capital. The state is almost entirely mountainous, with large valleys between its ranges. N Puebla is dominated by the Sierra Madre Oriental, and a volcanic belt stretches across the central part of the state. Mexico's three highest peaks—Orizaba in the east and Popocatépetl and Ixtacihuatl in the west—border on Puebla. The state's extreme northeastern section lies on the humid coastal plain of the Gulf of Mexico; the southern part is in drier upland valleys. Differences in climate and elevation permit the cultivation of a variety of agricultural products, including sugarcane, coffee (of which Puebla is a leading Mexican producer), cotton, tobacco, rice, and grains. Stock raising is also important. The great majority of the state's population is engaged in agriculture. Although gold, silver, copper, and lead are mined, Puebla's great mineral wealth remains largely untapped. The potential for a lumbering industry is also relatively undeveloped. Puebla is an important manufacturer of textiles. Communications within the state are excellent.

Puebla, city (1970 pop. 521,885), capital of Puebla state, E central Mexico. Its official name is Puebla de

Zaragoza, in honor of Gen. Ignacio Zaragoza, who defeated the French forces there in 1862. Located in a highland valley, it is an important agricultural, commercial, and manufacturing center, as well as a popular tourist spot. The site of Mexico's first textile-producing factory, Puebla now has cotton mills, onyx quarries, and pottery and food industries. The city is noted for the fine, colored tiles that decorate its buildings and numerous churches, as well as those of nearby Cholula. The cathedral, built between 1552 and 1649, is one of the finest in Mexico; the theater, constructed in 1790, is said to be the oldest on the continent. Puebla is also the seat of an archbishop. Founded c.1535 as Puebla de los Ángeles, the city was historically a link between the coast and Mexico City. It was taken (1847) by U.S. Gen. Winfield Scott during the Mexican War. French troops captured Puebla in 1863 but were ousted by Porfirio Díaz in 1867.

Pueblo (pwĕb'lō, pyo͞oĕb'lō), city (1970 pop. 97,453), seat of Pueblo co., S central Colo., on the Arkansas River in the foothills of the Rockies; inc. 1885. It is the center of shipping, trade, and industry for an extensive timber, coal, livestock, and irrigated-farm area. It has a huge steel industry. Wire, concrete, and lumber are also produced. A trading post, called Pueblo, was established there in 1842, followed by a temporary Mormon settlement (1846–47). The city was laid out in 1860. After a severe flood in 1921, levees were constructed and the Arkansas River was controlled. Construction on an ambitious Arkansas River reclamation project, designed to serve irrigation, rediversion, and power purposes, began in 1964. Pueblo is the seat of Southern Colorado State College. A large U.S. army ordnance depot, the state fairgrounds, and a state mental hospital are also there. The city is the headquarters for San Isabel National Forest.

Pueblo Indians, name given by the Spanish to the sedentary Indians who lived in stone or adobe community houses in what is now the SW United States. The term *pueblo* is also used for the villages occupied by the Pueblo Indians. Their prehistoric settlements, known as the Anasazi culture, extended southward from S Utah and S Colorado into Arizona, New Mexico, and adjacent territory in Mexico. By 2000 B.C. the earliest agricultural groups—known as the Cochise culture—were using corn, ground with a stone metate and mano; squash and beans were added by 1000 B.C. The trio of foods is still used by the Pueblos. The first village settlements of pit houses were built by the Mogollon peoples early in the 1st cent. A.D. Among North American Indians they had the first true pottery and bow and arrow. Contemporaries of the Mogollon, the basket makers, lived in the area around the juncture of the present-day states of Arizona, Colorado, New Mexico, and Utah. Finely made baskets served as cooking and carrying vessels. They lived in caves, using storage pits for grains; clothing, as well as stone, seed, and shell jewelry are found in graves. From 400 to 700, irrigation, pottery, and surface houses were developed; grave goods include flutes, pipes, and gaming sets. During that period some cultural changes occurred, including flattening of skulls (by cradleboard pressure) and multiroomed clan group houses. These developmental Puebloans performed rites in kivas that resembled the underground ceremonial chambers now used by Pueblo Indians; the apparent derivation is from the old pit houses. Cotton was grown and fabrics woven by loom. Drought-resistant corn produced a food surplus, allowing a large concentration of population. Multistoried cliff houses, as at Mesa Verde, mark the Great Pueblo Period from about 1050 to the end of the 13th cent., when the area was abandoned, it is believed, because of protracted drought conditions. The Spanish who entered the Rio Grande area in the 16th cent. found Pueblo villages over 200 years old. The seven Zuñi towns were exaggeratedly reported by the Franciscan Marcos de Niza to be the fabulous Seven Cities of Cibola, and this led to the first contacts—a Spanish exploration party under Francisco Vásquez de Coronado in 1540. Due to increasing pressure on the existing food supplies, the initially friendly Pueblos became hostile and then revolted; their resistance ended in a mass execution of Indians by Coronado. In 1598, Juan de Onate began full-scale missionary work and moved the provincial headquarters of the Spanish colonial government to Santa Fe. By 1630, 60,000 Pueblo Indians had been converted to Christianity, and 90 villages had chapels, according to Father de Benavides. Determined to put an end to the suffering caused by their Spanish oppressors, the Pueblos staged a successful revolt in 1680. POPÉ, a medicine man, led the band of Pueblos, who killed 380 settlers and 31 missionaries, and the Spanish retreated to El Paso. However, the Pueblos lost 347 of their number in one attack on Santa Fe. Fearing Spanish reprisal, villages were abandoned for better fortified sites; in 1692, De Vargas with the cooperation of some Pueblo leaders reconquered the Pueblos in New Mexico, but the Western Pueblos, including the Hopi, remained free. The Pueblo Indians have the oldest civilization N of Mexico, dating back 700 years for the still occupied Hopi, Zuñi and Acoma pueblos. They also had the highest civilization of any of the aboriginal peoples N of Mexico, perhaps because of their proximity to the advanced Aztec and Toltec Indians of Mexico. The Europeans who settled in the Southwest adopted the adobe structures and compact village plans of the Pueblos. The Pueblos, for their part, adopted many domestic animals and assorted crafts from the old world, including blacksmithing and woodworking, and were introduced to chili and to many new fruits. Pueblo Indians speak languages of at least two different families. Languages of the Tanoan branch of the Aztec-Tanoan linguistic stock (see AMERICAN INDIAN LANGUAGES) are spoken at 11 pueblos, including Taos, Isleta, Jemez, San Juan, San Ildefonso, and the Hopi pueblo of Hano. Languages of the Keresan branch of the Hokan-Siouan linguistic stock also are limited to Pueblo people—Western Keresan, spoken at Acoma and Laguna, and Eastern Keresan, at San Felipe, Santa Ana, Sia, Cochiti, and Santo Domingo. The Hopi language (which belongs to the Uto-Aztecan branch of the Aztec-Tanoan linguistic stock) is spoken at all Hopi pueblos except Hano. The Zuñi language may be connected with Tanoan and fall within the Aztec-Tanoan linguistic stock. Among the modern Pueblo Indians, men are the weavers and women make pottery and assist in house construction. The position of women among both the Western and the Eastern Pueblos is high, but there are differences related to the different social systems of each. The Western Pueblos, including the Hano, Zuñi, Acoma, Laguna, and, the best known, the Hopis, have exogamous clans with a matrilineal emphasis and matrilocal residence, and the houses and gardens are owned by women; the KACHINA cult has a major emphasis on weather control, and the Pueblos who follow this cult are governed by a council of clan representatives. Among the Eastern Pueblos, there are bilateral extended families, patrilineal clans, and male-owned houses and land; warfare and hunting as well as healing and exorcism are more important than among the Western Pueblos. The Spanish added new elements to the government, in the form of civil officers, but the de facto government and ceremonial organization remained native. In recent years the Bureau of Indian Affairs introduced elected officials in Santa Clara, Laguna, Zuñi, and Isleta. The Hopi have an elected council on the tribal level. The Kachina and other secret societies dealing with war, agriculture, and healing still carry out their complicated rituals and dances—to some of which the public is invited. The reservation population in Arizona and New Mexico was some 32,000 in 1968. See H. A. Tyler, *Pueblo Gods and Myths* (1964); E. P. Dozier, *The Pueblo Indians of North America* (1970); W. A. Longacre, ed., *Reconstructing Prehistoric Pueblo Societies* (1970); Robert Silverberg, *The Pueblo Revolt* (1970); J. U. Terrell, *Pueblos, Gods, and Spaniards* (1973).

Puelche (pwĕl'chā), name for various hunting groups of nomadic Indians who roamed the Argentine Pampa, hunting guanaco and rhea. Little is known of the Puelche prior to the 18th cent. Accomplished horsemen fighting with lance and bolo, they were not very numerous and were absorbed in the 18th cent. by the ARAUCANIAN INDIANS.

Puerto Barrios (pwār'tō bär'yōs), city (1971 est. pop. 29,425), E Guatemala, capital of Izabal dept., on the Bay of Amatique, an arm of the Caribbean Sea. It was named after the Guatemalan politician Justo Rufino Barrios. The port handles more trade than any other in Guatemala. Bananas and coffee are the leading exports. As the terminus of the International Railways of Central America, Puerto Barrios also serves as an eastern seaport for El Salvador.

Puerto Bello: see PORTOBELO, Panama.

Puerto Cabello (käbā'yō), city (1970 est. pop. 71,000), N Venezuela, a port on the Caribbean Sea. The second most important Venezuelan port, it ships meat, coffee, cacao, dyewoods, and copper ores. Near the city is one of Venezuela's most modern oil and chemical plants. Strategically located, Puerto Cabello was subject to attacks by buccaneers and was a favorite market for Dutch smugglers during the colonial era. The last Spanish royalist stronghold during Venezuela's war for independence, it was captured by José Antonio PÁEZ in 1823.

Puerto Cortés (kōrtās'), town (1961 pop. 17,000), NW Honduras, on the Caribbean Sea; founded c.1525. It is a principal banana port; other exports are hardwoods, abaca, and minerals. The town is also a rail and processing center.

Puerto de Santa Maria (thā sän'tä märē'ä), town (1970 pop. 42,111), Cádiz prov., S Spain, in Andalusia, on the Bay of Cádiz at the mouth of the Guadalete River. It is a commercial center, exporting sherry wine.

Puerto Montt (mōnt), city (1970 pop. 86,750), capital of Llanquihue prov., S central Chile, a port on Ancud Gulf, an inlet of the Pacific Ocean. It is the southern terminus of Chile's mainland railroads and the starting point for navigation through the inland waterways and among the islands to the south. The scenery—forested hills, lakes, narrow fjords, and peaks—helps make Puerto Montt a popular resort. Founded in 1853 and named for Chilean President Manuel Montt, the city was settled largely by Germans. Sheep farming and fishing are important, and there are minor industries. In 1960 the city was devastated by an earthquake.

Puerto Plata, city (1970 pop. 32,181), N Dominican Republic, on the Atlantic Ocean. It is the major northern port of the country, serving Santiago de los Caballeros and other inland towns. Dairy and cacao products are made there. Nearby are the ruins of Columbus' first settlement in the New World.

Puerto Rico (rē'kō), formerly **Porto Rico** (pôr'tō rē'kō), island (1970 pop. 2,712,033), 3,425 sq mi (8,871 sq km), West Indies, c.1,000 mi (1,610 km) SE of Miami, Fla. Officially known as the Commonwealth of Puerto Rico (a self-governing entity in association with the United States), it includes the offshore islands of Mona, Vieques, and Culebra. The capital is SAN JUAN; other important cities are PONCE and MAYAGÜEZ. Smallest and easternmost of the Greater Antilles, Puerto Rico is bounded by the Atlantic Ocean on the north and the Caribbean Sea on the south. Mona Passage to the northwest separates the island from the Dominican Republic, and the Virgin Islands lie to the east. Puerto Rico is crossed by mountain ranges, notably the Cordillera Central, which rises to 4,389 ft (1,388 m) in the Cerro de Punta. Although rivers are short and unnavigable, some provide irrigation or hydroelectric power. The climate is mildly tropical, with little seasonal change. Rainfall is plentiful, despite some arid regions in the south. Hurricanes are likely to occur between August and October. Puerto Rico's fertile soil supports one of the densest populations in the world. Sugarcane has long been the chief product; livestock raising (for meat and dairy production) ranks second among agricultural pursuits. Coffee, pineapples, and tobacco are other leading crops, and vegetable growing and canning are increasingly important. Reforestation has been undertaken to restore the tropical woods of the interior, where the Caribbean National Forest is set apart. Heavy industry and manufacturing have come to replace agriculture as the greatest contributors to Puerto Rico's national income largely because of "Operation Bootstrap," which since the 1940s has attracted U.S. firms through the use of tax exemptions. The metallurgical and chemical industries are among the most important, along with oil refining (using crude oil from Venezuela) and the production of petrochemicals. Tourism is also a major industry. Puerto Rico's mineral resources are limited and not fully exploited. The United States is by far Puerto Rico's chief trading partner. The leading exports are raw and refined sugar and sugar products (rum, candy, molasses). Imports consist mainly of food products as well as such consumer items as automobiles and home appliances. Although Puerto Rico is no longer dependent on a single-crop economy and has reduced its unemployment rate, overpopulation and insufficient jobs have contributed to social and economic problems and to heavy migration (mainly to New York). The Puerto Ricans are descended from Spanish colonists, with an admixture of Indian and African strains. Spanish is the official language, and Roman Catholicism the main religion. Before the Spanish arrived, the island was inhabited by Arawak Indians, who called the region Borinquén or Boriquén. Christopher Columbus discovered the island in 1493 and named it San Juan Bautista [St. John the Baptist], but he sailed on to Hispaniola to plant a settlement. Juan Ponce de León began the actual conquest in 1508, landing at San Juan harbor, which he called Puerto Rico [Span.,=rich port]. A settlement was founded in 1521 on the site of present-day San Juan. As hardship, disease, and Spanish reprisals

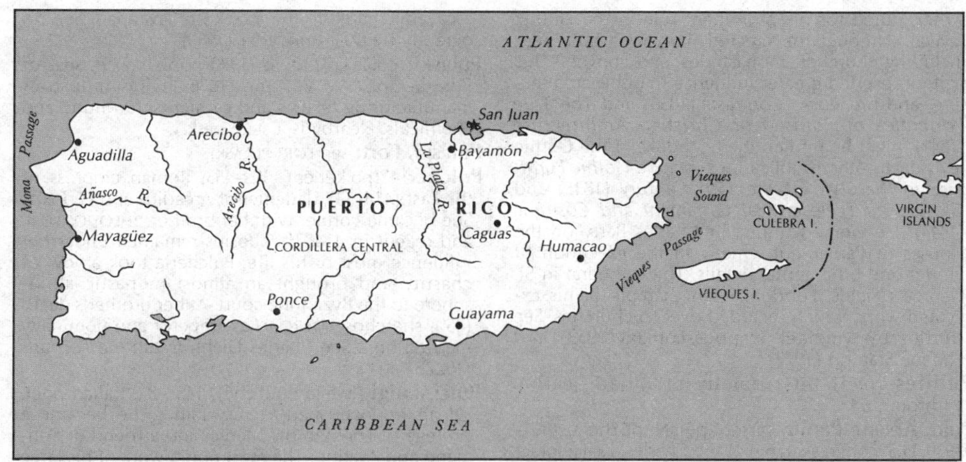

eliminated the Arawak Indians altogether, they were replaced as plantation workers by African slaves, first introduced in 1513. Deposits of placer gold were virtually depleted during the 1530s, after which the Spanish devoted their full attention to the sugar plantations. Raids by nearby Carib Indians and by British, French, and Dutch pirates, however, hampered agricultural prosperity. San Juan, meanwhile, became a leading outpost of the Spanish Empire. Treasure-filled Spanish galleons that anchored there on their long trip to Spain attracted buccaneers. George Clifford, earl of Cumberland, held Puerto Rico for five months in 1598, and the Dutch besieged the island in 1625. Spain's response was to build several fortresses (whose walls still stand) that made San Juan virtually impregnable. With external threats thus warded off, Puerto Rico settled down to a quiet plantation existence. Coffee was introduced in the 18th cent. to supplement sugar. Beginning in the 1820s there were some uprisings against Spanish rule, but all were quelled. Most notable was the Lares rebellion of 1868, the year Queen Isabella II was forced to abdicate and the first Spanish republic proclaimed. As part of a reform movement that extended to Puerto Rico, slavery was abolished in 1873, and the new Spanish constitution of 1876 granted Puerto Rican representation in Spain's parliament. A movement for self-government, supported by liberal groups in Spain, grew in Puerto Rico during the 1880s. Finally, in February, 1898, largely through the efforts of the Puerto Rican statesman Luis MUÑOZ RIVERA, Spain granted the island some autonomy. The new form of government had little chance to operate, however, for a few months later the Spanish-American War erupted. U.S. troops occupied the island without much difficulty. By the Treaty of Paris (Dec. 10, 1898), which ended the war, Puerto Rico was ceded to the United States. It remained under direct military rule until 1900, when the U.S. Congress passed the Foraker Act, setting up an administration with a U.S. governor, an upper legislative chamber appointed by the U.S. President, and an elected house of delegates; the U.S. Congress was given the right to review all legislation. Meanwhile, a movement for Puerto Rican independence gained strength as pressures to define the island's political status grew. In 1917 the Jones Act stipulated that Puerto Rico was a U.S. territory whose inhabitants were entitled to U.S. citizenship. The act provided for election of both houses of the Puerto Rican legislature, but the governor and other key officials were still to be appointed by the U.S. President, and the governor was empowered to veto any legislation. During World War I, U.S. holdings in Puerto Rico increased, and the change to a one-crop sugar economy was completed. The island's territorial status gave Puerto Rican sugar a ready market within U.S. tariff walls; however, large sugar corporations encroached on land where foods had been raised for subsistence, thus causing social upheaval in the countryside and necessitating greater food imports. Absentee ownership and one-crop culture aggravated the ills of overpopulation. Sanitary and health improvements under the U.S. occupation further accelerated population growth. Many Puerto Ricans criticized the American regime for its menace to the Hispanic roots of Puerto Rican culture. Criticism intensified when the sugar market dropped in the 1930s and many workers, always near the edge of starvation, became even more desperate. Recovery measures were taken during the presidency of Franklin Delano Roosevelt and especially under the governorship (1941–46) of Rexford G. TUGWELL. Military activities related to World War II also aided the economy. The Popular Democratic party, headed by Luis MUÑOZ MARÍN, adopted a program based on economic reform and expansion, but other political parties were more concerned with U.S.-Puerto Rican relations. The Conservative Republicans advocated statehood; the Independentists, led by Gilberto Concepción, and the Nationalists, headed by Pedro ALBIZU CAMPOS, favored immediate independence. In 1946, the U.S. government granted Puerto Rico increased local autonomy, exemplified by the appointment of the first native Puerto Rican governor, Jesus T. Piñero. The right of popular election of the governor followed, and Muñoz Marín won the 1948 election. His administration undertook a program of agricultural reform and industrial expansion. On July 25, 1952, the Commonwealth of Puerto Rico was proclaimed. The continuing Nationalist campaign for independence, however, was dramatized by an attempt to assassinate President Harry S. Truman in 1950 and by a shooting attack in the U.S. House of Representatives in 1954. Muñoz Marín was reelected in 1952, 1956, and 1960. Declining to run for reelection in 1964, he was succeeded by his Popular Democratic party's candidate, Roberto Sanchez Vilella. In the face of an increasingly active movement for statehood, the governor arranged for a plebiscite in 1967 in which Puerto Ricans could choose among independence, statehood, and maintenance of the commonwealth relationship. An overwhelming majority voted in favor of the status quo. In the 1968 gubernatorial election, Luis A. Ferré, candidate of the New Progressive party, which advocated statehood, emerged victorious. However, in 1972 the Popular Democratic party was returned to power with the defeat of Ferré and the election of Raphael Hernández Colón as governor. The election was regarded by many as a strong endorsement for continuation of commonwealth status. Puerto Rico's governor and both legislative houses are popularly elected for four-year terms. There are 27 senators and 51 representatives. An elected resident commissioner sits in the U.S. House of Representatives but cannot vote. The governor may serve an unlimited number of terms. On the local level, Puerto Rico is divided into municipalities, each with its own mayor and assembly. Puerto Ricans share all the rights and obligations of U.S. citizenship, including service in the armed forces; however, they do not pay Federal taxes and cannot vote in national elections. The U.S. government handles Puerto Rico's foreign affairs, and U.S. military installations are maintained on the island. Since Puerto Rico's relationship with the United States began, illiteracy has been greatly reduced. Although Spanish is the medium of instruction, English is a second language studied by all Puerto Ricans. By the late 1950s the commonwealth was able to provide a basic education for all children of elementary school age. The island's rural vocational schools are exemplary. Institutions of higher learning include the Univ. of Puerto Rico (with its main branch at Río Piedras), the Inter-American Univ. at San Germán, the Catholic Univ. at Ponce, and a Catholic college for women at San Juan. See Writers' Program, *Puerto Rico: A Guide to the Island of Boriquén* (1940); H. S. Perloff, *Puerto Rico's Economic Future* (1950); J. W. Pratt, *America's Colonial Experiment* (1950); Millard Hansen and Henry Wells, ed., *Puerto Rico: A Study in Democratic Development* (1953); Earl P. Hanson, *Transformation: The Story of Modern Puerto Rico* (1954) and *Puerto Rico: Land of Wonders* (1960); R. G. Tugwell, *The Stricken Land* (1946, repr. 1968); Henry Wells, *The Modernization of Puerto Rico* (1969); Kal Wagenheim, *Puerto Rico, a Profile* (1970); Francesco Cordasco and Eugene Bucchioni, comp., *The Puerto Rican Experience* (1973); M. J. Golding, *A Short History of Puerto Rico* (1973).

Puerto Rico, University of, mainly at Río Piedras, near San Juan; land grant and commonwealth; coeducational; founded 1903 as successor to a normal school. The College of Liberal Arts in Río Piedras has faculties of humanities, natural sciences, and social sciences, as well as a general studies program. At Mayagüez there is a college of arts and sciences (including agriculture and engineering) and a center for nuclear studies offering programs in nuclear technology, radiological physics, and mathematics. Another campus is located at Bayamon. The university also maintains a medical center at San Juan and two-year branches at Arecibo, Humacao, and Ponce.

Pueyrredón, Juan Martín de (hwän märtĕn' dā pwāĭrādōn'), 1776–1850, Argentine general, supreme director of the United Provinces of La Plata (1816–19). In 1806, when British troops under William Carr BERESFORD invaded the Río de la Plata, he organized a volunteer force, which, after a defeat outside Buenos Aires, united with the army of LINIERS to recapture the city (Aug. 12). Taking an important part in the revolutionary government, he was governor of Córdoba (1810) and of Charcas (1810–11), commander of the patriot Army of the North (1811–12), and a member of the triumvirate at Buenos Aires (1812). As supreme director, he assisted SAN MARTÍN in the Chilean campaign of 1817–18. In 1819 congress promulgated a unitarian constitution, which was rejected by the people. The demand for federalism brought Pueyrredón's resignation. His success in preventing anarchy was transient; the civil war of 1820 followed.

Pufendorf, Samuel, Baron von (zä'mo͞oĕl bärôn' fən po͞o'fəndôrf), 1632–94, German jurist and historian. He is especially noted as an early theorist of international law. Pufendorf maintained that the law of nations is a branch of NATURAL LAW and that to treat it as positive law (i.e., law decreed by men) is erroneous. The natural relations of nations (as of men) are peaceable, and war is justified only to punish an infraction of international law after attempts at pacific redress have failed. These views are developed in his *Elementa jurisprudentiae universalis* [elements of universal jurisprudence] (1661) and in *De jure naturae et gentium* [on the law of nature and of nations] (1672). His chief historical work was *De statu imperii Germanici* [on the condition of the German Empire] (1667), in which he described Germany as a monstrous aggregate lacking a strong imperial power. Pufendorf taught jurisprudence at the universities of Lund and Heidelberg, and in his later years he was royal historiographer at Stockholm and Berlin. See study by Leonard Krieger (1965).

puff adder: see VIPER.

puffball or **smokeball,** fungus in which the aboveground portion is typically a stemless brownish sac with an opening at the top through which issues the dustlike mass of ripe spores. The common puffball is *Lycoperdon gemmatum*. The giant puffball (*L. giganteum*) may reach a diameter of 1 ft (30 cm) or more. No puffballs are poisonous, and most forms are edible when young. They are related to the MUSHROOM and are similar in flavor. Puffballs are classified in the division FUNGI, class Basidiomycetes.

puffer, common name for some tropical marine fish of the family Tetraodontidae. The puffers and their allies, the boxfish, the porcupinefish, and the ocean sunfish or headfish, form an odd group (order Tetraodontiformes). The puffers, or swellfishes, named for their ability to inflate their bodies to three times normal size, are found all along the Atlantic coast, e.g., the northernpuffer (*Sphaeroides maculatus*), and in the Pacific. Their prickly skin is exaggerated into stout spines in the porcupinefish (family Diodontidae) and the spiny boxfish, or burrfish, which are also able to inflate themselves. Like the puffers, they feed on marine invertebrates. The ocean sunfish, or headfish (family Molidae), occurs widely in all seas, although it prefers warmer waters. Its appearance is that of a huge head with fins attached, as its body does not taper. It moves clumsily and is usually seen basking in the sun. The ocean sunfish is one of the largest of all fishes, the record weight being about one ton (900 kg). It is harpooned for sport; except for the oil from its liver, it is of little value as food. Puffers and their allies are classified in the phylum CHORDATA, subphylum Vertebrata, class Osteichthyes, order Tetraodontiformes.

puffin, common name for a diving bird of the family Alcidae (AUK family). Its large, triangular bill, brilliantly colored in yellow, blue, and vermilion, is adapted to carrying several fish at one time; it also gives the puffin its alternate name of sea parrot. During the mating season horny excrescences may develop over the eyes. Puffins have dumpy bodies, short legs set far back, and small wings; although expert swimmers, they are clumsy on land and in flight. They nest in colonies in burrows or rock cavities on northern islands and migrate regularly—the Atlantic puffin, *Fratercula arctica*, as far south as Long Island and the Pacific puffin, *Lunda cirrhata*, to California. The female lays a single egg, which is incubated mainly by the female. The chick is fed fish by both parents, and is abruptly deserted after 6 weeks. The adolescent puffin stays alone for another week, and then leaves the burrow alone. Puffins are classified in the phylum CHORDATA, subphylum Vertebrata, class Aves, order Charadriiformes, family Alcidae.

pug, breed of sturdy, compact TOY DOG that became popular in England during the 19th cent. It stands about 11 in. (27.9 cm) high at the shoulder and weighs from 14 to 18 lb (6.4–8.2 kg). Its short, smooth, glossy coat is either silver or apricot fawn in color with black mask and ears. As is true of most toy dogs that have short faces and tails curled tightly over their backs, the pug probably originated in China. Traders of the Dutch West India Company brought specimens of the breed back to Holland from the Orient and later introduced them into England, where they quickly became fashionable with the nobility. Today the pug is raised as a watchdog and pet. See DOG.

Pugachev, Emelian Ivanovich (yĭmĭlyän' ēvä'nəvĭch po͞ogəchôf'), d. 1775, Russian peasant leader, head of the peasant rebellion of 1773–74. An almost illiterate Don Cossack, he exploited the peasants' widespread belief that PETER III had not actually been murdered. Claiming (1773) to be Peter III, he soon found himself at the head of an army and of a revolutionary movement. His followers—Cossacks, peasants, runaway serfs, Tatar bands, and serfs from the mines and factories—all belonged to the lower classes, whose rights and liberties had been increasingly curtailed in the past two centuries. Pugachev announced the abolition of serfdom. His army overran the middle and lower Volga districts and the Ural region and took Kazan and several fortresses, committing barbarous excesses and threatening the throne of CATHERINE II, who was waging war on Turkey. However, the rebels lacked experienced leadership and were ultimately defeated. Pugachev was betrayed, taken to Moscow, and beheaded. As a result of the rebellion Catherine introduced the administrative reform (1775) that increased the central government's control over outlying areas and more firmly entrenched the institution of serfdom.

Puget, Pierre (pyĕr püzhā'), 1622–94, French painter and sculptor. At 17 he went on foot to Italy, where he worked for Pietro da CORTONA on the ceilings of the Barberini and Pitti palaces. Much of his work is in S France and in Italy, where he worked. His famous statue of St. Sebastian is in Genoa. He made paintings for the churches of Aix-en-Provence and Toulon, but gradually devoted himself wholly to sculpture. From 1655 to 1658, Puget carved the caryatids for the town hall of Toulon. He also executed commissions for Fouquet. Puget used skillful variations on the Italian baroque idiom, ranging from the expressive contortions of his caryatids to the controlled form of his *Milo of Crotona* (Louvre).

Puget Sound (pyo͞o'jĕt), arm of the Pacific Ocean, NW Wash., connected with the Pacific by Juan de Fuca Strait, entered through the Admiralty Inlet and extending in two arms c.100 mi (160 km) S to Olympia. The sound, which receives many streams from the Cascade Range, has numerous islands and is navigable for large ships. Along its shores are important ports and commercial cities. Puget Sound Naval Shipyard (est. 1891), at Bremerton, employs about 10,000 people in fleet repair and construction. The Puget Sound lowland, which extends south from the sound, is the most densely populated area of Washington; Seattle and Tacoma are the principal cities. Discovered in 1787, the sound was explored and named by English Capt. George Vancouver for his aide, Peter Puget, in 1792.

pugilism (pyo͞o'jəlĭz"əm): see BOXING.

Pugin, Augustus Charles (pyo͞o'jĭn), 1762–1832, English architectural draftsman and writer on medieval architecture, b. France. His writings furnished a mass of working material for the architects of the GOTHIC REVIVAL. Among them is *Specimens of Gothic Architecture* (2 vol., 1821–23). In some of his publications he was assisted by his son, **Augustus Welby Northmore Pugin,** 1812–52, English architect and writer, noted for his prominent role in the Gothic revival. Although he erected numerous buildings, including churches, monasteries, and convents, his writings exerted greater influence than his architecture, and his works *Contrasts* (1836) and *The True Principles of Pointed or Christian Architecture* (1841) might be termed the textbooks of the Gothic revival. His other publications include *Gothic Furniture in the Style of the 15th Century* (1835) and *Glossary of Ecclesiastical Ornament and Costume* (1844). He worked under Sir Charles Barry on the Houses of Parliament, chiefly in the execution of fittings and ornamental details. The cathedral in St. George's Fields, London, is an example of his executed work, which included over 65 churches. See studies by Michael Trappes-Lomax (1933) and Phoebe Stanton (1972).

Puhites (pyo͞o'hīts), family of Kirjath-jearim. 1 Chron. 2.53.

Pujo, Arsène Paulin (arsĕn' pôlăN' püzhō'), 1861–1939, U.S. congressman, b. Lake Charles, La. He practiced law in Louisiana before serving (1903–13) as a Democratic Congressman in the U.S. House of Representatives. From 1908 to 1912 he was a member of the National Monetary Commission, which was established to study international banking systems with a view to improving the American system. He became chairman of the House Banking and Currency Committee in 1911, and, dissatisfied with the monetary commission's report, he obtained congressional authorization in 1912 to investigate the "money trust." The hearings of the Pujo committee, which were highlighted by a spectacular interrogation of J. P. Morgan by the committee's counsel, Samuel Untermeyer, uncovered evidence that a few financial leaders had achieved an unhealthy control of the nation's money and credit. The committee's disclosures helped create a climate of public opinion that led to the passage of the Federal Reserve Act of 1913 and the Clayton Antitrust Act of 1914.

Pukaskwa National Park (pŭk'ăskwə), c.725 sq mi (1,890 sq km), central Ont., Canada, near Marathon; est. 1971. Stretching for c.50 mi (80 km) along the north shore of Lake Superior between the Pukaskwa and White rivers, the park has a rugged terrain with many lakes, rivers, and waterfalls. Tip Top mt. (2,120 ft/650 m high), one of the highest points in Ontario, is in the park.

puku: see MARSH ANTELOPE.

Pul (pŭl). **1** Assyrian king, invader of Israel, known as Tiglath-pileser III. 2 Kings 15.19; 1 Chron. 5.26. **2** African region. Isa. 66.19. Probably the same as PHUT or PUNT.

Pula (po͞o'lä), Ital. *Pola,* city (1971 pop. 70,079), NW Yugoslavia, in Croatia, on the Adriatic and at the southern tip of the Istrian peninsula. A major seaport and an industrial center, it has shipyards, docks, and varied manufactures. Captured (178 B.C.) by the Romans, it was destroyed by Augustus, but was rebuilt by him and named Pietas Julia. It passed to Venice in 1148, but in 1379 it was taken and destroyed by the Genoese. However, it remained a Venetian possession until the Treaty of Campo Formio (1797) transferred it to Austria. Under Austrian rule Pula became the chief naval base and arsenal of the Hapsburg empire. The city was ceded to Italy after World War I and to Yugoslavia after World War II. Pula has many well-preserved Roman ruins, notably a large amphitheater, the Porta Aurea (a triumphal arch of the 1st cent. B.C.), and the temple of Augustus and Roma (1st cent. A.D.).

Pulangi (po͞oläng'gē), river, c.200 mi (320 km) long, rising in the mountains of N Mindanao, the Philippines, and flowing SW to Liguasan Marsh then NW (as the Mindanao River) to Illana Bay at Cotabato. It drains a rich rice-growing area.

Pulaski, Casimir (kă'sĭmĕr pəlăs'kē), Pol. *Kazimierz Pułaski* (käzē'myĕsh po͞olä'skē), c.1748–1779, Polish patriot and military commander in the American Revolution. Born in Podolia of a noble family, he participated with his father in forming (1768) the Confederation of BAR to oppose Russian influence in Poland. In the unsuccessful rebellion against the Russian-dominated king of Poland, Stanislaus II, he gained military fame. After the Confederation was suppressed by Russian troops, he escaped (1772) to Prussia and later to France. There he met Benjamin Franklin, who gave him a letter of recommendation to George Washington. Joining the Revolutionary cause in 1777, he served at Brandywine and Germantown. In 1778 he resigned a cavalry command rather than continue in service under Gen. Anthony Wayne, and he organized his own cavalry unit, the Pulaski Legion, which saw a great deal of service before Pulaski was mortally wounded while leading a cavalry charge in the attack on Savannah. See biography by D. J. Abodaher (1969).

Pulaski (pəlăs'kē), town (1970 pop. 10,279), seat of Pulaski co., SW Va.; inc. 1886. It has industries manufacturing textiles and garments, furniture, and chemicals. Nearby is a state park.

Pulaski, Fort: see FORT PULASKI.

Pulcheria (pəlkĕr'ēə), 399–453, Roman empress of the East (414–53), daughter of Arcadius and Eudoxia. She became coruler with her brother, THEODOSIUS II, and regent in 414. Theodosius remained under her influence most of his life. Pulcheria took a vow of chastity and brought an almost monastic atmosphere to the Byzantine court. At her brother's death (450) she chose MARCIAN as emperor and nominally married him. See Charles Diehl, *Byzantine Portraits* (1927).

Pulci, Luigi (lwē'jē po͞ol'chē), 1432–84, Italian poet. Of an impoverished literary family, he became a protégé of Lorenzo de' Medici and a friend of Poliziano and Aretino. The most noted work of his large literary production is *Morgante Maggiore* (1483). A hodgepodge of comic incidents, scientific digressions, and lofty passages, it recounts the adventures of Orlando and the giant Morgante in the land of the infidel. The first canto was translated (1822) by Byron. See Leigh Hunt, *Stories from the Italian Poets* (4 vol., 1846–54).

puli (po͞ol'ē, pyo͞o'lē) (pl., pulik), a breed of wiry, medium-sized WORKING DOG developed nearly 1,000 years ago in Hungary. It stands from 16 to 18 in. (40.6–45.7 cm) high at the shoulder and weighs from 25 to 35 lb (11.3–15.9 kg). The weather-resistant double coat is composed of soft, woolly underhairs and a moderately harsh, long, slightly curled outercoat that tends to become tangled and matted, producing a characteristically corded appearance when not groomed. Its usual color is a faded black, but it may also be white or various shades of gray. Raised for centuries in its native Hungary to herd sheep, today the puli is kept principally as a watchdog and companion. See DOG.

Pul-i-Khumri (po͞ol-ĭ-kho͞omrē'), town (1967 pop. 10,000), central Afghanistan. It is a trading center and a stopping place for trucks and caravans traveling to N Afghanistan and the Soviet Union.

Pulitzer, Joseph (po͞o'lĭtsər, pyo͞o'-), 1847–1911, American newspaper publisher, b. Hungary. He emigrated to the United States in 1864, served a year in the Union army in the Civil War, and became a journalist on the *Westliche Post,* a German language newspaper. In 1869 he was elected to the Missouri legislature, where he earned a reputation as a liberal reformer. As owner and publisher after 1878, he made the St. Louis *Post-Dispatch* a successful paper, and in 1883 he bought the New York *World* from Jay Gould. His aggressive methods of building up this paper, its Sunday issue, and the *Evening World* (started 1887) included the use of illustrations, news stunts, crusades against corruption, and cartoons, as well as aggressive news coverage. William Randolph Hearst established his New York *Journal* in 1895 to vie with Pulitzer's papers in sensationalism and in circulation. The ensuing contest, with its banner headlines, lavish pictures, emotional exploitation of news—in short, "yellow journalism"—reached notorious heights in the treatment of the Spanish-American War. Later the *World* became more restrained and the outstanding Democratic organ in the United States, although it sometimes opposed party policies. In 1885, Pulitzer was elected to the U.S. House of Representatives, where he served briefly. After 1890 partial blindness kept Pulitzer from the editorial offices, but he directed his papers no less closely than before. He left funds to found what is now the graduate school of journalism at Columbia Univ. and endowed the Pulitzer Prizes. In 1931, Pulitzer's sons, Ralph (1879–1939) and Joseph (1885–1955), sold the New York papers to the Scripps-Howard chain, and the *Evening World* was merged with the New York *Telegram.* The *Post-Dispatch,* under his son Joseph and then under his grandson Joseph Pulitzer (1913–), was cited repeatedly for outstanding journalism and public service. Its editorial page maintained the Pulitzer tradition of independent liberalism. See biographies by W. J. Granberg (1966), G. Juergens (1966), and W. A. Swanberg (1967, repr. 1972).

Pulitzer Prizes, annual awards for achievements in American journalism, letters, and music. The prizes are paid from the income of a fund left by Joseph Pulitzer to the trustees of Columbia Univ. They have been awarded each May since 1917 on the recommendation of an advisory board comprising newspapermen and the president of the university, with a faculty member of the graduate school of journalism as secretary. Eight awards are given in journalism—$1,000 each for local reporting under deadline pressure, for local reporting free of deadline pressure, for national reporting, for international correspondence, for editorial writing, for the best cartoon, and for the best news photograph, and a gold medal for distinguished and meritorious public service by a newspaper. Special citations may also be presented for journalistic excellence and initiative in other categories. The prizes in letters, of $500 each, are for fiction, drama, history, biography, and poetry; works with American themes are preferred. The $500 musical composition award was added in 1943. Of four traveling scholarships (of $1,500 each), three are to graduates of the Columbia school of journalism and one is to an art student. Pulitzer directed that the winners "study social, political, and moral conditions of the people and the character and principles of the foreign press." See studies by John Hohenberg, ed. (1959) and W. J. Stuckey (1966).

Pulkovo (po͞ol'kəvə), observatory, S of Leningrad, NW European USSR. It is the major astronomical observatory of the Soviet Academy of Sciences and a leading center of Soviet astronomy. Pulkovo was built (1834–39) under a commission headed by F. G. W. von Struve. It was rebuilt (1946–54) after suffering severe damage in World War II. Equipment includes a 70-cm (27.6-in.) reflecting TELESCOPE, a 65-cm (25.6-in.) refracting telescope, and a Maksutov wide-angle camera telescope with a 70-cm mirror.

pulley, simple MACHINE consisting of a wheel over which a rope, belt, chain, or cable runs. A grooved pulley wheel like that used for ropes is called a sheave. A single sheave mounted in a block and fixed in place simply changes the direction of force exerted on the rope passing over it. If the end of the rope that ordinarily would attach to the load is passed around a second, unfixed pulley and back to the fixed pulley, a load attached to the free pulley can be raised with half the effort, or with a mechanical advantage of 2. Thus arranged, the device is called a block and tackle. The number of pulley wheels mounted in the fixed and free blocks can be increased indefinitely to get a higher and higher mechanical advantage, the mechanical advantage equalling the number of strands running to the free pulley. Therefore if the rope is run over the first fixed pulley wheel, around the free pulley, over a second pulley wheel in the fixed block, and back to the free block, the mechanical advantage is 3. A 300-lb load can be raised by a pull of 100 lb on the free end of the rope. To raise the load 10 ft, however, the free end of the rope must be pulled 30 ft. Disregarding friction, work output will always equal work input. If the action is reversed by attaching the load to the free end of the rope and pulling on the free block, the mechanical advantage becomes a mechanical disadvantage, but a speed advantage. A rope block and tackle is usually for hand operation.

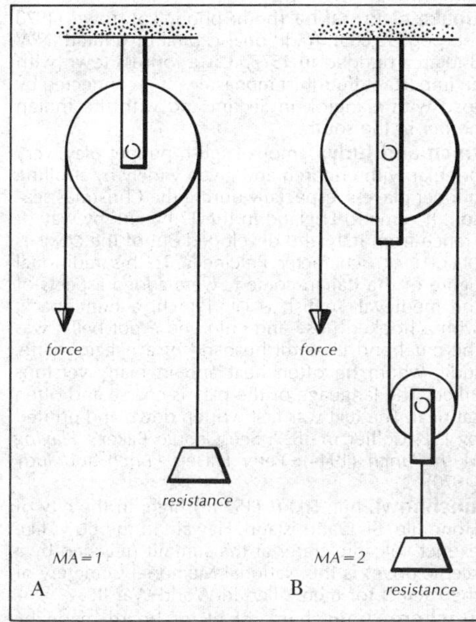

Pulleys: The mechanical advantage (MA) of a system of pulleys is equal to the number of supporting strands; in A the MA=1 and in B the MA=2.

To lift larger loads by hand, a chain is substituted for the rope and the pulleys have grooves for gripping the links. A differential pulley consists of two pulleys of different radii connected and rotating as one on a common axle. The pulleys have their circumferences grooved and spiked so that a chain will run in them without slipping. Over the pulleys an endless chain is run, forming two hanging loops. In one loop is placed a movable block, whose pulley is shaped to take the chain. The load is attached to the movable block and is raised by pulling on the other loop of the chain. Power-operated machinery usually has cables, as in vertical-lift drawbridges, power shovels, and cranes. Before the extensive use of electric motors, steam engines or water turbines often supplied the power for factory machinery. One engine or turbine might run a whole factory through a complicated system of shafts, pulleys, and belts. Pulleys for flat belts are crowned to keep the belt centered. Raised flanges will serve the same purpose, but they wear the edges of the belt. Drive pulleys for conveyor belts often have a covering, called lagging, to provide better grip. Individual electric motors usually provide drive by means of V belts, the pulleys having raised flanges to form slots that match the trapezoidal cross sections of the belts. Cone pulleys consist of a number of pulleys of varying diameters massed in the shape of a cone. They are used with belt drives for machines (e.g., lathes) requiring a variety of speeds.

Pullman, George Mortimer, 1831–97, American industrialist and developer of the railroad sleeping car, b. Brocton, N.Y. As a young man he became a cabinetmaker, and after he moved (1858) to Chicago he began converting (1859) old railroad coaches in order to facilitate long-distance traveling. Some five years later he built the *Pioneer,* the first modern sleeping car. Gaining great wealth from his invention, he founded (1867) the Pullman Palace Car Company. The town of Pullman, now part of Chicago, was built (1880) for the company and its workers. One of the most famous of all U.S. strikes was that at Pullman in 1894.

Pullman. 1 Former city, since 1889 part of Chicago, Ill. It was founded in 1880 by G. M. Pullman as a model community for workers of his sleeping-car company; all property was company owned, and administration policies were paternalistic. The residents voted for incorporation with Chicago, and Illinois courts later required the company to sell all property not used for industrial purposes. In 1894, Pullman was the site of one of the most memorable strikes in U.S. history. A protest against wage cuts led (May, 1894) to the strike, then to a boycott by the American Railway Union, and ultimately to the imprisonment of its president, Eugene V. Debs. A sharp contest ensued during the strike between Gov. John P. Altgeld and President Grover Cleveland over the sending of Federal troops to the area. The strike was broken in July. **2** City (1970 pop. 20,509), Whitman co., SE Wash., at the junction of the three forks of the Palouse River, near the Idaho line; inc. 1888. It is an agricultural center for a region that produces peas and wheat and that also has dairy farms. Washington State Univ. is in Pullman.

Pullman strike, in U.S. history, an important labor dispute. On May 11, 1894, workers of the Pullman Palace Car Company in Chicago struck to protest wage cuts and the firing of union representatives. They sought support from their union, the American Railway Union (ARU), led by Eugene V. DEBS, and on June 26 the ARU called a boycott of all Pullman railway cars. Within days, 50,000 rail workers complied and railroad traffic out of Chicago came to a halt. When the railroad owners asked the Federal government to intervene, Attorney General Richard Olney, a director of the Burlington and Santa Fe railroads, obtained (July 2) a court injunction. On July 4, President Cleveland dispatched troops to Chicago. Much rioting and bloodshed ensued, but the government's actions broke the strike and the boycott soon collapsed. Debs and three other union officials were jailed for disobeying the injunction. See Almont Lindsey, *The Pullman Strike* (1942, repr. 1964); Stanley Buder, *Pullman* (1967).

Pully (pülē'), town (1970 pop. 15,917), Vaud canton, W Switzerland, on the Lake of Geneva. It is a residential suburb of Lausanne. The town has a 15th-century church and a museum honoring Charles Ferdinand Ramuz, the 19th-century Swiss novelist.

Pulog, Mount (po͞o'lōg), peak, 9,606 ft (2,928 m) high, NW Luzon, the Philippines, in the Cordillera Central. It is the second highest point in the Philippines.

pulp: see PAPER.

pulpit, in churches, elevated platform with low enclosing sides, used for preaching the sermon. In the earliest churches the episcopal throne served this purpose. The boxlike elevated ambo of early medieval times, the apparent forerunner of the pulpit, was situated in the choir and served for reading and singing. In basilical churches there was usually an ambo at both the north and south sides of the choir. At an unknown date the north-side ambo came to be used for sermons, its location being a matter of favorable acoustics rather than ritual. The modern pulpit is ordinarily in the nave against the first pier outside the chancel and at the epistle side. Pulpits early became objects of fine craftsmanship. They were generally polygonal, supported by a single pillar or a group of columns or by brackets extending from a wall. In Italy there are many handsome examples, enriched with sculpture and mosaics. The hexagonal carved marble pulpit (1259) in the baptistery at Pisa, by the sculptor Nicola Pisano, displayed the first intimations of the Renaissance. The cathedral at Prato has the celebrated round outdoor pulpit sculptured by Donatello, who also designed in his last years two magnificent rectangular pulpits for the Church of San Lorenzo, Florence. With the Reformation the pulpit became the most conspicuous and important accessory in the Protestant church. Modern pulpits are, as a rule, of simple design.

pulque (po͞ol'kā), Mexican spirituous liquor, made from the sap of the maguey (see AMARYLLIS). The bud of the flower stalk is removed before it is well developed and a hollow is scooped in the heart of the plant; in this the sweet sap, aguamiel, collects. Fermentation of aguamiel produces pulque, a milky, highly intoxicating liquid. In use since pre-Columbian times, pulque is the ordinary drink among the poorer people of Mexico.

pulsar, in astronomy, a celestial object that emits brief, sharp pulses of radio waves instead of the steady radiation associated with other natural sources (see RADIO ASTRONOMY). The pulses recur at precise intervals, but successive pulses differ considerably in strength. The time between pulses ranges from 1/30 sec to 2 sec. Two pulsars, one in the CRAB NEBULA and the other in the constellation Vela, also emit pulses of visible light. Unlike many sources of natural radio emission, pulsars are not spread over a measurable region of the sky, but are pointlike sources. Pulsars are generally believed to be rotating NEUTRON STARS that are remnants of SUPERNOVAS, or exploding stars. The intense magnetic field and PLASMA that are believed to surround a neutron star provide an effective source of radio waves. The high-energy electrons of the plasma spiral around the magnetic field and emit radio waves and other forms of electromagnetic radiation. This so-called SYNCHROTRON RADIATION is highly directional, like a flashlight beam. If the neutron star is rotating, the beam of radio waves will sweep across the line of sight like a revolving beacon and produce the observed pulses.

pulse, alternate expansion and contraction of ARTERY walls as HEART action varies blood volume within the arteries. Artery walls are elastic. Hence they become distended by increased blood volume during systole, or contraction of the heart. During diastole, or relaxation of the heart, blood volume in the arteries decreases and the walls contract, propelling the blood farther along the arterial pathway. The effect is that of a pressure wave initiated by the heartbeat and traveling from the aorta, the major artery leaving the heart, along the walls of all the other arteries. It takes about a quarter of a second for this wave to travel from the aorta to the arteries in the soles of the feet. The rate of heartbeat is equivalent to the pulse rate. Usually the pulse rate is determined by counting the pulsations per minute in the radial artery at the wrist. It may also be determined at any other artery point near the surface of the body. The normal rate is 70 to 90 pulsations per min in adults, and 90 to 120 in children. Various diseases may be indicated by changes in the rate, rhythm, and force of the pulse.

pulse, in botany, common name for members of the Leguminosae, a large plant family, called also the pea, or legume, family. Numbering about 550 genera and 13,000 species, the family is second in size only to the composites and approximates that of the orchids. Some botanists divide the Leguminosae into three or more separate subfamilies, but most species share certain common and easily recognizable features. The leaves are usually compound; the fruit is a LEGUME (a type of pod); and the blossoms have an irregular butterflylike (papilionaceous) shape. Typically the flowers have 10 stamens, and the corolla and the calyx are formed of 5 petals and 5 sepals, respectively. Usually the uppermost petal (called the "standard") is large and conspicuous, the two lateral ones (the "wings") are smaller, and the two lower-

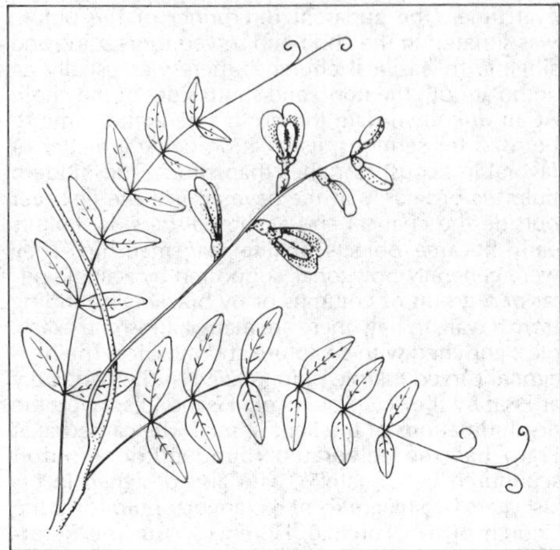

Sweet pea, Lathyrus odoratus, *a member of the pulse family*

most are pressed close together and are upturned (the "keel"). Many species have thorny branches. The Leguminosae include herbs, shrubs, and trees distributed throughout the world in a great variety of forms. Arboreal species occur in temperate and, frequently, in tropical zones, where epiphytic and climbing forms also thrive. Many leguminous shrubs and trees inhabit desert and semiarid regions, usually forming the characteristic vegetation—e.g., the acacias of the S African bushveld and of Australia, and the mesquite of the American Southwest. Economically the family is second only to the grasses in importance. Legumes provide valuable and nutritive foods because the food stored for the embryo in the seed (the pea) is rich in protein. In many regions, especially where meat is scarce or expensive, legumes—notably peas, beans, lentils, peanuts, carob, and soybeans—are staples of the diet. The Leguminosae are equally important as fodder and forage plants; clover, alfalfa, vetch, lupine, beggarweed, lespedeza, sainfoin, and soybeans are among the numerous valuable types. These food and forage legumes are chief among the plants used as "green manure" (see MANURE). Nitrogen-fixing bacteria dwelling in nodules of their roots fix free nitrogen from the air into the nitrogenous compounds needed by all forms of life for building protoplasm (see NITROGEN CYCLE). Rotation of leguminous crops with nonleguminous crops has long been a standard agricultural practice; the soil is enriched when their roots are left to decay after harvesting. The pulse family also provides gums and resins (e.g., tragacanth, copal, and acacia and carob gums), dyes and tannins (e.g., from the indigo plant, logwood, brazilwood, and types of acacia and broom), timber (e.g., rosewood, locust, honey locust, and acacia), medicines (e.g., from tamarind, licorice, and senna), perfume oils (e.g., from acacia, black locust, broom, and sweet pea), vegetable oils (e.g., soybean and peanut oils), and other commercial items such as flavorings, fibers, and insecticides. In many parts of the world native species of the Leguminosae are of great importance locally, if not commercially. Often every part of the plant finds some use—the pods and leaves for food, beverages, and forage; the wood and stems for building purposes, fiber, and household items; and the leaves, blossoms, and bark for domestic remedies. The blossoms of many of the Leguminosae are excellent honey sources. Species that grow in arid climates are particularly valuable because of the scarcity of the usual fodder, food, and timber crops; they are also important to wildlife for forage and cover. North American Indians have cultivated peanut and bean plants since antiquity and still rely on breadroot, redwood, mesquite, and many other species for food and other products. Among the native North American trees cultivated for shade or for their beautiful springtime blossoms are the locusts, the honey locust, the yellowwood, the redbud, and the acacias. The mimosas, sennas, laburnums, poincianas, Old World acacias, shrubby brooms, and wisteria have been introduced for the same purpose. The American lupines, the Old World sweet pea, and numerous types of clover are among the cultivated herbaceous species. In all, members of over 140 genera of the Leguminosae are grown for ornament. Furze from Europe and the kudzu vine from Asia have been introduced for erosion control (the latter has become a noxious weed). The locoweeds and lupines of the Western states are among the plants poisonous to livestock. The pulse family is classified in the division MAGNOLIOPHYTA, class Magnoliopsida, order Rosales. See articles on individual plants.

pulse code modulation: see MODULATION.

pulse position modulation: see MODULATION.

puma (pyo͞o'mə) or **cougar** (ko͞o'gər), New World member of the CAT family, *Felis concolor.* Also known as mountain lion, catamount, panther, and painter, it ranges from S British Columbia to the southern tip of South America. The puma is slenderly built, with a lionlike face. There is great variation both in size and in color, and pumas at the extremes of their geographic range are much larger than those of the tropics. Adult males of the cooler regions average about 7 ft (2.1 m) in length, including the 30-in. (76-cm) tail, and about 28 in. (71 cm) in shoulder height; they weigh up to 175 lb (80 kg). Females are smaller. The fur is yellow-brown, red-brown, or gray; the puma is distinguished from the other large New World cat, the jaguar, by its lack of spots. Pumas are found in almost every type of country, including mountain tops, grasslands, deserts, and temperate and tropical forests. They are solitary hunters, preying on animals up to the size of deer. Some individuals prey on livestock, and farmers have therefore waged extensive war on the species, which is nonetheless still numerous in Central and South America. In North America it is probably extinct in the eastern two thirds of the continent, except for a few survivors in Florida. Pumas avoid contact with humans, and seldom, if ever, attack them. They are classified in the phylum CHORDATA, subphylum Vertebrata, class Mammalia, order Carnivora, family Felidae.

Pumacagua, Mateo García (mätā'ō gärsē'ä po͞omäkä'gwä, -kä'wä), 1738–1815, Peruvian Indian leader. He aided in suppressing the insurrection (1780–81) of Tupac Amaru and later the first rebellion in the war against Spain; in 1814, however, he led an uprising. Beginning in Cuzco, the movement spread, gaining force from Pumacagua's great influence over the Indians. After initial successes the Indians were defeated, and Pumacagua was put to death.

pumice (pŭm'ĭs), volcanic glass formed by the solidification of lava that is permeated with gas bubbles. Usually found at the surface of a lava flow, it is colorless or light gray and has the general appearance of a rock froth. The viscosity of the lava, the quantity of water vapor and gas, and the rate of cooling together determine the fineness of the vesicular substance. Large amounts of gas result in a finer-grained variety known as pumicite. The chemical composition is that of granite. Coarser-grained rock, with fewer and larger air spaces, is called scoria; it is usually associated with dark-colored igneous rocks of diorite or gabbro composition. Pumice is used chiefly as an abrasive and is included in many scouring preparations. Ground pumice is also used in finishing furniture. Deposits are found in volcanic areas throughout the world. Because of its air chambers, pumice has a very low density and has been observed blowing off volcanic islands in strong winds. It usually floats and can be carried great distances by ocean currents.

pump, device to lift, transfer, or increase the pressure of a fluid (gas or liquid) or to create a vacuum in an enclosed space by the removal of a gas (see vacuum pumps under VACUUM). The centrifugal pump, the most common kind, consists basically of a rotating device, called an impeller, inside a casing. The fluid to be pumped enters the casing near the shaft of the impeller. Vanes attached to the spinning impeller give the fluid a high velocity so that it can move through an outlet. The reciprocating pump moves a fluid by using a piston that travels back and forth in a cylinder with valves to help control the flow direction. Examples are the lift pump and the force pump. In a lift pump the piston and cylinder are positioned vertically. When the piston moves upward, atmospheric pressure pushes water into the cylinder to fill the empty space beneath the piston. On the downward stroke, the water in the cylinder is forced to flow above the piston. Reversing direction, the piston moves up, allowing more water to come up under it into the cylinder and lifting the water held above it to an outlet pipe where the water flows out of the pump. Since atmospheric pressure will support a column of water no higher than about 33 ft (10 m), a lift pump can raise water no farther than this distance. The rotary pump is like the reciprocating pump in that it allows a fluid to fill a space that then decreases in volume, forcing the fluid out of the space. However, unlike a reciprocating pump, it has no valves and uses one or more rotating components in place of a piston. The jet pump has no moving parts; it uses a swiftly moving fluid to induce motion in another fluid. For example an atomizer, a type of jet pump, uses a high speed stream of air to pump a liquid, such as a perfume. Compressors are used to pump air or other gases into a closed container. They range from hand pumps to large power-driven devices that furnish compressed air for operating pneumatic machinery and for various other purposes. In nuclear reactors that use liquid radioactive metal, the nonmechanical electromagnetic pump is employed. An electric current is either induced in the liquid metal or is passed through it by electrodes. A magnetic field surrounding the pipe then propels the current-carrying liquid forward.

pumpkin, common name for the genus *Cucurbita* of the family Cucurbitaceae (GOURD family), a group that includes the pumpkins and squashes—the names may be used interchangeably and without botanical distinction. *C. pepo,* a species that includes varieties of pumpkin, vegetable marrow (a common European vegetable), and summer squash, has been cultivated so long that its wild form no longer exists and its place of origin is uncertain. If it is native to Asia it was introduced to America in prehistoric times; squashes, maize, and lima beans were the chief crops cultivated by pre-Columbian Indians. The pumpkin was among the fruits of the first Thanksgiving celebration of the Pilgrims; it has been a favorite pie filling for autumn festivities ever since, and its shell is carved into the Halloween jack-o'-lantern. The summer squashes include the pattypan, acorn, scallop, and summer crookneck squashes. Other squashes are varieties of *C. moschata,* including the crookneck squashes and the cheese pumpkin, and *C. maxima,* the winter squashes (e.g., the Hubbard and turban squashes), called pumpkins in Europe. Pumpkins are classified in the division MAGNOLIOPHYTA, class Magnoliopsida, order Violales, family Cucurbitaceae.

pumpkinseed: see SUNFISH.

pun, use of words, usually humorous, based on (a) the several meanings of one word, (b) a similarity of meaning between words that are pronounced the same, or (c) the difference in meanings between two words pronounced the same and spelled somewhat similarly, e.g., Thomas Hood's "They went and told the sexton and the sexton tolled the bell." Puns have also been used seriously, as in the Bible, Mat. 16.18: "Thou art Peter [Gr. *Petros*], and upon this rock [Gr. *petra*] I will build my church."

puna (po͞o'nä), high plateau region, 12,000 to 16,000 ft (3,658–4,877 m) high, between ridges of the Andes in Peru and Bolivia. Arid, cold, and in general, covered by short coarse grass, the puna has, nevertheless, long supported an Indian population. The icy wind sweeping the mineral-rich plateaus is also called puna.

Punaka or **Punakha** (both: po͞onŭ'kə), town (1970 est. pop. 12,000), traditional capital of Bhutan, NW Bhutan. Founded in 1577, it is a fortress town with an important Buddhist monastery. It is connected by road with Gangtok in Sikkim and with the Indian border in the south.

Punch and Judy, famous English puppet play, very popular with children and given widely by strolling puppet players, especially during the Christmas season. It came to England in the 17th cent. by way of France from Italy and developed out of the COMMEDIA DELL' ARTE character, Pulcinella. To this traditional figure of the Italian comedy were added aspects of the medieval English FOOL. Punch, a hunchback, with a hooked nose and chin and a pot belly, was the cruel and boastful husband of a nagging wife, Judy, whom he often beat and in many versions killed. The language of the play is coarse and often satirical. The text was first written down and printed by J. P. Collier in 1827. See George Baker's *Playing With Punch* (1944); Peter Fraser, *Punch and Judy* (1970).

Punchbowl, hill, 500 ft (152 m) high, in the city of Honolulu, SE Oahu island, Hawaii. In the bowl-like extinct volcanic crater at the summit (reached by a scenic drive) is the National Memorial Cemetery of the Pacific, for men killed in World War II.

puncheon (pŭn'chən), plank or board made by hewing instead of sawing. American pioneers who could not procure the products of sawmills made much use of puncheons in their log buildings. The puncheons used for floors were split logs hewn smooth on the split side only.

punctuation [Lat.,=point], device of writing supplementing the use of letters. In every language, besides the sounds of the words that are strung together there are other features, such as tone, accent, and pauses, that are equally significant (see GRAMMAR and PHONETICS). In English, stress, pausing, and tonal changes interlock in a set of patterns often called intonations. Such features are represented by punctuation, indicated by signs inserted usually between words, and often following the feature they mark. The intonations of declaration are classified in three types, symbolized by the comma (,), used to separate words or phrases for clarity; the semicolon (;), used to mark separation between elements in a series of related phrases, generally in a long sentence; and the full stop, or period (.), used to mark the end of a sentence. Other intonations are shown by the exclamation point (!); the interrogation point, or question mark (?); the parenthesis ( ), used to set off a word or phrase from a sentence that is complete without it; and the colon (:), typically used to introduce material that elaborates on what has already been said. Quotation marks (" ") indicate direct quotation or some borrowing, and usually demand special intonation. Punctuation of material intended to be read silently rather than aloud—the far more usual case today—has introduced refinements designed to help the reader: brackets ([ ]), a secondary parenthesis; capital letters; paragraphing; and indentation. The ellipsis (. . .) is used to indicate the place in a passage where material has been omitted or a thought has trailed off. The long dash (—) is especially used in handwriting for incomplete intonation patterns. Two other frequent signs are the apostrophe ('), marking an omission of one or two letters, or a possessive case, and the hyphen (-), marking a line division or an intimate joining, as in compound words. These last two are practically extra letters, and their use, belonging with spelling rather than with punctuation, is highly arbitrary. Each written language has its tradition of punctuation, often very different from that used in English; thus, in German nouns are capitalized, and in Spanish the beginnings of exclamations and of questions are marked with inverted signs. See also ACCENT. See *Words into Type* (1948, rev. ed. 1964); Univ. of Chicago Press, *A Manual of Style* (12th ed. 1969); W. D. Drake, *The Way to Punctuate* (1971).

Punic Wars, three distinct conflicts between CARTHAGE and ROME. When they began, Rome had nearly completed the conquest of Italy, while Carthage controlled NW Africa and the islands and the commerce of the W Mediterranean. When they ended, Carthage was ruined, and Rome was the greatest power W of China. The first war saw Rome fighting to break the tight hold that Carthage was gaining on the W Mediterranean. The last war was the final, desperate attempt of Carthage to preserve Punic (Carthaginian) liberty. But it was the second war that was the most spectacular and the most interesting. The initial area of conflict was Sicily, where the ambitions of the two commercial powers were directly opposed. The **First Punic War,** 264–241 B.C., grew immediately out of a quarrel between the Sicilian cities of Messana (now Messina) and Syracuse. One faction of the Messanians called on Carthage for help and another faction called on Rome. The Strait of Messana, which separates the Italian Peninsula from Sicily, was of extreme strategic importance, and both powers responded. The Punic army arrived in Sicily first, arranged a peace between Messana and Syracuse, and established a garrison. Upon its arrival, the Roman army ejected the Carthaginians from the garrison, and thus the war began. Roman legions occupied E Sicily without difficulty, and the newly created Roman fleet, after victories at Mylae (260) and off Cape Ecnomus (256), landed a force in Africa. This excursion was a failure, and its commander, REGULUS, was captured (255) by the Greek mercenary general Xantippus. In Sicily the Romans took Palermo (254) but were effectively blocked farther west by the brilliant guerrilla warfare of HAMILCAR BARCA, and they failed to take Lilybaeum, the chief Punic base. The Romans equipped a new fleet that destroyed (241) the Punic fleet off the Aegates (now Aegadian Isles), and Carthage sued for peace. The terms were the payment of an indemnity and the cession of Punic Sicily to Rome. The chief events of the next 20 years were the Roman entry into Sardinia and Corsica—a gross breach of treaty—and the conquests in Spain by Hamilcar. When Hamilcar's son Hannibal took (219) the Spanish city of Saguntum (present-day Sagunto), a Roman ally, Rome declared war. This **Second Punic War,** or Hannibalic War, 218–201 B.C., was one of the titanic struggles of history. Rome owed its success to various factors: its stubborn will and splendid military organization; its superior economic resources; its generals, Fabius and, above all, Scipio; the failure of supply from Carthage to Hannibal's Italian army; and the mountainous character of central Italy, which rendered the Punic superiority in cavalry nearly useless. For the course of the war, see HANNIBAL and SCIPIO AFRICANUS MAJOR. At the war's close, Carthage surrendered to Rome its Spanish province and its war fleet; Carthaginian commercial greatness never returned. The **Third Punic War,** 149–146 B.C., originated, like the others, in a deliberate Roman aggression, the result of years of agitation by CATO THE ELDER for the destruction of Carthage. Charging Carthage with a technical breach of treaty in resisting the encroachment of the Numidian king MASINISSA (a Roman ally), Rome declared war and blockaded the city. Carthage never surrendered. The younger Scipio (SCIPIO AFRICANUS MINOR) conquered it, house by house, and sold the surviving inhabitants into slavery. The city was razed and its site plowed up. The Latin accounts are biased, and there are no Punic ones; the best source is POLYBIUS. See H. H. Scullard, *Roman Politics 220–150 B.C.* (1951); T. A. Dorey and D. R. Dudley, *Rome against Carthage* (1971).

punishment: see CAPITAL PUNISHMENT; CORPORAL PUNISHMENT; CRIMINAL LAW; PRISON.

Punites (pyo͞o'nīts), descendants of PHUVAH.

Punjab (pŭn"jäb') [Sanskrit,=five rivers], historic region in the northwest of the Indian subcontinent. The Indus River bounds the region in part of the west and the Jumna River in part of the east. The five rivers that give Punjab its name, the Jhelum, the Chenab, the Ravi, the Sutlej, and the Beas, merge to form the Panjnad, which flows into the Indus. Except in the north, where there are forested mountains yielding salt and coal, the Punjab is a level alluvial plain. Rainfall is scant and irregular, but an extensive irrigation system using the waters of the great rivers has made possible enormous agricultural productivity. Wheat (by far the leading crop), millet, barley, cotton, and sugarcane are grown, and there are extensive fruit orchards. The Punjab has a large textile industry and much flour milling. Communications (by road, by rail, and on the rivers) are excellent. The region, situated athwart the main approaches to the Indian subcontinent, formed one of the centers of the prehistoric INDUS VALLEY CIVILIZATION, and after c.1500 B.C. it was the site of the earliest Aryan settlements. The Punjab was occupied by Alexander the Great and then by the MAURYA empire. Muslims occupied W Punjab by the 8th cent. and firmly implanted Islam. Not until the late 12th cent. did they conquer E Punjab, which even afterward remained predominantly Hindu. Under the Mogul empire the Punjab reached its cultural height. When the empire declined in the late 18th cent., the Sikhs rose to dominance. By the early 19th cent. their territorial aggrandizement brought conflict with the British, who emerged victorious in the two Sikh Wars (1846, 1849) and in 1849 annexed most of the Punjab and made it a province, though some of the princely states were retained. With the creation of Pakistan in 1947, the Punjab was partitioned approximately along the line between the main concentrations of the Muslim and the Hindu populations. The western portion became the Pakistan province of West Punjab (renamed simply Punjab in 1949; c.58,000 sq mi/150,220 sq km) with its capital at LAHORE. The Indian section (c.91,000 sq mi/235,690 sq km) of the Punjab was divided after partition into three areas. The numerous Punjab hill states were merged into the union territory of Himachal Pradesh (now a state), other princely states were formed into the Patiala and East Punjab States Union, and the remaining area became the Indian state of East Punjab. In 1956, however, the state of East Punjab, the union territory of Patiala, and East Punjab States Union were merged to form the state of Punjab. In a further reorganization in 1966, Punjab was divided into two states: Hindi-speaking HARYANA and Punjabi-speaking Punjab (1971 pop. 13,422,927), 19,764 sq mi (51,189 sq km). A third portion of the former Punjab was added to Himachal Pradesh. The capital of Punjab is CHANDIGARH. Other important cities in Punjab are AMRITSAR, JULLUNDUR, and LUDHIANA. The state of Punjab is governed by a chief minister and cabinet responsible to a bicameral legislature with one elected house and by a governor appointed by the president of India.

Punjabi (pŭnjä'bē), language belonging to the Indic group of the Indo-Iranian subfamily of the Indo-European family of languages. See INDO-IRANIAN LANGUAGES.

punkie: see MIDGE.

Puno (po͞o'nō), city (1969 est. pop. 31,200), alt. 12,648 ft (3,855 m), capital of Puno dept., SE Peru, on Lake TITICACA. It is a commercial and transportation center of SE Peru. Wool, alcohol, and cacao are exported. Historical landmarks include a cathedral and some Indian ruins. Puno is also an archaeological center for the exploration of ancient Indian villages.

Punon (pyo͞o'nŏn), unlocated desert resting place, E of Mt. Seir. Num. 33.42,43.

Punt (po͝ont), ancient land S of Egypt accessible by way of the Red Sea. Its exact location has not been identified, but it probably included the Somali coast. Temple reliefs at Deir el Bahari in W Thebes depict an Egyptian expedition to Punt in the reign of Hatshepsut. From Punt the Egyptians obtained slaves, as well as gold and incense.

Punta Arenas (po͞on'tä ärä'näs), city (1970 pop. 64,958), capital of Magallanes prov., in TIERRA DEL FUEGO, S Chile, the only city on the Strait of Magellan and southernmost of the world's cities. Punta Arenas was founded in 1847 to maintain Chile's claim to the strait. Until the building of the Panama Canal, Punta Arenas was a busy coaling station and has since been an important center for export of Patagonian wool and mutton. The region's coal and oil are exploited. Punta Arenas is popular with tourists in spite of a long rainy season. The city has one of the finest museums in South America.

Punta del Este (po͞on'tä thĕl ās'tā), city, E Uruguay, on the Atlantic Ocean. Located on a narrow peninsula surrounded by excellent beaches, Punta del Este is one of the largest and most fashionable seaside resorts of South America. In 1939 the German battleship *Graf Spee* was crippled by a British squadron in waters off Punta del Este. The city was the site of the conference (Aug., 1961) of the Inter-American Economic and Social Council, during which the charter of the ALLIANCE FOR PROGRESS was drafted, and there also the foreign ministers' conference of the Organization of American States met in Jan., 1962, and voted to impose a censure on Cuba. In 1967 the presidents of republics in the Americas met in Punta del Este to formulate economic assistance programs for Latin America.

Punta Gallinas, Colombia: see LA GUAJIRA.

Puntarenas (po͞ontärä'näs), town (1970 pop. 53,075), capital of Puntarenas prov., W Costa Rica, on the Gulf of Nicoya. It is the center of the country's banana industry and a major Pacific port. Bananas and coffee are the main exports. There is also a substantial coastal trade. Other industries are fishing (for shark and tuna) and fish processing.

pupa (pyo͞o'pə), name for the third stage in the life of an INSECT that undergoes complete metamorphosis, i.e., develops from the egg through the larva and the pupa stages to the adult. A complete metamorphosis is characteristic of members of the orders Coleoptera (beetles), Diptera (flies, mosquitoes, and gnats) and Lepidoptera (moths and butterflies). Before entering the pupa stage the insect is an active larva, usually wormlike in form. The pupa is a resting stage in which the insect is transformed into an adult. It does not feed or increase in size, and typically it is outwardly inactive and covered by a hard integument. Internally, however, a great deal of metabolic activity occurs. Some larval organs are destroyed and some adult organs are initiated during this stage. Other adult organs develop from structures already present in the larva. At the end of the pupa stage, the integument is shed and the imago, or adult form, emerges. Pupae of moths usually have an additional outer covering, called a cocoon, built by the larva (called a caterpillar) just before it enters the pupa stage. Cocoons may be made of bits of woody material held together by silk strands, or woven entirely of silk. Some cocoons are formed on or under the ground, some under tree bark; others are suspended from branches or twigs. Some moths form cocoons by wrapping leaves around themselves and gluing them together with silk. Cocoon building occurs in other insects, e.g., wasps; the material and design of the cocoon vary greatly from one group to another. Very few butterflies make cocoons, but the butterfly pupa, called a chrysalis, is usually suspended by a silk thread, and its integument is often sculptured and brightly colored. The chrysalis of the monarch butterfly is soft green with gold spots. A few insects, e.g., the MOSQUITO, have active pupae. The duration of the pupa stage varies in different insects from a few days to several months. Many insects pass the winter in the pupa stage, and the imago emerges in the spring.

pupil: see EYE.

Pupin, Michael Idvorsky (pyo͞opēn'), 1858–1935, American physicist and inventor, b. Idvor, Hungary (now in Yugoslavia), grad. Columbia (B.A., 1883). He came to the United States in 1874 and from 1889 was associated with Columbia (as professor of electromechanics, 1901–31). He is known for his researches in X rays and for his invention of numerous electrical devices used in telegraphy and telephony. Pupin wrote the Pulitzer Prize-winning autobiography, *From Immigrant to Inventor* (1923).

puppet, small human or animal figure performing on a miniature stage, manipulated by an unseen operator who also speaks the dialogue. A distinction is made between marionettes, moved by strings or wires from above, and hand puppets, in which the hand of the operator is concealed in the costume of the doll. The English PUNCH AND JUDY shows are an ancient and familiar form of the puppet show, and the Guignol puppet theaters are popular in France. Puppet theaters have been established in the Americas; old epic dramas, often based on the *Chanson de Roland,* and other medieval and modern pieces have drawn crowded houses. The puppet show itself is so ancient that it is impossible to tell with accuracy where it first appeared. The Greeks of the 5th cent. B.C. were familiar with it; in Java, China, and Japan it is almost immemorial; and in Europe of the Middle Ages it was the most popular form of entertainment for the masses. From the end of the 16th cent. to the end of the 18th, puppet or marionette shows, sometimes called motions, reached the summit of their vogue on the Continent and in England. During Puritan times in England they flourished after the theaters were prohibited. On the Continent great writers such as Goethe and major composers including Mozart and Haydn wrote for them. In 18th-century Japan the most celebrated dramatists wrote plays for the puppet theater. During the 1950s in the United States, Burr Tilstrom's hand puppet show *Kukla, Fran, and Ollie* was a popular television series. The successful children's series *Sesame Street* introduced an engaging and imaginative group of puppets, known as muppets, in the late 1960s. The art of ventriloquism (making the voice appear to come from a source other than the speaker) is associated with the puppet. The manipulator, in full view, converses with the "dummy," a large doll usually held in the lap of the manipulator. Edgar Bergen and Charlie McCarthy are a well-known American team of ventriloquist and dummy. Large numbers of amateur puppeteers and hobbyists have existed for centuries in many countries and have contributed much to the arts of puppet making and handling. See George Speaight, *The History of the English Puppet Theatre* (1955); C. W. Beaumont, *Puppets and Puppetry* (1959); Paul McPharlin, *The Puppet Theatre in America* (1949, repr. with supplement 1969); Bunraku, *Puppet Theatre* (1972).

Pur (pûr) [Heb.,=lot], lot cast by Haman to determine the time for the murder of the Jews. Esther 3.7; 9.15–32. See PURIM.

Puranas (po͞orä'nə): see SANSKRIT LITERATURE.

Purbeck, Isle of, peninsula, c.12 mi (20 km) long and c.8 mi (13 km) wide, Dorset, S England, between Poole Harbour and the English Channel. St. Albans Head is the most southerly point of the rocky shore. Ranges of chalk hills cross the peninsula from east to west. The region is noted for the production of Purbeck marble and china clay; Swanage and Corfe Castle are the leading towns. Purbeck was a favorite hunting ground of Saxon and Norman kings.

Purcell, Henry (pûr'səl), c.1659–1695, English composer and organist; pupil of John Blow. Often considered England's finest native composer, Purcell combined a great gift for lyrical melody with harmonic invention and mastery of counterpoint. He sang in the choir of the Chapel Royal until 1673 and became organist there in 1682. In 1677 he was appointed composer for the king's band, and from 1679 until his death he was organist at Westminster Abbey. His sole opera, *Dido and Aeneas* (1689), is an early masterpiece of the form, regarded by some as the best original opera in English. It is remarkable for its dramatic characterization, poignant melodies, and adherence of the music to the genuine rhythms of English speech. His other notable stage works include the masque *The Fairy Queen* (1692), based on Shakespeare's *Midsummer Night's Dream,* and music for Dryden's *King Arthur* (1691). Purcell also excelled at writing songs for public occasions, including several odes for St. Cecilia's Day and his famous birthday ode for James II, *Sound the Trumpets.* In his vocal music Purcell often employed the device of the ground bass, in which a bass melody is repeated while the upper parts pursue variations. He also composed outstanding instrumental works and music for the English church service, which is secular in tone. Purcell invigorated English music with Italian and French elements, creating at the same time a distinctively English baroque style. His importance in English musical life was overshadowed only by that of Handel, in whose choral works there are strong reflections of Purcell's influence. See biographies by J. A. Westrup (1947) and F. B. Zimmerman (1967).

Purchas, Samuel (pûr'kəs, -chəs), 1577?–1626, English clergyman and compiler of travel literature, b. Essex. Chaplain to the archbishop of Canterbury, he later was rector of St. Martin's Church, London. His first book, *Purchas His Pilgrimage* (1613), was designed as a survey of peoples and religions of the world. Its success led to his most famous compilation of travel literature, *Hakluytus Posthumus, or Purchas His Pilgrims* (4 vol., 1625) for which he used the papers of Richard Hakluyt, East India Company records, and many manuscripts he had collected, which have since been lost. See selections by H. G. Rawlinson (1931) and Cyril Wild (1939).

Purdue University (pərdyo͞o', -do͞o'), mainly at West Lafayette, Ind.; land-grant with state support; coeducational; chartered 1865, opened 1874. It maintains regional campuses at Calumet, Westville, and Fort Wayne. In 1969 the university's branch at Indianapolis merged with that of Indiana Univ. to form a joint campus. Purdue is noted for its engineering and agricultural programs and laboratories. Its libraries house noteworthy collections in the fields of engineering, agriculture, history, and literature.

pure-food laws: see FOOD ADULTERATION.

Pure Land Buddhism or **Amidism,** devotional sect of Mahayana BUDDHISM in China and Japan. It centers on the worship of the Buddha Amitabha, who, according to the *Pure Land Sutra,* vowed to save all sentient beings by bringing them to rebirth in his realm, the "Western Paradise," which is endowed with miraculous characteristics that ensure easy entry into NIRVANA for its inhabitants. Salvation can be attained by invoking the name of Amitabha with absolute faith in his grace and in the efficacy of his vow. It was believed that Amitabha would appear with his retinue to the faithful at the time of death and take them to his paradise. In both China and Japan the movement gained impetus from the theory of the "end of the Dharma." This doctrine divided the development of Buddhism into three ages, that of the true, the counterfeit, and the decaying dharma, or Buddhist teaching. Those living in the present (the final, degenerate age) are unable to achieve enlightenment by the original means of self-effort, austerity, and superior knowledge and must rely entirely on faith. There were devotees of Amitabha in China as early as the end of the 3d cent. A.D. The sect was officially founded in 402 by its first patriarch, Hui-Yuan. Later masters spread the faith among the masses, sometimes using evangelical methods of contrasting the torments of hell to the bliss of the "Western Paradise." In Japan, Pure Land Buddhism was established as a sect by Honen (1133–1212), who taught that even those who had mastered Buddhist philosophy "should behave themselves like simpleminded folk" and give up all practices except the *nembutsu,* recitation of the formula *Namu Amida Butsu* [hail to Amitabha Buddha]. His disciple Shinran (1173–1262) carried his teachings to their logical conclusion by abandoning monastic celibacy and marrying. He held that reliance on one's own effort or on any practice other than the *nembutsu* would show lack of faith in Amitabha. He broke with Honen's followers on these issues and became the leader of the True Pure Land Sect, which grew to be the largest Buddhist sect in Japan. Chinese and Japanese Buddhist art includes numerous representations of Amitabha with his attendant bodhisattvas and depictions of hell that show the influence of Pure Land Buddhism.

purgatory (pûrg'ətôr"ē) [Lat.,=place of purging], in the teaching of the Roman Catholic Church, the state after death in which the soul destined for heaven is purified. Since only the perfect can enjoy the vision of God (inferred from Mat. 12.36; Rev. 21.17), and some die in grace who have still unpunished or unrepented minor sins on their conscience, they must be purged of such sins. Those who have suffered already (especially the martyrs) may have undergone much or all of their punishment. Souls in purgatory are members of the church along with the living and the blessed in heaven and may be helped, as in life, by the prayers and works of their fellow members. This unity is the communion of saints. Prayers for the dead are therefore commonplace in Roman Catholic life; one form is the REQUIEM Mass (see also INDULGENCE). The duration of time and the nature of the state of purgatory are not defined; the suffering is different in kind from that of HELL, for the soul in purgatory knows that his punishment is temporary. The ancient Jews prayed for the dead (2 Mac. 12.43–46), and the Christians continued the practice, holding the concomitant belief in a middle state between life and heaven. The Eastern Orthodox Church maintains this position without adopting the Western terms developed in the Middle Ages. Protestants have generally abandoned it.

Puri (po͞o'rē), town (1971 pop. 72,712), Orissa state, E central India, on the Bay of Bengal. The life of the town centers around the cult of Juggernaut (Jagannath), a form of the Krishna incarnation of Vishnu. This cult, unique in HINDUISM, has no caste distinctions. The images of Juggernaut and his sister and brother repose within a vast temple compound. Every summer each statue is mounted on an enormous temple cart and dragged by hundreds of pilgrims to a summer home 1 mi (1.6 km) distant. Although pilgrims have hurled themselves to death beneath the wheels of the cart, this act, contrary to common belief, is not part of the ritual. Puri is a district administrative center. Limestone carving and toy making are the main industries.

purification, in religion, the ceremonial removal of what the religion deems unclean. The usual agents of purification are water (as in BAPTISM), bodily alteration (as in CIRCUMCISION), and fire. The origin of purification rites is a matter of dispute, but frequently the necessity for purification may result from violation of taboo or from defilement incurred while participating in critical events of life, such as childbirth, puberty, marriage, bloodshed or war, and death. The ancient Hebrew rites are described in the Bible, as in Num. 19. CANDLEMAS commemorates the purification of the Virgin Mary after the birth of Jesus, Luke 2.22.

Purim (po͞o'rĭm) [Heb.,=lots], Jewish festival celebrated on the 14th of Adar, the sixth month in the Jewish calendar (Feb.–March). According to the book of ESTHER (Esther 3.7; 9.24,26) it commemorated the deliverance of the Persian Jews from a general massacre; however, the festival may have arisen in the pagan celebration of the advent of spring. Although preceded by a day of fasting, Purim is almost completely lacking in religious features and is a day of joy, marked by merrymaking and feasting. The Book of Esther is read in the synagogue. Other features of the festival, which developed in medieval times, are the exchange of gifts, the obligatory giving of alms to the poor, and often the presentation of Purim plays. In Israel, a Purim carnival is held. See Philip Goodman, *Purim Anthology* (1949, repr. 1960); Hayyim Schauss, *Guide to Jewish Holy Days* (1938, repr. 1970).

purine, type of organic base found in the NUCLEIC ACIDS of plant and animal tissue. The German chem-

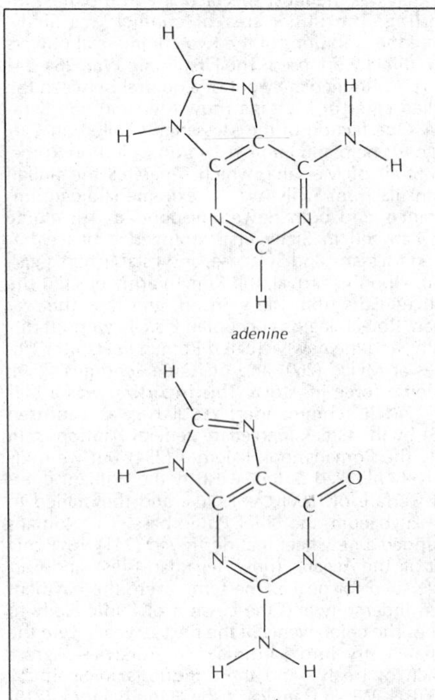

adenine

guanine

Purines found in deoxyribonucleic acid (DNA)

ist Emil Fischer did much of the basic work on purines and introduced the term into the chemical literature in the early 20th cent. The two major purines of almost universal distribution in living systems are ADENINE and GUANINE.

Puritanism, in the 16th and 17th cent., a movement for reform in the Church of England that had a profound influence on the social, political, ethical, and theological ideas of England and America. Historically it began early (c.1560) in the reign of Queen Elizabeth I as a movement for religious reform. The early Puritans felt that the Elizabethan ecclesiastical establishment was too political, too compromising, and too Catholic in its liturgy, vestments, and episcopal hierarchy. Calvinist in theology, they stressed PREDESTINATION and demanded scriptural warrant for all details of public worship. They believed that the Scriptures did not sanction the setting up of bishops and churches by the state. The aim of the early Puritans such as Thomas Cartwright was to purify the church (hence their name), not to separate from it. However, by 1567 a small group of lay rigorists was discovered meeting secretly in London to worship after the pattern of the service of the church in Geneva. Although Puritans believed that if they searched the Scriptures long enough they would eventually agree, they early differed on the nature of the church polity advised in the Bible. The parish was the unit of the Puritan church; the parochial group of church members elected ministers. The main body of Puritans, the Presbyterians (see PRESBYTERIANISM), favored a central church government, whereas the SEPARATISTS, INDEPENDENTS or Congregationalists (see CONGREGATIONALISM), defined the church as any autonomous congregation of believers, emphasized the point that a man could arrive at his own conclusions in religion, and opposed a national, comprehensive church. During the reign of James I, the Presbyterian majority unsuccessfully attempted to impose their ideas upon the Established Church at the Hampton Court Conference (1604). The result was mutual disaffection and a persecution of the Puritans, particularly by Archbishop William LAUD, that brought about Puritan migration to Europe and America (see MAYFLOWER). Those groups that remained in England grew as a political party and rose to their greatest power between 1640 and 1660 as a result of the ENGLISH CIVIL WAR; during that period the Independents gained dominance. The great Puritan apologist of this period was John Milton. During the Restoration the Puritans were oppressed under the Clarendon Code (1661–65), which secured the episcopal character of the Established Church and, in effect, cast the Puritans out of the Church of England. From this time they were known as NONCONFORMISTS. In New England, in the Puritan "Holy Commonwealth," some 35 churches had been formed by 1640. The Puritans in New England maintained the Calvinist distinction between the elect and the damned in their theory of the church, in which membership consisted only of the regenerate minority who publicly confessed their experience of conversion. Ministers had great political influence, and civil authorities exercised a large measure of control over church affairs. The CAMBRIDGE PLATFORM (1648) expressed the Puritan position on matters of church government and discipline. In 1662 it was made easier for the unregenerate majority to become church members in Massachusetts by the adoption of the HALF-WAY COVENANT. Clerical power was lessened by the expansion of New England and the opening of frontier settlements filled with colonists who were resourceful, secular, and engaged in a struggle to adapt to a difficult environment. In 1692 in Massachusetts a new charter expressed the change from a theocratic to a political, secular state; suffrage was stripped of religious qualifications. After the 17th cent. the Puritans as a political entity largely disappeared, but Puritan attitudes and ethics continued to exert an influence on American society. To the Puritan, man by nature was wholly sinful and could achieve good only by severe and unremitting discipline. Hard work was considered a religious duty and emphasis was laid on constant self-examination and self-discipline. Although profanation of the Sabbath day, blasphemy, fornication, drunkenness, playing games of chance, and participation in theatrical performances were penal offenses, the severity of the code of behavior of the early Puritans is often exaggerated. They made a virtue of qualities that made for economic success—self-reliance, frugality, industry, and energy—and through them influenced modern social and economic life. Their concern for education was important in the development of the United States, and the idea of congregational democratic church government was carried into the political life of the state as a source of modern democracy. Prominent figures in New England Puritanism include Thomas HOOKER, John COTTON, Roger WILLIAMS, Increase MATHER, and Cotton MATHER. See V. L. Parrington, *The Colonial Mind* (1927; vol. I of *Main Currents in American Thought*); H. W. Schneider, *The Puritan Mind* (1930); William Haller, *The Rise of Puritanism* (1938, repr. 1957); M. M. Knappen, *Tudor Puritanism* (1939, repr. 1965); Perry Miller, *The New England Mind* (1939); R. B. Perry, *Puritanism and Democracy* (1945, repr. 1964); T. F. Wertenbaker, *The Puritan Oligarchy* (1947); Alan Simpson, *Puritanism in Old and New England* (1955); J. E. Christopher Hill, *Society and Puritanism in Pre-Revolutionary England* (2d ed. 1967); H. C. Porter, *Puritanism in Tudor England* (1970); D. B. Rutman, *American Puritanism: Faith and Practice* (1970); Larzer Ziff, *Puritanism in America* (1973).

Puritan Revolution: see ENGLISH CIVIL WAR.

Purity: see PEARL, THE.

Purkinje, Johannes Evangelista (yōhän'əs ä"vänggālĭs'tä po͝or'kĭnyä), 1787–1869, Czech physiologist. While professor (1823–50) at the Univ. of Breslau he pioneered in establishing laboratory training in German universities. From 1850 he was professor at Charles Univ., Prague, and was active in the Czech nationalist movement. He improved microscope technique and made numerous contributions in the fields of histology and embryology. He discovered the apertures of the sweat glands and the large ramified nerve cells of the cerebellum now known by his name. In his research in ophthalmology he worked on the functions of the eye, studied subjective visual figures and recurrent images, and described important phenomena concerning the eye's sensitivity to color.

purple sail: see JELLYFISH; POLYP AND MEDUSA.

purse, receptacle for carrying money or belongings, which is attached to the belt or carried in the hand, over the arm, or over the shoulder. Excavations in Greece have revealed small linen bags decorated with embroidery; the tradition of the modern purse began, however, in the Middle Ages. Crusaders returning home wore little bags appended to their girdles. Called almsbags, they were of silk or leather and were used to carry coins for the poor. They were made larger to accommodate other belongings and were more highly decorated, often tasseled or hung with bells. Later some were square to hold a prayer book. After 1200 they became smaller and flatter, were worn at the belt, and were called pouches or purses. Decorative purses for men generally disappeared with the advent (c.1630) of pockets, but it became even more common for women to carry a purse, either in the hand or suspended from the belt by cord or ribbon. In the 18th cent. the beaded bag was first popular; the early 19th cent. saw a fashion for the small bag-shaped reticule. Such purses were frequently closed by drawstrings. As pockets became popular for women (c.1850), large purses were not so popular. In the latter part of the century they returned and were usually carried in the hand by a chain support. The 20th cent. brought forth a variety of purses—handbags, evening bags, clutch bags, shoulder bags, tote bags, cosmetic purses, coin purses, and wallets. The handbag is usually distinguished from the purse in that it is supplied with a handle and is large enough to contain the purse and other belongings.

purslane, common name for some plants of the Portulacaceae, a family of herbs and a few small shrubs, chiefly of the Americas. The portulacas or purslanes (genus *Portulaca*) include many species indigenous to the United States. The pussley, or common purslane (*P. oleracea*), is a common trailing weed in America; it and the upright European variety are sometimes used as potherbs and greens. Several species of *Portulaca* are cultivated in gardens, e.g., the small, showy-blossomed rose moss, or garden purslane (*P. grandiflora*), introduced from Brazil. Many North American wildflowers, sometimes also cultivated, are members of this family. The spring beauty (*Claytonia virginica*; for John Clayton) is an early spring flower of Eastern woods. Red maids, or rock purslanes (*Calandrinia ciliata*), range from British Columbia to Cape Horn and are also found in Australia. Bitterroot (*Lewisia rediviva*) is also a Western plant; it was found by Lewis and Clark on their expedition in the American West, and the genus was named for Lewis. The common name is applied to several Western landmarks, such as the Bitterroot Mountains; it is the state flower of Montana. Purslane is classified in the division MAGNOLIOPHYTA, class Magnoliopsida, order Caryophyllales.

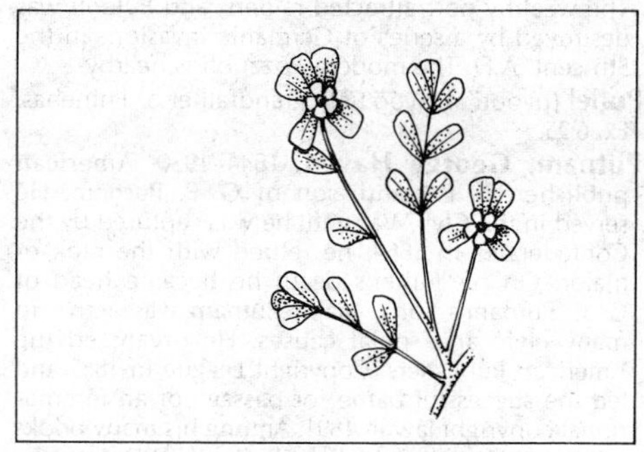

Purslane, Portulaca oleraceae

Purulia (po͝oro͞ol'yə), town (1971 pop. 57,721), West Bengal state, E central India. It is a district administrative center. An annual fair is held in September.

Purus (po͝oro͞oz'), river, c.2,100 mi (3,380 km) long, rising in the Andes Mts., E Peru. It flows generally northeast in a meandering course, across Acre and Amazonas states, NW Brazil, to the Amazon River. Mostly navigable, it traverses a rubber-producing region and receives the Acre River at Bôca do Acre.

Purva Mimamsa (po͝or'və mēmäm'sä): see INDIAN PHILOSOPHY.

Purvey, John, c.1354–c.1421, English scholar, who in support of the LOLLARDRY movement completed the first thorough translation of the Bible into English. Becoming associated with John WYCLIF at Oxford, he accompanied the Lollard leader to Lutterworth in 1382 and there perhaps finished a faulty translation of the Bible previously begun by others under Wyclif's inspiration. He completed (c.1395) a careful and scholarly translation entirely his own. These two versions were erroneously attributed to Wyclif himself until modern times. The second shows a prose style better than that of Wyclif's writings; portions of it were later used by the translators of the King James Version. Purvey continued active as a Lollard until his arrest in 1401. The following year he recanted under pressure and accepted a living from Archbishop Arundel. In 1403, however, he resigned and resumed Lollard activities until his arrest again in 1421, after which time nothing certain is known of his fate.

Purvits, Vilhelms (vĭl'hĕlms po͝or'vĭts), 1872–1945, Latvian landscape painter. He was director of the Latvian Academy of Art at Riga and was director of the city museums and professor at the Univ. of Latvia. A follower of the school of French impressionism, he developed a colorful style of his own. His work can be seen in museums of Riga, Tallinn, Stockholm, Leningrad, and Moscow.

pus, thick white or yellowish fluid that forms in areas of infection such as wounds and abscesses. It is constituted of decomposed body tissue, bacteria (or other micro-organisms that cause the infection), and certain white blood cells. These white cells form one of the defense mechanisms of the body. Known as phagocytes, they rush to the area of infection and engulf the invading bacteria in a process called phagocytosis. Many white cells themselves succumb in the process and become one of the constituents of pus.

Pusan (po͞o'sän), Jap. *Fusan,* city (1970 pop. 1,880,710), extreme SE South Korea, on the Korea Strait. It is the nation's second largest city and largest port, handling most of South Korea's foreign trade. Since 1963, Pusan has been a special city with the status of a province. Lying at the head of the Naktong River basin, it has served as a main southern gateway to Korea from Japan, which, during its rule over Korea (1910–45), developed Pusan's excellent natural harbor. The city is also the southern terminus of the main railroad line from Seoul. A leading industrial and commercial center, Pusan's manufactures include woolen, cotton, and silk textiles; iron and steel; tires and other rubber products; plywood; frozen seafood; fishing nets; and wigs. There are also important shipbuilding and ship repair facilities, railroad shops, and several thermal and hydroelectric power stations. Fishing and agriculture are carried on chiefly for local consumption. Nearby hot springs have made Pusan a popular resort city. The city became a major port under the Chinese Empire. It was invaded in 1592 by the Japanese, who had long maintained a trading post there; however, the Japanese forces were recalled in 1598. In 1876 the Koreans were compelled to sign a treaty opening Pusan to Japanese trade and immigration. In 1883 the port was opened to general foreign commerce. During the Korean War it was (Aug–Sept., 1950) the site of a United Nations beachhead (see INCHON).

Refugees from the war more than doubled Pusan's population. Historic landmarks include the Kyongbok Palace, built in 1394 by the first monarch of the Yi dynasty; the Changdok Palace, containing many valuable relics; and the Toksu Palace (1593), which houses the National Museum and Art Gallery. The city also has a national and a private university.

Pusey, Edward Bouverie (pyo͞o'zē), 1800–1882, English clergyman, leader in the OXFORD MOVEMENT. Having studied at Christ Church College, Oxford, Pusey was elected a fellow of Oriel College (1823) and thus became associated with John KEBLE, John Henry NEWMAN, and their group. He studied theology and Semitic languages at Göttingen and Berlin and then wrote (1828–30) a critical history of German theology; however, the work was misunderstood as a defense of German rationalism, and Pusey later withdrew it. In 1828 he was ordained an Anglican priest, was made regius professor of Hebrew at Oxford, and was appointed canon of Christ Church, a position he retained for the rest of his life. In late 1833 he formally aligned himself with the Oxford movement; the tracts on fasting (1834) and baptism (1836) in the series *Tracts for the Times* were Pusey's. As his tract on fasting was the first one not published anonymously the movement was sometimes known, usually derogatorily, as Puseyism. From 1836, Pusey was editor of the influential *Library of Fathers* and contributed several studies of patristic works. When Newman withdrew from the Oxford movement in 1841, Pusey became its leader. His influence in the High Church party was widened when he was suspended from preaching for two years because of the ideas expressed in his sermon, "The Holy Eucharist, a Comfort to the Penitent" (1843). He advocated the doctrine of the Real Presence, which holds that the body and blood of Christ are actually (and not symbolically or figuratively) present in the sacrament. In 1845 he assisted in the establishment of the first Anglican sisterhood and throughout his life continued his efforts toward establishing Anglican orders. His sermon "The Entire Absolution of the Penitent" (1846) claimed for the Church of England the right of priestly absolution, thus establishing the Anglican practice of private confession. His sermon "The Rule of Faith" (1851) was credited with checking the secessions to Roman Catholicism that had been accelerated by his suspension and by the controversy over the Gorham case, which involved the right of the privy council to adjudicate on matters of church doctrine. In the 1850s and 60s he published several works on the Real Presence and on the faults of rationalist methods of contemporary biblical scholarship. He strongly defended High Church doctrines that supported RITUALISM, although he was never a ritualist himself. His *Eirenicon* (3 parts, 1865–70), an endeavor to find some ground for reuniting Roman Catholicism and the Church of England, was answered by Cardinal Newman and generated considerable controversy. His name is perpetuated in Pusey House at Oxford, where his library is maintained. See biographies by H. P. Liddon (4 vol., 1893–97), Maria Trench (1900), and G. L. Prestige (1933); C. C. Grafton, *Pusey and the Church Revival* (1914); Geoffrey Faber, *Oxford Apostles* (1933).

Pushkin, Aleksandr Sergeyevich (po͞osh'kĭn, Rus. əlyĭksän'dər syĭrgā'yəvĭch po͞osh'kĭn), 1799–1837, Russian poet and prose writer, among the foremost figures in Russian literature. He was born in Moscow of an old noble family; his mother's grandfather was Abram Hannibal, the Negro general of Peter the Great. Pushkin showed promise as a poet during his years as a student in a lyceum for young noblemen. After a riotous three years in St. Petersburg society, Pushkin was exiled to S Russia in 1820. His offenses were the ideas expressed in his *Ode to Liberty* and his satirical verse portraits of figures at court. The same year his fairy romance *Russlan and Ludmilla* was published; Glinka later adapted it as an opera. In exile Pushkin was strongly moved by the beauty of the Crimea and the Caucasus. The poems *The Prisoner of the Caucasus* (1821) and *The Fountain of Bakhchisarai* (1822) describe his response to this beauty and reveal the influence of Byron. *The Gypsies* (1823–24) expresses Pushkin's yearning for freedom. In 1824 he was ordered to his family estate near Pskov, where he remained under the supervision of the emperor until pardoned in 1826. Pushkin established the modern poetic language of Russia, using Russian history for the basis of many works including the poems *Poltava* (1828) and *The Bronze Horseman* (1833), glorifying Peter the Great; *Boris Godunov* (1831), the tragic drama on which Moussorgsky based an opera; and two works on the peasant uprising of 1773–75, *The Captain's Daughter* (a short novel, 1837) and *The History of the Pugachev Rebellion* (1834). Pushkin's masterpiece is *Eugene Onegin* (1825–31), a novel in verse concerning twice-rejected love. A brilliant poetic achievement, the work contains witty and perceptive descriptions of Russian society of the period. Pushkin's other major works include the dramas *Mozart and Salieri* and *The Stone Guest* (both 1830); the folktale *The Golden Cockerel* (1833) on which Rimsky-Korsakov based an opera; and the short stories *Tales by Belkin* (1831) and *The Queen of Spades* (1834). Tchaikovsky based operas on both *Eugene Onegin* and *The Queen of Spades.* Pushkin died as a result of a duel with a young French nobleman who was accused, in anonymous letters to the poet, of being the lover of Pushkin's flirtatious young wife. He was buried secretly by government officials whom LERMONTOV, among others, accused of complicity in the affair. Most of Pushkin's writings are available in English. See Vladimir Nabokov's translation of *Eugene Onegin* (4 vol., 1964); biographies by E. J. Simmons (1937), David Magarshack (1968), W. N. Vickery (1968), and Henri Troyat (1946, tr. 1970); study by John Bailey (1971).

Pushkin (po͞osh'kĭn, Rus. po͞osh'kĭn), city (1969 est. pop. 73,000), NW European USSR, a residential and resort suburb of Leningrad. It produces road-building equipment and has an important botanical institute. Founded in 1708 under Peter I on the site of a Finnish village, it was first called Tsarskoye Selo [czar's village] and was renamed Detskoye Selo [children's village] after the Bolshevik Revolution. Pushkin served as a royal residence from 1725, with the huge baroque style summer palace of Catherine II (built 1748–62) and that of Alexander I (built 1792–96) in the classical mode. The vast park at Pushkin had innumerable rococo style grottoes, pavilions, canals, lakes, and bridges. The college where the poet Pushkin studied was opened in 1811 and is now a museum. In 1837 the city was joined with St. Petersburg (now Leningrad) by Russia's first railroad. Heavily damaged during World War II, Pushkin has since been restored.

Pushtu (pŭsh'to͞o), language belonging to the Iranian group of the Indo-Iranian subfamily of the Indo-European family of languages. It is also called Pashto and Afghan. See INDO-IRANIAN LANGUAGES.

Pushtunistan: see PATHAN.

pussley (pŭs'lē): see PURSLANE.

pussy willow: see WILLOW.

Puszta (po͞o'stä), arid grasslands that once covered a large part of the ALFÖLD, E Hungary. They were used for extensive cattle raising. With the irrigation and drainage projects of the late 19th cent., the Puszta disappeared except in the small Hortobagy region (c.100 sq mi/260 sq km), near Debrecen. Old customs of the Puszta are preserved there, mainly for the tourist trade.

Put, variant of PHUT.

put, in finance: see CALL.

Puteaux (pütō'), suburb W of Paris (1968 pop. 39,687), Hauts-de-Seine dept., N central France, on the Seine River. An important industrial center, Puteaux is the birthplace of the French automobile industry. Other manufactures include electric locomotives, electrical equipment, aircraft, rubber goods, and perfume.

Puteoli (pyo͞otē'əlī), ancient city of Campania, S Italy, 8 mi (13 km) W of Naples. Founded c.520 B.C. by Samian Greeks from Cumae, it came under Roman control by the end of the 4th cent. B.C. and was made a citizen colony in 194. It became famous as Rome's port of entry for Eastern trade, handling notably mosaics, pottery, and perfumes. The shops were rich, and the city was surrounded by handsome villas. When St. Paul visited the city there was already a large Christian community (Acts 28.13). The wealthy port attracted raiders, and Puteoli was destroyed by a series of Germanic invasions in the 5th cent. A.D. The modern Pozzuoli is nearby.

Putiel (pyo͞otī'əl, pyo͞o'tĭēl), grandfather of Phinehas. Ex. 6.25.

Putnam, George Haven, 1844–1930, American publisher, b. England; son of G. P. Putnam. He served in the Civil War until he was captured by the Confederates in 1864; he retired with the rank of major. On his father's death he became head of G. P. Putnam's Sons. Major Putnam was active in many civic and social causes. He organized the American Publishers' Copyright League in 1887 and led the successful battle for passage of an international copyright law in 1891. Among his many books are *Books and Their Makers during the Middle Ages* (2 vol., 1896–97), *Memories of My Youth* (1914), *Memories of a Publisher* (1915), and *Some Memories of the Civil War* (1924).

Putnam, George Palmer, 1814–72, American publisher, b. Brunswick, Maine; grandnephew of Israel Putnam. A member of the New York City bookselling firm of Wiley and Putnam, he established a branch in London in 1841. He later returned to New York to found (1848) G. P. Putnam's Sons. He was proprietor of *Putnam's Magazine* (1853–57), which was revived for brief periods in 1868–71 and 1906–10. One of the founders of the Metropolitan Museum of Art, he was its honorary secretary. George Haven Putnam and Herbert Putnam were his sons, and Mary Putnam Jacobi, a physician, was his daughter. See the memoir by his son G. H. Putnam (1912).

Putnam, George Palmer, 1887–1950, American author and explorer, b. Rye, N.Y.; grandson of G. P. Putnam, founder of the publishing firm. He led two expeditions to the Arctic—one in 1926, under the sponsorship of the American Museum of Natural History, up the west coast of Greenland and the other in 1927 to Baffin Island to collect specimens of wildlife. He married Amelia Earhart in 1931, and after she was lost at sea in 1937 he wrote her biography, *Soaring Wings* (1939). His autobiography, *Wide Margins,* appeared in 1942.

Putnam, Herbert, 1861–1955, American librarian, b. New York City; son of George P. Putnam. He served as librarian at the Minneapolis Athenaeum (1884–87) and of the Minneapolis Public Library (1887–91). In 1895, after practicing law in Boston, Putnam became librarian of the Boston Public Library, and in 1899 he began his 40 years of service as librarian of Congress. He built the collection of the Library of Congress into one of the finest in the world, reorganizing and introducing important procedures and establishing a classification system that has come into wide use. Putnam was twice the president of the American Library Association (1898 and 1904). See *Essays Offered to Herbert Putnam by His Colleagues and Friends* (1929).

Putnam, Israel, 1718–90, American Revolutionary general, b. Salem (now Danvers), Mass. A farmer at Pomfret, Conn., he fought in the French and Indian Wars, seeing action at Montreal (1760) and at Havana (1762). In 1764, he was commander of the Connecticut force sent to relieve Pontiac's siege of Detroit. At the outbreak of the American Revolution he joined the Continental army and was prominent in the battle of Bunker Hill. Putnam was in command at the unhappy battle of Long Island (1776) and in 1777 lost forts Montgomery and Clinton in the Hudson Highlands to the British. A paralytic stroke (1779) ended his military career. See biographies by William Cutter (4th. ed. 1850, repr. 1970) and I. N. Tarbox (1876, repr. 1970).

Putnam, Rufus, 1738–1824, American Revolutionary general, one of the founders of the OHIO COMPANY OF ASSOCIATES, b. Sutton, Mass.; cousin of Israel Putnam. In the French and Indian War he joined (1757) the army and saw action around Lake Champlain. In the American Revolution, Putnam was an engineering officer at Boston, New York, and West Point; he also served as a field officer, most notably under Horatio Gates in the Saratoga campaign (1777) and under Anthony Wayne at Stony Point (1779). He was made a brigadier general in 1783, after the war's end. In 1786 he, with other veterans, formed the Ohio Company of Associates. Putnam helped the passage of the Ordinance of 1787, and in 1788 he and Manasseh Cutler supervised the building of Marietta, Ohio. Putnam was appointed (1790) judge of the Northwest Territory and later was (1796–1803) U.S. surveyor general. See his memoirs, ed. by Rowena Buell (1903).

Putney (pŭt'nē), district of Wandsworth borough, London, England. It is the starting point of the Oxford-Cambridge boat races. Thomas Cromwell and Edward Gibbon were born in Putney, and Algernon Swinburne and William Pitt lived there. Putney Heath was the scene of a duel in 1798 between Pitt and George Tierney and of one in 1809 between Robert Castlereagh and George Canning.

Puto: see CHOU-SHAN ARCHIPELAGO, China.

putrefaction: see DECAY OF ORGANIC MATTER.

putrescine: see DECAY OF ORGANIC MATTER.

Putrid Sea: see SIVASH SEA, USSR.

Puttenham, George (pŭt'ənəm), d. 1590, English author. *The Arte of English Poesie* (1589), generally considered the best treatise on English versification of its time, has been attributed to him. The book, which shows discriminating taste and wide classical knowledge, has also been ascribed to his brother

Richard Puttenham, 1520?–1601. See edition by G. D. Willcock and Alice Walker (1936, repr. 1969).

putty, commonly a mixture of whiting (calcium carbonate) and boiled linseed oil. Other substances may be combined with the oil to make putties suitable for some specific purpose. For example, the red and white oxides of lead mixed with linseed oil form a putty used in sealing pipe joints. Putty hardens gradually when put in place, as along the edges of window panes to fasten them, in cracks in plaster walls, and in crevices in wood and other substances. The linseed oil absorbs oxygen from the air and, holding fast the calcium carbonate or metallic oxides, causes the mixture to harden. A powder composed of a mixture of lead and tin oxides, known as putty powder, is extensively used in polishing. Putty is gradually being replaced in some applications by caulking materials of butyl and silicone rubbers. The higher cost of these materials is offset by their greater durability.

Putumayo (po͞oto͞omä'yō) or **Içá** (ēsä'), river, c.1,000 mi (1,600 km) long, rising in the Andes, S Colombia, and flowing SE to the Amazon in NW Brazil. Mostly navigable, it marks part of Colombia's boundary with Ecuador and most of Colombia's frontier with Peru. The river valley, once a major source of rubber, has declined somewhat in economic importance, but rubber and balata are shipped to Manaus, Brazil. In the early 20th cent., during the peak of the wild-rubber bonanza, Roger Casement, a British consul, was appointed to head a group to investigate the treatment of Indian laborers in the region and made a report for the Peruvian government on the brutal exploitation of native labor; the report shocked the world.

Puukohola Heiau National Historic Site, Hawaii: see NATIONAL PARKS AND MONUMENTS, table.

Puvis de Chavannes, Pierre (pyĕr püvē' də shävän'), 1824–98, French mural painter, b. Lyons. In 1844 he went to Paris, where he studied under Delacroix and Couture. His painting *War* (Amiens), purchased by the state in 1861, established his reputation. From that time on he lived in Paris and painted mural decorations there and in other cities. Late in life he married his lifelong friend, Princess Marie Cantacuzène. They both died the following year. Although Puvis studied with the romanticists, his work is classical in inspiration. His chaste murals with their subdued color and allegorical figures are in the Hôtel de Ville, the Sorbonne, and the Panthéon, Paris, and in the Boston Public Library. His easel paintings can be found in many American and European galleries.

Puy, Le (lə püē'), city (1968 pop. 29,549), capital of Haute-Loire dept., S central France. A busy industrial city, Le Puy is the center of an old lace industry. It was an old capital of VELAY and an episcopal see from the 6th cent. The city grew after its shrine to the Virgin became (10th cent.) a major place of pilgrimage. The modern section of Le Puy lies below a bare rock, which, towering almost 500 ft (152 m) above the city, is capped by a bronze statue of the Virgin. Immediately at the foot of the rock lies the old city, with a cathedral (12th cent.) of extraordinarily daring construction, an 11th-century baptistery, and numerous Gothic buildings. Atop a lesser, needle-shaped rock is the Romanesque Church of St. Michel d'Aiguilhe, and at its foot is an 11th-century chapel.

Puyallup (pyo͞oăl'əp), city (1970 pop. 14,742), Pierce co., W Wash., on the Puyallup River; inc. 1890. It is located in a fertile farm valley noted for its berries and daffodil bulbs. A state fish hatchery and a Washington State Univ. agricultural experiment station are there. Of interest is the mansion home (1890) of Ezra Meeker, the city's founder. A daffodil festival and a nine-day fair are held there annually.

Puyallup Indians, North American Indians whose language belongs to the Salishan branch of the Algonquian-Wakashan linguistic stock (see AMERICAN INDIAN LANGUAGES). Puyallup culture was of the Pacific Northwest Coast area. In the early 19th cent. they occupied the region around the mouth of the Puyallup River in W Washington, near the site of Tacoma. By the Treaty of Medicine Creek (1854) they ceded their lands to the United States and moved to a small reservation on Puget Sound. They now number some 170. See M. W. Smith, *Puyallup-Nisqually* (1940, repr. 1969).

Puy-de-Dôme (püē-də-dōm), department (1968 pop. 547,743), S central France, in AUVERGNE. CLERMONT-FERRAND is the capital.

Puy de Dôme, extinct volcano of the Massif Central and the second-highest peak (4,806 ft/1,465 m) of the Auvergne mts., central France, W of Clermont-Ferrand. Crops are raised on the lower slopes; the highlands are used as pasturage. On its level summit (it has no crater) are a meteorological observatory and the ruins of a temple of Mercury. There Florence Périer conducted (1648), upon instructions of his brother-in-law, Blaise Pascal, the famous experiment that confirmed Torricelli's theory on air pressure (see PASCAL'S LAW).

Pu Yi, Henry (po͞o yē), Manchu *Aisin Gioro,* 1906–67, last emperor (1908–12) of China, under the reign name Hsuan T'ung. After his abdication, the new republican government granted him a large government pension and permitted him to live in the Forbidden City of Peking until 1924. After 1925, he lived in the Japanese concession in Tientsin. In 1934, reigning under the name K'ang Te, he became the sole emperor of the Japanese puppet state of MANCHUKUO, or Manchuria. He was captured by the Russians in 1945 and kept as their prisoner. In 1946, Pu Yi testified at the Tokyo war crimes trial that he had been the unwilling tool of the Japanese militarists and not, as they claimed, the instrument of Manchurian self-determination. In 1950 he was handed over to the Chinese Communists, and he was imprisoned at Mukden until 1959, when Mao Tse-tung granted him amnesty. See his autobiography, *From Emperor to Citizen* (tr. by W. J. F. Jenner, 1964–65); study by Henry McAleary (1963).

PVC: see POLYVINYL CHLORIDE.

Pyarnu: see PARNU, USSR.

Pyatigorsk (pyĭtyĕgôrsk'), city (1969 est. pop. 84,000), Stavropol Kray, SE European USSR, on the Podkumok River in the N Caucasus. It is a rail terminus and a health resort. The city has an electrotechnical industry, shops for the repair of agricultural equipment, and factories that produce food, clothing, footwear, and other items for resort visitors. The name Pyatigorsk [Rus.,=five mountains] derives from the five peaks of the Besh-Tau mts. that overlook the city. Founded in 1780, Pyatigorsk has been a spa since 1803. There is a museum devoted to the memory of the Russian poet M. Y. Lermontov, who was shot in a duel at Pyatigorsk in 1841.

Pydna (pĭd'nə), ancient town of Pieria, S Macedonia, near the Gulf of Salonica (now Thessaloníki). Nearby in 168 B.C. the Romans under Aemilius PAULLUS defeated the Macedonians under Perseus and thus ended the kingdom of Macedon.

Pye, John, 1782–1874, English engraver, founder of modern landscape engraving. As an illustrator for popular art annuals, he executed plates for landscapes by J. M. W. Turner, Claude Lorrain, and Gaspard Poussin. The British Museum has his impressions for Turner's *Liber Studiorum.* By his expert use of chiaroscuro, he translated works in color into effective black-and-white engravings. He wrote *Patronage of British Art* (1845).

Pye (pyä) or **Prome** (prōm), city (1953 pop. 36,997), Pegu, S central Burma, on the Irrawaddy River. It is a commercial town and port, with railroad connections to Rangoon. One of the oldest cities in Burma, Pye was founded in the 8th cent. by the Indianized Pyus, who were conquered and absorbed by the Mon kingdom of Pegu, probably in the 9th cent. It was incorporated into British Burma in 1852. The ruins of the old city are near its modern namesake.

pyelonephritis: see NEPHRITIS.

Pygmalion (pĭgmāl'yən). **1** In Greek mythology, king of Cyprus. He fell in love with a beautiful statue of a woman. When he prayed to Aphrodite for a wife like it, the goddess brought the statue to life and Pygmalion married her. In one version of the legend, the statue becomes Aphrodite; another states that Pygmalion sculptured the statue himself and that after coming to life it was called Galatea. **2** In Vergil's *Aeneid,* king of Tyre. He was the brother of Dido and killed her husband, Sychaeus, to get his riches.

Pygmy or **Pigmy** (both: pĭg'mē), anthropological term referring to any one of various geographic populations scattered from Africa to New Guinea whose adult males average less than 59 in. (150 cm) in height. Generally regarded as genetically related to the Negroids, the Pygmies nevertheless differ from them and from each other in many respects. The African Pygmies, often called Negrillos, are lighter in color than the Negroids among whom they live, with whom they have interbred, and whose languages they speak. Before agriculture was developed they were probably the sole inhabitants of the Congo valley; today they number about 35,000. Early extinction appears likely for these people because of low birth rates, high infant mortality, and extensive interbreeding. Among the larger groups are the Batwas in the great bend of the Congo. The Akkas of the upper Nile are probably the Pygmies known to the ancient Egyptians and to Homer and Herodotus. The Far Eastern Pygmies, sometimes called Negritos, include the Aetas of the Philippines, the Semangs of the Malay Peninsula, and several other small groups from the Andaman Islands eastward. There is also evidence of Pygmy admixture in the populations of Malaya and Melanesia. The Pygmies in this area average about 5 ft tall and have thick lips, skin color ranging from yellow to black, and scant body hair but thick head hair. They are settled mostly on poor land in isolated locales, where they live by primitive methods of food gathering, hunting, and fishing. Their numerous languages and dialects can be grouped into a few linguistic families. The theory that all Pygmies are of common stock, migrants from S Asia in prehistoric times, is unproved, as is the theory that they are survivors of the ancestral type of man. See A. E. Putnam, *Madami* (1954).

Pylades (pĭl'ədēz): see ORESTES.

Pyle, Ernie (Ernest Taylor Pyle), 1900–1945, American journalist, b. Dana, Ind. After working (1923–32) as a reporter, an editor, and an aviation writer, he became managing editor of the Washington *Daily News.* In 1935 he began writing a column syndicated by the Scripps-Howard chain to about 200 newspapers. Pyle captured America's affection by writing about the lives and hopes of typical citizens. During World War II he served as a war correspondent in Europe, N Africa, and the Pacific. He became the most popular of all correspondents because he wrote about the experiences of enlisted men rather than about battles or the exploits of officers. He was awarded the Pulitzer Prize for distinguished correspondence in 1944, and the next year he was killed by Japanese machine gun fire on Ie Shima. His columns were reprinted in *Ernie Pyle in England* (1941), *Here Is Your War* (1943), *Brave Men* (1944), *Last Chapter* (published posthumously, 1946), and *Home Country* (prewar writing published posthumously, 1947). See biography by Lee Graham Miller (1950).

Pyle, Howard, 1853–1911, American illustrator and writer, b. Wilmington, Del., studied at the Art Students League, New York City. His illustrations appeared regularly in *Harper's Weekly,* and in many other American magazines. He both wrote and illustrated tales of chivalry and adventure for young people, among them *The Merry Adventures of Robin Hood* (1883), *The Wonder Clock* (1888), *The Garden Behind the Moon* (1895), and *The Story of King Arthur and His Knights* (1903). His illustrations are of marked individuality. Scenes from both medieval folklore and American history are rendered with engaging simplicity and penetrating realism. Pyle's reconstructions of the past, of which he had an exhaustive knowledge, were uniquely believable. He also painted murals and taught painting. In 1894 he became director of illustration at Drexel Institute, Philadelphia. In 1900 he started the Howard Pyle School of Art next to his own studio in Wilmington, and classes were offered free to a limited number of students. A large collection of his pictures is preserved at the Wilmington Society of the Fine Arts. See biography by Elizabeth Nesbitt (1966); H. C. Pitz, *The Brandywine Tradition* (1969).

Pylos (pī'lŏs), ancient harbor, Messenia, SW Greece, on a bay of the Ionian Sea. Excavations have revealed a great Mycenaean palace of the 13th cent. B.C., perhaps the dwelling of King NESTOR. Six hundred clay tablets were found there which were important in the decipherment of the late Minoan script (see MYCENAEAN CIVILIZATION). The modern town of Pílos, formerly known as Navarino, grew up on the south shore of the bay. The Bay of Pylos was the scene of an Athenian naval victory over Sparta in 425 B.C. and of the battle of Navarino (1827) during the Greek War of Independence.

Pym, John (pĭm), 1583?–1643, English statesman. A Puritan opposed equally to Roman Catholicism and to Arminianism in the Anglican church, Pym early became prominent in the parliamentary opposition to CHARLES I. He organized the impeachment (1626) of George Villiers, 1st duke of Buckingham, and the passage (1628) of the Petition of Right. In the 11-year interval between Parliaments (1629–40), he supported the colonizing ventures of the Providence Island Company in the West Indies. Pym was the unquestioned leader of the House of Commons in the events leading up to the ENGLISH CIVIL WAR. His long speech in the Short Parliament (1640) listing popular grievances resulted in the dissolution of that Parliament. Resuming the attack in the Long Parliament (1640), he initiated the prosecution of Thomas Wentworth, earl of Strafford, and of Archbishop Laud; urged the abolition of the courts of high commission and the Star Chamber; proposed the abolition of episcopacy; and played a major role in drafting the Grand Remonstrance (1641). Pym was one of the five members of Commons whom Charles tried to remove (1642) by military arrest. After the outbreak (1642) of the civil war, Pym organized various taxation reforms for Parliament and imposed the first English excise duties. His last important act was the arrangement of an alliance with the Scots, based on English acceptance of the Solemn League and Covenant (1643; see COVENANTERS). See biographies by C. E. Wade (1912, repr. 1971), S. R. Brett (1940), and J. H. Hexter (1941).

Pynchon, John (pĭn'chən), c.1626–1703, American colonist and merchant, b. England; son of William Pynchon. He emigrated to Massachusetts Bay colony with his father in 1630. When his father returned to England in 1652, young Pynchon acquired a profitable business and an influential position in Springfield. He established trading posts at Westfield, Northampton, Hadley, Hatfield, and Deerfield and held a number of public offices. See J. C. Pynchon, *Record of the Pynchon Family in England and America* (1885; rev. by W. F. Adams, 1898).

Pynchon, Thomas, 1937–, American novelist, b. Glen Cove, N.Y., grad. Cornell Univ., 1958. He studiously avoids interviews; thus, little is known about him. He is thought to spend much of his time in California and Mexico. Considered a major American writer, Pynchon is noted for his extravagant imagination and wild sense of humor. He is often grouped with authors of BLACK HUMOR (such as Kurt Vonnegut, John Barth, and Joseph Heller), who have turned from realism to fantasy as the appropriate idiom for depicting 20th-century American life. Pynchon's fictive world is a dark, labyrinthine, and insanely energetic place, where unimaginable horrors are commonplace. His novels include *V.* (1963), *The Crying of Lot 49* (1966), and *Gravity's Rainbow* (1973).

Pynchon, William, c.1590–1662, American colonist and theologian, b. England. An original patentee and assistant in the Massachusetts Bay Company, he migrated to America in 1630, where he helped found Roxbury and served as treasurer of the colony (1632–34). In 1636 he settled, and was commissioned to govern, a plantation at the confluence of the Connecticut and Agawam rivers, which he called Agawam but which was renamed Springfield in 1641. Through a flourishing fur trade he increased an already considerable fortune. While visiting England (1650), he published *The Meritorious Price of Our Redemption,* which expressed his liberal views of the atonement. The book was denounced as heretical and ordered burned in Massachusetts. Relenting somewhat but refusing to retract all of his opinions, Pynchon left his property to his son John and other children and returned permanently (1652) to England.

Pynson, Richard (pĭn'sən), d. 1530, English printer, b. Normandy. He moved to England c.1482 and in 1491 or 1492 began printing books pertaining to law in London. He became king's printer (to Henry VIII) in 1508. In craftsmanship he surpassed William CAXTON, WYNKYN DE WORDE, and all other English printers of his time. He was the first English printer to use roman type.

Pyongyang (pyŭng'yăng'), Chin. *P'ing-jang,* Jap. *Heijo,* city (1966 est. pop. 1,364,000), capital of North Korea, NW Korea, on a high bluff above the Taedong River. It is a special city with the status of province. Pyongyang, located near large iron and coal deposits, is a major industrial center; products include iron and steel, machinery, armaments, aircraft, textiles, sugar, and various light manufactures. Korea's oldest city, Pyongyang was founded, according to legend, in 1122 B.C. by remnants of the Chinese Shang dynasty. Nearby is the reputed grave of the city's legendary founder, the Chinese scholar Ki-tze (Kija). As Lolang, the city served as capital of the Choson kingdom (300–200 B.C.) and later became (108 B.C.) a Chinese colony and an important cultural center. It was again capital under the Koguryo (77 B.C.–A.D. 668) and Koryo (10th–12th cent.) kingdoms. Pyongyang fell c.1594 to the Japanese, who hoped to use it as a base for an invasion of China, but who then destroyed the city. Japanese invaders again devastated Pyongyang in 1894 and 1904. It became the capital of North Korea in 1948. Captured (1950) by UN forces during the Korean War, Pyongyang later fell to the North Koreans. After being ravaged in the war, the city was rebuilt along modern lines. Only six gates remain of Pyongyang's former great walls. Other landmarks include three tombs (1st cent. B.C.) with remarkable murals, several old Buddhist temples, and a museum. Pyongyang also has a university (1946).

pyorrhea (pīərē'ə), inflammation and degeneration of the gums and other tissues surrounding the teeth. The onset of the disease is marked by bleeding of the gums. As the disease proceeds, the gums recede from the teeth, loosening of the teeth occurs, and the bone supporting the teeth is resorbed. Pus is discharged from pockets in the gums, which are formed as the jawbone recedes from the roots of the teeth. Pyorrhea, known medically as pyorrhea alveolaris, is most common in persons over 40. There are numerous possible causes, toward which therapy is directed, including poor nutrition, poor oral hygiene, ill-fitting dentures, and irritation of the tissues by dental tartar.

pyracantha (pĭr"əkăn'thə) or **firethorn,** any hardwood evergreen shrub of the genus *Pyracantha* of the family Rosaceae (ROSE family). Native from S Europe to W China, pyracanthas are now cultivated elsewhere (often as hedge plants or espaliered on walls) for their red fruits and spiny branches. *P. coccinea,* also called everlasting thorn, is the most popular; it now grows wild in parts of North America. Pyracantha is classified in the division MAGNOLIOPHYTA, class Magnoliopsida, order Rosales, family Rosaceae.

pyramid. The true pyramid exists only in Egypt, though the term has been applied also to similar structures in other countries. The Egyptian pyramids, usually of stone, are square in plan. Their triangular sides, directly facing the points of the compass, slope at an angle to the ground of about 50° and meet at an apex. The oldest remaining Egyptian tombs are the MASTABAS of the Old Kingdom (2680–2565 B.C.). From these the true pyramid was evolved about the IV dynasty, and continued to be the favored form of royal burial through the VI dynasty. The few pyramid tombs of later dynasties were in the nature of deliberate archaisms, lacking the splendor and significance of their predecessors. Each monarch built his own pyramid, in which his mummified body might be preserved for eternity from human view and sacrilege and into whose construction went years of time and measureless amounts of material and labor. Entrance into a pyramid is through an opening in the northern wall. A small passage, traversing lesser chambers, leads to the sepulchral chamber deep beneath the immense pile, excavated from the rock upon which the monument is built. Stone blocks forming a gable transfer the weight of the great masonry masses over these chambers. Though the pyramids were usually built of rough stone blocks laid up in horizontal courses, many were of mud bricks with a stone casing. The three pyramids of Gizeh, all of the IV dynasty, are the largest and finest of their kind. The Great Pyramid of Khufu or Cheops (2680 B.C.), at Gizeh near Cairo, is one of the Seven Wonders of the World and the largest pyramid ever built. A solid mass of limestone blocks covering 13 acres (5.3 hectares), it was originally 756 ft (230 m) along each side of its base and 482 ft (147 m) high. It has several passages, two large chambers in addition to one beneath the ground level, and two small air chambers for ventilation. Adjacent to each pyramid was a small funerary chapel for the performance of rites, as well as the smaller pyramids of the chief wives and lesser members of the royal family and the mastabas of the nobles who had lived under that particular monarch. Pyramidal structures, though not true pyramids, were built also by the Mesopotamians and by the Maya of Central America and Mexico. The Middle Eastern ZIGGURAT was square in plan and built up in receding terraces. The Maya pyramids, built in steep, receding blocks, also were topped by ritual chambers and in some cases possessed an interior tomb crypt. The Romans built small pyramid tombs. The Pyramid of Cestius (62 B.C.–12 B.C.) at Rome, of concrete faced with marble, has an interior tomb vault and is 116 ft (35 m) high. See I. E. S. Edwards, *The Pyramids of Egypt* (rev. ed. 1961); P. Tompkins, *Secrets of the Great Pyramid* (1971); Kurt Mendelssohn, *The Riddle of the Pyramids* (1974).

pyramid, in geometry, solid figure bounded by a POLYGON (the base, or directrix) and the surface generated by a moving line (the generator) passing through a fixed point (vertex) and continually intersecting the perimeter of the polygon. The surface, or lateral faces, of the pyramid are triangles having as a common vertex the vertex of the pyramid; in a regular pyramid the base is a regular polygon and the lateral faces are congruent triangles. The altitude of a pyramid is the perpendicular distance from the vertex to the base. The volume of a pyramid is equal to one third the product of the altitude and the area

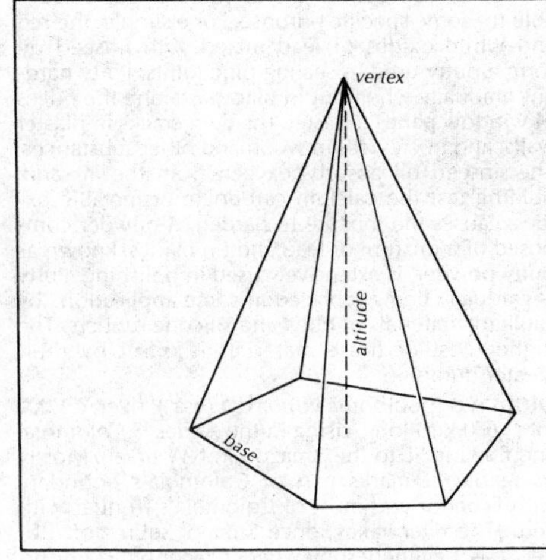

Pyramid

of the base. The frustum is the portion of a pyramid between the base and a plane parallel to the base cutting the pyramid into two parts.

Pyramid Lake, 188 sq mi (487 sq km), W Nev. The lake is a remnant of ancient Lake Lahontan. The Truckee River flows into the lake. Discovered in 1844 by U.S. explorer John Frémont, the lake was named for its large pyramidal rocks. It is located in Pyramid Lake Indian Reservation. In the lake is Anaho Island, a national wildlife refuge.

Pyramids, battle of, July, 1798, during the French Revolutionary Wars, battle fought between the French forces under Napoleon Bonaparte and the Egyptian Mamelukes led by Murad Bey. Napoleon's victory gave the French access to Cairo and brief control over EGYPT. See Alan Moorehead, *Blue Nile* (1962).

Pyramus and Thisbe (pĭr'əməs, thĭz'bē), in classical mythology, youth and maiden of Babylon, whose parents opposed their marriage. Their homes adjoined, and they conversed through a crevice in the dividing wall. On a night when they had arranged to meet at the tomb of Ninus, Thisbe, who was the first at the trysting place, was frightened by a lion with jaws bloody from its prey. As she fled, she dropped her mantle, which was seized by the lion. When Pyramus came, the torn and bloody mantle convinced him that she had been slain. He killed himself, and Thisbe, returning, took her own life with his sword. The white fruit of a mulberry tree that stood at the trysting place was dyed red with Pyramus' blood, and the fruit was ever after the color of blood.

pyranometer (pĭr"ənŏm'ətər), ACTINOMETER used to measure the total radiation incident on a surface.

Pyrenees (pĭr'ənēz), Span. *Pirineos,* Fr. *Pyrénées,* mountain chain of SW Europe, 21,380 sq mi (55,374 sq km), between France and Spain, a formidable barrier between the Iberian Peninsula and the European mainland. It extends in an almost straight line 270 mi (435 km) from the Bay of Biscay on the west to the Mediterranean Sea on the east; its maximum width is c.80 mi (130 km). About two thirds of its area is in Spain. Of the three main ranges of the Pyrenees, the central section is the highest. The Pico de Aneto, Spain (11,168 ft/3,404 m), is the tallest peak; other peaks include the Pic de Vignemale and the Pic du Midi d'Ossau (France) and Monte Perdido (Spain). The Cantabrian Mts. are a western extension of the Pyrenees. The Pyrenees were formed during the Tertiary period. Exposed crystalline rock is found in the uplands, while folded limestone composes the lower slopes. Glaciated in the distant past, the Pyrenees do not have any glaciers now. The permanent snowline is at an elevation of c.6,000 ft (1,830 m). Characteristic of the French Pyrenees, which are much steeper than the southern slopes, are the torrents called *gaves,* often falling in cascades, and the natural amphitheaters known as *cirques,* notably the famous Cirque de Gavarnie. The Pyrenees are a climatic divide. The northern slopes receive abundant rainfall while the southern slopes have a steppelike climate. On the French side are the best-known resorts, such as Pau and Tarbes, famed both for the beauty of their scenery and for their mineral waters. Lourdes, one of the world's chief places of pilgrimage, is also there. On the Atlantic shore, below the W Pyrenees, are the fashionable resorts of Biarritz and Saint-Jean-de-Luz (France) and San Sebastián (Spain). The Franco-Spanish border, unchanged since the Peace of the Pyrenees (1659), generally follows the watershed. The more important rivers—the Garonne, the Aude, and the Adour—run north; among the Spanish rivers rising in the Pyrenees are the Aragón, the Cinca, and the Segre. The Pyrenees are crossed by a railroad from Toulouse to Barcelona, via Puigcerdá, but the two chief rail lines connecting Spain with France skirt the Pyrenees in the west and east along the coastal lowlands. The mountain passes are high and difficult, but they were often crossed by invading armies and barbarian hordes and by innumerable medieval pilgrims on their way to Santiago de Compostela. The Col de Perthus, used by the Romans, and Roncesvalles, famous for the Roland legend, are the best known. The Pyrenees are rich in timber and in pastures, and the many streams are utilized by hydroelectric power stations. Bauxite, talc, and zinc are mined there. The population, partly of Basque and Bearnese stock, engages mostly in stock raising and agriculture. The high stage of civilization reached there by prehistoric man is evidenced by the cave paintings at Altamira and Aurignac. Parts of six French departments and six Spanish provinces are in the Pyrenees region. Perpignan, Bayonne, and Orthez in France and Gerona, Huesca, Pamplona, and Irún in Spain are other important cities. Wedged between France and Spain, in the E Pyrenees, is the small republic of Andorra.

Pyrénées, Hautes-: see HAUTES-PYRÉNÉES.

Pyrenees, Peace of the, 1659, treaty ending the warfare between France and Spain that, continuing after the Peace of Westphalia, had been complicated by Spanish intervention in the FRONDE. Together with the Peace of Westphalia, it marked the rise of France as the dominant European power. France received Roussillon and extensive territories in Flanders, while its Spanish border was set at the Pyrenees. A marriage contract between Louis XIV and Marie Thérèse, daughter of Philip IV of Spain, was included in the terms. The infanta renounced her claims to the Spanish throne in consideration of a large payment. The nonpayment of that dowry was the occasion for the War of DEVOLUTION and, indirectly, the War of the SPANISH SUCCESSION.

Pyrénées-Atlantique (pĕrānā'-zätläNtĕk'), department (1968 pop. 508,734), SW France; formerly Basses-Pyrénées dept. PAU is the capital.

Pyrénées-Orientales (pĕrānā'-zôryäNtäl'), department (1968 pop. 281,976), S France, in ROUSSILLON, on the Mediterranean Sea. PERPIGNAN is the capital.

pyrenoid: see CHLOROPLAST.

pyrethrin (pīrē'thrĭn): see INSECTICIDE.

pyrethrum (pīrē'thrəm): see CHRYSANTHEMUM.

Pyrgos, Greece: see PÍRGOS.

pyrheliometer (pīər"hēlēŏm'ĭtər), ACTINOMETER used to measure solar radiation.

pyridine (pĭr'ĭdēn) or **azine** (ăz'ēn), C_5H_5N, colorless, flammable, toxic liquid with a putrid odor. It melts at −42°C and boils at 115.5°C. Chemically, it is a heterocyclic aromatic tertiary amine (see under AMINO GROUP). Its molecule resembles that of benzene, one carbon-hydrogen unit in the benzene ring being replaced with a nitrogen molecule. It is miscible with water and with most organic solvents. Its aqueous solution is slightly alkaline. Pyridine is used as a solvent, as a denaturant for alcohol, and as a starting material in the synthesis of other compounds. Compounds that can be derived from pyridine include antihistamines and vitamins. Pyridine is obtained from bone oil or from coal tar by destructive distillation, which decomposes alkaloids that contain it. Alkaloids that contain pyridine include coniine, piperine (the alkaloid in pepper), and nicotine (present in tobacco); free pyridine is present in tobacco smoke.

pyridoxal phosphate (pĭr"ĭdŏks'əl): see COENZYME; VITAMIN.

pyridoxine: see COENZYME; VITAMIN.

pyrimidine (pīrĭm'ĭdēn"), type of organic base found in certain COENZYMES and in the NUCLEIC ACIDS of plant and animal tissue. The three major pyrimidines of almost universal distribution in living systems are CYTOSINE, THYMINE, and URACIL. (See diagram at right.)

pyrite (pī'rīt) or **iron pyrites** (pīrī'tēz, pə-, pī'rīts), pale brass-yellow mineral, the bisulfide of iron, FeS_2. It occurs most commonly in crystals (belonging to the isometric system and usually in the form of cubes and pyritohedrons) but is also found in massive, granular, and stalactite form. In spite of its nickname, "fool's gold," it often is associated with true gold; auriferous pyrite is a commercially important source of gold. Other metals that sometimes replace a part of the iron are cobalt, nickel, arsenic, and copper. The most common sulfide mineral, pyrite is widely distributed in rocks of all ages and types. Its chief use is as a source of sulfur in the manufacture of sulfuric acid. The term *pyrites* is applied to any of a number of metallic sulfides that strike fire with steel. Some minerals resembling pyrite in appearance or composition are ARSENOPYRITE, CHALCOPYRITE (copper pyrites), COBALTITE, MARCASITE (white iron pyrites or spear pyrites), and PYRRHOTITE (magnetic pyrites).

pyrogallol (pī"rōgăl'ōl) or **pyrogallic acid** (-ĭk), $C_6H_6O_3$, white, crystalline, aromatic compound with a biting taste; it is poisonous. It melts at 133°C and boils at 309°C. In alkaline solution it is an active reducing agent. Pyrogallol is widely used in photographic developing and in the manufacture of some dyes. Chemically it is a phenol; its IUPAC name is 1,2,3-trihydroxybenzene.

pyroligneous acid (pī"rəlĭg'nēəs), a dark liquid that is essentially a mixture of ACETIC ACID and METHANOL (wood alcohol) and is obtained in the destructive distillation of wood. It once served as a commercial source of acetic acid.

pyrolusite (pī"rōlōō'zīt), naturally occurring manganese dioxide, MnO_2, a black mineral that crystallizes in the tetragonal system but is usually found in earthy or massive deposits. It is the principal source of manganese and its compounds, and it is extensively used in steel smelting and in the manufacture of dry-cell batteries. The main producing countries are the USSR, Brazil, South Africa, Gabon, India, China, and Australia.

pyromania (pī"rōmā'nēə) [Gr.,=craze for fire], symptom of an emotional disorder characterized by a compulsion to set fires. In some states the irresistible impulse to set fires is considered a form of legal insanity. Pyromania must be distinguished from criminal motives for arson, e.g., to collect insurance.

pyrosis: see HEARTBURN.

pyrotechnics (pī"rōtĕk'nĭks, pī"rə-), technology of making and using fireworks. Gunpowder was used in fireworks by the Chinese as early as the 9th cent., and it was they who brought fireworks to a high stage of development. The use of fireworks for display has spread throughout the world. In many countries fireworks are used to celebrate national holidays, e.g., Independence Day in the United States and Bastille Day in France. Many combustibles and explosives and ingenious combinations of the two have been devised to produce impressive sounds and lights of many colors and to drive wheels and rockets. Fireworks are also widely used as signal devices, e.g., red flares to stop railroad trains and various colored flares and smoke grenades to denote distress or to locate targets in military operations. Powerful flares are also used in combat to illuminate enemy positions.

pyroxene (pī'rŏksēn), name given to members of a group of widely distributed rock minerals, metasilicates of magnesium, iron, and calcium, often with aluminum, sodium, lithium, manganese, or zinc. The pyroxene minerals crystallize in three different systems—orthorhombic, monoclinic, and triclinic—but all have a fundamental prism with angles of 87° to 93° and cleavages parallel to the prism angles. They are commonly white, gray white, green white, greenish black, black, or brown, but yellow, reddish, pink, purple, and blue varieties occur. The pyroxene minerals are found chiefly in igneous and metamorphic rocks. Varieties include enstatite, bronzite, hypersthene, diopside, diallage, wollastonite, augite, pectolite, spodumene, and rhodonite. Pyroxenes are abundant in lunar rocks.

thymine

cytosine

Pyrimidines found in deoxyribonucleic acid (DNA)

pyroxylin (pīrŏk'sĭlĭn), partially nitrated cellulose (see NITROCELLULOSE). It is used in lacquers, plastics, and artificial leathers. Pyroxylin lacquers are made by dissolving pyroxylin in a mixture of volatile solvents and adding a plasticizer and a pigment or dye. Pyroxylin plastics are made by colloiding pyroxylin with large amounts of a plasticizer such as camphor; such plastics (e.g., celluloid) are highly flammable. COLLODION is a solution of pyroxylin in ether and ethanol.

Pyrrha (pĭr'ə): see DEUCALION.

Pyrrho (pĭr'ō), c.360–270 B.C., Greek philosopher, a native of Elis, regarded as the father of SKEPTICISM. After accompanying Alexander's expedition to the Orient, he enjoyed great respect at Elis and Athens. His doctrines were preserved by his disciple, Timon of Phlius, in satires. Pyrrho taught that nothing can be known, because the contradictory of every statement can be maintained with equal plausibility. Hence the philosophic attitude is one of suspended judgment and imperturbability.

pyrrhotite (pĭr'ətīt) or **magnetic pyrites,** bronze-yellow to bronze-red mineral, a sulfide of iron sometimes containing nickel. It tarnishes easily and is somewhat magnetic. It crystallizes in the hexagonal system, but appears usually in massive form, and occurs chiefly in basic igneous rocks. In some areas, e.g., at Sudbury, Ont., Canada, it is associated with pentlandite, an important ore of nickel. It is found also in the United States, Europe, and South America.

Pyrrhus (pĭr'əs), c.318–272 B.C., Molossian king of Epirus. He fought at Ipsus in Asia Minor in the service of Demetrius Poliorcetes (later DEMETRIUS I) of Macedon, and by the aid of Ptolemy I he became (297 B.C.) joint king of Epirus with Neoptolemus. He removed (295) Neoptolemus from the throne, but before his kingdom was consolidated he went to war with Demetrius (291–286); Pyrrhus obtained half of Macedonia and Thessaly but was driven back (c.286) by LYSIMACHUS. He then went to S Italy with a large force to aid the Tarentines and defeated (280) the Romans at Heraclea. In the same year Pyrrhus' peace proposals were rejected by the Romans. In 279 he again defeated the Romans at Asculum in Apulia. His heavy losses caused him to declare, "one more such victory and I am lost," thus the origin of the term "Pyrrhic victory." At Beneventum (now Benevento) he was barely defeated (275) by the Romans. He again attempted to conquer Macedonia, defeating (273) Antigonus II. Turning his attention suddenly to the Peloponnesus, he failed to take Sparta by siege. He then fled to Argos, where he was killed by a mob in the street. He accomplished nothing beyond bringing Epirus to ruin.

Pyrrhus, in Greek legend: see NEOPTOLEMUS.

Pyrrophyta (pərŏf'ətə), division of the plant kingdom consisting of mostly unicellular, often flagellated, and usually photosynthetic organisms, extremely abundant in tropical oceans. The division includes the group commonly known as the dinoflagellates. The Pyrrophyta are unusual in that in each cell, the chromosomes remain compact between divisions, instead of stretching out into slender threads, as in most other organisms. The chromosomes are constricted at regular intervals and do not have centromeres, or fiber-attachment centers. There is no spindle, yet the very numerous chromosomes are divided equally at the time of MITOSIS. The cell chloroplasts have, in addition to the photosynthetic pigments chlorophyll *a* and chlorophyll *c*, a large proportion of xanthophylls. The xanthophyll peridinin, found only in members of this division, imparts a golden brown to golden green color to the cells. The cell wall, when present, is composed of cellulose and consists of two valves or interlocking plates; in some species the cell wall is absent. Food reserves are largely starch. Reproduction for most is asexual, through simple division of cells following mitosis. Pyrrophyta, and especially the dinoflagellates, are important primary food sources in the food chains of warmer oceans; they are largely responsible for the phosphorescence visible at night in tropical seas.

Pythagoras (pĭthăg'ərəs), c.582–c.507 B.C., pre-Socratic Greek philosopher, founder of the Pythagorean school. He migrated from his native Samos to Crotona and established a secret religious society or order similar to, and possibly influenced by, the earlier Orphic cult. We know little of his life and nothing of his writings. Since his disciples came to worship him as a demigod and to attribute all the doctrines of their order to its founder, it is virtually impossible to distinguish his teachings from those of his followers. The **Pythagoreans** are best known for two teachings: the TRANSMIGRATION OF SOULS and the theory that numbers constitute the true nature of things. The believers performed purification rites and followed moral, ascetic, and dietary rules to enable their souls to achieve a higher rank in their subsequent lives and thus eventually be liberated from the "wheel of birth." This belief also led them to regard the sexes as equal, to treat slaves humanely, and to respect animals. The highest purification was "philosophy," and tradition credits Pythagoras with the first use of the term. Beginning with the discovery that the relationship between musical notes could be expressed in numerical ratios (see GREEK MUSIC), the Pythagoreans elaborated a theory of numbers, the exact meaning of which is still disputed by scholars. Briefly, they taught that all things were numbers, meaning that the essence of things was number, and that all relationships—even abstract ethical concepts like justice—could be expressed numerically. They held that numbers set a limit to the unlimited—thus foreshadowing the distinction between form and matter that plays a key role in all later philosophy. The Pythagoreans were influential mathematicians and geometricians, and the theorem that bears their name is witness to their influence on the initial part of Euclidian geometry. They made important contributions to medicine and astronomy and were among the first to teach that the earth was a spherical planet, revolving about a fixed point. At the end of the 5th cent. B.C. the Pythagoreans were forced to flee Magna Graecia when people grew enraged at their interference with traditional religious customs; many were killed. A short-lived **Neo-Pythagoreanism** developed at the beginning of the Christian era; it borrowed some elements from Jewish and Hellenistic thought and greatly emphasized the mystical element in Pythagorean ideas. See John Burnet, *Greek Philosophy* (1960 ed, repr. 1968); J. A. Philip, *Pythagoras and Early Pythagoreanism* (1966).

Pythagoras of Rhegium (rē'jəm), fl. 5th cent. B.C., Greek sculptor. In a signature on a pedestal at Olympia he declares himself a Samian, but the period of his training and work belongs to Rhegium, Italy. As no works are known that can with certainty be identified as his, his fame depends upon the statements of those who saw his statues and named them. They were mainly of athletes and mark a step in the transition between the archaic and the classical styles. He is said to have been the first to represent hair, veins, and muscles naturally and the first to aim at rhythm and symmetry in sculpture. Among his statues were a portrait of the boxer Euthymus, a figure of a man singing to a lyre, and one of Apollo shooting the Python with his arrows.

Pythia: see DELPHI.

Pythian games (pĭth'ēən), in ancient Greece, games held at Delphi every four years (the third of each Olympiad). They included musical, literary, and athletic contests. The games honored Apollo and took their name from Pythia, the priestess of the oracle at DELPHI.

Pythias: see DAMON AND PYTHIAS.

python (pī'thŏn), name for nonvenomous constrictor snakes of the BOA family, found in the tropical regions of Africa, Asia, Australia, and the S Pacific islands. Pythons climb and swim expertly. They kill the birds and mammals on which they feed by squeezing them in their coils. Unlike boas, pythons are egg layers. The female coils her body over the eggs for the six to eight week incubation period. The reticulated, or royal, python, *Python reticulatus,* of SE Asia, Indonesia, and the Philippines is one of the largest snakes in the world and may reach a length of 30 ft (9 m) or more. It is often found in towns as well as in the forest. Pythons are classified in the phylum CHORDATA, subphylum Vertebrata, class Reptilia, order Squamata, family Boidae.

Python, in Greek mythology, a huge serpent. It was sent by Hera to harm LETO when she was with child. In some myths the infant Apollo gave chase to Python and slew it at the oracle of Gaea in Delphi; in others Apollo killed the serpent in order to claim the oracle for himself. The Pythian games celebrated the victory of Apollo over Python.

pyxie (pĭk'sē): see DIAPENSIA.

Q

Q, 17th letter of the ALPHABET, corresponding to the koppa of western Greek alphabets. *U* must follow the letter in English (e.g., *queen, question*), and the combination properly represents a sound much like the true voiceless labiovelar stop (also represented by the combination *kw*).

"Q": see QUILLER-COUCH, SIR ARTHUR THOMAS.

Qabis (käb'ĭs), city (1966 pop. 32,330), E central Tunisia, on the Gulf of Gabès (Khalij Qabis), an arm of the Mediterranean Sea. It is a fishing port and the center of an oasis noted for its date palms. The city was founded by the Romans and was held (c.1147–59) by the Normans of Sicily. It is also known as Gabès.

Qaddafi, Muammar al- (mo͞oäm-mär' äl-käd-dä'-fē), 1938–, Libyan army officer and political leader. He graduated (1963) from the University of Libya with a degree in history and then entered the Libyan military academy in Benghazi. He was commissioned an officer in 1965 and rose to the rank of captain within four years. Along with a group of fellow officers, he formed a secret revolutionary committee, and in 1969 the group led a coup against the monarchy of Idris I. Qaddafi established himself as Libya's commander in chief and chairman of the Revolutionary Command Council. Blending Arab nationalism, revolutionary socialism, and Islamic orthodoxy, Qaddafi proceeded to run Libya's government as a stridently anti-Western dictatorship. British and American military bases were closed in 1970; in the same year, the property of Libya's Italian and Jewish communities was confiscated. The ancient Koranic law of cutting off the hands of thieves was reinstituted, and Tripoli's major Christian church was transformed into a mosque. A fervent Arab nationalist, Qaddafi has used his nation's vast oil wealth to help support the Palestinian guerrilla movement. He has also sought to unify Libya with other Arab countries, including Egypt and Tunisia.

Qafsah (käf'sä), town (1966 pop. 32,408), W central Tunisia, in an oasis. It is in a region of thermal springs rich in phosphates. The town is a trade center for phosphates, dates, olives, and woolen goods. It is on the site of Capsa, a Numidian and later a Roman town. The region around Qafsah has yielded artifacts of an upper Paleolithic culture (Capsian) of N Africa and S Europe. The town is also known as Gafsa.

Qalyub (käl'yo͞ob), town (1966 pop. 49,300), N Egypt, on the Nile River, near Cairo. It is the trade center for a densely populated agricultural region.

Qantarah, Al (äl kän'tärä), town, NE Egypt, on the east bank of the Suez Canal. It is on the ancient military road between Egypt and Syria. Al Qantarah is the terminus of a railroad to Palestine constructed during World War I, when the British Expeditionary Force in Egypt was based there. Israel captured the town during the Arab-Israeli war of 1967 and in 1969 evacuated the civilian population. It was returned to Egyptian control in 1974. The town is also known as El Kantara.

Qarun, lake, Egypt: see MOERIS.

Qatar or **Katar** (both: kä'tär), sheikhdom (1973 est. pop. 160,000), c.4,400 sq mi (11,400 sq km), E Arabia, coextensive with the Qatar peninsula, which projects into the Persian Gulf. The capital is Doha, or Bida (1971 est. pop. 95,000). Qatar is largely barren. The inhabitants are mainly Arabs of the WAHABI (puritanic) sect of Islam. Fishing and work in the oil industry support most of the population; oil began to be produced commercially in 1949. The sheikhdom had close ties with Great Britain until Sept. 1, 1971, when it became independent. Qatar is a member of the Arab League and of the United Nations. Sheikh Khalifa ibn Hamad ath-Thani came to power in Feb., 1972.

Qattara Depression (kätär'ə) or **Munkhafad al-Qattarah** (mo͞ongkhäfäd' äl-kät-tärä'), desert basin, c.7,000 sq mi (18,130 sq km), NW Egypt, NE Africa, in the Libyan Desert. It contains the lowest point (436 ft/133 m below sea level) in Africa.

Qazvin (käzvēn'), city (1966 pop. 88,106), Tehran prov., NW Iran. A road and rail-transport center, the city has textile and flour mills, and wineries. Qazvin was probably founded by Shapur II, king of Persia, in the 4th cent. A.D. It was captured by the Arabs in 644. Hasan-i Sabbah, the founder of the secret Ismaili ASSASSIN order, seized (c.1090) the nearby fortress of Alamut and made it the headquarters of the order. Shah Tahmasp I embellished the city with many fine buildings. It was the capital of Persia from 1548 to 1598. In 1722 the city was temporarily captured by the Afghans. During World War I it was occupied by Russian forces. In 1941 the city was bombed by the Soviet air force and after World War II was a stronghold during the brief Soviet occupation of N Iran. The city is also known as Kazvin and Kasbin.

Qeshm or **Qishm** (both: kĕ'shəm), largest island of Iran, c.500 sq mi (1,300 sq km), S Iran, in the Strait of Hormoz. It is mostly rocky and has little vegetation; dates and fruits are raised. Qeshm, at the eastern end of the island, is the largest town.

Q fever: see RICKETTSIA.

Qift: see COPTOS.

Qina (kĭnə) or **Keneh** (kĕn'ə), town (1970 est. pop. 77,600), capital of Qina governorate, E central Egypt, on the Nile River. Sugarcane and grains are grown nearby, and pottery is made in the town. Qina was built on the site of ancient Caene (or Caenepolis), of which many ruins remain. During World War II, Qina took on strategic importance as the terminus of a road through the mountains from Al Quayr on the Red Sea coast.

Qishon: see KISHON.

Qom (kôm), city (1966 pop. 134,292), Tehran prov., W central Iran. Located in a semiarid region, it is an industrial and transportation center. Its manufactures include textiles, glass, pottery, and shoes. Large deposits of petroleum have been found in the area. Qom has been a center of the Shiite Muslims since early Islamic times and is the burial place of Fatima al-Masuma (d. 816), sister of Imam Riza. The city became a center of pilgrimage in the 17th cent., and an imposing shrine was erected over Fatima's tomb. Qom was pillaged by the Afghans in 1722, but in the 19th cent. its great shrine was lavishly restored and embellished. The city is also known as Qum and Kum.

Quabbin Reservoir (kwŏb'ĭn), 39 sq mi (101 sq km), in the Swift River valley, central Mass., NE of Springfield. The reservoir, formed by Winsor Dam and Quabbin Dike, is the largest reservoir in Massachusetts. It is fed by the Swift and Ware rivers. The water flows to the Wachusett Reservoir through Quabbin Aqueduct (25 mi/40 km long) and supplies the Boston area.

quack grass or **couch grass,** Old World perennial GRASS (*Agropyron repens*), now widely distributed and in the United States a troublesome weed. It somewhat resembles a beardless wheat and has creeping, yellowish rootstalks, the joints of which, even though detached, are capable of producing new plants; thus quack grass is a good soil binder

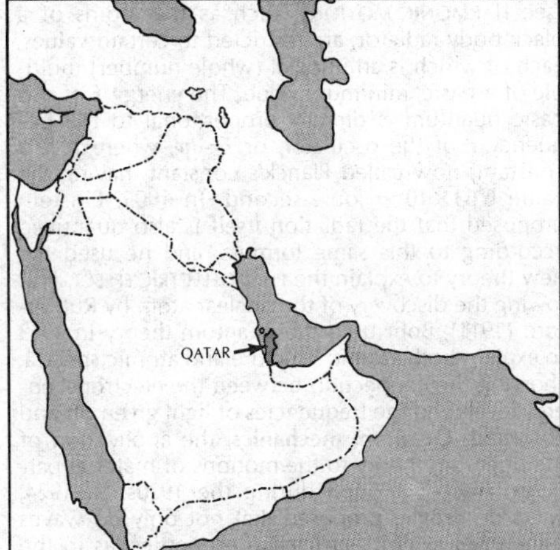

but extremely difficult to eradicate. The dried sweetish rootstalks have been used medicinally, and the foliage is useful for forage. Quack grass is classified in the division MAGNOLIOPHYTA, class Liliatae, order Cyperales, family Gramineae.

quadrant. 1 In analytic geometry, one of the four regions of the plane determined by two lines, the *x*-axis and the *y*-axis. Commonly these lines are drawn perpendicular to each other, and the quadrants, or regions, they determine are numbered counterclockwise, beginning with the upper right quadrant. **2** In geometry, a region of a plane determined by two perpendicular radii of a circle and the circle itself. Thus two perpendicular diameters of a circle divide it into four regions, or quadrants.

quadrant, in technology, angle-measuring device based on a scale of 90°. It is sometimes confused with the SEXTANT, a similar instrument based on a scale of 60°. The quadrant is rarely used today.

quadraphonic sound: see STEREOPHONIC SOUND.

quadratic, mathematical expression of the second degree in one or more unknowns (see POLYNOMIAL). The general quadratic in one unknown has the form ax^2+bx+c, where *a, b,* and *c* are constants and *x* is the variable. A quadratic equation $ax^2+bx+c=0$ always has two ROOTS; these may be real or imaginary (see NUMBER). The quadratic formula

$$x=\frac{-b\pm\sqrt{b^2-4ac}}{2a}$$

gives the roots of any quadratic equation in terms of its coefficients *a, b,* and *c.* The expression b^2-4ac is called the discriminant and can be used to determine the character of the roots: If the discriminant is zero, the roots are real and equal; if positive, they are real and unequal; if negative, they are imaginary.

quadrature, in astronomy, arrangement of two celestial bodies at right angles to each other as viewed from a reference point. If the reference point is the earth and the sun is one of the bodies, a planet is in quadrature when its ELONGATION is 90°. As viewed from the earth, the half-moon is in quadrature to the sun. The inferior planets (Mercury and Venus) never reach quadrature; the superior planets each have two points of quadrature in their orbits.

Quadros, Jânio (zhä'nyo͞o kwä'dro͞os), 1917–, president of Brazil (Jan.–Aug., 1961). A schoolteacher and lawyer, he served as mayor of the city of São Paulo (1953–54) and as governor of the state of São Paulo (1955–59). A political independent, he was elected president in 1960 by an unprecedented popular margin. He initiated reform measures, drastically cut government spending, and attempted to reduce economic dependence on the United States. Encountering opposition, especially in congress, he abruptly resigned (Aug., 1961), creating a national crisis before the controversial vice president, João GOULART, succeeded him. In 1964, after a military takeover in Brazil, Quadros was deprived of his political rights.

Quadruple Alliance, any of several European alliances. The Quadruple Alliance of **1718** was formed by Great Britain, France, the Holy Roman emperor, and the Netherlands when Philip V of Spain, guided by Cardinal ALBERONI, sought by force to nullify the peace settlements reached after the War of the Spanish Succession (see UTRECHT, PEACE OF). An English fleet landed Austrian troops in Sicily, which Spain had seized, while French and English forces entered Spain. Early in 1720, Spain yielded to the allies, but the peace terms thoroughly revised those signed at Utrecht. The Treaty of The Hague restored Naples to the house of Austria; Austria in turn promised that Philip's son Charles (later Charles III of Spain) would succeed to Parma, Piacenza, and Tuscany. Savoy, in exchange for yielding Sicily to the house of Austria, received the island of Sardinia and became the kingdom of Sardinia. Spain joined the alliance. A progressive rapprochement between Spain and France led to the FAMILY COMPACT of 1733 and a further redistribution of territories after the War of the POLISH SUCCESSION (1733–35). The Quadruple Alliance of March, **1814,** was concluded among Great Britain, Austria, Prussia, and Russia at Chaumont, France, in order to strengthen their coalition against Napoleon I. After Napoleon's first abdication the four powers made peace with France (see PARIS, TREATY OF, **1814**); after Napoleon's return from Elba, they defeated him in the Waterloo campaign and imposed on France the more severe Treaty of Paris of 1815. On the same day that treaty was signed (Nov. 20), the Quadruple Alliance was renewed in order to insure the treaty's execution. The so-called HOLY ALLIANCE, signed a few days earlier by Russia, Austria, and Prussia, became confused with the Quadruple Alliance, especially since the international congresses at Aachen (1818), Troppau (1820), Laibach (1821), and Verona (1822)—which were held according to provisions of the Quadruple Alliance—increasingly shaped the policy of the Holy Alliance, while England retired into "splendid isolation." In 1818, France joined the powers of the Quadruple Alliance to form a Quintuple Alliance. The Quadruple Alliance of **1834** was formed by Great Britain, France, Spain, and Portugal for the purpose of strengthening the constitutional government of Spain and the throne of Isabella II against the CARLISTS. The Spanish marriages (1846; see ISABELLA II) ended Franco-British cooperation in Spanish affairs.

quaestor or **questor** (both: kwĕs'tər), Roman magistrate, with responsibility for the treasury; in early times a quaestor also had judicial powers. At first there were two quaestors; when the office was opened (421 B.C.) to plebeians, there were four. Sulla named 20, and Caesar set 40 as the number (45 B.C.), but Augustus reduced them to 20. Quaestors were in theory deputies for consuls, praetors, or proconsuls. A quaestorship was the first magistracy sought by an ambitious young man.

quagga (kwăg'ə), extinct species of ZEBRA, *Equus quagga*. It formerly inhabited open plains in S Africa, where its range overlapped that of the common zebra (*E. burchelli*). Its coat was sandy brown and its legs and tail whitish; only its head, neck, and shoulders were striped with white in typical zebra fashion. Its shoulder height was about 4½ ft (1.4 m). Like other zebras, quaggas lived in herds. Hunted for their skins, they were exterminated in the 19th cent.; the last quagga died in 1883 in the Amsterdam Zoo. Some tamed quaggas were used to draw light vehicles. Quaggas are classified in the phylum CHORDATA, subphylum Vertebrata, class Mammalia, order Perissodactyla, family Equidae.

quahog: see CLAM.

Quai d'Orsay (kā dôrsā'), quay on the left bank of the Seine River in Paris, extending from the Eiffel Tower to the Palais Bourbon (housing the national assembly). Next to the Palais Bourbon stands the French ministry of foreign affairs, a vast palatial building, which is often referred to as simply the Quai d'Orsay.

quail, common name for a variety of small game birds related to the partridge, pheasant, and more distantly to the grouse. There are three subfamilies in the quail family: the New World quails; the Old World quails and partridges; and the true pheasants and seafowls. No species of New World quail is migratory; but some Old World quail represent the only migratory species of the order. The migratory quail of Eurasia has been known for its phenomenal migrations since biblical times. Quails have high reproductive potentials, with 12 to 15 eggs laid per clutch. The nests are built on the ground in vegetation. The female does the major portion of incubation and rearing. Quails are extremely popular game birds. The Old World quail has never been naturalized in America; in the central and S United States the BOBWHITE, *Colinus virginianus,* is commonly called quail (or partridge). The helmet and plumed quails, named for their crests, the Gambel's quail, and the valley and scaled quails are all western birds. They eat harmful insects and seeds and travel in flocks called coveys. Quails are classified in the phylum CHORDATA, subphylum Vertebrata, class Aves, order Galliformes, family Phasianidae.

quaker-ladies: see MADDER.

Quakers: see FRIENDS, RELIGIOUS SOCIETY OF.

quaking grass, any plant of the genus *Briza*, annuals or perennials of the Gramineae (GRASS family), cultivated for the graceful clusters of seeds, which vibrate in a breeze and are used in EVERLASTING bouquets. The plants are native to temperate regions of Europe and South America and now widely naturalized in North America. Quaking grass is classified in the division MAGNOLIOPHYTA, class Liliatae, order Cyperales, family Gramineae.

Quant, Mary: see under FASHION.

Quantrill, William Clarke (kwŏn'trĭl), 1837–65, Confederate guerrilla leader, b. Canal Dover (now Dover), Ohio. In the Civil War his band of guerrillas was active in Missouri and Kansas. He was given the rank of captain in the Confederate army. On Aug. 21, 1863, Quantrill, with about 450 men, pillaged Lawrence, Kansas, and wantonly killed some 150 citizens. He was mortally wounded by Federal troops in May, 1865. See W. E. Connelley, *Quantrill and the Border Wars* (new ed. 1956); biography by A. E. Castel (1962).

quantum theory, modern physical theory concerned with the emission and absorption of energy by matter and with the motion of material particles; the quantum theory and the theory of RELATIVITY together form the theoretical basis of modern physics. Just as the theory of relativity assumes importance in the special situation where very large speeds are involved, so the quantum theory is necessary for the special situation where very small quantities are involved, i.e., on the scale of molecules, atoms, and elementary particles. According to the older theories of classical physics, energy is treated solely as a WAVE phenomenon, while matter is assumed to occupy a very specific region of space and to move in a continuous manner. According to the quantum theory, energy is held to be emitted and absorbed in tiny, discrete amounts. An individual bundle or packet of energy, called a quantum (pl. quanta), thus behaves in some situations much like particles of matter; particles are found to exhibit certain wavelike properties when in motion and are no longer viewed as localized in a given region but rather as spread out to some degree. For example, the light or other radiation given off or absorbed by an atom has only certain frequencies (or wavelengths), as can be seen from the line SPECTRUM associated with the chemical element represented by that atom. The quantum theory shows that those frequencies correspond to definite energies of the light quanta, or PHOTONS, and result from the fact that the electrons of the atom can have only certain allowed energy values, or levels; when an electron changes from one allowed level to another, a quantum of energy is emitted or absorbed whose frequency is directly proportional to the energy difference between the two levels. The restriction of the energy levels of the electrons is explained in terms of the wavelike properties of their motions: electrons occupy only those orbits for which their associated wave is a standing wave (i.e., the circumference of the orbit is exactly equal to a whole number of wavelengths) and thus can have only those energies that correspond to such orbits. Moreover, the electrons are no longer thought of as being at a particular point in the orbit but rather as being spread out over the entire orbit. Just as the results of relativity approximate those of Newtonian physics when ordinary speeds are involved, the results of the quantum theory agree with those of classical physics when very large "quantum numbers" are involved, i.e., on the ordinary large scale of events; this agreement in the classical limit is required by the CORRESPONDENCE PRINCIPLE of Niels Bohr. The quantum theory thus proposes a dual nature for both waves and particles, one aspect predominating in some situations, the other predominating in other situations. While the theory of relativity was largely the work of one man, Albert Einstein, the quantum theory was developed principally over a period of thirty years through the efforts of many scientists. The first contribution was the explanation of BLACK BODY radiation in 1900 by Max Planck, who proposed that the energies of any harmonic oscillator (see HARMONIC MOTION), such as the atoms of a black body radiator, are restricted to certain values, each of which is an integral (whole number) multiple of a basic, minimum value. The energy E of this basic quantum is directly proportional to the frequency ν of the oscillator, or $E=h\nu$, where h is a constant, now called Planck's constant, having the value 6.63×10^{-34} joule-second. In 1905, Einstein proposed that the radiation itself is also quantized according to this same formula, and he used the new theory to explain the PHOTOELECTRIC EFFECT. Following the discovery of the nuclear atom by Rutherford (1911), Bohr used the quantum theory in 1913 to explain both atomic structure and atomic spectra, showing the connection between the electrons' energy levels and the frequencies of light given off and absorbed. **Quantum mechanics,** the application of the quantum theory to the motions of material particles, was developed during the 1920s. In 1924, Louis de Broglie proposed that not only do waves sometimes exhibit particlelike properties, as in the photoelectric effect and atomic spectra, but particles may also exhibit wavelike properties. This hypothesis was confirmed experimentally in 1927 by C. J. Davisson and L. H. Germer, who observed DIFFRACTION of a beam of electrons analogous to the diffraction of a beam of light. Two different formulations of quantum mechanics were presented following de Broglie's suggestion. The wave mechanics of Erwin Schrödinger (1926) involves the use of a mathematical entity, the wave function, that has no direct physical interpretation yet yields correct physical results. The matrix mechanics of Werner Heisenberg (1925) makes no mention of wave functions or similar concepts but was shown to be mathematically equivalent to Schrödinger's theory. Quantum mechanics was combined with the theory of relativity in the formulation of P. A. M. Dirac (1928), which, in addition, predicted the existence of ANTIPARTICLES. A particularly important discovery of the quantum theory is the UNCERTAINTY PRINCIPLE, enunciated by Heisenberg in 1927, which places an absolute theoretical limit on the accuracy of certain measurements; as a result, the assumption by earlier scientists that the physical state of a system could be measured exactly and used to predict future states had to be abandoned. Other developments of the theory include quantum statistics, presented in one form by Einstein and S. N. Bose (the Bose-Einstein statistics) and in another by Dirac and Enrico Fermi (the Fermi-Dirac statistics); quantum electrodynamics, concerned with interactions between charged particles and electromagnetic FIELDS; and quantum electronics. Aspects of the quantum theory have provoked vigorous philosophical debates concerning, for example, the uncertainty principle, the use of mathematical objects that have no physical meaning (e.g., Schrödinger's wave function), and the statistical nature of all the predictions of the theory. See Werner Heisenberg, *The Physical Principles of the Quantum Theory* (1930) and *Physics and Philosophy* (1958); George Gamow, *Thirty Years that Shook Physics: The Story of Quantum Theory* (1966); Victor Guillemin, *The Story of Quantum Mechanics* (1968); Eugen Merzbacher, *Quantum Mechanics* (2d ed. 1970); Max Jammer, *The Conceptual Development of Quantum Mechanics (1973).*

Quantz, Johann Joachim (yō'hän yō'äkhĭm kvänts), 1697–1773, German flutist and composer for the flute. He played several instruments and was in his early life a wandering bandsman and composer. In 1741 he became chamber musician and teacher of the flute to Frederick the Great, for whom Quantz wrote more than 500 pieces, many of which were published. He also wrote a famous textbook for the flute, *Versuch einer Anweisung die Flöte traversière zu spielen* (1752), which was translated into French, English, and Dutch, and invented several improvements upon the instrument.

Quapaw Indians (kwô'pô), North American Indians, also called the Arkansas, whose language belongs to the Siouan branch of the Hokan-Siouan linguistic stock (see AMERICAN INDIAN LANGUAGES). They once lived with the Omaha, the Kansa, the Ponca, and the Osage in the Ohio valley, but when the groups separated the Quapaw migrated down the Mississippi River. Jacques Marquette arrived at their village in 1673 and was the first of many French explorers to visit the Quapaw. They made a large land cession to the United States in 1818 and some years later moved to Oklahoma, where they later lived on a reservation. Today they number some 700. The Quapaw were essentially of the Plains culture, but they had other distinctive traits; they built temple and burial mounds and lived in longhouses.

Qu'Appelle (kăpĕl'), river, c.270 mi (430 km) long, rising in S Sask., Canada, NW of Moose Jaw and flowing generally E through Buffalo Pound Lake and Fishing Lakes, past Fort Qu'Appelle to the Assiniboine River, just over the Manitoba border. The river is noted for whitefish.

quarantine (kwŏr'əntēn), isolation of persons, animals, places, and effects that carry or are suspected of harboring communicable disease. The term originally referred to the 40 days of offshore wait during which incoming vessels could not discharge passengers or cargo in the era when plague and other great epidemics swept across Europe. The practice has been changed by developments in medical science. Usually the word of the ship's officer that the passengers are free of disease and presentation by the passengers of certificates of inoculation against certain diseases are now sufficient to permit passage of travelers from one country to another. Some nations still maintain extended periods of quarantine for cattle and household pets coming from another country to guard against such diseases as foot-and-mouth disease and rabies. Plant life may also be held for assurance that fungus and other plant diseases are not being introduced. Local quarantine regulations are also in effect to guard against the spread of communicable disease. Public health laws require that physicians report certain infections to the authorities. The patients may be isolated and their effects disinfected, condemned, or destroyed, if it is in the public interest, since quarantine laws supercede even property rights.

quark (kwôrk): see ELEMENTARY PARTICLES.

Quarles, Francis, 1592–1644, English poet. His best-known work is *Emblems* (1635), a book of moral and religious verse. Though not an ardent royalist, he wrote pamphlets during the Commonwealth upholding the divine right of kings. *Enchiridion* (1640) is his collection of prose aphorisms.

quarrying, open, or surface, excavation of rock used for various purposes, including construction, ornamentation, road building, and as an industrial raw material. Rock that has been quarried is commonly called stone. Quarrying methods depend chiefly on the desired size and shape of the stone and its physical characteristics. For industrial use (e.g., limestone for preparing cement), as the aggregate in concrete, or for road beds, the rock is shattered. Explosives are detonated in a series of holes drilled in the rock in a pattern designed to yield the greatest amount of fracturing. The rock fragments may be further reduced in crushing machines and sorted according to size by screening. For building stone, rocks that do not shatter are separated by blasting; for softer rocks or when explosives cannot be used (e.g., because they would disturb adjacent workings), a process known as broaching, or channeling, is used. In this process a line of holes is drilled perpendicular to the joints or cleavage planes of a formation; wedges are inserted into the holes and hammered until the stone splits off. This method was probably used in ancient times notably by the Incas and the Egyptians. Much quarrying of ornamental stone today is done by using pneumatically operated channelers. After the vertical cuts have been made, gadding machines (working on the same principle) are used to make horizontal cuts. Wedges are then used to split off the long blocks, which are subdivided and removed. Wire saws are also used; these consist of several pulleys over which passes an endless steel wire. Holes are drilled in the rock, each hole being made large enough to accommodate a pulley and the shaft to which it is attached. The wire, extending from one pulley to another, presses down against the rock between them. As the cut is deepened by the constantly moving wire the pulleys are continously lowered into the holes.

quart: see ENGLISH UNITS OF MEASUREMENT.

quarter horse, American breed of LIGHT HORSE that originated during the colonial era, partly from Arabian ancestry (see ARABIAN HORSE). The name refers to the horse's reputation for speed at the quarter-mile distance. It can spring into full speed and consequently is faster than the THOROUGHBRED for a short sprint. The breed was by far the most popular cattle horse in the early West. It continues in this role today and is also used almost exclusively for rodeo events such as cutting, roping, and barrel racing. Registered quarter horses are of solid colors, stand 15 to 16 hands (60–64 in./150–160 cm) high, weigh over 1,000 lb (450 kg), and have thick muscular shoulders and short necks.

Quartus (kwôr'təs), follower of Paul at Corinth. Rom. 16.23.

quartz, one of the commonest of all rock-forming minerals and one of the most important constituents of the earth's crust. Chemically, it is silicon dioxide, SiO_2. It occurs in crystals of the hexagonal system, commonly having the form of a six-sided prism terminating in a six-sided pyramid; the crystals are often distorted and twins are common. Quartz may be transparent, translucent, or opaque; it may be colorless or colored. Varieties are classified as crystalline and cryptocrystalline. Crystalline varieties include ordinary colorless crystallized quartz, or rock crystal; rose quartz; yellow quartz, sometimes used as imitation TOPAZ; smoky quartz, or cairngorm stone; milk-white milky quartz; aventurine quartz, which contains scales of hematite or mica; and AMETHYST. Varieties of cryptocrystalline quartz, the crystal structure of which can be seen only under the microscope, if at all, are CHALCEDONY, FLINT, hornstone, and chert. Colored varieties of chalcedony known by special names are CARNELIAN, SARD, CHRYSOPRASE, AGATE, ONYX, SARDONYX, and JASPER. Clastic quartzes are SAND and SANDSTONE.

quartzite, usually metamorphic ROCK composed of firmly cemented quartz grains. Most often it is white, light gray, yellowish, or light brown, but is sometimes colored blue, green, purple, or black by included minerals. It results from the metamorphism of pure quartz SANDSTONE. It is most easily distinguished from sandstone by the fact that it fractures across its constituent grains of sand, while sandstone fractures along the line of the cementing material between the grains of sand. Although most quartzites are metamorphic, some are sedimentary in origin, resulting from cementation of quartz sandstone by groundwater solutions containing pure quartz.

quasar (kwā'sär), one of a class of faint blue celestial objects having the appearance of stars when viewed through a telescope and currently believed to be the most distant and most luminous objects in the universe; the name is shortened from "quasi-stellar radio source." Quasars were discovered as the visible counterparts of certain discrete celestial sources of radio waves (see RADIO ASTRONOMY). Similar starlike objects that emit no radio waves were subsequently discovered and named quasi-stellar objects (QSO's). Although their visible light is faint, the quasars are optically brighter than the galaxies with which radio sources had been identified before 1963. Before their spectra were studied carefully, it was believed that the quasars were stars in or near our galaxy. However, the lines in their spectra have enormous RED SHIFTS that seem to imply that they are receding from the Milky Way with speeds as great as 80% of the speed of light. Only shifts toward the red end of the spectrum have been observed for quasars; there are no blue shifts that would indicate a quasar approaching our galaxy. If HUBBLE'S LAW for the expansion of the universe is extrapolated to include the quasars, they may be as far as 8 billion light-years away and consequently as luminous intrinsically as 100 galaxies combined. Because very distant objects are seen as they were when the light received today was emitted, astronomers can observe the quasars as they were shortly after the beginning of the universe (see COSMOLOGY). See G. R. and E. M. Burbidge, *Quasi-Stellar Objects* (1967).

Quasimodo, Salvatore (sälvätô'rā kwäzē'mōdō), 1901–68, Italian poet and translator, b. Sicily. Quasimodo worked first as a technical designer and civil engineer. His five volumes of verse published between 1930 and 1938, including *Acque e terra* (1930), established him as leader of Italy's "hermetic" poets, whose verbal complexity, derived from the French symbolists, was used in discreet opposition to Mussolini. His anti-Fascist activities during World War II led to his imprisonment. Quasimodo's poetic ripening and his commitment as poet to the plight of modern man brought him the 1959 Nobel Prize in Literature. His mature style is marked by increased clarity and sensitivity. He chose to interpret man's history and fate with an underlying lament for human defeat in a violent universe. His works include *Dare e avare: 1959–1965* (1966, tr. *To Give and to Have,* 1969) and *Debit and Credit* (tr. 1972). See his *Selected Writings* (tr. 1960) and *The Poet and the Politician and Other Essays* (tr. 1964).

quasi-stellar object: see QUASAR.

quassia (kwŏsh'ə), name for several tropical trees and for a bitter extract from their bark. The extract is used medicinally as a bitter tonic and a pinworm remedy; it is also used in insecticides, e.g., in flypaper and against aphids. Surinam quassia comes from the tree *Quassia amara* of N Brazil and surrounding regions; Jamaica quassia comes from *Picrasma excelsa* of the West Indies. Some Old World quassia species are similarly used. The trees are related to the ailanthus. Quassia is classified in the division MAGNOLIOPHYTA, class Magnoliopsida, order Geraniales, family Simaroubaceae.

Quaternary period (kwətûr'nərē), younger of the two geologic periods of the CENOZOIC ERA of geologic time (see GEOLOGIC ERAS, table). Comprising all geologic time from the end of the TERTIARY PERIOD to the present, it is divided into the Pleistocene and Holocene, or Recent, epochs. It was named (1759) by Giovanni Arduino, an Italian scientist who thought that the biblical great flood was responsible for its deposits. During the early Quaternary, Europe and North America were covered by the glaciers of the PLEISTOCENE EPOCH. In the Quaternary the climate and present physical features of the earth have been developed. The period has been characterized by erosion, the chief agent in shaping mountains and valleys to their present forms, and by extensive disturbances of the earth's crust, including earthquakes and the eruption of volcanoes. Significant changes in sea level within historic times are demonstrated by the submergence of the temple of Jupiter Serapis near Naples and by the rising of the shores of the Baltic. The life of the Quaternary has been marked by the rise and dominance of man.

quaternion (kwətûr'nēən), in mathematics, a type of higher complex number first suggested by Sir William R. Hamilton in 1843. A complex number is a number of the form $a+bi$ when a and b are real numbers and i is the so-called imaginary unit defined by the equation $i^2=-1$. The rules for operating with complex numbers are simply those of operating with the polynomial $a+bx$ except that i^2 is replaced by -1 whenever it occurs. A quaternion, an extension of this concept, is a number of the form $a+bi+cj+dk$ when a, b, c, and d are real numbers and i, j, and k are imaginary units defined by the equations $i^2=j^2=k^2=ijk=-1$. Quaternions, as well as VECTORS and TENSORS (later outgrowths of the concept of quaternions), have many important applications in mechanics.

Quatre Bras (kä'trə brä'), village, Brabant prov., central Belgium, between Charleroi and Brussels. There, on June 16, 1815, in a battle of the WATERLOO CAMPAIGN, the British under Wellington gradually repulsed the French under Marshal Ney. Nevertheless, Ney prevented Wellington's forces from aiding those of Blücher against Napoleon I at Ligny.

Quauhtémoc: see CUAUHTÉMOC.

Quay, Matthew Stanley (kwā), 1833–1904, American political leader, b. Dillsburg, Pa. He studied law in Pittsburgh and was admitted (1854) to the bar. He fought in the Civil War, and after the war he rose steadily in Pennsylvania politics until he became boss of the state Republican machine. His skill in organization and manipulation of patronage kept Pennsylvania thoroughly Republican. As chairman (1888) of the Republican National Committee, Quay secured large campaign contributions and played a leading role in Benjamin Harrison's presidential election. He served (1887–99) in the U.S. Senate, but serious charges of venality prevented his reelection in 1898. Quay was, however, able to block the election of anyone else. When a jury found him innocent of all charges, the governor appointed him Senator ad interim, but there was a great public protest, and the Senate refused to seat him. Quay was, however, reelected in 1901.

Quebec (kwēbĕk', kwə-, kē-, kə-), Fr. *Québec* (kābĕk'), province (1971 pop. 6,027,764), 594,860 sq mi (1,553,637 sq km), E Canada. The city of QUEBEC is the capital. MONTREAL is the largest city; other important centers are VERDUN, LAVAL, TROIS RIVIÈRES, SHERBROOKE, and HULL. Quebec is bounded on the N by Hudson Strait and Ungava Bay, on the E by Labrador and the Gulf of St. Lawrence, on the S by New Brunswick and the United States, and on the W by Ontario, James Bay, and Hudson Bay. The Canadian Shield comprises the northern nine tenths of the province, which is relatively unexplored and uninhabited; the region has been planed by glacial action into a pattern of rounded hills, swiftly flowing rivers, and numerous lakes and bogs. Dense forests cover much of the surface, and the area is rich in minerals. South of the Canadian Shield lies the great St. Lawrence River. On both sides of the river S of Quebec city are the lowlands that are the centers of agriculture, commerce, and industry. Quebec city and Trois Rivières are on the north bank of the river and Montreal, the leading industrial center of Canada, is situated on an island where the Ottawa River joins the St. Lawrence. In the southeast section of the province are the Appalachian Highlands, which run parallel to the St. Lawrence. The Gaspé Peninsula, on the south bank of the St. Lawrence, borders on the Gulf of St. Lawrence. Quebec's climate is generally temperate, with variations among the regions. Tourism is important throughout the province during the summer season, and in the winter the Laurentian Mts. are a skiing attraction. The small farming and fishing villages that dot the Gaspé coast charm tourists with their simplicity and self-sufficiency. Quebec has vast resources of water power. The forests of the north yield wood for the province's pulp, paper, and lumber industries, and throughout the north country copper, iron, zinc, silver, and gold are mined. The iron ore deposits in the Ungava Bay region have been exploited in recent decades. Asbestos is found in the far north, but more importantly, in the Thetford Mines region of the Appalachian Highlands. At Arvida, in the Saguenay valley, is one of the world's largest aluminum plants. The small farms of the lowlands yield dairy products, sugar beets, and tobacco. Quebec is second to Ontario among the Canadian provinces in

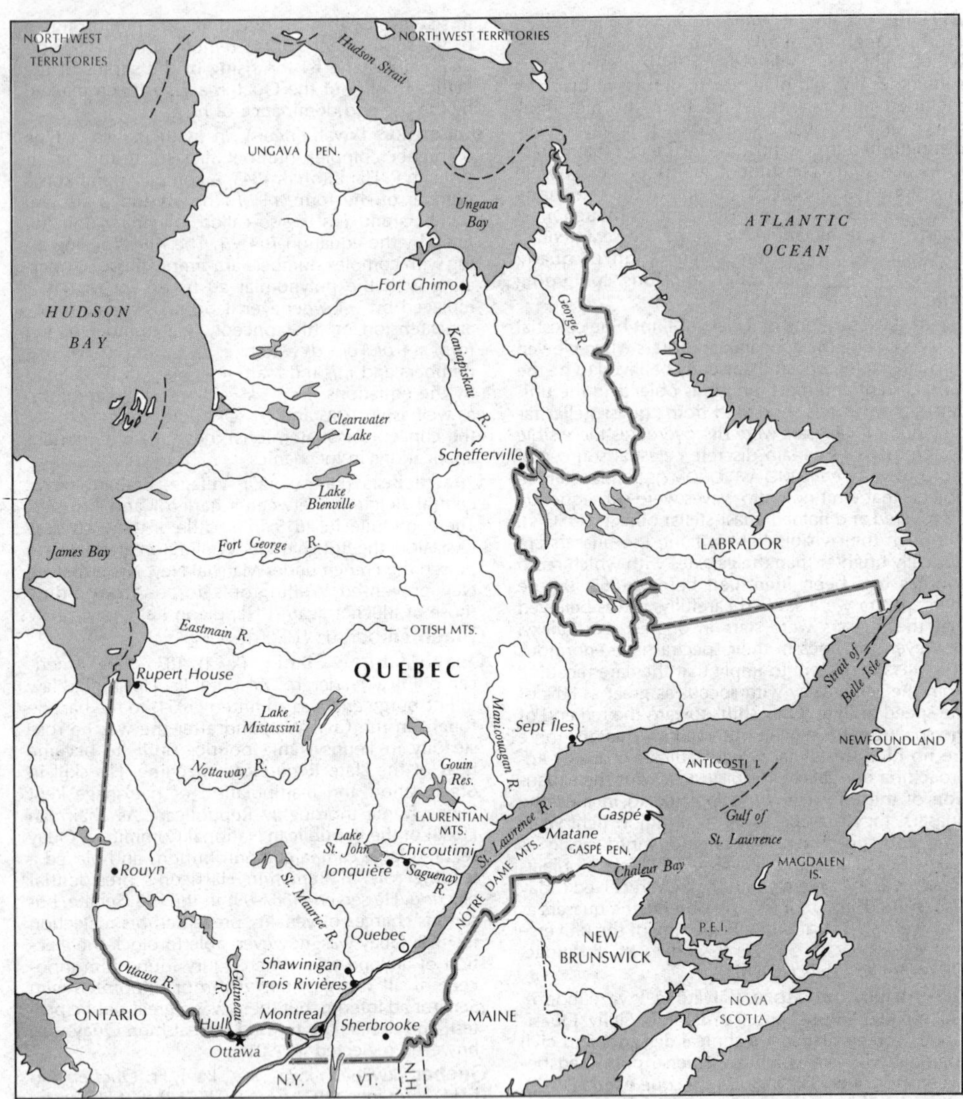

industrial production. Its main manufactures are food products, beverages, transportation equipment, chemicals, and metal and paper products. Since many continental explorations began in the region, Quebec has been called the cradle of Canada. In 1534, Jacques Cartier planted a cross on the Gaspé and the following year he sailed up the St. Lawrence. In 1608, Samuel de Champlain built a trading post on the site of the present-day Quebec city, and from this and subsequent settlements Catholic missionaries, explorers, and fur traders penetrated the American continent. The activities of private fur-trading companies ended in 1663 when Louis XIV made the region, known as New France, a royal colony and chose Jean Baptiste Talon to be intendant, or administrator. The long struggle to protect the colony and the fur trade against the hostile Iroquois Indians (other tribes were allies of the French) and the British were effectively lost in 1759 when the British defeated the French on the Plains of Abraham (see ABRAHAM, PLAINS OF). By the Treaty of Paris of 1763, Great Britain acquired New France. In an attempt to conciliate the French inhabitants, the British passed the Quebec Act of 1774, under which the colony was allowed to continue its semifeudal system of land tenure and to retain its language, religion, legal system, and customs. After the American Revolution, many British Loyalists came to settle in Quebec. By the Constitutional Act of 1791 the British detached the area west of the Ottawa River and made it the colony of Upper Canada (now Ontario). Quebec became known as Lower Canada, and in 1791 the first elective assembly was introduced. The resentment of leaders of the French community against the British precipitated a revolt in 1837 led by Louis PAPINEAU. Although the rebellion was crushed, the disturbances in Upper and Lower Canada caused the British to send the Earl of Durham (see DURHAM, JOHN GEORGE LAMBTON) to study conditions in the British North American colonies. His report led ultimately to internal self-government and the creation of the Canadian confederation. Upper and Lower Canada were reunited in 1841, and Quebec became known as Canada East. Responsible government was granted in 1849. With the formation of the confederation of Canada in 1867, Canada East became the province of Quebec. Its special, traditional institutions were specifically written into the Canadian constitution. English and French were made the official languages of both Quebec and the Canadian Parliament, and a dual school system was established within Quebec. However, in 1974 French was made the sole official language of the province, and all children were required to attend French language school. But the coexistence of majority-French and minority-English cultures within the province and the reverse situation within Canada as a whole have remained sources of tension. Attempts in Manitoba and Ontario at the beginning of the 20th cent. to curtail or abolish separate Catholic schools increased the French Canadian's feeling of isolation. In 1917 they vehemently opposed conscription for World War I. During the 20th cent. great economic growth in Quebec was coupled with increasing determination to maintain and broaden provincial rights. In the 1960s separatist groups, advocating an independent Quebec, gained attention. In 1970 separatist terrorists kidnapped a British diplomat, James R. Cross, and the Quebec Minister of Labour, Pierre Laporte. Cross was later released, but Laporte was found murdered. The incident led to the temporary curtailment on the part of the federal government of certain civil rights guaranteed in the Canadian constitution. It was the first time such powers had been used by the federal government during peacetime. See G. F. Stanley, *New France: The Last Phase, 1744–1760* (1968); C. C. Nish, ed., *Quebec in the Duplessis Era, 1935–1959* (1970); Nick Auf Der Maur and Robert Chodos, ed., *Quebec: A Chronicle, 1968–1972* (1972); Fernand Grenier, ed., *Quebec* (1972); John Saywell, *Quebec 70* (1972); Marcel Trudel, *The Beginning of New France* (1972).

Quebec, Fr. *Québec,* city (1971 pop. 186,088; metropolitan pop. 480,502), provincial capital, S Que., Canada, at the confluence of the St. Lawrence and St. Charles rivers. The population is largely French speaking. Quebec is an important port and is an industrial, cultural, and tourist center. Part of the city is built on the waterfront and is called Lower Town; that part called Upper Town is on Cape Diamond, a bluff rising c.300 ft (91 m) above the St. Lawrence. Winding, narrow streets link the two sections of the city. The chief industries are shipbuilding, and the manufacture of pulp and paper, leather products, textiles, clothing, machinery, and foods and beverages. The site of Quebec was visited by Cartier in 1535, and in 1608 Champlain established a French colony in the present Lower Town; this was captured (1629) by the English, who held it until 1632. In 1663, Quebec was made the capital of New France and became the center of the fur trade. The city was unsuccessfully attacked by the English in 1690 and 1711. Finally in 1759 English forces under Wolfe defeated the French under Montcalm on the Plains of Abraham (see ABRAHAM, PLAINS OF) and captured Quebec. During the American Revolution, Americans under Richard Montgomery and Benedict Arnold failed (1775–76) to capture the city, although Arnold briefly held the Lower Town. Quebec became the capital of Lower Canada in 1791. After the union (1841) of Upper and Lower Canada, it was twice the capital of the United Provinces of Canada (1851–55 and 1859–65). The QUEBEC CONFERENCE was held in the city in 1864. There are many notable old structures, including the Ursuline Convent (1639); the Basilica of Notre Dame (1647); Quebec Seminary (1663); and parts of the fortifications enclosing Old Quebec. The surrounding area also has many notable sights, such as Montmorency Falls, the Île d'Orléans, and the shrine of Ste Anne de Beaupré. See Mazo de la Roche, *Quebec, Historic Seaport* (1944); J. E. Morgan, *Castle of Quebec* (1949); W. P. Percival, *The Lure of Quebec* (rev. ed. 1965); Michel Gaumond, *Place Royale: Its Houses and Their Occupants* (tr. 1971).

Quebec, University of, at Quebec City, Que., Canada; provincially supported; French language; founded 1968. It has branches at Chicoutimi, Montreal, Three Rivers, and Rimouski. The university maintains a school of public administration and an institute of scientific research at Quebec City.

Quebec Act, 1774, passed by the British Parliament to institute a permanent administration in Canada replacing the temporary government created at the time of the Proclamation of 1763. It gave the French Canadians complete religious freedom and restored the French form of civil law. The Thirteen Colonies considered this law one of the INTOLERABLE ACTS, for it nullified many of the Western claims of the coast colonies by extending the boundaries of the province of Quebec to the Ohio River on the south and to the Mississippi River on the west. The concessions in favor of Roman Catholicism also roused much resentment among Protestants in the Thirteen Colonies. Although it thus helped to bring on the American Revolution, the act, for which Sir Guy Carleton was largely responsible, was very influential in keeping Canada loyal to the crown during the Revolution. It was replaced by the Constitutional Act of 1791. See studies by Reginald Coupland (1925) and H. B. Neatby (1972).

Quebec campaign, 1775–76, of the American Revolution. The Continental Congress decided to send an expedition to Canada to protect the northern frontier from British attack and to persuade Canada to join the revolt against England. Late in Aug., 1775, Gen. Philip SCHUYLER led troops up Lake Champlain and captured St. Johns; illness forced him to turn over his command to Gen. Richard MONTGOMERY, who proceeded to capture Montreal in Nov., 1775. In Sept., 1775, General Washington sent Benedict ARNOLD to lead an expedition against Quebec by way of the Kennebec and Chaudière rivers in Maine. When this force arrived, it was so weakened by the incredibly hard march, illness, desertion, and lack of supplies that Arnold was forced to wait for Montgomery before attacking. The unsuccessful assault was launched in the early morning of Dec. 31, 1775. The Continentals withdrew after Montgomery was killed, Arnold wounded, and Daniel MORGAN captured. Arnold and Montgomery's successor, David WOOSTER, continued the siege until spring, when British reinforcements enabled Sir Guy CARLETON to push the Americans, now commanded by Gen. John Thomas, back to Crown Point on Lake Champlain. See Harrison Bird, *Attack on Quebec* (1968).

Quebec Conference, name of two meetings held in Quebec, Canada, in World War II. The first meeting (Aug., 1943) was attended by President Franklin Delano Roosevelt of the United States, Prime Minister Winston Churchill of Great Britain, Prime Minister W. L. Mackenzie King of Canada, and Foreign Minister T. V. Soong of China. An important step toward unified Allied command was taken when the China-Burma-India theater of operations was created under the command of Lord Mountbatten. The United States extended limited recognition to Charles De Gaulle's French Committee of National Liberation. Approval was accorded to the Allied military plans for a landing in France; these plans were communicated to Marshal Stalin later in the year at the Teheran Conference. The second Quebec Conference (Sept., 1944), attended by Roosevelt, Churchill, and their chief military advisers, was concerned with the broad strategy of the war and with the future of Germany.

quebracho (kābrä'chō), name for a tanning substance and for the trees from which it comes, chiefly the red quebracho, or quebracho colorado (*Schinopsis lorentzii*), of the family Anacardiaceae (SUMAC family). This hardwood tree, native to the Paraguayan subtropics, supplies one of the most durable and heavy of timbers. It has been used as a source of tanning material for nearly 100 years but has been widely used only in the 20th cent.; today it provides most of the vegetable tannin for the leather industry. The heartwood, stripped of its bark and subjected to extraction processes, is about 30% tannin. Quebracho is obtained chiefly from wild trees of the forests of the Gran Chaco of Argentina, Paraguay, and Bolivia. White quebracho (*Aspidosperma quebracho blanco*) of the DOGBANE family is one of the other hardwoods similarly used and is native to the same region. Red quebracho is classified in the division MAGNOLIOPHYTA, class Magnoliopsida, order Sapindales, family Anacardiaceae.

Quechua, Kechua (both: kĕch'o͝oə, –wä), or **Quichua** (kēch'wä), linguistic family belonging to the Andean branch of the Andean-Equatorial stock of AMERICAN INDIAN LANGUAGES (mainly in South America). The languages of the Quechuan family are spoken by peoples in Peru, Ecuador, Bolivia, Brazil, Argentina, Colombia, and Chile. There is a modern standard language of this family spoken by half the people of Peru (some 7 million), and some 28 Quechuan languages still are in use. The official language of the ancient Inca empire, also called Quechua, was of this family. In the early 1400s, Quechua was dominant in S Peru. As the Incas' empire expanded, their language became the administrative and commercial tongue from N Ecuador to central Chile. After their conquest of the Incas in the 16th cent., the Spaniards spread the use of Quechua beyond the Inca empire. Grammatically, the Quechuan language is characterized by a high degree of regularity.

Quedlinburg (kvād'lĕnbo͝orkh), city (1970 pop. 30,829), Halle district, W East Germany, at the foot of the lower Harz mts. It is an industrial center and an agricultural market. Manufactures include food products, paper goods, and precision instruments. One of the oldest German cities, Quedlinburg was fortified in 922 by Henry I (Henry the Fowler). It later became a member of the Hanseatic League. In 1698 the city passed to Brandenburg. The beautiful castle, church, and convent (secularized 1803) dominate the city from a hill; the age of the structures varies from the 10th to the 14th cent. Henry I and his wife, St. Matilda (who with her son, Emperor Otto I, founded the celebrated convent in 936), are buried in the castle church. Other historic structures in Quedlinburg include 14th-century fortifications, several early Gothic churches, and a 17th-century city hall. The city is the birthplace of the poet Klopstock (1724) and the geographer Karl Ritter (1779).

Queen Anne's lace or **wild carrot,** herb (*Daucus carota*) of the family Umbelliferae (CARROT family), native to the Old World but naturalized and often weedy throughout North America. Similar in appearance to the cultivated carrot (which is believed to have been derived from this plant), it has feathery foliage but a woody root. The tiny white flowers bloom in a lacy, flat-topped cluster (called an umbel) until they wither, when the cluster becomes nest-shaped (whence another of its names, bird's nest). The plant was formerly used in folk medicine as a diuretic and a stimulant. Queen Anne's lace is classified in the division MAGNOLIOPHYTA, class Magnoliopsida, order Umbellales, family Umbelliferae.

Queen Anne's War: see FRENCH AND INDIAN WARS.

Queen Charlotte Islands, archipelago of several large and many small islands, off the coast of W British Columbia, Canada. Most of the inhabitants are Haida Indians. The main islands are Graham and Moresby. Masset on Graham Island is the main settlement. There are valuable timber and fishing resources and several good harbors. The archipelago was visited in 1774 by Juan Pérez and in 1778 by Capt. James Cook; in 1787 it was surveyed by Capt. George Dixon. Hecate Strait separates it from the mainland; Dixon Entrance lies between it and Alaska to the north; and Queen Charlotte Sound separates it from Vancouver Island to the south.

Queen Elizabeth Islands, northern part of the Arctic Archipelago, Franklin dist., Northwest Territories, N Canada. Ellesmere Island (the largest), the Parry group (Melville, Bathurst, Devon, Prince Patrick, and Cornwallis islands), and the Sverdrup group (Axel Heiberg, Ellef Ringnes, Amund Ringnes, and many smaller islands) are found there. The islands are underlain by oil-bearing rock; extensive drilling has been under way since the early 1960s. The British explorer Sir William Parry discovered (1819–20) many of the islands, and they were known (until 1954) as the Parry Islands.

Queen Mary Coast, region: see ANTARCTICA.

Queen Maud Land, region: see ANTARCTICA.

queen of the meadow or **queen of the prairie:** see SPIRAEA.

Queens, borough of New York City (1970 pop. 1,973,708), land area c.113 sq mi (293 sq km), at the western end of Long Island, SE N.Y., coextensive with Queens co.; settled by the Dutch 1635, chartered as a borough of New York City 1898. Having the largest area of the city's boroughs, it extends from the junction of the East River and Long Island Sound in the north, across Long Island to Jamaica Bay and the Atlantic Ocean in the south. It is connected with Manhattan by the Queensboro Bridge, the Queens-Midtown Tunnel, and railroad and subway tunnels; with the Bronx and Manhattan by the Triborough Bridge; with the Bronx by the Hell Gate railroad bridge and by the Bronx-Whitestone and Throgs Neck bridges. The borough has c.200 mi (320 km) of waterfront. It is heavily industrialized in Long Island City; there and at Sunnyside are extensive railroad yards. Astoria and Jamaica (seat of St. John's Univ.) are industrial and commercial centers. Among the many residential communities are Flushing (Queens College is there), Forest Hills, and Kew Gardens. The Rockaways, on a peninsula between Jamaica Bay and the Atlantic Ocean, are a popular beach area. The first settlements in the area were made by the Dutch in 1635. Queens co. was organized in 1683. Several buildings of the 17th and 18th cent. remain. One of the first commercial nurseries in the country was established c.1737, and the community's collection of trees still includes several rare species. In the American Revolution, British troops held the area after the battle of Long Island (1776). In the 20th cent. growth was spurred with the opening of the Queensboro Bridge (1909) and a railroad tunnel (1910). After World War II there was a great increase in housing construction. Queens is the site of La Guardia Airport and John F. Kennedy International Airport. Two New York World's Fairs (1939–40; 1964–65) were held in Flushing Meadow Park. Also in the borough are the Aqueduct racetrack and Shea Stadium, home of the New York Mets (baseball) and New York Jets (football) teams. Parts of Jamaica Bay and the Rockaway peninsula (including former U.S. Fort Tilden) are included in the Gateway National Recreation Area.

Queensberry, James Douglas, 2d **duke of,** 1662–1711, Scottish statesman. One of the early supporters of William III in Scotland, he held offices under him and Queen Anne, rising to become commissioner to the Scottish Parliament (1700) and a secretary of state for Scotland (1702). Duped by an intrigue of Baron LOVAT, he falsely accused John MURRAY, 2d marquess and 1st duke of Atholl, of Jacobite activities and for that mistake was dismissed in 1703. Restored to favor (1705) with the offices of lord privy seal and a lord of the treasury, he worked hard for the union with England as commissioner to the Scottish Parliament. In 1708 he was created duke of Dover (in the English peerage), and in 1709 he was made third secretary of state for Great Britain.

Queensberry, John Sholto Douglas, 8th **marquess of,** 1844–1900, British nobleman, originator of the code of rules that governs modern BOXING. He served in the British army and navy and later was a member of (1872–80) the House of Lords as representative peer from Scotland. He is famous for drafting (1865), with the aid of John G. Chambers, the Queensberry rules for the sport of boxing. This code of rules, superseding the London prize-ring rules that had been introduced (1743) by Jack Broughton, contained the basic provisions that govern boxing today. The rules were gradually adopted in both Britain and the United States and by 1889 they were standardized. In 1895, objecting to the liaison between his son, Lord Alfred Douglas, and Oscar WILDE, Queensberry left an insulting letter to Wilde in a public place and was sued for libel by the writer. In this libel suit, which Wilde dropped, information was brought to light that led to the conviction of Wilde for immoral conduct.

Queensberry, William Douglas, 4th **duke of,** 1724–1810, English nobleman, known in his later years as Old Q. Also 3d earl of March, he succeeded his cousin to the dukedom in 1778. A famous horse fancier and a boon companion of the prince of Wales (later George IV), he was notorious for his dissolute life. See biography by Henry Blyth (1967).

Queensberry rules: see QUEENSBERRY, JOHN SHOLTO DOUGLAS, 8TH MARQUESS OF.

Queensborough-in-Sheppey, municipal borough (1971 pop. 31,541), on the Isle of Sheppey, Kent, SE England, at the confluence of the Medway and Thames rivers. The borough was created in 1968 by the amalgamation of the municipal borough of Queensborough, the urban district of Sheerness, and the rural district of Sheppey. Radios, furniture, rubber products, and clothing are made. The borough has a beach resort. In Sheerness were government dockyards, built under Charles II, that closed in 1958. Sheerness was captured by the Dutch in 1667.

Queens College of the City Univ. of New York, at Flushing, in the borough of Queens, N.Y.; coeducational; chartered and opened 1937. See NEW YORK, CITY UNIV. OF.

Queen's County, Ireland: see LAOIGHIS.

Queensland, state (1971 pop. 1,827,065), 667,000 sq mi (1,727,530 sq km), NE Australia. BRISBANE is the capital; other important cities are TOOWOOMBA, IPSWICH, TOWNSVILLE, ROCKHAMPTON, and CAIRNS. Queensland is bounded on the NE and E by the Coral Sea and the Pacific Ocean and on the NW by the Gulf of Carpentaria and Torres Strait. The state comprises the entire northeastern part of the Australian continent, with the major part of its coastline sheltered by the Great Barrier Reef. Roughly half the state is in the tropical zone, with rain forests on Cape York Peninsula in the extreme north. Annual rainfall ranges from 5 in. (13 cm) in the southwestern desert area to 160 in. (406 cm) in parts of the northeast coast. The Great Dividing Range separates the fertile coastal strip from vast interior plains. The Great Artesian Basin (376,000 sq mi/973,840 sq km) in the interior provides water for a large livestock-raising area. Mainly an agricultural state, Queensland produces sugarcane (the chief crop), cotton, wheat (grown mostly on the Darling Downs), and tropical fruits. In addition, the state is Australia's leading producer of beef. Mining is also important, especially copper, coal, lead, zinc, and bauxite. Oil and natural gas were discovered in the 1960s and are being exploited. Almost half of Queensland's people live in the Brisbane metropolitan area. There are more than 8,000 aborigines in the state. In 1770, Capt. James Cook explored the coast of Queensland (then called Moreton Bay). Originally under the authority of New South Wales, Queensland served as a penal colony from 1824 to 1843. The area was separated from New South Wales and made a British colony in 1859. Queensland was federated as a state of the Commonwealth of Australia in 1901. The state government consists of a governor (the nominal chief executive), who is appointed by the British crown on advice of the cabinet; a premier and a cabinet; and a unicameral legislature (the upper house voted itself out of existence in 1922).

Queensland, University of, at Brisbane, Australia; founded 1909. It has faculties of agriculture, architecture, arts, commerce and economics, dentistry, education, engineering, law, medicine, music, science, and veterinary science.

Queensland nut: see BANKSIA.

Queenston, village, S Ont., Canada, just N of Niagara Falls. There the British defeated American invaders in the battle of Queenston Heights (Oct. 13, 1812) in the War of 1812. The British commanding general, Sir Isaac Brock, was killed in the fighting.

Queenstown, Republic of Ireland: see CÓBH.

Queenstown, town (1970 pop. 55,357), Cape Prov., SE South Africa. It is a wool-processing center and the commercial center for the surrounding sheep-grazing and grain-farming region. Queenstown was founded in 1853 by Sir George Cathcart, governor of the British Cape of Good Hope colony. A regional agricultural research institute is in the town.

Queen's University, at Kingston, Ont., Canada; nondenominational; coeducational; founded 1841 as Queen's College. It achieved university status in 1912. It has faculties of arts and sciences, education, law, medicine, and applied science and schools of graduate studies, business, and nursing. Queen's Theological College is affiliated with the university.

Queensway or **Mersey Tunnel:** see MERSEY, river, England.

Queiros, Pedro Fernandes de (pĕ'drōō fərnəN'-dəsh dĭ kārôsh'), c.1560–1614, Portuguese navigator. In Spanish service, he sailed (1595) as second in command of the expedition of Alvaro de Mendaña de Neira to the Pacific. The expedition discovered the Marquesas Islands and Solomon Islands, and after the death of Mendaña, Queiros continued in command. On a later expedition he discovered (1606) the Tuamotu Islands and the New Hebrides, but almost certainly not the Society Islands (as is sometimes claimed).

quelea (kwē'lēə), common name for an East African weaverbird, *Quelea quelea.* Less than 5 in. (13 cm) long and weighing slightly more than ½ oz (1.4 grams), these tiny birds are found throughout sub-Saharan Africa in areas receiving less than 30 in. (76 cm) of annual rainfall. With the spread of grain farming and irrigation, they have extended their natural habitats, generally picking new breeding grounds every year. Highly mobile, they often descend in a locustlike manner upon fields and in flight may indeed be mistaken for locusts. Queleas are often found in concentrations of more than a million birds; such a flock can destroy up to 60 tons of grain in a single day, consuming half and knocking the rest to the ground. Hence, they are hunted aggressively with poisons and fire, but, as with locusts, to little effect. Queleas nest in thick thornbushes and trees; a colony may cover up to 4 sq mi (10.4 sq km). The males build the simple grass nests, and a single thatched nest may house hundreds of females and their young, with only a few highly polygamous males. Queleas are persistent and prolific breeders, beginning as early as nine months of age. In addition to grain, queleas also feed on insects and, in the dry season, strip the leaves from trees. The size of their groups is sufficient to break branches and flatten plants. Queleas are classified in the phylum CHORDATA, subphylum Vertebrata, class Aves, order Passeriformes, family Ploceidae.

Quelimane (kĕlĭmä'nē), town (1960 pop. 66,301), capital of Zambézia district, E central Mozambique, a seaport on the Rio dos Bons Sinais near its mouth in the Indian Ocean. It is a trade center and terminus of a railroad extending c.100 mi (160 km) into the interior. Exports include palm products, sisal, and tea. The Portuguese founded a trading station at Quelimane in 1544, and the town was an important slave market in the 18th and 19th cent. The name is also spelled Quilimane, Kilimane, and Kilimani.

Quellinus or **Quellin, Artus** (är'təs kvĕlē'nəs, kvĕl'-ĭn), 1609–68, Flemish sculptor. His allegorical figures decorating the royal palace of Amsterdam are famous. Quellinus was the outstanding follower of the Rubens tradition in sculpture. In addition to his baroque architectural decorations, he made numerous fine busts and figurines. His cousin **Artus Quellin,** 1625–1700, worked under his direction at Amsterdam. The younger man soon showed an independent talent in works that he created for the cathedrals of Antwerp and Tournai. The refined elegance of his early art developed into a dramatic baroque illusionism in the figure of God the Father (1682) for the rood screen of the cathedral of Bruges.

Quemoy (kĭmoi'), Mandarin *Kinmen* or *Chin-men,* island group (1972 pop. 61,305, excluding military personnel), Formosa (Taiwan) Strait, just off Fukien prov., China. It is a Nationalist outpost c.150 mi (240 km) W of Taiwan. The group consists of the islands of Quemoy and Little Quemoy and 12 islets in the mouth of Amoy Bay. The town of Quemoy, on Quemoy island, is the chief population center. Farming is the main occupation; about half the land is under cultivation. Crops include sweet potatoes, peanuts, sorghum, barley, wheat, soybeans, vegetables, and rice. Fishing is also important. Quemoy island is heavily fortified; since 1949 it has been subjected to periodic bombardment from the Communist mainland, which it has returned in kind. A radio station there beams propaganda broadcasts to the mainland.

Queneau, Raymond (rāmôN' kĕnō'), 1903–, French author and critic. He was an advocate of SURREALISM during the middle and late 1920s. Queneau is best known for his manipulations of style and language and his use of street slang in literary works. He often parodied traditional literary forms, as in his pastiche *Exercices de style* (1947). His novels include *Le Chiendent* (1933; tr. *The Bark Tree,* 1968), *Un Rude Hiver* (1940; tr. *A Hard Winter,* 1948), *Pierrot, mon ami* (1943), *Le Dimanche de la vie* [the Sunday of life] (1952), and the comic best-seller *Zazie dans le Métro* (1959; tr. *Zazie,* 1960). He has also written a great deal of poetry, and many of his novels contain extended verse passages. See his *Selected Poems* (tr. 1970).

Quental, Antero de (äntĕ'rō dĭ kĕntäl'), 1842–91, Portuguese poet. A brilliant student at the Univ. of Coimbra, he led the Coimbra dissidents in their opposition to the monarchy and to romanticism. A socialist, he worked for a time in Lisbon organizing the Portuguese Socialist party. His poetry can be considered a search for abstract truth through inner experience. His volumes of poetry include the carefully restrained *Odes modernas* (1865) and the exquisitely fashioned *Sonetos* (1881). Quental was constantly plagued by ill health and psychological torment; he committed suicide in the public square of his birthplace, Ponta Delgada. Despite his limited output, Quental is one of the principal modern Portuguese poets. His first name was formerly written Anthero.

Que Que (kwā kwā), city (1973 est. pop., with suburbs, 40,000), central Rhodesia, founded 1900. It is a gold-mining center and the focal point of Rhodesia's iron and steel industry.

Quercia, Jacopo della (yä'kōpō dĕl'lä kwĕr'chä), c.1374–1438, Italian sculptor. His work shows the transition from medieval to Renaissance art. He is especially noted for his imposing allegorical figures for the Gaia Fountain in Siena. About 1425 he began to decorate the main portal of San Petronio, Bologna, with scenes from Genesis and the life of Christ. His grandeur of conception and vigorous modeling formed one of the sources of inspiration for Michelangelo. See study by Charles Seymour, Jr. (1973).

Quercy (kĕrsē'), region and former county, SW France, now divided between Lot and Tarn-et-Garonne depts. Cahors is the chief city. It consists of arid limestone plateaus (causses), cut by fertile valleys of the Lot, Dordogne, and Aveyron rivers. Sheep raising is the chief activity in the causses; the famous Rocamadour cheese is made from sheep's milk. Of Gallo-Roman origin, Quercy (also known as Cahorsin) became (9th cent.) a fief of the counts of Toulouse. It was savagely contested during the Hundred Years War, after which it was united (1472) with the French crown and included in Guienne prov.

Querétaro (kārā'tärō), state (1970 pop. 464,226), 4,432 sq mi (11,479 sq km), central Mexico. The city of QUERÉTARO is the capital. With mountains in the north and valleys and plains in the south, the state raises a variety of agricultural products, including sugarcane, cotton, tobacco, and grains. Extensive pasturelands make livestock breeding important. The state is famous for its opals; silver, iron, copper, and mercury are also mined. Generally poor communications have hindered industrialization, and most manufacturing is concentrated in the capital. The territory of Querétaro was conquered from the Chichimec Indians by the Spanish in 1531, but colonization did not begin until 1550, when the area was established as a buffer against Indians to the north. Later included in the intendancy of Guanajuato, Querétaro became a separate state in 1824.

Querétaro, city (1970 pop. 140,379) capital of Querétaro state, central Mexico. It is a distribution center with industries producing machinery and farm implements; the city's cotton mills are among the most important in Mexico. Querétaro is also a popular tourist center. An Aztec city, Querétaro was conquered by the Spanish in 1531. The conspiracy (1810) under Hidalgo y Costilla and Allende that led to the revolution against Spain was planned there. In 1867, Emperor Maximilian and his generals Miguel Miramon and Tomas Mejia were forced to surrender and then taken out and shot on a hill outside the city. Querétaro retains numerous colonial landmarks.

Quesada, Gonzalo Jiménez de: see JIMÉNEZ DE QUESADA, GONZALO.

Quesnay, François (fräNswä' kĕnā'), 1694–1774, French economist, founder of the physiocratic school. A physician to Louis XV, he did not begin his economic studies until 1756, when he wrote the articles "Fermiers" [farmers] and "Grains" for the *Encyclopédie.* His chief work was the *Tableau économique* [economic table] (1758), said to have been printed by the king's own hands. Quesnay and his followers believed that the *Tableau* summed up the natural law of economy. Quesnay and the other PHYSIOCRATS greatly influenced the thought of Adam Smith. Quesnay's works have been collected in *Œuvres économiques et philosophiques* (with biographical studies and introduction, 1888).

Quesnel, Pasquier (päskyā' kĕnĕl'), 1634–1719, French Jansenist writer. He entered the Congregation of the Oratory in 1657 and was made director of the seminary at Paris in 1662. His edition of the works of Pope Leo I was placed on the Index (1676) for its Gallicanism, and Quesnel left his congregation. In 1685 he refused to subscribe to the formulas condemning Jansenism (see under JANSEN, CORNELIS), and he escaped to Brussels. There he completed his *Réflexions morales,* a French New Testament with Jansenist commentary. He was imprisoned in 1703 by order of the king of Spain but escaped to Amsterdam. Quesnel's teachings were condemned by Pope Clement XI in 1708 and in 1713 (in the bull *Unigenitus*).

question mark: see PUNCTUATION.

questor: see QUAESTOR.

Quetelet, Adolphe (ädôlf' kĕtəlā'), 1796–1874, Belgian statistician and astronomer. He was the first director (1828) of the Royal Observatory at Brussels. As supervisor of statistics for Belgium (from 1830), he developed many of the rules governing modern census taking and stimulated statistical activity in other countries. Applying statistics to social phenomena, he developed the concept of the "average man" and established the theoretical foundations for the use of statistics in social physics or, as it is now known, sociology. Thus, he is considered by many to be the founder of modern quantitative social science. *A Treatise on Man* (1835; tr., 1842) is his best-known work. See study by F. H. Hankins (1908, repr. 1968).

Quetta (kwĕ'tə), city (1972 metropolitan area est. pop. 140,000), capital of Baluchistan prov., W central Pakistan, at an altitude of c.5,500 ft (1,675 m), ringed by mountains. Deriving its name from the Pushtu word *kawatah* [fort], it commands the entrance through the strategic Bolan Pass into Afghanistan and is a trade center for Afghanistan, Iran, and much of central Asia. Fruits, vegetables, hides, and wool are the chief items traded. The city's cottage industries produce textiles, foodstuffs, and carpets. Some coal and chromite are mined in the area. Quetta is also a summer resort. The city was occupied (1876) by the British following the Second Afghan War, and it gained prominence as the seat of British resident Sir Robert Sandeman. It became a strongly garrisoned British military station. Much of the present city was rebuilt after a disastrous earthquake in 1935. Quetta has a military staff college (est. 1907) and a geophysical observatory.

quetzal (kĕtsäl') or **quezal** (kāsäl'), common name for a magnificent bird of the family Trogonidae (TROGON family), found in the rain forests from S Mexico to Costa Rica at altitudes of up to 9,000 ft (2,745 m). It is strikingly beautiful, with a crested head, bronze-green back, and crimson and white underparts. Quetzals nest in holes, and lay from two to four eggs per clutch. The male shares incubation duties with the female. The nesting hole has a single entrance, not two as was once believed. The Aztec and Maya used the 2-ft (61-cm) shimmering green tail plumes of the breeding male ceremonially and worshipped the bird as the god of the air, associating it with the god QUETZALCOATL. The quetzal, *Pharomachrus mocino,* is the national bird of Guatemala, and a monetary unit of the country is also called a quetzal. Quetzals are classified in the phylum CHORDATA, subphylum Vertebrata, class Aves, order Trogoniformes, family Trogonidae.

Quetzalcoatl (kĕt"sälkôät'əl) [Nahuatl,=feathered serpent], ancient deity and legendary ruler of the TOLTEC in Mexico. The name is also that of a Toltec ruler, who is credited with the discovery of maize, the arts, science, and the calendar. It is unclear whether the ruler took his name from the god or as a great ruler was revered and later deified. Quetzalcoatl, god of civilization, was identified with the planet Venus, and with the wind; he represented the forces of good and light pitted against those of evil and darkness, which were championed by TEZCATLIPOCA. According to one epic legend, Quetzalcoatl, deceived by Tezcatlipoca, was driven from Tula, the Toltec capital, and wandered for many years until he reached his homeland, the east coast of Mexico—where he was consumed by divine fire, his ashes turning into birds and his heart becoming the morning star. Another version has him sailing off to a mythical land, leaving behind the promise of his return. Adopting the name, the AZTEC linked it with the worship of the war god Huitzilopotchtli and applied it to some of their ranking priests. MONTEZUMA viewed the Spanish invaders as the returning hosts of Quetzalcoatl. There is a great pyramid in honor of the deity at CHOLULA, and the sky-serpent motif in the mosaics at Mitla probably represents Quetzalcoatl. The famous Temple of Quetzalcoatl at TEOTIHUACÁN is now regarded by some authorities as having been consecrated to a different god. It is likely that the figure who gave rise to the legendary Quetzalcoatl was an ancestor of his Maya counterpart, Kulkulcán. The Toltec of Tula moved southward, settled in SW Campeche, and in the 10th cent. under the leadership of Kulkulcán, a historical figure, occupied CHICHÉN ITZÁ and founded the cities of Uxmal and Mayapán. Although probably assimilated into the MAYA culture by this time, the invaders still employed Mexican architectural motifs (especially the feathered serpent) extensively. After the death of Kulkulcán he became the patron deity of Chichén Itzá, and most of the temples were dedicated to him. The symbol for both Quetzalcoatl and Kulkulcán, the serpent with QUETZAL feathers, has an obvious connection with serpent worship. See Laurette Séjourné, *Burning Water* (tr. 1957).

Quevedo y Villegas, Francisco Gómez de (frānthēs'kō gō'māth dā kāvā'thō ē vēlyā'gās), 1580–1645, Spanish satirist, novelist, and wit, b. Madrid. In 1611 he fled to Italy after a duel and became involved in revolutionary plottings. When Philip IV ascended the Spanish throne, Quevedo narrowly avoided a long prison term. He was later imprisoned (1639–43) as the presumed author of a satire on the king and his favorite, the conde de Olivares. Quevedo was one of the great writers of the Spanish Golden Age. *Los sueños* [visions] (1627) is a brilliant and bitterly satiric account, after Dante and Lucan, of the inhabitants of hell. Other major works include the philosophical treatise *Providencia de Dios* (1641), the political essay *Política de Dios y gobierno de Cristo* (1626–55), and the picaresque novel *La vida del Buscón* (1626). Also a major poet, his verse was collected in *El Parnaso español* (1648). His *Epístola satírica y censoria* (1639), a poetic satire against Olivares, is well known. Quevedo was a determined opponent of Gongorism (see GÓNGORA Y ARGOTE, LUIS DE). See studies by D. W. Blesnick (1972) and Henry Ettinghausen (1972).

quezal: see QUETZAL.

Quezaltenango (kāsältānäng'gō), city (1971 est. pop. 54,475), SW Guatemala. The city is the metropolis of the western highlands (it is 7,500 ft/2,286 m above sea level) and the second city of Guatemala. The people of the surrounding country and suburbs are predominantly QUICHÉ, but those of the administrative and residential sections of the city are ladino (mestizo). The native market offers excellent textiles and handicrafts, and the city has many local manufactures. The development of hydroelectric power, has helped make it a leading industrial city of Central America. Quezaltenango was rebuilt after being severely damaged in 1902 by an eruption of nearby Santa María volcano (12,362 ft/3,768 m). The site of the city was the center of the ancient Quiché kingdom of Xelaju.

Quezon, Manuel Luis (mänwĕl lōōēs' kā'sōn), 1878–1944, first president of the Commonwealth of the Philippines (1935–44). While a law student, he joined (1899) Emilio AGUINALDO'S insurrectionary army and fought the U.S. forces until 1901. He was imprisoned briefly after the insurrection. Admitted (1903) to the bar, he was elected (1905) governor of Tabayas prov. (renamed Quezon in his honor in 1946). As a member (1907–9) of the first Philippine assembly, he became floor leader of the majority nationalist party. He served (1909–16) as resident commissioner to the United States, crusading tirelessly for Philippine independence, and was instrumental in securing (1916) passage of the Jones Act, which increased self-government in the Philippines and gave the islands a pledge of future independence. On his return to the Philippines, he was elected (1916) to the first Philippine senate and was unanimously chosen president of that body—at the time the highest elective office in the land. He continued his ardent crusade for independence, strongly opposing the high-handed administration (1921–27) of Governor General Leonard WOOD, and after Wood's death effecting the appointment of the more sympathetic Henry Stimson. In 1934 he helped bring about passage of the Tydings-McDuffie Bill, which established the Commonwealth of the Philippines and promised complete independence in 1946. Quezon was elected (1935) president of the new commonwealth. As president he initiated administrative reforms, undertook many defense measures, and greatly expanded his power. Reelected in 1941, he escaped to the United States after the Japanese invasion of the Philippines in World War II and conducted a government-in-exile there until his death. See his autobiography, *The Good Fight* (1946) and biographies by S. H. Gwekoh (1948), Elinor Goettel (1970), and Carlos Quirino (1971).

Quezon, province (1970 pop. 971,637), E central Luzon, the Philippines. Lucena is the capital. A long, narrow province bordering on the Philippine Sea and containing in part the rugged Sierra Madre mts., it is an excellent source of timber. It has plywood mills and major wood-product manufactures, most notably Manila elemi (an oleoresin). Formerly called Tayabas, its name was changed in 1946 to honor Pres. Manuel Quezon, who was born there, in the village of Baler.

Quezon City, city (1970 pop. 754,452), official capital of the Republic of the Philippines, central Luzon, adjacent to Manila. It is the second largest city in the Philippines. Although chiefly residential, it has a large textile industry. It is named for President Manuel Quezon, who in 1937 selected this site as the new capital of a free Philippines. It officially replaced Manila as capital in July, 1948, and government offices are still being transferred. The area was formerly a private estate. The Univ. of the Philippines is there.

Quiberon (kēbrôN'), peninsula, Morbihan dept., NW France, in BRITTANY, projecting into the Bay of Biscay. The town of Quiberon (1968 pop. 4,595), a fishing port and resort, is at the tip of the peninsula and is linked with the mainland by a thin stretch of sand. Sardine canning is the major industry. A force of some 3,000 French royalists was landed at Quiberon by British ships in 1795 in the hope of reviving the VENDÉE movement, an anti-Revolution peasant uprising. The local population failed to rally, and bad weather prevented the British ships from giving assistance. Thus, the invaders were forced to capitulate; but, contrary to the capitulation terms, the French government ordered all prisoners executed. Some 750 were shot, and the rest were allowed to escape. **Quiberon Bay** was also the scene (1759) of a victory by the British under Lord Hawke over a French fleet in the SEVEN YEARS WAR (1756–63).

Quiché (kēchā'), Indians of Mayan linguistic stock, in the western highlands of Guatemala; most important group of the ancient southern MAYA. The largest of the contemporary Indian groups of Guatemala, numbering some 340,000, they live principally in the region between QUEZALTENANGO and CHICHICASTENANGO. From their origins, as told in the POPOL VUH, the Quiché have retained many ancient traditions, blending them with Western customs to create a distinctive mode of life. Pedro de ALVARADO with the help of the Cakchiquel or Kakchiquel, a neighboring but rival group similar in language and stock, conquered them in 1524. Studies of modern Quiché communities include Ruth Bunzel, *Chichicastenango: A Guatemalan Village* (1952) and Manning Nash, *Machine Age Maya* (1958). See also R. M. Carmack, *Quichean Civilization* (1973).

quicklime: see CALCIUM OXIDE.

quicksilver: see MERCURY.

Quidde, Ludwig (lōōt'vĭkh kvĭd'ə), 1858–1941, German pacifist and historian. He was elected (1907) to the Bavarian diet, was a member (1919–22) of the national assembly at Weimar, and later served in the Reichstag. Indefatigable in his attacks on German imperialism, he was briefly imprisoned for his brochure, *Caligula: eine Studie über romischen Casarenwahnsinn* [Caligula: a study in Roman Caesarean madness] (1894), an obvious polemic in which Caligula represented Emperor William II. A leading supporter of the League of Nations, Quidde shared the 1927 Nobel Peace Prize with Ferdinand Buisson. He lived in exile in Switzerland during World War I and again after Hitler's rise to power.

Quidor, John (kĭdôr'), 1801–81, American painter, b. Tappan, N.Y., studied with J. W. Jarvis. Little appreciated in his own time, he was subsequently accorded a place among the best early American artists. He is represented in the Brooklyn Museum by three paintings, *Dorothea, Money Diggers,* and *Wolfert's Will.* He is probably best known for his scenes inspired by the writings of Washington Irving, e.g., *Ichabod Crane Pursued by the Headless Horseman* (Yale Univ.). Quidor often provided a mysterious romantic setting for scenes in which he mingled macabre elements with an earthy humor. See study by John Baur (1942).

Quids, in U.S. political history, an extreme states' rights group of Jeffersonian Republicans led by John RANDOLPH of Virginia. Feeling that Thomas Jefferson and James Madison had retreated from the states' rights position they had taken in the Kentucky and Virginia Resolutions and that they had in fact become nationalists, the Quids tried to deprive Madison of the Democratic-Republican presidential nomination in 1808. Their candidate, James Monroe, however, received sizable support only in Virginia, and Jefferson's prestige secured Madison's nomination.

quietism, a heretical form of religious mysticism founded by Miguel de Molinos, a 17th-century Spanish priest. Molinism, or quietism, developed within the Roman Catholic Church in Spain and spread especially to France, where its most influential exponent was Madame GUYON. She preached her doctrines to members of the French aristocracy, winning a convert and friend in Madame de Maintenon, Louis XIV's wife, and an ally in Archbishop FÉNELON. Another quietist was Antoinette BOURIGNON. The essence of quietism is that perfection lies in the complete passivity of the soul before God and the absorption of the individual in the divine love to the point of annihilation not only of will but of all effort or desire for effort. Molinos talked about an entire cessation of self-consciousness, and Madame Guyon maintained that she could not sin, for sin was self, and she had rid herself of self. Molinos and his doctrines were condemned by Pope Innocent XI in 1687. A commission in France found most of Madame Guyon's works intolerable, and in 1699 Pope Innocent XII prohibited the circulation of Fénelon's book, the *Maxims of the Saints.* See William Backhouse and James Janson, comp., *Guide to True Peace . . . Composed Chiefly of Writings of Fénelon, Guyon, and Molinos* (1946).

Quill, Michael Joseph, 1905–1966, American labor leader, b. Co. Kerry, Ireland. Quill was active (1919–23) in the movement for Irish independence before emigrating (1926) to the United States. He worked as a laborer and in the New York City subways, and in 1934 he helped to organize the Transport Workers Union of America, of which he became president in 1935. In 1937 the union became affiliated with the Congress of Industrial Organizations, and Quill succeeded, with the help of John L. Lewis, in getting closed-shop contracts with transit lines of New York City. He then led in expanding the activities of the union to other big cities in the United States. As a member (1937–39, 1943–49) of the city council of New York, Quill—a colorful and fiery speaker—fought for numerous municipal reforms. Quill died shortly after he led a transit strike that paralyzed New York City for 12 days.

quill: see PEN.

Quiller-Couch, Sir Arthur Thomas (kwĭl'ər-kōōch"), pseud. **Q,** 1863–1944, English author. Among the novels of his native Cornwall are *Dead Man's Rock* (1887) and *Hetty Wesley* (1903), which are romantic in spirit yet distinguished for their clear and colorful style. He also wrote essays, lectures, and poetry and was the editor of many anthologies, including the *Oxford Book of English Verse* (1900) and the *Oxford Book of English Prose* (1923). He was knighted in 1910. See his unfinished autobiography, *Memories and Opinions* (1945); biography by Fred Brittain (1947).

quillwort, common name for several species of the plant genus *Isoetes,* which grow in ponds, slow streams, and swampy places. See LYCOPODIOPHYTA.

Quilmes (kēl'mēs), city (1970 pop. 355,265), Buenos Aires prov., E Argentina, on the Río de la Plata estuary. It is a district administrative center and a major industrial city, with one of the world's largest breweries as well as numerous distilleries. Other important products include paper, metals, chemicals, textiles, and glass. The city's name derives from the Kilmes Indian tribe, which was settled on the site in 1666 by the governor of Río de la Plata prov.

Quilon (kwē'lŏn), city (1971 pop. 124,072), Kerala state, SW India, on the Arabian Sea. It is a market for coconut products, spices, tea, coffee, and rice. Tiles and electrical apparatus are manufactured, and fishing is an important industry. Quilon is the oldest city on the Malabar Coast. In the 7th cent. it was noted by a Nestorian patriarch as the southernmost point of Christian influence in India. By the time the Dutch occupied Quilon in 1662, the Portuguese had already established a factory there. Soon after the Dutch came, the British East India Company took control of Quilon.

quilting, form of needlework in which two layers of fabric over an interlining are sewn together, usually in a pattern of back or running (quilting) stitches. This method of securing warmth in covering and clothing has been practiced in N Asia and Europe for centuries. Quilting has been a feature of embroidery in the form of raised work. It was a distinctive type of needlework in pioneer American homes, at first utilitarian, later ornamental. Quilts were usually of the pieced, or patchwork, type until c.1750, when the appliquéd, or laid-on, quilt and the monotone quilt decorated by trapunto (padding or cording) became popular. A fad for quilted petticoats for women and coattails for men was at its height from 1688 to 1714. The art of quilting is still practiced by Southern mountaineers and in other rural districts and has been revived generally as ornamental needlework. Machine-quilted materials are used for wearing apparel and in interior decoration, particularly for bed and couch covers. See Averil Colby, *Quilting* (1971); Marilyn Lithgow, *Quiltmaking and Quiltmakers* (1974).

Quimby, Phineas Parkhurst, 1802-66, American mental healer, b. Lebanon, N.H. He became interested in mesmerism and gave exhibitions of that art in New England and New Brunswick. He then turned to mental healing and gained a large and important following. "Doctor" Quimby is, however, best known through the controversy that later arose as to the influence of his thought and his doctrines on Mary Baker EDDY and on Christian Science. The problem is unsolved. Quimby's *Questions and Answers* appeared in 1862. His name and teaching remained influential long after his death. See biography by Ann B. Hawkins (1970).

Quimper (kăNpĕr'), town (1968 pop. 57,678), capital of Finistère dept., NW France, in Brittany, near the Bay of Biscay. It is famous for its pottery (quimper or Brittany ware) and also has textile, food, and furniture industries. It was once the capital of the Breton county of CORNOUAILLE. It has a Gothic cathedral (13th-16th cent.).

Quin, James, 1693-1766, English actor. He made his London debut in 1714. The successor of Barton Booth, he was the last of the declamatory school. At his best in declaiming the great tragic roles, Quin was in constant rivalry with the young Garrick until Quin left the stage in 1751. He was regarded as one of the greatest interpreters of the role of Falstaff.

quinacrine (kwĭn'əkrēn, -krĭn), drug used to treat malaria. An acridine dye, quinacrine was synthesized in 1933 and along with other synthetic substances, has largely replaced QUININE as the antimalarial of choice. It inactivates cellular deoxyribonucleic acid (DNA) in certain susceptible stages in the life cycle of malaria parasites. Quinacrine is also effective in treating some forms of lupus, an autoimmune disease, some forms of cancer, and intestinal infestations by protozoa and flatworms. The drug is marketed under the trade names Atabrine and Mepacrine.

Quinault, Philippe (fēlēp' kēnō'), 1635-88, French dramatist. His tragedies and comedies are affected and undistinguished, but he found an outlet for his talent in the 14 opera librettos which he wrote for Lully. The charm and delicacy of his style is clearly apparent in his masterpiece, *Armide* (1686), a libretto used first by Lully and later by Gluck.

quince, shrub or small tree of the Asiatic genera *Chaenomeles* and *Cydonia* of the family Rosaceae (ROSE family). The common quince (*Cydonia oblonga*) is a spineless tree with edible fruits cultivated from ancient times in the Orient and in the Mediterranean area, where it was early naturalized. Its pome fruit is similar to that of the related apple and pear but is very astringent, and hence it is used chiefly cooked in preserves; MARMALADE is said to have first been made from quince. As a commercial fruit tree, the quince is cultivated more widely in the temperate zone of Europe than in the United States, where it is grown chiefly in California and New York. It is often used as a rootstock for dwarf fruit trees, especially the pear. The flowering quinces (genus *Chaenomeles*) are cultivated as ornamental shrubs for their profuse, usually thorny branches and attractive scarlet, pink, or white flowers. The fruit is too small and hard to be of commercial value but is sometimes used locally. Best known of this genus is *C. lagenaria,* the Japanese quince, or japonica. Some other Oriental shrubs (e.g., a camellia) are also called japonica. Quince is classified in the division MAGNOLIOPHYTA, class Magnoliopsida, order Rosales, family Rosaceae.

Quincy, Josiah (kwĭn'zē), 1744-75, political leader in the American Revolution, b. Boston. An outstanding lawyer, he wrote a series of anonymous articles for the Boston *Gazette in which he opposed the Stamp Act and other British colonial policies. Nevertheless, Quincy, along with John Adams, defended the British soldiers in the trial after the* BOSTON MASSACRE. In 1773 he went to South Carolina for his health and on his journey established connections with other colonial leaders. His *Observations on the Act of Parliament Commonly Called the Boston Port Bill* (1774) was an important political tract. He was sent (1774) as an agent to argue the colonial cause in England and died on the way home. His son, also named Josiah Quincy, wrote a memoir of him (1825, 2d ed. 1874). See study by R. A. McCaughey (1974).

Quincy, Josiah, 1772-1864, American political leader and college president, b. Braintree, Mass.; son of Josiah Quincy (1744-75). After studying law, Quincy became interested in politics and entered (1804) the state senate as a Federalist. He subsequently proceeded (1805-13) to the U.S. House of Representatives, where he became minority leader Speaking against admission of Louisiana as a state, he declared, in an extreme states' rights view, that passage of the bill without the specific consent of the original 13 states would be cause for dissolution of the Union. An opponent of the Embargo and Nonintercourse Acts prior to the War of 1812, he nevertheless advocated preparedness for political reasons, although he later violently opposed the war. On leaving Congress he returned to Boston, where he reentered (1813) the state senate and continued to oppose the war. The Federalists dropped him for insurgency in 1820 but Quincy was elected (1821) to the Massachusetts house of representatives, where he became speaker; he resigned to become a municipal court judge. In 1823 he was elected mayor of Boston and energetically labored for reforms. In 1829 he became president of Harvard, serving until 1845. While there he gave impetus to the law school, and wrote *The History of Harvard University* (1840) to silence traditionalist critics. His son, Edmund Quincy, edited his *Speeches Delivered in the Congress of the United States* (1874) and also wrote a biography (1867; 6th ed., 1874). See his memoirs (1825, repr. 1971).

Quincy. 1 (kwĭnt'sē) City (1970 pop. 45,288), seat of Adams co., W Ill., on a bluff above the Mississippi; inc. 1839. It is a trade, industrial, and distributing center in a grain and livestock area. The city and county were named for John Quincy Adams. Quincy has a good harbor and was an important river port in the mid-19th cent. Before the Civil War it was the scene of several proslavery-abolitionist struggles. The sixth Lincoln-Douglas debate was held there on Oct. 13, 1858. Quincy College and a state soldiers' and sailors' home are in the city. **2** (kwĭn'zē) City (1970 pop. 87,966), Norfolk co., E Mass., an industrial suburb of Boston, on Boston Bay; settled 1634, set off from Braintree 1792, inc. as a city 1888. It has a large shipbuilding industry and plants that make power transmissions, packaging machinery, soaps and detergents, and television tubes. The Plymouth Colony broke up (1627) a trading post established (1625) in the area by Thomas Morton, but a new settlement began in 1634. Ironworks began operation in 1644. Granite quarrying, started in 1750, became a large industry. The first railroad tracks in the United States were laid in Quincy in 1826. The city's large shipyards were of great importance in both world wars. John Adams and John Quincy Adams were born in Quincy. They and their wives are buried in the First Parish Church (built 1828), and their homes and places of birth are national historic sites (see NATIONAL PARKS AND MONUMENTS, table). John Hancock was also born in Quincy; the Adams Academy, gift of John Adams, was built on the site of Hancock's birthplace. Eastern Nazarene College and a junior college are in the city.

Quine, Willard Van Orman (kwīn), 1908–, American philosopher and mathematical logician, b. Akron, Ohio, grad. Oberlin, 1930. He studied at Harvard (Ph.D., 1932) under Alfred North Whitehead and in Europe, where he was influenced by Rudolf Carnap. He taught at Harvard from 1936, becoming Edgar Pierce professor of philosophy there in 1955. Much of Quine's philosophical work deals with the implications of viewing language as a logical system. He disputed the distinction, originating in Immanuel Kant, between analytic and synthetic statements. He argued that any statement can be held to be true no matter what is observed, provided that adjustments are made elsewhere in a language's system of reference. Quine drew attention to "ontic commitments" in language systems, i.e., their tendency to commit their users to the existence of certain things. In the field of logic Quine made important contributions to set theory. His writings include *A System of Logistic* (1934), *Mathematical Logic* (1940), *Word and Object* (1960), *Philosophy of Logic* (1969), *Set Theory and Its Logic* (1969), and *Methods of Logic* (3d ed. 1972). See Donald Davidson and Jaakko Hintikka, *Words and Objections* (1970).

Quinet, Edgar (ĕdgär' kēnā'), 1803-75, French historian. A romantic nationalist, he was much influenced by Johann Gottfried von Herder and was a close friend and associate of Jules Michelet. Praising the French Revolution for weakening the power of the Jesuits and the Roman Catholic Church, Quinet advocated complete elimination of church influence as the prerequisite for political freedom. His anti-Jesuit lectures at the Collège de France caused his dismissal from his teaching post in 1846. He opposed the regime of Napoleon III and was banished in 1852. After the French defeat (1870) in the Franco-Prussian War, he returned to France and entered the national assembly as a deputy. See study by R. H. Powers (1957).

Qui Nhon (kwē nyôn), city (1968 est. pop. 117,000), E South Vietnam, on the South China Sea coast. On the railroad and coastal highway, it was a naval station and military base during the Vietnam War. Its small fishing port was dredged and improved by the United States. The surrounding area was the scene of heavy fighting during the war, and the population of Qui Nhon was greatly swollen by refugees. The city has an airport. The neighboring city of An Nhon (formerly Binh Dinh) was an old Annamese capital. Ruins of the ancient Cham center of Chaban are nearby.

quinidine (kwĭn'ĭdēn''), heart muscle relaxant used to maintain regular heart rhythm patterns. It is an ALKALOID chemically similar to QUININE and, like quinine, occurs naturally in some species of cinchona trees. Quinidine slows the rate of blood flow in heart chambers and lowers the excitability of the muscle. Quinidine is a general relaxant of smooth muscle and acts as a dilator of larger blood vessels. It has also been used to reduce fever and to treat malaria. Synchronized electric shock has largely replaced quinidine as a method of establishing more normal heart rhythms.

quinine (kwī'nīn'', kwĭnēn'), white crystalline alkaloid with a bitter taste. Almost insoluble in water, it dissolves readily in alcohol and other organic solvents. It is derived from the bark, called *quina quina* by Peruvian Indians, of several species of *Cinchona* and is used in the form of a salt, especially the sulfate. Cinchona bark was brought to Europe from South America by the middle of the 17th cent. and quinine was isolated in 1820 by the French chemists J. B. Caventou and P. J. Pelletier; chemical synthesis was achieved in 1944 by R. B. Woodward and W. E. Doering, American chemists. Before the development in recent years of more effective synthetic drugs such as QUINACRINE, chloroquine, and primaquine, quinine was the specific agent in the treatment of MALARIA. It was also used to allay fever and pain, to induce uterine contractions during labor, and as a sclerosing, or hardening, agent in the treatment of varicose veins. Quinine is used in soft drinks called tonics, which are often mixed with alcoholic beverages. Excessive dosage or continuous use of quinine may cause cinchonism, characterized by ringing in the ears, headache, dizziness, changes in blood pressure, and even death.

quinoa (kēnō'ə), tall annual herb (*Chenopodium quinoa*) of the family Chenopodiaceae (GOOSEFOOT family), whose seeds have provided a staple food for peoples of the higher Andes since pre-Columbian times. The plant resembles the related lamb's-quarters of North America; its seeds are threshed, winnowed, and prepared like grain. Quinoa is eaten boiled like rice, used in soup or porridge, toasted in the form of tortillas, or mixed with wheat flour for bread. It is also used for poultry and livestock feed and is fermented to make an alcoholic beverage called chicha, more commonly made from maize. The foliage is used for salad greens. In the Inca Empire, where only the potato was more widely grown, quinoa is said to have been sacred; the year's first furrows were opened ceremoniously with a gold implement. Attempts to establish the crop outside of its native habitat have been unsuccessful. Quinoa is classified in the division MAGNOLIOPHYTA, class Magnoliopsida, order Caryophyllales, family Chenopodiaceae.

Quintana, Manuel José (mänwĕl' hōsā' kēntä'nä), 1772-1857, Spanish poet. He held high government posts and was tutor to Queen Isabella II. One of the last Spaniards to exemplify classical style, he is best known for his patriotic odes, among them *El Panteón del Escorial* (1805) and *A la batalla de Trafalgar* (1805). Longfellow translated some of his poetry into English in 1833.

Quintana Roo (kēntä'nä rō'ō), state (1970 pop. 91,044), 19,630 sq mi (50,842 sq km), SE Mexico, on the Caribbean. Occupying most of the eastern half of the YUCATAN peninsula, it is wild, sparsely settled, and populated almost entirely by Indians. With a hot climate and excessive rainfall, it remains undeveloped; the flat plain, with its almost impenetrable ebony and cedar forests, and the resistance of the Maya forced Francisco de MONTEJO to abandon his attempt (1527–28) to conquer Yucatán from the east. There are no important industries; some lumber, coconuts, and chicle are exported, and there is sponge and turtle fishing along the coast. Scandalous episodes involving the wholesale purchase of Indians for what amounted to slave labor in the chicle plantations tarnished the history of the territory in the late 19th and early 20th cent. Along the Caribbean coast is the famous Mayan archaeological zone of Tulum.

Quintanilla, Luis (lo͞oēs' kēntänē'lyä), 1895–, Spanish painter. Quintanilla worked as a muralist under the Spanish republican government and executed frescoes in the Ciudad Universitario in Madrid. In 1939 he was sent to the United States to paint a vast fresco for the Spanish pavilion at the New York World's Fair. He was not allowed to return to Franco's Spain, and much of his work in Spain was destroyed. In 1942 he settled in the United States, where his gently satirical paintings and etchings were widely exhibited.

Quinte, Bay of (kwĭn'tē), arm of Lake Ontario, S Ont., Canada, between the mainland and the peninsula of Prince Edward co. With its approach, Adolphus Reach, it is 60 mi (97 km) long. The Trent River, which is the lower portion of the Trent Canal between Lake Ontario and Lake Huron, flows into the head of the bay. Belleville and Trenton are on the north shore.

Quintilian (Marcus Fabius Quintilianus)(kwĭntĭl'-yən), A.D. c.35–A.D. c.95, Roman rhetorician, b. Calagurris (now Calahorra), Spain. He taught rhetoric at Rome (Pliny the Younger and possibly Tacitus were among his pupils) and, as a public teacher, was endowed with a salary by Vespasian, who also made him consul. His *Institutio oratoria,* a complete survey of rhetoric in 12 books, begins with a discussion of the education of the young and proceeds with the various principles of rhetoric. The last book deals with the life of the orator outside his profession, e.g., his morality and his deportment. The 10th book contains a list of great writers with brief but acute criticisms of their important works. Quintilian's style is among the most beautiful in his period; he succeeds in demonstrating what he sets out to inculcate—the necessity of good taste and moderation in rhetoric. He had great influence in antiquity and in the Renaissance. A number of declamations formerly assigned to him were falsely attributed. See study by George Kennedy (1970).

quipus (kē'po͞oz), groups of strings, knotted for tally, which were used by the Inca for keeping records and sending messages. The quipu was based on the decimal system. Small cords with knots in them were attached to a main cord or a top band; the color of the cord, its place, its size, and the knots in it were all of significance to the record or the message. The quipus had to be made up and deciphered by specially trained officials. The method of deciphering is not known today, although Andean shepherds still use a sort of quipu. See L. L. Locke, *The Ancient Quipu* (1923); C. L. Day, *Quipus and Witches' Knots* (1967).

Quiriguá (kērēgwä', kērēwä'), city of the Classic epoch of the MAYA, E Guatemala. It is famous for its zoomorphics. Its stone steles have fine hieroglyphs. Near the ruins the United Fruit Company maintains a hospital.

Quirinal (kwĭr'ĭnəl), one of the seven hills of Rome, NE of Capitoline Hill. It was the site of several ancient shrines and the quarter of the *quirites,* probably the aristocracy in the first centuries of Roman history. In the 16th cent. a papal palace was built there; known as Quirinal palace, it was the residence of the kings of Italy from 1870 to 1946 and is now the home of the president of Italy.

Quirino, Elpidio (ĕlpē'thyō kērē'nō), 1890–1956, Filipino statesman, b. Ilocos Sur prov., Luzon. He worked his way through the Univ. of the Philippines (LL.B., 1915), and after he was admitted (1915) to the bar he became a law clerk in the Philippine senate. Here he met Manual QUEZON, became his secretary, and for many years thereafter was his political aide. Quirino was elected (1919) to the Philippine house of representatives, and as senator (1925–35, 1941) he devoted himself to problems of finance. After the Japanese invasion in World War II he became a leader of the underground and was captured and imprisoned; his wife and three of his five children were killed by the conquerors. After the liberation (1945) of the Philippines, Quirino became president pro tempore of the senate and was elected (1946) first vice president of the independent Philippine republic. When President Manuel Roxas died (1948), Quirino succeeded to the presidency and was elected to that office in 1949. His administration was plagued by the Hukbalahap insurrection. Although ill, Quirino ran for reelection (1953), but he was overwhelmingly defeated by Ramon MAGSAYSAY.

Quirinus (kwĭr'ĭnəs), in Roman religion, an early god, possibly of war. Worshiped originally by the Sabines, he was one of the chief gods of ancient Rome, associated with Jupiter and Mars. In the late republic he was identified with Romulus, legendary founder of Rome.

Quiroga, Horacio (ôrä'syō kērō'gä), 1878–1937, Uruguayan short-story writer. Quiroga is considered a master of the short story. His work was deeply influenced by Kipling, Poe, Chekhov, and Maupassant as well as by the MODERNISMO movement. In 1900 he took a short trip to Paris, then went to Argentina, where he lived the rest of his life—a good deal of it as an unsuccessful agricultural pioneer. His collections of stories *Cuentos de la selva* (1918), *Anaconda* (1921), and *El desierto* (1924), which echo the tales of Kipling, reflect his life in the jungle. His concern with strange and morbid themes is evident in *Cuentos de amor, de locura, y de muerte* [tales of love, madness, and death] (1917). Quiroga's writings also include witty, sophisticated stories such as those in *Mas alla* [beyond] (1935). See Arthur Livingston, tr. and ed., *South American Jungle Tales* (1959).

Quiroga, Juan Facundo (hwän fäko͞on'thō), 1790–1835, Argentine CAUDILLO. One of the most brutal of the early gaucho chieftains, he was called *el tigre de los llanos* (the tiger of the plains). After a turbulent youth, Quiroga participated briefly in the 1810 revolution against Spain and then rose rapidly to become, by 1822, virtual overlord of the Andean provinces of Argentina. Anxious to preserve control over his fiefdoms, he became a supporter of federalism. With other provincial caudillos he rejected the unitarian constitution of 1826, thus contributing to the downfall of President Bernardino RIVADAVIA and to the installation (1827) of Manuel DORREGO, a federalist, as governor of Buenos Aires. When Juan LAVALLE rose against Dorrego and had him executed, Quiroga and Juan Manuel de ROSAS joined Estanislao López, caudillo of Santa Fe, in putting down the insurrection and in destroying temporarily but with ruthless thoroughness the unitarian cause. In 1834, Quiroga came to Buenos Aires, which was then ruled by Rosas. Quiroga was assassinated while returning from a mission to the northern provinces, and it was believed that Rosas, who was angered by the rival caudillo, had instigated the killing. A famous study of Quiroga and his era is Domingo F. Sarmiento's *Facundo* (tr. *Life in the Argentine Republic in the Days of the Tyrants,* 6th ed. 1961).

Quisling, Vidkun (kwĭz'lĭng, Nor. vĭd'ko͞on kvĭs'-lĭng), 1887–1945, Norwegian fascist leader. An army officer, he served as military attaché in Petrograd (1918–19) and Helsinki (1919–21) and later assisted Fridtjof Nansen in relief work in Russia. He was Norwegian minister of defense from 1931 to 1933. He then left the Agrarian party to found the fascist Nasjonal Samling [national unity] party. In 1940 he helped Germany prepare the conquest of Norway. Remaining at the head of the sole party permitted by the Germans, he was made premier in 1942. Despite his unpopularity and difficulties with his German masters and within his own party, he remained in power until May, 1945, when, after the Germans in Norway surrendered, he was arrested. He was convicted of high treason and shot. From his name came the word *quisling,* meaning traitor. See biography by P. M. Hayes (1972).

quitclaim: see DEED.

Quitman, John Anthony, 1798–1858, American general and politician, b. Rhinebeck, N.Y. He settled in Natchez, Miss., where he practiced law and held a series of political offices, serving in the state legislature and as acting governor (1835–36). As a brigadier general (promoted to major general in 1847) in the Mexican War, he distinguished himself at Monterrey, fought at Veracruz and Puebla, and led the assault on Chapultepec. He was governor of Mexico City during the American occupation (1847–48). On his return to Mississippi he became governor (1850–51), but resigned after indictment by the Federal government for aiding a filibustering expedition to Cuba planned by Narciso LÓPEZ. He was a member of the U.S. House of Representatives from 1855 until his death.

Quito (kē'tō), city (1970 est. pop. 528,100), N central Ecuador, capital of Ecuador and of Pichincha prov. After Guayaquil it is Ecuador's largest city. The setting of Quito is visually splendid: It lies at the foot of the Pichincha volcano in the hollow of a gently sloping, fertile valley. Only a short distance below the equator but at an elevation of 9,350 ft (2,850 m), Quito has a pleasant, balmy climate; however, it is subject to earthquakes and has been damaged several times. Quito has little economic importance, although there are textile mills and handicraft and other minor industries, but it is the educational and cultural as well as the political center of Ecuador. It is the seat of the Central Univ. of Ecuador and of the oldest art school in Latin America. The site was originally settled by the Quito Indians. It was captured by the Inca and became the capital of the Inca Kingdom of Quito a few decades before Sebastián de Benalcázar arrived and captured it for Spain (1534). In 1663, Quito became the seat of an audiencia, with boundaries foreshadowing that of present-day Ecuador. Quito was shifted back and forth between the viceroyalty of Peru and that of NEW GRANADA. There was an abortive uprising against Spain in 1809, and not until 1822 was the city liberated by Antonio José de Sucre. Quito has a Spanish colonial atmosphere, with many examples of fine early architecture, notably the great Church of San Francisco (see SPANISH COLONIAL ART AND ARCHITECTURE). Indians form a major part of the city's population.

Quivira (kēvē'rä), land sought and reached by Francisco Vásquez de Coronado in 1541 and explored by later Spanish expeditions (1593 and 1601). The records do not make it entirely clear exactly where Quivira was located. It is generally identified with villages of the Wichita Indians somewhere in Kansas, probably around Great Bend, but other sites have been suggested, including one in N Texas.

Qum, Iran: see QOM.

Qumran (ko͞omrän'), ancient village on the northwest shore of the Dead Sea, in present Jordan. It is famous for its caves, in some of which the DEAD SEA SCROLLS were found. Archaeological work at Qumran has yielded a profile of its history. In Israelite times it was the site of a small settlement and was probably called the city of Salt (Joshua 15.62). Between c.130 B.C. and c.110 B.C. Qumran was rebuilt by the Jewish sect whose library is represented by the Dead Sea Scrolls. It was destroyed (31 B.C.) by an earthquake and was rebuilt c.4 B.C. The Romans destroyed it (A.D. 68) and made use of the site as a military fortress. See C. T. Frisch, *The Qumran Community* (1956, repr. 1972); J. van der Ploeg, *The Excavations at Qumran* (1958).

quoits: see HORSESHOE PITCHING.

Quonset Point (kwŏn'sĭt), peninsula extending into Narragansett Bay, S R.I., in the town of North Kingstown.

Quran: see KORAN.

Quraysh: see KURAISH.

Qusayr, Al (äl ko͞osär'), town (1966 pop. 5,500), E Egypt, on the Red Sea. The ancient Leucus Limen, it was once a major Egyptian port and the focus of several trade routes. It was formerly known as Koseir.

Qutb Minar (ko͝o'təb mē'när), minaret near New Delhi, India. One of the earliest Muslim monuments in India, it was erected (c.1230) by Iltutmish of the DELHI SULTANATE. It is c.240 ft (73 m) high, covered with relief work, and was probably built to celebrate a victory. It is also spelled Kutb Minar.

R

R, 18th letter of the ALPHABET, corresponding to Greek rho. When in Latin alphabets the letters for *p* and *r* became similar in appearance, the rho form (P; which at first was used for the *r* sound) was restricted to the *p* sound, and an extra line was added for the *r* sound (R). In Greek, where no confusion developed, the rho continued to look like Latin P. A modification of R is the symbol ℞, used medically for *recipe* [Lat.,= take] and liturgically for *responsum* [Lat.,= response].

Ra (rä) or **Re** (rā), in EGYPTIAN RELIGION, sun god, one of the most important gods of ancient Egypt. Ra was chief of the cosmic deities and was sometimes called the creator and father of all things. Early Egyptian kings alleged descent from him and added his name to their own royal titles. Ra had several manifestations, the most common being those of the hawk and the lion. He was depicted as sailing across the sky in a celestial barge during the day and battling the forces of evil and darkness by night. Various other Egyptian gods were frequently identified with him, such as Amon and Atum.

Ra, chemical symbol of the element RADIUM.

Raab: see RÁBA, river, Hungary and Austria.

Raabe, Wilhelm (vĭl'hĕlm rä'bə), 1831–1910, German novelist, whose pseudonym was Jakob Corvinus. At 23 he began to write novels and tales of village life; the charming idyll *Die Chronik der Sperlingsgasse* (1857) first brought him acclaim. Raabe's humor often serves to cover a more bitter irony. He later turned to the historical past and wrote such tales as the tragic "Des Reiches Krone" [the imperial crown] (1870). His novels include *Der Hungerpastor* (1864, tr. 1885) and *Abu Telfan* (1867; tr. *Abu Telfan's Return from the Mountains of the Moon,* 1881). See study by Barker Fairley (1961).

Raamah (rā'əmə). **1** Founder of a tribe. Gen. 10.7; 1 Chron. 1.9. **2** Region on the Persian Gulf. Ezek. 27.22.

Raamiah (rā"əmī'ə), chief who returned with Zerrubbabel. Neh. 7.7. Reelaiah: Ezra 2.2.

Raamses (rāăm'sēz), in the Bible, city of the eastern delta of Egypt, built by Hebrew slave labor. Ex. 1.11. It was rebuilt by Ramses II. The Rameses of Gen. 47.11 and Num. 33.3,5 is the region of the central eastern delta.

Rab (räb), Ital. *Arbe,* island (1971 pop. 8,515), 40 sq mi (104 sq km) off Croatia, W Yugoslavia, in the Adriatic Sea. One of the Dalmatian islands, it is a popular seaside resort. The island was under Venetian rule from the 10th cent. until 1797, and it retains its ancient walls, the ruins of the palace of the Venetian governors, a 12th-century cathedral, and the medieval palace of the former archbishops.

Rába (rä'bŏ), Ger. *Raab,* river, c.160 mi (260 km) long, rising in the mountains of SE Austria. It flows SE to the Austria-Hungary line, then NE through W Hungary to the Danube River at Győr. There are many small hydroelectric plants on the river. The valley is extensively farmed.

Rabanus Maurus Magnentius (rəbā'nəs mô'rəs măgnĕn'shəs), c.780–856, German scholar and theologian. His name appears also as Hrabanus and Rhabanus. A student under ALCUIN, he was later abbot of Fulda (822–42); his zeal for learning and his excellent administration made the school and library at Fulda an outstanding source of intellectual light. He is sometimes called the preceptor of Germany. He retired from Fulda but in 847 was made bishop of Mainz. Rabanus had an immense stock of knowledge, and his works, notably biblical exegeses, were encyclopedic rather than original. *De universo* is a sort of encyclopedic dictionary, and *De institutione clericorum* is a course of study for clerics. His poetry and writings are today chiefly of linguistic interest, but his role in spreading the Carolingian revival was eminent. GOTTSCHALK and the poet Walafrid Strabo were his students.

Rabat (räbät'), city (1970 est. pop. 325,000), capital of Morocco, on the Atlantic Ocean at the mouth of the Bou Regreg estuary, opposite Salé. The city is a minor port and has textile industries. There have been settlements on the site since ancient times. It became a Muslim fortress A.D. c.700. Prior to independence (1956), it was capital of the French protectorate of Morocco. Points of interest in Rabat are the old walls and the ruins of a large, unfinished mosque with adjoining tower (similar to the GIRALDA); these were built during the reign of Yakub (1184–99). Rabat was a stronghold of corsairs in the 17th and 18th cent. Muhammad V Univ. was founded in the city in 1957.

Rabaul (rä'boul), town (1971 est. pop. 21,400), on NEW BRITAIN island, BISMARCK ARCHIPELAGO, a part of Papua New Guinea. The principal city and port of the archipelago, Rabaul has one of the finest harbors in the world. Copra is the chief export. The town is surrounded by active volcanoes and was nearly destroyed by eruptions in 1937. Rabaul was the territorial capital from 1920 to 1941. During World War II, it was the major Japanese naval and air base for the projected invasion of Australia. Totally destroyed by Allied bombing, it was rebuilt after the war.

Rabb, Ellis: see ASSOCIATION OF PRODUCING ARTISTS—PHOENIX.

Rabbah or **Rabbath:** see AMMAN, Jordan.

rabbi [Heb.,= my master or my teacher], the title of a Jewish minister. He was called *rav* [great] among certain Jews in Eastern Europe, where the word *rabbi* was used only for a scholar or teacher. This was the meaning of the title when it first came into common use among the Palestinian Jews in the late 1st cent. A.D. It had been used earlier (in the Gospels, Jesus was frequently addressed as rabbi), but without official connotation. It was during the Middle Ages that in addition to being a legal scholar, the rabbi began to assume the roles of teacher, preacher, and communal leader that characterized the modern rabbi. The first rabbi to receive a salary (c.1400) was Simon ben Zemah Duran (see under DURAN, family). There is a chief rabbinate in the state of Israel consisting of two chief rabbis, one of whom represents the Ashkenazic community, the other the Sephardic branch. The chief rabbinate was introduced during the British mandate and is modeled after the chief Ashkenazic Orthodox rabbinate of Great Britain.

Rabbi Ben Ezra: see IBN EZRA, ABRAHAM BEN MEIR.

rabbit, name for herbivorous mammals of the family Leporidae, which also includes the HARE and the PIKA. Rabbits and hares have large front teeth, short tails, and large hind legs and feet adapted for running or jumping. In most, the length of the ears is considerably greater than the width. Although usage varies, the term *rabbit* generally refers to small, running animals, with relatively short ears and legs, which give birth to blind, naked young, while *hare* refers to larger, hopping forms, with longer ears and legs, whose young are born furred and open-eyed. Rabbits are chiefly nocturnal, although they are sometimes seen in the daytime. They have acute senses of smell and hearing. They feed on a wide variety of vegetation and are responsible in many areas for the stunted nature of the ground cover. When feeding on green herbage, rabbits, like hares, excrete soft pellets which they reingest; the waste products of the redigested food are excreted as dry pellets. The European common rabbit, *Oryctolagus cuniculus,* is native to S Europe and Africa, but is now found, in its domestic varieties, throughout the world; wild varieties have also been introduced in some places, such as England. All domestic rabbits, including the so-called Belgian hare, belong to this species. Wild common rabbits are up to 16 in. (41 cm) long and usually weigh 2 to 3 lb (0.9–1.4 kg). They have soft, thick fur, usually grayish brown above and white below. The tail is usually carried upright when the animal runs, exposing the white undersurface. Common rabbits live in elaborate systems of adjoining burrows called warrens. The young are suckled in a special burrow, dug by the mother at a distance from the warren and lined with a nest of her own fur. The entrance to this burrow is plugged with earth when she is away. Domestic rabbits, which may be various colors but are commonly white, are bred for food and for their fur, which is much used in making fur trim and felt. They are also frequently used as laboratory animals and are kept as pets. The reproductive rate of rabbits is notorious. The common rabbit breeds from February to October; its gestation period is 30 days and there are five to eight young in a litter. In most regions its numbers are kept down by its many predators, such as the fox, the badger, and birds of prey. However, when domestic rabbits escaped in Australia, where they had few natural enemies, they ran rampant and stripped the countryside of vegetation in many regions. They were brought partially under control by the artificial introduction of a viral disease, myxomatosis. The New World genus *Sylvilagus* includes the many species of COTTONTAIL RABBIT, which resemble the European rabbit in appearance, as well as the marsh rabbit and swamp rabbit (*Sylvilagus palustris* and *S. aquaticus,* respectively), of the S United States. These rabbits do not burrow, although in winter they may shelter in a burrow abandoned by another animal. They usually rest, like hares, in hollows which they make in the ground or in vegetation. The Idaho pygmy rabbit, *Brachylagus idahoensis,* of the U.S. Great Basin, digs simple burrows. The many North American species called JACKRABBIT are actually hares, as is the snowshoe rabbit, or VARYING HARE. There are several species of short-eared rabbits in Asia and one, the volcano rabbit, or Mexican pygmy rabbit (*Romerolagus diazi*), in central Mexico, where it is in danger of extinction. Wild rabbits are frequently infected with TULAREMIA, which is dangerous to humans. Rabbits are classified in the phylum CHORDATA, subphylum Vertebrata, class Mammalia, order Lagomorpha, family Leporidae.

rabbitbrush, name for shrubby plants of the American genus *Chrysothamnus* of the family Compositae (COMPOSITE family). They grow in arid regions of the W United States and in Mexico and are characteristic chaparral plants. The latex found in many species has been suggested as a source of rubber. Attention was first drawn to them because the Paiute Indians chew the wood and bark as a crude chewing gum. Many rabbitbrushes are good browsing plants for sheep and wildlife. The flower buds have been gathered by the Indians for food. Rabbitbrush is classified in the division MAGNOLIOPHYTA, class Magnoliopsida, order Asterales, family Compositae.

rabbit fever: see TULAREMIA.

Rabbith (răb'ĭth), town, Palestine, probably identical with DABERATH. Joshua 19.20.

Rabboni (răbō'nī), title of respect addressed to Jesus. John 20.16.

Rabelais, François (răb'əlā, Fr. fräNswä' räblā'), c.1490–1533, French writer and physician, one of the great comic geniuses in world literature. His father, a lawyer, owned several estates, including "La Devinière," near Chinon, the presumed birthplace of Rabelais. Early becoming a novice in a Franciscan monastery, Rabelais went as a monk to Fontenay-le-Comte. He studied Greek and Latin, as well as science, law, philology, and letters, becoming known and respected by the humanists of his time, including Budé. Harrassed because of his humanist studies, Rabelais petitioned Pope Clement VII and received permission to leave the Franciscan order and enter the Benedictine monastery of Maillezais; the monastery's scholarly bishop became his friend and patron. The facts concerning Rabelais's study of medicine are obscure, but it is probable that he studied in Paris and at other universities before receiving (1530) his degree of bachelor of medicine at the Univ. of Montpellier. In 1532 he went to Lyons, then an intellectual center, and there, besides practicing medicine, he edited various Latin works for the printer Sebastian Gryphius. For another publisher he composed burlesque almanacs. At Lyons in 1532 there appeared *Gargantua—Les grandes et inestimables cronicques du grand et énorme géant Gargantua,* a chapbook collection of familiar legends about the giant Gargantua. Their popularity apparently inspired Rabelais to write a similar history of Pantagruel, son of Gargantua. *Pantagruel* appeared in 1532 or 1533. His book had great success and he followed it, in 1534, with a romance concerning Pantagruel's father: *Gargantua: la vie inestimable du grand Gargantua, père de Pantagruel.* The third book of the romance, which differed greatly from the first two, was published in 1546; an incomplete edition of the fourth book appeared in 1548 and a complete one in 1552. After Rabelais's death a fifth book appeared (1562); the question of its authorship remains unsettled. Rabelais's novel is one of the world's masterpieces, a work as gigantic in scope as the physical size of its heroes. Under its broad humor, often ribald, are serious discussions of education, politics, and philosophy. The breadth of Rabelais's learning and his zest for living are evident. Rabelais made several trips to Rome with his friend Cardinal Jean du Bellay; he lived for a time in Turin with du Bellay's brother, Guillaume. Francis I was for a time a patron of Rabelais. Rabelais apparently spent some time in hiding, threatened with persecution for heresy. Du Bellay's protection saved Rabelais after the condemnation of his novel by the Sorbonne. He taught medicine at Montpellier in 1537 and 1538 and after 1547, became curate of St. Christophe de Jambe and of Meudon, offices from which he resigned before his death in Paris in 1553. The classic translation of Rabelais is that of Sir Thomas Urquhart (Books I–II, 1653, Book III, 1693); Books IV and V were translated by Pierre Motteux. W. F. Smith made a translation of the five books, with other writings (1893, new ed. 1934). More recent translations include those by J. M. Cohen (1955) and Jacques Le Clercq (1936, repr. 1963). See biographies by Jean Plattard (1931, repr. 1969) and Arthur Tilley (1907, repr. 1970); studies by A. J. Krailsheimer (1963) and Dorothy G. Coleman (1971).

Rabi, Isidor Isaac (rŏb'ē), 1898–, American physicist, b. Austria, grad. Cornell Univ., 1919, Ph.D. Columbia, 1927. A teacher at Columbia from 1929, he became professor of physics in 1937. He is known for his work in magnetism, molecular beams, and quantum mechanics. For his discovery and measurement of the radio-frequency spectra of atomic nuclei whose magnetic spin has been disturbed, he was awarded the 1944 Nobel Prize in Physics. From 1952 to 1956 he was chairman of the general advisory committee to the Atomic Energy Commission. He was appointed (1957) chairman of the President's Science Advisory Committee and served as consultant to many national and international organizations. See his autobiography (1960); *Science: The Center of Culture* (ed. by Ruth N. Anshen, 1970).

rabies (rā'bēz, rā'-) or **hydrophobia** (hī"drəfō'bēə), acute infectious disease of mammals, principally the carnivores. It is caused by a filtrable virus transmitted from one animal to another or from animal to man via infected saliva, most often by biting but also by the contact of torn skin with infected saliva. The virus has an affinity for nervous tissue, traveling to the spinal cord and brain. In man the incubation period of rabies is extremely variable—it ranges from 10 days to 2 years or more. Symptoms are fever, uncontrollable excitement, and pronounced spasms of the muscles of the larynx and pharynx. Salivation is extreme and thirst is great, but the victim cannot swallow water; hence the misnomer hydrophobia (fear of water). Death is caused by convulsions, exhaustion, or paralysis. The only treatment, once the disease manifests itself, is rest and sedation to avoid convulsions. Humans usually develop the infection from the bite of a dog, although cats, foxes, skunks, bats, and many other animals can transmit the disease. Immunization of dogs was successfully demonstrated by Pasteur in 1884; since that time vaccination to protect dogs against rabies has become common. In 1885, Pasteur showed that prompt administration of his vaccine to a human or animal victim would prevent development of the disease.

Rabin, Yitzhak (yĭtskhäk' räbēn'), 1922–, Israeli general and statesman, b. Jerusalem, the first native-born prime minister of Israel. His extensive military experience began in 1940 when he joined the Haganah (Jewish militia) and thereafter fought in the British army. He rose in rank from brigade commander in the 1948 war to chief of staff in 1964, acquiring credit for Israel's military success in the Six Day War (1967). After serving as envoy to Washington (1968–73), Rabin was elected as a Labor representative to the Knesset (Israeli parliament). In March, 1974, he joined Golda Meir's cabinet as labor minister. On her resignation in May, he succeeded her as prime minister and formed a coalition government.

Rabinowitz, Solomon or **Shalom:** see ALEICHEM, SHOLOM.

Rab-mag: see NERGAL-SHAREZER.

Rab-saris (răbsā'rĭs), title of a high official at the Assyrian and Babylonian court, used of the times of Sennacherib and of Nebuchadnezzar. 2 Kings 18.17; Jer. 39.3,13.

Rab-shakeh (răb-shā'kē), Assyrian official sent by Sennacherib against Jerusalem. 2 Kings 18.17–19.8; Isa. 36.2–22; 37.8.

Raca (rā'kə), contemptuous word appearing only in Mat. 5.22.

Racan, Honorat de Bueil, seigneur de (ōnōrä' də bö'yə sänyör' də räkäN'), 1589–1670, French poet. A disciple of Malherbe, he wrote some lyric poetry and a charming pastoral drama, *Arthénice* (performed in 1619), published as *Les Bergeries* (1625).

raccoon, nocturnal New World mammal of the genus *Procyon.* The common raccoon of North America, *Procyon lotor,* also called coon, is found from S Canada to South America, except in parts of the Rocky Mts. and in deserts. It has a stocky, heavily furred body, a pointed face, handlike forepaws, and a bushy tail. It is 1½ to 2½ ft (46–76 cm) long, excluding the 8 to 12 in. (20–30 cm) tail, with mixed gray, brown, and black hair, a black face mask, and black rings on the tail. It lives mostly in wooded areas and usually feeds along lakes and streams. A good climber, it often nests in a hollow tree or climbs aloft for refuge. It has a highly omnivorous diet, including nuts, seeds, fruits, eggs, insects, frogs, and crayfish. When water is available it may dip its food before eating; the reason for this behavior is not known. Raccoons do not hibernate but sleep through cold spells in their dens. Their metabolism is normal during these periods and they wake easily. Adult males are usually solitary; females and young live in family groups. Raccoons have proved highly adaptable to civilization and are found even in large cities, where they feed on garbage. They are a minor nuisance in fields and gardens, but are valuable as destroyers of insects; their durable fur is used for coats and trimmings. The crab-eating raccoon, *P. cancrivorus,* is a semiaquatic, reddish-colored South American species. Other species are found on Caribbean islands. The raccoon family also includes the New World COATIMUNDI, CACOMISTLE (ring-tailed cat), and KINKAJOU as well as the Old World PANDA. Raccoons are classified in the phylum CHORDATA, subphylum Vertebrata, class Mammalia, order Carnivora, family Procyonidae.

race, one of the group of populations constituting humanity. The differences among races are essentially biological and are marked by the hereditary transmission of physical characteristics. Genetically a race may be defined as a group with gene frequencies differing from those of the other groups in the human species (see HEREDITY; GENETICS; GENE). However, the genes responsible for the hereditary differences between humans are few when compared with the vast number of genes common to all human beings regardless of the race to which they belong. All human groups belong to the same species (*Homo sapiens*) and are mutually fertile. The term *race* is inappropriate when applied to national, religious, geographic, linguistic, or cultural groups, nor can the biological criteria of race be equated with any mental characteristics such as intelligence, personality, or character. Races arose as a result of MUTATION, selection, and adaptational changes in human populations. Most scholars hold that there has been a common evolution for all races and that differentiation occurred relatively late in history. Even to classify humans on the basis of physiological traits is difficult, for the coexistence of races since earliest times through conquests, invasions, migrations, and mass deportations has produced a heterogeneous world population. Nevertheless, by limiting the criteria to such traits as skin pigmentation, color and form of hair, shape of head, and stature, and form of nose, most anthropologists agree on the existence of three relatively distinct groups: the Caucasoid, the Mongoloid, and the Negroid. The Caucasoid, found in Europe, N Africa, and the Middle East to N India, is characterized as pale reddish white to olive brown in color, of medium to tall stature, with a long or broad head form. The hair is light blond to dark brown in color, of a fine texture, and straight or wavy. The color of the eyes is light blue to dark brown and the nose bridge is usually high. The Mongoloid race, including most peoples of E Asia and the Indians of the Americas, has been described as saffron to yellow or reddish brown in color, of medium stature, with a broad head form. The hair is dark, straight, and coarse; body hair is sparse. The eyes are black to dark brown. The epicanthic fold, imparting an almond shape to the eye, is common, and the nose bridge is usually low or medium. The Negroid race is characterized by brown to brown-black skin, usually a long head form, varying stature, and thick, everted lips. The hair is dark and coarse, usually kinky. The eyes are dark, the nose bridge low, and the nostrils broad. To the Negroid race belong the peoples of Africa south of the Sahara, the Pygmy groups of Indonesia, and the inhabitants of New Guinea and Melanesia. Each of these broad groups can be divided into subgroups. General agreement is lacking as to the classification of such people as the aborigines of Australia, the Dravidian people of S India, the Polynesians, and the Ainu of N Japan. Attempts have been made to classify humans since the 17th cent., when scholars first began to separate types of flora and fauna. Johann Friedrich BLUMENBACH was the first to divide mankind according to skin color. In the 19th and early 20th cent., men such as Joseph Arthur GOBINEAU and Houston Stewart CHAMBERLAIN, mainly interested in pressing forward the supposed superiority of their own kind of culture or nationality, began to attribute cultural and psychological values to race. This approach, called racism, culminated in the vicious racial doctrines of Nazi Germany, and especially in ANTI-SEMITISM. This same approach complicated the INTEGRATION movement in the United States and underlies segregation policies in the Republic of South Africa (see APARTHEID). See Ruth Benedict, *Race: Science and Politics* (rev. ed. 1943, repr. 1968); C. S. Coon, *The Origin of Races* (1962) and *Living Races of Man* (1965); Margaret Mead et al., ed., *Science and the Concept of Race* (1968); S. M. Garn, ed., *Readings on Race* (2d ed. 1968) and *Human Races* (3d ed. 1971); J. C. King, *The Biology of Race* (1971); L. L. Cavalli-Sforza, *The Origin and Differentiation of Human Races* (1972).

racemic acid (rāsē'mĭk): see TARTARIC ACID.

racer, name for several related swift, slender snakes, especially those of the genus *Coluber.* All of the racers are nonpoisonous, nonconstricting, day-active snakes. The black racer, *C. constrictor,* is easily confused with the constricting black rat snake, or pilot black snake (*Elaphe obsoleta*), which may account for its misleading Latin name. The black racer is satiny black, with a white patch on the chin, and may reach a length of 6 ft (180 cm) and a diameter of 1½ in. (4 cm). It is found in E North America from Canada to Florida. It feeds primarily on small rodents, frogs, and young snakes, and is a valuable destroyer of vermin. One of the fastest-moving snakes, it has been clocked at over 3½ mi (5.6 km) per hr. An aggressive snake, it will bite repeatedly if cornered; however, it can be tamed. The young, hatched from eggs, are pale gray, spotted with brown. The name is also applied to the related indigo snake (*Drymarchon corais*) and to some of the coachwhip snakes (*Masticophis*). The speckled racers are species of the genus *Dryombius.* All of the racers are classified in the phylum CHORDATA, subphylum Vertebrata, class Reptilia, order Squamata, family Colubridae.

Rachab (rā'kăb), variant of RAHAB **1.**

Rachal (rā'kăl), town, S Palestine. Sam. 30.29.

Rachel (rā'chəl), wife of Jacob and mother of Joseph and Benjamin. She is one of the four Jewish matriarchs. Gen. 29–33;35; Mat. 2.18. Rahel: Jer. 31.15.

Rachel (räshĕl'), 1821–58, stage name of Elisa Félix, French actress, b. Switzerland. Exploited by her father in her childhood, she sang in the streets with her sister Sarah. In Paris, showing great promise at the Théâtre Molière school, she entered the Gymnase (1833) and in 1838 made her debut with great success at the Comédie Française in Corneille's *Horace.* In 1841–42, after a sensational success in London, Rachel gained acclaim throughout Europe. Her genius was applauded in all the major works of Racine and Corneille, Phèdre (1843) being her best role. She created the title role in Scribe's *Adrienne Lecouvreur* in 1849. Rachel appeared in the United States with fair success in 1855 (she knew little English) and on this visit aggravated the tuberculosis that led to her death three years later. She revived the great tragic tradition of the actor Talma and has been regarded as the greatest actress of her day. Her death is the theme of a poem by Matthew Arnold. See biographies by J. E. Agate (1928), Bernard Falk (1936), and Joanna Richardson (1957); March Cost, *I, Rachel* (1957).

Rachel, pseud. of Rachel Bluwstein, 1890–1931, Russian poet who wrote in Hebrew. She moved to Palestine in 1909 where she worked as a laborer. Her verse is simple and relates to the experience of Jewish settlement in Palestine and to the countryside itself.

Rachmaninoff, Sergei Vasilyevich (syĭrgā' vəsē'lyĭvĭch räkhmä'nēnôf), 1873–1943, Russian pianist, composer, and conductor. He became known as one of the greatest pianists of his generation, and he was also successful as a conductor and composer. From 1885 to 1892 he studied at the Moscow Conservatory, after which he began his career as a concert pianist. In Moscow he was conductor of the Imperial Opera (1905–6) and of the Philharmonic concerts (1911–13); he twice refused permanent conductorship of the Boston Symphony Orchestra. In 1917 he left Russia and never returned. After living in Switzerland until 1935, he immigrated to the United States and became a U.S. citizen shortly before his death. As a composer he was strongly influenced by his friend Tchaikovsky. Rachmaninoff's music, particularly his piano compositions, are characterized by their dark and massive chords, whose dramatic effects have made them enormously popular. His best-known works are the second (1901) of his four piano concertos, and the Prelude in C Sharp Minor (1892), for piano. Other compositions include Rhapsody on a Theme of Paganini (1934), for piano and orchestra; an orchestral tone poem, *The Isle of the Dead* (1907); *The Bells* (1913), for chorus and orchestra; three symphonies; and many piano pieces and songs. See his *Recollections* (tr. 1934); biographies by John Culshaw (1950), Victor I. Seroff (1950), and Sergei Bertensson and Jay Leyda (1956).

Racibórz (rätsē'bo͞osh), Ger. *Ratibor,* town (1970 pop. 40,418), S Poland, on the Oder River. A river port and rail junction, it also has industries producing machinery, machine tools, and electrical equipment. Chartered in 1217, it became (1288) the capital of a free imperial principality. It passed with Silesia to the house of Hapsburg in 1526 and to Prussia in 1745. It was (1822–1918) the capital of the principality, after 1840 the duchy, of Ratibor. It was heavily damaged in World War II and was incorporated into Poland in 1945.

Racine, Jean (zhäN räsēn'), 1639–99, French dramatist. Racine is the prime exemplar of French CLASSICISM. The nobility of his Alexandrine verse, the simplicity of his diction, the psychological realism of his characters, and the skill of his dramatic construction contribute to the continued popularity of his plays. Educated at Port-Royal, he broke with his Jansenist masters over his love for the theater. His first dramatic attempts, *La Thébaïde* (1664) and *Alexandre le Grand* (1665), were imitations of Corneille. With *Andromaque* (1667), a tragedy after Euripides, Racine supplanted Corneille as France's leading tragic dramatist. Corneille's friends, including Racine's former friend Molière, tried to ruin the young playwright, but the backing of Louis XIV and later of Boileau saved him. Racine's next play, *Les Plaideurs* (1668), wittily satirizes the law courts. His subsequent plays are milestones in French literature—*Britannicus* (1669); *Bérénice* (1670); *Bajazet* (1672), which, unlike most of Racine's plays, dealt with a contemporary scandal; *Mithridate* (1673); *Iphigénie en Aulide* (1674); *Phèdre* (1677). After a concerted attack on *Phèdre,* Racine, in a revulsion against his irregular life, gave up the theater. In the same year he married and was appointed official historiographer by Louis XIV. Mme de Maintenon persuaded him to write *Esther* (1689) and *Athalie* (1691) for performance at Saint-Cyr. These differ from the earlier plays in their Biblical subjects and use of a chorus and in the length of *Esther,* which has three acts instead of five. It is a truism among literary historians that Racine is the most French of French writers. The lesser appreciation of his plays in England and America is due perhaps to the difference between the dramatic concepts of classical TRAGEDY and of English drama. There are many English translations of Racine, among them those of John Masefield, Lacy Lockert, Kenneth Muir, and Robert Lowell. See biography by Geoffrey Brereton (rev. ed. 1974); studies by Roland Barthes (tr. 1964), Peter France (1966), and Martin Turnell (1972); Lytton Strachey, *Books and Characters (1922).*

Racine (rəsēn'), industrial city (1970 pop. 95,162), seat of Racine co., SE Wis., on Lake Michigan, at the mouth of the Root River; inc. 1848. It is a port of entry, and its manufactures include farm machinery, heavy construction equipment, automobile parts, machine tools, floor wax, furniture, and electrical equipment. The first permanent settlement was established in 1834. Improvement of the harbor (c.1844) and the coming of the railroad (1855) brought industrial growth. Three buildings in Racine were designed by Frank Lloyd Wright, and the reliefs at the county courthouse were designed by Carl Milles. The College of Racine is there.

racing: see HORSE RACING; AUTOMOBILE RACING; TRACK AND FIELD ATHLETICS; DOG RACING; for boat racing, see MOTORBOATING; ROWING; and SAILING; and for bicycle racing, see under BICYCLE.

Rackham, Arthur (răk'əm), 1867–1939, English illustrator and watercolorist. He is known for imaginative, delicately colored, and cheerful pen drawings, especially for children's books. Among these are *Peter Pan* (1906), *Alice in Wonderland* (1907), and *A Christmas Carol* (1915). See study by Derek Hudson (1960, repr. 1974).

Racovian Catechism: see SOCINIANISM.

racquets, game played by two or four persons on a court 60 by 30 ft (18.3 m by 9.1 m); it is surrounded by three walls 30 ft (9.1 m) high and a backwall 15 ft (4.6 m) high. The ball, 1 in. (2.54 cm) in diameter, is made of polyethylene with an adhesive tape cover. The gut-strung racket is 30 in. (76.2 cm) long, has a circular head about 8 in. (20 cm) in diameter, and weighs 8 to 10 oz (about .25 kg). A service line is painted horizontally across the front wall a little over 9.5 ft (2.9 m) from the ground, and a short-line is painted 36 ft (11 m) from, and parallel to, the front wall. A line also extends from the center point of the short-line into two service courts. The rules of the game are similar to those of SQUASH RACQUETS. The hardness and speed of the ball makes racquets one of the fastest and most dangerous games. It originated in 18th-century England, probably in debtors' prisons, but was soon adopted by the wealthier classes. Expensive racquets courts were built in England, and racquets was introduced into the United States in the 19th cent. by way of Canada. The United States Racquets Association annually conducts national championship matches. The sport's popularity is limited to the NE United States and certain areas of Great Britain.

Radama I (rädä'mə), c.1793–1828, founder of the kingdom of Madagascar. He succeeded (1810) his father, Andrianimpoinimerina, as king of Merina, a small kingdom on the central plateau of the island. With British aid, he trained his army along European lines and brought (1817–24) most of Madagascar under his rule. He encouraged Western learning and Christianity. His widow, Queen Ranavalona I, succeeded him. Radama is often called Radama the Great.

radar, system or technique for detecting the position, motion, and nature of a remote object by means of radio waves reflected from its surface. The term *radar,* a contraction of "radio detection and ranging," is also used to denote the apparatus for implementing the technique. Radar was developed (c.1935–40) independently in several countries. One of the earliest practical radar systems was devised (1934–35) by Sir Robert Watson-Watt, a Scots physicist. The information secured by radar includes the position and velocity of the object with respect to the radar unit. In some advanced systems the shape of the object may also be determined. Radar involves the transmission of pulses of electromagnetic waves by means of a directional antenna; some of the pulses are reflected by objects that intercept them. The reflections are picked up by a receiver, processed electronically, and converted into visible form by means of a cathode-ray tube. The range of the object is determined by measuring the time it takes for the radar signal to reach the target and return. The object's direction with respect to the radar unit is determined from the direction in which the pulse was transmitted. In most radar units the beam of pulses is continuously rotated at a constant speed, or it is scanned (swung back and forth) over a sector, also at a constant rate. The velocity of the object is measured by applying the Doppler principle: If the object is approaching the radar unit, the frequency of the returned signal is greater than the frequency of the transmitted signal; if the object is receding from the radar unit, the returned frequency is less; and if the object is not moving relative to the radar unit, the return signal will have the same frequency as the transmitted signal. Although most radar units use microwave frequencies, the principle of radar is not confined to any particular frequency range. There are some radar units that operate on frequencies well below 100 megahertz (megacycles) and others that operate in the infrared range and above. Radar improved immensely following World War II, the principal improvements being higher power outputs, greater receiver sensitivity, and improved timing and signal-processing circuits. Commercial airliners are equipped with radar devices that warn of obstacles in their path and give accurate altitude readings. Planes can land in fog at airports equipped with radar-assisted ground-controlled approach (GCA) systems, in which the plane's flight is observed on radar screens while operators radio landing directions to the pilot. A ground-based radar system for guiding and landing aircraft by remote control was developed in 1960. Radar is also used to measure distances and map geographical areas (shoran) and to navigate and fix positions at sea (LORAN). Meteorologists use radar to monitor precipitation; it has become the primary tool for short-term weather forecasting and is also used to watch for severe weather such as thunderstorms and tornados. In 1946 radar beams from the earth were reflected back from the moon. Radar contact was established with Venus in 1958 and with the sun in 1959, thereby opening a new field of astronomy—radar astronomy. Radar can be used to study the planets and the solar ionosphere and to trace solar flares and other moving particles in outer space. Various radar tracking and surveillance systems are used for scientific study and for defense. For the defense of North America the U.S. government developed (c.1959–63) a radar network known as the Ballistic Missile Early Warning System (BMEWS), with radar installations in Thule, Greenland; Clear, Alaska; and Yorkshire, England. See Gershon J. Wheeler, *Radar Fundamentals* (1967); William S. Burdic, *Radar Signal Analysis* (1968); Michael H. Carpentier, *Radars: New Concepts* (rev. ed. 1968); Merill I. Skolnik, *Introduction to Radar Systems* (1962) and (ed.) *Radar Handbook* (1970).

radar astronomy, application of RADAR to the determination of distances within the solar system. A short burst of radio waves is transmitted in the direction of the object under study. The object reflects the radio waves back to earth, where they are detected by the same antenna that sent the signal. The time between sending the signal and receiving the "echo" can be precisely measured by electronic apparatus. Since radio waves travel with the speed of light, the roundtrip distance from the earth to the object and back is then easily computed. This technique differs from RADIO ASTRONOMY in that the celestial object is here merely a passive reflector, rather than the actual source of the emission. The first yield of radar astronomy was a much improved value for the distance from the earth to the moon. Using more powerful transmitters, the distances to Venus and Mercury were also measured, as well as the planets' rotational periods and gross surface properties. Even greater precision can be obtained by replacing the radio transmitter with a LASER. During the Apollo project, special reflectors were installed on the moon; subsequently, by bouncing laser light off the moon the distance from the earth to the moon could be determined within centimeters.

Radcliffe, Ann (Ward), 1764–1823, English novelist, b. London. The daughter of a successful tradesman, she married William Radcliffe, a law student who later became editor of the *English Chronicle.* Her best works, *The Romance of the Forest* (1791), *The Mysteries of Udolpho* (1794), and *The Italian* (1797), give her a prominent place in the tradition of the GOTHIC ROMANCE. Her excellent use of landscape to create mood and her sense of mystery and suspense had an enormous influence on later writers, particularly Walter Scott. See studies by C. F. McIntyre (1920, repr. 1970) and E. B. Murray (1972).

Radcliffe, municipal borough (1971 pop. 29,320), Lancashire, N England. There are cotton and rayon mills and chemical, engineering, and paper plants. The parish church, founded in Norman times, has been restored. In 1974, Radcliffe became part of the new metropolitan county of Greater Manchester.

Radcliffe-Brown, Alfred Reginald, 1881–1955, British anthropologist. He did fieldwork in the Andaman Islands and in Australia. Radcliffe-Brown fostered the development of social anthropology as a science, and contributed to the study of kinship and social organization. See Meyer Fortes, *Kinship and the Social Order* (1969).

Radcliffe College: see HARVARD UNIV.

Raddai (răd'āī, rădā'ī), brother of David. 1 Chron. 2.14.

Radek, Karl (kärl rä'dyĭk), 1885–1939?, international Communist leader and journalist, b. Lvov (then in Austrian Poland); his original name was Sobelsohn. Radek participated in the 1905 revolution in Warsaw as a member of the Social Democratic party of Poland and Lithuania. He was a leading contributor (1906–17) to the social democratic press of central and Eastern Europe. During World War I he lived in Switzerland and was a staunch supporter of the Bolshevik proposal to turn the war into a revolutionary civil war. After the October Revolution in Russia (1917), Radek joined the Russian Communist party and participated in the Brest-Litovsk peace negotiations with Germany. In 1918 he was sent to Germany as a representative of the central committee of the Russian Communist party to help reorganize the German Communist movement. Jailed for a time in Berlin, he returned to Russia and became (1920) a leading official of the COMINTERN. The failure of the Comintern to effect a Communist takeover in Germany contributed to the decline of Radek's influence, and in 1924 he lost his seat on the central committee of the Communist party. Expelled from the party (1927), he recanted and was readmitted (1930). A brilliant writer for the government newspaper *Izvestia,* Radek was also coauthor of the 1936 Stalin constitution. In the party purges of the 1930s he was accused of treason; he confessed (as did his codefendants) in the so-called Trial of the Seventeen (1937). He is believed to have died in a prison camp. See Warren Lerner, *Karl Radek, the Last Internationalist* (1970).

Radetzky or **Radetzki, Joseph, Graf Radetzky de Radetz** (yō'zĕf rädĕt'skē grăf rädĕt'skē də ră'dĕts), 1766–1858, Austrian field marshal. In the war of 1848–49 against Sardinia (see RISORGIMENTO) he won the brilliant victories of Custozza (1848) and Novara (1849). He was governor of Upper Italy (1849–57). Johann Strauss (the elder) composed the famous *Radetzky March* in his honor.

Radford, city (1970 pop. 11,596), surrounded by but independent of Pulaski and Montgomery counties, SW Va., on the New River; settled 1756, inc. as a city 1892. Ammunition, textiles, and apparel are among the city's manufactures. Radford College is there. Jefferson National Forest and a state park are in the area.

Radhakrishnan, Sarvepalli (sŭr"vəpŭl'lē rä'dəkrĭsh"ən), 1888–, Indian philosopher, president of India (1962–67). The main part of his life was spent as an academic; he was a philosophy professor at Mysore (1918–21) and Calcutta (1921–31, 1937–41) universities and also held a professorship in eastern religion and ethics at Oxford (1936–52). His positions in academic administration included the vice chancellorship of Andhra Univ. (1931–36) and of Benares Hindu Univ. (1939–48) and the chancellorship of Delhi Univ. (1953–62). He was ambassador to the USSR (1949–52) and vice president of India (1952–62) before his election as president. He stressed the need for India to establish a classless and casteless society. As a philosopher, Radhakrishnan espoused a modern form of Hinduism that attempted to reconcile the world's religions. Among his works are *Indian Philosophy* (2 vol., 1923–27), *The Philosophy of the Upanishads* (1924), *Eastern Religions and Western Thought* (1939, 2d ed. 1969), *East and West: Some Reflections* (1955), and *Religion in a Changing World* (1967). He was knighted in 1931. See studies by S. J. Samartha (1964) and Kunduri Iswara Dutt, ed., (1966).

radial velocity, in astronomy, the speed with which a star moves toward or away from the sun. It is determined from the red or blue shift in the star's SPECTRUM.

radiant: see METEOR SHOWER.

radiant heating: see HEATING.

radiation (rā"dēā'shən), term applied to the emission and transmission of energy in the form of WAVES through space or through a material medium and also to the radiated energy itself. In its widest sense the term includes electromagnetic, acoustic, and particle radiation, and all forms of ionizing radiation. Commonly *radiation* refers to the electromagnetic SPECTRUM, which, in order of decreasing wavelength, includes radio, microwave, infrared, visible-light, ultraviolet, X-ray, and gamma-ray emissions. All of these travel through space at the speed of light (c.300,000 km/186,000 mi per sec) but differ in wavelength and frequency. According to the QUANTUM THEORY, the energy carried in the form of ELECTROMAGNETIC RADIATION may be viewed as made up of tiny bundles or packets, each bundle being known as a PHOTON. The sun is the source of much radiant energy in the form of sunlight and heat. Heat radiation is INFRARED RADIATION. All types of electromagnetic radiation are reflected and absorbed in the same manner as is visible light. Acoustic radiation, propagated as sound waves, may be sonic (in the frequency range from 16 to 20,000 cycles per sec), infrasonic, or subsonic (frequency less than 16 cycles per sec), and ultrasonic (frequency greater than 20,000 cycles per sec). Examples of particle radiation are alpha and beta rays in RADIOACTIVITY, and many kinds of atomic and subatomic particles such as electrons, mesons, neutrons, protons, and heavier nuclei (see COSMIC RAYS). Radiation is usually considered to travel from a source in straight lines, but its path may be affected by external factors; for instance, charged particles travel in curved paths in magnetic fields. The Van Allen radiation belts consist of charged particles trapped in the earth's magnetic field.

radiation chemistry: see RADIOCHEMISTRY.

radiation sickness, harmful effect produced on body tissues by exposure to radioactive substances. The biological action of radiation is not fully understood, but it is believed that a disturbance in cellular activity results from the chemical changes caused by ionization (see ION). Some body tissues are more sensitive to radiation than others and are more easily affected; the cells in the blood-forming tissues (bone marrow, spleen, and lymph nodes) are extremely sensitive. Radiation sickness may occur from exposure to a single massive emanation such as a nuclear explosion, or it may occur after repeated exposure to even very small doses in a plant or laboratory, since radiation effects are cumulative. Moreover, solar radiation in sufficient quantity is enough to cause tissue destruction; persons unduly exposed to sunlight, such as farmers and sailors, have a far greater incidence of skin cancer than has the general population. Radiation sickness may be fairly mild and transitory, consisting of weakness, loss of appetite, vomiting, and diarrhea. Since even in a mild dose of radiation the blood-forming tissue is destroyed to some extent, there is a reduction in the supply of blood cells and platelets. This increases the tendency to bleed and reduces the body's defense against infection. After a massive dose of radiation the reaction may be so severe that death quickly ensues. This is usually due to severe anemia or hemorrhage, to infection, or to dehydration. Extremely high doses damage the tissues of the brain, and death usually follows within 48 hr. There is no treatment for radiation sickness, although it is sometimes possible for persons to survive otherwise lethal doses of radiation if bone marrow transplants are performed. Exposure to radiation can cause genetic mutation; the progeny of those subjected to excessive radiation tend to show deleterious genetic changes. Persons working with radioactive materials or X rays protect themselves from excessive exposure to radiation by shields and special clothing usually containing lead. Processes involving radioactive substances are observed through thick plates of specially prepared glass that exclude the harmful rays. A dosimeter, a device measuring the amount of radiation to which an individual has been exposed, is always worn by persons working in radioactive areas.

radiator, device used to heat an area surrounding it or to cool a fluid circulating within it. The familiar radiators of steam and hot water heating systems in buildings are misnamed, as they operate principally by CONVECTION, in which heat is transferred by air currents, rather than by RADIATION, in which heat is transferred by waves that do not need air (or any other substance) as a medium for their transmission. Typically they are made of cast iron or of steel, aluminum, or copper. They are usually constructed in sections so that several can be joined together to give a sufficient surface area for efficient heat transfer. Heating efficiency is reduced if screens or shelves or even certain kinds of paint cover them. When steam is the heating agent, the radiator acts as a condenser; heat is given off at the rate of about .5 calories per gram of steam for each degree centigrade decrease in temperature and 540 calories for each gram of steam that changes to water (see VAPORIZATION). The condensate is returned to the boiler where it is reheated to form steam. In hot water systems there is a continuous circulation of hot water. The heat is given off by the hot water or steam to the inner wall of the radiator, from which it is transmitted to the outer wall by CONDUCTION; there it passes off chiefly by convection currents set up by raising the temperature of the air that is in contact with the heated surfaces and to a lesser extent by radiation. Coil radiators consist essentially of long steam pipes; they are used widely in factories, gymnasiums, auditoriums, and halls, being set on the walls or ceilings to conserve floor space. Gas radiators use a gas flame to heat air or water or to generate steam. Electric radiators have an electric resistance unit set in a reflector; heat is generated when an electric current flows through the unit. An appreciable fraction of this heat is transferred from the radiator by radiation. The automobile radiator is a part of the COOLING SYSTEM of the automobile engine. As its operation depends on a flow of air across it, it operates mainly by convection.

Radić, Stjepan, or **Radich, Stefan** (both: stĕ'făn ră'dĭch), 1871–1928, Croatian politician. Of peasant origin, he early became active in politics and founded (1905) the Croatian Peasant party. In 1918 he opposed the union of Croatia and Serbia (later Yugoslavia), fearing Serbian centralism, and favoring a Croat peasant republic. After World War I, Radić dominated Croatian politics, and fought for a federal state structure within Yugoslavia and for Croatian autonomy, as well as for land reform and reduced peasant taxes. Despite the electoral success of his party in Croatia, he refused to participate in the national parliament, thus allowing the premier, Nikola PAŠIĆ, to impose a centralized government on Yugoslavia. Leaving Yugoslavia in 1923, he visited Moscow. By affiliating his party with the Peasant International there, he exposed himself to charges of Communism and after his return to Yugoslavia he was imprisoned by Pašić on just such grounds; his party was disbanded. A temporary compromise with the government was reached, however, and Radić was released from prison and became (1925) Yugoslav minister of education. Resigning in 1926, he returned to the opposition. He died of wounds inflicted by an assassin on the floor of parliament.

radical, in chemistry, group of atoms that are joined together in some particular spatial structure and that take part in most chemical reactions as a single unit. Important inorganic radicals include ammonium, NH_4; carbonate, CO_3; chlorate, ClO_3, and perchlorate, ClO_4; cyanide, CN; hydroxide, OH; nitrate, NO_3; phosphate, PO_4; silicate, SiO_3 (meta) or SiO_4 (ortho); and sulfate, SO_4. The use of these radicals simplifies the naming and description of inorganic compounds, since such usage does not consider the electronic charge on the group. (When IONS are dealt with, electronic charge must be considered.) In organic chemistry, the term *radical* is sometimes used synonymously with *group;* e.g., the group CH_3 is sometimes called the methyl radical instead of the methyl group. This use is limited chiefly to ALKYL GROUPS and ARYL GROUPS; it is usually not applied to FUNCTIONAL GROUPS, such as carbonyl. Because the term *radical* easily could be taken to mean a FREE RADICAL, the term *group* is preferred by some.

radical, in mathematics, symbol placed over a number or expression, called the radicand, to indicate a ROOT of the radicand. When used without a sign or index number, as in $\sqrt{4}$, it designates the positive square root of the radicand, i.e., 2. If both square roots are meant, the radical sign is preceded by $\pm$ as in $\pm\sqrt{4}$. To indicate higher roots of the radicand, e.g., cube or fourth roots, an index number is used, as in $\sqrt[3]{27}$. The radical sign is generally taken to indicate the principal root of the radicand, i.e., $\sqrt[3]{27} = 3$, although any radicand will have *n* different *n*th roots. The term radical is sometimes used loosely to refer to the entire expression consisting of radical sign and radicand.

Radich, Stefan: see RADIĆ, STJEPAN.

Radiguet, Raymond (rāmôN' rădēgā'), 1903–23, French writer. In his brief career he wrote two penetrating novels—*The Devil in the Flesh* (1923, tr. 1932), a study of adolescence; and *Le Bal du comte d'Orgel* (1924, tr., *Count's Ball,* 1929, *Count d'Orgel,* 1953), a sophisticated novel of manners reflecting the disillusionment of the post-World War I period.

Radin, Paul (ră'dĭn), 1883–1959, American anthropologist, b. Poland, grad., College of the City of New York, 1902, Ph.D. Columbia, 1911. He was a student of Franz BOAS and did most of his work among the Winnebago Indians. Radin's studies center on the religion, philosophy, and psychology of primitive man as an individual. They include *Primitive Man as a Philosopher* (1927, rev. ed. 1958) and *The World of Primitive Man* (1953).

radio, transmission or reception of ELECTROMAGNETIC RADIATION in the RADIO FREQUENCY range. The term is commonly applied also to the equipment used, especially to the radio receiver. The prime purpose of radio is to convey information from one place to another through the intervening media (i.e., air, space, nonconducting materials) without wires. Its development is based on the studies of James Clerk Maxwell, who developed the mathematical theory of electromagnetic waves, and Heinrich Hertz, who devised the apparatus for generating and detecting them. Guglielmo Marconi, recognizing the possibility of using these waves for a wireless communication system, gave a demonstration (1895) of the wireless telegraph using Hertz's spark coil as a transmitter and Edouard Branly's coherer as the first radio receiver. The effective operating distance of this system increased as the equipment was improved, and in 1901, Marconi succeeded in sending the letter *S* across the Atlantic Ocean. In 1904, Sir John A. Fleming developed the first vacuum ELECTRON TUBE,

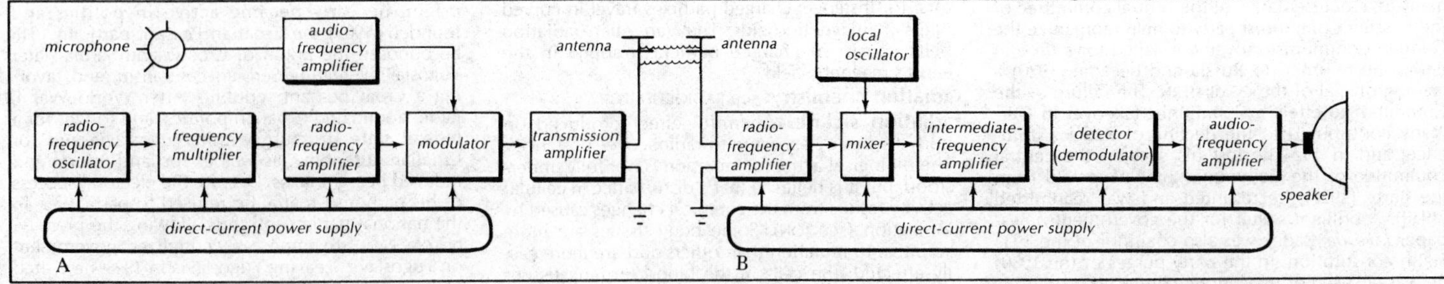

A. *AM transmitter* B. *AM receiver*

which was able to detect radio waves electronically. This marked the beginning of radio telephony— the transmission of music and speech. Two years later, Lee de Forest invented the audion, a type of triode, or three-element tube, which not only detected radio waves but also amplified them. However, it was not until Edwin H. Armstrong patented (1913) the circuit for the regenerative receiver that long-range radio reception became practicable. The major developments in radio initially were for ship-to-shore communications. Following the establishment (1920) of station KDKA at Pittsburgh, Pa., the first commercial broadcasting station in the United States, technical improvements in the industry increased, as did radio's popularity. Particularly in the United States, the radio receiver became a standard household fixture. Subsequent research gave rise to countless technical improvements and to such applications as FACSIMILE, RADAR, and TELEVISION. For the propagation and interception of radio waves, a transmitter and receiver are employed. A radio wave acts as a carrier of information-bearing signals; the information may be encoded directly on the wave by periodically interrupting its transmission (as in dot-and-dash telegraphy) or impressed on it by a process called MODULATION. In modulation, some characteristic of the radio wave is made to vary in accordance with the characteristics of a lower-frequency electrical signal. The actual information is contained in the SIDEBANDS, or frequencies added to the carrier wave, rather than in the carrier wave itself. The two most common types of modulation used in radio are amplitude modulation (AM) and frequency modulation (FM). Frequency modulation eliminates NOISE and provides greater fidelity than amplitude modulation, which is the standard method of broadcasting. In its most common form, radio is used for the transmission of sounds (voice and music) and pictures (television). The sounds and images are converted into electrical signals by a microphone (sounds) or camera tube (images), amplified, and used to modulate a carrier wave that has been generated by an OSCILLATOR circuit in a transmitter. The modulated carrier is also amplified, then applied to an ANTENNA that converts the electrical signals to electromagnetic waves for radiation into space. Such waves radiate at the speed of light and are transmitted not only by line of sight but also by deflection from the IONOSPHERE. Receiving antennas intercept part of this radiation, change it back to the form of electrical signals, and feed it to a receiver. The most efficient and most common circuit for radio-frequency selection and amplification used in radio receivers is the superheterodyne. In that system, incoming signals are mixed with a voltage from a built-in oscillator to produce an intermediate voltage whose frequency is equal to the arithmetical difference of the mixed voltages. The oscillator frequency is controlled usually by a variable capacitor mounted on the same shaft as the station-selecting capacitor, thus permitting equal increase or decrease in the signal and oscillator frequencies and maintaining the necessary constant intermediate frequency for all dial settings. If the incoming signals are above the threshold of sensitivity of the receiver and if the receiver is tuned to the frequency of the signal, it will amplify the signal and feed it to circuits that demodulate it, i.e., separate the signal wave itself from the carrier wave. There are certain differences between AM and FM receivers. In an AM transmission the carrier wave is constant in frequency and varies in amplitude (strength) according to the sounds present at the microphone; in FM the carrier is constant in amplitude and varies in frequency. Constant amplitude is the element responsible for FM's noise-reducing feature, since most noise is manifested in amplitude variations, and FM receivers are insensitive to those. That quality is achieved by including in the FM receiver limiter and discriminator stages whose circuits respond solely to changes in frequency. The ratio detector, which combines the two functions of limiter and discriminator, is often used as it saves space and materials. The other stages of the FM receiver are similar to those of the AM receiver but require more care in design and assembly to make full use of FM's advantages. FM is also used in television sound systems. In both radio and television receivers, once the basic signals have been separated from the carrier wave they are fed to a loudspeaker or cathode-ray tube, where they are converted into sound and visual images, respectively. Besides being used for transmitting sound and television signals, radio is used for the transmission of data in coded form. In the form of radar it is used also for sending out signals and picking up their reflections from objects in their path. Some celestial bodies and interstellar gases emit relatively strong radio waves that are observed with radio telescopes composed of very sensitive receivers and large directional antennas (see RADIO ASTRONOMY). Long-range radio signals enable astronauts to communicate with the earth from the moon and carry information from space probes as they travel to distant planets (see SPACE EXPLORATION). For navigation of ships and aircraft the RADIO RANGE, radio compass (or direction finder), and radio time signals are widely used. Various remote-control devices, including rocket and artificial satellite operations systems and automatic valves in pipelines, are activated by radio signals. The development of the transistor and other microelectronic devices (see MICROELECTRONICS) led to the development of portable transmitters and receivers. Those used in space vehicles are extremely small and use little power. Military applications of radio include the proximity fuse and the radio monitoring system used to detect missile launchings. Among the early communications satellites launched by the United States for improved long-range radio reception were the Echo, Telstar, and Syncom. See H. M. Watson and others, *Understanding Radio* (rev. ed. 1960); Abraham and William Marcus, *Elements of Radio* (6th ed. 1973).

radioactive dating: see DATING.

radioactive isotope or **radioisotope,** natural or artificially created ISOTOPE of a chemical element having an unstable nucleus that decays, emitting alpha, beta, or gamma rays until stability is reached. The stable end product is a nonradioactive isotope of another element, i.e., radium-226 decays finally to lead-206. Very careful measurements show that many materials contain traces of radioactive isotopes. For a time it was thought that these materials were all members of the ACTINIDE SERIES; however, exacting radiochemical research has demonstrated that certain of the light elements also have naturally occurring isotopes that are radioactive. Since minute traces of radioactive isotopes can be sensitively detected by means of the Geiger counter and other methods, they have various uses in medical therapy, diagnosis, and research. In therapy, they are used to kill or inhibit specific malfunctioning cells. Radioactive phosphorus is used to treat abnormal cell proliferation, e.g., polycythemia (increase in red cells) and leukemia (increase in white cells). Radioactive iodine can be used in the diagnosis of thyroid function and in the treatment of hyperthyroidism. Since the iodine taken into the body concentrates in the thyroid gland, the radioaction can be confined to that organ. In research, radioactive isotopes as TRACER agents make it possible to follow the action and reaction of organic and inorganic substances within the body, many of which could not be studied by any other means. They also help to ascertain the effects of radiation on the human organism (see RADIATION SICKNESS). In industry, radioactive isotopes are used for a number of purposes, including measuring the thickness of metal or plastic sheets by the amount of radiation they can stop, testing for corrosion or wear, and monitoring various processes.

radioactive waste, material containing the unusable radioactive by-products of the scientific and industrial applications of nuclear energy. Since its radioactivity presents a serious health hazard (see RADIATION SICKNESS) disposing of such material is a great problem. Methods of disposal include the dumping at sea of concrete-encased containers filled with radioactive waste, and pumping the waste underground into old mine workings.

radioactivity, spontaneous disintegration or decay of the NUCLEUS of an atom by emission of particles, usually accompanied by ELECTROMAGNETIC RADIATION. Natural radioactivity is exhibited by several elements, including radium, uranium, and other members of the ACTINIDE SERIES, and by some isotopes of lighter elements, such as carbon-14, used in radioactive DATING. Radioactivity may also be induced, or created artificially, by bombarding the nuclei of normally stable elements in a PARTICLE ACCELERATOR. Natural radioactivity was first observed in 1896 by A. H. Becquerel, who discovered that when salts of uranium are brought into the vicinity of an unexposed photographic plate carefully protected from light, the plate becomes exposed. The radiation from uranium salts also causes a charged electroscope to discharge. In addition, the salts exhibit PHOSPHORESCENCE and are able to produce FLUORESCENCE. Since these effects are produced both by salts and by pure uranium, radioactivity must be a property of the element and not of the salt. Marie and Pierre Curie extended the work on radioactivity, demonstrating the radioactive properties of thorium and discovering the highly radioactive element radium. It was found that the radiation produced during natural radioactivity is of three types, designated as alpha (α), beta (β), and gamma (γ) rays. These types differ in velocity, in the way in which they are affected by a magnetic field, and in their ability to penetrate or pass through matter. Alpha rays have the least penetrating power, move at a slower velocity than the other types, and are deflected slightly by a magnetic field in a direction that indicates a positive charge. Ernest Rutherford demonstrated that alpha rays are nuclei of ordinary helium atoms (see ALPHA PARTICLE). Beta rays are more penetrating, move at a very high speed, and are deflected considerably by a magnetic field in a direction that indicates a negative charge; analysis shows that beta rays are high-speed electrons (see BETA PARTICLE; ELECTRON). Gamma rays have very great penetrating power and are not affected at all by a magnetic field. They move at the speed of light and have a very short wavelength (or high frequency); thus they are a type of electromagnetic radiation (see GAMMA RADIATION). The nuclei of elements exhibiting radioactivity are unstable and are found to be undergoing continuous disintegration (i.e., gradual breakdown). The disintegration proceeds at a definite rate characteristic of the particular nucleus; that is, each RADIOACTIVE ISOTOPE has a definite lifetime. The lifetime of a radioactive substance is not affected in any way by any physical or chemical conditions to which the substance may be subjected. The rate of disintegration of a radioactive substance is commonly designated by its HALF-LIFE, which is the time

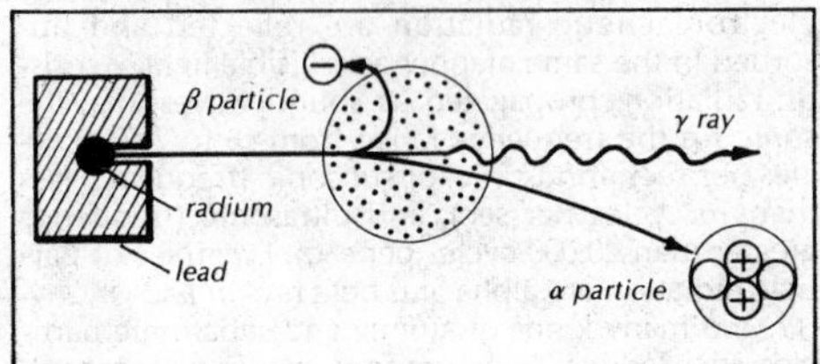

Effects of a magnetic field on the products of radioactivity

required for one half of a given quantity of the substance to decay. Alpha decay reduces the atomic weight, or mass number, of a nucleus, while beta and gamma decay leave the mass number unchanged. Thus, the net effect of radioactivity is to produce nuclei lighter than those of the original radioactive substance. For example, in the disintegration, or decay, of uranium-238 by the emission of alpha particles, radioactive thorium (formerly called ionium) is produced. The alpha decay reduces the atomic number of the nucleus by 2 and the mass number by 4: ${}^{238}_{92}\mathrm{U} \rightarrow {}^{234}_{90}\mathrm{Th} + {}^{4}_{2}\alpha$. In beta decay a neutron within the nucleus changes to a proton, in the process emitting an electron and an antineutrino (the ANTIPARTICLE of the NEUTRINO, a massless, neutral particle). The electron is immediately ejected from the nucleus, and the net result is an increase of 1 in the atomic number of the nucleus but no change in the mass number. The thorium-234 produced above experiences two successive beta decays: ${}^{234}_{90}\mathrm{Th} \rightarrow {}^{234}_{91}\mathrm{Pa} + {}^{0}_{-1}\beta + \bar{\nu}$; ${}^{234}_{91}\mathrm{Pa} \rightarrow {}^{234}_{92}\mathrm{U} + {}^{0}_{-1}\beta + \bar{\nu}$. Gamma rays result from the transition of nuclei from excited states (higher energy) to their ground state (lowest energy), and their production is analogous to the emission of ordinary light caused by transitions of electrons within the atom (see ATOM; SPECTRUM). Gamma decay often accompanies alpha or beta decay and affects neither the atomic number nor the mass number of the nucleus. Other, less common, types of radioactivity are electron capture (capture of one of the orbiting atomic electrons by the unstable nucleus) and positron emission—both forms of beta decay and both resulting in the change of a proton to a neutron within the nucleus—and internal conversion, in which an excited nucleus transfers energy directly to one of the atom's orbiting electrons and ejects it from the atom. It should be noted from the examples given that the product of a radioactive decay may itself be unstable and undergo further decays, by either alpha or beta emission. Thus, a succession of unstable elements may be produced, the series continuing until a nucleus is produced that is stable. Such a series is known as a radioactive disintegration, or decay, series. The original nucleus in a decay series is called the parent nucleus, and the nuclei resulting from successive disintegrations are known as daughter nuclei. There are four known radioactive decay series, the members of a given series having mass numbers that differ by jumps of 4. The series beginning with uranium-238 and ending with lead-206 is known as the $4n+2$ series because all the mass numbers in the series are 2 greater than an integral multiple of 4 (e.g., $238=4\times59+2$, $206=4\times51+2$). The accompanying illustration shows a portion of the uranium disintegration series, i.e., from radium-226 to lead-206. The series beginning with thorium-232 is the $4n$ series, and that beginning with uranium-235 is the $4n+3$ series, or actinide series. The $4n+1$ series, which begins with neptunium-237, is not found in nature because the half-life of the parent nucleus (about 2 million years) is many times less than the age of the earth, and all naturally occurring samples have already disintegrated. The $4n+1$ series is produced artificially in nuclear reactors. Because the rates of disintegration of the members of a radioactive decay series are constant, the age of rocks and other materials can be determined by measuring the relative abundances of the different members of the series. All of the decay series end in a stable isotope of lead, so that a rock containing mostly lead as compared to heavier elements would be very old. The energy produced by radioactivity has important military and industrial applications. However, the rays emitted by radioactive substances can cause RADIATION SICKNESS, and such substances must therefore be handled with extreme care (see RADIOACTIVE WASTE). See Sir James Chadwick, *Radioactivity and Radioactive Substances* (rev. ed. 1962); Alfred Romer, ed., *Radiochemistry and the Discovery of Isotopes* (1970).

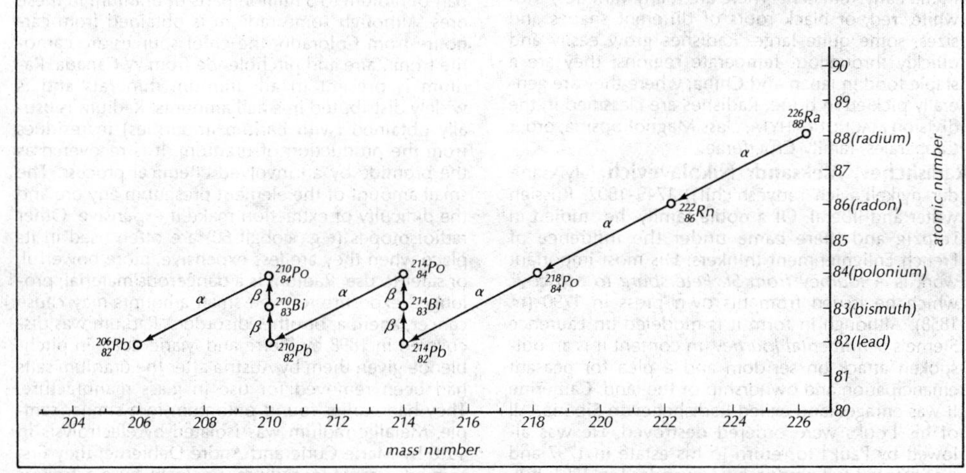

Disintegration series: Radioactive decay of radium-226 into lead-206

radio altimeter: see ALTIMETER.

radio astronomy, study of celestial bodies by means of the radio waves they emit and absorb naturally. These waves are received by specially constructed antennas, called radio TELESCOPES, whose use corresponds to that of the optical telescope in observing visible light. In the most common design, a parabolic "dish" of open metal latticework replaces the mirror of the reflecting optical telescope. This dish serves to focus the radio waves into a concentrated signal that is then filtered, amplified, and finally analyzed using a computer. The radio signals received from outer space are extremely weak, and long observing times are required to collect a useful amount of energy. Therefore, most radio telescopes are mounted so that they can automatically track a given object as its position changes because of the rotation of the earth. Naturally occurring radio emission from the sky was accidentally discovered in 1931 by Karl Jansky. An inexplicable source of radio noise exhibiting diurnal variations was eventually identified as originating from the center of our own galaxy, the MILKY WAY. This radiation is spread over a wide band of radio frequencies and originates in the ionized interstellar gases surrounding hot, bright stars. In these so-called H II regions, free electrons emit radio waves when they are scattered by collisions with the heavier ions. A prominent example of a radio-emitting H II region is the Horsehead Nebula in Orion. Other sources of radio waves within our galaxy are the remnants of SUPERNOVAS, or exploded stars. The most famous example of a supernova remnant is the CRAB NEBULA in Taurus. Because there are strong magnetic fields (see MAGNETISM) in the vicinities of supernova remnants, an additional mechanism is present for producing radio waves. This is the SYNCHROTRON RADIATION emitted by energetic electrons as they rapidly spiral around the magnetic lines of force, instead of simply being deflected by collisions with ions. A third source of radio waves within our own galaxy consists of the atoms and molecules in the INTERSTELLAR MATTER. This radiation is at discrete frequencies instead of over a broad band, or continuum, of frequencies. These definite frequencies are characteristic of the quantum jumps (see QUANTUM THEORY) made by electrons in the atoms and molecules. The first of these "radio lines" to be discovered was the line at a wavelength of 21 cm produced by the hydrogen atom (as opposed to the hydrogen molecule, which is composed of two atoms). The intensity of this line in the radiation from a given region is a direct measure of the amount of hydrogen there. Because hydrogen is a major constituent of the interstellar medium, the 21-cm line has provided astronomers with a means of mapping the spiral structure of the Milky Way. The visible light is blocked off by the same interstellar material in which the hydrogen giving rise to a 21-cm line lies, so that the view of the galaxy is obscured in certain directions, particularly in the direction of the center of the galaxy. Thus, before the advent of radio astronomy, the spiral structure of the Milky Way had not actually been observed but was only inferred from comparison with the ANDROMEDA GALAXY and from other indirect studies. Besides atomic hydrogen, certain simple organic (carbon-containing) molecules, including cyanogen (CN) and formaldehyde (H_2CO), have been discovered in the interstellar medium by means of their radio lines. Radio waves also come from outside the Milky Way. These extragalactic radio sources have great implications for COSMOLOGY, the theory of the overall structure of the universe. Normal spiral galaxies like the Milky Way are only weak sources of radio waves, but certain giant elliptical and irregular GALAXIES emit more than a million times as much radio energy as ordinary galaxies. Such galaxies are usually marked by dust lanes, which are unusual for galaxies lacking spiral arms. Some of these objects can be detected only by their radio emission, but in other cases the position of the radio source has been determined accurately enough to allow astronomers to identify the radio source with a galaxy visible in a photograph taken with a large optical telescope. Other radio sources were optically identified with what at first appeared to be faint blue stars. However, it was discovered that these "stars" had enormous red shifts (shifting of the spectral lines toward the red end of the spectrum) that implied, according to HUBBLE'S LAW, that they were the most remote objects ever detected and that their intrinsic intensities were about 100 times greater than an entire galaxy. These extraordinary objects were named quasi-stellar sources, which was soon shortened to QUASARS. Their nature is still not completely understood. At present, about 10,000 extragalactic radio sources are known. Of the 100 most intense sources, about two thirds are identified with visible objects. Of these optically identified radio sources, roughly one third (about 25) are quasars, and the remainder are radio galaxies. Quasars and radio galaxies show certain similarities that are not presently explained. For example, both show a "doublet" structure, with two regions of radio emission flanking, and in a straight line with, a visible object. In addition to these localized radio sources, there is uniform low-level radio noise from every direction in the sky. This cosmic background radiation is believed to be an indication that the universe began with an explosive big bang rather than having always existed in an unchanging steady state. More recently radio astronomy has discovered PULSARS, radio sources that radiate bursts of energy on and off regularly between 1 and 30 times a second. See studies by J. S. Hey (1973) and Bernard Lovell (1973).

radio beacon: see RADIO RANGE.

radiochemistry, chemistry of radioactive substances (see RADIOACTIVITY). RADIOACTIVE ISOTOPES are very useful as TRACERS to study the mechanisms of complex organic reactions, since even minute amounts of these isotopes are easily detected by means of a Geiger counter or photographic film. For example, by feeding plants carbon dioxide that contains the radioisotope carbon-14 and by monitoring the carbon compounds through the plants' life cycle, the intermediate stages of the photosynthetic process can be determined. A method developed by W. F. Libby uses carbon-14 to date archaeological discoveries and other samples containing organic matter (see DATING). Radioactive substances have also been used to investigate the properties of artificially produced elements and to measure the rates of electron transfers.

Radio City: see ROCKEFELLER CENTER.

radio compass: see RADIO RANGE.

Radio Free Europe, broadcasting complex providing a daily service to the people of Poland, Czechoslovakia, Hungary, Rumania, and Bulgaria in their own languages; founded 1950; privately operated; financed mainly by the U.S. government; headquarters are at Munich, West Germany. Half of its broadcasting consists of news, political commentaries, and press reviews and half of music, sports, and other features. The programs are written, produced, and broadcast by exiles from the five audience countries. The broadcasts originate in Western Europe and are estimated to reach about 31 million regular listeners. Much of its information comes from the monitoring of East European radio stations and wire services and from interviews with travelers from these countries. See Robert Holt, *Radio Free Europe* (1958); A. A. Michie, *Voices Through the Iron Curtain* (1963); Donald Shanor, *The New Voice of Radio Free Europe* (1968).

radio frequency, range of electromagnetic waves with a frequency or wavelength suitable for utilization in radio communication. Some of these waves serve as carriers of the lower-frequency audio waves generated in a microphone by sound. Short waves have relatively high frequencies; long waves have relatively low frequencies. Radio waves are identified by their frequencies, expressed in kilohertz (kHz), i.e., thousands of cycles per second, or in megahertz (MHz), i.e., millions of cycles per second. The waves regularly used in commercial broadcasting have frequencies ranging from 550 to 1,600 kHz. Waves and frequencies above 1,600 kHz are called short waves; those with frequencies of less than 550 kHz are called long waves. A range, or band, of radio frequencies is regularly assigned to a broadcasting station by the nation in which it operates. By international agreement, some of the frequencies are reserved for specific purposes, as for aircraft and ship communication and for amateur and experimental work. At an international conference in 1959 the radio frequency spectrum was divided as follows:

Frequency (kHz)	*Name*	*Abbr.*
10–30	Very low	VLF
30–300	Low	LF
300–3,000	Medium	MF
3,000–30,000	High	HF
30,000–300,000	Very high	VHF
300,000–3,000,000	Ultra high	UHF
3,000,000–30,000,000	Super high	SHF
30,000,000–300,000,000	Extremely high	EHF

radiography: see X RAY.

radioisotope: see RADIOACTIVE ISOTOPE.

radiology, branch of medicine specializing in the use of X rays, gamma rays, radioactive isotopes, and other forms of radiation in the diagnosis and treatment of disease. X rays are the principal form of radiation used for diagnostic purposes. X-ray machines and fluoroscopes are essential in diagnosing bone fractures, tumors, and other abnormalities of the internal organs. Radioactive isotopes are also employed in diagnosis, e.g., iodine-131 is used to confirm cases of suspected thyroid disorder. In radiotherapy, X rays, gamma rays (chiefly from cobalt-60), and other radiation sources are used in the treatment of CANCER and related diseases.

radiometer (rā"dēŏm'ətər), instrument for detection or measurement of ELECTROMAGNETIC RADIATION; the term is applied in particular to devices used to measure INFRARED RADIATION. One of the earliest experiments in radiometry was performed c.1800 by W. Herschel, who observed the heating of a mercury thermometer by sunlight; he was also able to detect heat radiated from hot but not incandescent bodies. E. Becquerel was able (c.1843) to detect near-infrared radiation by photographic means. Radiometers that function by an increase in the temperature of the device, such as Herschel's thermometer, are called thermal detectors. Commonly used thermal detectors include the thermocouple, which produces a voltage when heated, and the BOLOMETER, which changes in electrical resistance when heated. Devices that can, in principle, detect a single quantum of radiant energy, such as Becquerel's photographic plate, are called quantum detectors. Many current quantum detectors are based on the PHOTOELECTRIC CELL. The term *radiometer* is often used to refer specifically to a type of thermal detector invented by Sir William Crookes (c.1874). Because his device was somewhat insensitive and not readily calibrated, it is rarely used today as a scientific instrument. A Crookes radiometer consists essentially of two parts. The first part is a glass bulb from which most of the air has been removed, creating a partial vacuum. The second part is a rotor that is mounted on a vertical support inside the bulb. The rotor consists of four light, horizontal arms mounted at right angles to one another on a central pivot; the rotor can turn freely in the horizontal plane. At the outer end of each arm is mounted a metal vane, placed vertically. Each vane has one side polished and the other blackened; the vanes are arranged so that the polished side of one faces the blackened side of the next. When radiant energy strikes the polished surfaces, most of it is reflected away, but when it strikes the blackened surfaces, most of it is absorbed, raising the temperature of the surfaces. The air near a blackened surface thus becomes hotter, exerts a greater pressure on the blackened surface, and causes the rotor to turn. The rate of rotation provides an indication of the intensity of the radiation.

radio range, geographically fixed radio transmitter that radiates coded signals in all directions to enable aircraft and ships to determine their bearings. An aircraft or ship can determine its line of position and drift if it knows its bearing relative to the radio transmitter and the geographic location of the transmitter. By taking successive bearings on two or more radio ranges the craft can determine its geographic position. Radio ranges are usually unattended; they emit either repeated call letters or steady signals that are periodically interrupted by station identification letters in Morse code. The aircraft or ship obtains its bearings relative to the radio range by picking up these signals with a receiver having a directional antenna, usually a loop antenna. The strength of the signal received depends on the orientation of the antenna relative to the radio range. By varying the orientation of the antenna and observing the changes in signal strength, the bearing of the vehicle can be obtained. When the antenna is driven automatically, the instrument is called an automatic direction finder (ADF). Both manual and automatic direction finders are also called radio compasses, although in aircraft the radio compass usually means an ADF. Another type of radio range called an A-N range transmits two coded signals via directional antennas so that a pilot on one of four fixed courses hears a continuous tone in his receiver when his bearing is correct; if he veers off course either a Morse *A* or *N* is heard depending on the direction in which the error is made. A very high frequency (vhf) omnidirectional radio range transmits a reference signal and another signal that varies from the reference according to the bearing of the receiver.

radiosonde (rā'dēōsŏnd), group of instruments for simultaneous measurement and radio transmission of meteorological data, e.g., temperature, pressure, and humidity of the atmosphere. The instrument package is usually carried into the atmosphere by a balloon (see WEATHER BALLOON); balloon-borne radiosondes reach altitudes as great as 90,000 ft (27,400 m) above the earth's surface. A radiosonde may also be carried by a rocket, in which case it is known as a rocketsonde, or dropped by parachute (usually from an aircraft), in which case it is known as a dropsonde. Instruments included in a radiosonde are typically an aneroid BAROMETER for pressure measurement, a thermistor for temperature measurement, and a HYGROMETER for humidity measurement. Signals from these instruments modulate a radio signal, which is usually transmitted at an ultrahigh radio frequency to minimize power consumption. Power for the instruments and radio transmitter is usually provided by a small dry-cell battery. Radiosonde observations, made as often as four times daily at stations around the globe, provide meteorologists with much useful information about atmospheric conditions.

radio telescope: see RADIO ASTRONOMY.

radish, herbaceous plant (*Raphanus sativus*) belonging to the family Cruciferae (MUSTARD family), with an edible, pungent root used as a relish. It is thought to be native to China; it spread to the Mediterranean area before Greek times and to the New World in the early 16th cent. There are many varieties, with white, red, or black roots of different shapes and sizes, some quite large. Radishes grow easily and quickly throughout temperate regions; they are a staple food in Japan and China, where they are generally pickled in brine. Radishes are classified in the division MAGNOLIOPHYTA, class Magnoliopsida, order Capparales, family Cruciferae.

Radishchev, Aleksandr Nikolayevich (əlyĭksän'dər nyĭkəlī'əvĭch rədyēsh'chĭf), 1749–1802, Russian writer and liberal. Of a noble family, he studied in Leipzig and there came under the influence of French Enlightenment thinkers. His most important work is *A Journey from St. Petersburg to Moscow,* which he issued from his own press in 1790 (tr. 1858). Although in form it is modeled on Laurence Sterne's *Sentimental Journey,* in content it is an outspoken attack on serfdom and a plea for peasant emancipation and ownership of the land. Catherine II was enraged and exiled Radishchev to Siberia. All of his books were ordered destroyed. He was allowed by Paul I to return to his estate in 1797 and was granted full pardon by Alexander I in 1801, but, broken by exile, he committed suicide the next year. See biography by D. M. Lang (1959); studies by J. V. Clardy (1964) and A. McConnell (1964).

Radisson, Pierre Esprit (pyĕr ĕsprē' rädēsôN'), c.1632–1710, French explorer and fur trader in North America. He arrived in Canada in 1651. His journals, first published as the *Voyages of Peter Esprit Radisson* (1885), are confusing documents, often leaving great doubt as to the location of places and the time of events. The first journal tells of his capture (1652–53) by the Iroquois. Another asserts that he made (1655–56) a trip to the West with his brother-in-law, Médard Chouart, sieur des Groseilliers, his companion on the later trips; it is probable, however, that only Groseilliers undertook the journey mentioned in this journal. On the second trip (1659–60) the two men entered Lake Superior and went as far west as the Sioux villages near Isanti Lake, the first white men to enter the region that is now Minnesota. They returned with an immense cargo of furs, which were confiscated at Montreal because they had traded without a license. This episode led Radisson and Groseilliers to transfer their allegiance to the English, and, backed by Prince Rupert, they set sail in 1668 for Hudson Bay. Radisson's ship was turned back but Groseillers's continued, and he established Fort Charles at the mouth of Rupert River in James Bay. He returned to England with furs, and in 1670 both men were back at Hudson Bay, Radisson establishing Port Nelson on the Nelson River. It was thus largely because of their efforts and Radisson's stories of the wealth of the north in furs that the HUDSON'S BAY COMPANY was formed. Later Radisson returned to the French and led a plundering expedition against the English forts on Hudson Bay. He finally (1684) joined the English again and after a long lawsuit was pensioned by the Hudson's Bay Company in his old age. See G. L. Nute, *Caesars of the Wilderness* (1943, repr. 1969).

Raditch, Stefan: see RADIĆ, STJEPAN.

radium (rā'dēəm) [from Lat. *radius*=ray], radioactive metallic chemical element; symbol Ra; at. no. 88; mass no. of most stable isotope 226; m.p. 700°C; b.p. about 1100°C; sp. gr. about 6.0; valence +2. Radium is a lustrous white radioactive metal. It is an ALKALINE-EARTH METAL; in its chemical properties it closely resembles barium, the element above it in group IIa of the PERIODIC TABLE. When it is exposed to air, a black coating of nitride rapidly forms. It combines directly with water to form the hydroxide. It reacts with acids to form the commercially important chloride and bromide. The most important property of radium and its compounds is their RADIOACTIVITY; radiotherapy is used in medicine in the treatment of cancer. Mixed with a phosphor such as zinc sulfide, radium compounds are used in luminous paints. Radium is also used as a neutron source (mixed with beryllium) and as a gamma-ray source. Sixteen isotopes of radium are known, but only radium-226 (half-life 1,620 years) is used commercially. It is a product in the radioactive decay series of uranium-238; it is immediately preceded in this series by thorium-230 and followed by RADON-222 (a gas formerly called radium emanation). In its radioactive decay radium emits alpha, beta, and gamma rays and also produces heat (about 1,000 calories per gram per year). The curie is a unit of radioactivity defined as that amount of any radioactive substance that has the same disintegration rate as 1 gram of radium-226, i.e., 3.7×10^{10} disintegrations per sec. Radium decreases in radioactivity about 1% in 25 years. Radium is a rare metal. Its compounds are found in uranium ores; there is usually about 1 part of radium to 3 million parts of uranium in these ores. Although some radium is obtained from carnotite from Colorado, the chief sources are carnotite from Zaïre and pitchblende from W Canada. Radium is present in all uranium minerals and is widely distributed in small amounts. Radium is usually obtained (with barium impurities) in residues from the production of uranium. It is recovered as the bromide by an involved chemical process. The small amount of the element present in any ore and the difficulty of extraction make it expensive. Other radioisotopes (e.g., cobalt-60) are often used in its place when they are less expensive, more powerful, or safer to use. Radium is a dangerous material; prolonged exposure to even small amounts may cause cancer, anemia, or other disorders. Radium was discovered in 1898 by Pierre and Marie CURIE in pitchblende given them by Austria after the uranium salts had been removed for use in glass manufacture. They had earlier found polonium in a similar sample. Metallic radium was isolated by electrolysis in 1910 by Marie Curie and André Debierne; they first formed a mercury-radium amalgam by electrolysis and then removed the mercury by distillation.

radium emanation: see RADON.

radius, in anatomy: see ARM.

Radnorshire (răd'nər-shĭr), county (1971 pop. 18,262), 471 sq mi (1,220 sq km), E Wales. The county town is PRESTEIGNE, but the administrative offices are in Llandrindod Wells. The terrain is hilly, rising to more than 2,000 ft (610 m) in the Forest of Radnor, an extensive moorland area. The region is one of the most sparsely populated in Wales. The raising of sheep and cattle is the main occupation. There are no large towns or manufacturing centers. In 1974, Radnorshire became part of the new nonmetropolitan county of Powys.

Radom (rä'dôm), city (1970 pop. 158,640), SE Poland. It is a railway junction and has important engineering and machine-building industries. There are also tanneries, food and tobacco processing plants, and various manufacturing industries. One of the oldest Polish settlements, Radom probably originated as an assembly place for local diets. Its first church was built in 1187. Casimir the Great of Poland founded the town of New Radom on the site in 1364. It was the seat of Polish diets (14th-16th cent.), of a tribunal (1613-1766), and of the Confederation of Radom (1767), which asked Catherine II of Russia to guarantee the old Polish constitution. Radom passed to Austria in 1795 and to Russia in 1815. It reverted to Poland after World War I.

radon (rā'dŏn), gaseous radioactive chemical element; symbol Rn; at. no. 86; mass no. of most stable isotope 222; m.p. about −71°C; b.p. −61.8°C; density 9.73 grams per liter at STP; valence usually 0. Radon is colorless and the most dense gas known. Chemically unreactive, it is classed as an INERT GAS in group 0 of the PERIODIC TABLE. Synthesis of radon fluoride has been reported. Radon is highly radioactive and has a short half-life. The chief use of radon is in the treatment of cancer by radiotherapy. It has also found some use (mixed with beryllium) as a neutron source. All naturally occurring radon decays by the emission of alpha particles. The element is found in some spring waters, in streams, and to a very limited extent (about 1 part in 10^{21}) in air. Radon is produced by the disintegration of its precursors in minerals, from which it diffuses in small amounts. Twenty isotopes of radon are known, but only three occur naturally. Radon-222 (half-life 3.82 days) is produced by the decay of radium-226. Radon-220 (half-life 55 sec), also called thoron, is produced in the decay series of THORIUM-232. Radon-219 (half-life 4 sec), also called actinon, is produced in the decay series of URANIUM-235 (actinouranium). Ernest Rutherford discovered thoron in 1899. F. O. Dorn discovered radon-222 in 1900 and called it radium emanation. In about 1902, F. O. Giesel discovered actinon. In 1908 William Ramsay and R. W. Whytlaw-Gray isolated the element, which they called niton, and studied its physical properties. The name radon was adopted in the 1920s to refer to all the isotopes of the element, although the name *emanation* and symbol *Em* are sometimes used.

Rae, John, 1813-93, Scottish arctic explorer. A physician in the employ of the Hudson's Bay Company in N Canada, Rae made (1846-47) a journey of exploration from Fort Churchill to the Gulf of Boothia, which he described in his *Narrative of an Expedition to the Shores of the Arctic Sea* (1850). In 1847 he joined Sir John Richardson's expedition in search of the lost party of Sir John Franklin, the British explorer; later (1851) he commanded a search party which crossed the tundra and explored part of Victoria Island. It was not until his expedition of 1853-54, however, that he found evidence of Franklin's fate.

Raeburn, Sir Henry (rā'bərn), 1756-1823, Scottish portrait painter, b. near Edinburgh. He was apprenticed to a goldsmith at 15 and he showed considerable talent. In 1784 he went to London and there met Reynolds, who greatly influenced him. After living for two years in Italy, where he developed his virtuoso brush technique, Raeburn returned to Edinburgh in 1787. Establishing himself in that city, he portrayed the prominent persons of his native Scotland. His work was in constant demand, and he enjoyed many honors, including knighthood (1822). His portraits number over 700. At its best, Raeburn's work is distinguished by forcefulness, technical finesse, and a direct approach achieved without preliminary drawings. He is best represented in the National Gallery of Scotland, Edinburgh, which contains, among many others, his self-portrait and portraits of Mrs. Campbell, Dr. Adam, and Lord Newton. The Metropolitan Museum of Art and the Frick Collection in New York City and the Huntington Art Gallery in San Marino, Calif., have examples of his work. See biographies by E. R. Dibdin (1925) and J. Seligman (1938).

Raeder, Erich (ā'rĭkh rā'dər), 1876-1960, German admiral. As chief of staff to Admiral Franz von Hipper in World War I, he took part in the battles of Dogger Bank (1915) and Jutland (1916). Appointed (1928) commander of the German navy, Raeder secretly rebuilt the navy in violation of the Treaty of Versailles. He disagreed with Adolf Hitler on war strategy, and in 1943 Admiral Karl Doenitz succeeded him in command. Raeder was sentenced (1945) to life imprisonment as a war criminal but was released in 1955. His memoirs were published in 1957 (tr. 1960).

Rafa or **Rafah** (both: rä'fä), town in the present Gaza Strip on the Egyptian border. The ancient name was Raphia. There in 217 B.C., Ptolemy IV defeated Antiochus III.

Raff, Joseph Joachim (yō'zĕf yō'äkhĭm räf), 1822-82, Swiss-German composer and pianist, largely self-taught. He was a friend and follower of Liszt, who produced his opera *King Alfred* at Weimar in 1851. A prolific composer, Raff achieved a position of eminence in Germany during his late years, but is remembered only for a few salon pieces.

Raffet, Denis Auguste Marie (dənē' ōgüst' mārē' räfā'), 1804-60, French lithographer and illustrator; student of Charlet and of Gros. He attained an individual style in his series depicting Napoleon I and his soldiers. His most notable work was a series of lithographs (1850) of the French siege of Rome. An excellent draftsman, Raffet illustrated numerous works, among them the *Histoire de la révolution française* of Adolphe Thiers.

raffia (răf'ēə) or **raphia** (rā'fēə), fiber obtained from the raffia palm of Madagascar, exported for various uses, such as tying up plants that require support, binding together vegetables to be marketed, and weaving baskets, hats, and mats. It is also made into a native cloth that is exported as rabanna. The raffia palm (*Raphia ruffia*) is crowned with enormous leaves that may be as much as 65 ft (19.8 m) long and composed of 80 to 100 leaflets. The fiber, which is soft, pliable, strong, and nonshrinking when wet, is torn in thin strips from these leaves. After being dried in the sun, raffia takes on a yellowish-tan hue, but it is often dyed other colors.

Raffles, Sir Thomas Stamford Bingley, 1781-1826, British East Indian administrator. He was one of the founders of Britain's empire in the Far East. Beginning his career (1795) as a clerk in the British East India Company, he was sent to Pinang, Malaya (Malaysia), in 1805 as assistant secretary. Through his knowledge of the Malay language and customs he played a large part in planning the capture of Java from the Dutch. He ruled Java as lieutenant governor (1811-15) and reduced the power of native princes. Raffles also reorganized the administration, launched reforms in taxation, abolished forced labor and feudal dues, and provided security of land tenure. Recalled (1815) on the eve of Java's restoration to Holland, he returned to England, where his *History of Java* (1817) was published. While lieutenant governor of Bencooleen in Sumatra (1818-23), he introduced coffee and sugar cultivation and established schools. He secured the transfer (1819) of Singapore to the East India Company and initiated policies that contributed greatly to Singapore's vital role in the lucrative China trade. Raffles was outstanding for his liberal attitude toward peoples under colonial rule, his rigorous suppression of the slave trade, and his zeal in collecting historical and scientific information. He played the chief role in founding the Zoological Society of London and was its first president. He was knighted in 1817. See biographies by C. E. Wurtzberg (1954) and Maurice Collis (1966).

Rafinesque, Constantine Samuel (räfēnĕsk'), 1783-1840, American naturalist, b. near Constantinople, of French and German parentage. After a first visit (1802-5) to the United States, spent in making field trips near Philadelphia, he settled in America in 1815. Rafinesque taught botany and modern languages at Transylvania Univ. in Kentucky. Lauded by some for his theories on the evolution of species, which considerably predated Darwin's, he was criticized for scientific inaccuracy by others, including Asa Gray. His works include *Ancient History; or, Annals of Kentucky* (1824); *Medical Flora . . . of the United States* (2 vol., 1828-30), and *A Life of Travels and Researches in North America and South Europe* (1836). See biographies by R. E. Call (1895) and Huntley Dupre (1945).

raft, floating platform of wood, cork, or air-inflated rubber for conveying goods or people. Originally, several logs, bound together by vines, strips of animal skin, and later rope, formed a flat surface upon which goods and people could move across bodies of water. From prehistoric times to the 19th cent. rafting was an important means of transportation. Rafts were indispensable in the frontier period of American history; on rivers such as the Ohio and Mississippi they were used to convey settlers and transport supplies. Large rafts are still used occasionally on the Pacific coast to float lumber along the coastline. In recent times life rafts have come to replace lifeboats on many vessels. Because they are more easily handled and cannot capsize or crash in launching, life rafts can merely be thrown over the side of a ship or permitted to slide down into the water. They contain distress signals and other emergency paraphernalia to sustain the lives of persons awaiting rescue.

Ragau (rā'gô), variant of REU.

Ragaz, Bad (bät rä'gäts), town (1970 pop. 3,173), St. Gall canton, E Switzerland, at the confluence of the Rhine and Tamina rivers. It is a spa, with hot mineral waters conducted from the ancient springs of Pfäfers, a village c.2 mi (3 km) to the south.

Rages (rā'jēz) or **Rhagae** (rā'jē), ancient and medieval city of Persia, located on the site of modern-day RAY, N Iran, a suburb of Tehran. Rages is mentioned in the Avesta and in the inscriptions at Behistun. Because it controlled the NE Persian trade route, it was occupied by the Parthians and the Arabs. It flourished under the Seljuk Turks. Fierce religious conflict between Sunni and Shiite Muslims resulted in the destruction of much of the city in 1186; further damage was done by the Mongols in 1220, and by 1400 the city was deserted. There are ruins of walls and towers at the site. The city was the scene of some of the principal events in the Old Testament book of Tobit.

ragged robin: see PINK.

Raglan, Fitzroy James Henry Somerset, 1st **Baron,** 1788-1855, British general. He entered the army in 1804 and was made (1814) a lieutenant colonel for his services on the duke of Wellington's staff in the Peninsular War. He was secretary of the embassy in Paris when Napoleon reentered Paris (1815), and he lost an arm at the battle of Waterloo. Raglan became secretary to Wellington in 1818, retaining that position until the latter's death (1852) when Raglan succeeded him as master general of ordnance. He was raised to the peerage in the same year. As commander of the British force in the CRIMEAN WAR, Raglan again showed himself a brave officer and was made field marshal after the battle of Inkerman. However, he was handicapped by his joint command with the French commander, Marshal Saint-Arnaud, by weather conditions, and by the inefficiency of government departments and became the object of bitter criticism because of slow military progress and the sufferings of the troops. The failure of the attack on Sevastopol hastened his death from disease before the end of the war. The raglan, an overcoat in which the sleeves go directly to the neck without shoulder seams, was named for Lord Raglan. See Christopher Hibbert, *The Destruction of Lord Raglan* (1961, repr. 1963).

Ragnarok (räg'nərŏk''), in Norse mythology, the doom of the gods. According to prophecy the end of the world would follow a severe ice age, in which human civilization would be destroyed. Then the gods of Asgard, led by Odin, would clash with the devastating forces of evil and chaos, led by Loki and the giants. After a fierce battle the universe itself would be destroyed by fire and a new golden age would appear, ruled by the surviving gods, including Balder. See GERMANIC RELIGION.

ragtime: see JAZZ.

Raguel (rāgyo͞o'əl). **1** Same as JETHRO. **2** Father-in-law of Tobias in the book of Tobit.

Ragusa (rägo͞o'zä), city (1971 pop. 59,509), capital of Ragusa prov., SE Sicily, Italy. Petroleum, asphalt, cheese, and plastics are produced in the city. Nearby is the site of the ancient town of Hybla Heraea.

Ragusa: see DUBROVNIK, Yugoslavia.

ragweed, any plant of the genus *Ambrosia*, coarse, weedy herbs belonging to the family Compositae (COMPOSITE family), most of which are native to America. They have inconspicuous greenish flowers and soft subdivided leaves. Ragweeds are regarded as especially troublesome because their pollen is acknowledged as the primary cause of hay fever—especially the pollen of *A. artemisiifolia* (common ragweed) and *A. trifida* (great ragweed), the two most prevalent species in North America. The leaves of the common ragweed were formerly used as an astringent and hemostatic; they sometimes impart a bitter taste to milk if eaten by cattle. One variety (*elatior*) of this species has become widely naturalized in Europe. Ragweeds are classified in the division MAGNOLIOPHYTA, class Magnoliopsida, order Asterales, family Compositae.

ragwort: see GROUNDSEL.

Rahab (rā'hăb), in the Bible. **1** Harlot of Jericho whose protection of Joshua's two spies saved both her and her family from destruction. She may be the same as the woman mentioned in the Gospel genealogy as Rachab. Joshua 2; Mat. 1.5. **2** Monster, similar to a dragon. Isa. 51.9. The name is sometimes translated. Isa. 30.7; Job 26.12.

Raham (rā'hăm), Judahite. 1 Chron. 2.44.

Rahel (rā'hĕl), variant of RACHEL.

Rahimyar-Khan (rəhēm'yər-khän), city (1972 metropolitan area est. pop. 130,000), E central Pakistan, on the Karachi-Lahore railroad. It is a market for food grains and hides.

Rahman, Mujibur: see MUJIBUR RAHMAN.

Rahman, Tunku Abdul (to͝on'ko͞o äb'do͝ol rä'män), 1903–73, Malaysian political leader. A prince, he was the fifth son of Sultan Abdul Halim Shah of Kedah and was educated in England at Cambridge. Rahman entered the Kedah state civil service in 1931. In 1945 he helped found the United Malay National Organization, a nationalist political party of which he was president (1952–55). In 1955, after the Federation of Malaya's first elections, he was named chief minister; he vigorously opposed the Communist guerrillas in Malaya. When Malaya became independent on Aug. 31, 1957, Rahman was elected the country's first prime minister. An influential statesman in Southeast Asia, Rahman in 1961 put forward the plan for the Federation of Malaysia, approved in 1963. He retired as prime minister in 1970.

Rahway (rô'wā), industrial city (1970 pop. 29,114), Union co., NE N.J., on the Rahway River; settled c.1720 as part of Elizabethtown, inc. 1858. Chemicals, pharmaceuticals, and vacuum cleaners are among the city's manufactures. The British were routed in skirmishes there in 1777. One of the signers of the Declaration of Independence and 42 Revolutionary soldiers are buried in the Rahway cemetery.

Raiatea (rä"yätā'ä), volcanic island (1967 est. pop. 6,200), 92 sq mi (238 sq km), South Pacific, largest and most important of the Leeward group of the SOCIETY ISLANDS, FRENCH POLYNESIA. The island is mountainous, with Mt. Temehani (3,389 ft/1,033 m) the highest peak. Uturoa is the chief port and seat of government of the Leeward Islands; it has a fruit cannery, a government hospital, and a wireless station. Raiatea's chief products are copra, oranges, tobacco, kapok, and vanilla. Raiatea is believed to be the ancient Polynesian Maraiki, the religious and cultural center from which migrations to Hawaii, the Cook Islands, and New Zealand began c.600 years ago. The Maori of New Zealand still regard Raiatea as a venerable seat of learning.

Raibolini, Francesco: see FRANCIA.

Raichur (rī'cho͝or), town (1971 pop. 79,519), Karnataka state, S central India. It is a district administrative center and a market for sesame, sorghum, cotton, pulses, and chilies. Copper and iron mines are nearby. An inscription on the old fort at Raichur states that it was built in 1294. The area around the town was frequently a battleground in early Indian history.

Raiffeisen, Friedrich Wilhelm (frē'drĭkh vĭl'hĕlm rīf'ī"zən), 1818–88, German leader in the cooperative movement. Between 1845 and 1865 he was mayor of several German towns. After the agricultural crisis of 1846–47 Raiffeisen came to the conclusion that the chief need of the peasant was for credit. He used his own limited fortune to start a system of rural credit cooperatives and banks; in 1872 he founded a regional cooperative bank and in 1876 a national one; in 1877 he unified the entire system. It was an early form of CREDIT UNION.

Raikes, Robert (rāks), 1735–1811, English philanthropist. In 1780 he organized a SUNDAY SCHOOL, primarily for poor children, who were taught to read and to spell to enable them to read the Bible. The Raikes system spread rapidly through England and he became known as the founder of Sunday schools, although others had been concerned with similar undertakings. Raikes gave his project publicity in the Gloucester *Journal,* which he had inherited from his father. See biography by J. H. Harris (1899).

rail, common name for some members of the large family Rallidae, marsh birds that include the gallinule and the COOT, two specialized rails. Rails are cosmopolitan in distribution, except in polar regions. Although migratory, they have small wings and are weak fliers, escaping danger by concealment rather than flight. They are protectively colored in drab browns and reds and have extremely slender bodies (whence the expression "thin as a rail") and strong legs, enabling them to dart through thick marsh vegetation undetected. Rails, also called mud hens or marsh hens, are omnivorous, hunting their food at nightfall. They may be divided into two major types: the long-billed rails, which include the Virginia (*Rallus limicola*), king, clapper, and water rails; and those with short, conical bills, including the sora (*Porzana carolina*), yellow, and black rails (called crakes in Europe.) Gallinules are rails that have webbed toes; they are more aquatic and less timid than those members of the family specifically called rails. They have bright forehead shields and are widespread in temperate and tropical regions. The common American gallinule, *Gallinula chloropus,* and the similar Eurasian moorhen are drab in color; the gaudier purple gallinule, *Porphyrula martinica,* found from Texas to Ecuador, has blue-green plumage and yellow legs. Fifteen species of extinct flightless rails are known; recently a flightless gallinule (genus *Notornis*) was rediscovered in New Zealand. The rails are all considered good game birds and are perhaps the most widely distributed of all the avian families. Rails are classified in the phylum CHORDATA, subphylum Vertebrata, class Aves, order Gruiformes, family Rallidae.

railroad or **railway,** form of transportation most commonly consisting of steel rails, called tracks, on which freight cars, passenger cars, and other rolling stock are drawn by one LOCOMOTIVE or more. However, there are other types of railways, including those whose units consist of single self-propelled cars, cable-drawn railways used to ascend steep grades, and monorails whose cars are usually propelled along a single rail. As early as 1556, Georgius AGRICOLA, in his book on minerals, *De re metallica,* mentioned a mining railway running on wooden poles. The replacement of wooden poles by cast-iron rails in the late 18th cent. and the development by Richard TREVITHICK in 1804 of a locomotive capable of heavy haulage (20 tons) prepared the railroad for uses other than mining. But it was not until 1825 that steam-powered freight and passenger service started on the Stockton and Darlington Railway in England. In the United States, as in England, the first railroads, employing horse-drawn wagons, were used to haul minerals. The earliest such railroad, built from Quincy, Mass., to the Neponset River, dates from 1826, and in the next year another was built in Pennsylvania from the coal mines in Carbon co. to the Lehigh River. In 1829 two locomotives were imported from England, but they were found to be too heavy for the existing tracks. Thereafter, locomotives suited to the American railway were produced domestically; Matthias BALDWIN of Philadelphia soon took the lead in building them. The BALTIMORE & OHIO RR began operation in 1828 with horse-drawn cars, but after the successful run (1830) of the *Tom Thumb,* a locomotive built by Peter COOPER, steam power was used. While the stagecoach type of railroad car was giving way to the square type in the 1830s, many short-run railroads began to appear throughout the United States. The big cities on the Atlantic Coast became the nerve centers, while inland points were readily connected with one another. Only the ERIE RR was projected on a grand scale. Because of the long distances involved, the United States and Russia had sleeping cars earlier than other countries. A type of sleeping car containing three tiers of berths on one side of the coach appeared in 1836 on the Cumberland Railway's run between Philadelphia and Harrisburg. Sleeping cars of a more modern type were patented (1856) by George M. PULLMAN and soon put in operation. Separate compartments in cars first appeared in Europe in 1873 and in the United States in 1883. Cast iron proved too brittle in railway construction and was gradually replaced by wrought iron, which in turn, by 1863, was generally replaced by steel. The first all-steel car had appeared in 1859. In the United States a turnpike era and then a canal era had immediately preceded the coming of the railroads, which proved to be fast, direct, and reliable in all weather. After 1830 the railroads grew so quickly that within a decade their mileage surpassed that of the canals. The Atlantic Coast was connected with the Great Lakes in 1850, with Chicago in 1853, and with the western side of the Mississippi in 1856. Two acts of Congress (1862 and 1864) initiated the building of the first transcontinental railroad: the UNION PACIFIC RR built westward from Nebraska and the Central Pacific RR built eastward from California; the two met at Promontory Point, Utah, on May 10, 1869. For many years railroad tracks had varied in width, so that cars could not pass from one line to another. However, in the mid-1880s a standard gauge of 4 ft 8 1/2 in. (1.44 m) was adopted, mainly because the transcontinental railroad had, on Federal orders, used such a width for its tracks. Cars had also differed in design; in 1867 the car builders organized to plan standardized cars. George WESTINGHOUSE patented his air brake in 1872, but not until 1884 were all passenger cars provided with such equipment, and not until 1887 were air brakes being added to freight cars. Electric light, from power provided by storage batteries, was first used by a railroad in 1881 in England on the London, Brighton, and South Coast Railway. Automatic couplers were first added to cars in 1887; such equipment was in use on nearly all railroads in the country within little more than a decade. Subsequent developments included the introduction of steam heat (water was heated in the locomotive and conducted to the passenger cars through pipes) and the construction of refrigerator freight cars; large-scale use of such cars, originally cooled by salted ice, began in 1887. Subsequent years saw the development of mechanical refrigeration. In 1887 the INTERSTATE COMMERCE COMMISSION (ICC) was established to cope with abuses resulting in part from the rapid expansion of the railroads, whose steadily increasing political power, excessive rates, and REBATE policy caused much popular discontent. Overexpansion and unsound financing of the railroads had affected the national economy, contributing to several depressions, starting with the Panic of 1837, which was precipitated by the collapse of the railroad boom in England. During the turnpike- and canal-building booms the Federal and state governments had done much of the financing; consequently, during the panic many states found it necessary to repudiate the debts thus incurred. That experience discouraged government participation in the railroad boom that was just beginning and accounted in large part for private instead of public ownership of railroads in the United States. Growing sectionalism and the conflict between the North and the South before the Civil War had tended to block large-scale projects (e.g., that of Asa WHITNEY), but the war itself gave tremendous impetus to railroads (e.g., the PENNSYLVANIA RR), which aided in the transportation of troops and supplies. After the Civil War the great battles of the railway financiers began. Cornelius VANDERBILT consolidated the NEW YORK CENTRAL RR system, but he, like others—e.g., Jay GOULD, Daniel DREW, and James FISK—was accused of acting with complete disregard for the American public. The 1880s saw the revival of Southern railway construction and the last period of feverish expansion, attributable in part to such financiers as James J. HILL and Henry VILLARD; one of the greatest financial battles over American railways was fought by Hill and Edward H. HARRIMAN. For years the ICC sought to establish adequate controls over the railroads but lacked the necessary power. Its authority was accordingly increased by additional legislation until, in 1906, the Hepburn Act gave it, among other powers, that of fixing rates. Subsequent acts further expanded Federal regulatory powers. In 1917 the Federal government took over the railroads for the duration of World War I. Although the Transportation Act of 1920 returned the railroads to their private owners, it also granted the ICC general control over the lines, including the right to mediate labor disputes, which had become an important factor. Organization of railway labor began with the unionization (1864) of locomotive engineers; by 1900 railroad personnel was organized on an almost nationwide basis. The many unions were headed by the Big Four—the brotherhoods of the engineers, the firemen and enginemen, the conductors, and the trainmen. After 1920 the railroads failed to recapture their former prosperity largely because of added competition from the automobile, the bus, long-distance trucking, oil pipelines, and the airplane. Further improvements, including the widespread introduction in the 1930s of diesel power on long-distance passenger routes and the electrification of heavily traveled urban lines, still failed to revive the industry. Only for a brief period during World War II, when gasoline rationing forced many travellers to abandon the use of their cars, did railroads increase their passenger traffic. After the war, railroad companies tried to maintain their gains through the introduction of air conditioning and lighter, faster, more streamlined cars, built of steel and aluminum. In spite of the changes, however, business, especially passenger travel, continued to decline. By 1951 total American rail mileage had fallen below that of 1906. Railroad companies claimed deficits in their passenger service for every year from the end of World War II until the 1970s. Moreover, the shrinkage in revenue was aggravated by serious labor problems, especially disputes over "featherbedding" and other allegedly archaic work rules. To solve their difficulties the railroads first turned to large-scale consolidation. With the approval of the ICC, many competing lines merged, and hundreds of unprofitable short-run lines were discontinued. The consolidation movement reached its peak with the merger (1968) of the Pennsylvania and New York Central railroads, to create the Penn Central RR, by far the largest American railway in mileage, assets, and revenue. Consolidation, however, proved to be only a temporary solution, and after the huge Penn Central filed a bankruptcy petition (1970) many people came to believe that some form of direct government assistance would be the only real answer to the problems of the railroads. Many rail lines, in fact, made appeals for subsidies from public funds, and growing concern was shown by the Federal government for solving the problem. At that time some questions of ecology and convenience were working in favor of the railways. By the 1960s concern over air pollution caused by automobile use, overcrowding of highways and airports, and the inconvenient out-of-town location of many large airports caused many people to call for government support of large-scale railroad passenger service. Finally, by terms of the Rail Passenger Service Act (1970), a National Railroad Passenger Corp. was created to take over and operate virtually all intercity passenger rail lines in the United States. Known as AMTRAK, the quasi-public agency reduced the number of intercity passenger trains by one half in its first year of operation, retaining service only in areas of high-density travel. The modern railroad industry has been helped by many technological developments, especially in the area of freight service. Containers that adapt to truck, ship, or train travel, multilevel rack trains that carry up to 15 automobiles each, and piggyback carriers that allow trains to carry fully loaded trucks have all contributed to the modernization of freight service. Thus, while rail freight haulage has declined relative to trucks, airplanes, and other forms of transport, it has still managed to rise in absolute terms and maintain steady profits. Perhaps the most important technological development in passenger service is the creation of high-speed intercity railroads. The most famous such line is Japan's Tokyo-Osaka Railway, whose trains reach a maximum speed of 130 mi (209 km) per hr. Other nations with important railway lines include Great Britain, whose well-integrated railroad system, built mostly with private capital, was amalgamated into four lines by the Railway Act of 1921 and finally nationalized in 1948. In Canada, the promise of a transcontinental railroad was a major impetus to confederation (see CANADIAN PACIFIC RAILWAY). Railroads in France date from 1827, and after the 1840s France had one of the largest railroad systems in Europe. The first German railroad, running from Nuremberg to Furth, began operation in 1835. Soon Germany had a well-developed system, and by the beginning of the 20th cent. a majority of its railroads were owned by the state. By 1922 the entire system was under state control. The first monorail line began operation (1899) in Elberfeld-Barmen (now Wuppertal), Germany. In most other European countries, railroads date from about the middle of the 19th cent. and have come increasingly under government ownership and operation. In the Soviet Union railroad construction, also begun in the mid-19th cent., received a great stimulus following the 1917 revolution, when railroads were first extended into Siberia. British capital and American engineering skill laid the basis for many of the railroads of South America. Railroads of historical importance have included the Baghdad Railway, the Trans-Caspian RR, the Chinese Eastern Railway, the Transandine Railway, and the Trans-Siberian RR. See C. J. Allen, *Modern Railways* (1959); J. F. Stover, *The Life and Decline of American Railroads* (1970); Paul Hastings, *Railroads: An International History* (1972).

Raimar, Freimund: see RÜCKERT, FRIEDRICH.

Raimondi, Marcantonio (märkäntô'nyō rīmôn'dē), b. c.1480, d. before c.1534, Italian engraver. In Venice he was influenced by Dürer to such an extent that he plagiarized the German master's series, *Life of the Virgin* and the *Passion.* It is said that Dürer complained to the Venetian senate. Raimondi's art of imitation was appreciated more by Raphael, who selected him to copy his designs and paintings. Thus under Raphael's supervision (1510-20) he became the first eminent engraver of reproductions. He was quite free in his interpretation of original works, when compared with later, more literal engravers. However, his was a somewhat heavy-handed style. Among his most famous works after Raphael are *Lucretia, Pietà, Massacre of the Innocents, Death of Dido,* and *Adam and Eve.* Raimondi made engravings after other artists, including Michelangelo, Giulio Romano, and Baccio Bandinelli. In 1527, during the sack of Rome, he fled to Bologna. The rest of his life was spent in obscurity.

Raimund, Ferdinand (fĕr'dēnänt rī'mo͝ont), 1790–1836, Austrian actor and dramatist. From 1817 he was a popular comedian in Vienna, and in 1823 he began to produce his own plays. Raimund wrote fine comedies of Viennese life, among them *Der Bauer als Millionär* [the peasant millionaire] (1826), *Der Verschwender* (1833, tr. *The Spendthrift,* 1949), and *Der Alpenkönig und der Menschenfeind* (1828, tr. *The King of the Alps,* 1850). Blending humor with pathos, these plays raised the Viennese folk comedy to a high literary level. Subject to depression, Raimund shot himself at a time when his public favor had temporarily ebbed. See study by Dorothy Prohaska (1973).

rain, precipitation in liquid form. It consists of drops of water falling from clouds; if the drops are very small, they are collectively termed drizzle. Clouds contain huge numbers of tiny droplets of moisture. Raindrops are formed when these tiny droplets are enlarged, first by moisture from the surrounding air condensing on them and then by coalescing with other droplets during their descent. From the time they leave the bottom of the cloud, evaporation takes place and, if the cloud is high, the air warm and dry, and the raindrops small, so that they fall slowly, they may evaporate completely before they reach the earth. If they do so, the drops are called virga. Rainfall, one of the primary elements in CLIMATE and a factor of tremendous importance in the distribution of plant and animal life, varies from less than an inch annually in an arid DESERT to more than 400 in. (1,000 cm) where the monsoons strike the Khasi hills in Assam, India, and on the windward slopes of Hawaiian mountains. In the United States the range is from less than 2 in. (5 cm) in Death Valley, Calif., to more than 100 in. (250 cm) on the coast of Washington state; in most of the country the average rainfall is between 15 and 45 in. (38 and 114 cm) annually. Factors controlling the distribution of rainfall over the earth's surface are the belts of converging-ascending air flow (see DOLDRUMS; POLAR FRONT), air temperature, moisture-bearing winds, ocean currents, distance inland from the coast, and mountain ranges. Ascending air is cooled by expansion, which results in the formation of clouds and the production of rain. Conversely, in the broad belts of descending air (see HORSE LATITUDES) are found the great desert regions of the earth, descending air being warmed by compression and therefore absorbing instead of releasing moisture. If the temperature is low, the air has a small moisture capacity and, consequently, is able to produce little precipitation. When winds blow over the ocean, especially over areas of warm water (where evaporation of moisture into the air is active) toward a given coastal area, that area receives more rainfall than a similar area where the winds blow from the interior toward the oceans. Areas near the sea receive more rain than inland regions, since the winds constantly lose moisture and may be quite dry by the time they reach the interior of a continent. Windward slopes of mountain ranges generally receive heavy rainfall; the leeward slopes receive almost no rain. The southwest coast of Chile, the west coast of Canada, and the northwest coast of the United States receive much rain because they are struck by the moisture-bearing westerlies from the Pacific and are backed by mountains that force the winds to rise and drop their moisture. The territories immediately east of the regions mentioned are notably dry. There are thousands of stations throughout the world where rainfall observations and records are made. Included in such records is the fall of SNOW, reduced to its equivalent in rain. Rainfall is measured, in terms of inches or millimeters of depth, by means of a simple receptacle-and-gauge apparatus or by more complex electrical or weighing devices placed where eddies of air will not interfere with the normal fall of the raindrops. In addition to the daily, monthly, and annual totals, the depth of individual rainfalls and their intensity (amount of rain falling during a specific period of hours or minutes) and other pertinent facts are recorded. The need for rain at a particular time and the dangers attendant upon drought brought rain prominently into the religion of most agricultural peoples. Rain-gods and thunder-gods are more prominent in many mythologies than sun-gods, and they have been propitiated in various ways in different cultures. The rain dances of the American Indians may, however, be said to be generally typical of all in the elaborate symbolic gestures and patterns and in much use of drums and rattles (presumably sympathetic magic by imitation of the sounds of thunder and showering rain). Because the purpose is to make the fields bear crops, the connection of such rites with those of fertility is obvious. See WEATHER. See P. D. Thompson et al., *Weather* (rev. ed. 1969); R. J. Ordway, *Earth Science* (2d ed. 1972).

Rainaldi, Carlo (kär'lō rīnäl'dē), 1611-91, Italian architect of the high baroque. He followed in the steps of the great Roman masters of baroque building, Bernini, Borromini, and Cortona. Largely dependent upon them for his designs, Rainaldi developed a heavier and more austere style that was widely imitated. Most of his work is in Rome. One of his first important buildings was the Church of Santa Maria in Campitelli (1663-67). With the assistance of Carlo Fontana, he completed during this period the facade of Sant' Andrea della Valle, which had been begun by Carlo Maderno. His greatest project was the planning of the Piazza del Popolo and the twin churches at the focal point of the plaza. Bernini and then Fontana took over the design of the church at the left, Santa Maria di Monte Santo, but Rainaldi was mainly responsible for the construction (1675–79) of the other church, Santa Maria de' Miracoli.

Rainalducci or **Rainallucci, Pietro** (pyĕ'trō rīnäldo͞ot'chē, rīnäl-lo͞ot'chē), d. 1333, Italian churchman (b. Corvaro, near Rieti), antipope (1328–30) with the name Nicholas V. Having separated from his wife, he became a Franciscan (1310) and was made a penitentiary in Rome. In 1328, Holy Roman Emperor LOUIS IV in his struggle with Pope John XXII (at Avignon) invaded Italy and took Rome; he declared the pope deposed for heresy and set up Pietro instead. Within a year Pietro found his position untenable, and in 1330 he made submission to the pope, who pardoned him and kept him an honorable captive in the papal palace at Avignon thereafter.

rainbow, arc showing the colors of the SPECTRUM, violet inside and red outside, which appears when the sun shines through water droplets. It often appears while the sun is shining after a brief thundershower in the late afternoon. The sun, the observer's eye, and the center of the arc must be aligned—the rainbow appears in the part of the sky opposite the sun. The rainbow is an arc of 180° if the sun is at the horizon, and it cannot appear if the sun is high in the sky. It is caused by the REFRACTION and REFLECTION of rays from the sun: a ray is refracted as it enters the sphere of the raindrop, is reflected from the drop's opposite side, and is again refracted as it leaves the drop and passes to the observer's eye. When conditions are suitable, a double rainbow may be seen; a larger, paler, secondary rainbow with colors reversed (red inside) outside the primary arc is caused by two refractions and two reflections of the ray while it is inside a drop. The "rainbows" of mist, lawn spray, and spray from a waterfall are similarly caused. The lunary rainbow, seen much less often, is usually observable soon after dark following a brief summer storm or shower when the moon is nearly full. Aristotle was first to devote serious attention to the rainbow, but his mistaken explanation of it misled thinkers for centuries. Descartes in the 17th cent. also attempted to account for the phenomenon but the correct explanation of it could not be furnished until light and its reflection and refraction were understood and the spectrum explained. In religion and art the rainbow symbolizes God's promise of mercy to mankind after the Deluge (Gen. 9.13). The Greeks and Romans called the rainbow the sign of Iris, messenger of the gods. The Inca and other Indians regarded the rainbow as a gift from the sun-god. There are fairy tales of searches for the pot of gold at the foot of the rainbow. See C. B. Boyer, *The Rainbow: From Myth to Mathematics* (1959).

Rainbow Bridge National Monument, 160 acres (65 hectares), S Utah; est. 1910. Rainbow Bridge, the largest natural bridge in the world, is a symmetrical, pink, sandstone arch, 309 ft (94 m) high, 33 ft (10 m) wide, with a 278-ft (85-m) span. Located in one of the most rugged and remote regions of the United States, it was discovered in 1909 by an expedition that set out to find the great stone arch rumored by the Indians.

Rainbow Division, nickname of the 42d Division of the U.S. army. The first U.S. combat division to arrive in France in World War I, it participated in the second battle of the Marne, fought in the counteroffensive at Château-Thierry, and spearheaded attacks at Saint-Mihiel and in the Meuse-Argonne sector. Throughout the war the division suffered heavy losses. It later became a part of the National Guard. See Henry J. Reilly, *Americans All—The Rainbow at War* (1936).

rainbow fish: see KILLIFISH.

Raine, Kathleen, 1908–, English poet and critic, b. London, educated at Cambridge. In her poems and in her essays she puts forth the idea that the best poetry is always an expression of the reality of a spiritual order behind the material appearance of things. Her volumes of poetry include *The Pythoness* and *Collected Poems* (1966). She has also published *William Blake and Traditional Mythology* (1963).

Rainier III (rĕnyā'), 1923–, prince of MONACO (1949–). On the death of his grandfather, Louis II, he succeeded as ruler of Monaco. In 1956, Prince Rainier married the American actress Grace Kelly.

Rainier, Mount: see MOUNT RAINIER NATIONAL PARK.

rainmaking, production of rain by artificial means. Until recent times it was thought that rain might be induced by explosions, updrafts from fires, or by giving the atmosphere a negative charge. Research during the 1930s showed that rain forms in warm clouds when larger drops of condensed water grow at the expense of smaller ones until they are big enough to fall; also that in cold clouds supercooled water below 5°F (−15°C) freezes into ice crystals that act as nuclei for snow. On this basis the American physical chemist Irving Langmuir and his associates carried on Project Cirrus from 1940 to 1952 to find ways to produce rain. Three methods resulted. One way is to spray water into warm clouds. A second way is to drop dry ice into cold clouds. The dry ice freezes some water into ice crystals that act as natural nuclei for snow. The third way is to waft silver iodide crystals or other similar crystals into a cold cloud from the ground or from an airplane over the cloud. The crystals hasten the freezing of supercooled water between 27°F (−2.8°C) and 5°F. Overseeding can dissipate a cloud. It is probable that rainmaking hastens or increases rainfall from clouds suitable for natural rainfall. These techniques are only moderately successful; they cannot be relied upon in case of drought. Scientists feel that improved techniques will bring more conclusive and satisfactory results. See B. J. Mason, *Clouds, Rain and Rainmaking* (1962); Utah Water Research Laboratory, *Development of Cold Cloud Seeding Technology for Use in Precipitation Management* (1971).

Rainolds or **Reynolds, John** (both: rĕn'əldz), 1549–1607, English clergyman and biblical scholar. He was a fellow (1568–86) of Corpus Christi College, Oxford, and later president (1598–1607) of the college. He was a leading Puritan representative at the Hampton Court Conference (1604). He suggested to King James I that a new translation of the Bible be undertaken, and he assisted in translating the Prophets for the King James Version.

rainproof fabric: see WATERPROOF AND WATER-REPELLENT FABRICS.

rain tree, also called monkeypod, a large leguminous tropical tree (*Samanea saman*) belonging to the family Leguminosae (PULSE family), the leaves of which fold together in cloudy weather and in darkness. Rain trees may attain heights of 80 ft (24 m) with a branch spread of up to 100 ft (30 m). These flat-topped trees are widely cultivated throughout the tropics as shade trees for such crops as coffee and cacao. Their edible pods are used chiefly for stock feed. The durable wood has a deep, rich color and is used for furniture. Other species of *Samanea* are grown in warm climates for timber or food and sometimes as a source of gums and tannin. Rain trees are classified in the division MAGNOLIOPHYTA, class Magnoliopsida, order Rosales, family Leguminosae.

Rainy Lake, c.345 sq mi (890 sq km), on the U.S.-Canada border in N Minn. and W Ont. The lake, irregular in shape and dotted with islands, is located in rough woodlands. Its outlet, **Rainy River** (c.85 mi/140 km long), flows westerly along the international border to Lake of the Woods, passing International Falls (site of a power plant) and Baudette, Minn. The river is used for logging.

Raipur (rī'po͝or), town (1971 pop. 205,909), Madhya Pradesh state, E central India, on the Kharun River. It is a district administrative center and agricultural-processing town situated on the Nagpur-Bilaspur Railway.

Rais, Gilles de Laval, seigneur de: see RETZ, GILLES DE LAVAL, SEIGNEUR DE.

Raisin, river, 115 mi (185 km) long, rising in S Mich. and flowing E to Lake Erie at Monroe, Mich. After Detroit's surrender in the War of 1812, U.S. troops under Gen. James Winchester, sent to retake Frenchtown (the present Monroe), were crushed there by the British and their Indian allies. The Indians, after promising protection, massacred (Jan. 22, 1813) the remaining Americans, and "Remember the River Raisin" became the American rallying cry to the war's end.

raisin, dried fruit of certain varieties of grapevines bearing GRAPES with a high content of sugar and solid flesh. Although the fruit is sometimes artificially dehydrated, it is usually sun-dried. The culture of grapes for the production of raisins is limited to regions with a long, hot growing season because the grape must remain on the vine until fully mature in order to attain a high percentage of sugar and because enough time must elapse between harvesting and fall rains to permit sun-drying. Raisins are produced from grapes of the European type (*Vitis vinifera*). Most seedless raisins, especially in California, are produced from the Sultanina, or Thompson, variety of seedless grape, known in international trade as the Sultana. A different variety, produced in California, is known there as the Sultana. The Muscat, a very ancient variety, is noted for its flavor and meatiness, but it has seeds and is somewhat sticky; it is commonly marketed in clusters for table use. Raisins of sharp flavor and firm texture are often called currants (although unrelated to the true currant) and are preferred for certain bakery products. The best known of these is the Black Corinth, or Zante, currant of Greece; the variety is grown also in California. Grapes have been dried for out-of-season consumption from ancient times and were early important in Mediterranean trade. Spain, Asia Minor, and Greece were long the centers of cultivation, but in the 20th cent. Australia also became an important producer and California became the leading producer, over one third of its annual grape crop now being used to make raisins. Raisin production was introduced in California by Spanish missionaries in the late 18th cent. and began to assume importance after 1875; although grapes are cultivated over a large area, the region around Fresno is outstanding in the production of grapes for raisins. Clusters of fully ripened grapes are usually picked by hand, placed in trays between the rows of vines to dry in the sun for several days, then shipped to packing houses, where they are cleaned and stemmed by machine. Today most seed grapes are seeded, and many grapes are bleached and dipped in oil to improve their appearance. About 3½ lb (1.6 kg) of grapes yield 1 lb (.45 kg) of raisins. Raisins are valuable nutritionally because of their sugar, mineral (especially iron), and vitamin (B and A) content.

Raisuli, Ahmed ben Muhammad (äkh'mĕd bĕn mo͞ohäm'mäd rīso͞o'lē), 1875–1925, Berber bandit and tribal leader in NW Morocco. His kidnappings of foreigners for ransom created international incidents embarrassing to the Moroccan government. Defeated by the Spanish in 1919, he joined them later against ABD EL-KRIM, who captured him. He is also known as Raisuni.

Rajagopalachari, Chakravarti (chəkrəvär'tē rä"jəgōpä'ləchä"rē), 1878–1972, Indian political leader. He was educated in Bangalore and Madras and admitted to the bar in 1900. Following World War I, he joined the Indian National Congress, in which he rose to prominence. A close friend of Mohandas K. Gandhi, he served several terms in prison for his noncooperation with the British government of India. He was known for his tolerant views, and he accepted the right of the Muslims of India to demand special minority safeguards and even a separate state (Pakistan). After India became independent as a dominion, he served (1948–50) as the last governor general, resigning that office when India was declared a republic. He was home minister in the central government (1950–51) and chief minister of the Madras government (1952–1954). His increasing concern about the socialist program of the Congress party led him in 1959 to found the Swatantra [freedom] party, a conservative group, dedicated to a free enterprise economy.

Rajahmundry (rä'jəməndrē), city (1971 pop. 165,900), Andhra Pradesh state, central India, on the Godavari River. It is a center of the tobacco industry and headquarters of the Godavari irrigation works. The Pushkaram religious festival, attracting thousands of pilgrims, is held there every 12 years. In the 15th cent. Rajahmundry was a fortress town of the Bahmani and Vijayanagar kingdoms.

Rajasthan (rä'jəstän), state (1971 pop. 25,724,142), 132,150 sq mi (342,269 sq km), NW India, bordered on the W by Pakistan. The capital is JAIPUR; other large cities are AJMER, JODHPUR, BIKANER, KOTAH, and UDAIPUR. In the west of the state is the Thar (Indian) Desert, which is sparsely inhabited by pastoral nomads. In the east is part of the upland region of the Deccan, where, with the aid of irrigation, millet, wheat, and cotton are grown. The Aravalli range, which produces salt, sandstone, marble, coal, mica, and gypsum, crosses the state from the northeast to the southwest. Handicrafts are Rajasthan's leading industry, but there is also some cotton milling and cement making. The rail and road systems are poor. Hindus comprise about 75% of the population, which also includes Muslims, Jains, and primitive tribesmen. Rajasthani and Hindi are the principal languages. The state was formed in 1948 from several former principalities of Rajputana. Other small areas were added in 1949, 1950, and 1956. Rajasthan is one of the strongholds of the conservative Hindu Jan Sangh and Swatantra political parties, which are supported by many former Rajput princes. The state has numerous famous Buddhist, Jain, and Mogul monuments. In 1974 the desert region of Rajasthan was the site of the underground explosion of India's first nuclear device. Rajasthan is governed by a chief minister and cabinet responsible to an elected unicameral legislature and by a governor appointed by India's president.

Rajk, Laszlo (läs'lō roik), 1909–49, Hungarian Communist leader. After fighting in the Spanish civil war of 1936–39 he was interned (1939) in a French camp for Spanish Loyalists. Rajk returned to Hungary in 1941 and became first secretary of the illegal Communist party. He participated in the Hungarian underground movement during the German occupation in World War II and was imprisoned for a time by the Gestapo. After the war he was made minister of the interior and in 1948 became foreign minister. In 1949, Rajk was accused of conspiring with TITO and others to overthrow the Hungarian government. He was tried, confessed, and was executed. In March, 1956, the Hungarian government declared his trial to have been in error. See B. S. Szász, *Volunteers for the Gallows* (tr. 1971).

Rajkot (räj'kōt), city (1971 pop. 300,152), Gujarat state, W central India, on the Aji River. Formerly the capital of the Rajkot princely state and Saurashtra state, Rajkot is now a district administrative headquarters and an educational and cultural center. Textiles, hosiery, machine tools, plastics and electrical goods, and vegetable oil are produced. Poultry and cattle are raised nearby.

Rajputana (räj"po͞otä'nə), historic region, NW India; roughly coextensive with the modern Indian state of Rajasthan. The name means "land of the RAJPUTS." Rajput tribal power rose here between the 7th and 13th cent., and the princes resisted the early Muslim incursions which began in the 11th cent. Rajput power reached its peak in the early 16th cent., but the area fell to the Moguls when Akbar captured the fort of Chitor in 1568. From their seat at Ajmer the Moguls ruled Rajputana until the early 18th cent. The Marathas held feudatories in the region from c.1750 to 1818, when it passed to Great Britain. Under the British, Rajputana included more than 20 princely states, notably Bikaner, Jaipur, Jodhpur, Udaipur, and Ajmer. The internal autonomy of many of the states was guaranteed. Most of these states were incorporated into Rajasthan after India gained independence in 1947.

Rajputs (räj'po͞ots) [Sanskrit,=son of a king], dominant people of Rajputana, an historic region now almost coextensive with the state of Rajasthan, NW India. The Rajputs are mainly Hindus (although there are some Muslim Rajputs) of the warrior CASTE; traditionally they have put great value on etiquette and the military virtues and take great pride in their ancestry. They claim divine origin, and they are divided into four groups (Snake, Solar, Lunar, and Fire) and 32 exogamous clans, the major ones being Rahtor, Kashwaha, Chauhan, Jadu, Sisodhiya, and Ponwar. The Rajputs speak Rajasthani. Their power in Rajputana grew in the 7th cent., but by 1616 all the major clans had submitted to the Moguls. With the decline of Mogul power in the early 18th cent., the Rajputs expanded through most of the plains of central India, but by the early 19th cent. they had been driven back by the Mahrattas, Sikhs, and British. Under the British, many of the Rajput princes maintained independent states within Rajputana, but they were gradually deprived of power after India attained independence in 1947. See S. M. Rameshwar, *Resurgent Rajasthan* (1962); Leigh Minturn, *The Rajputs of Kahlpur* (1966); Dasharatha Sharma, *Lectures on Rajput History and Culture* (1970).

Rajshahi (räjshä'hē), formerly **Rampur Boalia** (räm'po͝or bōä'lēä), town (1969 est. pop. 76,000), W central Bangladesh, on the Ganges River. It is the administrative center for a district that produces practically all of the country's silk. In the town are oil-pressing plants, match factories, and sawmills. Rajshahi also houses the Varendra Research Museum, a silk institute, and a university (founded 1953) with several affiliated colleges.

rake, farm implement consisting of a row of straight or curved teeth of metal or wood attached to a bar or frame. It is used for gathering hay or grain into piles; for clearing fields, lawns, and yards; and for stirring and spreading soil. Horse-drawn rakes first appeared in the early 19th cent. but were not used generally until later. Of the several types of modern power-drawn hay rakes, the side-delivery rakes, which gather hay into continuous windrows by a rolling action, are the most popular. These include a reel type, which has raking teeth attached to rotating bars, and a finger-wheel type, which has teeth attached to large wheels. Lesser used rakes include the dump rake, which creates piles, and the sweep rake, which gathers and hauls a heavy load directly to the stack. See Claude Culpin, *Farm Machinery* (8th ed. 1969); Michael Partridge, *Farm Tools through the Ages* (1973).

Rakem (rā'kĕm), descendant of Manasseh. 1 Chron. 7.16.

Rakkath, city, on the shore of the Sea of Galilee. Joshua 19.35.

Rakkon (răk'ŏn), unidentified place, S Palestine. Joshua 19.46.

Rákóczy (rä'kôtsĭ), noble Hungarian family that played an important role in the history of TRANSYLVANIA and Hungary in the 17th and 18th cent. **Sigismund Rákóczy,** 1544–1608, was elected (1607) prince of Transylvania to succeed Stephen Bocskay. His son, **George I Rákóczy,** 1591–1648, was elected prince of Transylvania in 1630. He continued the anti-Hapsburg policy of his predecessors, Gabriel Báthory and Gabriel Bethlen, and like them he relied on alliances with the Protestant powers. In 1644 he declared war on Holy Roman Emperor Ferdinand III and overran Hungary. Peace was made (1645) at Linz, and the emperor granted religious freedom to the Hungarians and ceded territory to Rákóczy. George I's son, **George II Rákóczy,** 1621–60, succeeded his father on the throne of Transylvania but was deposed (1657) as a result of his unsuccessful invasion of Poland. He was mortally wounded when the Turks invaded Transylvania. He married Sophia, a niece of Gabriel Báthory. Their son, **Francis I Rákóczy,** 1645–76, was designated George's successor by the diet of Transylvania in 1652. However, he was never recognized. Having married a daughter of Peter ZRINYI, governor of Croatia, he entered with Zrinyi into an unsuccessful conspiracy against Holy Roman Emperor Leopold I. **Francis II Rákóczy,** 1676–1735, son of Francis I and of Helen Zrinyi, became the leader of the rebellion of the Hungarians against Hapsburg oppression. The outbreak (1701) of the War of the Spanish Succession was followed by an uprising (1703) of the Hungarian peasants, particularly the Calvinists. Rákóczy, at the head of the movement, soon controlled most of Hungary and in 1704 was elected "ruling prince" by the diet. He secured the support of King Louis XIV of France, who sent subsidies and troops. At the Diet of Onod (1707) the Hungarian nobles proclaimed the Hapsburg dynasty deposed in Hungary and set up an aristocratic republic. Rákóczy, however, suffered severe defeats in 1708 and 1710, and in 1711 the Hungarians and Austrians negotiated peace at Szatmar. The Hungarians were promised an amnesty and the restoration of religious and constitutional freedom. Rákóczy, who refused to accept the treaty, fled to Poland, then to France, and eventually to Turkey. He died in exile in Turkey, but his remains were brought back to Hungary in 1906. He left an autobiography. Francis II Rákóczy is a major national hero of Hungary. The stirring "Rákóczy March," named in his honor, was composed (1809) by John Bihari. It was used by Berlioz in his *Damnation de Faust* and by Liszt in the Hungarian Rhapsody No. 15. Playing the march was long forbidden in Hungary, where the tune was used as a national air by the independence movement.

Rákosi, Mátyás (mä'tyäs rä'kōshē), 1892–1963?, Hungarian Communist politician. An associate of Bela KUN and later a disciple of Joseph STALIN, Rákosi was one of the chief engineers of post-World War II Communist Hungary. He became premier in 1952, but was removed in 1953 as a Stalinist. His successor, Imre NAGY, was ousted in 1955 for Titoism, and Rákosi regained the premiership. In Aug., 1956, shortly before the anti-Soviet rebellion, Rákosi was again forced by anti-Stalinists to resign, and he fled to the Soviet Union. He was expelled from the Communist party in 1962 and was reported to have died in the Soviet Union in Aug., 1963.

Rakovsky, Christian Georgyevich (khrĭstyän' gēyôr'gyĭvĭch rəkôf'skē), 1873–?, Russian Communist diplomat. His early revolutionary activities extended from his native Bulgaria through Switzerland, Germany, France, and Rumania. In 1919 he briefly headed the Ukrainian Soviet government. A Soviet delegate at the Conference of Genoa (1922), he was later Russian chargé d'affaires at London (1924) and ambassador to France (1926–27). His opposition to Joseph Stalin's leadership caused his expulsion (1927) from the party. He later recanted (1934). In the public purge trial of March, 1938, Rakovsky was convicted of treason and sentenced to imprisonment for 20 years. He is believed to have died in prison.

Rale, Sébastien: see RASLES, SÉBASTIEN.

Raleigh or **Ralegh, Sir Walter** (both: rôl'ē, räl'ē), 1554?–1618, English soldier, explorer, courtier, and man of letters. As a youth Raleigh served (1569) as a volunteer in the Huguenot army in France. In 1572 he was listed as an undergraduate at Oxford, where he may also have studied before going to France, and his name appears in the register of the Middle Temple in 1575. Little is known of his activities in London, but the verses that he prefixed to George Gascoigne's *Steele Glas* (1576) indicate some literary connections. In 1578, Raleigh and his brother Carew joined their half brother Sir Humphrey GILBERT in outfitting a heavily armed fleet, ostensibly for a "voyage of discovery." Storms and desertions soon ended the project. In 1580, Raleigh served in Ireland, suppressing the rebels in Munster.

Courtier, Poet, and Adventurer. When he returned to England in 1581, Raleigh immediately went to court and soon became a favorite of Queen Elizabeth I. Whether he placed his cloak in the mud for her or not, it seems fairly certain that his personal charm had much to do with his friendship with the queen. As an important courtier he was granted (1583) a wine monopoly, was knighted (1585), and was given vast estates in Ireland. Made warden of the stanneries (the tin mines of Cornwall and Devon) in 1585, Raleigh exhibited a genuine talent for administration, but he had already alienated too many important people to achieve real political power. He was appointed captain of the queen's guard in 1587, an office significant because it required constant attendance on Elizabeth. Raleigh conceived and organized the colonizing expeditions to America that ended tragically with the "lost colony" on ROANOKE ISLAND, Va. He was later named a member of the commission for defense against Spain, but it is doubtful that he participated in the naval operations against the Spanish Armada (1588). Probably because of his conflict with Robert Devereux, 2d earl of ESSEX, Elizabeth's new favorite, Raleigh left court in 1589. At Kilcolman Castle, Ireland, he became a close friend of Edmund SPENSER, whose *Faerie Queene,* begun under the aegis of Sir Philip Sidney, was continued under Raleigh's patronage. After the queen's quarrel with Essex over the earl's marriage, Raleigh returned to prominence at court and was granted (1592) an estate at Sherborne. Later that year he set out on a privateering expedition, but he was recalled by Elizabeth and imprisoned in the Tower of London when she learned of his secret marriage to Elizabeth Throckmorton, a maid of honor at court. Late in 1592, Raleigh's expedition returned to England with a richly loaded Portuguese carrack. Disputes broke out over the division of the spoils, and Raleigh was sent to quell the disturbance, thereby winning his freedom. Barred from the court, Raleigh sat in Parliament. He achieved great notoriety for his connection with the poetic group known as the "school of night." Led by Thomas HARRIOT and including Christopher Marlowe and George Chapman, the group's skeptical attitude and critical interpretation of Scripture won them a reputation for atheism. In 1595, Raleigh embarked on an expedition with the adventurer-scholar Laurence Kemys to find the fabled city of EL DORADO. They penetrated 300 mi (480 km) up the Orinoco River into the interior of Guiana, bringing home specimens containing gold. Raleigh published his *Discovery of Guiana* the following year. In 1596 he commanded a squadron in the English expedition against Cádiz. The next year, on the expedition to the Azores, he captured Fayal without waiting for Essex; the incident precipitated a violent quarrel between the two.

Downfall. Raleigh was made governor of Jersey in 1600, but his fortunes ebbed when he drifted apart from his former ally Robert Cecil (later earl of Salisbury) in the political tempest over Essex's treason and death. He met his downfall upon the accession (1603) of James I, who had been convinced by Raleigh's enemies that Raleigh was opposed to his succession. Many of Raleigh's offices and monopolies were taken away, and, on somewhat insufficient evidence, he was found guilty of intrigues with Spain against England and of participation in a plot to kill the king and enthrone Arabella Stuart. Saved from the block by a reprieve, Raleigh settled down in the Tower and devoted himself to literature and science. There he began his incomplete *History of the World.* He was released in 1616 to make another voyage to the Orinoco in search of gold, but he was warned not to molest Spanish possessions or ships on pain of his life. Raleigh gathered all his resources to outfit the expedition, and he set out for South America with Kemys in 1617. The expedition failed to arrive at the reputed mine, but Kemys captured a Spanish town. Raleigh returned to England, where the Spanish ambassador demanded his punishment. Failing in an attempt to escape to France, he was executed under the original sentence of treason passed many years before. Raleigh was the author of a number of political essays and philosophical treatises and of a body of poetry that was highly praised by his contemporaries. Much of his verse is now lost, and a number of his prose works also appear to be missing. See his poems, ed. by Agnes Latham (1951). See also biographies by W. M. Wallace (1959), Philip Magnus (1968), J. H. Adamson and H. F. Folland (1969), S. J. Greenblatt (1973), and Robert Lacey (1974); A. L. Rowse, *Sir Walter Ralegh: His Family and Private Life* (1962); M. C. Bradbrook, *The School of Night* (1936, repr. 1965).

Raleigh, Sir Walter, 1861–1922, English teacher and critic, b. London. He taught in colleges in India, Liverpool, and Glasgow and at Oxford. An extremely popular teacher and brilliant conversationalist, he is now remembered for his criticism, distinguished by scholarship, wit, and eloquence. His critical works include *The English Novel* (1894), *Milton* (1900), *Wordsworth* (1903), *Shakespeare* (1903), and *Six Essays on Johnson* (1910).

Raleigh (rôl'ē, räl'ē), city (1970 pop. 123,793), state capital, and seat of Wake co., central N.C.; the site was selected for the capital in 1788, and the city was laid out and inc. 1792. It is a political, cultural, trade, and industrial center, with food, textile, and electrical manufactures. The first capitol (built 1792–94) burned in 1831 and was replaced by the present building, completed in 1840. In the Civil War, Sherman occupied the city on April 14, 1865. Raleigh is the seat of Meredith College, North Carolina State Univ. at Raleigh, Shaw Univ., St. Augustine's College, a technical institute, and two junior colleges. It has libraries, museums, a theater, and several 18th-century houses, including the birthplace of Andrew Johnson. The state prison is in Raleigh.

Raleigh, Fort: see ROANOKE ISLAND.

Ralik Chain: see MARSHALL ISLANDS.

Ralston, James Layton (rôl'stən), 1881–1948, Canadian cabinet minister, b. Nova Scotia. In the first Mackenzie King administration, he was minister of national defense (1926–30); in the second Mackenzie King government, he was made minister of finance (1939) but was transferred in 1940 to the post of minister of defense. When his demand that the cabinet invoke military conscription was rejected, Ralston resigned in Nov., 1944; the policy was shortly put in force by his successor, A. G. L. McNaughton.

Ram. 1 Ancestor of David. 1 Chron. 2.9,10; Ruth 4.19. Aram: Mat. 1.3,4; Luke 3.33. **2** Son of Jerahmeel. 1 Chron. 2.25,27. **3** Ancestor of Elihu. Job 32.2.

Ram, The, English name for ARIES, a CONSTELLATION.

Rama, hero: see RAMAYANA.

Rama (rä'mə), variant of RAMAH.

Ramadan (rämädän', răm"ədän'), in ISLAM, the ninth month of the Muslim year, during which all Muslims must fast during the daylight hours. Indulgence of any sort is forbidden during the fast. There are only a few who are exempt, e.g., soldiers and the sick. Because of the purely lunar calendar, Ramadan falls in different seasons. The first revelation of the Koran is commemorated in this month.

Ramadi: see AR RAMADI, Iraq.

Ramah (rā'mə). **1** Town, NE Palestine, allotted to Naphtali. Joshua 19.36. **2** Town of Asher. Joshua 19.29. **3** Unidentified town of Simeon, called Ramah of the south. Joshua 19.8. It is apparently intended by the Ramoth of 1 Sam. 30.27, by the Baal of 1 Chron. 4.33, and by Baalath-beer in Joshua 19.8. **4** Town of Palestine, on the border between Judah and Israel. Ramah is the traditional burial place of Rachel. Joshua 18.25; Judges 4.5; 19.13; 1 Sam. 22.6; 1 Kings 15.17; 2 Chron. 16.1; Ezra 2.26; Neh. 7.30; 11.33; Isa. 10.29; Jer. 31.15; 40.1; Hosea 5.8. Rama: Mat. 2.18. This is possibly the Ramah of Samuel: see RAMATHAIM-ZOPHIM. **5** Same as RAMOTH-GILEAD. The term *Ramathite* may refer to any of the above. 1 Chron. 27.27.

Ramakrishna or **Sri Ramakrishna Paramahansa** (shrē rä"məkrĭsh'nə pərä"məhän'sä), 1836–86, Hindu mystic. He was born of a poor Brahman family in Bengal, and his given name was Gadadhar Chatterjee. In about 1855 he became a devotee of the goddess Kali and lived for the rest of his life at her temple in Dakshineswar outside Calcutta. During a 15-year period of intense spiritual practice he mastered all the types of Hindu Yoga and also had mystical experience through Christian and Islamic worship. He concluded that all religions are valid means of approaching God. Ramakrishna had little formal learning, but his saintliness and wisdom attracted a large following. After his death his teachings were spread by his disciples and by his wife Sarada Devi. Ramakrishna's message of universal religion was carried to the West by Swami VIVEKANANDA. The Ramakrishna Mission, founded by Vivekananda, is represented by a large monastic order in India, devoted to both contemplation and social action, and by centers in major cities of Europe and the United States. Ramakrishna's sayings are contained in *The Gospel of Sri Ramakrishna* (tr. by Swami Nikhilananda, 1942). See biography by Swami Saradananda (3d ed. 1963); Christopher Isherwood, *Sri Ramakrishna and His Disciples* (1965).

Ramallah (rämä'lä), town, W Jordan, N of Jerusalem. It lies in a fertile farming region where olives, figs, and grapes are grown. Ramallah is inhabited chiefly by Christian Arabs. It was occupied by Israeli forces after the Arab-Israeli war of 1967.

Raman, Sir Chandrasekhara Venkata (chŭn'drəsĕkärə vĕng'kətə rä'mən), 1888–1970, Indian physicist. He was professor of physics at Calcutta Univ. from 1917 to 1933. In Bangalore he directed the Indian Institute of Science and, from 1946, the Raman Institute. For his research on the diffusion of light and for his discovery of the RAMAN EFFECT, he received the 1930 Nobel Prize in Physics. He is noted also for his studies of diamonds. In 1929 he was knighted.

Ramana Maharshi (rəmän'ə məhär'shē), 1879–1950, Indian mystic. He was born of a Brahman family in S India as Venkataraman Ayyar. In 1896 he left home as a renunciant and went to Tiruvannamalai, the site of Arunachala, the sacred mountain of Shiva. Two years later he took up permanent residence on the mountain and lived there until his death. Many devotees, both Indians and Westerners, sought him out there. Ramana Maharshi taught realization of the formless reality of the self, or atman, through the Yoga of self-enquiry, which is regarded by his followers as the truest application of the nondualist VEDANTA. See his collected works, ed. by Arthur Osborne (3d ed. 1968); *Spiritual Teaching of Ramana Maharshi* (1972); study by Arthur Osborne (1954, repr. 1970).

Raman effect (rä'mən), appearance of additional lines in the SPECTRUM of monochromatic light that has been scattered by a transparent material medium. The effect was discovered by C. V. Raman in 1928. The frequency and thus the wavelength of the scattered light changes as a result of a change in the rotational or vibrational energy of the scattering molecules. The line spectrum of the scattered light will have one prominent line corresponding to the original wavelength of the incident radiation, plus additional lines to each side of it corresponding to the shorter or longer wavelengths of the altered portion of the light. This Raman spectrum is characteristic of the transmitting substance. Raman spectrometry is a useful technique in physical and chemical research, particularly for the characterization of materials.

Ramanuja: see VEDANTA.

Ramanujan, Srinivasa (shrē"nĭvä'sə rämä'no͝ojən), 1889–1920, Indian mathematician. He was a self-taught genius in pure mathematics who made original contributions to function theory, power series, and number theory with the training gained from a single textbook. He was invited to Cambridge by G. H. Hardy, with whom he collaborated, and continued there his work in number theory. He died of tuberculosis at the age of 30.

Ramapithecus (rāməpəthē'kəs, -pĭth'ə-), extinct group of primates and a possible ancestor of AUSTRALOPITHECUS and, therefore, of modern man. Fossils of *Ramapithecus* were discovered in N India and in E Africa. Although it was generally an apelike creature, *Ramapithecus* is the earliest fossil distinguishing the hominid family of man from the pongid family of the apes on the basis of its dental characteristics. It dates from about 12 to 14 million years ago.

Ramapo Mountains, beautiful forested range of the Appalachian Mts., NE N.J. and SE N.Y. Elevations range from c.900 ft to 1,200 ft (270–370 m), and there are many trails for hikers.

Rama's Bridge: see ADAM'S BRIDGE.

Ramat Gan (rä'mät gän), city (1972 pop. 117,500), W central Israel, adjacent to Tel Aviv. Founded in 1921, Ramat Gan is an important industrial center and a health resort. Food processing is the chief industry; construction materials are also made there. Diamonds are processed on the city's outskirts. Bar Ilan Univ. and a technical school are in Ramat Gan, which is also the site of Israel's largest sports stadium. Parts of the quadrennial international Maccabiah Games for Jewish sportsmen are held at the stadium.

Ramathaim-zophim (răm"əthā'ĭm-zō'fĭm), birthplace of Samuel, usually called Ramah and later Ramathaim. 1 Sam. 1.1; 1.19; 7.17; 28.3. It has been variously identified with RAMAH **4**, with ARIMATHAEA, and with the modern RAMALLAH and RAMLA. The land of ZUPH is connected with the name.

Ramathite (rā'məthīt), pertaining to RAMAH.

Ramath-lehi (rā'măth-lē'hī), place, SW Palestine, where Samson slew the Philistines with the jawbone of an ass. Judges 15.9–20. Lehi: Judges 15.9,14.

Ramath-mizpeh (rā'măth-mĭz'pē), unidentified place, E of the Jordan River, identical with MIZPAH **6.** Joshua 13.26.

Ramayana (rämä'yənə) [story of Rama], classical Sanskrit epic of India, probably composed in the 3d cent. B.C. Based on numerous legends, it is traditionally the work of Valmiki, one of the minor characters. The epic was revised and set down in its best-known form by the poet Tulsi Das (1532–1623). The *Ramayana,* because of its single subject, has more unity and is far shorter than the *Mahabharata,* the other great Indian epic. In the many different recensions of the work, there are from 24,000 to 43,000 couplets of 16-syllable lines. Incorporating much earlier sacred material from the VEDA, the *Ramayana* relates the adventures of Rama, who, together with his three half brothers, collectively made up the seventh avatar (incarnation) of the Hindu god Vishnu. Rama was deprived by guile of the throne of Ajodhya and forced into a long exile with his wife, Sita, the prototype of noble womanhood. When Sita was abducted by a demon, Rama allied himself with the king of the monkeys, Sugriva, and the monkey general, Hanuman, and fought a mighty battle in Lanka (Sri Lanka). Finally, Sita was recovered, and Rama was restored to his kingdom. The *Adhyatma Ramayana,* a popular work of more recent date, tells how Sita's mother (the earth mother) rose from a great chasm to reclaim her daughter. The epic influenced many of the literatures of Southeast Asia. Its principal characters are still worshiped in India. See translation by H. P. Shastri (3 vol. 1952–59); study by Hermann Jacobi (tr. 1960).

Ramazzini, Bernardino (bärnärdē'nō rämät-tsē'nē), 1633–1717, Italian physician. He was professor at Modena (1682–1700) and at Padua until 1714. He is often called the father of industrial medicine, and his *De Morbis Artificium* was the first systematic exposition of occupational disease. Ramazzini saw the relationship between various metals and the symptoms of metallic poisoning that developed in the artisans who worked with them, and he recognized that paints were a factor in the poisoning of painters. He also made studies of diseases in other occupations (e.g., lung diseases of miners, eye conditions of printers). Although most physicians of that period prescribed cinchona bark (the source of quinine) for every type of fever, Ramazzini opposed such indiscriminate use of the drug and correctly reserved it for the treatment of malarial attacks only. He was also an epidemiologist; he described several plagues that occurred in his region.

Rambam: see MAIMONIDES.

Rambaud, Alfred Nicolas (älfrĕd' nēkôlä' räNbō'), 1842–1905, French historian and politician. He served in the administration of Jules Ferry, was elected senator (1895), and was minister of public instruction (1896–98). Rambaud taught at the universities of Caen, Nancy, and Paris. All his works are characterized by honest scholarship, insight, and lucidity. His studies in Byzantine history were major contributions, and his excellent short general works on French civilization appeared in numerous editions. Rambaud was also an authority on Russian history; his *Histoire de la Russie* (1877; tr., new ed. 1904) was for many years a standard work outside Russia. He edited, with others, a collection of instructions to the French ambassadors in Russia for the period 1648–1789. Some of Rambaud's most important writings, particularly on Byzantine history, are included in the monumental *Histoire générale,* which he edited jointly with Ernest LAVISSE.

Rambert, Dame Marie, 1888–, a founder of the English ballet, b. Warsaw as Miriam Rambam. Trained by Jacques Dalcroze in eurythmics, Rambert joined the Diaghilev Ballets Russes as an instructor in 1913. She danced with the company after studying ballet with Enrico Cecchetti. In 1920 she opened her own school in London; her Ballet Rambert became the first permanent school and company in England when, in 1930, she founded the Ballet Club at the Mercury Theatre. Rambert discovered and fostered the talents of many great dancers and major choreographers, including Frederick Ashton and Antony Tudor.

rambler rose: see ROSE.

Rambouillet, Catherine de Vivonne, marquise de (kätrēn' də vēvôn' märkēz' də räNbo͞oyā'), 1588–1665, famous Frenchwoman, whose salon exercised a profound influence on French literature. She retired from court life in 1608 and began to receive at her house the intellectuals of Paris. Her literary salon was the first of the kind, and her example was soon imitated throughout France and spread to the rest of the world. The height of her influence was between 1620 and 1645. Her circle included Mme de Sévigné, Mme de La Fayette, Mlle de Scudéry, the duchesse de Longueville, the duchesse de Montpensier, Jean Louis Guez de Balzac, Corneille, Richelieu, Malherbe, Racan, Voiture, Bossuet, Chapelain, Scarron, Vaugelas, and La Rochefoucauld. The conversation and literary criticism of the Hôtel de Rambouillet, as her house was called, aimed solely at refinement and good taste, although the marquise like to indulge in practical jokes on her guests. The name *précieux* (fem. *précieuse*) adopted by the members of her circle lacked at that time its derogatory connotation, but the preciosity made fashionable by her salon soon deteriorated into extravagance and was much ridiculed by Molière. The oldest daughter of the marquise de Rambouillet was Julie d'Angennes (later duchesse de Montausier), to whom the members of the circle addressed the cycle of verses *Guirlande à Julie.* A younger daughter, Angélique, was the first wife of the marquis de Grignan.

Rambouillet, town (1968 pop. 15,918), Yvelines dept., N France. It is a summer resort in the heart of a magnificent forest. Sheep are raised, and radio equipment and plastics are made. The nearby château (14th–18th cent.), set in a beautiful park, is the official summer residence of French presidents, and the vast forest is used for official hunting parties. A national farm there was established by Louis XVI.

Rambouillet sheep (răm'bo͞olā"), fine-wool breed developed in France from the Spanish MERINO SHEEP. It has become very popular in the United States and is the foundation of most of the Western range flocks. Intermediate to large in size, Rambouillets are the largest and strongest of the fine-wool sheep; the rams are horned, the ewes hornless. Besides being valued for their high-quality wool, Rambouillets are also good meat animals. The ewes are bred extensively on the range to coarser-wooled rams, especially of the Hampshire and Suffolk breeds.

Rameau, Jean Philippe (zhäN fēlēp' rämō'), 1683–1764, French composer and theorist. He was organist at the cathedral in Clermont and at Notre Dame de Dijon. In the early part of his career his wrote two treatises on harmony in which he introduced the important and influential theory of chord inversion. His first opera, *Hippolyte et Aricie* (1733), was produced when he was 50, and it was followed by more than 30 stage works, including the dramatic ballet *Les Indes gallantes* (1735) and his best opera, *Castor et Pollux* (1737). Rameau's career was marked by controversies; at first he was attacked for his Italianate departure from the classical style of Lully, and later he was criticized for his old-fashioned French style. His harpsichord works and chamber music are brilliant examples of the elegant rococo style of the mid-18th cent. See his *Treatise on Harmony* (tr. 1971); G. A. Brundett, *Rameau's Orchestration* (1962).

Ramée, Joseph Jacques (zhôzĕf' zhäk rämā'), 1764–1842, French architect. He left France in 1792 and was active in Germany (where he built the Hamburg Exchange) and in Denmark. He lived in the United States from 1811 to 1816 and drew the plan for Union College, Schenectady, N.Y.

Ramée, Pierre de La: see RAMUS, PETRUS.

Ramelli, Agostino (ägōstē'nō rämĕl'-lē), c.1531–c.1600, Italian engineer who served in the armies of the marquis de Marignan and of the duc d'Anjou (later Henry III of France). His book, *Le Diverse et Artificiose Machine* (1558), urged the application of mathematics to mechanics and contained many illustrations and explanations of water-powered machines such as pumps, derricks, grinding mills, sawmills, bridges, and engines for military uses. Ramelli's designs were very inventive and often required precise machining that was impossible in his day.

Rameses or **Ramesses:** see RAMSES. For Rameses in the Bible, see RAAMSES.

Ramiah (rəmī'ə), husband of a foreigner. Ezra 10.25.

ramie: see NETTLE.

Ramillies, battle of (răm'ĭlēz, Fr. rämēyē'), fought May 23, 1706, near the village of Ramillies-Offus, Brabant prov., Belgium, 12 mi (19 km) S of Tienen, in the War of the Spanish Succession. Here, in one of his most brilliant victories, Marlborough commanded British, Dutch, and Danish troops and defeated the French under Villeroi. The victory enabled the allies to capture Antwerp, Ghent, and Bruges and to overrun the Spanish Netherlands.

Ramiro I (rämē'rō), d. 1063, first king of Aragón (1035–63), illegitimate son of Sancho III of Navarre, from whom he inherited Aragón. After the death of his half brother Gonzalo he annexed Sobrarbe and Ribagorza and fought unsuccessfully against the Moorish king of Saragossa. He died while fighting the Castilians at Graus and was succeeded by his son, Sancho Ramírez.

Ramla or **Ramleh** (both: räm'lĕ) [Arab.,=sand], town, central Israel, in a farming area. Ramla may be the biblical RAMATHAIM-ZOPHIM, but more probably it was founded (c.716) by the Arabs. It became the capital of Palestine and was fought over constantly during the Crusades. After Israeli forces took it in 1948, Ramla was resettled with Jewish immigrants. Landmarks include the Great Mosque (originally a 12th-century Crusader church) and the Square Tower (1318).

Ramleh: see RAMLA, Israel.

rammed earth, material consisting chiefly of soil of sufficiently stiff consistency that has been placed in forms and pounded down. It has been used for buildings and walls since ancient times and was employed in some of the most ancient fortifications in the Near East. Pliny the Elder records the survival of a rammed-earth fort built by Hannibal 250 years earlier. The material has been recommended especially for subsistence homesteads and for farm buildings; it has been widely used in the Rhone valley. It is known in England by the French term *pisé de terre.* It is formed either into monolithic walls or into blocks, and in both forms it makes strong, durable walls with good insulating and fireproofing properties. Its resistance to water may be increased by stabilizing it with cement and by surfacing. Earth walls should rest on a foundation with a waterproof top and must be roofed immediately. The material usually costs nothing and does not require skilled labor. Adobe, unlike rammed earth, is sun-dried and is made without packing the earth down between forms. Cob and chalk mud are related building systems. The cob mixture consists of straw added to clay and water. It has been used in Japanese architecture and until recently was an important building material in some regions of Great Britain, particularly in Devonshire and South Wales. In the chalk-mud method, chalk is added to the earth and water. Sir Edwin Lutyens designed a monumental chalk building, Marsh Court in Hampshire, England. See R. L. Patty and L. M. Minium, *Rammed Earth Walls for Farm Buildings* (1938); Clough Williams-Ellis and John and Elizabeth Eastwick-Field, *Building in Cob, Pisé, and Stabilized Earth* (1947).

Ramón: see GÓMEZ DE LA SERNA, RAMÓN.

ramontchi, small tree or shrub (*Flacourtia indica*) belonging to the family Flacourtiaceae. It is cultivated in S Asia and in other tropical regions for its large edible berries. Dark purple to black in color and acid in taste, the fruit is used chiefly for preserves. The hard, durable wood is used locally for agricultural and other implements. In parts of tropical Africa the plant is considered a curative for jaundice. The ramontchi is called also governor's, or botoko, plum. Fruits of other species of *Flacourtia* are also gathered. The ramontchi is classified in the division Magnoliophyta, class Magnoliopsida, order Violales, family Flacourtiaceae.

Ramón y Cajal, Santiago (säntyä'gō rämōn' ē kähäl'), 1852–1934, Spanish histologist. He was a university professor at Valencia (1881–86), at Barcelona (1886–92), and at Madrid (1892–1922), where he founded the Cajal Institute. He described the terminal branchings of neurons, devised a method of staining nerve tissues, and made numerous discoveries in the structure of the nervous system. For this work he shared with Camillo Golgi the 1906 Nobel Prize in Physiology and Medicine. His works include *Studies of the Degeneration and Regeneration of the Nervous System* (tr. 1928) and the classic *Histology* (tr. 1933). See his autobiography (tr. 1937, repr. 1966); biography by D. F. Cannon (1949).

Ramoth (rā'mŏth), Jew who married a foreigner. Ezra 10.29. For places named Ramoth, see RAMAH **3;** RAMOTH-GILEAD; REMETH.

Ramoth-gilead (rā'mŏth-gĭl'ēăd) or **Ramoth in Gilead,** ancient city of Palestine, E of the Jordan. It is named in the Bible as a place of refuge and as Ahab's last battlefield. Deut. 4.43; Joshua 20.8; 21.38; 1 Kings 4.13; 22; 2 Kings 8.28; 9.1; 1 Chron. 6.80; 2 Chron. 18; 22.5. Ramah: 2 Kings 8.29; 2 Chron. 22.6.

Rampal, Jean-Pierre, 1922–, French virtuoso flutist. Rampal studied medicine for three years and subsequently studied flute at the Marseilles Conservatory with his father, Joseph. Although Rampal played briefly in opera orchestras and has been a member of several chamber groups, he is most celebrated as a soloist of great brilliance. His many recordings and tours have made him world-famous.

Rampolla del Tindaro, Mariano (märyä'nō rämpôl'lä dĕl tēn'därō), 1843–1913, Italian churchman, cardinal of the Roman Catholic Church. He was a nobleman. He was papal nuncio at Madrid (1882–87) and was made cardinal in 1887. On his return to Rome he was secretary of state for LEO XIII and played a distinguished part in reestablishing the papacy's relations with Germany.

Rampur (rämpŏŏr'), city and former princely state, 893 sq mi (2,313 sq km), N central India. In 1949 the state was merged with Uttar Pradesh state. **Rampur,** city (1971 pop. 161,802), formerly the capital of Rampur state and now a district administrative center, produces pottery, fabrics, and cutlery. Its library has more than 12,000 rare manuscripts and a fine collection of Mogul miniature paintings.

Ramsay, Allan, 1685?–1758, Scottish poet. An Edinburgh bookseller, he opened one of the first circulating libraries in Great Britain. *The Gentle Shepherd* (1725), a pastoral comedy, is his most famous poetic work. He compiled several collections of old Scottish poems and songs and is considered an important figure in the revival of Scottish vernacular poetry that culminated in the work of Robert Burns. See biography by Oliphant Smeaton (1896); study by Burns Martin (1931). His son, **Allan Ramsay,** 1713–84, was a noted portrait painter. After a successful career in Edinburgh he moved to London in 1767 and became principal painter to George III. See biography by Alastair Smart (1952).

Ramsay, Sir Bertram Home, 1883–1945, British admiral. A career naval officer who retired in 1938, he returned to the service in World War II to command British and Allied naval units in some of the most spectacular operations of the war. He directed the evacuation of Dunkirk (1940), led the Allied fleets in the invasions of Africa (1942), Sicily, and Italy, and commanded, under General Eisenhower, the naval operations in the invasion of France in 1944. He was killed in a plane crash.

Ramsay, Sir William, 1852–1916, Scottish chemist. He was professor of chemistry at University College, Bristol (1880–87), and at University College, London (1887–1912). In his early experiments he showed that the alkaloids are related to pyridine, which he synthesized (1876) from acetylene and prussic acid. He then turned to inorganic and physical chemistry. Investigating the inert gases of the atmosphere, he discovered helium; with Rayleigh he discovered argon, and with M. W. Travers, krypton, neon, and xenon. He also carried on research on radium emanation. In 1902 he was knighted. For his work on gases he received the 1904 Nobel Prize in Chemistry. His writings include *System of Inorganic Chemistry* (1891) and *Essays Biographical and Chemical* (1908). See biography by M. W. Travers (1956).

Ramses (răm'sēz), **Rameses** or **Ramesses** (both: răm'əsēz"), name of several kings of ancient Egypt of the XIX and XX dynasties. The kings of the XX dynasty, all named Ramses but the first, are often, on that account, called Ramessides or Ramessids. **Ramses I,** d. c.1314 B.C., succeeded HOREMHEB, the true founder of the XIX dynasty. He died after only one year as king. His son was SETI I, whose son in turn was **Ramses II,** d. 1225 B.C. Ramses was not the heir to the throne but usurped it from his brother. He reigned for 67 years (1292–1225 B.C.). Under him Egypt acquired unprecedented splendor. His empire extended from S Syria to near the Fourth Cataract of the NILE. The most notable incident of his reign was the battle near Kadesh on the Orontes, where the Egyptians were ambushed by the Hittites. Ramses, claiming to have saved his forces single-handed, had vast texts written about his personal valor. War continued with the Hittites for about 15 years until Ramses concluded a treaty of friendship (1280) with the Hittite king and married (1267) a Hittite princess. Ramses left monuments throughout Egypt. The principal ones are probably the temple at Karnak, which he completed; the Rameseum, his mortuary temple, at Thebes; the temple at Luxor; and the great rock temple at Abu Simbel with four seated figures of the king on the facade. The period was characterized by great luxury, increased slavery, and the growth of a mercenary army, all of which led to the final decline of Egypt. He was probably the pharaoh of the exile mentioned in the Old Testament. MERNEPTAH succeeded him. See J. D. Schmidt, *Ramsses II* (1973). The period of anarchy that followed Merneptah was ended by **Ramses III,** d. 1167 B.C., the last important Ramses (reigned c.1198–1167 B.C.) and second king of the XX dynasty. He fought off the attempted invasions of the Libyans and the threat of the sea peoples who were camping in Syria waiting to invade Egypt. Although he was able to maintain an Asiatic empire in Palestine, he was the last Egyptian king to hold territory in this region. The accumulation of slaves and riches in the temples and the tremendous wealth of the nobility weakened the Egyptian social structure so that it could not recover. The last year of Ramses III was darkened by the conspiracy of his wife TIY. The XX dynasty continued to be ruled by kings with the name Ramses, but little of significance occurred during their reigns. The dynasty ended with Ramses XI in 1090 B.C.

Ramsey, Arthur Michael, 1904–, archbishop of Canterbury (1961–74), b. Cambridge, England. He was educated at Repton School; Magdalene College, Cambridge; and Cuddesdon Theological College. After his ordination in 1928 he held various teaching posts. In 1940 he was appointed canon of Durham Cathedral and professor of divinity at the Univ. of Durham, and in 1950 he became regius professor of divinity at Cambridge. In 1952 he was consecrated bishop of Durham and from 1956 to 1961 was archbishop of York. In June, 1961, he succeeded Geoffrey Francis Fisher as archbishop of Canterbury. Although a member of the High-Church group, Ramsey pressed for increased autonomy for the Church of England and was active in the ecumenical movement. He retired as archbishop in 1974 and was succeeded by Donald Coggan. A noted scholar, his works include *The Gospel and the Catholic Church* (1931), *The Resurrection of Christ* (1945), *F. D. Maurice and the Conflict of Modern Theology* (1951), and *From Gore to Temple* (1960). See biography by J. B. Simpson (1962).

Ramsey, residential borough (1970 pop. 12,571), Bergen co., NE N.J.; settled 1846, inc. 1908. Dairy farms are in the area.

Ramsgate (rămz'gĭt), municipal borough (1971 pop. 39,482), in the Isle of Thanet, Kent, SE England. It is a resort and yachting harbor. Ramsgate began as a fishing settlement, and extensive trade with Baltic ports developed early in the 18th cent. Queen Victoria lived in Ramsgate as a young princess. There are fine examples of Regency architecture there. During World War II troops evacuated from Dunkirk (1940) landed at Ramsgate. Caves in the cliffs provided bombproof shelters during the war.

Ramus, Petrus (pē'trəs rā'məs) or **Pierre de La Ramée** (pyĕr də lä rämā'), 1515–72, French humanist and philosopher. Attempting to break through Aristotelian and scholastic traditions, Ramus wrote a number of works that became influential, among them *Dialecticae Institutiones* (1543) and *Aristotelicae Animadversiones* (1543). In consequence, his teaching position was threatened, but in 1551, through the efforts of Cardinal de Lorraine, Ramus was established in a chair of rhetoric and philosophy at the Collège de France. In the religious wars of the period Ramus attached himself to the reformers and fled (1568) to Germany. He returned to Paris in 1570 and was killed in the St. Bartholomew's Day massacre. Ramist logic, although faulted by modern thinkers, was exceedingly influential in the 16th and early 17th cent., holding sway in Protestant lands—Switzerland, Scotland, and much of Germany. From its English stronghold at Cambridge it markedly affected Francis Bacon, John Milton, and others. The emphasis of Ramist logic on clarity, precision, and testing and on definite boundaries between subjects can be said to have encouraged the scientific spirit. See studies by N. E. Nelson (1947) and W. J. Ong (1958, repr. 1974); W. S. Howell, *Logic and Rhetoric in England, 1500–1700* (1956, repr. 1961).

Ramusio, Giambattista (jäm″bät-tē′stä rämo͞o′-zyō), 1485–1557, Italian editor and compiler, b. Treviso. He served in diplomatic posts for the Venetian state and eventually in the Council of Ten. He is remembered for his monumental *Delle navigationi e viaggi* (1550–59), a collection of geographical accounts of explorations. This work provides many of the extant accounts of early voyages of exploration; it includes a fine edition of Marco Polo's account and an early description of Magellan's circumnavigation.

Ramuz, Charles Ferdinand (shärl fĕrdēnäN′ rämüz′), 1878–1947, Swiss novelist. His works deal with the simple people of his native canton of Vaud. Among his major novels are *Le Règne de l'esprit malin* (1917; tr. *The Region of the Evil One,* 1922), *Présence de la mort* (1922; tr. *The End of All Men,* 1944), *La Grand Peur dans la montagne* (1926), and *Derborence* (1935; tr. *When the Mountain Fell,* 1947).

Rancagua (rängkä′gwä, -kä′wä), city (1970 pop. 95,030), capital of O'Higgins prov., central Chile, in a fertile valley among the Andean foothills. Though one of Chile's largest copper mines (El Teniente) is nearby, Rancagua is primarily an agricultural center. The city was founded in 1743. At Rancagua on Oct. 1 and 2, 1814, Bernardo O'HIGGINS commanded a heroic defense of the plaza against a superior Spanish royalist force in an engagement that closed the first phase (1810–14) of the Chilean war against Spain.

Rancé, Armand Jean le Bouthillier de (ärmäN′ zhäN lə bo͞otēyā′ də räNsā′), 1626–1700, French religious reformer, founder of the TRAPPISTS. He was of a noble family, was well educated, and lived at court as a worldly priest. In 1664 he retired to the Cistercian abbey at LaTrappe, where he was already abbot *in commendam* (i.e., he received its revenues, but performed no duties). There, as regular abbot, he established a discipline stricter than the primitive Benedictine rule. In a few years LaTrappe was famous, and its reform spread; out of the movement came the Trappists.

ranch, large farm devoted chiefly to raising and breeding cattle, horses, sheep, and goats. The cattle ranch was introduced from Latin America to Texas and the plains of the W United States and Canada. The first ranchmen owned cattle, ponies, and camp equipment but no land, grazing their stock on the free public RANGE. When the fencing of land became compulsory, most ranges were broken up into smaller ranches. Cattle and sheep are often shipped from ranches to feed lots in the corn belt for fattening. The term *ranch* is applied in the W United States also to grain and fruit farms. The dude ranch offers horseback riding and other typically Western outdoor activities for the entertainment of paying guests. Some dude ranches are also "working" ranches, but most are devoted solely to vacationers.

rancheria (ränchä′rēäs), type of communal settlement characteristic of the Yaqui Indians of Sonora, Mexico, and of some Indians of the SW United States. These clusters of dwellings were less permanent than the pueblos (see PUEBLO INDIANS) but more so than the camps of the nomadic Indians. The form of the dwelling units varied, ranging from circular, dome-shaped, mat-covered houses of unknown size to rectangular, flat-roofed structures with woven cane or wattle and daub walls. Every cluster of dwelling units was also characterized by ramadas, or pole-supported roofs without walls, which served as shade for food preparation, lounging, and sleeping.

Ranchi (rän′chē), city (1971 pop. 176,225), Bihar state, E central India. It is a district administrative center and a health resort, 2,128 ft (647 m) above sea level, in a region of tea plantations and rich coal deposits. The city houses one of the largest machine-tool factories in India, and the Univ. of Ranchi is there.

Rancho Cordova (răn′chō kôrdō′və), uninc. residential town (1970 pop. 30,451), Sacramento co., N Calif.

Rand, Ayn (īn), 1905–, Russian-American novelist, b. Leningrad. She came to the United States in 1926 and worked for many years as a screenwriter. Her novels are romantic and dramatic, and they espouse a philosophy of rational self-interest that opposes the altruistic tendencies of the modern welfare state. Her best-known novels include *The Fountainhead* (1943) and *Atlas Shrugged* (1957). In *The New Intellectual* (1961) she summarizes her philosophy, which she calls "objectivism."

Rand, the: see WITWATERSRAND.

Randall, James Garfield, 1881–1953, American historian, b. Indianapolis, Ind. He taught history and political science at various colleges before joining (1920) the faculty of the Univ. of Illinois. A leading authority on Lincoln, Randall was a leader of the Civil War revisionists (who maintained that the war was not inevitable and came about as a result of the failures of American statesmanship). Randall wrote *Confiscation of Property during the Civil War* (1913), *Constitutional Problems under Lincoln* (1926), *The Civil War and Reconstruction* (1937; rev. by David Donald, 1961), *Lincoln the President: Springfield to Gettysburg* (4 vol., 1945–55; Vol. IV completed by R. N. Current), *Lincoln and the South* (1946), and *Lincoln the Liberal Statesman* (1947). He also edited, with T. C. Pease, *The Diary of Orville H. Browning* (2 vol., 1927–33) and, with Jeannette Nichols, *Democracy in the Middle West, 1840–1940* (1941).

Randall, Samuel Jackson, 1828–90, American politician, b. Philadelphia. A Democrat, he was a U.S. Representative from Pennsylvania from 1863 until his death. As speaker (1876–81), he presided over the sessions dealing with the disputed presidential election of 1876 and helped codify the House's rules of procedure. He was also chairman (1883–87) of the powerful appropriations committee. Because of Pennsylvania's industrial interests, Randall always opposed his party's traditional stand for a low tariff. He fell out (1887) with President Cleveland on this issue and thereafter lost most of his influence. See H. B. Fuller, *The Speakers of the House* (1909).

Rand Corporation, research institution in Santa Monica, Calif.; founded 1948 and supported by Federal, state, and local governments, as well as by foundations. Its principal fields of research are in the areas of national security and public welfare. Research in national security affairs includes studies in planning, procurement, support and operations of military forces, and studies of strategic and tactical forces, command and control, and logistics management. Research in domestic problems includes studies in health care, education, transportation, communication, racial discrimination, poverty, housing, and environmental pollution. See B. L. Smith, *Rand Corporation* (1966).

Randers (rä′nərs), city (1970 com. pop. 64,193), Århus co., N central Denmark, a seaport at the mouth of the Gudenå River in the Randers Fjord (an arm of the Kattegat). It is a commercial and industrial center and a rail junction. Manufactures include machinery, iron products, and gloves. The city is noted for its salmon fishing. Founded in the 11th cent., Randers was an important trade center in the Middle Ages. Noteworthy buildings include the Church of St. Morton (15th cent.) and the city hall (18th cent.).

Randfontein (rănt″făntān), city (1970 pop. 32,527), Transvaal, NE South Africa, near Johannesburg. Randfontein is a gold-mining center, and uranium is refined there.

Randolph, Asa Philip, 1889–, U.S. labor leader, b. Crescent City, Fla., attended the College of the City of New York. As a writer and editor of the black magazine *The Messenger,* which he helped to found, Randolph became interested in the labor movement. In 1917 he organized a small union of elevator operators in New York City. After an unsuccessful campaign for the office of New York secretary of state on the Socialist ticket, he devoted his energies to organizing the Pullman car porters, a group of black workers he had tried to organize earlier. Despite bitter opposition by the Pullman Company, Randolph eventually won recognition for the Brotherhood of Sleeping Car Porters, pay increases, and shorter hours. Randolph was elected president of the union when it was formed in 1925. An untiring fighter for civil rights, he organized (1941) the March on Washington Movement in protest against job discrimination. This movement, although it did not culminate in a march, is credited with hastening the establishment of the FAIR EMPLOYMENT PRACTICES COMMITTEE during World War II. Randolph was also one of the most prominent leaders in the fight against segregation in the armed forces. His election to a vice presidency of the AFL-CIO in 1955 was, in part, in recognition of his efforts to eliminate racial discrimination in the organized labor movement. In 1963, Randolph was director of the March on Washington for Jobs and Freedom, one of the largest civil rights demonstrations ever conducted in the United States. The A. Philip Randolph Institute was founded in 1964 by Randolph and others to serve and promote cooperation between labor and the black community. Randolph retired from the presidency of the union in 1968, although he continued in his position as a vice president of the AFL-CIO. See biographies by D. S. Davis (1972) and Jervis Anderson (1973).

Randolph, Edmund, 1753–1813, American statesman, b. Williamsburg, Va.; nephew of Peyton Randolph. He studied law under his father, John Randolph, a Loyalist who went to England on the outbreak of the American Revolution. He served briefly in the Continental army as aide-de-camp to George Washington. He was a member of the Virginia constitutional convention of 1776, state attorney general (1776–86), a delegate to the Continental Congress (1779–82), and governor of Virginia (1786–88). Randolph was prominent at the FEDERAL CONSTITUTIONAL CONVENTION in 1787, presenting the Virginia, or Randolph, Plan, which favored the large states. He at first vigorously opposed the Constitution as finally drafted, although his plan, more than any other, closely resembled it; later he urged its adoption in the Virginia ratifying convention (June, 1788). First Attorney General of the United States (1789–94), he left that post to succeed Thomas Jefferson as Secretary of State. Like Jefferson, he had difficulties because of Alexander Hamilton's constant pressure to secure a favorable treaty with England rather than one with France. In 1795 the British captured dispatches of the French minister to the United States, which implied (falsely) that Randolph would welcome French money, whereupon President Washington forced his resignation. Randolph returned to the practice of law in Virginia, and many years passed before his name was entirely cleared. In 1807 he was chief counsel for Aaron Burr in his trial for treason. See M. D. Conway, *Omitted Chapters of History Disclosed in the Life and Papers of Edmund Randolph* (1888, repr. 1971); H. J. Eckenrode, *The Randolphs* (1946).

Randolph, Edward, c.1632–1703, English colonial agent in America. In 1676 he carried royal instructions to Massachusetts Bay that required the colony to send representatives to England to satisfy complaints of the heirs of John MASON (1586–1635) and Sir Ferdinando GORGES; he also had orders to make a complete report on the colony. Rebuffed by the Massachusetts authorities, he made a personal investigation and upon his return to England wrote a denunciatory report based on facts but colored by his dislike for the Puritans. His attack on the legality of the Massachusetts Bay charter helped bring about the withdrawal (1679) of New Hampshire from the colony's administration as well as the order that the colony repeal all laws unfavorable to England and enforce the Navigation Acts. In 1679, Randolph settled in Boston as collector of customs for New England. His relations with the colonials were extremely bitter. After the annulment (1684) of the Massachusetts charter, an act to which he had devoted much energy, he became secretary and register for the Dominion of New England and also acted as a councilor under Joseph Dudley and Sir Edmund ANDROS. With the collapse (1689) of the Andros regime, Randolph was imprisoned for a time. In 1691 he became surveyor general of customs for North America. His letters and papers have been edited with a biographical commentary by R. N. Toppan and A. T. S. Goodrick (7 vol., 1898–1909, repr. 1967). See biography by M. G. Hall (1960, repr. 1969).

Randolph, John, 1773–1833, American legislator, known as John Randolph of Roanoke, b. Prince George co., Va. He briefly studied law under his cousin Edmund Randolph. He served in the U.S. House of Representatives (1799–1813, 1815–17, 1819–25, 1827–29), where he became a prominent and feared figure, and in the U.S. Senate (1825–27). After breaking (1805) with President Jefferson on the acquisition of Florida, which he opposed, Randolph lost his leadership in the House. He strongly opposed James Madison and the War of 1812, the second Bank of the United States, the Missouri Compromise, and the tariff measures. From 1820 he was a violent sectionalist. His impassioned denunciations of Henry Clay and John Quincy Adams led (1826) to a duel with Clay. Appointed (1830) by President Jackson minister to Russia, he resigned shortly after his arrival there because of ill health. Following his return he denounced Jackson's proclamation against nullification. An outspoken champion of individual liberty, he staunchly defended the Constitution and states' rights, and his views were influential in the South long after his death. A bizarre figure, Randolph numbered Pocahontas among his forebears. He became more eccentric in his later years and at times suffered from dementia. Chiefly remembered for his epigrammatic wit and caustic tongue, he also possessed a brilliant and scholarly mind and was celebrated as an orator. See biographies by Henry Adams (1882, repr. 1972) and W. C. Bruce (2 vol., 1922; repr. 1970); study by Russell Kirk (rev. ed. 1964).

Randolph, Peyton, c.1721–1775, American political leader, first president of the Continental Congress, b. Williamsburg, Va. After a general education at the College of William and Mary, he studied law in England. He was prominent in Virginia after his return there, was king's attorney for Virginia (1748–66), and was long a member of the house of burgesses (1748–49, 1752–75) and its speaker (1766–75). He wrote the protest for the house against the proposed Stamp Act in 1764, but he opposed Patrick Henry's radical resolutions against it in 1765. A moderate, and a personal friend of George Washington, Randolph worked for the cause of independence, headed the Virginia conventions of 1774 and 1775, and was elected to the First Continental Congress, of which he was briefly (Sept.–Oct., 1774) president. Elected (1775) to the Second Continental Congress, he was again chosen president, but resigned because of illness. See Jonathan Daniels, *The Randolphs of Virginia* (1972).

Randolph, Thomas, 1523–90, English diplomat. He was graduated from Oxford (1545) and served as principal of Broadgates Hall (later Pembroke College), Oxford, until forced because of his Protestant sympathies to flee to France upon the accession (1553) of Queen Mary I. He returned (1559) after the accession of Elizabeth I and served her in diplomatic missions to Scotland, where he acquired the friendship of MARY QUEEN OF SCOTS. He was directed to block the marriage of Mary to Lord Darnley, and in 1566 he was dismissed from Edinburgh, charged by Mary with giving money to support the rebellion of James Stuart, 1st earl of MURRAY. Randolph's letters during his service in Scotland are a valuable source for the history of the period. In 1568 he headed a special trade embassy to Russia. Subsequently he was sent on missions to France. In 1580 he was in Scotland intriguing on behalf of the imprisoned James Douglas, 4th earl of MORTON. His plot to abduct the young King James VI was discovered, and Randolph narrowly escaped death. In 1586, however, he successfully arranged a treaty with Scotland.

Randolph, Thomas, 1605–35, English poet and dramatist. After graduating from Cambridge in 1632, he went to London where he became a disciple of Ben Jonson. His best-known poems are "A Gratulatory to Ben Jonson" and "On the Death of a Nightingale." *Amyntas* (1631), *The Muses' Looking-Glass* (1630), and *The Jealous Lovers* (1632) are his most famous comedies. See edition of his works edited by W. C. Hazlitt (1875).

Randolph. **1** Community (1970 pop. 18,233), Montgomery co., W central Md., a suburb of Washington, D.C. **2** Town (1970 pop. 27,035), Norfolk co., E Mass.; settled c.1710, set off from Braintree and inc. 1793. It is chiefly residential.

Randolph-Macon College, at Ashland, Va.; United Methodist; primarily for men; chartered 1830, opened 1832 at Boydton, Va., moved 1868; named for John Randolph and Nathaniel Macon.

Randolph-Macon Woman's College, at Lynchburg, Va.; United Methodist; for women; est. 1891, opened 1893. Until 1953 it was a division of Randolph-Macon College at Ashland, Va.

Randwick, municipality (1971 pop. 123,404), New South Wales, SE Australia, part of the Sydney urban agglomeration. It has a large race track.

Rangabe (räNgäbā') or **Rhangavis, Alexandros Rizos** (ălĕk'sänthrôs rē'zôs räng"gävēs'), 1810–92, Greek scholar, author, and diplomat, b. Constantinople. After 1831 he held government posts at Athens, notably the ministry of education (1833), and he later served as a diplomat in various capitals, among them Washington, D.C. In 1844 he became professor of archaeology at the Univ. of Athens. Prominent in the Greek classicist revival, he was a leading representative of the classical trend in modern Greek literature. He was particularly successful as a dramatist; among his works (written in classical Greek) are the comedy *Tou Koutrouli o gamos* [the marriage of Koutroulis] (1845) and the tragedy *Triakontai tirani* [the Thirty Tyrants] (1866).

range, large stretch of land unsuited to crop cultivation but providing native grasses and other forage plants for livestock grazing. Originally the ranges of the W United States and Canada were unfenced public land; later, under the Homestead Act, more than 50% of the Western range land in the United States passed to private ownership and was fenced with barbed wire. The national forests of the West contain large unfenced ranges; grazing permits are purchased by ranch owners. Ranges are known as summer or winter ranges according to the time of year when grazing conditions are best. *Range management* is the term applied to efficient, productive utilization of range land to prevent overgrazing and misuse.

Rangoon (răn"gōōn'), city (1969 est. pop. 1,733,000), capital of Burma, S central Burma, on the Rangoon River near its entrance into the Gulf of Martaban. The largest city in Burma, Rangoon is the transportation hub of the country and its commercial and industrial center. The major exports are rice, teak, bran, petroleum, cotton, rubber, and copper; there are rice mills, sawmills, oil refineries, and shipyards. Probably founded in the 6th cent., it was until the 18th cent. a small fishing village, dominated—as is the modern city—by the most celebrated temple in Burma, the golden-spired Shwe Dagon Pagoda. Alaungapaya, the founder of the last line of Burmese kings, made the town his capital in 1753. Under his rule Rangoon was given its present name and was built up as the chief port of Burma. It was held briefly by the British in 1824–26; after it came under British rule in 1852, it was transformed into a modern city. Rangoon was heavily damaged by an earthquake and tidal wave in 1930, and again in World War II. The Univ. of Rangoon, Burma's center of higher learning was founded in 1920 and reorganized in 1948.

Rangpur (rŭng'pŏŏr), town (1961 est. pop. 40,400), NW Bangladesh, on the Little Ghaghet River. The administrative center of a tobacco-growing district, Rangpur manufactures cigarettes and cigars and is noted for its cotton carpets. In the city is a college affiliated with Rajshahi Univ.

Ranjit Singh (rŭn'jĭt sĭng), 1780–1839, Indian maharaja, ruler of the Sikhs. Seizing Lahore (1799) and Amritsar (1802), he established himself as the leading Sikh chieftain. In 1809 he made a treaty with the British, by which he agreed not to expand his domain south of the Sutlej River. However, he built up a formidable army with the help of European officers and rapidly expanded his holdings to the north and west. By the time of his death he controlled all of the Punjab north of the Sutlej as well as Kashmir. At the end (1849) of the Sikh Wars most of his kingdom fell to Great Britain.

Rank, Otto (ôt'ō rängk), 1884–1937, Austrian psychoanalyst; one of Sigmund Freud's first and most valued pupils. He early employed Freudian techniques to clarify the underlying significance of myths, producing the classic paper *Der Mythus von der Geburt des Helden* (1909; tr. *Myth of the Birth of the Hero,* 1914). Rank, in collaboration with Hanns Sachs, founded the psychoanalytic journal *Imago* in 1912. Rank's theoretical views, diverging from those of Freud, gave the birth trauma, rather than the Oedipus complex, the central position in the causation of psychoneurosis, claiming all neurotic anxiety to be a repetition of the physiological phenomenon of birth. As a therapist, he attempted to reduce the time required for a successful psychoanalysis to a few months. Rank emigrated to the United States a few years before his death. Among his writings are *The Trauma of Birth* (tr. 1929), *Art and Artist* (tr. 1932), *Modern Education* (tr. 1932), and *Will Therapy* (tr. 1936). See study by Jessie Taft (1958); F. B. Karpf, *The Psychology and Psychotherapy of Otto Rank* (1953).

Ranke, Leopold von (lā'ōpôlt fən räng'kə), 1795–1886, German historian, generally recognized as the father of the modern objective historical school. He applied and elaborated Barthold Niebuhr's scientific method of historical investigation. Ranke's aim was to reconstruct the unique periods of the past as they actually were and to avoid injecting the history of former times with the spirit of the present; this approach to historiography is known as historicism. To attain his goal, Ranke insisted that only contemporary accounts and related material be used as sources. His technique depended in large part on exhaustive archival research and on philological criticism of sources. It is difficult to say whether Ranke was more influential through his writing or through his teaching. As professor at the Univ. of Berlin (1825–71), he inaugurated the seminar system of teaching history and formed an entire generation of historians, who in turn spread his methods throughout the world. Outside Germany, his ideas were particularly influential in England and in the United States. The accumulation of facts and details, serving the purposes of preparatory research and practical training, was a prominent feature of Ranke's method. In his seminars originated the *Jahrbücher* [yearbooks], which grew into a tremendous repository of information on medieval Germany. It is implicit in Ranke's work that he regarded history as the result of the divine will. Since he saw power as the overt expression of that will, Ranke concentrated on political, and primarily on diplomatic, developments. He sought to apply his methods to the history of all European nations, and his investigations ranged over a wide field. One of his earliest works was *Zur Kritik neuerer Geschichtschreiber* [critique of modern historical writing] (1824), which set forth his method; the culmination of his life work was his *Weltgeschichte* [universal history] (9 vol., 1881–88). The great body of his writing is made up of particular histories of the 16th, 17th, and 18th cent. English translations include the enduring *Ecclesiastical and Political History of the Popes during the Sixteenth and Seventeenth Centuries* (3 vol., 1840), *Memoirs of the House of Brandenburg and History of Prussia during the Seventeenth and Eighteenth Centuries* (3 vol., 1847–48), *Civil Wars and Monarchy in France in the Sixteenth and Seventeenth Centuries* (1852), and *History of England* (6 vol., 1875). Important among his other writings are extensive histories of Prussia and of the rise of the Prussian state. The quantity of his work is as impressive as the quality; the German edition (1867–90) of his complete works numbered 54 volumes without the universal history. Politically a conservative and a monarchist, Ranke did not share the liberalism of some of his Prussian contemporaries. See G. P. Gooch, *History and Historians in the Nineteenth Century* (2d ed. 1952, repr. 1965); T. H. Von Laue, *Leopold Ranke, the Formative Years* (1950, repr. 1970).

Rankin, Jeannette, 1880–1973, American pacifist, b. Missoula, Mont. She was active in social work and campaigned for woman suffrage. A Republican, she was the first woman in the United States to serve (1917–19) in Congress and also was (1941–43) a member of the 77th Congress. She voted against the declaration of war on Germany in 1917 and in 1941 cast the only vote in the House against entering the war. A member of various antiwar organizations, she led (1968) the Jeannette Rankin Brigade, a peace group, to Washington to protest the Vietnam War. See biography by Hannah Josephson (1974).

Rankine, William John Macquorn (răng'kĭn), 1820–72, Scottish engineer and physicist. Serving as a professor of engineering at the Univ. of Glasgow from 1855, he made valuable contributions to civil and mechanical engineering as well as to thermodynamics. His manuals of applied mechanics and of civil engineering and one on the steam engine and other such engines went into many editions.

Rankine temperature scale: see KELVIN TEMPERATURE SCALE.

Ranković, Aleksandar (älĕksän'där ränkōvĭ'tyə), 1909–, Yugoslav political leader. A Serbian, he joined the Yugoslav Communist party in 1928 and later became (1937) a member of its central committee. In World War II, Ranković was active in the resistance. After the war, he was minister of the interior, heading the military and secret police. From 1948 to 1966 he also held the second highest post in the executive branch of the Yugoslav government, with the title of vice president of the republic from 1963 to 1966. Regarded as a possible successor to Josip Broz Tito, Ranković was accused in 1966 of abusing his position in the state security service and was deprived of his offices and expelled from the Yugoslav Communist party.

Rannoch, Loch (lŏkh răn'əkh), lake, 9½ mi (15.3 km) long and 1 mi (1.6 km) wide, Perthshire, central Scotland, in the Grampians. It is fed by the Ericht River and drained by the Tummel River to the Tay River. Part of a hydroelectric project, there is a power station at the west end. The lake is known for trout and salmon fishing. The Black Wood, a pine forest, is on the southern shore.

Rann of Kutch: see KUTCH.

Ransom, John Crowe, 1888–1974, American poet and critic, b. Pulaski, Tenn., grad. Vanderbilt Univ. and studied at Oxford as a Rhodes scholar. He is considered one of the great stylists of 20th-century American poetry. His verse, elegant and impersonal, is concerned with the breakdown of traditional order and stability in the modern world. His first volume of verse, *Poems about God*, appeared in 1919. It was followed by *Chills and Fever* (1924) and *Two Gentlemen in Bonds* (1926). He taught at Vanderbilt from 1914 to 1937, during which time he (with Allen Tate, Robert Penn Warren, and others) founded and edited the *Fugitive* (1922–25), a bimonthly literary magazine. One of the so-called new critics, he brought to 20th-century criticism a new respect for poetry as a medium, emphasizing close textual analysis and the importance of a poem as a poem. From 1937 to 1958 he taught at Kenyon College; there he founded the *Kenyon Review*, a magazine that established him as an influential and controversial critic and editor. In *The World's Body* (1938) and *The New Criticism* (1941) he voices his literary theories. See the revised and enlarged edition of his *Selected Poems* (1969) and *Beating the Bushes: Selected Essays 1941–1970* (1972). See studies by Robert Buffington (1967) and T. H. Parsons (1969).

ransom, price of redemption demanded by the captor of a person, vessel, or city. In ancient times cities frequently paid ransom to prevent their plundering by captors. The custom of ransoming was formerly sanctioned by law, and one of the rights of a feudal lord was to call upon his tenants to ransom him. Soldiers, given the right to kill or enslave their prisoners, frequently preferred to free their captives after receiving money payment. This mitigated bloodshed, for it was more profitable to capture the enemy and hold him for ransom than to massacre him. The amount of ransom varied with the rank of the captive, and the ransoming of a king or a noted warrior involved great sums. For the payment of the ransom of RICHARD I (Richard Coeur de Lion) a special tax was levied in England; the French sovereign paid heavy ransoms for Bertrand DU GUESCLIN; and Scotland was impoverished in paying for JAMES I. Merchant vessels captured by privateers were sometimes ransomed by their owners. After receiving the ransom, the privateer sometimes furnished a ransom bill, which allowed safe conduct for the ship to one of her native ports (see PRIVATEERING). Its present usage generally refers to the sum paid to a kidnaper for the release of an individual or to an airplane HIJACKER for the release of passengers, crew, and plane. In 1961, Cuba revived the practice of ransoming prisoners; Premier Fidel Castro released prisoners taken in the unsuccessful invasion of 1961 in exchange for large payments, partly in medical supplies.

Ranson, Charles Wesley, 1903–, British Methodist clergyman, b. Ireland. Educated at Queens Univ., Belfast, and Oxford, he was ordained and went (1929) as a missionary to India. There he became particularly interested in the social problems of the city of Madras and in the problems of creating an indigenous Christian ministry. After serving as secretary of the National Christian Council of India, Burma, and Ceylon, he became (1948) general secretary of the International Missionary Council, a position he held until 1958. He was founder and director (1958–64) of the Theological Education Fund, an ecumenical organization that fostered theological training in the churches of Asia, Africa, and Latin America. From 1964 to 1967 he was dean of the theology school of Drew Univ., Madison, N.J., where he was also (1962–68) professor of ecumenical theology. His writings include *A City in Transition* (1938), *The Christian Minister in India* (1946), and *That the World May Know* (1953).

Rantekombola (rän"təkŏm'bələ), mountain, 11,335 ft (3,455 m) high, on the southwest peninsula of Celebes island, Indonesia. It is the island's highest point.

Ranters, name given to the adherents of an antinomian movement in England about the time of the Commonwealth and Protectorate (1649–59). Its principal teaching was pantheistic, that God is present in nature. The Ranters appealed to the inner experience of Christ and denied the authority of Scripture. They were accused of fostering immorality and were legislated against by Parliament and vigorously suppressed. They were often confused with the Quakers. In the 19th cent. the Primitive Methodists were sometimes called Ranters.

Rantoul (răntōōl'), village (1970 pop. 25,562), Champaign co., E Ill., in a rich blackland farm area that yields corn and soybeans; inc. 1868. Chanute Air Force Base, a technical training center which first opened in 1917, is there.

ranz des vaches (räNz dā väsh), type of Alpine folk melody of irregular melodic and rhythmic form used to call cattle. It is played on the alphorn by Swiss herdsmen, or sung, with or without words. There are about 50 or more regional variations on the basic melodic pattern. Beethoven, in the *Pastoral* Symphony, and Rossini, in *William Tell*, are among the composers who have used the ranz des vaches in compositions.

Rao, Raja (rä'jə rou), 1909–, Indian novelist. Rao was educated in India and France and for many years has divided his time among India, Europe, and the United States. In 1965 he was appointed professor of philosophy at the Univ. of Texas at Austin. His three novels are considered to be among the foremost of Indian works written in English. The first, *Kanthapura* (1938), describes the daily life of Indian villages during a revolt against an overbearing plantation owner. Rao's commitment to Ghandian nonviolence is clearly revealed in his description of the peasants' conversion to the principle of civil disobedience. *The Serpent and the Rope* (1960) is a semi-autobiographical account of a marriage between intellectuals that is destroyed by philosophical discord. His metaphysical novel *The Cat and Shakespeare* (1965) is a tale of individual destiny. All three works, but particularly the latter two, are profoundly serious and reflect Rao's catholic concern with religion and philosophy. He has also published a collection of short stories, *The Cow of the Barricades and Other Stories* (1947). See biography by M. K. Naik (1972).

Raoul (räōōl'), d. 936, duke of Burgundy, king of France (923–36). Elected king to succeed his father-in-law, ROBERT I, Raoul fought the Normans and the Hungarians, who repeatedly invaded France. He also defended his crown against those nobles who supported the claims of the deposed Carolingian king, CHARLES III. The royal authority, lessened in part by objections to Raoul's taking the throne, remained weak under his Carolingian successor, LOUIS IV.

Raoult's law (räōōlz') [for F. M. Raoult] states that the addition of solute to a liquid lessens the tendency for the liquid to become a solid or a gas, i.e., reduces the freezing point and the VAPOR PRESSURE (see SOLUTION). For example, the addition of salt to water causes the water to freeze below its normal freezing point (0°C) and to boil above its normal boiling point (100°C). Qualitatively, depression of the freezing point and reduction of the vapor pressure are due to a lowering of the concentration of water molecules, since the more solute is added, the less the percentage of water molecules in the solution as a whole and therefore the less their tendency to form into a crystal solid or to escape as a gas. Quantitatively, Raoult's law states that the solvent's vapor pressure in solution is equal to its MOLE fraction times its vapor pressure as a pure liquid, from which it follows that the freezing point depression and boiling point elevation are directly proportional to the molality of the solute, although the constants of proportion are different in each case. This mathematical relation, however,is accurate only for dilute solutions. The fact that an appropriate solute can both lower the freezing point and raise the boiling point of a pure liquid is the basis for year-round antifreeze for automobile cooling systems. In the winter the antifreeze lowers the freezing point of the water, preventing it from freezing at its normal freezing point; in the summer it guards against boilover by raising the boiling point of the water.

Rapallo (räpäl'lō), town (1971 pop. 27,042), in Liguria, NW Italy, on the Ligurian Sea and on the Italian RIVIERA. It is a seaport and seaside resort.

Rapallo, Treaty of, 1920: see RIJEKA.

Rapallo, Treaty of, 1922, agreement signed by Germany and the USSR at Rapallo, Italy. It was reached by Walter Rathenau and G. V. Chicherin independently of the Conference of Genoa (see GENOA, CONFERENCE OF), which was then in session. Germany accorded the USSR de jure recognition (the first such recognition extended to the Soviet government), and the two signatories mutually canceled all prewar debts and renounced war claims. Particularly advantageous to Germany was the inclusion of a most-favored-nation clause and of extensive trade agreements. The treaty enabled the German army, through secret agreements, to produce and perfect in the USSR weapons forbidden by the Treaty of Versailles.

rape, name applied to each of the six obsolete territorial divisions (Hastings, Pevensey, Lewes, Bramber, Arundel, and Chichester) into which Sussex, England, is divided.

rape, in botany, annual herb (*Brassica napus*) of the family Cruciferae (MUSTARD family), belonging to the same genus as the cabbage, the mustard plant, and the turnip (which it resembles in appearance). The origin of the rape is uncertain, and it is now known only as a cultivated plant. The seeds have been valued since ancient times for their oil content (30% to 45%). The oil, expressed or extracted by solvents, is used for lubricating, cooking, and illuminating purposes, for fuel, and for the manufacture of soap and synthetic rubber. A cake made of the seed residue is a valuable stock feed and a good nitrogenous fertilizer. The chief producing areas, in order of importance, are China, India, and Europe; the United States is the chief importer of the oil. Rape is also grown for forage for hogs and sheep and sometimes for cattle, although it may cause bloating in stock other than swine; it is also sown as a cover crop (e.g., in orchards). Rape seed is used in birdseed mixtures. In North America the plant is cultivated chiefly for forage—especially in the northern states and in Canada, because it can be grown as a winter-hardy biennial. Other similar species of *Brassica* are sometimes cultivated, especially in Asia for oil production. Rape is classified in the division MAGNOLIOPHYTA, class Magnoliopsida, order Capparales, family Cruciferae. See bulletins of the U.S. Dept. of Agriculture.

rape, in law, the crime of sexual intercourse with a woman (other than one's wife) without her consent. A woman is deemed legally incapable of consenting if she is insane, intoxicated, drugged, or below the AGE OF CONSENT. In most jurisdictions failure to resist physically implies consent and exonerates the accused.

Rapha (rā'fə), variant of REPHAIAH.

Raphael (răf'ēəl, rā'–), archangel. He is prominent in the book of Tobit, as the companion of Tobias, as the healer of Tobit, and as the rescuer of Sara from Asmodeus. Milton made him a featured character of *Paradise Lost*. Feast: Sept. 29 (jointly with the other archangels).

Raphael Santi or **Raphael Sanzio,** Ital. *Raffaello Santi* or *Raffaello Sanzio* (räf"fäĕl'lō sän'tē, sän'tsyō), 1483–1520, major Italian Renaissance painter, b. Urbino. In Raphael's work is the clearest expression of the exquisite harmony and balance of High Renaissance composition. His father, Giovanni Santi, painter at the court of Federigo Montefeltro, Duke of Urbino, first taught him the elements of art. About six years after the death of his father (1494) he entered the workshop of Perugino, whose influence is seen in *The Crucifixion* and *The Knight's Dream* (both: National Gall., London); *Coronation of the Virgin* (Vatican); *The Three Graces* (Chantilly); and the *Sposalizio* (Brera, Milan). The Colonna altarpiece, representing the *Madonna and Saints* (Metropolitan Mus.), marks the end of the Perugian period of his work. The five predella scenes, *Agony in the Garden* (Metropolitan Mus.), *St. Anthony of Padua* and *St. Francis* (both: Dulwich), *Procession to Calvary* (National Gall., London), and *Pietà* (Gardner Mus., Boston), give evidence of the new influences of Leonardo, Michelangelo, Masaccio, and, especially, Fra Bartolomeo. Studying the intricacies of anatomy, perspective, and coloring, he achieved a freer, more able, and deeper interpretation than was seen in his earlier work. In Florence (1504–8) he produced numerous Madonnas that are renowned for their sweetness of expression. His self-portrait (Uffizi) and the penetrating portraits of Angelo and Maddalena Doni (Pitti Palace) are also from this period. At Rome his style matured, benefiting from Michelangelo's influence. In the Vatican, Raphael was wholly responsible for the Stanza della Segnatura (finished 1511); the two largest walls represent, respectively, the *School of Athens*, portraying the Greek philosophers, and the *Triumph of Religion*, also called *Disputà*. On the vault are *The Flaying of Marsyas* and *The Temptation of Eve*. The ceiling is devoted to the allegorical figures *Law, Philosophy, Poetry,* and *Theology*. Two large lunettes over the windows represent *Parnassus* and *Jurisprudence*. In the Stanza d'Eliodoro he painted (1511–14) *The Expulsion of Heliodorus from the Temple, The Miracle of Bolsena, The Repulse of Attila from Rome by Leo I,* and *The Deliverance of St. Peter*. He also designed the *Incendio del Borgo* and painted part of it. Other designs for the Vatican include *The Battle of Ostia, The Oath of Leo III before Charlemagne,* and *The Victory of Constantine over Maxentius;* the 52 religious subjects covering one ceiling and known as "Raphael's Bible" were executed by his pupils after his design. Among the other paintings of his Roman period are the *Madonna with the Fish* (Prado); *Madonna of the Chair* (Pitti Palace); the *Sistine Madonna* (Dresden); *Galatea* (Farnesina); the *Alba Madonna* (National Gall. of Art, Washington, D.C.); and the unfinished *Transfiguration,* completed by Giulio Romano. Portraits of that period include *Julius II,* long his patron; *Baldassare Castiglione* (Louvre); *Tommaso Inghirami* (Gardner Mus., Boston); and *Pope Leo X with Two Cardinals.* Having been named (1514) successor to Bramante as chief architect of the Vatican, Raphael also designed a number of churches, palaces, and mansions. For his patron, Leo X, he undertook (1518) a survey of ancient Rome showing the chief monuments. He also designed 10 tapestries with themes from the Acts of the Apostles for the Sistine Chapel; seven of the designs are in the Victoria and Albert Museum. Raphael was deeply indebted to the sculpture of antiquity for his mythological and biblical figures, and in his interpretation of classical art he achieved a harmony and monumentality emulated far into the 19th cent. See his complete paintings, introd. by Richard Cocke (1966); complete works by Mario Salmi et al. (1969); biography by Luciano Berti (tr. 1961); studies by A. P. Oppé (rev. ed. 1970), John Pope-Hennessy (1970), and Luitpold Dussler (tr. 1971).

Raphia: see RAFA.

raphia: see RAFFIA.

Raphu (rā'fyo͞o), father of Palti the spy. Num. 13.9.

Rapid City, city (1970 pop. 43,836), seat of Pennington co., SW S. Dak., on Rapid Creek, in an irrigated farm region served by the Bureau of Reclamation's Rapid Valley project; founded 1876 after the discovery of gold nearby, inc. 1882. It is the trade and transportation center of an extensive lumbering, ranching, and mining (gold, silver, feldspar, bentonite, mica, and uranium) area. The city has meatpacking houses, flour mills, and firms that make jewelry, cement, and lumber. Nearby Ellsworth Air Force Base, a strategic air command installation, is a major source of employment. The city is also the tourist center of the Black Hills and the gateway to many attractions, including Mount Rushmore National Memorial, the Badlands National Monument, and Wind Cave National Park. South Dakota School of Mines and Technology, two nursing schools, a business college, and a Federal Sioux museum are in Rapid City. In June, 1972, the city was struck by a severe flash flood after heavy rains caused the collapse of two nearby earth dams. More than 200 lives were lost and property damage was estimated at $120 million.

rapid transit, transportation system designed to allow passenger travel within or throughout an urban area, usually employing surface, elevated, or underground railway systems or some combination of these. Rapid transit systems are generally considered to be mass transit systems, capable of moving large numbers of passengers in a single train. The large capacities of such systems make them potentially more efficient, in terms of cost and environmental effects, than automobile transportation. The principal problem to be solved in an urban rapid transit system is that of providing extra capacity to handle the volume of traffic during the morning and evening rush hours without unreasonable delays. Basically a rapid transit train consists of a number of electrically powered, self-propelled cars, each of which draws electricity from a "third rail" that runs near the tracks. Since there is an engine in each car, greater traction is produced than would be generated by a locomotive pulling a series of unpowered cars. The controls for the car motors are arranged so that an operator at either end of the train can control all of them. This arrangement eliminates involved turnarounds at the terminals. While railways of any type may have portions of their tracks below, on, or above ground level, the term *subway* is generally reserved for systems using the arrangement of cars described above and having most of their track underground. London's subway, which went into service in 1863, is the oldest in the world. Other cities which have subway service include Boston (the first in the United States, 1898), Paris (1900), Berlin (1902), New York (1904), Madrid (1919), Tokyo (1927), Moscow (1935), and Chicago (1943). Toronto's subway, completed in 1954, was the first in Canada. Some subways consist of only a single line, but others, such as the *Métropolitain* in Paris, the New York City Transit system, and the London underground, are networks. By far the largest underground transportation system in the United States is that of New York City. It comprises over 200 mi (320 km) of lines. Moscow has an elaborate subway system with tunnels 15 to 20 ft (4.6 to 6.1 m) high instead of the usual 10 ft (3.1 m). Marble was used lavishly in constructing the stations, and Russia's best-known artists participated in their decoration. In recent years the crowding of major cities throughout the world with automobile traffic has stimulated public funding for the construction and expansion of many rapid transit systems. Some of the new lines, such as the Bay Area Rapid Transit system in California, are partially or fully automatic in operation. See A. J. F. Wrottesley, *Famous Underground Railways of the World* (rev. ed. 1960).

Rapoport, Solomon Seinwil: see ANSKY, SHLOIME.

Rapp, George, 1757–1847, German religious leader, known as Father Rapp, b. Württemberg. In 1803 he emigrated to the United States, where he and his followers, known as Rappites, formed the HARMONY SOCIETY.

Rappahannock (răpəhăn'ək), river, 212 mi (341 km) long, rising in the Blue Ridge Mts., N Va., and flowing generally SE to Chesapeake Bay. It is navigable to Fredericksburg. In the Civil War much fighting took place in the vicinity of the Rappahannock and the Rapidan, its largest tributary (see BULL RUN, SECOND BATTLE OF; FREDERICKSBURG, BATTLE OF; CHANCELLORSVILLE, BATTLE OF; BRANDY STATION; WILDERNESS CAMPAIGN).

Rapperswil (rä'pərsvēl), town (1970 pop. 8,713), St. Gall canton, NE Switzerland, on the Lake of Zürich. It has some diversified light industry. Allied with several Swiss cantons after the 15th cent., Rapperswil was included in St. Gall canton in 1803. It has a 14th-century castle, a 15th-century town hall, and a 17th-century Capuchin monastery. The town is the headquarters of the International Institute of Historic Castles.

rare-earth metals, in chemistry, group of metals including those of the LANTHANIDE SERIES, usually YTTRIUM, sometimes SCANDIUM and THORIUM, and rarely ZIRCONIUM. Promethium, which is not found in nature, is not usually considered a rare-earth metal. The metals usually occur together in minerals as their oxides (RARE EARTHS) and are somewhat difficult to separate because of their chemical similarity. A subgroup of the rare-earth metals, consisting of those with atomic numbers between 57 and 63 and ytterbium, is often called the cerium metals. Misch metal is an alloy of the cerium metals often used in lighter flints, in alloys with other metals (especially MAGNESIUM), and to remove residual gases in the manufacture of vacuum tubes. Individual metals may be isolated as their compounds by ion exchange methods, solvent extraction, or fractional crystallization, and chemically or electrolytically reduced to the pure metal. Uses are discussed in articles on individual elements. See F. H. Spedding and A. H. Daane, ed., *The Rare Earths* (1961, repr. 1971).

rare earths, in chemistry, oxides of the RARE-EARTH METALS. They were once thought to be elements themselves. They are widely distributed in the earth's crust and are fairly abundant, although they were once thought to be very scarce. Generally, the name of an earth is formed from the name of its element by replacing *-um* with *-a;* e.g., the earth of cerium is ceria. Mixed rare earths are used in glassmaking, ceramic glazes, glass-polishing abrasives, carbon arc-light electrode cores, and catalysts for petroleum refining. Individual purified rare earths have many uses, e.g., in lasers and as color-television picture tube phosphors. Important rare-earth minerals include bastnasite, cerite, euxenite, gadolinite, monazite, and samarskite.

rare gas: see INERT GAS.

Raritan, river, 85 mi (137 km) long, rising in N central N.J., and flowing generally SE to Raritan Bay, an arm of Lower New York Bay, at Perth Amboy. Coal, brick products, refined metals, petroleum, clay, and sand are transported on the river. The Delaware and Raritan Canal once connected the Raritan and Delaware rivers.

Rarotonga (rärōtông'gä, rărətŏng'gə), formerly **Goodenough's Island,** volcanic island (1968 est. pop. 10,900), 26 sq mi (67 sq km), South Pacific, capital of the COOK ISLANDS. It is the largest, most important, and most southwesterly of the group. Avarua is the administrative seat and chief town and port of Rarotonga. Citrus fruit, copra, and pearl shell are exported. Rarotonga was discovered in 1823 by the English missionary John Williams.

Ras Addar, cape, Tunisia: see BON, CAPE.

Ras al-Khaimah (räs äl-khī'mä), sheikhdom (1968 pop. 24,482), c.650 sq mi (1,680 sq km), part of the federation of UNITED ARAB EMIRATES, E Arabia, on the Persian Gulf. Previously affiliated with SHARJAH, Ras al-Khaimah became a separate sheikhdom under British protection in 1921. Oil production began in 1969. After some hesitation, the sheikhdom joined the United Arab Emirates in 1972.

Ras at Tib, cape, Tunisia: see BON, CAPE.

Ras Dashan (räs dä-shän'), highest peak of Ethiopia, 15,158 ft (4,620 m) high, N Amhara Plateau, E Africa. It is of volcanic origin and has many craters.

rash, nonspecific term for an eruption of the SKIN. It may result from skin allergy, skin irritation, or skin disease, or it may be a symptom of a systemic disease like measles, smallpox, or scarlet fever. A rash may appear as discolored spots or a general redness, or as blisters or pustules, either flat or raised above the surface of the skin. The rash may cause skin irritation—itching, tingling, burning, or pain—or it may not cause any discomfort. The appearance and distribution of a rash are often important factors for consideration in diagnosing a particular disease.

Rashi (rä'shē), 1040–1105, Jewish exegete, grammarian, and legal authority, b. Troyes, France. The name he is known by is an abbreviation of Rabbi Solomon bar Isaac. He studied in Worms, returning to Troyes c.1065. There, supported by income derived from the family vineyards, he taught and wrote his famous commentaries. Those on the Old Testament (on all but a few books) and the Talmud rank among the most inclusive and authoritative in Jewish exegesis and are still important in Jewish life. Rashi's commentary on the Pentateuch (printed 1475) was the first dated Hebrew book printed. His commentary on the Talmud covers the Mishna with the Gemara. Rashi used a cursive writing, the so-called Rashi script. His work influenced Christian thinking, being known to Martin Luther. It is distinguished by great clarity. See Maurice Liber, *Rashi* (1906, repr. 1970), Herman Hailperin, *Rashi and His World* (1957) and *Rashi and the Christian Scholars* (1963); Simon Noveck, ed., *Great Jewish Personalities in Ancient and Medieval Times* (1959).

Rashid: see ROSETTA, city, Egypt.

Rashid, El, Syria: see AR RAQQAH.

Rasht (răsht), city (1966 pop. 143,557), capital of Gilan prov., NW Iran, near the Caspian Sea. It is the trade center for a fertile agricultural region where rice, cotton, silk, and peanuts are produced. Manufactures include textiles, food products, and soap. Bandar-e Pahlavi serves as its port on the Caspian. Rasht was reached by British trading expeditions from Russia in the late 16th cent. Shah Abbas I had his eldest son, Safi Mirza, murdered in Rasht. Stenka Razin, at the head of a contingent of Cossacks, pillaged the city in 1636. It is also known as Resht.

Rasis: see RHAZES.

Rask, Rasmus Christian (räs'mo͞os krĭs'tyän räsk), 1787–1832, Danish philologist. Rask was a major linguistic pioneer. He published one of the first usable Anglo-Saxon and Icelandic grammars (translated into English). Rask also produced much valuable work on the relationship of the Indo-European languages.

Rasles, Sébastien (sābästyăN' räl), 1657?–1724, French Jesuit missionary in North America. Arriving in present-day Maine in 1689, he spent two years with the Abnaki Indians in ACADIA. He then became a missionary among the Illinois Indians. In 1693 he was recalled to take charge of the mission of the Abnaki, now at Norridgewock, Maine, which was then disputed territory of the French and British. When in 1721 the British invaded the camp, Father Rasles escaped, but his dictionary of the Abnaki language, which he had been carefully compiling, was carried off. It was not published until 1833. He was killed in 1724 when the British raided the settlement. His name also appears as Rale.

Rasmussen, Knud Johan Victor (kəno͞ot' yō'hän vĭk'tôr räs'mo͞osən), 1879–1933, Danish arctic explorer and ethnologist. Born in Greenland of Eskimo ancestry on his mother's side, he began in 1902 his 30 years of exploration and of study of the Eskimo, in which he sought confirmation of his theory that they are derived from the same stock as the North American Indians, having originally migrated from Asia. In 1910 he established at Cape York, Greenland, his noted Thule station, the base for seven expeditions, five of which Rasmussen himself led. He explored (1921–24) some 29,000 mi (46,000 km) of arctic North America, being the first to traverse the Northwest Passage by dog sled when he crossed the ice of Viscount Melville Sound, accompanied only by an Eskimo woman and youth. Rasmussen also disproved the existence of Peary Channel and Independence Bay. In 1932 he went on his last expedition, from Thule to SE Greenland for ethnological and archaeological data. His translated works include *Greenland by the Polar Sea* (1921) and *Across Arctic America* (1927) in addition to several studies of the Eskimo. See Peter Freuchen, *I Sailed with Rasmussen* (1958).

raspberry, name for several thorny shrubs of the genus *Rubus* of the family Rosaceae (ROSE family) and for their fruit (see BRAMBLE).

Rasputin, Grigori Yefimovich (răspyōō'tĭn, Rus. grĭgô'rē yĭfē'məvĭch rəspōō'tyĭn), 1872–1916, Russian "holy man," a notorious figure at the court of Czar Nicholas II. He was a semiliterate peasant and debauchee who preached and practiced a doctrine of salvation that mixed religious fervor with sexual indulgence. Because of his personal magnetism and his ability to check the bleeding of the czarevich Alexis, who suffered from hemophilia, Rasputin gained a powerful hold over Czarina ALEXANDRA FEODOROVNA and, through her, over the czar. Starting in 1911, Rasputin's appointees began to fill high positions. Rasputin never had a clear political program, but unscrupulous and reactionary officials, financiers, and ecclesiastics profited through his influence. During World War I, when the czar went (1915) to the front, Rasputin's influence predominated. Those who opposed him were often removed from their posts; fortune hunters and incompetents were appointed to replace them. Rasputin's disgraceful behavior, the czarina's attempts to shield him, and a series of scandals involving his appointees helped to undermine the imperial government. It was suspected at the time that Rasputin and the czarina were working for a separate peace with Germany. In Dec., 1916, a group of right-wing patriots, including Prince Felix Yussupov and the czar's cousin, Grand Duke Dmitri, conspired to assassinate Rasputin. A generous dose of poison failed to produce any visible effect, and the terrified conspirators riddled him with bullets and threw his body into the frozen Neva River. Later buried, Rasputin's corpse was exhumed and burned by the mob during the February Revolution of 1917. See study by M. V. Rodzianko (tr. 1927 and 1973); biographies by Prince F. F. Yussupov (1927) and René Fülöp-Miller (tr. 1928).

Rassam, Hormuzd (hôrmŏŏzd' räsäm'), 1826–1910, Turkish archaeologist. He assisted Sir Austen Henry LAYARD in Nineveh in 1845–47 and 1849–51, studying at Oxford in the years between. While in charge (1852–54) of excavations for the British Museum, he discovered at Nineveh the palace of Assurbanipal. Later during field work (1872–82) in Assyria and Babylonia he identified and partially excavated the site of Sippar. He wrote *Narrative of the British Mission to Theodore, King of Abyssinia* (1869) and *Asshur and the Land of Nimrod* (1897).

Ras Shamra: see UGARIT.

Rastatt (rä'shtät, -stät), city (1970 pop. 29,850), Baden-Württemberg, SW West Germany, on the Murg River, near the French border. Manufactures include railroad cars, machinery, precision instruments, and furniture. Rastatt was first mentioned in 1247. It was destroyed (1689) by the French, but was rebuilt soon thereafter and served as the residence of the margraves of Baden-Baden from 1705 to 1771. The Treaty of Rastatt (March, 1714) complemented the treaties signed at Utrecht and Baden in 1713–14 (see UTRECHT, PEACE OF); together they ended the War of the Spanish Succession. As a result of the Treaty of CAMPO FORMIO (1797), a congress of the states of the Holy Roman Empire (attended by France) was held (1797–99) at Rastatt in order to determine compensation for the member states that had lost territory near the Rhine River to France during the French Revolutionary Wars; the congress was prematurely adjourned after the resumption of hostilities against France. Noteworthy buildings of the city include a baroque palace (17th–18th cent.) and several 18th-century churches. The city's name is sometimes spelled Rastadt.

rat, name applied to various stout-bodied RODENTS, usually having a pointed muzzle, long slender tail, and dexterous forepaws. It refers particularly to the two species of house rat, *Rattus norvegicus,* the brown, or Norway, rat and *R. rattus,* the black, roof, or Alexandrine, rat. Both species originated in Asia, but have spread throughout the world, mostly on board ships. The black rat was common in Europe in the Middle Ages and was responsible for the spreading of plague. It has since been largely displaced in cooler regions by the brown rat, which reached Europe early in the 18th cent. and North America by 1775. The brown rat is the larger of the two, growing up to 10 in. (25 cm) long excluding the naked, scaley tail and sometimes weighing more than a pound (.5 kg). It is commonly brown with whitish underparts and pink ears, feet, and tail. It is a poor climber, but an excellent burrower and swimmer; it is found in the damp basements and sewers of most temperate zone cities. The laboratory white rat is an albino strain of the brown rat. The black rat is commonly dark gray. It reaches a maximum length of 8 in. (20 cm) and has a longer tail and larger ears than the brown rat. A good climber, the black rat inhabits attics and upper floors in warm areas; it is the common rat of the Mediterranean region, the SE United States, and Central and South America. Rats are omnivorous, aggressive, intelligent, adaptable, and extremely fecund. Females produce as many as 8 litters each year with as many as 20 young per litter. The gestation period is three weeks, and the young reach sexual maturity in about two months. Rats may live as long as four years. They are social animals but sometimes fight among themselves. They live mostly in and around human settlements, where they have few natural enemies and an abundant source of food. They invade food supplies and cause widespread destruction; they also spread human diseases such as typhus, tularemia, and rabies. Despite human efforts to exterminate rats, the house rat population is probably equal to the human population. Besides the house rats, the genus *Rattus* contains several hundred wild-living species. In addition, many other members of several different rodent families are called rats, e.g., the BANDICOOT RAT, the wood rat, or PACK RAT, the rice rat, the MUSKRAT, and the KANGAROO rat. House rats are classified in the phylum CHORDATA, subphylum Vertebrata, class Mammalia, order Rodentia, family Muridae. See also MOUSE. See Hans Zinsser, *Rats, Lice and History* (1935); S. A. Barnett, *The Rat, a Study in Behavior* (1963).

Ratak Chain: see MARSHALL ISLANDS.

ratchet and pawl, mechanical device that permits motion in one direction only. The ratchet is usually a wheel with slanting teeth. The pawl is a lever tangential to the wheel with one end resting on the teeth. When the wheel rotates one way, the pawl slides over the teeth; when the wheel rotates the other way, the pawl catches in the teeth.

Ratdolt, Erhard (ĕr'härt rä'tôlt), 1442–1528, printer in Venice from 1476 to 1486 and in Augsburg from 1487 to 1522. A sheet showing specimens of his sizes and designs of type, dated 1486, is the earliest known specimen sheet. Ratdolt's ornamental initials and borders, replacing the work of the illuminator, are still admired. His printing influenced that of William Morris.

ratel (rāt'əl): see HONEY BADGER.

ratfish: see CHIMAERA.

rath (rä, räth), circular hill fort protected by earthworks, used by the ancient Irish in the pre-Christian era as a retreat in time of danger. Some of the larger raths, such as that at TARA, were important in early Irish history and were used by chieftains or kings. Many raths remain throughout Ireland.

Rathenau, Walther (väl'tər rä'tənou), 1867–1922, German industrialist, social theorist, and statesman. Son of Emil Rathenau (1838–1915), founder of the German public utilities company *Allgemeine Elektrizitätsgesellschaft* (A.E.G.), Rathenau succeeded to the presidency of this corporation on his father's death. He directed the distribution of raw materials in World War I and became minister of reconstruction (1921) and later foreign minister (1922). He represented Germany at the Cannes and Genoa reparations conferences and negotiated the Treaty of Rapallo (see RAPALLO, TREATY OF) with Russia. A Jew, he was assassinated by nationalist and anti-Semitic fanatics, who opposed his attempts to fulfill reparations obligations. Rathenau's social philosophy was idealistic. He clearly realized the dangers of industrialization and feared that civilization was moving toward a stage of extreme mechanization, in which the human soul would be lost. Opposed to state socialism, Rathenau advocated a decentralized, democratic social order, in which the means of production and distribution would be administered by consumer-producer guilds. His translated works include *In Days to Come* (1921) and *The New Society* (1921). See studies by H. K. U. Kessler (1928, tr. 1930, repr. 1969) and David Felix (1971).

Rathlin Island (răth'lĭn), 5 sq mi (13 sq km), N Northern Ireland; part of Co. Antrim. Its cliffs, of limestone and basalt, rise at Slieveacarn to 449 ft (137 m). Farming and fishing are important. St. Columba is said to have founded a church there in the 6th cent., and there are ruins of a castle in which Robert the Bruce is reputed to have hidden.

Ratibor: see RACIBÓRZ, Poland.

ratio. The ratio of two quantities expressed in terms of the same unit is the fraction that has the first quantity as numerator and the second as denominator. For example, if in a group of 100 people 5 die, the ratio of deaths to the total number in the group is $5/100=1/20=.05$. Ratios are indicated also by writing the two values with a colon between them, e.g., the ratio of 4 to 8 can be expressed by 4:8 as well as by 4/8.

rationalism [Latin,=belonging to reason], in philosophy, a theory that holds that reason alone, unaided by experience, can arrive at basic truth regarding the world. Associated with rationalism is the doctrine of innate ideas and the method of logically deducing truths about the world from "self-evident" premises. Rationalism is opposed to empiricism on the question of the source of knowledge and the techniques for verification of knowledge. René Descartes, G. W. von Leibniz, and Baruch Spinoza all represent the rationalist position, and John Locke the empirical. Immanuel Kant in his critical philosophy attempted a synthesis of these two positions. More loosely, rationalism may signify confidence in the intelligible, orderly character of the world and in the mind's ability to discern such order. It is opposed by irrationalism, a view that either denies meaning and coherence in reality or discredits the ability of reason to discern such coherence. Irrational philosophies accordingly stress the will at the expense of reason, as exemplified in the existentialism of Jean Paul Sartre or Karl Jaspers. In religion, rationalism is the view that recognizes as true only that content of faith that can be made to appeal to reason. In the Middle Ages the relationship of faith to reason was a fundamental concern of SCHOLASTICISM. In the 18th cent. rationalism produced a religion of its own called deism (see DEISTS). See J. W. Smith, *Theme for Reason* (1957); Eduard Heimann, *Reason and Faith in Modern Society* (1961); T. F. Torrance, *God and Rationality* (1971).

rationalization, in psychology: see DEFENSE MECHANISM.

rational number: see NUMBER.

rationing, allotment of scarce supplies, usually by governmental decree, to provide equitable distribution. It may be employed also to conserve economic resources and to reinforce price and production controls. Originally used in community emergencies and in distributing supplies to sailors, rationing was first organized on a national scale in Great Britain during World War I, and during World War II it spread to most of the world. The methods used have varied according to the degree of rationing needed and to the products. Rationing methods include specific rationing, or allotment in terms of physical units; point rationing, the allotment of points (ration stamps) to be apportioned by the user among commodities of a given group; and value rationing, allotment in terms of expenditure. Rations may be allotted to individuals, institutions, and industrial users, or to communities, as in rural areas of undeveloped countries. In universal rationing, ration currency is issued to everyone in equal amounts; in differential rationing, the allocation is based on need and may vary according to occupation, age, sex, or health. In the so-called flow-back system, ration currency, usually distributed by the government to the consumer, moves upward from the consumer level to the manufacturer or processor as the product moves down. During World War II, rationing in the United States was administered by the OFFICE OF PRICE ADMINISTRATION. See W. A. Nielander, *Wartime Food Rationing in the United States* (1947).

Ratisbon: see REGENSBURG, West Germany.

Rat Islands: see ALEUTIAN ISLANDS.

ratite (răt'īt), common and general term for a variety of flightless birds characterized by a flat, raftlike sternum rather than the keeled sternum, designed to support flight muscles, typical of most birds. Once used more technically, *ratite,* or *Ratitae,* is today but a loose covering term for a number of bird orders whose members possess such a breast shape. It is generally recognized, however, that the common morphology shared by these assorted birds is the product of a shared adaptation to ground living rather than of a common evolutionary descent. While ratites were formerly thought to be ancestral to the carinates, or flying birds, they are now believed to be degenerate forms that have lost adaptation for flight. Indeed, they resemble permanent overgrown chicks with short, stubby wings and soft rather than stiff-vaned flight feathers. This condition, in which animals reach adult size and maturity while maintaining an infantile appearance, is called neoteny. In their own environment, however, the ratites are by no means inferior to other birds. With their strong, heavy legs and reduced toes, they are powerful runners, and their heavy, solid bones are sturdier than the hollow bones of flying birds. The ratites include the Afro-Asian OSTRICHES, (order Struthioniformes), and their South American counterparts the RHEAS (Rheiformes), as well as a number of orders now or recently native to Australia, New Zealand, and New Guinea—the EMUS and CASSOWARIES (Casuariiformes); the KIWIS (Apterygiformes); the extinct MOAS, (Dinornithiformes); the Madagascan elephant birds, (Aepyornithiformes); and several other extinct orders. The small, tropical New World TINNAMOU, (order Tinamiformes), has a keeled sternum and can fly, but shares some features with the ratites, such as the possession of a specialized bony palate. The flightless penguins are not ratites, since they have neither bony palate nor flat breastbone. In addition, their wings are powerful swim fins, and their chest muscles and sternum are as developed as those of any flying bird. The orders of ratites are classified in the phylum CHORDATA, subphylum Vertebrata, class Aves.

Ratlam (rətläm'), town (1971 pop. 118,625), Madhya Pradesh state, E central India, on the Bombay-Delhi RR. Capital of the former state of Ratlam, the town is now a district administrative center and a market for food grains, cotton, and oilseed. Manufactures include textiles, paper, straw products, and umbrellas. Ratlam stands c.1,580 ft (482 m) above sea level.

Ratnapura (rŭt'nəpo͞orə) [Sinhalese,=city of gems], town (1963 pop. 21,582), SW Sri Lanka (Ceylon). Located in a rubber- and rice-producing area, Ratnapura is Sri Lanka's major precious-stone center and has ruby and sapphire mines and an important gem-cutting industry. It is also an administrative and commercial town. A hill topped by a Portuguese fort dominates Ratnapura. Near the town is the noted temple of Maha Saman Dewal, sacred to Buddhists and Hindus.

rat snake: see BLACK SNAKE.

rattan (rătăn'), name for a number of plants of the genera *Calamus* and *Daemonorops,* climbing palms of tropical Asia, belonging to the family Palmae (PALM family). Rattan leaves, unlike those of most palms, are not clustered into a crown; they have long, whiplike barbed tips by which the plant climbs to the tops of trees. From the stem, noted for its extraordinary length (often several hundred feet) is obtained the rattan cane of commerce, a slender, flexible tough cane of uniform diameter, usually split for wickerwork, baskets, and chair seats and left entire for walking sticks, e.g., the Malacca cane. A resin that exudes from the fruit is known commercially as DRAGON'S BLOOD. Rattan plants are classified in the division MAGNOLIOPHYTA, class Liliatae, order Arecales, family Palmae.

Rattazzi, Urbano (o͞orbä'nō rät-tät'tsē), 1808–73, Italian premier (1862, 1867). A leader of the left in the Sardinian parliament, he was briefly (1849) minister of the interior and later held cabinet posts as a strong supporter of Cavour until the two quarreled (1857). Rattazzi was again minister of the interior (1859–60). After the unification of Italy in 1861, he was twice premier; both his resignations as premier arose from trouble with Garibaldi, who attempted to take Rome during Rattazzi's premierships.

Rattigan, Terence Mervyn, 1911–, British dramatist. One of England's most popular and commercially successful contemporary playwrights, he is the master of the so-called well-made play. Among his plays are *O Mistress Mine* (1945), *The Winslow Boy* (1947), *The Browning Version* (1948), *The Deep Blue Sea* (1952), *Separate Tables* (1954), *The Sleeping Prince* (1956), *Ross* (1960), *A Bequest to the Nation* (1970), and *In Praise of Love* (1973).

rattlesnake, poisonous New World snake of the PIT VIPER family, distinguished by a rattle at the end of the tail. The head is triangular, being widened at the base. The rattle is a series of dried, hollow segments of skin, which, when shaken, make a whirring sound. When the snake is alarmed, it shakes its tail, and the noise serves as a warning to the attacker. While the snake is young, three or four segments are usually added each year, one at each molt. After maturity fewer develop and old ones start to break off. Rattlesnakes feed on rodents, birds, and other warm-blooded animals. Like other pit vipers, they have heat-sensitive organs in pits on the sides of the head, which help them locate and strike at their prey. The erectile fangs are folded back in the mouth, except when the snake strikes. The venom is highly toxic to humans and occasionally proves fatal (see SNAKEBITE). Rattlesnakes bear live young. Most species are classified in the genus *Crotalus.* The timber rattlesnake, *C. horridus,* is found from S Maine to NE Florida and W to Iowa and Texas. It is from 3½ to 5 ft (105–150 cm) long and is yellow or tan with wide, dark crossbands. The largest and deadliest species is the eastern diamondback rattlesnake, *C. adamanteus,* of the S and SE United States, which reaches a length of 5 to 8 ft (1.5–2.4 m). The western diamondback, *C. atrox,* is shorter and thicker. The western, or prairie, rattlesnake, *C. viridis,* sometimes lives in prairie-dog burrows. The SIDEWINDER, *C. cerastes,* is a North American desert species. The approximately 30 *Crotalus* species range from S Canada to N Argentina. The genus *Sistrurus* comprises the three pygmy rattlesnake species of the United States and Mexico. The smallest, *S. miliarius,* of the SE United States, is under 18 in. (45 cm) long. Rattlesnakes are classified in the phylum CHORDATA, subphylum Vertebrata, class Amphibia, order Squamata, family Crotalidae. See study by L. M. Klauber (2d ed., 1972).

rattlesnake weed: see HAWKWEED.

Rattner, Abraham, 1895–, American painter, b. Poughkeepsie, N.Y. Rattner lived and worked in Paris from 1920 to 1940. His works are characterized by intense colors in bold designs, akin to those of stained glass, and an imagery of personal religious symbolism. Rattner has designed tapestries, mosaics, and windows for temples and other buildings, including Loop Synagogue, Chicago, and the Museum of Art, Flint, Mich. Among his many paintings in major museums is his *Self-Portrait* in the Detroit Institute of Arts. Rattner has taught at numerous universities and art schools. See biography by Allen Leepa (1974).

Ratzel, Friedrich (frē'drĭkh rät'səl), 1844–1904, German geographer. He traveled as a journalist in Europe (1869) and in Cuba, Mexico, and the United States (1872–75). Thereafter he devoted himself to geographical studies and taught geography at the polytechnical school in Munich (1876–86) and at the Univ. of Leipzig (from 1886). He was a pioneer in developing the school of anthropogeography and was a founder of modern political geography. He emphasized the importance of physical environment as a factor determining human activity. His geographic concepts had a profound influence on European and American geographers and he had many followers. The most noted of his many works are *Anthropogeographie* (2 vol., 1882–91), and *Politische Geographie* (1897).

Rauch, Christian Daniel (krĭs'tyän dä'nyĕl roukh), 1777–1857, German sculptor. After studying in Rome (1804–11 and again later), where his work was influenced by Thorvaldsen, he achieved a reputation as an outstanding sculptor of tombs, monuments, and portraits. His major works include monuments to Queen Louise, Emperor Alexander of Russia, and Frederick the Great (Berlin). The latter, Rauch's chief work, is a colossal bronze equestrian statue of Frederick on a pedestal, with groups of generals and soldiers and with bas-reliefs depicting various scenes from his life.

Rauma (rou'mä), Swed. *Raumo,* city (1970 pop. 25,672), Turku ja Pori prov., SW Finland, on the Gulf of Bothnia. It is Finland's leading western port and has wood, paper, chemical, and lace and embroidery industries. In the late 19th cent. it had one of the largest sailing fleets in Finland. Rauma was an early medieval trade center, chartered c.1445. Its 15th-century Franciscan church and the old city hall (1776), now a museum, are outstanding landmarks.

Rauschenberg, Robert (rou'shənbûrg''), 1925–, American painter, b. Port Arthur, Texas. Rauschenberg studied with Josef ALBERS. His paintings, incorporating images and objects from everyday life, are executed in a loose and spontaneous style. *Gloria* (1956; Cleveland Mus. of Art) and *Summer Rental III* (1960; Whitney Mus., New York City) are characteristic of his COLLAGES known as "combines."

Rauschenbusch, Walter (rou'shənbo͞osh), 1861–1918, American clergyman, b. Rochester, N.Y. In 1886 he was ordained and began work among German immigrants as pastor of the Second German Baptist Church in New York City. He studied (1891–92) economics and theology at the Univ. of Berlin and industrial relations in England, where he became acquainted with the Fabian Society. In 1902 he was appointed professor of church history at Rochester Theological Seminary. He was a leading figure in the SOCIAL GOSPEL movement, which sought to rectify economic and social injustice. His writings include *Christianity and the Social Crisis* (1907), *Christianizing the Social Order* (1912), *The Social Principles of Jesus* (1916), and *A Theology for the Social Gospel* (1917).

Ravel, Maurice (mōrēs' rävĕl'), 1875–1937, French composer, b. in the Pyrenees. He entered the Paris Conservatory in 1889, where he was later a student of Fauré. Ravel became a leading exponent of IMPRESSIONISM. Along with Debussy, with whom he had an affinity of style, he led French music away from Wagnerian romanticism. He composed highly original, fluid music within the outlines of classical forms. Ravel excelled at piano composition and orchestration, often scoring his own piano pieces and works by other composers. Among his piano compositions are *Pavane pour une infante défunte* (1899), *Jeux d'eau* (1901), *Gaspard de la nuit* (1908), *Valses Nobles et Sentimentales* (1911), *Le Tombeau de Couperin* (1917), and Concerto in D Major, for left hand (1931). His orchestral works include *Rhapsodie Espagnole* (1908) and *Bolero* (1928); he is also known for his orchestration of Modest Moussorgsky's *Pictures at an Exhibition* (1922). Other works are the song cycle *Shéhérazade* (1903) and ballets such as *Daphnis et Chloé* (1912), *Ma Mère l'Oye* (1915), and *La Valse* (1920). See biographies by Madeleine Goss (1940), Victor I. Seroff (1953), and H. H. Stuckenschmidt (tr. 1968); study by Arbie Orenstein (1975).

raven, common name for the largest member of the family Corvidae (CROW family), ranging throughout the arctic and temperate regions of the Northern Hemisphere. The raven, *Corvus corax,* is a glossy black scavenging bird about 26 in. (66 cm) long, with a call resembling a guttural croak. Long the subject of superstition and legend, the raven can be tamed and taught to mimic human speech. Ravens are classified in the phylum CHORDATA, subphylum Vertebrata, class Aves, order Passeriformes, family Corvidae.

Ravenna (rävĕn'nä), city (1971 pop. 131,878), capital of Ravenna prov., in Emilia-Romagna, N central Italy, near the Adriatic Sea (with which it is connected by a canal). It is an agricultural market and an industrial center. Manufactures include petroleum, furniture, cement, and processed food. Ravenna rose to importance under the Romans, who made Classis, its port, the station for their fleet in the N Adriatic. In A.D. 402, Honorius made Ravenna the capital of the Western Empire, and it was also the capital (5th–6th cent.) of the Ostrogoth kings Odoacer and Theodoric, who are responsible for some of the city's best buildings. Ravenna was the seat of the exarchs (governors of Byzantine Italy) from the late 6th cent. to 751, when its capture by the Lombards broke Byzantine power in Italy. Pope Stephen II claimed the exarchate and secured the help of Pepin the Short in wresting it from the Lombards. Pepin donated the lands of the exarchate to the pope in 756; this donation, confirmed by Charlemagne in 774, marked the beginning of the temporal power of the popes. The Da Polenta family—known as Dante's hosts—were lords in Ravenna from the 13th to the 15th cent. After a period of Venetian domination, the city returned to papal control in 1509. During the ITALIAN WARS the French defeated (1512) Spanish and papal forces at Ravenna; the French commander, Gaston de Foix, died in the battle. Ravenna is famous for its colorful mosaics (see MOSAIC) of the 5th and 6th cent., which show a strong Middle Eastern influence, and for its Roman and Byzantine buildings. Ornamented with mosaics are the mausoleum of Galla Placidia (5th cent.), the octagonal baptistery (formerly a Roman bath), the 6th-century churches of Sant' Apollinare Nuovo and Sant' Apollinare in Classe, and, richest of all, the Byzantine Church of San Vitale (consecrated 547). Also of note in Ravenna are the tombs of Theodoric and Dante, the Archbishop's Palace (with a museum), and the Academy of Fine Arts. Near the city, along the sea, are pinewoods celebrated since Roman times.

Ravenna (rĭvăn'ə, rəvĕn'ə), city (1970 pop. 11,780), seat of Portage co., NE Ohio, in a lake and farm area; settled 1799, inc. 1852. Its varied manufactures include rubber, electric, and plastic products.

Ravensberg (rä'vənsbĕrkh), former county, W West Germany, now in North Rhine-Westphalia. Bielefeld was a major town in the county. In 1346, Ravensberg came under the control of the counts of BERG. It passed, with Berg, to the dukes of Jülich in 1348 and, with Jülich, to the duchy of Cleves in 1521. In 1614 it was taken by Brandenburg.

Ravensburg (rä'vənsbo͞orkh), city (1970 pop. 32,068), Baden-Württemberg, S West Germany. Its manufactures include machinery, pharmaceuticals, textiles, clothing, and processed foods. Ravensburg was founded in the late 11th cent. under the protection of the Guelphs. The ruins of the Guelphic ancestral castle are nearby. It became a free imperial city in the 13th cent. and was a flourishing commercial center in the 15th and 16th cent. The city passed to Württemberg in 1810. It has retained much of the appearance of a medieval town.

Ravi (rä'vē), one of the five rivers of the Punjab, 475 mi (764 km) long, rising in the Himalayas, NW India, and flowing generally west to join the Chenab River, NE Pakistan. Its waters are used extensively for irrigation and were contested by India and Pakistan until 1960, when a treaty on the use of the Indus River waters was signed.

Rawalpindi (räwəlpĭn'dē), city (1972 metropolitan area est. pop. 508,000), NE Pakistan. It occupies the site of an old village inhabited by the Rawals, a tribe of Yogis. A railroad junction and an important industrial and commercial center, the city has an oil refinery, gasworks, an iron foundry, railroad yards, and factories making tents, textiles, hosiery, chemicals, ordnance, finished steel, furniture, plywood, slate, and flour. Sikhs settled the area in 1765 and invited nearby traders to live in Rawalpindi. After the British occupied the PUNJAB (1849), it became a major British military outpost. In 1919 a peace treaty ending the Third Afghan War was signed by British and Afghan representatives at Rawalpindi. The city, strategically located astride the road between the Punjab and Kashmir, is Pakistan's army headquarters. From 1959 to 1970, it was the interim capital of Pakistan. Several colleges affiliated with the Univ. of the Punjab, a polytechnic school, a police training institute, and an armed forces medical college are in Rawalpindi.

Rawdon-Hastings, Francis: see HASTINGS, FRANCIS RAWDON-HASTINGS, 1ST MARQUESS OF.

rawinsonde (rā'wĭnsŏnd''), RADIOSONDE whose position in the atmosphere is continuously determined by radar or radio direction finder. Use of the rawinsonde permits simultaneous measurement of temperature, pressure, humidity, and wind velocity at different altitudes in the atmosphere. The average wind velocity in a given atmospheric layer can be determined by trigonometric calculation from the balloon's observed positions upon entering and leaving the layer; the balloon is assumed to have a perfect and immediate response to the wind and to move with the flow of air, so that its computed horizontal velocity is equivalent to the wind velocity.

Rawlings, Marjorie Kinnan, 1896–1953, American author, b. Washington, D.C., grad. Univ. of Wisconsin, 1918. She was a journalist until 1928, when she moved to the Florida backwoods, where most of her novels are set. *Cross Creek* (1942) is a humorous autobiographical account of her life there. *The Yearling* (1938; Pulitzer Prize), is the story of a boy and his pet deer. Her other novels include *South Moon Under* (1933), *Golden Apples* (1935), and *The Sojourner* (1953).

Rawlins, John Aaron, 1831–69, Union general in the American Civil War, b. Galena, Ill. Admitted to the bar in 1854, he practiced law in Galena. In 1861 he joined the Union army at the request of his fellow townsman Ulysses S. Grant and was appointed a captain and assistant adjutant general of volunteers on Grant's staff. Rawlins remained with Grant throughout the war and was his most influential adviser. He was promoted to brigadier general of volunteers in 1863, was made chief of staff of the whole Union army in March, 1865, and became a major general in the regular army in April, 1865. On Grant's accession to the presidency in 1869, Rawlins became his Secretary of War, but he died of tuberculosis before the year was out. He was an ardent advocate of Cuban independence. See biography by J. H. Wilson (1916).

Rawlinson, George, 1812–1902, English Orientalist and historian, educated at Oxford. He is known for his long, authoritative, and still useful histories of the ancient world. His most famous history is that of *The Five Great Monarchies of the Ancient Eastern World* (4 vol., 1862–67). He and his brother, Sir Henry C. Rawlinson (of whom he wrote a biography), edited works by Herodotus.

Rawlinson, Sir Henry Creswicke, 1810–95, English Orientalist and administrator; brother of George Rawlinson. In the course of his service with the Persian army and as consul at Baghdad, Rawlinson became interested in deciphering the CUNEIFORM of the BEHISTUN INSCRIPTIONS of Darius I. The results of his investigation were published in *Journal of the Royal Asiatic Society* (1846). He also helped prepare *The Cuneiform Inscriptions of Western Asia* (5 vol., 1861–84) for the British Museum. See biography by his brother (1898).

Rawlinson, Henry Seymour Rawlinson, 1st **Baron,** 1864–1925, British general; son of Sir Henry Creswicke Rawlinson. He served in the Burma expedition of 1886–87, in the Sudan campaign (1898), and in the South African War (1899–1902). In World War I he commanded (1914–15) the IV Corps and became (1916) lieutenant general in command of the British 4th Army, which went through heavy fighting in the battle of the Somme (1917). In 1918 he was a member of the Supreme War Council at Versailles, and later, returning to his previous command, he achieved notable success in piercing the German line in a breakthrough between St. Quentin and Cambrai (Aug.–Nov., 1918). He was raised to the peerage in 1919 and commanded the British forces in India from 1920 until his death. Under him high army posts were assigned to Indians for the first time, and the northwest frontier was pacified. See biography by Frederick Maurice (1928).

Rawls, John, 1921–, American philosopher and political theorist, b. Baltimore, grad. Princeton (A.B. 1943, Ph.D. 1950). He taught at Princeton (1950–52), Cornell (1953–59), and Massachusetts Institute of Technology before becoming (1962) professor of philosophy at Harvard. Rawls's chief work is *A Theory of Justice* (1971), in which he attempts, within the social contract tradition of John Locke, Jean Jacques Rousseau, and Immanuel Kant, to offer an alternative to utilitarian political philosophy. His system is developed from two basic principles: Each person has a right to the most extensive basic liberty compatible with like liberty for others; and inequalities in the distribution of wealth and power are just only when they can be reasonably expected to work to the advantage of those who are worst off. For Rawls, justice does not require equality in social position, but it does require that men share one another's fate. By providing the social contract tradition with a formidable philosophic defense Rawls's book revived interest in systematic political theory. See study by B. M. Barry (1973).

Ray or **Wray, John,** 1627–1705, English naturalist. He was extremely influential in laying the foundations of systematic biology. With his pupil Francis Willughby, he planned a complete classification of the vegetable and animal kingdoms and toured Europe collecting specimens. On Willughby's death, Ray organized and published the material left by his friend. Ray's own work—the botanical part of the project—includes the important *Historia plantarum* (3 vol., 1686–1704). Ray was the first to name and make the distinction between monocotyledons and dicotyledons. He was also the first to define and explain the term *species* in the modern sense of the word. Ray studied and wrote on quadrupeds, reptiles, and birds. The Ray Society for the publication of scientific works was founded in his honor in 1844. See his *Correspondence*, ed. by Edwin Lankester (1848) and *Further Correspondence*, ed. by R. W. Gunther (1928); C. E. Raven, *John Ray, Naturalist* (2d ed. 1951).

Ray, Man, 1890–, American painter and photographer, b. Philadelphia. Ray was a founder of the DADA movement in New York and Paris. He is celebrated for his later surrealist paintings and photography. Among his inventions is the rayograph, a photograph obtained by the direct application of objects of varying opacity to a light-sensitive plate. His paintings include *The Rope Dancer Accompanies Herself with Her Shadows* (Mus. of Modern Art, New York City). Ray also made several surrealist films, of which *L'Étoile de Mer* (1928) is the best known. See his autobiography (1963).

Ray (rā), city (1966 pop. 102,835), Tehran prov., N Iran, a suburb of Tehran. The mausoleum of Hazrat Abd al-Azim, a major Shiite Muslim holy person, is there. The city was the site of the ancient and medieval city of RAGES. Ray is also known as Rai and Rey.

ray, extremely flat-bodied cartilaginous marine FISH, related to the SHARK. The pectoral FINS of most rays are developed into broad, flat, winglike appendages, attached all along the sides of the head; the animal swims by rippling movements of these wings. Most rays have slender whiplike tails. The eyes and spiracles are located on top of the head, the mouth and the GILL slits on the underside. Many rays are bottom dwellers, lying like rugs on the sea floor; others inhabit the upper waters. Bottom-dwelling rays breathe by taking in water through the spiracles, rather than through the mouth as most fishes do, and passing it out through the gills. Rays feed on a variety of smaller animals; the heavy, rounded teeth of most species are adapted to crushing the shells of snails and clams. The rays, which form the order Batoidea, are divided into seven families. The largest are the mantas, also called devil rays and devilfish (family Mobulidae). These are top-swimming forms which may weigh up to 3,000 lb (1360 kg), with a width of up to 22 ft (7 m). Unlike most rays, mantas are filter-feeders; the manta uses a pair of horns at the front of the head to drive small prey into its mouth; there the prey is caught in a strainer and swallowed, the water passing out through the manta's gills. Electric rays, or torpedos (family Torpedinidae), have electric organs in their wings that generate electric current, used to immobilize prey and for defense. The current is strong enough to stun humans, and it is said that the ancient Greeks used these fish for shock therapy. Skates (family Rajidae), which are sometimes caught for food, are bottom dwellers with nearly disk-shaped bodies and short tails; some species have electric organs in their tails. The stingrays, or whiprays (family Dasyatidae), have rows of spines along their tails, which are generally much longer than their bodies. The stingray inflicts wounds by lashing with its tail; the spines contain a poison that causes pain and can be fatal to humans. Most of the eagle rays and bat rays (family Myliobatidae) bear a single poison spine on the tail. The guitarfishes (family Rhinobatidae) are sharklike in form, having well-developed tails used for swimming and smaller pectoral fins than most rays; however, the fins are attached, as in all rays, above the gills, giving these fishes a broad-headed appearance. Sawfishes (family Pristidae) are similar in body form, but have long, flat snouts with a row of toothlike projections on either side. Some species reach a total length of 20 ft (6 m), with snouts 6 ft (1.8 m) long and 1 ft (30 cm) wide. They use these ponderous weapons to slash and impale small fishes and to probe in the mud for burrowing animals. Sawfishes should not be confused with saw sharks, which are true sharks. Fertilization is internal in rays. Most bear live young, but the skates lay flattened, rectangular eggs, enclosed in leathery shells, with tendrils at the corners for anchorage. Empty egg cases of this type are found on beaches and are known as mermaids' purses. Most ray families have a more or less cosmopolitan distribution in tropical and subtropical marine waters; some include temperate or cold-water species. Some rays can live in brackish bays and estuaries, and the sawfish enters freshwater rivers and lakes. Rays are classified in the phylum CHORDATA, subphylum Vertebrata, class Chondrichthyes, subclass Elasmobranchii, order Batoidea.

ray, in astronomy: see MOON.

ray, in physics, term denoting the straight line along which LIGHT or other form of radiation is propagated from its source. It generally refers to the line of propagation of waves but is also applied to streams of particles such as the electrons emitted from a cathode or particles emitted by substances exhibiting RADIOACTIVITY. See COSMIC RAYS; X RAY.

Rayburn, Sam, 1882–1961, U.S. legislator, b. Samuel Taliaferro Rayburn in Roane co., Tenn. After his family moved (1887) to Fannin co., Texas, he worked at cotton picking. He worked his way through school, studied law at the Univ. of Texas, and practiced in Bonham, Texas. He was (1907–12) a member of the Texas legislature and in 1913 entered the U.S. Congress. A middle-of-the-road Democrat, Rayburn soon became prominent in national politics. In the 1930s he was the man most directly responsible for the passage of New Deal legislation in the House. Rayburn held the office of speaker (1940–47; 1949–53; 1955–61) more than twice as long as any of his predecessors; his great political skill and his intimate knowledge of the House rules contributed to his unique prestige as a parliamentary leader. See biography by C. D. Dorough (1962); study by Booth Mooney (1971).

Rayleigh, John William Strutt, 3d **Baron** (rā'lē), 1842–1919, English physicist. He was professor at Cambridge (1879–84) and at the Royal Institution (1887–1905), and chancellor of Cambridge from 1908. He won the 1904 Nobel Prize in Physics for his discovery (with Sir William Ramsay) of argon. He is known for his extensive and important research in sound (resonance, vibration, diffraction, hearing) and light (scattering, polarization, optics, color vision); for his determinations of electrical units; and for his investigation of the application of Boyle's law to gases at low pressures. His works include *The Theory of Sound* (1877–78) and *Scientific Papers* (1899–1920).

Raymond IV, c.1038–1105, count of Toulouse (1093–1105), leader in the First Crusade (see CRUSADES). He was also count of Saint Gilles and marquis of Provence. The first great prince to take the Cross, he was the chief planner and organizer of the expedition. He refused to follow BOHEMOND I and GODFREY OF BOUILLON in swearing fealty to the Byzantine emperor ALEXIUS I, confining himself to a promise (1097) to do no injury to the emperor's life or honor. Raymond distinguished himself at the sieges of Nicaea, Antioch, and Jerusalem, but quarreled (in vain) with Bohemond over the possession of Antioch. Having refused the title king of Jerusalem, he fought at Ashkelon (1099). Unable to protect his city of Laodicea against Bohemond, he went to Constantinople to seek the aid of Alexius. Subsequently he was held prisoner by TANCRED, who was acting as regent for Bohemond. At the end of his life, with Byzantine support, he laid siege to Tripoli, which was finally formed into a county by his descendants. See biography by J. H. Hill and L. L. Hill (1962).

Raymond VI, 1156–1222, count of Toulouse (c.1194–1222). His tolerant attitude towards the ALBIGENSES resulted in his repeated excommunication, although he temporarily made peace with the church in 1209. Attacked (1211) by Simon de MONTFORT, he received the support of his brother-in-law Peter II of Aragón. In 1213 he and Peter were defeated at Muret, and Raymond went into exile in England. Although obliged to grant Toulouse and Montauban to Montfort and Provence to his own son, Raymond VI returned (1217) and fought with his son against Montfort and Montfort's son. By the time of his death, Raymond had recaptured almost all of his territory for his son.

Raymond VII, 1197–1249, count of Toulouse; son of Count Raymond VI. He fought with his father in the ALBIGENSIAN CRUSADE, assisting Raymond VI in his attempt to regain Toulouse from Simon de MONTFORT and Simon's son, Amaury. Continuing the war on his father's death (1222), he signed (1223) a truce with Amaury in which the latter renounced the countship of Toulouse. In 1226, King Louis VIII of France resumed the Albigensian Crusade. Defeated by the French, Raymond VII agreed in 1229 to a treaty that virtually transferred the major part of S France to the French crown, partly through cession, partly through the proposed marriage of his daughter to ALPHONSE of Poitiers, a brother of King Louis IX of France. Raymond was permitted to keep much of his lands during his lifetime. He was compelled, however, to allow the establishment of the Inquisition in his lands. In 1242, in alliance with King Henry III of England, he revolted against France. He was forced to sue for peace after Henry's defeat and agreed to destroy the Albigenses. He executed many heretics.

Raymond, c.1140–1187, count of Tripoli (1152–87), great-great-grandson of Raymond IV of Toulouse. He played a leading part in the last years of the Latin Kingdom of Jerusalem. Captured (1164) by the Muslims, he was released c.1173 and became (1174) regent for King BALDWIN IV of Jerusalem. He gave up that post in 1176, but in 1183 was appointed regent for Baldwin V. Leading the baronial faction in the kingdom, Raymond opposed GUY OF LUSIGNAN, who became king at the death (1186) of Baldwin, and he even entered into an alliance with SALADIN. However, in 1187 he became reconciled with Guy and valiantly led the Christians in the battle of Hattin. Saladin was victorious, and the Kingdom of Jerusalem soon fell entirely into the hands of the Muslims. Raymond died at Tyre soon after the battle. See M. W. Baldwin, *Raymond III of Tripolis and the Fall of Jerusalem* (1936).

Raymond, town (1971 pop. 2,156), S Alta., Canada, SE of Lethbridge, in a sugar beet area. Sugar is refined and honey is produced there. A provincial agricultural college is in the town.

Raymond Berengar IV (bĕr'əngär), d. 1162, count of Barcelona (1131–62). He married Petronilla, daughter and heir of King Ramiro II of Aragón, after whose abdication (1137) Raymond also ruled Aragón. Catalonia and Aragón remained united under Raymond's descendants. Raymond continued the fight against the Moors and took Tortosa (1148), Lérida (1149), and several other towns. He also took part in politics in S France. One of the greatest figures of the Catalan dynasty, Raymond was succeeded by his son Alfonso II.

Raynal, Guillaume Thomas François, Abbé (gēyōm' tômä' fräNswä' äbā' rānäl'), 1713–96, French historian and philosopher. Raynal was a priest, but he was dismissed from his parish in Paris; he then turned to writing and sought the society and collaboration of the philosophes. His history (6 vol., 1770) of political and commercial colonization in the Orient and the New World was condemned by the Parlement of Paris in 1781 because of its impiety and its dangerous ideas on the right of the people to revolt and to give or withhold consent to taxation.

rayon, synthetic fibers made from CELLULOSE or textiles woven from such fibers; more rayon is manufactured than any other synthetic fiber. The name was adopted (1924), in preference to "artificial silk," by the U.S. Dept. of Commerce and various commercial associations. As early as 1665 the English naturalist Robert Hooke had suggested the possibility of making artificial silk, but the first artificial textile fiber was produced in 1884 by a French scientist, Hilaire de Chardonnet, and was manufactured by him in 1889. Unpopular at first because it was too lustrous and laundered poorly, it has been steadily improved. Cellulose, originally from cotton linters but now chiefly from wood pulp, washed, bleached, and pressed into sheets, is dissolved by chemicals, then forced under pressure through minute holes in a metal cap (spinneret), emerging as filaments that unite to form one continuous strand solidified by passage through a suitable liquid or warm air. The spinning solution may be forced through a larger orifice or slit to produce a monofilament, a ribbon, or a sheet. Filaments are doubled and twisted into smooth, silklike yarns or cut into staple lengths and spun. Spun rayon can be treated to simulate wool, linen, or cotton. There are four methods of manufacturing rayon, using different materials and processes. In the nitrocellulose process developed by Chardonnet and no longer of commercial importance, cellulose is treated with nitric and sulfuric acids. In the VISCOSE PROCESS discovered in 1892, it is treated with carbon disulfide, then dissolved in caustic soda, forced through a spinneret, and hardened in sulfuric acid. Viscose rayon is the most important type commercially, being used in most kinds of wearing apparel, furniture fabric, and carpets. For cuprammonium rayon, the cellulose is dissolved in copper oxide and ammonia, forced through holes larger than the intended diameter, then, by a process known as stretch spinning, is elongated and twisted under tension to yield a very fine, strong yarn used for sheer fabrics and hosiery. Rayon produced by these three methods is classified as regenerated, since the final product, like the original material, is cellulose. The fourth type, saponified acetate rayon, originated in England in 1918, is an acetate derivative of cellulose made by steeping cellulose in acetic acid, then treating it with acetic anhydride. Acetate rayon is more resistant to stains and creasing, is plasticized by heat, and requires special dyes, thus allowing two-tone effects with a single dye when acetate is combined with other fibers. An acetate filler is used to make shatterproof glass.

Rayonnant style (rā'ənänt), the middle period (c.1240–1350) of French GOTHIC ARCHITECTURE, so termed from the characteristic radiating tracery of the ROSE WINDOW. In this period many of the great cathedrals were under construction; the builders became bolder and more proficient, emphasizing in every way the vertical elements of the structure. Light and soaring structural skeletons were erected, reducing the size of all supporting members; the enlargement of windows resulted in a drastic reduction of wall surfaces. Bar TRACERY, displaying elaborate geometrical patterns, supplanted plate tracery. Sculptural ornament turned to greater naturalism and was used more generously. Of this period are the cathedral at Amiens (begun 1220), the Sainte-Chapelle at Paris (1243–46), and the earlier portions of St. Ouen at Rouen (begun 1318). The Rayonnant style spread to other parts of Europe. The scheme was employed in the cathedrals at Cologne, Germany (begun 1248), and Leon, Spain (begun c.1255).

Raytown (rā'toun"), city (1970 pop. 33,306), Jackson co., W central Mo., a residential suburb of Kansas City; inc. 1950. It was the first stop on the Santa Fe Trail out of Independence, Mo.

Razak, Abdul (äb'dŏŏl rä'zäk), 1922–, prime minister of Malaysia (1970). He worked in the civil service and local government before his election to the national legislature in 1959. He was deputy prime minister and minister of defense from 1959 to 1970 and held other cabinet offices. He became prime minister and foreign minister in 1970, succeeding Tunku Abdul Rahman, and also retained his defense post.

Razin, Stenka (stĕng'kä rä'zēn), d. 1671, Cossack leader, head of the peasant revolt of 1670. As commander of a band of propertyless Cossacks of the Don, he raided and pillaged (1667–69) through the lower Volga valley and across the Caspian Sea. On his return (1670) to the Don, Razin rebelled against the authority of the czar. His force of some 7,000 men took Tsaritsyn (now Volgograd), Astrakhan, Saratov, and Samara (now Kuybyshev), and was joined by serfs, peasants, and non-Russian tribes of the middle and lower Volga region. However, he was defeated by government troops at Simbirsk (now Ulyanovsk) and fled to the Don, where the propertied Cossacks delivered him to the government. Razin was executed at Moscow. His exploits have long been celebrated in song and legend.

Rb, chemical symbol of the element RUBIDIUM.

Ré (rā), island, 33 sq mi (85 sq km), Charente-Maritime dept., off La Rochelle, W France, in the Bay of Biscay. The island is largely agricultural; it has oyster beds, some fishing, and a salt-extraction industry. There is also some tourism. The citadel, built (1681) by Vauban at Saint-Martin-de-Ré, is now a penitentiary. The name was formerly sometimes spelled Rhé.

Re: see RA, in Egyptian religion.

Re, chemical symbol of the element RHENIUM.

reactance: see IMPEDANCE.

reaction, chemical: see CHEMICAL REACTION.

reaction-formation: see DEFENSE MECHANISM.

reaction rate: see CHEMICAL REACTION.

reactor, nuclear: see NUCLEAR REACTOR.

Read, George, 1733–98, American jurist, signer of the Declaration of Independence, b. near Northeast, Cecil co., Md. He was admitted to the bar in 1753 and later (1763–74) was attorney general of the Lower Counties (Delaware) and a member of the Continental Congress (1774–77). Initially opposed to the resolution for independence, he later signed the Declaration of Independence. He was president of the Delaware constitutional convention in 1776 and president of Delaware (1777–78). Read was a member of the Federal Constitutional Convention (1787) and helped to make Delaware the first state to ratify the Constitution (Dec. 7, 1789). A U.S. Senator (1789–93), he resigned to become (1793) chief justice of Delaware. See W. T. Read, *Life and Correspondence of George Read* (1870).

Read, Sir Herbert, 1893–1968, English poet and critic. His studies at the Univ. of Leeds were interrupted by World War I, in which he served with a Yorkshire regiment. After the war he completed his education. His first volume of poems, *Naked Warriors* (1919), treats the horrors of war. An advocate of free verse, he published poetry all his life; his last volume of *Collected Poems* was published in 1966. Read was an important critic of both art and literature, and he influenced the treatment of these subjects in British education. As an art critic he defined and advocated various modern art movements and aided the careers of many British artists, notably Henry Moore. His works of art criticism include *The Innocent Eye* (1933), *Art and Industry* (1934), *Art and Society* (1936), *Education Through Art* (1943), *Art Now* (1948), *The Grass Roots of Art* (1961), and *Art and Alienation: The Role of the Artist in Society* (1967). As a literary critic, Read reasserted the importance of the 19th-century English Romantic authors, most notably in *The True Voice of Feeling: Studies in English Romantic Poetry* (1953). His other works of literary criticism include *Form in Modern Poetry* (1932), *Coleridge as Critic* (1949), and *Phases of English Poetry* (1950). Read also wrote many essays, some of which are collected in *The Cult of Sincerity* (1969). See his autobiographical *The Contrary Experience* (1974); studies by W. T. Harder (1972) and George Woodcock (1972).

Reade, Charles, 1814–84, English novelist and dramatist. He is noted for his historical romance *The Cloister and the Hearth*. After being elected a fellow of Magdalen College, Oxford, he was called to the bar. His interests, however, soon turned to the theater. He achieved his first success with *Masks and Faces* (1852), written in collaboration with Tom TAYLOR. The play, concerned with life in the theater, was used as the basis for his first novel, *Peg Woffington* (1853). An ardent reformer, he began a long series of propagandist novels with *It's Never Too Late to Mend* (1856), describing the cruelties of prison discipline. Others in the series included *Hard Cash* (1863), and *Put Yourself in His Place* (1870). He also wrote the novels *Griffith Gaunt* (1866), *Foul Play* (1869), and *A Terrible Temptation* (1871). *The Cloister and the Hearth* (1861), is a picaresque novel concerning the adventures of Gerard, the father of Erasmus. In 1879 Reade collaborated with Charles Warner in writing *Drink*, a dramatization of Zola's *L'Assommoir*. See biography by Malcolm Elwin (1931); study by Wayne Burns (1961).

Reading, Rufus Daniel Isaacs, 1st **marquess of** (rĕd'ĭng), 1860–1935, British statesman. Called to the bar in 1887, he achieved great success in his profession. He entered Parliament as a Liberal in 1904, became attorney general in 1910, and in 1912 was given a seat in the cabinet. Involved in charges of buying stock in the American Marconi Corp. while the government was contracting with the British branch of the firm, he was, however, exonerated and in 1913 was created lord chief justice. During World War I he served the government in financial operations, becoming (1915) president of an Anglo-French loan commission to the United States, where he subsequently served as special envoy (1917) and special ambassador (1918–19). In 1921 he was made viceroy of India at a time when the temper of the people, partly under the influence of Mohandas GANDHI and partly as a result of the massacre at AMRITSAR (1919), was roused against British rule. Faced with the passive resistance of the Gandhi adherents, Isaacs authorized the imprisonment of Gandhi and felt compelled to allow the hated salt tax. He returned to England in 1926 and was created a marquess (having already been created in succession baron, viscount, and earl), but he was much criticized for his administrative acts in India. He was (1931) foreign secretary in Ramsay MacDonald's National government. See biographies by Stanley Jackson (1936), his son G. R. Isaacs, 2d marquess of Reading (2 vol., 1943–45), and H. M. Hyde (1967).

Reading, county borough (1971 pop. 132,023), county town of Berkshire, S central England, on the Kennet River near its influx to the Thames. Reading is a market center with iron founding, engineering, malting, brewing, and biscuit and seed industries. It was occupied in 871 by the Danes, who burned it in 1006. A gateway and ruins of buildings, surrounded by a public park, remain of a Benedictine abbey founded in 1121 by Henry I, who is buried there. Several parliaments met in the abbey. In 1643 the town surrendered to the parliamentarians under the 3d earl of Essex. There are a 15th-century grammar school, the Reading College of Technology, and the Univ. of Reading (1926; formerly a college, founded 1892, of Oxford Univ.), with noted departments of agriculture and dairying. Oscar Wilde's *Ballad of Reading Gaol* was inspired by his imprisonment there, and Reading is the Aldbrickham of Thomas Hardy's *Jude the Obscure*.

Reading. **1** Town (1970 pop. 22,539), Middlesex co., NE Mass., a suburb of Boston; settled 1639, set off from Lynn and inc. 1644. Printing is the major industry. A 17th-century tavern is in the town. **2** City (1970 pop. 14,303), Hamilton co., SW Ohio, a suburb of Cincinnati; platted 1798, inc. 1851. It has diverse light manufacturing industries. **3** City (1970 pop. 87,643), seat of Berks co., SE Pa., on the Schuylkill River, in the Pennsylvania Dutch region; laid out 1748, inc. as a city 1847. It is an important commercial, industrial, and railroad center, with large railroad shops and a marketing point in a fertile farm area. Its many manufactures include textiles, clothing, leather goods, and iron and steel products. Reading was an early iron-producing town; cannons were made there during the Revolution, and it was a Union ordnance center during the Civil War. It is the seat of Albright College. Also in the city are the county historical society, a museum, and a planetarium. Nearby points of interest include the birthplace of Daniel Boone (now a state historic park) and the Pagoda, a Japanese-style observation tower on Mt. Penn.

reading, process of mentally interpreting written symbols. Facility in reading is an essential factor in educational progress, and instruction in this basic skill is a primary purpose of elementary education. The ability to read was not considered important for most laymen until sometime after Johann Gutenberg's invention of the printing press (c.1450), and the Protestant Reformation, with its emphasis on individual interpretation of the Bible. Until that time reading was generally restricted to the clergy and certain members of the nobility. Although ILLITERACY is still a problem in many areas of the world, compulsory childhood education laws have assured that most citizens of advanced industrial nations can read. Physiological and psychological studies suggest that the process of reading is based on a succession of quick eye movements, known as fixations, across the written line, each of which lasts for about a quarter of a second. In each fixation more than one word is perceived and interpreted, so that a skilled reader may take in more than three words per fixation when reading easy material. Depending on the rate of his fixations and the difficulty of the material, an adult can read and understand anywhere from 200 to 1,000 words per minute. There is considerable difference of opinion about the best method of teaching children to read. The central issue involves the relative merits of the whole-word and phonics approaches. Most educators, however, agree on the importance of remedial work for students whose progress is impeded by impaired vision, faulty eye movements, or personal handicaps resulting from poor teaching. See Gertrude Hildreth, *Teaching Reading* (1958); Ivor A. Richards, *How to Read a Page* (1959); George Cuomo, *Becoming a Better Reader* (1960); Hunter Diack, *Reading and the Psychology of Perception* (1960); Jeanne S. Chall, *Learning to Read: The Great Debate* (1967); Margaret Cox, *The Challenge of Reading Failure* (1968); Mortimer J. Adler and Charles Van Doren, *How to Read a Book* (rev. ed. 1972); M. C. Robeck and J. A. R. Wilson, *Psychology of Reading* (1974).

Reading, University of, at Reading, Berkshire, England; established 1892 as a university extension college affiliated with Oxford Univ. In 1926 it received its charter as an independent university. It has faculties of letters and social sciences, science, agriculture and food, urban and regional studies, as well as a school of education. The National Institute for Research in Dairying is part of the university.

Reagan, John Henninger (rē'gən), 1818–1905, American political leader, b. Sevierville, Tenn. He moved to Texas in 1839, became a lawyer, and held several state offices before serving (1857–61) as a Democrat in the U.S. House of Representatives. Reagan, a member of the Texas secession convention of 1861, was elected to the provisional congress of the Confederacy, and Jefferson Davis appointed him postmaster general in March, 1861. He ably administered that department throughout the Civil War. Urging Texans to accept the results of the war, he helped frame the state constitutions of 1866 and 1875. He was returned (1875–87) to the House, and served (1887–91) in the U.S. Senate. Reagan was joint author of the act (1887) that established the Interstate Commerce Commission. See his memoirs, ed. by W. F. McCaleb (1906, repr. 1968); biography by B. H. Procter (1962).

Reagan, Ronald Wilson, 1911–, governor of California (1967–75), b. Tampico, Ill. A motion-picture actor, he served six terms as president of the Screen Actors Guild (1947–51, 1959). In the 1950s he was among those Democrats who supported Dwight D. Eisenhower and Richard M. Nixon. After joining the Republican party in 1962 he championed right-wing causes. In the California gubernatorial election of 1966 he defeated the incumbent, Edmund G. "Pat" Brown. Reagan was reelected in 1970. As governor, he cut state welfare and medical services and aid to public schools and higher education. He did not run for reelection in 1974.

Reaia (rē"ā'ə, rēā'yə), son of Micah the Reubenite. 1 Chron. 5.5.

Reaiah (rē"ə'ə, rēā'yə). **1** Grandson of Judah. 1 Chron. 4.2. **2** Family that returned from the Exile. Ezra 2.47; Neh. 7.50.

real estate: see PROPERTY.

realgar (rēăl'gər), mineral, arsenic monosulfide, AsS, with a red to yellow color. It commonly occurs in association with other arsenic minerals, less often with ores of silver and lead. It is monoclinic, showing short prismatic crystals, and on prolonged exposure to light it disintegrates into a powder. Macedonia, Japan, Rumania, and Switzerland are sources of the mineral, and in the United States it is found in Utah and Nevada and in Yellowstone National Park.

realism, in art, specifically, the movement of the mid-19th cent. formed in reaction against the severely academic production of the French school. Realist painters sought to portray what they saw without idealizing it, choosing their subjects from what was the ugly and commonplace of everyday life. The major realists included Gustave COURBET, J. F. MILLET, and Honoré DAUMIER. In a broader sense the term is applied to an unembellished rendering of natural forms. In recent years realism has come to mean the presentation of forms and materials that are simply themselves, not primarily representations of things that already exist.

realism, in literature, an approach that attempts to describe life without idealization or romantic subjectivity. Although realism is not limited to any one century or group of writers, it is most often associated with the literary movement in 19th-century France, specifically with the French novelists Flaubert and Balzac. George Eliot introduced realism into England, and William Dean Howells introduced it into the United States. Realism has been chiefly concerned with the commonplaces of everyday life among the middle and lower classes, where character is a product of social factors and environment is the integral element in the dramatic complications (see NATURALISM). In the drama, realism is most closely associated with Ibsen's social plays. Later writers felt that realism laid too much emphasis on external reality. Many, notably Henry James, turned to a psychological realism that closely examines the complex workings of the mind (see STREAM OF CONSCIOUSNESS).

realism, in philosophy. **1** In medieval philosophy realism represented a position taken on the problem of UNIVERSALS. There were two schools of realism. Extreme realism, represented by WILLIAM OF CHAMPEAUX, held that universals exist independently of both the human mind and particular things—a theory closely associated with that of Plato. Some other philosophers rejected this view for what can be termed moderate realism, which held that universals exist only in the mind of God, as patterns by which he creates particular things. St. THOMAS AQUINAS and JOHN OF SALISBURY were proponents of moderate realism. **2** In epistemology realism represents the theory that particular things exist independently of our perception. This position is in direct contrast to the theory of idealism, which holds that reality exists only in the mind. Most contemporary British and American philosophy tends toward realism. Prominent modern realists have included Bertrand Russell, G. E. Moore, and C. D. Broad. See J. D. Wild, *Introduction to Realistic Philosophy* (1948); Henry Veatch, *Realism and Nominalism Revisited* (1954).

real number: see NUMBER.

Real Presence, the actual presence of the body and blood of Jesus Christ in the EUCHARIST. The term was defined in the 16th cent. at the Council of Trent; the doctrine is held especially by Roman Catholics and some Anglicans. For various Protestant interpretations, see LORD'S SUPPER.

real property: see PROPERTY.

reaper, farm machine of earlier years that was drawn by draft animals or by tractor and used to harvest grain. The historical predecessors of the reaper were the sickle and the cradle scythe, which are still used in some parts of the world. The earliest known reaper using animal power was described by Pliny the Elder as used in Gaul. It was pushed by an ox and consisted of a box on two wheels with a comb projecting from the front of the box. The heads of the grain were torn off by the comb and fell into the box. Modern attempts to make reaping machines began in England, where the first patent was issued in 1799. The first reaper to win general acceptance for practical field work was made by American inventor Cyrus Hall McCormick in 1831. The grain cut by this reaper fell on a platform, from which it was raked by a man who walked beside the machine. A number of improved reapers were developed later. The COMBINE, which threshes the grain as it is reaped, has virtually replaced the reaper, although a self-raking type is still used to a limited extent. The MOWER, used for cutting hay, was developed from the reaper in the 19th cent. See Cyrus McCormick, *The Century of the Reaper* (1931, repr. 1971).

reapportionment: see LEGISLATIVE APPORTIONMENT.

Reason, Age of: see ENLIGHTENMENT.

Réaumur, René Antoine Ferchault de (rā'əmyŏŏr, Fr. rənā' äNtwän' fĕrshō' də rāōmür'), 1683–1757, French physicist and naturalist, one of the foremost scientists of the 18th cent. He invented an alcohol thermometer (1731) and the Réaumur temperature scale, in which the freezing point of water is 0° and the boiling point 80°. In 1710 he directed the official description of arts and trades in France. He investigated gold-bearing rivers, turquoise mines, and forests. He did research on the composition of Chinese porcelain, which led him to develop an opaque glass, and on the composition and manufacture of iron and steel, including a means of tinning iron. As a naturalist he is best known for his exhaustive study of insects (6 vol., 1734–42; a 7th vol., part of the original manuscript, appeared in 1928); he also studied regeneration in crayfish and showed corals to be animals, not plants.

Reba (rē'bə), king of Midian killed by the Jews. Num. 31.8; Joshua 13.21.

rebate, partial refund of the total price paid for goods or services. In the United States, rebates were historically given by railroads to favored shippers as a return on transportation charges. The Elkins Act (1903), the Hepburn Act (1906), and the regulations of the INTERSTATE COMMERCE COMMISSION prohibit and penalize railroad rebates. A tax rebate from local, state, or federal governments may occur when unexpectedly large tax revenues create a budget surplus. The term is also used to refer to coupons, trading stamps, and other premiums used by retailers to stimulate sales.

rebec (rē'bĕk), one of the earliest European forms of the violin. It was pear-shaped, had from three to five strings, and possessed a strident tone. Its use, documented as early as the 8th cent., was to play melo-

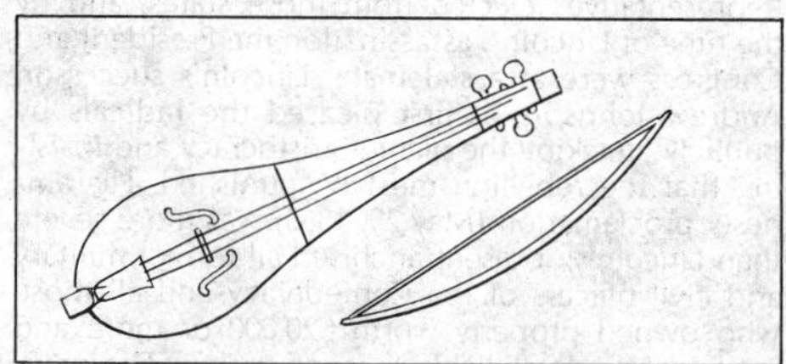

Rebec

dies of popular songs and dance music, accompanied by percussion. The rebec became obsolete because it lacked the volume needed for large ensembles.

Rebecca or **Rebekah** (both: rēbĕk'ə), wife of Isaac and mother of Jacob. One day, as was her custom, she drew water at the city well; while there she showed kindness to Eliezer, Abraham's servant. He had been sent to select a suitable wife for Abraham's son, Isaac, and he chose Rebecca. After years without children she bore the twins Jacob and Esau. Jacob was his mother's favorite, and for him she devised their deception of the blind Isaac. She is one of the four Jewish matriarchs. Gen. 24-27; 49.31; Rom. 9.10.

Récamier, Juliette (zhülyĕt' rākämyā'), 1777-1849, celebrated French beauty and social figure, née Jeanne Françoise Julie Adelaïde Bernard. At 15 she married Jacques Récamier, a wealthy middle-aged banker; their marriage was a mere formality. Her fashionable salon was, from the Consulate to the end of the July Monarchy, a gathering place for some of the most influential political and literary figures. Although many men fell in love with her, Mme Récamier, whose nature was ineffably gentle and unpassionate, probably never had any but platonic attachments. The most celebrated of her liaisons was that with Chateaubriand, to whom she devoted the later part of her life. Among her friends were Mme de Staël, Sainte-Beuve, and Benjamin Constant. The famous portrait of her by Jacques Louis David hangs in the Louvre. Her memoirs and correspondence have been published. See study by H. D. Sedgwick (1940); Maurice Levaillant, *The Passionate Exiles* (1956, tr. 1958).

recapitulation, theory, stated as the biogenetic law by E. H. HAECKEL, that the embryological development of the individual repeats the stages in the development of the race. Studies of embryos show that at certain stages the embryos of fish, birds, and mammals are very similar. The beginnings of gill clefts appear in both man and fish, but while they are elaborated and eventually function in the fish, in humans, except for the modified gill cleft that becomes the Eustachian tube, they disappear as the embryo develops. The significance of this theory—"ontogenesis recapitulates phylogenesis"—is that it lends support to the theory of EVOLUTION.

Recared (Recared I) (rĕk'ərĕd), d. 601, Visigothic king in Spain (586-601), son and successor of LEOVIGILD. Although before his accession he had greatly distinguished himself in warfare with the Franks, he did not pursue his father's policy of conquest. He did make war on the Basques and repulsed Frankish invasions, but in general he was pacific. He made peace with the Byzantine Empire, and he seems to have sought to conciliate his Roman subjects. The most important event of his reign was his conversion (c.587-589) to Roman Catholicism; this meant the conversion of the Visigoths, but only after the suppression of a number of Arian revolts and conspiracies. There is good reason for believing that Recared modified the Visigothic law even more than Euric or Leovigild. His work is, however, a matter of conjecture. His name is also spelled Reccared.

Recceswinth (rĕk'əswĭnth), d. 672, Visigothic king of Spain (653-72). He was the son of CHINDASWINTH, who in 649 admitted him to joint rule. Recceswinth succeeded to the throne without election, thereby violating the Visigothic tradition enjoining election of the king by the nobility. Almost immediately he was faced by an insurrection. Although he conquered the rebellious nobles, he nevertheless compromised by rejecting the principle of hereditary succession at the Eighth Council of Toledo. Like his father, he advocated a policy of assimilation between his Visigothic and Spanish-Roman subjects. Considered one of the greatest Visigothic lawmakers, Recceswinth completed and promulgated (c. 654) the law code begun by his father to replace the BREVIARY OF ALARIC of 506. Known as the *Liber iudiciorum* and later as the *Liber* or *Forum iudicum*, its 12 books fused Roman and Germanic law and were binding on both populations. The compilation was the basis of Spanish medieval law and served for centuries as a widely used legal handbook.

recession: see DEPRESSION.

Rechab (rē'kăb). **1** Eponym of the Rechabites. Jer. 35. **2** Murderer of Ish-bo-sheth. 2 Sam. 4.2.-12. **3** Father of a worker on the wall. Neh. 3.14.

Rechabites (rē'kəbīts), in the Bible, a family that practiced asceticism. Organized by Jonadab, who helped Jehu purge Israel of the Baal cult, they drank no wine, built no houses, sowed no seed, planted no vines, and lived in tents. Jer. 35. The Rechabites were apparently related to the Kenites. 1 Chron. 2.55.

Rechah (rē'kə), unidentified place. 1 Chron. 4.12.

recidivism: see CRIMINOLOGY.

Recife (rəsē'fī) [Port.,=reef], city (1970 pop. 1,060,-752), capital of Pernambuco state, NE Brazil, a port on the Atlantic Ocean. The city is also called Pernambuco by foreigners. The chief urban center of NE Brazil, it lies partly on the mainland and partly on an island. Dissected by numerous waterways, it is often called the Brazilian Venice. Its fine natural harbor, enclosed by a coral reef, has modern facilities. Recife exports great quantities of the hinterland's products, including sugar, cotton, and coffee. Sugar refining and cotton milling are the chief industries, but the majority of the labor force is employed in the service sector. The city is an important transportation center, with an international airport and good railroad and highway facilities. Founded by the Portuguese in 1548 as the port for nearby Olinda, Recife was settled by fishermen and sailors. The city was plundered by the British in 1595, and was occupied by the Dutch (1630-54), prospering under Maurice of Nassau. After the Dutch occupation, Recife replaced Olinda as capital of the Pernambuco captaincy. During World War II an Allied air base was there. The city is the seat of two universities and has long been famed for its intellectual groups and political ferment. In addition to its modern buildings, Recife has a 17th-century cathedral, an old Dutch fort, and an elaborate government palace.

reciprocal trade agreement, international commercial treaty in which two or more nations grant equally advantageous trade concessions to each other. It usually refers to treaties dealing with tariffs. For example, one nation may grant another a special schedule of TARIFF concessions in return for equivalent advantages. Originally reciprocity agreements involved bilateral tariff reductions that were not to be extended to third countries. In the 18th cent., England relaxed its Navigation Acts in return for similar action by other nations. In the 19th cent. the German ZOLLVEREIN was based on reciprocity, and the system of reciprocity fostered by Napoleon III worked strongly in favor of FREE TRADE. After the downfall of the French Second Empire (1870), most European countries began to follow a policy of high tariffs. In the United States reciprocity was advocated as part of the tariff policy after 1880. The use of the MOST-FAVORED-NATION CLAUSE after 1922 resulted in a widespread exchange of tariff concessions; it was followed by the Trade Agreements Act (1934). Since 1948 the general policy of the United States has been to negotiate reciprocal tariff concessions within the framework of the GENERAL AGREEMENT ON TARIFFS AND TRADE (GATT). The Trade Expansion Act (1962) provided for negotiations, under GATT auspices, to expand reciprocal trade agreements, especially with the European COMMON MARKET. The act resulted in the Kennedy Round (1967) of reciprocal tariff reductions, mainly between the United States and W Europe. In 1973 a new round of tariff meetings opened in Tokyo. Reciprocal agreements may also deal with such matters as rights of foreigners and consular relations. See Gottfried Haberler, *Theory of International Trade* (rev. ed. 1956).

recitative (rĕs"ĭtətēv'), musical declamation for solo voice, used in opera and oratorio for dialogue and for narration. Its development at the close of the 16th cent. made possible the rise of opera. The Florentine composers Peri, Caccini, and Galilei sought a style in which the words could be clearly understood, the rhythms of natural speech would be followed, and the music would convey the feeling of a whole passage. Toward the middle of the 17th cent. arose *recitativo secco*, which employed a quick succession of notes having little melodic character and serving only to advance the action, punctuated by occasional chords in a figured bass accompaniment. *Le Nozze di Figaro* by Mozart employs much recitative of this sort. In 18th-century opera greater importance was assumed by the *recitativo accompagnato* or *stromentato*, accompanied by the string section or the full orchestra, in which the music was more strictly measured. This type of recitative was used at the points of greatest dramatic interest and to introduce important arias. Robert Cambert and Lully developed a style of recitative suited to the French language; Purcell and Mozart attacked similar problems in English and German. Wagner, opposed to the Italian type of recitative, developed his *Sprechgesang*, in which the melody was completely molded to the text, upon which the accompaniment served as a sort of commentary.

Recklinghausen (rĕk'lĭnghou"zən), city (1970 pop. 125,237), North Rhine-Westphalia, W West Germany, an industrial center and transshipment point for the RUHR district. Manufactures include iron and steel, machinery, chemicals, and textiles. Recklinghausen was chartered c.1230 and was held until 1803 by the archbishopric of Cologne. In 1815 it came under Prussian sovereignty. The city retains part of its medieval fortifications and a Romanesque church.

Reclamation, United States Bureau of, agency set up in the Dept. of the Interior under the Reclamation Act of 1902, at first called the Reclamation Service. It is charged with promoting regional economies by developing water and related land resources in the West. The original purpose of developing and executing irrigation projects in arid and semiarid regions of the West has been expanded to include developing, and often executing, projects to provide municipal and industrial water supplies, hydroelectric power generation and transmission, water quality improvement, flood control, navigation, and river regulation and control. The bureau contracts for the project beneficiaries to reimburse the government for the cost of constructing and operating the project. In what is now the U.S. Southwest, Indians practiced irrigation before the coming of the Spanish. Catholic missionaries there, and more particularly in California, supervised agriculture under irrigation on a large scale. Modern irrigation practices may, however, be said to have begun in 1847 with the Mormons in Utah. By 1865 nearly 150,000 acres were under irrigation by various groups and individuals in the West. Strong moves to gain government help for reclamation schemes resulted in the CAREY LAND ACT (1894). Attention focused sharply on conservation of natural resources during the presidency of Theodore Roosevelt, and reclamation was advocated for lands ruined by injudicious farming, grazing, and deforestation as well as for lands with little rainfall. Representative (later Senator) Francis Griffith Newlands was the author of the Reclamation Act of 1902 (sometimes called the Newlands Act). It provided that the Federal government should plan and construct irrigation projects using the proceeds of PUBLIC LAND sales, and that the water users (usually organized in some type of cooperative) should liquidate the cost and purchase the irrigation works over a period of 10 years. The program was immediately and vigorously pushed by Secretary of the Interior Ethan Allen Hitchcock. Among the many projects started then were the Truckee-Carson project (see NEWLANDS PROJECT) and the Salt River project (see SALT RIVER VALLEY). The 1902 act had an acreage-limitation provision, but it did not halt the process of speculation in lands to be irrigated, which made costs to the actual farmers prohibitive. In 1914 the period of time for the water users to pay for the project was lengthened to 20 years (later raised to 40 years). Interest in reclamation quickened after terrible droughts in the late 1920s and early 30s, and in the public works program of the New Deal under Franklin Delano Roosevelt the reclamation program was linked with projects for flood control and for the development of power. The Bureau of Reclamation began to work alongside the U.S. Army Engineers Corps in building dams and forwarding many-purpose projects. The Flood Control Act of 1944 broadened the powers of the Federal government in these matters. The Bureau of Reclamation in many instances chooses the sites for dams to be used for power as well as irrigation, and it constructs them. It cooperates with the Federal Power Commission and other government agencies in distributing the power developed. Among such projects are the Bonneville Dam (with an enormous power project) and Grand Coulee Dam, together with a host of related activities on the Columbia, the Snake, and their tributaries (see COLUMBIA, river); the CENTRAL VALLEY PROJECT in California; the COLORADO-BIG THOMPSON PROJECT; and the MISSOURI RIVER BASIN PROJECT. Reclamation has created much new wealth in the United States by turning areas that had formerly been wasteland into thriving agricultural and industrial communities.

reclamation of land, practice of converting unproductive land (e.g., desert or swamp wasteland) into arable land by such methods as IRRIGATION, DRAINAGE, flood control, improving of the texture and of the mineral and organic content of soil (see FERTILIZER), and checking EROSION. In the United States, all these methods have been widely used, but the chief government effort has been directed toward reclamation by irrigation and by flood control. Federal sponsorship of reclamation projects dates from the Reclamation Act of 1902 and is carried on chiefly by the Bureau of Reclamation (see RECLAMATION, UNITED STATES BUREAU OF). See Paul Wagret, *Polderlands* (1968); Stuart Chase, *Rich Land, Poor Land* (1936, repr. 1969).

Reclus, Jean Jacques Élisée (zhäN zhäk ālēzā' rəklü'), 1830–1905, French geographer, b. Gironde, educated mainly in Germany, where he studied under Karl Ritter. Several times he was forced to leave France because of his political views, and he traveled in the British Isles, the United States, and South America and for many years lived in Switzerland. He was professor of comparative geography at the Univ. of Brussels from 1895 to 1905. The great work of Reclus is his *Nouvelle Géographie universelle* (19 vol., 1876–94; tr. *The Earth and Its Inhabitants,* 19 vol., 1876–94). *La Terre* (2 vol., 1868–69) was also translated into English (*The Earth,* 2 vol., 1871).

recognition, acknowledgment of the admission of new states into the international community by political action of states that are already members. Its derivation is found in the policy of the older European powers, which, after developing a system of binding diplomatic usage, refused to permit the admission of new states to the concert of nations unless the new power was properly qualified to assume its responsibilities under international law. Three kinds of recognition exist. Recognition of independence occurs when a new state is created, usually by a successful rebellion, and is accepted by members of the international community, either by a formal statement or by entering into diplomatic relations with the new state. Recognition of independence generally takes place after the new nation has demonstrated its ability to maintain itself; if a power recognizes an insurrectionary colony or dependency while the mother country is attempting to crush the rebellion, it is considered an offense to the dominant country that is being ousted. A second type of recognition may occur when a new form of government follows the establishment of a new political force in a country. A republic may be recognized as the successor of a monarchy, or a new president may be acknowledged after the overthrow of the previous incumbent. Recognition of belligerency, the third kind, was introduced into international law when that form of acknowledgment was given (1861) to the Confederate States of America by Great Britain. Such recognition grants the belligerents the rights and duties of a state as they concern war and commerce, but it does not grant the right to enter into official diplomatic relations with neutral nations. In recognizing belligerency, the nation offends the state against which the rebellion is directed. When recognition is *de facto* it involves a provisional acknowledgment that the government in power is exercising the function of sovereignty. Such recognition is revocable and implies a lesser degree of recognition than the formal recognition accorded *de jure* [Lat.,=as of right]. Recognition is retroactive to the actual date of the establishment of the state or the formation of the new government, and all its acts from that time are valid. The withholding of diplomatic recognition may be used in an attempt to force changes of policy on a new government, as illustrated by the nonrecognition of the Huerta (1913) and Obregón (1920) governments in Mexico and of the Communist government in China (1949) by the United States. The United States normally follows a policy known as the Stimson Doctrine (established by Secretary of State Henry Stimson in 1931), which states that the United States does not recognize territorial changes brought about by breach of international obligation. For this reason the United States did not recognize the Japanese-supported government in Manchukuo (1932) or the Italian government in Ethiopia (1936). This principle is implied in the Charter of the United Nations. See Hersch Lauterpacht, *Recognition in International Law* (1947); T. C. Chen, *The International Law of Recognition* (1951); Bernard Bot, *Nonrecognition and Treaty Relations* (1968).

recoilless rifle, light artillery piece, without recoil, usually operated by two men. An American invention, it was used as an infantry weapon for attacking fortifications such as pillboxes and bunkers during the last months of World War II and later in the Korean and Vietnam wars. Unlike standard artillery pieces it does not need a recoil mechanism and thus is light enough to be carried by one man. Recoilless rifles use a perforated artillery cartridge case that allows a portion of the propellent gases to escape through vents in the breech of the gun, thereby greatly reducing the recoil.

recombination, process by which an individual acquires new GENES, or hereditary material. In recombination through sexual reproduction, the offspring's complete set of genes results from the combination of both parents' genetic material and is different from the set of genes of either parent. In recombination by CROSSING OVER, paired, or allelic, genes are exchanged during MEIOSIS. This exchange results in the introduction of new alleles on segments of chromosomes, counteracting the tendency of linked genes, i.e., genes on the same chromosome, to be always transmitted as a group. Various mechanisms for introducing new genetic material have been discovered in bacteria. In transformation, a fragment of free deoxyribonucleic acid (DNA) is inserted in a recipient bacterium (see NUCLEIC ACID). The free DNA fragment comes from the CHROMOSOME of a bacterial cell that has been lysed, or dissolved. In transduction, genetic material is transferred from one bacterium to another by a carrier virus. When a virus enters a bacterium, its DNA is inserted into the bacterial chromosome, reproducing along with the host chromosome in cell division. Subsequently, sometimes many bacterial generations later, the viral particle is detached from the bacterial chromosome, taking some of the bacterial chromosomal material along with it. The bacterium then lyses, the viral particle enters a new bacterium, and the viral particle, together with the bacterial genes it carries, is inserted into the chromosome of the new host. In conjugation, which occurs between bacteria of the same species and also between some bacteria of different species, either an entire chromosome or a part of one is transferred from a bacterium of a donor-mating strain to a bacterium of a recipient-mating strain. Donor strains, denoted male, contain a sex-factor particle composed of a nucleic acid; recipient, or female, strains lack the particle (see EPISOME). The bacterial recombination mechanisms have been used extensively to study gene structure and function. Conjugation has been used to construct genetic maps, i.e., the ordering of genes along a chromosome. Evidence from transformation experiments was used to support the idea that DNA was the genetic material.

Recôncavo: see BAHIA, state; SALVADOR, Brazil.

Reconstruction, 1865–77, in U.S. history, the period of readjustment following the Civil War. At the end of the Civil War, the defeated South was a ruined land. The physical destruction wrought by the invading Union forces was enormous, and the old social and economic order founded on Negro slavery had collapsed completely, with nothing to replace it. The 11 Confederate states somehow had to be restored to their positions in the Union and provided with loyal governments, and the role of the emancipated Negroes in Southern society had to be defined. Even before the war ended, President Lincoln began the task of restoration. Motivated by a desire to build a strong Republican party in the South and to end the bitterness engendered by war, he issued (Dec. 8, 1863) a proclamation of amnesty and reconstruction for those areas of the Confederacy occupied by Union armies. It offered pardon, with certain exceptions, to any Confederate who would swear to support the Constitution and the Union. Once a group in any conquered state equal in number to one tenth of that state's total vote in the presidential election of 1860 took the prescribed oath and organized a government that abolished slavery, he would grant that government executive recognition. Lincoln's plan aroused the sharp opposition of the radicals in Congress who believed it would simply restore to power the old planter aristocracy. They passed (July, 1864) the Wade-Davis Bill, which required 50% of a state's male voters to take an "ironclad" oath that they had never voluntarily supported the Confederacy. Lincoln's pocket veto kept the Wade-Davis Bill from becoming law, and he implemented his own plan. By the end of the war it had been tried, not too successfully, in Louisiana, Arkansas, Tennessee, and Virginia. Congress, however, refused to seat the Senators and Representatives elected from those states, and by the time of Lincoln's assassination the President and Congress were at a stalemate. Lincoln's successor, Andrew Johnson, at first pleased the radicals by publicly attacking the planter aristocracy and insisting that the rebellion must be punished. His amnesty proclamation (May 29, 1865) was more severe than Lincoln's; it disenfranchised all former military and civil officers of the Confederacy and all those who owned property worth $20,000 or more and made their estates liable to confiscation. The obvious intent was to shift political control in the South from the old planter aristocracy to the small farmers and artisans, and it promised to accomplish a revolution in Southern society. With Congress in adjournment from April to Dec., 1865, Johnson put his plan into operation. Under provisional governors appointed by him, the Southern states held conventions that voided or repealed their ordinances of secession, abolished slavery, and (except South Carolina) repudiated Confederate debts. Their newly elected legislatures (except Mississippi) ratified the Thirteenth Amendment guaranteeing Negro freedom. By the end of 1865 every ex-Confederate state except Texas had reestablished civil government. The control of white over Negro, however, seemed to be restored, as each of the newly elected state legislatures enacted statutes severely limiting the freedom and rights of the Negroes. These laws, known as BLACK CODES, restricted the ability of Negroes to own land and to work as free laborers and denied them most of the civil and political rights enjoyed by whites. Many of the offices in the new governments, moreover, were won by disenfranchised Confederate leaders, and the President, rather than ordering new elections, granted pardons on a large scale. An outraged Northern public believed that the fruits of victory were being lost by Johnson's lenient policy. When Congress convened (Dec. 4, 1865) it refused to seat the Southern representatives. Johnson responded by publicly attacking Republican leaders and vetoing their Reconstruction measures. His tactics drove the moderates into the radical camp. The Civil Rights Act (April 9, 1866), designed to protect the Negro from legislation such as the black codes, and the Freedmen's Bureau Bill (July 16), extending the life of that organization (see FREEDMEN'S BUREAU), were both passed over Johnson's veto. Doubts as to the constitutionality of the Civil Rights Act led the radicals to incorporate (June, 1866) most of its provisions in the Fourteenth Amendment (ratified 1868). The newly created Joint Committee on Reconstruction reported (April 28, 1866) that the ex-Confederate states were in a state of civil disorder, and hence, had not held valid elections. It also maintained that Reconstruction was a congressional, not an executive, function. The radicals solidified their position by winning the elections of 1866. When every Southern state (except Tennessee) refused to ratify the Fourteenth Amendment and protect the rights of its Negro citizens, the stage was set for more severe measures. On March 2, 1867, Congress enacted the Reconstruction Act, which, supplemented later by three related acts, divided the South (except Tennessee) into five military districts in which the authority of the army commander was supreme. Johnson continued to oppose congressional policy, and when he insisted on the removal of the radical Secretary of War, Edwin M. STANTON, in defiance of the TENURE OF OFFICE ACT, the House impeached him (Feb., 1868). The radicals in the Senate fell one vote short of convicting him (May), but by this time Johnson's program had been effectively scuttled. Under the terms of the Reconstruction Acts, new state constitutions were written in the South. By Aug., 1868, six states (Arkansas, North Carolina, South Carolina, Louisiana, Alabama, and Florida) had been readmitted to the Union, having ratified the Fourteenth Amendment as required by the first Reconstruction Act. The four remaining unreconstructed states—Virginia, Mississippi, Texas, and Georgia— were readmitted in 1870 after ratifying the Fourteenth Amendment as well as the Fifteenth Amendment, which guaranteed the Negro's right to vote. The radical Republican governments in the South attempted to deal constructively with the problems left by the Civil War and the abolition of slavery. Led by CARPETBAGGERS (Northerners who settled in the South), SCALAWAGS (Southern whites in the Republican party), and freedmen, they began to rebuild the Southern economy and society. Agricultural production was restored, roads rebuilt, a more equitable tax system adopted, and schooling extended to Negroes and poor whites. The freedmen's civil and political rights were guaranteed, and Negroes were able to participate in the political and economic life of the South as full citizens for the first time. The bitterness engendered by the Civil War remained, however, and most Southern whites objected strongly to the Negro's new role in society. Organizations such as the KU KLUX KLAN arose. Their acts of violence kept Negroes and white Republicans from voting, and gradually the radical Republican governments were overthrown. Their collapse was hastened by the death of the old radical leaders in Congress, such as Thaddeus STEVENS and Charles SUMNER, and by the revelation of internal corruption in the radical Republican government; the Grant administration was compelled to lessen its support of them because of growing criticism in the North of corruption in the Federal government itself. By 1876 only Florida, South Carolina, and Louisiana remained under Republican domination. The Republican presidential candidate, Rutherford B. HAYES, promised to alleviate conditions in the South, but the feeling there had already led to the formation of the "solid South" in support of his Democratic opponent, Samuel J. TILDEN. In those three states the presidential contest was the occasion for a determined effort to throw off Republican rule, and on their electoral votes (and on one disputed electoral vote in Oregon) hung the fate of the famous disputed election of 1876. It is practically certain that at least one of the three gave a majority, and thus the presidency, to Tilden, but two sets of returns were sent in from each of the three states. A specially constituted electoral commission (composed of eight Republicans and seven Democrats) accepted the Republican returns, and Hayes was given the presidency. Reconstruction officially ended as all Federal troops were withdrawn from the South. White rule was restored, the Negro was once again deprived of many civil and political rights, and his economic position remained depressed. The radicals' hopes for a basic reordering of the social and economic structure of the South, beyond the abolition of slavery, died. The results, instead, were the one-party "solid South" and increased racial bitterness. The literature on the period is extensive and has shown sharp changes in interpretation. The first major historical writing on Reconstruction was done early in the 20th cent. It reflected the rising tide of nationalism that followed the Spanish-American War and incorporated the then current assumptions of Negro racial inferiority. Reconstruction was portrayed as a tragic era during which vindictive, scheming, radical Republicans imposed harsh military rule on a vanquished South and supported corrupt state governments dominated by unscrupulous carpetbaggers, scalawags, and uneducated freedmen. Typical examples of this school of historiography are J. W. Burgess, *Reconstruction and the Constitution* (1902, repr. 1970); W. A. Dunning. *Reconstruction, Political and Economic* (1907, repr. 1962); W. L. Fleming, *The Sequel of Appomattox* (1919, repr. 1921); C. G. Bowers, *The Tragic Era* (1929, repr. 1962); and E. M. Coulter, *The South During Reconstruction* (1947). The first major attack upon this interpretation came from W. E. B. Du Bois in *Black Reconstruction* (1935, repr. 1969). It stimulated a complete rethinking of the meaning of Reconstruction. The old Burgess-Dunning school of thought was revised and to a large extent discredited. The moral idealism of the radicals has been recognized and their sincere concern for the rights of the freedmen applauded. Historians agree that the radical state governments were no more corrupt than their predecessors and successors, and that they made notable contributions toward restoring a devastated Southern economy, protecting the rights of freedmen, and extending public education to whites and blacks alike. Some of the best examples of revisionist writing are C. V. Woodward, *Reunion and Reaction* (2d ed. 1956, repr. 1966); E. L. McKitrick, *Andrew Johnson and Reconstruction* (1960); J. H. Franklin, *Reconstruction* (1961); W. R. Brock, *An American Crisis* (1963); K. M. Stampp, *The Era of Reconstruction* (1965); J. P. Shenton, ed., *The Reconstruction* (1963); K. M. Stampp and L. F. Litwack, ed., *Reconstruction: An Anthology of Revisionist Writings* (1969); Robert Cruden, *The Negro in Reconstruction* (1969); H. L. Trefousse, *Reconstruction: America's First Effort at Racial Democracy* (1971); E. L. Thornbrough, comp., *Black Reconstructionists* (1972); LaWanda and J. H. Cox, *Reconstruction, the Negro, and the New South* (1973).

Reconstruction Finance Corporation (RFC), former U.S. government agency, created in 1932 by the administration of Herbert Hoover. Its purpose was to facilitate economic activity by lending money in the depression. At first it lent money only to financial, industrial, and agricultural institutions, but the scope of its operations was greatly widened by the New Deal administrations of Franklin Delano Roosevelt. It financed the construction and operation of war plants, made loans to foreign governments, provided protection against war and disaster damages, and engaged in numerous other activities. In 1939 the RFC merged with other agencies to form the Federal Loan Agency, and Jesse JONES, who had long headed the RFC, was appointed federal loan administrator. After Jones became (1940) Secretary of Commerce, Congress transferred (1942) the RFC to his department. When Henry Wallace succeeded (1945) Jones, Congress removed the agency from Dept. of Commerce control and returned it to the Federal Loan Agency. When the Federal Loan Agency was abolished (1947), the RFC assumed its many functions. After a Senate investigation (1951) and amid charges of political favoritism, the RFC was abolished as an independent agency by act of Congress (1953) and transferred to the Dept. of the Treasury to wind up its affairs, effective June, 1954. It was totally disbanded in 1957. RFC had made loans of approximately $50 billion since its creation in 1932. See J. H. Jones, *Fifty Billion Dollars* (1951).

recorder, musical wind instrument of the FLUTE family, made of wood, varying in length, and having an inverted conical bore (largest end near the mouthpiece). Its tone is produced by an air stream against an edge, like that of the flute, but the air is conducted by a mouthpiece through a channel to the edge; intonation is somewhat less flexible on the vertical recorder than on the transverse flute. The recorder has a soft, sweet timbre which makes it an ideal chamber instrument. It was known in Europe as early as the 10th cent., and at first was the principal flute instrument. By the 16th cent. it was made in a variety of sizes, and in the 17th and early 18th cent. it was a very important solo, chamber, and orchestral instrument. Until c.1750, the term *flute* referred to the recorder; the transverse flute was always distinguished by a qualifying adjective. After that time the recorder was too weak for the continually growing orchestra, and it fell into disuse until the revival of interest in older music and instruments in the early 20th cent. Since it lacks keys and a complicated embouchure, the recorder is one of the few instruments of artistic importance easily played by an amateur, a fact that has contributed to its growing popularity. It has a huge literature of solo and ensemble music from the 16th to 18th cent., to which many 20th-century composers have added. Related to the recorder is the FLAGEOLET, which differs mainly in that it has fewer holes, usually six, two of which are closed by the thumbs. It was known as early as the 16th cent. and has seldom figured in serious music.

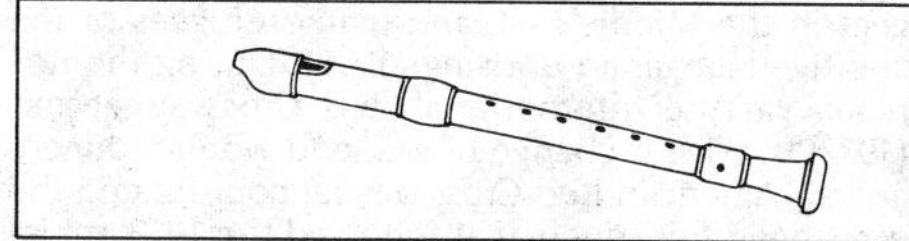

Alto recorder

record player or **phonograph,** device for reproducing sound that has been recorded as a spiral, undulating groove on a disk. This disk is known as a phonograph record, or simply a record (see SOUND RECORDING). In using a record player, a record is placed on the player's motor-driven turntable, which rotates the record at a constant speed. A tone arm, containing a pickup at one end, is placed on the record. The tone arm touches the groove of the record with its stylus, or needle. As the record revolves, the variations in its groove cause the stylus to vibrate. The stylus is part of the pickup, a device that also contains a TRANSDUCER to convert these mechanical vibrations into corresponding electrical signals. These signals are then increased in size by an AMPLIFIER. After leaving the amplifier, they are passed to a LOUDSPEAKER that converts them into sound. Although sound waves had been recorded in the middle of the 19th cent., the first machine to reproduce recorded sound, the phonograph, was built by Thomas A. Edison in 1877. Edison's records were made of tinfoil, upon which a groove of unvarying lateral direction but varying depth was cut; later this method became known as "hill-and-dale" recording. In 1887, Emile Berliner invented the disk record (patented 1896) having grooves of unvarying depth but of varying lateral direction. His method, called lateral recording, superseded the earlier method. Berliner also invented the matrix record, from which unlimited duplicate recordings could be pressed. In these early recordings the sound was directed into a horn that transmitted the vibrations, by means of a diaphragm, directly to the stylus that cut the groove. Only a limited frequency range and part of the overtones could be recorded. Orchestral recording was not attempted until c.1913 and even then was very unsatisfactory. The turntable was operated by a spring-driven motor that required rewinding for each record played; later the use of an electric motor made rewinding unnecessary. Automatic record changers were developed, and the quality of reproduction was greatly improved by high-fidelity amplification (popularly called hi-fi) and by complex speaker systems. Stereophonic reproduction is achieved by adapting the phonograph to reproduce two or four channels of sound (see STEREOPHONIC SOUND), in such a way that the different sections of an orchestra, for example, seem to be located as they are in a concert hall. From 1948 records were made to be played at slower speeds, thus lengthening the amount of material that could be recorded on a single disk. In addition to musical performances, records are used to reproduce sound effects for radio and the theater, transcriptions of radio broadcasts, "talking books" for the blind, and lessons for language study. See Roland Gelatt, *The Fabulous Phonograph* (rev. ed. 1966).

recreation, any activity voluntarily engaged in for the satisfaction it brings, whether through relaxation, fun, or the opportunity for self-expression. Suitable recreation may be a factor in promoting mental and bodily health, in developing personality, occupational skills, and social cooperation, and in preventing delinquency. Although the need for recreation has only recently been recognized, it has found expression since ancient times in games, festivals, dances, and music. In the United States a noncommercial recreation movement was initiated in the 19th cent. by the establishment of gymnasiums in schools and universities and by the opening of parks and playgrounds. The playground, fostered at first by social and philanthropic agencies in order to keep children off the streets, also received support in the 20th cent. from schools and municipal and state agencies. The National Recreation Association (organized in 1906 as the Playground Association of America) has been a leader in promoting playgrounds, training recreation leaders, and widening recreation opportunities for adults. The extension of community recreation facilities for adults was stimulated in World War I by the organization of recreation for the armed forces. In the 1930s the Federal government, as a means of relieving unemployment caused by the depression and as part of its conservation program, sponsored projects to maintain and expand national parks for recreation. The expansion of recreational facilities in the mid-20th cent. has been stimulated by the growth of cities, by the need to relieve tension resulting from the pressure of modern living and the specialization and mechanization of work, and by the increase of leisure time created by the general reduction of working hours. Commercial interests provide such recreations as moving pictures, radio, television, music, travel, and professional sports. The expansion of professional sports has been especially marked. For example, in just a ten-year period (1959-69) the number of American cities having major professional football teams more than doubled, growing from 12 to 26. See UNITED SERVICE ORGANIZATIONS; YOUNG MEN'S CHRISTIAN ASSOCIATION; YOUNG WOMEN'S CHRISTIAN ASSOCIATION. See Reuel Denney, *The Astonished Muse* (1957); G. D. Butler, *Playgrounds* (3d ed. 1960); Foster R. Dulles, *A History of Recreation* (2d ed. 1965); Richard G. Kraus, *Recreation and Leisure in Modern Society* (1971).

rectifier, component of an electric circuit used to change alternating current to direct current. Rectifiers are made in various forms, all operating on the principle that current passes through them freely in one direction but only slightly or not at all in the opposite direction. One type of rectifier is the diode ELECTRON TUBE. When low currents are to be rectified, a diode tube from which all gases have been removed can be used. When higher currents are to be rectified, a gas such as mercury vapor is enclosed in the tube; the gas aids conduction across the gap between cathode and anode. The industrial type for high current is called the mercury-arc rectifier. It uses a pool of mercury for the anode; the tube is in the form of a metal tank. A SEMICONDUCTOR rectifier is essentially a DIODE made large enough to safely dissipate the heat caused by current flow. For heavy currents, it is often equipped with cooling fins. Semiconductors used as rectifiers are crystalline materials such as selenium, copper oxide, germanium, and silicon. Silicon semiconductors are widely used because of their stability under high voltages and currents. There are two kinds of mechanical rectifiers. One, for polyphase alternating current, is a rotating switch that is synchronized with the fluctuations of the alternating current. The other uses a synchronized vibrating reed to change single-phase alternating current into pulsating direct current.

rectum: see INTESTINE.

recycling: see SOLID WASTE.

red algae: see SEAWEED; RHODOPHYTA.

Red Angus cattle: see ANGUS CATTLE.

Red Bank. 1 Borough (1970 pop. 12,847), Monmouth co., E N.J., on the Navesink estuary, in a fertile farm area; inc. 1908. An early shipping center, it is now a summer and winter resort with some light industry. Landmarks include Old Christ Church (1769) and the Allen House (1667). Albert Brisbane helped to establish a Fourierist phalanx there in 1843. 2 City (1970 pop. 12,715), Hamilton co., SE Tenn., a residential suburb of Chattanooga; inc. 1955.

redbird: see CARDINAL.

red blood cell: see BLOOD.

Redbridge, borough (1971 pop. 238,614) of Greater London, SE England. Redbridge was created in 1965 by the merger of the municipal boroughs of Ilford and of Wanstead and Woodford, part of the municipal borough of Dagenham, and part of the urban district of Chigwell. Although primarily residential, Redbridge is an important shopping and commercial center. Its industries include light engineering and the manufacture of electrical components, photographic materials, and chemicals. Much of Epping Forest lies within the borough. Wanstead and Woodford was represented in Parliament by Winston Churchill from 1924 to 1964.

redbud or **Judas tree,** name for trees and shrubs of the genus *Cercis*, handsome plants of the family Leguminosae (PULSE family), covered in the early spring with deep rose or (rarely) white flowers resembling pea blossoms. Species native to North America include the common redbud (*C. canadensis*), ranging through Mexico and the United States E of the Rockies, and the California redbud (*C. occidentalis*). According to tradition an Old World species was the tree on which Judas hanged himself. The bark of *C. chinensis* has been used in Chinese medicine as an antiseptic. The genus *Cercis* is classified in the division MAGNOLIOPHYTA, class Magnoliopsida, order Rosales, family Leguminosae.

red bug, name for various red insects. Chief among them are the cotton stainer of the S United States, which pierces the seeds of the cotton plant and discolors the fibers, and the larva of the harvest mite, or CHIGGER, the cause of red-bug dermatitis.

red cedar: see JUNIPER.

Red Cloud, 1822–1909, North American Indian chief, leader of the Oglala Sioux. He led the Indian warfare against the establishment of the Bozeman Trail (see BOZEMAN, JOHN M.). The Fetterman Massacre (see FETTERMAN, WILLIAM JUDD) in 1866 led to partial abandonment of the trail. Red Cloud's continual hostility led the government finally to abandon completely (1868) the trail and the forts built to protect it. After signing a treaty he lived in peace with the whites, although he was later charged with duplicity in encouraging hostile Indians. Deposed as chief in 1881, he lived thereafter in retirement on the Pine Ridge Reservation in South Dakota. See J. C. Olson, *Red Cloud and the Sioux Problem* (1965).

Red Cross, international organization concerned with the alleviation of human suffering and the promotion of public health. The creation of the agency was spurred by the publication of *Un Souvenir de Solférino* (1862), an account by Jean Henry Dunant (1828–1910) of the suffering endured by the wounded at the battle of SOLFERINO in 1859. Dunant, a Swiss citizen, urged the formation of voluntary aid societies for relief of such war victims. He also asked that service to military sick and wounded be neutral. The Société genovoise d'Utilité publique, a Swiss welfare agency, actively seconded Dunant's suggestion, the result being the formation (1863) of the organization that is today known as the International Committee of the Red Cross. The next year, delegates from 16 nations met in Switzerland, and the Geneva Convention of 1864 for the Amelioration of the Condition of the Wounded and Sick of Armies in the Field was adopted and signed by 12 of the nations represented. It provided for the neutrality of the personnel of the medical services of armed forces, the humane treatment of wounded, the neutrality of civilians who voluntarily assisted them, and the use of an international emblem to mark medical personnel and supplies. In honor of Dunant's nationality a red cross on a white background—the Swiss flag with colors reversed—was chosen as this symbol. The original Geneva Convention, its subsequent revisions, and allied treaties such as the Hague Convention for naval forces and the Prisoner of War Convention were signed but not always ratified by almost all countries and their dependencies. Today there are national Red Cross societies in over 100 countries of the world, each a self-governing organization, and two international groups with headquarters in Geneva: the International Committee of the Red Cross (name adopted 1880), composed of 25 Swiss citizens and serving as a neutral intermediary in time of war, with special interest in the welfare of prisoners of war; and the League of Red Cross Societies (founded 1919), a federation of national societies for mutual help, cooperation, and program development, especially in time of peace. The blanket agency for all Red Cross groups is known as the International Red Cross. It sponsors the International Red Cross Conference (instituted 1867), the highest deliberative body of the organization. The conference meets every four or six years, and its membership consists of representatives from each national society, from the International Committee of the Red Cross, from the League of Red Cross Societies, and from the nations signatory to the Geneva conventions. All societies are supported by membership fees and popular subscriptions, and a number receive government subsidies in addition. The work of the International Red Cross has been greatly expanded since the end of World War II, and it has moved into many fields. It has taken on extensive refugee relief activities, helping to care for the approximately 300,000 Arab refugees in the Middle East, and many refugees of the abortive Hungarian uprising (1956). During the Korean War the International Red Cross suggested (1952) the first exchange of sick and wounded men, and an American Red Cross official coordinated the exchange of prisoners that followed the 1953 armistice. The group also coordinated international relief efforts following the massive cyclone and tidal waves that hit East Pakistan (Bangladesh) in 1970 and left almost a half million dead and the hurricane that hit Honduras in 1974. The American Red Cross was organized (1881) by Clara BARTON and received its first Federal charter in 1900. In 1905 it was brought into closer relationship with the government when a new congressional charter was granted. The charter was revised in 1947. The organization, with headquarters in Washington, D.C., is supported entirely by voluntary contributions. The President of the United States is honorary chairman of the society and appoints its president and seven other members of a 50-man board of governors. The American Red Cross puts special emphasis on disaster relief, services to the armed forces and veterans, and public health and safety programs. The nationwide Red Cross blood program is a comprehensive system designed to collect, store, treat, and distribute blood and blood products to the ill and injured throughout the United States. The world-recognized symbol of mercy and absolute neutrality is the Red Cross flag or brassard (which in Muslim areas is replaced by a red crescent and in Iran by a red lion and sun). The International Red Cross was awarded the Nobel Peace Prize in 1917 and in 1944. See Clara Barton, *The Story of the Red Cross* (1904); F. R. Dulles, *The American Red Cross: A History* (1950); Charles Hurd, *The Compact History of the American Red Cross* (1959); J. A. Joyce, *Red Cross International* (1959); R. J. Berens, *The Image of Mercy* (1967).

Red Deer, city (1971 pop. 27,674), S central Alta., Canada, on the Red Deer River. It is the trade center for a region of dairying, mixed farming, and oil and gas production.

Red Deer, river, 385 mi (620 km) long, rising in the Rocky Mts. in Banff National Park, SW Alta., Canada, and flowing NE past Red Deer city, then SE and E across the plains to the South Saskatchewan River just over the Saskatchewan border.

red deer: see WAPITI.

Redding, city (1970 pop. 16,659), seat of Shasta co., N central Calif., on the Sacramento River; inc. 1872. A tourist center for a mountain and lake region, it also has lumbering and food-processing industries. A junior college is there. Nearby are Shasta Dam, Lake Shasta Caverns, Lassen Volcanic National Park, the Lava Beds National Monument (see NATIONAL PARKS AND MONUMENTS, table), Whiskeytown Lake, and Burney Falls state park.

Redditch, new town and urban district (1971 pop. 37,648), Worcestershire, central England. Redditch was designated one of the NEW TOWNS in 1964 to alleviate overpopulation in Birmingham and the BLACK COUNTRY. The planned population is 70,000. Its manufactures include needles, fishing tackle, springs, bicycles, and motorcycles. In 1974, Redditch became part of the new nonmetropolitan county of Hereford and Worcester.

Red Eagle: see WEATHERFORD, WILLIAM.

red eft: see NEWT.

Redfield, Robert, 1897–1958, American anthropologist and sociologist, b. Chicago, grad. Univ. of Chicago (B.A., 1920; Ph.D., 1928). He began teaching at the Univ. of Chicago in 1928, later becoming professor of anthropology and dean of the social science division. His field research in Mexico in the 1920s resulted in *Tepoztlán* (1930), a pioneer case study of a folk community that was the forerunner of a series of important studies. As research associate (1930–47) at the Carnegie Institution he directed anthropological investigations in Yucatán and Guatemala and evolved the concepts of folk society and folk culture, borrowing from sociological methods and concepts. He attempted a closer integration of the social sciences and the humanities. In his later years he turned increasingly to the comparative study of civilizations. His writings include *The Folk Culture of Yucatán* (1941), *The Primitive World and Its Transformations* (1953), and *The Little Community* (1955).

red fir: see PINE.

red giant, star that is relatively cool but very luminous because of its great size. All normal stars are expected to pass eventually through a red-giant phase as a consequence of STELLAR EVOLUTION. As a star uses up its hydrogen by converting it to helium, its central core contracts while the outer layers expand and cool; this process produces the low temperature and large size (from 10 to 100 times that of the sun) that characterize the red giant. Although most giant stars are red, some prominent giant stars are other colors near the red end of the spectrum, e.g., Arcturus (orange), Aldebaran (orange), and Capella (yellow). The largest and brightest stars (excluding SUPERNOVAS) are classed as supergiants. These stars have diameters between 100 and 1,000 times that of the sun. Blue supergiants, e.g., Rigel, are young stars on the main sequence of the HERTZSPRUNG-RUSSELL DIAGRAM, whereas red supergiants, e.g., Betelgeuse and Antares, are old, highly evolved stars.

Redgrave, family of English actors. **Sir Michael Redgrave,** 1908–, is an actor, director, and writer. Since his first professional performance in *Counsellor-at-Law* (1934), he has appeared in an enormous number of stage plays in London and Stratford and abroad and has made many films and television plays. He is especially adept at emotionally tense, cerebral roles. His major stage appearances include *As You Like It, Hamlet, Macbeth, The Family Reunion, Uncle Vanya,* and *Mourning Becomes Electra.* Among his films are *The Lady Vanishes* (1938), *The Browning Version* (1951), *The Hill* (1965), and *David Copperfield* (1969). Redgrave is married to the actress Rachel Kempson. See his *Mask and Face* (1953) and *The Actor's Ways and Means* (1954); biography by K. B. F. Bain (1956). Their elder daughter, **Vanessa Redgrave,** 1937–, is noted for her elegant and luminous presence. She has frequently appeared on the London stage (she created the title role in *The Prime of Miss Jean Brodie*), and in several films, including *Morgan!* (1966), *Isadora* (1968), *The Seagull* (1968), and *The Trojan Women* (1972). Her sister **Lynn Redgrave,** 1943–, has appeared on stage and in several films, notably *Georgy Girl* (1966). Their brother Corin has appeared on the English stage.

Redi, Francesco (frănchās'kō rā'dē), 1626?–1698?, Italian naturalist, poet, philologist, and court physician to the dukes of Tuscany. Through controlled experiments he demonstrated that certain living organisms, notably maggots in rotting meat, did not arise, as had been alleged, through spontaneous generation. His *Generation of Insects* (1668, tr. 1909) is included in the nine-octavo edition (1809–11) of his complete writings. His chief poetical work was the dithyrambic ode *Bacchus in Tuscany* (1685; tr. by Leigh Hunt 1825).

redistricting: see LEGISLATIVE APPORTIONMENT.

Red Jacket, c.1758–1830, chief of the Seneca Indians, b. probably Seneca co., N.Y. His Indian name was

Otetiani, changed to Sagoyewatha when he became a chief. His English name came from the British redcoat he wore as an ally of the English in the American Revolution. He had an excellent memory and was articulate and skillful in dealing with the whites, but he was accused of cowardice by other Indian leaders in active warfare. At an Indian conference (1786) at the mouth of the Detroit River, Red Jacket urged the continuance of hostilities against the whites, but in later years he attempted to make peace with the U.S. government. He was one of the Indian chiefs who visited President George Washington in 1792. In the War of 1812 he influenced his people to support the United States. An ardent advocate of the Indian mode of life, he resisted the introduction of white customs, especially Christianity and the work of the missionaries. Late in his life the growth of Christianity among Indians and opposition to his policies resulted in his being deposed as chief, but he appealed to the government, defended himself before a tribal council, and was restored.

Redlands, city (1970 pop. 36,355), San Bernardino co., S Calif., in the San Bernardino Valley; inc. 1888. Aircraft propulsion systems, furniture, and electrical vehicles are made. Citrus groves are in the area. The Univ. of Redlands is there, and Norton Air Force Base is nearby.

red lead, bright red to orange-red powder, also called minium, that is used in the manufacture of storage batteries, lead glass, and red pigments; a paint made with red lead is commonly used to protect iron and steel from rusting. Chemically, red lead is lead tetroxide, Pb_3O_4, a water-insoluble compound that is prepared by the oxidation of metallic lead or of LITHARGE (lead monoxide); the commercial product sometimes contains litharge as an impurity.

red maids: see PURSLANE.

Redmond, John Edward, 1856–1918, Irish nationalist leader. He was elected to Parliament as a HOME RULE member in 1881 at the height of the obstructionist program of Charles PARNELL. When the Irish nationalist group split as a result of Parnell's involvement in the O'Shea divorce case, Redmond became chief of the pro-Parnell group. On reunion with the majority (1900), he was chosen as chairman of the combined Irish party. He served on various commissions that led to the Wyndham Land Purchase Act of 1903 (see IRISH LAND QUESTION) and gradually gained the leadership as well as the chairmanship of the Irish party. When the Liberals came to power in Britain in 1905, Redmond had no choice but to support them even though the policy they then advocated was one of "devolution" or merely administrative Home Rule for Ireland. He gave them particularly strong support in their effort to limit the power of the House of Lords, which strongly opposed Home Rule. Passage of the Parliament Act of 1911, which accomplished this purpose, made feasible the introduction (1912) of the third Home Rule Bill. In the ensuing crisis caused by the militant opposition to the bill in Northern Ireland, Redmond reluctantly gave his support to the Irish Volunteer movement, a military organization raised to counter the threat of the newly formed Ulster Volunteers. When World War I broke out, Home Rule was approved (1914), although suspended until after the war. Redmond turned down a cabinet post in the coalition government of 1915. He had declared Ireland's loyalty to the Allied cause in the war, and the Easter Rebellion of 1916 was a great blow to him. He supported the plan to begin the operation of Home Rule with the temporary exclusion of Ulster, but his power and influence were declining, and at the end of his life he was opposed by the revolutionary SINN FEIN. See biographies by W. B. Wells (1919) and Denis Gwynn (1932); study by S. L. Gwynn (1919).

Redmond, city (1970 pop. 11,031), King co., W Wash., a suburb of Seattle, on Lake Sammamish; inc. 1912. Its economy centers around research and development industries and the manufacture of electronic components and building products. A Nike missile battery is there. Of interest are the preserved portions of the old brick Stevens Pass highway, and Marymoor Park, site of archaeological excavations and a historical museum.

Redon, Odilon (ôdĕlôN' rədôN'), 1840–1916, French painter and lithographer. He studied in Paris under Gérôme. Later his friend Fantin-Latour taught him lithography, but he was most influenced by Rodolphe Bresdin, an older artist who had created a world of fantastic imagery. Redon's first volume of lithographs, *Dans le rêve,* appeared in 1879. After 1889 he devoted himself to oil painting and especially pastels. Symbolically conceived, his work is related to that of writers such as Poe, Baudelaire, and Mallarmé. An artist of lyrical and mystical vision, he created translucent flower pieces and often depicted literary subjects. Redon stands as a precursor to surrealism, with his mysterious evocations of a dreamworld. Characteristic of his art are *Les Yeux clos* (Louvre) and *Le Silence* (Mus. of Modern Art, New York City). Excellent examples of his graphic work can be found at the Art Institute, Chicago, and at the Bibliothèque nationale, Paris. See his journal, *À Soi-Même* (1922); *Graphic Works* (tr. 1913, repr. 1969); studies by K. Berger (1965) and J. Selz (1971).

Redonda: see ANTIGUA, island.

Redondo Beach (rĭdŏn'dō), city (1970 pop. 57,425), Los Angeles co., S Calif., on the Pacific Ocean; inc. 1892. It is a residential and resort city, with boating facilities and fine beaches. There is some manufacturing.

redox (rē'dŏks): see OXIDATION AND REDUCTION.

red pepper: see PEPPER.

Red Poll cattle (pōl), breed of polled (hornless) cattle, originated in England c.1846. They are a medium-sized, hardy breed of cattle, light red to very dark red in color, and are raised for both milk and beef. Well established throughout the world, they are found in the United States chiefly in the Midwest.

Red River, Chinese *Yuan Chiang,* Annamese *Song Ca,* chief river of North Vietnam, 730 mi (1,175 km) long, rising in Yünnan prov., S China, and flowing southeast, in deep, narrow gorges, through North Vietnam to form a great delta before entering the Gulf of Tonkin. The river carries a large quantity of silt, rich in iron oxide, that gives it a red color. Northwest of Hanoi the river flows onto the coastal plain and receives the Clear and Black rivers, its chief tributaries. The Red River delta, c.75 mi (120 km) long and 75 mi wide, is the economic center of North Vietnam, whose chief port, Haiphong, is on the delta's north branch. Rice is the principal crop of the river valley; wheat, beans, rapeseed, corn, and subtropical crops are also grown. The Red River has an irregular flow and is subject to flooding, especially during the June-October high water period; dikes and canals protect the delta from flood waters. A railroad and highway follow the Red River valley, an important transportation route linking China and North Vietnam.

Red River. 1 River, 1,222 mi (1,967 km) long, southernmost of the large tributaries of the Mississippi River. It rises in two branches in the Texas Panhandle and flows SE between Texas and Oklahoma and between Texas and Arkansas to Fulton, Ark. It then turns southward, enters Louisiana, and crosses SE to the Atchafalaya and the Mississippi rivers. In Texas it flows rapidly through a canyon in semiarid plains, but later in its course it waters rich red-clay farm lands (whence the name Red). Dams on the river include the Denison Dam (completed 1943), which impounds Lake Texoma, one of the largest reservoirs in the United States. For many years navigation was difficult on the lower course of the Red River due to fallen trees that floated downstream and collected behind obstructions, forming rafts. The Great Raft, a 160-mi (257-km) log-jam built through the centuries, was cleared from the river in the mid-1800s. The river is now navigable for small ships to above Shreveport, La. There are many lakes along the lower part of the river, while reservoirs—such as Lake Texarkana, Wallace Lake, and the Bayou Bodcau reserves—serve as flood-control units on its tributaries. In the Civil War a Union military and naval expedition (1864) under Gen. N. P. Banks and Admiral Porter went up the Red River to open the way to Texas, but was defeated at Sabine Crossroads. **2** River, often called the **Red River of the North,** c.310 mi (500 km) long, formed N of Lake Traverse, NE S. Dak., by the confluence of the Bois de Sioux and the Otter Tail rivers. It flows N between Minnesota and North Dakota and crosses the Canadian border into Manitoba, emptying into Lake Winnipeg. The river drains the principal spring wheat- and flax-growing area of the United States and Canada—the rich Red River valley region, the bed of the ancient Lake Agassiz. Its chief tributary is the Assiniboine River.

Red River Rebellion: see RIEL, LOUIS.

Red River Settlement, agricultural colony in present Manitoba, North Dakota, and Minnesota. It was the undertaking of Thomas Douglas, 5th earl of SELKIRK. Wishing to relieve the dispossessed and impoverished in Scotland and Northern Ireland, he secured enough control of the HUDSON'S BAY COMPANY to obtain from it a grant of land called Assiniboia. This project met opposition from the very start, principally from the NORTH WEST COMPANY, but also from the fur traders in the Hudson's Bay Company. Despite efforts to discourage the colony, Miles Macdonnell, a Selkirk man, brought a small group to the colony in 1812. The determined hostility of the North West Company mounted, especially after the company men had won the half-breeds, or métis, entirely to their side. By cajolery and threat they persuaded settlers to desert, but a new group of settlers came, and the colony was restored in 1815. North West Company men and half-breeds now resorted to violence on a large scale, killing 22 in the massacre of Seven Oaks (June 19, 1816). On hearing the news of the massacre, Selkirk fell upon the North West Company post, Fort William, and seized it. Other attacks followed. The result of these moves was a series of court charges and countercharges that impoverished Selkirk and helped to bring about the union (1821) of the Hudson's Bay Company and the North West Company. Agriculture had by this time been firmly established on the Western plains, and the Red River settlements were to grow and flourish. See RIEL, LOUIS. See J. P. Pritchett, *The Red River Valley, 1811–1849* (1942); John M. Gray, *Lord Selkirk of Red River* (1964).

Red Rock chicken, the only chicken still popular to any large extent in the United States today for both meat and eggs. It resulted from a cross between a RHODE ISLAND RED male and a PLYMOUTH ROCK female. The breed recently acquired new value when it was discovered that the sex of the day-old chicks could be determined by the differences in the color of their down. The variety is raised primarily in New England.

Redruth, England: see CAMBORNE-REDRUTH.

Red Sea, ancient *Sinus Arabicus* or *Erythraean Sea,* narrow sea, c.170,000 sq mi (440,300 sq km), c.1,450 mi (2,330 km) long and up to 225 mi (362 km) wide, between Africa (Egypt, Sudan, and Ethiopia) and the Arabian Peninsula (Israel, Jordan, Saudi Arabia, and the Yemen Arab Republic); a part of the Great Rift Valley. The Gulf of Aqaba and the Gulf of Suez are the sea's northern arms; between them is the Sinai peninsula. The Red Sea is linked with the Gulf of Aden and the Arabian Sea by the straits of Bab el Mandeb. The flat coastal plains of the Red Sea slope gradually to the submarine central trough, more than 7,000 ft (2,134 m) deep. The sea is dotted with islands (the largest group is the Dahlak Archipelago in the southwest) and with dangerous coral reefs. It is surrounded by exceedingly hot and dry deserts and steppes; the summer water temperature exceeds 85°F (29°C), and the water has a high salt content. The Red Sea was probably named for the reddish algae that appear in it at certain times of the year. The Red Sea was an important trade route in antiquity. Its importance declined with the discovery of an all-water route around Africa in 1498. The opening of the Suez Canal in 1869 made the Red Sea one of the chief shipping routes connecting Europe with the Far East and Australia; however, the closing of the canal after the 1967 Arab-Israeli War, the building of pipelines to the Mediterranean Sea, and the construction of supertankers too large for the canal have combined to diminish the sea's importance as a commercial artery, especially for petroleum. Suez, Egypt; Elat, Israel; Jidda, Saudi Arabia; Hodeida, Yemen; Massawa, Ethiopia; and Port Sudan, Sudan, are the main ports on the Red Sea, but they are generally small and of relatively minor importance. The Bible, in recounting the crossing of the Red Sea by the Israelites, probably intended the Gulf of Suez between Sinai and Egypt proper.

red shift, in astronomy, the systematic increase in the wavelength of all light received from a celestial object; it is observed in the shifting of individual lines in the SPECTRUM of the object toward the red, or longer wavelength, end of the visible spectrum. Most observed red shifts are the result of the DOPPLER EFFECT, i.e., of the relative motion of the earth and the object away from each other. All distant galaxies show a red shift proportional to their distance from the earth as a result of the general expansion of the universe (see HUBBLE'S LAW); the most distant known galaxies have red shifts that indicate they are moving away from the earth at speeds approaching that of light. Red shifts are also produced by gravitation in accordance with the general theory of RELATIVITY. A strong gravitational field will cause all vibrations to be slowed, so that the frequency of the light emitted by atoms in a massive star will be lower and the wavelengths consequently longer; such effects have been observed in WHITE DWARFS.

red snapper: see SNAPPER.

red spider: see MITE.

red spruce: see SPRUCE.

red squill: see PESTICIDE.

redstart, common name for an Old World thrush of the genus *Phoenicurus,* family Turdidae. A small, slender-legged songbird, it is found in woodlands, parks, and heaths. The European redstart, *P. phoenicurus,* also known as the firetail, breeds as far north as Scotland but winters in Africa. It is red-tailed and black-throated, with a bay-colored breast and ash-blue back and cap. It is a solitary bird and is highly aggressive during its breeding season. The Japanese *P. aurorea* is the easternmost representative of the genus. Redstarts build crude, cup-shaped nests either near the ground or in the hole of a tree or building. They lay from five to seven greenish-blue, faintly red-spotted eggs per clutch. The common name redstart is also used for several species of small New World wood-warblers, family Parulidae, in the genera *Stetophaga* and *Myioborus.* These are aerial insect catchers with wide, flat bills surrounded by stiff whiskerlike bristles called vibrissae. Like the Old World redstarts, to which they are not related, they are songbirds. The North American redstart (*S. ruticillia*) breeds in the temperate United States and Canada but winters in N South America. It is glossy black with a white breast and has orange wings, tail, and side patches. In females, gray and yellow replace black and orange. In the painted redstart (*S. picta*) of Central America, both sexes are equally brightly colored, red where its North American cousin is white, and white where the cousin is orange. There are also approximately ten species of redstarts in the tropical genus *Myiobarus.* The New World redstarts inhabit deciduous forest areas, preferably near water. Their eggs, from three to five per clutch in the northern species and from two to four per clutch in the tropical species, are grayish-white with variously colored spots and speckles. Redstarts are classified in the phylum CHORDATA, subphylum Vertebrata, class Aves, order Passeriformes, families Turdidae and Parulidae.

Redstone Arsenal, U.S. rocket research and development center, 38,781 acres (15,694 hectares), N Ala., W of Huntsville; est. 1941. One of the state's largest industrial enterprises, it includes the Army Missile Command, responsible for the army's rocket and guided missile program; the Army Missile and Munitions Center and School; the NATIONAL AERONAUTICS AND SPACE ADMINISTRATION's George C. Marshall Space Flight Center which researches and develops large boosters for space vehicles; and several private contractors.

redtop: see BENT GRASS.

reduction, in chemistry: see OXIDATION AND REDUCTION.

reductions, Span. *reducciones,* settlements of Indians in colonial Latin America, founded (beginning in 1609) to utilize efficiently native labor and to teach the natives the ways of Spanish life. Best known were those established by the Jesuits in old Paraguay (many of them in present-day Argentina)—about 30 among the Guaraní Indians and about 7 in the Chaco wilderness. Each Jesuit reduction was directed by two priests, a spiritual overseer and an administrator; their rule was absolute but usually benevolent. The missions prospered in agriculture, trade, and manufactures, and printed thousands of volumes, contributing greatly to geographic and scientific knowledge about South America. Some reductions were established and run by civil authorities.

Red Wing, city (1970 pop. 10,441), seat of Goodhue co., SE Minn., on the Mississippi River at the head of Lake Pepin; inc. 1857. It is a commercial and manufacturing center in the Hiawatha valley farm area. Shoe manufacturing, leather processing, and flour milling are carried on in Red Wing. The early explorers found an Indian village there. From 1836 to 1840 it was the site of a Swiss mission to the Indians. The county historical museum is in Red Wing, and a state park is nearby.

redwood: see SEQUOIA.

Redwood City, city (1970 pop. 55,686), seat of San Mateo co., W Calif., on San Francisco Bay; inc. 1868. Food is processed there, and electronic products, wire and cables, cement, plastics, automotive equipment, and chemicals are made. The city's large chrysanthemum industry dates from 1900. Marine World, a large entertainment complex, is located nearby on several islands in San Francisco Bay.

Redwood National Park, 56,201 acres (22,745 hectares), along the Pacific coast, NW Calif.; est. 1968. Backed by coastal bluffs, 40 mi (64 km) of beach, lagoon, and rocky coast are preserved in their natural state; seals, sea lions, and birds live on offshore rocks. Inland, numerous stands of virgin California redwood, many over 2,000 years old, are found; the world's tallest tree, 367 ft (112 m) high, is located in the park.

Reed, Sir Carol, 1906–, English film director, b. London. He acted and directed on the stage before turning to films in the mid-1930s. Among his best-known works are *Night Train from Munich* (1940), *The Young Mr. Pitt* (1941), *Odd Man Out* (1946), *The Fallen Idol* (1948), *The Third Man* (1949), *Outcast of the Islands* (1951), *A Kid for Two Farthings* (1955), *The Key* (1958), *The Agony and the Ecstasy* (1965), and *Oliver!* (1968).

Reed, James Alexander, 1861–1944, American political leader, b. near Mansfield, Ohio. He moved to Iowa and was admitted (1885) to the bar, practicing there and later in Missouri. He was (1898–1900) an extremely successful prosecuting attorney of Jackson co., Mo., and then served (1900–1904) as mayor of Kansas City, Mo. As Democratic Senator (1911–29) from Missouri, he adamantly opposed national prohibition and U.S. participation in the League of Nations. In 1928 he was a contender for the Democratic presidential nomination, but lost it to Alfred E. Smith. See biography by Lee Meriwether (1948).

Reed, John, 1887–1920, American journalist and radical leader, b. Portland, Oregon. After graduating from Harvard in 1910, he wrote articles in the United States for various publications and from 1913 was attached to the radical magazine *The Masses.* His coverage of the Paterson, N.J., silk workers strike of 1913 profoundly affected him, and thereafter he became a proponent of revolutionary politics. The articles that he wrote from Mexico about the revolt of Pancho Villa established his reputation as a journalist and a radical. He served as a reporter in Europe in World War I and was in Petrograd (now Leningrad) when the Bolsheviks seized power in 1917; his book on the event, *Ten Days That Shook the World* (1919), is considered the best eyewitness account of the revolution. Expelled from the U.S. Socialist convention in 1919, he helped to organize the Communist Labor party, which was a left-wing splinter group of the Socialist party. He was indicted for sedition in New York City in 1918 and in Philadelphia in 1919, but both cases were dropped. Reed returned to the USSR, worked in the Soviet bureau of propaganda, and was appointed Soviet consul to New York. Upon protest from the U.S. government, Reed was withdrawn from the consulship. He died in Moscow of typhus and was buried at the Kremlin. A selection of his writings was edited by John Stuart (1955). See biographies by Granville Hicks (1936), Richard O'Connor and D. L. Walker (1967), and Barbara Gelb (1973).

Reed, Joseph, 1741–85, American Revolutionary political leader and army officer, b. Trenton, N.J. He studied law, was admitted (1763) to the bar, and then went to London to study at the Middle Temple. After returning (1765) to practice law in Trenton, he took an active part in pre-Revolutionary affairs. After settling (1770) in Philadelphia Reed became a member of the committee of correspondence (1774) and president of the Pennsylvania provincial congress (1775). In the war he served as military secretary to George Washington and as adjutant general and took part in a number of battles. He served in the Continental Congress (1777–78). As president (1778–81) of the supreme executive council of Pennsylvania he abolished slavery in Pennsylvania and caused (1778) Benedict ARNOLD to be prosecuted on charges of corrupt practices. He was a trustee and founder of the Univ. of the State of Pennsylvania (later the Univ. of Pennsylvania). See biography by J. F. Roche (1957, repr. 1968).

Reed, Stanley Forman, 1884–, Associate Justice of the U.S. Supreme Court (1938–57), b. Macon co., Ky. After receiving the B.A. degree from both Kentucky Wesleyan (1902) and Yale (1906), he studied law at the Univ. of Virginia and Columbia Univ. and then studied in France. A lawyer of Maysville, Ky., he became general counsel of the Federal Farm Board (1929–32) and of the Reconstruction Finance Corporation (1932–35). He was (1935–38) Solicitor General and presented the government arguments in numerous New Deal cases. Appointed to the Supreme Court by President Franklin Delano Roosevelt, Reed was generally considered a moderate there and often held the balance between the liberal and the conservative members of the court in split decisions.

Reed, Thomas Brackett, 1839–1902, American legislator, b. Portland, Maine. A lawyer, he served in the state assembly (1868–69) and state senate (1870) and became (1870–73) state attorney general before he was elected (1876) as a Republican to the U.S. Congress. Reed quickly took his place among the leaders of his party. As Speaker of the House (1889–91, 1895–99) he inaugurated the "Reed Rules" (1890)—one of which determined the House quorum by the count of members present rather than by the count of those voting. "Czar" Reed, as he was known, also arbitrarily used the speaker's power of recognition to prevent minority obstruction and to facilitate orthodox Republican legislation in the face of strong opposition. Reed was an advocate of high tariffs. He strongly opposed the war with Spain, the annexation of Hawaii, and the ensuing expansion program. Reelected in 1898, he retired from Congress in 1899 and then practiced law in New York City. See biographies by S. W. McCall (1914, repr. 1972) and W. A. Robinson (1930).

Reed, Walter, 1851–1902, American army surgeon, b. Gloucester co., Va. In 1900 he was sent to Havana as head of an army commission to investigate an outbreak of yellow fever among American soldiers. Following the earlier suggestion by C. J. Finlay that the disease was transmitted by a mosquito vector rather than by direct contact, Reed and his companions used human volunteers under controlled experimental conditions to prove this conclusively. In 1901 they published their findings that yellow fever was caused by a virus borne by the *Stegomyia fasciata* mosquito (later designated as *Aëdes aegypti*). See studies by H. A. Kelly (3d ed. 1923), A. E. Truby (1943), and L. N. Wood (1943).

Reed, Willis, 1942–, U.S. basketball player, b. Hico, La. After outstanding high school and college performances, Reed (6 ft 9½ in./207 cm) was drafted by the New York Knickerbockers in 1964 and played his entire professional career with them. Named "Rookie of the Year" for the 1964–65 season, he was elected the National Basketball Association's (NBA) most valuable player for 1969–70 and 1972–73, years in which the Knickerbockers won the NBA championship. His aggressive play and excellent defensive ability enabled the center to score 12,183 points and gain 8,414 rebounds in his career. He announced his retirement in 1974.

reed, name used for several plants of the family Graminae (GRASS family). The common American reed, also called reedgrass and canegrass, is a tall perennial grass (*Phragmites communis*), widely distributed in wet places. It has stout, creeping rootstalks and a large, plumelike panicle. In the SW United States this grass is called carrizo and is used in building adobe huts; it has also been used for thatching and cordage. Indians collected a sweet exudation from the plant and made arrows of the stalks. The leaves served as edible greens and the seeds as a cereal food. The giant reed (*Arundo donax*), of similar appearance, is native to the Mediterranean region but is now widely naturalized throughout tropical and warm climates, including the S United States. It is often cultivated for ornament, and in Europe the stems have been used to make reed instruments, bagpipes, and reed organs. This is the reed from which Pan was fabled to have made his Panpipe, or syrinx. The "reeds" of wickerwork are often RATTAN. Reeds are classified in the division MAGNOLIOPHYTA, class Liliatae, order Cyperales, family Gramineae.

reed bird: see BOBOLINK.

reedbuck: see MARSH ANTELOPE.

Reed College, in Portland, Oregon; coeducational; inc. 1908, opened 1911 through a bequest from Mr. and Mrs. Simeon G. Reed. Reed is noted for its program of natural sciences and for its system of tutorial and small-conference instruction.

reedfish: see BICHIR.

reed instrument, in music, an instrument whose sound-producing agent is a thin strip of cane, wood, or metal that vibrates as air is passed over it. The predecessor of these instruments is the Chinese SHENG. Single-reed instruments have one reed that is either free or beating. Free reeds, such as those in the REED ORGAN, ACCORDION, CONCERTINA, and HARMONICA, do not overlap the air passage; they are generally of metal. Beating reeds, such as those used in ORGAN pipes and in the CLARINET, strike the edges of the aperture while vibrating. Double-reed instruments, such as the OBOE, BASSOON, and ENGLISH HORN, have two reeds facing each other, between which air is forced into the instrument; thus the reeds are set vibrating.

reed mace: see CATTAIL.

reed organ, an ORGAN in which air is forced over free reeds by means of bellows, usually worked by pedals. It is played by the use of one or more keyboards. Variations in tone are produced by stops that control different sets of reeds or vary the manner in which the air acts upon them. Couplers add the upper or lower octave of each tone played. In the late 18th cent. C. G. Kratzenstein built a small reed organ, inspired by the Chinese SHENG. In 1810, G. J. Grenié of Paris invented the *orgue expressif,* also inspired by the sheng, and numerous similar instruments followed. Most of these, including the harmonium, as modified in 1840 by Alexandre Debain of Paris, had bellows that blew the air over the reeds, but c.1835 a workman conceived the idea of employing suction bellows. His idea was used by Jacob Estey of Brattleboro, Vt., and Mason Hamlin of Boston in the mid-19th cent. American organ, melodeon or melodium, and cabinet organ were the names generally applied to this type of instrument, although the terms harmonium and melodeon have sometimes been confused. Both types of instrument found wide use in churches and homes in the United States. Many larger modern reed organs are electrically powered and have pedal keyboards like those of the pipe organ.

reef: see CORAL REEF.

Reelaiah (rē″ĕlā'yə), same as RAAMIAH.

Reelfoot Lake, 20 mi (32 km) long, NW Tenn., near the Mississippi River; designated a national natural landmark by the National Park Service. It was formed when a depression created by earthquakes in the winter of 1811–12 was filled with Mississippi River water. The lake is in a beautiful wooded area, which attracts fishermen and hunters. A state park and two national wildlife refuges are nearby.

Reese, Lizette Woodworth (rēs), 1856–1935, American poet, b. Waverly, Md. She taught school for 45 years, 21 of them at the Western High School in Baltimore. Her poetry, remarkable for its intensity and concision, has been compared to that of Emily Dickinson. She is probably best remembered for the sonnet "Years." Her volumes of poetry include *A Branch of May* (1887), *A Handful of Lavender* (1891), *A Quiet Road* (1896), *Spicewood* (1920), and *Selected Poems* (1926). See her autobiographical *Victorian Village* (1929) and *The York Road* (1931).

Reeve, Clara (rēv), 1729–1807, English novelist. Her most famous work, *The Champion of Virtue: A Gothic Story* (1777), was written in imitation of Walpole's *Castle of Otranto.* After the first edition it was entitled *The Old English Baron.*

Reeve, Tapping, 1744–1823, American lawyer and jurist, b. Brookhaven, N.Y. In 1784 he opened his law school in Litchfield, Conn.; it was one of the first schools of law in the United States. Aaron Burr, John C. Calhoun, Horace Mann, and many other future senators, governors, and judges studied there.

referendum, referral of proposed laws or constitutional amendments to the electorate for final approval. This direct form of legislation, along with the INITIATIVE, was known in Greece and other early democracies. Today, these legislative devices are widely used in certain countries, most notably Switzerland. Their use in the United States reached a peak in the early part of the 20th cent. In the United States there are two main types of referendum—mandatory and optional. The mandatory referendum may be required by state constitutions and city charters for a variety of matters. It usually applies to constitutional amendments and bond issues, which by law have to be placed before the voters for approval. The optional referendum is applied to ordinary legislation. By the usual procedure implementation of a law is postponed for a certain length of time after it has been passed by the legislature; during this time, if a petition is presented containing the requisite number of names, the proposed legislation must be put to a vote at the next election.

refining, any of various processes for separating impurities from crude or semifinished materials. It includes the finer processes of metallurgy, the fractional distillation of petroleum into its commercial products, and the purifying of cane, beet, and maple sugar and many other substances. The nature of the refining process depends on such factors as the type of material involved, the value of the end product, and the degree of purity necessary. The purification of a metal is based upon physical or chemical differences between the metal and its accompanying impurities, including density, melting point, magnetic properties, and reaction to certain chemicals. It may be accomplished by a continuation of a process used in separating the metal from its ore. ELECTROLYSIS is much used in the refining of various metals (e.g., copper); the open hearth process (see STEEL) and the BASIC OXYGEN PROCESS are used in the refining of iron; the AMALGAMATION PROCESS and the CYANIDE PROCESS are chemical means of metal refining.

reflection, return of a wave from a surface that it strikes into the medium through which it has traveled. The general principles governing the reflection of light and sound are similar, for both normally travel in straight lines and both are wave phenomena. Objects are visible because of the light reflected from their surfaces, and their color depends upon their ability to reflect light of a certain wavelength and to absorb that of other wavelengths. The reflection of light follows certain definite laws. A ray of light striking a reflecting surface at right angles to it is returned directly along the path it has followed in reaching the surface. When, however, a ray strikes a reflecting surface at any other angle, it is reflected at an angle in an opposite direction. The incoming ray is called the incident ray. Its direction is usually described by the angle of incidence, which is the angle that it makes with the normal, or line perpendicular to the reflecting surface at the point of reflection. The angle formed by the reflected ray and the normal is called the angle of reflection and is equal to the angle of incidence. Furthermore, the reflected ray is always in the same plane as the incident ray, and this plane is perpendicular to the surface. Not all surfaces reflect light in the same way or to the same degree. Smooth surfaces give regular reflection, also called specular reflection, in which incident parallel rays remain parallel after reflection. Rough or uneven surfaces give diffuse reflection, since the reflected rays are scattered and not parallel. For example, reflection by a MIRROR is regular; by a highly polished but uneven piece of metal, it is diffused. Reflection of light is also brought about under certain conditions by the surfaces of transparent media through which light normally passes. An example is seen in the blazing glare of sunlight on a window or an automobile windshield when the sun's rays strike it at a very oblique angle. The phenomenon called total internal reflection is observed when light passing from one medium (e.g., a glass prism or water) to a less dense medium (e.g., air) reaches the boundary between the two media and is thrown back into the denser medium instead of passing outward as would be expected. This occurs when the light strikes at an oblique angle, greater than a certain degree. Up to that degree, REFRACTION (not reflection) takes place, and the greatest angle at which refraction is possible is called the critical angle; if the angle of incidence exceeds this angle, total reflection occurs. The fire of a faceted diamond is due to total internal reflection. Internal reflection accounts in part for a number of natural phenomena. Rays of sunlight striking raindrops are refracted upon entering them and then undergo internal reflection; since the sunlight is broken up into its colors, a rainbow appears. A MIRAGE is also partially the result of internal reflection. The reflection of sound waves from a surface is ECHO.

reflector: see TELESCOPE.

reflex: see NERVOUS SYSTEM.

Reformation, religious revolution that took place in Western Europe in the 16th cent. It arose from objections to doctrines and practices in the medieval church (see ROMAN CATHOLIC CHURCH) and ultimately led to the freedom of dissent (see PROTESTANTISM). The preparation for the movement was long. Opponents of orthodox views had asserted themselves over centuries, and in the 14th cent. John WYCLIF had led a dissident movement. His ideas were amplified later by John HUSS in Bohemia, who was burned (1415) at the stake by order of the Council of Constance. After his death his followers in Bohemia upheld his cause in the long and bitterly fought HUSSITE WARS. These dwindled into compromise, but Huss's challenge to the orthodox view of the Eucharist and the revolutionary effect of the wars did not disappear. New forces fanned discontent with the church and the medieval order of society. There had long been outcries against abuses in the church, especially the blatant worldliness of some of the clergy, the emphasis on money, and the oppressiveness, not only intellectual but economic, of members of the church hierarchy. In the 15th cent. the conciliar movement (i.e., the attempt to establish the superiority of the ecumenical council

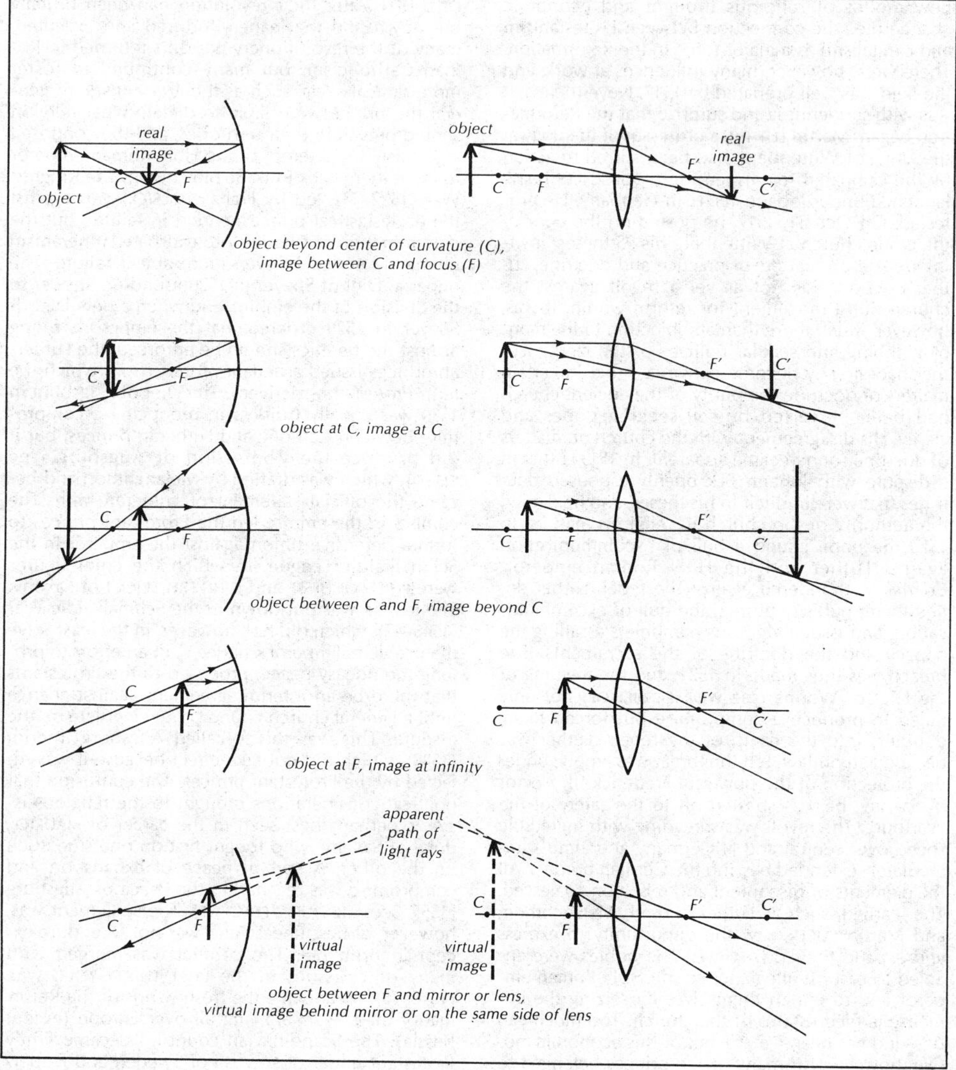

Image formation by curved mirrors and lenses

over the pope) heralded the growing internal church dissent. Although the movement failed, the number of those wishing reform nevertheless grew steadily. The desire for change was increased by the appearance of HUMANISM and the spirit of the RENAISSANCE. Study of the ancient Greek and Hebrew texts concentrated attention on the Bible and evoked a new critical spirit, exemplified in such men as Lorenzo VALLA and Johann REUCHLIN. The Renaissance also tended to develop an emphasis on the individual. The later humanists were outspoken in their attacks on the abuses in the church; Desiderius ERASMUS was, perhaps, the most prominent, but there were many others, including the humanists at Oxford. The intimate connection between the new learning and the Reformation itself is shown in the pursuits of men who were to be prominent in the Reformation in central Europe; Ulrich von HUTTEN and Philip MELANCHTHON were outstanding figures in humanism, and Huldreich ZWINGLI arrived at opposition to the church mainly through the study of Greek and Hebrew. The very founding of the Univ. of Wittenberg, which was to be the center of revolt, was part of the urge to humanism. The introduction of printing in Western Europe allowed more widespread dissemination of criticism. Printing was to hasten the Reformation, and the Reformation in turn was to spread printing further. In secular matters the opposition between church and state was centuries old, but it had begun to take a new turn with the building of strong nations. In Germany this opposition to the power of the church was coupled in the minds of many princes with opposition to that other supranational body, the Holy Roman Empire, and the princes were to play a decisive part in the ecclesiastical rebellion. The rise of the cities and of the power of merchants and the middle class generally not only upset the old medieval order of things but created much discontent with the scholastic views on finance and economic affairs that fettered the enterprise of the men in search of wealth. The economy of Europe was expanding and forcing cracks in the more or less rigid walls of the system. Scholars of the 20th cent. have put a great deal of emphasis on the connection between the new modes of religious thought and economic change (i.e., the connection between Protestantism and capitalism) as a major force in the Reformation. There were, however, many influences at work, and the field was well prepared by 1517. Nevertheless, it was with suddenness and surprise that the Reformation began. Martin LUTHER, a professor of theology at the Univ. of Wittenberg, had been stirred to action by the campaign for dispensing INDULGENCES being launched under Johann TETZEL in Germany. He protested. On Oct. 31, 1517, he posted on the door of the castle church at Wittenberg his 95 theses, inviting debate on matters of practice and doctrine. Luther's action was not as yet a revolt against the church but a movement for reform within. It was, however, much more than an objection to the money-grabbing and secular policies of the clergy. Luther had already become convinced that in certain matters of doctrine the purity of the ancient church had been perverted by self-seeking popes and clergy. His disagreement with the church on matters of doctrine soon became apparent. In 1519 Luther in a dispute with Johann Eck openly espoused doctrines that were implicit in his theses, and he denied the authority of the church in religious matters. In 1520 the pope issued a bull of excommunication against Luther and the Holy Roman emperor, Charles V, thundered against the rebel. Luther defied them, publicly burned the bull of excommunication, and issued vigorous pamphlets assailing the papacy and the doctrine of the sacraments. The breach was thus made in 1521, and the meeting of the Diet of Worms (see WORMS, DIET OF) not only failed to produce a compromise but forced many doubters into the camp of the rebels. Luther was declared an outlaw, but the threat was empty; under the protection of the powerful Frederick III, elector of Saxony, he was spirited off to the safety of the Wartburg. The revolt was spreading with incredible speed over central and N Germany and almost immediately extended beyond the German borders. All the elements of discontent and rebellion coalesced. The learned, such as Luther himself, Melanchthon, and Martin BUCER, saw the opportunity to express and expand their own views. The nobles were enabled to cast off allegiance to the Holy Roman emperor and to enrich themselves by seizing the immense landed estates of the church. Too much can be—and has been—made out of this economic motive, however, for many of the princes belonged to the intellectual group that had been stirred to critical rejection of church doctrines, and they were perhaps better aware than common men of the venality and money-mindedness of many of the clergy. Many of the pious, increased in number by a spontaneous religious revival in the late 15th cent., drank the doctrine of a new spirituality with pleasure, for Luther's doctrine of justification (i.e., salvation) by faith alone and not by sacraments, good works, and the mediation of the church placed man in naked and direct communication with God. The new insistence upon reading the word of God in the Bible placed a greater responsibility on the individual. Those who were feeling the first and welcome experience of nationalism were anxious to shake off the hand of Rome. Absolutist rulers, particularly in Scandinavia, welcomed the opportunity to end the interference of the church in state affairs; by creating national churches they were able to escape outside influence. Merchants and capitalists found the air of individual freedom exhilarating. The peasants, chafing under the old restrictions of feudalism, lifted up their heads in hope that the new dispensation would take away their burdens. In Zurich, Switzerland, Huldreich Zwingli had developed his own brand of dissent. In 1529 in the Colloquy of Marburg, Luther and Melanchthon on the one side and Zwingli and John OECOLAMPADIUS on the other discussed the nature of the sacrament of the LORD'S SUPPER (the Protestant form of the Catholic EUCHARIST) but failed to come to an agreement. The fundamental principle that every man could arrive at truth by study of the Bible also led many to more radical conclusions than those that Luther adopted. The preacher known as CARLSTADT (from the place of his birth) argued for a more thoroughgoing dismissal of old practices and doctrines in Wittenberg itself and caused Luther to emerge from his retirement to halt the progress of radicalism. The PEASANTS' WAR (1524–25) showed plainly the rifts within the ranks of the rebels, and Luther, forced to choose between the revolutionary peasants and their opponents, the princes, chose the princes and orderly governance. The lower classes then in large measure followed more revolutionary social leaders, such as the communistic Thomas MÜNZER and JOHN OF LEIDEN. After their revolution had been brutally put down and the leaders tortured and executed, many of the revolutionary peasants returned to Roman Catholicism, but many continued to foster more radical sects, such as the ANABAPTISTS. In general the princes were able to dictate what religion should prevail in their territories, and they opposed vigorously the attempt of the Holy Roman emperor to force them back into the old church. The Knights' War (1522–23), led by Franz von SICKINGEN against the ecclesiastical princes, ended in failure, but the determination of Charles V to extirpate Lutheranism ultimately ended in even more abject failure. The imperial Diet of Speyer in 1526 found no answer to the division of the empire, and when a new Diet of Speyer in 1529 ordered that the emperor's ruling against the heretics should be enforced, the Lutheran princes issued a defiant protest (from which the term *Protestant* is derived). The Diet of Augsburg in 1530 was equally fruitless in producing a compromise between Catholic and Lutheran princes, but it did produce the Confession of Augsburg (see CREED), which was drafted by Melanchthon and became the official statement of Lutheran faith. The conflict in the empire led the Protestant princes to form a defensive union against the emperor in the Schmalkaldic League, in which the chief figures were PHILIP OF HESSE and JOHN FREDERICK I of Saxony. The league was put down in the Schmalkaldic War (1546–47), which did not, however, in the least solve the problem. Emperor Charles V, in an effort to prolong the uneasy peace, proposed to the Protestants that there be an interim agreement against change until a general church council could legislate on the dispute. This was the so-called Augsburg Interim (1548), which did not take effect because it was rejected by the Protestant princes. The confusion that political considerations brought to the religious issue is perhaps best seen in the career of MAURICE, duke of Saxony, who fought first on one side, then on the other. A sort of peace of exhaustion and compromise was reached in the Peace of Augsburg (1555; see AUGSBURG, PEACE OF). The settlement was, however, at best uneasy and was not to endure except in principle. The conflict was merged with many other issues in the later THIRTY YEARS WAR (1618–48). Meanwhile the fresh winds of the Reformation had been blowing all over Europe (except Russia). The Scandinavian countries became firmly Protestant under GUSTAVUS I of Sweden and Frederick I of Denmark and Norway; later attempts to win them back to Catholicism failed. Geneva had become in 1536 the headquarters of John CALVIN, who is considered by many the greatest theologian of Protestantism. His *Institutes of the Christian Religion,* published at Basel in 1536, marked a new era in thought. He differed from Luther principally in the doctrine of predestination (the foregone choosing by God of the elect to be saved), in the austerity of the life of the godly, and in the emphasis on theocratic government (see CALVINISM). His influence was immediate and enormous. France, which had hardly been touched by Lutheranism, was fired by Calvinist doctrine, and the Protestant minority, called the HUGUENOTS, waged fierce battle against the Catholic majority in the Wars of Religion until toleration was won when the Huguenot leader Henry of Navarre turned Catholic, became King Henry IV, and issued (1598) the Edict of Nantes. Calvinism superseded Lutheranism in the Netherlands, where the religious revolt was coupled with revulsion at the policies of Charles V and his successor, PHILIP II of Spain. Through bloody wars independence and Calvinism gained the upper hand in the N Low Countries. Calvinism conquered Scotland, too, through the victory of John KNOX in his long duel with MARY QUEEN OF SCOTS. It spread also to Hungary and Poland and took root in parts of Germany. It proved quite impossible to reconcile the finely wrought theology of Calvinism with Lutheran doctrines, for Lutheranism rejected predestination and clung to part of the sacramental system (see LORD'S SUPPER). Calvinist thought did greatly influence the course of the Reformation in the British Isles and the present United States. There was also a conflict of Lutheranism and Calvinism with the more radical and emotional groups, and the enthusiasm of preachers who interpreted Scripture in their own way met with a cool reception among the Calvinists. The divisions within Protestantism were from the beginning sharp, and attempts to reconcile Calvinist, Lutheran, and other doctrine had only partial success. Moreover, in England the Reformation went its own course. It was there much more closely connected with the conflict of church and state than was the Reformation on the Continent. The conflict of King HENRY VIII with Rome led to the Act of Supremacy (1534), which firmly rejected papal control and created a national church (see ENGLAND, CHURCH OF). Currents of Calvinistic thought were, however, strong in England. The Reformation was begun with the creation of a state church and the dissolution of the monasteries. It was given Calvinist touches under Edward VI, suffered a complete reversal under Mary I, and reached a sort of balance under Elizabeth I with some persecution of both Catholics and Calvinists. The process was to work itself out slowly later in the ENGLISH CIVIL WAR, just as the fierce hatreds between Protestant and Protestant as well as between Catholic and Protestant were to be worked out later on the Continent. The burning of SERVETUS was a sample of the internal strife within Protestantism itself. The divisions within the churches of the Reformation also served to forward the counterreformation within the Roman Catholic Church (see REFORMATION, CATHOLIC), which rewon Poland, Hungary, most of Bohemia, and part of Germany for the Catholics. The end of the Thirty Years War in the Peace of Westphalia (see WESTPHALIA, PEACE OF) in 1648 brought some stabilization, but the force of the Reformation did not end then. It has continued to exert influence to the present day, with its emphasis on personal responsibility and individual freedom, its refusal to take authority for granted, and its ultimate influence in breaking the hold of the church upon life and consequent secularization of life and attitudes. See T. M. Lindsay, *History of the Reformation* (2 vol., 1906–7, repr. 1971); E. M. Hulme, *The Renaissance, the Protestant Revolution, and the Catholic Reformation in Modern Europe* (rev. ed. 1917); Preserved Smith, *The Age of the Reformation* (1920, repr. 1962); Albert Hyma, *The Christian Renaissance* (1924); R. H. Murray, *The Political Consequences of the Reformation* (1926, repr. 1960); R. H. Tawney, *Religion and the Rise of Capitalism* (1926); Max Weber, *The Protestant Ethic and the Spirit of Capitalism* (tr. 1930); Constantin Hopf, *Martin Bucer and the English Reformation* (1946); R. H. Bainton, *The Reformation of the Sixteenth Century* (1952, repr. 1965) and *Studies on the Reformation* (1963); G. G. Coulton, *Art and The Reformation* (rev. ed. 1958); H. S. Lucas, *The Renaissance and the Reformation* (2d. ed. 1960); H. J. Grimm, *The Reformation Era, 1500–1650* (rev. ed. 1965); G. R. Elton, *Reformation Europe, 1517–1559* (1966); A. G. Dickens, *The English Reformation* (1967); Norman Sykes, *The Crisis of the Reformation*

(1967); Philip Hughes, *A Popular History of the Reformation* (1969); H. J. Hillerbrand, *The World of the Reformation* (1973).

Reformation, Catholic, 16th-century reformation, known popularly as the Counter Reformation from the fact that it arose largely in answer to the Protestant Reformation. Although the Roman Catholic reformers shared the Protestants' revulsion at the corrupt conditions in the church, there was present none of the tradition breaking that characterized Protestantism; the Catholic Reformation was led by conservative forces whose aim was to secure the traditions of the church against the innovations of Protestant theology and against the more liberalizing effects of the Renaissance. Since the time of St. Catherine of Siena (14th cent.) there had been a growing demand for reform—of the clergy, of Christian life, and of ecclesiastical administration. Probably the Great SCHISM did more than anything else to prevent change, for in its duration ecclesiastical politics preoccupied those who might have been busy with reform. In the 15th cent. the PAPACY was too weak to lead any movement, much less a drastic reform of the kind called for by Girolamo SAVONAROLA. A key factor in the stagnation in Christendom was the general worldliness and negligence of the prelates who—with their kings and princes—really ran the church. Such was their power that in the only vigorous papal effort at reform of the century, the mission of Nicholas of Cusa in Germany (1451), the papal legate dared not touch the bishops. At the time the most publicized scandal was the immoral Renaissance papal court; but of all the evils this proved to be the easiest remedied, once it was attacked by PAUL IV. Before he became pope Paul (as Cardinal Carafa) was, with St. CAJETAN (1480–1547) and others, a member of a tight little reform party at Rome. The nucleus was a society of priests and laymen, the Oratory of Divine Love, founded (1497) at Genoa for charitable work and then extended as a spiritual movement in the Curia itself. The reformers in Rome were helped from abroad by men of the prestige of St. Thomas More, Erasmus, St. John Fisher, and Cardinal Jiménez. The first major reform efforts failed; these were the Fifth Lateran Council (see LATERAN COUNCIL, FIFTH) and the election of Adrian VI, who died too soon to accomplish anything. In the next pontificate (Clement VII, 1523–34) the reform party worked on quietly, forming the core of resistance to Lutheranism; they founded the Theatines (1524) and the Capuchins (1525), religious orders to evangelize the common people. Meanwhile Protestantism expanded, and the sack of Rome (1527) convinced even the most complacent cardinals that political gambling was a danger to the church. The influence of Holy Roman Emperor CHARLES V weighed on the side of reform. In 1534, PAUL III became pope, and St. IGNATIUS OF LOYOLA and his friends took the vows that founded the Jesuits (see JESUS, SOCIETY OF). Thus simultaneously (but quite independently) the reformers finally won the papacy, and the pope was provided with a resolute band of helpers. In 1545, after delay and miscarriage, the Council of Trent (see TRENT, COUNCIL OF) was convened by Paul III. This council (1545–47, 1551–52, 1562–63) was the central feature of the Catholic Reformation. The popes of the council were Paul III, Julius III, and PIUS IV. The reign of Pius's predecessor, Paul IV, an interlude in the council, was devoted to the purge of the papal court; from Paul's work dates the quasi-monastic air that has ever since characterized the Vatican. The end of the council (1563) opened the second period of the reformation, lasting until 1590, with the pontificates of St. PIUS V, GREGORY XIII, and SIXTUS V. The work of the council was given effect. The chief evil in church life, simony in many forms, including the preaching of some indulgences, was uprooted. Worship was standardized; the law of the church and the government of the Holy See were reorganized; new educational requirements for parish priests were introduced and provided for (by diocesan seminaries); religious orders were reformed; and the life of the clergy was scrutinized. A new spirit began to breathe in the church, as seen in the work of St. CHARLES BORROMEO. In the Papal States and in a few other lands the new INQUISITION was extended. A far-reaching local movement in the reformation was the Oratory (see ORATORY, CONGREGATION OF THE) of St. PHILIP NERI. Catholicism took the offensive in Europe, and the Jesuits and Capuchins helped win Austria, Poland, the S Netherlands, and parts of Germany, Hungary, and Bohemia back to the Roman Catholic Church. The Jesuits led in foreign missions; in America it was the spirit of the Catholic Reformation that led the missionaries to work strenuously for the Indians, often in opposition to the secular authorities. Spanish religion was deepened by the Carmelite reforms of St. THERESA of Ávila and by St. JOHN OF THE CROSS. In France the Catholic Reformation took root later, after the accession and conversion to Catholicism of Henry IV; the great French figures were St. FRANCIS OF SALES and St. VINCENT DE PAUL. In England the Catholic Reformation took effect less in the restoration of the Roman Catholic Church under Queen Mary (although Cardinal POLE was a reformer) than in the mission of the Jesuits (1580), led by St. Edmund CAMPION and Robert PERSONS. Diverse figures showing effects of the Catholic Reformation are Caesar Baronius, St. Robert Bellarmine, Pedro Calderón de la Barca, Richard Crashaw, St. Francis Borgia, Robert Southwell, and Torquato Tasso. See Pierre Janelle, *The Catholic Reformation* (1949, repr. 1963); A. G. Dickens, *Counter Reformation* (1969); J. C. Olin, *Catholic Reformation* (1969); M. R. O'Connell, *The Counter Reformation 1559–1610* (1974).

Reform Bills, in British history, name given to three major measures that liberalized representation in PARLIAMENT in the 19th cent. Representation of the counties and boroughs in the House of Commons had not, except for the effects of parliamentary union with Scotland (1707) and Ireland (1800), been materially altered since the 17th cent. The system was very irregular and greatly restricted the franchise; it failed to take into account the great shifts of population and the growth of new social classes that attended the Industrial Revolution. "Pocket boroughs," controlled by the crown or large landholders, and "rotten boroughs," whose populations had declined (the most notorious was OLD SARUM, which had virtually ceased to exist) were amply represented. Yet large cities such as Manchester and Birmingham returned no members of their own. Out of a population of about 24,000,000 in the British Isles (including Ireland), only about 435,000 were qualified to vote. Corruption and the sale of seats flourished. Reform agitation, beginning to develop in the 1760s, was supported by William Pitt and others, but the emergency period of the French Revolution interrupted it. Revived c.1807, it had become the leading issue of the day by 1830. The **Reform Bill of 1832,** enacted under the Whig administration of the 2d Earl Grey, redistributed seats in the interest of larger communities; it also extended the franchise in the boroughs to those who occupied premises of an annual value of £10 and in the counties to similar leaseholders—to the advantage of shopkeepers and other middle-class men—and it simplified registration and voting procedure. The bill was passed in the House of Lords only as a result of the government's threat to overcome opposition by creating enough Whig peers to ensure passage. The electorate was increased by about 50%, but the new distribution of seats still allowed the rural areas to retain their supremacy. Agitation by the advocates of CHARTISM and others for further reform produced no results until Benjamin Disraeli made a bid for the support of the working classes by enacting the **Reform Bill of 1867.** This act, which further redistributed the seats and more than doubled the electorate, gave the vote to many workingmen in the towns. The **Reform Bill of 1884,** passed during the administration of William Gladstone, removed the distinction between county and borough franchises and, by the reduction of rural qualifications, added about 2,000,000 more men to the electorate. A redistribution act in 1885 rendered representation nearly proportional to population. It was not, however, until the passage of the REPRESENTATION OF THE PEOPLE ACTS in the 20th cent. that the British Parliament adopted universal male and female suffrage. See studies of electoral reform by Charles Seymour (1915, repr. 1970) and H. L. Morris (1921, repr. 1971); Norman Gash, *Politics in the Age of Peel* (1953); I. R. Christie, *Wilkes, Wyvill and Reform* (1962); F. B. Smith, *The Making of the Second Reform Bill* (1966); Maurice Cowling, *1867: Disraeli, Gladstone and Revolution* (1967).

Reformed churches, in a general sense, all Protestant churches that claim a beginning in the Reformation. In more restricted and more usual historical usage, Reformed churches are those Protestant churches that had their ecclesiastical origin in the doctrines of John Calvin, as distinct from those that are Lutheran or Evangelical. Swiss and Dutch churches and many in Germany came to be denominated Reformed. The Reformed churches as a rule follow the polity of PRESBYTERIANISM. They tend toward a simple form of worship rather than elaborate ritual. In the United States, churches bearing the Reformed title include the REFORMED CHURCH IN AMERICA, generally known as the Dutch Reformed Church, the CHRISTIAN REFORMED CHURCH, the EVANGELICAL AND REFORMED CHURCH, and the Free Magyar Reformed Church in America. The first two trace their origin to Holland, the third to Germany and Switzerland, and the fourth to Hungary. See CALVINISM.

Reformed Church in America, Protestant denomination founded in colonial times by settlers from the Netherlands and formerly known as the Dutch Reformed Church. The Reformed Church in Holland emerged in the 16th cent., after the Calvinist Reformation movement gained influence in the northern provinces of the Netherlands. In 1571 a synod held at Emden laid the foundation for the Reformed Church. A liturgy was formulated along Reformation lines, and a modified presbyterian form of polity was adopted. The Belgic Confession of Faith (1561) and the Heidelberg Catechism (1563) were made the basis of the new church; later, the canons of the Synod of Dort (1619) were added. After 1581, when the northern provinces of the Netherlands declared their independence from Spain, the Reformed Church grew even stronger. In America, the early Dutch settlers in New Netherland held informal meetings for worship until Jonas Michaelius organized (1628) a congregation in New Amsterdam, called the Reformed Protestant Dutch Church. Four churches in New York City (the Fort Washington Collegiate Church, Middle Collegiate Church, Marble Collegiate Church, and West End Collegiate Church) are descendants of this early activity. Until the English conquest of New Netherland in 1664, the Reformed Church was the established church of the colony. After that, while still owing ecclesiastical allegiance to the classis (i.e., governing body) of Amsterdam in Holland, the church gave civil allegiance to England. However, the church continued to expand. Permission was given (1747) to form an assembly in America, which in 1754 declared itself independent of the classis of Amsterdam. This American classis secured a charter (1766) for Queens College (now Rutgers Univ.) in New Jersey. The appointment (1784) of John Henry Livingston as professor of theology marked the beginning of the New Brunswick Theological Seminary. In 1792 a formal constitution was adopted; in 1794 the Reformed Church held its first general synod, and in 1867 the present name became the official one. The church embraces many of the historic colonial churches of New York and New Jersey, the denominational stronghold; fresh immigration from the Netherlands in the mid-19th cent. led to the development of the church in the Midwest. Hope College and Western Theological Seminary were founded in Holland, Mich., and Central College at Pella, Iowa. In 1857 a group of Dutch settlers in Michigan separated from the Reformed Church and organized the CHRISTIAN REFORMED CHURCH; in 1922 that body received most of the American congregation of the Reformed Church of Hungary. A small part of the Eureka classis, organized in 1910 in South Dakota, continued as the Reformed Church in the United States after the majority of the body merged (1934) into the Evangelical and Reformed Church, which joined (1961) the Congregational Christian Churches to become the United Church of Christ. The Reformed Church in America, which has long been active in the foreign mission field, numbered about 380,000 in the early 1970s. Several attempts at unification between the Reformed Church and other Reformed and Presbyterian groups have proved unsuccessful. See M. G. Hansen, *The Reformed Church in the Netherlands, 1340–1840* (1884); J. J. Birch, *The Pioneering Church in the Mohawk Valley* (1955).

Reformed Church in the United States: see EVANGELICAL AND REFORMED CHURCH.

Reformed Episcopal Church, formed in 1873 by members of the Protestant Episcopal Church who withdrew from it because of sacramental and ritualistic dissensions. They have a membership of about 6,000.

Reformed Presbyterianism: see PRESBYTERIANISM; CAMERON, RICHARD.

Reform Judaism: see JUDAISM.

refraction, in physics, deflection of a wave on passing obliquely from one transparent medium into a second medium in which its speed is different, as the passage of a light ray from air into glass. Other forms of ELECTROMAGNETIC RADIATION, in addition to light waves, also experience refraction, as do sound waves. A light ray entering a different medium is called the incident ray; after bending, the ray is called the refracted ray. Refraction is commonly explained in terms of the wave theory of light and is based on the fact that light travels with greater velocity in some media than it does in others. When, for example, a ray of light traveling through air strikes the surface of a piece of glass at an oblique angle, one side of the wave front enters the glass before the other and is retarded (since light travels more slowly in glass than in air), while the other side continues to move at its original speed until it too reaches the glass. As a result, the ray bends inside the glass, i.e., the refracted ray lies in a direction closer to the normal (the perpendicular to the boundary of the media) than does the incident ray. The speed at which a given transparent medium transmits light waves is related to its optical density (not to be confused with mass or weight DENSITY). In general, a ray is refracted toward the normal when it passes into a denser medium, and away from the normal when it passes into a less dense medium. The law of refraction relates the angle of incidence (angle between the incident ray and the normal) to the angle of refraction (angle between the refracted ray and the normal). This law, credited to Willebrord Snell, states that the ratio of the sine of the angle of incidence, *i*, to the sine of the angle of refraction, *r*, is equal to the ratio of the speed of light in the original medium, v_i, to the speed of light in the refracting medium, v_r, or $\sin i/\sin r = v_i/v_r$. Snell's law is often stated in terms of the indexes of refraction of the two media rather than the speeds of light in the media. The index of refraction, *n*, of a transparent medium is a direct measure of its optical density and is equal to the ratio of the speed of light in a vacuum, *c*, to the speed of light in the medium: $n = c/v$. Indexes of refraction are always equal to or greater than 1; for air, $n = 1.00029$; for water, $n = 1.33$. Using indexes of refraction, Snell's law takes the form $\sin i/\sin r = n_r/n_i$, or $n_i \sin i = n_r \sin r$. If the original medium is denser than the refracting medium (n_i greater than n_r), sin *r* will be greater than sin *i*. Thus, there will be some acute angle less than 90° for the incident ray corresponding to an angle of refraction of 90°. This angle of incidence is known as the critical angle. For angles of incidence greater than the critical angle, refraction cannot take place and the incident ray is instead reflected back into the original medium according to the law of REFLECTION (angle of reflection equals angle of incidence). This phenomenon is known as total internal reflection. Refraction has many applications in optics and technology. A LENS uses refraction to form an IMAGE of an object for many different purposes, such as magnification. A PRISM uses refraction to form a SPECTRUM of colors from an incident beam of light. Refraction also plays an important role in the formation of a MIRAGE and other optical illusions.

refractor: see TELESCOPE.

refractory brick, brick that can withstand high temperatures; synonym for FIREBRICK.

refrigeration, process for drawing heat from substances to lower their temperature, often for purposes of preservation. Before the advent of modern refrigeration, perishable foods were kept in cool cellars or in buckets lowered into wells. A device still used in some areas is a room built with porous walls over which water is made to trickle. As the water evaporates the room is cooled. A spring of cold water often determined the site of an American pioneer's home. A springhouse was built over the flowing water, and the cooling fluid was led through troughs in which crocks of butter and cream were placed. In winter, farmers stored ice in icehouses for use in the summer. Similarly, natural ice from commercial icehouses was used in cities until artificial methods of producing ice were initiated in the middle of the 19th cent. The first patent for mechanical refrigeration was issued (1834) in Great Britain to the American inventor Jacob Perkins. Mechanical refrigeration systems are based on the principle that absorption of heat by a fluid (refrigerant) as it changes from a liquid to a gas lowers the temperature of the objects around it. In the compression system, which is employed in electric home refrigerators and commercial installations, a compressor, controlled by a thermostat, exerts pressure on a vaporized refrigerant (usually a Freon compound or ammonia), forcing it to pass through a condenser where it loses heat and liquefies. It then moves through the coils of the refrigeration compartment. There it vaporizes, drawing heat from whatever is in the compartment. The refrigerant then passes back to the compressor and the cycle repeats. In the absorption system, widely employed in commercial installations, ammonia is usually used as a refrigerant to cool brine (water containing calcium chloride or sodium chloride) that is then sent through pipes to cool the refrigerated space. The steam-jet system is used where temperatures below 32°F (0°C) are not required. Water is used as the refrigerant. Research and development is being carried out to apply the Peltier effect (see THERMOELECTRICITY) in various practical refrigeration systems. Wherever fresh or frozen food must be stored, processed, transported or sold, refrigeration is indispensable; thus appropriate refrigeration machinery was developed for trains, ships, factories, and cold-storage plants (used not only for foods but also for fur storage). An outgrowth of the preservation of foods by refrigeration was the development of a process for preparing frozen foods. Although a number of experimenters contributed to the discovery of a workable process, the name of American inventor Clarence Birdseye is associated with the early successful introduction of the method; one of his chief contributions was his system of freezing perishable foods (packed in individual containers ready for sale) between refrigerated metal plates. See AIR CONDITIONING and COOLING SYSTEM. See R. J. Dossat, *Principles of Refrigeration* (1961); G. H. Reed *Refrigeration* (1967); W. R. Woolrich, *The Men Who Created Cold: A History of Refrigeration* (1967).

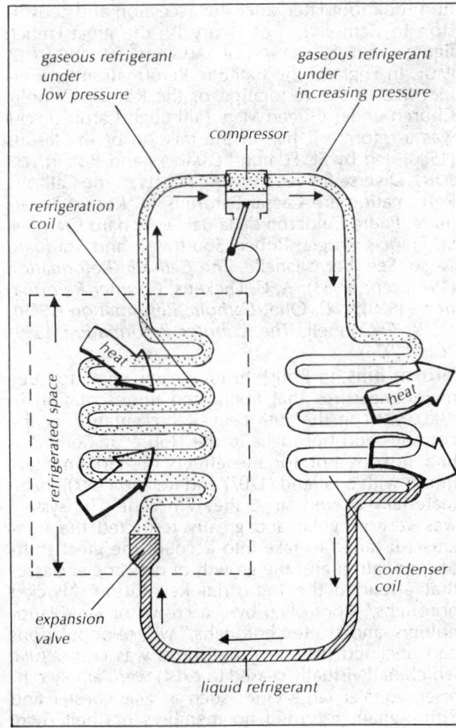

Compression system of refrigeration

refugee, one who leaves his native land either because of expulsion or to escape persecution. The legal problem of accepting refugees is discussed under ASYLUM; this article considers only mass dislocations. Early examples of the movement of refugees in considerable number include the expulsion of the Jews and the Moors from Spain in the late 15th cent., the flights from religious persecutions in Europe to the New World in the 16th and 17th cent., and the exodus of the émigrés in the French Revolution. Before the 20th cent. there was little or no systematic attempt to help refugees. After World War I, international organizations were created to give assistance. The Russian Revolution of 1917 forced the resettlement of about 1.5 million opponents of Communism. In the 1920s large numbers of Armenian and Greek refugees fled from Turkey, and many Bulgarians left their country. In 1921 the League of Nations appointed Fridtjof NANSEN its high commissioner for refugee work; later the INTERNATIONAL LABOR ORGANIZATION and the Nansen International Office for Refugees took charge. Nansen effected repatriation wherever possible; in other cases he arranged for the issuance of Nansen passports, which gave the holder the right to move freely across national boundaries; these passports were recognized by 28 countries. The refugee problem was revived after Adolf Hitler's accession to power in Germany (1933) and his annexation of Austria (1938) and Czechoslovakia (1939). The Loyalist defeat in Spain (1939) and anti-Semitic legislation in Eastern Europe added to the overall problem, with Jews being the largest group affected. Many asylum governments attempted to return refugees to their country of origin; they were often forbidden to work and sometimes imprisoned. Some progress was achieved with the establishment of a permanent committee for refugees in London after a conference of 32 nations held in France in 1938. World War II further dislocated civilian populations. At the war's end the UNITED NATIONS RELIEF AND REHABILITATION ADMINISTRATION (UNRRA) had the responsibility of caring for some 8 million displaced persons (persons removed from their native countries as prisoners or slave laborers.) The majority of those refugees were speedily repatriated, but about one million in Germany, Austria, and Italy refused to return to their native countries, which were by then under Communist governments. The number of Jewish refugees was in time greatly reduced by emigration to Israel, but uprooting the Arab population of that new state in its turn created some one million refugees. With the end of UNRRA, the United Nations created the INTERNATIONAL REFUGEE ORGANIZATION to carry on its work. After much debate the United States in 1948 adopted the Displaced Persons Act, which, despite numerous restrictions, eventually permitted the entrance of about 400,000 immigrants. The world refugee problem has remained acute. When the Indian subcontinent was partitioned in 1947, millions of people were forced to migrate. Steady streams of refugees left mainland China and East Germany, especially in the 1950s. The Korean War produced some 9 million refugees. During the years Algeria fought (1954–62) for independence from France, many people fled the country. In Africa south of the Sahara Desert, a massive refugee problem, rooted in the continent's colonial past, exists. In precolonial days, Africans had moved freely within their own tribal areas. However, the boundaries fixed by the colonial powers in dividing up the continent among themselves in the 19th cent. often cut across tribal areas, resulting, particularly after independence, in mass movements of refugees across national borders. By the early 1970s there were close to 2 million refugees in Africa. Other major refugee creating events of the 1950s include the Hungarian Revolution (1956), the expulsion of the Dutch from Indonesia (1957), the uprising in Tibet (1958–59), and the establishment of a Communist government in Cuba in 1959. The 1960s brought grave refugee problems to Africa and the Arab-Israeli War of 1967 expanded an already swollen refugee population in the Middle East. A tremendous refugee population has been created by the Vietnam War; the India-Pakistan War of 1971 produced about 10 million refugees, but most of these returned to their homes in the newly created Bangladesh. In 1972 the government of Uganda began expelling Asians. Numerous attempts have been made to alleviate the plight of these various refugee groups. Since 1951 the Office of the UNITED NATIONS HIGH COMMISSIONER FOR REFUGEES has coordinated international activities and worked for independent solutions cooperating closely with national and international voluntary organizations. Much money has been raised through voluntary contributions by these and other kinds of organizations. Despite these efforts to aid people once they become refugees, little has been accomplished in tackling the problems that produce refugees. See Jacques Vernant, *The Refugee in the Post-War World* (1953); J. G. Stoessinger, *The Refugee and the World Community* (1956); Robert Kee, *Refugee World* (1961); Peter Collins, *A Mandate to Protect and Assist Refugees* (1971); Paul Tabori, *The Anatomy of Exile* (1972); Louise Holborn, *The International Refugee Organization* (1956) and *Refugees, a Problem for Our Time: The Work of the United Nations High Commissioner for Refugees, 1950–1970* (1974).

refuse: see SOLID WASTE.

regatta: see ROWING; SAILING.

Regem (rē'gĕm), name in an obscure genealogical passage. 1 Chron. 2.47.

Regem-melech (rē'gĕm-mē'lĕk), messenger sent to Zechariah. Zech. 7.2.

régence style (räzhäNs'), transitional style in architecture and decoration originated in France during the regency (1715–23) of Philippe II, duc d'Orléans. The most important practitioners of the régence were Gilles Marie Oppenord and Robert de Cotte. In this period, curved lines and many motifs such as shells, masques, and sinuous foliated scrolls were introduced. These innovations were subsequently developed in ROCOCO design. The legs of furniture took bulging outlines and the corners of panels were curved. The use of gilt bronze was extended, and walnut, rosewood, and other woods largely replaced ebony in veneers.

Regency, in British history, the period of the last nine years (1811–20) of the reign of George III, when the king's insanity had rendered him unfit to rule and the government was vested in the prince of Wales (later GEORGE IV) as regent. The period witnessed the end (1815) of the Napoleonic Wars and growing social unrest, which was met by the Tory government of the time with harsh repression. Socially, the period took a distinctive coloration from the gay and dissolute regent and his companions. It was the time of a notable flowering in arts, letters, and architecture. In literature, the period marks the height of the romantic movement in the work of such poets as Lord Byron, John Keats, and Percy Bysshe Shelley and in the novels of Sir Walter Scott. Regency architecture culminated in the elegant simplicity of the REGENCY STYLE. Regency furniture shows a similar refinement of design and taste and a strong influence of the styles of the French Directoire. See Paul Emden, *Regency Parade* (1936); Arthur Bryant, *The Age of Elegance* (1950); J. B. Priestley, *The Prince of Pleasure and His Regency* (1969).

Regency style, in English architecture, flourished during the regency and reign of George IV (1811–30) and was chiefly represented by the court architect John Nash. The period is characterized by the diversity of the architectural styles of many countries and periods. For the prince regent, John Nash constructed at Brighton the Royal Pavilion (1815–22) in the Indian style; it included exotic Oriental furnishings. The preponderant trend, however, was neoclassical, as seen in the works of Sir John Soane and George Dance II and in the rigid geometric order of Nash's design for Regent's Park in London. During this time stucco was often used on the exterior of buildings, and bay windows and balconies were in vogue. Furniture design was eclectic and showed the influence of Greek, Roman, Gothic, Egyptian, and Oriental ornament. See Paul Reilly, *An Introduction to Regency Architecture* (1948); John Harris, *Regency Furniture Designs* (1961); Clifford Musgrave, *Regency Furniture* (1961).

Regensburg (rā'gənsbo͝orkh), city (1970 pop. 129,589), Bavaria, SE West Germany, a port at the confluence of the Danube (Donau) and Regen rivers. In English it is known as Ratisbon. The city is a commercial, industrial, and transportation center; its manufactures include machines, precision instruments, chemicals, leather goods, and printed materials. There are shipyards in the city. Regensburg, one of the oldest German cities, is a cultural center with many historic monuments. It was an important Roman frontier station, known as Regina Castra. An abbey was founded there in the mid-7th cent., and St. Boniface established an episcopal see in 739. Regensburg was captured (788) by Charlemagne when he subjugated Bavaria. The city was one of the most prosperous commercial centers of medieval Germany, trading especially with India and the Middle East. In 1245, Regensburg was made a free imperial city; part of the adjacent countryside, however, remained in ecclesiastical hands. The city proper accepted the Reformation in the 16th cent., but soon thereafter it was strongly influenced by the Roman Catholic Counter Reformation (late 16th cent.). Its commerce declined in the 15th and 16th cent., as a result of the shifting of international trade routes. In the Thirty Years War, Regensburg, garrisoned by Bavarian troops, was bombarded and captured (1633) by the Protestant general Bernhard of Saxe-Weimar, but it was recovered (1634) by imperial forces under Ferdinand of Hungary and Bohemia (later Emperor Ferdinand III). Regensburg was frequently the meeting place of the imperial DIET from 1532, and from 1663 to 1806 it was the permanent seat of the diet. The diet that met there from 1801 to 1803 under the influence of Napoleon Bonaparte completely reorganized the moribund Holy Roman Empire. The city and the bishopric of Regensburg (later raised to an archbishopric) were given, with Aschaffenburg, to K. T. von DALBERG. In 1810 the city passed to Bavaria and became the capital of the Upper Palatinate. Regensburg was badly damaged by the Allies in World War II, largely because it was an airplane-manufacturing center. Noteworthy structures of the city include the Gothic cathedral (13th–16th cent.); parts of the Porta Praetoria, a Roman gate (built A.D. 179); the Schottenkirche St. Jakob, a 12th-century church; an 11th-century chapel (with later decoration in the rococo style); the old city hall (14th–18th cent.), where the imperial diet met; and St. Emmeram, the episcopal residence (a former Benedictine convent founded in the 7th cent.). The church of the Benedictine convent, with foundations dating from the 8th cent. to the 12th cent. and with an 18th-century baroque interior, contains the tombs of Emperor Arnulf and of Louis the Child. Regensburg is the seat of a university (founded 1965) and schools of engineering and church music. The city was a residence of the painter Albrecht Altdorfer and the astronomer J. Kepler, both of whom died there.

Reger, Max (mäks rā'gər), 1873–1916, German composer; he studied with Hugo Riemann in Wiesbaden. Through his sensitive interpretations of Mozart and Bach he won acclaim as a pianist. In 1901 he settled in Munich, where he taught composition and organ, and from 1907 until his death he taught at the Leipzig Conservatory. In 1911 he became conductor of the court orchestra at Meiningen. He was highly esteemed in Germany for his organ music, which exhibits extreme polyphonic complexity and a consummate technique. Among his important compositions for the organ are *Fantasy and Fugue in C Minor* (Op. 29) and *Fantasy and Fugue on Bach* (Op. 46). His enormous output also includes *Improvisation* (Op. 18), for the piano; the *Symphonic Prologue to a Tragedy,* for orchestra; and more than 300 songs.

Reggio di Calabria (rĕd'jō dē kälä'brēä), city (1971 pop. 162,888), capital of Reggio di Calabria prov., Calabria, extreme S Italy, on the Strait of Messina opposite Sicily. It is a beach resort and an important agricultural market for fruits and tobacco. Bergamot essence (used in perfume) is produced there. Known as RHEGIUM in ancient times, the city became (12th cent.) part of the kingdom of Sicily and later (13th cent.) of Naples. Its strategic position has resulted in numerous foreign invasions and incursions. The city has also suffered many earthquakes—the worst came in 1783 and 1908. In 1970–71 there was considerable unrest in the city when the capital of Calabria was shifted from Reggio to Catanzaro. The National Museum in Reggio has rich collections of ancient art.

Reggio nell' Emilia (nĕl″āmē'lyä), city (1971 pop. 128,844), capital of Reggio nell' Emilia prov., in Emilia-Romagna, N central Italy, on the Aemilian Way. It is an agricultural and industrial center and a rail junction. Manufactures include food products, chemicals, and electrical equipment. Founded by Rome in the 2d cent. B.C., it later became a free commune and in 1289 came under the ESTE family. Points of interest include the 13th-century cathedral, the Renaissance Church of the Madonna della Ghiara, and the Parmeggiani art gallery. The poet Ariosto was born in Reggio in 1474.

regicides (rĕj'ĭsīdz) [Lat., =king-killers], in English history, name given to those judges and court officers responsible for the trial and execution of Charles I in 1649. After the Restoration (1660) of the monarchy they were excepted from the general pardon granted by the Act of Indemnity. At that time 41 of the 59 signers of the king's death warrant were still alive. Fifteen of them fled: William GOFFE, John Dixwell, and Edward WHALLEY went to New England; several went to Germany and Holland; and Edmund LUDLOW and four others went to Switzerland. Some were able to convince Charles II that they had had little to do with his father's trial and that they were loyal to the monarchy, and they were reprieved. Nine of those who signed the warrant and four others closely connected with the trial were hanged. Those deemed less politically dangerous were imprisoned for life, and some were later reprieved. See C. V. Wedgwood, *A Coffin for King Charles* (1964).

Regillus, Lake (rĭjĭl'əs), in ancient Latium, SE of Rome, possibly near Frascati. Traditionally it was the scene of a battle (499 or 496 B.C.) by which Rome gained supremacy in Latium.

Regina (rĭjī'nə), city (1971 pop. 139,468), provincial capital, S Sask., Canada, on Wascana Creek. The city is the distribution and service center for one of the world's largest wheat-growing plains. Industries include agricultural processing, meat-packing, printing, bookbinding, oil refining, and automobile manufacturing. Regina was founded in 1882 when a railroad line was constructed through the region. It was the capital of the Northwest Territories from 1883 to 1905, when it became the capital of the newly created Saskatchewan. From 1892 to 1920, Regina was the headquarters of the Northwest Mounted Police, and it is now western headquarters of the Royal Canadian Mounted Police, which maintains its crime detection laboratory there. Regina has a campus of the Univ. of Saskatchewan. See E. G. Drake, *Regina, the Queen City* (1955).

Reginald of Châtillon (shätēyôN'), d. 1187, Crusader, lord of Krak and Montreal in the Latin Kingdom of Jerusalem. He came to the Holy Land in the Second Crusade and married (1153) Constance, daughter of Bohemond II of Antioch. He was energetic, impulsive, and intolerant, and his quarrels with the Latin princes weakened the position of the Crusaders. In 1159, after plotting with the Armenian prince, Thoros, against Emperor Manuel II of Byzantium, he was forced to submit to the emperor. Captured (1160) by the Saracens, he remained a prisoner over 15 years. After his release he took as his second wife the heiress of Krak and Montreal, and in 1177 he became procurator of Jerusalem for a brief period. In 1182–83 he raided the Red Sea coast. With GUY OF LUSIGNAN, whom he influenced and also helped to install as king of Jerusalem in 1186, Reginald advocated a belligerent and disastrous policy against SALADIN and opposed the conciliatory attitude of RAYMOND of Tripoli. His attack (1187) on one of Saladin's caravans violated his truce with the sultan and helped to bring on Saladin's attack on the Christians. Reginald was captured at the battle of Hattin and was executed by the sultan's own hand.

Regiomontanus (rē″jēōmŏn″tā'nəs) [Lat., =belonging to the royal mountain, i.e., to Königsberg], 1436–76, German astronomer and mathematician, b. Königsberg. His original name was Johannes Müller. In 1461 he went to Rome with Cardinal Bessarion and learned Greek in order to translate Greek writings. In 1468 he was called to the court of the king of Hungary to make a collection of Greek manuscripts, and three years later he settled at Nuremberg, where, with his pupil and patron, Bernhard Walther, he established an observatory and a printing press. Among other works they published the *Ephemerides* for the years 1474–1506, calculated by Regiomontanus, and Georg von Purbach's *Theoricae planetarum novae.* Summoned by Pope Sixtus IV, Regiomontanus went to Rome in 1475 to assist in reforming the calendar and was made bishop of Regensburg. He died in Rome. He made improved instruments, both mathematical and astronomical, introduced algebra into Germany, and did much to further trigonometry.

regional planning: see CITY PLANNING.

Regium or **Rhegium Julium:** see RHEGIUM.

Regla (rā'glä), city (1970 pop. 35,966), La Habana prov., W Cuba, a commercial suburb of Havana. It grew up around the hermitage of Nuestra Señora de Regla (est. 1690) and was officially founded in 1765. During the colonial period, Regla was a smuggling center for Havana.

Regnard, Jean François (zhäN fräNswä' rənyär'), 1655–1709, French comic dramatist. He traveled widely in Europe; captured by Barbary pirates, he was held in slavery (1678–79) until ransomed. His best-known comedies, characterized by verve and mocking gaiety, are *Le Joueur* [the gamester] (1696), a comedy of character; *Les Folies amoureuses* [lover's madness] (1704); *Les Ménechmes* (1705), after Plautus; and *Le Légataire universel* (1708; tr. *The Sole Heir,* 1912).

Regnault, Henri Victor (äNrē' vĕktôr' rənyō'), 1810–78, French physicist and chemist. He was professor of chemistry at the École polytechnique, Paris, from 1840 and at the Collège de France from 1841; he became chief engineer of mines (1847) and director of the porcelain manufactory at Sèvres (1854). In chemistry he is known for his work on the halogen and other derivatives of the unsaturated hydrocarbons. In physics he is noted for his careful measurements of the specific heats and expansion coefficients of many gases, liquids, and solids. He showed that Boyle's law is only approximately true for real gases, and he did important research on the operation of steam engines.

Régnier, Henri de (äNrē' də rānyā'), 1864–1936, French poet, one of the young SYMBOLISTS of the circle of Mallarmé. His early *Poèmes anciens et romanesques* (1891) showed skill in free verse, but his style soon changed to follow classical models, chiefly through the influence of José Maria de Heredia, father of Régnier's wife, Marie Louise de Heredia de Régnier, herself a poet. The poetic volume *La Sandale ailée* (1906; tr. *Poems from the Wingèd Sandal,* 1933) represents Régnier's classical style. Régnier also wrote successful novels that reflected his interest in history.

Régnier, Mathurin (mätüräN'), 1573–1613, French poet. He wrote 16 vigorous, realistic, and often licentious verse satires in the manner of Latin authors, first published as a whole in 1613.

Rego, José Lins do: see LINS DO REGO, JOSÉ.

regrating: see ENGROSSING.

regression, in psychology: see DEFENSE MECHANISM.

Regulator movement, designation for two groups, one in South Carolina, the other in North Carolina, that tried to effect governmental changes in the 1760s. In South Carolina, the Regulator movement was an organized effort by backcountry settlers to restore law and order and establish institutions of local government. Plagued by roving bands of outlaws and angered by the assembly's failure to provide the western counties with courts and petty officers, the leading planters, supported by small farmers, created (1767) an association to regulate backcountry affairs. They brought criminals to justice and set up courts to resolve legal disputes. The assembly and the governor, recognizing the legitimacy of the grievances, did not attempt to crush the movement. By 1768, order was restored, and the Circuit Court Act of 1769, providing six court districts for the backcountry, led the Regulators to disband. The movement in W North Carolina, with different causes, arose at the same time. Led by small farmers protesting the corruption and extortionate practices of sheriffs and court officials, the Regulators, strongest in Orange, Granville, Halifax, and Anson counties, at first petitioned (1764-65) the assembly to recall its officers. When this failed, they formed (1768) an association pledged to pay only legal taxes and fees and to abide by the will of the majority. They won control of the provincial assembly in 1769, but with Gov. William TRYON, the provincial council, and the courts against them they were unable to secure relief. At first orderly, the Regulators resorted to acts of violence (especially at Hillsboro) after Edmund FANNING, a particularly despised official, was allowed to go unpunished. Those actions alienated large property holders and the clergy from the movement. On May 16, 1771, Tryon's militia completely routed a large body of Regulators in the battle of Alamance Creek. Seven of the leaders were executed, and the movement collapsed. One group of Regulators moved W to Tennessee, where they helped form the WATAUGA ASSOCIATION, but most of them submitted. Tensions remained, however, between the western farmers and the tidewater aristocracy. See R. M. Brown, *The South Carolina Regulators* (1963).

Regulus (Marcus Atilius Regulus)(rĕg'yōōləs), d. c.250 B.C., Roman general in the First Punic War. While consul (267 B.C.) he conquered the Sallentini and captured Brundisium (now Brindisi). He became consul a second time (256), defeated the Carthaginians at sea, and waged war against them in Africa, at first with success. Soon afterward the Carthaginians won a complete victory and captured (255) Regulus. He was sent on parole to solicit peace from the Romans, but instead he advised the senate against accepting the Punic terms or exchanging prisoners. Resisting persuasions to break his parole, he returned to Carthage, where he was supposedly tortured to death. The story made Regulus famous as a Roman patriot-martyr.

Regulus (rĕg'yələs), brightest star in the constellation LEO; Bayer designation Alpha Leonis; 1970 position R.A. 10ʰ06.8ᵐ, Dec. +12°17'. A bluish-white main-sequence star of SPECTRAL CLASS B7 V, its apparent MAGNITUDE of 1.35 makes it one of the 25 brightest stars in the sky. Its distance from the earth is about 85 light-years. Regulus is a visual triple star. Its name is Latin for "prince."

Rehabiah (rē"həbī'ə), Moses' grandson. 1 Chron. 23.17; 24.21; 26.25.

rehabilitation: see PHYSICAL THERAPY.

Rehan, Ada (rē'ən), 1860-1916, American actress, b. Ireland. Her original name was Crehan. Rehan came to the United States when she was five. From 1879 to 1899 she was a member of Augustin Daly's company and for a large part of this time was costarred with John Drew. Excelling in Daly's adaptations of German and French society comedies and in Shakespearean comedies, she won special acclaim in *The Taming of the Shrew.* See William Winter, *The Wallet of Time* (1913).

Rehnquist, William Hubbs (rĕn'kwĭst), 1924-, American public official, Associate Justice of the U.S. Supreme Court (1971-), b. Milwaukee, Minn. After receiving his law degree from Stanford Univ. in 1952, he served (1952-53) as law clerk to Supreme Court Justice Robert H. Jackson. The following year he went to Phoenix where he practiced law and became involved in conservative Republican politics. He was (1968-71) an assistant attorney general, heading the office of legal counsel in the Dept. of Justice before being named to the Supreme Court by President Nixon. Generally regarded as the most conservative member of the court, Rehnquist became known as a staunch advocate of law and order. He wrote several opinions reversing the liberal trend of the Earl Warren court, especially in criminal cases.

Rehnskiöld, Karl Gustaf (kärl gŭs'täv rān'shöld), 1651-1722, Swedish field marshal. One of the ablest lieutenants of Charles XII in the Northern War, he played an important part in the Polish campaign of 1701-3 and defeated (1706) the combined Russian, Polish, and Saxon forces at Fraustadt, SW of Poznan. He accompanied Charles on his Ukrainian campaign. When Charles was incapacitated by a wound just before the battle of Poltava (1709), he appointed Rehnskiöld commander in chief. The battle was disastrous for the hopelessly outnumbered Swedes; Rehnskiöld himself was captured by the Russians.

Rehob (rē'hŏb). **1** Hadadezer's father. 2 Sam. 8.3,12. **2** Sealer of the Covenant. Neh. 10.11. **3** See BETH-REHOB. **4** Town of Asher. Joshua 21.31; Judges 1.31; 1 Chron. 6.75. **5** Town of Asher. Joshua 19.28,30, probably the same as **4**.

Rehoboam (rē"əbō'əm), king of Israel, son of Solomon. Under him the northern tribes broke away from the rule of Jerusalem and set up a separate kingdom (called Israel) with JEROBOAM I as their king. Rehoboam's foolish insolence to the protesting tribesmen is celebrated. In Rehoboam's reign Palestine was invaded by SHESHONK I of Egypt. 1 Kings 11.43;12; 14.21-31; 2 Chron. 9.31; 12. Roboam: Mat. 1.7.

Rehoboth (rĭhō'bəth). **1** Well dug for Isaac. Gen. 26.22. **2** City of Assyria, or possibly a part of Nineveh. Gen. 10.11. **3** Probably a place by the Euphrates, home of Shaul, king of Edom. But as the home of an Edomite, such a location is strange. Gen. 36.37; 1 Chron. 1.48.

Rehoboth: see REHOVOT, Israel.

Rehovot (rĭhō'vōt) or **Rehoboth** (-bəth), town (1970 est. pop. 37,000), central Israel. It is the trade center for a large citrus-growing area, and its industries include fruit packing and the production of citrus concentrates. Plastic products, imitation leather, cereals, and pharmaceuticals are also manufactured. Rehovot was founded in 1890 by Jewish immigrants from Russia. Chaim Weizmann, Israel's first president, lived in the town during the British mandate period (1922-48) and is buried there. His house is preserved. Rehovot is the seat of the Weizmann Institute of Science, the Faculty of Agriculture of the Hebrew Univ. of Jerusalem, and the government-run Volcani Institute of Agricultural Research.

Rehum (rē'həm). **1** One of the returning exiles. Ezra 2.2. Nehum: Neh. 7.7. **2** Samaritan official who obstructed work on the Temple. Ezra 4.8,9,17,23. **3** Sealer of the Covenant. Neh. 10.25. **4** Levite who worked to rebuild Jerusalem. Neh. 3.17. **5** Same as HARIM **1**.

Rei (rē'ī), loyal adherent of David. 1 Kings 1.8.

Reich, Wilhelm (vĭl'hĕlm rīkh), 1897-1957, Austrian psychiatrist and biophysicist. For many years a chief associate at Freud's Psychoanalytic Polyclinic in Vienna, he later broke with Freud and the psychoanalytic movement. Forced to leave Nazi Germany, he resettled in New York City in 1939 to continue independent research in biophysics. He taught (1939-41) at the New School for Social Research, and in 1942 he founded the Orgone Institute. According to Reich's theories the universe is permeated by a primal, mass-free phenomenon that he called orgone energy; in the human organism the lack of repeated total discharge of this energy through natural sexual release is considered the genesis not only of all individual neurosis but also of irrational social movements and collective neurotic disorder. Reich invented the orgone box, a device that he claimed would restore energy but that was declared a fraud by the Food and Drug Administration. In 1956 he was tried for contempt of court and violation of the Food and Drug Act and sentenced to two years in a Federal penitentiary, where he died. See his selected writings (1960); studies by Charles Rycroft (1972) and David Boadella (1974).

Reichenbach (rī'khənbäkh) or **Reichenbach im Vogtland** (ĭm fôkt'länt), city (1970 pop. 28,818), Karl-Marx-Stadt district, S East Germany, at the foot of the Erzgebirge; chartered in the late 13th cent. Manufactures of this industrial city include textiles, clothing, plastics, and machinery.

Reichenbach: see DZIERŻONIÓW, Poland.

Reichenbach Falls, waterfalls, total drop 656 ft (200 m), S central Switzerland, where the Reichenbach River joins the Aare River. Upper Reichenbach Falls is one of the highest cataracts (c.300 ft/90 m high) in the Alps. The name Reichenbach Falls is familiar to readers of A. Conan Doyle.

Reichenberg: see LIBEREC, Czechoslovakia.

Reichenhall, West Germany: see BAD REICHENHALL.

Reichsregiment (rīkhs'rā"gēmĕnt') [Ger.,=government of the empire], imperial council created by the Diet of Augsburg in 1500. It was intended to form the executive branch of the government of the HOLY ROMAN EMPIRE. Headed by the emperor or by his deputy, it comprised 20 other members representing the ecclesiastic and secular princes, the various estates, and the free cities. The creation of the Reichsregiment (as well as of the imperial court of justice, of an imperial taxation, and of an imperial army) represented a serious but unsuccessful effort toward transforming the Holy Roman Empire into a unified national state. Holy Roman Emperor Maximilian I gave it little support and dissolved it in 1502. His successor, Holy Roman Emperor Charles V, was requested at the Diet of Worms (1521) to restore the Reichsregiment, but he merely gave the council full powers only in the emperor's absence and reduced it to an advisory body at other times. Lacking the support of the emperor, the council failed. It was formally dissolved in 1531.

Reichstadt, Napoleon, duke of: see NAPOLEON II.

Reichstag (rīkhs'täk) [Ger.,=imperial parliament], name for the DIET of the Holy Roman Empire, for the lower chamber of the federal parliament of the NORTH GERMAN CONFEDERATION, and for the lower chamber of the federal parliament of Germany from 1871 to 1945. Under the German Empire of 1871-1918 the Reichstag, which represented the country at large, had little real power; it was mainly a deliberative body. Election was on the basis of universal manhood suffrage. The republican Weimar Constitution of 1919 did not alter the structure of the Reichstag, but it introduced proportional representation and extended voting rights to women. The new Reichstag, however, was not powerless; it was the supreme legislative body of the republic. The states were represented by an upper chamber, the Reichsrat. The jurisdictions of the Reichstag and Reichsrat were limited to matters affecting Germany as a whole; in other matters the member states were sovereign. The Reichsrat had only a power of suspensive veto over legislation approved by the Reichstag. The federal cabinet, appointed by the president and headed by the chancellor, was responsible to the Reichstag and normally had to resign if it received a vote of no confidence. However, the president of the republic could, on the advice of his cabinet, dissolve the Reichstag and order new elections before the normal term (four years) had ended. After 1930, under President Paul von Hindenburg, the Reichstag was suspended several times at the instigation of successive chancellors, and rule by presidential emergency decree began to replace parliamentary rule. In Jan., 1933, when Adolf HITLER became chancellor without an absolute majority, the Reichstag was dissolved and new elections were set for March 5; a violent election campaign ensued. On Feb. 27, 1933, a fire destroyed part of the Reichstag building. Hitler immediately accused the Communists of having set the fire. President von Hindenburg proclaimed a state of emergency and issued decrees suspending freedom of speech and assembly. The elections gave a bare majority of seats to Hitler's National Socialists (Nazis) and their allies, the German Nationalists. Severe measures were taken against the Communist party and its deputies were barred from the Reichstag. On March 23 the Reichstag passed the Enabling Act, which gave the government, i.e., Hitler, dictatorial powers. Only the Social Democrats dissented. In the sensational Reichstag fire trial of 1933, a Dutchman named Marinus van der Lubbe was charged with having set the fire as part of a Communist plot. Several Communist leaders, including Georgi DIMITROV, were charged with complicity. Van der Lubbe was sentenced to death; the others were found not guilty. For many years it was assumed outside Germany that the Reichstag fire was carried out by the Nazis themselves as a propaganda maneuver to ensure the defeat of the Communists and other leftist parties in the elections. However, later evidence indicates that Van der Lubbe alone set the fire, and that Hitler merely used it as a pretext to launch a campaign against the Communists. During Hitler's rule, the Reichstag was merely summoned from time to time to approve important government measures. The Reichsrat was abolished in 1934, along with sovereignty of the German states. After World War II, the new constitutions (1949) of West Germany and East Germany replaced the Reichstag and Reichsrat with other legislative bodies.

Reichstein, Tadeus (tädĕ'ōōsh rīkh'shtīn), 1897-, Swiss organic chemist, b. Poland, educated at the technical school in Zurich. After teaching (1922-38) chemistry at the technical school, he became (1938) head of the department of pharmacy at the Univ. of Basel. For his work on the hormones of the cortex of the adrenal glands he shared with Edward C. Kendall and Philip S. Hench the 1950 Nobel Prize in Physiology and Medicine. Reichstein was also the first (1933) to synthesize ascorbic acid (vitamin C).

Reid, Thomas, 1710–96, Scottish philosopher. He taught at King's College, Aberdeen, and at the Univ. of Glasgow. He is known as the founder of the common-sense school of philosophy, also known as the Scottish school, a group that had considerable influence in Great Britain and the United States during the 19th cent. Common sense is regarded as self-evident knowledge, the means by which we know the objects of the external world. These objects are known by us in their true sense and not as copies or ideas. This is the theory of natural realism, and it is the point of difference with the theories of John Locke. Reid based morality on conscience or moral sense, the ethical position of intuitionism. He had considerable influence on Dugald Stewart and Sir William Hamilton. His writings include *An Inquiry into the Human Mind on the Principles of Common Sense* (1764), *Essays on the Intellectual Powers of Man* (1785), and *Essays on the Active Powers of Man* (1788). See his *Philosophical Works,* ed. with notes and supplementary dissertations by Sir William Hamilton (2 vol, 8th ed. 1895, repr. 1967); A. J. Ayer and Raymond Winch, ed., *British Empirical Philosophers* (1968); Normen Daniels, *Thomas Reid's Inquiry* (1974).

Reid, Thomas Mayne (Mayne Reid), 1818–83, British novelist, b. Ireland. He emigrated to the United States in 1840 and after various adventures in the West served as a lieutenant in the Mexican War. He returned to England and began writing adventure stories that were especially popular with boys. The first of these was *The Rifle Rangers* (1850). Others include *The Scalp Hunters* (1851), *The White Chief* (1855), and *The Headless Horseman* (1866). See memoir by his wife, E. M. Reid (1890).

Reid, Whitelaw, 1837–1912, American journalist and diplomat, b. near Xenia, Ohio. His distinguished correspondence during the Civil War for the Cincinnati *Gazette* led Horace Greeley to make him managing editor of the New York *Tribune* in 1868. After Greeley's death, Reid gained financial as well as editorial control of the paper and continued it as a leading journal of the nation. While publishing the *Tribune,* he was minister to France (1889–92), was the Republican candidate for Vice President in 1892, and was ambassador to Great Britain from 1905 until his death in London. Reid's many books reflect his journalistic and diplomatic activities. *After the War* (1866) and *Ohio in the War* (1868) relate to the Civil War; typical of several on foreign affairs is *Problems of Expansion* (1900). Whitelaw Reid's son, Ogden Mills Reid (1882–1947) was the next editor of the paper, assisted and succeeded (1947) by his wife, Helen Rogers Reid (1882–1970). The couple strengthened the paper by purchasing the New York *Herald,* creating the New York *Herald Tribune;* the deal included the Paris *Herald,* which has since been published as a European edition of the *Herald Tribune.* The Reids' sons, Whitelaw Reid (1913–) and Ogden Rogers Reid (1925–), directed the *Herald Tribune* from 1953 until 1958, when John Hay WHITNEY acquired control. Ogden Reid was U.S. ambassador to Israel (1959–61) and in 1962 was elected to the U.S. House of Representatives.

Reidsville (rēds'vĭl), industrial city (1970 pop. 13,636), Rockingham co., N N.C.; settled c.1815, inc. 1873. It is a port of entry and a leading tobacco center, with a cigarette factory and tobacco storage facilities.

Reigate (rī'gĭt), municipal borough (1971 pop. 56,088), Surrey, S England. It is largely residential. Numerous parks attract visitors from London. In the partly Norman church is the tomb of Lord Howard of Effingham, who defeated the Spanish Armada. There is a technical college in Reigate.

Reign of Terror, 1793–94, period of the FRENCH REVOLUTION. Directed by the Committee of Public Safety, the Terror was essentially a war dictatorship, instituted to rule the country in a national emergency. To preserve the reforms of the Revolution and the very existence of the republic, the Committee of Public Safety was created on April 6, 1793. Its membership took final form on Sept. 6, when J. N. BILLAUD-VARENNE and J. N. COLLOT D'HERBOIS were added to the committee. Among the other 10 members were Bertrand BARÈRE DE VIEUZAC, Lazare CARNOT, Georges COUTHON, M. J. HÉRAULT DE SÉCHELLES, Maximilien ROBESPIERRE, and Louis de SAINT-JUST. Robespierre became the dominant member. Their aim was to eliminate all internal counterrevolutionary elements, to raise new armies, and to regulate the national economy. Some of their measures were made necessary by the people of Paris, whose support was essential. Responsibility for the police measures taken during the Terror lay also with the Committee of General Security, which had control over the local committees formed to ferret out treason. The Law of Suspects (Sept. 17, 1793) defined those who could be arrested for "treasonable" activities; it was enforced by the Committee of General Security and the Revolutionary Tribunal. Estimates vary as to the number of victims; several thousand were guillotined, and more were arrested. Many were the victims of mass drownings called noyades. The machinery of government was centralized in the hands of the Committee of Public Safety. Military mobilization was largely the work of Carnot. Universal conscription, or the *levée en masse* (Aug. 23, 1793), was followed by a complete reorganization of the armed forces. That reorganization paid dividends in the FRENCH REVOLUTIONARY WARS. In the field of economics, the demands of the ENRAGÉS in Paris brought strict controls. The law of the maximum and other measures set price and wage ceilings, forbade hoarding and withholding from the market, requisitioned food and supplies for the army, and instituted rationing. Land purchase by the peasants was made easier. Despite these measures, economic problems continued to intensify. In June, 1794, the Committee of Public Safety introduced a new law, which strengthened the power of the Revolutionary Tribunal; the court could return verdicts of either acquittal or death. Executions increased greatly. When French military success began in June, 1794, popular discontent with the strong measures grew evident. By this time the members of the committee were at odds with one another and with the Committee of General Security. The members of the National Convention, fearing that the new law would be turned against them, joined forces with Robespierre's enemies on the committees and overthrew Robespierre on 9 THERMIDOR (July 27, 1794). The Reign of Terror was followed by the Thermidorian reaction under a reconstituted Committee of Public Safety (1794) and by the White Terror, in which many former terrorists were executed. While the Reign of Terror answered the need for a strong executive and saved France from anarchy and military defeat, its effect upon public opinion, especially foreign opinion, was harmful to the Revolutionary cause. See W. B. Kerr, *The Reign of Terror, 1793–1794* (1927); R. R. Palmer, *Twelve Who Ruled* (1941, repr. 1968).

Reik, Theodor (tā'ōdōr rīk), 1888–1969, American psychologist and author, b. Vienna, Ph.D. Univ. of Vienna, 1912. He was one of Sigmund Freud's earliest and most brilliant students; their association lasted from 1910 to 1938. In Europe, Reik conducted research and lectured at several psychoanalytic institutes before coming to the United States in 1938. He was naturalized in 1944. He founded (1948) the National Psychological Association for Psychoanalysis. His writings include *From Thirty Years with Freud* (tr. 1940), *Listening with the Third Ear* (1948, repr. 1972), *The Secret Self* (1952), *The Search Within* (1956, repr. 1968), *Of Love and Lust* (1957, repr. 1970), *Myth and Guilt* (1957, repr. 1970), *The Compulsion to Confess* (1959, repr. 1972), *Creation of Woman* (1960), *The Temptation* (1961), *Voices from the Inaudible* (1964), *Curiosities of the Self* (1965), and *The Many Faces of Sex* (1966). See the autobiographical *Fragments of a Great Confession* (1949, repr. 1965).

Reims, France: see RHEIMS.

Reinach, Joseph (zhôzĕf' rĕnäk'), 1856–1921, French publicist and lawyer. An associate of Léon Gambetta, he waged (1889) a campaign against General BOULANGER in the journal *République française.* He was elected a deputy in the same year, but lost his seat in 1898 as a result of his pro-Dreyfus campaign (which was the more courageous because Reinach himself was a Jew) in the DREYFUS AFFAIR. He was again a deputy from 1906 to 1914. During World War I he wrote widely praised military articles for *Le Figaro.* He also wrote *Histoire de l'affaire Dreyfus* (7 vol., 1901–11).

reincarnation (rē"ĭnkärnā'shən) [Lat.,=taking on flesh again], occupation by the SOUL of a new body after the death of the former body. Beliefs vary as to whether the soul assumes the new body immediately or only after an interval of disembodiment. Although some religions teach that it may inhabit a higher or lower form of life, most believe that the soul is consistently reincarnated in the same species. See TRANSMIGRATION OF SOULS. See Joseph Head and S. L. Cranston, ed., *Reincarnation: An East-West Anthology* (1961) and *Reincarnation in World Thought* (1967).

reindeer, ruminant mammal, genus *Rangifer,* of the deer family, found in arctic and subarctic regions of Eurasia and North America. It is the only deer in which both sexes have antlers. The Eurasian reindeer, *Rangifer tarandus,* is a small deer, the male standing about 4 ft (120 cm) high at the shoulder and weighing about 250 lb (113 kg), but it is extremely strong and has great powers of endurance. A reindeer can travel 40 mi (64 km) a day, pulling twice its own weight on a sled. Reindeer have long fur, light brown in summer and whitish in winter, with dense woolly undercoats. The antlers are many pronged, with characteristically curved main stems that sweep back and up from the forehead, then turn forward. The hooves are broad and rounded and in winter become concave, providing a good grip on icy ground. Reindeer are gregarious and migratory; they travel hundreds of miles between their summer and winter grounds in herds of up to 200,000 animals. They feed on a variety of plant matter, particularly grasses in summer and lichen in winter. Reindeer have been hunted for perhaps 30,000 years. They have been domesticated for many centuries in Lapland and N Siberia, where they provide meat, milk, clothing, and transportation. They are used both to pull sleds and to carry burdens and riders. The Laplanders until recently were completely dependent upon the reindeer for their livelihood and followed the herds on their annual migrations. Reindeer living in a wild state in Eurasia are probably descended in part from domesticated strains. The wild reindeer of North America, called CARIBOU, are larger than, but otherwise quite similar to, the Eurasian species. They have never been domesticated. Domesticated reindeer were introduced into Alaska from Siberia in the 1890s and became essential to the economy of the Alaskan Eskimo. Herds were established for the Canadian Eskimo in the 1930s. Reindeer are classified in the phylum CHORDATA, subphylum Vertebrata, class Mammalia, order Artiodactyla, family Cervidae. See P. S. Zhigunov, ed., *Reindeer Husbandry* (tr. 1968); D. F. Olson, *Alaska Reindeer Herdsmen* (1969).

Reindeer Lake, one of the largest lakes in Canada, 2,467 sq mi (6,390 sq km), NE Sask. and NW Man. The Reindeer River drains it S to the Churchill River. The lake has many islands and is noted for its commercial and sport fishing.

reindeer moss: see LICHEN.

Reinecke, Carl (kärl rī'nəkə), 1824–1910, German composer, pianist, and conductor. After serving as court pianist (1846–48) in Denmark, he taught at the Cologne Conservatory and the Univ. of Breslau. In 1860 he moved to Leipzig, where he conducted the Gewandhaus concerts until 1895 and taught composition at the conservatory until 1902. He toured extensively as a pianist, gaining particular acclaim for his interpretations of Mozart. His compositions, the best of which are for piano, are in the German romantic tradition.

Reinhardt, Ad (Adolph), 1913–1967, American painter, b. New York City. Both a painter and an art theorist, Reinhardt is best known for his black paintings, begun in 1960. Associated with minimalism (see MODERN ART), the paintings appear all black and exhibit only slight variations in hue and the presence of form on close scrutiny. In rejecting the conventional attributes of painting, he attempted to abstract the pure and contemplative qualities he admired in Eastern art.

Reinhardt, Django (Jean Baptiste Reinhardt), 1910–53, Belgian gypsy guitarist. While wandering through France and Belgium in a caravan, Reinhardt was severely burned so that two fingers of his left hand became useless. He adapted his guitar style to the handicap and thus was able to play with various bands. Reinhardt worked intermittently (1934–39) in the Quintet of the Hot Club in Paris where he gained recognition. He toured the United States with Duke Ellington in 1946 and spent his last years in France, touring and recording. His playing, influenced by his gypsy background, was notable for virtuosity and improvisation. He was the first foreign musician to exert an influence on American jazz.

Reinhardt, Max, 1873–1943, Austrian theatrical producer and director, originally named Max Goldmann. After acting under Otto Brahm at the Deutsches Theater in Berlin, he managed (1902–5) his own theater, where he produced more than 50 plays. He was director of the Deutsches Theater after 1905 and of the smaller Kammerspiele, which he built in 1906. Reinhardt often used the entire auditorium for a production, seeking to bridge the gap between actor and audience by placing the spectator within the action. He staged gigantic productions, full of pageantry and color, and was especially noted for his direction of mob scenes. His settings, which incorporated the ideas of Appia and Craig, were masterfully executed. Among his world-famous productions were *The Lower Depths, A Midsummer Night's Dream, Faust, Oedipus Rex,* and *The Miracle.* He was also one of the first to stage the plays of the expressionists after World War I. In 1919 he opened an enormous arena theater, the Grosses Schauspielhaus ("Theatre of the Five Thousand"), and in 1920 he founded the Salzburg Festival, where he annually staged *Everyman* with the Austrian Alps as his backdrop. In 1933 he was forced by the Nazis to flee Germany. In the United States he directed a movie version of *A Midsummer Night's Dream* (1935) and a stage pageant, *The Eternal Road* (1937). He became a U.S. citizen in 1940. See Huntley Carter, *The Theatre of Max Reinhardt* (1914, repr. 1964); O. M. Saylor, ed., *Max Reinhardt and His Theatre* (tr. 1924).

Reinmar von Hagenau (rīn'mär fən hä'gənou), called "Der Alte" [the old one], 12th-century German MINNESINGER. He was probably the teacher of WALTHER VON DER VOGELWEIDE, though Walther refers to him as a rival.

Reinmar von Zweter (tsvā'tər), c.1200–c.1260, German MINNESINGER. He is best known for his *Sprüche,* short and often satirical verses on politics, religion, morals, and courtly love.

Réjane (rāzhän'), 1857–1920, stage name of Gabrielle Réju, French actress. After her first success, in Meilhac's *Ma Camarade* (1883), she grew in reputation as a comedienne. She appeared in London in 1894. The next year, she re-created her most famous role, as Catherine in Sardou's *Mme Sans-Gêne,* in New York City (film, 1911). In 1905 she opened the Théâtre Réjane in Paris. She retired in 1915.

rejería (rāhārē'ä), the art of making iron screens and grilles, developed in Spain from the Romanesque period through the Renaissance. It employs chiseled and hammered metal as well as wrought iron. The screen makers, or *rejeros,* were often architects, armorers, or silversmiths. The individual screen (*reja*) securely enclosed but did not conceal the sacred treasures of the high altars. The *rejas* of the Romanesque period were built up of numerous scrolls topped by a cresting. By the early 15th cent. they were supplanted by the Gothic *rejas* composed of rows of upright bars strengthened by horizontal bands of pierced or repoussé ornament. In the early Renaissance, Corinthianesque pilasters were introduced, and later (16th cent.) the bars were replaced by rows of balusters and ornate crestings. The screen enclosing the Royal Chapel in the cathedral at Granada has a cresting composed of 10 biblical scenes with about 30 superb life-size figures in the round, hammered from iron. In the cathedral at Seville the 16th-century *rejas* of the high altar and choir are gilded plateresque creations.

Rekem (rē'kĕm). **1** Midianite king killed by the Jews. Num. 31.8; Joshua 13.21. **2** Son of Hebron. 1 Chron. 2.43. **3** Unidentified town of Benjamin. Joshua 18.27.

Relander, Lauri Kristian (lou'rē krĭs'tēän rĕlän'dər), 1883–1942, Finnish political leader. A leading agronomist, he was a member of the Finnish diet (1910–13, 1917–19), and governor of Viipuri prov. (1920–25). He served (1925–31) as Finland's second president.

relativity, physical theory, introduced by Albert Einstein, which discards the concept of absolute motion and instead treats only relative motion between two systems or frames of reference. One consequence of the theory is that space and time are no longer viewed as separate, independent entities but rather are seen to form a four-dimensional continuum called space-time. Full comprehension of the mathematical formulation of the theory can be attained only through a study of certain branches of mathematics, e.g., tensor calculus. The modern theory is an extension of the simpler Galilean or Newtonian concept of relativity, which holds that the laws of mechanics are the same in one system as in another system in uniform motion relative to it. Thus, it is impossible to detect the motion of a system by measurements made within the system, and such motion can be observed only in relation to other systems in uniform motion. The older concept of relativity assumes that space and time are correctly measured separately and regards them as absolute and independent realities. The system of relativity and mechanics of Galileo and Newton is perfectly self-consistent, but the addition of Maxwell's theory of electricity and magnetism to the system leads to fundamental theoretical difficulties related to the problem of absolute motion. It seemed for a time that the ETHER, an elastic medium thought to be present throughout space, would provide a method for the measurement of absolute motion, but certain experiments in the late 19th cent. gave results unexplained by or contradicting Newtonian physics. Notable among these were the attempts of A. A. Michelson and E. W. Morley (1887) to measure the velocity of the earth through the supposed ether as one might measure the speed of a ship through the sea. The null result of this measurement caused great confusion among physicists, who made various unsuccessful attempts to explain the result within the context of classical theory. The validity of concepts of absolute and independent time and space was challenged by H. A. Lorentz and others. Since absolute motion cannot be confirmed by objective measurement, Einstein suggested that it be discarded from physical reasoning; he explained the experimental results by means of the special relativity theory, which he enunciated in 1905. This theory accepts the Michelson-Morley experiments as evidence that the hypothesis that the laws of nature are the same in different moving systems applies also to the propagation of light, so that the measured speed of light is constant for all observers regardless of the motion of the observer or of the source of the light. Einstein deduced from these hypotheses the full logical consequences and reformulated the mathematical equations of physics, basing them in part on equations of H. A. Lorentz (see LORENTZ CONTRACTION) by which measurements made in one uniformly moving system can be correlated with measurements in another system if the velocity of one relative to the other is known. The theory resolves the conflict between Newton's mechanics and Maxwell's electrodynamics by introducing fundamental changes in Newton's theory. Einstein's relativity does not contradict Maxwell's equations but requires them to be expressed in a more general (tensor) form. In most phenomena of ordinary experience the results obtained from the application of the special theory approximate those based on Newtonian dynamics, but the results deviate greatly for phenomena occurring at velocities approaching the speed of light. In innumerable cases where the results predicted by these theories are incompatible, experimental evidence supports the Einstein theory. The theory is difficult to understand because it entails a long chain of mathematical reasoning and because it invalidates assumptions that have long seemed self-evident, e.g., the absolute character of time and space. Among its assertions and consequences are the propositions that the maximum velocity attainable in the universe is that of light; that mass appears to increase with velocity; that mass and energy are equivalent and interchangeable properties (this is spectacularly confirmed by nuclear fission, on which the atomic bomb is based); that objects appear to contract in the direction of motion; that the rate of a moving clock seems to decrease as its velocity increases; that events that appear simultaneous to an observer in one system may not appear simultaneous to an observer in another system; and that, since absolute time is excluded from physical reasoning because it cannot be measured, the results of observers in different systems are equally correct. Under classical physics, physical reality could be represented by mechanical models obeying Newton's laws; under modern relativity theory the changes cannot be visualized, but reality may be represented mathematically in a four-dimensional geometry of SPACE-TIME in which the order of events can be located by space and time coordinates and in which material particles can be charted by one-dimensional lines (world lines). Einstein expanded the special theory of relativity into a general theory (completed c.1916) that applies to systems in nonuniform (accelerated) motion as well as to systems in uniform motion. The general theory is principally concerned with the large-scale effects of GRAVITATION and therefore is an essential ingredient in theories of the universe as a whole, or COSMOLOGY. Although the special theory has been completely established and accepted into the structure of physics, the general theory has not, and experimental tests of it are of considerable interest. The available evidence, while inconclusive, is in no case inconsistent with the general theory. The theory recognizes the equivalence of gravitational and inertial MASS and substitutes a field concept for the Newtonian concept of gravitation as a force acting at a distance. It asserts that material bodies produce curvatures in space that form a gravitational field and that the path of a body in the field is determined by this curvature. From the equations of the general theory can be predicted the geometry of a given region of space and the motion in the field. Details of the motions of the planet Mercury had long puzzled astronomers; Einstein's computations explained them. He stated that the path of a ray of light is deflected by a gravitational field; observations of starlight passing near the sun, first made by A. S. Eddington during an eclipse of the sun in 1919, confirmed this. He predicted that in a gravitational field spectral lines of substances would be shifted toward the red end of the spectrum. This has been confirmed by observation of light from WHITE DWARF stars. Cosmological deductions from the general theory by Einstein and other scientists have resulted in theories, as yet not fully verified, that the universe is a finite but expanding system. Although the Einstein relativity theory has been subjected to repeated attacks and different formulations of relativity have been proposed by several scientists, notably E. A. Milne and, more recently, R. H. Dicke, the theory has proved its value as a tool in physics. Einstein sought for many years to incorporate the theory into a unified field theory valid also for subatomic and electromagnetic phenomena and in 1950 presented a unified theory that cannot as yet be evaluated. See Albert Einstein, *The Meaning of Relativity* (6th ed. 1956); Hans Reichenbach, *Philosophy of Space and Time* (tr. 1958); Martin Gardner, *Relativity for the Million* (1962); Lincoln Barnett, *The Universe and Dr. Einstein* (rev. ed. 1968); Bertrand Russell, *The A B C of Relativity* (rev. ed. 1970). For more advanced readers: Albert Einstein et al., *The Principle of Relativity* (1923, repr. 1958; a collection of original papers on the theory); David Bohm, *The Special Theory of Relativity* (1965).

relay, electromechanical SWITCH operated by a flow of electricity in one circuit and controlling the flow of electricity in another circuit. A relay consists basically of an electromagnet with a soft iron bar, called an armature, held close to it. A movable contact is connected to the armature in such a way that the contact is held in its normal position by a spring. When the electromagnet is energized, it exerts a force on the armature that overcomes the pull of the spring and moves the contact so as to either complete or break a circuit. When the electromagnet is de-energized, the contact returns to its original position. Variations on this mechanism are possible: some relays have multiple contacts; some are encapsulated; some, as in certain telephone circuits, advance through a series of positions step by step as they are energized and de-energized.

relics, part of the body of a saint or something closely connected with him in life. In traditional Christian belief they have had great importance, and miracles have often been associated with them. Members of the Orthodox Eastern Church have generally followed St. John of Damascus in teaching that the earthly body of the saint has a kind of permanent grace, but in the Roman Catholic Church the miracles are held to be performed by the intercession of the saint in heaven on the prayer of the living; relics therefore are only to be revered as memorials, and belief is not required in any particular relic as authentic or miraculous. Roman Catholic altars (even portable ones) contain a relic, a rule coming from the time of the persecutions in Rome, when Mass was said over the martyrs' graves. Protestants have abandoned relics. Veneration of relics as miraculous dates from the 3d cent. Famous relics include the pieces of the True Cross (see CROSS); the VERONICA; the Holy Nails in the iron crown of Lombardy (Monza, Italy), the Holy Lance (St. Peter's, Rome), the Holy Coat (Trier, Germany), and the Precious Blood of Bruges. These are all called relics of the Passion. Celebrated shrines are often depositories of relics, e.g., of St. Peter and St. Paul at St. Peter's, of St. James at Compostela, Spain, of St. Thomas à Becket at Canterbury, of St. Edward the Confessor at Westminster Abbey. Many relics are duplicated, i.e., there are rival claims of genuineness. Since the Middle Ages, close accounting of relics has been maintained in Western Christendom; the creation of false relics or the buying or selling of genuine relics is prohibited under penalty of excommunication.

relief, in sculpture, three-dimensional projection from a flat background. In alto-relievo, or high relief, the protrusion is great; basso-relievo, or bas-relief, protrudes only slightly; and mezzo-relievo is intermediate between the two. Ancient Egyptians and Etruscans also used cavo relievo, INTAGLIO, or sunken relief, in which the design is incised deeper than the background. High relief, although also used in ancient times, reached its climax in the baroque period. Bas-relief is commonly employed on coins and medals.

religion, a system of thought, feeling, and action that is shared by a group and that gives the members of that group an object of devotion; a code of behavior by which an individual may judge the personal and social consequences of his actions; and a frame of reference by which an individual may relate himself to his group and his universe. Usually, religion concerns itself with that which transcends the known, the natural, or the expected; it is an acknowledgment of the extraordinary, the mysterious, and the supernatural. The religious consciousness generally recognizes a transcendent, sacred order and elaborates a technique to deal with the inexplicable or unpredictable elements of human experience in the world or beyond it. The evolution of religion cannot be precisely determined owing to the lack of clearly distinguishable stages, but anthropological studies of isolated cultures in various periods of development have suggested a typology: the Australian aborigine practices MAGIC and fetishism (see FETISH) but considers the powers therein to be not supernatural but a natural aspect of the world. Inability or refusal to divide real from preternatural and acceptance of the idea that inanimate objects may work human good or evil is sometimes said to mark a prereligious phase of thought. This is sometimes labeled naturism or animatism. It is characterized by a belief in a life force that itself has no definite characterization (see ANIMISM). A second type of religion, represented by many Oceanic and African tribal beliefs, includes momentary deities (a tree suddenly falling on or in front of a man is malignant, although it was not considered "possessed" before or after the incident) and special deities (a particular tree is inhabited by a malignant spirit, or the spirits of dead villagers inhabit a certain grove or particular animals). In this category man has distinguished between natural and supernatural forces. This development is related to the emergence of objects of devotion, to rituals of propitiation, to priests and medicine men, and to an individual sense of group participation (where the individual or the group is protected by, or against, supernatural beings and is expected to act singly or collectively in specific ways when in the presence of these forces). See ANCESTOR WORSHIP; TOTEM; SPIRITISM. In a third class of religion—usually heavily interlaced with fetishism—magic, momentary and special deities, nature gods, and deities personifying natural functions (such as the Egyptian solar god Ra, the Babylonian goddess of fertility Ishtar, the Greek sea-god Poseidon, and the Hindu goddess of death and destruction Kali) emerge and are incorporated into a system of MYTHOLOGY and ritual. Sometimes they take on distinctively human characteristics (see ANTHROPOMORPHISM). Beyond these more elementary forms of religious expression there are what are commonly called the higher religions. Theologians and philosophers of religion agree that these religions embody a principle of transcendence, i.e., a concept, sometimes a godhead, that involves man in an experience beyond the satisfaction of his immediate personal and social needs, an experience known as "the sacred" or "the holy." In the comparative study of these religions certain classifications are used. The most frequent are POLYTHEISM (as in popular Hinduism and ancient Greek religion), in which there are many gods; DUALISM (as in Zoroastrianism and certain Gnostic sects), which conceives of equally powerful deities of good and of evil; MONOTHEISM (as in Christianity, Judaism, and Islam), in which there is a single god; supratheism (as in Hindu Vedanta and certain Buddhist sects), in which the devotee participates in the religion through a mystical union with the godhead; and PANTHEISM, in which the universe is identified with God. Another frequently used classification is based on the origins of the body of knowledge held by a certain religion: some religions are revealed as in Judaism (where God revealed the Commandments to Moses), Christianity (where Christ, the Son of God, revealed the Word of the Father), and Islam (where the angel Gabriel revealed God's will to Muhammad). Some religions are nonrevealed, or "natural," the result of human inquiry alone. Included among these and sometimes called philosophies of eternity are Buddhist sects (where Buddha is recognized not as a god but as an enlightened leader), Brahmanism, and Taoism and other Chinese metaphysical doctrines. See E. O. James, *Comparative Religion* (1930, repr. 1969); Joachim Wach, *Comparative Study of Religions* (1951, repr. 1958); J. G. Frazer, *The Golden Bough* (3d ed., 13 vol., 1955; repr. 1966); Mercea Eliade, *The Sacred and the Profane* (1958, repr. 1961); V. T. A. Ferm, *Encyclopedia of Religion* (1959); W. C. Smith, *The Meaning and End of Religion* (1962); John Hick, *The Philosophy of Religion* (1963); Jan de Vries, *The Study of Religion* (tr. 1967); John Middleton, *Gods and Rituals* (1967); Geoffrey Parrinder, ed., *Man and His Gods* (1971).

Religion, Wars of, 1562-98, series of civil wars in France, also known as the Huguenot Wars. The immediate issue was the French Protestants' struggle for freedom of worship and the right of establishment (see HUGUENOTS). Of equal importance, however, was the struggle for power between the crown and the great nobles and the rivalry among the great nobles themselves for the control of the king. The foremost Protestant leaders were, successively, Louis I de CONDÉ, Gaspard de COLIGNY, and Henry of Navarre (later HENRY IV); the Catholic party was dominated by the house of GUISE. A third party, called the Politiques and composed of moderate Catholics, sided with the Protestants, while CATHERINE DE' MEDICI and her sons, CHARLES IX, HENRY III, and FRANCIS, duke of Alençon, vainly sought to maintain a balance of power by siding now with the Catholics, now with the Huguenots. The Conspiracy of Amboise (1560), by which the Huguenots attempted to end the persecutions suffered at the hands of FRANCIS II, was a prelude to the first three civil wars (1562-63, 1567-68, 1568-70). The Treaty of Saint-Germain (1570), ending the wars, gave the Protestants new liberties and the wardenship of four cities, including La Rochelle. The fourth civil war (1572-73) began with the massacre of SAINT BARTHOLOMEW'S DAY, a general slaughter of Protestants throughout France. The fifth civil war (1574-76) ended with the Peace of Monsieur (named for Francis of Alençon, who then sided with the Huguenots), which, ratified by the Edict of Beaulieu, granted freedom of worship throughout France except Paris. When the Catholics retorted by forming the LEAGUE (1576) and persuaded Henry III to repeal the edict of toleration (1577), the Huguenots revolted once more and sought the aid of foreign Protestant states. This sixth civil war ended with the Peace of Bergerac (1577), which renewed most of the terms of the Peace of Monsieur; this Henry III never carried out. A seventh war (1580) was inconsequential, but in 1584 the recognition by Henry III of the Protestant Henry of Navarre as his heir presumptive led to the renewal of the League by Henri de Guise and to the War of the Three Henrys (1585-89). After the assassination of Henri de Guise (1588) and of Henry III (1589), the League, now headed by the duc de MAYENNE, invoked the aid of Spain against Henry's successor, Henry IV. Henry, after his victories at Arques (1589) and Ivry (1590) and his conversion to Catholicism (1593), entered Paris in 1594. With the Edict of Nantes (see NANTES, EDICT OF), which granted freedom of worship throughout France and established Protestantism in 200 towns, and with the Treaty of VERVINS with Spain (both in 1598), Henry IV brought the Wars of Religion to as successful a conclusion as the Protestants could desire. This result, however, was completely reversed in the 17th cent. by Cardinal Richelieu, who broke the political power of the Protestants, and by Louis XIV, who destroyed their religious privileges by his revocation (1685) of the Edict of Nantes. See study by J. W. Thompson (1958).

reliquary (rĕl'əkwĕr'ē), receptacle containing the relics of saints and other sacred objects of the Christian religion. Reliquaries were often designed in shapes that reflected the nature of their contents, such as hands, shoes, buildings, and heads. They were richly decorated with gold, silver, enamel, and jewels. Such relics as the splinters of the True Cross and the Crown of Thorns were manufactured in great numbers and became the objects of pilgrimages.

relocation center, in U.S. history, camp in which Japanese and Japanese-Americans were interned during World War II. Fearing a Japanese invasion, the military leaders, under authority of an executive order, defined (March, 1942) an area on the West Coast from which all persons of Japanese ancestry were to be excluded. That same month the War Relocation Authority (WRA) was created. After voluntary evacuation was prohibited, the army forcibly moved approximately 110,000 evacuees, most of whom were American citizens, to 10 relocation centers in Western states operated by the authority. Although food and shelter were provided and wages were paid to those who wished to work, living conditions were poor, and there were many riots during the war. Separation of the loyal and disloyal began in July, 1943. Persons who could prove their loyalty and had employment waiting for them were released to live anywhere except in the proscribed area, while those deemed disloyal by the Federal Bureau of Investigation were segregated in the Tule Lake center. The majority of evacuees remained in the relocation centers until after Dec., 1944, when the mass exclusion orders were revoked. The last of the centers, at Tule Lake, was closed in March, 1946. The WRA was terminated in 1946. The evacuees suffered property losses estimated at $400 million, and the government was severely criticized for depriving citizens of their civil liberties. See Audrie Girdner and Anne Loftis, *The Great Betrayal* (1969); Bill Hosokawa, *Nisei: The Quiet Americans* (1969); Roger Daniels, *Concentration Camps U.S.A.: Japanese Americans and World War II* (1971).

Remagen (rā'mä"gən), town (1970 pop. 13,590), Rhineland-Palatinate, W West Germany, on the Rhine River. It is a rail junction from which mineral water is shipped. U.S. troops used the Ludendorff bridge at Remagen when they first crossed (March, 1945) the Rhine in World War II.

Remah: see ISSERLES, MOSES BEN ISRAEL.

Remaliah (rĕməlī'ə), father of Pekah. 2 Kings 15.25; Isa. 7.1-9; 8.6.

Remarque, Erich Maria (ā'rĭkh märē'ä rəmärk'), 1897-1970, German-American novelist, whose original name was Erich Paul Remark. From his experience of trench warfare during World War I, Remarque drew a grimly realistic picture of the horror of battle in his first novel and masterpiece, *Im Westen nichts Neues* (1929; tr. *All Quiet on the Western Front,* 1929), an immediate international success. The Nazi regime ordered it burned. Remarque's next work was *The Way Back* (1931, tr. 1931), a sequel describing the attempt of Germans to come to terms with their postwar situation. Remarque lived in Switzerland after 1932 and emigrated to the United States in 1939. His later books include *Three Comrades* (1937, tr. 1938), *Arch of Triumph* (tr. 1946), *A Time to Love and a Time to Die* (tr. 1954), and *Shadows in Paradise* (1971, tr. 1972). See studies by R. O. Glaser (1972) and J. S. White (1972).

Rembrandt Harmenszoon van Rijn or **Ryn** (rĕm'brănt, Du. rĕm'bränt här'mənsōn vän rīn), 1606-69, Dutch painter, etcher, and draftsman, b. Leiden. Rembrandt is acknowledged as the greatest master of the Dutch school. A miller's son, he attended a Latin school and spent part of one year at the Univ. of Leiden, leaving in 1621 to study painting with a local artist, Jacob van Swanenburgh. His most valuable training was received during the six months of 1624 that he spent in the studio of Pieter LASTMAN in Amsterdam. Lastman's work affected Rembrandt's in his sense of composition and his frequent choice of religious and historical themes. Receptive to many influences at this time, Rembrandt sometimes reflected the dramatic chiaroscuro of Caravaggio in paintings such as *The Money Changer* (Berlin) or the more delicate and detailed manner of Elsheimer as in *The Tribute Money* (London). In 1625 Rembrandt returned to Leiden, where he developed his own distinct style, using the many possibilities of the oil medium, heavily layering the paint, and experimenting with diverse techniques. He showed an unusual preference for the faces of the old and the poor from his earliest works to his latest (e.g., *Two Philosophers,* Melbourne). In the Leiden years, he began the magnificent series of nearly 100 self-portraits that describe the continuing development of his profound self-understanding and self-awareness, as well as his stylistic growth. While in Leiden, he collaborated with Jan Lievens and began to teach. He devoted much of his life to teaching, and one of his foremost pupils in Leiden was Gerard DOU. Rembrandt moved to Amsterdam in 1632, where he became established as a portrait painter with his group portrait *Anatomy Lesson of Dr. Tulp* (1632; The Hague), a traditional subject to which he gave radical treatment. The prodigious output of his lifetime is known to embrace more than 600 paintings, about 300 etchings, and nearly 2,000 drawings. To each medium he gave his best effort. His commissioned portraits include those of Minister Johannes Elison and his wife (Mus. of Fine Arts, Boston) and Nicolas Ruts (Frick Coll., New York City). His position in Amsterdam was further solidified by the dowry and social connections gained by his joyous marriage to Saskia van Ulyenburgh, a burgomaster's daughter. Affluent and successful, he began to collect numerous works of art, costumes, and curiosities, always learning from the art and often using the costumes in his portraits. During this period his style acquired a new richness of color and greater plasticity of form. He incorporated the vigor, opulence, and drama of the baroque movement, best seen in *The Sacrifice of Abraham* (Leningrad) and *The Blinding of Samson* (1636, Frankfurt-am-Main). His studio was filled with pupils, including Jacob Backer, Govaert Flinck, Ferdinand Bol, and later the gifted Carel Fabritius and Nicholas Maes. Serious financial difficulties began for Rembrandt with his purchase of an impressive house in 1639. Saskia died in 1642 after the birth of their only surviving child, Titus, who was later to become Rembrandt's favorite portrait subject. During the same year he completed his most famous group portrait, *The Shooting Company of Capt. Frans Banning Cocq* (Rijks Mus.), traditionally called *The Night Watch* until it was cleaned in 1946–47, revealing a daylight setting. Instead of painting a conventional group portrait, Rembrandt made of it a crowd spectacle, sacrificing individual identities to dramatic, high-contrast lighting. His *Young Girl at a Half Door* (1645; Art Inst., Chicago) is more traditionally composed to reveal the expression of serene inner life. During the 1640s Rembrandt developed an enduring interest in landscape. He made numerous etchings, including *Three Trees* and *Christ Healing the Sick*, executed with exceptional spontaneity and vigor, and created many works solely for his own pleasure, an unusual practice for his time. This, together with his art collecting, eventually caused financial ruin. In 1660 his housekeeper and devoted love for many years, Hendrickje Stoffels, and Titus formed a business partnership to shield the bankrupt Rembrandt from his creditors. In the last two decades of his life Rembrandt, withdrawn from society and no longer fashionable, created many of his masterpieces. These works were more concerned with human character than with outward appearance and are the foundation of his unequaled reputation. *Aristotle Contemplating the Bust of Homer* (1653; Metropolitan Mus.) reveals his power to elicit a mood of profound mystery and meditation. Among the other remarkable paintings of this period are *Bathsheba* (Louvre) and *The Polish Rider* (Frick Coll., New York City); two of the notable etchings are *Three Crosses* (1653) and *Christ Presented to the People* (1655). The powerful night scene *The Conspiracy of the Batavians* (1661; Stockholm) is the remaining fragment of his most monumental historical work. To the late 1660s belong *The Family Group* (Brunswick) and *The Jewish Bride* (Rijks Mus.), both loosely structured, flamelike in color, and psychologically penetrating. *The Syndics of the Cloth Guild* (1662; Rijks Mus.) has been described as the culmination of Dutch portrait painting. Personal tragedy struck the master with the death of Hendrickje in 1663 and of Titus in 1668. Rembrandt lived for one more year, survived by Cornelia, his and Hendrickje's only child. The universal appeal of Rembrandt's art rests upon its profound humanity. His surpassing handling of light was recognized even when his critics considered that his subject matter was vulgar and indecorous. His work can be found in many European and American museums. The best collections are in Amsterdam, Berlin, The Hague, Leningrad, New York City, and Washington, D.C. The Louvre, the British Museum, and the Rijks Museum have good collections of his etchings and drawings. Comprehensive editions of his works have been compiled: his paintings by Abraham Bredius (rev. by Hearst Gerson, 3d ed. 1969), his etchings by A. M. Hind (2d ed. 1923, repr. 1967), and his drawings by Otto Benesch (6 vol., 1954–58). See studies of his life and works by Ludwig Goldscheider (3d ed. 1964), Kenneth Clark (1966, repr. 1968), Jakob Rosenberg (3d ed. 1968), Christopher White (1964; and 2 vol., 1969), Bob Haak (tr. 1969), and J. E. Muller (tr. 1969); Otto Benesch, *Essays on Rembrandt* (Vol. I of Benesch's *Collected Works*, tr. 1970).

Remeth (rēʹməth), town of Issachar, near the Sea of Galilee. Joshua 19.21. Jarmuth: Joshua 21.29. Ramoth: 1 Chron. 6.73.

Remington, Eliphalet (ĭlĭfʹəlĭt), 1793–1861, American inventor, gunsmith, and arms manufacturer, b. Suffield, Conn. Trained in blacksmithing, he turned to gunsmithing at an early age. With his father he founded a firearms firm at Ilion, N.Y., and took over the firm upon his father's death (1828). He supplied the U.S. army with rifles in the Mexican War. In 1856 the business was expanded to include the manufacture of agricultural implements. His son, **Philo Remington,** 1816–89, b. Litchfield, Herkimer co., N.Y., directed the business during the Civil War, when the firm held many government contracts. The Remington firm later supplied the armies of several European countries with breech-loading rifles. In 1870 it began making sewing machines, and in 1873 Philo Remington became interested in the manufacturing of typewriters. The first Remington typewriter was exhibited in 1876 at the Centennial Exhibition in Philadelphia. See Alden Hatch, *Remington Arms in American History* (1956).

Remington, Frederic, 1861–1909, American painter, sculptor, illustrator, and writer, b. Canton, N.Y., studied at the Yale School of Fine Arts and the Art Students League. His subjects, drawn largely from his life on the Western plains, are chiefly horses, soldiers, Indians, and cowboys, each modeled or painted with sympathetic understanding and usually in spirited action. His paintings are exciting and accurate portrayals of the West and have been extensively reproduced in color prints. Replicas of his 23 bronzes appear in many museums and private collections. Remington was war correspondent for the Hearst papers in the Spanish-American War. An indefatigable worker, he completed more than 2,700 paintings and drawings, including illustrations for *Century* magazine, *Collier's Weekly*, Harper publications, and other periodicals. He wrote *Pony Tracks* (1895), *Crooked Trails* (1898), *John Ermine of Yellowstone* (1902), and other books. There is a Remington Art Memorial Museum at Ogdenburg, N.Y. See catalog by Marta Jackson (1970); biography by Harold McCracken (1959); Douglas Allen, *Frederic Remington and the Spanish-American War* (1971).

Remington, Philo: see under REMINGTON, ELIPHALET.

Remizov, Aleksey Mikhailovich (əlyĭksyāʹ mēkhīʹləvĭch rĕʹmēzəf), 1877–1957, Russian novelist and short-story writer. Remizov's emphasis on style, especially his ornamentation of colloquial speech, influenced many Soviet writers (e.g., Babel and Pilnyak). In early novels such as *The Clock* (1908, tr. 1924) and *The Pond* (1908) he described the squalor and brutality of middle-class life in Russian provincial cities. Remizov also wrote many religious legends and grotesque fairy tales. He left Russia in 1921 and died in Paris.

Remmon (rĕmʹən): see EN-RIMMON.

Remmon-methoar (rĕmʹən-mēthōʹər), the same as RIMMON 5 .

Remojadas (rāmōhäʹthäs), archaeological site, central Veracruz, Mexico. It is known chiefly for remarkable clay figurines, presumably the work of Totonac-speaking Indians during pre-Aztec times. Some of the statuettes are plain in design and material, although often quite large. Another style is that represented by the so-called smiling head figures, which are often graceful and whimsical.

Remonstrants (rĕmŏnʹstrənts), Dutch Protestants, adherents to the ideas of Jacobus ARMINIUS, whose doctrines after his death (1609) were called Arminianism. They were Calvinists but were more liberal and less dogmatic than orthodox Calvinists and diverged from the teachings of the Dutch Reformed Church. After the death of Arminius and under the leadership of Simon EPISCOPIUS, they set forth their articles of faith for Holland and West Friesland in a petition that became known as the Remonstrance. Their main variations from orthodox views, as set forth, were conditional, rather than absolute, predestination; universal atonement; the necessity of regeneration through the Holy Ghost; the possibility of resistance to divine grace; and the possibility of relapse from grace. A movement to suppress the Remonstrants was led by Franciscus Gomarus and Prince MAURICE OF NASSAU, and finally, after a hearing at the Synod of Dort (1618–19), the orthodox position prevailed. Remonstrants were denied church services, and their leaders were persecuted and exiled. With the death of Prince Maurice in 1625 the ban was lifted and the religion was tolerated until 1795, when it was recognized as an independent church. The Remonstrants survive as a small group in the Netherlands. They have had a liberalizing influence on Calvinist doctrine as well as on other evangelical churches.

remora (rĕmʹərə), any of the several species of warmwater fishes of the family Echeneidae, characterized by an oval sucking disk on the top of the head. With this apparatus (a modification of the dorsal fin) the remora, or suckerfish, attaches itself to sharks, swordfishes, drums, marlins, and sea turtles. In this way it travels without effort, feeding on scraps from the prey of these larger creatures and in some cases on their crustacean parasites. Remoras sometimes attach themselves to small boats, but they can also swim well on their own. The adhesive power of their sucking disks is so great that the natives of some tropical regions use remoras to catch sea turtles by attaching lines to their tails. Different species prefer different hosts. The whalesucker, *Remilegia australis,* is usually found attached to whales. The smallest remora, the 7 in. (18 cm) *Remoropsis pallidus,* prefers swordfishes and tuna. Largest and most common is the shark remora, or sharksucker, which reaches 3 ft (90 cm) in length and attaches itself to sharks; it is found along the Atlantic coast N of Long Island in the summer. Remoras are classified in the phylum CHORDATA, subphylum Vertebrata, class Osteichthyes, order Echeniformes, family Echeneidae.

Remphan (rĕmʹfăn), same as CHIUN.

Remscheid (rĕmʹshīt), city (1970 pop. 136,419), North Rhine-Westphalia, W West Germany, on the Wupper River. It is the leading center of the West German tool and hardware industry; other products include textiles, household appliances, and machinery. Remscheid was chartered in 1808. Its masonry dam (completed 1891) is the oldest in Germany. The city was badly damaged (1943) during World War II.

Remus: see ROMULUS.

Rémusat, Charles, comte de (shärl kôNt də rämüzäʹ), 1797–1875, French philosopher and liberal politician. He was a deputy (1830–48) and minister of the interior (1840) under King Louis Philippe. In the Revolution of 1848 he was associated with Adolphe Thiers. Rémusat went into exile after the coup d'etat of Louis Napoleon (later Emperor NAPOLEON III), becoming politically active again when the emperor had to make concessions to the liberals toward the end of the Second Empire. After Napoleon's fall he served (1871–73) under Thiers as minister of foreign affairs. Among his works are *Essais de philosophie* (1842), *Histoire de la philosophie en Angleterre depuis Bacon jusqu'à Locke* (1875), and several biographies.

Renaissance (rĕnəsänsʹ, –zänsʹ) [Fr.,=rebirth], term used to describe the rich development of Western civilization that marked the transition from medieval to modern times. In Italy the Renaissance emerged by the 14th cent. and reached its height in the 15th and 16th cent. (Italian *quattrocento* and *cinquecento*); elsewhere in Europe it may be dated from the 15th to the mid-17th cent. The transition from the MIDDLE AGES stretched over a long period, and late medieval values were not sharply distinct from those of the early Renaissance; yet the age of the Renaissance can be clearly distinguished. In outlook the Renaissance brought new importance to individual expression, self-consciousness, and worldly experience; culturally it was a time of new currents and brilliant accomplishments in scholarship, in literature, and in the arts (see RENAISSANCE ART AND ARCHITECTURE). More generally it was an era of emerging nation-states, of exploration and discoveries, of the beginning of the COMMERCIAL REVOLUTION, and of a revolution in science.

The Renaissance in Italy. The Renaissance first appeared in Italy, where relative political stability, economic expansion, wide contact with other cultures, and a flourishing urban civilization provided the background for a new view of the world. The development of powerful, independent city-states, ruled by princes of commerce, came as the result of complex class conflicts within burgeoning urban centers. Their separate governments established diplomatic relations with one another to maintain a delicate balance of power, an uneasy alliance comparable to modern international relations. In the field of scholarship the continued investigation, begun in medieval times, of ancient learning was derived from Latin and Greek manuscripts and art and was newly stimulated by contact with the Arab world. It produced an increased knowledge of the classical age and its values, which permeated the works of PETRARCH. Classical Latin became an important field of study, and at the same time emphasis on grammar and orthography helped to purify the Tuscan vernacular as a more suitable vehicle for literature. An important result of the new learning was the establishment of fine libraries, among them the notable collection of PICO DELLA MIRANDOLA. Learned academies flourished, and the intellectual scope of the universities was gradually broadened. Scholars, poets, craftsmen, and artists received encouragement and material support from wealthy benefactors; the great patrons of the age included the MEDICI of FLORENCE, such Renaissance popes of ROME as JULIUS II and LEO X, the doges of VENICE, the SFORZA of MILAN, the ESTE of FERRARA, the GONZAGA of MANTUA, and the dukes of URBINO. As the Renaissance outlook took shape medieval scholasticism gave way to the more secular intellectual orientation of HUMANISM, exemplified in the works of Lorenzo VALLA. The Platonic idealism that underlay humanism was propounded by Marsilio FICINO and other scholars. In ITALIAN LITERATURE the rejection of medieval asceticism found full expression with BOCCACCIO, whose treatment of romantic and physical love introduced themes that became central to Renaissance literature. The works of MACHIAVELLI provided an enduring secular analysis of political power. The writing of BIOGRAPHY gained impetus from the lively interest in personality, and the concern with classical antiquity inspired the writing of secular and more objective works of HISTORY, viewed from a wider perspective. The humanist emphasis on the individual was typified in the ideal of the Renaissance man, the man of universal genius; the towering exemplar was LEONARDO DA VINCI. In society, emulation of this ideal brought the emergence, by the 15th cent., of the courtier, the polished gentleman whose manners and accomplishments were codified by Baldassare CASTIGLIONE. In Italian art new attention was given to individual face and form, and there was a departure from symbolic treatment to a more realistic imitation of nature, seen at its greatest expression in the works of Leonardo, MICHELANGELO, and RAPHAEL. The scientific system of PERSPECTIVE was explored; the effects of color were investigated, particularly by the Venetian school; subject matter was greatly expanded to include PORTRAITURE, LANDSCAPE PAINTING, GENRE, animal, and historical subjects, often within a religious context but increasingly independent of it. Renaissance architects turned to the splendid re-creation and adaptation of classical forms and produced important technical innovations. ALBERTI and VITRUVIUS set down the canons of the new building, the chief masters of which were Alberti himself, BRUNELLESCHI, Laurana, BRAMANTE, SANGALLO, and Michelangelo. Diverse artistic accomplishment came to be expected of the cultured individual. Through all the aspects of the Italian Renaissance there ran enthusiasm for worldly life and for human endeavor.

The Renaissance of Europe and England. As an economic base for cultural enrichment was developed elsewhere, the currents from Italy spread through Europe, often mingling with older interests and forces and flourishing variously in different lands. The role of the university became prominent; new universities, concerned with spreading the new learning, sprang up in France, in Spain, in England, and particularly in Germany. Perhaps the most important distinguishing aspect of the Renaissance outside Italy was its close interaction with the Protestant REFORMATION and also with the Catholic Reformation (see REFORMATION, CATHOLIC); the movements for religious change and reform in the Church came to dominate European political life in the 16th cent. In France, where Italian currents were perhaps most directly influential, the fine classical tone that burgeoned in FRENCH LITERATURE was exemplified in the works of RONSARD and Joachim DU BELLAY, while Renaissance sensual vitality was given its triumphant expression by RABELAIS. The classicist and humanist BUDÉ was but one of many writers and artists who enjoyed the abundant and enlightened patronage of King FRANCIS I. The Italian influence in the French Renaissance found particular reflection in French architecture and art. France and Flanders led in the development of new musical forms and styles; 15th-century composition was marked by a new clarity and by the evolution of artistic standards and principals. Among the great composers of the age were Guillaume MACHAUT, JOSQUIN DESPREZ, and Orlando di LASSO. With the 16th cent. came the flowering of POLYPHONY. In the broad German lands, which stretched across Europe from the Low Countries to Poland, Renaissance culture exhibited a degree of somber restraint not characteristic of Italy or France. Humanism merged with the older traditions of religious mysticism and purification and played a part in the development of the Reformation. Classical and humanist scholarship was furthered by REUCHLIN, and in the Netherlands ERASMUS, the most notable of all the humanists, gained international eminence. The invention of printing and movable TYPE facilitated the spread of the new learning. FLEMISH ART AND ARCHITECTURE flourished, and the current of the Italian Renaissance in DUTCH ART grew strong in the 16th cent. In S Germany Renaissance awareness and outlook were incorporated into the paintings and graphic works of Albrecht DÜRER and into the perceptive portraits by the younger Hans HOLBEIN. England became a center of humanist thought, influenced greatly by Erasmus and furthered by the group of humanists that included John COLET, John FISHER, and Sir Thomas MORE; these men not only advanced the new learning but were important in the early movement for the Catholic Reformation. The Elizabethan Age produced an overwhelming richness in ENGLISH LITERATURE; Shakespeare's unparalleled genius dwarfed the accomplishments of numerous extraordinarily gifted writers. Sir Philip SIDNEY was a paramount example of the English Renaissance intellectual. In England scholarship, art, and music gained the patronage of Henry VIII, who, with Henry IV of France and Philip II of Spain, typified the powerful monarchs who ruled the emerging nation-states of the Renaissance era. In Spain, which had its own rich heritage of close contact with the Arab world, Italian influence exerted great force during and after the 15th cent. Cardinal JIMÉNEZ promoted humanism, classical and Hebraic studies flourished, and the study of science became an important pursuit. The Italian mode of poetry was successfully introduced by GARCILASO DE LA VEGA, and the 16th cent. saw the beginning of the Golden Age of SPANISH LITERATURE, crowned by Cervantes' masterpiece, *Don Quixote.* Scandinavia was the last area of Europe to be reached by the currents of the Renaissance. In the 17th cent. Queen CHRISTINA of Sweden, the patron of DESCARTES, encouraged scholarship, literature, and the arts at her court. By this time Renaissance influence had reached its zenith in the field of science; here too classical studies were vital and the trend was toward a more secular world view. Thus the revolutionary theories of COPERNICUS, and GALILEO, which partly reflected ancient learning, were to impugn the church-supported concept of a static universe. Contact with strange lands and forms of life was to increase and focus the pursuit of such disciplines as BOTANY and ZOOLOGY. The scientific method, in an early form, was propounded by Francis BACON and others. Near the end of the Renaissance era the invention of the telescope and microscope opened to man the new worlds of the cosmos and the microcosm. The Renaissance intellectual outlook and its concomitant cultural manifestations were gradually replaced by that of the ENLIGHTENMENT. The secularism of the Renaissance was not yet part of a complete social and intellectual framework. Modern historians generally emphasize that religious questions and religious strife were of great importance in the era of the Renaissance; some have pointed out that the Renaissance scholars thought little of man's progress and that not until the Enlightenment did man begin to see himself as controlling his environment and mastering his future. Undeniably the Renaissance period produced an unequaled blossoming of the human creative spirit.

Bibliography. The classic portrayal of the Renaissance in Italy as a rebirth of the individual human spirit marking a distinctive break with the Middle Ages is Jacob BURCKHARDT'S *The Civilization of the Renaissance in Italy* (1860, in German; many English editions); the longer standard work, expanding Burckhardt's point of view, is J. A. Symonds's *The Renaissance in Italy* (7 vol., 1875–86; many later editions). Modern scholarship has greatly modified the interpretation of the age from a broad, general one to a much more complex and detailed view based on intensive and specific study of diverse aspects of the period. Medievalists, emphasizing the retention of medieval institutions and concepts, have frequently attacked the notion of a distinct Renaissance. The term *renaissance* is now often used more flexibly to designate the flowering of various civilizations and eras. See Wylie Sypher, *Four Stages of Renaissance Style* (1955); H. S. Lucas, *The Renaissance and the Reformation* (2d ed. 1960); Denys Hay, *The Italian Renaissance and Its Historical Background* (1961); P. S. Allen, *The Age of Erasmus* (1914, repr. 1963); Albert Hyma, *The Christian Renaissance* (1924, repr. 1965); Hans Baron, *The Crisis of the Early Italian Renaissance* (rev. ed. 1966); Bertrand Gille, *Engineers of the Renaissance* (1966); Douglas Bush, *The Renaissance and English Humanism* (1939, repr. 1968); Vincent Cronin, *The Flowering of the Renaissance* (1969); George Holmes, *The Florentine Enlightenment* (1969); W. K. Ferguson, *The Renaissance in Historical Thought* (1948) and *Renaissance Studies* (1963, repr. 1970); R. S. Lopez, *The Three Ages of the Italian Renaissance* (1970); P. O. Kristeller, *Renaissance Thought* (1961), *Renaissance Thought II* (1965), *The Classics and Renaissance Thought* (1955, repr. 1969), and *Renaissance Concepts of Man* (1972).

Renaissance art and architecture. A radical break with medieval methods of representing the visible world occurred in Italy during the second half of the 13th cent. The sculptor Nicola Pisano evoked an interest in the forms of classical antiquity. In painting Giotto led the way in restoring dignity and monumentality to the human figure. He also worked toward a more realistic depiction of space, and his efforts were expanded during the 14th cent. in Siena by the Lorenzetti brothers. However, after the Black Death of 1348 came a marked decline in artistic activity. Not until the second decade of the 15th cent. was there a decided break with the medieval pictorial tradition. Florence became the great center of quattrocento (15th-century) art and art theory. The artist began to emerge from the role of artisan to participate in the current of intellectual pursuits. Together with early humanists (see HUMANISM), artists turned from a veneration of the purely celestial realm to an appreciation of all aspects of physical nature. They shared a growing esteem for individual man and a vital enthusiasm for classical antiquity. The architects Brunelleschi and Alberti and the sculptor Donatello were among the first to visit Rome in order to study the ruins of antiquity and to incorporate many of the ancient principles into their work; at the same time they were intensely preoccupied with problems of representing the dimensions of nature on a flat surface. With Masaccio they pioneered in developing a scientific organization of space—the system of PERSPECTIVE. Masaccio and Uccello worked out a geometrical system, whereas Fra Angelico and Fra Filippo Lippi concentrated on a unifying color scheme. While the Florentines inclined toward an abstract simplicity of form, they never lost awareness of the visible world, particularly in their portrayal of the human figure. Antonio Pollaiuolo, Castagno, and above all Leonardo da Vinci were dedicated to the study of anatomy. During the 15th cent. artists came to be supported not only by churchmen but also by private collectors. Besides commissioning paintings of the traditional sacred themes, these patrons created a new demand for pictures of secular subjects. For the embellishment of private palaces, painters adorned cassone (chest) panels, plates, and walls with allegorical and mythological episodes often derived from literary sources, such as the works of Petrarch and Boccaccio. To fulfill the patrons' dreams of glory and perpetual fame, the art of PORTRAITURE began to flourish. In commemoration of notable citizens and events, medals were designed and struck by great metalworkers, such as Pisanello, in a revival of an ancient practice. Piero della Francesca, Mantegna, and Botticelli painted remarkable portraits of political leaders, at the same time emphasizing their individual characteristics and conveying an air of princely splendor. Chief among the Florentine patrons were the Medici, who fostered a group of poets, philosophers, and artists. Botticelli and Michelangelo were profoundly influenced by the Neoplatonic philosophy developed in the Medici circle. Outside of Florence there were bursts of artistic activity in Urbino, Mantua, Rimini, Milan, and Naples. Their courts attracted such artists as Piero della Francesca, Mantegna, Antonello da Messina, and Leonardo, as well as a number of Flemish artists who left their mark on N Italian painting. In the early 16th cent. the leadership in Italian art shifted from Florence to Rome. The works of Leonardo, Michelangelo, and Raphael were the culmination of all the qualities toward which quattrocento artists had been striving. These were the men who created the short-lived but glorious style of the High Renaissance (c.1490–1520). Conceived in a truly classical spirit, their paintings were imbued with a noble ideal, heroic proportions, and unequaled harmony. Once this equilibrium had been reached, their successors sought more diversified ideals. The style known as MANNERISM followed. Meanwhile, by the beginning of the 16th cent., Venetian art had come into its full glory. The great colorists Giovanni Bellini and Giorgione were succeeded by Titian, Veronese, and Tintoretto, who added a new freedom of brush stroke to the canvas. The superb coloring of the Venetians was achieved as the effects of the golden age of painting in the Low Countries were felt across Europe. In the 1420s the van Eyck brothers developed the technique of oil painting, and with it the ability to render the most subtle variation of light and color, to perfection. They did not practice the system of geometric perspective, but with their acute sense of observation they created a convincing appearance of reality. An exquisite sensitivity is reflected in their minute detailing of objects of daily life, which often assumed a symbolic value. The Master of Flémalle (Robert Campin), Roger van der Weyden, and Hugo van der Goes were among the most remarkable masters of the 15th cent. Netherlandish painting at the turn of the century was enriched by the wild fantasies of Bosch and the spirited peasant scenes of Pieter Brueghel, the elder. In Germany, Schongauer and above all Dürer made the first and greatest contributions in the media of woodcuts and engravings. Other important painters of the 16th cent. included Grünewald, Hans Holbein, the younger, and Lucas Cranach, the elder. Many artists in France continued to paint fine altarpieces in the Gothic tradition. The Renaissance spirit in France produced admirable portraitists such as Fouquet and Clouet. Francis I invited Italian painters and architects to his court, including Leonardo and Andrea del Sarto. In the 1530s the influence of mannerism began to be felt, particularly at Fontainebleau (see FONTAINEBLEAU, SCHOOL OF). Artists in England and Spain were influenced by Netherlandish painting until the 16th cent., when the Italian Renaissance began to permeate Europe. During the Renaissance the ideals of art and architecture became unified in the mutual acceptance of classical antiquity and in the belief that man was a measure of the universe. The rebirth of classical architecture, which took place in Italy in the 15th cent. and spread in the following century through Western Europe, terminated the supremacy of the Gothic style. Since the Gothic had never really taken root in Italy, a return to the classical was only natural and was manifested in a rediscovery and appropriation of the classical ORDERS OF ARCHITECTURE. Rome's structural elements, its arches, vaults, and domes, as well as its decorative forms, served as an open treasury, from which the designers of the 15th cent. unstintingly borrowed, adapting them to new needs in original combinations. Although built using Roman motifs, the churches, town halls, palaces, and villas showed new developments in plan and structure. The stone houses of Florence, of which the Medici-Riccardi Palace by Michelozzi is a principal example, are marked by a rugged simplicity. On the other hand, fondness for the free use of beautiful details led, particularly in Lombardy, to graceful designs, in which the more massive appearance of the building was submerged; the facade of the Certosa di Pavia exemplifies this spirit. Brunelleschi, the earliest great architect of the Renaissance, produced its first examples (c.1420) in the Florentine churches of San Lorenzo and Santo Spirito and in the revolutionary plan for the dome of the Cathedral of Florence. Alberti was the first important architectural theoretician of the Renaissance. In his works he was strongly influenced by the writings of the ancient Roman architect Vitruvius; the books of both men served as a basic source of inspiration for later architects. In ecclesiastical building there was a trend toward the centralized structure. Brunelleschi, Filarete, Francesco di Giorgio, and Leonardo designed many variations on the theme, creating polygonal and Greek-cross plans, but the greatest realization of the circular form was achieved by Bramante in his Tempietto (c.1502) in Rome. Numerous palaces and churches erected in Rome gave the city preeminence, and Raphael, Peruzzi, Vignola and Michelangelo worked there, as well as Antonio da Sangallo, the younger, whose Farnese Palace embodies the period's highest standards. Work on St. Peter's Church was begun by Bramante and carried on by a succession of the finest artists and architects that Italy produced. Deeper understanding of the monumental Roman works resulted in grand and unified designs with pure and well-integrated details. The classical orders, often on a monumental scale, now played the chief role in decoration. Palladio, Serlio, Vignola, and others codified the system of proportioning, and their ideas were extremely influential in the development of European architecture. In France in the 16th cent., Renaissance taste made one of its first tentative appearances in the Louis XII wing of the château of Blois. In the first period Gothic traditions persisted in plan, structure, and exterior masses, onto which fresh and graceful Renaissance details were grafted. The movement was sponsored by Francis I, a prolific builder. Handsome and livable châteaus replaced grim feudal castles. Fontainebleau, Chambord, and Azay-le-Rideau are famous examples. The beginning (1546) of the construction of the Louvre by Pierre Lescot usually serves as the opening date of the classical period. Classical proportions and methods of composition were assimilated, and the use of the orders became general. Although Italian models were followed, a distinctively French brand of classicism took form. The leading architects were Lescot, Philibert Delorme, and the Androuet du Cerceau family. Jean Goujon and others contributed fine sculptural adornments. In Germany, about the middle of the 16th cent., the medieval love for picturesque forms still dominated, although transferred to classical motifs. Freely interpreted and resembling the Elizabethan work in England, these gave full play to originality and craftsmanship. The style, however, lacking truly great architects, failed to achieve full development as in France and England. Nuremberg and Rothenburg ob der Tauber are rich in works of the early period. In the first period of the Renaissance in Spain, Gothic and Moorish forms (see MUDÉJAR) intermingled with the new classical ones. Under the leadership of Francisco de Herrera, the younger, who imported strictly classical principles from Italy, the second period was one of correctness and formality. The palace of Charles V at Granada (1527) is its finest product. In England the Renaissance flowered in the middle of the 16th cent. The Elizabethan style and the Jacobean style applied classical motifs while retaining medieval forms. The move toward a pure and monumental classical style was due to Inigo Jones, whose royal banqueting hall (1619) in London decisively established Palladian design in English architecture. See articles on individual artists, e.g., DONATELLO, and countries, e.g., ITALIAN ART. See Anthony Blunt, *Artistic Theory in Italy, 1450–1600* (1940); Erwin Panofsky, *Renaissance and Renascences in Western Art* (2d ed. 1965); Rudolf Wittkower, *Architectural Principles in the Age of Humanism* (3d ed. 1962, repr. 1965); E. H. J. Gombrich, *Norm and Form* (1966) and *Symbolic Images* (1972); Creighton Gilbert, *History of Renaissance Art* (1973).

Renan, Ernest (ĕrnĕst' rənäN'), 1823–92, French historian and critic. He began training for the priesthood but renounced it in 1845. His first trip to Italy (1849) influenced his interest in antiquity but did not change most of his basic ideas, formed by 1848 when he wrote *L'Avenir de la science* (1890, tr. 1891). Relativistic, concerned with fundamental problems of human nature, he studied religion from a historical rather than a theological point of view. He wrote *Histoire des origines du christianisme* (8 vol., 1863–83; tr. *The History of the Origins of Christianity*, 5 vol., 1888–90), of which the first volume, *Vie de Jésus*, became his most widely known book, and the *Histoire du peuple d'Israël* (5 vol., 1887–93; tr. *History of the People of Israel*, 1888–96). In 1878 he was elected to the French Academy, and in 1883 he was made director of the Collège de France. Renan turned to creative writing in later years and, with irony and poetic style, composed *Dialogues et fragments philosophiques* (1876) and the much-discussed *Drames philosophiques* (1888). His subtle irony and beautiful prose are blended, sometimes whimsically, in the *Souvenirs d'enfance et de jeunesse* (1883; tr. *Recollections of My Youth*, 1883). Renan's influence was widespread. See biographies by H. W. Wardman (1964) and R. M. Chadbourne (1968); studies by R. M. Chadbourne (1957) and V. V. Gaigalas (1972).

Renard, Jules (zhül rənär'), 1864–1910, French writer. His *Écornifleur* (1892) is a novel about a young writer's selfish exploitation of a bourgeois family. *Poil de carotte* (1894), an autobiographical novel about an unhappy child, reflects Renard's bitter memories. Both novels were dramatized by the author, the first as *Monsieur Vernet* (1903), the second with the original title (1900). Other plays include *Le Plaisir de rompre* (1897) and *Le Pain de ménage* (1898), one-act comedies. *Le Vigneron dans sa vigne* (1894) and *Les Bucoliques* (1898) are collections of essays and short descriptive tales. Renard's *Journal* (1925–27) gives a view of the literary figures of his day and shows his preoccupation with style and language.

Renart, Jean (zhäN rənär'), fl. 1212, French poet. He is believed to be the author of two charming *romans courtois*, or metrical romances—*Guillaume de Dole* and *L'Escoufle* [the hawk] as well as *Le Lai de l'ombre*. These works contain realistic sketches of medieval life and are marked by psychological insight. Renart's use of traditional songs in his verse novels was widely imitated. See study by P. H. Beekman (1935).

Renault, Louis (lwē rənō'), 1843–1918, French jurist, professor of international law at the Univ. of Paris. Renault was one of the founders of the scientific study of international law in France. He sat on the Hague Tribunal (the Permanent Court of Arbitration) and did much to advance the cause of international arbitration. He shared with E. T. Moneta the 1907 Nobel Peace Prize.

Renault, Mary, pseud. of **Mary Challens,** 1905–, English novelist, b. London. After receiving her R.N. from Radcliffe Infirmary, Oxford, in 1936, she emigrated to South Africa. She is noted for her historical novels about ancient Greece and Rome. They include *The King Must Die* (1958), *The Mask of Apollo* (1966), *Fire from Heaven* (1970), and *The Persian Boy* (1973). The theme of homosexuality is found in all these works; it is the central focus of *The Charioteer* (1955), a study of soldiers in World War II, widely regarded as her finest novel.

Rendsburg (rĕnts'bo͝orkh), city (1970 pop. 34,765), Schleswig-Holstein, N West Germany, a port on the Eider River and the Kiel Canal. The city's manufactures include machinery, and there are shipyards. Rendsburg passed to the counts of Holstein in 1252 and was chartered soon thereafter. When Schleswig-Holstein rose (1848–51) against Denmark, Rendsburg was made the provisional capital. The Danes, however, regained control of the city and razed (1852–56) its fortress. In 1866, Rendsburg was annexed by Prussia. It has a 13th-century church and a 16th-century city hall.

René (rənā'), 1409–80, king of Naples (1435–80; rival claimant to ALFONSO V of Aragón and FERDINAND I of Naples), duke of Anjou, Bar, and Lorraine, count of Provence. He was also called René of Anjou and Good King René. The second son of King Louis II of Naples, he was count of Guise when he married (1419) Isabella, heiress of Lorraine and Bar. He inherited Bar (1430) and Lorraine (1431), but the latter title was contested by a rival supported by Philip the Good of Burgundy. René was captured (1431) and held prisoner, although Holy Roman Emperor Sigismund awarded him Lorraine. At the death (1434) of his brother, LOUIS III of Naples, he inherited Anjou, Provence, and the claim to the succession of JOANNA II of Naples (d. 1435), who adopted him as heir. Released from his imprisonment in 1437, René arrived (1438) in Italy to take possession of his kingdom. Alfonso V, who had taken over the kingdom when Joanna died, defeated (1442) him; René returned to France and established a brilliant court at Angers. In 1445 his daughter, MARGARET OF ANJOU, married Henry VI of England. René about that time delegated his interests in Lorraine and Naples to his son John, whom he made duke of Lorraine and Bar in 1452. John's expedition to Naples ended with defeat (1462) at Troja, and he died in 1470. René was obliged by King Louis XI of France to make the French crown his heir in Anjou. In 1473 he retired to Provence and there devoted himself to poetry and painting, for which he acquired a certain reputation. His titles to Provence and Naples passed to his nephew Charles, count of Maine; they reverted to the French crown when the death (1481) of Charles ended the Angevin dynasty. Lorraine and Bar remained under René's descendants. Important in history for his dynastic connections, René was also remarkable as one of the last representatives of medieval chivalry and culture.

Renewed Church of the Brethren: see MORAVIAN CHURCH.

Renfrew (rĕn'fro͞o), burgh (1971 pop. 18,589), county town of Renfrewshire, W central Scotland, on the Clyde River, near Glasgow. It has shipyards and manufactures rubber, paint, and soap. A busy Clydeside port since the 12th cent., it became a burgh in the 14th cent. The title "baron of Renfrew" has been held by the Scottish sovereign's eldest son since 1404. In 1975, Renfrew became part of the Strathclyde region.

Renfrewshire, county (1971 pop. 362,144), 225 sq mi (583 sq km), central Scotland, on the Clyde River estuary. The county town is RENFREW but the administrative offices are in PAISELY. Besides the Clyde, the principal rivers are the Gryfe, the Black Cart, and the White Cart. Renfrewshire is one of the smallest but most populous counties of Scotland. It is an important industrial region, with shipbuilding, the manufacturing of boilers and electrical cables, sugar refining, and other industries. Chief towns include GREENOCK and PORT GLASGOW. Once part of STRATHCLYDE, Renfrewshire was not separated from Lanarkshire until 1404. In 1975, Renfrewshire became part of the Strathclyde region.

Reni, Guido (gwē'dō rĕ'nē), 1575–1642, Italian painter and engraver, b. Bologna. As a child he entered the studio of the Flemish painter Denis Calvaert. He was for a short time (c.1595) a pupil of the Carracci, who were then at the height of their popularity. By 1598 he had been commissioned by the government to execute decorative frescoes for the facade of the Palazzo Pubblico. Shortly after 1600 he made the first of his many trips to Rome, which was to become the center of his activities until 1614. He became a rival of Caravaggio, whose work clearly influenced his famous *Crucifixion of St. Peter* (Vatican). He worked (c.1608–c.1609) on frescoes in the Church of San Gregorio Magno (Rome). There, in his *God the Father above a Concert of Angels*, he displays the grandeur of style and glittering tonality characteristic of his most renowned work, the *Aurora* fresco of 1613, in the Rospigliosi Palace, Rome.

In 1620 he began the frescoes and the altarpiece *Israelites Gathering the Manna,* in the cathedral at Ravenna. During the latter part of his life he returned to Bologna, where he established his own academy. Among his many works in European museums are *Atalanta and Hippomenes* (Naples) and *Ecce Homo* (versions in the National Gall., London, and the Louvre) and *Mater Dolorosa* (versions in the Corsini Gall., Rome, and in Berlin). He made engravings of his own and others artists' works. In spite of his voluptuous sentimentality, Guido's abilities surpassed those of most of his Bolognese contemporaries. During the 17th and 18th cent. he was held in great esteem. See study by A. S. Harris (1967).

Rennell, James, 1742–1830, English cartographer, geographer, and oceanographer. He was surveyor general (1764–77) of Bengal and published *A Bengal Atlas* (1779). He constructed the first approximately correct map of India (1783). A specialist on the geography of W Asia and of North Africa, he wrote on the geographical knowledge of Herodotus (1800), on the topography of the plain of Troy (1814), and on Xenophon's retreat (1816). He was a pioneer in the scientific study of winds and of ocean currents.

Renner, Karl (kärl rĕn'ər), 1870–1950, Austrian socialist politician. A deputy after 1907, Renner became, following the abdication (Nov., 1918) of Emperor Charles I, the head of the provisional Austrian government and, after elections were held, the first chancellor (1919–20) of the Austrian republic. As leader of the Austrian delegation at the Paris Peace Conference, Renner signed the Treaty of Saint-Germain. He later served (1931–33) as president of the parliament. As World War II was ending in April, 1945, Renner became premier and minister of foreign affairs in the provisional Austrian government, and in Dec., 1945, he was elected president of the liberated Austrian republic. After his death he was succeeded by Theodor Körner. Renner wrote works in sociology, economics, and political science.

Rennes (rĕn), city (1968 pop. 188,515), capital of Ille-et-Vilaine dept., NW France, at the junction of the Vilaine and Ille rivers. Among the products of Rennes's many industries are textiles, leather goods, automobiles, electronic equipment, and petroleum. Rennes was an important Gallo-Roman town. In the 10th cent. it became the capital of the Breton county of Rennes and, in 1196, under the Angevin dukes, of Brittany. Under the ancien régime it was the seat of the provincial Breton estates, the powerful parlement of Rennes, and several courts of justice. The town was ravaged by the Norsemen and in the Hundred Years War and was swept by a fire in 1720. The Univ. of Rennes was founded in 1735. The National School of Public Health is in Rennes. General Boulanger was born in the city.

rennet, substance containing rennin, an enzyme having the property of clotting, or curdling, milk. It is used in the making of CHEESE and junket. Rennet is obtained from the stomachs of young mammals living on milk, especially from the inner lining of the fourth stomach (abomasum) of young calves. The preparation of rennet was formerly a part of the domestic function of making cheese; the inner membrane was kept in salt, dried, and, when rennet was needed, soaked in water. Now extract of rennet is made and sold commercially. It is usually prepared by soaking the tissues in warm, slightly salted water and straining and preserving the resulting liquid. Heat interferes with the action of rennet.

Rennie, John, 1761–1821, British civil engineer. In London he designed the Waterloo (1811–17) and Southwark (1815–19) bridges. London Bridge, also designed by him, was built (1824–31) by his son, **Sir John Rennie,** 1794–1874, who was knighted on its completion.

rennin: see RENNET.

Reno, Jesse Lee (rē'nō), 1823–62, Union general in the American Civil War, b. Wheeling, Va. (now W.Va.). He was twice brevetted for his service in the Mexican War. In the Civil War, Reno was made a brigadier general of volunteers (Nov., 1861) and commanded a brigade in Ambrose Burnside's expedition to North Carolina (1861–62). Promoted to major general (July, 1862), he led the 9th Corps at the second battle of Bull Run, at Chantilly, and at South Mt., where he was killed on Sept. 14, 1862. Reno, Nev., was named for him.

Reno, city (1970 pop. 72,863), seat of Washoe co., W Nev., on the Truckee River; inc. 1903. Tourism is the major industry. A crisp climate, extensive resort facilities (especially night entertainment), and free port privileges, in a state that permits quick divorce and legalized gambling, have promoted Reno's prosperity; the city's bustling air has resulted in its slogan "the biggest little city in the world." It has an international airport and is a major distributing center. Mining and agriculture are also important; irrigation is aided by the Truckee storage project. The site was once a popular campsite beside a ford on the Donner Pass route to California; in 1860 a bridge was built. The name Lake's Crossing was changed to Reno when the Central Pacific RR arrived in 1868 and the town was laid out. A rodeo, a national air race, and the state fair are held there annually. Reno is the site of a branch of the state university, a school of mines, and the museum and library of the state historical society. It has a planetarium, an extensive collection of antique cars, and a firearms exhibit. Lake Tahoe, Pyramid Lake, and other recreational areas and state parks are in the vicinity.

Renoir, Jean (zhäN rənwär'), 1894–, French film director and writer, b. Paris; son of Pierre Auguste Renoir. Renoir's *La grande illusion* (1937), a balanced, compassionate study of people in time of war, is considered one of the greatest motion pictures ever made. His films are noted for their integration of visual and narrative elements. They include *Le Crime de M. Lange* (1935), *Une partie de campagne* (1936), *La Bête humaine* (1938), *La Règle du jeu* (1939); the American films *The Southerner* (1944) and *Diary of a Chambermaid* (1945); *The River* (1951) and *C'est la revolution* (1967). Renoir has written the biography *Renoir, My Father* (tr. 1962) and a novel, *The Notebooks of Captain Georges* (tr. 1966). See his autobiography, *My Life and My Films* (1974); study by André Bazin (tr. 1973).

Renoir, Pierre Auguste (pyĕr ōgüst'), 1841–1919, French impressionist painter and sculptor, b. Limoges. Renoir went to work at the age of 13 in Paris as a decorator of factory-made porcelain, copying the works of Boucher. In 1862 he entered M. C. Gleyre's studio where he formed lasting friendships with Bazille, Monet and Sisley. His early work reflected myriad influences including those of Courbet, Manet, Corot, Ingres and Delacroix. He began to earn his living with portraiture in the 1870s; an important work of this period was *Madame Charpentier and her Children* (1876; Metropolitan Mus.). Simultaneously he developed the ability to paint joyous, shimmering color and flickering light in outdoor scenes such as *The Swing* and the festive *Moulin de la Galette* (both: 1876; Louvre). Renoir traveled in Algeria and in Italy (1881–82), returning to Paris where a successful exhibition (1883) established him financially. He had gone beyond impressionism. His ecstatic sensuality, particularly in his opulent, generalized images of women, and his admiration of the Italian masters removed him from the primary impressionist concern: to imitate the effects of natural light. After a brief period, often termed "harsh" or "tight," in which his forms were closely defined in outline (e.g., *The Bathers,* 1884–87; private coll.), his style of the 1890s changed, diffusing both light and outline, and with dazzling, opalescent colors describing voluptuous nudes, radiant children, and lush summer landscapes. From 1903, Renoir fought the encroaching paralysis of arthritis at the same time that his work attained its greatest sensual power and monumentality. Despite illness and personal tragedy he began to produce major works of sculpture (e.g., *Victorious Venus,* Renoir Mus., Cagnes-sur-Mer). Among his most celebrated paintings are: *Luncheon of the Boating Party* (1881; Phillips Coll., Washington, D.C.); *Dance at Bougival* (1883; Mus. of Fine Arts, Boston); *Lady Sewing* (Art Inst., Chicago); and *Bather* (1917–18; Philadelphia Mus. of Art). Renoir's work is represented in most of the important galleries in the world. The Art Institute of Chicago; the Barnes Collection, Merion, Pa.; Clark Institute, Williamstown, Mass.; and the Louvre have large collections. His son, the film director Jean RENOIR, wrote a biography (tr. 1962). See studies by W. Pach (1950), L. Hanson (1968), and W. Gaunt (2d ed. 1971).

Rensselaer (rĕnsəlĕr', rĕn'sələr), city (1970 pop. 10,136), Rensselaer co., E N.Y., on the east bank of the Hudson River opposite Albany; settled 1630 by Dutch, inc. 1897. Chemicals and concrete products are among its manufactures. The city was formed by the union of several villages within the tract granted to Kiliaen Van Rensselaer by the Dutch West India Company. At the 17th-century Fort Crailo, now a museum, the British surgeon Richard Shuckburg is said to have written "Yankee Doodle."

Rensselaer Polytechnic Institute, at Troy, N.Y.; coeducational; founded and opened 1824 as Rensselaer School; chartered 1826. It was called Rensselaer Institute from 1837 to 1861. The first private technical school in the United States, Rensselaer pioneered in the use of the laboratory method in teaching science. It granted the first U.S. engineering degrees in 1835. The university continues to maintain extensive laboratory facilities devoted to the study of science and technology. In 1955 a new division, the Hartford Graduate Center, was opened in Connecticut. See histories by P. C. Ricketts (3d ed. 1934) and Samuel Rezneck (1968).

rent, in law, periodic payment by a tenant for the use of another's property. Rent, in this sense, may be merely a token in recognition of the renter's ownership. In economics its meaning is more complex, but since the word *rent* means any income or yield from an object capable of producing wealth, its limitation to a more special sense is somewhat arbitrary and justified only by a general consensus of opinion and usage. The term *rent* is now ordinarily used in the broad sense and, besides the return from land, includes the return from such things as tools, machinery, and houses. Objects are rented for a limited period of time and must be returned in their original condition. The early English writers on economics (16th–18th cent.) used the word to mean interest on a loan, but its economic meaning gradually narrowed to the sense of the return on land. Modern rent doctrine began in the 18th cent. The PHYSIOCRATS centered their economic system on land. They believed that rent was measured by the net product, i.e., the surplus over the cost of production. Because they identified wealth with fixed material objects, the physiocrats considered rent not as the variable yield from the land but as a fixed value, which they called "current price of leases" and "disposable revenue." Adam Smith attempted to formulate a "natural rate" of rent based on the laws of supply and demand. This rate would be an amount high enough to induce the landowner to keep his land in cultivation and low enough to allow the tenant to subsist. The theory developed by David RICARDO (also by Thomas MALTHUS) was formulated in a period of great food scarcity. Ricardo held that the demand determined the amount of marginal land under cultivation and that rent was determined by this margin, which, since it was the poorest land, had the highest costs of production. Ricardo attacked Smith for putting rent on the same footing with wages and profits as one of the costs of production. Ricardo thought that high or low wages and profits were the cause of high or low prices, while high or low rents were the effect of these prices. The subsequent history of rent doctrine consists largely of hostile criticisms of the Ricardian theory. Henry GEORGE, for example, thought that monopolistic control of rent was the cause of poverty, which could only be cured by converting private rights into public by the medium of a single tax on land. See J. S. Keiper et al., *Theory and Measurement of Rent* (1961); William Alonso, *Location and Land Use: Toward A General Theory of Land Rent* (1964).

Renton, city (1970 pop. 26,648), King co., W Wash., an industrial suburb of Seattle, on Lake Washington; inc. 1901. It is a freshwater port of entry via the Lake Washington Ship Canal. Its clay works were established in 1901 and its iron foundry in 1905. A Boeing aircraft plant began operation there during World War II and has since greatly expanded. The city has a municipal airport, four flying schools, a seaplane base, and a racetrack.

Renwick, James, 1818–95, American architect, b. New York City, grad. Columbia, 1836. His design for Grace Church (1843–46) in New York City was followed by that for St. Patrick's Cathedral; he was chosen as architect for the cathedral in 1853, and it was dedicated in 1879, the most ambitious essay in Gothic that the revival of the style produced. In Washington he built the original Corcoran Gallery and the Smithsonian Institution. Other of his works were the first building of Vassar College and the distributing reservoir for the Croton Aqueduct in New York.

reparations, payments sought by the victorious nations of World War I and World War II as compensation for material losses and suffering caused by war. The Treaty of Versailles (1919) formally asserted Germany's war guilt and ordered it to pay reparations to the Allies. The United States did not ratify the treaty and waived all claims on reparations. A reparations commission fixed sums in money; some payments were to be in kind (i.e., coal, steel, ships). The chaotic conditions of the German economy after the war made it difficult for the Allies to collect the amounts due them, and they in turn declared it impossible to honor their WAR DEBTS to the United States. In 1923, French and Belgian troops occupied the RUHR district after Germany was declared in default. The DAWES PLAN (1924) and the YOUNG PLAN

(1929) sought to ease the strain of reparations payments. By 1931 the world economic situation had so deteriorated that a one-year moratorium, usually called the Hoover moratorium, on all intergovernmental debts was announced. The Lausanne Pact of 1932 substituted a bond issue for the reparation debt, and although the pact was not ratified, German payments were never resumed. Reparations were also demanded in treaties with Germany's allies in the war—Austria, Hungary, Bulgaria, and Turkey—but the amounts were never set and nothing was collected. In 1945 the Allies assessed Germany for damages suffered in World War II. Payments were to be effected chiefly through removal of assets and industrial equipment. The Western powers and the USSR came into conflict over reparations, and seizures of capital goods and of German assets in Allied or neutral countries proceeded unevenly. The Western powers ended reparations collections from West Germany in 1952, and the USSR ceased collection from East Germany a year later, although official renunciation of claims did not occur until 1954 in both cases. In 1953 the West German government agreed to pay reparations to Israel for damages suffered by the Jews under the Hitler regime. Lesser reparations claims were made against Germany's allies in the war—Bulgaria, Finland, Hungary, Italy, and Rumania. The Western powers did not support these claims, and payments to the nations that asked compensation were arranged through separate treaties. Japan also had to pay reparations after World War II. The United States administered removal of capital goods from Japan, and the USSR seized Japanese assets in the former state of Manchukuo. The United States ended collections from Japan in 1949 and renounced further claims in 1951. At that time Japan agreed to settle the reparations claims of Asian nations by individual treaties with those countries. These treaties were subsequently negotiated. See J. M. Keynes, *The Economic Consequences of the Peace* (1919); C. G. Dawes, *A Journal of Reparations* (1939); Benjamin Ratchford, *Berlin Reparations Assignment* (1947).

repartimiento (răpärtēmyĕn'tō), in Spanish colonial practice, usually, the distribution of Indians for forced labor. In a broader sense it referred to any official distribution of goods, property, services, and the like. From as early as 1499, deserving Spaniards were allotted pieces of land, receiving at the same time the Indians living on them; these allotments were known as *encomiendas* (see ENCOMIENDA) and the process was the *repartimiento;* the two words were often used interchangeably. The *encomienda* soon gave way to the *repartimiento de indios* (thereafter shortened to *repartimiento*), a system of forced labor and other assessments exacted from the Indians. The system endured and was the core of PEONAGE in New Spain. The assessment of forced labor was called the *mita* in Peru and the *cuatequil* in Mexico.

Rephael (rĕf'āĕl), gatekeeper of the Temple. 1 Chron. 26.7.

Rephah (rē'fə), ancester of Joshua. 1 Chron. 7.25.

Rephaiah (rĕf"ī'ə, rēfā'yə). **1** Descendant of Judah. 1 Chron. 3.21. **2** Chief whose followers defeated the Amalekites. 1 Chron. 4.42. **3** Son of Tola. 1 Chron. 7.2. **4** Repairer of the wall. Neh. 3.9. **5** Descendant of Saul. 1 Chron. 9.43. Rapha: 1 Chron. 8.37.

Rephaim (rĕfā'ĭm). **1** Pre-Israelite race of giants. Gen. 14.5; 15.20. They were also referred to simply as "giants." Deut. 2.11,20; 3.11,13; Joshua 12.4; 13.12; 17.15. **2** Valley, SW of Jerusalem. 2 Sam. 5.18,22; 23.13; 1 Chron. 11.15; 14.9; Isa. 17.5.

Rephidim (rĕf'ĭdĭm, rĕfĭd'ĭm), unlocated place in Sinai where Moses struck the rock and brought forth water. Ex. 17; 19.2; Num. 33.14.

Repin, Ilya Yefimovich (ēlyä' yĭfē'məvĭch ryĕ'pĭn), 1844–1930, Russian historical and genre painter and sculptor. He studied in St. Petersburg and abroad and became the foremost representative of the realistic style in Russia. In his *Volga Boatmen, The Arrest of a Political Offender,* and *The Terrorists* Repin expressed criticism of the social order. His large historical paintings, e.g., *Ivan the Terrible* and *The Cossacks Drafting a Letter to the Sultan,* are his best-known works. Most of his pictures are in the museums of Moscow and Leningrad.

replacement series: see ELECTROMOTIVE SERIES.

repoussé (rəpo͞osā'), the process or the product of ornamenting metallic surfaces with designs in relief hammered out from the back by hand. Gold and silver are most commonly used today for fine work, but copper and tin are suitable for the purpose, and bronze was extensively used in past times. The process is of ancient origin, having been employed by most early civilizations. Among the finest examples of repoussé are the famous bronze armor of Greece of the 4th cent. B.C., Byzantine religious works, and much of the gold and bronze work of Benvenuto Cellini. The process is distinct from EMBOSSING, in which the relief ornament is produced by use of dies.

Repplier, Agnes (rĕp'lēr), 1858–1950, American essayist, b. Philadelphia. Her essays, esteemed for their scholarship and wit, are collected in several volumes, including *Books and Men* (1888), *Points of Friction* (1920), and *To Think of Tea!* (1932). She also wrote biographical studies of Jacques Marquette (1929), Marie de l'Incarnation (1931), and Junípero Serra (1933), and a historical study of types of humor, *In Pursuit of Laughter* (1936).

representation, in government, the term used to designate the means by which a whole population may participate in governing through the device of having a much smaller number of people act on their behalf. Although an elective presidency and even a nonelective monarchy may possess psychological characteristics of representation for its people, the term is generally used to refer to the procedure by which a general population selects an assembly of representatives through VOTING. In the United States this assembly is the CONGRESS OF THE UNITED STATES, while in Great Britain it is PARLIAMENT. Historically, representation was first seen in the Roman republic, but it came into more general use in feudal times when a king would select representatives from each estate—the clergy, nobility, and burghers—so they might offer advice or petition him. Out of this system, as people gradually secured the right to choose their representatives themselves, grew the modern representative LEGISLATURE. Modern representation is usually based upon numbers and territorial groupings of the population, such as a congressional district in the United States. An election district in both the United States and Great Britain sends only a single member to the legislative body and is therefore called a single-member district. The representative is chosen on the basis of winning a plurality within the district. In contrast to this system is that of proportional representation, in which there are plural-member districts (in national elections, the country as a whole may form one constituency) and the seats in the assembly are distributed among the parties on the basis of the proportion of the vote that each party receives. This system gives more assurance that minority votes will be taken into account and tends to encourage the proliferation of parties. A controversy yet to be settled over representation concerns whether an elected representative should act according to the explicit desires of his constituents or according to his own personal judgment when it conflicts with those desires.

Representation of the People Acts, statutes enacted by the British Parliament to continue the extension of the franchise begun by the REFORM BILLS. As a result of the government's dependence on the unified efforts of the whole people in World War I the **Representation of the People Act of 1918** qualified as voters (with a few exceptions) women over 30 years of age and all men of 21 years or over who could establish short residence. The basis of representation in the House of Commons was fixed at 1 to 70,000. The **Representation of the People Act of 1928** qualified all women on the same terms as men. The **Representation of the People Act of 1949** reenacted and codified previous legislation relating to the conduct of elections and illegal electoral practices; it abolished the university constituencies and the additional vote given to the occupiers of business premises, thus eliminating plural voting. The **Representation of the People Act of 1969** lowered the voting age to 18.

Representatives, House of: see CONGRESS OF THE UNITED STATES.

repression, in psychology: see DEFENSE MECHANISM; PSYCHOANALYSIS.

repressor: see NUCLEIC ACID.

reprieve (rĭprēv'), in law, the temporary suspension of a sentence imposed after conviction of a crime. In the United States the power to reprieve generally is vested in the executive (President or governor), who may also grant a PARDON.

reprisal, in international law, the forcible taking, in time of peace, by one country of the property or territory belonging to another country or to the citizens of the other country, to be held as a pledge or as redress in order to satisfy a claim. A reprisal, technically, is not an act of war, because it is solely in response to conduct that violated international law. When, however, reprisals are taken against a power of equal strength, they may provoke war. The Covenant of the League of Nations and the Charter of the United Nations classify reprisals as acts endangering peace. Modern international law no longer recognizes private reprisal. This was the right of a private person to satisfy a legal claim against an alien by seizing property belonging to a person of the alien's nationality. The authority was contained in a letter of reprisal issued by the sovereign. Private reprisals all but disappeared by 1800, as the central authority of states grew stronger.

reproduction, capacity of all living systems to give rise to new systems similar to themselves. The term *reproduction* may refer to this power of self-duplication in a single cell, in groups of cells and organs, or in a complete animal or plant organism. In all cases reproduction consists of a basic pattern: the conversion by a parent organism of raw materials from the environment into offspring—or into cells that develop into offspring (see MEIOSIS)—of a similar or potentially similar constitution. The reproductive process always includes the transmission of a hereditary pattern or code (see NUCLEIC ACID) from the parents so that the offspring too can reproduce themselves. Although the methods and complexity of the reproductive process vary tremendously, two fundamental types may be distinguished: asexual reproduction, in which a single organism separates into two or more equal or unequal parts; and sexual

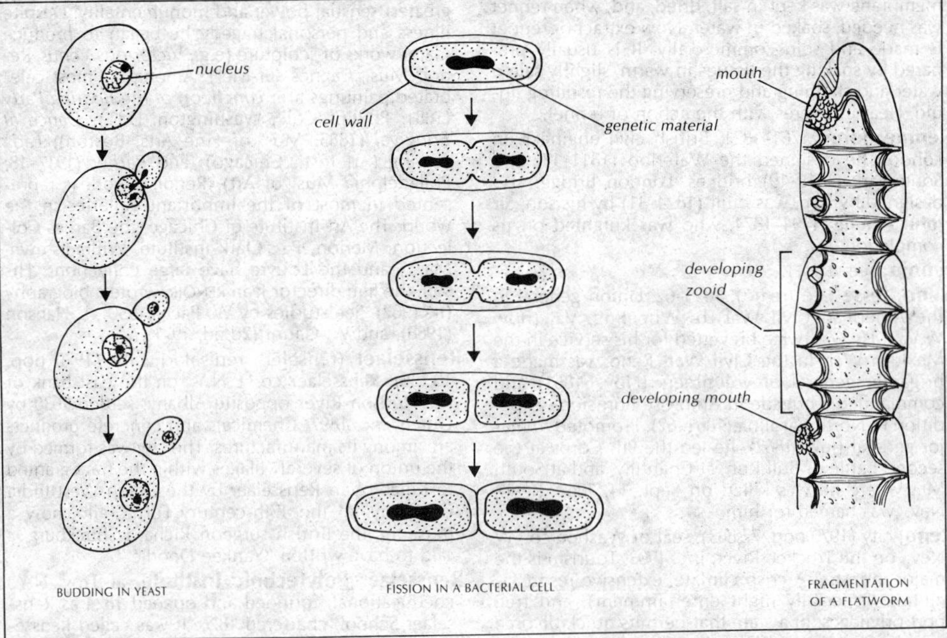

Examples of asexual reproduction

reproduction, in which a pair of specialized reproductive (sex) cells fuse. Asexual reproduction is advantageous in allowing beneficial combinations of characteristics to continue unchanged and in eliminating the often vulnerable stages of early embryonic growth. It is found in all plants and in some animals, e.g., one-celled forms (protozoa) and the lower invertebrates. In one-celled organisms it most commonly takes the form of fission, or MITOSIS, the division of one individual into two new and identical individuals. In some cases the cells thus formed remain clustered together to form filaments (as in many fungi) or colonies (as in staphylococci and Volvox). Fragmentation is the process in filamentous forms in which a piece of the parent breaks off and develops into a new individual. Sporulation, or SPORE formation, is another means of asexual reproduction among protozoa and many plants. A spore is a reproductive cell that gives rise to a new organism without fertilization. In some lower animals (e.g., hydra) and in yeasts, budding is a common form of reproduction; a small protuberance on the surface of the parent cell increases in size until a wall forms to separate the new individual, or bud, from the parent. The internal buds formed by sponges are called gemmules. Regeneration is a specialized form of asexual reproduction; by regeneration some organisms (e.g., the starfish and the salamander) can replace an injured or lost part, and many plants are capable of total regeneration—i.e., the formation of a whole individual from a single fragment such as a stem, root, leaf, or even a small slip from such an organ (see CUTTING; GRAFTING). In 1958, F. C. Steward showed that single phloem cells from a carrot plant, when grown on an AGAR medium, would form a complete carrot plant. Among animals, the lower the form, the more capable it is of total regeneration; no vertebrates have this power. Closely allied to regeneration (and sometimes synonymous with it) is vegetative reproduction, the formation of new individuals by various parts of the organism that are not specialized for reproduction. In some plants structures that form on the leaves give rise to young plantlets. Rhizomes, bulbs, tubers, and stolons are other examples. Sexual reproduction occurs in many one-celled organisms and in all multicellular plants and animals. In higher invertebrates and in all vertebrates it is the exclusive form of reproduction, except in the few cases in which PARTHENOGENESIS is also possible. Sexual reproduction is essentially cellular in nature, i.e., it involves the FERTILIZATION of one sex cell (gamete) by another, producing a new cell (called a zygote), which develops into a new organism. The union of two isogametes (structurally identical but differing physiologically) is called isogamy, or conjugation, and occurs only in some lower forms (e.g., Spirogyra and some protozoa). Heterogamy is the fusion of two clearly differing kinds of gametes, distinguished as the OVUM and the SPERM. Multicelluar plants alternate sexually reproducing, or GAMETOPHYTE, and asexually reproducing, or sporophyte, generations. The gametophyte produces gametes and the union of gametes results in the growth of a sporophyte; the sporophyte produces spores that give rise to a gametophyte. The prominent generation in lower plants (e.g., mosses, liverworts, and complex fungi) is the gametophyte; in the vascular plants (ferns, conifers, grasses, and flowering plants) it is the sporophyte. The less prominent generation may be an independent plant, as is the small inconspicuous gametophyte of ferns, or a reduced organism consisting of only a few cells and dependent for survival on the prominent form, like the pollen grain, which is the male gametophyte of seed plants. Many organisms exhibit special reproductive mechanisms to ensure fertilization; among higher plants the process of POLLINATION may involve extremely complex interaction between the flower and the pollen-bearing agent (e.g., the yucca plant and the yucca moth). Among land-dwelling animals internal fertilization (copulation) is necessary in order to provide the fluid environment essential to fertilization. Sexual reproduction is of great significance in that, because of the fusion of two separate parental nuclei, the offspring inherit endlessly varied combinations of characteristics that provide a vast testing ground for new variations that may not only improve the species but ensure its survival. This probably explains the predominance of sexual reproduction among higher forms. Even in those microorganisms that reproduce asexually (e.g., bacteria) exchanges of hereditary material take place; in the hermaphroditic plants and animals (e.g., the earthworm) self-fertilization is almost always prevented by anatomical specializations or by differing maturation times for male and female gametes. See also GENETICS and SEX.

reproductive system, in animals, the anatomical organs concerned with production of offspring. In humans and other mammals the female reproductive system produces the female reproductive cells (the eggs, or ova) and contains an organ in which development of the fetus takes place; the male reproductive system produces the male reproductive cells, the sperm, and contains an organ that deposits the sperm within the female. In the human female reproductive system, ova are produced in the OVARIES, two small organs set in the pelvic cavity below and to either side of the navel. The ovaries also secrete, in cyclic fashion, the hormones ESTROGEN and PROGESTERONE (see MENSTRUATION). After an ovum

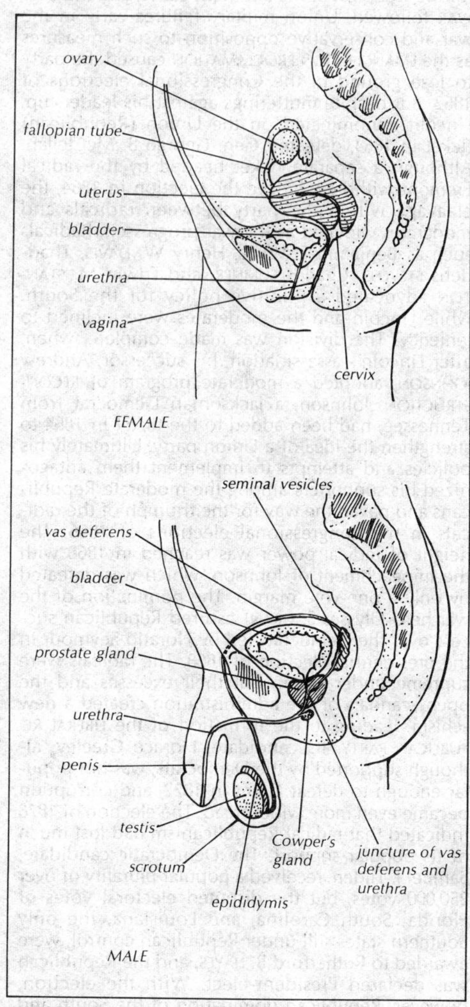

Reproductive system

matures, it passes into the uterine tube, or FALLOPIAN TUBE. If sperm are present as a result of sexual intercourse fertilization occurs within the tube. The ovum, either fertilized or unfertilized, then passes down the fallopian tube, aided by cilia in the tube, and into the womb, or UTERUS, a pear-shaped organ specialized for development of a fertilized egg. An inner uterine layer of tissue, the endometrium, undergoes cyclic changes as a result of the changing levels of the hormones secreted by the ovaries. The endometrium is thickest during the part of the menstrual cycle in which a fertilized ovum would be expected to enter the uterus and is thinnest just after menstruation. If no fertilized egg is present toward the end of the cycle, the thickened endometrium degenerates and sloughs off and menstruation occurs; if a fertilized egg is present it becomes embedded in the endometrium about a week after fertilization. The developing embryo produces trophoblastic cells and these, along with cells from the endometrium, form the placenta, the organ in which gas, food, and waste exchange between mother and embryo takes place. The embryo also forms the amniotic sac within which it develops. The lower end of the uterus is called the cervix; the vagina, a passage connecting the uterus with the external genitals, receives sperm during sexual intercourse and is also the exit passageway for menstrual blood and for the baby and placenta during BIRTH. The external genitals, or vulva, include the clitoris, erectile tissue that responds to sexual stimulation, and the labia, elongated folds of skin. After birth, the infant is fed with milk from the breasts, or MAMMARY GLANDS, which are also sometimes considered part of the reproductive system. In the male reproductive system sperm are produced in the seminiferous tubules of the TESTES, two organs contained in the scrotum, an external sac in the groin. The testes also produce the male hormone TESTOSTERONE and a portion of the seminal fluid, the liquid in which sperm are carried. The external location of the scrotum ensures the relatively low temperature that is necessary for the normal development of sperm. After formation, the sperm pass from the testes into the tubular epididymis, and from there into another passage, the vas deferens. The seminal vesicle, which produces nutrient seminal fluid, and the PROSTATE GLAND, which produces alkaline prostatic fluid, are both connected to the ejaculatory duct leading into the internal URETHRA. The first stage of the male sexual act, erection, results from nerve impulses from the autonomic nervous system that dilate the arteries of the penis, thus allowing arterial blood to flow into erectile tissues of the organ. During intercourse, contractions in the ducts of the testes, epididymis, and vas deferens cause expulsion of sperm into the internal urethra and their mixture with the seminal and prostatic fluids. These substances, together with mucus secreted by accessory glands known as Cowper's glands, form the semen, which is discharged from the penile urethra during ejaculation. Disorders of the reproductive system frequently affect fertility. See FERTILITY DRUG; STERILITY.

reptile, name for the dry-skinned, usually scaly, cold-blooded vertebrates (see CHORDATA) of the order Reptilia. Reptiles are found in a variety of habitats throughout the warm and temperate regions (except on some islands), with the greatest variety in the tropics. They range in size from 2-in.-long (5-cm) lizards to 30-ft-long (9-m) snakes. They typically have low-slung bodies with long tails, supported by four short legs that project outward from the sides of the body; however, all snakes are limbless. Reptiles are fundamentally a terrestrial group, although some are adapted to living in water. All breathe air by means of lungs and have thick, waterproof skins designed for retaining body moisture. Unlike AMPHIBIANS, they do not possess gills or breathe water at any stage of their development, and nearly all lay their eggs or bear their young on land. The reptilian egg has a porous shell and a system of membranes designed to protect the embryo from dessication. It also has a large quantity of yolk for nourishment. This type of egg is typical of terrestrial vertebrates, and is very different from the simple, unprotected eggs of fishes and amphibians, which are laid in the water. Fertilization is internal in reptiles, and males have copulatory organs. Females of most species lay eggs, but in some the egg is incubated and hatched internally. In a very few there is true live birth, with the young nourished by a primitive placenta instead of an egg yolk. Reptiles differ from other terrestrial vertebrates (birds and mammals) in that they are cold-blooded, that is, they lack an effective system for regulating their body temperature, which tends to approach that of the environment. For this reason reptiles are not found in the coldest regions of the world, and they hibernate in cool winter areas. Living reptiles are classified in four orders. The TURTLES, order Chelonia, have a protective bony shell, usually covered with horny plates. They are mostly aquatic in habits although some (see TORTOISE) are adapted to land. They are the oldest living reptiles, having existed nearly unchanged since the Triassic period. Members of the order Crocodilia, which includes ALLIGATORS, caimans, CROCODILES, and GAVIALS, are large, carnivorous reptiles of tropical and subtropical swamps and rivers. They constitute the only remaining order of the great reptilian subclass Archosauria, or ruling reptiles, which includes the extinct DINOSAURS. The order Squamata includes the LIZARDS (suborder Sauria) and SNAKES (suborder Serpentes). Nearly all members of this large and successful modern order are terrestrial. The order Rhynchocephalia has a single living member, the TUATARA, a lizardlike reptile of New Zealand. Reptiles first evolved from amphibians about 250 million years ago in the Carboniferous period and were dominant in the world's fauna during the Mesozoic era, sometimes called the Age of Reptiles. The dinosaurs, the marine ICHTHYOSAURUS and PLESIOSAURUS, and the flying PTEROSAURUS reached the peak of their development and distribution in the later part of this era (late Cretaceous period). Mammallike reptiles appeared very early in reptilian history and by the Triassic period had given rise to mammals. Bird ancestors arose from precursors of the dinosaurs; the first known birds lived in the Jurassic. The only reptiles that survived into the Cenozoic era belonged to the presently living orders. The approximately 6,000 living reptile species represent a very small fraction of this once vast class. See R. L. Ditmars, *Reptiles of the World* (1933) and *Reptiles of North America* (rev. ed. 1951); Roger Conant, *Field Guide to Reptiles and Amphibians* (1958); Angus Bellairs, *The Life of Reptiles* (2 vol., 1970); K. P. Schmidt and R. F. Inger, *Living Reptiles of the World* (1957, repr. 1972).

Repton, village (1971 pop. 32,667), Derbyshire, central England. It was once a capital of the kingdom of MERCIA. A monastery, the seat of the bishopric of Mercia, stood there in the 7th cent. but was later destroyed by the Danes. There are remains of a priory founded in 1172, and the Church of St. Wystan has a fine Saxon crypt. Repton is known chiefly as the site of a public school for boys (on the grounds of the priory), Repton School (1557).

republic [from Lat. *res publica,*=public affair], today understood to be a sovereign state ruled by representatives of a widely inclusive electorate. The term *republic* formerly denoted a form of government that was both free from hereditary or monarchial rule and that had some type of popular control of the state and a conception of public welfare. It is in this sense that we speak of the ancient Roman republic. Today, in addition to the above characteristics, a republic is also understood to be a state in which all segments of society are enfranchised and in which the state's power is constitutionally limited. Traditionally a republic is distinguished from a true DEMOCRACY in that, though both are controlled by the public, the republic operates through a representative assembly chosen by the citizenry, while in a democracy the populace participates directly in governmental affairs. In actual practice, however, most modern representative governments are closer to a republic than a democracy. The United States is an example of a federal republic, in which the powers of the central government are limited and the component parts of the nation, the states, exercise some measure of home rule. France is an example of a centralized republic, in which the component parts have more limited powers. The USSR, though in theory a group of federated and even autonomous regions, is also a centralized republic. See Ferdinand Hermens, *The Representative Republic* (1958) and *Introduction to Modern Politics* (1959).

Republican, river, c.420 mi (680 km) long, formed in S Nebr. by the junction of the North Fork and Arikaree rivers. It is joined by the South Fork at Benkelman and flows E across the rolling grasslands of Nebraska and SE across Kansas to join the Smoky Hill and form the Kansas River at Junction City. Its broad channel traverses a rich agricultural region. The river is included in the Missouri River basin project. Many dams and reservoirs have been built for flood control, irrigation, and power. Among them are the Bonny Dam on the South Fork in Colorado; the Trenton Dam, which creates Swanson Reservoir, and the Harlan County Dam in Nebraska; and two dams of the Bureau of Reclamation's Frenchman-Cambridge unit—the Enders, and the Medicine Creek, which creates Harry Strunk Lake. Further downstream at Superior, Nebr., is the Bureau of Reclamation's Bostwick Irrigation Project and nearby in Kansas is its Lovewell Reservoir on a branch of the Republican. Near the river's mouth are Milford Dam and its reservoir.

Republican party, American political party. The name was first used by Thomas Jefferson's party, later called the Democratic Republican party or, simply, the DEMOCRATIC PARTY. The name reappeared in the 1850s, when the present-day Republican party was founded. At that time the crucial issue of the extension of slavery into the territories split the Democratic party and the WHIG PARTY, and opponents of the KANSAS-NEBRASKA ACT of 1854 organized the new Republican party. Jackson, Mich., is called the birthplace of the party (July 6, 1854) and Joseph MEDILL is credited with having suggested its name, but these distinctions are also claimed for other places and other men. By 1855 the new party was well launched in the North. Anti-slavery Whigs such as William SEWARD and Thurlow WEED were dominant in the new grouping, but elements of the KNOW-NOTHING MOVEMENT, together with the FREE-SOIL PARTY, ABOLITIONISTS, and anti-Nebraska Democrats also supplied strength. The party's national organization was perfected at Pittsburgh in Feb., 1856, and its first presidential candidate, John C. FRÉMONT, made a creditable showing against victorious James Buchanan. The party opposed the repeal of the Missouri Compromise and the extension of slavery, denounced the Supreme Court's decision in the DRED SCOTT CASE, and favored the admission of Kansas as a free state. Generally belligerent towards the South, the Republicans were regarded by Southerners with mingled hatred and fear as sectional tension increased. They were successful in the elections of 1858 and passed over their better-known leaders to nominate Abraham LINCOLN in 1860. The party platform in 1860 included planks calling for a high protective tariff, free homesteads, and a transcontinental railroad; these were bids for support among Westerners, farmers, and eastern manufacturing interests. Lincoln's victory over Stephen A. Douglas, John C. Breckinridge, and John Bell was the signal for the SECESSION of the Southern states, and the CIVIL WAR followed. Union military failures early in the war and conservative opposition to such measures as the EMANCIPATION PROCLAMATION caused the party to lose ground in the Congressional elections of 1862. But despite mutterings against his leadership, Lincoln, renominated on the Union (Republican) ticket in 1864, defeated Gen. George B. McClellan. Although a separate ticket headed by the radical Frémont withdrew before the election in 1864, the cleavage within the party between radicals and moderates widened as the war progressed. Radicals such as Benjamin F. WADE, Henry W. DAVIS, Thaddeus STEVENS, Charles SUMNER, and Edwin M. STANTON advocated a punitive policy for the South, while Lincoln and the moderates were inclined to leniency. The division was made complete, when, after Lincoln's assassination, his successor, Andrew JOHNSON, adopted a moderate program of RECONSTRUCTION. Johnson, a Jacksonian Democrat from Tennessee, had been added to the ticket in 1864 to strengthen the idea of a Union party. Ultimately his policies and attempts to implement them antagonized his supporters among the moderate Republicans and paved the way for the triumph of the radicals in the congressional elections of 1866. The height of radical power was reached in 1868 with the impeachment of Johnson, which was defeated by only a one-vote margin. The nomination of the war hero Ulysses S. GRANT assured Republican success over the Democrats led by Horatio Seymour in the presidential election of 1868. The radicals were supreme under Grant, but their excesses and the open scandals of the administration created a new schism, leading to the formation of the LIBERAL REPUBLICAN PARTY. Its candidate, Horace Greeley, although supported by the Democrats, was not popular enough to defeat Grant in 1872, and corruption became even more widespread. The election of 1876 indicated that radical Republicanism had lost much of its popular support. The Democratic candidate, Samuel J. Tilden, received a popular plurality of over 250,000 votes, but the disputed electoral votes of Florida, South Carolina, and Louisiana, the only Southern states still under Republican control, were awarded to Rutherford B. HAYES, and the Republican was declared President-elect. With the election, however, Republican domination of the South and radical rule of the party were definitely ended. In the period that followed, the two parties differed little in their programs. Each party had numerous almost irreconcilable factions and each avoided taking any real stand on controversial issues, which were generally left to lesser political groups such as the GRANGER MOVEMENT and the GREENBACK PARTY. The Republicans favored a protective tariff and the Democrats a tariff for revenue only, but even this traditional distinction was not rigidly kept. However, the Republican tariff policy was the work of leaders of the new industrial capitalism, whose influence in party councils began to be strongly felt under Grant. The Republican "old guard," led by Roscoe CONKLING, while failing to secure a third nomination for Grant in 1880, nevertheless temporarily blocked the presidential aspirations of James G. BLAINE. Another ex-Union general, James A. GARFIELD, was nominated and was elected over a Democratic general, Winfield S. Hancock. Assassinated shortly after taking office, Garfield was succeeded by Vice President Chester A. ARTHUR. In these post-war elections, the party, always supported by the GRAND ARMY OF THE REPUBLIC, denounced all Democrats as former COPPERHEADS and claimed to have alone saved the Union. But "waving the bloody shirt," as this type of propaganda was styled, was not enough to elect Blaine in 1884. The reform wing of the party, led by Carl SCHURZ, deserted Blaine for the conservative Democrat Grover Cleveland, who was elected. This defection by the MUGWUMPS illustrated the lack of real issues between the two parties; it was the man and not the party that counted. Benjamin HARRISON defeated Cleveland in 1888 but lost to him in 1892. The growing POPULIST PARTY, with its radical program, had a peculiar position in those elections, receiving in each section of the country the support of the party not in power. When, in 1896, the Democratic party was captured by the radicals under William Jennings Bryan, its presidential candidate in 1896, 1900, and 1908, the Republican party became openly the champion of the gold standard and conservative economic doctrines. The conservatives, skillfully guided by national chairman Marcus A. HANNA, won with William MCKINLEY in 1896 and 1900, and under such leaders as Nelson W. ALDRICH, Thomas B. REED, Joseph G. CANNON, Thomas C. PLATT, and Matthew S. QUAY, the party prospered. Theodore ROOSEVELT, successor to the assassinated McKinley, easily defeated the conservative Democrat Alton B. Parker in 1904, and the vigorous foreign policy of his administration fostered the belief that the Republicans stood for the imperialism represented by the recent Spanish-American War. Under Roosevelt's Republican successor and friend, William Howard TAFT, "dollar diplomacy" flourished, but a new rift appeared in the party. INSURGENTS led by Senator Robert M. LA FOLLETTE balked at the party's conservatism and when the regulars renominated Taft in 1912, most of the dissidents withdrew and in the Bull Moose convention chose Roosevelt to lead the new PROGRESSIVE PARTY ticket. With this division, the Democratic candidate, Woodrow Wilson, was elected President, and, narrowly reelected in 1916 over Charles Evans HUGHES, he served through World War I. The party, however, won the Congressional elections of 1918, and Republican opposition was a large factor in defeating Wilson's peace program. By straddling the issue of the League of Nations and calling for a return to "normalcy," the party easily elected Warren G. HARDING in 1920. His administration rivaled Grant's for corruption, but after Harding died in office, his successor, Calvin COOLIDGE, was returned over John W. Davis and La Follette. The Republican victory with Herbert C. HOOVER in 1928 marked the first time since the end of Reconstruction that the party had carried states of the old Confederacy; this came about chiefly because the Democratic candidate, Alfred E. Smith, was a Roman Catholic and an opponent of prohibition. Hoover and the Republicans were blamed for the disastrous economic depression that soon enveloped the country, and the Democrats, under Franklin Delano Roosevelt, were swept into office in 1932. The frustrated Republicans were never able to break the remarkable hold of Roosevelt and the New Deal on the electorate and regularly went down to defeat every four years, with Alfred M. LANDON (1936), Wendell WILLKIE (1940), and Thomas E. DEWEY (1944). Isolationists held the upper hand in the party before World War II and in 1940 two Republicans, Henry L. STIMSON and Frank KNOX, were virtually read out of the party for accepting posts in Roosevelt's cabinet. But the party supported the nation's war effort and after the war, led by Senator Arthur H. VANDENBERG, joined the Democratic administration in a bipartisan foreign policy. In 1948 the Republican party was supremely confident of defeating Roosevelt's successor, Harry S. Truman. However, Dewey, the party's first unsuccessful candidate ever to be renominated, was defeated by a close margin. The more liberal element among the Republicans was able to deny the conservatives' choice, Robert A. TAFT, the presidential nomination in 1952, choosing instead the popular war hero, Gen. Dwight D. EISENHOWER. Campaigning against the domestic policy of the Truman administration and its prosecution of the war in Korea, Eisenhower swept to a landslide victory over the Democratic candidate, Adlai E. Stevenson. The domestic program of the Eisenhower adminstration was moderately conservative, and in foreign policy the internationalist approach of the previous Democratic administration was continued. Despite the President's overwhelming personal popularity and his landslide reelection over Stevenson in 1956, a feat that included carrying several Southern states for the second consecutive time, the Democrats retained control of Congress through the 1960 elections. In 1960, for the first time since 1836, the Republicans nominated the incumbent Vice President, Richard M. NIXON. Although the Republican party had become a minority in registration, Nixon failed by fewer than 200,000 votes to defeat John F. Kennedy. In 1964 the conservative wing of the party engineered the nomination of Senator Barry GOLDWATER, who was, however, defeated in a landslide by Lyndon B. Johnson. In 1968 the party rebounded and won a narrow victory with party stalwart Richard Nixon over Democratic candidate Hubert Humphrey, who was handicapped by disaffection over the Vietnam War. In 1972, President Nixon was triumphantly reelected, defeating George McGovern on a record of favoring a strong defense with a limited detente with the Soviet Union and Communist China, and a conservative domestic program featuring a decentralization of political power. The party, however, suffered a series of massive setbacks with the resignation of Vice President Spiro AGNEW upon his conviction for tax evasion and revelations of major White House involvement in the WATERGATE AFFAIR, which led finally to the resignation of President Nixon. Nixon's successor, Gerald R. FORD, attempted to disassociate the party from the scandals, but Watergate appeared to be a major factor in the substantial Republican losses in the 1974 elections. See C. O. Jones, *The Republican Party in American Politics* (1965); G. H. Mayers, *The Republican Party, 1854–1966* (2d ed. 1967); H. L. Trefousse, *The Radical Republicans* (1968); Eric Foner, *Free Soil, Free Labor, Free Men* (1970); R. D. Marcus, *Grand Old Party: Political Structure in the Gilded Age, 1880–1896* (1971); H. S. Merrill, *The Republican Command, 1897–1913* (1971); F. L. Burdette, *The Republican Party: A Short History* (2d ed. 1972).

Requesens, Luis de Zúñiga y (lwēs dā thōō'nyēgä ē räkāsäns'), 1528–76, Spanish general. Born into the highest nobility of Spain, he held high governmental and diplomatic posts and was chief adviser to John of Austria, with whom he took part in the battle of Lepanto (1571). In 1573, Philip II sent Requesens to the Netherlands to replace Alba as governor. Alba's terrorism had failed to subdue the Netherlanders, and Requesens at first tried to restore peace by negotiation. However, his overtures were rejected by WILLIAM THE SILENT, so warfare continued. Requesens was beset by financial difficulties, which led his unpaid troops to mutiny, and, after the long and successful siege (1574) of LEIDEN, he once more made peace overtures to William, who again rejected them. Despite his difficulties, Requesens began a victorious campaign in Zeeland, but he died before he could consolidate his gains. He was succeeded as governor by John of Austria.

requiem (rĕk'wēəm, rē'-, rā'-) [Lat.,=rest], proper MASS for the souls of the dead, performed on ALL SOUL'S DAY, at funerals, and at request. Its peculiarities include omission of the Gloria, the creed, and the blessing of the people. The variable parts are appropriate; the famous sequence the DIES IRAE is now optional. The opening words of the introit, "Eternal rest grant upon them, O Lord, and let perpetual light shine upon them," echo through all the prayers for the dead. The traditional Gregorian musical setting of the requiem is quite beautiful; other requiem music has been written (e.g., by Mozart and Verdi), but it is not often heard in churches. The reformation of Roman Catholic liturgy following the Second Vatican Council has modified the traditional requiem. Black vestments are no longer required, and white or purple may be worn; flowers are permitted; the hymnody, while still solemn in tone, is often joyful and reflects hope in the resurrection; and the service is conducted in the vernacular.

reredos (rēr'dŏs), ornamented wall or screen that rises behind the high altar of a church, forming a background for it. It may be placed against the apse wall at the extreme end or directly behind the altar, as in certain English churches where it serves to separate the choir and the retrochoir. Called dossal, or dorsal in its earliest form, it was a tapestry or a richly embroidered fabric suspended behind the altar. In the 11th and 12th cent. the reredos was generally a screen of gold, silver, or ivory adorned with sculptures in relief. It became a permanent architectural feature in the late Gothic in England and the Renaissance in Spain, where it was seen as a lofty decorative structure filling the entire width of the choir. Relief sculptures of the Passion and figures of angels and saints were enclosed by a rich framework of pilasters and pinnacles. Especially ornate were the marble and alabaster examples in Spain and those of polychromed and gilded wood in the baroque churches of Mexico. The reredos of Italy and Germany were primarily religious paintings within an architectural framework.

Resaca de la Palma (räsä'kä thä lä päl'mä), valley, an abandoned bed of the Rio Grande, N of Brownsville, Texas, where the second battle of the Mexican War was fought, May 9, 1846. Mexican troops under Gen. Mariano Arista, retreating south after the battle of PALO ALTO, were defeated by American forces led by Gen. Zachary Taylor.

Resen (rē'sĕn), unidentified city of Assyria, between Nineveh and Calah. Gen. 10.12.

Resende, Garcia de (gərsē'ə də rəzĕn'də), c.1470–1536, Portuguese poet and chronicler. Resende's *Cancioneiro geral* (1516) is a compilation of the court poetry of his day, the best of which is his own. His lament for the death of Inés de Castro is generally regarded as his finest poem. His chronicles, stories and descriptions of dress, manners, and court customs, are an invaluable historical source.

reserpine (rĕsûr'pēn), alkaloid isolated from the root of the snakeroot plant (*Rauwolfia serpentina*), a small evergreen climbing shrub of the dogbane family native to the Indian subcontinent. Known in India as Sarpaganda, it was used for centuries to treat insanity as well as physical illnesses such as fevers and snakebites. After its isolation in 1952 it was used to lower high blood pressure, but its property of producing severe depression as a side effect also made it useful in psychiatry as a tranquilizer in the control of agitated psychotic patients. It has largely been replaced in psychiatric use by the phenothiazine tranquilizers, although it is still used as an experimental tool in the study of psychosis. Reserpine causes many toxic side effects including nightmares, Parkinsonism, and gastrointestinal disturbances.

reservoir (rĕz'əvôr, -vwär), storage tank or wholly or partly artificial lake for storing water. Building an embankment or DAM to preserve a supply of water for IRRIGATION is an ancient practice; India and Egypt have many old and large reservoirs. In building artificial lakes for a municipal water supply it is necessary to consider all the aspects of a CATCHMENT AREA, including the amount and distribution of rainfall, evaporation, runoff, soil or rock conditions, and elevation (for its effect upon precipitation and upon the pressure in the conducting pipes). The ground of the reservoir may be naturally impervious enough to prevent excessive seepage, or a clay or other lining may have to be built. The embankments or retaining walls may be of earth, loose rock, or masonry. Earth forms a good embankment but must be sealed by a core of clay, and the face must be covered with masonry or a similar substance to prevent erosion. Distributing reservoirs in towns are sometimes built of masonry or of reinforced concrete. They serve to cope with fluctuations of demand and with interruptions of supply from the source. Reservoirs are also built on the headstreams of or along the courses of rivers to aid in flood control, on canals to maintain water level for navigation, and to insure water supply for hydroelectric plants. Some reservoirs are built on the tributaries of large rivers to act as catch basins for silt. In addition to seepage, the major loss of water from a reservoir is by evaporation; chemicals that form a film on a water surface are used to minimize such losses. Covered tanks made of prestressed concrete are used for limited local water supply.

Resheph (rē'shĕf), Ephraim's son. 1 Chron. 7.25.

Reshevsky, Samuel, 1911–, Polish-American chess player. A child prodigy, Reshevsky toured Europe in exhibition matches at the age of six. Emigrating to the United States in 1920, he took part in an exhibition at the U.S. Military Academy at West Point in that year. Exhibition tours followed this debut until he withdrew from them at the age of 12 to pursue a normal education. On his return to chess he won the title of grand master. He was the U.S. champion five times between 1936 and 1946. In 1945 he played in the first international team match conducted by radio. Subsequently he played in tournaments and gave exhibitions of simultaneous play throughout the United States and Europe. Among his writings are *Reshevsky on Chess* (1948), *How Chess Games Are Won* (1962), and *Reshevsky on the Fischer-Spassky Games . . . the Complete Match with Analysis* (1972).

Resht, Iran: see RASHT.

residence: see DOMICILE.

resin, any of a class of amorphous solids or semisolids. Resins are found in nature and are chiefly of vegetable origin. They are typically light yellow to dark brown in color; tasteless; odorless or faintly aromatic; translucent or transparent; brittle, fracturing like glass; and flammable, burning with a smoky flame. Resins are soluble in alcohol, ether, and many hydrocarbons but are insoluble in water. When heated, they soften and finally melt. Their chemical composition varies, but most are mixtures of organic acids and esters. Resins are generally classified according to their source or by such qualities as hardness or solubility. Natural resins are found as exudations, often as globules or tears, on the bark of various trees (mostly pines and firs) or on other living plants; they also occur as fossils or as exudations from the bodies of certain scale insects (see LAC). Some natural resins, called oleoresins, contain both a resin and an essential oil; they are often viscid, sticky, gummy, or plastic. Other resins are exceedingly hard and resistant to most solvents, softening only at high temperatures. The primary uses for most resins are in varnish, shellac, and lacquer, in medicine, in molded articles (e.g., pipe mouthpieces), and in electrical insulators. See AMBER; BALSAM; BENZOIN; CANADA BALSAM; COPAIBA; COPAL; DRAGON'S BLOOD; MASTIC; ROSIN; TURPENTINE.

Resina (räzē'nä), city, Campania, S Italy, on the Bay of Naples. Situated on the site of ancient Herculaneum, it has fine villas and gardens and an iron industry.

resistance, in biology: see IMMUNITY.

resistance, in psychiatry: see PSYCHOANALYSIS.

resistance, property of an electric conductor by which it opposes a flow of electricity and dissipates electrical energy away from the circuit, usually as heat. Optimum resistance is provided by a conductor that is long, small in cross section, and of a material that conducts poorly. Resistance is basically the same for alternating and direct current circuits (see IMPEDANCE). However, an alternating current of high frequency tends to travel near the surface of a conductor. Since such a current uses less of the available cross section of the conductor than a direct current, it meets with more resistance than a direct current. In circuit analysis an ideal RESISTOR, i.e., a circuit component whose only property is resistance, is called a resistance. It is thought that the phenomenon of resistance arises from electron interactions. The unit of resistance is the OHM. See SUPERCONDUCTIVITY; OHM'S LAW; CONDUCTION.

Resistencia (rāsēstän'syä), city (1960 pop. 84,036), capital of Chaco prov., NE Argentina. It is the nucleus of an area of frontier settlements extending into the sparsely inhabited northwest. The city, an important commercial center, carries on a lively trade from its port, Barranqueras, on the Paraná River. Cotton, cattle, leather, and quebracho (for tannin extraction) are the city's chief products; the economy of the surrounding region is based on farming, cattle raising, and lumbering. Resistencia was originally the site of an 18th-century Jesuit mission and Indian settlement. In 1876 during the wars against the Indians, the name *Resistencia* was officially adopted, and the city became an important military outpost.

resistor, two-terminal electric circuit component that offers opposition to an electric current and in so doing generates heat. Resistors are normally designed and operated so that, with varying levels of current, variations of their resistance values are negligible (see RESISTANCE). The most common forms of resistors are made from fine wires of special alloys wound onto cylindrical forms or from a molded composition material containing carbon and other substances in varying amounts. Film-type resistors are made by depositing a conductive film on an insulator base. Some resistors are made so that their values can be adjusted (see POTENTIOMETER; RHEOSTAT). Since resistors absorb power from a circuit and convert it into heat, they are normally rated for the maximum amount of power that they can safely handle. For electronic work 1/4 watt (W), 1/2 W, 1W, and 4W are common ratings. For power circuits resistors may be rated at many kilowatts. See INTEGRATED CIRCUIT.

Reşita (rĕ'shētsä), Hung. *Resiczabánya*, city (1970 est. pop. 68,000), W Rumania, in the Banat, in the western foothills of the Transylvanian Alps. It is a railroad terminus and a leading Rumanian mining and industrial center. The production of iron and steel, machinery, metals, and chemicals are the leading industries. Coal and iron are mined nearby. Reşita was known in Roman times as a mining center for precious metals. The modern city was founded in 1768, when the first foundry was established.

res judicata (rēz jōō"dĭkā'tə): see JEOPARDY.

Resolution Island, 387 sq mi (1,002 sq km), off SE Baffin Island, Canada, in SE Franklin dist., Northwest Territories, at the east entrance of Hudson Strait. At its southern extremity is a governmental radio direction-finding and meteorological station.

resolving power: see TELESCOPE.

resonance, in acoustics: see VIBRATION.

resonance, in chemistry: see CHEMICAL BOND.

resorcinol (rĭzôr'sĭnōl, - ŏl) or **resorcin** (rĭzôr'sĭn), $C_6H_4(OH)_2$, colorless, crystalline, aromatic compound that melts at 111°C and boils at 280°C. It turns pink on exposure to air. Resorcinol is soluble in water, ethanol, ether, and benzene. It is made synthetically by treating benzene with sulfuric acid and reacting the subsequent product with sodium hydroxide. Resorcinol is used in the manufacture of dyes, explosives, and antiseptics, and as an oxidant.

Respighi, Ottorino (ôttōrē'nō rāspē'gē), 1879–1936, Italian composer, studied at the music lyceum of Bologna and with Rimsky-Korsakov and Max Bruch. He was director (1924–25) of the Conservatory of St. Cecilia, Rome, afterward teaching advanced composition there until his death. Among his romantic symphonic poems are *The Fountains of Rome* (1917), *The Pines of Rome* (1924), and *Roman Festivals* (1929), which evoke Italian scenes and show him a master of orchestration. He wrote other orchestral works, chamber music, piano pieces, and operas, including *Belfagor* (1923; a comic opera), *La campana sommersa* (1927; based on Hauptmann's *The Sunken Bell*), *La fiamma* (1934), and the posthumously produced *Lucrezia* (1937), which was finished by his wife, Elsa. See biography by Elsa Respighi (1962).

respiration, process by which an organism exchanges gases with its environment. The term now refers to the overall process by which oxygen is abstracted from air and is transported to the cells for the oxidation of organic molecules, while carbon dioxide (CO_2) and water, the products of oxidation, are returned to the environment. In single-celled organisms, gas exchange occurs directly between cell and environment, i.e., at the cell membrane. In complex animals, where the cells of internal organs are distant from the external environment, respiratory systems facilitate the passage of gases to and from internal tissues. In such systems, when there is a difference in pressure of a particular gas on opposite sides of a membrane, the gas diffuses from the side of greater pressure to the side of lesser pressure, and each gas is transported independently of other gases. For example, in tissues where carbon dioxide concentration is high and oxygen concentration is low as a result of active metabolism, oxygen diffuses into the tissue and carbon dioxide diffuses out. In lower animals, gas diffusion takes place through a moist surface membrane, as in flatworms; through the thin body wall, as in earthworms; through air ducts, or tracheae, as in insects; or through specialized tracheal GILLS, as in aquatic insect larvae. In the gills of fish the blood vessels are exposed directly to the external (aquatic) environment. Oxygen-carbon dioxide exchange occurs between the surrounding water and the blood within the vessels; the blood carries gases to and from tissues. In other vertebrates, including man, gas exchange takes place in the LUNGS. Breathing is the mechanical procedure in which air reaches the lungs. During inhalation muscular action lowers the diaphragm and raises the ribs; atmospheric pressure forces air into the enlarged chest cavity. In exhalation the muscles relax and the air is expelled. This combined rhythmic action takes place about 16 times per minute when the body is at rest. The rate of breathing is controlled mainly by a respiratory center in the brain stem that responds to changes in the level of hydrogen ion and carbon dioxide in the blood, as well as to other factors such as stress, temperature changes, and motor activities. Some residual air always remains in the lungs, but with each breath an additional quantity of fresh air, called tidal air, is inhaled. ARTIFICIAL RESPIRATION is used for respiratory failure. In higher vertebrates, oxygen-poor, carbon dioxide-rich blood from the right side of the heart is pumped into the lungs and flows through the net of capillaries surrounding the alveoli, the cup-shaped air sacs of the lungs; oxygen diffuses across the capillary membranes into the blood, and carbon dioxide diffuses in the opposite direction. The oxygen combines with the protein hemoglobin in red blood cells, as the blood returns to the left side of the heart, is pumped throughout the body, and is released into tissue cells (see CIRCULATORY SYSTEM). Carbon dioxide passes in the opposite direction, from the cells of the tissues to the red blood cells. In the blood, carbon dioxide exists in three forms: as bicarbonate ion, in which form it serves as a buffer, keeping blood acidity fairly constant; combined with hemoglobin; and as the dissolved free gas. Of these, only free carbon dioxide gas is available for diffusion from the blood into the lungs. In plants, gas exchange with the environment occurs in special organs, the stomates, found mostly in the leaves (see LEAF; TRANSPIRATION). In biochemistry, respiration refers to the series of biochemical oxidations in which organic molecules are converted to carbon dioxide and water while the chemical energy thus obtained is trapped in a form useful to the cell. Biochemical respiration occurs in both plant and animal cells. Carbohydrates, amino acids, and fatty acids—the organic fuel molecules of the cell—can be converted to acetyl CoA, a derivative of acetic acid and COENZYME A. Acetyl CoA then enters a series of reactions in the mitochondria, organelles in the cell's cytoplasm. The series of reactions, known as the CITRIC ACID CYCLE, converts the acetic acid portion of acetyl CoA to carbon dioxide, protons, and hydride ions, the latter usually as part of the coenzyme NADH. This molecule is oxidized back to NAD when it donates the hydride ion to the series of enzymes known as the electron transport chain. In a process called oxidative PHOSPHORYLATION, each electron transport enzyme is in turn reduced (receives the hydride ion), then oxidized (donates a hydride ion to the next enzyme in the series), and the chemical energy liberated in this series of reactions is coupled to the synthesis of ADENOSINE TRIPHOSPHATE (ATP) from adenosine diphosphate (ADP) and phosphoric acid. ATP, the cell's form of energy storage and supply, furnishes the chemical energy needed for muscle contraction, protein synthesis, active transport of substances across membranes, and electrical impulses. At the end of the electron transport chain, a hydride ion is donated to an atom of oxygen; this pair, together with a proton from the surrounding solution, forms a molecule of water. Thus, in the overall process of cellular respiration, the fuel molecules are converted to carbon dioxide and water while the chemical energy gained is trapped in a useful form as ATP Organisms that utilize respiration to obtain energy are aerobic, or oxygen-dependent. Some organisms can live in the absence of oxygen and obtain energy from fuel molecules solely by FERMENTATION or GLYCOLYSIS; these anaerobic processes are much less efficient since the fuel molecules are merely converted to end products such as lactic acid and ethanol, with relatively little energy-rich ATP produced during these conversions. For individual respiratory organs, see separate articles.

respiratory system: see RESPIRATION.

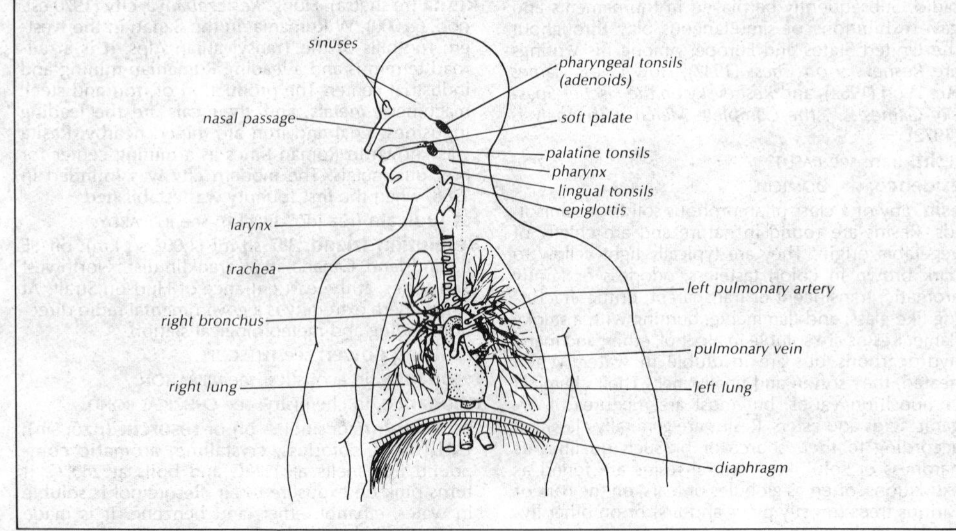

Respiratory system

rest, in music: see NOTE.

restaurant, public eating place. In the 16th cent. English inns and taverns began to serve one meal a day at a fixed time and price, at a common table, and usually distinguished by a special dish. The meal was called the ordinary, and inn dining rooms and eating places generally began to be called ordinaries. Famous among those in London were the Castle, much frequented by famous men, and Lloyd's, a meeting place for merchants and men interested in shipping. In the 17th cent. the ordinaries became fashionable clubs, gambling resorts, and eventually centers of such intense political activity that they were closed by Charles II in 1675. The name restaurant was first used (c.1765) for a Paris establishment serving light ("restoring") dishes. After the French Revolution many former chefs of aristocratic houses opened restaurants. Early American taverns and inns resembled those of England. Fraunces Tavern (see under FRAUNCES, SAMUEL) in New York was a famous meeting place. The first modern restaurant in New York City was opened (c.1834) by Lorenzo Delmonico. The self-service restaurant, or cafeteria, was originated in the United States by philanthropic organizations to help working women secure cheaper meals. The idea was rapidly adopted by commercial restaurants, business organizations, and schools. An outgrowth of the cafeteria is the fully automated vending area, in which prepackaged food and drinks are dispensed from coin-operated machines.

Restif de la Bretonne, Nicolas Edme (nēkôlä' ĕd'mə rĕstēf' də lä brətôn'), 1734–1806, French novelist. A printer by trade, he wrote and published over 250 novels, mostly based on incidents in his own rather libertine life. His detailed realism earned him the epithets "the Rousseau of the gutter" and "the Voltaire of the chambermaids." He was the author of many tracts on social reform. Outstanding among his novels are *Le Pied de Fanchette* (1769), *Le Paysan perverti* (1775), *Les Parisiennes* (1787), and *Monsieur Nicolas* (16 vol., 1794–97; tr., 6 vol., 1930–31). See study by C. A. Porter (1967).

Restigouche (rĕstĭgo͞osh'), river, c.130 mi (210 km) long, rising in NW N.B., Canada, E of Edmundston, and flowing generally NE to the Matapedia River, then past Campbellton to Chaleur Bay at Dalhousie. Its lower course forms part of the Quebec-New Brunswick boundary. The river is noted for salmon fishing.

Reston, James Barrett, 1909–, American journalist, b. Scotland. After working briefly for the Springfield, Ohio, *Daily News*, he joined the Associated Press in 1935. He moved to the New York *Times* in 1940 but took a leave to establish a U.S. office of war information in London (1942). Rejoining the *Times*, Reston was assigned to Washington, D.C., as national correspondent, then diplomatic correspondent and (1953) bureau chief and columnist. During these years Reston acquired a journalistic reputation for insight, fair-mindedness, and wit. He twice won the Pulitzer Prize for national reporting. Reston subsequently became associate editor of the *Times* (1967–68), executive editor (1968–69), and vice president (1969–74). His books include *The Artillery of the Press* (1967) and *Sketches in the Sand* (1967).

restoration, in art: see ART CONSERVATION AND RESTORATION.

Restoration, in English history, the reestablishment of the monarchy on the accession (1660) of CHARLES II after the collapse of the Commonwealth and the Protectorate. The term is often used to refer to the entire period from 1660 to the fall of James II in 1688, and in English literature the Restoration period (often called the age of Dryden) is commonly viewed as extending from 1660 to the death of John Dryden in 1700. After the death of Oliver Cromwell in Sept., 1658, the English republican experiment soon faltered. Cromwell's son and successor, Richard, was an ineffectual leader, and power quickly fell into the hands of the generals, chief among whom was George MONCK, leader of the army of occupation in Scotland. In England a strong reaction had set in against Puritan supremacy and military control. When Monck marched on London with his army, opinion had already crystallized in favor of recalling the exiled king. Monck recalled to the Rump Parliament the members who had been excluded by Pride's Purge in 1648; the reconvened body voted its own dissolution. The newly elected Convention Parliament, which met in the spring of 1660, was overtly royalist in sympathy. An emissary was sent to the Netherlands, and Charles was easily persuaded to issue the document known as the Declaration of Breda, promising an amnesty to the former enemies of the house of Stuart and guaranteeing religious toleration and payment of arrears in salary to the army. Charles accepted the subsequent invitation to return to England and landed at Dover on May 25, 1660, entering London amid rejoicing four days later. Control of policy fell to Charles's inner circle of old Cavalier supporters, notably to Edward Hyde, 1st earl of CLARENDON, who was eventually superseded by a group known as the CABAL. The last remnants of military republicanism, as exemplified in the FIFTH MONARCHY MEN, were violently suppressed, and persecution spread to include the Quakers. The Cavalier Parliament, which assembled in 1661, restored a militant Anglicanism (see CLARENDON CODE), and Charles attempted, although cautiously, to reassert the old absolutist position of the earlier Stuarts. Yet the crown was still dependent upon Parliament for its finances. The unwillingness of Charles and his successor, James II, to accept the implications of this dependency had some part in bringing about the deposition (1688) of James II, who was hated as a Roman Catholic as well as a suspected absolutist. The GLORIOUS REVOLUTION gave the throne to William III and Mary II. The Restoration period was marked by an advance in colonization and overseas trade, by the Dutch Wars, by the great plague (1665) and the great fire of London (1666), by the birth of the Whig and Tory parties, and by the Popish Plot and other manifestations of anti-Catholicism. In literature perhaps the most outstanding result of the Restoration was the reopening of the theaters, which had been closed since 1642, and a consequent great revival of the drama (see ENGLISH LITERATURE). The drama of the period was marked by brilliance of wit and by licentiousness, which may have been a reflection of the freeness of court manners. The last and greatest works of John Milton fall within the period but are not typical of it; the same is true of John Bunyan's *Pilgrim's Progress* (1678). The age is vividly brought to life in the diaries of Samuel Pepys and John Evelyn, and in poetry the Restoration is distinguished by the work of John DRYDEN and a number of other poets. See Allardyce Nicoll, *A History of Restoration Drama* (1923); Basil Willey, *The Seventeenth Century Background* (1934); David Ogg, *England in the Reign of Charles II* (2 vol., 2d ed. 1955); G. N. Clark, *The Later Stuarts* (2d ed. 1956); C. V. Wedgwood, *Seventeenth-Century English Literature* (2d ed. 1970).

Restoration, in French history, the period from 1814 to 1830. It began with the first abdication of Emperor Napoleon I and the return of the Bourbon king, Louis XVIII, but was interrupted (1815) by Napoleon's return (the HUNDRED DAYS). After Napoleon's defeat at Waterloo, Louis XVIII was again restored as king of France. The Bourbon regime was responsible for considerable French economic recovery and expansion and for the restoration of French prestige abroad. These years also saw the growth of the romantic movement in French literature and arts. However, the period marked the failure of the attempt to reconcile the royalist and Revolutionary traditions. Increasing political influence was exerted upon the moderate Louis XVIII by the ultraroyalists, dominated by his brother, the comte d'Artois, who succeeded (1824) Louis as King CHARLES X. The ultraroyalists sought a return to the ancien régime. They were aware, however, that this could not be achieved and acted instead to ensure their own political and social predominance. Their power was finally broken by the bourgeois JULY REVOLUTION of 1830. See Jean Lucas-Dubreton, *The Restoration and the July Monarchy* (tr. 1929, repr. 1968); F. B. Artz, *France under the Bourbon Restoration* (1931, repr. 1963); Nora Hudson, *Ultra-Royalism and the French Restoration* (1936); D. P. Resnick, *The White Terror and the Political Reaction after Waterloo* (1966); J. H. Stewart, *The Restoration Era in France* (1968).

resurrection (rĕz"ərĕk'shən) [Lat.,=rising again], arising again from death to life. The emergence of Jesus from the tomb to live on earth again for 40 days as told in the Gospels has been from the beginning the central fact of Christian experience and a cardinal feature of Christian doctrine (Mat. 28; Mark 16; Luke 24; John 20; Acts 4.2; Romans 6). It was the guarantee not only of Christ's mission and the seal of redemption but also of the resurrection of all men. The general resurrection or resurrection of the body has been understood in diverse ways, always in the light of St. Paul's teaching on the risen or glorified body. In the conventional theology the material body is identified with the glorified body (since the soul is the substantial form of each) and is in some way spiritualized so that it is made incorruptible and immortal. At the end of the world (see JUDGMENT DAY) the souls of all men will be reunited with their risen bodies. The Christian doctrine of resurrection of the body is thus fundamentally different from the resurrection beliefs of the ancient EGYPTIAN RELIGION and other ancient religions (see FERTILITY RITES). Belief in a resurrection of the body distinguished the Pharisees from the Sadducees. It is also a tenet of Muslim belief.

resurrection plant, name for several plants, usually of arid regions, that may apparently be brought back to life after they are dead. In reality they have hygroscopic qualities which cause them to curl up when dry and to unfold when moist. They are frequently sold in the dried condition as a novelty. The most common are the ROSE OF JERICHO and the bird's-nest moss, a CLUB MOSS (*Selaginella lepidophylla*), native to Mexico and Texas, which has a rosette of flattened branches and is capable of growing if it has not been dry too long. It is also sold in Mexican markets for use as a diuretic. These plants are classified in the division LYCOPODIOPHYTA (club mosses).

resuscitator (rĭsŭs'ĭtā"tər), device used to revive a person whose normal breathing has been disrupted. Several types are in wide use. The automatic tank resuscitator consists of a face mask that fits tightly over the nose and mouth and is connected by a tube to one or more tanks of gas. Pressurized oxygen enters the mask through the action of automatic valves. A second tank may contain carbon dioxide, small amounts of which are mixed with oxygen, serving to activate the respiratory center in the brain. In a similar device, the manual tank resuscitator, the oxygen flow is regulated by the operator. The self-inflating, bag-mask resuscitator consists of an airtight mask that fits over the nose and mouth, a self-inflating bag, and often an oxygen tube connector. When the bag is squeezed, air or oxygen enters the patient's lungs. The bag inflates automatically when released. Air from the lungs leaves the mask by an escape valve without returning to the bag.

Reszke, Jean de (zhäN də rĕsh'kē), 1850–1925, Polish singer. His voice, at first a baritone, developed into one of the finest tenors of the 19th cent. He first appeared as a tenor in Madrid in 1879, but it was after his debut (1885) at the Paris Opéra, where he created the leading roles in several of Massenet's operas, that he began to receive his greatest acclaim. Reszke sang (1888–1900) at Covent Garden, London, and from 1891 to 1901 was leading tenor of the Metropolitan Opera Company, New York City. From 1902 until his death he was a teacher in Paris. See biography by Clara Leiser (1934). His brother, **Edouard de Reszke,** 1853–1917, a bass, made his debut in Paris in 1876, sang (1880–84) in London, and from 1891 to 1903 was a leading bass of the Metropolitan Opera Company.

retable (rē'tābəl), frame for decorative panels at the back of an altar in European churches. Retables, often sumptuously decorated in alabaster and gold, generally contained scenes from the Bible. An altarpiece made of fixed panels may also be termed a retable.

Rethel, Alfred (äl'frĕt rā'təl), 1816–59, German historical painter and draftsman. He gained a reputation in Frankfurt, where he painted *Daniel in the Lions' Den* and *Guardian Angel of Emperor Maximilian.* His major work was half of a fresco cycle (1847–52) for the town hall of Aachen, depicting scenes from the life of Charlemagne. Rethel also made a series of remarkable drawings for wood engravings for *Another Dance of Death* (1849), in which he depicted events from the Revolution of 1848.

Rethel (rətĕl'), town (1968 pop. 8,342), Ardennes dept., N France, on the Aisne River. It is a farm trade center with textile industries and plants making farm machinery. It was (13th cent.) the seat of a county held by the courts of Champagne, and passed (1384) to the house of Burgundy. It was raised to a duchy (1581) and acquired by the house of Gonzaga. The title was sold (1663) to the Mazarin family. Strategically located, Rethel has been the scene of much fighting throughout history. It suffered extensive damage in both World Wars.

retina: see VISION; EYE.

retriever: see SPORTING DOG.

retrograde motion, in astronomy, real or apparent movement of a planet, moon, asteroid, or comet from east to west relative to the fixed stars. The most common direction of motion in the solar system, both for orbital revolution and axial rotation, is from west to east (counterclockwise as seen from the north CELESTIAL POLE); revolution or rotation in the opposite direction is actual retrograde motion. Bodies in the solar system with real retrograde orbits include four satellites of Jupiter, one of Saturn, one of Neptune, and some asteroids and comets. With the possible exception of the rotation of Venus, there is no real retrograde motion among the planets, although the plane in which Uranus rotates and its five satellites revolve is tilted slightly more than 90° to the plane of the ECLIPTIC, so that these motions are technically retrograde. All the planets exhibit apparent retrograde motion when they are nearest the earth; i.e., they appear to move backward (east to west) against the background of stars. The superior planets, whose orbits lie outside that of the earth, appear to move backward at OPPOSITION, because the earth is overtaking and passing them. (Of any two planets, the one closer to the sun has the greater orbital speed.) As a consequence, a superior planet's progress through the zodiac is interrupted by annual loops or switchbacks. Mercury and Venus, the inferior planets, exhibit apparent retrograde motion when at inferior CONJUNCTION. They are then passing between the earth and the sun, overtaking the earth, and thus seem to move east to west, relative to both the sun and the background stars. In the geocentric PTOLEMAIC SYSTEM, the retrograde motion of the planets was explained, using epicycles, as real retrograde motion; the modern heliocentric theory satisfactorily explains these motions as apparent, due to the relative speeds of the planets in their orbits about the sun.

Retz or **Rais, Gilles de Laval, seigneur de** (zhēl də läväl' sänyör' də rĕts, rĕs), 1404–40, marshal of France, a lord of the Breton marches. A noted soldier, he was at Orléans with Joan of Arc. He was a liberal patron of music, literature, and the arts. After his retirement, rumors spread of satanic and vicious doings in his castle. He was tried in an ecclesiastical court, and he confessed to kidnaping more than 100 children, mostly boys, and to murdering them after maltreating them. He was handed over by the Church to the civil authorities and was executed. There is no reason to doubt his confession. He has been supposed, probably wrongly, to be the original of BLUEBEARD. See Émile Gabory, *Alias Bluebeard* (tr. 1930); Tennille Dix, *Black Baron* (1930); Jean Benedetti, *Gilles de Rais* (1971).

Retz, Jean François Paul de Gondi, Cardinal de (zhäN fräNswä' pōl də gôNdē', də rĕts), 1613–79, French prelate and political leader. He was made coadjutor (and thus successor designate) to his uncle, the archbishop of Paris, in 1643. An enemy of Cardinal Mazarin (and coveting his position as chief minister for the regent ANNE OF AUSTRIA), Retz took a prominent part in the FRONDE against him. In an attempt to win Retz's support against the Frondeurs, Anne nominated him (1651) to be made cardinal; he received the red hat in 1652. At the close of the Fronde, Retz was imprisoned (1652). On the death of his uncle (1654), he became archbishop of Paris but was not allowed to take office. He escaped, fled to Rome, and appealed to the pope, but without much success. After Mazarin's death (1661) he resigned his see in return for several rich abbeys. He retired from Paris and occasionally represented the court at Rome. His memoirs (1717; tr., 4 vol., 1723) are classic. See biography by J. H. Salmon (1969).

Reu (rē'yōō), son of Peleg. Gen.11.18. Ragau: Luke 3.35.

Reuben (rōō'bən), Jacob's eldest son and ancestor of one of the 12 tribes. His intercession for Joseph's life and his guaranteeing the safe return of Benjamin indicate a kindly nature. At the occupation of Palestine his tribe, with that of Gad, was allotted the pasture lands E of the Jordan. To Reuben was given the region adjoining the Dead Sea and S of Gad. After this the Reubenites are unreported until, with Gad, they are carried captive by Tiglathpileser into Assyria. Gen. 29.32; 35.22; 37; 42.22,37; 46.8; 49.3,4; Num. 1.20,21; 2.10; 26.5–10; 32.37; Joshua 22; 1 Chron. 5.26.

Reuchlin, Johann (yō'hän roikh'lən), 1455–1522, German humanist and lawyer, a scholar of Greek and Hebrew, b. Baden. He taught jurisprudence at Tübingen. In 1492 he began the study of Hebrew, and his *Rudimenta Hebraica* (1506) was the first Hebrew grammar written by a Christian. His reputation as a scholar had already been established by the translations from the Greek that he made at Heidelberg. When Johann Pfefferkorn, a Jew who had converted to Christianity, advocated destruction of all Hebrew books, Emperor Maximilian requested Reuchlin's opinion in the matter. Reuchlin suggested that only those Hebrew books which calumniated Christianity should be suppressed and that the Jews should be required to furnish books for the universities, with two chairs of Hebrew learning to be set up in every university in Germany. His decision brought forth a storm of opposition from bigots and obscurantists, which Reuchlin met by his *Augenspiegel* [mirror of the eye] (1511). In this work he attacked Pfefferkorn and drew a distinction between classical works in Hebrew and anti-Christian polemics. A violent controversy developed between the humanists supporting Reuchlin and the clericals and powers of the Inquisition supporting Pfefferkorn. From the struggle emerged the famous defense of Reuchlin, *Episculae obscurorum virorum* [letters of obscure men] by Crotus Rubianus and Ulrich von HUTTEN. Reuchlin, himself, remained a Roman Catholic. In 1521 the Curia suppressed his writings against Pfefferkorn.

Reuel (rēyo͞o'əl). **1** See JETHRO. **2** Son of Esau and Bashemath. Gen. 36.4,10; 1 Chron. 1.35. **3** See DEUEL. **4** Descendant of Benjamin. 1 Chron. 9.8.

Reumah (ro͞o'mə), concubine of Nahor. Gen. 22.24.

Réunion (rāünyôN'), overseas department of France (1971 pop. 455,200), c.970 sq mi (2,510 sq km), one of the Mascarene Islands, in the Indian Ocean c.430 mi (690 km) E of Madagascar. Saint-Denis (the capital) and Le Port (the leading port) are the chief cities. The island is composed mainly of one active and several extinct volcanoes; its highest point is Le Piton des Neiges (10,069 ft/3,069 m). Settlement and cultivation are concentrated in the coastal lowlands. Since the 19th cent. sugar has been by far the island's chief product and export. Réunion was known to the Arabs and was visited by the Portuguese in the early 16th cent. The island was uninhabited until settled by the French c.1642; its present mixed population is descended from the Frenchmen and their East African, Indian, and Indochinese slaves (after 1848, when slavery was abolished, indentured laborers). Most of the inhabitants are Roman Catholic and speak a creole patois. At first a penal colony, Réunion became a post of the French East India Company in 1665. In the 18th cent. the island was an exporter of coffee. It was held by Great Britain from 1810 to 1814. After 1815, when coffee no longer could be produced competitively, sugarcane became the main crop. In 1947 the status of Réunion was changed from a colony to an overseas department. Most of the island's leaders are white, but there is no official system of segregation based on color.

Reus (rĕ'o͞os), city (1970 pop. 59,095), Tarragona prov., NE Spain, on the Mediterranean Sea, in Catalonia. Since the introduction (18th cent.) by English manufacturers of a cotton-spinning industry, Reus has grown into an important commercial and industrial center.

Reuter, Christian (krĭs'tēän roi'tər), 1665–c.1712, German writer of satiric fiction and drama. Reuter's *Schelmuffsky* (1696, tr. 1962) was among the first picaresque novels in German. His plays for the traveling theater, including *Graf Ehrenfried* (1700), *Die frohlockende Spree* [the rejoicing Spree] (1703), and *Letzter Zuruf* [last call] (1705), describe petty bourgeois weaknesses.

Reuter, Fritz (Heinrich Ludwig Christian Friedrich Reuter), 1810–74, German writer. His tales of Mecklenburg life are among the best of German provincial literature. Reuter's political views brought him a death sentence (1833), later commuted to 30 years' imprisonment. Released in the Prussian amnesty of 1840, he led a wretched life until, in the 1850s, he won recognition with novels, tales, and verse in Low German dialect, or Plattdeutsch. His works, characterized by compassion for the poor and acute understanding of provincial people, include *Ut de Franzosentid* (1860; tr. *In the Year '13*, 1867), *Ut mine Stromtid* (1862–64; tr. *Seedtime and Harvest*, 1871), and *Ut Mine Festungstid* [from my prison days] (1863).

Reuter, Baron Paul Julius von (bärōn' poul yo͞o'lyo͞os fən), 1816–99, founder of Reuter's Telegraph Company, b. Kassel, Germany. His original name was Israel Beer Josaphat. First a bank clerk, he started in 1849 a pigeon post service, which bridged a gap in the telegraph line between Aachen, Germany, and Verviers, Belgium. In 1851 he went to England, where he was later naturalized, and soon opened a news office in London. In 1858 he persuaded English newspapers to publish his foreign telegrams. He then extended his influence and soon had worldwide cable connections. In 1865 he converted the Reuters agency into a joint stock company, and he was governing director until 1878. He was named a baron by the duke of Saxe-Coburg-Gotha in 1871. See NEWS AGENCY.

Reuther, Walter Philip (ro͞o'thər), 1907–70, American labor leader, b. Wheeling, W.Va. A tool- and diemaker, he became shop foreman in a Detroit automobile plant, meanwhile completing his high school work and attending college. Discharged because of his union activities, he and his brother Victor spent some years (1932–35) in Europe (including the Soviet Union) and in the Far East. Active in the organization drives (1935–37) of the United Automobile Workers of America (UAW) and in the sit-down strikes, he became director of the union's General Motors department (1939) and union vice president (1942). In World War II, he favored active support of the war by labor and evolved a plan for airplane mass production in automobile plants. In 1946 he was elected president of the UAW and also became a vice president of the Congress of Industrial Organizations (CIO). After 1945 he led the auto workers in several major contests for wage increases and social welfare programs, while gaining undisputed control of the UAW. His importance as an anti-Communist labor leader grew. He was severely wounded by an unidentified assailant in 1948, as was his brother Victor the following year. Reuther succeeded (1952) Philip Murray as president of the CIO. An engineer of the merger (1955) of the CIO with the American Federation of Labor (AFL), he became a vice president, a member of its executive board, and head of its industrial union department. In the following years, Reuther had many disagreements with George Meany, the president of the AFL-CIO. For example, in 1963, Reuther strongly supported the civil rights march on Washington, but the AFL-CIO executive board, led by Meany, would only express sympathy with civil rights objectives; the board refused to endorse the march itself. By 1968, after a dispute with Meany over the direction and structure of the labor movement, Reuther led the UAW out of the AFL-CIO. In 1969, Reuther attempted an ill-fated merger with the Teamsters union (a union he had been instrumental in having removed from the AFL-CIO in 1957); known as the Alliance for Labor Action, it was dissolved in 1972. Reuther was killed in a plane crash. See Frank Cormier and W. J. Eaton, *Reuther* (1970); Jean Gould and Lorena Hickok, *Walter Reuther* (1972).

Reutlingen (roit'lĭng-ən), city (1970 pop. 79,534), Baden-Württemberg, SW West Germany. Manufactures include textiles, paper, leather goods, and machinery. Reutlingen was a free imperial city from the mid-13th cent. until it passed (1802–3) to Württemberg. In 1377 the Swabian League defeated Duke Ulrich of Württemberg there. Reutlingen was the first Swabian city to accept the Protestant Reformation (16th cent.). The Church of St. Mary (13th–14th cent.) is an outstanding example of late German Gothic architecture. The 19th-century economist Friedrich List was born in Reutlingen.

Reval: see TALLINN, USSR.

Revelation or **Apocalypse** (əpŏk'əlĭps), the 27th and last book of the New Testament. It was written A.D. c.95 on Patmos Island by one John, probably during the persecutions of the Roman emperor Domitian. Tradition has identified John with the disciple St. JOHN, but many scholars deny such authorship. Scholars also disagree as to whether this book has common authorship with the Gospel or with Second and Third John. The book is a mysterious prophetic work, consisting mainly of visions that show the overcoming of evil and persecution and the triumph of God and the martyrs. The plan is careful and depends heavily on patterns of sevens. It consists of the prologue (1.1–20); the letters to seven churches in Asia Minor, counseling and warning (2.1–3.22); the opening of the seven seals on the scroll in the hand of God, four of which reveal the Four Horsemen of the Apocalypse (5.1–8.1); the blowing of seven trumpets by angels standing before the throne of God (8.2–11.19); the seven visions, which include the war in heaven between St. Michael and the seven-headed dragon (Satan) and the rising from the sea of the beast with the number 666 (12.1–15.4); the seven plagues (15.5–16.21); the great seven-headed harlot named Babylon, who represents the Roman Empire (17.1–19.10); visions of heaven, including the defeat of Satan, the judgment, and the New Jerusalem (19.11–22.5); and the epilogue (22.6–21). The style is majestic. There is constant allusion to Old Testament prophecies, especially those of Ezekiel, Daniel, and Isaiah. One immediate goal of Revelation was to encourage Christians faced with persecution; but assurance of interpretation stops there. It is not even agreed as to whether the author expected an early fulfillment of his prophecies or intended a more spiritual interpretation. Every period of Christian history has produced new (often bizarre) explanations of the mysteries of the book. See APOCALYPSE. See G. E. Ladd, *A Commentary on the Revelation of John* (1972); D. H. Lawrence, *Apocalypse* (1972).

Revelstoke (rĕv'əlstōk), city (1971 pop. 4,867), SE British Columbia, Canada, on the Columbia River. The city is at the foot of the Selkirk Mts. and is the gateway to Mt. Revelstoke National Park. It is also a railroad division point and a distributing center for a mining and lumbering area.

Reventazón (rāvāntäsōn'), river, c.85 mi (140 km) long, rising in the Meseta Central, E Costa Rica, and flowing NE to the Caribbean Sea, N of Limón. The Reventazón is navigable for a short distance only, but its deep valley through the mountains offers the best access for the railway from San José, the capital, to Limón, the principal port of the country.

revenue: see FINANCE.

reverberatory furnace, horizontal furnace in which material is heated in a shallow hearth by a flame passing overhead. A substantial amount of the heat that the material, or charge, receives is reverberated, or reflected, down onto it from a vaulted furnace roof that is also heated by the flame. The flame is produced by burning coal, gas, or oil. Such furnaces are used to smelt copper and tin ore concentrates.

Revere, Paul, 1735–1818, American silversmith and political leader in the American Revolution, b. Boston. In his father's smithy he learned to work gold and silver, and he became a leading silversmith of New England. He also turned to various other skills—designing, engraving, printing, bell founding, and dentistry. In the French and Indian War he was a soldier, and in the period of growing colonial discontent with British measures after the Stamp Act (1765), he was a fervent anti-British propagandist. He early joined the SONS OF LIBERTY, took part in the BOSTON TEA PARTY, and was a courier (1774) for the Massachusetts committee of correspondence. Revere became a figure of popular history and legend, however, because of his ride on the night of April 18, 1775, to warn the people of the Massachusetts countryside that British soldiers were being sent out in the expedition that, as it turned out, started the American Revolution (see LEXINGTON AND CONCORD, BATTLES OF). William DAWES and Samuel PRESCOTT also rode forth with the news. Revere did not reach his destination at Concord but was captured by the British; nevertheless, it is Revere who is remembered as the midnight rider, chiefly because of the poem by Henry Wadsworth Longfellow. He designed the first seal for the united colonies, designed and printed the first Continental bond issue, and established (1776) a powder mill at Canton, Mass. His military career was not distinguished. On the ill-fated expedition against Penobscot he was arrested for disobeying orders (though a court-martial later acquitted him of the charges), and in 1780 he returned to silversmithing. His shrewdness in other enterprises, particularly the establishment of a copper-rolling and brass-casting foundry at Canton, helped to make his later years very prosperous. See biographies by E. G. Taylor (1930) and Esther Forbes (1942, repr. 1962).

Revere, city (1970 pop. 43,159), Suffolk co., E Mass., a residential suburb of Boston, on Massachusetts Bay; settled c.1630, set off from Chelsea and named for Paul Revere 1871, inc. as a city 1914. It has printing industries and varied manufactures. Revere Beach is a popular resort.

reversion: see ATAVISM.

Revilla Gigedo, Juan Francisco de Güemes y Horcasitas, conde de (hwän fränthēs'kō thā gwā'mās ē ôrkäsē'täs kōn'dā thā rävē'lyä hĕhā'thō), 1682?–1766, Spanish colonial administrator, viceroy of New Spain (1746–55). As captain general of Cuba he engaged in illicit trade in tobacco and amassed a fortune, which he increased in Mexico. His businesslike rule brought new revenues to the Spanish treasury. He encouraged the conquest and settlement of N Mexico, particularly under José de Escandón. His son, **Juan Vicente Güemes Pacheco de Padilla, conde de Revilla Gigedo**, 1740–99, b. Havana, was viceroy of New Spain (1789–94). He gave to the viceroyalty one of the finest administrations of the colonial era. He put the new administrative system of intendancies into working order, improved Mexico City, sent out an expedition that carried the Spanish territorial claims N of the California coast, and brought the revenues of the viceroyalty to their highest point.

Revillagigedo Islands (rāvē'yähĕhā'thō), archipelago in the Pacific Ocean, c.450 mi (720 km) W of Colima state, Mexico. Socorro (110 sq mi/285 sq km) is the largest island. A volcano on San Benedicto island rose suddenly in 1952. The Mexican flag was officially raised over the islands in 1957.

revival, religious, renewal of attention to religious faith and service in a church or community, usually following a period of comparative inactivity and frequently marked by intense fervor. As applied to the Christian religion, the phrase belongs to modern times, dating from the 18th cent.; but such experience is described in scriptural accounts. The development of the Protestant movements in the 14th, 15th, and 16th cent. was in the nature of a series of revivals under the leadership of John WYCLIF, Jan HUSS, Martin LUTHER, John CALVIN, Huldreich ZWINGLI, and others. But revivals, so called, began (c.1737) in Europe with the evangelical awakening in England under John and Charles WESLEY and George WHITEFIELD. Under their direction an army of itinerant and local workers and of missionaries spread the spirit of Methodist evangelism with amazing rapidity over Great Britain, into Ireland, and across the seas. Almost simultaneously with the Methodist movement, the GREAT AWAKENING began in America; given stimulus by Whitefield, revivals were started in 1720 by Theodore Frelinghuysen of New Jersey and in 1734 by Jonathan Edwards of Massachusetts. The newer settlements in the South and West experienced a wave of religious animation characterized by emotional excitement and physical manifestations. The movement was developed c.1797 in Kentucky under the preaching of James McGready. From these meetings held in the open developed the CAMP MEETING. Professional revivalists were Timothy Dwight, grandson of Jonathan Edwards, Lyman Beecher, Asahel Nettleton, and Charles Grandison Finney. The preeminent figure in modern revivalistic history in the United States and Great Britain was Dwight L. MOODY, who, with the singing evangelist Ira D. Sankey, moved vast audiences for more than 25 years. In recent years revival campaigns, which should be distinguished from those of practitioners of FAITH HEALING, have been conducted by B. Fay Mills, Sam Jones, J. Wilbur Chapman, R. A. Torrey, William A. (Billy) Sunday, Gipsy Smith, Aimee Semple McPherson, and Billy Graham. Modern psychologists have devoted particular attention to the states of mind represented in the conversions that result from revivalistic methods. See C. G. Finney, *Autobiography* (1876); William James, *Varieties of Religious Experience* (1902, repr. 1963); F. M. Davenport, *Primitive Traits in Religious Revivals* (1905, repr. 1968); W. W. Sweet, *Revivalism in America* (1944, repr. 1965); William Sargant, *Battle for the Mind* (1957, repr. 1961); T. L. Smith, *Revivalism and Social Reform in Mid-Nineteenth Century America* (1957); B. A. Weisberges, *They Gathered at the River* (1958, repr. 1966); W. G. McLoughlin, *Modern Revivalism* (1959).

revolution, in a political sense, fundamental and violent change in the values, political institutions, social structure, leadership, and policies of a society. The totality of change implicit in the definition of revolution distinguishes it from coups, rebellions, and wars of independence, which involve only partial change. Examples include the French, Russian, Chinese, and Cuban revolutions. The American Revolution, however, is a misnomer. The word *revolution*, borrowed from astronomy, took on its political meaning in 17th-century England, where, paradoxically, it meant a return or restoration of a former situation. It was not until the 18th cent., in the French Revolution, that the word began to be used to mean a new beginning. Since Aristotle, economic inequality has been recognized as an important cause of revolution. Tocqueville pointed out that it was not absolute poverty but poverty relative to other parts of society that contributed to revolutions. The fall of the old order also depends on the ruling elite losing its authority and self-confidence. These conditions are often present in a country that has just fought a debilitating war. Both the Russian and Chinese revolutions in the 20th cent. followed wars. Contemporary ideas about revolution are dominated by the ideas of Karl Marx in which revolution fulfills a crucial function in the development of society by transferring power from a reactionary class to a progressive one. See Crane Brinton, *Anatomy of Revolution* (1938); Hannah Arendt, *On Revolution* (1963); Chalmers Johnson, *Revolutionary Change* (1966); Samuel Huntington, *Political Order in Changing Societies* (1968); John Dunn, *Modern Revolutions* (1972).

revolutions of 1848, in European history. The FEBRUARY REVOLUTION in France gave impetus to a series of revolutionary explosions in Western and Central Europe. The stage was set when the unrest caused by the economic effects of severe crop failures in 1846-47 merged with the discontent caused by political repression of liberal and nationalist aspirations. In Germany, popular demonstrations and uprisings (Feb.-March, 1848) led to the calling of a national parliament (see FRANKFURT PARLIAMENT) to draft a constitution for a united Germany. While the constitution was debated at length, rulers of the German states were able to recover their authority. By 1849, the Frankfurt Parliament and the provisional government it established had collapsed and the old order was restored. The revolution within the Austrian empire followed a similar pattern of initial success and subsequent defeat. In contrast to the situation in Germany, however, revolutionists in the Hapsburg domains (see AUSTRIA, HUNGARY, and BOHEMIA) demanded less central authority and a more autonomous role for the national groups. Lack of cooperation among the revolutionary movements and the loyalty of the armies to old authorities permitted the suppression of the insurgents by armed might. In Italy (see RISORGIMENTO) the demand for expulsion of the Austrians and for national unification found a champion in King CHARLES ALBERT of Sardinia, but again the revolutions were put down by Austrian armies. The revolutions of 1848 failed notably because the two sets of demands—one social and economic, the other liberal and national—were not easily reconciled. Middle-class moderates gained control of the revolutionary movements and resisted the more radical demands of the lower classes, thus losing much of the popular support that was essential to their success. This contributed greatly to the class antagonism of succeeding decades. See studies by Sir L. B. Namier (1948) and Priscilla Robertson (1952).

revolver: see SMALL ARMS.

revue, a stage presentation that originated in the early 19th cent. as a light, satirical commentary on current events. It was rapidly developed, particularly in England and the United States, into an amorphous musical entertainment, retaining a small amount of satire and partaking increasingly of the elements of vaudeville and the pageant. In the United States the revue became noted for its extravagant staging and costumes, its display of showgirls, and its short comedy sketches and popular songs. The best known of this type was the annual *Follies* (1907-c.1930) produced by Florenz ZIEGFELD, which had as its chief rivals Earl Carroll's *Vanities* and George White's *Scandals*. In the late 1920s the revue reverted to its original form as the so-called intimate revue in the works of such writers as Noel Coward. The satirical revue has found extensive audiences in cabarets and coffeehouses as well as on the legitimate stage and on television. Elaborate showgirl revues and comedy acts, often of a satirical nature, are still popular in the casino nightclubs of Las Vegas, Nevada.

Rewa (rä'və), walled city (1971 pop. 69,197), Madhya Pradesh state, central India. It is the administrative center of a district rich in coal, corundum, and limestone. Rewa is a market for timber, cement, and limestone. It has a 19th-century palace and several temples set in a park.

Rewald, John (rē'wôld), 1912-, American art historian, b. Berlin. Rewald emigrated to the United States in 1941. He is recognized as a foremost authority on late 19th-century art. His books include studies of Maillol (1935), Gauguin (1938), Seurat (1943), Bonnard (1948), Cézanne (1948), Pissarro (1963), Manzù (1967), and the standard work, *The History of Impressionism* (1946). He has taught at the Univ. of Chicago since 1964.

Rex cat: see CAT.

Rexroth, Kenneth, 1905-, American poet and critic, b. South Bend, Ind. He was a resident of San Francisco and was associated with the BEAT GENERATION for a short time. Self-educated, he taught himself several languages and made translations, including *One Hundred Poems from the Japanese* (1956) and *The Orchid Boat: Women Poets of China* (with Ling Chung, 1973). He is best known, however, for his poetry, *In What Hour* (1940), *The Phoenix and the Tortoise* (1944), *In Defense of the Earth* (1956), and *New Poems* (1974). He also wrote one volume of verse plays, *Beyond the Mountains* (1951), and several volumes of essays, including *Bird in the Bush* (1959), *Alternative Society: Essays from the Other World* (1970), and *The Elastic Retort: Essays in Literature and Ideas* (1974). See study by Morgan Gibson (1972).

Reyer, Ernest (ĕrnĕst' rāyĕr'), 1823-1909, French composer and critic, whose name originally was Louis Étienne Ernest Rey. Largely self-taught, he was strongly influenced by Berlioz, whom he succeeded as critic of the *Journal des débats*. He composed little besides operas, the most successful of which was *Sigurd* (1884). His last opera, *Salammbô* (1890), was based on Flaubert's novel.

Reyes, Alfonso (älfôn'sō rä'yĕs), 1889-1959, Mexican writer, diplomat, and educator. Reyes is generally recognized as one of the greatest Spanish American writers of his time. After spending several years in Europe, Argentina, and Brazil as a diplomat, he became president of the Colegio de Mexico. Reyes gained international fame for his poetry, narratives, literary criticism, and essays. His *Visión de Anáhuac* (1917) is a long prose poem. His poetry also includes *Huellas* [traces] (1922), *Romance del Río de Enero* (1933), *Yerbas del Tarahumara* (1934), *Golfo de México* (1935), and *Romances* (1945). A classicist both in style and temperament, he brought grace, wit, and prodigious erudition to his essays. His prose works number in the hundreds; some of the most representative are *La experienca literaria* (1942), *El deslinde* [the frontier] (1944), *Mexican Heritage* (in English, 1946), and the series *Simpatías y diferencias* [sympathies and indifferences], *Burlas literarias* [literary spoofs], and *Marginalias*. His more recent works are *Ancorajes* (1951), *Albores* (1960), and *A campo traviesa* [open country] (1960). The complete works of Reyes were published in 14 volumes between 1955 and 1959. See his selected essays (tr. and ed. by Charles Ramsdell 1964); studies by J. W. Robb (1969) and B. B. Aponte (1972).

Reyes, Rafael (räfäĕl' rā'yās), 1850-1921, president of Colombia (1904-9). As a young man, he explored the upper Amazon wilderness with his brother. Later he distinguished himself in the civil wars of 1885 and 1895. Sent to Washington, D.C., in 1903, he was unable to secure redress from the United States for its part in the revolution in Panama. Elected president of Colombia, he assumed dictatorial powers and vigorously pushed the economic development of the country, improving communications, bringing order to the finances, beautifying Bogotá, and encouraging industry. He also put down opposition ruthlessly and remade the constitution to his liking. A treaty with the United States recognizing the independence of Panama awoke widespread popular opposition that brought about his downfall.

Reykholt (rāk'hôlt''), farm, SW Iceland, famous since the Middle Ages as the home of the historian SNORRI STURLUSON, author of the *Prose Edda* (see EDDA).

Reykjavík (rā'kyävēk, rā'kävēk), city (1970 pop. 81,684), capital of Iceland, SW Iceland, on the Faxaflói. It is the center of the cod-fishing industry and the chief commercial and industrial hub of Iceland. Publishing is an important industry. Reykjavík is the seat of the parliament (Althing), of the Lutheran bishop of Iceland, and of the supreme court; there is a university (founded 1911). Among the city's cultural institutions are the national theater and the national museum. One of the city's remarkable features is its heating system, which utilizes nearby hot springs. The founding of Reykjavík by Ingolfur Arnarson, thought to be the first settler in Iceland, is traditionally dated 874. Chartered in 1786, its modern growth began after 1904, when it became the capital. Among its monuments is a statue of Leif Ericsson, given by the Congress of the United States to the people of Iceland in 1930 to commemorate the 1,000th anniversary of the founding of the Althing. Reykjavík has a large airport, but international traffic uses the airport at nearby Keflavík.

Reyles, Carlos (kär'lōs rā'lās), 1868-1938, Uruguayan novelist. A wealthy breeder of horses, Reyles traveled extensively and devoted himself to writing. His impassioned, naturalistic novels include *La raza de Caín* [Cain's race] (1900), showing the influence of Zola. *Beba* (1894) and *El terruño* [the plot of earth] (1916) depict Uruguayan ranch life; *El embrujo de Sevilla* (1922, tr. *Castanets*, 1929) is a prose poem about the Andalusian city. Reyles lost his fortune by 1929. His masterwork, *El Gaucho Florida* (1932), deals with the social upheaval of ranch and GAUCHO life.

Reymont, Władysław Stanisław (vlädĭs' läf stänēs' läf rä'mônt), 1867?-1925, Polish short-story writer and novelist. Reymont's poverty-stricken farm childhood and his early manhood as a touring actor and worker in the provinces provided rich material for his writings. Among his major works are *The Comedienne* (1896, tr. 1920), a story of a wandering theatrical troupe; *The Promised Land* (1899, tr. 1927), a novel attacking modern industrial society; and *The Peasants* (4 vol., 1902-9; tr. 1924-25), the great prose epic of Polish village life. Reymont was awarded the 1924 Nobel Prize in Literature. See study by J. R. Krzyzanowski (1972).

Reynard the Fox (rĕ'nərd, rā'närd), celebrated hero of the medieval beast epics, works predominantly in verse which became increasingly popular after c.1150. They are found chiefly in Latin, French, Low German, Dutch and Flemish, High German, and English. The type probably originated in a German-speaking section of what is now Alsace-Lorraine, whence it passed into France, the Low Countries, and Germany. The summons of Reynard by King Noble (the Lion) to answer accusations by Isengrim the Wolf and other animals forms the nucleus and starting point of the loosely connected tales. Most of the stories reflect in biting satire the peasant's criticism and contempt for the upper classes and the clergy. An episode at once outstanding and typical is the funeral of Reynard, with the pious laments of his late enemies and his devastating resurrection from the grave. Professional minstrels and poets soon found these tales good entertainment and made them popular with the upper and middle classes. The French, who contributed most to the original story, produced *Le Roman de Renart* (c.1175–1250). Caxton translated from a Flemish version his *Historie of Reynart the Foxe* (1481). Modern English versions include T. J. Arnold's translation (1860) of Goethe's *Reinecke Fuchs*, a paraphrase of an older High German version, and William Rose's *Epic of the Beast* (1924). See Kenneth Varty, *Reynard the Fox* (1967); *The History of Reynard the Fox*, tr. by William Caxton, ed. by N. F. Blake (1970).

Reynaud, Paul (pōl rānō'), 1878–1966, French statesman and lawyer. He held several cabinet posts, and after Nov., 1938, as minister of finance in the cabinet of Édouard DALADIER, he pursued an extremely deflationary policy. During World War II he succeeded Daladier as premier in March, 1940. On May 18, as France faced military disaster, he called in Marshal PÉTAIN as vice premier to boost French morale. On June 16 he gave way to Pétain and others who wished to surrender to Germany, and resigned. Imprisoned later in 1940, he was among the defendants at the abortive RIOM war-guilt trial. After the war Reynaud served as finance minister (1948) and vice premier (1953).

Reynolds, John: see RAINOLDS, JOHN.

Reynolds, John Fulton, 1820–63, Union general in the American Civil War, b. Lancaster, Pa. He distinguished himself in the Mexican War. In the Civil War, Reynolds was made (Aug., 1861) a brigadier general of volunteers. In the Seven Days battles (July, 1862), he was captured at Gaines's Mill but was exchanged in time to command a division at the second battle of Bull Run (Aug., 1862). In November he was made commander of the 1st Corps of the Army of the Potomac and promoted to major general. He rendered able service in the battles of Fredericksburg (Dec., 1862) and Chancellorsville (May, 1863). In the GETTYSBURG CAMPAIGN Reynolds directed the fighting on the first day (July 1, 1863) until he was killed. See biography by E. J. Nichols (1958).

Reynolds, Sir Joshua, 1723–92, English portrait painter, b. Devonshire. Long considered historically the most important of England's painters, by his learned example he raised the artist to a position of respect in England. Reynolds studied painting in London and in 1742 began as a portraitist in Devon. He was able to study the Italian masters when Commodore Keppel, a friend, took him to Italy in 1749. After three years of study and travel, Reynolds returned and took London by storm. Intensely ambitious, Reynolds used his wit and charm as well as his artistic talents to advance himself, and within a year he was besieged with portrait commissions and was employing assistants. He maintained a gallery not only of his own works but also those of old masters whose paintings he bought and sold. He entertained the world of wealth and fashion and the great literary figures of the day. When the Royal Academy was founded in 1768, Reynolds was inevitably elected president and was knighted the following year. His annual discourses before the Academy have literary distinction and are a significant exposition of academic style, propounding eclectic generalization over direct observation, and allusion to the classical past over the present. The Grand Style, thus proclaimed, was of enormous influence in the development of English portraiture. At 59, Reynolds had a paralytic stroke but recovered sufficiently to continue his work for several years. Before he lost his sight (1789), his style had become warmer and less formal, having been influenced by Rubens. Reynolds painted more than 2,000 portraits and historical paintings, depicting almost every notable person of his time. He often used experimental painting methods, which resulted in works now poorly preserved. His portraits of Commodore Keppel, Dr. Johnson, Lady Caroline Howard, Mrs. Siddons, Sterne, Goldsmith, Garrick, Gibbon, and Edmund Burke are among the many fine examples that are of historical interest. Reynolds's works are in nearly every major museum in the western world. He is best represented in the National Gallery, London, but examples of his work are to be seen in the Metropolitan Museum of Art; the Museum of Fine Arts, Boston; the Cleveland Museum of Art; and the Art Institute of Chicago. See his letters (ed. by F. W. Hilles, 1929) and his *Discourses on Art* (ed. by R. Wark, 1959, repr. 1965); studies by Ellis Waterhouse (1941 and 1973).

Reynolds, Osborne, 1842–1912, British mechanical engineer. He was educated at Cambridge and became (1868) the first professor of engineering at the Univ. of Manchester, where his courses attracted a number of outstanding students. He developed the theory of the radiometer and determined by direct measurement the mechanical equivalent of heat. Reynolds made many contributions to theoretical engineering. His work on fluid dynamics includes the introduction of the dimensionless REYNOLDS NUMBER.

Reynoldsburg (rĕn'əlzbûrg''), city (1970 pop. 13,921), Franklin and Licking counties, central Ohio, a residential suburb of Columbus; inc. 1839, as a city 1961. It was settled (c.1805) on lands reserved for Canadian refugees who had supported Americans in the Revolutionary War.

Reynolds number [for Osborne Reynolds], dimensionless quantity associated with the smoothness of flow of a fluid. It is an important quantity used in aerodynamics and hydraulics. At low velocities fluid flow is smooth, or laminar, and the fluid can be pictured as a series of parallel layers, or lamina, moving at different velocities. The fluid FRICTION between these layers gives rise to VISCOSITY. As the fluid flows more rapidly, it reaches a velocity, known as the critical velocity, at which the motion changes from laminar to turbulent, with the formation of eddy currents and vortices that disturb the flow. The Reynolds number for the flow of a fluid of density ρ and viscosity η through a pipe of diameter d is given by $R=\rho d v_c/\eta$, where v_c is the critical velocity. The Reynolds number for laminar flow in cylindrical pipes is about 1,000.

Rezaiyeh (rĕzäē'yə), city (1966 pop. 110,749), capital of West Azerbaijan prov., NW Iran, near Lake Rezaiyeh. It is the trade center for a fertile agricultural region where fruit and tobacco are grown. An important town by the 9th cent., Rezaiyeh was seized by the Oghuz Turks (11th cent.), sacked by the Seljuk Turks (1184), and later occupied a number of times by the Ottoman Turks. Rezaiyeh was the seat of the first U.S. Christian mission in Iran (1835). Around 1900 Christians made up more than 40% of the city's population; however, most of the Christians fled in 1918, and many who remained were massacred by Kurds. The city was formerly called Urmia and is also known as Rezaieh.

Rezaiyeh, Lake, shallow salt lake, 1,815 sq mi (4,701 sq km), c.90 mi (140 km) long and 50 mi (80 km) wide, NW Iran; alt. 4,180 ft (1,275 m). The largest lake in Iran, it has no outlet and receives the drainage of the surrounding mountains. The lake was formerly called Urmia.

Rezanov, Nikolai Petrovich (nyĭkəlī' pētrô'vĭch ryĕzä'nəf), 1764–1807, Russian trader, an official of the RUSSIAN AMERICAN COMPANY. He headed an expedition to Alaska in 1803. There he found (1805) the settlement at Sitka in desperate need of food and decided to go to California to obtain supplies. He reached (1806) what is today San Francisco and succeeded in his mission partly because of a romantic attachment to Doña Concepción, daughter of the commandant, José Darío Argüello. He took the supplies to Sitka but died on his return trip to Russia. See Hector Chevigny, *Lost Empire* (1937, repr. 1958).

Reza Shah Pahlevi (rē'zä shä pä'ləvē), 1877–1944, shah of Iran (1925–41). He began his career as an army officer and gained a reputation for great valor and leadership. He headed a coup d'etat in 1921 and became prime minister of the new regime in 1923. He negotiated the evacuation (1921) of the Russian troops and (1924) of the British forces stationed in Iran since World War I. Virtually a dictator, Reza Khan deposed (1925) AHMAD MIRZA, the last shah of the Kajar, or Qajar, dynasty, and was proclaimed shah of Iran. He changed his name to Reza Shah Pahlevi, thus founding the Pahlevi dynasty, and in 1935 officially changed the name of Persia to its more traditional name, Iran. Reza Shah introduced many reforms, reorganizing the army, government administration, and finances. He abolished all special rights granted to foreigners, thus gaining real independence for Iran. Under his rule the Trans-Iranian RR was built, the Univ. of Tehran was established, and industrialization was stepped-up. In World War II his rapprochement with the Germans was protested by the Allies, and in 1941 British and Russian forces invaded and occupied Iran. Forced to abdicate in favor of his son, Muhammad Reza Shah, he died in exile in South Africa.

Rezekne (rä'zĕknə), Ger. *Rositten*, city (1967 est. pop. 29,000), NW European USSR, in Latvia, on the Rezekne River. It is a rail junction and agricultural market center and has food-processing, brickmaking, and linen industries. Rezekne developed around a castle that was built in 1285 by the LIVONIAN BROTHERS OF THE SWORD on the site of an ancient settlement. The city passed to the Polish-Lithuanian state in 1569 and to Russia during the first partition of Poland in 1772. It was incorporated into newly independent Latvia in 1918.

Rezeph (rē'zĕf), ancient city, probably to be identified with Rasafa, E of Palmyra in the Euphrates valley. 2 Kings 19.12; Isa. 37.12.

Rezia (rēzī'ə), son of Ulla the Asherite. 1 Chron. 7.39.

Rezin (rē'zĭn). **1** Syrian king who was defeated and killed by the Assyrian king Tiglathpileser. 2 Kings 15.37; 16.5–9. **2** Family that returned from the Exile. Ezra 2.48; Neh. 7.50.

Rezon (rē'zŏn), founder of a dynasty in Damascus and adversary of Solomon. 1 Kings 11.23–25.

Rh, chemical symbol of the element RHODIUM.

Rhadamanthus (răd''əmăn'thəs), in Greek mythology, son of Zeus and Europa. Renowned for his justice on earth, the gods made him one of the judges of Hades.

Rhaeto-Romanic (rē'tō-rōmăn'ĭk), generic name for several related dialects of the Romance group of the Italic subfamily of the Indo-European family of languages (see ROMANCE LANGUAGES). These dialects are now considered sufficiently similar to form a single unit in the Romance group. The principal Rhaeto-Romanic dialects are Romansh, Ladin, and Friulian. Romansh has about 40,000 speakers in SE Switzerland and was recognized in that country in 1937 as a national language, coofficial with German, French, and Italian. Ladin is the tongue of some 20,000 persons in the Italian Tyrol, and Friulian is spoken by approximately 500,000 in Friuli, a region of NE Italy.

Rhagae: see RAGES.

Rhangavis, Alexandros Rizos: see RANGABE.

Rhazes (rä'zēz) or **Rasis** (rä'sĭs,-zĭs), 860–932, Persian physician. He was chief physician at the Baghdad hospital. An observant clinician, he formulated the first known description of smallpox as distinguished from measles in a work known as *Liber de pestilentia* (tr. *A Treatise on Smallpox and Measles,* 1848). His works were widely circulated in Arabic and Greek versions and were published in Latin in the 15th cent. They include a textbook of medicine called *Almansor* and an encyclopedia of medicine compiled posthumously from his papers and known as *Liber continens.*

rhea (rē'ə), common name for a South American bird of the order Rheiformes, which superficially resembles the ostrich. Weighing from 44 to 55 lb (20–25 kg) and standing up to 60 in. (152 cm) tall, the rhea is slightly smaller than the ostrich and lacks that bird's extravagant plumelike tail feathers. The rhea also differs from the unrelated ostrich in structure of the palate, pelvis, and foot. It is yellow and gray above, with a black head and dirty-white underside. The common rhea (*Rhea americana*) is found from northeastern Brazil to Argentina. The somewhat smaller Darwin's rhea (*Pterocnemia pennata*) occurs from Patagonia to the high Andes. The rhea is typically a creature of the pampas and savannas and may often be found feeding in mixed herds along with cattle or guanaco, occupying an ecological niche similar to that of the ostrich and the zebra of Africa. Rheas feed on several kinds of plants, insects, and small vertebrates. While the old males tend to stay solitary, the young male is aggressive and highly polygamous, gathering about itself from three to seven hens. The nest is built in a dry and protected area, preferably near water. The male excavates a shallow hole with his bill, lines it with dry vegetable matter, and assumes all the incubation duties. He may incubate as many as 50 eggs, produced by a number of females over a period of weeks. Incubation takes from 35 to 40 days. The eggs, lemon yellow when laid, or greenish in the case of Darwin's rhea, weigh up to 2 lb (almost 1 kg) each. When hatched, the chicks are gray with darker stripes. The rhea is one of the flat-breastboned, or ratite, flightless birds. Rheas are classified in the phylum CHORDATA, subphylum Vertebrata, class Aves, order Rheiformes, family Rheidae.

Rhea, in astronomy, one of the 10 known moons, or natural satellites, of SATURN.

Rhea, in Greek religion, a Titan. She was the wife and sister of CRONUS, by whom she bore Zeus, Poseidon, Pluto, Hestia, Hera, and Demeter. She eventually helped Zeus overthrow Cronus. Her worship, which was orgiastic and associated with fertility rites, was particularly prominent in Crete. The Greeks often identified her with Gaea and Cybele. In Rome, Rhea was worshiped as Magna Mater and identified with Ops. See GREAT MOTHER OF THE GODS.

Rhea Silvia: see ROMULUS.

rhebok: see MARSH ANTELOPE.

Rhee, Syngman (sĭng'mən rē), 1875–1965, Korean statesman, president of the Republic of Korea (1948–60). Early an advocate of Korean independence, he led a demonstration against the Japanese in 1897 and was condemned to life imprisonment but was released under an amnesty. Rhee went to the United States, where he studied at Harvard and Princeton, and after returning to Korea went to Hawaii for a time. In 1919 a group of conspirators for Korean independence made him president of a government in exile, and he never ceased working for the cause. After World War II he became a leader in South Korea under the U.S. occupation, and in 1948 he became first president of the Republic of Korea, which claimed the right to rule over all Korea. He was reelected in 1952. When, on July 27, 1953, a truce was reached in the Korean War, Rhee maintained that all Korea should be united. In 1954 he visited the United States, and in 1956 he was elected to a third term as president. There was increasing opposition in Korea to his administration, however; economic conditions worsened, corruption in government was rampant, and Rhee became more autocratic. Reelected in 1960, Rhee was accused of rigging the election. In May, 1960, following rioting, he was forced out of office and into exile in Hawaii. See biographies by R. C. Allen (1960) and R. T. Oliver (1954, repr. 1973).

Rhegium (rē'jēəm), ancient city, S Italy, on the Strait of Messina. It is the modern REGGIO DI CALABRIA. Founded (c.720 B.C.) as a colony of Chalcis, many Messenians later settled there. It was powerful until its defeat and destruction (386 B.C.) by Dionysius the Elder of Syracuse. The Romans, who favored it, called the city Rhegium Julium. It is mentioned in Acts 28.13. The name is also spelled Regium.

Rheims (rēmz), Fr. *Reims* (răNs), city (1968 pop. 158,634), Marne dept., NE France, in Champagne. The center of the CHAMPAGNE industry, Rheims is situated amid large vineyards. Before the champagne industry took on its present proportions in the 18th cent., the chief products of Rheims were woolen textiles. They are still important, and there are many other industries. As Durocotorum, the city of Remi, it was one of the most important cities in Roman Gaul. The see of an archbishopric since the 8th cent., Rheims continued to play an exceptional role in French history. Clovis I was baptized and crowned (496) king of all Franks in the cathedral by St. Remi, the bishop of Rheims, and it became customary after Louis VII (1137) for the kings of France to be crowned there. In the present cathedral (13th–14th cent.), Joan of Arc stood next to Charles VII when, at her instance, he was crowned in 1429. The cathedral is a monument of French Gothic architecture. During World War I, heavy bombing, which nearly leveled the city, destroyed the interior, including most of the irreplaceable stained-glass windows. Restored, partly with funds from the Rockefeller Foundation, it was reopened in 1938. The town hall (17th cent.) and the old Church of St. Remi (11th–16th cent.) were also gravely damaged. In World War II, on May 7, 1945, German emissaries signed the unconditional surrender of Germany at Allied headquarters in Rheims. Rheims has a university founded by Pope Paul III in 1547. Jean Baptiste Colbert and St. John Baptist de la Salle were born in Rheims.

Rhein: see RHINE, river.

Rheinberger, Josef (yō'zĕf rīn'bĕrgər), 1839–1901, German composer; studied at the Munich Conservatory, where he later taught. An eclectic, late romantic composer, he wrote 20 organ sonatas and Masses, among them the eight-part Festive Mass for Pope Leo XIII. These have outlived his orchestral and stage works.

Rheinfelden (rīn'fĕldən), town (1970 pop. 6,866), Aargau canton, N Switzerland, on the Rhine River, opposite the German town of the same name. Although it has one of the largest hydroelectric plants in Europe, Rheinfelden is chiefly noted as a tourist center with saline baths. It was the scene of almost continuous fighting in the THIRTY YEARS WAR. There, in 1638, Bernhard of Saxe-Weimar defeated the imperial troops and Henri de Rohan was killed.

Rheinhausen (rīn'hou"zən), city (1970 pop. 69,430), North Rhine-Westphalia, W West Germany, a port on the Rhine River; chartered 1934. Manufactures of this industrial city include metal products, machinery, and textiles.

Rheinland: see RHINELAND.

Rheinsberg (rīns'bĕrk), town, Potsdam dist., N central East Germany. It is a tourist and manufacturing center. The rococo palace in Rheinsberg was the residence (1736–40) of Crown Prince Frederick, later FREDERICK II of Prussia, who devoted his quasi-exile there to music, literature, and study.

Rhenish Hesse: see HESSE, Germany.

Rhenish Palatinate: see PALATINATE.

Rhenish Prussia: see RHINE PROVINCE.

Rhenish Slate Mountains, Ger. *Rheinisches Schiefergebirge*, extensive mountainous plateau, W West Germany, lying between W Hesse state and the borders of Belgium and Luxembourg. It comprises the Eifel, Hunsrück, Taunus, and Westerwald mts., which flank both sides of the Mosel and Lahn rivers. The plateau is dissected by the Rhine River and its tributaries.

rhenium (rē'nēəm), metallic chemical element; symbol Re; at. no. 75; at. wt. 186.2; m.p. about 3180°C; b.p. about 5625°C; sp. gr. 21.02 at 20°C; valence −1, +2, +3, +4, +5, +6, or +7. Rhenium is a very dense, high-melting, silver-white metal. Of the elements, only carbon and tungsten have higher melting points and only iridium, osmium, and platinum are more dense. The chemical properties of rhenium are like those of technetium, the element above it in group VIIb of the PERIODIC TABLE. A number of rhenium compounds are known, among them halides, oxides, and sulfides. The heptavalent oxide, Re_2O_7, on dissolving in water forms perrhenic acid, $HReO_4$, from which many other compounds are prepared. Rhenium is not found uncombined in nature. It is widely distributed in the earth's crust in platinum and molybdenum ores and in many minerals, but is not abundant. In the United States rhenium is obtained commercially as a by-product of the roasting of copper sulfide ores from Arizona and Utah. Rhenium metal is obtained as a powder by reduction of its compounds with hydrogen. The powder is compacted, sintered, annealed, and formed into wire, foil, rods, or strips. Rhenium is used in alloys with tungsten; it gives improved ductility and high-temperature strength. These alloys are used for electrical contacts, electronic filaments, thermocouples, and in photographic flash lamps. Rhenium forms a superconductive alloy with molybdenum. Rhenium is used as a catalyst for hydrogenation and petroleum cracking. Based on his PERIODIC LAW, Mendelejeff predicted the existence of rhenium, which he called dvi-manganese. The accuracy of prediction of the properties of the element led to its discovery in 1925 by Walter Nodack, Ida Tacke, and Otto Berg in platinum ores and the mineral columbite.

rheology (rēŏl'əjē), branch of physics dealing with the deformation and flow of matter. It is particularly concerned with the properties of matter that determine its behavior when a mechanical FORCE is exerted on it. Rheology is distinguished from fluid dynamics (see FLUID MECHANICS) in that it is concerned with all three of the traditional STATES OF MATTER rather than only with liquids and gases. Unlike polymer physics it is concerned with macroscopic properties and behavior and not with molecular structure. The results of rheology provide a mathematical description of the viscoelastic behavior of matter (see ELASTICITY; VISCOSITY). Applications of rheology are important in many areas of industry, involving metals, plastics, and many other materials.

rheostat (rē'əstăt"), device whose resistance to electric current depends on the position of some mechanical element or control in the device. Typically a rheostat consists of a resistance element equipped with two contacts, or terminals, by which it is attached to a circuit: a fixed contact at one end and a sliding contact that can be moved along the resistance element. Electric current enters and leaves the resistance element through the contacts. By moving the sliding contact toward or away from the fixed contact, the length of the resistance element through which the current travels can be decreased or increased. In this way the current through the circuit can be increased or decreased. Rheostats are widely used for such purposes as controlling the speed of electric motors and dimming electric lights, but they are being replaced in many applications by systems based on semiconductor devices that waste far less power. See POTENTIOMETER.

Rhesa (rē'sə), ancestor of Joseph. Luke 3.27.

rhesus factor: see RH FACTOR.

rhesus monkey: see MACAQUE.

Rheticus (Georg Joachim von Lauchen) (rā'tĕko͝os, gā'ôrk yōä'khĭm fən lou'khən), 1514–76, German astronomer, mathematician, and first disciple of Copernicus. In 1540 he printed a summary of heliocentric ideas in the *Narratio prima* and in 1542 supervised publication of the trigonometric sections of Copernicus's masterpiece *De revolutionibus*. He subsequently persuaded Copernicus to publish (1543) the entire work. To mathematics he contributed *Opus palatinum de triangulis*, in which for the first time trigonometric functions were related to angles rather than to the arcs of circles.

rhetoric: see ORATORY.

Rhett, Robert Barnwell, 1800–1876, American politician, b. Beaufort, S.C. His family changed its name from Smith to Rhett (after a colonial ancestor) in 1837. A lawyer, he was a state legislator, state attorney general (1832), U.S. Representative (1837–49), and Senator (1850–52). Extremely pro-Southern in his views, he split (1844) with John C. Calhoun to lead the movement for separate state action on the tariff, an act indicative of his belief that the Federal government would not protect Southern interests. Rhett was one of the leading FIRE-EATERS at the Nashville Convention of 1850, which failed to endorse his aim of secession for the whole South. When South Carolina passed (1852) an ordinance merely declaring the state's right to secede, he felt repudiated by his state and resigned (1852) his Senate seat. He continued to express his rabid secessionist sentiments through the Charleston *Mercury*, edited by his son. Rhett was a member of the South Carolina secession convention in 1860 and a representative of his state to the Southern convention that drew up the Confederate constitution. Receiving no office in the Confederate government, he returned to South Carolina, where he sharply criticized the policies of President Jefferson Davis. See biography by L. A. White (1931, repr. 1965).

rheumatic fever (ro͞omăt'ĭk), systemic inflammatory disease, extremely variable in its manifestation, severity, duration, and aftereffects. It is frequently followed by serious heart disease, especially when there are repeated attacks. Rheumatic heart disease accounts for practically all heart disease in persons under 20 years of age. Rheumatic fever has its onset early in life and is closely related to a preceding streptococcal infection (e.g., streptococcal tonsillitis or pharyngitis). Some of its symptoms are tenderness and inflammation about the joints, fever, nosebleeds, and skin rash. If inflammation of the heart, or myocarditis, is mild, there is no permanent heart damage. But if the valves of the heart become inflamed, they may become scarred and deformed, permanently impairing their function. Such heart damage may sometimes be corrected by surgery. Treatment of rheumatic fever is with penicillin, salicylates, and cortisone; extended rest is usually necessary. Rheumatic fever may be prevented by prompt treatment of all streptococcal infections. Cardiac damage may possibly be avoided if prophylactic measures are taken after a first attack of rheumatic fever, i.e., maintenance doses of sulfa drugs or penicillin for as long as five years, or in some cases for life, to discourage streptococcal infections and recurrences of rheumatic fever.

rheumatism (ro͞o'mətĭzəm), general term for a number of disorders that cause inflammation and pain in muscles, bones, joints, or nerves. In common usage ARTHRITIS, BURSITIS, NEURITIS, and GOUT are frequently designated by this term.

Rheydt (rīt), city (1970 pop. 100,077), North Rhine-Westphalia, W West Germany. It forms a twin city with MÖNCHENGLADBACH. Rheydt is an industrial center; its manufactures include cotton, silk, and velvet textiles as well as machinery, chemicals, and shoes. It was first mentioned in 1180 but was not chartered until 1856. The city was heavily damaged in World War II. Nearby is the Renaissance-style Rheydt palace (1567–81), now a museum.

Rh factor, protein substance present in the red blood cells of most people, capable of inducing intense antigenic reactions. The Rh, or rhesus, factor was discovered in 1940 by K. Landsteiner and A. S.

Wiener, when it was observed that the injection of blood from a rhesus monkey into rabbits caused an antigenic reaction in the serum component of rabbit blood (see IMMUNITY). When blood from humans was tested with the rabbit serum, the red blood cells of 85% of the humans tested agglutinated (clumped together). It was determined that the red blood cells of the 85% (later found to be 85% of the white population and a larger percentage of blacks and Asians) contained the same factor present in rhesus monkey blood; such blood was typed Rh positive. The blood of the remaining 15% lacked the factor and was typed Rh negative. Under ordinary circumstances the presence or lack of the Rh factor has no bearing on life or health. It is only when the two blood types are mingled in an Rh-negative individual that difficulty arises, since the Rh factor acts as an antigen in Rh-negative persons, causing the production of antibodies. Besides the Rh factors, human red blood cells contain a large number of additional antigenic substances that have been classified into 19 known blood group systems (see BLOOD GROUPS); however, the Rh system is the only one, aside from the ABO system, that is of major importance in blood transfusions. If Rh-positive blood is transfused into an Rh-negative person, the latter will gradually develop antibodies called anti-Rh agglutinins, that attach to the Rh-positive red blood cells, causing them to agglutinate. Destruction of the cells (hemolysis) eventually results. If the Rh-negative recipient is given additional transfusions of Rh-positive blood, the concentration of anti-Rh agglutinins may become high enough to cause a serious or fatal reaction. The same type of immune reaction occurs in the blood of an Rh-negative mother who is carrying an Rh-positive fetus. (The probability of this situation occurring is high if the father is Rh positive.) Some of the infant's blood may enter the maternal circulation, causing the formation of agglutinins against the fetal red blood cells. Although the first baby is not harmed, if the mother's agglutinins pass into the circulation of subsequent fetuses, they may destroy the fetal red blood cells, causing the severe hemolytic disease of newborns known as ERYTHROBLASTOSIS FETALIS.

Rhine (rīn), Du. *Rijn,* Fr. *Rhin,* Ger. *Rhein,* Lat. *Rhenus,* principal river of Europe, c.820 mi (1,320 km) long. It rises in the Swiss Alps and flows generally north, passing through or bordering on Switzerland, Liechtenstein, Austria, West Germany, France, and the Netherlands before emptying into the North Sea. The river carries more traffic than any other waterway in the world and is navigable by ocean-going vessels as far as Mannheim, West Germany, by river barges to Basel, Switzerland, and by pleasure craft and sightseeing boats on navigable stretches as far as Rheinfelden, Switzerland. Its important tributaries are the Aare, Neckar, Main, Moselle, and Ruhr rivers; canals link the river with the Maas, Rhône-Saône, Marne, and Danube (via the Main) valleys. The Rhine's highest source, the Hinter Rhine, issues from the Rheinwaldhorn Glacier more than 11,000 ft (3,353 m) above sea level and joins the Vorder Rhine, flowing from Lake Tuma, to form the Rhine proper at Reichenau, S of Chur, Switzerland. From Chur the river flows N to the Lake of Constance and then W over the 65-ft (20-m) Rhine Falls at Schaffhausen (harnessed for hydroelectric power by the Swiss) to Basel, c.500 mi (800 km) from the North Sea. At Basel the Rhine becomes the Upper Rhine of the Germans and turns sharply N to Mainz across the broad-floored Rhine rift valley, a large graben, or down-faulted block, between the Black Forest and the Vosges mts. Navigation in this section is by way of a lateral canal through France as far as Strasbourg; below Strasbourg the river bed has been improved for navigation. Below Mainz, at Bingen, West Germany, the Rhine leaves the rift valley and flows for c.80 mi (130 km) across the Rhenish Slate Mts. in a steep gorge, famous for its scenery, vineyards and superb wines, castles surviving from times when tolls were levied on the river's traffic, and legendary landmarks such as the Lorelei and the Drachenfels. Beyond Bonn the river becomes the Lower Rhine of the Germans and emerges onto the North German Plain as a broad, sluggish, and increasingly polluted river flowing on a bed of ancient deltaic deposits left by ancestors of the modern river. Just below Emmerich, on the border with the Netherlands, the modern delta begins, and the Rhine breaks up into two major distributaries, the Lek and the Waal. The Lek, which becomes the Nieuwe Maas, continues W to Rotterdam and then by the canalized New Waterway enters the North Sea at Hoek van Holland (Hook of Holland). The Waal, which merges with the waters of the Maas to form the Merwede, also flows west; the Merwede and the Bergsche Maas join to form the Hollandschdiep, an arm of the North Sea, 6 mi (9.6 km) SE of Dordrecht. A third distributary, known as the Crooked Rhine, leads to Utrecht and continues west to the sea as the Old Rhine; it is linked with Amsterdam by the Amsterdam-Rhine Canal and thence by the North Sea Canal to the North Sea. The Rhine was declared free to international navigation in 1868, and in 1919 navigation of the river between Basel and Krimpen, on the Lek, and Gorinchem, on the Waal, was placed under the authority of the Central Rhine Commission, with headquarters at Strasbourg. Navigation above Basel is controlled jointly by Switzerland and West Germany. Coal, coke, grain, timber, and iron ore are the principal cargoes carried on the river. Rotterdam is the chief outlet to the North Sea, and Duisburg, the outlet for the Ruhr industrial region, is the leading river port. See Goronwy Rees, *The Rhine* (1967); Walter Marsden, *The Rhineland* (1973).

Rhine, Confederation of the: see CONFEDERATION OF THE RHINE.

Rhinebeck, village (1970 pop. 2,336), Dutchess co., SE N.Y., in the foothills of the Berkshire Mts. near the Hudson River; settled before 1700, inc. 1834. It is the site of Beekman Arms, said to be the oldest hotel in the United States, and of a pre-Revolutionary Dutch Reformed church and cemetery.

Rhine Canals. Among the chief canals linking the Rhine with other river systems are the Rhine-Rhône Canal, 217 mi (349 km) long (built 1784–1833, now unimportant), connecting with the Rhône River through the Saône River; the Rhine-Marne Canal, 195 mi (314 km) long (built 1841–52); and the Dortmund-Ems Canal, 165 mi (266 km) long (built 1892–99), and the Rhine-Herne Canal, 24 mi (39 km) long (built 1907–14), connecting the Rhine with the West German port of Emden. The Rhine-Main-Danube Canal (opened 1968) links waterway systems between the North Sea and the Black Sea.

Rhineland (rīn'lănd″), Ger. *Rheinland,* region of W West Germany, along the Rhine River. The term is sometimes used to designate only the former RHINE PROVINCE of Prussia, but in its general meaning it also includes the Rhenish PALATINATE, Rhenish and S HESSE, and W BADEN. (For a description, see RHINE.) Cologne, Mainz, and Ludwigshafen are among the chief cities. The Treaty of Versailles (1919) after World War I provided for the Allied occupation of most of the region; the RUHR district was occupied by French and Belgian forces from 1923 to 1925. Largely as a result of the efforts of the German foreign minister, Gustav STRESEMANN, the last occupation troops (who were French) withdrew from the Rhineland in June, 1930, five years before the terminal date set by the treaty. The Treaty of Versailles had also provided that after Germany recovered the occupied territories, it was to maintain no fortifications on the left bank of the Rhine and within a zone extending 31 mi (50 km) E of the Rhine. Germany specifically reaffirmed those conditions in the Locarno Pact of 1925. In March, 1936, however, the National Socialist (Nazi) government of Germany began to remilitarize the Rhineland, and at the same time Hitler denounced the Locarno Pact. The League of Nations censured Germany, but took no further action. The German fortifications in the Rhineland—the so-called Siegfried Line—were an extensive system of defenses in depth, which were penetrated by the Allies in World War II only after very heavy fighting. The Rhineland was the scene of the Rhenish separatist movement, whose leaders staged uprisings in Düsseldorf, Bonn, Koblenz, Wiesbaden, and Mainz, and proclaimed a Rhineland republic at Aachen in 1923; the movement, however, collapsed in 1924.

Rhineland-Palatinate (rīn'lănd pəlăt'ĭnĭt″), Ger. *Rheinland-Pfalz,* state (1970 pop. 3,645,000), 7,658 sq mi (19,834 sq km), W West Germany. Mainz is the capital. The state was formed in 1946 by the merger of the Rhenish PALATINATE, Rhenish Hesse, the southern portion of the former RHINE PROVINCE of Prussia (including Koblenz and Trier), and a small part of the former Prussian province of Hesse-Nassau. Rhineland-Palatinate borders on France and the Saarland in the south and on Luxembourg and Belgium in the west. It is drained by the Rhine and Moselle (Mosel) rivers and includes the Hunsrück and Eifel ranges and other divisions of the Rhenish Slate Mts. The majority of the working population is employed in industry, which is centered in Ludwigshafen, Pirmasens, Kaiserslautern, and Zweibrücken. Grain, potatoes, sugar beets, fruit, and tobacco are grown in the fertile Rhine plain. Some of the most famous West German vineyards are found in the Moselle and Rhine valleys in Rhineland-Palatinate; these include the celebrated stretch of vineyards, known as the Weinstrasse, that runs parallel to the Rhine. Bad Ems and Bad Kreuznach are noted spas. Although the state has as yet little historic unity, it does include the historic centers of Mainz, Speyer, Trier, and Worms.

Rhine Province, Ger. *Rheinprovinz,* former province of Prussia, W West Germany. The province was also known as Rhenish Prussia and as the RHINELAND. The northern section of the former province (which contained part of the industrial RUHR district) is now included in the state of North Rhine-Westphalia, and the southern section (with its famous wine districts along the Moselle and Rhine rivers) is in Rhineland-Palatinate. The province bordered in the W on the Netherlands, Belgium, and Luxembourg and in the S on France. Koblenz (the former capital), Cologne, Düsseldorf, Aachen, and Wuppertal were among the chief cities. The region is traversed by the Rhine, Moselle, and Wupper rivers and by the lower course of the Ruhr. The Rhenish Slate Mts. are in the south. After the breakup (11th cent.) of the duchy of Lower Lorraine (see LOTHARINGIA), of which the area was a part, the region split into more than 100 ecclesiastic and secular fiefs; Aachen and Cologne became free imperial cities. Chief among the territorial princes were the archbishops of Cologne and Trier and the dukes of Cleves, who also absorbed the duchies of Jülich and Berg. In 1614, Jülich and Berg passed to the dukes palatine of Neuburg (later electors palatine), while Cleves went to the electors of Brandenburg (later kings of Prussia). As a result of the French Revolutionary Wars, France annexed the entire territory W of the Rhine, while the territory E of the Rhine was constituted (1803) the duchy (after 1806, grand duchy) of Berg. The award of the entire territory to Prussia at the Congress of Vienna (1814–15) represented the greatest Prussian territorial gain since the Partitions of Poland. At first divided into two provinces, the entire region was constituted the Rhine Province in 1824. One of the strongholds of Roman Catholicism in Germany, the province played an important part in the Kulturkampf later in the century. Under the Treaty of Versailles (1919), the border territories of Eupen and of Malmedy and Moresnet were ceded to Belgium, and the southernmost corner of the province was included in the Saar Territory. These were recovered by Germany after 1935, but the status quo as of 1920 (with minor modifications) was restored in 1945 after World War II and prior to the formation of the Federal Republic of Germany.

Rhinns of Galloway: see GALLOWAY, Scotland.

rhinoceros, massive hoofed mammal of Africa, India, and SE Asia, characterized by one or two horns made of congealed hair on the snout. The rhinoceros family, along with the horse and tapir families, forms the order of odd-toed hoofed mammals. The skin of the rhinoceros is extremely thick, nearly hairless in most species, and deeply folded in some. The legs are stout and rather short and end in broad feet, each with three toes. Each toe bears a small hoof. Rhinoceroses are strictly vegetarian animals, browsers or grazers according to the species. Most live near water and bathe frequently; all swim well. They have poor vision but good hearing and a good sense of smell. Of low intelligence, they are generally placid, but they are unpredictable and may charge with great speed and force if irritated; there is a case on record of a black rhinoceros derailing a train. Mostly solitary animals, they feed by night and in the early morning and evening; they rest in shady spots during the heat of the day. They are often accompanied by small birds, called tickbirds, that feed on parasites in their skin and, by their cries, alert them to danger. Once much more widespread, rhinoceroses are rapidly diminishing in range and numbers; this is due in part to the encroachment of settlements and agriculture on the river valleys that have been their major habitat, and in part to the demand for their horns. These are believed, especially in China, to have aphrodisiac properties and have commanded a very high price for many centuries. There are five living species, two in Africa and three in Asia. Members of both African species have two horns, one behind the other, and their skins are smooth rather than folded. The black rhinoceros, *Diceros bicornis,* of E Africa, is still quite numerous although declining rapidly. It is dark gray and has a hooked upper lip, used for clipping shrubbery; its front horn may be over 18 in. (45 cm) long. The white, or square-lipped, rhinoceros (*D. simus*) of central and S Africa is a slightly lighter shade of gray; the term *white* is probably a corruption of the Africaans word for "wide," referring to its broad snout.

Also called ceratotherium, the white rhinoceros is the largest of all land mammals except the elephant; it stands 6½ ft (200 cm) at the shoulder and weighs 3 to 4 tons (2,700–3,600 kg). Members of two of the Asian species have a single horn. The great Indian rhinoceros, *Rhinoceros unicornis,* is the second largest rhinoceros and lives in reedy areas of Bengal, Assam, and Nepal. Its hide is so deeply folded in several places as to create the impression that it is divided into plates, like a coat of armor, and it is studded with bumps resembling rivets. The similar, smaller Javan rhinoceros, *R. sondaicus,* is nearly extinct. The Sumatran rhinoceros, *Didermocerus sumatrensis,* is the only rhinoceros with a hairy coat and the only Asian species with two horns. Smallest of the rhinoceroses, it stands 4½ ft (140 cm) and weighs about one ton (910 kg). It survives in limited numbers in secluded regions of SE Asia. The rhinoceros is classified in the phylum CHORDATA, subphylum Vertebrata, class Mammalia, order Perissodactyla, family Rhinocerotidae. See J. G. Davis, *Operation Rhino* (1972).

rhizome (rī'zōm) or **rootstock,** fleshy, creeping underground stem by means of which certain plants propagate themselves. Buds that form at the joints produce new shoots. Thus if a rhizome is cut by a cultivating tool it does not die, as would a root, but becomes several plants instead of one, which explains why such weeds as Canada thistle and crabgrass are so hard to eradicate. Ginger, the common iris, trillium, and Solomon's-seal all have rhizomes. True arrowroot is starch from the rhizome of a West Indian plant. See PERENNIAL.

rhobuck: see MARSH ANTELOPE.

Rhoda, servant of Mary, Mark's mother. Acts 12.13.

Rhode Island, state (1970 pop. 949,723), 1,214 sq mi (3,144 sq km), NE United States, in New England, one of the Thirteen Colonies. PROVIDENCE is the capital and the largest city; other large cities are WARWICK, PAWTUCKET, and CRANSTON. The smallest of the 50 states and the second most densely populated, Rhode Island is bounded on the N and the E by Massachusetts, on the S by the Atlantic Ocean, and on the W by Connecticut. The dominant physiographic feature of the state is the Narragansett basin, a shallow lowland area of Carboniferous sediments, extending into SE Massachusetts and, in Rhode Island, being partly submerged in Narragansett Bay. The bay cuts inland c.30 mi (50 km) to Providence, where it receives the Blackstone River; it contains several islands, including Rhode Island, the largest (and the site of historic Newport); Conanicut Island, with the resort of JAMESTOWN; and Prudence Island. The coastline between Point Judith and Watch Hill is marked by sand spits and barrier beaches, sheltering lagoons and salt marshes. Glaciation left many small lakes, and the rolling hilly surface of the state is cut by short, swift streams, with numerous falls. More than half the state is covered with forests, and agriculture is relatively unimportant to the economy. Most of the farm and pasture land is used for dairying and poultry raising, and the state is known for its Rhode Island Red chickens. Principal crops are potatoes, hay, apples, oats, and tomatoes. Commercial fishing is important. Narragansett Bay abounds in shellfish; flounder and porgy are also caught. Minerals found in the state are sand and gravel, stone, and gemstones. Eastern Rhode Island is intensively industrialized, and the concentration of the jewelry business in Providence is one of the largest in the world. Other products are silverware, textiles, primary and fabricated metals, machinery, electrical equipment, and rubber and plastic items. Rhode Island attracts summer tourists. Its coast is lined with resorts noted for their fine swimming and boating facilities, and windswept Block Island is a favorite vacation spot. Narragansett Bay is famous for its sailboats and yachts, and Newport was the site of a popular summer jazz festival. The state also has many historic attractions. Its official name is the State of Rhode Island and Providence Plantations, and its familiar name is taken from the island of Rhode Island. The region was probably visited (1524) by Verrazano, and in 1614 the area was explored by the Dutchman Adriaen Block. Roger Williams, banished (1635) from the Massachusetts Bay colony, established in 1636 the first settlement in the area at Providence on land purchased from the NARRAGANSETT INDIANS. In 1638, William Coddington, John Clarke, Anne Hutchinson, and other Puritan exiles bought, with Williams' aid, the island of Aquidneck (now Rhode Island) from the Narragansett Indians. There they established the settlement of Portsmouth (1638). Because of factional differences, Coddington and Clarke withdrew and founded (1639) Newport on the southwest side of the island, but the two towns later combined governments (1640–47). A fourth settlement, Warwick, was made on the western shore of Narragansett Bay by Samuel Gorton in 1642. In order to thwart claims made to the area by the Massachusetts Bay and Plymouth colonies, Williams, through influential friends, secured (1644) a parliamentary patent under which the four towns drew up a code of civil law and organized (1647) a government. The liberal charter granted (1663) by Charles II of England, through Clarke's instrumentality, ensured the colony's survival, although boundary difficulties with Massachusetts and Connecticut continued well into the 18th cent. The early settlers were mostly of English stock. Many of them were drawn to the colony by the guarantee of religious freedom, a cardinal principle with Williams, confirmed in the patent of 1644 and reaffirmed by the royal charter of 1663. Jews settled in Newport in the first year of Williams' presidency (1654), and Quakers followed in large numbers. All the early settlers owned land that, following Williams' practice, was bought from the Indians. Fishing and trade supplemented the living won from the soil. The inhabitants of "Rogues' Island," or "the sink of New England," as others styled it, were an extremely contentious lot who highly valued their liberties. Because of the colony's religious freedom, it was viewed with mixed loathing and fear by the more powerful neighboring colonies and was never admitted to the NEW ENGLAND CONFEDERATION. However, it bore equally the devastation of KING PHILIP'S WAR in 1675–76. The charter government was suspended while Sir Edmund Andros was (1686–89) governor of the Dominion of New England, but it was restored after his removal from power by the Bostonians. Between 1750 and 1770 there was bitter strife between Providence and Newport over control of the colony, resulting in a long feud between Stephen Hopkins of Providence and Samuel Ward of Newport. Livestock from the Narragansett county (South County), especially the famous Narragansett pacers, figured largely in the early commerce, which developed rapidly in the late 17th cent. Until the American Revolution, Newport was the commercial center of the colony, thriving especially on the triangular trade in rum, Negro slaves, and molasses. Rhode Island, like other colonies, objected to British mercantilist policies and consistently violated the Molasses Act of 1733 and the NAVIGATION ACTS. Narragansett Bay became a notorious haven for smugglers, and the British revenue cutter *Gaspee* was burned (1772) by patriots in protest against the enforcement of revenue laws. After the start of the American Revolution, Rhode Island militia under Nathanael Greene joined (1775) the Continental Army at Cambridge, and on May 4, 1776, the province renounced its allegiance to George III. British forces occupied parts of Rhode Island from 1776 to 1779, when they withdrew before the arrival of the French fleet. The Revolution won, Rhode Island, jealous of its independence, refused to sanction a national import duty; it therefore deprived the Continental Congress of a major source of revenue and became one of the states responsible for the failure of the Articles of CONFEDERATION. Rhode Island did not send delegates to the Constitutional Convention at Philadelphia and resisted ratifying the Constitution until the Federal government threatened to sever commercial relations with the state; even then, ratification passed (1790) by only two votes. The post-Revolutionary era brought bankruptcy and currency difficulties. Shipping, which continued to be a major factor in the state's economy until the first quarter of the 19th cent., was hard hit by Jefferson's EMBARGO ACT OF 1807 and by the competition of larger ports such as New York and Boston. However, this post-Revolutionary period also marked the beginning of Rhode Island's industrial greatness. Samuel Slater built his first successful cotton-textile mill in the United States at Pawtucket in 1790. An abundance of water power led to the rapid development of manufacturing, in which merchants and shipping magnates invested their capital. With the growth of industry the towns increased in population, and Providence surpassed Newport as the commercial center of the state. Since suffrage had long been restricted to freeholders, Rhode Island's increased urbanization resulted in the disenfranchisement of most of the townspeople. Frustrated in repeated attempts to amend the constitution, many Rhode Islanders joined Thomas Wilson Dorr in forcibly establishing an illegal state government in Providence in 1842. Dorr's Rebellion, though abortive, resulted in the adoption of a new constitution (1842) extending suffrage; however, the property qualification was not abolished until 1888. Antislavery sentiment was strong in Rhode Island, and the state firmly supported the Union in the Civil War. Until well into the 20th cent. Rhode Island's political and economic life was dominated by mill owners. (Nelson W. Aldrich was a power in the nation as well as the state.) The small mill town, with its company houses and company store and its large foreign-born population, were important elements in the social fabric. English, Irish, and Scottish settlers had begun arriving in large numbers in the first half of the 19th cent.; French Canadian immigration commenced around the time of the Civil War; at the end of the 19th cent. and the beginning of the 20th there was a large influx of Poles, Italians, and Portuguese. Sporadic labor troubles in the 19th cent. had little effect on the state's economy. However, after World War I there was a long textile strike, centering in the Blackstone valley; this, together with the gradual removal of the mills to the South—the source of the cotton supply where labor was cheaper—led to a continuing decline in the cotton-textile industry. Nevertheless, the manufacture of textile products is still an important industry in the state today and new industries such as electronics have been introduced. In 1973 the large naval installations at Quonset and Newport, which had been extremely important to the state's economy since World War II, were closed as part of a program of reduced Federal spending. Measures have been taken to prevent future damage from hurricanes that have ravaged the coast in the past; the Hurricane Barrier Dam, designed to prevent damage from ocean waters, was built in the 1960s. Politically, Rhode Island was generally controlled by Republicans until the 1930s, when the Democrats' insistence on reapportionment of representation (which had tended to favor small towns at the expense of urban areas) helped bring their party into power. In 1958 a Republican was elected governor for the first time in 30 years. Rhode Island's present constitution was adopted in 1842; it has been amended 36 times. The state's executive branch is headed by a governor elected for a two-year term and eligible for reelection. The bicameral legislature has a senate with 50 members and a house with 100, all elected for two-year terms. Local government is carried out on the city level; Rhode Island's counties have no political functions. The state sends two Senators and two Representatives to the U.S. Congress. It has four electoral votes. Philip W. Noel, a Democrat, was elected governor in 1972 and was reelected in 1974. The state's leading educational institutions are Brown Univ., in Providence, and the Univ. of Rhode Island, at Kingston. See E. C. Tanner, *Rhode Island: A Brief History* (1954); P. F. Gleeson, *Rhode Island: The Development of Democracy* (1957); D. S. Lovejoy, *Rhode Island Politics and the American Revolution, 1760–1776* (1958); P. J. Coleman, *Transformation of Rhode Island, 1790–1860* (1963); F. G. Bates, *Rhode Island and the Formation of the Union* (1967); Federal Writers' Project, *Rhode Island* (1937, repr. 1973).

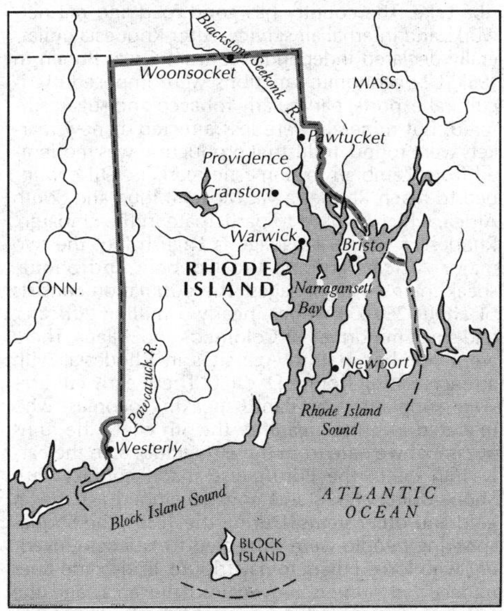

Rhode Island, island, 15 mi (24 km) long and 5 mi (8 km) wide, S R.I., at the entrance to Narragansett Bay. It is the largest island in the state, with bold cliffs and fine beaches. Known to the Indians and early colonials as Aquidneck (əkwĭd'nĕk), it was renamed Rhode Island (probably after the isle of Rhodes) in

1644. Newport, Middletown, and Portsmouth are on the island.

Rhode Island, University of, at Kingston; coeducational; land-grant and state supported; chartered 1888, opened as a school 1890, as an agricultural and mechanical college 1892. From 1909 to 1951 it was called Rhode Island State College. It operates the state agricultural research station (est. 1888) nearby. The university's other research centers include those in oceanography, engineering, and water resources.

Rhode Island Red chicken, American breed of POULTRY, no longer raised commercially, but still maintained for use in breeding programs. See RED ROCK CHICKEN.

Rhoden, Ausser and **Inner:** see APPENZELL, Switzerland.

Rhodes, Cecil John (sĕs'ĭl, rōdz), 1853–1902, British imperialist and business magnate. The son of a Hertfordshire clergyman, he first went to South Africa in 1870, joining his oldest brother, Herbert, on a cotton plantation in Natal. In 1871 the brothers staked a claim in the newly opened Kimberley diamond fields, where Cecil was to make most of his fortune. He returned to England in 1873 and entered Oxford, but his studies were repeatedly interrupted by visits to South Africa and he did not receive his degree until 1881. A trip in 1875 through the rich territories of Transvaal and Bechuanaland apparently helped to inspire him with the dream of British rule over all southern Africa; later he spoke of British dominion "from the Cape to Cairo." His power in the diamond-mining industry developed until, in 1880, he formed the De Beers Mining Company, which was second only to that organized by Barnett BARNATO. In 1881, Rhodes entered the Parliament of Cape Colony, in which he held a seat for the remainder of his life. In Parliament he stressed the policy of containing the northward expansion of the Transvaal Republic, and in 1885, largely at his persuasion, Great Britain established a protectorate over Bechuanaland. In 1888 he tricked LOBENGULA, the Matabele ruler, into an agreement by which Rhodes secured mining concessions in Matabeleland and Mashonaland. He exploited these through the British South Africa Company (organized 1889), which soon established complete control of the territory. In 1888, Rhodes had also secured a monopoly of the Kimberley diamond production by the creation (with Barnato) of the De Beers Consolidated Mines, which reputedly had the largest capital in the world. Rhodes became the prime minister, and virtual dictator, of Cape Colony in 1890. He was responsible for educational reforms and for restricting the franchise to literate persons (thereby reducing the African vote). His personal and business sympathies with the Uitlanders [Dutch,=foreigners] in the Transvaal, who were mostly British and the victims of discrimination, brought him to conspire for the overthrow of the government of Paul KRUGER. The result was the Jameson Raid (1895; see JAMESON, SIR LEANDER STARR). Although Rhodes did not approve the timing of the raid, he was so clearly implicated that he was forced to resign as prime minister in 1896. In 1897 a committee of the British House of Commons pronounced him guilty of grave breaches of duty as prime minister and as administrator of the British South Africa Company. Thereafter he devoted himself primarily to the development of the country that was called Rhodesia in his honor. In the South African War he commanded troops at Kimberley and was besieged there for a time. He died in South Africa. Rhodes left nearly all his fortune of £6,000,000 to public service. One of his chief benefactions was the Rhodes Scholarships to Oxford. There are some 170 scholarships for students from the (now former) British colonies, the United States, and Germany. See biographies by Philip Jourdan (1911); Sarah Millin (rev. ed. 1952, repr. 1971); Herbert Baker (1938, repr. 1969); Felix Gross (1957); J. G. Lockhart and C. M. Woodhouse (1963) and John Marlowe (1974).

Rhodes, James Ford, 1848–1927, American historian, b. Ohio City (now part of Cleveland). While studying in Europe he visited ironworks and steelworks in Germany and Great Britain, and upon his return he investigated for his father iron and coal deposits in Georgia, North Carolina, and Tennessee. In 1874 he became associated with his brother, Robert, and his brother-in-law Marcus A. Hanna, in an iron and coal business at Cleveland. Having made a considerable fortune, he retired in 1885 to devote himself to writing history. He moved to Cambridge, Mass., in 1891. His major work, *History of the United States from the Compromise of 1850* (7 vol., 1893–1906), which covered the years 1850–77, made him a national figure in historical literature. This work, upon which his fame rests, was highly praised by the critics, especially for its fair-mindedness, and has maintained its reputation fairly well. He was honored by numerous academic and literary institutions and societies. His other books include *Historical Essays* (1909); *Lectures on the American Civil War* (1913), delivered at Oxford in 1912; *History of the Civil War, 1861–1865* (1917), for which he received the 1918 Pulitzer Prize in history; *History of the United States from Hayes to McKinley, 1877–1896* (1919); and *The McKinley and Roosevelt Administrations, 1897–1909* (1922). See biographies by M. A. De Wolfe Howe (1929) and Robert Cruden (1961).

Rhodes (rōdz) or **Ródhos** (rô'thôs), island (1971 pop. 66,606), c.540 sq mi (1,400 sq km), SE Greece, in the Aegean Sea; largest of the DODECANESE, near Turkey. The island has fertile coastal strips where wheat, tobacco, cotton, olives, wine grapes, oranges, and vegetables are grown. The interior is mountainous, rising to 3,986 ft (1,215 m) on Mt. Atavyros. Shipbuilding, cattle raising, fishing, and sponge diving are important occupations. There is a large tourist industry. Rhodes was early influenced by the Minoan civilization of Crete and was colonized before 1000 B.C. by Dorians from Árgos. By the 7th cent. B.C. it was dominated by the three city-states of Camirus, Lindus, and Ialysus, all commercial centers. In the early 7th cent. Rhodes established Gela, in Sicily, as its principal colony; other colonies were founded on the eastern coast of Italy and in Spain. Rhodes retained its independence until the Persian conquest in the late 6th cent. B.C. and joined (c.500 B.C.) the Ionian revolt that led to the PERSIAN WARS. Rhodes later joined the DELIAN LEAGUE (led by Athens) but fell away from Athens in 411 B.C., during the Peloponnesian War. In 408 B.C. the three city-states of Rhodes united in a confederacy, whose capital was the newly founded city of Rhodes. The island was occupied by Macedon in 322 B.C., but it asserted its independence after the death of Alexander the Great (323 B.C.) and entered the period of its greatest prosperity, power, and cultural achievement. The arts and sciences flourished on the island; major figures included the painter Protogenes and the astronomer Hipparchus. However, in the 2d cent. B.C. its commerce—and hence its power—declined sharply, and Rhodes became a minor ally of Rome. The island became involved in Rome's civil wars of the 1st cent. B.C., and in 43 B.C. it was seized and sacked by Caius Cassius, the Roman conspirator. At the same time, Rhodes was the seat of a famous school of rhetoric. Julius Caesar studied on the island. Through the early Christian era Rhodes retained a reputation for the high quality of its literary output. Rhodes remained in the Byzantine Empire until the capture of Constantinople (1204) during the Fourth Crusade. It then passed under local lords, was held by Genoa (1248–50), was annexed (1256) by the emperor of Nicaea, and was conquered (c.1282) by the KNIGHTS HOSPITALERS. The knights defended the island against Ottoman attack until 1522–23, when it was captured by the forces of Sulayman I. The island had prospered under the knights, but it was neglected by the Ottoman Empire. Rhodes, along with the other Dodecanese, was taken by Italy from the Ottomans in 1912 and was ceded by Italy to Greece in 1947. The modern city of **Rhodes** or **Ródhos** (1971 pop. 32,092), located at the northeastern tip of the island, is the capital of the Dodecanese prefecture and is an industrial center and port. Its manufactures include cigarettes, soap, brandy, carpets, and processed foods. It is near the site of ancient Rhodes, planned in 408 B.C. by Hippodamus of Miletus. After repulsing a siege by Demetrius I of Macedon in 305 B.C., the citizens of ancient Rhodes erected (292–280 B.C.) in the harbor the Colossus of Rhodes (see under COLOSSUS), a bronze statue of Helios and one of the seven wonders of the ancient world. The colossus was destroyed in 224 B.C. by an earthquake. Rhodes declined in the 2d cent. B.C. with the rise of the free port of Delos. The present city was built largely by the Knights Hospitalers.

Rhodes, Knights of: see KNIGHTS HOSPITALERS.

Rhodesia (rōdē'zhə), republic (1973 est. pop. 5,900,000), 150,803 sq mi (390,580 sq km), S central Africa. SALISBURY is the capital. Rhodesia is bordered on the N by Zambia, on the NE and E by Mozambique, and on the SW and W by Botswana. The terrain is mainly a plateau of four regions. The highveld, above 4,000 ft (1,219 m), crosses the country from southwest to northeast. On each side of it lies the middle veld, 3,000 to 4,000 ft (914–1,219 m) high, and beyond it the lowveld, at elevations below 3,000 ft (914 m). The fourth region, the Eastern Highlands, is a narrow, mountainous belt along the Mozambique border, where the highest point in Rhodesia, Inyangani

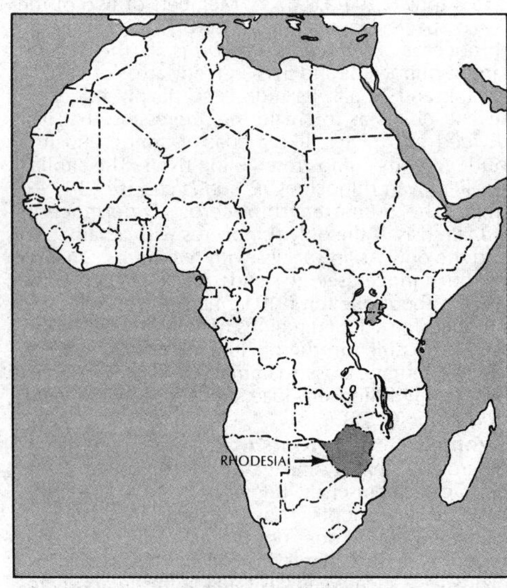

(8,503 ft/2,592 m), stands. Rainfall varies from about 70 in. (178 cm) in the Highlands to less than 25 in. (64 cm) in the south. The Rhodesian economy is basically agricultural, with tobacco the principal cash crop and maize the chief food source. Farms owned by whites produce, besides these crops, cotton, sugarcane, vegetables, and fruits. The major products of African farms include sorghum, millet, rice, groundnuts, and cassava, as well as maize. There are also numerous tea plantations in the country, and in the middle veld there is excellent ranching land. Forests in SE Rhodesia yield valuable hardwoods. The country is endowed with a wide variety of mineral resources, including gold, tin, iron, and coal. Among Rhodesia's industrial products are iron and steel, cement, food products, textiles, and consumer goods. Most of Rhodesia's power is generated by a hydroelectric station on Kariba Lake. The country has good road and rail networks and internal air service. After Rhodesia unilaterally declared independence from Great Britain in 1965, UN economic sanctions were imposed. Agricultural exports, particularly tobacco and sugar, suffered; but minerals were less affected as new markets were found. Industrial production was reoriented from Zambian to domestic markets. Oil continued to reach Rhodesia via Mozambique and South Africa, which refused to participate in the embargo. Rhodesia's official language is English, but the two major African groups, the Ndebele and Shona, speak their own languages. The population consists of about 250,000 whites, nearly 5 million Africans, and small minorities of Coloureds and Asians. There are a number of Iron Age sites in Rhodesia, with artifacts dating from A.D. c.180. These early cultures were supplanted by Bantu-speaking peoples, who migrated into the area after the 5th cent.; the ruins at Zimbabwe date from these migrations. In the early 16th cent., the Portuguese made contact with Shona-dominated states and developed a trade in gold and other items. During the 1830s, the Shona-speaking people were subjected to Ndebele invaders, who forced them to pay tribute. British and Boer traders and hunters moved into the area, and the London Missionary Society established a mission to the Ndebele in 1861. In 1889 the British South Africa Company, organized by Cecil Rhodes, obtained a charter to promote commerce and colonization in the region. Leander Starr Jameson, an associate of Rhodes, led a column of white South African and British pioneers deep into the interior, where they founded (1890) Fort Salisbury. Fighting in 1893 resulted in the defeat of the Ndebele and the takeover of their territory by Rhodes's company. Both the Ndebele and the Shona staged unsuccessful revolts against the British in 1896–97. The settlers pressed the company for political rights, and in 1914 the British government renewed the company's charter on the condition that self-government be granted to the settlers by 1924. In late 1922, settlers voted in a referendum to reject proposals for incorporation into the Union of South Africa and instead to make Rhodesia a self-governing colony under the British Crown, a status that became effective on Sept. 12, 1923. A series of white governments developed the Rhodesian economy but failed to share the resulting benefits with the African majority or to grant political rights to Africans. In 1953, Southern Rhodesia became a member of the Federation of Rhodesia and Nyasaland (see RHODESIA AND NYASALAND, FEDERATION OF), despite African objections to a white-dominated federal structure. In the early 1960s, under the relatively liberal leadership of the federal prime minister, Roy Welensky, and the Rhodesian prime minister, Edgar Whitehead, a new constitution was adopted that provided for limited African political participation; however, the Africans remained unappeased, while the white nationalists feared for their supremacy. In the 1962 elections Whitehead's United Federal party lost to the right-wing Rhodesian Front under Winston Field. In 1963 the federation broke up as African majority governments assumed control in Northern Rhodesia and in Nyasaland (renamed Malawi). After the federation's demise, conservative trends hardened in Southern Rhodesia (which became known simply as Rhodesia in the wake of Northern Rhodesia's independence as Zambia in 1964). Ian Smith, a staunch conservative, became prime minister in 1964, and the Rhodesian Front swept the 1965 elections. The Smith government proclaimed a unilateral declaration of independence on Nov. 11, 1965. Britain called the proclamation an act of rebellion but refused to reestablish control by force. When negotiations in Dec., 1966, failed to produce an agreement, Britain requested UN economic sanctions against Rhodesia. In Nov., 1969, Rhodesia voted to become a republic as of Mar. 2, 1970. The new republican constitution provided for complete separation of the franchise along racial lines. In 1971, Britain and Rhodesia reached an accord that provided for gradually increased African political participation, but without any guarantee of eventual black majority rule. However, after a British commission's hearings in Rhodesia revealed widespread African opposition to the terms, Britain refused to recognize Rhodesian independence on the basis of the accord. Despite nationalist guerrilla incursions from Zambia and other sanctuaries, the white Rhodesian government has retained complete control; the banned African nationalist organizations have seemed incapable of mounting a serious challenge to the regime. The Rhodesian constitution provides for a president as head of state. He is appointed by a cabinet, headed by a prime minister. Legislative authority is vested in a bicameral parliament. In the election of July, 1974, the Rhodesian Front won a sweeping victory. See B. V. Mtshali, *Rhodesia, Background to Conflict* (1967); Frank Clements, *Rhodesia* (1969); L. H. Gann, *A History of Southern Rhodesia: Early Days to 1934* (1969); George Kay, *Rhodesia: A Human Geography* (1970); David Randall-MacIver, *Mediaeval Rhodesia* (1906, repr. 1971); E. E. Mlambo, *Rhodesia: The Struggle for a Birthright* (1972); John Parker, *Rhodesia* (1972); L. W. Bowman, *Politics in Rhodesia* (1973).

Rhodesia and Nyasaland, Federation of, SE Africa, 1953–63, composed of the self-governing British colony of Southern Rhodesia and the British protectorates of Northern Rhodesia and Nyasaland. The capital was Salisbury, Southern Rhodesia. The federation, also called the Central African Federation, was formed on Britain's initiative. Under an appointed governor general, the federal government handled external affairs, defense, currency, intercolonial relations, and federal taxes for its constituent members, which, however, retained most of their former legislative structure. The Africans, fearing continued domination by the whites, demonstrated (1960–61) against the federation, and in 1962 there was a strong movement for its dissolution, particularly from the new African-dominated regime of Northern Rhodesia. Official dissolution came on Dec. 31, 1963, after which Northern Rhodesia became independent as Zambia and Nyasaland as Malawi. Southern Rhodesia refused to hand political control over to its African majority, and in 1965 the white government unilaterally proclaimed the colony's independence from Britain.

Rhodesian man: see NEANDERTHAL MAN.

Rhodesian ridgeback, sometimes called the African lion hound, breed of large, muscular HOUND developed in South Africa in the 16th and 17th cent. It stands from 24 to 27 in. (61.0–68.6 cm) high at the shoulder and weighs between 65 and 75 lb (29.5–34.0 kg). Its short, dense coat is glossy and usually tan or reddish tan in color. The ridge down its back is caused by the hair growing in the opposite direction from the rest of the coat. The original ridgeback stock was produced by the crossing of such dogs as mastiffs, bloodhounds, Great Danes, and terriers brought to South Africa by German and Dutch emigrants, and a half-wild, native hunting dog that contributed the characteristic ridge. In addition to its outstanding ability at hunting lions, the ridgeback was prized as a protector of farms from prowling animals. Today it is rapidly gaining popularity as a companion dog. See DOG.

rhodium (rō'dēəm), metallic chemical element; symbol Rh; at. no. 45; at. wt. 102.905; m.p. about 1965°C; b.p. about 3725°C; sp. gr. 12.41 at 20°C; valence +2, +3, +4, +5, or +6. Rhodium is a lustrous, silver-white, chemically resistant metal in the so-called platinum group of metals in group VIII of the PERIODIC TABLE. It has a face-centered cubic crystalline structure. It is insoluble in most acids, including aqua regia, but is dissolved in hot concentrated sulfuric acid. Rhodium compounds include halides, oxides, sulfates, sulfites, a nitrate, and a sulfide. The salts form rose-colored aqueous solutions. Rhodium is found associated with other platinum metals in river sands and in compounds in such minerals as rhodite and sperrylite. It is obtained as a by-product in the refining of nickel sulfide ores mined near Sudbury, Ont., Canada. The major use of the metal is in alloys with platinum and iridium; it gives improved high-temperature strength and oxidation resistance. These alloys are used in pen nibs, phonograph needles, high-temperature thermocouple and resistance wires, bearings, electrical contacts, and as a catalyst. The metal itself, because of its brilliance and resistance to tarnish, is used to plate jewelry and the reflectors of searchlights. Rhodium was discovered in 1804 by W. H. WOLLASTON in crude platinum ore.

rhododendron (rō"dədĕn'drən) [Gr.,=rose tree], any plant of the genus *Rhododendron,* shrubs of the family Ericaceae (HEATH family) found chiefly in mountainous areas of the arctic and north temperate regions and also of the tropics. They are particularly abundant in Asia, whence many of the popular cultivated species and hybrids derive. They commonly have large shining leathery evergreen leaves and clusters of large pink, white, or purplish flowers. Native American species include the great laurel, or rose bay (*R. maximum*), the common eastern species and the state flower of West Virginia; the mountain rose bay (*R. catawbiense*) of the southern mountains; and the western rhododendron (*R. californicum*), the state flower of Washington. The AZALEA and the rhodora are similar shrubs usually distinguished by their deciduous leaves. Rhododendrons are classified in the division MAGNOLIOPHYTA, class Magnoliopsida, order Ericales, family Ericaceae. See F. P. Lee, *The Azalea Book* (1965); C. L. Phillips, *The Rothschild Rhododendrons* (1967).

Rhodope (rŏd'əpē), Bulg. *Rodopi Planina,* Gr. *Rodope,* mountain range of the Balkan Peninsula, extending c.200 mi (320 km) from the Struma River, SE Bulgaria, to the lower Maritsa River, NE Greece. It consists of three sections—the Rhodope, Pirin Planina, and Rila Planina—and its highest peak, Musala, rises to 9,596 ft (2,925 m). The rugged range has few passes and has long hindered communications between the upper Maritsa valley and the coastal plain.

Rhodophyta (rōdŏf'ətə), division of the plant kingdom consisting of the photosynthetic organisms commonly known as red ALGAE. Members of the division have a characteristic clear red or purplish color imparted by the photosynthetic pigment phycoerythrin, unique to this division. Of the approximately 3,500 known species of red algae, nearly all are marine; a few species occur in fresh water. Although red algae are found in all oceans, they are most common in warm-temperate and tropical climates, where they may occur at greater depths than any other photosynthetic organisms. The plants are multicellular and are characterized by a great deal of branching, but without differentiation into complex tissues. The red algal cell wall has a firm inner layer and a mucilaginous or gelatinous outer layer. Cells may have one or more nuclei, depending on the species. Cell division is by MITOSIS. The red algae are remarkable in that none has motile cells of any kind. Cells of the Rhodophyta possess CHLOROPLASTS that, in addition to the pigment phycoerythrin, contain chlorophyll *a* and *d*, carotenes, and xanthophylls. At great ocean depths, where the wavelength of light available for photosynthesis is very different from that in shallow water, phycoerythrin becomes more active than the chlorophylls in absorbing light; this fact may explain the ability of red algae to exist at depths of up to 700 ft (210 m). The carbohydrate reserves of red algae are in the form of floridean starch, a specialized glucose polymer of different structure than the starch of higher plants. The life cycle of the red algae is extremely complex. Most marine red algae have soft and delicate plant bodies, or thalli; however, the coralline algae have thalli that become strongly calcified and contribute significantly to the growth of coral reefs in tropical seas. Because of the permanent nature of the structures that they produce, coralline algae are known far back in geological history and have been preserved and identified. Commercial AGAR, used as a culture medium for bacteria and other organisms as well as for other purposes, is produced from several genera of red algae. The so-called Irish moss is the source of carrageenin, a substance widely used as a stabilizing agent in emulsions.

rhodora: see AZALEA.

Rhoecus (rē'kəs) [Gr.*Rhoikos*], fl. 6th cent. B.C., Greek sculptor of Samos. He and Theodorus, another Samian, are said to have introduced better methods of casting bronze for sculpture. Rhoecus is recorded as architect (probably with Theodorus) of the early temple of Hera at Samos, which was destroyed by fire c.530 B.C.

Rhondda, David Alfred Thomas, 1st **Viscount** (rŏn'də), 1856–1918, British industrialist and public official. He entered his father's coal business in S Wales and eventually developed one of the largest coal combines in Britain. He sat in Parliament, as a Liberal, from 1888 to 1910. During World War I he served the government in facilitating the munitions output and arranging war contracts in the United States and Canada. In 1917 he was made food minister, instituted a compulsory rationing system of vital foodstuffs, and successfully curbed food profiteering. He was created baron in 1916 and viscount shortly before his death. See biography by his daughter (1921). That daughter, **Margaret Haig,** 2d **Viscountess Rhondda,** 1883–1958, by special provision inherited his title. She was active from 1906 to 1914 in the militant woman suffrage movement and was founder (1920) and editor of *Time and Tide,* a liberal and feminist weekly. She and her father were both on the *Lusitania* when it was sunk by the Germans in 1915.

Rhondda (rŏn'də, Welsh rôn'thə), municipal borough (1971 pop. 88,924), Glamorganshire, S Wales, on tributaries of the Taff River. Coal mining, the chief industry, has declined in importance since the 1920s and 1930s. There is also light manufacturing and quarrying in the district. Population has steadily decreased in recent decades. In 1974, Rhondda became part of the new nonmetropolitan county of Mid Glamorgan.

Rhône (rōn), department (1968 pop. 1,325,611), E central France, in parts of BEAUJOLAIS and LYONNAIS. LYONS is the capital.

Rhône, Lat. *Rhodanus,* river, 505 mi (813 km) long, rising in the Rhône glacier, NE Valais, Switzerland. It flows west through a narrow, flat valley that separates the Bernese Alps from the Pennine Alps and enters Lake Geneva near Montreux. Leaving the lake at Geneva, it enters E France and is joined by the Saône River at Lyons. Now navigable, it flows S past Valence and Avignon and separates the Massif Central from the French Alps. At Arles, at the head of the Rhône delta, the river separates into the Grand Rhône and the Petit Rhône, which join the Mediterranean Sea W of Marseilles and enclose the island of Camargue. Both branches are silted, and a canal has been built connecting the Rhône with the port of Marseilles. With its impetuous Alpine tributaries (Isère, Drôme, Durance, and others), the Rhône has the largest water flow of all French rivers. There are large hydroelectric power plants near Sion and Geneva (Switzerland); in France, the Génissiat Dam and allied projects are of great economic importance. Almost the entire Rhône valley S of Lyons is covered with excellent vineyards and fruit and vegetable gardens; in the extreme south silkworms are cultivated for the Lyons textile factories, and olives and flowers are important products. The Compagnie National du Rhône seeks to develop the Rhône for power production, irrigation and improved navigation. The Rhône-Saône valley is a principal north-south communications route in France. An extensive canal system links the Rhône with other river systems. The Rhône is the cradle of Provençal culture.

rhubarb: see BUCKWHEAT.

Rhyl (rĭl), urban district (1971 pop. 21,715), Flintshire, N Wales, at the mouth of the Clwyd River. It is a seaside resort. In 1974, Rhyl became part of the new nonmetropolitan county of Clwyd.

rhyme or **rime,** the most prominent of the literary artifices used in VERSIFICATION. Although it was used in ancient Oriental poetry, rhyme was practically unknown to the ancient Greeks and Romans. With the decline of the classical quantitative meters and the substitution of accentual meters, rhyme began to develop, especially in the sacred Latin poetry of the early Christian church. In the Middle Ages, end rhyme (rhyme at the end of a line), assonance (repetition of related vowel sounds), and alliteration (repetition of consonants, particularly at the beginning of words) were predominant in vernacular verse. After 1300 rhyme came to be the outstanding metrical mark of poetry until the introduction of blank verse in the 16th cent. Alliteration and assonance were both called rhyme by early writers, but today two words are said to rhyme only when the sound of the final accented syllable of one word (placed usually at the end of a line of verse) agrees with the final accented syllable of another word so placed. When the vowels in the final accented syllables of the two rhyming words and the consonants (if any) succeeding the vowel have exactly the same sound, it is called perfect rhyme, e.g., *shroud* and *cloud, mark* and *bark*. Many poets, however, particularly 20th-century poets, use imperfect or approximate rhymes, in which the rhymed vowels and even the consonants might be similar but not identical, e.g., *groaned* and *ground*. Two words cannot rhyme unless both are accented on the same syllable. When rhymes are of one syllable or end in a consonant with no mute *e* following, as *sad* and *bad*, they are said to be a single or masculine rhyme. This type predominates in English verse because of the great number of monosyllabic words in the language. When rhymes are of two syllables or, more properly, when they are not accented on the last syllable or end in a final mute *e* (*able* and *cable*), they are said to be weak endings, or double, or feminine, rhymes. Feminine rhyme predominates in Spanish and Italian poetry, while German and French use masculine and feminine rhyme equally. Triple rhymes, or three-syllable rhymes, as *cheerily* and *wearily*, are less common, especially in serious verse. Rhymes of more than three syllables are rare. Some rhymes, as *wind* (noun) and *kind*, are called eye-rhymes (words which are spelled alike but not pronounced alike) and have come into general use through "poetic license." Occasionally the initial words in a line may rhyme; more often there may be a rhyme within the line. Rhymes when used in a set pattern combine with other metrical elements to form such verse structures as the sonnet, the Spenserian stanza, and the heroic couplet. See rhyming dictionaries in English (which include discussions of versification) by John Walker (1775; revised and reprinted frequently), Burges Johnson (1931), and Clement Wood (1943; 1947); studies by Henry Lanz (1968) and Eva Guggenheimer (1972).

Rhyniophyta (rī″nēŏf′ətə), division of plants known only from fossil evidence, consisting of several genera, of which the genus *Rhynia* was perhaps the most important. These plants date from the Silurian and Devonian age. Relatively simple in structure, they resemble the PSILOTOPHYTA in many features, such as the lack of clearly developed roots. Like modern higher plants the Rhyniophyta had the specialized conducting tissues xylem and phloem. The Rhyniophyta are the most primitive group of vascular plants so far known and appear to be ancestral to most of the major divisions of vascular plants.

rhyolite, fine-grained light-colored volcanic ROCK. Rhyolite is chemically the equivalent of granite, and is thus composed primarily of quartz and orthoclase feldspar with subordinate amounts of plagioclase feldspar, biotite mica, amphiboles, and pyroxenes. Rhyolite lava exhibits a typical banded structure produced by its flow pattern. Volcanoes that extrude rhyolite lavas are found only on continental regions of the earth's crust. Rhyolite lavas are typically highly viscous and are explosively erupted from volcanoes. Rhyolites were formed in profusion in the Yellowstone Park area and throughout the southwestern portion of the United States.

Rhys, Jean (rēs), 1894–, English novelist. Her novels, written in the 1930s, were rediscovered in the 70s in an atmosphere of resurgent feminism. She frequently writes about pretty, no-longer-young women who are down and out in large European cities. Without work or funds, her characters must depend on men, chance encounters, or former lovers, for money to buy a hotel room, a drink, a pair of gloves. Rhys's vision is uncompromising and her literary style is spare. Her works include the novels *Quartet* (1929), *After Leaving Mr. Mackenzie* (1931), *Good Morning, Midnight* (1938), *Wide Sargasso Sea* (1966), and the short-story collection *Tigers Are Better-Looking* (1974).

Rhys ap Gruffydd (rēs äp grĭf′ĭth), 1132?–1197, ruler of South Wales and, after the death (1170) of OWAIN GWYNEDD, leader of the Welsh princes. The failure (1165) of the English troops under HENRY II in Wales and Henry's later domestic troubles contributed to Rhys's power. In 1171 he signed a pact with Henry, and he helped the king suppress the rebellion of 1173–74. After Henry's death, however, Rhys revolted against the absent Richard I. The first recorded EISTEDDFOD was held by Rhys in Cardigan in 1176.

rhythm, basic temporal element of music that is concerned with the duration of tones and with the stress or accent placed upon certain tones. The formulation in the late 12th cent. of the rhythmic modes—basic recurrent patterns that were adhered to in composition—led to the development of METER. In the centuries immediately following, music achieved a rhythmic complexity such as is found only in 20th-century works. The degree of rhythmic complexity and the types of rhythms used are major considerations in analysis of the style of a composer or a period. The rhythmic tension of music is of value in eliciting emotional response from the hearer. In the 20th cent., composers have been much interested in the possibilities of polyrhythm, the simultaneous use of several rhythmic patterns whose accents do not coincide. See SYNCOPATION and METRONOME. See Kurt Sachs, *Rhythm and Tempo* (1953).

rhythm, biological, cyclic pattern of physiological changes or changes in activity in living organisms, most often synchronized with daily, monthly, or annual cyclical changes in the environment. The exact nature of the internal mechanism, or "biological clock," that controls such rhythms is not understood. Rhythms that vary according to the time of day, called circadian rhythms, include such phenomena as the opening and closing of flowers and, in humans, changes in body temperature, blood pressure, and urine production. In diurnal animals, activity increases in daylight; in nocturnal animals nighttime activity predominates. Activity of many marine organisms varies according to the tide. Monthly rhythms include weight changes in men and the menstrual period in women. Annual cycles, or circannual rhythms, include bird migrations, reproductive activity, and mammalian hibernation. Daily cycles, or circadian rhythms, are in part a response to daylight or dark, and annual cycles in part responses to changes in the relative length of periods of daylight. However, environmentally determined cyclical changes, such as changes in daylight, temperature, and availability of food, serve primarily to refine and adjust physiologically determined circadian or circannual rhythms: in the absence of external cues, the internal rhythms gradually drift out of phase with the environment. Physiological rhythms are also present in the activity of individual organs, e.g., the beating of heart muscle and the activity of electrical waves of the brain. See G. G. Luce, *Biological Rhythms in Human and Animal Physiology* (1971).

Riad: see RIYADH, Saudi Arabia.

Rialto, city (1970 pop. 28,370), San Bernardino co., S Calif., a residential suburb of San Bernardino; inc. 1911. Grapes and citrus fruits are grown in the area.

Rialto Bridge (rēäl′tō), Ital. *Ponte di Rialto*, bridge of Venice, NE Italy, over the Grand Canal, connecting Rialto and San Marco islands. Built between 1588 and 1591, it consists of a single marble arch and has arcades lined with shops.

Riau Archipelago (rē′ou, rē′ō), island group (1961 pop. 278,966), 2,280 sq mi (5,905 sq km), Indonesia, at the entrance to the Strait of Malacca, separated from Malaya by the Strait of Singapore. Its largest island, Bintan, has extensive bauxite and tin deposits and is the site of Tanjung Pinang, chief city of the group. Together with the Lingga Archipelago to the south, it forms the Riau-Lingga Archipelago of Indonesia.

rib, one of the slender, elongated, curved bones that compose the chest cage in higher vertebrates. Ribs occur in pairs and are present in almost all vertebrates; however, in some lower vertebrates, including fishes, they run along the entire length of the backbone. The ribs of the snake are used in locomotion. In the human there are 12 pairs of ribs. Each rib is connected to the vertebral column by strong ligaments. In the front, a flexible section of cartilage connects the rib to the sternum, or breastbone. Below the 7th rib, the 8th, 9th, and 10th ribs are not attached directly to the sternum, but to the cartilage of the 7th rib. The 11th and 12th pairs of ribs are not attached in front at all, and hence are known as floating ribs. In birds and mammals, ribs enclose the lungs and heart and assist in the process of breathing. During inhalation the ribs move upward and farther apart, expanding the chest cavity. During exhalation their downward motion aids in expelling air from the lungs. See SKELETON.

Ribai (rī′bā, rĭbā′ī), father of one of David's valiant men. 2 Sam. 23.29; 1 Chron. 11.31.

Ribaut or **Ribault, Jean** (both: zhäN rēbō′), c.1520–65, French mariner and colonizer in Florida, b. Dieppe. When Gaspard de Coligny decided to plant a French colony as an asylum for Huguenots in the New World, he appointed Ribaut to lead the expedition. Ribaut sailed from France in Feb., 1562, with five vessels carrying 150 colonists. On May 1, after entering the St. Johns River, which he called the River of May, he landed in Florida and claimed the land for France. Sailing north, he established his colony on what is now Parris Island, S.C. (see SEA ISLANDS), naming it Charlesfort, and then returned to Dieppe in July, 1562. With the Roman Catholics and Huguenots at war in France, Ribaut fled to England and there published the English translation of his report to Coligny, *The Whole and True Discouerye of Terra Florida* (1563). Queen Elizabeth I of England, after urging him to join Thomas STUCLEY in establishing an English colony in Florida, accused Ribaut of planning to escape to France with the ships, and he was for some time imprisoned in the Tower of London. Meanwhile, Charlesfort had been abandoned, the colonists sailing for France when aid did not come. However, René de LAUDONNIERE in 1564 established a new post, Fort Caroline, near the mouth of the St. Johns. In 1565, Ribault sailed with seven ships and reinforcements for Fort Caroline. The Spanish, alarmed by the activities of these Frenchmen and heretics, dispatched Pedro MENÉNDEZ DE AVILÉS to drive them out. Ribaut's fleet avoided a fight with Menéndez at the mouth of the St. Johns, and the Spanish sailed to SAINT AUGUSTINE. Ribaut followed, intending to annihilate them. With Fort Caroline virtually undefended, Menéndez marched overland and killed most of the colonists. Ribaut's fleet, meanwhile, was wrecked in a tropical hurricane. He and his followers, stranded on the coast S of St. Augustine, were captured by Menéndez, who massacred most of them. Ribaut's narrative has been reprinted in facsimile with notes by H. M. Biggar and a biography by Jeannette T. Connor (1927, repr. 1964). See Francis Parkman, *Pioneers of France in the New World* (1865, repr. 1965).

Ribbentrop, Joachim von (yō′aäkhĭm fən rĭb′əntrôp), 1893–1946, German foreign minister (1938–45). After World War I he became a wealthy champagne merchant. He joined the National Socialist party in 1932 and impressed Adolf HITLER with his knowledge of foreign languages and countries; he soon became Hitler's foreign policy expert and set up his own office on foreign affairs, which often superseded the foreign office. At the same time, he was German ambassador at large (1935–36) and ambassador to Great Britain (1936–38), returning a violent Anglophobe. In 1938 he succeeded Constantin NEURATH as foreign minister. He was influential in the formation of the Rome-Berlin Axis (1936), in the conclusion of the Russo-German nonaggression pact of Aug., 1939, and in planning the attack on Poland that set off World War II. As foreign minister, he was subservient to Hitler. He was dismissed by Admiral Karl DOENITZ after Hitler's death. At the war crimes trials at Nuremberg he was convicted as a war criminal and hanged.

Ribble, river, c.75 mi (120 km) long, rising in the Pennines, North Yorkshire, N England, and flowing SW across Lancashire to the Irish Sea through a long, narrow estuary. Its chief tributary is the Hodder River. A dredged channel leads to Preston, the port city at the head of the estuary.

ribbon, relatively narrow width of woven fabric edged with selvage. Ribbons have been used for centuries as girdles, headdresses, badges, and for ornamentation. At first called ribbands, they were narrow strips of cloth which were attached to a garment to form borders. The modern ribbon with two selvages was known after 1500; at first it was reserved for the wealthy. In the 17th cent. ribbons were highly fashionable and were used profusely on every part of the costume. The blue and red ribbons, which have since become awards of merit, at first indicated the Orders of the Garter and the Bath, respectively, in England. The French Legion of Honor is symbolized by a watered red ribbon and a medal.

ribbon grass, ornamental perennial GRASS (*Phalaris arundinacea picta*), a variety of the reed canary grass. It has green leaves striped with white and is often cultivated in gardens; it is also known as gardener's-garters. It is classified in the division MAGNOLIOPHYTA, class Liliatae, order Cyperales, family Gramineae.

ribbon worm: see NEMERTINEA.

Ribe (rē'bə), city (1970 com. pop. 17,187), capital of Ribe co., SW Denmark, on the Ribe River. One of the oldest cities of Denmark, Ribe was mentioned in the 9th cent. and became an episcopal see in 948. Its cathedral (built c.1130; restored 1884-1904) is one of the finest examples of Danish Romanesque architecture. Other buildings, such as the Black Friars abbey (begun 1228), St. Catherine's Church (c.1230), and the city hall (c.1500), attest to the city's prosperity in the Middle Ages.

Ribeirão Prêto (rēbärouN' prā'tō), city (1970 pop. 212,300), São Paulo state, SE Brazil. The former "coffee capital" of Brazil, the city grew during the late 19th cent., with railroad construction and a large influx of Italian immigrants. During the 1930s coffee cultivation declined greatly, and the city became a processing center for a rich agricultural region producing chiefly sugarcane. Cotton and cereals are also grown, and cloth, cottonseed oil, food products, and alcoholic beverages are produced. Cattle breeding is also important. In recent years the coffee industry has been reviving.

Ribeiro, Bernardim (bərnərdēm' rēbā'rōō), 1482?-1552?, Portuguese poet. Ribeiro was a figure at the Lisbon court and is said to have gone mad after an unhappy love affair. *Saudades,* or *Menina e moça* (1554), recounts the affair. In part a tale of chivalry and in part a pastoral romance, it is remarkable for its prevailing tone of melancholy, for the music of its language, and for the haunting, romantic concept of love that it presents.

Ribera, Jusepe, José, or **Giuseppe** (hōōsā'pā rēbä'rä, hōsā', jōōzĕp'pā), c.1590-1652, Spanish baroque painter. He studied in Valencia and Rome but at an early age settled in Naples, then a Spanish possession. There, under the nickname of "Lo Spagnoletto" [little Spaniard], he achieved immense popularity and became court painter to the Spanish viceroy. In 1644 he was knighted by the pope. The influence of Caravaggio can be seen in Ribera's early works, somber in tone but dramatic in lighting contrasts and movement. Examples are *Drunken Silenus* (1626; Naples) and *Martyrdom of St. Andrew* (1628; Budapest). After c.1635, Ribera's art showed freer brushwork and brighter colors, often with silvery effects, in such works as *St. Joseph* (c.1635; Brooklyn Mus., N.Y.); *Trinity* (1636-37; Prado); and *Holy Family with St. Catherine* (1648; Metropolitan Mus.). He had the ability to combine Caravaggesque naturalism with a Spanish feeling of mysticism. Ribera often painted the single figure of an old saint or martyr stripped to the waist and modeled in strong light and shade against a dark background. These intensely realistic studies of aged and emaciated figures have extraordinary power, dignity, and beauty. Ribera also produced a number of fine etchings. He is well represented in American museums, including the Hispanic Society, New York City, which has *The Ecstasy of St. Mary Magdalen* and *St. Paul.* Ribera had many imitators in Italy and Spain. See studies by Elizabeth Trapier (1952) and Jonathan Brown (1973).

Ribičić, Mitja (mē'tyä rĭbĭchĭ'tyə), 1919-, Yugoslav politician. He participated in the revolutionary student movement and joined the Communist party in 1941. He was a member of the partisans of Josip Broz Tito in World War II. After the war he served as a member of the executive council of Slovenia, as a deputy of the Slovenian parliament (1951-63), and as a deputy of the federal parliament (1963-67, 1969). Ribičić was elected in May, 1969, to serve as president of the federal executive council, a position equivalent to that of premier. He is also a member of the presidium of the Yugoslav Communist party.

Ribicoff, Abraham Alexander (rĭb'ĭkôf), 1910-, American political leader, U.S. Senator (1963-), b. New Britain, Conn. A lawyer, he served (1949-53) as a U.S. Representative. In 1954 he was elected governor of Connecticut, and he was reelected in 1958. He resigned from the governorship to serve (1961-62) as Secretary of Health, Education and Welfare in the Kennedy administration. In 1962 he left the cabinet and was elected to the U.S. Senate. He was reelected in 1968 and 1974. A liberal Democrat, he nominated George McGovern for President at the 1972 Democratic national convention.

Riblah (rĭb'lə). **1** Unidentified boundary landmark, N Palestine. Num. 34.11. **2** City of ancient Syria, used by the Egyptians and later by the Neo-Babylonians as a headquarters in the west. It was on the Orontes at the foot of Lebanon and E of Tripoli. Situated at the beginning of the valley between Lebanon and Anti-Lebanon, it guarded the entrance to Syria and Palestine and was of strategic importance. 2 Kings 23.33; 25; Jer. 39.5,6; 52.9. Diblath: Ezek. 6.14.

riboflavin: see COENZYME; VITAMIN.

riboflavin mononucleotide (FMN): see COENZYME.

ribose (rī'bōs), monosaccharide CARBOHYDRATE of universal distribution in living tissue, found in ribonucleic acid (RNA; see NUCLEIC ACID), free NUCLEOTIDES, and various COENZYMES. Its close relative, deoxyribose, is a constituent of deoxyribonucleic acid (DNA); ribose has one more oxygen atom in its molecule than deoxyribose. Some of the best procedures for the laboratory preparation of ribose involve the hydrolysis of yeast nucleic acid.

ribosome: see CELL; NUCLEIC ACID.

Ribot, Théodule (rēbō'), 1839-1916, French psychologist. He was professor of experimental psychology at the Sorbonne and later at the Collège de France. His many works include *Heredity: A Psychological Study of Its Phenomena, Laws, Causes, and Consequences* (1873, tr. 1875), *The Diseases of the Will* (1884, tr. 1884), *The Diseases of Personality* (1885, tr. 1887), and *The Psychology of the Emotions* (1896, tr. 1897).

Ricardo, David, 1772-1823, British economist, of Dutch-Jewish parentage. At the age of 20 he entered business as a stockbroker and was so skillful in the management of his affairs that within five years he had amassed a huge fortune. He then turned much of his attention to scientific topics, and in 1799, after reading Adam Smith's *The Wealth of Nations,* began to study political economy. However, 10 years elapsed before the appearance of his first writings on the subject, a series of letters to the *Morning Chronicle.* A number of pamphlets and tracts followed, in turn succeeded by Ricardo's major work, *The Principles of Political Economy and Taxation* (1817). In that book he presented most of his important theories, especially those concerned with the determination of wages and value. For the problem of wages he proposed the "iron law of wages," according to which wages tend to stabilize around the subsistence level. Any rise in wage rates above subsistence will cause the working population to increase to the point that heightened competition among the glut of laborers will merely cause their market price, or wage, to fall back to the subsistence level. As far as value was concerned, Ricardo stated that the value of almost any good was, essentially, a function of the labor needed to produce it. According to his labor theory of value, a clock costing $100 required 10 times as much labor for its production as did a pair of shoes costing $10. Ricardo was also concerned with the subject of international trade, and for that he developed the theory of comparative advantage, still widely accepted among economists. In a now classic illustration, Ricardo explained how it was advantageous for England to produce cloth and Portugal to produce wine, as long as both countries traded freely with each other, even though Portugal might have produced both wine and cloth at a lower cost than England did. Although his publications were often turgidly written, with little of the social insight and breadth of knowledge that characterized Adam Smith's work, Ricardo was an enormously influential economic thinker. His rigidly deductive and scientific method of analysis served as a model for subsequent work in economics. See studies by J. H. Hollander (1910, repr. 1968), Oswald St. Clair (1957, repr. 1965), and Mark Blang (1958, repr. 1973).

Ricasoli, Bettino, Barone (bĕt-tē'nō bärô'nā rēkäzô'lē), 1809-80, Italian political leader. An active propagandist for Italian unity, he became (1859) head of the provisional government of Tuscany after the flight of Grand Duke LEOPOLD II. As a result of his skillful policy the annexation of Tuscany to the kingdom of Sardinia, which had taken the lead in the unification movement, was overwhelmingly voted in the plebiscite of 1860. Ricasoli succeeded Camillo Benso di Cavour as premier (1861-62) of the now unified kingdom of Italy. He was again premier in 1866-67.

Ricci, Matteo (mät-tā'ō rēt'chē), 1552-1610, Italian missionary to China. He entered the Society of Jesus, and in Rome he studied under Clavius. Ricci was sent to the Indies (1578), and he worked at Goa and Cochin until 1582, when he was called to Macao to enter China. In 1583 he and his companion, Father Michele Ruggieri settled in Kwangtung prov., studying the language and culture. They found ready acceptance among some officials, for the Chinese took an intense interest in their possessions, such as clocks and Western paintings. The missionaries wrote tracts on Christianity, including a dialogue. Father Ricci's aptitude for languages and his respect for the Chinese classics increased his standing among the officials; by 1589 he had adopted the dress of the literati. In 1595, Father Ricci, now alone, moved to Nan-ch'ang, a center of erudition, where he stayed until 1597, when he went to Nanking. He was twice turned away from Peking, but in 1601 he was allowed entrance to the capital. There he became a court mathematician and astronomer; he made few converts, but he brought Christianity into good repute. He helped translate many Western works on mathematics and the sciences into Chinese. His maps were eagerly perused by the Chinese, who gained from him their first notion of modern Europe. In return, Ricci sent back to Europe the first modern detailed report on China. He composed a number of treatises, the principal being a catechism, *True Doctrine of God,* which was widely printed in China. He made a careful study of the translation of Christian teachings into Chinese. Concerning the attitude Christians should have toward Chinese official ceremonies, he concluded that the rites expressed respect only, not worship, for Confucius and the imperial ancestors. See Henri Bernard, *Matteo Ricci's Scientific Contribution to China* (1937, repr. 1973); L. J. Gallagher, *China in the Sixteenth Century: The Journals of Matteo Ricci* (1953); Vincent Cronin, *The Wise Man from the West* (1955).

Riccio, Andrea: see BRIOSCO, ANDREA.

Riccio, David: see RIZZIO, DAVID.

Rice, Elmer, 1892-1967, American dramatist, b. New York City, LL.B. New York Law School, 1912. After the success of his first play, *On Trial* (1914), he turned his interests to the theater. Rice's first major contribution to the American stage was *The Adding Machine* (1923), an expressionistic play satirizing man in the machine age. *Street Scene* (1929; operatic version by Kurt Weill, 1947), one of his most compassionate works, is a realistic drama of tenement life in New York. His plays of the 1930s—including *Counsellor-at-Law* (1931), *We, the People* (1933), and *Between Two Worlds* (1934)—continued to express his social and political views. Although *Dream Girl* (1945), a romantic comedy, was a huge success, his later plays for the most part lack the power of his early works. He was also the author of novels and of essays, some of which were published as *The Living Theatre* (1959). During the 1930s Rice was regional director of the N.Y. Federal Theater project. See his autobiography *Minority Report* (1963).

rice, cereal GRAIN (*Oryza sativa*) of the family Gramineae (GRASS family), probably native to the deltas of the great Asian rivers—the Ganges, the Tigris, the Yangtze, and the Euphrates. It has been cultivated in China since ancient times and was introduced to India before the time of the Greeks. Chinese records of rice cultivation go back 4,000 years. In classical Chinese the words for agriculture and for rice culture are synonymous, indicating that rice was already the staple crop at the time the language was taking form. In several Eastern languages, the words for rice and for food are identical. Many ceremonies have arisen in connection with planting and harvesting rice, and the grain and the plant are traditional motifs in Oriental art. Thousands of rice strains are now known, both cultivated and escaped, in India and China, and the original form is not known. Rice cultivation has been carried into all regions having the necessary warmth and abundant moisture favorable to its growth, mainly subtropical rather than hot or cold. Modern culture makes use of irrigation, and a few varieties of rice may be grown with only a moderate supply of water. The plant is an annual, from 2 to 6 ft (61-183 cm) tall, with a round, jointed stem, long, pointed leaves, and seeds borne in a dense head on separate stalks. It has been estimated that half the world's population subsists wholly or partially on rice. Almost 90% of the world crop is grown in India, China, and Japan, and most of it is consumed domestically. Rice is the only major cereal crop that is primarily consumed by man directly as harvested. Only wheat and corn are produced in comparable quantity. In densely populated parts of the East all the original forest has been cleared for rice growing. Methods of growing differ greatly in different localities, but in most Asian countries the primitive methods of cultivating and harvesting rice, which have been followed for centuries, are still practiced. The fields are prepared by plowing (typically with simple plows drawn by water buffalo), fertilizing (usually with dung or sewage), and smoothing (by dragging a log over them). The seedlings are started in seedling beds and, after 30 to 50 days, are transplanted by hand to the fields, which have been flooded by rain or river water. During the growing season, irrigation is maintained by dike-controlled canals or by hand-watering. The fields are allowed to drain before cutting. Rice when it is still covered by the brown hull is known as paddy; rice fields are also called paddy fields or rice paddies. Before marketing, the rice is threshed to loosen the hulls—mainly by flailing, treading, or working in a mortar—and winnowed free of chaff by tossing it in the air above a sheet or mat. The practice of polishing the natural brown rice to a creamy whiteness is standard in the West but less common in the Orient. Brown rice has a greater food value than white, since the outer brown coatings contain the proteins and minerals; the white endosperm is chiefly carbohydrate. As a food, rice is low in fat and (compared with other cereal grains) in protein. In recent years, the so-called miracle rices have been developed by plant breeders; there is a much higher yield of grains that are richer in protein than the old varieties. In the East rice is eaten with sauces made from the SOYBEAN, which supply the lacking elements and prevent the deficiency diseases that a wholly rice diet would otherwise induce in greater measure. Since rice is deficient in gluten, it cannot be used to make bread unless it is mixed with the flour of other grains. In the United States and in many parts of Europe, rice cultivation has undergone the same mechanization at all stages of cultivation and harvesting as have other grain crops. The resulting decrease in the cost of growing has enabled these countries to undercut the world market prices of Oriental rice, which is raised by cheap coolie labor. Rice was introduced to the American colonies in the mid-17th cent. and soon became an important crop. Although U.S. production is less than that of wheat and corn, rice is grown in excess of domestic consumption and has been exported, chiefly to Europe, South America, and the West Indies. North American average annual consumption is about 6 lb (2.7 kg) per person, as compared with 200 to 400 lb (90-181 kg) per person in the Orient. Chief production areas of the United States are in the South, especially in Arkansas, Louisiana, Texas, and California. For feeding domestic animals the bran, meal, and chopped straw are useful, especially when mixed with the polishings or given with skim milk. The polishings are also an increasingly important source of FURFURAL and other chemurgic products. The straw, which is soft and fine, is plaited in the East for hats and shoes, and the hulls supply mattress filling and packing material. Laundry starch is manufactured from the broken grain, which is also used by distillers. A distilled liquor called ARRACK is sometimes prepared from a rice infusion, and in Japan the beverage SAKE is brewed from rice. Rice paper is made from a plant of the GINSENG family. WILD RICE is obtained from a different grass plant. Rice is classified in the division MAGNOLIOPHYTA, class Liliatae, order Cyperales, family Gramineae. D. H. Grist, *Rice* (4th ed. 1965); Food and Agricultural Organization, *Rice Reports* (1963, 1964, 1971, 1972).

rice bird: see BOBOLINK.

riceditch killifish: see CAVE FISH.

ricefish: see CAVE FISH.

rice-paper plant: see GINSENG.

Rice University, at Houston, Texas; coeducational; chartered 1891 as Rice Institute through a bequest of William Marsh Rice, opened 1912, renamed 1960. It offers university courses in engineering, science, architecture, and liberal arts. In addition to biology, chemistry, geology, and physics laboratories, Rice maintains a nuclear research laboratory and is associated with the National Aeronautics and Space Administration in connection with the Lyndon B. Johnson Space Center. Until 1965 there were no tuition fees.

Rich, Adrienne, 1929–, American poet, b. Baltimore, Md., grad. Radcliffe, 1951. The dominant theme of most of her poetry is revolution as a rebirth, an awakening to new possibilities. Such new American movements as black power, student activism, peace in Vietnam, and women's rights have been the source of her poems. Among her volumes of poetry are *A Change of World* (1951), *Necessities of Life: Poems 1962–1965* (1966), *Leaflets: Poems 1966–1968* (1969), *Will to Change* (1971), and *Diving Into the Wreck: Poems 1971–1972* (1973).

Rich, Edmund: see EDMUND, SAINT.

Rich, John, 1692–1761, English actor-manager. Rich introduced pantomime to England, himself playing (1717–60) the role of Harlequin in annual performances. His successful production of John Gay's *Beggar's Opera* (1728) enabled him to build COVENT GARDEN Theatre, which he opened in 1732.

Rich, Penelope, Lady, 1562–1607, the "Stella" of Sir Philip Sidney's *Astrophel and Stella* (1591). Daughter of Walter Devereux, first earl of Essex, she married (1581) Lord Rich (later earl of Warwick); after a divorce she married (1605) the earl of Devonshire.

Richard I, Richard Cœur de Lion (kör də lyôN'), or **Richard Lion-Heart,** 1157–99, king of England (1189–99); third son of HENRY II and ELEANOR OF AQUITAINE. Although enthroned as duke of Aquitaine in 1172, he was, like his brothers Henry and Geoffrey, discontented with his lack of authority and joined their revolt (1173–74) against their father. Later he fought (1183) against the same brothers when they intervened in support of a rebellion against Richard in Aquitaine. In 1189 he again warred with his father and defeated him, before Henry II's death brought him to the throne. Soon after his coronation, Richard set out (1190) on the Third Crusade (see CRUSADES). En route he captured Messina and Cyprus and married (1191) Berengaria of Navarre. With PHILIP II of France, he stormed Acre. Philip then returned to France, where he began plotting against Richard with the latter's brother JOHN. Richard remained but had to abandon his attempt to seize the strongly fortified city of Jerusalem. After concluding a treaty with SALADIN that allowed Christians access to the holy places of Jerusalem, he too started home. However, he was captured (Dec., 1192) by Leopold V of Austria, with whom Richard had quarreled on crusade, and was imprisoned in the castle of Dürnstein, where the troubadour BLONDEL DE NESLE is supposed (by legend) to have found him. Leopold delivered Richard to Holy Roman Emperor Henry VI, who released him (1194) only after Richard paid an enormous ransom, raised by his English subjects, and surrendered his kingdom, receiving it back as a fief of the empire. Richard returned (1194) briefly to England to complete the suppression of the revolt raised against him by his brother John and to raise funds. Thereafter he fought Philip in France, in the process building the famous Château Gaillard. He was killed in a minor engagement. Richard spent only six months of his reign in England, which he was concerned with chiefly as a source of revenue, but his ministers, William of LONGCHAMP and Hubert WALTER, were able to rule the kingdom effectively by the excellent administrative system set up by Henry II and extended by them. Richard's military prowess and reputation for chivalry have made him a central figure in English romance. He appears in Sir Walter Scott's novels *Ivanhoe* and *The Talisman*. See biographies by Philip Henderson (1958), Kate Norgate (1924, repr. 1969) and James Brundage (1974); A. L. Poole, *From Domesday Book to Magna Carta, 1087–1216* (2d ed. 1955); J. T. Appleby, *England without Richard, 1189–1199* (1965).

Richard II, 1367–1400, king of England (1377–99), son of Edward the Black Prince. After his father's death (1376) he was created prince of Wales and succeeded his grandfather, Edward III, to the throne. During his minority, his uncle JOHN OF GAUNT was the most influential single noble, but the struggle for power among several rival lords perpetuated the faction-ridden government inherited by Richard from his predecessor. In 1381, when Richard was 14, there occurred the uprising known as the Peasants' Revolt, led by Wat TYLER and John BALL. The young king acted with great courage in meeting with the insurgents, but the concessions that he made were immediately revoked and the rebels were ruthlessly persecuted. In 1382, Richard married ANNE OF BOHEMIA, to whom he became very much devoted. In the following years the king began to assert his independence from the barons who had dominated the government, gathering about him a new court party, led by Robert de Vere, earl of Oxford, and Michael de la Pole, earl of Suffolk (see POLE, family). He had a bitter quarrel with John of Gaunt, his uncle, while on an expedition to Scotland in 1385. The following year, however, when Gaunt went to Spain, Richard found himself at the mercy of a resentful baronial party led by another of his uncles, Thomas of Woodstock, duke of GLOUCESTER. In the so-called Wonderful Parliament (1386) that group forced the king to dismiss Pole from the chancellorship and imposed on him a baronial council. Richard did not submit for long. He obtained (1387) a statement from the royal judges declaring the proceedings of the Parliament to have infringed his prerogative and raised an army in N England. However, his supporters were defeated in battle at Radcot Bridge (1387), and the king, threatened with deposition, had to submit to the proceedings of the Merciless Parliament of 1388. His friends, Pole, de Vere, and others, were "appealed" (i.e., accused) of treason by five lords appellant—Gloucester, the earl of Arundel, Thomas de Beauchamp, earl of WARWICK, Thomas Mowbray, later 1st duke of NORFOLK, and the duke of Hereford (later HENRY IV); and those that did not escape the country were executed. The lords appellant ruled the country until 1389, when Richard quietly reasserted his authority. Aided by Gaunt, who returned from Spain later in 1389, Richard ruled in comparative peace for the next seven years. After Anne's death, he went (1394) to Ireland to settle troubles there and in 1396 married an eight-year-old French princess, Isabella, to obtain a truce in war with France. In 1397–98, Richard suddenly took his revenge on the lords appellant: Gloucester, Arundel, and Warwick were themselves "appealed" of treason and respectively murdered, executed, and banished; Norfolk and Hereford too were banished after a mysterious quarrel between them. The king became increasingly despotic in his methods of government, strengthening his personal army, imposing heavy taxes and fines, and possibly even planning to supersede Parliament. Finally, on the death (1399) of John of Gaunt, he took the fatal step of confiscating the Lancastrian estates, to which the exiled duke of Hereford was heir. While Richard was on another expedition in Ireland, Hereford landed in England and rapidly gathered support. Richard hurriedly returned from Ireland, but his cause was lost. He was forced to abdicate, and Hereford was crowned king as Henry IV in Sept., 1399. Richard was imprisoned in Pontefract Castle and there either starved himself to death or was murdered in 1400. Richard is possibly the most enigmatic of the English kings, and some historians have found the explanation for his behavior in the last years of his reign in madness. He appears to have been a sensitive and intelligent man, but it is clear that he lacked the strength of character and devotion to royal business that alone might have surmounted the political, economic, and religious tensions of his age. Geoffrey CHAUCER, John GOWER, William LANGLAND, and John WYCLIF made his reign outstanding in the literary and ecclesiastical history of England. Shakespeare's *Richard II* is a dramatic account of the king's fall from power. See biographies by Anthony Steel (1941, repr. 1963) and H. F. Hutchison (1961); May McKisack, *The Fourteenth Century* (1959); Anthony Tuck, *Richard II and the English Nobility* (1974).

Richard III, 1452–85, king of England (1483–85), younger brother of EDWARD IV. Created duke of Gloucester at Edward's coronation (1461), he served his brother faithfully during Edward's lifetime—fighting at Barnet and Tewkesbury and later invading Scotland. On the death (April, 1483) of the king, Edward's eldest son, then only 12 years old, was proclaimed king as EDWARD V. Richard, aided by Henry STAFFORD, 2d duke of Buckingham, seized custody of the young king from Edward IV's widow, Elizabeth WOODVILLE, and her relatives, and was able to assume the protectorship. Soon afterward, apparently suspecting a conspiracy against himself, he arrested and summarily executed Lord Hastings, a leading member of the council. He followed this provocative move by having Parliament declare his brother's children illegitimate. Edward V and his brother were placed in the Tower of London (where they were almost certainly murdered, probably on Richard's orders, although there is no conclusive evidence either way), and Richard had himself crowned king in July, 1483. A rebellion broke out in Oct., 1483, led by Richard's erstwhile supporter Buckingham, in favor of Henry Tudor (later HENRY VII). This revolt collapsed, and Buckingham was executed. In 1485, however, Henry landed in Wales, defeated and killed Richard in the battle of Bosworth Field, and ascended the throne. Despite his usurpation of the throne, Richard was not the total villain that tradition has made him. His evil reputation, perpetuated by Shakespeare's *Richard III,* was shaped at least in part by the efforts of Tudor propagandists to justify Henry VII's own usurpation. Richard was apparently an earnest and hardworking ruler, and his government was well intentioned. He sought to dispense justice fairly and to make himself accessible to appeals from all classes, and he instituted a number of administrative reforms. Few men, however, were close to him or understood him personally, and this obscurity has never been lifted. Richard was the last of the Yorkist kings, and his death ended the Wars of the Roses. See biography by Paul Kendall (1955, repr. 1972); E. F. Jacob, *The Fifteenth Century* (1961).

Richard, earl of Cornwall, 1209–72, second son of King John of England and brother of HENRY III. In 1227, following an expedition to Gascony and Poitou, Richard forced Henry to grant him the land and wealth he regarded as his right, as well as the title earl of Cornwall. He improved his position further by his marriage (1231) to Isabella, daughter of William Marshall, 1st earl of Pembroke. He went on a crusade in 1240 and concluded (1241) a truce with the sultan of Egypt. On Henry's expedition to Poitou in 1242, Richard was barely able to save his brother from complete military disaster. In the 1130s, Richard had often associated himself with the baronial opposition to Henry. Now, however, especially after his marriage (Isabella having died) to the queen's sister in 1243, he became a faithful supporter of the king and his most sensible adviser. He financed the reform of the coinage in 1247, adding greatly thereby to his already considerable wealth, and acted as regent when Henry was out of the country. Richard refused (1252) Pope Innocent IV's offer of the Sicilian crown (which Henry later accepted for his son Edmund), but in 1257 he had himself elected king of the Romans (i.e., emperor-elect of the Holy Roman Empire). The minority of electors who did not favor him adhered to their candidate, Alfonso X of Castile. Richard was crowned at Aachen and made three other visits to Germany, but he was never more than titular ruler there. When the BARONS' WAR broke out in earnest, Richard was one of Henry's chief supporters. He was captured at the battle of Lewes (1264) and held prisoner until after the battle of Evesham (1265). In the settlement after the war he advised moderation against the rebels. See biographies by Noel Denham-Young (1947) and T. W. E. Roche (1966).

Richard, Maurice, 1921–, Canadian hockey player, b. Montreal. Richard, nicknamed "the Rocket" by his admirers, played his entire career (1942–60) with the Montreal Canadiens, where he became a great hockey star. He established many National Hockey League records, including scoring records of 50 goals in a regular season, which was then 50 games, and eight points in one game. His career total was 544 goals in regular season play. After he retired (1960), Richard engaged in various business and sports enterprises.

Richard Cœur de Lion: see RICHARD I, of England.

Richard de Bury (bĕr'ē), 1287–1345, English bibliophile and bishop of Durham. His name was Aungerville, but he was called Bury from his birthplace, Bury St. Edmunds. Under Edward III he served as treasurer and as chancellor and went on numerous diplomatic missions. He founded a library in Durham College, Oxford. In *Philobiblon* he describes his experiences as a book collector. See edition of the Latin text with a translation by Michael Maclagan (1960).

Richard Lion-Heart: see RICHARD I, of England.

Richard of Devizes (dĭvī'zĭz), fl. late 12th cent., English chronicler and monk. He wrote a lively *Chronicon de rebus gestis Ricardi primi* [chronicle of the deeds of Richard I], a valuable historical source having information not found elsewhere. He may also have been the author of part (as far as 1202) of the annals of Winchester.

Richard of Saint Victor, d. 1173, Scottish monk and mystic, prior of the Abbey of St. Victor, Paris. His principal importance is in the history of mystical theology, in which he is a successor to HUGH OF SAINT VICTOR. In two works, *Benjamin Major* and *Benjamin Minor,* he defined anew the stages of mystic contemplation, which he divided into six. He also wrote on rational theology, especially on the Blessed Trinity and on the Incarnate Word.

Richards, Dickinson Woodruff, Jr., 1895–1973, American physician and physiologist, b. Orange, N.J., grad. Yale, 1917, M.D. Columbia, 1923. He joined the staff of the College of Physicians and Surgeons at Columbia in 1928 and became professor of medicine in 1945. He shared with André F. Cournand and Werner Forssmann the 1956 Nobel Prize in Physiology and Medicine for work in developing a technique whereby a catheter can be inserted through a vein into the heart. This technique facilitates study of the condition of the heart in health and in disease.

Richards, Ellen Henrietta Swallow, 1842–1911, American chemist, educator, and organizer of the home economics movement, b. Dunstable, Mass., grad. Vassar, 1870. In 1870 she began the study of chemistry at the Massachusetts Institute of Technology, being the first woman to enter that school, and from 1884 until her death was an instructor there in sanitary chemistry. She became a pioneer in the systematizing and simplifying of housekeeping to free women for other activities. The last 30 years of her life were given to the development of what she called euthenics, "the science of controlled environment." With the spur of her enthusiasm and scientific knowledge, the teaching of HOME ECONOMICS made rapid progress in the first decade of the 20th cent. She was an organizer and first president (1908) of the American Home Economics Association. Her publications include *Euthenics* (1910) and *Conservation by Sanitation* (1911).

Richards, Gordon, 1904–, British jockey. He began as a stable apprentice in 1919. From the mid-1920s until his retirement in 1954, he was the leading British jockey. In 1943 he became the all-time British winner, surpassing Fred Archer's record of 2,749 wins; in all he won more than 4,500 races. Richards was a horse trainer from 1955 to 1970, after which he became a racing manager. He was knighted in 1953. See his autobiography (1955).

Richards, I. A. (Ivor Armstrong Richards), 1893–, English literary critic. In the 1920s he conceived with Charles Kay Ogden a simplified language called Basic English, which consists of a primary vocabulary of 850 words. Richards has taught at both Cambridge and Harvard. Among his many works are *Foundations of Aesthetics* (with C. K. Ogden and James Wood, 1921), *The Meaning of Meaning* (with C. K. Ogden, 1923), *Basic English and Its Use* (1943), and *So Much Nearer: Essays Toward a World English* (1968). He has edited the *Iliad,* Plato's *Republic,* which he put into Basic English, and the works of Coleridge. Among his volumes of poetry are *Internal Colloquies: Poems and Plays* (1973) and *Beyond* (1974).

Richards, Thomas Addison, 1820–1900, American landscape painter, illustrator, and author, b. London. He emigrated to the United States in 1831. Richards organized and was first director of the School of Design for Women at Cooper Union (1858), and from 1867 taught art at New York Univ. His illustrations appeared in *Harper's Magazine* and other leading periodicals and in *Appleton's Illustrated Handbook of American Travel.* His paintings, which belong to the Hudson River school, include *Warwick Castle, Pennsylvania Homestead,* and *French Broad River.* Well-traveled in both Europe and America, he wrote and illustrated *The Romance of American Landscape* and *American Scenery* (1854).

Richards, William Trost, 1833–1905, American marine and landscape painter, b. Philadelphia, studied in Florence, Rome, and Paris, and settled in Germantown, Pa. About 1867 he turned from painting landscapes and still life to marine paintings. His luminous sea pictures were highly realistic. See H. S. Morris, *Masterpieces of the Sea* (1912).

Richardson, Dorothy M., 1882–1957, English novelist. Her important work is *Pilgrimage* (12 vol., 1915–38; omnibus ed., 1938), a novel that records in great detail the inner experience of one woman. In constructing the English novel as a series of images running through the mind of a character, Richardson prefigured Joyce and Woolf. She preferred the label "interior monologue" to STREAM OF CONSCIOUSNESS for her work. See biography by J. Rosenberg (1973); studies by C. R. Blake (1960) and Horace Gregory (1967).

Richardson, Elliot Lee, 1920–, U.S. government official, b. Boston. Admitted to the bar in 1949, he served (1957–59) as Assistant Secretary of Health, Education and Welfare under President Dwight D. Eisenhower. Richardson was later active as a Republican in Massachusetts state politics, serving as lieutenant governor (1965–67) and attorney general (1967–69). He became (1970) Secretary of Health, Education, and Welfare under President Richard M. Nixon, and supported the administration's cutbacks in social welfare programs and its conservative approach to school desegregation. After serving briefly (1973) as Secretary of Defense, Richardson was appointed Attorney General, but resigned abruptly on Oct. 20, 1973, in protest against President Nixon's order to fire Watergate special prosecutor Archibald Cox (see WATERGATE AFFAIR).

Richardson, Ernest Cushing, 1860–1939, American librarian and bibliographer, b. Woburn, Mass. He was assistant librarian at Amherst (1879–80), librarian and professor of bibliology at Hartford Theological Seminary (1884–90), and director of Princeton Univ. libraries and professor of bibliography (1890–1925). In 1925, Richardson became consultant to the Library of Congress. He was the author of many professional papers and books, including *Classification, Theoretical and Practical* (1901), *Special Collections in American Libraries* (1927), and *Some Aspects of Cooperative Cataloging* (1934).

Richardson, Henry Handel, pseud. of **Ethel Richardson Robertson,** 1870–1946, Australian novelist, b. Melbourne. Her years of study at the Presbyterian Ladies' College, Melbourne, were reflected in her book *The Getting of Wisdom* (1910). After studying piano at Leipzig she turned to writing, living mainly in Germany until 1903 and then in England. Her first novel, *Maurice Guest* (1908), is the story of a music student's disastrous infatuation. The trilogy *The Fortunes of Richard Mahony* (1930), which presents an accurate and outstanding picture of Australian life, is considered her major work. Her writing, clear and austere in style, has been characterized as combining romantic insights with scientific attention to detail. See her autobiographical fragment, *Myself When Young* (1948); study by Dorothy Green (1973).

Richardson, Henry Hobson, 1838–86, American architect, b. St. James parish, La., grad. Harvard, 1859, studied at the École des Beaux-Arts; great-grandson of Joseph Priestley. He was a major exponent of romanticism in American architecture and was noted for his revival of Romanesque design. After employment in Paris, he began practice (1866) in New York City but moved to Brookline, Mass., in 1874. Trinity Church in Boston (1872–77) was his first monumental, and his finest, work; its French Romanesque design was a departure from the Gothic revival that controlled contemporaneous American architecture. In it and in subsequent works Richardson developed a free and strongly personal interpretation of Romanesque design. The style, known as Richardson Romanesque, spread and won many followers, exerting a great influence upon the building arts of the period, especially in the young, growing cities of Chicago, Cleveland, Cincinnati, and St. Louis. Richardson's buildings showed strength, simplicity, and a skillful employment of varied materials. In his country houses of wood he produced a distinct American type. He elevated the position of the minor crafts in his work, and to artists such as Augustus Saint-Gaudens and John La Farge he entrusted the important units of decoration. Among Richardson's principal works are the New Brattle Square Church, Boston; public library, Woburn, Mass.; courthouse and jail, Pittsburgh; Sever Hall and Austin Hall, Harvard; parts of the state capitol at Albany, in association with Eidlety and Olmsted; Glessner House, Illinois Institute of Technology; and the Marshall Field wholesale store, Chicago. See H. R. Hitchcock, *The Architecture of H. H. Richardson and His Times* (1936, rev. ed. 1961).

Richardson, John, 1796–1852, first Canadian novelist to write in English. He fought in the War of 1812 and later served with the British army in England, Spain, and Barbados. His most famous works are two frontier romances, *Wacousta* (1832) and *The Canadian Brothers* (1840), both about the Indian chief Pontiac. His own experiences furnished material for *Personal Memoirs* (1838), *The War of 1812* (1842), and other vivid, historical works.

Richardson, Sir Ralph, 1902–, English stage and film actor. Since his first professional stage appearance in *Jean Valjean* (1921), Richardson has played in an enormous variety of roles, both classic and modern. He worked for several years with the Birmingham Repertory Theatre and with the Old Vic, which gave him wide Shakespearean experience. His New York stage appearances have included *King Henry IV* (parts I and II), *Uncle Vanya, Oedipus Rex, The School for Scandal,* and *Home.* Among his many films are *The Fallen Idol* (1948), *Richard III* (1956), *Long Day's Journey into Night* (1962), *The Wrong Box* (1966), and *David Copperfield* (1969).

Richardson, Samuel, 1689–1761, English novelist, b. Derbyshire. When he was 50 and established as a prosperous printer, Richardson was asked to compose a guide to letter writing. The idea of introducing a central theme occurred to him, and he interrupted his task to write and publish his novel of morals in letter form, *Pamela; or, Virtue Rewarded* (2 vol., 1740). The novel tells the story of a virtuous young maidservant who so successfully eludes the lecherous assaults of her employer's son that the young man finally marries her. The guide, known now as *Familiar Letters,* came out in 1741, just before Vol. III and IV of *Pamela.* Richardson wrote two more long, epistolary novels, *Clarissa Harlowe* (7 vol., 1747–48), the tragic story of a girl who runs off with her seducer, regarded today as his best work, and *The History of Sir Charles Grandison* (7 vol., 1753–54). All Richardson's novels were enormously popular in their day. Although he was a verbose and sentimental storyteller, his emphasis on detail, his psychological insights into women, and his dramatic technique have earned him a prominent place among English novelists. See his correspondence, ed. by A. L. Barbauld (6 vol., 1804; repr. 1966); biography by T. C. Duncan Eaves and B. D. Kimpel (1971); studies by J. W. Krutch (1930, repr. 1959), J. J. Carroll (1969), Mark Kinkead-Weekes (1973), and C. G. Wolff (1973).

Richardson, William Adams, 1821-96, American jurist and U.S. Secretary of the Treasury, b. Tyngsboro, Mass. Admitted to the bar in 1846, he helped to codify the statute law of Massachusetts in 1855. Appointed Assistant Secretary of the Treasury (1869), he became Secretary in 1873. Following an investigation into contracts awarded for tax collections by which the Treasury was defrauded, Richardson was censured and forced to resign. President Grant, however, appointed (1874) him to the U.S. Court of Claims, of which he became chief justice in 1885.

Richardson, city (1970 pop. 48,582), Dallas and Collins counties, N Texas, a residential suburb of Dallas; founded 1873, inc. 1925.

Richberg, Donald Randall, 1881-1960, American public official, b. Knoxville, Tenn. He practiced law in Chicago, served as attorney for the city and for Illinois, and became nationally known after specializing in railroad and labor legislation. He helped draft (1933) the act that established the National Recovery Administration and was (1933-35) adviser to the NRA before becoming (1935) its chief administrator. After the NRA was declared unconstitutional, he returned to law practice. His writings include *A Man of Purpose* (1922), *Tents of the Mighty* (1930), and *Government and Business Tomorrow: a Public Relations Program* (1943). See his autobiography, *My Hero* (1954); study by T. E. Vadney (1970).

Richelieu, Armand Emmanuel du Plessis, duc de (ärmäN' ĕmänüĕl' dü plĕsē' dük də rĕshəlyö'), 1766-1822, French statesman. An émigré from the French Revolution, he served Russia as governor of Odessa (1803) and of the Crimea (1805). Made chief minister of France by King Louis XVIII after the HUNDRED DAYS (1815), he secured the quick payment by France of the indemnity imposed by the second Treaty of Paris (1815) and thus hastened the evacuation of occupation troops. In his domestic policy, Richelieu favored leniency toward the ex-revolutionists and Bonapartists, thus displeasing the ultraroyalists headed by the king's brother, the comte d'Artois (later King Charles X). In 1816 Richelieu persuaded the king to dissolve the extreme reactionary chamber of deputies (the so-called *chambre introuvable*) rather than submit to its program. Richelieu resigned in 1818, but returned to power in 1820, after the murder of the duc de Berry caused the fall of Élie DECAZES. His measures against the radicals were not sufficient to suit the ultraroyalists, who applied pressure on Louis XVIII and secured (1821) Richelieu's dismissal. With Richelieu's successor, the comte de Villèle, the ultraroyalists came into power.

Richelieu, Armand Jean du Plessis, duc de (Cardinal Richelieu) (zhäN), 1585-1642, French prelate and statesman, chief minister of King Louis XIII, cardinal of the Roman Catholic Church. Consecrated bishop of Luçon (1607), he was a delegate of the clergy to the States-General (1614). In 1616, through the favor of the king's mother, MARIE DE' MEDICI, he became a secretary of state. He went into exile with Marie after the king freed himself from her influence with the aid of the duc de LUYNES. The death (1621) of Luynes and the reconciliation of Louis XIII and Marie restored Richelieu to favor. In 1622 he was made cardinal, and he became chief minister in 1624. The growing jealousy of Marie and the great nobles endangered his position, and in 1630 Marie supported a conspiracy against Richelieu. She was unable to win the king's support, however, and was exiled. Richelieu then had full control of the government. His domestic policy aimed at consolidating and centralizing royal authority, which had as its corollary the destruction of the power of the Huguenots and the great nobles. The HUGUENOTS were humbled by the capture of La Rochelle (1628); the peace of Alais (1629) ended their special political privileges—without, however, denying them religious toleration. Conspiracies of the nobles, who invariably found a figurehead in the king's brother Gaston d'ORLÉANS, were rigorously suppressed. In foreign affairs, Richelieu reacted against Marie de' Medici's pro-Hapsburg diplomacy in favor of the traditional French anti-Spanish and anti-Austrian policy. To this end he strengthened the army and the navy, made alliances with the Netherlands and the German Protestant states, and subsidized GUSTAVUS II of Sweden against the Holy Roman Emperor in the THIRTY YEARS WAR. In 1635 he formed an active alliance with Sweden and BERNHARD OF SAXE-WEIMAR, and France entered the Thirty Years War. Although Richelieu died before the peace was signed (1648; see WESTPHALIA, PEACE OF), the terms agreed to were in general conformity to his aims. In France, the war resulted in heavy taxation; this, combined with Richelieu's poor management of finances, depleted the treasury and caused dissatisfaction with his rule. Overseas, however, he encouraged commercial capitalism, organizing companies to trade in the Indies and Canada. He was a patron of the arts and the founder of the French Academy. Among his literary works are his memoirs (1650) and the *Testament politique* (1688, tr. 1961). See biographies by Richard Lodge (1896, repr. 1970), Auguste Bailly (1934, tr. 1936), and Carl Burckhardt (tr. 1940); F. C. Palm, *The Economic Policies of Richelieu* (1922, repr. 1970); C. V. Wedgwood, *Richelieu and the French Monarchy* (1949, rev. ed. 1962); G. R. R. Treasure, *Cardinal Richelieu and the Development of Absolutism* (1972).

Richelieu (rĭsh'əlōō), river, c.75 mi (120 km) long, issuing from the north end of Lake Champlain, near the N.Y.-Que. border, and flowing N across S Que. to the St. Lawrence River at Sorel. It is a link in the waterway connecting the Hudson and St. Lawrence rivers. Discovered (1609) by Samuel de Champlain, the French explorer, the river was the route of early explorers. It was an important military corridor in the French and Indian War, in the American Revolution, and in the War of 1812. There are pulp and paper mills along its banks. Ft. Lennox National Historic Park is on Île-aux-Noix near St. Jean, Que.

Richepin, Jean (zhäN rĕshpăN'), 1849-1926, French poet and dramatist. He was briefly imprisoned for an "offense to morals" in his frank poems about tramps, *La Chanson des gueux* (1876). Richepin's successful plays include *Par le glaive* (1892) and *Le Chemineau* (1897).

Richet, Charles Robert (shärl rōbĕr' rĕshā'), 1850-1935, French physiologist. From 1887 to 1927 he was professor at the Univ. of Paris. His special study was anaphylaxis, a term he used to describe a phenomenon noted earlier by Theobald Smith, i.e., a hypersensitive reaction (akin to allergy) to injections of foreign proteins, e.g., serums. For his work on anaphylaxis he received the 1913 Nobel Prize in Physiology and Medicine. He also worked on serum therapy, the nervous system, and animal heat and was interested in psychical research. Richet discovered that hydrochloric acid is the base of gastric juice.

Richfield, city (1970 pop. 47,231), Hennepin co., SE Minn., a residential suburb of Minneapolis; settled c.1851, inc. 1964. The Twin City International Airport adjoins Richfield on the east.

Richier, Germaine (rĕshyā'), 1904-59, French sculptor. She studied with Bourdelle (1925-29) and after 1940 developed a tortured awareness expressed in powerful, distorted figures. Richier's works embody a brittle tension between mass and surface that influenced numerous younger sculptors. *Don Quichotte de la Forêt* (Walker Art Center, Minneapolis) is characteristic of her macabre, surreal images.

Richier, Ligier (lēzhyā'), c.1500-c.1567, French sculptor. Most of his work is in the churches of his native Lorraine. The most famous is *The Entombment,* consisting of 13 life-size figures in marble in the Church of St. Étienne, Saint-Mihiel. The group is dramatically conceived and beautifully executed. Other works attributed to him are in the Church of St. Pierre, Bar-le-Duc, and in the Louvre.

Richland, city (1970 pop. 26,290), Benton co., S Wash., at the confluence of the Columbia and Yakima rivers; inc. 1958. It is the headquarters of the Atomic Energy Commission's Hanford Works (620 sq mi/1,606 sq km), on which the city's economy is based. The area was settled in 1910, and a small farming hamlet there was taken over (1942) by the U.S. government for an atomic bomb development plant. The city of Richland was built (1943-45) to house employees of the project. Federal ownership and management of the city were gradually relinquished after World War II (by 1958), and since 1961 the Hanford Works has been operated by an increasingly large number of private companies. With Kennewick and Pasco, Richland forms a tri-city community prospering in a farm and ranch area that is supported by the Columbia basin reclamation project.

Richler, Mordecai, 1931-, Canadian novelist. Reflecting his youth in Montreal, his novels often treat the unique experience of the Canadian Jew. They usually contain fantastic and wildly comic elements. *The Apprenticeship of Duddy Kravitz* (1959), his best-known work, chronicles the ascent to wealth of a poor and fiercely ambitious Jewish youth. Richler has written screenplays for several films, including *No Love for Johnnie* (1959) and *The Apprenticeship of Duddy Kravitz* (1974). His other works include the novels *The Acrobats* (1954), *Cocksure* (1968), and *St. Urban's Horseman* (1969); and *Notes on an Endangered Species* (1974), essays.

Richmond, former municipal borough, SE England. See RICHMOND UPON THAMES.

Richmond. 1 City (1970 pop. 79,043), Contra Costa co., W Calif., on San Pablo Bay, an inlet of San Francisco Bay; inc. 1905. It is a deepwater port and an industrial center with oil refineries and railroad repair shops. Varied manufactures include metal products, chemicals, canned foods, and electronics equipment. Originally part of a Spanish ranch founded in 1823, it was heavily settled with the coming of the railroad in 1899. It has a junior college. **2** City (1970 pop. 43,999), seat of Wayne co., E Ind., near the Ohio line; settled 1806 by Quakers from North Carolina, inc. as a city 1840. In the fertile Whitewater River valley, Richmond is primarily an industrial city. Buses and trucks, modular homes, and wire and cable are among its many manufactures. In the city are Earlham College and a state mental hospital. Richmond has a symphony orchestra, a historical museum, an art gallery, an arboretum, and a zoo. A state park is nearby. **3** City (1970 pop. 16,861), seat of Madison co., central Ky., in the bluegrass region; inc. 1800. It is a tobacco and livestock (cattle and thoroughbred horses) market. In the Civil War the battle of Richmond (Aug. 30, 1862) was a victory for the Confederates under Kirby Smith. Eastern Kentucky Univ. and a U.S. army depot are in the city. Cassius M. Clay is buried there. **4** Borough of New York City (1970 pop. 295,443), SE N.Y.: see STATEN ISLAND. **5** City (1970 pop. 249,430), state capital, E Va., at the head of navigation on the James River; settled 1637, inc. as a city 1782. It is a port of entry and a financial, commerical, shipping, and distribution center, with a deepwater port. It is a major tobacco market, and tobacco and tobacco products are its leading manufactures. Textiles and apparel, chemicals, foodstuffs, metal items, paper and paper goods, and machinery are also produced, and there are printing and publishing enterprises. The first permanent settlement was made in 1637. Fort Charles was built in 1645, and the site became a trading center. The city was laid out in 1737 under the patronage of William Byrd. It was made the capital of Virginia in 1779 and was raided by the British in 1781. During the Civil War Richmond was the capital of the CONFEDERACY and the constant objective of Federal forces. The city was seriously threatened in the PENINSULAR CAMPAIGN (1862), when it was saved by the SEVEN DAYS BATTLES, in the WILDERNESS CAMPAIGN (1864), and in Grant's campaign of 1864-65 around PETERSBURG, which culminated in Richmond's fall. Much of the city was burned during the Confederate evacuation, April 3, 1865. Richmond National Battlefield Park (see NATIONAL PARKS AND MONUMENTS, table) includes several of the battlefields. Places of interest include the state capitol (1785), which was designed by Thomas Jefferson; the Washington Monument (designed by Thomas Crawford); the Valentine Museum; the White House of the Confederacy, once the home of Jefferson Davis and now the Confederate Museum; St. John's Church (1741), where Patrick Henry made his famous "Give me liberty, or give me death" speech; the Edgar Allan Poe Shrine (the oldest building in the city, built c.1686); John Marshall's house (c.1790); the Robert E. Lee House (1844); Monument Ave., with its statues of Confederate leaders; Hollywood Cemetery (1847), burial place of James Monroe, John Tyler, Jefferson Davis, and some 18,000 Confederate soldiers; and the Virginia Museum of Fine Arts. The city is the seat of the Univ. of Richmond, Virginia Commonwealth Univ., Virginia Union Univ., Presbyterian School of Christian Education, and the Union Theological Seminary in Virginia. See W. A. Christian, *Richmond: Her Past and Present* (1912); M. N. Stanard, *Richmond: Its People and Its Story* (1923); P. S. Dulaney, *The Architecture of Historic Richmond* (1968); E. M. Thomas, *The Confederate State of Richmond* (1971).

Richmond and Derby, Margaret Beaufort, countess of: see BEAUFORT, MARGARET.

Richmond and Lennox, Charles Lennox, 3d **duke of,** 1735-1806, British statesman. He was secretary of state for the south (1766) and became a staunch defender of the cause of the American colonies. In 1780 he introduced a reform bill that advocated annual Parliaments, manhood suffrage, and equal electoral districts. His famous letter advocating universal suffrage was first published in 1783. Serving in the cabinet as master general of the ordnance (1782–83 and 1784–95), he gradually abandoned the cause of reform. See study by A. G. Olson (1961).

Richmond and Lennox, Frances Teresa Stuart or **Stewart, duchess of,** 1647–1702, mistress of Charles II of England. The daughter of an exiled Scottish physician, she was educated in France and returned to England as maid of honor to Charles's queen, Catherine of Braganza. Her beauty attracted the attention of Charles, and she became his mistress. In 1667 she declined Charles's offer to make her a duchess and eloped with and married Charles Stuart, duke of Richmond and Lennox, much to the king's displeasure. However, the duchess (known as La Belle Stuart) soon returned to court, and Charles renewed his attentions, dispatching her husband to Scotland (1670) and Denmark (1671), where he died.

Richmond College: see NEW YORK, CITY UNIV. OF.

Richmond Heights, city (1970 pop. 13,802), St. Louis co., E Mo., a residential suburb adjacent to St. Louis; inc. 1913.

Richmond National Battlefield Park: see RICHMOND, Va.; NATIONAL PARKS AND MONUMENTS (table).

Richmond-San Rafael Bridge, W Calif., c.4 mi (6 km) long, part of the network of bridges serving the SAN FRANCISCO BAY area; completed in 1957. It provides an essential link between the east side of San Francisco Bay and the north coastal counties on the west side of the bay.

Richmond upon Thames, borough (1971 pop. 173,592) of Greater London, SE England. The borough was created in 1965 by the merger of the municipal boroughs of Barnes, Richmond, and Twickenham. Richmond upon Thames is mainly residential, with more than 5,000 acres (2,023 hectares) of public recreation grounds. The annual Oxford-Cambridge boat race on the Thames takes place nearly entirely within the borough. Rugby matches between the two schools are also played there. Famous houses include Hampton Court Palace, the residence of Henry VIII, and Strawberry Hill, the home of Horace Walpole.

Richter, Conrad (rĭk'tər), 1890–1968, American novelist, b. Pine Grove, Pa. After newspaper work in Pennsylvania and Ohio, he moved to New Mexico. Richter's novels treat the American frontier experience in terms of everyday life. His best-known works are the novels *The Trees* (1940), *The Fields* (1946), and *The Town* (1950; Pulitzer Prize), which comprise a trilogy. His other novels include *The Sea of Grass* (1937), *The Light in the Forest* (1953), *The Lady* (1957), and *The Aristocrat* (1968).

Richter, Hans (häns rĭkh'tər), 1888–, American artist, b. Germany. A painter and filmmaker, Richter was influenced by CUBISM and DADA and was a member of the Dutch de Stijl group (see STIJL, DE). His preoccupation with continuity led him first to scroll painting and then to the making of abstract films. His film *Dreams That Money Can Buy* (1944–46), made in collaboration with several major artists, concerns the fantasies of a group of psychiatric patients.

Richter, Johann Paul Friedrich (yō'hän poul frē'drĭkh), pseud. **Jean Paul,** 1763–1825, German novelist. He studied theology at the Univ. of Leipzig and later taught in that city. His novels combine the idealism of Fichte with the romantic sentimentality of STURM UND DRANG. Among his romances are *Hesperus* (1795, tr. 1865); *Leben des Quintus Fixlein* (1796; tr. by Carlyle, *Quintus Fixlein,* 1827), a charming prose idyl about a village schoolteacher; and *Siebenkäs* (1796–97, tr. 1845), in which a sensitive husband ends his unhappy marriage by feigning death and burial. Other works include the novel *Titan* (1800–1803, tr. 1862) and *Levana* (1807, tr. 1848), a treatise on education. Richter's writings were extremely popular in his lifetime, admired for their idealism and warm portrayals of simple life, as well as for their humor and sentimentality. See study by Dorothea Berger (1973).

Richter, Ludwig (lo͞ot'vĭkh), 1803–84, German painter, illustrator, and etcher; son and pupil of the engraver Karl Richter (1770–1848). His characteristic paintings combine figure and landscape, as in *Bridal Procession in Springtime.* Richter made approximately 240 etchings, including scenes in Saxony and Rome, and over 1,000 drawings for woodcuts, including illustrations for Goldsmith's *Vicar of Wakefield,* Schiller's poem "Song of the Bell," and many German fairy tales. They are executed in a simple, often humorous manner.

Richter, Sviatoslav (svyä'tōsläf), 1915–, Soviet pianist. He studied at the Moscow Conservatory under Heinrich Neuhaus. After earning an impressive critical reputation, he was awarded the Stalin Prize in 1945. In 1960 he made the first of many international concert tours. Richter is known as a perfectionist who plays in a warm, romantic style. His repertoire is extensive, including works by Bach, Beethoven, Schubert, Debussy, Mozart, and Schumann.

Richter scale, scale of earthquake magnitude that describes the amount of energy released at the focus of an earthquake; devised in 1935 by the American seismologist Charles F. Richter. The scale is logarithmic; that is, the energy release increases by powers of ten in relation to the Richter magnitude numbers. Thus the energy released in an earthquake of magnitude 5 is about ten times the energy released in an earthquake of magnitude 4. Scale numbers for the Richter scale range from 0 to 9. However, since the scale is logarithmic, no theoretical upper limit exists. An earthquake whose magnitude is greater than about 4.5 on this scale can cause damage; severe earthquakes have magnitudes greater than 7. The Alaska earthquake of 1964 was 8.4 on the Richter scale, and the famous San Francisco earthquake of 1906 was 7.8. Like ripples formed when a pebble is dropped into quiet water, earthquake waves travel outward in all directions, gradually losing energy, and the intensity of earth movement and ground damage generally decreases at greater distances from the earthquake focus. In addition, the nature of the underlying rock or soil at a particular location affects ground movements. In order to give a rating to the effects of an earthquake in a particular place, the Mercalli scale, developed by the Italian seismologist Giuseppe Mercalli, is often used. It measures the severity of an earthquake in terms of its effects on the inhabitants of an area, e.g., how much damage it causes to buildings and whether or not sleeping persons are awakened by it.

Richthofen, Ferdinand, Baron von (fĕr'dēnänt bärōn' fən rĭkht'hōfən), 1833–1905, German geographer, geologist, and traveler. He took part in a Prussian expedition in E Asia (1860–62), worked as a geologist in W United States (1862–68), then made several exploring journeys in China and Japan (1868–72). His geographical, geological, economic, and ethnological findings in China were embodied in three volumes and an atlas (1877–85); three posthumous volumes appeared in 1911 and 1912. He was professor at the universities of Bonn (1875–83), Leipzig (1883–86), and Berlin (from 1886) and was the founder and the first director (1902–5) of the Institut für Meereskunde, Berlin.

Richthofen, Manfred, Baron von (män'frāt), 1892–1918, German aviator in World War I. He was credited with the spectacular achievement of shooting down 80 aircraft; he was killed in action on April 21, 1918. He was known as the "Red Baron." See biographies by F. P. Gibbons (new ed. 1964) and W. E. Burrows (1969).

Ricimer (rĭs'ĭmər), d. 472, Roman general of the tribe of the Suebi. After winning (456) two victories over the Vandals, he allied with the senate and deposed (456) Emperor AVITUS. Thereafter the true ruler of Italy, he erected a series of puppet emperors. The most able was MAJORIAN, whom Ricimer deposed and killed. Ricimer's power was strengthened by good relations with the East Roman Empire and with the senate.

Rickenbacker, Edward Vernon, 1890–1973, American war hero and airline executive, b. Columbus, Ohio. He became a car racing driver at 16 and set numerous speed records. In World War I he volunteered for the air service and became the leading U.S. ace by destroying 26 enemy planes. After serving as an executive of several airline companies, he became president and general manager (1938–53) and chairman of the board (1954–63) of Eastern Airlines, which he built into a major passenger and transport system. A political conservative, he often spoke on contemporary American affairs. His book *Seven Came Through* (1943) recounts his 22 days on a raft in World War II after being shot down while on an observation tour. He also wrote *Fighting the Flying Circus* (1919). See his autobiography (1967) and his *From Father to Son,* ed. by W. F. Rickenbacker (1970).

rickets or **rachitis** (rəkī' tĭs), bone disease caused by a deficiency of vitamin D. Essential in regulating calcium and phosphorus absorption by the body, vitamin D can be formed in the skin by ultraviolet rays contained in sunlight; it can also be consumed in such foods as fish oils, eggs, and butter. Since calcium and phosphorus are essential for the proper development and hardening of bones, the disease manifests itself in children as softening of bones, abnormal bone growth, and enlargement of cartilage at the ends of the long bones. In areas where bones must support weight, such as the legs and pelvis, the skeleton is likely to become bent or deformed. The result is often knock-knees, bowlegs, and deformities of the chest and pelvis. In temperate climates vitamin-D deficiency usually results from poor diet rather than from lack of exposure to ultraviolet rays of sunlight. Rickets is no longer common in the United States because milk is usually fortified with vitamin D and infants commonly receive the nutrient as a vitamin supplement. Treatment of rickets is largely preventive, i.e., by early recognition and by including adequate amounts of vitamin D in the diet.

Ricketts, Charles, 1866–1931, British illustrator, designer, writer, and connoisseur, b. Geneva. He and his lifelong friend, Charles Shannon, edited (1897–99) the *Dial.* He is best remembered as designer and manager of the VALE PRESS from 1896 to 1904. His contribution to fine bookmaking was very great. He also wrote on art. See *Self-Portrait: Letters and Journals of Charles Ricketts* (1939).

rickettsia (rĭkĕt'sēə), any of a group of very small BACTERIA, many disease-causing, that live in vertebrates and are transmitted by bloodsucking parasitic arthropods such as FLEAS, lice (see LOUSE), and ticks. Rickettsias are named after their discoverer, the American pathologist Harold Taylor Ricketts, who died of TYPHUS in Mexico after confirming the infectious agent of that rickettsial disease. Rickettsias are gram-negative, coccoid-shaped or rod-shaped bacteria; unlike other bacteria, they cannot be cultured outside living hosts, possibly because their cell membranes are more fragile than those of other bacteria. Rickettsias from infected vertebrates, usually mammals, live and multiply in the gastrointestinal tract of an arthropod carrier but do not cause disease there; they are transmitted to another vertebrate, possibly one of another species, by the arthropod's mouthparts or feces. *Rickettsia prowazekii* causes louse-borne typhus, carried from man to man by two species of lice. Flea, or murine, typhus, caused by *R. mooseri,* is transmitted from rodents to man by fleas. Trench fever, caused by *R. quintana,* was an epidemic disease in World War I; it is transmitted by the rat flea from rat to man or from man to man. Trench fever disease reservoirs (perpetuation of the disease in wild animal populations) exist in some parts of Europe and Mexico. Various typhuslike rickettsial diseases, such as ROCKY MOUNTAIN SPOTTED FEVER and African tick typhus, are transmitted by ticks from animal hosts to man. Mite-borne rickettsial infections include rickettsialpox, caused by *Rickettsia akari* and transmitted from house mice to man, and scrub typhus, or tsutsugamushi fever, caused by *R. tsutsugamushi* and found in Japan and SE Asia. Q fever, caused by *Coxiella burnetii,* a more hardy rickettsia viable outside the living host, is usually transmitted to man by inhalation of contaminated airborne particles or from contaminated materials, often from infected livestock; it is an occupational hazard among dairy farm and slaughterhouse workers. The similar symptoms of rickettsial infections often make it difficult to distinguish one disease from another. In man the organisms grow in cells lining blood and lymph vessels; a rash, fever, and flulike symptoms are usually present. Q fever also causes lung damage. All rickettsial diseases respond to treatment with TETRACYCLINES and CHLORAMPHENICOL. A group of organisms of a related bacterial family, the Chlamydiaceae, are responsible for the disease PSITTACOSIS. Rickettsias are classified in the phylum Schizophyta, class Schizomycetes, order Rickettsiales, family Rickettsiaceae.

rickettsialpox: see RICKETTSIA.

Rickmansworth, urban district (1971 pop. 29,510), Hertfordshire, SE England, at the confluence of the Colne, Gade, and Chess rivers. Rickmansworth is an old market town. The district is largely residential and has many recreation spots, including woods, lakes, and Moor Park (400 acres/162 hectares). Papermaking is the major industry. Basing House, a home of William Penn, is in the district.

Rickover, Hyman George, 1900–, American admiral, b. Russia. In World War II he served as head of the electrical section of the navy's Bureau of Ships. After the war he was assigned (1946) to the atomic submarine project at Oak Ridge, Tenn., and helped convince the navy that nuclear sea power was feasible. Rickover directed the planning and construction of the world's first atomic-powered submarine, the *Nautilus,* launched in 1954, and other of the U.S. navy's nuclear-powered ships. He was promoted to rear admiral in 1953 and vice admiral in 1958; on both occasions the navy was urged by Congress to make the promotions. Rickover later became chief of the Naval Reactors Branch of the Atomic Energy Commission and was in charge of the nuclear propulsion division of the navy's Bureau of Ships. His naval career was marked by a certain amount of controversy because of his outspoken opinions and unorthodox methods. He wrote *Education and Freedom* (1959), *Swiss Schools and Ours: Why They Are Better* (1962), and *American Education* (1963). See Clay Blair, *The Atomic Submarine and Admiral Rickover* (1954).

riddle, puzzling question, specifically one that consists of a fanciful description or definition of something to be guessed. A famous riddle was asked by the Sphinx: "What goes on four legs in the morning, on two at noon, on three at night?" OEDIPUS guessed the answer correctly: "Man—in infancy he crawls, at his prime he walks, in age he leans on a staff." Samson's riddle is also famous: "Out of the eater came forth meat, and out of the strong came forth sweetness" (Judges 14.14). It refers to a lion he had just killed, on which he saw bees and honey; he ate some of the lion and the honey. Punning riddles are common, as: "When is a door not a door?" The answer is, "When it's ajar." There is comparatively little riddle literature, but riddles do figure prominently in Old English. The Exeter Book contains many English verse riddles of uncertain date; they vary considerably in matter. There are also many riddles in Latin hexameters dating from Anglo-Saxon England. See Archer Taylor, *English Riddles from Oral Tradition* (1951); H. H. Abbott, ed., *The Riddles of the Exeter Book* (1968).

Rideau Canal (rēdō', rē'dō), 126 mi (203 km) long, S Ont., Canada, connecting the Ottawa River at Ottawa with Lake Ontario at Kingston. The canal, which has 47 locks, follows the course of the Rideau River. It was built (1826–32) by army engineers under the direction of Col. John By to provide access from the St. Lawrence to Lake Ontario without exposure to attack by American forces on the U.S. shore of the St. Lawrence. Little used as a commercial waterway, the canal system has become a popular recreation area and scenic attraction.

Ridgefield. 1 Residential town (1970 pop. 18,188), Fairfield co., SE Conn.; inc. 1709. The battle of Ridgefield (April 27, 1777) was fought there in an effort to stop William Tryon's men from retreating after a raid on Danbury. The town has many colonial homes and is noted for its quiet 18th-century charm. Cass Gilbert lived there. **2** Residential borough (1970 pop. 11,308), Bergen co., NE N.J.; inc. 1892. Several corporate headquarters are located there.

Ridgefield Park, village (1970 pop. 13,990), Bergen co., NE N.J., on the Hackensack River; inc. 1892. It is chiefly residential.

Ridgewood, residential village (1970 pop. 27,547), Bergen co., NE N.J.; inc. 1876. Various Revolutionary War historical sites are there.

Ridgway, Matthew Bunker, 1895–, U.S. general, b. Fort Monroe, Va. A West Point graduate, in World War II he was made (1942) assistant division commander and then commander of the 82d Infantry Division. This became the 82d Airborne Division, and Ridgway jumped with his men in the invasions of Sicily, Italy, and France (1942–44). He later commanded the 18th Airborne Corps. Appointed (1950) commander of the U.S. 8th Army in Korea, he replaced (1951) Douglas MacArthur as commander of the United Nations forces in Korea and of the Allied occupation forces in Japan. In June, 1952, Ridgway succeeded Dwight D. Eisenhower as supreme commander of the Allied Powers in Europe and held that post until he became army chief of staff in Aug., 1953. He protested vigorously but unsuccessfully against the Eisenhower administration's over-all military policy, which emphasized air and atomic power at the expense of the army and navy. Retiring from the army in June, 1955, with the permanent rank of general, Ridgway was (1955–60) chairman of the board of trustees of the Mellon Institute for Industrial Research in Pittsburgh. See his memoirs (1956) and book, *The Korean War* (1967).

Ridgway, Robert, 1850–1929, American ornithologist, b. Mt. Carmel, Ill. Curator of the division of birds at the U.S. National Museum from 1880, he is known for his work in systematic ornithology and color definition and as one of the founders and early presidents of the American Ornithologists' Union. His works include *Manual of North American Birds* (1887) and *Color Standards and Color Nomenclature* (1912).

Riding, East, North, West, England: see YORKSHIRE.

Riding Mountain National Park, 1,148 sq mi (2,973 sq km), SW Man., Canada, W of Lake Manitoba; est. 1929. A wooded region with small glacial lakes, on the highest part of the Manitoba escarpment, it is a recreation area and big-game sanctuary.

Ridley, Nicholas, c.1500–1555, English prelate, reformer, and Protestant martyr. In 1534, while a proctor of Cambridge, he signed the decree against the pope's supremacy in England. In 1537 he became chaplain to Thomas Cranmer, in 1540 master of Pembroke Hall, Cambridge, and in 1541 chaplain to Henry VIII and canon of Canterbury. As bishop of Rochester (1547), Ridley was chosen to strengthen and establish the Reformed teachings at Cambridge. In the reign of Edward VI, he took part in compiling (1548) the Book of Common Prayer, and he was a commissioner in the examination that resulted in the deposition of bishops Stephen Gardiner and Edmund Bonner. In 1550 he succeeded Bonner as bishop of London, where he did much to improve the condition of the poor by preaching on social injustices before the king. Ridley supported Lady Jane Grey's claims to the crown, and in 1553, shortly after Mary Tudor's accession as the Catholic Mary I, he was imprisoned. With Cranmer and Hugh LATIMER he took part (1554) in the Oxford disputations against a group of Catholic theologians and would not recant his Protestant faith. He was burned at the stake with Latimer before Balliol Hall, Oxford. Latimer's parting words to Ridley are often quoted: "Be of good courage, brother Ridley, and play the man; for we shall this day light such a candle by God's grace in England, as I trust shall never be put out." See his works (ed. by Henry Christmas, 1841); biography by J. G. Ridley (1957).

ridley: see SEA TURTLE.

Ridpath, John Clark, 1840–1900, American educator and author, b. Putnam co., Ind., grad. Indiana Asbury College (now DePauw Univ.), 1863. After teaching in Indiana schools, he was successively (1869–85) professor of belles lettres, of history, and of political philosophy at Indiana Asbury, serving also, after 1879, as vice president. He was instrumental in interesting the industrialist Washington Charles DePauw in the college, which was renamed in his honor. He wrote biographies of James G. Blaine, James A. Garfield, William E. Gladstone, and James Otis and popular histories of the United States and of the world, which have been frequently reissued. He was also editor in chief of the *Ridpath Library of Universal Literature* (25 vol., 1898; rev. ed. 1906).

Riduna: see ALDERNEY, island, England.

riebeckite (rē'bĕkīt"): see AMPHIBOLE.

Riego y Nuñez, Rafael del (räfäĕl' dĕl rēä'gō ē nōō'nyāth), 1785–1823, Spanish general and revolutionary. Taken captive (1808) by the French during Napoleon's Spanish campaign, he returned from imprisonment in France in 1814. In 1820 he assumed leadership of a revolutionary band of liberals and military officers that protested the monarchical absolutism of King Ferdinand VII and reinstated the Cortes constitution of 1812 in S Spain. Serving as commander of the revolutionary forces in Aragón during the ensuing civil war and later as president of the Cortes, Riego y Nuñez had mixed success against the invading French army that came to Ferdinand's assistance. He was captured in 1823 and executed for treason. Although his historic role was brief and ineffective, a favorite tune of his troops, the *Himno de Riego,* was used in 1931 for the national anthem of the Spanish republic.

Riehen (rē'ən), city (1970 pop. 21,026), Basel-Stadt canton, N Switzerland, on the Wiese River. It is a residential suburb of Basel.

Riel, Louis (lwē rēĕl'), 1844–85, Canadian insurgent, leader of two rebellions, b. Manitoba, of French and métis parentage. In 1869–70 he led the rebels of the Red River settlements and headed the provisional government they founded. His followers were mainly métis and Indians, who considered that in the transfer (1869) of the Hudson's Bay Company territory to Canada their land rights and other interests were threatened. Donald A. Smith (later Lord STRATHCONA) was sent by the government to treat with Riel. When troops were dispatched (1870) to face the rebels at Fort Garry, the Red River Rebellion collapsed without bloodshed, and Riel fled the country. In that year, under the Manitoba Act, the Red River settlements were accorded a provincial government and many of the rights that Riel had sought. He returned to Canada and was elected to the House of Commons, but he was expelled from it (1874) and declared an outlaw (1875). He then lived in Montana for several years, but in 1884 he was summoned back to Canada to lead a group of Indians and métis who were bent on securing titles to their lands in Saskatchewan. The uprising ended with an engagement (1885) at Batoche, his headquarters. He was captured, tried for treason, and hanged. See G. F. G. Stanley, *The Birth of Western Canada* (rev. ed. 1960); Richard Howard, *Riel* (1967)

Riel's rebellions: see RIEL, LOUIS.

Riemann, Georg Friedrich Bernhard (gā'ôrk frē'drĭkh bĕrn'härt rē'män), 1826–66, German mathematician. He studied at the universities of Göttingen and Berlin and was professor at Göttingen from 1859. His great contributions to mathematics include his work on the theory of the functions of complex variables and his method of representing these functions on coincident planes or sheets (Riemann surfaces). He laid the foundations of a non-Euclidean system of geometry (Riemannian geometry) representing elliptic space and generalized to *n* dimensions the work of C. F. Gauss in differential geometry, thus creating the basic tools for the mathematical expression of the general theory of relativity. Riemann also was interested in mathematical physics, particularly optics and electromagnetic theory.

Riemenschneider, Tilman (tĭl'män rē'mənshnī"-dər), c.1460–1531, German Renaissance sculptor, who worked in stone and wood. He was in Würzburg by 1483. In 1520 he was made burgomaster, but he was imprisoned in 1525 because of participation in the peasant insurrection, and little is known about his work in later years. He created slender figures with delicately carved, expressive faces, all arranged in clearly ordered, though not static, compositions. His stone tombs of Bishop Rudolf von Scherenberg in the cathedral at Würzburg and of Emperor Henry II and his wife in the cathedral at Bamberg are well known, as are his stone *Adam and Eve* (Würzburg Mus.) and his wooden altar in Rothenburg ob der Tauber. Examples of his work are in the National Gallery of Art, Washington, D.C., and in the Metropolitan and Cleveland museums.

Rienzi or **Rienzo, Cola di** (kô'lä dē rēĕn'tsē, rēĕn'tsō), 1313?–1354, Roman popular leader. In 1343 on a mission to Pope Clement VI at Avignon, he won the papal confidence. While there he befriended Petrarch. Returning to Rome as papal votary, he won great popular support and received (May, 1347) wide dictatorial powers, which he claimed to hold under the pope's sovereignty. He crushed the barons and began great reforms in an effort to rouse an Italian national conscience. Calling himself tribune of the sacred Roman republic, he sought to rally the support of the other Italian cities and dreamed of a popular Italian empire with Rome as the capital. The pope, aroused by his policies, incited the barons against him. Renzi was defeated (Dec., 1347) and fled. At Prague in 1350 he disclosed to Holy Roman Emperor Charles IV his conviction that they shared a call to regenerate the Roman Catholic Church and the world. Charles, however, responded by jailing him and in 1352 sent him to Avignon to face the Inquisition. The new pope, Innocent VI, subsequently absolved and freed Rienzi and sent him with Cardinal Albornoz to Italy. The cardinal made him senator, and Rienzi entered Rome in triumph, but his violent and arbitrary rule soon resulted in a popular uprising and in his murder. In modern times Rienzi has been idealized as a forerunner of Italian nationalism. See study by Victor Fleischer (1948, repr. 1970).

Riesa (rē'zä), city (1970 pop. 49,746), Dresden dist., SE East Germany, on the Elbe River. It is a river port and an industrial center. Manufactures include steel, furniture, and rubber goods. Riesa developed around a 12th-century Benedictine monastery (now in ruins).

Riesener, Jean Henri (zhäN äNrē' rēzənĕr'), 1734–1806, French cabinetmaker, one of the major artists who made important contributions to the formation of the Louis XVI style in France. Born in Germany, he early moved to Paris and joined the Arsenal workshop of J. F. Oeben, with whom he collaborated in the creation of Louis XV's writing desk, finished in 1769, one of the supremely fine achievements of 18th-century cabinetmaking. After Oeben's death (c.1765), Riesener became conductor of the Arsenal workshops and continued the production of sumptuous furniture for the court and fashionable society. Riesener's furniture pieces are distinguished for their architectural lines, finely executed adornments in chiseled bronze, and exquisite marquetries. Examples are in the Louvre, Compiègne, Fontainebleau, Windsor, and the Wallace Collection, London.

Riesengebirge: see KRKONOŠE, mountains.

Rietveld, Gerrit Thomas (gĕrĭt' tō'məs rēt'fĕlt), 1888–1965, Dutch architect and furniture designer. At first a cabinetmaker, Rietveld created (c.1917) a chair that was an important contribution to modern furniture design. Moving away from the established heavy, closed furniture style, he emphasized a dematerialized effect. From 1919 to 1931 he was a member of the STIJL movement, during which time he turned to architecture. His best-known building is the Schröder House, Utrecht (1924) in which he created an impression of weightlessness and equilibrium that are clearly related to Mondrian's painting style. See studies by Theodore Brown (1958) and A. Buffinga (tr. 1971).

rifampin (rĭfăm'pĭn), ANTIBIOTIC used in the treatment of TUBERCULOSIS. It is also used to eliminate the meningococcus microorganism from carriers and to treat LEPROSY, or Hansen's disease. Rifampin, or rifampicin, as it was formerly called, acts by inhibiting protein synthesis in sensitive cells. It is a toxic drug whose use is still largely experimental. Because resistant microorganisms emerge during treatment, rifampin is used along with other drugs, e.g., with ISONIAZID and ethambutol for tuberculosis treatment, and with sulfones (see SULFA DRUGS) in the treatment of leprosy.

Rif Atlas, range of the Atlas Mts., NE Morocco, NW Africa, curving along the Mediterranean coast from Ceuta to Melilla. Tidighin (8,056 ft/2,455 m) is the highest peak. Composed of sedimentary rocks and uplifted during the Alpine orogeny, the range is a continuation of the Sierra Nevada of Spain and is separated from it by the Strait of Gibraltar. The region is inhabited by Berber tribes, who generally were independent of any central authority until subdued (1925–26) by the campaign of France and Spain against Abd el-Krim.

rifle: see SMALL ARMS.

rift valley, elongated depression, trough, or graben in the earth's crust, bounded on both sides by normal faults. The central block forming the trough has slipped downward relative to the crustal blocks on either side. Because its general appearance is that of a fallen keystone in a broken arch, it was first thought that rift valleys were formed solely by tensional forces fracturing and pulling apart the earth's crust. Most geologists today believe that thermal currents in the earth's mantle break the earth's crust into vast slabs, or plates, that slide around upon a plastic region in the earth's mantle (the ASTHENOSPHERE). Sites where great slabs of crust are being arched upward and fractured become rift valleys. Volcanic activity associated with this rifting process produces new crustal material that is pushed upward from within the earth's mantle. Active rift valley zones such as the Red Sea and the African Rift Valleys (sections of the Great Rift Valley of SW Asia and E Africa) are centers of volcanic and earthquake activity and are thought to be regions that will become future oceans as the land is rifted apart. The rifting process is of critical importance to the theories of SEA-FLOOR SPREADING and PLATE TECTONICS.

Riga (rē'gə), city (1970 pop. 733,000), capital of the Latvian Soviet Socialist Republic, NW European USSR, on the Daugava (Western Dvina) River near its entry into the Gulf of Riga. A major Baltic port, it is also a rail junction, a military base, and one of the USSR's leading industrial and cultural centers. Among Riga's industries are machine building, metalworking, shipbuilding and repairing, woodworking, food processing, and the manufacture of diesel engines, streetcars, chemicals, pharmaceuticals, electrical apparatus, radio and telephone equipment, meteorological instruments, textiles, building materials, and paper. The site had long been occupied by Baltic tribes when the monk Meinhard built a monastery c.1190 among a settlement of Livs. German merchants established a community at Riga in 1158. Bishop Albert of Livonia transferred his seat there in 1201 and founded the LIVONIAN BROTHERS OF THE SWORD, or Livonian Knights, a German military religious order whose mission was to spread Christianity in the Baltic region. The knights also established a trading station at Riga. The city, which became an archiepiscopal see in 1254 and a member of the HANSEATIC LEAGUE in 1282, developed into a major commercial and handicraft center. Its favorable strategic location made it an intermediary in Russian trade with Western Europe. Although it belonged to the domain of the Livonian Knights, Riga maintained a semi-independent existence under its archbishops and German merchants, and it controlled a large part of Livonia. Riga's acceptance of the Reformation in 1522 definitively ended the power of the archbishops there. After the dissolution of the Livonian Order in 1561, Riga was briefly independent and then passed (1581) to Poland, despite attempts by Ivan IV of Russia to seize it. Polish efforts to reintroduce Catholicism made the capture of Riga in 1621 by King Gustavus II of Sweden a welcome event for the Protestant citizens. The Swedes granted self-government to the city. Captured (1710) by Czar Peter I during the NORTHERN WAR, Riga and the rest of Swedish Livonia were ceded to Russia by the Treaty of Nystadt in 1721. Having declined during the 17th cent., Riga's commercial importance revived in the 18th and particularly with the coming of the railroad in the 19th. The city became second only to St. Petersburg as Russia's leading port and was the center of Europe's timber trade. A leading Russian industrial center from the second half of the 19th cent., Riga had the third largest number of industrial workers (after Moscow and St. Petersburg) by the 1890s. The city was a stronghold of the Russian Social Democratic party and played an important role in the Revolution of 1905. German troops occupied Riga in 1917. After World War I, the independence of Latvia was proclaimed at Riga, which became the new country's capital. When Latvia was incorporated into the USSR in 1940, Riga was made the capital of the Latvian SSR. During World War II the city was again occupied (1941) by the Germans, from whom it was retaken (1944) by the Soviet army. Riga is the site of a university (est. 1919), the Latvian Academy of Sciences (1946), and numerous other educational and cultural institutions. The old section, or Hansa town, of Riga is circled by a park-lined moat and includes the ancient castle of the Livonian Knights (rebuilt at various periods), the 13th-century Lutheran cathedral (rebuilt 16th cent.), and the Parliament building (19th cent.). The famous Hanseatic Schwarzhaupter House (15th cent.) and the Church of St. Peter with a steeple 412 ft (126 m) high were largely destroyed during World War II. The old town, with its narrow, cobbled streets lined with gabled dwellings and warehouses, has retained much of its medieval character. Riga's new sections are spacious and modern.

Riga, Gulf of, eastern arm of the Baltic Sea, W European USSR, bordering on Estonia and on Latvia. At its mouth it is nearly closed off by the Estonian island of Sarema. The gulf, which is frozen from December to April, receives the Western Dvina River. Riga and Parnu are the chief ports.

Riga, Treaty of, either of two peace treaties signed at Riga, Latvia. By the Treaty of Riga of **1920,** between the USSR and Latvia, the USSR recognized Latvian independence. The Treaty of Riga of **1921,** between the USSR and Poland, followed a truce concluded late in 1920. The war between Poland and the USSR (1920) had been precipitated largely by the demand of POLAND that its eastern border of 1772 be restored. The treaty terms, which fixed the Russo-Polish border, did not satisfy the claims of the victorious Poles, but they awarded to Poland large parts of Belorussia and of Ukraine. Nullified by the German and Soviet invasion of Poland in 1939, the treaty was replaced in 1945 by a new Russo-Polish border agreement.

Rigaud, André (äNdrā' rēgō'), 1761–1811, Haitian mulatto general in the wars that liberated Haiti. Educated, but vain, he believed in the superiority of mulattoes. He sought (1798–1800) unsuccessfully to wrest the leadership from TOUSSAINT L'OUVERTURE. In 1802 he went to France, returned with General Leclerc and was sent back again as a prisoner. In 1810, once again on Haitian soil, he tried to overthrow Alexandre PÉTION in the south. Defeated, he died, presumably by starving himself to death.

Rigaud, Hyacinthe (Hyacinthe Rigaud y Ros) (yäsăNt'; ē rôs), 1659–1743, French portrait painter, b. Perpignan. From 1688 he became almost exclusively the official painter of the French court. His sitters included most of the royal family and distinguished visitors at Versailles. Much of his portrait style is based on Van Dyck and stresses social rank over the individuality of his subjects. He is best known for his portraits of Louis XIV, in which the regal bearing and splendid costume of the ruler are accentuated. Rigaud is well represented in the Louvre.

Rigel (rī'jəl), bright star in the constellation ORION; Bayer designation Beta Orionis; 1970 position R.A. $5^h31.1^m$, Dec. $-8°14'$. A huge, blue supergiant of SPECTRAL CLASS B8 Ia, Rigel has an intrinsic brightness about 40,000 times as luminous as that of the sun. It is an irregular VARIABLE STAR, with apparent MAGNITUDE ranging from 0.08 to 0.20, making it normally the seventh-brightest star in the sky. Its distance from the earth is nearly 1,000 light-years. Rigel is actually a four-star system consisting of a visual BINARY STAR, each component of which is itself a spectroscopic binary. Its name is from the Arabic word meaning "foot," indicating its position in the constellation.

rigging, the wires, ropes, and chains employed to support and operate the masts, yards, booms, and sails of a vessel. Standing rigging is semipermanent, consisting mainly of mast supports, the fore-and-aft stays, and the stays running from the masthead to each side of the vessel. Running rigging includes the ropes, blocks, and other apparatus needed to brace the yards, make or take in sails, and hoist cargo.

Riggs, Bobby (Robert Larimore Riggs), 1918–, U.S. tennis player, b. Los Angeles. Playing tennis from the age of 11, Riggs won several tournaments in the 1930s and helped the U.S. team win the Davis Cup in 1938. After winning the U.S. singles (1939, 1941), he turned professional (1941). He won the national professional singles championship in 1946, 1947, and 1949. In May, 1973, he emerged from retirement as a professional tennis competitor to play Margaret Court, whom he defeated in a nationally televised winner-take-all match. Proclaiming the superiority of the male athlete over the female no matter what the age, he challenged Billie Jean King to a match. Riggs was soundly defeated (Sept., 1973) by her before a national television audience and 30,492 spectators in Houston.

Riggs, Elias, 1810–1901, American missionary, noted for his mastery of the Semitic languages and of Greek, b. New Providence, N.J. For 67 years after his ordination (1832) to the Presbyterian ministry, Riggs was a missionary in Greece, Asia Minor, and Turkey. His translation of the Scriptures into Armenian (1853) was followed by his Bulgarian translation (1871), and he was a member of the committee that prepared the standard Turkish text (1878). He also prepared grammars of the Chaldee, modern Armenian, and Turkish languages.

right, in politics, the more conservative groups in the political spectrum, in contrast to the radical LEFT and the liberal CENTER. The designation stems from the seating of the nobility on the right side of the presiding officer in the French National Assembly of 1789. In some European legislative assemblies conservative members are still seated in that position.

Right, Petition of: see PETITION OF RIGHT.

right ascension, in astronomy, one of the coordinates in the EQUATORIAL COORDINATE SYSTEM. The right ascension of a celestial body is the angular distance measured eastward from the vernal equinox along the celestial equator to its intersection with the body's HOUR CIRCLE.

right-handedness: see HANDEDNESS.

right of way, in land and air traffic and in sea navigation, rules that determine precedence in the use of traffic lanes. The rules are framed in the simplest possible terms and with nearly absolute uniformity in order to minimize the possibility of collisions. In land traffic, railroad trains, military vehicles in convoy, government vehicles (e.g., mail trucks), and emergency vehicles have the right of way over ordinary private vehicles. Rules of sea and air navigation are largely governed by international conventions and law. The term "right of way" is also applied to an EASEMENT in gross (e.g., that of a railroad). See AIR, LAW OF THE; MARITIME LAW.

right whale, name for WHALES of the family Balaenidae. They were so named by whalers, who for centuries considered them "the right whales" to hunt, because they float when killed and because they yield enormous quantities of oil and of baleen. Baleen, or whalebone, is the substance forming the fringed, triangular plates that hang from the roof of the whale's mouth and serve as a filter for plankton. It commanded such a high price in the 19th cent. that baleen whales (right whales and rorquals) were nearly exterminated by hunting. Right whales are distinguished from rorquals by the lack both of a dorsal fin and of neck furrows. Their girth is great in proportion to their length, and they have two thick pectoral fins. The lower jaws are scooplike in shape; the upper jaws contain about 300 baleen plates. The black right whale (*Eubalaena glacialis*) is usually black all over; some individuals have white [...] sides. The female, larger than the male, av[...] to 60 ft (14–18 m) in length. There is a[...] shaped, horny growth, called the bon[...] snout. It has no known function a[...] an immense conglomeration of p[...]

three subspecies of black right whales, inhabiting the N Atlantic and N Pacific oceans and the Southern Hemisphere, respectively. The northern populations travel to the equator in winter, breeding on their way back to the poles. The bowhead, Greenland, or Arctic right whale (*Balaena mysticus*) remains near the ice front all year, following its seasonal advances and recessions. It is black with a white chin and often a white tail band; there is a bump on top of the head. Its baleen plates grow up to 13 ft (4 m) long, and it produces large quantities of oil. Like the black right whale, it appears to be near extinction. The 20-foot-long (6 m) pygmy sperm whale is found in the waters of Australia and New Zealand. Right whales are classified in the phylum CHORDATA, subphylum Vertebrata, class Mammalia, order Cetacea, family Balaenidae.

Rigi (rē'gē), mountain, in the Alps, N central Switzerland, between the lakes of Lucerne, Zug, and Lauerz, rising to 5,908 ft (1,801 m) at the Kulm, the highest peak. Ascended by rack-and-pinion railways (built in the 1870s), it commands one of the most famous views in the world—a panorama of nearly 180 mi (290 km).

Rigil Kent (rī'jəl): see ALPHA CENTAURI.

rigor mortis (rī'gər môr'tĭs), rigidity of the body that occurs after death. The onset may vary from about 10 min to several hours or more after death, depending on the condition of the body at death and on factors in the atmosphere. Rigor mortis affects the facial musculature first and then spreads to other parts of the body. It is caused by chemical changes in the muscle tissue. The state of rigor lasts about 24 hr; then bacterial decomposition and acid formation begin to exert their effects.

Rigsdag: see FOLKETING.

Rig-Veda (rĭg-vā'də): see VEDA.

Riihimäki (rē'hĭmă"kē), town (1970 pop. 22,862), Häme prov., S Finland. It is a railroad junction and industrial center with glass and chemical industries.

Riis, Jacob August (rēs), 1849–1914, Danish-American journalist and social reformer, b. Denmark. He emigrated to the United States in 1870. In 1877 he became a police reporter for the New York *Tribune* and later for the New York *Evening Sun*. His reports on slum dwellings and abuses of lower-class urban life culminated in his first book, *How the Other Half Lives* (1890), and earned him the friendship of Theodore Roosevelt. Together they worked to improve New York City. Riis founded a pioneer settlement house in New York (named for him in 1901). His association with the public park and playground movements was commemorated by the Jacob Riis Park on Long Island. See his autobiography, *The Making of an American* (1901; new ed. with epilogue by his grandson, J. Riis Owre, 1970); biography by L. Ware (1938).

Rijeka (rēĕ'kä) or **Fiume** (fēo͞o'mē, Ital. fyo͞o'mā), city (1971 pop. 132,933), NW Yugoslavia, in Croatia, on the Adriatic Sea and the Gulf of Quarnero. Yugoslavia's largest seaport, it exports ores, timber, and grain, and imports cotton, petroleum, and coal. The city's industries include shipbuilding and oil refining. Dating from Roman times, Rijeka was later held by the Franks. From the 9th to the 14th cent., Croatian dukes ruled the city. It passed to Austria in 1466. Rijeka, which became a free port in 1723, was united with Croatia in 1776, but three years later Austria transferred it to Hungary. It flourished as a major Hungarian port. The French held it briefly during the Napoleonic Wars, but in 1814 it was restored to Austria, which transferred it to Hungary in 1822. After World War I, Rijeka became an object of dispute between Italy and Yugoslavia. The secret Treaty of London (1915) promised it to Yugoslavia, but at the Paris Peace Conference Italy claimed it on the grounds that Italian-speaking inhabitants formed a majority of the population. While negotiations continued, the poet Gabriele D'ANNUNZIO at the head of an Italian free corps seized the city in Sept., 1919. By the Treaty of Rapallo (1920), Italy and Yugoslavia agreed to establish Rijeka as a free state. In 1922, however, a Fascist coup overthrew the local government, and Italian troops occupied Rijeka. The Treaty of Rome (1924) eased tensions by leaving Rijeka in Italian hands but awarding its eastern suburb, Susak (Ital. *Porto Barros*), to Yugoslavia. Susak was developed into a leading Yugoslav seaport. In 1945 Rijeka passed under Yugoslav administration, and in 1947 the Allied peace treaty with Italy formally transferred it to Yugoslavia, which reunited it with Susak as a single city.

Rijks Museum or **Ryks Museum** (both: rīks), Dutch national museum in Amsterdam, founded in 1808 by Louis Napoleon Bonaparte, King of Holland, as the Great Royal Museum in the Royal Palace. In the same year, 225 paintings from the National Museum in The Hague (est. 1798) were added to the collection, and the city of Amsterdam contributed seven paintings, including Rembrandt's *Shooting Company of Capt. Frans Banning Cocq* and *Syndics of the Drapers' Guild*. In 1815 the museum was named the Rijks Museum (state museum) and housed (1817–85) in the Trippenhuis. The present building, designed by P. J. H. Cuypers, was opened in 1885 to accommodate the fast-growing collection. The Nederlands Museum, containing the collection of sculpture, decorative arts, and historical objects, was housed in the same building and opened two years later. The Rijks Museum is famous for its outstanding collection of Dutch paintings and drawings, particularly of the 17th cent. Rembrandt, Frans Hals, Vermeer, Ruisdael, Jan Steen, the Dutch primitives, and many others are well represented. Most paintings done after 1850 have been transferred on loan to the Municipal Museum of Amsterdam.

Rijn: see RHINE, river.

Rijswijk (rīs'vīk), city (1971 pop. 50,482), South Holland prov., W Netherlands, near The Hague. It has varied industries. The Treaty of Ryswick (see RYSWICK, TREATY OF) was signed here in 1697. Ryswick is a former spelling.

Riksdag (rēks'däg, rēks'tä), national parliament of Sweden, formed in 1866. Originally a two-chamber legislature, it became a single chamber body in 1971. Representation in the chamber is proportional. Members are elected by universal suffrage for a term of three years. The cabinet is responsible to the Riksdag. A new constitution, effective in Jan., 1975, which eliminated the monarch's residual authority, gave the speaker of the Riksdag rather than the king the right to appoint a new premier.

Riley, Bridget, 1931–, English painter. Associated with the POP ART movement, Riley covers large canvases with interlocking bands, undulating curves, scattered discs, or repeated squares or triangles. Because of their sequential arrangement and the relationship of their color values, these patterns create optical sensations of rhythmically vibrating surfaces. Riley's work is represented in the Museum of Modern Art, New York City. See study by Maurice de Sausmarez (1970).

Riley, Charles Valentine, 1843–95, American entomologist, b. England. He emigrated to the United States in 1860 and served as state entomologist (1868–77) of Missouri and as entomologist (1878–79, 1881–94) in the Dept. of Agriculture. Riley has been called the father of modern economic entomology. His observations and suggestions helped control the destructive cottony cushion scale in California (by introducing parasites from Australia) and virtually saved the wine industry of France from the grape PHYLLOXERA. He founded the periodical *Insect Life* and served as editor from 1889 to 1894.

Riley, James Whitcomb, 1849–1916, American poet, b. Greenfield, Ind., known as the Hoosier poet. He was at various times a traveling actor, a sign painter, and finally a newspaperman. Under the name "Benj. F. Johnson of Boone" he began to write verse for the Indianapolis *Journal* in 1875, selections first collected in *"The Old Swimmin'-Hole" and 'Leven More Poems* (1883). This volume, containing the favorite "When the Frost is on the Punkin," was followed by many others, mostly written in Hoosier dialect. Riley's verse was extremely popular because of its humor, pathos, simplicity, and sentimentality. Especially well-known are his children's poems such as "Little Orphant Annie," "The Raggedy Man," and "The Runaway Boy." Among the collections of his verse are *Rhymes of Childhood* (1890) and *Knee Deep in June* (1912). See biography by Marcus Dickey (*Youth,* 1919; *Maturity,* 1922); study by Peter Revell (1970).

Riley, Fort: see FORT RILEY.

Rilke, Rainer Maria (rĭ'nər märē'ä rĭl'kə), 1875–1926, German poet, b. Prague, the greatest lyric poet of modern Germany. His youth at military school and business school was not happy. His relations with his father were difficult, and he was able to attend the Univ. of Prague only with the help of an uncle. Married only briefly (1901–2), Rilke preferred an unsettled, wandering life among literary people; he was greatly influenced by his travels, notably by trips to Russia (1899, 1900). The sculptor Rodin, a close friend of Rilke who employed him as secretary (1905–6), shaped the poet's career by introducing him to the craftsman's approach to creativity. After extensive travel in Italy, North Africa, and elsewhere, Rilke returned to Paris (1913), but World War I drove him back to Germany, where war service and chronic ill health frustrated his work. After 1919 he lived at Castle Muzot, in Valais canton, Switzerland. He died from blood poisoning, contracted from the prick of a rose thorn. Rilke was sensitive and introspective. His poetic style was rich, varying from the simple to the elaborate and profound. It is generally characterized by striking visual imagery, by musicality, and by a preponderant use of nouns. In tone Rilke's verse was often mystical and prophetic; he used symbolism as a means of expression and created poetry that bears a strong resemblance to medieval verse. This resemblance may reflect Rilke's religious outlook—his probing into the emotional and spiritual nature of man and his absorption with death as a poetic theme. Rilke was antimodern in many ways, an attitude particularly evident in his antipathy for large modern cities. His first book of poetry, *Leben und Lieder* [life and songs], appeared in 1894, but not until the stories of *Geschichten vom lieben Gott* (1904, tr. *Stories of God,* 1931) did his mature mysticism find expression. His visits to Russia inspired one of the three books of *Das Stundenbuch* (1905, tr. *Poems from the Book of Hours,* 1941), with which he achieved fame and in which he treated God as an evolutionary concept. His *Neue Gedichte* [new poems] (2 vol., 1907–8) are distinguished by the power and beauty of their verse, and critics often prefer them to Rilke's own favorite verse, his *Duineser Elegien* (1923, tr. *Duinese Elegies,* 1930, 1939), which are written in a purposely staccato style and contain his most positive praise of human existence. Rilke's reputation has ascended to great heights since his death. Most of his work has been translated. See his *Journal of My Other Self* (tr. 1930) and *Letter to a Young Poet* (rev. ed. 1954); biographies by H. F. Peters (1960) and E. M. Butler (1941, repr. 1973); studies by E. C. Mason (1961), K. A. Batterby (1966), J. Rolleston, and A. Stephens (tr. 1972).

rille (rĭl): see MOON.

Rímac (rē'mäk), river, c.80 mi (130 km) long, rising in the Andes of W Peru, and flowing W through Lima to the Pacific Ocean near Callao. It is used extensively for irrigation. The scenic Rímac valley affords one of the chief lines of communication to the high, interior mountain basins.

Rimbaud, Arthur (ärtür' răNbō'), 1854–91, French poet who had a great influence on the SYMBOLISTS and subsequent modern poets. A defiant and precocious youth, Rimbaud at 16 sent some poems to VERLAINE, who liked his work and invited him to Paris. In 1872–73 the two poets lived together in London and Brussels. In a drunken quarrel Verlaine fired a pistol, wounding Rimbaud, and their relationship ended. Rimbaud returned home and finished *Une Saison en enfer* (1873), a confessional autobiography in which he renounces his former hellish life and his work. At an undetermined time he produced *Les Illuminations,* consisting of prose poems that transcend all traditional syntax and narrative elements. He probably stopped writing poetry at the age of 19, and thereafter he wandered throughout Europe and N Africa, engaging in numerous business ventures. After the amputation of his leg he died in Marseilles at 37. Rimbaud's poetry has been called hallucinatory because the poet seems to write not of material reality but of his dreamworld; his technique anticipates the symbolists by its suggestiveness, its abstract verbal music, and its images drawn from the subconscious. *Le Bateau ivre* [the drunken boat] is an outstanding example. Rimbaud's works were published by Verlaine in several posthumous editions, the first complete collection appearing in 1898. See biographies by Elizabeth Hanson (1960) and Enid Starkie (3rd ed. 1961, repr. 1968); studies by W. M. Frohock (1963), W. Fowlie (1966), and R. G. Cohn (1974).

rime: see RHYME.

Rimini (rē'mēnē), anc. *Ariminum,* city (1971 pop. 119,541), in Emilia-Romagna, N central Italy, on the Adriatic Sea. It is a commercial, industrial, and railroad center and a fashionable beach resort. Food products and wine are manufactured, and there are fisheries. Located at the junction of the Flaminian and Aemilian Ways, the city was a Roman colony of strategic importance (founded in the mid-3d cent. B.C.). It later came under Byzantine rule and was a member of the Pentapolis. Rimini was included in Pepin the Short's donation to the popes (754). The MALATESTA family seized power in Rimini in the 13th cent. and later conquered neighboring cities. FRANCESCA DA RIMINI married (13th cent.) a Malatesta. In 1509 the city passed under papal control. The Tempio Malatestiana, a 13th-century church that Sigismondo Malatesta had renovated (c.1450) by Alberti to honor his wife Isotta, is a fine Renaissance-style building. Of note also are the Arch of Augustus (27 B.C.) and the Bridge of Tiberius (completed in A.D. 21).

Rimmer, William, 1816–79, American sculptor and writer, b. Liverpool, England. He was brought up in the United States and after working as a cobbler in Brocton, Mass., at the age of 30 began the study of medicine. He practiced medicine for a number of years, at the same time painting occasional portraits and religious subjects. In 1855 he began to carve in granite. Among his early works are *Despair* (Mus. of Fine Arts, Boston) and the *Falling Gladiator* (Metropolitan Mus.). His knowledge of anatomy and his imaginative power are apparent in the few pieces that survive. He completed statues of Alexander Hamilton (Boston) and Osiris in 1864. Other remaining sculptures are *The Dying Centaur* and *Fighting Lions* (Metropolitan Mus.). In 1876, Rimmer became professor of anatomy and sculpture at the School of the Museum of Fine Arts, Boston. He was director and chief instructor (1866–70) of the School of Design for Women, Cooper Union, New York City. He wrote *Elements of Design* (1864) and *Art Anatomy* (1877).

Rimmon (rĭm'ən). **1** Syrian god. 2 Kings 5.18. **2** Father of the murderers of Ish-bosheth. 2 Sam. 4.2–9. **3** Rock, E of Bethel. There the remnants of the Benjamites took refuge after the battle of Gibeah. Judges 20.45,47; 21.13. **4** See EN-RIMMON. **5** Levitical town, N Palestine, the modern Rummana (Israel), N of Nazareth. 1 Chron. 6.77. Remmon-methoar: Joshua 19.13. Dimnah: Joshua 21.35.

Rimmon-parez (rĭm'ən-pā'rĕz), unlocated resting place in the desert, S of the Dead Sea. Num. 33.19,20.

Rimouski (rĭmo͞o'skē), town (1971 pop. 26,887), S Que., Canada, on the south shore of the St. Lawrence River, NE of Quebec. It has lumber industries, dairy processing, and telecommunications-equipment plants. A Roman Catholic cathedral and seminary are there.

Rimsky-Korsakov, Nicolai Andreyevich (nyĭkəlī əndrā'əvĭch rĭm'skē-kôr'səkôf), 1844–1908, Russian composer; one of the group of nationalist composers called The FIVE. He prepared himself for a naval career, but after meeting BALAKIREV in 1861 he turned seriously to composing. In 1871 he became professor of composition at the St. Petersburg Conservatory, retiring from the navy two years later. In 1833 he became assistant to Balakirev, who was director of the Imperial Chapel. He conducted the St. Petersburg Symphony Concerts, 1886–1900. Although his first symphony (1865) and his symphonic poem *Sadko* (1867) were the first works in these forms by a Russian, more important are his operas, notably *The Snow Maiden* (1881), based on the play by Ostrovski; *The Maid of Pskov* (1873, rev. 1892; also known as *Ivan the Terrible*); *Sadko* (1895); and *Le Coq d'Or* (*The Golden Cockerel,* posthumously performed 1909). The best known of Rimsky-Korsakov's orchestral works is *Scheherezade* (1888), which was used by the Diaghilev ballet. It probably best exemplifies his romantic exoticism and mastery of orchestral color. Glazunov, Gretchanin, and Stravinsky were among his pupils. He wrote a treatise on orchestration and an autobiography, *My Musical Life* (tr., 3d ed., 1942).

Rinehart, Mary Roberts (rīn'härt), 1876–1958, American novelist, b. Pittsburgh. A graduate nurse, she married Dr. Stanley M. Rinehart in 1896. The first of her many mystery stories, *The Circular Staircase* (1908), established her as a leading writer of the genre; Rinehart and Avery Hopwood successfully dramatized the novel as *The Bat* (1920). Her other mystery novels include *The Man in Lower Ten* (1909), *The Case of Jennie Brice* (1914), *The Red Lamp* (1925), *The Door* (1930), *The Yellow Room* (1945), and *The Swimming Pool* (1952). Stories about "Tish," a self-reliant spinster, first appeared in the *Saturday Evening Post* and were collected into *The Best of Tish* (1955). See Rinehart's autobiography (1931, rev. ed. 1948).

Rinehart, William Henry, 1825–74, American sculptor, b. near Union Bridge, Md. A Baltimore stonecutter, he became one of the best of the early American sculptors, working in the classic vein. He lived in Italy after 1858. His works are best seen in the Peabody Institute, Baltimore, where there are casts of 42 of his figures, reliefs, and busts and 3 marble originals, including his masterpiece, *Clytie.* He left a fund for the education of American sculptors, first used in 1895.

ring, small ornamental hoop usually worn on finger or thumb, but it may be attached to the ear or the nose. Finger rings made of bronze, gold, and silver from the period c.2500–1500 B.C. have been found in the Indus valley in India; in Egypt rings from c.1600 B.C. served as a symbol of status and were exchanged as a pledge or seal of faith. They were often also used as money. The signet ring grew from the custom of wearing a cylindrical seal suspended from the arm or neck, developed in Egypt, and was widely adopted as a seal of authority. Numerous rings were worn by Egyptian women, sometimes as many as three on a finger. In Greece gold bands were worn; later they were engraved with cameos or intaglios. Talismanic rings, endowed with many charms and powers, were also worn. In the middle and latter part of the Roman civilization the type of ring worn was governed by law. Iron rings were worn by the mass of the people; gold rings were reserved for those of civil or military rank. Later the gold ring was permitted to freeborn citizens, silver to freedmen, and iron to slaves. The Romans also used poison rings for assassination or suicide in the case of capture by an enemy. In addition there were key rings, which, worn by a matron, symbolized her authority to carry the keys of the house. The betrothal ring, used by Egyptians, Greeks, and Romans, was adopted by early Christians in the 2d cent. and later evolved into the wedding ring. The engagement ring set with a precious gem came into use in the Middle Ages; the diamond attained popularity in the 15th cent. and became customary c.1800. From the Middle Ages rings have figured in the coronation of kings and the consecration of bishops as emblems of authority or mystical significance. Since that time a gold seal ring (Fisherman's ring) with an intaglio of St. Peter in a fishing boat has been given each pope and is destroyed when he dies. By the 16th cent. the extravagant use of rings had reached its height. Highly decorated with enamel and jewels, they were sometimes worn on every finger and on several joints. At that time, too, the gold wedding band became popular, and signet rings were engraved with the family crest. Later, memorial rings and mourning rings became fashionable. See William Jones, *Finger-Ring Lore* (1898, repr. 1968); J. R. McCarthy, *Rings Through the Ages* (1945).

ring, in mathematics, system consisting of a set of elements, or mathematical objects, and two binary operations, usually considered addition and multiplication, such that the following requirements are satisfied: (1) the set of elements is closed under both operations, i.e., for any two elements in the set the sum and product is also in the set; (2) the COMMUTATIVE LAW holds for addition; (3) the ASSOCIATIVE LAW holds for both addition and multiplication; (4) the DISTRIBUTIVE LAW holds for multiplication over addition; (5) there exists a zero element, 0, in the set such that for every element a in the set $a+0=a$; and (6) for every a in the set there exists an inverse of a, denoted as $-a$, such that $a+(-a)=0$. A commutative ring is one in which the commutative law also holds for multiplication. Examples of commutative rings are the set of rational numbers (see NUMBER) and the set of real numbers.

ringbone, bony outgrowth on the front and sides of the pastern bones of a horse's foot, resulting from inflammation or faulty conformation of the bones. The outgrowths increase with sprains and other injuries. Ringbone often produces lameness and is difficult to remedy. It may be controlled by keeping the feet of young animals in proper balance by correct trimming. In cases where swelling above the top edge of the hoof wall has developed and lameness is marked, the sensory nerves may have to be cut.

ring compound: see AROMATIC COMPOUND.

Ring des Nibelungen, Der: see NIBELUNGEN.

ringhals: see COBRA.

Ring nebula, planetary NEBULA in the northern constellation Lyra; cataloged as M57 or NGC 6720. It is perhaps the most famous and beautiful nebula of this type. Its name describes the appearance of the expanding shell of gas. The nebula is estimated to be more than 5,000 light-years distant.

Ringsted (rĭng'stĕth), city (1970 com. pop. 25,476), Vestsjaelland co., E Denmark. It is the commercial and processing center of a rich agricultural region. Ringsted was a place of pagan worship in ancient Sjaelland, but later became a center of Christianity. It was one of the most important towns in Denmark in the Middle Ages. The 12th-century Benedictine monastery there has a church containing the tombs of several Danish kings of the 12th–13th cent.

ringtail or **ring-tailed cat:** see CACOMISTLE.

ringtail monkey: see CAPUCHIN.

Ringwood, borough (1970 pop. 10,393), Passaic co., N N.J., in the Ramapo Mts. and on the Wanaque River near the N.Y. line. Iron was found nearby in 1730; mines and works were developed from 1764 by Peter Hasenclever, who made Ringwood Manor his headquarters. His successor, Robert Erskine, produced munitions for the patriots in the American Revolution. Other owners of the Ringwood properties included Peter Cooper and Abram S. Hewitt. Presented to the state in 1936, the estate (95 acres/38 hectares) became (1939) a park and the manor house was converted into a museum; Ringwood Manor has been designated a national historic landmark.

ringworm or **tinea** (tĭn'ēə), superficial eruption of the skin caused by a fungus, chiefly *Microsporum, Trichophyton,* or *Epidermophyton.* Any area of the skin may be affected, including the scalp and nails, but the most common site is the feet. That disorder is often called athlete's foot in the belief that the infection is contracted during the use of communal shower facilities. Actually, fungi are present on the bodies of most persons, but some individuals are more resistant to fungus invasion than others. Moreover, a prolonged moist, airless condition caused by excessive perspiration may subject a formerly resistant person to fungus invasion. Ringworm infection causes dry, scaly patches or blisterlike elevations, usually with burning or itching. Griseofulvin, a modified form of penicillin, is effective against scalp infection but is ineffective against foot fungi. In mild cases of athlete's foot, often the only treatment is to keep the feet scrupulously dry. In more persistent cases local antifungal ointments and soaks are recommended; however, overtreatment can cause more damage to the skin than the original eruption.

Rinnah (rĭn'ə), descendant of Judah. 1 Chron. 4.20.

Rinns of Galloway: see GALLOWAY, Scotland.

Río and **Rio,** respectively Spanish and Portuguese terms for river. For those not listed here, see under the second element of the name. Thus, for Río Lerma, see LERMA.

Riobamba (rēōbäm'bä), city (1970 est. pop. 53,700), capital of Chimborazo prov., central Ecuador, near CHIMBORAZO volcano, in a high basin of the Andes. Riobamba is a commercial center on the railroad from Quito to Guayaquil. It was founded c.1530 and was completely destroyed by earthquake in 1797. The convention that proclaimed Ecuador's independence from Greater Colombia met there in 1830. Riobamba has an open-air market where Indian artisans display their wares.

Rio Branco, José Maria da Silva Paranhos, barão do (zho͞ozĕ' mərē'ə də sēl'və pərä'nyo͞os bərouN' do͞o rē'o͞o brăng'ko͞o), 1845–1912, Brazilian statesman and diplomat. He was consul in Liverpool from 1876 to 1893, when he was appointed to plead Brazil's case in the border dispute with Argentina arbitrated by President Grover Cleveland. After winning his case in 1895, he worked on the dispute with French Guiana over the territory of AMAPÁ and again won (1900) a substantial victory. He served briefly as minister to Berlin and returned to Brazil in 1902 to become minister of foreign affairs. In this post, which he held until his death, he concluded some 30 treaties of arbitration. See study by E. F. Burns (1966).

Rio Branco, city (1970 pop. 84,344), capital of Acre state, NW Brazil, on the Acre River. Rubber and Brazil nuts are its chief products; there is also some farming. Rio Branco has air connections with the major cities of Brazil, but river travel is still an important means of transportation. Rio Branco was built on the site of a former rubber plantation.

Río Cuarto (rē'ō kwär'tō), city (1970 pop. 168,689), Córdoba prov., central Argentina, in the W Pampa, on the Río Cuarto. It is the commercial center for a large agricultural area yielding fruit and cattle. The city was settled in the 18th cent. The movement to overthrow Juan Perón in 1955 began at the air force base in Río Cuarto.

Rio de Janeiro (rē'ō də zhänā'rō, Port. rē'o͞o thĭ zhənē'ro͞o), state (1970 pop. 4,746,848), 16,568 sq mi (42,911 sq km), SE Brazil, on the Atlantic Ocean and enclosing the state of GUANABARA. The capital is NITERÓI.

Rio de Janeiro [Port.,=river of January], city (1970 pop. 4,252,009), capital of Guanabara state, SE Brazil, on Guanabara Bay of the Atlantic Ocean. The second largest city and former capital of Brazil, it is the cultural center of the country and a financial, commercial, and transportation hub. Rio, as it is popularly known, has one of the world's most beautiful natural harbors. The harbor is surrounded by low mountain ranges whose spurs extend almost to the waterside, thus dividing the city. Among its natural landmarks are Sugar Loaf Mt. (1,296 ft/395 m); Corcovado peak (2,310 ft/704 m), site of a colossal statue of Christ; and the hills of Tijuca (3,350 ft/1,021 m) and Gávea (2,760 ft/841 m). The city acquired its modern outline in the early 1900s, and extensive public sanitation and remodeling are continuing. Hills have been leveled, tunnels bored (the longest underground urban highway, linking the northern and southern sections of the city, opened in 1968), parts of the bay filled, parks laid out, and beautiful palm-lined drives built to connect the various districts. The harbor is deep enough for even the largest vessels to come alongside the wharves, which lie near the center of the city. Through the port of Rio flows the major portion of Brazil's imports as well as its exports (iron ore, manganese, coffee, cotton, meat, and hides). Rio is also a distribution center for the coastal trade. The city's manufactures include textiles, foodstuffs, household appliances, cigarettes, chemicals, leather goods, metal products, and printed material. There are two major airports. Rio's climate is warm and humid, and the city has a worldwide reputation as a tourist center. Of particular attraction are the crescent-shaped beaches, especially the Copacabana, with its famous mosaic sidewalks. The most popular holiday is the pre-Lenten carnival, with its colorful street processions and reveling Cariocas (citizens of Rio). The sports stadium is one of the world's largest. Examples of Rio's famous modern architecture are the ministry of education, the Brazilian press association headquarters, and the museum of modern art. Older buildings house the national library, the municipal opera house, and several museums. The Itamarati Palace is also noteworthy. Foremost among educational institutions are the Univ. of Guanabara (formed 1920 as the Univ. of Rio de Janeiro), the Univ. of Brazil (1937), now partly housed in the University City on Guanabara Bay, and the Catholic Univ. (1958); there are also military and naval academies, the Oswaldo Cruz biological research center, and other scientific institutes. Notable churches include the ornate Candelária Church, the 18th-century Church of Nossa Senhora da Glória, the 17th-century Franciscan convent, and a 16th-century Benedictine monastery. Rio has beautiful subtropical parks, including the Quinta da Boa Vista (a former estate of the emperors) and the botanical garden (founded 1808). According to tradition, the Rio de Janeiro area was visited in Jan., 1502, by Portuguese explorers who believed Guanabara Bay to be the mouth of a river; it was therefore named Rio de Janeiro. It is more likely that the region was discovered in 1504 by Gonçalo Coelho. In 1555 the French Huguenots established a colony, but they were driven out (1560–67) by Mem de Sá, governor general of the Portuguese colony of Brazil. At the same time the city of São Sebastião do Rio de Janeiro was founded by Mem de Sá's cousin. The settlement was captured and held for ransom by the French in 1711. Rio gained importance in the 18th cent., when it was designated the shipping point for all gold from the interior. It replaced Bahia (now Salvador) as the capital of Brazil in 1763 and subsequently became capital of the exiled royal court of Portugal (1808–21), the Brazilian empire (1822), and the federal republic (1889). It was superseded as capital by BRASÍLIA in 1960. See Hugh Gibson, *Rio* (1937); Marcel Gautherot, *Rio de Janeiro* (1965); L. E. da Costa, *Rio in the Times of the Viceroys* (tr. 1936, repr. 1971).

Río de Oro: see SPANISH SAHARA.

Rio Grande (rē'o͞o grän'dĭ), city (1970 pop. 116,827), Rio Grande do Sul state, S Brazil, on the Rio Grande River at the outlet of the Lagoa dos Patos (a tidal lagoon) to the Atlantic Ocean. It is an important outport for the city of Pôrto Alegre on the northern end of the lagoon. Rio Grande has refrigeration plants, oil refineries, and factories producing foodstuffs, spices, leather, and tires. The city was founded in 1737.

Rio Grande, name of several rivers of Brazil. The largest rises in S Minas Gerais state, SE Brazil, and flows c.650 mi (1,050 km) NW to the Paranaíba River, with which it forms the Paraná River. Its lower course forms part of São Paulo's northern boundary. The huge Furnas Dam with its reservoir near Passos, Minas Gerais, serves the industrial heart of Brazil with hydroelectricity.

Rio Grande (rē'ō grănd, rē'ō grän'dē), river, c.1,885 mi (3,000 km) long, rising in SW Colo. in the San Juan Mts. and flowing south through the middle of N.Mex., past Albuquerque, then meandering generally southeast as the border between Texas and Mexico, making a big bend (see BIG BEND NATIONAL PARK) and eventually emptying into the Gulf of Mexico at Brownsville, Texas, and Matamoros, Mexico. Other paired towns are Laredo, Texas, and Nuevo Laredo, Mexico, and El Paso, Texas, and Juárez, Mexico. The Rio Grande is unnavigable except near its mouth; Brownsville is the river's chief port. Indian pueblos were thriving on its banks N of Las Cruces, N.Mex., when Francisco Vásquez de Coronado, the Spanish explorer, came (1540), and the Indians were then practicing irrigation of the arid country. Dams on the Rio Grande are used for irrigation, flood control, and regulation of flow. Elephant Butte Dam (completed 1916) and Caballo Dam (completed 1938) in New Mexico create reservoirs that serve large areas. Further downstream N of Del Rio, Texas, is the Amisted Dam (completed 1969); it is 6 mi (9.7 km) long and impounds a huge reservoir. Amisted National Recreation Area is there. Below Laredo are Falcon Dam (completed 1954) and its large reservoir. Near the mouth of the Rio Grande is the citrus-fruit and truck-farm region commonly called the Rio Grande Valley and developed principally in the 1920s. An agreement between the United States and Mexico in 1945 provided for future projects to share the river's water. Shifts in the river's channel have led to border disputes between the United States and Mexico. Parts of its bed have been stabilized by canalization, and an international border commission mediates disputes. The 114-year controversy over the location of the border at El Paso was finally settled in 1968 when the water of the Rio Grande was diverted into a concrete channel. The river is known to the Mexicans as Río Bravo del Norte. See Paul Horgan, *Great River: The Rio Grande in North American History* (2 vol., 1954); Harvey Fergusson, *Rio Grande* (2d ed. 1955, repr. 1967).

Rio Grande do Norte (rē'o͞o grän'dĭ tho͞o nôr'tĭ), state (1970 pop. 1,552,158), 20,469 sq mi (53,015 sq km), NE Brazil, on the Atlantic Ocean. NATAL is the capital.

Rio Grande do Sul (rē'o͞o grän'dĭ tho͞o so͞ol), state (1970 pop. 6,670,382), 108,951 sq mi (282,183 sq km), S Brazil, bordering on Argentina and Uruguay and on the Atlantic Ocean. PÔRTO ALEGRE is the capital.

Rioja (rēō'hä), region, N Spain, in Old Castile, along the right bank of the Upper Ebro River. It is very fertile and is famous for its fine wines. Logroño is the chief center.

Riom (rēôN'), town (1968 pop. 16,562), Puy-de-Dôme dept., S central France, in Auvergne. It has distilleries, tobacco plants, and factories making electrical appliances. Of Gallic origin, the Roman Ricomagus grew around the collegiate Church of St. Amable (1077; restored). It was the capital of the dukes of Auvergne. In 1942, Riom was the scene of an abortive trial of French leaders (including Blum, Daladier, and Gamelin) by the Vichy government. The defendants, charged with plunging France into World War II unprepared, produced evidence placing the guilt on their accusers, and the trial was recessed.

Río Muni: see EQUATORIAL GUINEA.

Rion (rēôn'), ancient *Phasis,* river, c.195 mi (310 km) long, rising in the Caucasus near the Mamison Pass, W Georgian SSR, S European USSR, and flowing S and W past Kutaisi into the Black Sea at Poti. Its upper course is used to produce hydroelectric power. In its lower course it passes through the lowland of Mingrelia. The Ossetian Military Road follows the upper Rion valley.

Riopelle, Jean Paul (zhäN pōl rēōpĕl'), 1924–, Canadian painter in France, b. Montreal. Riopelle's inclination toward abstract painting was strengthened by his association with the *automatiste* group in Montreal (see CANADIAN ART AND ARCHITECTURE). In 1947 he settled in Paris and became a leading exponent of nonrepresentational art. The Museum of Modern Art, New York City, has his *Forest Blizzard.*

Río Piedras (pyā'thräs), suburb of San Juan, Puerto Rico, with which it was merged in 1951. It is an industrial and agricultural trading center and the seat of the Univ. of Puerto Rico.

riot, rout, and unlawful assembly, in law, varying degrees of concerted disturbance of the peace. At common law, an unlawful assembly is a gathering for a common purpose (whether lawful or unlawful) of at least three persons whose conduct causes nearby observers to reasonably fear that a breach of the peace will result. When the meeting is a furtherance of a criminal CONSPIRACY, the participation of only two persons will suffice to constitute the crime of unlawful assembly. A gathering, originally peaceable, may be transformed into an unlawful assembly if three or more persons behave in concert so as to palpably threaten disorder. Modern statutes have freed the crime of unlawful assembly from some of its technicalities. Thus there are municipal ordinances that make unlawful an unlicensed street assembly that blocks traffic even if there is no danger of tumult. An unlawful assembly becomes a rout when the participants take some step to achieve their common purpose; e.g., if three men who have assembled unlawfully to commit arson proceed toward the building that they intend to set on fire, they are guilty of a rout even if they never reach their goal. There is a riot if violence actually results from an unlawful assembly. If a police officer (or other officer of the peace) commands bystanders at a riot to help him in repressing it, they must obey on pain of themselves being deemed rioters.

riot-control gas: see POISON GAS; TEAR GAS.

Río Tinto, Ríotinto (both: rē'ō tēn'tō), or **Minas de Ríotinto** (mē'näs dā), town (1970 pop. 7,903), Huelva prov., SW Spain, in the Sierra Morena mts., in Andalusia. It is the center of the Río Tinto mining region, named for the river which crosses it. Known since Phoenician times, the area has some of the world's largest copper deposits and some iron and manganese.

Rio Treaty (Inter-American Treaty of Reciprocal Assistance), signed Sept. 2, 1947, and originally ratified by all 21 American republics. Under the treaty, an armed attack or threat of aggression against a signatory nation, whether by a member nation or by some other power, will be considered an attack against all (see PAN-AMERICANISM). The treaty provides that no member can use force without the unanimous consent of the other signatories, but that other measures against aggressors may be approved by a two-thirds majority. It differs from previous inter-American treaties in that it is a regional treaty within a larger international organization; it recognizes the higher authority of the Security Council of the United Nations.

Riouw Archipelago: see RIAU ARCHIPELAGO, Indonesia.

riparian rights: see WATER RIGHTS.

Riphath (rī'făth), grandson of Japheth. Gen. 10.3; 1 Chron. 1.6.

Ripley, George, 1802–80, American literary critic and author, b. Greenfield, Mass. After graduating from Harvard Divinity School in 1826, he entered the Unitarian ministry. He was one of the leaders of the TRANSCENDENTALISTS and a contributor to their magazine, the *Dial.* In 1841 his interest in social reform led him to resign from the ministry and help found BROOK FARM, where he remained as president until 1847. His edition, with F. H. Hedge, of *Specimens of Foreign Standard Literature,* in translation (14 vol., 1838–42), increased American knowledge of European literature. In his later life he became an influential literary critic on the New York *Tribune,* conducting the first regular book review department in a U.S. newspaper. See biography by O. B. Frothingham (1882, repr. 1970); study by C. R. Crowe (1967).

Ripon, Frederick John Robinson, 1st earl of (rĭp'ən), 1782–1859, British statesman, better known as Viscount Goderich. Entering Parliament as a Tory in 1806, he sponsored the unpopular CORN LAW of 1815 in the House of Commons. However, as president of the Board of Trade (1818–23) and chancellor of the exchequer (1823–27), his liberal policy of tariff reduction was an important step toward free trade. In 1827 he was created Viscount Goderich and was appointed secretary for war and the colonies. On George Canning's death within the same year he became prime minister, but internal strife and his own lack of resolution wrecked his ministry in 1828. Goderich (created earl of Ripon in 1833) served as secretary for war and the colonies (1830–33) and lord privy seal (1833–34). He was president of the Board of Trade (1841–43) and president of the India board of control (1843–46) in Sir Robert Peel's second ministry. By now an opponent of the corn laws, he resigned with Peel when repeal of the laws split the Tories in 1846. See biography by W. D. Jones (1967).

Ripon, George Frederick Samuel Robinson, 1st marquess of, 1827–1909, British statesman and colonial administrator; son of the first earl of Ripon. As a young man he was interested in the Christian Socialist movement and entered the House of Commons as a Liberal in 1853. He moved to the House of Lords after succeeding to his father's title in 1859. He served as secretary for war (1863–66), secretary for India (1866–68), and lord president of the council (1868–73). His successful chairmanship of the commission to negotiate settlement of the *Alabama* claims with the United States was rewarded (1871) with the title of marquess. Ripon resigned from public office in 1873, but in 1880 William Gladstone appointed him viceroy of India. He settled the situation in Afghanistan, introduced a system of local self-government in India, and ended restrictions on freedom of the vernacular press. However, his Ilbert Bill (1883), which would have allowed senior Indian judges to try Europeans, raised a storm of opposition among the Europeans and was drastically modified. After his return (1884) to England he served as first lord of the admiralty (1886), colonial secretary (1892–95), and lord privy seal (1905–8). See biography by Lucien Wolf (1921); study by Sarvepalli Gopal (1953).

Ripon, municipal borough (1971 pop. 10,987), West Riding of Yorkshire, N England, on the Ure River. It has foundries, varnish and paint factories, tanneries, and breweries and is a market town. Ripon is famous as an old cathedral city. There have been monasteries on the site since the 7th cent. The present cathedral dates from the 12th to the 15th cent. It has a Saxon crypt with a narrow passage called St. Wilfrid's Needle; the ability to pass through it was supposed to be an indication of chastity. The Wakeman's House (13th or 15th cent.), in the market place, was the residence of the mayor ("wakeman"). In 1640 a treaty signed in Ripon concluded the second of the BISHOPS' WARS. St. Wilfrid, founder of an early monastery, is commemorated in an annual pageant. In 1974, Ripon became part of the new nonmetropolitan county of North Yorkshire.

Rishon Leziyyon (rē'shōn ləzī'ən, rēshōn' lətsēōn'), town (1970 est. pop. 46,500), W central Israel. It has one of Israel's largest wineries. Rishon Leziyyon was founded in 1882 as the second modern Jewish village to be established in Palestine.

Risorgimento (rēsôr"jĕmĕn'tō) [Ital.,=resurgence], in Italian history, period of cultural nationalism and of political activism in Italy, leading to unification of the country. The Risorgimento's roots lie in 18th-century Italian culture in the works of such people as Ludovico Antonio MURATORI, Vittorio ALFIERI, and Antonio GENOVESI. Italy had not been a single political unit since the fall of the Western Roman Empire in the 5th cent., and from the 16th through the 18th cent. foreign domination or influence was virtually complete. During the French Revolutionary Wars and the period dominated by NAPOLEON I, the temporary expulsion of Austrian and other repressive regimes and the formation of new states in Italy (see CISALPINE REPUBLIC) encouraged hopes for unification. Secret societies such as the CARBONARI appeared and carried on revolutionary activity after the restoration of the old order by the Congress of Vienna (1814–15). The Carbonari engineered uprisings in the Two Sicilies (1820) and in the kingdom of Sardinia (1821). Despite severe reprisals inspired by the HOLY ALLIANCE, new uprisings occurred in 1831 in the Papal States, Modena, and Parma. Italian literature of this period, especially the novels of Alessandro MANZONI and the marchese d'AZEGLIO and the poetry of Ugo FOSCOLO and Giacomo LEOPARDI, did much to stimulate Italian nationalism. The Risorgimento was primarily a movement of the middle class and the nobility; since economic issues were virtually ignored, the peasantry remained indifferent to the political ideals. Political activity was carried on by three groups. Giuseppe MAZZINI led the radical faction through his secret society Giovine Italia [young Italy], founded in 1831. Its program was republican and anticlerical; it vaguely alluded to social and economic reforms. The conservative and clerical elements among the nationalists generally advocated a federation of Italian states under the presidency of the pope. The moderates—the propertied bourgeoisie and the north Italian promoters of industry—favored unification of Italy under a king of the house of Savoy. This monarch, as events later turned out, was VICTOR EMMANUEL II of Sardinia. Sardinia assumed the leadership of the Risorgimento in 1848 when the Lombardo-Venetian kingdom rose against Austrian rule and King CHARLES ALBERT intervened in favor of the rebels. After initial victories Charles Albert was defeated by the Austrians at Custozza and was forced to sign an armistice and withdraw his forces. Renewing his attack in 1849, he was again defeated by the Austrians at Novara and abdicated in favor of his son, Victor Emmanuel II, who made peace. Meanwhile, revolutions were suppressed in Venice (under Daniele MANIN), Parma, Modena, Tuscany, the Two Sicilies, and the Papal States, where a short-lived Roman Republic was proclaimed under the leadership of Mazzini. However, the liberal movement gradually coalesced around Victor Emmanuel II and the policies of his minister Camillo Benso di CAVOUR. Cavour realized that Sardinia could not defeat Austria without foreign aid. He set out to win French support and British sympathy by introducing sweeping social reforms within Sardinia, by inaugurating a free-trade policy, and by joining (1855) the allies in the Crimean War. Emperor Napoleon III met Cavour at Plombières (1858) and promised military aid against Austria. War broke out in 1859. The French and Sardinians defeated the Austrians at Magenta and caused them to retreat at Solferino. These victories were so costly, however, that Napoleon signed a separate armistice at VILLAFRANCA DI VERONA (ratified by the Treaty of Zurich). Austria retained Venetia, and Sardinia gained only Lombardy. It was also stipulated that Tuscany, Modena, Parma, Bologna, and the Romagna, where revolutionists had organized provisional governments, were to return to their former rulers. This provision was not fulfilled; plebiscites were held (March, 1860) in these states, resulting in a vote for union with Sardinia. In return for recognizing these plebiscites, Napoleon received Savoy and Nice. The spectacular conquest of the Two Sicilies (1860) by Giuseppe GARIBALDI was followed by Sardinia's annexation of Umbria and the Marches. After the Two Sicilies had voted for union with Sardinia, the kingdom of Italy was proclaimed in March, 1861. The remaining territorial objectives of the Risorgimento were Venetia, still in Austria's possession, and Rome and Latium, which the pope was able to retain because of French protection. Through its alliance with Prussia in the AUSTRO-PRUSSIAN WAR of 1866, Italy obtained Venetia. Italy seized the remainder of the papal possessions in 1870 when France withdrew its troops during the Franco-Prussian War. Italian unification was then complete, but unsatisfied nationalism continued to exist in the form of IRREDENTISM. See George Martin, *The Red Shirt and the Cross of Savoy: The Story of Italy's Risorgimento* (1969); D. M. Smith, *Victor Emanuel, Cavour, and the Risorgimento* (1971); C. M. Lovett, *Carlo Cattaneo and the Politics of the Risorgimento* (1972).

Rissah (rĭs'ə), unlocated resting place in the desert. Num. 33.21,22.

Ristić or **Ristich, Jovan** (both: yō'vän rē'stĭch), 1831–99, Serbian statesman. A leader of the liberal party, he was repeatedly foreign minister and was three times premier (1873, 1878–80, 1887). Ristić hoped to make Serbia the nucleus of a large South Slav state, and in the 1878 Treaty of Berlin, Serbia gained full independence and additional territory. After the abdication of King Milan, Ristić headed (1889–93) the council of regency for Milan's son, Alexander.

Ristich, Jovan: see RISTIĆ, JOVAN.

Ritchey, George Willis, 1864–1945, American astronomer, b. Meigs co., Ohio, studied at the Univ. of Cincinnati (1883–84, 1886–87). He was superintendent of instrument construction (1899–1904) at Yerkes Observatory and then (1905–9) was associated with the Solar Observatory of Carnegie Institution. From 1901 to 1905 he taught astronomy at the Univ. of Chicago. Ritchey was in charge of the designing and construction of the 60-in. (152-cm) and 100-in. (254-cm) reflecting telescopes at Mt. Wilson Observatory. Later he went to the Paris Observatory as director (1924–30) of the astrophotographic laboratory. He is coinventor of the Ritchey-Chrétien reflecting telescope, and he supervised (1931) the construction of a 40-in. (102-cm) telescope of that type for the U.S. Naval Observatory. The cellular type of optical mirror was also his invention.

Ritchie, Alexander Hay, 1822–95, American engraver and painter, b. Scotland. He came to the United States in 1841 and a few years later established a successful workshop in New York City. His engravings, mezzotints, and etchings were chiefly of historical or allegorical subjects, often very ambitious in scale. *Washington and His Generals,* after his own painting, is representative of his work.

Ritchie, Anne Isabella Thackeray, Lady, 1837–1919, English writer; eldest daughter of William Makepeace Thackeray. In 1877 she married a cousin, Richmond T. W. Ritchie (knighted 1907). She wrote several novels but is more notable as one of the last commentators who had known the famous Victorians. Her biographical writings include notes for an edition of Thackeray's works (25 vol., 1898–99), *Tennyson and His Friends* (1892), and *Chapters from Some Memoirs* (1894). See *Thackeray and His Daughter: Letters and Journals* (ed. by Hester Thackeray Ritchie, 1924).

Rithmah (rĭth'mə), unlocated resting place in the desert. Num. 33.18,19.

Ritschl, Albrecht (äl'brĕkht rĭch'əl), 1822–89, German Protestant theologian. He taught theology at Bonn (1851–64) and at Göttingen (from 1864). The Ritschlian theology, a reaction against rationalism, was influential in the 19th and early 20th cent. Ritschl held that God could be known only through the revelation contained in the works and person of Jesus Christ. His theology stressed ethics and the community of man and repudiated metaphysics. Ritschl's most characteristic work has been translated as *The Christian Doctrine of Justification and Reconciliation* (Vol. I and III, 1872 and 1900). His son Otto Ritschl wrote his biography (2 vol., 1892–96). See also E. A. Edghill, *Faith and Fact: A Study of Ritschlianism* (1910); P. J. Hefner, *Faith and the Vitalities of History* (1966); D. W. Lotz, *Ritschl and Luther* (1974).

Ritson, Joseph, 1752–1803, English antiquarian and scholar, b. Stockton-on-Tees. An industrious student of English literature, he attacked Thomas Warton's scholarship in *Observations on Warton's History* (1782) and disputed the originality of Bishop Percy's *Reliques.* He criticized Dr. Johnson, George Steevens, and Malone as editors of Shakespeare, and in 1802 he compiled a catalog of English poets from the 12th to the 16th cent. See biography by B. H. Bronson (1938).

Rittenhouse, David, 1732–96, American astronomer and instrument maker, b. near Germantown, Pa., self-educated. A clockmaker by trade, he developed great skill in the making of mathematical instruments. He was called upon to determine, with his own instruments, the boundary lines of several states and also part of the boundary known as the MASON-DIXON LINE. In 1769 he was asked by the American Philosophical Society to observe the transit of Venus. His contributions include the use of measured grating intervals and spider threads on the focus of the telescope. Active in public affairs, he was a member of the convention that framed Pennsylvania's constitution and was state treasurer (1777–89) and director of the U.S. mint (1792–95). After the Revolution he was an Anti-Federalist. He succeeded Benjamin Franklin as president (1791–96) of the American Philosophical Society; most of his writings appeared in its *Transactions.* See biography by Brooke Hindle (1964).

Ritter, Karl, 1779–1859, German geographer, a founder of modern human geography. He was a professor of geography at the Univ. of Berlin from 1820. He helped define the scope of geography and its relationship to other sciences, and he emphasized the influence of natural environment on the development and activities of man. His *Comparative Geography* (1852) was translated into English in 1865 and 1881. His most important work, *Die Erdkunde* (2 vol., 1817–18), was revised and enlarged in the second edition (19 vol., 1822–59).

ritual: see CEREMONY.

Ritz, Walter, 1878–1909, Swiss physicist. He taught at the universities of Zürich and Göttingen. Ritz's combination principle, confirmed by later research, stated that the frequencies of spectral lines could be expressed as differences between a relatively small number of "terms," later identified by Niels Bohr, a Danish physicist, as the permissible energy levels of the radiating atoms. Ritz also developed important theories of radiation, magnetism, and electrodynamics.

Riukiu Islands: see RYUKYU ISLANDS.

Riva or **Riva di Trento** (rē'vä dē trän'tō), town (1971 pop. 12,066), Trentino-Alto Adige, N Italy, beautifully situated at the north end of Lake Garda. It is a summer resort and excursion center. The town passed from Austria to Italy in 1919.

Rivadavia, Bernardino (bärnärthē'nō rēvä'thä'vyä), 1780–1845, Argentine statesman and diplomat, first president of the United Provinces of La Plata (1826–27). He served (1806–7) under Jacques de LINIERS against the British invaders and was a leading advocate of independence in 1810. As a member of the first triumvirate of the young republic (1811–12), he exerted a significant influence. After six years (1814–20) as a diplomat in Europe, he became a minister under Martín RODRÍGUEZ, governor of Buenos Aires, and was largely responsible for the progressive measures of that administration. He was envoy to Great Britain before becoming president of the republic. An ardent liberal, Rivadavia instituted many reforms and strove to impose centralistic government on the nation. A unitarian constitution, adopted in 1826, was rejected by QUIROGA and other chieftains, who revolted. Rivadavia resigned and went into exile.

Rivas, Ángel de Saavedra, duque de (äng'hĕl thä sä"ävä'thrä dōō'kä thä rē'väs), 1791–1865, Spanish romantic poet and dramatist. A liberal, Rivas was condemned to death and fled in 1823 to England. After the death of Ferdinand VII he returned to Spain, having inherited his title and fortune. He became ambassador to Naples and France and president of the Spanish Royal Academy of the language. In literature Rivas was the champion of Spanish romanticism. His *Don Álvaro; o, La fuerza del sino* [Don Alvaro; or, the power of destiny] (1835) emerged from heated literary controversy as the first romantic success in the Spanish theater. This play was used as the basis of Francesco Piave's libretto for Verdi's opera *La forza del destino* (1862). Rivas's best-known poems are the colorful *Romances históricos* (1841), renderings of popular legends in ballad form. See study by E. A. Peers (1923).

Rivas, town (1970 est. pop. 25,748), SW Nicaragua. It is on the Isthmus of Rivas, a narrow land strip between Lake Nicaragua and the Pacific Ocean. Rivas was the seat of an Indian civilization at the time of the Spanish Conquest. During the California gold rush it controlled the transit route across Nicaragua; its loss by William Walker in 1857 ended his Nicaraguan campaign. Rivas is strategically located near the route of the proposed Nicaragua Canal.

river, stream of water larger than a brook or creek. Land surfaces are never perfectly flat, and as a result the runoff after precipitation tends to flow downward by the shortest and steepest course in depressions formed by the intersection of slopes. Runoffs of sufficient volume and velocity join to form a stream that, by the EROSION of underlying earth and rock, deepens its bed; it becomes perennial when it cuts deeply enough to be fed by ground water or when it has as its source an unlimited water reservoir, for example, the St. Lawrence flowing from the Great Lakes. The lowest level to which a river can erode its bed is called base level. Sea level is the ultimate base level, but the floor of a lake or basin into which a river flows may become a local and temporary base level. Cliffs or escarpments and differences in the resistance of rocks create irregularities in the bed of a river and can thus cause rapids and WATERFALLS. A river tends to eliminate irregularities and to form a smooth gradient from its source to its base level. As it approaches base level, downward cutting is replaced by lateral cutting, and the river widens its bed and valley and develops a sinuous course that forms exaggerated loops and bends called meanders. A river may open up a new channel across the arc of a meander, thereby cutting off the arc and creating an OXBOW LAKE. The discharge, or rate of outflow, of a river depends on the width of its channel and on its velocity. Velocity is governed by the volume of water, the slope of the bed, and the shape of the channel (which determines the amount of frictional resistance). River volume is affected by duration and rate of precipitation in the drainage basin of the river. A river system may be enlarged by piracy, or the process by which one river, cutting through the divide that separates its drainage basin from that of another river, diverts the waters of the other into its own channel. Rivers modify topography by deposition as well as by erosion. River velocity determines quantity and size of rock fragments and sediment carried by the river. When the velocity is checked by changes of flow or of gradient, by meeting the water mass of lakes or oceans, or by the spreading of water when a stream overflows its banks, part of the load carried by the stream is deposited in the river bed or beyond the channel. Landforms produced by deposition include the DELTA, the FLOOD PLAIN, the channel bar, and the alluvial fan and cone. Traditionally, river systems have been classified according to their stage of development as young, mature, or old. The young river is marked by a steepsided valley, steep gradients, and irregularities in the bed; the mature river by a valley with a wide floor and flaring sides, by advanced headward erosion by tributaries, and by a more smoothly graded bed; and the old river by a course graded to base level and running through a peneplain, or broad flat area. The age classification of rivers is diminishing in popularity now that quantitative studies of river behavior are more common. River valleys have been important centers of civilization; they afford travel routes, and their alluvial soils form good agricultural lands. Navigable rivers are important in commerce and have influenced the location of cities. Rivers with sufficient velocity and gradient can be used to produce hydroelectric power. Among the most important river systems of the world are the Nile, the Congo, the Niger, the Zambezi, and the Orange-Vaal in Africa; the Amazon, the Orinoco, and the Paraguay-Paraná in South America; the Mississippi-Missouri, the St. Lawrence, the Rio Grande, the Colorado, the Columbia, the Mackenzie-Peace, and the Yukon in North America; the Danube, the Rhine, the Rhône, the Seine, the Po, the Tagus, the Thames, the Loire, the Elbe, the Oder, the Don, the Volga, and the Dnepr in Europe; the Tigris, the Euphrates, the Ob-Irtysh, the Yenisei, the Lena, the Syr Darya, the Amu Darya, the Amur, the Yellow River, the Yangtze, the Ganges, the Brahmaputra, the Indus, the Irrawaddy, and the Mekong in Asia; and the Murray-Darling in Australia. See FLOOD; WATER RIGHTS; WATERS, TERRITORIAL. See F. C. Lane, *Earth's Grandest Rivers* (1949); A. N. and A. H. Strahler, *Environmental Geoscience* (1973).

Rivera, Diego (thyā'gō rēvä'rä), 1886–1957, Mexican mural painter, studied as a youth with Posada and other Mexican painters. The native sculpture of Mexico deeply impressed him. In Europe (1907–9, 1912–21) he worked in several countries and was influenced by the paintings of El Greco and Goya. He had close association with Cézanne and Picasso and with communistic Russians in exile. He became convinced that a new form of art should respond to "the new order of things . . . and that the logical place for this art . . . belonging to the populace, was on the walls of public buildings." Returning in 1921 to Mexico, he painted, with the assistance of younger artists, large murals dealing with the life, history, and social problems of Mexico, in the Preparatory School and the Ministry of Education in Mexico City and the Agricultural School of Chapingo. To the peasants and workers he became a sort of prophet. He visited Moscow in 1927–28 and upon his return painted in the National Palace and in the Palace of Cortés at Cuernavaca. In the United States he painted frescoes in the luncheon club of the Stock Exchange and in the Fine Arts Building, both in San Francisco, and murals in the Detroit Institute of Arts, giving his interpretation of industrial America as exemplified in Detroit. A mural for Rockefeller Center, New York City, was destroyed by order of his sponsors because of the inclusion of a portrait of Lenin. The mural was reproduced in Mexico City at the Palace of Fine Arts. Rivera in 1936 interceded with President Cárdenas to permit Trotsky to come to Mexico. In 1956 the artist went to Moscow for an operation. Several months before his death he announced his affiliation with the Roman Catholic Church. See *Portrait of America* (1934) and *Portrait of Mexico* (1937), both with illustrations by Rivera and text by B. D. Wolfe; autobiography (1960); biography by B. D. Wolfe (1963); study by Florence Arquin (1971).

Rivera, Fructuoso (frōōktōō-ō'sō), 1790?–1854, first president of Uruguay (1830–34, 1839–42). After serving with ARTIGAS, he was one of the Thirty-three Immortals who raised the standard of independence under Juan Antonio LAVALLEJA. He was chosen president and was responsible for the succession of Manuel ORIBE, against whom he revolted in 1836. In the long civil strife, which was to characterize much of Uruguay's subsequent history, two factions appeared, distinguished by their badges, the Colorados [reds] of Rivera and the Blancos [whites] of Oribe. Rivera succeeded (1838) in routing Oribe, who fled to Buenos Aires. The following year Rivera declared war on Juan Manuel de ROSAS, ruler of the United Provinces of La Plata (Argentina). With the help of Rosas, Oribe besieged Montevideo from 1843 to 1851. Rivera, opposed by factions within his own party, was exiled from the invested city in 1847, taking refuge in Brazil. After the downfall of Rosas and the end of the siege, he was selected (1853) as one of the triumvirate to head the provisional government of Uruguay.

Rivera, José de (hōsā' dā rĭvĕr' ə), 1904–, American sculptor, b. West Baton Rouge, La. Rivera worked as an industrial designer and machine-tool maker in the 1920s, then studied drawing with John Norton in Chicago. Since the 1940s he has developed an abstract sculpture of curving, iridescent filaments and sheets of metal that revolve in space. One of his stainless steel constructions is in the courtyard of the Statler-Hilton Hotel, Dallas; his *Construction 1, Homage to the World of Minkowski* is in the Metropolitan Museum of Art.

Rivera, José Eustasio (hōsā' āōōstä'syō), 1889–1928, Colombian novelist. Rivera served on the commission to fix the Venezuelan boundary deep in the rain forest of the Amazon basin. The jungle became the setting and protagonist of his masterly novel, *La vorágine* (1924, tr. *The Vortex,* 1935). In fluid language he tells of the hardships and brutal sufferings of rubber gatherers. Rivera wrote sonnets in classical manner about the tropics in *Tierra de promisión* [promised land] (1921).

Rivera, Julio Adalberto (hōō'lyō ädälbār'tō), 1921–73, president of El Salvador (1962–67). An army lieutenant colonel, he headed the junta that overthrew the leftist government in Jan., 1961. His junta rule was unexpectedly progressive, enacting numerous measures, including a new income tax law. In 1962 the junta promulgated a new constitution under which Rivera was elected president for a five-year term. His administration was noteworthy for its social reforms, economic prosperity, and domestic tranquility. He was succeeded by Fidel Sánchez Hernández.

Rivera, Primo de: see PRIMO DE RIVERA, MIGUEL.

River Brethren, name used to designate certain Christian bodies originating in 1770 in a revival movement among the German settlers in E Pennsylvania. In the 1750s, Mennonite refugees from Switzerland had established their homes near the Susquehanna River. Their religious leaders, Jacob and John Engle, became associated with Philip William OTTERBEIN, Martin BOEHM, and others in the revival movement. The followers of the Engles came to be known as the River Brethren, either because they lived "down by the river" or because they were baptized in the Susquehanna upon joining the brotherhood. In 1843 a conservative group in York co., Pa., withdrew; these are known as the Old Order or Yorker Brethren. In 1852 another group left the main body, under the leadership of Matthias Brinser, adopting the name United Zion's Children (now known as the United Zion Church). The main body took the name Brethren in Christ, by which a group of Mennonites is also known. The Brethren are very similar to the Dunkards; they practice trine (triple, in allusion to the Trinity) immersion and foot washing, adhere to plain dress, and oppose war, alcohol, tobacco, and worldly pleasures. The Brethren carry out missionary work in Asia and Africa.

Riverdale, village (1970 pop. 15,806), Cook co., NE Ill., a suburb adjacent to Chicago; inc. 1892. It has a large steel mill.

River Edge, residential borough (1970 pop. 12,850), Bergen co., NE N.J., on the Hackensack River; inc. 1894.

River Forest, residential village (1970 pop. 13,402), Cook co., NE Ill., a suburb of Chicago, on the Des Plaines River; inc. 1880. It is the seat of Rosary College and Concordia Teachers College. Several homes there were designed by Frank Lloyd Wright. A forest preserve is adjacent to the village.

River Grove, village (1970 pop. 11,465), Cook co., NE Ill., a suburb of Chicago on the Des Plaines River; inc. 1888. Sports equipment and wire cables are made. County forest preserves and a junior college are there.

Riverina (rĭv"ərē'nə), region, 26,560 sq mi (68,790 sq km), New South Wales, SE Australia. Located S of the Lachlan River in the south central part of the state, Riverina is a rich agricultural area with associated processing industries. The Murrumbidgee River runs through the region, and much of the farming depends on irrigation. Chief towns are Albury, Wagga Wagga, Leeton, and Griffith.

River Rouge (rōōzh), city (1970 pop. 15,947), Wayne co., SE Mich., an industrial suburb of Detroit, on the Detroit and Rouge rivers; settled c.1817, inc. 1899. It is a port of entry, with automobile, shipbuilding, paper, and steel industries. The city grew in the 1920s with the expansion of the Ford Motor Company in the area.

Rivers, Larry, 1923–, American artist, b. New York City. Reacting against ABSTRACT EXPRESSIONISM, Rivers painted a series of nude studies in 1954, including *Double Portrait of Birdie.* He was a forerunner of the POP ART movement, being among the first to use popular images in his work. His themes range from eroticism to social concern, and his works are painted in a spontaneous manner. See study by Sam Hunter (1969).

Rivers, Richard Woodville, 1st Earl, d. 1469, English nobleman. He was knighted (1426) by Henry VI and acquired wealth and power by marrying (c.1436) Jacquetta of Luxemburg, widow of John of Lancaster, duke of Bedford. He served in the wars in France and helped suppress the rebellion (1450) of Jack Cade in England. In the Wars of the Roses, Rivers fought for Henry VI until the Lancastrian defeat at Towton (1461). He then transferred his loyalty to the Yorkist Edward IV, to whom he gave his daughter (see WOODVILLE, ELIZABETH) in marriage in 1464. He and his family soon received extensive royal favors, Rivers himself becoming treasurer and then constable (1467) of England. He was created earl in 1466. The favoritism shown the Woodville faction embittered Richard Neville, earl of WARWICK, who rebelled in 1469. Rivers was captured and executed after Edward's defeat at Edgecot. His eldest son, **Anthony Woodville, 2d Earl Rivers,** 1442?–1483, accompanied Edward into exile (1470–71) and later served him in various capacities. In 1473 he was appointed guardian of Edward, prince of Wales (later Edward V). On Edward IV's death, however, Rivers was arrested by Richard, duke of Gloucester (later RICHARD III), and executed. A somewhat romantic and otherworldly figure, Rivers wrote translations of various French works. His *Dictes and Sayengis of the Philosophres* (1477) was the first dated book printed in England by William Caxton.

Rivers, William Halse Rivers, 1864–1922, British anthropologist. He taught at Cambridge from 1893 until shortly before his death. Trained in medicine and psychology, he pioneered in the experimental study of mental functions among preliterate peoples, making his first field investigations in 1898 among the islanders of the Torres Strait, which separates Australia and New Guinea. Rivers also made a major contribution to social anthropology, introducing the genealogical method into sociological investigations. This method is applied with great success in his classic study, *The Todas* (1906). An expedition to Melanesia in 1908 resulted in his monumental work, *The History of Melanesian Society* (1914). His attempts to fuse ethnological facts and psychoanalytic theory led to such works as *Instinct and the Unconscious* (2d ed. 1922) and *Medicine, Magic, and Religion* (1924). Other writings include *Kinship and Social Organization* (1914), *Essays on the Depopulation of Melanesia* (1922), *Psychology and Politics* (1923), and *Social Organization* (ed. by W. J. Perry, 1924).

Riverside. **1** City (1970 pop. 140,089), seat of Riverside co., S Calif.; inc. 1883. It is famous for its orange industry. Other products include mobile homes, aluminum, aircraft and space components, and food machinery. The navel orange was introduced there in 1873; the original tree, still producing, is a tourist attraction. The first marketing cooperative, organized in Riverside in 1892, led to the founding of the California Fruit Growers Exchange. The city is the seat of the Univ. of California at Riverside (with a citrus research center, est. 1907); La Sierra campus of Loma Linda Univ.; California Baptist College; and a junior college. Mission Inn, a hotel in a unique mission setting, is in the city. Easter sunrise services are held on nearby Mt. Rubidoux, where a large cross stands in memory of Father Junípero Serra. March Air Force Base, headquarters of the 15th U.S. air force and a major Strategic Air Command installation, is to the southeast. **2** Village (1970 pop. 10,432), Cook co., NE Ill., a residential suburb of Chicago, on the Des Plaines River; inc. 1875. It was planned as a model suburb by Frederick Law Olmsted and Calvert Vaux. The city has a number of buildings designed by Frank Lloyd Wright. The old water tower (late 19th cent.) is a national historic landmark.

Riverview, city (1970 pop. 11,342), Wayne co., SE Mich., on the Detroit River, a suburb of Detroit; inc. 1959. Chemicals and steel wheels are among the manufactures of Riverview. Rich limestone deposits, quarried as early as 1763, contributed to the city's growth.

Rives, William Cabell (rēvz), 1793–1868, American politician and diplomat, b. Nelson co. (then part of Amherst co.), Va. A lawyer, he sat in the Virginia legislature (1817–21, 1822–23), was a U.S. Representative (1823–29), and served (1829–32) as minister to France. Rives was elected to three terms in the U.S. Senate (1832–34, 1836–39, 1841–45). Originally a Jacksonian Democrat, he opposed President Van Buren's Independent Treasury System and supported William H. Harrison for President in 1840; by 1844, when he backed Henry Clay, he was definitely a Whig. From 1849 to 1853 he was again minister to France. In 1861 he was a member of the peace convention at Washington sponsored by Virginia in an effort to avert the Civil War. He served in the provisional and then the regular congress of the Confederacy until 1862. His *History of the Life and Times of James Madison* (3 vol., 1859–68) covers Madison's life through 1797.

rivet, headed metal pin or bolt whose shaft is passed through holes in two or more pieces of metal, wood, plastic, or other material in order to unite them by forming the plain end into a second head. The button-head rivet has a hemispherical head; the countersunk-head rivet has a flat head made to fit a countersunk hole. A large rivet for building construction is first heated so that the pneumatic hammer used to set it can more easily squash the plain end into a head. When the hot rivet cools, it shrinks and pulls the parts tightly together. For critical work, holes are drilled and reamed to exact size; for most other work they are punched. Full tubular and split rivets can be driven through soft materials without the necessity of first making a hole; after passing through the materials, the rivets' plain ends spread out to form heads as they strike a hard substance. More complicated blind rivets are used when only one side of the work is accessible. The mandrel type is a tube in which a rod with an enlarged end is inserted. After the rivet is pushed into the hole, the rod is pulled back through, crushing the end of the rivet into a head and forcing the sides of the tube against the walls of the hole. The drive-pin type is a tube with an opening at the headless end smaller than at the head end. As the pin is driven through from the head end, it spreads the tube out over the edge of the hole. The explosive blind rivet is filled with an explosive; when the head is heated with an iron, the explosive ignites and expands the headless end over the edge of the hole. Rivets are made of steel, aluminum, copper, and many other metals, and of plastics.

Riviera (rĭvēâr'ə), narrow coastal strip between the Alps and the Mediterranean, extending, roughly, from La Spezia (Italy) to Hyères (France). Famous for its scenic beauty and for its mild winter climate, and dotted with fashionable resorts, hotels, and villas, the Riviera is a major international playground. Genoa is the center of the Italian Riviera and divides it into the Riviera di Levante (east) and the Riviera di Ponente (west). Among the well-known resorts on the Italian Riviera are Bordighera, San Remo, Portofino, and Rapallo. Also noteworthy is the rugged Cinqueterre coast near La Spezia. The French Riviera, also called the Côte d'Azur [azure coast], has the famous resorts of Nice, Cannes, Saint-Tropez, and Monte Carlo (in Monaco). Flowers for export and for use in the perfume industry are grown throughout the region, particularly at Crasse (near Cannes). A panoramic highway runs along the Riviera from end to end; its section (the CORNICHE DU LITTORAL) between Nice and Menton, France, which hugs the red cliffs of the coastline, is particularly famous.

Riviera Beach (rəvēr'ə), resort city (1970 pop. 21,401), Palm Beach co., SE Fla., on Lake Worth (a lagoon); inc. 1922. There are research and development firms and aerospace industries in the city.

Rivière du Loup (rēvyĕr' dü lo͞o), city (1971 pop. 12,760), E Que., Canada, on the south shore of the St. Lawrence River, NE of Quebec. It is a commercial and industrial center in a lumbering and agricultural region. There are saw and paper mills. It is also a resort and tourist center. Settled in 1833, it was originally called Fraserville.

Rivoli Veronese (rē'vōlē vārōnā'zā), village (1971 pop. 47,280), Venetia, NE Italy, on the Adige River. It was the scene in Jan., 1797, of a decisive French victory over the Austrians. Masséna, who participated in the battle under Napoleon I, was created duke of Rivoli in 1808.

Riyadh or **Riad** (both: rēäd'), city (1970 est. pop. 300,000), capital of Saudi Arabia, in the Nejd, central Saudi Arabia. It is situated in an oasis, c.240 mi (390 km) inland from the Persian Gulf. Riyadh is the focal point for desert travel and trade. Its architecture formerly represented the classic Arabic style, but in the oil boom of recent decades many buildings were torn down and replaced by large modern structures. The city was long the center of the WAHABI movement. It is the seat of Riyadh Univ. (1957) and other schools.

Rizal, José (hōsā' rēsäl'), 1861–96, Philippine nationalist, author, poet, and physician, b. Calamba, Laguna prov. He studied at a Jesuit school in Manila, at the Univ. of Madrid (M.D., 1884; Ph.D., 1885), and in Paris, Berlin, Heidelberg, and Leipzig. In Berlin he published his first novel, *Noli me tangere* (1886, tr. *The Lost Eden,* 1961), a diatribe against Spanish administration and the religious orders in the Philippines. Because of this attack he was compelled by Spanish officials to leave the islands soon after his return home in 1887. He lived successively in China, Japan, the United States, England, and France, before establishing himself in Hong Kong to practice medicine. In 1890 he published an annotated edition of Antonio Morgas's *Sucesos de las islas Filipinas,* and in 1891 he published his second novel, *El filibusterismo* (tr. *The Subversive,* 1962), a sequel to his first. Returning to Manila in 1892, he was arrested as a revolutionary agitator and banished to Dapitan on Mindanao. While on his way to Cuba in 1896, he was arrested and returned to Manila. There he was given a farcical trial and executed as an instigator of insurrection and founder of secret revolutionary societies. His martyrdom incited a full-scale rebellion against Spanish rule. He also wrote articles; *Mariang Makiling* (1890), a Philippine folk tale; and considerable poetry. See his letters, tr. by J. P. Apostol (1959); his reminiscences and travels, ed. by Encarnación Alzona (Vol. I, 1961); biographies by Carlos Quirino (1958), L. M. Guerrero (1963), and Austin Coates (1968).

Rizal, province (1970 pop. 2,781,081), central Luzon, the Philippines. The capital is Pasig. The province, which horseshoes around Manila and includes Quezon City, has had a huge population increase in recent years. It has cement plants and dairy farms and is a major mango-producing area. In 1968 an earth satellite station linking the Philippines into the worldwide communications network was established in Rizal. The province was hard hit by flooding in mid-1972.

Riza Shah Pahlevi: see REZA SHAH PAHLEVI.

Rizpah (rĭz'pə), Saul's concubine, Aiah's daughter, who held watch over her dead sons on Mt. Gibeah. 2 Sam. 3.7; 21.8–11.

Rizzio, David (rĭt'sēō), 1533?–1566, favorite of MARY QUEEN OF SCOTS. He was a Piedmontese musician (also called Riccio) who arrived (1561) in Scotland with the ambassador from Savoy. He came to the notice of Queen Mary and toward the end of 1564 became her secretary for French affairs. The trust that Mary placed in him, however, caused jealousy and hatred on the part of many great nobles. They persuaded Lord DARNLEY, Mary's husband, that Rizzio was Mary's lover. Then, in 1566, with Darnley's support, they broke into Mary's quarters in Holyrood Palace, seized Rizzio in the queen's presence, and killed him. There is no proof or disproof of the charge that Mary was his mistress, but it is clear that his murder was only part of a larger campaign by Scottish nobles against Mary.

Rjukan (rēo͞o'kän), town, Telemark co., S Norway, on the Rjukanfoss, one of several high waterfalls of the Måne River. Its large power stations supply electricity to saltpeter and chemical fertilizer factories. At nearby Vemork a plant for making heavy water was destroyed by Norwegian commandos (Feb., 1943) in World War II; this action helped prevent the Germans from manufacturing an atomic bomb. The plant was rebuilt after 1945.

Rn, chemical symbol of the element RADON.

RNA: see NUCLEIC ACID.

Roa, Raúl (räo͞ol' rō'ä), 1908–, Cuban minister of foreign affairs (1959–73). A lawyer, he was also a university professor in the 1940s and 1950s. He wrote prolifically as well. Appointed foreign minister by Fidel Castro, Roa gained international prominence with his blunt diplomacy. In the 1970s he worked to restore good relations with other Latin American countries, and in 1973 he signed an anti-hijacking agreement with the United States.

roach: see COCKROACH.

road, strip of land used for transportation. The history of roads has been related to the centralizing of populations in powerful cities, which the roads have served for military purposes and for the collection of supplies and tribute. In Persia, between 500 and 400 B.C., all the provinces were connected with the capital, Susa, by roads, one of them 1,500 mi (2,400 km) long. The ancient Greeks, cherishing the independence of their city-states and opposing centralization, did relatively little road making. The ROMAN ROADS, however, are famous. In Italy and in every region that the Romans conquered, they built roads so durable that parts of them yet remain serviceable. The Roman roads were generally straight, even over steep grades. The surface, made of large slabs of hard stone, rested on a bed of smaller stones and cement about 3 ft (91 cm) thick. From the fall of the Roman Empire until the 19th cent., European roads generally were neglected and hard to travel. People usually walked, rode horses, or were carried in sedan chairs. Goods were transported by pack animals. In France, Louis XIV and Napoleon built good roads for military purposes. Elsewhere on the Continent roads were not much improved before the middle of the 19th cent. In Great Britain two Scottish engineers, Thomas Telford and John L. McAdam, were responsible for the development of the macadam road (see PAVEMENT). The expansion of the Industrial Revolution brought this and other road improvements to the Continent, although the emphasis was on railroad construction until after the invention of the automobile. In the Americas the Inca empire was remarkable for its fine roads. In what is now the United States, however, the waterways were the normal mode of Indian travel, and the Indian trails, though many, were simply crude footpaths. These were used by white settlers and were eventually widened to make wagon trails. The increasing use of stagecoaches led to some improvement, and the TURNPIKE, or toll road, was introduced at the beginning of the 19th cent. Although the planning and building of road arteries, notably the NATIONAL ROAD, marked the early years of the century, canals and then railroads took precedence. It was not until the invention of the automobile that the road became paramount again. Hard-surfaced highways were stretched across the entire land in a relatively few years. The building of roads became a major branch of engineering, and even the most difficult obstacles were surmounted. Roads have helped greatly to equalize and unify American culture in the 20th cent. Most major cities of the United States are now connected by the Interstate Highway System, which consists of over 30,000 mi (48,000 km) of roads. The highways through Canada and the Pan American Highway are also serving to promote land travel in the Americas and increase understanding among peoples of different countries. See Jean Labatut and W. J. Lane, ed., *Highways* (1950); Geoffrey Hindley, *A History of Roads* (1972).

road runner: see CUCKOO.

Road Town, town in the British VIRGIN ISLANDS.

Roanne (rôän'), town (1968 pop. 54,748), Loire dept., E central France, on the Loire River. Cotton and metals are the chief products; other industries include tanning and the spinning of artificial silk. Roanne (then Rodumna) was a crossroads in Gallo-Roman times and was mentioned in ancient geography by Ptolemy. The Joseph-Dechelette Museum, noted for its ancient artifacts, is located in the town. Roanne also has several ruins from the Roman period, as well as remnants of a medieval château and several 15th- and 16th-century houses.

Roanoke (rō'ənōk), city (1970 pop. 92,115), independent and in no co., SW Va., on the Roanoke River; settled c.1740, inc. 1882. Situated between the Blue Ridge and Allegheny Mts., Roanoke is the southern gateway to the Shenandoah valley. A tiny village until the coming of the railroad in 1882, Roanoke has since developed into the region's commercial, transportation, and industrial center. It contains important railroad shops and factories that manufacture a great variety of products, including furniture, textile goods, electrical equipment, and metal products. Roanoke has a junior college, and Hollins College is nearby. Of interest are a transportation museum and Mill Mt. Park. Roanoke College is in nearby Salem.

Roanoke, river, c.410 mi (660 km) long, rising in SW Va. and flowing generally southeast across the Blue Ridge Mts. and into Albemarle Sound, NE N.C. The lower river is navigable for small craft. A comprehensive flood-control and hydroelectric-power scheme has been initiated on the river. John H. Kerr Dam impounds one of the largest reservoirs in the United States and has a 204,000-kw capacity. Gaston Dam, a non-Federal hydroelectric project, has a 177,900-kw capacity. Roanoke, Va., is the chief city on the river.

Roanoke Island, 12 mi (19 km) long and 3 mi (4.8 km) wide, NE N.C., off the Atlantic coast in Croatan Sound between Albemarle and Pamlico sounds. Manteo (1970 pop. 547) is the chief town, and tourism and fishing are the principal industries of the island. The English navigators Philip Amadas and Arthur Barlowe, exploring for Sir Walter Raleigh in 1584, brought back such glowing accounts of the island that Raleigh immediately dispatched a colonizing expedition under Sir Richard Grenville and Sir Ralph Lane. The colonists landed on Roanoke Island in Aug., 1585, and built the "Citie of Ralegh" (or New Fort); but, faring badly, they returned to England the next year. In 1587 Raleigh sent out another group under John White. Forced to return to England for supplies, White was unable to come back to Roanoke until 1591. Upon his return he found the colonists gone and the letters CROATOAN carved on a tree. This gave rise to a theory that the settlers had moved to Croatoan Island or had joined the Croatoan or Hatteras Indians. White was unable to search for the colonists because of bad weather. Another theory was later advanced with the discovery (1937-40) of some 40 stone tablets (now at Brenau College, Gainesville, Ga.), inscribed with what some believe to be the history of the "lost colony." The inscriptions tell of the death of many of the colonists (including Virginia Dare) from disease and Indian attacks and of the migration of others into the interior, as far away as present-day Atlanta, Ga. If the stones are not a hoax, as some think possible, they would seem to dispel forever the Croatoan theory of the colony's disappearance. In 1937 Paul Green's symphonic drama *The Lost Colony* was first presented to commemorate the 350th anniversary of the landing of White's colony, and in 1947 U.S. government archaeologists at Fort Raleigh National Historic Site (see NATIONAL PARKS AND MONUMENTS, table) announced that they had uncovered other artifacts of the colony. Roanoke Island fell to Union forces under Gen. A. E. Burnside in the Civil War (Jan., 1862).

Roanoke Rapids, industrial city (1970 pop. 13,508), Halifax co., N N.C., on the Roanoke River near the Virginia line; founded 1893, inc. 1931. Cotton textiles and paper products are manufactured there.

roaring forties, name applied, especially by sailors, to the latitudes between 40°S and 50°S, where the prevailing westerly winds are strong and steady. Unlike the winds in the Northern Hemisphere, those in the roaring forties are not impeded by large land areas.

Roatán: see BAY ISLANDS, Honduras.

robalo: see BASS.

Robbe-Grillet, Alain (älăN' rôb-grēyā'), 1922-, French novelist. Robbe-Grillet is considered the originator of the French "anti-novel," in which story is subordinated to structure and the significance of objects is stressed above that of human motivation or action. His first novel, *Les Gommes* (tr. *The Erasers*, 1964), was published in 1953. Among his many novels, most of them marked by violence, are *The Voyeur* (1955, tr. 1958), *Jealousy* (1957, tr. 1960), *In the Labyrinth* (1959, tr. 1960), *Snapshots* (1962, tr. 1968), *La Maison de Rendez-vous* (1965, tr. 1966), and *Project for a Revolution in New York* (1970, tr. 1972). Robbe-Grillet's film works include the screenplays for *Last Year at Marienbad* (1960), *L'Immortelle* (1962), and *Trans-Europe Express* (1966); he also directed the latter two. See his collection of essays *For a New Novel* (1963, tr. 1966); studies by B. F. Stoltzfus (1964) and Bruce Morrissette (1965).

Robbers, Herman (hĕr'män rô'bərs), 1868-1937, Dutch novelist. A representative of descriptive realism in Dutch literature, he wrote *De Roman van een Gezin* (1909-10; tr. *The Fortunes of a Household,* 1924).

Robber Synod: see EUTYCHES.

robbery, in law, felonious taking of property from a person against his will by threatening or committing force or violence. The injury or threat may be directed against the person robbed, his property, or the person or property of his relative or of anyone in his presence at the time of the robbery. There is no robbery unless force or fear is used to overcome resistance. Thus, surreptitiously picking a man's pocket or snatching something from him without resistance on his part is LARCENY, but not robbery. Robbery differs from EXTORTION, where force or fear are used to obtain the consent of the victim. The distinction, however, is tenuous. In some states there are several degrees of robbery with graduated penalties; aggravating circumstances—e.g., the use of firearms—result in a greater penalty.

Robbia, Italian sculptors: see DELLA ROBBIA.

Robbins, Frederick Chapman, 1916-, American physician, b. Auburn, Ala., grad. Univ. of Missouri, 1938, M.D. Harvard, 1940. He served on the staff of Children's Hospital, Boston, and at Harvard; from 1952 he was director of pediatrics at City Hospital, Cleveland, and professor of pediatrics at the medical school of Western Reserve Univ. He shared the 1954 Nobel Prize in Physiology and Medicine with J. F. Enders and T. H. Weller for their work in growing polio viruses in cultures of different tissues.

Robbins, Jerome, 1918-, American choreographer and dancer, b. New York City. Robbins began his career dancing in musical comedy (1937), and in 1940 he joined the Ballet Theatre. His first ballet, *Fancy Free* (1944), was expanded into the musical *On the Town*. He later gained distinction as choreographer of several Broadway musicals, including *High Button Shoes* (1947) and *The King and I* (1951). Among the musicals he directed were *Peter Pan* (1954) and *West Side Story* (1957). In 1949 Robbins became associate artistic director of the New York City Ballet where he remains as ballet master.

Robbinsdale, city (1970 pop. 16,845), Hennepin co., SE Minn., a residential suburb of Minneapolis; inc. 1893.

Robert I, c.865-923, French king (922-23), son of Count Robert the Strong and younger brother of King EUDES. He inherited from Eudes the territory between the Seine and the Loire rivers. In 922, Robert led a rebellion against King CHARLES III (Charles the Simple) and was crowned king by a party of nobles and clergy, but he was soon killed in battle. His son-in-law, Raoul of Burgundy, succeeded him. His son was HUGH THE GREAT.

Robert II (Robert the Pious), 970-1031, king of France (996-1031); son of Hugh Capet, with whom he was joint king after 987. Distinguished for his piety and learning, he also sought to strengthen the weak royal power, conquered several towns, and secured the duchy of Burgundy for the crown. His son and successor was Henry I.

Robert I or **Robert the Bruce,** 1274-1329, king of Scotland (1306-29). He belonged to the illustrious BRUCE family and was the grandson of that Robert the Bruce who in 1290 was an unsuccessful claimant to the Scottish throne. He became earl of Carrick in 1292 and on his father's death (1304) assumed the lordship of Annandale and of the Bruce lands in England. In 1296, Robert swore fealty to EDWARD I of England, but in the following year he joined the struggle for national independence. He appears to have taken part only intermittently until an obscure contest between him and John COMYN (d. 1306) for the adherence of the Scottish nationalists resulted in Comyn's murder (probably unpremeditated) by Bruce or his followers. In defiance of Edward I, Robert was then crowned king at Scone on March 27, 1306. Defeated by the English at Methven (1306), he fled to the west and apparently took refuge on the island of Rathlin, off the coast of Ireland. The Bruce estates were confiscated by Edward, and punishment was meted out to Robert's followers. From this time of discouragement stems the legend that Robert learned courage and hope from watching a spider persevere in spinning its web. Returning in 1307, he won a victory at Loudon Hill, which brought him new adherents. Edward I attempted to lead a new expedition against the rebellious Scots, but he died on the way and was succeeded by his son, Edward II, who failed to pursue the vigorous course of his father. Robert was able to consolidate his hold on Scotland and to recapture lands and castles from the English. Stirling was besieged by the Scots and so hard pressed that the English governor finally agreed to its surrender if relief from England did not arrive before June 24, 1314. On June 23 and 24, at nearby BANNOCKBURN, Robert overwhelmingly defeated the large English relief force led by Edward II. The war went on, and in 1318 the Scots recaptured Berwick. A truce, made in 1323, lasted only until 1327, when the bellicose young Edward III led an unsuccessful expedition to the north. Finally, by the Treaty of Northampton (1328), the English recognized the independence of Scotland and the validity of Robert's title to the throne. Robert spent the short remainder of his life in his castle at Cardross and died there, perhaps of leprosy. As he requested, his embalmed heart was given to Sir James de DOUGLAS, lord of Douglas, to be carried to Jerusalem for burial. Douglas was killed in Spain, but (according to tradition) Robert's heart was recovered, brought back to Scotland, and buried in Melrose Abbey. By his courage and skill Robert had freed Scotland from English rule. He was succeeded by his son, David II. See biographies by A. M. Mackenzie (1934, repr. 1957) and G. W. S. Barrow (1965).

Robert II, 1316-90, king of Scotland (1371-90), nephew and successor of DAVID II. He was the first sovereign of the house of Stuart, or Stewart (see STUART, family), which eventually succeeded to the English as well as the Scottish throne. The son of Walter the Steward and Marjory, daughter of Robert I, he was regent three times (1333-35, 1338-41, and 1346-58) for David II during the latter's exile and captivity. He thus led the resistance to Edward de BALIOL and Edward III of England. Robert rebelled against his uncle in 1363 when David recognized Edward III as his successor. On David's death (1371), however, he succeeded peacefully to the throne, in accordance with the succession law adopted in 1318. Robert's first marriage took place after the birth of several of his sons, but their succession to the throne was legitimized by an act of Parliament in 1373. Through most of his reign the government was dominated by two of these sons—John, earl of Carrick (later ROBERT III) and Robert STUART, later 1st duke of Albany. The Scots in alliance with France fought off several English invasions; they invaded England without assistance in 1388 and won a great victory at Otterburn. Robert was succeeded by Robert III.

Robert III, 1340?-1406, king of Scotland (1390-1406), eldest son and successor of Robert II. Known before his accession as John, earl of Carrick, he ruled for his father until 1389, when, having been crippled by a horse, he was supplanted by his brother Robert (see STUART, ROBERT, 1ST DUKE OF ALBANY). The latter continued as virtual ruler after Robert III came to the throne. War with England during his reign was marked by Henry IV's invasion (1400) of Scotland and a retaliatory expedition into England, led by Archibald DOUGLAS, 4th earl of Douglas, that met defeat at Homildon Hill (1402). The duke of Albany is thought to have been responsible for the death of the king's eldest son, David STUART, duke of Rothesay, in 1402. Robert III died soon after his second son (later JAMES I of Scotland) was seized and detained in England by Henry IV.

Robert I (Robert the Magnificent), d. 1035, duke of Normandy (1027–35); father of William the Conqueror. He is often identified with the legendary ROBERT THE DEVIL. He aided King HENRY I of France against Henry's rebellious brother and mother, intervened in the affairs of Flanders, and supported Edward the Confessor, then in exile at Robert's court. He also sponsored monastic reform in Normandy. After making his illegitimate son William his heir, he made a pilgrimage to Jerusalem and died at Nicaea.

Robert II (Robert Curthose), c.1054–1134, duke of Normandy (1087–1106); eldest son of King WILLIAM I of England. Aided by King Philip I of France, he rebelled (1077) against his father. Father and son became reconciled, but Robert was later exiled. At William's death he inherited Normandy. England fell to his younger brother William II, with whom Robert was intermittently at war (1090–96) until Robert went (1096–1100) on the First Crusade. While he was away, William II died and Henry I, youngest son of William I, was crowned. Robert invaded (1101) England but was forced to recognize Henry. In Normandy, Robert's misgovernment prompted an invasion by Henry (1105), who defeated (1106) Robert at Tinchebrai, seized Normandy, and kept Robert a prisoner. See biography by C. W. David (1920).

Robert, Henry Martyn, 1837–1923, American military engineer, b. Robertville, S.C., grad. West Point, 1857. He is best known as the author of a book on parliamentary law, *Pocket Manual of Rules of Order for Deliberative Assemblies* (1876), of which a revision appeared in 1915 as *Robert's Rules of Order Revised.* In the Civil War, Robert was assigned to the engineers and worked on the defenses of Washington, Philadelphia, and the New England coast. Almost continuously from 1867 until 1895 he was in charge of river, harbor, and coast improvements along the Pacific and Gulf coasts, on the Great Lakes, and on Long Island Sound. In 1901 he was appointed brigadier general, chief of engineers; soon afterward he retired.

Robert, Hubert (übâr′ rôbĕr′), 1733–1808, French painter and landscape architect. A follower of PIRANESI and PANNINI, Robert was known as a painter of idealized landscapes, fantastic ruins, and vistas of city plazas and parks. His decorations for the Château of Fontainebleau (1787) are now in the Louvre. Robert was one of the first curators of painting at the Louvre and a draftsman for the gardens at Versailles. Imprisoned during the French Revolution, he escaped death when another man of the same name went to the guillotine in his place. He later died in obscurity.

Robert, Léopold (lāôpôld′ rōbĕr′), 1794–1835, French genre painter, b. Switzerland; pupil of J. L. David. He excelled in depicting Italian folk life in a classical style. His two best-known paintings, *Pilgrimage of the Madonna of the Arc* and *Harvesters in the Pontine Marshes,* are in the Louvre.

Robert College: see BOSPORUS, UNIV. OF THE.

Robert Curthose: see ROBERT II, duke of Normandy.

Robert Grosseteste: see GROSSETESTE, ROBERT.

Robert Guiscard (gēskär′), c.1015–1085, Norman conqueror of S Italy, a son of Tancred de Hauteville (see NORMANS). Robert joined (c.1046) his brothers in S Italy and fought with them to expel the Byzantines. In 1057 he succeeded his brother Humphrey as count of Apulia, and in 1059 Pope Nicholas II invested him at Melfi with Apulia, Calabria, and Sicily. However, most of these lands remained to be conquered, and Robert set himself to the task with the help of his younger brother Roger, who wrested (1061–91) Sicily from the Arabs (see ROGER I). Calabria was occupied by 1060; Bari fell in 1071, Salerno in 1076. Robert's attacks on the duchy of Benevento, a papal fief, resulted in his excommunication (1074), but a reconciliation was brought about because the pope, GREGORY VII, needed Norman assistance against Holy Roman Emperor HENRY IV, who had invaded Rome (1081). Ultimately, virtually all of Benevento except the city itself fell to Robert; he then turned his eyes to the Byzantine Empire. Championing the cause of the deposed emperor, Michael VII, he sailed in 1081, conquered Corfu, and defeated (1082) Emperor ALEXIUS I. In 1083 he returned to aid Gregory VII, who was besieged in the Castel Sant' Angelo. Robert's troops sacked Rome for three days (1084), but were again expelled by those of Henry IV. Robert, with his elder son BOHEMOND I, resumed his conquests in the east. Robert died of fever during the siege of Cephalonia and was succeeded in Apulia by his younger son, Roger.

Robert-Houdin, Jean Eugène: see HOUDIN, JEAN EUGÈNE ROBERT.

Robert Joffrey Ballet, one of the major American dance companies. It was founded in New York City in 1954 by the dancer-choreographer Robert Joffrey. From 1956 to 1964 it made yearly tours of the United States. The company was dissolved in 1964 and then revived in 1965 by Joffrey, Alex Ewing, and Gerald Arpino. In 1966 it became affiliated with the New York City Center as the City Center Joffrey Ballet. The company has toured Europe, including the Soviet Union, and Asia. Its modern repertory has featured the work of outstanding choreographers, including George Balanchine, Antony Tudor, and Alvin Ailey.

Robert of Brunne: see MANNYNG, ROBERT.

Robert of Courtenay (kôrt′nē, ko͝ortənā′), d. 1228, Latin emperor of Constantinople (1218–28). His father, Peter of Courtenay, was elected by the Latin nobles to succeed Henry of Flanders as emperor, but shortly afterward he was captured (1217) by Theodore, despot of Epirus. Robert succeeded to the throne in the next year; his mother, Yolande, was regent until 1219. Disaster befell the Latin Empire in 1224, when Robert was defeated almost simultaneously by Theodore and by John III, emperor of Nicaea. The emperor's territories were reduced to little more than the city of Constantinople. Robert was deposed in 1228, and his brother Baldwin II succeeded him under the regency of John of Brienne.

Robert of Geneva, d. 1394, Genevan churchman, antipope (1378–94; see SCHISM, GREAT) with the name Clement VII. He was archbishop of Cambrai (1368) and was created (1371) a cardinal. He was subsequently papal legate in Italy, and he put down a rebellion at Cesena with great cruelty. In 1378, on the death of GREGORY XI, URBAN VI was elected, but the cardinals reconsidered and elected Robert instead. He went to Avignon at once, and the Great Schism had begun. He was recognized by France (his protector), Scotland (France's ally), Spain, and Naples. Several German states also recognized him. Portugal twice recognized and twice repudiated him. He was unsuccessful in trying to increase his support. He died just as the ideas that led to the conciliar theory (i.e., that councils, as opposed to the pope, have supreme authority) were being propagated from Paris. His successor at Avignon was Benedict XIII (see LUNA, PEDRO DE).

Robert of Gloucester (glŏs′tər), fl. 1260–1300, English chronicler. Possibly a monk of Gloucester, he is known only from the vernacular metrical chronicle of English history that bears his name. The chronicle, which covers the period from the legendary Brut to 1270, may have been written by more than one person, for the two recensions vary in fullness of treatment. It is important both for philological studies and as a historical source for the Barons' War in the reign of Henry III.

Robert of Jumièges (zhümyĕzh′), fl. 1037–52, Norman churchman in England, b. Normandy. As abbot of Jumièges he won the favor of Edward (later EDWARD THE CONFESSOR) during Edward's exile in Normandy. He went (1043) to England with the king and received the bishopric of London (1044), becoming archbishop of Canterbury in 1051. A leader of the Norman party of the king, Robert opposed the powerful Earl Godwin and helped send him into exile in 1051. Upon Godwin's return Robert fled to France, was later outlawed by the hostile English, and never succeeded in returning to his see, despite the support of the pope.

Roberts, Benjamin Titus, 1823–93, American clergyman, one of the founders of the Free Methodist Church, b. Gowanda, N.Y. In 1858 he was expelled from the Genesee Conference of the Methodist Episcopal Church of New York state, because of his criticisms of Church practices. He and other ministers of the same mind formed the Free Methodist Church of North America in 1860, of which he was general superintendent from 1860 to 1893.

Roberts, Sir Charles George Douglas, 1860–1943, Canadian author, b. New Brunswick. He was the first Canadian to be knighted for his work as a writer. He wrote over 67 works, of which the best-known are *Orion* (1880), *Divers Tones* (1886), *Selected Poems* (1936), and other volumes of lyrics and idyls; such tales of wildlife as *Watchers of the Trails* (1904) and *Hoof and Claw* (1913); and a popular *History of Canada* (1897).

Roberts, Elizabeth Madox, 1886–1941, American poet and novelist, b. Perryville, Ky., grad. Univ. of Chicago, 1921. She is best known for her novels and stories of the Kentucky mountain people, whose dialect and customs she carefully represented. All her work is distinguished by the beauty and rhythm of her prose. Her novels include *The Time of Man* (1926), *My Heart and My Flesh* (1927), *Jingling in the Wind* (1928), *The Great Meadow* (1930), and *Black Is My Truelove's Hair* (1938). Some of her short stories are collected in *The Haunted Mirror* (1932) and *Not by Strange Gods* (1941). Her volumes of poetry include *Under the Tree* (1922) and *Song in the Meadow* (1940).

Roberts, Frederick Sleigh, 1st **Earl Roberts of Kandahar** (kăndəhär′), 1832–1914, British field marshal. He joined the Bengal artillery in 1851 and fought with distinction in the Indian Mutiny (1857–58), earning the Victoria Cross. By 1875 he was quartermaster general of the Indian army and a strong advocate of the "forward" policy of controlling the Himalayan passes to forestall Russian encroachments; this became the general defensive policy of the British in India. He became a popular British hero for the relief of Kandahar in the second Afghan War (1878–80). Roberts was made commander in chief of the Madras army in 1880 and of the entire Indian forces in 1885. In 1893 he returned to England and wrote his reminiscences, *Forty-one Years in India* (1897). He became field marshal in 1895. In 1899, when the English were meeting reverses at the hands of the Boers in the SOUTH AFRICAN WAR, Roberts was appointed commander in chief. Aided by his chief of staff, Horatio Kitchener, Roberts reorganized the transport system, achieving a mobility that had been lacking. By late 1900 the war seemed near a successful conclusion, and Roberts was brought home, awarded an earldom, and appointed commander in chief of the British army. His office was abolished in 1904, and thereafter he devoted himself to the advocacy of compulsory military service for home defense. See biography by David James (1954).

Roberts, Kenneth Lewis, 1885–1957, American author, b. Kennebunk, Maine, grad. Cornell, 1908. Well known as staff correspondent for the *Saturday Evening Post* and as an author of travel books, Roberts retired in 1928 to write the *Chronicles of Arundel,* a series of American historical novels; the series eventually included *Arundel* (1930), *The Lively Lady* (1931), *Rabble in Arms* (1933), and *Captain Caution* (1934). All Roberts's novels are colorful, exciting, and historically accurate. His later novels include *Northwest Passage* (1937), *Oliver Wiswell* (1940), *Lydia Bailey* (1946), and *Boon Island* (1956). See the autobiographical *I Wanted to Write* (1949).

Roberts, Owen Josephus, 1875–1955, Associate Justice of the U.S. Supreme Court (1930–45), b. Philadelphia. After receiving (1898) his law degree from the Univ. of Pennsylvania, he practiced law in Philadelphia, taught (1898–1918) at the Univ. of Pennsylvania, and served as assistant district attorney (1901–4) of Philadelphia co. During World War I he was appointed by the U.S. Attorney General to prosecute cases involving espionage, and he became nationally known as a prosecuting attorney in the Teapot Dome scandal (1924). Appointed (1930) to the Supreme Court by President Hoover, Roberts faced with other justices the problems of legislation for a depression economy. After 1935 he allied himself with the conservative group, but later he supported New Deal legislation. He was appointed to investigate the Pearl Harbor disaster. After he resigned from the Supreme Court, he was (1948–51) dean of the Univ. of Pennsylvania law school. He wrote *The Court and the Constitution* (1951). See study by C. A. Leonard (1971).

Robertson, Sir Dennis, 1890–1963, British economist, grad. Trinity College, Cambridge. A professor at Cambridge for most of his working life, he also handled Anglo-American financial relationships during World War II and played an active part in the postwar Bretton Woods Monetary Conference. Robertson was an early associate of John Maynard Keynes, and his *Banking Policy and the Price Level* (1926) foreshadowed some of Keynes's later work, especially that part dealing with the relationship between saving and investment. Later, however, Robertson became a trenchant critic of Keynesian economics. He especially opposed government action to moderate inflation, although toward the end of his life he again changed his views, taking an interventionist and strongly anti-inflationary position. He was noted for his unique ability to present abstract economic analysis in highly readable form. See R. J. Saulnier, *Contemporary Monetary Theory* (1938, repr. 1970).

Robertson, Ethel Richardson: see RICHARDSON, HENRY HANDEL.

Robertson, James, 1742–1814, American frontiersman, a founder of Tennessee, b. Brunswick co., Va. He was reared in North Carolina. After the failure of the REGULATOR MOVEMENT, he led (1771) a group of settlers from Orange co., N.C., to Tennessee, where he became a leader of the WATAUGA ASSOCIATION. In 1779, Robertson explored the Cumberland River country for Richard HENDERSON and his TRANSYLVANIA COMPANY and in 1780 began the settlement of Nashborough, later renamed Nashville. Under the Cumberland Compact he became the chief civil and military officer of the community, and his wise leadership was largely responsible for its survival. When the state of Tennessee was organized in 1796, Robertson was prominent in drafting its first constitution. In his later years he served in the state senate (1798) and as agent to the Chickasaw. See biography by A. W. Putnam (1859; repr. 1971).

Robertson, Oscar, 1938–, U.S. basketball player, b. Charlotte, Tenn. Passionately devoted to basketball as a youth, Robertson led his high school team to 45 consecutive victories. After an athletically brilliant college career at the Univ. of Cincinnati, Robertson, known as the Big O, joined the Cincinnati Royals of the National Basketball Association. Robertson, only 6 ft 4 in. (193 cm) in height, scored over 26,000 points for the Royals (1960–70) and the Milwaukee Bucks (1970–). His total of more than 9,000 assists marks him as a superb playmaker.

Robertson, Thomas William, 1829–71, English dramatist and actor; brother of Madge Kendal. After spending several years as an actor, he turned to playwriting, initiating the "cup and saucer" school of drama, which was characterized by its realism and its contemporary, domestic setting. His first successful play, *David Garrick* (1864), was followed by *Society* (1865) and *Ours* (1866). With *Caste* (1867) he began a close association with Squire Bancroft and his wife, Marie Wilton BANCROFT, the actress, and they produced several of his plays. Although Robertson's plays were always criticized as being sentimental and shallow, they were very popular.

Robertson, William, 1721–93, Scottish churchman and historian. As moderator (1762–80) of the general assembly of the Church of Scotland, he led the moderate party and enforced the right of the state to make clerical appointments. Robertson was one of the first to approach history as an empirical science. His *History of Scotland during the Reigns of Queen Mary and King James VI* (1759), a factual, pragmatic history, was praised by Edmund Burke, David Hume, and others. Soon after its success, he became principal of the Univ. of Edinburgh and historiographer royal. His masterpiece was *The History of the Reign of Charles V* (3 vol., 1796; ed. by W. H. Prescott, 2 vol., 1857), though it has long been obsolete. His *History of the Discovery and Settlement of America* (1777) was the first sympathetic treatment in English of the Spanish in America. See J. B. Black, *The Art of History* (1926, repr. 1965).

Robertson, Sir William Robert, 1860–1933, British field marshal. He enlisted in the army in 1877 and became an officer in 1888. He was in the intelligence department in India (1892–96) and served in a similar capacity in the South African War (1899–1902). In World War I he served in France as quartermaster general of the British army and chief of staff (1915) to Gen. Sir John French. Appointed chief of the imperial general staff in 1915, he came into conflict with David Lloyd George because of his strong advocacy of concentrating forces on the Western Front. He was relieved of this command in 1918. He commanded (1919–20) the British army on the Rhine and was made a baronet (1919) and a field marshal (1920). He was the first British field marshal to come up through the ranks. He is the author of *From Private to Field-Marshal* (1921) and *Soldiers and Statesmen, 1914–1918* (1926). See biography by V. Bonham-Carter (1964).

Robert the Bruce: see ROBERT I, king of Scotland.

Robert the Devil, hero of a medieval legend. He was sold to the devil by his mother before his birth, but upon discovering the fact did penance and was able to purify himself of his many sins. The tale may have been derived from the life of Robert I, duke of Normandy. The story exists in several French and English versions and is the basis of Meyerbeer's opera *Robert le Diable.*

Robert the Strong, d. 866, French warrior, marquess of Neustria; father of the French kings Eudes and Robert I and ancestor of the Capetians. He joined the rebellious nobles against Charles II, Emperor of the West. They invited Louis the German to invade France (858). Becoming reconciled to Charles in 861, Robert was charged with the defense of the country between the Seine and the Loire, from which he repelled the Bretons and the Normans. He was killed fighting against the Normans.

Robeson, Paul (rōb'sən), 1898–, American actor and bass singer, b. Princeton, N.J. The son of a runaway slave who became a minister, Robeson graduated first from Rutgers (1919), where he was a four-letter man in athletics, and then from Columbia Univ. law school (1923). He began his acting career in 1924 with the Provincetown Players. His creation of the title role in Eugene O'Neill's *Emperor Jones* (1925; film, 1933) won wide acclaim. His other outstanding dramatic performances include Crown in DuBose Heyward's *Porgy* (1928) and *Othello* (in London, 1930, and New York, 1943–45). In 1925 he made his debut as a concert singer. He became known especially for his rendition of "Ol' Man River" in Jerome Kern's play *Show Boat* (1928; film, 1936) and for his interpretations of Negro spirituals. Robeson's association with Communist causes and his winning of the International Stalin Peace Prize (1952) made him a controversial figure in the United States. He moved to England in 1958, and continued to appear in concerts in Europe and the Soviet Union. He returned to live in the United States in 1963. See his *Here I Stand* (1958); biographies by his wife (1930) and Shirley Graham (1946).

Robespierre, Maximilien Marie Isidore (mäksēmēlyăN' märē' ēzēdôr' rôbĕspyĕr'), 1758–94, one of the leading figures of the FRENCH REVOLUTION. A poor youth, he was enabled to study law in Paris through a scholarship. He won admiration for his abilities, but his austerity and dedication isolated him from easy companionship. Returning to his native Arras, he practiced law and gained some reputation. He soon came under the influence of Rousseau's theories of democracy and deism, and Robespierre's emphasis on virtue—which in his mind meant civic morality—later earned him the epithet, the Incorruptible. Elected to the States-General of 1789, he remained in obscurity, but his influence in the Jacobin Club grew steadily until he became its leader (see JACOBINS). In the National Constituent Assembly (June, 1789–Sept., 1791), he unsuccessfully championed democratic elections and successfully backed the law that made members of the Constituent Assembly ineligible to sit in the Legislative Assembly, which succeeded it. In the spring of 1792 he opposed the war proposals of the GIRONDISTS and his opposition made him lose popularity. This was only temporary, however, and he was elected to the insurrectionary COMMUNE OF PARIS set up on Aug. 10, 1792. As a deputy from Paris in the National Convention, he played an important part in the struggle for power between the Girondists and the MOUNTAIN, as the Jacobins in the assembly were known. He demanded the execution of the king and was instrumental in finally suppressing (May–June, 1793) the Girondists. On July 27, 1793, he was elected to the Committee of Public Safety (the "Great Committee"), where his power and prestige grew. The dangers of foreign invasion and the urgent need to maintain order and unity led the committee to inaugurate the REIGN OF TERROR; although it was a collective effort, the name of Robespierre is always associated with it, because of his predominance on the committee. Robespierre opposed both the extreme left, under Jacques Hébert, and the moderates, led by Georges Danton and Camille Desmoulins. When these groups threatened the revolutionary government, each in turn was overthrown (March–April, 1794). By this time, however, Robespierre's position was becoming precarious; he was faced by divisions within the Committee of Public Safety and by opposition from the PLAIN in the Convention. His establishment of a new civic religion, partly to combat the atheism of the Hébertists, also provoked criticism. The law of 22 Prairial (June 10) gave the Revolutionary Tribunal greater power just when military successes convinced the moderates in the Convention that emergency measures were no longer necessary. In answer to a speech by Robespierre that seemed to threaten further purges, the forces of the right joined the Plain in a dramatic rising within the Convention on 9 THERMIDOR (July 27, 1794). Robespierre was placed under arrest, and although temporarily freed, was summarily tried and guillotined the next morning (July 28). Robespierre's character has been the subject of great controversy. However, his courage, integrity, and devoted republicanism are beyond debate. There are many biographies of Robespierre, notably that by J. M. Thompson (1935, repr. 1968). See also those by Ernest Hamel (3 vol., 1865–67, in French), Louis Gosselin (tr. 1927), Friedrich Sieburg (tr. 1937), Ralph Korngold (1937), and J. M. Eagan (1938, repr. 1970). In addition, see J. M. Thompson, *Robespierre and the French Revolution* (1952, repr. 1968).

robin or **robin redbreast,** common name for a migratory bird of the family Turdidae (THRUSH family).

Robin Hood, legendary hero of 12th-century England who robbed the rich to help the poor. Chivalrous, manly, fair, and always ready for a joke, Robin Hood reflected many of the ideals of the English yeoman. He lived in Sherwood Forest with Little John (his chief archer), Friar Tuck, Maid Marion (his beloved), and his band. Robin Hood was the hero of at least 30 Middle English ballads and of many later stories and plays. He is mentioned in such diverse works as *Piers Plowman, Ivanhoe* (1820) by Sir Walter Scott, and *The Once and Future King* (1958) by T. H. White.

Robinson, Boardman, 1876–1952, American painter, illustrator, and cartoonist, b. Somerset, N.S., studied at the Massachusetts School of Art, Boston, and in Paris. After four years of painting in San Francisco he went to New York City and was illustrator and cartoonist for the *Morning Telegraph* (1907–10) and for the *Tribune* (1910–14). He went with John Reed to the Balkans and Russia and served (1915) as war correspondent. Upon his return he contributed cartoons to various journals and was for several years at the Art Students League, where he gained a great following as a teacher. He also became known for his murals that decorate Rockefeller Center, New York City, the Dept. of Justice Building, Washington, D.C., and many other buildings. From 1936 to 1947 he was director of the Colorado Springs Fine Arts Center. Robinson is perhaps most famous for his satirical political cartoons and his illustrations, as for Dostoyevsky's works and Melville's *Moby Dick.* See study by Albert Christ-Janer (1946).

Robinson, Charles, 1818–94, American politician, first governor of the state of Kansas (1861–63), b. Hardwick, Mass. He studied medicine and began to practice in Massachusetts in 1843. In 1849 he joined the gold rush to California, where the next year he was elected to the California legislature; he opposed the establishment of slavery in California. He returned (1851) to Massachusetts, again practiced medicine, and for two years edited the Fitchburg *News.* In 1854, Robinson went to KANSAS as agent of the EMIGRANT AID COMPANY, began the settlement of Lawrence, and commanded free-state forces in the Wakarusa War. Under the free-state constitution adopted by the Topeka convention he was elected (Jan., 1856) governor. He attempted to avoid conflict with Federal authorities, but he ignored the laws passed by the proslavery territorial legislature of 1855. After taking office he was arrested for treason and usurpation of office by the proslavery party. A Federal grand jury acquitted him. Robinson was reelected in 1858 and again in 1859, under the Wyandotte Constitution, but he waited until Kansas was admitted (1861) to the Union before assuming the governorship. He was elected state senator in 1874 and 1876, was a regent of the state university (1864–74, 1893–94), and was superintendent of the Haskell Institute at Lawrence (1887–89). He wrote *The Kansas Conflict* (1892). See biography by F. W. Blackmar (1901, repr. 1971).

Robinson, Edward G., 1893–1973, American movie actor, b. Bucharest, Rumania; his real name was Emmanuel Goldberg. He made his stage debut in New York City in 1915. Robinson's most famous role was that of the snarling mobster in *Little Caesar* (1931). He played tough-guy roles in such movies as *Five Star Final* (1931), *Kid Galahad* (1937), and *Key Largo* (1948), and character parts in films like *Double Indemnity* (1944), *The Night Has a Thousand Eyes* (1948), *Nightmare* (1956), and *Soylent Green* (1973). See his autobiography (1974).

Robinson, Edwin Arlington, 1869–1935, American poet, b. Head Tide, Maine, attended Harvard (1891–93). At the time of his death Robinson was considered by many to be the greatest poet in the United States. He is now best remembered for his short poems characterizing various residents of "Tilbury Town." Robinson grew up in Gardner, Maine (the prototype for Tilbury Town). His first volume of verse, *The Torrent and the Night Before,* was published at his own expense in 1896. The following year some of these poems were published with additions as *The Children of the Night.* In 1899, Robinson settled in New York City and supported himself by various odd jobs. A third volume of poetry, *Captain Craig* (1902), was poorly received by critics. Robinson had, however, an admirer in President Theodore Roosevelt, who secured for the struggling poet a job in the New York customs house, where he worked from 1905 to 1909. From 1911 until his death Robinson spent his summers at the MacDowell Colony for artists and writers (in Peterborough, N.H.). He finally achieved critical recognition with *The Man Against the Sky* (1916). Thereafter he concentrated on long psychological narrative poems, such as *Avon's Harvest* (1921), *The Man Who Died Twice* (1924; Pulitzer Prize), *Dionysus in Doubt* (1925), *Cavender's House* (1929), *Talifer* (1933), *King Jasper* (1935), and the Arthurian romances *Merlin* (1917), *Lancelot* (1920), and *Tristram* (1928; Pulitzer Prize). A quiet, introverted man, Robinson never married and became legendary for his reclusiveness. His later poetry reveals a deep consciousness of social issues, an experimentation with symbolism, and an increasingly optimistic view of man's evolving destiny. Yet in spite of the greater profundity of the later poems, Robinson's most lasting work is probably his early verse—austere portraits exploring the paradoxes of human character and the frustration and pain of the human predicament. "Miniver Cheevy," "Richard Cory," "Cliff Klingenhagen," "Reuben Bright," and "Luke Havergal" are among the most famous of his brief, dramatic poems. Volumes of his collected poems were published in 1921 (Pulitzer Prize) and 1937. See his letters, comp. by Ridgely Torrence (1940), Denham Sutcliffe (1947), and Richard Cary (1968); biographies by C. P. Smith (1965) and L. O. Coxe (1969); studies by Wallace Anderson (1967) and Ivor Winters (rev. ed. 1971).

Robinson, Henry Crabb, 1775-1867, English diarist and journalist, a lawyer. In addition to practicing law occasionally, he served (1808-9) as war correspondent for the London *Times.* His voluminous correspondence and diaries are a mine of information about his literary acquaintances, among whom were Goethe, Schiller, the Wordsworths, Coleridge, and Lamb. Selections from his writings have been published since 1869; the most recent volumes were edited by E. J. Morley, who also wrote his biography (1935).

Robinson, Jackie (Jack Roosevelt Robinson), 1919-72, American baseball player, the first Negro to play in the major leagues, b. Cairo, Ga. He grew up in Pasadena, Calif., where he became an outstanding athlete in high school and junior college. While attending (1939-41) the Univ. of California at Los Angeles, he established a state-wide reputation at baseball, basketball, football, and track. Robinson left college to support his mother, and in 1941 he played professional football with the Los Angeles Bulldogs of the Pacific Coast League. He entered (1942) the army in World War II and was discharged as a lieutenant in 1945. In Oct., 1945, Branch Rickey, then president of the Brooklyn Dodgers baseball organization, signed Robinson to play for the Montreal Royals, a Brooklyn farm club of the International League. Despite several tense situations in spring training in the South and many inconveniences during the season, Robinson—the first Negro ball player in that league—excelled as second baseman and won the batting crown of the league for 1946. In 1947 major-league precedent was shattered when Robinson was brought up to the Brooklyn club. Negroes had never before played in big-league competition, but resistance against Robinson died down soon after he proved his worth. In 1949 he won the batting crown of the National League, hitting .342, and was named the most valuable player of the league. Robinson played his entire career (1947-56) with the Brooklyn team, where he set fielding and batting records and gained a reputation for base stealing. Other Negroes began playing in the major leagues soon after Robinson's debut. In 1962 Robinson became the first Negro to gain admission to the National Baseball Hall of Fame. See his autobiography (1972).

Robinson, James Harvey, 1863-1936, American historian, b. Bloomington, Ill. He taught history at the Univ. of Pennsylvania from 1891 to 1895 and at Columbia from 1895 to 1919, becoming a full professor in 1895. In 1919 he was one of the founders of the New School for Social Research, of which he was the first director. Through his writings and lectures, in which he stressed the "new history"—the social, scientific, and intellectual progress of mankind rather than merely political happenings—he exerted an important influence on the study and teaching of history. An editor (1892-95) of the *Annals* of the American Academy of Political and Social Science, he was also an associate editor (1912-20) of the *American Historical Review* and president (1929) of the American Historical Association. Among his many textbooks and books for the general public are *The Development of Modern Europe* (2 vol., 1907-8; rev. ed. 1929), with C. A. Beard; *The New History* (1911); *The Mind in the Making* (1921), which enjoyed a wide sale; *The Humanizing of Knowledge* (1923, rev. ed. 1926); *The Ordeal of Civilization* (1926); and *The Human Comedy as Devised and Directed by Mankind Itself* (1937). See biography by L. V. Hendricks (1946).

Robinson, John, 1576?-1625, English nonconformist pastor of the Pilgrim Fathers in Holland. In 1592 he entered Cambridge; in 1597 he received a fellowship and was ordained. Soon thereafter he became curate of a church at Norwich. He was a member of the group of separatists at Gainsborough and a little later (c.1606) was in the company of the separatists gathered around William Brewster at Scrooby. He became their pastor and was a leader in the removal (1608) of the Scrooby group to Amsterdam. In 1609 he and his flock moved to Leiden, where they set up a church. Robinson actively encouraged the projected emigration (1620) to America and would have accompanied the PILGRIMS had the majority of his congregation gone; with their settlement at Plymouth, CONGREGATIONALISM was founded in the New World. Robinson was the author of a number of essays and polemics on the separatists' position. See his works (ed. by Robert Ashton, 1851); biography by W. H. Burgess (1920); Champlin Burrage, *New Facts concerning John Robinson* (1910).

Robinson, Sir John Beverley, 1791-1863, Canadian jurist, b. Lower Canada (Quebec). After holding many important offices, he entered upon his long career (1829-62) as chief justice of Upper Canada; in this period he was also briefly president of the executive council and was speaker of the legislative council (1830-41). A man of great ability and integrity, he was, as a leading member of the unpopular and conservative FAMILY COMPACT group, an opponent of the union (1841) of Upper and Lower Canada and of the Reform party in its efforts to secure responsible representative government. He was created baronet in 1854.

Robinson, Joseph Taylor, 1872-1937, U.S. legislator, b. Lonoke co., Ark. He was admitted (1895) to the bar and served (1903-13) in the U.S. House of Representatives. In 1913 he became governor of Arkansas but resigned from this post within the year on being elected to the U.S. Senate. In 1928 he ran for Vice President on the Democratic ticket along with Alfred E. Smith. As majority leader (1933-37) in the Senate, Robinson steered many New Deal measures through the Senate and assumed (1937) leadership of the unsuccessful fight for President Franklin Delano Roosevelt's Supreme Court reorganization bill. He was cosponsor of the Robinson-Patman Act (1936) against price discrimination.

Robinson, Lennox, 1886-1958, Irish dramatist. From 1910 to 1923 he was manager of the Abbey Theatre in Dublin, and he served as director there from 1923 until his death. The comedy *The White Headed Boy* (1920) was his outstanding early success. His later dramas of Irish life, which include *The Big House* (1926) and *Drama at Inish* (1933; in America, *Is Life Worth Living?*), are characterized by a somber realism. He edited *The Irish Theatre* (lectures, 1939) and Lady Gregory's journals (1946), and he also wrote a study of W. B. Yeats (1939). See his autobiography (1942).

Robinson, Sugar Ray, 1921-, American boxer, b. Detroit. His real name is Walker Smith. He began boxing after three years of high school in New York City. Having won all his amateur fights (about 90), including the Golden Gloves featherweight title, Robinson turned professional in 1940. He won the welterweight championship in 1946 by defeating Tommy Bell and the middleweight championship for the first time in 1951 by knocking out Jake La Motta. When Robinson retired from boxing as middleweight champion in 1952 he had lost only three times in 137 bouts. Returning to boxing in 1955, he was the first boxer ever to regain a title after retiring. Robinson became the first man in boxing history to win a divisional (weight class) world championship five times when he regained the middleweight title in 1958 by defeating Carmen Basilio; he lost the title in 1960 to Paul Pender. In his prime, the swift, hard-punching Robinson was rated the best boxer, pound for pound, of his time.

Robinson, Theodore, 1852-96, American painter, b. Irasburg, Vt. Beginning his career as a realist, Robinson was profoundly influenced by his meeting with Monet in 1888. Translating the impressionist rendering of light, air, and broken color to the American landscape, Robinson combined contemporary American and European trends. His *Giverny: Bird's-Eye View* is in the Metropolitan Museum.

Robinson-Patman Act, passed by the U.S. Congress in 1936 to supplement the CLAYTON ANTITRUST ACT. The act, advanced by Congressman Wright Patman, forbade any person or firm engaged in interstate commerce to discriminate in price to different purchasers of the same commodity when the effect would be to lessen competition or to create a monopoly. Sometimes called the Chain-Store Act, this act was directed at protecting the independent retailer from chain-store competition, but it was also strongly supported by wholesalers eager to prevent chain stores from buying directly from the manufacturers. See G. H. Montague, *The Robinson-Patman Act and Its Administration* (1945, repr. 1958); D. J. Baum, *The Robinson-Patman* (1964).

robin's plantain (plăn'tĭn), common name of several plants belonging to the family Compositae (COMPOSITE family). Robin's plantain, also known as hawkweed, of the genus *Hieracium,* is mostly native to South America and Europe. The ancient Greeks believed that the hawks used the sap of these plants to sharpen their eyesight. Poor robin's plantain, also called fleabane, is the common name for the genus *Erigeron,* found worldwide, particularly in mountainous regions. The name comes from the Greek, meaning "old man in the spring." Robin's plantains are classified in the division MAGNOLIOPHYTA, class Magnoliopsida, order Asterales, family Compositae.

Rcboam (rōbō'əm): see REHOBOAM.

robot (rō'bət, rōb'ät) or **automaton,** mechanical device designed to perform the work generally done by a human being. Karel Čapek, a Czech dramatist, popularized the expression in his play *R. U. R. (Rossum's Universal Robots),* produced in Prague in 1921. Modern robots include automatic control systems such as those that keep an airplane or ship on course. Automatic systems have been developed that allow computers of staggering complexity to operate with minimal human intervention. The industrial trend toward automation in general has produced innumerable devices that replace human personnel, but the term *robot* is used less and less to designate most of this machinery. It is most often used in fiction, referring to a self-controlling machine that is shaped like a human being.

Rob Roy [Scottish Gaelic, = red Rob], 1671-1734, Scottish freebooter, whose real name was Robert MacGregor. He is remembered chiefly as he figures in Sir Walter Scott's novel *Rob Roy* (1818). Deprived of their estates as a result of proscription, the MacGregors lived largely by stealing cattle and selling "protection." Because of the proscription, which was renewed in 1693, Rob Roy assumed his mother's name, Campbell. He exploited the fact that his territory, Balquhidder, lay between the estates of the rival dukes of Montrose and Argyll. The duke of Montrose at first supported him in a cattle-farming business, but Montrose withdrew his support, forcing Rob into bankruptcy, in 1712. Rob then took to brigandage in earnest, particularly against Montrose. He took advantage of the Jacobite rising of 1715 to engage in plundering raids, but he did not espouse the Jacobite cause. In 1717, Montrose induced the duke of Atholl, previously friendly to Rob, to capture him, but he escaped to the protection of the duke of Argyll. Rob later attempted to make peace with Montrose and with the Hanoverians and to deny culpability for his activities during 1715. However, he was arrested, imprisoned in Newgate, and in 1727 sentenced to be transported. He was pardoned and returned to Balquhidder, where he remained until his death.

Robsart, Amy (rŏb'särt), 1532-60, maiden name of the wife of Robert Dudley, later earl of LEICESTER, a favorite of Queen Elizabeth I of England. When Lady Dudley was found dead at the foot of a staircase in Cumnor Hall, Berkshire, rumor had it that her husband had arranged her murder so that he might be free to wed the queen. An investigating jury returned a verdict of accidental death, but Leicester's innocence or guilt has never been definitely established. A version of the story appears in Scott's novel *Kenilworth.* See biography by Sir Bartle Frere, *Amy Robsart of Wymondham* (1937).

Robson, Mount, British Columbia: see MOUNT ROBSON PROVINCIAL PARK.

Robstown, city (1970 pop. 11,217), Nueces co., S Texas; inc. 1912. It is a packing and shipping center for a blackland region that produces cotton, grain, and oil. Its industries are based upon the area's products.

Robusti, Jacopo: see TINTORETTO.

Roca, Julio Argentino (ho͞o'lyō ärhäntē'nō rō'kä), 1843–1914, Argentine general and statesman, president of the republic (1880–86, 1898–1904). Minister of war under Nicolas AVELLANEDA, he drove (1878–79) the Patagonian Indians beyond the Río Negro, opening a vast territory for colonization. His first administration effected the federalization of Buenos Aires. It was a time of peace and growth, of rapid immigration, of railway construction, and of increased wealth. Speculation, however, flourished and later became flagrant. Roca's second administration was, indeed, marked by recovery from the crisis caused by the misgovernment of Miguel JUÁREZ CELMAN. Paper-currency redemption stabilized money. The boundary dispute with Chile was settled in 1902, and perpetual peace between the nations was symbolized in the CHRIST OF THE ANDES (dedicated March, 1904). Roca's foreign minister, Luis M. Drago, formulated the significant DRAGO DOCTRINE (1902).

Roca, Cabo da (kä'bo͞o thə rô'kə), cape, W Portugal, W of Lisbon. It is the western extremity of Europe.

Rocafuerte, Vicente (vēsān'tā rōkäfwār'tā), 1783–1847, president of Ecuador (1834–39). Rocafuerte headed (1833) the opposition to Juan José FLORES. Leader of a revolt at Guayaquil (1834), he was defeated and imprisoned, but was released after he and Flores settled their differences. As president he promulgated a new constitution and accomplished many liberal reforms, notably protection of the Indians and advancement and secularization of education. Protesting against the clerical policy and dictatorial practices of Flores, Rocafuerte went into exile in 1843.

Rochambeau, Jean Baptiste Donatien de Vimeur, comte de (zhäN bätēst', kôNt də rôshaNbō'), 1725–1807, marshal of France. He took part in the wars of King Louis XV and had been promoted to lieutenant general by 1780, when King Louis XVI sent him, with some 6,000 regulars, to aid General Washington in the American Revolution. He landed in Newport, R.I., and remained there a year because the French fleet was blockaded off Narragansett. In July, 1781, he joined Washington on the Hudson River and the two armies marched south against General Cornwallis. The result was the YORKTOWN CAMPAIGN, which ended the war. In the French Revolution, Rochambeau was made (1791) a marshal and commanded the Northern Army, but he resigned (1792) after a disagreement with General DUMOURIEZ. He was imprisoned in the Terror and barely escaped execution. Napoleon restored him to his rank. His memoirs of the American Revolution were translated in 1838. See biography by Arnold Whitridge (1965); J.-E. Weelen, *Rochambeau, Father and Son* (1936).

Rochdale (rŏch'dāl), county borough (1971 pop. 91,344), Lancashire, NW England, on the Roch River. The chief industry is the spinning and weaving of cotton and woolen yarns. Rayon, rubber, leather, and asbestos are also produced. The ROCHDALE SOCIETY OF EQUITABLE PIONEERS was founded there in 1844. There is a memorial to John Bright, who was born in Rochdale. The parish church of St. Chad dates from the 14th cent. In 1974, Rochdale became part of the new metropolitan county of Greater Manchester.

Rochdale Society of Equitable Pioneers, one of the first consumers' cooperatives, founded in 1844 in Rochdale, England, by 28 Lancashire weavers. Influenced by the theories of Robert OWEN, they opened a grocery store that was so successful that they were able to establish a cooperative factory and textile mill (see COOPERATIVE MOVEMENTS). Their rules combined a fixed interest on capital with a distribution of profits in proportion to purchases. This has remained the basic structure of consumers' cooperatives. See Joseph Reeves, *A Century of Rochdale Co-operation, 1844–1944* (1944).

Rochefort, Victor Henri, marquis de Rochefort-Luçay (vēktôr' äNrē' rôshfôr' märkē' də rôshfôr'lüsā'), 1831–1913, French journalist and politician. The editor of *Le Figaro* in 1863, he also founded and edited the bitterly anti-imperial journals *La Lanterne* (1868) and *La Marseillaise* (1869). After the Franco-Prussian War he founded *Le Mot d'ordre* (1871), supported the Commune of Paris, and was consequently sent (1873) to the penal colony of New Caledonia. He soon escaped and revived *La Lanterne* in Geneva, Switzerland. After the general amnesty of 1880 he returned to Paris and started *L'Intransigeant.* Twice elected a deputy, Rochefort, in a political switch from the extreme left to the extreme right, became an ardent supporter of Georges BOULANGER and was forced to flee France. Tried in absentia, he remained in exile from 1889 to 1895. Later, Rochefort's extreme nationalism led him to take a violent stand against Alfred Dreyfus in the Dreyfus Affair. See biography by R. L. Williams (1966).

Rochefort (rôshfôr') or **Rochefort-sur-Mer** (-sürmĕr), city (1968 pop. 34,780), Charente-Maritime dept., W France, on the Charente River near the Bay of Biscay. It is a fishing port with shipyards and aircraft and machine industries. An important naval base in the days of sailing ships, it was built (1666) by Colbert and fortified by Vauban. In 1815, Napoleon surrendered himself to a British warship off Rochefort. The port's importance declined after the advent of steamships. Today an air force technician school is there.

Rochelle, La (lä rôshĕl'), city (1968 pop. 75,497), capital of Charente-Maritime dept., W France, on the Bay of Biscay. Industries include naval, aircraft, and automobile construction. La Rochelle is the principal French fishing port on the Atlantic coast. Chartered in the 12th cent., it soon became one of the chief seaports of France. It was a Huguenot stronghold during the Wars of Religion and successfully resisted Catholic besiegers for half a year (1572–73). However, when Cardinal Richelieu resolved to crush the HUGUENOTS, La Rochelle fell after a siege of 14 months (1627–28). Louis XIV had the port refortified by Vauban; his revocation (1685) of the Edict of NANTES resulted in the foundation of New Rochelle, N.Y., by Protestant refugees. La Rochelle prospered again as it became the chief center of trade with Canada, but it suffered from the loss of Canada by France and from the Continental System under Napoleon. Although its fisheries, canneries, and shipyards still make it a busy port, La Rochelle never recovered its former importance. The principal harbor is now at La Pallice, some 3 mi (5 km) distant. The picturesque old fishing port in the heart of the city, the Renaissance town hall, and other old buildings make the city a favorite tourist center.

Rochelle salt, colorless to blue-white orthorhombic crystalline salt with a saline, cooling taste. It is also called Seignette salt after Pierre Seignette, an apothecary of La Rochelle, France, who was the first to make it (c.1675). Chemically, it is potassium sodium tartrate, KNa ($C_4H_4O_6$) · $4H_2O$. It is soluble in water and slightly soluble in alcohol, melts at about 75°C, has specific gravity 1.79, and exhibits double refraction. It is used in medicine as a mild purgative, often in the form of Seidlitz powders. It is an ingredient of FEHLING'S SOLUTION. It is used in silvering mirrors. Crystals of Rochelle salt are easily grown and are used in piezoelectric devices, e.g., crystal microphones and phonograph pickup cartridges (see PIEZOELECTRIC EFFECT).

Roches, Peter des (dā rōsh), d. 1238, English churchman and statesman, b. Poitou. He served as a chamberlain under Richard I of England and then entered the service of King JOHN, who gave him rich estates and made him (1205) bishop of Winchester. In John's struggle with Pope Innocent III, Peter took the part of the king as far as he could without endangering his office. He was made justiciar in 1214, but he was unpopular with the barons and was replaced in 1215 by Hubert de BURGH. On the accession (1216) of HENRY III, Peter became the young king's guardian, and after the death (1219) of the regent, William Marshal, 1st earl of Pembroke, he struggled for power with Hubert de Burgh. Hubert prevailed, and in 1227 Peter left to join a crusade under Holy Roman Emperor Frederick II. He returned to England in 1231, secured the fall (1232) of Hubert, and placed his nephew (or possibly his son), Peter des Rivaux, in charge of the royal household. The rule of the two Peters soon provoked a baronial revolt (1233–34), and Henry was forced by Edmund Rich, archbishop of Canterbury, to dismiss his Poitevin advisers. In 1235, Peter des Roches left England and entered the service of the pope. He returned in 1236 and eventually was reconciled with Hubert de Burgh.

Rochester, John Wilmot, 2d **earl of,** 1647–80, English poet and courtier, b. Ditchley, Oxfordshire. Most notorious and dissolute of the Restoration rakes, he lost the favor of Charles II on several occasions because of his recklessness. His most celebrated poem is his *Satyr Against Mankind* (1675). Although his poetry is primarily characterized by its wit, its polish, and its licentiousness, an undercurrent of piety runs through much of his work. In the last years of his life, Rochester underwent a religious conversion. See his *Complete Poems,* ed. by D. M. Vieth (1968); V. de S. Pinto, *Enthusiast in Wit* (1962); D. H. Griffin, *Satires Against Man* (1974); Graham Greene, *Lord Rochester's Monkey* (1974).

Rochester (rŏch'ĭstər), municipal borough (1971 pop. 55,460), Kent, SE England, on the Medway River. Cement, heavy machinery, electronic equipment, precision tools, and clothing are made. Rochester, Chatham, and Gillingham (the three Medway boroughs) form a conurbation. Rochester was the Roman Durobrivae and was important in Saxon times. St. Augustine founded a mission and bishopric in 604, and Bishop Gundulf built a cathedral on its site in the late 11th and early 12th cent.; most of the present cathedral is of 12th- to 14th-century construction. A Norman wall 12 ft (3.7 m) thick surrounds ruins of a 12th-century castle, which was besieged several times in the 13th and 14th cent. King's School for boys was refounded in 1542. From Rochester, in 1688, James II embarked in disguise. Charles Dickens's home at Gadshill is nearby.

Rochester (rŏch'ĕstər, -ĭstər). **1** City (1970 pop. 53,766), seat of Olmsted co., SE Minn.; inc. 1858. It is a farm trade center, and its manufactures include electronic and electrical equipment, medical supplies, business machines, foodstuffs, and plastic, metal, wood, and fiber glass products. The city is famous as the home of the Mayo Clinic, founded (1889) by Dr. W. W. Mayo, with his sons Charles Horace Mayo and William James Mayo. A state mental hospital and a junior college are also there. Rochester has a symphony orchestra, a municipal band, and museums of medical science, history, and antique vehicles. **2** City (1970 pop. 17,938), Strafford co., SE N.H., on the Cocheco River, near the Maine line; settled 1728, inc. as a city 1891. It has diverse industries. An annual fair has been held there since 1875. In the city are an art gallery and an antique aircraft museum. The White Mts. recreation area begins nearby. **3** City (1970 pop. 296,233), seat of Monroe co., W N.Y., a port of entry on the Genesee River and Lake Ontario, in a rich fruit and truck farm region; inc. 1817. It is a leading center in the production of photographic, optical, dental, and gear-cutting equipment, process control and recording instruments, and thermometers. It also ranks high in the manufacture of office machines and equipment, communications materials, electronics, machinery, automotive parts, wearing apparel and accessories, and jewelry. Permanent settlement by Col. Nathaniel Rochester and others began in 1812. The Erie Canal gave impetus to Rochester's growth, and flour milling became the first important industry. It is the seat of the Univ. of Rochester, Nazareth College of Rochester, the Rochester Institute of Technology (est. 1829), St. John Fisher College, and a junior college. The city's cultural features include the Rochester Philharmonic and Eastman School of Music orchestras, a large choral group, the Rochester Museum of Art and Sciences (with a planetarium), the Memorial Art Gallery, the historical society, a zoo, and the Rundell Memorial Building, which houses the public library and an art gallery. A state mental hospital is in the city. Prominent residents have been Susan B. Anthony, Frederick Douglass, and George Eastman. Numerous parks and nurseries have earned Rochester the name Flower City.

Rochester, University of, at Rochester, N.Y.; coeducational; chartered and opened 1850. It is noted for the Eastman School of Music (1918), the Memorial Art Gallery, its schools of dentistry and medicine (with Strong Memorial Hospital), and its library with its outstanding collections in history, music, and medicine. The university also maintains special programs in South Asian studies, East Asian studies, and brain research.

Roche-sur-Yon, La (lä rôsh-sür-yôN), city (1968 pop. 38,749), capital of Vendée dept., W France, on the Yon River. A transportation and agricultural trade center, it also has industries producing automobile and washing-machine parts, slippers, foundry products, and printed materials. Founded in 1804 by Napoleon I as a town for non-Royalists, it was first named Napoléon-Vendée; under the Restoration (1814–48) it was called Bourbon-Vendée.

Rochet, Waldeck (väldĕk' rôshā'), 1905–, French political leader. A member of the French Communist party, he was named to its central committee in 1936. He was imprisoned and sent to Algeria when the Communist party was declared illegal at the outbreak of World War II; freed in 1943, he worked with the Free French. For many years a member of the French assembly, he was (1964–72) secretary general of the French Communist party.

rock, aggregation of solid matter composed of one or more of the MINERALS forming the earth's crust. The term is applied not only to the solid rock, but also to the mantle rock—the fragments which have been detached from the solid rock and overlie it, such as clay, sand, gravel, and broken rock. Rocks are commonly divided, according to their origin, into three major classes—igneous, sedimentary, and metamorphic. Igneous rock originates from the cooling and solidification of molten matter from the earth's interior. If formed by rapid cooling and solidification on the earth's surface of lava from within the earth, it is called extrusive rock; igneous rock that has cooled and solidified slowly beneath the earth's surface is intrusive rock. Among the forms commonly taken by intrusive rocks are batholiths, which are enormous, irregular masses cutting or displacing older rocks; stocks, irregular and smaller than batholiths; necks, or plugs, columnar in form and probably the result of the hardening of magma in the necks of extinct volcanoes; dikes, more or less vertical, filling fissures in previously existing rock; sills, more or less horizontal, forced between layers of previously existing rock; and laccoliths, modified domelike sills that arch under the overlying rock. Igneous rocks are commonly divided into classes by texture. Some rocks are markedly granular (e.g., GRANITE, syenite, diorite, gabbro, peridotite, and pyroxenite), while others (e.g., BASALT, trachite, dacite, and andesite) are composed of grains visible only under a microscope. Both fine-grained and coarse-grained igneous rocks frequently contain grains called phenocrysts that are larger than the surrounding grains; such rocks are said to be porphyritic in texture (see PORPHYRY), while rocks with grains of uniform size are called equigranular. Igneous rocks are commonly light in color if their constituent minerals are predominantly alkali feldspars and dark in color if the feldspars are calcic or if magnesia and iron minerals are abundant. The glassy igneous rocks include obsidian, pitchstone, and PUMICE, which contain few or no phenocrysts, and vitrophyre, or glass porphyry, which does contain phenocrysts. Rocks such as tuff and volcanic breccia, which are formed from fragmental volcanic material, are sometimes grouped as pyroclastic rocks. Sedimentary rocks originate from the consolidation of sediments derived in part from living organisms but chiefly from older rocks of all classes (ultimately the mineral elements are derived from igneous rocks alone). The sediments of mineral origin are chiefly removed from older rocks and transported to the place of deposition by erosion; chemical precipitation from solution is a secondary cause of deposition of mineral matter. Sedimentary rocks are commonly distinguished, according to their place of deposition, by a great variety of terms, such as continental, marine, littoral, estuarine, lacustrine, and fluviatile. The characteristic feature of sedimentary rocks is their STRATIFICATION; they are frequently called stratified rocks. Sedimentary rocks made up of angular particles derived from other rocks are said to have a clastic texture, in contrast to pyroclastic sediments, which are particles of volcanic origin. Among the important varieties of sedimentary rock, distinguished both by texture and by chemical composition, are conglomerate, GRAVEL, SAND, SANDSTONE, grit, till, tillite, sedimentary breccia, CLAY, mud, SHALE, MARL, CHALK, LIMESTONE, COAL, PEAT, LIGNITE, GYPSUM, rock salt, and iron ore. Characteristic occurrences in sedimentary rocks are fossils, footprints, raindrop impressions, concretions, oolites, ripple marks, rill marks, and crossbedding. Some of these occurrences are useful in determining the antiquity of sedimentary formations and in interpreting geologic history. Metamorphic rocks originate from the alteration of the texture and mineral constituents of igneous, sedimentary, and older metamorphic rocks under extreme heat and pressure deep within the earth (see METAMORPHISM). Some (e.g., MARBLE and QUARTZITE) are massive in structure; others, and particularly those which have been subject to the more extreme forms of metamorphism, are characterized by foliation, i.e., the arrangement of their minerals in roughly parallel planes, giving them a banded appearance. A distinguishing characteristic of many metamorphic rocks is their slaty CLEAVAGE. Among the common metamorphic rocks are SCHIST (e.g., mica schist and hornblende schist), GNEISS, quartzite, SLATE, and marble. The scientific study of rocks is called petrology. See W. A. Deer et al., *Rock-forming Minerals* (5 vol., 1962–63); Harvey Blatt et al., *Origin of Sedimentary Rocks* (1972); A. F. Deeson, ed., *The Collector's Encyclopedia of Rocks and Minerals* (1973).

Rockaway, narrow peninsula, c.10 mi (16 km) long, SW Long Island, SE N.Y., in Queens borough of New York City. Separating Jamaica Bay from the Atlantic Ocean and isolated from the rest of New York City, the densely populated peninsula owes its growth to road and rail connections across the bay. There are fine sand beaches on Rockaway's southern side. A section of Gateway National Recreation Area, including Rockaway Beach, Fort Tilden, and Jacob Riis Park, is there.

Rockburne, Dorothea, 1938–, American artist, b. Quebec, Canada. The configurations of Rockburne's constructions are predetermined by the nature of her materials and by various limiting rules of her procedure, e.g., mathematical set theory or methods of folding paper. Her works are generally made of paper, including thick, industrial stock, often soaked in oil, and carbon paper. Some contain elements of drawing.

rock carvings and paintings, designs inscribed on rock surfaces and huge stone monuments in many parts of the world and attributed to primitive man. They have been found on every continent and are usually from prehistoric times. Petroglyphs (rock carvings) are more widespread than pictographs (rock paintings), which are preserved chiefly in dry regions, inside caves, and under overhanging cliffs. It is thought that these designs were created for purposes of religious propitiation and sympathetic magic. Whatever the motive, the prehistoric artist often reached great aesthetic heights, as in the PALEOLITHIC ART of Western Europe, the rock figures attributed to the San of S Africa, and the Tassili cliff paintings discovered in the central Sahara that suggest that this was once a fertile area. Similar evidence was found in the Alps of N Italy. Successive styles and phases were found, and several layers of designs were often superimposed. Wild animals and hunting scenes abound, while the scenes of daily life were depicted alongside representations of ceremonies and deities. In Neolithic times herdsmen and cows appeared, but rock art seems to have declined and disappeared with the advent of agriculture. In Europe and Africa the style was largely naturalistic, while in Australia and the Americas designs were more often symbolic and geometric, and sometimes approached a primitive form of writing. Carvings were usually incised or chipped out with a stone. Sometimes they were deeply gouged out in intaglio technique. The paintings, made with charcoal and earth pigments mixed with grease, gum, or water, vary from crude outlines to fully developed polychrome compositions. Engraving and painting techniques were sometimes combined. Stenciled human hands were found in numerous places. See D. S. Davidson, *Aboriginal Australian and Tasmanian Rock Carvings and Paintings* (1936); Leo Frobenius and D. C. Fox, *Prehistoric Rock Pictures in Europe and Africa* (1937, repr. 1972); J. D. Lajoux, *The Rock Paintings of Tassili* (tr. 1963); Herbert Kuhn, *The Rock Pictures of Europe* (tr. 1966); Campbell Grant, *Rock Art of the American Indian* (1967); D. N. Lee and H. C. Woodhouse, *Art on the Rocks of Southern Africa* (1970).

rock crawler, name applied to the slender, wingless INSECTS of the family Grylloblattidae in the order Orthoptera. They have long antennae and range in length from ½ to 1 in. (15–30 mm). Rock crawlers occur at altitudes of 1,500 to 6,500 ft (450–2,000 m), where they live in caves, under rocks, or on snow and ice; they thrive at temperatures just above freezing. They appear to be nocturnal and omnivorous. Rock crawlers were not discovered until 1911, and only five species are now known in the United States. Other species occur in Canada, Japan, and Siberia. They are very primitive insects, considered closely related to the basic stock from which the Orthoptera (including the cockroaches, mantids, and locusts) arose. Rock crawlers are classified in the phylum ARTHROPODA, class Insecta, order Orthoptera, suborder Grylloblattodea, family Grylloblattidae.

rock crystal: see QUARTZ.

Rockefeller, John Davison, 1839–1937, American industrialist and philanthropist, b. Richford, N.Y. He moved (1853) with his family to a farm near Cleveland and at the age of 16 went to work as a bookkeeper. Frugal and industrious, Rockefeller became (1859) a partner in a produce business, and four years later, with his partners, he established an oil refinery, thus taking part in an industry already thriving in Cleveland. In 1870 he and his associates—including S. V. Harkness, H. M. Flagler, and his brother William—organized the Standard Oil Company of Ohio, capitalized at $1 million. By enforcing strict economy and efficiency, by mergers and agreements with his able competitors, by ruthlessly crushing his less able opponents, and by accumulating large capital reserves, John D. Rockefeller soon dominated the American oil-refining industry. Rebate agreements, which he forced from the railroads, and the control of pipeline distribution of refined oil strengthened the monopoly of the Standard Oil Company. In 1882 the diverse holdings of the various members of Rockefeller's combination were tied together into the Standard Oil trust. Court action compelled the trust to dissolve 10 years later, but in a few years the Standard Oil Company of New Jersey was chartered as a holding company, with a capitalization of $110 million. In 1911 a decision of the U.S. Supreme Court required the holding company to be dissolved and its directors to relinquish their control over the numerous subsidiaries. Rockefeller personally ruled over the great petroleum business until 1911, when he retired with a fabulous fortune. When the United States Steel Corporation was formed (1901), Rockefeller was one of the directors. He was also prominent in the affairs of railroads and banks, being second only to J. P. Morgan in the domain of finance. Of a deeply religious nature, Rockefeller had an interest in philanthropy which was as deep as his interest in business. He gave generously to the Baptist Church, to the YMCA, and to the Anti-Saloon League. He founded (1892) the Univ. of Chicago. The most prominent of the philanthropic enterprises to which he eventually turned over some $500 million were the Rockefeller Institute for Medical Research, founded (1901) in New York City and since 1953 known as ROCKEFELLER UNIVERSITY; the General Education Board, organized (1902) to make gifts to various educational and research agencies; the ROCKEFELLER FOUNDATION, established (1913) to promote public health and to further the medical, natural, and social sciences; and the Laura Spelman Rockefeller Memorial Foundation, founded (1918) in memory of his wife, for the furthering of child welfare and the social sciences. He wrote *Random Reminiscences of Men and Events* (1909). See biographies by Allan Nevins (rev. ed. 1959) and Jules Abels (1965); J. T. Flynn, *God's Gold* (1932, repr. 1971). His son, **John Davison Rockefeller, Jr.,** 1874–1960, b. Cleveland, grad. Brown, 1897, took over active management of his father's interests in 1911 and engaged in numerous philanthropies. Riverside Church in New York City was built through his gifts. He gave vast sums of money for religious projects, for scientific investigation, and for the restoration of historic monuments. Among his most notable philanthropies were the restoration of colonial Williamsburg, Va., and the donation of the site for the United Nations headquarters in New York City. He founded (1931) and helped plan Rockefeller Center in New York City, which the Rockefeller interests completed in 1939. John D. Rockefeller, Jr., had six children, and his five sons have all become famous in various fields of human endeavor. See biography by R. B. Fosdick (1956). His son **John Davison Rockefeller, 3d,** 1906–, b. New York City, grad. Princeton, 1929, has been active in the management of family interests as well as numerous civic and philanthropic ventures, such as Lincoln Center for the Performing Arts, the United Negro College Fund, and the Population Council. Another son is Nelson Aldrich Rockefeller (see separate article). **Laurance S. Rockefeller,** 1910–, b. New York City, grad. Princeton, 1932, has been noted for his interest in conservation and the protection of wildlife. Among the organizations with which he has been active are the Palisades Interstate Park Commission and the executive committee of the Jackson Hole Wildlife Park. **Winthrop Rockefeller,** 1912–73, b. New York City, attended (1931–34) Yale and then went into investment management. Interested in agriculture, he became the owner of a farm in Arkansas noted for its experimental activities in animal husbandry. He served as Republican governor of Arkansas from 1967 to 1970. **David Rockefeller,** 1915–, b. New York City, grad. Harvard, 1936, Ph.D. Univ. of Chicago, 1940, was (1940–42) in the service of the government before entering (1942) the U.S. army. Active in banking (the Chase Manhattan Bank) after 1945, he has on several occasions been called upon to be the spokesman for the U.S. business community. See William Manchester, *A Rockefeller Family Portrait* (1959).

Rockefeller, Nelson Aldrich, 1908–, U.S. public official, governor of New York (1959–73), Vice President of the United States (1974–), b. Bar Harbor, Maine; grandson of John D. Rockefeller. A director of Rockefeller Center from 1931 to 1958, he also served in many government posts, including coordinator of the Office of Inter-American Affairs (1940–44), chairman of the International Development Advisory Board (1950–51), and chairman of the President's Advisory Committee on Government Organization (1952–58). A Republican, he defeated (1958) W. Averell Harriman for the governorship of New York; Rockefeller was reelected in 1962, 1966, and 1970. As governor he expanded state government services in such areas as education, transportation, housing, welfare, and environmental control. He unsuccessfully campaigned for the Republican presidential nomination in 1960, 1964, and 1968. On Dec. 18, 1973, he resigned from the governorship to serve full-time as chairman of the National Commission on Critical Choices for America. In 1974 President Ford nominated him for the vice presidency. Despite some criticism of the political uses to which he put his vast wealth, he was confirmed by Congress under the terms of the Twenty-fifth Amendment. Rockefeller wrote *The Future of Federalism* (1968), *Unity, Freedom and Peace* (1968), and *Our Environment Can Be Saved* (1970). See biographies by J. A. Morris (1960) and James Desmond (1964); W. H. Rodgers, *Rockefeller's Follies* (1966).

Rockefeller, William, 1841–1922, American financier, b. Tioga co., N.Y.; brother of John D. Rockefeller. He joined (1865) his brother in the oil-refining business. William was a successful stock market manipulator and was the New York representative of the Rockefeller interests until the Standard Oil Company of New Jersey was dissolved (1911) by the Supreme Court. He was associated with copper interests, railways, and public-utility corporations. With his vast resources he built up the National City Bank of New York.

Rockefeller Center, complex of buildings, in central Manhattan, New York City, between 48th and 51st streets and Fifth Ave. and the Ave. of the Americas (Sixth Ave.). Fourteen of the buildings, including the 70-story RCA (Radio Corp. of America) Building, were built between 1931 and 1939. The Time-Life Building (built 1960–61), the most recent addition to the group, extended the center's boundaries west of the Ave. of the Americas. The buildings are occupied by offices, shops, restaurants, exhibition rooms, broadcasting studios, and the Radio City Music Hall, New York City's largest movie theater. Five of the western buildings of Rockefeller Center in the broadcasting and entertainment section are known as Radio City. Many sculptors and painters are represented in the decoration of the buildings and grounds. Paul Manship designed the Prometheus of the central fountain, which overlooks an outdoor skating rink and mall. See Samuel Chamberlain, *Rockefeller Center; a Photographic Narrative* (1961).

Rockefeller Foundation, philanthropic institution established (1913) by John D. Rockefeller, Sr., with the general purpose of promoting "the well-being of mankind throughout the world." During its first 14 years the foundation received $183 million from Rockefeller. He was aided in the early years of the foundation's activities by his son John D. Rockefeller, Jr., and Frederick T. Gates. Gates was instrumental in channeling its early philanthropic activities into medical research and education and public health. Outstanding contributions in the form of funds, research, and field work were made by the foundation in the battle against hookworm, malaria, yellow fever, and other diseases throughout the world. It also helped finance relief measures after World War I. The consolidation (1929) of the Laura Spelman Memorial Fund (with its $58 million endowment) with the Rockefeller Foundation marked the organization's expansion into new areas of research including the natural and social sciences, humanities, and agriculture. The foundation financed the preparation of the *Encyclopaedia of the Social Sciences* (1932) and has helped support such independent research agencies as the National Bureau of Economic Research, the Brookings Institution, and the Social Science Research Council. The foundation has continued its worldwide philanthropic activities, concentrating in six major areas: hunger and the international food supply, overpopulation, education in underdeveloped areas, equal opportunity for all, cultural improvement, and ecology and the environment. By 1972 its endowment was estimated to be over $969 million. Other philanthropic foundations maintained by members of the Rockefeller family are the Rockefeller Brothers Fund (est. 1940), the Rockefeller Family Fund (est. 1967), and the Rockefeller Fund for Music (est. 1962).

Rockefeller University, philanthropic organization in New York City, founded 1901 as the Rockefeller Institute for Medical Research by John D. Rockefeller for furthering medical science and its allied subjects and to make knowledge of these subjects available to the public. Many millions of dollars allocated to the institute by its founder and members of his family enabled it to develop into one of the principal research organizations in the United States. Its first laboratory was opened in 1904; its hospital, established for the study of human diseases, opened in 1910. Two main departments were also organized—the departments of animal pathology (1914) and plant pathology (1931). The institute later added programs in the behavioral sciences, mathematics, physics, and philosophy. In 1954 the institute, becoming part of the Univ. of the State of New York, took on the status of a graduate university with authority to grant advanced degrees. In 1958 it became the Rockefeller Institute, and in 1965 its present name was adopted. Research projects in the biological and biomedical sciences are continually under way, including a program of advanced study in collaboration with the medical school of Cornell Univ. The university publishes several journals as well as conference reports and monographs.

rocket, in botany, popular name for several plants of the family Cruciferae (MUSTARD family). The dame's, or damask, violet, damewort, or sweet rocket is *Hesperis matronalis,* a hardy, herbaceous Old World perennial with four-petaled flowers, ranging from white to purple, that are especially fragrant in the evening. It grows wild in many parts of North America, where it has escaped from gardens. Rocket salad (*Eruca sativa*) is the roquette of France and Italy and is a coarse, weedy plant with whitish or creamy-yellow flowers that have an orange-blossom odor. Also known as tira and garden rocket, it is cultivated for salads. Yellow rocket (*Barbarea vulgaris*) is the name for a variety of winter cress or upland cress, a weedy plant sometimes cultivated for salads. Among the North American wild flowers called rocket are the prairie-rocket (*Erysimum asperum*), the purple rocket (*Iodanthus pinnatifidus*), and the sea rocket (*Cakile edulenta*). The latter, like related European species, grows along seacoasts. The unrelated dyer's rocket, or dyer's-weed, is *Reseda luteola,* a species of MIGNONETTE. Rockets are classified in the division MAGNOLIOPHYTA, class Magnoliopsida, order Capparales, family Cruciferae.

rocket, any vehicle propelled by ejection of the gases produced by combustion of self-contained propellants. The force acting on a rocket, called its thrust, is equal to the mass ejected per second times the velocity of the expelled gases. This force can be understood in terms of Newton's third law of motion, which states that for every action there is an equal and opposite reaction. In the case of a rocket, the action is the backward-streaming flow of gas and the reaction is the forward motion of the rocket. Another way of understanding rocket propulsion is to realize that tremendous pressure is exerted on the walls of the combustion chamber except where the gas exits at the rear; the resulting unbalanced force on the front interior wall of the chamber pushes the rocket forward. A common misconception, before space exploration pointed up its obvious fallacy, holds that a rocket accelerates by pushing on the atmosphere behind it. Actually, a rocket operates more efficiently in outer space, where there is no atmospheric friction to impede its motion. The invention of the rocket is generally ascribed to the Chinese, who as early as A.D. 1000 stuffed gunpowder into sections of bamboo tubing to make military weapons of considerable effectiveness. The English monk Roger Bacon introduced to Europe an improved form of gunpowder, which enabled rockets to become incendiary projectiles with a relatively long range. Rockets subsequently became a common if unreliable weapon. Major progress in design resulted from the work of William Congreve, an English artillery expert, who built a 20-lb (9-kg) rocket capable of traveling up to 2 mi (3 km). In the late 19th cent., the Austrian physicist Ernst Mach gave serious theoretical consideration to supersonic speeds and predicted the shock wave that causes sonic boom. The astronautical use of rockets was cogently argued in the beginning of the 20th cent. by the Russian Konstantin E. Tsiolkovsky, who is sometimes called the "father of astronautics." He pointed out that a rocket can operate in a vacuum and suggested that multistage liquid-fuel rockets could escape the earth's gravitation. The greatest name in American rocketry is Robert H. Goddard, whose pamphlet *A Method for Reaching Extreme Altitudes* anticipated nearly all modern developments. Goddard launched the first liquid-fuel rocket in 1926 and demonstrated that rockets could be used to carry scientific apparatus into the upper atmosphere. His work found its most receptive audience in Germany. During World War II, a German team under Wernher von Braun developed the V-2 rocket, which was the first long-range guided missile. The V-2 had a range greater than 200 mi (322

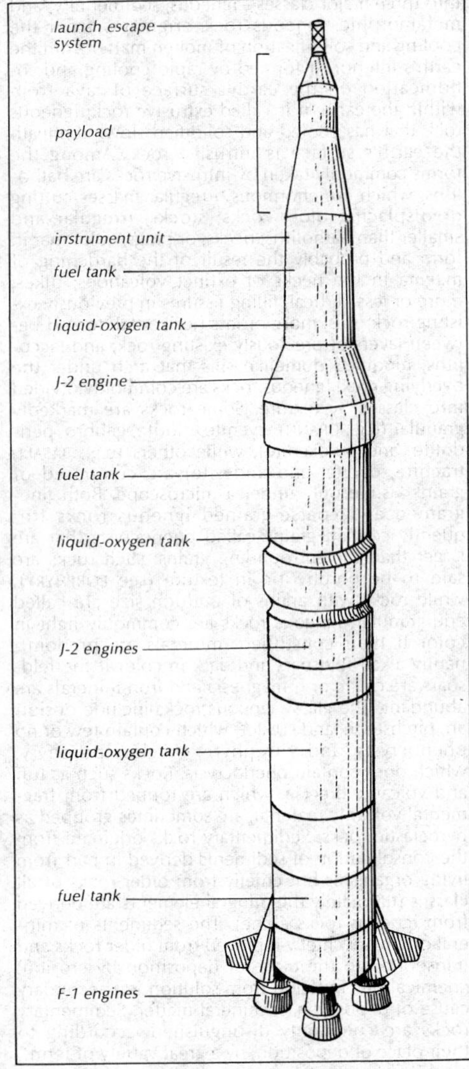

Relative positions of the components of the Saturn V rocket, the U.S. space vehicle used in the moon missions.

km) and reached velocities of 3,500 mi (5,600 km) per hr. After the war, rocket research in the United States and the Soviet Union intensified, leading to the development of the modern array of intercontinental ballistic missiles and spacecraft. Important U.S. rockets include the Redstone, Jupiter, Atlas, Titan, Agena, Centaur, and Saturn carriers. Saturn V, the largest rocket ever assembled, develops 7.5 million lb (3.4 million kg) of thrust. A three-stage rocket, it stands 300 ft (91 m) high exclusive of payload, e.g., satellite or space probe. During the Apollo program it delivered a payload of 44 tons to the moon. The most vital component of any rocket is the propellant, which accounts for 90% to 95% of the rocket's total weight. A propellant consists of two elements, a fuel and an oxidant; engines that are based on the action-reaction principle and that use air instead of carrying their own oxidant are properly called jets. Propellants in use today include both liquefied gases, which are more powerful, and solid explosives, which are more reliable. A typical liquid engine uses hydrogen as fuel and oxygen as oxidant; a typical solid propellant is nitroglycerine. In the liquid engine, the fuel and oxidant are stored separately at extremely low temperatures; in the solid engine, the fuel and oxidant are intimately mixed and loaded directly into the combustion chamber. A solid engine requires an ignition system, as does a liquid engine if the propellants do not ignite spontaneously on contact. The chemical energy of the propellants is released in the form of heat in the combustion chamber. A critical element in all rockets is the design of the exit nozzle, which must be shaped to obtain maximum energy from the exhaust gases moving through it. The nozzle usually converges to a narrow throat, then diverges, which shapes the hypersonic flow of exhaust gas most efficiently. The walls of the combustion chamber and nozzle must be cooled to protect them against the heat of the escaping gases, whose temperature may be as high as 3000°C—above the melting point of any metal or alloy. Although all known rockets currently in use derive their energy from chemical reactions, more exotic propulsion systems are being considered. In ion propulsion, a plasma (ionized gas consisting of a mixture of positively charged atoms and negatively charged electrons) would be created by an electric discharge and then expelled by an electric field. The engine could provide a low thrust efficiently for long periods; on a lengthy flight this would produce very high velocities, so that travel time to Mars, for example, could be cut from six to two months. The Nerva project has studied propulsion by nuclear fission using solid-core reactors. A gas-core nuclear rocket would be even more powerful. No single-stage rocket can reach orbital velocity (5 mi/8 km per sec) or the earth's escape velocity (7 mi/11 km per sec). Hence multistage rockets are necessary for space exploration. In these systems, two or more rockets are assembled in tandem and ignited in turn; once its fuel is exhausted, the lower stage detaches and falls back to earth. When extremely large thrust is required, several rockets may be clustered and operated simultaneously. The efficiency of a rocket engine is defined as the percentage of the propellant's chemical energy that is converted into kinetic energy of the vehicle. During the first few seconds after liftoff, a rocket is extremely inefficient, for at least two unavoidable reasons: High power consumption is required to overcome the inertia of the nearly motionless mass of the fully fueled rocket; and in the lower atmosphere, power is wasted overcoming air resistance. As the rocket gains altitude, however, it becomes more efficient. The trajectory, at first vertical, curves into a suborbital arc or into the desired orbit. Rocket navigation is usually based on inertial guidance; internal gyroscopes are used to detect changes in the position and direction of the rocket. See SPACE SCIENCE. See Willy Ley, *Rockets, Missiles, and Men in Space* (1968); Wernher von Braun and F. I. Ordway III, *History of Rocketry and Space Travel* (rev. ed. 1969); Michael Stoiko, *Soviet Rocketry* (1970).

rocketsonde, ROCKET with instrumentation capable of measuring and transmitting meteorological data to altitudes of 250,000 ft (76,200 m). See RADIOSONDE.

Rock Falls, city (1970 pop. 10,287), Whiteside co., NW Ill., on the Rock River opposite Sterling; inc. 1867. It is an industrial center in a farm region.

rockfish, member of the large family Scorpaenidae (rockfishes and scorpionfishes), carnivorous fish inhabiting all seas and especially abundant in the temperate waters of the Pacific. Rockfishes are found among rocks and reefs. Of commercial importance are the black and orange rockfishes and the bocaccio of the Pacific coast and the rosefish (called also red, or ocean, perch and the John Dory) of the Atlantic. In the West Indies are found the lion-fishes and the scorpionfishes, the latter vividly marked in red, blue, and green and equipped with poisonous dorsal fin spines, which have venom glands in their grooves. The name rockfish is also applied to various other fishes that frequent rocky places. Rockfishes and scorpionfishes are classified in the phylum CHORDATA, subphylum Vertebrata, class Osteichthyes, order Perciformes, family Scorpaenidae.

rockfoil: see SAXIFRAGE.

Rockford, industrial city (1970 pop. 147,370), seat of Winnebago co., N Ill., on the Rock River near the Wis. line; inc. 1839 with the merger of two settlements on opposite sides of the river. Rockford, the second largest city in the state, is the trade, processing, and shipping hub of an extensive agricultural region as well as an important manufacturing center. Machine tools, screws and fasteners, and airplane and automobile parts are produced. Rockford was founded (1834) on the site of a battlefield of the Black Hawk War. It is the seat of Rockford College and a junior college. The city has an extensive park and recreational system, a symphony orchestra, and several museums, including a notable clock museum. A state park is nearby.

rock garden, garden planned around natural rock formations or rocks artificially arranged to simulate natural (often mountainous) conditions. The concept of rock gardens is believed to have been introduced from China and Japan into the Western world in the 17th cent.; they have since gained wide popularity as an ideal method for the cultivation of mountain flora and for beautifying hilly, stony, or other awkward terrain. Rock plants usually have long roots that enable them to obtain moisture even when the surface is hot and dry. Low plants requiring well-drained conditions are suited to rock gardens: besides ALPINE PLANTS, these include stonecrops and species of columbine, phlox, bluebell, and rockrose. See H. Lincoln Foster, *Rock Gardening* (1968) and E. B. Anderson, *Rock Gardens* (1964).

Rockhampton, city (1971 pop. 49,141), Queensland, E Australia, on the Fitzroy River. It is a rail center and, with its port at Port Alma, the principal trade center for the pastoral and mining regions of central Queensland. The chief exports are wool, meat, and other farm products; copper and gold are also exported. There are cotton gins in the city and, in winter, a tourist trade. Rockhampton was founded in 1858.

Rock Hill, city (1970 pop. 33,846), York co., N S.C.; inc. 1870. An important textile center, it also has industries that produce fencing and plastics. A beautifully landscaped flower garden is in the center of the city. Rock Hill is the seat of Winthrop College and a junior college. The county fair and a county horse show are held in the city annually. A 25-mi (40-km) long impoundment of the nearby Catawba River provides water recreation. A former Catawba Indian reservation in the vicinity is now owned by the Indians. Andrew Jackson State Park is to the east.

Rockies, the: see ROCKY MOUNTAINS.

Rockingham, Charles Watson-Wentworth, 2d **marquess of** (rŏk'ĭng-əm), 1730–82, British statesman. In the early years of the reign of George III he became a leading opponent of the "king's friends," held several offices, and formed a coalition government in 1765. During his ministry the Stamp Act was repealed and conciliation with the American colonies attempted, but the administration fell in 1766. Rockingham continued to oppose the coercive colonial policy of the government. In 1782, at the fall of Lord North, he again formed a ministry. The war in America was already lost, and Rockingham died before the peace settlement could be reached. Rockingham's second ministry was marked by the repeal of Poynings's Law (see under POYNINGS, Sir Edward) and by measures to reduce corrupt practices in parliamentary elections. See study by R. J. S. Hoffman (1973).

Rock Island, town (1971 pop. 1,341), S Que., Canada, at the Vermont border. It is the seat of Stanstead College. Machine tools, dies, and textiles are made.

Rock Island, city (1970 pop. 50,166), seat of Rock Island co., NW Ill., on the Mississippi and Rock rivers, adjacent to Moline and opposite Davenport, Iowa; inc. 1841. These three cities, with East Moline, are called the Quad Cities. Rock Island is a trade, transportation, and industrial center. Farm equipment, machinery, metal and wood products, and rubber footwear are among its many manufactures. Railroad maintenance is also an important industry. On a 1,000-acre (405-hectare) island in the Mississippi River is a huge U.S. arsenal, established in 1862, one of the largest manufacturing arsenals in the world and a major source of local employment. Arsenal Island was fortified by the British in the War of 1812 and by the Americans in 1816. In 1833, George Davenport built a palatial house there, and it is still standing. During the Civil War, Arsenal Island was the site of a huge northern military prison. A Confederate cemetery and a national cemetery are on the island. Bridges connect Arsenal Island, the city, Davenport, and Moline. Rock Island is the seat of Augustana College. Black Hawk State Park adjoins the city.

Rockland, industrial town (1970 pop. 15,674), Plymouth co., E Mass.; settled 1673, set off from Abington and inc. 1874. Its products include abrasives, fiberglass boats, shoes, and sheet metal. A naval air base is in adjacent South Weymouth.

Rockledge, city (1970 pop. 10,523), Brevard co., E Fla., on Indian River (a lagoon).

rock music, type of music popular in the United States from 1954 to the mid-1970s. Essentially hybrid in origin, rock music includes elements of several black and white American music styles: black guitar-accompanied blues; black rhythm and blues, noted for saxophone solos; black and white GOSPEL MUSIC; white COUNTRY AND WESTERN MUSIC; and the songs of white popular crooners and harmony groups. Emerging in 1954–55, rock music was referred to as "rock 'n' roll," until 1964, after which it was called "rock music." The change in terminology indicates both a continuity with and a break from the earlier period; after 1964 the music was influenced by British groups such as The BEATLES. The first rock 'n' roll record to achieve national popularity was "Rock around the Clock" made by Bill Haley and the Comets in 1955. Haley succeeded in creating a music that appealed to youth because of its exciting off beat and the urgent call to dance and action of its lyrics. The melody was clearly laid down by amplified guitar; the lyrics were earthy and simple. Haley abruptly ended the ascendancy of the bland and sentimental ballads popular in the 1940s and early 50s. He also succeeded in translating black rhythm and blues into a form that adolescent white audiences could understand. Blues, and rhythm and blues, were too adult, sexual, angry, and solely identified with black culture to be acceptable either emotionally or commercially without adaptation. Major record companies had for years been producing records for black audiences called "race records." The emergence of rock 'n' roll signified a slight weakening in resistance to black culture. The unadulterated black rock 'n' roll that Haley transformed can be heard in the sexually adult work of such artists as Hank Ballard and the Midnighters ("Work With Me, Annie") or Joe Turner ("Shake, Rattle, and Roll"), the latter song adapted by Haley for white audiences and the former transformed into "Dance with Me, Henry." Rock 'n' roll was for and about adolescents. Its lyrics articulated teenage problems: school, cars, summer vacation, parents, and, most important, young love. The primary instruments of early rock 'n' roll were guitar, piano, drums, and saxophone. All aspects of the music—its heavy beat, loudness, self-absorbed lyrics, and raving delivery—indicated a teenage defiance of adult values and authority. Influential performers of the 1950s include Chuck Berry ("Johnny B. Goode"), Little Richard ("Keep A-Knockin'"), Sam Cooke ("You Send Me"), Buddy Holly ("Peggy Sue"), Jerry Lee Lewis ("Whole Lotta Shakin'"), and Carl Perkins ("Blue Suede Shoes"). The greatest exponent of rock 'n' roll from 1956 to 1963 was Elvis PRESLEY, a young white country blues singer from Memphis, Tenn., whose plaintive, wailing, dynamic delivery and uninhibited sexuality appealed directly to young audiences while horrifying older people. As rock 'n' roll became a financial success, record companies that had considered it a fad began to search for new singers; they generally succeeded in commercializing the music, robbing it of much of its gutsy, rebellious quality. In the late 1950s, for example, there was a fad for sentimentally morbid songs such as "Laura" and "Teen Angel." At the turn of the decade Detroit became an important center for black singers, and a certain type of sound known as "Motown" [motor town] developed. The style is characterized by a lead singer singing an almost impressionistic melody story line to the accompaniment of elegant, tight, articulate harmonies of a backup group. Popular exponents of this style are the Temptations, Smokey Robinson and the Miracles, and Diana Ross and the Supremes. Rock music again surged to popularity in 1962 with the emergence of The Beatles, a group of four lads from Liverpool, England. They were internationally acclaimed for their energy and appealing individual personalities rather than for any innovations in their music, which was derived from Berry and Presley. Their popularity inevitably produced other groups with extraordinary names. The most important of these was the Rolling Stones, who, in contrast to The Beatles, were raunchy and overtly sexual, their music deriving from the black blues tradition. These British bands instigated a return to the blues orientation of rock 'n' roll, albeit in ever louder and more electronic reincarnations. An important transformation of rock occurred in 1965 at the Newport Folk Festival when Bob DYLAN, noted as a composer and writer of poetic folk songs and songs of social protest like "Blowin in the Wind," appeared backed by a rock band. A synthesis of the folk revival and rock subsequently took place, with folk groups using rock arrangements and rock singers composing poetic lyrics for their songs (e.g., The Beatles' "Norwegian Wood," "Eleanor Rigby"). Performers like The Mamas and the Papas, Donovan, and The Lovin Spoonful sang a kind of music designated "folk rock." The influence of Eastern music added such instruments as the SITAR to the growing inventory of band equipment. The verbal content of rock songs turned toward rebellion, social protest, sex, and increasingly, drugs. Many groups, among them the Jefferson Airplane and the Grateful Dead, tried to approximate in music the aural experience of psychedelic drugs, producing long, repetitive, occasionally exquisite songs with abstruse lyrics (known as "acid rock"). In 1967, The Beatles again made history with their album *Sgt. Pepper's Lonely Hearts Club Band,* which, in addition to including drug-oriented songs, presented a body of interrelated pieces that constituted an organic whole. Subsequent products of this trend were rock musicals such as *Hair* (1968) and rock operas like *Tommy*, composed and sung by The Who. By the late 1960s rock was widely regarded as an important musical form. Musicians such as Miles DAVIS and John McLaughlin and groups like Cream or like Blood, Sweat, and Tears tried to unite rock and JAZZ, while such disparate artists as Leonard BERNSTEIN and Frank Zappa attempted to connect rock and classical music. Groups featuring virtuoso guitarists like Jimi Hendrix, Eric Clapton, and Duane Allman continued to perform variations on classic blues themes using the traditional instruments of rock 'n' roll. From about 1966 on, the rock festival was regarded as the ideal context in which to hear rock music, and thousands of fans attended. The most successful and peaceful rock festival was held near Woodstock, N.Y., in Aug., 1969. Later, however, a similar festival, featuring the Rolling Stones, was held at Altamont, Calif., and was marked by several violent incidents, including a murder. Altamont may have signaled the demise of rock. By 1970 several of its top performers—Janis Joplin, Jimi Hendrix—were dead, the victims of drugs. Violence and sadism, always a disturbing element in rock performances (The Who would smash their equipment for the benefit of each new audience) seemed to dominate it. The evil, bisexual quality projected by the Rolling Stones was taken to extremes by performers such as Alice Cooper and David Bowie, who were perhaps more famous for their sexual ambiguity and outrageous behavior than for their music. See Jonathan Eisen, ed., *The Age of Rock* (1969); Lillian Roxon, *Rock Encyclopedia* (1969); Pauline Rivelli and Robert Levine, ed., *The Rock Giants* (1970); Charlie Gillett, *The Sound of the City* (1970); Carl Belz, *The Story of Rock* (2d ed. 1972); Mike Jahn, *Rock* (1973).

Rockne, Knute Kenneth (no͞ot, rŏk'nē), 1888–1931, American football coach, b. Norway, B.S. Notre Dame, 1914. In 1893 he settled with his parents in Chicago. While a student at Notre Dame he excelled at football and in 1913, with Gus Dorais, scored a sensational upset of the heavily favored Army team through the use of the forward pass—a legal but then unused football tactic. Rockne became (1914) a chemistry instructor at Notre Dame and served (1918–31) as head football coach. In his 13 years as coach, Notre Dame won 105 games, lost 12, and tied 5; he had five undefeated, untied seasons. Rockne not only made Notre Dame the leading football center of the country but also revolutionized football theory. He stressed offense, developed the precision backfield or Notre Dame shift, perfected line play, and developed many stars, including the most famous football backfield of all time, the "Four Horsemen of Notre Dame" (Harry Stuhldreher, Don Miller, James Crowley, and Elmer Layden). He wrote *Coaching* (1925), *Four Winners* (1925), and *Football Problems* (1927). He died in an airplane crash. See his autobiography (1931); biographies by Harry Stuhldreher (1931), Warren Brown (1931), Arthur Daley (1960), and Francis Wallace (1960).

rock 'n' roll: see ROCK MUSIC.

rock rabbit: see PIKA.

Rock River, c.285 mi (460 km) long, rising in SE Wisc. and flowing SW through NW Ill. to the Mississippi River near Rock Island. It flows through a fertile farm area. Rockford, Ill., is the chief city on the river. Lake Koshkonong (c.20 sq mi/50 sq km) is a natural widening of the river. Lorado Taft's Black Hawk statue stands on a bluff overlooking the river near Oregon, Ill.

rock salt: see SODIUM CHLORIDE.

Rock Springs, city (1970 pop. 11,657), alt. c.6,270 ft (1,910 m), Sweetwater co., SW Wyo., on Bitter Creek; inc. 1888. It is a cattle and sheep shipping point and the center of large natural trona mines that produce soda ash. Oil and gas production, electric-power distribution, a revived coal industry, and tourism are also important. Rock Springs is the gateway to many recreational areas and natural wonders, and the surrounding area offers excellent trout fishing and antelope, deer, elk, and sagehen hunting. Rock Springs was settled around a trading post and stage station established on the Oregon Trail in the 1860s. The city boomed with the mining in the area and the coming of the transcontinental railroad. A junior college is there. The county fair is held in Rock Springs annually.

rock temple: see TEMPLE.

Rockville, city (1970 pop. 41,564), seat of Montgomery co., W central Md.; inc. 1860. It has several scientific-research laboratories. A junior college is there.

Rockville Centre, residential village (1970 pop. 27,444), Nassau co., SE N.Y., on SW Long Island; inc. 1893. Molloy Catholic College for Women is there. A state park is adjacent to the village.

Rockwell, Norman, 1894–, American illustrator, b. New York City. An enormously popular illustrator, Rockwell has specialized in warm and humorous scenes of everyday small-town life. Best known for his magazine covers, notably for the *Saturday Evening Post,* he developed a style of finely drawn realism with a wealth of anecdotal detail. Rockwell's poster series on the Four Freedoms was widely circulated during World War II. See his autobiography (1960); biographical study by T. S. Buechner (1970).

Rocky Hill, town (1970 pop. 11,103), Hartford co., central Conn., a suburb of Hartford, on the Connecticut River; settled c.1650, inc. 1843. Firearms, chemical coatings, and metal products are made there. Rocky Hill was an important river port from 1700 to 1820. The Congregational Church in the town was built in 1808. Also of interest is Dinosaur Park. A veterans home and hospital are in the city.

Rocky Mount, city (1970 pop. 34,284), Edgecombe and Nash counties, E N.C., on the Tar River; settled by 1818, inc. 1867. The city is the commercial and distribution center of a rich agricultural area (tobacco, cotton, and corn). It is also a transportation hub and a large tobacco market and processing point. Textiles, apparel, chemicals, and pharmaceuticals are manufactured there. North Carolina Wesleyan College is in the city.

Rocky Mountain elk: see WAPITI.

Rocky Mountain goat, hoofed ruminant mammal, *Oreamnos americanus,* found in the high mountains of S Alaska, W Canada, and the extreme NW United States. Although it is not a true goat it belongs to the same family (CATTLE family) and is goatlike in appearance, with a bearded chin, long face, and sharp, black horns 9 to 12 in. (22–30 cm) long, curved slightly backward. The head is large and the neck short. The coat is long, thick, and pure white. The male is about 3 ft (90 cm) high at the massively humped shoulder and weighs up to 200 lb (90 kg). Rocky Mountain goats live in small herds on steep mountain sides and cliffs, feeding on the stunted vegetation above the timberline. They are extremely sure-footed and nimbly traverse precipitous slopes and ledges. Related to the Old World CHAMOIS, the Rocky Mountain goat is classified in the phylum CHORDATA, subphylum Vertebrata, class Mammalia, order Artiodactyla, family Bovidae.

Rocky Mountain House, town (1971 pop. 2,968), S central Alta., Canada, at the foot of the Rocky Mts. and the confluence of the North Saskatchewan and Clearwater rivers. Founded in 1799 as a fortified post of the North West Company in Blackfoot Indian country, and known as Blackfoot post, it was taken over (1821) and operated by the Hudson's Bay Company until 1875. It is now the gateway to a big-game hunting area.

Rocky Mountains, major mountain system of W North America and easternmost belt of the North American cordillera, extending more than 3,000 mi (4,800 km) from central N.Mex. to NW Alaska; Mt. Elbert (14,431 ft/4,399 m) in Colorado is the highest peak. The Rockies are located between the Great Plains on the east (from which they rise abruptly for most of their length) and a series of broad basins and plateaus on the west. The mountains form the Continental Divide, separating rivers draining to the Atlantic and Arctic oceans from those draining to the Pacific. The major Atlantic-bound rivers rising in the Rockies include the Rio Grande, Arkansas, Platte, Yellowstone, Missouri, and Saskatchewan. Those draining to the Arctic include the Peace, Athabasca, and Liard rivers. Flowing to the Pacific Ocean are the Colorado, Columbia, Snake, Fraser, and Yukon rivers. The Rockies were formed in the Mesozoic and Early Cenozoic eras during the Cordilleran orogeny. They are geologically complex, with remnants of an ancestral Rocky Mt. system and evidence that uplift, which involved almost all mountain-building processes (see MOUNTAIN), occurred as a series of pulses over millions of years. The mountains have since been eroded to expose ancient crystalline cores flanked by thick upturned layers of sedimentary rocks. Glaciers and snowfields, which today cover the northern ranges and the high peaks of the south, were at one time more extensive; throughout the system the erosional features of alpine glaciation can be seen. Topographically, the Rockies are usually divided into five sections: the Southern Rockies, Middle Rockies, Northern Rockies (all in the United States), the Rocky Mountain system of Canada, and Brooks Range in Alaska. The Wyoming Basin, the system's principal topographic break, is sometimes considered a sixth section. The Southern Rockies, in New Mexico, Colorado, and S Wyoming, are dominated by two north-south belts of folded mountains that have been eroded to expose cores of Precambrian rocks rimmed by younger sedimentary rocks. The eastern belt comprises the Laramie, Medicine Bow, and Wet mts., and the Front Range. The principal ranges of the western belt are the Park, Gore, Mosquito, Sawatch, and Sangre de Cristo. Between the two belts are three basins known as the North, South, and Middle "parks." To the southwest are the San Juan Mts., a nonlinear group of uplands composed mainly of volcanic rocks. The Southern Rockies are the system's highest section and include many peaks above 14,000 ft (4,267 m), among them Mt. Elbert and Mt. Massive (14,418 ft/4,395 m), both in the Sawatch Mts. The Middle Rockies, chiefly in NE Utah and W Wyoming, lie N of the Southern Rockies and are separated from them by the Wyoming Basin. The ranges of this section are generally lower and less continuous than those to the south. The principal parts are the Wasatch and Teton ranges (which are both great tilted fault blocks), the Yellowstone Plateau and Absaroka Range (both developed on volcanic rocks), the Bighorn, Beartooth, Owl Creek, and Uinta mts., and the Wind River Range (all broad folded mountains). All of these component sections have been eroded down to their Precambrian cores and are rimmed by Paleozoic and Mesozoic sedimentary rocks. The highest peaks of the Middle Rockies are Gannet Peak (13,785 ft/4,202 m) in the Wind River Range and Grand Teton (13,766 ft/4,196 m) in the Teton Range. The Northern Rockies, in NE Washington, N and central Idaho, and NW Wyoming, extend N from Yellowstone National Park to the U.S.-Canadian border. They are composed of the Clearwater and Salmon mts., the Sawtooth and Lost River ranges (all of which developed in the batholith of central Idaho), and the Bitterroot Range along the Idaho-Mont. line. In the east are the Front Ranges of Montana. A series of north-south trending ranges separated by narrow trenches and valleys occupies most of N Montana and the Idaho panhandle. Two especially distinctive trenches are the Rocky Mountain Trench, which extends NW from Flathead Lake, and the Purcell Trench, which extends N from Coeur d'Alene Lake. The Okangan Highlands, in NE Washington, form the western edge of the Northern Rockies. The peaks of the Northern Rockies are generally lower than those to the south; among the highest are Borah Peak (12,655 ft/3,857 m) and Leatherman Peak (12,230 ft/3,728 m) in the Lost River Range. The Rocky Mt. system of Canada is composed of two major sections: the high rugged peaks of the Canadian Rockies proper, to the east, and the Columbia mts. group on the west. The Canadian Rockies are located along the British Columbia-Alta. border and include Mt. Robson (12,972 ft/3,954 m; highest peak of the Rocky Mts. in Canada), Mt. Columbia (12,295 ft/3,748 m), and Mt. Forbes (11,902 ft/3,628 m). The prominent, wide-floored Rocky Mountain Trench, west of the crest line, continues c.800 mi (1,290 km) into Canada from Montana and is drained by the headwaters of the Peace River and by sections of the Fraser, Columbia, and Kootenay rivers. The Purcell Trench to the west also crosses into Canada and joins the Rocky Mountain Trench c.200 mi (320 km) north of the border. Farther to the west is the Columbia mts. group, which includes the Selkirk, Purcell, Monashee, and Cariboo mts. The Rockies continue into the Yukon Territory and Northwest Territories as the Mackenzie, Richardson, and Franklin mts. In N Alaska, the Brooks Range, a cold and treeless region rising to Mt. Chamberlin (9,020 ft/2,749 m), forms the northernmost section of the Rocky Mts. Mining is important throughout the entire system; gold, silver, lead, zinc, copper, and molybdenum are the chief minerals. The principal mining centers are Leadville and Cripple Creek, Colo.; the Butte-Anaconda district of Montana; Coeur d'Alene, Idaho; and the Kootenay Trail region of British Columbia. The Rockies are also a year-round recreational attraction. The U.S. national parks in the system include Rocky Mountain, Yellowstone, Grand Teton, and Glacier (see NATIONAL PARKS AND MONUMENTS, table). In Canada are Jasper, Banff, Yoho, Glacier, Kootenay, and Mt. Revelstoke national parks. Vast forests, largely under government control and supervision, are a major natural resource. Lumbering and other forestry activities are limited mainly to Montana, Idaho, and British Columbia, where commercially valuable stands are most abundant and accessible. The Rockies are a major barrier to overland transcontinental travel. The principal U.S. pass across the mountains is South Pass (alt. c.7,500 ft/2,300 m) at the southern end of the Wind River Range, SW Wyoming, which links the Wyoming Basin and the Great Plains with the basins and plateaus W of the Rockies. This pass was followed by the Oregon, Mormon, and California trails; the Sante Fe Trail skirted the southern end of the Rockies. In Canada the important passes are Kicking Horse (alt. 5,539 ft/1,688 m), which carries the Trans-Canada Highway, Crowsnest Pass, and Yellowhead Pass. Explorers of the U.S. Rockies have included Vasquez de Coronado (1540), Meriwether Lewis and William Clark (1804-6), Zebulon Pike (1806-7), Stephen Long (1819-20), Benjamin Bonneville (1832-35), John Frémont (1843-44), Isaac Stevens (1853), John W. Powell (1868), and Ferdinand Hayden (1871). Leading Canadian explorers were sieur de la Vérendrye (1738-39), Sir Alexander Mackenzie (1792-93), David Thompson (1799-1803), and Simon Fraser (1803-7). See R. G. Thwaites, *A Brief History of Rocky Mountain Exploration* (1914); N. Fenneman, *Physiography of Western United States* (1931); W. W. Atwood, *The Rocky Mountains* (1945); D. S. Lavender, *The Rockies* (1968); O. P. Starkey and J. L. Robinson, *The Anglo-American Realm* (1969); Perry Eberhart and Philip Schmuck, *The Fourteeners, Colorado's Great Mountains* (1970); *The Magnificent Rockies*, pub. by American West (1973).

Rocky Mountain sheep: see BIGHORN.

Rocky Mountain spotted fever, infectious disease caused by a RICKETTSIA. The germ is harbored by wild rodents and other animals and is carried by infected ticks that attach themselves to humans. Rocky Mountain spotted fever is most prevalent in the NW United States, although it may be encountered in other tick-infested regions. Symptoms include chills and high fever; a rose-colored skin rash that appears first on the wrists and ankles and spreads to the trunk, the spots turning deep red and running together; headache; and pains in the back, muscles, and joints. In severe cases there may be delirium or coma. Spotted fever is a serious disease; however, it is not usually fatal if prompt antibiotic treatment is administered. Immunization with vaccine is effective.

Rocky River, city (1970 pop. 22,958), Cuyahoga co., NE Ohio, a suburb of Cleveland, on Lake Erie; settled 1815, inc. 1903. Chiefly residential, it has some light manufacturing.

rococo (rəkō'kō, rō-), style in architecture, especially in interiors and the decorative arts, which originated in France and was widely used in Europe in the 18th cent. The term may be derived from the French words *rocaille* and *coquille* (rock and shell), natural forms prominent in the Italian BAROQUE decorations of interiors and gardens. The first expression of the rococo was the transitional RÉGENCE STYLE. In contrast with the heavy baroque plasticity and grandiloquence, the rococo was an art of exquisite refinement and linearity. Through their engravings, Juste Aurèle Meissonier and Nicholas Pineau helped spread the style throughout Europe. The Parisian tapestry weavers, cabinetmakers, and bronze workers followed the trend and arranged motifs such as arabesque elements, shells, scrolls, branches of leaves, flowers, and bamboo stems into ingenious and engaging compositions. The fashionable enthusiasm for Chinese art added to the style the whole bizarre vocabulary of CHINOISERIE motifs. In France, major exponents of the rococo were the painters Watteau, Boucher, and Fragonard, and the architects Robert de Cotte, Gilles Marie Oppenord, and later Jacques Ange Gabriel. The rococo vogue spread to Germany and Austria, where Francois de CUVILLIÈS was the pioneer. Italian rococo, particularly that of Venice, was brilliantly decorative, exemplified in the paintings of Tiepolo. The furniture of Thomas CHIPPENDALE manifested its influence in England. During the 1660s and 1670s, the rococo competed with a more severely classical form of architecture, which triumphed with the accession of Louis XVI. See Fiske Kimball, *The Creation of the Rococo* (1943); Arno Schönberger and Halldor Soehner, *The Rococo Age* (tr. 1960); H. A. Millon, *Baroque and Rococo Architecture* (1961); Germain Bazin, *Baroque and Rococco* (tr. 1964); H. Hitchcock, *German Rococco* (1970).

rococo, in music, 18th-century reaction against the baroque style. Less formal and grandiose in structure, it was a graceful rather than a profound style, more hedonistic than venturesome. Extreme manifestations were in French keyboard music, the finest composer in the style being François Couperin (1668-1733). Jean Philippe Rameau represented the less frivolous French musical thought of the period. In Germany the style was adopted to some extent by Georg Philipp Telemann, Johann Mattheson (1681-1764), and the sons of J. S. Bach, and it was an element in the keyboard sonatas of Domenico SCARLATTI. Traces of rococo are present in the early works of Haydn and Mozart.

Rocourt (rôko͞or'), town (1970 pop. 4,882), Liège prov., E Belgium. There, in the War of the Austrian Succession, the French under Maurice de Saxe defeated (Oct., 1746) the allied English and Austrians.

Rod, Edouard (ădwär' rôd), 1857-1910, Swiss novelist and critic. Rod, who edited the *Revue contemporaine* in Paris and later taught comparative literature in Geneva, was an ardent follower of Stendhal. Among his novels are *La Course à la mort* (1885), *Le Sens de la vie* (1889), and *L'Incendie* (1906). His *Idées morales du temps présent* (1891) is an excellent critical survey of French literature.

rod: see ENGLISH UNITS OF MEASUREMENT.

Rodanim: see DODANIM.

Rodbertus, Karl Johann (kärl yō'hän rôdbĕr'to͞os), 1805-75, German economist and conservative socialist. He held several public offices, but after 1849 devoted himself to writing on economics. He believed that society would eventually attain, without violence, the socialist ideal of state-owned property. His books include *Overproduction and Crises* (1850-51, tr. 1898). See E. C. K. Gonner, *The Social Philosophy of Rodbertus* (1899).

Rodenbach, Georges (zhôrzh rôdĕnbäk'), 1855-98, Belgian symbolist poet and novelist. Living in Paris from 1887, he wrote about Flemish life. His works include the poems *Le Foyer et les champs* (1877), *La Jeunesse blanche* (1886), and *Les Vies encloses* (1896), and a novel, *Bruges-la-morte* (1892).

rodent, member of the mammalian order Rodentia, characterized by front teeth adapted for gnawing and cheek teeth adapted for chewing. The Rodentia is by far the largest mammalian order; nearly half of all mammal species are rodents. They are worldwide in distribution and are found in almost every terrestrial and freshwater habitat, from the shores of the Arctic Ocean to the hottest deserts. They are variously adapted for running, jumping, climbing, burrowing, swimming, and gliding. Many of them have dexterous forepaws, which they use as hands while sitting on their haunches in a position characteristic of many rodents. The great majority are under a few inches in length; the largest, the CAPYBARA, is about 4 ft (120 cm) long and 20 in. (50 cm) high at the shoulder. The approximately 1,800 rodent species are divided on the basis of their anatomy into three well-defined groups, or suborders. The Sciuromorpha, or squirrellike rodents, include the various species of SQUIRREL, CHIPMUNK, MARMOT, WOODCHUCK (or ground hog), PRAIRIE DOG, GOPHER (or pocket gopher), POCKET MOUSE, KANGAROO RAT, and BEAVER. The Myomorpha, or mouselike rodents, include a great variety of MOUSE and RAT species, as well as species of HAMSTER, LEMMING, VOLE, MUSKRAT, GERBIL, DORMOUSE, and JERBOA. This is the largest rodent group, containing about 1,100 species. The Hystricomorpha, or porcupinelike rodents, include the PORCUPINE, capybara, NUTRIA (or coypu), AGOUTI, CAVY (including the domestic GUINEA PIG), mara, and CHINCHILLA, as well as many species whose common names include the term *rat* (e.g., the South American bush rat). Rodents have enlarged, chisel-shaped upper and lower front incisors that grow throughout their lives. These have hard enamel on the front surface and soft dentine on the back surface, so that unequal wear keeps the chisel edge sharp. There is a gap between the front teeth and the cheek teeth. When the lower jaw is in a forward position, for gnawing, the upper and lower incisors are in contact but the upper and lower cheek teeth are not; thus, wear on the cheek teeth is avoided. The cheeks are drawn in behind the incisors when the animal is gnawing, so that bits of hard material cannot be swallowed. When the lower jaw is pulled back into the chewing position, only the cheek teeth make contact. The rabbits and hares were once classified as rodents because of their large, chisel-shaped incisors. However, they are quite distinct anatomically and have a long, separate evolutionary history; they are now classified in an order of their own, the Lagomorpha. See also MOUNTAIN BEAVER, GROUND SQUIRREL, FLYING SQUIRREL, PACK RAT, BANDICOOT RAT and JUMPING MOUSE. See Sir J. R. Ellerman, *The Families and Genera of Living Rodents* (2 vol., 1940, repr. 1965); B. S. Vindgradov and A. I. Argiropulo, *Key to Rodents* (tr. 1968).

rodenticide (rōdĕn'tĭsīd"): see PESTICIDE.

rodeo (rō'dēō, rōdā'ō), public exhibition of the skill of cowboys in various activities. Events include riding broncos, riding steers, "bulldogging" steers, roping and tying steers and calves, the use of the lasso, and other less closely related activities such as contests of marksmanship. The rodeo was originally merely an adjunct to the roundup, a contest of skill between various cow hands, but the spectacle became popular in the late 1880s and 90s and gradually took on more and more of the aspects of a circus. Today there are many professional rodeo performers who spend their time going from one exhibition to another. There are annual rodeos at many places in the West; in the East the rodeos normally travel like the circus and take place in indoor arenas. See C. P. Westermeier, *Man, Beast, Dust* (1947); Mary S. Robertson, *Rodeo: Standard Guide to the Cowboy Sport* (1961); Fred Schnell, *Rodeo* (1971).

Roderick (rŏd'ərĭk), d. 711?, last Visigothic king in Spain (710-711?). After the death of King Witiza, a group of nobles chose Roderick, duke of Baetica, as successor to the king. Having defeated Witiza's son, Roderick established himself on the throne. Little is actually known of his reign, but innumerable legends have developed around it. Most of the legends involve one Julian, governor of Ceuta, who—either for political motives or because his daughter had been violated by Roderick—joined the family of Witiza in requesting the help of the North African Muslims to overthrow Roderick. In any event, the Muslims under TARIK crossed (711) the Strait of Gibraltar, and Roderick, campaigning in the north against the Franks and the Basques, hastened south only to be defeated (711) by Tarik near Medina Sidonia. Roderick was probably killed in the battle, but according to some, he continued to resist the Muslim conquest of Spain until he was slain in 713. The colorful legends about this "last of the Goths" gained a permanent place in Spanish literature and passed into English writing, most notably in the works of Washington Irving, Robert Southey, and Walter Savage Landor.

Rodez (rôdĕz'), city (1968 pop. 26,398), capital of Aveyron dept., S France. It is a farm trade center. Gloves and plastics are made. It was an episcopal see since the 4th cent. and the historic capital of ROUERGUE. An impressive cathedral (13th-16th cent.) of northern Gothic style is there.

Rodgers, Christopher Raymond Perry, 1819-92, American naval officer, b. Brooklyn, N.Y. Appointed midshipman in 1833, he served in the Mexican War. In the Civil War he took part in the Union reduction of Port Royal, S.C., received the surrender of St. Augustine and other Florida and Georgia coastal towns, and commanded the naval forces in the trenches at the capture (April, 1862) of Fort Pulaski before Savannah, Ga. He was fleet captain commanding the *New Ironsides* in the attack on Charleston in April, 1863. From Oct., 1863, to the end of the war he commanded the *Iroquois* in its worldwide search for the *Shenandoah* and other Confederate cruisers. Promoted to captain in 1866 and rear admiral in 1874, he was chief of the Bureau of Yards and Docks (1871-74), superintendent of Annapolis (1874-78), and commander in chief of the Pacific squadron (1878-80).

Rodgers, John, 1773-1838, American naval officer, b. Harford co., Md. He had seen years of merchant service before he became (1798) a lieutenant in the new U.S. navy. He served in the TRIPOLITAN WAR, securing senior command in 1805. In 1811, Rodgers, in command of the *President,* was ordered to cruise off the U.S. coast to stop the impressment of American seamen by the British frigate *Guerrière.* He encountered a British ship, which he apparently took to be the *Guerrière,* and gave chase. Accounts of what happened vary, but a battle took place, and the British ship, the *Little Belt,* was defeated and cut to bits. The incident was one of those leading up to the War of 1812. Rodgers, at the outbreak of that war, at once set out to pursue British ships and captured several British merchantmen. In a battle with the frigate *Belvidera* he was wounded by an explosion of a gun on his own vessel. He later participated in the naval defense of Baltimore. After the war he was president of the board of naval commissioners (1815-24, 1827-37) and acting Secretary of the Navy in 1823. See biography by C. O. Paullin (1910, repr. 1967).

Rodgers, John, 1812-82, American naval officer, b. Harford co., Md.; son of John Rodgers (1773-1838). He became a midshipman in 1828 and saw varied service. He conducted (1852-56) exploring expeditions in the N Pacific, off the coast of China, and in the Arctic. In the Civil War he served on the Atlantic coast, taking part in the bombardment of Fort Darling (1862), in the attack on Fort Sumter (1863), and in the capture of the ironclad *Atlanta*. He commanded the Asiatic fleet (1870–72). Later he was in charge of the Mare Island navy yard (1873–77) and superintendent of the U.S. Naval Observatory (1877–82). See biography by R. E. Johnson (1967).

Rodgers, Richard Charles, 1902–, American composer, b. New York City. Rodgers studied at Columbia and at the Institute of Musical Art, New York City. He met both Lorenz HART and Oscar HAMMERSTEIN, 2d, while at Columbia. Rodgers and Hart began collaborating in 1919; among their outstanding musical comedies are *The Girl Friend* (1926); *A Connecticut Yankee* (1927; rev. 1943); *On Your Toes* (1936), containing the famous "Slaughter on Tenth Avenue"; *Babes in Arms* (1937); *I'd Rather be Right* (1937); *The Boys from Syracuse* (1938); *Pal Joey* (1940); and *By Jupiter* (1942). After Hart's death Rodgers and Hammerstein began their collaboration with the tremendously successful, Pulitzer Prize-winning *Oklahoma!* (1943). Many of their works were enormously popular, e.g., *Carousel* (1945), *South Pacific* (1949), and *The King and I* (1951). In 1962, Rodgers was named head of the Music Theater of the Lincoln Center for the Performing Arts in New York City. See biography by David Ewen (1963); Deems Taylor, *Some Enchanted Evening* (1953, repr. 1972).

Ródhos, Greece: see RHODES.

Rodilla or **Rodia, Simon:** see WATTS TOWERS.

Rodin, Auguste (ōgüst' rōdăN'), 1840–1917, French sculptor, b. Paris. He began his art study at 14 in the Petite École and in the school of Antoine Barye, earning his living by working for an ornament maker. In 1863 he went to work for the architectural sculptor A. E. Carrier-Belleuse, who had a great influence on him. From 1870 to 1875 he continued in the same trade in Brussels and then briefly visited Italy. In the Salon of 1877 he exhibited a nude male figure, *The Age of Bronze* (1876; Paris). It was both extravagantly praised and condemned; his critics unjustly accused him of having made a cast from life. From the furor Rodin gained the active support and patronage of Turquet, undersecretary of fine arts. His *Age of Bronze* and *St. John* (1878) were purchased for the Luxembourg Gardens, Paris. The government gave him a studio in Paris, where he worked the rest of his life with growing fame. From 1880, Rodin worked intermittently on studies for a huge bronze door for the Musée des Arts décoratifs. It was inspired by Dante's *Inferno* and was to be called the *Gate of Hell*. He never finished it. Among the 186 figures intended for it are *Adam* and *Eve* (1881) (Metropolitan Mus.), *The Thinker* (1879–1900), and *La Belle Heaulmière* (both: Paris). These, together with his group *The Burghers of Calais* (Calais), completed in 1894, are among his most famous creations. Other ambitious works are his monuments to Balzac (1897; Paris) and to Victor Hugo (1909; Paris). Rodin is also known for his drawings, his many fine portrait busts, and his figures and groups in marble, such as *Ugolino* (1882), *Danaïd* (1885), *The Kiss* (1886), and *The Hand of God* (1897–98) in the Rodin Museum, Paris, and *Pygmalion and Galatea* and *The Bather* in the Metropolitan Museum. He is best represented in the Rodin museums of Paris and Philadelphia, but fine examples of his work stand in many galleries throughout the world. Rodin's work is generally considered the most important contribution to sculpture of his century, although some recent critical opinion has found his allegorical works pretentious. Realistic in many respects, it is nevertheless imbued with a profound, romantic poetry. The Gothic, the dance, and the works of Dante, Baudelaire, and Michelangelo were major sources of inspiration. Rodin considered his work completed when it expressed his idea, and as a result his sculpture is varied in technique: some is polished, some is gouged and scraped, and some seems scarcely to have emerged from the rough stone. He worked long over his more important works, returning to them again and again but without injuring their essential vitality. See studies by S. Story (rev. ed. 1966), A. E. Elsen (1963, repr. 1967), R. Descharnes and J. F. Chabrun (tr. 1967), I. Jainu (1967), and Y. Taillandier (1967).

Rodney, Caesar, 1728–84, American political leader, signer of the Declaration of Independence, b. near Dover, Del. He was a member of the Delaware assembly (1761–70, 1772–76), its speaker (1769, 1773–76), and a delegate to the Stamp Act Congress (1765). As a member of the Continental Congress (1774–76), he advocated independence. Later, he was a general commanding Delaware militia in the Revolution and was (1778–81) president (i.e., governor) of Delaware. See his correspondence, ed. by G. H. Ryden (1933, repr. 1970).

Rodney, George Brydges Rodney, 1st **Baron,** 1719–92, British admiral. He served with distinction in the Seven Years War (1757–63), his most notable achievement being the capture (1762) of Martinique in the West Indies. Pressed by debts, he lived in France from 1775 to 1778. In 1778 he was recalled, made an admiral, and dispatched again to the West Indies. On the way he defeated (1780) a Spanish fleet off Cape St. Vincent, thus relieving Gibraltar, and became a national hero. In 1781 he captured St. Eustatius in the West Indies and confiscated large quantities of goods belonging to British merchants illegally trading with the American revolutionary forces. He was hounded with lawsuits for the rest of his life by the outraged merchants. Because of ill health, he resigned (1781) his command to Samuel HOOD, but he returned to the West Indies in 1782 and won a resounding victory over the French fleet of Admiral de Grasse off Dominica. He was rewarded with a peerage. See G. B. Mundy, *The Life and Correspondence of the late Admiral Lord Rodney* (1973); biographies by Donald Macintyre (1962) and David Spinney (1969).

Rodó, José Enrique (hōsā' ānrē'kā rôdō'), 1872–1917, Uruguayan essayist, literary critic, and philosopher. Rodó spent most of his life in Montevideo, where he taught at the university. He helped to found and edited *La revista nacional de literatura y ciencias sociales*. His essays, in the *modernista* manner, gained him acclaim in and beyond Spanish America. Rodó developed a new philosophy of ethics and sought to create a new spirit in politics. In *Ariel* (1900, tr. 1922), his best-known work, he calls upon Latin America (Ariel) to hold to spiritual values unsullied by the materialistic impact of the United States (Caliban). The influence of the book was enormous. Other collections of essays are *Los motivos de Proteo* (1909, tr. 1928) and *El mirador de Próspero* (1913) [Próspero's balcony].

Rodope or **Rodopi:** see RHODOPE, mountains.

Rodosto: see TEKIRDAĞ.

Rodríguez, Martín (rôthrē'gās), 1771–1844, Argentine general, governor of Buenos Aires prov. (1820–24). With Juan Martín de PUEYRREDÓN, he organized a force to expel the British invaders of the Río de la Plata, and later he served under Jacques de Liniers in the recapture (1806) and the defense (1807) of Buenos Aires. He was one of the leaders in the revolution of May, 1810, when the viceroy was deposed and a junta was established, and was active in the war against Spain. His administration as governor, following a period of anarchy, was progressive. Many measures of reform and administrative reorganization were undertaken, chiefly on the initiative of Bernardino RIVADAVIA. These served as an example to the other provinces, thus helping to lay the basis for the future national organization.

Rodriguez (rōdrē'gəs), island (1971 est. pop. 24,700), 42 sq mi (109 sq km), in the Indian Ocean, c.350 mi (560 km) E of Mauritius, of which it is an integral part. One of the Mascarene Islands, it is surrounded by coral reef. Port Mathurin is the chief town. Most of the inhabitants are of black African descent; some persons are of European, Indian, and Chinese descent. The population is largely French speaking and Roman Catholic. The main occupations are subsistence farming and fishing. Rodriguez was discovered in 1645 by the Portuguese, was briefly occupied (1691–93) by the Dutch, and was colonized (18th cent.) by the French from Mauritius. Britain took the island in 1810 and administered it as part of Mauritius, which became independent in 1968.

Rodríguez Francia, José Gaspar: see FRANCIA, JOSÉ GASPAR RODRÍGUEZ.

Rodríguez Larreta, Enrique: see LARRETA, ENRIQUE RODRÍGUEZ.

Roebling, John Augustus (rō'blĭng), 1806–69, German-American engineer, b. Mulhouse. He studied engineering in Berlin and in 1831 came to the United States. He demonstrated the practicability of steel cable and established a plant for manufacturing it at Trenton, N.J. A pioneer in the building of suspension bridges, he built the Allegheny Suspension Bridge (completed 1845) at Pittsburgh, the Niagara Falls Suspension Bridge (completed 1855), and the Cincinnati and Covington Bridge over the Ohio (completed 1867). His most ambitious project was the Brooklyn Bridge. It was scarcely begun when Roebling, directing operations, was injured in an accident and died a few days later. His son **Washington Augustus Roebling**, 1837–1926, b. Saxonburg, Pa., grad. Rensselaer Polytechnic Institute, 1857, had aided his father in building the Allegheny Suspension Bridge. During the Civil War he joined the Union army as a private, was transferred to Irvin McDowell's engineering staff, and rose to the rank of colonel. He went to Europe to study engineering and especially pneumatic caissons. After his father's death he directed the construction of the Brooklyn Bridge. Because of continuous underground work he was stricken (1872) with decompression sickness (caisson disease), but despite his invalidism he directed the project until the bridge was opened to traffic (1883). In 1888 he took over the management of the Roebling plant in Trenton. See biography by Hamilton Schuyler (1931); D. B. Steinman, *The Builders of the Bridge* (1945).

Roebuck, John, 1718–94, English physician, chemist, and inventor. He acted as a chemical consultant to local industries in Birmingham, and invented the lead chamber process of manufacturing sulfuric acid and a process for producing malleable iron. He was a friend and patron of English engineer James Watt, and at one time held a large interest in Watt's steam engine.

roe deer, small, short-horned deer, *Capreolus capreolus*, of Britain and Europe and as far east as China and Siberia. Its coat is golden red in summer, darkening to brown or even black in winter, with lighter undersides and a white rump patch. It stands from 26 to 30 in. (66–76.2 cm) at the shoulder and has small three-pronged horns. Roe deer are widely distributed in woods near fields and wooded valleys. They are nocturnal animals, traveling alone or in families and browsing on grass, leaves, and young shoots. The polygamous males fight over territory in early summer and rut in early fall. Females give birth the following June, usually to two spotted kids of opposite sexes. Roe deer often leave behind in the forest trampled areas in the shape of a figure-eight. Called roe rings, they are made during courtship rituals when the male chases the female, and also by the young at play. Roe deer are classified in the phylum CHORDATA, subphylum Vertebrata, class Mammalia, order Artiodactyla, family Cervidae.

Roehm or **Röhm, Ernst** (both: ĕrnst röm), 1887–1934, German National Socialist leader. An army officer in World War I, he met Adolf HITLER in 1919, and helped to launch his political career. Roehm organized the storm troops (*Sturmabteilung*, or SA), the militia of the National Socialist (Nazi) party. The role of the SA in the National Socialist movement provoked conflict between Roehm and Hitler, who wanted the SA to be an instrument of the Nazi party, rather than Roehm's private army. Roehm was imprisoned briefly for his participation in the abortive "beer-hall putsch" of 1923. After his release the conflict with Hitler flared again and Roehm resigned (April, 1925) his party posts. At the end of 1930, Hitler recalled him as commander of the SA. Within a year Roehm had developed a large army and had become Hitler's principal rival for power in the party. After Hitler became chancellor (Jan., 1933), Roehm pressed unsuccessfully for control by the SA over the regular army. Late in 1933 he was made minister without portfolio. In June, 1934, he was executed in Hitler's blood purge, ostensibly because he had been planning a coup by the SA.

Roelas or **Ruelas, Juan de las** (hwän dā läs rōä'läs, rōōä'läs), c.1558–1625, Spanish painter of the school of Seville. He has been called the Spanish Tintoretto, and there are stylistic analogies between the two artists. In Seville he was the first to combine a sense of realism and mysticism that became prevalent in 17th-century Spain. Among his most famous works are *Martyrdom of St. Andrew, St. Anne and the Virgin, Pentecost,* and *Circumcision* (all in the museums and churches of Seville).

Roemer, Olaus: see RØMER, OLAUS.

Roentgen or **Röntgen, Wilhelm Conrad** (both: rĕnt'gĭn, rŭnt'–, Ger. vĭl'hĕlm kôn'rät rönt'gən), 1845–1923, German physicist. His notable research in many fields of physics, especially thermology, mechanics, and electricity, has been overshadowed by his discovery (1895) of a short-wave ray, the Roentgen ray, or X ray, for which he received the first Nobel Prize in Physics (1901). He taught at several German universities, including those at Würzburg (1888–99) and Munich (1899–1920). See biography by W. R. Nitske (1971).

Roentgen ray: see X RAY.

Roerich, Nicholas Konstantin (nē'kōlous kənstəntyēn' rōr'ĭkh), 1874–1947, Russian artist, scene designer, and archaeologist. He was connected with the Moscow Art Theatre and the Diaghilev ballet. His stage sets for Stravinsky's *Sacre du printemps* (1913) revealed him as a brilliant colorist. He traveled to the United States where the Roerich Museum, New York City, was founded in his honor (1923). His exploration of the Himalayas resulted in 500 pictures. He is represented in the chief European collections and many American galleries. Among his books are *Heart of Asia* (1929) and *Realm of Light* (1931). See N. N. Selivanova, *The World of Roerich* (1924).

Roermond (rōōr'mônd), city (1971 pop. 36,715), Limburg prov., SE Netherlands, at the confluence of the Maas (Meuse) and Roer rivers. Manufactures include chemicals and electrical equipment. Roermond was an important center of the cloth trade in medieval times.

Roeselare (rōō'səlärə), Fr. *Roulers*, city (1970 pop. 40,428), West Flanders prov., W Belgium. It is an industrial center. At Roeselare, in 1794, the French under Pichegru defeated the Austrians.

Roethke, Theodore (rĕt'kə), 1908-63, American poet, b. Saginaw, Mich., educated at the Univ. of Michigan and Harvard. A poet of the American Midwest, Roethke combined a love of the land with his vision of the development of the individual. The moods of his poetry range from acid wit to simple feeling, his poetic technique from straightforward language and meters to free forms that approach the surreal. Among his volumes of poetry are *Open House* (1941), *The Lost Son and Other Poems* (1948), *The Waking* (1953, Pulitzer Prize), *Words for the Wind* (1957), *I Am! Says the Lamb* (1961), and *The Far Field* (1964). *On the Poet and His Craft* (1965) contains essays and lectures. See biography by Allan Seager (1968).

Rogaland (rō'gälän''), county (1972 est. pop. 273,000), c.3,540 sq mi (9,170 sq km), SW Norway, bordering on the North Sea. The main towns are Stavanger (the capital) and Haugesund. The northern part, called Ryfylke, is indented by several branches of the Boknafjord. Important industries include shipping, fishing, food processing, and dairy farming.

Rogation Days, in the calendar of the Western Church, four days traditionally set apart for solemn processions to invoke God's mercy. They are April 25, the Major Rogation, coinciding with St. Mark's Day; and the three days preceding Ascension Day, the Minor Rogations. The processions are Christian adaptations of Roman pagan ones; in rural districts they are regarded as blessing the fields. The prayers include the Litany of the Saints (see LITANY). Such liturgical usages are no longer prescribed in the universal Roman Catholic liturgical calendar; observance is left to the discretion of the national councils of bishops.

Rogelim (rōgē'lĭm), unidentified town of Gilead, E of the Jordan. 2 Sam. 17.27; 19.31.

Roger I (Roger Guiscard), c.1031-1101, Norman conqueror of Sicily; son of Tancred de Hauteville (see NORMANS). He went to Italy in 1058 to join his brother, ROBERT GUISCARD, in conquering Apulia and Calabria from the Byzantines. Between 1061 and 1091 he took Sicily from the Arabs. After the fall (1072) of Palermo he became count of Sicily under Robert's suzerainty. Robert's death (1085) left Roger the most powerful Norman lord in S Italy, and he ruled the various ethnic groups in his feudal domain justly and tolerantly. In 1098, Roger was made papal legate. His son succeeded him as Roger II. See J. J. Norwich, *The Other Conquest* (1967).

Roger II, c.1095-1154, count (1101-30) and first king (1130-54) of Sicily, son and successor of Roger I. He conquered (1127) Apulia and Salerno and sided with the antipope Anacletus II against Pope INNOCENT II. In 1130, Anacletus crowned Roger king. Innocent rallied Holy Roman Emperor Lothair II and other allies against Roger but was defeated in 1139. Naples and Capua recognized Roger's sovereignty; Innocent was obliged to invest him with the lands that, for the next seven centuries, were to constitute the kingdoms of Naples and Sicily. Roger also conquered the coast of Africa from Tunis to Tripoli. He established a strong central administration and attempted to fuse the disparate ethnic groups in his kingdom. Prosperity returned to Sicily, and Roger's brilliant court at Palermo was a center of the arts, letters, and sciences. Roger was succeeded by his son, William I. See Edmund Curtis, *Roger of Sicily* (1912, repr. 1973); J. J. Norwich, *Kingdom in the Sun* (1970).

Roger of Hoveden (hŏv'dən, hŭv'-), d. 1201; English chronicler. His chronicle, covering the years from 732 to 1201, is an original source only for the period from 1192 to 1201. His life as a member of the household of Henry II and the documents he included make his work important. It was translated by Henry T. Riley (1853).

Roger of Loria, c.1245-1304, Sicilian-Aragonese admiral. An adherent of MANFRED, last Hohenstaufen king of Sicily, he left Sicily for Aragón after Manfred's defeat (1266) by the Angevin claimant to the throne. There he held posts under Manfred's son-in-law, King PETER III. Peter was chosen king of Sicily after the SICILIAN VESPERS (1282), and in his service Roger commanded the Aragonese fleet in the long war against the Angevin rulers of Naples for possession of Sicily. He defeated the Angevins at Malta (1283) and in the Bay of Naples (1284), and in 1285 triumphed over the French fleet off Catalonia. Roger also served James (later JAMES II of Aragón), Peter's successor in Sicily. In 1295, James reversed his policy, ceding Sicily to the pope, who bestowed it on CHARLES II of Naples; James agreed to help Charles to gain possession of the island. Devoted to Aragón, Roger fought with the Angevins against the Sicilians. In 1302 he retired to Catalonia. Loria is also spelled as Lauria or Luria.

Roger of Wendover, d. c.1236, English chronicler, a monk of St. Albans. As historiographer of St. Albans, he began the *Flores historiarum* (see MATTHEW OF WESTMINSTER), a general chronicle starting with the creation. He drew the material from 1192 to 1201 from ROGER OF HOVEDEN, but that from 1201 to 1235 is original. His work contains many fantastic and distorted stories and judgments hostile to King John. He is in large part responsible for the negative picture of John (perpetuated by MATTHEW OF PARIS) that has come down through history.

Rogers, Bruce, 1870-1957, American typographer and book designer, b. Lafayette, Ind. As printing adviser to Cambridge Univ. Press and to Harvard Univ. Press, as well as to commercial houses specializing in limited editions and fine printing, he earned the reputation of being the leading American book designer of his time. Influenced by Nicolas Jenson's types, he designed the typeface called Centaur and the format of the Oxford Lectern Bible (1935). Rogers is the author of *Paragraphs on Printing* (1943) and *Pi* (1953), a collection of letters, papers, and addresses.

Rogers, Henry Huttleston, 1840-1909, American financier, b. Fairhaven, Mass. After he moved (1860) to Pennsylvania, he entered the oil business, experimented in the refining of petroleum, and, in partnership with Charles Pratt, became one of the important independent refiners. In 1874, when his company was absorbed by the Standard Oil Company, Rogers—who originated the idea of pipeline transportation for oil—became a lieutenant of John D. Rockefeller, Sr. His holdings steadily grew larger and more diverse; they included major interests in the Consolidated Gas Company and Amalgamated Copper and directorships of U.S. Steel and the Union Pacific and Santa Fe railroads. He was one of America's leading capitalists.

Rogers, James Gamble, 1867-1947, American architect, b. Kentucky. He designed many buildings for Yale, his alma mater. Among them are the Sterling Memorial Library, the Sterling School of Graduate Studies, Pierson College, and the Harkness Memorial Quadrangle. For 10 years he was architectural advisor to Yale. Among his other designs are the Columbia-Presbyterian Medical Center and the Butler Library of Columbia Univ., New York City; the New Haven (Conn.) post office; and the Deering Library of Northwestern Univ.

Rogers, James Harvey, 1886-1939, American economist, b. South Carolina, grad. Univ. of South Carolina (B.A., 1906) and Yale (B.A., 1909; Ph.D., 1916). He was professor of economics at the Univ. of Missouri (1923-30) and of political economy at Yale (from 1930), and he had written *Stock Speculation and the Money Market* (1927), *The Process of Inflation in France, 1914-1927* (1929), and *America Weighs Her Gold* (1931) before he was called to Washington as monetary adviser to President Franklin Delano Roosevelt. In 1933 he was sent to Europe to consult with British economists on stabilization and in 1934 went to the Orient to study, for the U.S. Treasury, the monetary systems of the world's largest silver-using countries. He was killed in an airplane crash at Rio de Janeiro.

Rogers, John, 1500?-1555, English Protestant martyr, grad. Cambridge, 1526. He became a Roman Catholic priest, but under the influence of William TYNDALE, whom he met in Antwerp, he turned (1535) to Protestantism. He employed himself in preparing for the press an English version of the Bible, which he published (1537) under the pseudonym Thomas Matthew. He contributed prefaces and marginal notes but most of the translation was the work of Tyndale and of Miles COVERDALE. Returning (1548) to England, Rogers became (1551) a prebendary of St. Paul's Cathedral, London. On the accession of Mary I he was deprived of his benefices because of anti-Catholic expression in the pulpit and was imprisoned (1554). He was tried and burned at Smithfield as a heretic.

Rogers, John, 1829-1904, American sculptor, b. Salem, Mass. Trained as an engineer, he was forced by failing eyesight to work as a machinist. He began modeling in clay as a pastime and studied sculpture in Rome for a short while. His early clay group, *The Slave Auction*, given publicity by the abolitionists, and "Rogers groups" had attained great popularity by the end of the Civil War. Thousands of copies were made by machine of such subjects as *One More Shot, Going to the Minister*, and *The Wounded Scout*. As accurate records of the period, they have regained a certain popularity. See study by David Wallace (1967).

Rogers, Lindsay, 1891-1970, American political scientist, b. Baltimore, grad. Johns Hopkins (B.A., 1912; Ph.D., 1915). He was (1914-15) a fellow in political science at Johns Hopkins before becoming (1915) professor at the Univ. of Virginia. In World War I he was attached (1918) to the general staff corps. He lectured (1920-21) on public law at Harvard and from 1920 to 1959 taught government and public law at Columbia. He was visiting lecturer at several colleges and universities and served with the New York state department of labor (1928), the National Recovery Administration (1933), and Public Works Administration (1934-36). He was director of the Social Science Research Council (1934-36) and a consultant to the U.S. Senate Committee on Foreign Relations (1952; 1956-59). His published work includes *The Postal Power of Congress* (1916), *The American Senate* (1926), *Crisis Government* (1934), and *The Pollsters* (1949).

Rogers, Robert, 1731-95, American frontiersman, b. Methuen, Mass. As a child he moved with his family to the New Hampshire frontier. In King George's War (1744-48) he served briefly as a scout. In the last of the FRENCH AND INDIAN WARS he was appointed (1758) major in command of all rangers. Rogers led (1759) his men in a daring expedition that resulted in the destruction of the SAINT FRANCIS INDIANS. In 1760 he was sent to receive the submission of the French posts on the Great Lakes, and in 1763 he served on the expedition to defend Fort Detroit, which was threatened by Pontiac's Rebellion. His many exploits made him a popular hero, but his participation in illicit trade with the Indians brought him into official disgrace. He went (1765) to England to obtain pay for his service. There he was much feted, and his *Journals* and *A Concise Account of North America* were published in 1765. He also wrote a crude play, *Ponteach* (1766), important primarily as an early American drama. Successful in securing an appointment as commander of the post at MACKINAC, he returned to the Northwest. His career there has been the subject of much speculation and discussion. Rogers, who was ambitious to find the Northwest Passage, sent out the mysterious expedition of Jonathan CARVER to the Northwest, quarreled with his associates, was accused of plotting to set up an independent state, and was arrested on charges of treasonable dealings with the French. Brought to Montreal in chains and court-martialed, he was acquitted of all charges. He went (1769) to England but returned (1775) to America and played such an equivocal role at the beginning of the American Revolution that he was imprisoned as a Loyalist spy. He escaped and openly joined the Loyalists, but his record in the war was anything but distinguished. In 1780 he returned to England, dying there in 1795 in obscurity. See his play, *Ponteach*, ed. with a biographical account by Allan Nevins (1914; repr. 1973); his journals, ed. by F. B. Hough (1883, repr. 1966); biography by J. R. Cuneo (1959).

Rogers, Samuel, 1763-1855, English poet. Independently wealthy, he owned a beautiful home on St. James Street, Westminster, which became the center of literary society. He was famous for his conversation and numbered Byron, Lamb, and Wordsworth among his friends. His poetry, which includes *Pleasures of Memory* (1792), *Jacqueline* (1814), and *Italy* (2 vol., 1822-28), is graceful but undistinguished. He also wrote *Table Talk* (1856) and *Recollections* (1859).

Rogers, Will (William Penn Adair Rogers), 1879-1935, American humorist, b. Oolagah, Indian Territory (now in Oklahoma). In his youth he worked as a cowboy in Oklahoma, and after traveling over the world, he returned to the United States and worked in vaudeville as a cowboy rope-twirler, joking casually with the audience. He was an immediate success when he joined the Ziegfeld *Follies* in 1915. Rogers gained a wide audience through motion pictures, books, the radio, and a syndicated newspaper column. His salty comments on the political and social scene made the "cowboy philosopher" widely known. A constant booster of airplane travel, Rogers made several long airplane trips; he was killed with Wiley Post when their plane crashed near Point Barrow, Alaska. See his autobiography (ed. by Donald Day, 1949) and writings (1973); biographies by Donald Day (1962) and E. P. Alworth (1974).

Rogers, William Barton, 1804–82, American geologist and educator, b. Philadelphia, grad. William and Mary, 1822. He was professor of geology at William and Mary (1828–35) and at the Univ. of Virginia (1835–53) and headed the Virginia geological survey. Rogers was the founder of the Massachusetts Institute of Technology, where he served as first president and as professor of physics and geology, laying the foundation of the institute's distinguished service to scientific education. In addition to his report on the Virginia survey, he wrote *Strength of Materials* (1838) and *Elements of Mechanical Philosophy* (1852).

Rogers, William Pierce, 1913–, U.S. government official, b. Norfolk, N.Y. Admitted to the bar in 1937, he served (1947–50) as chief counsel to two Senate investigating committees before becoming (1953) Deputy Attorney General under President Dwight D. Eisenhower. He lobbied vigorously for passage of the 1957 Civil Rights Act and later, as Attorney General (1957–61), set up the civil rights division of the Justice Department. As Secretary of State (1969–73) under President Richard M. Nixon, Rogers argued for restraint in the use of U.S. military power. In 1970 he arranged a ceasefire in the Middle East between Israel and Egypt.

Rogers, Woodes, 1679?–1732, British privateer and colonial administrator. A romantic figure, Rogers plundered (1708–9) Spanish commerce in the Pacific and rescued Alexander SELKIRK from the Juan Fernández islands. He later (1717) leased the Bahama islands and served as the first governor there, expelling pirates and bringing orderly government. See biography by Bryan Little (1960); A. F. MacLiesh and M. L. Krieger, *The Privateers: A Raiding Voyage to the Great South Sea* (1962).

Rogers, city (1970 pop. 11,050), Benton co., extreme NW Ark., in the Ozarks; inc. 1881. The city is located in a resort area and has meat-processing plants and factories making air rifles, plastic bags, and electric motors.

Roger van der Weyden: see WEYDEN, ROGER VAN DER.

Roger Williams National Memorial: see NATIONAL PARKS AND MONUMENTS (table).

Roget, Peter Mark (rōzhā'), 1779–1869, English physician and lexicographer. For 50 years while he practiced medicine and was secretary of the Royal Society (1827–49), Roget prepared his *Thesaurus of English Words and Phrases* (1852). In successive editions supervised by him, his son, and his grandson, it has remained a standard reference book. See biography by D. L. Emblen (1970).

Rogue, river, c.200 mi (320 km) long, rising in SW Oregon, in the Cascade Range N of Crater Lake. It flows southwest and west through a fertile valley (noted for its orchard fruits) and then across the Coast Range to the Pacific Ocean at Gold Beach. The Rogue and its tributaries irrigate lands around Grants Pass, Medford, and Ashland.

Rohan, Henri, duc de (äNrē' dük də rōäN'), 1579–1638, French Protestant general; son-in-law of the duc de Sully. A leader of the HUGUENOTS, Rohan took up arms against the French government in 1621–22 as a consequence of the reestablishment of Roman Catholicism in Béarn. With his brother, Benjamin de SOUBISE, Rohan led revolts in Languedoc and the Cévennes in 1625–26 and again in 1627–29 but was forced to submit to King Louis XIII's chief minister, Cardinal Richelieu, in the Peace of Alais (1629). He retired to Venice. In 1635 he was chosen by Richelieu to command the French troops in the VALTELLINA, which he subdued. Treachery and weak official support forced his retreat in 1637. Rohan subsequently joined the army of Bernhard of Saxe-Weimar and was killed at Rheinfelden during the Thirty Years War. He left memoirs (1644, enl. ed. 1646, tr. 1660) and other writings.

Rohan, Louis René Édouard, prince de (lwē rənā' ādwär' prăNs də), 1734–1803, French churchman and politician, cardinal of the Roman Catholic Church. Although he succeeded (1779) his uncle as archbishop of Strasbourg, he spent most of his career in Paris. As French ambassador to Vienna (1772) he aroused the dislike of Empress Maria Theresa. In France, his anti-Austrian attitude earned him the hostility of her daughter, the French queen Marie Antoinette. It was apparently in a desire to curry favor with the queen that he became involved in the Affair of the DIAMOND NECKLACE. For his inglorious part in this he was acquitted of guilt (1786) but lost his office of grand almoner and was banished from Paris. He was elected to the States-General (1789), refused to sign the Civil Constitution of the Clergy (1791), and emigrated.

Rohde, Ruth Bryan (rō'thə), 1885–1954, American public official, b. Jacksonville, Ill.; daughter of William Jennings Bryan. She studied (1901–3) at the Univ. of Nebraska, and, interested in politics from childhood, she was her father's secretary in his presidential campaign in 1908. She married (1910) Reginald Owen, a British army officer. After Owen's death in 1927 she served (1929–33) as a U.S. Representative (Democratic) from Florida and was appointed (1933) minister to Denmark, the first woman minister of the United States. In 1936 she married Boerge Rohde of the Danish army and resigned as minister. She was (1949–50) an alternate delegate to the United Nations. Her works include *Denmark Caravan* (1936) and *Caribbean Caravel* (1949).

Róheim, Géza, 1891–1953, Hungarian anthropologist and psychoanalyst. He was educated at the universities of Leipzig, Berlin, and Budapest (Ph.D., 1914). From 1928 to 1931 he did field work in central Australia, in Duau (Normanby Island), and in the SW United States. In 1939 he entered private psychoanalytic practice in New York City. Róheim was a creator of the first rank in the field of psychoanalytic study of society and culture and in the field of personality problems. His books include *The Origin and Function of Culture* (1943), *Psychoanalysis and Anthropology* (1950), and *The Gates of the Dream* (1952). See study by P. A. Robinson (1969).

Rohgah (rō'gə), Asherite. 1 Chron. 7.34.

Röhm, Ernst: see ROEHM, ERNST.

Rohtak (rō'tək), city (1971 pop. 124,072), Haryana state, N central India. Rohtak is a district administrative center and a market for grain and sugar. Sculpture from the Buddhist period (c.600 B.C.) has been uncovered there. The city contains five constituent colleges of Punjab Univ.

Rojas, Fernando de (färnän'dō thā rō'häs), 1465?–1541?, Spanish writer. Scanty records show him to have practiced law at Salamanca. He wrote *La Celestina,* published anonymously in 1499. An extended novel, in 22 acts, it is a graphic description of human passion recounted in exquisite Renaissance prose. It is considered a masterpiece of Spanish literature comparable to *Don Quixote.*

Rojas Pinilla, Gustavo (gōōstä'vō rō'häs pēnē'yä), 1900–, president of Colombia (1953–57). As head of the armed forces he led the coup that ousted President Laureano Gómez in 1953. He ruled as a dictator, brutally suppressing all opposition. His attempted fiscal reforms failed, and his administration was riddled with corruption. In 1957 he was deposed by a military junta backed by both liberals and conservatives. He and his daughter, María Eugenia Rojas de Moreno (a senator), subsequently organized the National Popular Alliance, a political party with broad support among the urban poor. He ran for president in 1970, losing by only 1½% of the vote. Ill health forced his retirement in 1973. His daughter ran unsuccessfully for president in 1974.

Rojas Zorrilla, Francisco de (fränthē'skō dā rō'häs thôrē'lyä), 1607–48, Spanish dramatist. He created a new type of *comedia de gracioso,* enlarging the role of the gracioso, or buffoon, to include a variety of fools taken from real life. Of the 40 to 45 plays attributed to him, the best known is the drama of honor *Del rey abajo ninguno* [none beneath the king] (1650). Rojas Zorrilla's plots were borrowed by others, including Corneille and Le Sage. See study by R. R. MacCurdy (1968).

Rokitansky, Karl (kärl rōkĭtän'skē), 1804–78, Austrian pathologist, b. Bohemia. From 1834 to 1873 he taught pathological anatomy at the Univ. of Vienna. He performed over 30,000 autopsies and out of his observations and deductions made many valuable contributions, including treatises on diseases of the arteries and on defects of the septum of the heart. He wrote *A Manual of Pathological Anatomy* (3 vol., 1842–46; tr., 4 vol., 1849–54).

Rokossovsky, Konstantin (kənstəntyēn' rōkōs-sôf'skē), 1896–1968, Soviet general, b. Warsaw. He entered the czarist army and in 1917 joined the Bolshevik forces in the Russian Revolution. Purged in 1937, he was rehabilitated in 1940. In World War II he distinguished himself at Moscow, Stalingrad (later Volgograd), and Kursk and became (1943) commander on the central front. His armies stood by without aiding the tragic Warsaw uprising of 1944 against the Germans. In 1949, Rokossovsky was made commander in chief and minister of defense of Poland and from 1952 he was deputy prime minister; in this capacity he was an important symbol of Soviet influence in Poland. After the assertion of Polish nationalism under GOMUŁKA as leader of the Polish Communist party in 1956, Rokossovsky resigned and was recalled to the Soviet Union. From 1956 to 1958 he twice served as Russian deputy minister of defense.

Roland (rō'lənd), the great French hero of the medieval Charlemagne cycle of *chansons de geste,* immortalized in the *Chanson de Roland* (11th or 12th cent.). Existence of an early Roland poem is indicated by the historian Wace's statement that TAILLEFER sang of Roland's deeds to inflame the men before the Battle of Hastings (1066). Historically Roland was Charlemagne's commander on the Breton border; he was killed in a pass in the Pyrenees when Basques cut off the rear guard of the Frankish army returning from its invasion of Spain in 778. Legend makes Roland one of Charlemagne's 12 peers and his nephew, changes the Basques into Saracens, and locates the pass at Roncesvalles. The poem is marked by its unified conception, its vivid and direct narrative, and its predominantly warlike spirit. Through the treason of Roland's stepfather, Ganelon, count of Mayence and a vassal of Charlemagne, Roland is left in command of Charlemagne's retreating rear guard, with his friend Oliver and with Bishop Turpin. Instigated by Ganelon, the Saracens attack, but Roland is too proud to blow his horn to summon aid. In the ensuing battle the valiant Franks are greatly outnumbered and, though Roland finally blows his horn, all are killed. The last to die, Roland attempts to break his sword, Durandal; before he dies he hears too late that Charlemagne is returning. Charlemagne disperses the pagans and defeats the reinforcing hosts of the emir Baligant, and Ganelon is tried and put to death. The poem is cast in the heroic mold. The contrast of character in the two heroic friends is famous—Oliver was prudent, Roland rash. The Roland epopee was long a favorite with French, Spanish, and Italian poets, and Roland was eventually transformed beyond recognition into the *Orlando* of the Italian Renaissance epics of BOIARDO and ARIOSTO. Translations of the *Song of Roland* include those by Merriam Sherwood (1938) and Dorothy L. Sayers (1957).

Roland de la Platière, Jean Marie (zhäN märē' rôläN' də lä plätyĕr'), 1734–93, French revolutionary. An inspector general of commerce at Rouen and Amiens, he went to Paris in 1791 and published the *Financier patriote.* Largely through the influence of his wife, Jeanne Manon Roland de la Platière, Roland rose to power with the GIRONDISTS and became (1792) minister of the interior. King Louis XVI dismissed him in July, 1792, but he was restored to office after the overthrow of the monarchy (Aug. 10, 1792). Accused of royalism in 1793, he resigned and fled Paris. When he learned that his wife had been executed, he committed suicide.

Roland de la Platière, Jeanne Manon Phlipon (Mme Roland) (zhän mänôN' flēpôN'), 1754–93, French revolutionary. Imbued with classical ideals and with the philosophy of Rousseau, she made her house the intellectual center of the GIRONDISTS, and her influence on Girondist policy was great. Her husband, Jean Marie Roland de la Platière, rose to prominence in the Revolution largely as a result of her ambition and political connections. When her party fell Mme Roland was arrested; as she walked to the guillotine she cried, "O Liberty, what crimes are committed in thy name!" See her letters (ed. by Claude Perroud, 1900–1902); biographies by Ida Tarbell (1896), M. C. Jacquemaire (1930), and Gita May (1970).

Roland Holst, Henriëtte (van der Schalk) (hĕnrēĕt'ə vän dĕr skhälk rō'länt hôlst), 1869–1952, Dutch writer. Her early *Sonnets and Poems Written in Terza Rima* (1895) won praise for outstanding lyric quality. Roland Holst became an ardent communist and wrote vigorous biographies of Rousseau (1912), Garibaldi (1920), and Rosa Luxemburg (1935) from a leftist viewpoint as well as studies of class war and capitalism. The Bolshevik victory (1917) in Russia inspired her *Submerged Bounds* (1918), an enthusiastic poetic vision of a new age.

Rolfe, Frederick William, 1860–1913, English novelist, also known as Baron Corvo. After a vain attempt to become a priest, Rolfe earned a living painting and teaching before he began to write under the name Baron Corvo. His most famous work is the novel *Hadrian the Seventh* (1904), which chronicles the life of Arthur Rose, who, although rejected for the priesthood, eventually becomes pope. One of the strangest novels in English, *Hadrian the Seventh* was dramatized by Peter Luke in 1967 and successfully produced in London and New York. Rolfe's bizarre, abusive, and erudite personality is revealed in his *The Desire and Pursuit of the Whole* (1934), which tells of his final sordid years in Venice. See his letters (3 vol., 1959–62); biographical studies by A. J. A. Symons (1955) and Donald Weeks (1971).

Rolfe, John (rŏlf), 1585–1622, English colonist in Virginia. He reached the colony in May, 1610, and introduced (1612) the regular cultivation of tobacco, which became Virginia's staple. A widower, he fell in love with and married (1614) POCAHONTAS, daughter of the Indian chief Powhatan. They went to England in 1616, and there she died (1617). He returned to Virginia, remarried, and held several offices. He was probably killed in the Indian massacre of 1622.

roll, in aviation: see AIRFOIL.

Rolla (rŏl'ə), city (1970 pop. 13,245), seat of Phelps co., S central Mo.; inc. 1861. It is in a livestock and farm region of the Ozarks. Fan blades and dog food are produced there. The Univ. of Missouri has a campus in the city. Many state and Federal agencies have offices in Rolla. An annual Ozark festival is held there. Caves and springs abound in the area.

Rolland, Romain (rômăN' rôlăN'), 1866–1944, French novelist, biographer, playwright, and musicologist. After studying in Paris he spent two crucial years in Rome, where he was influenced by German intellectuals. He wrote biographies of Beethoven (1903, tr. 1909), Michelangelo (1905, tr. 1915), Tolstoy (1911, tr. 1911), and Mahatma Gandhi (1924, tr. 1924). His 10-volume novel *Jean-Christophe* (1904–12, tr. 1910–13), established his reputation in the literary world. An example of the roman-fleuve, or continuous series of novels, it is a fictional biography of a German-born musician and a study of contemporary French and German civilization. Rolland was awarded the 1915 Nobel Prize in Literature. His genuine pacifistic philosophy and the courage of his convictions, reflected in *Above the Battle* (1915, tr. 1916), led to self-imposed exile in Switzerland, where he remained until 1938. Among his other works are the play *The Wolves* (1898, tr. 1937), inspired by the Dreyfus Affair; the seven-volume novel *The Soul Enchanted* (1922–33, tr. 1925–34); and a biography (1945) of Péguy. *Journey Within* (2d ed. 1959, tr. 1947) and *Mémoires* (1956) are autobiographical. See biography by William T. Starr (1972); study by Harold March (1973).

Rolle of Hampole, Richard (rōl), c.1300–c.1349, English religious writer, a Yorkshire hermit. He wrote mainly in Latin, but his English works are important for the history of the language. Some of Rolle's Latin works were translated after his death into English, thus becoming disseminated and influential as popular manuals of spiritual life. The most important of these were *De emendatio vitae* (tr. *The Mending of Life*) and *Incendium amoris* (tr. into Middle English, *The Fire of Love*, 1896; same, with modern spelling, 1913; new tr., 1935; the 1896 and 1913 editions include *The Mending of Life*). *The Form of Perfect Living* was composed in English. Besides some English lyrics there is a translation of the Psalms (ed. by H. R. Bramley, 1884) that circulated throughout England. Rolle is often regarded as typical of English mystics (see MYSTICISM); his writings are characterized by tender, burning love of God and of Jesus and Mary, with constant allusions to sweetness and music; there is much lyrical analogy with human affection. *The Pricke of Conscience*, a long, devout poem in Northern Middle English, was formerly ascribed to him, but some modern scholars consider his authorship doubtful. See Robert H. Benson, *A Book of the Love of Jesus* (several editions); F. M. M. Comper, *The Life of Richard Rolle with His English Lyrics* (1928, repr. 1969).

roller, common name for brightly colored Old World birds noted for performing somersaults in flight. They include the rollers proper (subfamily *Coraciinae*) and ground rollers (subfamily *Brachypteraciinae*) of the family Coraciidae, as well as the monotypic cuckoo roller (*Leptostomus discolor*) of another family, Leptostomatidae. The rollers comprise approximately a dozen species of solitary, jaylike birds, widespread throughout the tropical and temperate areas of the Old World. They are stout-bodied and large-headed birds, ranging from 9½ to 13 in. (24–33 cm) long, with long, straight beaks that end in hooked tips. Their colors run to greens, blues, and reddish or yellowish browns, with little distinction between sexes. Rollers are strong flyers and feed while on the wing, usually on insects and small birds but occasionally on fruit. They lay their three to six white eggs in tree or rock holes, to which they add bits of grass, straw, or feathers. The slightly smaller tropical broad-billed rollers (genus *Eurystomas*) do not actually tumble or roll in flight. The five species of ground rollers are confined to the island of Madagascar. They differ from the true rollers in being ground feeders and thus show the expected adaptations of this way of life: longer and stouter legs; shorter, more rounded wings; and less bright but more cryptic coloration. Four species inhabit the forest floor, and one, the 18-in.-long (46-cm) *Uratelornis chimaera*, dwells in arid scrub. Ground rollers feed on insects and small animals and build their hole nests in the ground. The cuckoo roller is also found on Madagascar, as well as on the nearby Comoro Islands. It is about 17 in. (43 cm) in length and somewhat resembles the cuckoo in its coloration and its crested head. It differs from all other rollers in the possession of an outer toe capable of being turned backwards and a bill overhung with large tufts of feathers. A creature of forest and brushland, it feeds on large insects and lizards and lays its eggs in a tree-hole nest. Rollers are classified in the phylum CHORDATA, subphylum Vertebrata, class Aves, order Coraciiformes, families Coraciidae and Leptostomatidae.

roller printing: see TEXTILE PRINTING.

roller skating: see SKATING.

Rolling Meadows, city (1970 pop. 19,178), Cook co., NE Ill., a suburb of Chicago; inc. 1955. It has research and development firms and some light manufacturing.

rolling mill: see STEEL.

Rollins College, at Winter Park, Fla.; coeducational; chartered and opened 1885 by Congregationalists. Primarily an undergraduate liberal arts institution, the college also offers graduate work in business and finance.

Rollo (rŏl'ō) or **Hrolf** (rŏlf), c.860–c.932, first duke of Normandy. As leader of the Norman pirates settled at the mouth of the Seine, he attacked (910) Paris and Chartres. By the Treaty of Saint-Clair-sur-Epte (911) with King Charles III of France, he received in fief the territory his men had occupied (part of the future duchy of Normandy) on condition that he defend it against attack and that he receive baptism. Rollo was baptized (912) as Robert. He supported Charles against RAOUL, from whom he obtained additional territory. He was succeeded by his son William Longsword. Rollo's direct descendants included William the Conqueror.

Rolph, John (rŏlf), 1793–1870, Canadian physician and politician, b. England. He studied law and medicine in England and served in the Legislative Assembly of Upper Canada (1824–30, 1836–37). A leader in the Reform party and a fomenter of the rebellion of 1837, he was not a participant in it. He fled to the United States after the uprising and practiced medicine there until the amnesty of 1843 permitted his return to Canada. He founded (1843) in Toronto a school of medicine (later part of Victoria Univ.). He was one of the founders of the Clear Grit Reform party and again sat in the Legislative Assembly (1851–57).

Rølvaag, Ole Edvart (ō'lə ĕd'värt röl'vôkh), 1876–1931, Norwegian-American novelist, b. Helgeland, Norway, grad. St. Olaf College, Northfield, Minn., 1905. He emigrated to the United States in 1896 and was head of the department of Norwegian at St. Olaf from 1906 to 1931. He is most famous for the trilogy consisting of the novels *Giants in the Earth* (1927), *Peder Victorius* (1929), and *Their Father's God* (1931); powerful and realistic, these novels treat the life of Norwegian pioneers in the American Northwest, emphasizing both their physical and psychological struggles with the new land. Rølvaag's other novels include *Pure Gold* (1930) and *The Book of Longing* (1933). He wrote all his novels in Norwegian and assisted in their translation into English. See study by Paul Reigstad (1972).

Romagna (rōmä'nyä), historic region, N central Italy, bordering on the Adriatic Sea in the east, now included in the regions of EMILIA-ROMAGNA, Marche, and Tuscany. Although its boundaries varied at different times, the Romagna is now understood to occupy Forlì and Ravenna provs. and parts of Arezzo and Pesaro e Urbino provs. The independent republic of San Marino is an enclave within the Romagna. The region was the center of Byzantine domination in Italy (540–751). RAVENNA was the seat of the Byzantine exarchs; RIMINI was a city of the Pentapolis. Despite the donations of Pepin the Short (754) and of Charlemagne (774), which gave the exarchate and the Pentapolis to the pope, later emperors continued to claim the territory. Otto IV recognized (1209) the papal rights, but effective papal rule was prevented at first by the free communes and later by the petty tyrants who ruled the cities. Cesare BORGIA, made duke of Romagna (1501) by Pope Alexander VI, tried unsuccessfully to make the Romagna the nucleus of his own state. Shortly thereafter, Pope JULIUS II effectively incorporated the Romagna into the Papal States. Papal rule, interrupted (1797–1814) by French occupation, ended in 1860, when the Romagna was annexed by the kingdom of Sardinia. Austrian troops had helped until 1859 to maintain the papal regime.

Romains, Jules (zhül rômăN'), 1885–1972, French writer, whose original name was Louis Farigoule. A brilliant student of philosophy, he became known as the chief exponent of unanimism, a literary theory positing the collective spirit or personality, e.g., the spirit of a city. This concept pervades an early collection of his poems, *La Vie unanime* (1908). Romain's principal work is the novel cycle *Men of Good Will* (27 vol., 1932–46, tr. 14 vol., 1933–46), which gives an intricate and panoramic view of French life from 1908 to 1933. Among his other novels are *Mort de quelqu'un* (1911, tr. *The Death of a Nobody*, 1914) and *Les Copains* (1913, tr. *The Boys in the Back Room*, 1937). His plays, considered masterpieces of French theater, include *Cromedeyre-le-Vieil* (1920), in which an isolated village returns to primitive ways, and the satirical farce *Knock; ou, Le Triomphe de la médecine* (1923, tr. *Doctor Knock*, 1925). See study by Denis Boak (1974).

Romamti-ezer (rō'mămtī-ē'zər), leader of a group of temple singers. 1 Chron. 25.4,31.

roman: see TYPE.

Roman, town (1970 est. pop. 43,000), NE Rumania, in Moldavia, at the confluence of the Prut and Siretul rivers. Steel and chemicals are among the industrial products. The town was founded in the late 14th cent. by the ruling prince of Moldavia.

Roman architecture. First inspired by the Greek post-and-lintel construction of the buildings of S Italy and Sicily, Roman architects later derived a more perfectly proportioned columnar form from Greece itself. Etruscan and Middle Eastern architecture provided models for the semicircular arch and the vault and dome. To these elements, which they adapted to their special needs, the Romans added the use of concrete which, after the 2d cent. B.C., led them to revolutionary structural forms. Of early Rome and of the republic (c.500 B.C.–27 B.C.) the aqueducts outside the city of Rome are the most impressive remains. The principal examples of Roman architecture belong chiefly to the period between 100 B.C. and A.D. 300. The reign of Augustus (30 B.C.–A.D. 14) initiated the centuries of far-flung building enterprises. The special feature of Roman design was the combined use of arches and columns. Although at first tentatively employed in the spaces between the classical columns, the arch eventually came to be the chief structural element; the flanking columns, usually engaged and superimposed, served merely as buttresses or for decoration. The cut-stone construction of the Greeks was largely replaced after the 2d cent. B.C. by CONCRETE. Although unfired brick was employed in all periods, under the empire baked bricks became popular as a facing for concrete walls. From early times stucco was used as a finish for important buildings. For luxurious finishing of exterior and interior walls sheathings of alabaster, porphyry, or marble were used. Vaults of sun-dried or baked brick were developed to their full capacities. The types employed were the barrel vault, the cross or groined vault, and the dome and semidome. Vault buttresses, instead of forming exterior projections, became an integral part of the interior. The immense vaulted halls, unencumbered by supporting columns or piers, created pure spatial effects, as in the domed interior of the Pantheon at Rome. Under Trajan (A.D. 98–A.D. 117) Roman architecture reached its climax; after his reign it declined, although constructive boldness remained. In all periods, however, splendor and utility were the Roman ideals, as opposed to the subtle refinements of the Greeks. Provincial towns were laid out according to logical plans, particularly in N Africa. In Syria arcaded streets were built. Each town's focus was the forum, or open public square, surrounded by colonnades and the principal buildings in axial arrangement. In Rome itself civic planning resulted in the series of great forums created by successive emperors to extend the crowded area of the Roman Forum (see FORUM), the most ancient in the city. That of Trajan was the last great forum and most splendid. Temples, conforming to Etruscan type, were usually elevated upon high bases with steps ascending to a deep portico. Designed to face the forums, they were adorned merely with pilasters or engaged columns along their sides instead of side porticoes. This pseudoperipteral type is seen in the Maison Carrée (1st cent. B.C.) at Nîmes, France. Examples of circular temples were the temple of Vesta at Tivoli (1st cent. B.C.) and the 3d-century temples of Jupiter at Split and of Venus at Baalbek. Most important among the buildings developed by the Romans themselves were basilicas, baths, amphitheaters, and triumphal arches. Theaters were derived from those of the Greeks, which were built into hillsides; the Roman theaters, however, were often freestanding structures, such as the COLOSSEUM. The auditorium was semicircular, with the orchestra at ground level arranged for the movable seats of distinguished spectators. A Roman innovation was the uniting of stage and auditorium as a single structure and the rich architectural embellishment of the stage itself. For the amphitheaters there are no known Greek precedents. The monumental or TRIUMPHAL ARCH was also a purely Roman invention. The BASILICA, probably a Roman development based on the Greek temple, provided a large and relatively open interior space; it formed a link from classical to Christian architecture, as it was easily converted from a Roman law court to a Christian church. The baths, while probably derived from Greek gymnasia, were constructed on a totally unprecedented scale, the complexity of their plan competing with the luxury of their detail. In the typical dwelling the rooms were grouped about the atrium, which, by means of an opening in its roof, also served as a court. Beginning in the 2d cent. B.C. the addition of a Greek peristyle provided garden space and a focus for the grouping of the more private apartments. In the large cities the houses suggested modern tenements, probably four or five stories high, with staircases, many large windows, and shops or warehouses on the ground floors. At Ostia there are remains of these, mostly from the 3d cent. A.D. A third type of Roman dwelling was the luxurious country establishment or VILLA. See M. Wheeler, *Roman Art and Architecture* (1964); W. L. MacDonald, *The Architecture of the Roman Empire* (1965); A. Boëthius, *Etruscan and Roman Architecture* (1970); Paolo Portoghesi, *Roma Barocca* (tr. 1970); G. T. Rivoira, *Roman Architecture* (1925, repr. 1972).

Roman art. From the 7th to the 3rd cent. B.C., ETRUSCAN ART flourished throughout central Italy, including Latium and Rome. It was strongly influenced by the early art of Greece, although it lacked the basic sense of rational order and structural composition of the Greek models. The influence of native Italic and Middle Eastern art was also strongly felt, particularly during the archaic period (before c.400 B.C.). Large polychrome terra-cotta images, such as the *Apollo of Veii* (Villa Giulia, Rome), sandstone tomb effigies, and tomb paintings reveal a native feeling for voluminous forms and bold decorative color effects and an exuberant, vital spirit. From c.400 B.C. through the Hellenistic age, the vitality of the archaic period gave way to imitation of the Greek classical models combined with a native trend toward naturalism (*Mars of Todi*, Vatican). The merging of these trends produced the establishment of Hellenistic realism in Roman Italy at the end of the republic and the beginning of the empire (*Orator*, Museo Archeologico, Florence; *Capitoline Brutus*, Conservatori, Rome.). After the conquest of Greece (c.146 B.C.), Greek artists settled in Rome, where they found a ready market for works executed in the Greek classical manner or in direct imitation of Greek originals. While the many works by these copyists are of interest principally for their reflection of earlier Greek art, they throw light on the eclecticism of Roman taste, and their influence was of paramount importance throughout the development of Roman art. Roman portraits, however, have an origin very remote and altogether Italianate. It was a Roman custom to have a death mask taken, which was then preserved along with busts copied from it in terra-cotta or bronze. By the time of the empire, the Roman conception of art had become allied with the political ideal of service to the state. In the Augustan period (30 B.C.–A.D. 14) there was an attempt to combine realism with the Greek feeling for idealization and abstract harmony of forms. This modification is seen in the famous *Augustus from Prima Porta* (Vatican), which represents the first of a long series of the distinctly Roman type of portrait. Under the emperors from Tiberius through the Flavians (A.D. 14–A.D. 96) portrait busts reveal in general a growing concern with effects of pictorial refinement and psychological penetration. The magnificent reliefs from the Arch of Titus, Rome, commemorating the conquest of Jerusalem in A.D. 70, mark a climax in the development of illusionism in historical relief sculpture. From the time of Trajan (A.D. 98–A.D. 117) the influence of the art of the Eastern provinces began to gain in importance. The spiral band of low reliefs on Trajan's Column (Rome), commemorating the wars against the Daci, employs a system of continuous narration suggestive of the influence of the Egyptian or Middle Eastern illustrative tradition. In the period of Hadrian (117–138) there was a reversion to the idealization of the Augustan style and at the same time an almost Oriental sense of voluptuousness. Major works from the later period of the Antonines (138–192) are the column and the equestrian statue of Marcus Aurelius (Rome). From the time of Caracalla to the death of Constantine I (211–337) the rapid assimilation of Oriental influence encouraged a tendency toward abstraction that later developed into the stiff iconographic forms of the early Christian and Byzantine eras. The reliefs of the friezes from the Arch of Constantine, Rome (c.315), may be regarded as the last example of monumental Roman sculpture. Roman painting, like sculpture, was strongly influenced by the art of Greece. Unfortunately, much of the painting has perished. What remains suggests that the art was conceived principally as one of interior decoration. Aside from ENCAUSTIC portraits chiefly of Alexandrian origin, the largest single group of Roman paintings is from Pompeii, although parallel work exists elsewhere. The Incrustation, or Architectonic Plastic, style extended to c.80 B.C.; it was characterized by flat areas of color broken by full-scale painted pilasters in apparent imitation of marble slabs. The Architectural style that followed lasted 70 years; it was largely influenced by stage design and employed painted columns, arches, entablatures, and pediments to frame landscapes and figure compositions, destroying the architectonic quality of the wall. Many famous paintings, such as the *Aldobrandini Wedding* and *Odyssey Landscapes* (Vatican), are believed to be Roman copies of Greek originals. By 10 B.C. the Architectural style yielded to the Ornate style, where the semblance of architectural construction became subordinate to decoration, and the paintings within the borders became prominent. Most surviving Pompeiian paintings date from the Intricate style period, which commenced about A.D. 50 and continued until the destruction of the city in A.D. 79 by the eruption of Vesuvius. Large areas of flat color enclose diminutive, graceful, and delicate scenes executed in brilliant color. The continued striving after three-dimensional illusionist effects revealed in the various phases of painting was duplicated in the development of mosaics, extensively produced throughout the empire. In general the Roman minor arts tend to emphasize sumptuousness of materials and ornamentation. Cameos and golden jewelry were extensively produced. Among the most famous is the large *Cameo of the Deified Augustus* (Paris). The famous pottery from Arretium (modern Arezzo) was mass-produced and widely exported. Early examples employed a black finish and aimed at imitation of metallic effects. From the time of Augustus, the ware was characterized by a deep red glaze with decorative figures in low relief applied to the body of the vase. During the 1st cent. A.D. new processes were invented for making glass, and techniques were developed for the imitation of precious stones that made possible the production of fine murrhine vases (e.g., the famous PORTLAND VASE, British Museum). See Mortimer Wheeler, *Roman Art and Architecture* (1964); J. M. C. Toynbee, *The Art of the Romans* (1965); Giovanni Becatti, *The Art of Ancient Greece and Rome* (1967); Ranuccio Bianchi Bandinelli, *Rome, the Centre of Power* (1970) and *Rome, the Late Empire* (1971).

Roman Catholic Church, Christian church headed by the pope, the bishop of Rome (see PAPACY and PETER, SAINT). Its commonest title in official use is Holy Catholic and Apostolic Church. "Roman Catholic" is a 19th-century British coinage and merely serves to distinguish that church from other churches that are "Catholic" (see CATHOLIC CHURCH). The term "Roman Church," when used officially, means only the archdiocese of Rome. Roman Catholics may be simply defined as Christians in communion with the pope. To belong to the church one must accept as factually true the gospel of Christ as handed down in tradition and as interpreted by the bishops in union with the pope. Fundamental in this divine tradition is the BIBLE, its text determined and disseminated by the church. Adherents must also accept the church as possessing the fullness of revelation, and the church, according to the Roman Catholic catechism, is the only Christian body that is "one, holy, catholic [universal], and apostolic." The doctrine of APOSTOLIC SUCCESSION is one of the keystones of the Catholic faith; it holds that the pope (the vicar of Christ) and the bishops have in varying degrees the spiritual authority Christ assigned to his apostles. The voice of the pope, either alone or in conjunction with his bishops in council, is regarded as infallible when speaking on matters of faith and morals taught in common with the bishops (see INFALLIBILITY). Many features of the traditional teaching (dogma) have been analyzed and restated, by the councils and by great theologians (see COUNCIL, ECUMENICAL; CREED; THOMAS AQUINAS, SAINT; TRENT, COUNCIL OF; VATICAN COUNCIL, FIRST; VATICAN COUNCIL, SECOND). The chief doctrines of the church held in common with most other Christian churchs are: God's objective existence; His interest in individual men, who can enter into relations with Him (through prayer); the TRINITY; the divinity of Christ; the immortality of the soul of each human being, each one being accountable at death for his actions in life, with the award of HEAVEN or HELL; the RESURRECTION of the dead; the historicity of the Gospels; and the divine commission of the church. In addition the Roman Catholic Church stresses that since the members, living and dead, share in each other's merits, the Virgin MARY and other saints and the dead in PURGATORY are never forgotten (see CHURCH and SAINT). The church has from God a system of conveying His GRACE direct to man (see SACRAMENT). The ordinary Catholic frequents the sacraments of PENANCE (required at least once a year) and the EUCHARIST (required once every Easter time; see also SIN). The Eucharist is the center of public worship, often embellished with solemn ceremony (see MASS). Private prayer is essential; contemplation is the ideal (see MYSTICISM), and all believers are expected to devote some time to prayer that is more than begging favors. Different methods of prayer are recommended (see ROSARY; IGNATIUS OF LOYOLA, SAINT; THOMAS À KEMPIS). Self-renunciation is a necessary part of prayer (see FASTING and LENT). The church teaches that the main motive for ethical behavior is the love of God. Everything lies in the intent; the things that God has created are not bad in themselves, but bad use may be made of them. The doctrine concerning persons not Catholic is that since God affords each human being light sufficient to his salvation, all will be saved who persevere in what they believe to be good, regardless of ignorance. Only those will be damned who persist in what they know to be wrong; among these are persons who resist the church when they know it to be the one, true church. There are within the church a number of rites, i.e., ancient, independent traditions of discipline and worship, differentiated through isolation (see also LITURGY). Besides the Roman rite, to which the vast majority belong, there are among Catholics five Eastern rites, used by a number of communities (Eastern Catholics or Uniates; see PATRIARCH). They are: the Byzantine (the rite also of the ORTHODOX EASTERN CHURCH, which is not in communion with Rome), to which belong many groups, including MELCHITES, Ruthenians, Rumanians, and the Italo-Albanians of S Italy; the Antiochene (also the rite of the autonomous JACOBITE CHURCH), to which belong the MARONITES, the Syrian Catholics, and the Malankarese of Malabar; the Alexandrian, to which belong the Catholic Copts and Ethiopians (see COPT); the Chaldean (also the rite of the autonomous NESTORIAN CHURCH), to which belong Chaldean Catholics and Syro-Malabarese; and the Armenian (also the rite of the autonomous ARMENIAN CHURCH). These rites and communities have their own organizations under the pope and are protected from attempts to "Latinize" them. Best known, perhaps of the non-Roman Western rites are the Ambrosian, the Dominican, and the Mozarabic. Apart from these rites and foreign missions, the organization of the church is by diocese, the territory of a bishop. Important sees have archbishops, who often supervise neighboring, suffragan bishops. With certain restrictions, the pope names the bishops. Dioceses are made up of parishes, each of which has a church and a priest (the pastor). The pope controls bishops mainly by general legislation. His government, which is run by the cardinals living at Rome, is concerned with matters of wide significance, such as MISSIONS and relations with states (see also CARDINAL; PAPAL ELECTION; VATICAN). Cutting across territorial lines are the religious orders of men and women; their field is monastic life, nonparish activities, and schools; they frequently run missions, hospitals, and colleges (see MONASTICISM). Their members generally receive subsistence only. The parish clergy support themselves, often with salaries fixed by the bishop. Most of the clergy are priests (see ORDERS, HOLY); they are trained (usually from four to six years) in seminaries maintained by the bishops, the orders, or the Vatican. Members of the clergy do not marry, unless they are parish priests of Eastern rites. There is no churchwide census, and there are various criteria for determining membership. However, the Roman Catholics in the world are estimated to be more than half the total number of Christians and make the church the largest single religion in the world.

The Past of the Church. For the first centuries of the church's history, see CHRISTIANITY. From the 9th cent. to 1520 the church was simply Western Europe taken in its religious aspect, and no clear line divided spiritual from temporal life. In the West (unlike the East) the religious organization was free for centuries from grave interference from civil rulers. Charlemagne was an exception, but his influence was benign. In the chaotic 9th and 10th cent. every part of the church organization, including the papacy, became the prey of the powerful. The restoration of order began in monasteries; from Cluny a movement spread to reform Christian life (see CLUNIAC ORDER). This pattern of decline of religion followed by reform is characteristic of the history of the Roman Catholic Church; the reform goals have varied, but they have included the revival of spiritual life in society and the monasteries, and the elimination of politics from the bishops' sphere and venality from the papal court. The next reform (11th cent.) was conducted by popes, notably St. Gregory VII and Urban II. Part of this movement was to exclude civil rulers from making church appointments—the first, bold chapter in a 900-year battle between the church and the "Catholic princes" (see CHURCH AND STATE; INVESTITURE). The 12th cent. was a time of great intellectual beginnings. St. Bernard of Clairvaux and the Cistercians revived practical mystical prayer. Gratian founded the CANON LAW, and civil law began its development. This double study was to provide weapons to both sides in the duel between the extreme papal claims of Innocent III and Innocent IV, and the antipapal theories of Holy Roman Emperor Frederick II. In the 12th cent., Peter Abelard pioneered in rationalist theology; from his thought and from the teachings of Aristotle developed the philosophies and theologies of St. Bonaventure and St. Thomas Aquinas (see SCHOLASTICISM). This was the work of the new 13th-century universities; to them, and to the friars—the Dominicans and Franciscans—who animated them, passed the intellectual leadership held by the monasteries. St. Dominic's order was formed to preach against the Albigenses (a campaign that also produced the INQUISITION). The vast popular movement of St. Francis was a spontaneous reform contemporary with the papal reform of the Fourth Lateran Council. The 13th cent. saw also the flowering of Gothic architecture. Meanwhile the contest of church and state went on. It ruined the Hohenstaufen dynasty, but in the quarrel between Boniface VIII and Philip IV of France it brought the papacy near ruin too. Then came the Avignon residence—the "Babylonian captivity" of the papacy (1309–78), a time of good church administration, but of excessive French influence over papal policy. Except for lonely voices, such as that of St. Catherine of Siena, the church seemed to lose energy, and a long period devoid of reform set in. A long-enduring schism and a series of ambitious councils (see SCHISM, GREAT) involved most churchmen in a welter of politics and worldliness. There were popular religious movements, characterized by revivalism and a tendency to minimize the sacraments (along with church authority); they encouraged private piety, and one group produced the inspirational *Imitation* ascribed to Thomas à Kempis. The popular tendencies were extreme in John Wyclif, who developed an antisacramental, predestinarian theology emphasizing Bible study—a Protestant movement 150 years before Protestantism. The 15th-century councils did nothing for reform, and the popes, shorn of power, were reduced to being Renaissance princes. Such men could not cope with the Protestant revolt of Martin Luther and John Calvin (see REFORMATION). The Protestants aimed to restore primitive Christianity (as described in the Bible), and they succeeded in weakening the hold of the church in all of N Europe, in Great Britain, and in parts of Central Europe and Switzerland. Politics and religion were completely intertwined (as in England, Scotland, and France); hence the admixture of religious issues in the Thirty Years War. Within the church there triumphed the most extensive of all the church's reform movements (see REFORMATION, CATHOLIC, and JESUS, SOCIETY OF). From it sprang a general revival of religion and much missionary activity in the new empires of Spain and Portugal and in the Far East. In France, Catholicism found new life, beginning with St. Francis of Sales and St. Vincent de Paul. There, too, began the cult of the Sacred Heart (i.e., God's love for men), which would affect Catholic prayer everywhere. A contrary influence was Jansenism (see under JANSEN, CORNELIS), an antisacramental middle-class movement. In all the Catholic countries the 17th cent. saw an increase of state control over the church (see GALLICANISM), and in the 18th cent. the Bourbons began a course openly aimed at eliminating the papacy. The suppression of the Jesuits was part of the campaign, which reached a climax in the legislation of Holy Roman Emperor Joseph II. The revolutionary movement eventually destroyed the Catholic princes, and the church had to live with secular states, some anti-Catholic, some tolerant. The facts of the change were not clear at once, and for much of the 19th cent. the popes (and other Catholics) would look back to an imaginary 18th-century golden age before "liberalistic" atheism and materialism. The last of these popes was Pius IX, who was forced to give up the Papal States; he deplored this event, not realizing the church was thereby freed of a millstone. In enouncing the dogma of papal infallibility Pius did much to cement church unity. In his successor, Leo XIII, the church found new leadership; he and his successors worked and preached to urge Catholics to take part in modern life as Catholics, abandoning reactionary dreams and seeking some social reform. In some countries Catholic political parties were formed. Meanwhile oppressive conditions and the development of a mass socialist movement combined to detach much of the working class from the church. Otto von Bismarck (in Germany) and "liberal" governments (in Italy, France, and Portugal) passed hostile measures, especially against religious orders, and in the 20th cent. came suppression of the church (as in the USSR, Mexico, Spain, the Baltic states, Yugoslavia, Hungary, Czechoslovakia, and China). Mussolini and Hitler also wrecked as much of the church as they could. In the 20th cent. new trends in the practice and outlook of the church have been evident. The encyclical of Leo XIII, *Rerum Novarum* (1891), was followed by the *Quadrigesimo Anno* (1931) of Pius XII, the *Mater et Magistra* (1961) of John XXIII, and the *Progressio Populorum* (1967) of Paul VI. The purpose of these is fundamental readjustment to the moral and social problems of modern life and an increasing stress upon the part of the laity in the church. Linked with this has been a movement for church "renewal" both by laymen and the clergy. This has been particularly strong in France, Germany, Great Britain, and the United States and embraces the movement for liturgical reform, recognition of the various regional contributions to the living existence of the church, and recognition of the nonpolitical internationalism of the church (although declarations of implacable opposition to atheistic Communism persisted and were particularly strong under Pius XII, who urged the church to oppose all antireligious totalitarianism). Another growing revival was the deliberate attempt to forward closer relations of the Roman Catholic Church with Eastern Orthodoxy and Protestantism. All these "progressive" moves came to a head in the Second Vatican Council (1962–65), which, under John XXIII and Paul VI, initiated broad reforms in the areas of public worship, government, and ecumenism. See Philip Hughes, *A Popular History of the Catholic Church* (1947, repr. 1961); Ludwig Hertling, *A History of the Catholic Church* (tr. 1956); Joseph McSorley, *Outline History of the Church by Centuries* (11th ed. 1961); *The New Catholic Encyclopedia* (15 vol., 1967); M. A. Fitzsimons, *The Catholic Church Today: Western Europe* (1969); J. L. McKenzie, *The Roman Catholic Church* (1969).

The Roman Catholic Church in the United States. The oldest Roman Catholic foundations on U.S. territory are of Spanish (mainly Franciscan) origin, in Florida, New Mexico, and California. The French left their main religious legacy in the United States at New Orleans. English-speaking Catholicism began with Maryland. Only there and in Pennsylvania could Roman Catholics worship in the colonial period. Independence brought toleration. In 1790, John Carroll was made bishop for the United States, with Baltimore as his see. The church grew with immigration. By 1840 there were 16 dioceses. Then in the late 1840s came a flood of Irish immigrants. They were followed by many German Catholics and later by Italians, Poles, and others. The church made a vigorous effort to keep up with the arrivals, building thousands of churches and schools (see PAROCHIAL SCHOOL). The fact that the Irish were the first Catholics to arrive en masse was what determined that Catholicism in the United States should be officially English speaking, but not without resentment from non-Irish Catholics, aggravated by Irish-American hegemony in the clergy. The Irish also began the heavy urban concentration of American Catholics. There have been several outbreaks of criticism of Catholicism—in the 1830s, led by Lyman Beecher and Samuel F. B. Morse; in the 1850s, the Know-Nothing movement; in the 1890s, the American Protective Association; in the 1920s, the Ku Klux Klan agitation culminating in the opposition to the presidential candidacy of Alfred E. Smith in 1928; in the late 1950s, before the election in 1960 of John F. Kennedy, the first Roman Catholic President; and in the late 1960s and 70s, concerning the church's opposition to birth control and its lobbying efforts against the legalization of abortion. The 20th cent. saw new tendencies, including the liturgical movement, the Catholic Youth Organization, Catholic social work, Catholic trade unions, and a great expansion of Catholic parochial schools and universities. The structure of the church in the United States consists of 31 archdioceses and 129 suffragan sees. There are almost 48 million Catholics in the United States. See A. G. Cicognani, *Sanctity in America* (1939); Theodore Maynard, *The Story of American Catholicism* (1941, repr. 1960) and *The Catholic Church and the American Idea* (1953); J. T. Ellis, ed., *Documents of American Catholic History* (2 vol., rev. ed. 1967); T. T. McAvoy, *A History of the Catholic Church in the United States* (1969); John Cogley, *Catholic America* (1973).

romance [O.Fr., = something written in the popular language, i.e., a Romance language]. The *roman* of the Middle Ages was a form of chivalric and romantic literature widely diffused throughout Europe from the 11th cent. With the Provençal TROUBADOURS the *roman* was a form of narrative, originally sung but later recited before courts. The TROUVERES lengthened these into the CHANSONS DE GESTE and the *romans d'aventures,* or romances of love and adventure. It is from the latter class that the modern romance descends (see NOVEL). See studies by A. B. Taylor (1930, repr. 1969), Gillian Beer (1970), and Eugène Vinaver (1971).

Romance languages, group of languages belonging to the Italic subfamily of the INDO-EUROPEAN family of languages (see ITALIC LANGUAGES). Also called Romanic, they are spoken by about 400 million people in many parts of the world, but chiefly in Europe and the Western Hemisphere. Among the more important Romance languages are Catalan, French, Italian, Portuguese, Provençal, Rhaeto-Romanic, Rumanian, and Spanish. The spread of some Romance languages to other parts of the world, especially the Western Hemisphere, accompanied the colonizing and empire-building of the mother countries of these languages, notably Spain, Portugal, and France. All of the Romance languages are descended from Latin (see LATIN LANGUAGE). They are called Romance languages because their parent tongue, Latin, was the language of the Romans. However, the variety of Latin that was their common ancestor was not classical Latin but the spoken or popular language of everyday usage, which is believed to have differed greatly from classical Latin by the time of the Roman Empire. This vernacular Latin, known as Vulgar Latin, was spread by the soldiers and colonists of Rome over the empire. It superseded the original native tongues of certain conquered European peoples, although it was also influenced by their local speech practices and by the linguistic characteristics of colonists and later of invaders. After the fall of the Western Roman Empire there was a degree of regional isolation. Germanic invasions from the north had a further disrupting effect, and Vulgar Latin was thus differentiated into local dialects which in time evolved into the individual Romance tongues. Because of their common source, the Romance languages have many similar features, both in grammar and vocabulary. The differences between them tend to be phonetical rather than structural or lexical. Even when the Romance languages differ grammatically from Latin, such changes frequently are but examples of a shared parallel development from the parent tongue. For example, although Latin had three grammatical genders (masculine, feminine, and neuter), the individual Romance tongues have only two (masculine and feminine). Moreover, all Romance languages except Rumanian have discarded the Latin scheme of six different cases for the noun, retaining only one case. As a result, the grammatical relationships of words are clarified chiefly by prepositions and word order instead of by inflections, as in Latin. On the other hand, verbs in the Romance languages have preserved a highly developed conjugational system, inherited from Latin, in which the inflections make clear person and number, tense and mood. See articles on individual languages mentioned. See W. D. Edcock, *The Romance Languages* (1960); C. M. Carlton, *Studies in Romance Lexicology* (1965); Iorgu Iordan and John Orr, *An Introduction to Romance Linguistics, Its Schools and Scholars* (2d ed. 1970).

Roman de la Rose, Le (lə rōmäN′ də lä rōz), French poem of 22,000 lines in eight-syllable couplets. It is in two parts. The first (4,058) was written (c.1237) by GUILLAUME DE LORRIS and was left unfinished. It is an elaborate allegory on the psychology of love, often subtle and charming. The second part was written (1275–80) by JEAN DE MEUN, who stressed reproduction of the human race as the achievement of God's purpose in the world and digressed into discussion of various subjects. The Middle English *Romaunt of the Rose* (1st ed. 1532) is a fragmentary translation of the *Roman.* Chaucer translated a portion of the work. An old standard translation into English is that by Frederick S. Ellis (1900); a later one is by H. W. Robbins (1962). See C. S. Lewis, *The Allegory of Love* (1936).

Roman Empire: see ROME; BYZANTINE EMPIRE; HOLY ROMAN EMPIRE.

Romanes, George John (rōmä′nĭz), 1848–94, English biologist, b. Kingston, Ont. As a youth he went to England and there became a friend of Darwin, who encouraged him to apply the theory of natural selection to mental evolution and to psychology. He taught at the Univ. of Edinburgh and at the Royal Institution, London, and in 1891 established the annual Romanes Lectures at Oxford. His works include *Mental Evolution in Animals* (1883), *Mental Evolution in Man* (1888), *Darwin and after Darwin* (3 vol., 1892–97), and *Mind and Motion and Monism* (1895). See biography by his wife, E. D. Romanes, (1896).

Romanesque architecture and art. The Romanesque style of architecture prevailed throughout Europe from the mid-11th to the mid-12th cent., although it persisted until considerably later in certain areas. The term *Romanesque* points to the principal source of the style, the buildings of the Roman Empire. In addition to classical elements, however, Romanesque architecture incorporates components of Byzantine and Eastern origin. The specific character of the style, however, can be understood only in the light of the development of early medieval architecture in the West, notably its Carolingian and Ottonian phases. Certain of the most characteristic features of Romanesque structures—the massive west facade crowned by a tower or by twin towers, the complex design of the eastern part housing the sanctuary, the rhythmic alternation of piers and columns in the nave—represent only the advanced stages in a lengthy and complex formal evolution marked by considerable trial and error. The development of Romanesque architecture owes much to the primacy accorded to vaulting. Masonry vaulting (see VAULT) since the beginning of Christian architecture had been confined to buildings of relatively small scale and to crypts. Large basilican structures, in a continuation of a tradition inaugurated by the early Christian BASILICA, were topped by wooden roofs. Romanesque churches, on the other hand, with notable exceptions in Normandy and Italy, sustained massive barrel vaults, making mandatory the reinforcement of load-bearing walls in order to parry the lateral outward thrust. The frequent presence of galleries above the aisles, sometimes with half-barrel vaults, is in all probability rooted in structural considerations connected with the problem of abutment. The limitation of wall openings to a minimum, related to the same concern, contributed to the sober yet somberly impressive character of the light. The major share of architectural activity was sponsored by the great monastic communities. The Cluniac order, at the peak of its power, played a primary role in the patronage of construction. Thus a number of significant Cluniac churches connected with great 12th-century pilgrimages—St. Martin in Tours, St. Sernin in Toulouse, and Santiago de Compostela in Spain—show great similarity in plan and overall design. This sameness is especially notable in the presence of spacious ambulatories with radiating chapels designed to facilitate the pilgrims' access to the precious relics. The design of the third church of Cluny, dedicated in 1095, is reflected in a number of Burgundian churches. The basilica of San Marco in Venice and other Byzantine structures help to account for the presence of domed vaulting in a group of churches in French Aquitaine. German Romanesque architecture on the other hand remained strongly tied to the heritage of OTTONIAN ART. The following structures are noted works of Romanesque architecture: France—the abbey churches of St. Madeleine Vézelay (c.1090–1130) and Paray-le-Monial (early 12th cent.); Germany—the Cathedral of Speyer, dedicated in 1060, but largely reconstructed after 1082, and the Church of St. Mary on the Capitol in Cologne (1049); Italy—the cathedral (1063–92) and baptistery (1153) in Pisa, the Church of San Miniato al Monte (c.1070) in Florence, and the Cathedral of Monreale in Sicily (1174). From the last third of the 12th cent., certain features of the churches in N France and in England began to point toward the development of the Gothic (see NORMAN ARCHITECTURE). Similarly, architecture in the Ile-de-France, particularly the ambulatory (1140) of the abbey of St. Denis, reveals such an advance in unified design and construction as to be considered the first monument of Gothic architecture. Romanesque art was characterized by an important revival of monumental forms, notably sculpture and fresco painting, which developed in close association with architectural decoration and which exhibited a forceful and often severely structural quality. At the same time an element of realism, which parallels the first flowering of vernacular literature, came to the fore. It was expressed in terms of a direct and naïve observation of certain details drawn from daily life and a heightened emphasis on emotion and fantasy. For many aspects of its rich imagery Romanesque art depended on the heritage of antiquity and of earlier medieval art, while the prestige of Byzantine art remained high in Western eyes. The pilgrimages and Crusades contributed to an unprecedented expansion of the formal vocabulary through the development of closer contacts between regional cultures and distant peoples. The first important monuments of Romanesque sculpture were created in the last decade of the 11th cent. and the first decades of the 12th cent. The primary source of artistic patronage was provided by the monastic institutions, for whom sculptors executed large relief carvings for the decoration of church portals and richly ornate capitals for cloisters. Romanesque sculpture produced an art of extraordinary ornamental complexity, ecstatic in expression, and abounding in seemingly endless combinations of zoomorphic, vegetal, and abstract motifs. In France, themes portrayed on tympanums of such churches as Moissac, Vézelay, and Autun emphasized the awesome majesty of Christ as ruler and judge of the universe. They often depicted terrifying spectacles of hell. English sculpture showed a tendency toward geometric ornamentation. However, with the introduction in England of continental influences in the mid-12th cent., there also appeared gruesome renditions of the *Last Judgment*, e.g., at Lincoln Cathedral. In contrast with the demonic nature and animated quality of sculpture in France and in England, there was an assertion of more massive and ponderous figures in N Italy, with the narrative reliefs from *Genesis* designed by Wiligelmo in Modena and by Niccolò in Verona. Another aspect of the Romanesque revival was the production of metalwork objects, of which many outstanding examples, such as crucifixes, reliquary shrines, and candlesticks, are still preserved in church treasuries. The most productive centers of this art were the regions adjacent to the Rhine and the Meuse rivers, where the art of bronze casting reached a level of technical mastery sufficient to permit the execution of works of considerable dimension. An outstanding example of Mosan bronze casting is the baptismal font of St. Barthelemy in Liège, a large vessel supported by 12 oxen and decorated with scenes in high relief, executed by Rainer of Huy between 1107 and 1118. It was during this same period that Limoges, in central France, became an extremely active center of metalwork production, specializing in enamelwork. Fresco painting has been more adversely affected by the accidents of time, but several large cycles, as well as numerous other fragments of Romanesque wall painting, have survived. The large and relatively unbroken expanses of wall space within Romanesque buildings presented an excellent ground for the work of the painter, and the basic forms of Romanesque fresco painting are typically monumental in scale and bold in coloristic effect. Among the foremost examples of this art still largely extant are the cycles of Saint-Savin in western France and Sant'Angelo in Formis in S Italy. Manuscript illumination of the Romanesque period was characterized by a vast enlargement of the traditional fund of pictorial imagery, although in terms of overall execution and calligraphic quality Romanesque illuminated books often show a certain carelessness and lack of refinement. The Psalter, as in the early Middle Ages, continued to be the most widely read volume for religious use, and numerous sumptuously illuminated copies of this work were executed. The Romanesque scriptorium also produced large editions of the Bible, often extending to several volumes. A splendid example of such a work is the Winchester Bible, executed in the course of several generations and decorated with numerous scenes from the Old and the New Testaments. Romanesque manuscripts are enlivened by elaborate and highly inventive initial letters, on which the artists of this period lavished their bent for rich ornamental display. See H. P. Swarzenski, *Monuments of Romanesque Art* (2d ed. 1967); G. Künstler, ed., *Romanesque Art in Europe* (1968); G. Nebolsine, *Journey into Romanesque* (1969); O. Demus, *Romanesque Mural Painting* (1970); G. Zarnecki, *Romanesque Art* (1971).

Romania: see RUMANIA.

Romania, name used by Westerners to refer to the Latin Empire of Constantinople (see CONSTANTINOPLE, LATIN EMPIRE OF) or by the Byzantines to refer to the lands under their rule. It is also a variant spelling of the present-day nation of Rumania.

Romanic: see ROMANCE LANGUAGES.

Roman law, the legal system of Rome from the supposed founding of the city in 753 B.C. to the fall of the Eastern Empire in A.D. 1453; it was later adopted as the basis of modern CIVIL LAW. Most authorities, however, disregard the largely static period following the reign of Justinian (527–65). Roman law in the earliest period known is typically expressed in the TWELVE TABLES with their marked formalism. The usual early procedure was also stereotyped; it was the *legis actio,* a form of charge and denial the words of which had to be followed exactly by the parties at the risk of losing the suit. Exact knowledge of the words constituting the *legis actiones* was limited to a body of patrician priests, the College of Pontiffs. The reduction of these forms to writing (c.250 B.C.) was a victory for the plebeians and a step in reducing the religious and formal element in the law. Soon the primary source of law became the *lex* (plural *leges*), a statutory enactment that was proposed by a magistrate and accepted by a popular assembly. Among the assemblies empowered to enact *leges* was that of the plebeians. In the late 3d cent. B.C., Roman law could no longer limit itself to the inhabitants of the republic but was forced to take account of the surrounding non-Roman peoples. Thus, to the *jus civile,* which governed relations among the Romans and those admitted to Roman status, was added the *jus gentium,* the law applied in dealings with a foreigner. The *jus gentium* incorporated much of the highly developed commercial law of the Greek city-states and of other maritime powers. Such provisions, being better adapted to Rome's expanding economic needs than the unyielding provisions of the *jus civile,* in time tended to be applied universally. The development of new principles was especially vigorous after c.100 B.C., an important source being the *jus honorarium,* i.e., the law of the praetors (chief magistrates). On assuming office the praetor announced the principles, sometimes novel, that would govern his decisions. The praetors also contributed greatly to making practice more flexible. In place of the *legis actiones,* they often used the formulary system. A *formula,* like a *legis actio,* was a device for determining the issue between the parties; but instead of being a mere interchange of prescribed speeches, it provided a structure for discussing the actual dispute. Whichever method was used, when the nature of the dispute was agreed upon, the parties brought their case before the *judex,* a private functionary, who considered the evidence and gave judgment. After the establishment of the empire, the development of law largely passed from the praetors (the practice of issuing new edicts ended A.D. c.125) and from the popular assemblies into the hands of the emperors, sometimes operating through the senate. Various types of imperial enactments called constitutions were issued in abundance. Legal problems attained great complexity, and the aid of a specially trained class of scholars was enlisted for their solution. Those jurists with a special license from the emperor could write *responsa* to guide the judges in deciding cases. Most prominent among the jurists was PAPINIAN; his work, with that of GAIUS, MODESTINUS, PAULUS, and ULPIAN, attained the highest authority. The employment of jurists was a step in making the whole of Roman procedure official; in this process the institution of *judex* was abolished and the trial placed entirely in the hands of a judge. By the early 4th cent. most branches of Roman law were fully developed. The system was generally responsive to legal needs and allowed sufficient variety to meet local customs. A grave disadvantage of the system, however, was that the vast corpus of legal matter included much that was confused, contradictory, or redundant; reduction to CODE form was required. The THEODOSIAN CODE (438), the earliest attempt, was followed by the BREVIARY OF ALARIC (506). Finally the task was accomplished with the culminating work of Roman legal scholarship, the CORPUS JURIS CIVILIS (completed 535) under the direction of TRIBONIAN. After this date, Roman law persisted as a part of the GERMANIC LAWS and was in effect in the Eastern Roman Empire. Revival of classical studies during the Renaissance prepared the way for the partial resurrection of Roman law as the modern civil law in a large part of the world. The *jus gentium* is perhaps the most widely represented in modern legal systems, for it is the basis of COMMERCIAL LAW even in those countries that follow COMMON LAW. See Leopold Wenger, *Institutes of the Roman Law of Civil Procedure* (tr. 1940); H. J. Wolff, *Roman Law: A Historical Introduction* (1951, repr. 1964); H. F. Jolowicz, *Historical Introduction to the Study of Roman Law* (2d ed. 1952); A. H. M. Jones, *Studies in Roman Government and Law* (1960); W. W. Buckland, *A Text-Book of Roman Law from Augustus to Justinian* (3d ed. 1964); Wolfgang Kunkel, *An Introduction to Roman Legal and Constitutional History* (tr. 1966); John Crook, *Law and Life of Rome* (1967); Alan Watson, *The Law of the Ancient Romans* (1970).

Roman literature: see LATIN LITERATURE.

Romano, Giulio: see GIULIO ROMANO.

Romanov (rō'mənôf, Rus. rəmä'nəf), ruling dynasty of Russia from 1613 to 1917. The name Romanov was adopted in the 16th cent. by a family of boyars (great nobles) that traced its origin to the 14th cent. Czar Ivan IV took as his first wife Anastasia Romanov. Anastasia's brother, Nikita, was a regent for her son, Czar Feodor I. Nikita's son, Philaret, whom Boris Godunov forced to take monastic vows, was patriarch of Moscow from 1619 until his death in 1633. MICHAEL, Philaret's son, was chosen in 1613 as czar of Russia; his election ended a turbulent period in Russian history. Except for the period from 1722 to 1797, the succession was thereafter regulated by the law of primogeniture. The direct successors of Michael were ALEXIS (1645–76) and Feodor III (1676–82). Ivan V and PETER I (Peter the Great) reigned jointly under the regency of their sister Sophia Alekseyevna until 1689, when Peter assumed sole rule. In 1721, Peter took the title emperor of Russia in addition to his title of czar; the title was borne by all his successors. His succession decree of 1722 denounced the law of primogeniture and declared that the choice of a successor lay solely with the ruling emperor. In 1723, Peter made his consort joint empress as CATHERINE I, and after his death (1725) she continued to rule until she died in 1727. Peter's son by his first marriage, Czarevich ALEXIS, had been executed in 1718. By his second marriage, with Catherine, there were two daughters—Anna, who married Duke Charles Frederick of Holstein-Gottorp, and Elizabeth. They were bypassed in the succession of 1727 in favor of PETER II (1727–30), son of Czarevich Alexis. Peter II was the last of the direct male Romanov line, and on his death ANNA, duchess of Courland, a daughter of Ivan V, ascended the throne. She died without heirs and was succeeded (1740) by Ivan VI, a great-grandson of Ivan V. He was a German, son of the duke of Brunswick and of Anna Leopoldovna, a princess of Mecklenburg. The rule of foreigners was unpopular, and Peter I's daughter ELIZABETH executed a coup d'etat in 1741 and was proclaimed czarina. Her nephew PETER III succeeded her in 1762 but was deposed (and probably assassinated) that year in a coup that made his consort, a princess of Anhalt-Zerbst, empress as CATHERINE II (Catherine the Great). There was some argument as to the paternity of Catherine's son and successor, PAUL I (1796–1801), but it is now generally believed that he was the son of Peter III. Paul, who was assassinated, restored the succession by primogeniture in 1797. His successors reigned as ALEXANDER I (1801–25), NICHOLAS I (1825–55), ALEXANDER II (1855–81; assassinated), ALEXANDER III (1881–94), and NICHOLAS II (1894–1917). The marriage of Nicholas II to Princess Alix of Hesse (Czarina ALEXANDRA FEODOROVNA) brought hemophilia into the family; their son, Czarevich Alexis (b. 1904), was afflicted with the disease. In 1918, after the Russian Revolution, Nicholas II and his immediate family were executed. The members of the Romanov family who escaped execution fled abroad. See studies by A. G. Mazour (1960), J. D. Bergamini (1969), Ian Grey (1970), and Virginia Cowles (1971).

Roman Question: see LATERAN TREATY.

Roman religion. The indigenous Italic religion, which was the nucleus of the religion of ancient Rome, was essentially animistic. It depended on the belief that forces or spirits, called *numina* (sing., *numen*), existed in natural objects and controlled human destiny. The spirits were held in awe and were placated with offerings and prayers. In the beginning of the historical period, when Italy was dotted with small agricultural communities, the family and the household were the basic religious units. Everything vital to the continuance of human life had its *numen* and appropriate rite. For the perpetuity of the family, the Italian farmer made offerings to the GENIUS of the family. For the safety of the household he worshiped VESTA, the guardian spirit of the hearth fire; the LARES and PENATES, guardians of the house; and JANUS, guardian of the door. To protect the boundaries of his property he honored TERMINUS. To insure an abundant harvest he held various festivals throughout the year. To placate the spirits of the dead he made offerings to the LEMURES, to the MANES, and to the deities of the underworld. In performing these religious ceremonies the head of the family acted as the priest and was assisted by his sons and daughters. When these families coalesced into tribes and then a state, the family cult and ritual formed the basis of the state cult and ritual. Vesta had a community hearth, the penates a community storeroom, Janus a holy door in the Forum. Rome, which was theoretically one family, was ruled by its king, who as such was head of the family and chief priest. The king was assisted in his duties by his "sons and daughters," the colleges of priests and priestesses. They elaborated and recorded the rituals necessary for the propitiation of the gods and regulated the state ceremonies and the ceremonial calendar. The official clergy included the PONTIFEX MAXIMUS, the *rex sacrorum* [king of the sacred rites], the pontifices, the flamens (see FLAMEN), and the vestal virgins. In the earliest period of Roman state religion, JUPITER, MARS, and QUIRINUS were the supreme triad. The Romans, however, tolerant of new gods and religions (provided that no harm was done to the state as such), adopted many foreign gods. Under the influence of the Etruscans and other Italic communities, new gods began to appear about the 7th cent. B.C. A wider and much more significant influence, however, was that of the Greek and Middle Eastern cults from about the 3d cent. B.C. Old Roman deities were equated with the Greek gods and accordingly endowed with their attributes and myths. Such important cults as the worship of DIONYSUS and APOLLO were brought to Rome. Greek philosophy, particularly that of the Epicureans (see EPICURUS) and the Stoics (see STOICISM), began to influence Roman religious thought. However, in the last two centuries of the republic—when the old basis of Roman religion had lost much of its importance, and when the state had grown so massive and distant that its ceremonies failed to satisfy the populace—religious feeling rapidly degenerated. The people, needing a new and emotionally more satisfying religion, turned toward the religious mysteries and the Middle Eastern cults. The most prominent were those of the Great Mother (see CYBELE), ISIS and OSIRIS, SOL, and MITHRA. Old Roman worship had been controlled, impersonal, and concerned with matters of the everyday world. The new cults, which centered around the individual, promised personal salvation and blessed afterlife. It was in this religious air that Christianity took root and eventually triumphed. See W. R. Halliday, *Lectures on the History of Roman Religion* (1922); Franz Altheim, *A History of Roman Religion* (1938); H. J. Rose, *Ancient Roman Religion* (1959).

Roman roads, ancient system of highways linking Rome with its most distant provinces. The roads often ran in a straight line, regardless of obstacles, and were efficiently constructed, generally in four layers of materials; the uppermost layer was a pavement of flat, hard stones, concrete, or pebbles set in mortar. Roads were built or rebuilt by the Romans throughout the empire in Europe, Asia, and Africa. Many modern roads are laid out on their routes, and some of the old bridges are still in use. Examples of Roman roads exist near Rome and elsewhere. Their primary purpose was military, but they also were of great commercial importance and brought the distant provinces in touch with the capital. In Italy roads led out of Rome in every direction. The most ancient were the Ostiense Road to Ostia at the mouth of the Tiber; the Praenestine Way SE to Praeneste; and the Latin Road or Latin Way to a point near Capua where it later joined the APPIAN WAY, which was the first of the great highways. The three roads from Rome to the north were connected with others crossing the Alps by the great Alpine passes—Alpis Cottia (Mont Genèvre), Alpis Graia (Little St. Bernard), Alpis Poenina (Great St. Bernard), the Brenner Pass, and others leading into Rhaetia and Noricum. The FLAMINIAN WAY was the most important northern route. It ran from Rome NE to Ariminium (Rimini); from that point it was extended (187 B.C.) as the Aemilian Way, which ran in a straight line NW through Bononia (modern Bologna) to the Po at Placentia (Piacenza); later it was extended farther to Mediolanum (Milan). Another northern route was the Aurelian Way from Rome along the Tyrrhenian coast to Pisae (Pisa) and Luna; from there it was extended to Genua (Genoa). The third northern route was the Cassian Way from Rome through Etruria to Faesulae (Fiesole) and Luca (Lucca); near Luca it joined the Aurelian Way. The chief roads leading from Rome to the regions across the Apennines and to the Adriatic were the Salarian Way to Ancona and the Valerian Way to Aternum (Pescara). There were other roads in Italy, most notable among them the Postumian Way, leading from Genua across the Po valley to Aquileia at the head of the Adriatic. A wide system of roads was also built and rebuilt by the Romans in Britain, mainly for military purposes. The best-known British roads were ERMINE STREET, FOSSE WAY, WATLING STREET, and the pre-Roman ICKNIELD STREET. See Thomas Ashby, *The Roman Campagna in Classical Times* (1927, repr. 1970); I. D. Margary, *Roman Roads in Britain* (2 vol., 1955–57, rev. ed. 1967); V. W. Von Hagen, *The Roads that Led to Rome* (1967).

Romans, epistle of the New Testament, the sixth book in the usual order. It was written by St. PAUL, probably from Corinth before his last trip to Jerusalem, A.D. c.58. It is a treatise addressed to the Christian church at Rome, apparently to introduce himself and his teaching before his expected visit. The subject treated is central in Paul's teaching, justification by faith, i.e., the doctrine that believers achieve salvation through faith. The same matter is the subject of GALATIANS. The letter opens with a solemn introduction (1.1–17), in which the doctrine is summarized (1.16–17). Paul then argues that faith in Jesus Christ is the only means of salvation for both Gentiles and Jews (1.18–4.25), explaining for the latter that reliance on the Mosaic Law is not enough (2.11–3.31); a chapter (4) on Abraham's faith closes the section. Next (5–9) Paul treats the state of the justified man, listing the fruits of the redemption as confidence due to the defeat of original sin by grace (5), freedom from sin because of death and resurrection "in Christ" (6), and freedom from the Law (7–8.11); then an eloquent passage deals with the future glory of the just (8.12–39). Finally Paul discusses God's apparent rejection of Israel (9–11); he argues that God has not broken His promise to His chosen people, rather He is working toward universal redemption. The rest of the epistle is mainly exhortation (12–15.13), beginning with a general admonition (12) to Christian virtue. The end contains remarks of St. Paul about his life (15.14–33), greetings to various Romans (16), and a fine doxology (16.25–27). Some scholars have rejected the last two chapters as belonging to some other, lost epistle. Romans, one of the longest and most important of St. Paul's works, is claimed as an authority by many divergent theologians; thus, Lutheran and Roman Catholic interpretations of justification, diametrically opposed, both depend on this epistle. See C. H. Dodd, *The Epistle of Paul to the Romans* (1933); Karl Barth, *The Epistle to the Romans* (1918, tr. 1933).

Romansh: see RHAETO-ROMANIC.

romanticism, term loosely applied to literary and artistic movements of the late 18th and 19th cent. Resulting in part from the libertarian and egalitarian ideals of the French Revolution, these movements had in common only a revolt against the prescribed rules of CLASSICISM. The basic aims of romanticism were various: a return to nature and to belief in the goodness of man, most notably expressed by Jean Jacques Rousseau—with the subsequent cult of "the noble savage," attention to the "simple peasant," and admiration of the violently self-centered "hero"; the rediscovery of the artist as a supremely individual creator; the exaltation of the senses and emotions over reason and intellect. In addition, romanticism was a philosophical revolt against RATIONALISM. Although in literature romantic elements were known much earlier, as in the Elizabethan dramas, many critics now date English literary romanticism from the publication of Wordsworth and Coleridge's *Lyrical Ballads* (1798); in the preface to the second edition of that work (1800), Wordsworth stated his belief that poetry results from "the spontaneous overflow of powerful feelings," and pressed for the use of natural everyday diction in literary works; Coleridge emphasized the importance of the poet's imagination and discounted adherence to arbitrary literary rules. Such English romantic poets as Byron, Shelley, Robert Burns, Keats, Robert Southey, and William Cowper often focused on the individual self, on the poet's personal reaction to life. This emphasis can also be found in such prose works as the essays of Charles Lamb and William Hazlitt, and in Thomas De Quincey's autobiographical *Confessions of an English Opium Eater* (1822). The interest of romantics in the medieval period as a time of mystery, adventure, and aspiration is evidenced in the GOTHIC ROMANCE and in the historical novels of Sir Walter Scott. William Blake was probably the most singular of the English romantics. Presenting a highly personal mystical vision, his poems and paintings are radiant, imaginative, and heavily symbolic, indicating the spiritual reality underlying earthly matter. In Germany the STURM UND DRANG school with its obsessive interest in medievalism prepared the way for romanticism. Friedrich Schlegel first used the term *romantic* to designate a school of literature opposed to classicism, and he also applied the philosophical ideas of Immanuel Kant and J. G. Fichte to the "romantic ideal." Major German writers associated with romanticism include G. E. Lessing, J. G. Herder, Friedrich Hölderlin, Schiller, and particularly Goethe, who had a mystic feeling for nature and for Germany's medieval past. The credo of French romanticism was set forth by Victor Hugo in the preface to his drama *Cromwell* (1828) and in his play *Hernani* (1830); Hugo proclaimed the right of the artist to liberty in both choice and treatment of a subject. The French romantics included Chateaubriand, Alexandre Dumas père, Alphonse de Lamartine, Alfred de Vigny, Alfred de Musset, and George Sand. Other leading romantic figures were Giacomo Leopardi and Allesandro Manzoni in Italy, and Aleksandr Pushkin and Mikhail Lermontov in Russia. In the United States romanticism had philosophic expression in TRANSCENDENTALISM, notably in the works of Emerson and Thoreau. Poets such as Poe, Whittier, and Longfellow all produced works in the romantic vein. Walt Whitman in particular expressed supreme concern with the individual self and with the democratic spirit. The works of James Fenimore Cooper reflected the romantic interest in the historical past, whereas the symbolic novels of Hawthorne and Melville emphasized the movement's concern with transcendent reality. In the visual arts *romanticism* is used to refer loosely to a trend that appears at any time, and specifically to the art of the early 19th cent. Nineteenth-century romanticism was characterized by the avoidance of classical forms and rules, emphasis on the emotional and spiritual, representation of the unattainable ideal, nostalgia for the grace of past ages, and a predilection for exotic themes. Romantic artists developed precise techniques in order to produce specific associations in the mind of the viewer. To convey verbal concepts they chose extravagant means such as endowing inanimate objects with human values (e.g., the wild trees and shimmery moonlight used in the paintings of Caspas David to suggest an infinity of human longing, the weltschmerz of his time). The result was often sentimental or ludicrous. Romanticism stood outside the mainstream of 19th-century realism, producing only two major masters: Delacroix and Turner. Delacroix evolved a painterly style and use of color that exalted the romantic attitude. Turner transformed romanticism into the expression of a visionary imagination. Rodin, whose bronze works combined realistic treatment with romantic subject matter, was later—in his marble sculptures—to fight the conceptual limitations of the sentimentality inherent in the romantic ideal. In England, landscape gardening was used to express the romantic aesthetic by means of deliberate imitation of the picturesque in nature. In architecture Wyatt's preposterous, mock medieval Fonthill Abbey displayed the romantic building style in extreme form. The host of lesser artists of the romantic tradition included the French Géricault, the Swiss-English Henry Fuseli, the Swiss Arnold Böcklin, the English PRE-RAPHAELITES, the German NAZARENES, and the American artists of the HUDSON RIVER SCHOOL. Romanticism in music was characterized by an emphasis on emotion and great freedom of form. It attained its fullest development in the works of German composers. Although elements of romanticism are present in the music of Beethoven, Weber, and Schubert, it reached its zenith in the works of Berlioz, Mendelssohn, Schumann, Chopin, Liszt, and Wagner. Less totally romantic composers usually placed in the middle period of romanticism are Brahms, Tchaikovsky, Dvořák, and Grieg; those grouped in the last phase include Elgar, Puccini, Mahler, Richard Strauss, and Sibelius. Many romantic composers, including Mendelssohn, Schumann, Chopin, and Brahms, worked in small forms that are flexible in structure, e.g., prelude, intermezzo, nocturne, ballad, and cappriccio, especially in solo music for the piano. Another romantic contribution was the art song for voice and piano, most notably the German lied (see SONG). Romantic composers, particularly Liszt, in combining music and literature, created the SYMPHONIC POEM. Berlioz also made use of literature; much of his work is described as PROGRAM MUSIC. Romantic opera began with Weber, included the works of the Italians Rossini, Bellini, Donizetti, and Verdi, and culminated in the work of Wagner, who aimed at a complete synthesis of the arts in his idea of *Gesamtkunstwerk* [total work of art]. While Tchaikovsky was inspired by a more universal romanticism, the movement in Russia was nationalist in nature, exemplified by the works of Mikhail Glinka. The music of Bedřich Smetana and Dvořák in Czechoslovakia and that of Grieg in Norway also expressed romantic nationalism. Toward the end of the 19th cent. interest in classical forms was revived by Bruckner, Brahms, Tchaikovsky, and Franck. The end of the romantic period—described as decadent, grandiose, and even megalomaniac in character—is often referred to as postromanticism and is represented by the works of Holst, Elgar, Mahler, and Richard Strauss. See separate entries on the individual authors, artists, and composers mentioned. See Jacques Barzun, *Romanticism and the Modern Ego* (1944); A. O. Lovejoy, *Essays in the History of Ideas* (1948); L. R. Furst, *Romanticism in Perspective* (1970); R. F. Gleckner and G. E. Enscoe, ed., *Romanticism* (2d ed. 1970); Mario Praz, *The Romantic Agony* (tr., 2d ed. 1970). For treatment of romanticism in the visual arts, see Peter Quennell, *Romantic England* (1970); Donald Sutherland, *On Romanticism* (1971); Kenneth Clark, *The Romantic Rebellion* (1974). In music, see Alfred Einstein, *Music in the Romantic Era* (1947); R. M. Longyear, *Nineteenth Century Romanticism in Music* (1969).

Romanus I (Romanus Lecapenus), d. 948, Byzantine emperor (920–44). An admiral, he usurped the throne during the minority of his son-in-law, CONSTANTINE VII. He defended Constantinople against the Bulgars under SIMEON I and in 927 made peace with Simeon's son. He also tried unsuccessfully to protect peasant and military holdings from absorption into the estates of the great landowners. In 944, Romanus was overthrown by his two surviving sons, who were in turn overthown by Constantine VII. See study by Steven Runciman (1929, repr. 1969).

Romanus II, 939–63, Byzantine emperor (959–63), son and successor of Constantine VII. A profligate, he came under the domination of his second wife, Theophano. She, along with the eunuch Joseph Bringus, ruled the empire. His reign was marked by the brilliant victories of Nicephorus Phocas over the Arabs. After the death of Romanus, Nicephorus married Theophano and became emperor.

Romanus III (Romanus Argyrus)(är'jĭrəs), c.968–1034, Byzantine emperor (1028–34). An aged senator, he married ZOË and thus succeeded to the throne. A capricious ruler, he depleted his treasury and abolished needed taxes. He was seriously defeated by the Muslims in Syria in 1030 but was saved by the great general George Maniaces, who took Odessa in 1032. He was perhaps murdered by Zoë and Michael IV, who succeeded him as emperor and husband of Zoë.

Romanus IV (Romanus Diogenes)(dīŏj'ənēz), d. 1072, Byzantine emperor (1068–71). A Cappadocian general, he succeeded Constantine X by marrying his widow, Eudocia Macrembolitissa. After some early successes against the Seljuk Turks he was crushingly defeated and captured (1071) by Alp Arslan at MANZIKERT. He was ransomed and promised to pay tribute, but he was deposed and blinded by his stepson, Michael VII, and soon died.

Romany (rŏm'ənē, rō'-), language belonging to the Dardic group of the Indo-Iranian subfamily of the Indo-European family of languages (see INDO-IRANIAN LANGUAGES). The mother tongue of the GYPSIES, Romany has about one million speakers, largely outside of India. The gypsies apparently began migrating from NW India westward before the 9th cent. A.D. and had reached SE Europe before the 14th cent. They now live principally in central and E Europe and in Spain. Romany has three main dialectal groups: Asiatic, Armenian, and European. In grammar it can be traced back to SANSKRIT. It has borrowed considerable vocabulary from the languages of the various peoples among whom its speakers have lived and roamed. There is no important literature in Romany, but some biblical translations into Romany exist, for which both the Roman and Cyrillic alphabets were used. See John Sampson, *The Dialect of the Gypsies of Wales* (1925); R. L. Turner, *Position of Romani in Indo-Aryan* (1927); Jan Kochanowski, *Gypsy Studies* (1963).

Romberg, Sigmund (rŏm'bûrg), 1887–1951, Hungarian-American composer, educated in Vienna. He came to the United States in 1910, played in restaurant and café orchestras, and soon had his own orchestra. He wrote the score for the musical *The Whirl of the World* (1914), and followed it with more than 70 operettas. Among the most successful were *Blossom Time* (1921; based on the life and music of Franz Schubert), *The Student Prince* (1924), *The Desert Song* (1926), and *The New Moon* (1928). These recalled the romantic, lyrical style of Viennese operettas. He later wrote scores for several films, some of them adaptations of his own stage works. See Elliott Arnold's *Deep in My Heart: a Story Based on the Life of Sigmund Romberg* (1949).

Rome, Ital. *Roma,* city (1971 com. pop. 2,799,836), capital of Italy and see of the pope, whose residence, Vatican City (see under VATICAN), is a sovereign state within the city of Rome. Rome is also the capital of Latium, a region of central Italy, and of Rome prov. It lies on both banks of the Tiber and its affluent, the Aniene, in the CAMPAGNA DI ROMA, between the Apennine mts. and the Tyrrhenian Sea. Called the Eternal City, it is one of the world's richest cities in history and art and one of its great cultural, religious, and intellectual centers. The rise of Rome from an insignificant pastoral settlement to perhaps the world's most successful empire—supreme as a lawgiver and organizer, holding sway over virtually all the then-known world, on which it left a permanent imprint of its material and cultural achievements—is one of the great epics of history. Whatever its fortunes throughout history, Rome has remained the symbol of European civilization. Because of the complexity of the subject matter, the following article is divided into several sections, and additional information will be found in the articles to which there are cross references. See also ROMAN ART; ROMAN ARCHITECTURE; LATIN LITERATURE; ROMAN RELIGION.

Rome before Augustus. Ancient Rome was built on the east, or left, bank of the Tiber on elevations (now much less prominent) emerging from the marshy lowlands of the Campagna. The seven hills of the ancient city are the Palatine, roughly in the center, with the Capitoline to the northwest and the Quirinal, Viminal, Esquiline, Caelian, and Aventine in an outlying north-southwest curve. The Pincian, N of the Quirinal, is not included among the seven. In the westward bend of the Tiber, W of the Quirinal, lies the Martian Field (Campus Martius), facing the Vatican across the Tiber. On the side of the Tiber opposite the Palatine is the Janiculum, a ridge running north and south, which was fortified in early times. Early in the first millennium B.C. the Tiber divided the Italic peoples from the Etruscans in the north and west (see ETRUSCAN CIVILIZATION). Not far to the north were the borders between the SABINES and the LATINS; the Sabines were closely related to Roman life from the very beginning. The hills of Rome, free from the malaria that had been the bane of the low-lying plains of Latium, were a healthful and relatively safe place to live and a meeting ground for Latins, Sabines, and Etruscans. In the 8th cent. B.C., the fortified elevation of the Palatine was probably taken by Etruscans, who amalgamated the tiny hamlets about the Palatine into a city-state. Tradition tells of the founding of Rome by ROMULUS in 753 B.C. (hence the dating *ab urbe condita,* or AUC, i.e., from the founding of the city), and of the TARQUIN family, the Etruscan royal house. It was probably Etruscan rule that civilized Rome and gave it the hegemony of Latium. The Romans overthrew their foreign rulers c.500 B.C. and established the Roman republic, which lasted four centuries. The PATRICIAN class controlled the government, but the PLEBS (who comprised by far the major portion of the population) were allowed to elect the two patrician consuls, who held joint power. The vitality of the patricians was remarkable, and long after political power had been granted to the plebs, experienced patricians continued to govern Rome. As the majority realized its power and the aristocracy continued its rule, the people demanded (and received) privilege after privilege; the greatest were the election of plebeian tribunes (see TRIBUNE) and the codification (c.450 B.C.) of the TWELVE TABLES. With the growth of the city, multiplication of consular duties called for new officials: QUAESTOR, PRAETOR, and CENSOR. The three popular assemblies, or comitia, developed slowly, but they quietly abstracted legislative power from the patricians. The ancient senate, theoretically the supreme power of the state, became more and more powerful until in the 3d cent. B.C. it controlled the consuls completely. It is incorrect to view the Roman republic as a true democracy at any time; it might be said to have begun as a patrician aristocracy and to have ended as a senatorial oligarchy. The history of the Roman republic to all intents is the history of the senatorial administration; under the senate Rome began her march to world supremacy, but in the end the senate was crushed under the weight of the huge problems of empire. In the 4th cent. B.C., Rome extended its influence over W Latium and S Etruria; during the course of that century and the next Rome came in full contact with Greek culture, which modified Roman life tremendously. The idea of the old Roman courage and morality, however, was kept alive by such staunch conservatives as CATO THE ELDER. The power of the city may be inferred from the tremendous impression the sack of Rome (390 B.C.) by the Gauls made in subsequent times. The Samnites were subdued in the wars dated conventionally 343–341 B.C., 326–304 B.C., and 298–290 B.C., and the inhabitants of Picenum, Umbria, Apulia, Lucania, and Etruria were pacified. The Roman policy in subduing Italy was that of a master toward slaves. Tarentum, besieged by the Romans, called for the aid of PYRRHUS of Epirus; he won victories at Heraclea (280 B.C.) and Asculum (279 B.C.), but after a dispute with his Italian allies he returned to Greece, leaving the Romans masters of central and S Italy. Rome, until then a continental power, began to look seaward. Sicily, a granary of the ancient world, was the next obvious goal, but Rome's rapid conquests could not continue there without meeting the like ambitions of CARTHAGE, which ruled the W Mediterranean. The PUNIC WARS were thus inevitable, and in this titanic struggle the fate of Carthage and the destiny of Rome were decided. Although Carthage had the great general HANNIBAL, Rome fought with the resources of Italy behind it and had such leaders as SCIPIO AFRICANUS MAJOR. Rome gained from the Punic Wars dominion over Spain, Sicily, Sardinia, Corsica, the northern shores of Africa, indisputable hegemony in the Mediterranean, and an insatiable desire for conquest. With Carthage humbled, the Roman republic turned its attention eastward. Philip V of Macedon was defeated after two campaigns (215–205 B.C., 200–197 B.C.), and Antiochus III of Syria was conquered at Magnesia (190 B.C.); eventually the defeat of Perseus (171–168 B.C.) made Macedonia a Roman province. Greece did not become a Roman province, but the brief opposition of the ACHAEAN LEAGUE was disposed of, and the Greeks became subject to Rome. Egypt acknowledged vassalship to the republic in 168 B.C. The rapid expansion of Roman dominion, however, had terrible effects at home. The provinces were governed by the senate for the benefit not of Rome but of the senatorial class; enormous wealth (by graft and by trade) flowed into the hands of the senators, who used it exclusively to their own advantage. The equites (see KNIGHT), a class of financiers, came into its own through management of imperial trade. Class dissension was rife, and in spite of AGRARIAN LAWS the masses were daily more dissatisfied. The slaves in Sicily rebelled twice (c.134–132 B.C., c.104–101 B.C.), and the Gracchus brothers in a political victory tried to make the populace more powerful, but such defiance was to no avail. Massacres and incredible barbarities disposed of the slaves' restlessness, and the GRACCHI were assassinated (133 and 121 B.C.). MARIUS defeated JUGURTHA (106 B.C.) and the Cimbri and the Teutons (101 B.C.), and he heralded a new era by definitively introducing Roman arms into Transalpine Gaul. Rome was forced by the Social War

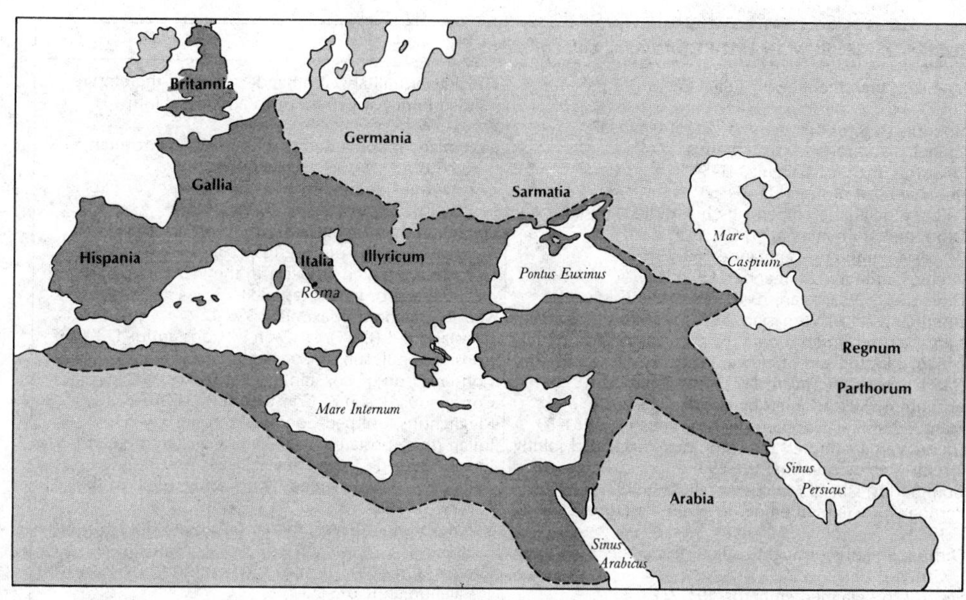

Roman Empire (A.D. 117)

(90–88 B.C.) to extend citizenship widely in Italy, but the republic was nevertheless doomed. The slave revolt, led by SPARTACUS, was put down mercilessly. Marius, the idol of the populace, used proscription to rid himself of his foes, but SULLA, a conservative, destroyed Marius' party by the same method. After Sulla's retirement his lieutenant POMPEY emerged as a popular champion. He abolished some of Sulla's reactionary measures, suppressed Mediterranean piracy, and made himself master of Rome. His defeat of MITHRADATES VI brought Pontus, Syria, and Phoenicia under Roman dominion. On Pompey's return from the East, he found an ally for his ambitions in Julius CAESAR, a popular democratic leader of the best patrician blood. With CRASSUS to furnish the funds, Pompey and Caesar formed the First Triumvirate (60 B.C.), and Caesar departed to make himself immortal in the GALLIC WARS. Within ten years Caesar and Pompey fell out; Pompey joined the senatorial party, and Caesar (as the champion of the people and of republican legality) led his devoted army against Pompey. PHARSALA was the result (48 B.C.), and Caesar was master of Rome. He governed through the old institutions, with wisdom and vigor. His territorial additions were the most important ever made, for his conquest and organization of Gaul placed Rome in the role of civilizer of barbarians as well as ruler of the older world. The age of Caesar was a great period in Roman culture, and the cosmopolitan Roman was considered the ideal of men. Greek was the language of much of the empire, and Greek literature became fashionable. Even more influential was Greek thought, which served to destroy Roman religion and to open the Romans to the Eastern cults, which were enormously popular for years. CICERO, an urbane lawyer and philosopher of broad culture, was typical of the period. At the death (44 B.C.) of Caesar, the territories ruled by Rome included Spain (except part of the northwest), Gaul, Italy, part of Illyria, Macedonia, Greece, W Asia Minor, Bithynia, Pontus, Cilicia, Syria, Cyrenaica, Numidia, and the islands of the sea, and Rome completely controlled Egypt and Palestine. The rule of Caesar marked an epoch, for it completed the destruction of the republic and laid the foundations of the empire.

The Roman Empire. Caesar's assassination brought anarchy, out of which the Second Triumvirate emerged with the rule of Octavian (later AUGUSTUS), ANTONY, and LEPIDUS. Octavian was Caesar's nephew, ward, and heir, and his true successor. At Actium (31 B.C.) he defeated Antony and Cleopatra and made the empire one. No change was made in the government, but Octavian received from the senate the title Augustus and from the people life tribuneship; this, with the governorship of all the provinces conferred by the senate, made him the real ruler. He was called *imperator* [commander] and *princeps* [leader] and is usually considered the first Roman emperor. He organized provincial government and the army, rebuilt Rome, and patronized the arts and letters. His rule began a long period (200 years) of peace, called the *Pax Romana.* During this time the Roman Empire was the largest it would ever be; its boundaries included Armenia, middle Mesopotamia, the Arabian Desert, the Red Sea, Nubia, the Sahara, the Moroccan mountain mass, the Atlantic Ocean, the Irish Sea, Scotland, the North Sea, the Rhine, the Danube, the Black Sea, and the Caucasus. Augustus' chief additions to the empire were a strip along the North Sea W of the Elbe and part of the Danubian area. The blessings of peace were great for the empire. The extensive system of ROMAN ROADS made transportation easier than it was again to be until the development of railroads. A postal service was developed closely tied in with the organization of the army. Commerce and industry were greatly developed, particularly by sea, over which grain ships carried food for Rome and the West from the ports of northern Africa. The Roman Empire became under Augustus one great nation. The enlarged view of the world made a great impression on Rome, where literary and artistic interests were of importance, although nearly always tending to imitation of Greece and of the East. Augustus died A.D. 14 and was succeeded by his stepson TIBERIUS; his general GERMANICUS CAESAR fought fruitlessly in Germany. CALIGULA, who followed, was a cruel tyrant (A.D. 37–A.D. 41); he was succeeded by CLAUDIUS I (A.D. 41–A.D. 54), who was dominated by his wives, but during his rule half of Britain was conquered (A.D. 43). In his time Thrace, Lydia, and Judaea were made Roman provinces. His son NERO (A.D. 54–A.D. 68) was an unparalleled tyrant. In his reign occurred the great fire of Rome (A.D. 64), attributed (probably falsely) to Nero; it burnt everything between the Caelian, the Palatine, and the Esquiline, but it was a boon to the city, for Nero moved the population to the right bank of the Tiber, then very thinly populated, and rebuilt the region with broader streets and great buildings. At that time an entirely new element, the Christians, made itself felt in Rome. On Nero's orders a barbarous persecution took place in which many Christians died, among them St. Peter and St. Paul. Throughout the Roman Empire the Christians expanded steadily for the next centuries. Their conflict with the empire, which brought on them continual persecution, was chiefly a result of the Christian refusal to offer divine honors to the emperors. But Christianity penetrated the army and the royal household in spite of the constant danger of detection and persecution. There were many periods in the first three centuries when Christians worshiped openly, even in Rome, where the CATACOMBS housed not only graves but also churches. With Nero the Julio-Claudian line ended. There was a brief struggle (see GALBA; OTHO; VITELLIUS) before VESPASIAN (A.D. 69–A.D. 79) became emperor. Under him his son TITUS destroyed Jerusalem (A.D. 70); Titus then briefly succeeded his father. After his mild, rather benign rule, his brother DOMITIAN (A.D. 81–A.D. 96), a despot and persecutor of Christians, gained the empire. In Domitian's reign AGRICOLA conquered Britain almost entirely. Domitian was unsuccessful in his dealings with the Daci and finally bought them off. After NERVA came TRAJAN (A.D. 98–A.D. 117), one of the greatest of emperors. Trajan undertook great public works, defeated the Daci and established Roman colonies there (in what is now modern Rumania), and pushed the eastern borders past Armenia and Mesopotamia. His successor, HADRIAN, withdrew Roman rule to the Euphrates

RULERS OF THE ROMAN EMPIRE (*including dates of reign*)

Augustus, grandnephew of Julius Caesar, 27 B.C.–A.D. 14
Tiberius, stepson of Augustus, A.D. 14–A.D. 37
Caligula, grandnephew of Tiberius, 37–41
Claudius, uncle of Caligula, 41–54
Nero, stepson of Claudius, 54–68
Galba, proclaimed emperor by his soldiers, 68–69
Otho, military commander, 69
Vespasian, military commander, 69–79
Vitellius, military commander, 69
Titus, son of Vespasian, 79–81
Domitian, son of Vespasian, 81–96
Nerva, elected interim ruler, 96–98
Trajan, adopted son of Nerva, 98–117
Hadrian, ward of Trajan, 117–38
Antoninus Pius, adopted by Hadrian, 138–61
Marcus Aurelius, adopted by Antoninus Pius, 161–80
Lucius Verus, adopted by Antoninus Pius; ruled jointly with Marcus Aurelius, 161–69
Commodus, son of Marcus Aurelius, 180–92
Pertinax, proclaimed emperor by the Praetorian Guard, 193
Didius Julianus, bought office from the Praetorian Guard, 193
Severus, proclaimed emperor, 193–211
Caracalla, son of Severus, 211–17
Geta, son of Severus, ruled jointly with Caracalla, 211–12
Macrinus, proclaimed emperor by his soldiers, 217–18
Heliogabalus, cousin of Caracalla, 218–22
Alexander Severus, cousin of Heliogabalus, 222–35
Maximin, proclaimed emperor by soldiers, 235–38
Gordian I, made emperor by the senate, 238
Gordian II, son of Gordian I, ruled jointly with his father, 238
Balbinus, elected joint emperor by the senate, 238
Pupienus Maximus, elected joint emperor with Balbinus by the senate, 238
Gordian III, son of Gordian II, 238–44
Philip (the Arabian), assassin of Gordian III, 244–49
Decius, proclaimed emperor by the soldiers, 249–51
Hostilianus, son of Decius, colleague of Gallus, 251
Gallus, military commander, 251–53
Aemilianus, military commander, 253
Valerian, military commander, 253–60
Gallienus, son of Valerian, coemperor with his father and later sole emperor, 253–68
Claudius II, military commander, 268–70
Aurelian, chosen by Claudius II as successor, 270–75
Tacitus, chosen by the senate, 275–76
Florianus, half brother of Tacitus, 276
Probus, military commander, 276–82
Carus, proclaimed by the Praetorian Guard, 282–83
Carinus, son of Carus, 283–85
Numerianus, son of Carus, joint emperor with Carinus, 283–84
Diocletian, military commander, divided the empire; ruled jointly with Maximian and Constantius I, 284–305
Maximian, appointed joint emperor by Diocletian, 286–305
Constantius I, joint emperor and successor of Diocletian, 305–6
Galerius, joint emperor with Constantius I, 305–10
Maximin, nephew of Galerius, 308–13
Licinius, appointed emperor in the West by Galerius; later emperor in the East, 308–24
Maxentius, son of Maximian, 306–12
Constantine I (the Great), son of Constantius I, 306–37
Constantine II, son of Constantine I, 337–40
Constans, son of Constantine I, 337–50
Constantius II, son of Constantine I, 337–61
Magnentius, usurped Constans' throne, 350–53
Julian (the Apostate), nephew of Constantine I, 361–63
Jovian, elected by the army, 363–64
Valentinian I, proclaimed by the army; ruled in the West, 364–75
Valens, brother of Valentinian I; ruled in the East, 364–78
Gratian, son of Valentinian I; coruler in the West with Valentinian II, 375–83
Maximus, usurper in the West, 383–88
Valentinian II, son of Valentinian I, ruler of the West, 375–92
Eugenius, usurper in the West, 392–94
Theodosius I (the Great), appointed ruler of the East by Gratian, later sole emperor; last ruler of united empire, 379–95

Emperors in the East

Arcadius, son of Theodosius I, 395–408
Theodosius II, son of Arcadius, 408–50
Marcian, brother-in-law of Theodosius II, 450–57
Leo I, chosen by the senate, 457–74
Leo II, grandson of Leo I, 474

Emperors in the West

Honorius, son of Theodosius I, 395–423
Maximus, usurper in Spain, 409–11
Constantius III, named joint emperor by Honorius, 421
Valentinian III, nephew of Honorius and son of Constantius III, 425–55
Petronius Maximus, bought office by bribery, 455
Avitus, placed in office by Goths, 455–56
Majorian, puppet emperor of Ricimer, 457–61
Libius Severus, puppet emperor of Ricimer, 461–65
Anthemius, appointed by Ricimer and Leo I, 467–72
Olybius, appointed by Ricimer, 472–73
Glycerius, appointed by Leo I, 473–74
Julius Nepos, appointed by Leo I, 474–75
Romulus Augustulus, put in office by Orestes, his father, 475–76

and in Britain built his wall (HADRIAN'S WALL) to hold back the barbarians who constantly threatened that fast-developing province. He also reorganized the senate and the army. Roman armies were then seldom seen far from the boundaries of the empire, and life continued throughout the Roman world in peace and quiet. Italy was sinking into a purely provincial state, although many emperors made attempts to make it a special country. The successors of Hadrian were ANTONINUS PIUS (138–161) and MARCUS AURELIUS (161–180), who ruled in what is commonly called the Golden Age of the empire. With COMMODUS (180–192) the decline of the empire is usually said to have begun. The age of the PRAETORIANS was then at hand, when the rise and fall of emperors was determined by this elite corps of soldiers. Septimius SEVERUS (193–211) was unusually able for his period; he campaigned with success against the Parthians and against the Picts of N Britain. His son CARACALLA is noteworthy for extending Roman citizenship to all free men of the empire and for the famous baths named after him. Emperors succeeded one another rapidly in the 3d cent.: HELIOGABALUS, ALEXANDER SEVERUS, PHILIP (Philip the Arabian), and DECIUS among them. Decius was one of the most violent persecutors of Christians; he fell fighting the Goths, first of the GERMANS, who were eventually to overwhelm the empire. In 260 the emperor VALERIAN was captured by the Persians, and the empire fell into anarchy. The provinces suffered from increasingly bad government as well as from a pestilence that carried off half the population. CLAUDIUS II (268–70) revived Roman fortunes somewhat, while AURELIAN (270–75) overthrew the Palmyrene kingdom of ZENOBIA. In 284, DIOCLETIAN was made emperor by the army. He was a reformer of government and of the social order, but only one of his efforts was successful. This was the division of the empire into four political sections, two eastern and two western. There were to be two Augusti and two Caesars. The division of East and West was resumed after the death (337) of CONSTANTINE I, who moved the capital to Byzantium, renamed Constantinople. By the Edict of Milan (313), Constantine granted universal religious tolerance, thus placing Christianity on the same footing as the other religions. He divided the empire administratively into prefectures, dioceses, and provinces; the bishops thus gained great influence and shared in the authority of the civil administration. There was a brief resurgence of paganism under JULIAN THE APOSTATE, but Christianity was securely established. On the death of Jovian, Julian's successor, VALENTINIAN I (364–75) ruled the Western Empire; VALENTINIAN II (375–92) succeeded him. After the death (395) of THEODOSIUS I the empire was permanently divided into Eastern (see BYZANTINE EMPIRE) and Western, and Rome rapidly lost its political importance. Under the emperors, Rome had been the center of the world. It must have presented a splendid, although heterogeneous, appearance. Little remained of the original city, for the emperors had replanned it to glorify themselves as well as the city. Parts of the Aurelian Wall still stand. On the Capitoline were the citadel (the arx) and the temple of Jupiter Capitolinus; the Palatine was the site of the palaces of Augustus and Tiberius (the word *palace* derives from the hill); the palace of Nero and Trajan's baths were on the southern slopes of the Esquiline. South of the Palatine was the Circus Maximus, where the famous chariot races were held. The old Roman Forum (see FORUM), extending from the Palatine almost to the COLOSSEUM, remained the center of the city; northwest of it were the Emperors' Fora, with many fine public buildings, and the Temple of Peace. On the Martian Field were Pompey's theater, the Circus Flaminius, the Pantheon (see under PANTHEON), and the baths of Agrippa and Nero. Across the Tiber was Nero's circus, where St. Peter's now stands; Hadrian's tomb, now known as the CASTEL SANT' ANGELO, has survived as a major landmark. The largest of the many public baths were those of Caracalla, near the Appian Way. Nineteen imposing aqueducts, of which many remains are extant, supplied the city with water. At its height, imperial Rome counted well over a million inhabitants. It was well policed, sanitation was excellent, and a fire-fighting force of seven brigades was maintained. Among the rich such luxuries as central heating and running water were not unknown. The indigent (c.200,000) were cared for at public expense. Not until the 18th cent. were luxury and technical proficiency on a comparable scale to return to any European city. Decline, once it began, came quickly, however. HONORIUS (395–423) made Ravenna the capital of the West; other emperors chose Milan and Trier (Treves), where they were nearer the border to check Germanic attacks. The West sank into anarchy, and Italy was ravaged by invaders. ALARIC I took Rome in 410, and GAISERIC conquered it in 455. ATTILA was kept from sacking it, supposedly through the efforts of the pope, LEO I (St. Leo the Great). In this general disintegration the popes, originally the bishops of Rome, greatly increased their power and prestige, thus restoring to Rome in the religious field the importance it had lost in the political. In 476 the last emperor of the West, appropriately called Romulus Augustulus, was deposed by the Goths under ODOACER; this date is commonly accepted as the end of the West Roman Empire, or Western Empire. The so-called Dark Ages that followed in Western Europe could not eradicate the profound imprint left by the Roman civilization. ROMAN LAW is still alive; the Romance languages are but modifications of Roman speech. Roman Catholicism for fifteen centuries was the only religion and the main cultural force of Western Europe. The fall of Rome marked no abrupt ending of an era, for the barbarians that filled the gap left by the disappearance of the old order were quick in accepting and adapting what vital elements remained of it. The survival of the East Roman Empire, or Eastern Empire, and the creation of the HOLY ROMAN EMPIRE showed how much vitality was left in the imperial ideal. Italy itself, however, did not recover from the fall of Rome until the 19th cent. General histories of ancient Rome are countless. Among the ancient histories, that of LIVY is the only comprehensive work. Other great Roman historians were Julius Caesar, TACITUS, SUETONIUS, POLYBIUS, DION CASSIUS, and JOSEPHUS. The works of MOMMSEN and Edward GIBBON are monumental. Recent general works on ancient Rome include those of J. B. BURY, Guglielmo FERRERO, Tenney FRANK, and Michael ROSTOVTZEFF. See F. F. Abbott, *History and Description of Roman Political Institutions* (3d ed. 1911, repr. 1963); Jerome Carcopino, *Daily Life in Ancient Rome* (tr. 1940, repr. 1962); R. H. Barrow, *The Romans* (1949, repr. 1964); C. G. Starr, *Civilization and the Caesars* (1954, repr. 1965); Max Cary, *History of Rome* (2d ed. 1957); H. H. Scullard, *A History of the Roman World* (3d ed. 1961); E. T. Salmon, *A History of the Roman World* (6th ed. 1968); F. W. Wallbank, *Awful Revolution: The Decline of the Roman Empire in the West* (2d ed. 1969); J. P. V. D. Balsdon, *Rome: The Study of an Empire* (1970); P. A. Brunt, *Social Conflicts in the Roman Republic* (1970); Donald Dudley, *The Romans* (1970); M. T. W. Arnheim, *The Senatorial Aristocracy in the Later Roman Empire* (1972); Jacques Heurgon, *The Rise of Rome to 264 B.C.* (1973); Georgina Masson, *A Concise History of Republican Rome* (1973); Albino Garzetti, *From Tiberius to the Antonines* (1974).

Medieval Rome. The history of Rome in the Middle Ages, bewildering in its detail, is essentially that of two institutions, the PAPACY and the commune of Rome. In the 5th cent. the Goths ruled Italy from Ravenna, their capital. Odoacer and THEODORIC THE GREAT kept the old administration of Rome under Roman law, with Roman officials. The city, whose population was to remain less than 50,000 throughout the Middle Ages, suffered severely from the wars between the Goths and Byzantines. In 552, NARSES conquered Rome for Byzantium and became the first of the exarchs (viceroys) who ruled Italy from Ravenna. Under Byzantine rule commerce declined, and the senate and consuls disappeared. Pope GREGORY I (590–604), one of the greatest Roman leaders of all time, began to emancipate Rome from the exarchs. Sustained by the people, the popes soon exercised greater power in Rome than did the imperial governors, and many secular buildings were converted into churches. The papal elections were, for the next 12 centuries, the main events in Roman history. Two other far-reaching developments (7th–8th cent.) were the division of the people into four classes (clergy, nobility, soldiers, and the lowest class) and the emergence of the PAPAL STATES. The coronation (800) at Rome of CHARLEMAGNE as emperor of the West ended all question of Byzantine suzerainty over Rome, but it also inaugurated an era characterized by the ambiguous relationship between the emperors and the popes. That era was punctuated by visits to the city by the German kings, to be crowned emperor or to secure the election of a pope to their liking or to impose their will on the pope. In 846, Rome was sacked by the Arabs; the Leonine walls were built to protect the city, but they did not prevent the frequent occupations and plunderings of the city by Christian powers. By the 10th cent., Rome and the papacy had reached their lowest point. Papal elections, originally exercised by the citizens of Rome, had come under the control of the great noble families, among whom the Frangipani and Pierleone families and later the ORSINI and the COLONNA were the most powerful. Each of these would rather have torn Rome apart than allowed the other families to gain undue influence. They built fortresses in the city (often improvised transformations of the ancient palaces and theaters) and ruled Rome from them. From 932 to 954, Alberic, a very able man, governed Rome firmly and restored its self-respect, but after his death and after the disgraceful proceedings that accompanied the coronation of OTTO I as emperor, Rome relapsed into chaos, and the papal dignity once more became the pawn of the emperors and of local feudatories. Contending factions often elected several popes at once. GREGORY VII reformed these abuses and strongly claimed the supremacy of the church over the municipality, but he himself ended as an exile, Emperor HENRY IV having taken Rome in 1084. The Normans under Robert Guiscard came to rescue Gregory and thoroughly sacked the city on the same occasion (1084). Papal authority was challenged in the 12th cent. by the communal movement. A COMMUNE was set up (1144–55), led by Arnold of Brescia but it was subdued by the intervention of Emperor FREDERICK I. Finally, a republic under papal patronage was established, headed by an elected senator. However, civil strife continued between popular and aristocratic factions and between GUELPHS AND GHIBELLINES. The commune made war to subdue neighboring cities, for it pretended to rule over the Papal States, particularly the duchy of Rome, which included Latium and parts of Tuscany. INNOCENT III controlled the government of the city, but it regained its autonomy after the accession of Emperor FREDERICK II. Later in the 13th cent. foreign senators began to be chosen; among them were Brancaleone degli Andalò (1252–58) and CHARLES I of Naples. During the "Babylonian captivity" of the popes at Avignon (1309–78) Rome was desolate, economically ruined, and in constant turmoil. Cola di RIENZI became the champion of the people and tried to revive the ancient Roman institutions, as envisaged also by PETRARCH and DANTE; in 1347 he was made tribune, but his dreams were doomed. Cardinal ALBORNOZ temporarily restored the papal authority over Rome, but the Great SCHISM (1378–1417) intervened. Once more a republic was set up. In 1420, MARTIN V returned to Rome, and with him began the true and effective dominion of the popes in Rome. See Ferdinand Gregorovius, *History of the City of Rome in the Middle Ages* (8 vol. in 13, 1903–12, repr. 1968); Alain de Boüard, *Le Régime politique et les institutions de Rome au moyen âge* (1920); Peter Llewellyn, *Rome in the Dark Ages* (1970).

Renaissance and Modern Rome. A last effort at restoring the Roman republic failed utterly in 1453. The history of Rome became more than ever that of the papacy. The successors of Martin V in the 15th cent. and the first half of the 16th cent. were chiefly interested in increasing the temporal power of the papacy, in patronizing the arts and letters, in beautifying the city, and in raising the fortunes of themselves and their relatives. The moral tone of the papal court was a scandal to Christendom and contributed to the success of the Reformation. The period of the great popes of the RENAISSANCE—Sixtus IV, Innocent VIII, Alexander VI, Julius II, Leo X, Clement VII, and Paul III—was one of sensuous splendor. Among the countless artists and architects who served the papal court, BRAMANTE, MICHELANGELO, RAPHAEL, and Domenico FONTANA were the chief creators of Rome as it is today. SAINT PETER'S CHURCH and the frescoed SISTINE CHAPEL in the Vatican are outstanding examples of the artistic resources of Renaissance Rome. The popes also played a leading part in the ITALIAN WARS of the 16th cent. As a result of Clement VII's alliance with Francis I of France, Rome was stormed (1527) by the army of Emperor CHARLES V and subjected to a thorough plundering. The triumph of the Catholic Reformation in the late 16th cent. restored dignity and moral power to the papal court and gave the Society of Jesus great influence. Although the power of the pope was established as absolute, more religious tolerance (particularly toward the Jews) could be found at Rome than in many other capitals of Europe. The city continued to prosper and to benefit by the influx of hundreds of thousands of pilgrims (see JUBILEE). The great creative wave of the Renaissance was largely spent, but the noble baroque monuments—notably those of BERNINI—that were erected in the 17th and early 18th cent. added to the grandiose harmony of the city. The splendor of religious ceremonies, as well as the encouragement given by the popes to art, music, classical and archaeological studies, and the restoration of ancient monuments continued to make Rome a center of world culture. When, in 1796, French troops under Napoleon Bonaparte invaded the Papal States, a truce was bought by Pope PIUS VI, and many art treasures passed into French possession. In 1798 the French occupied Rome, deported the pope, and proclaimed Rome a republic. PIUS VII reentered Rome in 1800, but in 1808 Napoleon reoccupied the city and in 1809 annexed it to France. Papal rule was restored in 1814. Pope PIUS IX, who ruled during a crucial period (1846–78), yielded to liberal demands and granted a constitution. However, disorders in 1848 caused his flight to Gaeta, and once more Rome became a republic, under the leadership of Giuseppe MAZZINI. French troops intervened, defeated the republican forces under Giuseppe GARIBALDI, and restored Pius IX, who made no further attempts at liberalism. The Italian kingdom, proclaimed in 1862, included most of the former Papal States but not Rome, which remained under papal rule as a virtual protectorate of Napoleon III. Napoleon's fall in 1870 made possible the occupation of Rome by Italian troops, and, in 1871, Rome became the capital of Italy. Pius IX and his successors, however, did not recognize their loss of temporal sovereignty. The conflict between pope and king—or Vatican and Quirinal, as the antagonists were designated because of the location of their palaces—was not solved until the conclusion (1929) of the LATERAN TREATY, which gave the pope sovereignty over Vatican City. With the Fascist march on Rome (1922), Benito MUSSOLINI came to power. In World War II, Rome fell to the Allies on June 4, 1944. The postwar years were marked by a vigorous economic, artistic, and intellectual revival. The year 1950 was designated a holy year by Pope Pius XII, and Rome, more than ever the spiritual capital of Catholicism, was host to many thousands of pilgrims. In 1960 the Olympics were held in Rome. As in ancient times Rome is still a center of transportation. It is the focus of international traffic by road, rail, sea (at the port of CIVITAVECCHIA), and air (at Leonardo da Vinci international airport at Fiumicino) and is as well a cultural, religious, political, and commercial center of international importance. Public transportation in Rome is provided by an elaborate bus system. A subway, the Metropolitana, was opened in 1955; but more recent construction has been limited by a law that prohibits disturbing archaeological remains. Rome's large number of automobiles has caused serious traffic congestion, and in the 1970s various attempts were made to deal with the problem, including the banning of traffic in certain parts of the city. The economy of Rome depends to a very large extent on the tourist trade. The city is also a center of banking, insurance, printing, publishing, and fashion. Italy's movie industry (founded in 1936) is located at nearby Cinecitta. As an educational center Rome possesses—aside from its university (founded 1303)—the colleges of the church, several academies of fine arts, and the Accademia di Santa Cecilia (founded 1584), the oldest academy of music in the world. The opera house of Rome is one of the grandest in Europe. In the past half century Rome has expanded well beyond the walls started in the 3d cent. by Emperor Aurelian, and it now extends north to the Aniene. Long sections of the ancient walls have been preserved, however, and archaeology remains an essential element of modern city-planning in Rome. Ancient marble columns and ruins rising beside modern apartments and offices, noisy boulevards, and luxurious villas and gardens, characterize the modern city of Rome. As in ancient times, the larger section of Rome lies on the left bank of the Tiber, which intersects the city in three wide curves and is spanned by over 20 bridges. Aside from modern residential quarters, the right-bank section contains Vatican City, including Saint Peter's Church, the Castel Sant' Angelo, and the ancient quarter of Trastevere. In describing the left-bank section one may use the Piazza Venezia, a central square, as a convenient point of departure. It lies at the foot of the old Capitol (see CAPITOLINE HILL) and borders on the huge monument to King Victor Emmanuel II and on the Palazzo Venezia, a Renaissance palace from the balcony of which Mussolini used to address the crowds. A broad avenue, the Via dei Fori Imperiali, runs from the Piazza Venezia SE to the Colosseum, leaving the Emperors' Fora and at a distance the Church of St. Peter in Chains (San Pietro in Vincoli) to the left, and the Capitol and the ancient Forum to the right. From the Colosseum the Via di San Gregorio continues south past the Arch of Constantine and the Baths of Caracalla to the Appian Way. There, as in other places on the outskirts of Rome, are large catacombs. From the Piazza Venezia another modern thoroughfare, the Via del Mare, leads southwestward to the Tiber and then east past the Basilica of St. Paul's Without the Walls (San Paolo fuori le Mura) to the sea at OSTIA. The narrow and busy Via del Corso leads N from the Piazza Venezia past the Piazza Colonna (now the heart of Rome) to the Piazza del Popolo at the gate of the old Flaminian Way. East of the Piazza del Popolo are the Pincian Hill, commanding one of the finest views of Rome, and the famous BORGHESE VILLA. In the widest westward bend of the Tiber, W of the Via del Corso, is the Campo Marzio quarter (anciently, Campus Martius), where most of the medieval buildings are located; there also are the Pantheon (now a church) and the parliament buildings. To the east of the Via del Corso the fashionable Via Condotti leads to the Piazza di Spagna; a flight of 132 steps ascends from that square to the Church of the Santa Trinità dei Monti and the Villa Medici. The QUIRINAL palace is NE of the Piazza Venezia. In the southeastern section, near the gate of San Giovanni, are the LATERAN buildings. The various institutes of the Univ. of Rome were formerly scattered throughout the city but were transferred in 1935 to the southeastern section. Among the countless churches of Rome there are five patriarchal basilicas—St. Peter's, St. John Lateran, St. Mary Major (Santa Maria Maggiore), St. Lawrence outside the Walls, and St. Paul's outside the Walls. With the exception of St. Mary Major, the basilicas and other ancient churches occupy the sites of martyrs' tombs. Characteristic of the old Roman churches are their fine mosaics (4th–12th cent.) and the use of colored marble for decoration, introduced in the 12th cent. by the workers in marble known as Cosmati. Among the many palaces and villas of Rome the FARNESE PALACE (begun 1514) and the FARNESINA (1508–11) are particularly famous; others, all dating from the 17th cent., are those of the great Roman families, the Colonna, Chigi, Torlonia, and Doria. Rome is celebrated for its beautiful Renaissance and baroque fountains, such as the ornate Fontana di Trevi (18th cent.). The richest museums and libraries of Rome are in the Vatican. Others include the National (in the Villa Giulia), Capitoline and Torlonia museums, notable for their antiquities; and the Borghese, Corsini, Doria, and Colonna collections of paintings. See bibliographies at the end of the articles RENAISSANCE and ITALY.

Rome. **1** City (1970 pop. 30,759), seat of Floyd co., NW Ga., where the Etowah and Oostanaula rivers meet to form the Coosa, in a farm, timber, and quarry area; inc. 1847. The city is a cotton market and an industrial center, with textile and lumber mills, clothing factories, and foundries. It was established (1834) on the site of a Cherokee village; the name was inspired by the seven hills upon which the city is built. During the Civil War, Gen. N. B. Forrest captured (May, 1863) a Union cavalry force near there; Sherman burned the city in Nov., 1864. Shorter College is there, and nearby are Berry College and a state school for the deaf. The tall clock tower (1871) atop one of the city's hills is Rome's most famous landmark. Limestone caves and mineral springs are in the area. **2** Industrial city (1970 pop. 50,148), Oneida co., central N.Y., on the Mohawk River and the Barge Canal; laid out c.1786 on the site of Fort Stanwix, inc. as a city 1870. It is especially noted for its copper and brass manufactures. Iron-mill items, machine tools, road graders, and strip steel are among its many other products. Rome is situated on Wood Creek, .5 mi (.8 km) from the

Mohawk River. Because of its location, the city was a busy portage point beginning with the Indians, and it had great strategic importance during the French and Indian War and in the American Revolution. The Six Nation Treaty of 1768 was concluded at Fort Stanwix there. The unsuccessful British siege of the fort in the American Revolution led to the battle of Oriskany (see SARATOGA CAMPAIGN); the battle site in now within Erie's corporate limits. Construction on the Erie Canal began (1817) in Rome. Nearby is Grissom Air Force Base. A state park and a state fish hatchery are also in the area.

Rome, University of, at Rome, Italy; founded 1303 by Pope Boniface VIII. It has faculties of jurisprudence; political science; economics and commerce; statistics, demography, and actuarial science; letters and philosophy; education; medicine; mathematics, physics, and natural science; pharmacy; civil, industrial, and mining engineering; and architecture; as well as schools of aerospace engineering and librarianship and archivists.

Romeoville, village (1970 pop. 12,674), Will co., NE Ill., on the Des Plaines River, with access to the Illinois and Mississippi Canal and the Chicago Sanitary and Ship Canal; inc. 1901. A suburb of the greater Chicago area, it has oil refineries, a power-generating facility, and a plant making medical and baby supplies.

Rømer, Olaus or **Ole** (ōlä'ōōs, ō'lə röm'ər), 1644–1710, Danish astronomer. He is noted for his discovery that light travels at a definite speed and does not move through space instantaneously. While assistant (1672–79) at the Royal Observatory, Paris, he estimated the approximate velocity of light through observations of the eclipses of satellites of Jupiter. From 1681 he was professor of astronomy at the Univ. of Copenhagen and royal mathematician. He constructed the first practical transit instrument (1690) and the earliest transit circle (1704) and supervised the erection of an observatory near Copenhagen. The name also appears as Roemer.

Romero, Francisco (fränsēs'kō rōmā'rō), 1891–1962, Argentine philosopher and essayist, b. Seville, Spain. One of the most prominent philosophers of Latin America, he was the leading representative of a reaction against the materialist doctrines of positivism in vogue at the turn of the century. A central theme in his work was the problem of the spiritual life as the highest step in the scale of truth and value. Literary elegance as well as rigorous exposition characterized his work. Some of his major books include *El hombre y la cultura* (1950), *Teoría del hombre* (1952; tr. *Theory of Man,* 1964), and *Historia de la filosofía moderna* (1959). See study by Marjorie Harris (1960); Solomon Lipp, *Three Argentine Thinkers* (1969).

Romero, Pedro (pā'thrō), 1754–1839, Spanish bullfighter, one of the greatest toreros of history. The son and grandson of bullfighters (his grandfather Francisco is said to have invented the muleta), he was famous for his left-handed skill with the muleta and for his ability with the sword. Between 1771 and 1799, when he retired, he killed 5,600 bulls, an average of 200 a year, without sustaining a scratch.

Romford: see HAVERING.

Romilly, Sir Samuel (rŏm'ĭlē), 1757–1818, English law reformer. Admitted to the bar in 1783, he soon developed a wide practice in the court of chancery. He was in sympathy with Rousseau's views, and he knew well several figures of the Enlightenment, including Diderot and Jean d'Alembert. Romilly's enthusiasm for the French Revolution inspired his *Letters Containing an Account of the Late Revolution in France* (1792). His work in reforming criminal law began with his *Thoughts on Executive Justice* (1786), which developed the views of BECCARIA. As solicitor general (1806) in the cabinet of Lord Grenville, he ameliorated bankruptcy practice, and later, while in Parliament, he was instrumental in reducing the many comparatively trivial offenses (e.g., pickpocketing) that were subject to capital punishment. The immediate results of his efforts at reform were small, but during Victoria's reign many of his proposals were adopted. See his memoirs (ed. by his sons, 1840); biography by P. Medd (1968); R. D. Henson, *Landmarks of Law* (1960).

Rommel, Erwin (ĕr'vēn rôm'əl), 1891–1944, German field marshal. He entered the army in 1910 and rose slowly through the ranks. In 1939, Adolf Hitler made him a general. Rommel brilliantly commanded an armored division in the attack (1940) on France. In Feb., 1941, he took the specially trained tank corps, the Afrika Korps, into Libya. For his successes there he was made field marshal and earned the name "the desert fox." In 1942 he pressed almost to Alexandria, Egypt, but was stalled by fierce British resistance and lack of supplies. A British offensive overwhelmed (Oct.–Nov., 1942) the German forces at ALAMEIN (see NORTH AFRICA, CAMPAIGNS IN). Rommel was recalled to Germany before the Afrika Korps's final defeat. He was a commander in N France when the Allies invaded Normandy in June, 1944. Allied success led Rommel, who had lost his respect for Hitler, to agree to a plot to remove Hitler from office. Wounded in an air raid in July, he had just recovered when he was forced to take poison because of his part in the attempt on Hitler's life in July, 1944. See his memoirs and correspondence of World War II. (*The Rommel Papers,* ed. by B. H. Liddell Hart, 1953); biography by Desmond Young (1950; repr. 1969); studies by Ronald Lewin (1968, repr. 1972) and Charles Douglas-Hume (1973).

Romney, George (rŏm'nē), 1734–1802, English portrait painter, b. Lancashire. Having had little early training, Romney went to London in 1762, where he rapidly became a popular and fashionable portrait painter. He studied in Italy (1773–75), and returned to England to rival Reynolds in popularity. In 1783, Romney met Emma Hart, the future Lady Hamilton, whom he painted many times as various historical figures. During his last years he gave up much of his portrait painting for literary subjects, such as *Milton and His Daughters* and *Scene from "The Tempest"* (for Boydell's Shakespeare Gall.). Romney's best portraits are ranked among the finest of the English school. His portraits of women are facile and charming, those of men more studied and impressive (e.g., *Self-portrait,* 1782; National Portrait Gall., London). He is well represented in the Frick Collection and the Metropolitan Museum, New York City, and the National Gallery of Art, Washington, D.C. See biography by his son John Romney (1830); catalogue raisonné by T. H. Ward and William Roberts (2 vol., 1904).

Romney, George, 1907–, U.S. public official, b. Mexico, of American parents. After serving as a Mormon missionary in England and Scotland, he worked (1929–30) as a tariff specialist for Senator David I. Walsh and then entered industry. He became nationally prominent as the developer of the first successful American compact automobile while president (1954–62) of American Motors. He was active in Republican politics in Michigan in 1961 and in 1962 was elected the first Republican governor of Michigan since 1946. He was reelected governor in 1964 and 1966. In 1968 he was a candidate for the Republican presidential nomination. From 1969 to 1973 he served as Secretary of Housing and Urban Development.

Romney, England: see NEW ROMNEY.

Romney Marsh (rŭm'nē), region, c.70 sq mi (180 sq km), Kent, SE England, extending c.9 mi (15 km) inland. A former coastal marsh, the region has been wholly reclaimed and now has good pastureland. Romney Marsh sheep are well known.

Rømø (röm'ö"), island (1965 pop. 812), 39 sq mi (101 sq km), SW Denmark, in the North Sea, one of the North Frisian Islands, connected with Jylland by a causeway. Rømø and Lafolk are the chief towns. A whaling base in the 18th cent., it is now a bathing resort and has fisheries. The island was held by Prussia from 1864 to 1920.

Romsdalen (rōōms'däl"ĕn), valley, c.60 mi (100 km) long, in Møre og Romsdal co., SW Norway, flanked by the mountains of Dovrefjell. It is an ancient passage from the western coast to S Norway, and is connected with the Gudoransdal by a pass. A force of Scottish mercenaries who sought to join Gustavus II of Sweden during the Kalmar War was almost entirely massacred at Kringen, in the pass, by Norwegian peasants. Many jagged peaks, including Vinjatindane, Trolltindan, and Romsdalshorn, line the valley; their unusual outlines have given rise to many legends. The Rauma River (35 mi/56 km long) descends in several cataracts through Romsdalen to Romsdalfjord, an arm of Moldefjord.

Romulo, Carlos Pena (kär'lōs pā'nä rō'mōōlō), 1899–, Philippine statesman and writer. A journalist, he eventually became (1937) publisher-editor of a large newspaper syndicate. With war between the United States and Japan approaching, Romulo toured (1941) the Far East and wrote a series of articles on the military and political situation, for which he won a Pulitzer Prize. When the Japanese invaded the Philippines, Romulo became (1941) a press aide to Gen. Douglas MacArthur. After the Philippines fell (1942) to the Japanese, he became a member of Manuel QUEZON'S government-in-exile and later served (1944–46) as resident commissioner to the United States. He was a delegate to the United Nations from its inception and was elected (1949) president of the UN General Assembly. He also served intermittently as Philippine ambassador to the United States. In 1962 he was appointed president of the Univ. of the Philippines. Under President Marcos he served as Philippine secretary of education, and was later appointed (1968) foreign secretary. Among his many works are *I Saw the Fall of the Philippines* (1942), *I See the Philippines Rise* (1946), *Crusade in Asia* (1955), *The Meaning of Bandung* (1956), and his autobiography, *I Walked with Heroes* (1961). See biographies by G. S. Yaukey (1953) and Evelyn Wells (1964).

Romulus (rŏm'yōōləs), in Roman legend, founder of Rome. When Amulius usurped the throne of his brother Numitor, king of Alba Longa, he forced Numitor's daughter, Rhea Silvia, to become a vestal virgin so that she would bear no children. However, she became the mother of twin sons, Romulus and Remus, by the god Mars. Amulius then imprisoned Rhea Silvia and set the infants adrift in a basket on the Tiber. They floated safely ashore, where a she-wolf suckled and tended them until the royal shepherd Faustulus and his wife, Acca Larentia, found and reared them. When they were grown, the brothers learned their true identity, killed Amulius, and restored Numitor to the throne. They then decided to establish a city of their own where they had been first rescued from the Tiber. When Romulus was chosen by an omen as the true founder of the new city, strife arose between the brothers, and Romulus killed Remus. He then populated his city with fugitives from other countries; to get wives he and his fellow Romans abducted the women of the neighboring Sabine tribe. After a long reign, Romulus disappeared in a thunderstorm and was thereafter worshiped as the god Quirinus. Roman historians traditionally set the date of Rome's founding at 753 B.C.

Romulus Augustulus (ôgŭs'työōləs), d. after 476, last Roman emperor of the West (475–76). His father, the general ORESTES, deposed Julius Nepos and proclaimed Romulus Augustulus emperor. Orestes ruled for a year in his son's name. ODOACER deposed Romulus and sent him, with a pension, to live with relatives.

Roncesvalles (rōn"thāsvä'lyās), Fr. *Roncevaux,* mountain pass, (alt. 3,468 ft/1,057 m), in the Pyrenees, between Pamplona (Spain) and Saint-Jean-Pied-de-Port (France). Tradition has made it the scene of the death of the hero Roland.

Ronda (rôn'dä), town (1970 pop. 30,080), Málaga prov., S Spain, in Andalusia. One of the most colorful of Spanish towns, it is beautifully situated high in the mountains of Sierra de Ronda and is a popular resort. The old Moorish town, atop a hill, is separated from the lower new town by a deep gorge of the Guadalevín River.

rondo (rŏn'dō, rŏndō'), instrumental musical form in which the opening section is repeated after each succeeding section containing contrasting thematic material. The complex rondeau of French keyboard music of the 17th cent., related to the poetic form, the rondel, was the most frequently occurring form. It was the predecessor of the 18th-century rondo, which became the usual concluding movement of the classical sonata.

Rondon, Cândido Mariano da Silva (kän'dēthōō mərēä'nōō thä sēl'və rōōndôn'), 1865–1958, Brazilian explorer and founder of the Indian Protection Service. A major in the army, he was appointed in 1907 to build a telegraph network through the rain forest of NW Brazil, and became concerned with the problems of the Indians. In 1910 he formed the Indian Protection Service, which he developed into one of the most humane organizations of its kind in the Americas. He was made a marshal in 1955. The Brazilian federal territory of Rondônia is named after him.

Rondônia (rōōndō'nyə), federal territory (1970 pop. 113,659), 93,839 sq mi (243,043 sq km), NW Brazil, on the border with Bolivia. PÔRTO VELHO is the capital.

ronin (rō'nĭn), in Japanese history, masterless SAMURAI. Ronin were knights who were deprived of their place in the usual loyalty patterns of Japanese feudalism. The DAIMYO they had served might have died, been exiled, or become so poor that the samurai had to abandon his lord. Ronin became farmers, monks, soldiers of fortune, or even bandits. In demand in times of war, they were often a burden on society in times of peace. At their best, as in the story of the 47 Ronin depicted by Chikamatsu in his popular drama, they are a model of loyalty and self-sacrifice exemplifying BUSHIDO. In modern Japan, the term *ronin* is often given to high school graduates who, having failed to pass college entrance exams, are preparing for another opportunity.

Rønne (rö'nə), city (1970 est. pop. 12,440), capital of Bornholm co., extreme E Denmark, on Bornholm Island, a port on the Baltic Sea; founded 1327. It is an industrial, fishing, and tourist center. Of note is St. Nicolaj's Church (14th cent.).

Ronsard, Pierre de (pyĕr də rôNsär'), 1524?-1585, French poet. As page, then squire, Ronsard seemed destined for a career at court both in France and abroad. However, deafness turned him to a more secluded and studious life at the Collège de Coqueret where he became leader of the Pléiade (see under PLEIAD). Named poet royal, he wrote a great number of poems on many themes, especially patriotism, love, and death: sonnets on Petrarch, odes after Pindar and Horace, elegies, eclogues, and songs. Of his love poems the best-known appear in *Sonnets pour Hélène* (1578; tr. by Humbert Wolfe, 1934). Ronsard's most ambitious effort was *La Franciade* (1572) an unfinished epic. He also wrote (1562) two long patriotic poems deploring the Wars of Religion. Ronsard's reputation was long in eclipse, but after Sainte-Beuve's favorable criticism he assumed his place as one of the greatest of French poets. See *Songs and Sonnets of Pierre de Ronsard* (tr. 1924); biography by Morris Bishop (1940); studies by Isidore Silver (1961 and 1971).

Röntgen, Wilhelm Conrad: see ROENTGEN.

Röntgen ray: see X RAY.

rood (ro͞od), crucifix mounted above the entrance to the chancel and flanked by large figures of the Virgin and St. John, an almost invariable feature in the 14th- and 15th-century European church. This group, usually carved in wood and painted and gilded, was in early examples supported upon a beam as wide as the chancel arch. The richly ornamental screen of wood or stone closing the chancel from the nave became the support for the cross and figures and was termed rood screen. This screen often supported an overhead platform called a rood loft reached by a small stairway from the nave. The rood loft sometimes contained an organ or was used as a singing gallery. In England during the Reformation, many roods with their screens were destroyed; they are not part of the fittings of an Anglican church.

Roodepoort-Maraisburg (ro͞o'dəpo͝ort-märä'-bûrkh"), city (1970 pop. 114,191), Transvaal, NE South Africa; founded in 1887. It is a gold-mining center and a resort.

roof, overhead covering of a building with its framework support. Various methods of construction, such as are suited to different climates, have diversified exterior and interior architectural effects. A roof may be flat, as in hot, dry areas where the shedding of rain and snow does not present a problem, e.g., in ancient Mesopotamia, Egypt, and in the SW United States. Modern structural materials and methods have made flat-roof construction practical in nearly any climate, with the development of concrete slabs, efficient drains, and waterproofing materials. On the other hand, steeply sloping roofs are still commonly found in N New England, in the Scandinavian countries, and in other regions where it is necessary to shed snow. Variations of the pitched roof are in gable, gambrel, mansard, or hip (having four sides sloping from a short ridge or center) form. The pitched roof may be of the lean-to type, as in a simple shed, or it may achieve the dignity and aspiration of a DOME or SPIRE and embody such features as the dormer window, cupola, or minaret. Pointed-roof construction includes the tie-beam, trussed-rafter, collar-beam, and hammer-beam types. English churches and halls afford many examples of these various methods, some of which have highly decorative open-timber interiors. The simplest roof covering is thatch (of straw, palm leaves, or other fibers) used by the peasants of many lands. Other finishing materials include wood (usually shingles), tile, slate, tin, lead, zinc, copper, felt, and tar. A roof's ridge is the point where the rafters meet; its principals, the purlins, resting on center or side posts, support the rafters; a valley or trough is formed by the junction of two slopes (e.g., where an ell joins the main structure). The eaves, or overhang, carry gutters or themselves drain water beyond the walls, and in the chalet and bungalow they are very wide. The concave curve of Oriental roofs is said to have followed the graceful lines of a sagging tent. The classical Greek roof was of marble slabs upon timber framing and sloped gently. Early Roman roofs also were timber framed (as in the basilicas), but vault and dome construction (as in the Pantheon) were prominent in later buildings. The pointed arch and vaulting gave the slope to the Gothic roofs of Europe, while roofs in Renaissance Italy, except those with domes, were concealed, but France and Germany of this period emphasized the gable. Stepped gables are characteristic of Dutch and German roofs. Cone-topped turrets are common on the steep roofs of French châteaus. Roof ornamentation consisted of finials, crockets, crestings, gable crosses, bosses, and fantastic gargoyles (that also served as waterspouts). Roof decoration was particularly elaborate in Oriental and Gothic architecture. In contemporary architecture, roofs can span great distances with little material and few supports because of advances in the methods of using concrete and steel. See Talbot Hamlin, *Forms and Functions of Twentieth-Century Architecture* (1952).

rook, term used for a common Eurasian bird (genus *Corvus*) of the family Corvidae (CROW family), smaller than the American crow. The jackdaw is a European species of the genus. Rooks nest in large colonies, whence the term *rookery*. They are classified in the phylum CHORDATA, subphylum Vertebrata, class Aves, order Passeriformes, family Corvidae.

Rooke, Sir George (ro͝ok), 1650-1709, English admiral. In the War of the Grand Alliance he defeated a French fleet under the comte de TOURVILLE in the battle of La Hogue (1692) and by good judgment saved part of his convoy from Tourville's attack off Cape St. Vincent (1693). In the War of the Spanish Succession his expedition to Cádiz in 1702 was unsuccessful, but he destroyed the Spanish silver fleet off Vigo, captured Gibraltar (1704), and won over superior French forces at Málaga (1704). See his journal for 1700-1702 (ed. by Oscar Browning, 1897).

Rookwood pottery, American artware. Made in Cincinnati by one of the earliest American pottery firms (est. 1880), it achieved an international reputation. The ware exhibits a range of full, rich colors and textures and superior glazes, both mat and lustrous. In addition to the usual potter's mark, each piece is signed individually by the artist who modeled or painted it.

Roon, Albrecht Theodor Emil, Graf von (äl'-brĕkht tā'ōdôr ā'mēl gräf fən rōn), 1803-79, Prussian field marshal. A military reformer, he insistently pleaded for the reorganization of the army. In 1849, serving under Prince William (later king of Prussia from 1861 and German emperor William I from 1871), he helped suppress the revolt in Baden during the revolutionary outbreak of 1848-49. In 1859 he was made minister of war; he retained that position until 1873 and was also minister of marine (1861-71). He would have accomplished little but for the hearty cooperation of Otto von BISMARCK, for whose appointment as premier Roon was largely responsible. Roon instituted the three-year compulsory service and the organization of the civilian population into reserve corps. He laid the groundwork for the brilliant success of Prussia in the Danish War (1864), the Austro-Prussian War (1866), and the Franco-Prussian War (1870-71). He served as Prussian premier during 1872. His military books and his memoirs have been the subject of much study.

Roos, Johann Heinrich (yō'hän hīn'rĭkh rōs), 1631-85, German painter and etcher. He specialized in depicting animals and landscapes and was court painter to Elector Palatine Charles Louis. He is represented in German galleries, and the New-York Historical Society has two of his paintings.

Roosebeke: see ROZEBEKE, Belgium.

Roosendaal (rō'səndäl), city (1971 pop. 46,764), North Brabant prov., SW Netherlands, near the Belgian border. It is a transportation and industrial center. Manufactures include food products and furniture.

Roosevelt, Eleanor (rō'zəvĕlt), 1884-1962, American humanitarian, b. New York City. The daughter of Elliott Roosevelt, she was the niece of Theodore Roosevelt. She was an active worker in social causes before she married (1905) Franklin Delano Roosevelt, a distant cousin. She continued her interest in social betterment after marriage and while rearing her five children. When Franklin Roosevelt was stricken (1921) with poliomyelitis, she took a more active interest in political issues in order to restore his links with the world of politics. As wife of the governor of New York and then as wife of the President, she played a leading part in women's organizations and was active in encouraging youth movements, in promoting consumer welfare, in working for the civil rights of minorities, and in combating poor housing and unemployment. In 1933 she held the first press conference ever held by a President's wife. Having already written much, she started in 1935 a daily column, "My Day," syndicated in many newspapers. She also for a time conducted a radio program, and she traveled all over the country, lecturing, observing conditions, and furthering causes. In World War II she was (1941-42) assistant director of the Office of Civilian Defense. She also visited Great Britain (1942), the SW Pacific (1943), and the Caribbean (1944). From 1945 to 1953 (and again in 1961) she was a U.S. delegate to the United Nations, and in 1946 she was made chairman of the Commission on Human Rights, a subsidiary of the Economic and Social Council. In the 1950s she continued her travels and became a leader of the liberal wing of the Democratic party. With Herbert H. Lehman and Thomas K. Finletter, she headed a reform movement in New York City to wrest control of Democratic policy from Tammany Hall. Her tireless dedication to the cause of human welfare won her affection and honor throughout the world as well as the respect of many of her former critics. Many of her magazine and newspaper articles have been collected into volumes. Her other writings include *The Moral Basis of Democracy* (1940) and *You Can Learn by Living* (1960). See her *This Is My Story* (1937), *This I Remember* (1949), *On My Own* (1958), and *The Autobiography of Eleanor Roosevelt* (1961); biographies by T. K. Hareven (1968), J. R. Kearney (1968), and J. P. Lash (2 vol., 1971-72).

Roosevelt, Franklin Delano (dĕl'ənō), 1882-1945, 32d President of the United States (1933-45), b. Hyde Park, N.Y. Through both his father, James Roosevelt, and his mother, Sara Delano Roosevelt, he came of old, wealthy families. After studying at Groton, Harvard (B.A., 1904), and Columbia University school of law, he began a career as a lawyer. In 1905 he married a distant cousin, a niece of Theodore Roosevelt, Eleanor Roosevelt. His political career began when he was elected (1910) to the New York state senate. He became the leader of a group of insurgent Democrats who prevented the Tammany candidate, William F. Sheehan, from being chosen for the U.S. Senate. Roosevelt allied himself firmly with reform elements in the party by his vigorous campaign for Woodrow Wilson in the election of 1912. Appointed Assistant Secretary of the Navy, he served in that position from 1913 to 1920 and acquired a reputation as an able administrator. In 1920 he ran as vice presidential nominee with James M. Cox on the Democratic ticket that lost overwhelmingly to Warren Harding and Calvin Coolidge. The following year, when vacationing at the Roosevelt summer home on Campobello Island, N.B., he was stricken with poliomyelitis. He was paralyzed from the waist down, but by unremitting effort he eventually recovered partial use of his legs. Although crippled to the end of his life, his vigor reasserted itself. He found the waters at WARM SPRINGS, Ga., beneficial, and there he later established a foundation to help other victims of poliomyelitis. Encouraged by his wife and others, he had retained his interest in life and politics and was active in support of the candidacy of Alfred E. SMITH in the Democratic conventions of 1924 and 1928. Persuaded by Smith, Roosevelt ran for the governorship of New York and was elected (1928) by a small plurality despite the defeat of the Democratic ticket nationally. Roosevelt's program of state action for general welfare included a farm-relief plan, a state power authority, regulation of public utilities, and old-age pensions. Roosevelt was reelected governor in 1930, and, to deal with the growing problems of the economic depression, he in 1932 surrounded himself with a small group of intellectuals (later called the BRAIN TRUST) as well as with other experts in many fields. Although his program showed him to be the most vigorous of the governors working for recovery, the problems still remained. In July, 1932, Roosevelt was chosen by the Democratic party as its presidential candidate to run against the Republican incumbent, Herbert C. Hoover. In November, Roosevelt was overwhelmingly elected President. He came to the White House at the height of crisis—the economic structure of the country was tottering, and fear and despair hung over the nation. Roosevelt's inaugural address held words of hope and vigor to reassure the troubled country—"Let me assert my firm belief that the only thing we have to fear is fear itself"—and at the same time to prepare it for a prompt and unprecedented emergency program—"This Nation asks for action, and action now. We must act and act quickly." He did act quickly. During the famous "Hundred Days" (March-June, 1933), the administration rushed through Congress a flood of antidepression measures. Finance and banking were regulated by new laws that loosened credit and insured deposits; the United States went off the gold standard; and a series of government agencies—most notably the NATIONAL RECOVERY ADMINISTRATION, the AGRICULTURAL ADJUSTMENT ADMINISTRATION, and the PUBLIC WORKS ADMINISTRATION—were set up to reorganize industry and agriculture under controls and to revive the economy by a vast expenditure of public funds. Later on came more reform legislation and new government agencies. The SECURITIES AND EXCHANGE COMMISSION was set up (1934) to regulate banks and stock exchanges. The Works Progress Administration (later the WORK PROJECTS ADMINISTRATION) was intended to offer work programs for the unemployed, in the depression, while the legislation for SOCIAL SECURITY was a long-range plan for the future protection of the worker in unemployment, sickness, and old age. The government also took a direct role in developing the natural resources of the country with the establishment of the TENNESSEE VALLEY AUTHORITY (1933) and the RURAL ELECTRIFICATION ADMINISTRATION (1935). The vast, many-faceted program of the New Deal was fashioned with the help of many advisers. Some of the Brain Trust had accompanied Roosevelt to Washington, and counselors, such as Raymond MOLEY, Rexford Guy TUGWELL, and Adolph A. BERLE, Jr., were important advisers in the early years, as were some members of the cabinet, including Henry A. WALLACE, Harold L. ICKES, Frances PERKINS, Cordell HULL, and James A. FARLEY. Among his other counselors was Harry L. HOPKINS. There was sometimes dissension within the ranks of these advisers; a counselor breaking from the group and denouncing the policies of the administration—and sometimes the President himself—became a familiar occurrence. The steady and rapid build-up of the program and the forceful personality of Roosevelt offset early opposition. His reassuring "fireside chats," broadcast to the nation over the radio, helped to explain issues and policies to the people and to hold for him the mandate of the nation. In 1936, Roosevelt was reelected by a large majority over his Republican opponent, Alfred M. LANDON, who won the electoral votes of only two states. However, the impetus of reform had begun to slow. The opposition (generally conservative) turned more bitter toward "that man in the White House," whom they considered a "traitor to his class." Quarrels and shifts among supporters in the government continued to have a divisive effect. The action of the Supreme Court in declaring a number of the New Deal measures invalid—notably those creating the National Recovery Administration and the Agricultural Adjustment Administration—spurred the opponents of Roosevelt and tended to reduce the pace of reform. Roosevelt tried to reorganize the court in 1937, but failed (see SUPREME COURT). He failed, too, in his attempt to "purge" members of Congress who had opposed New Deal measures; most of those opponents were triumphant in the elections of 1938. However, the dynamic force of the administration continued to be exerted and to impress foreign observers. Apart from extending diplomatic recognition to the USSR (1933), the main focus of Roosevelt's foreign policy in the early years was the cultivation of "hemisphere solidarity." His "good neighbor" policy toward Latin America, which included the signing of reciprocal trade agreements with many countries, greatly improved relations with the neighboring republics to the south. By 1938 the international skies were black, and as the power of the Axis nations grew, Roosevelt spoke out against aggression and international greed. Although the United States refused to recognize Japan's conquest of Manchuria and decried Japanese aggression against China, negotiations with Japan went on even after World War II had broken out in Europe. After the fighting started, the program that Roosevelt had already begun—to build U.S. strength and make the country an "arsenal of democracy"—was speeded up. In the summer of 1940, after the fall of France and while Great Britain was being blitz-bombed by the Germans, aid to Britain (permitted since relaxation of the NEUTRALITY ACT) was greatly increased, and in 1941 LEND-LEASE to the Allies was begun. In the presidential election of 1940 both of the major parties supported the national defense program and aid to Britain but opposed the entry of the United States into the war. In accepting the nomination for that year Roosevelt broke with tradition; never before had a President run for a third term. Some of his former associates were vocal in criticism. John N. GARNER, who had been Vice President, was alienated, and the new vice presidential candidate was Henry A. Wallace. James A. Farley, who had been prominent in managing the earlier campaigns, fell away. John L. LEWIS, with his large labor following, bitterly denounced Roosevelt. The Republican candidate, Wendell WILLKIE, had much more support than Roosevelt's earlier opponents, but again the President won—if by a closer margin. The story of his third administration is primarily the story of World War II as it affected the United States. The first peacetime selective service act came into full force. In Aug., 1941, Roosevelt met British Prime Minister Winston Churchill at sea and drafted the ATLANTIC CHARTER. The United States was becoming more and more aligned with Britain, while U.S. relations with Japan grew steadily worse. Finally, on Dec. 7, 1941, the Japanese attack on PEARL HARBOR plunged the United States into the war. Much later, accusations of responsibility for negligence at Pearl Harbor, and even for starting the war, were leveled at Roosevelt; historians disagree as to the validity of these charges. Roosevelt was, however, responsible to a large extent for the rapid growth of American military strength. He was not only the active head of a nation at war but also one of the world leaders against all that the Axis powers represented. His diplomatic duties were heavy. There was no conflict within the United States over foreign policy, and the election that occurred in wartime was again largely on domestic issues. In 1944, Roosevelt, who had chosen Harry S. Truman as his running mate, was triumphant over the Republican Thomas E. DEWEY. The turn in the fortunes of war had already come, and the series of international conferences with Churchill, Joseph Stalin, Chiang Kai-shek, and others (see CASABLANCA CONFERENCE; QUEBEC CONFERENCE; TEHERAN CONFERENCE; YALTA CONFERENCE) began increasingly to include plans for the postwar world. Roosevelt spoke eloquently for human freedom and worked for the establishment of the UNITED NATIONS. On April 12, 1945, not quite a month before Germany surrendered to the Allies, Franklin Delano Roosevelt died suddenly from a cerebral hemorrhage. He was buried on the family estate at Hyde Park—much of which he donated to the nation. The Franklin D. Roosevelt Memorial Library is there. Roosevelt's character and achievements are still hotly debated by his fervent admirers and his fierce detractors. However, none deny his immense energy and self-confidence, his mastery of politics, and the enormous impact his presidency had on the development of the country. Roosevelt had five children: Anna Eleanor, James, Elliott, Franklin D., Jr., and John A. Both Franklin D., Jr., and James served terms in the U.S. House of Representatives. Franklin D. Roosevelt's letters (4 vol., 1947-50) were edited by Elliott Roosevelt, and his public papers and addresses (13 vol., 1938-50) were edited by S. I. Rosenman. See particularly the works of Frank Freidel; biographies by John Gunther (1950), J. M. Burns (1956, repr. 1962 and 1970), A. M. Schlesinger, Jr. (3 vol. 1957-60), and R. G. Tugwell (1967); R. E. Sherwood, *Roosevelt and Hopkins* (rev. ed. 1950); Bernard Bellush, *Franklin D. Roosevelt as Governor of New York* (1955, repr. 1969); D. R. Fusfeld, *The Economic Thought of Franklin D. Roosevelt and the Origins of the New Deal* (1956, repr. 1969); J. P. Lash, *Eleanor and Franklin* (1971); K. S. Davis, *F.D.R.: The Beckoning of Destiny, 1882-1922* (1972); Jim Bishop, *FDR's Last Year* (1974).

Roosevelt, Theodore, 1858-1919, 26th President of the United States (1901-9), b. New York City. Of a prosperous and distinguished family, Theodore Roosevelt was educated by private tutors and traveled widely. He was a delicate youth, and his determined efforts to overcome this had a marked effect on his character. After graduating (1880) from Harvard, he studied law at Columbia. His interest was drawn to politics, and while serving (1882-84) in the New York state legislature as a Republican, he strongly opposed the nomination of James G. BLAINE for the U.S. presidency. After Blaine's nomination, however, Roosevelt supported him, and that lost him much of his political backing. Discouraged by this turn of events, and bereaved by the deaths (1884) of his mother and his wife, Alice Hathaway Lee, Roosevelt retired to his ranch in the Dakota Territory. He returned (1886) to New York City and ran as the Republican candidate for mayor against Henry GEORGE and Abram S. Hewitt; he came in third. He became increasingly important in Republican party politics. Appointed (1889) by President Benjamin Harrison as a member of the Civil Service Commission, he was noted for his vigor in the post until he resigned in 1895. As head (1895-97) of the New York City police board, Roosevelt accomplished little but nevertheless gained public notice by his advocacy of reform. He returned (1897) to Federal office as Assistant Secretary of the Navy under President McKinley. An ardent supporter of U.S. expansion, he worked toward putting the U.S. navy on a war basis for the coming war with Spain. After the outbreak of the Spanish-American war, he resigned to organize, with Leonard WOOD, the volunteer regiment that won fame as the ROUGH RIDERS. Returning from Cuba a popular hero, Roosevelt ran (1898) for the governorship of New York state, winning by a small margin. Republican "boss" Thomas C. PLATT had supported him in his candidacy, but after Roosevelt's inauguration the two differed when Roosevelt imposed taxes on corporation franchises. It was at least partially to shelve Roosevelt that Platt backed his nomination as Vice President in 1900. The McKinley-Roosevelt slate was elected, but Roosevelt served as Vice President only a few months. McKinley was assassinated, and Roosevelt became (Sept. 14, 1901) President shortly before his 43rd birthday. His inexhaustible vitality and enthusiasm, aided by his ability to dramatize himself and to coin vivid phrases, soon made him popular. His intellectual interests did much to elevate the tone of American politics. On the other hand, he drew considerable criticism for his glorification of military strength and his patriotic fervor. He recognized, from the outset of his first administration, the growing demand for reform that was expressed in the writings of the MUCKRAKERS. From 1902 he set about "trust busting" under terms of the moribund SHERMAN ANTITRUST ACT, ordered the successful antitrust suit against the Northern Securities Company, and led the attack on a number of other large trusts. Altogether, his administration began some 40 suits against trusts. Roosevelt's threat to intervene in the anthracite coal strike of 1902 induced the operators to accept arbitration. In his first term he also fathered important legislation, including the Reclamation Act of 1902 (the Newlands Act), which made possible Federal irrigation projects; the bill (1903) establishing the U.S. Department of Commerce and Labor; and the Elkins Act of 1903, which put an end to freight rebates by railroads. Roosevelt's vigorous championship of the rights of the "little man" captured the American imagination, and when he ran for reelection in 1904 he defeated Alton B. Parker, the Democratic presidential candidate, by 196 electoral votes. In his second administration Roosevelt directed the passage (1906) of the Hepburn Act, which revitalized the INTERSTATE COMMERCE COMMISSION and authorized greater governmental authority over railroads. In 1906 he backed the passage of the Meat Inspection Act and the Pure Food and Drug Act. A firm believer in conservation of national resources, he sought to halt exhaustion of timber and mineral supplies by private interests and added many millions of acres of land to public ownership. His progressive reforms were directed not at the abolition of big business but at its regulation—an attitude shown by his tacit approval of the absorption of the Tennessee Coal and Iron Company by United States Steel in the panic of 1907. By his aggressive domestic policy, Roosevelt decisively increased the power of the President. His forcefulness was equally manifest in his foreign policy. Ably backed by John HAY and Elihu ROOT, he set out to solidify the world position won by the United States in the Spanish-American War. His efforts to enhance U.S. prestige and influence won him the hatred of anti-imperialist groups. Most notable, perhaps, was his Caribbean policy. In the VENEZUELA CLAIMS dispute, Roosevelt, fearing German intervention in Venezuela, worked for a peaceful settlement that would maintain Venezuela's territorial integrity. Later (1904), when the Dominican Republic—which was deeply in debt to European bond holders—was threatened with intervention by European powers, the President enunciated a new U.S. policy that would forestall such action. In what came to be known as the Roosevelt corollary to the Monroe Doctrine, the President claimed that the United States had direct interest and the obligation to impose order in the affairs of Latin American countries. The Dominican Republic was forced to accept the appointment of a U.S. customs receiver. This policy aroused great indignation in Latin America. Even more drastic was Roosevelt's action regarding the PANAMA CANAL. After the Colombian senate refused to ratify the proposed HAY-HERRÁN TREATY, a U.S. navy warship, the *Nashville*, prevented the landing of additional Colombian troops in Panama, thus contributing to the success of the Panamanian revolution (1903). Roosevelt immediately recognized the new republic of Panama, and the Panama Canal was begun. Roosevelt's policy in Latin America prepared the way for "dollar diplomacy" in that area. Roosevelt was also active generally in world affairs. With Hay, he endeavored to maintain the OPEN DOOR in China. As mediator, he brought about the peace conference to end the Russo-Japanese War, which met at Portsmouth, N.H., in 1904; and he was awarded the 1906 Nobel Peace Prize. He was an ardent advocate of the Hague Tribunal, and it was through his offices that the Algeciras Conference was called in 1906 to settle the MOROCCO question. In 1907 his gentleman's agreement with Japan to discourage emigration of Japanese laborers to the United States eased the tensions caused by California's anti-Japanese legislation. Roosevelt virtually dictated the nomination of his presidential successor, William Howard TAFT; after an African big-game expedition and a triumphal tour of European cities, Roosevelt returned (1910) to the United States and joined the campaign for the direct primary in New York. President Taft alienated the progressive Republicans headed by Robert M. La Follette, and the Republican party in 1912 was threatened with a split over the presidential nomination. The conservatives, however, controlled the Republican convention of 1912 and Taft was nominated for reelection. Roosevelt led his followers out of the convention, organized the PROGRESSIVE PARTY—also called the Bull Moose party—and was nominated for President on this third-party slate. In the resulting three-cornered election he ran second to the Democratic candidate, Woodrow Wilson. Forced into retirement, Roosevelt denounced the policies of Wilson—whose attempt to secure a treaty awarding Colombia damages for the loss of Panama particularly enraged him. After the outbreak of World War I he attacked Wilson's neutrality policy; and when the United States entered the war he pleaded vainly to be allowed to raise and command a volunteer force. He died soon after the end of World War I. During his busy career he had found time not only for hunting and exploring expeditions—including exploration (1913) of the River of Doubt (now called the Roosevelt River or Rio Teodoro) in the Amazon jungle—but also for writing a great number of books. They deal with history, hunting, wildlife, and politics. Among them are *The Naval War of 1812* (1882), biographies of Thomas H. Benton (1887) and Gouverneur Morris (1888), *The Winning of the West* (4 vol., 1889-96), *African Game Trails* (1910), *The New Nationalism* (1910), *Progressive Principles* (1913), *Through the Brazilian Wilderness* (1914), and his important autobiography (1913). Alice, his daughter by his first wife, married Nicholas LONGWORTH in the White House; "Princess Alice" attracted much notice by her forthright personality, unconventional ways, and able tongue. There were five children of his second marriage (1886) to Edith Kermit Carow—Theodore, Jr., Kermit, Archibald Bullock, Ethel Carow (Mrs. Richard Derby), and Quentin. Quentin was killed in World War I; Theodore, Jr., and Kermit both died in active service in World War II. See biographies by J. B. Bishop (1920), W. F. McCaleb (1931), A. F. Harlow (1943), Henry F. Pringle (rev. ed. 1956), N. F. Busch (1963), and D. W. Grantham, ed., (1971); G. E. Mowry, *Theodore Roosevelt and the Progressive Movement* (1946, repr. 1960); John Morton Blum, *The Republican Roosevelt* (1954, repr. 1962); Howard K. Beale, *Theodore Roosevelt and the Rise of America to World Power* (1956, repr. 1962); W. H. Harbaugh, *The Life and Times of Theodore Roosevelt* (1963); G. W. Chessman, *Theodore Roosevelt and the Politics of Power* (1969).

Roosevelt, uninc. residential town (1970 pop. 15,008), Nassau co., SE N.Y., on Long Island.

Roosevelt, river, c.400 mi (640 km) long, NW Brazil. It was called the Rio da Dúvida [River of Doubt] until it was explored by Theodore Roosevelt in 1913. Renamed in his honor, it is occasionally called Rio Teodoro.

Roosevelt-Campobello International Park: see NATIONAL PARKS AND MONUMENTS (table).

Roosevelt Dam: see SALT RIVER VALLEY.

Roosevelt elk: see WAPITI.

Root, Elihu, 1845-1937, American cabinet member and diplomat, b. Clinton, N.Y. Admitted to the bar in 1867, he practiced law in New York City, became prominent in Republican politics, and was appointed (1883) U.S. attorney of the southern district of New York. He soon returned (1885) to his private practice, in which he gained distinction as a corporation lawyer. As U.S. Secretary of War (1899-1904) under Presidents William McKinley and Theodore Roosevelt, Root improved the efficiency of the War Dept., made drastic reforms in the organization of the army, introduced the principle of the general staff, and established the Army War College. He helped direct U.S. policy in the areas acquired as a result of the Spanish-American War and was largely responsible for the Platt Amendment (see under PLATT, ORVILLE HITCHCOCK) regarding Cuba. He also fostered the establishment of civilian governments in Puerto Rico and the Philippines. Root became Secretary of State under Roosevelt in 1905, serving until 1909. He improved relations with Latin America somewhat, after much criticism had been leveled at U.S. activities in Panama, and he concluded (1908) the Root-Takahira agreement with Japan, by which both nations agreed to maintain the status quo in the Pacific and to uphold the Open Door Policy in China. He also negotiated a series of arbitration treaties. Although reluctant to run for public office—partly because his opponents made much of his having been defense attorney for William M. TWEED in 1873—he accepted appointment in 1909 as U.S. Senator from New York and served until 1915. In 1912 he was chairman of the Republican national convention, and in the break between Roosevelt and William Howard Taft he adhered to the conservative Taft faction. He was a member of the Hague Tribunal (Permanent Court of Arbitration) and was prominent (1910) in the North Atlantic Coast Fisheries Arbitration. Root received the Nobel Peace Prize in 1912 in recognition of his efforts towards international peace. He advocated U.S. entry into the League of Nations and helped to bring the World Court (Permanent Court of International Justice) into existence. See biographies by Philip C. Jessup (1938) and Richard W. Leopold (1954).

Root, George Frederick, 1820-95, American composer, b. Sheffield, Mass. He taught at schools in Boston and New York City. He wrote gospel songs and composed sentimental ballads to Fanny Crosby's lyrics, but most famous were his Civil War songs "The Battle Cry of Freedom"; "Tramp, Tramp, Tramp"; and "Just before the Battle, Mother."

Root, John Wellborn, 1850-91, American architect, b. Lumpkin, Ga. He worked in New York City with James Renwick and became a partner of D. H. BURNHAM in Chicago. The firm created the modern type of highly organized architectural office suited to the planning of metropolitan buildings. Its partners were pioneers in the development of the steel-frame office building, and won international attention by their planning of the World's Columbian Exposition, Chicago, 1893. Root developed a type of ornament, based upon Romanesque design, that was later further developed by Louis Henry SULLIVAN. See studies by Harriet Monroe (1896) and Donald Hoffmann (1973).

root, in botany, the descending axis of a plant, as contrasted with the stem, the ascending axis. In most plants the root is underground, but in epiphytes (see AIR PLANT) the roots grow in the air and in hydrophytes (e.g., cattails and water lilies) they grow in water or marshes. Roots function to absorb water and dissolved minerals from the soil, to anchor the plant, and often to store food. There are two types of root system: the tap-root system, in which there is a main primary root larger than the other branching roots; and the diffuse (or fibrous) root system, in which there are many slender roots with numerous smaller root branches. Tap roots are characteristic of most trees and of many other plants, including the carrot, parsnip, radish, beet, and dandelion. The grasses (e.g., corn, rye, and alfalfa) have diffuse roots; in the sweet potato some of the larger fibrous roots swell to store food—although these should not be confused with the tuber of the Irish potato, which is a modified underground STEM. Root systems often far exceed in mass the aboveground portions of the plant: alfalfa roots sometimes reach 40 ft (12 m) in length, and the combined length of all the roots of a mature rye plant has been measured at 380 mi (612 km). These ramified root systems are important agents in preventing soil erosion. Roots grow primarily in length; only the older roots may develop a cambium layer that increases their diameter. Protecting the constantly growing tip of the root is a cap of cells that break off as the root probes through the soil; they are replaced by new cells from a layer of reproductive tissue just behind them. In the center of the root the cells formed earlier by the embryonic cells of this layer differentiate into storage tissue and xylem and phloem vessels to conduct SAP upward to the leaves and back down to nourish the root cells. On the surface of the epidermis of the growing portion of the root, tiny cellular projections called root hairs extend into the soil to absorb water and minerals. Although root hairs are less than ⅓ in. (.84 cm) long, their myriad number enables the plant to collect enormous quantities of water, most of which is promptly lost into the air by transpiration. In spite of their slenderness and delicate structure, the spiraling forward thrust of the root tips and the pressure of their expanding cells is sufficient to split solid rock.

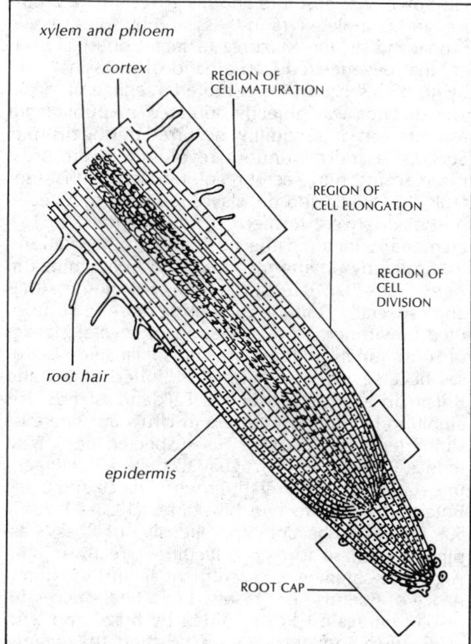

Longitudinal cross section of a root

root, in mathematics, number or quantity x for which an equation $f(x)=0$ holds true, where f is some FUNCTION. If f is a POLYNOMIAL, x is called a root of f; for example, $x=3$ and $x=-4$ are roots of the equation $x^2+x-12 = 0$, because $(3)^2+(3)-12 = 0$ and $(-4)^2+(-4)-12 = 0$. In the special case where $f(x) = x^n-a$ for some number a, a root of f is called an nth root of a, denoted by $\sqrt[n]{a}$ or $a^{1/n}$. For example, 2 is the third, or cube, root of 8 ($\sqrt[3]{8}= 2$), since it satisfies the equation $x^3-8 = 0$. Every number has n different (real or imaginary) nth roots; e.g., there are two square roots of 9 (3 and -3) since $(3)(3) = 9$ and $(-3)(-3) = 9$. Finding the root of a number is called evolution and is the inverse process of involution, or raising a number to a power (see EXPONENT).

root crop, vegetable cultivated chiefly for its edible roots, e.g., the beet, turnip, mangel-wurzel, carrot, and parsnip. All root crops have a large water content and grow best in deeply cultivated soil in cool, overcast weather when the plant's loss of water through transpiration is lowest. Because they require thorough cultivating they are often desirable in a rotation of crops—beets and turnips being most frequently so used. Root crops, especially beets, turnips, and carrots, are also grown as food for livestock.

rootstock: see RHIZOME.

rope: see CORDAGE.

Rops, Félicien (fālēsyăN′ rôps), 1833-98, Belgian painter, etcher, and lithographer. In 1857 he founded a satirical journal, *Uylenspiegel*, for which he made lithographs and caricatures. From c.1862 he lived principally in Paris and became noted as an illustrator of unusual imagination and an artist of great technical skill. Today Rops is best known for the erotic nature of his work and his pictorial explorations into the world of vice. He illustrated the poems of Baudelaire. His etchings include the series of the *Sataniques* and the *Album of 100 Sketches.*

roque: see CROQUET.

Roquefort cheese (rōk′fərt), semihard cheese, made solely from the milk of ewes in the region around Roquefort, Aveyron dept., S France, and matured in the natural limestone caves there. Its distinctive flavor and its greenish-blue veined appearance are produced by a penicillium mold, which is added to the unheated curds. Although the cheese is made in Roquefort, much of the milk comes from all over France.

Roraima (rōōrī′mə), federal territory (1970 pop. 40,915), 88,843 sq mi (230,103 sq km), NW Brazil, on the border of Venezuela and Guyana. BOA VISTA is the capital. Located almost entirely in the Guiana Highlands, the region is drained by the Rio Branco, a tributary of the Amazon. The climate is equatorial, with wet winters and dry summers. During the rainy season transportation is almost impossible. The economy is based on the exploitation of tropical-forest products (largely rubber and Brazil nuts) and on the region's minerals (diamonds, gold, bauxite, quartz, and some oil). Cattle breeding is also important. There is little agriculture. The region was first penetrated in the late 17th cent. by *bandeiras* seeking to enslave the Indians. By the mid-18th cent. the Portuguese had fortified some areas to prevent penetration by the Spanish, English, and Dutch. The federal territory was created in 1943 from land formerly belonging to the state of Amazonas. Until 1962 it was named Rio Branco. Roraima is administered by a governor appointed by the president of Brazil.

Roraima, mountain, 9,219 ft (2,810 m) high, at the junction of the boundaries of Brazil, Guyana, and Venezuela. A giant table mountain, it is the highest point in the Guiana Highlands.

Rore, Cipriano de (sēprēä'nō dā rō'rə), 1516–65, Flemish composer. Rore was a pupil of Adrien Willaert. Much of his mature life was spent in Italy, where his madrigals (eight books) were much admired. Other works by Rore include three books of motets and a setting of the St. John Passion.

Røros (rö'rōs), town (1970 pop. 5,147), Sør-Trøndelag co., E Norway, near the Swedish border. It is a tourist spot and a winter sports center. The copper mines in the vicinity, opened in 1644, were for many years the most important in Norway.

rorqual: see WHALE.

Rorschach (rôr'shäkh), town (1970 pop. 11,963), St. Gall canton, NE Switzerland, on the Lake of Constance. A prosperous commercial town in the Middle Ages, Rorschach is a resort and the largest Swiss port on the lake.

Rorschach test: see PSYCHOLOGICAL TESTS.

Rosa, Salvator (sälvätōr' rô'zä), 1615–73, Italian baroque painter, etcher, and poet of the Neapolitan school. In 1635, Rosa went to Rome, where he established his reputation with his painting *Prometheus* (Corsini Palace, Rome). He satirized the great Roman sculptor and architect G. L. BERNINI and moved to Florence in 1640 to avoid Bernini's wrath and to work for the Medici family, painting, writing poems and satires, composing music, and acting. He returned permanently to Rome in 1649. Rosa is best known for his spirited battle pieces painted in the style of Falcone, for his marines, and especially for his landscapes. His large historical works are considered less successful. His landscapes are usually desolate scenes, painted in a tempestuous manner. His works are in many major European museums; a self-portrait is in the Metropolitan Museum. He began etching in 1660 and produced over 100 fine plates. Several of his satiric poems are well known. See E. W. Manwaring, *Italian Landscape* (1925, repr. 1965).

Rosa, Monte (mōn'tā rô'zä), massif, in the Pennine Alps, on the Swiss-Italian border. Its highest peak, the Dufourspitze, 15,217 ft (4,638 m), is the highest point in Switzerland. The Swiss side is covered by glaciers.

Rosamond (rŏz'əmənd), fl. c.570, wife of the Lombard king ALBOIN. The daughter of King Kunimund of the Gepidae, a Germanic people, she was captured by Alboin, who had defeated and killed her father. When Alboin forced her to drink from a cup made from her father's skull, she had him murdered by two of his own courtiers and took refuge with the Byzantine prefect at Ravenna. Although married to one of her fellow conspirators, Helmechis, she preferred the prefect, Longinus. When Rosamond offered Helmechis a poisoned drink, he swallowed half and forced her to drink the remainder. Her story, neither confirmed nor disproved by historical research, is the subject of two tragedies, Swinburne's *Rosamund* and Alfieri's *Rosmunda.*

Rosamond (Rosamond Clifford), d. 1176, mistress of Henry II of England. She was not openly acknowledged by the king until 1174, after he had imprisoned his wife, Eleanor of Aquitaine. On Rosamond's death soon afterwards she was buried in Godstow Abbey, but her remains were removed to the chapter house after Henry's death. A considerable body of legendary material was written about Rosamond by later chroniclers. The best-known stories are variations on a tragic death. She was supposedly murdered at Woodstock by Eleanor of Aquitaine, either by poison, stabbing, beheading, or being bled to death in her bath. See V. B. Heltzel, *Fair Rosamond* (1947, repr. 1970).

Rosario (rôsär'yō), city (1970 pop. 798,292), Santa Fe prov., E central Argentina, a port on the Paraná River, on the eastern margin of the Pampa. The second largest city of Argentina, it is primarily the import and export center for the central and northern provinces. Sugar refining and flour milling are the principal industries, and there are large meat-processing plants. Rosario is the terminus of several railroads and has excellent port facilities. It was settled in the late 17th cent. but grew mainly after 1870 with the rapid development of the Pampa.

rosary [rose garden], prayer of Roman Catholics, in which beads are used as counters. The term, applied also to the beads, is extended to Muslim, Hindu, and Buddhist prayers that use beads. The Catholic rosary is a series of 15 meditations on events (mysteries) in the lives of Jesus and Mary. The joyful mysteries are (Luke 1-2) the Annunciation, the Visitation, the birth of Jesus, the Purification of the Virgin, and the finding of the child Jesus among the doctors. The sorrowful mysteries are (Mat. 26–27) the agony of Jesus in the garden, His scourging, the crowning with thorns, the carrying of the Cross, and the Crucifixion. The glorious mysteries are the Resurrection (Luke 24), the Ascension (Acts 1.1—11), the descent of the Holy Ghost (Acts 2), the assumption of the Virgin, and her coronation as Queen of Heaven. As one dwells on a mystery in thought one recites prayers—the Lord's Prayer once, Hail Mary (Ave Maria) 10 times, and Glory Be to the Father (Gloria Patri) once. Count is kept by slipping beads through the fingers; the beads have no other significance. The usual string—formerly called the chaplet—has five sets of 10 beads (decades); between the decades a single bead is set apart, for the Glory of one mystery and the Our Father of the next. There is a pendant with crucifix and beads for introductory prayers. The rosary is often said in common, but it remains an individual prayer. Its popularity is often ascribed to the combination of simplicity of method with solidity of subject matter. In one form or another it has been in use some 600 years. There is a feast of the rosary, Oct. 7, on the anniversary of the victory of the Christians over the Turks at the battle of LEPANTO. See DOMINIC, SAINT. See F. B. Thornton, *This Is the Rosary* (1961).

Rosas, Juan Manuel de (hwän mänwĕl' dā rô'säs), 1793–1877, Argentine dictator, governor of Buenos Aires prov. (1829–32, 1835–52). As a boy he served under Jacques de Liniers against the British invaders of the Rio de la Plata (1806–7), but most of his youth was spent in the cattle country, where he laid the foundations of his fortune through large-scale ranching. As a full-fledged CAUDILLO he began his political career in 1820 by leading his well-trained force of GAUCHOS in support of the conservatives and federalism, and after the deposition and execution (1828) of Manuel DORREGO he became the federalist leader. In conjunction with Estanislao López, Rosas defeated Juan LAVALLE, thereby increasing his prestige, and soon became governor of Buenos Aires. Aided by López and Quiroga, he waged a brutal, sanguinary campaign against the unitarians, destroying, at least temporarily, their movement. He surrendered office in 1832, but maintained his prestige by a successful expedition against Indians. In 1835 he again became governor; by machinations and arrangements with other provincial chiefs, he soon assumed the dictatorship of most of Argentina. His power was absolute and his government a ruthless and complete tyranny. Assisted by spies, servile propagandists, the Mazorca (a secret political society that degenerated into a band of assassins), and by his own sagacity, he instituted a regime of terror. The dictator was abjectly adulated in public, but few intervals of tranquillity occurred during his rule. Successive and continuous revolutions were organized against him, secret revolutionary groups—notably the Asociación de Mayo, founded by Esteban ECHEVERRÍA—were formed, and his conduct of foreign affairs incurred the hostility of other nations. Ironically, by driving into exile the finest minds in Argentina—Juan Bautista ALBERDI, Bartolomé MITRE, and especially Domingo F. SARMIENTO—he contributed unwittingly to the creation of several classics of South American literature and social analysis. Rosas became involved with the United States and Britain in a dispute over the Falkland Islands. His ambition led him to interfere in Uruguay, where he supported Manuel ORIBE. His suspected designs to reduce Paraguay and Uruguay to dependent Argentine states worsened relations with France and Great Britain, resulting in two blockades (1838–40, 1845–50). Brazil also became apprehensive of Rosas's aspirations. These foreign difficulties greatly injured Argentine commerce. Resentment against the dominance of Buenos Aires resulted in a final, successful revolution against Rosas. Aided by Brazil and Uruguay, Justo José de URQUIZA crushed the tyrant's army at Monte Caseros (1852), and the dictator fled to England, where he lived in exile until his death. Despite all, Rosas contributed greatly to the unification of Argentina. See study by J. F. Cady (1929, repr. 1969).

Roscelin (rŏs'əlĭn), c.1045–c.1120, French scholastic philosopher, also called Roscellinus, Johannes Roscellinus, and Jean Roscelin. Roscelin was one of the first thinkers of the Middle Ages to deal with the problem of universals, or general concepts (see REALISM). Although very little of his writing has survived, he seems to have been an extreme nominalist, teaching that universals were nothing more than words. Roscelin's position was attacked by his pupil, Peter ABELARD, but Abelard's own viewpoint on this question showed a considerable debt to Roscelin. Accused of the heresy of tritheism (teaching that the Three Persons of the Trinity are separate individuals), Roscelin was ordered (1092) by the Synod of Soissons to recant, but he escaped condemnation.

Roscher, Wilhelm (vĭl'hĕlm rôsh'ər), 1817–94, German economist. Criticizing classical economic theorists, he founded the historical school of economics. His chief work is *System der Volkswirtschaft* (5 vol., 1854–94; tr. of 13th ed., *Principles of Political Economy,* 1878).

Roscius, Quintus (kwĭn'təs rŏsh'əs), c.126 B.C.–62 B.C., Roman actor. Born a slave at Solonium, he became the greatest comic actor of his time. From the dictator Sulla, Roscius received the honor of the gold ring signifying equestrian rank. In a lawsuit, Cicero, whom he had taught elocution, defended him by an extant oration, *Pro Q. Roscio Comoedo.* The title "the young Roscius" or "the new Roscius" has been bestowed on several English actors as a mark of supreme distinction.

Roscoe, Sir Henry Enfield (rŏs'kō), 1833–1915, English chemist. He was professor (1857–87) at Owens College, Manchester. He is known for his work, with R. W. Bunsen, in photochemistry and for his study and analysis of vanadium compounds and his isolation of the metal. He was knighted in 1884. He wrote two standard works, *Lessons in Elementary Chemistry* (1870) and, with Carl Schorlemmer, *A Treatise on Chemistry* (3 vol., 1878–95). See his autobiography (1906); study by T. E. Thorpe (1916).

Roscoe, William, 1753–1831, English historian and author. He was called to the bar in 1774, and later, as a member of Parliament, fought against the slave trade (1806). *The Life of Lorenzo de' Medici* (1795), his principal historical work, received praise, but his *Life of Leo X* (4 vol., 1805) was severely criticized. In 1806 he contributed a children's classic, *The Butterfly's Ball and the Grasshopper's Feast,* to the *Gentleman's Magazine.* See study by George Chandler (1953).

Roscommon, Wentworth Dillon, 4th **earl of** (rŏskŏm'ən), 1633?–1685, English poet and scholar, b. Ireland. He was one of the first to praise Milton's genius. Besides making a blank-verse translation (1680) of Horace's *Ars poetica,* he wrote an *Essay on Translated Verse* (1684).

Roscommon (rŏskŏm'ən), county (1971 pop. 53,497), 951 sq mi (2,463 sq km), central Republic of Ireland. The county town is ROSCOMMON. A part of the central plain of Ireland, the region is low-lying and contains many lakes (Lough Allen and Lough Ree) and bogs. The Shannon, which forms the eastern border, and the Suck, which borders the county on the west, are the principal rivers. It is an agricultural county, given over chiefly to the pasturage of cattle and sheep. Several coal mines are operated in the northeast.

Roscommon, county town (1971 pop. 18,256) of Co. Roscommon, central Republic of Ireland. Noted for its Dominican priory and the remains of a castle, both dating from the 13th cent., Roscommon is a tourist center and market town.

Rose, Barbara, 1937–, American art critic, b. Washington, D.C. Among the most influential art critics of the 1960s, Rose contributed to the literature of color-field painting (see POST-PAINTERLY ABSTRACTION) and contemporary sculpture. Her books include *American Art Since 1900* (1967) and *Claes Oldenburg* (1969).

Rose, Gustav (gŏŏs'täf rō'zə), 1798–1873, German mineralogist. He served as professor at the Univ. of Berlin from 1839. Noted especially as a crystallographer, he advanced the scientific study of rocks. His brother, **Heinrich Rose,** 1795–1864, an analytical chemist, was professor at the Univ. of Berlin from 1823. He demonstrated (1844) that niobium (columbium) and tantalum are different elements.

rose, common name for some members of the Rosaceae, a large family of herbs, shrubs, and trees distributed over most of the earth. The family is especially abundant in E Asia, Europe, and North America, where species of almost half of the family's genera are indigenous, especially in the Pacific coastal area. Many of the Rosaceae are thorny, and most are

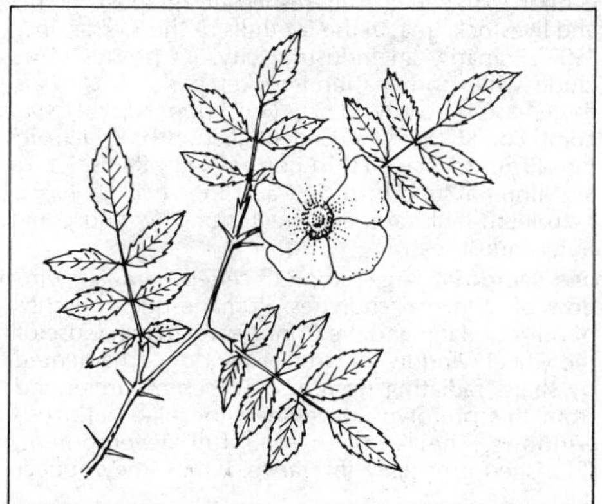

Pasture rose, Rosa carolina

characterized by the presence of stipules on the leaf, by flowers having five sets of parts, by a fleshy fruit, such as a rose hip or an apple, that is derived in large part from a cup-shaped enlargement of the flower stalk, and by the near absence of endosperm in the seed. Although some groups of these plants are sometimes classed as separate families, most botanists consider them all to be a single family that represents a natural phylogenetic classification, i.e., most or all members have evolved from common ancestors. The largest of the approximately 115 genera (comprising a total of some 3,200 species) are *Rubus* (including the raspberry, blackberry, dewberry, loganberry, and other types of BRAMBLE), *Spiraea* (including the bridal wreath, meadowsweet, and hardhack), *Rosa* (the roses), *Crataegus* (HAWTHORN), and *Prunus* (including the ALMOND, APRICOT, BLACKTHORN or sloe, CHERRY, NECTARINE, PEACH, and PLUM). Economically the rose family is of enormous importance. It provides numerous temperate fruits including (besides species of *Rubus* and *Prunus*) the APPLE, LOQUAT, MEDLAR, PEAR, QUINCE, and STRAWBERRY. The typically fragrant and beautiful flowers make many members of the family prized as ornamentals, e.g., the fruit trees and bushes mentioned and also the ANTELOPE BRUSH, CHRISTMASBERRY, MOUNTAIN ASH, NINEBARK, PYRACANTHA, and SHADBUSH. Many genera have species that are native wild flowers of the United States; in addition to many of those above are *Agrimonia* (AGRIMONY), *Potentilla* (CINQUEFOIL), and *Sanquisorba* (BURNET), which are also sometimes cultivated. The most popular ornamentals of the family, and among the most esteemed of all cultivated plants, are the true roses. *Rosa* occurs indigenously in the north temperate zone and in tropical mountain areas, usually as erect or climbing shrubs with five-petaled, fragrant flowers. Sometimes the foliage also is fragrant, as in the European SWEETBRIER, or eglantine. From many of the wild species have been developed the large number of cultivated varieties and hybrids, having single or double blossoms that range in color from white and yellow to many shades of pink and red. Since many species are highly variable and hybridize easily, the classification of *Rosa* is sometimes difficult, and the wild type of some modern forms is not always known. The rose has been a favorite flower in many lands since prehistoric times. It appears in the earliest art, poety, and tradition. It has been used in innumerable ways in decoration. In ancient times it was used medically—Pliny lists 32 remedies made of its petals and leaves. Formerly it was eaten in salads and conserves. It was sacred to Aphrodite and was a favorite flower of the Romans, who spread its culture wherever their armies conquered. Among the old species are the cabbage rose and the damask rose, both native to the Caucasus; the latter especially is cultivated for the perfume oil ATTAR OF ROSES. The famous roses of England include the white rose that was the emblem of the house of York and the red rose of the house of Lancaster in the Wars of the Roses, as well as the variegated red and white rose (now called the York and Lancaster). The rambler rose, frequently grown on trellises and porches, and the tea and hybrid tea roses are of more recent origin, the result of modern rose culture, which really began when the East India Company's ships brought new everblooming or monthly roses from the Orient. The rose is the emblem of England and the flower of New York state; the wild rose, of Iowa; the prairie rose, of North Dakota; and the American Beauty, of the District of Columbia. Rose shows are held annually in many cities and rose carnivals in several; rose gardens are often important parts of civic parks and private gardens. Practical uses of roses, besides their importance as a source of perfume, include a delicate-flavored jelly made from the fruits, called rose hips, of some wild species. Thorny rambling roses, such as the Oriental multiflora rose, are much used as hedge and erosion control plants in agriculture, highway landscaping, and wildlife preserves. Roses are classified in the division MAGNOLIOPHYTA, class Magnoliopsida, order Rosales, family Rosaceae. See the *American Rose Annual,* issued by the American Rose Society; Roy Genders, *The Rose: A Complete Handbook* (1965); S. M. Gault and P. M. Synge, *The Dictionary of Roses in Color* (1971).

Rosebery, Archibald Philip Primrose, 5th **earl of** (rōz'bərē), 1847–1929, British statesman. He succeeded his grandfather as earl in 1868. A Liberal, Rosebery was undersecretary for home affairs (1881–83), entered the cabinet as lord privy seal (1885), and served (1886, 1892–94) as foreign secretary. His imperialist views brought him into frequent conflict with the prime minister, William Gladstone, but he was able to secure the establishment of a British protectorate in Uganda. When Gladstone retired in 1894, it was expected that Sir William HARCOURT would succeed him, but Queen VICTORIA called on Rosebery to become prime minister. That caused a split in the Liberal party, and Rosebery was forced to resign in 1895. He became the leader of the Liberal Imperialist division of the party, but retired from politics in 1905 when Henry Campbell-Bannerman was chosen as Liberal prime minister. He wrote a number of historical monographs, including *William Pitt* (1891), *Napoleon: The Last Phase* (1900), and *Chatham* (1910). See biographies by his son-in-law, the 1st marquess of Crewe (1931), and R. R. James (1963).

Roseburg, city (1970 pop. 14,461), seat of Douglas co., SW Oregon; inc. 1872. A railroad and trade center, it has an important lumbering industry and handles the produce of nearby ranches (sheep and cattle) and fruit orchards. Tourism is also important; Roseburg is the headquarters for Umpqua National Forest, and the area is known for its good hunting and fishing. A junior college and a U.S. veterans hospital are there.

Rosecrans, William Starke (rōz'krănz), 1819–98, Union general in the American Civil War, b. Kingston, Ohio. He served in the army from 1842 to 1854 and in April, 1861, rejoined as a volunteer. He became aide-de-camp to Gen. George B. McClellan and helped to organize the Ohio Home Guards. Made a brigadier general (May, 1861), he operated successfully against the Confederates in W Virginia (July, 1861–April, 1862). As commander of the Army of the Mississippi, he was victorious at Iuka and CORINTH (Sept.–Oct., 1862). In Nov., 1862, Rosecrans succeeded to command of the Army of the Cumberland (formerly called the Army of the Ohio) and one month later opposed Braxton BRAGG in the battle of MURFREESBORO, which ended in a Confederate retreat. In the CHATTANOOGA CAMPAIGN, he ably outmaneuvered Bragg for a time, but the Confederates thoroughly defeated him at Chickamauga (Sept., 1863). Relieved of his command, Rosecrans for a time directed operations in Missouri. After resigning from the army in 1867, he became minister to Mexico (1868–69), Congressman from California (1881–85), and register of the Treasury (1885–93). See biography by W. M. Lamers (1961).

Roselle (rōzĕl'), borough (1970 pop. 22,585), Union co., NE N.J.; set off from Linden 1890 and inc. 1894. It is chiefly residential, but there is some industry. Thomas Edison had a laboratory there, and Abraham Clark, a signer of the Declaration of Independence, was born in Roselle.

Roselle Park, borough (1970 pop. 14,277), Union co., NE N.J.; founded c.1700, inc. 1901. It is mainly residential.

rosemary [ultimately from Lat.,=dew of the sea], widely cultivated evergreen and shrubby perennial (*Rosmarinus officinalis*) of the family Labiatae (MINT family), fairly hardy and native to the Mediterranean region. It has small light-blue flowers. The aromatic leaves, whitish beneath, are used for seasoning, and the oil is used in perfume and medicine. From ancient times rosemary has been regarded as a token of constancy and remembrance. In *Hamlet* (iv:5) Ophelia says, "There's rosemary, that's for remembrance." There is a prostrate variety. Rosemary is classified in the division MAGNOLIOPHYTA, class Magnoliopsida, order Lamiales, family Labiatae.

Rosemead, city (1970 pop. 40,972), Los Angeles co., S Calif., a suburb of Los Angeles; founded 1867, inc. 1959.

Rosenberg, Alfred (äl'frĕt rō'zənbĕrk), 1893–1946, German Nazi leader. He was born in Reval (now Tallinn, Estonia), and studied architecture in Riga, and later in Moscow. Returning to Reval, he became active as a political ideologist until he fled (1919) to Germany to escape arrest for counterrevolutionary speeches. There he joined the National Socialist party and became the editor of the party organ, *Völkischer Beobachter.* The author of an anti-Christian, anti-Semitic, and neopagan book, *Der Mythus des 20. Jahrhunderts* [the myth of the 20th cent.] (1930), he supplied Adolf Hitler with the spurious philosophical and scientific basis for his racist doctrine (see NATIONAL SOCIALISM). Rosenberg was made (1933) foreign affairs secretary of the party and distinguished himself as the foremost anti-Bolshevik among its leaders. In 1941 he was appointed minister for the occupied Eastern territories. Convicted as a war criminal at the Nuremberg trials, he was executed. See his memoirs (tr. 1949) and his *Selected Writings,* ed. by Robert Pois (1970); Robert Cecil, *The Myth of the Master Race: Alfred Rosenberg and Nazi Ideology* (1972).

Rosenberg, Isaac, 1890–1918, English poet, b. Bristol. He studied painting at the Slade School (1911–14) and had an exhibition of his work at the Whitechapel Gallery. Although he wrote on other topics, his best poems grew out of his experience as a private during World War I. He was killed in action in France. A volume of his *Collected Works* was published in 1937.

Rosenberg (rō'zənbərg), city (1970 pop. 12,098), Fort Bend co., S Texas, on the Brazos River, in an oil and natural gas area; inc. 1902. Rosenberg and its sister city of Richmond are for all practical purposes one community. Their economic activities center around sulfur, salt, agricultural products (especially sugar), and oil, with related processing and manufacturing. Rosenberg was founded with the coming of the railroad in 1883 and grew as a farm-marketing and shipping center. It attracted many German and Czech immigrants, and the community today reflects that strong ethnic background.

Rosenberg Case, in U.S. history, a lengthy and controversial espionage case. In 1950, the Federal Bureau of Investigation arrested Julius Rosenberg (1918–53), an electrical engineer who had worked (1940–45) for the U.S. army signal corps, and his wife Ethel (1916–53); they were indicted for conspiracy to transmit classified military information to the Soviet Union. In the trial that followed (March, 1951), the government charged that in 1944 and 1945 the Rosenbergs had persuaded Ethel's brother, David Greenglass—an employee at the Los Alamos atomic bomb project—to provide them and a third person, Harry Gold, with top-secret data on nuclear weapons. The chief evidence against the Rosenbergs came from Greenglass and his wife, Ruth. Both Julius and Ethel Rosenberg were found guilty (1951) and received the death sentence; Morton Sobell, a codefendant, received a 30-year prison term, as did Harry Gold; and David Greenglass was later sentenced to 15 years imprisonment. Despite many court appeals and pleas for executive clemency, the Rosenbergs were executed on June 19, 1953. They became the first U.S. civilians to suffer the death penalty in an espionage trial. The case aroused much controversy. Many claimed that the political climate made a fair trial impossible and that the only seriously incriminating evidence had come from a confessed spy; others questioned the value of the information transmitted to the Soviet Union and argued that the death penalty was too severe. Communists in the United States and abroad organized a campaign to save the Rosenbergs and received the support of many liberals and religious leaders. See Jonathan Root, *The Betrayers* (1963); Walter and Miriam Schneir, *Invitation to an Inquest* (1965, repr. 1973); and Louis Nizer, *The Implosion Conspiracy* (1973).

Rosenfeld, Morris (rō'zənfĕlt), 1862–1923, Jewish poet, b. Russian Poland. His name was originally Moshe Jacob Alter. He worked as a tailor in London and as a diamond grinder in Amsterdam before emigrating to the United States in 1886. He settled in New York City, working 14 hours a day as a tailor while he wrote poetry for the Yiddish press. He later became editor of the *New Yorker Morgenblatt* and the *Jewish Annals.* His *Lieder Buch* (1897) was translated into English by the Harvard philologist Leo Wiener as *Songs from the Ghetto* (1898). It has also been translated into a number of European languages. Rosenfeld wrote of the hell of the sweatshop in such poems as "Mein Ingele" and "Cradle Song." He died in increasing blindness, illness, and poverty, despite the fame he had won. See Leo Wiener's *History of Yiddish Literature* (1899).

Rosenquist, James, 1933–, American painter, b. Grand Forks, N.Dak. Identified with the POP ART movement, Rosenquist incorporates disparate and fragmented images of everyday life into huge canvases. Although they are realistically painted, they appear abstract because of their vast scale and color. Rosenquist has borrowed from his earlier experience as a billboard painter for these works. His painting *F-111* (1965) is a 51-panel work occupying the walls of an entire room.

Rosenthal, Moriz (mō'rĭts rō'zəntäl), 1862–1946, Polish pianist; pupil of Liszt. He made his debut in Vienna in 1876, and later made many tours of the United States, settling there in 1938. He was considered one of the greatest pianists of his time, retaining his powers almost until the end of his life.

Rosenwald, Julius (rō'zənwôld), 1862–1932, American merchant and philanthropist, b. Springfield, Ill. He was president (1910–25), and later chairman of the board, of the mail-order house of Sears, Roebuck & Company. He established in 1917 the Julius Rosenwald Fund, which was largely used to establish rural schools for Negroes. His many philanthropies also included Jewish relief in the Middle East and Russia, funds for YMCA and YWCA buildings in cities with large Negro populations, and grants to educational institutions. See biography by M. R. Werner (1939).

Rosenzweig, Franz (fränts rō'zəntsvīkh"), 1886–1929, German-Jewish philosopher, b. Kassel. As a youth he was thoroughly trained in German philosophy and, after a near conversion to Christianity, dedicated himself to Jewish scholarship. His chief work, *The Star of Redemption* (1921, tr. of 2d ed. 1971), begun while he was a soldier in World War I, proved him to be one of the most original of modern Jewish thinkers. He drew from Orthodox, Reform, and Zionist views and created a philosophy that greatly attracted Jewish youth. Later, with his friend Martin Buber, he translated the Hebrew Scriptures into German. Other works in English include *On Jewish Learning,* ed. by N. N. Glatzer (1955). See *Franz Rosenzweig: His Life and Thought,* presented by N. N. Glatzer (2d ed. 1961); Bernard Martin, comp., *Great Twentieth-Century Jewish Philosophers: Shestov, Rosenzweig, Buber* (1969).

rose of Jericho, common name for two plants belonging to different families in the plant kingdom. One, an annual desert plant (*Anastatica hierochuntica*) of the family Cruciferae (MUSTARD family), is native to Asia Minor. It is a RESURRECTION PLANT. The branches curl into a ball at maturity, after which the plant, in its native habitat, is blown about by the wind and the seeds are dispersed. The other, *Odontospermum pygmaeum,* is native to the same region and also called rose of Jericho because of its similar properties. It is a member of the family Compositae (COMPOSITE family). Both families are classified in the division MAGNOLIOPHYTA, class Magnoliopsida. The Cruciferae is in the order Capparales, and the Compositae is in the order Asterales.

Rose of Lima, Saint, 1586–1617, Peruvian Dominican religious mystic, of Spanish family. She was remarkable for pious austerities. St. Rose was canonized in 1671 (the first canonized saint of the New World), and her shrine is at Lima. Feast: Aug. 30.

rose of Sharon, common name for several plants, especially *Hibiscus syriacus,* of the family Malvaceae (MALLOW family), and for ST.-JOHN'S-WORT, i.e., any species of the genus *Hypericum* of the family Hypericaceae (St.-John's-wort family). The rose of Sharon of the Scriptures (Song 2.1) is thought to be either a narcissus or the meadow saffron. The Malvaceae are classified in the division MAGNOLIOPHYTA, class Magnoliopsida, order Malvales. The Hypericaceae are similarly classified, but in the order Theales.

Roses, Wars of the, traditional name given to the intermittent struggle (1455–85) for the throne of England between the noble house of YORK (whose badge was a white rose) and the noble house of LANCASTER (later associated with the red rose). About the middle of the 15th cent. Richard, duke of YORK, came to the fore as leader of the opposition to the faction (William de la POLE, duke of Suffolk, Edmund Beaufort, duke of SOMERSET, and the queen, MARGARET OF ANJOU) that controlled the weak Lancastrian king HENRY VI. The Yorkists gained popular support as a result of discontent over the failure of English arms in the Hundred Years War and over the corruption of the court, discontent reflected in the rebellion of Jack CADE in 1450. Also in that year Suffolk was murdered, and the duke of York forced the king to recognize his claim as heir to the throne. In 1453 the king became insane, and the birth of a son to Margaret of Anjou displaced York as heir. The duke was appointed protector, but when the king recovered in 1454, York was excluded from the royal council. He resorted to arms. The opposing factions met (1455) at St. Albans—usually taken as the first battle of the Wars of the Roses. Somerset was killed, leaving Queen Margaret at the head of the defeated royal party, and York again served as protector for a short period (1455–56). By 1459 both parties were once more in arms. The following year the Yorkists defeated and captured the king at the battle of Northhampton. The duke of York hurried to London to assert his claims to the throne, which were, by laws of strict inheritance, perhaps better than those of the king himself. A compromise was effected by which Henry remained king and York and his heirs were declared successors. Queen Margaret, whose son was thus disinherited, raised an army and defeated (1460) the Yorkists at Wakefield. York was killed in this battle, and his claims devolved upon his son Edward, but Richard Neville, earl of WARWICK, became the real leader of the Yorkist party. Margaret's army rescued the king from captivity in the second battle of St. Albans (Feb., 1461), but Edward meanwhile secured a Yorkist victory at Mortimer's Cross, marched into London unopposed, and assumed the throne as EDWARD IV. The Lancastrians, after their defeat at Towton (March, 1461), continued (with Scottish aid) to raise resistance in the north until 1464. The deposed Henry was captured (1465) and put into the Tower of London. Although the Lancastrian cause now seemed hopeless, a quarrel broke out between Warwick and Edward IV after the latter's marriage to Elizabeth Woodville in 1464. Warwick and the king's brother George, duke of CLARENCE, allied against Edward, fled to France (1470), and there became reconciled with Margaret of Anjou. Supported by Louis XI of France, they crossed to England and restored Henry VI to the throne. Edward fled, but with the aid of Charles the Bold, duke of Burgundy, returned to England in 1471, regained London, and recaptured Henry. In the ensuing battles of Barnet and Tewkesbury (1471), Warwick and Henry's son, Edward, were killed. Margaret was imprisoned. Soon thereafter Henry VI died, probably slain at the orders of Edward IV. After 12 relatively peaceful years, Edward IV was succeeded (1483) by his young son EDWARD V, but soon the boy's uncle Richard, duke of Gloucester, usurped the throne as RICHARD III. Opposition to Richard advanced the fortunes of Henry Tudor, earl of Richmond, now the Lancastrian claimant. In 1485, Henry landed from France, defeated and killed Richard at Bosworth Field, and ascended the throne as HENRY VII. His marriage to Edward IV's daughter, Elizabeth, united the houses of Lancaster and York. Except for various efforts during Henry's reign to place Yorkist pretenders on the throne, the Wars of the Roses were ended. It is generally said that with them ended the era of feudalism in England, since the nobles who participated suffered heavy loss of life and property and were too weak, as a class, to contest the strong monarchy of the Tudors. The middle and lower classes were largely indifferent to the struggle and relatively untouched by it. See E. F. Jacob, *The Fifteenth Century* (1961); P. M. Kendall, *The Yorkist Age* (1962, repr. 1965); S. B. Chrimes, *Lancastrians, Yorkists, and Henry VII* (1964); J. R. Lander, *The Wars of the Roses* (1965).

Rosetta (rōzĕt'ə), Arabic *Rashid,* city (1966 pop. 36,700), N Egypt, in the Nile River delta. Rice is cultivated nearby, and rice milling and fish processing are the city's main industries. Founded in the 9th cent., Rosetta was formerly an important port but declined after the building (1819) of the Mahmudiya Canal, which diverted its trade to ALEXANDRIA. The **Rosetta stone,** a basalt slab inscribed by priests of Ptolemy V in hieroglyphic, demotic, and Greek, was found by Napoleon's troops near the city in 1799. It was taken by the British in 1801 and is now in the British Museum. It gave Jean-François CHAMPOLLION, Thomas Young, and others the key to Egyptian hieroglyphic.

Rosetti, Constantin (kōnstäntēn' rōsĕt'), 1816–85, Rumanian statesman, b. Bucharest. A radical editor, he took part in the Revolution of 1848 and subsequently fled to Paris, where he published a review favoring the establishment of a national unitary state. He returned in 1861 to Rumania, was elected deputy, and in 1866 was minister of public instruction. A supporter of the deposition (1866) of Alexander John Cuza, Rosetti headed the chamber of deputies in 1877 and was minister of the interior (1881–82).

Roseville. 1 City (1970 pop. 18,221), Placer co., N central Calif., in a fruit (especially grapes), grain, and livestock area, in the foothills of the Sierras; inc. 1909. Primarily an industrial city, its products include wine, formica, and rocket parts. A U.S. air force base is nearby. **2** City (1970 pop. 60,529), Macomb co., SE Mich., a residential suburb of Detroit; inc. 1926. **3** Village (1970 pop. 34,518), Ramsey co., SE Minn., a suburb of St. Paul; inc. 1948. It has a petroleum tank farm and steel, trucking, and computer industries.

rose window, large, stone-traceried, circular window of medieval churches. Romanesque churches of both England and the Continent had made use of the wheel window—a circular window ornamented by shafts radiating from a small center circle; and from this prototype developed the elaborate rose windows. The latter, in their full development, flourished especially in France, where they appear

Rose window (Cathedral of Notre-Dame, Paris)

in practically every important Gothic cathedral, either over the center portal of the west front or on at least one of the transept ends. Stained glass was usually placed in them. The early examples, as on the west facade of the cathedral at Chartres (12th–13th cent.), were filled with plate TRACERY, pierced from a stone slab. With the perfection of bar tracery, the typical rose, as in the cathedral at Rheims (13th–14th cent.) and in Notre-Dame de Paris (12th–14th cent.), was filled with numerous radiating bars and intermediate bars, joining to form pointed arches at the outer edge. In the final or flamboyant period the bars were arranged in wavy curves and more intricate patterns. This rich and closely packed tracery, as in the fine transept window of St. Ouen at Rouen, suggests the design of an open rose.

rosewood, popular name for the ornamental wood of several species of tropical trees, especially for the heartwood of certain leguminous trees of the genus *Dalbergia* of the family Leguminosae (PULSE family). Brazilian rosewood, or jacaranda (*D. nigra*), is one of Brazil's finest woods, important in its commerce for 300 years. It is obtained from the purplish-black heartwood of old trees, is rather oily, fragrant—whence the name—and durable and is used whole or in veneers for piano casings and other kinds of cabinetwork and for tools, instruments, brush backs, and other articles. Honduras rosewood (*D. stevensoni*) is now used chiefly in percussion instruments (e.g., the marimba and the xylophone) where Brazilian rosewood was formerly employed. Among Old World species are the East Indian rosewood, or black rosewood (*D. latifolia*), which is a deep, rich purple streaked with golden yellow to black, and the very hard African blackwood (*D. melanosylon*), which is used as a substitute for ebony. Rosewoods are sometimes used locally for domestic remedies, and several—including trees of other genera also called rosewood—have been introduced into the S United States as ornamentals and for lumber. The genus is classified in the division MAGNOLIOPHYTA, class Magnoliopsida, order Rosales, family Leguminosae.

Rosh (rŏsh), son of Benjamin. Gen. 46.21.

Rosh ha-Shanah (hə-shä'nə) [Heb.,=head of the year], the Jewish New Year, also known as the Feast of the Trumpets. It is a holy day second in solemnity only to the Day of Atonement (Yom Kippur; see ATONEMENT, DAY OF). It is observed on the first day of the seventh month, Tishri, occurring usually in September. Rosh ha-Shanah is held in great reverence as the Day of Judgment (Yom ha-Din), the beginning of the 10-day period concluding with Yom Kippur and known as the "Days of Awe," during which, according to tradition, all the people of the earth pass before the Lord and are marked in the "Book of Life" or in the "Book of Death." A distinguishing feature of the New Year is the blowing of a trumpet (shofar—a ram's horn), which summons Jews to their penitential observance. See S. J. Agnon, *Days of Awe* (1965); Hayyim Schauss, *Guide to Jewish Holy Days* (1938, repr. 1966); Louis Jacobs, *A Guide to Rosh ha-Shanah* (1969).

Rosicrucians (rōzĭkro͞o'shənz), members of an esoteric society or group of societies, who claim that their order has been in existence since the days of ancient Egypt and has over the course of time included many of the world's sages. Their secret learning deals with occult symbols—notably the rose and the cross, the swastika, and the pyramid—and with mystical writings containing cabalistic, Hermetic, and other doctrines. Most scholars trace modern Rosicrucianism to Johan Valentin Andreä (1586-1654), who used the pseudonym Christian Rosenkreuz [rose cross]. In 1614 he published *Fama fraternitatis,* which caused great excitement in Europe, and, in 1615, the *Confessio rosae crucis.* In these works Andreä described the development of the Rosicrucian society, mainly from Eastern and Arab origins. Some scholars believe that the name was used by Andreä and later theological reformers to gain attention, and that the description of the society was a work of imagination having symbolic or satiric intent. However, some of the ideas attributed to the Rosicrucians seem to have been current earlier. The society was variously called Brothers of the Rosy Cross, Rosy-Cross Knights, and Rosy-Cross Philosophers; its adepts are called Illuminati. There seems to have been some connection between the Rosy Cross and Freemasonry. Rosicrucian symbolism figures in the writings of William Butler Yeats, particularly in the collection of poems entitled *The Rose.* American Rosicrucians are largely followers of theosophical doctrines. The Rosicrucian Order (Ancient Mystical Order Rosae Crucis) has headquarters at San Jose, Calif.; the Rosicrucian Brotherhood (Fraternitas Rosae Crucis) has headquarters in Quakertown, Pa.; and the Society of Rosicrucians (Societas Rosicruciana in America) has a center in New York City. See A. E. Waite, *Real History of the Rosicrucians* (1887); H. S. Lewis, *Rosicrucian Questions and Answers* (1929, 8th ed., 1965); R. Swinburne Clymer, *The Book of Rosicruciae* (3 vol., 1946-48); F. A. Yates, *The Rosicrucian Enlightenment* (1972).

rosin or **colophony,** hard, brittle, translucent RESIN, obtained as a solid residue from crude TURPENTINE. Usually pale yellow or amber, its color may vary from brownish-black to transparent depending on the nature of the source of the crude turpentine. Rosin has no taste but often has a faint odor of pine. It is soluble in alcohol, ether, turpentine, and several other organic solvents, and in solutions of various metal hydroxides. Rosin is not a pure substance but a mixture of several compounds, chiefly abietic acid. It is used in making cements, varnishes, paints, sealing wax, adhesives, and some soaps; for treating violin bows; as a dressing for machine belting; as a sizing material for paper; in the preparation of certain metals for soldering; and, in pharmacy, in some ointments, plasters, and similar preparations. Athletes commonly rub it (in the form of dust) upon their hands or the soles of their shoes to prevent slipping.

rosinweed: see COMPASS PLANT.

Rositten: see REZEKNE, USSR.

Roskilde (rôs'kĭlə), city (1970 com. pop. 50,189), capital of Roskilde co., E Denmark, a port on the Roskilde Fjord (an arm of the Isefjord). Manufactures of this industrial city include processed food, liquor, machines, leather goods, and pharmaceuticals. One of the oldest Danish cities, Roskilde was the capital of Denmark from the 10th cent. until 1443, when it was replaced by Copenhagen (which had been chartered by the bishop of Roskilde). The city was the country's ecclesiastical center from 1020 to 1536, when the see of Roskilde was suppressed during the Reformation. Subsequently, the city declined rapidly. The Lutheran bishops of Sjaelland resided at Copenhagen, but their cathedral continued to be that of Roskilde. It is a magnificent edifice (late 12th cent.) containing about 40 royal tombs, including those of most Danish kings. The commercial prosperity of Roskilde revived in the 19th cent., and in 1923 it again became an episcopal see. By the Treaty of Roskilde (1658) Denmark ceded its lands in S Sweden to Charles X of Sweden. Roskilde has a museum of Viking ships, and nearby is an atomic research center.

Roslavl (rô'slävəl, rəslä'vəl), city (1967 est. pop. 46,000), W central European USSR, on the Oster River. It is a road and rail junction and a market town. Rail lines and trucks are serviced, vegetables are dried and processed, and knitted goods and rope are manufactured. Known from the 12th cent., Roslavl was chartered under Lithuanian rule in 1408 and ceded to Russia in 1667.

Roslyn (rŏz'lĭn), uninc. community (1970 pop. 18,317), Montgomery co., SE Pa.

Rosminians: see ROSMINI-SERBATI, ANTONIO.

Rosmini-Serbati, Antonio (äntō'nyō rōzmē'nē-sĕrbä'tē), 1797-1855, Italian theologian. He was ordained a priest in 1821. He attempted to establish a philosophical system based on a strong belief in Roman Catholicism but incorporating modern political and social ideas. Politically, he believed in a form of Italian nationalism in which the pope would head the combined states as a perpetual president. In 1828 he founded the Institute of the Brethren of Charity (Rosminians), whose members were laymen and clergy devoted to education and charity, a movement that spread to England and the United States. In 1830, Rosmini wrote *Nuovo saggio sull origine delle idee* (tr. *Origin of Ideas,* 1883-86), which presented some of his basic philosophical beliefs. In 1848 his *Cinque piaghe della Santa Chiesa* (tr. *The Five Wounds of the Holy Church,* 1883) appeared. This book, however, aroused instant opposition, particularly from the Jesuits, and it was placed on the Index, although later released. The institutions started by Rosmini still are in operation. See J. F. Bruno, *Rosmini's Contribution to Ethical Philosophy* (1916); biography by Claude Leetham (1959).

Ross, Alexander, 1783-1856, Canadian fur trader and pioneer, b. Scotland. He went to Canada in 1805, taught school in Upper Canada, and in 1810 left for Oregon as a clerk in John Jacob Astor's Pacific Fur Company. In the founding (1811) of Astoria, Ross played a part. When that fur-trading post was sold (1813) to the North West Company, he entered their employ and was a member of the expedition that established (1818) Fort Nez Percé (also called Fort Walla Walla); he was in charge of this post until 1823, two years after the amalgamation (1821) of the North West Company with Hudson's Bay Company. His account of these years on the Pacific slope is related in his *Adventures of the First Settlers on the Oregon or Columbia River* (1849, new ed. 1923) and *The Fur-Hunters of the Far West* (1855, new ed. 1956). He was head of an expedition (1823-24) in the Snake River country. In 1825 Ross settled in the Red River district; in Assiniboia he was sheriff and a member of the council. His *Red River Settlement* was published in 1856.

Ross, Barney, 1909-67, American boxer, b. New York City. His original name was Barnet Rosofsky. After an amateur career, Ross turned professional in 1929 and lost only four decisions in 82 fights. He won the world lightweight championship in 1933 but relinquished it in 1935 when he failed to make the weight. In three bouts with Jimmy McLarnin, he gained the world welterweight crown in 1934, lost it the same year, and regained it in 1935. Ross lost the title to Henry Armstrong in 1938. During World War II, in action in Guadalcanal in 1942, Ross won the Silver Star for gallantry in action by saving three wounded fellow Marines. He was a victim of shell shock, minor shrapnel wounds, and malaria. Drugs administered to him caused addiction and he voluntarily entered a Federal Narcotics Sanitarium in Lexington, Ky., where he was cured. With Martin Abramson, he wrote *No Man Stands Alone* (1957).

Ross, Betsy, 1752-1836, American seamstress, b. Philadelphia. Her full name was Elizabeth Griscom Ross. She is known to have made flags during the American Revolution, although the long-accepted story that she designed and made the first American national flag (the Stars and Stripes) is generally discredited.

Ross, Edward Alsworth, 1866-1951, American sociologist, b. Virden, Ill., Ph.D. Johns Hopkins, 1891. He taught economics (1893-1900) at Stanford Univ., from which he was ousted in a controversy over academic freedom. From 1906 to 1937 he was professor of sociology at the Univ. of Wisconsin. He analyzed collective behavior and social control and wrote voluminously on population and other problems. His chief works are *Social Control* (1901, new ed. 1969) and *Principles of Sociology* (1921). See his autobiography, *Seventy Years of It* (1937); study by Julius Weinberg (1972).

Ross, George, 1730-79, political leader in the American Revolution, signer of the Declaration of Independence, b. New Castle, Del. He was a lawyer in Lancaster, Pa., and a member of the colonial assembly (1768-74) before serving as delegate (1774-77) to the Continental Congress.

Ross, Sir George William, 1841-1914, Canadian political leader, b. Ontario. He sat (1872-83) in the House of Commons and then entered the Ontario government as minister of education. He was Liberal prime minister of Ontario from 1899 to 1905. In 1907 he was appointed to the Canadian Senate and in 1910, the year he was knighted, became Liberal leader in the Senate. He was a notable public speaker, and many of his addresses have been published. See biography by Margaret Ross (1923).

Ross, Sir James Clark, 1800-1862, British polar explorer and rear admiral. In 1818 he accompanied his uncle, Sir John Ross, in search of the Northwest Passage and commanded the *Erebus.* He later studied Eskimo life while on several arctic voyages (1819-27) with W. E. Parry. In another expedition (1829-33) with his uncle, he located (1831) in Boothia Peninsula the north magnetic pole (now located in Prince of Wales Island). In command of an expedition (1839-43) to study earth magnetism in Antarctica, Ross discovered Ross Sea, reaching Ross Island and following the Ross Shelf Ice eastward for c.350 mi (560 km). He also discovered Victoria Land and much of North Graham Land. He recorded his experiences in his *Voyage of Discovery and Research to Southern and Antarctic Regions* (1847). In 1848-49 he made another visit to the arctic regions in search for Sir John Franklin. See E. S. Dodge, *The Polar Rosses* (1973).

Ross, Sir John, 1777-1856, British arctic explorer and rear admiral. In 1818 he went in search of the Northwest Passage but turned back after exploring Baffin Bay. Financed by Sir Felix Booth, he commanded a second search expedition (1829-33), in the course of which he discovered Boothia Peninsula, the Gulf of Boothia, and King William Island and explored Smith, Jones, and Lancaster sounds. Ross was knighted in 1833. His last trip to the arctic regions was made in 1850-51, when he went to the Lancaster Sound region to search for Sir John Franklin. He wrote two books describing his quest for the Northwest Passage. See E. S. Dodge, *The Polar Rosses* (1973).

Ross, John, whose name in Cherokee is **Koowes-koowe** (ko͞o"wĭs"ko͞owē'), 1790-1866, Indian chief, b. near Lookout Mt., Tenn., of Scottish and Cherokee parents. He was educated at Kingston, Tenn., and in the War of 1812 served under Andrew Jackson against the Creeks. Elected principal chief of the eastern Cherokee in 1828, Ross struggled valiantly to hold the ancestral lands of his people but was unable to withstand the constant pressure of the state of Georgia for removal. In a treaty (1835) of questionable validity, a small minority of the Cherokee ceded the lands and moved west. Ross and the majority refused to acknowledge the cession, but resistance was unsuccessful, and in 1838-39 he led them on the long, hard journey to present-day Oklahoma. Thousands died on the trip, known in Indian lore as the "trail of tears." From 1839 until his death Ross was chief of the united Cherokee nation (the western Cherokee had migrated at the beginning of the century). He counseled neutrality in the U.S. Civil War, but the Cherokee ultimately supported the Confederacy. See biography by R. C. Eaton (1921).

Ross, Robert, 1766-1814, British general. He served against the French in the Netherlands, in Egypt, and in the Peninsular War. In the War of 1812 he defeated a U.S. force at BLADENSBURG, and on the same day (Aug. 24, 1814) he surprised and captured Washington, burning all the public buildings. Spurred by victory, Ross decided to attempt the capture of Baltimore. On Sept. 12, in a thick wood near North Point, his army encountered the American militia. A skirmish ensued, and Ross was killed.

Ross, Sir Ronald, 1857-1932, English physician, b. Almora, India. He studied malaria in India as a member (1881-99) of the Indian Medical Service, was professor of tropical medicine at University College, Liverpool, from 1902, and directed the Ross Institute and Hospital for Tropical Diseases, London, from 1926. In 1898 he demonstrated the malarial parasite (*Plasmodium*) in the stomach of the *Anopheles* mosquito; in W Africa he discovered the mosquito that transmits African fever. He received the 1902 Nobel Prize in Physiology and Medicine for his work on malaria and was knighted in 1911. He also published poems, novels, and mathematical studies. See his memoirs (1923); J. Rowland, *The Mosquito Man* (1958).

Ross and Cromarty (krŏm'ərtē), county (1971 pop. 58,267), 3,089 sq mi (8,001 sq km), N Scotland. The county town is DINGWALL. Located in the Highlands region, the county extends from the North Sea to the Atlantic and includes the district of Lewis on Lewis with Harris island and many smaller islands. The irregular shoreline is indented by Moray, Cromarty, and Dornoch firths on the east and by a series of sea lochs on the west. Except for the fertile Black Isle district on the east coast, it is a mountainous region of moors and barren rocks, reaching its highest point at Mam Soul or Mam Sodhail (3,862 ft/ 1,178 m) on the southern border. Sheep grazing, crofting, distilling, and fishing are the main occupations. Tweeds are made in Lewis. The history of the county is largely that of feuds among the local clans. Ross-shire, once independent, was incorporated with Cromarty in 1889. In 1975, Ross and Cromarty was divided between the Highland and Western Isles regions.

Rossbach (rôs'bäkh), village, Halle dist., S central East Germany. At Rossbach on Nov. 5, 1757, Frederick II of Prussia defeated the imperial army and the French under Soubise in the Seven Years War. One of Frederick's most brilliant victories, it was followed by another at Leuthen one month later.

Ross Dam, Wash.: see SKAGIT, river.

Rosse, William Parsons, 3d **earl of** (rôs), 1800–1867, British astronomer and constructor of telescopes. He served as member of Parliament for King's Co., Ireland (1821–34), Irish representative peer (from 1845), president of the British Association (1843), president of the Royal Society (1849–54), and chancellor of the Univ. of Dublin (from 1862). His greatest interest was the construction of specula of large size for reflecting telescopes; he overcame defects caused by warping and cracking of surfaces in the cooling process and counteracted to a considerable degree other defects. His great reflecting telescope, with a speculum 6 ft (1.8 m) in diameter, the largest up to that time, was mounted in his park at Parsonstown (now Birr), Ireland, in 1845. For many years it was chiefly devoted to the study of the nebulas. Some nebulas that had eluded Sir William Herschel were resolved into groups of stars, many binary and triple stars were discovered, and the moon was more completely described.

Rosselli, Cosimo (kô'zēmō rōs-sĕl'lē), 1439–1507, Florentine painter. He was one of the artists summoned to Rome by Sixtus IV to assist in decorating the Sistine Chapel. He painted *The Last Supper* and other subjects for it. Of his many works in Florence the most famous is *The Miracle-working Chalice* in Sant' Ambrogio, a work that includes many contemporary portraits. He ran a large workshop. Among his pupils were Piero di Cosimo and Fra Bartolomeo. There are paintings by Rosselli in the Louvre; the National Gallery of Art, Washington, D.C.; and in the Walters Art Gallery, Baltimore.

Rossellini, Roberto (rōbĕr'tō rōs-sĕl-lē'nē), 1906–, Italian film director and producer. He began working in films in 1935 and first received international attention in 1946 with his daring *Open City,* which became the key film of the Italian neorealist movement. His *Paisan* (1946) and *Stromboli* (1949) were also notable films. Rossellini often drew memorable performances from nonprofessional actors. His significant later work includes *The Rise of Louis XIV* (1966). Rossellini was married to Ingrid BERGMAN.

Rossellino, Antonio (äntô'nyō rōs-sĕl-lē'nō), 1427–c.1478, Florentine sculptor, whose name was Antonio di Matteo di Domenico Gamberelli. He was the youngest and most celebrated of four brothers, of whom the eldest was the architect Bernardo Rossellino, who designed the Rucellai Palace and who carved the sculpture for Leonardo Bruni's tomb in Santa Croce, Florence. Antonio was well known for his tomb monuments. In such works as his monument to the cardinal of Portugal in San Miniato al Monte, Florence, and the tomb of Mary of Aragon (Naples) he created masterful combinations of sculpture and architecture. He carved vigorous portraits, such as those of Matteo Palmieri (Bargello Mus., Florence) and Giovanni Chellini (Victoria and Albert Mus., London). Rossellino also produced many picturesque reliefs, exemplified by the *Nativity* (Mt. Oliveto, Naples) and scenes for the cathedral pulpit at Prato. Two Madonnas in the Metropolitan Museum and the Pierpont Morgan Library, New York City, are ascribed to him as well.

Rossetti, Christina Georgina (rōsĕt'ē), 1830–94, English poet; sister of Dante Gabriel Rossetti. She is probably the greatest female poet in English literature. Publication of some of her poems in her brother William's magazine the *Germ* was her only contribution to Pre-Raphaelite activities. Of a very religious nature, she was a devout member of the Church of England and lived the last 15 years of her life as a recluse in her home. Much of her poetry is religious, some of it melancholy, and such poems as her famous "Uphill" and "When I Am Dead, My Dearest" are written about death. Her life and her spontaneous lyric gift seem perhaps comparable to those of Emily DICKINSON, though the comparison can go no further, for Christina Rossetti, who came close to technical perfection in traditional poetic forms, experimented very little. Her gay and simple songs, especially those in *Sing-Song* (1872), are favorites with children. Some of her volumes of poetry are *Goblin Market and Other Poems* (1862), probably her best work; *The Prince's Progress* (1866); and *A Pageant and Other Poems* (1881). See biographies by Marya Zaturenska (1949), Lona Mosk Packer (1963), and M. Bell (4th ed., 1971).

Rossetti, Dante Gabriel (dăn'tē gā'brēəl), 1828–82, English poet and painter; son of Gabriele Rossetti and brother of Christina Rossetti. He was one of the founders of the PRE-RAPHAELITES. In addition to attending the Royal Academy he studied painting briefly with Ford Madox Brown. In 1848 he became acquainted with W. Holman HUNT and John Everett MILLAIS and with them formed the brotherhood of Pre-Raphaelites. In an effort to spread their ideas the group published in 1850 a short-lived magazine, the *Germ,* edited by Rossetti's brother William Michael Rossetti (1829–1919). In it was printed "The Blessed Damozel" by Dante Gabriel, written when he was 19 and considered by many to be his best poem. In 1851, John Ruskin championed the Pre-Raphaelites, and shortly thereafter made an arrangement with Rossetti to buy all of Rossetti's paintings that pleased him; thus, Rossetti became financially solvent. In 1860 he married his model Elizabeth Siddal, a former milliner's assistant whom he loved and had been more or less engaged to for nearly 10 years. Melancholic and tubercular, she took an overdose of laudanum and died in 1862. Rossetti, in a fit of guilt and grief, buried with her a manuscript containing a number of his poems. Some years later he permitted her body to be exhumed and the poems recovered. The first edition of his collected works appeared in 1870. The last years of his life were marked by an increasingly morbid state of mind (he became addicted to alcohol and chloral), and for a time he was considered insane. Although he began his career as a painter, Rossetti's lasting reputation rests upon his poetry. He never really mastered the technique of painting, and although his pictures are extremely sensuous, they are also somewhat two-dimensional. His best artistic efforts are his drawings, particularly the pen-and-ink portraits of his mother, his sister, and his wife. Almost inseparable in tone and feeling from his paintings, his poetry is noted for its pictorial effects and its atmosphere of luxurious beauty. Although there is always passion in his verse, there is also always thought. He was a master of the sonnet form, and his sonnet sequence "The House of Life" is one of his finest works. His other notable works include the ballad "Sister Helen" and the dramatic monologues "Jenny" and "A Last Confession." His translations from the Italian appeared as *Dante and His Circle* (1861). There are examples of his paintings in the Tate Gallery and the Victoria and Albert Museum, London, and in many collections in England and the United States. See his poems (ed. by Oswald Doughty, 1957); biographies by Oswald Doughty (2d ed. 1963) and Evelyn Waugh (1928, repr. 1969); studies by S. A. Brooke (1908, repr. 1964), G. H. Fleming (1967), and Robert S. Fraser, ed. (1972).

Rossetti, Gabriele (gäbrēē'lā), 1783–1854, Italian poet and critic; father of Dante Gabriel Rossetti and of Christina Rossetti. Exiled in 1821, he fled first to Malta, where he stayed for three years, and then to England, where he lived until his death. There he wrote patriotic and liberal verse in Italian and a curious study attempting to show that Dante had written as spokesman for a vast secret, ritualistic society opposed to tyranny. He was professor of Italian at King's College, London, from 1831 until he retired in 1845. His long romantic poem *Il veggente in solitudine* [the seer in solitude] was published in 1846 and his autobiography in 1849. See R. D. Waller, *The Rossetti Family* (1932).

Rossi, Pellegrino Luigi Edoardo, Conte (pĕl"-lāgrē'nō lwē'jē ādōär'dō kôn'tā rôs'sē), 1787–1848, Italian political leader and jurist. As a supporter of Joachim MURAT, Rossi was obliged to flee Italy (1815) when Murat fell. He went first to Geneva, where he became a noted professor of law and an active politician, then to Paris (1833), where he taught at the Collège de France, became a citizen, and was raised to the peerage. Louis Philippe sent him as ambassador to the Holy See, where he favored the election of Pope PIUS IX. After the upheaval (1848) in France, Rossi became president of the council in the pope's first constitutional government. A moderate reformer, he was the target of both radicals and reactionaries. He was assassinated by radicals. Rossi wrote treatises on economics.

Rossini, Gioacchino Antonio (jōäk-kē'nō äntô'-nyō rōs-sē'nē), 1792–1868, Italian operatic composer, one of the great masters of the Italian opera buffa. His parents were both musicians, and he began his career in childhood as a singer. He received his first formal musical education at the Liceo Comunale of Bologna, where one of his early cantatas was performed. Rossini's first comic opera, *La Cambiale de Matrimonio,* was produced in Venice in 1810, and it was followed by a series of lively works, culminating in his masterpiece, *Il Barbiere di Siviglia* (*The Barber of Seville,* 1816). Based on the comedy by Beaumarchais, the opera resounds with Rossini's brilliant arias, ensemble numbers, and his famous crescendos. Among his many other operas are *L'italiana in Algeri* (1813), *La Cenerentola* (1817), and *Semiramide* (1823). In 1824, Rossini became the director of the Théâtre-Italien in Paris. After the production of his *William Tell* at the Paris Opéra in 1829, he stopped composing operas, and during the remaining 39 years of his life he wrote only songs, piano pieces, and a setting of the *Stabat Mater* (1842), in which his operatic style is still evident. See biographies by Stendhal (1822, repr. 1971), Francis Toye (1934, repr. 1963), and Herbert Weinstock (1968).

Rossiter, Thomas Pritchard, 1818–1871, American historical painter, b. New Haven, Conn. He spent many years in Europe, studying and painting, and settled finally in Cold Spring, N.Y., where he devoted himself chiefly to religious and historical painting. *Washington and Lafayette at Mount Vernon* (Metropolitan Mus.), also called *Palmy Days,* is one of his better-known works.

Ross Lake National Recreation Area: see NATIONAL PARKS AND MONUMENTS (table).

Rosso, Il (ēl rôs'sō), 1495–1540, Italian painter, one of the founders of mannerism, b. Florence. His real name was Giovan Battista di Iacopo di Gasparre. Influences of Andrea del Sarto and Pontormo are evident in his first work, *The Assumption* (the Annunziata, Florence), a painting in which there is already a distorted treatment of space and a dissonant use of color. Rosso's figures become more elongated and entwined in the *Deposition from the Cross* (Volterra) and in the startling *Daughters of Jethro* (Uffizi). In 1523 he went to Rome. After the sack of Rome (1527) he worked in various towns of Italy and then traveled to France. By 1532 he had become the official painter to King Francis I. Together with PRIMATICCIO, he worked on the decoration of the royal château at Fontainebleau. They were both influential in bringing the artistic currents of Italy to France.

Rosso, Medardo (mādär'dō), 1858–1928, Italian sculptor. A painter until 1883, he turned to sculpture and worked periodically in Paris but lived mainly in Milan. He was a friend of Degas and Rodin, but he quarreled with the latter in 1898 about which of them had introduced impressionism into sculpture. Rosso showed brilliance in his ability to capture the play of light on a surface. He preferred to work in wax, since the material lends itself to effects of suppleness and fluidity. A characteristic portrait is his *Bimbo ebreo* (Univ. of Nebraska). In Barzio the Rosso Museum houses much of his work.

Rosso di San Secondo, Piermaria (pyĕr"märē'ä rôs'sō dē sän sĕkôn'dō), 1887–, Italian writer, b. Sicily. His many sophisticated plays include *Marionette, che passione!* (1918) and *La bella addormentata* [sleeping beauty] (1919). His novel *La fuga* [flight] appeared in 1917 and *Banda municipale,* short stories, in 1954.

Ross Sea, arm of the Pacific Ocean, ANTARCTICA, between Victoria Land and Marie Byrd Land. It was discovered in 1841 by Sir James Clark Ross, a British explorer. Ross Island with Mt. Erebus, an active volcano, is in the western part of the sea; Roosevelt Island is in the east. The Ross Sea's southern extension is the Ross Ice Shelf, a great frozen area whose 400-mi (644-km) seaward side is the source of huge icebergs. The **Bay of Whales,** the ice shelf's best known inlet, lasted for c.50 years and was the site of Norwegian explorer Roald Amundsen's base for his trek to the South Pole in 1911; Little America, a U.S. base, was located nearby. **McMurdo Sound,** on the western side of Ross Sea, is usually free of pack ice in late summer; it has been the most important staging point for exploration and scientific investigation.

Rostand, Edmond (ĕdmôN′ rôstäN′), 1868–1918, French poet and dramatist. In 1890 appeared his first volume of verse, *Les Musardises.* His first plays were light, fanciful, and charmingly poetic, though of slight substance—*Les Romanesques* (1894, tr., *The Romancers,* 1899); *La Princesse lointaine* (1895, tr. *The Princess Faraway,* 1899), written for Sarah Bernhardt; and *La Samaritaine* (1897, tr. *The Woman of Samaria,* from his *Plays,* 1921). They were followed by *Cyrano de Bergerac* (1897, tr. 1923), a tour de force of dramatic poetry. The role of Cyrano was made memorable by the acting of Coquelin aîné, Richard Mansfield, and, on the screen (1950), Jose Ferrer. In 1900 Rostand wrote *L'Aiglon,* whose central figure is the pathetic duke of Reichstadt (Napoleon II), a role long played by Sarah Bernhardt. His barnyard fable *Chantecler* (1910) was played in the United States by Maude Adams.

Rostock (rôs′tôk) or **Rostock-Warnemünde** (-vär″nəmün′də), city (1970 pop. 198,396), capital of Rostock district, N East Germany, on the Baltic Sea. It is an industrial center and a major seaport, with petroleum tank installations and shipyards. Manufactures include agricultural machinery, chemicals, watches, processed food, and furniture. There is a large fishing fleet based at Rostock. The city is a terminus of a train ferry to Gedser, Denmark. Originally a Slavic fortress, Rostock was chartered in the 13th cent. It became one of the chief members of the Hanseatic League. Its university (founded 1419) was an important center of learning for N Germany and Scandinavia. The city was heavily damaged in World War II. Historic structures include the 13th-century Church of St. Mary and parts of the medieval city walls and gates. Gebhard von Blücher, the Prussian general, was born (1742) in Rostock.

Rostopchin, Feodor Vasilyevich, Count (fyô′dər vəsē′lyəvĭch, rəstəpchēn′), 1763–1826, Russian general and statesman. He rose rapidly under Czar Paul I, serving as foreign minister from 1798–1800. He was made a count in 1799. In 1812, Czar Alexander I appointed him governor-general of Moscow. He was later held responsible for the burning of Moscow, which occurred when French forces entered the city in Sept., 1812. He was dismissed from office in 1814 and went into exile. Rostopchin denied the accusation in his pamphlet *The Truth Concerning the Fire of Moscow* (in French, 1823); the cause of the conflagration is still in doubt.

Rostov (rŏ′stŏv, Rus. rəstôf′), city (1967 est. pop. 31,000), E European USSR, on Lake Nero. It is a road and rail junction and has food-processing and flax-spinning plants. Linen is produced, and an old enamel-painting craft is still practiced. One of Russia's oldest cities, Rostov has been known since 862 and still retains its medieval aspect. It became the capital of the Rostov-Suzdal principality in 1207, was annexed by the grand duchy of Moscow in 1474, was made the seat of an Orthodox metropolitan in 1587, and served as an important commercial center from the 16th to 19th cent. Trade, however, was of less economic importance to the city than agriculture and handicrafts. Rostov's ancient kremlin contains the Uspenski Cathedral and other splendid 13th-century churches with precious murals. The palace of the metropolitan is now a museum. The city was also known as Rostov-Veliki (Great Rostov) and Rostov-Yaroslavski.

Rostov-na-Donu (rəstôf′-nə-dənoo͞′), city (1970 pop. 789,000), capital of Rostov oblast, SE European USSR, on the Don River near its entrance into the Sea of Azov. It is a major port and rail hub and an important industrial, cultural, and scientific center. Grains and wool are the chief exports. One of the USSR's leading producers of agricultural machinery, Rostov-na-Donu also has ship and locomotive repair yards, plants processing food and tobacco, mechanical engineering works, and factories that manufacture chemicals, building materials, electrical equipment, road-making machinery, furniture, clothing, footwear, and leather goods. A customs house was built on the site in 1749, but the city grew around a fortress erected in 1761 and named for St. Dmitri of Rostov. Chartered in 1797, it was named Rostov-na-Donu to distinguish it from the older city of Rostov. It grew rapidly after the opening of its port in 1834 and was a major grain-exporting center throughout the 19th cent. Its position as a center for trade between European Russia and the Caucasus area also gave it the name "Gateway to the Caucasus." The city suffered much damage in World War II and had to be rebuilt after the war.

Rostovtzeff, Michael Ivanovich (rŏstŏv′tsĕf), 1870–1952, American historian, b. Kiev, Ukraine. He studied at the Univ. of St. Petersburg (Leningrad), where he was professor of Latin and of Roman history from 1898 to 1918. He emigrated to the United States during the Russian Revolution, taught ancient history at the Univ. of Wisconsin (1920–25), and was appointed (1925) Sterling professor of ancient history and archaeology at Yale. From 1939 to 1944, when he received emeritus status, Rostovtzeff was director of archaeological studies at Yale. One of the most distinguished modern scholars of ancient history, Rostovtzeff won his chief reputation through his *Social and Economic History of the Roman Empire* (1926) and *A History of the Ancient World* (Vol. I, *The Orient and Greece,* 1926; Vol. II, *Rome,* 1927). The first of these was a pioneering effort in its application of the most recent archaeological research to an aspect of Roman history that until then had been neglected. It has taken its place among the chief modern contributions to Roman historiography. The two volumes of his *History of the Ancient World* are admirable condensations and place the cultural, economic, and social aspects of ancient life on the same level of importance as political and military events. Among Rostovtzeff's other works in English are *A Large Estate in Egypt in the Third Century B.C.* (1922) and *Iranians and Greeks in South Russia* (1922).

Rostow, Eugene Victor Debs, 1913–, U.S. lawyer, brother of Walt Whitman Rostow, b. Brooklyn, N.Y. Admitted to the bar in 1938, Rostow joined the Yale law school faculty and became (1944) full professor of law. As dean of the law school (1955–65), he launched a major curricular revision intended to emphasize the relationship of law to other academic disciplines and the workings of society. Rostow served (1966–69) as Undersecretary of State for political affairs under President Lyndon B. Johnson. He is the author of numerous articles and books including *Planning for Freedom* (1959), *Law, Power and the Pursuit of Peace* (1968), and *Peace in the Balance* (1972).

Rostow, Walt Whitman, 1916–, economist and government official, b. New York City; brother of Eugene Debs Rostow. A Rhodes scholar, he served (1942–45) with the Office of Strategic Services during World War II and later was (1950–60) a professor of economic history at Massachusetts Institute of Technology. As chairman (1961–66) of the policy planning council of the State Dept., and later as special assistant (1966–69) to President Lyndon B. Johnson, Rostow exerted a major influence on U.S. foreign policy. An anti-Communist, he advocated military intervention in Vietnam, and he was in large part responsible for the decision (1965) to bomb North Vietnam. He became (1969) professor of economics and history at the Univ. of Texas. An important economic theorist, Rostow wrote *The Stages of Economic Growth* (1960, 2d ed. 1971). He is also the author of *The United States in the World Arena* (1960); *Politics and the Stages of Growth* (1971); and *The Diffusion of Power* (1972).

Roswell (rŏz′wĕl), city (1970 pop. 33,908), seat of Chaves co., SE N. Mex., near the Pecos River; settled 1869 as a trading post, inc. 1903. It is the trade, marketing, and rail center of an irrigated farm area. The city grew rapidly after the discovery (1891) of artesian wells, with the coming (1894) of the railroad, and with the later discovery of oil. Eastern New Mexico Univ. has a campus in Roswell; and New Mexico Military Institute, a state-supported junior college, is also there. Nearby are a state park, Bitter Lake National Wildlife Refuge, Lincoln National Forest, and the ranch of John S. Chisum, the 19th-century cattleman.

Roszak, Theodore (rô′shäk), 1907–, American sculptor, b. Poland. Commencing his artistic career as a painter, Roszak began in the late 1930s to create constructions in plastics and metal. In the postwar period his style underwent an abrupt change in the direction of irregular and explosive forms, symbolic and fantastic in content. Roszak's *Thorn Blossom* (Whitney Mus., New York City) and *Whaler of Nantucket* (1952; Art Inst. of Chicago) are representative examples that carried sculpture toward ABSTRACT EXPRESSIONISM. See study by H. H. Arnason (1956).

rotary engine, internal-combustion engine whose cycle is similar to that of a piston engine, but which produces rotary motion directly without any conversion from reciprocating motion. A major problem associated with engines of this type is preventing the leakage of combustion gases. The only type of rotary engine currently considered to be of practical value is the Wankel engine (see INTERNAL-COMBUSTION ENGINE). Although the gas turbine produces rotary motion directly, it is not generally considered a rotary engine because it functions differently.

Rotary International, organization of business and professional men, founded (1905) by Paul Percy Harris, a Chicago lawyer. Beginning with one club in Chicago, it spread to other cities, and in 1910 the National Association of Rotary Clubs was formed. After other branches were established in many countries throughout the world, the name was changed (1922) to Rotary International. Each club contains no more than one representative of each business or profession in its locality. The name was derived from the original custom of meeting in rotation at the members' places of business. The organization promotes friendly cooperation and high standards of service among businessmen, supports charities and welfare activities, and encourages international friendship. Its membership exceeds 700,000. Its official publication is the *Rotarian.*

rotation of crops, agricultural practice of varying the crops on a piece of land in a planned series, to save or increase the mineral or organic content of the soil, to increase crop yields, and to eradicate weeds, insects, and plant diseases. In a rotation, it is often desirable to alternate a cultivated crop (e.g., corn) with a legume (e.g., clover), which adds nitrogen to the soil.

rotenone (rō′tənōn″): see INSECTICIDE.

Roth, Cecil, 1899–1970, Jewish historian and educator, b. London. He was educated at Oxford (Ph.D., 1924) and was reader in Jewish Studies there from 1939 to 1964. Thereafter he was visiting professor at Bar-Ilan Univ., Israel (1964–65), and at the City University of New York (1966–69). He was editor of *Encyclopedia Judaica* from 1965 until his death. His works number over 600 items, including histories of the Jews in England (1941) and Italy (1946), *A History of the Marranos* (3d ed. 1966), *The Jews in the Renaissance* (1959), *Jewish Art* (1961), and *The Dead Sea Scrolls* (1965). See bibliography of his writings in J. M. Shaftesley, ed., *Remember the Days* (1966).

Roth, Frederick George Richard, 1872–1944, American animal sculptor, b. Brooklyn, N.Y., educated at Bremen, Germany, and studied art in Vienna and Berlin. His elephants, dogs, and horses, whether in small bronzes or life size, are presented in an original and sympathetic manner.

Roth, Joseph (yō′zĕf rōt), 1894–1939, Austrian novelist, essayist, journalist, and publisher. Roth was an outspoken critic of Hitler and militarism. His novels, though basically conservative, reflect political awareness and skepticism. They include *Hotel Savoy* (1924) and *Die Flucht ohne Ende* (1927; tr. *Flight without End,* 1930). *Hiob* (1930; tr. *Job,* 1933), concerning the struggle of East European Jews, and *Radetzkymarsch* (1932), an ironic portrait of the Danube monarchy, are his best-known works.

Roth, Philip, 1933–, American author, b. Newark, N.J., grad. Univ. of Chicago (M.A., 1955). Roth's writings, noted for their perceptive wit and irony, deal chiefly with middle-class Jewish-American life. *Portnoy's Complaint* (1969), his most famous novel, is an outrageously comic account of a contemporary man torn between his Jewish background, as represented by his mother, and his lust for WASP women. Roth's other works include the short-story collection *Good-bye Columbus* (1959); and the novels *Letting Go* (1962); *When She Was Good* (1967); *Our Gang (Starring Tricky and His Friends)* (1971), a satire of the Nixon administration; *The Breast* (1972); *The Great American Novel* (1973); and *My Life As A Man* (1974).

Rothamsted Experimental Station (rŏth′əmstĭd), world's oldest and England's most important agricultural experiment station. It was founded in 1843 by John Bennet Lawes on his estate at Harpenden, in Hertfordshire, where he had been experimenting with fertilizers. In 1842 a patent had been granted him for the development of superphosphate—bone meal, or calcium phosphate, treated with sulfuric acid—an artificial fertilizer which his factory soon produced in large quantities. The station continued experimenting with fertilizers and expanded its activities to include crop-production studies and animal nutrition experiments. Expansions started in 1902 provided new facilities and added to the staff botanists, bacteriologists, chemists, and writers, which increased the value of the station to Great Britain's varied agricultural interests, distributed as they were throughout the world. In 1934 a public appeal brought forth the funds needed to buy the grounds used by the station. The experimental work, which had once been financed entirely by Lawes, came to be sustained by government grants, supplemented by contributions of private interests. The departments among which the station's functions are divided are chemistry, soil microbiology, physics, botany, entomology, insecticides and fungicides, plant pathology, and statistics. Their work is recorded in the ongoing *Rothamsted Memoirs on Agricultural Science* and *Rothamsted Monographs on Agricultural Science.* These publications are distributed to major libraries, agricultural colleges, and other stations throughout the world. An important function of the station now is the training of postgraduate research workers. See A. D. Hall, *The Book of the Rothamsted Experiments* (2d ed. 1917); Sir Edward John Russell, *British Agricultural Research: Rothamsted* (rev. ed. 1947); catalogue of the station's publications, ed. by D. H. Boalch (1954).

Rothe, Richard (rĭkh'ärt rō'tə), 1799–1867, German Lutheran theologian. Rothe, a disciple of Schleiermacher, was influenced by Pietism while professor at Wittenberg Theological Seminary. His insistence on the close connection between ethics and religion is presented in *Theoligische Ethik* (3 vol., 1845–48).

Rothenburg ob der Tauber (rō'tənbo͝orkh ôp dĕr tou'bər), town (1970 pop. 11,662), Bavaria, S West Germany, on the Tauber River. One of the best-preserved and most picturesque medieval towns in West Germany, it is primarily a tourist center. The town is entirely walled (the walls dating from the 14th and 15th cent.), and it contains numerous Gothic and Renaissance-style buildings. The town hall (13th–16th cent.) is considered one of the most beautiful in S West Germany. Noteworthy churches include St. Jakobskirche (1373–1436) and St. Johanniskirche (1393–1403). First mentioned in the 10th cent., Rothenburg was a free imperial city from the late 13th cent. until 1803, when it passed to Bavaria.

Rothenstein, Sir William (rō'thənstīn), 1872–1945, English painter and writer. He was well known for his portraits of famous people and for his pictures of Jewish subjects, including *Jews Mourning in the Synagogue* (Tate Gall., London). There is a self-portrait in the Metropolitan Museum. He worked as an artist in both World Wars. Rothenstein wrote biographical sketches that appear in *English Portraits* (1898) and *Twenty-four Portraits* (1920–23). His *Men and Memories* (2 vol., 1922–38) and *Since Fifty* (1940) are autobiographical.

Rotherham (rŏth'ərəm), county borough (1971 pop. 84,646), West Riding of Yorkshire, N England, at the confluence of the Don and Rother rivers. It lies in a coal district. Manufactures include steel, brass, electrical equipment, glass, and chemicals. On an old bridge over the Don is a 15th-century chapel. There are technical and art colleges. In 1974, Rotherham became part of the new metropolitan county of South Yorkshire.

Rothermel, Peter Frederick (rŏth'ərmĕl), 1817–95, American painter, b. Nescopeck, Pa., studied in Paris. His noted historical works include a colossal *Battle of Gettysburg* (Capitol building, Harrisburg, Pa.).

Rothermere, Harold Sidney Harmsworth, 1st Viscount (rŏth'ərmēr), 1868–1940, English publisher. He was the financial wizard of the publishing firm headed by his brother Alfred, Viscount NORTHCLIFFE. In 1915 he founded the *Sunday Pictorial* and after his brother's death in 1922 gained control of the vast newspaper empire. He was created viscount in 1919. Though long friendly to Fascism and a proponent of appeasement in 1938, he wholeheartedly supported the British cause in World War II.

Rothesay, David Stuart, duke of: see STUART, DAVID, DUKE OF ROTHESAY.

Rothko, Mark (rŏth'kō), 1903–1970, American painter, b. Russia. Rothko emigrated to the United States in 1913. He was a student of Max WEBER, then came under the influence of the surrealists. In the mid-1940s Rothko experimented with abstraction, arranging intense colors in irregular shapes. His later works (e.g., *No. 10,* 1950; Mus. of Modern Art, New York City) frequently consist of floating rectangles of luminous color on enormous canvases. He was considered a leading exponent of ABSTRACT EXPRESSIONISM. Rothko committed suicide at 67. See study by Peter Selz (1961, repr. 1972).

Rothschild (rŏth'chīld, Ger. rōt'shĭlt), prominent family of European bankers. The first important member was Mayer Amschel Rothschild (1743–1812), son of a money changer in the Jewish ghetto of Frankfurt, Germany. His first names are also variously spelled as Meyer and Anselm. It was he who laid the foundation of the family fortune by his skillful operations as financial agent for the landgrave of Hesse-Kassel, later known as Elector William I. His five sons were Amschel Mayer Rothschild (1773–1855), who remained at Frankfurt with his father; Salomon Rothschild (1774–1855), who established the Vienna branch of the family; Nathan Meyer Rothschild (see separate article), who founded the London branch; Karl Rothschild (1788–1855), who established the Naples branch (discontinued in 1860 after the Italian annexation of Naples); and Jacob Rothschild (1792–1868), who settled in Paris. After the Napoleonic Wars the house of Rothschild, which remained a single-family enterprise, attained increasing power, and in 1822 all five brothers were created barons by Emperor Francis I of Austria. Because of their position as creditor of many European governments, the Rothschilds were undoubtedly one of the world's chief financial powers in the 19th cent., but the improvement in state financing late in the century greatly reduced their influence. The Rothschild family has made it a tradition to cling to the Jewish faith and to engage in large-scale philanthropies, both for Jews and non-Jews. Many later and contemporary members of the family distinguished themselves as patrons of the arts, sportsmen, writers, and doctors. See E. C. Corti, *Rise of the House of Rothschild* (1928, repr. 1972) and *Reign of the House of Rothschild* (1928); M. E. Ravage, *Five Men of Frankfurt* (1929); Frederic Morton, *The Rothschilds* (1962); V. S. Cowles, *The Rothschilds: A Family of Fortune* (1973).

Rothschild, Nathan Meyer, 1777–1836, British banker, b. Frankfurt, Germany; of the famous Rothschild family. He went to England in 1797, was naturalized in 1804, and opened a business house in London in 1805. He acted as agent of the British government in supplying subsidies to the powers opposing Napoleon I and was of vital help in the defeat of the French emperor. Aside from his financial acumen, Rothschild was aided in his transactions by a very efficient information service. Thus he was informed of the allied victory at Waterloo by carrier pigeons and, in a single day, made a fortune and saved the London stock exchange from collapse by buying up all the shares sold by frightened investors. In 1822 he became Austrian consul general in England but never carried the title of baron presented to him by Austria. His loans to France, Russia, and other countries (particularly in South America) were popular in England because they required repayment in sterling, thereby avoiding disadvantageous exchange-rate fluctuations. After his death the house of Rothschild was dominated by his son, **Baron Lionel Nathan de Rothschild,** 1808–79, who established a virtual family monopoly for the flotation of large international loans. He handled the Irish famine loan (1847) and the Crimean War loan (1856). First elected to the House of Commons in 1847, he was not able to assume his seat until 1858, when he was finally allowed to take the parliamentary oath in a manner acceptable to his Jewish faith. Aside from being the first Jewish member of Parliament, he was also active in public life as a generous philanthropist.

Rothstein, Arnold (rôth'stēn), 1883–1928, American gambler, b. New York City. Supposedly beginning his gambling career at the age of 12, Rothstein became a professional gambler and operated gambling houses in New York City, Saratoga Springs, N.Y., and Long Beach, N.Y. He had a reputation for betting large amounts of money, and he once bet $140,000 on a horse and $100,000 on a single throw of dice. Besides running gambling houses, he operated a racing stable, a real estate business, and a bail bond operation. Rothstein was believed to have contacts in high places and was often accused of being the mastermind behind large gambling scandals (such as the "Black Sox" baseball scandal of 1919, where eight members of the Chicago White Sox confessed to accepting bribes to throw the world series of that year to Cincinnati); however, the charges remain unproved. While playing cards in a hotel room he was murdered—allegedly for reneging on a bet. His murderer or murderers were never identified. See Donald Henderson Clark, *In the Reign of Rothstein* (1929); Carolyn Rothstein, *Now I'll Tell* (1934); Leo Katcher, *The Big Bankroll* (1959).

Roth vs. United States, case decided in 1957 by the U.S. Supreme Court. Samuel Roth of New York City was convicted of mailing obscene materials. On appeal his conviction was affirmed by the Supreme Court, which held that obscenity was not protected by the First Amendment to the U.S. Constitution. The court ruled that material is obscene if, to the average person applying contemporary community standards, the dominant overall theme appeals to prurient interest. In later decisions in 1973 and 1974 the Court held that community standards need not be national; a state can establish its own standards if it defines them explicitly.

Rotifera, class of organisms belonging to the phylum ASCHELMINTHES.

rotogravure: see PRINTING.

rotor: see GENERATOR; MOTOR, ELECTRIC.

Rotorua (rōtəro͞o'ə), city (1971 pop. 31,265), central North Island, New Zealand. It is located in a region of lakes and hot springs. The area is also important for timber and wood pulp.

Rotrou, Jean de (zhäN də rôtro͞o'), 1609–50, French dramatist. One of the *Cinq auteurs,* five playwrights commissioned by Cardinal Richelieu, Rotrou wrote many plays, including the noble and effective tragedies *Saint-Genest* (1646) and *Venceslas* (1647). He was a friend and rival of Corneille.

Rotterdam (rŏt'ərdăm", Dutch rôtərdäm'), city (1971 pop. 679,032), South Holland prov., W Netherlands, on the Nieuwe Maas (New Meuse) River near its mouth on the North Sea. One of the largest and most modern ports in the world, Rotterdam is the major foreign-trade center of the Netherlands and its second-largest city. The city's inner port, which lies mainly on the left bank of the Nieuwe Maas, is connected to HOEK VAN HOLLAND, its outer port, by the New Waterway. Europoort, a large harbor area opposite Hoek van Holland built largely in the 1960s, is designed chiefly for unloading and storing petroleum. Rotterdam owes its importance mainly to the transit trade with the Ruhr district of NW Germany, with which it is connected by several waterways and oil pipelines. The city is also a center of industry, with shipyards, oil refineries, automobile assembly plants, and factories that manufacture clothing, paper, electronic equipment, and food products. Rotterdam was chartered in 1328. Although it grew considerably because of the efforts of the Dutch statesman Johan van Oldenbarneveldt (1547–1619), the city was long overshadowed by neighboring Delft and its port Delfshaven (now a suburb of Rotterdam), from where the Pilgrims sailed for America. The separation (1830) of Belgium from the Netherlands diverted much trade from Antwerp to Rotterdam. However, Rotterdam experienced its greatest growth with the construction (1866–90) of the New Waterway, which made the port accessible to the largest oceangoing vessels; with the major expansion of industry in NW Germany from the late 19th cent.; and with the European economic boom after World War II. During World War II the entire center of the city was destroyed by German air bombardment (May 14, 1940), several hours after it had capitulated. Most of the old houses of Rotterdam (including the birthplace of Erasmus) were destroyed; the Groote Kerk (a 15th-century church) was damaged. Among the noteworthy buildings that survived the raid were the stock exchange (18th cent.), the city hall (1920), and the Boymans-Van Beuningen Museum, with its collection of paintings by Dutch masters. Rotterdam is the site of a school of economics. The city is the birthplace of the 17th-century painter Peter de Hooch.

Rotterdam, town (1970 pop. 25,214), Schenectady co., E N.Y.; settled c.1670, inc. 1821.

Rottweiler (rŏt'wīlər), breed of sturdy WORKING DOG developed from a Roman cattle dog introduced into S Germany more than 1,900 years ago. It stands from 21¾ to 27 in. (55.3–68.6 cm) high at the shoulder and weighs from 75 to 90 lb (34.0–40.8 kg). Its short, flat-lying, coarse coat is black with markings ranging in shade from tan to mahogany on the cheeks, muzzle, chest, and legs and over both eyes. The tail is docked close to the body. Named for the German township of Rottweil, a livestock center in the Middle Ages, the Rottweiler was used both as a cattle drover and as a guardian of traveling merchants. When the driving of cattle by dogs was outlawed in Germany at the turn of the 20th cent., the Rottweiler was used as a draft animal and, increasingly, as a police dog. Its police-dog ability saved the breed from extinction. Today the breed is still much used in police work and is also raised as a pet. See DOG.

Roty, Louis Oscar (lwē ôskär' rôtē'), 1846–1911, French medalist and engraver, one of the greatest medalists of the 19th cent. His best-known commemorative medals include those for the death of President Sadi Carnot and for the 25th anniversary of the Franco-Prussian War. He also designed French coins. The originality of his graceful designs won him high honors.

Rouault, Georges (zhôrzh ro͞o-ō′), 1871–1958, French expressionist artist. First apprenticed to a stained-glass maker, Rouault studied after 1891 under Gustave MOREAU. He exhibited several paintings with the fauves in 1905. His sorrowful and bitter delineations of judges, clowns, and prostitutes caused a great stir in Paris. The suffering of Christ was his frequent subject. His thickly encrusted, powerfully colored images, outlined heavily in black, have the effect of icons and a pattern suggestive of stained glass. About 1916, Rouault began more than a decade of work for the publisher Vollard. Using a variety of graphic techniques, he executed a series of about 60 prints called *Miserere.* He continued to paint the themes he had used earlier, but in a more tranquil style. Rouault's works are unequalled in the religious art of our time. Examples of his art can be found in many European and American collections. The Museum of Modern Art, New York City, owns his *Three Judges* and *Christ Mocked by Soldiers.* See catalog by Pierre Courthion (1962); studies by Giuseppe Marchiori (1967), J. B. Kind (1969), Jacques Maritain (1969), and W. A. Dyrness (1972).

Roubaix (ro͞obā′), city (1968 pop. 114,774), Nord dept., N France, in French Flanders. With adjacent Tourcoing, it is one of the largest textile (chiefly wool) centers in France; a national textile school is there.

Rouen (ro͞oäN′), city (1968 pop. 124,577), capital of Seine-Maritime dept., N France. Situated on the Seine near its mouth at the English Channel, Rouen functions as the port of Paris, handling an enormous volume of traffic. Among its many manufactures are metal products, chemicals, drugs, textiles, paper, and leather goods. Rouen is also an old commercial, administrative, and cultural center. Of pre-Roman origin, Rouen was the victim of repeated raids (9th cent.) by the Norsemen. By the 10th cent. it was the capital of Normandy and a leading European city. It was held (1419–49) in the Hundred Years War by the English. Joan of Arc was tried and burned there in 1431. From 1499 to 1789, Rouen was, with interruptions, the seat of a provincial parlement. A judicial center, it furnished many magistrates to France. Rouen has been an archiepiscopal see since the 5th cent. and is particularly rich in ecclesiastical buildings (see GOTHIC ARCHITECTURE AND ART). Rouen suffered severe damage in World War II; its port and much of the city had to be reconstructed. Damaged, but since restored, are the cathedral of Notre Dame (12th–15th cent.) with its famous Tour de Beurre [butter tower]; the Church of St. Maclou and the palace of justice (both 15th–16th cent.); and the Grosse Horloge, a Renaissance clock tower. The houses where Pierre Corneille and Gustave Flaubert were born are both museums. A university opened in Rouen in 1966.

Rouergue (ro͞oĕrg′), region of S France, in the S MASSIF CENTRAL, coextensive with the present Aveyron dept. RODEZ, the historic capital, and MILLAU are the chief towns. One of the most mountainous areas of France, it is traversed by the Aveyron, Tarn, and other rivers, which form many deep gorges. Sheep are raised in great quantity and furnish milk for the Roquefort cheese industry. The county of Rouergue (or Rodez) and the viscounty of Millau were formed in the feudal period as dependencies of the counts of TOULOUSE. They passed to the French crown in 1271 but were ceded to England by the Treaty of Brétigny (1360); they reverted to France in 1368. The lands passed eventually to the Bourbon family and were inherited in 1607 by Henry IV, who united them with the royal domain.

Rougé, Emmanuel, vicomte de (ĕmänüĕl′ vēkôNt′ də ro͞ozhā′), 1811–72, French Egyptologist. Rougé was curator of the Egyptian section of the Louvre and professor of Egyptology at the Collège de France. He and LEPSIUS produced a consistent system for the interpretation of discoveries, and he worked out fundamental principles for studying Egyptian texts. Rougé sought to prove that the Semitic alphabet had an Egyptian origin.

Rouge (ro͞ozh), river, c.30 mi (50 km) long, rising in S Michigan and winding S and SE to the Detroit River at the city of River Rouge. Dearborn and part of Detroit also lie on the river, which carries much of the raw materials used by Detroit's industries.

rouge: see COSMETICS and POLISHES.

Rougemont, Denis de (dənē′ də ro͞ozhmôN′), 1906–, French philosopher and critic, b. Switzerland. He moved to Paris in 1936 and published numerous articles on EXISTENTIALISM, some of which are collected in *Les Personnes du drame* (1945; tr. *Dramatic Personages,* 1964). From 1940 to 1947, Rougemont lectured in the United States, where he wrote *La Part du diable* [the devil's portion] (1944), about the European crisis of conscience. He is also the author of the psychological-historical study *L'Amour et l'occident* (1939; tr. *Love in the Western World,* 1956).

Rough Riders, popular name for the 1st Regiment of U.S. Cavalry Volunteers, organized largely by Theodore ROOSEVELT in the Spanish-American War (1898). Its members were mostly ranchers and cowboys from the West, with a sprinkling of adventurous blue bloods from the Eastern universities. Roosevelt resigned his post as Assistant Secretary of the Navy to enter active fighting. The command of the regiment went, however, to a man of more military experience, Leonard WOOD. Roosevelt was made lieutenant colonel. Transportation difficulties caused the regiment's horses to be abandoned in Florida, and it fought chiefly on foot in Cuba. It took part in the battles about Santiago; its exploits, especially at San Juan Hill, were highly publicized. See Theodore Roosevelt, *The Rough Riders* (1899, repr. 1961); Charles Herner, *The Arizona Rough Riders* (1970).

Roulers: see ROESELARE, Belgium.

roulette (ro͞olĕt′), game of chance popular at Monte Carlo, Las Vegas, and other gambling resorts, and in a simplified form elsewhere. In gambling houses the roulette wheel is set into the middle of an oblong table. Its outer area is marked off into 37 (in Europe) or 38 (in the United States) spaces, each of which has retaining walls so that a small ivory ball may come to rest in one. The sectors, alternately red and black, are numbered 1 to 36; there is also a green (or sometimes white) 0 and in the United States an additional 00. On either side of the table is an arrangement of red and black squares numbered in correspondence with the wheel. In addition, there are spaces for other types of bets: manque, that the winning number will be 1–18; passe, that it will be 19–36; pair, that it will be an even number; impair, that it will be odd; rouge, that it will be red; noir, that it will be black. All bets are placed against the house and are indicated by placing stakes on the layout. The croupier spins the wheel and tosses the ball onto it; its final place of rest indicates the winning bets. Many betting combinations are allowed, with varying odds and maximum stakes. Roulette dates from the late 18th cent.

Roumania: see RUMANIA.

Roumelia: see RUMELIA.

round, in music, a CANON on a simple tune in which all the voices enter at the unison or the octave. An example is SUMER IS ICUMEN IN. Rounds were popular in 17th-century England, particularly during the reign of Charles II, when the catch reached its height. The catch was originally just a simple round, e.g., *Three Blind Mice,* written in a single line with the effect gained by having another singer come in ("make the catch") at the right time. Later, comic effects, often quite bawdy, were added, using the interweaving of the parts. *The Rounds, Catches and Canons of England* (1864) by E. F. Rimbault is a comprehensive collection. The term *round* was also used to designate a dance performed in a circle and, by extension, to the tunes for such dances.

Roundheads, derisive name for the supporters of Parliament during the ENGLISH CIVIL WAR. The name, which originated c.1641, referred to the short haircuts worn by some of the Puritans in contrast to the fashionable wigs worn by many of the supporters of King Charles I, who were called Cavaliers.

Round Table, in ARTHURIAN LEGEND, the table at which King Arthur and his knights held court. It was allegedly fashioned at the behest of Arthur to prevent quarrels among the knights over precedence. According to one version it was given to Arthur as a wedding gift by his father-in-law. A round table of undetermined antiquity hangs now in the castle at Winchester. Traditionally King Arthur's, it may be a relic of one of the medieval jousts also called round tables.

Round Tops: see GETTYSBURG CAMPAIGN.

roundworm, another name for a nematode. See phylum ASCHELMINTHES, class Nematoda.

Rourkela (rôrkä′lə), city (1971 pop. 125,427), Orissa state, E central India, at the confluence of the Koel and Lankh rivers. The city is built around large iron and steel plants. Other products are heavy machinery, fertilizers, and chemicals.

Rous, Francis Peyton, 1879–1970, American pathologist, b. Baltimore, educated at Johns Hopkins (B.A., 1900; M.D., 1905). He taught (1906–08) pathology at the Univ. of Michigan and in 1909 joined the Rockefeller Institute (now Rockefeller Univ.), in New York City. His long career included research in the physiology of the liver and blood (he helped develop blood banks). The 1966 Nobel Prize in Physiology and Medicine was awarded jointly to C. B. Huggins and Rous. The latter's award recognized his discovery of tumor-inducing viruses. The first report of this work in 1910 was received with disbelief by scientists, but subsequent research justified Rous's findings and added to the understanding of one of the causes of cancer.

Rousseau, Henri (äNrē′ ro͞osō′), 1844–1910, French primitive painter, b. Laval. He was, from the first, entirely self-taught, and his work remained consistently naive and imaginative. Rousseau was called *Le Douanier* because before he retired to paint (1885), he held a minor post in the Paris customs service. Although, by his own account, he had lived in Mexico in his youth, his remarkable landscapes have no counterpart in nature. His jungles are an organized profusion of carefully defined yet fantastic plants, half-concealing various wild animals with staring eyes. These scenes are rendered in a vivid, almost hypnotic folk style. The finest ones include *The Snake Charmer* (1907; Louvre) and *The Dream* (1910; Mus. of Modern Art, New York City). With the same approach Rousseau employed in painting the familiar (e.g., *Village Street Scene,* 1909, Philadelphia Mus. of Art), he painted the haunting and dreamlike *Sleeping Gypsy* (1897; Mus. of Modern Art, New York City). His fantastic gypsy sleeps in a nighttime desert, closely observed by a lion—the entire absurdity rendered in a compelling, straightforward manner. The painting thus combines the unique elements of Rousseau's art to their most startling effect. Rousseau exhibited at the Salon des Indépendants from 1886. See R. Shattuck, *The Banquet Years* (1958, repr. 1968); studies by D. Vallier (1964) and D. C. Rich (1946, repr. 1970).

Rousseau, Jean Jacques (zhäN zhäk), 1712–78, Swiss-French philosopher, author, political theorist, and composer. He was born at Geneva, the son of a watchmaker. His mother died shortly after his birth, and his upbringing was haphazard. At 16 he set out on a wandering, irregular life that brought him into contact (c.1628) with Louise de Warens, who became his patroness and later his lover. She arranged for his trip to Turin, where he became an unenthusiastic Roman Catholic convert. After serving as a footman in a powerful family, he left Turin and spent most of the next dozen years at Chambéry, Savoy, with his patroness. In 1742 he went to Paris to make his fortune with a new system of musical notation, but it turned out to be a failure. Once in Paris, however, he became an intimate of the circle of Denis Diderot (to whose *Encyclopédie* Rousseau contributed music articles), Melchior Grimm, and Mme d'Épinay. At this time also began his liaison with Thérèse Le Vasseur, a semiliterate servant girl who became his common-law wife. In 1749, Rousseau won first prize in a contest, held by the Academy of Dijon, on the question: "Has the progress of the sciences and arts contributed to the corruption or to the improvement of human conduct?" Rousseau took the negative stand, contending that man was good by nature and had been corrupted by civilization. His essay made him both famous and controversial. Although it is still widely believed that all of Rousseau's philosophy was based on his call for a return to nature, this view is an oversimplification, due to an excessive importance attached to this first essay. A second philosophical essay, *Discours sur l'origine de l'inégalité des hommes* (1754), is one of Rousseau's most mature and daring productions. After its publication, Rousseau returned to Geneva, reverted to Protestantism in order to regain his citizenship, and returned to Paris with the title "citizen of Geneva." Mme d'Épinay lent him a cottage, the Hermitage, on her estate at Montmorency. But Rousseau began to quarrel with Mme d'Épinay, Diderot, and Grimm, all of whom he accused of complicity in a sordid plot against him, and left the Hermitage to become the guest of the tolerant duc de Luxembourg, whose château was also at Montmorency. There he finished his novel, *Julie, ou La Nouvelle Héloïse* (1761), written in part under the impact of his love for Mme d'Houdetot, the sister-in-law of Mme d'Épinay; his *Lettre à d'Alembert sur les spectacles* (1758), a diatribe against the suggestion that Geneva would be better off for having a theater; his *Du contrat social* (1762); and his *Émile* (1762), which offended both the French and Genevan ecclesiastic authorities and was burned at Paris and at Geneva. Rousseau, with the connivance of highly placed friends, escaped, however, to the Swiss canton of Neuchâtel, then a Prussian possession. His house was stoned, and Rousseau fled once more, this time to the canton of Bern, settling on the small island of Saint-Pierre, in the Lake of Biel. In

1765 he was expelled from Bern and accepted the invitation of David Hume to live at his house in England; there he began to write the first part of his *Confessions,* but after a year he quarreled violently with Hume, whom he believed to be in league with Diderot and Grimm, and returned to France (1767). His suspicion of people deepened and became a persecution mania. After wandering through the provinces, he finally settled (1770) at Paris, where he lived in a garret and copied music. The French authorities left him undisturbed, while curious foreigners flocked to see the famous man and be insulted by him. At the same time he went from salon to salon, reading his *Confessions* aloud. In his last years he began *Rêveries du promeneur solitaire,* descriptions of nature and man's feeling about it, which was unfinished at the time of his death. Shortly before his death Rousseau moved to the house of a protector at Ermenonville, near Paris, where he died. In 1794 his remains were transferred to the Panthéon in Paris.

Rousseau's Thought. Few people have equaled Rousseau's influence in politics, literature, and education. His political thought is contained in *Du contrat social,* but it must be supplemented by other works, notably the *Discours sur l'origine de l'inégalité* and his drafts of constitutions for Corsica and for Poland. Rousseau is fundamentally a moralist rather than a metaphysician. As a moralist, he is also, unavoidably, a political theorist. His thought begins with the assumption that man is by nature good, and with the observation that in society man is not good. The fall of man was, for Rousseau, a social occurrence. "But human nature does not go backward, and we never return to the times of innocence and equality, when we have once departed from them." Although he locates the cause of man's deformity in society, Rousseau is not a primitivist. In *Émile* and *Du contrat social,* he proposed, on an individual and a social level, what might be done. What was new and important about his educational philosophy, as outlined in *Émile,* was its rejection of the traditional ideal: Education was not seen to be the imparting of all things to be known to the uncouth child, rather it was seen as the "drawing out" of what is already there, the fostering of what is native. Rousseau's educational proposal is highly artificial, the process is carefully timed and controlled, but with the end of allowing the free development of human potential. Similarly, with the social order, Rousseau's aim is freedom, which again does not involve a retreat to primitivism but perfect submission of the individual to what he termed the general will. The general will is what rational men would choose, for the common good. Freedom, then, is obedience to a self-imposed law of reason, self-imposed because imposed by the natural laws of man's being. The purpose of civil law and government, of whatever form, is to bring about a coincidence of the general will and the wishes of the people. Society gives government its sovereignty when it forms the social contract to achieve liberty and well-being as a group. While this sovereignty may be delegated in various ways (as in a monarchy, a republic, or a democracy) it cannot be transferred and resides ultimately with society as a whole, with the people, who can withdraw it when necessary. Rousseau's political philosophy assumes that there really is a common good, and that the general will is not merely an ideal, but can, under the right conditions, be actual. And it is under such conditions, with the rule of the general will, that Rousseau sees man's full development taking place, when "the advantages of a state of nature would be combined with the advantages of social life." Because he had such faith in the existence of the common good and the rightness of the general will, Rousseau was extreme in the sanctions he was willing to allow for its achievement: "If anyone, after publicly recognizing these dogmas, behaves as if he does not believe them, let him be punished by death: He has committed the worst of all crimes, that of lying before the law." Finally, Rousseau advocates a civil religion. Rousseau's thought sometimes rings of Calvinist Geneva, even though he reacted against its vision of man and had his books burned by its ecclesiastic authorities. In its time his epistolary novel *Héloïse* was immensely popular, but it is scarcely read today, while the *Confessions* remains widely read. Proposing to describe not only his life, but his innermost thought and feelings, hiding nothing be it ever so shameful, Rousseau followed the model of St. Augustine's *Confession,* but he created a new, intensely personal style of autobiography. The *Nouvelle Héloïse, Émile,* the *Confessions,* and the *Rêveries* all transfer to the domain of literature Rousseau's longing for a closeness with nature. His sensitive awareness apprehended the subtle nuances of the influence of landscape, trees, water, birds, and other aspects of nature on the shifting state of the human soul. Rousseau was the father of Romantic sensibility; the trend existed before him, but he was the first to give it full expression. His influence on German and English romanticism—and thus, indirectly, on romanticism in general—cannot be overestimated. Rousseau's style, in all his writings, is always personal, sometimes bizarre, sometimes rhetorical, sometimes bitterly sarcastic, sometimes deliberately plebeian, and often animated by a tender and musical quality unequaled in French prose. Although self-taught, he possessed a thorough knowledge of musical theory, but his compositions exerted no direct influence on music. Rousseau's influence on posterity has been equaled by only a few, and it is by no means spent. Men as diverse as Immanuel Kant, Johann Goethe, Maximilien de Robespierre, Johann Pestalozzi, and Leo Tolstoy have been his disciples. His doctrine of popular sovereignty had a profound impact on French revolutionary thought. Although he did not advocate collective ownership, his ideas also had their effect on socialist thought. It is probably more correct to say that he anticipated rather than influenced many insights of modern social psychology. Rousseau's principal works are available in English translations. See biographies by F. C. Green (1955, repr. 1970), Jean Guéhenno (2 vol., tr. 1966), and L. G. Crocker (2 vol., 1968–73); Irving Babbitt, *Rousseau and Romanticism* (2d ed. 1947, repr. 1965); Ernst Cassirer, *The Question of Jean Jacques Rousseau* (tr. 1963); Alfred Cobban, *Rousseau and the Modern State* (2d ed. 1964); Joan MacDonald, *Rousseau and the French Revolution, 1762–1791* (1965); William Blanchard, *Rousseau and the Spirit of Revolt* (1967); R. D. Masters, *Political Philosophy of Rousseau* (1968); Jacques Maritain, *Three Reformers: Luther, Descartes, Rousseau* (1970); Ronald Grimsley, *The Philosophy of Rousseau* (1973).

Rousseau, Théodore (tāōdôr'), 1812–67, French landscape painter; leader of the BARBIZON SCHOOL. He first received recognition in the Salon of 1848 and was commissioned by the state to paint his *Sortie de la forêt de Fontainebleau* (Louvre). Thereafter he enjoyed a modest success and lived simply in Barbizon near his friend J. F. Millet. Rousseau's landscapes are grave and full of a deep love of solitude. He is best represented in the Metropolitan Museum and in the Louvre.

Roussel, Albert (älbĕr' rōōsĕl'), 1869–1937, French composer, studied with Vincent D'Indy. His early works, such as the piano suite *Des Heures passent* (1898) and his First Symphony (*Le Poème de la forêt,* 1904–6), show the influence of impressionism. An interest in the 18th-century tradition is apparent in his *Divertissement* (1906), which anticipates the neoclassicism of Poulenc, Milhaud, and Stravinsky. Following a trip to the Orient he experimented with exoticism, using Eastern scales and rhythms. With the symphonic poem *Pour une fête de printemps* (1920) and his Second Symphony (1919–21) he achieved a highly personal style marked by subtlety of melodic inflection, sharp dissonance, and contrapuntal agility.

Roussillon (rōōsēyôN'), small region and former province, S France, bordering on Spain along the Pyrenees and on the Mediterranean. It is now roughly coextensive with Pyrénées-Orientales dept. Perpignan is the historical capital. Wine, fruit, and olives are the chief products of this fertile and densely populated region, which also has a tourist industry. The area has changed hands many times, from the Romans, who arrived c.121 B.C., through the Visigoths, the Arabs, the Carolingians, the Spaniards, the counts of Barcelona, and the kings of Aragón, France, and Majorca. Louis XIII conquered it from Spain in 1642, and French possession was confirmed by the Treaty of the Pyrenees (1659).

rout: see RIOT, ROUT, AND UNLAWFUL ASSEMBLY.

Rouvray, battle of: see HERRINGS, BATTLE OF THE.

Roux, Jacques (zhäk rōō), d. 1794, French revolutionary. A priest in Paris, he abandoned the priesthood at the start of the French Revolution. Roux was a member of the Commune of Paris of Aug., 1792, and was elected to the Convention. As a leader of the ENRAGÉS, he helped to instigate (Feb. and March, 1793) food riots in Paris. He was arrested in Sept., 1793, was condemned by the Revolutionary Tribunal, and committed suicide (Jan., 1794).

Roux, Pierre Paul Émile (pyĕr pōl āmēl'), 1853–1933, French physician and bacteriologist. He was a pupil of and co-worker with Pasteur. In 1888 he and A. E. J. Yersin demonstrated that the diphtheria bacillus produces a toxin; this led to the development by E. A. von Behring of methods of producing a specific antitoxin, which revolutionized the treatment of diphtheria. Roux worked with the veterinarian E. I. C. Nocard in the study (1898) of bovine pneumonia and with Élie Metchnikoff on syphilis.

Roux, Wilhelm (vĭl'hĕlm), 1850–1924, German anatomist, a founder of experimental embryology. He was a pupil of Ernst Haeckel and a professor (1895–1921) at the Univ. of Halle. In his studies of the relationship of embryology to evolution he developed specialized research techniques that he called "developmental mechanics," and in 1894 he founded as its organ the *Archiv für Entwicklungsmechanik.*

Rouyn (rōō'ĭn, Fr. rōōăN'), city (1971 pop. 17,821), extreme W Que., Canada. With its twin city, Noranda, Rouyn is the commercial and service center of a copper, gold, zinc, and silver mining district.

Rovaniemi (rô'vänē"ĕmē), city (1970 pop. 27,774), capital of Lappi prov. (Lapland), N Finland, at the confluence of the Ounas and Kemi rivers. Commercial and agricultural fairs and winter sports events are held in the city. It is the starting point of the Great Arctic Highway. Rovaniemi was chartered in 1929. Retreating German troops destroyed it (1944) in World War II.

Rovereto (rōvārĕ'tō), town (1971 pop. 29,585), in Trentino-Alto Adige, N Italy, on the Adige River. It is an agricultural and industrial center. Manufactures include machinery, silk, and forest products. Rovereto was taken (15th cent.) from the bishopric of Trent by Venice, which ceded it to Austria in 1517. A part of the S Tyrol, it passed to Italy in 1919. Of note are a 14th-century castle and the Church of San Marco (15th–17th cent.).

Rove Tunnel (rōv, Fr. rôv), southern section of the Marseilles-Rhône Canal, 4.5 mi (7.2 km) long and 72 ft (22 m) wide, Bouches-du-Rhône dept., SE France; opened 1927. Starting near the village of Le Rove, it cuts through the Chaîne de l'Estaque at sea level. It is considered one of the greatest pieces of engineering since the Panama Canal.

Rovigo (rōvē'gō), city (1971 pop. 49,701), capital of Rovigo prov., Venetia, N Italy, between the Adige and the Po rivers. It is an agricultural market and an industrial center. Manufactures include dyes, beer, and leather goods. First mentioned in the 9th cent., Rovigo belonged to the Este family from 1194 to 1482, when it passed to Venice. Of note in the city are the octagonal Church of the Madonna del Soccorso (late 16th cent.) and an excellent art gallery.

Rovinj (rô'vēnyə), Ital. *Rovigno d'Istria,* town (1971 pop. 16,402), NW Yugoslavia, in Croatia, on the Istrian coast of the Adriatic Sea. It is a seaport with shipbuilding and fishing industries. Rovinj belonged to Venice from 1283 until 1797, when it passed to Austria. Italy acquired it in 1918, and it was ceded to Yugoslavia in 1947. The town has an institute of marine biology and an 18th-century cathedral.

Rovno (rôv'nə), Pol. *Równe,* Ukr. *Rivne,* city (1970 pop. 116,000), capital of Rovno oblast, SW European USSR, in the Ukraine, on the Ustye River. It is a road and rail junction and an industrial center producing reinforced concrete and other building materials, high-voltage apparatus, machinery, metal goods, clothing, soap, and foodstuffs. An old Ukrainian settlement, Rovno was first mentioned in 1282 and grew into an important trade center. It passed to Russia in 1793 and to Poland in 1921, reverting to the Ukraine in 1939. The city has ruins of a medieval palace.

Rovuma (rōvōō'mə), river, c.450 mi (724 km) long, rising in N Mozambique, near Lake Nyasa and flowing E to the Indian Ocean. It forms most of the Tanzania-Mozambique border. In its lower course it is navigable for small craft.

Rowan, Andrew Summers (rou'ən), 1857–1943, American army officer, b. Monroe co., Va. (now W.Va.). At the outbreak (1898) of the Spanish-American War he was sent to communicate with the Cuban revolutionary leader General García y Íñigues in order to find out the strength of the revolutionary army. His exploit was described in Elbert Hubbard's essay "A Message to Garcia"; Rowan wrote his own account in *How I Carried the Message to Garcia* (1923). After the war he served in the Philippines and the United States, retiring in 1909.

rowan tree: see MOUNTAIN ASH.

Rowe, Nicholas (rō), 1674–1718, English dramatist. An ardent Whig, he was able to gain various government posts during the course of his life. In 1715 he became poet laureate. His first two plays, *The Ambitious Stepmother* (1700) and *Tamerlane* (1701), established his reputation as a popular playwright. Soon afterward he wrote his best plays, *The Fair Penitent* (1703) and *Jane Shore* (1714); both are stories of men's cruelty to women that prefigure the domestic tragedies popular later in the 18th cent. Rowe is also well known for his edition of Shakespeare (1709), which supplied valuable textual and biographical data and divided the plays into acts and scenes.

Rowell, Newton Wesley (rou'əl), 1867–1941, Canadian jurist and statesman, b. Ontario. He was elected (1911) to the Ontario legislature and then served in the Canadian House of Commons (1917–21) and as a member of Sir Robert Borden's Union government (1917–20). In 1936 he became chief justice of Ontario, and in 1937 he was appointed by William Lyon Mackenzie King to head the royal commission on dominion-provincial relations. Ill health forced him to resign in 1938, and he was replaced as chairman by Joseph Sirois. The commission's findings, commonly called the Rowell-Sirois Report (1940), showed the need for an enlargement of dominion responsibilities—contrary to earlier Liberal party policies.

rowing, the art of propelling a boat by means of oars operated by hand. Boats propelled by oars (e.g., the GALLEY) were used in ancient times for both war and commerce. Rowing is now generally used only for propelling small boats or for sport. One of the oldest continuous sporting events in the world is the Doggett's Coat and Badge rowing race, held in London every year since 1716 and named for Thomas Doggett, a popular actor of early 18th cent. England. The most famous of all rowing races are the Thames River competitions between Oxford and Cambridge, first held at Henley in 1829. The first collegiate rowing regatta in the United States took place in 1852 between Harvard and Yale. In modern racing, each member of the rowing team, or crew, uses both hands to pull one oar through the water. The oars, attached to riggings jutting out from the side of the boats to increase leverage, are positioned alternately on opposite sides of the vessel. The boat, or shell, is sometimes steered by a coxswain, who sits at the back of the vessel and manipulates tiller ropes attached to a rudder; the coxswain also directs the speed and rhythm of the crew's strokes. Sculling is a variant of rowing in which the oarsman controls two oars, one in each hand. Sculling teams consist of one, two, or four members; rowing crews have two, four, or eight members, with or without a coxswain. Rowing and sculling events have been included in the Olympic games since 1900. See studies by J. G. P. Williams and A. C. Scott, ed. (1967) and P. C. Wilson (1969).

Rowland, Henry Augustus (rō'lənd), 1848–1901, American physicist, b. Honesdale, Pa., grad. Rensselaer Polytechnic Institute, 1870. He was professor of physics at Johns Hopkins from 1875. Rowland is known especially for his invention of a dividing engine for ruling diffraction gratings on curved surfaces and for accurately determining the value of the ohm and the mechanical equivalent of heat. He also did important work in the field of electrical power.

Rowlandson, Thomas (rō'ləndsən), 1756–1827, English caricaturist, b. London. He studied at the Royal Academy and in Paris, but his passion for gambling prevented him from producing much until c.1782, when he was obliged to earn a living. As a humorous caricaturist and critical commentator of the social scene, Rowlandson quickly gained celebrity. His drawing *Vauxhall Gardens* (1784) was a great success, as was his series of drawings *The Comforts of Bath* that was reproduced in 1789. This was followed by the famous *Tour of Dr. Syntax* (series in 3 vol., 1812–21), *Dance of Death* (1814–16), and *Dance of Life* (1822)—all with text by William Combe. Rowlandson also illustrated Smollett, Goldsmith, Sterne, and Swift. Most of his drawings were first done in ink with a reed pen and given a delicate wash of color. The fluidity of his line is likened to the French ROCOCO, but the spirited humor of his work, sometimes almost coarse, is in the English style. His work is represented in the British Museum, the Victoria and Albert Museum, and the Metropolitan Museum. See studies by Ronald Paulson (1972) and John Hayes (1972).

Rowley, William (rou'lē), 1585?–1642?, English playwright and actor. He collaborated with many noted dramatists, including Dekker, Ford, and Webster; his best work, notably *The Changeling* (1622), was written with Thomas MIDDLETON. Of Rowley's own plays, *All's Lost by Lust* (1622) is considered to be his best.

Rowley Regis: see WARLEY.

Rowson, Susanna Haswell (rou'sən), 1762–1824, American author and actress, b. England. She was brought to America as a young child, but after the Revolution, the family returned to England. Her first novel, *Victoria*, appeared in 1786, the same year she married William Rowson. Having acted for a short time in England, the Rowsons emigrated to the United States in 1793, joining a theatrical company in Philadelphia. Retiring from the stage in 1796, Mrs. Rowson opened a school for girls in Boston, one of the best of its day, which she directed for 25 years. She wrote novels, poetry, and plays, but is remembered for one novel, *Charlotte: a Tale of Truth* (1791), called in later editions *Charlotte Temple*, a sentimental and didactic story, which went through more than 150 editions.

Rowton, Montagu William Lowry Corry, 1st Baron (rôt'ən, rou'-), 1838–1903, English philanthropist. He was called to the bar in 1863. From 1866 until 1881 he served as private secretary to Disraeli, who recommended him for the title of Baron Rowton (1880) and made him his literary executor. Lord Rowton became interested in London housing conditions and promulgated a scheme for a poor man's hotel, which was opened in Vauxhall in 1892. Its success led to the formation of a company that constructed a number of similar establishments, known as Rowton Houses.

Roxana (rŏksăn'ə) or **Roxane** (-săn'ē), d. 311 B.C., wife of ALEXANDER THE GREAT. She was the daughter of Oxyartes, a Bactrian baron, and Alexander married her (327) to consolidate his power in Persia. She and Alexander's posthumous son, Alexander IV, were, after Alexander's death, embroiled in the wars of the DIADOCHI and were imprisoned by CASSANDER at Amphipolis in Macedonia. They were later killed.

Roxas, Manuel (mänwĕl' rō'häs), 1894–1948, Philippine statesman, b. Capiz, Panay. In 1921 he was elected to the Philippine house of representatives and in the following year he became speaker. After the Commonwealth of the Philippines was established (1935), Roxas became a member of the national assembly, served (1938–41) as secretary of finance in President Manuel Quezon's cabinet, and was elected (1941) to the Philippine senate. In World War II he was captured (1942) by the Japanese invasion forces. Ostensibly a supporter of the Japanese occupation, Roxas participated in the puppet government but was actually an intelligence agent for the Philippine underground. In 1946 he became the first president of the Republic of the Philippines and upon his death was succeeded by Elpidio Quirino.

Roxburghshire (rŏks'bərəshĭr), county (1971 pop. 41,942), 665 sq mi (1,722 sq km), S Scotland. JEDBURGH is the county town. The principal rivers are the Tweed, the Teviot, and the Liddel Water. Textiles are made at HAWICK and elsewhere. Sheep are the most important livestock. Roxburghshire, once part of the ancient kingdom of NORTHUMBRIA, suffered severely in the border wars between England and Scotland. An invasion was repelled at Ancrum Moor in 1545. Ruins of 12th-century abbeys are at MELROSE, Kelso, and Jedburgh. Hermitage Castle (13th cent.) was a border fortress of the Douglas and Hepburn families. Sir Walter Scott's mansion is at Abbotsford. The area around Melrose is known as "the Scott country." An old name of the county is Teviotdale. Under the Local Government Act of 1973, Roxburghshire became part of the Borders region.

Roxelana: see SULAYMAN I, Ottoman sultan.

Roy, Rammohun (räm-mō'hən roi), 1772–1833, Indian religious and educational reformer. Sometimes called the father of modern India, Roy was born to a wealthy and devout Brahman family in Bengal. He early mastered several languages and subsequently employed them in a study of the religions of the world. After a successful administrative career in the British East India Company, he retired (1815) and devoted himself to rejuvenating Hindu culture. He sought to preserve essential Hinduism, which he recognized as a strong unifying force in India, while removing from it the elements of idolatry, discrimination against women, and the caste system. Thus, he founded in Calcutta the Atmiya Sabha [friendly association], an organization that served as a platform for his liberal ideas. Roy formulated, notably in *The Precepts of Jesus* (1820), an adaptation of Christianity that accepted its ethical and humanitarian teachings while rejecting its theology. To spread his teachings, Roy founded newspapers in English, Persian, and Bengali and established several secondary schools that used English educational methods. He felt that India would have to absorb Western ideas to become a modern state. In 1828 he replaced the Amityo Sabha with the Brahmo Samaj [society of god], an organization that exerted a deep and continuing influence on Indian intellectual, social, and religious life. In 1830, Roy became one of the first Indians to travel to England, and he died there. See biographies by U. N. Ball (1933) and Iqbal Singh (1958).

Roy, city (1970 pop. 14,356), Weber co., N Utah, near Great Salt Lake; settled by Mormons 1877, inc. 1937. Many residents work at nearby Hill Air Force Base.

Royal Academy of Arts, London, the national ACADEMY OF ART of England, founded in 1768 by George III at the instigation of Sir William Chambers and Benjamin West. Sir Joshua REYNOLDS was the Academy's first president, holding the office until his death in 1792. His *Discourses* defined the scope of the Academy. The king himself chose the original 36 Academicians and fixed the number at 40. Until 1867 their successors were elected by the Academicians only and since that date by the Academicians and associates, whose number was increased from 20 to 30 in 1876, together. Since its inception the Academy, a notably conservative body, has maintained biennial exhibitions—one being of the works of masters of the past and one of contemporary art; has maintained a free school (women students have been admitted only since 1861); and has administered funds (partly derived from its exhibitions) for the relief of distressed artists and their families and for prizes and scholarships. In 1867 the academy was given a lease of 999 years on Burlington House and the adjoining gardens, where its galleries and school have since been erected. See W. R. M. Lamb, *The Royal Academy* (2d ed. 1952).

royal antelope: see ANTELOPE.

Royal Ballet, the principal British ballet company, based at the Royal Opera House, Covent Garden, London. Granted a royal charter in 1956, the company was formed from the Sadler's Wells Ballet and its satellite, the Sadler's Wells Theatre Ballet, founded in 1946. The former had its origins in the Academy of Choreographic Art, founded by Dame Ninette de VALOIS in 1926. Dancers from the Academy achieved renown in the 1930s as the Vic-Wells Ballet, performing at the Old Vic and Sadler's Wells theaters. The company's principal ballerina was Dame Alicia MARKOVA; when she left in 1935, Margot FONTEYN, who had made her debut that year at age 15, was trained to become prima ballerina, a rank she held until, in 1959, she became guest artist with the company. Many other celebrated dancers developed with the Royal Ballet, as well as such choreographers as Sir Frederick ASHTON, Antony TUDOR, Kenneth MacMillan, and John Cranko. The company toured during World War II, then settled in the Royal Opera House in 1946. Its touring section has traveled widely abroad since 1949 bringing international acclaim to the company as one of the finest in existence. It is noted for lavish dramatic productions, a superbly disciplined corps de ballet, and brilliant performances from its principals. De Valois directed the company for more than 35 years, retiring in 1963. She was succeeded by Ashton, the company's chief choreographer.

Royal Canadian Mounted Police, constabulary organized (1873) as the Northwest Mounted Police to bring law and order to the Canadian west and especially to prevent Indian disorders. In 1904 the name was changed to Royal Northwest Mounted Police and in 1920 to the present title. The corps, which gained a romantic reputation for daring exploits and persistence in trailing criminals, originally numbered 300 men; they came to be known as Red Coats, Riders of the Plains, and, most popularly, Mounties. The force later absorbed the provincial police forces of all the provinces except Ontario and Quebec. Numbering about 14,000, the force performs police functions throughout Canada.

Royal Danish Ballet, one of the oldest major ballet companies, established at the opening of Denmark's Royal Theater in Copenhagen in 1748. The company was developed over the centuries by three great masters. The first, Vincenzo Galeotti (1733–1816), who brought from Italy and France an international repertoire, led the company from 1775 until his death. One of his works, *Amors og Balletmasterens Luner* [*the whims of Cupid and the ballet master*] (1786), is the world's oldest ballet retaining its original choreography. The next great leader was Auguste BOURNONVILLE, who directed the company for 51 years (1828–79). The more than 50 ballets he created included many parts intended to show off his own brilliant dancing, and these later became vehicles to establish and display the excellence of Danish male dancing in general. After his death the Danish Ballet declined until 1932, when Harald Lander returned from studying dance in the Soviet Union and the United States to become the company's ballet master (1932–51). He trained many fine dancers, including Erik BRUHN. Lander choreographed and adapted many ballets for the company and promoted its tours abroad; it continued to tour widely in the 1960s and 70s.

Royal George, British naval vessel that sank on Aug. 29, 1782, while undergoing repairs at Spithead. Its commander, Admiral Richard Kempenfelt, and about 800 sailors and visitors were drowned. The incident is commemorated in William Cowper's poem "On the Loss of the Royal George."

Royal Gorge, 10 mi (16 km) long, narrow canyon cut by the Arkansas River, S central Colo., often called the Grand Canyon of the Arkansas. The gorge was discovered in 1806 by an expedition led by U.S. explorer Zebulon Pike. Its near-vertical walls are more than 1,000 ft (305 m) high. One of the world's highest suspension bridges, 1,053 ft (321 m) above the river, crosses the canyon, and a cable railway ascends the canyon wall.

Royal Greenwich Observatory, astronomical OBSERVATORY established in 1675 by Charles II of England; formerly known as the Royal Observatory and located at Greenwich, it was moved to Hurstmonceaux Castle, Sussex, beginning in 1948, when its name was changed. The observatory was under the Board of Ordnance until 1818 and under the Board of Admiralty until 1965, when it came under the direction of the Science Research Council. Its equipment includes the 98-in. (248.9-cm) Isaac Newton reflecting telescope, 36-in. (91.4-cm) and 30-in. (76.2-cm) reflecting telescopes, 26-in. (66-cm) and 13-in. (33-cm) refracting telescopes, and an 8-in. (20.3-cm) reversible transit circle. The observatory is administratively responsible for the Radcliffe Observatory, Pretoria, South Africa, where there is a 74-in. (188-cm) reflector. The Royal Greenwich Observatory also includes the Nautical Almanac Office, which publishes the national navigational almanacs, and is responsible for the national time service, on which is based the worldwide system of time zones. The zero meridian, from which longitude is measured, passes through the observatory's former location at Greenwich. Other principal programs include measurement of the proper motions and radial velocities of stars, studies of the dynamics of the solar system and the Milky Way, and studies of the abundances of chemical elements in stars. From the appointment of John Flamsteed as its first director until 1972, the director of the observatory held the title of astronomer royal. Among the noted directors have been Flamsteed, Edmond Halley, James Bradley, Nevil Maskelyne, G. B. Airy, and E. Margaret Burbidge, who was the first director not to be astronomer royal.

Royal Highlanders: see BLACK WATCH.

Royal Leamington Spa (lĕm'ĭngtən), municipal borough (1971 pop. 44,987), Warwickshire, central England, on the Leam River, a tributary of the Avon. The borough has ironworks and brick factories but is primarily a health resort, largely of 19th-century growth. There are mineral springs in the borough.

Royal Oak, residential city (1970 pop. 86,238), Oakland co., SE Mich., a suburb of Detroit; settled c.1820, inc. as a city 1921. The Detroit Zoological Park is there.

Royal Shakespeare Company, a British repertory theater. The company, established in 1960, was based on the earlier Shakespeare Memorial Theatre at Stratford-upon-Avon. The organization consists of two companies, one based at Stratford and the other at the Aldwych Theatre in London. Other than Shakespeare's works, the company has mounted such plays as *Ondine, Becket, Marat/Sade,* and *The Caucasian Chalk Circle.* See also OLD VIC. See studies ed. by John Goodwin (1964) and Michael Kustow et al. (1968).

Royal Society, oldest scientific organization in Great Britain and one of the oldest in Europe. The Royal Society was first incorporated in 1662 as the Royal Society of London for Improving Natural Knowledge. It was founded in 1660 by a group of learned men in London who met to promote scientific discussion, particularly in the physical sciences. It stimulates research in that field and acts in the capacity of adviser on scientific matters to the government, from which it receives annual subsidies. The Royal Society ranks as the foremost organization of its kind; its membership always includes leading scientists of the world. One of its activities is the publication of its *Proceedings* and *The Philosophical Transactions.* Among those who served as president of the Royal Society are Samuel Pepys, Sir Isaac Newton, Sir Joseph Banks, Sir Humphry Davy, Sir William Huggins, Lord Rayleigh, Sir Archibald Geikie, Sir William Crookes, Sir Joseph John Thomson, Sir Charles Sherrington, Lord Rutherford, Sir Frederick Gowland Hopkins, and Sir William Henry Bragg. See Thomas Sprat, *History of the Royal Society* (1667, ed. by J. I. Cope and H. W. Jones, 1959) and Sir Harold Hartley, ed., *Royal Society: Its Origins and Founders* (1960).

Royal Tunbridge Wells, municipal borough (1971 pop. 44,506), Kent, SE England. Mineral springs were discovered in 1606, and the town developed as a fashionable inland resort. Noted visitors have included many of the royal dignitaries and great literary figures of England. There are various light industries. Nearby Toad Rock and High Rocks are curious sandstone formations.

Royal Victoria College: see MCGILL UNIV.

Royce, Josiah, 1855–1916, American philosopher, b. California, grad. Univ. of California, 1873. After studying in Germany and at Johns Hopkins, he returned to California to teach (1878–82). From 1882 until his death he was at Harvard, becoming a professor in 1892. Among his works are *The Spirit of Modern Philosophy* (1892), *The World and the Individual* (1900–1901), *The Philosophy of Loyalty* (1908), and *Lectures on Modern Idealism* (1919). Royce, thoroughly grounded in history and cognizant of scientific thought, was the foremost American idealist. He held that reality is the life of an absolute mind. Man knows truth beyond himself because he is a part of the logos, or world-mind. Science successfully depends on description, but appreciation must precede description and consequently ideals must be deeper than the mechanism of science. The natural order of the world must be also a moral order. Man's ethical obligation is to the moral order and takes the form of loyalty to the great community of all individuals. See biography by Bruce Kuklick (1972); studies by Gabriel Marcel (tr. 1965), P. L. Fuss (1965), T. F. Powell (1967), and B. B. Singh (1973); Clifford Barrett, *Contemporary Idealism in America* (1932, repr. 1964).

Roycroft Press: see HUBBARD, ELBERT.

Royden, Agnes Maude, 1876–1956, English preacher and social worker, studied at Oxford. The first woman to preach (1917–20) in an established Anglican church, she was also active in social reforms, notably the woman suffrage and social hygiene movements. Among her many books are *Sex and Common Sense* (1922), *I Believe in God* (1927), *Women's Partnership in the New World* (1941), and her autobiography, *The Threefold Cord* (1947).

Royer-Collard, Pierre Paul (pyĕr pōl rwäyä'-kôlär'), 1763–1845, French statesman and philosopher. After entering the law, he took part in the French Revolution and became a constitutional monarchist. During the Consulate he devoted himself entirely to philosophy, and from 1811 to 1814 he lectured at the Sorbonne. Becoming active in government after the Bourbon restoration, he sat in the chamber of deputies almost continuously from 1815 to 1839. From 1815 to 1820 he was president of the commission for public instruction. Royer-Collard was a leader of the Doctrinaires, a middle-of-the-road group that included François Guizot, Camille Jordan, Charles de Rémusat, and the duc de Broglie. In philosophy he opposed the sensationalism of Étienne Bonnot de Condillac and helped to introduce the ideas of Thomas Reid into France.

Rozas, Juan Martínez de: see MARTÍNEZ DE ROZAS, JUAN.

Rozebeke (rō'zəbā''kə), formerly **Roosebeke,** village, East Flanders prov., W Belgium, near Oudenaarde. There, in 1382, the French under Olivier de Clisson defeated the Flemings under Philip van Artevelde. The battle restored Louis de Maële's control over the county of FLANDERS.

Rozhdestvenski, Zinovi Petrovich (zēnô'vē pētrô'vĭch rəzhdyĭstvyĕn'skē), 1848–1909, Russian admiral. Commander of the Baltic fleet at the time of the Russo-Japanese War of 1904–5, he was ordered to take his fleet to the Far East. In the battle of TSUSHIMA (1905), Rozhdestvenski's fleet was destroyed by Admiral Togo. The Russian disaster led to an armistice with Japan shortly afterward.

RR Lyrae: see VARIABLE STAR.

RSFSR: see RUSSIAN SOVIET FEDERATED SOCIALIST REPUBLIC.

Ru, chemical symbol of the element RUTHENIUM.

Ruad: see ARADUS.

Ruanda-Urundi (ro͞oän'dä-o͝oro͞on'dē), former colonial territory, central Africa, now divided between the independent states of RWANDA and BURUNDI. The original inhabitants of the area were the Twa, a PYGMY people, who around the 12th cent. A.D. were driven into the forests by the numerically superior Hutu, a Bantu-speaking agricultural people who immigrated from the east. Probably in the 15th cent., the pastoral TUTSI entered the area from the north. Although greatly outnumbered by the Hutu, the Tutsi gained dominance over them and by the 19th cent. had established two centralized states, Rwanda and Burundi. The first Europeans to explore the region were Oskar BAUMANN (in 1892) and Graf von Götzen (in 1894). Germany had gained rights to the region at the Conference of Berlin (1884–85), but only began to administer (as parts of GERMAN EAST AFRICA) Burundi in 1897 and Rwanda in 1907. During World War I, Belgium conquered (1916) the region, and, in 1924, Ruanda-Urundi was formally constituted a mandate of the League of Nations under Belgian rule. In 1946 it became a UN trust territory. Under neither the German nor the Belgian administrations was the social structure of Burundi altered, but in Rwanda the Hutu in 1960–61 gained dominance over the Tutsi. There was little economic development during the colonial period, but missionaries gained many adherents for Christianity. When Ruanda-Urundi achieved independence on July 1, 1962, it was split into two territories, Rwanda and Burundi, and by 1964 all common administrative bodies had been dissolved.

Ruapehu (ro͞oəpä'hō͞o), dormant volcanic peak, 9,175 ft (2,797 m) high, on North Island, New Zealand; highest point of North Island. A lake occupies its crater, and ski trails are on its slopes.

Rub al Khali (ro͞ob äl khä'lē) [Arabic,=empty quarter], great desert of the Arabian Peninsula, c.225,000 sq mi (582,750 sq km); one of the largest sand deserts in the world. The desert occupies much of the southern interior of the peninsula, from the highlands of the Nejd (to the north) to the plateaus of HADHRAMAUT (to the south); it slopes from an altitude of 3,300 ft (1,006 m) in the west to near sea level in the east. Sand dunes rise to c.660 ft (200 m) in the southwest; there are salt marshes and pans in the southeast. Rub al Khali is connected to the NAFUD desert in the north by the Dahna, a narrow corridor, 800 mi (1,287 km) long. The desert is usually considered part of Saudi Arabia, but, because it is waterless and cannot support life, its ownership is of little consequence. Rub al Khali was first explored by English explorer Henry Philby in 1932.

rubber, any solid substance, usually elastic, that can be vulcanized (see VULCANIZATION) so that it will stretch and then contract; the term includes both natural rubber, or CAOUTCHOUC, which is obtained from the milky secretion (latex) of various plants, and a wide variety of synthetic rubbers, which have similar properties. The term *elastomer* is sometimes used to designate synthetic rubber only and is sometimes extended to include caoutchouc as well. All rubberlike materials are compounds of high molecular weight; each consists of a series of one kind of molecule, the monomer, hooked together in a long chain to form a larger molecule, the POLYMER. The chain forms a loose coil that will return to its short coiled form after it is extended. Carbon and hydrogen make up most of the molecule, although some synthetics also have other elements such as chlorine, fluorine, nitrogen, or silicon. Natural rubber differs from synthetic rubber in the arrangement of hydrogen and carbon. Until 1955 this arrangement could not be duplicated synthetically; in that year two different synthetics were produced that closely duplicated natural rubber. Pure natural rubber is made up of molecules of isoprene linked into loosely twisted chains. Its properties of elasticity, toughness, impermeability, adhesiveness, and electrical resistance make it useful as an adhesive, a coating composition, a fiber, a molding compound, and an electrical insulator. Rubber is water repellent and resistant to alkalies and weak acids but is soluble in a number of hydrocarbons, including benzene, toluene, gasoline, and lubricating oils. Chemically, natural rubber is classified as a polyterpene, i.e., a polymer of isoprene. Studies have shown that the carbon chain in the polymer is in a *cis* arrangement (see ISOMER) and that this is responsible for the high elasticity of natural rubber; GUTTA-PERCHA exists in the *trans* configuration and is not nearly as elastic as natural rubber. A large variety of plants contain latex, a milky fluid with globules of rubber in an aqueous suspension, but only a few, chiefly of tropical or subtropical species, have been commercial sources. The most important source of natural rubber is the PARÁ RUBBER TREE. Rubber is also obtained from the Castilla tree (or caucho); the Ceará

$H_2C{=}C(CH_3){-}CH{=}CH_2$ *isoprene* NATURAL RUBBER	$H_2C{=}CH{-}CH{=}CH_2$ + $H_2C{=}CH{-}C_6H_5$ *butadiene* *styrene* BUNA S	$H_2C{=}C(Cl){-}CH{=}CH_2$ *chloroprene* NEOPRENE
$CH_2{=}C(CH_3)_2$ *isobutylene* BUTYL RUBBER	$H_2C{=}CH{-}CH{=}CH_2$ + $H_2C{=}CH{-}C{\equiv}N$ *butadiene* *acrylonitrile* NITRILE (BUNA N)	$(H_3C)_2Si(OH)_2$ *dimethysilanediol* A SILICONE RUBBER

Basic molecules in rubber

tree (*Manihot*); guayule, a shrubby plant native to the arid regions of Mexico and the SW United States; a few African vines; and, in the USSR, a Siberian dandelion. Most of the rubber imported into the United States is used in tire and inner-tube manufacture; other items that account for large quantities are belting, hose, tubing, insulators, valves, gaskets, and footwear. Most of the Pará rubber is exported as crude rubber and prepared for market by rolling slabs of latex coagulated with acid into thin sheets of crepe rubber or into heavier, firmly pressed sheets that are usually ribbed and smoked. An increasing quantity of latex, treated with alkali to prevent coagulation, is shipped for processing in manufacturing centers. Much of it is used to make foam rubber by beating air into it before pouring it into a vulcanizing mold. Other products are made by dipping a mold into latex (e.g., rubber gloves) or by casting latex. Sponge rubber is prepared by adding to ordinary rubber a powder that forms a gas during vulcanization. For most purposes rubber is ground, dissolved in a suitable solvent, and compounded with other ingredients, e.g., fillers and pigments such as carbon black for strength, and whiting for stiffening; antioxidants; plasticizers, usually in the form of oils, waxes, or tars; accelerators; and vulcanizing agents. The compounded rubber is sheeted, extruded in special shapes, applied as coating or molded, then vulcanized. Uncoagulated latex, compounded with colloidal emulsions and dispersions, is extruded as thread, coated on other materials, or beaten to a foam and used as sponge rubber. Used and waste rubber may be reclaimed by grinding followed by devulcanization with steam and chemicals, refining, and remanufacture. The four leading types of synthetic rubber are: Buna S, neoprene, butyl, and nitrile. Raw materials come from coal, oil, natural gas, and acetylene; alcohol made from grain and potatoes was used during World War II. By choosing the proper synthetic rubber the following advantages over natural rubber can be obtained: better aging and weathering, more resistance to oil, solvents, oxygen, ozone, and certain chemicals, and resilience over a wider temperature range. Natural rubber has other advantages: less build-up of heat from flexing and greater resistance to tearing when hot; these are properties important in tires, which use more rubber than any other product. Natural rubber, although it has been duplicated synthetically, is cheaper than synthetic rubber, and ways have been found to overcome some of its shortcomings. However, new and important synthetic varieties possessing special properties have been developed. Silicone rubbers are organic derivatives of inorganic polymers, e.g., the polymer of dimethysilanediol. They are very stable and remain flexible over a wide temperature range; they are used in wire and cable insulation. Polyurethanes have chemical stability and resist abrasion; they are used in tires, in shoes, and as foams. *Cis*-1,4-polyisoprene almost duplicates natural rubber. Hypalon and *cis*-1,4-polybutadiene are other new types. Older types are still used, however, because of properties peculiar to them. Buna S is a copolymer of butadiene and styrene, which are polymerized together in a mole ratio of about 7 to 1 of butadiene to styrene. It resists weathering and abrasion, and is used in tires and flooring. Neoprene is a polymer of chloroprene. The polymerization can be catalyzed by light to give a linear polymer similar in structure to natural rubber but with a *trans* arrangement of the carbon chain like that of gutta-percha. This linear polymer changes to a cross-linked, hard, nonplastic polymer unless inhibitors are added. Neoprene resists ozone, weathering, oil, flame, and a variety of chemicals; because of its resistance to oil it is used in making hose and tank linings. Butyl rubber is a polymer of isobutylene. It is highly impervious to gases and is a good insulator; it is used in inner tubes and as insulation on wire and cable. Nitrile, or Buna N, is a copolymer of butadiene and acrylonitrile; the acrylonitrile content of nitrile varies from about 18% to about 45%. By increasing the acrylonitrile content, oil resistance, tensile strength, and high-temperature resistance are improved at the expense of elasticity and low-temperature flexibility. Nitrile resists heat, oil, and fuels and is used to a limited extent to seal containers and to cover cables. Although natural rubber and synthetic rubber have specific qualities that make them preferable for certain purposes, in a large proportion of rubber goods the cost factor is decisive and determines which of the two is used.

History. Pre-Columbian Indians of South and Central America used rubber for balls, containers, and shoes and for waterproofing fabrics. Although it was mentioned by Spanish and Portuguese writers in the 16th cent., rubber did not attract the interest of Europeans until reports about it were made (1736–51) to the French Academy of Sciences by Charles de la Condamine and François Fresneau. Pioneer research in finding rubber solvents and in waterproofing fabrics was done before 1800, but rubber was used only for elastic bands and erasers, and these were made by cutting up pieces imported from Brazil. Joseph Priestley is credited with the discovery c.1770 of its use as an eraser, whence the name *rubber.* The first rubber factory in the world was established near Paris in 1803, the first in England by Thomas Hancock in 1820. Hancock devised the forerunner of the rubber masticator, and in 1835 Edwin Chaffee, an American, patented a mixing mill and a calender (a press for rolling the rubber into sheets). In 1823, Charles Macintosh found a practical process for waterproofing fabrics, and in 1839 Charles Goodyear discovered vulcanization, which revolutionized the rubber industry. In the latter half of the 19th cent. the demand for rubber insulation by the electrical industry and the invention of the pneumatic tire extended the demand for rubber. In the 19th cent. wild rubber was harvested in South and Central America and in Africa; most of it came from the Pará rubber tree of the Amazon basin. Despite Brazil's legal restrictions, seeds of the tree were smuggled to England in 1876. The resultant seedlings were sent to Ceylon and later to many tropical regions, especially the Malay area and Java and Sumatra, beginning the enormous Far Eastern rubber industry. Here the plantations were so carefully cultivated and managed that the relative importance of Amazon rubber diminished. American rubber companies, as a step toward diminishing foreign control of the supply, enlarged their plantation holdings in Liberia and in South and Central America. The cutting off of Far Eastern rubber during World War II gave impetus to the development of synthetic rubber. During World War I, Germany had made a synthetic rubber that was too expensive for peacetime use. In 1927 a less costly variety was invented, and in 1931 neoprene was made, both in the United States. German scientists developed Buna rubber just prior to World War II. When importation of natural rubber from the East Indies was cut off during World War II, the United States began large-scale manufacture of synthetic rubber, concentrating on Buna S. Today synthetic rubber accounts for most of the world's rubber production. See P. W. Allen, *Natural Rubber and the Synthetics* (1972); Maurice Morton, *Rubber Technology* (2d ed. 1973).

rubber plant, name for any plant that yields rubber, specifically the India-rubber tree (*Ficus elastica*), an Asiatic FIG.

rubella or **German measles,** acute infectious disease of children and young adults. It is caused by a filterable virus that is spread by droplet spray from the respiratory tract of an infected individual. Rubella is a much milder infection than rubeola (measles) and the rash, appearing after an incubation period of two to three weeks, rarely lasts more than three days. The lymph nodes behind the ears become tender and swollen, but otherwise German measles is almost always uncomplicated. However, during the first trimester of pregnancy it is associated with an increased risk of congenital damage to the fetus, producing stillbirths, abortion, low birth weight, and such malformations as cardiac defects, eye defects (especially cataracts), and mental retardation. During the first 16 weeks of pregnancy the infection has been estimated to carry a risk of fetal damage of between 30% and 35%. Pregnant women who have been exposed to rubella are given gamma globulin in an effort to prevent the disease. Research to develop a vaccine that would confer immunity was spurred by an epidemic of rubella in 1964 and the evidently related rise in the number of birth deformities. A live attenuated vaccine has been developed and is given to girls before they reach puberty and often to boys as well. Before the vaccine is administered to an adult woman it is determined that she is not pregnant, and the test for the presence of rubella antibodies (which would indicate immunity to the disease from previous exposure) is given. Birth control should be practiced for at least three months after receiving the vaccine.

Rubens, Peter Paul, 1577–1640, foremost Flemish painter of the 17th cent., b. Siegen, Westphalia, where his family had gone into exile because of his father's Calvinist beliefs. After his father's death in 1587, the family returned to Antwerp. There the young Rubens attended a Jesuit school, served as court page, and became an accomplished linguist. After 1591 he was apprenticed to several minor painters. In 1600 he went to Italy, where he spent eight years painting in the service of the duke of Mantua, who sent him on a mission to Spain in 1603. While there he painted the magnificent equestrian portrait of the Duke of Lerma (Conde Valdelagrana Coll., Madrid). In Italy he painted and traveled, learning by making copies from the masters. The altar paintings for the Santa Maria Nuova, Rome, are among his finest works of this period. In 1608, after the death of his mother, he returned to Antwerp, where within five years he became known as the greatest painter of his country. Much sought after as a teacher, Rubens set up an elaborate studio. He married Isabella Brant and prospered, being deluged with commissions, especially for church decorations and altarpieces of large dimensions. To complete them he organized an enormous workshop of skilled apprentices and associates, among whom were VAN DYCK and JORDAENS. *Raising of the Cross* and *Descent from the Cross* (1610 and 1611; cathedral, Antwerp) date from this time and are works with which Rubens already rivaled the grandiose creations of Italian art that had dominated the imagination of Northern artists for almost a century. From 1622 to 1625 he executed numerous commissions for the French court, including an imposing series of large, allegorical paintings of the life of Marie de' Medici for the Luxembourg Palace that are now in the Louvre. Although his assistants did much of the work on them, it was Rubens who designed them and added the finishing touches. In this way his workshop produced numerous monumental works (e.g., *The Assumption*, cathedral, Antwerp). In 1626, after the death of his wife, he entered the diplomatic service, for which his pleasing personality, knowledge of languages, and acquaintance with royalty fitted him well. In 1628 he went to Spain on a mission for England, and during his nine months in Madrid he became acquainted with Velázquez and painted the royal family. Thereafter in London, he was idolized and knighted for his peacemaking efforts. While in England he painted the *Allegory of War and Peace* (National Gall., London). On his return to Antwerp in 1630, Rubens, then 53, married the 16-year-old Helen Fourment. His portraits of her (Vienna Mus. and Louvre), and of himself with her (Alte Pinakothek, Munich), are among his most joyous and personal paintings. During the last 10 years of his life Rubens worked with incredible energy, producing many of his finest pictures. Among these were the paintings for the ceiling at Whitehall for Charles I, finished in 1635. He painted more than 100 works for the Spanish court alone. *The Judgement of Paris* and *Three Graces* (Prado) and *Venus and Adonis* (Metropolitan Mus.) belong to this period. Many of his last years were spent on his princely estate, Castle Steen, near Brussels. At the age of 63, at the height of his powers and popularity, Rubens died of gout, which had crippled him periodically for three years. Under his direction or influence a whole school of first-rate artists flourished in Antwerp. The volume of Rubens's work is enormous, and though he did little but supervise much of the work attributed to him, his domination was so absolute that almost everything proceeding from his workshop shows the mark of his genius. The influence of the Italians is clear in his monumental composition, his freedom of handling, and his large conception; but his color, technique, and lusty spirit were Flemish. He delighted in painting scenes of mythical battles and abductions, in which nude figures struggle in attitudes of superabundant vitality. Despite his superb religious paintings, a pagan joy of life is his most characteristic quality. He explored all fields of painting. In landscape, portrait, genre, and animal painting he was as supremely successful as in his large religious and allegorical works. Some of his small pictures, such as *Helen Fourment and Her Children* (Louvre) and *Peasant Dance* (Prado), are among his greatest masterpieces. Contemporaries doubted the durability of his delicate glazes, but his pictures are singularly well preserved. More than 2,000 paintings have been attributed to Rubens's studio. Almost every principal gallery of Europe contains fine examples. The Art Institute of Chicago; the Nelson Gallery, Kansas City, Mo.; the National Gallery, Washington, D.C.; the Metropolitan Museum; the Cleveland Museum; and the Gardner Museum, Boston, all have work by Rubens. See his letters, ed. by R. S. Magurn (1955); selected drawings, ed. by J. S. Held (2 vol., 1959); biographies by Emil Michel (2 vol., 1899), Pierre Cabanne (1967), and N. B. Gerson (1973); studies by Wolfgang Stechow (1968), Jennifer Fletcher (1969), J. R. Martin (1969), and Jacques Thuillier (tr. 1970); Roger Avermaete, *Rubens and his Time* (tr. 1968).

rubeola: see MEASLES.

Rubicon (ro͞o'bĭkŏn), Lat. *Rubico*, small stream that flows into the Adriatic and in Roman times marked the boundary between Cisalpine Gaul and ancient Italy. In 49 B.C., after some hesitation, Julius Caesar crossed the Rubicon to march against Pompey in defiance of the senate's orders. He thus committed himself to conquer or to perish, and "to cross the Rubicon" now means to take an irrevocable step.

rubidium (ro͞obĭd'ēəm), metallic chemical element; symbol Rb; at. no. 37; at. wt. 85.47; m.p. 38.89°C; b.p. 688°C; sp. gr. 1.53 at 20°C; valence +1. Rubidium is a very soft silver-white metal. One of the ALKALI METALS, it is directly below potassium in group Ia of the PERIODIC TABLE. It is extremely reactive, combining violently with water to form the hydroxide. It oxidizes rapidly, and may ignite when exposed to air. It forms numerous compounds, e.g., halides, oxides, sulfates, and sulfides. Its salts color a flame red. Rubidium is not found uncombined in nature but occurs widely distributed in lepidolite (the major source), carnallite, pollucite, and some rare minerals, and with lithium in seawater, brines, and natural spring waters. Although rubidium is much more abundant in the earth's crust than chromium, copper, lithium, nickel, or zinc, and about twice as abundant in seawater as lithium, it did not become available commercially until the early 1960s as a by-product of the manufacture of LITHIUM chemicals. The metal is obtained by electrolysis or chemical reduction of the fused chloride. It must be kept out of contact with air and water. Rubidium and its salts have few commercial uses. The metal is used in the manufacture of photocells and in the removal of residual gases from vacuum tubes. Rubidium salts are used in glasses and ceramics. Rubidium-87, a radioactive isotope (half-life about 5×10^{11} years), makes up about 28% of natural rubidium; the balance is the stable isotope rubidium-85. Fifteen other isotopes are known. Rubidium was discovered with cesium in 1861 by R. W. BUNSEN and G. R. KIRCHHOFF; these were the first elements discovered by spectroscopic analysis.

Rubinstein, Anton Grigoryevich (əntôn' grĭgôr'yəvĭch ro͞o'bĭnstīn), 1829–94, Russian pianist, composer, and educator. As a piano virtuoso he was celebrated for his perfect technique and emotional power, and was rivaled only by Liszt. He made his debut in Moscow at nine and later performed in Europe, where he won the admiration of Mendelssohn, Chopin, and Liszt. In 1872, Rubinstein founded the St. Petersburg Conservatory and was its director (1862–67, 1887–91). During 1872–73 he made a triumphant tour of the United States. He was once highly esteemed as a composer, but little of his music is performed today. His brother, **Nicholas Grigoryevich Rubinstein,** 1835–81, also a brilliant pianist and teacher, founded (1864) the Moscow Conservatory, which he headed for the rest of his life. See Catherine D. Bowen, *"Free Artist": the Story of Anton and Nicholas Rubinstein* (1939).

Rubinstein, Arthur, 1887–, Polish-American pianist, b. Łódź. Rubinstein studied in Warsaw and Berlin, making his debut in 1898 with the Berlin Symphony Orchestra, conducted by Joachim. He first played in the United States in 1906, achieving great acclaim there in 1937, especially for his superb lyric interpretations of Chopin's music and his ardent championship of Spanish works. Rubinstein's enormous popularity has spanned many decades. See his autobiography (1973).

ruby, precious stone, the transparent red variety of CORUNDUM, found chiefly in Burma, Thailand, and Sri Lanka (Ceylon) and classified among the most valuable of gems. The Burmese stones are blood red, the most valued tint being the "pigeon's blood." The Thai stones are darker and the Ceylonese stones lighter than the Burmese specimens. Star rubies, i.e., those that show an internal star-shaped formation when cut in cabochon (with a rounded top), are rare. Stones sometimes confused with the ruby are spinel ("balas ruby"), rubellite (pink TOURMALINE), and pyrope GARNET. Synthetic rubies are manufactured, especially in Europe and the United States, by the fusion of pure aluminum oxide. Chromium oxide is added to provide the appropriate color.

Rückert, Friedrich (frē'drĭkh rük'ərt), pseud. **Freimund Raimar** (frī'mo͝ont rī'mär), 1788–1866, German scholar and poet. An editor and professor of Oriental languages, he wrote imitations of Oriental poetry and made fine translations of Arabic, Persian, and Chinese verse. He also wrote lyric romantic poems in a simple German style. Among these are the patriotic and anti-French *Geharnischte Sonette* [sonnets in armor] (1814), *Liebesfrühling* [springtime of love] (1823), and *The Wisdom of the Brahmins* (6 vol., 1836–39; tr. 1882), a long, contemplative work. Several of Rückert's works were set to music by Schumann and Mahler.

rudbeckia (rədbĕk'ēə): see BLACK-EYED SUSAN.

rudder, mechanism for steering an AIRPLANE or a ship. In ships it is a flat-surfaced structure hinged to the stern and controlled by a helm. When the ship is on a straight course, the rudder is in line with the vessel; if the rudder is turned to one side or the other it offers sufficient resistance to the water to deflect the stern, thus changing the direction of the ship. In earliest times, as in small boats today, a paddle or oar hand-operated at the stern served to turn a boat. Later, Greek and Roman vessels required two rudders, one at each end, in order to maintain course when the prow or stern lifted out of the water. Vikings placed the rudder not directly on the stern but on the right side near it; thus the term *starboard* (steerboard) is used for the right side of a vessel. By the early 14th cent. the stern rudder had generally replaced the side rudder, and in the latter half of the 19th cent. wooden rudders gave way to iron and steel. Large modern liners have rudders that are 60 ft (18 m) or more in height and weigh 100 tons.

rudderfish, common name for members of the family Kyphosidae, small-mouthed fishes of warm seas throughout the world. Also called sea chubs, rudderfishes commonly follow vessels (whence their name), scavenging on refuse. Best known is the Bermuda chub, averaging 3 to 4 lb (1.3–1.8 kg), common off the Florida coasts. Rudderfishes are classified in the phylum CHORDATA, subphylum Vertebrata, class Osteichthyes, order Perciformes, family Kyphosidae.

Rude, François (fräNswä' rüd), 1784–1855, French sculptor. As a Bonapartist, he left Paris after the battle of Waterloo and spent 12 years in Brussels. Rude is best known for his monumental relief on the Arc de Triomphe de l'Étoile, *The Departure of the Volunteers,* known also as *La Marseillaise.* This work has been much admired for its patriotic fervor and force of execution. Other examples of his art are the portrait of J. L. David (Louvre) and the statue of Marshal Ney in Paris.

Rüdesheim (rü'dəs-hīm"), town (1966 pop. c.7,500), Hesse, central West Germany, on the Rhine River. Vineyards in the area produce some of the most noted Rhine wines. Rüdesheim was first mentioned in the 9th cent. Nearby is the Brömserburg (10th cent.), a castle (now a museum) once used by the archbishops of Mainz.

Rudini, Antonio Starrabba or **Starabba, marchese di** (äntô'nyō stäräb'bä märkā'zä dē ro͞odēnē'), 1839–1908, Italian political leader. A Sicilian revolutionist, he was mayor of Palermo (1864), prefect of Naples (1868), minister of the interior (1869), and twice premier (1891–92, 1896–98) as the leader of the right. He renewed the Triple Alliance (1891) and attempted a rapprochement with France. He was obliged to resign in 1898 after having severely suppressed a series of bread riots.

Rudolf I or **Rudolf of Hapsburg** (ro͞o'dŏlf), 1218–91, German king (1273–91), first king of the HAPSBURG dynasty. Rudolf's election as king ended the interregnum (1250–73), during which time there was no accepted German king or Holy Roman emperor. The election was prompted by Pope Gregory X, who needed the support of a strong German ruler to counter the power of CHARLES I of Anjou in Italy. Rudolf's election was contested by the powerful King OTTOCAR II of Bohemia. Rudolf finally defeated Ottocar at Marchfeld (1278) and invested (1282) his own sons Albert (later King ALBERT I) and Rudolf with Austria, Styria, and Carniola, which he had won from Ottocar; these lands became the core of the Hapsburg possessions. Rudolf thus laid the foundations for a strong kingship based on large dynastic holdings. In Germany, Rudolf attempted to recover the rights lost to the crown during the interregnum. He issued local land peaces to overcome internal anarchy and imposed taxes on the imperial towns in order to strengthen the central government, but these measures had little success. In his Italian policy Rudolf attempted to conciliate the new pope, Nicholas III (reigned 1277–80), in the hope of securing the pope's approval for his coronation as Holy Roman emperor; Rudolf renounced his sovereignty over the Papal States and sought to bring about the withdrawal of the house of Anjou from central Italy. With Nicholas's death, however, and the election of an anti-German pope, Rudolf's plans for imperial coronation fell through. He also failed to have his son Albert elected king, which would have insured Albert's succession as emperor. Instead, Adolf of Nassau succeeded Rudolf.

Rudolf II, 1552–1612, Holy Roman emperor (1576–1612), king of Bohemia (1575–1611) and of Hungary (1572–1608), son and successor of Holy Roman Emperor Maximilian II. Acceding to the Hapsburg lands, he reversed his father's tolerant policy toward Protestantism and gave assistance to the Catholic Reformation. Although Rudolf was a learned man, he was incapable of ruling because he was plagued by melancholy and later became subject to occasional fits of insanity. Other members of his family began to intervene in imperial affairs. Following a revolt in Hungary (1604–6) by Stephen BOCKSAY and his Turkish allies, most of the actual ruling power passed to Rudolf's brother MATTHIAS; the revolt was provoked by Rudolf's attempt to impose Roman Catholicism in Hungary. In 1608, Matthias forced Rudolf to cede Hungary, Austria, and Moravia to him. Seeking to gain the support of the Bohemian estates, Rudolf issued (1609) a royal charter that guaranteed religious freedom to the nobles and cities. This effort was in vain, and Rudolf was forced to give up Bohemia to Matthias in 1611. Rudolf's turbulent reign was a prelude to the Thirty Years War.

Rudolf, 1858–89, Austrian archduke, crown prince of Austria and Hungary; only son of Emperor Francis Joseph and Empress Elizabeth. Upon his mysterious death at Mayerling near Vienna (officially declared a double suicide with his mistress, Baroness Maria

Vetsera), his cousin Francis Ferdinand became heir to the Austro-Hungarian throne.

Rudolf, Lake, c.2,500 sq mi (6,475 sq km), NW Kenya and SW Ethiopia, E Africa, in the Great Rift Valley; alt. 1,230 ft (375 m). Surrounded by desolate, volcanic mountains, the 170-mi- (274-km-) long lake is the focus of interior drainage and has no outlet; it is becoming increasingly saline.

Rudolf of Hapsburg: see RUDOLF I.

Rudolph: see RAOUL, king of France.

Rudolph, Paul Marvin, 1918–, American architect, b. Elkton, Ky. Rudolph has taught at a number of universities and in 1958 became chairman of the architecture department at Yale. He planned the Jewett Art Center (1959) at Wellesley College, the Greeley (Colo.) Forestry Building (1959), the Art and Architecture Building (1963) at Yale, and the Oriental Masonic Gardens Housing in New Haven (1970). His sculptural facades and use of sunscreens are reminiscent of the work of Le Corbusier. See his book on architecture (1970); study by Rupert Spade (1971).

Rudolstadt (ro͞o'dôlshtät"), city (1970 pop. 31,539), Gera district, S East Germany, on the Thuringian Saale River. Manufactures include china, glass, machinery, and leather and metal goods. It is also a tourist resort. Founded by A.D. 800, Rudolstadt was (1574–1918) the seat of the rulers of Schwarzburg-Rudolstadt. The Heidecksburg Palace, rebuilt in 1735, is now a museum.

rue, common name for various members of the family Rutaceae, a large group of plants distributed throughout temperate and tropical regions and most abundant in S Africa and Australia. Most species are woody shrubs or small trees; many are evergreen and bear spines. The family is characterized by the presence of glands producing an essential oil, and the foliage, fruits, and flowers are noticeably aromatic and fragrant. The aromatic principle is widely utilized for flavorings, perfume oils, and drugs. Chief in importance are the CITRUS FRUITS, source of numerous extracted oils but best known as a major tropical-fruit industry, rivaled only by the banana and, to a lesser extent, the pineapple. Also of value medicinally are angostura bark and the rues (both now more commonly used for flavoring) and the poisonous jaborandi. Several species of the Rutaceae yield lumber used for cabinetwork, e.g., the orange and the species called SATINWOOD. The PRICKLY ASH, native to North America, is used in domestic brews and is often planted as a fragrant garden ornamental, as are the citrus trees and the varieties of dittany or fraxinella (*Dictamnus alba*), Old World woody perennials with a strong, lemonlike aroma. The gas plant (var. *ruber*), called also Moses' burning bush and candle plant, yields a volatile and flammable oil that may be ignited around the plant on hot, calm evenings. The name *rue* is properly restricted to the shrubby herbs of the genus *Ruta*, ranging from the Mediterranean to E Siberia. The common rue of history and literature is *R. graveolans*, which has greenish-yellow flowers and blue-green leaves sometimes variegated, with a very strong odor and a bitter taste. The leaves are now sometimes used in flavorings, beverages, and herb vinegars and in the preparation of cosmetics and perfumes. In medieval times rue was much used as a drug. Its use as a condiment was thought to prevent poisons from affecting the system, and it was strewn about law courts in parts of Great Britain as a preventive against diseases carried by criminals. It was sometimes associated with witches but also symbolized grace, repentance, and memory. Shakespeare in *Richard II* refers to it as the "sour herb of grace." It is also mentioned in *Hamlet, A Winter's Tale,* and many other great works of literature including Milton's *Paradise Lost.* The family Rutaceae is classified in the division MAGNOLIOPHYTA, class Magnoliopsida, order Linales.

Rueda, Lope de: see LOPE DE RUEDA.

Ruef, Abraham (Abe Ruef)(ro͞of), 1864–1936, American political boss, b. San Francisco. He practiced law in San Francisco after 1886 and became a familiar figure in San Francisco ward politics. He was active in the local Republican party and later became the leader of the Union Labor party. After securing the election (1901) of Eugene Schmitz, a musician, as mayor of San Francisco, Ruef gained political control of the city and directed it with shocking corruption until he was indicted in 1906. In a sensational trial—Prosecutor Francis J. Heney was shot in the courtroom and replaced by Hiram Johnson—Ruef was convicted (1908) of bribery and was sentenced to a 14-year prison term. He was released on parole in 1915. See Walton Bean, *Boss Ruef's San Francisco* (1952); Lately Thomas, *A Debonair Scoundrel* (1962).

Rueil-Malmaison (rüĕ'yə-mälmāzôN'), town (1968 pop. 62,933), Hauts-de-Seine dept., N central France. It is an industrial center where metals, armaments, photographic equipment, film, pharmaceuticals, and automobile accessories are produced. Food products are also manufactured there. The town was originally a resort of the MEROVINGIAN kings (5th–7th cent.). It was bought by Cardinal Richelieu, who built an estate there and who carried on extensive construction during the early 17th cent. Napoleon lived there from 1800 to 1804 and the Empress Josephine and her daughter are buried in the town. Napoleon's home, the famous Malmaison, is now a museum housing artifacts from the Napoleonic period.

ruellia: see ACANTHUS.

ruffed grouse: see GROUSE.

Ruffin, Edmund (rŭf'ĭn), 1794–1865, American agriculturist, one of the Southern FIRE-EATERS, b. Prince George co., Va. His interest in improving impoverished land led him to become a pioneer in soil chemistry. Against much opposition he advocated the benefits of marl and proved its value. His arguments were propounded in *An Essay on Calcareous Manures* (1832, 5th rev. ed. 1852). He founded (1833) and edited until 1842 an excellent agricultural publication, the *Farmers' Register.* An ardent supporter of states' rights and secession, he left Virginia for the more congenial political milieu of South Carolina, where on April 12, 1861, he was given the privilege of firing the first shot against Fort Sumter. With the surrender of Robert E. Lee at Appomattox he committed suicide. See his *Diary*, ed. by W. K. Scarborough (Vol. I, 1972); study by A. O. Craven (1932, repr. 1964).

Ruffo, Fabrizio (fäbrē'tsēō ro͞of'fō), 1744–1827, Neapolitan general, cardinal of the Roman Catholic Church. In the French Revolutionary Wars he led the royal Neapolitan army against the PARTHENOPEAN REPUBLIC, set up at Naples under French protection. He promised the republicans full immunity from reprisals and obtained their surrender in June, 1799. Cardinal Ruffo sympathized with the grievances of the revolutionists, but in granting full pardon he possibly exceeded his authority. Even before Naples capitulated, Admiral Horatio NELSON appeared with his fleet, called the cardinal to task for his leniency, and revoked the terms of surrender. The rebels, who had been only vaguely informed of the change, surrendered nevertheless. Their leader, Caracciolo, was executed on Nelson's flagship, and a general massacre of the rebels followed.

Rufiji (ro͞ofē'jē), river, c.375 mi (600 km) long, rising in the highlands of SW Tanzania, E Africa, and flowing NE then E to the Indian Ocean opposite Mafia Island. The Ruaha River is its chief tributary. There are irrigation and flood-control projects on the river. Cotton is raised in the delta.

Rufinus (ro͞ofī'nəs), d. 395, Roman statesman, minister of THEODOSIUS I and ARCADIUS. After Theodosius' death (395) he virtually ruled the Eastern Empire for Arcadius, but his attempt to marry his daughter to the young emperor was thwarted by EUTROPIUS (d. 399). Rufinus was assassinated by Gothic mercenaries, who acted possibly on the orders of his rival STILICHO.

Rufus. 1 Son of Simon of Cyrene. Mark 15.21. **2** Christian in Rome. Rom. 16.13. Perhaps the same as **1.**

rug: see CARPET.

Rugby, municipal borough (1971 pop. 59,372), Warwickshire, central England. It is an important railroad junction and engineering center, with a prominent radio-transmitting station. Rugby is the largest cattle market in the Midlands, but is known chiefly as the seat of one of the great English public schools. Rugby School was founded in 1567 under the terms of the will of Laurence Sheriff, a wealthy London merchant born in Rugby. Its present buildings date from the early 19th cent., when Rugby became famous under the headmastership of Thomas Arnold. His son Matthew Arnold wrote of the school in his poetry, and another Rugbeian, Thomas Hughes, wrote the great schoolboy classic *Tom Brown's School Days,* which deals with life at Rugby. Rugby football originated at the school in 1823. Among Rugby's fine buildings is the war-memorial chapel, which commemorates the 682 Old Rugbeians who died in World War I.

rugby, game that originated (1823) on the playing fields of Rugby in England. It has many of the characteristics of SOCCER and American FOOTBALL. The game is said to have been started quite by accident when a Rugby student playing soccer picked up the ball and ran downfield with it instead of kicking it. Games of that sort were soon seen frequently at Rugby, and when other English schools and universities adopted the style of play in the mid-19th cent., the name rugby was given to the game. In 1871 the English Rugby Union was formed to standardize the game, and the sport was soon organized in other sections of the British Isles. The game was introduced (1875) into the United States, where it made relatively little headway. The rugby field is roughly 160 yd (146 m) long and 75 yd (69 m) wide, with goal lines 110 yd (101 m) apart and two in-goals (corresponding to football's end zones) 25 yd (23 m) deep. A halfway line divides the field, which is further subdivided by other lines parallel to the goal line. The goal posts have measurements similar to those used in American football, and the ball, although larger and more rounded, is similar to the American football. A team consists of 15 players (8 forwards and 7 backs), and no substitution is permitted. If a player is seriously injured, the team must play shorthanded. The ball may be kicked, carried, or passed (to the sides or to the rear); though tackling is permitted, blocking is forbidden. Unlike American football, play is almost continuous in rugby; after penalties and out-of-bounds plays, however, a scrum (in which the two opposing lines of forwards kick the ball thrown between them) starts play again. A try (carrying the ball into the opponent's in-goal) counts three points, a conversion (kicking the ball between the goal posts after a try is scored) two points, a field goal kick three points, and a penalty kick three points. A rugby match is divided into halves of 40 min, and there is no overtime period in case of a tie. Professional rugby, known as Rugby league, was organized in England in 1895. It is played by 13-man teams, and has somewhat different rules from the amateur Rugby union game. It is played chiefly in the North of England and in Australia, New Zealand, and France. See F. N. Creek, *Rugby Football* (rev. ed. 1970); Wallace Reyburn, *History of Rugby* (1971).

Rügen (rü'gən), island (1970 pop. 86,216), 358 sq mi (927 sq km), Rostock district, N East Germany, in the Baltic Sea, separated from the mainland by the Strelasund. The chief towns are Bergen (1970 pop. 11,046) and Sassnitz (1970 pop. 13,456), the largest port and the terminus of a train ferry to Trelleborg, Sweden. The island is also connected by ferry with Stralsund on the East German mainland. Agriculture and fishing are the main occupations on Rügen. There are many popular seaside resorts. The famous chalk cliffs rise on the eastern shore. Rügen was conquered by Denmark in 1168, passed to Pomerania in 1325, and shared the history of Swedish Pomerania from 1648 to 1815, when the island was taken by Prussia. It is the largest island of East Germany.

Ruggles, Carl, 1876–1971, American composer, b. Marion, Mass. Ruggles studied music at Harvard and was a friend of Charles Ives. His works are highly original, characterized by complex textures and jagged outlines. He wrote relatively little and later disavowed the music he had written before 1918. His best-known pieces include *Men and Mountains* (1924) and *Sun-Treader* (1932), for orchestra; *Angels,* for muted brass (1921); and *Evocations* (1934–43), for piano.

Ruggles, Samuel Bulkley, 1800–1881, American public figure, b. New Milford, Conn. He was a successful lawyer in New York City, but between 1831 and 1851 gave up his practice to devote himself to public affairs. He enthusiastically promoted real-estate development in the city and was mainly responsible for the laying out of Gramercy Park, for which he gave the land, and Union Square. Ruggles promoted the new Croton water system for the city and other improvements and served as a state assemblyman. He helped to organize the Erie RR and the Union Pacific RR. As a trustee (1836–81) of Columbia College he was to a large extent responsible for the beginning of its development into a great university. Interested in international affairs, he was a delegate to the International Monetary Conference in 1867. See biography by D. G. B. Thompson (1946).

Ruhamah (rühā'mə), daughter of Hosea. Hosea 2.1.

Ruhr (ro͝or), region, c.1,300 sq mi (3,370 sq km), W West Germany; the principal manufacturing center of West Germany and one of the world's greatest industrial complexes. It lies along, and north of, the Ruhr River (145 mi/233 km long), which rises in the hills of N central West Germany and flows generally west to the Rhine River at Duisburg. The Ruhr's principal cities are, in the west, Duisburg, Mülheim, Essen, Oberhausen, Bottrop, Gladbeck, and Gelsenkirchen; and in the east, Bochum, Dortmund, and the smaller cities of Wattenscheid, Recklinghausen, Herne, and Witten. Extensive coal deposits, especially the high quality coking coal required in steel manufacturing, underlie the region in basins that are near the surface along the Ruhr River (where the oldest mines and steel plants are located), and at greater depths to the north along the Lippe River (where most of the modern mines are found). Iron ore, oil, chemicals, and other raw materials are imported into the region by way of the Rhine, the Ruhr (navigable below Witten), the Rhine-Herne Canal, the Dortmund-Ems Canal, and a dense network of rail and road connections. The Ruhr Planning Authority (est. 1921) protects designated farmlands and green areas from encroachment by the cities and enforces pollution legislation. The development of the Ruhr district began in the 19th cent. when the KRUPP and Thyssen concerns built large integrated coal and steel empires. The Ruhr was occupied (1923) by French and Belgian forces during the dispute over REPARATIONS. The troops evacuated (1925), but the occupation greatly embittered German nationalist feeling. Some of the chief Ruhr industrialists helped Hitler to power in 1933. The Ruhr was a major bombing target for Allied forces during World War II. The International Authority for the Ruhr was set up in 1949 with responsibility for development of the region. Control passed to the European Coal and Steel Community in 1952 and to West Germany in 1954. Coal production has suffered from competition from other fuels, but the overall industrial strength of the region is greater now than prior to 1945.

Ruisdael or **Ruysdael, Jacob van** (both: yä'kōp vän rois'däl), c.1628–1682, Dutch painter and etcher, the most celebrated of the Dutch landscape painters. He studied with his father Isack and, later, with his uncle Salomon van Ruysdael, a well-known Haarlem landscapist. He first worked in Haarlem and moved to Amsterdam in 1656. Late in life, he obtained a medical degree and practiced as a physician in Amsterdam. Ruisdael's characteristic work shows northern nature in a somber mood. His skies are usually overcast, throwing a restless flux of light over the countryside. Gnarled, knotted oak and beech trees are rendered with extraordinary accuracy. Ruisdael's later works show great breadth of stroke, dramatizing mankind's insignificance amid the splendor of nature. Important later paintings include *Jewish Cemetery* (Detroit Inst. of Art) and *Wheatfields* (Metropolitan Mus.). He also produced some very fine etchings. Ruisdael anticipated and inspired many of the great French and English landscapists of the next two centuries. Of his pupils, Meindert Hobbema was the most outstanding. The Rijks Museum, the National Gallery, London, and many American collections have examples of his work. See W. Stechow, *Dutch Landscape Painting of the Seventeenth Century* (1968).

Ruiz, Juan (hwän rōōeth'), 1283?–1350?, Spanish poet, musician, and archpriest of Hita. Ruiz suffered 13 years in prison, during which time he revised his masterpiece, *El Libro de buen amor* (c.1330, tr. *The Book of Good Love*, 1933). This is a miscellany in verse of fables; autobiographic adventures in the picaresque style; and adaptations of medieval, classical, and oriental stories and apologues—all forming a vivid and unified satirical panorama of medieval society. He is considered the Spanish Chaucer.

Ruiz de Alarcón y Mendoza, Juan: see ALARCÓN Y MENDOZA, JUAN RUIZ DE.

Ruiz de Apodaca, Juan: see APODACA, JUAN RUIZ DE.

Rukeyser, Muriel (rōō'kīsər), 1913–, American poet, b. New York City. Her poetry expresses the beauty and passion in the confrontation of the individual and his constantly changing world. *Theory of Flight*, her first volume of poems, appeared in 1935. It was followed by *U. S. 1* (1938), *Beast in View* (1944), *The Green Wave* (1948), *Body of Waking* (1958), *Waterlily Fire: Poems 1935–1962* (1962); and *Speed of Darkness* (1968). Her writings include children's books, essays, and biographies of the scientist Willard Gibbs (1942) and the astronomer Thomas Harlot (1971).

rules of order: see PARLIAMENTARY LAW.

Rulfo, Juan (hwän rōōl'fō), 1918–, Mexican writer. In his novels and short stories he recreates the desolation, sadness, and abandonment of his native southern Jalisco and brings to life its simple and joyless people. He has written one book of short stories, *El llano en llamas* (1955; tr. *The Burning Plain and Other Stories*, 1967), and one novel, *Pedro Páramo* (1955; tr. 1959), a complex work with many episodes that are out of chronological order and are narrated by people who are already dead.

rum, spirituous liquor made from fermented sugarcane products. Prepared by fermentation, distillation, and aging, it is made from the molasses and foam that rise to the top of boiled sugarcane juice. An inferior rum is made from the waste products. Although rum is produced in most places where sugarcane is grown in quantity (e.g., Cuba, Brazil, Trinidad, the Malagasy Republic, Indonesia, and Puerto Rico), Jamaica is generally thought of as the home of rum. Naturally colorless, rum acquires by the addition of caramel a rich brown color deepened by storage in casks. Rum has been produced in the United States from colonial times.

Rumah (rōō'mə), unidentified place, home of Pedaiah, the grandfather of King Jehoiakim. 2 Kings 23.36.

Rumania (rōōmān'ēə, -yə) or **Romania** (rō-), republic (1971 pop. 20,478,658), 91,699 sq mi (237,500 sq km), SE Europe, bordering on Hungary in the northwest, on Yugoslavia in the southwest, on Bulgaria in the south, on the Black Sea in the southeast, and on the USSR in the east and north. BUCHAREST is the capital and largest city of the country, which is divided into 40 administrative districts. Rumania includes 7 historic and geographic regions: WALACHIA, MOLDAVIA, TRANSYLVANIA, and parts of BUKOVINA, CRIȘANA-MARAMUREȘ, the DOBRUJA, and the BANAT. The Danube River, which forms part of the border with Yugoslavia and almost all of the frontier with Bulgaria, traverses Rumania in the southeast; its tributary, the Prut, constitutes most of the border with the USSR. The Carpathian Mts., of which the Transylvanian Alps are a part, cut through Rumania in a wide arc from north to southwest; the Carpathians'

highest peaks in Rumania are Moldoveanu (8,343 ft/2,543 m) and Negoiu (8,317 ft/2,535 m). The country's climate is continental, with hot, dry summers and cold winters; severe droughts are common during the summer. The great majority of the inhabitants speak Rumanian, although there are also sizable minorities speaking Hungarian and German. By far the largest religious body is the Rumanian Orthodox Church, which is independent of, but similar in dogma to, the Eastern Orthodox Church. Traditionally an agricultural country rich in fertile soil, Rumania greatly expanded its industrial base after World War II so that in the early 1970s industry contributed more than half of the national product. The economy is almost entirely controlled and planned by the state. The chief farm products are wheat, maize, sugar beets, potatoes, sunflower seeds, and barley. There are extensive vineyards, and much wine is produced. Rumania is Europe's largest producer of petroleum and natural gas (methane) outside the USSR, with large oil fields around PLOIEȘTI (in Walachia) and on the Carpathian slopes in Moldavia. Other major resources include anthracite, lignite, iron and copper ores, salt, bauxite, gold, and chromium. About 25% of the country is forested, and large quantities of timber are cut, especially in Transylvania. The country's main industrial centers are ARAD, Bucharest, BRAȘOV, HUNEDOARA, IAȘI, ORADEA, REȘITA, and TIMIȘOARA. The leading manufactures include refined petroleum, iron and steel, chemicals, textiles, cement, forest products, processed food, tires, and electronic and electric equipment. BRĂILA, GALAȚI, and GIURGIU are the main Danubian ports; CONSTANȚA is the chief Black Sea port. Rumania's leading exports are petroleum and petroleum products, farm produce, cement, and tractors; the main imports are iron ore, coked coal, metals, and electric equipment. The principal trading partners are the USSR, West Germany, Czechoslovakia, and East Germany. There are universities at Brașov, Bucharest, Cluj, Craiova, and Timișoara.

History to 1881. Rumania occupies, roughly, ancient DACIA, which was a Roman province in the 2d and 3d cent. A.D. The ethnic character of modern Rumania seems to have been formed in the Roman period; Christianity was introduced at that time as well. After the Romans left the region, the area was overrun successively by the Goths, the Huns, the Avars, the Bulgars, and the Magyars. After a period of Mongol rule (13th cent.), the history of the Rumanian people became in essence that of the two Rumanian principalities—Moldavia and Walachia—and of Transylvania, which for most of the time was a Hungarian dependency. The princes of Walachia (in 1417) and of Moldavia (mid-16th cent.) became vassals of the Ottoman Empire, but they retained considerable independence. Although the princes were despots and became involved in numerous wars, their rule was a period of prosperity as compared with the 18th and 19th cent. Many old cathedrals in the country still testify to the cultural activity of the time. MICHAEL THE BRAVE of Walachia defied both the Ottoman sultan and the Holy Roman emperor and at the time of his death (1601) controlled Moldavia, Walachia, and Transylvania. However, Michael's empire soon fell apart. An ill-fated alliance (1711) of the princes of Moldavia and Walachia with Peter I of Russia led to Turkish domination of Rumania. Until 1821 the Turkish sultans appointed governors, or hospodars, usually chosen from among the Phanariots (see under PHANAR), Greek residents of Constantinople. The governors and their subordinates reduced the Rumanian people (except for a few great landlords, the boyars) to a group of nomadic shepherds and poor, enserfed peasants. At the end of the 18th cent. Turkish control was seriously challenged by Russia and by Austria; at the same time, a strong nationalist movement was growing among the Rumanians. The treaty of KUCHUK KAINARJI (1774) gave Russia considerable influence over Moldavia and Walachia. When, in 1821, Alexander Ypsilanti raised the Greek banner of revolt in Moldavia, the Rumanians (who had more grievances against the Greek Phanariots than against the Turks) helped the Turks to expel the Greeks. In 1822 the Turks agreed to appoint Rumanians as governors of the principalities; after the Russo-Turkish War of 1828–29, during which Russian forces occupied Moldavia and Walachia, the governors were given life tenure. Although the two principalities technically remained within the Ottoman Empire, they actually became Russian protectorates. Under Russian pressure, new constitutions giving extensive rights to the boyars were promulgated in Moldavia (1832) and in Walachia (1831). At the same time, a renewed national and cultural revival was under way, and in 1848 the Rumanians rose in rebellion against both foreign control and the power of the boyars. The uprising, secretly welcomed by the Turks, was suppressed, under the leadership of Russia, by joint Russo-Turkish military intervention. Russian troops did not evacuate Rumania until 1854, during the Crimean War, when they were replaced by a neutral Austrian force. The Congress of Paris (1856) established Moldavia and Walachia as principalities under Turkish suzerainty and under the guarantee of the European powers, and it awarded S BESSARABIA to Moldavia. The election (1859) of Alexander John CUZA as prince of both Moldavia and Walachia prepared the way for the official union (1861–62) of the two principalities as Rumania. Cuza freed (1864) the peasants from certain servile obligations and distributed some land (confiscated from religious orders) to them. However, he was despotic and corrupt and was deposed by a coup d'etat in 1866. CAROL I of the house of Hohenzollern-Sigmaringen was chosen as his successor. A moderately liberal constitution was adopted in 1866. In 1877, Rumania joined Russia in its war on Turkey. At the Congress of Berlin (1878), Rumania gained full independence but was obliged to restore S Bessarabia to Russia and to accept N Dobruja in its place. In 1881, Rumania was proclaimed a kingdom.

1881 to the Present. After becoming a kingdom, Rumania continued to be torn by violence and turmoil, caused mainly by the government's failure to institute adequate land reform, by the corruption of government officials, and by frequent foreign interference. There was no real attempt to curb the anti-Semitic excesses through which the peasants, encouraged by demagogues, vented their feelings against the Jewish agents of the absentee Rumanian landlords, the boyars. A major peasant revolt in 1907 was directed against both the Jews and the boyars. Rumania remained neutral in the first (1912) of the BALKAN WARS but entered the second war (1913), against Bulgaria, and gained S Dobruja. Although Rumania had adhered (1883) to the Triple Alliance, it proclaimed its neutrality when World War I broke out in 1914. In the same year FERDINAND succeeded Carol as king. Rumanian irredentism in Transylvania helped to bring Rumania into the Allied camp, and in 1916 Rumania declared war on the Central Powers. Most of the country was overrun by Austro-German forces, and in Feb., 1918, by the Treaty of Bucharest, Rumania consented to a harsh peace. On Nov. 9, 1918, Rumania again entered the war on the Allied side, and the general armistice of Nov. 11, 1918, annulled the Treaty of Bucharest. Shortly thereafter, Rumania annexed Bessarabia from Russia, Bukovina from Austria, and Transylvania and the Banat from Hungary. Rumanian armed intervention (1919) in Hungary defeated the Communist regime of Bela Kun and helped to put Admiral Horthy into power. Rumania's acquisition of Bukovina, Transylvania, part of the Banat (the rest going to Yugoslavia), and Crişana-Maramureş (until then a part of Hungary) was confirmed by the treaties of Saint-Germain (1919) and Trianon (1920), but the USSR did not recognize Rumania's seizure of Bessarabia. A series of agrarian laws beginning in 1917 did much to break up the large estates and to redistribute the land to the peasants. The large Magyar population as well as other minority groups were a constant source of friction, and Rumania entered the LITTLE ENTENTE (1921) and the BALKAN ENTENTE (1934) largely to protect itself against Hungarian and Bulgarian revisionism. Internal Rumanian politics were undemocratic and unfair. Electoral laws were revised (1926) to enable the party in power to keep out opponents, and assassination was not unusual as a political instrument. Political conflict became acute after the death (1927) of Ferdinand, when the royal succession was thrown into confusion. Ferdinand's son, Carol, had renounced the succession and Carol's son MICHAEL became king, but in 1930 Carol returned, set his son aside, and was proclaimed king as CAROL II. The court party, led by the king and by Mme Magda LUPESCU, was extremely unpopular, but its opponents were divided. The Liberal party, headed first by John Bratianu (see under BRATIANU, family) and later by Ion Duca, was bitterly opposed by the Peasant party, led by Iuliu MANIU. A right wing of the Peasant party joined with other anti-Semitic groups in the National Christian party, which was linked with the terrorist IRON GUARD. There was a frequent turnover of cabinets, and the only figure of some permanence was Nicholas TITULESCU, who was foreign minister from 1927 to 1936, when the increasingly powerful Fascist groups forced him to resign. In 1938, Carol II assumed dictatorial powers and promulgated a corporative constitution, which was approved in a rigged plebiscite. Later in 1938, after CODREANU and 13 other leaders of the Iron Guard were shot "while trying to escape" from prison, Carol proclaimed the Front of National Renascence as the sole legal political party. In foreign affairs, Rumania after 1936 drew closer to the Axis powers. The country remained neutral at the outbreak (1939) of World War II, but in 1940 it became a neutral partner of the Axis. Rumania was powerless (1940) to resist Soviet demands for Bessarabia and N Bukovina or to oppose Bulgarian and Hungarian demands, backed by Germany, for the S Dobruja, the Banat, Crişana-Maramureş, and part of Transylvania. The Iron Guard rose in rebellion against Carol's surrender of these territories. Carol was deposed (1940) and exiled, and Michael returned to the throne. The army gained increased influence. Ion Antonescu became dictator, and in June, 1941, Rumania joined Germany in its attack on the Soviet Union. Rumanian troops recovered Bessarabia and Bukovina and helped to take Odessa, but they suffered heavily at Stalingrad (now Volgograd) in late 1942 and early 1943. In Aug., 1944, two Soviet army groups entered Rumania. Michael overthrew Antonescu's Fascist regime, surrendered to the USSR, and ordered Rumanian troops to fight on the Allied side. The peace treaty between Rumania and the Allies, signed at Paris in 1947, in essence confirmed the armistice terms of 1944. Rumania recovered all its territories except Bessarabia, N Bukovina, and S Dobruja. Politically and economically, the country became increasingly dependent on the Soviet Union. A Communist-led coalition government, headed by the non-Communist Peter Groza, was set up in 1945. In Dec., 1947, Michael was forced to abdicate, and Rumania was proclaimed a people's republic. The first constitution (1945) was superseded in 1952 by a constitution patterned more directly on the Soviet model. Nationalization of industry and natural resources was completed by a law of 1948, and there was also forced collectivization of agriculture. Control over the major industries, notably petroleum, was shared with the USSR after 1945, but an agreement in 1952 dissolved the joint companies and returned them to full Rumanian control. In 1949, Rumania joined the Council of Mutual Economic Assistance (COMECON), and in 1955 it became a charter member of the Warsaw Treaty Organization and also joined the United Nations. From 1945 to 1965 Gheorghe GHEORGHIU-DEJ was head of the Rumanian Workers' (Communist) party; he was succeeded by Nicholas Ceauşescu as leader of the party, renamed the Rumanian Communist party. In 1965, Rumania was officially termed a socialist republic, instead of a people's republic, to denote its alleged attainment of a higher level of Communism, and a new constitution was adopted. Beginning in 1963, Rumania's foreign policy became increasingly independent of that of the USSR. In early 1967, Rumania established diplomatic relations with West Germany. It maintained friendly relations with Israel after the Arab-Israeli War of June, 1967, whereas the other East European Communist nations severed diplomatic ties. In 1968, Rumania did not join in the invasion of Czechoslovakia, and in 1969, Ceauşescu and President Tito of Yugoslavia affirmed the sovereignty and equality of socialist nations. However, Rumania maintained close economic ties with the USSR and in the early 1970s appeared to be drawing closer again in other matters as well.

Government. Under the constitution adopted in 1965, the grand national assembly, consisting of 465 elected members, is the chief legislative body. In March, 1974, the government was reorganized; authority was concentrated in the new office of president of the republic (which replaced the 28-member state council). The president is also the head of state. In practice, power in Rumania is controlled by the Rumanian Communist party, whose leading members are also the country's chief officials. The permanent presidium, led by the general secretary, is the party's highest body. See R. W. Seton-Watson, *A History of the Roumainians* (1963); S. A. Fischer-Galati, *Twentieth Century Rumania* (1970); Nicolae Iorga, *A History of Roumania* (tr. 1925, repr. 1970); J. A. Hale, *Ceauşescu's Romania* (1971); T. W. Riker, *The Making of Roumania* (1931, repr. 1971); Vlad Georgescu, *Political Ideas and the Enlightenment in the Romanian Principalities, 1750-1831* (1972); E. K. Keefe and others, *Area Handbook for Romania* (1972).

Rumanian language, member of the Romance group of the Italic subfamily of the Indo-European family of languages (see ROMANCE LANGUAGES). It is spoken by about 17 million people in Rumania, where it is the official language, by 2.5 million people in the USSR, and by an additional 500,000 persons scattered in Albania, Bulgaria, Greece, Hungary, Italy, and Yugoslavia. At the present time Rumanian is written in the Roman alphabet, to which have been added the symbols ă, â, î, ş, and ţ. In the USSR, however, Cyrillic characters are used for Rumanian. A distinctive feature of Rumanian is the attachment of the definite article to the noun as a suffix, as in *omul* (literally, "man-the"). The oldest surviving Rumanian texts are from the 16th cent., and there are four major dialects of the language. See James E. Augerot and Florin D. Popescu, *Modern Romanian* (1971); Emanuel Vasiliu and Sanda Golopentia-Ertescu, *Transformational Syntax of Romanian* (1973).

Rumanian literature. Until the 16th cent. most writing among the Rumanians was in Slavonic. An exception was a crude translation of the Acts of the Apostles and the Psalms, done by a Transylvanian cleric under the influence of Hussite propaganda. In 1541 a catechism in Rumanian was issued at Sibiu, and from 1560 liturgical works were published in Rumanian to meet the needs of the local Calvinist Church. Translations of the legend of Alexander the Great appeared c.1600, and in 1673 the Moldavian Bishop Dositheiu published the first volume of poetry in Rumanian, a verse translation of the Psalms. Dositheiu also started a movement in 1679 for the use of the vernacular in the liturgy. Early historical works were the *Moldavian Chronicle* of Miron Costin (1633-91) and the famous *Moldo-Wallachian Chronicle* (1710) of Demetrius Cantemir (1673-1723), a great scholar who also wrote a philosophical treatise in Rumanian on the old theme of body versus soul. Cantemir's *Chronicle* laid the foundation of a movement that, starting in Transylvania under George Lazan (1779-1823), had as its purpose the emphasis of the Latin as opposed to the Slavic element in the Rumanian national character. The mainspring of this movement was Ion Eliade (1802-72, known as Radulescu), and its culminating product was a dictionary of the Rumanian language produced (1871-76) by August Laurianu and others, in which all words of non-Latin origin were eliminated. In 1860 the Latin replaced the Cyrillic as the official Rumanian alphabet (the church used the Cyrillic until 1890), and 1860 thus marks the beginning of modern Rumanian literature. Just as first the Slavic and later, in the Phanariot period (1711-1821), the Greek influence had been strong, in the early 19th cent. that of France predominated. The native Rumanian spirit had therefore to struggle to become articulate. The efforts of Vasile ALECSANDRI in the ballad *Little Lamb* (1852) gave Rumanian literature its starting point. Drama played a major part in the rise of Rumanian literature, from the time of Eliade and George Asachi (1788-1869), cofounders (1833-36) of the Rumanian national theater. Other outstanding names in the drama are Ion Luca CARAGIALE, a master of the comedy of manners; Ronetti Roman (1853-1908), author of the tragedy *Manasse* (1900), dealing with the conflict of Jew and Christian in Rumania; Victor Eftimiu, who experimented with poetic drama; and Lucian Blaga. Poetry flourished in 1867 when at Jassy in Moldavia Titu Maiorescu (1840-1917) founded the cosmopolitan journal *Convorbiri literare* [literary conversations], which soon began to publish the lyrics of Mihail EMINESCU. The peasant and folk tradition had as its spokesman the historian Nicolae Iorga (1871-1940). In poetry this school produced George Cosbuc (1866-1918) and in prose Ion Slavici (1848-1945), who collected native tales, and Ion Creanga (1837-89), a pioneer in the field of the novel. Themes of social concern were treated by Alexandru Vlahuta (1858-1919) in the novel *Dan* (1894) and by Duiliu Zamfirescu (1858-1922) in *Country Life* (1894). The contrast between rural and urban life was detailed in the realistic novels *Dinu Millian* by Constantin Mille and *Parasites* (1893) by Barbu Delavrancea (1858-1919). From the "back to the soil" movement in Rumanian letters came the novel *Ion* (1920) by Liviu Rebreanu, known also for his novel of World War I, *The Forest of the Hanged* (1922). Major Rumanian poets of the 20th cent. include Dimitrie Anghel (1872-1914) and Octavian Goga (1881-1938), an outspoken and often partisan advocate of Transylvanianism. Rumanian writers have been under Soviet influence since 1945. The prolific novelist Mihail Sadoveanu (1880-1961), a compassionate spokesman for the humble, is perhaps the foremost modern Rumanian literary figure; the poets Tudor Arghezi and Mihai Beniuc (1907-44) have also produced outstanding work. Some significant younger writers are the novelists Zaharia Stancu, Marin Preda, and Titus Popovici and the poets Veronica Porumbacu, Alexandu Jar, and Maria Banusi. See Leon Feraru, *The Development of Rumanian Poetry* (1929); Basil Munteano, *Modern Rumanian Literature* (tr. 1939); E. D. Tappe, *Rumanian Prose and Verse* (1956); Jacob Steinberg, ed., *Introduction to Rumanian Literature* (1966).

Rumelia or **Roumelia** (both: ro͞omē'lēə), region of S Bulgaria, between the Balkan and Rhodope mts. Historically, Rumelia denoted the Balkan possessions (particularly Thrace and Macedonia) of the Ottoman Empire. The Ottoman province of Rumelia comprised much of present-day Yugoslavia, Bulgaria, European Turkey, N Greece, and part of Albania. SOFIA was the seat of the governors of Rumelia until 1878. In that year the Treaty of San Stefano, ending a war between Russia and Turkey, created a huge Bulgarian state; but the European powers, fearing that Bulgaria would become a Russian dependency, agreed (see BERLIN, CONGRESS OF) to make N Bulgaria an autonomous principality owing nominal allegiance to the Turkish sultan and to create an autonomous province of **Eastern Rumelia.** This province, with its capital at PLOVDIV, comprised, roughly, the part of present Bulgaria situated S of the Balkan mts. It remained under Turkish sovereignty but enjoyed considerable autonomy and was ruled by a governor appointed by the Ottoman Empire with the approval of the European powers. Resentment at the partition of Bulgaria sparked a revolution at Plovdiv in 1885, and Prince Alexander of Bulgaria annexed Eastern Rumelia, thus incurring the wrath of Russia and Serbia. The Serbians, who also claimed the area, declared war on Bulgaria but were forced to make peace (1886) on the basis of the status quo, while the sultan agreed to name Alexander governor of Eastern Rumelia. This arrangement amounted to a tacit Turkish surrender of the province, which henceforth remained part of Bulgaria, although it was nominally under Ottoman rule until Bulgaria became officially independent in 1908.

Rumford, Benjamin Thompson, Count, 1753-1814, American-British scientist and administrator, b. Woburn, Mass. In 1776 he went to England, where he served (1780–81) as undersecretary of the colonies, conducting significant experiments with gunpowder in his spare time. Later he entered the service of the elector of Bavaria as an administrator. He was knighted in 1784 and in 1791 was created count of the Holy Roman Empire. He chose his title from the name of the town Rumford (later Concord), N.H., where his wife was born. Returning to England (1795), he introduced improved methods of heating and cooking, and developed a more accurate theory of heat. In contrast to the prevalent belief that heat was a substance, he presented, in a paper (1798) to the Royal Society, the theory that heat was produced by the motion of particles. He founded the Royal Institution in England, established the Rumford medal of the Royal Society, and founded the Rumford professorship of chemistry at Harvard. See biographies by Egon Larsen (1953) and W. J. Sparrow (1964).

Rumi, Jalal ed-Din or **Jalal ud-Din** (jäläl' ĕd-dēn' ro͞o'mē, o͝od-dēn'), 1207–73, Persian poet. He was a native of Balkh, but lived at Rum (ancient Iconium, modern Konya), whence his name. He was a Sufi, and his lyrics express mystic thought in finely wrought symbols. He is considered by many as the greatest of the brilliant school of Sufist poets. Rumi's main work is the *Mathnawi*, a poetic exposition of Sufism in eight books (tr. 1925–40). He founded a Sufist sect that still survives. See a selection of his mystical poems, tr. by A. J. Arberry (1968); critical biographies by R. A. Nicholson (1950) and A. R. Arasteh (1965).

ruminant, any of a group of hooved mammals that chew their cud, i.e., that regurgitate and chew again food that has already been swallowed. Ruminants have an even number of toes on each foot and a stomach with either three or four chambers. In the first chamber, called the rumen, the food is mixed with fluid to form a soft mass, the cud, or bolus. The regurgitated cud, after having been slowly chewed, is swallowed again, and passes through the rumen into the other stomach chambers for further digestion. The group, a suborder of the mammalian order Artiodactyla, includes goats, sheep, cows, camels, and antelope.

Ruml, Beardsley (rŭm'əl), 1894–1960, American economist, b. Cedar Rapids, Iowa, grad. Dartmouth, 1915, Ph.D. Univ. of Chicago, 1917. He was an executive of philanthropic societies, dean (1931–33) of the social science division of the Univ. of Chicago, and after 1934 he was active in the administration of the Federal Reserve Bank of New York and a department store. Ruml was the author of the withholding tax plan ("pay-as-you-go plan"), which was adopted by the U.S. Congress in 1943. His works include *Tomorrow's Business* (1945).

rummy, card game played by two to six players with a standard deck. The cards usually rank from king down through ace. Seven cards are dealt to each player in the three- or four-hand game, one card is turned up on the table, and the remaining cards are left face down in a stock pile. Players, in order, each draw one card from stock and then discard one card from their hands into the discard pile, face up. They have the option of drawing the top card from the discard pile. The object is to meld, that is to put down sets of cards—either three or four cards of the same rank or a sequence of three or more in the same suit. The first player to meld all his cards wins. A variation is knock rummy, in which a player may wait to meld his seven cards for higher stakes, but may also knock after he draws from stock and discards. By knocking he lays down his cards, and if the nonmelded cards have a total less than the nonmelded cards of each of the other players, he wins. Aces are counted 1 point, each face card 10, and all others for their pip values. Gin rummy, a variant invented in 1909, became immensely popular in the early 1940s. Two may play and each is dealt 10 cards; knocking is permitted only with unmatched cards totaling 10 points or less. Gin is scored when all cards are melded. The game continues until 100 points are scored. Scoring is relatively complicated, for it involves box tallies and a system of bonus points. Between 1949 and 1951 a rummy variation from Argentina, canasta, became the biggest game fad in the United States since Mah-Jongg in the early 1920s. The Argentinian import for a time even surpassed contract bridge in popularity. It is played with two standard decks, plus four jokers, which, with the eight deuces, are wild cards. Red threes are counted as bonus cards and black threes may be used as defensive discards. It also is similar to some other (but by no means all) forms of rummy in that a card is turned up to form the basis of a discard pile and the whole pile may be drawn by a player. Furthermore, sequences have no value and suits no meaning. A player's object is to score the most points by making canastas (seven or more cards of the same rank or four or more cards of one rank plus wild cards to total seven cards constitute a canasta) and melding cards of the same rank. To go out of the game a player must lay at least one canasta on the table with the remaining cards in melded form. Canasta variants include Bolivia and Samba. Other popular varieties of rummy are five-hundred rummy, continental rummy, and panguingue. See Oswald Jacoby, *How to Win at Gin Rummy* (1959); W. L. Richard, *The Complete Gin-Rummy* (1959).

Rumor, Mariano (märyä'nō ro͞o'mōr), 1915–, Italian political leader. He entered politics after World War II and was elected to parliament in 1948 as a member of the Christian Democratic party. He rose rapidly in party and government circles. Leader of a moderate Christian Democratic faction, he became head of the Christian Democrats in Dec., 1963. After serving as minister of agriculture and minister of the interior, he became premier in Dec., 1968, and served, except for a brief interruption, until July, 1970. He was interior minister in 1972 before becoming premier again in July, 1973. His government fell in Oct., 1974, but he continued to serve in a caretaker capacity.

Rump Parliament: see ENGLISH CIVIL WAR.

Runciman, Walter Runciman, 1st **Viscount** (rŭn'sĭmən), 1870–1949, British shipping magnate and public official. He inherited his father's large shipping business. As a Liberal he served in Parliament, with two interruptions, from 1899 to 1937 and held a number of governmental administrative positions, including the presidency of the Board of Trade (1914–16, 1931–37). He was made viscount in 1937. In July, 1938, he was sent to Czechoslovakia to mediate between the Czech government and the Sudeten Germans. The unsuccessful mission was a prelude to the MUNICH PACT.

Runcorn, urban district (1971 pop. 35,953), Cheshire, W England, on the Mersey River. It is on the Manchester Ship Canal and is the terminus of the Bridgewater Canal, which connects with the Mersey by a series of locks. Runcorn has shipyards, iron foundries, and tanning factories, and industries that manufacture pharmaceuticals and chemicals. It owes its development chiefly to the construction of the Bridgewater Canal in the 18th cent. It was the site of a castle of Æthelflæd in the 10th cent. The district includes Runcorn New Town, which was designated in the 1960s to accommodate overpopulation in the Liverpool and N Merseyside areas.

Rundstedt, Karl Rudolf Gerd von (kärl ro͞o'dôlf gĕrt fən ro͞ont'shtĕt), 1875–1953, German field marshal. He proved his exceptional abilities in World War I. In World War II he commanded in the Polish campaign (1939), in the French campaign (1940), and in Russia (June–Dec., 1941). From March, 1942, to March, 1945, except for a brief period in 1944, he was supreme commander in the West. He launched a deadly counteroffensive on Dec. 16, 1944 (see BATTLE OF THE BULGE). After the war he was held by the British for possible prosecution as a war criminal. In 1949 he was released because of ill health.

Runeberg, Johan Ludvig (yo͞o'hän lŭd'vĭg rü'nəbĕryə), 1804–77, Finnish national poet. In 1837 he became professor of Latin at Porvoo near Helsinki. Runeberg's simple and realistic style helped to check the tendency toward false rhetoric in Scandinavian literature. His first long work was the realistic peasant epic *The Elkhunters* (1832). The excellent lyric epic *King Fjalar* (1844, tr. 1912), an unrhymed verse cycle based on Scandinavian legend, is pervaded by a sense of inexorable tragedy. The first song from Runeberg's great poem on the Russo-Swedish War of 1808–9, "The Tales of Ensign Stål" (1848–60, tr. 1925, 1938), has been adopted as the Finnish national anthem. Like other Finnish authors of his day, Runeberg wrote in Swedish.

runes, ancient characters used in Teutonic, Anglo-Saxon, and Scandinavian INSCRIPTIONS. They were probably first used by the East Goths (c.300), who are thought to have derived them from Helleno-Italic writing. The runes were adapted to carving on wood and stone; they consisted of perpendicular, oblique, and a few curved lines. The first six runic signs were for *f, u, th, o* (*a*), *r, c* (*k*), hence the name *Futhorc* for the runic alphabets. There were two alphabets, one of 16 signs and the other of 24 (the same 16 with 8 additional signs). They were used extensively throughout N Europe, Iceland, England, Ireland, and Scotland until the establishment of Christianity. From then on the use of runes was reviled as a pagan practice. In Scandinavia their use persisted even after the Middle Ages; there they were used for manuscripts as well as inscriptions. The word *rune* is derived from an early Anglo-Saxon

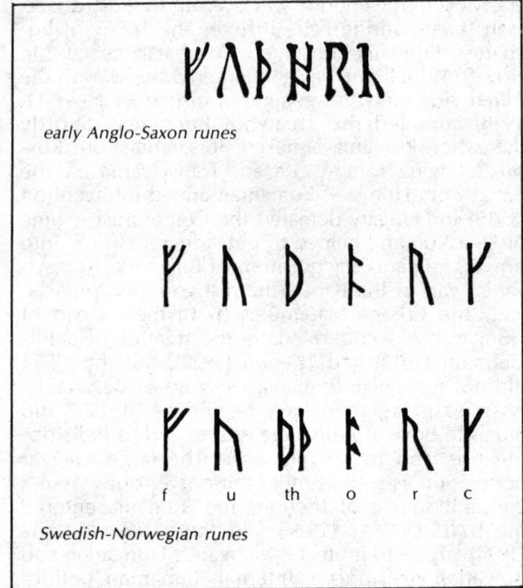

Examples of runes

word meaning *secret* or *mystery*. See A. F. Brodeur, *The Riddle of the Runes* (1932, repr. 1973); R. I. Page, *An Introduction to English Runes* (1973).

Runge, Philipp Otto (fē'lĭp ôt'ō ro͝ong'ə), 1777–1810, German painter. Immersed in the mysticism of the romantic movement in Germany, Runge became a leading figure of romantic painting. He was influenced by C. D. FRIEDRICH and by Goethe to seek universal harmonies through his art. His *Rest on the Flight into Egypt* (c.1805) is in the Kunsthalle in Hamburg.

Runnemede (rŭn'ĭmēd), residential borough (1970 pop. 10,475), Camden co., SW N.J.; settled 1683 by Friends as New Hope, inc. 1926.

runner or **stolon,** slender, creeping stem capable of taking root where its nodes touch the ground and thereby producing new shoots. The runner itself usually dies at the end of the season, leaving independent new plants. Among the plants that propagate by means of runners are the strawberry, the black raspberry, white clover, and some grasses.

running pine, common name for the plant species *Lycopodium clavatum,* also called ground pine. See LYCOPODIOPHYTA.

Runnymede or **Runnimede** (rŭn'ĭmēd), meadow, in Egham, Surrey, S England, on the south bank of the Thames River, W of London. Either on this meadow or on nearby Charter Island, King John accepted the MAGNA CARTA (1215), which is commemorated by a memorial. There is also a memorial to John F. Kennedy on Runnymede.

runway: see AIRPORT.

Runyon, Damon (Alfred Damon Runyon), 1884–1946, American short story writer and journalist, b. Manhattan, Kansas. He is best known for his humorous stories—written in a picturesque, slangy journalistic idiom (often referred to as Runyonese)—about New York City's Broadway and underworld characters. Collections of his works include *Guys and Dolls* (1931), *Blue Plate Special* (1934), *Money from Home* (1935), and *Runyon à la Carte* (1944). The musical *Guys and Dolls* (1950) was based on Runyon's stories. See biography by Damon Runyon, Jr. (1954).

Rupert, 1352–1410, German king (1400–1410), elector palatine of the Rhine. He was elected German king after the deposition of WENCESLAUS. Seeking the imperial crown, Rupert went to Italy. He attempted to intervene in Italian affairs and regain the former imperial city of Milan from Gian Galeazzo VISCONTI, but he was defeated and returned impoverished to Germany in 1402. Recognized (1403) by the Roman Pope Boniface IX, he adhered to the Roman popes in the Great SCHISM. When he sent envoys to plead for Gregory XII at the Council of Pisa, the council refused to recognize his title. Rupert was unable to exercise any control over the warring cities and nobles. At his death, two successors were elected, but in 1411 he was succeeded by SIGISMUND.

Rupert, Prince, 1619–82, count palatine of the Rhine. Born in Prague, he was the son of Frederick the Winter King, elector palatine and king of Bohemia, and Elizabeth, daughter of James I of England.

Rupert grew up in the Netherlands and studied at Leiden. Active in the later part of the Thirty Years War against the Holy Roman Empire, he was at the siege of Breda (1637) and was taken prisoner (1638). Released in 1641, he went to the aid of his uncle, King Charles I of England, in the civil wars. Despite his youth Rupert became an outstanding royalist general. His cavalry was generally successful, and he was created earl of Holderness and duke of Cumberland. Despite his defeat at Marston Moor (1644) he was made a general of the king's army. However, Rupert's support of peace proposals and his surrender of Bristol (1645) to Sir Thomas Fairfax resulted in his dismissal by the king, and in 1646 he was ordered to leave England. He went to France, soon became reconciled with Charles, and commanded a fleet assisting the king's forces in Ireland. After the triumph of Parliament over the monarchy, Rupert went (1654) to Germany, where he remained until the Restoration of the Stuart kings under Charles II (1660). Returning to England, he became a privy councillor to Charles II, and, as an admiral, played an important part in the DUTCH WARS. A man of many artistic and scientific interests, Rupert also took part in colonial and commercial schemes, notably in the ventures of the Hudson's Bay Company. See biographies by Eva Scott (1899), Bernard Fergusson (1952), and Frank Knight (1967).

Rupert House, village and trading post, W Que., Canada, on the Rupert River east of its mouth on James Bay. Founded in 1668 as Fort Charles by the explorer Groseilliers and later called Fort Rupert, then Rupert's House or Rupert House, it is the oldest fur-trading post of the HUDSON'S BAY COMPANY. In the struggle between the English and French in Canada, the post was captured in 1686 by the French and alternately held by the French and British until the Peace of Utrecht (1713) restored it permanently to the Hudson's Bay Company. The post is the center of a large beaver sanctuary.

Rupert's Land, Canadian territory held (1670–1869) by the HUDSON'S BAY COMPANY, named for Prince Rupert, first governor of the company. Under the charter granted (1670) to the company by Charles II, the region comprised the drainage basin of Hudson Bay. The area embraced what is today the provinces of Ontario and Quebec N of the Laurentians and W of Labrador; all of Manitoba; most of Saskatchewan; the southern half of Alberta; the eastern part of the Northwest Territories; and portions of Minnesota and North Dakota in the United States. In 1869 the Hudson's Bay Company transferred Rupert's Land to Canada for £300,000 but retained certain blocks of land for trading and other purposes.

rupture, in medicine: see HERNIA.

Rural Electrification Administration (REA), agency of the U.S. Dept. of Agriculture charged with administering loan programs for electrification and telephone service in rural areas. The REA was created (1935) by executive order as an independent Federal bureau, authorized by the Congress in 1936, and later (1939) reorganized as a division of the U.S. Dept. of Agriculture. The REA undertook a program to provide farms with inexpensive electric lighting and power and to improve farming equipment. To implement those goals the administration made long-term, self-liquidating loans to state and local governments, to farmers' cooperatives, and to nonprofit organizations; no loans were made directly to consumers. In 1944, Congress liberalized the terms of the REA loans and removed the time limitation from the lending program. In 1949 the REA was authorized to make loans for the purpose of furnishing and improving telephone service. The success of REA is supported by the fact that by the early 1970s about 98% of all farms in the United States had electric service. See C. T. Ellis, *A Giant Step* (1966).

Rurik (ro͞o'rĭk), d. 879, semilegendary VARANGIAN warrior, regarded as the founder of the princely dynasty of medieval Russia. Rurik and his two brothers, at the head of an armed band, apparently seized Novgorod and nearby districts (c.862). According to unreliable early accounts, they had been invited by the local Slavs. Rurik's successors founded the powerful Kievan state, which lasted until the 13th cent. The house of Rurik also came to rule the grand duchy of Moscow, and later all Russia, until the death of Feodor I in 1598.

Ruschuk: see RUSE, Bulgaria.

Ruse (ro͞o'sĕ), city (1968 est. pop. 145,300), NE Bulgaria, on the Danube River bordering Rumania. The chief river port of Bulgaria, it is also an industrial and communications center. It has shipyards, a petroleum refinery, and varied manufactures. Ruse is the seat of an Eastern Orthodox metropolitan and of a Roman Catholic bishop. Founded (2d cent. B.C.) as Prista, it became a Roman naval station. Under Turkish rule (15th–19th cent.) Ruse, known as Ruschuk, served as a military base. The city has a polytechnic institute and is noted for its old churches and mosques.

Rush, Benjamin, 1745?–1813, American physician, signer of the Declaration of Independence, b. Byberry (now part of Philadelphia), Pa., grad. College of New Jersey (now Princeton), 1760, M.D. Univ. of Edinburgh, 1768. On his return to America (1769) he became professor of chemistry, the first in the colonies, at the College of Philadelphia. A member of the Continental Congress (1776–77), he served for a time in the Continental Army. In 1786 he established in Philadelphia the first free dispensary in the United States. He was a member of the Pennsylvania convention that ratified the Federal Constitution. In 1792 he became professor of the institutes of medicine and clinical practice at the Univ. of Pennsylvania (which had absorbed the College of Philadelphia), later becoming professor of theory and practice. His reliance upon the bleeding and purging of patients, particularly in the yellow-fever epidemic of 1793 (in which he worked heroically), aroused a bitter controversy. Popular as a teacher, he made notable contributions to psychiatry, was a founder of the first American antislavery society, and helped in the founding of Dickinson College. From 1797 to his death he was treasurer of the U.S. mint at Philadelphia. Rush Medical College, Chicago, was named for him. His principal writings were *Medical Inquiries and Observations* (5 vol., 1794–98), *Essays, Literary, Moral, and Philosophical* (1798), and *Medical Inquiries and Observations upon the Diseases of the Mind* (1812). See his letters (ed. by L. H. Butterfield, 1951); autobiography (ed. by G. W. Corner, 1948); biographies by N. G. Goodman (1934) and D. F. Hawke (1971).

Rush, Richard, 1780–1859, Amercian statesman and diplomat, b. Philadelphia, Pa.; son of Benjamin Rush. He studied law and became (1811) attorney general of Pennsylvania, resigning the same year to become comptroller of the U.S. Treasury, and from 1814 to 1817 was U.S. Attorney General. While serving temporarily as Secretary of State (1817), he helped negotiate the RUSH-BAGOT CONVENTION and in the same year was made minister to Great Britain. He signed (1818) a convention with the British providing for joint occupation of the Oregon country. His preliminary negotiations with George Canning, British foreign minister, on policy toward Latin America led to the enunciation (1823) of the Monroe Doctrine. In 1825 he became Secretary of the Treasury and in 1828 was the vice presidential candidate on the unsuccessful John Quincy Adams ticket. Rush spent from 1836 to 1838 in England obtaining the Smithson bequest for the establishment of the Smithsonian Institution. Later, he was (1847–49) minister to France. See biography by J. H. Powell (1942).

Rush, William, 1756–1833, American sculptor, one of the earliest in the country, b. Philadelphia. His wood carvings, clay models, and figureheads were famous in their day. Of his other works, carved in wood, the statue of George Washington is in Independence Hall in Philadelphia, and a bronze replica of his graceful *Spirit of the Schuylkill* (1812) is in Fairmount Park in Philadelphia. Thomas Eakins painted Rush at work on this figure (1877; Philadelphia Mus. of Art). Rush was a leader in founding the Pennsylvania Academy of the Fine Arts, which owns many of his works including a plaster cast of a vigorous self-portrait. He also did portraits of Joseph Wright, Samuel Morris, Washington, Lafayette, and others. The Philadelphia Museum of Art contains some of his sprightly allegorical figures, among them *Comedy* and *Tragedy*. See catalog by Henri Marceau (1937).

rush, name for tall, grasslike plants of various families, many of which have hollow stems. The true rushes belong to the family Juncaceae, one of the oldest families of plants, closely related to the family Liliaceae (LILY family). Most rushes grow in swamps. Among them are the common or bog rush (*Juncus effusus*), widely distributed in swamps and moist places of the Northern Hemisphere, and the slender rush (*J. tenuis*), found in drier surroundings. Rushes are used for basketwork, mats, chair seats, and other articles. Wicks for candles known as rushlights are made from the pith of some rushes. The wood rush (*Luzula*) grows on dry ground, and some species are relished by livestock. Other plants often called rushes are the bulrush; the Dutch or scouring rush, a horsetail (*Equisetum hyemale*), still used in some regions for scouring; and the sweet flag, or sweet rush (*Acorus calamus*), of the arum family. Rushes were formerly strewn on the floors of churches, castles, and other buildings. True rushes are classified in the division MAGNOLIOPHYTA, class Liliatae, order Juncales, family Juncaceae. Sweet rushes, family Araceae, belong to the same class as the true rushes, but in the order Arales. Scouring rushes are classified in the division EQUISETOPHYTA.

Rush-Bagot Convention (rŭsh-băg'ət), 1817, agreement between the United States and Great Britain concerning the Canadian border. It consisted of the exchange of notes signed by Richard RUSH, Acting Secretary of State of the United States, and Charles Bagot, British minister in Washington. In 1818 the U.S. Senate gave its consent to the notes, thus giving them the authority of a treaty. The convention provided for practical disarmament on the U.S.-Canadian frontier; each nation should have no more than four warships, none to exceed 100 tons, on the Great Lakes. The agreement, a result of negotiations begun after the signing of the Treaty of Ghent, was important because it set a precedent for the pacific settlement of Anglo-American difficulties and because it inaugurated a policy of peace between the United States and Canada. Only one move was made to abrogate it—during the Civil War strained relations with Canada caused the Secretary of State, William H. Seward, to announce (1864) that the United States intended to abrogate, but before the six months of grace had elapsed the announcement was canceled (1865).

Rushmore, Mount: see MOUNT RUSHMORE NATIONAL MEMORIAL.

Rusk, David Dean, 1909–, U.S. Secretary of State (1961–69), b. Cherokee co., Ga. After teaching (1934–40) and serving in World War II, he entered (1946) the Dept. of State. In 1950 he became Assistant Secretary of State for Far Eastern Affairs and played a major role in the U.S. decision to take military action in the Korean War. After serving (1952–61) as president of the Rockefeller Foundation, Rusk became (1961) Secretary of State in President John F. Kennedy's Cabinet and continued to hold the post under President Lyndon B. Johnson. He supported economic aid to underdeveloped nations, low tariffs to encourage world trade, and the 1963 nuclear test ban treaty with the Soviet Union. A firm believer in the use of military force to prevent Communist expansion, Rusk strongly defended the VIETNAM WAR. In 1970 he became professor of law at the Univ. of Georgia. See *The Winds of Freedom,* selections from his speeches, ed. by E. K. Lindley (1963).

Rusk, Jeremiah McLain, 1830–93, American political leader, b. Malta, Ohio. He became a farmer in Wisconsin, where he entered politics and held numerous offices. After serving in the Civil War, he was a U.S. Representative (1871–77) and then served (1882–89) as Republican governor of Wisconsin. President Benjamin Harrison appointed (1889) Rusk to the newly created cabinet post of Secretary of Agriculture, and he served in this position until his death.

Rusk, Thomas Jefferson, 1803–57, American political leader, U.S. Senator from Texas (1846–57), b. Pendleton District, S.C. He studied law under John C. Calhoun and practiced in Clarksville, Ga., for 10 years before moving to Texas in 1835. Rusk was a member of the convention that declared the independence of Texas (1836) and became secretary of war in the provisional government of the new republic. He distinguished himself at the battle of San Jacinto and, when Sam Houston was wounded there, commanded the Texas army for a brief period. He was (1838–40) chief justice of the Texas supreme court and president of the convention that confirmed the annexation of Texas (1845). The following year, he was elected Democratic Senator from Texas. He remained in the U.S. Senate until, despondent over the death of his wife, he committed suicide.

Ruskin, John, 1819–1900, English critic and social theorist. During the mid-19th cent. Ruskin was the virtual dictator of artistic opinion in England. Educated by his wealthy, evangelical parents, Ruskin was prepared for the ministry, and until 1836 he spent his mornings with his domineering mother, reading and memorizing the Bible. In 1833 the family went on the first of its many tours of Europe, and the boy ardently studied nature and painting. His stay (1836–40) at Oxford resulted in his winning the Newdigate Prize for poetry and in his determining not to enter the ministry. A breakdown of health in 1840 forced him to travel. In 1843 appeared the first volume of *Modern Painters.* This work started as a defense of the painter J. M. W. Turner and developed into a treatise elaborating the principles that art is based on national and individual integrity and morality and also that art is a "universal language." He finished the five volumes in 1860. *The Seven Lamps of Architecture* (1849) applied these same theories to architecture. In 1848, Ruskin married Euphemia Gray, a beautiful young woman with social ambitions; the union, which apparently was never consummated, was annulled in 1854, and Mrs. Ruskin subsequently married the painter John Everett Millais. From his position as the foremost English art critic, Ruskin in 1851 defended the work of the Pre-Raphaelite group. His third great volume of criticism, *The Stones of Venice* (1851-53), maintained that the Gothic architecture of Venice reflected national and domestic virtue, while Venetian Renaissance architecture mirrored corruption. About 1857, Ruskin's art criticism became more broadly social and political. He wrote *Unto This Last* (in *Cornhill Magazine*, 1860) and *Munera Pulveris* (in *Fraser's Magazine*, 1862-63). These works attacked bourgeois England and charged that modern art reflected the ugliness and waste of modern industry. Ruskin's positive program for social reform appeared in *Sesame and Lilies* (1865), *The Crown of Wild Olive* (1866), *Time and Tide* (1867), and *Fors Clavigera* (8 vol., 1871-84). Many of his suggested programs—old age pensions, nationalization of education, organization of labor—have become accepted doctrine. He was made the first professor of art in England (Slade professor, Oxford, 1870) and his lectures were well attended. His multifarious activities broke down his health, however, and in 1878 he suffered his first period of insanity. Recurrences of unbalance became more frequent, though some of his greatest prose, the autobiography *Praeterita* (1885-89), was written in the lucid intervals. Ruskin's reputation declined after his death, and he has been treated harshly by 20th-century critics. Although it is undeniable that he was an extravagant and inconsistent thinker (a reflection of his lifelong mental and emotional instability), it is equally true that he revolutionized art criticism and wrote some of the most superb prose in the English language. See his works (39 vol., 1903-12); Mary Lutyens, *The Ruskins and the Grays* (1972); biographies by Peter Quennell (1949), E. T. Cook (2 vol., 1911, repr. 1969); studies by J. D. Rosenberg (1961), Joan Evans (1952, repr. 1970), and J. C. Sherburne (1973).

Russell, English noble family. It first appeared prominently in the reign of Henry VIII when **John Russell, 1st earl of Bedford,** 1486?-1555, rose to military and diplomatic importance. He was lord high steward and lord keeper of the privy seal under Henry VIII and Edward VI, was created 1st earl of Bedford in 1550, and had a part in arranging the marriage of Mary I to Philip II of Spain. He died possessing great wealth and lands, which have remained in the family until the 20th cent.; these now include Woburn Abbey and large parts of Bloomsbury in London. His son, **Francis Russell, 2d earl of Bedford,** 1527?-1585, was an influential privy councilor under Elizabeth I and president of the council of Wales. **Francis Russell, 4th earl of Bedford,** 1593-1641, was the most important opponent of Charles I in the House of Lords and was the brightest hope for reconciliation between king and Parliament when he suddenly died in 1641. He also began the draining of the Fens. **William Russell, 5th earl** and **1st duke of Bedford,** 1613-1700, fought first for Parliament and then for the king in the civil war. His son was Lord William Russell (see separate article). In 1694, when his son's attainder was reversed, the 5th earl was made duke of Bedford, a title that had been held in the 15th cent. by John of Lancaster, brother of King Henry V. **John Russell, 4th duke of Bedford,** 1710-71, was one of the politicians who attacked Robert Walpole and served in the cabinets of Henry Pelham, duke of Newcastle, Lord Bute, and George Grenville. He was the leader of a faction of Whig politicians, known as the Bedford group, which had considerable electoral power. **Francis Russell, 5th duke of Bedford,** 1765-1802, was a follower of Charles James Fox and one of the friends of the prince of Wales (later George IV). His criticism of Edmund Burke's pension elicited Burke's *Letter to a Noble Lord* (1796). Bedford was a notable stockbreeder. One of the most outstanding members of the family was the 5th duke's nephew, John Russell, 1st Earl Russell (see separate article). His grandson Bertrand Russell (see separate article) became 3d Earl Russell. John Robert Russell became 13th duke of Bedford in 1953. See various studies of the family to 1771 by Gladys Thomson, especially *Two Centuries of Family History* (1930); Christopher Trent, *The Russells* (1966).

Russell, Bertrand Arthur William Russell, 3rd Earl, 1872-1970, British philosopher, mathematician, and social reformer, b. Trelleck, Wales. He had a distinguished background: His grandfather Lord John Russell introduced the Reform Bill of 1832 and was twice prime minister; his parents were both prominent freethinkers; and his informal godfather was John Stuart Mill. Orphaned as a small child, he was reared, despite his parents' wishes to the contrary, by his paternal grandmother under stern puritanic rule. That experience, although failing in its intended effect, powerfully affected his thinking on matters of morality and education. Russell studied at Trinity College, Cambridge (1890-94), where later he was a fellow (1895-1901) and a lecturer (1910-16). It was during this time that he published his most important works in philosophy and mathematics, *The Principles of Mathematics* (1903) and, with A. N. Whitehead, *Principia Mathematica* (3 vol., 1910-13), and also had as his student Ludwig WITTGENSTEIN. World War I had a crucial effect on Russell: until that time he had thought of himself as a philosopher and mathematician; although he had arrived at pacifism before that time, it was in reaction to the war that he became passionately concerned with social issues. His active pacifism at the time of the war inspired public resentment, caused him to be dismissed from Cambridge, attacked by former associates, and fined by the government (which confiscated and sold his library when he refused to pay), and led finally to a six-month imprisonment in 1918. From 1916 until the late 1930s, Russell held no academic position and supported himself mainly by writing and by public lecturing. In 1927 he founded with his wife, Dora, the experimental Beacon Hill School, which influenced the founding of other schools in Britain and America. He succeeded to the earldom in 1931 and in 1938 began teaching in the United States, first at the Univ. of Chicago and then at the Univ. of California at Los Angeles. In 1941 he went to teach at the Barnes Foundation in Merion, Pa., following the cancellation of his appointment to the College of the City of New York as a result of a celebrated legal battle occasioned by protest against his liberal views, particularly those on sex. These views, much distorted by his critics, had appeared in *Marriage and Morals* (1929), where he took liberal positions on divorce, adultery, and homosexuality. In 1944 he was restored to a fellowship at Cambridge. In 1950 he received the Nobel Prize in Literature. Prior to World War II, in the face of the Nazi threat, Russell abandoned his pacifist stance; but after the war he again became a leading spokesman for pacifism, and especially for the unilateral renunciation (by Great Britain) of atomic weapons. In 1961 his activity in mass demonstrations to ban nuclear weapons led once more to his imprisonment. He organized, but was unable to attend, what was called the war crimes tribunal, held in Stockholm in 1967, presided over by Jean-Paul Sartre, and directed against U.S. activities in Vietnam. Almost until his death he was active in social reform. Throughout his life his dissent had scorned easy popularity with either the right or the left. Untamable, he had profound trust in the ultimate power of rationality, which he voiced with an undogmatic but quenchless zeal. Philosophically and ethically Russell's thought grew in reaction against the extremes he encountered. He answered the idealism of F. H. Bradley and J. M. E. McTaggart with a logical atomism founded on a rigorous empirical base: he was deeply convinced of the logical independence of individual facts and the dependence of knowledge on the data of original experience. His emphasis on logical analysis influenced the course of British philosophy in this century. One of his most important notions was that of the logical construct, the observation that an object normally thought of as a unity was actually constructed from various, discrete, simpler empirical observations. The technique of logical constructionism was first employed in his mathematical theory. Under the influence of the symbolic logic of Giuseppe Peano, Russell tried to show that mathematics could be explained by the rules of formal logic. His demonstration involved showing that mathematical entities could be "constructed" from the less problematic entities of logic. Later he applied the technique to concepts such as physical objects and the mind. Although he came to have misgivings about logical atomism and never assented to all the propositions of empiricism, he never ceased trying to base his thought—mathematical, philosophical, or ethical—not on vague principle but on actual experience. This can be seen in his pacifism as well as in his philosophy: he objected to specific wars in specific circumstances. So, in the circumstances preceding World War II he could abandon pacifism and, following the war, resume it. Similarly, in ethics he described himself as a relativist. Good and evil he saw to be resolvable in (or constructed from) individual desires. He did distinguish, however, between what he called "personal" and "impersonal" desires, those founded mainly on self-interest and those formed regardless of self-interest. He admitted difficulties with this ethical stance, as well as with his logical atomism. As much as anything, his thought was characterized by a pervasive scepticism, toward his own thought as well as that of others. As with his philosophical stance, Russell's positions on social issues grew as a reaction against extremes in his own experience. He believed that cruelty and an admiration for violence grew from inward or outward defects that were largely an outcome of what happened to people when very young. Pacifism could not be effected politically; a peaceful and happy world could not be achieved without deep changes in education. "I believe that nine out of ten who have had a conventional upbringing in their early years have become in some degree incapable of a decent and sane attitude toward marriage and sex generally." His objections to religion were similarly based. What he tried to draw attention to was the destructiveness of accepting propositions on faith—in the absence of, or even in opposition to, any evidence. "The important thing is not what you believe, but how you believe it." The person who bases his belief on reason will support it by argument and be ready to abandon the position if the argument fails. Belief based on faith concludes argument to be useless and resorts to "force either in the form of persecution or by stunting and distorting the minds of the young whenever [it] has the power to control their education." If Russell's logic was not always unassailable, his life showed that ethical relativism could be combined with a passionate social conscience and that passionate commitment could be stated without dogmatism. In his autobiography (3 vol., 1967-69) Russell summarized his personal philosophy by saying, "Three passions, simple but overwhelmingly strong, have governed my life: the longing for love, the search for knowledge, and unbearable pity for the suffering of mankind." See American Civil Liberties Union, *The Story of the Bertrand Russell Case* (1941); John Dewey and H. M. Kallen, eds., *The Bertrand Russell Case* (1941, repr. 1972); D. F. Pears, *Bertrand Russell and The British Tradition in Philosophy* (1967); E. D. Klemke, ed., *Essays on Bertrand Russell* (1970); John Watling, *Bertrand Russell* (1970); A. J. Ayer, *Russell and Moore: The Analytic Heritage* (1971) and *Bertrand Russell* (1972); Ronald Jager, *The Development of Bertrand Russell's Philosophy* (1972).

Russell, Charles Edward, 1860-1941, American author, b. Davenport, Iowa. He was a prominent newspaper editor (1894-1902) in New York and Chicago. A member of the Socialist party before World War I, he declined the party's presidential nomination in 1916. His many books include *The Uprising of the Many* (1907), *Why I Am a Socialist* (1910), *These Shifting Scenes* (1914), and the biography *The American Orchestra and Theodore Thomas* (1927, Pulitzer Prize). See his autobiography, *Bare Hands and Stone Walls* (1933).

Russell, Charles Marion, 1864-1926, American painter, b. Oak Hill, Mo. Together with Frederic REMINGTON, Russell was one of the two greatest and most popular painters of the American West. A stalwart individualist, he first earned his living as a trapper and cowboy, later translating his passion for adventure and American wildlife onto canvas for his own amusement. Russell's works are filled with the movement of cowboys, Indians (with whom he lived for a time), and galloping horses. His mural *Lewis and Clark Meeting the Flathead Indians* (1912) is in the Montana State Capitol, Helena. A museum was built to honor Russell's work in Great Falls, Mont.

Russell, Charles Taze, 1852-1916, founder of the movement whose followers are known as Russellites, as Bible Students, and (since 1931) as JEHOVAH'S WITNESSES, b. Pittsburgh, Pa. There he predicted (1872) the second coming of Christ and the millennium. In 1878 he organized his followers as an independent church. His teachings were spread through the *Watch Tower*, which Russell began to publish in 1879. In 1909 he moved his headquarters to the Brooklyn Tabernacle, New York City. Russell was involved in scandals, which somewhat tarnished his reputation, but his sect, nonetheless, flourished. His writings are contained in a series of books under the title *Millennial Dawn* (6 vol., 1886–1904).

Russell, Francis, dukes and earls of Bedford: see RUSSELL, family.

Russell, George William, pseud. **A.E.,** 1867–1935, Irish author, b. Lurgan, educated in Dublin. An active member of the Irish nationalist movement, he edited the *Irish Homestead* (1904–23) and the *Irish Statesman* (1923–30). He worked with Sir Horace Plunkett for Irish agricultural improvement, and he was also a talented amateur painter and a renowned conversationalist. Russell was one of the major writers in the IRISH LITERARY RENAISSANCE. His poems and plays are noted for their mystical tone, their delicate melodious style, and their view of man's spiritual nature. Among his works are *Homeward: Songs by the Way* (1894), *The Candle of Vision* (1918), and *Selected Poems* (1935). See his prose collection *The Living Torch* (ed. by Monk Gibbons, 1937); memoir by John Eglinton (1937).

Russell, Henry Norris, 1877–1957, American astronomer, b. Oyster Bay, N.Y., grad. Princeton, 1897. In 1902 he went to Cambridge, England, to study. He returned to Princeton in 1905, was professor of astronomy there (1911–27), research professor (1927–47), and director of the observatory (1912–47). In 1947 he became research associate at the Harvard Observatory. Russell established a method of determining the dimensions of eclipsing binary stars. With Ejnar Hertzsprung he devised the HERTZSPRUNG-RUSSELL DIAGRAM. His spectroscopic studies resulted in his development of a theory of stellar evolution. He wrote *Determinations of Stellar Parallax* (1911), *Astronomy* (1926–27), *Fate and Freedom* (1927), *The Solar System and Its Origin* (1935), and *The Masses of the Stars* (with C. E. Moore, 1940).

Russell, James Earl, 1864–1945, American educator, b. Hamden, N.Y., grad. Cornell Univ., 1887, Ph.D. Leipzig, 1894. From 1895 to 1897 he was professor of philosophy and pedagogy at the Univ. of Colorado. In 1897 he became professor of education at Teachers College, Columbia, and in the following year was appointed dean. Under Russell's leadership Teachers College developed from a small normal school into a major professional training center. In 1927 he became dean emeritus, but he remained professor of education until 1931. His writings include *The Extension of University Teaching in England and America* (1895), *Trend in American Education* (1922), and *Founding Teachers College* (1937).

Russell, John, dukes and earls of Bedford: see RUSSELL, family.

Russell, John Russell, 1st **Earl,** 1792–1878, British statesman; younger son of the 6th duke of Bedford, known most of his life as Lord John Russell. He became a Whig member of Parliament in 1813 and soon began his long career as a liberal reformer. He worked for Catholic Emancipation, leading the attack on the Test and Corporation acts, which were repealed in 1828. As paymaster general in the ministry of the 2d Earl Grey, Russell helped prepare and introduce the REFORM BILL of 1832. His advocacy of the reduction of Irish church revenues helped bring down the Whig government in 1834, but when the Whigs returned to power (1835), Russell became home secretary and later secretary for war and the colonies (1839). In the meantime he had given the name to the newly emerging LIBERAL PARTY and become one of its chief spokesmen. Russell led the opposition during the second ministry (1841–46) of Sir Robert Peel and, following the repeal of the corn laws (which Russell supported), succeeded him as prime minister. During his ministry Russell used public works, grants, and other relief to help the Irish during the potato famine and supported the bill (1847) that limited the working day to 10 hr for many laborers. In 1851 he demanded the resignation of his foreign secretary, Viscount PALMERSTON, for his unauthorized approval of Napoleon III's coup d'etat in France, and the following year Palmerston helped secure the fall of Russell's ministry. Russell served (1852–55) in Lord Aberdeen's coalition government and represented (1855) England at Vienna in an unsuccessful conference to end the Crimean War. He was reconciled with Palmerston and, as his foreign secretary (1859–65), vigorously advocated neutrality in the American Civil War and supported the Risorgimento in Italy. He had been made an earl in 1861 and became prime minister again on Palmerston's death in 1865. For many years an advocate of further parliamentary reform, he attempted to push through a new Reform Bill, but the bill was defeated and caused the fall of his ministry in 1866. Among Russell's literary and historical writings are a translation of Schiller's *Don Carlos* and biographies of Lord William Russell (1819) and of Charles James Fox (3 vol., 1853–57). See his *Recollections and Suggestions, 1813–1873* (1875); early correspondence (ed. by Rollo Russell; 2 vol., 1913) and later correspondence (ed. by G. P. Gooch; 2 vol., 1925); biographies by Spencer Walpole (2 vol., 1889, repr. 1968) and John Prest (1972); W. P. Morrell, *British Colonial Policy in the Age of Peel and Russell* (1930, repr. 1966).

Russell, Lillian, 1861–1922, American singer and actress, b. Clinton, Iowa. Her original name was Helen Louise Leonard. She first appeared in light opera in 1879. In the early 1880s her introduction by Tony Pastor at his casino in New York City launched her career as "The American Beauty." After 1899 she appeared at Weber and Fields's Music Hall, with the McCaull Opera Company, and later with her own company. She was noted for her flamboyant personality and for her love of jewelry. Her affair with "Diamond Jim" Brady has become a legend. See biography by Parker Morell (1940).

Russell, Mary Annette (Beauchamp) Russell, Countess, pseud. **Elizabeth,** 1866–1941, English novelist, b. Sydney, Australia; cousin of Katherine Mansfield. In 1890 she married Count Henning von Arnim and went to live in Germany. There she wrote her first novel, *Elizabeth and Her German Garden* (1898), which was immediately successful, and its successors, including *The Solitary Summer* (1899), *Adventures of Elizabeth in Rügen* (1904), and *The Pastor's Wife* (1914). Highly autobiographical, her novels are witty, gay, and gently satirical. Her husband died in 1910, and in 1916 she married the 2d Earl Russell, brother of Bertrand Russell. Among her later works are *The Enchanted April* (1922); *Love* (1925); *Jasmine Farm* (1934); and *Mr. Skeffington* (1940).

Russell, Morgan, 1886–1953, American painter, b. New York City. Russell, together with Stanton MACDONALD-WRIGHT, founded synchromism in Paris in 1913. Structuring his paintings on interlocking planes of color, Russell created volume and mass with color alone, as in *Synchromy in Orange: To Form* (1913–14).

Russell, William, 5th **earl** and 1st **duke of Bedford:** see RUSSELL, family.

Russell, Lord William, 1639–83, English statesman; younger son of the 1st duke of Bedford. He entered Parliament in 1660. Contempt for the dissolute court and fear of Roman Catholicism and of France led him to join the opposition to Charles II. However, he was prepared to negotiate (1678) with his relative, the marquis de Ruvigny, agent of Louis XIV, for aid to secure the dissolution of Parliament and the overthrow of the earl of DANBY. In the excitement over the Popish Plot (1678) he joined the 1st earl of SHAFTESBURY in demanding the indictment of the duke of York (later James II) and in pressing the bill to exclude him from the succession. With the temporary Whig success he became (1679) a privy councilor, but he was arrested (1683), tried, and convicted of treason for his supposed implication in the RYE HOUSE PLOT. Executed in 1683, he was vindicated by the reversal of attainder under William III.

Russell, William Fletcher, 1890–1956, American educator, b. Delhi, N.Y., grad. Cornell Univ., 1910, Ph.D. Columbia, 1914; son of James Earl Russell. He was dean (1917–23) of the College of Education, State Univ. of Iowa, and professor of education (1923–54) and associate director of the International Institute (1923–27) at Teachers College, Columbia. In 1927 he succeeded his father as dean of Teachers College, and he was later appointed (1949) president of the school. He retired in 1954. Russell wrote *Economy in Secondary Education* (1916), *Education in the United States* (1917), and *The Meaning of Democracy* (with T. H. Briggs, 1941) and edited *The Rise of a University* (Vol. I, 1937).

Russell Cave National Monument: see NATIONAL PARKS AND MONUMENTS (table).

Russell of Killowen, Charles Russell, 1st **Baron** (kĭlō'ən), 1832–1900, British jurist, b. Ireland. He practiced law in Belfast and London before his election to Parliament as a Liberal in 1880. In the Commons he worked for the conciliation of Ireland, and he was the leading counsel for Charles Stewart Parnell before the Parnell Commission (1888–90). He served as William Gladstone's attorney general (1886, 1892–94) and in 1894 became lord chief justice, the first Roman Catholic to hold that office since the Reformation. Russell served as counsel (1893) in the Bering Sea Fur-Seal Controversy and in 1899 was one of the Venezuela Boundary Arbitration Tribunal. See biography by R. B. O'Brien (1909).

Russellville, city (1970 pop. 11,750), seat of Pope co., central Ark., in an area yielding coal, timber, and diverse agricultural products; settled 1835, inc. 1870. Arkansas Polytechnic College and the headquarters of the Ozark National Forest are there. A man-made lake adjoins the city, and Mt. Nebo State Park and a national wildlife refuge are nearby.

Rüsselsheim (rüs'əls-hīm), city (1970 pop. 59,861), Hesse, central West Germany, on the Main River. It is a center for the assembly of automobiles. Rüsselsheim was chartered in 1437 and passed to Hesse in 1479.

Russia, Rus. *Rossiya.* In its political meaning, the term *Russia* applies to the Russian Empire until 1917 and to the RUSSIAN SOVIET FEDERATED SOCIALIST REPUBLIC, largest and most important member of the USSR. The name is often loosely used to mean the whole Union of Soviet Socialist Republics. It is also used to designate the area inhabited by the Russian people as distinguished from other Eastern Slavs and from non-Slavic peoples. The following article deals with the formation and history of the Russian state and empire until 1917.

RUSSIAN RULERS FROM 1462 TO 1917 (*including dates of reign*)
House of Rurik
Ivan III (the Great), 1462–1505 Vasily III, 1505–33 Ivan IV (the Terrible), 1533–84 Feodor I, 1584–98
House of Godunov
Boris Godunov, 1598–1605 Feodor II, 1605
Usurpers
Dmitri, 1605–6 Vasily IV, 1606–10
Interregnum, 1610–13
House of Romanov
Michael, 1613–45 Alexis, 1645–76 Feodor III, 1676–82 Ivan V and Peter I (the Great), 1682–96 Peter I (the Great), 1696–1725 Catherine I, 1725–27 Peter II, 1727–30 Anna, 1730–40 Ivan VI, 1740–41 Elizabeth, 1741–62 Peter III, 1762 Catherine II (the Great), 1762–96 Paul I, 1796–1801 Alexander I, 1801–25 Nicholas I, 1825–55 Alexander II, 1855–81 Alexander III, 1881–94 Nicholas II, 1894–1917

Early Russia. Numerous remains indicate that Russia was inhabited in the Paleolithic period. By the 7th cent. B.C. the northern shore of the Black Sea and the Crimea were controlled by the Scythians (see under SCYTHIA); in the 3d cent. B.C. the Scythians were displaced by the Sarmatians (see under SARMATIA). Later the open steppes of Russia were invaded by numerous peoples, notably the Germanic Goths (3d cent. A.D.), the Asian HUNS (4th cent.), and the Turkic AVARS (6th cent.). The Turkic KHAZARS built up (7th cent.) a powerful state in S Russia, and the Eastern BULGARS established (8th cent.) their empire in the Volga region. By the 9th cent. the Eastern SLAVS had settled in N Ukraine, in Belorussia, and in the regions of Novgorod and Smolensk, and they had established colonies to the E on the Oka and upper Volga rivers. The chief Slavic tribes in S Russia were dominated by the Khazars. The origin of the Russian state coincides with the arrival (9th cent.) of Scandinavian traders and warriors, the VARANGIANS. Tradition has it that one of their leaders, RURIK, established himself peaceably at Novgorod by 862 and founded a dynasty. The name *Russ* or *Rhos* possibly originally designated the Varangians, or some of them, but it was early extended to the Eastern Slavs and became the name of their country in general. Rurik's successor, OLEG (reigned 879–912), transferred (882) his residence to Kiev, which remained the capital of KIEVAN RUSSIA until 1169. He united the Eastern Slavs and freed them from Khazar suzerainty, and signed (911) a commercial treaty with the Byzantine Empire. Under SVIATOSLAV (reigned 964–

72) the duchy reached the peak of its power. Christianity was made the state religion by VLADIMIR I (reigned 980–1015), who adopted (988–89) the Greek Orthodox rite. Thus Byzantine cultural influence became predominant. After the death of YAROSLAV (reigned 1019–54), Kievan Russia was divided in a rotation system among his sons. Political supremacy shifted, passing from Kiev to the western principalities of Galich and Vladimir (see VLADIMIR-VOLYNSKY and VOLHYNIA) and to the northeastern principality of Suzdal-Vladimir (see VLADIMIR). In 1169, Kiev was stormed by the Suzdal prince Andrei Bogolubski (reigned 1169–74), who made Vladimir the capital of the grand duchy. In 1237–40 the Mongols (commonly called TATARS) under Batu Khan invaded Russia and destroyed all the chief Russian cities except Novgorod and Pskov. In S and E Russia the Tatars established the empire of the GOLDEN HORDE, which lasted until 1480. BELORUSSIA, most of the UKRAINE, and part of W Russia were incorporated (14th cent.) into the grand duchy of LITHUANIA. Thus NE Russia became the main center of economic and political life. At the end of the 13th cent. Tver was the most important political center, but in the 14th cent. the Muscovite princes of the grand duchy of Vladimir, although still tributary to the Tatars, began to consolidate their position. Under Ivan I (Ivan Kalita; reigned 1328–41), Moscow took precedence over the other cities. After the victory of DMITRI DONSKOI (reigned 1359–89) over the Tatars at KULIKOVO in 1380, the grand duchy of Vladimir was bequeathed, without the sanction of the Golden Horde, to his son Vasily (reigned 1389–1425), and its rulers began to be called grand dukes of Moscow or Muscovy (see MOSCOW, GRAND DUCHY OF).

Consolidation of the Russian State. Under IVAN III (1462–1505) and his successor, VASILY III (1505–33), the Muscovite state expanded, and its rulers became more absolute. The principality of Yaroslav was annexed in 1463 and Rostov in 1474; Novgorod was conquered in 1478, Tver in 1485, Pskov in 1510, and Ryazan in 1521. The peoples of Mari, Yurga, and Komi were subjugated at the end of the 14th cent. and the Pechora and Karelians at the end of the 15th cent. Ivan ceased to pay tribute to the Tatars, and in 1497 he adopted the first code of laws. Having married the niece of the last Byzantine emperor, Ivan considered Moscow the "third Rome" and himself heir to the tradition of the Byzantine Empire. In 1547, at the age of 17, IVAN IV (Ivan the Terrible; reigned 1533–84) was crowned czar of all Russia. He conquered the Tatar khanates of KAZAN (1552) and ASTRAKHAN (1556), establishing Russian rule over the huge area of the middle and lower Volga; thus he laid the basis for the colonization and annexation of SIBERIA, begun by the Cossack YERMAK in 1581. The conquered border territories were colonized by Russian settlers and defended by the COSSACKS. At home, Ivan crushed the opposition of the great feudal nobles—the boyars—and set up an autocratic government. After the reign of the sickly Feodor I (1584–98), state power passed to Boris GODUNOV (reigned 1598–1605), who was elected czar by a *zemsky sobor* [national council]. With the death of Boris in 1605 began the "Time of Troubles"—a political crisis marked by the appearance of pretenders (see DMITRI) and the intervention of foreign powers. In 1609, SIGISMUND III of Poland invaded Russia, and in 1610 Polish troops entered Moscow according to an agreement concluded with the boyars. However, in 1612, Russian forces led by Prince Dmitri Pozharski took Moscow, and in 1613 a *zemsky sobor* unanimously chose Michael Romanov as czar (see MICHAEL; reigned 1613–45). Thus began the ROMANOV dynasty, which ruled Russia until 1917. Michael was succeeded by ALEXIS (reigned 1645–76), who gained E Ukraine from Poland. Russia in the 17th cent. was still medieval in culture and outlook, and it was not regarded as a member of the European community of nations. In its economic development it was centuries behind Western Europe; distrust of foreign ways and innovations kept its inhabitants ignorant and isolated. The consolidation of central power was effected not with the help of the almost nonexistent middle class or by social reforms but by forcibly depriving the nobility and gentry of their political influence. The nobles were compensated with land grants and with increasing rights over the peasants. Thus serfdom (see SERF), which became a legal institution in Russia in 1649, included growing numbers of persons and became increasingly oppressive. The process of enserfment, which reached its peak in the 18th cent., resulted in several violent peasant revolts, notably those led by Stenka RAZIN (1667–71) and by PUGACHEV (1773–75).

Empire and European Eminence. During the reign (1689–1725) of PETER I (Peter the Great) Russian politics, administration, and culture were altered considerably. However, the trend of increased autocracy and enserfment of peasants was accelerated by the changes. Peter, who assumed (1721) the title of emperor, "Westernized" Russia by using stringent methods to force on the people a series of reforms. He created a regular conscript army and navy. He abolished the patriarchate of Moscow (see ORTHODOX EASTERN CHURCH) and created (1721) the Holy Synod, directly subordinate to the emperor, thus depriving the church of the last vestiges of independence. He recast the administrative and fiscal systems, creating new organs of central government and reforming local administration, and he also founded the first modern industries and made an attempt to introduce elements of Western education. Seeking to make Russia a maritime power, Peter acquired LIVONIA, INGERMANLAND (Ingria), ESTONIA, and parts of Karelia and Finland as a result of the NORTHERN WAR (1700–1721), thus securing a foothold on the Baltic Sea. As a symbol of the new conquests he founded (1703) St. Petersburg (now LENINGRAD) on the Gulf of Finland and transferred (1712) his capital there. Russia was rapidly becoming a European power. Peter also began the Russian push to the Black Sea, taking AZOV in 1696, but his war with Turkey from 1711 to 1713 ended in failure and the loss of Azov. In addition, he sent (1725) Vitus BERING on an exploratory trip to NE Siberia. The RUSSO-TURKISH WARS of the next two centuries resulted in the expansion of Russia at the expense of the Ottoman Empire and in the growing influence of Russia on Ottoman affairs (see EASTERN QUESTION). Russia also took an increasing part in European affairs. The immediate successors of Peter the Great were CATHERINE I (reigned 1725–27), PETER II (reigned 1727–30), ANNA (reigned 1730–40), and IVAN VI (reigned 1740–41). Empress ELIZABETH (reigned 1741–62) successfully sided against Prussia in the SEVEN YEARS WAR, but her successor, PETER III, took Russia out of the war. Peter's wife successfully seized power from him (1762), and when he was murdered shortly thereafter she became empress as CATHERINE II (Catherine the Great; reigned 1762–96). Under her rule Russia became the chief power of continental Europe. She continued Peter I's policies of absolute rule at home and of territorial expansion at the expense of neighboring states. The three successive partitions of Poland (1772, 1793, 1795; see POLAND, PARTITIONS OF), the annexations of the CRIMEA (1783) and of COURLAND (1795), and the treaties of Kuchuk Kainarji (1774) and Jassy (1792) with Turkey gave Russia vast new territories in the west and south, including Belorussia, the Ukraine W of the Dnepr River, and the Black Sea shores. Catherine's administrative reforms further centralized power. The suppression of Pugachev's rebellion strengthened the privileged classes and lessened the chances of social reform. However, under her "enlightened despotism," Russian writers, scientists, and artists began the great creative efforts that culminated in the late 19th and early 20th cent. Russia became involved in the French Revolutionary Wars under Catherine's successor, the demented PAUL I, who was murdered in 1801. His son, ALEXANDER I (reigned 1801–25), joined the third coalition against Napoleon I, but made peace with France at Tilsit (1807) and annexed (1809) FINLAND from Sweden. In wars with Turkey and Persia, Alexander gained BESSARABIA by the Treaty of Bucharest (1812) and Caucasian territories by the Treaty of GULISTAN (1813). In 1812, Napoleon began his great onslaught on Russia and took Moscow, but his army was repulsed and nearly annihilated in the winter of that year. Napoleon's downfall and the peace settlement (see VIENNA, CONGRESS OF) made Russia and Austria the leading powers on the Continent at the head of the HOLY ALLIANCE.

Reaction, Reform, and Revolution. Liberal ideas gained influence among the Russian aristocracy and educated bourgeoisie despite Alexander's growing intransigence. They found an outlet in the unsuccessful Decembrist Conspiracy of 1825 (see DECEMBRISTS), which sought to prevent the accession of NICHOLAS I. Under Nicholas (reigned 1825–55), Russia became the most reactionary European power, acting as the "policeman of Europe" in opposing liberalism and helping Austria to quash the Hungarian revolution (1848–49). Russian POLAND, nominally a kingdom ruled by the Russian emperor, lost its autonomy after an unsuccessful rising there in 1830–31. A clash of interests between Russia and the Western powers over the Ottoman Empire led to the CRIMEAN WAR (1854–56), which revealed the inner weakness of Russia. ALEXANDER II (reigned 1855–81), who acceded one year before the war ended, passed important liberal reforms during the first decade of his reign, after which time he became increasingly conservative. Just as he seemed to be entering another liberal phase, Alexander was assassinated in 1881. Among his reforms, the liberation (1861) of the serfs (see EMANCIPATION, EDICT OF) was the most far-reaching, but significant changes were also made in local government, the judicial system, and education. During the second half of the 19th cent., Russia continued its territorial expansion, and industrialization was accelerated. The remainder of the CAUCASUS was acquired and pacified; the territories of what is now Soviet Central Asia, including TURKISTAN, were taken during 1864–65; and the southern section of the Far Eastern Territory (see SOVIET FAR EAST) was acquired from China. Russia thus reached the frontiers of Afghanistan and China and the shores of the Pacific Ocean. VLADIVOSTOK was founded in 1860; in the early 20th cent. it became an important naval base. The TRANS-SIBERIAN RAILROAD (constructed 1891–1905) opened much of Siberia to colonization and exploitation. ALEXANDER III (reigned 1881–94), who succeeded Alexander II, pursued a reactionary domestic policy, guided by the influential POBYEDONOSTZEV. Alexander was followed by NICHOLAS II (reigned 1894–1917), the last Russian emperor, a generally incompetent ruler surrounded by a reactionary entourage. However, there was considerable financial and industrial development, directed largely by Count Witte. Russia, having suffered a severe diplomatic setback at the Congress of Berlin (see BERLIN, CONGRESS OF, 1878), eventually abandoned the THREE EMPERORS' LEAGUE with Germany and Austria-Hungary and in 1892 entered into an alliance with republican France. This alliance led to the Triple Entente (see TRIPLE ALLIANCE AND TRIPLE ENTENTE) of England, France, and Russia. The disastrous and unpopular RUSSO-JAPANESE WAR (1904–5) led to the Revolution of 1905 (see RUSSIAN REVOLUTION). Nicholas was forced to grant a constitution, and a parliament (see DUMA) was established. Soon, however, the new democratic freedoms were curtailed, as the government again became reactionary. As a result, there was renewed agitation by revolutionaries; the emperor countered with police terror and attempted to channel popular discontent into anti-Semitic outbreaks (see POGROM). At the same time, STOLYPIN (prime minister during 1906–11) tried to create a class of independent landowning peasants by breaking up and redistributing the land held by village communities (see MIR); however, he refused to split up the estates held by large landlords and generally ignored the peasant masses. Although the Russian economy was mainly agricultural and underdeveloped, industry—largely financed by foreign capital—was growing rapidly in a few centers, notably St. Petersburg, Moscow, and the Baku oil fields. It was particularly among the industrial workers, who because of their geographic concentration possessed great political strength, that the leftist Social Democratic party found its adherents. The formal split of the party into BOLSHEVISM AND MENSHEVISM in 1912 had crucial consequences after the outbreak of the Russian Revolution of 1917. By promoting PAN-SLAVISM in the Balkan Peninsula and in Austria-Hungary, Russia played a leading role in the events that led to the outbreak (1914) of WORLD WAR I. Ill-prepared and cut off from its allies in the west, the country suffered serious reverses in the war at the hands of the Germans and Austrians. Inflation, food shortages, and poor morale among the troops contributed to the outbreak of the February Revolution of 1917. Nicholas abdicated in March, 1917 (he was executed in July, 1918). A provisional government under Prince LVOV, a moderate, tried to continue the war effort, but was opposed by the soviets (councils) of workers and soldiers. KERENSKY, who succeeded Lvov as prime minister in July, 1917, was also unable to enforce the authority of the central government. Finally, on Nov. 7, 1917 (Oct. 25 O.S.) the Bolsheviks, led by LENIN, seized the government. Russia ended its involvement in World War I by signing the humiliating Treaty of BREST-LITOVSK (March, 1918), under which it lost much territory to the Central Powers. Shortly thereafter, and partly because of the reaction to the poor terms of the treaty, civil war (complicated by foreign intervention) broke out in Russia; it continued until 1920, when the Soviet regime emerged victorious. (For a more detailed account of the intellectual and political background of the Russian Revolution and for the events of the revolution and the civil war, see RUSSIAN REVOLUTION.) Poland, Finland, and the Baltic countries emerged as independent states in the aftermath of the civil war; the Ukraine, Belorussia, and the Transcaucasian countries of Azerbaijan, Georgia, and Armenia proclaimed their independence, but by 1921 were conquered by the Soviet armies. In 1917, Russia was officially proclaimed as the Russian Soviet Federated Socialist Republic, which in 1922 was united with the Ukrainian, Belorussian, and Transcaucasian republics to form the UNION OF SOVIET SOCIALIST REPUBLICS. See V. O. Kliuchevskii, *A History of Russia* (tr., 5 vol., 1911–31; repr. 1960); Hugh Seton-Watson, *The Russian Empire, 1801–1917* (1967); S. S. Harcave, *Russia, a History* (6th ed. 1968); Ronald Hingley, *The Tsars: Russian Autocrats, 1533–1917* (1968) and *A Concise History of Russia* (1972); P. N. Miliukov et al., *History of Russia* (tr., 3 vol., 1968–69); A. G. Cross, comp., *Russia under Western Eyes, 1517–1825* (1971); Marc Raeff, *Imperial Russia, 1682–1825* (1971); R. E. Zelnik, *Labor and Society in Tsarist Russia* (2 vol., 1971–); P. H. Avrich, *Russian Rebels, 1600–1800* (1972); Martin Gilbert, *Russian History Atlas* (1972); George Vernadsky et al., *A Source Book for Russian History, from Early Times to 1917* (3 vol., 1972); S. F. Starr, *Decentralization and Self-Government in Russia, 1830–1870* (1972); Shmuel Galai, *The Liberation Movement in Russia, 1900–1905* (1973); G. A. Hosking, *The Russian Constitutional Experiment: Government and Duma, 1907–1914* (1973); Taras Hunczak, *Russian Imperialism from Ivan the Great to the Revolution* (1974).

Russia Company: see MUSCOVY COMPANY.

Russian American Company, colonial trading company, chartered by Czar Paul I in 1799. The charter granted the merchant-dominated company monopoly trading privileges in Russian America, which included the Aleutian Islands, Alaska, and the territory down to 55° N lat. (a second charter, granted in 1821, extended its domain to 51°); one third of all profits were to go to the czar. Under Aleksandr BARANOV, who governed the region (1800–1818), a permanent settlement was established on the mainland at Sitka and a thriving fur trade organized. The company failed, however, in its intention to create a large, settled population of Russians. The inhospitable climate, persistent shortages of food and supplies, and the unwillingness of the czar to send serfs to North America kept the colony weak and small. In the 1840s, as the profits from the fur trade began to decline, the czarist government took control of the Russian-American Company from the merchants. The company was officially dissolved in 1867 when Alaska was sold to the United States. See S. B. Okun, *The Russian-American Company* (1951).

Russian art and architecture. With the Christianization of Russia in the late 10th cent., the Russian church and its art became subject to Constantinople (see BYZANTINE ART AND ARCHITECTURE). Major artistic centers developed in Kiev, Novgorod, and Pskov. Although the early churches were made largely of wood (with strong Norse stylistic influences), stone was already in use in the Cathedral of Sancta Sophia (1018–37) in Kiev. A distinctive Russian style soon emerged, marked by steeply sloping roofs and high walls, a proliferation of domes, and later a compartmentalization of interior space into many aisles and apses. The typical onion-shaped dome made an early appearance (mid-12th cent.) in the rebuilding of the Cathedral of Sancta Sophia in Novgorod. In the 12th cent. the Vladimir-Suzdal region became an important cultural center. There the Western Romanesque was combined with Byzantine elements, as in the palace of Andrei Bogolyubsky. The earliest painters of religious art in Russia were Greeks or Greek-trained Russians, who generally followed the form and iconography of the Byzantine school (see ICON). Within the framework of the highly schematic Byzantine rendering of the human figure, Russian art (11th–14th cent.) ranged from an extremely hieratic and intellectual concept to a softer, more devotional image. The Russians added a number of saints to the Byzantine hierarchy. Among those frequently depicted were saints Vladimir, Olga, Boris, Gleb, and later Alexander Nevsky. From the mid-13th through the 14th cent. little art flourished under the Tatar invaders except in Novgorod and Pskov, which remained free and were the dominant cultural centers until the rise of Moscow at the end of the 15th cent. After the fall of Constantinople in 1453 the Russian church became independent of the Greek Orthodox faith, and the Moscow school of art and architecture became the official liturgical and court art of Russia, maintaining this status until the 18th cent. ICON painting was brought to its highest achievement as a Russian art form in the late 14th and 15th cent. with the expressive frescoes of the Greek painter Theophanes, in the church of the Transfiguration in Novgorod (1378), and with the Hellenized works of the Russian artist Andrei Rublev (e.g., *Trinity*, c.1410; Tretyakov Gall., Moscow). The master Dionysius introduced new iconographical motifs, scenes of miracles, which he imbued with great vitality. In the 16th cent. art was first pressed into the service of the government. Frescoes such as *The Heart of the Czar Is in the Hand of God* decorated the palace walls of Ivan IV. A high level of quality was maintained in icon painting until the 17th cent., when it deteriorated into an ornate, extremely detailed, convention-ridden art. In architecture a new period began in the 15th cent., when the first of many Italian architects were invited to work on the Kremlin in Moscow (see under KREMLIN). The Cathedral of the Dormition (1475–79), planned by Aristotele Fioravanti, is notable for a new rationality of proportions, and Italian High Renaissance elements can also be seen in the decoration (pilasters, scallop shells, and arches) of the Cathedral of St. Michael (1505–9), built by Alevisio Novi. On the other hand, the Russo-Byzantine style was still very much in favor under Ivan IV. The Cathedral of St. Basil (1555–60) was designed by two Russian architects, Postnik and Barma, who combined several chapels into one unique and splendid church. It served as a model for Russian churches until the 17th cent., with its profusion of oddly shaped cupolas, gilt and polychrome arches, and air of fairy-tale fantasy. During the 17th cent. influences from Lithuania and Poland brought about a humanistic interest in classical antiquity that was to culminate in the Westernization of Russia under Peter the Great. In 1712 Peter moved his capital from Moscow to St. Petersburg (now Leningrad) and began the transformation of a mud flat on the coast of Finland into a sparkling European city. A host of Western architects was imported for the enterprise and continued to work under successive reigns. The outstanding architect of the period was Conte Bartolomeo Francesco Rastrelli. Working in a ROCOCO style, he designed the Winter Palace (now part of the HERMITAGE), Smolny Cathedral, and the facade at Peterhof, one of the most beautiful buildings in Leningrad. Catherine the Great preferred a more dignified manner. The Italian Antonio Rinaldi (c.1709–c.1790), the French architect Jean Baptiste Vallin de la Mothe (1729–1800), and the Scottish Charles Cameron (c.1740–c.1815) were responsible for the neoclassical architecture that Catherine promoted as the official court style. Prominent Russian architects during her reign included V. I. Bazhenov (1737–99) and I. Y. Starov (1744–1808); the latter built the splendid Tauride Palace in St. Petersburg. In the 18th cent. the infiltration of European painting styles began, and for the first time since the introduction of Christianity sculpture became a major Russian art form. European artists, such as Falconet and Vigée Le Brun, came to St. Petersburg, while Russian artists started to receive their training abroad. Portrait and historical painting predominated. Under Alexander I foreign architects were still imported, including Thomas de Thoman (1754–1813), who built the Bolshoi Theatre. The Greek revival came into vogue, revealed in the buildings of M. F. Kazakov (1733–1812), A. D. Zakharov (1761–1811), and V. P. Stasov (1769–1848). During the 19th cent. there was a revival of medieval Russian architecture. A romantic school of painting arose in the early years of the century, and pictorial epics were produced by Karl Briullov (1799–1852), F. A. Bruni (1800–1875), and A. A. Ivanov (1806–58). The second half of the 19th cent. saw the introduction of ideological realism, particularly in the works of V. G. Perov (1833–82) and I. Y. REPIN, who is now hailed as one of the first artists of the revolution. Mikhail Vrubel (1856–1910), a tormented original and one of the foremost modern Russian masters, painted a remarkable series of decorations for the monastery of St. Cyril at Kiev. Around the turn of the century *Mir Iskusstva* (World of Art Group) was initiated, a movement akin to ART NOUVEAU. It served as the background for some of the first truly abstract artists who prevailed briefly in Russia after 1917 (see CONSTRUCTIVISM and SUPREMATISM). Among the more radical modern artists were Casimir Malevich, Vladimir Tatlin, Chaim Soutine, Aleksey von Jawlensky, Antoine Pevsner, Naum Gabo, Wassily Kandinsky, Mikhail Larinov, Marc Chagall, and Alexander Archipenko. Most of them left the country after 1923 and settled in Western Europe and America. The Ministry of Culture took over the direction of Russian art, and a standardized literal style known as SOCIALIST REALISM was enforced, abstraction having been renounced as decadent. Artists of this school include Georgi Nisski and Vera Mukina. Only since the death of Stalin has there been a slight relaxation of government strictures, although artists working in an abstract idiom are rarely exhibited and harshly criticized. Architecture, after a brief phase of constructivist experimentation in the 1920s, has tended toward an unimaginative combination of neoclassicism and skyscraper construction. See articles on individual artists, e.g., Naum GABO. See G. H. Hamilton, *The Art and Architecture of Russia* (1954); Richard Hare, *The Art and Artists of Russia* (1965); Arthur Voyce, *The Art and Architecture of Medieval Russia* (1967); K. V. Kornilovich, *Arts of Russia* (2 vol., tr. 1967–68); Camilla Gray, *The Russian Experiment in Art, 1863–1922* (1971).

Russian Blue cat: see CAT.

Russian Church: see ORTHODOX EASTERN CHURCH.

Russian language, also called Great Russian, member of the East Slavic group of the Slavic subfamily of the Indo-European family of languages (see SLAVIC LANGUAGES). The principal language of administration in the Soviet Union, Russian is spoken by about 142 million people as a first language in the USSR. It reaches many additional millions as a second language in European and Asian Russia and in the East European countries. About 1.5 million speakers of Russian live in the United States. Closely related to Russian are the other East Slavic tongues, Ukrainian (also called Little Russian or Ruthenian) and White Russian (or Belorussian). The former is spoken by about 38 million people, mainly in the Ukrainian SSR (where it is the official language), and is written in a modified version of the Cyrillic alphabet. The latter, which also uses a form of the Cyrillic alphabet, is the tongue of about 7 million persons, most of whom live in the Belorussian SSR. Because of its large number of speakers and its leading position in the increasingly powerful Soviet Union, Russian today has become one of the chief languages of the world. Used officially by the United Nations (along with English, French, Spanish, and Chinese), it is gaining importance in the field of scientific writing as well. The great literature in Russian makes that language also one of major cultural significance. It is difficult to master Russian pronunciation because the accent is free; that is, it can be placed on any syllable. Thus, there being no set rules for stress, the accent of each word has to be learned separately. In fact, the position of the accent on a given word may vary as the word's case and number change when it is declined. Some words that are spelled alike are distinguished only by a different stress. In addition, no significant differentiation is made between long and short vowels. Grammatically, Russian is highly inflected. The noun has six cases (nominative, genitive, dative, accusative, instrumental, and locative), with an occasional seventh case, the vocative. There are three declensional schemes and three genders, masculine, feminine, and neuter. Although the verb has only three tenses (past, present, and future), it is enabled by a feature called aspect to express numerous subtle shades of meaning, some of which cannot be rendered even in English. In addition the Russian verb has five moods and four voices. The historical development of Russian is not easy to trace because until the 17th cent. the religious and cultural language of the Russian people was not Russian, but CHURCH SLAVONIC. However, within Russia the latter language became sufficiently altered by the vocabulary and pronunciation of spoken Russian to be transformed into a Russian form of Church Slavonic adapted to Russian needs; this change began in early times. The earliest extant document containing Russian elements is an Old Church Slavonic text from the 11th cent. Ukrainian texts can be distinguished from Russian by the late 13th cent., but White Russian does not definitely appear as a separate language before the 16th cent. When Peter the Great tried to westernize Russia in the early 18th cent., the Russian language was subjected to Western influences and absorbed a number of foreign words. Peter was the first to reform and simplify the Cyrillic alphabet used for Russian. In the late 18th and early 19th cent., partly as a result of the work of the great Russian writer Aleksandr Pushkin, the Russians succeeded in throwing off the dominance of Church Slavonic and in developing their own tongue into a literary language, which was, nevertheless, influenced and even enriched by the Church Slavonic legacy. Literary Russian is based on the dialect used in and around the city of Moscow, which became the leading cultural center of the country in the 15th cent. Extensive reforms, aimed at simplifying and standardizing Russian writing and grammar, took place after the Revolution of 1917. See S. K. Boyanus, *A Manual of Russian Pronunciation* (1935); John Turkevich and Ludmilla B. Turkevich, *Russian for the Scientist* (1959); C. R. Townsend, *Russian Word Formation*

(1968); G. O. Vinokur, *Russian Language: A Brief History* (tr. 1971).

Russian literature was first produced after the introduction of Christianity from Byzantium in the 10th cent.; Byzantine influence, which suffused Kievan Russian culture, explains the adoption of CHURCH SLAVONIC as the religious and literary language. Early Church Slavonic literature was overwhelmingly religious in character and didactic in intent, although some movement toward a literary purpose marked the chronicles attributed to the friar NESTOR. Far superior were the BYLINY, oral folk lays, which fused Christian and pagan traditions and at times achieved the level of great epic poetry. The first written masterpiece of Russian literature was *The Song of Igor's Campaign* (c.1187; see IGOR), which towered above the general cultural desolation under Tatar domination. A few notable sermons and lives of saints were written in this period, and in the early 15th cent. the priest Sophonia of Ryazan wrote the epic *Beyond the River Don* to commemorate the victory over the Tatars at Kulikovo (1380). Athanasy Nikitin (d. 1472) wrote a distinguished account of his *Journey beyond Three Seas* to distant lands. The rise of the grand duchy of Moscow and the overthrow of the Tatars was followed by an expansion of literary activity, still largely in a religious vein. Russian literature in general was hampered by the autocratic regime of the czars and by political and religious turmoil, although these conditions generated the few exceptional works of the 16th and 17th cent. The recriminatory correspondence between Czar Ivan IV and Prince Andrei Mikhailovich Kurbsky (c.1528–1583), who had deserted to the Poles, showed polemical and linguistic mastery; the great schism which rent the Russian Church in the mid-17th cent. produced the memorable autobiography of the archpriest Avvakum (martyred 1682), the first work in colloquial Russian. Western influence was manifest in the 17th cent. in numerous translations and in the establishment (1662) of the first theater in Russia. Under Peter I the westernizing process was enormously accelerated; at the same time the Russian alphabet was revised and Russian works began to be published in the vernacular. Close contact with Europe began a century of the application of Western literary modes to Russian materials. Prince Antioch Kantemir (1708–44) blended European neoclassicism with portraiture of Russian life and wrote poetry in the syllabic system common to French and Polish. Poetry in tonic form, more suitable to Russian, was written by V. K. Tredyakovsky and was brought to a brilliant level by M. V. Lomonosov. A. F. Sumerokov, the founder of Russian drama, combined European forms and Russian themes in his fables and plays. The literature of the reign of Catherine II revealed the influence of the European Enlightenment; Catherine's own dramas compounded classical style and satirical tone, as did the journals of N. I. Novikov and the grandiose odes of G. R. Derzavhin. Satire was combined with realistic motifs in the plays of D. I. Fonzivin (1745–92), author of Russia's first truly national drama, *The Minor* (produced 1782), and in the fables of I. I. Khemnitser. Near the end of the century the beginning of political radicalism was given expression in tandem with Rousseauean sentimentalism by A. N. Radishchev. Sentimentality was developed by Vladislav Ozerov (1770–1816) in the drama and found its principal prose exponent in Nikolai Karamzin, who also initiated the Russian short story. V. A. Zhukovsky introduced European romantic idealism into Russian poetry. Increasing interest in national characteristics was expressed in the fables of I. A. Krylov, and literary nationalism rose to a high pitch during the wars against Napoleon I. In the 1820s a modern Russian literary style, realistic and nationally conscious, if to some degree shaded by romanticism and by European influence, was advanced by the versatile Aleksandr Pushkin, generally considered the greatest of Russian poets. M. Y. Lermontov's poetry maintained this stylistic excellence for a brief time. The despair detailed in the works of the romantic poet and novelist Yevgeny Baratinsky reflects the repressive atmosphere that existed during the reign of Czar Nicholas I. In the 1830s cultural schism was manifested in the conflict between SLAVOPHILES AND WESTERNIZERS; the leader of the Westernizers, the critic V. G. Belinsky, stressed the importance of literature's relationship to national life, thus furthering the development of Russian literary realism. Nikolai Gogol, considered the primary initiator of realistic prose, also revealed aspects of romantic and morbid fantasy in his satirical and humanitarian tales. At mid-century a merciless realism, not devoid of humor, was developed by I. A. Goncharov, while N. A. Ostrovsky, who first made the merchant world a subject of Russian literary works, wrote a vast number of plays, most of which are no longer performed. The poetry of F. I. Tyuchev conferred philosophic significance upon everyday events. N. A. Nekrasov created verses of social purpose. The works of Russia's golden age of prose literature were written against a background of czarist autocracy. Falling generally within the realist framework, the masterworks of this era exhibit a strong bent toward mysticism, brooding introspection, and melodrama. I. S. Turgenev achieved world stature with sophisticated novels that were profoundly critical of Russian society. Great critical and popular acclaim were bestowed upon the tormented genius and moral and religious idealism expressed in the works of Feodor Dostoyevsky, and upon the monumental, socially penetrating novels of Leo Tolstoy; these two authors stand among the giants of world literature. With the brilliantly sensitive stories and plays of Anton Chekhov the golden age essentially came to a close, passing into a time noted for poetic works. A reaction against realism manifested itself in the rise of symbolism, which flourished from the 1890s to about 1910 in the works of Feodor Sologub, V. K. Brynsov, I. F. Annensky, Andrei Bely, A. A. Blok, K. D. Balmont, and A. M. Remizov. The reaction was also evident in the religious and philosophical works of Vladimir Soloviev and in the historical novels of D. S. Merezhkovsky. In 1912 the Acmeist school, led by N. S. Gumilev and S. M. Gorodetsky, proclaimed a return to more concrete poetic imagery. The poets Osip Mandelstam and Anna Akhmatova belonged to this group also. In fiction the outstanding figures included V. M. Garshin and V. G. Korolenko. Maxim Gorky dominated fictional literature just prior to the Revolution of 1917. His passionate realism was echoed in the stories and dramas of his disciple Leonid Andreyev, while Ivan Bunin, also a member of Gorky's circle, wrote in a more conservative realistic vein.

Soviet Russian Literature. After the triumph of the Bolsheviks in the Russian Revolution (1917), many writers emigrated and were active abroad (Bunin, Kuprin, Merezhkovsky, Aldanov, and Vladimir Nabokov, among others). Some writers remained in Russia but published no new works; others became Communists; some adapted their talents to the needs of the new system while remaining partly aloof from its doctrines. Literary forms developed under the Bolshevik regime were at first similar to those appearing in Western Europe at the same time. In the first period after the revolution (to 1921) poetry flourished; principal figures included the symbolist Blok, the imagist S. A. Yesenin, and the iconoclast V. V. Mayakovsky. The older novelist Boris Pilnyak chronicled the new scene, and Isaac Babel wrote colorful short stories. In the era of the New Economic Policy (1922–28) there was much debate over literary dictatorship, with the "On Guard" group arguing for it and the Mayakovsky group against it. The Serapion Brothers (a group including K. A. Fedin, M. M. Zoshchenko, Vsevolod Ivanov, V. A. Kaverin, Yevgeny Zamyatin, and Lev Lunts), proclaimed their credo of artistic independence, and the formalists emphasized the structure of a poem rather than its content. This period saw the rebirth of the novel in the satirical works of Ilya Ilf and Y. P. Petrov and in the psychological and romantic novels of L. M. Leonov, Yuri Olesha, and Kaverin. M. A. Sholokhov gave the revolution-oriented novel an epic breadth, and in 1928 Gorky returned to enormous popularity. A general dissolution of the various literary groups took place from 1929 to 1932, and there was a marked trend toward political mobilization of writers. This trend was strengthened in the 1930s during Stalin's purges of the intelligentsia, and SOCIALIST REALISM was proclaimed as the guiding principle in all writing. In the drama, a form greatly encouraged and widely used as a means of propaganda, outstanding figures since the revolution include Yevgeny Schvartz, Nikolai Erdman, M. A. Bulgakov, S. M. Tretyakov, V. P. Katayev, V. M. Kirshon, A. N. Afinogenov, and Alexei Arbuzov. Boris Pasternak and Nikolai Tikhonov became the leading poets, and the novels of Ostrovsky, Aleksey Tolstoy, and Ilya Ehrenburg were widely read. V. B. Shklovski gained great influence as a critic. During World War II, Ehrenburg and Simonov were outstanding reporters. The spirit of friendliness toward the West ended abruptly in 1946 with a campaign initiated by Andrei Zhdanov, a Communist party secretary. Cultural isolationism and rigid party dictatorship of literature were enforced, and the effects on literature were disastrous. After the death of Stalin in 1953 some writers, previously in disgrace, were returned to favor; those still living were again permitted to publish. Ehrenburg's celebrated novel *The Thaw* (1954) described the despair of authors condemned to write in accordance with official doctrines. During this period cultural exchange with foreign countries was encouraged. In opposition to patriotic propaganda from orthodox party spokesmen, literature critical of Soviet society was, for a time, warmly received. Andrei Voznesensky and Yevgeny Yevtushenko were widely acclaimed for their nonconformist poetry. Voznesensky was praised for remarkable innovation in poetic form and use of language. Among Yevtushenko's most admired works is *Babi Yar,* an eloquent protest against Soviet anti-Semitism. In 1963 the government and the Union of Soviet Writers issued severe reprimands to these and other dissident writers. Pasternak's epic novel *Doctor Zhivago* (1957), published and received with critical accolades throughout the Western world, was refused publication in the USSR, and the author was compelled by official pressure to decline the Nobel Prize. Since Khrushchev's fall from grace in 1964, the struggle to liberate Soviet writing from political control has intensified. Famous writers such as Voznesensky and Aleksandr Solzhenitsyn have publicly asked for an end to government censorship. Others, including Andrei Sinyavsky and Yuri Daniel, have been imprisoned for permitting pseudonymous foreign publication of works critical of the Soviet regime. Solzhenitsyn's first novel, *One Day in the Life of Ivan Denisovich* (1962), described life in a concentration camp; its anti-Stalinism was in line with the political climate of 1962. His subsequent works earned him exile from Russia in 1974. See articles about individual writers, e.g., Maxim GORKY. See D. S. Mirsky, *A History of Russian Literature* (rev. ed. 1949); E. J. Simmons, ed., *Through the Glass of Soviet Literature* (1953, repr. 1963); Marc Slonim, *The Epic of Russian Literature* (1950, repr. 1964) and *Soviet Russian Literature* (rev. ed. 1967); H. E. Segel, ed., *The Literature of Eighteenth-Century Russia* (2 vol., 1967); E. J. Brown, *Russian Literature since the Revolution* (rev. ed. 1969); Olga Carlisle, ed., *Poets on Street Corners* (1969); N. K. Gudzii, *History of Early Russian Literature* (1949, repr. 1970); Gleb Struve, *Russian Literature under Lenin and Stalin* (1971); W. E. Harkins, *Dictionary of Russian Literature* (1956, repr. 1971); John Ferrell and Antony Stokes, *Early Russian Literature* (1973); Janko Lavrin, *A Panorama of Russian Literature* (1973).

Russian Platform: see BALTIC SHIELD.

Russian Revolution, violent upheaval in Russia in 1917 that overthrew the czarist government. The revolution was the culmination of a long period of repression and unrest. From the time of PETER I (Peter the Great), the czardom increasingly became an autocratic bureaucracy that imposed its will on the people by force, with wanton disregard for human life and liberty. As Western technology was adopted by the czars, Western humanitarian ideals were acquired by a group of educated Russians. Among this growing intelligentsia, the majority of whom were abstractly humanitarian and democratic, there were also those who were politically radical and even revolutionary. The university became a seat of revolutionary activity; NIHILISM, ANARCHISM, and later MARXISM were espoused and propagated. The reforms of ALEXANDER II brought the emancipation of the serfs (1861; see EMANCIPATION, EDICT OF) and opened the way for industrial development. However, emancipation imposed harsh economic conditions on the peasants and did not satisfy their craving for land. Rural discontent provided good material for revolutionary propaganda. Industrialization brought a concentration of population in urban centers, where the exploited working class provided a receptive audience for radical ideas. A reactionary and often ignorant clergy kept religion static and persecuted religious dissenters. Pogroms were instituted against the Jews, which turned many radical Jews to ZIONISM. Subject nationalities in the empire were repressed. By 1903, Russia was divided into several political groups. The autocracy was upheld by the landed nobility and the higher clergy; the capitalists desired a constitutional monarchy; the liberal bourgeoisie made up the bulk of the group that later became the Constitutional Democratic party; peasants and intelligentsia were incorporated into the SOCIALIST REVOLUTIONARY PARTY; and the workers, influenced by Marxism, were represented in the Bolshevik and Menshevik wings of the Social Democratic Labor party (see BOLSHEVISM AND MENSHEVISM). The corruption and incompetence of the czarist regime was glaringly revealed by the Russo-Japanese War (1904–5).

The Revolution of 1905. The Russian Revolution of 1905 began in St. Petersburg on Jan. 22 (Jan. 9, O.S.) when troops fired on a defenseless crowd of workers, who, led by a priest, were marching to the winter palace to petition Czar NICHOLAS II. This "bloody Sunday" was followed in succeeding months by a series of strikes, riots, assassinations, naval mutinies, and peasant outbreaks. These disorders, coupled with the disaster of the Russo-Japanese War, forced the government to promise the establishment of a consultative DUMA, or assembly, elected by limited franchise. However, unsatisfied popular demands provoked a general strike, and in a manifesto issued in October the czar granted civil liberties and a representative duma to be elected democratically. The manifesto split the groups that collectively had brought about the revolution. Those who were satisfied with the manifesto formed the Octobrist party. The liberals who wanted more power for the duma consolidated in the Constitutional Democratic party. The Social Democrats, who had organized a SOVIET, or workers' council, at St. Petersburg, attempted to continue the strike movement and compel social reforms. The government arrested the soviet and put down (Dec., 1905) a workers' insurrection in Moscow. As soon as order was restored, the czar promulgated the Fundamental Laws, under which the power of the duma was limited. Some attempt at economic reform was made by the czar's minister, STOLYPIN, but his efforts failed. At the same time Stolypin ruthlessly suppressed the revolutionary movement. When World War I broke out in 1914, most elements of Russia (except the Bolsheviks) united in supporting the war effort. However, the repeated military reverses, the acute food shortage, the appointment of inept ministers, and the intense suffering of the civilian population created a revolutionary climate by the end of 1916. The sinister influence of RASPUTIN over Czarina ALEXANDRA FEODOROVNA, whom Nicholas had left in charge of the government when he took personal command of the armed forces in 1915, destroyed all support for the czar except among extreme reactionaries.

The February Revolution. By March, 1917 (the end of Feb., 1917, O.S., thus the name February Revolution), most of the workers in Petrograd (Leningrad) and Moscow were striking and rioting for higher food rations. Many of the soldiers refused to suppress the insurgents; military insubordination and mutiny spread. Nicholas II ineffectually sought to put down the workers by force and also dissolved (March 11, N.S./Feb. 26, O.S.) the Duma. The Duma refused to obey, and the Petrograd insurgents took over the capital. Nicholas was forced to abdicate (March 15, N.S./March 2, O.S.) at Pskov after the Duma had appointed a provisional government composed mainly of moderates; it was headed by Prince LVOV and included MILYUKOV and KERENSKY. Although most Russians welcomed the end of autocracy, that was the only point on which they agreed. The provisional government had little popular support, and its authority was limited by the Petrograd workers' and soldiers' soviet, which controlled the troops, communications, and transport. The soviet furthered the military breakdown by establishing soldiers' committees throughout the army and making officership elective. Despite its strength, the soviet at first did not openly seize power; the Socialist Revolutionaries and Mensheviks who initially dominated it believed that at this stage of the revolution the bourgeois provisional government should rule. The government's program called for a general amnesty, broad civil liberties, and a constituent assembly to be elected by universal suffrage. This failed to meet two burning issues—continuation of the war and redistribution of land. The government announced that the question of land distribution could only be handled by the future constituent assembly. In March the soviet demanded peace. Milyukov, the foreign minister, was forced to resign in May after demonstrations against his insistence on continuing the war. The cabinet was reorganized and several other socialists, in addition to Kerensky, were added. Kerensky took over as minister of war, and Viktor CHERNOV, a Socialist Revolutionary, became minister of agriculture. In April, LENIN and other revolutionaries returned to Russia after having been permitted by the German government to cross Germany. The Germans hoped that the Bolsheviks would undermine the Russian war effort. Lenin galvanized the small and heretofore cautious Bolshevik party into action. The courses he advocated were simplified into the powerful slogans "end the war," "all land to the peasants," and "all power to the soviets." The failure of the all-out military offensive in July increased discontent with the provisional government. Disorders and violence in Petrograd led to popular demands for the soviet to seize power. The Bolsheviks assumed direction of this movement, but the soviet still held back. The government then took strong measures against the Bolshevik press and leaders. Nevertheless, the position of the provisional government was precarious. Prince Lvov resigned in July because of his opposition to Chernov's cautious attempts at land reform. He was replaced by Kerensky, who formed a coalition cabinet with a socialist majority. Army discipline deteriorated after the failure of the July offensive. The provisional government and the Menshevik and Socialist Revolutionary leaders in the soviet lost support from the impatient soldiers and workers, who turned to the Bolsheviks. Although the Bolsheviks were a minority in the first all-Russian congress of soviets (June), they continued to gain influence. The more conservative and even some moderate elements, who wished to limit the power of the soviets, rallied around General KORNILOV, who attempted (September, N.S./August, O.S.) to seize Petrograd by force. At Kerensky's request, the Bolsheviks and other socialists came to the defense of the provisional government and the attempt was put down. From mid-September (Aug. 31, O.S.) on the Bolsheviks had a majority in the Petrograd soviet, and Lenin urged the soviet to seize power.

The October Revolution. On the night of Nov. 6 (Oct. 24, O.S.), the Bolsheviks staged an armed coup d'etat, engineered by TROTSKY; aided by the workers' Red Guard and the sailors of Kronstadt, they captured the government buildings and the winter palace in Petrograd. A second all-Russian congress of soviets met and approved the coup after the Mensheviks and Socialist Revolutionaries walked out of the meeting. A cabinet, known as the Council of People's Commissars, was set up with Lenin as chairman, Trotsky as foreign commissar, RYKOV as interior commissar, and Stalin as commissar of nationalities. The second congress immediately called for cessation of hostilities, gave private and church lands to village soviets, and abolished private property. Moscow was soon taken by force, and local groups of Bolshevik workers and soldiers gained control of most of the cities of Russia. The remaining members of the provisional government were arrested (Kerensky had fled the country). Old marriage and divorce laws were discarded, the church was attacked, workers' control was introduced into the factories, the banks were nationalized, and a supreme economic council was formed to run the economy. The long-promised constituent assembly met in Jan., 1918, but was immediately disbanded by Bolshevik troops, its composition being predominantly non-Bolshevik. The Cheka (political police), directed by DZERZHINSKY, was set up to liquidate the opposition. Negotiations with the Central powers, which had begun late in 1917, resulted in the Russian acceptance (March, 1918) of the humiliating Treaty of Brest-Litovsk (see BREST-LITOVSK, TREATY OF). Most of the lands ceded to Germany under the treaty belonged to the subject nationalities of the Russian Empire; these lands, including Finland, Estonia, Latvia, Lithuania, the Ukraine, Georgia, Armenia, and Azerbaijan had proclaimed their independence from Russia after the Bolshevik coup. Following the German defeat by the Allies and the withdrawal of German troops, the Bolsheviks regained some of their former territory (the Ukraine, Georgia, Armenia, and Azerbaijan) during the Russian civil war.

The Civil War of 1918–20. The civil war between the Reds and the anti-Bolsheviks, known as the Whites, ravaged Russia until 1920. The Whites represented all shades of anti-Communist groups, including members of the constituent assembly; several of their leaders sought to set up a military dictatorship, but few were outspoken czarists. Armed opposition to the Soviet regime centered at first in the south, where the volunteers under Kornilov (succeeded by DENIKIN) joined forces with the Don Cossacks. The UKRAINE was the scene of fighting after the Germans evacuated it as a result of the general armistice of Nov. 11, 1918; it was seized by the Bolsheviks (early 1919), by the forces of Denikin (Aug.–Dec., 1919), again by the Bolsheviks (Dec. 1919), and finally by the Poles (May, 1920), with whom war had broken out over the Russo-Polish frontier question. Denikin in the meantime had turned over his command to General P. N. WRANGEL, who after the conclusion of the Russo-Polish armistice was driven by the Bolsheviks into the Crimea and was obliged to evacuate his forces to Constantinople (Nov., 1920). The civil war in the east was equally fatal to the Whites. A government was organized at Samara (now Kuybyshev) by a group of Socialist Revolutionaries who had been members of the constituent assembly. It received the support of the CZECH LEGION, which controlled the Trans-Siberian RR, but it merged (Sept., 1918) with a more conservative government set up at Omsk, in Siberia, and a few weeks later fell under the dictatorship of Admiral KOLCHAK. Although at first successful, Kolchak's forces were eventually driven to the Far East; by January, 1920, all Siberia except VLADIVOSTOK and some other Far Eastern territory was in Bolshevik hands. The civil war was complicated by Allied intervention. In N Russia, British, French, and American forces occupied (March, 1918) Murmansk and later Archangelsk with the stated purpose of protecting Allied stores against possible seizure by the Germans; they were evacuated only in Nov., 1919. In the Far East the Allies occupied Vladivostok, which the Japanese held until 1922. The Bolshevik military victory was due partly to the lack of cooperation among the various White commanders, partly to the remarkable reorganization of the Red forces after Trotsky became commissar for war. It was won, however, only at the price of immense sacrifice; Russia by 1920 was ruined and devastated. Atrocities were committed throughout the civil war by both sides. For the history of Russia after the civil war, see UNION OF SOVIET SOCIALIST REPUBLICS and LENIN, VLADIMIR ILYICH. See Leon Trotsky, *The History of the Russian Revolution* (tr. 1932); W. H. Chamberlin, *The Russian Revolution* (1935); John Reed, *Ten Days That Shook the World* (1935); Sir Bernard Pares, *The Fall of the Russian Monarchy* (1939); E. H. Carr, *The Bolshevik Revolution, 1917–1923* (3 vol., 1950–53); Adam Ulam, *The Bolsheviks* (1955, repr. 1968); David Footman, *Civil War in Russia* (1962); Marc Ferro, *The Russian Revolution of 1917* (tr. 1972).

Russian Soviet Federated Socialist Republic (RSFSR), constituent republic (1970 pop. 130,079,000), 6,591,100 sq mi (17,070,949 sq km), USSR. It is by far the largest, most populous, and economically most important of the 15 union republics that make up the USSR. Moscow, the capital of the USSR, is also the capital of the RSFSR. The republic occupies most of E Europe and N Asia, extending for c.5,000 mi (8,000 km) from the Baltic Sea in the west to the Pacific Ocean in the east and for 1,500 to 2,500 mi (2,400–4,000 km) from the Arctic Ocean in the north to the Black Sea, the Caucasus, the Altai and Sayan mts., and the Amur and Ussuri rivers in the south. The Urals form the conventional geographic boundary between the European and Siberian parts of the RSFSR. The RSFSR is bounded by Norway and Finland in the northwest; by the Estonian, Latvian, Belorussian, and Ukrainian republics in the west; by the Georgian and Azerbaijan republics in the southwest; and by the Kazakh Republic, Mongolia, and China along the southern land border. The Kaliningrad oblast is an exclave separated by Lithuania and bordering on Poland. The RSFSR occupies about 76% of the total land area and contains about 54% of the total population of the USSR. Its dominant relief features are (from west to east) the East European plain, the Urals, the West Siberian lowland, and the central Siberian plateau. Mt. Elbrus (18,481 ft/5,633 m), in the Caucasus, is the highest peak in the republic. The chief rivers draining the European RSFSR are the Don (into the Black Sea), the Volga (into the Caspian Sea), the Northern Dvina (into the White Sea), and the Pechora (into the Barents Sea). (For the main physical features of the Siberian RSFSR, see SIBERIA.) The climate of the RSFSR, generally continental, varies from extreme cold in N Russia and Siberia (where Verkhoyansk, the coldest place on earth, is situated), to subtropical along the Black Sea shore. The soil and vegetation zones include the entire TUNDRA and TAIGA belts of the USSR, nearly the entire wooded STEPPE and the northern black-earth steppes, and isolated sections of the semidesert, desert, and subtropical zones. The majority of the population are Russians (83%). There are also Ukrainians and such non-Slavic linguistic and ethnic groups as Tatars, Bashkirs, Chuvash, Komi, Komi Permyaks, Udmurts, Mari, Mordvinians, Jews, and various groups of the Far North and the Caucasus. Administratively, each area with a predominantly Russian population is constituted as a KRAY or OBLAST; non-Russian nationalities are constituted, in descending order of importance, as autonomous republics, autonomous oblasts, and national okrugs. The RSFSR has 16 autonomous republics: Bashkir, Buryat, Chechen-Ingush, Chuvash, Dagestan, Kabardino-Balkar, Kalmyk, Karelian, Komi, Mari, Mordvinian, North Ossetian, Tatar, Tuva, Udmurt, and Yakut; 6 krays: Altai, Khabarovsk, Krasnodar, Krasnoyarsk, Primorsky (Maritime), and Stavropol; 5 autonomous oblasts:

Adyge, Gorno-Altai, Jewish (Birobidzhan), Karachay-Cherkess, and Khakass; 10 national okrugs: Agin-Buryat, Chukchi, Evenki, Khanty-Mansi, Komi-Permyak, Koryak, Nenets, Taymyr, Ust-Orda Buryat, and Yamalo-Nenets; and 49 oblasts. The RSFSR may be conveniently divided into 9 physio-economic regions as follows:

Central European Area. This flat, rolling country, with Moscow as its center, forms a major industrial region. Besides Moscow, major cities include Gorky, Smolensk, Yaroslavl, Vladimir, Tula, Dzerzhinsk, and Rybinsk. Trucks, ships, railway rolling stock, machine tools, electronic equipment, cotton and woolen textiles, and chemicals are the principal industrial products. The Volga and Oka rivers are the major water routes, and the Moscow-Volga and Don-Volga canals link Moscow with the Caspian and Baltic seas. Many rail lines serve the area.

North and Northwest European Area. Leningrad, the industrial center of this area, has industries producing machine tools, electronic equipment, chemicals, ships, and precision instruments. Other cities include Pskov, Kaliningrad, Murmansk, Archangelsk, and Vologda. The hills, marshy plains, lakes, and desolate plateaus contain rich deposits of coal (Pechora Basin), oil (Ukhta), iron ore, and bauxite, and the area is a prime source of lumber. The chief water routes are the Baltic-Belomorsk Canal and the Volga-Baltic Waterway.

Volga. This area, stretching along the greatest river of European Russia, has highly developed hydroelectric power installations, including major dams at Volgograd (formerly Stalingrad), Kazan, Kuybyshev, and Balakovo. Farm machinery, ships, chemicals, and textiles are manufactured, and extensive oil and gas fields are worked. Agricultural products include wheat, vegetables, cotton, hemp, oil seeds, and fruit. Livestock raising and fishing are also important.

North Caucasus. In this area, descending northward from the principal chain of the Caucasus mts. to a level plain, are found rich deposits of oil, natural gas, and coal. The major cities are Rostov-na-Donu, Krasnodar, Grozny, and Novorossiysk. Sochi is a popular resort. Farm machinery, coal, petroleum, and natural gas are the chief products. The Kuban River region, a fertile black-earth area, is one of the chief granaries of the RSFSR. Wheat, sugar beets, tobacco, and rice are grown, and cattle are raised. Other rivers include the Don, the Kuma, and the Terek, and the Volga-Don Canal is a major transportation route.

Ural Area. The southern half of the Ural region is a major center of Soviet iron and steel production. A substantial share of Soviet petroleum is produced there, mainly in the Bashkir Autonomous Republic. Large deposits of iron ore, manganese, and aluminum ore are mined. The major industrial centers are Magnitogorsk, Sverdlovsk, Chelyabinsk, and Nizhni Tagil. Several trunk railroads serve the area, and rivers include the Kama and Belaya in the west and the Ural in the south.

Western Siberia. This vast plain—marshy and thinly populated in the north, hilly in the south—is of growing economic importance. At Novosibirsk and Kamen-na-Obi are large hydroelectric stations. Other principal cities include Kemerovo and Novokuznetsk. The Kuznetsk Basin in the southwest is a center of coal mining, oil refining, and the production of iron, steel, machinery, and chemicals. The Ob-Irtysh drainage system crosses this area, which is also served by the Trans-Siberian and South Siberian rail lines. Barnaul is a major rail junction. Agricultural products include wheat, rice, oats, and sugar beets, and livestock is raised.

Eastern Siberia. In this area of plateaus, mountains, and river basins, the major cities—Krasnoyarsk, Irkutsk, Ulan-Ude, and Chita—are located along the TRANS-SIBERIAN RAILROAD. A branch line links Ulan-Ude with Mongolia and Peking, China. There are hydroelectric stations at Bratsk, Krasnoyarsk, and Irkutsk. Coal, gold, graphite, iron ore, aluminum ore, zinc, and lead are mined in the area, and livestock is raised.

Northern and Northeastern Siberia. Covering nearly half of Soviet territory, this is the least populated and least developed area of the USSR. The Ob, Yenisei, and Lena rivers flow to the Arctic. Through the use of atomic-powered icebreakers, the Northern Sea Route has gained increasing economic importance. The Kolyma gold fields are the principal source of Soviet gold, and industrial diamonds are mined in the Yakut Autonomous Republic, notably at Mirny. Fur trapping and hunting are the chief activities in the taiga and tundra regions.

Far East. Bordering on the Pacific Ocean, the region has Komsomolsk, Khabarovsk, and Vladivostok as its chief cities. Machinery is produced, and lumbering, fishing, hunting, and fur trapping are important. The Trans-Siberian RR follows the Amur and Ussuri rivers and terminates at the port of Vladivostok.

Note on History. The RSFSR was formed in 1917 and was joined with the Ukraine, Belorussia, and Transcaucasia in 1922 to constitute the USSR. See RUSSIA; UNION OF SOVIET SOCIALIST REPUBLICS.

Russian thistle: see GOOSEFOOT; TUMBLEWEED.

Russian Turkistan: see TURKISTAN.

Russian wolfhound: see BORZOI.

Russo-Finnish War, 1939–40: see FINNISH-RUSSIAN WAR.

Russo-Japanese War, 1904–5, imperialistic conflict that grew out of the rival designs of Russia and Japan on MANCHURIA and KOREA. Russian failure to withdraw from Manchuria and Russian penetration into N Korea were countered by Japanese attempts to negotiate a division of the area into spheres of influence. The Russian government, however, was inflexible, and it was willing to risk an armed conflict in the belief that Japan was bound to be defeated and that a Russian victory would head off the growing threat of internal revolution in Russia. Japan broke off negotiations and severed (Feb. 6, 1904) diplomatic relations with Russia. Two days later, without a declaration of war, Japan attacked Port Arthur and bottled up the Russian fleet. A series of quick Japanese victories, which astounded the world, culminated in the fall of Port Arthur (Jan., 1905), the victory of General Oyama at Mukden (Feb.–March, 1905), and the destruction of the Russian fleet under ROZHDESTVENSKI at TSUSHIMA by Admiral TOGO (May, 1905). Through the mediation of U.S. President Theodore Roosevelt, peace was made in September at Portsmouth, N.H. (see PORTSMOUTH, TREATY OF). The disastrous outcome of the war for Russia was one of the chief immediate causes of the Russian Revolution of 1905. Japan gained the position of a world power and continued its imperialistic expansion. See R. Hargreaves, *Red Sun Rising: the Siege of Port Arthur* (1962); J. A. White, *The Diplomacy of the Russo-Japanese War* (1964); H. P. Hoyt, *The Russo-Japanese War* (1967).

Russo-Turkish Wars. The great eastward expansion of Russia in the 16th and 17th cent. still left the shores of the Black Sea in the hands of the Ottoman sultans and their vassals, the khans of CRIMEA. The Russo-Turkish Wars were the result of Russian attempts to find an outlet on the Black Sea and—in later stages—to conquer the Caucasus, dominate the Balkan Peninsula, gain control of the Dardanelles and Bosporus straits, and retain access to world trade routes. Warfare between the Russians and the Crimean Tatars was a chronic condition in the 16th and 17th cent. In 1696, PETER I won the first major Russian victory over the Turco-Tatars by capturing the fortress of Azov. In the Northern War (1700–1721) Sultan Ahmed III openly entered the conflict against Russia in 1710 and regained Azov by the Peace of the Pruth (1711). France, the traditional ally of Turkey, had a share in instigating this and later Turkish attempts at stemming the Russian advance. In 1736 war again broke out between Turkey and Russia, allied with Austria. The Russians recaptured Azov and won a spectacular success in Moldavia, where General Münnich entered Jassy (1739). However, Austria became alarmed by Russian ambitions in the Balkans and concluded the separate Treaty of Belgrade (1739), in which Russia was forced to join. Russia agreed to demilitarize Azov and not to build a Black Sea fleet. The first major Russo-Turkish War, that of 1768–74, was an indirect result of Russian interference in Poland. Sultan Mustafa III, alarmed by Russia's action and encouraged by France, declared war on CATHERINE II of Russia. The Russians conquered (1771) the Crimea, where a pro-Russian khan was installed, and overran Moldavia and Walachia. The Treaty of KUCHUK KAINARJI (1774) declared the Crimean khanate independent of the sultan, gave Russia considerable territorial gains, conceded to Russia the role of protector of the sultan's Greek Orthodox subjects, and allowed Russian merchantmen to navigate the Black Sea and pass through the Straits. A general partition of the Ottoman Empire was contemplated in the treaty of alliance (1781) between Catherine II and Emperor Joseph II; the fate of Turkey thus became a major concern of the Western powers and created the explosive EASTERN QUESTION. In 1783, Catherine annexed the Crimea outright. A new Russo-Turkish War broke out in 1787, and in 1788 Joseph II entered the war as Catherine's ally. Although Austria was forced, chiefly by Prussian exertions, to withdraw from the alliance in 1791, Russian successes under SUVAROV enabled Catherine to reach a favorable settlement in the Treaty of Jassy (1792). In 1806 the energetic Sultan Selim III deposed the Russophile governors of Moldavia and Walachia, an act that led to the Russo-Turkish War of 1806–12. This was brought to a close by Kutuzov's lightning campaign of 1811–12 and resulted in the gain of BESSARABIA by Russia in the Treaty of Bucharest (1812). The Greek War of Independence (see GREECE) precipitated the Russo-Turkish War of 1828–29, which ended with the Treaty of Adrianople (see ADRIANOPLE, TREATY OF). When, in 1853, Russia sought to obtain further concessions from Turkey, the Turks, backed by England and France, declared war; their allies entered the conflict in 1854, and the CRIMEAN WAR resulted. The peace of 1856 (see PARIS, CONGRESS OF) brought no major territorial changes but marked a severe setback to Russian influence. The last Russo-Turkish War came as a result of the anti-Turkish uprising (1875) in Bosnia and Hercegovina. Serbia and Montenegro joined, on Russian instigation, the rebels in their war on Turkey; after securing Austrian neutrality, Russia openly entered the war (1877). The Treaty of SAN STEFANO in 1878 so thoroughly revised the map in favor of Russia and of Russian-influenced Bulgaria that the European powers called a conference to revise its terms (see BERLIN, CONGRESS OF). In 1878 a thorough realignment of alliances took place. In World War I, Russia and Turkey faced each other once more; Russia sided with the traditional allies of Turkey—England and France—while Turkey fought with the former partners of Russia—Austria and Bulgaria. By the separate Russo-Turkish treaty of 1921, the USSR returned the districts of Kars and Ardahan, acquired in 1878, to Atatürk's Turkish government.

rust, in botany, name for various parasitic fungi of the order Uredinales and for the DISEASES OF PLANTS that they cause. Rusts form reddish patches of spores on the host plant. About 1,000 species are known in North America. Some grow entirely on one plant; others require two hosts, plants of two species, in order to complete their life cycles. Cedar rust, for instance, grows on cedar and on apple trees, needing both for development. Blister rust of pine grows on pines and either currant or gooseberry bushes. The stem rust *Puccinia graminis* is one of the most destructive to wheat, rye, and other grasses. Barberry is an alternate host. Rusts attack all cereal crops and many fruits, vegetables, forage crops, ornamental plants, and forest trees. Rusts are hard to eradicate; control measures are the use of rust-resistant varieties of seed and the elimination of alternate hosts in agricultural areas. Rusts are classified in the division FUNGI, class Basidiomycetes, order Uredinales.

Rustavi (ro͞ostä'vē), city (1970 pop. 98,000), SE European USSR, in Georgia, on the Kura River. It is a new industrial center of Georgia, with ironworks and steelworks and chemical plants. The city, developed after 1948, is near the site of the ancient town of Rustavi, which was destroyed c.1400 by Tamerlane.

rustication (rŭstĭkā'shən), method of creating textures upon masonry wall surfaces, chiefly upon those of stone, by projecting the blocks beyond the surface of the mortar joints. Each joint thus lies in a channel or in a V-shaped groove, between adjoining stones, and a separating shadow line is produced. The degree of projection, whether slight or bold, permits varying effects. The Romans occasionally built rusticated walls. This device was used by Renaissance architects in the palace facades at Florence, a favorite treatment being that of a ground floor with stones of strong projection and roughly textured surface, surmounted by upper stories in which both forms were more refined. Often columns and pilasters also were rusticated. The basement story of the Pitti Palace (mid-15th cent.) exhibits a celebrated example of rustication, some of its enormous and roughly quarried blocks of stone projecting as much as 2 ft 6 in. (76.2 cm) beyond the surface of the joints. The garden architecture of the Italian baroque VILLA shows many grotesquely textured examples. Rustications also appeared frequently in the Georgian style and in American Colonial architecture. In these and also in modern work often only the corners of a building are rusticated, thus contrasting with the smooth surface of the remainder.

Rustico di Filippo (ro͞o'stēkō dē fēlēp'pō), 13th cent. Italian poet. He was perhaps one of the first to use the Tuscan dialect in literature. Some 60 of his sonnets, most of them in a burlesque vein, are extant. He was a friend of Brunetto LATINI.

rusting: see CORROSION.

Ruston (rus'tən), city (1970 pop. 17,365), seat of Lincoln parish, N La.; settled 1884 as a railroad town and inc. the same year. It is the trading center of a rich farm, dairy, and natural-gas region. Wood products are made there. Louisiana Tech Univ. is located in the city.

rutabaga: see TURNIP.

Rutebeuf (rütəböf'), fl. between 1254 and 1285, French poet. He was the author of an early miracle play, *Le Miracle de Théophile*, and of fabliaux, allegories, saints' lives, and satires. Skillfully using legend, he eloquently attacked social abuses and mocked the flaws of all classes.

Rutgers University, mainly at New Brunswick, N.J.; land-grant and state supported; coeducational; chartered 1766 as Queen's College, opened 1771. Rutgers was the eighth colonial college, receiving a royal charter from George III in response to a petition of leaders in the Dutch Reformed Church. In 1825 the name was changed to Rutgers College in honor of Col. Henry Rutgers, a benefactor. It became a university in 1924. The Rutgers Scientific School was redesignated (1864) as a state college and, in 1917, as the state university of New Jersey. In 1945 the entire institution became the State Univ. of New Jersey. The corporate title was changed to the State Univ. of Rutgers in 1956. Rutgers operates Douglass College (est. 1918 as the New Jersey College for Women; renamed 1955) and Livingston College (opened 1969), at New Brunswick; Newark Colleges at Newark (formerly the Univ. of Newark; absorbed by Rutgers 1946); and the College of South Jersey, at Camden (absorbed by Rutgers 1950). Extension centers are at Jersey City and Paterson. The university's large agriculture program includes an agricultural experiment station (est. 1880) and a university farm system. Its research facilities include microbiology, radiation, engineering, ceramics, economics, biological science, and labor relations institutes. The university's library includes specialized collections in science, medicine, and microbiology as well as rare books and research materials relating to English literature and early Americana.

Ruth, Babe (George Herman Ruth), 1895–1948, American baseball player, considered the greatest of all baseball players, b. Baltimore. When he was seven years old his parents placed him in St. Mary's Industrial School (Baltimore), an institution for underprivileged boys. His days at St. Mary's were spent learning the tailor's trade and practicing baseball in his spare time. He began to play semiprofessional ball in Pennsylvania and was soon signed by the Baltimore Orioles (International League) in 1914. That same year he was sold as a pitcher to the Boston Red Sox of the American League. Ruth, a left-hander, proved to be (1914–19) a formidable pitcher for the Red Sox and one of the most successful in major league baseball, winning 87 and losing 44 games and winning three world series games (one in 1916, two in 1918). However, because pitchers do not play every day, in 1919 Ruth was shifted to the outfield, where his hitting prowess could be used more consistently. The following year he was sold to the New York Yankees of the American League, and because of his batting feats and attractive personality he greatly helped to salvage baseball's popularity, weakened by revelations that gamblers and players, in the so-called Black Sox scandal, had successfully conspired to influence the results of the 1919 World Series. Ruth hit the most home runs per season for several years (1919–21, 1923–24, 1926–30), tied for the home run lead in 1918 and 1931, and set the existing record of 60 home runs for one season in 1927 (Roger Maris hit 61 in the present extended game schedule). Ruth hit 714 home runs in major league play, a record that held until 1974. He led the Yankees to seven pennants (1921–23, 1926–28, 1932), and Yankee Stadium, built in 1923, came to be known as "the house that Ruth built." Ruth was an unmistakable figure with his large frame and spindle-thin legs, and his talented and colorful play captured the baseball fan's imagination. For example, in the third game of the 1932 world series he appeared to indicate a spot in the stands of the Chicago Cubs' ball park where he would hit the ball and promptly blasted it there for a home run. Off the playing field "the Bambino," as he was affectionately called, made headlines by his charitable actions, such as visiting sick children in hospitals. He was the highest-paid player of his era, but he took several salary cuts before he was traded by the Yankees to the Boston Braves (National League) in 1935. He played with the Braves while serving as assistant manager but soon (June, 1935) was released. In 1936, Ruth became the second player to be elected to the National Baseball Hall of Fame; Ty Cobb was the first. A year before he died he established and endowed the Babe Ruth Foundation to aid underprivileged youth. He wrote *How to Play Baseball* (1931). See biographies by R. B. Considine (1948), D. M. Daniel (2d ed. 1963), and Robert W. Creamer (1974).

Ruth, book of the Old Testament, 8th in order in the Authorized Version. It tells a story, set in the days of the judges, of the fidelity of a Moabite widow (Ruth) to her widowed mother-in-law (Naomi). After the death of her husband in Moab Ruth returns with Naomi to Bethlehem. There Ruth marries Naomi's kinsman, Boaz. Boaz and Ruth were ancestors of David. This idyll is one of the most popular of scriptural stories. The book has been variously dated, but in its final form it appears to have been written between 450 B.C. and 250 B.C. See G. T. Bull, *Love-Song in Harvest* (1972); see also bibliography under OLD TESTAMENT.

Ruthenia (ro͞othē'nēə), Latinized form of the word *Russia.* The term was applied to the Ukraine in the Middle Ages when the princes of Galich briefly assumed the title kings of Ruthenia. Later, in Austria-Hungary, the term *Ruthenians* was used to designate the Ukrainian population of W Ukraine, which included GALICIA, BUKOVINA, and Carpathian Ukraine. After 1918 the term Ruthenia was applied only to the easternmost province of Czechoslovakia, which was also known as Carpathian Ukraine, or by its Czech name, *Podkarpatská Rus* [Sub-Carpathian Russia]; for the history of this area from 1918, see ZAKARPATSKAYA OBLAST. There is no ethnic or linguistic distinction between Ukrainians and Ruthenians. Culturally, however, the Ruthenians were distinct from the Ukrainians, especially after 1596, when the Orthodox Church of the Western Ukraine entered into union with the Roman Catholic Church, and after 1649, when a similar union was effected in Hungary. The Ruthenian Uniate Church of the Byzantine (see ROMAN CATHOLIC CHURCH) thus included the majority of the Ruthenians in the Austro-Hungarian Monarchy, while the Greek Orthodox Church was fully restored (17th cent.) in the Russian part of the Ukraine. When all Ruthenians were united (1945) in the Soviet Ukraine, government pressure resulted in the secession of the Ruthenian Uniate Church from Rome and its reunion with the Russian Orthodox Church.

ruthenium (ro͞othē'nēəm), metallic chemical element; symbol Ru; at. no. 44; at. wt. 101.07; m.p. about 2310°C; b.p. about 3900°C; sp. gr. 12.41 at 20°C; valence commonly +2, +3, +4, +6, or +8. Ruthenium is a hard, lustrous, silver-gray metal with a close-packed hexagonal crystalline structure. It is found directly above osmium in group VIII of the PERIODIC TABLE. Below about 100°C ruthenium is insoluble in acids, including aqua regia, but reacts violently if potassium chlorate is added. It reacts with the halogens and with fused alkali hydroxides. When heated above 800°C it oxidizes, but it does not react with air at room temperature. It forms compounds with silicon and sulfur. Its compounds resemble those of osmium. Ruthenium is found in nature with other metals of the so-called platinum group in river sands, in minerals such as laurite (the sulfide) and osmiridium, and in association with certain ores containing platinum, copper, and nickel. It is obtained commercially as a by-product of the refining of nickel sulfide ores mined near Sudbury, Ont., Canada. Ruthenium metal powder is obtained as the final product of a complex chemical process. It is used as a catalyst in hydrogenation, isomerization, nitrogenation, oxidation, and reforming reactions. The metal is used as a hardener in electrical contact alloys and filaments, in jewelry, in pen nibs, and in instrument pivots. It is usually alloyed with other metals. It is a very good hardener for palladium and platinum, and vastly improves the corrosion resistance of titanium when added in small amounts. It is also used in alloys with cobalt, molybdenum, nickel, tungsten, and other metals. Ruthenium compounds are used to color ceramics and glass. Ruthenium was discovered in 1827 in an impure form by G. W. Osann in residues of crude platinum ores from the Ural Mts. of Russia. Pure ruthenium was first prepared by K. K. Klaus in 1845; he showed that Osann's sample contained at least one other metal.

Rutherford, Ernest Rutherford, 1st **Baron,** 1871–1937, British physicist, b. New Zealand. After working under J. J. Thomson at Cambridge he was professor of physics at McGill Univ. (1898–1907), professor and director of the physical laboratory at the Univ. of Manchester (1907–19), and in 1919 succeeded Thomson as professor and director of the Cavendish Laboratory at Cambridge. He is known for his studies of RADIOACTIVITY and for his discovery of the atomic NUCLEUS. He discovered and named alpha and beta radiation and with Frederick Soddy proposed a theory of radioactive transformation of atoms; for this work he was awarded the 1908 Nobel Prize in Chemistry. On the basis of experiments with alpha rays carried out under his direction by H. Geiger and E. Marsden he was led (1911) to a description of the atom as a small, heavy nucleus surrounded by orbital electrons; this nuclear model of the atom was taken by Niels Bohr (1913) and combined with the new quantum theory to provide the basic description of the atom still accepted today. In the course of his researches, he produced hydrogen by bombarding atoms of various elements, e.g., nitrogen, with helium nuclei (alpha rays); these results, published in 1919, were the first evidence of artificially produced splitting of atomic nuclei. In addition to his own work, Rutherford was known for his outstanding leadership in directing the research of others. Rutherford was knighted in 1914 and elevated to the peerage in 1931. His works include *Radioactive Transformations* (1906), *The Electrical Structure of Matter* (1926), *The Artificial Transmutation of the Elements* (1933), and *The Newer Alchemy* (1937). The first volume of his collected papers appeared in 1962. See biography by Norman Feather (1949, repr. 1973); study by Edward Andrade (1964).

Rutherford, Joseph Franklin, 1869–1942, American sectarian leader, b. Missouri. He became leader of the JEHOVAH'S WITNESSES (then called Russellites) after the death of the sect's founder, Charles T. RUSSELL, in 1916. Under the direction of Rutherford the Witnesses' attack on the existing social order took on an increasingly revolutionary tone. In 1918 he served a year's imprisonment in Atlanta, Ga., for his encouragement of conscientious objectors. His writings were widely distributed among Witnesses in the United States and abroad.

Rutherford, Mark: see WHITE, WILLIAM HALE.

Rutherford, Samuel, 1600–1661, Scottish clergyman. His *Exercitationes apologeticae pro divina gratia* (1636), urging a Calvinist view of grace against ARMINIANISM, caused his suspension from his living at Anwoth on the charge of nonconformity to the Acts of Episcopacy. Banished to Aberdeen until the National Covenant was drawn up in 1638, he then was made professor of divinity at St. Mary's College, St. Andrews, and rector of the university in 1651. In 1643 he was chosen a commissioner from Scotland to the Westminster Assembly, and was attacked by name in John Milton's sonnet "On the New Forcers of Conscience under the Long Parliament." His *Lex Rex* (1644) brought him wide attention as a political theorist; it was burned by the public hangman after the Restoration, and Rutherford was removed from his official positions and summoned (1661) by Parliament on a charge of treason. He died before he could be tried. Rutherford's letters, first published as *Joshua Redevivus* (1664), edited by A. A. Bonar with a life (2 vol., 1863), have passed through a number of editions.

Rutherford (rŭth'ərfərd), borough (1970 pop. 20,802), Bergen co., NE N.J., a residential suburb of the New York City–N New Jersey metropolitan area; inc. 1881. It is the seat of Fairleigh Dickinson Univ. Several pre-Revolutionary houses remain.

Rutherfurd, Lewis Morris (rŭth'ərfərd), 1816–92, American physicist, b. New York City, grad. Williams, 1834. From 1837 to 1849 he practiced law. Rutherfurd studied and experimented in celestial photography, especially in spectral analysis, in which he was a pioneer, and he invented several instruments for his work, including a micrometer for measuring positions on photographs, an apparatus for ruling diffraction gratings, and a telescope specially fitted for astronomical photography. He gave his instruments and collections of photographs to Columbia Univ., of which he was a trustee (1858–84).

Rutherglen (rŭth'ərglĕn), burgh (1971 pop. 24,728), Lanarkshire, S central Scotland, on the Clyde River. Manufactures include chemicals, paper, textiles, and metal products. Rutherglen became a royal burgh in 1126 and was for some time one of the leading Clyde ports. There, in 1679, the COVENANTERS published the Declaration and Testament which preceded the battles of Drumclog and Bothwell Bridge. In 1975, Rutherglen became part of the Strathclyde region.

Ruthven (rĭv'ən, ro͞oth'vən), Scottish noble family, believed to trace its ancestry to Thor, a Saxon or Dane, who settled in Scotland in the reign of David I. The name is derived from lands in Perthshire held by the family, several members of which were earls of Gowrie in the 16th cent. **Sir William Ruthven,** 1st

lord of Ruthven, d. 1528, received his title from James III in 1488. His grandson, **Patrick Ruthven,** 3d **lord of Ruthven,** 1520?-1566, was a firm supporter of Protestant doctrines. He acted on various commissions appointed by the lords of the congregation to deal with the queen regent, Mary of Guise, and with Elizabeth I of England, and he served later as privy councilor to MARY QUEEN OF SCOTS. He took a leading part in the murder (1566) of David Rizzio and wrote a memoir of the affair, which still exists in manuscript in the British Museum. He fled to England, where he died shortly after. Associated with him in the murder was his son, **William Ruthven,** 4th **lord of Ruthven** and 1st **earl of Gowrie,** 1541?-1584. He also fled to England and remained there until pardoned (1567). Returning to Scotland, he took part in the opposition to the queen and the earl of Bothwell. He was created earl of Gowrie in 1581. He was head of the group of nobles who planned and carried out in 1582 what came to be known as the raid of Ruthven, in which they seized the young King James VI (later JAMES I of England) and brought about the dismissal of Esmé STUART, 1st duke of Lennox. Although pardoned in 1583, Gowrie began plotting again. He was tried for high treason and beheaded. Two of his sons, **John Ruthven,** 6th **lord of Ruthven** and 3d **earl of Gowrie,** 1578?-1600, and **Alexander Ruthven,** 1580?-1600, were involved in the mysterious Gowrie conspiracy of 1600. All that is known for certain of the incident is that while James VI was dining privately with the two brothers, some kind of fight occurred in which the Ruthvens were killed. James alleged that Gowrie and his brother had plotted to murder him, but the king's account of the incident was both inconsistent and improbable, and it was widely disbelieved at the time. On the other hand, there is no real evidence to support the hypothesis that the incident was a deliberate plot on James's part to get rid of the Ruthvens. The result, however, was that the titles and dignity of the Ruthven family were extinguished and its estates annexed to the crown. Descended in collateral line was **Patrick Ruthven,** 1573?-1651, who won distinction in the service of Gustavus II of Sweden. Later he supported the cause of Charles I in Scotland and England, eventually serving as general in chief of the royalist forces (1643-44). He was created Lord Ruthven of Ettrick in 1639, earl of Forth in 1642, and earl of Brentford in 1644. He had no sons, and his titles became extinct.

Ruthven Castle: see HUNTINGTOWER.

rutile (ro͞o'tēl, -tīl), mineral, one of the three forms in which titanium dioxide, TiO_2, is found. It crystallizes in the tetragonal system, crystals being common; twins frequently occur, and rosettes (sixlings and eightlings) are not unusual. Iron is generally present. The mineral is typically brownish red, though there are black varieties. A common titanium mineral, rutile is of wide occurrence in igneous rocks, e.g., granite, and metamorphic rocks, e.g., gneiss and mica schist. Fine specimens are found in Switzerland, Norway, and some other parts of Europe, in various parts of the United States, and in Brazil.

Rutland, county (1971 pop. 27,463), 152 sq mi (394 sq km), central England. The county town is Oakham. It is drained by the Welland River, which forms the southern boundary with Northamptonshire. Smallest of the English counties in both area and population, Rutland has a rolling terrain and is largely devoted to tillage and pasturage. Iron ore and limestone are extracted. Cement, clothing, and plastics are made. In 1974, Rutland became part of the new nonmetropolitan county of Leicestershire.

Rutland, city (1970 pop. 19,293), seat of Rutland co., W Vt., at the junction of Otter and East creeks; settled c.1770, inc. as a city 1892. It is a railroad and trade center with many small industries. Products include medical supplies, awnings, and flags. Marble quarrying, which began c.1845, still flourishes in the area. The headquarters of the Green Mountain National Forest, Rutland is surrounded by picturesque mountains, lakes, and streams; numerous skiing and recreational areas are nearby. The College of St. Joseph the Provider and an art museum are in Rutland. A state fair is held there annually.

Rutledge, Ann, 1813?-1835, American historical figure, alleged fiancée of Abraham Lincoln. Her father kept the inn at New Salem, Ill., where Lincoln lived from 1831 to 1837. Ann's sudden death from brain fever on Aug. 25, 1835, grieved Lincoln deeply, and from this one known fact William H. HERNDON, Lincoln's biographer, wove the story of Lincoln's alleged love for her. Lincoln's wife, Mary Todd Lincoln, insisted that the story was false, and most historians have found Herndon's evidence unconvincing. Actually, Ann was engaged to Lincoln's friend John McNamar. In 1890, Ann's remains were removed from the old Concord cemetery near New Salem and reinterred in Oakland cemetery near Petersburg, Ill. There in 1921 was erected a monument bearing a passage from Edgar Lee Master's poem about her in *Spoon River Anthology.*

Rutledge, Edward, 1749-1800, political leader in the American Revolution, signer of the Declaration of Independence, b. Charleston, S.C.; brother of John Rutledge. He studied law at the Middle Temple, London, and was admitted (1772) to the English bar. He returned to America and was (1774-77) a member of the Continental Congress. Rutledge later held many official posts at both the national and state level. He was captured (1780) by the British at the fall of Charleston. He was governor of South Carolina from 1798 to 1800.

Rutledge, John, 1739-1800, American jurist and political leader, 2d Chief Justice of the United States, b. Charleston, S.C.; brother of Edward Rutledge. After studying law in London he began practice in Charleston, S.C., in 1761. He rose to prominence when quite young, was a member (1762) of the provincial assembly, attorney general of South Carolina (1764-65), and a delegate (1765) to the Stamp Act Congress. He twice (1774-76, 1782-83) was a member of the Continental Congress and meanwhile held strong sway as president (1776-78) of his state and later (1779-82) as governor. As delegate (1787) to the Federal Constitutional Convention, Rutledge played an important role in the drafting of the U.S. Constitution, and then (1788) was a member of the state ratifying convention. After serving (1789-91) as Associate Justice of the U.S. Supreme Court he was chief justice of South Carolina. In July, 1795, he was appointed interim Chief Justice of the United States and presided at the August term of the Supreme Court, but the Senate (Dec., 1795) refused to confirm the appointment because of his bitter attacks on JAY'S TREATY. See biography by R. H. Barry (1942; repr. 1971).

Rütli (rüt'lē) or **Grütli** (grüt'lē), meadows, Uri canton, central Switzerland, on the shore of the Lake of Lucerne. Here, according to the legend of William Tell, representatives of Uri, Schwyz, and Unterwalden met in 1307 to swear the **Rütli Oath,** on which Swiss freedom was founded. However, the discovery in the 19th cent. of a written alliance of the three cantons, dated Aug. 1, 1291, has detracted from the historic importance of the Rütli meeting. The meadows and a nearby chalet are national monuments.

Ruwenzori (ro͞o"wənzō'rē), mountain range, E central Africa, on the Uganda-Zaïre border, in the western arm of the Great Rift Valley between lakes Albert and Edward. This fault-block range is composed of ancient crystalline rock; Uganda's Kilembe copper mine is located in the range's eastern foothills. The snowcapped summits of the Ruwenzori include Mt. Margherita (16,798 ft/5,120 m) and Mt. Alexandra (16,750 ft/5,105 m). The peaks are invariably shrouded in mist, presenting an eerie aspect, and there are extensive glaciers and glacial lakes. The range may be the semifabulous "Mountains of the Moon," erroneously supposed by the ancients to be the source of the Nile. Discovered in 1889 by Henry Stanley, the British explorer, the range was first climbed (1906) by the duke of the Abruzzi, the Italian explorer.

Ruysbroeck, John, Dutch *Jan van Ruusbroec* (yän vän rois'bro͝ok), 1293-1381, Roman Catholic mystic, b. Brabant (now in Belgium and the Netherlands). He was an Augustinian canon. In middle age he retired to a hermitage at Groenendael (near Brussels), where he was prior of a small community. His sanctity and good counsel attracted visitors from afar, and Johannes TAULER and Gerard GROOTE were among his followers. His influence on Groote was so great that John is regarded as a forerunner of the Brothers of the Common Life. His mystical treatises are classics of Middle Dutch literature and of Christian mysticism. There are English translations of *The Seven Steps of the Ladder of Spiritual Love* (1944) and *The Spiritual Espousals* (1953). His cult is widespread among Roman Catholics of N Europe. He was beatified in 1908. See Vincent Scully, *A Mediaeval Mystic* (1911); Stephanus Axters, *Spirituality of the Old Low Countries* (1954).

Ruysdael, Jacob van: see RUISDAEL, JACOB VAN.

Ruyter, Michiel Adriaanszoon de (mēkhēl' ä'drēänsōn" də roi'tər), 1607-76, Dutch admiral. His life was spent in the Dutch mercantile and naval service. He fought under Maarten TROMP in the first (1652-54) of the DUTCH WARS and distinguished himself in the second DUTCH WAR (1664-67) by the capture of English holdings on the Gold and Guinea coasts. He saved the Dutch fleet in a brilliant withdrawal after defeat at North Foreland (Aug. 4, 1666) and burned English ships (1667) in the Medway. With Cornelis TROMP he led the Dutch fleet in the third Dutch War (1672-78) and saved Dutch ports (1672) from attack by the English and French. Despite his protests over the conditions of the Dutch fleet, he was sent to the Mediterranean (1675), where he was mortally wounded at Messina.

Ruzicka, Rudolph (ro͞ozĭ'kə), 1883-, American artist, b. Bohemia. Ruzicka studied at the Art Institute of Chicago and established himself early as a distinguished etcher and wood engraver. He gained acclaim as a leading book illustrator and designer. Ruzicka designed the Fairfield typeface. He was the author of *Thomas Bewick, Engraver* (1943) and *Studies in Type Design* (1968).

Rwanda (ro͞oän'dä), republic (1973 est. pop. 4,000,000), 10,169 sq mi (26,338 sq km), E central Africa, bordering on Zaïre in the west, on Uganda in the north, on Tanzania in the east, and on Burundi in the south. KIGALI is the capital and largest town; other towns include Butare, Nyanza, and Gisenyi. The country is divided into 10 prefectures. Most of Rwanda is situated at 5,000 ft (1,520 m) or higher, and the country has a rugged relief made up of steep mountains and deep valleys. The principal geographical feature is the Virunga mountain range, which runs N of Lake Kivu and includes Rwanda's loftiest point, Volcan Karisimbi (14,787 ft/4,507 m). There is some lower land (at elevations below 3,000 ft/910 m) along the eastern shore of Lake Kivu and the Ruzizi River in the west and near the Tanzanian border in the east. The ethnic composition of the

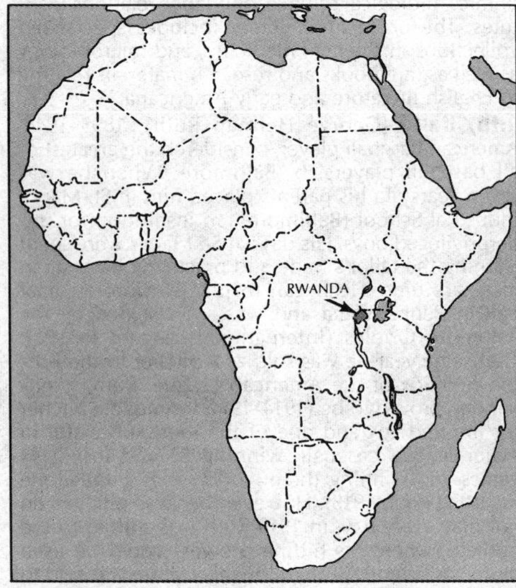

population is similar to that of Burundi. About 90% of the inhabitants are Hutu, agriculturalists who speak a Bantu language; 9% are Tutsi, who speak a Nilotic language; and 1% are Twa, who are a Pygmy group. Rwanda is the most densely populated country in Africa, and its population has a high annual growth rate that is usually between 3% and 3.5%. About half of the population follows traditional religious beliefs, and most of the rest are Roman Catholic. A small number of Tutsi are Muslim. Kinyarwanda and French are the official languages. The economy of Rwanda is overwhelmingly agricultural, with most of the workers engaged in subsistence farming. Economic development in Rwanda is hindered by the needs of its large and growing population and by its lack of easy access to the sea (and thus to foreign markets). The chief food crops are plantains, cassava, sweet potatoes, pulses, sorghum, and potatoes. The principal cash crops are coffee, tea, and pyrethrum. Large numbers of cattle, goats, and sheep are raised; most of the cattle are owned by the Tutsi, for whom they are a symbol of wealth and status more than a source of food. Tin ore (cassiterite), wolframite, beryl, and colombo-tantalite are mined in significant quantities, and natural gas (methane) is produced at Lake Kivu. Rwanda's industries are limited to small factories that manufacture textiles, chemicals, and basic consumer goods such as processed food, beverages (especially beer), clothing, and footwear. The country has a good road network but no railroads. The annual value of Rwanda's imports is usually considerably higher than its earnings from exports. The main imports are foodstuffs, textiles, clothing, machinery, motor vehicles, and fuel; the principal exports are coffee, tin ore, wolframite, tea, and pyrethrum. The chief trading partners are Belgium and Luxembourg, Uganda, Japan, West Germany, and Kenya. Rwanda depends on aid from Belgium and international agencies to balance its national budget, to finance foreign purchases, and to fund development projects. The early history of Rwanda is similar to that of BURUNDI. By the late 18th cent. a single Tutsi-ruled state occupied most of present-day Rwanda. It was headed by a *mwami* (king), who controlled regionally based vassals who were also Tutsi. They in turn dominated the Hutu, who, then as now, made up the vast majority of the population. Rwanda reached the height of its power under Mutara II (reigned early 19th cent.) and Kigeri IV (reigned 1853–95). Kigeri established a standing army, equipped with guns purchased from traders from the E African coast, and prohibited most foreigners from entering his kingdom. However, in 1890, Rwanda accepted German overrule without resistance and became part of GERMAN EAST AFRICA. A German administrative officer was assigned to Rwanda only in 1907; in fact the Germans had virtually no influence over the affairs of the country and initiated no economic development. During World War I, Belgian forces occupied (1916) Rwanda, and in 1919 it became part of the Belgian League of Nations mandate of RUANDA-URUNDI (which in 1946 became a UN trust territory). Until the last years of Belgian rule the traditional social structure of Rwanda was not altered; however, considerable Christian missionary work was undertaken. In 1957 the Hutu issued a manifesto calling for a change in Rwanda's power structure that would give them a voice in the country's affairs commensurate with their numbers. Two Hutu political parties were formed: the Association for the Social Improvement of the Masses, led by Joseph Gitera, and the Party of the Hutu Emancipation Movement (Parmehutu), led by Grégoire Kayibanda. In 1959, Mutara III died and was succeeded by Kigeri V. The Hutu contended that the new *mwami* had not been properly chosen and fighting between the Hutu and the Tutsi (who were aided by the Twa) broke out. The Hutu emerged victorious, and some 100,000 Tutsi, including the new *mwami*, fled to neighboring countries. The Hutu parties won the election of 1960, and Kayibanda became interim prime minister. In early 1961 a republic was proclaimed, and it was confirmed in the UN-supervised referendum later in the year. Under pressure from the UN trusteeship council, Belgium granted independence to Rwanda on July 1, 1962. Under the constitution adopted in Nov., 1962, Rwanda was headed by a president, who was also prime minister and whose considerable power included effective control of the 47-member national assembly. Kayibanda was elected as the first president and was re-elected in 1965 and 1969. In 1964, following an incursion from Burundi, which continued to be controlled by its Tutsi aristocracy, many Tutsi were killed in Rwanda, and numerous others left the country. In 1967–68 relations with Zaïre were temporarily strained when some white mercenaries involved in fighting in that country took refuge in Rwanda. In 1971–72, relations with Uganda were bitter after President Idi Amin of Uganda accused Rwanda of aiding groups trying to overthrow him. In Feb. and March, 1973, there was renewed fighting between the Hutu and Tutsi, and some 600 Tutsi fled to Uganda. On July 5, 1973, on the eve of presidential elections in which Kayibanda was the only candidate, a military group toppled Kayibanda without violence and replaced him as head of state with Maj. Gen. Juvénal Habyalimana, the commander of the national guard. The Parmehutu party (since independence known officially as the Republican Democratic Movement-Parmehutu), the only legal party in the country, was suspended and the national assembly dissolved. Habyalimana, a Hutu from the northern part of the country, tried to improve relations between the Hutu and the Tutsi and to distribute power more evenly among the Hutu. See Jan Vansina, *Évolution du Royaume Rwanda des origines à 1900* (1962); William Roger Louis, *Ruanda-Urundi, 1884–1919* (1963); René Lemarchand, *Rwanda and Burundi* (1970).

Ryan, Loch (lŏkh rī'ən), inlet, 9 mi (14.5 km) long and 3½ mi (5.6 km) wide, at the mouth of the Firth of Clyde, Wigtownshire, SW Scotland. The port of Stranraer is at the head of the sheltered loch.

Ryazan (ryəzän'yə), city (1970 pop. 357,000), capital of Ryazan oblast, E central European USSR, on the Oka River. Industries include oil refining, lignite processing, and the manufacture of machine tools and agricultural and transport equipment. The city has extensive piers, and river trade is carried on in agricultural products. One of Russia's oldest cities, Ryazan was founded in 1095 and became the capital of the Ryazan principality when the Mongols destroyed Old Ryazan (see SPASSK-RYAZANSKI) in 1237. It was annexed by Moscow in 1521 and was called Pereyaslavl-Ryazan until 1778, when it became a city. Ryazan retains much medieval architecture and has picturesque churches with many-colored domes and gilded ornaments. A kremlin wall, dating from 1208, surrounds two former monasteries built in the 15th and the 17th cent. Ryazan has the Archangel Cathedral (late 15th–early 16th cent.) and the Uspenski or Assumption Cathedral (1693–99). The former archiepiscopal palace is now a museum.

Rybinsk (rĭ'bĭnsk), city (1970 pop. 218,000), NE European USSR, on the upper Volga and the RYBINSK RESERVOIR. The site of a hydroelectric station, it is a major inland port with shipyards and factories producing road-building equipment, cables, and printing presses. Known since 1137, it has been a trade and shipping center for traffic between Moscow and Arkhangelsk since the 16th cent. In the 1870s it developed as a shipping point to St. Petersburg (now Leningrad). The construction of the Volga-Neva canal system increased its importance as a river port. Between 1946 and 1958 the city was called Shcherbakov.

Rybinsk Reservoir, artificial lake, c.2,000 sq mi (5,200 sq km), NW European USSR. It was formed in 1941 between the upper Volga River and its tributaries, the Mologa and Sheksna rivers, with the completion of the dam and hydroelectric station at Rybinsk. The reservoir is the southernmost component of the VOLGA-BALTIC WATERWAY.

Rybnik (rĭb'nēk), town (1970 pop. 43,415), S Poland. It is a railway junction and industrial center with industries manufacturing mining machinery, metal products, and chemicals. There are coal mines and coke plants nearby. Originally a fish hatchery (established c.1100) noted for its carp, it was chartered in the 14th cent. Rybnik passed from Germany to Poland in 1921. The town has a feudal castle and an 18th-century city hall.

Rydberg, Abraham Viktor (ä'brähäm vĭk'tôr rüd'bĕryə), 1828–95, Swedish philosopher and writer. *Singoalla* (1857), a romantic and mystical story of medieval times, was his first major work. His polemical novel *The Last Athenian* (1859, tr. 1869) contrasted Hellenic tolerance and humanism with Christian dogmatism and bigotry. In *The Teaching of the Bible about Christ* (1862), he opposed fundamentalist Christian views. Rydberg's verse is distinguished for its majestic lyricism and for its sense of the mystery of man's existence.

Rydberg, Johannes Robert (yo͞o'hänəs rô'bərt rüd'bĕryə), 1854–1919, Swedish physicist. Rydberg was a professor at Lund from 1901 to 1919. He is best known for his grouping of the frequencies of certain lines of the emission spectra of the elements into simple series characterized by a running integer and a universal "Rydberg" constant. These series helped guide the development of atomic physics. Rydberg also wrote on the structure of the periodic table of the elements.

Rydberg constant (rĭd'bərg), physical constant used in studies of the SPECTRUM of a substance. Its value for hydrogen is 109,678 cm^{-1}.

Ryde (rīd), municipal borough (1971 pop. 23,171), on the Isle of Wight, S England, on Spithead channel. It is one of the leading resorts of the island.

Ryder, Albert Pinkham, 1847–1917, American painter, b. New Bedford, Mass. In 1867 his family moved to New York City. There he studied with W. E. Marshall, the engraver, and at the National Academy of Design, but he was largely self-taught. Except for several brief trips abroad, most of his life was spent in New York. He devoted all his energy to his paintings, on which he worked over and over, often for years. He experimented constantly with the oil medium, loading his canvases with layers of paint, often not allowing surfaces time to dry. Unfortunately, many of his experiments were unsuccessful, and his paintings have deteriorated markedly. Ryder produced only about 160 canvases, now considered among the finest American works of art. Although small in size, they have grandeur of design and feeling, great luminosity, and subtle color. Moonlight and the sea predominate in Ryder's highly imaginative paintings, which are remarkable in their power to evoke a lonely and poetic mood. His later works appear to be painted dreams. All his life Ryder was afflicted with an eye malady that made focusing on small details or looking at bright light painful. Freeing himself, therefore, from the literal depiction of the natural world, Ryder expressed the mysterious forces of nature in rhythmic and somber masses. His tendency toward abstraction has linked him with the modern movement. Notable examples of his art are in most of the important American galleries; the Brooklyn and Metropolitan museums, New York City, and the National and Phillips Memorial galleries, Washington, D.C., have the largest collections. *Toilers of the Sea* (Metropolitan Mus.), *Death on a Pale Horse* (Cleveland Mus.), and *The Flying Dutchman* (National Gall., Washington, D.C.) are much loved and characteristic works. In American painting Ryder's works were among those most often forged. See catalog by Whitney Museum (1947); studies by F. M. Price (1932) and Lloyd Goodrich (1959).

Rydz-Śmigły or **Śmigły-Rydz, Edward** (rĭts'-shmē̆g'lĭ), 1886–1941, Polish politician. He served under Pilsudski in the Polish Legions (1914–17), in the war with the USSR (1920), and in the coup d'etat of 1926. At Pilsudski's death and in accordance with his wish, Rydz-Śmigły succeeded him (1935) as inspector general of the army; in 1936 he was named "first citizen after the president" and marshal of Poland. A virtual dictator, he fostered the Ozon [Camp of National Unity], a government party that dominated parliament. When Germany and the USSR invaded Poland, he fled (Sept., 1939) to Rumania.

Rye, municipal borough (1971 pop. 4,434), East Sussex, SE England, on the Rother River. It is a tourist resort and small port. There are boatbuilding and netmaking industries. Rye was one of the "ancient towns" added to the CINQUE PORTS. It had a thriving trade in the 17th cent. but decayed after the recession of the sea early in the 19th cent. There are remains of an ancient friary, a large Norman and Early English church, the 12th-century Ypres Tower, and Pocock's school (1636). The dramatist John Fletcher was born in Rye.

Rye, city (1970 pop. 15,869), Westchester co., SE N.Y., a suburb of New York City, on Long Island Sound; settled 1660, inc. as a city 1942. It is chiefly residential, with a cancer-research center, a hardware and locks manufacturing company, and several corporate offices. In colonial times it was the first stop on the Boston Post Road after New York City. The old Square House, an inn where many Revolutionary notables stayed, is now a museum. Playland, a large county-owned amusement park, is on the beach there. Chief Justice John Jay is buried in Rye.

rye, cereal GRAIN of the family Gramineae (GRASS family). The grain, *Secale cereale*, is important chiefly in Central and N Europe. It seems to have been domesticated later than wheat and other staple grains; cultivated rye is quite similar to the wild forms and no traces of it have been found among Egyptian ruins or Swiss lake dwellings. Where it grows well, wheat is preferred, but rye will produce a good crop on soil too poor or in a climate too cool to produce a good crop of wheat. The standard *schwarzbrot*, or pumpernickel, of Europe was formerly the major rye product. A bread of lighter color, called rye bread, is made of rye flour mixed with wheat flour. Today rye is used mostly as a stock feed (usually mixed with other grains), for hay and pasturage, for green manure, and as a cover crop. The Soviet Union leads in world production. Rye is much used as a distillers' grain in making whisky and gin. The tough straw of rye is valued for many purposes, e.g., thatching for roofs and stuffing for horse collars. ERGOT is a fungus disease of rye; the fungus is poisonous and may make the rye unsafe to use. Wild rye and lyme grass are names for several grasses of the genus *Elymus*, some of which are occasionally planted as ornamentals or used for binding sand. Rye is classified in the division MAGNOLIOPHYTA, class Liliatae, order Cyperales, family Gramineae.

rye grass, short-lived perennial, leafy, tufted plant belonging to the family Gramineae (GRASS family). Two species are grown in the United States—Italian rye grass (*Lolium multiflorum*), the leading hay grass of Europe, and English, or perennial, rye grass (*L. perenne*). In parts of the United States where winters are mild, both are sowed, often mixed with other grains, for pasturage. Italian rye grass is much used for lawns in warmer regions of the United States. Perennial rye grass was probably the first of all perennial grasses to be cultivated pure for forage. Poison rye grass, or darnel (*L. temulentum*), reputed to be poisonous, grows in grain fields and waste places; it is thought to be the tare of the Bible. Rye grass is classified in the division MAGNOLIOPHYTA, class Liliatae, order Cyperales, family Gramineae.

Rye House Plot, 1683, conspiracy to assassinate Charles II of England and his brother James, duke of

York (later James II), as they passed by Rumbold's Rye House in Hertfordshire on the road from Newmarket to London. However, the king did not make the journey on the expected day; the plot, an offshoot of earlier insurrection plots hatched by the 1st earl of SHAFTESBURY, was revealed. Although the actual conspirators were only minor figures, the great Whig leaders Lord William RUSSELL and Algernon SIDNEY were executed on flimsy evidence of guilt by association.

Ryerson, Egerton (Adolphus Egerton Ryerson), 1803–82, Canadian clergyman and educator, b. Ontario. He was a founder (1829) and the first editor of the *Christian Guardian*, a Methodist periodical that achieved wide circulation under his guidance. His attack (1826) on the powerful Church of England clergyman John Strachan, exponent of clergy reserves and ecclesiastical control of education, was the beginning of many years of political controversy. Ryerson founded and was first president (1841) of Victoria College, Cobourg (later Victoria Univ.). He was superintendent (1844–76) of public schools in Upper Canada. The school system of Ontario, largely his creation, served as a model for other provincial school systems. See biography by Clara Thomas (1969); J. H. Putnam, *Egerton Ryerson and Education in Upper Canada* (1912).

Rykov, Aleksey Ivanovich (əlyĭksyā' ēvä'nəvĭch rē'kôf), 1881–1938, Russian revolutionary and Communist leader. A Bolshevik, he became commissar for the interior after the October Revolution of 1917 and a member of the Politburo in 1922. On Lenin's death (1924) he succeeded as chairman of the council of commissars (i.e., premier of the USSR). However, the real political power was exercised by the triumvirate of STALIN, KAMENEV, and ZINOVIEV. Rykov was accused (1930) of "rightist deviation" because of his opposition to Stalin's drastic collectivization program, and he was expelled from the Politburo. Molotov succeeded him as premier. Rykov recanted in 1931 and received a secondary post. He was a victim of the party purges of the 1930s and was executed after a public trial for treason.

Ryks Museum: see RIJKS MUSEUM.

Ryle, Gilbert, 1900–, British philosopher. A graduate of Oxford, he became a tutor at Christ Church, Oxford, and later was Waynflete professor of metaphysical philosophy (1945–68) there. From 1947 to 1971 he was editor of the philosophical journal *Mind*. Like Ludwig Wittgenstein, Ryle was concerned with problems caused by the confusion of grammatical with logical distinctions. He pointed out the so-called "category mistake," in which, usually because of a grammatical equivalence, two things are mistakenly treated as belonging to equivalent logical categories. In his *Concept of Mind* (1949), Ryle argued against the common categorization of the mind and the body as separate but equivalent. He held that the mind is not a theoretical counterpart to the body, "a ghost in a machine," but a part of the body's activity; all references to the mental must be understood in terms of, at least theoretically, witnessable activities. His other works include *Dilemmas* (1954), *Plato's Progress* (1966), and *Collected Papers* (2 vol., 1971). See study by Laird Addis and Douglas Lewis (1965).

Rymer, Thomas (rī'mər), 1643?–1713, English critic and historiographer. Educated at Cambridge and Gray's Inn, he was called to the bar in 1673 but turned his efforts instead to literature, especially drama. Although in 1678 he did publish *Edgar, or the English Monarch*, a play in rhymed verse, he was especially interested in drama criticism. In his treatise *The Tragedies of the Last Age* (1677) he was fanatically hostile toward contemporary dramatists, and in *A Short View of Tragedy* (1692) he labeled Shakespeare's *Othello* "a bloody farce without salt or savour." Made historiographer royal in 1692, Rymer began (1693) to edit a work bringing together all public documents showing relations between England and other nations from 1101 to 1654. This work, called *Foedera* (1704–35), was modeled after Leibniz's *Codex juris gentium diplomaticus*; the last 5 of the 20 volumes were edited by Robert Sanderson. See preface to T. D. Hardy's *Syllabus of Rymer's "Foedera"* (1869–85); C. A. Zimansky, ed., *The Critical Works of Thomas Rymer* (1956, repr. 1971).

Ryswick, Netherlands: see RIJSWIJK.

Ryswick, Treaty of, 1697, the pact that ended the War of the GRAND ALLIANCE. Its signers were France on one side and England, Spain, and the Netherlands on the other. It was a setback for LOUIS XIV, who kept Strasbourg but lost most other conquests made after 1679. Commercial concessions were granted the Dutch, the independence of Savoy was recognized, and William III was acknowledged king of England.

Ryti, Risto (rē'stō rü'tē), 1889–1956, Finnish political leader. In 1919 he was elected to the Finnish diet. He later served as minister of finance (1921–24) and as governor of the Bank of Finland (1923–44), winning admiration for improving the country's international credit despite its war debt and the effects of the depression. Prime minister during the Russo-Finnish War of 1939 and 1940, he became president of Finland in late 1940. Ryti's alliance with Germany against the Soviet Union in World War II resulted in his resignation in 1944 after Finland's defeat. The following year, in a Soviet-sponsored trial, he was convicted as a war criminal. In 1949, Ryti's 10-year sentence was commuted because of his deteriorating health.

Ryukyu Islands (rēōō'kyōō), Jap. *Ryukyu-retto* or *Nansei-shoto* [southwest group], archipelago (1970 est. pop. 1,235,000), c.1,850 sq mi (4,790 sq km), SW Japan, in the W Pacific Ocean. The chain stretches about 650 mi (1,050 km) between Taiwan and Japan, separating the East China Sea from the Philippine Sea. The Ryukyus are composed of three principal groups: they are, from north to south, the Amami Islands (part of Kagoshima prefecture), the Okinawa Islands, and the Sakishima Islands (both part of Okinawa prefecture). OKINAWA is the largest and most important island of the Ryukyus. The islands are the exposed tops of submarine mountains and are of volcanic or coral origin; there are several active volcanoes in the group. Although the islands are low, with few points above 2,000 ft (610 m), they have rugged hills and little flatland. The Ryukyus have a subtropical climate with much rain and are often hit by typhoons. The chief agricultural products are sugarcane, sweet potatoes, pineapples, and rice. Fishing is also important to the economy. Some light industry is found in NAHA, Okinawa, the Ryukyus' largest city. Sugar and canned pineapples account for most of the exports. The inhabitants speak a language said to be related to Ainu. The islands were the site of an ancient independent kingdom that had its capital at Shuri, on Okinawa. The Chinese reached the islands in the 7th cent. but did not exact tribute until the 14th cent. In the 17th cent. the Japanese prince of Satsuma invaded the islands, which thereafter paid tribute to both Japan and China. Commodore Matthew Perry of the U.S. navy landed in the Ryukyus in 1853. The entire archipelago was incorporated into the Japanese empire in 1879, but the islands were generally neglected by Japan. During World War II the Ryukyus were the scene of fierce fighting between U.S. and Japanese forces, with the United States winning control of the islands in 1945. After the war the islands south of lat. 30°N were placed (Aug., 1945) under a U.S. military governor at Naha. The Ryukyus became a key salient of the U.S. Pacific defense perimeter, and major military bases were established on Okinawa. In 1951, at the San Francisco Peace Conference, the Japanese were given residual sovereignty over the islands, but the United States retained actual control. The Amami group was returned to Japan in 1953. The Japanese desire to regain the remaining U.S.-held islands was a source of friction between the two countries for nearly two decades. In 1962 the occupation administration was liberalized, and in 1968, after a series of negotiations, the United States permitted the popular election of the governor of the Ryukyus and the seating of Ryukyu representatives in the Japanese Diet. The archipelago was returned to Japan in May, 1972. The United States was allowed to retain its military bases subject to certain limitations. Other forms of the name are Luchu, Loo-choo, Liu-kiu, and Riukiu.

Ryun, Jim (James Ronald Ryun), 1947–, American track runner, b. Wichita, Kan. One of the greatest milers in the history of track, Ryun, who did not make the team in his freshman year in high school, was voted athlete of the year by three different groups in 1966. In that year he set a world record for the mile (3 min 51.3 sec), and in 1967 he surpassed his own record with a time of 3 min 51.1 sec. Ryun quit running in 1969, but returned to the sport in 1971 and became a professional shortly afterward.

Rzeszów (zhĕ'shōōf), city (1970 pop. 82,192), capital of Rzeszów prov., SE Poland. It is a railway junction and an important industrial center, whose major industries produce rolling stock, machinery, metals, building materials, foodstuffs, and clothing. An old commercial settlement, Rzeszów was chartered c.1340. Casimir the Great of Poland later awarded the city to a nobleman in return for military service during Mongol raids. Rzeszów passed to Austria in 1772; it reverted to Poland in 1919. Its many historic buildings include a 17th-century castle and an 18th-century town hall. The city also has two colleges and numerous cultural facilities.

Rzhev (ərzhĕf'), city (1970 pop. 61,000), NW European USSR, on the Volga River and on a major rail line to Moscow. It has textile plants and repair shops for railroad equipment. Rzhev, an ancient trade center, was controlled by the Smolensk principality in the 12th cent. and taken by Novgorod in 1216. During World War II it was fortified by the Germans as a major bastion on their northern defense line.

S

S, 19th letter of the ALPHABET, representing the common sibilant, voiceless in *spur,* voiced in *rose.* Its Greek equivalent is sigma. In former times the nonterminal *s* was written or printed much like an *f* without the right half of the cross bar. In chemistry S is the symbol of the element SULFUR.

Sá, Mem de (mãN dĭ sä), d. 1572, Portuguese colonial official, governor general of Brazil (1557?–1572). He drove (1567) the French colony from Guanabara Bay and founded the city of Rio de Janeiro at its site.

Saadi: see SADI.

Saadia ben Joseph al-Fayumi (sä'dēä, äl-fīyo͞o'mē), 882–942, Jewish scholar, b. Egypt. He was known as Saadia Gaon. He was the head of the great Jewish Academy at Sura, Babylonia, which under his leadership became the highest seat of learning among the Jews, and a vigorous opponent of the KARAITES. Saadia's *Book of Language* laid the foundation of Hebrew grammar; he also wrote a Hebrew dictionary, called the *Agron,* and made an Arabic translation of the Old Testament that became the standard version for all Arabic-speaking Jews and exerted an important influence upon Muslims as well. His great philosophical work, *The Book of Beliefs and Opinions,* was translated by Samuel Rosenblatt (1948). See David Druck, *Saadya Gaon* (1942); S. L. Skoss, *Saadia Gaon, the Earliest Hebrew Grammarian* (1955); Henry Malter, *Saadia Gaon: His Life and Works* (1926, repr. 1969); Israel Efros, *Studies in Medieval Jewish Philosophy* (1974).

Saale (zäl'ə), river, c.265 mi (430 km) long, rising in the Fichtelgebirge, E West Germany, and flowing generally N through SW East Germany, past Jena, Naumberg (the head of navigation), and Halle, to the Elbe River SE of Magdeburg. The Weisser Elster, Ilm, and Unstrut are the chief tributaries. The Saale's picturesque course is flanked by numerous medieval castles. Sugar beets are grown in the fertile lower valley. There are two large reservoirs on the upper part of the river in East Germany. It is also called the Sächsische (Saxonian) or Thüringer Saale to distinguish it from the Fränkische (Franconian) Saale, which flows 84 mi (135 km) SW from the Thüringer Wald, through central West Germany, to the Main River.

Saalfeld (zäl'fĕlt), city (1970 pop. 33,405), Gera district, S East Germany, on the Thüringer Saale River. Manufactures include machine tools, electrical equipment, and dyes. Iron is mined and slate is quarried nearby. Saalfeld was founded c.1200 and in the 16th cent. was a silver-mining center. It was the capital of the duchy of Saxe-Saalfeld from 1680 to 1735. In 1806 the French defeated the Prussians there during the Napoleonic Wars. The duke of SAXE-COBURG exchanged (1826) Saalfeld for Gotha with the duke of Saxe-Meiningen. Noteworthy buildings of the city include a 14th-century church, a 16th-century city hall, a 13th-century Franciscan monastery (now a museum), a 13th-century castle, and an 18th-century palace.

Saar, Ferdinand von (fĕr'dēnänt fən zär), 1833–1906, Austrian writer. His best works are his short stories, among them the two collections (1876, 1897) of *Novellen aus Österreich* [tales from Austria]. Saar was of the decadent school, and the people he portrayed were generally weak failures. Some of his later writings place him with the more sympathetic naturalists.

Saar, region: see SAARLAND.

Saar (zär), Fr. *Sarre,* river, c.150 mi (240 km) long, rising in the Vosges mts., NE France, and flowing N past Sarrebourg and Sarreguemines. It enters Saarland, W West Germany, and continues NW past Saarbrücken into the Moselle River near Trier. The river flows through a heavily industrialized region; it carries much barge traffic.

Saarbrücken (zär"brük'ən), Fr. *Sarrebruck,* city (1970 pop. 127,989), capital of Saarland, W West Germany, on the Saar River near the French border. It is the leading industrial center of the Saar coal basin and is a rail junction. Manufactures include precision instruments, machinery, metal goods, printed materials, and beer. Located on the site of earlier Celtic, Roman, and Frankish settlements, Saarbrücken was chartered in 1321. It was the capital of the counts of Nassau-Saarbrücken, a dependency of the Walramian counts of Nassau, from 1381 until its occupation (1793) by the French. The city passed to Prussia in 1815. From 1919 to 1935 and again from 1945 to 1957, Saarbrücken was included in and was the capital of the French-administered Saar Territory (see SAARLAND). Although badly damaged in World War II, the city retains the 15th-century late Gothic Castle Church, the old city hall (1750), and a baroque church, the Ludwigskirche (1762–75). The city is the site of the Univ. of the Saarland.

Saare: see SAREMA, island, USSR.

Saaremaa: see SAREMA, island, USSR.

Saarinen, Eero (ā'rō sä'rĭnĕn), 1910–61, Finnish-American architect, son of Eliel Saarinen. Saarinen's reputation was established with his design of the General Motors Technical Center, Warren, Mich. (1951–55). His innovations are significant, particularly in domical construction. At the Massachusetts Institute of Technology he built in 1955 the circular brick chapel and also the auditorium, notable for its thin-shelled concrete dome. He followed the principles of suspension bridge construction in the David S. Ingalls Hockey Rink at Yale (1958) and created soaring intersecting concrete vaults for the Trans World Airlines Terminal at Kennedy International Airport, New York City. He erected many collegiate buildings, including those at Concordia Senior College, Fort Wayne, Ind.; Vassar; and the Univ. of Chicago. He also designed the American embassies at London and Oslo. Saarinen died before the completion of two of his greatest projects, the Dulles International Airport at Chantilly, Va., and two polygonal college buildings at Yale. See *Eero Saarinen On His Work,* ed. by A. Saarinen (rev. ed. 1968).

Saarinen, Eliel (ĕl'ēĕl), 1873–1950, Finnish-American architect and city planner, resident of the United States after 1923. In Finland, Saarinen's most celebrated building was the railway station in Helsinki. He took second prize in the Chicago *Tribune* Tower competition in 1922. At the Cranbrook Foundation he designed several buildings and also headed the Academy of Art. His other major works include the Crow Island Elementary School, Winnetka, Ill. (1939); two churches in Columbus, Ind. (1941–42), and Minneapolis, Minn. (1949), and the music shed for the Berkshire Festival at Tanglewood, Mass. His later designs were made in collaboration with his son, Eero Saarinen.

Saarland (zär'länt), state (1970 pop. 1,120,000), 991 sq mi (2,567 sq km), SW West Germany. The region encompassed by the state was formerly called the Saar or the Saar Territory. Saarbrücken is the capital; other cities include Völklingen, Saarlouis, and Sankt Ingbert. The state is bounded by France in the south and west, by Luxembourg in the northwest, and by Rhineland-Palatinate in the north and east. A region of low, partly wooded hills, Saarland is drained by the Saar River. The state is highly industrialized, with a large iron and steel industry based on vast coal fields. The Warndt deposit, in the south, is particularly valuable for its coking coal, necessary in the production of steel; iron ore is imported from the neighboring Lorraine basin in France. Other manufactures of the Saarland include metal goods, glass, chemicals, and textiles. Agricultural production is limited. The state is served by a dense rail net and is connected with the Rhine-Marne Canal. The population is German-speaking and largely Roman Catholic. There is a university at Saarbrücken. The Saarland possessed little unity before the 20th cent. Until 1797, when it was ceded to France by the Treaty of Campo Formio, it was divided among France (which held the city of Saarlouis and the adjacent territory), the county of Saarbrücken (a dependency of Nassau), and the palatine duchy of Zweibrücken. The Treaty of Paris of 1815 divided the territory between Bavaria (i.e., the Bavarian or Rhenish Palatinate) and Prussia. The Saar Territory came into existence as a political unit when the Treaty of Versailles (1919) made it an autonomous territory, administered by France under League of Nations supervision, pending a plebiscite to be held in 1935 to determine its final status. France also received the right to exploit its coal fields until that time. When more than 90% of the votes cast in the plebiscite favored its reunion with Germany, the Saar was restored (March, 1935) to Germany and constituted the Saarland prov. During World War II, Hitler incorporated it (1940) with Lorraine (annexed from France) into the province of Westmark. The scene of heavy fighting at the close of the war (1944–45), the Saarland was placed under French military occupation in 1945 and in 1947 was given an autonomous government. In a referendum (1947) the population voted for economic union with France, and in 1948 a customs union went into effect. Strong West German claims to the Saar, however, were a serious cause of friction in postwar Franco-German relations. An agreement between France and West Germany in 1954 (see PARIS PACTS) provided for an autonomous Saar under a neutral commissioner to be named by the Western European Union; the economic union with France was to be maintained for 50 years. However, the agreement was rejected (Oct., 1955) by the Saarlanders in a popular referendum, and, in accordance with subsequent Franco-German agreements (1956), the Saar Territory became (Jan. 1, 1957) a state (Saarland) of the Federal Republic of Germany. The agreements permitted France to extract coal from the Warndt deposit until 1981, but the customs union with France was dissolved in July, 1959, whereupon the Saarland became economically integrated with West Germany.

Saarlouis (zär"lo͞o'ē), Fr. *Sarrelouis,* city (1970 pop. 37,741), Saarland, W West Germany, on the Saar River near the French border. It is a commercial and industrial center. Manufactures include steel, furniture, tobacco products, and bells. Coal is mined in the area. Founded (1680) by Louis XIV, for whom it was named, Saarlouis was fortified (1680–85) by Vauban and became a major French frontier fortress. It was awarded (1815) to Prussia at the Congress of Vienna. As part of the Saar Territory (see SAARLAND), it was administered by France from 1919 to 1935 and from 1945 to 1957. From 1935 to 1945 the city was known as Saarlautern. Marshal Ney of France was born there in 1769.

Saar Territory: see SAARLAND.

Saavedra, Ángel de, duque de Rivas: see RIVAS, ÁNGEL DE SAAVEDRA, DUQUE DE.

Saavedra, Hernandarias de: see ARIAS DE SAAVEDRA, HERNANDO.

Saavedra Lamas, Carlos (kär'lōs sävä'thrä lä'mäs), 1880–1959, Argentine statesman, foreign minister (1932–38). An advocate of Pan-Americanism and of the League of Nations (he was president of the Assembly in 1936), he presided over several international conferences. He drafted (1932) an antiwar pact adopted (1933–34) by many American republics, and together with Argentine president Agustín Pedro JUSTO he was instrumental in bringing an end to the war over the CHACO. Saavedra Lamas received the 1936 Nobel Peace Prize.

Saavedra y Fajardo, Diego de (dyā'gō thā sävā'thrä ē fähär'thō), 1584–1648, Spanish writer and diplomat in the reign of Philip IV. His chief works are *Empresas políticas* [political maxims] (1640), a political treatise widely translated and read in the 17th cent., and *República literaria* [the literary republic] (1655), a work of literary criticism.

Saaz, Johannes von: see JOHANNES VON SAAZ.

Saaz: see ŽATEC, Czechoslovakia.

Saba: see SHEBA.

Saba (sä'bə), island (1969 est. pop. 972), 5 sq mi (13 sq km), Netherlands Antilles (see CURAÇAO), one of the NW Leeward Islands. The rugged island is actually the cone of an extinct volcano rising to c.2,800 ft (850 m). Spiral roads winding up through steep cliffs and lush greenery make Saba a scenic island, but there are no sheltered harbors, and landing is difficult. The chief settlement, called The Bottom, is in the crater of the volcano. Fishing and boat building are the principal occupations. The Dutch settled the island in 1632.

Sabadell (säbäthĕl'), city (1970 pop. 159,408), Barcelona prov., NE Spain, in Catalonia. Since medieval times, it has been a leading textile center. Diesel engines, electrical equipment, and fertilizers are also made.

Sabae (säbä'ā), city (1970 pop. 52,614), Fukui prefecture, central Honshu, Japan. It is an agricultural market with textile and chemical industries.

Sabaeans: see SHEBA.

Sabah (sä'bä), state (1971 pop. 655,622), 29,545 sq mi (76,522 sq km), Malaysia, N Borneo, on the South China and Sulu seas. It is bordered on the south by Kalimantan (Indonesian Borneo). The capital is KOTA KINABALU; other important towns are SANDAKAN and Victoria (on Labuan Island). The terrain is densely forested and mountainous; Mt. Kinabalu, the highest peak in Malaysia, is 13,455 ft (4,101 m) high. Forest products, rubber, and copra are exported. Formerly called North Borneo or British North Borneo, the area was made a British protectorate in 1882. In 1963 it joined the Federation of Malaysia and assumed its present name. The Philippines have also claimed Sabah.

Sabalan or **Savalan** (sä"vəlän'), volcanic cone, 15,592 ft (4,752 m) high, NW Iran, near Ardabil. The prophet Zoroaster reputedly wrote the *Avesta* there.

Sabaoth (săb'āōth, -ōth, săbā'əth), Hebrew term used in the New Testament (Rom. 9.29; James 5.4) and in Christian hymns (e.g. SANCTUS and *Te Deum*) in the title of God, translated in the Old Testament "Lord of Hosts" (Isa. 1.9).

sabatia: see GENTIAN.

Sabatier, Auguste (ôgōōst' säbätyä'), 1839–1901, French Protestant theologian. He was professor (1867–72) of reformed dogmatics at Strasbourg, and from 1877 until his death he was a member of the Protestant theological faculty of the Sorbonne, Paris. Sabatier became noted as a liberal theologian, stressing the subjective, symbolic nature of religious knowledge and the need for continual revision of religious dogmas in the light of personal experience. Among English translations of his works are *The Apostle Paul* (1891), *Religion and Modern Culture* (1897), *Outlines of a Philosophy of Religion* (1897), and *Religions of Authority and the Religion of the Spirit* (1904). See Thomas Silkstone, *Religion, Symbolism and Meaning* (1968).

Sabatier, Paul, 1858–1928, French Protestant clergyman and historian; brother of Auguste Sabatier. Ill-health required his withdrawal from the active ministry, and he went to Assisi, Italy; there he studied the life of St. Francis. His subsequent *Life of St. Francis of Assisi* (1893) was widely translated and has passed through a number of editions. In 1919, Sabatier became professor of Protestant theology at Strasbourg.

Sábato, Ernesto (ārnās'tō sä'bätō), 1911–, Argentinian novelist and literary critic. Trained in physics, he was a professor of mathematical physics until 1945, when he turned to writing. His novels, *El túnel* (1948; tr. *The Outsider,* 1950) and *Sobre héroes y tumbas* [on heroes and tombs] (1962) treat man's inability to free himself from his psychological complexities. His volumes of literary criticism include *El escritor ye sus fantasmas* [the writer and his phantoms] (1963). See study by H. D. Oberhelman (1970).

Sabbatai Zevi (säbätī' zä'vē), 1626–76, Jewish mystic and pseudo-Messiah, founder of the Sabbatean sect, b. Smyrna. After a period of study of Lurianic Cabala (see LURIA, ISAAC BEN SOLOMON), he became deeply influenced by its ideas of imminent national redemption. In 1648 he proclaimed himself the Messiah, named the year 1666 as the millennium, and gathered a host of followers. In 1666 he attempted to land in Constantinople, was captured, and to escape death embraced Islam. Nevertheless, the influence of the Sabbatean movement survived for many years; it had secret adherents in the 18th cent. and was revived under Jacob FRANK. The name is also spelled Shabbatai Zvi. See G. G. Scholem, *Major Trends in Jewish Mysticism* (3d rev. ed. 1954, repr. 1967), *The Messianic Ideas in Judaism* (tr. 1971), and *Sabbatai Sevi, the Mystical Messiah* (tr. 1973).

Sabbatarians, persons who insist upon strict observance of Sunday as the SABBATH. Societies promoting Sabbatarian objectives include the Lord's Day Alliance of the United States and the Lord's Day Observance Society in England. In the United States, Sabbatarian laws, known as blue laws, which bar certain business and sporting activities on Sunday, are still effective in many states and localities. The term is also applied to those who observe the seventh day (Saturday) as the Sabbath, such as certain ADVENTISTS and the SEVENTH-DAY BAPTISTS.

Sabbath [Heb.,=repose], last day of the week (Saturday), observed as a rest day by the Jews. In the biblical account of creation (Gen. 1) the seventh day is set as a Sabbath to mark God's rest after his work. In Jewish law, starting with the Ten Commandments, the rules for the Sabbath are given in careful detail. Early Christians had a weekly celebration of the liturgy on the first day (Sunday), observing the Resurrection. Hence, in the Christian tradition, which survives among Roman Catholics and Orthodox, Sunday is a liturgical feast, and most penitential rules are relaxed then. Protestants, applying the idea of the Jewish Sabbath to Sunday, forbade all but pious activity then. The term "Lord's Day" was used, especially by Sabbatarians, to promote such observance (see BLUE LAWS). Some sects (e.g., SEVENTH-DAY BAPTISTS and Seventh-Day ADVENTISTS) replaced Sunday with Saturday. In Islam, Friday is the weekly day of public prayer.

Sabeans: see SHEBA.

Sabelli (səbĕl'ī), people of ancient Italy who spoke Oscan. They were a loose group and seemed to have had little or no political unity. Oscan-speaking tribes expanded over central Italy, and by the 5th cent. B.C. they seem to have taken ancient Campania and Lucania. The Samnites and Sabines were probably Sabelli. So-called Old Sabellic dialects were not Oscan but other non-Etruscan dialects.

Sabellius, fl. 215, Christian priest and theologian, b. probably Libya or Egypt. He went to Rome, became the leader of those who accepted the doctrine of modalistic MONARCHIANISM, and was excommunicated by Pope St. Calixtus I in 220. Opposing the orthodox teaching of "essential Trinity," Sabellius advanced the doctrine of the "economic Trinity." God, he held, was one indivisible substance, but with three fundamental activities, or modes, appearing successively as the Father (the creator and lawgiver), as the Son (the redeemer), and as the Holy Spirit (the maker of life and the divine presence within men). The term **Sabellianism** later was used to include all sorts of speculative ideas that had become attached to the original ideas of Sabellius and his followers. In the East, all monarchians came to be labeled Sabellians.

Sabians: see MANDAEANS.

Sabin, Albert Bruce (sā'bĭn), 1906–, American physician and microbiologist, b. Bialystock, Russia, grad. New York Univ. (B.S., 1928; M.D., 1931). He emigrated to the United States in 1921 and was naturalized in 1930. He conducted medical research for several organizations before joining (1939) the faculty at the Univ. of Cincinnati college of medicine; there he became (1946) professor of research pediatrics. He is known for his research on virus and other infectious diseases and for his development (c.1959) of a live-virus vaccine for immunization against POLIOMYELITIS. The Sabin vaccine may be taken orally and provides longer immunity than the killed-virus vaccine. Also, the killed-virus vaccine protects only against paralyzation, whereas the live vaccine guards against both paralyzation and infection.

Sabin, Joseph (săb'ĭn), 1821–81, American bibliophile, b. England. Sabin came to the United States in 1848 and established himself as a dealer in rare books in New York City and Philadelphia. He published the *American Bibliophilist* (1869–75), *Bibliography of Bibliography* (1877), and *Bibliotheca Americana,* better known as *A Dictionary of Books Relating to America* (begun in 1868 and continued by others after his death until 1892).

Sabine (săbēn'), river, c.575 mi (925 km) long, rising on the prairies NE of Dallas, Texas. It flows SE across Texas, then south to mark the Texas-Louisiana line. Near its mouth it broadens to form Sabine Lake (c.17 mi/27 km long; c.7 mi/11.3 km wide), then goes through Sabine Pass to the Gulf of Mexico. The Neches River flows into the lake. Port Arthur, Texas, is on Sabine Lake, and Orange, Texas, is on the river. The Sabine-Neches Canal divides above Port Arthur, the west branch leading up the Neches River to Beaumont and the east branch flowing to Orange. Part of the Intracoastal Waterway, it permits ocean-going vessels to reach these cities.

Sabine Crossroads (săb"ēn'), locality, De Soto parish, NW La., near Mansfield. There in the Civil War, Union forces under Nathaniel P. BANKS, advancing on Shreveport, were defeated and driven back by Gen. Richard TAYLOR on April 8, 1864.

Sabines (sā'bīnz), ancient people of central Italy, centered principally in the Sabine Hills, NE of Rome. Not much dependable information on them can be gathered. They were probably Oscan-speaking and therefore may be classed among the Sabelli. From the earliest days there was a Sabine element in Rome (the story of the rape of the Sabine women to supply wives for the womanless followers of Romulus is a legend explaining this fact); many Roman religious practices are said to have Sabine origins. Rome was involved in numerous wars with the inland Sabines; Horatius is supposed to have defeated them in the 5th cent. B.C., and Marcus Curius Dentatus conquered them in 290 B.C. The Sabines became (268) Roman citizens. The Samnites were possibly a branch of the Sabines.

Sablé, Madeleine de Souvré, marquise de (mädəlĕn' də sōōvrā', märkēz' də säblā'), 1599–1678, French woman of letters. Her salon was in vogue after the decline of the salon at the Hôtel de Rambouillet; its circle included Mme de La Fayette, Philippe I, duc d'Orléans, and La Rochefoucauld. Mme de Sablé's maxims were published in 1678.

sable, species of MARTEN, *Martes zibellina,* found in Siberia, N Russia, and N Finland. This carnivorous mammal is highly valued for its thick, soft fur, which is dark brown or black, sometimes with white underparts and sometimes flecked with silver. Unrestricted hunting for several centuries has exterminated the sable in some regions and dangerously reduced it in others; it now survives chiefly in the mountains of the northernmost parts of its former range. Protection is now afforded in parts of Russia, and it is raised on farms. The fur of the American marten, *M. americana,* sometimes called the American sable, also commands a price, although not as high as that of the true sable. Sables are classified in the phylum CHORDATA, subphylum Vertebrata, class Mammalia, order Carnivora, family Mustelidae.

Sable, Cape, S Fla., southernmost extremity of the U.S. mainland. It is part of Everglades National Park.

Sable Island, low, sandy island, 25 mi (40 km) long and 1 mi (1.6 km) wide, off N.S., Canada, SE of Halifax. It is the exposed part of a sand shoal that stretches northeast-southwest for more than 100 mi (160 km). The island was known to mariners in the early 16th cent., and a small French semimilitary colony was there from 1598 to 1603. Known as the "graveyard of the Atlantic," Sable Island is a major hazard to navigation and has been the scene of many shipwrecks; it now has a lighthouse, a lifesaving station, and a radio beacon. The island is also a breeding place for seals, which are protected by the government.

Saboraim (säbōrä'ĭm) [Heb.,=expositors], title given to the Jewish scholars of the Babylonian academies in the period (6th–7th cent. A.D.) immediately following the AMORAIM and preceding that of the GAONIM. The Saboraim further explained the legal decisions of their predecessors and attempted to clarify certain ambiguities still found in the Talmudic text. They were responsible for the final redaction of the Babylonian Talmud, completing the work undertaken by the Amoraim. See H. L. Strack, *Introduction to the Talmud and Midrash* (1931, repr. 1969).

sabotage [Fr., *sabot*=wooden shoe; hence, to work clumsily], form of DIRECT ACTION by workers against employers through obstruction of work and/or lowering of plant efficiency. Methods range from peaceful slowing of production to destruction of property. In 1897, French workers adopted sabotage as a general strategy. It was also used by the syndicalists (see SYNDICALISM) and by the Industrial Workers of the World in the United States. It has been condemned by Communists and Socialists as counterrevolutionary because it often results in a wave of repressive measures. The term has also been used, notably by Thorstein Veblen, to refer to limitation of output by businessmen to enhance profits by maintaining scarcity of goods. In wartime it connotes nonmilitary enemy activity, by either foreign agents or native sympathizers, especially the physical damage of vital industries (see GUERRILLA WARFARE). Citizens of the Republic of South Africa, in opposition to the government, initiated over 200 incidents of sabotage between 1961 and 1964. See Émile Pouget, *Sabotage* (1910, tr. 1913); S. B. Mathewson, *Restriction of Output among Unorganized Workers* (1931); Edward Feit, *Urban Revolt in South Africa, 1960–1964: A Case Study* (1971).

Sabrina: see SEVERN, river, England.

Sabta or **Sabtah** (both: săb'tə), son of Cush. His descendants occupied a region of S Arabia. Gen. 10.7; 1 Chron. 1.9.

Sabtecha or **Sabtechah** (both: săb'tēkə, săbtē'-), son of Cush. His descendants apparently occupied regions near the Persian Gulf. Gen. 10.7; 1 Chron. 1.9.

Sabzevar (säbzĕvär′), city (1971 est. pop. 45,000), Khurasan prov., NE Iran. It is the trade center of a cotton-growing region. The city's manufactures include textiles and rugs.

Sacajawea (săk″əjəwē′ə, səkä″-), **Sacagawea** (-gəwē′ə), or **Sakakawea** (-kəwē′ə), c. 1784-1884?, North American Indian woman guide on the LEWIS AND CLARK EXPEDITION and the only woman to accompany the party. She is generally called the Bird Woman in English, although this translation has been challenged, and there has been much dispute about the form of her Indian name. She was a member of the Shoshone Indians, had been captured and sold to a Mandan Indian, and finally was traded to Toussaint Charbonneau, one of whose wives she became. He was interpreter for the expedition. She proved invaluable as a guide and interpreter when Lewis and Clark reached the upper Missouri River and the mountains from which she had come. On the return journey she and Charbonneau left (1806) the expedition at the Mandan villages. While some historians date Sacajawea's death around 1812, there are others who claim that she was discovered by a missionary in 1875 and that she actually died in Wyoming in 1884. See biography by H. P. Howard (1971).

Sac and Fox Indians, closely related North American Indians of the Algonquian branch of the Algonquian-Wakashan linguistic stock (see AMERICAN INDIAN LANGUAGES). For a long period they dwelt around Saginaw Bay in E Michigan, but in the early 17th cent. they were driven from this area by the allied Ottawa and Neutral groups. The Sac (also commonly written Sauk) and the Fox fled N across the Strait of Mackinac, then S into present Wisconsin. Thus in 1667, when visited by Father Claude Jean Allouez, they were settled around Green Bay in NE Wisconsin. They then numbered some 6,500. The Sac were enterprising farmers but spent much time hunting and raiding, although they never developed a soldier society to the degree that the Fox did. The Fox were fierce warriors and constantly waged war with the Ojibwa. Together, the Sac and Fox fought wars against the Sioux and the Illinois, as well as the French. The French, harassed by the Fox, waged a war of extermination; by 1730 they had reduced the Fox to a mere handful. The remnants of the tribe incorporated with their longstanding allies, the Sac, and from that time the two tribes have been known as the Sac and Fox. After the war with the Illinois (c.1765), the Sac and Fox moved into Illinois territory. In 1804 a fraudulent treaty was extracted from them, and they were told to move W of the Mississippi. Most of them refused to go, but by 1831 they were induced to cross the river into Iowa. By 1832, however, they were back on the east side of the river, attacking frontier settlements. This started the BLACK HAWK WAR. After that war they moved west, eventually settling on reservations in Iowa, Kansas, and Oklahoma. Today they number some 1,500. Sac and Fox culture was of the Eastern Woodlands area with some Plains area traits. See W. T. Hagan, *The Sac and Fox Indians* (1958); F. O. Gearing, *The Face of the Fox* (1970).

Sacar (sā′kər). **1** Father of Ahiam. 1 Chron. 11.35. Sharar: 2 Sam. 23.33. **2** Son of Obed-edom: 1 Chron. 26.4.

saccharin (săk′ərĭn), $C_7H_5NSO_3$, white, crystalline, aromatic compound. It was discovered accidentally by I. Remsen and C. Fahlberg in 1879. Pure saccharin tastes several hundred times as sweet as sugar. It is not readily soluble in water, but its sodium salt, which is sold commercially, dissolves readily. Saccharin has no nutritive value and is excreted unchanged by the body. It is used as a sweetener by persons who must limit their consumption of sugar.

Saccharomyces: see YEAST.

Sacchetti, Franco (frăng′kō säk-kĕt′tē), c.1330-1400, Italian author. He held a number of public offices in Florence and wrote lyric verse and moral discourses. He is best remembered for his *Novelle* (c.1378-c.1395), a collection of tales in the manner of the *Decameron*.

Sacchi, Andrea (ändrĕ′ä säk′kē), 1599-1661, Italian baroque painter, b. Rome. He studied in Rome and in Bologna under Francesco Albani. His masterpiece, an allegory of *Divine Wisdom* (c.1629-33; ceiling fresco, Barberini Palace, Rome) typifies his classical treatment of composition. Inspired by Raphael's ideal art, Sacchi was associated with Poussin and Algardi in the championing of classical theory, in contrast to the dynamic approach of Pietro da Cortona and Bernini. Sacchi's foremost pupil was MARATTI.

Sacchini, Antonio Maria Gasparo (äntô′nyō märē′ä gä′spärō säk-kē′nē), 1730-86, Italian operatic composer of the Neapolitan school. He wrote numerous operas, which were graceful and popular. His best work, *Oedipe à Colone* (1786) was in the repertory of the Paris Opéra for more than half a century. He also composed chamber music and oratorios.

Sacchis, Giovanni Antonio de: see PORDENONE.

Sacco-Vanzetti Case (săk′ō-vănzĕt′ē). On April 15, 1920, a paymaster for a shoe company in South Braintree, Mass., and his guard were shot and killed by two men who escaped with over $15,000. It was thought from reports of witnesses that the murderers were Italians. Because Nicola Sacco and Bartolomeo Vanzetti had gone with two other Italians to a garage to claim a car that local police had connected with the crime, they were arrested. Both men were anarchists and feared deportation by the Dept. of Justice. Both had evaded the army draft. On their arrest they made false statements; both carried firearms; neither, however, had a criminal record, nor was there any evidence of their having had any of the money. In July, 1921, they were found guilty after a trial in Dedham, Mass. and sentenced to death. Many then believed that the conviction was unwarranted and had been influenced by the reputation of the accused as radicals when antiradical sentiment was running high. The conduct of the trial by Judge Webster Thayer was particularly criticized. Later much of the evidence against them was discredited. In 1927 when the Massachusetts supreme judicial court upheld the denial of a new trial, protest meetings were held and appeals were made to Gov. Alvan T. Fuller. He postponed the execution and appointed a committee to advise him. On Aug. 3 the governor announced that the judicial procedure in the trial had been correct. The execution of Sacco and Vanzetti on Aug. 22, 1927, was preceded by worldwide sympathy demonstrations. They were—and continue to be—widely regarded as martyrs. However, new ballistics tests conducted with modern equipment in 1961 seemed to prove conclusively that the pistol found on Sacco had been used to murder the guard. This has led some authorities to conclude that Sacco was probably guilty of the crime, but that Vanzetti was innocent. The case was the subject of Maxwell Anderson's play *Gods of the Lightning* and is reflected in his *Winterset.* It is also the subject of Upton Sinclair's novel *Boston* and of sonnets by Edna St. Vincent Millay. See Felix Frankfurter, *The Case of Sacco and Vanzetti* (1927, repr. 1961); M. A. Mustamanno, *After Twelve Years* (1939); G. L. Joughin and E. M. Morgan, *The Legacy of Sacco and Vanzetti* (1948, repr. 1964); R. H. Montgomery, *Sacco-Vanzetti: The Murder and the Myth* (1960, repr. 1965); Francis Russell, *Tragedy in Dedham* (1962, repr. 1971); David Felix, *Protest: Sacco and Vanzetti and the Intellectuals* (1965); H. B. Ehrmann, *The Case that Will Not Die* (1969).

Sacheverell, Henry (səshĕ′vərəl), 1674?-1724, English clergyman, the center of a religio-political incident in the reign of Queen Anne. In two sermons (1709) Dr. Sacheverell attacked the Whig government, lashing out especially against its toleration of religious dissenters. He was charged with seditious libel, tried, convicted, and sentenced (1710) to a three-year suspension from preaching. The trial created a furor, and the light sentence made Sacheverell the victor in the eyes of the public. The Whigs were severely humiliated by the trial. See study by Geoffrey Holmes (1973).

Sachs, Hans (häns zäks), 1494-1576, German poet, leading MEISTERSINGER of the Nuremberg school. A shoemaker and guild master, he wrote more than 4,000 master songs in addition to some 2,000 fables, tales in verse (*Schwanke*), morality plays, and farces. His Shrovetide plays, humorous and dramatically effective, present an informative picture of life in 16th-century Nuremberg. An ardent follower of Luther, Sachs wrote the poem "The Nightingale of Wittenberg" in Luther's honor. Many of his melodies were later adapted as Protestant hymn tunes. Hans Sachs is a principal character in several operas, notably in Richard Wagner's *Die Meistersinger von Nürnberg.*

Sachs, Julius von, 1832-97, German botanist. A professor at the Univ. of Würzburg from 1868, he was a founder of experimental plant physiology. He demonstrated the importance of transpiration in plants and the role of chlorophyll; his researches on plant metabolism were a conspicuous contribution to botanical knowledge. He was the teacher of many eminent European botanists. Among his works are the famous *Textbook of Botany* (1868, tr. 1882), which first brought together the results of the work of various branches of modern botany; *Lectures on Physiology* (1882, tr. 1887); and *History of Botany* (1875, tr. 1890).

Sachs, Nelly, 1891-1970, German poet and translator who lived after 1940 in Sweden. Sachs describes her own experiences and the sufferings of the European Jews in the collections *In den Wohnungen des Todes* [in the apartments of death] (1947), *Das Leiden Israels* [Israel's suffering] (1969), and *Die Suchende* (1966; tr. *The Seeker and Other Poems,* 1970). The selection of her poems in English, *O the Chimneys* (1967), incorporates the verse mystery play *Eli* (written 1943-44; publ. 1951). Sachs shared the 1966 Nobel Prize in literature with S. Y. Agnon.

Sachs, Paul J., 1878-1965, American art teacher and collector, b. New York City. As Professor of Fine Arts at Harvard, Sachs influenced and inspired many art historians and curators during the years of growth in the history of American art museums. His major publications include *Drawings in the Fogg Museum* (3 vol., 1940) and *Modern Prints and Drawings* (1954). Part of Sach's graphic arts collection is exhibited at the Museum of Modern Art, New York City.

Sac Indians: see SAC AND FOX INDIANS.

sackbut (săk′bət), medieval name for the trombone, probably derived from the old French word *sacqueboute,* which means "pull-push." The instrument achieved its present form in the 15th cent., the only

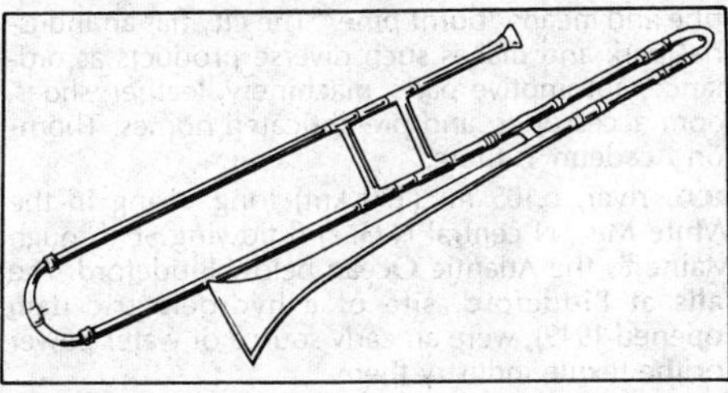

Sackbut

differences being a narrower bore and a smaller bell. These differences lent the sackbut, sometimes called a *posuane,* a mellower tone than its modern counterpart.

Sackville, Charles, 6th **earl of Dorset,** 1638-1706, English poet and courtier. After the restoration, he became a member of the intimate circle of young rakes and wits at the court of Charles II, writing epigrams, caustic satires, and songs, of which the best known is the ballad "To All You Ladies Now at Land." In 1652 he was given the courtesy title Lord Buckhurst.

Sackville, George Sackville Germain, 1st **Viscount:** see GERMAIN, GEORGE SACKVILLE.

Sackville, Lionel Sackville-West, 2d **Baron,** 1827-1908, British diplomat. He served in numerous diplomatic posts before being appointed (1881) ambassador to the United States. He helped to settle (1887-88) the quarrel between the United States and Canada over fishing rights in the North Atlantic. In 1888 he was tricked, by a letter falsely purporting to come from a nonpolitical source, into making a statement implying that the reelection of Grover CLEVELAND would be to the British interest. His reply was publicized to further the Republican campaign for Benjamin HARRISON. He was recalled (1888) to London upon President Cleveland's demand. He succeeded to his brother's title in 1888 and retired the following year.

Sackville, Thomas, 1st **earl of Dorset,** 1536-1608, English statesman and poet. A barrister of the Inner Temple, Sackville entered Parliament in 1558, gained favor with Elizabeth I, and was created Baron Buckhurst in 1567. He was sent on several diplomatic missions to France and served as a commissioner of state trials. In 1586 he told Mary Queen of Scots of her sentence of death. Elizabeth was angered at his conduct in a mission (1587) to the Low Countries, but he soon regained her favor and rose rapidly in rank. He was made lord treasurer (1599) and lord high steward (1601). After the accession of James I, he was appointed lord treasurer for life and created earl of Dorset (1604). Sackville is important in English literature as the author, with Thomas Norton and others, of *Gorboduc* (first acted 1561), a drama in blank verse, generally considered the earliest English tragedy. His most important poems are the "Induction" and the "Complaint of the Duke of Buckingham," which were included in the second edition (1563) of *The Mirror for Magistrates,* a collection of verse tragedies in the form of dramatic monologues. His works were edited by Reginald Sackville-West (1859). See *Gorboduc*, ed. by Irby Cauthen, Jr. (1970); John S. Farmer, ed., *The Dramatic Writings of Richard Edwards, Thomas Norton, and Thomas Sackville* (1966).

Sackville, town (1971 pop. 3,180), SE N.B., Canada, near the head of Chignecto Bay, an arm of the Bay of Fundy. The early French Acadian settlers diked and reclaimed the nearby Tantramar marshes, creating fertile agricultural land. The first Baptist church in Canada was established there in the 1770s. Sackville is the seat of Mt. Allison Univ.

Sackville-West, Victoria Mary, 1892–1962, English writer; wife of Sir Harold Nicolson and granddaughter of the 2d Baron Sackville. Both she and Nicolson were members of the BLOOMSBURY GROUP. Her poems in *The Land* (1926), *Selected Poems* (1941), and *The Garden* (1946) won praise, but she is better known for her novels, *The Edwardians* (1930) and *All Passion Spent* (1931). Among her other works are *Knole and the Sackvilles* (1922), about her family's past, and her charming fictional portrait of her grandmother, *Pepita* (1937). All Sackville-West's books reveal her wit, her vocation as a poet, and her aristocratic heritage. See *Portrait of a Marriage* (1973) by her son Nigel Nicolson; studies by S. R. Watson (1972) and Michael Stevens (1974).

Saco (sô'kō), city (1970 pop. 11,678), York co., SW Maine, on the Saco River; settled 1631, inc. as Pepperellboro 1762; name changed to Saco 1805; inc. as a city 1867. Saco is named for the Sawatucke Indian tribe and means "burnt pine." The city has an industrial park and makes such diverse products as ordnance, automotive parts, machinery, leather, shoes, loom accessories, and prefabricated homes. Thornton Academy is there.

Saco, river, c.105 mi (170 km) long, rising in the White Mts., N central N.H. and flowing SE through Maine to the Atlantic Ocean below Biddeford. The falls at Biddeford, site of a hydroelectric dam (opened 1949), were an early source of water power for the textile industry there.

sacrament [Lat.,=something holy], an outward sign of something sacred. In Christianity, the generally accepted definition of a sacrament is that it was instituted by Christ and that it consists of a visible sign of invisible grace. Christianity is divided as to the number and operation of sacraments. The traditional view held by Orthodox, Roman Catholics, and certain Anglicans counts the sacraments as seven—EUCHARIST, BAPTISM, CONFIRMATION, PENANCE, ANOINTING OF THE SICK, matrimony (see MARRIAGE), and holy orders (see ORDERS, HOLY). These are held to produce grace in the soul of the recipient by the very performance of the sacramental act (*ex opere operato*); the recipient need only have the right intention. Most Protestant denominations recognize two sacraments—baptism and communion, or the LORD'S SUPPER. Protestants hold generally that it is the faith of the participant, itself a gift of God, rather than the power of the sacramental act that produces grace. A conventional division of the seven sacraments sets apart the "sacraments of the dead," i.e., baptism and penance, because they are for souls in a state of sin; the rest, "sacraments of the living," are conferred on souls in a state of grace.

sacramental, in the Roman Catholic Church, aid to devotion that is not a sacrament. Sacramentals are commonly divided into six classes: prayer, anointing, eating, confession, giving, and blessings. According to church teaching, sacramentals are not founded by God but by the church, and therefore do not convey grace. Examples are HOLY WATER, many blessings, and the ROSARY.

Sacramento (săkrəmĕn'tō), city (1970 pop. 257,105), state capital and seat of Sacramento co., central Calif., on the Sacramento River at its confluence with the American River; settled 1839, inc. 1850. A deepwater port via a 43-mi (69-km) channel to Suisun Bay (opened 1963), it is the shipping, rail, processing, and marketing center for the truck and fruit farms of the rich Sacramento valley. Food processing is the city's major industry. There are large canneries, frozen-food plants, meat-packing houses, flour and rice mills, beet-sugar refineries, and almond-shelling establishments. The city lies on a part of a Mexican land grant that belonged to John A. Sutter, who in 1839 began a settlement called New Helvetia and in 1840 built a fort. The discovery of gold in 1848 at nearby Sutter's Mill (now Coloma) led to the platting of the town, and its population soon reached 10,000. Sacramento was made the state capital in 1854. It is the seat of California State Univ. at Sacramento and three junior colleges. Points of interest include the capitol building in a beautiful park, the governor's mansion (occupied 1903–1968; now a museum), Sutter's Fort, and the Crocker Art Gallery. The city is known for its camellias. Mather Air Force Base, McClellan Air Force Base, and an army depot are in the vicinity.

Sacramento, longest river of Calif., c.380 mi (610 km) long, rising near Mt. Shasta, N Calif., and flowing generally SW to Suisun Bay, an arm of San Francisco Bay, where it forms a large delta with the San Joaquin River. Its chief tributaries are the Pit, Feather, and American rivers. At high water the river is navigable by small steamers c.260 mi (420 km) to Red Bluff. The valley saw the great gold strike of 1848, and many of the cities on or near the river and its tributaries sprang up in the gold rush; Sacramento is the largest. This northern part of the Central Valley of California has been developed as a fertile agricultural region. In recent years the CENTRAL VALLEY PROJECT has been developed to use the waters of the Sacramento with greater efficiency, particularly for use in the fertile but dry San Joaquin section of the Central Valley. Shasta Dam and Keswick Dam on the Sacramento are major units of the project; they also generate electricity.

Sacré-Cœur (säkrā-kör'), basilica in Paris, dedicated to the Sacred Heart of Jesus. It is a famous landmark atop the MONTMARTRE, from which it dominates the city. Built (1875–1914) by subscriptions as a votive offering after the Franco-Prussian War, it was consecrated in 1919 after World War I and has a patriotic as well as religious symbolic significance. Designed by the architect Paul Abadie, the basilica is a huge and harmonious edifice in the Byzantine-Romanesque style. Behind its tall dome rises a bell tower 276 ft (84 m) high.

sacrifice [Lat. *sacrificare*=to make holy], an element in religion found in many cultures and in diverse forms. It is an act whereby an offering is made to a god or divine being, and thus the object offered is made holy. The purpose of this act is either to establish or sustain a proper relationship with the god or gods or to appease divine wrath kindled by man's transgression of these arrangements. Sacrifices are performed both on a regular basis, according to established patterns of daily, monthly, or seasonal acts; they are also performed on special occasions, notably at important times in an individual's life (birth, puberty, marriage, death), to insure a successful harvest, in the face of extraordinary conditions, at times of war, and as thanksgiving for divine aid. Biblical accounts of sacrifices begin with Cain's sacrifice of the fruit of the ground, not acceptable to God, and Abel's rightful sacrifice of the firstlings of his flock (Gen. 4.2–5). The release of Abraham from the vow to sacrifice Isaac (Gen. 22) is said to mark an end of human sacrifice in Hebrew tradition; however, the story of Jephthah's daughter is an example of human sacrifice (Judges 11–12). The chief sacrifices of Old Testament worship were the paschal lamb (Ex. 12) and the scapegoat (Lev. 16.20–26); in the Temple there was a regular offering of incense also. Among Samaritans, the paschal lamb is still sacrificed at the time of the Passover. In the New Testament the symbolization of Jesus by the sacrificial lamb is frequent, and his death on the cross became the supreme sacrifice of history (Heb. 8–10). In the ancient liturgies the EUCHARIST is regarded as a real continuation of this sacrifice of Calvary; hence Roman Catholics call the Mass "the holy sacrifice." *Ex-voto*, or votive, offerings (performed to fulfill a vow or in gratitude) are common in the Christian tradition, e.g., offerings of candles or of ships' models hung up in churches in thanksgiving. The other ancient cultures of the Middle East, the Far East, and Europe also had religions with sacrificial rituals. Perhaps the most fully developed was that of the Vedic religion in India, as worked out in great detail in the Brahmanic texts (see HINDUISM). The Maya and the Aztec developed a particularly bloody and elaborate ritual of human sacrifice. Human sacrifice in simpler forms (e.g., cannibalism, headhunting, killing of prisoners) has also been widespread. See E. O. James, *Origins of Sacrifice* (1933, repr. 1971) and *Sacrifice and Sacrament* (1962); Henri Hubert, *Sacrifice, Its Nature and Function* (tr. 1964); G. B. Gray, *Sacrifice in the Old Testament* (1971).

Sacrobosco, Johannes de (yōhän'əs də săkrōbŏs'kō), or **John of Hollywood,** c.1200–1256, English mathematician and astronomer. He wrote several widely read and influential books: *Algorismus*, a study of arithmetic; a treatise on the calendar; and the most popular medieval introductory textbook on astronomy, the *Tractatus de sphaera*. See Lynn Thorndike, ed., *The Sphere of Sacrobosco and its Commentators* (1949).

sacrum: see SPINAL COLUMN.

Sacsahuamán (säksäwämän'), stronghold of the Incas outside Cuzco, Peru. Built in the 15th cent., Sacsahuamán is an imposing terraced fortress more than one third of a mile long; it is a masterpiece of stone construction. Cyclopean blocks (one is 38 ft/11.6 m long; 18 ft/5.5 m high; and 6 ft/1.8 m thick) were brought from some distance over rugged terrain without wheeled vehicles and then were fitted precisely. It was captured by the Spanish garrison besieged (1536–37) in Cuzco by MANCO CAPAC. The loss hastened the defeat of the Indians.

Sacy, Antoine Isaac, Baron Silvestre de (äNtwän' ēzäk' bärôN' sēlvĕ'strə də säsē'), 1758–1838, French Orientalist. Sacy's works on Arabic were pioneering, and he was one of the founders of modern Arabic studies in France.

Sadat, Anwar al- (änwär' äl-sädät'), 1918–, Egyptian political leader and president (1970–). He entered (1936) Abbassia Military Academy, where he became friendly with Gamal Abdal NASSER and other fellow cadets committed to Egyptian nationalism. A German agent during World War II, he was imprisoned (1942) by the British but escaped after two years in jail. He was again jailed (1946–49) for participating in terrorist acts against pro-British Egyptian officials. Sadat took part in the bloodless coup (1952) that deposed King Farouk. Between 1952 and 1968, he held a variety of government positions, including director of army public relations; secretary-general of the National Union, Egypt's only political party; and president of the national assembly. In 1969 he was chosen to be Nasser's vice president, and after Nasser's death (1970), he succeeded to the presidency. Less charismatic than his predecessor, Sadat was nevertheless able to establish himself as Egypt's strongman and a leader of the Arab world. He assumed the premiership in 1973 and in October of that same year led Egypt into war with Israel. He became an Arab hero when Egyptian troops recaptured a small part of the Sinai Peninsula, taken by the Israelis in 1967. A pragmatist, Sadat has indicated his willingness to consider a negotiated settlement with Israel; he supported the 1974 Egyptian-Israeli troop disengagement accord.

saddle, seat or pad to support the rider on an animal, chiefly the horse. The saddles mentioned in the Bible are generally considered to have been saddlecloths. The ancient Greeks sometimes used saddlecloths, but they had no saddles and often rode bareback. The Romans did not use a saddle until near the end of the empire. The Indians of the Great Plains of North America were famous horsemen, and usually rode without saddles. To riders accustomed to the saddle, however, its advantages are decisive. Probably it developed either in France during the early Christian era or in the steppe region of Asia. In Europe the saddle came into general use in the Middle Ages. The exploits of medieval knights would have been difficult without the saddle. Saddles of various types include the packsaddle, to which the load of a pack animal is secured; the camel saddle; the howdah used by riders of elephants; and the saddle used by riders of horses. There are two main types of horse saddles, the Hungarian and the Moorish. The Moorish saddle, which was used extensively by cowboys in the United States, has a horn; the Hungarian saddle, of which the English saddle is an example, the McClellan saddle, and the racing saddle have no horns. The English saddle is padded, and the stirrup is hung farther forward than on the Moorish saddle or the McClellan saddle, neither of which is padded. For constant use, the hard saddle is believed in North America to be better for both the horse and the rider. The padded saddle has advantages in brief and occasional rides. The horn of the cowboy's saddle is essential in using the lasso. To hold it in place under the strain of the lasso, this saddle has two strong girths, each tightened by a cinch strap. See also HORSEMANSHIP; STIRRUP.

Sadducees (săj'o͞osēz, săd'yo͞o-), sect of Jews formed c.200 B.C. It was drawn largely from the upper classes, especially of the city. The Sadducees accepted only the Hebrew Scriptures and not the oral tradition held by the Pharisees. They did not believe in immortality, resurrection, the existence of demons and angels, or the coming of the Messiah. They were a smaller group than their rivals, the Pharisees, and more conservative and literal in their interpretations of Scripture. Their legal decisions were sometimes quite harsh, and they were less popular. Their life was centered on the cult of the Temple, and they ceased to exist after its destruction in A.D. 70. See bibliography under PHARISEES.

Sade, Donatien Alphonse François, comte de (dônäsyäN' älfôNs' fräNswä' kôNt də säd), 1740–1814, French writer and libertine. He is known as the **marquis de Sade**—the title he held before becoming count on his father's death (1767). Famous for his licentious prose narratives, he also wrote many essays, antireligious pamphlets, and plays. He fought in the Seven Years War, and after his marriage in 1763 he pursued a life of pleasure and was imprisoned for his scandalous conduct. Charged with numerous sexual offenses, he spent a total of 27 years of confinement in several institutions, including the Bastille, the dungeon at Vincennes, and at Charenton asylum.During this time he wrote such ribald romances as *Justine; ou, Les Malheurs de la vertu* (1791), *La Philosophie dans le boudoir* (1793), and *Histoire de Juliette; ou, Les Prosperités du vice* (6 vol., 1797). Released for a time during the French Revolution, he succeeded in having some plays produced by the Comédie Française, and during his final confinement at Charenton he directed theatrical performances by the inmates. De Sade brought to light the controversial theory that since both sexual deviation and criminal acts exist in nature, they are therefore natural. This was in violent opposition to the spirit of his times but made him a precursor of modern psychological thought. The sexual aberration in which cruelty is inflicted in order to attain sexual release is termed *sadism* after him. Generally banned for obscenity, de Sade's works were almost all published in expurgated or unofficial editions. The complete works, edited by Gilbert Lély, appeared in 1966–68 (8 vol.). See biography by Gilbert Lély (tr. 1961, repr. 1970), essay by Simone de Beauvoir (tr. 1953); studies by Geoffrey Gorer (rev. ed. 1953, repr. 1963) and Norman Gear (1963).

Sá de Miranda, Francisco de (fränsēsh'kō də sä də mērän'dä), 1481–1558, Portuguese writer. A noble and a courtier, he lived for a time in Italy and became acquainted with the literature of the Italian Renaissance. He was impressed by the new classic style and introduced it to Portugal on his return. His sonnets and other Italian-patterned poems, written in Portuguese and in Spanish, are disillusioned and moralistic. Two comedies, *Estrangeiros* [strangers] (1559) and *Vilhalpandos* (1560), laid the foundation for the Portuguese classical theater.

Sadi or **Saadi** (both: sä'dē), 1184–1291, Persian poet, b. Shiraz. Sadi is thought to have studied in Baghdad, made the pilgrimage to Mecca more than once, and traveled widely before returning to Shiraz. He was a mystical poet of great power, one of the finest of the Sufi writers. His *Bustan* [garden of fruits] (1257) is a long didactic poem. *Gulistan* [garden of roses] (1258), generally considered his masterpiece, is a miscellany of prose and various kinds of poetry. The work is suffused with warmth of feeling and lofty religious thought. His tomb in Shiraz is a shrine.

sadism (săd'ĭzəm, sā'–), sexual abnormality in which pleasure is derived from inflicting pain on others. More broadly it refers to a tendency toward acts of humiliation and cruelty in which unconscious needs are satisfied. In psychoanalysis the term refers to a destructive drive that is turned on other people. The word *sadism* derives from the comte de SADE.

Sadler or **Sadleir, Sir Ralph** (both: săd'lər), 1507–87, English diplomat. Through the influence of Thomas Cromwell, he secured (c.1536) the favor of Henry VIII, for whom he went on numerous missions to Scotland to try to counteract the influence of David, Cardinal BEATON. Sadler distinguished himself at the battle of Pinkie (1547). He retired during the reign of Queen Mary I, but after Elizabeth I's accession (1558) he became an agent of William Cecil (later Lord Burghley) and was sent (1559) to form an English alliance with the Protestant party in Scotland. In 1568 he was a member of the tribunal appointed to adjudicate between MARY QUEEN OF SCOTS and her subjects. He was frequently employed to carry messages to the captive queen, and in 1584 he reluctantly undertook the guardianship of Mary. He was relieved of the task the following year.

Sado (sä'dō), island, 330 sq mi (855 sq km), in the Sea of Japan, off the west coast of N Honshu, Japan. Mt. Kimpoku (3,872 ft/1,180 m) is the highest point. The fertile central lowlands are an important rice-growing region; fishing and tourism are also important. Aikawa, the administrative center of the island, is the site of gold and silver mines which have been worked since 1601. In feudal times the Emperor Juntoku and the priest Nichiren were exiled there.

Sadoc (sā'dŏk), name appearing in the Gospel genealogy. Mat. 1.14.

Sadová (sä'dôvä), village, N Czechoslovakia, in Bohemia, near Hradec Králové. It was the site of a decisive Prussian victory over the Austrians in 1866, during the AUSTRO-PRUSSIAN WAR. The German name for the village was Königgrätz.

Saenredam, Pieter Jansz (pē'tər yäns sän'rədäm), 1597–1665, Dutch painter. Saenredam, a painter of architecture, and especially of Dutch gothic church interiors, is known for his austere, meticulously executed work. The geometry of buildings serves as the focus of his works, in which tiny figures move through great, spacious halls filled with diffused light (e.g., *Interior of St. Janskerk*, 1645; Centraal Mus., Utrecht).

Sáenz Peña, Roque (rō'kā sä'āns pā'nyä), 1851–1914, Argentine statesman, president of the republic (1910–14); son of an earlier president (1892–95), Luis Sáenz Peña. He had an active career as soldier, legislator, diplomat, and cabinet official before he was inaugurated president (Oct., 1910) for a six-year term. His administration was significant for electoral reform. Because of these measures a peaceful revolution occurred when, in the presidential election of 1916, the landowning oligarchy was replaced by a new group, the Radicals, headed by Hipólito IRIGOYEN. Sáenz Peña, however, did not live to see the full results of his reform.

Safad: see ZEFAT, Israel.

Safaqis (säfä'kīs) or **Sfax** (sfäks), city (1966 pop. 70,472), E Tunisia, on the Gulf of Gabès (Khalij Qabis), an arm of the Mediterranean Sea. It is Tunisia's second largest city and has exports of phosphates, olive oil, cereals, and sponges. Safaqis was the site of Phoenician and Roman colonies. It was briefly held by Roger II of Sicily (c.1150) and by the Spanish (16th cent.). Later it became a stronghold of the Barbary pirates.

Šafařik, Pavel Josef (pä'vĕl yô'zĕf shä'fär-zhĕk), 1795–1861, Czech philologist and archaeologist. Šafařik advanced the theory that the Slavs originally were a composite people with a common language that later had split into separate dialects. In his *Slavonic Antiquities* (1836–37) he maintained that the Slavs had been indigenous to Europe since the 5th cent. B.C. His theories, though now obsolete, were of great significance in the advance of Slavic studies; they also gave intellectual impetus to Pan-Slavism.

Safdie, Moshe (mōshā' säf'dē), 1938–, Israeli architect. Designer of Montreal's revolutionary "Habitat" for Expo 67, Safdie worked on the master plan for the exposition as well. His several housing systems of the Habitat type are based on three-dimensional prefabricated MODULES, mobile units stacked around prefabricated or site-built utility cores (see PREFABRICATION). Safdie has designed a 4,500-unit housing complex in Israel and a 300-unit hillside cluster in Puerto Rico. He believes that technology can make industry as flexible as nature. Safdie is the author of *Beyond Habitat* (1970).

Safed: see ZEFAT, Israel.

Safed Koh (säfād' kō), mountain range on the Pakistan-Afghanistan border, SE of Kabul; rises to 15,620 ft (4,761 m) at Mt. Sikaram. The range is crossed by the Khyber Pass and parallels the Kabul River. The northern slopes are nearly barren; pine and deodar grow on the main range, and the valleys support some agriculture.

Safety Islands: see ÎLES DU SALUT.

safety lamp, oil lamp designed for safe use in mines and other places where flammable gases such as firedamp (see DAMP) may be present. Its invention (c.1816) is usually attributed to Sir Humphry Davy. The Davy lamp is based upon the principle that to be ignited a substance must first be heated to its kindling temperature and that if such heating is prevented combustion will not occur. The flame in the lamp is surrounded by a metal-gauze screen that distributes the heat over a large area so that the maximum temperature of the screen is below the ignition temperature of the flammable gas mixture (e.g., firedamp). Improvements devised by K. G. Bischof and others include special locks to prevent the accidental opening of the lamp and devices to permit the lamp to be held upside down without danger. If firedamp or related gas mixtures are present in a mine, the Davy lamp flame burns higher and with a blue halo; the height of the flame and color of the halo indicate the amount of combustible gas in the air. If the mine air is deficient in oxygen, the lamp flame is extinguished. Coal miners often place the safety lamp close to the ground to detect gases, e.g., carbon dioxide, that are denser than air and thus collect in poorly ventilated depressions in the mine. Other gas-detecting devices are now used as well, e.g., the methanometer; as a light source the Davy lamp has been largely replaced by electric lighting.

safety movement, widespread effort to prevent accidents that followed the increasing number of casualties in industry, traffic and transportation, and homes arising out of the Industrial Revolution and the growth of cities. Large manufacturing companies, public utilities, railroads, steamship lines, and insurance companies were particularly concerned with reducing the number of injuries and deaths as well as with cutting the cost of workmen's compensation, other damage payments, and litigation arising out of accidents. Humanitarianism and the evolution of an awareness of public responsibility were other factors in the initiation of the safety movement, which took the form of educating the public in accident prevention by way of safety clubs, posters, magazines, and other means. A vital part of the safety movement was the passing of laws, such as those requiring that buildings be constructed in accord with fire prevention laws, that ships be equipped with ship-to-shore radios and enough lifeboats to accommodate all persons on board, that fire drills be held, that automobiles meet certain basic safety requirements, that halls be well lighted in certain classes of buildings, that theater exits be marked, that machinery be properly guarded, that food conform to specified standards, that poisonous materials be so marked, and that elevators be equipped with safety devices. In the United States the National Safety Council, founded in 1913, collects and distributes information and statistics regarding safety in industry, the home, travel, and schools; it also publishes several magazines and numerous pamphlets and newsletters. The Royal Society for the Prevention of Accidents performs similar functions in Great Britain. On an international level, world congresses have met periodically since 1955 to discuss programs for the prevention of occupational accidents and diseases. See R. P. Blake, ed., *Industrial Safety* (3d ed. 1963); C. L. Gilmore, *Accident Prevention and Loss Control* (1970).

safety valve, device attached to a BOILER or other vessel for automatically relieving the pressure of steam before it becomes great enough to cause bursting. The common spring-loaded type is held closed by a spring designed to open the valve when the internal pressure reaches a point in excess of the calculated safe load of the boiler. Safety valves are installed on boilers according to strict safety regulations.

Saffi: see SAFI, Morocco.

safflower, Eurasian thistlelike herb (*Carthamus tinctorius*) of the family Compositae (COMPOSITE family). Safflower, or false saffron, has long been cultivated in S Asia and Egypt for food and medicine and as a costly but inferior substitute for the true SAFFRON dye. In the United States, where it is sometimes called American saffron, it is more important as the source of safflower oil, which has recently come into wide use as a cooking oil. Safflower is classified in the division MAGNOLIOPHYTA, class Magnoliopsida, order Asterales, family Compositae.

saffron, name for a fall-flowering plant (*Crocus sativus*) of the family Iridaceae (IRIS family) and also for a dye obtained therefrom. The plant is native to Asia Minor, where for centuries it has been cultivated for its aromatic orange-yellow stigmas (see PISTIL). The stigmas, handpicked and dried, yield saffron powder, the source of the principal yellow dye of the ancient world. The plant is still grown in limited quantities for this powder, which is used in medicinals and perfumes and for flavoring, especially in Mediterranean cooking. It has been estimated that the stigmas of about 4,000 flowers are required for one ounce of saffron powder. Saffron is mentioned in classical writings and in the Bible (Cant. 4.14). It is one of the crocuses sometimes cultivated for ornament; its blossoms are white or lilac in color. The SAFFLOWER, sometimes used as a substitute for saffron and called false, or American, saffron, and the MEADOW SAFFRON, or autumn crocus (*Colchicum autumnale*) are unrelated plants. True saffron is classified in the division MAGNOLIOPHYTA, class Liliatae, order Liliales, family Iridaceae.

Safi or **Saffi** (both: sä'fē), city (1970 est. pop. 130,000), W central Morocco, on the Atlantic Ocean. It is a center of the Moroccan fishing and canning industries. Phosphates are exported. Safi was a Portuguese base in the early 16th cent.; it then became (until 1660) the chief port, being close to the capital, Marrakesh, of the Sadian dynasty. In World War II, Allied forces landed there on Nov. 8, 1942.

Safid Kuh, mountains, Afghanistan: see PARAPAMISUS.

Safid Rud (säfēd' rōōd), river, c.450 mi (720 km) long, rising in NW Iran and flowing generally east to meet the Caspian Sea at Rasht. A storage dam on the river was completed in 1962. The Safid Rud has cut a water gap through the Elburz mts., capturing two headwater tributaries and widening the valley between the Talesh Hills and the main Elburz range. The gap provides a major route between Tehran and the Caspian lowlands.

Saga (sä'gä), city (1970 pop. 143,426), capital of Saga prefecture, W Kyushu, Japan. It is a railroad and coal-distributing center. Cotton textiles and ceramics are produced in the city. A castle town in feudal times, Saga was the center of a rebellion in 1874. Saga prefecture (1970 pop. 838,442), 946 sq mi (2,450 sq km), is known for its porcelain ware and yields large crops of rice.

saga, in OLD NORSE LITERATURE, especially Icelandic and Norwegian, narrative in prose or verse, centering on a legendary or historical figure or family. Sagas may be divided into sagas of the kings, mainly of early Norwegian rulers; Icelandic sagas, both biographical and historical; contemporary sagas, which were also Icelandic and were written about living persons; legendary sagas of the distant past; and sagas that were translations of foreign romances. Sagas were composed from about the early 11th to the mid-14th cent. and were first written down c.1200. Scholars disagree as to the extent to which written versions borrowed from earlier oral compositions. The sagas vary greatly in length. The greatest attention has been given to the history sagas (e.g., *Sturlungasaga*), the family sagas (e.g., *Njala,* tr. by G. W. Dasent, 1861; M. Magnusson and P. Palsson, 1960), and the mythical heroic sagas (e.g., *Volsungasaga,* tr. by William Morris, 1870). In all these the epic element is strong, and the milieu of a heroic society is made vivid. Historical accuracy was often a major aim of the saga, although reworking, interjection of the supernatural, and other changes caused distortion. The historical approach is felt in the careful selection of events and the great emphasis on cause and effect. Among other noted sagas are the *Heimskringla* of SNORRI STURLUSON (tr. by L. Hollander, 1964); the *Laxdœla,* translated in *Earthly Paradise* by William Morris; the *Grettla,* translated by the same author; the *Frithjof,* translated by Esaias TEGNÉR; and *Gisli,* translated by R. B. Allen. See Stefán Einarsson, *A History of Icelandic Literature* (1957); Peter Hallberg, *The Icelandic Saga* (tr. 1962).

Sagamihara (sägämē'härä), city (1970 pop. 278,326), Kanagawa prefecture, central Honshu, Japan. It is a suburb of Tokyo with chemical, food processing, and metallurgical industries.

Sagamore Hill National Historic Site: see NATIONAL PARKS AND MONUMENTS (table).

Sagan: see ŻAGAŃ, Poland.

Sagar (sä'gər), town (1971 pop. 127,458), Madhya Pradesh state, central India. Sagar is a district administrative center and a market for wheat, cotton, and oilseed.

Sagarra, Josep Maria de (Sagarra i Castellarnau) (hōsĕp' märē'äthä sägä'rä ē kästälyär'nou), 1894–1961, Catalonian poet, novelist, and playwright. He published his first poems at the age of 12 and later, on the advice of his mentors Miquel COSTA I LLOBERA and Joan MARAGALL I GORINA, abandoned law for writing. Among his important poetic works are *Cançons d'abril i novembre* [songs of April and November] (1918), which makes graceful use of regional idioms, and the epic poem *El Comte Arnau* [Count Arnau] (1928), which emphasizes the human aspects of myth. His numerous plays, which were enormously popular, are noted for their originality and grace of language; they include *L'estudiant i la pubille* (1921) and *L'hostel de la glòria* (1931). His novels are largely social satires.

Sagasta, Práxedes Mateo (präk'sāthās mätā'ō sägä'stä), 1825–1903, Spanish statesman. A leader of the Progressive party in the Cortes, he was twice exiled for his opposition to the government of Isabella II. In 1868 he led, with Juan Prim, the revolution that resulted in the queen's deposition. He served as premier (1871–72) under King Amadeus and as cabinet minister under the first Spanish republic but retired after the restoration (1875) of Alfonso XII. In 1880 the Liberal party was founded under his leadership, and Sagasta returned to power as premier (1881–83, 1885–95, 1897–99, 1901–2). In 1897, Sagasta granted autonomy to Cuba, which had been in revolt since 1895, but he was unable to prevent U.S. intervention and the defeat of Spain in the Spanish-American War of 1898. He was generally blamed for the Cuban disaster.

Sage, Russell, 1815–1906, American financier, b. Oneida co., N.Y. He was successful in the grocery business in Troy, N.Y. Active in public affairs, he became (1845) alderman of Troy and served (1853–56) as a Whig member of Congress. He continued to amass great wealth by banking, and after moving (1863) to New York City he engaged in stock speculation. In association with Jay Gould, he gained extensive financial control in several Western railroads, in the elevated railway system in New York City, and in the Western Union Telegraph Company. An attempt to assassinate him in 1891 failed. Upon his death, the distribution of his fortune was left in the hands of his widow, **Margaret Olivia Slocum Sage,** 1828–1918. She made large gifts to the Emma Willard School and to the Rensselaer Polytechnic Institute in Troy and donated money to other educational organizations and to benevolent societies. Marsh Island in the Gulf of Mexico was bought by her in 1912 and given to Louisiana as a bird sanctuary. The great single benefaction was the establishment (1907) of the Russell Sage Foundation in New York City. This institution, endowed with a total of $15 million for "the improvement of social and living conditions" in the United States, did pioneer work in cooperating with various social agencies. In addition to conducting research activities in social welfare, public health, education, government, and law, the foundation has also been concerned with the possibilities of increased use of social-science techniques in the practicing professions. See John M. Glenn et al., *Russell Sage Foundation, 1907–1946* (1947); biography by Paul Sarnoff (1965).

sage, any species of the large genus *Salvia,* aromatic herbs or shrubs of the family Labiatae (MINT family). The common sage of herb gardens is *S. officinalis,* a strongly scented shrubby perennial, native from S Europe to Asia Minor. The dried leaves are used as seasoning, especially in dressings for meat and poultry and also in sage cheese; sage tea, once popular as a beverage, has also been used as a domestic remedy for colds and other ailments and as a hair rinse; the oil is used in medicinals and flavorings and sometimes in perfumery. Prized since ancient times, common sage was thought to prolong life and to increase wisdom by strengthening the memory—whence the name. The ornamental sages are often popularly called salvia. Of these the scarlet sage (*S. splendens*), native to Brazil, is best known. It is cultivated as an annual bedding plant for its neat spikes of red blossoms; there are also varieties in other colors. Clary (*S. sclarea*), native from the Mediterranean region to Iran, is a biennial sage whose seeds were once used to "clear the eye"; it has bluish or pinkish flowers, and its oil is sometimes used similarly to that of the common sage. The seeds of some species of W North America, e.g., the thistle sage (*S. carduacea*) of California, were used by the Indians for a flour and a beverage. Another species is *S. carnosa,* the purple sage of the western deserts. Most sages are good honey plants. One of the lantanas (see VERVAIN) is sometimes called red or yellow sage. Sage is classified in the division MAGNOLIOPHYTA, class Magnoliopsida, order Lamiales, family Labiatae.

sagebrush, name for several species of *Artemesia,* deciduous shrubs of the family Compositae (COMPOSITE family), particularly abundant in arid regions of W North America. The common sagebrush (*A. tridentata*), called also big sagebrush, is a silvery-gray low shrub with a pungent odor of sage, although it is unrelated to the true SAGE. It is one of the most common shrubs of the West, where it is important as a forage plant on many cattle ranges and is often indicative of good soil. This species has been employed as a domestic remedy and tonic, and the seeds were used for food by Indians. The wood ignites easily and burns well so that it has been valuable for starting fire by friction. Sagebrush is the state flower of Nevada, which is sometimes called the Sagebrush State. The pasture, or mountain, sagebrush (*A. frigida*) has also been used medicinally. It is native both to Siberia and to North America, from Alaska to Texas. The word *sagebrush* is often shortened to *sage.* Other species of *Artemesia* include TARRAGON, WORMWOOD, and the plants yielding santonin. Sagebrush is classified in the division MAGNOLIOPHYTA, class Magnoliopsida, order Asterales, family Compositae.

sage grouse, sage hen, or **sage cock:** see GROUSE.

Saghalien: see SAKHALIN, USSR.

Saginaw (săg'ĭnô), city (1970 pop. 91,849), seat of Saginaw co., S Mich., on the Saginaw River, 15 mi (24 km) from its mouth on Saginaw Bay (an inlet of Lake Huron); settled 1816, inc. 1857. Situated in an extensive agricultural area, Saginaw is also a port of entry and an industrial center. Indian trails crossed there, and Indian villages were in the vicinity. Lewis Cass negotiated a treaty there (1819) with the Indians, who ceded much of Michigan to the United States. Fur trade was followed by a great pine-lumbering industry, which thrived until about 1890. The old Schuch Hotel (1868) has a collection of antiques and curios.

Saginaw, river, 22 mi (35 km) long, formed by the confluence of eight branches, SE Mich. The river drains a large area of lower Michigan and flows into **Saginaw Bay** (c.60 mi/100 km long and 15–25 mi/24–40 km wide), an arm of Lake Huron. Bay City, a port, is located at the bayhead near the mouth of the river, and Saginaw, an industrial center, is located upstream. Coal, pig iron, stone, and oil are transported on the river.

Sagittarius (săjĭtâr'ēəs) [Lat.,=the archer], CONSTELLATION lying on the ECLIPTIC (the sun's apparent path through the heavens) between Scorpius and Capricornus; it is one of the constellations of the ZODIAC. It is traditionally depicted as a centaur drawing his bow to release an arrow. The constellation contains a configuration of stars known as the Milk Dipper. It also contains the Lagoon, Horseshoe, and Trifid nebulas. The center of our galaxy, the MILKY WAY, lies in Sagittarius. The constellation reaches its highest point in the evening sky in August.

sago (sā'gō) [Malay], edible starch extracted from the pithlike center of several Indonesian palms (chiefly *Metroxylon sago*) or sometimes of cycads. The starch is an important item in the diet of the Indonesians and is exported for use in foods (e.g., puddings) and for stiffening textiles. Sago is obtained by grinding the stem content of a mature sago palm into powder and washing the starch free. For local use it is pulverized, but for the market it is usually sieved and then heated to form granules. The florists' sago palm is not a true palm but a cycad of the American genus *Zamia. Z. floridana,* called wild sago or coontie, yields Florida ARROWROOT.

Sagua la Grande (sä'gwä lä grän'dā), city (1970 pop. 35,809), Las Villas prov., central Cuba, on the Sagua la Grande River. It is a road and rail hub and the commercial and processing center for the surrounding area, which raises sugarcane and cattle. The city's origins date back to the 17th cent.

saguaro: see CACTUS.

Saguaro National Monument: see NATIONAL PARKS AND MONUMENTS (table).

Saguenay (săg'ənā, săg''ənā'), river, c.125 mi (200 km) long, S Que., Canada. It issues from Lake St. John (c.375 sq mi/970 sq km) in two channels, the Grande Décharge and the Petite Décharge, separated by the Île d'Alma, and flows generally SE past St. Joseph d'Alma, Arvida, and Chicoutimi, to the St. Lawrence River at Tadoussac. Navigable below Chicoutimi, it flows through a picturesque gorge whose banks rise to more than 1,500 ft (457 m) at Eternity and Trinity capes. The Peribonca River is its chief tributary. The Saguenay was first visited (1535) by Cartier, and Champlain explored its lower reaches in 1603. For more than three centuries it was a route traveled by explorers, missionaries, and fur traders; later it became a major lumber transportation route and the approach to noted hunting and fishing areas. In the 20th cent. pulp and paper mills and important hydroelectric stations (especially those at Shipshaw and Chute à Caron) were built on the banks of the river and some of its tributaries, and at Arvida is one of the world's largest aluminum plants. Excursions up the Saguenay by steamer from Quebec have long been a tourist attraction.

Sagunto (sägōōn'tō), Latin *Saguntum,* town (1970 pop. 47,026), Valencia prov., E Spain, on the Palencia River, in Valencia. A seaport on the Mediterranean, it is an important metallurgical center, with iron and steel foundries. Saguntum was an ally of Rome when it was besieged and captured (219–218 B.C.) by the Carthaginians under Hannibal. This led to the Second Punic War (see PUNIC WARS). Saguntum was conquered by the Romans (214 B.C.) and made a *municipium.* On a ridge above the present city are important Roman remains, notably a well-preserved theater. The city fell to the Moors and was called Murviedro until its old name was restored in 1877. In 1874 the restoration of the Spanish Bourbon dynasty was proclaimed there.

Saha, Meghnad (māgnäd' sä'hä), 1893–1956, Indian physicist. He was a professor at Allahabad University from 1923 to 1938 and a professor and physics department head at Calcutta Univ. from 1938. His theory of high-temperature ionization of elements and its application to stellar atmospheres, expressed in the Saha equation, is fundamental to modern astrophysics; subsequent development of his ideas has led to increased knowledge of the pressure and temperature distributions of stellar atmospheres.

Sahand (sähänd'), peak, 12,140 ft (3,700 m) high, NW Iran, S of Tabriz. It is snow-covered most of the year and is traditionally associated with the prophet ZOROASTER.

Sahaptin Indians: see NEZ PERCE INDIANS.

Sahara (səhâr'ə) [Arabic, = desert], world's largest desert, c.3,500,000 sq mi (9,065,000 sq km), N Africa; the western part of a great arid zone that continues into SW Asia. Extending more than 3,000 mi (4,830 km), from the Atlantic Ocean to the Red Sea, the Sahara is bounded on the N by the Atlas Mts., steppelands, and the Mediterranean Sea; it stretches south c.1,200 mi (1,930 km) to the SAHEL, a steppe in W and central Africa that forms its southern border. The desert includes most of Spanish Sahara, Mauritania, Algeria, Niger, Libya, and Egypt; the southern portions of Morocco and Tunisia; and the northern portions of Senegal, Mali, Chad, and Sudan. The E Sahara is usually divided into three regions—the LIBYAN DESERT, which extends west from the Nile valley through W Egypt and E Libya; the ARABIAN DESERT, or Eastern Desert, which lies between the Nile valley and the Red Sea in Egypt; and the NUBIAN DESERT, which is in NE Sudan. Regions of sand dunes (erg) occupy only about 15% of the Sahara; "stone deserts," consisting of plateaus of denuded rock (hammada) or areas of coarse gravel (reg), cover about 70% of the region; mountains, oases, and transition zones account for the remainder. High mountain massifs rise in the central regions; they are the Ahaggar (Hoggar) in S Algeria, which rises to more than 9,000 ft (2,740 m); the Tibesti Massif in N Chad, which rises to more than 11,000 ft (3,350 m); and the Aïr Mountains (Azbine) in N Niger, which rise to more than 6,000 ft (1,830 m). The mountains are deeply dissected and were in the past infamous for the shelter they provided to marauders preying on desert traffic. The Sahara has one of the harshest climates in the world. Located in the trade winds belt, the region is subject to winds that are frequently strong and that blow constantly from the northeast between a subtropical high pressure cell and an equatorial low pressure cell. As air moves downward from the high pressure into the low pressure cell, it becomes warmer and drier. The desiccating and dust-laden winds are sometimes felt north and south of the desert, where they are variously known as sirocco, khamsin, simoom, and harmattan. The northern slopes of the Atlas Mts. intercept most of the moisture from winds blowing inshore from the Mediterranean Sea. Border zones on the north and south, where the desert merges with the steppe, receive about 10 in. (25 cm) of rain a year with some seasonal regularity, but over most of the region rainfall is sparse, with an average annual total of less than 5 in. (12.7 cm); rainfall is usually torrential when it occurs after long dry periods that sometimes last for years. The region's low relative humidity rarely exceeds 30% and is often in the 4% to 5% range. Daytime temperatures are high; Azizia, Libya, recorded the world's highest official temperature in the shade (136°F/58°C) in Sept., 1922. Heat loss is rapid at night and a diurnal range of 86°F (30°C) is common. Freezing temperatures are not uncommon at night from December to February. Sparse vegetation is found in most parts of the Sahara, with the exception of the sand dune regions. The Nile and Niger rivers, both fed by rains outside of the desert, are the only permanent rivers in the region. Water is present at or just below the surface gravel in wadis (intermittent streams) that radiate from the mountain massifs, in scattered oases where the water table comes to the surface, and at greater depths in huge underground aquifers. The aquifers are believed to be filled with water dating from the Pleistocene epoch, when the Sahara was much wetter than it is today; the more than 20 lakes (called chotts in the north) and areas of salt flats and boggy salt marshes are also considered relics from this pluvial period. There is dispute as to whether the desiccation of the region has continued into historic time. Those who support this theory contend that increasing aridity is the reason for the recorded advance of desert conditions into areas under cultivation in Roman times in the north and more recently (since the late 1960s) in the south. Opponents of this view explain such changes as being the result of alterations in land-use practices and neglect of water-supply and irrigation systems. Two thirds of the Sahara's estimated 2 million inhabitants (excluding those in the Nile valley) are concentrated in oases where date palms, fruits, vegetables, grains, and other crops are produced under irrigation. Nomads, with herds of sheep and goats and with camels for transportation, predominate in drier areas and continue to use oases (including modern oases created by the drilling of wells), as in centuries past, for water, trade, and provisioning stops. The principal ethnic groups of the Sahara are the Tuareg (of Berber origin), who dominate the mountains of the central Sahara; the peoples of mixed Berber and Arab origin in W Sahara; and the Tibu (Tébu) of mostly Negroid origin, who dominate the Tibesti Massif. Salt is still mined, as in the past, at Taoudenni, Mali, and at Bilma, Niger, and is transported, as in the days of the great medieval kingdoms of W Africa, by camel caravans across the desert. Extensive iron ore deposits are worked in the Fort Gouraud area of Mauritania, and there are huge oil and gas deposits in Algeria and Libya. At the time of the European Ice Age (c.50,000–100,000 years ago), the Sahara was a region of extensive shallow lakes, well-vegetated, and occupied by a predominantly Negroid population. By Roman times most of the vegetation had long since disappeared and there was little knowledge or exploration of the region. The camel was introduced probably in the 1st cent. A.D. and facilitated occupation by nomads (first the Berbers, later the Arabs), who lived in interdependence with the oasis dwellers, providing protection against enemies in exchange for supplies of food and water. A profitable trans-Saharan trade in gold and slaves from W Africa, salt from the desert, and cloth and other products from the cities on the Mediterranean coast, was carried on by the nomads from the 10th through 19th cent. The first European explorers to travel in the Sahara were Friedrich Horneman in 1805 and Mungo Park in 1806; René Caillié was the first to cross (1822–24) the desert and emerge alive. Among others who contributed to knowledge of the desert were Heinrich Barth, Gustav Nachtigal, Dixon Denham, and Hugh Clapperton. Some areas of the Sahara remain unexplored, although a network of air and modern automobile routes now crosses the desert and links the major oases and mining areas. From west to east the four principal land routes across the desert are from Colomb-Bechar to Dakar; from Colomb-Bechar to Gao and Timbuktu by way of Reganne; from Touggourt to Agadès and Kano by way of In-Salah; and from Tripoli to Ghat. See E. F. Gautier, *Sahara: The Great Desert* (1928; tr. 1935, repr. 1970); L. C. Briggs, *Tribes of the Sahara* (1960); J. H. Wellard, *The Great Sahara* (1965); Christoph Kruger et al., *Sahara* (tr. 1969); H. T. Norris, *Saharan Myth and Saga* (1972).

Saharanpur (səhä'rənpo͝or''), city (1971 pop. 225,698), Uttar Pradesh state, N central India, on the Dharmaula River. Once a summer resort of the Mogul court, Saharanpur is now a district administrative center. Wood products and furniture are manufactured. The region is noted for its mangoes.

Sahel (sähĕl'), name applied to the semiarid region of Africa between the Sahara to the north and the savannas to the south, extending from Senegal, on the west, through Mauritania, Mali, Upper Volta, Niger, N Nigeria, Sudan, to Ethiopia on the east. Beginning in the late 1960s the Sahel was afflicted by a prolonged and devastating drought that further reduced the region's normally meager water supplies, shattered its agricultural economy, contributed to the starvation of hundreds of thousands of people, and forced the mass migration southward of many tribes. Many parts of the Sahel received heavy and prolonged periods of rainfall in mid-1974.

Sahiwal (sä'hĭväl), city (1972 metropolitan area est. pop. 118,000), N Pakistan, on the Jhelum River. It is a district administrative headquarters and a market for food grains and cotton. Two colleges affiliated with the Univ. of the Punjab are in Sahiwal.

Said, Sayyid (both: säēd'), 1791?–1856, ruler of Oman and Zanzibar. He became ruler of Oman in 1806, when he was about 15. After defeating opposition in Oman, with British help he determined to reassert Oman's traditional claims in E Africa. He eventually succeeded and in about 1840 shifted his capital to Zanzibar, where he introduced the cloves that became the foundation of the island's economy. He also controlled the Arab traders that brought back slaves and ivory from the African interior.

saiga: see ANTELOPE.

Saigo, Takamori (täkä'mōrē sī'gō), 1828–77, Japanese soldier and statesman noted for his obstinate conservatism. He was an early opponent of the Tokugawa shogunate. He was exiled (1859–64) but returned to train Satsuma warriors. In 1867 his troops supported the emperor in the Meiji Restoration. In the new government he was an imperial adviser, and in 1873 he advocated war with Korea and opposed the Westernization of Japan. When his advice was rejected, he and a group of dissidents retired from the government. He spent four years training a military force, and in 1877 he led the Satsuma revolt; his samurai followers were defeated by imperial troops, drawn from the peasantry and equipped with modern arms. Saigo committed suicide. He later became a symbol of devotion to principle. See biography by Saneatsu Mushakoji (tr. 1942); Moriaki Sakamoto, *The Fall of Shiroyama* (1962).

Saigon (sīgŏn', sī'gŏn, Fr. säēgôN'), city (1970 est. pop. 1,760,000), capital of South Vietnam, on the right bank of the Saigon River, a tributary of the Dong Nai. Together with CHOLON, Saigon is the largest city, the greatest port, and the commercial and industrial center of South Vietnam. It has an international airport and is the focus of the country's highways, railroads, and of the Mekong delta waterways. Almost all of South Vietnam's industry is located in the Saigon metropolitan area. There are textile mills, canneries, glassworks, paper mills, shipyards, machine-assembling plants, and establishments processing the food and industrial crops of the country (rice, sugarcane, rubber) and manufacturing plastics, pharmaceuticals, feathers, building materials, and handicrafts. Known for its beauty throughout the East, Saigon has a European atmosphere and is laid out in rectilinear fashion with wide, tree-lined avenues and parks (Cholon, on the other hand, is Chinese in aspect). An ancient Khmer settlement, Saigon passed (17th cent.) to the Annamese. It was captured by the French in 1859 and ceded to France in 1862. A small village at the time of French conquest, Saigon became a modern city under French rule. It was capital of COCHIN CHINA and from 1887 to 1902 was capital of the Union of Indochina. In 1932, Saigon and Cholon were merged for administrative purposes, and in 1956 the two cities were included in the new prefecture of Saigon. Saigon became the capital of the newly created state of South Vietnam in 1954. In the VIETNAM WAR it served as military headquarters for U.S. and South Vietnamese forces. It suffered considerable damage during the 1968 Tet offensive. Throughout the 1960s and early 1970s at least a million refugees from the rural areas poured into the city, creating serious problems of housing and overcrowding. Saigon has a symphony orchestra and is the seat of the Univ. of Saigon, Van Hanh Univ., and several colleges.

Saijo (sījō'), city (1970 pop. 51,127), Ehime prefecture, W Shikoku, Japan, on the Hiuchi Sea. It is an agricultural center.

Saiki (sī'kē), city (1970 pop. 50,698), Oita prefecture, NE Honshu, Japan. It is a fishing port and agricultural market.

sail: see SAILING.

Sailendra (sīlĕn'drä), name, meaning king of the mountain, given to a dynasty in Indonesia and SE Asia. Possibly of Indian origin, the dynasty appeared in central Java in the 7th cent. and had consolidated its position by the mid-8th cent. The Sailendras, who adopted Buddhism, extended their power over the Sumatran domains of Sri Vijaya and the Malay Peninsula and exerted influence in Siam and Indochina. After their eclipse in Java (late 9th cent.), they retained control of Sri Vijaya, with important centers at Palembang (their capital) and in Kedah and Patani on the Malayan Peninsula. The Sailendra power was badly shaken by the Chola war of the 11th cent., but endured in some form until the Javanese invasion of Sumatra and the Malay Peninsula in the 13th cent.

sailfin: see MOLLIE.

sailfish, common name for a marine game and food fish belonging to the family Istiophoridae and related to the SWORDFISH and the MARLIN. It is named for its high, wide dorsal fin, colored deep blue with black spots. Like the marlin it has a pikelike upper jaw and small scales embedded in its skin. The average length is 6 ft (180 cm), though it may reach 10 ft (305 cm). The Atlantic sailfish, *Istiophorus americanus,* found north to Cape Cod in summer, averages 60 lb (27 kg) in weight, while the Pacific sailfish, *I. orientalis,* grows to 100 lb (45 kg). Sailfish are classified in the phylum CHORDATA, subphylum Vertebrata, class Osteichthyes, order Perciformes, family Istiophoridae.

sailing, as a sport, the art of navigating a sailboat for recreational or competitive purposes. Although sailing as a means of transportation dates back to prehistoric times, sailing for sport did not appear until the 17th cent., in Holland. From there it was introduced into England by King Charles II (c.1660) and eventually spread to the American Colonies. Then, as now, it was common for sport sailors to join together for social and recreational purposes in groups known as yacht clubs. The world's first such club was founded (1720) in Ireland as the Water Club of Cork Harbor. The oldest continuously existing yacht club in the United States is the New York Yacht Club (founded 1844). In 1851 the New York Yacht Club sent the schooner *America* across the Atlantic to compete in a race for the Hundred-Guinea Cup. After the victory of the U.S. boat over her British competitors, the trophy was brought back to the United States, and thus was born the *America*'s Cup, the oldest and most prestigious event in international sailboat racing. Limited to relatively large vessels, 70 to 145 ft (21.34-44.19 m) long, the event has been won by the United States in every competition held since 1851. Other important sailboat races are the Sewanhaka Cup and Canada's Cup of the Great Lakes, both for smaller craft, and various transoceanic races including the United States to Bermuda, the Trans-Atlantic, and the Trans-Pacific. Sailboat racing has also been an event in the Olympic Games since 1900. Compared to most other racing vehicles, the sailboat is rather slow. The fastest recorded time in the *America*'s Cup series is only about 15 mi (24 km) per hr; and the American inland lake scow, probably the world's fastest sailing boat, travels at a maximum speed of about 20 mi (32 km) per hr. In all major races, competition is generally restricted to boats of the same class and similar size. Boats are classified according to the arrangement, shape, size, and number of their sails and masts. The most common types are the sloop (one mast, two sails), schooner (usually two masts and five sails), yawl (two masts, four sails), and ketch (two masts, five sails). Sloops, from 10 to 70 ft (3.05-21.34 m), are generally used for racing, and schooners, yawls, and ketches, usually more than 20 ft (6.1 m) long, are used for noncompetitive recreational cruising. Sailboats originally had wooden hulls with sails made of sailcloth, a form of canvas that is commonly called duck. Today, however, most hulls are made of fiber glass, while synthetic fibers, especially Orlon, nylon, and Dacron, have replaced sailcloth. Although sport sailing in the 19th cent. was largely a sport of the wealthy, modern methods of boatbuilding have in the 20th cent. allowed many of the less affluent to participate with small, relatively inexpensive sport craft. Especially popular are the 16 to 23 ft (4.88-7.01 m) so-called one-design boats; these are mass-produced craft made from a single blueprint and intended for the sailor of modest means. Included among these crafts are the Star, Snipe, Comet, Mercury, and Lightning; the Star (designed 1911) is the earliest and most popular of the one-design vessels. Races between one-design boats of the same type are thought to be a particularly good test of a crew's ability, because any variation in speed must, at least in theory, be attributable to the skill of the crew rather than to the design of the boat. Although sailing is popular throughout the world, the United States, Great Britain, Australia, and the Soviet Union have dominated international racing competition since World War II. See NAVIGATION. See Juan Baader, *The Sailing Yacht* (tr. 1965); J. M. Lewis, *Sailing and Small Boats* (1965); E. L. Bloomster, *Sailing and Small Craft down the Ages* (2d ed. 1969).

sailplane: see GLIDER.

Saimaa (sī'mä), lake system c.1,850 sq mi (4,790 sq km), occupying the heavily glaciated plateau of S central Finland. It comprises more than 120 connecting lakes; the large southern basin of the system constitutes Lake Saimaa proper (c.500 sq mi/1,290 sq km). The system drains SE into Lake Ladoga (USSR) through the Vuoskijoki (c.100 mi/160 km long). There are numerous canals to facilitate steamship and lumber-raft traffic through the **Saimaa Canal** (c.37 mi/60 km long; completed 1856), which terminates at Vyborg, USSR, on the Gulf of Finland. The cities of Joensuu, Kuopio, Lappeenranta, and Mikkeli are on the lakes.

sainfoin (sān'foin) [Fr.,=holy hay], leguminous perennial herb (*Onobrychis viciaefolia*) of the family Leguminosae (PULSE family) indigenous in S Europe and in temperate W Asia. Sainfoin has for centuries been widely cultivated in Europe as a forage crop. Although it was introduced into the United States about 160 years ago, it has never become agriculturally important there. It thrives on calcareous soils too dry or too barren for clover or alfalfa. The plant is sometimes associated with the Christmas story of the Infant Jesus in the manger. Sainfoin is also called esparcet and holy clover. It is classified in the division MAGNOLIOPHYTA, class Magnoliopsida, order Rosales, family Leguminosae.

Saint. For canonized and uncanonized saints, see under the proper name, e.g., AMBROSE, SAINT. For surnames and place names beginning thus, see in alphabetical position here: thus, SAINT EXUPÉRY, ANTOINE DE; SAINT LOUIS.

saint [O.Fr., from Latin *sanctus*=holy]. In the Hebrew Scriptures God is "the Holy One" or "one who is holy" (Isa. 1.4; 5.19; 41.14). "His people share His holiness" (Ex. 19.6). To the New Testament authors the church is the community of saints (Acts 9.13 and the Pauline epistles). Although the creeds, with the phrase "communion of saints," maintain that usage, in later Christianity the term saint came to be used for those who live in heaven. In traditional belief, as taught by Roman Catholics and Orthodox Eastern, faithful Christians on earth and the saints in heaven are all members of the church, and just as living members seek the prayers of others and share in the merits of others, so the living ask those in heaven for their prayers and share in their merits (see INDULGENCE). An aspect of the same cooperation of the living and the saints is prayer for those dead who are not yet saints (i.e., in PURGATORY). The Virgin MARY is the chief saint. Angels are counted as saints. Prayer to the saints ("veneration" or "honor") is distinct in kind from prayer to God ("worship" or "adoration"), who is the source of all their glory. In the liturgy a saint is commemorated and his intercession sought on a special day ("saint's day"; see also ALL SAINTS DAY), usually the anniversary of his death. In the ancient churches each member has at least one PATRON saint from baptism, and in the West another is adopted at confirmation; patrons are expected to have a mutual relation of affection with their earthly charges. Saints vary in popularity: St. Joseph, very popular today among Catholics and Orthodox, had scarcely any cultus 1,000 years ago; St. Nicholas, for centuries a favorite in the West, has today few devotees among Roman Catholics. Examples of nonliturgical devotions to saints are pilgrimages (see PILGRIM), many forms of LITANY, images and icons, novenas, and annual celebrations in honor of patron saints. Accounts of saints' lives have been favorite reading material for many, and at times their composition (hagiography) has become a real art. Apart from those that are simple, contemporary records, they often become miracle-studded tales. Two immortal collections of saints' lives are the GOLDEN LEGEND and the *Little Flowers of St. Francis* (see FRANCIS, SAINT). In the modern Roman Catholic Church the BOLLANDISTS have been charged with the task of separating the true from the false in hagiography. The effort entails the revision of official books, e.g., the Roman Martyrology, a compendium of saints' lives. The addition of the name of a person to the official list of saints is called CANONIZATION. Generally in the Roman Catholic Church the title *saint* is limited to the canonized if they lived after the year 1000; otherwise the title is used according to custom. In East and West criteria for recognition of sainthood are martyrdom, holiness of life, miracles in life and after death (e.g., with RELICS), and a popular cultus. In 1969 the Roman Catholic Church dropped a number of saints from its liturgical calendar because of doubt that they ever lived; among them was the popular St. Christopher. See G. H. Gerould, *Saints' Legends* (1916, repr. 1969); Herbert Thurston and Donald Attwater, ed., *Butler's Lives of the Saints* (4 vol., 1956, repr. 1965); Phyllis McGinley, *Saint-Watching* (1969); Donald Attwater, *The Penguin Dictionary of Saints* (1970).

Saint Albans (sŭnt ôl'bənz), municipal borough (1971 pop. 52,057), Hertfordshire, E central England. A market town, it has printing and engineering industries and produces clothing and seeds. Many residents work in London. St. Albans is the site of the Roman Verulamium. King Offa of Mercia founded an abbey there in 793 to house the relics of Saint Alban, an early British martyr. The abbey and attached school (replaced by St. Alban's School in the 16th cent.) were made famous by Mathew of Paris and other chroniclers. The present cathedral was built mostly in the 11th cent. by Paul of Caen, the first Norman abbot, who used Roman materials from Verulamium. Extensions and alterations were made in the 13th, 14th, and 19th cent. Part of nearby St. Michael's Church dates from the 10th cent.; the church contains a memorial to Francis Bacon. In the Wars of the Roses, St. Albans was the scene of a Yorkist victory in 1455 and a Lancastrian victory in 1461. Sarah Jennings, 1st duchess of Marlborough, was born in nearby Holywell House.

Saint Albans (sānt ôl'bənz), city (1970 pop. 14,356), Kanawha co., W.Va., at the junction of the Coal and the Kanawha rivers; settled c.1790, inc. 1868. It is chiefly residential, and most of the residents work at chemical plants in surrounding cities. The battle of Scary Creek (1861) was fought nearby. West Virginia State College is in the vicinity.

Saint-Amant, Marc-Antoine de Gérard, Sieur de (märk-äNtwän' də zhärär', syör də săNtämäN'), 1594-1661, French lyric poet. After establishing himself through public readings in Parisian cabarets, Saint-Amant traveled to Warsaw, Rome, and London and performed on commission in many royal courts. His best-known works, noted for their vivid realism, are the sonnet *Les Goinfres* [the drinkers] (c.1630) and the satire *Rome ridicule* [ridiculous Rome] (1633).

Saint Andrews, burgh (1971 pop. 11,633), Fife, E Scotland, on the North Sea. A summer resort, it is famous for its golf courses. It was an archbishopric from 908 and the ecclesiastical capital of Scotland until the Reformation. St. Andrews Cathedral, the largest in Scotland, but now a ruin, was founded in 1160 and vandalized by Protestants in 1559. At St. Andrews the Protestant reformers Patrick Hamilton and George Wishart were burned. Protestants, among them John Knox, seized the bishop's palace (now also a ruin) in 1546 and held it for a year against siege by the French forces of Mary of Guise. The Univ. of St. Andrews, which dates from 1410, is the oldest in Scotland.

Saint Andrews, University of, at St. Andrews, Scotland; founded 1410. It is the oldest university in Scotland. It has faculties of arts, science, and divinity. St. Salvator's College was founded in 1450 and St. Leonard's College in 1512. St. Mary's College (1537) has been restricted since 1579 to the teaching of theology.

Saint Ann, city (1970 pop. 18,215), St. Louis co., E Mo., a suburb of St. Louis; inc. 1948. Lambert-St. Louis Municipal Airport is nearby.

Saint-Arnaud, Armand Jacques Leroy de (ärmäN' zhäk lərwä' də săNtärnō'), 1798?-1854, marshal of France. After serving in the French Foreign Legion in Algeria from 1837, he was one of the generals summoned from Africa by Louis Napoleon (later Napoleon III) to support his coup d'etat of Dec., 1851. As minister of war, Saint-Arnaud supported bloody repression of workers' resistance to the coup. He commanded the French troops in the Crimean War and won the victory of the Alma shortly before he died of cholera.

Saint Augustine (sānt ô'gəstēn), city (1970 pop. 12,352), seat of St. Johns co., NE Fla.; inc. 1824. Located on a peninsula between the Matanzas and San Sebastian rivers, it is separated from the Atlantic Ocean by Anastasia Island; the INTRACOASTAL WATERWAY passes through the city. St. Augustine is a port of entry, a shrimping and shipping center, and a popular year-round resort; food-processing and aircraft-repair industries are also important. The oldest city in the United States, it was founded in 1565 by the Spanish explorer Pedro Menéndez de Avilés on the site of an ancient Indian village and near the place where Ponce de Léon, the discoverer of Florida, had landed in 1513. It was named for St. Augustine, on whose feast day (Aug. 28) Menéndez entered the harbor. The town was burned and sacked by the English buccaneers Sir Francis Drake (1586) and Capt. John Davis (1665). St. Augustine repelled attacks by South Carolinians in 1702-3 and in 1740 by James Oglethorpe, the founder of Georgia, but it passed to the English in 1763 at the end of the French and Indian Wars. In the American Revolution, Tories flocked to the city from the North but left when it reverted to Spain in 1783. In 1821, Spain ceded Florida to the United States, and St. Augustine grew rapidly until the Seminole War (see SEMINOLE INDIANS) in the 1830s. Union troops occupied the city in March, 1862, and held it throughout the Civil War. Much of St. Augustine's colonial atmosphere remains. Among the old landmarks is **Castillo de San Marcos** (kästē'yō də săn mär'kəs), now a national monument (see NATIONAL PARKS AND MONUMENTS, table). The oldest masonry fort in the country (built 1672-96), it was Spain's northernmost outpost in the Americas and guarded the shipping lane to Spain. **Fort Matanzas** (mətăn'zəs), also a national monument, was built by Spain in 1742 near the site where Menéndez massacred a French force (1565), led by Jean Ribaut, which was guarding the southern entrance to the Matanzas River, S of St. Augustine. The Castillo, Fort Matanzas, and the old city gates (built 1804 to replace earlier ones) were all built of native coquina rock. Other places of interest in the city are the old schoolhouse, the house reputed to be the oldest in the United States (said to date from the late 16th cent.), the slave market, the cathedral (built 1793–7; partly restored), and the Flagler Memorial Church.

Saint Austell with Fowey (sŭnt ô'stəl; foi), municipal borough (1971 pop. 32,252), Cornwall, SW England, at the mouth of the Fowey River on St. Austell Bay. The municipal borough of Fowey and the urban district of St. Austell were amalgamated in 1968 to form the new borough. China clay is produced and exported, and tourism and fishing are also important. Fowey was an important port in the 14th cent. The valuable china clay was discovered c.1755 by William Cookworthy. The Haven was the residence of the writer Sir Arthur Quiller-Couch. Nearby at Pridmouth are fossils and minerals of geological interest. Castle Dore, to the north, is believed to be the castle of King Mark of Cornwall and thus is associated with the story of Tristram and Isolde.

Saint Barthélemy: see GUADELOUPE.

Saint Bartholomew's Day, massacre of, murder of French Protestants, or HUGUENOTS, that began in Paris on Aug. 24, 1572. It was preceded, on Aug. 22, by an attempt, ordered by CATHERINE DE' MEDICI, on the life of the Huguenot leader Admiral COLIGNY. The failure of the attempt led to formulation of the plan for a general massacre. The opportunity was furnished by the presence in Paris of many of the Huguenot nobility for the wedding of Henry of Navarre (later King HENRY IV) and Catherine's daughter, Margaret of Valois. Involved with Catherine in the scheme were the duc d'Anjou, later King HENRY III; Henri, 3d duc de Guise (see under GUISE); and the reluctant King CHARLES IX. Coligny was the first victim; his death was followed by the killing of minor leaders and of all Huguenots within reach of the soldiery and the mob. The massacre spread from Paris into other sections of France. Its result was the resumption of civil war (see RELIGION, WARS OF). See studies by Philippe Erlanger (tr. 1962) and N. M. Sutherland (1973).

Saint Bernard, two Alpine passes, both used since antiquity. The **Great Saint Bernard** (alt. 8,110 ft/2,472 m), on the Italian-Swiss border, links Valais canton, Switzerland, with Valle d'Aosta, Italy. Frequented by the Gauls and Romans, the pass also was crossed by Charlemagne, Emperor Henry IV, Frederick Barbarossa, and Napoleon I. The hospice, founded by St. Bernard of Menthon, is in the charge of Augustinian friars. The St. Bernard dogs bred by them were formerly used to search for lost travelers. A ruined temple of Jupiter stands at the summit. Nearby are a hotel, a church, a library, and a scientific institute. The Great St. Bernard Road Tunnel, c.4 mi (6.4 km) long, linking Switzerland and Italy, was opened in 1964. The **Little Saint Bernard** (alt. 7,178 ft/2,188 m) connects Savoie dept., France, with Valle d'Aosta, Italy. It also has a hospice founded by St. Bernard of Menthon.

Saint Bernard, breed of massive WORKING DOG developed in Switzerland in the 18th cent. and perfected by British breeders during the 19th cent. It stands from 25 to 29 in. (64–74 cm) high at the shoulder and weighs from 140 to 170 lb (64–77 kg). There are two varieties of St. Bernard, the smooth-coated, with very dense, short hair, and the rough-coated, with medium-length, straight or slightly wavy hair. In color the coat may be white with red markings, red with white markings, white with brindle, or brindle with white. The muzzle is white and the face characteristically marked with black. The St. Bernard was originally bred by the monks at the Hospice of the St. Bernard Pass in the Swiss Alps for rescue and guide work. Early in its history, the St. Bernard became a legendary figure as a result of the widespread stories of its valiant missions to save the lives of snowbound travelers in the pass. This rescue work, however, has undoubtedly been overemphasized. Endowed with an uncanny sense of direction, the St. Bernard was used primarily to guide the monks over trails often obliterated by windblown snow. Today it is gaining popularity as a show competitor and family companion. See DOG.

Saint Boniface (sānt bŏn'ĭfās), city (1971 pop. 46,714), SE Man., Canada, on the Red River opposite Winnipeg. It is an industrial center, with large stockyards and meat-packing plants, oil refineries, flour mills, and breweries. St. Boniface was founded in 1818 as a Roman Catholic mission. Many of the inhabitants are French-speaking. A Roman Catholic cathedral is there, as is St. Boniface College, affiliated with the Univ. of Manitoba.

Saint-Brieuc (săN-brēō'), town (1968 pop. 54,763), capital of Côtes-du-Nord dept., NW France, on the Gouet River near its mouth on the Bay of Saint-Brieuc, an arm of the English Channel. Metallurgy and textiles are the chief industries. Saint-Brieuc was probably founded in the 5th cent. and grew rapidly after St. Briomach, the Welsh missionary for whom the town was named, built a monastery there (6th or 7th cent.). An episcopal see since the 9th cent., the town was the meeting place for the provincial estates of Brittany in the 17th and 18th cent. Many old houses remain, and there is a Gothic cathedral.

Saint Catharines, city (1971 pop. 109,722), S Ont., Canada, on the Welland Ship Canal. An industrial center in a rich fruit-growing region, it has canneries and wineries as well as textile and paper mills; motor vehicle parts, machinery, electrical products, and farm implements are manufactured. St. Catharines was founded in 1790. Brock Univ. (1964) is in the city. The Royal Henley Regatta is held annually in Port Dalhousie, part of St. Catharines since 1961.

Saint-Chamond (săN-shămăN'), city (1968 pop. 38,406), Loire dept., SE France, at the confluence of the Gier and Janon rivers. The city grew in the 19th cent. as a coal-mining center. Other products besides coal include weapons, textiles, bicycles, and toys. The remains of a Roman aqueduct are in Saint-Chamond.

Saint Charles. 1 City (1970 pop. 12,928), Kane co., NE Ill., on the Fox River, in a farm and resort area; inc. 1850. Its manufactures include iron castings and furniture. **2** City (1970 pop. 31,834), seat of St. Charles co., E Mo., on the low bluffs along the north bank of the Missouri River, in an industrial area; settled by French traders 1769, inc. as a city 1849. It is the trade and distribution center of a rich farm area. Shoes and metal products are manufactured. Coal mines are nearby. The earliest permanent white settlement on the Missouri River, St. Charles was an important trading post, a starting point on the westward Boone's Lick Trail, and the state capital from 1821 to 1826. The Lindenwood Colleges and the Sacred Heart Convent (1818) are there. Of interest is the old capitol building.

Saint Christopher, British West Indies: see SAINT KITTS-NEVIS.

St. Clair, Arthur, 1734–1818, American general, b. Thurso, Caithness co., Scotland. He left the Univ. of Edinburgh to become (1757) an ensign in the British army and served in the French and Indian War at Louisburg and Quebec. In 1762 he resigned his commission and settled in Pennsylvania, where he purchased a vast estate and held a number of civil offices. In the American Revolution he served in the expedition to Canada as colonel of a regiment of militia which he had raised (1775). He was made a brigadier general and, authorized by George Washington to organize the New Jersey militia, fought in the battles of Trenton and Princeton. As major general, St. Clair took command (1777) at Fort Ticonderoga, which he evacuated without a fight to superior British forces. A court-martial in 1778 cleared him of blame, and he served afterward in several minor capacities. After serving as a delegate to Congress (1785–87), St. Clair was appointed (1787) the first governor of the Northwest Territory. He established its capital at Cincinnati and became (1791) commander in chief of the forces fighting the Indians. The Indians, led by LITTLE TURTLE, surprised and defeated St. Clair near the Miami villages. The defeat led him to resign his commission (1792), although a congressional investigating committee later exonerated him. St. Clair's arbitrary rule as governor gained him many enemies, and in 1802 he was removed by Thomas Jefferson after condemning the act making Ohio a state. He published in 1812 a defense of his conduct in the Indian wars and spent his later years in poverty. See W. H. Smith, ed., *The St. Clair Papers* (2 vol., 1882, repr. 1971); biography by F. E. Wilson (1944).

Saint Clair, Lake, c.490 sq mi (1,270 sq km), 27 mi (43 km) long, on the U.S.-Canadian border, between SW Ont. and SE Mich. The St. Clair River (41 mi/66 km long) flows into the lake from Lake Huron; the Detroit River drains it S into Lake Erie. The lake is one of the busiest sections of the St. Lawrence Seaway.

Saint Clair Shores, city (1970 pop. 88,093), Macomb co., SE Mich., a residential suburb adjacent to Detroit, on Lake St. Clair; settled 18th cent. by the French, inc. 1925. It is a boating center.

Saint-Claude (săN-klōd), town (1968 pop. 13,117), Jura dept., E France, in Franche-Comté, at the confluence of the Bienne and Tacon rivers. It is a resort and an industrial center where brier pipes, plastic products, glasses, and toys are manufactured. First a Gallic, then a Roman town, it took its name from Bishop Claude of Besançon, who died there in the 7th cent. Serfdom survived in the town at the abbey of Saint-Claude until the abbey was suppressed by the French Revolution in 1789.

Saint-Cloud (săN-klōō'), town (1968 pop. 28,560), Hauts-de-Seine dept., N central France, a suburb W of Paris on the Seine River. It is a residential town and resort, with a famous racetrack. Aeronautic equipment, carburetors, radio equipment, motors, and cosmetics are produced. The town was named after Clodoald (or Cloud), grandson of Clovis I. The palace of Saint-Cloud (built 1572; destroyed during the Franco-Prussian War in 1870), of which the picturesque park remains, was a residence of many rulers of France. Napoleon I proclaimed the Empire at Saint-Cloud in 1804.

Saint Cloud, city (1970 pop. 39,691), seat of Stearns co. and also in Benton and Sherburne counties, central Minn., on the Mississippi River, in a dairy farm region; inc. 1856. Granite has been quarried there since 1868, and granite finishing is still a leading industry. Refrigeration equipment, lenses, paper products, valves, tanks and processing equipment, and generators are also made. St. Cloud State College and a U.S. veterans hospital are there.

Saint Croix, (sānt kroi), island (1970 pop. 31,779), 80 sq mi (207 sq km), the largest of the U.S. VIRGIN ISLANDS, in the West Indies. Christiansted (1970 pop. 2,966), on the northeast coast, is the island's leading town.

Saint Croix. 1 River, 75 mi (121 km) long, rising in the Chiputneticook Lakes and flowing SE to Passamaquoddy Bay, forming part of the U.S.-Canada border; navigable to Calais, Maine. The river is used for power and to float logs downstream. In 1604, French explorer Samuel de Champlain and colonist Pierre du Gua, sieur de Monts, established a colony on St. Croix (Dochet) Island (now a national monument) near the river's mouth; it was abandoned in 1605. In 1798 the British insisted that the St. Croix was the Penobscot River, some miles to the west, and not the international boundary. However, the discovery of ruins of the French settlement on St. Croix Island verified the river as the St. Croix and therefore the border. **2** River, 164 mi (264 km) long, rising in the lake district of NW Wis. and flowing generally S to the Mississippi River at Prescott, Wis.; forms part of the Wis.-Minn. line. The Dalles, a scenic gorge, is located in Interstate Park. A hydroelectric plant at St. Croix Falls supplies power to Minneapolis-St. Paul.

Saint Croix Island National Monument: see NATIONAL PARKS AND MONUMENTS (table).

Saint Croix National Scenic Riverway: see NATIONAL PARKS AND MONUMENTS (table).

Saint-Cyr, Laurent Gouvion, marquis de: see GOUVION-SAINT-CYR, LAURENT, MARQUIS DE.

Saint-Cyran, Abbé de: see DUVERGIER DE HAURANNE, JEAN.

Saint-Cyr-l'École (săN-sēr-lākôl'), town (1968 pop. 17,037), Yvelines dept., N central France. A school for the daughters of impoverished noblemen was founded there in 1685 by Louis XIV and Mme de Maintenon. The building later housed the famous military academy (the West Point of France) founded by Napoleon in 1808. It was destroyed in World War II, and the school was moved to Coëtquidan in Brittany. A new military school was opened in 1966.

Saint David's, village, Pembrokeshire, SW Wales. The village cathedral, the most famous and one of the finest in Wales, is mainly Transitional Norman in style, built of red-violet stone. Among its features is the late 13th-century shrine of St. David (St. David is the patron saint of Wales). The cathedral, after numerous additions and alterations, was restored by Sir George Gilbert Scott in 1878. Across the Alun brook, which flows past the cathedral, are the imposing ruins of the Bishop's Palace (14th cent.). St. David's (ancient Menevia) was for centuries one of the most important places of pilgrimage in Great Britain; it is the focal point of several old roads. **Saint David's Head,** 2½ mi (4.2 km) northwest of the village, is the westernmost point of Wales.

St. Denis, Ruth (sānt dĕn'ĭs), 1877–1968, American dancer, b. Newark, N.J., whose name was originally Ruth Dennis. After her debut (c.1893) she toured with David Belasco. In 1906 she began her recitals of highly imaginative and spectacular Oriental dances, performing in Europe (1906–8) and in the United States (after 1909); these had widespread influence on modern dance. With Ted Shawn, whom she married in 1914, she founded the Denishawn Schools in Los Angeles and in New York City (1920). A divergence in their views after 1931 led her to found (1940) a separate school. Her dances include *Radha, Incense, Cobras,* and *Nautch.* See her autobiography (1939); biography by Walter Terry (1969); study by C. L. Schlundt (1962).

Saint-Denis (săN-dənē'), city (1968 pop. 100,060), Seine-Saint-Denis dept., N central France. It is an industrial suburb N of Paris. Metals, chemicals, machinery, glass, paper, soap, and food products are the major manufactures. Saint-Denis was founded early in the Christian era (presumably on the site where St. Denis fell and was buried) and grew rapidly as a place of pilgrimage. In 626, King Dagobert I built a Benedictine abbey near the chapel housing the tomb; this abbey became the richest and most famous in France. Around 750 a new sanctuary was begun by Pepin the Short and finished by Charlemagne. Joan of Arc blessed her weapons at the abbey, and it was there that Abelard became a monk. The abbey's banner, the oriflamme, was the royal standard of France from the reign of Louis VI (early 12th cent.) to that of Charles VI (early 15th cent.). In the 12th cent. the famous basilica was built under the supervision of Abbé Suger, the abbot of Saint-Denis and a minister of Louis VI and Louis VII. Devastated during the French Revolution, the abbey was restored, with later work by the architect Eugène Viollet-le-Duc. Saint-Denis was the first cathedral considered essentially Gothic in construction and was the prototype of SENLIS, CHARTRES, and other cathedrals. Within the cathedral are the tombs of many kings and leading personages of France. Particularly remarkable are the tombs of Francis I by Philibert Delorme and of Henry II by Germain Pilon. Louis XVI and Marie Antoinette are buried in the crypt. The abbey is now a school for daughters of members of the Legion of Honor. Other points of interest in the city include a museum of gold and silver wares.

Saint-Denis, city (1971 est. pop. 94,000), capital of the French overseas department of Réunion. It is a port on the Indian Ocean at the mouth of the St.-Denis River and exports sugar and rum. St.-Denis is Réunion's largest city and its administrative, communications, and economic center. Industry is related to food processing for local consumption. Arabs play a leading role in the city's commerce. The Institute for Legal, Economic, and Political Studies (1950) is there. St.-Denis was founded in the late 17th cent. as a French way station to the Orient.

Saint-Dié (săN-dyā), city (1968 pop. 26,340), Vosges dept., E France, in LORRAINE, on the Meurthe River. It is an industrial center where wire, foundry products, chemical products, and machinery are manufactured. The city grew around a monastery founded in the 7th cent. In World War II the Germans destroyed many of Saint-Dié's landmarks and deported much of the population. The *Cosmographiae introductio* by Martin Waldseemüller, a geographic work that for the first time referred to the newly discovered continent as America, was printed in Saint-Dié in 1507.

Saint-Dizier (săN-dēzyā'), town (1968 pop. 39,014), Haute-Marne dept., NE France, on the Marne River. It is a trading and transportation center; its manufactures include machinery, musical instruments, and metals. Saint-Dizier has many structures dating from the 15th to the 18th cent. There is also a museum with Roman, Carthaginian, and early Christian artifacts.

Sainte Agathe des Monts (săNtägät' dā môN), town (1971 pop. 5,532), S Que., Canada, on the North River, NW of Montreal. It is a resort center.

Sainte Anne de Beaupré (săNtăn' də bōprā', Fr. săNtăn'də bōprā'), village (1971 pop. 1,797), S Que., Canada, on the St. Lawrence River and NE of Quebec. It is the site of a famous shrine established in 1620 by sailors who had been shipwrecked. A chapel was built in 1658 and a large church in 1876. Burned in 1922, the church was magnificently rebuilt; it houses relics and is one of Canada's foremost pilgrim resorts. Many miraculous cures are ascribed to prayers at the shrine. Mountains, a river, and falls near the village are also named for the saint.

Sainte Anne de Bellevue (săNtăn' də bĕlvü'), town (1971 pop. 4,976), S Que., Canada, on Montreal Island, SW of Montreal. The town has woodworking plants and a publishing house. In fur-trading days it was the point of departure for canoes going west, and it is referred to in Thomas Moore's "Canadian Boat Song." The agricultural faculty of Macdonald College, McGill Univ., is there.

Sainte-Beuve, Charles Augustin (shärl ōgüstăN' săNt-böv), 1804–69, French literary historian and critic. The first major professional literary critic, he developed the art of appreciating literature through psychological and biographical insight. He studied medicine but abandoned it for literature, and began contributing reviews to the *Globe* in 1824. After attempts at writing poetry, *Vie, poésies, et pensées de Joseph Delorme* (1829), and a semiautobiographical psychological novel, *Volupté* (1834), which was inspired by his love for Mme Victor Hugo, he turned to criticism. His weekly articles in reviews were collected as the *Causeries du lundi* (15 vol., 1851–62, tr. *Monday Chats,* 1877). He considered his great work to be *Port-Royal* (1840–59), taken in part from his lectures in 1837 at Lausanne. This work, comprised of six books, is a history not only of Jansenism but of a whole section of 17th-century French society. Made a member of the French Academy in 1844, Sainte-Beuve taught (1848–49) at Liège, and in 1857 he became a professor at the École normale supérieure. He was appointed senator in 1865. His vast literary output reveals a critic of great taste, vast memory and learning, and a passion for truth in judgment. See studies by L. F. Mott (1925) and Andrew Lehmann (1962); biography by Harold Nicolson (1957).

Sainte-Chapelle (săNt-shäpĕl'), former chapel in Paris. Forming part of the buildings of the Palais de Justice (once the royal palace) on the Île-de-la-Cité, it was built by Pierre de Montreuil (1243–46) for Louis IX (St. Louis) to enshrine the Crown of Thorns and other sacred relics brought back from the Crusades. It was admirably restored in the 19th cent. by J. B. Lassus and Viollet-le-Duc. Now a museum, the Sainte-Chapelle is one of the finest examples of medieval art. It consists of two chapels, one above the other, and a spire. A winding staircase leads from the painted and gilded lower chapel to the porch of the upper chapel. The elegant proportions and airiness of the upper chapel, its 15 magnificent stained-glass windows, separated only by thin colonnettes and reaching nearly from floor to ceiling, and its vividly painted columns and panels combined to create the effect of a sheer blaze of color and light. The Sainte-Chapelle is a superb example of the RAYONNANT STYLE in Gothic architecture.

Saint Elias, Mount (ĭlī'əs), 18,008 ft (5,489 m) high, in the St. Elias Mts. on the U.S.-Canadian border between SW Yukon Territory and SE Alaska; fourth highest peak of North America. It was first seen by Vitus Bering, the Danish explorer, on July 16, 1741; the duke of the Abruzzi, an Italian explorer, was the first (1897) to climb it. Malaspina Glacier rises there.

Saint Elias Mountains, section of the Coast Ranges, SW Yukon Territory, Canada, and SE Alaska, rising to 19,850 ft (6,050 m) at Mt. Logan, Canada's highest peak. Kluane National Park is there.

Saint Elmo's fire, luminous discharge of electricity extending into the atmosphere from some projecting or elevated object. It is usually observed (often during a snowstorm or a dust storm) as brushlike fiery jets extending from the tips of a ship's mast or spar, a wing, propeller, or other part of an aircraft, a steeple, a mountain top, or even from blades of grass or horns of cattle. Sometimes it plays about the head of a person, causing a tingling sensation. The phenomenon occurs when the atmosphere becomes charged and an electrical potential strong enough to cause a discharge is created between an object and the air around it. The amount of electricity involved is not great enough to be dangerous. The appearance of St. Elmo's fire is regarded as a portent of bad weather. The phenomenon, also known as corposant, was long regarded with superstitious awe. See also PETER GONZALES, SAINT.

Saintes (săNt), town (1968 pop. 28,138), Charente-Maritime dept., W France, on the Charente River. It is a market for grains, brandy, and leather. The town, probably the capital of the Celtic Santones and later occupied by the Romans, was the capital of old SAINTONGE. Louis IX defeated Henry III of England there in 1242. In Saintes are the ruins of a Roman amphitheater and triumphal arch and the two partially restored Romanesque churches of St. Eutrope (11th–12th cent.).

Saintes, Les: see GUADELOUPE.

Sainte Thérèse (săNt tārĕz'), city (1971 pop. 17,175), S Que., Canada, on the St. Lawrence River, NW of Montreal. It has factories producing automobiles, pianos, furniture, plywood, and clothing.

Saint-Étienne (săNtātyĕn'), city (1968 pop. 216,020), capital of Loire dept., SE France, in the MASSIF CENTRAL. It is a major steel and textile center in the heart of one of France's great industrial areas. Other manufactures include ribbons (famous since the 15th cent.), silk, firearms, bicycles, automobile parts, and textile machinery. The textile and silk industry began in the 11th cent.; the first firearms were produced in the 16th cent. for Francis I. The first steel plant was built in 1815, and in 1827 the city became the terminus of the first railroad in France. Points of interest include a medieval church and abbey, the 17th-century Church of St. Louis and Notre Dame, and a Palace of Arts.

Saint Eustatius (sānt yōōstā'shəs), island (1969 est. pop. 1,341), 8 sq mi (20.7 sq km), Netherlands Antilles (see CURAÇAO), one of the Leeward Islands. The mountainous island thrives on agriculture and a growing tourist trade. Orangetown, the chief port, has a colorful history. Settled by the Dutch in 1632, it became a center of contraband trade with the American colonies before and during the American Revolution. According to tradition, it was the first foreign port to salute (1776) the American flag. The island changed hands frequently. During the 18th cent. pirates and smugglers made it one of the leading trade centers of the West Indies. The island is called Statia by its inhabitants.

Saint-Évremond, Charles de Marguetel de Saint-Denis de (shärl də märgətĕl' də săN-dənē' də săNtāvrəmôN'), 1616?–1703, French critic, writer, and soldier. He served under Condé at Rocroi and Nördlingen, was made *maréchal de camp* in 1652, and was later exiled for expressing hostility to the Peace of the Pyrenees (1659). His exile was divided between Holland and England. Refusing permission given in 1689 to return to France, he died in England and was buried in Westminster Abbey. Saint-Évremond contributed to the skeptical, freethinking current of his century. He revealed his mordant wit in his *Comédie des académistes* and his originality as a critic in his essays and dissertations on tragedy, poetry, religion, and history. His correspondence (tr. 1930) is a valuable source for events and persons of his time.

Saint Exupéry, Antoine de (äNtwän' də săNtĕgzüpārē'), 1900–1944, French aviator and writer. He became a commercial pilot in 1926 and flew in Europe, Africa, and South America; in World War II he was a military pilot. He was lost in action. His writings reflect his feeling for the open skies and desert and embody his love of freedom of action. *Courrier Sud* (1929, tr. *Southern Mail,* 1933), *Vol de nuit* (1931, tr. *Night Flight,* 1932), and *Terre des hommes* (1939, tr. *Wind, Sand, and Stars,* 1939) are impressionistic, poetic narratives expressing his highly individualistic philosophy. *Pilote de guerre* (1942, tr. *Flight to Arras,* 1942) tells of a hopeless French reconnaissance flight in 1940. His fable *Le Petit Prince* (1943, tr. *The Little Prince,* 1943) is read by adults as well as children. See biographies by M. A. Smith (1956) and Curtis Cate (1970).

Saint Francis, city (1970 pop. 10,489), Milwaukee co., SE Wis., a residential suburb of Milwaukee on Lake Michigan; inc. 1951. A power plant and a school for the deaf are there.

Saint Francis, river, Canada: see SAINT FRANÇOIS.

Saint Francis, river, c.470 mi (760 km) long, rising in the hills of SE Missouri and flowing S through NE Arkansas to join the Mississippi River near Helena, Ark. The river forms part of the Arkansas-Missouri line. Wappapello Dam (completed 1941), near Poplar Bluff, Mo., forms a reservoir which is a popular recreational area.

Saint Francis, Lake, an expansion of the St. Lawrence River, SE Ont. and S Que., Canada, SW of Montreal, extending between Cornwall and Valleyfield. It is part of the St. Lawrence Seaway.

Saint Francis Indians, group of the ABNAKI INDIANS, attacked by Robert Rogers and his Rangers in 1759. The group, after warfare with New Englanders along the Kennebec River, were forced into Canada and settled chiefly at St. Francis, a village on the St. Francis River near its confluence with the St. Lawrence River. Rogers's troops were sent out against the Indians, burned the town of St. Francis, killed 200 Indians, and took several children as prisoners. Despite the damage to the settlement, it remained the principal home of the remnants of the tribe.

Saint Francis Xavier University (zā'vyər), at Antigonish, N.S., Canada; Roman Catholic; coeducational; opened as a college 1853, chartered as a university 1866. The woman's college is Mt. St. Bernard (Congregation of Notre Dame). The university has a faculty of arts and science, an institute for social leadership, and an affiliated school of nursing.

Saint François (săN fräNswä') or **Saint Francis.** **1** River, 165 mi (266 km) long, rising in Lac St. François, SE Que., Canada, and flowing SW through Lac Aylmer to Sherbrooke, then NW past Drummondville to Lac St. Pierre of the St. Lawrence River. There are several hydroelectric stations on its course. **2** River, c.60 mi (100 km) long, rising in the Notre Dame Mts., SE Que., Canada, and flowing generally SE to the St. John River. It forms part of the Quebec and New Brunswick boundary with N Maine.

Saint Gall (sānt gôl, găl, gäl), Ger. *Sankt Gallen,* canton (1970 pop. 384,475), 777 sq mi (2,012 sq km), NE Switzerland. Bordering on the Lake of Constance in the north and on the Rhine River in the east, it surrounds the entire canton of Appenzell. The south is fairly mountainous, and the north is mainly a meadowland. Wine and fruit are produced. The canton is especially known for its embroideries and silk and cotton textiles. Its inhabitants are mainly German-speaking. The canton and its capital city, **Saint Gall** (1970 pop. 80,852), take their name from the Benedictine abbey erected (8th cent.) on the site of the hermitage of St. Gall, an Irish monk, around which the town grew. The city is the center of the textile industry of E Switzerland. The abbots of St. Gall, who also ruled APPENZELL, became princes of the Holy Roman Empire in the early 13th cent. The town became a free city of the Holy Roman Empire in 1311. Rebelling against the abbot, the city made an alliance with the Swiss Confederation (1454). The Reformation, accepted by the town but suppressed in the districts controlled by the abbot, brought about a long series of disturbances (notably the War of the TOGGENBURG) until 1718. In 1803 the town and the abbot's domains (secularized in 1798) were consolidated as a canton of the Swiss Confederation under Napoleon's Act of Mediation. One of the oldest scholastic centers north of the Alps, St. Gall has a library with a world-famous collection of medieval manuscripts. An episcopal see since 1846, it also has a noted 18th-century cathedral (formerly the abbey church). There are several museums, schools, and institutes.

Saint Gall, former Benedictine abbey, at St. Gall, Switzerland. Originating in a cell built c.614 by St. Gall, an Irish missionary (see COLUMBAN, SAINT), it became an abbey under Charles Martel (8th cent.). It gained large landholdings and acquired universal fame as a center of learning in the early Middle Ages. In its library invaluable classic manuscripts were copied and preserved. Among the teachers were NOTKER BALBULUS, NOTKER LABEO, and four monks named EKKEHARD. The abbey was secularized in 1798. The present buildings date mainly from the 18th cent. See J. M. Clark, *The Abbey of St. Gall* (1926).

Saint-Gaudens, Augustus (sānt-gôd'ənz), 1848–1907, American sculptor, b. Dublin, Ireland. An apprentice in cameo cutting, he gained mastery over sculpture in low relief. He had an unusual genius for plastic expression and an unfailing enthusiasm and industry. He was trained at the École des Beaux-Arts, Paris, and gained knowledge of the Italian Renaissance from his stay (1870–73) in Italy. Saint-Gaudens became the foremost sculptor in the United States and a strong influence in the development of American sculpture. In 1881 his statue of Admiral Farragut for Madison Square, New York City, set a new standard for public monuments. Stanford WHITE collaborated on the pedestal for this figure and several others. In 1887 the figure of Lincoln in Lincoln Park, Chicago, was completed. Other works that followed are Deacon Samuel Chapin (*The Puritan*), Springfield, Mass.; the Shaw Memorial, Boston Common; General Logan, Chicago; General Sherman, entrance to Central Park, New York City; and the seated Lincoln for the Chicago lake front. Of the portrait tablets and plaques, most notable are Dr. McCosh, Princeton, N.J.; Robert Louis Stevenson for St. Giles, Edinburgh, Scotland; and charming low reliefs of children. Among ideal figures is the Adams Memorial, Rock Creek Cemetery, Washington, D.C., one of his most splendid works. See his portrait reliefs (1969); biography by L. H. Tharp (1969). His brother, Louis, 1854–1913, was also a sculptor of talent.

Saint-Gaudens National Historic Site: see NATIONAL PARKS AND MONUMENTS (table).

Saint-Gelays or **Saint-Gelais, Mellin de** (mĕlăN də săN-zhəlā'), c.1490–1558, French poet. He lived in Italy for many years, and he helped to introduce the Italian sonnet form as well as the spirit of the Renaissance into French literature.

Saint George, town (1970 pop. 1,604), on St. George's Island, Bermuda. It was the capital of Bermuda until 1815, when it was replaced by HAMILTON. During the American Civil War it harbored Confederate blockade-runners.

Saint George's or **Saint George,** town (1970 pop., 6,657), capital of GRENADA, in the West Indies. A port town on a deep and beautiful harbor, it is administrative headquarters of the country. Chief exports are cacao, nutmeg, and mace. St. George's was the capital of the former British colony of the Windward Islands.

Saint George's Channel, strait, c.100 mi (160 km) long and 50 to 95 mi (80–153 km) wide, linking the Atlantic Ocean and the Irish Sea. It separates SE Ireland from Wales.

Saint-Germain, Treaty of (săN-zhĕrmăN'), any of several treaties signed at Saint-Germain-en-Laye, near Paris, France. The Treaty of Saint-Germain of **1570** terminated the first phase of the French religious wars (see RELIGION, WARS OF). The Treaty of Saint-Germain of **1679** made peace between France and the elector of Brandenburg at the end of the third of the Dutch Wars. Frederick William the Great Elector had to restore nearly all his conquests in Pomerania to Charles XI of Sweden, who was allied to France. The Treaty of Saint-Germain of Sept. 10, **1919,** was signed by the victorious Allies of World War I on the one hand and by the new republic of AUSTRIA on the other. Like the Treaty of Versailles with Germany, it contained the Covenant of the League of Nations and as a result was not ratified by the United States. The treaty declared the Austro-Hungarian Monarchy dissolved. The new republic of Austria, consisting of most of the German-speaking part of the former Austrian Empire, recog nized the independence of Hungary, Czechoslovakia, Poland, and Yugoslavia (then called the kingdom of Serbs, Croats, and Slovenes). Austria was reduced not only by the loss of crownlands incorporated into Czechoslovakia, Poland, and Yugoslavia (the "successor states") but by the cession of S Tyrol, Trieste, Istria, several Dalmatian islands, and Friuli to Italy and the cession of Bukovina to Rumania. BURGENLAND, then a part of Hungary, was awarded to Austria. Austria assumed the responsibility of the imperial Austrian government for its share in bringing about the war, but its reparations payments to the Allies actually were never exacted because of the obvious insolvency of the Austrian state. An important article of the treaty required Austria to refrain from directly or indirectly compromising its independence, which meant that Austria could not enter into political or economic union (see ANSCHLUSS) with Germany without the agreement of the council of the League of Nations. The Austrian army was limited to a force of 30,000 volunteers. There were numerous provisions dealing with Danubian navigation, the transfer of railroads, and other details involved in the breakup of a great empire into several small independent states. The Treaty of TRIANON in 1920 between Hungary and the Allies completed the disposition of the former Dual Monarchy.

Saint-Germain-des-Prés (săN-zhĕrmăN'-dā-prā), historic abbey and church of Paris, on the left bank of the Seine. It was founded (6th cent.) by Childebert I; several Merovingian kings were buried there. Both church and abbey were several times destroyed; the present church, in Romanesque style, dates from the early 11th cent. The architect Pierre de Montreuil made some notable additions in the 13th cent., but they were destroyed in the French Revolution.

Saint-Germain-en-Laye (săN-zhĕrmăN'-äN-lā), town (1968 pop. 41,190), Yvelines dept., N central France, on the Seine River, a residential suburb W of Paris. The town, a resort, is known primarily for its 16th-century Renaissance château, built by Pierre Chambiges, which was a royal residence until the French Revolution and now houses the major museum of pre-Christian antiquities in France. Henry II and Louis XIV were among the kings born in the château; Louis and his court resided there until 1682. The magnificent château park was designed by André Lenôtre. Several important treaties (most notably the 1919 Treaty of SAINT-GERMAIN) were signed in the town. Claude Debussy was born there.

Saint Gotthard (sānt gŏt'hərd, gŏt'ərd), mountain group of the Lepontine Alps, S central Switzerland, rising to Pizzo Rotondo (10,472 ft/3,192 m high). The Reuss, Rhine, Ticino, and Rhône rivers rise there. It is crossed by the **Saint Gotthard Pass,** 6,935 ft (2,114 m) high. The pass, first extensively used in the 11th cent., has been important since then. It is crossed by the St. Gotthard Road (built 1820–30). The St. Gotthard Railway (built 1872–80), which links the northern and southern parts of Switzerland, passes through St. Gotthard Tunnel (9¼ mi/15 km long; maximum alt. 3,786 ft/1,154 m), one of the longest of Alpine tunnels.

Saint Gotthard: see SZENTGOTTHARD, Hungary.

Saint Helena (həlē'nə), island (1971 pop. 5,056), 47 sq mi (122 sq km), in the S Atlantic Ocean, 1,200 mi (1,931 km) W of Africa. Together with the islands of ASCENSION and TRISTAN DA CUNHA, it comprises the British dependency of St. Helena. The capital and port is Jamestown. Mountainous and of volcanic origin, the island rises to a height of 2,685 ft (818 m) on Mt. Actaeon. Hemp, vegetables, sweet potatoes, and livestock are raised. Discovered uninhabited by the Portuguese navigator João da Nova Castella in 1502, St. Helena was annexed by the Dutch in 1633. In 1659 it was annexed and occupied by the British East India Company, and in 1834 it became a British crown colony. The island served as a prison for South African Boers from 1900 to 1902. St. Helena is best known as the place of exile of Napoleon I, who was sent there in 1815 and who died at Longwood, near Jamestown, in 1821. His home has been maintained as a memorial.

Saint Helena Island: see SEA ISLANDS.

Saint Helens, county borough (1971 pop. 104,173), Lancashire, NW England. It is the chief center of glass manufacture in England and also has iron and brass foundries, chemical and soap factories, and potteries. Coal mining, although declining, is still carried on. There is a college of technology in the borough. In 1974, Saint Helens became part of the new metropolitan county of Merseyside.

Saint Helens, Mount, volcanic peak, 9,677 ft (2,950 m) high, SW Wash., in the Cascade Range.

Saint Helier (sānt hĕl'yər, Fr. săNtālyā'), town (1971 pop. 28,135), capital of Jersey, Channel Islands, Great Britain, on St. Aubin's Bay. It is a residential town, resort, and point of export for local produce. Royal Square was the scene of a battle (1781), when the French unsuccessfully attempted to regain Jersey. The parish church dates partly from the 14th cent. A museum, an art gallery, a zoo, and an observatory are in the town. On an adjacent island, protecting the harbor and connected with the mainland at low tide, is Elizabeth Castle, built in the late 16th cent. Near the castle is a rock that was supposedly the hermitage of St. Helier or St. Helerius, the early missionary for whom the town was named. On the rock are the ruins of a 12th-century chapel. Fort Regent is east of the harbor.

Saint-Hilaire, Étienne Geoffroy: see GEOFFROY SAINT-HILAIRE, ÉTIENNE.

Saint-Hubert (săNtübĕr'), town (1970 pop. 3,091), Luxembourg prov., SE Belgium, in the Ardennes. It is a tourist resort. Of note is a former Benedictine abbey (reputedly founded in the 7th cent.), now housing a juvenile reformatory; St. Hubert, patron of the hunt, is buried in the abbey church (16th cent.).

Saint Hyacinthe (sānt hī'əsĭnth, Fr. săNtyäsăNt'), city (1971 pop. 24,562), S Que., Canada, on the Yamaska River, NE of Montreal. It is an industrial center, with textile mills and plants manufacturing rubber and paper products, furniture, shoes, and leather goods. The famous Casavant organ factory (est. c.1860) is there. There are institutions for religious education and schools of dairy husbandry, textile technology, and veterinary medicine.

Saint James, uninc. town (1970 pop. 10,818), Suffolk co., SE N.Y., on Long Island, in a farm and resort area.

Saint James's Palace, in Westminster, London, England, on St. James's Street and fronting on Pall Mall. The site was once occupied by St. James's hospital for leprous women. Henry VIII built the palace and established the park about it. It was the London royal residence after the burning of Whitehall in 1697 until the time of Queen Victoria. The palace was damaged by bombing during World War II. Although the palace is now seldom used except for certain ceremonials, the British court is still designated as the Court of St. James.

Saint Jean (săN zhäN) or **Saint Johns,** city (1971 pop. 32,863), S Que., Canada, on the Richelieu River, SE of Montreal. It is an industrial center with textile and hosiery mills, food-canning plants, and varied light manufactures. A fort was built on the site in the 17th cent. A later post, Fort St. Jean, changed hands several times during the American Revolution. The city was the terminus of the first Canadian railroad (1836) from Lapprairie. It is the seat of a bilingual military school, the Collège Militaire Royal de Saint Jean.

Saint-Jean d'Acre: see AKKO, Israel.

Saint-Jean-de-Luz (săN-zhäN-də-lüz), town (1968 pop. 11,035), Pyrénées-Atlantiques dept., SW France, in the BASQUE PROVINCES, on the Bay of Biscay. It is a beach resort and a sardine- and tuna-fishing port. Louis XIV married (1660) Marie Thérèse of Austria there. Saint-Jean-de-Luz has a 16th-century Basque church.

Saint Jérôme (săN zhārōm'), city (1971 pop. 26,524), S Que., Canada, on the North River, NW of Montreal. It is an industrial center with woolen and paper mills. Rubber and wood products are also manufactured. Saint Jérôme is a commercial center for the Laurentian resort area.

St. John, Henry, Viscount Bolingbroke (sĭn jŭn, bŏl'ĭngbrŏŏk), 1678–1751, English statesman. Entering Parliament in 1701, he associated himself with Robert HARLEY and eventually came to rival Harley as a Tory leader. After the accession (1702) of Queen ANNE he became a favorite of the powerful duke of MARLBOROUGH and was appointed (1704) secretary for war. However, he resigned when Harley was forced out of his post by the Marlborough-Godolphin faction in 1708. When the unpopularity of the War of the Spanish Succession and the Henry SACHEVERELL incident brought in a Tory ministry (1710) under Harley, St. John became a secretary of state. He used the London Tory clubs and writers such as Jonathan SWIFT to influence public opinion in favor of his policies and carried on, despite protests from England's allies, separate peace negotiations with France. In 1712 he was created Viscount Bolingbroke, and by the influence of Abigail MASHAM, Queen Anne's favorite, he gradually rose to become the leading figure in the government. The Peace of Utrecht (1713) and Bolingbroke's intrigues preceding it were denounced by the Whigs, whose political influence he sought to weaken by the Occasional Conformity and Schism acts, directed against religious dissenters. He now broke completely with Harley, who was dismissed in 1714. Bolingbroke's true intent is not known, but it is sure that, in anticipation of the succession of a pro-Whig Hanoverian to the throne, he negotiated with James Francis STUART, the Old Pretender, and began replacing Whig officers, especially in the army, with Tories. Whatever plans he had were thwarted by the sudden death (1714) of Queen Anne and the peaceful succession of George I, who promptly dismissed Bolingbroke. He was impeached, but he fled to France before the trial and was then attainted by Parliament. In France, Bolingbroke helped plan the uprising of the JACOBITES in 1715, but in 1716 he was dismissed from the service of the Old Pretender on suspicion of having given secret Jacobite plans to the English government. He abjured the Jacobite cause, but only in 1723 did he receive (with the help of a generous bribe) a pardon from George I. On his return to England, although excluded from the House of Lords, he exerted great political influence, at first supporting but later organizing strong opposition to Robert WALPOLE. He initiated new methods of opposition to the government, such as the use of parliamentary inquiries, and attacked the government in the pages of a new periodical, the *Craftsman,* to which he contributed a famous series of letters, including a "Dissertation upon Parties" (1735), under the signature of Occasional Writer. He retired from politics in 1735 and spent most his remaining years on his estates in France, where he devoted himself to political and philosophical writing. His numerous writings, in a lucid but rhetorical style that was greatly admired at that time, include *Idea of a Patriot King* (1749), *Letters on the Study and Use of History* (privately printed, 1735–36), and *The True Use of Retirement* (1738). Although he was one of England's great orators, Bolingbroke was also an unstable profligate, and he was generally distrusted. Yet he apparently believed sincerely in a kind of "Tory democracy," for which he was later much admired by Benjamin Disraeli. His works were edited by David Mallet (5 vol., 1754) and several times thereafter. See his correspondence (ed. by Gilbert Parke, 1798); biographies by Sir Charles Petrie (1937) and H. T. Dickenson (1970); J. P. Hart, *Viscount Bolingbroke, Tory Humanist* (1965); I. Kramnick, *Bolingbroke and His Circle* (1968).

St. John, John Pierce, 1833–1916, American political reformer, b. Brookville, Ind. He traveled in the West and in South America, fought in the Union army in the Civil War, and after 1869 practiced law in Kansas. As governor of Kansas (1879–83) he successfully supported a prohibition amendment to the state constitution. In 1884 he was the Prohibition party candidate for President. He later joined the free-silver movement and championed woman suffrage.

St. John, Oliver (sĭn'jən), 1598?–1673, English politician. He married (1638) a cousin of Oliver Cromwell. In 1637–38 he was, by his brilliant defense of John HAMPDEN in the ship money case, drawn into the opposition to Charles I. Although Charles appointed (1641) him solicitor general, St. John remained a conspicuous opposition leader in the Long Parliament, taking a leading part in the attainder (1641) of Thomas Wentworth, earl of Strafford. He supported Cromwell and the army against Parliament in 1647 and was made (1648) chief justice of common pleas. He refused to take part in the trial (1649) of Charles I. St. John was one of the commissioners who negotiated (1652) the union with Scotland. His friendship with Cromwell cooled during the Protectorate, and he cooperated with Gen. George Monck in effecting the Restoration (1660) of the monarchy. In his *Case of Oliver St. John* (1660) he denied complicity in the execution of Charles I and the establishment of the Commonwealth. He was punished only with exclusion from holding office. He lived abroad after 1662.

Saint John, city (1971 pop. 89,039), S N.B., Canada, at the mouth of the St. John River on the Bay of Fundy. A major year-round port, it has an excellent harbor, large dry docks, and terminal facilities and maintains extensive shipping connections with Europe, North and South America, and the West Indies. The city is the commercial, manufacturing, and transportation center of New Brunswick, with pulp and paper mills, oil and sugar refineries, and food-processing plants. The site was visited (1604) by Champlain, and a fort and trading post was built (1631–35) by Charles de la Tour. In the struggle between France and England for possession of ACADIA, the fort was captured and recaptured several times, finally becoming British in 1758. Growth of the city dates from 1783, when a large party of LOYALISTS from the United States established themselves there on land grants. The settlement was called Parr Town and in 1785 was incorporated with Carleton and named St. John, becoming the first incorporated city in Canada. Benedict Arnold lived and conducted a business there from 1786 to 1791. Much of the old city was destroyed by fire in 1877. Among notable features in St. John are Market Slip (1783), the old Loyalist Burying Ground (1783), Martello Tower (fortification; built 1812), the old court house (1830), the Roman Catholic cathedral and bishop's residence (1853), the New Brunswick Mus., and the Reversing Falls rapids.

Saint John, Virgin Islands: see VIRGIN ISLANDS of the United States.

Saint John, river, 418 mi (673 km) long, rising in N Maine and flowing NE to New Brunswick, Canada, then SE below Edmundston, past St. Leonard, Grand Falls, Woodstock, and Fredericton to the Bay of Fundy at St. John. It forms part of the border between Maine and New Brunswick. Its chief tributaries are the Aroostook and Tobique rivers. At Grand Falls the river drops 75 ft (23 m) in a great cataract. At its mouth, within the city of St. John, are the Reversing Falls Rapids, caused by the strong tides of the Bay of Fundy, which force the river to reverse its flow at high tide. The river was discovered (1604) by the French explorers Samuel de Champlain and Sieur de Monts. In the 17th and 18th cent. it was an important route for French, Indian, and English traders, and several trading posts were established on its banks. It later became a major lumber transportation route. There are major hydroelectric power plants at Grand Falls, Beechwood, and Mactaquac. The river is navigable to Fredericton. The valley of the St. John is fertile, and potatoes are raised there.

Saint John, Lake, Canada: see SAGUENAY, river.

Saint John of Jerusalem, Knights of: see KNIGHTS HOSPITALERS.

Saint John's, city (1966 pop. 24,367), capital of ANTIGUA, in the British West Indies. St. John's, at the head of a harbor formed by an inlet, is the commercial center of Antigua. Tourism is important. The harbor is limited to shallow-draft vessels. In the 18th cent. St. John's served as a headquarters for the Royal Navy in the West Indies.

Saint John's, city (1971 pop. 88,102), provincial capital, SE N.F., Canada, on the northeast coast of the Avalon Peninsula. Built on hills overlooking a fine harbor, it is the commercial and industrial center of the province and the base of its great fishing fleet. The city's industries are chiefly related to fishing and include shipbuilding, the manufacturing of fishing equipment and marine engines, and the storing, preserving, and processing of fish. Although the exact date of its first settlement is not known, St. John's is one of the oldest settlements in North America. In 1583, Sir Humphrey Gilbert took possession of the region for England. Since that time fishing boats from many countries have based there. The settlement was captured and recaptured by France and England, becoming permanently British in 1762 and serving as a naval base during the American Revolution and in the War of 1812. It was at St. John's that Marconi heard (1901) the first transatlantic wireless message and from there that the first nonstop transatlantic flight was made in 1919. The city has been partially destroyed by fire several times. It is the site of the provincial government offices, of Roman Catholic and Anglican cathedrals, of the Newfoundland Mus., and of Memorial Univ.

Saint Johns, Que., Canada: see ST. JEAN.

Saint Johns, river, 285 mi (459 km) long, rising in the swampy region of SE Fla., N of Lake Okeechobee, and flowing N to Jacksonville, where it turns abruptly eastward and enters the Atlantic Ocean 28 mi (45 km) away. It passes through eight lakes and receives many tributaries; the Oklawaha River (120 mi/193 km long), which receives the Silver Springs, is the most important. The dredged river is navigable c.170 mi (270 km) upstream; there is a 30-ft (9-m) channel from Jacksonville to the ocean. The lower third of the river forms part of the Intracoastal Waterway.

St.-John's-bread: see CAROB.

Saint John's College, mainly at Annapolis, Md.; coeducational; founded 1696 as King William's School, chartered 1784, opened 1786 as St. John's College. Its curriculum is built around the "great books" program advocated by the educator R. M. Hutchins. In 1964 a campus was opened at Santa Fe, N.Mex.

Saint John's University, at Jamaica, New York City; Roman Catholic; St. John's College for men, other divisions coeducational; established 1870 as St. John's College. Its present name was adopted in 1954. There is a branch on Staten Island.

St.-John's-wort, any species of the large and widespread herbaceous genus *Hypericum* of the family Hypericaceae (St.-John's-wort family), usually found in moist, open places and often having bright yellow flowers and dotted leaves. A St.-John's-wort is said to have been associated with the sun god Balder, because of its golden flowers, and when Balder's Day became St. John's Day the plant was likewise transferred to St. John. It was supposed to ward off evil spirits and thunderbolts, for which it was worn on St. John's Eve. It was also considered to have curative powers, and some species are still used in the Old World for treating wounds. Of the North American species a few are cultivated and some are noxious weeds, poisonous to livestock. Several naturalized American plants are Asiatic species that were introduced by way of Europe. A species of *Hypericum* is one of several plants called Aaron's-beard, in this case because of the beardlike aspect of its many stamens. See ROSE OF SHARON. St.-John's-wort is classified in the division MAGNOLIOPHYTA, class Magnoliopsida, order Theales, family Hypericaceae.

Saint John the Divine, Cathedral of, New York City. The charter for the building was granted to the Episcopal diocese in 1873, the first stone was laid in 1892, and the crypt was opened for worship in 1899. In 1941 the entire length of the cathedral was first opened. Begun in the Romanesque style after designs by G. L. Heins and C. Grant La Farge, the plans were altered (1911) and a Gothic style adopted according to the design of Ralph Adams Cram. Part of the east end of the nave remains unfinished. The grounds include a complete close, with a bishop's house, cathedral house, diocesan house, synod house and the Cathedral School for Boys and Girls of All Faiths.

Saint Joseph (sānt jō'zəf). **1** City (1970 pop. 11,042), seat of Berrien co., SW Mich., on Lake Michigan at the mouth of the St. Joseph River; inc. 1834. A resort with beaches and mineral springs, it is also a port and a trade center for a fruit-growing region. Household appliances, refrigerators, automobile parts, and rubber goods are manufactured there. Indian villages, a Jesuit mission, Fort Miami (a French trading fort built by Robert Cavelier, sieur de La Salle, in 1679), and a fur-trading post occupied this site before permanent American settlement began c.1830. **2** City (1970 pop. 72,691), seat of Buchanan co., NW Mo., on the Missouri River; inc. 1845. A port of entry, it is a railroad center and the hub of a rich farming area. The city is a large market for livestock and grain, and has meat-packing and food-processing plants. Among its manufactures are electrical products, wire rope, and wood products. The city was laid out c.1843 on the site of a trading post founded (1826) by Joseph Robidoux. In 1860 it became the eastern terminus of the pony express. Of interest are the pony-express stables (now a museum), the house in which Jesse James was killed, Eugene Field's home, and a museum of pioneer and Indian relics. Missouri Western College is there.

Saint Joseph, river, 210 mi (338 km) long, rising in S Mich. and flowing generally westward in wide curves to Lake Michigan at Benton Harbor, Mich. South Bend, Ind., is on the river, which was an important link to the Ohio River and Lake Erie for pioneer travelers.

Saint-Just, Louis de (lwē' də săN-zhüst'), 1767–94, French revolutionary. A member of the Convention from 1792, he became a favorite of Maximilien Robespierre and was (1793–94) a leading member of the Committee of Public Safety (see REIGN OF TERROR). As commissioner (1793) with the army of the Rhine, he contributed to the successful operations that drove the allies beyond the French border. On his return he served as president of the Convention. He supported Robespierre in the destruction of the Hébertists and Dantonists (see HÉBERT, JACQUES; DANTON, GEORGES); in doctrinaire interpretation of Rousseau's political teachings he was more radically idealistic than Robespierre. Saint-Just believed fanatically in the perfect state, based on rigorous Spartan virtue, and brooked no opposition to this political philosophy. During the coup d'etat of 9 THERMIDOR (1794), which overthrew Robespierre and other members of the Committee of Public Safety, Saint-Just was prevented from delivering a speech in defense of Robespierre. Saint-Just's arrest was ordered, and he was guillotined with Robespierre. See biographies by Geoffrey Bruun (1932, repr. 1966), E. N. Curtis (1935, repr. 1973), and J. B. Morton (1939).

Saint Kitts or **Saint Christopher:** see SAINT KITTS-NEVIS.

Saint Kitts-Nevis, island state (1970 est. pop. 45,800), 120 sq mi (311 sq km), British West Indies, in the Leeward Islands. The state consists of the islands of St. Kitts or St. Christopher (68 sq mi/176 sq km), Nevis (50 sq mi/130 sq km), and Sombrero (2 sq mi/5.2 sq km). The capital is BASSETERRE on St. Kitts. The chief settlement on Nevis is Charlestown, the birthplace of Alexander Hamilton. A narrow strait separates the two larger islands, which are volcanic

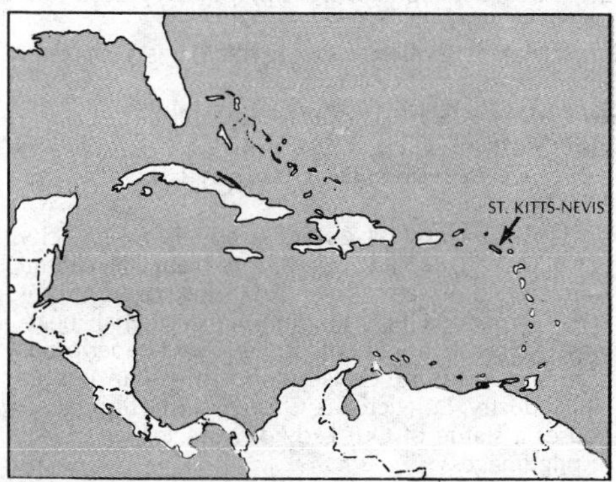

in origin, mountainous, and renowned for their scenery. Sugar, molasses, cotton, and coconuts are exported. St. Kitts and Nevis were discovered by Columbus in 1493, but settlement did not begin until the British arrived on St. Kitts in 1623. French settlers came to the island two years later. Nevis was first settled by the British in 1628. The Treaty of Paris of 1783 definitively awarded the islands to Britain. They were part of the colony of the Leeward Islands (1871–1956) and of the West Indies Federation (1958–62). In 1967, together with ANGUILLA, they became a self-governing state in association with Great Britain. Anguilla seceded later that year.

Saint Lambert (sānt lăm'bərt), city (1971 pop. 18,616), S Que., Canada, on the St. Lawrence River. It is a residential suburb of Montreal.

St. Laurent, Louis Stephen (săN lôrăN'), 1882–1973, Canadian political leader. A well-known lawyer, he entered (1941) political life as minister of justice and attorney general in the Mackenzie KING government; he was later minister of external affairs (1946–48). He was elected to the House of Commons in 1942 and succeeded King as Liberal party leader, taking office (Nov., 1948) as prime minister after King's retirement. His party failed to obtain a majority of votes in 1957, and John G. Diefenbaker, a Conservative, succeeded him as prime minister. On his retirement in 1958 Lester B. Pearson became Liberal party leader. See biography by D. C. Thomson (1968).

Saint-Laurent, Yves: see under FASHION.

Saint Lawrence, one of the principal rivers of North America, 744 mi (1,197 km) long. It issues from the northeastern end of Lake Ontario and flows northeast, first along the U.S.-Canadian border, then into S Que., Canada, past Montreal and Quebec city, to the Gulf of St. Lawrence, N of Cape Gaspé. It is the outlet of the Great Lakes and together with them forms a c.2,300-mi (3,700-km) waterway from the western end of Lake Superior to the Atlantic Ocean. The river is an integral part of the SAINT LAWRENCE SEAWAY (opened 1959). In its upper course the river cuts through a part of the Canadian Shield; there, just downstream from Lake Ontario, are found the THOUSAND ISLANDS. Below Cornwall, Ont., the river widens into Lake St. Francis. Shortly it widens again into Lake St. Louis, then descends through the Lachine Rapids to Montreal, head of navigation for very large ocean-going vessels. Between Sorel and Trois Rivières is Lake St. Peter, another widened section. Below the city of Quebec the river is tidal. It gradually increases in width to c.90 mi (140 km) at its mouth. The river's principal tributaries are the Richelieu (linking the St. Lawrence with Lake Champlain and the Hudson River), St. Francis, Ottawa, St. Maurice, and Saguenay rivers. The St. Lawrence River is an important source of hydroelectric power; one of the world's largest facilities is the Beauharnois power plant (capacity 1,641,000 kilowatts) near Montreal. Agreements between the United States and Canada govern power distribution and navigation in the international section of the river. Canals have been constructed around the rapids, making the entire river navigable to all but the largest of vessels. The river is the chief trade artery of Canada. The upper part is not navigable during the winter months because of ice accumulation. The most important cities and ports along the St. Lawrence are Ogdensburg, N.Y.; Kingston, Brockville, and Cornwall, Ont.; and Montreal, Sorel, Trois Rivières, Quebec city, and Lévis, Que. The many bridges that cross the St. Lawrence River include the Thousand Islands International Bridge (1938), the Roosevelt International Bridge (1934), and the Seaway Skyway Bridge (1960), all between Ontario and New York; the Victoria Bridge (remodeled 1898) at Montreal; and the Quebec Bridge (1917), near Quebec city. The St. Lawrence valley, long inhabited predominantly by French Canadians, is an agricultural region; potatoes, grains, hay, vegetables, and dairy cattle are raised. The St. Lawrence River was visited in 1534 by Jacques Cartier, the French explorer; in 1535 he ascended it as far as Montreal. Quebec was settled (1608) by Samuel de Champlain. The river system was long a highway for explorers, fur traders, and missionaries. The valley remained in the possession of the French until Canada was surrendered to the British at the close of the French and Indian Wars in 1763. After the establishment of the independence of the United States, the river became an international boundary, but British influence was generally dominant over the whole St. Lawrence valley and most of its southern tributaries until after the War of 1812. See D. G. Creighton, *The Empire of the St. Lawrence* (1958); A. S. Malkus, *Blue-Water Boundary* (1960). See also bibliography under SAINT LAWRENCE SEAWAY.

Saint Lawrence, Gulf of, arm of the Atlantic Ocean, c.100,000 sq mi (259,000 sq km), SE Canada, extending c.250 mi (400 km) from the mouth of the Saint Lawrence River to Newfoundland on the east. At its greatest width (northeast-southwest) it is c.500 mi (800 km). It is bounded by Nova Scotia, New Brunswick, and Quebec; in the Gulf are Prince Edward Island, Anticosti Island, the Magdalen Islands, and numerous small islands near its north shore. Chaleur Bay, a west inlet, lies between the Gaspé Peninsula and New Brunswick. The Strait of Belle Isle, Cabot Strait, and the Strait of Canso lead to the Atlantic. The Gulf is subject to frequent fog and is closed to navigation by ice from early December to mid-April. It was visited by explorers before the 16th cent., and it has important fishing grounds, especially for cod.

Saint Lawrence Island, c.90 mi (145 km) long and from 8 to 22 mi (13–36 km) wide, off W Alaska, in the Bering Sea. It is a barren island, inhabited by Eskimo engaged in whaling and fox trapping. It was discovered by Vitus Bering on St. Lawrence's Day, 1728. See H. B. Collins, Jr., *Archeology of St. Lawrence Island, Alaska* (1937).

Saint Lawrence Islands National Park, 1,000 acres (405 hectares), S Ont., Canada, in the Thousand Islands; est. 1904. It includes 17 wooded Canadian islands and some adjacent mainland between Kingston and Brockville. It is popular with summer campers.

Saint Lawrence Seaway, international waterway, 2,342 mi (3,769 km) long, consisting of a system of canals, dams, and locks in the St. Lawrence River and connecting channels between the Great Lakes; opened 1959. It provides passage for large ocean-going vessels into central North America. The seaway includes a 27 ft (8 m) deep waterway, a canal, and seven locks between the port of Montreal and Lake Ontario; a 27 ft (8 m) channel and eight locks through the WELLAND CANAL; and the SAULT STE MARIE CANALS and locks. The seaway has created a fourth seacoast accessible to the industrial and agricultural heartland of North America and has brought ocean-going vessels to lake ports such as Buffalo, Cleveland, Toledo, Detroit, Chicago, Milwaukee, Duluth, and Toronto. The present maximum vessel size is 730 ft (223 m) in length with a cargo capacity of 28,000 tons. The shipping season has been extended to 250 days (mid-April to mid-December) by increased use of icebreakers and air pumps to control ice formation in the locks. Iron ore, wheat, and coal are the principal cargoes carried on the seaway. Construction of the project was authorized by Canada in 1951 and by the United States in 1954. The St. Lawrence Seaway Authority was charged with construction and maintenance of required facilities in Canadian territory; the St. Lawrence Seaway Development Corporation was responsible for facilities in U.S. territory. The principal new locks on the St. Lawrence River section of the seaway are, from east to west, the St. Lambert (18 ft /5.5 m lift); Côte Ste Catherine (30 ft/9.1 m), which enables vessels to bypass the Lachine Rapids; Lower and Upper Beauharnois (82 ft/25 m, including the Beauharnois Canal built in 1932); Bertrand H. Snell (45 ft/13.7 m); Dwight D. Eisenhower (38 ft/11.6 m); and the Iroquois Guard Lock (3 ft/91 cm). Hydroelectric facilities were integrated with the project and developed and operated by the Power Authority of the State of New York and the Hydro-Electric Power Commission of Ontario. The seaway was included in the binational Water Quality Agreement of 1972 to prevent further pollution and improve water quality in the Great Lakes and the international section of the Seaway. See Angelika Roemer, *The St. Lawrence Seaway* (1971); Lowell Thomas, *Story of the St. Lawrence Seaway* (1972).

Saint Lawrence University, at Canton, N.Y.; coeducational; chartered 1856.

St. Leger, Barry, 1737–89, British officer in the American Revolution. In the French and Indian Wars he served at Louisburg (1758) and with Gen. James Wolfe at Quebec. He was given (1777) command of the Mohawk valley wing of the British attack that was ended by the SARATOGA CAMPAIGN. St. Leger's force, composed mostly of Indians and Tories, was intended to come down the valley to meet General Burgoyne at Albany. St. Leger laid siege to Fort Stanwix (Fort Schuyler), where Continental troops barred his way to Albany; meanwhile a relief force led by Nicholas HERKIMER was ambushed at Oriskany Creek. However, when St. Leger's Indian allies heard that a Continental force under Benedict Arnold was moving to relieve Fort Stanwix, they deserted the British, and St. Leger was forced to make a retreat to Canada.

Saint-Lô (săN-lō), town (1968 pop. 19,613), capital of Manche dept., NW France, in Normandy. It is an agricultural center and has famous horse stables. Wood products, plaster, and clothing are manufactured. An old Gallo-Roman town, Saint-Lô was a medieval fortress and was the scene of a massacre of HUGUENOTS in the 16th cent. Saint-Lô has been rebuilt since its virtual destruction during the Allied invasion of Normandy in 1944.

Saint Louis (lo͞o'ĭs), city (1970 pop. 622,236), independent and in no county, E Mo., on the Mississippi River below the mouth of the Missouri; inc. as a city 1822. It is the largest city of the state, a great river-freight handler, and a major rail center. A market for furs, livestock, grain, and other farm produce, St. Louis is also a wholesale, banking, and financial center. Its industries produce a wide variety of manufactures, including shoes and leather goods, beer, machinery, chemicals, aircraft, space capsules, and automotive vehicles and parts. The site of the present city was chosen (1763) by Pierre LaClede for a fur-trading post. To honor Louis XV of France, it was named for his "name" saint, Louis IX of France. Transferred to the Spanish in 1770 in accord with an earlier treaty agreement, it was retroceded to France in the time of Napoleon I and then sold to the United States along with the other lands of the Louisiana Purchase. However, the population and customs remained predominantly French until well into the 19th cent. St. Louis, the gateway to the Missouri and the West, was the market and supply point for fur traders, mountain men, and explorers (including Lewis and Clark). The town did not grow rapidly until after the War of 1812, when immigrants came in numbers to settle the West. St. Louis grew to be one of the greatest U.S. river ports. Even after the railroads came, the river steamers were at the peak of their glory. After the Civil War—in which St. Louis was Unionist in sympathy—industry in the city expanded greatly. There are many bridges across the Mississippi; the oldest was constructed by James B. Eads in 1874. The city has a symphony orchestra, a municipal opera, and many educational institutions, including Saint Louis Univ., Washington Univ., three theological seminaries, and a branch of the Univ. of Missouri. The St. Louis *Post-Dispatch* is one of the distinguished newspapers of the country. Forest Park, the largest of many city parks, has an open-air theater, a notable art museum, a zoo, a planetarium, and the Jefferson memorial building, which recalls the Louisiana Purchase Exposition of 1904 (the "St. Louis Fair") and now houses the Missouri Historical Society. The National Museum of Transport is in the city, and the Shaw Botanical Garden (officially named the Missouri Botanical Garden) is well known. Eugene Field, the poet and journalist, was born in St. Louis, and his house is now a museum. New Cathedral is one of the largest Roman Catholic cathedrals in the country. The civic center has many imposing public buildings, including the Busch Memorial Stadium (opened in 1966), home of the St. Louis Cardinals professional football and baseball teams (the city also has a major league hockey team). The Jefferson National Expansion Memorial National Historic Site (91 acres/37 hectares) was established in 1935 to preserve such historical buildings as the old courthouse (1839–64) and the old cathedral (1831–34). Its major attraction is Gateway Arch, a giant stainless steel arch, 630 ft (192 m) high, designed by Eero Saarinen. The arch, which stands on the banks of the Mississippi, symbolizes St. Louis as the gateway to the West. Near the arch on the riverfront is a replica of the *Santa Maria.* In 1973, St. Louis was besieged by floodwaters from the Mississippi River for 77 days. An extensive system of levees prevented major inundations in the city although some suburban areas to the north and south were flooded. See M. Quigley, *St. Louis, The First Two Hundred Years* (1964); E. M. Coyle, *Saint Louis: Portrait of a River City* (2d ed. 1970).

Saint-Louis (săN-lwē), city (1969 est. pop. 75,000), NW Senegal, a port on an island in the Senegal River. The terminus of a railroad from DAKAR, it is a trade and export center for peanuts, hides, and skins. Meat is processed. The oldest French colonial settlement in Africa, Saint-Louis was founded as a trade base in 1638. In 1659 a French fort was built there. Except for brief periods (1758–79 and 1809–15) of British ownership, Saint-Louis was long the capital of all French possessions in W Africa and was the capital of FRENCH WEST AFRICA from its inception in 1885 until 1902. From 1902 to 1958, Saint-Louis served as the capital of both Senegal and Mauritania. The city has a research institute.

Saint Louis Park, city (1970 pop. 48,922), Hennepin co., SE Minn., a suburb of Minneapolis; settled 1854, inc. 1886. The manufactures of its industrial park include electronic equipment; machinery; metal, rubber, and plastic products; and processed foods.

Saint Louis University, mainly at St. Louis, Mo.; Jesuit; coeducational; opened 1818 as an academy, became a college 1820, chartered as a university 1832. Parks College of Aeronautical Technology (est. 1927) in Cahokia, Ill., has been part of the university since 1946. The university's research facilities include a computer center, seismographic stations, and meteorological and geophysical laboratories. Its library houses valuable copies of documents from the Vatican Library.

Saint Lucia (sānt lo͞o'shə, -sēə), island (1970 pop. 101,100), 238 sq mi (616 sq km), British West Indies, one of the Windward Islands. The capital is CASTRIES. Mountains, rising abruptly from the sea, create startlingly lovely scenic effects. Morne Gimie (3,145 ft/959 m high) and the twin pyramidal cones known as the Pitons are the most imposing landmarks. The forests of the mountain slopes yield fine cabinet woods, and the volcanic soil is rich. Bananas and a host of other tropical agricultural products are exported. Columbus probably discovered the island in 1502. The British, in the first attempt at colonization early in the 17th cent., were beaten back by the fierce Carib Indians. The island was later settled by the French, who signed a treaty with the Caribs in 1660. Thereafter St. Lucia was much contested by the two powers until the British regained it definitively in 1803. In 1958 it joined the short-lived Federation of the West Indies and formed part of the British Windward Islands colony until 1959, when the colony was dissolved. In 1967, St. Lucia became one of the six Associated States of the West Indies, with internal self-government. The British commissioner resides on the island. French culture has left an indelible mark, and the population, largely of black African descent, speak a French patois.

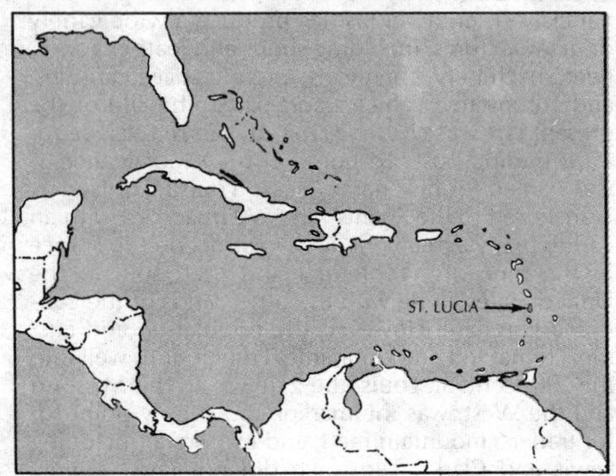

Saint-Malo (săN-mälō'), town (1968 pop. 43,722), Ille-et-Vilaine dept., NW France, on the English Channel. Built on a rocky promontory, Saint-Malo is a fishing port and one of the great tourist centers of Brittany. The major industries are deep-sea fishing, the drying of cod, and boatbuilding. A Welsh monk built a monastery nearby in the 6th cent., and in the 9th cent. refugees fleeing Norman raids on nearby Saint-Servan settled at the site of the present-day Saint-Malo. The town was made a part of France in 1491; it became a prosperous commercial seaport in the 1500s. Between the 17th and 19th cent., French corsairs operated out of Saint-Malo, despite repeated English efforts to destroy the port and corsair fleet. Saint-Malo is famous for its ramparts and its 17th-century architecture. Points of interest include the main gate to the city (15th cent.) and a château (15th cent.) that is now a municipal museum. In World War II, German forces, retreating before the U.S. army, set the city ablaze. In 1966 a tidal-power station, harnessing the energy from the channels' high tides, was opened. The nearby towns of Saint-Servan and Paramé were annexed by Saint-Malo in 1967. The city was the birthplace of Jacques Cartier and François Chateaubriand, whose tomb is near the harbor.

Saint Mark's Church, Venice, named after the tutelary saint of Venice. The original Romanesque basilical church, built in the 9th cent. as a shrine for the saint's bones, was destroyed by fire in 967. Byzantine architects assisted in its reconstruction, the main fabric being completed c.1071. In the 12th and following centuries through alterations and elaborate adornments it became a splendid Byzantine monument, reflecting Venice's preeminent position in trade with the East. In the 14th cent. the facade received Gothic additions. The present structure is thus a mixture of Byzantine and Gothic and incorporates materials taken from temples and Eastern ruins. Its plan is a Greek cross, with a dome over the center and one over each arm of the cross. Across the west front extends a vestibule from which five portals open upon the Piazza San Marco. The facade is incrusted with marble slabs and mosaics. In the interior the lower walls are sheathed with veined marbles. The vaults and domes are completely covered with beautifully colored mosaics spread on a golden background. These varied materials combine into a unique harmonic architectural polychromy, effectively illuminated by a hazy light admitted through narrow openings in the domes. The Four Horses of St. Mark's, in gilded bronze, stand upon the gallery over the main entrance. The only existing specimen of an ancient quadriga, or monumental four-horse chariot, they may have originally adorned a Roman triumphal arch. They were found in Constantinople and in 1204 were brought to Venice. In 1797, Napoleon carried them off to Paris but in 1815 the horses were returned to Venice. In recent years they have suffered from the effects of atmospheric pollution. See Giovanni Musolino, *The Basilica of St. Mark in Venice* (1956).

Saint-Martin, Louis Claude, marquis de (lwē klōd märkē' də săN-märtăN'), 1743–1803, French mystic philosopher. He wrote under the name of *le Philosophe inconnu* [the unknown philosopher]. Influenced at first by the Spanish mystic Martínez Pasquales, Saint-Martin was later affected by the mysticism of Jakob BOEHME, whose work he translated. His own writings include *Des erreurs et de la vérité* (1775), *L'Homme de désir* (1790), and *Le Nouvel Homme* (1792). See biography by A. E. Waite (1901, repr. 1970).

Saint Martin (săN märtăN'), Du. *Sint Maarten,* island, 37 sq mi (96 sq km), West Indies, one of the Leeward Islands. Since its occupation in 1648 by the Dutch and the French, it has been divided; the northern part (1967 pop. 5,061; 20 sq mi/52 sq km), with the capital at Marigot, belongs to French Guadeloupe, and the southern part (1968 pop. 6,881; 17 sq mi/44 sq km) belongs to the Netherlands Antilles (see CURAÇAO). The chief town on the Dutch side is Philipsburg. Both towns are free ports. A hilly, scenic island provided with good harbors, Saint Martin is a tourist resort. Cotton, sugarcane, and tropical fruits are raised.

Saint Martin's, England: see SCILLY ISLANDS.

Saint Martin's-in-the-Fields, church in London, England, on Trafalgar Square; built 1721–26 by James Gibb. It has a Corinthian portico and elaborate spire. The crypt is kept open all night for the use of the homeless; in World War II it was an air-raid shelter.

Saint Mary's, England: see SCILLY ISLANDS.

Saint Marys. 1 River, c.175 mi (280 km) long, rising in Okefenokee Swamp, SE Ga., and flowing, with a great southern bend, E to the Atlantic Ocean. It forms part of the Georgia-Florida line. The lower river is dredged for navigation. **2** River, 63 mi (101 km) long, flowing generally SE from Lake Superior to Lake Huron and forming part of the U.S.-Canada line. The cities of Sault Sainte Marie, Mich. and Ont., are on the river. The rapids there are circumvented by the Sault Sainte Marie Canals. Although frozen for about five months each year, the river and canal together form one of the world's busiest waterways.

Saint Marys City, village (1970 pop. 540), St. Marys co., S Md., on the St. Marys River; est. 1634 as Maryland's first town. English colonists, after purchasing a small village from the Indians, renamed it St. Marys and built Fort St. George. The first state assembly met there in 1635, and the village remained the provincial capital until Annapolis replaced it as capital in 1694.

Saint Mary's College: see NOTRE DAME, UNIVERSITY OF.

Saint Mary's Island: see BANJUL, Gambia.

Saint Matthews, city (1970 pop. 13,152), Jefferson co., N Ky., a residential suburb of Louisville; inc. 1950.

Saint-Maur-des-Fossés (săN-mōr-dā-fôsā'), city (1968 pop. 70,681), Val-de-Marne dept., N central France, on the Marne River. An industrial suburb of Paris, it manufactures automobile parts, ball bearings, electrical equipment, asbestos and paper products, and furniture. Construction is also an important industry. St. Nicholas Church (12th–14th cent.) houses a statue of Our Lady of Miracles, an object of pilgrimages.

Saint Maurice (sānt môr'ĭs, Fr. săN mōrēs'), river, c.325 mi (520 km) long, rising in the Laurentian Mts., S Que., Canada, and flowing SE and S to the St. Lawrence River at Trois Rivières. It passes La Tuque, Grand' Mère, and Shawinigan Falls, where waterfalls furnish hydroelectric power. The river is important for the transportation of lumber.

Saint Michael's Mount, pyramid-shaped rocky islet, 21 acres (8.5 hectares), Cornwall, SW England, in Mounts Bay; it rises to more than 200 ft (61 m). A natural causeway connects it at low tide with the mainland. Its Christian history began in 495 when fishermen claimed to see a vision of St. Michael appearing on its summit. A priory built in the 11th cent. and a castle are there.

Saint Michel, Mont: see MONT-SAINT-MICHEL.

Saint-Mihiel (săN-mēyĕl'), town (1968 pop. 5,382), Meuse dept., NE France, in Lorraine, on the Meuse River. Its chief manufactures are eyeglasses, furniture, plywood, and copper products. Saint-Mihiel grew around a Benedictine abbey founded in 709. Abbey buildings constructed in the 17th and 18th cent. are now used as a courthouse, library, and school. Points of interest include St. Michel church (17th cent.), with a door from Roman times, and the Church of St. Etienne, designed by Ligier Richier. In Sept., 1918, Saint-Mihiel was recovered from the Germans in the first battle of World War I in which American forces fought independently.

Saint Moritz (sānt môr'ĭts, mərĭts'), Ger. *Sankt Moritz,* town (1970 pop. 5,699), Grisons canton, SE Switzerland, in the Upper Engadine, on the Lake of St. Moritz. One of the largest winter sports centers in the world, it is also a famous year-round resort. It is surrounded by magnificent peaks and has long-frequented mineral springs. The Olympic winter games were held there in 1928 and in 1948.

Saint-Nazaire (săN-näzĕr'), city (1968 pop. 64,003), Loire-Atlantique dept., W France, at the mouth of the Loire River on the Bay of Biscay. Saint-Nazaire is an important seaport (mainly for trade with the Antilles and Central America) and a great shipbuilding and industrial center with aeronautical, metallurgical, chemical, and food industries. Built on the site of an ancient Gallo-Roman town, Saint-Nazaire belonged to the dukes of Brittany in the 14th and 15th cent. A major German submarine base during World War II, Saint-Nazaire was nearly destroyed by Allied bombing.

Saint-Nicolas: see SINT-NIKLAAS, Belgium.

Saint Olaf College, at Northfield, Minn.; American Lutheran; coeducational; founded 1874 by Norwegians as a school, became a college 1886, chartered 1889. It offers special programs on Scandinavian, especially Norwegian, culture.

Saint-Omer (săNtômĕr'), city (1968 pop. 19,597), Pas-de-Calais dept., N France, in Flanders, on the Aa River. The chief manufactures are metals, textiles, telephone equipment, and beer. The city grew around a monastery founded in the 7th cent. by St. Omer, the bishop of Thérouanne. In medieval times the abbey of Saint-Bertin was famous. Points of interest include the church (now basilica) of Notre Dame (13th–15th cent.), which contains the tomb of St. Omer; the Museum of Fine Arts; and the ruins of the abbey.

Saintonge (săNtôNzh'), region of W France, on the Bay of Biscay. It is now part of the Charente-Maritime dept. Cattle and sheep raising, dairying, and the manufacture of cognac from the grapes grown along the Charente River are the major occupations; oysters are harvested along the coast. Known as the country of Santones, the region was conquered by the Romans and was occupied by the VISIGOTHS in 419 and by Clovis I in 507. As a fief of AQUITAINE, it became part of England (1154) following the marriage of Eleanor of Aquitaine to Henry of Anjou (later Henry II of England). During the WARS OF RELIGION (1562–98), Saintonge was a Protestant stronghold, especially at the city of La Rochelle. The region was incorporated into the French crown lands in 1372 and was a province of France until the Revolution in 1789.

Saint-Ouen (săNtōōä'), city (1968 pop. 52,103), Seine-Saint-Denis dept., N central France, on the Seine River. It is an industrial suburb N of Paris and a terminal point for river shipping. Electrical equipment, metal products, pharmaceuticals, and perfumes are among the chief manufactures. In 1814, Louis XVIII signed the Declaration of Saint-Ouen, by which he became a constitutional monarch. The city retains a villa from the MEROVINGIAN period.

Saint Pancras: see CAMDEN.

Saint Patrick's Cathedral, New York City, largest Roman Catholic church in the United States. The Gothic building at Fifth Ave. between 50th and 51st St. replaces an earlier cathedral at Mott St. The original plans, by James Renwick, were executed in 1853; the cornerstone was laid in 1858; in 1879 the building was dedicated. The Lady Chapel behind the high altar was added later, using the plans of Charles T. Matthews. The cathedral is of marble in the traditional cruciform shape and has 12 side chapels, many stained-glass windows, and a chime of 19 bells.

Saint Patrick's Purgatory, place where St. Patrick had a vision of Purgatory, traditionally located on Station Island in Lough Derg, Co. Donegal, Ireland. It has been a place of pilgrimage since the early Middle Ages, although its connection with St. Patrick is not accepted by modern scholars. The wild, rough scenery is also alleged to suggest Purgatory.

Saint Paul, city (1970 pop. 309,828), state capital and seat of Ramsey co., E Minn., on bluffs along the Mississippi River, contiguous with Minneapolis; inc. 1854. A port of entry at a great bend in the Mississippi and a major railroad hub, St. Paul is the industrial, commercial, and cultural center for a vast fertile region. Major manufactures are tapes and abrasives, computers, and electronic materials. Among the city's many other products are automobiles, machinery, chemicals, paper, food products, beer, furniture, and steel and iron goods. A fur-trading post was established (early 1800s) at the confluence of the Mississippi and Minnesota rivers in what is now the historic village of Mendota (6 mi/9.7 km SW of St. Paul), and Fort Snelling was built there. Traders, missionaries, and explorers were the first inhabitants; settlers came from the east after treaties with the Indians officially opened the area to farming and to profitable lumbering. By 1823 the landing at the head of navigation on the Mississippi was an important debarkation point and trading port. In 1841, Father Galtier established St. Paul Church, from which the city (platted along the river in 1846) took its name. St. Paul became territorial capital in 1849 and state capital when Minnesota was admitted to the Union in 1858. It was a booming river port and transportation center, especially after the arrival of the railroad in 1862. Later it became the center of the railroad empire of James J. Hill. Its population was swelled by immigrants, notably Irish and German Roman Catholics; Bishop Ireland was long their leader. Like many of the upper Mississippi River towns, St. Paul's oldest streets are narrow and crooked, conforming to the hills and to the river frontage; but as the city grew, new residential sections were laid out with wide, tree-shaded streets and many parks and playgrounds. Several fine parks (the largest of which are Como and Phalen) and many lakes (over 900 in the general metropolitan area), public beaches, and nearby ski areas provide excellent recreational facilities. Indian Mounds Park contains several Indian tumuli. An annual Winter Carnival is held in the city, and the state fairgrounds are in the Midway district, between St. Paul and Minneapolis. The capitol, completed in 1904 and designed by Cass Gilbert, has the largest unsupported marble dome in the world; it was modeled after St. Peter's in Rome. Near the capitol are the Cathedral of St. Paul; the state historical society building, containing a museum and library; and the St. Paul Arts and Science Center. In the concourse of the city hall and county courthouse (1932) is a notable peace monument designed by Carl Milles. Other points of interest in the area are Fort Snelling State Park and the Sibley House Museum (1835), home of the first territorial governor. St. Paul's many educational institutions include Bethel College, The College of St. Catherine, College of St. Thomas (1855), Hamline Univ. (1854), Macalester College, William Mitchell College of Law, and several theological seminaries. St. Paul shares an international airport with Minneapolis. See Carol Brink, *The Twin Cities* (1961); H. F. Koeper, *Historic St. Paul Buildings* (1964).

Saint Paul's Cathedral, London, masterpiece of Sir Christopher Wren and one of the finest church designs of the English baroque. It stands at the head of Ludgate Hill, where, according to tradition, a Roman temple once stood. In the early 7th cent. King Æthelbert of Kent dedicated the first church to St. Paul. The Saxon cathedral was destroyed by fire in 1087 and was replaced by a Norman structure, completed in the 13th cent. In 1258 the choir was enlarged in the Gothic style. The notable architect William Ramsay added the cloister and chapter house (begun 1332), which were among the first structures in the Perpendicular style. In 1561, St. Paul's was again struck by fire. Major rebuilding was not undertaken until 1628, when Inigo Jones was employed to restore it. He appended a classical facade. Plans for further repairs were next prepared by Wren, but the great fire of London (1666) almost destroyed the church, and in 1668 he was granted authority to demolish the badly damaged structure and to build an entirely new one. Wren's design, in the shape of a Greek cross, with a dome over the center, was modified to provide the long nave and choir of the traditional medieval plan. In 1675, Wren himself laid the first foundation block of the building, and 35 years later he set the final stone in place. The interior of the church consists of a three-aisled nave and choir, of equal lengths, extending east and west from a great central space at the crossing. Porticoes project north and south at the center of the building. The mosaic decorations are modern work and accord with Wren's original program for the interior adornment. The crossing is covered by a great dome, pierced at the crown to allow a view of the lantern above. Over this dome rises a concealed conical dome of brick that acts as support for the timber framework of the exterior dome, the entire domical feature thus being constructed in three shells. The western front of the church has as central motif a double-storied portico of coupled columns, flanked by two finely designed towers. The exterior dome, which ranks as one of the great domes of the world, rises above a colonnaded drum and supports a stone lantern terminating with a cross. Wren's scheme for an open, colonnaded piazza to furnish a setting for St. Paul's was not executed because of the high value of the requisite space. The cathedral was severely damaged by bombings in World War II, and reconstruction according to Wren's original plan was not completed until 1962. See W. R. Matthews and W. M. Atkins, *A History of St. Paul's Cathedral* (1957).

Saint Paul's Church National Historic Site: see NATIONAL PARKS AND MONUMENTS (table).

Saint Peter Port, town, capital of Guernsey, Channel Islands, Great Britain. Its shallow harbor is protected by piers; vegetables, fruits, and flowers are exported. Hauteville House, the residence of Victor Hugo from 1856 to 1870, contains memorials of the author. The 13th-century Castle Cornet is on an islet near the town, and the Church of St. Peter, partly 14th cent., is the finest on the islands. Elizabeth College for boys was founded in 1563.

Saint Petersburg: see LENINGRAD, USSR.

Saint Petersburg, city (1970 pop. 216,232), Pinellas co., W Fla., on Tampa Bay and the Gulf of Mexico at the southern end of the Pinellas peninsula; settled in the mid-1800s, inc. 1892. A port of entry with a large harbor, it is one of the state's most popular winter resorts and year-round residential communities. Because of its annual average of 360 sunny days, it is called the Sunshine City. Manufactures include boats, trailers and campers, air conditioners, electronic equipment, and cement. The city also has citrus-fruit and commercial-fishing industries. Among places of interest are the yacht basin, the municipal pier, the historical museum, the museum of fine arts, and the auditorium-arena, all on the bay waterfront. Florida Presbyterian College, a junior college, the Stetson College of Law, and a military academy are there, as well as an international airport and a U.S. coast guard base. Two bridges cross the bay to Tampa, and a third bridge, the twin-span Sunshine Skyway, links the peninsula with the mainland near Bradenton. The chain of narrow islands and beaches to the west of the city on the Gulf are connected by several causeways.

Saint Peter's Church, Rome, principal and largest church of the Christian world. The present structure was built mainly between 1506 and 1626. Originally it was the site of the Vatican cemetery and an early shrine to St. Peter. In the 4th cent. Emperor Constantine built the first church of St. Peter, a wood-roofed basilica, with transepts, five aisles, and an atrium. It was said to be built over the grave of St. Peter. Here Charlemagne and many other emperors and popes were crowned. In the 15th cent. Pope Nicholas V undertook the rebuilding of the choir and transepts after a design by Bernardo Rossellino. In 1452 the work was begun, and part of the choir was built. Pope Julius II decided that the entire church should be rebuilt and in 1506 appointed Bramante as the architect. He appears to have originally planned a symmetrical Greek cross with a great dome over the center. Bramante was succeeded by Raphael (1514), Antonio da San Gallo (1520), and Michelangelo (1547), who completed the building up to the drum of the great dome. Giacomo della Porta modified the design and completed the dome. Throughout the 16th cent. there was controversy over the final form in which the church would be built—the centralized Greek cruciform plan or the shape of a Latin cross. The problem was resolved in favor of the Latin cross plan, when Carlo Maderno added the nave and facade (1607–14). Unfortunately his additions obscured the dome. The church was dedicated by Urban VIII in 1626. Between 1629 and 1662 BERNINI completed the great composition of St. Peter's, creating a forecourt preceded by a majestic elliptical piazza bounded by quadruple colonnades. The great obelisk of Heliopolis, brought to Rome by Caligula, was moved by Domenico Fontana, and now adorns the center of the piazza. A monumental avenue leading to the piazza was added by Mussolini. The huge scale of all the elements of the interior prevents any accurate notion of its magnitude, and its effectiveness is chiefly due to the dome, which is 404 ft (123 m) high from the pavement. The interior diameter of the dome, 137 ft (42 m) is one of the largest in the world. Beneath it is the high altar covered by Bernini's superb bronze baldachino. At this altar only the pope may read Mass. The interior with its colored marbles, its sculptures, and its gilt and fresco decorations gives an effect of multicolored space. See James Lees-Milne, *Saint Peter's* (1967); Thea and Richard Bergere, *The Story of St. Peter's* (1967); Irving Lavin, *Bernini and the Crossing of St. Peter's* (1968).

Saint-Pierre, Charles Irénée Castel, Abbé de (shärl ērānā' kästĕl' äbā' də săN-pyĕr'), 1658–1743, French social philosopher. An advocate of natural religion and toleration, he favored the economic theories of the PHYSIOCRATS. His ideas combined utilitarian and philanthropic motives; he felt that the state should institute an equitable tax system, including a graduated income tax, and that the services of the state should include free public education, for women as well as men, and improved transportation to further commerce. In *Projet de paix perpetuelle* (1713) he described his plan for an international court and league of states. His *Discours sur la polysynodie* (1718), which advocated a constitutional monarchy, to be aided by a system of councils and an academy of experts, caused him to be expelled from the French Academy, of which he had been a member from 1694. He was a founder of the Club de l'Entresol (c.1720–1734), which furthered interest in direct action to improve social conditions. Saint-Pierre's numerous writings were all animated by faith in human nature, progress, and *bienfaisance* [benevolence], a word he coined. See study by M. L. Perkins (1959).

Saint-Pierre, Jacques Henri Bernardin de: see BERNARDIN DE SAINT-PIERRE, JACQUES HENRI.

Saint-Pierre, town (1961 pop. 5,434), Martinique, French West Indies. Founded by Esnambuc in 1635 and once the chief commercial city of the island, it was engulfed by a mass of flame, lava, and ash in the eruption (1902) of Pelée. Of the city's inhabitants (about 28,000), only one person survived, and many thousands more were killed in the surrounding region. The town's present activity revolves around tourists visiting the ruins.

Saint Pierre and Miquelon (săN pyĕr, mēkəlôN'), French territory (1971 est. pop. 5,600), 93 sq mi (241 sq km), consisting of nine small islands, S of Newfoundland, Canada, in the Gulf of St. Lawrence. The capital is St. Pierre on the island of the same name. Miquelon (83 sq mi/215 sq km) is the largest island. The population consists mainly of fishermen, most of whom live in or near the capital. The islands are barren, rocky, and often fogbound, but their proximity to the Grand Banks makes them a valuable base for fishermen. Probably first settled by Basques, they were colonized by France in 1604. They were taken by the British (1713) but returned to France in 1763; twice retaken by the British, they were restored to France in 1814, with the provision that they be unfortified. They were granted local autonomy in 1935. In April and October, Norman and Breton fishermen come there from France to fish.

Saint-Quentin (săN-känTăN'), city (1968 pop. 66,161), Aisne dept., N France, on the Somme River. Foundry products, machinery, textiles, furniture, rubber, and food products are manufactured. Saint-Quentin was famous for its cloth during the Middle Ages. Of Roman origin, the city was chartered in 1080 and was the capital of the medieval county of VERMANDOIS. It became part of the royal domain in 1191 and was ceded briefly to Burgundy (1435–77). The city has a long history of sieges and captures, most notably by the Spanish (1557) during the Wars of Religion. The Musée Lécuyer contains pastels by Maurice Quentin de La Tour, who was born in Saint-Quentin. In the city is the Collégiale Saint-Quentin (dating from the 13th to the 15th cent.), a large Gothic church.

Saint-Raphaël (săN-räfäĕl'), town (1968 pop. 18,339), Var dept., SE France, on the French RIVIERA. It is an elegant resort and a small commercial port as well as an important naval air base and the site of a naval school. Napoleon Bonaparte landed at Saint-Raphaël on his return from Egypt in 1799.

Saint Regis (sānt rē'jĭs), settlement of Roman Catholic Iroquois on the south bank of the St. Lawrence River, on both sides of the boundary line between Canada and the United States, partly in Huntingdon co., Que., and partly in Franklin co., N.Y. The village was named after St. John Francis Regis (1597–1640), a French nobleman, philanthropist, and priest, canonized in 1737. It was established c.1755 by a party of Catholic Iroquois from Caughnawaga, Que. See IROQUOIS CONFEDERACY.

Saint-Saëns, Charles Camille (shärl kämē'yə săN-säNs), 1835–1921, French composer. A child prodigy, he made his debut as a pianist at 10 and entered the Paris Conservatory in 1848. He was a prolific composer, writing in almost every form, and he was organist at the Madeleine for 20 years. Saint-Saëns is best known for his biblical opera, *Samson et Dalila* (1877); other works include the Third Symphony (1886), with organ and piano; the *Introduction and Rondo Capriccioso* (1863), for violin and orchestra; the piano concertos in G minor (1868) and C minor (1875); and symphonic poems, notably *Le Rouet d'Omphale* (1871) and *Danse macabre* (1874). His works are marked by unfailing craftsmanship and brilliant orchestration, but they frequently lack imaginative force. He was a champion of instrumental music in France when it was extremely low in popular esteem. In his later years, Saint-Saëns became highly conservative, strenuously opposing modern music. See his *Musical Memories* (tr. 1919); biographies by Arthur Hervey (1921, repr. 1970) and Watson Lyle (1923, repr. 1970); J. Harding, *Saint-Saëns and His Circle* (1965).

Saintsbury, George Edward Bateman (sānts'bərē), 1845–1933, English critic and historian. His many works on English and French literature, notable for their breadth of knowledge and spirited style, include *A Short History of English Literature* (1898), *A History of Criticism* (1900–1904), and *A History of the French Novel* (1917–19). He also wrote biographies of Dryden (1881), Sir Walter Scott (1897), Matthew Arnold (1899), and others. From 1895 to 1915 he was professor of rhetoric and English literature at Edinburgh.

Saint-Simon, Claude Henri de Rouvroy, comte de (klōd äNrē də ro͞ovrwä' kôNt də săN-sēmôN'), 1760–1825, French social philosopher; grand nephew of Louis de Rouvroy, duc de Saint-Simon. While still a young man, he served in the American Revolution as a volunteer on the side of the colonists. He took no part in the French Revolution, but used the opportunity to make a fortune through land speculation. He lavished his wealth on a salon for scientists and spent his later years in poverty, sustained by the faith that he had a message for mankind. Foreseeing the triumph of the industrial order, Saint-Simon called for the reorganization of society by scientists and industrialists on the basis of a scientific division of labor that would result in automatic and spontaneous social harmony. In *Le Nouveau Christianisme* [the new Christianity] (1825), he proclaimed that the concept of brotherhood must accompany scientific organization. His writings contain ideas foreshadowing the positivism of Auguste COMTE (for a time his pupil), socialism, federation of the nations of Europe, and many other modern trends. Around him gathered a small group of brilliant young men. After his death, they modified and elucidated his principles into a system of thought known as **Saint-Simonianism.** Partly because of their eccentricities, the Saint-Simonians achieved brief fame. Led by Barthélemy Prosper ENFANTIN and Saint-Amand BAZARD, they organized a series of lectures (published in 1828–30 as *L'Exposition de la doctrine de Saint-Simon*), calling for abolition of individual inheritance rights, public control of means of production, and gradual emancipation of women. Although the movement developed into a moral-religious cult and had split and was disintegrated by 1833, it exerted much influence, especially on later socialist thought. See Saint-Simon's *Social Organization, The Science of Man and Other Writings*, ed. and tr. by F. Markham (1964); *Historical Memoirs*, ed. and tr. by Lucy Norton (3 vol., 1969–72); studies by M. M. Dondo (1955), Émile Durkheim (tr. 1958), and F. E. Manuel (1956, repr. 1963).

Saint-Simon, Louis de Rouvroy, duc de (lwē də ro͞ovrwä' dük), 1675–1755, French writer of memoirs and courtier. He resigned (1702) from the army after his arrogance had involved him in a quarrel with Marshal Luxembourg. Although disliked by Louis XIV, in 1710 he was allowed to establish himself at the court of Versailles, where he associated with LOUIS, duke of Burgundy, until the duke's death (1712). Between 1715 and 1723 he served ineffectually as a member of the regency council and as a special ambassador to Madrid. After the regency he retired to his estates. Saint-Simon's fame is due entirely to his memoirs, written in the years 1739–51. They are based on his own notes, begun in 1691, and on contemporary journals and memoirs. Despite their uneven quality and their disregard for literary technique and even grammar, the memoirs are a monument of French literature. Saint-Simon's account of the court of Louis XIV is the intensely personal and emotional apology of a grand seigneur who was prevented, by his proud temperament and his limited intelligence, from accepting the rise of the bourgeoisie. He vented his resentment against Louis XIV, whose victory over the great nobles he refused to recognize. Though full of errors, the memoirs are an indispensable historical source and are remarkable for their psychological observation and brilliant sketches. First published in 1788, the memoirs subsequently appeared in several enlarged editions, notably that of Arthur de Boislile and L. Lecestre (41 vol., 1879–1928). See abridged edition of his memoirs ed. and tr. by Lucy Norton (Vol. I and II, 1968; Vol. III, 1972).

Saint Sophia: see HAGIA SOPHIA.

Saint Stephen, town (1971 pop. 3,409), SW N.B., Canada, on the St. Croix River opposite Calais, Maine. The two towns, connected by an international bridge, form virtually a single community. St. Stephen was founded by Loyalists after the American Revolution.

Saint Stephens: see GAINES, George S.

Saint Thomas, city (1971 pop. 25,545), S Ont., Canada, S of London. The city is located in a rich agricultural area, and has automobile plants and other factories.

Saint Thomas, island (1970 pop. 28,960), 32 sq mi (83 sq km), one of the U.S. VIRGIN ISLANDS, West Indies. Charlotte Amalie, the capital of the U.S. Virgin Islands, is on St. Thomas. Tourism is the main economic activity.

Saint Thomas National Historic Site: see NATIONAL PARKS AND MONUMENTS (table).

Saint-Trond: see SINT-TRUIDEN, Belgium.

Saint-Tropez (săN-trôpā'), town (1968 pop. 6,151), Var dept., SE France, on the French RIVIERA. It is a popular beach resort and a picturesque small fishing port. From the 15th to the 17th cent. it was an independent republic.

Saint Valentine's Day, Western European Christian holiday, originally the Roman feast of Lupercalia. It was christianized in memory of the martyrdom of St. Valentine in A.D. 270, who, in medieval times, came to be associated with the union of lovers under conditions of duress. The holiday is celebrated on Feb. 14th by the exchange of romantic or comic verse messages called "valentines." The first commercial valentine greeting cards produced in the United States were created in the 1840s by Esther A. Howland. Today millions of such cards are sold annually.

Saint-Vallier, Jean Baptiste de la Croix (zhäN bätēst' də lä kro͞oä' săN-välyā'), 1653–1727, Roman Catholic bishop of Quebec, b. France. He succeeded François Xavier de LAVAL in 1688 after serving as his vicar general. Austere and aggressive, he formulated a strict ecclesiastical discipline and came into conflict with the civil governors, especially the comte de Frontenac. Quarrels also arose between Saint-Vallier and Laval with regard to diocesan organization, the seminary, and the new bishop's expenditures. From 1700 to 1713 Saint-Vallier was in France and, as a prisoner, in England. He did much for the people of Quebec, notably founding the Hôpital Général for the poor.

St. Vincent, John Jervis, earl of: see JERVIS, JOHN, EARL OF ST. VINCENT.

Saint Vincent, island state (1971 est. pop. 90,000), 150 sq mi (388 sq km), British West Indies, in the Windward Islands. It comprises the island of St. Vincent (140 sq mi/363 sq km) and the small Grenadine islands to the north. The capital is KINGSTOWN. St. Vincent island is mountainous, rising to 4,048 ft

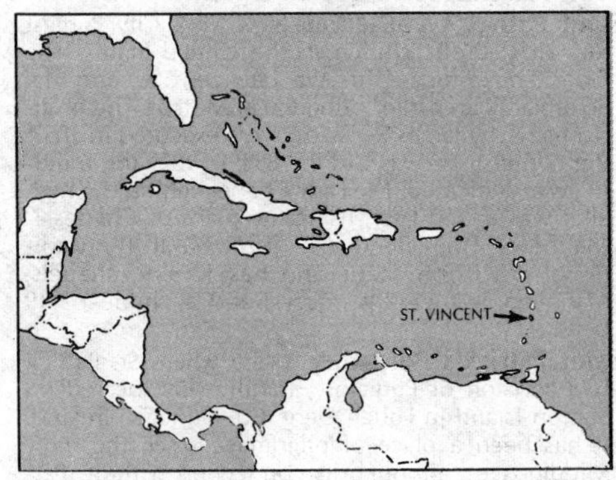

(1,234 m) at the now inactive Soufrière volcano, and well forested, with a healthful climate and abundant rainfall. Bananas, arrowroot, and copra are the chief exports, followed by other agricultural products including fine sea-island cotton. Tourism is also economically important. Presumably discovered by Columbus in 1498, St. Vincent remained uncolonized until a British settlement was made in 1762. The French captured it in 1779 but it was restored to Britain in 1783. Attempts to subdue the warlike Carib Indians failed, and the British deported most of them in 1797. Portuguese and East Indian laborers were introduced in the 19th cent. The population is predominantly of black African descent with an admixture of Carib. In 1902 much of the island was destroyed by an eruption of Soufrière. St. Vincent was part of the British colony of the Windward Islands (1880–1958) and of the West Indies Federation (1958–62). In 1969 it became a self-governing state in association with Great Britain.

Saint Vincent, Cape, Port. *Cabo de São Vicente,* high and rocky promontory at the southwestern extremity of Portugal. Several historic sea battles were fought nearby, the most notable in 1797, when the British under John Jervis defeated a large Spanish fleet and Commodore Horatio Nelson distinguished himself. To the Portuguese the cape symbolizes the dreams and plans of Prince Henry the Navigator, the Portuguese patron of exploration, who lived nearby.

Saint Vincent, Gulf, inlet of the Indian Ocean, 90 mi (145 km) long and 45 mi (72 km) wide, SE South Australia state, Australia. Port Adelaide is on the eastern shore. Salt is obtained from the shores of the gulf by solar evaporation.

Saint-Vith (săNvĕt'), Ger. *Sankt Vith,* town (1970 pop. 3,001), Liège prov., E Belgium, in the Malmédy district and near the West German border. An important road and rail junction in World War II, it was captured (Dec., 1944) by the Germans early in the BATTLE OF THE BULGE and was later taken (Jan. 23, 1945) by U.S. forces. The town was severely damaged in the fighting.

St. Vitus' dance: see CHOREA.

Saionji, Kimmochi, Prince (kēmō'chē sīōn'jē), 1850–1940, Japanese statesman. He took part in the Meiji restoration, then spent 10 years in France, absorbing many democratic ideas. In 1882 he accompanied his friend and patron, Prince Ito, to Europe to study foreign governments. He served in several cabinets under Ito and was president of the privy council (1900–1903). He succeeded Ito as president of the Seiyukai party in 1903 and, as Ito's protégé, was prime minister (1906–8, 1911–12). He retired from party politics in 1914 and refused to form a cabinet in 1918, but in 1919 he headed the delegation to the Paris Peace Conference. As a genro [elder statesman] he continued to enjoy tremendous prestige and influence until his death. He escaped assassination in the military coup of Feb., 1936. See Bunji Omura, *The Last Genro* (1938).

Saipan (sī'păn, sīpän'), volcanic island (1970 pop. 7,967), 47 sq mi (122 sq km), W Pacific, in the MARIANAS ISLANDS, U.S. Trust Territory of the PACIFIC ISLANDS. It is mountainous; the highest peak is Mt. Tagpochau (1,526 ft/465 m). Trust Territory headquarters are located at Capitol Hill on Saipan; the town of Susupe is the district headquarters of the Marianas; and Chalan Kanoa is the island's commercial center. Copra and scrap metal are the only exports, but sugarcane, coffee, and citrus fruits are grown, and the island has phosphate and manganese deposits. Saipan, with the other Marianas, was mandated to Japan in 1920 by the League of Nations. In World War II the island (site of a Japanese airbase) was taken by U.S. forces in 1944 and became a base for air attacks on the Japanese mainland. From 1953 to 1962 Saipan was used to train Nationalist Chinese guerrillas for infiltration of the Chinese mainland.

Saïs (sā'ĭs), ancient city of Egypt, in the west central region of the Nile delta. It was the royal residence of the XXVI dynasty and much visited as a shrine of Neith and Osiris.

Saishu: see CHEJU, South Korea.

Saisset, Bernard (bĕrnär' sĕsā'), d. 1314, French churchman. In 1295 he became bishop of Pamiers (near Foix, S France). He was sent (1301) by Pope BONIFACE VIII as papal legate to King Philip IV of France to protest the king's anticlerical measures. He also urged the king's support for Boniface's projected crusade. On his return to Pamiers, Saisset, who was openly hostile to Philip, was arrested for seeking to incite rebellion against the king. Philip asked Boniface to depose Saisset; the pope replied by asking that Saisset be sent to Rome for trial by an ecclesiastic court. Philip refused and had Saisset indicted by a civil court. This strictly illegal measure revived and intensified the struggle between church and state. In the meantime, Saisset, the relatively unimportant figure in the struggle, was forgotten. He was allowed to go to Rome and in 1308 was restored to his see.

Saitama (sī'tämä), prefecture (1970 pop. 3,866,472), E central Honshu, Japan. URAWA (the capital), Omiya, and KAWAGUCHI are the chief cities. Largely a fertile plain, Saitama is an agricultural region.

Saito, Makoto (mäkō'tō sī'tō), 1858–1936, Japanese admiral and statesman. A moderate militarist, his selection as prime minister (1932–34) to replace Ki Inukai, who had been assassinated, signaled the end of prewar party cabinets. Saito's cabinet was torn by the struggle between the war minister, who advocated expansionist aims in China, and the finance minister, who unsuccessfully opposed greater military expenditures. In 1936, Saito became keeper of the privy seal, a position close to the emperor. During the abortive military uprising of Feb. 26, 1936, he was assassinated by young militarists.

Sakai (säkī'), city (1970 pop. 594,369), Osaka prefecture, S Honshu, Japan, on Osaka Bay at the mouth of the Yamato River. An industrial center, it has engineering, iron, and steel works, chemical plants, machine factories, and textile mills. Sakai was a major port from the 15th to the 17th cent.

Sakakawea: see SACAJAWEA.

Sakartvelo: see GEORGIAN SOVIET SOCIALIST REPUBLIC, USSR.

Sakarya (säkäryä'), anc. *Sangarius,* river, c.490 mi (790 km) long, rising on the Anatolian plateau, NW Turkey. It flows generally north in a series of huge bends past Adapazarı to the Black Sea at Karasu. There are hydroelectric-power plants on the river. The Porsuk and Ankara rivers are its chief tributaries.

sake (sä'kē), Japanese fermented liquor, from 12% to 16% alcohol. Made principally from rice, it is fermented by a kind of mold cake called *koji.* Sake is yellowish and sherrylike in flavor. When distilled it forms a variety of ARRACK. Sake is usually served warm in porcelain cups.

Sakhalin (səkhəlyēn'), formerly **Saghalien** (sägälyĕn'), island (c.29,500 sq mi/76,400 sq km), off the coast of the Soviet Far East, USSR, between the Sea of Okhotsk and the Sea of Japan; separated from the Soviet mainland on the west by the Tatar Strait and from Hokkaido, the northernmost island of Japan, by the Soya Strait. With the Kuril Islands it forms the Sakhalin oblast (1970 pop. 616,000) of the SOVIET FAR EAST. Two parallel mountain ranges, separated by a central valley, run the length of this elongated and heavily forested island. The climate is severe, but grains, beets, and potatoes are grown in the south. Lumbering, coal mining, herring fishing, and paper milling are the principal industries. There are oil fields in the northeast and a pipeline runs to Nikolayevsk on the Soviet mainland. Despite their small size, the coal and iron deposits are vital to the Soviet Far East region, where these minerals are scarce. Coastal shipping is also important to Sakhalin's economy. The island's population is predominantly Russian, with the indigenous tribe of Gilyaks the largest minority. Sakhalin was explored by Russians in the 17th cent. and colonized by Russia and Japan in the 18th and 19th cent. It was under joint Russo-Japanese control (formalized by the Treaty of Shimoda, 1855) until it passed entirely to Russia in 1875, when Japan obtained the Kuril Islands in return. Sakhalin became a czarist place of exile. By the Treaty of Portsmouth (1905), Russia retained the portion of Sakhalin north of lat. 50° N and Japan obtained the remainder. The Japanese territory was named Karafuto, and this name was sometimes applied to the whole island. Both countries colonized extensively and reduced the native population to a minority. After World War II the Japanese holdings were transferred to the USSR and nearly all the Japanese population was repatriated. In the peace treaty signed (1951) with the USSR, Japan renounced all claims to Sakhalin. See J. J. Stephan, *Sakhalin: A History* (1971).

Saki: see MUNRO, HECTOR HUGH.

saki: see MONKEY.

Sakkara (säkä'rä), necropolis (burial place) of ancient MEMPHIS, Egypt, 3 mi (5 km) from the Nile and on the border of the Libyan desert. Zoser had his famous step-pyramid built there in the III dynasty, and on the grounds are many pyramids that date from the V and VI dynasties. The Serapeum, burial place of the Apis bulls, dates from the later period. The oldest dated papyrus (VI dynasty) was discovered there in 1893.

Sakkuth: see SICCUTH.

Sakuntala: see KALIDASA.

Sakura-jima (säkōō'rä'-jīmä), peninsula, Kagoshima prefecture, S Kyushu, Japan, opposite Kagoshima. Formerly an island, Sakura-jima became a peninsula in 1914 when lava from its three volcanic cones closed the channel. The fruits and turnips raised there are famous throughout Japan.

Sala (sā'lə), variant of SALAH.

Sala (sä'lä''), city (1970 pop. 10,476), Västmanland co., E Sweden; chartered 1624. It is a mining center for sphalerite and silver-bearing lead ore.

salad, herbs or fruit, vegetables, meat, poultry, eggs, or fish, served cold and usually with a dressing. Green salads, served raw, usually consist of endive, escarole, lettuce, spinach, or watercress; these may be used singly or in combination. Often other raw vegetables are used, e.g., carrot, celery, cucumber, onion, and tomato. Cooked vegetables typically used in salads include asparagus, beets, beans, cauliflower, and potatoes. Light salads are usually served as an accompaniment to a meat course or as a separate course; the heartier salads are served as a main course. Frozen and jellied salads may use fruits, vegetables, or both. The important salad dressings are oil (preferably olive) and vinegar or lemon, with various mixtures of seasonings and cheese and mayonnaise.

Saladin (săl'ədĭn), Arabic *Salah ad-Din,* 1137?–1193, Muslim warrior and Ayyubid sultan of Egypt, the great opponent of the Crusaders, b. Mesopotamia, of Kurdish descent. He lived for 10 years in Damascus at the court of NUR AD-DIN, where he distinguished himself by his interest in Sunni theology. He accompanied his uncle, Shirkuh (or Shirkoh), a lieutenant of Nur ad-Din, on campaigns (1164, 1167, 1168) against the Fatimid rulers of Egypt. Shirkuh became vizier there and on his death (1169) was succeeded by Saladin. Saladin later caused the name of the Shiite Fatimid caliph to be dropped from the Friday prayer, thus deposing him. After the death of Nur ad-Din, who was planning to campaign against his too-powerful subordinate, Saladin proclaimed himself sultan of Egypt, thus beginning the Ayyubid dynasty. He spread his conquests westward on the northern shores of Africa as far as Qabis and also conquered Yemen. He took over Damascus after Nur ad-Din's death and undertook to subdue all Syria and Palestine. He had already come into conflict with the Crusaders (see CRUSADES), and he put the rulers of the Latin Kingdom of Jerusalem on the steadily weakening defensive. He was unsuccessful in his efforts to conquer the Assassins in their mountain strongholds, but he took Mosul, Aleppo, and wide areas from rival Muslim rulers and became the principal warrior of Islam. Gathering a large force of Muslims of various groups—but all called Saracens by the Christians—he set out to attack the Christians. Raymond of Tripoli was at first his ally, but then joined the other Crusaders, and the great battle of Hattin (near Tiberias—now Teverya) in 1187 found Christians matched solely against Muslims. Saladin won brilliantly, capturing GUY OF LUSIGNAN and REGINALD OF CHÂTILLON. Jerusalem fell to him, and the Christians seemed lost. The Third Crusade was gathered (1189) and came to the Holy Land to try to recover the Holy City. Thus it was that Richard I of England and Saladin met in the conflict that was to be celebrated in later chivalric romance. The reputation that Saladin had among the Christians for his generosity and chivalry does not seem to have been a legend, and there seems no doubt that Saladin admired Richard as a worthy opponent. The Crusaders, however, failed in their purpose and succeeded only in capturing Akko. In 1192, Saladin came to agreement with the Crusaders upon the Peace of Ramla, which left the Latin Kingdom only a strip along the coast from Tyre to Yafo. The Christians were never to recover from their defeat. Saladin was not only a warrior but a builder. He restored the irrigation systems and erected fine mosques. He was also a cultivated man and a patron of literature and learning as well as an able theological disputant in his own right. See biographies by G. E. T. Slaughter (1955), S. Lane-Poole (2d ed. 1964), A. S. Ehrenkreutz (1972), and A. R. H. Gibb (1973).

Salado, Río (rē'ō sälä'thō) [Sp.,=salty river], name of several South American rivers, including more than 10 in Argentina. The most important is the Río Salado del Norte (c.1,250 mi/2,010 km long), rising in the Andes near Salta, N Argentina, and flowing SE through a livestock-raising region, to the Paraná River at Santa Fe. Salt and sulfur are mined along its upper course.

Salah (sā'lə), descendant of Shem. Gen. 10.24; 11.12,14. Shelah: 1 Chron. 1.18,24. Sala: Luke 3.35.

Salair Ridge (səlaēr'), range, c.200 mi (320 km) long, E Siberian USSR. Extending along the northern border of the Altai Kray, it rises to more than 2,000 ft (610 m) and forms the western edge of the Kuznetsk Basin; to the south it merges with the Kuznetsk Ala-Tau range. The Salair Ridge has iron, lead, silver, and zinc deposits.

Salamanca (sälämäng'kä), city (1970 pop. 103,740), Guanajuato state, W central Mexico. Chiefly an oil center, it also serves as the commercial and distribution point for the surrounding agricultural region. The city lies on major national highway and rail systems. The first important battle between liberals and conservatives in the 19th-century War of the Reform (see MEXICO) was fought at Salamanca.

Salamanca, city (1970 pop. 125,220), capital of Salamanca prov., W central Spain, in León, on the

Tormes River, c.2,600 ft (790 m) above sea level. There are food-processing and other industries. An ancient city, it was taken by Hannibal in 220 B.C. The Moors were driven out in 1085. Salamanca became world famous after the foundation (c.1230) of its university by Alfonso IX. The university soon rivaled Bologna, Paris, and Oxford, and it made Arabic philosophy available to the Western world. In the late Middle Ages and throughout the Renaissance, Salamanca was the center of Christian Spanish cultural life and the fountainhead of Spanish theology. In the Peninsular War the city was in part demolished (1811) by the French. It was (1937–38) the capital of the Insurgents in the Spanish civil war. Salamanca is rich in architectural interest; there is a Roman bridge in the city. The Plaza Mayor is among the finest colonnaded squares in Spain. Adjoining the old Gothic cathedral (12th cent.) is the imposing new cathedral (1513–1733), in which the Gothic, plateresque, and baroque styles are combined. The university building (15th cent.) has a richly adorned facade and possesses a library with precious manuscripts. There are many splendid palaces, notably the Casa de las Conchas, named for the scallop shells on its facade, and the Casa de la Salina, with a picturesque patio.

Salamanca, University of, at Salamanca, Spain; founded 1218 by Alfonso IX of León, reorganized 1254 by Alfonso X of Castile and León. It has faculties of philosophy and letters, law, science, and medicine.

salamander, an AMPHIBIAN of the order Urodela, or Caudata. Salamanders have tails and small, weak limbs; superficially they resemble the unrelated lizards (which are reptiles), but they are easily distinguished by their lack of scales and claws, and by their moist, usually smooth skins. Salamanders are found in damp regions of the northern temperate zone and are most abundant in North America. Most are under 6 in. (15 cm) long, but the giant salamander of Japan (*Megalobatrachus japonicus*) may reach a length of over 5 ft (1.5 m). Most salamanders are terrestrial as adults, living near water or in wet vegetation, but some are aquatic and a few are arboreal, burrowing, or cave-dwelling. Most are nocturnal, and all avoid direct light. Salamanders are able to regenerate a lost limb or tail. They feed on small animals, such as insects, worms, and snails. Most salamanders breed in water and are gregarious at breeding time, when there is usually a courtship display. In most species fertilization is internal. The male deposits sperm packets, which the female picks up with the cloaca; the sperm is then stored until fertilization can take place. The eggs, surrounded by gelatinous material, are usually laid in ponds or brooks, where they develop into aquatic larvae that breathe water by means of gills. Most salamanders, including most that remain in an aquatic environment, go through a typical amphibian metamorphosis into air-breathing adults. Generally the adults have lungs, but in the large family of lungless salamanders (Plethodontidae) breathing occurs entirely through the skin and the lining of the throat. A few salamanders breed on land, laying their eggs under rotting vegetation; the young pass through the gilled stage in the egg, emerging as miniature adults. Such strictly terrestrial forms are the red-backed salamander *(Plethodon cinereus)* and slimy salamander *(P. glutinosus)* of E United States and the slender salamander *(Batrachoseps attenuatus)* of the Pacific coast. The North American blind salamanders (several genera in the family Plethodontidae) live in underground streams, caves, and wells in S United States. As adults they have whitish, translucent skin, which covers their eyes. The olm is a European blind salamander related to the MUD PUPPY. The giant salamander *(Dicamptodon ensatus)* of the NW United States grows to 12 in. (30 cm) in length. The hellbender *(Cryptobranchus alleganiensis)* of E United States and the so-called Congo eel *(Amphiuma means)* are large aquatic species. The former, of the same family as the Japanese giant salamander, grows to 20 in. (50 cm); the latter, slender and eellike in appearance, with tiny legs, may reach 30 in. (75 cm). In a few salamanders growth occurs without metamorphosis, and the gilled, juvenile form is able to reproduce. This phenomenon (called NEOTENY) is found in the sirens (family Sirenidae) of S United States and N Mexico, in the mud puppies (family Protidae), and in the Mexican AXOLOTL. It may also occur in the Western varieties of the North American tiger salamander *(Ambystoma tigrinum)* under certain environmental conditions. The NEWTS are a large, widely distributed family of salamanders; North American species include the red-spotted newt, which goes through a terrestrial stage known as the red eft. There are over 200 salamander species, classified in approximately 60 genera and 8 families of the phylum CHORDATA, subphylum Vertebrata, class Amphibia, order Urodela.

Salamis (săl'əmĭs), ancient city on Cyprus, once the principal city. St. Paul visited it on his first missionary journey (Acts 13.5). Excavations there revealed the ruins of a Greek theater; there are also many Roman ruins. At nearby Enkomi, which preceded Salamis as the principal city of Cyprus, important Mycenaean remains have been found.

Salamis, island, E Greece, in the Saronic Gulf (now Saronikós Kólpos), W of Athens. It early belonged to Aegina but was later under Athenian control, except for a brief period after it was occupied (c.600 B.C.) by Megara. In the PERSIAN WARS the allied Greek fleet, led by THEMISTOCLES, decisively defeated (480 B.C.) the Persians off Salamis.

sal ammoniac: see AMMONIUM CHLORIDE.

Salandra, Antonio (äntō'nyō sälän'drä), 1853–1931, Italian premier (1914–16). He entered parliament as a moderate conservative (1886), held various cabinet posts from 1891 to 1910, and succeeded Giolitti as premier in 1914. He immediately declared Italian neutrality in World War I but undertook active military preparations. After the failure of his negotiations with Austria, he signed the Treaty of London (1915) with Great Britain, France, and Russia, denounced the Triple Alliance, and finally declared war on Austria. He resigned in 1916 after the Italian retreat in the Trentino. Salandra was a delegate at the Paris Peace Conference (1919) and was the Italian delegate to the League of Nations. He at first supported Fascism, but then opposed it. In 1928, however, he was made a senator.

Salang: see PHUKET, Thailand.

Salathiel (sālā'thēəl), variant of SHEALTIEL.

Salazar, António de Oliveira (əntô'nyōō thĭ ōōlēvā'rə sələzär'), 1889–1970, Portuguese statesman and dictator. After studying at the Univ. of Coimbra, he became professor of political economy there. Profoundly religious, Salazar was the leader of a political group committed to putting into action the social principles expressed in the encyclicals of Pope Leo XIII. He was elected a deputy in 1921 but withdrew from the chamber immediately, viewing its proceedings as futile. After the military coup d'etat of 1926 Salazar was briefly minister of finance, and in 1928 he was recalled to office by Gen. António de Fragoso CARMONA. Given the full financial control that he demanded, he put Portuguese finances on a stable footing for the first time in the 20th cent. As premier after 1932, Salazar was generally considered a dictator. He introduced (1933) a new constitution that established a corporative and authoritarian state. Political opposition was effectively suppressed. Salazar supported the Nationalists during the Spanish civil war (1936–39), but he maintained relations with Portugal's traditional ally, Britain, and permitted the Allies to use the Azores as a base during World War II. After the war he set in motion several economic-development programs, but there were signs of increasing opposition to his regime. In his final years he devoted considerable resources to the attempt to suppress revolts in Portugal's African colonies. In 1968, Salazar suffered a severe stroke and was replaced as premier by Marcello Caetano. See study by H. Kay (1970).

Salazar Bridge, vehicular suspension bridge across the estuary of the Tagus River, S Estremadura prov., Portugal, between Lisbon and the Setual Peninsula; opened 1966. Its main span, 3,323 ft (1,013 m) long, is the longest in Europe and one of the longest in the world.

Salcah or **Salchah** (both: săl'kə), ancient fortress, SE Syria, E of the Jordan and on the boundary of Bashan. Deut. 3.10; Joshua 12.5; 13.11; 1 Chron. 5.11.

Sale, Australia: see GIPPSLAND.

Sale, municipal borough (1971 pop. 55,623), Cheshire, W England. It is a residential suburb of Manchester. Biscuits are made there. In 1974, Sale became part of the new metropolitan county of Greater Manchester.

Salé (sälā'), Arab. *Sla,* city (1960 pop. 75,799), NW Morocco, near Rabat. It has industries producing flour and fine carpets. The harbor was long a haven for pirates, who came to be called Sallee rovers.

sale, in law, transfer of ownership in return for money. An exchange of goods for goods is termed barter, but the distinction between sale and barter is mainly technical; laws that govern one govern the other equally. Sale and barter are distinguished from the giving of a GIFT, which involves no valuable consideration. Laws governing sales distinguish fundamentally between sales of real PROPERTY and sales of personal property. If nothing is said to the contrary, the law of sales is understood to be the law of sales of personal property, sales of real property being governed by real-estate law. Delivery of goods sold passes TITLE to the goods, even though full payment has not been made; the seller may sue for the amount due him, but cannot recover the goods. A contract may provide, however, that the goods, though delivered, remain the property of the seller until full payment for them has been made. By a contract, one may purchase goods not yet in existence, e.g., the crop that a farmer will grow in his field. Sales are governed by the Uniform Commercial Code in all U.S. jurisdictions, except Louisiana.

Salegard: see SALEKHARD, USSR.

Salekhard (səlyĭkhärt'), city (1970 pop. 22,000), capital of Yamalo-Nenets National Okrug, NW Siberian USSR, on the lower Ob River. It is a river port and has fish canneries, lumber mills, and shipyards. The population is mainly Russian. Founded as Obdorsk in 1595, the city was renamed in 1930. It is also spelled Salegard.

Salem (sā'ləm), in the Bible. **1** Royal city of Melchizedek, in tradition identified with **2.** Gen. 14.18; Heb. 7.1, 2. **2** Abbreviation used for Jerusalem. Ps. 76.2.

Salem, city (1971 pop. 308,303), Tamil Nadu state, SE India. Iron and manganese mining, mineral processing, and textile manufacturing are the major economic activities.

Salem. 1 City (1970 pop. 40,556), seat of Essex co., NE Mass., on an inlet of Massachusetts Bay; inc. 1629. Its once famous harbor has silted up, and it is now only nominally a port of entry. The city has electrical, leather, and precision machine industries. Its many historical landmarks are tourist attractions. In 1626, Roger Conant led a group from Cape Ann to this site, called Naumkeag by the Indians. Salem's early history was darkened by the witchcraft trials of 1692, in which Samuel Sewall was a judge. From colonial days through the clipper ship era, Salem was world famous as a port and a wealthy center for the China trade. It was a privateering base in the American Revolution and in the War of 1812. Nathaniel Hawthorne was overseer of the port from 1846 to 1849. Shipping declined after the War of 1812, and the city turned to manufacturing. Mansions designed by Samuel McIntire recall the days of commercial glory. A great fire in 1914 leveled 250 acres (101 hectares), but many fine old buildings remain. Hawthorne's birthplace dates from the 17th cent., and the House of Seven Gables (1668) is preserved. Also of interest are Pioneer Village (the reproduction of a 1630 settlement) and Salem Maritime National Historic Site, which preserves the aspect of the old shipping days. The Essex Institute (est. 1848) has an excellent library and historical collections. The Peabody Museum, founded (1868) by George Peabody, contains exhibits of a museum organized in 1799 by the Salem East India Marine Society. Salem State College is in the city. See history by J. D. Phillips (4 vol., 1933–49); R. D. Paine, *Ships and Sailors of Old Salem* (1909); Paul Boyer and Stephen Nissembaum, comp., *Salem-Village Witchcraft* (1972). **2** Town (1970 pop. 20,142), Rockingham co., SE N.H.; settled 1652, inc. 1750. It is a marketing and distributing center, with steel-fabricating, printing, electronic, shoe, and wood-product industries. It has a racetrack and a large glider airport. Of interest is Mystery Hill, site of large man-made structures believed to date from 2,000 B.C. **3** City (1970 pop. 14,186), Columbiana co., NE Ohio, in a rich coal region; inc. 1806. Tools and dies, industrial machinery, pumps, and water systems are among its many and diverse manufactures. Settled (1803) by Quakers, Salem was an early abolitionist center and an important station on the Underground Railroad. A branch of Kent State Univ. is there. **4** City (1970 pop. 68,296), state capital and seat of Marion co., NW Oregon, on the Willamette River; inc. 1857. In a dairying, stock-raising, and farming area, it has numerous food-processing plants and a paper mill. Founded 1840–41 by Methodist missionaries, it became capital of Oregon Territory in 1851 and remained the capital when Oregon became a state in 1859. Salem is the seat of Willamette Univ., various state and Federal government buildings, state hospitals, and the state penitentiary. A U.S. Indian school is at nearby Chemawa. The annual state fair is held at Salem. **5** City (1970 pop. 21,982), seat of Roanoke co., SW Va., on the Roanoke River, between the Blue Ridge and the Allegheny mts.; first inc. 1806, inc. as a city 1967. Electrical equipment, rubber tires, fork lifts, steel items, locks, and tools and dies are made. Roanoke College is there.

Salem Church: see CHANCELLORSVILLE, BATTLE OF.

Salem Maritime National Historic Site: see NATIONAL PARKS AND MONUMENTS (table).

Salerno (sälär'nō), city (1971 pop. 154,481), capital of Salerno prov., Campania, S Italy, on the Gulf of Salerno, an inlet of the Tyrrhenian Sea. It is an agricultural, commercial, and industrial center. Manufactures include machinery, textiles, paper, and processed food. Originally a Greek settlement and later a Roman colony (founded 197 B.C.), Salerno became (6th cent.) a part of the duchy of Benevento and in the 9th cent. the seat of an independent principality, which fell to Robert Guiscard in 1076. In Sept., 1943, there was fierce fighting on the beaches near Salerno between the Allied landing forces and the Germans, who were pressed to retreat toward Naples. Of note in Salerno is the Sicilian-Norman cathedral (11th cent; redone in the 18th cent.), with the tomb of Pope Gregory VII and an impressive 12th-century pulpit. The famous medical school of Salerno (founded in the 9th cent., closed in the early 19th cent.) is believed to have been the first of its kind and reached its height in the 12th cent.

sales tax, levy on the sale of goods or services, generally calculated as a percentage of the selling price, and sometimes called a purchase tax. It is usually collected in the form of an extra charge by the retailer, who remits the tax to the government. It may be levied each time a commodity changes hands—as from manufacturer to wholesaler, from wholesaler to retailer—and is then called a transactions, or turnover, tax. Many oppose the tax as being regressive, i.e., as placing a disproportionately heavy burden on the poor; but it yields a large revenue, and governments find it easy to collect. As of 1972, 45 states and the District of Columbia, a number of cities and counties, and many foreign countries levied sales taxes. A modern variant of the sales tax is the VALUE-ADDED TAX.

Salford (sŏl'fərd, sôl'-), county borough (1971 pop. 130,641), Lancashire, NW England, on the Irwell River. It is a textile center and has an unusual number of parks and recreation grounds. Many Port of Manchester docks are in Salford, as is the Manchester racecourse. Made a free town in 1230, Salford included Manchester in the Middle Ages. The Univ. of Salford specializes in science and technology. In 1974, Salford became part of the new metropolitan county of Greater Manchester.

Salgótarján (shŏl'gōtŏr"yän), city (1970 pop. 37,212), N Hungary, near the Czechoslovak border. It is an industrial center with ironworks, steelworks, and manufactures of agricultural machinery and glass. Salgótarján was a small settlement that grew rapidly after the discovery of coal there in the early 19th cent. Nearby, on a basaltic hill, are the ruins of a medieval fortress.

Salian Law: see GERMANIC LAWS.

Salians: see FRANKS.

Salic Law: see GERMANIC LAWS.

Salic law (sā'lĭk), rule of succession in certain royal and noble families of Europe, forbidding females and those descended in the female line to succeed to the titles or offices in the family. It is called the Salic law on the mistaken supposition that it was part of the *Lex Salica* (see GERMANIC LAWS); provisions of that code forbade female succession to property but were not concerned with titles or offices. The rule was most prominently enforced by the house of Valois and the succeeding house of Bourbon in France. At the time of PHILIP V it was introduced to Spain; when it was rescinded there in favor of Isabella II, the Carlists rose in revolt on the grounds of the law. The rule was also involved in the rivalry of STEPHEN and MATILDA for the throne of England and in the claim of EDWARD III to the French succession (one cause of the HUNDRED YEARS WAR). Because the GUELPHS followed the Salic law, the union of Great Britain and Hanover—begun when the elector of Hanover ascended the British throne as George I—had to be discontinued when VICTORIA ascended the British throne.

salicylate (səlĭs'əlāt"), any of a group of ANALGESICS, or pain-killing drugs, that are derivatives of salicylic acid, e.g., ASPIRIN (acetylsalicylic acid). Methyl salicylate is the main component of oil of wintergreen; the compound is used in rubbing LINIMENTS to soothe muscular aches and is used as a flavoring agent. Sodium salicylate is used in dyes and as a nonedible preservative. Salicylates, especially aspirin, are used medically to reduce fever and inflammation and to relieve headache, menstrual pain, and pain in nerves, muscles, and joints. Because they cause increased excretion of uric acid, salicylates are useful in the treatment of gout. Salicylic acid is used topically to remove calluses and warts and to control acne. Salicylates are useful, relatively safe, frequently used drugs, but large doses may cause hearing and vision difficulties and gastrointestinal disturbances.

salicylic acid or **2-hydroxybenzoic acid,** $C_6H_4(OH)CO_2H$, a colorless, crystalline organic carboxylic acid that melts at 159°C; it is soluble in ethanol and ether but is only slightly soluble in water. It is prepared commercially by heating sodium phenolate (the sodium salt of phenol) with carbon dioxide under pressure to form sodium salicylate, which is treated with sulfuric acid to liberate salicylic acid. Salicylic acid and its derivatives are toxic when consumed in large amounts. Sodium salicylate is used to a small extent as a food preservative and as an antiseptic in mouthwashes and toothpastes. The major use of salicylic acid is in the preparation of its ester derivatives; since it contains both a hydroxyl ($-OH$) and a carboxyl ($-CO_2H$) group, it can react with either an acid or an alcohol. The hydroxyl group reacts with acetic acid to form the acetate ester, acetylsalicylic acid (see ASPIRIN). Several useful esters are formed by reaction of the carboxyl group with alcohols. The methyl ester, methyl salicylate, (also called oil of wintergreen since it produces the fragrance of wintergreen), is formed with methanol; it is used in food flavorings and in liniments. The phenyl ester, phenyl salicylate, or salol, is formed with phenol; it is used in medicine as an antiseptic and antipyretic. This ester hydrolyzes, not in the acidic stomach, but in the alkaline intestines, releasing free salicylic acid. The menthyl ester, menthyl salicylate, which is used in suntan lotions, is formed with menthol.

Salieri, Antonio (äntô'nyō sälyä'rē), 1750–1825, Italian composer and conductor. He received his first training in Italy, going afterward (1766) to Vienna, where he remained as conductor of the opera and later (1788–1824) as court conductor. He was a friend of Haydn, and he taught Beethoven, Schubert, and Liszt. The most successful of his 43 operas were *Les Danaïdes* (1784) and *Tarare* (1787). He also wrote instrumental pieces and church music.

Salim (sā'lĭm), unlocated place, Palestine, near the scene of John's last baptizing. John 3.23.

Salina (səlī'nə), city (1970 pop. 37,714), seat of Saline co., central Kansas, on the Smoky Hill River; founded 1858 by antislavery people, inc. 1870. It is the marketing and shipping center for an area that produces grain, livestock, oil, and natural gas, and a leading hub of the great hard-winter-wheat belt. The city has grain elevators, flour mills, and factories that make farm implements, lamps, and aircraft. Kansas Wesleyan Univ., Marymount College, and a military school are there. Nearby is a noted Indian burial pit.

Salinas (səlē'nəs), city (1970 pop. 58,896), seat of Monterey co., W Calif.; inc. 1874. It is the shipping and processing center of a fertile valley famous for its lettuce. Fruits, sugar beets, and dairy goods are also produced, and spices, candy, and jams and jellies are made in Salinas. The Alisal area (formerly called East Salinas), which was annexed by Salinas in 1964, was settled (1933) principally by migratory farm workers. The city is the scene of an annual rodeo and the seat of a junior college. John Steinbeck was born in Salinas, and his home is open to the public.

Salinas, river, c.150 mi (240 km) long, rising in the Santa Lucia Mts., S Calif., and flowing (partly underground) past King City, Paso Robles, and Salinas, NW to Monterey Bay. The irrigated valley is highly productive and is the chief lettuce-producing region in the United States.

Salinas Grandes (sälē'näs grän'dās), salt desert, c.3,200 sq mi (8,290 sq km), in Córdoba and Santiago del Estero provs., N Argentina. The Córdoba-Tucumán RR crosses the desert. Sodium and potassium are mined there.

Salinger, J. D. (Jerome David Salinger) (săl'ĭnjər), 1919–, American novelist and short-story writer, b. New York City. Combining pathos with humor, Salinger depicts the loneliness and frustration of individuals caught in a world of banalities and restricting conformity. His best-known work, *The Catcher in the Rye* (1951), is a picaresque novel that describes the adventures of Holden Caulfield, a schoolboy at odds with a "phoney" society. The novel was extremely popular among high school and college students of the 1950s and early 1960s; Caulfield was, to them, a symbol of the purity and honesty of youth. Many of his short stories concern the Glass family, presented by Salinger as overly sensitive people in a materialistic world. Collections of his stories, most of which first appeared in the *New Yorker* magazine, include *Nine Stories* (1953); *Franny and Zooey* (1961); and *Raise High the Roof Beam, Carpenters* and *Seymour: An Introduction* (1963). See H. A. Grunwald, ed., *Salinger: A Critical and Personal Portrait* (1962); Marvin Laser and Norman Fruman, ed., *Studies in J. D. Salinger* (1963).

salinity of ocean water: see OCEAN.

Salisbury, John of: see JOHN OF SALISBURY.

Salisbury, Robert Arthur Talbot Gascoyne-Cecil, 3d **marquess of** (sôlz'bərē), 1830–1903, British statesman. He entered Parliament in 1853 as a Conservative and devoted himself for 50 years to a program of cautious imperialism and implacable resistance to sweeping parliamentary and franchise reforms. He became (1866) secretary for India in Lord Derby's government but resigned (1867) in protest against the Reform Bill sponsored and passed by Benjamin DISRAELI. Salisbury (who succeeded to his father's title in 1868) returned to the India Office in 1874 and in 1878 became Disraeli's foreign secretary. His "Salisbury Circular" outlined British policy concerning the Eastern Question and led to the Congress of Berlin (1878), which he attended with Disraeli. The Conservatives lost office in 1880, and on Disraeli's death (1881) Salisbury became leader of the opposition to the administration of William GLADSTONE. In 1885 he entered upon the first of his three ministries. His government fell early in 1886, but Salisbury returned to power within the year, following the defeat of Gladstone's bill for Irish Home Rule. Salisbury's second government lasted six years (until 1892); his third, seven years (1895–1902). In each of his ministries he acted as his own foreign minister. Salisbury avoided alignments in European affairs, maintaining the policy of what was later called "splendid isolation." Colonial affairs, however, brought difficulties with some of the European powers. An Anglo-German agreement (1890) resolved conflicting claims in East Africa; Great Britain received Zanzibar and Uganda in exchange for Helgoland. A treaty with Portugal (1891) gave Britain further rights in E Africa. The FASHODA INCIDENT (1898) brought Britain and France to the verge of war but ended in a diplomatic victory for Britain. Difficulties with the Boers, however, resulted in the South African War (1899–1902). Salisbury conciliated the United States at the time of the Venezuela Boundary Dispute, in the Spanish-American War, and in the Panama negotiations. He attempted with some success to maintain the Open Door in China. Although preoccupied largely with foreign affairs, Salisbury did carry several land purchase acts for Ireland. His governments were also responsible for such reforms as the reorganization of local government (1888), free public education (1891), and workmen's compensation (1897). He relinquished the foreign office in 1900 and resigned as prime minister after the conclusion of the South African War in 1902. Salisbury designated his nephew, Arthur Balfour, as his successor. See biographies by his daughter, Lady Gwendolen Cecil (4 vol., 1921–32, repr. 1971) and A. L. Kennedy (1953).

Salisbury, Robert Cecil, 1st **earl of,** 1563–1612, English statesman; son of William Cecil, Baron BURGHLEY. He entered Parliament and came gradually to rank second only to his father as adviser to Queen Elizabeth I. About 1589 he began to perform the duties of secretary of state, and he was officially appointed to that position in 1596. He became chancellor of the duchy of Lancaster in 1597 and in 1598 succeeded his father as principal secretary, despite the rivalry of Francis Bacon and the 2d earl of ESSEX. The fall and execution of Essex in 1601 cleared the way for Cecil to enter into secret negotiations with James VI of Scotland and arrange the latter's peaceful accession to the English throne as JAMES I on the death of Elizabeth (1603). After the accession of James, Cecil was created Baron Cecil (1603), Viscount Cranborne (1604), and earl of Salisbury (1605). His influence over James was due to his abilities, not, as in the case of the earl of Somerset and the 1st duke of Buckingham, to a personal ascendancy over the king. For the remainder of his life virtually the entire administration of the government was in his care. The duties of lord treasurer devolved upon Salisbury in 1608. He exhibited great financial skill, reducing the king's debt and attempting to restrain James's extravagance. However, his practice of levying impositions (customs duties) without parliamentary consent raised a storm in Parliament. In 1610, Salisbury negotiated the so-called Great Contract with Parliament, by which James was to receive a settled income in return for abandoning his feudal revenues. The agreement was broken off, however, because of mutual suspicions. In foreign affairs Salisbury ended (1604) the war with Spain and thereafter attempted to maintain a balance of power between France and Spain. After 1604 he received a pension from Spain, but his hope that England might lead a Protestant alliance led him to support the marriage (1612) of James's daughter Elizabeth to the elector palatine. Salisbury planned and had built the great Jacobean mansion Hatfield House in Hertfordshire. He managed to restrain the king from serious error during his lifetime, but Salisbury's adherence to outmoded Elizabethan policies and principles of government prevented him from developing satisfactory solutions for the new problems facing James I. See P. M. Handover, *The Second Cecil* (1959).

Salisbury (sôlz'bərē) or **New Sarum** (sâr'əm), municipal borough (1971 pop. 35,271), county town of Wiltshire, S England. A market town with varied industries, Salisbury was founded in 1220 when the bishopric was moved there from OLD SARUM. Squares or "checkers" are characteristic of the regular plan of the city. The great cathedral, a splendid example of Early English architecture with the highest spire in England (404 ft/123 m), was built mainly between 1220 and 1260, some of the materials being brought from the razed cathedral of Old Sarum. The 13th-century palace of the bishops, numerous medieval churches and other old buildings, and the Salisbury and South Wiltshire Museum are of interest. There is a teacher-training college and a theological college. The city is the Melchester of Thomas Hardy's Wessex novels. STONEHENGE is 10 mi (16 km) to the north.

Salisbury, city (1973 est. pop., with suburbs, 502,000), alt. 4,865 ft (1,483 m), capital of Rhodesia, NE Rhodesia. One of Africa's most modern cities, Salisbury is Rhodesia's largest city and its administrative, commercial, and communications center. It has a mild climate and is the trade center for an agricultural region whose main products are tobacco, maize, cotton, and citrus fruits. Manufactures include textiles, clothing, processed food and tobacco, beverages, steel, chemicals, furniture, fertilizers, and construction materials. Gold is mined in the area. Salisbury is connected by rail with Bulawayo, SW Rhodesia, and with BEIRA, Mozambique, a port on the Indian Ocean. Salisbury was founded in 1890 as a fort by the Pioneer Column, a mercenary force organized by Cecil J. Rhodes to seize Mashonaland. The city was named for R. A. Salisbury, then British prime minister. It became a municipality in 1897 and a city in 1935. Salisbury was the capital of the Federation of Rhodesia and Nyasaland (1953–63). Since World War II many black Africans have migrated to Salisbury; by the early 1970s they made up about three fourths of the city's population, while persons of European background constituted about one fourth. Salisbury is the site of the Univ. of Rhodesia, of Rhodes National Gallery, which has collections of African soapstone carvings, and of the National Museum, known for its archaeological holdings.

Salisbury. 1 City (1970 pop. 15,252), seat of Wicomico co., Md., on the Eastern Shore, at the head of the Wicomico River; settled 1732, inc. 1872. Poultry raising and processing is the city's major industry. The city is also a trade and service center for the Eastern Shore and has varied light manufacturing industries. Salisbury State College is there. Of interest are several early colonial homes. **2** City (1970 pop. 22,515), seat of Rowan co., W central N.C., in the Piedmont industrial region; inc. 1770. The production of textiles and garments is the major industry. Structural steel, brick, furniture, aluminum foil, and mobile homes are among the many other manufactures. Granite quarries are nearby. Salisbury is the seat of Catawba College, Livingstone College, a technical institute, and a large veterans hospital. The city has a great number of 18th- and 19th-century buildings, churches, and homes. The beautiful old county courthouse (1857) has been designated a historic site. The "Old Stone House" (1766) served as a fort in the French and Indian War. A nearby mill (built c.1816) is still in operation. The national cemetery in Salisbury was the site of one of the largest Confederate prison camps during the Civil War; approximately 11,700 Federal soldiers are buried there. Andrew Jackson studied law in Salisbury from 1784 to 1787.

Salisbury Plain, undulating, mostly barren chalk plateau, c.300 sq mi (780 sq km), Wiltshire, S England. It is noted chiefly as the site of ancient monuments, of which Stonehenge is the most famous. The region is an important army training ground.

Salishan (sā'lĭshən, săl'-), branch of the Algonquian-Wakashan linguistic family, or stock, of North America and spoken by American Indians of the NW United States and W Canada. See AMERICAN INDIAN LANGUAGES.

Salish Indians: see FLATHEAD INDIANS.

salivary glands (săl'əvâr"ē), in humans, three pairs of glands that secrete the alkaline digestive fluid, saliva, into the mouth. Most animals have salivary glands that resemble those in humans, however, in some animals these glands perform other functions. For example, the salivary glands of many blood-sucking species secrete a substance that prevents blood coagulation. In man the largest pair of salivary glands is situated just below and in front of each ear (parotid glands), the second pair is below the jaw (submaxillary), and the third is under the tongue (sublingual). Ducts carry the secretions of the salivary glands into the mouth cavity. Together with the mucus secreted by the membrane of the mouth and the secretions of other small glands in the mouth, saliva helps to keep the mouth moist, softens the food as it is chewed, and by means of salivary AMYLASE—the digestive enzyme contained in saliva—converts starch to sugar, thus initiating the process of digestion (see DIGESTIVE SYSTEM). The flow of saliva is stimulated by the presence of food in the mouth, or even the sight and smell of food. A lack of salivary flow from a gland may be caused by the formation of a calculus, or mineral concretion, that blocks a duct. The parotid glands are subject to growths, usually benign, and to infection (see MUMPS).

Salk, Jonas Edward, 1914–, American physician and microbiologist, b. New York City, B.S. College of the City of New York, 1934, M.D. New York Univ. College of Medicine, 1939. He did research on the influenza virus at the Univ. of Michigan, in 1946 became assistant professor of epidemiology there, and in 1947 went to the Univ. of Pittsburgh. In 1963 he became director of the Salk Institute for Biological Studies at the Univ. of California, San Diego. He is known for his work in developing a vaccine against POLIOMYELITIS. The **Salk vaccine** is made by cultivating three strains of the virus separately in monkey tissue. The virus is separated from the tissue, stored for a week, and killed with formaldehyde; tests are then made to make certain that it is dead. A series of three or four injections with the killed virus vaccine is required to confer immunity.

Salkhat: see SALCAH.

Sallai (săl'āī). **1** Man who returned from the Exile. Neh. 11.8. **2** Same as SALLU **1.**

Sallu (săl'yo͞o). **1** One who returned with Zerubbabel. Neh. 12.7. Sallai: Neh. 12.20. **2** Benjamite. 1 Chron. 9.7; Neh. 11.7.

Sallust (Caius Sallustius Crispus) (săl'əst), 86 B.C.–c.34 B.C., Roman historian. He was tribune of the people (52 B.C.) and praetor (46). He was ejected (50) from the senate ostensibly for adultery, but more probably because of his partisanship for Caesar. He served with Caesar after his praetorship and was his governor in Numidia; he was subsequently accused of misusing his governorship for personal gain. His principal work is the *Bellum Catilinarium,* or *Catilina,* on the conspiracy of CATILINE. Sallust's account of the Jugurthine War, *Bellum Jugurthinum,* or *Jugurtha,* is of little value as history. His history of Rome is extant only in fragments; it probably covered the period 78 B.C. to 67 B.C. There are also two letters, in rhetorical style, from Sallust to Caesar, the authenticity of which has been greatly disputed. As a historian Sallust was inaccurate and strongly biased, but he was important as one of the first to write historical monographs dealing with sharply limited events and periods. Although his style is consciously archaic, it is distinguished by its terseness and directness. His character sketches are particularly impressive and vivid, and his work has found as many imitators as critics. See studies by D. C. Earl (1961, repr. 1966) and Ronald Syme (1964); bibliography by A. D. Leeman (rev. ed. 1965).

Salma (săl'mə), variant of SALMON **1.**

Salmasius, Claudius (klôd'ēəs sălmā'shəs), 1588–1653, French humanist and philologist. Salmasius is known in French as Claude de Saumaise. After studying Latin and Greek with his father, he began a law career at Dijon in 1610. He turned to the study of theology, Hebrew, Arabic, and Persian when his Protestantism impeded his advancement in law. In 1631 he was called to the Univ. of Leiden to succeed Joseph SCALIGER. There he produced 80 books and became widely known as a scholar of the first rank. Supporting the Stuarts, he wrote *Defensio regia pro Carlo I* (1649), upholding the divine right of monarchy, which brought a celebrated dissenting reply from John Milton. Salmasius' major works include an important commentary on Pliny (1629), and *Observationes in jus Atticum et Romanum* (1645).

Salmerón y Alonso, Nicolás (nēkōlās' sälmārōn' ē älōn'sō), 1838–1908, Spanish statesman and philosopher. A professor at Oviedo and Madrid universities and a convinced republican, he became, after the expulsion (1868) of Isabella II, a member of the revolutionary junta, of the constituent assembly (1869), and of the Cortes (1871). After Amadeus's abdication, he was minister of justice and then president of the republic (1873). He restored some order, but he was unable to handle the confused political situation and soon resigned. He opposed the coup (1874) that brought Serrano to power and fled to Paris after the restoration of Alfonso XII. Returning to Spain, he regained (1884) his chair of philosophy at Madrid Univ. and was reelected (1886) to the Cortes, where he led the federalist republicans.

Salminen, Sally (säl'lē säl'mĭnĕn), 1906–, Finnish novelist, writing in Swedish. While working in Massachusetts as a housemaid, Salminen entered her first novel, *Katrina* (1936, tr. 1937), in a Finnish-Swedish literary competition; it won first prize and became an international best-seller. Her novels, which also include *Mariana* (1939, tr. 1940) and *New Lands* (1945), are fresh and ingenuous, projecting a powerful view of nature's harshness and man's endurance.

Salmon (săl'mŏn). **1** Father of Boaz. Ruth 4.21; Mat. 1.5; Luke 3.32. Salma: 1 Chron. 2.11, 51, 54. **2** Place, probably the same as ZALMON **2.**

Salmon, river, c.425 mi (680 km) long, rising in many branches in the Sawtooth and the Salmon River mts., central Idaho. It flows northeast and is joined, at Salmon, by the Lemhi River, after which it flows west and is joined by the Middle Fork and the South Fork, then goes north to join the Snake River. The river's canyon, c.1 mi (1.6 km) deep and 10 mi (16.1 km) wide in some places, threads through a wilderness preserve. In 1935 a party sponsored by the National Geographic Society explored the canyon. Though the swift waters and rapids are navigable downstream, it is impossible to return by the water route, thus giving the Salmon the name River of No Return. Salmon travel up the river to spawn. See R. G. Bailey, *The River of No Return: The Salmon* (1935).

salmon (săm'ən), member of the Salmonidae, a family of marine fish that spawn in fresh water, including the salmons, the trouts, and the chars. Many authorities place the whitefish and the GRAYLING among the Salmonidae, so similar are they in structure and habits. The Salmonidae are the most highly developed of the herringlike fishes, characterized by soft, rayless adipose fins, and are denizens of cold, oxygen-rich waters. In general they are uniform and silvery in color in the sea and more brightly hued in brooks and lakes. There are three genera of Salmonidae: *Salmo, Oncorhynchus,* and *Salvelinus.* Unfortunately, the common names of the species do not correspond to the natural divisions. The "true", or black-spotted, trout is actually a *Salmo,* and the speckled, or brook, trout of the E United States is a *Salvelinus* and should more properly be called a char, as are similar fishes in Europe. The American species of *Salmo* were originally split by the Mississippi basin, and were represented in the east by the Atlantic salmon and in the west by the rainbow and cutthroat trouts. The Atlantic salmon was a plentiful source of food for the Indians and the colonists, but its ranks are now much depleted because of water pollution, damming, and overfishing. This salmon is a large fish (15 lb/6.8 kg average) found along the Atlantic coast of NE America, in Greenland, and in Europe. While in the sea it feeds on crustaceans, but as it approaches the shores en route to the large rivers to spawn, it changes its diet to small fish. A landlocked species, the Sebago salmon, is found in Maine. Of the many races of cutthroat trout, some are now extinct; the greenback trout of the Colorado Rockies was recently rediscovered. It is thought that the more aggressive rainbow trout, with the same range (N California to British Columbia and Alaska), is partially responsible for the diminution in the variety of cutthroat species. The steelhead trout is believed to be the silvery saltwater phase of the colorful rainbow trout. Rainbows and cutthroats are known to hybridize, and a new species, the Gila trout, combining characteristics of both, has been discovered in New Mexico. The brown trout, introduced from Europe in 1883, requires warmer waters than the native species and for this reason is important in fish-management programs. The genus *Oncorhynchus* is comprised of the five species of Pacific salmon, found from S California to Alaska. These fish are the most important commercial species. Canning centers are located on the Columbia River and on Puget Sound and in British Columbia, Siberia, and N Japan; Alaska alone produces over half the world's supply of canned salmon. The largest and commercially most important of the Pacific salmon is the chinook (or quinnat or king) salmon, which averages 20 lb (9 kg) and may reach 100 lb (45 kg). It is found from the Bering Sea to Japan and S California and is marketed fresh, smoked, and canned. The blueback salmon (called sockeye in Oregon and redfish in Alaska) has firm reddish flesh and forms the bulk of the canned salmon. Also of economic importance are the humpback, or pink, salmon, the smallest of the group, and the silver, or coho, salmon, important in the fall catch because of its late spawning season. The meat of the dog salmon is too mushy for canning but is palatable when fresh or smoked. The genus *Salvelinus* includes the various European chars; the common brook, or speckled, trout, a popular game fish of E North America, introduced in the West; and the Dolly Varden, or bull, trout, a similar western form. A fourth genus, *Cristivomer,* contains one species, the common lake trout, and one subspecies, the siscowet, or fat trout. These are deepwater fishes of North American lakes, more sluggish, less migratory, and bulkier than the other Salmonidae; individuals have been recorded at 100 lb (45 kg). A fish called the splake has been produced by crossing the speckled trout and the lake trout. The basic life pattern of the Salmonidae begins when, within the first year or two of life, the fish travels downstream to the sea, where it grows to its full size. After reaching maturity (one to nine years) it returns to its hatching site to spawn. The Pacific salmon are famed for their gruelling journeys of hundreds of miles to their headwater breeding grounds. When they begin this trip, months before the spawning period, they are in prime condition, but they cease eating when they leave the sea and arrive exhausted and battered by their fight upstream against swift currents and over rapids and falls. Those that survive the trip and escape fishermen and predatory animals spawn with their last strength and then die. These salmon are taken at the mouths of large rivers, as they begin their upstream migration. The Atlantic salmon and the trouts spawn more than once. Most trouts migrate to the sea if there is a cold-water connection but will also live and reproduce if landlocked—though there is considerable variation on this point between species and even between individuals of the same species. Salmon are classified in the phylum CHORDATA, subphylum Vertebrata, class Osteichthyes, order Clupeiformes, family Salmonidae. See Anthony Netboy, *The Salmon: Their Fight for Survival* (1973).

Salmone (sălmō'nē), cape, E Crete, now called Pláka. It is mentioned in the account of Paul's voyage to Rome (Acts 27.7).

salmonellosis (săl"mənĕlō'sĭs), infection caused by intestinal bacteria of the genus *Salmonella.* The most common form of salmonellosis is an intestinal disease, gastroenteritis, caused by *Salmonella typhimurium* and other *Salmonella* species (see FOOD POISONING). Sometimes salmonella infection takes the form of a generalized bacterial infection. The generalized form of the disease resembles another *Salmonella* infection, TYPHOID FEVER, and is often known as paratyphoid fever. The pathogenic organisms carried by the bloodstream may cause formation of ABSCESSES in bones, joints, lungs, and other sites. The more serious forms of the disease are treated by CHLORAMPHENICOL. Salmonella outbreaks occasionally result from contaminated institutional or other mass-prepared food, or from contact with animal carriers such as pet turtles.

Salmoneus (sălmō'nēəs), in Greek mythology, king of Elis; son of Aeolus. Pretending to be Zeus, he demanded sacrifices, threw torches to imitate lightning, and made noises like thunder with his chariot. For this impiety Zeus destroyed him and his kingdom with a thunderbolt.

salmon fly: see MAYFLY.

salol: phenyl salicylate; see SALICYLIC ACID.

Salome (səlō'mē). **1** Daughter of Herod Philip and Herodias. She is generally supposed to be the daughter who danced to obtain the head of John the Baptist. Mat. 14.3, 11; Mark 6.16–28. **2** One of the women who ministered to Jesus, who beheld his crucifixion, and who brought offerings to his tomb. Mark 15.40; 16.1. Many identify her with the wife of Zebedee. Mat. 27.56.

Salome Alexandra: see MACCABEES, Jewish family.

Salomon, Haym (hīm), 1740–85, American Revolutionary financier, b. Lissa (now Leszno), Poland. A Jewish emigrant from Poland, he was imprisoned (1778) by the British in New York City for aiding the Revolutionaries and was condemned to death, but he escaped to Philadelphia. There he started a successful brokerage business. He aided Robert MORRIS in obtaining loans from France and pledged his own fortune to the new government to maintain its credit. Salomon was never recompensed and he died impoverished. See biographies by C. E. Russell (1930) and H. M. Fast (1941).

Salon, annual exhibition of art works chosen by jury and presented by the French Academy since 1737; it was originally held in the Salon d'Apollon of the Louvre. By the mid-19th cent. the Salon had become an expression of conservative, established tastes in art. Until 1863 it was the only major public art exhibition held in Paris. That year the Salon des Refusés was organized in protest by artists whose works were rejected by the Salon jury. See ACADEMIES OF ART.

Salona (səlō'nə), Latin *Salonae,* ancient city of Dalmatia, 3 mi (5 km) NE of modern Split, Yugoslavia. A port on the Adriatic, it was used as a base for Roman conquest and was made a Roman colony and the capital of Illyricum in the 1st cent. B.C. The busy commercial city gained prestige when Diocletian, after retiring in A.D. 305, built a magnificent palace nearby. Salona became an episcopal see in the 4th cent., but in the 7th cent. the people fled before invaders to Diocletian's palace, which they transformed into the city of Spalato (now Split, Yugoslavia). Salona was destroyed. Considerable portions of the palace remain. Salona is also called Solim.

Salon-de-Provence (sälôN'-də-prôväNs'), town (1968 pop. 31,732), Bouches-du-Rhône dept., SE France. Its major manufactures are olive oil, electrical equipment, coffee, and soap. In the town are churches dating from the 12th to the 14th cent.

Salonica, Greece: see THESSALONÍKI.

Salonica campaigns. In the summer of 1915, Bulgaria entered World War I on the side of the Central Powers; in September, Bulgaria attacked Serbia. An Allied expeditionary force that landed at Salonica in an effort to aid Serbia attempted to join forces with the Serbians but was thwarted by the Bulgarian victory at Babuna pass. The Allies retreated to the vicinity of Salonica. Meanwhile the Greek government under VENIZELOS, which had decided to support the Allies, fell when it was repudiated by King CONSTANTINE I. The Allies fostered the establishment at Salonica of a rival Greek government, under Venizelos, which declared war on the Central Powers. After the Allies began an invasion of Greece, Constantine abdicated (June, 1917) and Greece formally joined the Allies. A number of unsuccessful Allied campaigns were launched against the German and Bulgarian forces. Finally, in Sept., 1918, a new offensive was launched, and the Allies advanced northward along the entire front. Bulgaria capitulated on Sept. 30, Serbia was recovered by Nov. 1, and on Nov. 10 Rumania was captured. The armistice of Nov. 11, 1918, ended the campaign.

Salop, England: see SHROPSHIRE.

salp: see TUNICATE.

salpiglossis (săl"pəglŏs'əs), any plant of the genus *Salpiglossis* of the family Solanaceae (NIGHTSHADE family), herbs native to Chile and widely cultivated elsewhere as garden annuals for their richly variegated, funnel-shaped blossoms in a variety of colors. Painted tongue (*S. sinuata*) is the most common in gardens. The genus is classified in the division MAGNOLIOPHYTA, class Magnoliopsida, order Polemoniales, family Solanaceae.

Salsette Island, India: see BOMBAY.

salsify, common name for a tall, narrow-leaved biennial (*Tragopogon porrifolius*) of the family Compositae (COMPOSITE family), native to S Europe but now naturalized and sometimes growing as a weed in North America. Known also as purple goatsbeard, oyster plant, and vegetable oyster, it is widely cultivated for its long edible root, oysterlike in flavor. The roots may be left in the ground through winter and dug as needed. The related meadow salsify or yellow goatsbeard (*T. pratensis*) is sometimes called John-go-to-bed-at-noon because the flower heads of salsifies close at midday. It is similar to the common salsify but has a large, flat head of yellow (rather than purple) flowers; it is seldom cultivated. The common name goatsbeard—a translation of the Greek generic name *Tragopogon*—refers to the long, feathery, dandelionlike hairs on the seeds. Among other plants with similar names are an ornamental Eurasian perennial, *Aruncus sylvester,* called goatsbeard but related to the spiraea and usually cultivated under that name, and the black salsify (*Scorzonera hispanica*), a composite with an edible root like that of the common salsify. Salsify is classified in the division MAGNOLIOPHYTA, class Magnoliopsida, order Asterales, family Compositae.

sal soda: see SODIUM CARBONATE.

Salt, Sir Titus, 1803–76, English textile manufacturer and inventor. He invented a machine for making worsted from coarse wool and a process for spinning and weaving alpaca. In 1851 he started to build, on the Aire River, extensive textile works and a model manufacturing town, called Saltaire, in which he attempted to embody his conceptions of ideal factory conditions for workers.

salt, chemical compound (other than water) formed by a chemical reaction between an acid and a base (see ACIDS AND BASES). The most familiar salt is SODIUM CHLORIDE, common table salt. Sodium chloride, NaCl, and water, H_2O, are formed by NEUTRALIZATION of sodium hydroxide, NaOH, a base, with hydrogen chloride, HCl, an acid: $HCl + NaOH \rightarrow NaCl + H_2O$. Most salts are ionic compounds (see CHEMICAL BOND); they are made up of IONS rather than molecules. The chemical FORMULA for an ionic salt is an empirical formula; it does not represent a molecule, but shows the proportion of atoms of the elements that make up the salt. The formula for sodium chloride, NaCl, indicates that equal numbers of sodium and chlorine atoms combine to form the salt. In the reaction of sodium with chlorine, each sodium atom loses an electron, becoming positively charged, and each chlorine atom gains an electron, becoming negatively charged (see OXIDATION AND REDUCTION); there are equal numbers of positively charged sodium ions and negatively charged chloride ions in sodium chloride. The ions in a solid salt are usually arranged in a definite crystalline structure, each positive ion being associated with a fixed number of negative ions, and vice versa. Salts are also prepared by methods other than that defined above. A metal can combine directly with a nonmetal to form a salt; e.g., sodium metal reacts with chlorine gas to form sodium chloride. A metal may react with a dilute acid to form a salt and release hydrogen gas; e.g., zinc reacts with dilute sulfuric acid to form zinc sulfate and hydrogen. A metal oxide may react with an acid to form a salt and water; e.g., calcium oxide reacts with carbonic acid to form calcium carbonate and water. A base can react with a nonmetallic oxide to form a salt and water; e.g., sodium hydroxide reacts with carbon dioxide to form sodium carbonate and water. Two salts may react with one another (in solution) to form two new salts; e.g., barium chloride and sodium sulfate react in solution to form barium sulfate (as an insoluble precipitate) and sodium chloride (which remains in solution). A salt may react with an acid to form a different salt and acid; e.g., sodium chloride and sulfuric acid react when heated to form sodium sulfate and release hydrogen chloride gas (which in solution forms hydrochloric acid). A salt undergoes DISSOCIATION when it dissolves in a polar solvent, e.g., water, the extent of dissociation depending both on the salt and the solvent. A salt that has neither hydrogen (H) nor hydroxyl (OH) in its formula, e.g., sodium chloride, NaCl, is called a normal salt. A salt that has hydrogen in its formula, e.g., sodium bicarbonate, $NaHCO_3$, is called an acid salt. A salt that has hydroxyl in its formula, e.g., basic lead nitrate, $Pb(OH)NO_3$, is called a basic salt. Since a salt may react with a solvent to yield different ions than were present in the salt (see HYDROLYSIS), a solution of a normal salt may be acidic or basic; e.g., trisodium phosphate, Na_3PO_4, dissolves in and reacts with water to form a basic solution. In addition to classifying salts as normal, acid, or basic, salts are classified as simple salts, double salts, or complex salts. Simple salts, e.g., sodium chloride, contain only one kind of positive ion (other than the hydrogen ion in acid salts). Double salts contain two different positive ions, e.g., the mineral dolomite, or calcium magnesium carbonate, $CaMg(CO_3)_2$. ALUMS are a special kind of double salt. Complex salts, e.g., potassium ferricyanide, $K_3Fe(CN)_6$, contain a complex ion that does not dissociate in solution. A HYDRATE is a salt that includes water in its solid crystalline form; Glauber's salt and Epsom salts are hydrates. Salts are often grouped according to the negative ion they contain, e.g., BICARBONATE or CARBONATE, CHLORATE, CHLORIDE, CYANIDE, FULMINATE, NITRATE, PHOSPHATE, SILICATE, SULFATE, or SULFIDE.

Salta, city (1970 pop. 182,535), capital of Salta prov., NW Argentina, in the Lerma valley. It is the commercial center of a region rich in agricultural produce, minerals (chiefly oil), and forest products. Sugar, tobacco, wine grapes, and livestock are shipped through the city. Salta has retained its colonial atmosphere. The cathedral is well known, and ruins of many 17th-century buildings dot the surrounding countryside. Founded in 1582, Salta was a military outpost in the fight against the Indians. It became an important commercial and cultural center during the 17th cent.

Saltaire: see SHIPLEY.

Saltillo (sältē'yō), city (1970 pop. 191,879), capital of Coahuila state, N Mexico. It is located in an alluvial valley almost surrounded by mountains. The growing of cereal and cattle raising are the chief occupations, but textile manufacturing and food processing are also important. Founded in 1575, the city was known in colonial times for its annual fair, at which imports from Spain and the Philippines were exchanged for products made in Mexico. Saltillo was taken by Zachary Taylor's forces in the Mexican War and was occupied by French troops several times during the French intervention in Mexico. The city has a university and other institutions of higher learning.

Salt Lake City, city (1970 pop. 175,885), alt. c.4,330 ft (1,320 m), state capital and seat of Salt Lake co., N central Utah, on the Jordan River and near the Great Salt Lake, at the foot of the Wasatch Range; inc. 1851. The largest city in the state, it is a great regional center, world headquarters of the Church of Jesus Christ of Latter Day Saints, and processing point for the products of an irrigated farm region which is also rich in minerals. Major industries include food processing; silver, lead, and copper smelting; the development and production of missiles and electronic equipment; oil refining; and printing and publishing. Founded in 1847 by Brigham Young as the capital of the MORMON community, the city achieved greatness as its economic hub; the prominence of the gigantic Temple (built 1853–93) on Temple Square at the city's heart shows that Salt Lake City is still preeminently a Mormon city. The first Mormon irrigation used the water of City Creek, and the city (called Great Salt Lake City until 1868) initiated most enterprises in Utah. After 1849 it was a supply point for overland travel to California and was connected with the first transcontinental railroad by a line built (1869–70) by Brigham Young to Ogden. It is the seat of the Univ. of Utah, Westminster College, Stevens Henager College, and a two-year technical college. Of interest are the state capitol (1914), Brigham Young's home (the "Beehive House"; restored to its 1877 appearance), the Brigham Young Monument (1897), and a planetarium. Also in the city are a veterans hospital, the state prison, and Fort Douglas, which was founded in 1862.

Salto (säl'tō), city (1963 pop. 57,958), capital of Salto dept., NW Uruguay, on the Uruguay River. Salto is a thriving cultural and commercial center for a farming and livestock region. There are boatbuilding and meat-packing industries. In the surrounding region are extensive orange and tangerine orchards as well as vineyards.

Salto Ángel, falls, Venezuela: see ANGEL FALL.

Salton Sea (sôl'tən), saline lake, 370 sq mi (958 sq km), northern part of the Imperial Valley, SE Calif.; 232 ft (71 m) below sea level. Salton Sea was formed as the Colorado River delta grew across the Gulf of California, severing its northern part. The area was a salt-covered depression known as Salton Sink until 1905, when a flood on the Colorado broke through an irrigation gap in its levee; the river flowed into the sink for two years before being checked. The Salton Sea's water level has gradually risen due to runoff from surrounding mountains and irrigation systems, thus flooding out some settlements and natural formations along its shores. The Salton Sea is a major S California recreation and fishing area. A state park and a national wildlife refuge are on its shores. The U.S. Atomic Energy Commission has an experimental station on the western shore at Seaview Beach.

Salton Sink: see SALTON SEA.

Saltonstall, Sir Richard (sôl'tənstôl), 1586–1658, early English colonist in Massachusetts. Of a prominent Yorkshire family (he was knighted in 1618), Saltonstall became a member and was appointed an assistant of the Massachusetts Bay Company in 1629. With his five children he accompanied John Winthrop (1588–1649) to America in 1630 and was a founder of Watertown, Mass. In 1631 he returned to England, where he helped secure the grant at the mouth of the Connecticut River that led to the settlement of Saybrook.

saltpeter or **saltpetre:** see POTASSIUM NITRATE.

Salt River valley, irrigated region around the lower course of the Salt River, which rises in mountain streams near the Mogollon Rim of the Mogollon Plateau and flows southwest to join the Gila River in S central Arizona. Phoenix is the main city of the region. Indians used the Salt River for irrigation many centuries ago. In the 19th cent. American settlers began irrigated farming in the valley, and the Mormons used some of the old Indian canals at Mesa, Ariz. The **Salt River project,** the first large irrigation scheme undertaken under the Federal Reclamation Act of 1902, is one of the most economically successful projects in North America. It began in 1903 when construction started on the Roosevelt Dam in a canyon E of Phoenix. The dam, forming Roosevelt Lake behind it, impounds enough water to irrigate fields for about two years even if no rain falls. Other dams were built between 1922 and 1946 to supply water and power. The region is a rich producer of alfalfa, citrus fruits, lettuce, melons, and other crops. Short-staple cotton is the chief cash crop. A major factor in the Salt River project's success is the long season without frost; the climate also makes this area an attractive winter resort.

Saltykov-Shchedrin, Mikhail Evgrafovich (mēkhəyēl' yĭvgrä'fəvĭch säl'tĭkôf-shchĕ'drēn), 1826–89, Russian novelist and satirist. Saltykov-Shchedrin was a master of the satirical sketch, which he used to attack the bourgeoisie, the gentry, and the officials of the civil service, of which he was a member. His greatest satirical work is *The History of a Town* (1869–70), directed against Russian officials and citizens alike. His masterpiece is his only novel, *The Golovyov Family* (1876, tr. 1931), a study of decaying gentry. *Fables* (1885, tr. 1931), a collection of pointedly critical tales in the manner of Aesop, revealed his genius for circumventing the censor. See Nikander Strelsky, *Saltykov and the Russian Squire* (1940).

Salu (sā'lyo͞o), father of ZIMRI **2.** Num. 25.14.

Saluda, river, c.200 mi (320 km) long, rising in the Blue Ridge, W S.C., and flowing southeast across the Piedmont to the Broad River (with which it forms the Congaree) near Columbia. The Saluda Dam (completed 1930) impounds Lake Murray; its power plant has a 208,750-kw capacity.

Saluki (səlo͞o'kē), breed of tall, slender HOUND whose origins may be traced back to the Sumerian empire of 6,000 B.C. It stands between 23 and 28 in. (58.4–71.1 cm) high at the shoulder, although females may reach only 18 in. (45.7 cm), and weighs between 45 and 60 lb (20.4–27.2 kg). Its smooth, silky coat is short except for fringes of longer hair, or feathers, on the ears, back of legs, and tail. It may be colored cream, white, fawn, red, golden, grizzle and tan, black and tan, or black, white, and tan. Possibly the oldest breed of domesticated dog, the Saluki has been used down through the centuries as a sight hunter of gazelles, boars, jackals, foxes, and hares. Still used to hunt hares today, it is also commonly bred for racing on a round or oval track equipped with a mechanical rabbit. See DOG.

Saluzzo (sälo͞ot'tsō), town (1971 pop. 17,828), Piedmont, NW Italy. It is an agricultural and industrial center. Manufactures include textiles, machinery, and processed food. It was the capital of the marquisate of Saluzzo from the 12th cent. to 1548, when it passed to France. The town came under the house of Savoy in 1601. The Gothic cathedral (c.1481–1511) contains sculptured tombs of the marquises.

Salvador: see EL SALVADOR.

Salvador (săl'vədôr", Port. səlvəthôr') or **Bahia** (bəē'yə), formerly **São Salvador** (souN), city (1970 pop. 1,007,744), capital of Bahia state, E Brazil, a port on the Atlantic Ocean. It is the commercial center of a fertile crescent (the *Recôncavo*) and a shipping point for the cacao district to the south. Other exports include tobacco, sugar, hardwoods, industrial diamonds, and oil. Salvador is also a fashionable tourist center. Despite the abundance of electrical energy, industrialization has proceeded slowly. Food processing is a leading industry. Founded in 1549, Salvador flourished with the development of sugar plantations and became the leading center of colonial Brazil. Because of an influx of black African slaves, the area is noted for its African heritage in music, dance, folk customs, and cuisine. Briefly under Dutch occupation (1624–25), the city was the capital of the Portuguese possessions in America until 1763. It still contains many buildings and fortifications from the colonial period. In the early 19th cent. it was a center of the Brazilian independence movement and in 1912 was bombarded and heavily damaged by federal forces. Salvador's intellectual and cultural vitality was manifested by such famous *bahianos* as Ruy Barbosa, the statesman, and Antônio de Castro Alves, the poet. The city, built on a peninsula, is divided into two sections connected by graded roads, elevators, and cable cars. Points of interest include a 16th-century cathedral (one of the city's many notable churches), a state university, and agricultural institutes. Salvador has a naval base.

salvage, in maritime law, the compensation that the owner must pay for having his vessel or cargo saved from peril, such as shipwreck, fire, or capture by an enemy. Salvage is awarded only when the party making the rescue was under no legal obligation to do so. A claim for salvage ordinarily is allowed if the salvor's activities had some effect in averting the threatened peril even if they were not indispensable. In the United States, salvage is granted for rescues made on navigable streams and lakes as well as on the open sea. Salvage includes a reward designed to encourage rescue operations besides the payment for the value of the services. In setting the amount of the salvage, courts consider relevant factors such as the expense and hazard of the rescue and the price of the ship or goods saved. Salvage is distributed by the court to the owner, the master, and the crew of the rescuing ship, usually according to fixed ratios. Salvage money is not payable to the captain and crew of ships commissioned by a government specifically for rescue operations.

Salvation Army, Protestant denomination and international nonsectarian Christian organization for evangelical and philanthropic work. It was founded by William Booth, with the assistance of his wife, Catherine Booth. Booth, a Methodist minister, began independent evangelistic work in Cornwall, England, in 1861. In 1865 he began his movement by holding outdoor meetings and revivals in tents and theaters in London. The movement was originally known as the East London Revival Society, shortly renamed the Christian Mission, and finally in 1878 designated the Salvation Army. A military form of organization, with uniforms and other distinctive features, was adopted in the interest of a more effective "warfare against evil." Members believe that they are "saved to save," and the organization enjoins complete self-denial on its followers. From its inception the organization sought to minister to physical as well as spiritual human needs. Soup kitchens were first in a long line of widely varied projects designed to provide physical assistance to the destitute. Although the members often met opposition, the value of Salvation Army services had been generally acknowledged by 1890, when General Booth set forth his plan of procedure in his book *In Darkest England and the Way Out.* The organization has established branches in more than 75 countries throughout the world. On his death William Booth was succeeded by his son, Bramwell, as head of the organization; but in 1929 his removal was voted by the high council of the Army, and Edward J. Higgins was elected to that post. Salvation Army work in the United States dates from 1880, when Commissioner George Railton and seven women workers from England founded a branch in Pennsylvania. In 1904, Evangeline Booth, daughter of the founder, was put in command of the work in the United States; in 1934 she became general of the International Salvation Army. The Army's ministers are ranked as officers and its members are called "soldiers"; women have equal position and responsibility with men. High commands may be attained by promotion from lower offices. Each country has its divisions and its local corps, with a commander at the head of all. In the United States, where the movement is strong, headquarters are in New York City. International headquarters are in London. Officers are prepared in training colleges for their varied responsibilities. The Army operates hospitals, community centers, alcoholic and drug rehabilitation programs, emergency and disaster services, social work centers, and recreation facilities. Support of the vast undertakings in all parts of the world depends upon voluntary contributions and profits from the sale of publications. *The War Cry* is the official organ. The beliefs of the Army as set forth in the *Handbook of Salvation Army Doctrine* (1926) generally agree with those of most Protestant evangelical denominations, but the sacraments of baptism and the Lord's Supper are not considered essential to salvation and are not practiced. Great emphasis is placed upon the experience of salvation and purity of life. In conducting the meetings officers are allowed great freedom, as no form of service is required; bands and singing are important features. The Salvation Army distinguished itself by its work with the armed services in both World Wars and by its aid to the suffering in disasters, such as floods and earthquakes, all over the world. See VOLUNTEERS OF AMERICA. See Robert Sandall, *The History of the Salvation Army* (4 vol., 1947–64); H. A. Wisbey, *Soldiers without Swords* (1955); Pamela Search, *Happy Warriors* (1956); Sallie Chesham, *Born to Battle* (1965); Richard Collier, *The General Next to God* (1965).

Salvator Rosa: see ROSA, SALVATOR.

Salvemini, Gaetano (gäätä'nō sälvämē'nē), 1873–1957, Italian historian. He taught at the universities of Messina, Pisa, and Florence and also served (1919–21) in parliament. After being arrested in 1925 as an anti-Fascist, he left Italy. He lectured (1930–48) on history at Harvard Univ., became (1940) a U.S. citizen, and in 1954 retired to Italy. Although Salvemini wrote chiefly on recent and contemporary history, he is also noted for his study of the medieval Italian commune. A prolific author, he wrote *Italian Fascism* (1938, in English), *Prelude to World War II* (tr. 1953), and *The French Revolution, 1788–1792* (tr. 1954).

Salve Regina (säl'vā räjē'nə) [Lat.,=hail, queen], prayer or hymn to the Virgin Mary, traditionally said, usually in the vernacular, after Low Mass and also, during part of the year, at vespers (in Latin) as an antiphon. It begins, "Hail, holy queen, mother of mercy."

Salvi, Giovanni Battista: see SASSOFERRATO.

salvia: see SAGE.

Salvian (săl'vēən), fl. 5th cent., Christian writer of Gaul. His Latin name was Salvianus. He was a monk and priest of Lérins (from c.424) and became a renowned preacher and teacher of rhetoric. Of his several works two treatises and nine letters are extant. *De gubernatione Dei* [on the governance of God] is in eight books, of which the first five are Salvian's. Incomplete as it is, it is a moving indictment of contemporary Roman and Gallic society and a call to true Christian living. The other work, usually called *Contra avaritiam* [against avarice], is a plea for generosity to the Church. See tr. by E. M. Sanford (1930) and J. F. O'Sullivan (1947).

Salviati, Francesco de' Rossi (fränchās'kō dā rôs'sē sälvēä'tē), 1510–63, Italian painter. Salviati studied with Andrea Del Sarto and was greatly influenced by Parmigianino and Michelangelo. His elegant portraits (e.g., *Portrait of a Gentleman,* c.1541; Metropolitan Mus.) were popular, and his reputation spread to France where he was employed by Francis I. Salviati's works, such as his decorations for the Palazzo Farnese in Rome, were characteristic of the mannerist style in their extreme complexity, display of chiaroscuro technique, elongated figures, and spatial and pictorial ambivalence (see MANNERISM).

Salvini, Tommaso (tōm-mä'zō sälvē'nē), 1829–1915, Italian actor. The son of actors, he became a leading tragedian after joining Adelaide Ristori's company in 1847. His tours brought him to the United States, where, in 1866, he played Othello, his best role, to the Iago of Edwin Booth. He retired in 1890. See his autobiography (tr. 1893).

Salween (săl"wēn'), Chin. *Nu Chiang,* Tibetan *Chiama Ngu Chu,* river of SE Asia, c.1,750 mi (2,820 km) long, rising in E Tibet, China, and flowing SE through Yünnan prov. in deep, narrow gorges parallel to the Mekong, Yangtze, and Irrawaddy rivers, into Burma, where it cuts through the Shan Plateau and Karenni Hills and then empties into the Gulf of Martaban, E Burma, near Moulmein. Because of rapids, it is navigable only for about 75 mi (120 km) upstream. Flowing through gorges for nearly its entire length, the Salween is an obstacle to east-west transportation; it is crossed by the Burma Road and several road ferries. The river's depth varies c.65 ft (20 m) between wet and dry seasons, making it useless except for floating logs downstream.

Salza, Hermann von (hĕr'män fən zäl'tsä), d. 1239, grand master (1210–39) of the TEUTONIC KNIGHTS. A friend and adviser of Holy Roman Emperor Frederick II, he often mediated between the emperor and Pope Gregory IX. In 1226, Duke Conrad of Masovia asked the Teutonic Order for aid against the heathen Prussians, who had taken his territory of Chelmno (Kulm); he offered Chelmno to the order in return. In the same year Hermann obtained from Frederick II vast privileges for his order and recognition of his lordship over Chelmno. Thus, the Knights carried Christianization and Germanization eastward. Hermann formally received the territory from Conrad c.1230 by treaty, with the promise of all further territory conquered. In 1234 Hermann placed these lands under papal suzerainty. Hermann's masterful diplomacy had gained future Prussia for the Teutonic Order. In 1237, Hermann effected the union of his order with the LIVONIAN BROTHERS OF THE SWORD.

Salzburg (zälts'bo͝ork), province (1971 pop. 399,000), c.2,760 sq mi (7,150 sq km), W central Austria. The province borders on West Germany in the north and northwest. It is a predominately mountainous region, with parts of the Hohe Tauern mts. and Salzburg Alps, and it is drained by the Salzach River. There are famous salt deposits that have long been worked, as well as gold, copper, and iron mines. Precious stones are also found there. Salzburg province is a scenic area, noted for its numerous Alpine resorts and spas. The industry is varied; manufactures include machinery, aluminum, textiles, and forest products. Cattle and horses are raised. Kaprun dam, on the Salzach high up in the mountains, includes one of the largest hydroelectric facilities in Europe. Originally inhabited by Celts, the territory was conquered by the Romans and became part of the province of Noricum. After the fall of the Roman Empire, its history followed that of its capital and chief city, **Salzburg** (1971 pop. 128,800). An ancient Celtic settlement, and later a Roman trading center named Juvavum, the city is an industrial, commercial, and tourist center and a transportation hub. Salzburg developed in the early 8th cent. around the late 7th-century monastery of St. Peter. By c.798 it was the seat of an archbishopric, and for almost 1,000 years it was the residence of the autocratic archbishops of Salzburg, the leading ecclesiastics of the German-speaking world. They became princes of the Holy Roman Empire in 1278 and wielded their power with extreme intolerance. In the late 15th cent. the Jews were expelled, and in 1731–32 some 30,000 Protestants migrated to Prussia after a period of severe persecution. Secularized in 1802, Salzburg was transferred to Bavaria by the Peace of Schönbrunn (1809). The Congress of Vienna (1814–15) returned it to Austria. Present-day Salzburg is an architectural gem. Picturesquely situated on both banks of the Salzach River, the city is bounded by two steep hills, the Capuzinerberg (left bank) and the Mönchsberg, on the southern tip of which is the 11th-century fortress of Hohensalzburg (right bank). The city's most noteworthy buildings are a late 7th-century Benedictine abbey, which was for many years the center of missionary activities; the Franciscan church, consecrated in 1223; the early 17th-century cathedral, modeled after St. Peter's in Rome; the Residenz (16th–18th cent.), formerly the archiepiscopal palace; Mirabell castle (early 18th cent.), situated in a beautiful garden; and the Festspielhaus (1960), the city's chief concert hall. There is a monument to the physician and alchemist Paracelsus, who died in Salzburg in 1541. The city's university (founded 1623), except for its theological seminary, was closed in 1810 but was reopened in 1963. The composer Mozart, Salzburg's most distinguished son, met scant recognition in the city during his stay there. However, he is now honored by an annual summer music festival (est. 1925), which constitutes an important source of tourist revenue for Salzburg. Part of the house where Mozart was born is now a museum, and there is a commemorative statue on the quaint little square, the Mozart Platz. Since 1920 the morality play *Everyman,* written by Hugo von Hofmannsthal, has been performed annually in the cathedral square (now during the Mozart festival). The Salzburg Seminar in American Studies is centered in Schloss Leopoldskron (18th cent.), a rococo castle.

Salzburg Festival, annual festival of music and drama held in Salzburg, Austria, for five weeks starting in late July. The festival may be considered a descendant of the Salzburg Music Festival Weeks that the Vienna Philharmonic gave irregularly between 1877 and 1910. After World War I several leading German-speaking cultural figures—including Hermann Bahr, Richard Strauss, Max Reinhardt, and Hugo von Hofmannsthal—developed the idea of an annual summer cultural festival to be held in Salzburg. The modern series of festivals began on Aug. 22, 1920, when Hofmannsthal's adaptation of the medieval English morality play *Everyman* was given in a production by Reinhardt in the cathedral square. The following year Mozart operas were added to the festival program. In 1926 the former archiepiscopal stables were converted into the Festival Hall, and concerts by the Vienna Philharmonic became a regular feature. In succeeding years, as the festival became internationally celebrated, performances of spoken drama in German declined in prominence in favor of music programs. The festival probably achieved its greatest brilliance in the 1930s, when Arturo Toscanini and Bruno Walter were its leading conductors. Vienna State Opera productions directed by these maestros of works by Mozart, Beethoven, Wagner, and Verdi were especially distinguished. When the Nazis took over Austria in 1938, the festival declined in significance, as many musicians could not (Walter) or would not (Toscanini) participate. Nevertheless the festival continued through 1943. It was revived as an international event in the summer of 1945, immediately following the Allied victory in Europe, and has been held every summer since then. Performances of music and drama are given in the "Old" Festival Hall, the "New" Festival Hall (built 1960), and an arena that can be roofed over. The residence palace of the archbishop is also used for music. Performances of *Everyman* are still held in front of the cathedral.

Salzgitter (zälts'gĭt'ər), city (1970 pop. 118,201), Lower Saxony, E West Germany. Situated in one of the richest iron-ore producing regions in West Germany, it has blast furnaces, steel plants, and industries producing chemicals, textiles, machinery, and petroleum. The city was created in 1942 by the merger of 29 towns and until 1951 was known as Watenstedt-Salzgitter.

Salzkammergut (zälts'käm'ərgo͞ot"), resort area in Upper Austria, Styria, and Salzburg provs., W Austria. Known since antiquity for its salt mines, the region was banned to visitors until the early 19th cent. because the government, which held a monopoly on salt mining there, wanted to prevent salt from being smuggled out. Salzkammergut is a beautiful Alpine lake district and is a summer and winter tourist center with such resorts as Bad Ischl, Sankt Wolfgang, Hallstatt, and Gmunden (all in Upper Austria) and Altaussee (in Styria). Among its lovely lakes are the Wolfgangsee or Abersee, the Traunsee or Gmundnersee, the Mondsee, the Halstätter See, and the Attersee or Kammersee. The Dachstein (9,883 ft/3,012 m), covered with glaciers, is the principal peak.

Samadhi (səmä'dē), a state of deep absorption in the object of meditation, and the goal of many kinds of YOGA. In Buddhism the term refers to any state of one-pointed concentration. In Hinduism it signifies the highest levels of mystical contemplation, in which the individual consciousness becomes identified with the Godhead.

Samain, Albert (älbĕr' sämăN'), 1858–1900, French poet. He was a founder (1890) of the literary periodical *Mercure de France.* His first collection of verse, *Au jardin de l'infante* (1893, reissued with *L'Urne penchée,* 1897), was in a symbolist vein, but he was subsequently influenced by the PARNASSIANS. Some of his best work appeared as *Le Chariot d'or* (1901). Samain's verse is distinguished by its melancholy tone and musical quality.

Samar (sä'mär), island (1970 pop. 1,024,336), 5,050 sq mi (13,079 sq km), 3d largest of the Philippines, one of the Visayan Islands, NE of Leyte (from which it is separated by the narrow San Juanico Strait). It has commercial coconut plantations and is a leading banana producer. There are important lumbering, fishing, and mining industries; copper and iron ore are extracted.

Samara: see KUYBYSHEV, USSR.

Samara (səmä'rə), river, c.360 mi (580 km) long, rising in the foothills of the S Urals, E European USSR. It flows generally northwest, and joins the VOLGA River at Kuybyshev, at the eastern extremity of the Samara Bend.

Samarai (săm'ărī), small island (59 acres/23.9 hectares), at the southeastern tip of Papua New Guinea, New Guinea island. It is a commercial and shipping center and a port of entry. An important European settlement before World War II, it was totally destroyed by Japanese bombing in 1942 and never regained its former prominence.

Samaras, Lucas (lo͞ok'əs sämär'əs), 1936–, American artist, b. Kastoria, Greece. Samaras is noted for his unusual use of such materials as straight pins, multicolored string, plastics, chicken wire, feathers, and mirrors. He has created remarkable variations on everyday forms, notably boxes, scissors, chairs, eyeglasses, and X rays. His work is often considered harsh and self-obsessed.

Samaria (səmâr'ēə), ancient city, central Palestine, on a hill NW of Nablus (Shechem). The site is now occupied by a village, Sabastiyah (Jordan). Samaria (named for Shemer, who owned the land) was built by King Omri as the capital of the northern kingdom of Israel in the early 9th cent. B.C. The scene of the wickedness of Omri's son Ahab and Ahab's wife Jezebel, Samaria was considered a place of iniquity by the Hebrew prophets. In the expansion of Assyria, Samaria fell in 721 B.C. to Sargon. The native population was deported, others were settled in its place, and the city was made the capital of an Assyrian province. (1 Kings 16.23-33; 20.1-21; 2 Kings 6.24-33; 10.17-28; 13.9-13; 17). It was destroyed in 120 B.C. by John Hyrcanus and was rebuilt by Herod the Great, who called it Sebaste in honor of Emperor Augustus [Gr.,=Sebastos]. There Philip the Evangelist (see PHILIP, SAINT) preached and the incident of Simon Magus occurred (Acts 8.5-24). According to tradition St. John the Baptist is buried there. Remains of a church of the Crusaders are in the city. Excavations (1908-10, 1931-35) uncovered fortifications and the palace of Omri, as well as ostraca, or potsherds, and ivories probably made by Phoenician artists. There are also extensive Roman remains. The city has given its name to the **Samaritans,** of whom a small remnant still live at Nablus and Jaffa, Israel. The Samaritans are the descendants of non-Jewish colonists from Babylonia, Syria, and elsewhere who were settled in Samaria when the Israelites were deported (722 B.C.) In the Bible the Samaritans recognize only the Pentateuch and are even more scrupulous about observing its ordinances than are Orthodox Jews. They worship on Mt. GERIZIM, where they had a temple in ancient times. The continual hatred between Jew and Samaritan apparently governed the choice of characters in the parable of the Good Samaritan (Luke 10.30-37). The Samaritan language is a variety of Palestinian Aramaic (a Semitic language). The Samaritan manuscripts, although pre-Masoretic (see MASORA) are not believed to be ancient, but they supply some useful variants of biblical passages. See J. W. Crowfoot, et al., *The Buildings of Samaria* (1942) and *The Objects from Samaria* (1958); André Parrot, *Samaria* (tr. 1958).

samarium (səmâr'ēəm), metallic chemical element; symbol Sm; at. no. 62; at. wt. 150.35; m.p. 1072°C; b.p. about 1800°C; sp. gr. 7.54 at 20°C; valence +2 or +3. Samarium is a lustrous silver-white metal. It is one of the RARE-EARTH METALS of the LANTHANIDE SERIES in group IIIb of the PERIODIC TABLE. It has two crystalline forms (see ALLOTROPY). The metal does not oxidize at room temperature but ignites when heated above 150°C. Samarium is found widely distributed in nature; it is obtained commercially from the minerals MONAZITE and bastnasite. Naturally occurring samarium is a mixture of seven isotopes, three of which are radioactive with extremely long half-lives. The metal was not isolated in relatively pure form until recently, although it has long been used in pyrophoric alloys used in cigarette lighter flints. Samarium is used as a catalyst in certain organic reactions. A samarium-cobalt compound, $SmCo_5$, is used to make magnets for use in computer memories. The oxide, samaria, is used in special infrared absorbing glass and cores of carbon arc-lamp electrodes. Since one isotope of samarium is a good neutron absorber, the element has found use in nuclear reactor control rods. Samarium was discovered in 1879 by P. E. Lecoq de Boisbaudran by spectroscopic analysis of the mineral samarskite.

Samarkand (sămərkănd', Rus. səmərkänt'), city (1970 pop. 267,000), capital of Samarkand oblast, Central Asian USSR, in Uzbekistan, on the Trans-Caspian RR. It is one of the oldest existing cities in the world and the oldest of central Asia. Built on the site of Afrosiab, which dated from the 3d or 4th millennium B.C., it was known to the ancient Greeks as Marakanda; ruins of the old settlement remain north of the present city. The chief city of Sogdiana, on the ancient trade route between the Middle East and China, Samarkand was conquered (329 B.C.) by Alexander the Great and became a meeting point of Western and Chinese culture. The first paper mill outside China was established there in 751. The Arabs took Samarkand in the 8th cent. A.D., and under the Umayyad empire it flourished as a trade center on the route between Baghdad and China. In the 9th and 10th cent., as capital of the Abbasid dynasty in central Asia, Samarkand emerged as a center of Islamic civilization. The tomb of Bukhari (d. 870), near Samarkand, is a major Muslim shrine. Samarkand continued to prosper under the Samanid dynasty of Khurasan (874-999) and under the subsequent rule of the Seljuks and of the shahs of KHOREZM. In 1220, JENGHIZ KHAN captured and devastated the city, but it revived in the 14th cent. when TAMERLANE made it the capital of his empire. Under his rule the city reached its greatest splendor; sumptuous palaces were erected, and mosques and gardens laid out. Under Tamerlane's successors, the Timurids, the empire soon was much reduced; it broke up in the late 15th cent. and was ruled by the Uzbeks for the following four centuries. Samarkand eventually became part of the emirate of Bukhara (see BUKHARA, EMIRATE OF) and fell to Russian troops in 1868, when the emirate passed under Russian suzerainty. In 1925, Samarkand became the capital of the Uzbek SSR, but in 1930 it was replaced by Tashkent. The old quarter of Samarkand with its maze of narrow, winding streets occupies the eastern part of the city and centers on the Registan, a great square. It contains some of the most remarkable monuments of central Asia, built during the reign of Tamerlane and his successors. The most famous of these is Tamerlane's mausoleum, surmounted by a ribbed dome and faced with multicolored tiles; the conqueror's tomb was opened in 1941. Other buildings include the Bibi Khan Mosque, with its turquoise cupola, erected by Tamerlane to the memory of his favorite wife; several other magnificent mosques; the mausoleums of the Timurid cemetery (Shah-i-Zinda); and the ruins of the observatory built by Ulugh-Beg, a grandson of Tamerlane. At the time of its greatest splendor medieval Samarkand was a fabulous city of palaces and gardens, with paved and tree-lined streets and a water system that supplied most of the individual houses. It had great silk and iron industries and was the meeting point of merchants' caravans from India, Persia, and China. Modern Samarkand still is a major cotton and silk center. Wine and tea are produced, and there are industries producing metal products, motor vehicle parts, leather goods, clothing, and footwear. The irrigated surrounding region has orchards and gardens and wheat and cotton fields. Samarkand is the seat of the Uzbek state university and of medical, agricultural, and teachers' institutes and the site of a regional museum.

Samaroff, Olga (səmä'rôf), 1882-1948, American pianist and educator, whose real name was Hickenlooper, b. San Antonio, Texas; studied at the Paris Conservatory. Her American debut (1905) was in New York City. She taught at the Juilliard School of Music and at the Philadelphia Conservatory. She was music critic (1927-29) for the New York *Evening Post* and in 1933 founded the Layman's Music Course, Inc. She was the wife of Leopold Stokowski from 1911 to 1923. Her writings on music include *The Layman's Music Book* (1935) and *A Music Manual* (1936). See her autobiography, *An American Musician's Story* (1939).

Samarra (sämär'rä), town, N central Iraq, on the Tigris River. It is on the site of an ancient settlement and has given its name to a type of Neolithic pottery of the 5th millennium B.C. The present town was founded (836) by the Abbasid caliphs. The 17th-century mosque with its golden dome is sacred to Shiite Muslims. There are notable ruins of many palaces, mosques, and other buildings.

Sama-Veda: see VEDA.

sambar: see WAPITI.

Sambourne, Edward Linley, 1844-1910, English caricaturist and illustrator. He was associated with *Punch* from 1867, when he began contributing, until the end of his life, and he followed Sir John Tenniel as chief cartoonist in 1901. Among other works he illustrated was Charles Kingsley's *Water Babies* (1885).

Sambre (säN'brə), river, 120 mi (193 km) long, rising in N France and flowing NE to the Meuse River at Namur, SE Belgium. Canalized along most of its length, the river traverses the important Franco-Belgian coal basin and industrial district. During World War I heavy fighting occurred along the river.

Samchok (säm'chŭk'), city (1966 pop. 26,000), E South Korea, a port on the Sea of Japan. It is a large industrial center in the heart of a rich coal and iron ore mining area. Samchok has metallurgical, chemical, cement, carbide, and fertilizer plants.

Samchonpo (säm'chŭn'pô'), city (1970 pop. 54,945), S South Korea, on the Korea Strait. It is a fishing port and processing center.

Samgar-nebo (săm'gär-nē'bō), Babylonian prince with Nebuchadnezzar at Jerusalem. Jer. 39.3.

Samkhya (säng'kyə): see INDIAN PHILOSOPHY.

Samlah (săm'lə), king of Edom. Gen. 36.36,37; 1 Chron. 1.47,48.

Sammartini, Giovanni Battista (jōvän'nē bät-tēs'tä säm-märtē'nē), 1701-75, Italian composer. Sammartini lived most of his life in Milan. He is said to have composed more than 2,000 works and was influential in the development of the symphony, the string quartet, and the galant style of composition generally. Gluck studied with him. Sammartini's brother Giuseppe (c.1695-c.1750) was also a composer.

Samnites (săm'nīts), people of ancient Italy. Their country was SAMNIUM. The Samnites were Oscan-speaking and therefore should be included among the Sabelli. The loose confederation of agricultural tribes, expanding in the 4th cent. B.C., came into conflict with the Romans over Campania. There was probably a good deal of warfare before the three Samnite Wars (343-341 B.C., c.326-304 B.C., 298-290 B.C.), in which the Romans won control of central and S Italy. The Samnites declined rapidly. They sided with Marius in the Social War and were crushed (82 B.C.) by Sulla before the gates of Rome; most of them were killed. Some survivors were sold into slavery; the rest were Romanized.

Samnium (săm'nēəm), ancient country of central and S Italy, mostly in the S Apennines. It was E of Campania and Latium and NE of Apulia. The desire of the SAMNITES to expand Samnium at the expense of Campania led to the Samnite Wars (343-290 B.C.).

Samoa, chain of volcanic islands in the South Pacific, comprising the independent nation of WESTERN SAMOA, and E of long. 171° W, the islands of AMERICAN SAMOA, under U.S. control. The Samoan islands extend c.350 mi (560 km), with a total land area of c.1,200 sq mi (3,110 sq km), and lie midway between Honolulu, Hawaii, and Sydney, Australia. The major islands are volcanic and mountainous and are surrounded by coral reefs. Soil in the interior is rocky; most cultivation takes place along the coast. Temperatures range from 90°F (32.2°C) in December, the hottest month, to 75°F (23.9°C) in August; the annual rainfall is 190 in. (483 cm), with the rainy season occurring between December and March. The natives are Polynesians who may have arrived in the islands as early as 1000 B.C. From Samoa they swept out across the Pacific (c.1200 A.D.), carrying Polynesian civilization to innumerable other islands. The Dutch explorer Jacob Roggeveen was the first European to discover (1722) Samoa. Subsequent European expansion into the islands led to disorder and violence, which was compounded by tribal warfare. The first European missionaries arrived in 1830. Between 1847 and 1861, the United States, Great Britain, and Germany sent representatives to Samoa, and in 1878 the United States and the Samoan kingdom signed a treaty giving the United States certain trade privileges and the right to establish a naval station at PAGO PAGO. Germany and Great Britain were accorded similar privileges in 1879. A tripartite treaty in 1899 between Great Britain, the United States, and Germany recognized U.S. interests east of long. 171°W; Germany was granted the western islands, and Great Britain withdrew from the area in consideration of rights in TONGA and the SOLOMON ISLANDS. New Zealand seized the German islands in 1914 during World War I and received a mandate to administer them from the League of Nations in 1920. In 1946 they became a UN trust territory held by New Zealand. In 1962 the independent nation of Western Samoa was created from the New Zealand territory; the eastern islands remained under U.S. control.

Samory (sä'mərē), 1835?-1900, Muslim religious leader of W Africa. Of humble origin, he was able to unite the tribes of the hinterlands of Guinea and the Ivory Coast. His activities brought him into conflict with the French. After a long struggle (1883-98) he was captured. He died in exile.

Sámos (sā'mŏs, Gr. sä'môs), island (1971 pop. 32,664), c.181 sq mi (469 sq km), SE Greece, in the Aegean Sea; one of the Sporades, near Turkey. Largely mountainous, it rises to c.4,725 ft (1,440 m) on Mt. Kerki. The main towns are Karlóvasi and Vathi, the capital of Sámos prefecture. The island has much fertile soil; grapes, tobacco, citrus fruits, and currants are grown. Cigarettes and wine are manufactured, and shipbuilding is carried on. Sámos was inhabited in the Bronze Age, and about the 11th cent. B.C. it was colonized by Ionian Greeks. By the 6th cent. B.C., when it was ruled by the tyrant Polycrates, the island was a commercial and maritime power and a cultural center. The poet Anacreon, the sculptor Rhoecus, and (according to legend) the fabulist Aesop lived on Sámos; Pythagoras and Conon were born there. Sámos was conquered by the Persians toward the end of the 6th cent. B.C. but regained its independence after the battle of Mycale (479 B.C.). It joined the Delian League and was a loyal supporter of Athens during the Peloponnesian War. The island declined after 322 B.C., when it fell out of Athenian hands. In the Middle Ages, Sámos was held by a Genoese trading company from 1304 to 1329 and from 1346 to 1475, when it was captured by the Ottoman Empire. It was a semi-independent principality from 1832 until it passed to Greece in 1913.

Samosata (səmŏs'ətə), ancient city of N Syria, on the Euphrates. It was founded c.150 B.C. as the capital of the Commagene kingdom. Taken by the Romans in

A.D. 72, it was of some importance in later Roman times. The Arabs took it in the 7th cent. Lucian was born there.

Samothrace (săm′ōthrās″) or **Samothráki** (sämōthrä′kē), island (1971 pop. 3,012), c.71 sq mi (184 sq km), NE Greece, in the Aegean Sea. The main town is Samothrace, or Samothráki (1971 pop. 1,214), located on the northwest shore. The island is largely mountainous, rising to c.5,575 ft (1,700 m) on Mt. Fengari. In ancient times Samothrace was an important center of worship. There are ruins of a religious sanctuary, some of which date to the 6th cent. B.C. The famous statue of the winged *Nike* (or *Victory*) *of Samothrace,* built c.200 B.C. to adorn a ship and later transferred to the island, was discovered on Samothrace in 1863 and is now in the Louvre in Paris. The island was ceded to Greece by the Ottoman Empire in 1913. Samothrace was the first stop in St. Paul's Macedonian itinerary (Acts 16.11).

Samoyed (săm′əyĕd), breed of hardy, muscular WORKING DOG developed in N Siberia many centuries ago. It stands from 19 to 23.5 in. (48.3–59.7 cm) high at the shoulder and weighs from 35 to 65 lb (15.9–29.5 kg). The weather-resistant double coat is composed of dense, woolly underhairs and a long, harsh, curl-free outercoat that stands straight out from the body. It may be pure white, white and biscuit, pure biscuit, or cream in color. Raised by the Samoyed people near the White Sea thousands of years before the Christian era, this hardy arctic dog was used to herd reindeer and haul sledges, at the same time being welcomed into the home as a family companion. Today the Samoyed is popular principally as a show dog and pet. See DOG.

Samoyedes or **Samoyeds** (both: săm′əyĕdz″), partly nomadic, partly settled agricultural tribes found in N Siberia and the Taimyr Peninsula, especially in the basin of the Ob and Yenisei rivers. Traditionally they hunted reindeer and held shamans in high repute. The Samoyede language, included in the Uralic family, is distantly related to Finno-Ugric. The Samoyedes today live mainly by raising reindeer and fishing. See Peter Hajdú, *The Samoyed Peoples and Languages* (1963).

samp: see HOMINY.

sampler, sample piece of needlework or embroidery, of silk, cotton, or worsted, for the preservation of some pattern or as an example of the ability of a child or a beginner. In museums and private collections there are samplers dating from as early as 1643. It was long the custom for each little girl to work her own sampler as soon as her needlework showed a proper degree of skill. Certain features of the sampler remained constant—the name of the maker, the date, the alphabet, texts from Scripture, proverbs or bits of verse, and a conventional border framing the whole.

Sampson, William Thomas, 1840–1902, American naval officer, b. Palmyra, N.Y. After serving with Union naval forces in the Civil War, he saw varied naval service and was (1886–90) superintendent of the U.S. Naval Academy at Annapolis. As chief of the bureau of ordnance (1893–97), he made important changes in naval gunnery. Sampson was president of the board of inquiry on the destruction of the MAINE in Havana harbor. With the outbreak of the Spanish-American War (1898), he was made commander of the N Atlantic squadron. He commanded the blockade of Cuba and the attack on San Juan. Although he was not present for most of the battle of Santiago de Cuba, where the Spanish fleet was destroyed, he claimed credit for the victory, since he had laid down the general instructions for the attack; his claim was contested by Winfield Scott SCHLEY, who actually commanded in the engagement. Public opinion favored Schley, and Sampson never received due recognition for his part in the victory. In 1899 he attained the rank of rear admiral and from then until his death commanded the Boston navy yard.

samsara: see BUDDHISM; KARMA; NIRVANA.

Samson, judge of Israel. His long hair was a symbol of his vows to God, and because of this covenant Samson was strong. The enemies of his people, the Philistines, accomplished his destruction through the woman Delilah. By cutting his hair she forced him to break his vow and thus destroyed his might. Captured and blinded and chained in the temple of the Philistines, he regained his strength as his hair grew long again, and with his bare hands he pulled down the temple, destroying himself along with his enemies (Judges 13–16). The Samson cycle was probably drawn from popular oral folk tales and may be a myth connected with the cult of sun worship. Milton's *Samson Agonistes* is a celebrated English poem on the blinded Samson.

Samsonov, Aleksandr Vasilyevich (əlyĭksän′dər vəsē′lyəvĭch səmsô′nəf), 1859–1914, Russian general. Early in World War I, when his army advanced into East Prussia (see MASURIA) in order to relieve German pressure on the French, it was virtually annihilated by German field marshal Hindenburg in the battle of TANNENBERG (Aug., 1914). His defeat was partly caused by the failure of General Rennenkampf to bring his forces to Samsonov's aid. Samsonov shot himself on the field of battle.

Samsun (sämsōōn′), city (1970 pop. 134,272), capital of Samsun prov., N Turkey, on the Black Sea. The most important Turkish port on the Black Sea, it is also a major tobacco-processing center and an agricultural market. The ancient Amisus, it was founded (6th cent. B.C.) by Greek colonists, became an important city of the kingdom of Pontus, and was much favored under the Roman Empire. In the Middle Ages it was held by the Byzantines, the Seljuk Turks, the Genoese, and the empire of Trebizond before falling (14th cent.) to the Ottoman Turks. On May 19, 1919, Kemal Atatürk landed at Samsun to organize a nationalist movement in Turkey. A statue commemorates this event.

Samuel, Herbert Louis Samuel, 1st Viscount, 1870–1963, British statesman. Entering Parliament as a Liberal in 1902, he was postmaster general (1910–14, 1915–16) and home secretary (1916). He lost his seat in Parliament in 1918 but served as first British high commissioner in Palestine (1920–25) and chairman of the royal commission of inquiry into the coal industry (1925–26). He played an important role in negotiating an end to the general strike of 1926. In the Commons again (1929–35), Samuel was home secretary (1931–32) and leader of the Liberal party (1931–35). He was created a peer in 1937. Samuel's writings include *Practical Ethics* (1935), *Belief and Action: an Everyday Philosophy* (1937), and *In Search of Reality* (1957). See his memoirs (1945).

Samuel, two books of the Old Testament, originally a single work in the Hebrew canon, called First and Second Samuel in the Authorized Version, where they occupy the 9th and 10th place, First and Second Kingdoms in the Septuagint, and First and Second Kings in the Western canon. They are a consecutive historical narrative of events of Hebrew history, covering substantially the careers of Samuel, Saul, and David (roughly the 11th cent. B.C.) as follows: first, Samuel's career and judgeship (1 Sam. 1–7); second, the establishment of the Hebrew monarchy (1 Sam. 8–31), which begins with the anointing and subsequent success of Saul (1 Sam. 8–15), followed by the anointing of David and the bitter rivalry between David and Saul (1 Sam. 16–31); third, the reign of David, first at Hebron (2 Sam. 1–4), then at Jerusalem (2 Sam. 5–20); and, fourth, an appendix of various materials out of order (2 Sam. 21–24). Scholars have detected two main strands in the composition of the book, based on divergent attitudes toward the establishment of the monarchy; some scholars divide it further. One section (2 Sam. 9–20) was apparently written by a contemporary of David, which makes it the oldest piece of narrative in the Bible. The prophet Samuel (fl. 1050 B.C.) was the last judge of Israel and the first of the prophets after Moses. The circumstances of his birth, childhood, and vocation are told in 1 Sam. 1–3. His judgeship was dominated by war with the Philistines, who captured the Ark of the Covenant (1 Sam. 4–7). In his old age he agreed, at the divine behest, to the establishment of a king and anointed Saul (1 Sam. 8–12). He remained chief prophet in Saul's reign (1 Sam. 13.11–16; 15; 19.18–24). In this role he anointed David, and after dying, appeared to Saul at Endor (1 Sam. 28). Samuel, a great leader, became a national hero and eventually a popular figure of Jewish legend. Ecclus. 46.16–23. For critical views on the composition of First and Second Samuel and for bibliography, see OLD TESTAMENT.

Samuelson, Paul A., 1915–, American economist, b. Gary, Ind., grad. Univ. of Chicago (B.A., 1935), Harvard (M.A., 1936; Ph.D., 1941). Appointed a professor of economics at the Massachusetts Institute of Technology in 1941, he later (1966) became institute professor, the highest professorial rank at the school. A liberal and a supporter of applied Keynesian economics, Samuelson has held a variety of governmental positions. He has been a consultant to the National Resources Planning Board (1941–43), the U.S. Treasury (1945–52), and the Federal Reserve Board (1967–). An adviser to Presidents John F. Kennedy and Lyndon B. Johnson, he had a major role in shaping the tax legislation and antipoverty efforts of the early 1960s. In addition, he was president of the Econometric Society (1951), the American Economics Association (1961), and the International Economics Association (1966–68). In 1970, Samuelson received the Nobel Memorial Prize in Economics on behalf of his efforts to "raise the level of scientific analysis in economic theory." His contributions to the systematization of economic theory's underlying mathematical structure are probably unequaled by any other 20th-century economist. His introductory textbook, *Economics* (9th ed. 1973), is the standard work in its field. Originally published in 1948, it has been translated into almost every modern language. Samuelson's other writings include *Foundations of Economic Analysis* (1947), *Collected Scientific Papers* (3 vol., 1966), and numerous articles in *Newsweek* magazine, of which he is a contributing editor and columnist.

samurai (sä′mōōrī′), knights of feudal Japan, retainers of the DAIMYO. This aristocratic warrior class arose during the 12th cent. wars between the Taira and Minamoto clans and was consolidated in the Tokugawa period. Samurai were privileged to wear two swords, and at one time had the right to cut down any commoner who offended them. They cultivated the martial virtues, indifference to pain or death, and unfailing loyalty to their overlords (see BUSHIDO). Samurai were the dominant group in Japan, and the masterless samurai, the RONIN, were a serious social problem. Under the TOKUGAWA shogunate (1603–1867), the samurai were removed from direct control of the villages, moved into the domain castle towns, and given government stipends. They were encouraged to take up bureaucratic posts. As a result, they lost a measure of their earlier martial skill. Dissatisfied samurai from the Choshu and Satsuma domains of W Japan were largely responsible for overthrowing the shogun in 1867. When feudalism was abolished after the MEIJI RESTORATION, some former samurai also took part in the Satsuma revolt under Takamori SAIGO in 1877. As statesmen, soldiers, and businessmen, former samurai took the lead in building modern Japan. See H. P. Varley, *The Samurai* (1970).

San (săn), people of S Africa, consisting of several groups and numbering about 50,000 in all. They are generally short in stature; their skin is yellowish brown in color; and they have broad noses, flat ears, bulging foreheads, and prominent cheekbones. The San have been called Bushmen by whites in South Africa, but the term is now considered a derogatory one. Although many now work for white settlers, about half are still nomadic hunters and gatherers of wild food in desolate areas like the Kalahari desert of SW Africa. Their social unit is the small hunting band; larger organizations are loose and temporary. Caves and rock shelters are used as dwellings. They possess only what they can carry, using poisoned arrowheads to fell game and transporting water in ostrich shells. The San have a rich folklore, are skilled in drawing, and have a remarkably complex language characterized by the use of click sounds, related to that of the KHOIKHOI. For thousands of years the San lived in S and central Africa, but by the time of the Portuguese arrival in the 15th cent., they had already been forced into the interior of S Africa. In the 18th and 19th cent., they resisted the encroachment on their lands of Dutch settlers, but by 1862 that resistance had been crushed. See E. M. Thomas, *The Harmless People* (1959, repr. 1969); Laurens Van der Post, *The Lost World of the Kalahari* (1958) and *The Heart of the Hunter* (1961); J. B. Wright, *Bushmen Raiders of the Dakensberg, 1840–1870* (1971).

San (sän), town (1967 est. pop. 14,900), central Mali, a port on the Bani River. It is the trade center for a region where peanuts, cotton, fruit, and vegetables are grown. The town manufactures bricks and has lime kilns and cotton ginneries.

Sana or **San'a** (both: sŏnä′), city (1970 est. pop. 125,000), capital and principal city of Yemen. The city, the largest in S Arabia, lies inland on a high plain (alt. 7,250 ft/2,210 m) and is connected to the Red Sea port of Hodeida by road. Sana is an Islamic cultural center, and there is a Muslim university, other institutions of learning, and many mosques. It is a commercial and marketing center and is noted for the grapes grown nearby. Sana has been settled from pre-Islamic times and has an ancient wall. It was under Ethiopian control in the 6th cent. In the 17th cent. and again from 1872 to 1918 it was occupied by Turkey. After 1918, when Yemen's independence was reestablished, Sana became its capital.

Sanandaj (sän″ändäj′), city (1971 est. pop. 58,000), tal of Kurdistan prov., W Iran. It is the trade center of a grain and sheep-raising region and is known for its rugs and fine woodwork. It was formerly known as Sinneh and Sehna.

San Andreas fault, great fracture (see FAULT) of the earth's crust in California. It is the principal fault of an intricate network of faults extending more than 600 mi (965 km) from NW California to the Gulf of California. The San Andreas fault, a strike-slip fault, also extends vertically at least 20 mi (30 km) into the earth. It is located on the boundary between two sections of the earth's lithosphere—the North American plate and the Pacific plate (see PLATE TECTONICS)—and separates SW California from the North American continent. The Pacific plate is moving northwest in relation to the North American plate, and it is believed that the total displacement along the fault since its formation more than 30 million years ago has been about 350 mi (560 km). Movement along the fault causes earthquakes; several thousand occur annually, although only a few are of moderate or great magnitude. The destructive San Francisco earthquake of 1906 was caused by a movement in which land surfaces on either side of the fault were displaced horizontally up to 21 ft (6.4 m).

San Angelo (săn ăn'jəlō), city (1970 pop. 63,884), seat of Tom Green co., W Texas, where two forks join to form the Concho River; laid out 1869, inc. 1903. It is an important wool and mohair market and a trade and shipping point for a wide area of sheep, goat, and cattle ranches, irrigated farms, and oil and natural gas fields. Meat and dairy items, leather footwear, and oil field equipment are also produced. Founded beside a border military post, Fort Concho (1866; now restored as a museum), San Angelo was a rough frontier town of cattle trails and overland traffic in the 1870s; it grew after the coming of the railroad in 1888. Angelo State Univ. is there. Goodfellow Air Force Base adjoins the city, and Lake Nasworthy (the municipal reservoir) and San Angelo Reservoir are nearby.

San Anselmo (săn ănsĕl'mō), city (1970 pop. 13,031), Marin co., W Calif., near San Francisco; inc. 1907. It is mostly residential. San Francisco Theological Seminary is there.

San Antonio (săn ăntō'nēō, əntōn'), city (1970 pop. 654,153), seat of Bexar co., S central Texas, at the source of the San Antonio River; inc. 1837. It is one of the nation's largest military centers; Fort Sam Houston and Brooke Army Medical Center are in the city, and nearby are Lackland and Randolph air force bases, both training command centers; Brooks Air Force Base, an aerospace medical headquarters; and Kelly Air Force Base, an air material and security service post. San Antonio is also the industrial, trade, and financial center of a large agricultural area. Its manufactures include processed foods, aircraft, building materials, chemicals, wood products, clothing, and machinery. The city's green and flowered streets and parks, the tree-lined river meandering through its center, the huge Mexican quarter, the many reminders of its past, as well as the warm winter sun, attract thousands of tourists annually. The site had been visited by the Spanish long before the expedition under Martín de Alarcón founded a mission (San Antonio de Valero) and a presidio (San Antonio de Béjar or Béxar) there in 1718. Other missions were opened along the river—San José (1719), Concepción (1731), San Francisco de la Espada (1731), and San Juan Capistrano (1731)—and the neighboring town of San Fernando (now the heart of San Antonio) was founded in 1731. San Antonio was the most important Texas settlement in Spanish and Mexican days. During the Texas Revolution it was captured by the Texans (Dec., 1835) and was the scene of the Mexican attack on the ALAMO in March, 1836. Later a group of Comanche Indians were killed (1840) in the "council house fight," and in 1842 the city was taken and held briefly by Mexicans. After the Civil War and especially after the coming of the first railroad in 1877, San Antonio prospered as a roaring cow town with a Spanish flavor, which it still retains. In addition to its many missions (including the Alamo, which is now in the center of town), points of interest include La Villita, the reconstruction of a 250-year-old Spanish-speaking settlement; the Spanish governor's palace (c.1749); the Paseo del Río, a downtown river walk; the Hertzberg Circus Collection; and numerous old homes. The Hemisfair Plaza, site of the 1968 world's fair, contains the Institute of Texan Cultures and the 750-ft (229-m) Tower of the Americas, with a revolving restaurant at its top. Among San Antonio's educational institutions are Trinity Univ., St. Mary's Univ., Incarnate Word College, Our Lady of the Lake College, the Univ. of Texas Medical School at San Antonio, and two junior colleges. The Southwest Research Institute is notable for its research into the technical problems of the southwest region. The city has artists' colonies, a symphony orchestra, an art institute, and numerous museums. See G. P. Wertenbaker, *San Antonio, City in the Sun* (1946); Charles Ramsdell, *San Antonio; a Historical and Pictorial Guide* (1959); Sam Woolford, ed., *San Antonio; a History for Tomorrow* (1963); Boyce House, *San Antonio* (1968); Joseph Gallegly, *From Alamo Plaza to Jack Harris's Saloon* (1970).

Sanballat (sănbăl'ət), one of the Persian officials in Palestine who consistently opposed Nehemiah in his restoration of Jerusalem. He is called a Horonite, a designation perhaps from the name Bethhoron. Neh. 2.10,19; 4; 6; 13.28.

San Benito (săn bənē'tō), city (1970 pop. 15,176), Cameron co., extreme S Texas; inc. 1911. San Benito is chiefly a processing center for citrus fruit and vegetables grown in the irrigated region of the lower Rio Grande valley. Truck trailers, electric equipment, and other products are manufactured in the city's industrial park. San Benito is also a retirement and winter tourist spot.

San Bernardino (săn bûr"nədē'nō), city (1970 pop. 104,783), seat of San Bernardino co., S Calif., at the foot of the San Bernardino Mts.; inc. 1854. It is the center of a thriving metropolitan area that includes the cities of Ontario and Riverside. The city's many manufactures include steel, iron, and related products; propellants and rocket motors; electric golf carts; cement; and food items. The adjacent Norton Air Force Base is a major employer. The area was explored (1772), named (1810), and first settled by Spanish explorers. A colony of Mormons arrived in the early 1850s and plotted the present city. It is the seat of California State College at San Bernardino and a junior college. San Bernardino National Forest is to the northeast.

San Bernardino (sän bĕrnärdē'nō), Alpine pass, 6,770 ft (2,063 m) high, between Mesocco Valley and Rheinwald Valley, Grisons canton, SE Switzerland. Used possibly since prehistoric times, it is crossed by a road (built 1818-23) that passes through the resort village of San Bernardino.

San Bernardino Mountains, part of the Coast Range, S Calif., extending c.60 mi (100 km) NW and SE through San Bernardino and Riverside counties. Notable peaks are San Bernardino Mt. (10,630 ft/3,240 m) and Mt. San Gorgonio (11,485 ft/3,501 m). This region embraces the mountain resort and recreational areas around Gregory, Arrowhead, and Big Bear lakes, in the San Bernardino National Forest.

Sanborn, Franklin Benjamin, 1831-1917, American journalist, author, and philanthropist, b. Hampton Falls, N.H., grad. Harvard, 1855. An active abolitionist, he was a friend and agent of John Brown, although he disapproved of the Harpers Ferry raid. He was a correspondent of the Springfield *Republican*, editor (1863-67) of the Boston *Commonwealth*, and a founder of the American Social Science Association and editor (1867-97) of its journal. He served as secretary of the Massachusetts Board of Charities and helped found the Massachusetts Infant Asylum, the Clarke School for Deaf Mutes, and the National Prison Association. Long a resident in Concord, he wrote valuable biographies of Bronson Alcott, Ralph Waldo Emerson, W. E. Channing, Nathaniel Hawthorne, Henry David Thoreau, and others. See B. P. Broadhurst, *Social Thought, Social Practice, and Social Work Education* (1971).

San Bruno (săn broo'nō), city (1970 pop. 36,254), San Mateo co., W Calif., a residential suburb on San Francisco Bay; inc. 1914. A junior college, a Federal archives center, a naval engineering command, and a U.S. marine corps reserve base are in the city.

San Carlos (săn kär'lōs), residential city (1970 pop. 25,924), San Mateo co., W Calif.; inc. 1925. The chief manufactures are electronic and communications equipment.

Sánchez, Florencio (flōrän'syō sän'chās), 1875-1910, Uruguayan playwright. His many plays concern pastoral life in the region of the Río de la Plata. Sánchez's style owes much to the naturalism of Ibsen, although it has none of its refinements. His major plays include *La gringa* [the foreign girl] (1904) and *Barranca abajo* [down the cliffs] (1905).

Sánchez Ferlosio, Rafael (răfäĕl' sän'chĕth fărlō'syō), 1927-, Spanish novelist, b. Rome. He has published two novels. *Industrias y andanzas de Alfanhuí* [the ingenuity and wanderings of Alfanhuí] (1951) is a work of fantasy about a child's wanderings through Spain. *El Jarama* (1956) has no single protagonist but many insignificant characters whose personalities are revealed in the realism of their dialogue.

Sánchez Hernández, Fidel (fēdĕl', ārnän'dās), 1917-, president of El Salvador (1967-72). An army general, he served as minister of interior under President Rivera. As president, he named a largely civilian cabinet and continued Rivera's progressive programs. He faced new economic difficulties, however, after the brief but serious war with Honduras in July, 1969. Sanchez directed military operations of the war from the field, with considerable success; after a cease-fire was arranged by the Organization of American States, he withdrew his troops from Honduras despite opposition from many of his military leaders. Sanchez was succeeded by his hand-picked successor, Col. Arturo Armando Molina.

Sánchez Vilella, Roberto (rōbār'tō, vēlā'yä), 1913-, governor of Puerto Rico (1965-69). A civil engineer, he graduated from Ohio State Univ., entered politics, and, with Luis Muñoz Marín, was a founding member of the Popular Democratic party. Muñoz's closest adviser, he served as secretary of state (1952-64) and was elected governor (1964) as Muñoz's hand-picked successor. He concentrated on urban problems, created new jobs, and presided over a booming economy. His divorce and remarriage in 1967 cost him renomination by his party in 1968. He ran as an independent, splitting the votes of his party and giving the election to Luis Ferré.

Sancho I (Sancho Ramírez) (sän'chō rämē'rĕth), 1045?-1094, king of Aragón (1063-94) and, as Sancho V, king of Navarre (1076-94); son and successor of Ramiro I. He continued the war against the Moors and at the death of Sancho IV of Navarre was proclaimed king of Navarre. He died in the siege of Huesca. Peter I succeeded him.

Sancho III or **Sancho the Great,** c.970-1035, king of Navarre (1000-1035). Having inherited the kingdom of Navarre, which included Aragón, he launched an annexation campaign that made him the leading power in Christian Spain. After conquering (c.1015-25) the territories of Sobrarbe and Ribagorza from the Moors, he took possession of Castile, Vizcaya, and Álava (1028) as his wife's inheritance from her deceased brother, the count of Castile, for whom he had been protector since 1017. Sancho the Great also claimed overlordship of Barcelona, forcing Berengar Raymond I to become his vassal. He occupied the eastern part of León and was crowned in its capital in 1034. Although his kingdom was the largest Christian political unit in Spain, Sancho regarded it as his personal domain, to be divided at will. Its unity was thus broken at his death when he bequeathed his lands to his four sons. Navarre passed to García; Castile and Aragón, made into kingdoms, went respectively to Ferdinand I and Ramiro I; Sobrarbe and Ribagorza, joined as a separate kingdom, were given to Gonzalo.

Sancho I, c.1154-1211, king of Portugal (1185-1211), son and successor of Alfonso I. He was associated in his father's government from c.1170. Sancho undertook to restore and repeople the lands devastated in the wars against the Moors; thus he became known as *Sancho o Povoador* [Sancho the settler or populator]. Early successes against the Moors in Algarve were canceled by new Moorish attacks. He was succeeded by his son Alfonso II.

Sancho II, d.1072, Spanish king of Castile (1065-72), son and successor of Ferdinand I. He conquered (1072) León from his brother ALFONSO VI, but his sister Urraca rebelled against him at Zamora, and Sancho was assassinated while beseiging the city. He was succeeded by Alfonso VI.

Sancho IV (Sancho the Brave), 1257?-1295, Spanish king of Castile and León (1284-95), son and successor of ALFONSO X. On the death (1275) of his elder brother, Ferdinand de la Cerda, Sancho was designated as Alfonso's successor by a coalition of nobles. Throughout his reign Sancho was forced to defend his throne against the claims of Ferdinand de la Cerda's heirs, who at times received the support of Aragón. He conquered (1292) Tarifa from the Moors. His son, Ferdinand IV, succeeded him under the regency of Sancho's widow, María de Molina.

San Clemente (săn klĭmĕn'tē), city (1970 pop. 17,063), Orange co., S Calif., on the Pacific coast; inc. 1928. Camp Pendleton, a large U.S. marine base, adjoins the city. San Clemente is a popular vacation spot, with several missions, a state park, and a national forest nearby. President Nixon maintained a "Western White House" there.

San Cristóbal (sän krēstō'bäl), city (1970 pop. 25,829), S Dominican Republic, on a Caribbean coastal plain. The city was founded in the late 16th cent. The first Dominican constitution was signed in San Cristóbal in 1844. The dictator Rafael TRUJILLO was born there in 1891. Nearby is an agricultural institute.

San Cristóbal, city (1971 est. pop. 157,000), capital of Táchira state, W Venezuela, in a mountainous region near the Colombian border. It is a commercial and industrial center. Textiles, leather products, ceramics, cement, and tobacco are produced, and coffee, sugar, and corn are exported. San Cristóbal was founded in 1561 and was severely damaged by an earthquake in 1875.

Sancroft, William (săng'krôft), 1617-93, English prelate, archbishop of Canterbury. His opposition to Calvinist doctrine caused him to remain abroad during the latter part of the Commonwealth. After the Restoration, he returned to England in 1660 and advanced through various ecclesiastical offices to become (1678) archbishop of Canterbury. Earlier, as dean of St. Paul's, London, he directed the building of the famous cathedral designed by Sir Christopher Wren. He crowned James II at his accession, but refused to serve on the newly reconstituted court of high commission. In 1687, with six of his bishops, he signed a petition asking that the declaration of indulgence, which suspended the penal laws directed against non-Anglicans, be withdrawn, on grounds that it represented an illegal use of the royal dispensing power. The imprisonment, trial, and acquittal of the seven bishops greatly heightened religious tension prior to the deposition of James. Sancroft refused to take the oath of allegiance to William and Mary. He was suspended (1689) and deprived (1690) of his office, and in his retirement became leader of the NONJURORS.

sanction, in law and ethics, any inducement to individuals or groups to follow or refrain from following a particular course of conduct. All societies impose sanctions on their members in order to encourage approved behavior. These sanctions range from formal legal statutes to informal and customary actions taken by the general membership in response to social behavior. A sanction may be either positive, i.e., the promise of reward for desired conduct, or negative, i.e., the threat of penalty for disapproved conduct, but the term is most commonly used in the negative sense. This is particularly true of the sanctions employed in international relations. These are usually economic, taking the form of an EMBARGO or BOYCOTT, but may also involve military action. Under its Covenant, the League of Nations was empowered to initiate sanctions against any nation resorting to war in violation of the Covenant. Its declaration of an embargo against Paraguay (1934) derived from this power. Economic sanctions were applied against Italy during its invasion of Ethiopia (1935) in the League's most famous, and notably ineffective, use of its power. Under its Charter, the United Nations also has the power to impose sanctions against any nation declared a threat to the peace or an aggressor. Once sanctions are imposed they are binding upon all UN members. However, the requirement that over half of the total membership of the Security Council and all five permanent members agree on the decision to effect a sanction greatly limits the actual use of that power. UN military forces were sent to aid South Korea in 1950, and in the 60s economic sanctions were applied against South Africa and Rhodesia. See C. K. Webster, *Sanctions: The Use of Force in International Organization* (1956); Richard Arens and Harold Lasswell, *In Defense of Public Order* (1961); Ronald Segal, ed., *Sanctions Against South Africa* (1964); M. P. Doxey, *Economic Sanctions and International Enforcement* (1971).

Sanctis, Francesco de: see DE SANCTIS, FRANCESCO.

Sancti-Spíritus (sängk'tē-spē'rētōōs), city (1970 pop. 57,703), Las Villas prov., central Cuba, on the Yayabo River. It is the commercial and processing center of an area that raises sugarcane, tobacco, and cattle. Founded in 1514, the city was moved to its present site in 1522. It experienced several pirate attacks. During the 19th cent., it became one of Cuba's most aristocratic cities. Sancti-Spíritus was the first important city to be captured by Fidel Castro's guerrilla forces (late 1958). Declared a historic monument on its 450th anniversary, the city retains some of its colonial atmosphere; landmarks include a 16th-century bridge over the Yayabo River, a 16th-century church, and a theater dating back to 1839.

Sanctorius (săngktôr'ēəs), Ital. *Santorio,* 1561-1636, Italian physiologist. He was a professor at Padua (1611-24). By his quantitative experiments in temperature, respiration, and weight, he measured what he called "insensible perspiration" and laid the foundation for the study of metabolism. Among the instruments that he designed was a clinical thermometer. He wrote *De statica medicina* (1614; tr. 5th ed. 1737).

sanctuary, sacred place, especially the most sacred part of a sacred place. In ancient times and in the Middle Ages, a sanctuary served as ASYLUM, a place of refuge for persons fleeing from violence or from the penalties of the law. To injure a person in sanctuary or to remove him from it forcibly was considered sacrilege. In Egypt the temples of Osiris and Amon offered the right of sanctuary. Under the Greeks all temples enjoyed this privilege, and certain ones, like the Temple of Apollo at Delphi, were known throughout the Mediterranean world as a haven for fugitives. In Rome sanctuary was often sought by fugitive slaves. Christian churches were given the right of sanctuary by Constantine I. Abuses of sanctuary, tending to encourage crime, led to its curtailment and abolition. Modern penal codes no longer recognize the right of sanctuary.

Sanctus [Lat.,=holy], hymn of the Roman Catholic MASS, beginning, "Holy, holy, holy," from Isa. 6.3; Mat. 21.9. It is the solemn choral ending of the preface. In the old liturgy the second part of the hymn, called *Benedictus,* was sometimes sung after the elevation. The *Sanctus* (sometimes called *Tersanctus*) also includes the *Hosanna.*

Sand, George (sănd, Fr. zhôrzh säN), pseud. of **Amandine Aurore Lucie Dupin, baronne Dudevant** (ämäNdēn' ôrôr' lüsē' düpăN, bärôN' düdväN'), 1804-76, French novelist. Other variant forms of her maiden name include Amantine Lucile Aurore Dupin. Born of an aristocratic father and a lower-class mother, she was reared by her austere paternal grandmother on a country estate in Berry. After entering a convent in Paris, she returned to the countryside and led an unconventional life, donning the male clothes that became a mark of her rebellion. In 1831, after eight years of a marriage of convenience with Baron Dudevant, a country squire, she went with her two children to Paris, obtaining a divorce in 1836. She wrote some 80 novels, which were widely popular in their day, supporting herself and her children chiefly by her writing. Her earlier novels were romantic; later ones often expressed her serious concern with social reform. Her liaisons—with Jules Sandeau, Musset, Chopin, and others—were open and notorious, but were only part of her life. She demanded for women the freedom in living that was a matter of course to the men of her day. Her first novel, *Rose et Blanche* (1831), was in collaboration with Jules Sandeau (a shortening of his last name provided her with the pseudonym which she kept all her life), with whom she had previously written articles for the journal *Figaro.* Of her own novels, *La Mare au diable* (1846, tr. *The Haunted Pool,* 1890) and *Les Maîtres sonneurs* [the master bell-ringers] (1853) are considered masterpieces. Notable also are *Indiana* (1832, tr. 1881), *Mauprat* (1837), *Consuelo* (1843, tr. 1846), *François le champi* (1848, tr. *Francis the Waif,* 1889), *La Petite Fadette* (1849, tr. *Fanchon the Cricket,* 1864), and *Contes d'une grand'mère* (1873, tr. *Tales of a Grandmother,* 1930), a collection of Breton fairy tales. All these books are distinguished by a romantic love of nature as well as an extravagant moral idealism. She also wrote a number of plays. Much of her work was autobiographical, notably *Histoire de ma vie* (1854); *Elle et lui* [she and he] (1859), which concerns her life with Musset; and *Un Hiver à Majorque* [a winter in Majorca] (1842), about her life with Chopin. See her *Intimate Journal* (1929, tr. 1929); biographies by André Maurois (1951, tr. 1953) and Frances Winwar (1945, repr. 1972); study by René Doumie (1910, repr. 1972).

sand, rock material occurring in the form of loose, rounded or angular grains, varying in size from .06 mm to 2 mm in diameter, the particles being smaller than those of GRAVEL and larger than those of SILT or CLAY. Sand is formed as a result of the WEATHERING and decomposition of igneous, sedimentary, or metamorphic rocks. Its most abundant mineral constituent is silica, usually in the form of QUARTZ, and many deposits are composed almost exclusively of quartz grains. Many other minerals, however, are often present in small quantities, e.g., the amphiboles, the pyroxenes, olivine, glauconite, clay, the feldspars, the micas, iron compounds, zircon, garnet, tourmaline, titanite, corundum, and topaz. Some sands—e.g., coral sands, shell sands, and foraminiferal sands—are organic in origin. Sand grains may be rounded or more or less angular, and differences in shape and size account chiefly for differences in such important properties as porosity (proportion of interstices to the total mass), permeability to gases and liquids, and viscosity, or resistance to flow. Permeability and viscosity are also affected by the proportion of clayey matter present. The chief agents in accumulating sands into deposits are winds, rivers, waves, and glaciers; sand deposits are classified according to origin as fluviatile, lacustrine, glacial, marine, and eolian. The most extensive superficial deposits are seen in the DESERT and on beaches. The surface of a sand deposit may be level or very gently sloping, or the sand may be gathered by wind action into ridges called dunes. SANDSTONE and QUARTZITE rocks are indurated masses of sand, and sand deposits are sometimes formed by the weathering of sandstone and quartzite formations. Sand is used extensively in the manufacture of bricks, mortar, cement, concrete, plasters, paving materials, and refractory materials. It is also used in the metallurgical industry, in the filtration of water, in pottery making, in glassmaking, in the manufacture of explosives, and as an abrasive. Other industrial uses are numerous. Although soils entirely composed of sand are too dry and too lacking in nourishment for the growth of plants, a soil that is to some extent sandy (a "light" soil) is favorable to certain types of agriculture and horticulture, as it permits the free movement of air in the soil, offers less resistance than a clay soil to growing roots, improves drainage, and increases ease of cultivation. Sand to which nutrient solutions have been added is often used in soilless gardening.

Sandakan (səndəkän'), city (1971 pop. 28,806), Sabah, Malaysia, on N Borneo, on Sandakan Harbor, an inlet of the Sulu Sea. It is the trade hub for a rubber-producing and lumbering region. Sandakan was the capital of British North Borneo (now Sabah) until 1947, when it was supplanted by KOTA KINABALU (Jesselton).

sandalwood, name for several fragrant tropical woods, especially for *Santalum album,* an evergreen partially parasitic tree either native to India or introduced there centuries ago. It is used for joss sticks in Buddhist religious ceremonies and funeral rites and is made into ornamental wares. Oil distilled from the wood is used extensively as a perfume and has a place in medicine. About 19 species of *Santalum* are distributed over the Hawaiian and other Pacific islands. Red sandalwood obtained from a leguminous tree (*Adenanthera pavonina*), also native to India, was probably the almug of the Bible. It is used chiefly as the source of a dye.

Sandalwood Island: see VANUA LEVU.

Sandalwood Island: see SUMBA, Indonesia.

Sanday, William, 1843-1920, English theologian and biblical scholar. He was professor of exegesis (1883-95) at Oxford and from 1895 to 1919 Lady Margaret professor of divinity and canon of Christ Church, Oxford. He was joint editor of the *Variorum Bible* (1880) and won acceptance for new methods of New Testament study among Anglican clergy. Besides commentaries, his many writings include *The Authorship and Historical Character of the Fourth Gospel* (1872), *The Gospels in the Second Century* (1876), and *The New Testament Background* (1918).

sandblast, stream of sand or other abrasive particles driven by a jet of COMPRESSED AIR or water or by centrifugal force against a surface to clean or abrade it. When centrifugal force is used, the abrasives are whirled in a rapidly rotating device before being directed against the surface. Powdered quartz, emery, chilled iron globules, and other hard granular substances are used as the abrasive material. The sandblast is used for cleaning castings in foundries; for preparing metal surfaces for painting, enameling, and galvanizing; and for cleaning the stonework of buildings. Frosted designs are worked on glass by placing a stencil or suitable pattern over the surface so that the blast affects only the uncovered parts.

sandbur or **bur grass,** any species of the genus *Cenchrus* of the family Gramineae (GRASS family), sandy-soil plants of tropical and temperate regions. At maturity the sharp spines and burlike seeds make the plant a troublesome weed, especially to sheepgrowers. The name *sandbur* is sometimes used for the buffalo bur and the horse nettle of the family Solanaceae (NIGHTSHADE family). The family Gramineae is classified in the division MAGNOLIOPHYTA, class Liliatae, order Cyperales. The Solanaceae is in the class Magnoliopsida, order Polemoniales.

Sandburg, Carl, 1878-1967, American poet and biographer, b. Galesburg, Ill. Sandburg is among the major figures of 20th-century American literature. The son of poor Swedish immigrants, he left school at the age of 13 and became a day laborer. He served in the Spanish-American War and, after returning to Galesburg, put himself through Lombard College (now Knox College). He graduated in 1902, then went to work as a newspaperman in Milwaukee. In

1908 he married Lillian Steichen, sister of the photographer Edward Steichen. From 1910 to 1912 he was secretary to the Socialist mayor of Milwaukee. Sandburg later moved to Chicago, where he continued his journalism career, becoming in 1917 an editorial writer for the Chicago *Daily News*. His poetry first began to attract attention in Harriet Monroe's magazine *Poetry*. With the appearance of his *Chicago Poems* (1916), *Cornhuskers* (1918), *Smoke and Steel* (1920), and *Slabs of the Sunburnt West* (1922), his reputation was established. Among his later volumes of verse are *Good Morning, America* (1928), *The People, Yes* (1936), *Complete Poems* (1950; Pulitzer Prize), *Harvest Poems, 1910-1960* (1960), and *Honey and Salt* (1963). Sandburg drew most of his inspiration from American history and was profoundly influenced by Walt Whitman. His verse is vigorous and impressionistic, written without regard for conventional meter and form, in language both simple and noble. Much of his poetry celebrates the beauty of ordinary people and things. Sandburg's most ambitious work was his six-volume biography of Abraham Lincoln (1926-39; Pulitzer Prize); this monumental work exalts Lincoln as the symbol and embodiment of the American spirit. At 70, Sandburg produced his first work of fiction, the novel *Remembrance Rock* (1948), a panoramic epic of America. His other works include *The American Songbag* (1927), a collection of folk ballads and songs; children's books, such as *Rootabaga Stories* (1922); and the autobiographical *Always the Young Strangers* (1953). See his letters, ed. by Herbert Mitgang (1968); biographies by Joseph Haas and Gene Lovitz (1967) and North Callahan (1970); studies by Richard Crowder (1963) and H. B. Durnell (1965).

Sandby, Paul (sănd'bē), 1725-1809, English watercolorist and draftsman. He was employed to survey the Highlands of Scotland after the 1745 rebellion. During his years in Scotland (1746-51) he learned to interpret landscape with delicacy and precision of detail. Most of his paintings of landscapes are done in watercolor or gouache; many of his most important drawings he reproduced in aquatint, a process that he introduced in England. Windsor Castle is the subject of a number of his drawings, which have sometimes been confused with those of his brother, Thomas (1721-99), also a fine draftsman. Much of Paul's work is in the Victoria and Albert Museum. See A. P. Oppé, *The Drawings of Paul and Thomas Sandby . . . at Windsor Castle* (1947).

Sand Creek, Colorado, site of a massacre (1864) of CHEYENNE INDIANS by Col. John M. Chivington and his Colorado Volunteers. The Cheyennes, led by their chief, BLACK KETTLE, had offered to make peace with the white men and, at the suggestion of military personnel, had encamped at Sand Creek near Fort Lyon while awaiting word from the governor of the territory. There they were attacked in a surprise dawn raid on Nov. 29, 1864. Chivington and his men, choosing to ignore the white flag Black Kettle had raised over his tent, indiscriminately slaughtered and mutilated hundreds of men, women, and children. The atrocity has been the subject of much controversy. See Stan Hoig, *The Sand Creek Massacre* (1961).

sand dollar, common name for a marine animal in the same phylum as the starfish (see SEA STAR). The sand dollar has a rigid, flattened, disk-shaped test, or shell, made of firmly united plates lying just beneath the thin skin. Small spines that densely cover the test enable the animal to burrow in sand just below the surface. Like other members of its class, the sand dollar is radially symmetrical. It also shows evidence of a secondary bilateral symmetry, i.e., the mouth is centered on the oral (under) surface, but the anus lies near the rear edge of the test. Tube feet are similar to those in other echinoderms and are used for locomotion and to convey small food particles, mostly organic matter found in sand, to the mouth. Tube feet on the upper surface are used for respiration. Sand dollars differ from the closely related heart urchins by their shorter spines and more flattened shape. More convex, short-spined sand dollars are called sea biscuits. Sand dollars are abundant on the sandy bottom of deeper waters on both the Atlantic and Pacific coasts. They are classified in the phylum ECHINODERMATA, class Echinoidea, order Clypeastroida.

Sandeau, Jules (zhül săNdō'), 1811-83, French novelist. His best-known work is the romance *Mademoiselle de la Seiglière* (1848), dramatized in 1851. He collaborated several times with authors better known than he; with the baronne Dudévant, who took her pen name George Sand from Sandeau's name, he wrote *Rose et Blanche; ou, La Comédienne et la religieuse* (1831).

Sandefjord (sä'nəfyôr), town (1970 pop. 32,066), Vestfold co., SE Norway, near the mouth of the Oslofjord. An important shipping center since the 14th cent., it is also the base for a large whaling fleet operating in arctic waters. The town has shipyards, chemical works, and food-processing plants.

Sandemanians (săn"dəmā'nēənz), name in England and America for the Glassites, a religious sect founded by John GLAS. Robert Sandeman, for whom the movement was named, was a co-worker of Glas.

Sander, August (ou'go͝ost zän'dər), 1876-1964, Austrian photographer. During his long life Sander made a remarkable composite portrait of the German people. He began his immense work in the early 1890s, making pictures of young men who wanted mementos to give to their families before they emigrated to the United States. He opened a portrait studio in Linz (1904), but a great percentage of his masterful, perceptive portraits were made in the homes and working environments of his sitters. He produced a realistic picture of the daily life and look of a vast cross-section of German society. His subjects included country people, craftsmen, laborers, technicians, artists, professionals, politicians, aristocrats, and family groups of every sort, the total work comprising an extraordinary human document in which the photographer himself is particularly unobtrusive. See his *Men Without Masks: Faces of Germany, 1910-1938* (tr. 1973).

Sanders or **Sander, Nicholas,** 1530-81, English Roman Catholic churchman. He became prominent at Oxford as an ally of Cardinal Pole and had to flee on the accession of Elizabeth I. He attended the Council of Trent and traveled in Poland and Lithuania. He rose to prominence as a leader of the exiled English Catholics. From 1573 to 1578 he worked on plans to restore Catholicism by deposing Elizabeth, and in 1579 he sailed with a Spanish troop to join in the revolt of the earl of DESMOND. Disaster overtook them, and in 1581 he died of the hardships he had undergone. His *De origine ac progressu schismatis Anglicani* is the prime source for the state of Roman Catholics in England under Elizabeth I.

Sanders, Otto Liman von: see LIMAN VON SANDERS, OTTO.

Sanderson, Nicholas: see SAUNDERSON, NICHOLAS.

Sanderson, Robert, 1587-1663, English clergyman. Gaining William Laud's favor, he was appointed a royal chaplain in 1631 and regius professor of divinity at Oxford in 1642. Imprisoned during the civil war, he was reinstated to his professorship and named bishop of Lincoln in 1660. The second preface of the Anglican prayer book and the General Thanksgiving are attributed to him. His published writings include *Logicae artis compendium* (1618) and *De obligatione conscientiae praelectiones decem* (1660). See his works (6 vol., 1854); biographies by Izaak Walton (1678) and George Lewis (1924).

sand fly: see MIDGE.

sandgrouse, common name for pigeon-sized, seed-eating, terrestrial birds of the genera *Pteroclida* (approximately 14 species) and *Syrrhaptes* (2 species). They are birds of the Old World deserts and steppes, and are protectively colored and mottled to blend in with their backgrounds. Colors are typically fawn and gray in the desert-dwelling species and striped or mottled orange and brown in those of the steppe. Sandgrouse are structurally similar to pigeons, but have thicker skin. They have long, pointed wings and tails, and feathers all the way down their short legs. They range in length from 9 to 16 in. (22.5-40 cm). Sandgrouse are especially remarkable for their drinking habits, descending upon water in flocks of as many as 80,000 birds. With their beaks continuously in the water, they can swallow until full without pausing. They must have water daily, and desert species may make a round trip journey as great as 75 mi (120 km) a day just to reach water. They are strong flyers and can reach speeds up to 40 mi (64 km) per hr. Aground, sandgrouse are not very graceful, progressing with a rapid waddle on their short, feathered legs. Lacking a first toe, they do not perch. They forage on berries and seeds and sometimes on insects. They lay their round, spotted eggs, usually three, in ground nests or shallow depressions. The precocious young leave the nest soon after hatching, incubation taking 23 to 28 days, and being shared by the male and female. The newly hatched young are fed by regurgitation of the parents. Several species of sandgrouse are known to be migratory. Sandgrouse are classified in the phylum CHORDATA, subphylum Vertebrata, class Aves, order Columbiformes, family Pteroclidae.

Sandhurst, village, Berkshire, S central England. It is the site of the Royal Military Academy.

San Diego (săn dēā'gō), city (1970 pop. 697,027), seat of San Diego co., S Calif., on San Diego Bay; inc. 1850. With an excellent natural harbor, it is an important port of entry; a shipping and receiving point for S California, Arizona, New Mexico, and Lower California; and headquarters for the 11th U.S. naval district. Major naval and marine training bases are located there. San Diego has large aerospace, electronic, and shipbuilding industries, and is an important center for scientific research, especially in the field of oceanography. It is also a distributing and processing point for a highly productive agricultural area. Tuna are caught and canned, and sporting goods, clothing, rugs, furniture, and office equipment are among its manufactures. Tourism is an important element in San Diego's economy; the city's delightful climate, its 17 mi (27 km) of ocean beaches, and many historic attractions, as well as its proximity to Mexico, draw visitors, convention groups, artists, and retirees. Juan Rodríguez Cabrillo sailed into San Diego Bay in 1542 and claimed the land for Spain. Don Sebastian Viscaino encamped on Ballast Point in 1602, and in 1769 Junípero Serra established Mission San Diego de Alcalá, the first of a chain of 21 California missions. That same year Father Serra dedicated the Presidio, the first Spanish fort in California. Indian attacks kept the first settlers within the Presidio walls, but as fear of the Indians abated, the town slowly expanded down the hill. By 1830 most of the people were living in what is now Old Town. They traded in cattle hides, and from 1850 to 1870 whaling was a major enterprise. Parts of Old Town are now a state historical park. Also of interest are Cabrillo National Monument and Mission San Diego de Alcalá (restored). San Diego is a cultural, educational, and medical center. Its many health facilities include large naval and veterans hospitals. It is the seat of the Univ. of California at San Diego, United States International Univ., the Univ. of San Diego, Electronic Technical Institute, and three junior colleges. Balboa Park contains a fine art gallery, several museums (including an aerospace museum), and the enormous San Diego zoo. Some buildings from the Panama-California International Exposition (1915-16) and the California Pacific International Exposition (1935-36) remain, and there is also a spectacular aquatic park. The new San Diego Stadium is home for the city's professional baseball and football teams. The city also has an international airport. San Diego includes the unincorporated communities of LA JOLLA and Spring Valley. CORONADO is across the Bay.

Sandino, Augusto César (ougo͞os'tō sä'sär sändē'nō), 1895-1934, Nicaraguan revolutionary general. A farmer and a mining engineer, he joined the liberal revolution (1926) against the conservative government headed by Adolfo Díaz and Emiliano Chamorro. He protested against the new U.S. intervention in Nicaragua in 1926 and rejected the Stimson-Moncada agreement for the elections of 1927. On this score Sandino broke with the liberal leader, José María Moncada, and conducted vigorous guerrilla campaigns (1927-33) against the U.S. marines. Never captured but finally reconciled after the withdrawal of the marines, he headed a cooperative farming scheme. In 1934 he was invited to meet with Gen. Anastasio SOMOZA, and when he did so, he was seized and executed.

Sandomierz (sändô'myĕsh), Rus. *Sandomir,* town (1968 pop. 15,800), SE Poland, on the Vistula. A river port and agricultural center, it also has industries producing glass, industrial porcelain, and wool products. Founded probably before Poland accepted Christianity, Sandomierz became the capital of a duchy in 1139. It was razed by the Tatars in 1241 and again in 1259, but was rebuilt (14th cent.) by Casimir III and became (16th cent.) a flourishing trade and cultural center and one of the most beautiful Polish towns. A synod (known as the Consensus Sandomiriensis) held there in 1570 united all Polish Protestants. The town was heavily damaged by the Swedes in 1656 and lost its importance. It passed to Austria in 1772, to Russia in 1815, and reverted to Poland in 1919. Its most notable buildings are a 13th-century town hall and a 14th-century castle.

sandpaper, abrasive originally made by gluing grains of sand to heavy paper sheets. Today sandpaper is made primarily with quartz, aluminum oxide, or silicon carbide grains, and is graded according to the size of the grains. It is used for smoothing and polishing, for removing old paint or varnish, and for otherwise preparing wood surfaces for refinishing or other treatment.

sandpiper, common name for some members of the large family Scolopacidae, small shore birds, including the SNIPE and the CURLEW. Sandpipers are wading birds with relatively long legs and long, slender bills for probing in the sand or mud for their prey—all sorts of small invertebrates. Their plumage is dull, usually streaked brown or gray above and buff with streaks or spots below. Most sandpipers are found in flocks on seacoasts throughout the Northern Hemisphere, but some frequent inland waters and marshes. Except for three species, all sandpipers nest on the ground. The three exceptions, the solitary sandpiper of the New World, and the green and wood sandpipers of the Old World, usually use the abandoned nests of other birds, and nest in trees. Sandpipers fly in irregular, large flocks, with no apparent leader. Among the North American sandpipers are the spotted and solitary sandpipers, found by streams; the Baird's, least, semipalmated, western, and white-rumped sandpipers, collectively called "peeps"; the red-backed sandpiper, or dunlin, and the greater and lesser yellow-legs, the willet, the knot, and the sanderling. Sandpipers are classified in the phylum CHORDATA, subphylum Vertebrata, class Aves, order Charadriiformes, family Scolopacidae.

Sandrart, Joachim Von (yōä'khĭm fən zänt'rärt), 1606–88, German painter. An academic painter fond of chiaroscuro effects, Sandrart is best remembered for his comprehensive history of art (1675). This history records invaluable information on Sandrart's German contemporaries.

Sandringham (săn'drĭngəm), village, Norfolk, E England, near the Wash River. Sandringham House, with its large estate, was purchased in 1861 by Edward VII, then prince of Wales. It has been used as a royal residence by Queen Alexandra, King George V, King George VI, and Queen Elizabeth II.

Sandrocottus: see CHANDRAGUPTA.

Sand Springs, city (1970 pop. 10,565), Tulsa co., NE Okla., an industrial suburb of Tulsa, on the Arkansas River; founded 1907. There are oil and natural gas wells and textile and glass industries. Lorado Taft designed a memorial group there.

sandstone, sedimentary ROCK formed by the cementing together of grains of sand. The usual cementing material in sandstone is calcium carbonate, iron oxides, or silica, and the hardness of sandstone varies according to the character of the cementing material; quartz sandstones cemented with quartz are the hardest. Sandstones are commonly gray, buff, red, or brown although green and some other colors are also found. Green sandstones often contain, in addition to sand and glauconite, fossil shells and iron oxides; those that break apart easily are known as greensands and are sometimes used to replenish depleted potash in soils. Sandstones are widely used in construction and industry. Varieties of sandstone include arkose, which contains feldspar and resembles granite, and graywacke, a gray or sometimes greenish or black rock composed of quartz and feldspar with numerous fragments of other rocks, such as shale, slate, quartzite, granite, and basalt. Sandstone may be crushed to the form of loose sand grains, which can then be put to the same industrial uses as sand. See BROWNSTONE.

sandstorm, strong dry wind blowing over the desert that raises and carries along clouds of sand or dust often so dense as to obscure the sun and reduce visibility almost to zero. Such a wind is usually the result of convection currents created by intense heating of the ground. The wind is strong enough to move dunes, and it often interferes with travel, sometimes obliterating roads in flat dry regions such as those of the W United States. The simoom (or simoon) is the dust- and sand-laden desert wind of N Africa and Arabia that contributes largely to the atmospheric dust over Europe. The haboob is a sandstorm prevalent in the region of the Sudan around Khartoum. Haboobs, the leading edges of which often appear as solid walls of dust as much as 5,000 ft (1,525 m) high, also occur, although less frequently, in the SW United States. One that occurred near Tucson, Arizona, on July 16, 1971, was extensively documented by meteorologists.

Sandusky (səndŭs'kē, săn-), industrial city (1970 pop. 32,674), seat of Erie co., N central Ohio, a port of entry on Sandusky Bay of Lake Erie; inc. 1824. Its natural harbor has major coal-loading docks; sand, gravel, and salt are also shipped. Sandusky has a fishing industry and many assorted manufactures, and it has been a tourist center since the 1880s. Nearby are Cedar Point, a popular summer resort; Kelleys Island and numerous other small islands; Blue Hole Spring; Crystal Rock Caves; and Marblehead Peninsula.

Sandusky, river, c.120 mi (190 km) long, rising in N Ohio and flowing W through Bucyrus, then N past Tiffin to Sandusky Bay, an arm of Lake Erie. This landlocked bay, 18 mi (29 km) long, is one of the best harbors on the lake.

Sandviken (sänd'vē''kən), city (1970 pop. 27,137), Gävleborg co., S central Sweden. A planned industrial city, it has ironworks and steelworks (founded 1862) that produce large quantities of high quality steel.

Sandwich, Edward Montagu, 1st earl of (mŏn'təgyōō), 1625–72, English admiral. He fought in the parliamentary army during the civil war, became (1653) a member of the council of state of the Commonwealth, and was appointed (1656) general at sea. After the collapse of the Protectorate, however, he assisted in the Restoration (1660) of Charles II and escorted the king home from Holland. Created (1660) earl of Sandwich and admiral of the narrow seas, he negotiated (1661) the marriage between Charles and Catherine of Braganza, secured English possession of Tangier as part of her dowry, and brought Catherine to England. He fought with distinction at the battle of Lowestoft (1665) in the second DUTCH WAR and was killed in the battle of Southwold Bay in the third war. Samuel Pepys was his secretary at the admiralty. See biography by F. R. Harris (2 vol., 1912).

Sandwich, John Montagu, 4th earl of, 1718–92, British politician. He served variously as secretary of state (1763–65, 1770–71) and first lord of the admiralty (1748–51, 1763, 1771–82). He earned (1763) great unpopularity for his charges of obscenity against John WILKES, because not only had he been Wilkes's friend but he was himself notoriously dissolute. His reputation has suffered chiefly, however, and somewhat unjustly, because he presided at the admiralty over the British defeats of the American Revolution. In fact, he was an able, if corrupt, administrator, and his naval policy was apparently sound. He was shackled, however, by the stringent economies of Lord North and unable to expand the navy as needed. The Sandwich (Hawaiian) Islands were named after him by Capt. James Cook. The SANDWICH was also named after him; he supposedly ate food in that form rather than leave the gaming table.

Sandwich, Ont., Canada, part (since 1935) of the city of WINDSOR.

Sandwich, municipal borough (1971 pop. 4,467), Kent, SE England, on the Stour River. It is a resort and market center with some light industries. One of the CINQUE PORTS, Sandwich was the chief military port of the kingdom in the late 15th cent. Silting in the 16th cent. ruined the harbor. There are many interesting medieval buildings.

sandwich, a piece of meat or other food placed between two slices of bread. Although food in this form has long been used, the term sandwich originated in the 18th cent. It is named for John Montagu, the 4th earl of Sandwich, an inveterate gambler who ate informally at the gaming table rather than stopping for the set meal.

Sandwich Islands: see HAWAII.

sand worm, name applied to a number of marine sand-dwelling WORMS. Several species are used as bait by fishermen. See *Class Polychaeta* under ANNELIDA.

Sandy Hook, low, sandy peninsula, NE N.J., projecting 5 mi (8 km) N toward New York and separating Sandy Hook Bay from the Atlantic Ocean. At the northern end is Fort Hancock, which was built to protect New York harbor and was once used as a proving ground for heavy artillery. The Sandy Hook Lighthouse (85 ft/25.9 km high; built 1763) is the oldest in service in the United States. Henry Hudson's men explored this region in 1609. The British held the peninsula during the Revolution. Sandy Hook is part of Gateway National Recreation Area.

Sandys, Edwin (săndz), 1516?–1588, English prelate, archbishop of York (1576–88). While a student at Cambridge he turned to Protestantism. On the death (1553) of Edward VI, Sandys supported Lady Jane Grey as candidate for the throne. As a result he was imprisoned by Mary I, but he was released and fled to the Continent. He returned (1559) after the accession of Elizabeth I and was made bishop of Worcester (1559), bishop of London (1570), and archbishop of York (1576). He was one of the translators of the Bishops' Bible (1568).

Sandys, Sir Edwin, 1561–1629, English statesman, leading promoter of the colony in Virginia; son of Archbishop Edwin Sandys. He studied law and was first returned to Parliament in 1586. His *Europae Speculum* (1605), published after an extended tour abroad beginning in 1593, revealed a remarkably tolerant attitude toward Roman Catholics for an Englishman of that period. Sandys was knighted (1603), reentered Parliament (1604), and became a leading figure in the parliamentary opposition to King James I. He was a member of several chartered companies, including the LONDON COMPANY, of which he became treasurer in 1619. As leader of the liberal faction within the company, Sandys was responsible for many of the progressive features that characterized the last years of the company's control over Virginia, including the introduction of representative government in the first house of burgesses (1619). The king prevented his reelection as treasurer in 1620, but despite opposition from this and other formidable quarters he continued to wield great influence until the king annulled the company's charter in 1624.

Sandys, George, 1578–1644, English poet and traveler, b. Yorkshire, son of Archbishop Edwin Sandys. He was educated at Oxford and in 1610 began an extended tour of Europe and the Middle East, which he wrote about in *A Relation of a Journey* (1615). In 1621 he became a treasurer of the London Company. He accompanied (1621) the new governor, Sir Francis Wyatt, to Virginia, where he remained until 1631, serving three terms on the governor's council. While in Virginia, Sandys produced his most famous work, a translation of Ovid's *Metamorphoses* (1626). His other works include paraphrases of the Psalms, hymns, and a translation of a work of Grotius under the title *Christ's Passion: A Tragedy* (1640). See his works, ed. by Richard Hooper (1968); biography by R. B. Davis (1955).

San Felipe (săn fəlē'pā), pueblo (1970 pop. 1,187), Sandoval co., N central N.Mex., on the Rio Grande; founded early 18th cent. The inhabitants are Pueblo Indians of the Keresan linguistic stock. Ceremonial dances are held in May and December.

San Fernando (săn fərnăn'dō), city (1970 pop. 119,565), Buenos Aires prov., E Argentina. It is a district administrative center in the Greater Buenos Aires area. The city was established in 1806 to replace the port of Las Conchas, which had been destroyed by a storm. An important landmark is the Juan N. Madero museum and library.

San Fernando (sän färnän'dō), city (1970 pop. 60,167), Cádiz prov., S Spain, in Andalusia. An Atlantic port, it has a naval academy and arsenal, naval workshops, and an observatory. Much salt is obtained from nearby marshes by evaporation.

San Fernando (săn fərnăn'dō), city (1970 pop. 37,313), Trinidad and Tobago, on the Gulf of Paria. It is the country's second largest city and a commercial center for S Trinidad.

San Fernando, city (1970 pop. 16,571), Los Angeles co., S Calif., in the San Fernando valley; inc. 1911. It has garment and electronic industries. The valley was first entered by white men in 1769, and from early days it was used for journeys to N California. Gold was found in 1842 before the big gold strike. Founded in 1874, the city is the oldest in the valley. San Fernando suffered extensive damage in the 1971 earthquake. To the southeast is Hansen Dam, and San Fernando Mission (1797) is nearby.

Sanford. 1 City (1970 pop. 17,393), seat of Seminole co., central Fla., on Lake Monroe and the St. Johns River; inc. 1877. It is an agricultural center where citrus fruit and vegetables (chiefly celery) are processed. Electronic equipment, boats, clothing, and aluminum products are also manufactured. The city was founded (1871) on the site of a trading post established (1837) near old Fort Mellon. A naval academy and a junior college are there. **2** Industrial town (1970 pop. 15,812), York co., SW Maine, on the Mousam River; inc. 1768. It was formerly a textile and garment manufacturing center, but there are now diversified industries. The town includes the unincorporated village of Springvale, seat of Nasson College. Nearby ocean beaches and recreational facilities attract summer vacationers. **3** City (1970 pop. 11,716), seat of Lee co., central N.C.; inc. 1874. It is a processing center in a rich agricultural region. The city has a large tobacco market and is also one of the country's major brick-manufacturing cities. Sanford is in a popular year-round golf resort area. A technical institute is there.

Sanford National Recreation Area, former name of Lake Meredith National Recreation Area; see NATIONAL PARKS AND MONUMENTS (table).

San Francisco (săn frănsĭs'kō), city (1970 pop. 715,674), coextensive with San Francisco co., W Calif., on the tip of a peninsula between the Pacific Ocean and San Francisco Bay, which are connected by the strait known as the Golden Gate; inc. 1850. It is the center of the web of busy industrial cities in the San Francisco Bay area, the marketplace for a large agricultural and mining region, the focus of many transportation routes, and the financial and insurance center of the West Coast. San Francisco and the bay area form the largest port on the West Coast and are a major center of trade with the Orient, Hawaii, and Alaska. Industries include food processing, shipbuilding, petroleum refining, and the manufacture of metal products and chemicals. With its educational institutions, theaters, publishing firms, and musical organizations, the San Francisco area is a major cultural center of the West Coast and one of the greatest in the nation. On his voyage around the world, Sir Francis Drake stopped (1579) in what is now the San Francisco Bay area. The city was founded in 1776, when a Spanish presidio and a mission were established at a location chosen by Juan Bautista de Anza. The little settlement called Yerba Buena, although much visited by ships en route to the Far East, was still a village when the Mexican War broke out and a naval force under Commodore John D. Sloat took it (1846) in the name of the United States. It was then named San Francisco. When gold was discovered in California in 1848, San Francisco had a population of c.800; two years later it was incorporated with a population of c.25,000. The rush of gold seekers, adventurers, and settlers brought a period of lawlessness, when the wicked BARBARY COAST flourished and the VIGILANTES were organized to keep peace. The city took on a cosmopolitan air, with newcomers arriving from all over the world. In this period the first Chinese settled in the city, and today San Francisco's famous Chinatown is the largest settlement of Chinese in the United States. In the years after the gold rush, San Francisco continued to grow as California became linked overland with the East, by the pony express in 1860 and by the transcontinental railroad in 1869. On the morning of April 18, 1906, the great San Andreas fault, which extends up and down the California coast, settled violently; and San Francisco was shaken by an earthquake which, together with the sweeping three-day fire that followed, all but destroyed the city. It was one of the most spectacular disasters in the nation's history. The city was quickly rebuilt. The opening of the Panama Canal, a boon to the city's trade, was celebrated by the Panama-Pacific Exposition of 1915. By the time of the Golden Gate International Exposition (1939-40) the whole San Francisco Bay area was heavily industrialized, and it had become the leading commercial center of the West Coast. In World War II, San Francisco was the major mainland supply point and port of embarkation for the war in the Pacific. The United Nations Charter (1945) was drafted at San Francisco, and the Japanese Peace Treaty (1951) was signed there. The spectacular SAN FRANCISCO-OAKLAND BAY BRIDGE was opened in 1936, and the GOLDEN GATE BRIDGE in 1937. San Francisco is one of the most gracious and picturesque cities in the country. Its natural beauty and mild climate make it particularly attractive as a residential city, and many homes with dramatic views of the city and surrounding waters dot the steep hills upon which San Francisco is situated. The individuality of the city, almost legendary in the United States, is compounded of such things as the San Francisco fogs; soaring bridges; cable cars (now operated chiefly for tourists); busy Market St., with its department stores and office buildings; the Embarcadero, crowded with docks, ships, and cargoes; Fisherman's Wharf, famous for its seafood restaurants and the center of the city's seafood industry; Chinatown, with its Oriental architecture, tearooms, and temples; Telegraph Hill, where in earlier times a signal tower sent word to the city of the arrival of ships; Nob Hill, once the home of millionaires; and Russian Hill. The city is also noted for its many fine restaurants, serving both foreign and domestic cuisine; and atop the Mark Hopkins Hotel is one of the most famous cocktail lounges in the world. Also of interest to the visitor are Mission Dolores (1782; at first called San Francisco de Asís); many old mansions built by railroad and mining kings; Golden Gate Park, where the California Academy of Sciences has two natural history museums, an aquarium, and a planetarium; the Cliff House on Point Lobos, overlooking the Pacific and the rocks, 100 ft (30.5 m) offshore, inhabited by sea lions; the San Francisco Zoological Gardens (Fleishhacker Zoo); and the civic center, with a distinctive Renaissance-style city hall, a public library, and the municipally owned opera house, where performances of the symphony orchestra and ballet and opera companies are held. Art museums include the SAN FRANCISCO MUSEUM OF ART, the M. H. De Young Memorial Museum, and the Palace of the Legion of Honor. Institutions of higher learning in the city include California State Univ., San Francisco, the Univ. of San Francisco, the Hastings College of Law, the Univ. of California, San Francisco, Lone Mountain College (formerly San Francisco College for Women), and several theological seminaries and junior colleges. The Presidio of San Francisco, the largest (1,542 acres/624 hectares) military encampment within the confines of an American city, is the headquarters of the Sixth U.S. Army, as well as the site of Letterman General Hospital and a national military cemetery. Continuously fortified since its establishment in 1776, the Presidio still contains remnants of the original Spanish adobe buildings, now incorporated into the officers' club. See Federal Writers' Project, *San Francisco: The Bay and Its Cities* (rev. ed. 1973); Samuel Dickson, *San Francisco Profiles* (3 vol., 1947-55); Harold Gilliam, *The Face of San Francisco* (1960); H. G. Bolton, *An Outpost of an Empire* (1930, repr. 1966); and O. Lewis, *San Francisco: Mission to Metropolis* (1966).

San Francisco Bay, 50 mi (80 km) long and from 3 to 13 mi (4.8-21 km) wide, W Calif.; entered through the Golden Gate, a strait between two peninsulas. The bay is as deep as 100 ft (30 m) in spots, with a channel 50 ft (15 m) deep maintained through the sand bar off the Golden Gate. San Francisco is on the southern peninsula; on the northern peninsula are the residential cities of Marin co., while on the eastern shore of the crescent-shaped bay are such industrial cities as Alameda, Oakland, Berkeley, and Richmond. The Santa Clara Valley, part of a great depression paralleling the coast, is the landward extension of the bay. Angel Island, Alcatraz, and Yerba Buena Island are in the bay. With San Pablo Bay and Suisun Bay, the natural harbor of San Francisco Bay is one of the best in the world. On those secondary bays and on Carquinez Strait, which connects them, are the cities of Vallejo, Benicia, Martinez, and Pittsburg. The bay area is served by a network of bridges, most important of which are the Golden Gate, San Francisco-Oakland Bay, Richmond-San Rafael, and San Mateo bridges. The Trans-Bay Tube, a tunnel 3.5 mi (5.6 km) long between San Francisco and Oakland, is the longest underwater rapid transit tube in the world. The tunnel was especially constructed to absorb earthquake tremors. Several U.S. navy facilities are located in the region. The English navigator Sir Francis Drake discovered the bay in 1579, but the Spanish explored it more fully in the late 18th cent.

San Francisco de Macorís (thä mäkōrēs'), city (1970 pop. 43,941), N Dominican Republic. It is the commercial and processing center for an agricultural region. Its port is Sanchez.

San Francisco-Oakland Bay Bridge, double-decked structure, W Calif.; built 1933-36. It has a total length of 8.25 mi (13.2 km). From San Francisco it crosses the bay to Yerba Buena Island, where a tunnel connects with spans leading to Oakland and Berkeley.

San Francisco Peaks, N Ariz., N of Flagstaff, consisting of Mt. Humphreys, 12,670 ft (3,862 m); Mt. Agassiz, 12,340 ft (3,761 m); and Mt. Fremont, 11,940 ft (3,639 m).

San Gabriel (săn gā'brēəl), residential city (1970 pop. 29,336), Los Angeles co., S Calif.; inc. 1913. Toys are manufactured there. An annual three-day fiesta celebrates the founding (1771) of the San Gabriel mission, which was partly rebuilt after an earthquake in 1812.

San Gabriel Mountains, S Calif., E and NE of Los Angeles, running c.50 mi (80 km) westward from Cajon Pass. San Antonio Peak (10,080 ft/3,072 m) is the highest of the range. Citrus fruits are raised on the southern foothills.

Sangallo (säng-gäl'lō), three Italian Renaissance architects, two brothers and their nephew. **Giuliano da Sangallo,** 1445-1516, designed the Church of Santa Maria delle Carceri at Prato and palaces in Florence. After Bramante's death Giuliano worked on St. Peter's in Rome with Raphael and Fra Giocondo. He was a late follower of Brunelleschi, interested in clarity and elegance of form. His brother, **Antonio da Sangallo,** the elder, 1455-1534, moved from reminiscences of Giuliano's manner to a High Renaissance massiveness, seen in the domed Church of the Madonna di San Biagio at Montepulciano. **Antonio da Sangallo,** the younger, 1485-1546, their nephew, whose real name was Antonio Cordiani, was the most noted of the three. He collaborated with Bramante in the latter's final years. For Cardinal Alessandro Farnese (later Pope Paul III) he designed the Farnese Palace, the architectural epitome of Roman Renaissance palaces. After Raphael's death Antonio was appointed (1520) to succeed him in the construction of St. Peter's, although his complex plan for its completion was not accepted. At the Vatican he designed the Sala Regia and the Pauline Chapel. He developed a severe, logical, and weighty style.

Sanger, Frederick (săng'ər), 1918-, British biochemist, grad. Cambridge Univ. (B.A., 1939; Ph.D., 1943). He continued his research at Cambridge after 1943. He won the 1958 Nobel Prize in Chemistry for isolating and identifying the amino acid components of which the insulin molecule, a protein, is constituted.

Sanger, Margaret (Higgins), 1883-1966, American leader in the BIRTH-CONTROL movement, b. Corning, N.Y. Personal experience and work as a public-health nurse convinced her that family limitation, especially where poverty was a factor, was a necessary step in social progress. She studied in London with Havelock Ellis and others and, back in the United States, began her campaign almost single-handed. Indicted in 1915 for sending birth-control information through the mails and arrested the next year for conducting a birth-control clinic in Brooklyn, Sanger gradually won support from the public and the courts. A clinic opened (1923) in New York City functioned until the 1970s. She organized the first American (1921) and international (1925) birth-control conferences and formed (1923) the National Committee on Federal Legislation for Birth Control. She was president of the committee until its dissolution (1937) after birth control under medical direction was legalized in most of the states. She visited many countries in Europe, Africa, and Asia, lecturing and helping to establish clinics. Her books include *Woman and the New Race* (1920), *Happiness in Marriage* (1926), and an autobiography (1938). See D. M. Kennedy, *Birth Control in America: The Career of Margaret Sanger* (1970).

Sanger, city (1970 pop. 10,088), Fresno co., S central Calif., in the San Joaquin Valley; inc. 1911. It is a shipping and processing center for agricultural products.

San Germán (sän härmän'), town (1970 pop. 11,613), SW Puerto Rico. It is the site of the Porta Coeli Convent (built 1511), one of the oldest churches in the Americas; it now serves as a museum. San Germán is also the seat of the Inter American Univ. of Puerto Rico.

San Germano: see CASSINO, Italy.

sangha: see BUDDHISM.

Sangihe Islands (säng-gē'ə) or **Sangi Islands** (säng'ē), volcanic group (314 sq mi/813 sq km), Indonesia, NE of Celebes. Tahuna is the chief town and port. The islands are mountainous, forested, and fertile; tropical woods, rattan, copra, and nutmeg are produced. The largest island, also called Sangihe, has an active volcano, Mt. Awu, 6,002 ft (1,829 m) high. The area came under Dutch control in 1677.

San Gimignano (sän jēmēnyä'nō), town (1971 pop. 7,652), Tuscany, central Italy. It is a tourist center that has fully preserved its medieval aspect. The city walls, the palaces, and the celebrated 14 towers (out of an original 72) still stand as they did in the 13th cent. Also of note in the town are the cathedral (12th cent.; damaged in World War II), which is rich in works of art, and the Church of St. Augustine (13th cent.), with frescoes by Benozzo Gozzoli.

Sangli (säng'glē'), town (1971 pop. 115,052), Maharashtra state, SE India, on the Krishna River. It is an agricultural market.

Sangre de Cristo Mountains (săng'grē də krĭs'tō), part of the S Rocky Mts., extending c.220 mi (350 km) from S central Colo. into N central N.Mex. Noted elevations in Colorado are Blanca Peak (14,317 ft/4,364 m), the highest, lying in the Sierra Blanca section, and Kit Carson Peak (14,100 ft/4,298 m); the Truchas peaks are in New Mexico. Most of the range is included in national forests.

Sangster, Charles, 1822-93, Canadian poet, b. Ontario. At first an imitator of Byron, he became with the publication of *Hesperus and Other Poems and Lyrics* (1860) the first notable Canadian poet to make use of native themes and settings. See biography by W. D. Hamilton (1971).

Sanhedrin (sănhĕd'rĭn), ancient Jewish legal and religious institution in Jerusalem that exercised the functions of a court. The accounts of it in the Mishna do not correspond to those in Josephus or in the New Testament; most scholars, following the theory of Adolf Büchler, maintain that there probably were two Sanhedrins—one political and civil, the other, known as the Great Sanhedrin, purely religious. The former, consisting of 23 members, was like a legal court; the latter, with 71 members, was presided over by a *nasi* [prince]. The political court perished after the destruction of the Temple (A.D. 70), but the religious Sanhedrin continued in existence as the rabbinic patriarchate until about A.D. 425. In 1807, Napoleon appointed a "French Sanhedrin" of 71 members, made up of both rabbis and laymen, to consider questions of relationship between Jews and the state. See S. B. Hoenig, *The Great Sanhedrin* (1953); Hugo Mantel, *Studies in the History of the Sanhedrin* (1961).

San Ildefonso (sän ēldāfōn'sō) or **La Granja** (lä gräng'hä), town (1970 pop. 4,164), Segovia prov., central Spain, in Old Castile. Near the town is the Spanish royal summer residence, called La Granja, built by Philip V (1721-23) in imitation of Versailles. It consists of the palace, the collegiate church, and the celebrated gardens, laid out by French landscape architects.

San Ildefonso (săn ēl"dəfōn'sō), pueblo (1970 est. pop. 375), N central N.Mex., on the Rio Grande, established in the early 1700s. The inhabitants speak a language of the Tanoan family. The pueblo is famous for its excellent pottery and paintings, and many of its artists have won individual fame. On Jan. 23, the day of fiesta, ceremonial dances (e.g., the buffalo and Comanche dances) are performed. The Puye cliff dwellings are to the north. See William Whitman, *The Pueblo Indians of San Ildefonso* (1947, repr. 1969).

San Ildefonso, Treaty of, any of several treaties signed at the royal residence of San Ildefonso, Spain. The Treaty of San Ildefonso of **1796** was an alliance of France with Spain against Great Britain in the French Revolutionary Wars. The secret Treaty of San Ildefonso of **1800** was actually a draft confirmed by two later treaties (March, 1801; Oct., 1802). Spain retroceded Louisiana to France and was compensated by the creation in Tuscany of the kingdom of Etruria, which was given to the duke of Parma, son-in-law of Charles IV of Spain. Although Napoleon Bonaparte agreed never to alienate Louisiana, he disregarded the treaty and sold Louisiana to the United States three years later.

San Isidro (sän ēsē'thrō), city (1970 pop. 250,008), Buenos Aires prov., E Argentina. It is a district administrative center in the Greater Buenos Aires area. San Isidro grew around a chapel built in 1706. The city is known for its cathedral and historical museums.

sanitary landfill: see SOLID WASTE.

sanitary science, principles of health preservation, embracing HYGIENE, on an individual level, and PUBLIC HEALTH, on a communal level. Those who specialize in sanitary science are sanitary engineers. They endeavor to eliminate or reduce health hazards associated with the supply of water and milk, the collection and disposal of sewage and refuse, and the prevalence of rodents and insects. Conditions of noise, air pollution, and improper food handling that threaten the well-being of the public are also their concern. Sanitary engineers have had to develop methods for safely disposing of radioactive waste material at sea and on land. See REFUSE. See G. E. Mitchell, *Sanitation, Drainage and Water Supply* (6th ed. 1960). E. S. Hopkins et al., *Practice of Sanitation* (4th ed. 1970); J. A. Salvato, *Environmental Engineering and Sanitation* (2d ed. 1972).

sanitation: see PLUMBING; SANITARY SCIENCE.

San Jacinto, river, c.130 mi (210 km) long, rising in SE Texas as the West Fork and flowing S to Galveston Bay. Its chief tributary is Buffalo Bayou, and both the bayou and the lower river are used for the Houston ship channel. In 1836, Texans under Sam Houston surprised and defeated a larger force of Mexicans in the final and decisive battle of the Texas Revolution on the San Jacinto near the mouth of Buffalo Bayou. The battlefield, a national historic landmark, is in San Jacinto State Park, which has a monument 570 ft (173 m) high; April 21, San Jacinto Day, is a Texas holiday. The U.S.S. *Texas* is moored near the park. Dams on tributaries include the Barker Dam (39 ft/12 m high; 14 mi/23 km long; completed 1945) on Buffalo Bayou and Addicks Dam (50 ft/15 m high; 12 mi/19 km long; completed 1948) on South Mayde Creek.

San Joaquin (săn wäkēn'), river, c.320 mi (510 km) long, rising in the Sierra Nevada, E Calif., and flowing W then N through the Central Valley to form a large delta with the Sacramento River near Suisun Bay, an arm of San Francisco Bay. The San Joaquin is navigable c.40 mi (60 km) for oceangoing vessels to Stockton. The Mokelumne, Tuolumne, Merced, and Fresno are its chief tributaries. The wide southern part of the basin between the Sierra Nevada and the Coast Range is usually called the San Joaquin Valley, although it includes independent rivers such as the Kings and the Kern. Between Stockton in the north and Bakersfield in the south are many cities, notably Fresno, Modesto, and Merced. The CENTRAL VALLEY PROJECT, undertaken largely to bring surplus water from the north to make the San Joaquin Valley more fertile, has as one of its units Friant Dam on the San Joaquin; the San Luis Dam is on the San Luis River.

San José (sän hōsā'), city (1968 est. pop. 198,523), central Costa Rica, capital and largest city of Costa Rica. San José is the economic, political, and social center of Costa Rican life, dominating the central plateau and the nearby towns, ALAJUELA and HEREDIA. During colonial times the main industry of the region was tobacco raising; by the mid-19th cent. the city had become the center of a coffee-producing area. It is the national distribution point for imports. San José was founded (c.1738) at the beginning of the westward expansion from CARTAGO; with independence from Spain (1821) it became the center of the country's liberal element and, in 1823, the capital. A modern city, with parks and fine public buildings, including the elaborate National Theater, it has a mixture of Spanish and North American architecture, with many houses set back to have lawns and gardens fronting the street. Often seen in the city are tiny, brightly painted oxcarts characteristic of the region. San José is a stop for international air lines, the hub of the highway system, and the center of the Pacific and Caribbean railroads. It has a university (founded 1844). In 1960 it was the site of two conferences of foreign ministers of the member states of the Organization of American States.

San José, town (1964 pop. 17,956), SW Guatemala, on the Pacific Ocean. It is a rail terminus and, although the harbor is exposed and cargoes are handled by lighters, the major Pacific port of Guatemala.

San Jose (sănəzā', săn hōzā'), city (1970 pop. 445,779), seat of Santa Clara co., W Calif.; founded 1777, inc. 1850. It is in a rich fruit-growing area and has wineries and a large number of food-processing industries. Business machines, atomic-power equipment, and food machinery are among the manufactures. The first state legislature (1849) met there, and San Jose was the state capital from 1849 to 1851. Among the city's parks are Alum Rock Park, with mineral springs; Kelley Park, with a zoo and a Japanese garden and tea house; and Rosicrucian Park, with an Egyptian museum, a science museum, and a planetarium. California State Univ. at San Jose and a junior college are in the city. To the north lies Mission San Jose de Guadalupe (1797) and to the west is Mission Santa Clara de Asís (1777). Lick Observatory is on nearby Mt. Hamilton.

San José or **San José de Mayo** (sän hōsā'; -thā, mä'yō), city (1963 pop. 27,478), capital of San José dept., S Uruguay, on the San José River. It is a commercial center for a large grain and livestock region. The city was founded in 1783 by settlers from Spain, and was Uruguay's provisional capital in 1825-26. San José is noted for its architecture. Landmarks include a monument to Uruguayan patriots.

San Jose Mission National Historic Site: see NATIONAL PARKS AND MONUMENTS (table).

San Jose scale, common name for a SCALE INSECT, *Aspidiotus perniciosus,* introduced from China into San Jose, Calif., c.1870 on nursery stock. The insect has since spread throughout much of the United States and Canada. It is found in the commercial fruit-growing areas throughout the world and is a serious pest of apples, pears, peaches, plums, sweet cherries, gooseberries, and many other trees and shrubs. Only the winged males and young scales are mobile. The young nymphs, or crawlers, move about for a few hours in search of a good feeding spot; then they molt, lose their functional legs and antennae, and secrete a resinous waxy shell, or armor, under which they feed by sucking the sap of the host plant until they become adults. The sedentary female mates and gives birth to several hundred living young while still securely under the protection of the scale, which it never leaves. Two to six generations are produced per year, with an estimated 30 million progeny possible from a single female during one year. Infested trees show a decrease in vigor, take on a gray appearance from the low, conical, overlapping scales, and eventually die if the scale is not controlled. The pest is dispersed by being carried on the bodies of larger insects, on the feet and beaks of birds, by wind, and by shipment of infested nursery stock. The San Jose scale is classified in the phylum ARTHROPODA, class Insecta, order Homoptera, family Diaspididae.

San Juan (săn wän, Span. sän hwän), city (1970 pop. 112,500), capital of San Juan prov., W Argentina. It is a commercial and industrial center in an agricultural region. Wine is the chief product, and vineyards dot the picturesque landscape. Fruits and grains are grown, cattle are raised, and the province is rich in minerals. Founded in 1562, San Juan figured prominently in the civil wars of the 19th cent. Many Argentine statesmen, including Domingo Faustino Sarmiento, were born in San Juan.

San Juan, city (1970 pop. 452,749), capital and chief port and commercial center of Puerto Rico, NE Puerto Rico. Sugar, tobacco, coffee, and fruit are exported, mainly to the United States. San Juan's industries include tourism, sugar refining, rum distilling, metalworking, publishing, and the manufacture of jewelry, clothing, shoes, textiles, furniture, pharmaceuticals, electronic equipment, machine tools, and plastics. The city's old section, situated on two rocky islets guarding one of the finest harbors in the West Indies, is linked by bridges with the mainland. The bay was named Puerto Rico [rich port] by Ponce de León, who in 1508 founded a settlement at nearby Caparra. In 1521 the settlement was moved across the bay to the site of present-day San Juan. Strongly fortified, it withstood attacks by the English buccaneers Drake and Hawkins in 1595 but succumbed for a few months in 1598 to George Clifford, earl of Cumberland, and was sacked by the Dutch in 1625. San Juan gained increasing importance as a West Indian port during the 18th and 19th cent. U.S. troops occupied the city during the Spanish-American War in 1898. In the old city, whose narrow streets, small shops, and houses with overhanging balconies recall a colonial atmosphere, there are impressive historic buildings: El Morro castle (begun 1539), which commands the harbor entrance and is a national monument; San Cristóbal castle (begun 1631), originally a Spanish fort; and La Fortaleza (begun 1529), a former fort now used as the governor's official residence. Other San Juan landmarks include San José Church (founded c.1523), the oldest church in continuous use in the Western Hemisphere; Casa Blanca (1523); and the Cathedral of San Juan Bautista, which contains the tomb of Ponce de León. Also in the city are the Univ. of Puerto Rico and its School of Tropical Medicine, the College of the Sacred Heart, the Institute of Puerto Rican Culture, and the Carnegie Library. Nearby are several fine resort beaches (notably the Condado and Isla Verde), which attract winter tourists from North America. San Juan has an international airport and is the site of a U.S. air base.

San Juan, pueblo (1970 est. pop. 1,100), Rio Arriba co., N N.Mex., on the Rio Grande; settled 1598 by Juan de Oñate. A Franciscan mission was later established. It was the home of Popé, the medicine man who led the Indians in the Pueblo revolt of 1680. Today the inhabitants are still Pueblo Indians who speak a language of the Tanoan family and produce Indian arts and crafts. The principal festival is held on June 24 in honor of St. John the Baptist.

San Juan (sän hwän), river, c.110 mi (180 km) long, flowing from the southeast corner of Lake Nicaragua E to the Caribbean Sea, near the port of San Juan del Norte. The lower course is the boundary between Nicaragua and Costa Rica. The deep navigable river would be a vital link in the often proposed Nicaragua Canal.

San Juan (săn wän), river, c.400 mi (640 km) long, rising in the San Juan mts., SW Colo., and flowing generally W through N. Mex. and Utah to Lake Powell on the Colorado River. NAVAJO DAM is on the river. The San Juan is used extensively for irrigation; vegetables, fruits, and grains are grown in the river valley.

San Juan Bautista (săn wän bətē'stə), city (1970 pop. 1,164), San Benito co., W Calif., in the fertile San Juan valley; inc. 1869. The town, which is rich in history, is a tourist center. The nearby mission of San Juan Bautista (1797), largest of the California missions, draws thousands of visitors every year.

San Juan Boundary Dispute, controversy between the United States and Great Britain over the U.S.-British Columbia boundary. It is sometimes called the Northwest Boundary Dispute. The difficulty arose from the faulty wording of the treaty of 1846 that established the northern boundary of the Oregon Territory. That instrument set the boundary as a line through the middle of the channel between the mainland and Vancouver Island and through the middle of Juan de Fuca Strait. The strait, however, breaks into several channels, and between the two main ones—Haro Strait and Rosario Strait—lie the San Juan Islands. Ownership of the islands, especially San Juan Island, was disputed. The quarrel, unsettled by diplomatic negotiations, was brought to a crisis in 1859, when George E. PICKETT and U.S. troops occupied San Juan Island. British war vessels promptly appeared. No armed conflict resulted because Gen. Winfield Scott, commander in chief of American armies, went to the scene and arranged with the British for joint occupation of San Juan. Until 1872 there were soldiers of both powers on the island. Attempts to appoint a neutral arbitrator were defeated by the U.S. Senate until the Washington Treaty of 1871. Emperor William I of Germany, as arbitrator in 1872, decided upon Haro Strait as the line, thus giving the San Juan archipelago to the United States.

San Juan Capistrano (săn wän kăpĭsträ'nō), city (1970 pop. 3,781), Orange co., S Calif.; inc. 1961. Although San Juan Capistrano has a small industrial park that manufactures sailboats, plastics, novelty clothing, and other items, the economy is based chiefly on tourism. Padre Junípero Serra founded a mission there in 1776 and named it after St. John of Capistrano, a Crusader. The mission church, completed in 1806, was ruined by an earthquake in 1812, but the chapel where Father Serra said Mass is still in daily use. Mexico nationalized mission lands in the early 1840s; President Abraham Lincoln returned the mission to the Roman Catholic Church in 1865. It is said that swallows come to the ruins of the church every March 19, the Feast Day of St. Joseph, and depart on Oct. 23, the death date of St. John of Capistrano. An annual fiesta celebrates the arrival of the swallows.

San Juan del Norte (săn hwän dĕl nôr'tä), small town, SE Nicaragua, on the Caribbean Sea. Small quantities of bananas and hardwoods are exported. Also called Greytown, it was occupied (1848) by the British to secure control of the MOSQUITO COAST and to check the U.S. efforts to build an interoceanic canal. The port became the thriving eastern terminus of a transisthmian transport company operated by Cornelius VANDERBILT in the gold rush to California. In 1854 it was bombarded by the U.S. warship *Cyane* in retaliation for insults to the U.S. minister and damage to U.S. property in Nicaragua. San Juan was important in the filibustering activities of William WALKER.

San Juan del Sur (dĕl so͞or), town, SW Nicaragua, on the Pacific Ocean. It was the Pacific terminus of the transit route across the isthmus during the California gold rush and is today connected by a short railroad to RIVAS. Coffee, sugar, cocoa, and balsam are exported from San Juan del Sur.

San Juan Hill (săn wän, Span. sän hwän), Oriente prov., E Cuba, near the city of Santiago de Cuba. It was the scene (July, 1898) of a battle in the Spanish-American War, in which Theodore Roosevelt and the Rough Riders took part.

San Juan Islands (săn wän), archipelago of 172 islands constituting San Juan co. (1970 pop. 3,856), NW Wash., E of Vancouver Island. The islands were discovered and named c.1790 by Spanish explorers. The islands were the subject of the SAN JUAN BOUNDARY DISPUTE between Great Britain and the United States; their ownership was decided in 1872. San Juan, Orcas, and Lopez islands are the largest of the group. San Juan Island is a national historical park (see NATIONAL PARKS AND MONUMENTS, table).

San Juan National Historic Site: see NATIONAL PARKS AND MONUMENTS (table).

Sankt Pölten (zängkt pöl'tən), city (1971 pop. 43,300), Lower Austria prov., N central Austria. It is an industrial center and rail junction. Manufactures include machinery, textiles, and paper. Chartered in the 12th cent., Sankt Pölten has a Romanesque cathedral (consecrated 1150; rebuilt in the 18th cent.) and a town hall of the 16th–17th cent.

Sankt Wolfgang (vôlf'gäng), town, Upper Austria prov., in the SALZKAMMERGUT, on the Wolfgang See, a lake. It is a popular resort, famous for the White Horse Inn. A noteworthy attraction is the great altar carved (1481) by Michael Pacher for the parish church (15th–16th cent.).

San Leandro (săn lēăn'drō), residential and industrial city (1970 pop. 68,698), Alameda co., W Calif., on San Francisco Bay; inc. 1872. Food products, metal items, transportation equipment, electronic products, containers, and furniture are among its many manufactures. There are also notable orchid, gardenia, and rose greenhouses. Settled by José Joaquin Estudillo in 1837, it was county seat from 1854 to 1871.

San Lorenzo, uninc. city (1970 pop. 24,633), Alameda co., W Calif. It is chiefly residential.

Sanlúcar de Barrameda (sänlo͞o'kär dā bärämä'thä), city (1970 pop. 41,072), Cádiz prov., S Spain, on the Guadalquivir River estuary, in Andalusia. Manzanilla, a white wine, is a noted product. The port of Bonanza, 3 mi (4.8 km) upstream, has an active trade. Sanlúcar flourished after the discovery of America when all ships passed it to reach Seville. Columbus sailed from Sanlúcar in 1498, and Magellan in 1519. A medieval castle, the palace of the dukes of Medina Sidonia, and a 14th-century church are of interest.

San Luis, city (1970 pop. 59,113), capital of San Luis prov., W central Argentina. The city is the commercial center of an area producing cattle, grain, and wine. It is also a popular resort. Founded in 1594, San Luis was burned and sacked by Indians in 1712 and 1720.

San Luis Obispo (săn lo͞o'ĭs ōbĭs'pō), city (1970 pop. 28,036), seat of San Luis Obispo co., S Calif., near San Luis Obispo Bay; inc. 1856. Furniture, electronics, building materials, and food items are among its products. In 1846, Frémont seized the city for the United States. To escape torrential rains he quartered in the Franciscan mission, San Luis Obispo de Tolosa (1772), which is now a state landmark. Many historic buildings are preserved in the mission plaza. The city is the seat of California Polytechnic State Univ., San Luis Obispo. Los Padres National Forest is to the east.

San Luis Potosí (sän lo͞oēs' pōtōsē'), state (1970 pop. 1,257,028), 24,417 sq mi (63,240 sq km), central Mexico. SAN LUIS POTOSÍ is the capital. Most of the state lies on the eastern tablelands of Mexico's central plateau. Except in the humid tropical Pánuco River valley in the extreme east, near the Gulf of Mexico, the climate is mild and dry. Generally level, with a mean elevation of 6,000 ft (1,829 m), the plateau is broken by spurs of the Sierra Madre Oriental; it is largely desert in the north. Rainfall is light, and rivers are few; thus, despite fertile soil, agriculture is practiced mainly for subsistence. Livestock raising is important in the uplands. Hides, tallow, and wool are exported. Some timber is cut, but the state's tropical forests remain mostly unexploited. San Luis Potosí has rich silver, gold, copper, zinc, and bismuth deposits and is one of Mexico's leading mining states and oil producers.

San Luis Potosí, city (1970 pop. 207, 176), capital of San Luis Potosí state, central Mexico. Situated on a plain almost entirely surrounded by low mountains, the city is a mining and agricultural distribution center and a rail junction. Industries include foundries, smelters, and factories producing clothing, leather goods, and beverages. Founded in 1576, San Luis Potosí was strategically important in colonial times and during the wars of the republican period. The patriot Francisco I. Madero, who was briefly imprisoned in the city in 1910, later named his revolutionary call to arms the Plan of San Luis Potosí. The city has narrow cobbled streets and solid colonial architecture. Among its major landmarks is the San Francisco convent.

San Marcos (săn mär'kəs), city (1970 pop. 18,860), seat of Hays co., S central Texas, on the San Marcos River; inc. 1877. Meat is packed, and cattle feed, plastic products, heating equipment, and furniture are among the manufactures. The city is situated on the Balcones fault, where prehistoric earthquakes split the earth, releasing spring water to the surface (the San Marcos River was thus formed) and creating underground caves. Aquarena Springs, a major tourist attraction, features rides in glass-bottom boats and an underwater theater. Also of interest are Wonder Cave and many historic 19th-century homes. San Marcos is the seat of Southwest Texas State Univ., a large job training center, a military academy, and a U.S. fish hatchery.

San Marcos, University of, at Lima, Peru; the first university in South America; founded 1551 by the Spanish king Charles I (Holy Roman Emperor Charles V) and recognized by papal bull in 1571; closed at the time of the establishment of the republic of Peru and reinaugurated in 1861. It has programs in medicine; pharmacy and biochemistry; dentistry; veterinary science; chemistry and chemical engineering; education; mathematics and physics; geology and geography; biology; social science; law and political science; philosophy, psychology, and art; linguistics, literature, and philology; education; administrative science and accountancy; and economics.

San Marino (sän mărē'nō), republic (1972 est. pop. 18,320), 24 sq mi (62 sq km), in the Apennines near the Adriatic Sea, SW of Rimini, N central Italy. It is the world's smallest republic and claims to be Europe's oldest existing state. The capital is San Marino (1971 est. pop. 4,350); Serravalle is the only other town. Virtually all of the republic's inhabitants speak Italian and are Roman Catholic. Farming is the main occupation; cereals and fruit are grown, and

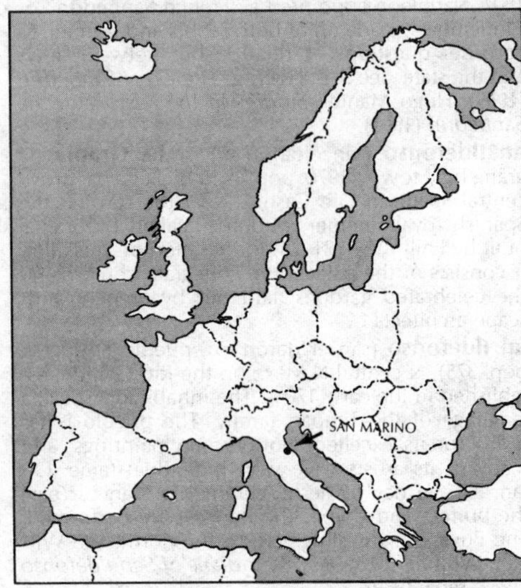

cattle and hogs are raised. Major sources of revenue are tourism and the sale of postage stamps, mainly for collectors. Woolens, wine, and limestone are exported. The republic receives an annual subsidy from Italy in return for having renounced certain rights, such as establishing a broadcasting station and growing tobacco. Although San Marino mints its own coins, Italian and Vatican City currency is in general use. There are highway and rail connections with Italy. According to tradition, Marino, a Christian stonecutter from Dalmatia, took refuge (early 4th cent.) on Mt. Titano (2,300 ft/701 m), the chief geographical feature of present-day San Marino. By the mid-5th cent., a community was formed; because of its relatively inaccessible location and its poverty, it has succeeded, with a few brief interruptions, in maintaining its independence. In 1631 its independence was recognized by the papacy. In 1849, San Marino gave refuge to Garibaldi, the Italian patriot and soldier. Italy and San Marino signed a treaty of friendship and economic cooperation in 1862 (renewed and expanded several times). Volunteers from San Marino served with the Italians in World Wars I and II; Allied aircraft bombed the republic in 1944. Of note in San Marino are the Basilica of Santo Marino; towers (14th-16th cent.) built on each of the three peaks of Mt. Titano; the Gothic government house; and several museums of art. There is a bust of Abraham Lincoln, who in 1861 accepted the honorary citizenship of the republic. Legislative power in San Marino is vested in the popularly elected grand council (made up of 60 members elected to five-year terms); every six months the council appoints two regents (*Capitani reggenti*), who in conjunction with the 10-member council of state form the executive. Following a period of Communist rule (1947–57), a coalition of Christian Democrats and Social Democrats came to power. After the 1969 elections the coalition held 38 of the 60 seats in the grand council. In 1973, the Social Democrats left the coalition and were replaced by the Socialists and the tiny Movement for Statutory Liberties. In 1960 women were given the right to vote, and in 1973 they were granted the right to hold public office.

San Marino (săn mərē'nō), residential city (1970 pop. 14,177), Los Angeles co., S Calif.; inc. 1913. The Henry E. Huntington Library and Art Gallery are there.

San Martín, José de (hōsā' thā sän märtēn'), 1778–1850, South American revolutionist, b. Yapeyú, in present-day Argentina. After service with the Spanish army in Europe, he returned (1812) to join the revolution against Spain in his native country. He superseded Manuel BELGRANO in command of the army against royalist forces in Upper Peru and decided, after some experience, that the attack on the royalist stronghold could best be made through Chile. After training his troops at Mendoza, San Martín accomplished the difficult feat of leading an army across the Andes through Los Patos and Uspallata passes. Ably seconded by Bernardo O'HIGGINS, he defeated (1817) the Spanish at Chacabuco. San Martín was offered the governorship of Chile, which he refused. After a setback at Cancha Rayada, the patriots defeated (1818) the royalists at Maipú and completed the liberation of Chile. San Martín, with the aid of Thomas Cochrane (earl of DUNDONALD), prepared to conquer Peru. Lima was taken (1821), and San Martín became protector of Peru. When Simón BOLÍVAR advanced with the intention of driving out the Spanish, San Martín interviewed (July, 1822) him at Guayaquil and then resigned, leaving the conquest of Peru to Bolívar. San Martín retired from public life and in 1824 went to Europe, where he spent his remaining years in exile and comparative poverty. See Bartolomé Mitre, *The Emancipation of South America* (tr. 1893, repr. 1969); J. C. Metford, *San Martín the Liberator* (1950, repr. 1971).

San Mateo (săn mətā'ō), city (1970 pop. 78,991), San Mateo co., W Calif., on San Francisco Bay; inc. 1894. It is a commercial and retail center. San Mateo, Spanish for St. Matthew, was named by a Spanish expedition in 1776. The area was a Mexican colony from 1822 to 1846. San Mateo's main growth dates from the start of railroad service in 1863. Refugees from the 1906 San Francisco earthquake greatly increased San Mateo's population. The College of San Mateo, a junior college, is in the city. San Mateo Bridge spans San Francisco Bay.

Sanmicheli, Michele (mēkĕ'lā sänmēkĕ'lē), c.1484-1559, Italian architect and engineer. He was influenced by Bramante's works in Rome, and after 1527 worked primarily in Verona, where his manner changed from a harmonious High Renaissance style toward the more complex and discordant rhythms of mannerist art. Typical of his later style is the Palazzo Bevilacqua, Verona. Other examples of his highly refined style include the Church of the Madonna di Campagna near Verona, the Petrucci Chapel in the Church of San Domenico at Orvieto, the Palazzo Grimani in Venice, and the Canossa and Pompei palaces at Verona. See study by E.J. Langenskiold (1938).

San Miguel (sän mēgĕl'), city (1970 est. pop. 52,000), E El Salvador, at the foot of San Miguel volcano (6,996 ft/2,132 m). It has textile and dairy-products industries. The region produces cotton, henequen, and vegetable oil. San Miguel was founded in 1530.

Sannar (sänär') or **Sennar** (sĕn-), town, E Sudan, on the Blue Nile. It was the capital of the Muslim kingdom of Sannar, traditionally known as the "Black Sultanate," which was founded in the 16th cent. Under its strongest rulers, Sannar extended over most of the eastern part of the present Sudan. The kingdom declined in the 18th cent. and was annexed in 1821 by Egypt, then a part of the Ottoman Empire. The old capital lies abandoned near modern Sannar.

Sannazaro, Jacopo (yä'kōpō sän-nätsä'rō), 1456?-1530, Italian humanist. He lived briefly (1501-4) in France, a follower of the exiled Frederick III of Naples. On Frederick's death, he returned to Naples and a life of study and literary fame. His *Arcadia*, a pastoral idyll in prose and verse, was the first of a long line of idylls on the subject of Arcadia, including one by Sir Philip Sidney. Sannazaro's work *Epigrammatica* (3 vol.) is pungent; his *Piscatoriae* enlarged the literary uses of the eclogue by substituting fishermen for shepherds.

San Nicolás de los Garzas (sän nēkōläs' dā lōs gär'säs), city (1970 pop. 111,502), Nuevo León state, N Mexico, in the Santa Catarina valley. It is situated on a major highway in a predominantly poor rural area where oranges are grown.

San Pablo (săn păb'lō), city (1970 pop. 21,461), Contra Costa co., W Calif., on San Pablo Bay, in a farm region; inc. 1948. One of the oldest Spanish settlements in the region, the city is now a commercial and medical center. A junior college is there.

San Pablo Bay: see SAN FRANCISCO BAY.

San Pedro, Diego de (dyā'gō thā sän pā'thrō), fl. 1450, Spanish writer. He is best known for two sentimental novels that influenced the later development of the Spanish novel. They are *Tratado de amores de Arnalte y Lucena* [treatise on the loves of Arnalte and Lucena] (1491) and *Cárcel de amor* [prison of love] (1492).

San Pedro de Macorís (sän pā'thrō thā mäkōrēs'), city (1970 pop. 42,473), SE Dominican Republic, on the Caribbean Sea at the mouth of the Higuamo River. It is the nation's leading sugar port. Textiles and alcohol are produced there.

San Pedro Sula (säm pā'thrō sōō'lä), city (1969 est. pop. 96,341), capital of Cortés dept., NW Honduras. It is the second largest city in the country. San Pedro Sula and Puerto Cortés are the principal ports of Honduras and serve the northwestern banana and sugar plantations.

San Quentin (săn kwĕn'tən), peninsula extending into San Francisco Bay, W Calif., N of San Francisco. The state prison there was begun in 1852. San Quentin is the western terminus of the Richmond-San Rafael Bridge.

San Rafael (săn rəfĕl'), residential city (1970 pop. 38,977), seat of Marin co., W Calif., a suburb of San Francisco on the northern portion of San Francisco Bay; inc. 1913. Several large companies have their regional headquarters there. Electrical equipment and metal, plastic, and wood products are manufactured. It is the seat of the restored Mission San Rafael Arcángel (est. 1817) and the Dominican College of San Rafael. The county civic center there was designed by Frank Lloyd Wright.

San Remo (sän rĕ'mō), city (1971 pop. 62,198), in Liguria, NW Italy, on the Ligurian Sea and on the Italian RIVIERA. It is a fashionable resort and gaming center and a major flower market.

San Remo, Conference of, 1920, meeting with the purpose of ratifying decisions made at the Paris peace conference of May, 1919. Representatives of Great Britain, France, Italy, Japan, Greece, and Belgium met at San Remo, Italy, in April, 1920, to discuss problems arising from World War I. Members of the supreme council of the Allies took leading parts. Methods of executing the Treaty of Versailles (1919) were discussed, the basic features of a peace treaty with Turkey (see SÈVRES, TREATY OF) were adopted, and Class A MANDATES in the Middle East were allotted.

San Salvador (sän sälväthōr'), city (1970 est. pop. 359,000), central El Salvador, capital and largest city of the country. It is the center of El Salvador's trade and communications. Beer, tobacco products, clothing, textiles, and soap are produced there. Built on the volcanic slope that parallels the Pacific coast (nearby is San Salvador volcano, 6,398 ft/1,950 m), the city has suffered from recurrent and severe earthquakes and has been frequently rebuilt. The most disastrous quake (1854) led to the founding of SANTA TECLA. The city is high enough to escape the excessive heat of the tropics but has a year-round summer climate. It has several fine parks, broad avenues, and modern houses (particularly in outlying sections). San Salvador was founded early in the 16th cent. and for a time (1831-38) was the capital of the CENTRAL AMERICAN FEDERATION.

San Salvador, one of the Bahama Islands (1970 pop. 897), British West Indies. It was the first land discovered by Columbus in the New World in 1492. Indian inhabitants called it Guanahani, and it has also been named Watling or Watlings Island. It was formerly confused with what is now known as Cat Island.

Sansannah (sănsăn'ə), town, S Palestine.

sans-culottes (säN-külôt') [French,=without knee breeches], general term applied to the lower classes in France during the French Revolution. The name, derived from the fact that these people wore long trousers instead of the knee breeches worn by the upper classes, was usually applied to the extreme republicans of Paris who were connected with the JACOBINS. The ENRAGÉS were a distinct group of sans-culottes.

sans-culottides (säN-külôtēd'), the last five days of the year in the FRENCH REVOLUTIONARY CALENDAR, thus named in honor of the SANS-CULOTTES.

San Sebastián (sän sābästyän'), city (1970 pop. 165,829), capital of Guipúzcoa prov., N Spain, on the Bay of Biscay at the mouth of the Urumea River, in the Basque Provinces near the French frontier. Picturesquely situated at the foot of Mt. Urgull, it was a summer residence of the Spanish court in the 20th cent. and still is one of the most fashionable seaside resorts in Spain. There are fishing, steel, and paper industries. The city was rebuilt in the 19th cent. after its virtual destruction in the Peninsular War, when it was the scene of a bloody battle between Wellington and the French (1813). The San Sebastián pact, or republican manifesto, which precipitated the fall of the Spanish monarchy, was signed there in 1930.

Sanskrit (săn'skrĭt), language belonging to the Indic group of the Indo-Iranian subfamily of the Indo-European family of languages (see INDO-IRANIAN LANGUAGES). Sanskrit was the classical standard language of ancient India, and some of the oldest surviving Indo-European documents are written in Sanskrit; however, Hittite is probably the earliest recorded Indo-European tongue with at least one text dated c.17th cent. B.C. The oldest known stage of Sanskrit is Vedic or Vedic Sanskrit, so-called because it was the language of the VEDA, the most ancient extant scriptures of Hinduism. The Veda probably date back to about 1500 B.C. or earlier, many centuries before writing was introduced into India. Vedic Sanskrit was current c.1500 B.C. to c.200 B.C. However, Sanskrit in its classical form, a development of Vedic, was spoken c.400 B.C. as a standard court language. It became the literary vehicle of Hindu culture and as such was employed until A.D. c.1100 (see SANSKRIT LITERATURE). Even today Sanskrit survives in liturgical usage. Although it is a dead language, it is one of the languages recognized in the Indian constitution of 1950 because of its association with the religion and literature of India. Study of grammar by Indian scholars began early. The oldest existing Sanskrit grammatical work was written by the Indian grammarian Panini (c.4th cent. B.C.), who analyzed and commented on the Sanskrit language with amazing perceptiveness. Grammatically, Sanskrit has eight cases for the noun (nominative, accusative, genitive, dative, ablative, instrumental, vocative, and locative), three genders (masculine, feminine, and neuter), three numbers for verbs, nouns, pronouns, and adjectives (singular, dual, and plural), and three voices for the verb (active, middle, and passive). The language is very highly inflected. The ancient Indian scripts known as the Brahmi and Kharosthi alphabets have been employed to record Sanskrit. Both Brahmi and Kharosthi are thought to be of Semitic origin. The Devanagari characters, which are descended from Brahmi, also were, and still are, used for writing Sanskrit. The comparison of Sanskrit with the languages of Europe, especially by Sir William JONES, opened the way to the scientific study of language in Europe in the 18th cent. See Jules Bloch, *Indo-Aryan, from the Vedas to Modern Times* (rev. ed., tr. 1965); Thomas Burrow, *The Sanskrit Language* (2d ed. 1965).

Sanskrit literature, main body of the classical literature of India. The literature is divided into two main periods—the Vedic (c.1500-c.200 B.C.), when the Vedic form of Sanskrit generally prevailed, and the Sanskrit (c.200 B.C.-A.D. c.1100), when classical Sanskrit (a development of Vedic) predominated. Sanskrit had, however, become the standard language of the court by 400 B.C., and its early literature overlapped the Vedic. The word *Sanskrit* means "perfected," and the language was adopted as an improvement of the Vedic. The first part of the Vedic period (c.1500-c.800 B.C.), that of the VEDA, was a poetic and creative age, but afterward (c.800-c.500 B.C.) the priestly class transferred its energies to sacrificial ceremonial. They produced the *Brahmanas*; these are prose commentaries, in a later form of Vedic, explaining the relations of the Vedas (which had become sacred texts) to the ceremonials of the Vedic religion. In time the *Brahmanas*, like the Vedas, came to be considered sruti [Skt.,=hearing, i.e., revealed]. All later works, in contrast, are called smriti [Skt.,=memory or tradition] and are considered to be derived from the ancient sages. The later portions of the *Brahmanas* are theosophical treatises; since they were meant to be studied in the solitude of the forest, they are called *Aranyakas* [forest books]. The final parts of the *Aranyakas* are the philosophical *Upanishads* [secret doctrine] (see VEDANTA). In language structure the *Aranyakas* and the *Upanishads* approach classical Sanskrit. The *Sutras* [Skt.,=thread or clue] were written in the third and final stage (c.500-c.200 B.C.) of the Vedic period. They are treatises dealing with Vedic ritual and customary law. They were written to fulfill the need for a short survey in mnemonic, aphoristic form of the past literature, which by this time had assumed massive proportions. There are two forms of sutra; the *Srauta Sutras*, based on sruti, which developed the ritualistic side, and the *Grihya Sutras*, based on smriti. Those *Grihya Sutras* dealing with social and legal usage are the *Dharma Sutras*, the oldest source of Indian law (see MANU). The body of works composed in the *Sutra* style was divided into six *Vedangas* [members of the Veda]—*Siksha* [phonetics], *Chhandas* [meter], *Vyakarana* [grammar], *Nirukta* [etymology], *Kalpa* [religious practice], and *Jyotisha* [astronomy]. A sutra well-known in the West is the *Kamasutra* of Vatsyayana concerning the art and practice of love. Linguistic standards were stereotyped in the middle of the *sutra* period by the grammar of Panini (c.350 B.C.), regarded as being the starting point of the Sanskrit period. Nearly all Sanskrit literature, except that dealing with grammar and philosophy, is in verse. The first period (c.500 B.C.-c.50 B.C.) of the Sanskrit age is one of epics. They are divided into two main groupings—the natural epics, i.e., those derived from old stories, and those which come from artificial epics called kavya. The oldest and most representative of the natural school is the MAHABHARATA, while the oldest and best-known of the artificial epics is the RAMAYANA. The *Puranas*, a group of 18 epics, didactic and sectarian in tone, are a direct offshoot of the *Mahabharata*. In the court epics (c.200 B.C.–A.D. c.1100), most of which were derived from the *Ramayana*, the matter gradually became subordinated to the form, and elaborate laws were set up to regulate style. The lyric poems are artificial in technique and are mainly stanzaic. The most common form, the sloka, developed from the Vedic *anushtubh*, a stanza of four octosyllabic lines. Part of the lyric poetry is comprised of gemlike miniatures, portraying emotion and describing nature; most of it is erotic. There are, however, many lyrics that are ethical in tone. These reflect the doctrine of the TRANSMIGRATION OF SOULS in a prevailing melancholy tone and stress the vanity of human life. Sanskrit drama (A.D. c.400–1100) had its beginnings in those hymns of the *Rig-Veda* which contain dialogues. Staged drama probably derives from the dance and from religious ceremonial. It is characterized by the complete absence of tragedy; death never occurs on the stage. Other typical features are the alternation of lyrical stanzas with prose dialogue and the use of Sanskrit for some characters and Prakrit for others (see PRAKRIT LITERATURE). The stories were borrowed from legend, and love is the usual theme. The play almost always opened with a prayer and was followed by a dialogue between the stage manager and one of the actors, referring to the author and the play. There were no theaters, so the plays were performed in the concert rooms of palaces. The most famous drama was the *Sakuntala* of KALIDASA. Other major dramatists were Bhasa, Harsa, and Bhavabhuti (see ORIENTAL DRAMA). There is a didactic quality in all of Sanskrit literature, but it is most pronounced in fairy tales and fables (A.D. c.400–1100). Characteristically, different stories are inserted within the framework of a single narration. The characters of the tale themselves tell stories until there are many levels to the narrative. The PANCHATANTRA is the most important work in this style. The sententious element reached its height in the *Hitopadesa*, which was derived from the *Panchatantra*. The Sanskrit literature of the modern period consists mainly of academic exercises, while the main body of modern Indian literature is written in various vernacular languages as well as in English. Translations of many of the important texts of Sanskrit literature are in *The Sacred Books of the East*, the famous collection edited by Max Müller. See the histories of Sanskrit literature by A. B. Keith (1928) and A.A. Macdonell (1962); H. H. Gowen, *A History of Indian Literature* (1931, repr. 1968); R. W. Frazer, *A Literary History of India* (1898, repr. 1970).

Sansovino, Andrea (ändrĕ'ä sänsōvē'nō), c.1460–1529, Florentine sculptor and architect of the High Renaissance, b. Monte Sansavino. His real name was Andrea Contucci. He trained under Antonio Pollaiuolo and worked in Florence, Rome, and Loreto. His tombs of Cardinals Sforza and Basso in Rome and his statues and reliefs for church decoration, such as the graceful *Virgin and Child with St. Anne* (1512) at San Agostino, were greatly admired.

Sansovino, Jacopo (yä'kōpō), 1486–1570, Italian sculptor and architect of the Renaissance. His surname was taken in place of his own, Tatti, as homage to the Florentine sculptor Andrea Sansovino, under whom he was apprenticed. After early years devoted to sculpture, he was architect of several buildings in Rome and in 1527 moved to Venice, importing to that city the classic manner of Roman architecture. In Venice, besides his masterpiece, the Library of St. Mark's (designed 1536) in the Piazza San Marco, he built the Palazzo Corner della Ca' Grande, the mint, the loggia at the base of the great campanile, and several churches. His versatility as a sculptor is realized in his creation of the supple figure *Apollo* and the three other imposing statues in the niches of the campanile: *Minerva, Mercury*, and *Peace*. Among his other sculptural works are the gigantic *Mars* and *Neptune* outside the Doge's palace.

Sans Souci (säN sōōsē') [Fr.,=without care], palace built (1745–47) at Potsdam, Germany, by Frederick II, who lived there for 40 years. Over 300 ft (91 m) long, it is believed to have been conceived by Frederick himself and executed by Knobelsdorff. The palace is interesting chiefly for the relics it contains of Frederick II. His apartments are shown as they were when he occupied them; there are also rooms that were Voltaire's during his long visit. The library and the magnificent park, the audience chamber with its fine paintings, the orangery, the statue of Frederick, and the great fountain are especially remarkable.

San Stefano, Treaty of (săn stĕf'ənō), 1878, peace treaty between Russia and the Ottoman Empire (Turkey), at the conclusion of the last of the RUSSO-TURKISH WARS; it was signed at San Stefano (now Yeşilköy), a village W of İstanbul, Turkey. Turkey ceded to Russia parts of Armenia and the DOBRUJA; agreed to pay a very large indemnity; recognized the independence of Rumania, Serbia, and Montenegro; and increased the territories of Serbia and Montenegro. Bulgaria was made an autonomous principality and was immensely enlarged, and Turkey promised reforms for Bosnia and Hercegovina. Because the treaty modified the Treaty of Paris of 1856 (see PARIS, CONGRESS OF) and greatly increased Russian influence in SE Europe, the other great powers obtained its revision at an international conference (see BERLIN, CONGRESS OF).

Santa Ana (sän"tä ä'nä), city (1970 est. pop. 105,000), W El Salvador. It is the second largest city in the country and the commercial and processing center for a sugarcane, coffee, and cattle region. There are textile and foodstuffs industries. Nearby rises Santa Ana volcano (7,828 ft/2,386 m), the highest in El Salvador.

Santa Ana (săn'tə ăn'ə), city (1970 pop. 156,601), seat of Orange co., S Calif., in the fertile Santa Ana valley; inc. 1886. It is the governmental, business, medical, and industrial center of the large Anaheim-Santa Ana-Garden Grove metropolitan area. Among its many products are radios, electrical connectors, nuclear and aircraft components, and sporting goods. Insurance companies are also major employers. Santa Ana has a junior college and a museum that displays early Indian and Spanish artifacts. El Toro Marine Corps Air Station is to the south.

Santa Ana (sän"tä ä'nä), pueblo, central N.Mex., on the Jemez River. The inhabitants are Pueblo Indians of the Keresan linguistic stock. Their church, Santa Ana de Alamillo, dates from 1692.

Santa Anna, Antonio López de (äntō'nyō lō'pās dā sän'tä ä'nä), 1794–1876, Mexican general and politician. He fought in the royalist army, but later joined ITURBIDE in the struggle that won independence for Mexico (1821). Santa Anna then entered upon a long and tortuous political career. His actions were governed by opportunism rather than by any fixed principle, and he shifted his allegiance from party to party, his fortunes rising and falling with bewildering rapidity. He led the revolution against Iturbide (1823); aided, then revolted against, Vicente GUERRERO; and turned against Anastasio BUSTAMANTE after helping him to power. His victory over the Spanish when Guerrero was in power gained for him a popularity which he turned into political capital; he was ever afterward "the hero of Tampico." Elected president for a term beginning in 1833, he struggled with the vice president for power and established himself as a reactionary dictator in 1834. He went to Texas to crush the revolution there and became a sort of ogre in American eyes because of the slaughter at the ALAMO and the brutality of the massacre at Goliad, which was carried out under his orders. His defeat and capture by Samuel HOUSTON at San Jacinto (1836) put a temporary halt to his political career in Mexico, but his shrewd political sense, aided by the not unhappy accident of losing a leg in an attempt to repulse the French at Veracruz (1838), restored his prestige. Driven from power after a wasteful, corrupt presidential administration (1841–44), he returned from exile—with U.S. aid apparently—and again became president (1846–47). He commanded in the Mexican War, but his defeats at Buena Vista, Cerro Gordo, and Puebla and the loss of Mexico City sent him again into exile. He returned and ruled (after Dec., 1853) as "perpetual dictator" until the revolution of AYUTLA again drove him into exile (1855) and brought Benito JUÁREZ to the fore. After several attempts, he was allowed to return to Mexico (1874). See his memoirs, *Mi historia militar y política* (1905); biographies by W. H. Callcott (1936, repr. 1968) and O. L. Jones (1968); R. G. Santos, *Santa Anna's Campaign Against Texas 1835–1836* (1968).

Santa Barbara (săn"tə bär'brə, -bərə), city (1970 pop. 70,215), seat of Santa Barbara co., S Calif., on the Pacific Ocean; inc. 1850. A beautiful residential and resort city with many recreational facilities, it also has electronics and aerospace research and development firms, and an orchid industry. Oil fields are in the area and offshore. The region was discovered by Juan Cabrillo in 1542 and explored and named in 1602. A Spanish presidio, remnants of which remain, was founded there in 1782. The Spanish mission (established in 1786; present building completed in 1820) is a major tourist attraction and is considered one of the most beautiful of all of the California missions. An Old Spanish Days Fiesta is held there for four days every August. Santa Barbara is known for its prevalent Spanish architecture; the county courthouse is patterned after a Moorish castle. Other points of interest include a "street in Spain" shopping area, an undersea aquarium, and many beautiful parks and gardens. A junior college is in the city, as are the Brooks Institute of Photography and the Music Academy of the West. The Univ. of California at Santa Barbara and Westmont College are outside the city limits. Los Padres National Forest is in the Santa Ynez Mts., which rise behind the city. In Feb., 1942, oil tanks in Santa Barbara harbor were the object of a Japanese submarine attack. In Jan., 1969, an oil leak in an offshore drilling platform in the Santa Barbara Channel brought great destruction to the city's harbor and beaches.

Santa Barbara Islands (săn'tə bär'brə, -bərə), or **Channel Islands,** chain of eight rugged islands and many islets, extending c.150 mi (240 km) along the S Calif. coast from Point Conception to San Diego. The islands were discovered in 1542 by Juan Rodriguez Cabrillo, a Portuguese explorer in the service of Spain. Located from 13 to 68 mi (21–109 km) west of the mainland, they are divided into two groups: to the north, the Santa Barbara group including San Miguel, Santa Rosa, Santa Cruz, and Anacapa islands; and to the south, the Santa Catalina group including San Nicolas, Santa Barbara, Santa Catalina, and San Clemente islands. The Santa Barbara group is separated from the mainland by the Santa Barbara Channel and the Santa Catalina group by the San Pedro Channel and the Gulf of Santa Catalina. The islands are the exposed tops of low mountains; the highest point (2,471 ft/753 m) is on Santa Cruz Island rising from the continental shelf. They are in an earthquake region. The Santa Barbara Islands have a Mediterranean-type climate, with warm summers and mild winters. The surrounding waters are noted for sport fishing. Santa Cruz (98 sq mi/254 sq km) is the largest island of the chain; sheep and cattle are raised there. San Miguel Island is uninhabited and has been badly eroded. On its western point are large sea-elephant and sea-lion herds. Anacapa and Santa Barbara, the smallest islands in the chain, constitute CHANNEL ISLANDS NATIONAL MONUMENT (est. 1938). Santa Catalina Island is the most economically developed of the islands and is a popular tourist center. In 1969 leakage from an oil well in the Santa Barbara Channel created an 800 sq mi (2,072 sq km) oil slick that destroyed much aquatic life.

Santa Catalina (săn'tə kăt"əlē'nə) or **Catalina Island,** S Calif., one of the Santa Barbara Islands, off Huntington Beach, Calif. It is a resort island, 22 mi (35 km) long and 1 to 8 mi (1.6–12.9 km) wide, with a picturesque, irregular coastline dotted with coves and beaches. It was discovered in 1542 by Juan Rodríguez Cabrillo, and given its present name by Vizcaíno in 1602. In 1919, William Wrigley bought the island and constructed vacation and sports facilities. Avalon, the only city on the island, is the center of activities. The casino on Sugar Loaf Mt. is the island's principal landmark.

Santa Catarina (săn'tə kətərē'nə), state (1970 pop. 2,903,360), 37,060 sq mi (95,985 sq km), S Brazil. The capital is FLORIANÓPLIS.

Santa Clara (sän'tä klä'rä), city (1970 pop. 131,504), capital of Las Villas prov., central Cuba. It is a communications and commercial center located on major rail and highway junctions, and it has an airport. Cattle raising was the traditional industry until the 19th cent., when sugarcane became important. Tobacco processing and trading are carried on there. Santa Clara was founded in 1689. It was captured by guerrilla forces in late 1958 during Fidel Castro's revolution against Fulgencio Batista.

Santa Clara (săn'tə klâr'ə), city (1970 pop. 87,717), Santa Clara co., W Calif.; inc. 1852. Electronic equipment, fiber glass, and plastic products are among the many manufactures. Points of interest include the Santa Clara de Asís Mission, founded in 1777. The Univ. of Santa Clara is there.

Santa Clara (sän"tä klä'rä), pueblo (1970 est. pop. 770), N N.Mex., on the Rio Grande. Its inhabitants are Pueblo Indians of the Tanoan linguistic stock. They have their own elected government, and they farm, raise cattle, or work at the nearby Los Alamos testing grounds. Some are noted painters and pottery makers. The feast day of Santa Clara is celebrated on Aug. 12; Mass is accompanied by ceremonial dances. Near Santa Clara are Puye ruins, consisting of the remains of a pueblo (abandoned c.1700) that included cliff dwellings, kivas, and four-terraced community houses; pictographs and pottery shards have been found there. There is an annual public festival, in which Indians dance atop Puye Mesa for two days.

Santa Claus: see NICHOLAS, SAINT.

Santa Cruz, Álvaro de Bazán, marqués de (äl'-värō thā bäthän' märkās' dā sän'tä krōōth), 1526–88, Spanish admiral. He fought in various actions against the Turks and distinguished himself at Lepanto (1571). In Philip II's war for the crown of Portugal, Santa Cruz decisively defeated (1582) the French, who were supporting the Portuguese pretender, off the Azores. The leading promoter of an invasion of England, he was to have commanded the Spanish Armada, but he died before the expedition began.

Santa Cruz, Andrés (ändrās' sän'tä krōōs), 1792?–1865, president of Bolivia (1829–39). In 1820 he joined the revolutionists against Spain and, as Bolívar's chief of staff, participated in the decisive liberating battles of Junín and Ayacucho. To achieve his one great aim of a Peru-Bolivia confederation, Santa Cruz, elected president shortly after the resignation of Antonio José de SUCRE, energetically set about establishing Bolivia on a sound footing. At the same time he carried on intrigues to foster trouble in Peru and Chile so that his confederation might be realized. When the opportunity came with internal disorder in Peru in 1835, Santa Cruz invaded and established himself as protector. However, at the battle of Yungay (1839) he was defeated by a coalition of his enemies under Manuel BULNES of Chile and barely escaped to spend the remainder of his life in Europe in exile.

Santa Cruz (sän'tä krōōs), city (1971 est. pop. 135,000), capital of Santa Cruz dept., central Bolivia, on the Piray River. A trade and processing center for sugar, coffee, rice, cattle, and lumber, it is of strategic and commercial importance because of its central location. A rail line completed in 1962 has given the city access to both the Atlantic and Pacific oceans. Santa Cruz was founded in the 16th cent. and was an early Jesuit missionary center.

Santa Cruz (săn'tə krōōz), city (1970 pop. 32,076), seat of Santa Cruz co., W Calif., on Monterey Bay; inc. 1866. It is a seaside city with many fine beaches and is surrounded by hills and redwoods. The huge municipal wharf (built in 1913) is one of its most popular attractions. In addition to tourism, there are electronic and food-processing industries. Agriculture flourishes in the area. Points of interest include a replica of a mission established there in 1791. The Univ. of California at Santa Cruz is in the city.

Santa Cruz de Tenerife (dā tānārē'fā), city (1970 pop. 151,361), capital of Tenerife prov., Spain, a port on Tenerife island in the Canary Islands. Vegetables, sugarcane, tobacco, and bananas are exported. The city's splendid scenery and mild subtropical climate make it a favorite tourist resort.

Santa Fe, city (1970 pop. 312,427), capital of Santa Fe prov., NE Argentina, a river port near the Paraná, with which it is connected by canal. On the eastern margin of the Pampa, it is an important shipping point for the agricultural products of much of NW Argentina. The city also has some industry. Founded by the Spanish conquistador Juan de Garay (1573), Santa Fe was the site of the promulgation of the 1853 Argentine constitution. There are several notable churches and a national university.

Santa Fe (săn'tə fā), city (1970 pop. 41,167), alt. c.7,000 ft (2,130 m), state capital and seat of Santa Fe co., N N.Mex., at the foot of the Sangre de Cristo Mts. It is an administrative, tourist, and resort center, and a shipping point for Indian wares, minerals, and farm products. Founded c.1609 by the Spanish, on the site of ancient Indian ruins, it was a center of Spanish-Indian trade for over 200 years. A seat of government since its founding, it is the oldest capital city in the United States. In the Pueblo revolt of 1680, the Spanish colonists were driven out; in 1692 they returned under Diego de Vargas. Shortly after Mexico gained independence from Spain (1821), extensive commerce with the United States developed by way of the Santa Fe Trail. In 1846, Gen. S. W. Kearny and his troops entered the city; he met no resistance, and the region became a province of the United States. The railroad reached Lamy (the station for Santa Fe, 16 mi/26 km distant) in 1879. The see of an archbishopric since 1875, the city is a center of Roman Catholicism in North America. Among its churches are San Miguel Mission Church (c.1636); the Cathedral of St. Francis, built (1869) on the site of a monastery erected (1622) by Alonzo de Benavides; and Cristo Rey Church, the largest adobe building in the United States. Among the many other points of interest are the Palace of the Governors (c.1610; occupied in turn by Spanish, Indian, Mexican, and American administrators), which now houses a state museum; the Laboratory of Anthropology; museums of international folk art and of Navaho ceremonial art; and a state-owned art gallery. Also in the city are artists' and writers' colonies, an opera house, St. John's College, the College of Santa Fe, two Indian schools, headquarters for the Santa Fe National Forest, regional headquarters for the National Park Service, and the state penitentiary. An annual rodeo is held there in July. There are many Indian pueblos in the region, and Bandelier National Monument (see NATIONAL PARKS AND MONUMENTS, table) is nearby. See R. E. Twitchell, *Old Santa Fe* (1963).

Santa Fe Railroad, chartered in 1863 as the Atchison, Topeka, and Santa Fe RR; opened to traffic in 1864. Construction continued and, in 1880 it reached Santa Fe, N.Mex.; the following year the railroad connected with the Southern Pacific RR. The railroad acquired several small lines, and further construction followed; by the early 1890s the Santa Fe, with its 9,000 mi (14,480 km) of track and connections to Chicago and Los Angeles, became one of the world's longest railroad systems. Poor management and a reckless dividend policy combined with the depression of 1893, however, to bankrupt the railroad company, which in 1895 was reorganized as the Atchison, Topeka & Santa Fe Railway Company. In the 20th cent. the railroad increased its holdings.

Santa Fe Springs, city (1970 pop. 14,750), Los Angeles co., S Calif., in an oil and natural gas region; inc. 1957.

Santa Fe Trail, important caravan route of the W United States, extending c.780 mi (1,260 km) from Independence, Mo., SW to Santa Fe, N.Mex. Independence and Westport, Mo., were the chief points where wagons, teams, and supplies were obtained. From there, the trail led 150 mi (241 km) SW to Council Grove, Kansas, which was the main wagon train organization point. Crossing the Kansas plains to the Arkansas River, the trail then followed the river to its fork near Dodge City, Kansas. The Mountain Division of the trail in the north continued to hug the river W to Bents Fort (now a national historic site); turning south, it passed over its most rugged part, including the Raton Pass. The Cimarron or Cutoff Division of the trail in the south, a more direct route, crossed the Great Plains from the Arkansas River to Fort Union, N.Mex., where it rejoined the northern route. Although less rugged, the Southern route was dry, with poor grass and little wildlife. By the early 19th cent., small trapping parties had reached Santa Fe, then under Spanish rule; but they were forbidden to trade. In Nov., 1821, William Becknell, a trader, returned with news that Mexico was free and Santa Fe welcomed trade. Early in 1922 he left Missouri for Santa Fe with the first party of traders. From then on, annual wagon caravans, usually leaving in early summer, made the 40- to 60-day trip over the trail and returned after a 4- to 5-week stay in Santa Fe. An increasing amount of goods (valued at $5 million in 1855) was taken to Santa Fe each year. In 1850 a monthly stage line was started between Independence and Santa Fe over the northern route. In 1880 the Santa Fe Railroad reached Santa Fe and marked the death of the trail, which, in part, the line parallels.

Santa Gertrudis cattle, breed of beef cattle derived from crosses between Shorthorn cows (see SHORTHORN CATTLE) and Brahman bulls (see BRAHMAN CATTLE); the breed was developed by Robert J. Kleberg, Jr., of the King Ranch in S Texas, in the early 1900s. The breed has been widely distributed in the United States, particularly in the South, and has been extensively exported.

Santa Isabel: see MALABO, Equatorial Guinea.

Santa María, Domingo (dōmēng'gō sän'tä märē'ä), 1825–89, Chilean historian and statesman, president of Chile (1881–86). A liberal statesman, scholar, and author of several historical works, he took part in revolutions against the conservative regime of Manuel Montt and was twice exiled (1852–53, 1859–60). In his administration the separation of church and state was fostered, the War of the Pacific brought to a successful end, and the last serious uprising of Araucanian Indians suppressed.

Santa Maria (sän'tə mərē'ə), city (1970 pop. 156,929), Rio Grande do Sul state, S Brazil. It is a major railroad terminus and the site of an important military base. Leather goods, beer, and foodstuffs are produced. Santa Maria was established in 1797.

Santa Maria, city (1970 pop. 32,749), Santa Barbara co., S Calif., near San Luis Obispo Bay; inc. 1905. The economy is based largely on agriculture and oil. Other industries produce phonograph records, wire cables, marine equipment, and tire molds. Santa Maria, founded in 1874 as Central City, received its present name in 1882. A junior college is in Santa Maria. Vandenberg Air Force Base is nearby.

Santa Marta (sän'tä mär'tä), city (1968 est. pop. 129,200), capital of Magdalena dept., N Colombia, a port on the Caribbean Sea. The city's banana industry, operated by the United Fruit Company, is one of the most important in South America. Santa Marta also has fine beaches and is a tourist center. Founded by the Spanish explorer Rodrigo de Bastidas in 1525, it was often sacked by corsairs in the 16th cent. During colonial times the city was important as an outlet for the Magdalena River valley. It remained royalist during the revolution and was liberated in 1821. Simón BOLÍVAR died on an estate nearby.

Santa Maura, Greece: see LEVKAS.

Santa Monica (săn'tə mŏn'ĭkə), city (1970 pop. 88,289), Los Angeles co., S Calif., on Santa Monica Bay; inc. 1886. Missiles, aircraft parts, electronic equipment, ceramics, chemicals, leather goods, furniture, and optical instruments are among the manufactures. A junior college and the J. Paul Getty museum are located there. The city has a 3-mi (4.8-km) oceanfront beach; nearby are several state parks.

Santana, Pedro (pā'thrō säntä'nä), 1801–64, president of the Dominican Republic (1844–48, 1853–56, 1858–61). He joined the revolution that in 1844 freed his nation from Haiti and became its first president. He and his bitter rival, Buenaventura BÁEZ, alternated in power. Santana was unscrupulous and dictatorial. He repulsed later Haitian attacks, but the republic did not fare well under his repressive rule. Convinced that security was possible only with foreign protection, Santana in 1861 placed his country again under Spanish rule, converting it into an overseas province of which he became governor. Intense opposition forced him to resign.

Santander, Francisco de Paula (fränsē'skō dā pou'lä säntändär'), 1792–1840, Colombian revolutionist. Given command of the guerrillas of the llanos by Simón BOLÍVAR, Santander materially contributed to the victory at BOYACÁ. In Oct., 1821, he became vice president of Colombia and ably administered the country during Bolívar's long absences. A believer in constitutional government, Santander led the federalist opposition to Bolívar, who, on Sept. 24, 1828, suspended him from office. That night Bolívar barely escaped assassination. Convicted without proof of complicity in the plot, Santander was sentenced to death, but was instead banished. After Bolívar's death and the dissolution of the republic of Greater Colombia, he returned and served (1832–36) as president of New Granada. His administration was competent, but there were plots against his life and he maintained control only by force. See study by David Bushnell (1970).

Santander, city (1970 pop. 149,704), capital of Santander prov., N Spain, in Old Castile, on the Bay of Biscay. It is a seaport and a popular resort. On the nearby peninsula of Magdalena is a former royal summer palace. An ancient port, Santander became, after the discovery of America, one of the busiest ports of N Spain. The exploitation of nearby mines has favored the development of industries (ironworks and shipyards). The 13th-century cathedral and the business district were destroyed by fire in 1941, but have been restored. There is an international summer university named for the writer Marcelino Menéndez y Pelayo.

Santa Paula (săn'tə pôl'ə), city (1970 pop. 18,001), Ventura co., S Calif., on the Santa Clara River in a fertile valley that yields citrus fruits, avocados, and walnuts; laid out 1875, inc. 1902. Fruit packing and oil production are major industries, and there are plants that manufacture paper products, building materials, clothing, ceramics, and plastics. The Union Oil Company, which was founded in Santa Paula in 1890, operates a notable oil museum there.

Santarém (səntərĕm'), town (1970 municipal pop. 57,292), capital of Santarém dist. and Ribatejo, W central Portugal, above the right bank of the Tagus River. Agricultural produce is exported. The town has been important since Roman times because of its strategic location along the approaches to Lisbon. It was retaken from the Moors by the first king of Portugal, Alfonso I, in 1147.

Santarosa, Santorre Annibale De Rossi di Pomarolo, conte di (säntôr'rā än-nē'bälā dā rôs'sē dē pōmärō'lō kôn'tā dē sän"tärō'zä), 1783–1825, Italian revolutionary. A supporter of CHARLES ALBERT, heir to the throne of Sardinia, he organized an unsuccessful revolution in Piedmont in 1821. He fled to Switzerland, then lived in France and England, and died while fighting for Greek independence.

Santa Rosa, city (1970 pop. 37,893), capital of La Pampa prov., central Argentina. It is a modern city and road junction surrounded by a rich agricultural and cattle-raising area. First settled in 1889, Santa Rosa attracted many Spanish, Italian, and French immigrants.

Santa Rosa (săn'tə rō'zə), city (1970 pop. 50,006), seat of Sonoma co., W Calif.; inc. 1868. It is an industrial city and a retail, financial, and medical center for the fertile Sonoma Valley. Luther Burbank lived there, and his gardens are preserved as a monument. Of interest also is the Church of One Tree, built (1874) from a single redwood, and now housing the Robert L. Ripley Memorial Museum. A junior college is in the city and California State College, Sonoma, is nearby. In the vicinity are the Jack London "Wolf House" and memorial museum, Armstrong Redwoods State Park, and many other state parks and historic and natural attractions.

Santa Rosa Island, narrow barrier beach between the Gulf of Mexico and Santa Rosa Sound, NW Fla., extending c.50 mi (80 km) parallel to the coast. It is the site of Fort Pickens and of a missile-launching station. The island is also a resort area.

Santa Sophia: see HAGIA SOPHIA.

Santa Tecla (sän'tä tā'klä), city (1970 est. pop. 38,000), central El Salvador. It was founded in 1854 after the capital, San Salvador, was destroyed in an earthquake. San Salvador, 9 mi (14.5 km) away, was rebuilt, and Santa Tecla became a wealthy suburb. It is situated among coffee farms. The city is also called Nueva San Salvador.

Santayana, George (säntäyä'nä), 1863–1952, American philosopher and poet, b. Madrid, Spain. He emigrated to the United States in 1872. A graduate of Harvard (1886), he taught in the department of philosophy from 1889 until 1912. After resigning from Harvard he returned to Europe, eventually settling in Italy, where he lived in a convent after the outbreak of World War II until his death. He detached himself from the social turmoil of the 20th cent., secluding himself from relationship with either people or events. Santayana's philosophic stance has been given the apparently opposite descriptions of materialism and Platonism. The contradiction is partly understandable as resulting from his view of the mind as being firmly placed in and responsive to a physical, biological context, and his simultaneous emphasis on and high evaluation of the mind's rational and imaginative vision of physical reality. In an important early work, *The Sense of Beauty* (1896), he enunciated a qualified hedonism that placed high value on aesthetic pleasure; it was a pleasure that was understood to be an irrational expression of vital interests but was distinguished from direct, sensual pleasures. *The Life of Reason* (1905–6) investigates the mind's evolving attempts to define its relationship to its natural context. In that work he saw the relationship of thought and reality as one of ideal correspondence. Santayana's earlier work is marked by a psychological approach to the life of the mind; with the publication of *Scepticism and Animal Faith* (1923) and *The Realms of Being*, a four-volume work (*The Realm of Essence*, 1927; *The Realm of Matter*, 1930; *The Realm of Truth*, 1937; *The Realm of Spirit*, 1940; 1-vol. ed. 1942) he adopted a more classical philosophic approach, making ontological distinctions between the objects of mental activity. Against Cartesian skepticism and idealism he advanced the notion of "animal faith" as the basis of the life of reason. Religion he viewed as an imaginative creation of real value but without absolute significance. Although he continued to value imaginative and rational consciousness he warned against the mind's tendency to confer substantial reality and causal efficacy on its own creations. His personal withdrawal from active life was paralleled in his philosophy by a decided moral detachment. The whole of Santayana's philosophic writing displays a characteristic richness of style; he also wrote poetry, a volume of which appeared in 1923. His only novel, *The Last Puritan* (1935), had great popular success. His *Dominations and Powers*, on political philosophy, was published in 1951. See *The Works of George Santayana* (15 vol., 1936–40) and *The Philosophy of Santayana*, ed. by Irwin Edman (rev. ed. 1953, repr. 1973); his letters (ed. by Daniel Cory, 1955; repr. 1973); his memoirs, *Persons and Places* (3 vol., 1944–53). See also P. A. Schilpp, ed., *The Philosophy of George Santayana* (1951); Richard Butler, *The Mind of Santayana* (1955, repr. 1968) and *The Life and World of George Santayana* (1960); T. N. Munson, *The Essential Wisdom of George Santayana* (1962); Daniel Cory, *Santayana: The Later Years* (1963); B. J. Singer, *The Rational Society* (1970).

Santee (săntē'), river, 143 mi (230 km) long, formed by the confluence of the Congaree and Wateree rivers, central S.C., and flowing SE to the Atlantic Ocean. The Santee-Wateree-Catawba system (c.440 mi/710 km long) is the chief waterway of South Carolina. A navigable canal (built 1792–1800) connects the Santee with the Cooper River. The Santee has been extensively developed for power and navigation. Santee Dam (48 ft/14.6 m high; c.8 mi/12.9 km long; completed 1941) impounds Lake Marion (172 sq mi/445 sq km), the largest lake in South Carolina. Pinopolis Dam, impounding Lake Moultrie, has a 132,615-kw capacity. See Henry Savage, *River of the Carolinas: The Santee* (1956, repr. 1968).

Sant' Elia, Antonio (äntō'nyō sänt ā'lēä), 1888–1916, Italian architect. Associated with the movement known as FUTURISM, he created visionary drawings of futurist houses that he likened to gigantic machines. His projects for urban complexes suggest the functional architecture of the 1920s. He died on the battlefield before his plans could be realized.

Santerre, Jean Baptiste (zhäN bätēst' säNtĕr'), 1651–1717, French figure and portrait painter. He was known for allegorical portraits and his ROCOCO use of nude figures. He founded a drawing academy for women at Versailles. Among his works are *Susanna at the Bath* (Louvre) and *Adelaide d'Orléans* (Versailles).

Santiago (säntēä'gō), city (1970 pop. 2,661,920), central Chile, capital of Chile and of Santiago prov., on the Mapocho River. It is the political, commercial, and financial heart of the nation. The city was founded and named Santiago de Nueva Estremadura on Feb. 12, 1541, by Pedro de Valdivia. Laid out according to Valdivia's plan in a gridiron pattern between the hill of Santa Lucía and the Mapocho, a mountain torrent, Santiago has spread over a broad valley plain and is today one of the largest cities in South America. Low foothills encompass the valley, and the snow-capped Andes, forming a superb backdrop, rise in the eastern distance. For most of the year the capital (alt. c.1,700 ft/520 m) has a nearly perfect climate—warm days and cool nights. Much of Chile's industry is distributed among other cities, but Santiago is an active manufacturing center. Textiles, foodstuffs, clothing, footwear, and other goods are produced. There are also large iron and steel foundries in the city. While some structures from the colonial era remain, the atmosphere of Santiago is fairly modern (much construction took place in the late 19th cent.), with neoclassical government offices, modern office buildings, and sumptuous residences. Spacious parks, plazas, gardens, and wide avenues (the Avenida Bernardo O'Higgins extends 2 mi/3.2 km in a straight line through the city) are characteristic features. Focal point of the intellectual and cultural development of Chile from colonial times to the present, Santiago has many national establishments—the library, the museum, the theater, and (besides other institutions of higher learning) the National Univ., which is the successor to the Univ. of San Felipe, founded by a royal decree of 1738. Santiago has experienced several catastrophes. In Sept., 1541, the Araucanian Indians nearly wiped out the new settlement; it was completely leveled by an earthquake in 1647; and the Mapocho has frequently flooded the city. In 1863 the Campania Church, with doors that opened inward, caught fire from a falling lamp, and 2,000 worshipers perished. In the early 1970s, Santiago was the scene of mass political demonstrations for and against the regime of Chilean President Salvador Allende, who died there during the coup d'etat of Sept., 1973.

Santiago (säntyä'gō), city (1970 pop. 14,595), W central Panama. Santiago is a communications and commercial center in the Pacific lowlands. It is a provincial and district capital.

Santiago, Río Grande de, river, Mexico: see LERMA.

Santiago de Compostela (säntyä'gō thā kōmpōstä'lä) or **Santiago,** city (1970 pop. 70,893), La Coruña prov., NW Spain, in Galicia, on the Sar River. The city owes its importance to its role as one of the chief shrines of Christendom. There in the early 9th cent. the supposed tomb of the apostle St. JAMES the Greater was reputedly discovered by a miracle, and Alfonso II of Asturias had a sanctuary built on the site. The city grew around the shrine and became, after Jerusalem and Rome, the most famous Christian place of pilgrimage in the Middle Ages. Santiago de Compostela still thrives as a pilgrimage and tourist center. It is an archiepiscopal see and has a university (founded 1501). Its most remarkable building is the cathedral, which replaced the earlier sanctuary after its destruction (10th cent.) by the Moors. Originally built (11th–13th cent.) in Romanesque style, the cathedral has had baroque and plateresque additions and restorations. Other historic buildings include the Hospital Real (1501–11), built by Ferdinand and Isabella for the accommodation of poor pilgrims, and the Colegio Fonseca (16th cent.), a part of the university.

Santiago de Cuba (thā kōō'bä), city (1970 pop. 275,970), capital of Oriente prov., SE Cuba. Cuba's second largest city, Santiago is situated on a cliff overlooking a bay. Minerals, agricultural produce, and woods are exported. The city is also the terminus of a major highway. Founded in 1514 by Diego de Velázquez and moved to its present site in 1588, Santiago served for some time as Cuba's capital. In its early days, it was captured by French and English buccaneers and was a center of the smuggling trade with the British West Indies. Frenchmen fleeing the slave revolt in Haiti in the early 19th cent. settled in Santiago and heavily influenced the city's development. During the Spanish-American War of 1898, U.S. ships established a blockade in Santiago's harbor; when the Spanish admiral Pascual Cervera y Topete, bottled up in the harbor, made a desperate attempt to escape, his fleet was destroyed. Heavy fighting preceded the city's surrender. Fidel Castro began his revolutionary struggle against Fulgencio Batista by attacking the Moncada army garrison in Santiago on July 26, 1953. The city retains many colonial landmarks, notably its cathedral (the largest in Cuba) and the crumbling forts that stand on high cliffs above the harbor. It also has a university.

Santiago del Estero, city (1970 pop. 119,127), capital of Santiago del Estero prov., N Argentina. It is a transportation hub of the Argentine Chaco and a commercial center for cattle raised in the region. Founded in 1553, Santiago del Estero is one of the oldest cities of Argentina. Nearby thermal springs have made the city a health resort. There are two 16th-century churches.

Santiago de los Caballeros (dā lōs käbäyä'rōs), city (1970 pop. 155,151), N Dominican Republic, on the Yaque del Norte River. The second most important city in the country, it is a rail and road junction in the center of the fertile region known as the Cibao lowland. The region produces subsistence crops, sugarcane, tobacco, coffee, and cotton. Tobacco products, beeswax, and honey are made in the city. Santiago is the commercial center and distribution point for the most densely populated part of the country. It was founded in 1495 and in 1844 was the site of a decisive battle in the Dominican Republic's war of independence.

Santillana, Iñigo López de Mendoza, marqués de (ēnyē'gō lō'pĕth dā mändō'thä märkās' dā säntēlyä'nä), 1398–1458, Spanish poet and literary patron, of a wealthy and distinguished literary family. Influenced by Dante, Petrarch, and Boccaccio, he is considered the chief Spanish literary figure of his century. The first to write sonnets in Spanish, he also wrote the first Spanish ars poetica; a humanistic dialogue, *Diálogo de Bias contra Fortuna* (c.1450); an allegorical poem, *Comedieta de Ponza* (1436); and several songs called *serranillas*. Santillana's *refranes*, or proverbs, were translated into English in 1579. His philosophical poetry is still read. See study by D. W. Foster (1971).

Santo, New Hebrides: see ESPIRITU SANTO.

Santo André (sän'tōō ändrĕ'), city (1970 pop. 418,578), São Paulo state, S Brazil, a suburb of São Paulo. The city houses the offices of many international firms and has industries that produce textiles, metal products, rubber goods, porcelain, foodstuffs, furniture, airplanes, munitions, and printed material.

Santo Domingo (sän'tō dōmēng'gō), former Spanish colony on the island of HISPANIOLA. The name is also given to the DOMINICAN REPUBLIC, and in early days it applied to HAITI. Columbus discovered the island in 1492 and established a settlement on the northern coast, but when he returned in 1493 the settlers had vanished. He administered a new colony there until complaints against his rule caused him to be replaced (1500) by Francisco de Bobadilla. In 1509, Diego Columbus became governor. Failing to find mineral wealth in quantity, the colonists became farmers; the work was done for them under the ENCOMIENDA system by Indians. Before the adoption (1542) of the New Laws urged by Bartolomé de las Casas for protection of the Indians, most of the natives had perished and importation of Negro slaves had been sanctioned. Santo Domingo was subject to frequent raids by English and French buccaneers. Although Spain nominally owned the whole island, colonization had not been undertaken in the west; French buccaneers used the ports there (in present Haiti) as a rendezvous, and later French planters were able to establish settlements. In the latter half of the 18th cent. sugarcane was introduced and sugar plantations became dominant. Unable to enforce its claims to the whole island, Spain ceded (1697) the western part (then called Saint-Domingue) to France and in 1795 gave up the whole island. Spanish rule was restored in the east when the inhabitants, aided by the British, rebelled against the French in 1808–9. The Spanish themselves were ousted in 1821 but in 1822 the Haitians extended their rule over the entire island. The Haitians were driven out in 1844 and the Dominican Republic was proclaimed. The capital is **Santo Domingo** (1970 pop. 671,402), S Dominican Republic, on the Caribbean Sea, at the mouth of the Ozama River. It is the country's largest city and leading port. Founded Aug. 4, 1496, by Bartholomew Columbus, brother of Christopher Columbus, it is the oldest continuously inhabited settlement in the Western Hemisphere. Shortly after its founding it became the base from which Diego de Velázquez set out to conquer Cuba. Prior to the conquest of Mexico and Peru, Santo Domingo was the seat of Spain's colonial administration in the New World. The city was sacked by Sir Francis Drake in 1586. Santo Domingo was almost totally destroyed by a hurricane in 1930 but was rebuilt and renamed Ciudad Trujillo after dictator Rafael Leonidas Trujillo; the original name was restored in 1961 after his death. Although replete with historic sites, Santo Domingo today is a city of broad avenues and modern buildings. The cathedral, begun in 1514, is the oldest in the Western Hemisphere; it contains the reputed tomb of Christopher Columbus.

Santo Domingo (sän″tə dəmĭng′gō), pueblo (1970 pop. 1,662), Sandoval co., N central N.Mex., on the Rio Grande; founded c.1700 after earlier pueblos were destroyed by floods. Its inhabitants are Pueblo Indians of the Eastern Keresan linguistic family. Its principal ceremony, a magnificent Green Corn (or Busk) dance, is held on the feast of St. Dominic, Aug. 4. See L. A. White, *The Pueblo of Santo Domingo* (1935).

Santorin, Greece: see THÍRA.

Santos (sän′tŏŏs), city (1970 pop. 346,096), São Paulo state, SE Brazil, on the island of São Vicente in the Atlantic just off the mainland. It is 40 mi (64 km) SE of the city of São Paulo, with which it is linked by rail and by the Via Anchieta highway. Santos is the world's greatest coffee port and the chief shipping point for the rich interior of São Paulo state. It handles the major share of Brazilian exports, including, besides coffee, oranges, bananas, cotton, and industrial products. Along its spacious harbor there are more than 4 mi (6 km) of modern wharves. Santos was founded c.1540 near the settlement of São Vicente. It was sacked by the English in 1591. Santos is a fashionable residential area and resort center with fine beaches.

Santos-Dumont, Alberto (älbĕr′tŏŏ sän′tŏŏzh-dü-môN′), 1873–1932, Brazilian aeronaut. From 1891 to 1928 he lived in France. A pioneer in the development of aircraft, he was the first to construct and fly (1898) a gasoline-motored airship. He built several other lighter-than-air craft, winning in one a prize for a round-trip flight between Saint-Cloud and the Eiffel Tower (1901). At Neuilly, France, he established in 1903 the first airship base. In 1905 he turned to the construction of airplanes and in 1909 built a successful small monoplane. See his autobiography (tr. 1973).

Santo Tomás, University of (sän′tō tōmäs′), at Manila, the Philippines; Roman Catholic, coeducational; founded 1611 by Dominican priests. It is the oldest institution of higher learning in the country. It has faculties of sacred theology, canon law, philosophy, civil law, medicine and surgery, pharmacy, arts and letters, and engineering, as well as colleges of education, science, commerce and business administration, architecture and fine arts, and nursing.

Sanusi or **Senussi** (both: sənōō′sĭ), Arabic *Sanusiyya,* Muslim brotherhood in N Africa and W Arabia, chief nationalistic movement in Libya in the 20th cent. It was founded as a Sufi order (see SUFISM) in Mecca in 1837 by an Algerian, Sayyid Muhammad Ali as-Sanusi (1787?–1859), known as the Grand Sanusi. The order took firm root in Cyrenaica in 1843 and spread to Jaghbub, Kufra, Wadai, and Central Africa. The Sanusi unsuccessfully fought (1902–13) French expansion in the Sahara, and in 1911 the Italian invasion of Libya forced them to concentrate there. During World War I they attacked British-occupied Egypt. The Sanusi continued to oppose the Italians in Libya until the end of World War II. The leader of the order at that time became (1951) IDRIS I, the first king of Libya. See E. E. Evans-Pritchard, *The Sanusi of Cyrenaica* (1949, repr. 1963).

San Vicente (sän vēsān′tā), city (1968 est. pop. 19,000), central El Salvador. Among its manufactures are shawls, hats, and tobacco products. San Vicente is the commercial center of a region that produces coffee, sugarcane, and indigo. From the nearby volcano San Vicente (7,360 ft/2,243 m) a wide vista of Central America may be seen.

Sanzio, Raphael: see RAPHAEL SANTI.

São Caetano do Sul (souN kĭtä′nōō thōō sōōl), city (1970 pop. 150,171), São Paulo state, SE Brazil, an industrial suburb southeast of the city of São Paulo. Because of their integration into São Paulo's industrial zone, São Caetano do Sul and nearby Santo André and São Bernardo do Campo are sometimes collectively referred to as "ABC". Headquarters for General Motors in Brazil, São Caetano do Sul assembles motor vehicles and produces metal products, electrical and communications equipment, chemicals, pharmaceuticals, textiles, clothing, and food products. The city was founded c.1631.

São Francisco (souN frəsēsh′kōō), river, c.1,800 mi (2,900 km) long, rising in the Serra de Canastra, SW Minas Gerais state, Brazil, and flowing northeast, then southeast through the sertão region of E Brazil to the Atlantic Ocean. The river's flow varies with the season. The São Francisco, an ancient river that is embedded in the Brazilian Plateau, probably once entered the sea near Cape São Roque, northeast of its great bend. The near right-angle bend near Cabrobó is believed to be caused by stream piracy (see RIVER). Paulo Afonso falls (275 ft/84 m high), east of the great bend, blocks navigation into the interior; a railroad circumvents the falls. The river is navigable along c.900 mi (1,450 km) of its middle course. The São Francisco valley, linking Brazil's northeastern and southeastern regions, is the object of a large-scale river development and control scheme. The harnessing of Paulo Afonso falls and the building of Três Marias Dam have improved economic conditions in the potentially rich but drought-ridden and sparsely settled region.

São Gonçalo (souN gōōnsä′lōō), city (1970 pop. 430,349), Rio de Janeiro state, SE Brazil, on Guanabara Bay opposite the city of Rio de Janeiro. It is a distribution point and a manufacturing center.

São João de Meriti (souN zhwouN thĭ mərē′tĭ, də mĭrētē′), city (1970 pop. 303,108), Rio de Janeiro state, SE Brazil, a residential suburb northwest of the city of Rio de Janeiro. Most of the labor force commutes to Rio.

São Luís (souN lōōēsh′), city (1970 pop. 265,595), capital of Maranhão state, NE Brazil. It is a port city located on São Luís Island in São Marcos Bay of the Atlantic Ocean. São Luís is a trading and distribution center for the state's agricultural products and for the products of Teresina, in Piauí state. Industries in the city produce babassu oil, cacao, sugar, rum, and canned fruits. Founded in 1612 by the French and named in honor of Louis XIII, São Luís was captured in 1615 by the Portuguese and was occupied by the Dutch from 1641 to 1644. A noted cultural center in the 19th cent., it was also considered a bourgeois stronghold and merchant's center, in contrast to the aristocratic city of Alcantara (an abandoned city that is now a national historic monument) across São Marcos Bay.

São Miguel (souN mēgĕl′), island (288 sq mi/746 sq km), one of the E AZORES, in Ponta Delgada dist., Portugal. It is the largest island of the archipelago, and its principal city, PONTA DELGADA, is the largest city of the islands. The soil yields pineapples, oranges, tea, and other produce. The island's volcanic features, including a crater with a large lake, attract tourists.

Saône (sōn), river, 268 mi (431 km) long, rising in the Vosges mts. near Épinal, E France, and flowing SW past Gray, Chalon-sur-Saône, and Mâcon to join the Rhône River at Lyons. An important transportation link between Paris and Marseilles, it is connected by canals to the Moselle, Marne, Yonne, and Loire rivers. Because of its even and gentle flow, the Saône carries more traffic than the Rhône. There are famous vineyards along its course.

Saône-et-Loire (sōn-ā-lwär′), department (1968 pop. 550,362), E France, in BURGUNDY. MÂCON is the capital.

São Paulo (souN pou′ lōō), state (1970 pop. 17,775,-889), 95,713 sq mi (247,897 sq km), SE Brazil. The capital is the city of SÃO PAULO.

São Paulo, city (1970 pop. 5,186,752; metropolitan area 5,921,796), capital of São Paulo state, SE Brazil, on the Tietê River. The largest city of Brazil and of South America, São Paulo is an ultramodern metropolis with skyscrapers, palatial homes, and spacious parks and recreational facilities. Its tropical climate is moderated by the city's altitude (2,700 ft/6,823 m). São Paulo, which dominates the vast hinterland of Brazil's wealthiest agricultural state, is the commercial, financial, and industrial center of Brazil. Through its Atlantic Ocean port of SANTOS, it ships the farm produce of the interior. São Paulo's chief manufactures are textiles, processed foods, motor vehicles, heavy machinery, metal products, electrical equipment, pharmaceuticals, chemicals, furniture, clothing, shoes, paper, synthetic rubber, and tobacco products. Printing and publishing are also important. Abundant hydroelectric power has spurred industrial growth. The city is a major road, rail, and air transportation hub and has a modern subway system. São Paulo was founded by Jesuit priests on Jan. 25, 1554, on the site of an old Indian village. In the 17th cent. it became a base for penetration into the Brazilian interior by expeditions (*bandeiras*) seeking mineral wealth and Indian slaves. In 1681, São Paulo was made the administrative capital of the surrounding area, and in 1711 it achieved city status. The independence movement was strong in the city; in 1822 at São Paulo, Brazilian emperor Dom Pedro I proclaimed the country independent of Portugal. The city, however, remained a minor commercial center for a sugarcane and diversified agricultural region until the 1880s, when widespread coffee cultivation in São Paulo state brought sudden growth, prosperity, and an influx of European immigrants. The city has been a prominent cultural and intellectual center since the 19th cent. It has four universities, a medical school, a law school, and the noted Butantan institute, where snake serums are prepared. The art museum features a fine collection of old masters, and the museum of modern art is famed for its *Bienal,* an international competition held every two years. Near the Ipiranga Museum is a monument commemorating Dom Pedro's independence proclamation. See R. M. Morse, *From Community to Metropolis* (1958).

São Salvador, Brazil: see SALVADOR, city.

São Thomé and Principe: see SÃO TOMÉ AND PRINCIPE.

São Tiago: see CAPE VERDE ISLANDS.

São Tomé (souN tōōmĕ′), town (1960 pop. 7,364), capital of the Portuguese overseas province of São Tomé and Principe and a port on São Tomé island, in the Gulf of Guinea. It is the province's largest town, administrative center, commercial center, and main port. The chief exports are cocoa, coffee, copra, and palm products. An international airport is there, and a railroad runs to the interior of São Tomé Island. The town has been the seat of a Roman Catholic bishop since 1534.

São Tomé and Principe (souN tōōmĕ′, prēn′sēpə), overseas province of Portugal (1970 pop. 73,811), 372 sq mi (964 sq km), W Africa, in the Gulf of Guinea, consisting of the islands of São Tomé (c.330 sq mi/860 sq km), Principe (c.40 sq mi/100 sq km), Pedras Tinhosas, and Rolas. SÃO TOMÉ is the capital and chief town. The province is run by an appointed governor. Located just north of the equator, the islands are of volcanic origin and rise to 6,640 ft (2,024 m) on São Tomé. They have a tropical rain forest climate and a thick vegetation cover. The native inhabitants are mainly descendants of slaves imported from the mainland; there is a sizable population of migrant workers and contract laborers. Plantation-grown tropical produce, notably cocoa, copra, coconut, coffee, and cinchona, are exported. São Tomé island has a good road and railroad system. The islands were discovered (1471) by Pedro Escobar and Jaõa Gomes, the Portuguese explorers, and in 1483 the São Tomé settlement was founded. They were proclaimed a colony of Portugal in 1522. The Dutch held the islands from 1641 to 1740, when they were recovered by the Portuguese. Until the establishment of a plantation economy in the 18th cent., the islands were used mainly as supply stations on the shipping routes to Brazil and India. By 1974, in the wake of Portugal's recognition of the right of its African holdings to independence, the political future of the islands remained uncertain. The name also appears as São Thomé and Principe.

São Vicente (souN vēsĕn′tĭ), city (1970 pop. 116,625), São Paulo state, SE Brazil, off the mainland on an island in the Atlantic. It was the first permanent Portuguese settlement (1532) in Brazil and during the 16th and parts of the 17th cent. was capital of the São Vicente captaincy. It was sacked in 1591 by the English pirate Thomas Cavendish. São Vicente is now a residential suburb of Santos (which is also on the island) and an ultramodern beach resort.

São Vicente, Cabo de: see SAINT VINCENT, CAPE.

sap, fluid in plants consisting of water and dissolved substances. Cell sap refers to this fluid present in the large vacuole, or cell cavity, that occupies most of the central portion of mature plant cells. The term *sap* is generally applied to all the fluid that travels through the vascular tissues (xylem and phloem) of higher plants. Water containing dissolved minerals enters the plant through the root hairs by osmosis and is transported upward through the xylem to the parts containing chlorophyll, usually the leaves. There, large amounts of excess water leave the plant by transpiration, although some is used in photosynthesis to produce food materials. The phloem carries the resulting highly concentrated colloidal solution down to the other plant parts for storage. Sap ascends at a rate of from 1 to 4 ft (30–122 cm) per hr; in the coast redwood it rises easily to a height of almost 400 ft (120 m). The exact mechanisms behind this enormous lifting force are not certain, although several principles are thought to be involved. Chief among them is the pull of transpiration; as water evaporates from the leaf cells, they draw in liquid osmotically from the xylem tubes to replace it. Because of the great cohesiveness of water molecules, the resulting tension affects the entire continuous column of water down to the root tips, which in turn absorb more water from the soil. Root pressure is another factor, although it can force the sap up only a limited distance and operates chiefly in the nongrowing season, which explains the sap flow when a leafless tree is tapped in winter. Atmospheric pressure and capillary attraction, which could apply only to the lowest part of the xylem system, are minor factors. The sap of some plants (e.g., sugarcane and the sugar maple) contains much sugar and is an article of commerce. The name sap is sometimes applied to latex (e.g., rubber) and other specialized plant fluids.

Sapele (səpä'lē), city (1969 est. pop. 71,000), S Nigeria, a port in the Niger delta. The center of the Nigerian timber industry, Sapele has sawmills and a large plywood and veneer factory; rubber is processed there, and shoes are manufactured. After the British established a vice consulate in the city in 1892, Sapele grew in importance as a port; in 1894 it came under British protection and served as a local administrative center.

Saph (săf), Philistine giant killed by one of David's men. 2 Sam. 21.18. Sippai: 1 Chron. 20.4.

Saphir (sā'fər), unidentified village denounced by Micah. Micah 1.11.

Sapir, Edward (səpēr'), 1884–1939, American linguist and anthropologist, b. Pomerania. Sapir was brought to the United States in 1889. After teaching at the Univ. of California and the Univ. of Pennsylvania, he served (1910–25) as chief of the division of anthropology of the Canadian National Museum. He was professor of anthropology at the Univ. of Chicago (1925–31), and of anthropology and linguistics at Yale from 1931 until his death. His studies on the ethnology and linguistics of various Indian groups of the United States contributed greatly to the development of descriptive linguistics. Among his books are *Wishram Texts* (1909), *Time Perspective in Aboriginal American Culture* (1916), *Language: An Introduction to the Study of Speech* (1921), and *Nootka Texts* (1939).

sapodilla: see CHICLE.

saponin: see SOAP PLANT.

Sapor: see SHAPUR.

sapote (səpō'tā), name for several Central American trees and their fruits. Sapotes, sweet and pulpy, are commonly seen in tropical markets and are usually eaten fresh, although some are also used in preserves, e.g., the green sapote (*Calocarpum viride*) and *C. sapota,* also called marmalade-plum. These and the yellow sapote (*Lucuma salicifolia*) are of the sapodilla family. The white sapote (*Casimiroa edulis*), of the rue family, has been introduced throughout the Caribbean area and is sometimes grown in S California. The various sapotes are classified in the division MAGNOLIOPHYTA, class Magnoliopsida. *Calocarpum* and *Lucuma* are classified in the order Ebenales, class Sapotaceae, *Casimiroa* in the order Sapindales, family Rutaceae.

Sapphira (səfī'rə), wife of ANANIAS **1.**

sapphire, precious stone. A transparent blue CORUNDUM, it is classified among the most valuable of gems. Sapphires are found chiefly in Thailand, India, Ceylon, and Burma and also in Australia and in the United States (in Montana). The sapphires from Kashmir are of a beautiful cornflower blue and are highly valued. The Ceylonese varieties are paler; those from Montana have a metallic luster; and the Australian sapphires are of a dark blue shade approaching black. The terms yellow sapphire, purple sapphire, and green sapphire are used alternatively with Oriental topaz, Oriental amethyst, and Oriental emerald for other varieties of corundum. Like rubies of similar structure, some sapphires display a six-pointed star when cut to a cabochon (round-topped) shape and exposed to direct sunlight. Such star sapphires are usually obtained from Ceylon. Synthetic sapphires are made by the fusion of aluminum oxide, with titanium oxide added as a coloring agent.

Sappho (săf'ō), fl. early 6th cent. B.C., greatest of the early Greek lyric poets (Plato calls her "the tenth Muse"), b. Mytilene on Lesbos. Facts about her life are scant. She was an aristocrat, and apparently she was a member of a society of girls. There is reason to believe she was married and had a daughter. The legend that she fell in love with the youth Phaon and committed suicide by leaping from a cliff is almost certainly pure fiction. She and ALCAEUS may have exchanged responsive lyrics. The ancients had seven or nine books of her poetry (the first book originally consisted of 330 Sapphic stanzas). Only fragments survive, the longest (seven stanzas) is an invocation to Aphrodite asking her to help the poet in her relation with a beloved girl. She wrote in Aeolic dialect in a great many meters, one of which has been called, after her, the Sapphic. Her verse, the classic example of the "pure" love lyric, is characterized by passion, a love of nature, a direct simplicity, and perfect control of meter. She influenced many later poets, e.g., Catullus, Ovid, and Swinburne. See translations by J. M. Edmonds (3 vol., 1958–59), Mary Barnard (1962), Willis Barnstone (1965), and S. Q. Groden (1967); studies by D. M. Robinson (1930, repr. 1963) and D. L. Page (1965).

Sapporo (säp-pō'rō), city (1970 pop. 1,010,122), capital of Hokkaido prefecture, SW Hokkaido, Japan. It is one of Japan's most rapidly growing urban centers. Food processing, lumbering, woodworking, and printing are the major industries. Sapporo is also a tourist center. It is famous for its annual snow festival and played host to the 1972 winter Olympics. Hokkaido Univ. and Sapporo Agricultural School are in the city.

saprophyte (săp'rəfīt''), any plant that depends on dead plant or animal tissue for a source of nutrition and metabolic energy, e.g., most fungi (molds) and a few flowering plants, such as Indian pipe and some orchids. Most saprophytes do not produce chlorophyll and therefore do not photosynthesize; they are thus dependent on the food energy they absorb from the decaying tissues, which they help to break down.

sapsucker: see WOODPECKER.

Sapulpa (səpŭl'pə), city (1970 pop. 15,159), seat of Creek co., E central Okla; inc. 1898. It is the trade center of a farm and oil region. Pottery and glass products are the chief manufactures; steel tanks and oil-drilling equipment are also made. Heyburn Reservoir is nearby.

sapwood, relatively thin, youngest, outer part of the woody stem of a tree, the part that conducts water and dissolved materials. In the cross section of a tree, the sapwood is recognizable by its texture and color; it is softer and lighter than the inner HEARTWOOD. As the tree grows in diameter, the innermost layers of sapwood become heartwood, and new sapwood is produced on the outside of the woody column. See WOOD.

Sara or **Sarah,** wife of Abraham and mother of Isaac. She was one of the four Jewish matriarchs. Her name was originally Sarai. She was Abraham's lifelong companion; she was childless until, by divine favor, she gave birth to Isaac in her old age. After his birth, jealous of her handmaid Hagar, who was Abraham's concubine, she drove Hagar and her son Ishmael into the desert to die. Sarah died in Hebron at the age of 127 and was buried in the cave of Machpelah. Gen. 11.29–31; 23.19; Rom. 4.19; 9.9; Heb. 11.11; 1 Peter 3.6. The Sarah of Num. 26.46 is the same as SERAH.

saraband (sâr'əbănd), dance of Oriental origin that first appeared in Spain in the 16th cent. At that time it was characterized by alternate 3–4 and 3–8 meter and was accompanied by castanets and tambourines. Cervantes denounced it for its indecent gestures, and it was suppressed at the end of the reign of Philip II. In the 17th and 18th cent. it had a slow triple meter and a more dignified form. It then began to appear as a movement in the instrumental suite.

Saracens (sâr'əsənz), term commonly used in the Middle Ages to designate the Arabs and, by extension, the Muslims in general, whether they were Arabs, Moors, or Seljuk Turks. Strictly, the term applied only to the people of NW Arabia. In Spain and Portugal, the Muslims were known as Moors, rather than Saracens. The Saracens invaded France in the 8th cent., where they were defeated by Charles Martel. Their cultural influence in Europe is particularly noticeable in Sicily, which they held from the 9th to the 11th cent., and in S Italy. Palermo and Monreale have fine examples of the fused architectural styles of the Saracens, Byzantines, and Normans.

Saracoğlu, Şükrü (shükrü' säräj'ōlōō''), c.1890–1953, Turkish premier (1942–46). A lawyer, he became a political protégé of Kemal ATATÜRK and held many ministerial posts, including those of justice (1932–38) and foreign affairs (1938–42). As premier, his skillful diplomacy kept Turkey out of World War II until Feb., 1945, when it joined the Allies.

Saragat, Giuseppe (jōōsĕp'pē särä'gät), 1898–, Italian political leader. He joined the Socialist party in 1922 but left Italy after the Fascists came to power. He lived in exile, first in Vienna and then in Paris, returning to Rome after the Italian armistice with the Allies in 1943. In 1946 he became president of the constituent assembly that framed Italy's republican constitution. In 1947 he broke with the Socialist party headed by Pietro Nenni and founded (1951) the anti-Communist Democratic Socialist party. After serving as deputy premier and cabinet minister in several postwar governments, he was elected in 1964 as Italy's president. His term ended in 1971.

Saragossa, Spain: see ZARAGOZA.

Sarah or **Sarai:** see SARA.

Sarah Lawrence College, at Bronxville, N.Y.; primarily for women; chartered 1926, opened 1928 as Sarah Lawrence College for Women; renamed 1947. It is noted for its creative arts program.

Sarai (sərī'), former city, SE European USSR, near present-day Volgograd. Founded in 1241 by Batu Khan, it was (13th–15th cent.) the capital of the Tatar GOLDEN HORDE, to which the Russians paid tribute for more than 200 years. The city declined after Czar Ivan III threw off the Tatar yoke in 1480.

Sarajevo (sâr''əyā'vō), city (1971 pop. 292,241), capital of Bosnia and Hercegovina, S central Yugoslavia, on the Bosnia River. An important industrial and railway center, it has industries that manufacture metal products, electrical equipment, textiles, and tobacco. Lignite, iron ore, and manganese are mined nearby. The city is the seat of an Orthodox Eastern metropolitan, a Roman Catholic archbishop, and the chief ulema of the Yugoslav Muslims, who constitute a majority of the population. Founded in 1263, Sarajevo, then a citadel known as Vrh-Bosna, fell to the Turks in 1429 and was renamed Bosna-Saraj, or Bosna-Seraj. The town established around the citadel became an important Turkish military and commercial center and reached the peak of its prosperity in the 16th cent. The Congress of Berlin (1878) gave Sarajevo and the rest of BOSNIA AND HERCEGOVINA to Austria-Hungary, where it remained until its incorporation in 1918 into Yugoslavia. The city was a center of the Serbian nationalist movement. The assassination in Sarajevo of Archduke FRANCIS FERDINAND and his wife on June 28, 1914, was an immediate cause of World War I. The city has a university (founded in 1946), several Muslim seminaries, and various institutes of higher education. It is noted for its Muslim architecture, including its Oriental marketplace and more than 100 mosques, the most important one dating from 1450.

Saran, trademark for a man-made thermoplastic resin fiber that can be quickly and economically molded. Because it can be softened and reshaped again and again, little waste is occasioned. Saran is made in filaments and fabrics. Properties include resistance to chemicals, stains, abrasion, corrosion, and moisture. It is nonflammable, tough, and quite flexible. Its principal uses are in screen cloth, draperies, luggage, shoes, and upholstery.

Saranac Lake, village (1970 pop. 6,086), Essex and Franklin counties, N N.Y., in the Adirondacks; settled c.1819 as a lumbering town, inc. 1892. It is a major summer and winter resort community. It was developed as a health center after Edward L. Trudeau founded a tuberculosis sanatorium there in 1884. The sanatorium was closed in 1954, but its research center is still in operation. The Will Rogers Memorial Sanatorium (built 1930) is there.

Saransk (səränsk'), city (1970 pop. 191,000), capital of the Mordvinian Autonomous Republic, central

European USSR. Machine building and food processing are the major industries. Saransk was founded as a fort in 1680.

Saraph (sā'răf), Judahite. 1 Chron. 4.22.

Sarapis: see SERAPIS.

Sarapul (sərä'po͝ol), city (1969 est. pop. 94,000), E European USSR, in the Udmurt Autonomous Soviet Socialist Republic, on the Kama River. It has important dock facilities and is a rail junction on the Moscow-Sverdlovsk line. Industries include food processing, woodworking, tanning, and the production of oil field machinery, machine tools, radio equipment, steel, and aircraft parts. Founded in the late 16th cent., Sarapul was devastated in the Pugachev rebellion of 1773. During the early 19th cent. it served as a trade center on the route to Siberia.

Sarasate, Pablo de (pä'blō thā säräsä'tā), 1844–1908, Spanish violin virtuoso. He made difficult arrangements that displayed his brilliant technique and wrote violin pieces that effectively popularized what came to be known as the Spanish idiom. His most popular composition was *Zigeunerweisen.* Lalo, Bruch, and Saint-Saëns wrote concertos for him.

Sarasota (sâr"əsō'tə), city (1970 pop. 40,237), seat of Sarasota co., SW Fla., on Sarasota Bay; settled c.1884, inc. 1914. It is a yachting and fishing resort with a construction industry, varied light manufacturing, and packing houses handling the citrus fruit, celery, and beef raised in the area. Sarasota is the former winter home of the Ringling Brothers and Barnum & Bailey Circus and is the site of the beautiful John and Mable Ringling Museum of Art, which is reputed to have the largest Rubens collection in the United States. Other attractions are the Circus Hall of Fame and the Cars of Yesterday Museum. New College is in Sarasota. Nearby, on the keys off the Gulf of Mexico, are many beautiful white-sand beaches. The Sarasota Jungle Gardens and a state park are also in the area.

Sarasvati: see HINDUISM.

Saraswati, Dayananda (däyənŭn'də särŭs'wətē), 1824–83, Indian religious reformer, founder of the Arya Samaj movement. He was a Brahman from Gujarat who became the major spokesman for the 19th-century Hindu revival that placed exclusive authority in the Vedas. He condemned idol worship, untouchability, child marriage, and the low station of women, which he said were not sanctioned by the Vedas. In 1875 he founded the Arya Samaj [society of nobles] in Bombay to spread the doctrines of the newly reinterpreted Vedas. Although he was little concerned with politics, his message reawakened the Hindu traditionalists and reinforced the division between Muslim and Hindu in India.

Saratoga, residential city (1970 pop. 27,110), Santa Clara co., W Calif., in a vineyard and orchard area, in the foothills of the Santa Cruz mts.; inc. 1956. Wine is produced in the city; local attractions include tours of the champagne cellars. The Villa Montalvo estate (1912), home of the late Senator James Phelan, is a cultural center; its extensive facilities include art galleries, theaters, gardens, and an outdoor amphitheater.

Saratoga campaign, June–Oct., 1777, of the American Revolution. Lord George GERMAIN and John BURGOYNE were the chief authors of a plan to end the American Revolution by splitting the colonies along the Hudson River. Burgoyne was to advance S from Canada along Lake Champlain to Albany, where he would join Sir William HOWE, advancing N from New York City up the Hudson, and Barry ST. LEGER, coming E along the Mohawk River. Howe, however, became engaged in the campaign against Philadelphia, and Sir Henry CLINTON, who assumed the command in New York City, never reached Albany. Burgoyne had no trouble in taking TICONDEROGA (July 6), but his march south proved difficult. The column of Hessians (German mercenaries) he sent to raid Bennington was badly beaten (Aug. 14–16) by troops (including the GREEN MOUNTAIN BOYS) under John STARK and Seth WARNER. Meanwhile, the force under St. Leger besieged the Revolutionary forces at Fort Stanwix (Fort Schuyler). An American party under Nicholas HERKIMER, which had come to relieve the fort, was ambushed (Aug. 6, 1777) when crossing Oriskany Creek; Herkimer was mortally wounded, and the force dispersed. The British siege did not prosper, however, and when rumors came that a large Revolutionary force was approaching under Benedict ARNOLD, the Indians deserted the British service. St. Leger had to abandon (Aug. 22) the siege and retreated to Canada. Burgoyne continued southward, crossed the Hudson (Sept. 13), and halted near the present Saratoga Springs, where, on Bemis Heights, the Americans had taken up position. With Benjamin LINCOLN threatening his rear and his supplies running low, Burgoyne tried to break through at Freeman's Farm (Sept. 19) and at Bemis Heights (Oct. 7). Both attempts were stopped by Benedict Arnold, Daniel MORGAN, and Horatio GATES, who had replaced Philip J. Schuyler as American commander. The British commander then tried to retreat, but, finding himself outnumbered and surrounded, he surrendered on Oct. 17, 1777. The battle of Saratoga was the first great American victory of the war, and it is considered by many the decisive battle of the Revolution. Besides the heartening effect on the patriots, the campaign also encouraged the French, who had helped the victory by unofficial supplies and funds, to send official aid. See studies by Hoffman Nickerson (1928, repr. 1967), C.E. Bennett (1933), Harrison Bird (1963), and Rupert Furneaux (1971).

Saratoga National Historical Park: see NATIONAL PARKS AND MONUMENTS (table).

Saratoga Springs, resort and residential city (1970 pop. 18,845), Saratoga co., E N.Y.; inc. as a village 1826, as a city 1915. Skidmore College is the largest source of employment. Lingerie, electronic and electrical supplies, farm equipment, and food products are among the city's manufactures. The last battle of the SARATOGA CAMPAIGN was fought near the city in 1777. The nearby Saratoga National Historical Park embraces the battlefield. After the Revolution, as the fame of its carbonated mineral waters spread, the village became a health and pleasure resort. In the 19th cent. Saratoga Springs was one of the most popular social and sporting centers in America. Horse racing, which continues to be one of its major attractions, was begun after 1863. Of interest are the racing museum and many old buildings and homes, including the Casino (1867), a former gambling house that now houses two museums. An elaborate state-owned spa (1935) preserves and utilizes the waters and offers curative baths; there is also a research laboratory named for Simon Baruch. Saratoga Spa state park and a state tree nursery are south of the city. Petrified gardens are to the west, and to the north is the cottage on Mt. McGregor where President Ulysses S. Grant completed his memoirs and spent the last weeks of his life. See C. Amory, *The Last Resorts* (1952); and G. Waller, *Saratoga* (1966).

Saratov (sərä'təf), city (1970 pop. 785,000), capital of Saratov oblast, E European USSR, on the Volga River. It is a major industrial, transportation, and cultural center of the lower Volga region. Its river port is a transfer point for the agricultural products of the lower Volga valley and for petroleum from Baku. Saratov's industries produce precision instruments, building materials, construction equipment, and electric generators. There are oil refineries, ship-repairing docks, gas plants, and chemical factories. The city was founded c.1590 as a Russian sentry post on the Volga. Although its military importance declined in the 18th cent., the city retained significance for its river trade. In the late 19th cent. railroad construction tied Saratov to central European Russia. The city has a museum and a university named in honor of the literary critic N. G. Chernyshevsky, who was born there.

Sarawak (sərä'wäk), state (1971 pop. 977,013), 48,342 sq mi (125,206 sq km), Malaysia, in NW Borneo and on the South China Sea. It is bordered on the NE by Brunei and on the S and W by Kalimantan (Indonesian Borneo). KUCHING is the capital, and Sibu is an important port. Petroleum is the chief mineral, and sago, rice, and rubber are important commercial crops. Sometimes called the Land of the White Rajahs, Sarawak was ceded (1841) by the sultan of Brunei to James BROOKE, an Englishman, who became rajah of the independent state. It became a British protectorate in 1888, but remained under the control of the Brooke family. In World War II the area was occupied by the Japanese. The Brookes ceded Sarawak to the British in 1946, and it became a crown colony. A leftist revolt (Dec., 1962) in nearby Brunei spread to Sarawak, and rebels, who opposed the formation of the proposed Federation of MALAYSIA, occupied several towns. The revolt was quelled by British troops. However, sporadic activity by the rebels, who apparently were supported by Indonesia, continued into 1963, when Malaysia was formed. The name of the state is sometimes spelled Serawak.

Sarazen, Gene (sā'rəzən), 1902-, American golfer, b. Harrison, N.Y. He became a caddie at Rye, N.Y., and later taught golf at Fort Wayne, Ind. In 1922—at the age of 20—Sarazen won the U.S. Open championship. He won it again in 1932, the year he also won the British Open crown. He won the Professional Golfers Association championship three times (1922, 1923, 1933) and for several years played on the U.S. Ryder Cup teams. One of the great golfers of all time, Sarazen briefly returned to the sport in the 1950s and won the Professional Golfers Association Seniors championship in 1954 and 1958.

Sarcelles (särsĕl'), city (1968 pop. 51,803), Val-d'Oise dept., N central France. Mostly residential, it has some light industry. A church dating partly from the 12th cent. and partly from the Renaissance is in Sarcelles.

sarcoma (särkō'mə), highly malignant tumor arising in connective-cell tissue. It may affect bone, cartilage, blood vessels, lymph nodes, and skin. Its rapid development results in circulatory failure and degeneration of tissue, with ensuing infection and sepsis. See CANCER; NEOPLASM.

sarcophagus (särkŏf'əgəs) [Gr.,=flesh-eater], name given by the Greeks to a special marble found in Asia Minor, near the territory of ancient Troy, and used in caskets. It was believed to have the property of destroying the entire body, except for the teeth, within a few weeks. The term later generally designated any elaborate burial casket not sunk underground. The oldest known examples are from Egypt; they are box-shaped with a separate lid, which sometimes has sculptured effigies of the corpses. The sarcophagus of Tutankhamen (14th cent. B.C.), which was rediscovered in 1922, is of red granite and ornamented with reliefs of spirits with outspread wings. Later Egyptian sarcophagi were sometimes shaped to the body they contained. Sarcophagi were not in common use in Greece earlier than the 6th cent. B.C. because of the previous custom of cremation. After that time they became numerous. Records reveal that tne majority of sarcophagi were made of wood, but those that remain are of stone and terra-cotta, as evidenced in the early 6th-century examples (British Mus.) from Clazomenae. Many Greek and Etruscan sarcophagi are in the shape of a couch; others, such as the sarcophagus of Alexander the Great, are carved and painted in imitation of temple architecture. The marble sarcophagi (excavated in 1877) from Sidon, a chief city of ancient Phoenicia, are among the finest examples of Greek art. In Rome sarcophagi became popular before the Punic Wars. The earliest known example is that of the consul Cneius Cornelius Scipio of the 3d cent. B.C., now in the Vatican. Under the rule of the emperors Roman sarcophagi became elaborate, with mythological scenes carved on the sides and statues of the deceased on the lid. The early Christians also used sarcophagi for their distinguished dead. The carvings, usually representing Bible stories, are the chief source of early Christian sculpture. In the Middle Ages sarcophagi proper were used only in rare instances for especially elaborate entombments. Although memorials in the shape and decoration of sarcophagi were erected during the Renaissance and later, the body itself was almost always buried underground. See Erwin Panofsky, *Tomb Sculpture* (1964).

sard, semiprecious stone, a color variety of CHALCEDONY. It is very similar to carnelian but appears brownish red by reflected light and deep red by transmitted light, while carnelian is a brighter red. The color is believed to be caused by the presence of ferric oxide. It has been valued from ancient times.

Sardanapalus (särdənăp'ələs), in the *Persica* of CTESIAS, an Assyrian monarch who lived in great luxury. He was besieged in Nineveh by the Medes for two years, at the end of which time he set fire to his palace and burned himself and his court to death. Byron wrote a tragedy on the theme. The identity of Sardanapalus is a complete mystery, as the facts given in the legend certainly do not fit those of the life of ASSURBANIPAL, with whom some have tried to identify him.

Sardes: see SARDIS.

sardine: see HERRING.

Sardinia (särdĭn'ēə), Ital. *Sardegna,* region (1971 pop. 1,468,737), 9,302 sq mi (24,092 sq km), W Italy, mostly on the Mediterranean island of Sardinia, which is separated in the north from Corsica by the Strait of Bonifacio. The region also includes Asinara, Caprera, San Pietro, and La Maddalena islands. CAGLIARI is the capital of Sardinia, which is divided into the provinces of Cagliari, Nuoro, and Sassari (named for their capitals). The highest point of the mostly mountainous island is Mt. Gennargentu (6,016 ft/1,834 m). The main agricultural area is the large Campidano Plain, located in the southwest and watered by the Manno and Tirso rivers. Natural pastures cover more than half the area of Sardinia; sheep and goats are widely raised. Wheat, barley, grapes, olives, cork, and tobacco are produced. Sardinia is rich in minerals, including zinc, lead, antimony, lignite, copper, iron, and salt. Fishing for tuna, lobster, and sardines is important. There is still little industry, although hydroelectric plants, all-weather roads, and reclamation projects have been completed since 1945. Manufactures include processed food, wine, refined petroleum, paper, cement, and textiles. An early center of trade, Sardinia was mentioned in Egyptian sources in the 13th cent. B.C., and many traces of its prehistoric inhabitants remain. Phoenicians (c.800 B.C.) and Carthaginians (c.500 B.C.) settled there before Rome conquered (238 B.C.) the island. Sardinia was a source of grain and salt for the Romans, who governed the island harshly. After the fall of Rome, Sardinia passed to the Vandals (mid-5th cent. A.D.) and then to the Byzantines (early 6th cent.). The Byzantines neglected Sardinia, and the popes gained considerable power there; they claimed suzerainty over it and helped repel Arab attacks (8th–11th cent.). Later, Pisa and Genoa often fought (11th–14th cent.) for supremacy over the island, but neither held sway for long. Pisa had much influence on the art and architecture of Sardinia. In 1297, Pope Boniface VIII bestowed the island on the house of Aragón, from which it passed (late 15th cent.) to Spain. By the Peace of Utrecht (1713) Spain ceded it to Austria, but in 1717 Cardinal ALBERONI sent a Spanish force to occupy the island. The settlement of 1720 awarded Sardinia to VICTOR AMADEUS II of Savoy (who styled himself king of Sardinia) in exchange for Sicily, which was given to Holy Roman Emperor Charles VI. The kings of Sardinia usually resided at Turin. They tried to establish some order out of chaos on Sardinia with judicial, agrarian, and ecclesiastic reforms. Feudal privileges caused much unrest until they were abolished in 1835. Administrative autonomy was ended in 1847; however, the region received some autonomy under the Italian constitution of 1947. There are universities at Cagliari and Sassari.

Sardinia, kingdom of, name given to the possessions of the house of Savoy (see SAVOY, HOUSE OF) in 1720, when the island of Sardinia was awarded (by the Treaty of London) to Duke Victor Amadeus II of Savoy to compensate him for the loss of Sicily to Austria. Besides Sardinia, the kingdom included Savoy, PIEDMONT, and NICE; LIGURIA, including Genoa, was added by the Congress of Vienna in 1815. During the RISORGIMENTO the kingdom expanded to include almost all Italy. Lombardy was added in 1859. In 1860, Parma, Modena, Bologna, Marche, and the Romagna (i.e., the Papal States except Rome and Latium) were annexed by the kingdom. After the annexation (1861) of the Two Sicilies, Victor Emmanuel II of Sardinia was proclaimed king of Italy. Although the name of the kingdom of Sardinia was derived from the island, Turin was its capital except from 1799 to 1814, when the mainland territories were annexed by France. During that period, Cagliari, on Sardinia, was the royal residence.

Sardis (sär'dĭs) or **Sardes** (-dēz), ancient city of Lydia, W Asia Minor, at the foot of Mt. Tmolus, 35 mi (56 km) NE of the modern Izmir, Turkey. As capital of Lydia, it was the political and cultural center of Asia Minor from 650 B.C. until the death of CROESUS (c.547 B.C.). The first coins were minted there in the 6th cent. B.C. An almost impregnable citadel, Sardis was nevertheless captured in 499 by the Ionians in the Persian Wars. In 133 it passed to the Romans. An early seat of Christianity, Sardis was one of the SEVEN CHURCHES IN ASIA (Rev. 3.1). The city was destroyed by TAMERLANE in the 14th cent. Excavations uncovered the temple of Artemis (dating from the 4th cent. B.C.) and inscriptions in old Lydian. The actual site of the city was not discovered until 1958. In 1962 a large synagogue was uncovered.

Sardites (sär'dīts), descendants of SERED.

sardonyx (sär'dənĭks), banded variety of cryptocrystalline quartz. It has parallel layers of sard or of carnelian alternating with bands of onyx or of white chalcedony.

Sardou, Victorien (vĕktôryăN' särdo͞o'), 1831–1908, French dramatist. Author of some 70 plays, he won great popularity with his light comedies and pretentious historical pieces, but his reputation later declined. His best farce comedy is *Divorçons!* (1880, tr. 1881). Among his semihistorical melodramas are *Patrie!* (1869, tr. 1915) and *Fédora* (1882, tr. 1883), in which Sarah Bernhardt made her triumphant return to the Paris stage. Sardou's other plays written for her are *La Tosca* (1887, tr. 1925), the source of Puccini's opera, and *Cléopâtre* (1890). Two plays written for Sir Henry Irving, *Robespierre* (1899) and *Dante* (1903), were never given in French. Also among his plays in a lighter vein is *Madame Sans-Gêne* (1893, tr. 1901). Sardou was attacked for plagiarism but defended himself successfully. He was elected to the French Academy.

Sarema or **Saaremaa** (both: sä'rĕmä), Swed. *Ösel,* Rus. *Ezel,* 1,048 sq mi (2,714 sq km), island off the mainland of Estonia, W USSR, in the Baltic Sea, across the mouth of the Gulf of Riga. It is irregular in shape and has a level terrain. Dairy farming, stock raising, and fishing are the chief occupations. Kingisepp (formerly Kuressaare) is the main town and port. It is also a health resort. The island was ruled by the Livonian Knights until 1560, when it passed to Denmark, which in turn ceded (1645) it to Sweden. Sarema passed to Russia in 1710 and was incorporated into newly independent Estonia in 1917. It is also called Saare.

Sarepta (sərĕp'tə), variant of ZAREPHATH.

Sargasso Sea (särgăs'ō), part of the N Atlantic Ocean, lying roughly between the West Indies and the Azores and from about lat. 20°N to lat. 35°N, in the HORSE LATITUDES. The relatively still sea is the center of a great swirl of ocean currents and is a rich field for the marine biologist. It is noted for the abundance of gulfweed (see SEAWEED) on its surface. The Bermuda islands are in the northwestern part of the sea.

Sargassum (särgăs'əm), genus of brown algae that has given its name to the Sargasso Sea, where it is found in great abundance. See PHAEOPHYTA; SEAWEED.

Sargent, Henry, 1770–1845, American genre and portrait painter, b. Gloucester, Mass., studied in London with Benjamin West. He was skilled in the rendering of textures and accessories. Fine examples are his two conversation pieces *The Tea Party* and *The Dinner Party* (c.1840–42; Mus. of Fine Arts, Boston). The portrait of Peter Faneuil at Faneuil Hall in Boston is also attributed to him.

Sargent, John Singer, 1856–1925, American painter, b. Florence, Italy, of American parents, educated in Italy, France, and Germany. In 1874 he went to Paris, where he studied under Carolus-Duran. There he remained for 10 years except for visits to the United States, Spain, and Africa. From his first exhibit in the Salon of 1878 he received early recognition, and in 1884, when he moved to London, he already enjoyed a high reputation as a portrait painter. There he spent most of the remainder of his life, painting the dashing portraits of American and English social celebrities for which he is famous. In 1890 he was commissioned to paint a series of murals, *The History of Religion,* for the Boston Public Library. He completed them in 1916. An untiring and prolific painter of great facility, Sargent was particularly brilliant in his treatment of textures. In his portraiture he showed great virtuosity in his handling of the brushstroke, quickly capturing the likeness and vitality of his subject. His portraits nearly always flattered his sitters; he remarked upon this once, saying his was a pimp's profession. During his youth, and again after 1910, he deserted portrait painting long enough to produce a large number of brilliant impressionistic landscapes in watercolor, many of them painted in Venice and in the Tyrol. Of these, fine collections are in the Museum of Fine Arts, Boston, and the Brooklyn Museum. His portraits and figure pieces are housed in many private and public collections in England and the United States. Well-known examples are the portrait of Isabella Stewart Gardner and *El Jaleo* (Gardner Mus., Boston); the portraits of Mme X, the Wyndham sisters, Henry Marquand, and William Merritt Chase (Metropolitan Mus.); *The Fountain* (Art Inst., Chicago); and *Children of E. D. Boit* (Mus. of Fine Arts, Boston). See biography by C. M. Mount (3d ed. 1969); studies by D. F. Hoopes (1970) and Richard Ormond (1970).

Sargent, Sir Malcolm, 1895–1967, English conductor, whose original name was Harold Malcolm Watts-Sargent. He was a composer and organist prior to his debut as a conductor at Queen's Hall in 1921. He served as conductor with the D'Oyly Carte Opera Company and with Diaghilev's Ballets Russes (1927–30). An orthodox interpreter adhering to 19th-century tradition, Sargent was especially noted as a choral conductor. He served as conductor with the Royal Choral Society (after 1928), the Cortauld-Sargent Concerts (after 1929), and with the NBC Symphony Orchestra in his American debut. He was knighted in 1947. From 1950 to 1957 he was conductor of the BBC Symphony Orchestra.

Sargodha, city (1972 metropolitan area est. pop. 225,000), E Pakistan, on the lower Jhelum Canal. It is a center for trade in cotton and other agricultural commodities. Sargodha has a steel-rolling mill and railroad repair shops.

Sargon (sär'gŏn), king of Akkad in Mesopotamia (reigned c.2340–c.2305 B.C.). By conquest he established a great empire that included the whole of Mesopotamia and extended over Syria and Elam, and he controlled territories W to the Mediterranean and N to the Black Sea. Documents now support the theory that Sargon and his successors sent expeditions into SE Arabia as well as Asia Minor. The dynasty founded by Sargon lasted approximately 160 years; it was destroyed (c.2180 B.C.) by the Gutian barbarians from the Zagros mts. Sargon's dynasty did much to spread Semitic and Sumerian civilization. His name appears also as Sharukkin.

Sargon, d. 705 B.C., king of ASSYRIA (722–705 B.C.), successor to Shalmaneser V. He completed Shalmaneser's siege of Samaria in 721 B.C., thus destroying the northern Israelite kingdom forever. In 720 he defeated a coalition of enemies at Raphia. He captured Carchemish, subdued Babylonia, and advanced eastward to Kurdistan. He founded the last great Assyrian dynasty. Excavations of his palace at Dur Sharrukin (Khorsabad) have uncovered his personal annals, in which he recorded in detail his destruction of Samaria (2 Kings 17.6). His name appears also as Sharrukin.

Sari (särē'), city (1971 est. pop. 50,000), capital of Mazanderan prov., N Iran, near the Caspian Sea. It is the trade center for a farm region where citrus fruit, rice, and sugarcane are grown. The city is served by roads and a railroad.

Sarid (sā'rĭd), location, N Palestine, on the border of Zebulun. Joshua 19.10,12.

sarin (zärēn'), volatile liquid used as a NERVE GAS. It boils at 147°C but evaporates quickly at room temperature; its vapor is colorless and odorless. Sarin is more toxic than tabun or soman; however, a gas mask provides adequate protection, since the toxic effects arise chiefly from inhalation rather than from absorption through the skin. Chemically, sarin is fluoroisopropoxymethylphosphine oxide.

Sark, Fr. *Sercq* (sĕrk), island (1971 pop. 584), 2 sq mi (5 sq km), in the English Channel, E of Guernsey, one of the CHANNEL ISLANDS. It is divided into Great Sark and Little Sark, which are connected by a natural causeway, the Coupée. The interior is reached through tunnels from Creux Harbour, the landing place, on the east. The island belongs to Guernsey bailiwick; its local government is a survival of the feudal system. The economy is agricultural.

Sarmatia (särmā'shə), ancient district between the Vistula River and the Caspian Sea, occupied by the Sarmatians [Lat. *Sarmatae*] from the 3d cent. B.C. through the 2d cent. A.D. The term is vague and is also used to refer to the territory along the Danube and across the Carpathians where the **Sarmatians** were later driven by the Huns. The Sarmatians, who until c.200 B.C. lived E of the Don River, spoke an Indo-Iranian language and were a nomadic pastoral people related to the Scythians, whom they displaced in the Don region. The main divisions were the Rhoxolani, the Iazyges, and the Alans or Alani. They came into conflict with the Romans but later allied themselves with Rome, acting as buffers against the Germans. They were scattered or assimilated with the Germans by the 3d cent. A.D. See study by Tadeusz Sulimirski (1970).

Sarmiento, Domingo Faustino (dōmēng'gō foustē'nō särmyān'tō), 1811–88, Argentine statesman, educator, and author, president of the republic (1868–74). An opponent of Juan Manuel de ROSAS, he spent years of exile in Chile, becoming known as a journalist and an educational reformer. He toured Europe and North America and was impressed by the school system and the political organization of the United States. He helped URQUIZA to overthrow Rosas in 1852 and became active in politics. In Oct., 1868, he succeeded Bartolomé MITRE as president. His administration was marked by the conclusion of the War of the Triple Alliance against Paraguay, by material progress, and, especially, by the organization of schools and the reform of educational methods. Sarmiento was succeeded by Nicolás AVELLANEDA. His essays on education and politics, historical studies, and critical works are distinguished by crisp style. Best known is *Facundo, o Civilización i barbarie* (1845; tr. *Life in the Argentine Republic in the Days of the Tyrants,* new ed. 1961), nominally a biography of Juan Facundo QUIROGA, but actually an in-depth study of *caudillismo,* personalism in politics. See *Sarmiento's Travels in the United States in 1847,* tr. by M. A. Rockland (1970); *A Sarmiento Anthology* (tr. and ed. by S. E. Grummon and A. W. Bunkley, 1948); biographies by A. W. Bunkley (1952) and F. G. Crowley (1972).

Sarmiento de Acuña, Diego: see GONDOMAR, DIEGO SARMIENTO DE ACUÑA, CONDE DE.

Sarnath (särnät'), archaeological site, SE Uttar Pradesh, India, 4 mi (6.4 km) N of Varanasi (Benares). It is the site of the deer park (mrigadawa) where, according to tradition, Buddha first preached. Buddhist monuments include an inscribed pillar (3d cent. B.C.) of Emperor Asoka and a stupa (7th cent. A.D.), c.140 ft (42 m), high.

Sarnia, city (1971 pop. 57,644), S Ont., Canada, on the St. Clair River, at the south end of Lake Huron and opposite Port Huron, Mich. The two cities are connected by a railroad tunnel, and there is a bridge between Port Huron and Point Edward, just N of Sarnia. The city is a port and handles a large volume of freight for transshipment from railroads to lake steamers. There are grain elevators, machinery plants, oil refineries, and chemical and synthetic-rubber industries.

Sarnoff, David, 1891-1971, American pioneer in radio and television, b. Russia. Emigrating to the United States in 1900, he worked for the Marconi Wireless Co., winning recognition as the narrator of the news of the Titanic disaster (1912). The Radio Corporation of America absorbed the Marconi firm in 1921, and Sarnoff became general manager. As president (after 1930), he played a major role in the development of television. In 1947 he became the chairman of the board. He served Dwight D. Eisenhower in World War II as adviser on communications. Active in public affairs, he was often a spokesman for the broadcasting industry.

Saron (sā'rən), variant of SHARON.

Saronic Gulf (sərŏ'nĭk), arm of the Aegean Sea, indenting SE Greece and separated from the Gulf of Corinth by the Isthmus of Corinth. The Saronic Gulf is the eastern terminus of the Corinth Canal, which cuts across the isthmus. Athens, Piraiévs, Elevsís, and Mégara are on or near the gulf, which also contains many islands, notably Aegina and Salamís. It is also known as the Gulf of Aegina.

saros: see ECLIPSE.

Saroyan, William (səroi'ən), 1908–, American author, b. Fresno, Calif. An extremely prolific writer, Saroyan produces works that combine optimism, sentimentality, and a rhapsodic love of country. His major works include plays such as *The Time of Your Life* (1939; Pulitzer Prize), *My Heart's in the Highlands* (1939), and *The Cave Dwellers* (1957); novels, including *The Human Comedy* (1942) and *Boys and Girls Together* (1963); short-story volumes, notably *The Daring Young Man on the Flying Trapeze* (1934) and *My Name is Aram* (1940); and such autobiographical works as *Here Comes, There Goes, You Know Who* (1961) and *Places Where I've Done Time* (1972). See biography by H. R. Floan (1966).

Sarpedon (särpē'dən), in Greek mythology, son of Zeus and Laodamia, who was the daughter of Bellerophon. In the *Iliad*, as an ally of the Trojans, Sarpedon courageously led the Lycians against the Greeks in the Trojan War. He was killed by Patroclus, and Zeus had him carried back to Lycia for a hero's burial. According to post-Homeric legend, Sarpedon was the son of Zeus and Europa who, after a quarrel with his brother Minos, fled to Lycia.

Sarpi, Paolo (pä'ōlō sär'pē), 1552-1623, Venetian councillor, theologian, and historian. In 1565 he became a Servite friar and later theologian and adviser to the republic. In the conflict that developed in 1606 between Venice and Pope PAUL V he staunchly defended the right of the state to control ecclesiastic matters. In his writings against the papal interdict he showed intransigence. In 1607 his prestige was increased when he was wounded in an attempt, said to be sponsored by the pope, to seize him by force. His most important work is his history of the Council of Trent, in which he viewed the council as the triumph of papal absolutism and centralization. The work was published in London in 1619; many editions and translations followed.

Sarpsborg (särps'bôr), city (1970 pop. 13,363), Ostfold co., SE Norway, a port on the Glåma River near its mouth in the Oslofjord. Manufactures include forest products, chemicals, and textiles. There is a large hydroelectric plant. Sarpsborg was founded in 1016 by Olaf II, was burned by the Swedes in 1567, and was rebuilt in 1839. Skjeberg Church, a medieval stone structure, is nearby.

Sarraut, Albert Pierre (älběr' pyěr särō'), 1872-1962, French leader, a Radical Socialist. A member of the chamber of deputies from 1902, he was governor general (1911-14, 1916-19) of French Indochina, and from 1920 to 1940 he was almost continuously a member of French cabinets. Briefly premier in 1933 and 1936, Sarraut favored military action against the German occupation (1936) of the Rhineland but was unable to implement the policy. During World War II, he was arrested (1944) and deported to Germany, but was freed by the Allies in 1945. After the war he was editor of the powerful newspaper *Dépêche de Toulouse* and president (1959-60) of the FRENCH UNION.

Sarraute, Nathalie (nätälē' särōt'), 1902–, French novelist, b. Russia. Sarraute's *Tropismes* (1939, tr. 1967) and *Portrait d'un inconnu* (1949, tr. 1958) were revolutionary in technique. Sartre brought them to public attention. Termed "antinovels," they focus upon psychological preoccupations, giving subconscious impulses surrealistic and analytic treatment. Her later novels, *Martereau* (1953), *Le Planétarium* (1959, tr. 1960), and *Do You Hear Them?* (1972, tr. 1973) show some compromise with traditional form. Sarraute's essays on the novel were published in *Age of Suspicion* (1956, tr. 1963). See study by R. Z. Temple (1968).

Sarrazin or **Sarazin, Jacques** (zhäk särăzăN'), 1588-1660, French sculptor and painter, a founder (1648) and rector (1654) of the Académie royale. He spent much time in Rome (1610-c.1627) and was one of the first to carry the classicizing trend to France. Examples of his work are the caryatids for Lemercier's Pavillon de l'Horloge at the Louvre and the tomb of Henri II, prince de Condé (Chantilly). He was an influential teacher of many sculptors.

Sarre: see SAAR, river; SAARLAND.

Sarrelouis: see SAARLOUIS, West Germany.

sarrusophone (sərŭs'əfōn), brass keyed wind instrument, played with a double reed, thus a member of the OBOE family. Invented in 1856 by Sarrus, a French bandmaster, it is made in several sizes and was once much used in French bands to replace the weaker-toned oboes and bassoons. Only the contrabass was very successful, replacing the contrabassoon in French orchestras for a time.

sarsaparilla (särs"pərĭl'ə, săs"-), common name for various plants belonging to two different classes and also for an extract from their roots, much used in medicine and in beverages. True sarsaparilla is obtained from various tropical American species of the genus *Smilax* (which also includes the greenbrier) of the family Liliaceae (LILY family). These have thick rootstalks and thin roots several feet long. Other plants used as substitutes for sarsaparilla include the wild sarsaparilla (*Aralia nudicaulis*) and the American spikenard (*A. racemosa*), both North American plants of the family Araliaceae (GINSENG family). The Liliaceae are classified in the division MAGNOLIOPHYTA, class Liliatae, order Liliales. The Araliaceae are in the class Magnoliopsida, order Umbellales.

Sarsechim (särsē'kĭm, sär'sēkĭm), general with Nebuchadnezzar at Jerusalem. Jer. 39.3.

Sarsfield, Patrick, earl of Lucan (särs'fēld, lo͞o'kən), d. 1693, Irish Jacobite general. A firm supporter of James II, he went with him into exile. He commanded James's forces in Ireland and had some successes, but defeat by William III in the battle of the Boyne (1690) destroyed the Jacobite hopes in Ireland. He was forced (1691) to arrange the disadvantageous treaty of Limerick, surrendering that city. Allowed to go to France, he took thousands of Irish soldiers with him into French service in the War of the Grand Alliance. He fought at Steenkerke (1692) and was mortally wounded at Neerwinden.

Sarsi Indians (sär'sē), North American Indians whose language belongs to the ATHABASCAN branch of the Nadene linguistic stock (see also AMERICAN INDIAN LANGUAGES). They are also known as the Sarcee Indians. At the beginning of the 19th cent., their hunting grounds were on the upper Saskatchewan River. Attacks by the Cree and other Indians caused the Sarsi to ally themselves with the BLACKFOOT INDIANS for protection. Although their customs were greatly modified by association with this Plains tribe, their language remained uncorrupted. In 1877 they ceded their lands to the Canadian government and in 1880 moved to a reservation at Calgary, Alberta.

Sartain, John (sārtān'), 1808-97, American engraver, b. London. Shortly after his arrival in the United States in 1830, he received important commissions for prints after paintings by leading artists. He is known for having introduced pictorial illustration as an important feature of American periodicals, most notably in *Graham's Magazine* and in *Sartain's Union Magazine of Literature and Art*, which he founded in 1849. He pioneered in mezzotint engraving in the United States, and produced many fine engravings after such painters as Benjamin West and Thomas Sully. His daughter, **Emily Sartain,** 1841-1927, b. Philadelphia, was an engraver and painter. She studied with her father and in Paris. Her painting *The Reproof* was exhibited at the Centennial Exposition, Philadelphia, in 1876. She executed some mezzotint engravings and in 1886 became principal of the Philadelphia School of Design for Women. A son, **Samuel Sartain,** 1830-1906, b. Philadelphia, was also an engraver. He studied mezzotint engraving with his father and engraved after paintings by C.W. Peale, Thomas Sully, and others. Another son, **William Sartain,** 1843-1924, b. Philadelphia, engraver and painter, studied with his father and in Paris. Achieving success in Europe with his romantic landscapes and genre and allegorical scenes, he returned to the United States (1877), where he divided his time between painting and teaching in New York City and Philadelphia. Among his highly popular canvases are *Street in Dinon, Brittany* (Corcoran Gall.) and *Algerian Water Carrier* (National Gall. of Art, Washington, D.C.).

Sarthe (särt), department (1968 pop. 461,839), NW France. Le MANS is the capital.

Sarto, Andrea del (ändrĕ'ä dĕl sär'tō), 1486-1531, Florentine painter of the High Renaissance. He painted chiefly religious subjects. In 1509 he was commissioned by the Servites to decorate their Cloisters of the Annunziata in Florence. His five frescoes there, illustrating the life of St. Philip, won him the title "the faultless painter." Also in this court are *Nativity of the Virgin, Procession of the Magi,* and a lunette, *Madonna del Sacco*. His notable scenes from the life of St. John the Baptist in monotone are in the Cloisters of the Scalzo, Florence, and the *Last Supper* is in the refectory of the Convent of San Salvi. His oils include two *Annunciations, Deposition from the Cross,* two *Assumptions, Madonna in Glory* (Pitti Palace, Florence); *Madonna of the Harpies* (Uffizi); *Holy Family* and *Charity* (Louvre); *Holy Family* (Metropolitan Mus.); *Madonna and Child with St. John* (National Gall. of Art, Washington, D.C.); and others in London and Madrid. Del Sarto is noted for his harmonious coloring and consonance of figures and background. Toward the end of his career, his representations tended toward mannerism. He was the teacher of the great mannerist Pontormo. See studies by S. J. Freedberg (2 vol., 1963) and John Shearman (2 vol., 1965).

Sarton, May, 1912–, American poet and novelist, b. Belgium. Her father was the science historian George Sarton. Although cast in traditional molds, her poetry is modern in its wit and avoidance of dogmatism. Among her volumes of poetry are *Encounter in April* (1937), *In Time Like Air* (1957), *A Durable Fire* (1972), and *Collected Poems 1930–1973* (1974). Her novels, which often analyze intense but civilized relationships, include *Faithful Are The Wounds* (1955), *Kinds of Love* (1970), and *As We Are Now* (1973). See her autobiographical *Plant Dreaming Deep* (1969) and *Journal of a Solitude* (1973); biography by Agnes Sibley (1972).

Sartre, Jean-Paul (zhäN-pôl sär'trə), 1905–, French existential philosopher, playwright, and novelist. Influenced by German philosophy, particularly that of Heidegger, Sartre has become a leading exponent of 20th-century EXISTENTIALISM. His writings examine man as a responsible but lonely being, burdened with a terrifying freedom to choose and set adrift in a meaningless universe. His first novel, *Nausea* (1938, tr. 1949), was followed by *Intimacy* (1939, tr. 1949), a collection of short stories. Sartre served in the army during World War II, was taken prisoner, escaped, and became a resistance leader. During the occupation he wrote his first plays, *The Flies* (1943, tr. 1946) and *No Exit* (1944, tr. 1946), and the monumental treatise *Being and Nothingness* (1943, tr. 1953). His plays express his philosophy and have been successful as theater. After the war Sartre's writings became increasingly influential, and his ideas began to reflect his interest in Marxism. In 1945 he founded the periodical *Les Temps modernes.* His other major works include the trilogy of novels *The Age of Reason, The Reprieve* (both: 1945, tr. 1947), and *Troubled Sleep* (1949, tr. 1951); and the plays *The Respectful Prostitute* (1947, tr. 1949), *Dirty Hands* (1948, tr. 1949), *The Devil and the Good Lord* (1951, tr. 1953), and *The Condemned of Altona* (1956, tr. 1961). He has written several major studies of literary figures; a nine-volume collection of his literary and philosophical essays was published as *Situations* (1947-65; tr. in part, 1968). His essay collections in translation include *The Philosophy of Jean-Paul Sartre* (ed. by R. D. Cumming, 1965), *Essays in Aesthetics* (1963), and *Of Human Freedom* (1967). Among his later individual essays are *What Is*

Literature? (1948, tr. 1965), *The Ghost of Stalin* (tr. 1968), and *On Genocide* (1968). Sartre declined the 1964 Nobel Prize in Literature on the grounds that such awards lend too much weight to a writer's influence. Simone de BEAUVOIR, his close associate of many years, wrote about him in her autobiography, *The Prime of Life* (tr. 1962). See his autobiographical *The Words* (1964); studies by Benjamin Suhl (1970), Liselotte Richter (tr. 1970), R. D. Laing and D. G. Cooper (1971), H. E. Barnes (1973), and M. G. Grene (1973).

Saruch (sā'rək), variant of SERUG.

Sasebo (säsā'bō), city (1970 pop. 247,845), Nagasaki prefecture, W Kyushu, Japan. It is a port and naval base on the East China Sea. Shipbuilding, machine building, and food processing are the chief industries.

Saskatchewan (səskăch'əwən, -wän", săs"-), province (1971 pop. 926,242), 251,700 sq mi (651,903 sq km), W Canada. REGINA is the capital and largest city; other important cities are PRINCE ALBERT, SASKATOON, and MOOSE JAW. Saskatchewan is bounded on the N by the Northwest Territories, on the E by

Manitoba, on the S by North Dakota and Montana, and on the W by Alberta. Its desolate northern third is part of the Laurentian Plateau. The principal rivers are the Churchill, the North and South Saskatchewan, and the Qu'Appelle. Between the Saskatchewan and Churchill rivers lies a mixed forest belt containing much marketable timber; a section is reserved as Prince Albert National Park. Only in S Saskatchewan has there been any substantial settlement or development. Except for a semiarid section in the southwest used for grazing and an area in the east and central portion given over to mixed farming and dairying, the land is devoted to the raising of hard wheat. The vast expanses of unbroken plain are well-suited to large-scale mechanized farming. Oats, barley, rye, and flax are also grown throughout this region. Saskatchewan is rich in minerals. The region north of Lake Athabaska has been exploited for ores yielding uranium. The region around Flin Flon, in the northeast, is mined for copper, zinc, and gold. Coal is mined in the southwest, and in the prairie land oil and natural gas have been discovered. Potash mining was begun in the 1950s near Saskatoon and Esterhazy, and Canada is now the world's leading producer of this mineral. Most of the province's industries process raw materials. A steel mill was opened in Regina in 1960. The historic occupation of fur trapping is still practiced. Henry Kelsey of the Hudson's Bay Company was probably the first white man to see the area of Saskatchewan (c.1690). The earliest trading posts were established by the French (c.1750), but the first permanent settlement was made at Cumberland House in 1774 by the Hudson's Bay Company. Subsequently many other posts were set up by British fur traders along the region's waterways. In 1870 the Hudson's Bay Company, which had merged with the North West Company in 1821, ceded its rights to the Canadian government, and the area became part of the Northwest Territories. The construction of a rail line (1882) brought many settlers from E Canada and later from Europe and opened up trade through the Great Lakes ports. Most Indians in the Northwest Territories sold their lands to the government in the 1870s and were placed on reservations. Other Saskatchewan Indians and métis, people of mixed French and Indian ancestry, led by Louis RIEL, rebelled in 1884–85 and were suppressed. Saskatchewan became a province in 1905. In the early 20th cent. Saskatchewan farmers formed cooperative organizations to stabilize grain marketing. During the drought and depression of the 1930s the province's population declined as immigration almost stopped and many families left the area. Conservation programs and the increased demand for grain during World War II revived the economy. Except for the period from 1964 to 1971, when the Liberals were in power, Saskatchewan has been governed since 1944 by the socialist New Democratic Party (until 1961 called the Cooperative Commonwealth Federation). Among the socialists' achievements has been the enactment of compulsory hospital and medical insurance. See M. W. Campbell, *The Saskatchewan* (1950); J. F. Wright, *Saskatchewan* (1955); E. A. McCourt, *Saskatchewan* (1968); J. W. Bennett, *Northern Plainsmen* (1969); S. M. Lipset, *Agrarian Socialism* (new and enl. ed. 1972).

Saskatchewan, river, c.340 mi (550 km) long, formed by the confluence of the North Saskatchewan (c.760 mi/1,220 km long) and the South Saskatchewan (c.550 mi/890 km long) rivers near Prince Albert, central Sask., Canada; the system drains most of the Canadian prairie provinces. It flows generally east past Nipawin, across the Manitoba line, then past The Pas and through Cedar Lake to Lake Winnipeg. The North Saskatchewan River rises in the Columbia ice field at the foot of Mt. Saskatchewan, SW Alta., and flows generally east past Edmonton, into Saskatchewan prov., and then past North Battleford to Prince Albert. Its chief tributaries are the Clearwater, Brazeau, Vermillion, and Battle rivers. The South Saskatchewan River is formed in S Alberta by the junction of the Bow and Oldman rivers. It flows east past Medicine Hat, then northeast into Saskatchewan prov., past Saskatoon, to Prince Albert; it receives the Red Deer River. The Bow–South Saskatchewan–Saskatchewan system is c.1,200 mi (1,930 km) long. Completion (1967) of the Gardiner and Qu'Appelle Valley dams, major elements of the South Sasketchewan River Project, impound Lake Diefenbaker, a huge reservoir. The dams and reservoir provide hydroelectric power and irrigation for a large region south of Saskatoon. The Saskatchewan River and its branches were once important thoroughfares for explorers and trappers.

Saskatchewan, University of, at Saskatoon and Regina, Sask., Canada; provincially supported, coeducational; chartered 1907, opened 1909. It has faculties of agriculture, arts and science, commerce, education, engineering, law, music, pharmacy, medicine, home economics, graduate and research studies, dentistry, veterinary medicine, administration, nursing, and physical education.

Saskatoon (săskətōōn'), city (1971 pop. 126,449), S central Sask., Canada, on the South Saskatchewan River. The second largest city in the province, it is the chief manufacturing and distributing center for central and N Saskatchewan. There are grain elevators, grain and flour mills, stockyards, meat-packing plants, oil refineries, and potash-processing plants in the city. Saskatoon was settled in 1883 and grew rapidly after the coming of the railroad (1890). The Univ. of Saskatchewan with its affiliated colleges is there, and a dominion forestry station is nearby. The name derives from a Cree Indian word for a berry found in the area.

sassaby: see DAMALISK.

sassafras: see LAUREL.

Sassafras Mountain, peak, 3,560 ft (1,085 m) high, NW S.C., in the Blue Ridge mts., near the N.C. and Ga. lines; highest point in South Carolina.

Sassanid (săs'ənĭd) or **Sassanian** (săsā'nyən), last dynasty of native rulers to reign in Persia before the Arab conquest. The period of their dominion extended from A.D. c.224, when the Parthians were overthrown and the capital, Ctesiphon, was taken, until c.640, when the country fell under the power of the Arabs. The last Sassanian king died a fugitive in 651, but he had been forced to yield Ctesiphon to the Arabs in 636. Under the Sassanids, who revived Achaemenid tradition, the ancient Zoroastrianism was reestablished as the state religion. The name of the dynasty was derived from Sassan, an ancestor of the founder of the dynasty, ARDASHIR I, who took possession of Ctesiphon in 224 and reigned until 240. During his reign and many of those that followed, war with the Romans occupied much attention. Sassanian persecution of the Christians led to wars with Byzantium. Syria and Armenia suffered particularly from invading armies. Ardashir I was succeeded by his son SHAPUR I who was victorious over Roman Emperor Valerian and ruled until 272. The next reign of importance was that of SHAPUR II, from 309 to 379, a period of particular significance and glory. Bahram V, ruling 420 to 438, was defeated by the Emperor Theodosius, but was successful against the White Huns. The Armenians were overwhelmed by Yazdagird II in 451, and their land was overrun by the Sassanians under KHOSRU I, who reigned from 531 to 579 and who also invaded Syria. Both countries were again invaded by KHOSRU II, reigning 590 to 628, whose conquest of Egypt was the final victorious achievement of the dynasty. The last representative of the family on the throne was Yazdagird III, who began his reign in 632. His struggle against the Arabs ended in the fall of the Sassanid dynasty. See PERSIA.

Sassari (säs'särē), city (1971 pop. 107,200), capital of Sassari prov., NW Sardinia, Italy. It is an agricultural trade center, handling cheese, wine, fruit, and olive oil. Zinc and lead are mined nearby. Sassari was an important center in the Middle Ages and was held (13th cent.) by Genoa and (14th cent.) by the Aragonese. It passed to Piedmont in the early 18th cent. There is a cathedral (11th–13th cent.) with a baroque facade; a university (founded in the early 17th cent.); and an Aragonese castle.

Sassetta (säs-sĕt'tä), c.1400–1450, Italian painter of the Sienese school, whose original name was Stefano di Giovanni. A popular artist, he painted many large altarpieces, scenes from the life of St. Anthony (Yale Univ.; Philip Lehman Coll., New York City; National Gall. of Art, Washington, D.C.), and *Journey of the Magi* (Metropolitan Mus.), although the authenticity of some of the works attributed to him is dubious.

Sassnitz, East Germany: see RÜGEN.

Sassoferrato (säs"sōfär-rä'tō), 1605–85, Italian painter; pupil of Domenichino. His original name was Giovanni Battista Salvi. He is best known for his sentimental Madonnas, reminiscent of Raphael's, such as the *Madonna of the Rosary* (Santa Sabina, Rome) and *Madonna* (Metropolitan Mus.).

Sassoon, Siegfried, 1886–1967, English poet and novelist. An officer in World War I, he expressed his conviction of the brutality and waste of war in grim, forceful, realistic verse—*The Old Huntsman* (1917), *Counter-Attack* (1918), *Satirical Poems* (1926), *Vigils* (1935), *Sequences* (1957), and others. His fictional, semiautobiographical trilogy—*Memoirs of a Fox-hunting Man* (1928), *Memoirs of an Infantry Officer* (1930), *Sherston's Progress* (1936)—was collected as *The Memoirs of George Sherston* (1937). Sassoon also wrote several autobiographical works—*The Old Century and Seven More Years* (1938), *The Weald of Youth* (1942), and *Siegfried's Journey* (1945)—and a biography of George Meredith (1948). See his *Collected Poems, 1908–1956* (1961).

Sastre, Alfonso (älfōn'sō sä'strā), 1926–, Spanish dramatist, essayist, and critic, b. Madrid. He favors the problems of society's needy and rejected and pleads for justice in a world free of violence and hatred. His best-known plays include *Escuadra hacia la muerte* [squad toward death] (1953), *La mordaza* [the gag] (1954), *La sangre de Dios* [the blood of God] (1956), and *La cornade* [the thrust] (1960). See study by Farris Anderson (1971).

Satalia or **Satalieh,** variants of ANTALYA.

Satan [Heb.,=adversary]. In Judaeo-Christian terminology, *devil* and *demon* are used interchangeably to mean all evil supernatural beings, whereas *the Devil* has specific reference to Satan, the great adversary of man. In Christian tradition, Satan and the other devils (as the minor fallen angels were called) were originally created good but chose to become evil by their own free will, rebelled against God, and were cast out of heaven (Rev. 12.7–9). They became the tempters of men and the source of evil in the world. The Christian Church also has held that the fall of man was the result of Satan's actions, although this is not implied in Gen. 2 itself. Further, in Job, Satan is seen as a collector of information for the divine tribunals, suggesting that his role of adversary may be in terms of jurisprudence. The original offense of Satan against God is not clearly stated in the Scriptures but is generally held to be a result of his desire to be independent of God and to be His equal. Jude 6 and Revelation. The idea of Satan is closely related to ideas of the dualism of good and evil, light and dark, in ancient religions of the East. For example, the Egyptians considered the diabolical Seth to be the brother of the supreme solar deity, Ra: among the Zoroastrians, Ahriman, the principle of evil, was generated from the mind of Ormazd, the god of creativity and justice. Another aspect of Satan may be traced to various myths of gift-bearing deities. According to the Greek legend, Prometheus gave fire to man, whereas Satan gave man the knowledge of good and evil. The Satanic flaw, his pride and desire to be God, is a familiar myth in many cultures. Generally it was the Middle Ages that gave Satan his familiar attributes in folk tale—his hooves, his sulfurous odor, his horns, and, paradoxically, his polished, gentlemanly manners. Much of his appearance, however, and many of his actions can be traced back to the pre-Christian nature deities of Europe, such as the two-headed god Janus and a variety of Panlike nature and fertility deities. Scholars have frequently argued that WITCHCRAFT surrounding Satan was basically the continuation of pagan worship into Christian times. The names and nicknames of Satan are countless. Besides Satan (1 Chron. 21.1; Job 1-2; Zech. 3.1,2; Luke 10.18; Acts 26.18; 2 Cor. 2.11; 11.14) and Lucifer (Isa. 14.12), there are Abaddon and Apollyon (Rev. 9.11), Asmodeus (Tobit 3.17), Beelzebub or Baalzebub (Mat. 10.25; 12.22-30; Mark 3.22-30; Luke 11.14-26), and Belial. Antichrist is not properly a name for Satan. English names are Dragon, Serpent (Rev. 12.9; 20.2), Evil One, God of This World (2 Cor. 4.4), Prince of Darkness, Prince of the Devils (Mat. 9.34), Prince of Power of the Air (Eph. 2.2), Prince of This World (John 12.31; 14.30; 16.11), Tempter (1 Thess. 3.5), and Wicked One (Mat. 13.19). See Daniel Defoe, *History of the Devil* (1819, repr. 1972); William Woods, *A History of the Devil* (1974).

Satanism. The cult of Satan, or Satan worship, is in part a survival of the ancient worship of demons and in part a revolt against Christianity or the church. It rose about the 12th cent. in Europe and reached its culmination in the blasphemous ritual of the Black Mass, a desecration and perversion of the Christian rite. The history of Satanism is obscure. It was revived in the reign of Louis XIV in France and is said to be still practiced occasionally throughout the world. See WITCHCRAFT.

satellite, artificial, man-made object placed in orbit around the earth or other celestial body. The satellite is lifted from the earth's surface by a rocket and, once placed in orbit, maintains its motion without further rocket propulsion. If placed high enough to escape the frictional effects of the earth's atmosphere, the motion of the satellite is controlled by the same laws of celestial mechanics that govern the motions of natural satellites, and it will remain in orbit indefinitely. At heights less than 200 mi (320 km) the drag produced by the atmosphere will slow it down, causing it to descend into the denser portion of the atmosphere where it will burn up like a meteor. To attain an orbit, multistage rockets are used, with each stage falling away as its fuel is exhausted; the effect of reducing the total mass of the rocket while maintaining its thrust is to increase its speed, thus allowing it to achieve the required escape velocity of 7 mi per sec (11.3 km per sec). Once above the lower atmosphere, the rocket bends to a nearly horizontal flight path, until it reaches the orbital height desired for the satellite. Unless corrections are made, orbits are usually elliptical; perigee is the point on the orbit closest to the earth, and apogee is the point farthest from the earth. Besides this eccentricity (see ORBIT) an orbit of a satellite about the earth is characterized by its plane with respect to the earth. An equatorial orbit lies in the plane of the earth's orbit. A polar orbit lies in the plane passing through both the north and south poles. A satellite's period (the time to complete one revolution around the earth) is determined by its height above the earth; the higher the satellite, the longer the period. At a height of 200 mi (320 km), the period of a circular orbit is 90 min; at 500 mi (800 km), it increases to 100 min. At a height of 22,300 mi (35,888 km), a satellite has a period of exactly 24 hr, the time it takes the earth to rotate once on its axis; such an orbit is called synchronous. If the orbit is also equatorial, the satellite will remain stationary over one point on the earth's surface. Since more than one thousand satellites are presently in orbit, identifying and maintaining contact requires precise tracking methods. Optical and radar tracking are most valuable during the launch; radio tracking is used once the satellite has achieved a stable orbit. Optical tracking uses special cameras to follow satellites illuminated either by the sun or laser beams. Radar tracking directs a pulse of microwaves at the satellite, and the reflected echo identifies both its direction and distance. The majority of advanced satellites carry radio transmitters that broadcast their positions to tracking antennas on the earth. In addition, the transmitters are used for telemetry, the relaying of information from the scientific instruments aboard the satellite. To track, monitor, and control artificial satellites, NASA maintains a worldwide network of ground stations called STADAN (Satellite Tracking and Data Acquisition Network). The first artificial satellite, Sputnik I, was launched on Oct. 4, 1957, by the USSR; the first U.S. satellite, Explorer I, was launched on Jan. 31, 1958, and was responsible for the discovery of the Van Allen radiation belts surrounding the earth. Satellites can be divided into five principal types: research, communications, meteorological, navigational, and applications. Research satellites measure fundamental properties of outer space, e.g., magnetic fields, the flux of cosmic rays and micrometeorites, and properties of celestial objects that are difficult or impossible to observe from the earth. Of great scientific importance have been the multipurpose satellites called orbiting observatories. The orbiting solar observatory (OSO) studies the intensity of the X-ray, ultraviolet, and infrared radiation from the sun and their effects on the earth. The orbiting astronomical observatory (OAO) carries a 36-in. (91-cm) telescope that can be trained on any star or planet, allowing it to be viewed without the distortions caused by the atmosphere. The orbiting geophysical observatory (OGO) carries about twenty separate experiments to study the earth's atmosphere, ionosphere, magnetic field, and radiation belts. A fourth type of scientific satellite, scheduled for the late 1970s and 1980s, is the high-energy astronomical observatory (HEAO), which will study the X rays and gamma rays from galaxies, and other celestial bodies. Communications satellites provide a worldwide linkup of radio, telephone, and television. Because electromagnetic radiation travels in straight lines at most frequencies the range of a communications signal is limited by the curvature of the earth. If the signal is relayed by satellites orbiting thousands of miles above the earth's surface, this problem is avoided. The first communications satellite was Echo (launched August, 1960), a large metallized balloon that reflected radio signals striking it. This passive mode of operation has given way to the active or repeater mode, in which complex electronic equipment aboard the satellite receives a signal from the earth, amplifies it, and transmits it to another point on the earth. Telstar and Relay were early active communications satellites. Later communications satellites were placed in synchronous orbit. In principle, three such satellites located symmetrically in the plane of the earth's equator can provide complete coverage of the earth's surface. In practice, more are used in order to increase the system's message handling capacity. The Syncom project was the first attempt at a synchronous communications satellite. Meteorological satellites provide continuous, up-to-date information about large-scale atmospheric conditions such as cloud cover and temperature profiles. Tiros, the first weather satellite (launched April, 1960), transmitted infrared television pictures of the earth's cloud cover; it was able to detect the development of hurricanes and to chart their paths. The Nimbus series, which followed Tiros, carried six cameras for more detailed scanning. The Itos series was sensitive to infrared radiation emitted by the earth, making night photography possible. It is expected that eventually, through the use of satellites, accurate weather forecasts will be made two weeks in advance. Navigation satellites, such as Transit, provide the means for aircraft and ships to determine their positions with great accuracy. Applications satellites are designed to test ways of improving satellite technology itself. Areas of concern include structure, instrumentation, controls, power supplies, and telemetry for future communications, meteorological, and navigation satellites. Five applications satellites were launched between 1965 and 1970. Satellites have been used for a number of military purposes. The Vela series carries radiation-detecting equipment to monitor nuclear testing within the atmosphere. Such series

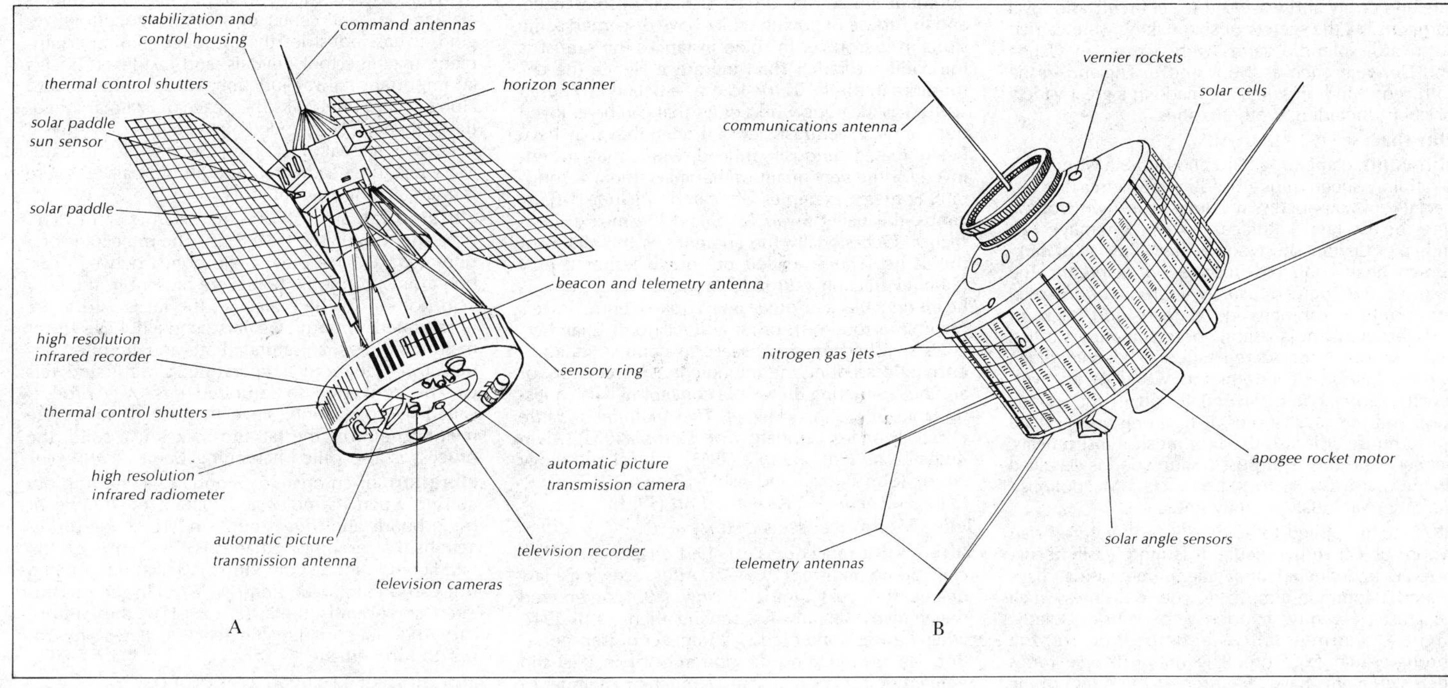

A. *A Nimbus weather satellite* B. *A Syncom communications satellite*

as MIDAS [from MIssile Defense Alert System] using optical and infrared detecting methods, and SAMOS [from Satellite And Missile Observation System] using photographic and electronic devices, are employed for military surveillance.

satellite, natural, celestial body orbiting a planet or star of a larger size. The most familiar natural satellite is the earth's MOON; thus, satellites of other planets are often referred to as moons. Within the solar system the moon is the largest satellite in relation to its primary, although with a diameter of 2,160 mi (3,457 km) it is not the largest in actual size. Ganymede of Jupiter ranges over 3,000 mi (4,828 km) in diameter and is larger than the planet Mercury. In comparison some satellites are quite small, e.g., Deimos, the outer satellite of Mars that is c.4 mi (6 km) in diameter. Neither of the inferior planets, Mercury or Venus, has a satellite; all of the superior planets (those whose orbits lie beyond the orbit of the earth) except Pluto have at least 2 known satellites each (Mars and Neptune, 2; Uranus, 5; Saturn, 9; and Jupiter, 12). A number of satellites, e.g., Phoebe of Saturn and Triton of Neptune, have RETROGRADE MOTION, i.e., orbital motion opposite to that of their primaries. Any successful theory of the origin of the solar system must explain these motions.

Satie, Erik (ārĕk' sätē'), 1866–1925, French composer, studied at the Paris Conservatory; pupil of Vincent D'Indy and Albert Roussel at the Schola Cantorum. He early realized that the romantic Wagnerian style was incompatible with the expression of French sensibility, and he developed a restrained, abstract, and deceptively simple style. In such piano pieces as *Sarabandes* (1887) and *Gymnopédies* (1888) he anticipated some of the harmonic innovations of the impressionists Debussy and Ravel; but in later works such as *Socrate* (1918; a setting of Plato's *Dialogues* for four sopranos and chamber orchestra) he foreshadowed the neoclassicism of Stravinsky and others writing in the early 20th cent. An eccentric, Satie often concealed his serious artistic intent with droll humor, adding nonsense programs or facetious titles such as *Three Pieces in the Shape of a Pear* (1903). In 1918 there gathered around him a group of young composers—Honegger, Georges Auric, Louis Durey, and Germaine Tailleferre—who were united in the reaction against impressionism. They were joined in 1919 by Milhaud and Poulenc, and were called *les six.* A ballet, *Les Mariés de la tour Eiffel* (1921), which had music by all except Durey, was the one work in which the group collaborated. Jean Cocteau, their literary prophet, wrote the scenario. See biographies by P. D. Templier (1932, repr. 1970) and Rollo H. Myers (1948, repr. 1974).

satin, lustrous silk in which the filling is so arranged as to bind the warp as seldom as possible and so spaced that practically nothing shows but the warp. Satin was first woven by the ancient silk weavers of China and was greatly desired by early Greeks and Romans. In the Middle Ages satin, known as *zatoni* (from the name of a Chinese town) and samite, was rare and costly and was used for churchly and royal garments. As the secrets of silk making were carried westward, splendid satins were woven in Genoa and Florence, then at Lyons and in England in the 15th cent. Modern satins are made in a great variety of fibers, including synthetic ones.

satin spar: see CALCITE; GYPSUM.

satinwood, name for a hard and durable wood with a satinlike sheen, much used in cabinetmaking, especially in MARQUETRY. It comes from two tropical trees of the family Rutaceae (ORANGE family). East Indian or Ceylon satinwood is the yellowish or dark-brown heartwood of *Chloroxylon swietenia.* The lustrous, fine-grained, usually figured wood is used for furniture, cabinetwork, veneers, and backs of brushes. West Indian satinwood, sometimes called yellowwood, is considered superior. It is the golden yellow, lustrous, even-grained wood of an evergreen (*Zanthoxylum flavum*) found in the Florida Keys and the West Indies. It has long been valued for furniture. It is also used for musical instruments, veneers, and other purposes. Satinwood is classified in the division MAGNOLIOPHYTA, class Magnoliopsida, order Sapindales, family Rutaceae.

satire, term applied to any work of literature or art whose objective is ridicule. It is more easily recognized than defined. From ancient times satirists have shared a common aim: to expose foolishness in all its guises —vanity, hypocrisy, pedantry, idolatry, bigotry, sentimentality—and to effect reform through such exposure. The many diverse forms their statements have taken reflect the origin of the word satire, which is derived from the Latin *satura,* meaning "dish of mixed fruits," hence a medley. A single satirical work may aim to correct several vices; or several satirical forms—poem, play, cartoon—may share one target. Outstanding among the classical satirists was the Greek dramatist Aristophanes, whose play *The Clouds* (423 B.C.) satirizes Socrates as the embodiment of atheism and sophistry, while *The Wasps* (422) satirizes the Athenian court system. The satiric styles of two Roman poets, Horace and Juvenal, became models for writers of later ages. The satire of Horace is mild, gently amused, yet sophisticated, whereas that of Juvenal is vitriolic and replete with moral indignation; Shakespeare later wrote Horatian satire and Jonathan Swift wrote Juvenalian satire. From the beast fables, fabliaux, and Chaucerian caricatures to the extended treatments of John Skelton, Shakespeare, Ben Jonson, Erasmus, and Cervantes, the satirical tradition flourished throughout the Middle Ages and the Renaissance, culminating in the golden age of satire in the late 17th and early 18th cent. The familiar names of Swift, Samuel Butler, John Dryden, Alexander Pope, Richard Steele, Henry Fielding, and William Hogarth, in England, and of Nicolas Boileau-Despréaux, La Fontaine, Molière, and Voltaire, in France, suggest not only the nature of the controversies that provided a target for the satirist's darts in both nations, but also the rediscovery and consequent adaptation of the classical models to individual talents. Pope, for example, wrote *The Rape of the Lock* (1714), a mock epic about the crisis that occurs when a lock of Lady Belinda's hair is snipped off by a suitor as she sips her coffee. The poem is based upon an actual happening, and Pope's Horatian tone gently castigates the frivolous life of London society. Swift, on the other hand, echoes Juvenal's "savage indignation." In *Gulliver's Travels* (1726), Swift exposes man in all his baseness and cruelty. Throughout his encounters with the inhabitants of imaginary lands, starting with the Lilliputians and ending with the Houyhnhnms—the latter are horses endowed with noble attributes, while their servants are bestial, filthy humanoids called Yahoos—Gulliver's (and Swift's) misanthropy grows, culminating in his refusal, once he is reunited with his family, to eat with creatures so closely resembling Yahoos. In the 19th cent. satire gave way to a more gentle form of criticism. Manners and morals were still ridiculed but usually in the framework of a longer work, such as a novel. However, satire can be found in the poems of Lord Byron, in the librettos of William S. Gilbert, in the drama of Oscar Wilde and G. B. Shaw, and in the fiction of W. M. Thackeray, Charles Dickens, Samuel Butler, and many others. American satirists have included Washington Irving, James Russell Lowell, Oliver Wendell Holmes, and Mark Twain. Contemporary satirists of note are Sinclair Lewis, James Thurber, Aldous Huxley, Evelyn Waugh, W. H. Auden, and Philip Roth. Although 20th-century satire continues to register Horatian or Juvenalian reactions to the enormities of an age dominated by fear of the atom bomb and plagued by pollution, racism, drugs, planned obsolescence, and the abuse of power, critics have discerned some shifts in its source. In some instances the satirist is the audience rather than the artist. Hence the enthusiasm in the 1960s for "camp"—defined by Susan SONTAG as meaning works of art that can be enjoyed but not taken seriously, even though they may have been created seriously, indeed, works that are enjoyed for the very qualities that make them second-rate. Sontag's examples of "camp" include Tiffany lamps, the ballet *Swan Lake,* and the movie *Casablanca.* Occasionally the audience is the victim of the satire. The so-called put-on, whether a play (Samuel Beckett's *Breath,* in which breathing is heard on a blacked-out stage), a joke (Lenny Bruce's night club routines), or an artifact (John Chamberlain's smashed-up cars), seeks to confuse its audience by presenting the fraudulent as a true work of art, thus rendering the whole concept of "art" questionable. See Gilbert Highet, *The Anatomy of Satire* (1962); Leonard Feinberg, *The Satirist* (1963); Alvin Kernan, *The Plot of Satire* (1965); critical anthology ed. by John Russell and Ashley Brown (1967); J. R. Clark, ed., *Satire—That Blasted Art* (1973).

Satire Ménippée: see SATYRE MÉNIPPÉE.

Sato, Eisaku (āsä'kōō sä'tō), 1901–, Japanese politician, prime minister (1964–72). After receiving a law degree from Tokyo Imperial Univ. (1924) he entered the ministry of railways, serving there until 1947, when he was appointed vice minister of transportation. He left the transportation ministry in 1948 and entered politics as a Liberal-Democratic member of the lower house of the Diet. He held a variety of ministerial posts in the next several governments, including minister of construction (1952–53), minister of finance (1958–60), and minister of science and technology (1963–64). In 1964 he succeeded Hayato Ikeda as prime minister when ill health forced the latter to resign. Although inexperienced in international affairs, Sato pursued a vigorous foreign policy during his term in office. He negotiated an agreement (1965) that called for the normalization of South Korean-Japanese relations, and in 1969 he signed a treaty with the United States that led to the reestablishment (1972) of Japanese sovereignty in Okinawa. However, Sato did not anticipate the public outcry against a provision in the Okinawa agreement that allowed U.S. forces to remain on the island, and he was forced to resign in 1972 shortly after the treaty took effect. Sato was awarded the Nobel Peace Prize for 1974.

satrap (sā'trăp), governor of a province (satrapy) of the ancient Persian Empire. He was nominated by the king and given extensive powers. DARIUS I reorganized the privileges and duties of his satraps in the 6th cent. B.C.; the number of satraps varied from 20 to 28 during his reign. To prevent the concentration of power in one man's hands, certain officials, responsible only to the king, checked up on the satrap. The king also regulated the taxes and imposed a fixed sum upon each satrap. Alexander the Great revised the system, replacing Persians with Macedonians and reducing their powers. The command of the troops was taken from the satraps, who lost the right to engage mercenaries and to issue coinage.

Satsuma (sätsōō'mä), peninsula, Kagoshima prefecture, SW Kyushu, Japan. It gives its name to a famous porcelain, Satsuma ware, which was first manufactured there by Korean artisans in the 16th cent. As a feudal province, Satsuma was controlled by the powerful Shimazu clan, which exacted tribute from the Ryukyu Islands from the 17th to the 19th cent. and developed Satsuma into one of the most advanced areas in 19th-century Japan. Kagoshima, the capital of Satsuma, was a center of Western influence in Japan. In 1877, Takamori Saigo led the Satsuma clansmen in a rebellion against the imperial government. This rebellion, suppressed by the imperial army, was the last serious internal threat to the Meiji restoration.

Satterlee, Henry Yates, 1843–1908, American Episcopal bishop, b. New York City. In 1896 he was consecrated as the first bishop of the diocese of Washington, D.C. The National, or Washington, Cathedral, whose cornerstone was laid before his death, has its origin in his plans and work. The most important of his several books is *A Creedless Gospel and the Gospel Creed* (1895), in which he argues that the dramatic self-revelation of God was not confined to the person of Christ but is manifest in present experience.

Satu-Mare (sä'tōō-mä'rĕ), Hung. *Szatmárnémeti* or *Szatmár,* city (1970 est. pop. 79,000), NW Rumania, in Crişana-Maramureş, on the Someşul River, near the Hungarian border. The administrative, commercial, and cultural center of a fertile agricultural region, it has industries that produce mining equipment, machine tools, metals, and textiles. It is also an important railway junction, with connections to Hungary and the USSR. The peace of Szatmár, negotiated there in 1711, ended the rebellion of Francis II Rakoczy. The seat of a Roman Catholic bishop, Satu-Mare has three cathedrals and an old palace. There is a large Hungarian minority.

saturated fat, any solid fat that is an ESTER of GLYCEROL and a saturated FATTY ACID. The molecules of a saturated fat have only single bonds between carbon atoms; if double bonds are present in the fatty acid portion of the molecule, the fat is said to be unsaturated. Unsaturated fats generally have lower melting points than saturated fats and are often liquids (oils) at room temperature. Unsaturated fats can be converted to saturated fats by a process called hydrogenation; since this usually raises the melting point of the fat and makes it a solid, the process is also called hardening. See FATS AND OILS.

saturation, of an organic compound, condition occurring when its molecules contain no double or triple bonds and thus cannot undergo addition reactions. For example, ethane ($H_3C{-}CH_3$) is a saturated compound. A compound is called unsaturated if it can undergo addition reactions. In the unsaturated compound ethene ($H_2C{=}CH_2$), the carbon-carbon double bond readily reacts, e.g., with hydrogen to form ethane.

saturation, of a solution: see SOLUTION.

Saturday: see WEEK; SABBATH.

Saturn, in astronomy, 6th planet from the sun, with an orbit lying between those of Jupiter and Uranus; its mean distance from the sun is c.886 million mi (2.4 billion km), almost twice that of Jupiter, and its period of revolution is about 29½ years. Saturn appears in the sky as a yellow, starlike object of the first magnitude. When viewed through a telescope, it is seen as a golden sphere, crossed by a series of lightly colored bands parallel to the equator. Its most remarkable feature is the system of thin, concentric rings lying in the plane of its equator. This system consists mainly of two bright outer rings, denoted A and B, separated by a dark rift known as Cassini's division, plus a third, faint inner ring known as the crepe ring. The inner edge of the crepe ring is c.8,800 mi (14,100 km) from the planet's visible surface, while the outer edge of ring A is c.47,000 mi (75,000 km) from the surface, so that the entire ring system has a width of c.40,000 mi (64,000 km). In 1859, J. C. Maxwell showed that the rings must consist of countless tiny particles each orbiting the planet in accordance with the laws of gravitation. Their total mass is found to be about 25% of that of the moon. Estimates of their thickness do not exceed 10 mi (16 km), and recent measurements indicate that their thickness may be no more than inches. When edgewise to the earth the rings appear as a nearly imperceptible ribbon of light across the planet; this occurs twice during the 29½-year period of revolution. Twice during each orbit the rings reach a maximum inclination to the line of sight, once when they are visible from above and once when visible from below. Saturn, like the other giant planets (Jupiter, Uranus, and Neptune), is covered with a thick atmosphere composed mainly of hydrogen and helium, with some methane and ammonia; its temperature is believed to be about −270°F (−168°C), suggesting that the ammonia is in the form of ice crystals that constitute the clouds. Scientists have yet to determine what solid surface, if any, exists below the obscuring layers of this atmosphere. Because no permanent markings on the planet are visible, the planet's exact period of rotation has not been determined. However, the period of each atmospheric band varies from 10 hr 14 min at the equator to about 10 hr 38 min at higher latitudes. This rapid rotation causes the largest polar flattening among the planets (over 10%). Saturn's equatorial diameter is c.75,000 mi (120,000 km), and its volume is more than 700 times the volume of the earth. Its mass is about 95 times that of the earth, making Saturn the only planet in the solar system with a density less than that of water. Saturn has 10 known natural satellites; the largest, Titan, is c.2,980 mi (4,770 km) in diameter and has the size and cold temperatures necessary to retain a methane atmosphere. It is the only satellite known to have an atmosphere. The other satellites range in diameters from c.800 mi (1,300 km) down to 100 mi (160 km). The outermost satellite, Phoebe, orbits with RETROGRADE MOTION, i.e., motion opposite to that of the planet's rotation.

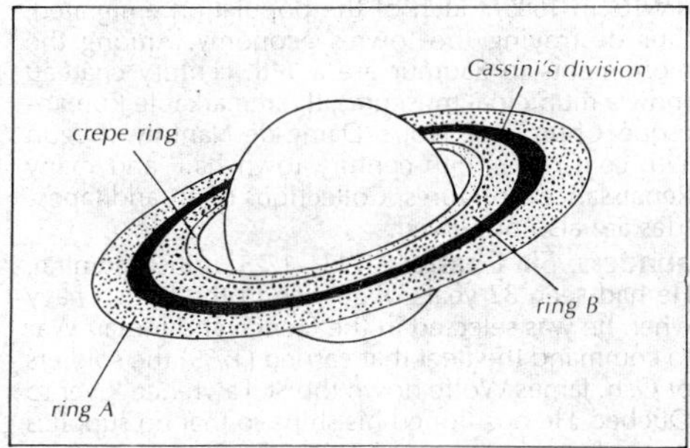

Saturn and its ring system

Saturn, in Roman religion, god of harvests, later identified with the Greek CRONUS. Little is known of the origins of his cult. His reign was regarded as the Golden Age (see AGE). He was the husband of Ops and the father of Jupiter, Juno, Ceres, Pluto, and Neptune. It was said that after the fall of the Titans, Saturn fled to Italy, where he settled on the Capitoline Hill, civilized the people, and taught them the arts of agriculture. At his festival, the Saturnalia, held at first on Dec. 17 but later extended for several days thereafter, gifts were exchanged, schools and courts were closed, war was outlawed, and slaves and masters ate at the same table.

Saturnalia: see SATURN, in Roman religion.

Saturninus (Lucius Appuleius Saturninus) (săt″ərnī′nəs), d. 100 B.C., Roman statesman. He was quaestor in 104 and later tribune of the people. He was violently opposed to the senatorial party and allied himself with MARIUS to procure the banishment of Metellus Numidicus (see under METELLUS, family), the passage of a grain law, and the establishment of new colonies in Sicily, Achaia, and Macedonia. With the demagogue Glaucia he instigated the murder of Caius Memmius, Glaucia's rival for the consulship; for this the senate proscribed them. He and Glaucia fled from the Forum to the Capitol, where they surrendered to Marius after the water supply was cut off. While they were being held for security, the mob stoned them to death with roofing tiles.

satyr (sā′tər, săt′ər), in Greek mythology, part bestial, part human creature of the forests and mountains. Satyrs were usually represented as being very hairy and having the tails and ears of a horse and often the horns and legs of a goat. An important part of Dionysus' entourage, they were lustful, fertile creatures, always merrily drinking and dancing. The satyr was similar in appearance to the SILENUS and FAUNUS.

Satyre Ménippée or **Satire Ménippée** (sätĕr′ mānĕpā′), anonymous French political pamphlet (1st ed. 1594) circulated in Paris in the 1590s. A brilliant lampoon attacking the leaders of the League at the 1593 States-General, it helped sway Parisian opinion to the side of Henry IV. A canon, Le Roy, had the principal part in writing it. The title of the lampoon derives from *Saturae Menippeae*, lost work of Varro based on satires by the Greek cynic Menippus.

sauce, seasoning or flavoring composition, usually in liquid or semiliquid form, used as an appetizing accompaniment for meat, fish, vegetables, and desserts. Sauces, an important feature of quality cookery, especially in France, have often been named for the chefs who created them. Sauces may be classed as hot and cold; and divided again, the hot as white and brown, the cold as the mayonnaise type and the type used for coating cold foods and often containing gelatin. Hot sauces, made with a base of flour, fat, and milk or stock, may be varied by seasonings and added ingredients. Stewed fruits, such as apple and cranberry, are sometimes classified as sauces. Commercial sauces, which are finely blended extracts of various fruits and vegetables with vinegar and condiments, include Worcestershire sauce, Leicester sauce, chili sauce, creole sauce, soy sauce, Tabasco, and catsup. Sauces for puddings and desserts include syrup, custard, fruit, and creamed sauces (hard sauce and wine and brandy sauce).

Saud (Abd al-Azizas-Saud) (äbd äl-äzēz′äs-säo͞od′), 1902–69, king of Saudi Arabia (1953–64), son of Ibn Saud. Saud, who had distinguished himself in several of his father's early campaigns, became viceroy of Nejd in 1926 and heir apparent in 1933. In 1953 he became foreign minister and minister of defense, and the same year, following his father's death, he assumed the throne. A poor administrator, Saud nearly bankrupted his country by his fiscal mismanagement and lavish personal spending. He surrendered some of his powers in 1958 to his brother Feisal, with whom he had disagreed over policy matters. In 1960 he reasserted his royal prerogatives but was formally deposed and replaced by his brother four years later. He died in exile in Athens.

Saud, Ibn: see IBN SAUD.

Sauðárkrókur (sö′ŭthourkrō″kür), town (1970 pop. 1,600), N Iceland, at the head of the Skagafjorður. It is a commercial center and a fishing port.

Saudi Arabia (säo͞o′dē ərā′bēə, sou′-, sô-), kingdom (1973 est. pop. 7,200,000), 829,995 sq mi (2,149,690 sq km), comprising most of the Arabian peninsula. RIYADH is the capital. Saudi Arabia is bounded on the W by the Gulf of Aqaba and the Red Sea, on the E by the Persian Gulf and Qatar, and on the N by Jordan, Iraq, a neutral zone, and Kuwait. To the southwest lies Yemen. The south and southeast of the country are occupied entirely by the great Rub al Khali desert. Through the desert run largely undefined boundaries with Southern Yemen, Oman, and the United Arab Emirates. In addition to the Rub al Khali, Saudi Arabia has four major regions. The largest is the Nejd, a central plateau, which rises from c.2,000 ft (610 m) in the east to c.5,000 ft (1,520 m) in the west. Riyadh is located in the Nejd. The Hejaz stretches along the Red Sea from the Gulf of Aqaba S to Asir and is the site of the holy cities of MECCA and MEDINA. Asir, extending S to the Yemen border, has a fertile coastal plain. Inland mountains in the Asir region rise to more than 9,000 ft (2,743 m). The Eastern Province extends along the Persian Gulf and is the oil region of the country. The oasis of Al Hasa, located there, is probably the country's largest. Saudi Arabia's climate is generally hot and dry, although nights are cool, and there may be frosts in winter. The humidity along the coasts is high. The population is predominantly Muslim Arab of the WAHABI sect. Nomads and seminomads, who comprise about 60% of the population, raise camels, sheep, goats, and horses. Because of the scarcity of water, agriculture has been restricted to Asir and to oases strung along the wadis, but recent irrigation projects have reclaimed many acres of desert, particularly at Al Kharj, SE of the Hejaz, and HOFUF, in the eastern part of the country. Mecca, Medina, and the port of Jidda have derived much income from religious pilgrims. The oil industry, located in the NE along the Persian Gulf, dominates the economy. Oil is sent by pipeline (the Tapline) to Sidon, Lebanon, and by ship to Bahrain for refining. In Saudi Arabia there are refineries at Ras Tanura on the Persian Gulf. The oil boom after World War II led to the construction of the Ad-Dammam–Riyadh railroad, the development of Ad-Dammam as a deepwater port, and the bringing of electricity to the towns. Schools, hospitals, and new homes, particularly for the oil workers, have been built. In 1957 a university was opened at Riyadh. The country is virtually an absolute monarchy, ruled under Muslim law. As a political unit, Saudi Arabia is of relatively recent creation. Its origins lay with the puritanical Wahabi movement (18th cent.), which gained the allegiance of the powerful Saud family of the Nejd, in central Arabia. Supported by a large Bedouin following, the Sauds brought most of the peninsula under their control, except for Yemen and the Hadhramaut in the extreme south. The Wahabi movement was crushed (1811–18) by an Egyptian expedition under the sons of Muhammad Ali. After reviving in the mid-19th cent., the Wahabis were defeated in 1891 by the Rashid dynasty, which gained effective control of central Arabia. It was Ibn Saud, a descendant of the first Wahabi rulers, who laid the basis of the present Saudi Arabian state. Beginning the Wahabi reconquest at the turn of the century, he took Riyadh in 1902 and was master of the Nejd by 1906. On the eve of World War I he conquered the Al Hasa region from the Turks and soon extended his control over other areas. He was then ready for the conquest of the Hejaz, ruled since 1916 by Husayn ibn Ali of Mecca. The Hejaz fell to Saud in 1924–25 and in 1932 was combined with the Nejd to form the kingdom of Saudi Arabia. In much of the country, King Ibn Saud compelled the Bedouins to abandon their tribal vendettas and encouraged their settlement as farmers. Oil was discovered in 1936, and commercial production began in 1938. Saudi Arabia is a charter member of the United Nations. It joined the Arab League in 1945, but it played only a minor role in the Arab wars with Israel in 1948, 1967 and 1973. An agreement with the United States in 1951 provided for an American air base at Dhahran, which was maintained until 1962. Ibn Saud died in 1953 and was succeeded by his eldest son, Saud, who soon came to rely on his brother, Crown Prince Faisal, to administer financial and foreign affairs. King Saud at first supported the Nasser regime in Egypt, but in 1956, in opposition to Nasser, he entered into close relations with the Hashemite rulers of Jordan and Iraq, until then the traditional enemies of the Saudis. He opposed the union in 1958 of Egypt and Syria as the United Arab Republic and became a bitter foe of Nasser's pan-Arab and reform program. When, in Sept., 1962, pro-Nasser revolutionaries in neighboring Yemen deposed the new imam and declared a republic, King Saud, together with King Hussein of Jordan, dispatched aid to the royalist troops. Prince Faisal deposed Saud and became king in Nov., 1964. Relations with Egypt were

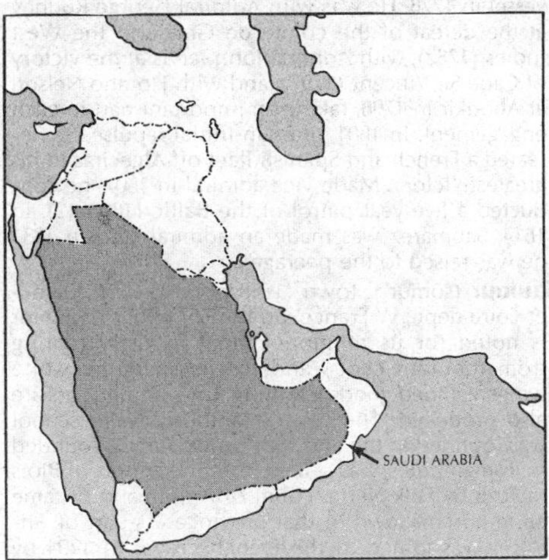

severed in 1962, but after the defeat of Egypt by Israel in June, 1967, an agreement was concluded between King Faisal and President Nasser. According to the agreement, the Egyptian army was to withdraw from Yemen and Saudi Arabia was to cease aiding the Yemeni royalists. By 1970, Saudi Arabia had withdrawn all its troops, and relations with Yemen were resumed. Saudi Arabia also agreed to give $140 million a year to Egypt and Jordan, which had been devastated in the 1967 war with Israel. In view of Britain's withdrawal from the Persian Gulf area, King Faisal pursued a policy of friendship with Iran, while encouraging the Arab sheikhdoms that had been under British rule to form the United Arab Emirates. King Faisal, however, maintained claims to the Buraimi oases, which were also claimed by the Sheikh of Abu Dhabi. In the 1970s, attention centered increasingly on Saudi Arabia and the other oil-producing countries because of the oil shortage in the United States and the attempts of Arab nations to lessen U.S. support of Israel. In 1972 the government of Saudi Arabia demanded participation in the oil concessions of foreign companies. Aramco (a conglomerate of several oil companies) and the government reached an agreement in June, 1974, whereby the Saudis would take a 60% majority ownership of the company's concessions and assets. The concept of participation was developed by the Saudi Arabian government as an alternative to nationalization. Relations with the United States improved dramatically with the signing (1974) of ceasefire agreements between Israel and Egypt and Israel and Syria (both mediated by U.S. Secretary of State Henry Kissinger) and by the visit (June, 1974) of President Richard M. Nixon to Jidda. For additional history and geography see ARABIA; HEJAZ; NEJD. See K. S. Twitchell et al., *Saudi Arabia* (3d ed. 1958, repr. 1969); N. C. Walpole et al., *Area Handbook for Saudi Arabia* (1971); H. S. Philby, *Sa'udi Arabia* (1955, repr. 1972); C. L. Riley, *Historical and Cultural Dictionary of Saudi Arabia* (1972).

Sauer, Christopher: see SOWER, CHRISTOPHER.

Sauer (zou'ər), principal river of Luxembourg, c.100 mi (160 km) long, rising in the Ardennes, SE Belgium. It flows east through Luxembourg, then south (forming part of the Luxembourg-West German border) to join with the Moselle (Mosel) River. With its tributaries, the Our, the Clerf, and the Alzette (which passes through the city of Luxembourg), the Sauer drains all of Luxembourg.

sauerkraut (sou'ərkrout") [Ger.,=sour cabbage], finely shredded cabbage fermented and preserved in a brine composed of its own juice and salt. Layers of cabbage and salt are placed under pressure in large vats, inoculated with a lactic acid culture, kept at a temperature of about 80°F (27°C) for two months, and then sold in bulk or canned. The juice is also canned and is used as an appetizer, alone or in vegetable cocktails.

Saugus (sô'gəs), town (1970 pop. 25,110), Essex co., NE Mass., a suburb of Boston on the Saugus River near the Atlantic Ocean; settled before 1637, set off from Lynn and inc. 1815. There are machine shops in the town. The Saugus ironworks (1646-c.1670; restored 1954) were the first successful enterprise of the kind in the colonies. See E. N. Hartley, *Ironworks on the Saugus* (1957).

Saugus Iron Works National Historic Site: see NATIONAL PARKS AND MONUMENTS (table).

Sauk Indians: see SAC AND FOX INDIANS.

Saul, first king of the ancient Hebrews. He was a Benjamite. Samuel anointed him king. Saul's territory was probably limited to the hill country of Judah and the region to the north, and his proximity to the Philistines brought him into constant conflict with them. The Bible tells his story dramatically, for it is really the story of DAVID, first the protégé, then the rival, finally the successor, of the king. Saul's son JONATHAN was David's friend—a fact that adds pathos to the story of Saul's attempts to destroy David. David would not harm Saul, who nevertheless met a melancholy end after he went to the witch of Endor and heard his defeat and death prophesied. Saul, defeated and wounded in battle with the Philistines on Mt. Gilboa, committed suicide rather than be captured. 1 Sam. 10-31. Though Saul was unsuccessful in defeating the Philistines he paved the way for national unity under David. The Saul of Gen. 36.37 is elsewhere called SHAUL.

Saul of Tarsus: see PAUL, SAINT.

Sault Sainte Marie (so͞o sānt mərē'), city (1971 pop. 80,332), S Ont., Canada, on the St. Marys River opposite Sault Ste Marie, Mich. A bridge connects the two cities. Sault Ste Marie is an important port and manufacturing center. Iron and steel, lumber, pulp and paper products, and chemicals are made there. It is a tourist center and the gateway to hunting and fishing resorts in nearby lake and forest regions. A fur-trading post was built on the site in 1783, and a canal and lock to bypass the St. Marys rapids was constructed by 1798. Americans destroyed the post and lock during the War of 1812; a new lock was opened in 1895. There are two forest research stations.

Sault Sainte Marie, city (1970 pop. 15,136), seat of Chippewa co., N Mich., Upper Peninsula, on the St. Marys River opposite Sault Ste Marie, Ont.; inc. as a city 1887. Birch veneers, tools, dies, and stampings are made; there are also welding and ship-repair services. Because of the distance from markets, competition from other products, and the harsh winter weather, most of the city's larger industries closed during the 1960s, and its population declined. Tourism remains the economic mainstay. The famous "Soo" locks, the world's busiest locks, on the St. Marys River are a major attraction. Hundreds of thousands of visitors come each year to watch heavy-laden ocean vessels and Great Lakes freighters pass through the intricate system that links lakes Superior and Huron. Four mammoth basins empty and fill as many as 80 times a day during the height of the shipping season. Particularly impressive is the 21-ft (6.4-m) lift to the level of Lake Superior. Excellent hunting and fishing in the area also draw sportsmen. The region at the rapids of the St. Marys River (known as "the Soo") was discovered by Etienne Brule in 1615. Father Jacques Marquette established a Jesuit mission there in 1668, and trading posts followed, flourishing with the fur trade. French occupation ended in 1763, and the British remained in control until Gov. Lewis Cass of Michigan arrived (1820), raised the American flag, and negotiated an Indian treaty. U.S. Fort Brady was built shortly thereafter. The decline of the fur trade coincided with the discovery of great mineral deposits in the northwest, and the Sault Ste Marie Canal was built in 1855 to facilitate the flow of ore. Since 1855 the locks have been enlarged and rebuilt many times. Other attractions in the city are the site of Father Marquette's mission; several historic homes, including that of H. R. Schoolcraft; and the new 21-story Shrine of the Missionaries with its 61-bell carillon and Crypt Museum. A giant international bridge connects Sault Ste Marie with its Canadian counterpart. Lake Superior State College is in the city, and Kincheloe Air Force Base, a strategic air command installation, is nearby.

Sault Sainte Marie Canals, two ship canals bypassing the rapids on the St. Marys River between Lake Superior and Lake Huron, at the cities of Sault Ste Marie, Mich. and Ont. The Canadian canal (1.4 mi/2.3 km long and 60 ft/18 m wide), which has one lock, was opened in 1895. It follows the route of the first canal constructed around the rapids (1797-98) by a fur company. The U.S. canal (1.6 mi/2.6 km long and 80 ft/24 m wide) was constructed (1853-55) by the state of Michigan and has since been reconstructed by the Federal government to accommodate larger vessels; it has four locks. Although closed by ice during the winter, the toll-free canals are among the busiest in the world and are a vital link in the Great Lakes Waterway. Most of the ships pass through the larger and deeper U.S. canal. The waterways are popularly called the Soo Canals.

Saumaise, Claude de: see SALMASIUS, CLAUDIUS.

Saumarez, James Saumarez, baron de (sŏm'ərĕz), 1757-1836, British admiral, b. Guernsey. He entered the navy in 1770 and attained command of a vessel in 1778. He was with Admiral George Rodney at the defeat of the comte de Grasse in the West Indies (1782), with Admiral John Jervis at the victory of Cape St. Vincent (1797), and with Horatio Nelson at Aboukir in 1798, taking an important part in each engagement. In 1801, after an initial repulse, he defeated a French and Spanish fleet off Algeciras in his greatest victory. Made vice admiral in 1807, he conducted a five-year patrol of the Baltic (1808-12). In 1814, Saumarez was made an admiral, and in 1831 he was raised to the peerage.

Saumur (sōmür'), town (1968 pop. 23,175), Maine-et-Loire dept., W France, on the Loire River. Saumur is noted for its religious-medal industry (dating from the 17th cent.) and for its sparkling white wines. Canned goods, clothing, toys, and liquors are also produced. The town's famous cavalry school was founded in the late 18th cent. Saumur, founded in Roman times, was seized from the counts of Blois in 1026 by Fulk Nerra, count of Anjou, and became an important town in that province. As part of Anjou it was joined to the French crown in 1204 by Philip II. In the 16th cent. Saumur was given by Henry III to the then Protestant Henry of Navarre (later Henry IV). Under Philippe de Mornay, the governor, a famous Protestant academy was founded (1599), and the town became a bastion of the HUGUENOT movement. With the revocation of the Edict of NANTES in 1685, much of the population emigrated, thus destroying the town's economy. Among the monuments in Saumur are a 14th-century château (now a municipal museum), the remarkable Romanesque Church of Notre-Dame-de-Nantilly (begun 12th-cent.), the 15th-century town hall, and many Renaissance structures. Collections of art and tapestries are also preserved.

Saunders, Sir Charles, 1713?-1775, British admiral. He had seen 32 years of service in the British navy when he was selected in the French and Indian War to command the fleet that carried (1759) the soldiers of Gen. James Wolfe down the St. Lawrence River to Quebec. He positioned his ships so that no supplies or reinforcements could reach the French garrison there, a maneuver that was a key factor in the fall of the city (see ABRAHAM, PLAINS OF). Saunders was knighted in 1761; he became first lord of the admiralty in 1766 and an admiral in 1770.

Saunderson or **Sanderson, Nicholas,** 1682-1739, English mathematician. He was blind from infancy. A lecturer (1707) on Newtonian philosophy at Cambridge Univ., in 1711 he became Lucasian professor of mathematics. To enable himself to accomplish figuring by touch, he invented a calculating machine. He was a fellow of the Royal Society. He wrote *Elements of Algebra* (1740).

sausage, food consisting of finely chopped meat mixed with seasonings and, often, other ingredients, all encased in a thin membrane. Although sausages were made by the ancient Greeks and Romans, they were usually plain and unspiced; in the Middle Ages people began to use the various spices and meats that led to the modern sausage. Many of the sausages that became famous were named for the localities where they were first made: the frankfurter in Frankfurt, Germany; the bologna in Bologna, Italy; the genoa salami in Genoa, Italy. Black pudding, an ancient dish in England and Scotland, was made of oatmeal, suet, and hog's blood. White pudding was suet with toasted oatmeal. Sausages are of two types, dry and wet, according to whether the casing is filled with fresh (wet) or cooked (dry) meat. Pork sausage is an example of the wet. Dry sausages are made from fresh meats and curing substances, and then smoked (e.g., peperoni). Salami, most common in Italy and Germany, contains beef and pork and is highly seasoned. The large bologna sausage is of veal and pork and is smoked. Frankfurters and wienerwursts are small, smoked varieties containing lean pork and beef. Sausage is usually packed in casings made either of the cleaned and salted intestines of the slaughtered animals or of synthetic cellulose.

Sausalito (sô"səlē'tō), residential city (1970 pop. 6,158), W Calif., N of San Francisco; inc. 1893. It is the northern terminus of the Golden Gate Bridge. The artists' colony there is a tourist attraction.

Saussure, Horace Bénédict de (ōrās' bānādĕkt' də sōsür'), 1740-99, Swiss physicist and geologist. He was professor at the Univ. of Geneva from 1762 to 1786. He is famous for his studies of the geology, meteorology, and botany of the mountainous regions of Europe, particularly the Alps. These are described in his great work, *Voyages dans les Alpes* (4 vol., 1779-96).

sauterne: see WINE.

Sava (sä'vä), Hung. *Száva,* longest river of Yugoslavia, c.580 mi (930 km) long, rising in two headstreams in the Julian Alps, NW Yugoslavia, and flowing generally SE across N Yugoslavia, past Ljubljana and Zagreb, to the Danube River at Belgrade. The Drina is its chief tributary. The Sava is navigable to Sisak; its valley is an important transportation corridor. The Sava basin is a fertile agricultural region.

Savage, Edward, 1761-1817, American portrait painter and engraver. He was probably self-taught, although he may have studied with Benjamin West during a brief visit to London. He at one time operated art galleries in Boston, Philadelphia, and New York City. His most famous painting is *The Washington Family* (National Gall. of Art, Washington, D.C.), which exhibits facility in the spatial organization of stiffly executed figures. The portrait of Abraham Whipple (U.S. Naval Academy) is another of his works often reproduced.

Savage, Minot Judson (mī'nət), 1841-1918, American Unitarian clergyman and writer, b. Norridgewock, Maine. After serving for nine years in the ministry of the Congregational Church, he became a Unitarian. He was pastor of the Third Unitarian Church, Chicago (1873–74); of the Church of the Unity, Boston (1874–96); and of the Church of the Messiah, New York City (1896–1906). An active advocate of Darwinian evolutionistic optimism and social reform, he also preached a spiritualistic faith in personal survival after death (see *Life Beyond Death,* 1899). Other writings include *Christianity, the Science of Mankind* (1873), *The Religion of Evolution* (1876), *The Morals of Evolution* (1880), *Social Problems* (1886), and *Immortality* (1906).

Savage, Richard, 1697?–1743, English poet. The now discredited story of his illegitimate descent from a noble line and of his persecutions, which are set forth in a biography by Samuel Johnson, won him a reputation that his works scarcely merited. His output includes two poems, *The Bastard* (1728) and *The Wanderer* (1729), and two comedies. In 1727 he killed a man in a tavern brawl and was sentenced to death but later was pardoned. He died in poverty. See biography by Clarence Tracy (1953).

Savage's Station: see SEVEN DAYS BATTLES.

Savai'i (sävī'ē), volcanic island (1971 pop. 40,572), WESTERN SAMOA. It is the largest (c.700 sq mi/1,810 sq km) and most westerly of the Samoan islands. Savai'i, fertile and mountainous, has the highest peak in Samoa, Mauga Sili (6,094 ft/1,857 m). Bananas, copra, and cocoa are exported. The largest town is Tuasivi. Savai'i was formerly called Chatham Island.

Savalan, mountain, Iran: see SABALAN.

savanna or **savannah** (both: səvăn'ə), tropical or subtropical grassland lying on the margin of the TRADE WIND belts. The climate of a savanna is characterized by a rainy period during the summer when the area is covered by grasses, and by a dry winter when the grasses wither. Parklike savannas near the equatorial belt, e.g., in Nigeria, support clumps of trees. The most extensive savannas—all important pasture lands—are in Africa; others include the llanos and the campos of South America.

Savannah, city (1970 pop. 118,349), seat of Chatham co., SE Ga., a port of entry on the Savannah River near its mouth; inc. 1789. It is a rail, fishing, and industrial center. Shipping is its major industry; manufactured goods are imported in great quantity, and exports include tobacco, cotton, sugar, clay, rosin, liner board, and wood pulp. Chemicals, petroleum, rubber, lumber, plastics, and paper are among the city's many products. Savannah is Georgia's oldest city; it was founded by James Oglethorpe in 1733 and served as the colonial seat of government. During the American Revolution the British took Savannah on Dec. 29, 1778, and held it until July, 1782. A land-sea force of French and Americans led by D'Estaing and Benjamin Lincoln tried to retake the city in 1779, first by siege and then by direct assault (on Oct. 9), but failed dismally. Savannah was the state capital from 1782 to 1785. With the growth of trade, and especially after the invention of the cotton gin and the construction of railroads extending to the cotton fields of central Georgia, the city became a rival of Charleston as a commercial center. The first steamship to cross the Atlantic, the *Savannah,* sailed from there to Liverpool in 1819. In the Civil War, Fort Pulaski, on an island near the mouth of the Savannah River, was captured by Federals in 1862, but the city did not fall until Dec. 21, 1864, when Sherman entered it on completing his march to the sea. Savannah, well planned at its founding, has beautiful, wide, shaded streets and many parks. Magnolias, pines, and ancient oaks are indigenous there. Despite devastating fires in 1796 and 1820, many old homes and buildings remain, including the Pirates' House (1754), an old seaman's inn mentioned in Stevenson's *Treasure Island*; the Herb House (1734), the oldest existing building in Georgia; and the Pink House (1789), which became Georgia's first bank in 1812. The mansion birthplace of Juliette Gordon Low (built 1819–21) is owned and operated by the Girl Scouts of the U.S.A. as a memorial to their founder. The city's historic district was designated a national historic landmark in 1966; many of its 18th- and 19th-century homes have been restored. The monument and grave of Nathanael Greene are in Johnson Square. The city has numerous fine old churches. The Lutheran Church of the Ascension dates back to 1741. The Independent Presbyterian Church (1890s), which is a replica of an earlier church destroyed by fire, was the scene of Woodrow Wilson's marriage to Ellen Axson. The original Christ Episcopal Church housed the colony's first congregation (1733); one of its clergymen was John Wesley (1736–37). The Cathedral of St. John the Baptist (1876) is one of the largest Roman Catholic churches in the South. Savannah is the seat of Savannah State College, Armstrong State College, a Benedictine school, several museums, and the Telfair Academy of Arts and Sciences, with its fine art gallery. An air force base and a U.S. coast guard station are there, and several beach and island resorts are nearby.

Savannah, river, 314 mi (505 km) long, formed by the confluence of the Tugaloo and Seneca rivers and flowing SE to the Atlantic Ocean; with the Tugaloo it forms the entire S.C.–Ga. boundary. Savannah, Ga., the largest port on the river, is the head of navigation for oceangoing ships. Clark Hill Dam (completed 1954) and Hartwell Dam (1961) above Augusta, Ga., are part of the Savannah River basin development plan; the U.S. Atomic Energy Commission's Savannah River plant is also on the river.

Savarkar, Vinayak Damodar (vĭnä'yək dä'mōdär səvär'kər), 1883–1966, Indian nationalist. Educated in Poona, he quickly became militantly anti-British and anti-Muslim. He founded a terrorist organization in London while ostensibly studying for a law degree and was later arrested when a plot on the life of Lord Curzon and the assassination (1909) of a British government official were traced to the group. In 1911 he was sentenced to life imprisonment on the Andaman Islands but was released in 1924. He was legally restricted from taking part in public life, but he was, nevertheless, elected president of the Hindu Mahasabha, an extremist Hindu party, for seven consecutive years. In 1948 he was implicated in the assassination of Gandhi and arrested. He was later acquitted for lack of evidence.

Savary, Anne Jean Marie René (än zhäN märē' rənā' sävärē'), 1774–1833, French general in the Napoleonic Wars. He presided (1804) at the trial of the duc d'ENGHIEN and was created (1808) duke of Rovigo. In 1808 he lured King FERDINAND VII of Spain into France, thus preparing the way for Napoleon's takeover there. Succeeding (1810) Joseph FOUCHÉ as minister of police, Savary did not approach his predecessor's skill and efficiency. After the Bourbon restoration he was condemned to death, but he escaped and in 1819 was allowed to return to France. After the Revolution of 1830 he commanded an expedition to Algeria. See his letters (4 vol., 1914–24, in French).

Savery, Thomas, c.1650–1715, English engineer. He became a military engineer, rising to the rank of captain by 1702. He spent his free time performing experiments in mechanics, inventing such devices as a machine for polishing plate glass and a contrivance employing paddle wheels to move becalmed ships. His most important invention, patented in 1698, was a machine designed to lift water for such purposes as keeping mines dry and supplying towns with water. Although not a steam engine in the modern sense, this machine was the first to provide mechanical power by harnessing steam.

Savery, William (sā'vərē), 1721–87, American cabinetmaker. He is believed to have lived in Philadelphia from c.1740. Savery is noted for his artistic and original interpretation of 18th-century English furniture designs, especially the Queen Anne style, and for his fine workmanship. Examples of his work are at the Metropolitan Museum.

Savigny, Friedrich Karl von (frē'drĭkh kärl fən sä'vĭnyē), 1779–1861, German jurist and legal historian, a founder of the historical school of jurisprudence. He taught (1810–42) Roman law at the Univ. of Berlin, of which he was the first rector. In 1814, Savigny wrote *The Vocation of Our Time for Legislation and Jurisprudence* (tr. 1831), which developed the view that the legal institutions of a people are, like their art or music, an indigenous expression of their culture, and cannot be externally imposed. Savigny's thought was very much a part of the German romantic movement, with its emphasis on the *Volksgeist* [spirit of the people], folk culture, and national history. Thus, he opposed the movement for legal codification on the grounds that it represented an arbitrary interference with the natural product of the national consciousness. Savigny's juristic theories had great significance in the 19th cent. in England, France, and Italy, as well as in Germany. His work as a legal historian had even greater influence, however. His studies of Roman law are models of historical research, notable for their treatment of the historical and social factors that were involved in the development of the Roman legal system. The greatest is *Geschichte des römischen Rechts im Mittelalter* [history of Roman law in the Middle Ages] (6 vol., 1815–31). His books on the modern European system of Roman law include *The Law of Possessions* (1803, tr. 1848) and the uncompleted *System of Modern Roman Law* (1840–53, partial tr. 1867–94).

Savile, George: see HALIFAX, GEORGE SAVILE, 1ST MARQUESS OF.

savings and loan association, type of financial institution that accepts savings from the public and invests those savings in mortgages. They are also known as building and loan associations, building associations, cooperative banks, and homestead associations. Savings and loan associations, the primary source for home mortgages in the United States, are corporations and may be organized either as mutual or capital stock institutions. A mutual organization is similar in operation to a mutual SAVINGS BANK. The first U.S. savings and loan association was founded in 1831; the associations grew steadily until after World War II, when they began a period of rapid expansion. Since 1933 the Federal government has chartered savings and loan associations, although they are not required to be federally chartered. See Alan Teck, *Mutual Savings Banks and Savings and Loan Associations* (1968); Alfred Nichols, *Management and Control in the Mutual Savings and Loan Association* (1972).

savings bank, financial institution that receives savings deposits of individuals, invests them, and provides a modest return to its depositors in the form of interest. Mutual savings banks are the only type that accept savings deposits exclusively, and in the United States they are concentrated in the Northeast. They are state-chartered institutions, owned by their depositors, and are managed for their mutual benefit by self-perpetuating boards of trustees. Other banks that accept savings deposits are national and state commercial banks and stock savings banks; unlike mutual savings banks, these institutions also offer checking accounts and a wide variety of other banking services (see BANKING). A great many mutual savings banks as well as commercial banks are insured by and operate under the regulations of the Federal Deposit Insurance Corporation (FDIC). Savings deposits may also be received by a CREDIT UNION. A SAVINGS AND LOAN ASSOCIATION, which is a corporation, may be organized like a mutual savings bank or as a capital stock institution. See Alan Teck, *Mutual Savings Banks and Savings and Loan Associations* (1968).

Savoie (sävwä'), department (1968 pop. 288,921), SE France, bordering Italy. CHAMBÉRY is the capital.

Savona (sävô'nä), city (1971 pop. 79,618), capital of Savona prov., in Liguria, NW Italy, on the Riviera. It is a major seaport and an industrial center. Manufactures include iron and steel, machinery, and chemicals. The seat of a marquessate in the Middle Ages, Savona was a flourishing commercial center until it was badly defeated and annexed by Genoa in 1528. The city has a 16th-century castle and a cathedral (16th–19th cent.).

Savonarola, Girolamo (jērō'lämō sävōnärō'lä), 1452–98, Italian religious reformer, b. Ferrara. He joined (1475) the Dominicans. In 1481 he went to San Marco, the Dominican house at Florence, where he became popular for his eloquent sermons, in which he attacked the vice and worldliness of the city, as well as for his predictions (several of which, including the death date of Innocent VIII, turned out to be true). In 1491 he became prior of San Marco, and after the death of Lorenzo de' Medici, who was his enemy, and the subsequent exile of the Medici (1494) he became the real spiritual ruler of the city. He was uncompromisingly severe in his condemnation of what he considered the paganism of the times and called for a regeneration of spiritual and moral values and a devotion to asceticism. When Charles VIII of France invaded Italy in 1494 (as Savonarola had predicted), Savonarola supported him, hoping that Charles would lead the way to the establishment of a democratic government in Florence and to the reform of the scandalously corrupt court of Pope Alexander VI. Alexander, understandably infuriated, ordered Savonarola to refrain from preaching; however, he continued to preach, and the pope excommunicated him for disobedience in 1497. Savonarola now declared Alexander no true pope, being elected by simony. The people of Florence, who had for a time staunchly supported Savonarola, tired of his rigid demands. Hostility toward him grew, led especially by local Franciscans, and in March, 1498, the government, threatened by a papal interdict, asked him to stop preaching. His ruin came suddenly when one of his disciples accepted an ordeal by fire to prove Savonarola's holiness. Rain prevented the event. Nevertheless, there were riots, and Savonarola and two disciples were arrested by the city. Under torture he confessed to being a false prophet, or so it was announced. The three were hanged for schism and heresy; papal commissioners had passed on the sentence, which was assured by Alexander's vindictiveness. See biographies by Pasquale Villari (2 vol., tr. 1888; repr. 1972), Roberto Ridolfi (1959), and R. R. Renner (1965); study by Donald Weinstein (1970).

Savonlinna (sä'vōnlĭn"nä), Swed. *Nyslott*, city (1970 pop. 17,942), Mikkeli prov., SE Finland. Situated in the Saimaa lake region, it is a resort, inland port, and road and railroad junction, with a large plywood industry, machine shops, and sawmills. It was built around the 15th-century fortress of Olavinlinna and was chartered in 1639.

savory, name for any plant of the genus *Satureja*, aromatic herbs and subshrubs of the family Labiatae (MINT family). Commonly cultivated as border ornamentals or potherbs are two species of the Mediterranean region and surrounding areas: summer savory (*S. hortensis*) and winter, or spring, savory (*S. acinos*). Summer savory is the plant most frequently grown commercially and in herb gardens for its foliage, used as savory spice. The aromatic oil is extracted for flavoring processed foods, sausages, and catsup. Winter savory is sometimes used medicinally as an aromatic and carminative. Savory is classified in the division MAGNOLIOPHYTA, class Magnoliopsida, order Lamiales, family Labiatae.

Savoy, house of, dynasty of Western Europe that ruled Savoy and Piedmont from the 11th cent., the kingdom of Sicily from 1714 to 1718, the kingdom of Sardinia from 1720 to 1861, and the kingdom of Italy from 1861 to 1946. Its first historical member was Count Humbert the Whitehanded, a powerful feudal lord of the kingdom of Arles (in SE France) in the 11th cent. He held possessions in SAVOY and acquired, through marriage, several fiefs in PIEDMONT, including TURIN. Through marriage, diplomacy, and conquest his successors expanded their holdings in France, Switzerland, and Italy, acquiring BRESSE and Bugey, Chablais (on the south shore of the Lake of Geneva), Lower VALAIS, Gex, IVREA, PINEROLO, NICE, parts of VAUD and of GENEVA, and other seigniories and towns. CHAMBÉRY, acquired in 1232, became the seat of the counts, whose scattered possessions were gradually consolidated. AMADEUS VIII acquired the ducal title in 1416. His son Louis (d. 1465) married Anne de Lusignan, titular heiress to the kingdoms of Jerusalem, Cyprus, and Armenia; these were titles later borne by ruling members of the house. The expansion of Switzerland and the ITALIAN WARS resulted in the temporary disintegration of the duchy. The Swiss took the lower Valais (1475) and Vaud (1536); Geneva became independent (1533); and the rest of the duchy was occupied (1536) by Francis I of France. In 1559, however, Duke EMMANUEL PHILIBERT, called Ironhead, obtained the restoration of his duchy—except the larger part of the Swiss conquests—at the Treaty of Cateau-Cambrésis. Emmanuel Philibert made Turin his capital, thus shifting the center of his duchy from France to Italy. The language and tone of the court, however, remained French until the late 18th cent. Emmanuel Philibert's son and successor, CHARLES EMMANUEL I, unsuccessfully sought to reconquer Geneva. He gained (1601) the marquisate of Saluzzo in Piedmont from France in exchange for Bresse, Bugey, and Gex. Charles's successor, VICTOR AMADEUS II, expanded his territories by advantageous alliances. In the War of the Spanish Succession he sided first with France, then with the forces of the Holy Roman emperor, and by the peace of Utrecht (1713–14) he was made king of Sicily and enlarged his Piedmontese territories. His cousin, EUGENE OF SAVOY, headed the imperial forces in the war. Spain reconquered Sicily in 1718 but was forced by the QUADRUPLE ALLIANCE to cede Sardinia to Victor Amadeus in exchange for Sicily. The political history of the dynasty became that of the kingdom of Sardinia (see SARDINIA, KINGDOM OF) and of Italy. Victor Amadeus II was succeeded by Charles Emmanuel III (reigned 1730–73), Victor Amadeus III (reigned 1773–96), and Charles Emmanuel IV, who lost all but the island of Sardinia to Napoleon I and abdicated (1802) in favor of his brother, VICTOR EMMANUEL I. Restored to his possessions in 1814, Victor Emmanuel I abdicated in 1821, after the outbreak of a revolution in Piedmont. His brother and successor, Charles Felix, died without issue in 1831, and the cadet line of Savoy-Carignano, descended from a younger son of Charles Emmanuel I, came to the throne in the person of CHARLES ALBERT. In his reign the house of Savoy became the center of the RISORGIMENTO, the movement that led to the unification of Italy under his son, VICTOR EMMANUEL II. Savoy itself, however, was ceded to France in 1860. HUMBERT I, who succeeded (1878) Victor Emmanuel II as king of Italy, was assassinated in 1900. His son and successor, VICTOR EMMANUEL III, also took the titles emperor of Ethiopia (1936) and king of Albania (1939); after the Italian armistice (1943) with the Allies in World War II he delegated (1944) his powers to his son, who briefly ruled (1946) as HUMBERT II from Victor Emmanuel's abdication until the establishment of the Italian republic. Collateral branches of the house of Savoy include that of Nemours. A younger son of Victor Emmanuel II, AMADEUS, was given the title duke of Aosta; he was king of Spain from 1870 to 1873. His ducal title descended to Emmanuel Philibert, duke of AOSTA. See Robert Katz, *The Fall of the House of Savoy* (1971); E. L. Cox, *The Eagles of Savoy* (1974).

Savoy, Prince Eugene of: see EUGENE OF SAVOY.

Savoy (savoi'), Fr. *Savoie*, Alpine region of E France. The boundaries of old Savoy have changed with time, but presently the region comprises the departments of SAVOIE and HAUTE-SAVOIE. It is bounded on the N by Lake Geneva, on the W by the Rhône River, on the S by DAUPHINÉ, and on the E by the Alpine crest on the Swiss and Italian borders. CHAMBÉRY is the historic capital of French Savoy. The region commands many important passes connecting France and Italy (notably the historic Little SAINT BERNARD and the Mont CENSIS) and includes the French portion of the highest Alpine peak, Mont Blanc. Agriculture and dairying have long been the region's chief occupations. Tourism is also important, and there are many spas, the most notable at ÉVIAN-LES-BAINS. Savoy was inhabited by the ALLOBROGES at the time Julius Caesar conquered the region. It became part of the first kingdom of BURGUNDY (5th cent.) and later of the kingdom of ARLES (10th cent.), after which it was ceded to the Holy Roman Empire. In the 11th cent., Humbert the Whitehanded, a lord of Arles, consolidated the various feudal territories of the region, and from then on the region's history is closely linked with the house of Savoy (see SAVOY, HOUSE OF). Under Amadeus VIII, Savoy became (early 15th cent.) a duchy extending far into France, Italy, and Switzerland. By the beginning of the 16th cent. the rule of the dukes had grown weak, and Savoy fell under French and Swiss dominance. Emmanuel Philibert greatly restored the territory and fortunes of the region and moved the ducal residence to Turin (1559), after which Savoy became essentially an Italian rather than a French state. When Victor Amadeus II became king of Sardinia in 1713, Savoy became a part of that new state (see SARDINIA, KINGDOM OF). Annexed by France in 1792, Savoy was returned to Sardinia in 1815. Finally, by the Treaty of Turin (1860), PIEDMONT, then the ruling part of Savoy, ceded French Savoy to France. The region was annexed after a plebiscite.

Savoy, the, chapel in London, between the Strand and the Thames River. Its name is derived from the palace of Peter of Savoy, uncle of Eleanor of Provence, wife of Henry III. Destroyed (1381) in the Peasants' Revolt, the palace was rebuilt (1505) as the Hospital of St. John of Jerusalem by Henry VII and finally destroyed when its foundations were removed in 1810 before the Waterloo Bridge was built. The chapel, which was connected with the hospital, is maintained by the crown. The **Savoy Conference** of 12 bishops of the Church of England and 12 Puritan divines was convened in 1661. They tried to revise the Book of Common Prayer but could not reach agreement. Near the chapel is the **Savoy Theatre,** erected in 1881 by Richard D'Oyly CARTE for the production of Gilbert and Sullivan operettas.

Savoy Conference: see SAVOY, THE.

Savoy Theatre: see SAVOY, THE.

sawfish: see RAY.

sawfly, common name for INSECTS of several families of the order Hymenoptera, which also includes the ANTS, WASPS, and BEES. Sawflies are named for the two sawtoothed blades of the female's ovipositor that are used for slitting leaves or stems in order to deposit the eggs. The insects have two pairs of membranous wings and chewing mouthparts. Both the sawfly and the closely related horntail, whose burrowing larvae are the hosts of the ICHNEUMON FLY, lack the characteristic constricted abdomen of other hymenopterans. Sawfly larvae resemble caterpillars; some are leaf and stem borers, many feed on the surface of foliage, and others produce GALLS. Various species are destructive to larch, spruce, broadleaved fruit and shade trees, shrubs, and grasses. Most species have a single generation a year; they pass the winter either as larvae or as pupae in a cocoon or in some protected place. Sawflies are classified in the phylum ARTHROPODA, class Insecta, order Hymenoptera.

Sawhaj (sô'häj) or **Sohag** (sō'hăg), town (1970 est. pop. 85,300), capital of Sawhaj governorate, central Egypt, on the Nile River. It is located in a densely populated agricultural region. Products of the town include ginned cotton and woven textiles. Two Coptic monasteries are there. Nearby is Bayt Khallaf, the site of a mastaba built under King Zoser (III dynasty).

sawmill, installation or facility in which cut logs are sawed into standard-sized boards and timbers. The saws used in such an installation are generally of three types: the circular saw, which consists of a disk with teeth around its edge; the band saw, which consists of a hoop of flexible metal that runs over pulleys and has teeth along one edge; and the log gang saw, which consists of saw blades separated by desired distances in a frame that oscillates as a log is fed into it. Logs are fed to gang saws through pressure rollers that ensure straight cutting. With other saws the log rides on a conveyor or carriage. Provision is made for placement of the log in a new position for each cut, by the worker who rides the carriage or by the one who operates the saw. Recently it has been discovered that a jet of water at a pressure of several thousand pounds per square inch is capable of cutting a log at a rate comparable to that of sawing. Despite the fairly exotic hardware necessary for this method, it reduces the kerfs, or widths of cuts, thus wasting less material, and it does not produce the flammable dust created by sawing. In sawmills that use their waste as raw material for wood pulp, logs are passed through machines that remove their bark prior to sawing. A large sawmill may have a capacity of several hundred thousand board feet per day.

Saxe, Maurice, comte de (mōrēs' kôNt də säks), 1696–1750, marshal of France, one of the greatest generals of his age. He was the illegitimate son of AUGUSTUS II of Poland and Saxony and Countess Maria Aurora von KÖNIGSMARK. When very young he entered the Saxon army, and in 1720 he went into French service. In 1726 he obtained leave to make good his claim to the duchy of Courland, but in 1727 the attempt failed. He fought under the duke of Berwick in the War of the Polish Succession. In the War of the Austrian Succession, he led the successful attack on Prague (1741) and later, after becoming (1744) marshal, made his reputation by victories at Fontenoy (1745) and Raucoux (1746) and by the capture of Maastricht (1748). In recognition of his services Louis XV gave him life tenure of the castle of Chambord and (1747) the title of marshal general. His *Mes Rêveries* (1757) is a remarkable work on the art of war. Maurice de Saxe was notorious for his amorous exploits and for his tragic liaison with Adrienne LECOUVREUR. Among his descendants was George Sand. L. H. Thornton has translated (1944) *Mes Rêveries*. See L. H. Thornton, *Campaigners Grave and Gay* (1925); J. E. M. White, *Marshal of France: The Life and Times of Maurice, Comte de Saxe* (1962).

Saxe-Altenburg (săks-ăl'tənbərg), Ger. *Sachsen-Altenburg*, former duchy, Thuringia, central Germany. Altenburg was the capital. Created a separate duchy in 1603, it was ruled by an Ernestine line of the house of WETTIN. It passed (1672) to the dukes of Saxe-Gotha, but from 1826 to 1918 it was again a separate duchy under the collateral line of Saxe-Hildburghausen. In 1920 it was incorporated into Thuringia.

Saxe-Coburg (săks-kōbərg), Ger. *Sachsen-Coburg*, former duchy, central Germany. A possession of the Ernestine branch of the house of WETTIN, it was given by Ernest the Pious (d. 1675) of SAXE-GOTHA to his son Albert. On Albert's death (1699) it passed to his younger brother, John Ernest, duke of Saxe-Saalfeld, whose descendants ruled the duchy of Coburg until 1918 and the duchy of Saalfeld until 1826. The extinction (1825) of the related line of Saxe-Gotha-Altenburg resulted in a general redivision of the Ernestine possessions in 1826. The duchy of Saalfeld passed to the duke of Saxe-Meiningen, while Ernest III of Saxe-Coburg received the duchy of Gotha and assumed the style ERNEST I, duke of **Saxe-Coburg-Gotha**. Ernest I's brother was crowned (1831) as Leopold I, king of the Belgians, and his younger son was Prince Albert, consort of Queen Victoria of England. Thus the house of Saxe-Coburg-Gotha became the ruling dynasty of Belgium and of England (where the name was changed to Windsor in World War I). His elder son, Ernest II, sided with Prussia in the Austro-Prussian War of 1866. He was succeeded (1893) by Alfred, duke of Edinburgh, a son of Queen Victoria and the father of Queen Marie of Rumania. On Alfred's death (1900) the duchy passed to his nephew, Charles Edward, who abdicated in 1918. In 1920 Saxe-Gotha was incorporated into Thuringia, and Saxe-Coburg into Bavaria.

Saxe-Eisenach: see SAXE-WEIMAR.

Saxe-Gotha (săks-gō'thə), Ger. *Sachsen-Gotha,* former duchy, Thuringia, central Germany. A possession of the Ernestine branch of the house of WETTIN, it passed in the 16th cent. to the dukes of Saxe-Weimar. After the death (1605) of Duke John of Weimar, his territories were divided among his heirs. Saxe-Gotha, along with Coburg, Meiningen, Saalfeld, and other territories, gradually came under the control of Ernest the Pious, one of John's younger sons, who inherited Saxe-Altenburg in 1672. On Ernest's death (1675), the succession was divided among his seven sons; the eldest, Frederick I, received Gotha and Saxe-Altenburg, which his descendants ruled until the male line failed in 1825. Saxe-Gotha was awarded in 1826 to Ernest III of Saxe-Coburg (Ernest I of Saxe-Coburg-Gotha; see under SAXE-COBURG). Saxe-Altenburg became a separate duchy under a collateral line. In 1920 Saxe-Gotha was incorporated into Thuringia.

Saxe-Meiningen (săks-mīn'ĭng-ən), Ger. *Sachsen-Meiningen,* former duchy, Thuringia, central Germany. The capital was MEININGEN. A possession of the Ernestine branch of the house of WETTIN, it became a separate duchy in 1681 under Bernard, third son of Ernest the Pious of SAXE-GOTHA. In the dynastic rearrangement that followed the extinction (1825) of the male line of Saxe-Gotha, the duke of Saxe-Meiningen received (1826) Saxe-Saalfeld from the duke of Saxe-Coburg (who obtained Gotha instead) and Saxe-Hildburghausen (whose duke was compensated with Saxe-Altenburg). Saxe-Meiningen sided (1866) with Austria in the Austro-Prussian War. The last duke abdicated in 1918, and in 1920 Saxe-Meiningen was incorporated into Thuringia. For the theatrical company organized by Duke George II of Saxe-Meiningen, see MEININGEN PLAYERS.

Saxe-Saalfeld: see SAXE-COBURG.

Saxe-Weimar (săks-vī'mär), Ger. *Sachsen-Weimar,* former duchy, Thuringia, central Germany. The area passed in the division of 1485 to the Ernestine branch of the WETTIN dynasty and remained with that branch after the redivision of the Wettin lands in 1547, when Elector JOHN FREDERICK I of Saxony was captured by Holy Roman Emperor Charles V at the battle of Mühlberg. John Frederick's heirs divided the Ernestine lands into the duchies of Weimar, Gotha, Coburg, Eisenach, and Altenburg. Duke John of Weimar, who died in 1605, left several sons; one of them was the celebrated Protestant general, BERNHARD OF SAXE-WEIMAR, who served in the Thirty Years War. The cadet lines of Coburg, Gotha, and Eisenach having failed by 1640, their lands passed to the sons of Duke John. Ernest the Pious, who had Gotha and Coburg, also inherited Altenburg in 1672; his possessions were again divided among his seven sons (see SAXE-GOTHA; SAXE-COBURG; SAXE-MEININGEN). An elder brother of Ernest the Pious, William, received Weimar and Eisenach; those duchies, however, were again separated under his heirs until the failure of the Eisenach line in 1741, when its territory (including Jena) reverted to Duke Ernest Augustus I of Saxe-Weimar. Small as it was, the duchy of **Saxe-Weimar-Eisenach**, which resulted from the reunion in 1741, was the most important of the Thuringian principalities. It gained its greatest prosperity and cultural importance under Duke CHARLES AUGUSTUS, the patron and friend of Johann Wolfgang von Goethe, who made WEIMAR, the ducal capital, an intellectual center of Europe. Charles Augustus sided against Napoleon I in the War of the Third Coalition, but was forced in 1806 to join the Confederation of the Rhine. The Congress of Vienna raised him (1815) to the rank of grand duke. Grand Duke Charles Alexander sided (1866) with Prussia in the Austro-Prussian War. His grandson, William Ernest, abdicated in 1918, and in 1920 Saxe-Weimar-Eisenach was incorporated into Thuringia.

saxhorn, any of a family of valved brass wind instruments with conical bore designed by Adolphe Sax from 1842 to 1845. They are mainly band instruments, so closely resembling many other earlier and later instruments that they are not distinctive. The term now often refers to other instruments as well as those designed by Sax. Each of them is a TRANSPOSING INSTRUMENT.

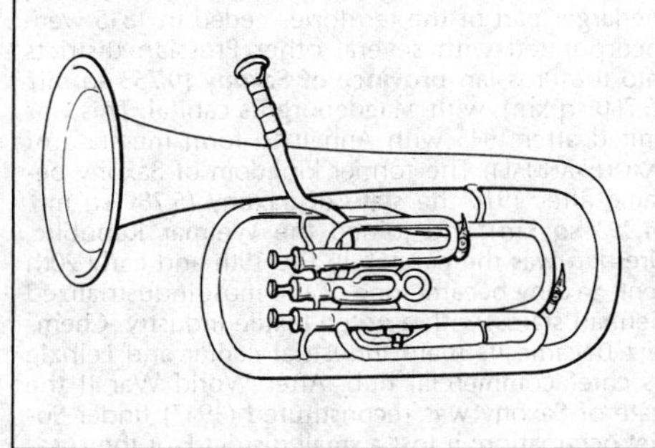

Alto saxhorn

saxifrage (săk'sĭfrĭj), common name for several members of the Saxifragaceae, a family of widely varying herbs, shrubs, and small trees of cosmopolitan distribution. They are found especially in north temperate zones and include many arctic and alpine species. Most American species are native to the West. The true saxifrages (genus *Saxifraga* and some species of other genera), also called rockfoils, comprise a large group of low rock plants including several species cultivated as rock-garden and border plants—e.g., the strawberry geranium (*S. sarmentosa*) native to E Asia, which propagates by runners like the strawberry. Among American wildflowers are the Eastern early saxifrage (*S. virginiensis*) and a Western species called umbrella plant (*S. peltata*). The genus also includes the arctic and alpine *S. oppositifolia*, one of the northernmost (found, e.g., on Ellesmere Island) of flowering plants. The golden saxifrage of the E United States is *Chrysosplenium americanum*. In the old doctrine of botanical naming, the saxifrage [Lat., =rock-breaker], because of its apparent ability to split rocks in rooting, was prescribed medicinally for calculous formations, e.g., gallstones. Other American wildflowers of the family include the miterwort, or bishop's cap (genus *Mitella*), named for its cap-shaped fruit capsule; the false miterwort, or foamflower (*Tiarella*); the grass-of-Parnassus (*Parnassia palustris*) of swamps and moist meadowlands; and the alumroot (genus *Heuchera*). *H. sanguinea*, called coral-bells, is a delicate ornamental with bright red flowers, native to New Mexico and Arizona. The other wildflowers of this group grow chiefly in rich woodland areas of the Northeast and the far West. The mock orange, or syringa, is a genus (*Philadelphus*) of deciduous shrubs native to Eurasia and North America. It is easily cultivated and has white blossoms generally similar to orange blossoms. One of the most popular fragrant species is the common, or sweet, mock orange (*P. coronarius*). Syringa [New Lat., from Gr., = pipe], an early name for mock orange, is now the scientific name for the unrelated lilac; both bushes are also sometimes called pipe tree. Among other shrubs of the saxifrage family cultivated as ornamentals are the deutzia, any species of the Asiatic genus *Deutzia*; and the hydrangea, American and Asiatic plants of the genus *Hydrangea* with flat-topped clusters of white, pink, or blue flowers. (The blue flowers are sometimes obtained by putting alum or iron in the soil.) Of minor economic importance is the genus *Ribes*, a group of berry-bearing shrubs—e.g., the gooseberry and the CURRANT. The Saxifragaceae are classified in the division MAGNOLIOPHYTA, class Magnoliopsida, order Rosales.

Saxo Grammaticus (săk'sō grəmăt'ĭkəs), c.1150–c.1220, the first important Danish historian. He was in the service of ABSALON, archbishop of Lund, at whose suggestion Saxo wrote the *Gesta Danorum* (or *Historia Danica*). The first nine books, translated (1893, repr. 1967) *Danish History,* are mostly composed of oral tradition and legends concerning the early Danes, including the story of Hamlet. The remaining seven books, dealing more with contemporary events, are an extremely valuable source for Danish history. The cognomen *grammaticus* [learned] was probably bestowed on Saxo after his death. See R. G. Latham, *Two Dissertations on the Hamlet of Saxo Grammaticus and Shakespear* (1872, repr. 1973).

Saxons, Germanic people, first mentioned in the 2d cent. by Ptolemy as inhabiting the southern part of the Cimbric Peninsula (S Jutland). Holding the area at the mouth of the Elbe River and some of the nearby islands, they gradually extended their territory southward across the Weser River. A politically unified people, the Saxons were ruled by princes or chieftains. Their assemblies, in which all classes except slaves were represented, were consulted on all issues of war and peace. In the 3d and 4th cent. the Saxons were active in raiding expeditions along the coasts of the North Sea. The European coast from the Loire to the Scheldt rivers and the southeastern coast of Britain, where defenses were erected against their piratical raids, were known to the Romans as *litora Saxonica* [Saxon shores]. By the 5th cent. Saxons had established settlements along the north shore of Gaul, especially at the mouth of the Loire, and eventually these Saxons came under Frankish domination. As the Roman occupation of Britain weakened, the Saxons increased their marauding attacks and also began (c.450) to make settlements there, resisting all efforts to drive them off. By the end of the 6th cent. they and their neighbors the Angles were firmly established in the island, laying the foundations of the Anglo-Saxon kingdoms (see ANGLO-SAXONS). Wessex, the kingdom of the West Saxons, became dominant. After the migration to Britain, the Saxons on the Continent came to be identified by historians as the Old Saxons. By virtue of their conquest (531) of Thuringia, they occupied NW Germany. In 566 they were subjugated by the Franks and forced to pay tribute. The Old Saxons waged intermittent war with the Franks until the end of the 8th cent., when they were conquered by Charlemagne and absorbed into his empire. After this conquest they were forcibly converted to Christianity. In the division of the empire by the Treaty of Verdun (843), the lands of the Saxons were included in the section that formed the basis for modern Germany.

Saxony (săk'sənē), Ger. *Sachsen,* Fr. *Saxe.* The geographic concept of Saxony has undergone great shifts and has acquired many meanings in the past 15 centuries. The land of the Saxons (see separate article), Saxony was in Frankish times roughly the area in NW Germany between the Elbe and Ems rivers; it also included part of S Jutland. (This area corresponds in part to the state of LOWER SAXONY, created after World War II.) After Charlemagne's conquest (772–804) of the Saxons, their land was incorporated into the Carolingian empire, and late in the 9th cent. the first **duchy of Saxony,** one of the five basic or stem duchies of medieval Germany, was created. Including the four divisions of Westphalia, Angria, Eastphalia, and Holstein, it occupied nearly all the territory between the Elbe and Saale rivers on the east and the Rhine on the west; it bordered on Franconia and Thuringia in the south. Duke Henry I (Henry the Fowler) of Saxony was elected German king in 919, and his son, Emperor Otto I, established the Holy Roman Empire, which he and his descendants ruled until the death (1024) of Henry II. Shortly before his imperial coronation, Otto I bestowed (961) Saxony on Hermann Billung (d. 973), a Saxon nobleman, whose descendants held the duchy until the extinction of the male line in 1106. Lothair of Supplinburg was invested with the vacant duchy and after becoming emperor as LOTHAIR II bestowed it on his Guelphic son-in-law, HENRY THE PROUD, who was already duke of Bavaria. Emperor Conrad III deprived Henry of Saxony, which he gave (1138) to ALBERT THE BEAR of Brandenburg, but in 1142 the duchy was restored to Henry the Proud's son, HENRY THE LION. The struggle between Henry the Lion and Emperor Frederick I ended with Henry's loss of all his fiefs in 1180. The stem duchy was broken up into numerous fiefs. The Guelphic heirs of Henry the Lion retained only their allodial lands—the duchy of BRUNSWICK, from which emerged the duchies of Brunswick-Wolffenbüttel and of Brunswick-Lüneburg (the later kingdom of Hanover). Vast territories passed to ecclesiastic princes—notably to the archbishops of Bremen, of Magdeburg, and of Cologne (who received the duchy of Westphalia) and the bishops of Münster, of Osnabrück, of Paderborn, of Minden, of Halberstadt, and of Hildesheim. The counties of Holstein, Oldenburg, and Lippe also became immediate fiefs of the empire. The ducal title of Saxony went to Bernard of Anhalt, a younger son of Albert the Bear of Brandenburg and founder of the Ascanian line of Saxon dukes. Besides Anhalt, Bernard received Lauenburg and the country around Wittenberg, on the Elbe. These widely separate territories continued after 1260 under separate branches of the Ascanians as Saxe-Lauenburg and Saxe-Wittenberg. The Golden Bull of 1356 raised the duke of Saxe-Wittenberg to the permanent rank of elector. **Electoral Saxony,** as his territory was called, was a relatively small area, and it lay outside the original stem duchy, being a part of the eastern march of Saxony, which was conquered from the Slavs in the 13th cent. To the S of Electoral Saxony extended the margraviate of Meissen, ruled by the increasingly powerful house of WETTIN. The margraves of Meissen acquired (13th–14th cent.) the larger parts of THURINGIA and of Lower LUSATIA and the intervening territories, and in 1423 Margrave Frederick the Warlike added Electoral Saxony; he became (1425) Elector FREDERICK I. Thus, Saxony had shifted to E central and E Germany from NW Germany. In 1485 the Wettin lands were partitioned between two sons of Elector Frederick II. Ernest, founder of the Ernestine branch of Wettin, received Electoral Saxony with Wittenberg and most of the Thuringian lands. Albert, founder of the Albertine branch, received ducal rank and the Meissen territories, including Dresden and Leipzig. Elector Ernest was succeeded by his son, FREDERICK III, who protected Martin Luther. His brother and successor, John (reigned 1525–32), and John's son JOHN FREDERICK I actively supported the Reformation. One of the leaders of the SCHMALKALDIC LEAGUE, John Frederick was defeated by Emperor Charles V at the battle of Mühlberg (1547). By the Capitulation of WITTENBERG, in the same year, John Frederick was deprived of the electorate, and the Ernestine branch retained only the Thuringian duchies, which were split among its various lines (see SAXE-ALTENBURG; SAXE-COBURG; SAXE-GOTHA; SAXE-MEININGEN; SAXE-WEIMAR). Duke MAURICE of Saxony, a grandson of Albert and a Protestant, received the electoral title, which remained in the Albertine branch until the dissolution (1806) of the Holy Roman Empire. Although Maurice had helped Charles V in conquering the Schmalkaldic League, he soon (1552) turned against the emperor. Despite his Protestant sympathies, Elector John George I (reigned 1611–56) sided with the emperor during the first part of the Thirty Years War. In 1631, however, he joined in an alliance with Gustavus II of Sweden; in 1635, at the Peace of Prague, he made peace with the emperor and obtained both Upper and Lower Lusatia. John George's failure to reach an understanding with Sweden led to the resumption of war in the same year, with the Saxons taking the field against Sweden and on the imperial side. Electoral Saxony was occupied by Swedish troops and thoroughly devastated, until in 1645 John George made a truce with Sweden. At the Peace of Westphalia (1648) he emerged—despite his military reverses and despite, or possibly because of, his frequent shifts of allegiance—as one of the two most powerful Protestant princes of Germany, the other being the elector of Brandenburg. The old rivalry between Saxony and Brandenburg (after 1701 the kingdom of Prussia) was a decisive factor in later Saxon history, as was the election (1697) of AUGUSTUS II (who was Frederick Augustus I as elector of Saxony) as king of Poland. In the NORTHERN WAR (1700–1721) against Sweden Augustus lost and regained the Polish throne. His son and successor, AUGUSTUS III (Frederick Augustus II in Saxony), retained the Polish crown in the War of the POLISH SUCCESSION (1733–35). In the War of the AUSTRIAN SUCCESSION, Saxony adhered to what had become its traditional wavering policy, changing sides in the middle of the conflict. It lost no territory at the Treaty of Dresden (1745) but paid a heavy indemnity to Frederick II of Prussia, who in 1756 opened the Seven Years War by invading Saxony once more. In the Treaty of Hubertusburg (1763), Saxony was restored to its prewar boundaries. Its prestige was much diminished. The death (1763) of Augustus III ended the union with Poland, where Stanislaus II became king. The period of Saxon rule in Poland marked a time of economic and social decay but of cultural and artistic flowering. During that period the electors had reverted to Roman Catholicism, but the population of Saxony remained staunchly Lutheran. Augustus II and Augustus III were lavish patrons of art and learning and greatly beautified their capital, DRESDEN. The universities of Wittenberg and Leipzig had long been leading intellectual centers, and 18th-century Leipzig led in the rise of German literature as well as in music, which reached its first peak in J. S. Bach. Saxony sided with Prussia against France early in the French Revolutionary Wars, but changed sides in 1806. For this act its elector was raised to royal rank, becoming King FREDERICK AUGUSTUS I. His failure to change sides again before Napoleon's fall cost him (1815) nearly half his kingdom at the Congress of Vienna. The **kingdom of Saxony** lost Lower Lusatia, part of Upper Lusatia, and all its northern territory including Wittenberg and Merseburg to Prussia. Its principal remaining cities were Dresden, Leipzig, Chemnitz (now Karl-Marx-Stadt), and Plauen. Saxony sided (1866) with Austria in the AUSTRO-PRUSSIAN WAR, was defeated, and was forced to pay a large indemnity and to join the North German Confederation. From 1871 until the abdication (1918) of Frederick Augustus III, it was a member state of the German Empire. Meanwhile, the larger part of the territories ceded in 1815 were incorporated with several other Prussian districts into the Prussian **province of Saxony** (9,753 sq mi/25,260 sq km), with Magdeburg its capital. This was united after 1945 with Anhalt to form the state of SAXONY-ANHALT. The former kingdom of Saxony became after 1918 the **state of Saxony** (5,789 sq mi/14,993 sq km) and joined the Weimar Republic. Dresden was the capital. In the 19th and early 20th cent. Saxony became one of the most industrialized German states, with a noted textile industry. Chemnitz became its main industrial center and Leipzig its chief commercial hub. After World War II the state of Saxony was reconstituted (1947) under Soviet occupation; it lost a small district E of the Lusatian Neisse, but gained a part of Silesia W of the Neisse. The post-war state (6,561 sq mi/16,993 sq km) joined the German Democratic Republic in 1949. It was abolished as an administrative unit in 1952 and was divided among the districts of Halle, Magdeburg, Leipzig, and Cottbus.

Saxony-Anhalt (săk'sənē-än'hält), Ger. *Sachsen-Anhalt*, former state, c.10,000 sq mi (25,900 sq km), S East Germany. Halle was the capital. As constituted in 1947 under Soviet military occupation, Saxony-Anhalt consisted, roughly, of the former state of ANHALT, the former Prussian province of SAXONY, and several small territories of the former state of BRUNSWICK. Saxony-Anhalt was abolished as an administrative district in 1952, and its territory was included in the districts of Halle, Magdeburg, Leipzig, and Cottbus.

saxophone, musical instrument invented in the 1840s by Adolphe Sax. Although it uses the single reed of the clarinet family, it has a conical tube and is made of metal. By 1846 there was a double family of 14 saxophones, seven in F and C for orchestral

Saxophone

use and seven in E flat and B flat for bands. The latter are by far most common today, the alto, tenor, and baritone being used most frequently. The saxophone has a powerful tone, between woodwind and brass in quality and blending well with both. Valuable to bands and occasionally used in the orchestra, it is now best known for its extensive use in dance and jazz music. It has a small serious solo literature. All saxophones except those in C are TRANSPOSING INSTRUMENTS.

Say, Jean Baptiste (zhäN bätēst' sā), 1767–1832, French economist. In *A Treatise on Political Economy* (1803, tr. from the 4th ed. 1821) he effectively reorganized and popularized the theories of Adam Smith. Say also developed a noted theory of markets and the concept of the entrepreneur. His works include *Cours complet d'économie politique pratique* (6 vol., 1828–29). See study by Thomas Sowell (1972). His grandson, **Léon Say,** 1826–96, was also an economist. As minister of finance under several governments he accomplished the payment of war debts to Germany ahead of schedule. He edited and wrote several works on finance.

Say, Thomas, 1787–1843, American naturalist, b. Philadelphia. He went on collecting expeditions to Georgia and Florida and, with Stephen H. Long, to the Rocky Mts. and up the Mississippi and Minnesota rivers. He was professor of natural history at the Univ. of Pennsylvania from 1822 to 1828 and spent the rest of his life at Robert Owen's colony in New Harmony, Ind. Called the father of American descriptive entomology, he wrote on paleontology and conchology as well. His complete entomological papers were collected by J. L. Le Conte (2 vol., 1859), and his complete writings on conchology were edited by W. G. Binney (1858). See biography by H. B. Weiss and G. M. Ziegler (1931).

Sayama (säyä'mä), city (1970 pop. 60,886), Saitama prefecture, E central Honshu, Japan, on Lake Sayama. It is a resort and center for various mechanical industries.

Sayan Mountains (säyän'), central Asia, chiefly in Central Asian USSR, in S Siberia. The Eastern Sayan Mts. extend c.680 mi (1,090 km) from the lower Yenisei River to the southwest end of Lake Baykal and rise to 11,686 ft (3,562 m) in the Munku-Sardyk; they form part of the USSR-Mongolian People's Republic border. The Western Sayan Mts., rising to 10,206 ft (3,111 m) in the Kyzyl-Tayga, extend c.400 mi (640 km) NE from the Altai range to the central section of the Eastern Sayan Mts. There are a variety of mineral deposits in the Sayan Mts. Lumbering, agriculture, and hunting are the chief occupations there.

Saybrook Platform: see CAMBRIDGE PLATFORM.

Saye and Sele, William Fiennes, 1st **Viscount** (fīnz, sā'ənsēl), 1582–1662, English politician and promoter of colonization in America. He was a Puritan in religious sympathy and a leader in the House of Lords of the opposition to James I and Charles I. From 1630, Saye, with Robert Greville (2d Baron Brooke), John PYM, and others, entered into several colonization schemes. The first of these was on Providence Island (now Providencia) in the Caribbean. The second was at Saybrook (named for the two lords), Conn., settled in 1635 on the basis of a deed obtained from the 2d earl of Warwick. John WINTHROP the younger (1606–76) was their governor at Saybrook. In 1633 they bought a plantation at Cocheco (now Dover, N.H.). The lords planned to settle in New England, but their plan for establishing a hereditary aristocracy in the colonies met with disfavor in New England, and after a few years they lost interest in the settlements. In 1641 they sold the Dover establishment to Massachusetts, and three years later they sold Saybrook to Connecticut. Providence Island was taken by the Spanish in 1641. In the English civil war Saye remained in the parliamentary party and played a decisive role in securing the adoption of the Self-Denying Ordinance (1645). In the dispute between the army and Parliament in 1647 he supported the army. He did not, however, desire the abolition of the monarchy, and he was one of the parliamentary commissioners who negotiated with Charles at Newport in 1648. He retired from public life after the king's execution (1649).

Sayers, Dorothy Leigh (sā'ərz), 1893–1957, English writer, grad. Somerville College, Oxford, 1915. Taking first-class honors in medieval literature, she was one of the first women to receive an Oxford degree. In 1926 she married Oswald A. Fleming, a well-known war correspondent. For a time she worked as a copy writer in a London advertising agency—the setting for her *Murder Must Advertise* (1933). Her first detective novel was *Whose Body?* (1923), in which appeared her nobleman-detective, Lord Peter Wimsey; he reappeared in 10 novels including *The Nine Tailors* (1934) and *Gaudy Night* (1935), with an Oxford setting. Her short stories featuring Wimsey were collected in *Lord Peter* (1972). Sayers is considered one of the masters of the detective story. Her novels are brilliantly plotted, and they are written with great vitality, wit, and erudition. She later wrote religious dramas and theological essays, which included *Begin Here* (1941) and *Creed or Chaos?* (1949). She translated most of Dante's *Divine Comedy* (1949, 1955) and wrote studies of Dante (1954 and 1957).

Sayreville, borough (1970 pop. 32,508), Middlesex co., E N.J., on the Raritan River; inc. 1919. Its manufactures include titanium, chemicals, plastics, photographic products, and ceramics.

Sazonov, Sergei Dmitreyevich (sĭrgā' dəmē'trēəvĭch səzô'nəf), 1861–1927, Russian statesman. As minister of foreign affairs (1910–16) he played a leading role in the crisis that led to WORLD WAR I. Sazonov and Russian military leaders urged the czar to order (July 30, 1914) a general rather than a partial mobilization of Russian armed forces. In response to the Russian move, the Austro-Hungarian emperor ordered immediate mobilization; war broke out several days later. After the Bolshevik Revolution (Nov., 1917, N.S.), Sazonov represented the anti-Bolshevik groups in Paris. See his memoirs, *Fateful Years* (tr. 1928, repr. 1971).

Sb, chemical symbol of the element ANTIMONY.

Sc, chemical symbol of the element SCANDIUM.

scabies (skā'bēz), highly contagious parasitic skin disease caused by the itch mite (*Sarcoptes scabiei*). The disease is also known as itch. It is acquired through close contact with an infested individual or contaminated clothing and is most prevalent among those living in crowded and unhygienic conditions. The female mite burrows her way into the skin, depositing eggs along the tunnel. The larvae hatch in several days and find their way into the hair follicles. Itching is most intense at night because of the nocturnal activity of the parasites. Aside from the burrows, which are usually clearly visible, there are a variety of skin lesions, many of them brought on by scratching and infection. All clothing and bedding of the victim and his household should be disinfected. Disinfestation of the skin is accomplished by applying creams or ointments containing gamma benzene hexachloride or benzyl benzoate. A variety of *S. scabiei* causes MANGE in animals.

scabiosa: see TEASEL.

Scaevola (Caius Mucius Scaevola) (sĕv'ôlə, -vələ), fl. 6th cent.? B.C., quasi-historical Roman hero. According to tradition he tried to murder Lars Porsena, who was besieging the city, and was condemned to be burned at the stake. When Scaevola put his right hand into the blaze and held it there, Porsena was so impressed he liberated him. Scaevola's warning that many Romans would follow his example persuaded Porsena to raise the siege.

Scaevola (Quintus Mucius Scaevola), d. 82 B.C., Roman jurist. He was tribune of the people (106 B.C.) and consul (95) with Lucius Licinius Crassus (see under CRASSUS, family); together they collaborated on a law that caused a purge of the rolls of citizenship. The wholesale disfranchisement of allies under this law brought on the Social War. He was proconsular governor of Asia, where the people esteemed him highly. Later he was elected pontifex maximus, but his sacred inviolability did not prevent his murder in the proscription of MARIUS. He made a systematic compilation of the civil law.

Scafell (skô'fĕl') or **Scaw fell,** mountain group, Cumberland, NW England, in the Lake District, in the Cumbrian Mts. It includes the peaks Scafell Pike (3,210 ft/978 m; highest in England), Scafell, and Great End. The region is a tourist resort.

Scala, Can Francesco della or **Can Grande della Scala** (kän fränchās'kō dĕl'lä skä'lä; käng grän'dā), 1291-1329, lord of Verona, the greatest member of the pro-imperial, or Ghibelline, family that ruled Verona from 1277 to 1387 (see GUELPHS AND GHIBELLINES). Can Grande was made imperial vicar by Holy Roman Emperor Henry VII and participated in the struggles against the Guelphs, the papal party, extending his territories to include Vicenza, Padua, Feltre, Belluno, and Treviso. His was one of the important states of N Italy. A typical Italian tyrant, he was also a great patron of the arts and letters and a protector of Dante, who mentioned him in the *Paradiso.* The tombs of the Della Scala (or Scaligeri) family are among the landmarks of Verona.

Scala, La [Teatro alla Scala], one of the world's great opera houses, located in Milan, Italy. It opened in 1778 with a production of Antonio Salieri's *Europa Riconosciuta.* Built on the site of the Church of Santa Maria della Scala, the opera house was designed by Giuseppe Piermarini. The building was remodelled in 1867, modernized in 1921, and restored in 1946 after having been bombed in World War II. La Scala has been the scene of many famous opera premieres, among them Verdi's *Otello* and *Falstaff,* Puccini's *Turandot* and *Madame Butterfly,* and Bellini's *Norma.*

scalar, quantity or number possessing only sign and magnitude, e.g., the real numbers (see NUMBER), in contrast to VECTORS and TENSORS; scalars obey the rules of elementary algebra. Many physical quantities have scalar values, e.g., length, area, mass, energy, and electric charge. Such quantities as velocity, force, momentum, and spin are vectors and follow different algebraic rules.

scalawags (skăl'əwăgz), derogatory term used in the South after the Civil War to describe native white Southerners who joined the Republican party and aided in carrying out the congressional RECONSTRUCTION program. A Republican who came from the north was called a CARPETBAGGER.

scaldic or **Skaldic poetry:** see OLD NORSE LITERATURE.

scale, in cartography, the ratio of the distance between two points on a map to the real distance between the two corresponding points portrayed. The scale may be expressed in three ways: numerically, as a ratio or a fraction, e.g., 1:100,000 or 1/100000; verbally, e.g., "one inch to one mile" (not "one inch equals one mile"); and graphically, by marking distances on a sample line. The last method has the advantage that the scale remains true even if the map is enlarged or reduced mechanically. The first method is particularly useful since any unit of measurement may be used; e.g., if one uses metric units, a scale of 1:100,000 would mean that one centimeter on the map represents one kilometer on the earth's surface (since 100,000 centimeters equals one kilometer). The more the size of features on the map approaches the features' actual size on the earth's surface, the larger the scale of the map is said to be. A large-scale map usually shows more detail than does a small-scale map, but covers a smaller area than does a small-scale map of the same size.

scale, in music, any series of tones arranged in a step-by-step rising or falling order of PITCH. A scale defines the INTERVAL relationship of each TONE to the others upon which the composition depends. Scales further serve to classify and catalogue the tonal material used in composition. There is an enormous variety of scales that have been used in the past and that are still being used; no single interval is common to all of them. In the 6th cent. B.C., Pythagoras defined the mathematical relationship of the perfect tone intervals (the octave, fourth, and fifth) and of the intervals between them. The resulting major scale, called diatonic, has five whole tones (*t*) and two semitones (*s*) arranged thus: *ttsttts* (as in the white notes on the keyboard); this scale, with certain modifications, became the basis of Western musical TONALITY until the end of the 19th cent. The Greek system was taken up by the Christian church, which adapted its note series to a number of MODES used in medieval music, especially in PLAINSONG. The dissemination and influence of the diatonic scale was therefore very great. Akin to the modes, the concept of KEY was developed, whereby a home tone, or tonic, is the principal focus of a composition, and the various other tones assume importance according to their relationship to the tonic. The increasing complexity of instruments demanded more refined TUNING SYSTEMS. By J. S. Bach's time equal TEMPERAMENT had become established. The resulting scale, called chromatic, consisted of 12 notes divided by semitone intervals (the white and black notes of the keyboard). Although the diatonic scale is basically heptatonic, music that is in a major or minor tonality usually employs the remaining five tones of the chromatic scale as auxiliary or ornamental tones. Music that employs them freely is said to be highly chromatic, while music that employs them sparingly is said to be diatonic. For purposes of HARMONIC variation, the minor scale or mode in the arrangement *tstttts* was adopted. The 12 scales, one for each note, and the 12 concomitant minor scales remained the basic organizing structure of Western music until the system was challenged by the dodecaphonic composers, in particular Arnold SCHOENBERG, who worked into the mid-20th cent. (see ATONALITY; SERIAL MUSIC). The whole-tone scale, which divides the octave into six equal whole tones (C, D, E, F sharp, G sharp, and A sharp, on the piano), gives a feeling of vagueness that made it adaptable to impressionism, but its possibilities seem to have been exhausted in the works of Debussy. The pentatonic scale (the black keys of the piano illustrate one form) has long been thought of as having an Oriental character because of the prevalence of pentatonic scales in Chinese, Japanese, and Javanese music. The most highly developed scales known belong to ARABIAN MUSIC and HINDU MUSIC. See Nicholas Slonimsky, *Thesaurus of Scales and Melodic Patterns* (1947).

scale, in weights and measures, instruments for determining weight, generally for other than laboratory use. For the principles of operation of all weighing devices, see BALANCE. Platform scales utilize a succession of multiplying levers that transmit the weight to a beam or other registration device. They are used where massive objects or large quantities are to be weighed. For example, a railway car or truck moves onto a platform scale before and after unloading or loading, in each case the difference between the weighings being the weight of its cargo. As the name implies, counter scales are used in commercial establishments where weighing can be most conveniently done on a counter. Cylinder, drum, or barrel scales show their calibrations on a rotatable chart. These find wide use because of the ease with which the cost of a given weight may be read from them through the juxtaposition of fixed and rotating charts. The same purpose is served by the fan-type scale, in which an indicator moves through an arc marked from zero to the maximum capacity of the scale. Both the indicator and the fan expanse are calibrated for automatic computation. A great variety of scales are specially constructed for industrial uses in which weighing of a continuous flow of material is required. The scale in such cases is part of the machinery that carries the weighed material to a succeeding operation. Many scales provide printed records of each reading, and some keep a cumulative registration of a succession of readings. See A. W. Green, *How We Weigh and Measure* (1961); Bruno Kisch, *Scales and Weights* (1965).

scale, in zoology, an outgrowth, either bony or horny, of the skin of an animal. The major component of the scales of fishes is bone, and they are formed directly in the skin membrane as the fish grows. The number of rows of scales, as well as the kind, figures in the identification of a species. The growth of the scales is marked by rings, which aid in determining the age of the fish. The placoid scales of sharks, which have a dentine base with a pulp cavity, are thought to be similar to the forms from which the teeth of the higher vertebrates evolved. Ganoid scales, found in primitive fishes such as the gar pike and the sturgeon, are heavy and platelike. Other fishes have either rough scales (ctenoid) with comblike edges or smooth scales (cycloid). The horny scales, or scutes, of most reptiles develop embryologically as outpushings of the epidermis. In some lizards the scales are modified to form tubercles or granules. Other lizards and snakes have overlapping scales, highly developed in the snakes as aids to locomotion. The crocodile has both horny and bony scales. Among turtles and their relatives scales are usually found on the head, neck, limbs, and tail; in most of the group horny scales also form a pattern of flat plates overlying the bony dermal skeleton of the back and belly. Birds have horny scales on the feet and sometimes on the legs. Some mammals, e.g., the mouse and the rat, have scales on the tail; the pangolin and the armadillo have a body covering of large horny scales.

scale insect, common name for members of a highly modified group of insects belonging to several families of the superfamily Coccoidea. Scales possess antennae and are characterized by reduced legs. Only the males have wings; females are always wingless. Scales are popularly subdivided into three groups; the armored scales, the unarmored scales, and the MEALYBUGS. The armored scales secrete a wax covering, the shape of which is characteristic for any given species. Under this coat, the insects develop and feed, sucking the sap of plants with their thin tubular mouthparts. The females never leave the protection of the scale after once forming it, but the adult males, which do not feed, develop a single pair of wings, leave the scale, and seek out the females, fertilizing them after the females are under the shell. Among the important armored scale pests of citrus, other fruits, and ornamentals are the SAN JOSE SCALE, the oyster scale, the purple scale, and the California and Florida red scales. The unarmored scales (or soft scales) are similar to the armored scales except that only a small amount of wax is secreted, which adheres to the insect. Unarmored scale pests of citrus fruits include the black scale and citricola scale. Mealybugs appear as white cottony clusters on citrus, ornamentals, and greenhouse plants. Like other scale insects, newly hatched nymphs, called crawlers, have legs and actively seek out food. When they find a suitable spot, they settle down to feed. Some scales secrete a resinous covering, which is used in the commercial production of shellac, varnish, and paints (see LAC). Control of scale insects has been largely by use of natural enemies, especially ladybird beetles and small parasitic wasps, which are natural predators of these pests. Scale insects have proved difficult to control by chemical means. Scale insects are classified in the phylum ARTHROPODA, class Insecta, order Homoptera, superfamily Coccoidea.

Scaliger, Joseph Justus (skăl'ĭjər), 1540-1609, French classical scholar. He was the son of Julius Caesar Scaliger, from whom he acquired his early mastery of Latin. He adopted Protestantism in 1562, served as companion of a Poitevin noble (1563-70), studied under Cujas at Valence (1570-72), and was professor of philosophy at Geneva (1572-74). After 1593 he held a research professorship at Leiden. Renowned in his own day for his erudition, he was learned in mathematics, philosophy, and many languages, and he was a promoter of scientific methods for textual criticism and the study of the classics. His *De emendatione temporum* [on the correction of chronology] (1583) surveyed all the ways then known of measuring time, and placed the study of ancient calendars and dates on a scientific basis. He discovered and restored the content of the lost original of the second book of Eusebius' chronicle. The chronological foundation for the modern study of ancient history was summed up in his *Thesaurus temporum* [repertory of dates] (1606). A brief autobiography, extending to 1594, supplemented by a selection from his letters, was edited and translated by G. W. Robinson (1927). See biography by Jacob Bernays (1885, repr. 1965).

Scaliger, Julius Caesar, 1484–1558, Italian philologist and physician in France. Scaliger studied medicine and settled in France (1526), where he worked as a physician. A scholar of profound erudition, Scaliger was nevertheless contentious and arrogant and made many enemies, including Erasmus and Jerome Cardan. In his *De causis linguae Latinae* (1540), he analyzed Cicero's style, criticizing the earlier studies of his humanist predecessors. He wrote commentaries on the medical and botanical writings of Hippocrates, Theophrastus, and Aristotle and urged an improved classification of plants according to their unique characteristics. In his famous *Poetics* (1561, tr. 1905) he extolled Vergil and Seneca.

scallion: see ONION.

scallop or **pecten,** marine BIVALVE mollusk. Like its close relative the oyster, the scallop has no siphons, the mantle being completely open, but it differs from other mollusks in that both mantle edges have a row of steely blue "eyes" and tactile projections. The rounded shells have radiating ribs with flared "ears" or "wings" at the hinge. Scallops are capable of swimming or leaping about by snapping their shells, which are controlled by a powerful adductor muscle, the only part of the animal that is eaten. Scallops are more common on the Atlantic coast than the Pacific. The common scallop is about 2 in. (5 cm) long. Found abundantly in shallow and offshore waters and in eelgrass and mud flats from Cape Cod to Texas, it is taken in large numbers around Long Island. The giant scallop, found in deeper waters from Labrador to New Jersey, attains a length of 5 in. (12.7 cm). Scallops are classified in the phylum MOLLUSCA, class Pelecypoda, order Filibranchia, family Pectinidae.

scalp, the integument covering the top of the head. It consists of three layers of tissue: the SKIN, an underlying layer of tissue and blood vessels, and the occipitofrontalis muscle stretching from the eyebrows to the back of the head. Except for its abundant growth of HAIR, the skin of the scalp resembles that of the rest of the body but is especially rich in blood vessels. Hence profuse bleeding may be associated with scalp injuries.

scalping, taking the scalp of an enemy. The custom, comparable to HEAD-HUNTING, was formerly practiced in Europe and Asia, but it is mainly associated with the North American Indians, although many Indian tribes did not take scalps. To some Indians, the scalp was not merely a trophy; it bestowed the possessor with the powers of the scalped enemy. In scalping, a circular cut was made around the crown of the head and the skin raised at one side and torn off. The scalping of a living person was not always fatal. In their early wars with the Indians the colonists of North America retaliated by taking scalps and heads of Indians, and bounties were offered for them.

scaly anteater: see PANGOLIN.

Scamander (skəmăn'dər), ancient name of the Küçük Menderes River, c.60 mi (95 km) long, NW Turkey. It flows W and NW from the Kaz Dağı through the TROAS into the Mediterranean Sea. It is frequently mentioned in the *Iliad.*

scammony: see MORNING GLORY.

Scanderbeg or **Skanderbeg** (both: skăn'dərbĕg), c.1404–1468, Albanian national hero. His original name was George Castriota or Kastriotes, but the Turks called him Iskender Bey [Lord Alexander], and this was corrupted into Scanderbeg. The son of a prince of N Albania, he was educated in the Muslim faith as a hostage at the court of Sultan Murad II. The sultan showered favors on him and gave him the title bey and an army command. In 1443, when the Turks indicated they would attack Albania, Scanderbeg escaped to his homeland, abjured Islam, and formed a league of princes among the quarreling Albanian chiefs. He proclaimed himself prince of Albania. To resist the Turks under Sultan Muhammad II, Scanderbeg received aid at various times from Venice, Naples, Hungary, and the pope. He had success in these wars partly because of the rugged Albanian terrain and partly because he employed a mobile defense force using guerrilla methods. He withstood repeated attacks and forced the sultan to conclude a 10-year truce in 1461. Scanderbeg broke the truce in 1463 when Pope Pius II called for a new crusade. The pope's death (1464) forced abandonment of the crusade; Scanderbeg, left without allies, had to retreat to his fortress of Kroia. After he died the chiefs resumed their quarrels, resistance collapsed, and Albania fell to the Turks. Scanderbeg's life has furnished Albania with a great fund of popular lore.

Scandinavia (skăn"dĭnā'vēə), region of N Europe. It consists of the kingdoms of Sweden, Norway, and Denmark; Finland and Iceland are usually considered part of Scandinavia. Physiographically, Denmark belongs to the North European Plain rather than to the geologically distinct Scandinavian peninsula (which is part of the ancient Baltic Shield), occupied by Norway and Sweden. The peninsula (c.300,000 sq mi/777,000 sq km) is c.1,150 mi (1,850 km) long and from 230 to 500 mi (370–805 km) wide and is bordered by the Gulf of Bothnia, the Baltic Sea, the Kattegat and Skagerrak straits, the North Sea, the Atlantic Ocean, and the Arctic Ocean. It is mountainous in the west (rising to 8,104 ft/2,470 m at Glittertinden, S Norway) and slopes gently in the east and the south. The region was heavily glaciated during the Ice Age; Jostedalsbreen (W Norway), the largest glacier of mainland Europe, is a remnant of the great ice sheet. The peninsula's western coast is deeply indented by fjords. Short, swift-flowing streams drain to the west, while long parallel rivers and numerous lakes are found in the east; Vänern and Vättern, both in S Sweden, are among Europe's largest lakes. Nearly a quarter of the peninsula lies N of the Arctic Circle, reaching its northernmost point in Cape Nordkyn, Norway. The climate varies from tundra and subarctic in the north, to humid continental in the central portion, and to marine west coast in the south and southwest. The region's best farmland is in S Sweden. The peninsula is rich in timber and minerals (notably iron and copper), and has a great hydroelectricity generating capacity. Its coastal waters are important fishing grounds. Population is concentrated in the southern part of the peninsula; Stockholm and Göteborg (both in Sweden) and Oslo (Norway) are the largest cities. Except for the Lapps and Finns in the north and east, the Scandinavian peoples speak a closely related group of Germanic languages—Norwegian, Danish, Icelandic, Faerose, and Swedish. The oldest Germanic literature (see OLD NORSE LITERATURE) flourished in Scandinavia, especially in Iceland.

Scandinavian art and architecture. The Scandinavian countries are rich in artifacts and objects of archaeological interest dating from the end of the Ice Age through the Bronze Age, the Celtic and Germanic Iron Ages, and the Viking period. Viking art (c.800–c.1050) is characterized by dynamic, geometric design of considerable complexity and sophistication and the ingenious use of animal forms. It bears a clear relationship to other European trends, particularly to Hiberno-Saxon ILLUMINATION. Numerous fine examples of early Scandinavian art are exhibited at the museums of Copenhagen and Stockholm. Church building became the principal artistic activity when Scandinavia was christianized in the 11th cent. The wooden STAVKIRKE is unique to this region; examples remain only in Norway where it was most prevalent. The cathedral at Lund, Sweden, begun in 1085, reveals Lombard influence; Gothic elements predominate in the cathedrals of Linköping and Skara. The island of Gotland produced numerous sculptural and architectural masterworks of the Gothic period. The cathedral at Trondheim, begun in the 12th cent., bears a resemblance to English Gothic architecture, particularly to Lincoln Cathedral. Uppsala Cathedral was built by French architects. Foreign stylistic influence persisted through the Renaissance and baroque periods, the North German school of Lübeck becoming more and more the chief source for Scandinavian styles. Castles such as Gripsholm exemplify this borrowing. Great castle-building activity was instigated by the Danish and Swedish rulers of the 16th to 18th cent; outstanding examples include Kronborg (c.1570–1590) and Fredriksborg (c.1560–1620) castles and the rebuilt castle of Stockholm (1690–1708; 1727–53). In the 18th and 19th cent. native artists began to gain international prestige. From Denmark the neoclassicist sculptor A. B. THORVALDSEN taught and worked in Rome, wielding enormous stylistic influence. The painters Christoffer ECKERSBERG and N. A. ABILDGAARD were prominent, as were the architects C. F. Harsdorff and C. E. Hansen. The academy of Copenhagen attracted students from Germany, including the painters P. O. Runge and C. D. Friedrich. Norway produced its best-known artists late in the 19th cent.—the sculptors Stephan Sinding and A. G. VIGELAND and the protoexpressionist painter Edvard MUNCH. Notable Swedish artists include the sculptor J. T. SERGEL and, in the late 19th and early 20th cent., the painters A. L. ZORN and Carl LARSSON and the modern sculptor Carl MILLES, who has worked extensively in the United States. Since World War II various strains of abstraction have been developed by Scandinavian artists. The inventive use of traditional and regional forms within the plain vocabulary of brick construction led to a rejuvenation of Scandinavian architecture in the early 20th cent. with the works of P. V. J. Klint of Denmark and Ragnar Ostberg, Sigfrid Ericsson, and, above all, E. G. ASPLUND of Sweden. The Finnish architects Eliel SAARINEN and Alvar AALTO have influenced Scandinavian design profoundly and have won international acclaim for establishing an unquestionably new architecture. Modern Scandinavian furniture and applied arts, particularly glassmaking, metalwork, woodwork, and ceramics, have been widely imitated for their simplicity and purity of line. See Thomas Paulsson, *Scandinavian Architecture* (1958); *The Art of Scandinavia,* Vol. I by Peter Anker (tr. 1970), Vol. II by Aron Andersson (tr. 1970).

scandium (skăn'dēəm), metallic chemical element; symbol Sc; at. no. 21; at. wt. 44.956; m.p. about 1800°C; b.p. about 2870°C; sp. gr. 2.99 at 20°C; valence +3. Scandium is a soft silver-white metal. It is a member of group IIIb of the PERIODIC TABLE; because of its chemical and physical properties, its scarcity, and the difficulty in extracting the metal, it is sometimes regarded as one of the RARE-EARTH METALS. At ordinary temperatures it crystallizes in a hexagonal close-packed structure. It tarnishes slightly when exposed to air. It reacts with many acids. It forms an oxide and a number of colorless salts. Its compounds are found widely distributed in minute amounts in nature. It is a major component of the rare Norwegian mineral thortveitite. It is found in many of the rare-earth minerals and in certain tungsten and uranium ores. Scandium is found in relatively greater abundance in the sun and certain stars than on earth. The metal has little commercial importance. In 1970 pure scandium cost several thousand dollars per pound. Scandium oxide (scandia) finds use as a catalyst and in making crucibles and other ceramic parts. Scandium sulfate in very dilute aqueous solution is used in agriculture as a seed treatment to improve the germination of corn, peas, wheat, and other plants. Scandium was discovered by L. F. Nilson in 1879 by spectroscopic analysis of euxenite and gadolinite. It was later shown by P. T. Cleve to correspond to the ekaboron predicted in 1871 by Mendelejeff from his periodic law.

Scania: see SKÅNE, Sweden.

Scapa Flow (skăp'ə), area of water, 15 mi (24 km) long and 8 mi (12.9 km) wide, in the Orkney Islands, off N Scotland. It is bounded by the islands of Mainland, Graemsay, Burray, South Ronaldsay, and Hoy. Scapa Flow was Britain's main naval base in both world wars. Lyness, on Hoy, was the headquarters. The British vessel *Vanguard* was torpedoed in Scapa Flow in July, 1917, and the German fleet was scuttled there in 1919. In Oct., 1939, a German submarine slipped in and sank the *Royal Oak,* causing the British fleet to withdraw until 1940. The Churchill Barrier was begun the same year to block the eastern entrance to Scapa Flow by sinking 250,000 tons of rock in the sounds linking Mainland, Burray, South Ronaldsay, and two smaller eastern islands. The barrier now forms a causeway linking Mainland to South Ronaldsay. The naval base was closed in 1957.

scaphopod: see MOLLUSCA.

scar, fibrous CONNECTIVE TISSUE that forms at the site of injury or disease in any tissue of the body. Scar tissue may replace injured skin and underlying muscle, damaged heart muscle, or diseased areas of internal organs such as the liver. Dense and thick, it is usually paler than the surrounding tissue because it is poorly supplied with blood, and although it structurally replaces destroyed tissue, it cannot perform the functions of the missing tissue. It may therefore limit the range of muscle movement or block circulation in a crucial area such as a heart valve. Extensively scarred tissue may lose its ability to function normally.

scarab beetle or **scarab,** name for members of a large family of heavy-bodied, oval BEETLES (the Scarabaeidae), with about 30,000 species distributed throughout most of the world and over 1,200 in North America. North American scarab beetles range in length from less than ½ in. to more than 2 in. (5–50 mm); members of some tropical species grow several inches long. Many scarab beetles are brightly colored and many are iridescent. A large group of scarab beetles are scavengers, feeding on decaying vegetation or on the dung of grazing animals. Most of these lay their eggs in underground chambers supplied with dung, where the larvae feed and pupate, emerging as adults. These scarabs, called dung beetles, play an extremely important role in the rapid recycling of organic matter and the disposal of disease-breeding wastes. Australia, which has few native dung beetle species, has imported African species to help dispose of cattle dung. Some of the dung beetles, known as tumblebugs, form balls of dung that they roll about with their hind legs, sometimes for long distances and sometimes working in pairs. Eventually they bury the ball and lay eggs in it. One such ball-roller is the sacred scarab *(Scarabaeus sacer)*, a black scarab beetle of the Mediterranean region. In ancient Egypt the periodic appearance of this beetle in great numbers on the surface of the Nile mud led men to associate the sacred scarab with resurrection and immortality. It was believed that all scarabs were males capable of reproducing their kind. Their ball-rolling activities were associated with the diurnal movement of the sun. Other species of scarab beetles feed on living plants. Members of these groups include such major crop and garden pests as the JAPANESE BEETLE, the rose chafer, and the JUNE BEETLE (also called June bug and May beetle). Cockchafers are Old World species similar to June beetles. Adult plant-eating scarab beetles attack leaves, flowers, and fruits, while the larvae, which develop from eggs laid in the ground, attack roots. The largest scarab beetles in North America are the plant-eating Hercules beetles and their close relatives, the rhinoceros beetles and elephant beetles. In most species of this group the males are prominently horned. The Hercules beetles of the S United States may grow 2½ in. (6.4 cm) long; their tropical relatives may attain a length of 6 in. (15 cm) including the horns. Despite their ferocious appearance these beetles are harmless to people. The term *scarab* is also applied to representations of scarab beetles made of stone, metal, or other materials. Finely carved scarabs were used as seals in ancient Egypt; inscribed scarabs were issued to commemorate important events or buried with mummies. Roman soldiers wore scarab rings as military symbols. Scarab beetles are classified in the phylum ARTHROPODA, class Insecta, order Coleoptera, family Scarabaeidae.

Scaramouche: see COMMEDIA DELL' ARTE.

Scarborough, municipal borough (1971 pop. 44,370), North Riding of Yorkshire, NE England, on the North Sea. The town is primarily a resort. Sports tournaments are held annually. The site was recognized at an early time for its strategic importance. There are vestiges of a 4th-century Roman signaling station and a 12th-century castle. The ancient Church of St. Mary is on the site of a Cistercian priory. St. Martin's has artwork by Burne-Jones, D. G. Rossetti, and William Morris. In 1974, Scarborough became part of the new nonmetropolitan county of North Yorkshire.

Scarlatti, Alessandro (älĕs-sän'drō skärlät'tē), 1660–1725, Italian composer. He probably studied with Carissimi in Rome, where his first opera was produced in 1679. In 1684 he went to Naples as master of the royal chapel and there composed operas for the royal palace and chamber music for the aristocracy. Later he was also active in Florence, Rome, and Venice. He wrote more than 100 operas, of which *Mitridate Eupatore* (1707) and *Il Tigrane* (1715) are considered the finest. As a leader of the Neapolitan school, he helped establish the conventions of the *opera seria*, perfecting the *aria da capo* and the three-part overture. His church music includes motets and masses; he also wrote serenades and madrigals, and he composed almost 700 chamber cantatas, which represent the highest development of his art. See biography by E. J. Dent (1905, new ed. 1960). His son, **(Giuseppe) Domenico Scarlatti,** 1685–1757, was a harpsichord virtuoso and composer. Domenico was first taught by his father and later by Gasparini in Venice. As a young man he engaged in friendly keyboard competition with his contemporary Handel, and thereafter the two had lifelong admiration for each other. From 1709 to 1714, Scarlatti was composer to the Polish Queen Maria Casimira in her court at Rome, and then for a time he was chapel master of St. Peter's. About 1719 he went to Lisbon as music master of the royal chapel and teacher of the Princess Maria Barbara. He accompanied her to Madrid in 1729, and spent the rest of his life at the Spanish court. Scarlatti wrote operas, oratorios, and cantatas, but his fame rests chiefly on his harpsichord sonatas, of which he wrote well over 500. They exploit the instrument to its fullest capacity, exemplifying his mastery of the homophonic "free style" of composition. His works display the vivacity, grace, and ornamentation of the rococo, and at the same time show boundless invention and originality. Scarlatti is widely considered to be the founder of modern keyboard technique. See biography by Ralph Kirkpatrick (1953); S. Sitwell, *A Background for Domenico Scarlatti* (1935, repr. 1970).

scarlet fever, acute, communicable infection caused by hemolytic streptococci. It occurs in young children, usually between two and eight years of age, and is spread by droplet spray from carriers and from individuals who have contracted the disease, and by contaminated articles, food, and milk. The incubation period is from three to five days and infectivity lasts about two weeks. Scarlet fever may be so mild as to go unrecognized or occasionally it may be severe, but it is rarely fatal if treated. Typical symptoms are sore throat, headache, fever, flushed face with a ring of pallor about the mouth, red spots in the mouth, coated tongue with raw beefy appearance and inflamed papillae underneath it (strawberry tongue), and a characteristic eruption on the body. The streptococcal bacterium that causes scarlet fever is identical to the streptococcal pharyngitis (strep throat) organism, the difference in the two conditions being the production of a toxin to which the patient is susceptible in the case of scarlet fever. Severe infections are occasionally complicated by rheumatic fever, kidney disease, ear infection, pneumonia, meningitis, or encephalitis. Mild scarlet fever requires only bed rest and symptomatic treatment. Antibiotics, immune serum, and antitoxin may be required for severe cases.

scarlet runner: see BEAN.

scarp: see ESCARPMENT.

Scarpanto, Greece: see KÁRPATHOS.

Scarron, Paul (pōl skärôN'), 1610–60, French writer. His picaresque novel *Le Romant comique* (1651) vividly portrays the lives of a company of strolling players. He also wrote short stories, collected as *Les Nouvelles tragi-comiques* (1655), satires, and burlesque poems and plays. Scarron married (1652) Françoise d'Aubigné, known later as Mme de Maintenon. He was long bedridden with paralysis. See N. F. Phelps, *The Queen's Invalid* (1951).

Scarsdale, village (1970 pop. 19,229), Westchester co., SE N.Y., a residential suburb of New York City; settled c.1701, inc. 1915. Scarsdale is often considered typical of upper-class suburban communities. See Harry Hansen, *Scarsdale: From Colonial Manor to Modern Community* (1954).

Scawfell: see SCAFELL, mts., England.

scene design and stage lighting. The Greek open-air theater was first a circular, flat orchestra located in the hollow between two hillsides. In 465 B.C. a small wooden hut called a *skene* (hence, scene), in which the actors changed costumes, was erected behind the playing area. When stone structures were erected the seating area was cut to little more than a semicircle and the *skene* became a two-story building with three doorways in front and an entrance by either side. It thus served additionally as the scenic background of the play. The floor in front of the *skene* was elevated, with steps leading down to the orchestra; this narrow playing level was called the *proskenion* (hence, proscenium). Sophocles is thought to have first employed scene painting; such devices as *periaktoi* (revolving prisms with painted scenery), *eccyclema* (wagons for tableaus), and *mechane* (flying machines) were also used. Greek plays were performed in daylight, and the dramas were frequently designed to take advantage of the position of the sun. Also, theater sites were well-placed to gain the best effects of the natural light. In the Roman theater the apron of the stage was created by extending the playing area over the orchestra. The entire structure was often enclosed and built on level ground. The background, the three-door *skene*, was always a street, with off left indicating the town or adjacent points and off right indicating an exit to the country or distant points. A curtain was sometimes used to open the play; it was dropped into a trough as the play began. The Romans were probably the first to use torches and lamps at evening performances. The religious plays of the Middle Ages were performed at first within, and later in front of, the church, with the separate scenes organized around an open space in a simultaneous setting. This form of staging continued when the plays were moved into the street, but the individual platform scenes became more elaborately built up, and there was widespread use of machinery and traps. Information about medieval lighting is uncertain although it seems likely that torches, both moving and stationary, were utilized. The renaissance of scene design began in Italy. Sebastiano Serlio, in his *Architettura*, Book II (1545), interpreted what he thought were classic ideas on perspective and the *periaktoi* and published the first designs on the definitive types of sets to be used—for tragedy, palaces; for comedy, street scenes; for satyr plays, the countryside. The first permanent theater in Italy, the Teatro Olimpico at Vicenza (1584), was an attempt to recreate the Roman *scaenae frons* with five permanent perspectives. In his *teatro all'antico*, built (c.1589) at Sabbioneta, Vincenzo Scamozzi employed a "solid drop" background and enlarged the central stage arch to make one perspective. In the early 17th cent., Giovanni Battista Aleotti was the first to use flats (painted canvas stretched over wooden frames) with decorative props painted on them, and in 1618 he introduced the proscenium arch. The realistic stage setting was not known; designs were always symmetrical and in perspective. Later in the century the mechanical innovations of Giacomo Torelli facilitated the simultaneous rapid shift of all the flats. Nicolo Sabbattini and Leone de' Sommi wrote on the use of lighting in the 16th cent.; in addition, they developed footlights and techniques for colored lights and for the dimming of lights. From the Renaissance period until the triumph of gas lighting in the mid-19th cent., great use was made of lamps, candles, and torches. Although they caused much work, odor, and smoke, ingenious effects were produced. A revolution in scene design came in the late 17th cent. with the initiation of multiple or oblique perspective by Ferdinando Galli da BIBIENA. He used either two points of perspective or only one placed indiscriminately. The great scene designers of the period were the great architects and artists. Their designs, baroque and heavy with movement and detail, became increasingly fussy; the set, in conflict with the actor, became the main attraction. In France the first permanent theater had been the Hôtel de Bourgogne (1548), and in England, the Theatre (1576; later known as the Globe). The early English designer Inigo JONES was influenced by the Italians, although in his time scenery was reserved for court spectacles; Shakespeare's plays were given on a bare stage. The Restoration period saw the development of a "popular" theater, although it was still primarily for the upper classes. With the Enlightenment in the mid-18th cent. there was a revival of classicism, and the unity of place was strictly observed by designers. They experimented with strong darks and lights and tried for the first time to infuse their designs with atmosphere. Toward the end of the century the curtain was first lowered to change the scene, and the scrim (gauze drop that becomes transparent when lit from behind) came into use. Lighting became a problem only when the theaters were entirely enclosed. At that time lights (torches, candles, oil lamps) and reflectors surrounded the stage, and footlights came into use. Later chandeliers and candelabras became fashionable. Much use was made of colored lights made with mirrors reflecting colored water; shadows were painted on the flats. The auditorium itself was not darkened for the performance. The 19th cent. brought extensive changes. Gaslight was first introduced (1817) in England. Although it was responsible for many theater fires, gaslight had, by 1849, the advantages of being centrally controlled. Sir Henry IRVING, at the end of the century, was first to darken the auditorium completely. He also was first to experiment with the color and intensity of gaslight. The first spotlight was the limelight (1816); it was followed by the arc light (1846). In 1840, Mme VESTRIS successfully employed the box set (three solid walls joined together) complete with a ceiling. The concept of the invisible "fourth wall" forced the acting area behind the proscenium arch, thus eliminating the need for a wide apron and glaring footlights. Decorative props were still painted on the flats, but as the naturalistic movement (in the theaters of André ANTOINE, Otto BRAHM, J. T. Grein, and Constantin STANISLAVSKY) gained impetus, realistic and even actual objects were used. This trend toward realism and historical accuracy culminated in the photographic realism of David BELASCO, who even incorporated smells into several productions. The invention (1839) of the photograph was a further influence toward realistic settings. With the invention (1879) of the incandescent bulb, light became the primary scene painter. Through the efforts of Adolphe APPIA, modern stage lighting was born. Scene designers in the early 20th cent., opposed to naturalism, strove to show the essence of a play through simplification, suggestion, and, often, stylization; selective realism was the keynote. The scene designer was directly responsible to the director who was by now the unifying head of a production. Edward Gordon CRAIG with his stage of many levels, Jacques COPEAU with suggestive forms and screens, Vsevolod MEYERHOLD with his constructivistic sets of skeletal structures and geometric forms, Max REINHARDT with his expressionistic sets of abstract distortion, and Erwin PISCATOR with his theatricality and educational approach—all brought imagination and creativeness to realistic design, which had become cluttered and uninteresting. The technical innovations of Steele MACKAYE also came into general use. In 1902 the cyclorama or sky-dome, a semicircular backing of whitewashed plaster or cement used to reflect light and thus create an illusion of depth, was invented. After 1912 lights were placed in the auditorium to allow for more natural angles of illumination for both the actor and the set. The projector lamp, a spotlight that could be dimmed, was invented in 1914; after 1919 colored "gels," or gelatine, were placed over the lights. By 1922 stage lighting had become a scientific study. After World War I the United States became a leader in the field of scene design with the work of such men as Robert Edmond JONES, Lee Simonson, Joseph Urban, Norman Bel GEDDES, and Mordecai Gorelik; more recently, Donald Oenslager, Jo MIELZINER, Oliver SMITH, Cecil BEATON, and Peter Larkin have gained prominence. Since World War II, with the rise of the "theater of the absurd," trends in scene design have become eclectic, ranging from realism to surrealism. Some set designers, such as Ralph Keltai, try to capture the major mood of a play through abstract expression. Others attempt to re-create the sense of a period in which the play is set or set old plays in modern surroundings. If there is a unifying element it is the acceptance of Gordon Craig's insistence upon unification of the various theatrical arts. Therefore, whether the set and lighting are naturalistic or surrealistic, the attempt is made to integrate these elements with the acting, movement, and text of the play. See DRAMA, WESTERN; ORIENTAL DRAMA; THEATER; DIRECTING; ACTING. See Lee Simonson, *The Art of Scenic Design* (1950); James Laver, *Drama, Its Costume and Decor* (1951); A. S. Gillette, *An Introduction to Scenic Design* (1967); Allardyce Nicoll, *The Development of the Theatre* (5th ed. 1967); Barnard Hewitt, ed., *The Renaissance Stage* (1958); Harold Burris-Meyer et al., *Scenery for the Theatre* (rev. ed. 1971); Jean Rosenthal and Lael Wertenbaker, *The Magic of Light* (1972); Sybil Rosenfeld, *A Short History of Scene Design in Great Britain* (1973).

Sceva (sē'və), chief priest of Ephesus. Acts 19.14.

Scève, Maurice (mōrēs' sĕv), c.1510–c.1564, French poet. While studying at Avignon he discovered the tomb of Laura, to whom Petrarch directed many of his sonnets. Scève was the leader of the so-called Lyons school of poets, which was the first to bring the influence of the Italian literary renaissance into France. He is best known for his own poems, including *Delie, object de plus haulte vertu* [Delie, object of highest virtue] (1544), a long and sometimes obscure celebration of courtly love in 10-line stanzas. It was supposedly inspired by the young poetess Pernette du Guiller, who died in 1545, and contains many passages of fresh beauty and charm. His other works include celebrations of rustic life.

Schacht, Hjalmar Horace Greeley (yäl'mär shäkht), 1877–1970, German financier. He held executive positions in several major German banks before becoming (1923) commissioner of currency. Inflation had reached its height and the paper mark had become worthless. Schacht substituted the rentenmark, in theory secured by a mortgage on all land and industry. By various stringent deflationary measures the rentenmark was stabilized and the budget balanced. In 1924, Germany obtained a foreign loan under the Dawes Plan, and in 1925 the rentenmark was replaced by the reichsmark, based on a gold standard. Appointed president of the Reichsbank in Dec., 1923, Schacht resigned in 1930 because of his opposition to continued German reparations payments. A nationalist and representative of conservative capitalism, Schacht after 1931 supported the National Socialist (Nazi) party. He was appointed president of the Reichsbank (1933) and minister of economy (1934) and was given wide powers. Through bartering agreements with Balkan and Middle Eastern countries, he enabled Germany to secure raw materials for its rearmament and developed German trade. Conflict with Hermann GOERING, who had been made virtual economic dictator, led to Schacht's resignation from the ministry in 1937. Schacht continued as president of the Reichsbank until 1939, when he was dismissed for opposing the huge armament program, which he felt would cause inflation. He remained minister without portfolio until 1943. In 1944 he was placed in a concentration camp for his alleged part in the plot against Hitler's life. Acquitted (1946) by the war-crimes tribunal at Nuremberg, he twice won (1948, 1950) appeal from a German "denazification" court's sentence. In 1953 he established a private bank in Düsseldorf. See his autobiography, *Confessions of the Old Wizard* (1953, tr. 1956); A. E. Simpson, *Hjalmar Schacht in Perspective* (1969).

Schadow, Johann Gottfried (yō'hän gôt'frēt shä'dôf), 1764–1850, German sculptor of the neoclassical school. He studied in Rome. In 1788 he returned to Berlin, where he became court sculptor. Among his best-known works are the tomb of Count Alexander von der Mark in Berlin; the *Quadriga* on the Brandenburg Gate, Berlin; statues of Leopold von Dessau and Frederick the Great; and monuments to Blücher at Rostock and to Luther at Wittenberg. His son **Rudolph Schadow,** 1786–1822, also a sculptor, was a follower of Canova and Thorvaldsen. Another son, **Friedrich Wilhelm von Schadow-Godenhaus,** 1789–1862, German religious and historical painter, was one of the NAZARENES. He was (1826–59) director of the Düsseldorf Academy.

Schafarik, Pavel Josef: see ŠAFAŘIK, PAVEL JOSEF.

Schaff, Philip (shäf), 1819–93, biblical scholar and church historian in America, b. Switzerland. He went to the United States in 1844 to teach in the Theological Seminary of the Reformed Church, Mercersburg, Pa. His importance as an interpreter of German theology and (in his writings) as a conveyor of the religious thought of America to Germany gained wide recognition. From 1870 until his death he was professor at Union Theological Seminary, New York City, where he held the chair of sacred literature (1874) and of church history (1887). Schaff was president of the American branch of the English Bible Revision Committee. He edited the first edition (1882–84) of the *Schaff-Herzog Encyclopedia of Religious Knowledge* and wrote *A History of the Christian Church* (7 vol., 1858–90). His literary work embraced the writing or editing of some 80 publications.

Schaffhausen (shäfhou'zən), canton (1970 pop. 72,854), 115 sq mi (298 sq km), N Switzerland. Entirely on the right (northern) bank of the Rhine River, the canton consists of three noncontiguous agricultural and forested areas, which are largely surrounded by West German territory. Its inhabitants, who are German-speaking and largely Protestant, raise cereals, fruit, and vegetables and produce a fine wine. Nearly all of the canton's industry is concentrated in the town of Neuhausen and in the adjoining city of **Schaffhausen** (1970 pop. 37,035), the original settlement and capital of the canton. Schaffhausen is an old city, picturesquely situated on the Rhine. Iron and steel, metal goods, chemicals, leather, woolen textiles, and watches are produced. The Rheinfall, a cataract of the Rhine, plunges c.70 ft (20 m) just southwest of the city and is harnessed for hydroelectric power. Originally a Benedictine abbey (founded c.1050), Schaffhausen became (c.1208) a free city of the Holy Roman Empire, ruled first by its abbots, then by the Hapsburgs, and, after c.1415, by its local trade guilds. It joined the Swiss Confederation in 1501. With an 11th-century minster, a hilltop castle (the Munot), and several old houses, Schaffhausen retains much of its medieval character.

Schäffle, Albert (äl'bĕrt shĕf'lə), 1831–1903, German economist and sociologist. He taught economics at the universities of Tübingen and Vienna. His views were based partly on the idealism of Hegel and Schelling, partly on Comtian and Darwinian ideas. His work was characterized by the use of organic analogies and the concept of value as indicating the elements of intelligence and spirituality. Schäffle was interested in socialism, which he believed would evolve out of capitalism. He made important contributions to the theory of taxation. His most popular book was *Die Quintessenz der Socialismus* (1875, tr. 1901); his most elaborate was *Bau und Leben des sozialen Körpers* [structure and life of the social body] (4 vol., 1875–78, rev. ed. 1896).

Schaffner, Jacob (yä'kôp schäf'nər), 1875–1944, Swiss novelist. His autobiographical novels, including *Konrad Pilater* (1910), *Johannes* (1922), and *Eine deutsche Wanderschaft* (1933), vividly describe European scenery and experience. Their primary note, however, is one of rebellion against Swiss bourgeois conventions, a reflection of Schaffner's personal disaffection. In an attempt to find a solution to what he considered Switzerland's problems, he actively supported National Socialism and thus destroyed his personal and literary reputations.

Schafřík, Pavel Josef: see ŠAFAŘIK, PAVEL JOSEF.

Schapiro, Meyer (shəpĭr'ō), 1904–, American art historian, b. Lithuania. Schapiro came to the United States in 1907 and later attended Columbia Univ. where he has taught since 1928, becoming a full professor in 1952. Schapiro first gained prominence in the 1930s as a critic and champion of modern art. Since then he has made pioneering investigations into the nature and aesthetics of early Christian, medieval, and modern art, exploring such areas as the history of style and the relationship of art to folk art traditions, to sociology, and to psychoanalysis. Schapiro's major essays include "The Nature of Abstract Art" (1937), "On the Aesthetic Attitude in Romanesque Art" (1948), and "Leonardo and Freud" (1956). Among his books are studies on Van Gogh (1950), Cézanne (1952), and *Israel, Ancient Mosaics* (1960, with M. Avi-Yonah).

Scharnhorst, Gerhard Johann David von (gĕr'härt yō'hän dä'vēt fən shärn'hôrst), 1755–1813, Prussian general. A Hanoverian army officer, military writer, and director of the war college, he entered Prussian service in 1801. He fought in the disastrous war of 1806–7 against Napoleon I, and he headed the commission for reorganizing the army and controlled the war ministry from 1807. He resigned his posts early in 1812, when Prussia was forced into an alliance with Napoleon I against Russia. When the French defeat in Russia enabled Prussia to break its alliance with France and join the anti-French coalition (1813), Scharnhorst served as chief of staff to the commander of the army, Field Marshal Blücher. As a military reformer Scharnhorst transformed the Prussian army from a mercenary one into a people's army. Every Prussian was considered liable to military service. However, since the introduction of general conscription was impossible under Napoleonic rule, Scharnhorst invented the *Krümpersystem* under which a larger number of men than that allowed to Prussia could be trained in the use of arms; citizens were called to service for a short training period to be then replaced by another group. Although the system was highly acclaimed, in reality only a small number exceeding the 42,000 man limit were trained in the use of arms. The abolition of physical punishment and the admission of nonnobles into the officers' corps further helped to popularize the cause of the army. General conscription, however, was introduced formally only in 1814 after Scharnhorst's death. His military reforms were aided by August Neithhardt von GNEISENAU and Karl vom und zum STEIN.

Scharoun, Hans (häns shär'oun), 1893–1972, German architect. Scharoun approached his building designs in terms of the special needs of each project. He conceived the Geschwister Scholl High School in Westphalia (1962) as a complex of apartmentlike classrooms, built to create for its students a continuity between home and school environments. Scharoun was also noted for theater and concert-hall designs.

Scharwenka, Franz Xaver (fränts ksävâr' shärvĕng'kä), 1850–1924, Polish-German pianist and composer. He founded conservatories in Berlin (1881) and New York City (1891). Beginning in 1874 he toured in Europe and the United States. Of his compositions, only a few piano pieces are still popular. His brother **Ludwig Philipp Scharwenka,** 1847–1917, was associated with him in teaching and composed several orchestral works, chamber music, and choral music.

Schaudinn, Fritz (frĭts shou'dĭn), 1871–1906, German zoologist. He confirmed the work of Sir Ronald Ross and G. B. Grassi on malaria, investigated amoebic dysentery, and in his research on protozoa discovered (1905) with Erich Hoffmann the *Treponema pallidum* (or *Spirochaeta pallida*) of syphilis.

Schaulen: see SIAULIAI, USSR.

Schaumburg-Lippe (shoum'bŏŏrkh-lĭp'ə), former state, N West Germany, E of the Weser River. In 1946 it was placed in Lower Saxony. Bückeburg was the capital. It was situated in a fertile agricultural region. The county of Schauenburg (as Schaumburg was originally called) included a considerable part of Westphalia in the 12th cent., and its lord, Count Adolf, was invested with HOLSTEIN in 1111. The direct line died out in 1459, and the branch line that succeeded retained only Schaumburg and the seigniory of Pinneberg in Holstein. When it in turn became extinct (1640), Pinneberg passed to the Danish crown and part of Schaumburg was divided between Brunswick-Lüneburg (later the electorate of Hanover) and Hesse-Kassel. The remainder of Schaumburg passed to Count Philip of LIPPE, thus forming the county of Schaumburg-Lippe. The county became a principality in 1807. The last prince abdicated in 1918, and Schaumburg-Lippe joined the Weimar Republic.

Schechter, Solomon (shĕkh'tər), 1847–1915, Hebrew scholar. Born in Rumania and educated in Berlin and Vienna, he went to England in 1882. In 1890 he was made lecturer in Talmud at Cambridge; he became professor of Hebrew at University College, London, in 1899. Schechter's identification of the hitherto missing Hebrew version of Ecclesiasticus made him known as a scholar of international reputation. In 1902 he became president of the Jewish Theological Seminary in New York City, which he developed into a center of learning and a spiritual home of the Conservative movement. He was also the founder of the United Synagogue of America, the association of Conservative congregations. Among his books are *Studies in Judaism* (1896; 2d series 1908; 3d series 1924) and *Some Aspects of Rabbinic Theology* (1909). See biography by N. de M. Bentwick (1938); Moshe Davis, *The Emergence of Conservative Judaism* (1963).

Scheel, Walter (väl'tər shāl), 1919–, German political leader, president of West Germany (1974–). After serving in World War II, Scheel became interested in politics and joined the Free Democrats, a liberal party. In 1953 he entered the Bundestag, or lower house of parliament, and he continued to be reelected. Late in 1967 he became chairman of the Free Democrats. When the Social Democrat-Free Democrat coalition government was formed in 1969 by Chancellor Willy Brandt, Scheel became foreign minister and vice chancellor. As foreign minister he helped improve relations with East Germany and the Soviet Union. He was elected to the largely ceremonial presidential office in May, 1974, for a five-year team.

Scheele, Karl Wilhelm (kärl vĭl'hĕlm shā'lə), 1742–86, Swedish chemist, b. Stralsund. He is known as the discoverer of many chemical substances. He was a pharmacist in Stockholm, in Uppsala (1770–75), and then in Köping. He prepared and studied oxygen c.1773, but his account in *Chemical Observations and Experiments on Air and Fire* (1777, tr. 1780) appeared after the publication of Joseph Priestley's studies. He discovered nitrogen independently of Daniel Rutherford and showed it to be a constituent of air. His treatise on manganese (1774) was influential in leading to the discovery of that element as well as to the discovery of barium and chlorine. He also isolated glycerin and many acids, including tartaric, lactic, uric, prussic, citric, and gallic. See his *Collected Papers* (tr. 1931, repr. 1971).

scheelite (shā'līt, shē'–), heavy white or yellow mineral, calcium tungstate, $CaWO_4$, crystallizing in the tetragonal system. It is found in granite pegmatites, in contact-metamorphic deposits (especially limestones intruded by granites), and in quartz veins. It is an important ore of tungsten and is mined in many parts of the world. Scheelite fluoresces bright bluish-white in ultraviolet radiation, a distinguishing feature utilized in prospecting and mining.

Schefferville, town (1971 pop. 3,271), E central Que., Canada, on the Labrador border. It is an iron-mining center. The town was founded in the 1950s as Knob Lake.

Scheffler, Johannes: see ANGELUS SILESIUS.

Scheherazade: see THOUSAND AND ONE NIGHTS.

Scheidemann, Philipp (fē'lĭp shī'dəmän), 1865–1939, German Social Democratic leader. A member of the Reichstag from 1898, he became (1918) secretary of state without portfolio in the cabinet formed by MAXIMILIAN, PRINCE OF BADEN just before Germany's defeat in World War I. After Emperor William II had fled (Nov., 1918), Scheidemann proclaimed the German republic and served as its first chancellor. He resigned (1919) in protest over the Treaty of Versailles. With the rise of Nazism, he left Germany in 1933 and died in exile in Denmark. See his memoirs, *The Making of New Germany* (tr. 1929, repr. 1970).

Scheiner, Christoph (krĭs'tôf shīn'ər), 1579?–1650, German astronomer and mathematician, a Jesuit priest. He taught at Ingolstadt, Rome, and elsewhere and became rector of a Jesuit college at Neisse, Germany, in 1622. His observation of sunspots in 1611 was recorded in two works (1612) and resulted in a controversy with Galileo, who claimed that he was the first to discover sunspots. Scheiner made over 2,000 observations of the sun and embodied the results of his studies in *Rosa ursina* (1630). His pioneer research on the physiology of vision appeared in his *Oculus* (1619).

Schelde, river: see SCHELDT.

Scheldt (skĕlt), Dutch and Flemish *Schelde*, Fr. *Escaut*, river, c.270 mi (435 km) long, rising in N France and flowing generally NE across W Belgium and into the North Sea through the Western Scheldt (De Honte) estuary, SW Netherlands. It receives its chief tributary, the Lys, at Ghent (Gent). Navigable for most of its length, the river is connected with a dense network of canals in N France and Belgium. The upper Scheldt valley is one of the most important steel-producing regions of N France. From the Peace of Westphalia in 1648 until 1863 (except during the Napoleonic period) the Netherlands possessed the right to close the Scheldt estuary and thus had a stranglehold over the port of Antwerp.

Scheler, Max (mäks shā'lər), 1874–1928, German philosopher. He taught at the universities of Jena (1901–7) and Munich (1907–10), where he was influenced by Franz Brentano and the followers of Edmund HUSSERL. From 1910 he concentrated on writing, but he returned to university teaching at Cologne and Frankfurt after World War I. Scheler was concerned with the permanent values in human personality and human action; this concern brought him to important work in PHENOMENOLOGY, which spread beyond Germany, chiefly through his influence. In his early thought, for which he is best known, Scheler taught that love is the great principle of human association, and he regarded God as the source of all love. His most basic work is *Formalism in Ethics and Non-Formal Ethics of Values* (2 vol., 1913–16; tr. 1973); other important works include *On the Eternal in Man* (1921; tr. 1960) and *Man's Place in Nature* (1928; tr. 1961). See his *Selected Philosophical Essays,* tr. with an introd. by D. R. Lachterman (1973); biography by J. R. Staude (1967); studies by E. W. Ranly (1966), A. R. Luther (1972), and Alfons Deeken (1974).

Schelling, Friedrich Wilhelm Joseph von (frē'drĭkh vĭl'hĕlm yō'zĕf fən shĕ'lĭng), 1775–1854, German philosopher. After theological study at Tübingen and two years of tutoring at Leipzig, he became in 1798 a professor at Jena, where he helped found the romantic movement in philosophy. There he was closely associated with August and Friedrich von Schlegel and J. G. FICHTE, from whom he drew apart when he left Jena for a professorship at Würzburg in 1803. He later taught at the Univ. of Berlin. Schelling's early essays were a development of the Fichtean science of knowledge, though in *Ideen zu einer Philosophie der Natur* (1797) he had already differed somewhat in holding that nature cannot be subordinated to mental life. The difference between the forces of nature and mind must be only a matter of degree or level, and the problem of knowledge is absorbed in the ultimate unity of mind and matter in the Absolute. In his later period, Schelling attempted to explain the origin of different degrees or levels within this unity. Schelling maintained that history is a series of stages progressing toward harmony from a previous fall and that differences are aspects of this development. Schelling argued that God also partakes of this process of development; that deity, to have personality, must hold within itself the limiting factors that define personality. Among his other notable works is *Die Weltalter* (1854; tr. by Frederick Bolman, *The Ages of the World,* 1942). See studies by P. C. Hayner (1967), E. D. Hirsch (1971), and F. G. Nauen (1972).

Schenck, Robert Cumming (skĕngk), 1809–90, American politician and diplomat, Union general in the Civil War, b. Franklin, Ohio. He studied law and practiced in Dayton. Schenck was a Whig in Congress (1843–51) and minister to Brazil (1851–53). During the Civil War he fought at both battles of Bull Run and in W Virginia. He resigned as major general of volunteers in 1863 and reentered Congress, where he was one of the leading radical Republicans (1863–70). While minister to Great Britain (1871–76), Schenck, for a consideration, allowed the Emma Silver Mining Company to use his name in promoting its stock, which soon proved fraudulent. A congressional investigation ultimately forced his resignation. Later he practiced law in Washington.

Schencker, Heinrich (hīn'rĭkh shĕngk'ər), 1867–1935, Austro-Polish music theorist, b. Wisniowczyki, Poland. Educated at the Vienna Conservatory, he devoted his life to teaching and research. Schencker developed the concept of structural levels and coherence in tonal music. He conceived of all tonal pieces as generated from a basic cell, the triad (major or minor chord). The interest and singularity of a composition was ascribed to the imagination and consistency with which the composer elaborated the triad into a complete piece. Schencker's theories have been successfully applied to nontonal music.

Schenck vs. United States, case decided in 1919 by the U.S. Supreme Court. During World War I, Charles T. Schenck produced a pamphlet maintaining that the military draft was illegal. He was convicted under the Espionage Act of attempting to cause insubordination in the military and to obstruct recruiting. In his opinion for the Supreme Court, Justice Oliver Wendell Holmes rejected the argument that the pamphlet was protected by the First Amendment to the U.S. Constitution and enunciated the clear and present danger test. Under this doctrine, speech may be suppressed if it creates a clear and present danger that it will produce a "substantive evil" that can be legally prevented. The doctrine was used in the late 1930s and the 40s, primarily to sustain convictions of persons considered politically subversive.

Schenectady (skənĕk'tədē), city (1970 pop. 77,958), seat of Schenectady co., E N.Y., on the Mohawk River and the Barge Canal; founded 1661 by Arent Van Curler, inc. 1798. It is the home of the huge General Electric Company, established there in 1886. Several other companies also manufacture electrical equipment, and the production of chemicals is also important. The early inhabitants were victims of a bloody French and Indian massacre in 1690, but the community grew again, prospering as a stopping place for traders and settlers traveling W on the Mohawk River. The city's growth was particularly spurred by the opening (1820s) of the Erie Canal and the building (1830s) of the railroads. The manufacture of locomotives, begun in 1848, was long an important industry. Schenectady is the seat of Union College and Univ. The city has a symphony orchestra, a light-opera company, and a civic playhouse. A science museum is maintained by the state in the former home and laboratory of Charles P. Steinmetz. Notable among Schenectady's historic buildings are the homes in the old stockade area, which date from the early 1700s, and the pre-Revolutionary St. George's Episcopal Church.

Scherchen, Hermann (hĕr'män shĕr'khĕn), 1891–1966, German conductor. Scherchen was largely self-taught. He played viola in the Berlin Philharmonic (1907–10) and made his debut there as a conductor in 1911. Scherchen conducted and taught throughout Europe and gained a reputation as an outstanding exponent of modern music. He was associated with Arnold Schoenberg in the first performances of *Pierrot Lunaire* (1912). Scherchen made his American debut in 1964 with the Philadelphia Orchestra. He wrote *Handbook of Conducting* (6th ed. 1949) and *The Nature of Music* (1950).

Scherer, Wilhelm (vĭl'hĕlm shĕr'ər), 1841–86, German philologist, b. Austria. Scherer held professorships at the universities of Vienna, Strasbourg, and Berlin. His *History of German Literature* (1883, tr. 1886) and his history of the German language (1868) are his best-known works. Through his writings ran a strong sense of nationalism. Scherer was one of the first to maintain that the phonetic development of language follows set rules that do not admit of exception.

scherzo (skĕr'tsō) [Ital.,=joke], in music, term denoting various types of composition, primarily one that is lively and presents surprises in the rhythmic or melodic material. In 1628 a group of light pieces for voice were published by Monteverdi as *scherzi musicali.* In the symphonies of Haydn the scherzo was a development of the minuet, and in Beethoven's works it replaced the minuet as the third movement of a work in sonata form. Mendelssohn gives the scherzo an airy grace, while the four piano scherzos of Chopin are works of boldness and strength.

Scheveningen (skhā'vənĭng"ən), urban district, South Holland prov., W Netherlands, on the North Sea and near The Hague, of which it is a part. It is a popular bathing resort and fishing center.

Schiaparelli, Elsa: see under FASHION.

Schiaparelli, Giovanni Virginio (jōvän'nē vērjē'nyō skyäpärĕl'lē), 1835–1910, Italian astronomer. He was director (1862–1900) of the Brera Observatory, Milan. He is especially noted for having detected (1877) on the surface of the planet Mars the markings that he called canals. He showed that meteor swarms travel through space in cometary orbits and suggested that Mercury and Venus rotate on their axes. He discovered the asteroid Hesperia (1861) and several double stars.

Schick, Béla (bā'lə shĭk), 1877–1967, American pediatrician, b. Hungary, M.D. Karl Franz Univ., Graz, 1900. After having taught at the Univ. of Vienna (1902–23), he came to the United States. From 1923 he was a pediatrician at Mt. Sinai Hospital, New York. In 1929 he became a naturalized American citizen. He devised (1910–11) the SCHICK TEST to determine susceptibility to diphtheria. He also made important studies of allergy and wrote, with others, *Scarlet Fever* (1912) and *Child Care Today* (1933). See biographies by Antonio Gronowicz (1954) and Iris Noble (1963).

Schick test, diagnostic test designed to evaluate susceptibility to DIPHTHERIA. A small amount of diphtheria TOXIN is injected into the skin; the injection will produce an area of redness and swelling in individuals with low levels of ANTIBODY (i.e., little IMMUNITY) against the toxin. If the individual is immune to diphtheria, the antibody in the system will neutralize the toxin and no skin reaction will occur.

Schiedam (skhē″däm′), city (1971 pop. 83,313), South Holland prov., W Netherlands, on the Nieuwe Maas (New Meuse) River, near Rotterdam. It is famous for its gin, which is widely exported. There are also shipyards and factories that manufacture chemicals, glass, and machinery. The city's noteworthy structures include a 14th-century church, the 16th-century town hall, and the ruins of a 13th-century castle.

Schiehallion (shĭhăl′yən), mountain, 3,547 ft (1,081 m) high, Perthshire, central Scotland, near Loch Rannoch. In 1774, Nevil Maskelyne experimented there to determine the density of the earth.

Schiele, Egon (ā′gôn shē′lə), 1890–1918, Austrian expressionist painter and draftsman. Influenced by the French impressionists, then by Gustav Klimt, Schiele developed a taut, linear style, emphasizing anatomical structure. With Kokoschka, he was in the forefront of the Austrian expressionist movement until his sudden death at 28 of influenza. A portrait by him is in the Minneapolis Institute of Arts. See study by Rudolf Leopold (1973).

Schiff, Jacob Henry, 1847–1920, American banker and philanthropist, b. Frankfurt, Germany. He emigrated to the United States in 1865 and became a partner in a brokerage house in New York City. At the age of 38 he was head of the banking house of Kuhn, Loeb and Company. Schiff became associated with E. H. Harriman in notable contests with the house of Morgan for control of Western railroads. His numerous philanthropies included the endowment of the Jewish Theological Seminary, the Montefiore Home, both in New York, and a museum at Harvard. See biography by Cyrus Adler (1928).

Schildkraut, Rudolph (shĭlt′krout), 1862–1930, Austrian actor. He was a member of Max Reinhardt's Deutsches Theater, Berlin. In 1911 he came to the United States and until 1922 was a star of the Yiddish Art Theater in New York City. His son, **Joseph Schildkraut,** 1896–1964, first achieved fame in a Theatre Guild production of *Liliom* (1931). He appeared in many motion pictures after 1921. His performance as the father in *The Diary of Anne Frank* (1955) was outstanding. See his autobiography, *My Father and I* (1959).

Schiller, Ferdinand Canning Scott (shĭl′ər), 1864–1937, British philosopher. Schiller studied at Oxford and was professor of philosophy there (1897–1926) and at the Univ. of Southern California (1929–37). His philosophical position is closely related to the pragmatism of William JAMES. Schiller called his system humanism, holding that "man is the measure of all things." Among his works are *Riddles of the Sphinx* (1891), *Humanism* (1912), *Problems of Belief* (1924), and *Logic for Use* (1929); *Our Human Truths* (1939), a collection of his last writings, was published posthumously. See studies by Reuben Abel (1955) and Kenneth Winetrout (1967).

Schiller, Friedrich von, 1759–1805, German dramatist, poet, and historian, one of the greatest of German literary figures, b. Marbach, Württemberg. The son of an army captain, Schiller attended the duke of Württemberg's military academy, the Karlsschule, and was forced by the domineering duke to study medicine. After graduating in 1780 he became an army surgeon, attached to a military life he abhorred. Turning to writing, he created a striking attack on political tyranny in *Die Räuber* (1781), one of the great plays of the STURM UND DRANG period. Its performance (1782) in Mannheim won him public acclaim as well as the wrath of the duke, who forbade him to write. Schiller fled from his post in Stuttgart and, after great deprivation, worked as a dramatist (1783–84) for the Mannheim theater. His second youthful success, *Don Carlos,* appeared in 1785 and was performed in revised form in 1787. While living in the great cultural center of Weimar, Schiller wrote a history (1788) of the revolt of the Netherlands against Spain. This work, together with the mediation of Goethe, gained him (1789) a professorship of history at the Univ. of Jena. In 1790, Schiller married the gifted writer Charlotte von Lengefeld. Plagued by poor health, he rejected subsequent offers of positions and from 1793 to the end of his life lived in Weimar, enjoying the friendship of Goethe, with whom he edited the literary periodicals *Horen* (1795–97) and *Musenalmanach* (1796–1800). He wrote several significant treatises on aesthetics and created his finest plays and poetry in this period; he also translated Shakespeare's *Macbeth* (1801), Racine's *Phèdre* (1805), and other works. Schiller's great dramas are alike in being tragedies or epics with historical and political backgrounds; they exemplify his idealism, high ethical principles, and insistence on freedom and nobility of spirit. In *Die Räuber* and other early works his heroes are pure idealists who perish because of the villainy of evil opponents. As Schiller moved from the phase of Sturm und Drang, he saw dangers in rampant individualism and even in fanatic idealism; thus his later *Don Carlos* has been interpreted both as a cry for political liberty and as a plea against excessive idealistic zealousness. Under the influence of the philosophy of Kant, Schiller developed his aesthetic theories, which stressed the sublime and emphasized the creative powers of man. These views and his concept of historical inevitability are manifest in the outstanding dramatic trilogy *Wallenstein* (1798–99, tr. of last two parts by S. T. Coleridge, 1800), in which the general, ennobled by Schiller as a great creative statesman, bows before inexorable fate. *Wallenstein* reflects his labors on his large historical study (1791–93) of the Thirty Years War. *Mary Stuart* (1800, tr. by Stephen Spender, 1959), his most popular play, and *Die Jungfrau von Orleans* (1801) deal with guilt and redemption. *Wilhelm Tell* (1804), which places history and hero in favorable conjunction, shows Schiller's technical mastery at its best. Schiller's interest in classical antiquity, inspired by Winckelmann, is reflected in the play *Die Braut von Messina* (1803), essays, and poems. An unfinished novel, *Die Geisterseher*, and the "Ode to Joy" (1785), used by Beethoven for the finale of his Ninth Symphony, indicate the range and quality of his literary activity. Also noteworthy are his ballades and philosophical lyrics—graceful, compelling, often pathetic in mood. The poets of German romanticism were strongly influenced by Schiller, and he ranks as one of the founders of modern German literature, second only to Goethe. See biography by Thomas Carlyle (1899, repr. 1974); studies by E. L. Stahl (1954), Thomas Mann (tr. 1959), R. M. Longyear (1966), and Ilse Graham (1974).

Schiller Park, village (1970 pop. 12,712), Cook co., NE Ill., a residential suburb of Chicago; inc. 1914. It has some light industry. O'Hare International Airport is to the west, and the county forest preserve is to the east.

Schilling, Johannes (yōhän′əs shĭl′ĭng), 1828–1910, German sculptor. He is represented by many monuments in Germany, including the colossal *Germania* (1883), a national monument in the Niederwald, which is considered his masterpiece.

Schimper, Karl Friedric (shĭm′pər), 1803–67, German botanist. He did important work in plant morphology and originated the theory, called phyllotaxis, that there is a fixed order to the arrangement of leaves on plant stems. His grandson, **Andreas Franz Wilhelm Schimper,** 1856–1901, wrote on plant ecology, gathering materials for his works in North America, Asia, and the West Indies as well as in Europe. In 1898 he prepared the first map of plant distribution. Among his work is *Plant-Geography upon a Physiological Basis* (1898, tr. 1903).

Schinkel, Karl Friedrich (kärl frē′drĭkh shĭng′kəl), 1781–1841, German architect and painter. He studied in Berlin and spent two years in Italy copying classical works. Upon his return he turned to landscape painting, embodying architectural features in his compositions. A member of the Berlin Academy, he became a professor in 1820. He also worked in lithography, etching, and illustration, but attained real distinction as an architect of the classical tradition. Among the public buildings, castles, and country residences he designed are the Royal Guard House (1816–18), Royal Theater (1818–21), and Old Museum (1822–30) in Berlin and the New Gate, Church of St. Nicholas, and Casino in Potsdam.

Schipa, Tito (tē′tō skē′pä), 1889–1965, Italian operatic tenor. He made his debut in 1911 in Vercelli. After many appearances in Europe, he came to the United States in 1919, joining the Chicago Opera Company. He sang with the Metropolitan Opera Company from 1932 to 1935. Possessing a beautiful voice and impeccable artistry, he sang the leading lyric tenor roles in all the principal operas of the French and German repertory and appeared in the major opera houses of Spain, Italy, and South America.

schipperke (skĭp′ərkē), a breed of small NONSPORTING DOG developed in Belgium several hundred years ago. It stands about 13 in. (33 cm) high at the shoulder and weighs from 14 to 18 lb (6.4–8.2 kg). Its weather-resistant double coat consists of a short, dense underlayer and a relatively short, abundant, slightly harsh topcoat that is longer around the neck and on the chest and hindquarters. It is solid black in color and is born tailless or with a very short tail. The probable ancestor of the schipperke was the Leauvenaar, a black sheepdog native to the Flemish provinces. The schipperke was popular as a watchdog and pet, as it is today, and was frequently kept as a companion on Belgian barges. It was from this latter role that the breed acquired its name, *schipperke,* being the Flemish word for "little captain." See DOG.

Schism, Great, or **Schism of the West,** division in the Roman Catholic Church from 1378 to 1417. There was no question of faith or practice involved; the schism was a matter of persons and politics. Shortly after GREGORY XI had returned the PAPACY from Avignon to Rome, he died (March 27, 1378). The Romans feared that the papal court might be returned to Avignon, and there was rioting, with the mob demanding a Roman, or at least an Italian, pope. On April 8 the 16 cardinals present elected URBAN VI. The new pope was soon acting very offensively to all in the church. The cardinals met at Agnani and on Aug. 2 declared Urban's election null. At Fondi on Sept. 20 they elected ROBERT OF GENEVA pope as Clement VII. The next year Clement fled to Avignon, where he reigned surrounded by the former Roman court. There were thus two lines of popes. The popes at Rome were Urban VI (1378–89), BONIFACE IX (1389–1404), Innocent VII (1404–6), and GREGORY XII (1406–15). Those of the rival line at Avignon were Clement VII (1378–94) and Benedict XIII (1394–1417; see LUNA, PEDRO DE). Schism within schism ensued. France withdrew from obedience to Benedict XIII and recognized no pope (1398–1403, 1408–9). Theologians of the Univ. of Paris, led by Pierre d'AILLY and John GERSON, were anxious to end the schism, and they developed the theory that popes are subject to general councils. The Council of Pisa (1409; see PISA, COUNCIL OF) was the result. This meeting declared that Gregory XII of the Roman (or Urbanist) line and Benedict XIII of the Avignon (or Clementine) line were not popes and elected another, Alexander V. He died soon after, but his energetic successor, Baldassarre COSSA (John XXIII, 1410–15), detached most of Europe from his rivals. In 1414 John reluctantly convened the Council of Constance (see CONSTANCE, COUNCIL OF). Gregory XII resigned. John XXIII and Benedict XIII, who refused to resign, were declared deposed by the council. MARTIN V was elected, and the schism was at an end. The main effects of the schism were to delay needed reforms in the church and to give rise to the conciliar theory, which was revived at the Council of Basel (see BASEL, COUNCIL OF). It is generally agreed by Roman Catholic scholars that the line of popes from Urban to Gregory was the canonical one. See Walter Ullmann, *Origins of the Great Schism* (1948, repr. 1972); Brian Tierney, *Foundations of Conciliar Theory* (1955, repr. 1969); E. F. Jacob, *Essays in the Conciliar Epoch* (3d ed. 1963); Marzieh Gail, *The Three Popes* (1969); J. H. Smith, *The Great Schism* (1970).

Schism of East and West, division between the ORTHODOX EASTERN CHURCH and the ROMAN CATHOLIC CHURCH. See CHRISTIANITY; FERRARA-FLORENCE, COUNCIL OF; LEO IX, SAINT; LYONS, SECOND COUNCIL OF; PAPACY; PHOTIUS.

Schism of the West: see SCHISM, GREAT.

schist (shĭst), metamorphic ROCK having a foliated, or plated, structure called schistosity in which the component flaky minerals are visible to the naked eye. Schists are distinguished from the other foliated rocks, slates and gneisses, by the size of their mineral crystals; these are larger than those of slates, being visible to the naked eye, but smaller than those of gneisses, which are coarsely foliated rocks as opposed to finely foliated, or schistose, rocks. As contrasted with the folia of slates, the folia of schists are rough-surfaced and irregular. Schists split readily along their planes of schistosity, like slates along cleavage lines. Like other foliated rocks, schists owe their origin to the metamorphism of other, preexisting rocks. The commonest of the schists is mica schist, the essential minerals of which are QUARTZ and MICA (biotite or muscovite). Other schists are hornblende schist, talc schist, chlorite schist, and graphite schists. Schists are abundant in the Precambrian (Archeozoic and Proterozoic) rocks.

schistosomiasis (shĭs'təsōmī'əsĭs), parasitic disease caused by blood flukes, trematode worms of the genus *Schistosoma.* Three species are human parasites: *S. mansoni, S. japonicum,* and *S. haematobium.* The disease is prevalent in the Orient, some Pacific islands, Africa, the West Indies, South America, Spain, and Cyprus. The larvae of the parasite are harbored by snails, which serve as intermediate host, and infect humans who bathe in or otherwise come in contact with infested waters. The larvae enter through the skin, migrate via the blood vessels, and mature in the bowel, bladder, and portal veins where they deposit eggs, many of which pass out in the feces. Other eggs are carried into the liver and may also lodge in the bladder, genitals, lungs, spinal cord, or other tissues. The disease is characterized by a skin eruption at the site of entry, fever, diarrhea, and other symptoms, depending on the tissues affected; cirrhosis of the liver is common. Treatment is usually with compounds containing antimony. Such drugs, however, are toxic and produce severe side effects; other drugs can sometimes bring relief in mild cases. Even with treatment, outlook in severe cases is poor. Although symptoms vary according to the species of infecting fluke, all forms can result in general weakening and eventual death. Control of the disease is difficult but attempts have been made to eradicate the snail hosts. Proper sanitation and disposal of human wastes is also important.

schizophrenia (skĭt"səfrē'nēə), severe mental disorder, or PSYCHOSIS, characterized by unrealistic behavior dominated by private fantasy. In 1896, the German psychiatrist Emil Kraepelin grouped what were previously considered unrelated mental diseases under the term *dementia praecox,* using four subdivisions (simple, hebephrenic, catatonic, and paranoid), which are still widely used. It was not, however, until 1911 that the Swiss psychiatrist Eugen Bleuler, preceded by the work of Freud, C. G. Jung, and others, wrote the highly influential *Dementia Praecox oder die Gruppe der Schizophrenien,* which corrected the Kraepelin theory that the disease is incurable. In it he introduced the term *schizophrenia* to replace *dementia praecox,* as the former emphasized the dissociative, or splitting, phenomena in the mind and avoided the implication regarding age of onset and outlook for deterioration. Schizophrenia commonly, though not always, occurs in late adolescence or early adulthood in the withdrawn, seclusive type of person. Among its basic symptoms are faulty thought processes, bizarre actions, tendency to live in an inner world, and incapacity to maintain normal interpersonal relationships. In simple schizophrenia, the individual becomes increasingly passive and indifferent to the environment; in hebephrenic schizophrenia, the individual's behavior is bizarre, exaggerated, and inappropriate; in catatonic schizophrenia, the individual is overly excited or stuporous; and in paranoid schizophrenia, the individual is dominated by the delusional systems of PARANOIA and sometimes suffers HALLUCINATIONS. Because of the crippling nature of the psychosis, a high percentage of sufferers must be hospitalized. It is roughly estimated that half the psychotics in mental hospitals are schizophrenic. It is possible that a hereditary predisposition to the disorder makes some individuals likely to develop schizophrenia when exposed to particular environmental stresses. In recent years tranquilizer drugs have largely replaced insulin coma treatment and electroconvulsive shock. Psychotherapy has been increasingly used, and the outlook for the remission of schizophrenia is much more hopeful than it was formerly.

Schizophyta (skĭzŏf'ədə), division of the plant kingdom that consists of all the BACTERIA and blue-green ALGAE. The organisms, which generally lack a well-defined nucleus, divide by fission without a true mitotic division. The plant body, or thallus, varies from unicellular to many-celled and, with the exception of some of the blue-green algae, is microscopic in size. In a strict sense reproduction is asexual, since no zygote (product of fertilization) is formed. Exchange of genetic material between cells also occurs (see RECOMBINATION).

Class Schizomycetes (bacteria). Bacteria usually consist of a single cell, although some form filaments or cell masses. They have no CHLOROPLASTS; although some carry out photosynthesis, the chlorophyll they contain is different from the kinds found in higher plants. Many bacteria contain other pigments and are green, purple, red, or brown in color. Many are motile, swimming about by means of one, two, or several whiplike flagella; others are completely nonmotile. The cytoplasm of bacteria, less complex in its organization than that of higher plants, lacks such cell organelles as plastids and mitochondria (see CELL). Bacterial cytoplasm contains various kinds of granules, including polysaccharide food reserves and ribonucleic acid, or RNA. Bacteria were long thought to be without a nucleus, but the more refined cytological techniques of recent decades have made it possible to establish the presence of a body, containing deoxyribonucleic acid, or DNA, that divides before cell division. Many bacteria produce thick-walled resting cells, or spores, which are highly resistant to extremes of heat, cold, and drought. When suitable conditions for growth occur, the spore swells and germinates, the old wall is split, and an active vegetative cell with its own new wall emerges. Spore formation is a mechanism of survival under adverse conditions; when environmental conditions become favorable, the cell is able to divide and establish a new population. Cell division occurs as often as once every 20 min under optimal conditions. Bacteria are extremely diverse in the ways they carry out chemical transformations to gain energy, and their taxonomic classification depends more on their biochemical capabilities than on their morphology. Further information on bacteria can be found in the article of that title.

Class Cyanophyceae (blue-green algae). The blue-green algae are relatively simple plants that resemble bacteria. However, unlike bacteria, their cells contain photosynthetic pigments, especially chlorophyll *a,* that are found in higher plants. Some blue-green algae are unicellular, but most are filamentous or colonial. They usually possess a definite cell wall and are additionally surrounded by a gelatinous sheath. Reproduction occurs through cell division, fragmentation of filaments or colonies, and spore formation. Blue-green algae, ubiquitous in their distribution, are found in nearly every habitat, including hot springs. They are especially abundant in soils, where some of them are able to fix nitrogen (see NITROGEN CYCLE). Because the organisms are able to produce so many individuals in a short time, they often produce noxious odors and tastes in stagnant and overly fertile bodies of water; some produce compounds toxic to fish (see EUTROPHICATION).

Schlegel, August Wilhelm von (ou'go͝ost vĭl'hĕlm fən shlā'gəl), 1767–1845, German scholar and poet. With his brother, Friedrich von Schlegel, he founded the *Athenaeum,* which he edited (1798–1800). He served as secretary to Bernadotte (later Charles XIV of Sweden) and became professor (1818–45) of art and literary history at Bonn. Schlegel was one of the first critics to see the importance of social evolution in the history of art, and he was a champion of the *Nibelungenlied.* He is most noted for his extraordinary translations of Shakespeare (1797–1810), later completed by Ludwig Tieck and others, which established Shakespeare's greatness in Germany.

Schlegel, Friedrich von (frē'drĭkh), 1772–1829, German philosopher, critic, and writer, most prominent of the founders of German ROMANTICISM. Educated in law at Göttingen and Leipzig, he turned to literature, writing *Die Griechen und Römer* (1797). It was followed by experimental literary works, notably *Lucinde* (1799) and *Alarcos* (1802). With his brother, August Wilhelm von Schlegel, he founded and edited the *Athenaeum,* the principal organ of the romantic school. His lectures at Jena (1800) and in Paris (1802) had a widespread influence. His study in Paris of Sanskrit and of Indian civilization later contributed to his outstanding work, *Über die Sprache und Weisheit der Indier* [on the language and wisdom of India] (1808). From 1808 to 1819 he engaged in political and diplomatic activities and also wrote works in history and literature. At Vienna, after 1818, he edited *Concordia,* issued his collected works (1822–25), and lectured on philosophy. Schlegel, during his early period, held that comprehension of life depends on the richness and variety of experience. He called it "romantic irony" that truth changes from experience to experience and that wisdom depends on the recognition of the fickleness of truth. Later, after he and his wife, Dorothea von Schlegel, had joined (1808) the Roman Catholic Church, he became more conservative. Among his translated lectures are *The Philosophy of History* (tr. 1835), *The Philosophy of Life and the Philosophy of Language* (tr. 1847), and *The History of Literature* (tr. 1859).

Schleicher, August (ou'go͝ost shlī'khər), 1821–68, German philologist. A professor at the universities of Prague and Jena, Schleicher wrote studies of the Lithuanian language (1856–57), the German language (1860), and the language of the Polabian Slavs (1871). His most important work on comparative philology, published in German (1861–62), was translated as *A Compendium of the Comparative Grammar of the Indo-European, Sanskrit, Greek, and Latin Languages* (2 vol., 1874–77).

Schleicher, Kurt von, 1882–1934, German general. A leading *Reichswehr* (army) figure after World War I, Schleicher wielded great power in the years before Adolf HITLER came to power (1933). He was war minister in the cabinet of Franz von Papen, whom he succeeded as chancellor of Germany in Dec., 1932. Trying to prevent Hitler from seizing power, Schleicher demanded authority from President HINDENBURG to dissolve the Reichstag and to assume emergency powers. Hindenburg refused and, after Schleicher's resignation (Jan. 28, 1933), appointed Hitler chancellor. Schleicher retired from public life but was shot with his wife in Hitler's 1934 "blood purge."

Schleiden, Matthias Jakob (mätē'äs yä'kôp shlī'dən), 1804–81, German botanist. He was professor at the universities of Jena (1839–63) and Dorpat (1863–64). With Theodor Schwann, he is credited with establishing the foundations of the cell theory. Schleiden's paper *Beitrage zur Phytogenesis* (1838), although mistaken in some aspects, recognized the significance of the nucleus in the propagation of cells.

Schleiermacher, Friedrich Daniel Ernst (frē'drĭkh dä'nyĕl ĕrnst shlī'ərmäkh"ər), 1768–1834, German Protestant theologian, b. Breslau. He broke away from the Moravian Church and studied at Halle. Ordained in 1794, he accepted a post as a Reformed preacher in Berlin. There he came into contact with the German Romantic movement and became a friend of Friedrich Schlegel. In 1799 he published his eloquent *Religion: Speeches to Its Cultured Despisers* (tr. 1893). The work showed his closeness to the Romantics as well as the influence of his Pietist background. He defined religion as an absolute dependence on a monotheistic God, reached through intuition and independent of dogma. From 1804 to 1807, Schleiermacher taught at Halle. When war led to the closing of that university he returned to Berlin, where he was made professor in 1810. Through his stirring sermons he played a prominent part in the Prussian war against Napoleon. From 1819 he was occupied with his major work, *The Christian Faith,* published in 1821–22 (tr. of 2d ed. 1928). Here he developed systematically his earlier ideas, viewing Christianity as the highest manifestation of religion. The work exhibits the influence of Kant, Spinoza, and Leibniz and shows Schleiermacher's aversion to both German rationalism and theological orthodoxy. His thought exerted an enormous and lasting influence on Protestant theology. He is also known for his attempt to secure the liberation of the church from the state and for his translations of Plato. See studies by R. B. Brandt (1941, repr. 1968), R. R. Niebuhr (1964), Gerhard Spiegler (1967), Stephen Sykes (1971), and Martin Redeker (1973).

Schlemmer, Oskar (ôs'kär shlĕm'ər), 1888–1943, German painter and stage designer. Known for his mechanical, geometricized forms, Schlemmer taught painting, sculpture, and stage design at the BAUHAUS (1920–29). He created the *Triadic Ballet* to Hindemith's music. In sculpture he experimented with plastic relief in a style related to CONSTRUCTIVISM.

Schlesinger, Arthur Meier (shlĕs'ĭnjər), 1888–1965, American historian, b. Xenia, Ohio. After teaching at Ohio State Univ. and the State Univ. of Iowa, he was a professor of history (1924–54) at Harvard and in 1928 became an editor of the *New England Quarterly.* His well-known works in the field of colonial history include *The Colonial Merchants and the American Revolution, 1763–1776* (1918) and *Prelude to Independence: The Newspaper War on Britain, 1764–1776* (1958). He is also known for his interest in the interpretation of social history, as in *The Rise of the City, 1878–1898* (1933) and *Political and Social Growth of the American People, 1865–1940* (1941). His other books include *New Viewpoints in American History* (1922), essays on American historiography. With Dixon Ryan Fox he edited the "History of American Life" series (13 vol., 1927–48), which remains a valuable examination of U.S. social and cultural life.

Schlesinger, Arthur Meier, Jr., 1917–, American historian and public official, b. Columbus, Ohio, son of Arthur Meier Schlesinger (1888–1965). He achieved early success as a historian with the publication of his Harvard honors thesis, *Orestes A. Brownson: a Pilgrim's Progress* (1939). In World

War II he served with the Office of War Information (1942–43) and the Office of Strategic Services (1943–45), and he was professor of history at Harvard from 1946 to 1961. His *Age of Jackson* (1945), a brilliant reinterpretation of the social, political, and economic aspects of the era, stimulated numerous American historians to reexamination of the Jacksonian period and won for Schlesinger the Pulitzer Prize. *The Age of Roosevelt* (Vols. I–III, 1957–60) is a sweeping narrative and analysis of the New Deal period in U.S. history, written from a strongly sympathetic viewpoint. Active in liberal politics, Schlesinger was a cofounder of the Americans for Democratic Action (1947). He served as an assistant to Democratic presidential candidate John F. Kennedy, and in 1961 President Kennedy appointed him special assistant for Latin American affairs. His study of Kennedy's White House Years, *A Thousand Days* (1965), won the Pulitzer Prize for biography. Since 1966 he has taught at the City University of New York. His other works include *The Bitter Heritage* (1968), *The Politics of Hope* (1963), and *The Imperial Presidency* (1973).

Schlesinger, James Rodney, 1929–, U.S. Secretary of Defense (1973–), b. New York City. After graduating from Harvard (A.B., 1950; A.M., 1952; Ph.D., 1956), he taught economics (1955–63) at the Univ. of Virginia and was then (1963–69) a specialist in strategic studies for the RAND Corp. In 1969 he was appointed assistant director of the Bureau of the Budget by President Richard Nixon, under whom he later assumed the offices of chairman of the Atomic Energy Commission (1971), director of the Central Intelligence Agency (Feb., 1973), and Secretary of Defense (July, 1973).

Schleswig (shlĕs'vĭkh), Dan. *Slesvig,* former duchy, N Germany and S Denmark, occupying the southern part of Jutland. The Eider River separates it from Holstein. German Schleswig forms part of SCHLESWIG-HOLSTEIN. Danish Schleswig, known as North Schleswig (Dan. *Nordslesvig* or *Sønderjylland*) includes the cities of Åbenrå, Haderslev, Sønderborg, and Tønder. Unlike HOLSTEIN, which was part of the Holy Roman Empire even after its union with the Danish crown, the duchy of Schleswig, created in 1115, was a hereditary fief held from the kings of Denmark. King Waldemar III (who had been duke of Schleswig as Waldemar V) conferred Schleswig on his uncle, Gerhard, and granted a charter forbidding the union of Schleswig and Denmark under a single overlord. In 1386 the count of Holstein received Schleswig as a hereditary fief. His descendant, Christian I of Denmark, inherited (1460) both Schleswig and Holstein, but he was obliged to recognize the inseparability of the two territories and to affirm that they were bound to the Danish crown by a personal union only. In the 16th cent. Schleswig and Holstein (which had also become a duchy) underwent complex subdivisions, although theoretically the principle of the inseparability of the two duchies was not violated. The three main divisions were: a ducal portion, including parts of both duchies, which was conferred on Adolphus, duke of Holstein-Gottorp, younger brother of Christian III of Denmark, and on his descendants, the dukes of Holstein-Gottorp; a royal portion, including parts of both duchies, ruled directly by the Danish kings; and a common portion, ruled jointly by the Danish kings and the dukes of Holstein-Gottorp. The arrangement was complicated by a number of factors, including the creation, within the royal portion of Schleswig, of the duchy of Sonderburg (see SØNDERBORG) in favor of John, youngest brother of Frederick II of Denmark. The Sonderburg branch later split into the Augustenburg line and the cadet Glücksburg line. By the Treaty of Roskilde (1658) the Danish crown renounced its suzerainty over ducal Schleswig; the resulting quarrels between Denmark and the duke of Holstein-Gottorp were a major factor in the NORTHERN WAR (1700–1721), which ended with the dispossession of Duke Charles Frederick of Holstein-Gottorp and the union of the ducal portion of Schleswig with the Danish crown. Charles Frederick's son became (1762) emperor of Russia as Peter III; his heir, Grand Duke Paul (later Emperor Paul I), renounced (1773) the ducal portion of Holstein, yielding it to the Danish crown, in exchange for OLDENBURG. Thus all Schleswig and Holstein were once more united under the Danish kings. The events related in the article SCHLESWIG-HOLSTEIN led to the annexation (1866) of both duchies by Prussia. After World War I, North Schleswig passed to Denmark after a plebiscite (1920) held in accordance with the Treaty of Versailles.

Schleswig, city (1970 pop. 32,518), Schleswig-Holstein, N West Germany, on the Schlei, an inlet of the Baltic Sea. The city's economy is based on the production of food products and leather and on fishing. One of the oldest cities in N Germany, Schleswig was known by c.800. It was a Roman Catholic episcopal see from 947 until the Reformation (16th cent.). The city was the residence of the dukes of Schleswig and (1514–1713) of the dukes of Holstein-Gottorp. It was the capital of Schleswig-Holstein from 1866 to 1917, when it was replaced as capital by Kiel. The fortified Gottorf, or Gottorp, castle (16th–18th cent.) in Schleswig now houses museums of art and early history. The Gothic Cathedral of St. Peter (12th–15th cent.) contains a fine carved reredos by Hans Brüggemann (16th cent.) and the tomb of Frederick I of Denmark.

Schleswig-Holstein (shlĕs'vĭkh-hôl'shtīn), state (1970 pop. 2,494,000), c.6,050 sq mi (15,670 sq km), N West Germany. Kiel (the capital and chief port), Lübeck, Flensburg, and Neumünster are the major cities. Flanked on the west by the North Sea and on the east by the Baltic Sea, Schleswig-Holstein occupies the southern part of the Jutland peninsula and extends from the Elbe River northward to the Danish border. It includes some of the North Frisian Islands of the North Sea and the island of Fehmarn in the Baltic. The Kiel Canal links the North Sea and the Baltic. Schleswig-Holstein is drained by the Eider River, which forms the historic border between the former duchies of Schleswig (in the north) and Holstein (in the south). A low-lying region, with excellent natural harbors along the Baltic coast, the state has fertile agricultural land except in the center, where heaths and moors predominate. Farming (grain, potatoes, and vegetables) and cattle raising are widely pursued; shipping and fishing are important along the coasts. Manufactures of Schleswig-Holstein include ships, processed food, textiles, clothing, and machinery. There are oil fields in the Dithmarschen region in the southwest. The islands of Sylt and Föhr and the southern Baltic coast are popular tourist resorts, while Eutin, Lübeck, and Schleswig are historic centers. There is a university in Kiel. With respect to the history of Schleswig-Holstein, Lord Palmerston once proclaimed it to be so complicated that only three men had ever fully understood it—one being Prince Albert, who was dead; the second, a professor, who had become insane; the third, Palmerston himself, who had forgotten it. (For the history of the area to the late 18th cent. see the articles HOLSTEIN and SCHLESWIG.) From 1773 the kings of Denmark held both duchies—Schleswig as full sovereigns, Holstein as princes of the Holy Roman Empire; both duchies were in personal union with, but not part of, Denmark. The Congress of Vienna (1814–15) did not change the status of the two duchies, except that the German Confederation had succeeded the Holy Roman Empire in its suzerainty over Holstein. A constitution for Holstein was guaranteed by the German Confederation. Because of the growing national consciousness of the predominantly German population in the two duchies, any change in their status that would tie them more closely to Denmark was a potentially explosive issue. Thus, when King Christian VIII announced (1846) that succession by females was to apply not only to the Danish throne but to Schleswig as well, there was violent opposition among German nationalists, who feared the complete incorporation of Schleswig into Denmark. Nevertheless, on the pressure of the Danish nationalists, Frederick VII, who succeeded Christian, declared the complete union of Schleswig with Denmark in 1848. Revolution broke out in both duchies, a provisional government was established in Kiel, and the German Confederation came to the aid of the rebels and occupied the duchies. British intervention led to an armistice in the German-Danish fighting, but in 1849 the war was resumed. After inconclusive fighting, peace was made in 1850 between Prussia (which had been commissioned by the Confederation to conduct the war) and Denmark; both sides reserved their rights. The fact that Frederick VII was childless made the Schleswig-Holstein succession a burning European issue. The question was taken up by the powers in a conference at London, and in 1852 Prussia, Austria, and other major powers (but not the German Confederation as a body) signed the Treaty of London. The treaty guaranteed the territorial integrity of Denmark, and settled the succession to Denmark and both duchies on the Glücksburg branch of the Danish royal house, which derived its claim through the female line. Duke Christian Augustus of Augustenburg, who represented a collateral line, renounced his claim to the duchies and accepted a money indemnity; Denmark in turn guaranteed the inseparability of the duchies and their continued status in personal union with Denmark. However, once more the pressure of the Danish nationalists forced Frederick VII to proclaim (1855) the Danish constitution as valid for both duchies. The protest of the German Confederation led to the withdrawal (1858) of that measure, but in Nov., 1863, just before Frederick's death, a common constitution for Denmark and Schleswig was drawn up. His successor, Christian IX, signed the constitution, which the German diet declared in violation of the protocol. In Jan., 1864, Prussia and Austria declared war on Denmark, which was easily defeated. The disposal of the duchies was still at issue. Austria favored the claims of the duke of Augustenburg, who denounced the surrender of the Augustenburg claim by his father in 1852; but Bismarck, who was guiding Prussian policy, had already resolved to annex the duchies and had encouraged the Danish War with that end in view. By the Treaty of Gastein (1865) with Austria, Bismarck deliberately imposed a solution which was bound to create friction with Austria. Schleswig was placed under Prussian administration and Holstein under Austrian administration, while the duchy of Lauenburg (also lost by Denmark in 1864) went to Prussia in return for a money payment to Austria. The dual administration led, as Bismarck had anticipated, to such tension that Austria could easily be maneuvered into a war with Prussia. The AUSTRO-PRUSSIAN WAR of 1866 ended with a swift (7 weeks) Prussian victory; Schleswig, Holstein, and Lauenburg were annexed to Prussia and became the province of Schleswig-Holstein. After World War I the Danish majority of N Schleswig determined by plebiscite (1920) the return of that part of the province to Denmark. The former free city of Lübeck and the Lübeck district of Oldenburg were incorporated into Schleswig-Holstein in 1937. After World War II, Schleswig-Holstein was constituted (1946) as a state.

Schley, Winfield Scott (slī), 1839–1911, American naval officer, b. Frederick co., Md. After serving with Union naval forces in the Civil War, he held various naval posts. In 1884 he commanded the third, and successful, relief expedition to rescue the arctic explorer Adolphus W. GREELY. Schley was promoted to the rank of commodore in 1898 and in the Spanish-American War commanded the "flying squadron," ordered to seek out the Spanish under Admiral Pascual Cervera. There was some ill feeling between Schley and William Thomas SAMPSON, who had been advanced to chief command. When the battle of Santiago was fought and the Spanish fleet destroyed, Sampson was absent and Schley had command, thus giving rise to a bitter controversy over the credit for the victory. Schley was made a rear admiral and resigned from the navy in 1901. A court of inquiry, requested by Schley to investigate charges leveled against him of negligence and misconduct in the battle of Santiago, was generally adverse toward him but recommended that no action be taken. He wrote *The Rescue of Greely* (with J. R. Soley, 1895) and also memoirs, *Forty-five Years under the Flag* (1904).

Schlick, Moritz (mō'rĭts shlĭk), 1882–1936, German philosopher, b. Berlin, grad. Univ. of Berlin (1904). He taught at Rostock and Kiel before he became (1922) professor of the philosophy of inductive sciences at the Univ. of Vienna; there he was the leader of the Vienna Circle, a group of logical positivists (see LOGICAL POSITIVISM). Influenced by Ludwig WITTGENSTEIN and Rudolf CARNAP, Schlick emphasized experience as the means of establishing the truth of claims to knowledge. His works include *General Theory of Knowledge* (2d ed. 1925) and *Problems of Ethics* (tr. 1939).

Schlieffen, Alfred, Graf von (äl'frāt gräf fən shlē'fən), 1833–1913, German field marshal and strategist. In the tradition of the Prussian officer corps, Schlieffen was a professional soldier who considered political questions beyond his responsibility. As chief of the German general staff from 1891 through 1905 he developed the famous **Schlieffen plan.** According to the plan, Germany could solve the problem of war on two fronts by first defeating France in a lightning campaign and then throwing its full weight against Russia. The plan called for a flanking movement by an overwhelmingly strong right (i.e., northern) wing, which was to advance through Belgium and Holland and, in an enveloping move, compel the bulk of the French forces either to fight with their backs to the frontier fortresses or to flee into Switzerland. Much weaker contingents were to be used to hold back the French in the south and the Russians in the east. The plan (which disregarded Belgian and Dutch neutrality) demanded boldness for its execution. When World War I broke out in

1914 the Schlieffen plan was employed in a modified form, but a number of factors—including Russian military strength, German lack of mobility, effective French delaying action, and the reluctance of Schlieffen's successor, H. J. L. von MOLTKE, to weaken his eastern front—led to its failure. In World War II, unhampered by a Russian threat in the east and possessing highly mobile forces, the German command successfully employed (May–June, 1940) a variation of the Schlieffen plan to defeat France. See Gerhard Ritter, *The Schlieffen Plan* (1956; tr. 1958, repr. 1968).

Schliemann, Heinrich (hīn'rĭkh shlē'män), 1822–90, German archaeologist, discoverer of the ruins of TROY. He accumulated a fortune in business, chiefly in Russia. A student of Homer from childhood, he retired from business in 1863 to dedicate himself to his dream of finding Troy and other Homeric sites. After several years of study and travel, in 1871 he undertook at his own expense excavations at Hissarlik which resulted in his discovery of four superimposed towns. Schliemann related every object he found to the verses of Homer, which he knew by heart. He made other notable excavations at Mycenae (1876–78), Ithaca (1878), Orchomenus, Boeotia (1881–82), and Tiryns (1884–85), and was assisted by Wilhelm Dörpfeld from 1882. Schliemann wrote several books describing his discoveries and left a vast collection of personal papers, records, and an autobiography published in 1892. He acquired American citizenship because he was living in California when it became a state (1850). See biographies by Emil Ludwig (1931), Robert Payne (1958), and A. C. Brackman (1974).

Schlüsselburg: see PETROKREPOST, USSR.

Schlüter, Andreas (ändrā'äs shlü'tər), 1664–1714, German sculptor. After studying in France and Italy, he became architect and sculptor to the Hohenzollern at Berlin, where the principal examples of his decorative work were in the royal castle. He was the most important German exponent of the baroque style. Most noted among his sculptures were the statue of King Frederick I in front of the castle at Königsberg and the *Great Elector*, an equestrian group on the Long Bridge, a pulpit in the Marienkirche, and the tombs of King Frederick I and his consort in the cathedral, all in Berlin. At the end of his life, having lost the favor of his patron, King Frederick I, Schlüter entered the service of Peter the Great of Russia.

Schmalkalden (shmäl'käl"dən), town (1970 pop. 14,103), Suhl district, SW East Germany. It has been a metalworking center since the Middle Ages, and its manufactures include tools, kitchen utensils, and machinery. Schmalkalden was chartered in the 13th cent., passed in 1583 to Hesse-Kassel, and, with it, passed to Prussia in 1866. In the town hall (built 1419) the SCHMALKALDIC LEAGUE was founded in 1531. The inn where Luther drew up (1537) the Schmalkaldic Articles, outlining the Protestant viewpoint, has been restored. Other noteworthy structures in Schmalkalden include the Church of St. George (15th cent.) and parts of the town's medieval fortifications.

Schmalkaldic League (shmälkäl'dĭk), alliance formed in 1531 at Schmalkalden by Protestant princes and delegates of free cities. It was created in response to the threat (1530) by Holy Roman Emperor CHARLES V to stamp out Lutheranism. Led by PHILIP OF HESSE and JOHN FREDERICK I of Saxony, the league grew rapidly. Under its protection the Reformation spread through most of Germany. In an effort to crush the independence of the states of the empire and to restore unity to the Roman Catholic Church, Charles initiated the so-called Schmalkaldic War against the league. At the battle of Mühlberg (1547), the league was defeated.

Schmidt, Helmut (hĕl'mo͞ot shmĭt), 1918–, German political leader, chancellor of West Germany (1974–). After serving in World War II, he entered politics and joined the Social Democratic party. He was elected to the Bundestag in 1953 and continued to serve in it except for the period between 1962 and 1965. Schmidt was Social Democrat leader in the Bundestag (1967–69) and in 1968 became party vice chairman. When the Social Democrat–Free Democrat coalition government was formed in 1969, he became minister of defense under Chancellor Willy Brandt. In 1972 he was made finance minister. Schmidt was elevated to the post of chancellor in May, 1974, in the wake of Brandt's resignation as a result of a spy scandal.

Schmidt, Wilhelm, 1868–1954, German linguist and anthropologist, a Roman Catholic priest. Educated at the universities of Berlin and Vienna, he entered the Society of the Divine Word in 1890. Residing mainly in Austria, he taught at the Univ. of Vienna, founded and directed an anthropological institute at Mödling, and, after 1938, was a professor at the Univ. of Freiburg. Schmidt devoted particular attention to the languages of S Asia, Australia, and Oceania. His books available in English translation are *The Origin and Growth of Religion* (1931), *High Gods in North America* (1933), *The Culture Historical Method of Ethnology* (1939), and *Primitive Revelation* (1939).

Schmidt camera telescope: see TELESCOPE.

Schmidt-Rottluff, Karl (shmĭt-rŏt'lo͝of), 1884–, German painter and woodcut artist. Schmidt-Rottluff cofounded and named the BRÜCKE in 1905. After moving to Berlin in 1911, he developed an art of compelling color and mystical intensity influenced by FAUVISM, CUBISM, and primitive art. His vigorous graphic technique is best realized in his woodcuts (e.g., *The Way to Emmaus*, 1918; Philadelphia Mus. of Art).

Schmitz, Ettore: see SVEVO, ITALO.

Schmoller, Gustav (go͝os'täf shmôl'ər), 1838–1917, German economist. He was the leader of the younger school of German historical economists, who tried to interrelate economics with the other social sciences. Selections from his chief writings have been translated by Walter Abraham and Herbert Weingast as *The Economics of Gustav Schmoller* (1942).

Schnabel, Artur (är'to͝or shnä'bəl), 1882–1951, Austrian-American pianist, b. Lipnik, at that time in Austria. He studied (1891–97) with Leschetizky and began his concert tours in Europe in 1896. Schnabel made his first tour of the United States in the 1921–22 season and appeared there regularly beginning in 1936. Schnabel is best known for his dynamic interpretations and editions of Beethoven's piano works. He made records of all 32 Beethoven sonatas and many other works. Among his own compositions are his First Symphony (1946) and his Rhapsody for Orchestra (1948). His writings include *Reflections on Music* (tr. 1934) and *Music and the Line of Most Resistance* (1942). In 1945 he became a U.S. citizen. See his *My Life and Music* (ed. by Edward Crankshaw, 1961); biography by César Saerchinger (1957, repr. 1973).

Schnabel, Johann Gottfried (yō'hän gôt'frēt), b. 1692, d. after 1742, German author, whose pseudonym was Gisander. He fought in the War of the Spanish Succession. Schnabel's popular novel *Die Insel Felsenburg* [Felsenburg island] (4 vol., 1741–43) was modeled on *Robinson Crusoe* but was primarily concerned with utopian ideals.

schnauzer (shnou'zər), a sturdy, wirehaired dog developed in S Germany. There are three separate breeds of schnauzer distinguished by their size. The standard schnauzer is a medium-sized dog whose existence in Germany dates back to the 15th cent. It stands from 17 to 20 in. (43.1–50.8 cm) high at the shoulder and weighs from 27 to 37 lb (12.3–16.8 kg). The giant schnauzer, developed at the end of the 19th cent. by crossing the standard schnauzer with various native sheepherding and farm dogs and later the Great Dane, stands from 21½ to 25½ in. (54.6–64.8 cm) high at the shoulder and weighs from 65 to 78 lb (29.5–35.4 kg). The miniature schnauzer, also developed around the end of the 19th cent., resulted from the crossing of standard schnauzer to affenpinscher. It stands from 12 to 14 in. (30.5–35.6 cm) high at the shoulder and weighs from 13 to 15 lb (5.9–6.8 kg). The coat of all three breeds may be pepper and salt, silver, or black in color. The standard schnauzer, listed by the American Kennel Club in the WORKING-DOG group, was originally used as a ratter, farm dog, and guardian. Later, both it and the giant schnauzer, also a working dog and bred especially for driving cattle, were used in police work. The miniature schnauzer is classified in the TERRIER group and has been raised primarily as a pet. See DOG.

Schneidemühl: see PIŁA, Poland.

Schneider, Alexander, 1908–, Russian-American musician, b. Vilna, Lithuania. Schneider studied at the Frankfurt Conservatory in West Germany and was concertmaster (1925–33) of the Frankfurt orchestra. He emigrated to the United States in 1933. From that year until 1944 and from 1957 until its dissolution in 1969, Schneider was second violinist in the Budapest Quartet. As both violinist and conductor Schneider has been closely associated with Pablo Casals and Rudolf Serkin.

Schneiderman, Rose (shnī'dərmən), 1884–1972, American labor leader, b. Poland. She emigrated to the United States in 1890. After working as a lining stitcher in a cap factory, she was instrumental in getting women admitted to the United Cloth, Hat, and Cap Makers Union and participated (1905) in a successful strike. Probably the best-known American woman trade unionist, she was elected (1907) vice president of the New York branch of the Women's Trade Union League and was its sole organizer (1917–19) in the Eastern states. She was subsequently elected president (1918) of the New York branch and became (1928) national president of the National Women's Trade Union League. She served also as secretary (1937–44) of the New York state department of labor. In addition she was an official of the National Recovery Administration in the 1930s and a member of President Franklin Delano Roosevelt's brain trust.

Schnitzer, Eduard: see EMIN PASHA.

Schnitzler, Arthur (är'to͝or shnĭts'lər), 1862–1931, Austrian dramatist and novelist. The son of a prominent Jewish Viennese physician, he studied and practiced medicine until he attracted critical notice with his drama *Anatol* (1893, tr. 1911), seven one-act plays about a philanderer. He achieved considerable success with *Liebelei* (1895, tr. *The Reckoning*, 1907; *Light-o' Love*, 1912). With several other Viennese writers opposed to German naturalist drama, he formed (c.1900) a group known as Young Vienna. His plays, *Novellen*, and novels are distinguished for their sparkling wit and brilliant style, unique mixture of melancholy and cheerfulness, and clinical observations of the pathological. His concern is with individual happiness, and his dramatic problems are often focused on love and sexual faithfulness. Among his translated dramas are *The Lonely Way* (1903, tr. 1915), on artistic dedication; *The Vast Domain* (1911, tr. 1923); *Professor Bernhardi* (1912, tr. 1913), a tragedy about a Jewish doctor, mirroring the anti-Semitic problem; and a number of one-act plays, collected in *Stories and Plays* (1934). Of his novels, *The Road to the Open* (1908, tr. 1923) is autobiographical. See biography by S. Liptzin (1932); studies by M. Swales (1971) and Reinhard Urbach (tr. 1973).

Schnorr von Carolsfeld, Julius (yo͞o'lyo͝os shnôr fən kä'rôlsfĕlt), 1794–1872, German religious and historical painter and draftsman. He studied with his father, Veit Hans Schnorr von Carolsfeld (1764–1841), a painter and engraver, and in Vienna. In 1817 he went to Rome and joined the NAZARENES; with them he worked on the frescoes of the Villa Massimo, contributing his *Orlando Furioso*. In 1827 he was summoned by King Louis I of Bavaria to Munich, where he was professor and later director of the academy and decorated the palace with his *Nibelungen* frescoes. Schnorr is best known, however, for his vigorous drawings for the illustrated Bible, *Bibel in Bildern* (1851–60).

Schober, Johann (yō'hän shō'bər), 1874–1932, Austrian chancellor (1921–22, 1929–30). A respected career civil servant, he held the key post of head of the Vienna police after July, 1918. As chancellor, he gained passage (1929) of constitutional reforms that strengthened the presidency, though the changes were far more liberal than those urged by Ignaz SEIPEL. As vice chancellor and foreign minister (1930–32) he promoted the customs-union pact with Germany, a project that failed because of French opposition.

Schobert, Johann (yō'hän shō'bərt), 1720–67, German composer. Schobert was born in Silesia and grew up in Strasbourg. He was a renowned harpsichord player and wrote many pieces for that instrument, generally in the homophonic Mannheim style initiated by Johann STAMITZ. Schobert died in Paris from eating poisonous mushrooms.

Schoelcher, Victor (vēktôr' shölshĕr'), 1804–93, French humanitarian and statesman. Long involved in the abolition movement, he presided (1848) over a commission that secured the abolition of slavery in French territory. He opposed the coup d'etat of Louis Napoleon (later Napoleon III) of Dec., 1851, and was forced into exile in England until Napoleon's fall in 1870. Elected to the national assembly, he sat with the extreme left. He became senator for life in 1875.

Schoenberg, Arnold (är'nôlt shön'bĕrkh), 1874–1951, Austrian composer. Before he became a U.S. citizen in 1941 he spelled his name Schönberg. He revolutionized modern music by abandoning tonality and developing a 12-tone, "serial" technique of composition (see SERIAL MUSIC). Except for periods in Berlin in 1901–3 and 1911–18, he lived until 1925 in Vienna. In 1918 he founded his famous private seminar in composition and the Society for Private Performances, at which neither critics nor applause were allowed. Though he himself had little formal instruction in music, teaching was a major activity throughout his life. Among his many students the most noted were Alban Berg and Anton von Webern. He taught at the Prussian Academy of Fine Arts in Berlin from 1925 to 1933, when he came to the United States and taught for one year at the Malkin Conservatory, Boston. He then went to Hollywood and was professor of music at the Univ. of Southern California in 1935–36 and at the Univ. of California at Los Angeles from 1936 to 1944. In his early works—*Verklärte Nacht* (1899), a string sextet; *Gurrelieder* (1901–2), a cantata for chorus and orchestra; and *Pelleas und Melisande* (1905), a symphonic poem—he expanded the chromatic style established by Wagner and Mahler. His later works are thinner in texture and highly contrapuntal. In 1908 in a set of piano pieces and the song cycle *Das Buch der hängenden Gärten,* to poems of Stefan George, he completely abandoned tonality (see ATONALITY). His use of *Sprechstimme,* halfway between song and speech, caused a sensation at the first performance in 1912 of the song cycle *Pierrot Lunaire.* His 12-tone technique, used to some extent in five piano pieces and a *Serenade* in 1923, was first employed throughout a work in the Suite for Piano (1924). Though he did not invent serial technique, he established it as an important organizational device in music. His other works include two chamber symphonies (1906; 1906–40) and Variations for Orchestra (1928); string quartets, a woodwind quintet (1924), and Suite for 7 Instruments (1927); a violin concerto (1936) and a piano concerto (1942); the monodrama *Erwartung* (1909) and an unfinished opera, *Moses und Aron* (1932–51; produced 1957), considered his masterpiece; *Ode to Napoleon* (1941), to Byron's poem, for male speaker, piano and strings; *A Survivor from Warsaw* (1947), for narrator, chorus and orchestra; and *Fantasia* (1949), for violin and piano. See his *Style and Idea* (tr. 1951) and *Structural Functions of Harmony* (tr. 1954); biographies by H. H. Stuckenschmidt (tr. 1959), A. Payne (1968), and W. Reich (tr. 1971); studies by M. Kassler (1961), G. Perle (rev. ed. 1968), and B. Boretz (1968).

Schoenbrunn Village State Memorial (shān'brən, -bro͞on), E Ohio, S of New Philadelphia; site of the first town in Ohio, est. 1772 by Moravian missionary David Zeisberger and his Indian converts. During the American Revolution, the town was abandoned because of the British and Indian menace; later the town was burned by Indians. Restoration of the site to its original appearance began in 1923. A museum is there.

Schöffer, Peter: see FUST, JOHANN.

Schofield, John McAllister (skō'fēld), 1831–1906, Union general in the American Civil War, b. Gerry, N.Y. He taught at West Point (1855–60) and on the outbreak of the Civil War became chief of staff to Nathaniel Lyon in Missouri. He was brigadier general commanding Missouri troops (Nov., 1861–April, 1863) and commander of the Dept. of the Missouri (May, 1863–Jan., 1864). In Feb., 1864, he was given command of the Army of the Ohio, which he led in the ATLANTA CAMPAIGN. He opposed John B. HOOD in Tennessee (Oct.–Dec., 1864), fighting at Franklin and Nashville. Schofield was Secretary of War under Andrew Johnson (1868–69) and held various commands until 1888, when he became commander of the U.S. army. He was appointed lieutenant general shortly before he retired in 1895. See his *Forty-six Years in the Army* (1897); study by J. L. McDonough (1972).

scholasticism (skōlăs'tĭsĭzəm), philosophy and theology of Western Christendom in the Middle Ages. Virtually all medieval philosophers of any significance were theologians, and their philosophy is generally embodied in their theological writings. There were numerous scholastic philosophies in the Middle Ages, but basic to all scholastic thought was the conjunction of faith and reason. For the greatest of the scholastics, this meant the use of reason to deepen the understanding of what is believed on faith and ultimately to give a rational content to faith. It was in the course of applying reason to faith that medieval thinkers developed and taught important philosophical ideas not directly related to theology. The greatest of earlier Christian philosophers had been St. AUGUSTINE, who saw in Plato (or in NEOPLATONISM) a system congenial with Christianity. This influence combined with that of the Pseudo-Dionysius (see DIONYSIUS THE AREOPAGITE, SAINT) to color the speculations of Western thinkers with Neoplatonic ideas. Much knowledge of ancient philosophy came to the early scholastics through the writings of BOETHIUS. John Scotus ERIGENA continued the tradition of Neoplatonism in the 9th cent., adding to it certain mystical notions of his own. But it is with St. ANSELM in the late 11th cent. that the formal beginnings of scholasticism can be identified. Taking as his life's motto "fides quaerens intelligentiam" [faith seeking understanding], Anselm sought to use reason to illuminate the content of belief. An example of this is his famous ontological proof of the existence of God, based upon the assertion that the highest being of which our minds can conceive must exist in reality. The most important philosophical problem in the 12th cent. was the question of the universal (see REALISM). Opposing both the extreme nominalism of ROSCELIN and the realism of WILLIAM OF CHAMPEAUX, Peter ABELARD taught a moderate doctrine; he recognized the universal as a symbol to which human beings have attached a commonly agreed significance, based on the similarity they perceive in different objects. Abelard's emphasis on the powers of reason, which he exaggerated in his early years, led to his condemnation by BERNARD OF CLAIRVAUX. JOHN OF SALISBURY, an English scholar noted for his humanistic studies, was representative of the important work done at the noted school at Chartres. Hugh of St. Victor, a German scholar and mystic, urged the study of every branch of learning. His treatise *On Sacraments* was the first summa, an important medieval literary genre. The summae were comprehensive, intricately arranged works on theology and philosophy; they were characterized by their wide scope and vast learning. The *Book of Sentences,* however, assembled by PETER LOMBARD in the early 12th cent., was to become the classical source book for medieval thinkers. It was a compilation of sources from the church fathers, especially St. Augustine, and in subsequent years virtually every great medieval thinker wrote a commentary on the *Sentences.* The 13th cent. is generally regarded as the golden age of medieval philosophy. It was marked by two important developments: the growth of universities, especially at Paris and Oxford (see COLLEGES AND UNIVERSITIES), and the introduction of ARISTOTLE into the West. Until then, only the early works of Aristotle had been known to Western scholars; between 1120 and 1220 virtually the whole body of Aristotle's work was rendered into Latin, mainly from Arabic translations. The impact on Western thinkers of this vast body of systematic thought and organized research and analysis was enormous; only slightly less important was the influence of AVICENNA and AVERROËS, the two Arabic commentators whose interpretations of Aristotle were translated as well. The Univ. of Paris became a leading center for the study of Aristotle and attracted scholars from all over Europe; the Dominicans and Franciscans, popular new religious orders, played a leading role in the expansion of the universities and the development of scholasticism. It was in the universities that the two traditional forms of scholastic literature were developed: the question (a thesis that is posed and defended against objections) and the commentary. Although Aristotle's work was of central significance in the development of scholasticism, it did not make its way without difficulties. In 1210 and 1215 papal authority prohibited the teaching of some of Aristotle's works at the Univ. of Paris, although by 1240 the ban was no longer enforced. The first Western Aristotelian was ALBERTUS MAGNUS, who was an important student of the natural sciences as well. But the leading figure in the movement to "Christianize Aristotle" was St. THOMAS AQUINAS, a Dominican and one of the greatest intellectual figures of the Middle Ages. He produced a vast body of philosophical work, which was remarkably precise, detailed, and organized. Denying any basic conflict between faith and reason, St. Thomas sought to demonstrate that reason could lead man to many of the great spiritual truths and could help him to understand those truths that he accepted on faith. He combated secular interpretations of Aristotle, especially "Latin Averroism," the doctrines of SIGER DE BRABANT. In particular, St. Thomas attacked the Averroist teaching that denied the immortality of the individual soul. St. Thomas himself was vigorously opposed by the Franciscans, led by St. BONAVENTURE. Bonaventure, rooted in an older theological tradition, feared the excesses of reason in its contact with faith and almost succeeded in having St. Thomas's teachings condemned at Paris. Another opponent of St. Thomas was DUNS SCOTUS, who developed a new scholastic synthesis. WILLIAM OF OCCAM, another Franciscan, is generally regarded as the last of the great medieval thinkers. By firmly separating philosophy and religion and insisting that there is no rational ground for faith, he brought an end to that synthesis of faith and reason that characterized the greatest scholastic thought. After the 15th cent. the reputation of medieval philosophy declined. But the break between medieval philosophy and Renaissance thought was mainly in the area of metaphysics; scholastic tradition and methods continued to be followed in politics and law—in canon law, civil law, and common law and, later, in the development of international law. In the late 15th cent. the Dominicans began a Thomistic revival; its brilliant leader was the former CAJETAN. There was also a living Scotist tradition, and every Catholic university had Thomists and Scotists in its theological faculty. After the 18th cent. the secularization of the universities resulted in the suppression of the theological faculties, and the old tradition was broken. The Scotists always suffered from the very bad state of the text of Duns Scotus' works, and in the 20th cent. the Franciscan order undertook a complete and authoritative edition of them. Contemporary interest in scholasticism, particularly among the neoscholastics, began as a concerted effort toward the end of the 19th cent. at the Univ. of Louvain. Impetus was given to the movement by the papal encyclical of Leo XIII, *Aeterni Patris* (1879), which called upon Roman Catholics to renew the study of the scholastics, especially St. Thomas Aquinas. Neoscholastics are not unanimous in their approach, but do generally agree that their philosophical study must not proceed in a manner that is neglectful of their Christian faith. Among the foremost neoscholastics have been the Frenchmen Jacques Maritain and Étienne Gilson. See Erwin Panofsky, *Gothic Architecture and Scholasticism* (1951, repr. 1963); Étienne Gilson, *History of Christian Philosophy in the Middle Ages* (1955); Josef Pieper, *Scholasticism* (tr. 1960, repr. 1964); J. R. Weinberg, *A Short History of Medieval Philosophy* (1964).

Scholem, Gershom Gerhard (gĕr'shôm gĕr'härt shō'ləm), 1897–, Jewish scholar, b. Berlin. He studied at the universities of Berlin, Jena, Berne, and Munich. Scholem received (1922) his doctorate for a dissertation on the earliest extant and one of the most obscure cabalistic works, *Sefer ha-Bahir.* This translation and commentary, published as *Das Buch Bahir* (1923), began a career that was to make the study of the history of cabala and Jewish mysticism an important scholarly discipline. He was the librarian of the Hebrew Univ. of Jerusalem and National Library (1923–27), lecturer at the university (1925–32), and professor of Jewish mysticism and cabala there from 1933 until his retirement in 1965. Scholem was the author of over 500 articles and books; his major works in English include *Major Trends in Jewish Mysticism* (1941), *Jewish Gnosticism, Merkabah Mysticism and the Talmudic Tradition* (1960), *On the Kabbalah and Its Symbolism* (tr.1965), *The Messianic Idea in Judaism* (tr.1971), *Sabbatai Zevi, the Mystical Messiah* (1973), and *Kabbalah* (1974).

Schomberg, Frederick Herman, 1st **duke of** (schŏm'bərg), Ger. *Friedrich Hermann von Schönberg,* 1615–90, German soldier of fortune. After serving on the Protestant side in the Thirty Years War, he entered French service in the early 1650s during the Fronde. From 1659 to 1668 Schomberg commanded a French army helping Portugal win independence from Spain. Schomberg distinguished himself in the Third Dutch War (1672–78) and was created marshal of France and duke by King Louis XIV. After the revocation of the Edict of Nantes (1685), Schomberg, a Protestant, left France and entered the service of the elector of Brandenburg, who made him commander in chief of the army of Brandenburg in 1687. He assisted (1688) William III of Orange, who was allied with Brandenburg, in the Glorious Revolution. Created (1689) duke of Schomberg in the English peerage, he was given command of the English forces in Ireland. He was killed there in the battle of the Boyne.

Schomburgk, Sir Robert Hermann (shŏm'bərk), 1804–65, English traveler and explorer, b. Germany. Under the direction of the Royal Geographical Society he went in 1835 on a trip of botanical and geographical exploration to British Guiana. For the British government he later (1841–43) surveyed that colony, outlining the Schomburgk line, a boundary that played a prominent part in subsequent boundary disputes with Venezuela. Knighted in 1844, Schomburgk was appointed British consul at Santo Domingo (1848) and at Bangkok (1857). He wrote books on British Guiana and Barbados and edited (1848) Sir Walter Raleigh's journal of his second voyage to Guiana.

Schönbein, Christian Friedrich (krĭs'tyän frē'drĭkh shön'bīn), 1799–1868, German chemist. From 1828 he taught at the Univ. of Basel (as professor from 1835). He discovered ozone (1840) and, through his work on nitrocellulose, developed guncotton and collodion.

Schönbrunn (shönbro͞on'), former royal palace in Vienna, built during the reigns of Emperor Charles VI and Maria Theresa. Mainly designed by FISCHER VON ERLACH, it is a splendid example of Austrian baroque. Its beautiful park, emulating Versailles, has a large zoological and botanical garden. Both palace and park were damaged during World War II. By the **Peace of Schönbrunn** (1809), imposed by NAPOLEON I, Austria temporarily lost W Galicia to the grand duchy of Warsaw, and Illyria to France.

Schongauer, Martin (mär'tĕn shōn'gou-ər), 1430–91, German engraver and painter, son of a goldsmith of Colmar, Alsace. Schongauer's only certain painting is *Madonna of the Rose Arbor* (1473; Church of St. Martin, Colmar). The strong figures and faces are treated with the almost metallic sharpness and linearity that later characterized his engravings. There also exist fragments of a mural in the Church of St. Stephen, Breisach, where he lived (1488–91). His work shows Flemish influences, particularly of Roger van der Weyden and Dierick Bouts. Schongauer is best known for his remarkable engravings of religious subjects. He produced 115 engravings signed with his monogram, M+S. Executed with amazing virtuosity, they were of great importance for the development of German art and were particularly admired by Dürer. Outstanding examples of Schongauer's engraving are *The Wise and Foolish Virgins, The Passion, Bearing the Cross, Death of the Virgin, Adoration of the Magi, Christ Enthroned,* and *Temptation of St. Anthony.* Schongauer was one of the earliest engravers to use copper for reproduction and contributed much to the development of the art. See his complete engravings, ed. by Alan Shestack (1970).

school, term commonly referring to institutions of pre-college formal education. It also properly includes colleges, universities, and many types of special training establishments (see ADULT EDUCATION; COLLEGES AND UNIVERSITIES; VOCATIONAL EDUCATION). In the United States the standard school system has developed from an uncoordinated conglomeration of dame schools, reading and writing schools, private academies, Latin grammar schools, and colleges into a well-organized system in which a child may progress from KINDERGARTEN to college in a continuous and efficient free public system. By 1890 there had evolved the now common twelve-grade system whereby the child enters kindergarten at the age of five, goes to grammar or elementary school for grades one through eight, high or secondary school for grades nine through twelve, and then enters college. To meet the psychological and social stresses of early adolescence, the junior high school was introduced (1890–1920) in many systems for grades seven through nine. This organization, sometimes called the six-three-three plan, is designed to ease the transition period by having the junior high school introduce its students to many aspects of the high school, such as student government and separate classes for different subjects. Critics of the junior high school, however, have contended that it merely copies the program of the high school, which they believe to be inappropriate for the age group that attends the junior high. In response, many districts have established intermediate schools, usually encompassing grades five through eight. Compulsory attendance at school has been legislated in all states, although standards of age and length of the school year vary considerably. To provide opportunity for advanced training beyond high school without a full college course, the junior or COMMUNITY COLLEGE, which generally includes the first two years of college, has been widely instituted. A number of states and municipalities have OPEN ENROLLMENT policies, whereby any high school graduate may enter a specified institution of higher education. Although in the United States schools are the responsibility, primarily, of state and local authorities, the Federal government has passed a number of measures intended to assist schools and their students. The National Defense Education Act (1958) and the Higher Education Act (1965) were designed to provide financial assistance to college and university students. The Elementary and Secondary Education Act (1965, amended 1966, 1967) was the first national general-aid education program in the United States. It provided funds for school library and textbook services, the education of poor and handicapped children, and educational innovations and construction by local school districts. Public school services have been extended, in some communities, into the sponsorship of community centers, adult education, summer schools, and recreation programs. Special programs are established for the deaf, the blind, and the mentally and physically handicapped and in some instances for the gifted. In large cities special high schools are sometimes set up to serve special student needs; e.g., there may be separate schools for artistic, industrial, scientific, and classical subjects. The free public school system is paralleled in many areas by a relatively small number of private and PAROCHIAL SCHOOLS. Preparatory schools are private schools operated primarily to prepare students for college. They correspond to English public schools, which are in fact private, endowed institutions. See also EDUCATION; GUIDANCE; PROGRESSIVE EDUCATION. See E. P. Cubberly, *Public Education in the United States* (rev. ed. 1962); Martin Mayer, *The Schools* (1961); Vivian T. Thayer and Martin Levit, *The Role of the School in American Society* (2d ed. 1966); Grace Graham, *The Public School in the New Society* (1969); Colin Greer, *The Great School Legend* (1972).

Schoolcraft, Henry Rowe, 1793–1864, American ethnologist, b. near Albany, N.Y. He gave enormous impetus to the study of the American Indian and may be regarded as the foremost pioneer in Indian studies. As a young man, Schoolcraft abandoned his family's glassmaking business and made a journey down the Ohio River to Missouri. There in 1818–19 he made valuable geographical, geological, and mineralogical surveys. His journal and findings were recorded in *A View of the Lead Mines of Missouri,* completed in 1819. As geologist on the expedition of Gen. Lewis Cass, Schoolcraft made topographical surveys of the country of present N Michigan and about the upper Great Lakes. The expedition reached Lake Itasca, which they incorrectly supposed to be the source of the Mississippi River. This voyage was described in *A Narrative Journal of Travels . . . from Detroit through the Great Chain of American Lakes to the Sources of the Mississippi River* (1821). In 1822 he was appointed Indian agent with headquarters at Sault Ste Marie and began his ethnological researches. Having married the half-Ojibwa daughter of a fur trader, Schoolcraft learned the Ojibwa language and a great deal of Ojibwa lore. His area of administration as Indian agent was later considerably increased, with new headquarters at Mackinac. He made another journey to the Mississippi in 1832 and served in the territorial legislature from 1828 to 1832. When the Whigs came to power in 1841, Schoolcraft lost his Indian agency and moved to the East, where he continued the Indian studies begun with *Algic Researches* (1839). He wrote voluminously on the Indians, the chief result being his *Historical and Statistical Information Respecting . . . the Indian Tribes of the United States* (6 vol., 1851–57).

school of Paris. The center of international art until after World War II, Paris was a mecca for artists who flocked there to participate in the most advanced aesthetic currents of their time. The school of Paris is not one style; the term describes many styles and movements. The practitioners and adherents of FAUVISM, CUBISM, and ORPHISM all belonged to the school of Paris, as well as many artists whose styles fit into no one category. After the war, when New York City challenged Paris's preeminence in the art world, the school of Paris continued to produce major figures and styles in art: Jean Dubuffet and the Art Brut school are recent examples.

schooner (sko͞o'nər), sailing vessel, rigged fore-and-aft, with from two to seven masts. Schooners can lie closer to the wind than square-rigged sailing ships, need a smaller crew, and are very fast. They were first constructed in colonial America and because of their speed became one of the favorite craft of the United States and Canada in the latter half of the 18th cent. and the first half of the 19th cent. Schooners were widely used in the North Atlantic fisheries and the North American coastal trade until World War I, when they were replaced by power-driven craft. See Howard I. Chapelle, *The History of American Sailing Ships* (1935); J. F. Leavitt, *Wake of the Coasters* (1970); Neale Haley, *The Schooner Era* (1972).

Schopenhauer, Arthur (är'to͞or shō'pənhou"ər), 1788–1860, German philosopher, b. Danzig (now Gdansk). The bias of his own temperament and experience was germinal to the development of his celebrated philosophy of pessimism, which he presented with such clarity and skill as to gain eventual recognition as one of the great philosophers. He studied at Göttingen, Berlin, and Jena, and he traveled throughout Europe. In Berlin he opposed the teachings of G. W. Hegel and attempted unsuccessfully to establish himself as a lecturer. After 1831, Schopenhauer lived and worked in retirement, chiefly in Frankfurt am Main. He had no friends, never married, and was estranged from his mother, a woman of considerable intellectual ability. Schopenhauer's most important work is *The World as Will and Representation* (1818, tr. 1958). His other works, mainly elaboration and commentary upon his original thesis, include *On the Will in Nature* (1836, tr. 1889), *The Basis of Morality* (1841, tr. 1903), *Essays from the Parerga and Paralipomena* (1851, tr. 1951), and many lesser essays. Schopenhauer considered himself the true successor of Immanuel Kant. However, he interpreted Kant's unknowable thing-in-itself as a blind, impelling force that is manifest in individuals as a will to live. Intellect and consciousness, in Schopenhauer's view, arise as instruments in the service of the will. Conflict between individual wills is the cause of continual strife and frustration. The world, therefore, is a world of unsatisfied wants and of pain. Pleasure is simply the absence of pain; unable to endure, it brings only ennui. The only possible escape is the renunciation of desire, a negation of the will reminiscent of Buddhism. Temporary relief, however, can be found in philosophy and art. Schopenhauer held that music was unique among the art forms in that it expressed will directly. The ethical side of Schopenhauer's philosophy is based upon sympathy, where the moral will, feeling another's hurt as its own, makes an effort to relieve the pain. His stress on the strength of the impelling will influenced Friedrich Nietzsche and the psychology of Sigmund Freud. See biography by William Wallace (1890, repr. 1970); V. J. McGill, *Schopenhauer, Pessimist and Pagan* (1931, repr. 1971); Patrick Gardiner, *Schopenhauer* (1963).

Schoreel, Jan van: see SCOREL, JAN VAN.

Schouler, James (sko͞o'lər), 1839–1920, American historian and lawyer, b. West Cambridge (now Arlington), Mass. Admitted to the bar in 1862, he served in the Union army and returned to Boston in 1863 to practice law. From 1871 to 1873 he published the *United States Jurist* in Washington, D.C. He lectured on law at Boston Univ. (1883–1902) and at the National Univ., Washington, D.C. (1888–1908), and on American history at Johns Hopkins (1891–1908). His *History of the United States of America under the Constitution* (7 vol., 1880–1913, repr. 1970), covering the period 1783–1877, is primarily a political and constitutional interpretation. Other works, aside from a number of treatises on legal subjects, include *Thomas Jefferson* (1893), *Alexander Hamilton* (1901), and *Ideals of the Republic* (1908). His *Historical Briefs* (1896) in part covers his own experience as a historian.

Schouten, Willem Cornelis (vĭl'əm kôrnā'lĭs skhou'tən), 1567?–1625, Dutch navigator. In 1615 he sailed from Texel island, Holland, in command of an expedition whose objective was to evade the trade restrictions of the Dutch East India Company by finding a new route to the Pacific. Avoiding the Strait of Magellan, in 1616 he rounded Cape Horn, which he named for his birthplace, Hoorn. He followed the north coasts of New Ireland and New Guinea and visited adjacent islands, including what became known as the Schouten Islands. Although he had opened an unknown route, the East India Company claimed infringement of its monopoly, arrested Schouten (who was later released) and confiscated his ship in Java.

Schreckhörner (shrĕk'hör"nər), two peaks of the Bernese Alps, S central Switzerland. Gross Schreckhorn (grōs"shrĕk'hôrn") is 13,387 ft (4,080 m) high; Klein Schreckhorn (klīn") reaches a height of 11,473 ft (3,497 m).

Schreiner, Olive (shrī'nər), pseud. **Ralph Iron,** 1855–1920, South African author and feminist, b. Wittebergen Reserve, Cape Colony. After several years as a governess, she went to England in 1881, taking with her the manuscript of her famous novel, *The Story of an African Farm* (1883). The novel, which has been likened to Emily Brontë's *Wuthering Heights,* is an intense story of two children living in the African veldt; it was controversial because of its feminist and anti-Christian sentiments. Her later works included *Dreams* (1921), a collection of allegories; *Women and Labour* (1911); and a significant novel, unfinished, *From Man to Man* (1926). Her letters were edited (1924) by her husband, S. C. Cronwright-Schreiner, who also wrote her biography (1923, repr. 1973).

Schröder, Friedrich Ludwig (frē'drĭkh lo͞ot'vĭkh shrō'dər), 1744–1816, German actor, manager, and dramatist. He introduced Shakespeare in Germany. The son of actors, Schröder had a difficult, demanding childhood and youth. On the stage from the age of three, he lived for a time in a deserted theater, learning acrobatics from traveling companies that occasionally worked there. Greatly influenced by the acting of Konrad Eckhof, Schröder further developed the realistic school and became the most celebrated German actor of his day. He raised the standard of taste in Germany with his excellent ensemble productions, initiating reforms in costume, scenery, and acting. In 1771 he and his mother assumed the management of the Hamburg National Theater. He produced his own translations of 11 plays by Shakespeare (1776–80), as well as his own plays and those of the new STURM UND DRANG movement.

Schrödinger, Erwin (ĕr'vĭn shrö'dĭng-ər), 1887–1961, Austrian theoretical physicist. He was educated at Vienna, taught at Breslau and Zürich, and was professor at the Univ. of Berlin (1927–33), fellow of Magdalen College, Oxford (1933–36), and professor at the Univ. of Graz (1936–38), the Dublin Institute for Advanced Studies (1940–57), and the Univ. of Vienna (1957–61). Schrödinger is known for his mathematical development of wave mechanics (1926), a form of quantum mechanics (see QUANTUM THEORY), and his formulation of the wave equation that bears his name. The Schrödinger equation is the most widely used mathematical tool of the modern quantum theory. For this work he shared the 1933 Nobel Prize in Physics with P. A. M. Dirac.

Schubert, Franz Peter (fränts pā'tər shōō'bərt), 1797–1828, Austrian composer, one of the most gifted musicians of the 19th cent. His symphonic works represent the best legacy of the classical tradition, while his songs exemplify the height of romantic lyricism. Displaying remarkable talent in childhood, he was first taught to play the violin and piano by his father and his brother, and then studied the organ and singing at a local church. His beautiful voice gained him admittance in 1808 to the imperial chapel choir and the Royal Seminary, where he later studied composition with SALIERI. Schubert wrote his first symphony in 1813, and in that year he left the Seminary. From 1814 to 1816 he taught at his father's elementary school, devoting his spare hours to composing lieder that give evidence of his inexhaustible melodic genius. He wrote more than 600 of these songs, many to the lyrics of such German poets as Goethe, Schiller, and Heine. In addition to individual lyrics, such as the famous *Erlkönig,* set to a ballad by Goethe, Schubert wrote such song cycles as *Die schöne Müllerin* (1823) and *Die Winterreise* (1827), both to poems of Wilhelm Müller. Schubert's symphonies are the final extension of the classical sonata forms, and three of them—the Fifth, in B Flat (1816), the Eighth, in B Minor (the *Unfinished,* 1822), and the Ninth, in C Major (1828)—rank with the finest orchestral music. The Quartet in D Minor (*Death and the Maiden,* 1824) and the Quintet in A Major (*The Trout,* 1819) are the best known of his mature chamber works. He also composed music for the stage, overtures, choral music, masses, and much piano music, including 21 sonatas and shorter waltzes, scherzos, and impromptus. Except for a circle of admirers who were among the leading artists of the period, he gained little recognition before his death. He held only one musical appointment, that of music teacher to the children of a Hungarian nobleman, and he lived in poverty. See O. E. Deutsch, *The Schubert Reader: A Life . . . in Letters and Documents* (tr. 1947); biographies by Alfred Einstein (1951), M. J. E. Brown (1958), and P. Young (1970); studies by M. J. E. Brown (1966) and J. A. Westrup (1969).

Schulberg, Budd, 1914–, American writer, b. New York City, grad. Dartmouth, 1936. Because his father worked for Paramount Studios, Schulberg could observe the corruption of the film industry. His novel *What Makes Sammy Run?* (1941) is about the rise of a ruthless film magnate. Among his other novels are *The Disenchanted* (1950) and *Sanctuary V* (1969). He wrote the screenplay for *On the Waterfront* (1954).

Schulenburg, Ehrengard Melusina von der, duchess of Kendal (ā'rəngärt mälōōzē'nä fən dĕr shōō'lənbōōrkh), 1667–1743, German mistress of George I of England. She became his mistress at the Hanoverian court and followed him to England c.1714. She exerted great influence over the king, but was unpopular with the English people because of her foreign birth and manners and the wealth she acquired through bribery and corrupt public transactions. She was created duchess of Kendal in 1719.

Schultze, Max Johann Sigismund (mäks yō'hän zē'gĭsmōōnd shōōl'tsə), 1825–74, German biologist, director of the Anatomical Institute at Bonn from 1859. He established that the cells of all organisms are composed of protoplasm and contain a nucleus. He also studied protozoa, sense organs, muscles, and nerve endings.

Schulz, Charles M., 1922–, American cartoonist, b. Minneapolis, Minn. Creator of the enormously popular syndicated comic strip "Peanuts," Schulz expresses a droll philosophy through the children of his strip who behave like adults. Among his principal characters are Charlie Brown, a puzzled, victimized boy and Snoopy, a romantic, self-deluded beagle. One of the many collections of "Peanuts" comic strips published in book form is *Peanuts Classics* (1970). A theological analysis of "Peanuts" is presented in Robert M. Short's *The Gospel According to Peanuts* (1964).

Schulze-Delitzsch, Hermann (hĕr'män shōōl'tsə-dā'lĭch), 1808–83, German liberal politician and economic reformer. Believing in economic self-help by cooperative associations, he founded peoples' banks, mercantile and consumers' cooperatives, and, in 1859, a general association of German cooperatives. In 1867 he obtained passage of a Prussian law protecting associations. A nationalist, he was one of the founders of the Nationalverein, an organization that favored German unification. He was a member of the Prussian lower house from 1861, of the North German diet from 1867, and of the Reichstag from 1871.

Schumacher, Peder, Count Griffenfeld: see GRIFFENFELD, PEDER SCHUMACHER, COUNT.

Schuman, Robert (rōbĕr' shōōmăN'), 1886–1963, French statesman and lawyer, b, grand duchy of Luxembourg. A member of the Catholic Mouvement Républicain Populaire (MRP), he was finance minister (1946, 1947) and premier (1947–48). He continued as foreign minister (1948–53), and as such, did much to promote European unity. In 1950 he proposed the creation of a West European coal and steel pool. This so-called Schuman Plan, which had been drafted by Jean Monnet, became effective in 1952 with the formation of the European Coal and Steel Community, the first step toward the creation of a EUROPEAN COMMUNITY. Schuman was president (1958–60) of the European Parliamentary Assembly.

Schuman, William (shōō'mən), 1910–, American composer, b. New York City. Schuman taught at Sarah Lawrence College (1935–45), leaving to become president of the Juilliard School of Music. Twice a Guggenheim Fellow (1939 and 1940), he became president of Lincoln Center for the Performing Arts in 1962. His outstanding compositions are his Third Symphony and his Fourth Symphony (both 1941); his American Festival Overture (1939); Symphony for Strings (1943); *Newsreel* (1941); two secular cantatas, *This is Our Time* (1940) and *A Free Song* (1942; awarded the first Pulitzer Music Prize, 1943); the ballet *Undertow* (1945); the opera *The Mighty Casey* (Hartford, 1953); and several chamber works. His music is highly contrapuntal and often employs complex rhythms suggestive of jazz. See study by F. R. Schreiber and Vincent Persichetti (1954).

Schumann, Robert Alexander (shōō'män), 1810–56, German composer. Both as a composer and as a highly articulate music critic he was a leader of the romantic movement. He studied theory with Heinrich Dorn and piano with Friedrich Wieck, whose daughter Clara he married. Forced by a hand injury to abandon a career as a pianist, he served as editor of the *Neue Zeitschrift für Musik* from its inception in 1834 until 1844. In his articles he championed younger composers, particularly Chopin and Brahms. Schumann's brilliant compositions for piano, including *Papillons, Die Davidsbündlertänze, Carnaval, Fantasiestücke, Études symphoniques, Kinderszenen,* and *Kreisleriana,* occupied him until 1840, when he began to write songs and orchestral music. In his lieder he set to music lyrics by such poets as Heine, Goethe, Eichendorff, and Kerner, achieving a superb fusion of vocal melody and piano accompaniment. Among his best song cycles are *Frauenliebe und -Leben* [*Woman's Love and Life,* on verses by Chamisso] and *Dichterliebe* [*Poet's Love,* verses by Heine]. His Piano Concerto in A Minor (1841–45), *Spring* Symphony (1841), and Third, or *Rhenish,* Symphony (1850) are his outstanding orchestral works. They exemplify his infusion of classical forms with intense, personal emotion. His one opera, *Genoveva* (1847–48), was unsuccessful. After a nervous breakdown, he entered (1854) a sanitarium, where he died two years later. See his essays, *On Music and Musicians* (1946); his letters, tr. by M. Herbert (1888, repr. 1970); biographies by J. Chissell (1967) and H. Bedford (1933, repr. 1971); studies by T. A. Brown (1968), S. Walsh (1972), and Alan Walker, ed. (1974). His wife, **Clara Josephine (Wieck) Schumann,** 1819–96, was one of the outstanding pianists of her time. After bitter opposition from her father she married Schumann in 1840 and eventually bore him eight children. She made her debut in 1832 and later performed with great success on the Continent, in England, and in Russia. She was noted for the intellectual brilliance and sensitivity of her playing, and was an outstanding interpreter of Schumann's and Brahms's works. Her own compositions were mainly piano pieces and songs. From 1878 to 1892 she taught at the Frankfurt Conservatory. See biographies by J. N. Burk (1940) and B. Harding (1961).

Schumann-Heink, Ernestine (shōō'mən-hīngk), 1861–1936, Austrian-American contralto, b. near Prague. Her voice was distinguished for its richness and wide range. She studied with Marietta Leclair, made her concert debut in 1876 and her operatic debut two years later in Dresden in *Il Trovatore.* For many years she sang at Hamburg and Bayreuth, also appearing at London's Covent Garden in Wagnerian roles. After making her American debut in Chicago in 1898, she sang regularly (1899–1904) with the Metropolitan Opera Company, becoming a U.S. citizen in 1905. She toured (1904–5) with great success in a comic opera, *Love's Lottery,* which was written for her. Afterward she sang mainly in concerts until 1926 and appeared once more at the Metropolitan in 1932. She had a repertory of 150 roles and was a fine actress, popular even when her voice had diminished.

Schumpeter, Joseph Alois (yō'zĕf ä'lōēs shōōm'-pā"tər), 1883–1950, Austrian-American economist, LL.D. Univ. of Vienna, 1906. He began practicing law but turned to teaching two years later. He was professor of economics at the Univ. of Graz from 1911 to 1914 and at Bonn from 1925 to 1932, when he went to the United States; thereafter he was professor of economics at Harvard. He served (1919–20) as Austrian minister of finance. His major contributions to economics were the theory of the entrepreneur as the dynamic factor in fostering the business cycle and the theory of economic development of capitalism. His most important books are *Theory of Economic Development* (1911, in German; tr. 1934), *Business Cycles* (1939), *Capitalism, Socialism, and Democracy* (1942, 3d ed. 1950), and *History of Economic Analysis* (1954). See study ed. by S. E. Harris (1951, repr. 1969).

Schurman, Jacob Gould (shûr'mən), 1854–1942, American educator and diplomat, b. Freetown, Prince Edward Island. His education was completed in London, Edinburgh, and, as Hibbert fellow, in Heidelberg, Berlin, and Göttingen. In 1886 he became head of the philosophy department at Cornell Univ. Schurman won a notable reputation as teacher, speaker, founder and editor of the *Philosophical Review,* and author of *The Ethical Import of Darwinism* (1887) and other philosophical works. In 1892 he succeeded Charles K. Adams as president of Cornell. In that office until 1920, he helped in the expansion of the university. He headed the first U. S. Philippines Commission (1899), was joint author of its report, and wrote *Philippine Affairs* (1902). Schurman served (1912–13) as minister to Greece, returning to write *The Balkan Wars, 1912–1913* (1914); later he was envoy to China (1921–25) and ambassador to Germany (1925–30).

Schurz, Carl (shōōrts), 1829–1906, American political leader, b. Germany. He studied at the Univ. of Bonn and took part in the revolutionary uprisings of 1848–49 in Germany. Compelled to flee to Zürich after the collapse of the movement, he went on to Paris and London and, in 1852, emigrated to the United States. For a few years he lived in Philadelphia, but in 1856 he settled in Watertown, Wis., and soon associated himself with the newly formed Republican party. He campaigned for Abraham Lincoln in the latter's senatorial contest with Stephen A. Douglas in 1858 and again in the presidential contest of 1860. For his services Lincoln appointed him (1861) U.S. minister to Spain. Made restive, however, by the prolongation of the Civil War, Schurz resigned this position and was commissioned brigadier general of volunteers in 1862. Promoted to major general in 1863, he fought in the battles of Chancellorsville, Gettysburg, and Chattanooga and served with Gen. William T. Sherman's army in North Carolina in 1865. Between 1865 and 1868, Schurz was Washington correspondent of the New York *Tribune,* editor of the Detroit *Post,* and joint editor and owner of the St. Louis *Westliche Post,* a German daily. He was U.S. Senator (1869–75) from his adopted state of Missouri. Antagonized by the radical Republican Reconstruction program and opposed to the administration of President Grant,

Schurz aided in forming (1872) the LIBERAL REPUBLICAN PARTY, which, though short-lived, had some effect in checking the cause of the radicals in Congress. In 1876, Schurz supported Rutherford B. Hayes, whose hard money views he approved, for the presidency. He served (1877–81) in Hayes's cabinet as Secretary of the Interior. He was an editor (1881–83) of the New York *Evening Post* and wrote editorials (1892–98) for *Harper's Weekly*. In 1884, convinced of James G. Blaine's unfitness for office, Schurz led the MUGWUMPS in their opposition to Blaine's nomination and candidacy. Schurz supported the Democrat Grover Cleveland in that year and again in 1888 and 1892. He turned to William McKinley in 1896 because of William Jennings Bryan's currency views, but in 1900 he supported Bryan because of his anti-imperialist views. Because of his honesty and fearlessness, Schurz exercised wide influence through his writings and speeches. He wrote *Life of Henry Clay* (2 vol., 1887), *Abraham Lincoln: an Essay* (1891), and his own reminiscences (3 vol., 1907–8; abridged vol. by Allan Nevins, 1961). See Frederic Bancroft, ed., *Speeches, Correspondence, and Political Papers of Carl Schurz* (6 vol., 1913); Joseph Schafer, ed., *Intimate Letters of Carl Schurz, 1841–1869* (1928); C. V. Easum, *The Americanization of Carl Schurz* (1929); biographies by Joseph Schafer (1930), C. M. Fuess (1932, repr. 1963), and J. P. Terzian (1965).

Schuschnigg, Kurt von (ko͝ort fən sho͞osh'nĭk), 1897–, Austrian chancellor. He served (1932–34) as minister of justice and education and helped Engelbert DOLLFUSS repress the Social Democrats and organize the CORPORATIVE STATE. After Dollfuss's assassination (1934) he became chancellor. In 1936, Schuschnigg forced the resignation of E. R. von STARHEMBERG as vice chancellor and became sole head of the semi-fascist state. Schuschnigg's efforts to prevent German absorption of Austria were successful until he lost (1937) the support of Benito Mussolini. In Feb., 1938, Hitler forced him to take the Austrian Nazi leader Arthur Seyss-Inquart into his cabinet. When German troops massed on the border in March, Seyss-Inquart became chancellor, and the troops marched into Austria unopposed. A Nazi prisoner until 1945, Schuschnigg settled (1947) in the United States and taught at St. Louis Univ. He wrote *My Austria* (1937, tr. 1938), *Austrian Requiem* (1946, tr. 1947), and *The Brutal Takeover* (1969, tr. 1971). See biography by R. K. Sheridon (1942).

Schuster, Sir Arthur, 1851–1934, English physicist, b. Germany. At Owens College, Manchester Univ., he was professor of applied mathematics (1881–88) and professor of physics (1888–1907). He is known for his work in spectroscopy (he was a leading authority in the field), electricity in gases, terrestrial magnetism, radiometry, calorimetry, and the mathematical theory of periodicity. In 1875 he led the Royal Society's expedition to Siam (now Thailand) to observe the solar eclipse. He was knighted in 1920. Among his works are *An Introduction to the Theory of Optics* (1904) and *Biographical Fragments* (1932).

Schütt, Great (shüt), Slovak *Velký Žitný Ostrov* (vĕl'kē zhĭt'nē ô'strôf), island, c.725 sq mi (1,880 sq km), SW Czechoslovakia, in the Danubian lowlands between the Danube River and its northern arm. It extends c.55 mi (90 km) from Bratislava to Komárno. The island's fertile soil produces a variety of crops. Opposite the Great Schütt lies Szigetköz (sĭ'gĕtkûz), or the **Little Schütt,** an island c.30 mi (50 km) long and up to c.10 mi (16 km) wide, in NW Hungary between the Danube River and its southern arm. Wheat, rye, and dairy products are produced there. In 1954 a disastrous flood submerged much of the island.

Schütz, Heinrich (hīn'rĭkh shüts), 1585–1672, German composer; pupil of Giovanni Gabrieli. From 1617 until his death he was director of music at the Dresden court. His first German work was his *Psalmen Davids* (1619), in which he used the new monodic, or declamatory, style. In 1627 he set to music a German translation of *Dafne*, set earlier in Italian by Jacopo Peri. Schütz's work (no longer extant) has been called the first German opera. Most of his works that have been preserved were written for the church, and they mark him as the outstanding master of 17th-century church music. His *Symphoniae sacrae* (1619, 1647, 1650) show the influence of Monteverdi. Later, in his oratorios and his settings of the Passion as narrated in each of the four Gospels, he combined the Venetian style of alternating choirs and the dramatic declamation of Florentine monody with the German polyphonic tradition. The resultant choral style influenced German music through the time of Handel and Bach. See biographical study by H. J. Moser (tr. 1967).

Schuyler, Philip John (skī'lər), 1733–1804, American Revolutionary general, b. Albany, N.Y. He was a member of one of the wealthiest colonial New York families. After serving in the French and Indian Wars he was a member of the New York assembly (1768–75) and of the Second Continental Congress (1775). He was a strong advocate of the colonial cause, and in the Revolution he was appointed (1775) a major general and head of the Northern Dept. After Ethan Allen and the Green Mountain Boys captured Ticonderoga, Schuyler helped to plan the Quebec campaign (1775–76), but illness forced him to give his command to Gen. Richard MONTGOMERY. When Gen. Arthur St. Clair surrendered (1777) Ticonderoga without a shot, Schuyler was accused of negligence and Horatio Gates was given the high command in the Saratoga campaign (1777–78). At his own insistence, Schuyler was brought before a court-martial and acquitted by it, but he then resigned (1779) from the army. He was (1779–80) a member of the Continental Congress, he favored adoption of the Constitution, and he was (1789–91, 1797–98) U. S. Senator. He advocated a canal (eventually the Erie Canal) and helped found Union College. His house (built 1777) in Schuylerville, N.Y., is a national monument. Schuyler's daughter, Elizabeth, married Alexander Hamilton. See biography by Bayard Tuckerman (1903, repr. 1969); studies by D. R. Gerlach (1964) and M. H. Bush (1969).

Schuyler, Fort: see FORT SCHUYLER.

Schuylkill (sko͞ol'kĭl", sko͞o'kəl) [Dutch, = hidden creek], river, c.130 mi (210 km) long, rising in Schuylkill co., E central Pa. and flowing generally SE to the Delaware River at Philadelphia. The Schuylkill is navigable by shallow-draft boats, and there are many industrial cities along its banks.

Schwab, Charles Michael (shwäb), 1862–1939, American steel magnate, b. Williamsburg, Pa. He started as a stake driver in Andrew Carnegie's steelworks and rose to become (1897) president of the Carnegie Steel Company and then the first president (1901) of the U.S. Steel Corp. He resigned (1903) to run the Bethlehem Steel Company, which under his direction became the largest independent producer in the field.

Schwabach (shvä'bäkh), city (1970 pop. 25,884), Bavaria, S West Germany. Manufactures include wire, needles, chemicals, and processed foods. Schwabach was chartered in the late 14th cent. It passed to Prussia in 1791 and to Bavaria in 1806. Noteworthy buildings include the late Gothic church (1469–95), which contains carvings by Veit Stoss and a tabernacle by Adam Kraft, and the city hall (1528). The **Articles of Schwabach,** drawn up in the city in 1529, were used in drafting (1530) the Augsburg Confession of the Lutheran faith. The Articles emphasized differences between Luther and Zwingli, and therefore many cities in S Germany refused to take part in the Augsburg discussions.

Schwabe, Samuel Heinrich (zä'mo͞oĕl hīn'rĭkh shväb'ə), 1789–1875, German apothecary and amateur astronomer. In the hope of discovering a new planet between Mercury and the sun, he made daily observations and tallies of sunspots. In 1843, after 17 years of sunspot counts, he noted a periodicity of 10 or 11 years in their totals. His discovery initiated modern solar studies and investigations of the effects of sunspots on terrestrial magnetism, weather, and plant and animal growth rates.

Schwäbisch Gmünd (shvĕb'ĭsh gəmünt') or **Gmünd,** city (1970 pop. 44,407), Baden-Württemberg, S West Germany, on the Rems River, at the northern foot of the Swabian Jura mts. It has long been known as a gold-working and silver-working center; other manufactures include machinery and glass. Founded by the mid-12th cent., Schwäbisch Gmünd was a free imperial city from 1268 until 1803, when it passed to Württemberg. Noteworthy buildings include the city hall (1783–85) and the St. Johanniskirche (1210–30), a late Romanesque church.

Schwäbisch Hall (shvĕb'ĭsh häl) or **Hall,** city (1970 pop. 23,505), Baden-Württemberg, S West Germany, on the Kocher River. It is a rail junction and has an iron and steel construction industry. The city is also a popular tourist center and, because of its saline baths, a health resort. Chartered in the 12th cent., Schwäbisch Hall was a free imperial city until 1803 and ruled considerable surrounding territory. Noteworthy buildings include the baroque city hall (1728–35) and St. Michael's Church (15th cent.). Nearby is Comburg, a former fortified Benedictine abbey (founded 1075; now a teachers college).

Schwann, Theodor (tā'ōdōr shvän), 1810–82, German physiologist and histologist. He was a student of J. P. Müller and professor at the universities of Louvain (1838–48) and Liège (from 1848). A cofounder (with Matthias Schleiden) of the cell theory, Schwann extended the work of Schleiden and demonstrated that the cell is the basis of animal as well as of plant tissue, and because he recognized the physiological and the morphological significance of the cell in advance of other 19th-century biologists he may be called the father of cytology. He described the nerve sheath known by his name and demonstrated the living nature of yeasts. Of great influence was his *Microscopical Researches . . . in the Structure and Growth of Animals and Plants* (1839, tr. 1847).

Schwann cell: see NERVOUS SYSTEM.

Schwanthaler, Ludwig von (lo͞ot'vĭkh fən shvän'tälər), 1802–48, German sculptor. Though he was a neoclassicist, his later works were more in the romantic manner and devoted to themes that appealed to the growing national sentiment. Overwhelmed by commissions for monuments and large decorative sculptures for the new palace, the Ruhmeshalle, and other buildings erected in Munich by King Louis I of Bavaria, he left the execution to a great extent in the hands of apprentices. In Munich there is a museum devoted to his work. His portrait of Mozart stands at Salzburg. The Metropolitan Museum owns his bronze *Dancing Girl*.

Schwartz, Delmore, 1913–66, American poet, b. Brooklyn, N.Y., grad. New York Univ., 1935. He was an editor of the *Partisan Review* (1943–55). His first work, *In Dreams Begin Responsibilities*, appeared in 1938. Among his later writings are *Shenandoah* (1941), a verse play; *Genesis* (1943), a prose poem on the growth of a human being; *World Is a Wedding* (1948), a collection of short stories; *Vaudeville for a Princess and Other Poems* (1950); *Summer Knowledge* (1959); and *Successful Love and Other Stories* (1961). See study by Richard McDougall (1974).

Schwarz, Berthold (bĕr'tôlt shvärts), fl. 14th cent., German Franciscan monk and alchemist. It was formerly widely believed, especially in Germany, that he invented gunpowder and was the first to construct bronze cannon. It is now known, however, that gunpowder was discussed by Roger Bacon in the 13th cent. and was probably known to the Chinese much earlier.

Schwarzenberg, Felix, Fürst zu (fā'lĭks fürst tso͞o shvär'tsənbĕrk), 1800–1852, Austrian premier; nephew of Karl Philipp zu Schwarzenberg. A soldier and diplomat, he was named (Nov., 1848) premier at the urging of his brother-in-law, Prince WINDISCHGRÄTZ, who had crushed the REVOLUTIONS OF 1848 in Prague (June) and Vienna (October). Schwarzenberg persuaded Emperor Ferdinand to abdicate in favor of the young Francis Joseph and in 1849 suppressed the revolutionaries in Hungary with the aid of the Russians. At the Convention of Olmütz (1850), he humiliated Prussia by gaining recognition of a restored German Confederation under Austrian leadership. See biography by Adolph Schwarzenberg (1946).

Schwarzenberg, Karl Philipp, Fürst zu (kärl fē'lĭp), 1771–1820, Austrian field marshal and diplomat. In 1810 he was made ambassador to France, and he led the Austrian forces sent to aid Napoleon I in the Russian campaign of 1812. When Austria joined (1813) the allies against Napoleon, Schwarzenberg was the senior general of the victorious coalition. He commanded at Leipzig (1813) and entered Paris in 1814.

Schwarzkopf, Elisabeth (shwärts'kôpf), 1915–, German lyric soprano. After studying music in Berlin she was trained by Maria Ivogün. After World War II she gained a reputation for subtlety and versatility in recitals, oratorios, and opera. She has performed with the Vienna Opera and at Covent Garden, London, and La Scala, Milan. In 1951, Schwarzkopf sang the leading role in the premiere of *The Rake's Progress* by Igor Stravinsky. Since 1954 she has performed and recorded extensively in the United States, becoming especially renowned for her lieder interpretations.

Schwarzwald: see BLACK FOREST.

Schwatka, Frederick (shwŏt'kə), 1849–92, American explorer, b. Galena, Ill.; grad. West Point, 1871, and later studied law and medicine. Sponsored by the New York *Herald*, he commanded, with William H. Gilder, an arctic expedition (1878–80) to King William Island to search for the traces of Sir John Franklin's party. The evidence he unearthed largely answered the last questions as to the fate of the Franklin expedition. Later (1883–84) he explored the

Yukon River in Alaska. Resigning from the army in 1885, he commanded (1886) an Alaskan expedition financed by the New York *Times*. Schwatka wrote several books and articles on Alaska and the Eskimo; *In the Land of Cave and Cliff Dwellers* (1893) described his explorations in the Southwest and Mexico. See W. H. Gilder, *Schwatka's Search* (1966).

Schweidnitz: see ŚWIDNICA, Poland.

Schweinfurt (shvīn'fo͝ort), city (1970 pop. 58,390), Bavaria, E central West Germany, on the Main River. Manufactures include ball bearings, small motors, dyes, soap, and leather goods. The compound Paris green is also known as Schweinfurt green. Schweinfurt was known c.791. It was a free imperial city from 1282 to 1803, when it passed to Bavaria. The city was heavily bombed by the Allies during World War II, largely because it was the center of the German ball-bearing industry. Of note is the Renaissance style town hall (1570–72). The orientalist and poet Friedrich Rückert was born there in 1788.

Schweitzer, Albert (äl'bĕrt shvī'tsər), 1875–1965, Alsatian theologian, musician, and medical missionary. Determined to become a medical missionary, he obtained a doctorate in medicine at the Univ. of Strasbourg and in 1913 established a hospital at Lambaréné, Gabon (then in French Equatorial Africa). Except for frequent trips to Europe to raise money and a visit to the United States in 1949 to address the Goethe Festival in Colorado, he remained in Gabon, establishing extensive medical facilities that received financial support throughout the world. Schweitzer was honored in many countries for his work as a scientist and humanitarian, his artistry as an organist, and his contributions as a theologian; he was awarded the 1952 Nobel Peace Prize. His biography of Bach (1905), considered one of the best studies of the master, along with his edition (with C. M. Widor, 1912–14) of Bach's organ music, made him an outstanding authority on Bach. *On the Edge of the Primeval Forest* (1920, tr. 1922) is an account of his early years at Lambaréné, supplemented later by *More from the Primeval Forest* (1925, tr.1931) and *From My African Notebook* (1936, tr. 1938). Schweitzer's philosophy is developed in *Philosophy of Civilization* (*The Decay and the Restoration of Civilization,* 1923, tr. 1923; *Civilization and Ethics,* 1923, tr. 1923; and *Reverence for Life,* tr. 1969). "Reverence for life" is the term Schweitzer used for a universal concept of ethics. He believed that such an ethics would reconcile the drives of altruism and egoism by requiring a respect for the lives of all other beings and by demanding the highest development of the individual's resources. A profound Christian, Schweitzer was unorthodox in that he rejected the historical infallibility of Jesus while following him spiritually. His theological works include *The Quest of the Historical Jesus* (1906, tr. 1910) and *The Mysticism of Paul the Apostle* (1930, tr. 1930). See his autobiography, *Out of My Life and Thoughts* (1932, tr. 1933) and *Albert Schweitzer: An Anthology* (ed. by C. R. Joy, 1947); biographies by Jacqueline Berrill (1965), I. L. Ice (1971), G. N. Marshall and David Poling (1971), and Norman Cousins (1960, repr. 1973); study by Henry Clark (1962).

Schwellenbach, Lewis Baxter (shwĕl'ənbäk), 1894–1948, American cabinet officer, b. Superior, Wis. After serving (1935–40) in the U.S. Senate, he was appointed (1940) U.S. district judge in Washington state. As Secretary of Labor (1945–48) under President Truman, he reorganized the Dept. of Labor and opposed congressional legislation curbing labor union activity. He died in office.

Schwenkfeld, Kaspar von (käs'pär fən shvĕngk'fĕlt), 1490–1561, German religious reformer. Schwenkfeld was in court service with the duke of Liegnitz from 1510 to c.1522. He visited Wittenberg during Martin Luther's absence at the Wartburg and there met the radical reformers Thomas Münzer and Carlstadt. Returning to Liegnitz, he devoted himself to the reform movement in Silesia. Luther suspected Schwenkfeld of Anabaptist leanings and opposed his belief that the Eucharist was only a spiritual symbol (see LORD'S SUPPER). After Lutheranism became dominant in Silesia, Schwenkfeld was forced to move to Strasbourg and later to Ulm. An anathema was proclaimed against him by the Lutherans at Schmalkald, and his books were banned. He offered a full statement of faith in *Konfession und Erklärung* (1540) and enunciated the differences between Luther and Huldreich Zwingli. An important part of his belief was the distinction between the outward and transitory word of God as given in the Scriptures and an inward spirit, divine, eternal, and necessary for salvation. His followers, known as **Schwenkfeldians** or **Schwenkfelders,** were persecuted, and in the 18th cent. many of them fled to other parts of Europe and to North America. Some Schwenkfeldians emigrated to Pennsylvania in the 18th cent., and there the sect still exists.

Schwerin, Kurt Christoph, Graf von (ko͝ort krĭs'tôf gräf fən shvārēn'), 1684–1757, Prussian field marshal. He was one of the most brilliant lieutenants of King Frederick II of Prussia in the War of the Austrian Succession and the Seven Years War. In Swedish service before entering (1720) the Prussian army, he served with King CHARLES XII. His most famous victory was the defeat (1741) of the Austrians at Mollwitz in the War of the Austrian Succession, after Frederick II had fled the field. He was killed in the battle of Prague.

Schwerin (shvārēn'), city (1970 pop. 96,949), capital of Schwerin district, NW East Germany, on Schwerin Lake. It is the commercial, industrial, and transportation center of an agricultural and dairying region. Manufactures include chemicals, pharmaceuticals, ceramics, and tobacco products. Originally a Wendish settlement, Schwerin was chartered in 1161 by Henry the Lion and shortly thereafter became an episcopal see. It was the capital of the county of Schwerin and with it passed to MECKLENBURG in 1358. In the early 17th cent. the city became the capital of Mecklenburg-Schwerin. It was occupied (1624–31) in the Thirty Years War by imperial troops under Wallenstein. The Peace of Westphalia (1648) secularized the bishopric and gave its territories to the duke of Mecklenburg-Schwerin. Schwerin became the capital of the former state of Mecklenburg in 1934. Noteworthy buildings include the Gothic Protestant cathedral (14th–15th cent.) and the former grand ducal palace, built (19th cent.) on an island in Schwerin Lake.

Schwind, Moritz von (mō'rĭts fən shvĭnt), 1804–71, Austrian historical painter and illustrator of the romantic school. Best known for the imagination and strength of his draftsmanship, Schwind created a gay world of dream figures. This air of fantasy was not fully realized in the monumental frescoes commissioned by the king of Bavaria. The scenes illustrating Mozart's *Zauberflöte* in the Vienna Opera, however, were outstanding.

Schwitters, Kurt (ko͝ort shvĭt'ərs), 1887–1948, German artist. Influenced by Kandinsky, by Picasso's reliefs, and by DADA constructions, he invented *Merz* [trash] constructions—arrangements of diverse materials and objects. Schwitters created gigantic architectural structures out of rubbish. His COLLAGES are among the outstanding creations in this medium.

Schwyz (shvēts), canton (1970 pop. 92,072), 351 sq mi (909 sq km), central Switzerland, one of the FOUR FOREST CANTONS. Bordering on the Lake of Zürich in the north and the Lake of Lucerne in the southwest, Schwyz is a mountainous and forested region, with meadows supporting livestock and orchards in the valleys. Cotton and silk textiles and wood products are manufactured, and there are large hydroelectric plants in the north. The population is German-speaking and Roman Catholic. In the early 13th cent. the rights to Schwyz passed to the counts of Hapsburg, but in 1240 Emperor Frederick II granted Schwyz a charter making it immediately subject to the Holy Roman Empire. The charter was revoked in 1274 by Rudolf I of Hapsburg, and in 1291 Schwyz concluded with URI and UNTERWALDEN the pact which became the basis of Swiss liberty. (The name *Switzerland* derives from Schwyz.) The canton rejected the Reformation and in 1845 joined the Catholic SONDERBUND. Its capital, **Schwyz** (1970 pop. 12,194), one of the oldest towns in Switzerland, is a summer resort. The Swiss federal archives there contain the original pact of 1291. The town has a 16th-century town hall with historic paintings, several baroque churches, and numerous patrician houses (17th–18th cent.).

sciatica (sīăt'ĭkə), severe pain in the leg along the sciatic nerve and its branches. It may be caused by injury or pressure to the base of the nerve in the lower back, or by metabolic, toxic, or infectious disease. Treatment is for the underlying condition; measures for the relief of pain include bed rest, immobilization of the leg, heat, and sedation.

science [from Lat. *scientia*=knowledge]. For many the term *science* refers to the organized body of knowledge concerning the physical world, both animate and inanimate, but a proper definition would also have to include the attitudes and methods through which this body of knowledge is formed; thus, a science is both a particular kind of activity and also the results of that activity. The scientific method has evolved over many centuries and has now come to be described in terms of a well-recognized and well-defined series of steps. First, information, or data, is gathered by careful observation of the phenomenon being studied. On the basis of that information a preliminary generalization, or hypothesis, is formed, usually by inductive reasoning, and this in turn leads by deductive LOGIC to a number of implications that may be tested by further observations and experiments (see INDUCTION; DEDUCTION). If the conclusions drawn from the original hypothesis successfully meet all these tests, the hypothesis becomes accepted as a scientific theory or law; if additional facts are in disagreement with the hypothesis, it may be modified or discarded in favor of a new hypothesis, which is then subjected to further tests. Even an accepted theory may eventually be overthrown if enough evidence comes to light, as in the case of Newtonian mechanics, which was shown after more than two centuries of acceptance to be an approximation valid only for speeds much less than that of light. All of the activities of the scientific method are characterized by a scientific attitude, which stresses rational impartiality. MEASUREMENT plays an important role, and when possible the scientist attempts to test his theories by carefully designed and controlled experiments that will yield quantitative rather than qualitative results. Theory and experiment work together in science, with experiments leading to new theories that in turn suggest further experiments. Although these methods and attitudes are generally shared by scientists, they do not provide a guaranteed means of scientific discovery; other factors, such as intuition, experience, good judgment, and sometimes a little luck, also contribute to new developments in science.

Branches. Science may be roughly divided into the natural sciences and the social sciences. For the latter, such as psychology, economics, political science, anthropology, and sociology, which are not discussed in this article, see separate articles. The natural sciences are divided into the physical sciences, the earth sciences, and the life sciences. MATHEMATICS is often considered one of the physical sciences, because those sciences are characterized by their extensive use of mathematics; but it might also be viewed as the language of science, the most important and objective means for communicating the results of science. The physical sciences include PHYSICS, CHEMISTRY, and ASTRONOMY; the earth sciences (sometimes considered a part of the physical sciences) include GEOLOGY, PALEONTOLOGY, OCEANOGRAPHY, and METEOROLOGY; and the life sciences include BIOLOGY and MEDICINE. Each of these subjects is itself divided into different branches—e.g., mathematics into arithmetic, algebra, geometry, and analysis; physics into mechanics, thermodynamics, optics, acoustics, electricity and magnetism, and atomic and nuclear physics; biology into botany, zoology, taxonomy, physiology, anatomy, genetics, and microbiology. In addition to these separate branches, there are numerous fields that draw on more than one branch of science, e.g., astrophysics, biophysics, biochemistry, geochemistry, and geophysics. All of these areas of study might be called pure sciences, in contrast to the applied, or engineering, sciences, i.e., technology, which is concerned with the practical application of the results of scientific activity. Such fields include mechanical, civil, aeronautical, electrical, architectural, chemical, and other kinds of ENGINEERING; agronomy, horticulture, and animal husbandry; and many aspects of medicine. Finally, there are distinct disciplines for the study of the history and philosophy of science.

Early History. Science as it is known today is of relatively modern origin, but the traditions out of which it has emerged reach back beyond recorded history. Technology has its roots in early toolmaking and other crafts, while scientific theory was once a part of philosophy and religion. The early civilizations of the Tigris-Euphrates valley and the Nile valley made advances in both areas, but separate groups within each culture were responsible for the progress. Practical advances in metallurgy, agriculture, transportation, and navigation were made by the artisan class, such as the wheel makers and ship builders. The priests and scribes were responsible for record keeping, land division, and calendar determination, and they developed written language and early mathematics for this purpose. The Babylonians devised methods for solving algebraic equations, and they compiled extensive astronomical records from which the periods of the planets' revolution and the eclipse cycle could be calculated; they used a year of 12 months and a week of 7 days, and also originated the division of the day into hours, minutes, and seconds. In Egypt there were also developments in mathematics and astronomy and the beginnings of the science of medicine. Wheeled vehicles and bronze metallurgy, both known to the Sumerians in Babylonia as early as 3000 B.C., were imported to Egypt c.1750 B.C. Between 1400 B.C. and 1100 B.C. iron smelting was discovered in Armenia and spread from there, and alphabets were developed in Phoenicia. The early Greek (Hellenic) culture marked a different approach to science. The Ionian natural philosophers removed the gods from the personal roles they had played in the cosmologies of Babylonia and Egypt and sought to order the world according to philosophical principles. Thales of Miletus (6th cent. B.C.) was one of the earliest of these and contributed to astronomy, geometry, and cosmology. He was followed by Anaximander, who extended Thales' ideas and proposed that the universe is composed of four basic elements, i.e., earth, air, fire, and water; this theory was also taught by Empedocles (5th cent. B.C.) in Sicily. The philosophers Leucippus and Democritus (both 5th cent. B.C.) held that everything is composed of tiny, indivisible atoms. In the school founded at Croton, S Italy, by the Greek philosopher Pythagoras of Samos (6th cent. B.C.) the principal concept was that of number. The Pythagoreans tried to explain the workings of the universe in terms of whole numbers and their ratios; in addition to contributions to mathematics and philosophy, they also made notable studies in the area of biology and anatomy, e.g., by Alcmaeon of Croton (fl. c.500 B.C.). The most important developments in medicine were made by Hippocrates of Cos (4th cent. B.C.), known as the Father of Medicine, who formulated the science of diagnosis based on accurate descriptions of the symptoms of various diseases. The greatest figures of the earlier Greek period were the philosophers Plato (427-347 B.C.) and Aristotle (384-322 B.C.), each of whom exerted an influence that has extended down to modern times. The later Greek, or Hellenistic, culture was centered not in Greece itself but in Greek cities elsewhere, particularly Alexandria, Egypt, which was founded in 332 B.C. by Alexander the Great. The so-called first Alexandrian school included Euclid (fl. c.300 B.C.), who organized the axiomatic system of geometry that has served as the model for many other scientific presentations since then; Eratosthenes (3d cent. B.C.), who made a remarkably accurate estimate of the size of the earth; and Aristarchus (3d cent. B.C.), who showed that the sun is larger than the earth and suggested a heliocentric model for the solar system. Archimedes (287-212 B.C.) worked at Syracuse, Sicily, and made contributions to mathematics and mechanics that were surprisingly modern in spirit. The second Alexandrian school flourished in the first centuries of the Christian era, after Rome had become the leading power in the Mediterranean; it included Ptolemy (2d cent. A.D.), who presented the geocentric system of the universe that was to dominate astronomical thought for 1400 years, and his contemporary Heron, who contributed to geometry and pneumatics. Galen (2d cent. A.D.) studied at Pergamum and Alexandria and later practiced medicine and made important anatomical studies at Rome. The Romans took over the more practical scientific accomplishments of the Greeks but added relatively little of their own. With the collapse of the Roman Empire in the 5th cent. and the coming of the Dark Ages, science ceased to develop in the West.

Oriental Science. In the East some accomplishments in science had been made paralleling the early developments in the West. In China scientific theories were subservient to the main schools of philosophy and theology, particularly those of Confucianism, Taoism, and, later, Buddhism. The agricultural society, which endured until modern times, encouraged the separation of theory and experiment, the former falling to the educated, scholar classes and the latter to the lower, craftsman classes. Astronomy and mathematics were used for practical purposes, such as calendar determination, and there was little interest in theory in these fields. Theories of metallurgy, alchemy, and medicine were all tied to the prevailing religious and philosophical doctrines. Nevertheless, many important practical discoveries were made. Paper was invented in the 2d cent. A.D.; block printing was known in the 7th cent. A.D., with movable clay type by the 11th cent. and cast metal type in Korea by the beginning of the 15th cent.; gunpowder was invented in the 3d cent. A.D. and firearms were in use by the 13th cent.; and the magnetic compass came into use during the 11th and 12th cent. In India an alphabetic script was developed, as well as a numeral system based on place value and including a zero; this latter Hindu contribution was adopted by the Arabs and combined with their numeral system. Important Hindu scientists flourished in the 6th and 7th cent. A.D. and also in the 12th cent., making contributions to astronomy and mathematics. Many of these early Indian works showed the influence of Greek science, as in the geocentric systems of astronomy, or of Babylonian science, as in their development of algebraic methods for solving many problems. Nevertheless, Oriental science remained inhibited by the stratification of societies that discouraged the interaction of theory and experiment.

Medieval Science. With the eclipse of the Greek and Roman cultures, many of their works passed into the hands of the Muslims, who by the 7th and 8th cent. A.D. had extended their influence through much of the world surrounding the Mediterranean. All of the Greek works were translated into Arabic, and commentaries were added. Important developments from the East were also transmitted, and the Hindu numeral system was introduced, as well as the manufacture of paper and gunpowder, learned from the Chinese. Scholars gathered at cities like Damascus, Baghdad, and Cairo, at one end of the Mediterranean, and at Cordova and Toledo, in Spain, at the other end. Many astronomical observations were made at different locations, but there was little effort to improve or modify the Greek model of Ptolemy. In medicine important contributions were made by Al-Razi (Rhazes, 865-925) and Ibn-Sina (Avicenna, 980-1037), and in alchemy and pharmacology by Jabir (Geber, 9th cent.), whose work was expanded in the 10th cent. by a mystical sect aligned with the Sufi tradition. At Cairo, Al-Hazen (965-1038) studied optics, particularly the properties of lenses, and Maimonides (1135-1204), the Jewish philosopher, came there from Spain to practice medicine as physician to Saladin, the Sultan. The Arabs thus preserved the scientific works of the Greeks and added to them, and also introduced other contributions from the Orient. This body of learning first began to be discovered by Europeans in the 11th cent. Centain technical innovations during the Dark Ages, e.g., development of the heavy plow, the windmill, and the magnetic compass, as well as improvements in ship design, had increased agricultural productivity and navigation and contributed to the rise of cities, with their craft guilds and universities. These changes were more pronounced in N Europe than in the south. The introduction of papermaking (12th cent.) and printing (1436-50) made possible the recording of craft traditions that had been handed down orally in previous centuries. This served to reduce the gap between the artisan classes and the scholar classes and contributed to the development of certain individuals who combined elements of both traditions—the artist-engineers such as Leonardo da Vinci, whose studies of flight and other technological problems were far beyond their time, and the artist-mathematicians, such as Albrecht Dürer, who examined the laws of perspective and wrote a textbook on geometry. Many artists came to study anatomy in detail. Beginning in the 12th cent. the Arabic versions of Greek works were translated into Latin, an edition of Ptolemy's *Almagest* being translated at Toledo, and one of Aristotle's biological works in Sicily. Leonardo da Pisa (Fibonacci) presented some of the new Hindu-Arabic mathematics in the early 13th cent., and the medical and alchemical works were also translated. Also in the 13th cent., a trend toward empiricism was promoted by Roger Bacon and others, but this was short-lived. The dominant philosophy of science and other fields was the Christianized version of Aristotelian philosophy created by Albertus Magnus and Thomas Aquinas in the 13th cent. This view tended to treat scientific theories as extensions of philosophy and, for example, postulated the existence of angelic agents to account for the movements of the heavenly bodies. Even so, the craft traditions continued to develop in an independent manner, particularly medieval alchemy, and certain schools grew up that were not dominated by the main scholastic philosophy. The rebirth, or Renaissance, of learning spread throughout the West from the 14th to the 16th cent. and was further enhanced by the great voyages of discovery that began in the 15th cent.

The Scientific Revolution. Science, in the modern sense of the term, came into being in the 16th and 17th cent., with the merging of the craft tradition with scientific theory and the evolution of the scientific method. The feeling of dissatisfaction with the older philosophical approach had begun much earlier and had produced other results, such as the Protestant Reformation, but the revolution in science began with the work of Copernicus, Paracelsus, Vesalius, and others in the 16th cent. and reached full flower in the 17th cent. Copernicus broke with the long tradition, supported by both scientists and theologians, that the earth was at the center of the universe; his work, finally published in the year of his death (1543), proposed that the earth and other planets move in circular orbits around the sun. Paracelsus rejected the older alchemical and medical theories and founded iatrochemistry, the forerunner of modern medical chemistry. Andreas Vesalius, like Paracelsus, turned away from the medical teachings of Galen and other early authorities and through his anatomical studies helped to found modern medicine and biology. The philosophical basis for the scientific revolution was expressed in the writings of Francis Bacon, who urged that the experimental method play the key role in the development of scientific theories, and of René Descartes, who held that the universe is a mechanical system that can be described in mathematical terms. The science of mechanics was established by Galileo, Simon Stevin, and others. The astronomical system of Copernicus gained increasing support from the accurate observations of Tycho Brahe; the modification of Johannes Kepler, who used Tycho's work to show that the planetary orbits are elliptical rather than circular; and the writings of Galileo, who based his arguments on his own mechanical theories and observations with the newly invented telescope. Other instruments were also of major importance in the discoveries of the scientific revolution. The microscope extended man's knowledge of living things around him just as the telescope had extended his knowledge of the heavens. The mechanical clock was perfected in the late 16th cent. by Christian Huygens, who also made improvements in the telescope, and thus events, both celestial and terrestrial, could be timed with greater precision—an essential factor in the development of the exact sciences, such as mechanics. Another important factor in the scientific revolution was the rise of learned societies and academies in various countries. The earliest of these were in Italy and Germany and were short-lived. More influential were the Royal Society in England (1660) and the Academy of Sciences in France (1666). The former was a private institution in London and included such men of science as Robert Hooke, John Wallis, William Brouncker, Thomas Sydenham, John Mayow, and Christopher Wren (who contributed not only to architecture but also to astronomy and anatomy); the latter, in Paris, was a government institution and included as a foreign member the Dutchman Huygens. In the 18th cent. important royal academies were established at Berlin (1700) and at St. Petersburg (1724). The societies and academies provided the principal opportunities for the publication and discussion of scientific results during and after the scientific revolution. The greatest figure of the period, Sir Isaac Newton, was a fellow of the Royal Society. To earlier discoveries in mechanics and astronomy he added many of his own and combined them in a single system for describing the workings of the universe; the system is based on the concept of gravitation and uses a new branch of mathematics, the calculus, that he invented for the purpose. All of this was published in his *Philosophical Principles of Natural Philosophy* (1687), which marks the beginning of the modern period of mechanics and astronomy. Newton also discovered that white light can be separated into a spectrum of colors, and he theorized that light is composed of tiny particles, or corpuscles, whose behavior can be described by the laws of mechanics. A rival theory, holding that light is composed of waves, was proposed by Huygens about the same time. However, Newton's influence was so great and the acceptance of the mechanistic philosophy of Descartes and others so widespread that the corpuscular philosophy was the dominant one for more than a century. The 17th cent. also saw the discovery of the circulation of the blood by William Harvey and the founding of modern chemistry by Robert Boyle.

Classical Science. The history of science during the 18th and 19th cent. is largely the history of the individual branches as they developed into the traditional forms by which they are still recognized today. In mathematics the calculus invented by Newton and G. W. Leibniz was developed by the Bernoullis, Leonhard Euler, and J. L. Lagrange into a powerful tool that was to be used not only in mathematics but also in physics and astronomy. Newtonian physics spread to the Continent slowly, its acceptance being hindered by adherents of the older Cartesian philosophy and by disputes over priority in the invention of the calculus. However, by the late 18th cent. it was firmly established. Other branches of physics came into their own during this period. The study of electricity expanded to include electric currents and magnetism, and it was finally synthesized in the theory of electromagnetic radiation of J. C. Maxwell in the second half of the 19th cent. These discoveries provided the foundation for the technological advances in communications and in other fields using electrical energy. The wave theory of light was revived at the beginning of the 19th cent. by Thomas Young and developed by others; Maxwell's theory showed that light was one form of electromagnetic energy. In the 18th cent. scientists thought that heat was a kind of fluid called caloric. However, by the early 19th cent. it became apparent that heat is a form of motion—the motion of the particles of which substances are composed. The classical theory of heat and thermodynamics was developed by J. P. Joule, Lord Kelvin, R. J. E. Clausius, and others, who showed the relation between heat and other forms of energy and formulated the law of conservation of energy. Maxwell, Ludwig Boltzmann and others developed statistical mechanics, which treats matter as a large aggregate of many particles and applies statistical methods to the prediction of its behavior. Chemistry became increasingly quantitative and experimental during the 18th cent. Joseph Priestley and other English scientists made a number of discoveries which served as the basis for A. L. Lavoisier's explanation of the role of oxygen in combustion and respiration. John Dalton proposed the modern version of the atomic theory in the early 19th cent. and Dmitri Mendeleev, in his periodic table, showed how the chemical elements described by the atomic theory could be arranged in a systematic way. In the mid-19th cent. R. W. Bunsen and G. R. Kirchhoff developed spectroscopy as a tool for chemical analysis. Also in the 19th cent., the synthesis of urea by Friedrich Wöhler (1828) established that organic substances are composed of the same kinds of atoms as inorganic substances, thus opening a new era in the study of organic chemistry. Astronomy progressed on the theoretical level through the contributions to celestial mechanics of P. S. Laplace and others, and on the observational level through the work of many scientists. They included William Herschel, who built telescopes and discovered Uranus (1781), the first planet found in modern times, and his son John Herschel, who extended his father's observations to the Southern Hemisphere skies and pioneered in astrophotography, which in modern astronomy is the chief method of observation. Another tool that found important application in astronomy was the spectroscope. Increasingly astronomers made use of the instruments, techniques, and theories of other fields, particularly physics. Modern geology may be said to date from the work of James Hutton, who postulated (1785) that the geologic processes and forces that had shaped the earth were still in operation and could be observed directly. Georges Cuvier, the French naturalist, founded the field of comparative anatomy and applied its principles to geology in the study of the fossil remains of animals of the distant past, thus also founding the field of paleontology. In biology Carolus Linnaeus instituted a system of classification of animals and plants, and improvements in this system helped scientists to arrange different forms of life according to complexity, suggesting to some that organisms may evolve from simple to complex forms. In the 19th cent. K. E. von Baer founded the field of embryology, the study of the earliest stages of different forms of life, and Matthias Schleiden and Theodor Schwann identified the cell as the basic unit of living matter. In medicine the treatment of disease was furthered by the introduction of smallpox vaccination by Edward Jenner and the recognition of the role of germs and viruses in causing diseases. A number of ways of reducing the growth of such organisms were introduced, including pasteurization of foods and antiseptic surgery. Anesthetics were introduced in the 19th cent. by several scientists, and new medications were developed through chemistry that aimed at treatment of specific ailments. Some of the greatest changes were in the area of technology, in the development of new sources of energy and their application in transportation, communications, and industry. Among the important aspects of this industrial revolution were the invention of the steam engine by James Watt and its use in factories, mines, ships, and railroad engines; the development of the internal combustion engine and the companion growth of petroleum technology to provide fuel for it; the invention of many different kinds of agricultural machinery and the resulting enormous increase in productivity; the improvement of many metallurgical processes, particularly those involving iron and steel; and the invention of the electric generator, electric motor, and numerous electric devices that are now commonplace. These are only the broadest outlines of the enormous growth of classical science during this period; it engendered an optimistic attitude on the part of many that all the major scientific discoveries had been made and that all that remained was the working out of minor details. Faith in the absolute truth of science was in some ways comparable to the faith of earlier centuries in such ancient authorities as Aristotle and Ptolemy.

Modern Science. This optimism was shattered in the late 19th and early 20th cent. by a number of revolutionary discoveries. These in turn served to attract ever-increasing numbers of workers into science, so that where a particular problem might have been studied by a single individual a century ago, or by a small group of scientists only a few decades ago, today a problem is attacked by a virtual army of scholars, each trained to a high degree of technical proficiency. To say that the growth of science in the 20th cent. has been unprecedented is at the least an understatement. Physics in particular was shaken to the core around the turn of the century. The atom had been presumed indestructible, but evidence in the form of the discoveries of X rays (1895), radioactivity (1896), and the electron (1897) could not be explained by the classical theories. The discovery of the atomic nucleus (1911) and of numerous subatomic particles in addition to the electron opened up the broad field of atomic and nuclear physics. Atoms were found to change not only by radioactive decay but also by more dramatic processes—nuclear fission and fusion—with the release of large amounts of energy; these discoveries found both military and peaceful applications. The explanation of atomic structure required the abandonment of older, commonsense, classical notions of the nature of space, time, matter, and energy in favor of the new view of the quantum theory and the theory of relativity. The first of these two central theories of modern physics was developed by many scientists during the first three decades of the 20th cent.; the latter theory was chiefly the product of a single individual, Albert Einstein. These theories, particularly the quantum theory, revolutionized not only physics but also chemistry and other fields. Knowledge of the structure of matter enabled chemists to synthesize a sweeping variety of substances, especially complex organic substances with important roles in life processes or with technological applications. Radioactive isotopes have been used as tracers in complicated chemical and biochemical reactions and have also found application in geological dating. Chemists and physicists have cooperated to create many new chemical elements, extending the periodic table beyond the naturally occurring elements. In biology the modern revolution began in the 19th cent. with the publication of Charles Darwin's theory of evolution (1859) and Gregor Mendel's theory of genetics, which was largely ignored until the end of the century. With the work of Hugo de Vries around the turn of the cent. biological evolution came to be interpreted in terms of mutations that result in a genetically distinct species; the survival of a given species was thus related to its ability to adapt to its environment through such mutations. The development of biochemistry and the recognition that most important biological processes take place at the molecular level led to the rapid growth of the field of molecular biology, with such fundamental results as the discovery of the structure of deoxyribonucleic acid (DNA), the molecule carrying the genetic code. Modern medicine has profited from this explosion of knowledge in biology and biochemistry, with new methods of treatment ranging from penicillin, insulin, and a vast array of other drugs to pacemakers for weak hearts and implantation of synthetic or living organs. In mathematics a movement toward the abstract, axiomatic approach began early in the 19th cent. with the discovery of two different types of non-Euclidean geometries and various abstract algebras, some of them noncommutative. While there has been a tendency to consolidate and unify under a few general concepts, such as those of group, set, and transformation, there has also been considerable research in the foundations of mathematics, with a close examination of the nature of these and other concepts and of the logical systems underlying mathematics. In astronomy ever larger telescopes have assisted in the discovery that the sun is a rather ordinary star in a huge collection of stars, the Milky Way, which itself is only one of countless such collections, or galaxies, that in general are expanding away from each other. The study of remote objects, billions of light-years from the earth, has been carried out at all wavelengths of electromagnetic radiation, some of the most notable results being made in radio astronomy, which has been used to map the Milky Way, study quasars, pulsars, and other unusual objects, and detect relatively complex organic molecules floating in space, raising new questions about the origin of life and the possible existence of intelligent life elsewhere in the universe. Throughout much of modern science the idea of progressive change, or evolution, has been of fundamental importance. In addition to biological evolution, astronomers have been concerned with stellar and galactic evolution, and astrophysicists and chemists with nucleosynthesis, or the evolution of the chemical elements. The study of the evolution of the universe as a whole has involved such fields as non-Euclidean geometry and the general theory of relativity. Geologists have discovered that the continents are not static entities but are also evolving; according to the theory of plate tectonics, some continents are moving away from each other while others are moving closer together. The technological advances of modern science, which in the public mind are often identified with science itself, have affected virtually every aspect of life. The electronics industry, born in the early 20th cent., has advanced to the point where a complex device, such as a computer, that once might have filled an entire room can now be carried in a suitcase. The electronic computer has become one of the key tools of modern industry. Electronics has also been fundamental in developing new communications devices (radio, television, laser). In transportation there has been a similar leap of astounding range, from the automobile and the early airplane to the modern supersonic jet and the giant rocket that has taken men to the moon. Perhaps the most overwhelming aspect of modern science is not its accomplishments but its magnitude in terms of money, equipment, numbers of workers, scope of activity, and impact on society as a whole. Never before in history has science played such a dominant role in so many areas. Modern science holds out a number of promises, as well as a number of problems. In the foreseeable future man may solve the riddle of life and create life itself in a test tube. Most diseases may be brought under control. Science is also working toward control over the environment, e.g., dispersing hurricanes before they can endanger life or property. New sources of energy are being developed, and these together with the capacity to manipulate alien environments may make life possible on the moon or other planets. Among the problems raised by modern science are such practical ones as the development and distribution of enough energy to meet increased demands and the elimination or reduction of pollutants in the environment. Some of these problems are political and sociological as well as scientific, as are such problems as control over nuclear and other forms of weapons (biological, chemical) and regulation of the use of computers and other electronic devices that may seriously infringe on individual privacy and freedom. Some have profound ethical implications, e.g., those associated with gene manipulation, organ transplantation, and the capacity to prolong life artificially. There are also philosophical problems raised by science, as in the uncertainty principle of the quantum theory, which places an absolute limit on the accuracy of certain physical measurements and thus on the predictions that may be made on the basis of such measurements; in the quantum theory itself, with its suggestion that at the atomic level much depends on chance; and in certain paradoxical discoveries in mathematics and mathematical logic. Even a detailed account of the history of science cannot be complete, for scientific activity is not isolated but takes place within a larger matrix that also includes, for example, political and social events, developments in the arts, philosophy, and religion, and forces within the life of the individual scientist. In other words, science is a human activity and is affected by all that affects human beings in any way. See J. W. N. Sullivan, *The Limitations of Science* (1933, repr. 1950); Henri Poincaré, *Science and Hypothesis* (1902, tr. 1905, repr. 1952); Jacob Bronowski, *The Common Sense of Science* (1953); Ernest Nagel, *The Structure of Science* (1961); Bentley Glass, *Science and Ethical Values* (1965); C. J. Singer, *A Short History of Scientific Ideas to 1900* (1959, repr. 1966); Alexandre Koyré, *Metaphysics and Measurement* (1968); George Sarton, *Intro-*

duction to the History of Science (3 vol., 1927–48; repr. 1968); Barry Commoner, *Science and Survival* (1966, repr. 1969); C. D. Broad, *Scientific Thought* (1923, repr. 1969); T. S. Kuhn, *The Structure of Scientific Revolutions* (2d ed. 1970); Jacques Monod, *Chance and Necessity* (tr. 1971).

science fiction, literary genre in which a background of science or pseudoscience is an integral part of the story. Although science fiction is a form of fantastic literature, many of the events recounted are within the realm of future possibility, e.g., robots, space travel, interplanetary war, invasions from outer space. Science fiction is generally considered to have had its beginnings in the late 19th cent. with the romances of Jules Verne and the novels of H. G. Wells. There was very little writing in the field until 1926, when Hugo Gernsback founded the pulp magazine *Amazing Stories,* which was devoted exclusively to science fiction, particularly to serious explorations into the future. There followed a gradual increase in popularity, climaxing when John W. Campbell, Jr., founded *Astounding Science Fiction* in 1937. In this magazine much attention was paid to literary and dramatic qualities, theme, and characterization; Campbell "discovered" and popularized many important science fiction writers, including Isaac Asimov, Frederic Brown, A. E. Van Vogt, Lewis Padgett, Eric Frank Russell, Clifford Simak, Theodore Sturgeon, Fritz Leiber, Murray Leinster, Robert Heinlein, and Raymond F. Jones. Interest diminished during World War II, but with the sweeping technological advancements that ensued there was a corresponding upsurge in enthusiasm, and the number of science fiction periodicals rose considerably. Subsequently science fiction has established itself as a legitimate branch of fantasy literature. It has been recognized that many of the predictions advanced in early science fiction works have been realized by science itself. Aldous Huxley's *Brave New World* (1932), George Orwell's *Nineteen Eighty-four* (1949), Ray Bradbury's *Farenheit 451* (1953), Kurt Vonnegut, Jr.'s *Cat's Cradle* (1963), and Michael Crichton's *Terminal Man* (1972) all demonstrate the particular effectiveness of science fiction as an instrument of social criticism. The singular use of science fiction as a vehicle for theological speculation is found in C. S. Lewis's *Out of the Silent Planet* (1938). Popular authors of science fiction are Poul Anderson, Alfred Bester, William Tenn, Arthur C. Clarke, Richard Matheson, John Wyndham, Damon Knight, C. M. Kornbluth, Walter M. Miller, Jr., Chad Oliver, Margaret St. Clair, and Peter Phillips. See the annual collections ed. by Harry Harrison and B. W. Aldiss, and their *Astounding-Analog Reader* (1973); B. W. Aldiss, *Billion Year Spree: The History of Science Fiction* (1973).

scientific empiricism: see LOGICAL POSITIVISM.

scientific management: see INDUSTRIAL MANAGEMENT.

scientific notation, means of expressing very large or very small numbers in a compact form that is easy to use in computations. In this notation, any number is expressed as a number between 1 and 10 multiplied by a power of 10 that indicates the correct position of the decimal point in the original number; numbers greater than 10 are expressed by positive powers of 10 and numbers less than 1 are expressed by negative powers of 10 (see EXPONENT). For example, 43,700 is written in scientific notation as 4.37×10^4 and 0.00526 as 5.26×10^{-3}. The larger the converted number, the more compactness is achieved: for example, the speed of light, about 30,000,000,000 cm per sec, becomes 3×10^{10} cm per sec. Calculations are greatly simplified by use of scientific notation: the first parts of a pair of numbers to be multiplied or divided are combined manually or by slide rule and the powers of 10 are added or subtracted in accordance with the rules for exponents. If the first part of the result is greater than 10, an adjustment is made. For example, in order to multiply 832,000 by 0.00035, one converts first to scientific notation as follows: $(832{,}000) \times (0.00035) = (8.32 \times 10^5) \times (3.5 \times 10^{-4}) = 8.32 \times 3.5 \times 10^5 \times 10^{-4} = 29.12 \times 10^1 = 2.912 \times 10^2$ (in scientific notation) or 291.2 (in ordinary notation).

Scilly Islands (sĭl'ē), officially Isles of Scilly, archipelago of more than 150 isles and rocky islets (est. pop. 2,000), rural district of the county of Cornwall, off SW England, 28 mi (45 km) from Lands End. On the rocky coasts, now marked by lighthouses and lightships, scores of ships were wrecked, notably Sir Clowdisley Shovell's fleet in 1707. The climate is mild, and the rainfall is heavy; subtropical plants flourish. The growing of flowers for Bristol and London markets is one of the leading occupations. Tourism and vegetable growing are also important. Five isles are inhabited—St. Mary's, Tresco, St. Martin's, St. Agnes, and Bryher. On the largest, St. Mary's, is the capital, Hugh Town, with the 16th-century Star Castle at which Prince Charles (later Charles II) stopped in 1645 on his flight to Jersey. On Tresco are Oliver Cromwell's Tower, ruins of a 10th-century abbey, and the residence of the lord proprietor of the islands. The isle of Samson has ancient stone monuments.

scintillation counter, device for detecting and measuring RADIATION by means of tiny visible flashes produced by the radiation when it strikes a sensitive substance known as a phosphor (see PHOSPHORESCENCE). Phosphors used in scintillation counters include zinc sulfide, sodium iodide, various liquids, and organic phosphors. The individual flashes are caused by absorption and reemission of radiation by the phosphor. They may be amplified by photomultiplier devices or amplified and converted to an electrical signal by photoemissive substances (see PHOTOELECTRIC EFFECT). Scintillation counters may be used to detect the various types of RADIOACTIVITY (alpha, beta, and gamma rays), cosmic rays, and various ELEMENTARY PARTICLES.

Scioto (sīō'tə), river, 237 mi (381 km) long, rising in W Ohio near Indian Lake and flowing east, then turning south to pass through Columbus and Chillicothe and enter the Ohio River at Portsmouth. It receives numerous tributaries and has many multipurpose dams.

Scipio (sĭp'ēō), ancient Roman family of the Cornelian gens. They were patricians. During the 3d and 2d cent. B.C. they were distinguished by their love of Greek culture and learning. Their wealth and extravagance were detested by the family of Cato the Elder, who worked hard to ruin them. **Cneius Cornelius Scipio Calvus,** d. 211 B.C., consul in 222, was sent to Spain (218) to destroy the supply lines of HANNIBAL, who was invading Italy. He and his brother Publius defeated Hasdrubal (215) and captured Saguntum (212). They were killed in separate engagements. **Publius Cornelius Scipio,** d. c.211 B.C., brother of Calvus, was consul in 218. He tried vainly to intercept Hannibal in Gaul, then rushed back to Italy, where he failed to hold the enemy at the Ticino River. He fought (against his judgment) at Trebbia, where Hannibal won (218) his great victory. The next year he joined Calvus in Spain. Publius was the father of the conqueror of Hannibal, Scipio Africanus Major (see separate article). Africanus Major's wife was the sister of Aemilius Paullus, his daughter CORNELIA was the mother of the Gracchi, and his eldest son was the adoptive father of Scipio Africanus Minor (see separate article). Africanus Minor was the son of Aemilius Paullus. **Publius Cornelius Scipio Nasica Serapio,** d. c.132 B.C., consul in 138, and pontifex maximus, was a son of Africanus Major's daughter; despite the family connections he led the mob of senators that murdered Tiberius Gracchus. He left Rome to escape popular hatred. A descendant of Nasica Serapio was adopted by Quintus Caecilius Metellus Pius (see under METELLUS) and named **Quintus Caecilius Metellus Pius Scipio,** d. 46 B.C. He early became a leader of the senatorial conservatives and was allied with POMPEY from 53 B.C., when he ran against Milo for the consulship. In 52, Pompey made Scipio his colleague in the consulship, and Scipio threw all his influence against Julius CAESAR. He backed the measure in the senate of 49, designed to wrest the army from Caesar. In 49 B.C.–48 B.C. he was governor of Syria, where he displayed a rapacity unusual even in the Roman Empire. He commanded the center at Pharsala and fled after the battle to Africa. He fought Caesar and lost at Thapsus and took to the sea to escape. He was met by a fleet under one of Caesar's lieutenants, and, foreseeing capture, he stabbed himself.

Scipio Africanus Major (Publius Cornelius Scipio Africanus) (ăfrĭkā'nəs), 234?–183 B.C., Roman general, the conqueror of HANNIBAL in the PUNIC WARS. He was the son of Publius Cornelius Scipio, and from a very early age he considered himself to have divine inspiration. He was with his father at the Ticino (218), and he survived Cannae (216). The young Scipio was elected (c.211) to the proconsulship in Spain. He conquered New Carthage (Cartagena) almost at once (209) and used the city as his own base; within several years he had conquered Spain. As consul in 205, Scipio wanted to invade Africa, but his jealous enemies in the senate granted him permission to go only as far as Sicily and gave him no army. He trained a volunteer army in Sicily. In 204 he received permission to go to Africa, where he joined his allies the Numidians and fought with success against the Carthaginians. In 202, Hannibal crossed to Africa and tried to make peace, but Scipio's demands were so extreme that war resulted; Scipio defeated Hannibal at Zama (202), returned home in triumph, and retired from public life. He was named Africanus after the country he conquered. His pride aggravated the hatred of his enemies, especially CATO THE ELDER, who accused the Scipio family of receiving bribes in the campaign against Antiochus III in which Scipio had accompanied (190) his brother. It was only through the influence of his son-in-law, Tiberius Sempronius Gracchus, that Scipio was saved from ruin. He retired into the country and ordered that his body might not be buried in his ungrateful city. Later he revealed his great magnanimity by his attempt to prevent the ruin of the exiled Hannibal by Rome. See studies by B. H. Liddell Hart (1927, repr. 1971) and H. H. Scullard (1970).

Scipio Africanus Minor (Publius Cornelius Scipio Aemilianus Africanus Numantinus), c.185–129 B.C., Roman general, destroyer of Carthage. He was the son of Aemilius Paullus, under whom he fought at Pydna. He was adopted by the eldest son of Scipio Africanus Major (see under SCIPIO, family). He earned a great reputation as a patron of Greek literature and of Roman writers, notably Terence and Laelius, and he was the lifelong friend of Polybius, his protégé. His friendship with Laelius has been immortalized by Cicero in *De amicitia.* He served in the army in Spain (151), and he visited Masinissa of Numidia. As consul (147) he went to Africa and terminated the Third Punic War with the capture and destruction of Carthage. In 142 he was censor. He was consul again (134) and went to Spain, where he ended the rebellion with the destruction of Numantia. On his return to Rome he openly rejoiced at the murder of his adoptive cousin and own brother-in-law, Tiberius Gracchus (Scipio's wife, Sempronia, was sister of the GRACCHI), and led the conservatives in attempting to destroy the Gracchan reforms. This culminated in a measure introduced by Scipio to deprive the Gracchan land commission of its powers and thus vitiate the agrarian law. A great public quarrel arose, and Scipio was found dead in his bed. No inquiry was made, and it was generally said that he was murdered by his wife, his mother-in-law, or some other of the Gracchan party. Cicero praises Scipio in the *Dream of Scipio,* a splendid passage in his *De republica.*

Scipione (Gino Bonichi) (shēpyō'nā; jē'nō bōnē'kē), 1904–33, Italian painter. Together with Mario Mafai, Scipione was a cofounder of the Roman school, an expressionist movement, in 1928. His highly personal symbolism depicts fantasy tinged with violence. *Roman Courtesan* (1930; Mattioli Coll., Milan) is a characteristic work.

scissor-tailed flycatcher: see FLYCATCHER.

Scituate (sĭch'o͞owāt, -wĭt), resort town (1970 pop. 16,973), Plymouth co., SE Mass., on the Atlantic coast about midway between Boston and Plymouth, in an area of poultry, fruit, and truck farms; settled c.1630, inc. 1636.

sclera: see EYE.

scleroprotein, large class of PROTEIN molecules that are ordinarily insoluble in water. The scleroproteins are employed principally for architectural purposes in the living cell and are localized in the structural tissues of bone, hair, skin, wool, silk, nails, hooves, and feathers. The major subclasses of scleroproteins include the COLLAGENS, elastins, and KERATINS.

Scodra: see SHKODËR, Albania.

Scofield, Paul, 1922–, English actor. Scofield joined the Birmingham Repertory Theatre in 1945, having his first major success in *King John.* At the Stratford Memorial Theatre he won wide acclaim for his *Hamlet* and *King Lear.* His portrayal of Sir Thomas More in the stage (1961) and film (1966) versions of *A Man for All Seasons* gained him international renown. Noted for his strong, sculptured face and unusual voice, Scofield has made several films, including *The Train* (1964), *King Lear* (1969), and *A Delicate Balance* (1973). See study by J. C. Trewin (1956).

Scone (sko͞on), village, Perthshire, central Scotland. Old Scone, west of the modern village of New Scone, was the repository of the Coronation Stone (see under CORONATION) and the coronation place of Scottish kings from Kenneth I to Charles II. The 12th-century abbey, razed by Protestants in 1559, stood on the site of the present-day Scone Palace (built 1803–8).

scooter: see MOTORCYCLE.

Scopas (skō'pəs), Greek sculptor, fl. 4th cent. B.C., b. Paros. Although numbered among the Athenians, he wandered from place to place and did not attach himself to any school. He was the first to express violent feeling in marble faces. Some mutilated fragments from the temple of Athena Alea at Tegea, of which he is recorded as architect, furnish evidence of his style and method. They are in the national museum at Athens. He is also credited with work on the temple of Artemis at Ephesus and the Mausoleum of Halikarnassos. Of his nonarchitectural work, known through Roman copies, are a statue of Meleager (Fogg Mus., Cambridge, Mass.); an *Apollo Citharoedus* (Villa Borghese, Rome); and the celebrated *Ludovisi Ares* (Rome).

Scopes trial, Tennessee legal case involving the teaching of evolution in public schools. A statute was passed (March, 1925) in Tennessee that prohibited the teaching in public schools of theories contrary to accepted interpretation of the biblical account of man's creation. John T. Scopes, a biology teacher, was tried (July, 1925) for teaching DARWINISM in a Dayton, Tenn., public school. Clarence DARROW was one of Scopes's attorneys, while William Jennings BRYAN aided the state prosecutor. Darrow argued that academic freedom was being violated and claimed that the legislature had indicated a religious preference, violating the separation of church and state. He also maintained that the evolutionary theory was consistent with certain interpretations of the Bible, and in an especially dramatic session he sharply questioned Bryan on the latter's literal interpretation. Scopes was convicted, partly because of the defense, which refused to plead any of the technical defenses available, fearing an acquittal on a technical rather than a constitutional basis. Scopes was, however, later released by the state supreme court on a technicality. Although the outcry over the case tended to discourage enactment of similar legislation in other states, the law was not repealed until 1967. See Ray Ginger, *Six Days or Forever?* (1958, repr. 1969); S. N. Grebstein, *Monkey Trial* (1960); J. T. Scopes, *Center of the Storm* (1967); L. Sprague de Camp, *The Great Monkey Trial* (1968).

scopolamine (skōpŏl'əmēn, -mĭn) or **hyoscine** (hī'əsēn", -sĭn), alkaloid drug obtained from plants of the nightshade family (Solanaceae), chiefly from HENBANE, *Hyoscyamus niger*. Structurally similar to the nerve substance ACETYLCHOLINE, scopolamine acts by interfering with the transmission of nerve impulses by acetylcholine in the parasympathetic NERVOUS SYSTEM and produces symptoms typical of parasympathetic system depression: dilated pupils, rapid heartbeat, and dry skin, mouth, and respiratory passages. Because scopolamine depresses the central nervous system, it is used as a SEDATIVE prior to anesthesia and as an antispasmodic in certain disorders characterized by restlessness and agitation, e.g., delirium tremens, psychosis, mania, and Parkinsonism. When combined with MORPHINE, the effect produced is a tranquilized state known as TWILIGHT SLEEP; this combination of drugs was formerly used in obstetrics but is now considered too dangerous. Overdosage of scopolamine causes delirium, delusions, paralysis, and stupor. The alkaloid is found in a variety of nonprescription sedatives.

Scopus, Mount (skō'pəs), peak, 2,736 ft (834 m) high, NNE of Jerusalem. Dominating Jerusalem, it has always held strategic importance in the defense of the city. Roman legions camped there in A.D. 70 as did the Crusaders in 1099. From the Arab-Israeli war of 1948 until Israel recaptured all of Jerusalem in 1967, Mt. Scopus was an Israeli-held enclave in Jordanian territory. It is the site of the Hebrew Univ. and the Hadassa Medical Center.

score, in MUSICAL NOTATION, manuscript or printed music in which the various parts are placed one above the other so that notes that are to be played simultaneously are in vertical alignment. Early polyphony was notated in score until about the 12th cent., when choir books, in which the parts were written out separately one after another, came into use. Part books, with a separate book for each part, were employed in the 15th and 16th cent. With the rise of orchestral music around the beginning of the baroque period, the modern score came into being, with bar lines scored from top to bottom through all the staffs. A full score is one such as an orchestral conductor uses, in which each part is on a separate staff, while in a condensed score two or more parts are written on a single staff. Full scores are also printed in miniature pocket editions. In a vocal score or piano-vocal score of an opera or a choral work, the vocal parts are written out in full but the accompaniment is reduced to two staffs.

Scorel, Jan van (yän vän skō'rəl), 1495–1562, Dutch portrait and religious painter, influenced by Gossaert in Utrecht and by Dürer in Nuremberg. About 1521 he visited Palestine and later Rome, where he acted as overseer of the Vatican gallery. On his return to Utrecht, he became a priest and later a canon. Many of his major religious paintings have perished. Well known are his *Virgin and Child* (Berlin), portraits of pilgrims from the Holy Land (museums in Utrecht and Haarlem), and *Magdalen* (Rijks Mus.). Scorel was the master of Antonio Moro and of Heemskerk. His style is characterized by a combination of northern interest in realistic observation and effects of light and shadow with the feeling for statuesque dignity imparted by the Italian High Renaissance.

Scoresby, William (skôrz'bē), 1789–1857, English arctic explorer and scientist. He made yearly voyages (1803–22) to Greenland, at first on his father's whaler, later as captain on other ships. Preparing himself by study between voyages, he mapped, charted, made deep-sea temperature soundings, noted the flora and fauna, and collected other valuable data along the little-known and hitherto unknown coasts of Greenland, giving special attention to terrestrial magnetism. His last trip to the Arctic was made in 1822. In 1825 he entered the Anglican ministry. He maintained his interest in exploration and encouraged the search for the Northwest Passage. He made a voyage to Australia (1856) to study terrestrial magnetism. Scoresby's several books on his arctic experiences helped lay the foundations of modern arctic geography.

Scoresby Sound, arm of the Greenland Sea, E Greenland. It has numerous fjords that branch out generally westward to the ice cap. Some of the branches extend more than 180 mi (290 km) inland. At its mouth is the settlement of Scoresbysund (1969 pop. 339), the center of the district of Scoresbysund (1969 pop. 539). The town is a fishing and hunting base.

scoria: see PUMICE.

Scorpio (constellation): see SCORPIUS.

scorpion, any arachnid of the order Scorpionida with a hollow poisonous stinger at the tip of the tail. Scorpions vary from about 1/2 in. to about 6 in. (1-15 cm) long; most are from 1 to 3 in. (2.5–7.6 cm) long. They are predominantly tropical or subtropical, but some species live in temperate regions. During the day they hide in crevices or under objects, emerging at night to feed, mostly on other arthropods. The body is composed of a prosoma (head) covered by a solid protective covering, or carapace, and a segmented opisthosoma (body) divided into a broader mesosoma and a narrower metasoma, which ends in a sting. There are six pairs of appendages located on the prosoma: short, pincerlike appendages called chelicera, which are used to tear up food for swallowing; large appendages called pedipalps, equipped with powerful pincers used to grasp prey (which is then immobilized by stinging if necessary); and four pairs of walking legs. The first segment of the opisthosoma has vestigial appendages in the form of a genital opening (operculum), and the second segment bears unique, comblike sensory appendages known as pectines. The next four opisthosomal segments each bear a pair of respiratory structures known as BOOKLUNGS, which open into the body by way of a hole, or spiracle. The metasoma is carried high in the air, in preparation for a quick stinging thrust. Although scorpion stings are painful, they are not usually dangerous to man. Exceptions are the greatly feared scorpion *Androctonus australis* of the Sahara Desert, whose sting causes death in 6 to 7 hr if the victim is not treated with antivenom, and several species of the genus *Centruroides,* found in Mexico, which have been responsible for the deaths of a number of persons, mostly children. The scorpion neurotoxin causes convulsions; death results from respiratory or cardiac failure. Complex courtship rituals precede mating. The young scorpions are born alive and are carried for a time by the mother, leaving her after the first molt. About a year is required to reach maturity. Scorpions are classified in the phylum ARTHROPODA, class Arachnida, order Scorpionida.

Scorpion, The, English name for SCORPIUS, a CONSTELLATION.

scorpionfish: see ROCKFISH.

Scorpius (skôr'pēəs) or **Scorpio** (-pēō) [Lat.,=the scorpion], conspicuous southern CONSTELLATION lying on the ECLIPTIC (the sun's apparent path through the heavens) between Sagittarius and Libra; it is one of the constellations of the ZODIAC. Scorpius contains the bright stars ANTARES (Alpha Scorpii) and SHAULA (Lambda Scorpii); a recurrent nova that flared up in 1863, 1906, and 1936; and Scorpius XR-1, the strongest X-ray source in the sky. The constellation reaches its highest point in the evening sky in July.

Scot, Michael, c.1175–c.1234, medieval scholar, b. Scotland. He served as astrologer and physician at the court of Holy Roman Emperor Frederick II, where with other scholars he translated Artistotle and Averroës into Latin. Scot was best known as a magician, however, famed for his occult learning and reputed supernatural powers. Numerous legends arose concerning his miraculous feats. He figures in Dante's *Inferno* and Scott's *Lay of the Last Minstrel.* See biography by J. Wood Brown (1897); study by Lynn Thorndike (1965).

Scotch broom: see BROOM.

Scotia (skō'shə), Latin name for Scotland, used in the Middle Ages. Today it is used poetically.

Scotland, political division of Great Britain (1971 pop. 5,227,706), 30,414 sq mi (78,772 sq km), comprising the northern portion of the island of Great Britain and many surrounding islands. Scotland, England, and Wales have been united since 1707 under the name of the United Kingdom of Great Britain. They share one Parliament, but Scotland retains its own system of laws (based on Roman law rather than the common law of England) and education. Its governmental departments are under the direction of a secretary of state for Scotland, who is a member of the British cabinet. The Church of Scotland, which is Presbyterian, is established, but there are no restrictions on religious liberty. The eight universities are Edinburgh, Glasgow, Aberdeen, St. Andrews, Dundee, Stirling, Strathclyde, and Heriot-Watt. Fewer than 1,000 people, primarily in the far north, still speak only Gaelic, and fewer than 80,000 speak Gaelic in addition to English. In 1973 local government in Scotland was thoroughly revised by act of Parliament. Nine regional authorities—Highland, Grampian, Tayside, Fife, Lothian, Central, Borders, Strathclyde, and Dumfries and Galloway—divided into districts, and three island authorities—Orkney Islands, Shetland Islands, and Western Isles—were established to replace the existing 33 counties. Scotland is separated from England by the Tweed River, the Cheviot Hills, the Liddell River, and Solway Firth. It is bounded on the N and W by the Atlantic Ocean and on the E by the North Sea. Because of Scotland's highly irregular outline (its breadth ranges from 154 mi/248 km to only 26 mi/42 km) and the deeply indented arms of the sea—usually called lochs when narrow and firths when broad—it has c.2,300 mi (3,700 km) of coastline. The Orkney and Shetland islands lie off the northern coast of the mainland and the Hebrides (see HEBRIDES, THE) off the western. Scotland's principal rivers are the Clyde, the Forth, the Dee, the Tay, and the Tweed. The largest freshwater loch is Loch Lomond. Scotland may be divided into three main geographical regions. The southern uplands, a region of high, rolling moorland cut by numerous valleys, comprises the former counties of WIGTOWNSHIRE, KIRKCUDBRIGHTSHIRE, BERWICK, DUMFRIESSHIRE, SELKIRKSHIRE, and ROXBURGHSHIRE. The central lowlands, Scotland's most populous district and the locus of its commercial and industrial cities, includes the former counties of PERTHSHIRE, ANGUS, BUTESHIRE, KINCARDINESHIRE, DUNBARTONSHIRE, STIRLINGSHIRE, CLACKMANNANSHIRE, KINROSS-SHIRE, FIFE, RENFREWSHIRE, AYRSHIRE, LANARKSHIRE, WEST LOTHIAN, MIDLOTHIAN, EAST LOTHIAN, and PEEBLESSHIRE. Separated from the lowlands by the Grampian mts. are the HIGHLANDS of the north, a rough, mountainous region divided by the Great Glen and containing Ben Nevis (4,406 ft/1,343 m) the highest peak in Great Britain. The former Highland counties are CAITHNESS, SUTHERLANDSHIRE, ROSS AND CROMARTY, INVERNESS-SHIRE, NAIRNSHIRE, MORAYSHIRE, BANFFSHIRE, ARGYLLSHIRE, ABERDEENSHIRE, and the island counties of SHETLAND and ORKNEY.

Economy. Most Scottish industry and commerce is concentrated in a few large cities on the waterways of the central lowlands. EDINBURGH, on the Firth of Forth, is the administrative and cultural capital of Scotland and a center of paper production and publishing. GLASGOW, one of the largest cities in Great Britain, lies on the Clyde; it is a thriving seaport and a center of shipbuilding, metalworks and engineering works, and varied light industry. The coal and iron deposits of Lanarkshire, the Lothians, and Fife support the diverse industries of Glasgow, DUNDEE, and several other manufacturing cities. Other important industries are textile production (woolens, worsteds, silks, and linens), distilling, and fishing. Textiles, beer, and whisky, which are among Scotland's chief exports, are produced in many towns throughout the country. Salmon is taken from the Tay and the Dee, and numerous coastal towns and villages are supported by the herring catch from the North Sea. Only about one fourth of the land is under cultivation (principally in cereals and vegetables), but sheep raising is important in the mountainous regions.

Early History. The PICTS, of obscure origin, inhabited Scotland from prehistoric times. The Romans attempted vainly to penetrate Scotland, and their successive lines of forts and walls proved inadequate to contain the northern tribes of Picts and Celts. Although the Romans had little influence on Scottish life, Christianity had been introduced into Scotland before they left by St. Ninian and his disciples in the 5th cent. In the century and a half after the Roman evacuation (mid-5th cent.), four Scottish kingdoms came into being—that of the Picts in the north; that of the Scots who came from Ireland and founded Dalriada in what is now Argyllshire and the island of Iona; that of the Britains in STRATHCLYDE; and that of NORTHUMBRIA, founded by the Angles and settled largely by Germanic immigrants. The mission of St. COLUMBA (563) from Ireland reintroduced Christianity to Scotland. The usages of the CELTIC CHURCH differed in various details from those of Rome, introduced in the S of Britain by St. Augustine. Conflict between the two was settled in favor of Roman usage decided at the Synod of Whitby in 663, but Scottish Christianity only slowly adopted the Roman forms. After the decline of the Northumbrian power in Scotland began the raids of the Norsemen, who harried the country from the 8th to the 12th cent. In 794 they attacked the islands off Scotland and soon returned to live in the Hebrides; by 870 they were established in what is now Caithness and Sutherlandshire. In the mid-9th cent. KENNETH I established his rule over nearly all the land N of the Firth of Forth. His descendants pushed into Northumbria and by the 11th cent. ruled all of present Scotland except N Pictland and the islands. Under MALCOLM III, who married St. MARGARET OF SCOTLAND (an English princess), there began a reorganization of the Scottish church and a gradual anglicization of the Lowland peoples. Malcolm invaded England after rejecting the claim of William II of England to sovereignty over Scotland, but peace followed the marriage of Malcolm's daughter to Henry I of England and allowed the process of feudalization in Scotland to continue. Although the clan system, based on blood relationships and personal loyalty to a chieftain, survived in the Highlands, feudal property laws were generally adopted in the Lowlands in the 11th and 12th cent. DAVID I (1124–53) supported feudalism with land grants from the crown, encouraged the growth of self-governing burghs, and backed his bishops in their refusal to recognize the supremacy of the archbishop of York.

The Struggle with England. In the reign of WILLIAM THE LION Scotland became a fief of England by a treaty extorted (1174) from William by Henry II. In 1189 Richard I sold the Scots their freedom, but he couched the agreement in ambiguous terms that allowed later English kings to revive the claim. The Norsemen were gradually pushed out of Scotland and finally defeated in 1263; only Orkney and Shetland remained in Norse hands until the 15th cent. When Alexander III died in 1286, his heiress was the infant MARGARET MAID OF NORWAY; she was betrothed to the son of Edward I of England but died (1290) as a child. In the ensuing struggle among many claimants to the throne, Edward I declared for John de BALIOL (1249–1315), who was crowned (1292), with Edward acknowledged as overlord of Scotland. In Edward's war (late 13th cent.), with Philip IV of France, the Scots allied with Philip, thus beginning the long relationship with France that characterizes much of Scottish history. Edward won Scottish submission, but Scotland rose in revolt, first under Sir William WALLACE, then under Robert the Bruce (later ROBERT I). Robert was crowned king at SCONE in 1306, recaptured Scottish castles and raided across the English border, and finally defeated Edward II at BANNOCKBURN in 1314. Edward III in 1328 signed a treaty acknowledging Scotland's independence, but during the troubled minority (1329–41) of David II he supported the pretender, Edward de BALIOL, and invaded Scotland. The reigns of David II and his successors (of the royal house of STUART) were years of dissension and turbulence among the nobles and royal heirs and of repeated attacks from England. Social chaos was compounded by the scourge of the Black Death plague epidemic, which killed nearly a third of the population. In 1424 JAMES I, who had spent his youth a prisoner at the English court, returned to Scotland. James vigorously attempted to revamp the laws and to establish control over his nobles. His murder in 1437 threw Scotland back into the old pattern of civil conflict during long royal minorities over the next century (see JAMES II, JAMES III, and JAMES V). A brief respite of internal peace in this period of strife was provided by the reign of JAMES IV, who perished with the flower of Scottish nobility at the battle of Flodden Field (1513). James V perpetuated the French alliance by marrying MARY OF GUISE, who brought a large French contingent to Scotland with her. The Reformation came to Scotland primarily through the efforts of John KNOX (1505–1572; see also PRESBYTERIANISM and SCOTLAND, CHURCH OF). The religious issue was inextricably connected with opposition to the French Roman Catholic party of Mary of Guise (queen regent after James's death in 1542) and of her daughter MARY QUEEN OF SCOTS, who lived in France as dauphine and then as queen. By the time Mary Queen of Scots arrived (1561) in Scotland, Catholicism had almost disappeared from the Lowlands. The turbulent career of the young queen hinged primarily on her personal involvements and on the conflict between the crown and the nobility, now divided into pro-French (Catholic) and pro-English (Protestant) parties. Elizabeth I of England maintained the Protestant party with money and arms. Mary's struggle ended in her loss of the throne (1567), imprisonment in England, and execution (1587). Her son, James VI, broke away from his guardians in 1583 and accomplished the difficult task of subduing the nobility and establishing once and for all the supremacy of royal authority. In 1603, on Elizabeth's death, he succeeded to the English throne as JAMES I of England. United under one crown, Scotland and England were finally at peace.

Scotland to the Union. Scotland enjoyed comparative peace for a few years, as many of the nobility followed the court to England. Presbyterianism and its maintenance now became the great question. The desire to bar episcopacy (governance of the church by bishops), which was favored by the Stuarts, shaped every political move of the Scottish Parliament (Estates). The COVENANTERS declared their opposition to the liturgical forms imposed by Charles I and stoutly resisted his attempt to bring them to heel in the BISHOPS' WARS (1639–40). These wars led directly to the ENGLISH CIVIL WAR. Although Scotland, like England, was somewhat divided in opinion, the great majority opposed the king, and Charles's efforts to win the Scots by yielding rights to Presbyterianism in 1641 came too late to sway the 8th earl of ARGYLL and his Covenanters. Yet James Graham, earl of MONTROSE, almost succeeded, with his wild Highlander troops, in winning Scotland for the king in 1644–45. Meanwhile, the Covenanters sought to force Presbyterianism on England, and the English Parliament proclaimed that form of religion in 1643. But the English army under Oliver Cromwell ultimately prevailed over Parliament, and the Scottish religion gained only toleration, not supremacy, in England. Charles I surrendered to the Scots, who handed him over to the English Parliament. Scottish sympathies shifted to Charles, however, and their army fought for him in 1648. The execution of the king in 1649 caused a revulsion of feeling in Scotland, and the junction with England imposed by Cromwell (see PROTECTORATE) was extremely unpopular. Many Scots rallied to CHARLES II, who was crowned at Scone in 1651, and the Restoration (1660) was cause for great rejoicing. The Stuarts, however, sought once more to restore episcopacy, and the Covenanters were, for many decades, subjected to severe persecution. The Scots hated the Roman Catholic James II even more bitterly than the English did, and the accession in 1689 of William III and Mary II was met with widespread support, if not enthusiasm. With the GLORIOUS REVOLUTION (1688–89) Presbyterianism once more became the national church. But the JACOBITES, supporters of the exiled Stuarts, caused great disruption, particularly in the Highlands, and the massacre of a Highland clan at GLENCOE (1692) tended to discredit the new government. Scotland's commercial interests nursed economic grievances against William, primarily for his failure to support the DARIEN SCHEME and for the discriminatory NAVIGATION ACTS. Constitutional union of England and Scotland, which had been considered ever since the junction of the crowns, was rejected at this time by the English, but its desirability became increasingly apparent. The question of succession to the throne was a burning issue in the reign of Queen Anne (1702–14), whose children predeceased her, in face of assiduous Jacobite activity in both kingdoms. Finally, in order to assure the Hanoverian succession (provided in the Act of Settlement, 1701) after Anne's death, the union was voted by both Parliaments in 1707, providing for Scottish representatives in a Parliament of Great Britain. Equality of trading privileges and toleration of episcopacy, along with recognition of a Presbyterian Established Church of Scotland, were among the terms of the union.

Modern Scotland. The Jacobites attempted in 1715 and again in 1745 to destroy the union, but without success, and Scotland had peace at last. In the 18th cent. Scotsmen such as David HUME and Adam SMITH stood in the forefront of the European Enlightenment. Educational standards, from elementary to university level, were high, and many English religious dissenters, barred from Oxford and Cambridge, received excellent educations in Scotland. From its intellectually vibrant atmosphere came many practical inventions to further the Industrial Revolution, including the work of James WATT. The economic results of the union eventually proved wholly favorable to Scotland, and the people gradually enjoyed a higher standard of living. Feudal land tenture slowly gave way to modern leases. Thriving commerce within the British Empire led to expansion of shipping and shipbuilding, and Glasgow achieved eminence as a commercial center. The increasing market for meat and wool spurred new developments in agriculture and cattle breeding but unfortunately led also to the disposession of a large part of the population in the Highland grazing lands during the INCLOSURE actions of the later 18th and early 19th cent. The resultant emigration of Highlanders to Canada, the United States, and Australia nearly depopulated parts of Scotland. Early in the 18th cent. linen manufacture and, to a lesser extent, woolcloth manufacture, came to be of major importance in the Lowland towns. Toward the end of the 18th cent. cotton spinning and weaving on the new power machinery of the Industrial Revolution became Scotland's leading industries. By the end of the 19th cent., however, metallurgical industry had come to dominate the economy; the exploitation of rich coal and iron fields resulted in a concentration of heavy industry in a central belt running from Ayrshire to Fife. The rise of a new middle class and an urban working class necessitated the same reform of corrupt and outmoded local institutions that occurred in England. Industrialization also produced severe social and economic distress, for which traditional private philanthropy proved inadequate, and led to outbreaks of unrest in city and countryside alike—such as the Crofters' War of hard-pressed tenant farmers in the 1880s. From Scotland emerged some of the first leaders of the British labor movement. Under Alexander MacDonald a powerful miners union developed in the 1860s. The first labor representatives in Parliament came from Scottish mining areas. James Keir HARDIE, founder of the Independent Labour party, and James Ramsay MACDONALD, first Labour prime minister, were Scotsmen. Concentration on heavy industry meant that Scotland was an important arsenal in World War I. It also meant that Scotland suffered heavily in the depression between the wars. In World War II, despite the fact that its industry supplied a great deal of the British war material, Scotland was not extensively damaged by bombing. After the war the steady exodus of population from the Highlands continued; in an effort to make the Highlands again profitably habitable, a program of reforestation and hydroelectric development, begun in a small way as early as 1922, was increased. Immigration from Ireland added to Scotland's urban population. Many new diversified industries were started to relieve the strong emphasis on heavy industry that had unbalanced the Scottish economy. Efforts to attract tourists led to the construction of many modern hotels and the development of the Edinburgh festival of arts. Scotland's participation in the benefits of the modern British welfare state has not lessened a persistent nationalist movement that urges greater autonomy for Scotland in the determination of local affairs. See GREAT BRITAIN. The oldest detailed history of Scotland is William Robertson, *The History of Scotland during the Reigns of Queen Mary and of King James VI* (1759). Two standard general histories are by P. Hume Brown (3 vol., 1900–1909) and Andrew Lang (4 vol., 1900–1907). Invaluable also are four studies by W. L. Mathieson—*Politics and Religion: A Study in Scottish History* (1902), *Scotland and the Union* (1905), *The Awakening of Scotland* (1910), and *Church and Reform in Scotland* (1916). Six self-contained volumes (1935–41) by A. M. Mackenzie make up a history of Scotland to 1939. There are several good short histories, among them those by A. M. Mackenzie (rev. ed. 1957), J. D. Mackie (1964), Eric Linklater (1968), and Rosalind Murchison (1970). See also V. G. Childe, *Prehistoric Scotland* (1940); D. H. McNeill, *The Scottish Realm* (1947); Gordon Donaldson, *The Scottish Reformation* (1960); W. C. Dickinson and G. S. Pryde, *A New History of Scotland* (2 vol., 2d ed. 1965); Gordon Donaldson, *Scottish Kings* (1967); J. G. Kellas, *Modern Scotland* (1968); T. C. Smout, *The History of the Scottish People, 1560–1830* (1969); I. G. McIntosh, *The Face of Scotland* (1970); N. T. Phillipson, ed., *Scotland in the Age of Improvement* (1970); Donald Cowie, *Scotland* (1973).

Scotland, Church of, the established national church of Scotland, Presbyterian (see PRESBYTERIANISM) in form. The first Protestants in Scotland, led by Patrick HAMILTON, were predominantly Lutheran. However, with the return of John KNOX from Geneva, the Scottish Reformation came under the influence of Calvinism. Following the signing of the First Covenant in 1557 by the great barons and other nobles, Parliament abolished (1560) the jurisdiction of the Roman Catholic Church in Scotland. A Reformed confession of faith was adopted, and the church was organized along Presbyterian lines. The first general assembly of the church met in Edinburgh, and the *First Book of Discipline* (1560) was drawn up. The *Second Book of Discipline* (1581) was ratified by Parliament in 1592. This definitely settled the Presbyterian form of polity and the Calvinistic doctrine as the recognized Protestant establishment in the country. But under James VI (from 1603, James I of England) and the other Stuart rulers who followed, periods of restored episcopacy interrupted the progress of the new organization and were accompanied by confusion and protest. In 1638 the National Covenant, a solemn promise to defend the Reformed religion, was signed; in 1643 the Solemn League and Covenant was signed in England as well as Scotland. In 1647 the Westminster Confession was accepted. In 1689, with William and Mary on the throne of England, religious liberty was secured, and the Act of Settlement (1690) ensured the establishment of the Presbyterian Church of Scotland. Confirmation of its status was made in 1707, when the kingdoms of Scotland and England were united. Questions on the connection between church and state caused division and resulted in secessions from time to time, but there was no diversity in faith. The notable early secessions were the Original Secession in 1733 and the Relief in 1761. The most extensive break occurred in 1843, when the Free Church of Scotland was formed under the leadership of Thomas CHALMERS. In 1847 the secessionists of the 18th cent. united to form the United Presbyterian Church of Scotland. In 1900 this body merged with the Free Church to form the United Free Church of Scotland, which in 1929 was rejoined with the Church of Scotland. However, some remnants of the Free Church and the United Free Church did not rejoin. Milestones in the separation of the church from the state were the transfer (1872) of church schools to civil authorities and the abolition (1874) of ecclesiastical patronage. The spiritual independence of the Church of Scotland was recognized by Acts of Parliament in 1921 and 1925. Although merger talks between representatives of the Church of England, the Church of Scotland, the Presbyterian Church of England, and the Episcopal Church of Scotland took place in the 1960s, these talks did not result in a merger. The church has about 1.2 million members. See C. S. Black, *The Scottish Church* (1952); J. H. S. Burleigh, *A Church History of Scotland* (1960); R. S. Louden, *The True Face of the Kirk* (1963), Gordon Donaldson, *Scotland—Church and Nation through Sixteen Centuries* (2d ed., 1972).

Scotland, Free Church of, in general acceptance, the secession Presbyterian church established as a result of the great disruption of 1843 in the Church of Scotland. The cause of the separation lay in the question of patronage, which by that time had developed into a problem of civil in relation to spiritual jurisdiction. In 1712 under Queen Anne an act was passed restoring patronage, previously abolished; protests and remonstrances resulted. In cases brought up for decision, civil and ecclesiastical courts disagreed with each other. The intrusion of ministers upon unwilling congregations became a serious issue. Congregations everywhere were divided. In 1843, after 10 years of conflict, a body of nonintrusionists in the General Assembly of the Church of Scotland signed a protest, withdrew, and constituted themselves the first Assembly of the Free Church. Thomas CHALMERS was their leader and organizer. Over 400 ministers and professors who formed the center of the movement signed a deed of demission, giving up their claims to any benefits of the Established Church. There was no divergence from the accustomed doctrine, discipline, and worship. New College at Edinburgh was established. All but a minority of the Free Church in 1900 entered a union with the United Presbyterian Church as the United Free Church of Scotland. In 1929 the body rejoined the Church of Scotland, except for a few congregations; the present membership is about 25,000.

Scotland Yard, headquarters of the Criminal Investigation Department (CID) of the London Metropolitan Police. Named after a short street in London, the site of a palace used in the 12th cent. as a residence of visiting Scottish kings, it became London's police center in 1829. New and separate headquarters for the CID were built in 1890 along the Thames embankment and were referred to as New Scotland Yard. In 1967, Scotland Yard moved to new headquarters also in the Westminster area. See H. R. Scott, *Scotland Yard* (1954); D. G. Browne, *The Rise of Scotland Yard: A History* (1956, repr. 1973); Ronald Howe, *The Story of Scotland Yard* (1965).

Scott, Duncan Campbell, 1862–1947, Canadian poet, b. Ottawa. He was a civil servant in the Dept. of Indian Affairs from 1879 to 1932, becoming its head in 1913. Scott began publication with *The Magic House and Other Poems* in 1893. Many of his narrative poems, such as "The Forsaken," deal with Indian life. Among his volumes of poetry are *New World Lyrics and Ballads* (1905) and *The Green Cloister* (1935). He also wrote short stories.

Scott, George C., 1926–, American actor, b. Wise, Va. Scott played his first major roles in *Richard III, The Merchant of Venice,* and *As You Like It* for the New York Shakespeare Festival. Thereafter he appeared in *Children of Darkness* (1957), *The Andersonville Trial* (1959), *General Seeger* (which he directed and coproduced, 1961), and *Uncle Vanya* (1973). His performances in the films *Anatomy of a Murder* (1959), *The Hustler* (1962), *Dr. Strangelove* (1964), *Patton* (1969, for which he won an Academy Award that he refused), and *Hospital* (1972) enhanced his image of intelligent toughness.

Scott, Sir George Gilbert, 1811–78, English architect. He was prominent in the Gothic revival as the designer of many public structures and director of a vast amount of restoration work upon Gothic edifices. His restorations began with renovations of Ely Cathedral in 1847 and included Westminster Abbey (where he worked upon the north front and the chapter house) and many other cathedrals and churches. His design for the Church of St. Nicholas at Hamburg, Germany, won first place in competition in 1844. Among his other designs were the buildings (1860–70) for the home office and the foreign office, the Albert Memorial, and St. Pancras Station, London. He was buried in Westminster Abbey. His grandson, **Sir Giles Gilbert Scott,** 1880–1960, English architect, while still a pupil submitted designs in the competition for the proposed Liverpool Cathedral. They were accepted (1903), but because of the winner's young age G. F. Bodley was placed in partnership with him. After his associate's death (1907), Scott redesigned the cathedral and created a monumental modern Gothic structure. King Edward VII laid the foundation stone in 1904, and it was consecrated in 1924. Subsequently, Scott was knighted. His many works, chiefly ecclesiastical, include new buildings for Clare College, Cambridge; several buildings at Oxford; a number of war memorials; and the Waterloo Bridge over the Thames River.

Scott, Hugh Lenox, 1853–1934, U.S. army officer, b. Danville, Ky., grad. West Point, 1876. He was assigned (1876) to military service in the West and took part in the Sioux, Nez Percé, and Cheyenne campaigns. In the Sioux territory he learned the sign language and therefore headed many scouting parties and was called upon to settle misunderstandings between whites and Indians. After serving (1898–1902) as adjutant general of Cuba, he was sent (1903) to the Philippines where he was governor of the Sulu Archipelago. He was (1906–10) superintendent of West Point and (1913–14) head of a Texas border patrol before serving (1914–17) as army chief of staff. After service on a Russian mission, he saw action in France in World War I and retired in 1919. Later he was a member of the Board of Indian Commissioners. He wrote an autobiography, *Some Memories of a Soldier* (1928), and various monographs on the Plains Indians.

Scott, James Brown, 1866–1943, American lawyer and educator, b. Ontario. He studied international law at Harvard and at Berlin, Heidelberg, and Paris. He was dean of the law schools of the Univ. of Southern California (1896–99) and the Univ. of Illinois (1899–1903) and professor of law at Columbia and George Washington universities and the Univ. of Chicago. He was solicitor of the Dept. of State (1906–10), delegate to the Second Hague Peace Conference (1907), and a prominent arbitrator in international disputes. One of America's most noted experts on international law, Scott was a trustee and secretary of the Carnegie Endowment for International Peace from 1910 to 1940, as well as director of its division of international law. He edited (1907–24) the *American Journal of International Law* and was president (1915–40) of the American Institute of International Law. His books include *The Hague Peace Conference of 1899 and 1907* (2 vol., 1909) and *Law, the State, and the International Community* (2 vol., 1939).

Scott, John: see ELDON, JOHN SCOTT, 1ST EARL OF.

Scott, Robert Falcon, 1868–1912, British naval officer and antarctic explorer. He commanded two noted expeditions to ANTARCTICA. The first expedition (1901–4), in the *Discovery,* organized jointly by the Royal Geographical Society and the Royal Society and well equipped for scientific research, was concerned with exploration of the region around the Ross Sea. Scott's achievements included sounding the sea, discovering King Edward VII Land (now known as Edward VII Peninsula), surveying the coast of Victoria Land, and making a long, important exploring trip on the antarctic continent itself; he reached a new "farthest South" of 82° 17'. On his return to England, Scott was promoted to captain in the navy and wrote an account of his expedition, *The Voyage of the "Discovery"* (1905). In 1910 he again set forth for Antarctica, this time in search of the South Pole. His *Terra Nova* reached its base on the Ross Sea in 1911, and in November he started southward on foot toward the pole. Scott and his four companions pulled their heavy sledges by hand across the high polar plateau, proceeding in subzero weather the entire way. When they reached the South Pole on Jan. 18, 1912, they found that Roald AMUNDSEN, the Norwegian explorer, had preceded them by about one month. On their retreat the heroic party was beset by illness, lack of food, frostbite, and blizzards. All five members died, the last three overwhelmed by a blizzard when only a few miles from their depot. Their bodies were later recovered, together with Scott's diaries, the records, and the valuable scientific collections. Scott's journey constitutes one of the epic events of British exploration. His diaries and the scientific findings of the expedition are contained in *Scott's Last Expedition* (2 vol., 1913). See biographies by Reginald Pound (1967) and Peter Brent (1974); E. A. Wilson, *Diary of the Terra Nova Expedition to the Antarctic* (1972).

Scott, Thomas, 1747–1821, English clergyman and biblical scholar. Ordained a priest in 1773, he served in several curacies. In Olney he succeeded (1781) John Newton, through whose influence his views had been changed from Unitarianism to Calvinism. That experience Scott recorded in *The Force of Truth* (1779), which was revised by William Cowper and passed through a number of editions. In 1801 he became vicar of Aston Sandford, Buckinghamshire. His most notable work is a commentary on the Bible (4 vol., 1788–92), many times reissued. His works (10 vol., 1823–25) and his letters and papers (1824) were edited by his son. See biography by A. C. Downer (1909).

Scott, Thomas Alexander, 1823–81, American railroad president, b. Fort Loudon, Pa. He was employed by the Pennsylvania RR as a station agent in 1850 and rose to become general superintendent (1858) and first vice president (1860). His efficiency in transporting Pennsylvania troops at the beginning of the Civil War won him a lieutenant colonelcy of volunteers, and from Aug., 1861, to June, 1862, he was Assistant Secretary of War (an office newly created by Congress) in charge of all government railroads and transportation lines. Later at various times he was called on to advise the government on the operation of its railroads. After the war he was active in promoting the enormous expansion of the Pennsylvania system, of which he was president (1874–80). His interest in a Southern transcontinental railroad route deeply involved him in politics; Scott was instrumental in obtaining the Southern support that made Rutherford B. Hayes President after the disputed election of 1876. He was also president of the Union Pacific (1871–72) and of the Texas Pacific (1872–80). See S. R. Kamm, *The Civil War Career of Thomas A. Scott* (1940).

Scott, Sir Walter, 1771–1832, Scottish novelist and poet, b. Edinburgh. He is considered the father of both the regional and the historical novel. After an apprenticeship in his father's law office Scott was admitted (1792) to the bar. In 1799 he was made sheriff-deputy of Selkirkshire. His first published works (1796) were translations of two German ballads by Bürger, followed by a translation (1799) of Goethe's *Götz von Berlichingen.* His *Ministrelsy of the Scottish Border* (2 vol., 1802; enl. ed., 3 vol., 1803) was an impressive collection of old ballads with introductions and notes. *The Lay of the Last Minstrel,* his first major poem, appeared in 1805 and was followed by *Marmion* (1808) and *The Lady of the Lake* (1810). In 1812, Scott received a court clerkship that assured him a moderate, steady income. His first novel, *Waverley* (1814), was an immediate success. There followed the "Waverley novels"—romances of Scottish life that reveal Scott's great storytelling gift and his talent for vivid characterization; they include *Guy Mannering* (1815), *The Antiquary* (1816), *The Black Dwarf* (1816), *Old Mortality* (1816), *Rob Roy* (1818), *The Heart of Midlothian* (1818), *The Bride of Lammermoor* (1819), and *The Legend of Montrose* (1819). *Ivanhoe* (1820), Scott's first prose reconstruction of a time long past, is a complicated romance set in 12th-century England. His public acclaim grew, and in 1820 Scott was made a baronet. Most of his following novels were of the *Ivanhoe* style of reconstructed history; they include *The Monastery* (1820), *The Abbot* (1820), *Kenilworth* (1821), *The Pirate* (1822), *The Fortunes of Nigel* (1822), *Peveril of the Peak* (1822), *Quentin Durward* (1823), *The Betrothed* (1825), and *The Talisman* (1825). With *St. Ronan's Well* (1824), Scott abandoned the historical style and attempted a novel of manners, but in *Redgauntlet* (1824) he reverted to the background and treatment of his early novels. In 1825, Scott was ruined financially; he had assumed responsibility for the Ballantyne printing firm in 1813 (previously, for a brief time, he had run it as a publishing house), and subsequently he had met Ballantyne's expenses out of advances from his publishers, Constable and Company. In 1825 an English depression brought ruin to both Constable and Ballantyne's. Refusing to go through bankruptcy, Scott assigned to a trust his property and income in excess of his official salary and set out to pay his debt and much of Constable's. The next few years' work included *Woodstock* (1826), a life of Napoleon (1827), *Chronicles of the Canongate* (1827), *The Fair Maid of Perth* (1828), and *Anne of Geierstein* (1829). His health began to fail in 1830; after finishing (1831) *Count Robert of Paris* and *Castle Dangerous,* he went abroad, returning to Abbotsford, his estate, in 1832, the year of his death. The remainder of the debt he had assumed was paid from the earnings of his books. Scott's narrative poems introduced a form of verse tale that won great popularity; his lyrics and ballads, such as "Lochinvar" and "Proud Maisie," are masterly in feeling and technique. Although the heroes of his novels now seem wooden and his plots mechanical, he excelled in recreating the spirit of great historical events and in painting realistic pictures of Scottish life. See his journal, ed. by W. E. K. Anderson (1972); his letters, ed. by Sir H. J. C. Grierson (12 vol., 1932–37); biographies by his son-in-law, J. G. Lockhart (10 vol., 1902) and Edgar Johnson (2 vol., 1970); studies by A. O. J. Cockshut (1969) and Robin Mayhead (1973).

Scott, Walter, 1867–1938, Canadian journalist and political leader, b. Ontario. A newspaper editor and publisher, he became (1900) a member of the House of Commons from Assiniboia West and was instrumental in securing the creation of the provinces of Saskatchewan and Alberta. An outstanding Liberal, he served as premier of Saskatchewan from 1905 until his retirement in 1916. He also acted as president of the council and minister of education.

Scott, Winfield, 1786–1866, American general, b. near Petersburg, Va. He attended the College of William and Mary briefly in 1805 before studying law at Petersburg. Abandoning law, he was commissioned a captain of light artillery in 1808 and was made a lieutenant colonel at the outbreak of the War of 1812. He was captured at Queenston Heights (Oct., 1812), but after his exchange he returned to the Niagara frontier and led a successful assault of Fort George (May, 1813). He was made a brigadier general in March, 1814. The thorough training he gave his troops paid off in July when his brigade pursued the British at Chippewa and bore the brunt of the fighting at LUNDY'S LANE, where Scott was severely wounded. Scott became a hero and was brevetted major general. The rest of his army career was long and varied. In 1815–16 he visited Europe, where he studied French army practices. He was to participate in the Black Hawk War (1832), but cholera broke out among his troops. Later that year, however, President Andrew Jackson personally dispatched him to Charleston, S.C., during the nullification troubles, and Scott ably handled the potentially explosive situation. He served in the Seminole and Creek campaigns and in 1838 supervised the removal of the Cherokee to the Southwest. His talent for peacemaking was further revealed in 1838, when he was sent to the Canadian border in the CAROLINE AFFAIR, and again in 1839, when he went to Maine during the so-called AROOSTOOK WAR. In 1841, Scott was appointed supreme commander of the U.S. army. In the MEXICAN WAR, Scott approved the northern campaign of Gen. Zachary Taylor; then he himself accepted command of the southern expedition. With the cooperation of the navy, he took Veracruz early in 1847 and then began the long march inland to Mexico City. CERRO GORDO fell in April, 1847, and Scott's army entered Puebla, where it remained inactive for several months. In August the Americans resumed their advance. Fighting at CONTRERAS and Churubusco preceded the attack on the outposts of Mexico City. An engagement at Molino del Rey was followed by the storming of CHAPULTEPEC, which fell on Sept. 13, 1847, and the way was clear to the capital. The campaign was a triumph for Scott's daring strategy and confirmed his reputation as a bold fighter. Scott had quarreled violently with the U.S. envoy Nicholas P. Trist over the peace negotiations when the army was at Puebla; the conflict caused some embarrassment at home, but after the capture of Mexico City the two men made up their differences. Scott was now very much a national hero. However, he was also a Whig and as such was disliked by the Democratic administration of James K. Polk. As a result Scott was recalled to the United States early in 1848. A court of inquiry, however, dismissed charges leveled at him by some of his subordinate officers, and he was brevetted a lieutenant general. In 1852, Scott was nominated as the Whig candidate for President, but the Whig party was disintegrating, and he made a poor showing against his Democratic opponent, Franklin PIERCE. In 1859, Scott once more took a hand in a boundary dispute, going to Washington Territory in an effort to settle the SAN JUAN BOUNDARY DISPUTE. The outbreak of the Civil War brought onerous burdens to the general, who, though a Southerner by birth, opposed secession and was loyal to the Union. He wished some delay before any military action was taken, so that the Union's civilian army could be more adequately trained. The disastrous first battle of Bull Run, fought despite his wishes, bore out his views. Old and in failing health, Scott was compelled to retire on Nov. 1, 1861. President Lincoln and his whole cabinet paid him a formal call, in fitting tribute to his long and honorable service to the nation. Many of the leading commanders on both sides in the Civil War, notably Robert E. Lee and Ulysses S. Grant, had received their most valuable training under him in Mexico. He is buried at West Point, an institution he did much to foster. Although vain and pompous (he was called "Old Fuss and Feathers"), Scott was also generous, fair-minded, and considerate of his officers and solicitous for the welfare of his men. In nonmilitary matters, excluding his diplomatic ventures, his tendency to be quarrelsome and his faculty for "putting his foot in it" made him far less successful. However, it is hard to dispute the statement that he was the greatest American general between Washington and Lee. His memoirs (2 vol.) appeared in 1864. See biographies by C. W. Elliott (1937) and A. D. Howden-Smith (1937).

Scotti, Antonio (äntô'nyō skôt'tē), 1866–1936, Italian operatic baritone. He made his debut in Malta in 1889, his London debut as Don Giovanni at Covent Garden in 1899, and his American debut in Chicago the same year. From 1899 to 1933 he was immensely popular at the Metropolitan Opera, both for his acting and for his vocal artistry. Among his outstanding roles were Iago in *Otello;* Scarpia, a role he created, in *La Tosca;* and Hans Sachs in *Die Meistersinger.*

Scottish deerhound, breed of tall HOUND developed in Scotland in the 16th and 17th cent. It stands from 28 to 32 in. (71.1–81.3 cm) high at the shoulder and weighs from 75 to 110 lb (34.0–49.9 kg). Its medium-length coat is harsh and wiry and may be colored blue gray, brindle, red, or fawn, sometimes with white markings on the toes and chest. The deerhound was originally owned and bred exclusively by the aristocracy, who perfected its scenting ability and its combined speed and strength for hunting and bringing down deer. Today it is most commonly raised as a companion dog. See DOG.

Scottish Gaelic language and literature: see CELTIC LANGUAGES; GAELIC LITERATURE.

Scottish terrier, breed of short-legged TERRIER perfected in Scotland in the mid-19th cent. It stands about 10 in. (25 cm) high at the shoulder and weighs from 18 to 22 lb (8.2–10.0 kg). Its dense, hard, wiry coat is about 2 in. (5 cm) long and may be steel gray, brindle, grizzle, black, sandy, or wheaten in color. A very strong dog for its size, the scottie was originally used to hunt small game, particularly badgers. Today it is raised chiefly as a family pet. See DOG.

Scottsbluff (skŏts'blŭf"), city (1970 pop. 14,507), Scotts Bluff co., W Nebr., on the North Platte River near the Wyo. line; inc. 1900. It is the market, distribution, and processing point of an extensive irrigated farm region. There are beet-sugar refineries, canneries, meat-packing plants, and flour mills. The city is named for a nearby butte, Scotts Bluff (alt. 4,649 ft/1,417 m), a landmark to travelers on the Oregon and Mormon trails. The first white men known to have seen this bluff were Robert Stuart and six companions, bearing dispatches to John Jacob Astor from his fur post in Oregon. In 1864, Fort Mitchell was established there as an outpost of Fort Laramie. Oregon Trail Museum is in Scotts Bluff National Monument, and Agate Fossil Beds National Monument is to the north (see NATIONAL PARKS AND MONUMENTS, table).

Scottsboro Case. In 1931 nine black youths were indicted at Scottsboro, Ala., on charges of having raped two white girls in a freight car passing through Alabama. In a series of trials the boys were found guilty and sentenced to death or to prison terms of 75 to 99 years. The U.S. Supreme Court reversed convictions twice on procedural grounds (that the youths' right to counsel had been infringed and that no blacks had served on the grand or trial jury). At the second trial one of the girls recanted her previous testimony. The Alabama trial judge set aside the guilty verdict as contrary to the weight of the evidence and ordered a new trial. (The judge was defeated for reelection the next year.) In 1937 charges against five were dropped and the state agreed to consider parole for the others whose last convictions had stood up. Three were freed in the 1940s. When the fourth escaped to Michigan in 1948 the state refused to return him to Alabama. The belief that the case against them was unproved and that the verdicts were the result of antiblack feelings in Alabama caused liberals and radicals to come to the defense of the youths. The Scottsboro Case became a cause célèbre. The fact that Communists used the case for propaganda purposes further complicated the affair. See Haywood Patterson and Earl Conrad, *Scottsboro Boy* (1950, repr. 1969); A. K. Chalmers, *They Shall Be Free* (1951); D. T. Carter, *Scottsboro: A Tragedy of the American South* (1969).

Scottsdale, city (1970 pop. 67,823), Maricopa co., central Ariz.; inc. 1951. It is a resort and retirement center. Electronic equipment is manufactured and Arabian horses are bred in Scottsdale. The Taliesin West School, a school of architecture founded by Frank Lloyd Wright, is in the city. There is also a junior college.

Scotus: see ERIGENA, JOHN SCOTUS; DUNS SCOTUS.

scouting: see BOY SCOUTS; GIRL SCOUTS.

Scranton, George Whitefield, 1811–61, American manufacturer, b. Madison, Conn. With his brother Selden he bought (1839) the lease and stock of the ironworks of Oxford Furnace, near Washington, N.J. The next year, with several other businessmen, Scranton formed a company to obtain large tracts of coal-bearing lands in the Lackawanna valley, including the site of Scranton, Pa., which he laid out. By 1842 he had developed the use of anthracite for smelting ore. Later he organized and was president of the Northumberland division of the Delaware, Lackawanna & Western RR and was a Republican Congressman from 1859 until his death.

Scranton, William Warren, 1917–, American politician, b. Madison, Conn. After a career as a lawyer and business executive in Pennsylvania, he entered politics. He made an impressive showing in his election to the U.S. House of Representatives in 1960 and soon became the recognized leader of the Republican party in Pennsylvania. In 1962 he was elected governor of the state and in 1964 he was an unsuccessful candidate for the Republican presidential nomination. After completing (1967) his term as governor, he retired from politics.

Scranton, city (1970 pop. 103,564), seat of Lackawanna co., NE Pa., in a mountain region, on the Lackawanna River; settled in the 1700s, inc. 1866. Named for George W. Scranton, it is the commercial and industrial center of the anthracite coal section of NE Pennsylvania. Iron was first forged there in 1797. Early products were coal-mining machinery, locomotives, and rails. Mining decreased after World War II; the unemployment that resulted was largely offset by a successful citizens' program for industrial improvement and expansion. Today the city has a great variety of manufactures, including plastics, heavy machinery, tanks, textiles and related items, metal tools and parts, glass products, electronic equipment, and dental and medical supplies. It is the seat of the Univ. of Scranton, Marywood College, the International Correspondence Schools, and a state school for the deaf. In Nay Aug Park are the Everhart Museum of Natural History, Science, and Art; a zoo; and a model coal mine. Other points of interest include a large Masonic temple-Scottish rite cathedral and historic blast furnaces. Nearby are a large army depot and two raceways. Many lakes, state forests, and recreational sites are in the area.

screamer, common name for gregarious, aquatic birds comprising three species in the family Anhimidae. Although they are related to the ducks and geese, they do not resemble them in outward appearance. Screamers possess some unusual anatomical features, such as a layer of insulating air cells that separate the outer skin from the body. This feature is also seen in the pelicans. They share another peculiarity solely with colies, penguins, and ostriches—their feathers grow over the body without any bare spaces (called apteria) in between. Another peculiarity of the screamers is their hollow bones. Finally, they lack particular rib bones that are functional as strengthening elements in all other birds except the extinct *Archaeopteryx.* The turkey-sized horned screamer (*Anhima cornuta*) is the largest of the family. It is distinguished by a 3- to 4-in. (8- to 10-cm) hornlike projection on its forehead and by two sharp wing spurs. A creature of the wetlands and tropical rainforest, it is found throughout most of South America. The slightly smaller crested screamer (*Chauna torquata*) is native to swamps and plains from Brazil to N Argentina. It is distinguished by a short, feathered neck crest. The swan-sized black-necked screamer (*C. chavaria*) of N Colombia and Venezuela is the smallest and darkest of the family. Using their short, conical, fowllike bills, screamers feed primarily on a vegetable diet of succulent grasses and seeds, although the horned screamer occasionally eats insects as well. Screamers are strong fliers and generally roost in trees. However, their delicate, shallow nests of rushes are built on the water or in marshes. Their white or buffy eggs number from two to six per clutch. Both sexes share incubation duties. The chicks are downy and resemble baby swans. Screamers are classified in the phylum CHORDATA, subphylum Vertebrata, class Aves, order Anseriformes, family Anhimidae.

screen, in architecture, partition or enclosure not extending to the ceiling; usually a structure in stone, wood, or metal. It frequently serves to mark the boundaries of portions of churches and cathedrals. The choir screen or chancel screen, the most usual form, separates the choir or CHANCEL from the body of the church. In many medieval cathedrals the choir screen was a richly decorated structure of pierced stonework, often with sculpture. The screens of the cathedrals of Chartres and Albi in France and of York, Lincoln, and Durham in England are especially noteworthy. Many English parish churches contain fine screens of carved and painted wood. In the basilican churches of Italy, such as St. Mark's, Venice, the chancel front was often marked by an elaborate inlaid marble parapet wall. With the coming of the Renaissance the constructing of chancel screens became rare except in Spain, where rejas of ironwork or bronze were extensively employed (see GRILLE and REJERÍA). In Greek Christian churches, the choir screen takes the form of a solid partition, the iconostasis, decorated with holy images (whence its name) and usually provided with three doors. It entirely separates the sanctuary from the body of the church and conceals from the congregation the altar and the celebration of Mass. The rood screen is a more elaborate form of choir screen that bears the ROOD or crucifix. A jube is a choir screen equipped with balconies for reading or preaching. A REREDOS is a wall or screen behind the high altar. As an article of furniture, the folding screen is of great antiquity, dating in China from the 2d cent. B.C. Widely used to adorn palaces and mansions, the screens of China and Japan were often gorgeous conceptions with carved wood frames, their panels of rich textiles or inlaid with jade and precious metals. The use of the folding screen, often showing Oriental influences in its construction, materials, and design, has continued to the present day. The term *screen* is applied loosely to various forms of covered frameworks, often portable, whose purpose is to conceal or shield from injury, e.g., the fire screen or the window screen. The term is also used of diverse kinds of openwork barriers, e.g., a bank screen, a low partition of glass or metal used to separate the public space from the teller's cage. See Francis Bond, *Screens and Galleries in English Churches* (1908); Aymer Vallance, *English Church Screens* (1936).

screw, simple MACHINE consisting essentially of a solid cylinder, usually of metal, around which an INCLINED PLANE winds spirally, either clockwise or counterclockwise. It is used to fasten one object to another, to lift a heavy object, or to move an object by a precise amount. The ridge forming the inclined plane is called the thread; in cross section the ridge may be approximately triangular, square, or rounded. The vertical distance from any point on one thread to a corresponding point on the next successive thread is called the pitch. A thread can also be placed on the inner surface of a hollow cylinder. Two screws of the same pitch and diameter, one on the outer surface of a solid cylinder and the other on the inner surface of a hollow cylinder, can be arranged so that one may be driven spirally into the other, as in the common nut and bolt. The thread on the surface of the bolt is called the external, or male, screw; that on the inner surface of the nut, the internal, or female, screw. The common jackscrew used to lift automobiles, houses, and other heavy objects is an application of this principle. The internal screw is situated in the base, the external screw on a metal cylinder; at the top of the cylinder a lever or handle is fastened. As the handle is rotated, the external screw moves up the internal screw and the object placed on top of the jack is lifted. The mechanical advantage of the jackscrew, as of any other screw, is theoretically the ratio between the circumference through which the end of the handle moves and the pitch of the screw. Since, however, there is much friction in the operation of a screw, the amount of WORK put into this machine is much greater than the amount done, and the efficiency is small. On the other hand, the small effort necessary to turn the handle, when compared to the enormous load raised, makes such a device of great value. The screw is often used for making delicate adjustments of tools and machines, e.g., in the micrometer screw and in the carburetor of the gasoline engine (for regulating the flow of gasoline). The self-tapping screw has notches in the first few threads that can cut female threads in a hollow cylinder. Wood and metal screws, the carpenter's and machinist's vise, the propeller of a boat or airplane, Archimedes' screw, and many other devices are applications of the screw.

screwpine, any plant of the genus *Pandanus,* tropical shrubs or trees characterized by aerial prop roots, ranging throughout the Old World tropics, especially in the Pacific. The usually spiral arrangement of clusters of long, slender leaves gives the genus its common name. Locally, screwpines are an important source of thatch, matting, clothing, and edible fruit. Although none are indigenous to the United States, several species (especially *P. candelabrum,* the candelabrum tree) are cultivated as ornamentals in the South and in greenhouses. The genus is classified in the division MAGNOLIOPHYTA, class Liliatae, order Pandanales, family Pandanaceae.

screwworm: see BLOWFLY.

Scriabin, Aleksandr Nikolayevich (əlyĭksän′dər nyēkəlī′əvĭch skrēäbēn′, skrēä′bĭn), 1872–1915, Russian composer and pianist. The name is sometimes spelled Skriabin. He studied at the Moscow Conservatory, where he later taught (1898–1903). In his piano compositions, including nine sonatas and such pieces as *Satanic Poem,* he introduced chords built in fourths instead of the conventional major and minor triads, producing an exotic, mystical effect. He aspired toward a fusion of the arts, and his *Divine Poem* (1903), a programmatic orchestral work, attempts to unite music and philosophy. *Prometheus: a Poem of Fire* (1909–10) calls for a color organ that produces a play of lights upon a screen during the performance. A projected composition, *Mystery,* that would have employed the media of all the arts, including colors and scents, was never realized. See biography by Faubion Bowers (2 vol., 1969); M. D. Calvocoressi and Gerald Abraham, *Masters of Russian Music* (1936).

Scribe, Augustin Eugène (ōgüstăN′ özhĕn′ skrēb), 1791–1861, French dramatist and librettist. He began his prolific and highly successful writing career with vaudeville sketches. One of the first playwrights to mirror bourgeois morality and life, he infused 19th-century French opera and drama with liberal political and religious ideas. Among the best of his comedies, which are notable for their well-structured plots, is *Bataille de Dames* (1851). His historical drama *Adrienne Lecouvreur* (1849) was later adapted as an opera. Scribe wrote librettos for about 60 operas by such composers as Auber, Meyerbeer, Jacques Halévy, Vincenzo Bellini, and Verdi. See study by N. C. Arvin (1924).

scribe (skrīb), originally a Jewish scholar who knew the art of writing, later one of the official teachers (called in Hebrew, *Soferim*) of Jewish law as based upon the Old Testament and accumulated traditions. The work of the scribes developed into the Oral Law, as distinct from the Written Law of the Torah. The name in its official designation of teacher was first applied to Ezra, c.444 B.C. These scribes were followed in succession by the TANNAIM, the AMORAIM, the SABORAIM, and the GAONIM.

Scriblerus Club, English literary group formed about 1713 to satirize "all the false tastes in learning." Among its chief members were Arbuthnot, Gay, Thomas Parnell, Pope, and Swift. Meetings of the club were discontinued after 1714. The club's major production, "Memoirs of . . . Martinus Scriblerus," was published in Pope's prose works in 1741, although it is considered to be primarily the work of Arbuthnot. The influence of the club is seen in Swift's *Gulliver's Travels* and Pope's *Dunciad.* See Alexander Pope et al., *Memoirs of the Extraordinary Life, Works and Discoveries of Martinus Scriblerus* (ed. by Charles Kerby-Miller, 1950; repr. 1966).

Scribner, Charles, 1821–71, American publisher, b. New York City. He founded in 1846 the publishing house that in 1878 became Charles Scribner's Sons and in 1870 he began *Scribner's Monthly,* which in 1881 became the *Century Magazine.* His son, **Charles Scribner,** 1854–1930, became head of the firm in 1879 and founded *Scribner's Magazine,* a literary periodical, in 1887. He was the donor of the Princeton University Press building.

scrip, temporary substitute for money, securities, or other valuable claims. Business enterprises and municipalities have at times, especially when short of cash, paid employees in scrip, and communities have facilitated trade by using it. Various devices have made it acceptable, e.g., a store that would receive it in exchange for goods. The term *scrip* has also been applied to money of fractional denominations.

Scripps, Edward Wyllis, 1854–1926, American newspaper publisher, b. Rushville, Ill. He began (1873) his career on the staff of the Detroit *Evening News,* a paper founded and edited by his half brother James Edmund Scripps. His first independent venture was starting the Cleveland *Penny Press* (later the *Press*) in 1878. He purchased several additional papers and in 1895, with his manager, Milton A. McRae, and his half brother George Scripps as partners, he set up the Scripps-McRae League, a powerful chain of newspapers. The first such chain in the United States, the Scripps-McRae League was liberal in politics and a crusader for labor. It developed its own news service, and in 1907 Scripps set up the United Press Association, with Roy W. Howard as manager. Scripps also organized the Newspaper Enterprise Association to furnish his papers with features, cartoons, and illustrations. In 1920 he started the Science Service for newspapers; later he endowed a foundation for population research at Miami Univ. at Oxford, Ohio, and the Scripps Institution of Oceanography at La Jolla, Calif. Scripps's son, Robert P. Scripps, became the partner of Roy Howard in 1922, and the newspaper chain was known as the Scripps-Howard papers. See Edward Scripps's writings, *Damned Old Crank* (ed. by C.R. McCabe, 1951); biography by Gilson Gardner (1932, repr. 1971).

Scripps College: see CLAREMONT COLLEGES.

Scripps Institution of Oceanography: see CALIFORNIA, UNIV. OF.

scrod: see COD.

Scroggs, Sir William, 1623?–1683, English jurist. Educated at Oxford and trained in law at Gray's Inn, he became (1669) a king's sergeant, was made (1676) justice in common pleas through the influence of the earl of Danby, and became (1678) lord chief justice. In the early trials for the alleged Popish Plot (see OATES, TITUS) Scroggs discriminated against and abused Roman Catholic defendants notoriously. In the case of Sir George Wakeman (1679), the queen's physician, who was accused of plotting to poison the king, Scroggs changed his stand, impugned the testimony of Oates and his fellow conspirators, and brought about the acquittal of Wakeman. Subsequently, Scroggs was one of the justices who discharged the grand jury that was to consider the impeachment of the duke of York (later James II) as a Roman Catholic recusant. Scroggs was attacked by fanatical Protestants as having yielded to court pressure. An effort was made to impeach and try him, but it failed (1681) when Charles II dissolved Parliament. Scroggs was supplanted on the bench, however, and retired on a pension from the crown.

Scrooby, village, Nottinghamshire, central England. It was the home of William Brewster, the Plymouth colonist, and other founding members of the group later called the Pilgrims.

Scrope, Richard Le (lə skro͞op), 1350?–1405, English archbishop. He probably studied law at both Oxford and Cambridge. Having taken priest's orders in 1377, he rose steadily in church rank. In 1386 he became bishop of Coventry and Lichfield, and in 1398 at the request of Richard II the pope made Scrope archbishop of York. Scrope at first supported Henry IV, but in 1405 he issued an indictment of Henry's government and raised an armed body of supporters. By the guile of the leader of the king's forces, the earl of Westmoreland, Scrope was arrested and imprisoned. He was convicted, and his execution, held at York as an example to the people, tended to elevate him as a martyr.

scrotum: see TESTIS.

scrub typhus: see RICKETTSIA; TYPHUS.

scruple: see ENGLISH UNITS OF MEASUREMENT.

scuba: see DIVING, DEEP-SEA.

Scudder, Janet, 1873–1940, American sculptor, b. Terre Haute, Ind., studied at the Art Academy of Cincinnati, with Lorado Taft at the Art Institute of Chicago, and in Paris. Her fountains and other garden figures, usually joyous, playful children, are widely known. Among them are the *Frog Fountain* (Metropolitan Mus.); the *Tortoise Fountain* (Peabody Inst., Baltimore); and *Seated Faun* (Brooklyn Mus., N.Y.). See her autobiography, *Modeling My Life* (1925).

Scudder, Samuel Hubbard, 1837–1911, American entomologist, b. Boston, grad. Williams (B.A., 1857) and Harvard (B.S., 1862). The founder of American insect paleontology and an authority on Orthoptera and Lepidoptera, he was assistant to Louis Agassiz (1862–64), custodian of the Boston Society of Natural History (1864–70), assistant librarian of Harvard (1879–82), and paleontologist of the U.S. Geological Survey (1886–92). His works include *A Century of Orthoptera* (1879), *Butterflies: Their Structure, Changes, and Life-Histories* (1881), and *Fossil Insects of North America* (1890).

Scudéry, Madeleine de (mädəlĕn' də skü̇därē'), 1607?–1701, French novelist. Prominent at the Rambouillet salon, she later had one of the chief literary salons of Paris. Her two principal works, *Artamène; ou, Le Grand Cyrus* (1649–53) and *Clélie* (1654–60), are long pseudohistorical novels, full of fashionable sentiment and preciosity. They were extremely popular and all were translated into English. On the title pages appeared only the name of her brother, **Georges de Scudéry** (zhôrzh), 1601–67, who was probably only a secondary collaborator. Georges wrote plays and other works and actively attacked Corneille's *Cid.*

sculling: see ROWING.

sculpin, common name for a member of the large family Cottidae, bizarre fishes with large, spiny or armored heads and short, tapering bodies, found in both marine and freshwater habitats. The family includes the muddlers and some species called bullheads. Sculpins are cosmopolitan in arctic and northern waters. They feed at the bottom on crabs and small fishes. Of little food value, they are occasionally used as bait. The longhorned sculpin (1 ft/30 cm) and the shorthorned sculpin have sharp spines on the head. Sculpins have no scales, but are variously adorned with prickles on the head and fins. The sea raven has large teeth and a prickly skin and swells when caught. The cabezon of the Pacific reaches a weight of 25 lb (11.3 kg). The muddlers are a widespread freshwater group found in northeastern and Mississippi basin streams with gravel bottoms. They have huge pectoral fins shaped like butterfly wings with which they hang onto stones. The grotesque sea robins and flying gurnards, with fins modified into "wings" and "talons" for creeping on the ocean floor, resemble the sculpins but are of a different family. Sculpins are classified in the phylum CHORDATA, subphylum Vertebrata, class Osteichthyes, order Perciformes, family Cottidae.

sculpture, art of producing in three dimensions representations of natural or imagined forms. It includes sculpture in the round, which can be viewed from any direction, as well as incised RELIEF, in which the lines are merely cut in a flat surface. It embraces such varied techniques as modeling, carving, casting, and construction—techniques that materially condition the character of the work. Whereas modeling permits addition as well as subtraction of the material and is highly flexible, carving is strictly limited by the original block from which material must be subtracted. Carvers, therefore, have sometimes had recourse to construction in which separate pieces of the same or different material are mechanically joined together. Casting is a reproduction technique that duplicates the form of an original whether modeled, carved, or constructed, but it also makes possible certain effects that are impractical in the other techniques. Top-heavy works that would require external support in clay or stone can stand alone in the lighter-weight medium of hollow cast metal. The principal sculptural techniques have undergone little change throughout the ages. Hand modeling in wax (see WAX FIGURES), PAPIER-MACHÉ, or clay remains unaltered, although the firing of the clay from simple terra-cotta to elaborately glazed ceramics has varied greatly. Carving has for centuries made use of such varied materials as stone, wood, bone, and, more recently, plastics, and carvers have long employed many types of hammers, chisels, drills, gauges, and saws. For carrying out monumental works from small studies, various mechanical means have been developed for approximating the proportions of the original study. Bronze casting is also a technique of extreme antiquity (see BRONZE SCULPTURE). The Greeks and Chinese mastered the CIRE PERDUE (lost-wax) process, which was revived in the Renaissance and widely practiced until modern times. Little Greek sculpture in bronze has survived, apparently because the metal was later melted down for other purposes, but the material itself resists exposure better than stone and was preferred by the Greeks for their extensive art of public sculpture. Metal may also be cast in solid, hammered, carved, or incised forms. The MOBILE, a construction that moves and is intended to be seen in motion, utilizes a wide variety of materials and techniques (see also STABILE). Contemporary practice emphasizes the beauty of materials and the expression of their nature in the work. Sculpture has been a means of human expression since prehistoric times. The ancient cultures of Egypt and Mesopotamia produced an enormous number of sculptural masterworks, frequently monolithic, that had ritual significance beyond aesthetic considerations (see EGYPTIAN ART; ASSYRIAN ART; SUMERIAN AND BABYLONIAN ART; HITTITE ART; PHOENICIAN ART). The sculptors of the ancient Americas developed superb, sophisticated techniques and styles to enhance their works, which were also symbolic in nature (see PRE-COLUMBIAN ART AND ARCHITECTURE; NORTH AMERICAN INDIAN ART). The freestanding and relief sculpture of the ancient Greeks developed from the rigidity of archaic forms. It became, during the classical and Hellenistic eras, the representation of the intellectual idealization of its principal subject, the human form. The concept was so magnificently realized by means of naturalistic handling as to become the inspiration for centuries of European art. Roman sculpture borrowed and copied wholesale from the Greek in style and techniques, but it made an important original contribution in its extensive art of PORTRAITURE, forsaking the Greek ideal by particularizing the individual (see GREEK ART; ETRUSCAN ART; ROMAN ART). In the Orient sculpture has been a highly developed art form since antiquity (see CHINESE ART; JAPANESE ART; INDIAN ART AND ARCHITECTURE). In Europe the great religious architectural sculptures of the Romanesque and Gothic periods form integral parts of the church buildings, and often a single cathedral incorporates thousands of figural and narrative carvings. Outstanding among the Romanesque sculptural programs of the cathedrals and churches of Europe are those at Vézelay, Moissac, and Autun (France); Hildesheim (Germany); and Santiago de Compostela (Portugal). Remarkable sculptures of the Gothic era are to be found at Chartres and Rheims (France); Bamberg and Cologne (Germany). Most of this art is anonymous, but as early as the 13th cent. the individual sculptor gained prominence in Italy with Nicola and Giovanni Pisano, who preceded a long line of famous Italian Renaissance sculptors from Della Quercia to Giovanni da Bologna. The center of the art was Florence, where the great masters found abundant public, ecclesiastical, and private patronage. The city was enriched by the masterpieces of Ghiberti, Donatello, the Della Robbia family, the Pollaiuolo brothers, Cellini, and Michelangelo. The northern Renaissance also produced important masters who were well known individually, such as the German Peter Vischer the elder, the Flemish Claus Sluter, and Pilon and Goujon in France. There a courtly and secular art flourished under royal patronage during the 16th and 17th cent. In Italy the essence of the high baroque was expressed in the dynamism, technical perfection, originality, and unparalleled brilliance of the works of the sculptor-architect Bernini. The sculpture of Puget in France was more consistently Baroque in style and theme than that of his contemporaries Girardon and the Coustous. The 18th cent. modified the dramatic and grandiose style of the baroque to produce the more intimate art of Clodion and Houdon, and it also saw the birth of neoclassicism in the work of Canova. This derivative style flourished well into the 19th cent. in the work of Thorvaldsen and his followers, but concurrent with the neoclassicists, and then superceding them, came a long and distinguished line of French realist sculptors from Rude to Rodin. Rodin's innovations in expressive techniques helped many 20th-century sculptors to free their work from the extreme realism of the preceding period and also from the long domination of the Greek ideal. In the work of Aristide Maillol, that ideal predominates. The influence of other traditions, such as those of African Negro sculpture and Aztec sculpture (in both of which a more direct expression of materials, textures, and techniques is found), has contributed to this liberation (see AFRICAN ART). Among the gifted 20th-century sculptors who have explored different and highly original applications of the art are sculptors working internationally, including Pablo Picasso, Constantin Brancusi, Jacques Lipschitz, Naum Gabo, Antoine Pevsner, Ossip Zadkine, Alberto Giacometti, and Ivan Meštrović. Important contributions have also been made by the sculptors Jacob Epstein, Henry Moore, and Barbara Hepworth (English); Aristide Maillol, Charles Despiau, and Jean Arp (French); Ernst Barlach, Wilhelm Lehmbruck, and Georg Kolbe (German); Julio González (Spanish); Giacomo Manzù and Marino Marini (Italian); and Alexander Calder, William Zorach, David Smith, Richard Lippold, Eva Hesse, and Louise Nevelson (American). A new element of much recent sculpture is movement: In kinetic works the sculptures are so balanced as to move when touched by the viewer; others are driven by machine. Large moving and stationary works in metal are frequently manufactured and assembled by machinists in factories according to the sculptor's design specifications. See also articles on individual sculptors, e.g., Naum GABO, and articles on special techniques, e.g., MODEL AND MODELING. See Jean Selz, *Modern Sculpture* (1963); Sir Herbert Read, *A Concise History of Modern Sculpture* (1964); Hans Koepf, *Masterpieces of Sculpture* (1966); Germain Bazin, *The History of World Sculpture* (tr. 1968); Sheldon Cheney, *Sculpture of the World* (1968); A. M. Hammacher, *The Evolution of Modern Sculpture* (1969).

Scunthorpe, municipal borough (1971 pop. 70,880), in the Parts of Lindsey, Lincolnshire, E England. Situated on an ironstone field, it is a center of iron and steel manufacture. Light engineering and the production of tar and clothing are other industries. In 1974, Scunthorpe became part of the new nonmetropolitan county of Humberside.

scup: see PORGY.

scurvy, deficiency disorder resulting from a lack of vitamin C (ascorbic acid) in the diet. Vitamin C is widespread in plant tissues, with particularly high concentrations occurring in citrus fruits (oranges, lemons, limes, grapefruits); tomatoes, potatoes, cabbages, and green peppers are also good sources of this vitamin. Scurvy was a serious problem in the past when fresh fruits and vegetables were not available during the winter in many parts of the world. It was especially common among sailors in the days when only nonperishable foods could be stocked aboard ship. More than half the crew of Vasco da Gama died from scurvy on his first trip (1497–99) around the Cape of Good Hope. In 1747 the Scottish naval surgeon James Lind treated scurvy-ridden sailors with lemons and oranges and obtained dramatic cures. In 1795 the British navy began to distribute regular rations of lime juice during long sea voyages (hence the name *limeys* for British sailors), a measure that was largely successful in preventing scurvy. It was probably the first disease to be definitely associated with a dietary deficiency. Scurvy results in the weakening of capillaries, which causes hemorrhages into the tissues, bleeding of the gums, loosening of the teeth, anemia, and general debility. In infants there is also interference with bone development. Severe phases of the disorder can result in death. Scurvy is treated with large doses of vitamin C. Modern methods of transporting and preserving foods have made a diet rich in vitamin C available everywhere throughout the year, and even infants' diets include orange juice. The vitamin is also available in tablet or syrup form.

scutage (skyo͞o'tĭj), feudal payment, usually in cash, given in lieu of actual military service due from a vassal to an overlord. It applied especially to the vassals of the king. Scutage collection increased noticeably in the later 12th cent., no doubt partly because of the rise of a professional military class of knights, with the consequent trend to commutation of military service. Subinfeudation (the system by which a vassal himself became an overlord, granting part of his fief to one who in turn became his vassal) may also have complicated the collection of military service and made money payments more feasible. In England the wars of the king for his French territories in the 12th, 13th, and 14th cent. were a great drain on the kingdom. The king obtained the necessary funds by scutages on his vassals and their subvassals. The barons resisted the imposition of scutage, and one of their major demands against King John concerned scutage. In the Magna Carta (1215), John pledged himself to collect scutage only with the "common counsel" of his barons. In later times the more important vassals collected the scutage from their subvassals, acting as tax farmers. The growth of taxes after the time of Edward III of England entirely displaced the feudal tax of scutage.

Scutari: see SHKODËR, Albania.

Scutari, Turkey: see ÜSKÜDAR.

Scutari, Lake (sko͞o'tərē), Albanian *Ligeni i Shkodrës*, Serbo-Croatian *Skadarsko Jezero*, c.25 mi (40 km) long and from 4 to 8 mi (6.4–12.9 km) wide, SE Europe, on the Yugoslav-Albanian border. The largest lake of the Balkan Peninsula, it varies seasonally in size (c.150–200 sq mi/390–520 sq km) and depth, and usually floods the surrounding area in the winter. Once an inlet of the Adriatic Sea, the lake is now separated from the sea by an alluvial isthmus. It is fed by the Morača River and drained by the Bojana southeastward to the Drin River. The lake is navigable by small steamers, and it abounds in fish.

Scylla (sĭl'ə), in Greek mythology. **1** Sea monster. According to one legend Circe, jealous of the sea god Glaucus' love for Scylla, changed her from a beautiful nymph into a horrible doglike creature with six heads and twelve feet; according to another, Amphitrite, jealous of Poseidon's love for her, transformed her into the ugly monster. Scylla lived on the rocks on the Italian side of the Strait of Messina, where she seized sailors from passing ships and devoured them. On the other side of the strait was the whirlpool Charybdis. Odysseus in his wanderings passed between them, as did Jason and the Argonauts. **2** Daughter of Nisus, king of Megara. She betrayed her father to his enemy Minos, but when she sought Minos' love, he scorned her. Later, Nisus was changed into a sea eagle and Scylla into a sea bird eternally pursued by him.

Scyllis: see DIPOENUS AND SCYLLIS.

Scyros, Greece: see SKÍROS.

Scythia (sĭth'ēə), ancient region of Eurasia, extending from the Danube on the west to the borders of China on the east. The **Scythians** flourished from the 8th to the 4th cent. B.C. They spoke an Indo-Iranian language but had no system of writing. They were nomadic conquerors and skilled horsemen. The so-called Royal Scyths established a kingdom in the E Crimea before the 9th cent. B.C. They seem to have maintained themselves as a ruling class while others (probably native inhabitants) worked the grain fields. The Scythians are traditionally associated with the area between the Danube and the Don, but modern excavations in the Altai Mts., particularly at the site of Pazirik, suggest that their origins were in W Siberia before they moved E into S Russia in the early 1st millennium B.C. Scythian power was maintained in the 8th cent. B.C. in obscure warfare with the Cimmerians. The Scythians, considered barbarians by the Greeks, traded (7th cent. B.C.) grain and their service as mercenaries for Greek wine and luxury items. They invaded (7th cent. B.C.) upper Mesopotamia and Syria. They threatened Judah but never actually occupied Palestine. They also made incursions into the Balkan Peninsula, and a century later the mysterious campaign of Darius I against them (c.512 B.C.) may have checked their expansion, although it was no conquest. They destroyed (c.325 B.C.) an expedition sent against them by Alexander the Great. After 300 B.C. they were driven out of the Balkans by the invading Celts. In S Russia they were displaced (2d or 1st cent. B.C.) by the related Sarmatians, and part of their empire became SARMATIA. See E. H. Minns, *Scythians and Greeks* (1913, repr. 1965); Tamara Rice, *The Scythians* (1957).

Scythopolis: see BETH-SHAN.

Se, chemical symbol of the element SELENIUM.

sea, term used as synonymous with OCEAN, or a subdivision of an ocean (Caribbean Sea, Yellow Sea), or erroneously designating a large salt LAKE (Caspian Sea, Dead Sea, Aral Sea).

sea, law of the: see MARITIME LAW.

sea anemone (ənĕm'ənē''), any of the relatively large, predominantly solitary polyps (see POLYP AND MEDUSA) of the class Anthozoa, phylum Cnidaria. Unlike the closely related corals, these organisms do not have a skeleton. Sea anemones occur everywhere in the oceans, at all depths, but are particularly abundant in coastal waters. Many are beautifully colored (reds, pinks, yellows) and look like flowers when the oral, or feeding, end, equipped with many extensions called tentacles, is fully open. Some anemones are tiny, but most are from one to several inches (2.5–10 cm) long; the genus *Stoichactis* in the Great Barrier Reef off the coast of Australia may reach 3 ft (90 cm) in diameter at the expanded oral end. Most sea anemones attach temporarily to submerged objects; a few thrust themselves into the sand or live in furrows; a few are parasitic on other marine organisms. Some anemones feed on small particles, which are caught with the aid of a mucus secretion and moving currents that are set up by the tentacles. Most sea anemones are predaceous, immobilizing their prey with the aid of specialized stinging cells called nematocysts. *Metridium* is the genus most often studied in classrooms. The burrowing anemone, *Cerianthuss*, occurs on both Pacific and Atlantic coasts; some may reach nearly 2 ft (60 cm) in length. Sea anemones are classified in the phylum CNIDARIA, class Anthozoa, subclass Zoantharia.

sea bass: see BASS.

Seaborg, Glenn Theodore, 1912–, American chemist, b. Ishpeming, Mich., grad. Univ. of California at Los Angeles, 1934, Ph.D. Univ. of California at Berkeley, 1937. In 1939 he began teaching at Berkeley, where he became professor of chemistry (1945) and chancellor of the university (1958). During World War II he was associated with the Univ. of Chicago, where he worked on the development of the atomic bomb. He served as chairman of the U.S. Atomic Energy Commission from 1961 to 1971. For discoveries concerning the chemistry of transuranium elements, he shared with Edwin M. MCMILLAN the 1951 Nobel Prize in Chemistry. Known for his work in nuclear chemistry and physics and artificial radioactivity, Seaborg is codiscoverer of the elements plutonium (and its isotope Pu-239), americium, curium, berkelium, californium, einsteinium, fermium, mendelevium, and nobelium. For his discoveries of these elements and for his "leadership in the development of nuclear chemistry and atomic energy," Seaborg received the 1959 Enrico Fermi award.

Seabury, Samuel, 1729–96, American clergyman, first bishop of the Protestant Episcopal Church, b. Connecticut, grad. Yale, 1748. He studied medicine at the Univ. of Edinburgh, then turned to theology and was ordained (1753) a priest in the Church of England before returning to America as a missionary in New Brunswick, N.J. He was then rector at Jamaica (Long Island) and in Westchester co., New York, until 1775. He then avowed himself a Loyalist in the American Revolution, and for a time he had to practice medicine in New York City, which was under British occupation. He later became (1778) a chaplain to a royal regiment. After the war he was chosen bishop of Connecticut in 1783. The English bishops withheld consecration because of a legal difficulty, but in 1784 he was consecrated at Aberdeen by bishops of the Scottish Episcopal Church. In 1789 the General Convention of the Episcopal Church in the United States confirmed his position, and he became presiding bishop. See biographies by Herbert Thoms (1963) and B. E. Steiner (1972).

Seabury, Samuel, 1873–1958, American jurist, b. New York City; great-great-grandson of Samuel Seabury (1729–96). He served on the supreme court (1907–14) and on the court of appeals (1914–16) of New York state. He became nationally prominent when he headed (1930–31) investigations of New York City's magistrate courts and the city's politics. As a result of these investigations, Mayor James WALKER resigned in 1932. The Tammany faction was defeated in the ensuing elections by Fiorello LaGuardia, whom Seabury had supported. He wrote *The New Federalism* (1950). See Herbert Mitgang, *The Man Who Rode the Tiger* (1970).

sea canary: see BELUGA.

sea cow: see SIRENIAN.

sea cucumber, any of the flexible, elongated echinoderms belonging to the class Holothuroidea. Although sea cucumbers have the basic echinoderm radial symmetry, they do not have arms like starfish. Instead the oral-anal distance is greatly increased, resulting in the typical cucumber-shaped body. Sea cucumbers live with one side facing permanently down. Like other echinoderms, sea cucumbers have a water-vascular system; the locomotor tube feet are concentrated in three areas on the ventral, or under, side, in some species forming a muscular, creeping sole. Some species burrow in sand or mud and have lost all tube feet. The leathery body wall contains minute, scattered skeletal ossicles, or bonelike plates; a few species have an armor of close-set plates. Some species eat bottom material, while others use tube feet modified as branched oral tentacles to capture particles or plankton and transfer them to the mouth. Most sea cucumbers have highly branched tubes called respiratory trees attached to the intestine near the anus. Water is pumped in and out, facilitating respiratory exchange and excretion. In some species, branches called tubules of Cuvier, attached to or near the bases of the respiratory trees, are ejected when the organism is attacked; they swell and become sticky, entangling the pursuer. Many sea cucumbers eject most of the internal organs when sufficiently irritated, later regenerating a new set. Sea cucumbers have a single, branched gonad. Eggs are usually expelled into the sea where, after fertilization, free-swimming larvae develop. After a second larval stage, metamorphosis occurs, and the adult body shape appears. Sea cucumbers occur in all seas and at all depths. Most do not exceed 1 ft (30.5 cm) in length, but *Stichopus variegatus* from the Philippines may reach 3 ft (91 cm) in length. Known as trepang or bêche-de-mer, a number of species are caught along warm coasts of Australia and the East Indies. They are dried and sold in China for soup. Sea cucumbers are classified in the phylum ECHINODERMATA, class Holothuroidea.

sea fan, colonial marine animal forming erect, flattened, branching colonies in tropical and subtropical waters. Colonies may be several feet high and are often colorful, with purples, reds, and yellows predominating. The individuals, or polyps (see POLYP AND MEDUSA), have eight feathery tentacles and feed on plankton organisms. Sea fans are classified in the phylum CNIDARIA, class Anthozoa, order Gorgonacea.

sea-floor spreading, theory of crustal evolution which holds that the ocean floors are spreading outward from vast underwater ridges. First proposed in the early 1960s by the late American geologist Harry H. Hess, its major tenets gave great support to the theory of CONTINENTAL DRIFT and provided a conceptual base for the development of the PLATE TECTONICS theory of crustal evolution. Development of highly sophisticated seismic recorders and precision depth recorders in the 1950s led to the discovery in the mid-1960s that the Mid-Atlantic Ridge, a vast, sinuous undersea mountain chain bisecting the Atlantic Ocean, was in fact only a small segment of a globe-girdling undersea mountain system some 40,000 mi (64,000 km) in length. This midocean ridge was found to contain a gigantic cleft, or rift, 20 to 30 mi (32–48 km) wide and c.1 mi (1.6 km) deep, extending along the crest of the ridge. The ridge itself does not form a smooth path, but is instead offset in many places. The offsets are called fracture zones, or transform FAULTS. Rifts are characteristic of places where the earth's crust is subjected to tensional forces, and indeed the rift and its associated transform faults are the locus of nearly all shallow earthquakes occurring in midocean areas. In 1962 a theory was put forth to explain the rifts. It proposed

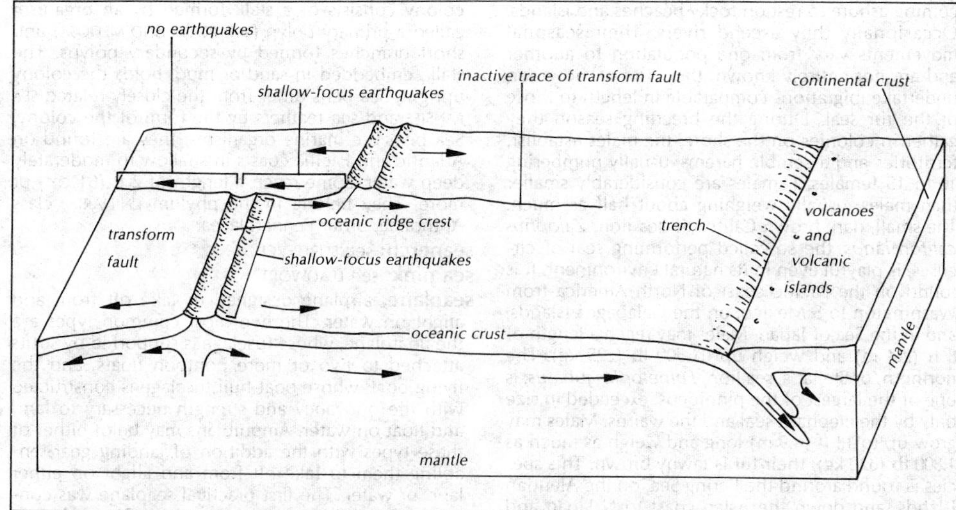

Schematic model of the oceanic crust, showing sea-floor spreading

that the sea floor itself is in motion, spreading in both directions from the midocean ridge system. This results in the widening of the rift at the ridge crest, which in turn becomes partly filled by the upwelling of a liquid rock called basaltic magma from the earth's mantle. When the magma hardens, it forms new oceanic crust that becomes welded to the crust on each side of the rift. Movement of the oceanic crust away from the center line of the ridge causes new rifting and the generation of still more oceanic crust. The oceanic trenches bordering the continents mark regions where the oldest oceanic crust is reabsorbed into the mantle through steeply inclined, earthquake-prone subduction zones. Abundant evidence supports the major contentions of the sea-floor spreading theory. First, samples of the deep ocean floor show that basaltic oceanic crust and overlying sediment become progressively younger as the midocean ridge is approached, and the sediment cover is thinner near the ridge. Second, the rock making up the ocean floor is considerably younger than the continents, with no samples found over 160 million years old, as contrasted with maximum ages of over 3 billion years for the continental rocks. This confirms that older ocean crust has been reabsorbed in ocean trench systems. Finally, by the mid-1960s studies of the earth's magnetic field showed a history of periodic reversals in polarity (see PALEOMAGNETISM). A time scale for "normal" and "reversed" polarity was established, showing 171 magnetic "flip-flops" in the past 76 million years. Magnetic surveys conducted near the midocean ridge showed elongated patterns of normal and reversed polarity of the ocean floor in bands paralleling the rift and symmetrically distributed as mirror images on either side of it. The magnetic history of the earth is thus recorded in the spreading ocean floors as in a very slow magnetic tape recording, forming a continuous record of the movement of the ocean floors. Other supportive evidence involves a study of the fracture zones that offset the sections of the ridge. See J. Coulomb, *Sea Floor Spreading and Continental Drift* (1972).

Seaford, uninc. hamlet (1970 pop. 17,379), Nassau co., SE N.Y., on the southern shore of Long Island, on Great South Bay; settled 1643. It is a residential suburb of New York City and a resort village, with marinas and boatyards. The county museum of natural history is there.

sea gooseberry, common name for members of the phylum CTENOPHORA. Sea gooseberries are also called comb jellies.

sea grapes: see TUNICATE.

Seaham (sē'əm), urban district (1971 pop. 23,410), Durham, NE England, on the North Sea. Mining and shipping coal are major industries. Engineering and the manufacture of clothing and pottery are also fairly important.

seahorse, common name for certain small fishes of the family Syngnathidae, inhabiting warm waters but sometimes found as far north as Cape Cod. The elongated head and snout of a seahorse, flexed at right angles to the body, suggest those of a horse. Members of different species range in size from 2 to 8 in. (5–20 cm); all feed on minute organisms. Protected by thin bony plates that are derivatives of the scales found in most fishes, the seahorse swims weakly in an upright position by means of rapid, hummingbirdlike beats of its fins; at rest it curls its thin, prehensile tail around seaweed. The pipefishes, belonging to the same family, comprise about 50 species, whose members range in size from 4 to 12 in. (10–30 cm) long. They are slightly more fishlike in appearance but have the long snout and unusual breeding habits of the seahorse. While linked in the mating embrace (during which the seahorses utter musical sounds) the female forces the eggs into a pouch on the underside of the male, where they are fertilized and where they remain, feeding on nutrients provided by the vascular lining of the pouch, until they are expelled as miniature versions of the adult. Pipefishes are able to change color. Some seahorses have deceptive leaflike appendages, and others are poisonous. Despite their poor locomotion, these fishes are more highly evolved than the streamlined varieties. Seahorses are classified in the phylum CHORDATA, subphylum Vertebrata, class Osteichthyes, order Gasterosteiformes, family Syngnathidae.

Sea Islands, chain of more than 100 low islands off the Atlantic coast of S.C., Ga., and N Fla., extending from the Santee River to the St. Johns River. The ocean side of the islands is generally sandy; the side facing the mainland is marshy. The islands have a humid, subtropical climate, with hot summers, warm winters, and rain throughout the year. Some islands remain uninhabited; others are resorts and wildlife sanctuaries. The Intracoastal Waterway passes through the Sea Islands. The Spanish discovered and were the first to inhabit the islands, setting up missions and garrisons in the 16th cent. These were abandoned as the English steadily advanced in the area. James Oglethorpe, founder of the Georgia colony, built Fort Frederica on St. Simons Island between 1736 and 1754, during the English-Spanish struggle for control of the present SE United States. The ruins of the fort now constitute a national monument. The Sea Islands were the first important cotton-growing area in North America. In the early 19th cent., St. Helena and Port Royal Island became the seats of large plantations that grew long-staple sea-island cotton. The Union invasion in the Civil War and the distribution of land by the Federal government to newly freed slaves after the war ruined the wealth of the planters. The Carolina islands are still largely inhabited by blacks. Of almost pure black African descent and virtually isolated until the 1920s, they developed distinct customs and dialects (especially GULLAH). With the coming of the boll weevil (c.1920), cotton culture gave way to diversified farming, including the growing of corn, potatoes, and peanuts; poultry raising, oyster gathering, and fishing are also important. Morris Island, Fort Sumter, and other islands lie in and around Charleston harbor. Beaufort (1970 pop. 9,434), on Port Royal Island, is the main city of the Sea Islands and is a center of menhaden fishing. Parris Island is the Atlantic coast recruit-training center for the U.S. marine corps. St. Simons Island, Sea Island, and Jekyll Island (also called the Golden Isles), near Brunswick, Ga., are popular resorts. St. Simons is joined to the mainland at Brunswick by a causeway. Jekyll Island, once the site of a club for Northern millionaires, is now a state park. Cumberland Island, largest of the Sea Islands, c.22 mi (35 km) long and from 1 to 5 mi (1.6–8 km) wide, has been designated a national seashore (see NATIONAL PARKS AND MONUMENTS, table). Other notable islands are the Isle of Palms, Johns, Edisto, and Hilton Head.

seal, carnivorous aquatic mammal with front and hind feet modified as flippers, or fin-feet. The name seal is sometimes applied broadly to any of the fin-footed mammals, or pinnipeds, including the WALRUS, the eared seals (SEA LION and FUR SEAL), and the true seals, also called earless seals, hair seals, or phocid seals. More narrowly the term is applied only to true seals. The so-called performing seal of circuses is actually a sea lion. Pinnipeds have streamlined bodies, rounded in the middle and tapered at the ends, with a thick layer of fat beneath the skin. Their limbs are short and their feet are long and webbed, forming flippers. Nearly all are marine, and most inhabit cold or temperate regions. Some spend most of the year in the open ocean, while others inhabit coastal waters and spend varying amounts of time on shores, islands, or ice floes. Occasionally they ascend rivers. All pinnipeds leave the water at least once a year, at breeding time. In nearly all species the females give birth a year after mating, so that the births take place on land, just before breeding begins. The pups are nursed during the period, usually of several months duration, spent on land. Some species spend most of the year far from their breeding grounds; the northern fur seals make particularly lengthy migrations each year. Most pinnipeds have diets of fish and shellfish; many are bottom feeders, with physiological adaptations for deep diving. They have acute hearing and some, if not all, make use of echolocation (sonar) for underwater navigation. The sea lions and fur seals (family Otariidae) and the walrus (family Odobenidae) are able to turn their hind flippers forward for walking on land; they swim chiefly by a rowing action of the long front flippers. The true seals (family Phocidae) are unable to rotate the hind flippers. They progress on land by wriggling on their bellies, pulling themselves with the short front flippers; in the water they are propelled by a side-to-side sweeping action of the hind flippers. True seals are called earless seals because they lack external ear projections; they have functional inner ears. They have short, coarse hair, usually with a close, dense undercoat. Their color and pattern vary with the species; many are spotted. The pups of most species have fluffy coats of a light color. True seals are generally polygamous and gregarious, but most do not form harems at breeding time, as do the eared seals. Some species have definite migrations, but in most the seals spread out after breeding, singly or in groups, over a wide area of ocean. Some polar species migrate in winter to avoid the advancing ice; members of other species winter under the ice, surfacing through holes to breathe. Most true seal species fall into one of three geographical groups: northern, antarctic, and warm water species. Nearly all are marine, but the Baikal seal (*Pusa siberica*) is confined to the freshwater Lake Baikal of Siberia and the Caspian seal (*P. caspica*) to the brackish Caspian Sea. In addition several populations of the normally marine harbor seals and ring seals are found in freshwater lakes. The northern seals include two species of temperate coastal waters: the common seal, or HARBOR SEAL, of the N Atlantic and N Pacific, and the larger gray seal of the N Atlantic. The former is the only seal frequently seen off U.S. coasts. The Greenland seal, or HARP SEAL, is found in the arctic Atlantic; the ribbon seal in the arctic Pacific. The small ringed seal and the larger bearded seal are circumpolar arctic species. Antarctic seals include the voracious leopard seal, which feeds on penguins and other sea birds, and the Ross, Weddell, and crabeater seals. The warm water seals are the Mediterranean, Caribbean, and Hawaiian species of monk seal. A fourth group includes the ELEPHANT SEAL and hooded seal. There are two elephant seal species, one of the Northern and one of the Southern Hemisphere. They are distinguished by their immense size and trunklike snouts. The hooded seal, distinguished by an inflatable bladder over the snout is found in the arctic Atlantic. Seals have been used by the Eskimo and other northern hunting peoples for food, oil, and hides. Commercial sealing has been largely confined to a few species, most notably the fur seal. Commercially important species of true seals are the harp seal, whose pups are valued for their fluffy white coats, and the ring seal. The hunting of these seals is regulated by international treaties, and they are not in danger of extinction. The elephant seals were formerly hunted for oil and almost exterminated, but they are now protected and are increasing in numbers. The monk seals have been greatly depleted by hunting in past centuries and their survival is threatened, although they are no longer of commercial importance. The ribbon seal and Ross seal are not much hunted, but appear to have been rare since before their existence was first recorded. Seals are classified in the phylum CHORDATA, subphylum Vertebrata, class Mammalia, order Carnivora, suborder Pinnipedia. See Brian Davies, *Savage Luxury: The Slaughter of the Baby Seals* (1971); V. B. Scheffer, *The Year of the Seal* (1972).

seal, stamp made from a die or matrix of metal, a gem, or other hard substance, that yields an impression on wax or other soft substance. The use of seals is very ancient, examples of great antiquity occurring in China, Egypt, Greece, Rome, and other places. The most common form was the seal ring, of which the GEM formed the seal. Ecclesiastical seals, used in the 9th cent., reached their highest perfection in the 13th and 14th cent. The use of seals with emblematic designs antedates the development of the escutcheon and is therefore important in the history of HERALDRY. Edward the Confessor was the first English king to adopt a Great Seal for the kingdom. Heraldic or emblematic seals are in wide use by national, state, and local authorities, by institutions of all kinds, and in the certification of legal documents. A committee was appointed by the Continental Congress on July 4, 1776, to prepare a device for the Great Seal of the United States (see UNITED STATES, GREAT SEAL OF THE).

Seal Beach, city (1970 pop. 24,441), Orange co., S Calif., on the Pacific coast; inc. 1915. Aerospace items and salad dressings are produced there. It is a beach city with an active art colony. A U.S. naval weapons station is there.

sea lettuce, common name for algal species of the genus *Ulva*. See SEAWEED; CHLOROPHYTA.

sea level, the level of the sea, which serves as the datum used for measurement of land elevations and ocean depths. Theoretically, one would expect sea level to be a fixed and permanent horizontal surface on the face of the earth, and as a starting approximation, this is true. However, a number of factors operate to cause variations in sea level ranging up to several meters from place to place and to cause secular variations through the passage of time, often severe enough to cause flooding and damage to coastal zones. The level of the surface of the world's oceans is disturbed by wind-driven waves and TIDES. Sea level therefore fluctuates in periods ranging from seconds to a year as a result of these factors. Thus for some purposes it is necessary to know the mean sea level in a particular area, determined by averaging the elevations of the sea's surface as measured by mechanical tide gauges over long periods of time. A number of other factors result in sea-level differences between one place or time and another. These may complement or counteract one another to result in a net rise or fall in mean sea level at a particular time and place. These factors include water temperature and salinity, air pressure, change of season, the amount of runoff from streams, and the amount of water stored as ice or snow on land.

sea lily, stalked echinoderm of the class Crinoidea. Sea lilies are ancient, having reached their peak in the Middle Mississippian period; about 5,000 fossil species are known. About 80 modern species remain. Marine animals, like all echinoderms, they are largely restricted to fairly deep water, from about 35 to 1,000 fathoms (60–300 m). Small organisms and particles are trapped in mucus in the water-vascular (ambulacral) grooves located on the feathery, branching arms, and are conveyed to the mouth. Unlike the free-swimming FEATHER STARS to which they are related, sea lilies remain permanently attached to the ocean bottom. Two genera, *Rhizocrinus* and *Cenocrinus,* occur at moderate depths in the Atlantic and Caribbean. Sea lilies are classified in the phylum ECHINODERMATA, class Crinoidea.

sea lion, fin-footed marine mammal of the eared seal family (Otariidae). Like the other member of this family, the FUR SEAL, the sea lion is distinguished from the true SEAL by its external ears, long, flexible neck, supple forelimbs, and hind flippers that can be turned forward for walking on land. It differs from the fur seal in having a thin coat of short, coarse hair rather than soft, thick fur. Sea lions swim by rowing movements of the forelimbs, with the hindlimbs stretched out behind the body as a rudder. They feed primarily on fish and squid and are known to dive as deep as 600 ft (180 m) for food. They are found in the oceans of the Southern Hemisphere and in the N Pacific Ocean. When not breeding they inhabit waters close to shore, sometimes coming ashore to rest on rocky beaches and islands. Occasionally they ascend rivers. Their seasonal movements vary from one population to another and are not entirely known; they do not, however, undertake migrations comparable in length to those of the fur seal. During the breeding season they gather in colonies on the shore; the males establish territories and assemble harems, usually numbering 10 to 15 females. Females are considerably smaller than males, usually weighing about half as much. The small, dark brown California sea lion, *Zalophus californianus,* the so-called performing seal of circuses, is playful even in its natural environment. It is found on the Pacific coast of North America from Washington to S Mexico, on the Galapagos Islands, and in the Sea of Japan. Males may reach a length of 8 ft (2.4 m) and weigh up to 500 lb (225 kg). The northern, or Stellar's, sea lion, *Eumetopias jubatus,* is one of the largest of the pinnipeds, exceeded in size only by the elephant seal and the walrus. Males may grow up to 13 ft (4.9 m) long and weigh as much as 1,800 lb (820 kg); their fur is tawny brown. This species is found around the Bering Sea, on the Aleutian Islands, and down the Asian coast to N Japan and the American coast to S California. The South American sea lion, *Otaria byronia,* is found on the Pacific coast and S Atlantic coast of South America, and the Falkland Islands. The Australian sea lion, *Neophoca cinerea,* is found off S Australia; Hooker's sea lion, *Phocarctos hookeri,* lives on subantarctic islands of New Zealand. Sea lions have been hunted for blubber and hide and have also been killed in large numbers because fishermen blamed them for robbing their nets. There is now very little hunting of sea lions and the northern sea lion is under government protection. Sea lions are classified in the phylum CHORDATA, subphylum Vertebrata, class Mammalia, order Carnivora, suborder Pinnipedia, family Otariidae.

Seal of the United States, Great: see UNITED STATES, GREAT SEAL OF THE.

Sealyham terrier (sē'lēhăm"), breed of short-legged TERRIER developed in Wales in the second half of the 19th cent. It stands about 10 in. (25 cm) high at the shoulder and weighs about 20 lb (9 kg). Its weather-resistant double coat consists of a dense, soft underlayer and a hard, wiry topcoat. It may be solid white or white with lemon or tan markings on the head and ears. The Sealyham takes its name from the Welsh country estate of Captain John Edwardes, who originated the breed. Used for years to hunt badger, otter, and fox, today it has come to be a popular house pet. See DOG.

sea mink: see CROAKER.

sea mouse, marine worm of the genus *Aphrodite* with a short, broad, segmented body, found in moderately deep water. The upper, or dorsal, surface of a sea mouse bears 15 pairs of raised scales; the space between the scales and the body surface forms a channel for the flow of water carrying oxygen for respiration. The entire dorsal surface, including the scales, is covered by long, feltlike threads called setae, which produce a brilliant iridescence; heavier, bristlelike setae project through them. Sea mice commonly reach 6 to 8 in. (15–20 cm) in length and 2 in. (5 cm) in width. They are classified in the phylum ANNELIDA, class Polychaeta, family Aphroditidae.

sea nettle, any one of several species of stinging jellyfish, common along coasts and much feared by swimmers. Most stings are painful but are not dangerous to man; however, certain jellyfish of the order Cubomedusae and especially an Australian species, *Chironex fleckeri,* have caused many deaths. The sting, produced by nematocysts located in the tentacles, is used to kill or stun prey. Sea nettles are classified in the phylum CNIDARIA, class Scyphoza.

sea otter: see OTTER.

sea pansy, fleshy, leaf-shaped colony of marine organisms belonging to the genus *Renilla* in the same phylum as the jellyfish. The colony consists of a stalk formed by a large organism called a primary polyp (see POLYP AND MEDUSA) that is thrust into soft bottom material; the upper part of the stalk is composed of several kinds of secondary polyps. Sea pansies are handsome creatures; the reddish to purple upper stalk is studded with white polyps and is brilliantly luminescent. The colonies occur in the warmer regions of the Atlantic and Pacific coasts. Sea pansies are classified in the phylum CNIDARIA, class Anthozoa, order Pennatulacea.

sea peach: see TUNICATE.

sea pen, long, slender colonial organism of the same phylum as the jellyfish. Sea pen colonies are formed by several genera of the order Pennatulacea. The colony consists of a stalk formed by an organism called a primary polyp (see POLYP AND MEDUSA) and short branches formed by secondary polyps. The stalk, embedded in sand or mud, holds the colony upright. Sea pens differ from the closely related SEA PANSIES and sea feathers by the form of the colony. Sea pens are marine organisms; they are found on Atlantic and Pacific coasts in shallow to moderately deep water. Some reach a length of 2 ft (61 cm) or more. They belong in the phylum CNIDARIA, class Anthozoa, order Pennatulacea.

seaperch: see SURFPERCH.

sea pink: see LEADWORT.

seaplane, airplane designed to take off from and alight on water. The two most common types are the floatplane, whose fuselage is supported by struts attached to two or more pontoon floats, and the flying boat, whose boat-hull fuselage is constructed with the buoyancy and strength necessary to land and float on water. Amphibians may be of either of these types with the addition of landing gear, enabling them to take off from and alight on either land or water. The first practical seaplane was constructed and flown by the American Glenn H. Curtiss in 1911. The seaplane developed rapidly in the 1920s and 30s, and for a time it was the largest and fastest aircraft in the world. Because the flotation structures offered greater resistance to the air than wheel-type landing gear, seaplanes were until recently less efficient and slower for any given horsepower requirement than land-based aircraft. However, developments in small and retractable flotation structures have eliminated that inefficiency and have made possible supersonic jet-powered seaplanes.

sea pork: see TUNICATE.

search, right of, in international law, right of a warship to detain and search a private vessel belonging to a foreign national. In peacetime, this right is ordinarily exercised only within the territorial waters (see WATERS, TERRITORIAL) of a state and merely as an incident of the power to police such waters. A search on the high seas usually is not justified in peacetime except where piracy, violation of fishing regulations, or interference with telephone cables is suspected or where a vessel that has fled territorial waters is being hotly pursued. In wartime, a belligerent may search neutral vessels on the high seas in order to capture the property of enemy nationals or to remove CONTRABAND bound for enemy ports. Forcible resistance to search allows the warship to attack or destroy the vessel or its cargo or to take them as a PRIZE. The right of search in wartime occasioned bitter controversy between Great Britain and the United States just before the War of 1812. The United States objected to the British navy's practice of stopping American merchant ships at sea to impress into naval service any seaman that the British captain believed to be a British subject. Impressment virtually ended after the War of 1812. The right of search is also called the right of visit and search.

searchlight, device, usually swiveled, using a lens and reflecting surface to direct a powerful beam of light of nearly parallel rays. In 1892 such apparatus was used along the English Channel in coastal defense and later, in the South African War, as an aid to infantry movement. It was also used to illuminate vessels in order to identify them and for possible bombardment, for dazzling the enemy, for illuminating the coast in an attack, and to locate targets, at sea or ashore, for the guns. After 1900 acetylene came into use as an illuminant, and in 1916 Edison invented a portable electric apparatus powered by storage batteries. During World War I powerful searchlights mounted on trucks and railroad cars came into use. The electric arc was generally employed after the American inventor E. A. Sperry introduced (1915) his high-intensity arc lamp based on principles that still predominate in modern searchlight equipment. Searchlights of 1,500 million candle power visible for 150 mi (241 km) have become common. Revolving searchlights as beacons spaced along air routes have yielded to radio beacons, but the use of powerful lights coordinated with antiaircraft guns developed considerably during World War II. Small searchlights, which are usually employed for signalling, use incandescent lamps. These lamps are often of the quartz-halogen type in which the filament is run at very high temperatures.

search warrant, in law, written order by an official of a court directing an officer to search in a specified place for specified objects and to seize them if found. The objects sought may be stolen goods or physical evidences of the commission of crime (e.g., narcotics). The Fourth Amendment of the U.S. Constitution provides, in effect, that a search warrant may be issued only on oath or affirmation that a crime was probably committed. Courts exclude from evidence in a trial information obtained by tapping telephone conversations without a court order or objects obtained by an illegal search. See also MAPP VS. OHIO.

Searle, Ronald, 1920–, English artist. Searle is celebrated for his sardonic cartoons, drawn in a free, graphic style, that have appeared in *Punch* and *New Yorker* magazines. A series of film comedies was based on his St. Trinian's cartoons. Collections of his works include *Searle's Cats* (1968) and *Hello, Where Did All the People Go?* (1970).

sea robin: see SCULPIN.

Sears, Isaac, c.1730–86, American Revolutionary leader, b. West Brewster, Mass. A merchant sea captain, Sears won a reputation as a daring privateer during the French and Indian War. He was a leader in the resistance to the Stamp Act in New York City, helped organize (1766) the Sons of Liberty, and remained prominent in the agitation against the British during the next decade. Arrested (1775) for anti-British activities, he was rescued at the prison door by his comrades. When news of the battle of Lexington reached New York, Sears led a mob that drove prominent loyalists from the city and seized the British arsenal. After the British capture (1776) of New York, Sears went to Boston and promoted privateering for the remainder of the war. He was later elected (1784, 1786) to the New York state assembly.

seas, freedom of the, in international law, the principle that outside its territorial waters (see WATERS, TERRITORIAL) a state may not claim sovereignty over the high seas except with respect to its own vessels. This principle, first established by the Romans, gives to all nations in time of peace unrestricted use of the seas for navigation (both naval and commercial), for fishing, and for the laying of submarine cables. For long periods, leading naval powers have repudiated the principle. From the late 15th to the early 19th cent., Spain, Portugal, and Great Britain attempted to exclude commercial rivals from parts of the open sea. Protests by other nations led to a revived acceptance of freedom of the seas. One of its strongest advocates was the United States, especially in its dispute with Great Britain preceding the War of 1812. In time of peace freedom of the seas cannot be restricted lawfully except by international agreements, such as those regulating fisheries or the right of visit and search (see SEARCH, RIGHT OF). During war, however, belligerents often assert limitations of the principle in order to facilitate the more effective conduct of hostilities, and it is then that the sharpest disagreements arise, e.g., the case of the *Lusitania* in World War I. Subjects of contention between neutrals and belligerents include the right to seize neutral property and persons aboard an enemy ship (see PRIZE), the mining of sea lanes, and the exclusion of neutral vessels from enemy ports by blockade. See J. B. Potter, *The Freedom of the Seas in History, Law, and Politics* (1924).

seasickness: see MOTION SICKNESS.

Seaside, city (1970 pop. 35,935), Monterey co., W Calif., on Monterey Bay, in a fruit region; founded 1887, inc. 1954. Its economy is based upon tourism and nearby U.S. Fort Ord.

sea slug, name for a marine GASTROPOD mollusk that lacks a shell as an adult and is usually brightly colored. Sea slugs, or nudibranchs, are distributed throughout the world, with the greatest numbers and the largest kinds found in tropical waters. They creep along the bottom or cling to submerged vegetation, usually in water just below the low tide line. Members of a few species swim on the surface in open ocean. Most sea slugs are under 1 in. (2.5 cm) long, although the largest, found in the Great Barrier Reef of Australia, reaches 12 in. (30 cm). Regarded by many people as the most beautiful of marine animals, sea slugs display a great array of solid colors and patterns. Many have feathery structures (cerata) on the back, often in a contrasting color. Most sea slugs have two pairs of tentacles on the head, used for tactile and chemosensory reception, with a small eye at the base of each tentacle. Sea slugs graze on small sessile animals such as coelenterates, sponges, and bryozoans. Certain sea slugs that feed on corals and sea anemones ingest the stinging cells of their prey without discharging them; these then pass from the slug's digestive tract to the cerata, where they are used by the slug for its own defense. Sea slugs are classified in the phylum MOLLUSCA, class Gastropoda, subclass Opisthobranchia, order Nudibranchiata.

sea snake, name for any of the venomous marine SNAKES of the family Hydrophidae, found in tropical waters of the Indian and Pacific oceans. The sea snake's body is flattened laterally and its oarlike tail is used as a scull. A specialized lung and nostrils with valves enable it to remain submerged for periods of up to 8 hr. Most species are dark above and lighter below, or ringed with black and grayish green. They feed on small fish and are preyed upon by sea birds, sharks, and larger fish. Their potent venom quickly immobilizes their prey; however, they are not aggressive and rarely strike at humans when caught. Most sea snakes are completely marine and lack the enlarged ventral scales that enable land snakes to grip the ground. These snakes bear live young at sea. Most inhabit the shallow waters of the Indonesian region, but the common sea snake, *Pelamis platurus,* ranges from Madagascar E to Mexico and is sometimes found swarming by the thousands in open ocean. It is black or dark brown above and yellow below and grows up to 3 ft (90 cm) long. A few sea snake species leave the water to lay eggs on coral reefs. These snakes have ventral plates like those of land snakes. Sea snakes are classified in the phylum CHORDATA, subphylum Vertebrata, class Reptilia, order Squamata, family Hydrophidae.

seasons, divisions of the year characterized by variations in the relative lengths of day and night and in the amount of heat received from the sun. These variations depend on the inclination of the equator to the plane of the ECLIPTIC and on the revolution of the earth around the sun. The amount of heat received at a given point on the earth's surface depends chiefly on the angle at which the sun's rays strike the earth at that point and on the daily duration there of exposure to the sun's rays; the more vertical the rays and the longer the exposure, the more heat will be received. Seasonal change varies greatly with latitude. Near the equator there is little change; in high latitudes spring and autumn are very short. In the temperate zones there are four well-defined seasons; in the north temperate zone, spring begins about March 21, the vernal EQUINOX; summer, about June 22, the summer SOLSTICE; autumn, about Sept. 23, the fall equinox; and winter, about Dec. 22, the winter solstice. However, the weather lags somewhat behind the seasons because, at the time of maximum sunlight (summer solstice for the Northern Hemisphere) the ground is still too cold to radiate as much heat as it receives, so average temperatures usually continue to rise for several weeks until a balance is reached between reception and radiation of heat. In low latitudes and in certain other areas (e.g., India) where oceans and winds are the chief factors governing seasonal changes, the terms "wet season" and "dry season" are used. The seasons play an important part in mythology and folklore; many holidays are connected with the changes of season.

sea spider, common name for members of the class Pycnogonida, long-legged, rather spiderlike organisms of the phylum Arthropoda, widely distributed in marine waters. Most are tiny, from 1 to 9 mm (0.04–0.36 in.), and live in littoral regions, crawling about over the surface of sessile animal colonies or seaweeds. Some live on or in clams. There are deep-sea forms, some becoming quite large; *Colossendeis colossea* has a leg span of nearly 2 ft (91 cm). Their unusual body form makes their relationships to other arthropods obscure. Nearly all of the body is composed of the anterior region (prosoma); a tiny tubular posterior region (opisthosoma) projects behind. A large proboscis is used to suck in food. At the base of the proboscis is a pair of modified appendages (chelicera) used to pick off bits of food and hold them in front of the mouth. The next appendages are a pair of leglike pedipalps, followed by a pair of specialized legs used by the male to carry eggs until they hatch. Four pairs of walking legs follow, but sometimes additional pairs are found. Members of this class are relatively common and widely distributed; well over 400 species are known. Sea spiders are classified in the phylum ARTHROPODA, class Pycnogonida.

sea squirt: see TUNICATE.

sea star, also called starfish, echinoderm of the class Asteroidae, common in tide pools. The body of most species consists of a central disk from which radiate a number of tapering arms—usually five, but up to 25 in some species. Some sea stars are pentagonal, the points of the disk not extending into arms. Each arm contains an extension of the body cavity and body organs. A network of calcareous plates located beneath the skin forms an external skeleton; the plates are joined by connective tissue and muscle, giving the apparently rigid sea star considerable flexibility. Calcareous spines, some of them moveable, project from the skin. The underside of the body bears a mouth, at the center, and a groove running along each arm. The grooves contain rows of tiny, flexible appendages called tube feet. Sea stars move by means of the tube feet, which are operated by a hydraulic, or water-vascular, system unique to echinoderms. Sea water, circulated through the radiating canals of this system, enters and extends the tube feet. Each tube foot can be withdrawn by its attached muscles. The tube feet are equipped with suction cups, and the animal moves in any direction by gripping with some of its tube feet and pulling itself forward. A sea star that is turned upside down can right itself by turning an arm under and walking with the tube feet. Each arm has a short sensory tentacle at its end that responds to chemicals and vibrations in the water, and a red photosensitive eyespot. A sea star often lifts the end of an arm to perceive light and movement. Sea stars are carnivorous. Members of many species have protrusible stomachs and prey largely on bivalves, such as clams and oysters; they are extremely destructive to commercial oyster beds. The sea star wraps its arms around the bivalve, grips the shell

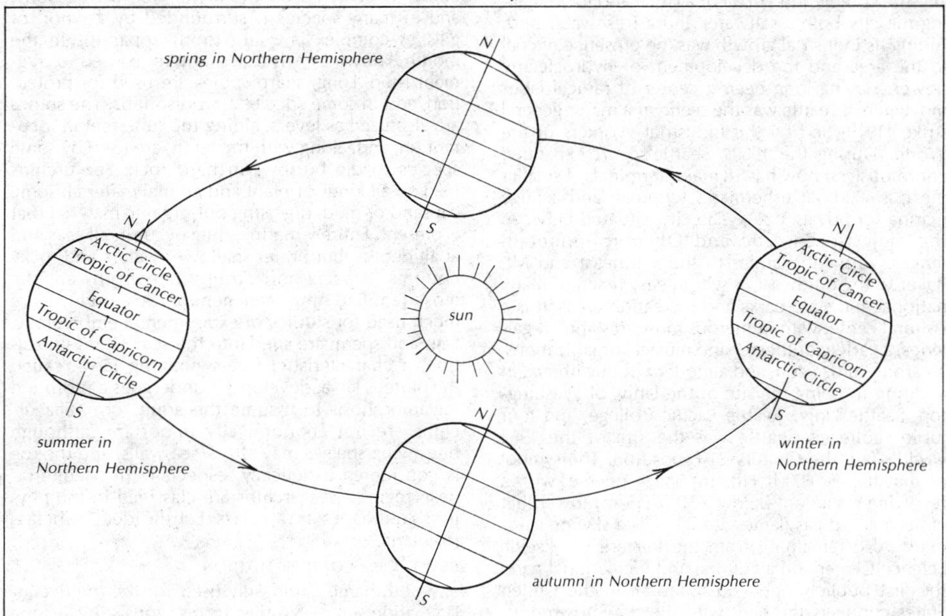

The seasons are caused by the tilt of the earth's axis to the plane of its orbit about the sun. The Northern Hemisphere is tilted toward the sun in the summer and receives more direct rays than in the winter, when it is tilted away from the sun.

with its tube feet, and opens it by sustained powerful suction. The shell needs to open only about 1/100 in. (0.25 mm). The sea star then extrudes its stomach through its mouth and inserts it inside the shell of the prey, where it digests and absorbs the soft inner tissues. Sea stars shed their eggs and sperm into the water, and fertilization occurs externally, producing a swimming, bilaterally symmetrical larva. The larva settles and undergoes a sessile (attached) period while metamorphosing into the free-living, radially symmetrical adult form. A single female may produce over 2 million eggs in one spawn, but the eggs and larvae form part of the plankton on which many marine animals feed, and few survive. Sea stars vary in size from under ½ in. (1.3 cm) to over 3 ft (90 cm) in diameter. They are commonly dull shades of yellow or orange, but there are many brightly colored ones as well. There are about 2,000 species distributed throughout the world, mostly in shallow water along rocky coasts. The BRITTLE STARS, of a different echinoderm class, have long, slender, jointed arms and are found in deeper waters. Sea stars are classified in the phylum ECHINODERMATA, class Asteroidae.

SEATO: see SOUTHEAST ASIA TREATY ORGANIZATION.

Seaton, John Colborne, 1st Baron, 1778–1863, British soldier and colonial administrator. He served in Egypt (1801) and Sicily (1806), participated (1808–14) in the Peninsular War, and helped to defeat Napoleon's "Old Guard" at Waterloo. He was appointed lieutenant governor of Guernsey (1825) and lieutenant governor of Upper Canada (1828), serving in the latter post until 1836. In 1835 he was made commander in chief of Canadian forces, and he suppressed the rebellions of 1837 and 1838. He was governor in chief of British North America in 1839, the year he was made a baron. After he left Canada he served as lord high commissioner of the Ionian Islands (1843–49) and commanded the forces in Ireland (1855–60). He was made a field marshal in 1860.

sea trout: see CROAKER.

Seattle (sēăt'əl), city (1970 pop. 530,831), seat of King co., W Wash., built on seven hills, between Elliott Bay of Puget Sound and Lake Washington; inc. 1869. Seattle, the largest city in the Pacific Northwest, is the region's commercial, transportation, and industrial hub and a major port of entry, important in the Alaskan and Far Eastern trade. In addition to being a center of aircraft manufacturing and shipbuilding since World War II, the city has major food-processing and lumber industries; chemical products, metal goods, machinery, textiles and apparel, and paper, stone, clay, and glass items are also produced. Settled in 1851–52, Seattle remained a small lumber town until the coming of the railroad in 1884. Despite strikes, anti-Chinese riots, and the great fire of 1889, subsequent growth was rapid. The city became a boom town with the 1897 Alaska gold rush and developed into the nation's chief link with Alaska. It grew further with the Alaska-Yukon-Pacific Exposition (1909), the opening of the Panama Canal (1914), and the completion (1917) of a canal and locks making the city both a saltwater and a freshwater port. Aiding its industrial growth was the presence of coal in the area and the development of hydroelectric power. Having long been a center of radical labor movements, Seattle was the scene of a major general strike (1919), led by the Industrial Workers of the World. During the 1960s, Seattle's port expanded enormously; it now has 18 major terminals, 4 smaller piers, a 600-boat fisherman's terminal, and a huge marina for private boats. The city, situated between the majestic Cascade and Olympic mountain ranges, with Mt. Rainier to the southeast and Mt. Baker to the northeast, is within easy reach of many national and state parks and recreation areas. It is a cultural center with numerous museums and art galleries, a variety of theater and musical organizations, an arboretum, a zoo, and a modern public library, in addition to being the site of the Univ. of Washington, Seattle Univ., Seattle Pacific College, and four junior colleges. Seattle was the site of the 1962 world's fair, the Century 21 Exposition. The symbol of that fair—a 600-ft (183-m) space needle, with a revolving restaurant below a 50-ft (15-m) tower that emits colored gas flames at night—is a skyline landmark. Also remaining from the fair are the Pacific Science Center and a cultural and recreational park; the first publicly operated monorail in the United States connects the park with the downtown area. Sand Point Naval Air Station, headquarters for the 13th Naval District, is nearby. Seattle has an international airport. See M. C. Morgan, *Skid Road* (rev. ed. 1960); Nard Jones, *Seattle* (1972).

sea turtle, name for several species of large marine TURTLES found in tropical and subtropical oceans. These turtles are modified for life in the ocean by having flipperlike forelimbs without toes and lightweight shells. Their heads are too large to be withdrawn into the shell. They spend most of their lives in the water, but come ashore to lay their eggs. All sea turtle species are declining in numbers, owing in large part to the destruction of the eggs, which are widely used as food in tropical regions. Sea turtle meat is also eaten, and there is a market for turtle oil, hide, and shell. In a few places, such as Sarawak, harvesting of eggs is regulated by law to insure propagation of the species. The size of sea turtles has also decreased, owing to the hunting of large specimens. Nearly all species have a circumglobal distribution although there are differences between the Atlantic and the Pacific populations. Most sea turtles are found in North American waters as far N as the U.S. S Atlantic coast and Baja California. All but one species belong to the family Chelonidae. The green turtle, *Chelonia mydas,* with greenish to brownish skin and shell, formerly reached weights of 1,000 lb (450 kg); the largest now found are about 4 ft (120 cm) long and weigh about 500 lbs (225 kg). The green turtle feeds chiefly on marine vegetation and is most abundant in shallow water. The loggerhead, *Caretta caretta,* is a large-headed brown to reddish turtle. Chiefly carnivorous, it ranges from open oceans to coastal salt marshes and stream mouths. Like the green turtle it sometimes comes ashore to bask in uninhabited places. The hawksbill, or tortoiseshell turtle, *Eretmochelys imbricata,* may reach 30 in. (75 cm) in length and weigh 100 lbs (45 kg). The horny plates of its shell are translucent and have a variegated color pattern, chiefly brown and yellow. These plates have long been valued for the making of ornamental objects. Although tortoiseshell has to a large extent been replaced in many applications by plastic, a renewed demand for the genuine material poses a serious threat to the hawksbill. The ridleys, the smallest sea turtles, inhabit shallow offshore waters. The 2-ft (60-cm) long, gray Atlantic ridley, *Lepidochelys kempii,* breeds only in the Gulf of Mexico, although the young are often carried by the Gulf Stream to the Carribean Sea and Europe. The slightly larger, greenish Pacific ridley, or oliveback (*L. olivacea*), is found in the Indian and Pacific oceans. The LEATHERBACK is the largest of all turtles and, although a marine turtle, belongs to a separate family. All sea turtles other than the leatherback are classified in the phylum CHORDATA, subphylum Vertebrata, class Reptilia, order Chelonia, family Chelonidae.

sea urchin, spherical-shaped echinoderm with movable spines covering the body. The body wall is a firm, globose shell, or test, made of fused skeletal plates and marked by regularly arranged tubercles to which the movable spines are attached. Five rows of the skeletal plates are pierced by pores for the tube feet of the water-vascular system; these are typical of echinoderms and are used for locomotion. The mouth is centered on the lower side of the body, and in many species is surrounded by a whorl of gills. A complex jaw and tooth apparatus in the mouth, known as Aristotle's lantern, is used to fragment food. Long, sharp spines are used for protection, and in some species are poisonous. The spines are also used as levers, aiding the tube feet in locomotion, and, along with the teeth, are used by some species to dig burrows in hard rock. Sea urchins feed on all kinds of plant and animal material; some eat sand or mud, digesting out organic material that is present. Entirely marine, they occur in all seas and at all depths, but prefer shallower waters and rocky bottoms. *Arbacia* and *Strongylocentrotus* are the most familiar American genera. Sea urchins are much used for studies of experimental embryology. Eggs and sperm are shed into the sea. After fertilization, a characteristic, free-swimming larva, called the pluteus larva, develops; it undergoes a profound metamorphosis to assume the adult form. Sea urchins are not economically important, although burrowing species may attack sea walls, and the roe is considered a delicacy, especially in Mediterranean regions. Sea urchins are classified in the phylum ECHINODERMATA, class Echinoidea, subclass Regularia.

seawall: see COAST PROTECTION.

seaweed, name commonly used for the multicellular marine ALGAE. Simpler forms, consisting of one cell (e.g., the DIATOM) or of a few cells, are not generally called seaweeds; these tiny plants help to make up plankton. The more highly developed types of seaweed usually have a basal disk, called a holdfast, and a frond of varying length and shape, which often resembles higher plants in having stemlike, leaflike, and berrylike parts. The simplest of these seaweeds are among the blue-green algae (division SCHIZOPHYTA, class Cyanophyceae) and green algae (division CHLOROPHYTA), found nearest the shore in shallow waters and usually growing as threadlike filaments, irregular sheets, or branching fronds. The brown algae (division PHAEOPHYTA), in which brown pigment masks the green of the chlorophyll, are the most numerous of the seaweeds and are the most common marine forms. They grow at depths of 50 to 75 ft (15–23 m). The red seaweeds (division RHODOPHYTA), many of them delicate and fernlike, are found at the greatest depths (100–200 ft/30–61 m); their red pigment enables them to absorb the blue and violet light present at those depths. Seaweeds reproduce in a variety of ways. Lower types reproduce asexually. More advanced kinds produce motile zoospores that swim off, anchor themselves, and grow into new individuals, or they reproduce sexually by forming sex cells (gametes) that, after fusing, follow the same pattern. Sometimes pieces of a seaweed break off and form new plants; in a few species there is a cycle of asexual and sexual reproduction foreshadowing the alternation of generations, which is characteristic of higher plants. The largest of the green algae, *Ulva* (sea lettuce), grows to a ribbon or sheet 3 ft (91 cm) long. It provides food for many sea creatures, and its broad surface releases a large amount of oxygen. *Fucus,* called rockweed or bladderwrack, is a tough, leathery brown alga (though it often looks olive-green), which clings to rocks and has flattened, branched fronds buoyed by air bladders at the tips. Seaweeds, especially species of the red algae *Porphyra* and *Chondrus,* form an important part of the diet and are farmed for food in China and Japan; other species (often called laver) are eaten in the British Isles and Iceland. Commercial AGAR (vegetable gelatin) is obtained from species of red algae and is the most valuable seaweed product. Irish moss or carrageen (*Chondrus crispus*), a red alga, is one of the few seaweeds used commercially in the United States, where it is gathered chiefly by Massachusetts Bay fishermen. After being bleached in the sun the fronds contain a high proportion of gelatin, which is used for cooking, textile sizing, making cosmetics, and other purposes. In Japan it is made into a shampoo to impart a gloss to the hair. The kelps generally include the many large brown seaweeds and are among the most familiar forms found on North American coasts. Some have fronds up to 200 ft (61 m) long, e.g., the Pacific coast *Nereocystis* and *Macrocystis,* found also off the Cape of Good Hope. Common Atlantic species include *Laminaria* and *Agarum* (devil's apron). The kelps are a source of salts of iodine and potassium and, to a lesser extent, other minerals. When the seaweed is burned, the soluble mineral compounds are removed from the ashes (also called kelp) by washing. They are used chiefly as chemical reagents and for dietary deficiencies in men and in livestock. Kelp is also a commercial source of potash, fertilizer, and, recently, medicines made from the plant's vitamin and mineral content. Kelps are especially abundant in Japan, and various foods known as *kombu* are made from them. The brown algae of the genus *Sargassum* are called gulfweed. They inhabit warm ocean regions and are commonly found floating in large patches in the Sargasso Sea and in the Gulf Stream. Gulfweed was observed by Columbus. Although it was formerly thought to cover the whole Sargasso Sea, making navigation impossible, it has since been found to occur only in drifts. Numerous berrylike air sacs keep the branching plant afloat. The thick masses of gulfweed provide the environment for a distinctive and specialized group of marine forms, many of which are not found elsewhere.

sea whip, erect colony of marine animals of the phylum Cnidaria, with whiplike branches. The skeleton consists of a horny axis, overlaid with small calcareous bodies called spicules. Often beautifully colored, sea whips and the closely related SEA FANS and sea feathers add to the beauty of tropical or subtropical shallow-water marine communities. Sea whips are classified in the phylum CNIDARIA, class Anthozoa, order Gorgonacea.

Seba (sē'bə), grandson of Ham. Gen. 10.7; 1 Chron. 1.9; Ps. 72.10.

sebaceous gland (səbā'shəs), gland in the SKIN of mammals that secretes an oily substance called sebum. In humans, sebaceous glands are primarily found in association with HAIR follicles but also occur in hairless areas of the skin, except for the palms of the hand and soles of the feet. Sebum is a mixture of fat and the debris of dead fat-producing cells. These cells are constantly replaced by new growth at the base of the glands. Generally the sebum is deposited on the hairs inside the follicles and is brought up to the surface of the skin along the hair shaft. In hairless areas, the sebum surfaces through ducts. Sebum lubricates and protects the hair and skin and prevents drying and irritation of membranes. Sebum may collect excessively as a result of poor hygiene, a diet rich in fats, or accelerated glandular activity, especially during adolescence. Excessive secretions of sebum may be related to ACNE, certain forms of BALDNESS, and other skin disorders.

Sebago Lake (sĭbā'gō), c.12 mi (20 km) long and from 1 to 8 mi (1.6–12.9 km) wide, SW Maine, in a resort area. It is the second-largest lake in Maine and is the source of Portland's water supply. Sebago State Park is on the lake.

Sebaste or **Sebastia:** see SIVAS.

Sebastian, Saint, fl. 3d cent.?, Roman martyr. Little is known of his life. According to tradition he was an officer of the Praetorian guards much favored by Emperor Diocletian, who did not know that Sebastian was a Christian. When the emperor learned of it, he ordered Sebastian killed by archers. Left for dead with arrows in his body, Sebastian recovered but was later beaten to death on the order of Diocletian. He was a favorite subject of Renaissance painters. Feast: Jan. 20.

Sebastian, 1554–78, king of Portugal (1557–78), grandson and successor of John III. He was under the regency first of his grandmother (until 1562) and then of his uncle Henry (a cardinal and later king) until declared of age in 1568. Weak and sickly, Sebastian was imbued by his Jesuit training with fanatic religious fervor, which he combined with a tremendous admiration for the military. Thus he viewed himself as a Christian knight and became determined to win glory by fighting the Muslim infidels in Africa. An appeal for help from a pretender to the Moroccan throne gave Sebastian his opportunity. Having secured (1576) a promise of aid from Philip II of Spain (his uncle), he spent vast sums of money in preparation for an expedition against Morocco. In 1578, Sebastian set out with a large force of foreign mercenaries (but no Spanish) and landed in Morocco. His headstrong desire to command and his lack of experience led to defeat in the Battle of the Three Kings at ALCAZARQUIVIR. His army was wiped out, and he himself was killed. However, it was not known at the time that he was dead, and rumor had it that he had been captured. The legend that he would return persisted, and Sebastianism (a messianic religious belief) lasted well into the 19th cent. His uncle Henry succeeded him and was the last of the Aviz kings. The crown then went to Philip II, and Spanish control of Portugal began.

Sebastiano del Piombo (sābästyä'nō dĕl pyôm'bō), c.1485–1547, Italian painter of the Venetian school, whose real name was Sebastiano Luciani. Although he was trained by Giovanni Bellini, his early work was influenced by Giorgione. His first important work is the frescoed altarpiece representing St. Chrysostom in the Church of San Giovanni Crisostomo, Venice. Called to Rome (c.1510), he painted a series of lunettes in the Farnesina. He allied himself with Michelangelo, under whose influence he painted the *Raising of Lazarus* (National Gall., London); *Pietà* (Church of San Francesco, Viterbo); *Martyrdom of St. Agatha* (Pitti Palace, Florence); *Flagellation* and *Transfiguration,* the latter a fresco (Church of San Pietro in Montorio, Rome). In 1531 he was appointed to the lucrative office of the *piombo* (keeper of the papal seals) and painted little thereafter. Piombo's portraits are famous for their characterization and coloring. Noted examples include Doge Andrea Doria (Doria Palace, Rome), Cardinal Pole (Hermitage, Leningrad), Christopher Columbus (Metropolitan Mus.), and portraits of cardinals (Vienna; Sarasota, Fla.).

Sebastopol: see SEVASTOPOL, USSR.

Sebat (səbät') or **Shebat** (shə–), the 11th month of the Jewish calendar, the fifth from New Year's. Zech. 1.7.

seborrhea (sĕb"ərē'ə), hypersecretion of the sebaceous glands (oil glands) of the skin. This condition occurs as a symptom of certain ailments of the skin, which are usually localized. More generalized disorders include seborrheic ECZEMA, which is accompanied by a rash, and seborrhea of the scalp, which accompanies some types of DANDRUFF. The tendency toward outbreaks of seborrhea is usually a lifelong, inherited phenomenon. It is treated by applications of local ointments and the maintenance of a well-balanced diet.

sebum: see SEBACEOUS GLAND.

Secacah (sĕk'əkə, sĕkā'kə), unidentified place in the wilderness. Joshua 15.61.

secant, in mathematics. **1** In geometry, a secant is a straight line cutting a curve or surface. If it intersects the curve in two different points, as in the secant of a CIRCLE, the segment of the secant between the points is called a chord. The limiting position of a secant, if such a limit exists, is called the TANGENT to the curve or surface at that point. **2** In trigonometry, the secant function is a relation defined in a right triangle for one of the acute angles (A) as the ratio of the length of the hypotenuse (c) to the length of the side (b) adjacent to the angle, or sec $A = c/b$. See TRIGONOMETRY.

Secaucus (sēkô'kəs), town (1970 pop. 13,228), Hudson co., NE N.J., on the Hackensack River, adjoining Jersey City; inc. 1917.

Secchi, Pietro Angelo (pyĕ'trō än'jālō sĕk'kē), 1818–78, Italian astronomer, a Jesuit priest. He was director of the observatory of the Gregorian Univ., Rome, from 1849. He is known especially for his work in spectroscopy and was a pioneer in classifying stars by their spectra. In 1860 he made some notable solar-eclipse photographs. His works include a star catalog (1867) and *Le stelle* (1877).

secession, in art, any of several associations of progressive artists, especially those in Munich, Berlin, and Vienna, who withdrew from the established academic societies or exhibitions. The artists of Munich formed a secession in 1892 that spread to other German cities. The Berlin Secession split away from the *Verein Berliner Künstler* in 1892; in 1899 it held its first exhibition in its own building. The group was led by Max Liebermann and included Lovis Corinth, Hans van Marées, and Franz von Stuck. When, in 1910, young artists of the Brücke group were excluded from the Berlin Secession exhibition, Max Pechstein led the rejected painters and organized the New Secession group. The Vienna Secession was organized in 1897 by 19 leading Austrian artists. Their leader was Gustav Klimt, whose decorative, exotic murals exemplify *Secessionstil,* the Viennese version of *art nouveau.* The Photo-Secession group was an American association of modern photographers founded in 1902 by Alfred Stieglitz and Edward Steichen in New York City in reaction against pictorial photography.

secession, in political science, formal withdrawal from an association by a group discontented with the actions or decisions of that association. The term is generally used to refer to withdrawal from a political entity; such withdrawal usually occurs when a territory or state believes itself justified in establishing its independence from that political entity of which it was once a part. By so doing, it assumes SOVEREIGNTY. An early example of secession is that of northern Israelite tribes from the larger Davidian kingdom after the death of Solomon (933 B.C.). Venezuela and Ecuador were created in 1830 when they seceded from Gran Colombia. Military action by Finnish nationalists enabled Finland to secede from a weakened Russia after 1917. In the 1960s the attempt of Katanga (now SHABA) to secede from the newly independent Republic of the Congo (now ZAÏRE) and that of BIAFRA to break away from NIGERIA were both crushed in long and bloody civil wars. By contrast, the secession (1971) of BANGLADESH (formerly East Pakistan) from the state of Pakistan was accomplished successfully with the help of India. Perhaps the best-known example of a secession taking place within the borders of a formerly unified nation was the withdrawal (1860–61) of the 11 Southern states from the United States to form the CONFEDERACY. This action, which led to the CIVIL WAR, brought to a head a constitutional question that had been an issue in the United States since the formation of the union. It was the most important point in the controversy over STATES' RIGHTS. The secessionists argued that the union created by the Constitution was only a compact of sovereign states and the power given to the Federal government was only a partial and strictly limited power, not paramount over the states and effective only in the limited field assigned it. The states, being sovereign, therefore had the legal right to withdraw from the voluntary union. The opponents of the right of secession believed that the Constitution created a sovereign and inviolable union and that withdrawal from that union was impossible. Prior to the Civil War secessionist sentiments were evidenced in both the North (see HARTFORD CONVENTION) and South, but as the North grew more powerful, talk of secession became more common in the South. The NULLIFICATION movement, which held that any state could declare null and void any Federal law that infringed upon its rights, was an attempt to eradicate the need for secession by giving the states complete sovereignty. Measures such as the MISSOURI COMPROMISE and the COMPROMISE OF 1850 were merely delays in solving the crucial problem of whether the states or the Federal government was to possess sovereignty. Desiring to maintain the slave system and threatened by the North socially and economically, the South finally seceded from the Union soon after the election of Abraham LINCOLN. The defeat of the Confederacy in the bloody war that followed settled the constitutional controversy permanently. See D. W. Howe, *Political History of Secession, to the Beginning of the Civil War* (1914); J. T. Carpenter, *The South as a Conscious Minority* (1930); D. L. Dumond, *The Secession Movement, 1860–1861* (1931, repr. 1963) and (ed.), *Southern Editorials on Secession* (1931, repr. 1964); U. B. Phillips, *The Course of the South to Secession* (1939, repr. 1964); H. C. Perkins, ed., *Northern Editorials on Secession* (1942, repr. 1964); D. M. Potter, *Lincoln and His Party in the Secession Crisis* (1942); K. M. Stampp, *And the War Came* (1950).

Secession, War of: see CIVIL WAR.

Sechu (sē'kə), unlocated place, N of Jerusalem. 1 Sam. 19.22.

second, abbr. sec or s, fundamental unit of TIME in all systems of measurement. In practical terms, the second is 1/60 of a minute, 1/3,600 of an hour, or 1/86,400 of a day. Since the length of the DAY varies, however, the second must be defined in more precise terms. For many years it was defined as 1/86,400 of the mean solar day (see MEAN SOLAR TIME), thus eliminating seasonal variations. Because the rotation of the earth itself is not constant, the second was redefined (1956) in terms of ephemeris time (ET), which is calculated from the motions of celestial bodies in accordance with the laws of motion; 1 sec is 1/31,556,925.9747 of the length of the tropical year for 1900. More recently, it has been calculated by atomic standards to be 9,192,631,770 periods of vibration of the radiation emitted at a specific wavelength by an atom of cesium-133.

Second Adventists: see ADVENTISTS.

secondary school: see SCHOOL.

Second Shepherd's Play, an English miracle play by the Wakefield Master (fl. 1425–50). The play portrays the adoration of Christ by the shepherds. Its singularity, however, lies in its introduction, a dramatically astute burlesque about a sheep stealer.

second sight, faculty of seeing as a vision events that are distant in time or space. It is closely related to various forms of divination, particularly CLAIRVOYANCE. The most curious aspect of second sight is the belief that it is experienced by domestic animals, who manifest their uncanny knowledge by signs of fear and distress when nothing startling is visible or audible to human beings.

Secord, Laura (Ingersoll) (sē'kôrd), 1775–1868, Canadian heroine of the War of 1812. Born in Massachusetts, she was taken by her parents to Canada after the American Revolution. In 1813 she learned from U.S. troops billeted in her house at Queenston of a planned surprise attack on the British at Beaver Dams on the Niagara frontier. She made her way through the American lines and gave warning to James Fitzgibbon at Beaver Dams. See biography by W. S. Wallace (1932).

secretary bird, common name for a long-legged African bird, *Sagittarius serpentarius,* related to the HAWK and about 4 ft (122 cm) tall. Its crest of black feathers suggested the quill pens behind the ear of a 19th-century male secretary. The bird hunts on foot, zigzagging toward its prey and flapping its wings, and is valued as a destroyer of snakes and other reptiles. Secretary birds are classified in the phylum CHORDATA, subphylum Vertebrata, class Aves, order Falconiformes, family Sagittariidae.

secretion, in biology, substance elaborated by the living material of an animal or plant. Secretions in man can be produced by a single cell or by a group of cells commonly called a gland. Some secretions perform special functions in the body (true secretions); others are eliminated as waste products (excretions). Digestive secretions include saliva, gastric juice, intestinal juice, pancreatic juice, and bile. Certain secretions serve as lubricants, e.g., the synovial fluid in joints or the secretions from mucous membranes and from the lachrymal (tear) glands. The mammary glands secrete milk. The endocrine (ductless) glands secrete hormones that enter directly into the bloodstream (see GLAND). Among the excretions from the body are urine (from the kidneys), perspiration (from the sweat glands), and bile pigments (from the gall bladder). Plant secretions include nectar and various enzymes concerned with the digestion of nutrients within the plant cells.

secret police, policing organization operating in secrecy for the political purposes of its government, often with terroristic procedures. The enforcement of the law has required, in nearly all societies, a certain amount of secrecy, particularly in that phase of law enforcement that is connected with the investigation of crime rather than with the apprehension and conviction of the criminal. The emergence of a uniformed, clearly recognizable police force is of much more recent origin than secret bodies formed by societies for their protection from internal and external attack. In its wider meaning, the term *secret police* embraces all those members of any police force that operate, often out of uniform, without giving warning to the suspected criminal that he is being investigated. However, in democratic nations, the role of the secret police ordinarily ends once the investigation is closed; either no sufficient ground for supposing guilt has been found, or the criminal is indicted and confronted with the full evidence against him. The limitation of the role of the secret police to investigation only and the right of the indicted offender to an open trial and to complete access to the evidence against him—these two conditions are basic guarantees of individual freedom in democratic societies. Wherever these interrelated conditions are not fulfilled, a secret police in the narrower sense of the term either exists or is in process of developing. In the narrow sense, the secret police is a body officially or in fact endowed with authority superior to other law-enforcing agencies. It investigates, apprehends, and sometimes even judges the suspect in secrecy, and it is accountable only to the executive branch of the government. In extreme cases such a secret police force may even have its own courts and prisons, and its activities are kept secret not only from the mass of the population but also from the legislative, judiciary, and executive authorities of the state, except at the topmost level. Like any ordinary police force, a secret police force may operate either in a recognizable uniform or in civilian clothes; the distinction does not lie there. It is sometimes assumed that secret police forces (in the narrower sense) have always been primarily concerned with the security of the state and that they are invariably created by governmental action, but this is not the case. Thus the formidable VEHMGERICHT of medieval Germany was a spontaneous creation of a segment of the people to protect its interests; it may be argued that the Vehme and similar institutions were secret societies rather than bodies of secret police, but the distinction is not always easy to make. It is certain that the institution of a secret police has reached its most menacing aspect in the modern totalitarian state—largely because of the improved technology at its disposal. Yet the institution is in no way exclusively limited to totalitarianism. It has existed in most societies where a minority has exercised an uneasy rule over a majority. Thus, in ancient Sparta, a well-organized secret police controlled the helots and ruthlessly suppressed any sign of rebellion. In Rome, particularly under the Julian emperors, a professional class of informers who received a share of their victims' confiscated fortunes, was employed by the state. Among the earliest secret police forces organized along modern lines were the Venetian Inquisition (see TEN, COUNCIL OF) and the Oprichina of Czar IVAN IV of Russia. Two 20th-century examples illustrate the workings of modern secret police forces.

Russia and the Soviet Union. After the abortive Decembrist coup of 1825, a powerful secret police was again organized in Russia at the order of the repressive Nicholas I. This force, the notorious Third Section (thus named because it was the third department of the czar's chancery), established a rigid and complicated system of censorship and sought to suppress not only subversive activity but even subversive thought. (The culmination of this trend, typical of police states, was symbolized by the name of the Japanese secret police before 1945—Thought Police.) The use of agents provocateurs by the czarist police led to such extremes that secret police, posing as revolutionists, actually helped to assassinate government officials. After the Russian Revolution of 1917 the Soviet government instituted its own secret police, the Cheka (the Russian acronym for All-Russian Extraordinary Commission for the Suppression of Counterrevolution and Sabotage), under Felix DZERZHINSKY. This was reorganized (1922) as the GPU, later the OGPU (United State Political Administration). In 1934 the functions of the OGPU were transferred to the NKVD (People's Commissariat for Internal Affairs), which was also responsible for all places of detention (e.g., forced labor camps) and for the regular police. Its first head, Genrikh Yagoda, was at first Stalin's chief agent in the purges that followed the murder of Sergei KIROV, but in 1936, Stalin replaced him with Nikolai Yezhov. Under Yezhov's direction the purges culminated in the wave of terror (1936–38) known as the Yezhovshchina. Yagoda himself was convicted, in the 1938 Moscow treason trials, of having been a leader in a conspiracy against Stalin. In 1938, Yezhov was succeeded by Lavrenti BERIA, and under Beria's long tenure the vast apparatus of the Soviet security organs became the most powerful and the most feared section of society. The NKVD was split (1943) into the NKVD and the NKGB, (People's Commissariat for State Security), the former retaining responsibility for internal security; in 1946 the NKVD became the MVD (Ministry of Interior), and the NKGB became the MGB (Ministry of State Security). After Stalin's death in 1953 the two ministries were fused into a new MVD under Beria. Later in the year Beria was arrested on charges of conspiracy and was killed; the charges illustrated the inherent danger of a strong secret police and its potential for overthrowing the very state that it is supposed to protect. After Beria's fall the Soviet security service was placed under the KGB (Committee of State Security). Although the KGB's functions resemble those of its predecessors, it has employed terror to a far lesser degree. It is subordinated to party control, and its main duties are concerned with internal intelligence.

Nazi Germany. Although the secret police in Italy during Mussolini's rule was notorious, probably the most extreme and terrible example was that in Germany under Adolf Hitler. Under NATIONAL SOCIALISM, Germany became a police state, i.e., a state where the power of the police, and especially the secret police, over security and justice was tyrannically applied with virtually no procedural checks. The German secret police had its genesis in the SS, or *Schutzstaffel* [defense echelon], created as Hitler's bodyguard under the SA (the military arm of the Nazi party), and in the SD, or *Sicherheitsdienst* [security service], organized in 1931 as the intelligence branch of the SS. From 1929, Heinrich HIMMLER controlled the SS. The Gestapo (secret state police) originated in 1933 under Hermann GOERING as the Prussian political police. Expanded and officially placed under Himmler in 1936, the Gestapo was effectively absorbed into the SS and was ultimately merged with the SD under Reinhard Heydrich. Just as the Gestapo had its secret ramifications among the mass of the population, the SD had agents, known only to the chief SD officers, in every department of the German government, in the armed forces, in the Nazi party, among the chief industrial executives, and among the Gestapo itself. While the existence of the Gestapo was common knowledge, the existence of the SD was known to few. The powers of the Gestapo, the SS, and the SD were vast; virtually any person suspected of disloyalty to the regime or of social aberration could be summarily arrested, executed, or interred in a concentration camp. The SS, which formed a separate army, was responsible to Himmler alone; thus, probably for the first time in history, a secret police wielded virtually absolute power. The crimes and atrocities of the Nazi authorities in Germany itself and throughout German-occupied Europe during World War II were largely carried out by the SS and the Gestapo, who controlled the concentration and extermination camps, and who set up their subsidiary agencies in every conquered country. See Brian Chapman, *Police State* (1970); P. S. Deriabin, *Watchdogs of Terror* (1972); Boris Levytski, *The Uses of Terror* (tr. 1972).

Secret Service, United States, law enforcement division of the Dept. of the Treasury. It was established in 1865 to investigate and prevent counterfeiting of currency. The Secret Service enforces Federal laws relating to coins, obligations, and the securities of the United States and foreign governments. After the assassination of President William McKinley in 1901, the force was charged with protecting the President. This protection was later extended to the members of the immediate family of the President, Vice President, the President-elect, the Vice President-elect, major presidential and vice presidential candidates, former Presidents and their wives, widows of former Presidents until their death or remarriage, minor children of a former President until they reach age 16, and visiting heads of state. See Michael Dorman, *The Secret Service Story* (1967).

secret society, organization of initiated persons whose members, purposes, and rituals are kept secret. Human groups throughout history have maintained secret societies. The ceremonies of initiation into such a society typically begin with an oath pledging secrecy as to all proceedings of the society, assuming special obligations to its members, and assenting to penalties for violation of the oath. This is followed by tests of the candidate's worthiness. In preliterate groups physical courage is stressed especially, and the tests at times include painful mutilations. A dominant theme in the initiation trials of most of these societies is the symbolism of death and rebirth. After the candidate has passed the prescribed tests, the secret knowledge is transmitted to him. One function of secret societies is to serve as schools in which the elders instruct the young men in the ways of their society. These initiations are essentially coming-of-age ceremonies. Women have comparable societies, but theirs have never matched those of men in number or importance. (A notable exception was the Hung Society of China, a secret society of women that lasted over 1,500 years.) The MYSTERIES, or secret rites and doctrines, of the Egyptians, the Persians, the Greeks, the Romans, and other ancient peoples were transmitted solely through secret societies. In modern civilizations secret societies are numerous. They usually offer various types of mutual aid for their members; there are, for example, special obligations to members who are ill and to the families of deceased members. Some churches oppose secret societies, as do some governments, which suspect them of being centers of disloyalty and subversion. Some secret societies, e.g., the MAFIA, under the guise of fraternal benevolence have defended the interests of their members by violence. See also FRATERNAL ORDERS, FRATERNITY, and FREEMASONRY. See J. H. Lepper, *Famous Secret Societies* (1932); Arkon Daraul, *A History of Secret Societies* (1962); J. M. Roberts, *The Mythology of the Secret Societies* (1972).

Secunderabad (sĭkŭn'dərəbăd"), town (1970 pop. 250,941), Andhra Pradesh state, S central India. A suburb of Hyderabad, the town is a major Indian army base.

Secundus (sēkŭn'dəs), companion of Paul on his third journey. Acts 20.4.

securities, in finance, instruments giving to their legal holders rights to money or other property. Securities include stocks, bonds, notes, mortgages, bills of lading, and bills of exchange. See SPECULATION and STOCK EXCHANGE.

Securities and Exchange Commission (SEC), agency of the U.S. government created by the Securities Exchange Act of 1934 and charged with protecting the interests of the public and investors in connection with the public issuance and sale of corporate securities. The five members of the SEC are appointed by the President and confirmed by the Senate for terms of five years. The SEC administers a number of the most important reform measures of the New Deal: the Securities Act of 1933, the Securities Exchange Act of 1934, the Public Utility Holding Company Act of 1935, the Trust Indenture Act of 1939, the Investment Company Act of 1940, and the Investment Advisers Act of 1940. In addition it may act as a participant in corporate reorganizations in the Federal courts under the National Bankruptcy Act. The first three of these statutes were passed in response to the pressure for greater protection of investors that developed as a result of the drastic decline in values of securities after Oct., 1929, the revelation of fraudulent and unfair practices in the sale of stocks and bonds, and the widespread belief that such practices had contributed to the severity of the GREAT DEPRESSION of the 1930s. The Securities Act of 1933 is intended to compel full disclosure to investors of material facts about securities offered and sold in interstate commerce or through the mails. It requires that before an issue of securities may be offered for public sale the issuer must file with the SEC a registration statement giving complete information on such securities and on the issuing company. Dealers in securities must provide their customers with a condensation of the data in the statement. The SEC examines the statement and may refuse registration if it appears to be misleading, inaccurate, or incomplete. If registration is denied, the securities may not be offered for sale. However, an approval of the statement is not a finding by the SEC that the securities have investment value, or even a guarantee that the disclosures are accurate. The Securities Exchange Act of 1934 is designed to increase the information available to investors and to prevent unfair practices in U.S. stock exchanges. It requires that certain current information be made public on the financial and managerial condition of corporations whose securities are traded in the exchanges. A registration statement containing such data for each listed security must be submitted to the SEC. The act also places the stock exchanges and over-the-counter markets under the SEC's supervision. Stock exchanges, brokers, and dealers must file information about themselves with the commission. Manipulative practices and false and misleading statements are prohibited. Other practices, such as short sales and market pegging, are regulated. Officers, directors, and principal stockholders of corporations whose securities are registered must report all their transactions in equity securities of their companies. The Board of Governors of the Federal Reserve System is responsible for regulating by means of margin requirements the use of bank credit to finance trading in securities. The Public Utility Holding Company Act regulates the financial practices of holding-company systems controlling electric and gas utilities. It provides for registration of holding companies, elimination of uneconomic holding-company structures, and supervision of their transactions in securities and of certain of their financial practices. The SEC must pass upon all plans for reorganization of such companies or their subsidiaries and must require the corporate simplification and geographic integration of holding-company systems. However, it does not regulate public-utility rates. This act was upheld by the Supreme Court in 1946. The Trust Indenture Act requires that securities of trustees meet satisfactory standards, and it also sets up qualifications for trustees. The Investment Company and Investment Advisers acts provide for registration and regulation of investment trusts, investment companies, and investment advisers. The various laws administered by the SEC are intended to give investors a greater degree of safety in entrusting their money to enterprises than was previously afforded them. With these laws the emphasis in determining responsibility for the quality and condition of goods sold has shifted from the buyer to the seller. However, the statutes do not guarantee investors against loss. It is perhaps no more difficult for them to lose their money than before. The regulatory measures were at first bitterly opposed by the financial community, on the ground that they imposed such severe limitations and liabilities on security issuers and dealers as to impede the financing of industry. Persons aggrieved by the decisions of the SEC have a right of review by a U.S. circuit court of appeals. The original penalties of the Securities Act of 1933 were softened in 1934. Governmental supervision has won generally increasing acceptance by the interests concerned. See annual reports of the SEC.

security, in international relations, state of safety from the effects of aggression. A nation that possesses security considers itself competent to protect itself through political, economic, and military means from foreign aggression. Typical expressions of the search for security are the maintenance of technologically modern military forces, the use of espionage, the establishment of a healthy national economy, and participation in military and political alliances. Since the end of World War I the attempt has been made to attain security through the collective efforts of many nations assembled together in international organizations by mobilizing the moral and physical resources of the great majority of nations against aggression. The LEAGUE OF NATIONS, the first of such bodies offering collective security, failed in its primary goal of maintaining international peace and was succeeded after World War II by the UNITED NATIONS. Difficulty in physically preventing the aggression of one UN member against another and the sharpening of the cold war during the 1950s led to the creation of important regional security organizations such as the North Atlantic Treaty Organization (NATO), the Southeast Asia Treaty Organization (SEATO), and the Warsaw Treaty Organization. The term "collective security" is, at present, generally used to refer to this type of military alliance. The proliferation of nuclear weapons and, consequently, the fear engendered by an increased threat of nuclear war, has given renewed importance to disarmament (see DISARMAMENT, NUCLEAR) as a means of attaining international security.

Security Council: see UNITED NATIONS.

Sedalia (sĭdā'lyə), city (1970 pop. 22,847), seat of Pettis co., W central Mo.; inc. 1864. A rail center in a farm area, it has railroad shops, meat-packing plants, and a great variety of manufactures. The huge state fairgrounds, a state workshop for the handicapped, a large children's therapy center, and a junior college are there. Whiteman Air Force Base is west of the city.

Sedan (sədäN'), town (1968 pop. 24,499), Ardennes dept., NE France, on the Meuse River. A noted textile center since the 16th cent., Sedan also has metal and brewing industries. The town became part of French crown lands in 1642. It was a Protestant stronghold in the 16th and 17th cent., and a noted Calvinist academy was located there. Sedan was the site of the decisive French defeat (1870) in the FRANCO-PRUSSIAN WAR and the surrender of Napoleon III. The town saw heavy fighting in World War I and was the point of the first German breakthrough (1940) in the invasion of France in World War II.

sedative, any of a variety of drugs that relieve anxiety. Most sedatives act as mild DEPRESSANTS of the nervous system, lessening general nervous activity or reducing the irritability or activity of a specific organ. Sedatives taken in small quantities are useful in relieving coughing, nausea, or convulsions, and in lessening anxiety. In increasing doses sedatives act as hypnotics (see HYPNOTIC DRUGS), i.e., they induce sleep, and as anesthetics. All sedatives, including BARBITURATES, MEPROBAMATE (Miltown), and chlordiazepoxide (Librium and Valium), are habit forming and should be taken only under medical direction. The term *sedative* is sometimes applied to drugs that alleviate pain but these are more properly known as ANALGESICS. TRANQUILIZERS are compounds that calm without excessively reducing mental alertness.

sedge, common name for members of the Cyperaceae, a family of grasslike and rushlike herbs found in all parts of the world, especially in marshes of subarctic and temperate zones. The name *sedge* is also used specifically for species of the genus *Carex* of the same family. Sedges differ from true grasses in having solid, angular (usually triangular) stems. Most are perennial, reproducing by rhizomes. Some sedges are woven into mats and chair seats, and a few provide coarse hay. The pith of *Cyperus papyrus* was the source of the PAPYRUS of ancient Egypt and other Mediterranean countries. Bulrushes, often called clubrushes, are sedges of the genus *Scirpus;* various other similar plants are also called bulrushes. The bulrushes in which the infant Moses was hidden (Ex. 2.8) were probably papyrus. The Oriental water chestnut (*Eleocharis tuberosa*) is cultivated extensively among the Chinese for its edible tubers. An unrelated Oriental aquatic plant, *Trapa natans,* also called water chestnut (or water caltrop or hornnut) and sometimes also used for food, is now naturalized in the United States. Many genera of the sedge family have indigenous and abundant species in America. Sedge is classified in the division MAGNOLIOPHYTA, class Liliatae, order Cyperales, family Cyperaceae.

Sedgemoor, marshy tract in Somerset, SW England. The forces of James II defeated the duke of Monmouth at Sedgemoor in 1685.

Sedgwick, Adam, 1785–1873, English geologist. He was a professor at Cambridge from 1818. His most important work was a study, made with R. I. Murchison, of the rock formation of Devonshire, which they named the Devonian system. Sedgwick also introduced the term *Cambrian.* See J. W. Clark and T. M. Hughes, *The Life and Letters of the Rev. Adam Sedgwick* (2 vol., 1890).

Sedgwick, Ellery, 1872–1960, American editor, b. New York City; brother of Henry Dwight Sedgwick. As editor (1908–38) of the *Atlantic Monthly* and president of its publishing company, he continued the literary traditions of the magazine and broadened its popularity. See his reminiscences, *The Happy Profession* (1946).

Sedgwick, Theodore, 1746–1813, American lawyer and statesman, b. West Hartford, Conn. He practiced law in Massachusetts after being admitted (1766) to the bar. In the American Revolution he acted (1776) as military secretary to Gen. John Thomas on the Canadian expedition. After serving in the state legislature for several years, he became a member of the Continental Congress, was concerned with the suppression of Shays's Rebellion, and was a delegate to the Massachusetts convention that ratified the Constitution (1788). A Federalist, from 1789 to 1801 he served both in the U.S. House of Representatives, where he was speaker (1799–1801), and in the Senate. He was afterward judge of the Supreme Judicial Court of Massachusetts until his death. See biography by R. E. Welch, Jr. (1965).

sediment, solid mineral or organic particles that have been deposited above or below sea level by the action of wind, water, or glacial ice. Sediments are commonly subdivided into three major groups—mechanical, chemical, and organic. Mechanical, or clastic, sediments are formed by the breakdown and erosion of earlier formed rocks on the earth's surface. These are then carried by streams, winds, or glaciers to the site where they are deposited. Streams may deposit sediment in flood plains along their courses or may carry these particles all of the way to the ocean, where they may be deposited to form part of a delta at the mouth of a river or part of a beach. They may also be deposited offshore on the continental shelf or deep ocean floor. Stream and wave action usually tend to sort the particles according to size, so that any given layer, or stratum, will tend to be composed primarily of particles of similar size. Thus, names given to these clastic deposits reflect the dominant size of particles making up the sediment. Particles larger than 2 mm (0.079 in.) in diameter are called, in order of increasing size, pebbles, cobbles, or boulders. Sand consists of particles ranging in size from 0.06 to 2 mm (0.0024–0.079 in.) in diameter and most commonly consists of the mineral quartz. Silt particles range from 0.004 to 0.06 mm (0.00016–0.0024 in.) in diameter. Clay consists of particles smaller than 0.004 mm (0.00016 in.) in diameter. Wind is usually capable of carrying only the finest particles, and most wind deposits are dunes composed of fine sands and silts. The finer clays are usually too widely dispersed to form a recognizable deposit except in deep lakes and deep ocean basins. Glaciers carry sediment frozen within the mass of the ice and are capable of carrying even huge boulders (erratics). Glacial deposits usually do not display evidence of size sorting unless the deposits are washed by meltwater streams. Chemical sediments are formed by chemical reactions in sea water that result in the formation and precipitation of minute mineral crystals. They settle to the floor of the sea, grow larger, and ultimately interpenetrate to form a more or less chemically pure layer of sediment. For example, limestone can form from the accumulation of tiny crystals of calcite, which may precipitate either by an increase in calcium carbonate concentration caused by the evaporation of sea water or by the loss of dissolved carbon dioxide from the sea water. Silica precipitates of chert also form directly from sea water. The nearly total evaporation of sea water, usually in shallow basins in land, results in the formation of a sequence of evaporite sediments, which includes gypsum and rock salt. Organic sediments are formed as a result of plant or animal actions. Peat and coal are formed by the incomplete decay of vegetation and its later compaction, during which process water and volatile substances are driven out. Lime deposits (marl) and limestone are most commonly formed by the aggregation of calcite shells of animals and some plants. Many limestones are coarse-grained because they are composed of rather large shells. Important deposits of lime are forming today as CORAL REEF deposits along tropical coasts. Lime muds form on the ocean floors as the calcium carbonate shells of microscopic planktonic organisms fall to the bottom. Foraminiferal oozes are composed of tiny coiled shells of single-celled zooplankton called Foraminifera. They are formed in regions of the ocean where biologic productivity is high and water depths are less than c.3,700 m (2.3 mi). Beyond that depth the increased carbon dioxide content, increased pressure, and lower temperature cause the calcite to dissolve. Sediments eventually may become lithified to form sedimentary rock by processes of compaction and cementation of the particles. Thus, coarse sediments gradually become CONGLOMERATE; sands become SANDSTONE; muds become SHALE; and reef debris becomes limestone. Sedimentary rocks make up only about 5% of all rocks of the earth's crust, yet they cover 75% of the land area in a veneer that averages 2.26 km (1.4 mi) in thickness, ranging from 0 to 12.9 km (0–8 mi). Shales are the most abundant sedimentary rock, making up over 80% of all sedimentary rocks. Sandstone and limestone each comprise slightly less than 10% of the sedimentary rock total. See W. H. Twenhofel, *Principles of Sedimentation* (2d ed. 1950); F. J. Pettijohn, *Sedimentary Rocks* (2d ed. 1957).

sedimentary rock: see ROCK; SEDIMENT.

sedition (sĭdĭ'shən), in law, acts or words tending to upset the authority of a government. The scope of the offense was very wide in early common law, which even permitted prosecution for a remark insulting to the king. Although there have been several statutes in the United States forbidding seditious utterances and writings, the protection guaranteed to speech and press by the First Amendment to the Constitution has made Congress reluctant to enforce them except in periods of great national stress. The Sedition Act of 1798 generated so much opposition (see ALIEN AND SEDITION ACTS) that similar statutes were not enacted until the 20th cent. During World War I the Espionage Act (1917) and the Sedition Act (1918) punished speeches and writings that interfered with the war effort or caused contempt for the government. Vaguely worded and broadly interpreted, they resulted in over 2,000 prosecutions, mostly against radicals and the radical press. The Smith Act of 1940, restricted in scope to the advocacy of violence against the government, was invoked only infrequently during World War II.

Sedition Act: see ALIEN AND SEDITION ACTS.

Sedley, Sir Charles, 1639?–1701, English dramatist and poet, b. London. Famous for his wit, he was a member of the intimate circle of young rakes at the court of Charles II. He wrote several plays, the best of which are the comedies *The Mulberry Garden* (1668) and *Bellamira* (1687). He also wrote amorous lyrics. See biography by V. de S. Pinto (1927, repr. 1973).

sedum: see STONECROP.

Seebeck effect: see THERMOELECTRICITY.

Seebohm, Frederic (sē'bōm), 1833–1912, English historian. His earliest historical studies were on aspects and results of the Reformation. Economic history claimed his attention, and in the discussion among historians of the village or MARK, Seebohm's *The English Village Community* (1883) upheld the theory that the feudal village had its origin in a semipastoral system probably influenced strongly by the Roman villa. He also wrote studies of original, pre-Roman customs in Britain.

Seeckt, Hans von (häns fən zākt), 1866–1936, German general. He fought in Poland, Serbia, Rumania, and Turkey during World War I. In 1920 he was made chief of the Reichswehr—the German army, which was limited to 100,000 men under the terms of the Treaty of Versailles. He commanded the Reichswehr until 1926 and made it an efficient nucleus capable of serving as cadre for a larger army. After the Treaty of Rapallo, Seeckt concluded (1923) a secret agreement with the USSR to obtain weapons forbidden by the Treaty of Versailles. He was (1930–32) a member of the Reichstag, representing the conservative People's party. In 1934–35 he was a military adviser to Chiang Kai-shek in China. Among his writings are *The Future of the German Empire* (tr. 1930) and *Thoughts of a Soldier* (1929, tr. 1930).

seed, ripened ovule of the PISTIL of a flower, consisting of the plant embryo, varying amounts of stored food material (endosperm), and a protective outer seed coat. Seeds are frequently confused with the FRUIT enclosing them, as in the grains and nuts. The seed-bearing plants are the highest in the evolutionary scale; in lower plants (e.g., mosses and ferns) the spore is the agent of propagation. Some plants (e.g., the banana) reproduce by vegetative means (see REPRODUCTION). True seeds vary in size from the dustlike seeds of some orchids to the large seed contained in the coconut. The period of dormancy undergone by many seeds before germination also varies; the mangrove seed may sprout inside a fruit still hanging on the tree, while the seeds of the Indian lotus are viable for about 400 years and the seeds of the arctic American lupine for 10,000 years when frozen in permafrost. Long dormancy in some seeds is ensured by their extremely hard coats, which commercially have to be scratched or split to force sprouting. In plant BREEDING, pollination is carefully controlled to produce the desired qualities in seed; under natural conditions a plant grown from seed may be quite different genetically from its maternal plant (see FERTILIZATION).

Seeger, Alan, 1888–1916, American poet, b. New York City, grad. Harvard, 1910. During World War I he served in the French Foreign Legion and was killed in battle in 1916. He is famous for his war poem, "I Have a Rendezvous with Death." See his *Collected Poems* (1916) and his letters and diary (1917).

Seeger, Pete, 1919–, American folksinger and composer, b. New York City. Seeger, son of a violinist mother and musicologist father, left Harvard in 1938 and made a journey through the United States, collecting songs and meeting Woody GUTHRIE and Huddy LEDBETTER. He served in World War II (1942–45) and entertained U.S. troops by singing folk songs. In 1940, Seeger organized the Almanac Singers, and in 1948 he formed the Weavers, thus helping to revive national interest in folk music. Always active in left-wing politics, Seeger was investigated by the House Committee on Un-American Activities in 1955. He was convicted on 10 counts of contempt of Congress, but the charges were dismissed in 1962. As a performer, Seeger is intimate and casual, often inviting his audience to sing along with him. He has influenced many younger singers, notably Joan BAEZ. Among the many songs he has composed are "Where Have All the Flowers Gone," "Turn, Turn, Turn," and "If I Had a Hammer."

seeing, in astronomy, the clarity with which stars and other celestial objects can be observed. It is primarily determined by the atmosphere of the earth. The most obvious phenomenon is twinkling, when the brightness of a star seems to fluctuate. Twinkling is caused by thermal motion of the air, which swirls air layers of different temperature and density. This motion causes minute alterations in the path of light from a star because different densities of air will bend light by different amounts. Twinkling is most obvious near the horizon because the light path from a star passes through more of the atmosphere. Since a planet is a disk and not, as a star, a point source, it will not show twinkling, but undulations across its surface can be viewed when it is near the horizon owing to the same effect. In addition, the atmosphere is denser at the bottom than at the top and thus continually bends a ray of light from a star more and more toward the vertical. As a result, all stars except those directly overhead appear to be closer to the zenith than they actually are; this is most pronounced for stars near the horizon. This effect causes the sun (or moon) to appear elliptical when it is rising or setting because its bottom edge is raised more by the refraction of the atmosphere than its top. Seeing is also affected by the amount of night light, which determines the length of time photographic plates can be exposed before fogging. This night light can be caused by the moon or other natural sources or by scattered light from artificial sources. Astronomical observatories are located in areas where seeing is good, usually on mountains where they are above some of the more turbulent layers of the atmosphere and also removed from cities' lights.

seeing-eye dog: see GUIDE DOG.

Seekonk (sē'kŏngk), town (1970 pop. 11,116), Bristol co., SE Mass., at the R.I. line; settled 1636, set off from Rehoboth 1812. It is residential.

Seeland: see SJAELLAND, Denmark.

Seely, John Edward Bernard, 1st **baron of Mottistone,** 1868–1947, British politician. He served in the South African War and entered Parliament as a Conservative in 1900. Having switched to the Liberal party, he became (1912) secretary of war in Herbert Asquith's cabinet. In 1914, when officers stationed at the Curragh military camp in Ireland asserted that they would not serve against the Ulster Unionists in the Home Rule crisis, Seely assured them that they would not be required to do so. This unauthorized concession complicated an already difficult situation, and Seeley was forced to resign. After serving in World War I, he was undersecretary for air (1919). In *Adventure* (1930) and *Fear and Be Slain* (1931) he tells the story of his life. He was created baron in 1933.

Seelye, Julius Hawley (sē'lē), 1824–95, American clergyman and educator, b. Bethel, Conn., grad. Amherst, 1849, and Auburn Theological Seminary, 1852, and studied in Germany; brother of L. C. Seelye. After serving as pastor of the First Reformed Church in Schenectady, N.Y., he became professor of mental and moral philosophy at Amherst in 1858; he was president of the college from 1876 to 1890. He inaugurated at Amherst what is said to be the first instance of student self-government on record in any American college. Seelye also served (1874–77) in Congress, to which he was elected in a nonpartisan movement. His writings include *The Way, the Truth, and the Life* (1873), *Duty* (1891), and *Citizenship* (1894).

Seelye, Laurenus Clark, 1837–1924, American educator and Congregational clergyman, b. Bethel, Conn., grad. Union College, 1857, and studied at Andover Theological Seminary and in Germany; brother of J. H. Seelye. From 1865 to 1873 he was professor of rhetoric, oratory, and English literature at Amherst. In 1873 he became first president of Smith College, retiring in 1910. See his *Early History of Smith College* (1923); biography by H. C. S. Rhees (1929).

Seferis, George (sĕfĕr'ēs), pseud. of Giorgos Sefiriades, 1900–1971, Greek poet. Educated at the Univ. of Paris, he returned to Greece, where he had a distinguished career as a diplomat, including service as ambassador to the United Nations (1956–57) and Great Britain (1957–62). His poetry is surrealistic and highly symbolic—at times cryptic—invoking classical Greek themes. Many of his poems explore the 20th-century Greek consciousness and way of life. His volumes of poetry include *Strophé* (1931) and *Mithistoríma* (1935, tr. 1960). He also produced a volume of essays on Greek poets and poetry, *Dokimés* (1944; tr. *On the Greek Style*, 1960). Seferis won the 1963 Nobel Prize in literature, the first Greek to do so. See his *Collected Poems, 1924–1955* (1967); *Three Secret Poems* (tr. 1969); *A Poet's Journal* (tr. 1974).

Sefiriades, Giorgos: see SEFERIS, GEORGE.

Segal, George, 1924–, American sculptor, b. New York City. A member of the POP ART movement, Segal is famed for his tableaux of life-sized white plaster human figures placed in everyday situations. Two major examples are *Woman in Restaurant Booth* (1961) and *Bus Driver* (Mus. of Modern Art, New York City). See study by W. C. Seitz (1972).

Segantini, Giovanni (jōvän'nē sägäntē'nē), 1858–99, Italian painter, b. in the Tyrol. A herdsman in his youth, he is known for his portrayal of Alpine peasant scenes. Well known among his works are *The Punishment of Luxury* (Liverpool) and *At the Watering Place* (Basel). The Segantini Museum is in Maloja, Switzerland.

Segesta (sĭjĕs'tə), ancient city of NW Sicily. Traditionally called a Trojan colony, it was the longstanding and bitter rival of Selinus. Athens undertook (415–413 B.C.) the disastrous expedition against Syracuse as an ally of Segesta in troubles growing out of a quarrel with Selinus. After this failure, Segesta got the help of Carthage, and Selinus was sacked (409). Thereafter Segesta was a Carthaginian dependency with some interruptions until the First Punic War, when it surrendered to the Romans. It declined in the 1st cent. B.C. The ruins, with a fine temple to Ceres, are near modern Alcamo.

Seghers, Anna (ä'nä sēgərs), 1900–, German novelist, whose original name was Netty Reiling Rádvanyi. She won fame with her first novel of social protest, *The Revolt of the Fishermen,* (1929, tr. 1930), but in 1933 she was forced to leave Germany. In Mexico she wrote *The Seventh Cross* (1939, tr. 1942), a poignant story of escape from a concentration camp. Other works include *Transit* (1942, tr. 1944) and a study of Tolstoy and Dostoyevsky (1963). After the war she settled in East Berlin.

Seghers, Hercules (hĕr'külĕs zā'gərs), c. 1590–c.1638, Dutch landscape painter and etcher. Seghers's work greatly influenced early 17th-century Dutch landscape painting. He studied with the painter Coninxloo (1544–1607) and may have traveled to Italy and in the Alps. Some of the frenzy of his personal life can be seen in his rare paintings and his more numerous masterly etchings. His landscapes consist of vast, often desolate, panoramas and powerful, smaller scenes rendered with drama and pathos. Rembrandt owned eight paintings by him, and his own landscape style was influenced by Seghers. The best collection of his work is at the Rijks Museum. See study by Leo C. Collins (1953).

Segni, Antonio (äntô'nyō sĕn'yē), 1891–1972, Italian political leader. A lawyer, he entered national politics in 1919 as a leader of the Popular party, the forerunner of the Christian Democratic party. For many years he was a professor at various universities. After World War II he was elected to the constituent assembly and then to parliament in 1948. He held numerous ministerial posts, serving twice as premier (1955–57, 1959–60). Elected president of Italy in 1962 he resigned in Dec., 1964, after suffering a cerebral hemorrhage.

sego lily (sē'gō), ornamental plant (*Calochortus nuttallii*) of the family Liliaceae (LILY family), also known in parts of the West as mariposa lily. It is native to the region W of the Rocky Mts., especially Utah, of which it is the state emblem. It has narrow leaves, beautiful tuliplike white flowers marked with purple, lilac, or yellow, and bulbous roots that were used by the early settlers for food. It is used in Mormon church symbolism. It is classified in the division MAGNOLIOPHYTA, class Liliatae, order Liliales, family Liliaceae.

Segonzac, André Dunoyer de (äNdrā' dünwäyā' də səgôNzäk'), 1884–1974, French painter and graphic artist. Segonzac was a member of the group known as the *section d'or,* which stressed geometric aspects in cubism. After 1920 his painting style became more lyrical and naturalistic. His watercolors, lithographs, and etchings include landscapes, dancers, figures, and still lifes, executed with great spontaneity and elegance.

Ségou or **Segu** (both: sāgōō'), town (1967 est. pop. 32,000), SW Mali, a port on the Niger River. It is the administrative and commercial center for an area where cotton, rice, millet, and peanuts are grown and cattle are raised. Cotton textiles are made in Ségou. In the late 17th cent. Ségou developed as the capital of a Bambara kingdom that reached its peak in the 18th cent. In 1861 the town was captured by Al-hajj Umar, a militant Muslim reformer. Umar (d.1864) and his son and successor Ahmadu, who ruled to 1890, made Ségou their capital. In 1890 the town was occupied by the French. It is the headquarters of a large-scale agricultural development project on the Niger River that was begun in 1932 by the French.

Segovia, Andrés (ändrās' sāgō'vyä), 1893–, Spanish guitarist. Segovia studied at the Granada Musical Institute. He is famous for his transcriptions of early contrapuntal music, which have shown the possibilities of the guitar as a concert instrument. Through concerts and recordings he is largely responsible for the 20th-century resurgence of interest in the guitar and its music. Composers who have written works for him include de Falla, Ponce, Roussel, and Villa-Lobos. See Roland Galatt, *Music Makers* (1953); Vladimir Bobri, *The Segovia Technique* (1972).

Segovia, city (1970 pop. 41,880), capital of Segovia prov., central Spain, in Old Castile, on the Eresma River. It stands on a rocky hill (3,297 ft/1,005 m high) crowned by the cathedral and the turreted alcazar (fortified palace). Under the Moors, it was a flourishing textile center but has since declined. There are light industries, and tourism is important. Segovia is of ancient origin and was favored by the Romans, who built (probably 1st cent.) the aqueduct (c.900 yd/820 m long) that still carries water to the city; it is built of uncemented limestone blocks and is one of the greatest Roman monuments in Spain. The city was repeatedly taken and lost by the Moors from 714 until Alfonso VI conquered it in 1079. It was a favorite residence of the kings of Castile. Isabella I was proclaimed queen in the alcazar (begun in the 11th cent.; built mostly in the 15th cent.; restored in the 19th). The late Gothic cathedral (16th cent.) has fine cloisters. Of the many medieval churches and palaces, the Romanesque churches of San Martín and San Esteban are the most notable. Spain's artillery academy is in Segovia.

Segovia, river, c.300 mi (480 km) long, rising in NW Nicaragua and flowing NE to the Caribbean Sea. Part of the MOSQUITO COAST region, once the object of dispute between Honduras and Nicaragua, the Segovia now forms the boundary between the two countries. It is also known as the Coco River.

segregation: see APARTHEID; INTEGRATION.

Segub (sē'gəb). **1** Son of Hiel the restorer of Jericho. 1 Kings 16.34. **2** Son of Hezron. 1 Chron. 2.21,22.

Séguier, Pierre, duc de Villemor (pyĕr sāgyā' dük də vēlmôr'), 1588–1672, chancellor of France. Beginning as counselor to the Parlement of Paris, he rose to become chancellor in 1635. He crushed a revolt in Normandy in 1639, presided (1642) over the trial of the marquis de CINQ MARS, and in 1661 arraigned Nicholas FOUQUET on charges of embezzlement at the start of a trial that ended in Fouquet's being condemned (1664) to banishment and eventually life imprisonment. A friend of Cardinal Mazarin, he was instrumental in having the Parlement accept Anne of Austria as regent for her infant son, Louis XIV.

Seguin (səgēn'), city (1970 pop. 15,934), seat of Guadalupe co., S central Texas, on the Guadalupe River; inc. 1853. Among its industrial products are bumpers, insulation, bricks, structural steel, fiber glass cloth, flour, packed meats, ditching machinery, furniture, and processed poultry. The city was founded (1831) by members of the Texas Rangers and named after Col. Juan Seguin, a hero of the Texas Revolution. It was once a plantation center and still keeps the appearance given it by later German settlers. The Guadalupe River and nearby Lake McQueeney attract vacationers. Texas Lutheran College is there.

Segura (sāgo͞o'rä), river, c.200 mi (320 km) long, rising on the northeastern slopes of the Sierra de Segura, SE Spain, and flowing generally East into the Mediterranean Sea. It is used for irrigation and hydroelectric-power generation.

seiche: see WAVE, in oceanography.

Seignette salt: see ROCHELLE SALT.

Seignobos, Charles (shärl' sānyōbō'), 1854–1942, French historian. He taught at the Univ. of Paris and wrote many works on French and European history and civilization, some being contributions to the series edited by Ernest LAVISSE and Alfred Rambaud. A number of these are widely used as textbooks in France. Seignobos's most outstanding book is his *Histoire politique de l'Europe contemporaine* (1897). Noted for his clear and unbiased narrative, Seignobos emphasized political history rather than social and economic change.

seignorial system: see MANORIAL SYSTEM; FEUDALISM.

Seillière, Ernest, Baron (ĕrnĕst' bärôN' sāyĕr'), 1866–1955, French critic and philosopher. He is best known as an opponent of romanticism and for his philosophy of "imperialism." His theories were expounded in many works, notably in *La Philosophie de l'impérialisme* (4 vol., 1903–8). A collection of his essays was translated as *Romanticism* (1929).

Seine, Lat. *Sequana,* river, c.480 mi (770 km) long, rising in the Langres Plateau and flowing generally NW through N France. It passes Troyes, Melun, and Paris, whence it meanders in large loops through Normandy, past Rouen, and empties into the English Channel in an estuary between Le Havre and Honfleur. With its tributaries (the Aube, Marne, Oise, Yonne, Loing, and Eure) and connecting canals, it drains the entire Paris basin. One of the most navigable rivers in France, it has been a great commercial artery since Roman times. The channel of the Seine is dredged and oceangoing vessels can dock at Rouen. Much of France's internal and foreign trade moves on the Seine. Paris, Rouen, and Le Havre owe their prosperity to their favorable location on the river.

Seine-et-Marne (sĕn-ā-märn), department (1968 pop. 604,340), N central France, in BRIE. MELUN is the capital.

Seine-Maritime (sĕn-märētēm'), formerly **Seine-Inférieure** (sĕn"-ăNfārēûr'), department (1968 pop. 1,113,977), N France, on the English Channel, mainly in Normandy. Cities include ROUEN (the capital) and Le Havre (see HAVRE, LE).

Seine-Saint-Denis (sĕn-săNd"nē'), department (1968 pop. 1,251,792), N central France, adjoining Paris. BOBIGNY is the capital.

Seipel, Ignaz (ĭg'näts zī'pəl), 1876–1932, Austrian chancellor (1922–24, 1926–29). A Roman Catholic priest, he was elected to the Austrian parliament in 1919 and became leader (1921–29) of the Christian Socialist party. As chancellor he did much to stabilize finances by introducing stringent economies and securing an international loan guaranteed by the League of Nations. His criticism of parliamentary democracy and his support of the Heimwehr, the Austrian fascistic militia, are thought to have paved the way for the quasidictatorial rule of DOLLFUSS and SCHUSCHNIGG.

Seir (sē'ər). **1** Mountainous region, S Palestine, S of the Dead Sea. Mt. Hor is the highest point. Seir is identical with EDOM, which is mentioned frequently in the Bible as Mt. Seir. The eponym appears at Gen. 36.20, 1 Chron. 1.38. **2** Mountain, at the border of Judah. Joshua 15.10.

Seirath (sē'ĭrăth, sēī'–), mountainous region, E central Palestine. Judges 3.26.

Seishin: see CHONGJIN, North Korea.

seismic sea wave: see TSUNAMI.

seismology (sīzmŏl'əjē, sīs–), scientific study of EARTHQUAKES and related phenomena. Instruments used to detect and record seismic disturbances are known as seismographs. Those in use today vary somewhat in design and function, but generally a heavy mass, either a pendulum or a large permanent magnet, is an essential part of the detecting instrument. A mechanical or optical recording device is connected with the pendulum or the magnet. A mechanical system consists of a rotating drum having either a smoke-covered surface marked by a stylus or a roll of paper marked by a pen or pencil. In an optical system a beam of light is reflected by a mirror on photographic paper or film. When tremors of the earth occur, the pendulum or the magnet, because of inertia, remains still as the earth moves beneath. The relative motion between the earth and the instrument is magnified by a system of levers or by electrical amplifying apparatus. For interpretation of the record the time intervals must be accurately marked on the drum. From the graphic record, called the seismogram, much information about an earthquake, e.g., its severity and distance, can be obtained. By using three instruments, each set to respond to motions from a different direction (north-south horizontal, east-west horizontal, and vertical), both the distance and the direction of the earth movement can be found. In some observatories a single instrument is used to make a simultaneous record of movement in all three directions. Three or more widely spaced seismographic stations are required to pinpoint the location of earthquakes in remote regions. An important commercial application of seismology is its use in prospecting for oil deposits. The first oil field to be discovered by this method was found in Texas in 1924. A portable seismograph is set up in the area to be investigated and a high explosive charge is detonated in a hole drilled nearby. From an interpretation of the waves created by the explosions and recorded on the seismograph the detection of geological structures in which oil may be trapped is possible. The waves generated by the explosions are received by detectors known as geophones, which are commonly placed in a fan-shaped pattern on the ground. Seismic methods are sometimes used to locate subsurface water and to determine the configuration and depth of the ocean floor. With the development of underground testing of nuclear devices, seismographic stations for their detection were set up throughout the world. Often called the founder of seismology, the American scientist John Winthrop (1714–79) was one of the first to make scientific studies of earthquakes. See C. F. Richter, *Elementary Seismology* (1958); K. E. Bullen, *An Introduction to the Theory of Seismology* (3d ed. 1963); Beno Gutenberg and C. F. Richter, *Seismicity of the Earth and Related Phenomena* (2d ed. 1954, repr. 1965); see also bibliography under EARTHQUAKE.

Seistan (sāstän') or **Sistan** (sē–), border lowland region of SW Afghanistan and E Iran, c. 6,000 sq mi (15,540 sq km), fed mainly by the spring flood of the Helmand River and other streams. At low water, the region is reduced to two lagoons (Hamun-e Helmand and Gowd-e Zereh), and wheat, barley, and cotton are grown on the exposed land. Seistan's c.300,000 inhabitants live mainly on three deltas. Seistan corresponds roughly to ancient Drangiana. In the 2d–3d cent. A.D. it was held by the Scythians and was called Sakastan, from which the modern name derives. From the 4th–7th cent. the region was the center of Zoroastrian worship. Seistan prospered under the Arabs from the 8th cent. A.D. until 1383, when Mongol conquerors destroyed the Helmand River control system and ended Seistan's prosperity. The area was disputed between Persia and Afghanistan from the 16th to early 20th cent.; in times of drought, water rights are still contested.

Seitz, Karl (kärl zīts), 1869–1950, Austrian politician. He was a deputy from 1901 and became (1907), with Viktor Adler, co-leader of the socialist group in parliament. He was (1919–20) acting president of Austria. As mayor of VIENNA (1923–34) he increased social services. When the Social Democrats were suppressed in 1934, he was arrested but was later released on parole. He was imprisoned by the Nazis in 1944. When Austria was restored after World War II, Seitz was elected (1945) to parliament.

Seiyukai (sā'yo͞okī"), Japanese political party, founded in 1900. It was derived, via the Kenseito (see MINSEITO) from the Jiyuto, organized by Taisuke Itagaki in 1881. Under the astute political leadership of Takashi HARA, it was the most powerful party in Japan from 1900 to 1921. Hirobumi ITO was its first president, and Kimmochi SAIONJI its second, but these great statesmen were more powerful in their own right than as party leaders. The first real party cabinet, marking the decline of the old GENRO oligarchy, was formed by Takashi Hara in 1918. Party governments prevailed from 1924 to 1932, the Seiyukai cabinets of Giichi Tanaka (1927–29) and Ki Inukai (1931–32) alternating with Minseito governments. After this the influence of political parties steadily declined as that of the militarists increased. Japanese parties have been based more on factionalism and personal loyalty than on divisions of principle. The Seiyukai was generally conservative and acceded to bureaucratic and military control more willingly than the Minseito. After World War II, the Seiyukai reappeared, under the leadership of Kijuro Shidehara, as the Progressive party, the most conservative major political party in postwar Japan. The Progressives were later absorbed into the business-oriented Liberal-Democratic party. The Seiyukai was traditionally identified with the Mitsui financial interests. See Peter Duus, *Party Rivalry and Political Change in Taishō Japan* (1968).

Sejanus (Lucius Aelius Sejanus) (sĭjā'nəs), d. A.D. 31, Roman statesman; son of Sejus Strabo, Praetorian prefect. When his father went to Egypt as governor, he succeeded to the command of the Praetorian Guards and obtained great ascendancy over Emperor TIBERIUS. He was suspected of conspiring (A.D. 23) with Livilla in a successful plot to poison her husband, the emperor's son Drusus. He obtained (A.D. 29) the arrest of AGRIPPINA I. Sejanus was put to death by Tiberius, who feared that he was plotting against him.

Sekondi-Takoradi (sĕk'əndē-täkôrä'dē), city (1970 pop. 89,686), capital of the Western Region, SW

Ghana, on the Gulf of Guinea. An important seaport and commercial city, Sekondi-Takoradi has shipbuilding, railroad repair, and cigarette industries. The two parts of the city developed around Dutch and English forts built in the 17th cent. Sekondi, the older and larger of the two, prospered after the construction (1903) of a railroad to the mineral and timber resources of the hinterland. A deepwater harbor was constructed at Takoradi in 1928. The two parts were amalgamated in 1946.

Sela or **Selah** (sē'lə) [Heb.,=rock], unidentified town, S of the Dead Sea. Amaziah captured it and renamed it Joktheel. Some identify Sela with PETRA. Num. 20.8; 2 Kings 14.7; Isa. 16.1. Sela in Judges 1.36 seems to be another rock.

Selah (sē'lə), obscure Hebrew word occurring many times in Psalms and in Hab. 3.3,9,13. Its derivation is unknown. It may be a musical notation signifying a pause or the end of a phrase.

Sela-hammahlekoth (sē'lə-hăm"əlē'kŏth), unlocated place associated with Saul's pursuit of David. 1 Sam. 23.28.

Selangor (səlăng'ər), state (1971 pop. 1,629,386), 3,150 sq mi (8,159 sq km), Malaysia, S Malay Peninsula, on the Strait of Malacca. KUALA LUMPUR, its capital, is also capital of Malaysia. Port Swettenham is the chief port. Tin and coal are mined; rubber, rice, pineapples, and oil palms are grown; and there are numerous fisheries. Both the Chinese and Indian groups in the population exceed the native Malay group; together the Chinese and Indians constitute about two thirds of the inhabitants. Before the 16th cent. the territory of Selangor was subject to the powers that in turn dominated the Malay Peninsula. After the fall of Malacca (1511), it was nominally ruled by the sultans of Riau and Johor, but in the early 18th cent. it was conquered by Bugis tribesmen from Celebes, who for a time threatened to dominate the Malay Peninsula from Selangor. Selangor became a British protectorate in 1874, one of the Federated Malay States in 1896, and part of the Federation of Malaya in 1948.

Selassie, Haile: see HAILE SELASSIE.

Selborne, Roundell Palmer, 1st **earl of** (sĕl'bôrn), 1812–95, British jurist and statesman. Called to the bar in 1837, he entered Parliament in 1847 as a nominal Conservative. He soon was associated more with the Liberals, however, and served Lord Palmerston as solicitor general (1861–63) and Palmerston and Lord John Russell as attorney general (1863–66). As lord chancellor under William Gladstone (1872–74, 1880–85), Selborne secured passage of the Judicature Act of 1873, a landmark reform of the British courts. He broke with Gladstone in 1885 on the question of Irish Home Rule and joined the Liberal Unionists. Selborne was a conservative writer on problems of church history and doctrine. He was created an earl in 1882. His son, **William Waldegrave Palmer,** 2d **earl of Selborne,** 1859–1942, was first lord of the admiralty (1900–1905) and worked closely with Sir John Fisher (later 1st Baron FISHER) on the important naval reforms of the period. As high commissioner (1905–10) for South Africa, he proposed and worked out the details for the formation of the Union of South Africa. He was president of the Board of Agriculture in 1915–16 but held no further offices.

Selden, John, 1584–1654, English jurist and scholar. He studied at Oxford, was called to the bar in 1612, and was elected to Parliament in 1623. He had already assisted in preparing the protestation of Commons in 1621, asserting to King James I Parliament's rights in the affairs of state, and he had briefly been held in custody as a result. He continued to support the rights of Parliament in its struggle with the crown, was prominent in the trial of George Villiers, 1st duke of Buckingham, and helped to draw up the Petition of Right in 1628. For his activity in the recalcitrant Parliament of 1629 he was imprisoned and not released until 1631. He represented Oxford Univ. in the Long Parliament from 1640 to 1649. Selden was considered one of the most erudite men of his time. His *England's Epinomis* and *Jani Anglorum* (1610) established him as the father of legal antiquarianism. The preface to his edition of the *Fleta* (1647) summarizes his lifelong study in the origins of British law. Selden's reputation as an Orientalist was begun with his *De Diis Syris* (1617), and he prepared a number of studies of rabbinical law. His *History of Tithes* (1618) involved him in a conflict with the clergy, and the work was suppressed. Among his other works is *Mare Clausum* (1635), a defense of England's right to sovereignty over the seas between that country and the Continent, written in response to Hugo Grotius's *Mare Liberum*. He is popularly best remembered for the record of his conversations kept by his secretary, Richard Milward, and published as *Table Talk* (1689, ed. by Frederick Pollock, 1927). See G. W. Johnson, *Memoirs of John Selden* (10 vol., 1883–84).

Selden, uninc. village (1970 pop. 11,613), Suffolk co., SE N.Y., on Long Island.

selection. In DARWINISM, the mechanism of natural selection is considered of major importance in the process of EVOLUTION. As a result of various factors in the environment (e.g., temperature and the quantity of food and water available) and of the geometrically increasing overproduction of plants and animals that results from the process of reproduction, a struggle for existence arises. In this struggle, according to Darwin, those organisms better adapted to the environment survive and reproduce, while those least fitted do not. The selection is therefore based on adaptation. A special form of natural selection, sexual selection, is also stressed in Darwinism. It attempts to account for secondary sexual characteristics that are not necessarily valuable in the struggle for existence. It assumes that the female selects as a mate one having the most highly developed of such characteristics, e.g., elaborate plumage or superior song, thereby perpetuating those characteristics. However, this interpretation is now questioned by many scientists. Artificial selection, the selection by man of individuals best suited for his purpose, is common in plant and animal breeding.

selective service, in U.S. history, term for CONSCRIPTION. Conscription was established (1863) in the Civil War, but Congress authorized release from service to anyone who furnished a satisfactory substitute and, at first, to those who paid $300. General conscription was introduced in World War I. The Selective Service Act of 1917 required all men from 21 to 30 years of age, inclusive, to register. The age limits were extended to 18 and 45 in 1918. Exemptions from service were granted to men who had families dependent on them, who were physically unfit, who were indispensable for duties at home, or who belonged to religious organizations with pacifist principles. By the end of World War I about 2,800,000 men had been inducted into service under the selective service system. The United States adopted peacetime conscription for the first time in its history by the Selective Training and Service Act of 1940. This act provided that not more than 900,000 men were to be in training at any one time, and it limited service to 12 months—later (1941) extended to 18 months. After the United States entered World War II a new selective service act was passed that made men between 18 and 45 liable for military service and required all men between 18 and 65 to register. The terminal point of service was extended to six months after the war. From 1940 until 1947—when the wartime selective service act expired after extensions by Congress—over 10,000,000 men were inducted into the armed forces. A new selective service act was passed in 1948 that required all men between 18 and 26 to register and that made men from 19 to 26 liable for induction for 21 months' service, which would be followed by 5 years of reserve duty. When the Korean War broke out the Selective Service Act of 1948 was replaced (1951) by the Universal Military Training and Service Act. The length of service was extended to 24 months, and the minimum age for induction was reduced to 18½ years. The Reserve Forces Act of 1955 had as its main purpose the strengthening of the reserve forces. It required six years of duty, including both reserve and active duty. The Military Selective Service Act of 1967 required all men between the ages of 18 and 26 to register for service. Exemptions were allowed for the handicapped, and educational deferments were granted. The educational deferment tended to discriminate against working-class and poor men, and thus a higher percentage from these groups were called upon for military service; for this reason and others, conscription became a major social issue during the Vietnam War. In 1973 conscription was abolished in favor of an all-volunteer army.

Seled (sē'lĕd), descendant of Jerahmeel. 1 Chron. 2.30.

Selene (səlē'nē), in Greek mythology, moon goddess; daughter of the Titans Hyperion and Theia and sister of the sun god Helios. There was no known moon cult among the Greeks, but Selene was a significant figure in Greek poetry and sorcery and was often identified with Hecate and Artemis.

Selenga (sĕlĕng-gä'), river, 616 mi (992 km) long, rising in the Khangai mts., NW Mongolian People's Republic, and flowing east, then north, across the Mongolia-USSR border to Lake Baykal; the Orkhon River is its main tributary. The Selenga, navigable from May to October, is Mongolia's chief river; its role as a transportation artery decreased with the advent of the Trans-Baykal RR. Ulan-Ude, an important Soviet rail junction, river port, and industrial center, is the largest city on the river.

selenite (sĕl'ĭnīt, səlē'nīt) [Gr.,=of the moon], transparent variety of GYPSUM. When pure, it is clear and colorless. It occurs commonly in nature and is found in the United States (New York, Utah, and Ohio), in Canada, and in Europe (France, Italy, and Switzerland). Crystals of great beauty have been discovered in Sicilian sulfur mines. Selenite crystallizes in the monoclinic system. Chemically it is hydrated calcium sulfate, $CaSO_4 \cdot 2H_2O$.

selenium (səlē'nēəm), nonmetallic chemical element; symbol Se; at. no. 34; at. wt. 78.96; m.p. 217°C; b.p. about 685°C; sp. gr. 4.81 at 20°C; valence −2, +4, or +6. Selenium is directly below sulfur in group VIa of the PERIODIC TABLE. In chemical activity and physical properties it resembles sulfur and tellurium. Selenium exhibits allotropy, appearing in a number of forms, including a red amorphous powder, a red crystalline material, and a gray crystalline metallike form called "metallic" selenium. A remarkable property (discovered by Willoughby Smith in 1873) of the gray metallic form is that its electrical conductivity is greater in light than in darkness, and it increases as the illumination increases. This property has led to use of the metallic form in the junction rectifier and as a cathode in the photoelectric cell rectifier. Selenium is extensively used in the vulcanization of rubber, in the manufacture of red glass and some enamels, as a decolorizer of glass to counteract the green of iron compounds, in electronics, and in xerography. Selenium forms the oxides SeO_2 and SeO_3, the selenious (H_2SeO_3) and selenic (H_2SeO_4) acids and their respective selenite and selenate salts, a nitride, carbide, hydride, two sulfides, and various halides and oxyhalides. Selenium sometimes occurs in conjunction with sulfur deposits and often occurs as the selenide (especially of copper, lead, silver, and iron) in sulfide ores. Commercially it is obtained chiefly as a by-product in the refining of copper. In the Great Plains region and certain other areas, selenium is absorbed from the soil by vegetation in quantities sufficient to poison livestock, thus rendering the land useless for grazing. The element was discovered by Berzelius in 1817.

Seleucia (səlo͞o'shə), ancient city of Mesopotamia, on the Tigris below modern Baghdad. Founded (c.312 B.C.) by Seleucus I, it soon replaced Babylon as the main center for east-west commerce through the valley. The city was the eastern capital of the Seleucids until the Parthians conquered it. The Seleucids then moved their capital across the river to Ctesiphon, and Seleucia was thus superseded. In a Parthian campaign Trajan burned the city, and in 164 B.C. it was destroyed by Romans. Another Seleucia was founded by Seleucus I in Syria as the seaport for Antioch on the Orontes. St. Paul sailed from there (Acts 13.4).

Seleucus I (Seleucus Nicator) (səlyo͞o'kəs), d. 280 B.C., king of ancient Syria. An able general of Alexander the Great, he played a leading part in the wars of the DIADOCHI. In the new partition of the empire in 312 B.C. he received Babylonia. Conquest of Susiana and Media enlarged his holdings, and he invaded NW India. Later (c.305) he yielded part of present Afghanistan to SANDRACOTTUS. Seleucus was drawn into the league against ANTIGONUS I, and when Antigonus was defeated at Ipsus in 301 B.C., Seleucus gained a large part of Asia Minor and all of Syria. Of the Macedonian generals he was the one who tried hardest to set up a kingdom following Alexander's ideas. He founded Greek colonies such as Seleucia and Antioch. He also tried to govern the subject people according to the methods of the Persian Empire. He finally won Asia Minor by defeating Lysimachus in the battle at Corupedion in Lydia in 281, an event that marked the end of the Diadochi. Seleucus was murdered before he could achieve his ambition of seizing the vacant throne of Macedonia as well. He was succeeded by Antiochus I. See E. R. Bevan, *The House of Seleucus* (2 vol., 1902; repr. 1966).

Seleucus II (Seleucus Callinicus), d. 226 B.C., king of ancient Syria (247–226 B.C.), son of Antiochus II. On his father's death there was a struggle for the throne between Seleucus and his stepmother, Berenice (on behalf of her infant son). Seleucus seems to have murdered both Berenice and her son before her brother Ptolemy III of Egypt could arrive. A long war with Ptolemy ensued. Seleucus also had to wage war with his own brother, Antiochus Hierax, for Asia Minor. Bactria and Parthia revolted and threw off Seleucid control. He was succeeded by his son Seleucus III, who was killed after a three-year reign; another son, ANTIOCHUS III, then became king.

self-heal or **heal-all,** weedy perennial (*Prunella vulgaris*) with the typical angular stems and bluish flowers of the family Labiatae (MINT family). Although it probably originated in the Old World, self-heal is now distributed throughout temperate climates and is a common plant of North American pastures and open woods. It was formerly used as a domestic remedy for sore throats and other minor ailments. *Prunella* is classified in the division MAGNOLIOPHYTA, class Magnoliopsida, order Lamiales, family Labiatae.

self-portrait: see PORTRAITURE.

Seligman, Edwin Robert Anderson (sĕl'ĭgmən), 1861–1939, American economist, b. New York City, Ph.D. Columbia, 1885. As professor (1885–1931) at Columbia, he edited the "Columbia University Studies in History, Economics, and Public Law" and the *Political Science Quarterly.* He was editor in chief of the *Encyclopaedia of the Social Sciences* (15 vol., 1930–35). An expert on public finance, he acted on many tax commissions and in 1931 was financial adviser to the Cuban government. His works include *The Shifting and Incidence of Taxation* (1892, 5th ed. 1927), *Essays in Taxation* (1895, 10th ed. 1925), *The Economic Interpretation of History* (1902, 2d ed. 1924), *Principles of Economics* (1905, 12th ed. 1929), and *The Economics of Farm Relief* (1929). See R. G. Hoxie and others, *History of the Faculty of Political Science, Columbia University* (1955).

Selim I (Selim the Grim) (sĕlĭm'), 1467–1520, Ottoman sultan (1512–20). He ascended the throne of the Ottoman Empire (Turkey) by forcing the abdication of his father, BEYAZID II, and by killing his brothers. A religious controversy (see SUNNI and SHIITES) and Persian support for his brother Ahmed led Selim, a Sunnite, to attack Persia. In 1514 he defeated the Shiite conqueror of Persia, Shah Ismail, annexing Diyarbekır and Kurdistan. This began the enduring rivalry between Persians and Ottomans. Aided by his superior artillery, he defeated (1516–17) the Mamelukes in Syria and Egypt, which he added to the Ottoman Empire. By assuming the CALIPHATE, Selim made himself and his successors spiritual as well as temporal heads of the empire and gained control over the holy cities, Mecca and Medina. Selim died while preparing the conquest of Rhodes. A bloodthirsty and inflexible despot, Selim was also an able organizer and reformer. Under him the Ottoman Empire entered the period of its greatest power. He supported literature and wrote poetry in Persian. His son, Sulayman I, succeeded him.

Selim II (Selim the Drunkard), c.1524–1574, Ottoman sultan (1566–74), son and successor of SULAYMAN I. During his reign the Ottoman Empire (Turkey) was dominated by Sokolli, his grand vizier (chief executive officer). Although the Turks conquered Cyprus from Venice and recovered Tunis from Spain, the Ottoman Empire received its first severe setback by Christians during Selim's reign in the naval defeat at LEPANTO in 1571. He was succeeded by his son Murad III.

Selim III, 1761–1808, Ottoman sultan (1789–1807), nephew and successor of Abd al-Hamid I to the throne of the Ottoman Empire (Turkey). He suffered severe defeats in the second of the RUSSO-TURKISH WARS with Catherine II, but suffered no major territorial losses when peace was made at Jassy in 1792. An ardent reformer, Selim set out to rebuild the Turkish navy on European lines, to reform the army, and to curb the JANISSARIES. In 1798 Selim joined the second coalition against France in the French Revolutionary Wars. Turkish forces lost Jaffa to Napoleon Bonaparte, who had invaded (1799) Syria after taking Egypt, but they held out at Acre and forced Napoleon to retreat. In 1801 the French left Egypt, which was restored to the sultan. In 1804 the Serbs under KARAGEORGE revolted. In 1806 war with Russia broke out again. A revolt of the Janissaries and conservatives who opposed his reforms led to Selim's deposition and imprisonment in 1807. MUSTAFA IV was placed on the throne. A loyal army marched on Constantinople to restore Selim. It entered the city in 1808, just after Selim had been strangled on Mustafa's orders. Mustafa was executed and another of Selim's cousins, Mahmud II, was put on the throne. During Selim's reign Egypt became virtually independent under MUHAMMAD ALI, as did Albania under ALI PASHA. Selim's well-intentioned and efficient reforms came too late to arrest the decay of the Ottoman Empire.

Selinus (sĭlī'nəs), ancient city of Sicily. It was founded (628? B.C.) by Dorian Greeks. The constant rival of neighboring Segesta, Selinus got Syracuse to interfere in a quarrel, which led to the unsuccessful Athenian expedition in Sicily (415–413 B.C.). Segesta invoked the aid of the Carthaginians, who sacked Selinus in 409 B.C. The city was rebuilt, but it did not prosper and was finally destroyed by Carthage in 250 B.C. The ruins of the five Doric temples on the Acropolis of Selinus have been excavated, revealing some of the finest examples of archaic Greek sculpture and architecture.

Seljuks: see TURKS.

Selkirk, Alexander (sĕl'kərk), 1676–1721, Scottish sailor, whose adventures suggested to Daniel Defoe the story of *Robinson Crusoe* (1719). In 1704, as a sailing master, Selkirk quarreled with the captain of his ship in the Juan Fernández Islands and asked to be put ashore. He remained on Más a Tierra Island for four years and four months before he was rescued (Feb., 1709) by an English privateer. See John Howell, *The Life and Adventures of Alexander Selkirk* (1829).

Selkirk, Thomas Douglas, 5th **earl of,** 1771–1820, Scottish philanthropist, founder of the RED RIVER SETTLEMENT. Emigration to America seemed to him the best solution for the poverty of his countrymen, especially the Highlanders who had been evicted from their small holdings. He obtained land on Prince Edward Island and supervised (1803) the founding of a successful settlement there. In 1811 he acquired a large tract in Rupert's Land from the Hudson's Bay Company, in which he had bought a controlling interest, and established the Red River Settlement. The planting (1812–16) of this colony led to bloodshed between the settlers and the North West Company, a rival of the Hudson's Bay Company. After Selkirk's return to Upper Canada, lawsuits were brought against him by the North West Company, and he was forced to pay damages. Having sacrificed his health and most of his fortune to his philanthropic enterprises, he returned home in 1818 and died in France two years later. He wrote *Observations on the Present State of the Highlands of Scotland* (1805) and *A Sketch of the British Fur Trade in North America* (1816). See his *Diary, 1803–1804,* ed. by P. C. White (1958); biography by J. M. Gray (1963); Chester Martin, *Lord Selkirk's Work in Canada* (1916); George Bryce, *Mackenzie, Selkirk, Simpson* (rev. ed. 1926); Hartwell Bowsfield, *Selkirk* (1968).

Selkirk, town (1971 pop. 9,331), SE Man., Canada, on the Red River. Just S of Lake Winnipeg, it is a port for products from N Manitoba. There are steel mills and foundries in the town. It is named for the 5th earl of Selkirk, who established (1812) the RED RIVER SETTLEMENT in the region.

Selkirk Mountains, rugged range of the Rocky Mts., SE British Columbia, Canada, near the Alta. border and extending northwest c.200 mi (320 km) from the U.S. border. Mt. Sir Sanford (11,590 ft/3,533 m) is the highest peak. The range is almost encircled by the Columbia River which loops around the northern edge.

Selkirkshire (sĕl'kərkshĭr), county (1971 pop. 20,868), 268 sq mi (694 sq km), SE Scotland. Selkirk is the county town. Hilly (the county is almost wholly in the southern uplands) and wooded, the county is watered by the Ettrick and Yarrow rivers. Sheep and cattle raising are the main occupations; woolens are manufactured at Selkirk and GALASHIELS. There is also a tanning industry. Once part of the Saxon kingdom of NORTHUMBRIA, the county was annexed to Scotland in 1018. It suffered severely in the prolonged border wars between England and Scotland. COVENANTERS defeated the 5th earl of Montrose in 1645 at Philiphaugh. The county was a royal hunting forest for many years. It has literary associations with Sir Walter Scott, once its sheriff, and James Hogg, the "Ettrick Shepherd." Under the Local Government Act of 1973, Selkirkshire became part of the Borders region.

Selma, city (1970 pop. 27,379), seat of Dallas co., S central Ala., on the Alabama River, in a fertile farm area; inc. 1820. Farm implements, foundry products, batteries, paper items, lumber, furniture, textiles, and clothing are among its manufactures. A Confederate arsenal and supply point, Selma was ravaged in 1865; however, a number of antebellum houses remain—notably Sturdivant Hall (1853). Sen. William Rufus King, who named the town, lived and is buried there. A historical museum and a zoo are in the city. Nearby are Craig Air Force Base (est. 1941) and the site of Cahaba, capital of Alabama from 1819 to 1826. In 1965, Selma was the center of a black voter registration drive led by Dr. Martin Luther King.

Selous Game Reserve, one of Africa's largest game reserves, 11,512 sq mi (29,816 sq km), S Tanzania; est. c.1900. It is located in the Rufiji River basin and includes grasslands and forests. There are many elephants in the reserve.

seltzer water, mineral water containing free carbon dioxide, obtained originally from springs at Niederselters, Germany. Reputed to have curative value in treating several diseases, it became very popular in the 19th cent. In the 20th cent. it was produced synthetically and, as soda water, is widely used as a beverage as well as a component of other beverages.

Selwyn, George Augustus (sĕl'wĭn), 1809–78, English prelate. In 1841 he was appointed to the colonial diocese of New Zealand, becoming the first Anglican bishop of the island. Having prepared himself on the voyage by studying navigation and the Maori language, he visited many of the South Sea islands during his 26-year episcopate by sailing his own vessel. He set up a synodical church government in New Zealand and was a pioneer in encouraging the growth of a native ministry. Returning to England, Selwyn became (1868) bishop of Lichfield. In 1882, Selwyn College, Cambridge, a tribute to his memory financed through popular subscription, was incorporated. See biographies by Louise Creighton (1923) and J. H. Evans (1964).

Selznick, David O., 1902–1965, American film producer, b. Pittsburgh. He worked for studios in Hollywood before founding Selznick International Pictures in 1936. Selznick's most famous movie is *Gone with the Wind* (1939). His other important films include *A Star Is Born* (1937), *The Prisoner of Zenda* (1937), *Rebecca* (1940), *Spellbound* (1945), *Duel in the Sun* (1946), *The Third Man* (1949), and *Tender Is the Night* (1962). His second wife was the actress Jennifer Jones. See Bob Thomas, *Selznick* (1970).

Sem, variant of SHEM.

Semachiah (sĕm"əkī'ə), temple doorkeeper. 1 Chron. 26.7.

semantics [Gr.,=significant] in general, the study of the relationship between words and meanings. The empirical study of word meanings in existing languages is a branch of linguistics; the abstract study of meaning in relation to language or symbolic logic systems is a branch of philosophy. Both are called semantics. The field of semantics has three basic concerns: the relations of words to the objects denoted by them, the relations of words to the interpreters of them, and, in symbolic logic, the formal relations of signs to one another (syntax). Semantics in linguistics had its beginnings c.1825 in France and Germany, when the meanings of words as significant features in the growth of language was recognized. Among the foremost linguistic semanticists of the 20th cent. are Gustaf Stern, Jost Trier, B. L. Whorf, Uriel Weinreich, Stephen Ullmann, Thomas Sebeok, Noam CHOMSKY, Jerrold Katz, and Charles Osgood. In linguistics in recent years an offshoot of transformational GRAMMAR theory has reemphasized the role of meaning in linguistic analysis. This new theory, developed largely by George Lakoff and James McCawley, is termed generative semantics. Within anthropology a new theoretical orientation related to linguistic semantics has been developed. Its leading proponents include W. H. Goodenough, F. G. Lounsbury, and Claude LÉVI-STRAUSS. In philosophy, semantics has generally followed the lead of symbolic logic, and many philosophers do not make a distinction between logic and semantics. The object of semantics in philosophy is to develop a formalized, symbolic language that will hold meaning and, through this, to find a theory of the relation between signs and what they mean. The leading practitioners have been Gottlob FREGE, Lady Welby, Bertrand RUSSELL, Otto Neurath, Rudolf CARNAP, Alonzo Church, Alfred Tarski, C. I. LEWIS, Ludwig WITTGENSTEIN, J. L. Austin, W. V. Quine, P. F. Strawson, John Searle, H. P. Grice, Saul Kripke, Donald Davidson, and Gilbert Harman. Since the publication of the influential *The Meaning of Meaning* (1925) by C. K. Ogden and I. A. RICHARDS, semantics has also become important to literary criticism and stylistics, in which the way that metaphors evoke feelings is investigated and differences between ordinary and literary language are studied. A related discipline, general semantics (so called to distinguish it from semantics in linguistics or philosophy), studies the ways in which meanings of words influence human behavior. General semantics was developed by Alfred KORZYBSKI. The key term in Korzybski's system is evaluation, the mental act that is performed by the hearer when a word is spoken.

Among the most prominent followers of Korzybski are Stuart CHASE, S. I. Hayakawa, and H. L. Weinberg. A useful introduction to general semantics is H. L. Weinberg, *Levels of Knowing and Existence* (1959). For semantics in linguistics, see Paul Ziff, *Semantic Analysis* (1960); Stephen Ullman, *Semantics* (1962) and *The Principles of Semantics* (1957, repr. 1967); Noam Chomsky, *Studies on Semantics in Generative Grammar* (1972); Jerrold Katz, *Semantics Theory* (1972); and Geoffrey Leach, *Semantics* (1974). For semantics in philosophy, see R. M. Martin, *Truth and Denotation* (1958); Rudolf Carnap, *Meaning and Necessity* (2d ed. 1956) and *Introduction to Semantics and Formalization of Logic* (1959); W. V. Quine, *Word and Object* (1960); Keith and Adrienne Lehrer, *The Theory of Meaning* (1970); J. F. Rosenberg and C. Travis, ed., *Readings in the Philosophy of Language* (1971); and Donald Davidson and Gilbert Harman, ed., *Semantics of Natural Language* (2d ed. 1973). For semantics in literary criticism, see Kenneth Burke, *A Rhetoric of Motives* (1950) and *A Grammar of Motives* (1955) and the works of William Empson and Philip Wheelwright.

semaphore (sĕm'əfôr″), device for the visible transmission of messages. The marine semaphore, used by day between ships or between a ship and the shore, consists essentially of a post at the top of which are two pivoted arms. The arms are connected by light gearing to two operating levers. Each letter of the alphabet and each numeral is indicated by a different placing of the arms. The system can also be used by the signalman through motions of his own arms, with or without small flags as indicators. In the railroad semaphore a single projecting arm pivoted at one end and attached to a vertical post is devised to take three positions. Horizontal indicates stop, and vertical, all clear; the inclined position indicates that the locomotive may go ahead under control expecting to be stopped. See SIGNALING.

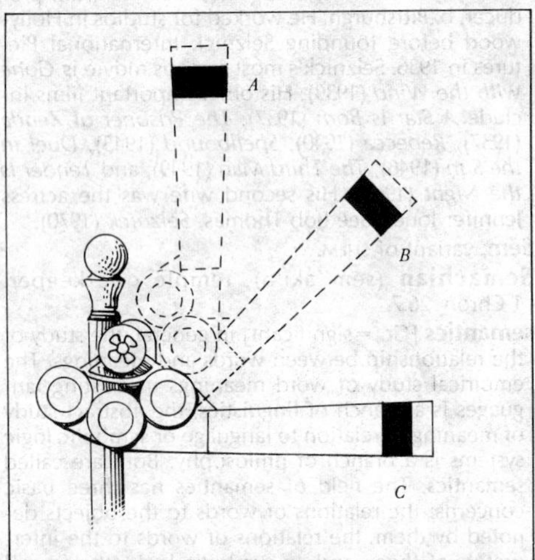

Positions of railroad semaphore: (A) clear, (B) caution, (C) stop

Semarang (səmä'räng), city (1961 pop. 503,153), capital of Central Java prov., N Java, Indonesia, on the Java Sea and at the mouth of the Semarang River. An important port, it is one of the major commercial centers of Java. Tobacco, sugar, rubber, coffee, and kapok are exported. There are textile and shipbuilding industries. The city has a television station and is the seat of Diponegoro Univ.

Sembrich, Marcella (sĕm'brĭk), 1858–1935, stage name of Praxede Marcelline Kochanska, Polish coloratura soprano. She studied piano and violin at the Lemberg Conservatory. Urged by Liszt to train her voice, she studied in Vienna and Italy and made her operatic debut in Athens in 1877. After singing in Dresden and in London, she made her American debut (1883) at the Metropolitan Opera, New York City, where she sang regularly from 1898 to 1909. She gave concerts until 1917; afterward she taught at the Curtis Institute in Philadelphia and at the Juilliard School of Music. She was considered the greatest coloratura of her day.

Semei (sĕm'ēī), ancestor of Joseph in the Gospel genealogy. Luke 3.26.

Semele (sĕm'ĭlē), in Greek mythology, mother of Dionysus, daughter of Cadmus and Harmonia. Zeus, who loved her, appeared to her as a man. Semele asked him to come to her in his divine form, but when he did, the fire of his thunderbolts killed her. Zeus snatched his unborn son from her ashes and thrust him into his thigh, from which Dionysus was finally born. Later Dionysus rescued Semele from Hades and made her a goddess on Olympus.

Semeru (səmĕr'ōō), volcanic peak, 12,060 ft (3,676 m) high, E Java, Indonesia. Formerly called Mt. Mahameru, it is the island's highest point.

semicircular canal: see EAR.

semicolon: see PUNCTUATION.

semiconductor, solid material whose electrical conductivity at room temperature is between that of a conductor and that of an insulator (see CONDUCTION; INSULATION). At high temperatures its conductivity approaches that of a metal, and at low temperatures it acts as an insulator. In a semiconductor there is a limited movement of electrons, depending upon the crystal structure of the material used. The substances first used for semiconductors were the elements germanium, silicon, and gray tin. It was found that the incorporation of certain impurities in them enhances their conductive properties. The impurities either add free electrons or create holes (electron deficiencies) in the crystal structures of the host substances by attracting electrons. Thus there are two types of semiconductor: the N-type (negative), in which the current carriers (electrons) are negative, and the P-type (positive), in which the positively charged holes move and carry the current. The process of adding these impurities is called doping; the impurities themselves are called dopants. Dopants that contribute mobile electrons are called donor impurities, those that cause holes to form are acceptor impurities. Undoped semiconductor material is called intrinsic semiconductor material. Certain chemical compounds, including indium antimonide, gallium arsenide, and aluminum phosphide are semiconductors. Use is made of semiconductors in various electronic devices, such as computers, rectifiers, transistors, and photoelectric cells. The field of solid-state physics includes the study of semiconductors. See TRANSISTORS.

Seminole Indians, North American Indians whose language belongs to the Muskogean branch of the Hokan-Siouan linguistic stock (see AMERICAN INDIAN LANGUAGES). They separated (their name means "separatist") from the Creek Indians in the early 18th cent. and settled in the former territory of the Apalachee Indians in Florida. They gradually grew in strength, absorbing many runaway Negro slaves and the remnants of the Apalachee. While still under Spanish rule the Seminoles became involved in war with the United States, particularly in the War of 1812 and again in 1817–18. In the retaliatory expedition of 1817–18 Gen. Andrew Jackson with over 3,000 men invaded Florida to punish the Seminoles. By the Treaty of Paynes Landing in 1832 the Seminoles were bound to move W of the Mississippi River within three years. Most Seminoles, led by OSCEOLA, refused to go and prepared for resistance. In 1835 began the Seminole War, which proved to be the most costly Indian war in which the United States engaged. The war, which lasted for nearly eight years, cost the lives of 1,500 U.S. soldiers and at least $30 million. The Seminoles, finally subdued (1842), consented to move to the West, although some remained isolated in the Everglades. In Oklahoma the Seminoles are one of the Five Civilized Tribes. There are some 1,200 Seminoles in Florida and about 3,000 in Oklahoma. See E. C. McReynolds, *The Seminoles* (1957); J. K. Mahon, *History of the Second Seminole War* (1967); Frank Laumer, *Massacre* (1968); M. S. Garbarino, *Big Cypress* (1972).

Seminole War, in U.S. history, armed conflict between the U.S. government and the Seminole Indians. In 1832 the U.S. government signed a treaty with the Seminole Indians, who lived in Florida, providing for their removal to Oklahoma in 1835 in exchange for a small sum of money. However, opposition to the treaty soon appeared among the Seminoles; under the leadership of the young chief,

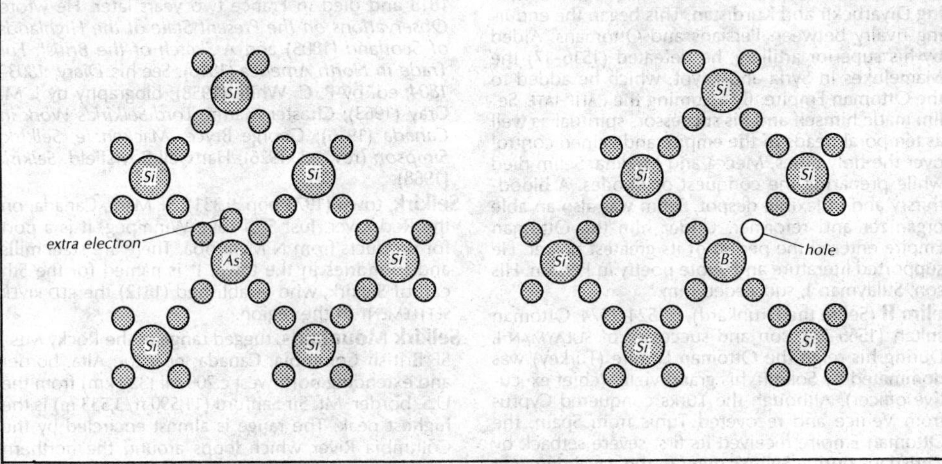

N-type and P-type crystals: In a pure silicon crystal each silicon atom (Si) is surrounded by four electrons. In the N-doped semiconductor, illustrated in the left-hand figure, some silicon atoms are replaced by arsenic atoms (As), which have one extra electron. In the P-doped semiconductor, illustrated in the right-hand figure, some silicon atoms are replaced by boron atoms (B), which have only three electrons, resulting in a deficiency, or hole. In N-type semiconductors the extra electrons move as free negative charges and in P-type semiconductors the holes move as free positive charges.

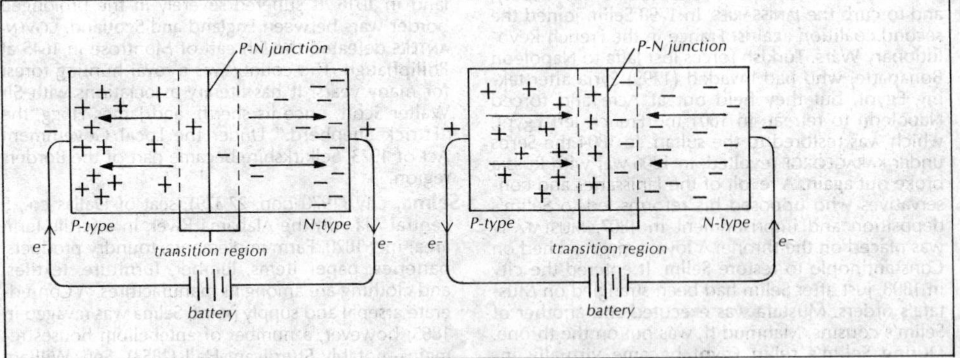

Semiconductor diode: In the figure on the left, electrons and holes are attracted away from the P-N junction. The transition region, with a low concentration of charges, is a layer of high resistance and no charge crosses the junction, i.e., no internal current exists. With the battery reversed, as in the figure on the right, the concentration of charges in the transition region is increased and an internal current is created.

Osceola, the Seminoles organized small raiding parties that attacked the American troops. The U.S. army was rendered helpless by the raiding tactics of the Indians and suffered heavy casualties. Although Osceola was captured in 1837 and died in prison a few months later, resistance continued. When Gen. William J. Worth became (1841) commander of U.S. forces, a new strategy was adopted. The Seminole's crops were systematically burned and their villages destroyed. As winter approached and starvation was imminent, the Seminoles surrendered. A peace treaty was signed in 1842 and the Indians were removed westward. The war resulted in 1,500 U.S. soldiers killed, and cost more than $20 million.

Semipalatinsk (syĭmē"pəlä'tyĭnsk), city (1970 pop. 236,000), capital of Semipalatinsk oblast, Central Asian USSR, in Kazakhstan, on the Irtysh River and the Turkistan-Siberia RR. It is a river port, rail terminus, and commercial center, with large freight depots for river and rail transport. Semipalatinsk has one of the USSR's biggest meat-packing plants; other industries include food processing, metal working, ship repairing, wool processing, and the manufacture of building materials. The name *Semipalatinsk* [seven palaces] derives from the seven ancient stone structures whose remains are nearby Founded as a fort in 1718, the city was finally established on its present site in 1778 after flooding by the Irtysh necessitated periodic movement of the fort. During the 19th cent. Semipalatinsk was a center for trade between Russians and the Kirghiz, Bukharans, and Chinese; it also lay on the caravan route from Mongolia to Europe.

Semi-Pelagianism: see PELAGIANISM.

semiprecious stone: see GEM.

Semiramis (sĕmĭr'əmĭs), mythical Assyrian queen, noted for her beauty and wisdom. She was reputed to have conquered many lands and founded the city of Babylon. After a long and prosperous reign she vanished from earth in the shape of a dove and was thereafter worshiped as a deity, acquiring many of the characteristics of the goddess ISHTAR. The historical figure behind this legend is probably Sammuramat, who acted as regent of Assyria from 810 to 805 B.C.

Semite (sĕm'īt, sē'mīt), originally one of a people believed to be descended from Shem, son of Noah. Later the term came to include the following peoples: Arabs; the Akkadians of ancient Babylonia; the Assyrians; the Canaanites (including Amorites, Moabites, Edomites, Ammonites, and Phoenicians); the various Aramaean tribes (including Hebrews); and a considerable portion of the population of Ethiopia. These peoples are grouped under the term *Semite,* chiefly because their languages were found to be related, deriving presumably from a common tongue, Semitic. The Semites were largely nomadic pastoralists, although settled in villages. At least as early as 2500 B.C., the Semites had begun to leave the Arabian peninsula in successive waves of migration that took them to Mesopotamia, the Mediterranean coast, and the Nile delta. They were organized into patrilineal tribes, occupying defined territories and ruled by hereditary leaders, or sheiks. In Mesopotamia, Semitic people from the earliest times were in contact with Sumerian civilization and with the rise of Sargon of Agade (Akkad) and Hammurabi of Babylon were able to dominate it completely (see SUMER). In PHOENICIA the Semitic population developed a widespread maritime trade and became the first great seafaring people. That group of Hebrews that had been diverted through Sinai into the Nile delta settled at last with other Semitic inhabitants in Palestine. These southern or Judean Hebrews became the leaders of a new nation and religion (see JEWS and JUDAISM). See W. R. Smith, *History of the Semites* (1956, repr. 1972); Sabatino Moscati, *The Semites in Ancient History* (1959).

Semitic languages, subfamily of the Hamito-Semitic family of languages. See HAMITO-SEMITIC LANGUAGES.

Semliki (sĕm'lĭkē), river, c.130 mi (209 km) long, E Zaïre, E central Africa, flowing N from Edward Nyanza to Albert Nyanza. It forms part of the Zaïre-Uganda border.

Semmelweis, Ignaz Philipp (ĭg'näts fē'lĭp zĕm'əlvīs), 1818–65, Hungarian physician. He was a pioneer in employing asepsis. While on the staff of the general hospital in Vienna, he recognized the infectious nature of PUERPERAL FEVER and insisted that attendants in obstetrical cases thoroughly cleanse their hands; he thus greatly reduced the mortality rate from infection in childbirth. Ridicule of his belief caused him to leave Vienna (1854) for Pest, Hungary, and ultimately drove him to insanity and suicide. He recorded his results in *The Cause, Concept, and Prophylaxis of Childbed Fever* (1861, tr. 1941), but the value of his work was not fully recognized until c.1890. See biographies by L. F. Destouches (tr. 1937) and Josephine Rich (1961).

Semmering (zĕm'ərĭng), scenic resort region of the Eastern Alps, E Austria. The Alps there are crossed by the **Semmering Pass,** 3,215 ft (980 m) high and 275 ft (84 m) long. Beneath it runs the first mountain railroad in the world (built 1848–54). It passes through 15 tunnels and over 16 viaducts.

Semmes, Raphael (sĕmz), 1809–77, American naval officer, b. Charles co., Md. He was appointed (1826) midshipman in the U.S. navy, and although he was admitted to the bar (1834), he continued in the service. He took part in the Mexican War, practiced law at Mobile, Ala., and was in the Lighthouse Service from 1856 to Feb., 1861, when he resigned his commission as commander. He soon took the same rank in the Confederate navy. His first ship, the *Sumter,* did considerable damage to Northern commerce before she was bottled up at Gibraltar in Jan., 1862. In Aug., 1862, Semmes, now a captain, took command of the *Alabama* (see CONFEDERATE CRUISERS), and a two-year cruise made him the naval hero of the Confederacy. After the *Alabama* was sunk by the *Kearsarge,* Semmes returned to the South. He was promoted to rear admiral (Feb., 1865) and charged with the naval defense of Richmond. After the war Semmes taught, edited a newspaper, lectured, and again practiced law in Mobile. See biographies by Colyer Meriwether (1913) and W. Adolphe Roberts (1938); H. A. Gosnell, *Rebel Raider* (1948); C. G. Summersell, *The Cruise of C.S.S. Sumter* (1965).

Semnan (sĕmnän'), city (1971 est. pop. 35,000), capital of Semnan governorate, Mazanderan prov., N Iran. It is the trade and transportation center of a fertile agricultural region. Manufactures of the city include textiles and carpets. Semnan was destroyed by the Oghuz Turks (1036) and by the Mongols (1221). There are many historical remains, including the ruins of several old castles.

Semonides of Amorgos (sĭmŏn'ĭdēz, əmôr'gŏs), fl. c.650 B.C., Greek iambic poet, b. Samos. He led a colony to the island of Amorgos in the SE Cyclades c.630 B.C. In one of the few extant fragments of his work, he satirizes women and likens their natures to the sea, mud, and various animals. The fragments reveal his sense of humor. His name also appears as Simonides.

Sempach (zĕm'päkh), town (1970 pop. 1,619), Lucerne canton, N central Switzerland, on the Lake of Sempach. Near Sempach the Swiss decisively defeated the Austrians in 1386.

Semper, Gottfried (gôt'frēt zĕm'pər), 1803–79, German architect, skillful in adapting the Italian Renaissance style to the German environment. He taught (1834–49) architecture at the Dresden Academy and became (1855) director of the architectural section of the Polytechnische Schule, Zurich. Because of his part in the Revolution of 1848, he was forced to leave Germany and was for a time in London. Among the buildings he designed are the New Synagogue and Hoftheater, Dresden; Polytechnicum, Zurich; and two museums and the imperial palace, Vienna. His chief written work was on style in the technical arts (1878).

Semple, Ellen Churchill, 1863–1932, American geographer, b. Louisville, Ky., grad. Vassar, 1882, and studied at the Univ. of Leipzig. A follower of the German geographer Ratzel, she helped develop the study of anthropogeography (or human geography, the science of geographical distribution of mankind) and lectured (1906–23) on the subject at the Univ. of Chicago. From 1921 to 1932 she was professor of anthropogeography at Clark Univ. Semple was an environmental determinist, and many of her ideas are now discounted as being too one-sided. She was a frequent contributor to geographical journals; her writings include *American History and its Geographic Conditions* (1903, rev. ed. 1933), *Influences of Geographic Environment* (1911), and *The Geography of the Mediterranean Region* (1931).

Sena (sä'nə), town, central Mozambique, on the Zambezi River. Founded by the Portuguese in the 16th cent., it developed as a distribution center for local products, especially sugar. A fort was built there in the 18th cent.

Senaah (sēnā'ə), same as HASSENAAH.

Senanayake, Don Stephen (sĕnənä'yəkə), 1884–1952, prime minister (1947–52) of Ceylon (later Sri Lanka). He entered politics in 1922 and became a prominent leader before independence from Great Britain (1948), serving as minister of agriculture and lands (1931–47) and as leader of the council of state (1942–47). He was succeeded as prime minister by his son **Dudley Senanayake** (1911–73), who had followed his father as minister of agriculture and lands (1947–52). Dudley Senanayake served three times as a right-of-center prime minister (1952–53, 1960, 1965–70) and led the opposition United National party in 1960–65.

Senancour, Étienne Pivert de (ātyĕn' pēvĕr' də sənäNōōr'), 1770–1846, French writer. He is known principally for his autobiographical epistolary novel *Obermann* (1804, tr. 1903). The sentimental attitude toward nature and the morbid melancholy of this novel without a plot are reminiscent of Rousseau, but a pervasive preoccupation with intellectual problems sets it apart from other works of the same genre and period.

Senate, United States: see CONGRESS OF THE UNITED STATES.

senate, Roman, governing council of the Roman republic. It was the outgrowth of the council of the kings. By the 3d cent. B.C. the senate was a group of 300 men with legislative and administrative control of Rome. There were serious checks on its power, especially in the hands of the tribunes. The members were chosen by the censors, and included theoretically the best citizens; but as it worked out, the senate consisted of ex-magistrates, almost entirely members of a small number of old families from either the patrician or plebeian classes. In the expansion of Rome in the 3d and 2d cent. B.C. the senate sent out the armies, made the treaties, organized the new domain, and controlled finance. The senatorial conduct of Roman affairs was fairly successful until c.130 B.C. After that the senate's provincial administration of the huge empire was increasingly inefficient and graft-ridden. However, the authority of the senate was not called into question until the growth of party-class division that developed with the agitation of the GRACCHI. The leaders of the senate became also the leaders of the most reactionary group and would yield on no point, economic or political. The fatal development in the republic of two parties, optimates (the senatorial conservatives) and populares, grew out of this resistance to change. The optimates tried to foster the idea that they represented constitutionalism versus subversion, but after SULLA, who combined the bloodiest illegality with the strictest defense of the senate (which he raised to 600 members), such a claim by optimates was hypocritical and cynical. Julius CAESAR, a populare, did not make his famous move across the Rubicon until the senate had defied him with a clearly unconstitutional decree. Caesar enlarged the number of the senate to 900. The ruin of the optimates and the senate was accomplished in the proscription of 43 B.C. after Caesar's assassination (the work of optimates). After the proscription what was left of the senate was docile and ineffectual. AUGUSTUS lowered the number to 600. As an administrator he found he had to reduce senatorial control in the provinces. Nevertheless, he made much of senatorial prestige, and for generations the emperor's chief title was *princeps senatus* [leader of the senate]. There was an important revival of the senate late in the 1st cent. A.D., often attributed to the influx of non-Roman Italians. Nerva and his successors emphasized the role of the senate, but even this shadow of former authority was obviously only possible if the monarch willed it. The ancient senate is not heard of after the 6th cent.

Sendai (sĕndī'), city (1970 pop. 545,065), capital of Miyagi prefecture, N Honshu, Japan, on Inshinomaki Bay. A major industrial and commercial city, it has industries that manufacture chemicals, metal goods, silk yarn, and machinery. Long an educational center, Sendai is the seat of Tohoku Univ. and the Industrial Art Institute. In the 17th cent. the city was the stronghold of the powerful feudal lord Date Masamune. The Osaki Hachiman Shrine (built 1606) is there.

Sender, Ramón José (rämōn'hōsā'sāndĕr'), 1902–, Spanish novelist. A journalist, Sender fought on the side of the Loyalists in the Spanish civil war. He left Spain in 1938 and became a U.S. citizen in 1946. Sender's novels, which have received international attention, are marked by profound compassion and by acute consciousness of social injustice; his early style is one of vigorous realism, while later works are in a more symbolic vein. Among his novels are *Imán* (1930, tr. 1934), *Seven Red Sundays* (1932, tr. 1936), *The Sphere* (1947, tr. 1949), and *The Affable Hangman* (1952, tr. 1954). His other works include a collection of short stories, *Relatos fronterizos* (1970), and *Before Dawn* (tr. 1958), an autobiographical novel.

Seneca, the elder (Lucius, or Marcus, Annaeus Seneca) (lo͞o'shəs, mär'kəs ənē'əs sĕn'ĭkə), c.60 B.C.–c.A.D. 37, Roman rhetorician and writer, b. Corduba (present-day Córdoba), Spain; grandfather of Lucan and father of Seneca the younger. He spent most of his life in Spain but made frequent trips to Rome, where he observed the leading orators of the day. Seneca the elder wrote two major works, the *Controversies,* a collection of imaginary legal cases as they might be argued before a court of law; and *Persuasions,* model orations on various subjects. The prefaces to the *Controversies* contain valuable material on famous Roman orators. He also wrote a history of Rome from the time of the civil wars to the 1st cent. A.D.

Seneca, the younger (Lucius Annaeus Seneca), c.3 B.C.–A.D.65, Roman philosopher, dramatist, and statesman, b. Corduba (present-day Córdoba), Spain. He was the son of Seneca the elder. The younger Seneca went to Rome in his childhood, studied rhetoric and philosophy, and earned renown as an orator when still a youth. He was exiled by Claudius (A.D. 41) ostensibly because of his intimacy with Julia, Claudius' brother Germanicus' daughter. In A.D. 49 he was recalled at the urgings of AGRIPPINA I to become tutor of the young NERO. In the first years of Nero's reign Seneca was virtual ruler with Afranius Burrus, and their influence on the emperor was probably for the best. But the ascendancy of Poppaea, Nero's wife, brought about first the death of Agrippina (A.D. 59), then that of Burrus (A.D. 62). Seneca asked to retire. He had amassed a huge fortune and wanted no more of court life. Accusations of conspiracy were finally leveled at Seneca, who, instructed to commit suicide, slashed his veins. His death scene was considered remarkably noble by the Romans. Seneca was a Stoic, and his writings show a high, unselfish nobility considerably at variance with his own life, in which greed, expediency, and even connivance at murder figured. His *Epistolae morales ad Lucilium* are essays on ethics written for his friend Lucilius Junior, to whom he also addressed *Quaestiones naturales,* philosophical—rather than scientific—remarks about natural phenomena. The so-called *Dialogi* of Seneca include essays on anger, on divine providence, on Stoic impassivity, and on peace of soul. Other moral essays have also survived, notably *De elementia,* on the duty of a ruler to be merciful, and *De beneficiis,* on the award and reception of favors. The *Apocolocyntosis* is a satire on the apotheosis of Claudius. The most influential of his works, at least in so far as European literature is concerned, were his tragedies. It is generally agreed that his plays were written for recitation and not for stage performance. Nine plays, based on Greek models, are accepted as his—*Hercules Furens, Medea, Troades, Phaedra, Agamemnon, Oedipus, Hercules Oetaeus, Phoenissae,* and *Thyestes.* A tenth, *Octavia,* is now ascribed to a later imitator. Although his drama has been deprecated in modern times, no author had a stronger influence on Renaissance tragedy than did Seneca. His atmosphere of gloom, his horrors, his rhetoric and bombast, his stoicism, were all essential contributions to the forming of Renaissance tragedy. The most significant play influenced by Seneca was Thomas Kyd's *The Spanish Tragedy.* See F. L. Lucas, *Seneca and Elizabethan Tragedy* (1922, repr. 1969); C. W. Mendell, *Our Seneca* (1941, repr. 1968).

Seneca Indians: see IROQUOIS CONFEDERACY.

Senefelder, Aloys (zā'nəfĕl"dər), 1771–1834, German lithographer, b. Prague. Senefelder invented lithography in Munich c.1796. In 1818 he published a full account of the nature and the history of his invention. The English translation, *A Complete Course of Lithography,* appeared in 1819.

Seneffe or **Seneff** (both: sənĕf'), town (1970 pop. 3,183), Hainaut prov., S central Belgium, near Charleroi. At Seneffe, the French under Louis II de Condé defeated (1674) the Dutch, and the French under Marceau defeated (1794) the Austrians.

Senegal (sĕnĭgôl', sĕn'ĭgôl), republic (1973 est. pop. 4,100,000), 76,124 sq mi (197,161 sq km), W Africa, bordered by the Atlantic Ocean in the west, by Mauritania in the north, by Mali in the east, and by Guinea and Guinea-Bissau in the south. The Republic of the Gambia is an enclave in the southwest. The capital of Senegal is DAKAR; other cities include DIOURBEL, KAOLACK, LOUGA, M'BOUR, Rufisque, SAINT-LOUIS, THIÈS, and ZIGUINCHOR. Most of the country is low-lying, with a maximum altitude of c.200 ft (60 m). However, the southeast, which forms a small part of the Fouta Djallon region, rises to c.1,400 ft (430 m). Senegal's coast (c.250 mi/400 km long) is sandy from Saint-Louis to Dakar, situated near the tip of the Cape Verde peninsula, and is swampy or muddy S of Dakar. The country is mostly covered with savanna, which becomes semidesert in the Sahel region of the north and northeast; the southwest

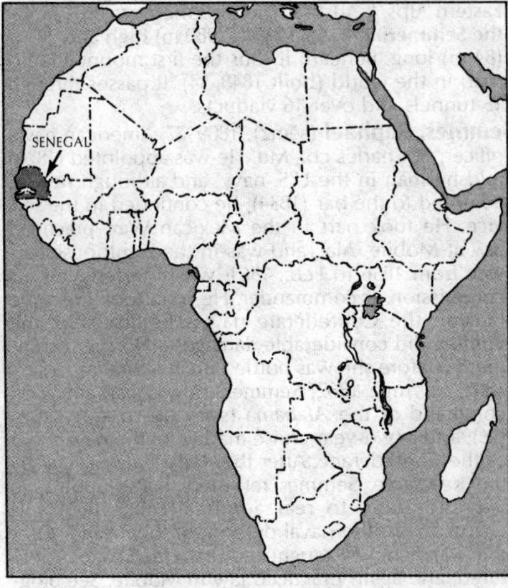

is forested. The chief rivers of the country are the Sénégal (which forms the boundary with Mauritania), the Falémé, the Gambia or Gambie, and the Casamance. Lake Guiers is located in the north. The inhabitants of Senegal are almost exclusively black Africans. The chief ethnic groups are the Wolof (about 35% of the population), Fulani (17%), Serer (16%), Tukolor (8%), Lebu (8%), Mande (7%), and Diola (4%). There are small numbers of Berbers, Europeans (mostly French), and Lebanese. French is the country's official language. About 80% of the people are Muslim, most of whom belong to either the Tijaniyya or the Qadiriyya Sufi brotherhoods. About 10% are Christian, mostly Roman Catholic, and the rest follow traditional religious beliefs. Senegal is primarily an agricultural country, but industry in the cities, especially Dakar, is growing. About 40% of the country's land area is arable, but only about 10% is actually cultivated; much of the rest is used for pasturing livestock. The principal food crops are millet, manioc, sorghum, rice, maize, and pulses. Groundnuts are the chief cash crop; they are grown mainly on small farms in the region between the Siné and Saloum wadis near Kaolack and Diourbel. Some of Senegal's largest industrial establishments process the groundnuts into oil and oilcake, and groundnuts, oil, and oilcake account for about 35% of Senegal's annual exports by value. Large numbers of cattle, sheep, and goats are raised. There is a sizable coastal fishing industry. The principal minerals extracted are phosphate rock, limestone, high-grade iron ore, and gold. Manufactures (besides groundnut products) include cement, chemicals, processed food, beverages, textiles, clothing, leather, footwear, and metal goods. The west-central part of Senegal, which includes Saint-Louis, Louga, Dakar, Thiès, and Kaolack, is well served by railroads and major highways; a rail line runs from Dakar to Mali. Dakar is the country's leading port and also has a major international airport where transatlantic flights are serviced. The annual cost of Senegal's imports is usually considerably higher than its earnings from exports. The chief imports are foodstuffs (especially rice), machinery, textiles, transportation equipment, and petroleum products; the main exports (in addition to groundnuts and groundnut products) are calcium phosphate, processed fish, and hides and skins. France is by far Senegal's leading trade partner; West Germany, the Netherlands, and Ivory Coast also carry on a considerable trade with the country. Archaeologists have found the remains of Paleolithic and Neolithic civilizations in the region now occupied by Senegal. The Wolof and Serer migrated into the area from the northeast around the middle of the first millennium A.D. The Tukolor settled in the Sénégal River valley in the 9th cent., and during the period from the 10th to 14th cent. their strong state of Tekrur dominated the valley. The Tukolor were converted to Islam; in the mid-11th cent. a group of them participated in establishing the ALMORAVID state, centered in Morocco, which conquered the empire of Ghana, located to the E of Senegal. In the 14th cent. the Mali empire expanded westward from the region of the upper Niger River and conquered Tekrur. In the 15th cent. the Wolof established the Jolof empire in the region between the Sénégal River and the Siné wadi. Jolof was made up of a number of states (including Wolof, Cayor, Baol, and Walo) and internal rivalries led to its breakup in the 17th cent. In 1444–45, Portuguese explorers reached the mouth of the Sénégal and Cape Verde. Portuguese traders used the Sénégal and Gambia rivers as routes to the interior, exchanging cloth and metal goods for gold dust, gum arabic, ivory, and small numbers of black African slaves. Trading stations were established at the mouths of the Sénégal and Casamance rivers and on Gorée Island and at Rufisque, both located near present-day Dakar. In the 17th cent. the Portuguese were displaced by the Dutch and the French. The French established a post at the mouth of the Sénégal in 1638, and in 1659 founded Saint-Louis on an island there. In 1677, the French captured Gorée from the Dutch, and it was for a time the main French naval base in W Africa. From 1697 until 1720, André Brüe was director of the Royal Company of Senegal, and he extended French influence far into the interior, increased the export of slaves, ivory, and gum, and encouraged with little success the cultivation of cotton and cacao. After Brüe the French companies active in Senegal handled less trade, partly because of competition from Fulani and Mande merchants. During the Seven Years War (1756–63), Great Britain captured all the French posts in Senegal, returning only Gorée in 1763, and joined them with its holdings along the Gambia River to form the short-lived colony of Senegambia, Britain's first colony in Africa. During the American Revolutionary War (1775–83), France regained its posts, but surrendered Gorée to Britain under the Treaty of Paris (1783). During the Napoleonic Wars, Britain again captured France's holdings in Senegal, but they were returned in 1815. At this time, the French presence was limited to Saint-Louis, Gorée, and Rufisque, and during the first half of the 19th cent. there was little contact with the interior, whose trade was oriented to the north and east. As part of a French policy of assimilation, black African (along with the French-born) inhabitants of Saint-Louis and Gorée elected a deputy to the national assembly in Paris from 1848 to 1852 and (joined by the inhabitants of Rufisque and Dakar) from 1871 to independence in 1960. During the period from 1854 to 1865 (except for 1862) Capt. Louis FAIDHERBE was governor of Senegal, and he extended French influence up the Sénégal and along the Casamance and conquered Walo and Cayor. Faidherbe established schools for the black Africans and encouraged the cultivation of groundnuts. He halted the westward expansion of al-Hajj Umar, the Tukolor leader of the Tijaniyya brotherhood, who waged a large-scale holy war from a base in what is now Guinea beginning in the early 1850s. After Faidherbe's tenure French activity in Senegal waned, but in 1880, when the scramble for African territory among the European powers was beginning, France held most of the Sénégal valley and the lower Casamance valley. In 1895, Senegal was made a French colony, with its capital at Saint-Louis; it was part of FRENCH WEST AFRICA, headquartered from 1902 at Dakar. In 1914, Blaise Diagne became the first black African elected from Senegal to the French national assembly, and he served until 1934. Under the French, Senegal's trade was reoriented toward the coast, its output of groundnuts increased dramatically, and railroads were built. During World War II, Senegal was aligned with the Vichy regime from 1940 to 1942, but then joined the Free French. In 1946, Senegal, together with the rest of French West Africa, became part of the FRENCH UNION and French citizenship was extended to all Senegalese. Politics in Senegal were led by its two deputies in the French national assembly, Lamine Gueye, whose base was in the coastal cities, and Léopold Sédar SENGHOR, whose political strength was derived from the rural areas of the interior. In 1948, Senghor founded the Senegalese Democratic Bloc, which dominated politics in Senegal in the 1950s. Under the French *loi cadre* [Fr.,=outline law] of 1956, a national assembly was set up in Senegal. In late 1958, after Charles de Gaulle had come to power in France, Senegal became an autonomous republic within the FRENCH COMMUNITY. In Jan., 1959, Senegal joined with Soudan (now Mali) to form the Mali Federation, which became independent in June, 1960. On Aug. 20, 1960, Senegal withdrew from the federation, becoming an independent state within the French Community. At the time of independence, power was fairly evenly divided between the country's president, who was Senghor, and its prime minister, Mamadou Dia, who with his cabinet was responsible to the 60-member national assembly. In

Dec., 1962, Dia staged an unsuccessful coup d'etat and was arrested; early in 1963 a new constitution was promulgated giving the president much additional power. Under the 1963 constitution and later revisions, the president is directly elected to a 5-year term; he appoints the prime minister and other ministers, and they are responsible to him Legislative power is vested in a 100-member national assembly. In 1966 the Senegalese Progressive Union (UPS), headed by Senghor, became the country's only political party. Senghor was reelected overwhelmingly in 1968 and 1973. From the mid-1960s there was considerable unrest in the country caused by dissatisfaction with the growing concentration of power in Senghor's hands and by a declining economic situation resulting from lower world prices for groundnuts and reduced aid from France. The economic situation was worsened by a long-term drought in the Sahel region of N Senegal that began in the late 1960s, continued into the early 1970s, but eased somewhat in 1974. Major demonstrations, often organized at the Univ. of Dakar, and strikes became an almost annual occurrence and were particularly virulent in 1968, 1971, and 1973. In early 1967 there was an unsuccessful attempt on Senghor's life. In the early 1970s, about 70,000 black Africans from neighboring Portuguese Guinea fled to S Senegal as a result of fighting in the colony between the Portuguese and black Africans; in May, 1973, Portuguese troops carried out a major raid on guerrilla bases in S Senegal. Also in the early 1970s, relations with Guinea were strained after President Sekou Touré of Guinea accused Senegal of supporting a mercenary raid on Conakry in 1970; Senegal severed its diplomatic ties with Guinea in Sept., 1973. Senghor was a leading force in establishing (1974) the West African Economic Community, which linked six former French territories. See W. J. Foltz, *From French West Africa to the Mali Federation* (1965); Michael Crowder, *Senegal: A Study in French Assimilation Policy* (2d ed. 1967); M. A. Klein, *Islam and Imperialism in Senegal: Sine-Saloum, 1847–1914* (1968); L. C. Behrman, *Muslim Brotherhoods and Politics in Senegal* (1970); G. W. Johnson, *The Emergence of Black Politics in Senegal: the Struggle for Power in the Four Communes, 1900–1920* (1971); D. B. Cruise O'Brien, *The Mourides of Senegal: the Political and Economic Organization of an Islamic Brotherhood* (1971); W. A. Skurnik, *The Foreign Policy of Senegal* (1972).

Senegal, river, c.1,000 mi (1,610 km) long, formed in SW Mali, W Africa, by the confluence of the Bafing and Bakoy rivers, both of which rise in the Fouta Djallon, N Guinea. The river flows north, then generally west to form the Mauritania-Senegal border before entering the Atlantic Ocean at St. Louis. The Falémé River, which forms the Senegal-Mali border, is its chief tributary. Entrance to the river from the sea is impeded by sand bars and a complex delta region. The river is tidal c.300 mi (480 km) upstream, and during the rainy season it is navigable to Kayes, Mali. The river is an important source of irrigation water; rice is grown on the floodplain.

senega snakeroot: see MILKWORT.

Seneh (sĕ'nē), in the Bible: see BOZEZ.

Senghor, Léopold Sédar (lāôpôld' sādär' säNgôr'), 1906–, African statesman and poet; president (1960–) of the republic of Senegal. The son of a rich landowner, Senghor was extraordinarily gifted in literature and won a scholarship to study in Paris. There he met writers such as Aimé CÉSAIRE and Léon DAMAS with whom he formulated the concept of negritude, which asserted the importance of their black African heritage (see AFRICAN NEGRO LITERATURE). He served in the French army in World War II, and after the war he represented Senegal (1945–58) in the French legislature. He then held a series of offices in Senegal and became one of the founders of the African Regroupement party. He was president of the legislative assembly in the Mali Federation, formed in 1959, but Senegal withdrew from the federation (1960), and Senghor became president of the republic of Senegal. He continued to work for African unity, and, in 1974, Senegal joined six other nations in the West African Economic Community. He was reelected president in 1963, 1968, and 1973. A distinguished intellectual, he has written numerous volumes of poetry and essays in French, including *Chants d'Ombre* (1945), *Hosties noires* (1948), *Chants pour Naëtt* (1949), and *Éthiopiques* (1956). These reflect his concept of negritude, an assertion of black African cultural values. Among his works in English translation are *On African Socialism* (1964) and *Selected Poems* (1964). See biographies by I. L. Markovitz (1969) and J. L. Hymans (1972); studies by S. W. Bâ (1973) and S. O. Mezu (1973).

Senherib: see SENNACHERIB.

Senigallia (sānēgäl'lyä), city (1971 pop. 37,911), in the Marche, central Italy, on the Adriatic Sea. It is a port, a seaside resort, and an industrial center. Manufactures include textiles, processed food, and construction materials. Made a Roman colony in the 3d cent. B.C., it was later (6th cent. A.D.) one of the cities of the Byzantine Pentapolis. Although included in the territories donated (8th cent.) by Pepin the Short to the popes, it became (12th cent.) a free commune and then was a papal fief under various rulers. Cesare Borgia had several rebellious lords slain there (1502). The city has walls and a castle dating from the 15th cent. and two Renaissance churches.

senility (sənil'ətē), deterioration of body and mind associated with old age. Indications of old age vary in the time of their appearance. Stooped posture, wrinkled skin, decrease in muscle strength, changes in the lens and muscles of the eye, brittleness of bone and stiffness of the joints, and hardening of the arteries (ARTERIOSCLEROSIS) are among the physical changes associated with old age. The mental changes associated with senility include impairment of judgment, loss of memory, and sometimes childish behavior. The psychological changes are thought to be related to aging of the cortical brain cells. Whereas the physical changes associated with aging occur in all individuals to some extent, evidence of psychological degeneration is not universal. In common usage, the term *senility* is applied only to mental deterioration. See GERIATRICS.

Senior, Nassau, 1790–1864, English economist. A graduate of Oxford, he was called there in 1825 to fill the first chair of political economy in England. In *An Outline of the Science of Political Economy* (1836) he sought to carry classical economic principles closer to scientific formulation. He also promulgated a famous theory stating that capital is a productive factor and that interest and profit accrue to the capitalist as a result of his "abstinence" (i.e., saving). Senior served on several commissions to investigate social problems and helped produce the report that was the basis for the poor-law amendment of 1834. See studies by Marian Bowley (1937, repr. 1967) and S. L. Levy (new ed. 1970).

Senir (sē'nər) or **Shenir** (shē'nər), Amorite name for Mt. HERMON and its surroundings. Deut. 3.9; 1 Chron. 5.23; Cant. 4.8; Ezek. 27.5.

Senlis (säNlēs'), town (1968 pop. 11,169), Oise dept., N central France, on the Nonette River. Wood products and mechanical and electrical equipment are the chief manufactures. Senlis has some of the best preserved monuments in France, including walls and towers from Gallo-Roman times and medieval ramparts and bastions. The Church of Notre Dame (12th–13th cent.) is one of the early masterpieces of Gothic architecture. Senlis also has a 15th-century town hall and the ruins of a château once inhabited by the first kings of France.

senna, any plant of the genus *Cassia,* leguminous herbs, shrubs, and trees of the family Leguminosae (PULSE family), most common in warm regions. Some species are cultivated for ornament, but sennas are best known as medicinal plants. The dried leaves are used as a purgative and are chiefly obtained from *C. acutifolia* (Alexandria senna) and *C. augustifolia* (Indian senna); both trees are cultivated especially in S India. The wild senna (*C. marylandica*), a perennial of the E United States, has been similarly used. Golden shower (*C. fistula*) of India yields canafistula, a purgative extracted from the fruit pulp. The young shoots of several wild species are used for food and the seeds for a coffee substitute. *C. nictitans,* a North American herb, is sometimes called wild sensitive plant because its leaves respond to touch as do those of the true sensitive plant, a mimosa. Cassia or cassia bark is the common name for a CINNAMON, unrelated to the genus *Cassia.* Senna is classified in the division MAGNOLIOPHYTA, class Magnoliopsida, order Rosales, family Leguminosae.

Sennacherib (sĕnăk'ərĭb) or **Senherib,** d. 681 B.C., king of Assyria (705–681 B.C.). The son of Sargon, Sennacherib spent most of his reign fighting to maintain the empire established by his father. It is difficult to determine the exact sequence of his conquests, but his first campaign seems to have been waged against Babylonia. Later he marched against an uprising of the western nations (Phoenicia, Palestine, and Philistia), who were supported by Egypt. He defeated the Egyptians at Eltekeh (701 B.C.) and prepared to take Jerusalem. Isaiah had warned HEZEKIAH not to join the uprising against Assyria, but the king had refused the advice. Thus, Sennacherib destroyed many Judaean cities and besieged Jerusalem, forcing the king to pay a heavy tribute. Hezekiah built the famous Siloam Tunnel when the water supply was threatened by the approach of the Assyrian forces. The prism of Sennacherib tells his version of the expedition against Hezekiah. It is uncertain whether the biblical account of the plague that ravaged Sennacherib's army occurred at this time or at a later date. Byron's poem, "The Destruction of Sennacherib," relies on the account in 2 Chron. 32. Disturbances in Babylonia called the king to that area, and he waged a naval campaign against the Chaldaeans. He laid Elam waste and finally fought both the Chaldaeans and the Elamites at the battle of Halulina (Khaluli) (c.691 B.C.). The exact outcome of the battle is uncertain. Two years later Sennacherib captured and destroyed Babylon. He constructed canals and aqueducts and built a magnificent palace at Nineveh. Two of his sons, jealous of their brother Esar-haddon, murdered Sennacherib. Esar-haddon succeeded to the throne. Isaiah 36; 37; 2 Kings 18; 19. See L. L. Homor, *Sennacherib's Invasion of Palestine* (1926, repr. 1966); B. S. Childs, *Isaiah and the Assyrian Crisis* (1967).

Sennar: see SANNAR, Sudan.

Sennett, Mack (sĕn'ĭt), 1884–1960, American movie director and producer, b. Danville, Que. In 1909 he began working for D. W. Griffith at the Biograph Company, and in 1912 he organized his own Keystone Company. Sennett's films, rarely more than one or two reels long, were slapstick comedies noted for their fantastic chases and custard pie warfare. His Keystone cops and bathing beauties became American institutions. In 1916 he became the third producer of the Triangle Corporation with D. W. Griffith and Thomas Ince. The Keystone Company, after some years of difficulty, went bankrupt in 1933, and slapstick became the property of the animated cartoon. See his autobiography, *King of Comedy* (1954); Gene Fowler, *Father Goose* (1934).

Senones (sĕnō'nēz, sĕn'ōnēz), ancient people of GAUL. There were two groups, one of which settled in NE Italy S of the Po in the 4th cent. B.C. The others lived in the valley of the Seine.

senryu (sĕnrēōō'), a Japanese poem structurally similar to the HAIKU but primarily concerned with human nature. It is usually humorous or satiric. Used loosely, the term means a poem similar to the haiku that does not meet the criteria for haiku.

Sens (säNs), town (1968 pop. 24,563), Yonne dept., N central France, on the Yonne River. Leather tanning and the manufacture of safes, electrical equipment, gears, and plastics are the chief industries. Sens was the capital of the Senones, a Gallic tribe, and was later a Roman metropolis. The town was attacked by the Saracens in 731 and by the Normans in 886 and was annexed by the French crown in 1055. Sens was an archiepiscopal see almost without interruption from the 8th cent; its prelates had jurisdiction over Paris until 1622 when that city became a separate archdiocese. A council held in Sens in 1121 condemned the teachings of Peter Abelard. The town was a stronghold of the HOLY LEAGUE during the early 16th cent. A massacre of Huguenots took place at Sens in 1562. The Cathedral of Saint-Étienne (begun 1140), one of the oldest Gothic cathedrals, was largely built by William of Sens, who also reconstructed much of Canterbury Cathedral in England.

sensationalism, in philosophy, the theory that there are no innate ideas and that knowledge is derived solely from the sense data of experience. The idea was discussed by Greek philosophers and is shown variously in the works of Thomas HOBBES, John LOCKE, George BERKELEY, David HUME, Julien de LA METTRIE, Baron d'HOLBACH, Claude HELVETIUS, Étienne de CONDILLAC, Ernst MACH, and others. See also EMPIRICISM.

sense, faculty by which external or internal stimuli are conveyed to the brain centers, where they are registered as sensations. The four commonly known special senses (sight, hearing, smell, and taste) are concerned with the outer world, and external stimuli are received and conducted by sensory receptors concentrated in the eye, ear, olfactory organ, and the taste buds. The so-called somatic senses respond to both external and internal stimuli. Although most of the somatic receptors are located in the skin (conveying the external sensations of touch, heat, cold, pressure, and pain), others are located in internal organs (e.g., the heart and the stomach). Somatic sensations such as hunger, thirst, and fatigue are thought to originate in specific areas of the nervous system.

sensitive plant: see MIMOSA.

sensitivity training: see GROUP PSYCHOTHERAPY.

Senta (sĕn'tä), Hung. *Zenta,* city (1971 pop. 31,407), NE Yugoslavia, in the Vojvodina region of Serbia, on the Tisza River. A river port and an agricultural center, it has industries that produce foodstuffs, soap, and textiles. At Senta in 1697, Prince Eugene of Savoy won a decisive victory over the Turks, who as a result of the defeat had to accept (1699) the Treaty of Passarowitz.

sentence, in criminal law, punishment that a court orders imposed on a person convicted of criminal activity. Sentences may consist of a fine, imprisonment for varying periods including life, or execution. In the United States exile and forfeiture of property by heirs are not used as punishment. A fine and imprisonment may both be imposed, or (especially in MISDEMEANORS) payment of a fine may be the alternative to a prison sentence. The sentence to be imposed is generally fixed by statute. In some cases the duration is exactly prescribed and in others the judge has a limited discretion. If a person is convicted of more than one crime at his trial, his sentences may run concurrently (i.e., all begin at the same date) or consecutively. Sentences may be determinate (of fixed duration) or indeterminate. In the latter a minimum and a maximum term is set, and if the convict's behavior is good he may be released on PAROLE any time after the expiration of the minimum term. In many states successive convictions of FELONY bring longer sentences. See VERDICT and JURY.

Sentinum (sĕntī'nəm), ancient town of Umbria, E central Italy, near the modern town of Sassoferrato. In 295 B.C. the Romans (led by Publius Decius Mus) defeated the Gauls and the Samnites there. The city wall and the remains of houses have been preserved.

Senuah (sēnyo͞o'ə), Benjamite. Neh. 11.9.

Senussi: see SANUSI.

Seorim (sēō'rĭm), chief priest of David's time. 1 Chron. 24.8.

Seoul (sā'o͞ol, sā'o͞ol, sōl) or **Kyongsong** (kyŭng'sŭng'), Jap. *Keijo,* city (1970 pop. 5,536,377), capital of South Korea, NW South Korea, on the Han River. It has special status equivalent to that of a province. The political, commercial, industrial, and cultural center of the nation, Seoul is also a highway and railroad hub. It is linked by rail with Inchon, its port, and there is an international airport at Kimpo. Before the partition of Korea in 1945, Seoul's easy access to industrial raw materials stimulated the establishment of iron, steel, and other primary industries; with most of the raw materials now in North Korea, the city has emphasized textile manufacturing, agricultural processing, and varied consumer industries. There are also tanneries, railroad repair shops, and large power plants. Founded in 1392, Seoul was an early fortress and trade center and served as the capital of the Yi dynasty, which ruled Korea until the country became (1910) a colony of Japan. The Japanese governor general made Seoul his headquarters. When the country was partitioned after World War II, Seoul became the seat of the U.S. occupation forces. It became the capital of South Korea in 1948. North Korean forces captured the city on June 28, 1950, only three days after the Korean War began; it then changed hands several times until UN troops took it in March, 1951, and it became the headquarters of the UN command in Korea. Heavily damaged during the war, the city was rebuilt along modern lines. Its population was greatly increased by refugees. In the center of Seoul is a huge bronze bell that was cast in 1468. The city retains three gates of the ancient wall that once surrounded it and three imperial palaces. It has a Roman Catholic cathedral and numerous other Christian churches; there are also several universities, an art museum, and zoological and botanical gardens.

sepal, a modified leaf, part of the outermost of the four groups of FLOWER parts. The sepals of a flower are collectively called the calyx and act as a protective covering of the inner flower parts in the bud. Sepals are usually green, but in some flowers (e.g., the lily and the orchid) they are the same color as the petals and may be confused with them. In a few flowers (e.g., the marsh marigold and the anemone) they are absent. The small green leaves at the base of the flower head in the composite family are not true sepals but bracts; the sepals are modified into a circle of tiny white hairs on the ovary (the pappus). The sepals are sometimes fused into a tube around the base of the petals, as in the mint family.

separation, in law, either the voluntary agreement of husband and wife to live apart or a partial dissolution of the marriage relation by court order. The marriage bond remains, and remarriage of either party is criminal. The separated parties will ordinarily be bound by the provisions of an agreement respecting the amount to be paid for separate maintenance and the adjustment of their property rights. Separation by court decree is a DIVORCE *a mensa et thora* [from bed and board]; the parties are forbidden to live together, and the wife may have a right to ALIMONY. The laws of the states of the United States vary greatly as to separation; generally jurisdictions where divorce is difficult to obtain have a more lenient policy toward legal separation than do jurisdictions with easier divorce laws. The main grounds for legal separation are adultery, cruelty, and desertion.

separatists, in religion, those bodies of Christians who withdrew from the Church of England. They desired freedom from church and civil authority, control of each congregation by its membership, and changes in ritual. In the 16th cent. a group of early separatists were known as Brownists after their leader, Robert BROWNE. The name Independents came into use in the 17th cent. Among other separatist groups were the Pilgrims, the Quakers, and the Baptists. See CONGREGATIONALISM.

separator, cream, dairy machine used to separate fresh whole milk into cream and skim milk. Formerly the separation was made by the gravity method, allowing the cream to rise to the top of a pan and then skimming it off. C. G. de Laval of Sweden devised the first mechanical cream separator c.1880, based on the principle of centrifugal force. Whole milk is conducted into a bowl, commonly through a central tubular shaft. A spindle rotates the bowl at a rate of from 6,000 to 9,000 rpm, and a series of identical conical disks separates the milk into vertical layers. The heavier skim milk collects on the outer circumference of the rapidly whirling bowl, and the lighter cream tends to remain in the center. The pressure of the whole-milk supply above the bowl then forces the cream and skim milk out of the machine and into separate collecting vessels. The cream separator makes it possible to control the amount of fat (called butterfat) remaining in the milk. The gravity method ordinarily leaves one fourth of the fat in the milk, while the cream separator leaves only 0.01% to 0.02% of the fat in the skim milk. Since the latter process is much faster than the gravity method, there is less chance for harmful bacterial action. All major parts of the machine are made of stainless steel, which is not affected by milk acids, does not rust, and is easily kept clean and polished.

Sephar (sē'fər), unidentified boundary of Joktan's territory, probably in S Arabia. Gen. 10.30.

Sepharad (sĕf'ərăd), unlocated place peopled with Jews in captivity. Obad. 20.

Sephardim (səfär'dəm), one of the major divisions of the Jewish people, made up of those Jews who in the Middle Ages resided in the Iberian Peninsula, as distinguished from those who lived in German lands, who came to be known as Ashkenazim (see ASHKENAZ). The name comes from the place-name Sepharad (Obad. 20), which early biblical commentators identified with Iberia. Sephardic ritual and liturgy followed the Babylonian tradition as a result of the influence of the GAONIM upon the Mediterranean area during the early period of Muslim domination. (The Ashkenazim followed the basics of the Palestinian tradition.) With the migration of the Iberian Jews, particularly following their formal expulsion from Spain in 1492, Sephardic traditions were transferred to N Africa and the Middle East and adopted by the local Jewish populations. Today the term *Sephardim* is employed to refer to those Jews who are native to the Middle East, even when Spanish descent is not present. Sephardic Jews spoke a dialect called Ladino (Judeo-Spanish or Spanioli); it consisted of medieval Castilian combined with Hebrew, Turkish, Arabic, and other elements, depending upon the period and geographic area in which it was used. Originally reserved for religious works (e.g., the early Bible translations of the 14th and 15th cent.), it came to be the vehicle for folktales, songs (*romanceros*), essays, and journalism. Those Sephardim who were forced to convert to Christianity during the period lasting from the 1391 massacres in Spain to the 1497 forced baptisms in Portugal, and who secretly maintained a Jewish life, were given the pejorative title of Marrano [pig] by the Christian populace. As time passed, many made their way to more tolerant lands, where they openly returned to Judaism, ending their double lives. They or their descendants founded the Jewish communities of Amsterdam, Hamburg, London, and New Amsterdam (New York City), among others. See Cecil Roth, *A History of the Marranos* (1932, repr. 1966) and *The Spanish Inquisition* (1937, repr. 1964); M. J. Bernadete, *Hispanic Culture and Character of the Sephardic Jew* (1953); David De Sola Pool, *An Old Faith in the New World* (1955); I. J. Baer, *The Jews in Christian Spain* (2 vol., 1961); Moshe Lazar, ed., *The Sephardic Tradition* (1972); Joachim Prinz, *The Secret Jews* (1973).

Sepharvaim (sē″färvā'ĭm), unidentified place, near RIBLAH **2.** Its inhabitants were sent to colonize Samaria. 2 Kings 17.24,31. It may be the same place given in 2 Kings 18.34; 19.13; Isa. 37.13.

Sepik, river, c.700 mi (1,130 km) long, N New Guinea, rising near the border of West Irian and Papua New Guinea. It flows east through a large swampy basin to the Bismarck Sea. The river drains a vast mountainous region of central New Guinea and is navigable for small craft c.300 mi (480 km) upstream.

sepiolite: see MEERSCHAUM.

Sepoy Rebellion: see INDIAN MUTINY.

seppuku: see HARA-KIRI.

septarium: see CONCRETION.

September: see MONTH.

September massacres: see FRENCH REVOLUTION.

septicemia (sĕptĭsē'mēə), invasion of the bloodstream by virulent bacteria that multiply and discharge their toxic products. The disorder is commonly known as blood poisoning. The invasive organisms are usually streptococci or staphylococci but may be any type of bacteria. The primary causes of septicemia are infection within the walls of the blood vessels, rapidly progressing tissue infections (osteomyelitis, cellulitis), virulent systemic disease (meningitis, typhoid), and local infections (abscess, carbuncle) that the defense mechanisms of the body are unable to contain. The microorganisms usually spread to other organs such as the lungs, liver, and brain. Symptoms of septicemia are fever (usually quite high), chills, prostration, and a hemorrhagic or other type of skin eruption. The condition is very grave and requires massive doses of antibiotics in its treatment. In contrast, bacteremia is the transient invasion of the blood by bacteria with no overt clinical evidence of an infection. It may occur as a result of tooth extraction or a traumatic wound; the invading bacteria are quickly removed by phagocytic cells.

septic tank, underground sedimentation tank in which sewage is retained for a short period while it is decomposed and purified by bacterial action. The organic matter in the sewage settles to the bottom of the tank, a film forms excluding atmospheric oxygen, and anaerobic bacteria attack the solid matter, causing it to disintegrate, liquefy, and give off gases. The gases are discharged from a vent and the liquids overflow through an outlet into a disposal field where they can leach into the soil. Here aerobic bacteria purify the liquid. The Imhoff septic tank, an improvement over the ordinary septic tank, is still used in the United States; it is a two-story structure with the upper compartment used for settling the sewage, the lower one for the anaerobic disintegration of sludge. A sloping floor enables solid material to slide to the lower compartment, where, since the sludge is separated from the material in the sedimentation compartment, the action is more rapid. A cesspool is a simpler underground structure that allows the liquids to leach directly into the soil while retaining the solids. The solids are not as efficiently decomposed as in a septic tank and more frequent cleaning is necessary. Also, as the effluent is likely to contain more coliform bacteria than that of a septic tank, cesspools pose a greater threat to water supplies. Septic tanks and cesspools are usually used in rural areas. For urban sewage-disposal systems, see SEWERAGE.

Sept-Îles (sĕtēl'), city (1971 pop. 24,320), E Que., Canada, on the St. Lawrence River near its mouth. It is a major port exporting iron ore. The harbor was visited by Jacques Cartier in 1535, and a trading post was built on the site in 1650.

Septimius Severus: see SEVERUS.

Septuagint (sĕp'tyo͞oəjĭnt) [Lat.,=70], oldest extant Greek translation of the Old Testament made by Hellenistic Jews, possibly from Alexandria, c.250 B.C. Legend, according to the fictional letter of Aristeas, records that it was done in 72 days by 72 translators for Ptolemy Philadelphus, which accounts for the name. The Greek form was later improved and altered to include the books of the Apocrypha and some of the pseudepigrapha. It was the version used by Hellenistic Jews and the Greek-speaking Christians, including St. Paul; it is still used in the Greek Church. The Septuagint is of importance to critics because it is translated from texts now lost. No copy of the original translation exists; textual difficulties abound. The symbol for the Septuagint is LXX.

Sepulcher, Holy: see HOLY SEPULCHER.

Séquard, Charles Édouard Brown-: see BROWN-SÉQUARD, CHARLES ÉDOUARD.

sequence, in mathematics, ordered set of mathematical quantities called terms. A sequence is said to be known if a formula can be given for any particular term using the preceding terms or using its position in the sequence. For example, the sequence 1, 1, 2, 3, 5, 8, 13, . . . (the Fibonacci sequence) is formed by adding any two consecutive terms to obtain the next term. The sequence −1/2, 1, 7/2, 7, 23/2, 17, . . . is formed according to the formula $(n^2-2)/2$ for the nth, or general, term. A sequence may be either finite, e.g., 1, 2, 3, . . . 50, a sequence of 50 terms, or infinite, e.g., 1, 2, 3, . . ., which has no final term and thus continues indefinitely. Special types of sequences are commonly called PROGRESSIONS. The terms of a sequence, when written as an indicated sum, form a SERIES; e.g., the sum of the sequence 1, 2, 3, . . ., 50 is the series 1+2+3+. . .+50.

sequoia (sĭkwoi'ə), name for the redwood (*Sequoia sempervirans*) and for the big tree, or giant sequoia (*Sequoiadendron giganteum*), both huge, coniferous evergreen trees of the BALD CYPRESS family, and for extinct related species. Sequoias probably originated over 100 million years ago. Once widespread in temperate regions of the Northern Hemisphere, the trees were almost exterminated by the ice sheets of the glacial ages. Several species are known only by fossil remains; some such fossils have been found in the Petrified Forest in Arizona. The two living species survive only in a narrow strip near the Pacific coast of the United States. The redwood occurs along the coast of California and S Oregon, often in easily lumbered, pure stands. Growing 100 to 385 ft (30–117 m) high, it is probably the tallest tree in the world. Its trunk is 20 to 25 ft (6.1–7.6 m) in diameter. It usually has bluish-green, needlelike leaves. Some redwoods are believed to be over 2,000 years old. The big tree, 150 to 325 ft (46–99 m) tall and with a trunk 10 to 30 ft (3–9.1 m) in diameter, grows on the western slopes of the Sierra Nevada in California. It reaches an even greater age than the redwood; some big trees are believed to be 3,000 to 4,000 years old. The leaves are small, overlapping scales. Both trees have deeply grooved, reddish bark and soft, straight-grained, reddish heartwood whose resistance to decay makes it especially valuable for outdoor building purposes, e.g., for shingles, siding, and flumes. Although the sequoias are protected in parks, e.g., in Sequoia National Park of California, their existence elsewhere is threatened by exploitation. China's deciduous dawn redwood tree (*Metasequoia*) is believed to be a related species and is perhaps an ancestor of the California redwood. This genus was named and described from fossil remains five years before the few living specimens were discovered in 1946. Fewer than 1,000 trees were found, and they were on the verge of extinction by lumbering. Dawn redwoods are now propagated elsewhere, chiefly in California. The tree sometimes called South American redwood is the unrelated BRAZILWOOD. The sequoia is classified in the division PINOPHYTA, class Pinopsida, order Coniferales, family Taxodiaceae. See Norman Taylor, *The Ageless Relicts* (1963); Robert Silverberg, *Vanishing Giants* (1969).

Sequoia National Park, 386,863 acres (156,563 hectares), E central Calif.; est. 1890. In the park are 35 groves of giant sequoias, spectacular granite mountains, and deep canyons. The General Sherman Tree, 272 ft (83 m) high and 37 ft (11 m) in diameter at its widest point, is the largest and one of the oldest living things in the world, estimated to be more than 3,500 years old. Within the area are Mt. Whitney, the highest point in the conterminous United States; Kern River canyon; and the Great Western Divide, which separates westerly flowing waters from easterly flowing waters. Marble Falls drops 2,000 ft (610 m) in seven cascades. Kings Canyon National Park (see NATIONAL PARKS AND MONUMENTS, table) adjoins Sequoia National Park in the north; the two are administered as a single park.

Sequoyah (sĭkwoi'ə), c.1766–1843, North American Indian leader, creator of the Cherokee syllabary, b. Loudon co., Tenn. Although many historians believe that he was the son of a Cherokee woman and a white trader named Nathaniel Gist, his descendants dispute this claim. To most Americans he was known as George Guess; to the Cherokee he was known as Sogwali. The name Sequoyah was given to him by missionaries. A silversmith and a trader in the Cherokee country in Georgia, he set out to create a system for reducing the Cherokee language to writing, and he compiled a table of 85 characters; he took some letters from an English spelling book and by inversion, modification, and invention adopted the symbols to Cherokee sounds. There is some dispute as to when the syllabary was completed. Many historians date its completion at about 1821; Cherokee tradition holds that it was created much earlier and was actually in use as early as the late 18th cent. In 1822, Sequoyah visited the Cherokee in Arkansas, and soon he taught thousands of the Indians to read and write. He moved with them to present-day Oklahoma. Parts of the Bible were soon printed in Cherokee, and in 1828 a weekly newspaper was begun. His remarkable achievement helped to unite the Cherokee and make them leaders among other Indians. The giant tree, sequoia, is named for him. See biographies by Grant Foreman (1938, repr. 1970) and C. C. Coblentz (1946, repr. 1962); Traveller Bird, *Tell Them They Lie: The Sequoyah Myth* (1971).

Seraglio: see ISTANBUL, Turkey.

Serah (sē'rə), daughter of Asher. Gen. 46.17. Sarah: Num. 26.46.

Seraiah (sĕr"ərī'ə), **1** See SHAVSHA. **2** High priest under Zedekiah. 2 Kings 25.18–21; 1 Chron. 6.14; Ezra 7.1; Jer. 52.24. **3** Companion of Zedekiah. Jer. 51.59. **4** Captain at Mizpah. 2 Kings 25.23; Jer. 40.8. **5** Father of Joab. 1 Chron. 4.13,14. **6** Grandfather of Jehu. 1 Chron. 4.35. **7** Leader in the return with Zerubbabel. Ezra 2.2; Neh. 12.1,12. Azariah: Neh. 7.7. **8** Same as AZARIAH **24.** **9** Officer of Jehoiakim. Jer. 36.26. **10** Sealer of the covenant. Neh. 10.2.

Seraing (sərĕN'), city (1970 pop. 40,545), Liège prov., E Belgium, on the Meuse River, near Liège. A major center of heavy industry, it is the seat of the Cockerill steel and locomotive works (founded in the early 19th cent. by an Englishman, John Cockerill). Nearby is Val Saint Lambert, one of the world's leading glassware-manufacturing centers.

Serampur or **Serampore** (both: sē"rəmpôr'), town (1971 pop. 101,597), West Bengal state, E central India, on the Hooghly River, just N of Calcutta. Founded in 1799, Serampur was the center of Danish colonialism in India. Great Britain purchased the town from Denmark in 1845. Serampur's college (opened 1818) grants degrees in Christian theology.

Seran or **Serang:** see CERAM, Indonesia.

seraph (sĕr'əf), plural **seraphim** (-ĭm), kind of ANGEL, surrounding God's heavenly court. According to the Bible seraphim have six wings. Isa. 6.2–7. From ancient times they have been associated with the cherubim (see CHERUB), with whom they share many attributes. Thus in art, seraphim are usually differentiated only in the surrounding color, red. In the Christian liturgy they go together, e.g., in the preface of Mass and the *Te Deum*.

Serapis (sĕrā'pĭs) or **Sarapis** (sărā'pĭs), Egyptian god whose devotees united the worship of the Apis bull and the god Osiris. His cult, which originated at Memphis, rose to its greatest significance at Alexandria during the reign of Ptolemy I. He was adopted as the universal godhead by some Gnostic sects. In Greece during Hellenistic times and later during the Roman Empire his worship rivaled that of other Middle Eastern and Mediterranean cults.

Serawak: see SARAWAK, Malaysia.

Serbia (sûr'bēə), Serbo-Croatian *Srbija* (sŭr'bēā), constituent republic of Yugoslavia (1971 pop. 8,436,-547), 34,107 sq mi (88,337 sq km), E Yugoslavia, the largest and most important of the republics. BELGRADE is the capital of both Serbia and Yugoslavia. The republic consists of Serbia proper with the cities of Belgrade and NIŠ, the autonomous VOJVODINA prov. with SUBOTICA and NOVI SAD, and the autonomous KOSSOVO-METOHIJA region with PRIŠTINA. Serbia is largely mountainous in the west and south, but the northeast is part of the fertile Danubian plain, drained by the Danube, Sava, Tisza, and Morava rivers. Vojvodina and Serbia proper, the "breadbasket" of Yugoslavia, provide about half the country's total agricultural produce. Wheat, corn, hemp, sugar beets, and flax are the chief crops. Serbia proper has extensive vineyards and is one of Europe's major regions for fruit-growing (notably plums). It is also an important mining area. The republic's population consists primarily of Serbs, with Slovenian, Croatian, Magyar, Montenegrin, Albanian, and Macedonian minorities. The Serbs distinguish themselves culturally from the closely related Croats and Slovenes through their membership in the Orthodox Eastern Church and use of the Cyrillic rather than the Roman alphabet.

Consolidation of a People. Serbs settled in the Balkan Peninsula in the 6th and 7th cent. and accepted Christianity in the 9th cent. Their petty principalities were theoretically under a grand *zhupan*, who usually recognized Byzantine suzerainty. Civil strife and constant warfare with their Bulgarian, Greek, and Magyar neighbors characterized the early history of the Serbs. Rascia, the first organized Serbian state, was probably founded in the early 9th cent. in the Bosnian mountains; it steadily expanded from the 10th cent. Bulgaria, meanwhile, challenged Byzantium for suzerainty over the Serbs. Stephen Nemanja, whom the Byzantine emperor recognized as grand *zhupan* of Serbia in 1159, founded a dynasty that ruled for two centuries. His son and successor assumed the title king of all Serbia in 1217 with the Pope's blessing. However, the king's brother, Sava, archbishop of Serbia, succeeded in having papal influence eliminated from the kingdom; in 1219 he won recognition from the patriarch of Constantinople of an autocephalous Serbian Orthodox Church. The Serbian kingdom was at first overshadowed by the rapid rise of the Bulgarian empire under IVAN II (Ivan Asen), but under STEPHEN DUSHAN, who became king in 1331 and czar in 1346, Serbia became the most powerful empire in the Balkan Peninsula, much of which it absorbed. Its might contrasted sharply with the decadent Byzantine Empire. Even among European states, Serbia was noted for its high economic, social, and cultural level. After Stephen's death in 1355, however, the empire decayed and fell victim to the onslaught of the Ottoman Turks. The Serbs suffered defeat at the Maritsa River in 1371; that same year the last czar, Stephen Urosh V, died without male issue. His successor, Lazar, contented himself with the title prince of Serbia. Lazar was slain in 1389 during the battle of KOSSOVO FIELD, in which the cream of Serbian nobility was massacred and the fate of independent Serbia sealed. Lazar's son, Stephen, was allowed to rule (1389–1427) over a diminished and divided Serbia by Sultan Bayazid I, to whom he paid tribute. Although he and his successor, George Brankovich (reigned 1427–56), received the title despots (lords) from the Byzantine Empire, the Turks gradually absorbed their lands. The quarrel over the Brankovich succession facilitated the complete annexation of Serbia by Sultan Muhammad II in 1459. Belgrade, then held by Hungary, fell to the Turks in 1521. During the centuries-long Turkish occupation of Serbia, national traditions and the memory of the Dushan's empire were preserved by the Serbian Orthodox Church.

Turkish Rule. Serbia became a Turkish province, with its pashas residing at Belgrade. Turkish rule in Serbia was more oppressive than in most Turkish provinces. The Serbian nobility was annihilated and its lands distributed to the Turkish military aristocracy, while the Christian peasants (*rayas*) were treated like virtual slaves. Although the Serbs were forbidden to possess weapons, frequent insurrections erupted. No attempt was made to curb Christianity; but the Serbian Church was placed in the hands of unpopular Greek Phanariots (see under PHANAR). Many Serbs fled to Hungary and Austria to help those countries fight the sultans. Turkish reverses in 17th- and 18th-century wars against Austria and Russia revived Serbian hopes for independence. The liberation struggle began in 1804, when KARAGEORGE ("Black George") led a rebellion that eventually freed the pashalik (province) of Belgrade from the Turks. Russia, also at war with Turkey, then formed an alliance with Serbia. The Treaty of Bucharest (1812) forced Turkish recognition of Serbian autonomy, but Russian preoccupation with Napoleon's invasion allowed the Turks to renew their tyranny in Serbia. A revolt flared in 1815 under Miloš Obrenović, who in 1817 procured the assassination of his rival Karageorge and became prince of Serbia. Turkey proved unable to challenge his power. In 1829, Russia forced the Treaty of Adrianople upon the sultan, who had to grant Serbian autonomy under Russian protection and to recognize Miloš as hereditary prince. Except for garrisons in Belgrade and other fortresses, the Turks evacuated Serbia.

Restoration of Serbia. Much of Serbia's ensuing history revolved around the bloody feud between the Karadjordjević and Obrenović families. Miloš's absolutist tendencies caused popular resentment and forced his abdication in 1839; his son shared the same fate. In 1842, Alexander Karageorge was recalled to the throne. The Congress of Paris, meeting in 1856 at the conclusion of the Crimean War, placed Serbia under the collective guarantee of the European powers while continuing to acknowledge Turkish suzerainty. In 1867 the last Turkish troops left Serbia. Prince Milan Obrenović liberalized the constitution in 1869, granting more power to the Skupchtina (lower house of Parliament). He also supported the rebellion of BOSNIA AND HERCEGOVINA against Turkish rule and in 1876 declared war on Turkey. The rout of the Serbs led Russia to enter the war on the Serbian side. The Congress of Berlin (1878) recognized Serbia's complete independence and substantially increased its territory. The placing of Bosnia and Hercegovina under Austro-Hungarian administration disappointed the Serbs, however. Serbia's championship of PAN-SLAVISM in the Balkans engendered bitter rivalry with Bulgaria and Austria-Hungary. Milan, who was proclaimed king in 1882, harmed Serbian prestige by fighting an unsuccessful war with Bulgaria in 1885 over the question of Eastern RUMELIA. The assassinations of King ALEXANDER Obrenović (reigned 1889–1903) and his unpopular queen marked the end of the Obrenović dynasty; with the accession of PETER I in 1903, the Karadjordjević dynasty entrenched itself. Peter restored the liberal constitution of 1889 and in 1904 appointed as premier Nikola Pašić, leader of the strongly nationalist and pro-Russian Radical party. The strengthening of parliamentary government and expansion of the economy greatly raised Serbia's prestige and exerted a powerful attraction on the South Slavs who remained under Austro-Hungarian rule. Austria-Hungary's annexation of Bosnia and Hercegovina in 1908 was designed to quell sentiment in that region for union with Serbia. The angry Serbs retaliated by creating a Balkan League (Montenegro, Bulgaria, and Greece) to liberate the Balkan Slavs from both Austro-Hungarian and Turkish rule. In 1912 the league declared war on and defeated Turkey, but the allies could not agree on division of the spoils. Dissatisfied with its failure to secure a major portion of MACEDONIA in the first of the BALKAN WARS, Serbia in 1913 turned against and defeated its former Bulgarian ally in the Second Balkan War. Serbia's victory made it the foremost Slavic power in the Balkans but greatly increased tensions with Austria-Hungary. When a Serbian nationalist (acting without governmental collusion) assassinated Austrian archduke FRANCIS FERDINAND in 1914, the empire declared war on Serbia, thus precipitating World War I. The Serbian army fought bravely; but in 1915, when Bulgaria joined the Central Powers and Germany reinforced the Austrians, Serbia was overrun. The Serbian troops and government were evacuated to Kérkira (Corfu), where in 1917 Serbian, Croatian, Slovenian, and Montenegrin representatives proclaimed the union of South Slavs. In 1918 the kingdom of the Serbs, Croats, and Slovenes, headed by Peter I of Serbia, officially came into existence. After that, the history of Serbia is essentially that of YUGOSLAVIA.

Serbia within Yugoslavia. Serbia's predominant position in the new kingdom was a major cause for unrest in Croatia and Macedonia in the period between World Wars I and II. After the conquest and dismemberment of Yugoslavia in World War II, German occupation forces set up a puppet government in a much-diminished Serbia. The Serbs waged guerrilla warfare under the leadership of Draža MIHAJLOVIĆ. Later, Marshal TITO and his pro-Communist partisans attracted the majority of the Yugoslav resistance fighters, while Mihajlović's following became mostly restricted to the Serbian nationalists. The federal constitution of Yugoslavia, adopted in 1946, stripped Serbia of Macedonia, Bosnia and Hercegovina, and Montenegro, which became autonomous republics. See L. S. Stavrianos, *The Balkans Since 1453* (1958); H. W. Temperly, *History of Serbia* (1917, repr. 1970); William Miller, *The Balkans, Roumania, Bulgaria, Servia, and Montenegro* (1896, repr. 1972).

Serbian literature: see YUGOSLAV LITERATURE.

Serbo-Croatian (sûr'bō-krōā'shən), language belonging to the South Slavic group of the Slavic subfamily of the Indo-European family of languages (see SLAVIC LANGUAGES). Although it is actually one language, Serbo-Croatian is designated as Serbian when spoken by Serbs (mostly belonging to the Orthodox Eastern Church) and written in a form of the Cyrillic alphabet, but as Croatian when spoken by Croats (mostly Roman Catholics) and written in a modified version of the Roman alphabet. This divergence in writing is the principal difference between the Serbian and Croatian versions of Serbo-Croatian. The major official language in Yugoslavia, Serbo-Croatian is the native tongue of about 15 million people in that country, of whom 8 million are Serbs and 4 million are Croats. The language is not spoken to any extent outside of Yugoslavia. A feature that sets Serbo-Croatian apart from other Slavic languages is its use of musical pitch or intonation. It possesses four kinds of musical ACCENT: two rising inflections, one long and one short, and two falling inflections, one long and one short. This musical intonation apparently reflects the earlier Indo-European pitch accent. Grammatically, Serbo-Croatian resembles Polish. The oldest extant texts in Serbo-Croatian date from the 12th cent. For a number of centuries the literary language of the Serbs was a variant of CHURCH SLAVONIC, and in Catholic Croatia it was usually Latin, although in the 13th cent. the Croats began to write down their spoken language. In the 19th cent. the Serbian philologist Vuk Stefanovíc KARADŽIĆ, through his writings and efforts, accomplished several major linguistic reforms. The most important one instituted the spoken tongue as the basis of the literary language. Karadžić also worked for a more phonetic spelling and consequently for a revision of the alphabet to that end. See also YUGOSLAV LITERATURE. For grammars see those by Monica Partridge (1964) and Oton Grozdić (1969).

Sered (sē'rĕd), Zebulunite, the ancestor of the Sardites. Gen. 46.14; Num. 26.26.

Seremban (sərĕmbän'), city (1971 pop. 79,915), capital of Negeri Sembilan, Malaysia, S Malay Peninsula, on the Linggi River. It is linked by rail with Port Dickson on the Strait of Malacca. Seremban is the commercial center of a rubber-growing area. There are tin mines nearby.

Serena, La: see LA SERENA.

serenade [Ital. *sera*=evening], term used to designate several types of musical composition. Opera and song literature yield numerous examples of the serenade sung or played by a lover at night beneath his beloved's window; outstanding is *Deh, vieni alla finestra* from Mozart's *Don Giovanni*. In the late 18th cent. the serenade became a light instrumental suite, whose movements were numerous and short and usually included a march and a minuet. The lover's song is known in German as *Ständchen,* while the suite is usually designated *Nachtmusik,* an example being Mozart's *Eine kleine Nachtmusik.* The Italian *serenata,* while the equivalent of the French term *serenade,* had an additional usage in the late 18th cent. in designating a short opera or dramatic cantata written to celebrate a special event in the household of the composer's patron.

Sereth, river: see SIRETUL.

serf, under FEUDALISM, peasant laborer, who can be generally characterized as hereditarily attached to the manor in a state of semibondage, performing the servile duties of the lord (see also MANORIAL SYSTEM). Although serfs were usually bound to the land, many exceptions are found in the medieval economy of Western Europe, in which serfdom is best known. Serfdom is distinguished from slavery chiefly by the body of rights the serfs held by a custom generally recognized as inviolable and by the strict arrangement that made the peasants servile in a group rather than individually. Serfdom sometimes arose from the conquest of a people by victors who did not reduce the natives to slavery but only depressed them to tributaries; these tributaries held their lands as of old, but paid dues (especially labor dues) to the conquerors. Thus serfdom was established in some Aegean regions by Greek conquests. More generally it may be said that serfdom arose only under a local agricultural economy, connected with a political system based on personal contract—some form of feudalism. Serfdom was known in the Hellenistic civilization, and in the Roman Empire economic maladjustment led to the appearance of the servile class, the coloni. In the Middle Ages, serfdom developed in France, Italy, and Spain, later spread to Germany, and in the 15th cent. was carried to Slavic countries. It developed separately in England (where serfs were more commonly referred to as VILLEINS), but underwent a great change with the Norman Conquest, when most of the freemen were depressed to serfdom. The status of manorial peasants was regulated by local custom, and a wide diversity of names was applied to the various types of tenancy, which extended from the completely servile tenant to the freeholder who paid only a form of rent. The tendency in the Middle Ages was for all tenants to approximate the same status and foı all landholding to be held by labor service (a mark of servile tenure) as well as by fixed payments. The true serf was theoretically subject to labor service at the will of his lord, but all such matters came to be governed by set customs. One distinguishing mark of servile tenure was the lord's control of the marriage of his serf's children. In legal theory the serf's holding was granted at the will of the lord, but in practice the right to hold came to be hereditary. In Western Europe the breakdown of the manorial system made serfdom anachronistic, and one of the principal questions of modern European reform was the emancipation of serfs. Serfdom disappeared in England before the end of the Middle Ages. In the Hapsburg monarchy, it was ended (1781) by Emperor JOSEPH II, but feudal labor service *(robot)* continued in some provinces until 1848. In France, where it survived in outlying provinces, serfdom was swept away by the French Revolution. The repercussions of the Napoleonic Wars helped to destroy it elsewhere, the most notable example being the reforms of Karl vom und zum STEIN in Prussia. In Russia and the other Slavic countries serfdom took different forms and persisted in some cases as late as the 19th cent.

Russian Serfdom. In Russia serfdom originated during the 16th cent. when Ivan IV created a new landholding aristocracy, the *pomiestchiks,* whose tenure was based on service to the czar. Beginning in 1581, laws were passed inhibiting the free movement of the peasant tenants of the *pomiestchiks;* however, at this time the peasants still retained their civil rights. In the reign of Peter I the peasants were definitely bound to the landowner rather than to the land; their condition became virtual slavery. There were also real slaves in the Muscovite state, and in the 18th cent. all real distinction between slaves and serfs was abolished. As can be seen, the institution was more akin to slavery in the United States than to serfdom under feudalism. It reached its peak in the late 18th cent. under Catherine II, but was somewhat limited by reforms under Alexander I and Nicholas I. Serfdom was regarded by the majority of Russians as the major defect in the Russian state and as contrary to the interests of the rising industrial class and of the great landowners. It was the small landowners who risked losing everything if serfdom were abolished, and it was that class that most stubbornly resisted reform. The serfs were freed only in 1861 by Alexander II (see EMANCIPATION, EDICT OF). Serfdom also appeared with feudalism in China, Japan, India, pre-Columbian Mexico, and elsewhere. See also SLAVERY; PEONAGE. See W. R. Brownlow, *Lectures on Slavery and Serfdom in Europe* (1892, repr. 1969); Jerome Blum, *Lord and Peasant in Russia From the Ninth to the Nineteenth Century* (1961); R. H. Hilton, *Decline of Serfdom in Medieval England* (1969).

sergeanty: see SERJEANTY.

Sergel, Johan Tobias (yo͞o'hän to͞obē'äs sĕr'yəl), 1740–1814, Swedish sculptor. He studied (1767–79) in Rome, and much of his sculpture is in the neoclassical style. His subjects, other than portraits, are drawn from classical history and mythology. Among his works are *Cupid and Psyche* and a monument to Gustavus III. He is known also for his lively caricatures and scenes illustrating daily life. In addition to their importance as works of art, these sketches are valuable as a record of late 18th-century Swedish history.

Sergipe (sərgē'pĭ), state (1970 pop. 901,618), 8,321 sq mi (21,551 sq km), NE Brazil, on the Atlantic Ocean. ARACAJU is the capital.

Sergius Paulus (sûr'jəs), proconsul in Cyprus, friendly to Paul. Acts 13.7.

serial music, also called twelve-tone music, the body of compositions whose fundamental syntactical reference is a particular ordering (called series or row) of the twelve pitch classes—C, C#, D, D#, E, F, F#, G, G#, A, A#, B—that constitute the equal-tempered scale. In contrast to tonal music, whose unity is perceived in the primacy of a single construct, the triad (the major or minor chord), serial music is not pitch centric, i.e., there is no home key. Instead, the presence of harmonic successions resulting from controlled juxtaposition of various row forms gives serial pieces their coherence. These forms are the prime, retrograde (pitch order reversed), inversion (interval direction reversed), and retrograde inversion, and the twelve transpositional degrees of the foregoing. Thus, the row functions as an ordering of intervals and not of absolute pitches. In practice, the row can be presented linearly or chordally. The twelve-tone system evolved in the 1920s in the works of Arnold Schoenberg, Anton von Webern, and Alban Berg as the result of efforts to establish a unifying principle for nontonal music. Classic serial pieces include Schoenberg's Piano Suite, Op. 25 (1924) and von Webern's String Quartet, Op. 28 (1938). Pierre Boulez and Milton Babbitt have led efforts toward "total serialization," the application of serial technique to rhythm, dynamics, and timbre, in addition to pitch. Important composers of serial music include Igor Stravinsky, Ernst Krenek, Egon Wellesz, and Walter Piston. For further information see separate articles on all composers mentioned in this article. See Joseph Rufer, *Composition with Twelve Notes* (tr. 1952); George Perle, *Serial Composition and Atonality* (3d ed. 1972).

sericulture: see SILK; SILKWORM.

series, in mathematics, indicated sum of a SEQUENCE of terms. A series may be finite or infinite. A finite series contains a definite number of terms whose sum can be found by various methods. An infinite series is a sum of infinitely many terms, e.g., the infinite series $\frac{1}{2}+\frac{1}{4}+\frac{1}{8}+\frac{1}{16}+\ldots$. The dots mean that the remaining terms are formed according to the rule made evident by the first few terms, in this case doubling the denominator of the preceding term to form that of the next term; the *n*th term of this series is $\frac{1}{2}^n$. Some infinite series converge to a certain value called its limit; i.e., as one adds together progressively more terms, these sums (called the partial sums of the series) form a sequence of values that progressively approach the limit. For example, the series given above converges to the value 1 because the partial sums form the sequence $\frac{1}{2}$, $\frac{3}{4}$, $\frac{7}{8}$, $\frac{15}{16}$, ... Many series, however, do not converge, i.e., have no value that their partial sums approach. Such a series is $\frac{1}{2}+\frac{1}{3}+\frac{1}{4}+\ldots$, for even though the terms become very small, enough of them added together will give a value greater than any number that can be named. A series that does not converge is said to diverge; various tests exist for determining whether or not a given series converges and for determining its limit if it does converge. See also PROGRESSION.

series circuit: see ELECTRIC CIRCUIT.

serigraphy: see SILK-SCREEN PRINTING.

serine (sĕr′ēn), organic compound, one of the 22 α-AMINO ACIDS commonly found in animal proteins. Only the L-stereoisomer appears in mammalian protein. It is not essential to the human diet, since it can be synthesized in the body from other metabolites, including GLYCINE. Serine is important in metabolism in that it participates in the biosynthesis of PURINES and PYRIMIDINES, CYSTEINE, TRYPTOPHAN (in

CH_2OH
$H_2N—C—C(=O)OH$
H

serine

bacteria), and a large number of other metabolites. When incorporated into the structure of enzymes, serine often plays an important role in their catalytic function. It has been shown to occur in the active sites of CHYMOTRYPSIN, TRYPSIN, and many other enzymes. The so-called nerve gases and many substances used in insecticides have been shown to act by combining with a residue of serine in the active site of acetylcholine esterase, inhibiting the enzyme completely. Without the esterase activity that usually destroys ACETYLCHOLINE as soon as it performs its function, dangerously high levels of this neurotransmitter build up, quickly resulting in convulsions and death. Serine was first obtained from silk protein, a particularly rich source, in 1865; its structure was established in 1902.

serjeanty or **sergeanty** (both: sär′jĕntē), a type of TENURE in English feudalism in which the tenant held his lands from the king or overlord in return for the performance of some personal, often menial, service. Examples of such duties ranged from that of king's constable or chamberlain to that of supplying arrows for an overlord when he went hunting. This method of landholding was less widespread than other forms of tenure, such as knight service (see KNIGHT 2) and socage, by which serjeanty was largely superseded. Such tenures were nontransferable and indivisible but could be inherited. A remnant of the custom survives in certain ceremonial offices at royal coronations.

Serkin, Rudolf, 1903–, Austrian-American pianist, b. Bohemia. Serkin was musically precocious and was sent to Vienna at nine for his musical training. He studied composition with Arnold Schoenberg (1918–20). Serkin gave joint recitals with Adolf Busch (his father-in-law) and made his U.S. debut (1933) with the Busch chamber players. He was a soloist (1934) with the New York Philharmonic-Symphony Orchestra under Toscanini. Serkin and Busch brought the entire cycle of Beethoven piano-and-violin sonatas to New York audiences in 1938. In 1939 he joined the staff of the Curtis Institute in Philadelphia. He became director of the Marlboro School of Music in Vermont in 1951. His son **Peter Serkin,** 1947–, b. New York City, is also a noted concert pianist.

Serlio, Sebastiano (sä″bästyä′nō sĕr′lyō), 1475–1554, Italian Renaissance architect and theoretician, b. Bologna. He was in Rome from 1514 until the sack in 1527 and worked under Baldassare Peruzzi. Few traces exist of his buildings in Venice, where he lived from 1527 to 1540. Invited to France by Francis I, he appears to have served in an advisory capacity for the construction of the palace at Fontainebleau. He designed several châteaus in France; the only one that has survived, despite alterations, is that of Ancy-le-Franc (c.1546), near Tonnerre in Burgundy. Serlio's major contribution was his treatise on architecture (eight books, 1537–75). Intended as an illustrated handbook for architects, the volumes, separately published, were highly influential in France, the Netherlands, and England as a conveyor of the Italian Renaissance style; the treatise was also an influence in theatrical SCENE DESIGN AND STAGE LIGHTING. An early manuscript of it is preserved in the Avery Architectural Library, Columbia.

Serna, José de la (hōsā′ thā lä sär′nä), 1770–1832, Spanish general, viceroy of Peru (1821–24). In 1821 the military leaders, dissatisfied with Viceroy PEZUELA and his conduct of the war against José de SAN MARTÍN, deposed Pezuela and named José de la Serna in his place; he was confirmed in the office by Spain. Forced to evacuate Lima, he made Cuzco his capital and preserved some show of royal government until the defeat at AYACUCHO, where he was captured.

serotine: see BAT.

serotonin (sĕr″ətō′nĭn), organic compound that was first recognized as a powerful vasoconstrictor occurring in blood serum. It was partially purified, crystallized, and named in 1948, and its structure was deduced a year later. Independent work indicated that serotonin was widely distributed in nature and occurred in tissues other than blood. It has been shown to be in many representatives of the animal kingdom, in wasp stings and scorpion venom, in various fruits, such as pineapples, bananas, and plums, and in various nuts. It has been estimated that an adult human contains about 5 to 10 mg of serotonin, 90% of which is in the intestine and the rest in blood platelets and the brain. The role of the compound, in spite of intensive investigation during the last two decades, remains obscure. It has been suggested that it contributes to the regulation of peristalsis (the rhythmic contractions of the intestine) and that it can function as a neurotransmitter (see ACETYLCHOLINE) in the central nervous system. The structural similarity of serotonin and several drugs known to cause mental aberrations, such as lysergic acid diethylamide (LSD), has prompted much speculation as to the role of serotonin in naturally occurring mental disorders such as schizophrenia. The function of serotonin in blood platelets is not clear; it seems to have no important role in the clotting mechanism. Its function in stings and venoms might be that of an irritant, since intravenous injections of serotonin in man produce pain at the site of injection, gasping, coughing, a general tingling and prickling sensation, nausea, cramps, and other unpleasant symptoms.

Serov (syĕ′rəf), city (1970 pop. 101,000), E European USSR, in the eastern foothills of the Urals, on the Kakvy River. A metallurgical center, Serov produces cast iron and quality steel. Founded in 1894 in connection with the building of the Trans-Siberian RR, the city was called Nadezhdinsk until 1939.

Serowe (sĕrō′wā), town (1971 pop. 15,723), E central Botswana. Located in a fertile, well-watered area, it is a trade center and the seat of the Ngwato tribe. There is a memorial to Khama III, chief of the Ngwato in the late 19th and early 20th cent.

serpent, term sometimes used to designate the larger species of SNAKES in mythology and folklore, a name often applied to any sinuous crawling creature, chiefly to a snake. No sea serpents have been discovered to substantiate the legends about them, although some accounts, such as stories of the so-called Loch Ness monster in Scotland, have received wide publicity. Large squids, octopuses, whales, dolphins, seals, and other sea animals are sometimes described as sea serpents. In religion and art, the serpent sometimes symbolizes Satan (Rev. 20.2), or the phallus (see PHALLIC WORSHIP). See also DRAGON.

serpentine (sûr′pəntēn, -tīn), hydrous silicate of magnesium. It occurs in crystalline form only as a pseudomorph having the form of some other mineral and is generally found in masses that may be granular, fibrous, or foliated. It is commonly some shade of green, but may also be reddish, yellowish, black, or nearly white. It has a greasy or silky luster and is often translucent, even in large masses. Serpentine is a secondary mineral, usually resulting from the alteration of minerals or rocks containing magnesium, and it occurs very widely throughout the world. Serpentine rocks are classified as common serpentine and precious serpentine, the common serpentine being darker, less translucent, and sometimes impure. When serpentine is mixed with calcite, dolomite, or magnesite, a mottled or veined rock called verd antique is produced. A fibrous variety of serpentine is chrysotile, or commercial ASBESTOS. Serpentine is sometimes used as a gem, and the massive varieties are quarried and used like marble for decorative purposes, although the masses are frequently jointed and only small slabs can be secured. Serpentine takes a beautiful high polish, but it is easily cracked and discolored by exposure to the weather and is consequently of little value for exterior use.

serpent star: see BRITTLE STAR.

Serpotta, Giacomo (jä′kōmō sĕrpôt′tä), 1659–1732, Italian sculptor. Patriarch of a family of stucco workers, Serpotta was employed on extensive decorations for the churches of Palermo. Most of his work was religious in nature and heavily influenced by antique sculpture.

Serpukhov (syĕr′po͝okhəf), city (1970 pop. 124,000), central European USSR, on the Oka River. It is an important textile center. A fortress town since 1339, it retains a stone kremlin (16th cent.), the Church of St. Gregory and St. Dmitri (16th cent.), and the Vysotsk monastery (17th cent.).

Serra, Junípero (ho͞onē′pārō sĕ′rä), 1713–84, Spanish Franciscan missionary in North America, b. Majorca. His name was originally Miguel José Serra, and Junípero was his name in religion. For 15 years he taught philosophy in the college at Palma. In 1749 he was sent to America with Francisco Palou, his lifelong friend and biographer, and proceeded to Mexico City, where he taught briefly at the College of San Fernando. For three years he worked successfully among the Indians of the Sierra Gorda and then returned to Mexico City for seven more years, working half of each year in the surrounding villages. His passionate preaching and stern asceticism won him a large and respectful following. It was at this time that his self-mortification began and that legends began to grow up about him. In 1769, Serra went with the second expedition to California, which was commanded by Gaspar de Portolá. When the party reached San Diego, Serra remained to found (1769) the mission there, while most of the rest of the party went on in search of the harbor of Monterey. When they returned unsuccessful, Serra was one of those responsible for the sending of another expedition, which he accompanied. When Monterey was reached and the mission San Carlos Barromeo founded (1770), Serra remained there as president of Alta California missions; in 1771 he moved the mission to Carmel-by-the-Sea, which became his headquarters for the rest of his days. Under his presidency were founded the missions San Antonio de Padua (1771), San Gabriel Arcángel (1771), San Luis Obispo (1772), San Jaun Capistrano (1776), San Francisco de Asís (1776), Santa Clara de Asís (1777), and San Buenaventura (1782). The source material on Father Serra is chiefly in Francisco Palou's *Life and Apostolic Labors of the Venerable Father Junípero Serra* (tr. 1958) and *The Founding of the First California Missions under the Spiritual Guidance of the Venerable Padre Fray Junípero Serra* (tr. 1934). See biographies by Theodore Maynard (1954), Dudley Gordon (1969), and Katherine Ainsworth and E. M. Ainsworth (1970); study by M. F. Sullivan (1971).

Sérrai (sâ′râ), **Siris** (sĭ′rĭs), or **Serres** (sĕr′əs), Lat. *Serrae* or *Serrhae,* city (1971 pop. 39,897), capital of Sérrai prefecture, NE Greece, in Macedonia. It is a trade center for tobacco, grain, and livestock. Textiles and cigarettes are manufactured. The city was fortified under the Byzantine Empire and in the 14th cent. became a capital of Czar Stephen Dushan of Serbia. Sérrai was held by the Ottoman Empire from 1383 to 1913, when it passed to Greece. The city was occupied and damaged by Bulgaria in both World Wars.

Serrano Súñer, Ramón (rämōn′ sĕrä′nō so͞onyĕr′), 1901–, Spanish politician. A conservative member of the Cortes (1933–36), he joined his brother-in-law, Francisco Franco, early in the Spanish civil war of 1936–39 and became Nationalist minister of the interior (1937–40), of the press and propaganda (1939–40), and of foreign affairs (1940–42). Serrano Súñer played a major role in the political construction of the Franco state. A leading advocate of Spanish collaboration with the Axis during World War II, he had to resign as foreign minister and as president of the political council of the Falange when Franco adopted a cooler attitude toward Germany and Italy. He retired from public life in 1947.

Serrano y Domínguez, Francisco (fränthēs'kō särä'nō ē dōmēng'gāth), 1810-85, Spanish general and statesman. In 1834-39 he distinguished himself in the war against the Carlists. He at first supported ESPARTERO but later worked for his overthrow (1843). He was appointed captain general of Granada (1847), then of Cuba (1859). On his return he was created duque de La Torre and a grandee of Spain. After the death of his friend Leopoldo O'Donnell (1867), he led the Liberal Union party. He participated with Juan Prim in the overthrow (1868) of Isabella and was named regent by the constituent assembly. Serrano was premier (1870-71) under King Amadeus, and after the latter's abdication (1873) he opposed the newly established republic. In 1874 a military coup d'état placed him at the head of the provisional government. Serrano was excluded from office when Alfonso XII was restored (1875) to the Spanish throne.

Serres, Greece: see SÉRRAI.

sertão (sər'touN) [Port.,=backlands], semiarid hinterland of NE Brazil; c.250,000 sq mi (647,500 sq km). Its characteristic landscape is the caatinga, or thorny scrub forest. The chief occupation of the region is stock raising. The sertão area, in the "polygon of drought," covers parts of the states of Piauí, Ceará, Rio Grande do Norte, Paraíba, Pernambuco, Alagoas, Sergipe, and Bahia. The periodic droughts have caused large-scale migrations to the Amazon basin and to the urban centers of SE Brazil. Official reclamation activities began in the early 20th cent., and were intensified in the 1950s and 60s with the construction of numerous dams and hydroelectric projects, especially on the São Francisco River. In the 1960s a successful extensive regional economic development program was begun there. The area remains a focal point of social unrest. Its harsh and picturesque history, peopled by leather-garbed cowboys, bandits (*cangaceiros*), and religious fanatics, has been a source of inspiration for numerous Brazilian writers (notably Euclides da Cunha). See Preston James, *Latin America* (1969); B. J. Chandler, *The Feitosas and the Sertão dos Inhamuns* (1972).

Sertorius, Quintus (sûrtôr'ēəs), d. 72 B.C., Roman general. He was a general under MARIUS but did not take part in Marius' proscriptions. Sertorius was appointed governor of Farther Spain in 83 B.C. but fled to Africa to escape the reprisals of SULLA. He later was summoned (80 B.C.) to Spain by the Lusitani, who were in rebellion. He was successful even after Metellus Pius and Pompey were sent out with new armies, but he was assassinated by Perperna, a disaffected officer. Sertorius had attempted to build a stronger national feeling among the local leaders by founding a senate and a school for their sons. He thus expanded the work of Viriatus. The identification of Sertorius with local interests led, long after, to a mistaken glorification of him as a Portuguese patriot.

Serug (sē'rəg), ancestor of Abraham. Gen. 11.20-27. Saruch: Luke 3.35.

serum: see BLOOD.

serum sickness, hypersensitive response that occurs after injection of a large amount of foreign protein. The condition is named for the serum taken from horses or other animals immunized against a particular disease, e.g., tetanus or diphtheria. Such serum, which contains ANTIBODIES against the disease TOXINS, was formerly widely used to temporarily immunize humans. However, the antibodies from the animal serum are also foreign proteins that can act as antigens when injected into humans. The recipient's body responds by producing, within 8 to 12 days, antibodies that react against the animal serum proteins; the reaction causes injury to blood vessel walls and such allergic symptoms as rash, itching, and swelling of the lymph nodes. Fever, joint pain, spleen enlargement, and even shock may occur (see ALLERGY; HYPERSENSITIVITY). The reaction subsides as continued production of antibodies removes foreign protein from circulation. A person who has once had a serum injection is sensitized to the serum antigens, and a second injection can bring on the acute reactions typical of ANAPHYLAXIS. Today, serum preparations are rarely used. Instead, inoculations of tetanus and diphtheria TOXOIDS are given in childhood; they confer active immunity against those diseases. Serum sickness may occur in response to proteins other than those found in serum.

Sérusier, Paul (pōl sārōōsyā'), 1863-1927, French painter. In 1888 at Pont-Aven, Sérusier met Gauguin whose style he adhered to, particularly in his paintings of Breton landscapes. With Maurice Denis, Sérusier was a founder and spokesman of the NABIS. Sérusier had a highly methodical approach to art; he expressed his theories in *ABC de la peinture* (1921).

serval, medium-sized African CAT, *Felis serval,* found S of the Sahara in scrub country close to water. The serval is lightly built with very long legs; it has a small head with large eyes and ears, set on a long neck. Its coat is yellow-orange with black spots. The head and body are about 3 ft (91 cm) long and the ringed tail about 12 in. (30 cm) long. The serval is among the swiftest and most agile of cats and catches birds flying as much as 6 ft (1.8 m) from the ground. It also hunts insects, lizards, rodents, hares, and small antelopes. It is classified in the phylum CHORDATA, subphylum Vertebrata, class Mammalia, order Carnivora, family Felidae.

Servetus, Michael (sərvē'təs), 1511-53, Spanish theologian and physician. His name in Spanish was Miguel Serveto. In his early years he came in contact with some of the leading reformers in Germany and Switzerland—Johannes OECOLAMPADIUS, Martin BUCER, Wolfgang Fabricius CAPITO, and probably Martin LUTHER. But he held views, concerning the Trinity in particular, that brought condemnation from the theologians of the Reformation as well as from those of the Roman Catholic Church. When he published *De trinitatis erroribus* (1531) and *De trinitate* (1532), the feeling of opposition was so strong that he assumed the name of Michel de Villeneuve, from the family home, Villanueva, and spent some time in Lyons, working on an edition of Ptolemy's geography and other scientific works, then in Paris studying medicine. There he is said to have seen John CALVIN. He became well-known for his ability in dissection and had unusual success as a physician; he discovered that some of the blood circulates through the lungs. From 1541 to 1553 he lived in the palace of the archbishop of Vienne as his confidential physician. When (1553) he had a work setting forth his ideas of Christianity secretly printed, investigation was begun by the Inquisition. Servetus, arrested, tried, and condemned, escaped from prison. Several months later, while making his way to Italy, he was seized in Geneva by Calvin's order. There, after a long trial, in which Calvin's condemnation was a stern factor, he was burned on Oct. 27, 1553. See biographies by R. H. Bainton (1953) and J. F. Fulton (1954).

Service, Robert William, 1874-1958, Canadian verse writer and novelist, b. England, educated at the Univ. of Glasgow. He went to Canada in 1897 and held odd jobs in British Columbia and at White Horse in the Yukon. His famous ballad "The Shooting of Dan McGrew" appeared in *Songs of a Sourdough* (1907, repr. 1915 as *The Spell of the Yukon*). Celebrations of the rough ways of Klondike life continued in *Ballads of a Cheechako* (1909) and in the novel *The Trail of '98* (1910). Service became a foreign correspondent in 1912 and drove an ambulance during World War I, an experience that gave him material for *Rhymes of a Red Cross Man* (1916). He spent the rest of his life, except during World War II, in France and Monte Carlo. His later works did not win the tremendous popularity of the earlier ones. His autobiography was issued in two volumes, *Ploughman of the Moon* (1945) and *Harper of Heaven* (1948).

serviceberry: see SHADBUSH.

Servile Wars, name given in Roman history to three slave uprisings. The agricultural slaves were exploited by their owners, who had extreme powers and were never averse to using them. The first of the Servile Wars was fought in Sicily from 134 to 132 B.C. (or from 135 to 133 B.C.); the second, more serious, also occurred in Sicily from 104 to 101 B.C. (or from 105 to 102 B.C.). The third took place in Campania and was led by the gladiator SPARTACUS. He and his men gained control over most of S Italy in 73 B.C. and were finally put down with great cruelty by Crassus and Pompey in 71 B.C.

servomechanism, automatic device for the control of a large power output by means of a small power input or for maintaining correct operating conditions in a mechanism. It is a type of FEEDBACK control system. The constant speed control system of a DC motor is a servomechanism that monitors any variations in the motor's speed so that it can quickly and automatically return the speed to its correct value. Servomechanisms are also used for the control systems of guided missiles, aircraft, and manufacturing machinery.

sesame (sĕs'əmē), herb (*Sesamum indicum* or *orientale*) cultivated for its seeds since ancient times, found chiefly in the tropics of Africa and Asia. Sesame seeds, also called bennes or gingellies, are black or white and yield an oil that resists turning rancid. The oil (known also as teel oil) is used extensively in India for cooking, soap manufacture, food, and medicine and as an adulterant for olive oil. The seeds are also popularly added to cookies and other baked goods and are made into candy (e.g., benne cakes). Sesame was introduced by the Negroes into the U.S. South, where it sometimes becomes a weed. The sesame was once credited with mystic powers; the phrase "Open sesame," from the Arabian Nights tale of the forty thieves, has come to mean a magical password. Sesame is classified in the division MAGNOLIOPHYTA, class Magnoliopsida, family Pedaliaceae.

Sesostris I (sīsōs'trĭs), d. 1926 B.C., king of ancient Egypt, 2d ruler of the XII dynasty; son and successor of AMENEMHET I. He was coregent with his father from 1980 B.C.; from 1971 to 1926 he was sole ruler. His reign was notable for successful campaigns in Nubia. Sesostris' son and successor, AMENEMHET II, was his coregent during the last three years of his reign. **Sesostris II,** d. 1878 B.C., was the son of Amenemhet II, first his coregent (1900 B.C.), then his successor (1897-1878). **Sesostris III,** d. 1840 B.C., succeeded (1878 B.C.) his father Sesostris II. He fixed the southern boundary of Egypt above the Second Cataract of the NILE not far from Wadi Halfa and curbed the power of the Egyptian nobles. The name also appears as Sen-Vsert.

Sesshu (sĕs'shōō''), 1420-1506, foremost Japanese master of ink painting (*suiboku*) and Zen Buddhist priest, also known as Sesshu Toyo. He may have studied under Shubun in Kyoto. He made a trip to China (c.1467), visiting many Zen monasteries and studying the works of old masters. Adapting the Chinese style of landscape painting, he set the standard in ink painting for later Japanese artists. His brilliant, abstract interpretations of nature include the ink-splash landscape (1495) in the National Museum of Tokyo. Two sets of screens attributed to him are in the Museum of Fine Arts, Boston, and the Freer Gallery, Washington, D.C. See T. Nakamura, ed., *Sesshu Toyo* (1959); *Sesshu's Long Scroll: a Zen Landscape Journey* (1959).

Sessions, Roger, 1896-, American composer and teacher, b. Brooklyn, N.Y. Sessions was a pupil of Horatio Parker at Yale and of Ernest Bloch. He taught (1917-21) at Smith, leaving to teach at the Cleveland Institute of Music as Bloch's assistant. With Aaron Copland he organized (1928) the Copland-Sessions Concerts for contemporary music. In 1935, after years abroad, Sessions joined the faculty of Princeton. He was professor of music at the Univ. of California from 1944 to 1952, when he retruned to Princeton. His first major work was his incidental music (1923) for Leonid Andreyev's *Black Maskers.* Other important works are chorale preludes for organ; four symphonies (1927, 1947, 1957, 1958); a violin concerto (1931-35); a piano concerto (1956); and two string quartets (1936, 1950). Sessions's music, at first romantic and harmonic, became austere, complex, and highly individual. He has written two operas, a harmony textbook, and several essays.

Sestos (sĕs'tōs), ancient town on the Thracian shore of the Hellespont (now Dardanelles) opposite Abydos (in present-day Turkey). It was the scene of the story of HERO and Leander. It was there that Xerxes entered Thrace on his invasion of Greece, crossing the Hellespont on a bridge of boats. The city was later controlled by Athens and remained important in Roman times, but declined after the founding of Byzantium (now İstanbul).

Sesto San Giovanni (sĕ'stō sän jōvän'nē), city (1971 pop. 90,838), Lombardy, N Italy; an industrial suburb of Milan. Manufactures include iron, machinery, chemicals, and textiles.

Sestriere (sĕs''trēē'rā), Fr. *Sestrières* (sĕstrēâr'), village, alt. 6,670 ft (2,033 m), Piedmont, NW Italy, in the Alps. It is a fashionable winter sports center, located near the French border and the Montgenèvre Pass.

Sestri Ponente (sĕ'strē pōnän'tā), industrial suburb of Genoa, N Italy, on the Ligurian Sea. Manufactures include iron and steel, machinery, and tools. It is also the site of the noted Ansaldo shipyards.

Set or **Seth** (both: sĕt or sāt), in Egyptian religion, god of evil. Set was a sun god of predynastic Egypt, but he gradually degenerated from being a beneficent deity into being a god of evil and darkness. In a widespread Egyptian myth he murdered his brother OSIRIS and was in turn defeated by Horus, the son of Osiris. The Greeks identified Set with Typhon.

set, in mathematics, collection of entities, called elements of the set, that may be real objects or conceptual entities. A set must be well defined; i.e., for any given object, it must be possible to decide whether or not the object is an element of the set. For example, if a set contains all the chairs in a designated room, then any chair can be determined either to be in or not in the set. If there were no chairs in the room, the set would be called the empty, or null, set, i.e., one containing no elements. A set is usually

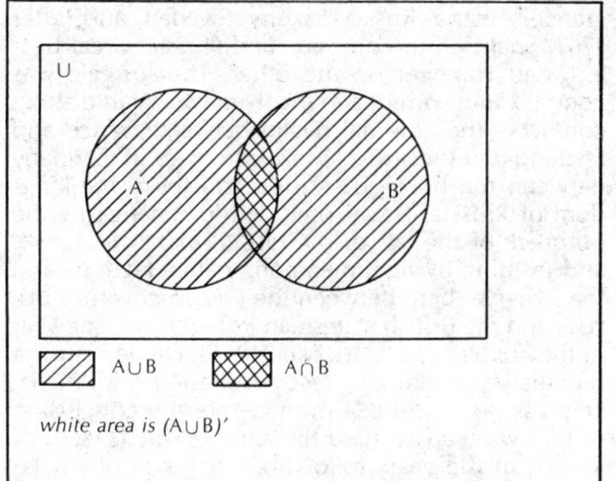

Union and intersection of sets A *and* B: *The union of* A *and* B, A∪B, *contains all members belonging to either* A *or* B. *The intersection of* A *and* B, A∩B, *contains all members common to both* A *and* B.

designated by a capital letter. If A is the set of even numbers between 1 and 9, then $A=\{2,4,6,8\}$. The braces, {}, are commonly used to enclose the listed elements of a set. The elements of a set may be described without actually being listed. If B is the set of real numbers that are solutions of the equation $x^2=9$, then the set can be written as $B=\{x{:}x^2=9\}$ or $B=\{x|x^2=9\}$, both of which are read: B is the set of all x such that $x^2=9$; hence B is the set $\{3,-3\}$. There are three basic set operations: intersection, union, and complementation. The intersection of two sets is the set containing the elements common to the two sets and is denoted by the symbol $\cap$. The union of two sets is the set containing all elements belonging to either one of the sets or to both, denoted by the symbol $\cup$. Thus, if $C=\{1,2,3,4\}$ and $D=\{3,4,5\}$, then $C\cap D=\{3,4\}$ and $C\cup D=\{1,2,3,4,5\}$. These two operations each obey the ASSOCIATIVE LAW and the COMMUTATIVE LAW, and together they obey the DISTRIBUTIVE LAW. In any discussion the set of all elements under consideration must be specified, and it is called the universal set. If the universal set is $U=\{1,2,3,4,5\}$ and $A=\{1,2,3\}$, then the complement of A (written A') is the set of all elements in the universal set that are not in A, or $A'=\{4,5\}$. The intersection of a set and its complement is the empty set (denoted by ϕ), or $A\cap A'=\phi$; the union of a set and its complement is the universal set, or $A\cup A'=U$. Membership in a set is indicated by the symbol ε and nonmembership by $\not\varepsilon$; thus, $x\varepsilon A$ means that element x is a member of the set A (read simply as "x is a member of A") and $y\not\varepsilon A$ means y is not a member of A. The symbols $\subset$ and $\supset$ are used to indicate that one set A is contained within or contains another set B; $A\subset B$ means that A is contained within, or is a subset of, B; and $A\supset B$ means that A contains, or is a superset of, B. Set theory not only is involved in many areas of mathematics but has important applications in other fields as well, e.g., computer technology and atomic and nuclear physics. See also BOOLEAN ALGEBRA.

Sète, formerly **Cette** (both: sĕt), town (1968 pop. 41,044), Hérault dept., S France, in Languedoc, on the Mediterranean. It is one of the most important commercial and fishing ports of S France, a wine-shipping center, with major gasoline refineries and plants making clothes, liqueurs, and chemical products. The city is crossed by numerous canals. The old harbor was designed by Colbert in 1666 and built by Vauban and Riquet. Paul Valéry was born and is buried there. The town has a school of hydrography and a zoology station of the Univ. of Montpellier.

Setesdal (sā'təsdäl), narrow valley, S Norway, in Aust-Agder co. It is drained by the Otra River (150 mi/241 km long) and contains several lakes. Communication with the rest of the country has, until recently, been difficult; as a result the Setesdalers have retained their ancient dress, speech, customs, and handicrafts. Agriculture, stock raising, and fishing are the chief occupations.

Seth, son of Adam and Eve, father of Enos. Gen. 4.25,26; 5.3. In Luke's chronology he is an ancestor of Jesus Christ. Luke 3.38. Sheth: 1 Chron. 1.1.

Seth, in Egyptian religion: see SET.

Seth, Andrew (Andrew Seth Pringle-Pattison), 1856–1931, Scottish philosopher, b. Edinburgh. He was professor of philosophy at University College, Cardiff (1883–87), and then professor of logic and metaphysics at St. Andrews (1887–91) and at Edinburgh (1891–1919). He added Pringle-Pattison to his name in 1898 to meet the conditions of a bequest. He was an influential teacher, and in his writings he examined philosophy through critical interpretations of the great philosophers. He wrote *Hegelianism and Personality* (1887), *Man's Place in the Cosmos* (1897), *The Idea of God in the Light of Recent Philosophy* (1917), *The Idea of Immortality* (1922), and *Studies in the Philosophy of Religion* (1930). See study by J. A. Vander Waal (1953).

Sethur (sē'thər), one of the spies sent by Moses into Canaan. Num. 13.13.

Seti I (sē'tī, sā'tē), d. 1290 B.C., king of ancient Egypt, of the XIX dynasty; son and successor of Ramses I. He succeeded to the throne c.1302 B.C. Invading Palestine and Syria, Seti I reduced them again to tributary status, and defeated the Libyans. He built temples at Thebes and Abydos and a magnificent tomb in the Valley of the Kings at Thebes. His successor was Ramses II. **Seti II,** d. 1205 B.C., one of the kings who reigned briefly after MERNEPTAH in the XIX dynasty, seems to have ruled for about four years. After his reign anarchy set in for a few years until the accession of Ramses III.

Sétif (sātēf'), ancient *Sitifis,* city (1966 pop. 98,337), capital of Sétif dept., NE Algeria. It is the commercial center of a region where native textiles and phosphates are manufactured and cereals are grown. Sétif was built by the French on the ruins of the Roman town of Sitifis, founded in the 1st cent. A.D. There is a Roman mausoleum on the outskirts of the city.

Seto (sā'tō), city (1970 pop. 92,682), Aichi prefecture, central Honshu, Japan. It has been an important porcelain center since the 13th cent.

Seton, Elizabeth Ann, 1774–1821, American Roman Catholic leader, usually called Mother Seton, b. Elizabeth Ann Bayley, New York City. She was the daughter of a prominent physician. Her husband, William Seton, a substantial merchant, died (1803) in Italy, leaving her with five young children. Soon afterward she became (1805) a Roman Catholic. This conversion severed her from her relatives, and she started a school in New York City to support her family. In 1808, invited by Bishop Carroll, she opened a school in Baltimore, then moved (1809) to Emmitsburg, Md., already the seat of a Catholic school for boys, Mt. St. Mary's. There she opened the first Catholic free school, the beginning of American parochial education and also founded St. Joseph's College (for women). About her she formed a community of women, which soon adopted the rule of the Daughters of Charity of St. Vincent de Paul, the great sisterhood centered in Paris. This was the first American congregation of Daughters of Charity (or Sisters of Charity). Mother Seton was superior of her community; this had grown into 20 communities before her death. She was beatified in 1963 and her canonization was announced in 1974, thereby making her the first native-born American saint. Her journals, letters, and memoirs have been published. See biography by J. I. Dirvin (1962).

Seton, Ernest Thompson, 1860–1946, American writer and artist, b. England. His name was originally Ernest Seton Thompson. His stories and paintings of wildlife, especially *Wild Animals I Have Known* (1898, new ed. 1942), were standard works on nature study and wood lore for boys and girls in the first quarter of the 20th cent. In 1902 he organized the Woodcraft Indians (later the Woodcraft League), much in the spirit of the later Boy Scout movement. See his autobiography, *The Trail of an Artist-Naturalist* (1940) and extracts from his journals, ed. by his widow, J. M. Seton (1967).

Seto-naikai, sea: see INLAND SEA, Japan.

Seton Hall University, mainly at South Orange, N.J.; Roman Catholic; coeducational; opened 1856, chartered 1861 as a college, became a university 1950. It has branches at Jersey City, Newark, and Paterson.

setter: see SPORTING DOG.

Settignano, Desiderio da: see DESIDERIO DA SETTIGNANO.

Settle, Elkanah, 1648–1724, English dramatist and poet. Thanks to the patronage of the earl of Rochester, Settle's heroic dramas for a time rivaled those of Dryden. His most successful play, the elaborate and bombastic *Empress of Morocco* (1671), provoked a long quarrel with Dryden, who satirized Settle as Doeg in *Absalom and Achitophel.*

Settlement, Act of, 1701, passed by the English Parliament, to provide that if William III and Princess Anne (later Queen Anne) should die without heirs, the succession to the throne should pass to SOPHIA, electress of Hanover, granddaughter of James I, and to her heirs, if they were Protestants. The house of HANOVER, which ruled Great Britain from 1714, owed its claim to this act. Among additional provisions, similar to those in the BILL OF RIGHTS, were requirements that the king must join in communion with the Church of England, that he might not leave England without parliamentary consent, and that English armies might not be used in defense of foreign territory without parliamentary consent. The act also prohibited royal pardons for officials impeached by Parliament. A clause providing that no appointee or pensioner of the king should sit in the House of Commons was repealed (1705) before the act became effective. The unpopularity of William's pro-Dutch policy, the lack of an heir to William or Anne, and fear of the JACOBITES prompted the act.

settlement house, neighborhood welfare institution generally in an urban slum area, where trained workers endeavor to improve social conditions, particularly by providing community services and promoting neighborly cooperation. The idea was developed in mid-19th-century England when such social thinkers as Thomas Hill GREEN, John RUSKIN, and Arnold TOYNBEE (1852–83) urged university students to settle in poor neighborhoods, where they could study and work to better local conditions. The pioneer establishment was Toynbee Hall, founded in 1884 in London under the leadership of Samuel Augustus BARNETT. Before long, similar houses were founded in many cities of Great Britain, the United States, and continental Europe. Some of the more famous settlement houses in the United States have been Hull House and Chicago Commons, Chicago; South End House, Boston; and the University Settlement, Henry Street Settlement, and Greenwich House, New York City. Settlements serve as community, education, and recreation centers. Sometimes known as social settlements, they are also called neighborhood houses, neighborhood centers, or community centers. The settlement house differs from other social welfare agencies; the latter provide specific services, while the former is aimed at improving neighborhood life as a whole. Its role has gradually altered as some of its varied functions have been assumed by state and municipal authorities and by other organizations. Kindergartens, formerly an important adjunct of the settlement house, are now operated by the public schools; municipal health departments have taken over its clinical services; and labor unions now sponsor educational and recreational activities for workers. The early leaders of settlement houses in the United States met from time to time and in 1911 founded the National Federation of Settlements and Neighborhood Centers; Jane Addams served as the first president. In 1926 the International Federation of Settlements and Neighbourhood Centres was established to coordinate community work on an international level. See Lorene Pacey, ed., *Readings in the Development of Settlement Work* (1951); Arthur Hillman, *Neighborhood Centers Today* (1960); A. F. Davis, *Spearheads for Reform* (1967, repr. 1970).

Settsu (sāt'tso͞o), city (1970 pop. 59,756), Osaka prefecture, SW Honshu, Japan. It is a suburb of Osaka.

Setúbal (sətoo͞'bəl), city (1970 pop. 64,531), capital of Setúbal district, S central Portugal, on the Bay of Setúbal at the mouth of the Sado River, in Estremadura. One of Portugal's most important ports, it handles wine, oranges, and cork. It has a fishing fleet and shipyards and is a major sardine-canning center. Setúbal was a royal residence (1481–95) under John II.

Seurat, Georges (zhôrzh sörä'), 1859–91, French neo-impressionist painter. He devised the pointillist technique of painting in tiny dots of pure color. His method, called divisionism, was a systematic refinement of the broken color of the impressionists. His major achievements are his *Baignade* (Tate Gall., London), shown in the Salon des Independants in 1884, and his masterpiece, *Un Dimanche à la Grande Jatte* (Art Inst., Chicago), completed two years later. He died of pneumonia at 31. Seurat is recognized as one of the most intellectual artists of his time and was a great influence in restoring harmonious and deliberate design and a thorough understanding of color combination to painting at a time when sketching from nature had become the mode. Other examples of Seurat's work are in the Barnes Foundation, Merion, Pa., and in the Louvre. See catalog (ed. by A. Blunt and R. Fry, 1965); drawings (ed. by R. L. Herbert, 1966); study by Pierre Courthion (tr. 1969).

Sevan (syĭvän'), lake, c.540 sq mi (1,400 sq km), SE European USSR, in Armenia, at an altitude of 6,280 ft (1,914 m); it is 324 ft (99 m) deep. The largest lake of the Caucasus, it is fed by some 30 streams, but the Razdan River is its only outlet. Lake Sevan is free of ice in winter. The Sevan-Razdan hydroelectric project has drained part of the lake. Several hydroelectric stations have been built along the Razdan. The steep gradient of the river and the great volume of Lake Sevan make possible such an extensive hydroelectric system. On Sevan Island, in the northwest, stands an ancient Armenian monastery, now a rest home.

Sevastopol (sĭvăs'təpōl", Rus. syĕ"vəstô'pəl), city (1970 pop. 229,000), SE European USSR, in the Ukraine, on the Crimean peninsula and the Bay of Sevastopol, an inlet of the Black Sea. The city is a port, a major naval base, and a strategic strong point. Commercial vessels no longer use the deep natural harbor, which guards the Black Sea entrance to the Ukraine and Transcaucasia. The city's industries include shipbuilding, lumber milling, food processing, and the production of bricks and furniture. Sevastopol stands near the site of the ancient Greek colony of Chersonesus or Cherson, founded in 421 B.C. A democratic city-state, Chersonesus was the most important Greek colony in the Crimea until Scythian invasions forced it to become (179 B.C.-63 B.C.) a protectorate of King Mithridates VI. In the 1st cent. A.D. the cities of the Crimea became part of the Roman Empire, and in the 4th cent. Chersonesus became the city of Korsun in the Byzantine Empire. In the Middle Ages it remained a large trading and political center and played an important role in the economic and cultural life of the Crimea, the Black Sea area, and Russia. The city survived as a Genoese trade colony until it was destroyed (1399) by a Tatar invasion. Sevastopol was founded as a city and port by Catherine II on the site of the Tatar village of Akhtiar after the Russian annexation (1783) of the Crimea. It was strongly fortified and became (1804) the chief base of the Russian Black Sea fleet. In the CRIMEAN WAR Sevastopol resisted the besieging British, French, Turks, and Sardinians for 349 days (1854-55). The hero of the land defense was Gen. E. I. TOTLEBEN; the Russian fleet was sunk by the Russians themselves to block the entrance to the harbor. In Sept., 1855, the French successfully stormed the fortress of Malakhov, on the south shore of the bay, and three days later the Russians were forced to abandon Sevastopol. A record of the spirit and sufferings of Sevastopol's defenders has been preserved in *The Tales of Sevastopol* by Tolstoy, who fought in the ranks of the besieged. Sevastopol declined as a military fortress after the Crimean Peace Conference (1856), and its fortifications were razed. After 1871, however, they were rebuilt, and in 1890 the city again became a chief naval base. The Sevastopol sailors mutinied during the 1905 revolution. In the Russian civil war Sevastopol was the headquarters of Gen. P. N. Wrangel during the last stand of the Whites (1920). The heroic resistance of Sevastopol in 1854-55 was, if possible, eclipsed by the stand the city made against the Germans in World War II. During a siege lasting more than eight months, the city was virtually destroyed. For three weeks the defenders fought on in the rubble, against all hope, until July 3, 1942, when German and Rumanian troops at last entered the city. After its recapture (May, 1944) by the Russians reconstruction began. The city was formerly spelled Sebastopol.

Seven against Thebes, in Greek legend, seven heroes—Polynices, Adrastus, Amphiaraüs, Hippomedon, Capaneus, Tydeus, and Parthenopaeus—who made war on Eteocles, king of Thebes. After the banishment of Oedipus, his sons, Eteocles and Polynices, agreed to reign alternately. When after the first year Eteocles refused to relinquish the throne, Polynices, assisted by Adrastus, king of Argos, organized the expedition known as the Seven against Thebes. All were killed except Adrastus. When Creon, Eteocles' uncle and successor to the throne of Thebes, would not permit the burial of the slain, Theseus marched against Thebes and gave them burial. Euripides' *Phoenician Women* and Aeschylus' *Seven against Thebes* are based on this legend.

Seven Churches in Asia, addressed in the preface of the REVELATION (1-3). They are the churches of Ephesus, Smyrna, Pergamum, Thyatira, Sardis, Philadelphia (Lydia), and Laodicea (Phrygia). They are in W Asia Minor.

Seven Days battles, in the American Civil War, the week-long Confederate counter-offensive (June 26-July 2, 1862) near Richmond, Va., that ended the PENINSULAR CAMPAIGN. After the battle of Fair Oaks the Union general George B. MCCLELLAN moved his army so that only the 5th Corps under Fitz-John PORTER remained N of the Chickahominy River. Gen. Robert E. LEE, commanding the Confederate Army of Northern Virginia, planned to attack Porter and cut McClellan off from his base at White House Landing on the Pamunkey River. Thomas J. (Stonewall) JACKSON, who was on his way from the Shenandoah Valley to join Lee, was to advance from the north and turn Porter's strong position behind Beaver Dam Creek. A. P. Hill was then to attack the Union advance lines at Mechanicsville, a village c.5 mi (8 km) NE of Richmond. Jackson failed to arrive; nevertheless, Hill's troops attacked and were severely repulsed in the battle of Mechanicsville (or Beaver Dam Creek) on June 26. Porter then fell back to another strong position at Gaine's Mill, a locality near Old Cold Harbor, c.10 mi (16 km) NE of Richmond. There on June 27, Longstreet, Jackson, A. P. Hill, and Daniel H. Hill led the Confederates against Porter's greatly outnumbered forces and at nightfall finally broke the Union resistance. With a good part of his corps, Porter crossed the river and joined the bulk of McClellan's army, which had remained inactive. McClellan decided to move his base to the navigable James River in order to add naval support. His march from the Chickahominy River was well executed, and Lee was unsuccessful in intercepting him in the battles of Savage's Station on June 29 and Frayser's Farm (or Glendale) on June 30. McClellan posted his army on Malvern Hill, a strong defensive position on the north bank of the James c.18 mi (29 km) SE of Richmond. In the battle of Malvern Hill on July 1, the Union troops repeatedly repulsed the Confederate attacks in some of the hardest fighting of the war. On the next day, however, McClellan, declining to take the offensive, withdrew to Harrison's Landing on the James River, and the Peninsular campaign was over. Lee had suffered the heavier losses, and he had been unsuccessful in his attempts to dismember McClellan's retreating army. However, by taking the offensive Lee had saved Richmond, and not until 1864 did Union forces again come so near the Confederate capital. See Clifford Dowdey, *The Seven Days* (1964).

Seveneh, biblical name: see ASWAN, Egypt.

Seven Hills, city (1970 pop. 12,700), Cuyahoga co., N Ohio, a residential suburb of Cleveland, in a hilly area; inc. as a city 1961. Part of its city hall is an old schoolhouse, built in 1861.

Seven Pines: see PENINSULAR CAMPAIGN.

Seven Sleepers of Ephesus (ĕf'ĭsəs), in a Christian version of a widespread story, martyrs immured in a cave near Ephesus during the persecutions by Decius (c.250). Long afterward, in the 5th cent., they awoke (as from sleep) and were taken before Theodosius II, Roman emperor of the east. Their story reassured the emperor, who had been wavering in his faith. The youths returned to their cave, to sleep again until Judgment. The story, thought to be of Syrian origin, was popularized by Gregory of Tours. Feast: July 27.

seventeen-year locust: see CICADA.

Seventh-Day Adventists: see ADVENTISTS.

Seventh-Day Baptists, Protestant sect holding the same doctrines as other Calvinistic Baptists but observing the seventh day of the week as the Sabbath. In the Reformation in England the observance was adopted by many, and in the 17th cent. there were Seventh-Day Baptists among the followers of Oliver Cromwell. In America the first Seventh-Day Baptist church in the country was organized (1671) in Rhode Island. Another group, the German Seventh-Day Baptists, under the leadership of Johann Conrad BEISSEL, established (c.1728-1733) at Ephrata, Pa., a semimonastic religious society, famous in colonial times. Among their industries was a noted print shop. Their teaching and practice are closely related to the BRETHREN Church.

Seven Weeks War: see AUSTRO-PRUSSIAN WAR.

Seven Wise Men of Greece, list of men drawn from among the outstanding politicians and political philosophers of ancient Greece. Although such listings differed widely, a usual one included BIAS, CHILON, CLEOBULUS, PERIANDER, PITTACUS, SOLON, and THALES.

Seven Wonders of the World, in ancient classifications, were the Great Pyramid of Khufu (see PYRAMID) or all the pyramids with or without the SPHINX; the Hanging Gardens of Babylon, with or without the walls; the MAUSOLEUM at Halicarnassus; the Artemision at EPHESUS; the Colossus of Rhodes (see under COLOSSUS); the Olympian *Zeus,* statue by PHIDIAS; and the PHAROS at Alexandria, or, instead, the walls of Babylon. See Leonard Cottrell, *Wonders of the World* (1959).

Seven Years War, 1756-63, worldwide war fought in Europe, North America, and India between France, Austria, Russia, Saxony, Sweden, and (after 1762) Spain on the one side and Prussia, Great Britain, and Hanover on the other. The struggle was complex in its origin and involved two main distinct conflicts—the colonial rivalry between France and England and the struggle for supremacy in Germany between the house of Austria and the rising kingdom of Prussia. It was preluded in America by the outbreak of the last of the FRENCH AND INDIAN WARS and in India by fighting among native factions and the struggle there between the French governor DUPLEIX and the British statesman Robert CLIVE. The War of the AUSTRIAN SUCCESSION (1740-48) had left Austria humiliated. Seeking to recover Silesia from Prussia, Empress MARIA THERESA even before the conclusion of that war had secured the alliance of ELIZABETH of Russia. In the years following the Treaty of Aix-la-Chapelle (1748), KAUNITZ, as Austrian ambassador to France and then as chancellor, worked for a rapprochement with France. In 1755, when hostilities broke out in North America, George II, king of England and elector of Hanover negotiated the Treaty of Westminster with FREDERICK II of Prussia, who guaranteed the neutrality of Hanover. This event hastened the alliance (1756) of France and Austria, sometimes called the "diplomatic revolution." Shortly afterward Frederick II opened hostilities by invading Saxony. In Jan., 1757, war was declared on the aggressor in the name of the Holy Roman Empire. Austria concluded alliances with France and Russia and was joined by Sweden. The main European phase of the war began with the Prussian invasion of Bohemia early in 1757. Victorious at first, Frederick was severely defeated by the Austrians under Daun at Kolin (June, 1757) and had to evacuate Bohemia. The fighting was carried into Saxony and Silesia, where Frederick gained the great victories of Rossbach (Nov., 1757) and Leuthen (Dec., 1757) over the French and Austrians. The Russians, who had invaded Prussia, were defeated by Frederick at Zorndorf (Aug., 1758). The English and Hanoverians, at first unsuccessful against the French in NW Germany, began a vigorous effort when the younger Pitt (later earl of CHATHAM) came into power; the troops then won the victories of Krefeld (June, 1758) and Minden (Aug., 1759). However, Frederick soon found himself in an almost desperate situation. He was badly beaten by Daun at Kunersdorf (Aug., 1759) and in Nov., 1759, Daun captured a Prussian army of 13,000 at Maxen. In Oct., 1760, the Russians took Berlin. Days later, as Frederick's army approached, they evacuated it, and in November, Frederick defeated Daun at Torgau, but his situation remained critical, especially after the fall of Pitt (1761) deprived him of British subsidies. The death (Jan., 1762) of Elizabeth of Russia and the accession of PETER III, Frederick's ardent admirer, helped save him from defeat. By the Treaty of St. Petersburg (1762) Russia made peace and restored all conquests; Sweden made peace in the same year. Now fighting alone in the east, the Austrians were soundly defeated at Burkersdorf (July, 1762). The French, too, had suffered severe reverses. In America, they had lost Louisburg (1758), Quebec (1759), and some possessions in the West Indies; in India, the British victories at Plassey (1757) and Pondichéry (1761) had destroyed French power; on the sea, the French took Port Mahón from the British (1757) but were defeated by Hawke in Quiberon Bay (1759). The entry of Spain into the war under the terms of the Family Compact of 1761 was of little help to France, where the war had never been popular. After protracted negotiations between the war-weary powers, peace was made (Feb., 1763) among Prussia, Austria, and Saxony at HUBERTUSBURG, and among England, France, and Spain at Paris (see PARIS, TREATY OF, 1763). The treaty of Hubertusburg, though it restored the prewar status quo, marked the ascendancy of Prussia as a leading European power. Through the Treaty of Paris, Great Britain emerged as the world's chief colonial empire, which was its primary goal in the war, and France lost most of its overseas possessions. For Russia, the Seven Years War was the first great venture into purely European affairs. See studies by L. J. Oliva (1964), Reginald Savory (1966), and H. H. Kaplan (1968).

Severing, Wilhelm Karl (vĭl'hĕlm kärl zā'vəring), 1875-1952, German statesman. A Social Democrat, he served (1907-33) in the Reichstag, was German minister of the interior (1928-30), and was Prussian minister of the interior during most of the period from 1920 to 1932. He supported the Weimar Republic.

Severini, Gino (jē'nō sāvārē'nē), 1883-1966, Italian painter. In 1906 he settled in Paris. First associated with the cubist painters, he later became a principal figure in the movement known as FUTURISM. Severini was greatly influenced by Seurat and theories of neo-impressionism. The most lyrical and decorative of the futurists, he occasionally sprinkled his canvases with sequins, as in *Hieroglyph of the Bal Tabarin* (1912; Mus. of Modern Art, New York City).

Severn, Joseph, 1793-1879, English portrait and landscape painter. He was consul at Rome from 1861 to 1872. He is best known for his devotion to Keats during the poet's last days. He became a popular portraitist, especially among the friends and associates of Keats. See biography by William Sharp (1892, repr. 1973); Sheila Smith, Countess of Birkenhead, *Against Oblivion* (1944) and *Illustrious Friends* (1965).

Severn (sĕv'ərn). **1** River, c.420 mi (680 km) long, rising in W Ont., Canada, and flowing NE through Severn Lake to Hudson Bay. Fort Severn, a Hudson's Bay Company trading post established (1689) at the mouth of the river, was captured (1690) by Pierre le Moyne, sieur d'Iberville. The post was rebuilt in 1759 and has been in continuous operation since. **2** River, c.20 mi (30 km) long, rising from the north end of Lake Couchiching, S Ont., Canada, and flowing NW to Georgian Bay of Lake Huron. It drains Lake Couchiching and Lake Simcoe and forms part of the inland waterway system linking Georgian Bay with Lake Ontario via the Trent Canal. There are two large hydroelectric stations on its course.

Severn, Lat. *Sabrina,* one of the principal rivers of Great Britain, c.200 mi (320 km) long, rising on Plinlimmon Mt., W Wales, and flowing NE and E to Shrewsbury, W England, and thence SE, S, and SW—through a great estuary—to the Bristol Channel. Worcester, Gloucester, and many smaller towns are on its banks. The tributaries include the Teme, Avon, and Stour. It is connected by canal with the Thames, Mersey, Trent, and other rivers. A railroad tunnel (opened 1886) more than 4 mi (6.4 km) long passes under the estuary. The Severn Road Bridge (opened 1966) is one of the world's longest (3,240 ft/988 m) suspension bridges. The river is important as a transportation route. Because of the conformation of the estuary, a great tidal bore occurs up to Gloucester.

Severna Park, uninc. town (1970 pop. 16,358), Anne Arundel co., central Md., a suburb of Baltimore.

Severnaya Zemlya (syĕ'vĭrnĭə zĭmlyä') [Rus.,= northern land], archipelago, c.14,300 sq mi (37,010 sq km), between the Kara and Laptev seas, Krasnoyarsk Kray, N Siberian USSR, off the Taymyr Peninsula. Extending N of lat. 80°N, it is composed of four major islands—October Revolution, Bolshevik, Komsomolets, Pioneer—and several smaller ones. Glaciers are found on the larger islands. Discovered in 1913, it was first named Nicholas II Land.

Severus or **Septimius Severus** (Lucius Septimius Severus) (sĕptĭm'ēəs sēvē'rəs), 146-211, Roman emperor (193-211), b. Africa. He was campaigning in Pannonia and Illyria when the emperor PERTINAX was murdered. He marched to Rome ostensibly to avenge Pertinax and had the usurper DIDIUS JULIANUS murdered. Proclaimed emperor, Severus went to the East to overthrow Pescennius Niger, the governor of Syria, who had also been proclaimed emperor by his legions. Severus defeated (194) the pretender. He took (196) Byzantium and subdued the rebellious Arabs of Mesopotamia. Returning to the West, he defeated (197) Clodius Albinus, another pretender, in Gaul and, returning eastward, attacked and expelled (198) the Parthians from Mesopotamia. In 208, Severus went to Britain. From there he harassed Scotland, but he died at York before completing his plans for a large invasion. Severus ruled with vigor, always favoring the army. During his reign Rome was adorned with new buildings, such as the Arch of Septimius Severus in the Old Forum, and when he was in Great Britain he repaired HADRIAN'S WALL. To finance his projects he debased the coinage. He was the patron of Papinian. Caracalla succeeded him. See studies by Maurice Platnauer (1918, repr. 1965), G. J. Murphy (1945), and A. R. Birley (1971).

Severus (Flavius Valerius Severus), d. 307, Roman emperor (306-7). He participated with GALERIUS in an unsuccessful attempt to overthrow MAXENTIUS. Surrendering to Maximian (father of Maxentius) at Ravenna on the condition that his life be spared, Severus was taken to Rome. He was later, however, treacherously killed by Maxentius.

Severus, Alexander: see ALEXANDER SEVERUS.

Sevier, John (səvēr'), 1745-1815, American frontiersman and political leader. He was born near the site of New Market, Va., the town he founded in his young manhood. In 1773 he moved with his family to W North Carolina, where he became a leader of the WATAUGA ASSOCIATION. In the American Revolution, Sevier, a supporter of independence and a veteran of many Indian campaigns, was prominent as one of the frontier leaders in the American victory at Kings Mountain (1780) in the CAROLINA CAMPAIGN. After the war, when North Carolina ceded (1784) its western lands to the United States, Sevier served (1785-88) as governor of a separate, short-lived state organized by the settlers (see FRANKLIN, STATE OF). For this he was arrested (1788) by the North Carolina government on a charge of treason, but he escaped. Following his election (1789) to the North Carolina senate, he was pardoned by the governor. He voted for the U.S. Constitution in the state ratifying convention of 1789, and he was elected (1789) to represent the western districts in Congress. In 1791 he was made a brigadier general in the "Territory South of the River Ohio" and in 1794 was appointed to its 10-man legislative council. The new state of Tennessee was organized (1796) out of this territory, and Sevier, elected the first governor, served from 1796 to 1801 and again from 1803 to 1809. The rising young Andrew Jackson unsuccessfully tried to curb Sevier's political power, and the two men became bitter personal enemies. Sevier ended his distinguished career by returning to Congress (1811-15). See his Letters in C. B. Sevier and N. C. Madden, *Sevier Family History* (1961); biographies by J. R. Gilmore (1887) and C. S. Driver (1932).

Sevier, river, c.280 mi (450 km) long, formed in SW Utah by the junction of Panguitch Creek and Assay Creek. It flows northward through canyons, then leaves the mountains and flows SW through the Sevier Desert to the salt Sevier Lake. Extensive diversion of the river's water for irrigation has dried up Sevier Lake.

Sévigné, Marie de Rabutin-Chantal, marquise de (märē' də räbütăN'-shäNtäl' märkēz' də sāvēnyā'), 1626-96, French woman of letters. Her correspondence of more than 1,500 letters is a monument of French literature. After her husband's death (1651) she devoted herself to her two children. To her daughter, the comtesse de Grignan, who lived in Provence, the marquise wrote long letters on personal, literary, and social news, full of witty comment. These letters constitute the greater part of the Sévigné correspondence. Her writing is distinguished by the unaffected elegance of her style and the acuteness of her observation. But the letters are also of great interest for the revelation of the personality of their author, a principled, intelligent, and delightful woman, and for their chronicle of her times. She counted among her friends Turenne, La Rochefoucauld, and Mme de La Fayette. The first edition of her letters appeared posthumously in 1725; a later definitive collection was published in 1953-57 (3 vol.). Among English translations of her letters is the partial edition by Richard Aldington (1937). Edward FitzGerald compiled a useful *Dictionary of Madame de Sévigné* (1914). See studies by Arthur Tilley (1937) and A. I. T. Ritchie (1881, repr. 1973).

Seville (səvĭl', sĕ'-), Span. *Sevilla,* city (1970 pop. 548,072), capital of Seville prov. and leading city of Andalusia, SW Spain, on the Guadalquivir River. Connected with the Atlantic by the river and by a canal accessible to oceangoing vessels, Seville is a major port as well as an important industrial and cultural center. Wines, fruit, olives, cork, and minerals are exported. Its industries include the manufacture of tobacco, armaments, explosives, perfume, porcelain, pharmaceuticals, chemicals, textiles, and machinery. It has a university (founded 1502). The ancient Hispalis, Seville was important in Phoenician times. It was favored by the Romans, who made it a judicial center of Baetica prov. and who built the nearby city of Italica (where the emperors Trajan and Hadrian were born), of which some ruins remain. Seville continued as the chief city of S Spain under the Vandals and the Visigoths. In the 6th cent. Seville was a center of learning. Falling to the Moors in 712, it was (c.1023-1091) the seat of an independent emirate under the ABBADIDS and a flourishing commercial and cultural center under the Almoravids and the Almohads. In 1248, Ferdinand III of Castile conquered it after a long siege and made it his residence. It is said that 300,000 Moors, the majority of its population, left Seville at that time. With the discovery of the New World, Seville entered its greatest period of prosperity, being the chief port of trade with the new colonies until 1718, when it was superseded by Cádiz. Its economic recovery from the subsequent decline is only recent. Yellow fever killed thousands in 1800. In 1810 the French sacked the city. Seville was held by the insurgents throughout the civil war (1936-39). Seville was the seat of a flourishing school of painting to which Velázquez, Murillo (both natives) and Pacheco belonged. The colorful life of the city was the subject of many of the best-known paintings of Murillo, who is generously represented in the art gallery and in the cathedral. Seville has kept much of its Moorish aspect. Its old quarters are crossed by tortuous, narrow streets, interrupted by fine squares, and lined with white-washed houses with patios and balconies trimmed with iron filigree work. The Gothic cathedral (1401-1519), one of the world's largest, occupies the site of a former mosque, of which two parts remain—the Court of Oranges and the beautiful GIRALDA tower. The interior of the cathedral is extraordinarily rich and contains invaluable works of art and the tomb of Christopher Columbus. During Holy Week the cathedral is the scene of unique and colorful pageantry. Adjoining the cathedral is the alcazar, built (14th cent.) in Moorish style by Moorish artisans on the order of Peter I (Peter the Cruel) and rivaling the Alhambra in its exquisite decorations and splendid halls. Among the many other notable buildings of Seville are the city hall (16th cent.); the Casa de Pilatos, a palace in Mudéjar style; the Torre del Oro, a 13th-century tower; the Colombina library, containing manuscripts by Columbus and many volumes; the former *lonja,* or exchange, which contains the archives of Spanish America; the university buildings, which were formerly a large tobacco factory (scene of part of the action of Mérimée's and Bizet's *Carmen*); and numerous churches and private palaces. One of the world's most beautiful cities, summarizing all that has made S Spain a land of romance, Seville is also renowned for the gay and spirited charm of its people. It is, moreover, the capital of bullfighting in Spain and a center of the Andalusian gypsies, famed for their songs and dances.

sevin: see INSECTICIDE.

Sèvres (sĕv'rə), town (1968 pop. 20,228), Hauts-de-Seine dept., N central France, on the Seine River; a residential suburb SW of Paris. The famous SÈVRES WARE porcelain is made in the town, which has a ceramics museum founded by Alexandre Brongniart and a ceramics school. Explosives, surgical supplies, and beer are also produced. Sèvres is the headquarters of the International Bureau of Weights and Measures and the International Center for Pedagogic Studies.

Sèvres, Treaty of, 1920, peace treaty concluded after World War I at Sèvres, France, between the Ottoman Empire (Turkey), on the one hand, and the Allies (excluding Russia and the United States) on the other. The treaty, which liquidated the Ottoman Empire and virtually abolished Turkish sovereignty, followed in the main the decisions reached at San Remo (see SAN REMO, CONFERENCE OF). In Asia, Turkey renounced sovereignty over Mesopotamia (Iraq) and Palestine (including Trans-Jordan), which became British mandates; Syria (including Lebanon), which became a French mandate; and the kingdom of HEJAZ. Turkey retained Anatolia but was to grant autonomy to Kurdistan. ARMENIA became a separate republic under international guarantees, and Smyrna (now İZMIR) and its environs was placed under Greek administration pending a plebiscite to determine its permanent status. In Europe, Turkey ceded parts of E Thrace and certain Aegean islands to Greece, and the Dodecanese and Rhodes to Italy, retaining only Constantinople and its environs, including the Zone of the Straits (see DARDANELLES), which was neutralized and internationalized. The Allies further obtained virtual control over the Turkish economy. The treaty was accepted by the government of Sultan Muhammad VI at Constantinople but was rejected by the rival nationalist government of Kemal ATATÜRK at Ankara. Ataturk's separate treaty with the USSR and his subsequent victories against the Greeks forced the Allies to negotiate a new treaty in 1923 (see LAUSANNE, TREATY OF).

Sèvres ware, porcelain made in France by the royal (now national) potteries established (1745) by Louis

XV at Vincennes, moved (1756) to Sèvres after changing hands. Before 1770 it was a soft-paste porcelain (*pâte tendre*), of underglaze decoration and alkaline glaze; subsequently it was a hard infusible porcelain, made of kaolin, with a feldspar glaze and an overglaze decoration. Delicacy and perfection of technique are dominant characteristics. Tableware shows flower and figure subjects on a white ground; clocks, vases, and plaques display panels or medallions on white with figures enclosed by ornate gold frames, the main ground being a brilliant color. Sometimes a diaper design in gold enriches the background. Generally the pattern of Sèvres ware followed the styles from the period of Louis XV through those of the 19th cent. In 1876 the factory was moved to new buildings near Saint-Cloud and is still in operation. Soft-paste porcelain was revived, and many new wares were introduced.

Sewall, Samuel (syōō'əl), 1652–1730, American colonial jurist, b. England. He was taken as a child to Newbury, Mass., and was graduated from Harvard in 1671. He became a minister but gave up the cloth to assume management of a printing press in Boston and entered upon a public career. He was elected (1683) to the general court and was a member of the council. As one of the judges who tried the Salem witchcraft cases in 1692, he shared responsibility for the condemnation of 19 persons. However, he became convinced of the error of these convictions and in 1697 in Old South Church, Boston, publicly accepted the "blame and shame" for them; thereafter he annually spent a day of repentance in fasting and prayer. Sewall served (1692–1728) as judge of the superior court of the colony, being chief justice during the last 10 years. His diary (3 vol., 1878–82) is very revealing of the man and of the period. See his diary (1973); biographies by O. E. Winslow (1964) and T. B. Strandness (1967); N. H. Chamberlain, *Samuel Sewall and the World He Lived In* (1897, repr. 1967).

Sewanee: see SOUTH, UNIV. OF THE.

Seward, Anna (sē'wərd), 1742–1809, English poet, called the Swan of Lichfield. A member of the Lichfield literary group which included Thomas Day and Erasmus Darwin, she was acquainted also with Dr. Johnson and James Boswell. She bequeathed her literary works to Sir Walter Scott, who edited them (3 vol., 1810). See selected letters, with short biography (ed. by Hesketh Pearson, 1936).

Seward, William Henry, 1801–72, American statesman, b. Florida, Orange co., N.Y. A graduate (1820) of Union College, he was admitted to the bar in 1822 and established himself as a lawyer in Auburn, N.Y., which he made his lifelong home. He was active in the ANTI-MASONIC PARTY and later joined the WHIG PARTY. Seward and his close personal and political friend, Thurlow WEED, became the two most influential Whigs in New York state. A state senator from 1830 to 1834, he ran unsuccessfully for the governorship in 1834. In 1838, however, he won that office, and he was reelected in 1840. As governor, he worked for educational reforms and internal improvements; he also secured legislation to better the position of immigrants and to protect fugitive slaves. He returned to his law practice in 1843 but was elected to the U.S. Senate in 1849. Reelected in 1855, Seward was one of the Senate's most prominent members in the troubled years preceding the Civil War. A genial, gregarious man with intellectual interests, he was generally well liked, even by his political opponents. Seward was an uncompromising foe of slavery, and, although he apparently tempered his public expressions so as not to alienate votes, he nevertheless made two remarks that became catch phrases of the antislavery forces. Voicing his opposition to the Compromise of 1850 in the Senate, he said (March 11, 1850), "there is a higher law than the Constitution which regulates our authority over the domain." In a speech at Rochester on Oct. 25, 1858, he declared that there would exist "an irrepressible conflict" until the United States became either all slave or all free. With the disintegration of the Whig party, Seward and Weed joined (1855) the new Republican party. Prominent as he was, Seward, despite (or possibly because of) the efforts of Weed's machine, was never able to secure the Republican presidential nomination. His friendship toward immigrants, especially the Irish, alienated members of the former Know-Nothing movement within the Republican party. In 1861, Seward became Secretary of State under Abraham Lincoln, and many expected him to be the real power in the administration. He revealed his own desire to dominate the President in a peculiar memorandum (April 1, 1861) to Lincoln in which he proposed waging war against most of Europe so as to unite the nation. Seward also did some unwarranted meddling during the Fort Sumter crisis. After the Civil War broke out, however, he showed himself an able statesman, although it took all of Lincoln's ingenuity to keep both Seward and his rival, Salmon P. CHASE, eternally ambitious for the presidency, in the same cabinet. Seward's handling of delicate matters of diplomacy with Great Britain, particularly in the TRENT AFFAIR, was notably adept. He also protested French intervention in Mexico and after the Civil War helped bring an end to it. The plot of John Wilkes BOOTH to assassinate Lincoln also included a stabbing attack on Seward, but he recovered from his wounds and retained his cabinet position under the new President, Andrew JOHNSON. He supported Johnson's Reconstruction policy and, like the President, was roundly denounced by the radical Republicans. Seward's most important act in this administration was the purchase of Alaska from Russia in 1867. His foresight was not generally acknowledged, however, and Alaska was long popularly called "Seward's folly." He also tried to purchase the two most important islands in the Danish West Indies (the Virgin Islands), but the Senate refused to approve his action. See G. E. Baker, ed., *The Works of William H. Seward* (5 vol., 1853–84); F. W. Seward, ed., *Autobiography of William H. Seward . . . to 1834 . . . and Selections from His Letters* (3 vol., 1891); biographies by T. K. Lothrop (1896), Frederic Bancroft (1900, repr. 1967), E. E. Hale, Jr. (1910), and G. G. Van Deusen (1967).

Seward, city (1970 pop. 1,587), Kenai Peninsula borough, S Alaska, on Kenai Peninsula, at the head of Resurrection Bay; inc. 1912. It was founded in 1902 as the ocean terminus of the Alaska RR (built 1915–23). The airfield and ice-free harbor make it an important shipping and supply center for the Alaskan interior. It has a seafood cannery and freezer plant and a saw mill. Seward was almost completely devastated by an earthquake in 1964 (90% of its waterfront industry was destroyed) but by the early 1970s there had been some reconstruction. In Seward are a Univ. of Alaska maritime research station and two military rest and recreation camps. An annual salmon derby is held, and a race up nearby Mt. Marathon every July 4th attracts athletes from a wide area.

Seward Peninsula, W Alaska, projecting c.200 mi (320 km) into the Bering Sea between Norton Sound and Kotzebue Sound, just below the Arctic Circle. The region is mostly bleak tundra, with long, cold winters. Placer-gold mining and trapping are the chief occupations of its sparse population. Nome is on the southern coast. Cape Prince of Wales is located at the western tip of the peninsula.

Sewell, Anna (sōō'əl), 1820–78, English author. Her only work, *Black Beauty* (1877), the story of a horse, became a children's classic and has gone into many reprints. See study by M. J. Baker (1957). Her mother, **Mary Wright Sewell,** 1797–1884, was also a popular writer for children.

Sewell, Jonathan, 1766–1839, Canadian jurist, b. Cambridge, Mass. He was educated in England and emigrated to Canada in 1785. A lawyer, he became attorney general of Lower Canada (Quebec) in 1795 and sat in the Legislative Assembly (1796–1808). While chief justice (1808–38) of Lower Canada, he made a decision (1818) that was the basis for drawing the boundary between Upper Canada (Ontario) and Lower Canada. President (1808–29) of the executive council and speaker (1809–39) of the legislative council, he was one of the earliest advocates of confederation.

sewellel beaver: see MOUNTAIN BEAVER.

sewerage, system for the removal and disposal of chiefly liquid wastes and of rain water, which are collectively called sewage. Domestic sewage, produced in urban residences, institutions, and businesses, is usually collected by pipes and conduits called sanitary sewers, which lead to a central discharge point. In rural residences domestic sewage is often collected in a SEPTIC TANK on the property. Industrial wastes, which consist of liquids produced in manufacturing processes, are sometimes collected in sanitary sewers, but the nature of many industrial wastes may make it dangerous or difficult to do so. Often industries dispose of their own wastes. Storm sewage, which comes from rain and ground water, is collected either in a storm sewer or, with domestic sewage and industrial wastes, in what is called a combined sewer. Materials used for sewer pipe include plastics, vitrified clay, cast iron and steel, corrugated iron, concrete, and asbestos cement. Sewer pipe must be strong enough to withstand the structural stresses to which it is subjected by being buried in the ground. In addition, the pipe itself and the joints between sections of pipe must be capable of withstanding at least moderate water pressure without significant leakage of sewage into the environment. The velocity of flow in such a system must be sufficient that suspended solids do not accumulate. Sewer pipes are usually inclined downward toward the central collection point so that sewage will flow to it naturally, although pumping stations may be required. Sewage is eventually discharged into underground or surface watercourses that naturally drain an area. In the past the dilution produced by discharging sewage into large bodies of water was considered sufficient to render harmless any toxic substances contained in it. However, the volume of sewage is now so great that dilution is no longer considered an adequate safeguard. The biochemical processes that take place in water bodies have also been relied on to neutralize sewage. Aerobic, or oxygen-requiring, bacteria feed on the organic material in sewage, decomposing it. However, this process uses the oxygen that is dissolved in water. Often the concentration of organic waste is so great that the biochemical oxygen demand (BOD) depletes the water's oxygen supply, killing fish and plants. In order to avoid these problems, it is now recognized that sewage must be treated before it is discharged. The only exception is storm sewage that has not been mixed with other wastes. Industrial wastes are treated by a number of methods, depending on the specific nature of the waste. Increasingly, governments are forcing industries to process effluents either chemically or mechanically, or both ways, so that harmful substances are removed. Domestic sewage is treated to produce discharge water that is free of odors, suspended solids, and objectionable bacteria. (Coliform bacteria, which inhabit the lower intestines of mammals, while not pathogenic of themselves, are taken as an index of contamination of watercourses.) One simple method of removing suspended solids involves storing sewage in a holding tank, e.g., a septic tank; naturally occurring anaerobic bacteria can decompose the solids, which then settle to the bottom. While suitable for small systems, this method has several disadvantages. First, anaerobic decomposition produces noxious gaseous effluents, and it is fairly slow. Second, harmful bacteria may still be present in the liquid effluent. Decomposition can be speeded by forcing air through the mass so that aerobic bacteria can be used. In large plants, where it is impractical to retain enormous volumes of water, the solids are removed mechanically, as by filtering or screening, and treated separately. The liquid is discharged, often after being disinfected with chlorine. Another method of removing solids is to allow the liquid to stand in large tanks until the solids fall out and form a sediment, but the process is slow and requires the accumulation of large volumes of liquid. Once solids are removed, they are treated in one of several ways. Most often they are removed in a semiliquid mass referred to as sludge. Sludge may be transferred to tanks where it is digested by aerobic or anaerobic bacteria. Gaseous by-products of this digestion are collected for use as fuels. After digestion solids may be dried and enriched with plant nutrients for use as fertilizer. In other cases, with or without digestion, they may be dried and incinerated. In other cases solids are buried in landfills or dumped far at sea, although there are serious questions concerning the impact of this on oceanic flora and fauna. Sewage treatment is classified as primary, secondary, or tertiary, depending on the degree to which the effluent is purified. Primary treatment is removal of floating and suspended solids. Secondary treatment uses biological methods such as digestion. Complete, or tertiary, treatment removes all but a negligible portion of bacterial and organic matter. One of the earliest known sewers was the Cloaca Maxima in Rome, built (c.6th cent. B.C.) to drain the site of the Forum. Although London's drainage system dates from the 13th cent., the discharge of offensive waste into it was illegal until 1815. In Paris sewers were constructed before the 16th cent., but by 1893 fewer than 5% of the city's houses were connected to the system. As early as 1701, Boston had drains. Generally, however, systematic sewage disposal was not widely introduced until the mid-19th cent. See POLLUTION. See E. W. Steel, *Water Supply and Sewerage* (4th ed. 1960); W. A. Hardenbergh and E. R. Rodie, *Water Supply and Waste Disposal* (2d ed. 1963); W. W. Eckenfelder, *Industrial Water Pollution Control* (1966); R. L. Bolton and Louis Klein, *Sewage Treatment* (1961, repr. 1971).

sewing: see NEEDLEWORK.

sewing machine, device that stitches cloth and other materials. An attempt at mechanical sewing was made in England (1790) with a machine having a forked, automatic needle that made a single-thread chain. In 1830, B. Thimonnier, a French tailor, patented a wooden device with a hooked needle. In 1841 he used 80 of these machines to make uniforms for the French army. His factory was wrecked by a mob, but in 1848 he placed another machine on the market. A needle with an eye at its point that made a chain stitch was tried about the same time for glove making. Inventor Walter Hunt of New York City is said to have devised in 1832 a machine using an eye-pointed needle but failed to patent it. American inventor Elias Howe made the first successful machine (1846) using an eye-pointed needle and an intermittent feed. After perfecting various features and defending his patents, he made a fortune from his machine. Before 1850 all machines were operated by hand and the cloth was fed by various clumsy devices, such as a separately moved belt with projecting steel spikes. American inventor A. B. Wilson devised in 1850 an automatic feed and later perfected the four-motion feed, an essential feature of later machines. He also invented the rotary bobbin and hook. American inventor Isaac M. Singer, who is credited with the invention of the foot treadle and the yielding presser foot, finally coordinated previous attempts into the modern machine, gave it a commercial status, and began large-scale manufacturing. Two types of machines, the lockstitch and the chain-stitch, operate on the same principle; an eye-pointed needle, raised and lowered at great speed, pierces the material lying on a steel plate, casting a loop of thread on the underside of the seam. In the lockstitch machine a second thread, fed from a shuttle under the plate, passes through the loop and is interlocked with the upper thread as it is drawn tightly up by the rising needle. In the chain-stitch machine, which uses a single thread, the loop is held under the seam while the needle rises, the cloth is fed forward, and the needle descends again, engaging the loop and drawing it flat under the cloth. Both lockstitch and chain-stitch machines are made in two classes, domestic and industrial. Most domestic machines are the lockstitch type. Electrification and attachments for hemming, tucking, quilting, embroidering, making buttonholes, and similar operations have widened the applications of the household machine. Power-driven, highly specialized machines for industrial use include many used in clothing manufacture, such as those for buttonholing and button sewing, seam finishing, and embroidery. Shoes, gloves, hats, books, upholstery, hosiery, tents, awnings, flags, and sails are sewn on specially devised machines.

sex, term used to refer both to the two groups distinguished as males and females and to the anatomical and physiological characteristics associated with maleness and femaleness. Sex is associated with the type of REPRODUCTION in which specialized reproductive cells (gametes) are produced and, when united by FERTILIZATION, form a zygote (fertilized egg) that develops into a new individual. The female gamete is called an egg or OVUM and the male gamete a SPERM. Differentiation into two sexes is observable in some members of all divisions of both the plant and animal kingdoms, and even in species where little or no sexual difference is detectable anatomically there is an implied separation in forms in which conjugation occurs (e.g., among different strains in paramecia and between plus and minus strains in molds). Many lower forms produce within the one individual two different kinds of cell that unite to form a new individual; in others, male and female cells are produced by different individuals. Among the higher animals (the vertebrates) the sexes are usually readily distinguishable by their primary sexual characteristics, i.e., the structure of their reproductive organs. In the highest group of plants (the spermatophytes, or seed-bearing plants) the female organ is the PISTIL and the male organ is the STAMEN. The stamens and pistil may appear in the same flower (as in most seed plants, e.g., the lily or tomato), in different flowers of the same plant (e.g., squash or corn), or in the flowers of separate plants (e.g., species of holly and willow). Secondary sexual characteristics also serve to distinguish the sexes. Among these are the bright coloration of many male birds and fish, the antlers of male deer, the beard and deepened voice of human males, and the mammary glands of female mammals. In higher animals hormones released by the sexual organs under stimulation from the pituitary hormones play a dominant role in the control of sexual characteristics and the sexual processes of reproduction. The factors that determine the sex of offspring have a long and colorful history of superstitious beliefs; it was not until the modern science of genetics that a scientific explanation was provided, based on the discovery that among the CHROMOSOMES present in the body cells there is a special pair, called the sex chromosomes, that bear the genes determining the sex of the offspring. In the human female these chromosomes are identical and are called X chromosomes (indicated by XX). In the male there is one X chromosome and one smaller Y chromosome, which is dominant for maleness. During the process of producing reproductive cells (see MEIOSIS), each of these chromosomes is segregated into a different gamete; thus, when fertilization occurs, according to Mendelian law 50% of the offspring will be XX (female) and 50% XY (male). Although there are deviations from this rule, for which explanations have yet to be established, it generally holds true. It also helps to explain the inheritance of sex-linked characteristics such as hemophilia and red-green color blindness, since the X chromosome also carries genes for nonsexual traits. The Y chromosome carries very few genes for nonsexual traits; those few (including one for hairy ears) are called holandric genes. The greatest significance of sex lies in its genetic role. Because of the myriad genes in the nucleus of every parent cell, the probability of two individuals' inheriting identical characteristics is almost zero; thus, innumerable new variations (see MUTATION) are constantly being tested for survival advantages in the individual's environment. The evolutionary flexibility that results from sexuality at some stage of the reproductive cycle seems not only beneficial but necessary in maintaining the adaptability of the species.

sextant, instrument for measuring the altitude of the sun or another celestial body; such measurements can then be used to determine the observer's geographical position or for other navigational, surveying, or astronomical applications. The term *sextant* is used generally to include related devices such as the quadrant, quintant, and octant. The sextant was

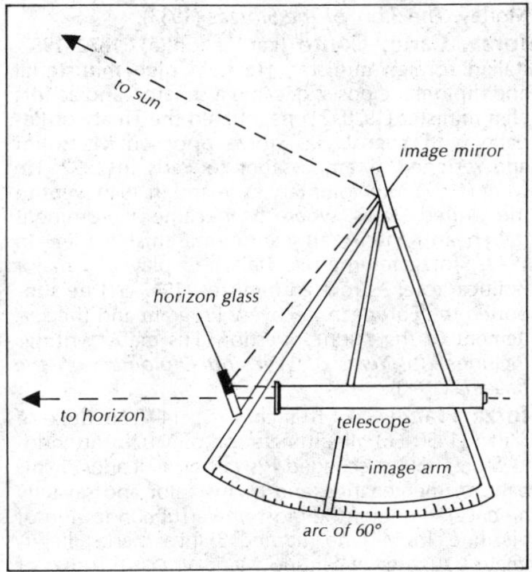

Sextant

invented independently in England and America in 1731. Its construction is based on the principle that a reflected ray of light leaves a plane surface at the same angle at which the direct ray strikes the surface. The sextant consists basically of a triangular frame, the bottom of which is a graduated arc of 60°; a telescope is attached horizontally to the plane of the frame. A small index mirror is mounted perpendicular to the frame at the top of a movable index arm or bar, which swings along the arc. In front of the telescope is the horizon glass, half transparent and half mirror. The image of the sun or other body is reflected from the index mirror to the mirror half of the horizon glass and then into the telescope. If the index (or image) arm is then adjusted so that the horizon is seen through the transparent half of the horizon glass, with the reflected image of the sun lined up with it, the sun's altitude can be read from the position of the index arm on the arc. By reference to navigational tables, the geographical position can then be determined. A sextant may be used on land with an "artificial horizon"—a small, shallow receptacle containing mercury, which gives a truly horizontal surface. In aerial navigation a bubble octant—sometimes called a bubble sextant—is used, in which a spirit level is reflected into the field of view in such a way that the center of the bubble indicates the true horizon.

Sexton, Anne (Harvey), 1928–74, American poet, b. Newton, Mass. Educated at Garland Junior College and at Radcliffe, she worked briefly as a fashion model in Boston. Her poems are highly autobiographical and often marked by irony and lyrical emotion. Her first work, *To Bedlam and Part Way Back* (1960) deals in personal terms with her efforts to retain her sanity. Other works include *Selected Poems* (1964), *Live or Die* (1966; Pulitzer Prize), *Love Poems* (1969), *Transformations* (1971), *The Book of Folly* (1973); and *The Death Notebooks* (1974). Sexton died at 46, an apparent suicide.

sexual selection: see SELECTION.

Seychelles (sāshĕlz′), British crown colony (1972 est. pop. 54,000), c.110 sq mi (285 sq km), comprising approximately 85 islands in the Indian Ocean, c.600 mi (970 km) N of Madagascar and c.1,000 mi (1,600 km) E of Mombasa, Kenya. The capital and only urban center and port is Victoria, located on the largest island, Mahé (c.55 sq mi/140 sq km), where about 65% of the population lives. Mahé and the other principal islands (Praslin, La Digue, Silhouette, and Curieuse) are granitic; there are also 45 coralline islands. The population is mainly of mixed European and black African descent; most of the inhabitants are Roman Catholic and speak a creole patois as their first language, although English is the official language. Copra, coconuts, cinnamon, patchouli, vanilla, and tea are exported; fishing is an important local industry. Tourism is growing. Probably known earlier to the Arabs, the Seychelles were discovered by Vasco da Gama in 1502. In 1756 the French claimed the islands, and colonization by French planters and their slaves from Mauritius (Île de France) began in 1768. Britain took possession of the Seychelles in 1794 and gained permanent control of them by the Treaty of Paris (1814). The islands were administered as part of Mauritius until 1903, when they were constituted a crown colony. The first elections to a legislative council were held in 1948, and gradual gains in self-government have since been made. Under the 1970 constitution, the Seychelles are run by a council of ministers presided over by a governor and a 19-member legislative assembly. The majority Seychelles Democratic party favors independence from Great Britain as does the minority Seychelles People's United party, which in 1973 was recognized as a liberation movement by the Organization of African Unity (OAU). Early in 1974, Chief Minister James Mancham announced his intention to lead the Seychelles to independence in 1975. In 1965 several outlying islands administered by the Seychelles were incorporated into the British Indian Ocean Territory.

Seydlitz, Friedrich Wilhelm, Freiherr von (frē′drĭkh vĭl′hĕlm frī′hĕr fən zīd′lĭts), 1721–73, Prussian general under Frederick II. He helped restore the effectiveness of the Prussian cavalry and fought in the most important battles of the War of the Austrian Succession and the Seven Years War, notably at Hohenfriedberg (1745), Kolin (1757), Rossbach (1757), Zorndorf (1758), and Freiberg (1762).

Seyhan (sāhän′), river, c.320 mi (515 km) long, rising in the Anti-Taurus Mts., central Turkey. It flows SW past Adana to the Mediterranean Sea. Cotton and grapes are grown in its valley. A dam on the river provides flood control, irrigation and municipal water, and electricity.

Seyðisfjörður (sā′thĭsfyör″thür), town (1970 pop. 884), E Iceland, at the head of the Seyðisfjörður, an arm of the Norwegian Sea. It is a trade center and a fishing port.

Seymour, Charles: see SOMERSET, CHARLES SEYMOUR, 6TH DUKE OF.

Seymour, Horatio (sē′môr, sē′mər), 1810–86, American politician, b. Pompey Hill, N.Y. He studied law at Utica, N.Y. and was admitted to the bar in 1832. A Democrat, he was military secretary to Gov. William L. Marcy (1833–39), was thrice elected to the New York state assembly (1841, 1844, 1845), and was chosen mayor of Utica in 1842. Elected governor in 1852, he was criticized for vetoing a prohibition bill and was defeated for reelection. Again elected (1862) governor, Seymour declared the Emancipation Proclamation unconstitutional, opposed Federal conscription as an unwarranted invasion of states' rights (but vigorously promoted voluntary enlistments), and denounced the military arrest of Clement L. VALLANDIGHAM. His conciliatory speech in New York City on the occasion of the DRAFT RIOTS (July, 1863) played into Republican hands and was a factor in his defeat (1864). He was the Democratic presidential candidate in 1868, and after his defeat by Ulysses S. Grant he assumed the role of elder statesman in his party. See biography by Stewart Mitchell (1938, repr. 1970).

Seymour, Jane, 1509?–1537, third queen consort of Henry VIII of England. She served as a lady in waiting to both of Henry's first two queens, Katharine of Aragón and Anne Boleyn. Henry became interested in her c.1535, but Jane refused to accept any proposal other than marriage. This was a strong factor in the institution of trial proceedings against Anne Boleyn. Jane and Henry were married (1536) less than two weeks after Anne's execution. Jane was a partisan of Katharine of Aragón and strove to reunite the king with Princess Mary. Parliament vested succession to the throne in Jane's issue, and in 1537 she gave birth to a son, later Edward VI. She died 12 days later.

Seymour, William: see HERTFORD, WILLIAM SEYMOUR, 1ST MARQUESS AND 2D EARL OF.

Seymour. 1 Town (1970 pop. 12,776), New Haven co., SW Conn., on the Naugatuck River; settled c.1678, inc. 1850. The industrial village of Seymour has metallurgical manufactures. **2** City (1970 pop. 13,352), Jackson co., SE Ind.; inc. 1864. A shipping center for a farm area, it is also a manufacturing city.

Seymour of Sudeley, Thomas Seymour, Baron, 1508?–1549, English nobleman. After the marriage (1536) of his sister Jane to Henry VIII, he served on various diplomatic missions, was in command of the English army in the Netherlands in 1543, and was admiral of the fleet in 1544. When, on the death of Henry in 1547, his brother Edward Seymour, duke of SOMERSET, became the protector of the young Edward VI, Thomas was made lord high admiral and Baron Seymour of Sudeley. Thereafter he tried to supplant his brother as guardian of the king. In 1547 he married the dowager queen, Catherine Parr. He was influential in securing an act of Parliament (1547) that made the duration of the protectorate dependent on the king's pleasure instead of being fixed until the king was 18, and he carefully cultivated the friendship of Edward. He also used his position as admiral to come to an understanding with pirates, in the hope of securing their support. After his wife's death (1548) he sued unsuccessfully for the hand of Princess Elizabeth (later Elizabeth I), to whom he had already made advances. His activities provoked questioning by the council, and he was convicted of high treason and executed.

Seyss-Inquart, Arthur (är'to͝or zīs'-ĭng'kvärt), 1892–1946, Austrian National Socialist leader. In Feb., 1938, Chancellor SCHUSCHNIGG of Austria was forced by German pressure to appoint him minister of the interior. Seyss-Inquart became chancellor a few hours before German troops entered (March 11) Austria. The *Anschluss* [union] of Austria and Germany was announced on March 15, and Seyss-Inquart was made governor of Austria. In 1940 he was appointed German high commissioner in the occupied Netherlands, where he ruthlessly exterminated the Dutch Jews and deported many thousands to slave-labor camps. He was convicted as a war criminal and was hanged.

Sfax: see SAFAQIS, Tunisia.

Sforza (sfôr'tsä), Italian family that ruled the duchy of MILAN from 1450 to 1535. Rising from peasant origins, the Sforzas became condottieri and used this military position to become rulers in Milan. The family governed by force, ruse, and power politics. Under their rule the city-state flourished and expanded. Similar to the Medici in their use of personal power, the Sforzas differed in that they were warriors, not bankers. In the family history, the first prominent member was **Muzio Attendolo Sforza,** 1369–1424, a farmer from the Romagna who became a noted condottiere and took the surname Sforza [the forcer]. He fought in the service of several Italian states, then became involved in the struggles for the succession to the kingdom of Naples and died while serving Queen Joanna II in her efforts to retain the throne. His illegitimate son, Francesco I Sforza (see separate article), became duke of Milan in 1450 through his marriage to Bianca Maria Visconti, daughter of the last Visconti duke of Milan. He was succeeded by his eldest son, **Galeazzo Maria Sforza,** 1444–76, a highly educated but dissolute and cruel man; he was a patron of the arts and had the architect Bramante work for him. He was assassinated in the Church of San Stefano at Milan by republican conspirators. The popular uprising anticipated by the assassins did not materialize. Another of Francesco's sons, **Ascanio Maria Sforza,** 1455–1505, was a cardinal of the Roman Catholic Church and a patron of the arts. He secured the election of Rodrigo Borgia (Pope ALEXANDER VI) as pope. Galeazzo's daughter Bianca Maria married Holy Roman Emperor Maximilian I, and his illegitimate daughter **Caterina Sforza,** 1463?–1509, became the wife of Gerolamo Riario, lord of the cities of Imola and Forlì, a nephew of Pope Sixtus IV. After Gerolamo was murdered (1488), Caterina ruled both cities until she lost them to Cesare Borgia in 1499. Her second husband, Giovanni de' Medici, a grandnephew of Cosimo de' Medici, died in 1498; to him she bore a son who became the famous condottiere Giovanni delle Bande Nere (see MEDICI, GIOVANNI DE'). Galeazzo's wife, Bona of Savoy, acted as regent for their son, a minor, **Gian Galeazzo Sforza,** 1469–94, who succeeded to the duchy on his father's assassination. However, in 1480, Galeazzo's brother Ludovico Sforza (see separate article) deprived his nephew of the duchy and assumed its control. Gian Galeazzo died a virtual prisoner. His daughter, Bona Sforza, married SIGISMUND I of Poland. In the ITALIAN WARS Milan was claimed by Louis XII of France, great-grandson of Gian Galeazzo Visconti. Ludovico lost Milan to Louis in 1499, but in 1512 the Swiss, as members of the Holy League against France, stormed Milan and installed Ludovico's son, **Massimiliano Sforza,** 1493–1530, as its duke. The Swiss actually controlled Milan until their defeat at Marignano (1515), which obliged Massimiliano to surrender Milan to Francis I of France. Massimiliano retired to France, and Holy Roman Emperor Maximilian conferred the title of duke of Milan on Massimiliano's brother, **Francesco II Sforza,** 1495–1535. Francesco took possession of his duchy after the French defeat (1522) by the army of Holy Roman Emperor Charles V at Bicocca. Accused by the imperial general PESCARA of plotting against Charles, Francesco was deprived (1525) of most of his duchy. He joined (1526) the League of Cognac against the emperor, but was obliged to surrender to the imperial troops who besieged him in Milan. After the Treaty of Cambrai (1529), Francesco was restored as duke and ruled until his death. He had no heirs, and the succession to Milan once more was contested by France and Spain, with Spain emerging victorious in the Treaty of Cateau-Cambrésis (1559). See C. M. Ady, *History of Milan under the Sforza* (1907); Lacy Collison-Morley, *The Story of the Sforzas* (1933).

Sforza, Carlo, Conte (kär'lō kōn'tā), 1872–1952, Italian foreign minister. He held high ministerial and diplomatic posts, became a senator, and as foreign minister (1920–21) negotiated the Treaty of Rapallo with Yugoslavia. Sforza opposed Mussolini and resigned as ambassador to Paris in 1922. He went (1927) into voluntary exile and in 1940 went to the United States, where he became a prominent Italian anti-Fascist and antimonarchist leader. In 1943, Sforza returned to Italy and played a major political role. As foreign minister (1947–51) he supported the European Recovery Program and the settlement of the TRIESTE question. His many writings include *Fifty Years of War and Diplomacy in the Balkans* (1940).

Sforza, Francesco I (frănchās'kō), 1401–66, duke of Milan (1450–66); illegitimate son of Muzio Attendolo Sforza. He succeeded his father as leader of his band of mercenaries, and by his valor and sagacity he became one of the most powerful condottieri of his time. In 1441 he married Bianca Maria, illegitimate daughter of Filippo Maria VISCONTI, duke of Milan. On Filippo's death (1447) the so-called Ambrosian republic was set up in Milan. Francesco, who commanded the Milanese troops, made himself master of the republic and was proclaimed duke in 1450 with the support of the Medici of Florence. He consolidated the power of Milan and in 1464 seized Genoa. An able prince, he patronized arts and letters and beautified Milan. His son, Galeazzo Maria Sforza, succeeded him as duke.

Sforza, Ludovico or **Lodovico** (lo͞odōvē'kō, lō–), b. 1451 or 1452, d. 1508, duke of Milan (1494–99); younger son of Francesco I Sforza. He was called Ludovico il Moro [the Moor] because of his swarthy complexion. In 1480 he deprived his sister-in-law, Bona of Savoy, of the regency for her infant son, Gian Galeazzo Sforza (see SFORZA, family), and from that date his actual rule may be reckoned. In 1494, Gian Galeazzo died, a virtual prisoner, and Ludovico was formally invested with Milan by Holy Roman Emperor MAXIMILIAN I. Partly in order to divert French ambitions from Milan, partly in order to protect himself from the hostility of the king of Naples, Ludovico concluded an offensive alliance with CHARLES VIII of France, whose invasion (1494) of Italy was the beginning of the ITALIAN WARS. In 1495, however, Ludovico reached an understanding with Charles's enemies and turned against the French, who were expelled from Italy. In 1499, LOUIS XII of France, who had a hereditary claim to the duchy of Milan (he was a great-grandson of Gian Galeazzo Visconti), invaded Italy and expelled Ludovico from his duchy. Ludovico's attempt, with the aid of Swiss mercenaries, to recover his lands was defeated at Novara (1500); he was captured and died a prisoner in France. Before his fall, Ludovico Sforza was one of the wealthiest and most powerful princes of Renaissance Italy. He was a subtle diplomat and an unscrupulous intriguer. With his wife, Beatrice d'ESTE, he held a brilliant court and spent immense sums of money to further the arts and sciences. He is remembered especially for his patronage of LEONARDO DA VINCI and of the architect Bramante.

sgraffito: see GRAFFITO.

's Gravenhage, Netherlands: see HAGUE, THE.

Shaalabbin (shā"ălăb'ĭn) or **Shaalbim** (shāăl'bĭm), town, W central Palestine. The related adjective is Shaalbonite. Joshua 19.42; Judges 1.35; 2 Sam. 23.32; 1 Kings 4.9; 1 Chron. 11.33.

Shaaph (shā'ăf). **1** Descendant of Judah. 1 Chron. 2.47. **2** Son of Caleb and Maachah. 1 Chron. 2.49.

Shaaraim (shā"ərā'ĭm). **1** Unidentified town, S Palestine. Joshua 15.36; 1 Sam. 17.52. **2** Location in Simeon. 1 Chron. 4.31. Shilhim: Joshua 15.32. Sharuhen: Joshua 19.6.

Shaashgaz (shāăsh'găz), chamberlain of King Ahasuerus. Esther 2.14.

Shaba (shä'bä), formerly **Katanga** (kätăng'gə, kə–), province (1969 est. pop. 2,174,400), c.200,000 sq mi (518,000 sq km), SE Zaïre. Shaba borders Angola on the southwest, Zambia on the southeast, and Lake Tanganyika on the east. The capital and chief city is Lubumbashi (formerly Elisabethville). The province encompasses the fertile Katanga Plateau (3,000–6,000 ft/914–1,829 m high), where profitable farming and ranching are carried on. In the eastern part of the province is an enormously rich mining region, which supplies most of the world's cobalt as well as extensive quantities of copper, tin, radium, uranium, and diamonds. The province's considerable industrial plant is largely concerned with the processing of minerals. Shaba is well connected by rail with the rest of Zaïre and with Angola and Zambia. There is also steamer service on Lake Tanganyika between Kalemi, in Shaba, and Kigoma, Tanzania. Copper has been mined and exported by the region's inhabitants for centuries. From the 17th to the 19th cent. much of the province was controlled by the Luba and Lunda kingdoms. In the late 19th cent. M'Siri, a Nyamwezi trader from what is now central Tanzania, founded a kingdom in the area that lasted until he was killed by the Belgians in 1891. Under Belgian rule (1884–1960), mineral resources were exploited by Belgian firms and the province was developed much more rapidly than the rest of the country. In July, 1960, after the Democratic Republic of the Congo (now Zaïre) became independent, Katanga proclaimed itself a republic and seceded from the central government. Under the leadership of its president, Moise Tshombe, and with Belgian aid, Katanga fought off repeated attempts by the central government to seize control. Disorder was widespread, and the central government invoked the help of the UN. In 1960, President Tshombe reluctantly allowed a small UN force to enter Katanga. Later a considerable number of UN troops, committed to a policy of nonintervention, were stationed in Katanga to oversee the withdrawal of foreign troops. The Belgian troops were slowly withdrawn, but white mercenary officers continued to command in the army of Katanga. There was recurrent trouble between the UN force and the Katangese, and attempts at reconciliation with the central government proved fruitless. The situation grew steadily more volatile until early 1961, when the former premier Patrice Lumumba was murdered in Katanga. Under a new, stronger UN mandate the international force took control (1961) of Elisabethville and other strongpoints. An agreement (Dec., 1961) for reintegrating Katanga into the country proved abortive. In Jan., 1963, UN troops routed Tshombe's forces and ended the Katanga secession. In 1966 the central government nationalized Union Minière du Haut Katanga, the Belgian firm that had controlled most of Katanga's mining interests.

Shabbatai Zvi: see SABBATAI ZEVI.

Shabbethai (shăbĕth'āī, shăb"ĕthā'ī), name of three Levites returned from exile. Ezra 10.15; Neh. 8.7; 11.16.

Shachia (shəkī'ə), descendant of Benjamin. 1 Chron. 8.10.

Shackleton, Sir Ernest Henry, 1874–1922, British antarctic explorer, b. Ireland. The first of his four voyages to Antarctica was made as a member of the expedition (1901–4) of Robert F. SCOTT. Although Shackleton was invalided home in 1903, he was determined to prove himself a skilled explorer. The valuable experience in antarctic exploration he had gained on the Scott expedition aided him greatly as commander of a south polar expedition (1907–9). In the course of this expedition Mt. Erebus was ascended, the south magnetic pole was located, and the polar plateau was crossed to a point less than 100 mi (160 km) from the South Pole. The scientific results of the expedition were of vast importance. Knighted in 1909, Shackleton published that year an account of his expedition, *The Heart of the Antarctic.* As commander of a transantarctic expedition, he set out in 1914, planning to enter the Weddell Sea and cross over the south polar region to the Ross Sea, a distance of c.2,000 mi (3,200 km). When his ship was crushed in the ice in 1915, he led (1916) his party to safety at Elephant Island, some 180 mi (290 km) distant; from there Shackleton and several companions made a voyage of c.800 mi (1,290 km) through wild seas and across the unknown, rugged interior of South Georgia Island to a whaling station on its north coast, where he received aid. He managed to rescue his Elephant Island party and later returned to the Weddell Sea to pick up a sledging party which he had left there earlier in the expedition. His *South* (1919) is an account of the whole expedition. In 1921 he sailed on the *Quest* to study Enderby Land but died and was buried on South Georgia Island. See biographies by H. R. Mill (1923) and James Fisher (1958); studies by D. B. Chidsey (1967) and Michael Brown (1969).

shad, fish, *Alosa sapidissima,* of the family Clupeidae (HERRING family), found along the Atlantic coast from Newfoundland to Florida and successfully introduced on the Pacific coast. The shad is one of the largest (6 lb/2.7 kg average) of the herrings and has delicious but bony flesh; its roe is valued as a delicacy. Shad ascend rivers to spawn in the spring; water pollution and indiscriminate netting have cut down their numbers. The gizzard shad, *Dorosoma* (named for its muscular gizzard-like stomach), a swift, silvery fish, 1 ft (30 cm) long, is found along the Atlantic coast from New Jersey to Texas and up the Mississippi to the Great Lakes. Shads are classified in the phylum CHORDATA, subphylum Vertebrata, class Osteichthyes, order Clupeiformes, family Clupeidae.

shadbush, Juneberry, or **serviceberry,** any species of the genus *Amelanchier* of the family Rosaceae (ROSE family), chiefly North American shrubs or trees conspicuous in the early spring for their white blossoms. The bush is more often called shadbush on the East Coast (it is said to bloom when the shad are running); serviceberry is in general a Western name. The huckleberrylike fruits of native species were eaten by the Indians and are still sometimes collected. They are an important wildlife food. Some kinds of shadbush are cultivated for ornament. The wood is very hard. Shadbushes are classified in the division MAGNOLIOPHYTA, class Magnoliopsida, order Rosales, family Rosaceae.

shaddock: see GRAPEFRUIT.

shad fly: see MAYFLY.

Shadow Mountain National Recreation Area: see NATIONAL PARKS AND MONUMENTS (table).

Shadrach (shā'drăk), one of the THREE HOLY CHILDREN.

shaduf or **shadoof** (both: shədo͞of', shä'do͞of), primitive device used to lift water from a well or stream for irrigation purposes. Essentially the device consists of a long boom balanced across a horizontal support from 8 to 10 ft (2.4–3 m) above the ground. The beam has a long, thin end and a short, stubby end. From the long end a bucket or similar container is suspended, and on the shorter end there is a counterweight. The operator pulls on a rope that lowers the long end of the boom so that the bucket submerges and is filled with water. He then releases the rope, allowing the counterweight to raise the bucket to the desired level, and then empties the bucket and repeats the process. Shadufs can be used in a series where it is desired to raise water to a height exceeding the range of a single one. It has been suggested that the massive stones used in building the pyramids of Egypt were raised by an ancient variant of this device.

Shadwell, Thomas, 1642?–1692, English dramatist and poet. His plays, written in the tradition of Jonson's comedy of humours, are distinguished for their realistic pictures of London life and for their frank and witty dialogue. They include *The Sullen Lovers* (1668), *Epsom Wells* (1672), and *The Squire of Alsatia* (1688). His devotion to Jonson instigated his feud with Dryden, whom he succeeded as poet laureate in 1689. Shadwell attacked Dryden in *The Medal of John Bayes* (1682) and was himself lampooned in Dryden's *Absalom and Achitophel* and *Mac Flecknoe.* See his works (ed. by Montague Summers, 5 vol., 1927); biography by A. S. Borgman (1928, repr. 1968).

Shaffer, Peter (shăf'ər), 1926–, English playwright, b. Liverpool, grad. Cambridge, 1950. His first successful play, *Five Finger Exercise* (1958), deals quietly with the tensions in a civilized, upper-middle-class family. *The Royal Hunt of the Sun* (1964), is an epic of the confrontation between Europe and the New World in the personages of Pizarro and the Inca priest-god Atahualpa. Shaffer's other plays include *The Private Ear and The Public Eye* (1962), *Black Comedy* (1965), *The Battle of Shrivings* (1970), and *Equus* (1973).

Shafter, William Rufus, 1835–1906, American general, b. Galesburg, Mich. He served in the Union army during the Civil War and in 1867 joined the regular army, rising to become brigadier general (1897). In the Spanish-American War he was placed in command of the army that in June, 1898, invaded Cuba. After hard fighting at El Caney and San Juan Hill, the expedition entered Santiago on July 17. Shafter was much criticized, however, because the expedition had been poorly prepared and ill-equipped and the mortality rate from disease was high. Shafter retired in 1899 and was advanced to major general on the retired list in 1901.

Shaftesbury, Anthony Ashley Cooper, 1st **earl of,** 1621–83, English statesman. In the English civil war he supported the crown until 1644 but then joined the parliamentarians. He was made a member of the Commonwealth council of state and supported Oliver Cromwell until 1654, when he turned against the Protectorate because of his distrust of autocratic rule. He supported the Rump Parliament against John LAMBERT and then participated in the Restoration (1660) of CHARLES II. Made a privy councilor and Baron Ashley (1661), he assisted in the trial of the REGICIDES but otherwise worked for a lenient settlement. The same year he became chancellor of the exchequer and gained royal favor by his support of religious toleration. Named one of the proprietors of Carolina, he took considerable interest in plans for the colony, commissioning his friend John LOCKE to draw up a constitution for it. He joined the opposition to the 1st earl of CLARENDON and, when the latter fell (1667), became a member of the CABAL administration. Created earl of Shaftesbury, he became lord chancellor in 1672. Shaftesbury had not been party to the secret Treaty of Dover (1670), and he gradually became suspicious of the king's efforts to improve the position of Roman Catholics. Renouncing his earlier belief in toleration, he supported the TEST ACT (1673). He was dismissed from office in the same year. Out of favor at court and embittered by his imprisonment in 1677 for opposing the prorogation of Parliament, he made use of the Popish Plot (see OATES, TITUS) to promote opposition to the earl of DANBY and to encourage anti-Catholic feeling. Using the Green Ribbon Club as his headquarters, Shaftesbury built up a party organization, and his followers, soon to be designated WHIG, dominated the three Parliaments of 1679 to 1681. On Danby's fall (1679) Shaftesbury became president of the privy council and began to press for the exclusion bill to keep the Roman Catholic James, duke of York (later James II), from the throne. He supported instead the claims of the duke of MONMOUTH. Again dismissed (1679), he continued the fight for exclusion until Charles dissolved the 1681 Parliament. Shaftesbury's position was now precarious, since his party was discredited and the king in complete control of the government. An indictment for treason failed, but he fled (1682) to Holland and soon died. Aided by his wealth and an exceptional mind, Shaftesbury has been called the most skillful politician of his day. He was bitterly satirized in John Dryden's *Absalom and Achitophel.* See biographies by L. F. Brown (1933) and K. H. D. Haley (1968); J. R. Jones, *The First Whigs: The Politics of the Exclusion Crisis, 1678–83* (1961).

Shaftesbury, Anthony Ashley Cooper, 3d **earl of,** 1671–1713, English philosopher. The philosopher John LOCKE, adviser to the 1st earl, his grandfather, was in charge of Shaftesbury's education, which was largely classical. Ill health restricted his political life, although he served (1695–98) in the House of Commons and in the House of Lords after his accession to his title in 1699. Shaftesbury's chief contributions were in the fields of moral philosophy and aesthetics. He reacted against rationalism as an ethical basis and found true morality in a balance between egoism and altruism. That balance is possible because there is a harmony between society and the individual that makes the general welfare identical with individual happiness. Man is innately equipped with spontaneous instincts or affections to promote such harmony. In the ethical field Shaftesbury called those instincts the moral sense, the first use of that term. His influence, especially in Germany, was considerable; his ideas were further developed by the British philosopher Francis HUTCHESON. Shaftesbury collected most of his important essays in *Characteristicks of Men, Manners, Opinions, Times* (1711). See F. M. Higham, *Lord Shaftesbury* (1945); Stanley Grean, *Shaftesbury's Philosophy of Religion and Ethics* (1967); see also G. B. Walters, *The Significance of Diderot's Essai sur le merite et la vertu* (1971), a study of Diderot's translation of a work by Shaftesbury.

Shaftesbury, Anthony Ashley Cooper, 7th **earl of,** 1801–85, English social reformer. He was known as Lord Ashley until 1851, when he succeeded his father as earl. Entering the House of Commons in 1826, he became a leading advocate of government action to alleviate the injustices caused by the Industrial Revolution. Notable legislation introduced by him included acts prohibiting employment of women and children in coal mines (1842), providing for care of the insane (1845), and establishing a 10-hr day for factory workers (1847). He promoted the building of model tenements and the "ragged schools" for waifs. See biographies by J. W. Bready (1926), J. L. Hammond and Barbara Hammond (4th ed., 1936), and G. F. Best (1964).

shaft sinking, excavation from the surface of an opening in the earth. Shafts, which are generally vertical, are usually distinguished from TUNNELS, which are horizontal. Little difficulty is experienced in shaft sinking through solid rock, which contains little water. When loose, water-bearing strata have to be contended with, careful shoring and sealing of the shaft lining becomes necessary, and pumping facilities are needed. Shafts are usually circular or rectangular and are generally lined with wood, masonry, concrete, steel, or cast iron. Shafts sunk in loose water-bearing soils, where there is great external pressure on the shaft sides, are nearly always circular; rectangular shafts with wood lining are often used in mining work, as the shafts are frequently of a temporary nature. Shaft sinking through rock is generally accomplished by blasting. When the loose surface material has been removed, holes are drilled, and the charges are placed and are fired by electricity. The broken rock is removed and the process is repeated. In an ordinary rectangular shaft the lining consists of timbers 8 or 12 in. (20 or 30 cm) square placed horizontally around the shaft. Shafts of a more permanent nature are generally circular in form and lined with cast iron or with concrete masonry 1 to 2 ft (30–61 cm) thick, built in sections as the work advances. When excessive quantities of water are met with, cast-iron tubbing is sometimes used. This consists of heavy cast-iron rings made in segments, with flanges for connecting, and bolted together in place. Cement grout is forced into the space between the outside of the tubbing and the surrounding earth to form a seal. Shaft sinking by the freezing process in very watery soil is accomplished by sinking pipes in the area to be excavated and circulating brine at low temperature in them until the earth is frozen and hard so that it can be excavated in the same manner as rock. In the grouting method, liquid cement is forced into the water-bearing earth under very high pressure. On mixing with the water, the cement solidifies the adjacent area, and it is removed by drilling and blasting as with rock.

Shagall, Marc: see CHAGALL, MARC.

Shage (shā'gē): see SHAMMAH.

Shah Alam (shä ä'ləm), 1728–1806, Mogul emperor of India (1759–1806). Driven out of Delhi in 1758, he nonetheless proclaimed himself emperor after the murder (1759) of his father, Alamgir II. He was under the protection of the nawab of Oudh, however, and when the nawab was defeated by the British at Buxar (1764), Shah Alam was forced to become a pensioner of the British East India Company. In 1765 he officially ceded to the company control of Bengal, Bihar, and Orissa. With the support of the Mahrattas, he was able to return to Delhi in 1772, but in 1788 the city was captured by the Rohillas, who blinded and deposed him. The British restored him to the throne in 1803 when they captured Delhi.

Shahaptin Indians: see NEZ PERCÉ INDIANS.

Shaharaim (shā"hərā'ĭm), descendant of Benjamin. 1 Chron. 8.8.

Shahazimah (shāhăz'īmə, shā"həzī'mə), unidentified town, N Palestine, between Mt. Tabor and the Jordan. Joshua 19.22.

Shahi (shähē'), city (1966 pop. 38,898), Mazanderan prov., N Iran. Manufactures include textiles and food products. It is a road and rail transport center.

Shah Jahan or **Shah Jehan** (both: shä jəhän'), 1592–1666, Mogul emperor of India (1628–58), son and successor of Jahangir. His full name was Khurram Shihab-ud-din Muhammad. He rebelled against his father in 1622 but was pardoned. On Jahangir's death, Shah Jahan won his way to the throne by having his male collateral relatives killed. He was an able, although ruthless, ruler, and during his reign Islam was restored as the state religion of the Mogul empire. In the course of his long reign he conquered most of the Deccan and temporarily (1638–49) recovered Kandahar from the Persians. Shah Jahan's reign is considered the golden age of MOGUL ART AND ARCHITECTURE. Among the buildings he erected were the unsurpassed TAJ MAHAL and the Pearl Mosque, both at Agra, and most of the great buildings of DELHI, which he made his capital. Literature also flourished at his magnificent court. Shah Jahan fell seriously ill in 1657, and this led to a war of succession among his sons. In 1658 he was deposed and imprisoned for the rest of his life by his son AURANGZEB. See B. P. Saksena, *History of Shahjahan of Dihli* (rev. ed. 1958, repr. 1962).

Shahjahanpur (shäjəhän'po͝or), city (1971 pop. 135,492), Uttar Pradesh state, N central India, on the Garra River. Founded by the Mogul emperor Shah Jahan (or Shah Jehan) in 1647, it was named in his honor. It is now a district administrative center, a railway junction, and an agricultural market town (especially for sugar).

Shahn, Ben, 1898–1969, American painter and graphic artist, b. Lithuania. Shahn emigrated to the United States in 1906. After working in lithography until 1930, his style crystallized in a series of 23 paintings concerning the Sacco-Vanzetti trial, among them *The Passion of Sacco and Vanzetti* (Whitney Mus., New York City). Shahn dealt consistently with social and political themes. He developed a strong and brilliant sense of graphic design revealed in numerous posters. His painting *Vacant Lot* (Wadsworth Atheneum, Hartford, Conn.) exhibits a poetic realism, whereas his more abstract works are characterized by terse, incisive lines and a lyric intensity of color. *The Blind Botanist* (Wichita Art Mus.) is characteristic of his abstractions. Shahn's murals include a series for the Bronx Central Annex Post Office, New York City. From 1933 to 1938 he worked as a photographer for the Farm Security Administration, producing masterful images of impoverished rural areas and their inhabitants. Shahn's later works are concerned with the loneliness of the city dweller. See his writings, ed. by J. D. Morse (1972); biography by his wife, Bernarda Bryson Shahn (1972); studies by J. T. Soby (1947 and 1957); K. W. Prescott, *The Complete Graphic Works of Ben Shahn* (1973).

Shah Nahmah: see FIRDAUSI.

Shaka: see CHAKA.

Shaker Heights, city (1970 pop. 36,306), Cuyahoga co., NE Ohio, a residential suburb of Cleveland; inc. 1912. Founded (1905) as a suburban development by the Van Sweringens, it takes its name from a Shaker community that existed there from 1822 to 1889. Today it is a beautiful community of imposing houses, squares, and wide boulevards, part of "the Heights" area, which also includes the cities of Beachwood, Cleveland Heights, South Euclid, and University Heights. A Shaker historical museum is maintained.

Shakers, popular name for members of the United Society of Believers in Christ's Second Appearing, also called the Millennial Church. Members of the movement, who received their name from the trembling produced by religious emotion, were also known as Alethians. The movement originated in a Quaker revival in England in 1747, and was led by James and Jane Wardley. However, the sect, then known as the Shaking Quakers, grew strong only after the appearance of Ann Lee. Imprisoned for her zeal, she believed herself the recipient of the mother element of the spirit of Christ. Following a vision, she and eight followers emigrated (1774) to New York state and in 1776 founded a colony at Watervliet, near Albany. Mother Ann, as she was known, gained a number of converts, who after her death (1784) began the formation of Shaker communities. By 1826 there were 18 Shaker communities in eight states, as far west as Indiana. After 1860, Shakerism began to decline; by the early 1970s the movement was all but extinct. One of the fundamental doctrines of the society was belief in the dual nature of the Deity. The male principle was incarnated in Jesus; the female principle, in Mother Ann. Other tenets were celibacy, open confession of sins, communal ownership of possessions in the advanced groups, separation from the world, pacifism, equality of the sexes, and consecrated work. Singing, dancing, and marching characterized phases of Shaker worship. The community was organized into groups, called families, of between 30 and 90 individuals. The believers donated their services and possessions but were always free to leave. Shaker furniture and handcrafts are noted for their fine design and workmanship. See E. D. Andrews and Faith Andrews, *Shaker Furniture* (1937, repr. 1964) and *The People Called Shakers* (2d ed. 1963); J. G. Shea, *American Shakers and their Furniture* (1970); H. C. Desroche, *The American Shakers* (tr. 1971).

Shakespeare, William, 1564–1616, English dramatist and poet, b. Stratford-on-Avon. He is considered the greatest playwright who ever lived.

Life. Shakespeare's father, John Shakespeare, was a successful businessman during Shakespeare's early childhood but later met with financial difficulties. During his prosperous years he was also involved in municipal affairs, holding the offices of alderman and bailiff during the 1560s. While little is known of Shakespeare's boyhood, he probably attended the grammar school in Stratford, which offered a competent grounding in the classics. Thus Ben Jonson's famous comment that Shakespeare had "small Latine, and less Greeke" could very well be untrue. In 1582, Shakespeare married Anne Hathaway, eight years his senior and pregnant at the time of the marriage. They had three children: Susanna, born in 1583, and twins, Hamnet and Judith, born in 1585. Nothing is known of the period between the birth of the twins and Shakespeare's emergence as a playwright in London in 1592. However, various suggestions have been made regarding this time, including those that he fled Stratford to avoid prosecution for stealing deer, that he joined a group of traveling players, and that he was a country schoolteacher. The last suggestion is given some credence by the academic style of his early plays, which are modeled after Roman comedy. In 1594, Shakespeare became an actor and playwright for the Lord Chamberlain's Men, the company that later became the King's Men under James I. Until the end of his London career Shakespeare remained with the company; it is thought that as an actor he played supporting roles, such as that of the ghost in Hamlet. By 1597 he was prosperous enough to buy New Place in Stratford, which later was the home of his retirement years. In 1599 he became a partner in the ownership of the Globe Theatre and in 1608 was part owner of the Blackfriars Theatre. Shakespeare retired and returned to Stratford in 1613. He undoubtedly enjoyed a comfortable living throughout his career and in retirement, although he was never a wealthy man.

The Plays. The chronology of Shakespeare's plays is uncertain, but dates of publication, references in contemporary writings, allusions in the plays to contemporary events, thematic relationships, and metrical and stylistic comparisons give a reasonable approximation of their order. His first plays are believed to be the three parts of *Henry VI,* although there is some question as to whether Part I was written before or after Parts II and III. In any case, it is thought that Part I is not completely Shakespeare's work. After these come *Richard III, The Comedy of Errors, Titus Andronicus, The Taming of the Shrew, The Two Gentlemen of Verona, Love's Labour's Lost,* and *Romeo and Juliet.* The comedies of this early period are classical imitations with a strong element of farce, while the histories and tragedies lack depth of characterization and tend toward bombast. Although it has traditionally been argued that *Titus Andronicus* could not be all Shakespeare's work be-

Shakespeare's Plays *(arranged by approximate date of composition)*

Play	*Approximate date of composition*	*Date of first publication*	*Sources*	*Major characters*	*Genre*
Henry VI, Part II	1590	1594	Edward Hall, *Union of the Two Noble and Illustre Families of Lancaster and York* (1548); Raphael Holinshed, *Chronicles of England, Scotland, and Ireland* (1587)	King Henry VI Queen Margaret Richard Plantagenet, Duke of York	History
Henry VI, Part III	1590	1595	Hall; Holinshed	King Henry VI Queen Margaret Edward, Prince of Wales Richard, Duke of Gloucester Richard Nevil, Earl of Warwick	History
Henry VI, Part I	1590	1623	Hall; Holinshed	King Henry VI Lord Talbot Joan of Arc Richard Plantagenet, Duke of York	History
Richard III	1592	1597	Hall; Holinshed; Sir Thomas More, *History of Richard III*	King Richard III Queen Elizabeth Duke of Buckingham Lady Anne George, Duke of Clarence	History
The Comedy of Errors	1592	1623	Plautus, *Menaechmi* and *Amphitruo*	Antipholus of Syracuse Antipholus of Ephesus Dromio of Syracuse Dromio of Ephesus	Comedy
Titus Andronicus	1593	1594	*History of Titus Andronicus* (chapbook); John Gower, *Appolonius of Tyre*	Titus Andronicus Tamora Aaron the Moor	Tragedy
The Taming of the Shrew	1593	1623	George Gascoigne, *Supposes* (1566); Earlier play *The Taming of a Shaw*	Petruchio Katherine	Comedy
The Two Gentlemen of Verona	1594	1623	Jorge de Montemayor, *Diana* (1559?)	Valentine Proteus Julius Silvia	Comedy

Shakespeare's Plays (Continued)

Play	*Approximate date of composition*	*Date of first publication*	*Sources*	*Major characters*	*Genre*
Love's Labour's Lost	1594	1598	Specific source not established	King of Navarre Princess of France Holofernes Don Adriano de Armado	Comedy
Romeo and Juliet	1594	1597	Arthur Brooke, *The Tragicall Historye of Romeus and Iuliet* (1562); Matteo Bandello, *Novelle* (tr. by William Painter in *Palace of Pleasure,* 1566–67)	Romeo Juliet Mercutio Tybalt Friar Laurence Nurse	Tragedy
Richard II	1595	1597	Holinshed, *Chronicles* (1587)	King Richard II Henry Bolingbroke Edmund of Langley, Duke of York	History
A Midsummer Night's Dream	1595	1600	Specific source not established	Hermea Lysander Theseus Helena Demetrius Oberon Titania Puck Bottom	Comedy
King John	1596	1623	Anon. play, *The Troublesome Raigne of King John* (1591)	King John Philip the Bastard Arthur, Duke of Britain Constance	History
The Merchant of Venice	1596	1600	Giovanni Fiorentino, *Il Pecarone* (1558)	Bassanio Shylock Antonio Portia	Comedy
Henry IV, Part I	1597	1598	Holinshed, *Chronicles* (1587)	King Henry IV Falstaff Henry, Prince of Wales (Prince Hal) Henry Percy ("Hotspur")	History
Henry IV, Part II	1597	1600	Holinshed	King Henry IV Falstaff Henry, Prince of Wales	History
Much Ado About Nothing	1598	1600	Ariosto, *Orlando Furioso* (1516)	Prince of Arragon Beatrice Benedick Claudio Hero	Comedy
Henry V	1598	1600	Holinshed, *Chronicles* (1587)	King Henry V Archbishop of Canterbury Fluellen Pistol	History
Julius Caesar	1599	1623	Plutarch, *Lives* (tr. by Sir Thomas North, 1579)	Brutus Cassius Marc Antony Caesar	Tragedy
As You Like It	1599	1623	Thomas Lodge, *Rosalynde* (1590)	Rosalind Orlando Touchstone	Comedy
Twelfth Night	1599	1623	Barnabe Riche, *Riche his Farewell to Militarie Profession* (1581)	Sir Toby Belch Viola Sebastian Duke Orsino Olivia	Comedy
Hamlet	1600	1603	François de Belleforest, *Histoires Tragiques* (1576)	Hamlet Horatio Ophelia Laertes Claudius Polonius Gertrude	Tragedy
The Merry Wives of Windsor	1600	1602	Specific source not established	Falstaff Mrs. Page Mr. Ford	Comedy

cause of its many inferior passages, critics today are more willing to accept the weaknesses in his early work as his own. *Romeo and Juliet* contains a hint of significant advance in Shakespeare's versification, evidenced particularly by the speeches of the Nurse; rather than use a uniform meter to serve various emotions and characters, Shakespeare here allows the state of mind of the speaker to control the rhythm, a technique that he developed more fully and with increasing subtlety in later years. After these early plays, and before his great tragedies, Shakespeare wrote *Richard II, A Midsummer Night's Dream, King John, The Merchant of Venice,* Parts I and II of *Henry IV, Much Ado About Nothing, Henry V, Julius Caesar, As You Like It,* and *Twelfth Night.* The comedies of this period grow away from farce toward idyllic romances, while the history plays successfully integrate political elements with individual characterization. In the two parts of *Henry IV* and in *Henry V* a sense of greater unity results from imagery and character being bound up with plot in an organic whole; these elements tended to exist in isolation from one another in Shakespeare's earlier work. The period of his great tragedies and the "problem plays" begins in 1600 with *Hamlet.* Following this are *The Merry Wives of Windsor* (a play written at the special request of Queen Elizabeth and not thematically typical of the period), *Troilus and Cressida, All's Well That Ends Well, Measure for Measure, Othello, King Lear, Macbeth, Antony and Cleopatra, Coriolanus,* and *Timon of Athens.* Although *Timon* is thematically related to the plays of this time, it is generally thought not to be entirely Shakespeare's work because of incoherence of plot and unevenness of style. Beginning with *Othello,* Shakespeare was at last able to dramatize successfully the moral and philosophical oppositions that earlier plays had only indicated. *Othello, Lear,* and *Macbeth* present clear oppositions of order and chaos, good and evil, and spirituality and animality on familial, state, and cosmic levels. Stylistically the plays of this period become increasingly compressed and symbolic. *Coriolanus* and *Antony and Cleopatra* amalgamate the political study with the portrait of a personal tragic hero. Of Shakespeare's last six plays, only three are considered entirely his work. The last two, *Henry VIII* and *The Two Noble Kinsmen,* are accepted as collaborations with John Fletcher. *Pericles,* the first of this final group, is only certainly Shakespeare's work in the verse portions of the final three acts. *Pericles* and the remaining three plays—*Cymbeline, The Winter's Tale,* and *The Tempest*—are tragicomedies. They develop in terms of situations and characters of full tragic potential but find a harmonious resolution through *grace,* a term embodying divine, humanistic, and artistic implications. Since his death Shakespeare's plays have been almost continually performed, in non-English-speaking nations as well as those where English is the native tongue. His works are quoted more than the works of any other single author and are constantly being rediscovered by critics. Critics and scholars continually attempt to define the perennial appeal of Shakespeare's plays. Initially, it would not appear to derive from their philosophical profundity. Indeed, Shakespeare has been castigated for propounding neither a philosophy nor the tenets of any particular religion. His universe is, however, a moral one. He recognized evil as being inevitable, pervasive, and fascinating, and he saw the triumph of good in its many forms as absolutely essential. In Shakespeare's view, man knows nothing of life, yet must still behave well and combat evil. This modest, human vision may be called a philosophy and cited as one reason for the persistent appeal of Shakespeare's plays. In addition, the plays tell splendid stories and are replete with superb characters. It has often been noted that Shakespeare's characters are living beings, neither wholly good nor wholly evil, and that it is their flawed, inconsistent nature that makes them memorable. Hamlet is fascinating because he is complex, cerebral, unable to make up his mind; he would not be half so interesting if, like Laertes, he could act in hot blood. Falstaff in *Henry IV* would not be beloved if, in addition to being genial, openhearted, and witty, he were not also boisterous, cowardly, and, ultimately, poignant. Finally, Shakespeare's plays are distinguished by an unparalleled use of language. The playwright had a tremendous vocabulary, and he was master of poetry, prose, and blank verse. Of course, it is not any of these separate elements alone that explains the greatness of Shakespeare's plays, but rather all of them and the extraordinary way in which they augment one another.

Editions and Sources. The first collected edition of Shakespeare is the First Folio, published in 1623 and including all the plays except *Pericles* and *The Two Noble Kinsmen* (the latter play also generally not appearing in modern editions). Eighteen of the plays exist in earlier quarto editions, eight of which are extremely corrupt, probably having been reconstructed from an actor's memory. The first edition of Shakespeare to divide the plays into acts and scenes and to mark exits and entrances is that of Nicholas Rowe in 1709. Other important early editions include those of Alexander Pope (1725), Lewis Theobald (1733), and Samuel Johnson (1765). Shakespeare used two main sources in writing his plays. Raphael Holinshed's *Chronicles of England, Scotland, and Ireland* (1587) was an important source for the English history plays, although Shakespeare did not hesitate to transform a character when it suited his dramatic purposes. For his Roman tragedies he used Sir Thomas North's translation (1579) of Plutarch's *Lives.* Many times he rewrote old plays, and twice he turned English prose romances into drama (*As You Like It* and *The Winter's Tale*). He also used the works of contemporary European authors. For further information on Shakespeare's sources, see table accompanying this article.

Shakespeare's Poetry. Shakespeare's first published works were two heroic narrative poems, *Venus and Adonis* (1593) and *The Rape of Lucrece* (1594). In 1599 a volume of poetry entitled *The Passionate Pilgrim* was published and attributed entirely to Shakespeare. However, only five of the poems are definitely considered his, two appearing in other versions in the *Sonnets* and three in *Love's Labour's Lost.* A love poem, *The Phoenix and the Turtle,* was published in 1601. Shakespeare's sonnets are by far his most important nondramatic poetry. They were first published in 1609, although many of them had certainly been circulated privately before this, and it is generally agreed that the poems were written sometime in the 1590s. There has been considerable question over the order of the poems and the degree of autobiographical content. The first 126 of the 154 sonnets are addressed to a young man whose identity has long intrigued scholars. The publisher, Thomas Thorpe, wrote a dedication to the first edition in which he claimed that a person with the initials W. H. had inspired the sonnets. Some have thought these letters to be the transposed initials of Henry Wriothesley, 3d earl of Southampton, to whom Shakespeare dedicated *Venus and Adonis* and *The Rape of Lucrece;* or they are possibly the initials of William Herbert, 3d earl of Pembroke, whose connection with Shakespeare is more tenuous. The identity of the dark lady addressed in sonnets 127–152 has also been the object of much conjecture but no proof. Certainly more important than the biographical questions is the contribution that the sonnets made to the development of Shakespeare's art. They represent an exercise in discipline, a development in that compression of meaning that is so fully realized in Shakespeare's later work. Furthermore, the sonnets often treat time, mutability, death, and their transcendence through love and art—themes that occupied Shakespeare in much of his dramatic work.

Critical Opinion. There has been a great variety of critical approach to Shakespeare's work since his time. During the 17th and 18th cent., Shakespeare was both praised and blamed. Much of the adverse criticism is not considered relevant today, although certain issues have continued to interest critics throughout the years. For instance, charges against his moral propriety were made by Samuel Johnson in the 18th cent. and by George Bernard Shaw in the 20th. However, early criticism was directed primarily at questions of form. It was charged that Shakespeare mixed comedy and tragedy and failed to observe the unities of time and place prescribed by the classical rules of drama. Critics also claimed that he had corrupted the language with false wit, puns, and ambiguity. While some of his early plays might justly be charged with a frivolous use of such devices, modern criticism has come to praise their use in later plays as adding depth and resonance of meaning. Generally the 17th and 18th cent. accused Shakespeare of a want of artistic restraint while praising him for a fecund imagination. Samuel Johnson, while agreeing with many earlier criticisms, defended Shakespeare on the question of classical rules. On the issue of unity of time and place he argued that no one considers the stage play to be real life anyway. Also, Johnson began the criticism of Shakespeare's characters that reached its culmination in the late 19th cent. with the work of A. C. Bradley. The German critics Gotthold Lessing and Augustus Wilhelm von Schlegel saw Shakespeare as a romantic, different in type from the classical poets,

Shakespeare's Plays (Continued)

Play	Approximate date of composition	Date of first publication	Sources	Major characters	Genre
Troilus and Cressida	1601	1609	Geoffrey Chaucer, *Troilus and Criseyde* (c.1386); William Caxton, *Recuyell of the Historyes of Troye* (1474)	Troilus Ulysses Pandarus Cressida	Comedy
All's Well That Ends Well	1602	1623	William Painter, *Palace of Pleasure* (1566–67)	Bertram Helena Parolles King of France	Comedy
Measure for Measure	1604	1623	George Whetstone, *Promos and Cassandra* (1578)	Vincentio Angelo Isabella Claudio Mariana	Comedy
Othello	1604	1622	Giovanni Battista Giraldi ("Cinthio"), *Ecatommiti* (1565)	Othello Desdemona Iago Cassio	Tragedy
King Lear	1605	1608	Holinshed, *Chronicles* (1587); Anon., *The True Chronicle History of King Leir* (before 1594)	King Lear Cordelia Earl of Gloucester Edgar Earl of Kent Edmund Goneril Regan Duke of Albany Lear's Fool	Tragedy
Macbeth	1605	1623	Holinshed	Duncan Macbeth Lady Macbeth Malcolm Macduff	Tragedy
Antony and Cleopatra	1606	1623	Plutarch, *Lives* (tr. 1579)	Mark Antony Cleopatra Octavius Caesar	Tragedy
Coriolanus	1607	1623	Plutarch	Coriolanus Tullus Aufidius Caius Marcius Menenius Agrippa Volumnia	Tragedy
Timon of Athens	1607	1623	Plutarch; Lucian, *Misanthropos* (2d cent. A.D.)	Timon of Athens Apemantus Alcibiades Flavius	Tragedy
Pericles	1608	1609	John Gower, *Confessio Amantis* (c.1390)	Pericles Thaisa Marina Simonides Lysimachus	Tragicomedy
Cymbeline	1609	1623	Holinshed, *Chronicles* (1587); Giovanni Boccaccio, *Decameron* (1348–53)	Cymbeline Imogen Posthumus Iachimo	Tragicomedy
The Winter's Tale	1610	1623	Robert Greene, *Pandosto* (1588)	Leontes Hermione Paulina Autolycus Perdita Florizel Polixenes	Tragicomedy
The Tempest	1611	1623	Specific source not established	Prospero Miranda Ferdinand Ariel Caliban	Tragicomedy
Henry VIII (probably written in collaboration with John Fletcher)	1612	1623	Holinshed, *Chronicles* (1587); John Foxe, *Book of Martyrs* (1563)	King Henry VIII Queen Katherine Cardinal Wolsey Duke of Buckingham Anne Boleyn	History
Two Noble Kinsmen (of doubtful authorship; may have been written in collaboration with John Fletcher)	1612	1634	Geoffrey Chaucer, "The Knight's Tale" in *Canterbury Tales* (c.1387)	Palamon Arcite	Comedy

but on equal footing. Schlegel first elucidated the structural unity of Shakespeare's plays, a concept of unity that is developed much more completely by the English poet and critic Samuel Coleridge. While Schlegel and Coleridge were establishing Shakespeare's plays as artistic, organic unities, such 19th-century critics as the German Georg Gervinus and the Irishman Edward Dowden were trying to see positive moral tendencies in the plays. The 19th-century English critic William Hazlitt, who continued the development of character analysis begun by Johnson, considered each Shakespearean character to be unique, but found a unity through analogy and gradation of characterization. While A. C. Bradley marks the culmination of romantic 19th-century character study, he also suggested that the plays had unifying imagistic atmospheres, an idea that was further developed in the 20th cent. The tendency in 20th-century criticism has been to abandon both the study of character as independent personality and moral considerations as separate from their dramatic and aesthetic context. The plays have been increasingly viewed in terms of the unity of image, metaphor, and tone. Caroline Spurgeon began the careful classification of Shakespeare's imagery, and although her attempts are now considered by some to be somewhat naive and morally biased, her work is a landmark in Shakespearean criticism. Other important trends in 20th-century criticism include the Freudian approach, such as Ernest Jones's Oedipal interpretation of *Hamlet;* the consideration of the plays primarily as stage vehicles; the study of Shakespeare in terms of the Elizabethan world view and Elizabethan stage conventions; and the study of the plays in mythic terms. For editions of his work see the Globe edition (1864, rev. ed. 1911), the New Variorum edition (27 vol., 1871–1955; repr. 1965–), the Kittredge edition (25 vol., 1966–68), and the Arden edition (26 vol., rev. ed. 1951–71); biographies by E. K. Chambers (2 vol., 1930), G. E. Bentley (1961), F. E. Halliday (1964), Anthony Burgess (1970), Samuel Schoenbaum (1970), J. O. Halliwell-Phillipps (1848, repr. 1973), and A. L. Rowse (1973); bibliographies ed. by G. R. Smith (1963), Edward Quinn et al. (1973), and Stanley Wells (1974); E. K. Chambers, *The Elizabethan Stage* (4 vol., 1923); Allardyce Nicoll, *Shakespeare: An Introduction* (1952); Geoffrey Bullough, ed., *Narrative and Dramatic Sources of Shakespeare* (8 vol., 1957–75); O. J. Campbell and E. G. Quinn, ed., *The Reader's Encyclopedia of Shakespeare* (1966); M. R. Martin and R. C. Harrier, *The Concise Encyclopedic Guide to Shakespeare* (1972); Maurice Morgan, *Shakesperian Criticism,* ed. by D. A. Fineman (1972); A. L. Rowse, *Shakespeare's Sonnets* (1973); Marvin Spevack, *A Complete and Systematic Concordance to the Works of Shakespeare* (6 vol., 1970) and *The Harvard Concordance to Shakespeare* (1973).

Shakhmatov, Aleksey Aleksandrovich (əlĭksyä' əlĭksän'drəvĭch shôkmətôf'), 1864–1920, Russian philologist and historian. Shakhmatov's many books on the history of the Russian language and the chronicles, among them *Studies in Ancient Russian Chronicles* (1908) and *Outline of the Ancient Period of the Russian Language* (1915), brought him international renown. He used the historical method of textual criticism to determine the original version of the chronicle of Nestor.

Shakhty (shäkh'tē), city (1970 pop. 205,000), SW European USSR; a major anthracite-mining center of the Donets Basin. Shakhty, founded in 1829 as a coal-mining settlement, was known as Aleksandrov-Grushevski until 1920. In 1928 a "show" trial of engineers was held, at which they were accused of sabotaging production in Shakhty on orders from the Germans. The trial initiated a period of terror against technicians and engineers.

Shakspere, William: see SHAKESPEARE, WILLIAM.

Shakti (shŭk'tē) [Skt.,=power], in Hinduism, name given to the female consorts of male deities. The Shakti personifies the dynamic, manifesting energy that creates the universe, while the male god represents the static, unmanifest aspect of the divine reality. The concept is related to that of *prakriti* in Samkhya metaphysics (see INDIAN PHILOSOPHY) and of MAYA in VEDANTA philosophy. The idea of Shakti is prominent in TANTRA where the Kundalini energy (see YOGA) is regarded as a goddess, and the theme of male-female polarity is developed. The term *Shakti* is often used to refer to the spiritual partner or consort of a spiritual master, a relationship often without the emotional and sexual components of ordinary marriage.

Shakuntala: see KALIDASA.

shale, sedimentary ROCK formed by the consolidation of mud or clay, having the property of splitting into thin layers parallel to its bedding planes. Shale tends to be fissile, i.e., it tends to split along planar surfaces between the layers of stratified rock. Shales comprise an estimated 55% of all sedimentary rocks. The composition of shale varies widely. Shales with very high silica content may have been formed when large quantities of DIATOMS and volcanic ash were present in the original sediment. Large numbers of FOSSILS in shales may give them a high calcium content; such shales may grade into LIMESTONES. Shales that contain a large percentage of ALUMINA are used as a source of that mineral in the manufacture of CEMENT. Shales containing abundant carbonaceous matter grade into bituminous COAL. Oil shales are widely distributed in the W United States and may be a future source of petroleum.

Shalem (shā'lĕm), unidentified town, near Shechem. Gen. 33.18.

Shalim, Land of (shā'lĭm), unidentified region, perhaps N of Jerusalem. 1 Sam. 9.4.

Shalisha (shăl'ĭshə), region of Palestine, probably W of Shiloh. 1 Sam. 9.4. BAAL-SHALISHA may have been in the region.

Shallecheth (shăl'ēkĕth, shălē'kĕth), gate of the Temple. 1 Chron. 26.16.

shallot: see ONION.

shallu: see SORGHUM.

Shallum (shăl'əm). **1** King of Israel for a month. He killed King Zachariah for the throne and was himself killed by Menahem. 2 Kings 15.8–15. **2** King of Judah: see JEHOAHAZ **2.** **3** Husband of Huldah. 2 Kings 22.14. **4** Chief of a family of porters. 1 Chron. 9.17. Meshullam: Neh. 12.25. **5** See MESHELEMIAH. **6** Ruler over part of Jerusalem. Neh. 3.12. **7** Priest. 1 Chron. 6.12,13; Ezra 7.2. Meshullam: 1 Chron. 9.11; Neh. 11.11. **8** See SHILLEM. **9** Simeonite. 1 Chron. 4.25. **10** Ephraimite. 2 Chron. 28.12. **11, 12** Men who had foreign wives. Ezra 10.24,42. **13** Descendant of Jerahmeel. 1 Chron. 2.40. **14** Eponymous head of a clan of Naphtali. 1 Chron. 7.13. **15** Uncle of Jeremiah. Jer. 32.7.

Shallun (shăl'ən), one who rebuilt the walls of Jerusalem. Neh. 3.15.

Shalmai (shăl'māī, shăl'mā), family returned from exile. Ezra 2.46; Neh. 7.48.

Shalman (shăl'măn), name occurring in a prophecy, perhaps for Shalmaneser. Hosea 10.14.

Shalmaneser I (shălmənē'zər), d. 1290 B.C., king of Assyria. He restored the temple at Assur, established a royal residence at Nineveh, and removed the capital from Assur to Calah, c.18 mi (29 km) S of Nineveh. **Shalmaneser III** (859–824 B.C.), son of Ashurnasirpal, claimed to have defeated (c.854 B.C.) Benhadad and AHAB, king of Israel, at Karkar (Kirharaseth) on the Orontes. His victory was probably indecisive, since he failed to reach Damascus or fight his other enemies. He received presents from Jehu of Judah. The black obelisk of Shalmaneser III, found at Calah and now in the British Museum, pictures Jehu prostrate before the king and is believed to be the only surviving picture of an Israelite king. Shalmaneser was defeated by the Chaldaeans in Armenia. In Calah he built an enormous ziggurat. **Shalmaneser V,** d. 722 B.C., succeeded Tiglath-pileser IV (728 B.C.). He attacked Hosea, king of Israel, and besieged Israel's capital, Samaria (2 Kings 17.3–6), but died during the siege. Sargon II finally destroyed Samaria.

Shama (shā'mə), one of David's mighty men. 1 Chron. 11.44.

shaman (shä'mən, shā'-, shă'-), among tribal peoples, a magician, medium, or healer. The name originated among Siberian tribes and literally means "he who knows." Like that of the American Indian MEDICINE MAN and the African witch doctor, the power of the shaman is contingent upon his ability to achieve mystical communion with the spirit world. It is not through supplication or through knowledge of tribal lore that he obtains his status. Rather, he is born to it, receiving a call from the spirit who has selected him and whom he cannot refuse. His training is usually at the side of another shaman, although it is said that the spirit who has chosen him is his real teacher. Shamanism is based on the belief that the visible world is pervaded by invisible forces or spirits that affect the lives of the living (see ANIMISM). The role of the shaman is to shield man from these spirits by coming into contact with the mysterious spirit world and rendering the destructive power of these spirits harmless. By supernatural or mediumistic means, he is supposed to control and manipulate nature. Shamans are specifically identified by their ability to enter into autohypnotic trances, during which time they are said to be in contact with the spirit world. Among certain tribes, the shaman has a familiar, usually the spirit of a departed shaman, who aids him in performing his magic and divination. The shaman usually enjoys great power and prestige in the community and is often a person of superior intellect and ability. He may serve as physician, priest, educator, civil magistrate, or war chief. Although most shamans are men, the male shaman frequently denies his own sexual identity by assuming the dress and attributes of a woman. Shamanism is a characteristic especially of the Siberian tribes, but it is found in varying forms among the Eskimos and some American Indian tribes and in SE Asia and Oceania. See Mircea Eliade, *Shamanism: Archaic Techniques of Ecstasy* (tr. 1964); M. J. Harner, ed., *Hallucinogens and Shamanism* (1973).

Shamariah (shăm"ərī'ə), son of Rehoboam. 2 Chron. 11.19.

Shamash (shä'măsh), sun god of Semitic origin, worshiped in Babylonia and Assyria. He was one of the great deities of ancient Middle Eastern religions, god of law, order, and justice. The chief center of his cult was Sippar. In Sumerian civilization he was called Utu.

Shamed (shā'mĕd), son of Elpaal. 1 Chron. 8.12.

Shamer (shā'mər). **1** Temple singer. 1 Chron. 6.46. **2** Grandson of Heber. 1 Chron. 7.34. Shomer: 1 Chron. 7.32.

Shamgar (shăm'gär), deliverer and apparently a judge of Israel. He slew 600 Philistines with an ox goad. Judges 3.31; 5.6.

Shamhuth (shăm'həth): see SHAMMAH.

Shamir (shā'mĭr). **1** Levite serving in the Temple. 1 Chron. 24.24. **2** Unidentified town, S Palestine. Joshua 15.48. **3** Unidentified place, E Palestine, home of the judge Tola. Judges 10.1,2.

Shamma (shăm'ə), Asherite. 1 Chron. 7.37.

Shammah (shăm'ə). **1** Jesse's third son. 1 Sam. 16.9; 17.13. Shimea: 1 Chron. 20.7. Shimeah: 2 Sam. 13.3,32. Shimma: 1 Chron. 2.13. **2** Duke of Edom, grandson of Esau. Gen. 36.13,17; 1 Chron. 1.37. In the confusing list of David's mighty men the name Shammah occurs several times, and the references may be to the same man. 2 Sam. 23.11,25,33. The correspondences with the parallel list in 1 Chron. 11 are also obscure, but Shammoth of 1 Chron. 11.27 seems to be the same as Shammah of 2 Sam. 23.25—as well as the captain Shamhuth of 1 Chron. 27.8—and the Shage of 1 Chron. 11.34 seems the same as Shammah of 2 Sam. 23.33.

Shammai (shăm'āī). **1** Jerahmeelite. 1 Chron. 2.28. **2, 3** Descendants of Caleb. 1 Chron. 2.44; 4.17.

Shammai (shä'mī), c. 50 B.C.–c. A.D. 30, in Jewish history, one of the leaders of the Sanhedrin. He is known for his opposition to the liberal teachings of HILLEL. Shammai's interpretation of the Law was extremely rigorous. The conflict between the schools of Shammai and Hillel continued long after their leaders' deaths. The school of Hillel ultimately won, although some 20 of Shammai's decisions were adopted by all as authoritative. See Louis Ginzberg, *On Jewish Law and Lore* (1955).

Shammoth (shăm'ŏth): see SHAMMAH.

Shammua or **Shammuah** (both: shăm'yo͞oə). **1** Son of David and Bathsheba. 1 Chron. 14.4; 2 Sam. 5.14. Shimea: 1 Chron. 3.5. **2** Reubenite spy. Num. 13.4. **3** Father of ABDA **2.** Neh. 11.17. Shemaiah: 1 Chron. 9.16. **4** Priest. Neh. 12.18.

Sha-mo, desert, Asia: See GOBI.

Shamokin (shəmō'kĭn), city (1970 pop. 11,719), Northumberland co., E Pa.; settled c.1835, inc. 1864. Shamokin is a mining center for anthracite coal, and textiles, shoes, and trailers are produced there.

shamrock, a plant with leaves composed of three leaflets. According to legend it was used by St. Patrick in explaining the doctrine of the Trinity; it is now used as the emblem of Ireland. An artificial or real shamrock leaf is customarily worn on St. Patrick's Day. The actual species of the true shamrock has long been debated, but the plants most often favored and used are the white clover (*Trifolium repens*), the black medic (*Medicago lupulina*), the wood sorrel (*Oxalis acetosella*), and a hop clover (*Trifolium minus*). All are classified in the division MAGNOLIOPHYTA, class Magnoliopsida. *Trifolium* and *Medicago* are in the order Rosales, family Leguminosae; *Oxalis* is in the order Sapindales, family Oxalidaceae.

Shamsherai (shăm"shērā'ī, shăm'shērī), descendant of Benjamin. 1 Chron. 8.26.

Shamyl (shä'mĭl), 1798?–1871, imam (religious and political leader) of the E Caucasus. From 1834 to 1859, he led the Muslim tribes of the E Caucasus in their holy war to resist Russian conquest, waging guerrilla warfare with great skill. During the Crimean War (1853–56) he became known to the European public as an exotic ally of England and France. After the war, Russia was able to send sufficient troops to the Caucasus to finally crush the Muslim holy war. Shamyl was captured in 1859. Taken first to St. Petersburg (now Leningrad) and later to Kaluga, he was allowed to make a pilgrimage (1870) to Mecca, where he died. See Lesley Blanch, *The Sabres of Paradise* (1960).

Shang (shäng) or **Yin,** dynasty of China, which ruled, according to traditional dates, from c.1766 B.C. to c.1122 B.C. or, according to some modern scholars, from c.1523 B.C. to c.1027 B.C. It is the first historic dynasty of China; its legendary founder, T'ang, is said to have defeated the last HSIA ruler, Chieh. His successors ruled over a city-state in modern Honan prov. and may have controlled other smaller states on the North China Plain. They warred against the Huns and against the CHOU, who finally defeated the last Shang king, Shou. Archaeological remains at one of the capitals, near modern AN-YANG, suggest (along with later records) that the Shang had a complex agricultural civilization of peasants and city-dwelling craftsmen, with a priestly class, nobles, and a king, who was also high priest. Shang religion was characterized by ancestor worship, sacrifices to nature deities, and divination. Stylized inscriptions on bone and bronze artifacts probably reveal the earliest examples of Chinese writing. Bronze casting under the Shang reached a height of artistic achievement rarely equaled anywhere in the world. There was a highly organized bureaucracy, and the patriarchal Chinese family system seems to have already been developed. See H. G. Creel, *The Birth of China* (1954); Cheng Te-k'un, *Archaeology in China:* Vol. II, *Shang China* (1960).

Shanghai or **Shang-hai** (shăng'hī', shăng'hī'), city (1968 est. pop. 11,000,000), in, but independent of, Kiangsu prov., E China, on the Whangpoo (Huang-p'u) River where it flows into the Yangtze estuary. It is administered directly by the central government. One of the world's great seaports, Shanghai is the largest city of China and the most populous on the continent of Asia. The only large port of central China not cut off from the interior by mountains, it is the natural seaward outlet of, and the gateway to, the productive Yangtze basin, one of China's richest regions. It handles the major share of the country's foreign shipping and a large coastwise trade. Great sums are expended to keep open its continually silting harbor. Despite a lack of fuel and raw materials, Shanghai is the leading industrial city of China, with large steelworks, textile mills, shipbuilding yards, oil-refining and gas-extracting operations, and plants making a great variety of light and heavy machinery, electrical and electronic equipment, machine tools, turbines, chemicals, pharmaceuticals, aircraft, tractors, motor vehicles, plastics, and assorted consumer goods. Shanghai is also a major publishing center. The commercial section of the city, the former International Settlement, is modern and Western in appearance, with broad streets and spacious boulevards lined with imposing buildings, many of skyscraper height. The Bund (which runs along the waterfront), Nanking Road, and Bubbling Well Road are the most noted thoroughfares. Typical Oriental buildings are found only in the original Chinese town (no longer walled), known as the Chapei quarter. There has been much rebuilding and expansion; new factories ring the city, and the northwest section is being developed into an industrial district. Shanghai has annexed a large part of the surrounding rural area (over 2,000 sq mi/5,180 sq km); there peasant communities and collective farms produce the food crops (wheat, barley, vegetables, fruits, etc.) that support the city's population. Though water transport is of prime importance to Shanghai, new highways radiate to the countryside, and there are rail connections with Nanking and Hangchow, with links through those cities to the N and S China networks. Shanghai has an international airport. A submarine base is in the harbor. The name *Shanghai* dates from the Sung dynasty (11th cent.), but the town, which became a walled city in the 16th cent., was unimportant until it was opened to foreign trade by the Treaty of Nanking in 1842. The ensuing Western influence launched the city on its phenomenal growth. The greater part of the city was incorporated into the British concession (1843), just north of the old walled city, and into the U.S. concession of Hongkew (1862). In 1863 the United States and Great Britain consolidated into the International Settlement the areas that had been conceded to them. The French, who had obtained a concession in 1849, continued it as a separate entity. The foreign zones, which were under extraterritorial administration, maintained their own courts, police system, and armed forces. Thus Shanghai until World War II was a divided city. In 1927, Chiang Kai-shek, at the head of the Nationalist army and with the support of the Chinese Communists, captured Shanghai. The Chinese section was immediately placed under the Kuomintang government. Japan invaded and attacked the Chinese city in 1932 to force the government to break an unofficial boycott of Japanese goods. In Aug., 1937, as part of the Second Sino-Japanese War, the Japanese again attacked the Chinese city, and gallant resistance was overcome in November. The foreign zones were occupied by the Japanese after Dec. 7, 1941. In 1943 the United States and Great Britain renounced their claims in Shanghai, as did France in 1946. The city was restored to China at the end of World War II, and the Chinese central government for the first time gained control of the entire city. In May, 1949, it fell to the Communists. Next to Peking, Shanghai is the country's foremost educational center. Its many institutions of higher learning include Futan Univ., Chiao-tung Univ., Shanghai Univ. of Science and Technology, Tungchi Univ., three medical colleges, and numerous technological and scientific institutes. Shanghai has an astronomical observatory, several museums, an opera, a performing arts group, and many research institutes and learned societies. See F. L. H. Pott, *A Short History of Shanghai* (1928, repr. 1973).

Shan-hai-kuan or **Shanhaikwan** (both: shän-hī-kwän) [Chin.,=mountain sea door], city, NE Hopeh prov., China, on the Po Hai. It has fertilizer and food-processing plants. Strategically situated where the Great Wall meets the sea and on the narrow coastal route to Manchuria, it has been the site of many battles and the route of many invasions. It now lies on a double-track railroad linking Tientsin with Shen-yang (Mukden). The city was known as Hai-yang until 1949. Another name is Lin-yü.

Shankar, Ravi, 1920–, Indian sitarist and composer. He is the first Indian instrumentalist to attain an international reputation. As a youth Shankar was a noted solo dancer with his brother Uday's Indian dance troupe in Paris. In 1938 he became a pupil of the great Indian instrumentalist Ustad Allauddin Khan, whose daughter, Annapurna, he later married. Proficient on many instruments, Shankar became a virtuoso of the SITAR, and in 1957 he made the first of several concert tours of the United States. In 1962 he founded the Kinnara School of Music in Bombay. For a few months in 1965, George Harrison of The Beatles studied sitar with Shankar, and Beatle performances began featuring Harrison playing the instrument. Other rock groups followed suit, and for a time the sound of the sitar was a staple of rock music. As the foremost interpreter of the instrument, Shankar was catapulted to fame. His 1967 concert tour of the United States was an overwhelming success, and he was invited to hold classes at various American colleges and universities. Although Americans were not familiar with the classical sitar music Shankar played, his masterly performances were received enthusiastically by students, critics, and general audiences alike. In 1968 he was named artist of the year by *Billboard* magazine. Among Shankar's many musical compositions are the scores for the motion pictures *Pather Panchali* (1954) and *Charly* (1968). See his autobiography, *My Music, My Life* (1969).

Shankara (shŭng'kərə): see VEDANTA.

Shannon, principal river of the Republic of Ireland and longest (c.240 mi/390 km) in the British Isles. It rises near Cuilcagh Mt., NW Co. Cavan, and flows S through the Central Plain to Limerick, where it turns west in a broad estuary (c.70 mi/110 km) to the Atlantic Ocean between Loop Head and Kerry Head. Loughs Allen, Boderg, Ree, and Dreg are expansions of the river. The Shannon with its many tributaries drains a region of farmland and peat bogs. Towns along the Shannon include Carrick-on-Shannon, Athlone, and Limerick. The river is connected with E Ireland by the Royal Canal and the Grand Canal. Large vessels, however, cannot ascend the river above Foynes, and Limerick is the head of estuary navigation. There is an important hydroelectric plant between Lough Derg and Limerick. The fisheries of the river are valuable. **Shannon Airport Industrial Estate** (opened 1945), a duty-free international terminal on the river, 15 mi (24 km) W of Limerick, has been developed by the government into an important industrial center.

Shansi (shän'sē'), Mandarin *Shan-hsi* [west of the (T'ai-hang) mountains], province (1967 est. pop. 18,000,000), c.60,000 sq mi (155,400 sq km), NE China. The capital is T'AI-YÜAN. It is bounded on the W and the S by the Huang Ho (Yellow River) and on the N by Inner Mongolia. Much of Shansi is a high plateau region. The soil is fertile loess, but scant rainfall and widespread erosion hamper the raising of sufficient food, and there have been recent droughts. Reforestation and irrigation projects have been instituted. The main food crops are winter wheat, corn, kaoliang, soybeans, millet, barley, and fruit. Cotton, tobacco, and grapes are grown as commercial crops. Livestock is raised in the northern grazing areas, and wool and hides are exported. Forestry is important in the mountainous regions. Shansi has rich and extensive coal and iron deposits. A salt lake in the southwestern part of the province is one of China's major inland sources of salt. The best communication system of the province is its rail network with connections to central and N China. There are few good roads, and of the rivers only the Fen (the longest) is partly navigable; it is ice-bound in winter. From 1911 until the Communist takeover in 1949, a warlord, Yen Hsi-shan, ruled Shansi as an almost independent province; he made notable internal improvements and brought a degree of prosperity. Shansi's strategic position in the northeast made it a center of Communist activity in the 1940s.

Shan State (shän), state (1969 est. pop. 2,725,000), c. 60,000 sq mi (155,400 sq km), E central Burma. Taunggyi, the capital, and LASHIO are its principal cities. It borders on China in the north, Laos in the east, and Thailand in the south. Most of the Shan State is a hilly plateau; there are higher mountains in the north and south. The gorge of the Salween River cuts across the state. Silver, lead, and zinc are mined, notably at the Bawdwin mine, and there are smelters at Namtu. Teak is cut, and rice and other crops are grown. The valleys and tableland are inhabited by the Shans, who in language and customs resemble the Thais and the Laos. They are largely Buddhists and are mainly engaged in agriculture. Among the Shans live Burmans, Chinese, and Karens. The hills are inhabited by primitive tribes, notably the Wa, formerly head-hunters, who are numerous in the north and along the Chinese border. The Shans dominated most of Burma from the 13th to the 16th cent. In the 19th cent., long after their power declined, they were distributed among more than 30 petty states; most of them paid tribute to the Burman king. Under British rule in Burma, the Shan States were ruled by their hereditary chiefs (sawbwas) as feudatories of the British crown. In 1922 most of these small states were joined in the Federated Shan States, under a commissioner who also administered the Wa states. This arrangement survived the constitutional changes of 1923 and 1937 in Burma proper. A single Shan state, including the former Wa states, was established by the 1947 Burmese constitution. In 1959 the sawbwas relinquished much of their power to the Burmese government.

Shantar Islands (shəntär'), archipelago, c.980 sq mi (2,540 sq km), Khabarovsk Kray, Far Eastern USSR, in the Sea of Okhotsk. Discovered in 1645, the islands are used as a fishing base and for fur trapping and lumbering.

Shan-t'ou (shän-tō) or **Swatow** (swä'tou'), city (1970 est. pop. 400,000), SE Kwangtung prov., China, a port on the South China Sea, in the Han River delta. When it was opened to foreign trade after the second OPIUM WAR, it was a minor fishing village. Today it is a trade and industrial center, with shipbuilding yards and machine shops. Fishing is still important.

Shantung or **Shan-tung** (both: shăn-tŭng, shän-dōōng) [east of the (T'ai shan) mountains], province (1967 est. pop. 57,000,000), c.54,000 sq mi (139,860 sq km), NE China. CHI-NAN is the capital. The eastern half of the province is a peninsula, situated between the Po Hai on the north and the Yellow Sea on the east and south. The mountain chain that forms the Liaotung peninsula in Manchuria continues into east and central Shantung. The western portion of the province, a level area, is part of the delta of the Huang Ho (Yellow River), which crosses Shantung to empty into the Po Hai. Although the soil is very fertile, rainfall is inadequate, and famines used to occur. Much of the land has been reclaimed, however, and half of the province is now under cultivation. Shantung is an important wheat-producing and cotton-producing province; kaoliang, millet, corn, soybeans, peanuts, sweet potatoes, fruits, and tobacco are also grown. Forest products are made, and pongee silk is produced by wild silkworms fed on oak leaves. Fishing is excellent along the rocky coast and offshore islands. Salt is also produced in the province. Oil, recently discovered, is extracted near the mouth of the Huang Ho (Yellow River). Abundant coal and iron reserves are also exploited, and Shantung has deposits of gold, copper, and kaolin. CH'ING-TAO and Chi-nan are leading light- and heavy-industrial centers. Chi-nan is on the north-south railway system that connects Shanghai and Nanking with Tientsin; a branch line extends to Ch'ing-tao and Yen-t'ai. There are many paved roads throughout the province. Strategically located near Manchuria and with excellent harbors, Shantung has often been subjected to foreign encroachment. Kiaochow was held by Germany until 1914 and by Japan until 1922, and Great Britain leased the territory of Wei-hai-wei from 1898 to 1930. In recent years many Chinese have migrated from Shantung to Manchuria to escape extreme overcrowding. Shantung is venerated by the Chinese as the birthplace of the ancient philosophers Confucius and Mencius, and as the site of Tai, a sacred peak. Shantung Univ. is in Ch'ing-tao.

shanty, in music: see CHANTEY.

Shaohing: see SHAO-HSING, China.

Shao-hsing (shou-shĭng) or **Shaohing** (shou'hĭng'), city (1970 est. pop. 225,000), N Chekiang prov., SE China, on the south shore of Hangchow Bay. It is a marketing center handling rice, silk, and tea. The most famous export is Shao-hsing rice wine. Silk textiles, paper products, and handicrafts are made. A small coal mine is nearby. In the 5th cent. B.C. it was the seat of a powerful king.

Shao-kuan (shou-gwän) or **Kükong** (kük'gông'), town (1970 est. pop. 125,000), N Kwangtung prov., SE China, on the North River and the Canton-Han-K'ou RR. It is a trade center with coal and tungsten mining, a lead-zinc plant, and factories making chemicals, machine tools, rubber products, and cement.

Shao-yang or **Shaoyang** (both: shou-yäng), city (1970 est. pop. 275,000), S Hunan prov., China. It is the trade center for the upper Tze valley and has coal and iron mines. It was formerly called Paoking.

Shapham (shā'făm), chief Gadite. 1 Chron. 5.12.

Shaphan (shā'făn). **1** Trusted secretary of King Josiah. He was the father of friends of Jeremiah and grandfather of Gedaliah. 2 Kings 22.3–14; 2 Chron. 34.8,15–22; Jer. 26.24; 29.3; 36.10–12; 39.14; 40.5. **2** Father of the idolatrous Jaazaniah. Ezek. 8.11.

Shaphat (shā'făt). **1** Prince of the blood in Judah. 1 Chron. 3.22. **2** Father of Elisha. 1 Kings 19.16,19; 2 Kings 3.11; 6.31. **3** One of the spies. Num. 13.5. **4** Officer under David. 1 Chron. 27.29. **5** Gadite. 1 Chron. 5.12.

Shapher, Mount (shā'fər), unlocated desert resting place. Num. 33.23,24.

Shapiro, Karl, 1913–, American poet and critic, b. Baltimore, studied at the Univ. of Virginia and Johns Hopkins. His interest in the aesthetics and artifice of modern poetry and in the role of the poet as cultural spokesman is expressed in his poems as well as in his criticism. Shapiro's early volumes of verse—*Person, Place, and Thing* (1942), *Place of Love* (1943), and *V-Letter* (1944; Pulitzer Prize)—were written while he was a soldier in World War II. Later volumes include *Trial of a Poet* (1947), *Poems, 1940–1953* (1953), *Poems of a Jew* (1958), and *Selected Poems* (1968). His critical essays were published in such volumes as *Essay on Rime* (in verse, 1945), *Beyond Criticism* (1953), *In Defense of Ignorance* (1960), *Prose Keys to Modern Poetry* (1962), and *To Abolish Children and Other Essays* (1968). His first novel, *Edsel*, appeared in 1971.

Shapley, Harlow (shăp'lē), 1885–1972, American astronomer, b. Nashville, Mo., grad. Univ. of Missouri, 1910, Ph.D. Princeton, 1913. He was astronomer at Mt. Wilson Observatory from 1914 to 1921, when he became director of Harvard Observatory. He did notable research work in photometry and spectroscopy, devoting particular study to the structure of the universe. He determined the size of the Milky Way and the position of its center as well as the position of the sun in the galaxy. Among his other distinguished contributions were his investigations in the fields of Cepheid variables (he established that they are pulsating stars rather than eclipsing binaries) and globular clusters. Shapley's works include *Galaxies* (1943) and *Of Stars and Men* (1958).

Shapur I (shäpo͝or') or **Sapor I** (sā'pôr), d.272, king of Persia (241–72), son and successor of Ardashir I, of the Sassanid or Sassanian dynasty. He was an able warrior king. Although he was defeated by the Roman emperor, Gordian III, in 242, Gordian's successor, PHILIP (Philip the Arabian), concluded a peace with him guaranteeing Shapur's power in Armenia and Mesopotamia. In 260 he achieved his greatest triumph by defeating the Roman emperor VALERIAN at Edessa—a landmark in the decline of Rome. The rise of ODENATHUS of Palmyra cut into Shapur's territories and even threatened Ctesiphon. Yet, Shapur not only maintained Persian power in the west but also rebuilt Persian economy. He promoted a program of public works, and in later years he commissioned the translation of numerous Greek and Indian writings. He placed Mani, the founder of Manichaeism, under his protection.

Shapur II or **Sapor II,** 310–79, king of Persia (310–79), of the Sassanid, or Sassanian, dynasty. He was the posthumous son of Hormuz II and therefore was born king. His long reign was marked by great military success. Central Asian tribes had taken advantage of his minority to regain much of their former territory, then held by Persia. Later, however, Shapur crushed their kingdom in the east and annexed the area as a new province. Cultural expansion followed on this victory, and Sassanian art penetrated Turkestan, reaching as far as China. Having removed the threat from the east, Shapur resumed warfare against the Romans over the control of Armenia. Although driven back at first, the Roman army counterattacked and threatened Ctesiphon. But when the emperor Julian the Apostate was killed (363) in battle, the Romans withdrew. The emperor JOVIAN made a humiliating peace, and Shapur recovered Armenia, which he placed under military occupation. Armenia had in the meantime accepted Christianity, and Shapur, an orthodox Zoroastrian, at first persecuted the Christians but later recognized their autonomy and respected their religion. He had a large rock sculpture made near Shapur to commemorate his victory over the Romans.

Shapur III or **Sapor III,** d. 388, king of Persia (383–88), of the Sassanid, or Sassanian, dynasty; son of Shapur II; successor of his uncle, Ardashir II. He made a new attempt to settle the long-lasting dispute with Rome over Armenia. A compromise was reached (384), and he surrendered part of that territory. He had a rock sculpture made at Taq-e Bostan near Kermanshah to commemorate his reign.

Sharai (shăr'āī, shərā'ī), Jew who had a foreign wife. Ezra 10.40.

Sharaim (shārā'ĭm), unidentified town, SW Palestine. Joshua 15.36.

Sharaku Toshusai (shä'räko͞o tōsho͞oshī'), fl. 1794, Japanese artist. He was a professional performer of No dance and was attached to a noble family. His prints of actors were all made between May, 1794, and Feb., 1795. During these ten months, he produced at least 136 prints, portraying actors of the Kabuki, or popular, stage. His drawing is individual and vigorous, but often exaggerated. See H. G. Henderson and L. V. Ledoux, *The Surviving Works of Sharaku* (1939); biography by Ichitaro Kondo (1955); study by Juzo Suzuki (1968).

Sharar (shā'rär), same as SACAR **1.**

share, in agriculture: see PLOW.

share, in finance: see STOCK.

share cropping, system of farm tenancy once common in some parts of the United States. In the United States the institution arose at the end of the Civil War out of the plantation system. Many planters had ample land but little money for wages. At the same time most of the former slaves were uneducated and impoverished. The solution was the share-cropping system, which continued the workers in the routine of cotton cultivation under rigid supervision. Economic features of the system were gradually extended to poor white farmers. The cropper brought to the farm only his own and his family's labor. Most other requirements—land, animals, equipment, and seed—were provided by the landlord, who generally also advanced credit to meet the living expenses of the cropper family. Most croppers worked under the close direction of the landlord, and he marketed the crop and kept accounts. Normally in return for their work they received a share (usually half) of the money realized. From this share was deducted the debt to the landlord. High interest charges, emphasis on production of a single cash crop, slipshod accounting, and chronic cropper irresponsibility were among the abuses of the system. Farm mechanization and a marked reduction in cotton acreage have virtually put an end to the system. See D. E. Conrad, *The Forgotten Farmers: The Story of Sharecroppers in the New Deal* (1965); A. F. Raper and I. D. Reid, *Sharecroppers All* (1941, rep. 1971); Robert Coles, *Migrants, Sharecroppers, Mountaineers* (1972).

Sharett, Moshe (mō'shə shərĕt'), 1894–1965, Israeli statesman, b. Russia, originally named Shertok. In 1906 he emigrated to Palestine where he was active in the labor movement. In 1933 he became head of the political department of the Jewish Agency for Palestine. Sharett was Davin Ben-Gurion's closest associate in the struggle for an independent Jewish state. In 1948 he was appointed foreign minister of Israel and from 1953 to 1955 served as prime minister. He resigned from the government in 1956. Sharet sought to strengthen Israel's position by statesmanship rather than confrontation, emphasizing "caution" rather than "courage." His replacement as premier by Ben-Gurion in 1955 and retirement in 1956 reflected the movement in Israel toward confrontation that resulted in the 1956 Arab-Israeli War. See biography by M. Z. Rosensaft (1966).

Sharezer (shərē'zər), brother of ADRAMMELECH **2.**

Shari, river, Chad: see CHARI.

Sharjah (shärjä'), sheikhdom (1968 pop. 31,480), c.1,000 sq mi (2,590 sq km), part of the federation of UNITED ARAB EMIRATES, E Arabia, on the Persian Gulf and the Gulf of Oman. The town of Sharjah (pop. 19,198), on the Persian Gulf, is, after Abu Dhabi, the largest town in the federation. Oil has been produced in Sharjah since 1961. Formerly a British protectorate, Sharjah was the site of a British base until 1971, when the British withdrew from the Persian Gulf area. In that year Sharjah joined the United Arab Emirates.

shark, member of a group of almost exclusively marine and predaceous fishes. Sharks are heavy fishes, possessing neither lungs nor swim bladders (see FISH). Their skeletons are made of cartilage rather than bone, and this, along with large deposits of fat, partially solves their weight problem; nevertheless, most sharks must keep moving in order to breathe and to stay afloat. They are good swimmers; the wide spread of the pectoral fins and the upward curve of the tail fin provide lift, and the sweeping movements of the tail provide drive. Their tough hides are studded with minute, toothlike structures called denticles. Sharks have pointed snouts; their crescent-shaped mouths are set on the underside of the body and contain several rows of sharp, triangular teeth. They have respiratory organs called GILLS, usually five on each side, with individual gill slits opening on the body surface; these slits form a conspicuous row and lack the covering found over the gills of bony fishes. Like most fishes, sharks breathe by taking water in through the mouth and passing it out over the gills. Usually there are two additional respiratory openings on the head, called spiracles. A shark's intestine has a unique spiral valve, which increases the area of absorption. Fertilization is internal in sharks; the male has paired organs called claspers for introducing sperm into the CLOACA of the female. Members of most species bear live young, but a few of the smaller sharks lay eggs containing much yolk and enclosed in horny shells. There are about 250 species of sharks, ranging from the 2-ft (60-cm) pygmy shark to 50-ft (15-m) giants. They are found in all seas, but are most abundant in warm waters. Some may enter large rivers, and one ferocious freshwater species lives in Lake Nicaragua. Most are predatory, but the largest species, the WHALE SHARK and the BASKING SHARK, are harmless plankton eaters. Only a small number of the predatory species are definitely known to engage in unprovoked attacks on humans. The largest and most feared of these is the great WHITE SHARK, or man-eater, which may reach 20 ft (6 m) in length and is probably responsible for more such attacks than any other species. Other sharks reputed to be especially dangerous are the tiger and blue sharks and the MAKO. Sharks are extremely sensitive to motion and to the scent of blood. Swimmers in areas where dangerous varieties occur should leave the water quietly if they are cut; divers should remove bleeding fish immediately. In some places bathing areas are guarded by nets. A number of substances have been used as shark repellents, including maleic acid, copper sulfate, and decaying shark flesh, but their effectiveness is variable. Sharks usually circle their prey before attacking. Since they seldom swim near the surface, an exposed dorsal fin is more likely to be that of a swordfish or ray than that of a shark. DOGFISH is the name for members of several families of small sharks; these should not be confused with the bony dogfishes of the mud minnow and BOWFIN families. Shark meat is nutritious and is used in some tropical areas for human food; in the Orient a gelatinous soup is made from the fins of certain species. The flesh is also sold for poultry feed, and shark oils are used in industry; shark-liver oil was formerly used as a source of vitamin A. The rough skin is used as a sandpaper called shagreen, and tanned sharkskin is a durable leather. Sharks, RAYS (including skates), and CHIMAERAS together form the vertebrate class Chondrichthyes, the cartilagenous fishes (see CHORDATA). The sharks and rays form the subclass Elasmobranchii, and the sharks form the order Selachii. See also HAMMERHEAD SHARK and THRESHER SHARK. See T. H. Lineaweaker and R. H. Backus, *The Natural History of Sharks* (1970); Paul Budker and P. J. Whitehead, *The Life of Sharks* (tr., rev. ed. 1971); P. E. Pope, *A Dictionary of Sharks* (1973).

sharksucker: see REMORA.

Sharm el Sheikh: see SINAI.

Sharon (shā'rən, shâr'ən), plain between the Samarian Hills of central Israel and the Mediterranean Sea, extending c.50 mi (80 km) from Jaffa to Caesarea. 1 Chron. 5.16; Isa. 33.9; 35.2; 65.10. Saron: Acts 9.35. See also ROSE OF SHARON. Famous for its fertility in ancient times, Sharon later became swampland. In the 20th cent. Zionist efforts transformed it into farmlands with many settlements.

Sharon (shâr'ən). **1** Town (1970 pop. 12,367), Norfolk co., E Mass.; settled c.1650, inc. 1775. It is residential. **2** City (1970 pop. 22,653), Mercer co., NW Pa., on the Shenango River, near the Ohio line; settled c.1800, inc. as a city 1920. An industrial city, its chief manufactures are steel and electrical appliances. A great variety of metal products are also made. A campus of Pennsylvania State Univ. is there, and Shenango Dam and Reservoir (completed 1965) are nearby.

Sharonville, city (1970 pop. 10,985), Hamilton co., SW Ohio, a suburb of Cincinnati; surveyed 1796, inc. 1911.

Sharp, Cecil James, 1859–1924, English musician, best known for his researches in English folk music. In 1911 he founded the English Folk Dance Society. In the United States he collected (1914–18) folk songs in the Appalachian Mts., where he found many songs of English origin. His numerous anthologies include *English Folk Songs from the Southern Appalachian Mountains* (with O.D. Campbell, 1917; 2d ed. by Maud Karpeles, 1952) and *American-English Folk Songs* (1918). He wrote *English Folk Song: Some Conclusions* (1907, 3d ed. 1954) and, with A. P. Oppe, *The Dance: An Historical Survey of Dancing in Europe* (1924). See biography by A. H. Fox Strangways and Maud Karpeles (rev. ed. 1967).

Sharp, Granville, 1735–1813, English reformer, scholar, and abolitionist. In 1772 he won a case establishing the principle that any slave would become free upon reaching British land. Sharp continued his abolitionist activities, notably the promotion of a Negro colony in Sierra Leone, which was unsuccessful. In 1776 he began agitation against the impressment of seamen. Later he founded a Bible society. Self-taught in Greek and Hebrew, he was noted for his studies in biblical texts. He also wrote many pamphlets on political questions. See Prince Hoare, *Memoirs of Granville Sharp* (1820, 2d ed. 1828); study by E. C. P. Lascelles (1928, repr. 1969).

Sharp, James, 1613–79, Scottish prelate. As a Presbyterian minister, Sharp became (1650) a leader of the moderate wing of the Scottish church called the Resolutioners. He was captured (1651) by Oliver Cromwell's forces and imprisoned until 1652. Sent (1657) to London to represent the interests of the Resolutioners, Sharp became involved with George MONCK in his schemes for the restoration of the monarchy and secretly shifted his loyalties to the restoration of episcopacy in Scotland. After the Restoration of Charles II he was appointed (1661) archbishop of St. Andrews and primate of Scotland and thereupon embarked on a policy of severe repression of the principles of the COVENANTERS. He was murdered by a group of Covenanters on Magus Moor. In Scottish history Sharp is usually pictured as a hated figure.

Sharp, William, pseud. **Fiona Macleod** (fē'nə məkloud', fēō'nə), 1855–1905, Scottish poet and man of letters. Under his own name he wrote literary biographies; poems, including the volume *Earth's Voices* (1884); and novels, notably *Silence Farm* (1899). With his wife he compiled the anthology *Lyra Celtica* (1896). Under the name Fiona Macleod, supposedly a talented Celtic lady, Sharp wrote his best novels and poems, including *Pharais* (1894), *The Mountain Lovers* (1895), and *The Washer of the Ford* (1896), as well as two plays, *The House of Usna* (1903) and *The Immortal Hour* (1908). Delicate and romantic, these works treat life in Scotland, evoking a haunting, almost supernatural atmosphere. See biography by Flavia Alaya (1970).

Sharuhen (shăro͞o'hĕn), variant of SHAARAIM.

Shashai (shăsh'āī, shā'shī), Jew who had a foreign wife. Ezra 10.40.

Shashak (shā'shăk), descendant of Benjamin. 1 Chron. 8.14,25.

Sha-shih (shä-shûr) or **Shasi** (shä'sē), city (1970 est. pop. 125,000), S Hupeh prov., China, on the Yangtze River. It is an important trade center for the N Tung-t'ing lake basin and the site of a massive reservoir built to protect the central Hupeh plains from floods. Textile mills are there. Sha-shih is connected to Hunan prov. by canal.

Shasi: see SHA-SHIH, China.

Shasta, Mount (shăs'tə), volcanic peak, 14,162 ft (4,317 m) high, N Calif., in the Cascade Range. Discovered c.1827 by Peter Skene Ogden, a British fur trader and explorer, Mt. Shasta has long been extinct except for hot sulfurous springs near the top. The resort town of Mt. Shasta is at the southwest foot of the mountain.

Shasta Dam, 602 ft (183 m) high and 3,460 ft (1,055 m) long, on the Sacramento River, N Calif.; built 1938–45. One of the largest concrete dams in the world, it is a major unit in the CENTRAL VALLEY PROJECT. The dam restores navigable depths to the Sacramento River, provides flood control, electric power (379,000-kw capacity), and irrigation and reclamation development. Its reservoir, **Shasta Lake,** 46 sq mi (119 sq km), is formed by the impounded waters of the Sacramento, Pit, and McCloud rivers. The lake is included in Whiskeytown-Shasta-Trinity National Recreational Area (see NATIONAL PARKS AND MONUMENTS, table).

Shastri, Shri Lal Bahadur (shrē läl bähä'do͝or shäs'trē), 1904–66, Indian political leader. He joined Mohandas Gandhi's noncooperation movement in 1921 and studied at the nationalist Kashi Vidyapeth school, where he was given the title *Shastri* [learned in the scriptures]. Elected to the central legislature in 1952, he served as minister for railways (1952–56), minister of commerce and industry (1957–61), and minister of home affairs (1961–63) before succeeding Jawaharlal Nehru as prime minister in 1964. Following the India-Pakistan War of 1965, Shastri met in Tashkent with President Ayub Khan of Pakistan and signed a "no-war" declaration. He died the next day (Jan. 11, 1966). See biography by J. N. Yadav (1971); study by R. C. Gupta (1966).

Shatt al Arab (shät äl ä'răb), tidal river, 120 mi (193 km) long, formed by the confluence of the Tigris and Euphrates rivers, SE Iraq, and flowing SE to the Persian Gulf, forming part of the Iraq-Iran border; the Karun is its chief tributary. The Shatt al Arab flows through a broad, swampy delta that contains the world's largest date-palm groves. The river supplies fresh water to S Iraq and Kuwait and is navigable for oceangoing vessels as far as Basra, Iraq's chief port. Iraq and Iran have disputed navigation rights on the Shatt al Arab since 1935, when an international commission gave Iraq total control of the Shatt al Arab, leaving Iran with control only of the approaches to Abadan and Khorramshahr, its chief ports, and unable to develop new port facilities in the delta. To preclude Iraqi political pressure and interference with its oil and freight shipments on the Shatt al Arab, Iran has built ports on the Persian Gulf to handle foreign trade.

Shatt el Arab: see SHATT AL ARAB.

Shaul (shôl). **1** Son of Simeon, eponym of the Shaulites. Gen. 46.10; Ex. 6.15; Num. 26.13; 1 Chron. 4.24. **2** King of Edom. 1 Chron. 1.48. Saul: Gen. 36.37. **3** Same as JOEL **13.**

Shaula, bright star in the constellation SCORPIUS; Bayer designation Lambda Scorpii; 1970 position R.A. $17^h31.6^m$, Dec. −37°05′. A bluish-white star of SPECTRAL CLASS B1 V, its apparent MAGNITUDE of 1.62 makes it one of the 25 brightest stars in the sky. Shaula is a spectroscopic BINARY STAR. Its distance from the earth is about 300 light-years. Its name is from the Arabic, meaning "raised part of the scorpion's tail."

Shaveh (shā'vē), unidentified valley, near Jerusalem. Gen. 14.17. This is possibly the same as the king's dale where Absalom placed his commemorative pillar. 2 Sam. 18.18.

Shaveh Kiriathaim (kĭr'ēəthā'ĭm) [Heb.,=plain of KIRIATHAIM], unidentified place. Gen. 14.5.

Shavli: see SIAULIAI, USSR.

Shavsha (shăv'shə), David's scribe. 1 Chron. 18.16. Seraiah: 2 Sam. 8.17. Sheva: 2 Sam. 20.25. Shisha: 1 Kings 4.3.

Shavuot (shəvo͞o'ət) [Heb.,=weeks], Jewish feast celebrated on the 6th of the month of Sivan (usually some time in May) in Israel and on the sixth and seventh days in the Diaspora. Originally an agricultural festival celebrating the end of the winter grain harvest (which began at Passover), Shavuot later commemorated the giving of the Ten Commandments to Moses on Mt. Sinai. See PENTECOST. See Hayyim Schauss, *Guide to Jewish Holy Days* (1938, repr. 1970).

Shaw, Anna Howard, 1847–1919, American woman-suffrage leader, b. England. She emigrated (1851) to the United States in early childhood and grew up on a farm in Michigan. She received a degree in theology (1878) and one in medicine (1885) from Boston Univ. Although the Methodist Episcopal Church refused to allow her to preach, she was ordained (1880) by the Methodist Protestant denomination. She had filled several pastorates in Massachusetts when, in 1888 she met Susan B. Anthony and from then on devoted her life to working for woman suffrage. She was vice president at large (1892–1904) and president (1904–15) of the National American Woman Suffrage Association. In Anthony's last years, she was her constant associate. Dr. Shaw campaigned in every state where a suffrage measure was under consideration; she was one of the most effective speakers of the movement. See her autobiography, *The Story of a Pioneer* (1915).

Shaw, George Bernard, 1856–1950, Irish playwright and critic, widely considered the greatest British dramatist since Shakespeare. He revolutionized the Victorian stage, then dominated by artificial melodramas, by presenting vigorous dramas of ideas. The lengthy prefaces to Shaw's plays reveal his mastery of English prose. His music and theater criticism is among the finest ever written. In 1925 he was awarded the Nobel Prize in Literature. Born in Dublin, Shaw was the son of an unsuccessful merchant; his mother was a singer who eventually left her husband to teach singing in London. Shaw left school at 14 to work in an estate agent's office. In 1876 he went to London and for nine years was largely supported by his parents. He wrote five novels, several of them published in small socialist magazines. Shaw was himself an ardent socialist, a member of the FABIAN SOCIETY, and a popular public speaker on behalf of socialism. Work as a journalist led to his becoming a music critic for the *Star* in 1888 and for the *World* in 1890; his enthusiasm for Wagner proved infectious to his readers. As drama critic for the *Saturday Review* after 1895, he won readers to Ibsen; he had already written *The Quintessence of Ibsenism* (1891). In 1898, Shaw married Charlotte Payne-Townshend, a wealthy, wellborn Irishwoman. By this time his plays were beginning to be produced. Although Shaw's plays focus on ideas and issues, they are vital and absorbing, enlivened by memorable characterizations, a brilliant command of language, and dazzling wit. In addition to being produced, his early plays were published as *Plays Pleasant and Unpleasant* (2 vol., 1898). The "unpleasant" plays were *Widower's Houses* (1892), on slum landlordism; *The Philanderer* (written 1893, produced 1905); and *Mrs. Warren's Profession* (written 1893, produced 1902), a jibe at the Victorian attitude toward prostitution. The "pleasant" plays were *Arms and the Man* (1894), satirizing romantic attitudes toward love and war; *Candida* (1893); and *You Never Can Tell* (written 1895). In 1897, *The Devil's Disciple,* a play on the American Revolution, was produced with great success in New York City. It was published in the volume *Three Plays for Puritans* (1901) along with *Caesar and Cleopatra* (1899), notable for its realistic, humorous portraits of historical figures, and *Captain Brassbound's Conversion* (1900). During the early 20th cent. Shaw wrote his greatest and most popular plays: *Man and Superman* (1905), in which an idealistic, cerebral man succumbs to marriage (the play contains an explicit articulation of a major Shavian theme—that man is the spiritual creator, whereas woman is the biological "life force" that must always triumph over him); *Major Barbara* (1905), which postulates that poverty is the cause of all evil; *Androcles and the Lion* (1912; a short play), a charming satire of Christianity; and *Pygmalion* (1913), which satirizes the English class system through the story of a cockney girl's transformation into a lady at the hands of a speech professor. The latter has proved to be Shaw's most successful work—as a play, as a motion picture, and as the basis for the musical *My Fair Lady* (1956). Of Shaw's later plays, *Saint Joan* (1923) is the most memorable; it argues that Joan of Arc, a harbinger of Protestantism and nationalism, had to be killed because the world was not yet ready for her. Among Shaw's other plays are *John Bull's Other Island* (1904), *The Doctor's Dilemma* (1906), *Fanny's First Play* (1911), *Heartbreak House* (1921), *Back to Methuselah* (1922), *The Apple Cart* (1928), *Too True to Be Good*

(1932), *The Millionairess* (1936), *In Good King Charles's Golden Days* (1939), and *Bouyant Billions* (1949). Perhaps his most popular nonfiction work is *The Intelligent Woman's Guide to Socialism and Capitalism* (1928). See his collected plays, ed. by D. H. Laurence (6 vol., 1970-73); his letters, particularly those to Ellen Terry (1931), Mrs. Patrick Campbell (1952), Granville Barker (1957), and Molly Tompkins (1960); his collected letters, ed. by D. H. Laurence (2 vol., 1972); his autobiography, reconstructed by Stanley Weintraub (2 vol., 1969-70); semiofficial biographies by Archibald Henderson (3 vol., 1911-56), Frank Harris (1931; called an unauthorized biography), and Hesketh Pearson (1942 and 1950); studies by E. R. Bentley (2d ed. 1967), Louis Crompton (1969), M. M. Morgan (1972), and Maurice Valency (1973).

Shaw, Henry Wheeler: see BILLINGS, JOSH.

Shaw, Leslie Mortier, 1848-1932, U.S. Secretary of the Treasury (1902-7), b. Morristown, Vt. Admitted to the Iowa bar in 1876, he organized (1880) a banking firm that specialized in agricultural credit. His strong defense of the gold standard in the 1896 presidential campaign won for him the Republican nomination for governor of Iowa the following year; he served (1898-1902) two terms. As Treasury Secretary under President Theodore Roosevelt, Shaw used government revenues to help expand the nation's money supply. After 1907, he returned to banking, and engaged in extensive writing and public lecturing. Shaw wrote *Current Issues* (1908) and *Vanishing Landmarks* (1919).

Shaw, Richard Norman, 1831-1912, English architect. Breaking away from contemporary Victorian house designs and returning to the Queen Anne and Georgian styles and to traditional English craftsmanship and use of materials, Shaw became the leader of a revolution in domestic architecture. He designed numerous London and country houses. The economical small houses that he designed in the late 1870s for the Bedford Park housing development had beneficial influence throughout England. His most important work was the New Scotland Yard (1887-90). Shaw wrote *Architectural Sketches from the Continent* (1858). See study by Sir R. T. Blomfield (1940).

Shaw, Robert Gould, 1837-63, Union hero in the American Civil War, b. Boston. An ardent white abolitionist, he was colonel of the 54th Massachusetts Regiment, the first body of Negro troops raised in a free state. He was killed leading the regiment in the attack on Fort Wagner, Charleston, S.C. A sculptured figure of him by Augustus Saint-Gaudens is on Boston Common. See study by Peter Burchard (1970).

Shawano Indians: see SHAWNEE INDIANS.

Shawinigan (shəwĭn'ĭgŭn), city (1971 pop. 27,792), S Que., Canada, on the St. Maurice River. Just north are the falls of the St. Maurice, 150 ft (46 m) high, with a hydroelectric station supplying power for the city's pulp and paper mills and plants that produce aluminum, abrasives, chemicals, cellulose, and textiles. Most of the inhabitants speak French.

shawl, a wrap, usually a square or oblong cloth worn loosely over the shoulders, used in most parts of the world at different periods and known by different names. A direct descendant of the ancient mantle, it enjoyed particular popularity in the Western world in the 19th cent., when it was used for ornamentation rather than warmth. The term is of Persian origin, and the shawl was first made in Persia, India, and central Asia; by 1789 oriental shawls were being imported into Europe. The cashmere shawl was most famous for its beauty and workmanship. Made in the Vale of Kashmir, from the underwool of the Tibetan or Kashmir goat, it was of the finest texture. It is characterized by an intricate cone pattern of large and small floral motifs; the borders are also patterned and are of varying widths. The shawl was often woven in one piece, but more often it was woven in sections and joined together with invisible stitches. Another type of cashmere shawl was embroidered with a design that imitated weaving. At Paisley, Scotland, hand looms turned out (c.1820) beautiful shawls patterned after Indian models. Broché shawls, with strips of different colors joined, were made about the same time, as were the printed shawl and the PLAID or tartan. Elsewhere, shawls were made in many styles of crepe, silk, wool, and lace; they were embroidered, fringed, and printed with cashmere designs. Men adapted the shawl to their outfits after 1840. The Spanish shawl of silk with long knotted fringe and gay silk embroidery, though made in China and fringed in Spain, has become a Spanish trademark. The shawl effect was continued in the fur and feather boas of the turn of the century and is still seen in the saris of Hindu women, in the blanket of the American Indian, and in scarves, stoles, and mufflers.

shawm (shôm), double-reed woodwind instrument used in Europe from the 13th through the 17th cent. The term denotes a family of instruments of different sizes. The shape and tone of the soprano shawm is comparable to that of the OBOE, of which it is a precursor. The shawm was constructed from a single piece of wood that was conically bored.

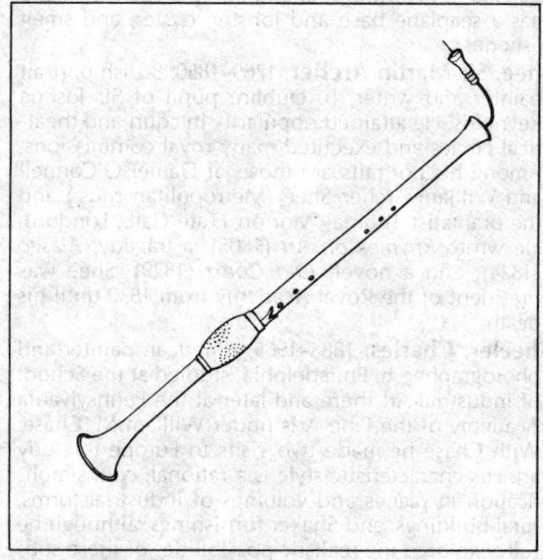

Tenor shawm

Shawnee (**1** shô'nē", shô"nē'; **2** shô"nē'). **1** City (1970 pop. 20,482), Johnson co., NE Kansas, a suburb of Kansas City; founded 1857, inc. 1922. Kitchenware is made in the city, and an animal pharmaceutical laboratory is there. Shawnee was the original site of the Shawnee Indian Methodist Mission (1830). The re-creation of an old Shawnee town is in Bluejacket Park. **2** City (1970 pop. 25,075), seat of Pottawatomie co., central Okla., on the North Canadian River; inc. 1894. Shawnee boomed with the discovery of oil there in 1926 and is now the trade and rail center for a rich farm, dairy, and oil area. Shawnee is the seat of Oklahoma Baptist Univ. and a junior college. Also in the city are an art museum and gallery.

Shawnee Indians or **Shawano Indians** (shô'wənō), North American Indians whose language belongs to the Algonquian branch of the Algonquian-Wakashan linguistic stock (see AMERICAN INDIAN LANGUAGES). Their earliest known home was in the present state of Ohio. In the mid-17th cent. part of the tribe was settled in W South Carolina and part in N Tennessee. These two bodies, divided by the Cherokee, migrated constantly, from South Carolina to S New York, then to W Pennsylvania and into Ohio, where they finally united in the mid-18th cent. They then numbered some 1,500. After their reunion in Ohio the warlike Shawnee participated in almost every war of the Old Northwest. By the Treaty of Greenville (1795) they were obliged to give up their lands in Ohio and move to Indiana. About 1800 the Shawnee Prophet (Tenskwatawa) arose. He and his followers, cooperating with TECUMSEH, established themselves in a village at the mouth of the Tippecanoe River in Indiana. It was this village that William Henry Harrison destroyed in the battle of Tippecanoe. The Shawnee were thereafter moved to Missouri, to Kansas, and finally to Oklahoma. Today they live on reservations in Oklahoma where they number some 2,250. See Henry Harvey, *History of the Shawnee Indians, 1681-1854* (1855, repr. 1970).

Shawnee Prophet, 1775?-1837?, North American Indian of the Shawnee tribe; brother of TECUMSEH. His Indian name was Tenskwatawa. He announced himself as a prophet bearing a revelation from the Indian master of life. The message urged the renunciation of the acquired ways of the whites and the return to Indian modes and customs in all matters. His doctrines were widespread among Indians, and his prestige was enhanced when he foretold a solar eclipse in 1806. His influence gave rise to the plan to confederate all the Indians in opposition to the whites—a plan that inspired the Creek War of 1813. In 1811 he led the Indian forces in the battle of TIPPECANOE. The movement inspired by him provided many recuits for the British in the War of 1812, after which Tenskwatawa retired to Canada with a British pension. He returned to Ohio in 1826 and accompanied his people to Missouri and farther west into Kansas, where he died. See Benjamin Drake, *The Life of Tecumseh and of his Brother the Prophet* (1841, repr. 1969).

Shays, Daniel (shāz), c.1747-1825, American soldier and insurrectionist, b. probably in Hopkinton, Mass. A farmer from W Massachusetts, he fought the British in the American Revolution and was made a captain of the 5th Massachusetts Regiment in 1777. After the war he settled at Pelham, Mass., and became a leader in the revolt of small farmers that resulted from postwar economic depression; the uprising became known as Shays's Rebellion. After the defeat of the insurgents in Feb., 1787, Shays fled to Vermont. He was finally pardoned in June, 1788, and later moved to New York state.

Shays's Rebellion, 1786-87, armed insurrection by farmers in W Massachusetts against the state government. Debt-ridden farmers, struck by the economic depression that followed the American Revolution, petitioned the state senate to issue paper money and to halt foreclosure of mortgages on their property and their own imprisonment for debt as a result of high land taxes. Sentiment was particularly high against the commercial interests who controlled the state senate in Boston, and the lawyers who hastened the farmers' bankruptcy by their exorbitant fees for litigation. When the state senate failed to undertake reform, armed insurgents in the Berkshire Hills and the Connecticut valley, under the leadership of Daniel Shays and others, began (Aug., 1786) forcibly to prevent the county courts from sitting to make judgments for debt. In September they forced the state supreme court at Springfield to adjourn. Early in 1787, Gov. James Bowdoin appointed Gen. Benjamin Lincoln to command 4,400 men against the rebels. Before these troops arrived at Springfield, Gen. William Shepard's soldiers there had repelled an attack on the Federal arsenal. The rebels, losing several men, had dispersed, and Lincoln's troops pursued them to Petersham, where they were finally routed. Shays escaped to Vermont. Most of the leaders were pardoned almost immediately, and Shays was finally pardoned in June, 1788. The rebellion influenced Massachusetts's ratification of the Federal Constitution; it also swept Bowdoin out of the office and achieved some of its legislative goals. See G. R. Minot, *History of the Insurrections in Massachusetts in 1786* (1788, repr. 1971); R. J. Taylor, *Western Massachusetts in the Revolution* (1954, repr. 1967); M. L. Starkey, *A Little Rebellion* (1955).

Shcherbakov: see RYBINSK, USSR.

Sheal (shē'əl), Jew with a foreign wife. Ezra 10.29.

Shealtiel (sheăl'tēĕl), father of Zerubbabel. Ezra 3.2,8; 5.2; Neh. 12.1; Hag. 1; 2. Salathiel: 1 Chron. 3.17; Mat. 1.12; Luke 3.27.

shear: see STRENGTH OF MATERIALS.

Shearer, Hugh, 1923-, prime minister of Jamaica (1967-). Formerly a journalist, he became active in the Jamaican Labour party and in the trade union founded by Alexander Bustamante. He was Jamaican delegate to the United Nations and served as foreign minister under prime ministers Bustamante and Donald Sangster. Following the death of Sangster shortly after his designation as prime minister, Shearer was chosen (April, 1967) as his successor.

Sheariah (shē"ərī'ə), one of the descendants of Saul. 1 Chron. 8.38; 9.44.

Shear-jashub (shē'ər-jā'shəb), son of Isaiah. Isa. 7.3.

shearwater, common name for members of the family Procellariidae, gull-like sea birds related to the PETREL and the albatross and including the fulmar. Shearwaters are found on unfrozen salt waters all over the world, with 35 species in North America. They have tubular nostrils, hooked bills enlarged at the tip, short tails, and long, pointed wings. They feed on marine animals and oily matter on the open seas, coming to shore only to breed. Shearwaters are 15 to 25 in. (37.5-62.5 cm) long, dark above and light below—except for the grayish-bellied sooty shearwater of the Southern Hemisphere. Most common in the North Atlantic are the greater shearwater and Cory's shearwater. The slender-billed shearwater of Australia, *Puffinus tenuirostris,* which migrates over the entire Pacific, is a game bird known also as muttonbird or Tasmanian squab. The two fulmars, one of the North Atlantic and the other, the silver-gray fulmar, of antarctic regions, have thick, stubby yellow bills. Shearwaters are classified in the phylum CHORDATA, subphylum Vertebrata, class Aves, order Procellariiformes, family Procellariidae.

sheatfish: see CATFISH.

Sheba (shē'bə). **1** Descendant of Shem, Eber's grandson. Gen. 10.28; 1 Chron. 1.22. **2** Descendant of Shem, Abraham's grandson. Gen. 25.3. Either may be the eponym of the Sabaeans; and textual confusion may explain the difference of ancestry of **1** and **2.** **3** Rebel against David. 2 Sam. 20.1–22. **4** Place. Joshua 19.2.

Sheba, biblical name of a region of S Arabia. This region, also called Saba, included present-day Yemen and the Hadhramaut, and its inhabitants were called Sabaeans or Sabeans. It is believed that the Sabaeans migrated south at an early date from NW Arabia. The Semitic colonization of Ethiopia was made in the 10th cent. B.C. from Sheba. In the same century the biblical queen of Sheba (called in Muslim tradition Balkis) made her famous visit to Solomon (1 Kings 10). The country of Sheba, situated along the trade route from India to Africa, was known as a region of great wealth. The mention of Saba in Assyrian documents of the 8th cent. B.C. shows that at an early age Sheba was a social and political entity. The culture of Sheba, which was at its height from the 6th to the 5th cent. B.C., is evidenced by the remains of engineering works such as the dam near Marib, the capital of Sheba, and by the many inscriptions found throughout Sheba. The inscriptions are written in a Semitic language (Himyaritic) akin to Ethiopic and Akkadian, in characters derived from Phoenician script. Ethiopia, after a short occupation in the 4th cent. A.D., conquered (c.525) Sheba. Sheba became (572) a Persian province and, with the rise of Muhammad, came under Islamic control and lost its separate identity. See H. St. J. B. Philby, *The Background of Islam* (1947); Wendell Phillips, *Qataban and Sheba* (1955); Richard Le Baron Bowen et al., *Archaeological Discoveries in South Arabia* (1958).

Shebam (shē'băm), town in the pasture land E of the Jordan. Num. 32.3. Shibmah: Num. 32.38. Sibmah: Joshua 13.19; Isa. 16.8,9; Jer. 48.32.

Shebaniah (shĕb"ənī'ə). **1, 2** Two signers of the Covenant. Neh. 9.4; 10.10, 12. **3** Priestly signer of the Covenant. Neh. 10.4; 12.14. Shechaniah: Neh. 12.3. **4** Musician. 1 Chron. 15.24.

Shebarim (shĕb'ərĭm, shēbā'rĭm), place, central Palestine. Joshua 7.5.

Shebeli, Webi (wĕ'bē shābĕl'ē) or **Webi Shibeli** (shēbā'lē), river, c.1,000 mi (1,610 km) long, rising near Mt. Guramba, central Ethiopia, E Africa, and flowing SE into central Somali Republic. It comes within c.20 mi (30 km) of the Indian Ocean near Mogadisho, but turns southwest and parallels the coast for c.200 mi (320 km) before entering a swamp N of the Juba River. The river is usually dry in February and March. The river's lower valley is part of the chief agricultural region of Somali; sugarcane, cotton, and bananas are grown.

Sheber (shē'bər), son of Caleb. 1 Chron. 2.48.

Shebna (shĕb'nə), official of Hezekiah's court denounced by Isaiah. 2 Kings 18; 19; Isa. 22.15; 36; 37.

Sheboygan (shĭboi'gən), city (1970 pop. 48,484), seat of Sheboygan co., E Wis., a port of entry on Lake Michigan at the mouth of the Sheboygan River; inc. 1853. Plastics, stainless-steel products, leather goods, enamelware, furniture, knitted goods, and paper boxes are manufactured there. Dairying and beer brewing are also important industries. The North West Company established a fur-trading post there in 1795. Permanent settlement began c.1835, and Sheboygan grew into a shipping and industrial center. Many of its people are of German descent; a colorful German Days festival is held there every August. A Univ. of Wisconsin extension center and a technical school are in the city. An Indian-mound park featuring a great number of excavated burial mounds is just south of the city. The surrounding area is popular resort country.

Shebuel (shĕb'yo͞oəl, shēbyo͞o'əl) or **Shubael** (sho͞o'bāl, sho͞obā'əl). **1** Descendant of Moses. 1 Chron. 23.16; 24.20; 26.24. **2** Leader of temple singers. 1 Chron. 25.4, 20.

Shecaniah or **Shechaniah** (both: shĕk"ənī'ə). **1, 2** Two chief priests. 1 Chron. 24.11; 2 Chron. 31.15. **3** Father-in-law of Tobiah. Neh. 6.18. **4** See SHEBANIAH **3.** Additional mention of this name is in 1 Chron. 3.21,22; Ezra 8.3,5; 10.2; Neh. 3.29.

Shechem (shĕk'əm, shē'-). **1** Hivite prince. Gen. 34. **2** Manassite chief. Num. 26.31; Joshua 17.2; 1 Chron. 7.19.

Shechem (shē'kəm), town, central Palestine, the modern Tell Balatan, between mounts Gerizim and Ebal, near NABLUS (Jordan). There Jacob lived; his well is still a landmark. Joseph was buried at Shechem. It was the first northern capital, before Samaria. Excavations in the 20th cent. indicate that an early village was there c.3500 B.C. Shechem's greatest period began c.1700 B.C. when the Hyksos rebuilt it. The Canaanites captured it and in the 13th cent. B.C. it fell to the Israelites. Sichem and Sychem are variants of the name. Gen. 12.6; 33.18; 34; Joshua 21.20,21; 24.32; Judges 9.6; 1 Kings 12; Acts 7.16.

Shedeur (shĕd'ēər), father of ELIZUR.

Shediac (shĕd'ēăk), town (1971 pop. 2,203), SE N.B., Canada, on Northumberland Strait. It is a resort and has a seaplane base and lobster, oyster, and smelt fisheries.

Shee, Sir Martin Archer, 1769–1850, British portrait painter and writer, b. Dublin; pupil of Sir Joshua Reynolds. He attained popularity in court and theatrical circles and executed many royal commissions. Among his portraits are those of Daniel O'Connell and William Archer Shee (Metropolitan Mus.) and the dramatist Thomas Morton (Tate Gall., London). He wrote *Rhymes on Art* (1805); a tragedy, *Alasco* (1824); and a novel, *Old Court* (1829). Shee was president of the Royal Academy from 1830 until his death.

Sheeler, Charles, 1883–1965, American painter and photographer, b. Philadelphia, studied at the School of Industrial Art there and later at the Pennsylvania Academy of the Fine Arts under William M. Chase. With Chase he made two visits to Europe to study art. His characteristic style is a rational, cool simplification in planes and volumes of industrial forms, rural buildings, and Shaker furnishings, although he fully explored the realistic possibilities of these subjects as well. His photographs exhibit a similar simplification and impersonality. *Rolling Power* (Smith College) exemplifies Sheeler's most realistic painting style; *Midwest, 1954* (Walker Art Center, Minneapolis) is an example of his later, more abstract manner. See biography by Constance Rourke (1938, repr. 1969).

Sheen, Fulton John, 1895–, American Roman Catholic clergyman, b. El Paso, Ill., grad. St. Viator College, Bourbonnais, Ill. (B.A., 1917; M.A., 1919). After receiving (1920) his baccalaureates in sacred theology and canon law at the Catholic Univ. of America, he studied at the Univ. of Louvain (Ph.D., 1923) in Belgium and at the Univ. of Rome (D.D., 1924). Ordained a priest in 1919, he joined the faculty of Catholic Univ. in 1926. He was appointed a papal chamberlain in 1934 and a domestic prelate in 1935. An outstanding orator, he won an increasingly large radio audience after he began broadcasting in 1930. In 1950 he was appointed national director of the Society for the Propagation of the Faith, and in 1951 he was consecrated titular bishop of Caesariana and auxiliary bishop of New York. He became bishop of Rochester, N.Y., in 1966 and on leaving (1969) that post he was named titular archbishop of Newport, England. Bishop Sheen is known for his strong stands on many issues, including his attacks on Communism, Freudianism, and birth control and his support of compulsory religious exercises in schools. He is the author of numerous books, including *God and Intelligence in Modern Philosophy* (1925), *The Cross and the Crisis* (1938), *Preface to Religion* (1946), *Communism and the Conscience of the West* (1948), *Philosophy of Religion* (1948), *Peace of Soul* (1949), *Life Is Worth Living* (5 vol., 1953–57), *Life of Christ* (1958), *The Power of Love* (1965), *Guide to Contentment* (1967), and *Children and Parents* (1970).

sheep, common name for many species of wild and domesticated ruminant mammals of the genus *Ovis* of the Bovidae, or cattle, family. The male is called a ram (if castrated it is a wether), the female is called a ewe, and their offspring is a lamb. Wild sheep, found in mountainous parts of Asia, North America, and the Mediterranean region, are agile rock climbers with large, spiraling horns. They do not bear wool. Among those species are the Asian argali, the Barbary sheep, or aoudad, of North Africa, and the North American BIGHORN, or Rocky Mountain sheep, found from Alaska to Mexico. Sheep were first domesticated c.7,000 years ago, and the first use of their fleeces for wool is dated at c.4000 B.C. Descendants of Roman flocks figured in the evolution of the Merino type in Spain. The present-day breeds of domesticated sheep—which vary greatly because they were developed for different purposes and environments—are all thought to be derived chiefly from the wild mouflon of Sardinia and Corsica and from the urial of Asia. Sheep are bred for their WOOL, meat (MUTTON or lamb, according to age), skins, and, in certain parts of Europe and the Middle East, their milk, from which cheese is made. They are found mostly in temperate climates and thrive on roughages. Most sheep mate in the fall, and the lambs, born five months later, are called spring lambs. Among the important breeds are the COLUMBIA, COTSWOLD, DORSET, HAMPSHIRE, KARAKUL, LEICESTER, LINCOLN, MERINO, OXFORD, RAMBOUILLET, SHROPSHIRE, SOUTHDOWN, and SUFFOLK sheep. Sheep are classified in the phylum CHORDATA, subphylum Vertebrata, class Mammalia, order Artiodactyla, family Bovidae. See M. E. Ensminger, *Sheep and Wool Science* (4th ed. 1970); N. D. May, *The Anatomy of the Sheep* (3d ed. 1970); publications of the U.S. Dept. of Agriculture.

sheepdog: see WORKING DOG.

sheep laurel: see MOUNTAIN LAUREL.

Sheepshead Bay, residential area in S Brooklyn borough of New York City, SE N.Y., on Sheepshead Bay. It was once famous for its horse and automobile races and as a resort center. The bay is an anchorage for commercial and pleasure fishing craft. A number of restaurants specialize in sea food.

Sheerness, England: see QUEENSBOROUGH-IN-SHEPPEY.

Sheffield, county borough (1971 pop. 519,703), West Riding of Yorkshire, N England, at the confluence of the Don River and four tributaries. Sheffield is one of the leading industrial cities of England. It has been a center of cutlery manufacture since the 14th cent. The Cutlers' Company, the governing body of cutlery manufacturers, was founded there in 1624. Silver and electroplate goods, tools, and heavy steel goods, including plates for artillery and rails, are also made. The first Bessemer steel works were built in Sheffield in 1859. In Weston Park are an observatory, City Museum, and the famous Mappin Art Gallery. Graves Art Gallery is also notable. Educational institutions include the Univ. of Sheffield (1905) and Sheffield Polytechnic. In 1974, Sheffield became part of the new metropolitan county of South Yorkshire.

Sheffield, industrial city (1970 pop. 13,115), Colbert co., NW Ala., on the Tennessee River near Muscle Shoals, in an iron and coal area; inc. 1885. It is a railroad center and has plants that make agricultural chemicals, aluminum, stoves, and lingerie. Nearby points of interest include Wilson Dam (1925), with one of the world's highest single-lift locks, and the home of Helen Keller in Tuscumbia.

Sheffield, University of, at Sheffield, England; founded 1905. It has faculties of arts, pure science, medicine, law, engineering, materials, social sciences, architectural studies, and educational studies; a school of librarianship and information science; and an institute of education.

Sheffield plate, metalware of copper, silver-plated by fusion, originated at Sheffield, England. This process of plating was discovered c.1742 by a Sheffield cutler, Thomas Boulsover, who found while doing repair work on silver and copper that they fused at high temperature and could be hammered and shaped as one metal. He used his discovery to make buttons and buckles, but an apprentice, Joseph Hancock, grasped the broader application and began the production of tableware and other domestic articles that won wide popularity as substitutes for the more expensive solid silver. The manufacture spread not only in England, where Birmingham became an active center of production, but to the Netherlands, Russia, and Poland, where English methods and patterns were adopted. Similar ware was produced in France by a different process. Sheffield plate followed, in general, the contemporary styles in silver, but some original designs were used and in the 19th cent. characteristic flat-chased pieces developed. Early ware was plated on one side only, but c.1765 a method for plating both sides was introduced. Edges were at first soldered, then concealed with plated wire and finally with applied silver edges. Additional silver was embedded in areas to be engraved. German silver, an alloy of nickel, zinc, and copper, came into common use c.1835 and was preferred to copper as a base, since it showed less where the plating wore off. Special hallmarks were used after 1784. Sheffield plate was superseded c.1840 by the cheaper electroplating method.

Shehariah (shē"hərī'ə), descendant of Benjamin. 1 Chron. 8.26.

Sheherazade: see THOUSAND AND ONE NIGHTS.

Shehu, Mehmet (mĕmĕt' shĕ'ho͞o), 1913–, Albanian political leader, premier (1954–). A member of the Communist party, he was active in the anti-Fascist resistance in Albania during World War II. In 1944 he became a member of the Albanian provisional government and, following military study in Moscow, was appointed (1946) chief of staff of the Albanian army. He later became minister of the interior, head of the secret police, and deputy premier. In 1954 he replaced Enver Hoxha as chairman of the council of ministers, or premier. He was one of the architects of the Sino-Albanian alliance that triggered Albania's formal break with the Soviet Union in Dec., 1961.

Sheki (shĕk'ē), city (1970 pop. 43,000), S European USSR, in the Azerbaijan Republic, on the southern slope of the Caucasus. It is a major center of silk production in a district that grows fruit and rice. Until its annexation (1805) by Russia it was the capital of a khanate under Persian sovereignty. It was formerly known as Nukha.

Shekinah (shēkī'nə) [Heb.,=dwelling, presence], term used in the Targum (Aramaic translation of the Old Testament) and elsewhere to indicate the manifestation of the presence of God among men. Whenever the Hebrew text speaks of the presence of God in a way that implies certain human limitations, the Targum paraphrases by substituting the word *Shekinah* for the word *God* (e.g., "And I will cause my Shekinah to dwell," in the Targum Onkelos). Although the Shekinah is rarely intended by the rabbis in the Talmud and Midrash as an intermediary between God and man, the word is sometimes used in such a manner that it cannot be identical with God, e.g., "God allows his Shekinah to rest." The medieval Jewish philosophers, however, wishing to avoid the problems of anthropomorphic interpretation of this concept, posited a separate existence for the Shekinah, which played a minor role at best in their systems. In the cabala and other mystical works of the later medieval and modern periods, the Shekinah is often treated as the consort of God who can only be reunited with God through man's fulfillment of all the divine commandments, which would likewise signal the messianic age. See Solomon Schechter, *Aspects of Rabbinic Theology* (1909, repr. 1961); Gershom Scholem, *Major Trends in Jewish Mysticism* (1946, repr. 1961); Raphael Patai, *The Hebrew Goddess* (1967).

Shekki: see CHUNG-SHAN, China.

Sheksna (shĭksnä'), river, c.100 mi (160 km) long flowing S between Lake Beloye and the Rybinsk Reservoir, NW European USSR. Cherepovets is on the river. The Sheksna forms a link in the VOLGA-BALTIC WATERWAY.

Shelah (shē'lə). **1** Son of Judah and ancestor of the Shelanites. Gen. 38.5; 46.12; 1 Chron. 2.3; 4.21; Num. 26.20. This tribe is the same as the Shilonites of 1 Chron. 9.5 and as the Shiloni of Neh. 11.5. **2** Same as SALAH.

Shelburne, William Petty Fitzmaurice, 2d **earl of,** 1737–1805, British statesman. He served briefly (1763) as president of the Board of Trade in George Grenville's cabinet but then became a supporter of William Pitt, later earl of Chatham. Appointed (1766) secretary of state in Chatham's cabinet, he adopted a policy of conciliation toward the North American colonies, but he was supported neither by his colleagues nor George III, and he resigned in 1768. In 1782 he became secretary of state again under Lord Rockingham and succeeded as head of the ministry on Rockingham's death. Shelburne concluded the Treaty of Paris in 1783, granting independence to the new United States, but he was driven from office (1783) by the coalition of Charles James Fox and Lord North. One of the most consistently liberal statesmen of his day, he was also one of the most consistently unpopular. He was created marquess of Lansdowne in 1784. The JUNIUS letters have been attributed to him.

Shelby, Isaac, 1750–1826, American frontiersman, b. Washington co. (then part of Frederick co.), Md. Around 1773 he settled in the Holston River country in what is now E Tennessee. In the American Revolution he was one of the frontier leaders who defeated the British at Kings Mt. (1780) in the CAROLINA CAMPAIGN. Shelby moved to Kentucky in 1783, helped secure its separation from Virginia, and was the first governor (1792–96) of the new state. During his second term (1812–16) he organized and commanded a body of volunteers under Gen. William Henry Harrison at the battle of the Thames River (Oct., 1813) in S Ontario, one of the few American land victories in the War of 1812. In 1818, with Andrew Jackson, he was a member of the special commission that purchased the remaining lands of the Chickasaw Indians in Kentucky and Tennessee.

Shelby, Joseph Orville, 1830–97, Confederate cavalry commander in the American Civil War, b. Lexington, Ky. He made a considerable fortune in rope manufacturing in Kentucky and Missouri. While in Missouri he participated in the Kansas-Missouri border war on the proslavery side. When the Civil War broke out he organized a cavalry brigade in Missouri. He participated in numerous raids in the Southwest, was wounded at Helena, Ark. (July, 1863), but joined Sterling Price in his invasion of Missouri in 1864. Shelby and his men had sworn never to surrender; after Appomattox his forces crossed the Rio Grande into Mexico and offered their services to the French puppet ruler, Emperor Maximilian. Shelby ultimately returned to the United States. From 1893 to 1897 he served as U.S. marshal for the Western District of Missouri. See biography by Daniel O'Flaherty (1954).

Shelby, city (1970 pop. 16,328), seat of Cleveland co., W N.C., in a rich piedmont farming (mostly cotton) area; inc. 1843. Natural and synthetic textiles are made. A junior college is in nearby Boiling Springs, and to the south (in South Carolina) is Kings Mountain National Military Park, site of a battle fought on Oct. 7, 1780, between a party of backwoodsmen under Isaac Shelby, John Sevier, and William Campbell and a British and Tory force led by Patrick Ferguson (see CAROLINA CAMPAIGN).

Shelbyville. 1 City (1970 pop. 15,094), seat of Shelby co., central Ind., in a rich corn and livestock area; platted 1822, inc. as a city 1860. It is a farm-trade and manufacturing center. **2** City (1970 pop. 12,262), seat of Bedford co., central Tenn., on the Duck River, in a farm and timber area; inc. 1819. Pencils, erasers, and pencil parts are its leading manufactures. The region is noted for the breeding of the Tennessee Walking Horse. Shelbyville was one of the country's early planned cities; many of its 19th-century buildings remain. A state vocational technical school is there.

Sheldon, Charles Monroe, 1857–1946, American Congregational clergyman and novelist, b. Wellsville, N.Y. He filled a long pastorate (1889–1919) at Topeka, Kansas, and edited the *Christian Herald* from 1920 to 1925. His religious novels grew out of his Sunday evening services. Of them, *In His Steps* (1896) was world famous. He was a well-known lecturer and an extreme pacifist. See Gene DeGruson, *Kansas Authors of Best Sellers* (1970).

Sheldon, Edward Austin, 1823–97, American educator, b. Wyoming co., N.Y., studied at Hamilton College. After illness forced him to cut short his own education, he held a variety of positions in the education field, including superintendent of public schools in Syracuse, N.Y. From 1862 until his death Sheldon served as principal of the Oswego Primary Teachers' Training School (from 1866, the Oswego State Normal and Training School), which was the first urban teacher training school in the United States. His curriculum, based on the theories of Johann PESTALOZZI, was one of the first to employ practice teaching. His system of teacher training served as a model for other normal schools in New York state. Sheldon's writings include several spelling books as well as a series of readers. See his autobiography (1911).

Sheldon, Gilbert, 1598–1677, English divine, archbishop of Canterbury. He attended Charles I at Oxford and Newmarket and in the Isle of Wight, remaining thereafter in retirement until the Restoration, when he became (1660) bishop of London and later (1663) archbishop of Canterbury. Sheldon was an influential adviser to Charles II. While chancellor of Oxford he built (1699) the Sheldonian Theatre at his own expense.

Shelekhov, Grigori Ivanovich (grĭgô'rē ēvä'nəvĭch shĕ'lyĭkhəf), 1747–95, Russian fur trader in North America, b. Rylsk, Ukraine. He had built up a large fur business in Siberia when profitable trading ventures in the Aleutian Islands led to his resolve to open a new fur-trading area. In 1783–84 he led a company to Kodiak Island and at Three Saints Bay founded the first permanent settlement in Alaska. From there the mainland was explored, and other fur-trade centers were established. In 1786, Shelekhov set out for Russia, unsuccessfully seeking a grant to his company of monopoly of the fur trade. To manage his interests in Alaska he dispatched (1790) Aleksandr Baranov, who later dominated affairs there. Shelekhov's company was the nucleus for the noted Russian American Company, which was formed several years after his death. His *Journal of the Voyages . . . to the Coast of America in 1783–87* was published in London in 1795. Shelikof Strait is named for him.

Shelemiah (shĕl"əmī'ə). **1** Father of Hananiah. Neh. 3.30. **2** Treasurer. Neh. 13.13. **3** Father of Irijah. Jer. 37.13. **4** See MESHELEMIAH. These identifications are not all certain; other appearances of the name may refer to some of the same persons. Ezra 10.39,41; Jer. 36.14,26; 37.3.

Sheleph (shē'lĕf), ancestor of a tribe of S Arabia. Gen. 10.26; 1 Chron. 1.20.

Shelepin, Aleksandr (əlyĭksän'dər shĕlĕ'pĭn), 1918–, political leader in the USSR. Active in the Young Communist League from the early 1940s, he became its head in 1952. In the same year he became a member of the Communist party central committee. A supporter of Premier Nikita Khrushchev, Shelepin was made head of the state security committee (1958–61), the Soviet secret police. From 1962 to 1965 he was deputy chairman of the council of ministers. An astute politician, he participated in Khrushchev's ouster in 1964; the same year he became a member of the presidium (later renamed the politburo). In 1967 he was appointed head of the central council of trade unions.

Shelesh (shē'lĕsh), Asher's descendant. 1 Chron. 7.35.

shell, in zoology, hard outer covering secreted by an animal for protection. It is also called the test, crust, or carapace. The term usually refers to the calcareous shells of the many species of mollusk but is also applied to the exoskeleton of the crab and other crustaceans, to the bony covering of the turtle, and to the hard exterior of a bird's egg. Man has made use of mollusk shells since early times as receptacles for food and water, as currency (see SHELL MONEY), and for ornament. The scientific study of shells is called conchology. See J. E. Rogers, *The Shell Book* (1951); P. A. Morris, *A Field Guide to the Shells* (of the Atlantic coast, 1951; the Pacific, 1952); R. T. Abbott, *Sea Shells of the World* (1962) and *Kingdom of the Seashell* (1972).

shellac, solution of LAC in alcohol or acetone. In commerce the name is applied to the resinous substance (lac) itself rather than to the solution. It ranges in color from orange to light yellow depending upon the extent to which it has been purified; the darker shellacs are the less pure. When bleached it is known as white shellac. Applied to surfaces such as wood and plaster, the solution forms a hard coating upon evaporation of the solvent. Shellac is widely used as a spirit VARNISH, as a protective covering for drawings and plaster casts, for stiffening in the manufacture of felt hats, in making sealing wax, and in electrical insulation.

Shelley, Mary Wollstonecraft, 1797–1851, English author; daughter of William Godwin and Mary Wollstonecraft. In 1814 she fell in love with the poet Percy Bysshe Shelley, accompanied him abroad, and after the death of his first wife in 1816 was married to him. Her most notable contribution to literature is her novel of terror, *Frankenstein,* published in 1818. It is the story of a German student who learns the secret of infusing life into inanimate matter and creates a monster that ultimately destroys him. Included among her other novels are *The Last Man* (1826) and the partly autobiographical *Lodore* (1835). After Shelley's death in 1822, Mary devoted herself to caring for her aged father and educating her only surviving child, Percy Florence Shelley. In 1839–40 she edited her husband's works. See her journal (ed. by F. L. Jones, 1947); her letters (ed. by Muriel Spark and Derek Stamford, 1953); biography by Muriel Spark (1951); studies by Elizabeth Nitchie (1953) and W. A. Walling (1972).

Shelley, Percy Bysshe (bĭsh), 1792–1822, English poet, b. Horsham, Sussex. He is ranked as one of the great English poets of the romantic period. The son of a prosperous squire, he entered Oxford in 1810, where readings in philosophy led him toward a study of the empiricists and the modern skeptics, notably William GODWIN. In 1811 he and his friend Thomas Jefferson HOGG published their pamphlet, *The Necessity of Atheism,* which resulted in their immediate expulsion from the university. The same year Shelley eloped with 16-year-old Harriet Westbrook, by whom he eventually had two children, Ianthe and Charles. Supported reluctantly by their fathers, the young couple traveled through Great Britain. Shelley's life continued to be dominated by his desire for social and political reform, and he was constantly publishing pamphlets. His first important poem, *Queen Mab,* privately printed in 1813, set forth a radical system of curing social ills by advocating the destruction of various established institutions. In 1814, Shelley left England for France with Mary Godwin, the daughter of William Godwin. During their first year together they were plagued by social ostracism and financial difficulties. However, in 1815, Shelley's grandfather died and left him an annual income. *Laon and Cynthna* appeared in 1817 but was withdrawn and reissued the following year as *The Revolt of Islam;* it is a long poem in Spenserian stanzas that tells of a revolution and illustrates the growth of the human mind aspiring toward perfection. After Harriet's suicide in 1816, Shelley and Mary officially married. In 1817, Harriet's parents obtained a decree from the lord chancellor stating that Shelley was unfit to have custody of his children.

The following year Shelley and Mary left England and settled in Italy. By this time their household consisted of their own three children and Mary's half-sister Claire Claremont and her daughter Allegra (whose father was Lord Byron). Shelley composed the great body of his poetry in Italy. *The Cenci*, a tragedy in verse exploring moral deformity, was published in 1819, followed by his masterpiece, *Prometheus Unbound* (1820). In this lyrical drama Shelley poured forth all his passions and beliefs, which were modeled after the ideas of Plato. *Epipsychidion* (1821) is a poem addressed to Emilia Viviani, a young woman whom Shelley met in Pisa and with whom he developed a brief but close friendship. His great elegy, *Adonais* (1821), written in memory of Keats, asserts the immortality of beauty. *Hellas* (1822), a lyrical drama, was inspired by the Greek struggle for independence. His other poems include *Alastor* (1816) and the shorter poems "Ode to the West Wind," "To a Skylark," "Ozymandias," "The Indian Serenade," and "When the Lamp Is Shattered." On July 8, 1822, Shelley was drowned while sailing in the Bay of Spezia, near Lerici. Most of his poetry reveals his philosophy, a combination of belief in the power of human love and reason, and faith in the perfectibility and ultimate progress of man. His lyric poems are superb in their beauty, grandeur, and mastery of language. Although Matthew Arnold labeled him an "ineffectual angel," 20th-century critics have taken Shelley seriously, recognizing his wit, his gifts as a satirist, and his influence as a social and political thinker. See his complete poetical works, ed. by Neville Rogers (4 vol., 1973–); letters, ed. by F. L. Jones (2 vol., 1964); *Shelley and his Circle*, ed. by K. N. Cameron (4 vol., 1961–70); biographies by E. C. Blunden (rev. ed. 1965), J. O. Fuller (1969), and N. I. White (2 vol., 1940; repr. 1972); studies by Neville Rogers (2d ed. 1967), Harold Bloom (2d ed. 1969), Desmond King-Hele (2d ed. 1971), E. R. Wasserman (1971), and K. N. Cameron (1974). See also biography of Mary Shelley by N. B. Gerson (1973).

shellfish, popular name for certain edible mollusks (see MOLLUSCA), e.g., oysters, clams, and scallops, and for certain edible CRUSTACEANS, e.g., crabs, lobsters, and shrimps. All are aquatic invertebrates with shells; they are not fish.

shell money, medium of exchange consisting of shells, the most widely distributed type of primitive currency. Shells are particularly useful as money because they may be strung in long strips of proportionate value or they may be used to provide a single unit value in exchange. Relative scarcity of the type of shell used or the way the shell is fashioned often determines its value. COWRIE shells have been the most common shell media and are probably the oldest in usage as money. WAMPUM was usually fashioned from thick-shelled clams; dentalia, or tooth shells, were popular with the Indians of the west coast of North America. Mother-of-pearl and tortoise shell are said to have been used as money in ancient China. Oceanic peoples in particular use a variety of shells in trade. As a rule the uses of shell money are more restricted than those of money in contemporary civilizations, i.e., shells can be exchanged only for specified items.

shell mound, in archaeology, a mound consisting largely of the shells of edible mollusks. It is a kind of KITCHEN MIDDEN found in various parts of the world.

Shelomi (shĕl'ōmī, shēlō'mī), father of Ahihud, a prince of Asher. Num. 34.27.

Shelomith (shĕl'ōmĭth, shēlō'-) or **Shelomoth** (-mŏth). **1** Woman whose son was stoned for blasphemy. Lev. 24.10–16. **2** Zerubbabel's daughter. 1 Chron. 3.19. **3** Kohathite Levitical family. 1 Chron. 23.18; 24.22; 26.25,26,28. **4** Gershonite Levite. 1 Chron. 23.9. **5** Family that returned from Exile. Ezra 8.10.

Shelter Island (1970 pop. 1,644), 7 mi (11.2 km) long and 6 mi (9.7 km) wide, between the two peninsulas of E Long Island, SE N.Y. Settled in the 17th cent. by English colonists, the island has been a summer resort since the 1870s. Its much-indented coast provides harbors for small boats.

Shelton, city (1970 pop. 27,165), Fairfield co., SW Conn., on the Housatonic River opposite Derby; settled 1697, set off from Stratford 1789, inc. as a city 1915. Textiles, wire, pins and fasteners, and furniture are among the city's manufactures. A state park is there.

Shelumiel (shēlōō'mĭəl), Simeonite prince at the time of the Exodus. Num. 1.6; 2.12; 7.36,41; 10.19.

Shem, eldest son of Noah and eponym of the Semites. Gen. 5.32; 7.13; 9.25–27; 11.10. Sem: Luke 3.36.

Shema (shē'mə). **1** Reubenite. 1 Chron. 5.8. Shemaiah: 1 Chron. 5.4. **2** ADAIAH **3.** **3** Son of Hebron. 1 Chron. 2.43,44. **4** Companion of Ezra. Neh. 8.4. **5** Unidentified town, S Palestine. Joshua 15.26.

Shemaah (shēmā'ə), father of two warriors. 1 Chron. 12.3.

Shemaiah (shĕm"āī'ə). **1** Prophet at the time of Rehoboam. 1 Kings 12.22–24; 2 Chron. 11.2–4; 12.5–7. **2** False prophet during the Captivity. Jer. 29.24–32. **3** False prophet hired to discredit Nehemiah. Neh. 6.10. **4** Descendant of Zerubbabel. 1 Chron. 3.22. **5** Scribe. 1 Chron. 24.6. **6** Korahite. 1 Chron. 26.4,6,7. **7** Levite in the time of Jehoshaphat. 2 Chron. 17.8. **8, 9** Levites in the time of Hezekiah. 2 Chron. 29.14; 31.15. **10, 11** Chief Levites. 1 Chron. 15.8,11; 2 Chron. 35.9. **12, 13** Chief men in the Exile. Ezra 8.13,16. **14, 15, 16, 17** Men present at the dedication of the wall. Neh. 12.34,35,36,42. **18** Father of URIJAH **2.** **19** Father of DELAIAH **4.** **20** Merarite Levite. 1 Chron. 9.14; Neh. 11.15. **21** A sealer of the Covenant. Neh. 10.8; 12.6,18. **22** Same as SHAMMUA **3.** **23, 24** Men who had foreign wives. Ezra 10.21,31. **25** Repairer of the wall. Neh. 3.29. **26** Simeonite. 1 Chron. 4.37. **27** Same as SHEMA **1.**

Shemakha (shĕməkhä'), city (1970 pop. 18,000), SE European USSR, in Azerbaijan, at the foot of the Caucasus. Its chief product is wine. Known since ancient times, Shemakha was an important silk center in the 16th cent., trading especially with Venice. It was the capital of the khanate of Shirwan until the 17th cent., and it passed to Russia in 1805. Its importance as a silk center declined after an earthquake in 1902. The city has ruins of the tomb of the Shirwan shahs.

Shemariah (shĕm"ərī'ə). **1** Benjamite warrior of David. 1 Chron. 12.5. **2, 3** Men who married foreigners. Ezra 10.32,41.

Shemeber (shĕm'əbər, shēmē'bər), king of Zeboiim. Gen. 14.2.

Shemer (shē'mər). **1** Owner and eponym of the hill of Samaria. 1 Kings 16.24. **2** Founder of a clan in the tribe of Asher. 1 Chron. 7.34. Shamer: 1 Chron. 7.34. Shomer: 1 Chron. 7.32.

Shemida or **Shemidah** (shēmī'də), Gileadite. Num. 26.32; Joshua 17.2; 1 Chron. 7.19.

Sheminith (shĕm'ĭnĭth): see ALAMOTH.

Shemiramoth (shēmĭr'əmŏth"). **1** Temple musician. 1 Chron. 15.18,20; 16.5. **2** Teacher of the Law. 2 Chron. 17.8.

Shemuel (shēmyōō'əl). **1** One who helped apportion Canaan. Num. 34.20. **2** Son of TOLA **1.**

Shen, place, perhaps close to Bethel, near which Samuel set up the stone Ebenezer. 1 Sam. 7.12.

Shenandoah, river: see SHENANDOAH VALLEY.

Shenandoah: see CONFEDERATE CRUISERS.

Shenandoah National Park, 193,537 acres (78,324 hectares), N Va., extending 80 mi (129 km) along the crest of the Blue Ridge; est. 1935. Skyline Drive, a north-south highway, extends for 105 mi (169 km) through the park. The Blue Ridge, Shenandoah valley, Massanutten Mt., and Allegheny mts. can be viewed from 75 overlooks on the drive. Elevations in the park range from 595 ft (181 m) at Front Royal to 4,049 ft (1,234 m) at the top of Hawksbill Mt. Heavily forested, the park contains a series of ridges and valleys, hollows, small hills, numerous streams, waterfalls, and trout-filled pools. The APPALACHIAN TRAIL follows the crest.

Shenandoah valley, part of the Great Appalachian Valley, c.150 mi (240 km) long, N Va., located between the Blue Ridge and the Allegheny mts. The valley is divided into two parts by Massanutten Mt., a ridge c.45 mi (70 km) long and c.3,000 ft (915 m) high. The Shenandoah River, c.150 mi (240 km) long, rises in two forks on either side of the ridge, uniting near Front Royal, Va., and flowing northeast to enter the Potomac at Harpers Ferry, W.Va. The Shenandoah valley was first explored in the early 1700s; the first white settlement was established in 1730. The valley was an important corridor in the westward pioneer movement, and it became a rich agricultural area with fertile farm land, orchards, and pastures. During the Civil War, the valley was the ideal avenue of approach for the Southern invasion of the North. Having strong Southern leanings, it served as one of the Confederates' principal storehouses. Shenandoah figured in the brilliant "valley campaign" of T. J. (Stonewall) JACKSON in 1862; Lee retreated through the valley after being checked in the Antietam campaign (1862) and the Gettysburg campaign (1863). The first conspicuous Union success in the Shenandoah valley was achieved by David Hunter in 1864, but he was defeated by J. A. Early. Early was driven from the valley by P. H. Sheridan, who then laid waste to the countryside. By early 1865, the valley was completely lost to the South. The principal cities are Winchester, Front Royal, Staunton, and Waynesboro. There are many recreational areas, including SHENANDOAH NATIONAL PARK, in the surrounding uplands.

Shenazar (shēnā'zər), descendant of Josiah. 1 Chron. 3.18. See SHESHBAZZAR.

Shen Chou (shĕn jō), 1427–1509, Chinese painter of the Ming dynasty. He lived withdrawn from worldly pursuits and is by tradition called the founder of the Wu school, a group of leading *literati* artists who lived in the region around Wuhsien. Although he faithfully copied the works of the Yüan dynasty masters, he developed his own distinctive style, creating hazy, atmospheric effects with light, transparent washes. Two of his album leaf landscapes are in the Nelson-Atkins Museum of Art, Kansas City, Mo.

sheng, Chinese musical instrument consisting of a gourd into which is fastened a set of graduated tubes with free reeds. These are set in motion by the player's breath, blown through a mouthpiece. Each

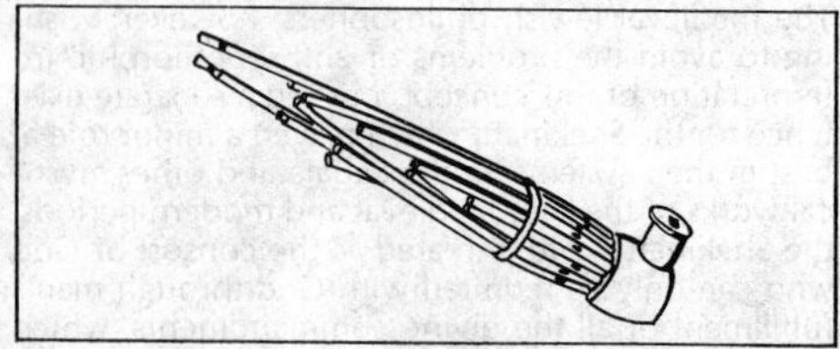

Sheng

tube has a hole that must be stopped in order to sound. The sheng was introduced into Europe in the 18th cent. and is thought to have been the predecessor of other free-reed instruments, such as the reed organ, accordion, and concertina. The spelling *cheng* is sometimes used.

Shenir (shē'nər), variant of SENIR.

Shensi (shĕn'sē'), Mandarin *Shan-hsi* [west of the mountain passes], province (1968 est. pop. 21,000,000), c.76,000 sq mi (196,840 sq km), N central China. HSI-AN is the capital. From north to south Shensi has four main regions—the loess plateau, fertile but dry; the Wei River valley, rich agriculturally and the center of population; the Tsingling divide, the highest range of the province; and the upper Han River valley. The valleys of the Wei and Han rivers and newly irrigated areas in the northwest are the main farming regions. Extensive reforestation, terracing, and irrigation have reclaimed much eroded land and increased agricultural output. Wheat, millet, cotton, soybeans, and corn are the chief crops. Rice, tea, and tung oil are produced in the south, and fruit orchards are cultivated in the upland areas. Livestock (notably sheep) are raised, and lumbering is important. Shensi has rich coal and iron deposits. Oil is extracted at Yen-ch'ang, just E of Yen-an, and salt is obtained from lakes. China's main east-west railroad traverses Shensi through the Wei valley. A branch line links the west with Ch'eng-tu in Szechwan prov. A highway ties the Wei valley to the northwest. Important population centers are Hsi-an, PAO-CHI, Tung-ch'uan, Hsien-yang, and YEN-AN. Since the 1960s, Shensi has developed industrially; cotton, once sent to Shanghai for processing, is spun and woven in the province. Shensi, especially the Wei River valley, was one of the early major political and cultural centers of N China. The founders of the Chou and T'ang dynasties built their power there, and the Manchus gave the province its present boundaries. There was a widespread Muslim rebellion in Shensi in the 1860s. In 1935 the Communist army came to Shensi on its "long march," and from 1935 until the assumption of power in 1949, Shensi was the seat of the Chinese Communists.

Shenstone, William, 1714–63, English poet and landscape gardener. *The Schoolmistress* (1742), his best-known poem, was written in imitation of Spenser. His home, "Leasowes," in Shropshire, was a notable example of 18th-century landscaping. See his life and works, ed. by George Gilfillan (1854, repr. 1968).

Shen-yang (shŭn-yäng), formerly **Mukden** (mōōk'dŭn), city (1970 est. pop. 3,750,000), capital of Liaoning prov., NE China, on the Hun River. It is China's fourth largest city and the leading manufacturing hub in a highly industrialized area. Manufactures include heavy machinery, aircraft, tractors, automotive parts, cables, machine tools (Shen-yang has one of the largest machine-tool plants in China), transformers, textiles, chemicals, paper products, medicines, and cement. The city is connected by rail with all the major cities of Liaoning prov. and with Peking and North Korea. Farm communes have recently been established; the introduction of rice, improved agricultural techniques, and the intensive cultivation of wheat, corn, soybeans, and vegetables have made Shen-yang virtually self-sufficient in food, despite a short growing season. During the Russo-Japanese War (1904–5), Shen-yang was an important military objective, which fell to the Japanese on March 10, 1905, after a 15-day battle. Following the establishment of the Chinese republic (1912), Shen-yang was the headquarters of several war lords, notably Chang Tso-lin, who was assassinated outside the city in 1928. There, in Sept., 1931, occurred the Mukden or Manchurian Incident, when the Japanese army used an explosion on the railroad N of Shen-yang as a pretext for occupying the city and beginning the occupation of all Manchuria. After 1931 the Japanese developed the city as an industrial center. Shen-yang fell to the Communists on Nov. 1, 1948, after a 10-month siege during which time thousands starved; the defending Nationalist force was annihilated during a breakout attempt. The city has three sections—the old Chinese city, which is the administrative center; the new city, developed by the Japanese around the railroad; and a residential section beyond the railroad. The area doubled in population in the 1950s and 1960s, with a striking increase in both city and suburban population. Shen-yang is the seat of Liaoning Univ., Northeastern China Technical Univ., a medical college, a conservatory of music, and numerous other specialized institutes.

Sheol: see HELL.

Shepard, Alan Bartlett, Jr., 1923–, American astronaut, b. East Derry, N.H., grad. Annapolis, 1944. On May 5, 1961, under the U.S. space program Project Mercury, he became the first American to be launched into space. His flight was a suborbital trip of 302 mi (486 km) down the Atlantic missile range. He reached a height of 115 mi (185 km) and performed several maneuvers of his capsule, *Freedom 7*, during the 15-min flight. In 1971 he commanded the Apollo 14 Lunar Landing Mission, becoming the fifth man to walk on the moon. An admiral in the navy, he had served on a destroyer during World War II and had later had extensive experience as a test pilot.

Shepham (shē'făm), unidentified boundary town, NE Palestine. Num. 34.10,11. See SHIPHMITE.

Shephatiah (shĕfətī'ə). **1** One of David's mighty men. 1 Chron. 12.5. **2** Chief Simeonite under David. 1 Chron. 27.16. **3** Son of David. 2 Sam. 3.4. **4** Son of Jehoshaphat. 2 Chron. 21.2. **5** Prince in Jeremiah's time. Jer. 38.1. **6** Shephathiah: Benjamite. 1 Chron. 9.8. **7** Judahite. Neh. 11.4. **8, 9** Families of returning exiles. Ezra 2.4,57; 8.8.

shepherd's-purse, annual herb (*Capsella bursa-pastoris*) of the family Cruciferae (MUSTARD family), indigenous to Europe but now a nearly cosmopolitan weed in temperate regions. It is also called pickpocket, and both the Latin and common names derive from the peculiarly shaped triangular seed pods. A decoction from the plant, containing the alkaloid bursin, has been used medicinally as an antidysenteric, a diuretic, and a febrifuge. *Capsella* is classified in the division MAGNOLIOPHYTA, class Magnoliopsida, order Capparales, family Cruciferae.

Shephi (shē'fī) or **Shepho** (-fō), Seir's descendant. 1 Chron. 1.40; Gen. 36.23.

Shephuphan (shĕfyōō'făn), variant of SHUPHAM.

Sheppard, Jack, 1702–24, English criminal. Raised in a workhouse, he ran away with Bess Lyon, known as Edgeworth Bess, who, with another girl known as Poll Maggott, incited him to a short but spectacular career as a thief and robber. He achieved his greatest fame for his many and astonishing escapes from custody, climaxed by an amazing escape (1724) from Newgate. He was soon apprehended and hanged at Tyburn. His exploits became the subject of numerous narratives and plays, one or two attributed to Daniel Defoe, and he is the hero of W. H. Ainworth's novel *Jack Sheppard* (1839). See Christopher Hibbert, *The Road to Tyburn* (1957).

Sheppard, Morris, 1875–1941, American legislator, b. Morris co., Texas. He practiced law in Texas and was elected (1902) to Congress to succeed his father. He was in the House until his election (1913) to the Senate, where he served until his death. A Democrat, his name is connected with the Sheppard-Towner Act, which provided for Federal and state cooperation toward maternity and infant welfare. Sheppard was an ardent prohibitionist and helped draw up the Webb-Kenyon Act (1913) to control interstate shipment of liquor and also wrote the Sheppard Bill (1916) to make the District of Columbia dry. He fathered the Senate resolution that eventually became the Eighteenth Amendment, and he helped frame the Volstead Act.

Sheppey, Isle of, c.30 sq mi (80 sq km), Kent, SE England, at the mouth of the Thames, separated from the mainland by The Swale, a narrow strait. It is largely flat, with wave-eroded cliffs to the north. Vegetables and grain are grown on the fertile soil, and sheep are raised. The chief towns are Sheerness, a resort, and Minister, where there is a church founded in the late 7th cent. containing the tomb of Sir Robert Shurland, the protagonist of a story in R. H. Barham's *Ingoldsby Legends.*

Sherah (shē'rə), daughter of Ephraim. She built Beth-horon and the unidentified Uzzen-sheerah. 1 Chron. 7.24.

Sher Ali: see SHERE ALI.

sherardized iron: see GALVANIZING.

Sheraton, Thomas, 1751–1806, English designer of furniture and author. He may have been apprenticed to a cabinetmaker, and as an earnest Baptist he wrote religious books and preached. Records show that he was in London from c.1790 and supplemented the meager earnings from his books by giving drawing lessons. Although he may have supervised the making of some furniture, his designs became influential through his manuals, especially the *Cabinet-Maker and Upholsterer's Drawing-Book* (1791–94). Sheraton's style is marked by a graceful delicacy and simplicity, emphasis on straight, vertical lines, and a preference for inlay decoration, reeded legs, and classical motifs. He is also the author of *The Cabinet Dictionary* (1803). See Ralph Fastnedge, *Sheraton Furniture* (1962).

Sherbrooke, Robert Lowe, Viscount (shûr'brŏŏk), 1811–92, British statesman. He emigrated (1842) to Australia and achieved recognition as a reform politician. Returning (1850) to England, he entered (1852) the House of Commons, distinguished himself as a speaker, and held subordinate offices in the ministries of Lord Aberdeen and Lord Palmerston. In 1866 he led the "cave of Adullam," the insurgent Liberals who attacked and defeated their government's reform bill. Despite this action, he served William Gladstone as chancellor of the exchequer (1868–73). In his first budgets Sherbrooke successfully reduced taxes, but he carried the Liberal policy of retrenchment too far and was transferred (1873) to the post of home secretary. He was created viscount in 1880. See biography by A. P. Martin (1893); study by Ruth Knight (1966).

Sherbrooke, city (1971 pop. 80,711), S Que., Canada, at the confluence of the Magog and the St. François rivers, E of Montreal. It is the commercial and market center for the surrounding farm region and is an industrial city, with textile mills and plants producing mining machinery, rubber products, and leather goods. The Univ. of Sherbrooke (1954) is in the city.

Sherbrooke, University of, at Sherbrooke, Que., Canada; French language; founded 1954. It has faculties of arts, science, administration, law, applied science, medicine, education, and theology.

Shere Ali (shēr älē', shâr) or **Sher Ali** (shâr), 1825–79, emir of Afghanistan (1863–79), son of Dost Muhammad. His succession was opposed by other members of his family, notably his brothers. Shere Ali turned from his friendship with the British toward friendly relations with Russia, which was then extending its power into central Asia. Trouble with the British finally brought on the second of the Afghan Wars. Shere Ali's forces were defeated by the British, and he had to flee the country. He died in exile, and his entire party was ousted from Afghanistan in 1880. His pro-British nephew, Abdar-Rahman Khan, became emir.

Sherebiah (shĕr"ēbī'ə), companion of Ezra and signer of the covenant. Ezra 8.18,24; Neh. 8.7; 9.4,5; 10.12; 12.8,24.

Sheresh (shē'rĕsh), Manassite. 1 Chron. 7.16.

Sherezer (shərē'zər), one of a group sent to ask the priests about fasting. Zech. 7.2.

Sheridan, Frances: see SHERIDAN, RICHARD B.

Sheridan, Philip Henry, 1831–88, Union general in the American Civil War, b. Albany, N.Y. After graduation from West Point (1853), he saw varied service on the frontier. In the Civil War, Sheridan, made colonel of the 2d Michigan Cavalry (May, 1862), took part in the Union advance on Corinth, Miss., under General Halleck and won a victory over Confederate cavalry at Booneville, Miss., on July 1, 1862. Made a brigadier general of volunteers and given command of a division of the Army of the Ohio, Sheridan distinguished himself under Don Carlos Buell at Perryville (Oct., 1862) and was promoted to major general of volunteers (Dec., 1862) for his able conduct under William S. Rosecrans at Murfreesboro. In the CHATTANOOGA CAMPAIGN (1863) he aided George H. Thomas in holding off the Confederates at Chickamauga and had a prominent part in the Union victory at Missionary Ridge. Ulysses S. Grant recognized his ability and appointed Sheridan commander of the cavalry corps of the Army of the Potomac (April, 1864). In a notable raid (May 9–24, 1864) in the Wilderness campaign, he destroyed communications and supplies behind Robert E. Lee's lines and defeated J. E. B. STUART at Yellow Tavern. The success of the Confederate general Jubal A. EARLY in the Shenandoah Valley prompted Grant to give Sheridan command of the Union forces there in Aug., 1864. At Winchester (Sept. 19) and Fishers Hill (Sept. 22) Sheridan roundly defeated Early and drove him up the valley. Sheridan then slowly withdrew, systematically laying waste to the Shenandoah so that, as he reported, even a crow flying over the place would have to take his rations with him. But Early advanced again, and on the morning of Oct. 19, while Sheridan was at Winchester, 15 mi (24 km) away, he surprised the Union forces at Cedar Creek and drove them back. Upon hearing of the defeat Sheridan hurried to the field, rallied his men, and, counterattacking, won a decisive victory. (This success was highly dramatized by Thomas Buchanan Read in his poem, "Sheridan's Ride.") Sheridan was made a major general in the regular army in Nov., 1864. In March, 1865, Gen. George CUSTER of Sheridan's army defeated the remains of Early's command at Waynesboro. Sheridan then moved eastward, destroying Confederate communications as he went. After his victory at FIVE FORKS (April 1, 1865), he pursued Lee vigorously and cut off the Confederate retreat at APPOMATTOX, forcing Lee's surrender. After commanding the Military Division of the Gulf (May, 1865–March, 1867), Sheridan commanded the 5th Military Dist. (Texas and Louisiana) from March until Sept., 1867, when President Andrew Johnson transferred him to the command of the Dept. of the Missouri because of differences over Reconstruction policy. There he led military operations against the Cheyennes, Comanches, and other Indian tribes. In the Franco-Prussian War he was a military observer with the Prussian army. Sheridan was again sent to Louisiana in 1875, when the revolt against Republican rule created great public disturbance. On William T. Sherman's retirement (1884), Sheridan was made commanding general of the U.S. army, and shortly before his death he was promoted to general. Although not a brilliant general, Sheridan's flair for leadership and his ready fighting ability made him the outstanding Union cavalry commander. See his *Personal Memoirs* (1888); biographies by Joseph Hergesheimer (1931) and Richard O'Connor (1953).

Sheridan, Richard Brinsley, 1751–1816, English dramatist and politician, b. Dublin. His father, Thomas Sheridan, was an actor and teacher of elocution and his mother, Frances Sheridan, published two novels and a successful play. Sheridan was educated by tutors and at Harrow. After his elopement in 1773 with Elizabeth, daughter of the composer Thomas Linley, Sheridan began writing for the theater and in 1776 became part owner and director of the Drury Lane Theatre. His masterpieces are *The Rivals* (1775) and *The School for Scandal* (1777), comedies of manners that blend the brilliant wit of the Restoration with 18th-century sensibility. Both plays affectionately satirize fashionable society with its materialism, gossip, and hypocrisy. Although each ridicules sentimentalism, neither is itself entirely free of that attribute. *The Critic* (1779) was a dramatic burlesque modeled on *The Rehearsal* by the 2d duke of Buckingham. Sheridan's other works include the comic opera *The Duenna* (1775) and *A Trip to Scarborough* (1777), an adaptation of *The Relapse* by Vanbrugh. Entering Parliament in 1780, he allied himself with the Whigs and became one of the most brilliant orators of his time. He played a prominent part in the impeachment of Warren Hastings and with Charles James Fox defended the French Revolution. During the course of his political career he was secretary of the treasury (1783), treasurer of the navy (1806), and member of the Privy Council (1806). A close friend of the prince regent, he was a leader of London society. The burning in 1809 of the new Drury Lane Theatre virtually ruined Sheridan financially. He was arrested and imprisoned for debt in 1813. After his death, he was given a splendid funeral by his wealthy former friends. See his plays ed. by Cecil Price (2 vol., 1973); his letters ed. by C. Price (3 vol., 1966); biographies by Walter Sichel (1909) and Madeleine Bingham (1972).

Sheridan, city (1970 pop. 10,856), seat of Sheridan co., N Wyo., on Goose Creek E of the Bighorn Mts., in a mineral, livestock, and irrigated farm region; inc. 1884. The largest city in N Wyoming, it is a railroad division point and a regional trade and market hub. It is the tourist center of an excellent hunting and fishing region, and headquarters of the spectacularly beautiful Bighorn National Forest. A rodeo and an Indian celebration are annual events. The city was named after Gen. Philip Sheridan, who led troops in the area. The old inn there (1893) is a national historic landmark. Sheridan has a junior college and an historical museum. A U.S. veterans' hospital is on the site of Fort MacKenzie. To the south are several historic places, including a reproduction of Fort Phil Kearny (a post in the 1860s); the site of the Fetterman massacre, where Indians wiped out a force of soldiers; and the Brinton Memorial Ranch, which commemorates Western art and culture.

Sheriffmuir (shĕr'ĭfmyo͝or"), battlefield in Perthshire, central Scotland, near Dunblane. It was the scene, Nov. 13, 1715, of an indecisive battle between the JACOBITES under John Erskine, 6th earl of Mar, and George I's forces under John Campbell, 2d duke of Argyll.

Sher Khan (shär khän) or **Sher Shah** (shä), 1486–1545, Afghan ruler in N India. He enlisted in the service of the Mogul leader Babur when the latter invaded India and became governor of Bihar. After Babur's death, however, he asserted his independence of the Moguls, and in 1537, when HUMAYUN, son of Babur, was elsewhere engaged, he overran Bengal. A brilliant strategist, Sher Khan routed the army of Humayun in 1539, and a year later decisively defeated a fresh army at Kanauj. Humayun fled to Sind and thence to Persia, and Sher Khan as Sher Shah took control of the Mogul empire. During the five years of his reign (1540–45), Sher Shah proved himself a gifted administrator as well as an able general. His reorganization of the empire laid the foundations for the later Mogul emperors, notably Akbar, son of Humayun.

Sherley, Sir Anthony: see SHIRLEY, SIR ANTHONY.

Sherman, James Schoolcraft, 1855–1912, Vice President of the United States (1909–12), b. near Utica, N.Y. A lawyer, he was (1884–85) mayor of Utica. Sherman served (1887–91, 1893–1909) as a Republican member of the U.S. House of Representatives and was a skillful parliamentarian. In 1908 he was elected Vice President on the Republican ticket along with William Howard Taft. Sherman was renominated in 1912 but died shortly thereafter. Nicholas M. Butler ran in his place.

Sherman, John, 1823–1900, American statesman, b. Lancaster, Ohio; brother of William Tecumseh Sherman. He studied law, was admitted (1844) to the bar, and practiced law several years in Mansfield, Ohio, before he moved (1853) to Cleveland. He had been a delegate to the Whig national conventions of 1848 and 1852 and in 1855 presided over the first Republican state convention. A moderate opponent of slavery expansion, he served (1855–61) in the House of Representatives and quickly rose to prominence. Sent (1861) to the Senate to fill a vacancy, he served there until 1877. Sherman became (1867) chairman of the Senate finance committee and played a leading role in government finance in the Reconstruction period. He had supported the Legal Tender Act of 1862 and the National Banking Act of 1863, but he opposed Secretary of the Treasury Hugh McCulloch's plan to retire the GREENBACKS in circulation and pushed a compromise plan for resuming specie payment. Later, however, he forced the Resumption Act of 1875 through the Senate, and as Secretary of the Treasury (1877–81) under President Hayes, he directed the implementation of the act. In 1880, 1884, and 1888 he was considered as a candidate for the Republican nomination for President. Again in the Senate (1881–97), he was associated in 1890 with the passage of the SHERMAN ANTITRUST ACT and the SHERMAN SILVER PURCHASE ACT. In 1897 he resigned from the Senate to provide a seat for Marcus A. Hanna and was appointed Secretary of State by President McKinley. He retired to private life in 1898. He wrote *Recollections of Forty Years in the House, Senate, and Cabinet* (1895). See *The Sherman Letters* (ed. by R. S. Thorndike, 1894); biographies by T. E. Burton (1906, repr. 1972) and W. S. Kerr (1908).

Sherman, Roger, 1721–93, American political leader, b. Newton, Mass. Sherman helped to draft and signed the Declaration of Independence. He was long a member (1774–81, 1783–84) of the Continental Congress, helped to draw up the Articles of Confederation, and after serving as a member of the Federal Constitutional Convention was one of the strongest proponents of the new Constitution. He was prominent in Connecticut colonial and state politics and was mayor of New Haven and treasurer of Yale College. Sherman was a U.S. Representative (1789–91), and U.S. Senator (1791–93). See biographies by L. H. Boutell (1896) and R. S. Boardman (1938, repr. 1971); Christopher Collier, *Roger Sherman's Connecticut* (1971).

Sherman, Stuart Pratt, 1881–1926, American critic and editor, b. Anita, Iowa, grad. Williams, 1900, Ph.D. Harvard, 1906. Professor of English at the Univ. of Illinois from 1907 to 1924, he resigned to edit the literary section of the New York *Herald Tribune*. His conservative, chauvinistic views involved him in a lengthy quarrel with H. L. Mencken; in later years his beliefs became more liberal. Among his critical works are a biography of Matthew Arnold (1917), *Americans* (1922), and *The Emotional Discovery of America and Other Essays* (1932). Sherman was also an editor of *The Cambridge History of American Literature*.

Sherman, William Tecumseh, 1820–91, Union general in the American Civil War, b. Lancaster, Ohio. After the death of his father (1829) he lived as a member of the family of Thomas EWING. In 1850 he married Ewing's daughter Eleanor Boyle Ewing, well known for her many philanthropic activities. After graduating (1840) from West Point, he spent several years at various Southern garrisons, served in the Mexican War, and was later stationed at St. Louis and at New Orleans. Resigning from the army in 1853, he was a banker in San Francisco and New York (1853–57) and a lawyer in Leavenworth, Kansas (1858–59), before he became superintendent of the state military academy at Alexandria, La. (now Louisiana State Univ. at Baton Rouge). When Louisiana seceded he resigned (Jan., 1861), and in May he rejoined the U.S. army as a colonel. Sherman commanded a brigade in the first battle of Bull Run (July) and in August was made a brigadier general of volunteers and sent to Kentucky. There he succeeded Robert Anderson in command of the Dept. of the Cumberland (Oct.), but in November he was transferred to the Dept. of the Missouri. Sherman distinguished himself as a division commander at Shiloh (April, 1862) and was promoted to major general in May. He took part in the operations about Corinth, occupied Memphis (July), and commanded the Dist. of Memphis (Oct.–Dec., 1862). After his defeat at Chickasaw Bluffs in the first advance of the VICKSBURG CAMPAIGN, he served under John A. MCCLERNAND in the capture of Arkansas Post (Jan., 1863). In the successful move on Vicksburg, Sherman ably led the 15th Corps. In July he was made a brigadier general in the regular army. When Ulysses S. Grant assumed supreme command in the West, Sherman became commander of the Army of the Tennessee (Oct., 1863). He commanded the Union left at Missionary Ridge in the CHATTANOOGA CAMPAIGN (Nov.), went to the relief of Ambrose E. Burnside at Knoxville (Dec.), and destroyed Confederate communications and supplies at Meridian, Miss., in Feb., 1864. On Grant's becoming commander in chief, Sherman succeeded him as supreme commander in the West (March). His ATLANTA CAMPAIGN (May–Sept., 1864) resulted in the fall of that city on Sept. 2. The Confederate attempt to draw him back failed, and Sherman burned (Nov. 15) most of Atlanta and the next day, with 60,000 men, began his famous march to the sea. With virtually no enemy to bar his way, he was before Savannah in 24 days, leaving behind him a ruined and devastated land. Savannah fell on Dec. 21, and in Feb., 1865, Sherman started northward to close in on Robert E. Lee from the rear. Every step now reduced the area upon which the Confederates in Virginia could depend for aid. His advance through South Carolina (the state that in the eyes of Sherman's men had provoked the war) was slower but even more destructive than the march through Georgia. In North Carolina, Joseph E. Johnston opposed Sherman in engagements at Averasboro and Bentonville, but after hearing of Lee's surrender, he asked for terms. Sherman, understanding the South and the devastation it had suffered better than any other Union general, offered him generous terms, but Secretary of War Stanton repudiated them. Johnston then surrendered (April 26, 1865) the last major Confederate army on the same terms as Lee. Sherman was promoted to lieutenant general in 1866 and to general in 1869, when he succeeded Grant as commander of the U.S. army. He retired in 1884. Sherman saw more clearly than any other Civil War general that modern warfare was completely unlike its 18th-century counterpart. Since the Civil War was a war between free peoples, Sherman maintained that only by breaking the war spirit of the enemy, noncombatant as well as combatant, could victory be won—hence the march through Georgia and South Carolina. His famous statement "War is hell" epitomizes his sentiments. He resisted all efforts to draw him into politics, vetoing Republican attempts to make him a presidential candidate in 1884 with the words: "If nominated I will not accept; if elected I will not serve." Sherman is said by many to be the greatest of the Civil War generals. See his memoirs (1875; ed. with foreword by B. H. Liddell Hart, 1957), *The Sherman Letters* (correspondence with his brother John Sherman, ed. by R. S. Thorndike, 1894), and *Home Letters of General Sherman* (ed. by M. A. DeWolfe Howe, 1909); biographies by B. H. Liddell Hart (1929, repr. 1960), Lloyd Lewis (1932; with appraisal by Bruce Catton, 1958), R. G. Athearn (1956), and J. M. Merrill (1971); Anna McAllister, *Ellen Ewing, Wife of General Sherman* (1936); T. H. Williams, *McClellan, Sherman, and Grant* (1962); J. B. Walters, *Merchant of Terror* (1973).

Sherman, city (1970 pop. 29,061), seat of Grayson co., N Texas, near the Red River; inc. 1858. Originally on a stagecoach route, it is now a highway and railroad junction. It has flour and feed mills, cotton gins, and textile factories. Business machines, instruments, and surgical dressings are also made. Despite these industries, the city has somewhat the air of a wealthy farm market. Austin College is there.

Sherman Antitrust Act, 1890, first measure passed by the U.S. Congress to prohibit trusts; it was named for Senator John Sherman. Prior to its enactment, various states had passed similar laws, but they were limited to intrastate businesses. Finally opposition to the concentration of economic power in large corporations and in combinations of business concerns led Congress to pass the Sherman Act. The act, based on the constitutional power of Congress to regulate interstate commerce, declared illegal every contract, combination (in the form of trust or otherwise), or conspiracy in restraint of interstate and foreign trade. A fine of $5,000 and imprisonment for one year were set as the maximum penalties for violating the act. The Sherman Act authorized the Federal government to institute proceedings against trusts in order to dissolve them. Its effectiveness was greatly reduced by Supreme Court decisions, particularly the E. C. Knight Company case in 1895. However, as a result of President Theodore Roosevelt's "trust-busting" campaigns, the Sherman Act was later invoked with some success, and in 1904 the Supreme Court upheld the government in its suit for dissolution of the Northern Securities Company. The act was further employed by President Taft in 1911 against the Standard Oil trust and the American Tobacco Company. In the Wilson administration the CLAYTON ANTITRUST ACT (1914) was enacted to supplement the Sherman Antitrust Act, and the FEDERAL TRADE COMMISSION was set up (1914). Antitrust action sharply declined in the 1920s, but under President Franklin Delano Roosevelt new acts supplementary to the Sherman Antitrust Act were passed (e.g., the ROBINSON-PATMAN ACT), and antitrust action was vigorously resumed. Subsequently, the Supreme Court generally upheld the Federal government's prosecution of trusts.

Sherman Silver Purchase Act, 1890, passed by the U.S. Congress to supplant the BLAND-ALLISON ACT of 1878. It not only required the U.S. government to purchase nearly twice as much silver as before, but also added substantially to the amount of money already in circulation. The Sherman Silver Purchase Act (supported by John Sherman only as a compromise with the advocates of FREE SILVER) threatened, when put into operation, to undermine the U.S. Treasury's gold reserves. After the panic of 1893 broke, President Cleveland called a special session of Congress and secured (1893) the repeal of the act.

Sherriff, Robert Cedric, 1896–, English dramatist. His best-known work is the war play *Journey's End* (1929). His other dramas include *St. Helena* (with Jeanne de Casalis, 1936) and *Home at Seven* (1950). Sherriff also wrote novels and film scripts such as *Goodbye Mr. Chips* (1936) and *Odd Man Out* (1945).

Sherrington, Sir Charles Scott, 1857–1952, English neurophysiologist, educated at Cambridge. He was professor of physiology at the universities of Liverpool and London and at Oxford. He contributed major concepts in his field, among them that of proprioception, that of the function of the synapse (a term he introduced), and the process described in his *Integrative Action of the Nervous System* (1906,

2d ed. 1948). As a physician, he did important work in the study of cholera and of diphtheria and tetanus antitoxins, and played an important role in the improvement of health and safety conditions in British factories during World War I. He was knighted in 1922 and with E. D. Adrian shared the 1932 Nobel Prize in Physiology and Medicine for their discoveries regarding the function of the neuron. Among his other works are *Mammalian Physiology* (1919, rev. ed. 1929), *The Brain and Its Mechanism* (1933), and *Man on His Nature* (1940, 2d ed. 1952). He was also known as a philosopher and poet. See biography by Ragnar Granit (1967).

sherry [from Jérez], naturally dry fortified wine, pale amber to brown in tint. The term *sherry* originally referred to wines made from grapes grown in the region of Jérez de la Frontera, Andalusia, Spain; today it may refer to any of the fortified wines from S Spain and is also applied to similar wines produced in the United States, Latin America, and South Africa. After fermentation the wine is fortified with brandy. Matured in cask for several years, the wine when mature is classed as *palma*, very dry; *raya*, full and rich; or *palo cortado*, an intermediate variation. The big sherry houses blend the wines with reserves from the Soleras, collections of flavoring wines from very fine vintages, kept in dated casks and maintained for long periods by exact replenishment of the blending wine withdrawn from the oldest cask with wine from the next oldest. The varieties of sherry include amontillado and manzanilla, apéritif wines of the *palma* type; the fairly sweet, fruity oloroso and amoroso, blended from *palo cortado;* and the very sweet golden or brown sherries, *raya* blends. The dessert sherries are usually colored and sweetened by the addition of dark, syrupy wines. Sherry contains from 15% to 23% alcohol, the more highly fortified wines being for export. Sherry must be long matured in wood and bottle to acquire the mellowness demanded of brandied wines. It is a widely used flavoring in fine cookery.

Sher Shah: see SHER KHAN.

's Hertogenbosch (sĕr″tōkhənbōs′), Fr. *Bois-le-Duc,* municipality (1971 pop. 81,401), capital of North Brabant prov., S central Netherlands, at the confluence of the Dommel and Aa rivers. It is an industrial and transportation center and has a large cattle market. Chartered in 1184, 's Hertogenbosch was a fortress city until 1876. It is the site of St. John's Cathedral, a beautiful Gothic structure. Hieronymus Bosch was born there (c.1450).

Sherwood, Robert Emmet, 1896–1955, American dramatist, b. New Rochelle, N.Y., grad. Harvard, 1918. After serving in World War I, he wrote for *Vanity Fair* and *Life,* serving as editor of the latter from 1924 to 1928. His first play, the historical comedy *The Road to Rome* (1927), was an immediate success. It was followed by *The Love Nest* (1927), *Waterloo Bridge* (1930), and *Reunion in Vienna* (1931), a nostalgic comedy of the exiled Hapsburgs. His next plays—*The Petrified Forest* (1935), a melodrama set in the Arizona desert; *Idiot's Delight* (1936; Pulitzer Prize), an antiwar drama; and *There Shall Be No Night* (1940; Pulitzer Prize), about the Russian invasion of Finland—depict a civilization on the brink of disaster. *Abe Lincoln in Illinois* (1938; Pulitzer Prize), one of his most notable efforts, concerns Lincoln's early years. During World War II, Sherwood was director of overseas operations in the Office of War Information and a speech writer for President Franklin D. Roosevelt. On the basis of the papers of Harry Hopkins he wrote a memoir, *Roosevelt and Hopkins* (1948; Pulitzer Prize), one of the most important documents on World War II. Sherwood also adapted Jacques Deval's comedy *Tovarich* (1936); wrote film scripts, including *The Best Years of Our Lives* (1946); and completed Philip Barry's last play, *Second Threshold* (1951). See biographical studies by J. M. Brown (1965; ed. by Norman Cousins, 1970), and W. J. Meserve (1970).

Sherwood Forest, formerly a large royal forest, mainly in Nottinghamshire, central England. Today remnants of the forest (c.150 sq mi/390 sq km) exist near Mansfield and Hucknall. The forest is most celebrated as the haunt of Robin Hood and his famous band.

Sheshach (shē′shăk), cryptic name apparently meaning Babylon. Jer. 25.26; 51.41.

Sheshai (shē′shī), son of ANAK.

Sheshan (shē′shăn), descendant of Judah. 1 Chron. 2.31,34,35.

Sheshbazzar (shĕsh″băz′ər), governor of Jerusalem, commissioned by Cyrus to carry back the sacred vessels. Ezra 1.8,11; 5.14,16. He may be identical with ZERUBBABEL and SHENAZAR.

Sheshonk I (shē′shŏngk), d. c.929 or 924 B.C., king of ancient Egypt, founder of the XXII (Libyan) dynasty. Originally a commander of mercenaries at Heracleopolis, he assumed (c.950 B.C.) royal authority when the weak dynasty at Tanis died out. A contemporary of Solomon, he offered Jeroboam I refuge (1 Kings 11.40). Later Sheshonk overran Palestine. He enlarged the temple at Karnak and on its walls recorded the tribute paid him in Palestine and Nubia. His temple court, fronted by a huge pylon, was the largest ever built. The king's body was found (1938–39) in his burial chamber at Tanis. Sheshonk is the Shishak of the Bible (1 Kings 9.16; 11.40; 14.25, 26). The name also occurs in English as Shoshenk.

Sheth. 1 See SETH. **2** Otherwise unknown person mentioned in an obscure passage. Perhaps "children of Sheth" refers to Moabites. Num. 24.17.

Shethar (shē′thər), prince and counselor of King Ahasuerus. Esther 1.14.

Shethar-Boznai (shē′thər-bŏz′nāī), Persian who tried to obstruct the building of the second Temple. Ezra 5.3,6; 6.6,13.

Shetland (shĕt′lənd) or **Zetland** (zĕt′-), county (1971 pop. 17,298), 551 sq mi (1,427 sq km), extreme N Scotland, consisting of the **Shetland Islands**, an archipelago c.70 mi (110 km) long, NE of the Orkneys. The group consists of some 100 islands. About one fourth of them are inhabited. Mainland, Yell, Unst, Fetlar, Whalsey, and Bressay are the largest islands. LERWICK, on Mainland, is the county town and the only large one. It is also the chief port of the islands. The surface of the islands is generally low and rocky, with few trees and spare soil. In places cliffs rise above 1,000 ft (305 m). The climate is humid and, despite the northern latitude, rather mild. Oats and barley are the chief crops, but fishing and cattle and sheep raising are more important. The region is famous for its knitted woolen goods. The small, sturdy Shetland pony is bred there. Tourism is also significant. By the late 9th cent. the islands were occupied by the Norsemen, and traces of their speech and customs survive. Shetland was not annexed to Scotland until 1472, when the islands were taken over as an unredeemed pledge of King Christian I of Norway and Denmark for the dowry of his daughter, Margaret, who married James III of Scotland. Shetland is famous for its ancient relics. Pictish forts are scattered throughout the islands, and a village from the Bronze Age has been unearthed at Jarlshof on Mainland.

Shetland pony, smallest breed of HORSE, originating in the Shetland Islands some 200 mi (322 km) N of Scotland. The Shetland resembles a miniature DRAFT HORSE and has long been used for working purposes. The most popular of the ponies, it has a gentle disposition and is therefore a favorite mount for children. Its official size is less than 46 in. (117 cm) high, and some Shetlands are scarcely more than 2 ft (61 cm). The coat is characteristically long and shaggy and may be any color, although many Shetlands have irregular dark and white patches.

Shetland sheepdog, breed of small, agile WORKING DOG perfected in the Shetland Islands in the 19th cent. It stands from 13 to 16 in. (33.0–40.6 cm) high at the shoulder and weighs about 15 lb (7 kg). Its double coat consists of a very dense, furry underlayer and a long, straight, harsh outercoat. It is usually colored a combination of black, blue merle, and sable, with white and tan markings. Although of obscure origin, the sheltie is probably a descendant of small specimens of the Scottish collie and the King Charles spaniel. It was developed to tend the diminutive sheep of the Shetland Islands, whose rugged, stormy shores have produced other small-statured animals such as the Shetland pony. Today it is raised as a farm dog and family pet. See DOG.

Sheva (shē′və). **1** Son of Caleb. 1 Chron. 2.49. **2** David's scribe: see SHAVSHA.

Shevchenko, Taras (tä′rəs shĭvchĕn′kō), 1814–61, Ukrainian poet and artist. Born a serf and orphaned early, Shevchenko passed a wretched childhood in the service of a brutal sexton. He was apprenticed to icon and mural painters until he was bought and freed in 1838 by a group of intellectuals who recognized his talent. Shevchenko became a prominent realist painter and his Ukrainian ballads, dealing with peasant life, were published in Russian. He joined a Ukrainian nationalist society, writing bitterly against serfdom and Russian autocracy. *The Heretic* (1845) professed his dream of a free brotherhood of all Slavs. Banished to an appalling military existence in Central Asia for his liberal ideas, he wrote exquisite lyric poetry and numerous novels in exile (1847–57). Dogged by terrible misfortune in love and life, the poet died seven days before the Emancipation of Serfs was announced. Shevchenko had tremendous influence on Ukrainian literature. See editions in English of his work by C. A. Manning (1945) and C. H. Andrusyshen and Watson Kirkconnell (1964); Roman Smal-Stocki, *Shevchenko Meets America* (3d ed. 1964).

Shiahs: see SHIITES.

Shibata (shĭbä′tä), city (1970 pop. 74,459), Niigata prefecture, W central Honshu, Japan, on the Kaji River. It is a distribution point for rice and a center for iron, steel, and chemical industries.

Shibboleth (shĭb′ōlĕth), test word that the Gileadites made the Ephraimites pronounce. As Ephraimites could not say *sh* but only *s* as in "Sibboleth," this was regarded as a test of an Ephraimite; 42,000 Ephraimites were thus detected. Judges 12.

Shibin al-Kom (shĭbēn′ äl-ko͞om), city (1970 est. pop. 75,600), capital of Munufiyah governorate, N Egypt, in the Nile River delta. It is an agricultural market and a cotton-processing center.

Shibmah (shĭb′mə), variant of SHEBAM.

Shickshock Mountains, range of the Appalachian system, E Que., Canada, a continuation of the Notre Dame Mts., extending c.100 mi (160 km) east-west near the north coast of the Gaspé Peninsula. Tabletop Mt., or Mt. Jacques Cartier (4,160 ft/1,268 m), is the highest point in SE Canada.

Shicron (shī′krŏn), unlocated landmark, on the boundary of N Judah. Joshua 15.11.

Shidehara, Kijuro (kē″jo͞orō′ shēdā′härä), 1872–1951, Japanese statesman. A career diplomat, he was ambassador to the Netherlands (1914–15), vice foreign minister (1915), and ambassador to the United States (1919–22). He served (1924–27, 1929–31) as foreign minister, pursuing a conciliatory policy toward both China and the Soviet Union contrary to the desires of the militarists. After World War II he became head of the Progressive party and was prime minister from Oct., 1945, to May, 1946; his conservative economic policies and family ties to the Mitsubishi interests made him unpopular with the leftist movement. When in 1947 he opposed nationalization of the coal industry, he was ousted from the party. He became speaker of the diet in 1949.

Shiel, Loch (lŏkh shēl), lake, 17 mi (27 km) long and 1 mi (1.6 km) wide, between Inverness-shire and Argyllshire, W Scotland. It is drained by a short stream into Loch Moidart. Prince Charles Edward Stuart raised his standard (1745) at Glenfinnan, at the head of Loch Shiel.

shield, piece of defensive ARMOR, worn on the arm to ward off weapons during combat, used prior to the introduction of gunpowder. The ancient Greeks and the early Romans carried circular shields, a later type being square and curved to the body. In the 9th and 10th cent. a shield comparable in shape to a child's kite came into general use in Europe, and it was on shields of this type that armorial designs were first represented. With the disuse of shields in war resulting from the use of offensive weapons that required both hands, the increase in body armor, and the introduction of firearms, the form of shields carrying armorial bearings became varied.

shield, in geology: see CONTINENT.

Shiga (shē′gä), prefecture (1970 pop. 889,768), S Honshu, Japan. OTSU (the capital) and Hikone are the chief cities. It is predominantly an agricultural region, with rice the principal crop. Textile manufacturing is important. Shiga includes part of Biwa, Japan's largest lake.

Shigatse: see JIH-K'A-TSE, China.

Shiggaion (shĭgā′yən), plural **Shigionoth** (shĭgī′-ōnŏth), in Ps. 7.1 and Hab. 3.1, terms perhaps describing the character of the psalm.

Shih-chia-chuang (shûr-jēä-jwäng), city (1970 est. pop. 1,500,000), capital of Hopeh prov., China, near the Shansi province border. A small village until the turn of the century, when it became a railroad junction, it is now at the intersection of north-south and east-west highways and railroads. It has textile, fertilizer, pharmaceutical, automotive, and paper industries.

Shihon (shī′hŏn), town, N Palestine, probably near Nazareth. Joshua 19.19.

Shihor (shī′hôr), variant of SIHOR.

Shihor-libnath (shī′hôr-lĭb′năth), unidentified boundary mark of Asher. Joshua 19.26.

Shih Tzu (shē dzo͞o), breed of active, alert TOY DOG originating in Tibet centuries ago. It stands from 8 to 11 in. (20.3–27.9 cm) high at the shoulder and weighs from 9 to 18 lb (4.1–8.2 kg). Its double coat consists of a soft, woolly underlayer and a long, dense, luxurious topcoat that may be any color. A probable descendant of the Lhasa apso, the Shih

Tzu was sent as a gift by the Tibetan Dali Lamas to the Chinese emperors as early as the 16th cent. In China it was crossed with the Pekingese, both breeds being referred to there as "lion dogs." In its relatively short history in the United States, the Shih Tzu is gaining in popularity as a house pet and watchdog. See DOG.

Shiites (shē'īts) [Arabic, = sectarians], members of one of the great divisions of ISLAM, the other, much more numerous, group being the SUNNI. The Shiites (also called Shiahs) may be said to represent a Persian variation of the religion of Muhammad, while the Sunni are considered the orthodox of Islam. The cause of the schism occurred during the UMAYYAD dynasty, when a dispute arose over Muhammad's successor, or caliph. The Shiites were the partisans of ALI, Muhammad's cousin and son-in-law, and of Ali's two sons HASAN and HUSEIN. After the murder of Ali and the assassinations of Hasan and Husein, who were all elevated to the rank of sacred martyrs after their death, the Shiites regarded the caliphate as in the hands of usurpers. The Shiites hold the view that the divine line of descent from Muhammad includes Ali, Hasan, Husein, and their nine successors, the last of whom, the twelfth IMAM, remains hidden from the usurpers but will appear on the last day as the MAHDI. The Shiites have rejected most of the oral traditions (Sunna) of Islam and have also come to differ from the Sunni in matters of law and ceremony. The zeal of some Shiites, further intensified by Persian nationalism, has given rise to the ISMAILIS and such fanatic sects as the FATIMIDS and ASSASSINS. They have also produced many more dervishes than other Muslims; mystic SUFISM was also greatly influenced by Shiite beliefs. Iran, as in earlier times, remains the Shiite center, but there are important Shiite communities in Iraq (which has the most sacred shrines at KARBALA and AN NAJAF), Yemen, Pakistan, and Oman. BABISM and BAHAISM have Shiite bases

Shikoku (shĭkō'kōō), island (1970 pop. 3,904,014), 7,247 sq mi (18,770 sq km), S Japan, separated from Honshu and Kyushu by the Inland Sea. The smallest of the major islands of Japan, it has a dissected topography with high mountains and steep slopes that limit agriculture and impede communication; there are no volcanoes. Shikoku's climate is humid subtropical. Rice, grains, mulberry, palms, and camphor are the chief products. A large copper mine is located at Besshi. Industry is found on the northern side of the island. Population is concentrated along the coast; Takamatsu and Matsuyama are the largest cities.

Shilhi (shĭl'hī), grandfather of King Jehoshaphat. 1 Kings 22.42.

Shilhim (shĭl'hĭm), variant of SHAARAIM.

Shilka (shēl'kə), river, c.345 mi (560 km) long, formed E of Chita, Far Eastern USSR, by the confluence of the Onon and Ingoda rivers, both of which rise along the Mongolian-USSR border. It flows NE past Shilka, Sretensk (head of navigation), and Ust-Karsk, joining the Argun River to form the Amur River on the USSR-China border.

Shillem (shĭl'ĕm), son of Naphtali. Gen. 46.24; Num. 26.49. Shallum: 1 Chron. 7.13.

Shillong (shĭlông'), town (1971 pop. 73,529), capital of Assam and Meghalaya states, NE India. It is a summer resort c.5,000 ft (1,525 m) high in the Khasi Hills. There are two colleges. Primitive tribes inhabit the surrounding district.

Shiloah (shīlō'ə), variant of SILOAM.

Shiloh (shī'lō), in the Bible. **1** Town, central Palestine, the modern Khirbet Seilun (Jordan), NNE of Jerusalem. It was the home of the prophets Eli and Ahijah and the place where the Ark rested after the conquest of Judah. Here Samuel spent his boyhood. It was the sanctuary and general meeting place of the Levites until the Philistines captured the Ark of the Covenant. Joshua 18.1; Judges 18.31; 21.19; 1 Sam. 3; 4; 1 Kings 11.29; 12.15; 14.2; Jer. 7.12 **2** Name appearing in a passage where the text is obscure. Gen. 49.10.

Shiloh, battle of, April 6-7, 1862, one of the great battles of the American Civil War. The battle took its name from Shiloh Church, a meetinghouse c.3 mi (5 km) SSW of Pittsburg Landing, which was a community in Hardin co., Tenn., 9 mi (14.5 km) S of Savannah on the west bank of the Tennessee River. After the fall of Fort Donelson to the Union army, Gen. Ulysses S. Grant advanced up the Tennessee River and established headquarters for his Army of the Tennessee (some 40,000 men) at Savannah. Five divisions were placed in the vicinity of Pittsburg Landing and one at Crump's Landing, c.5 mi (8 km) north. Meanwhile, General Buell, commanding the Army of the Ohio (35,000 men), was marching W from Nashville to join Grant and crush the Confederate army at Corinth, Miss., a strategic railway point. Gen. A. S. Johnston, about to make a stand after leading the retreat from original Confederate positions in the West, commanded the army at Corinth (40,000 men), with Gen. P. G. T. Beauregard second in command. Johnston's plan was to defeat Grant before Buell could arrive. He moved to attack on April 3, but because of delay in the 20-mi (32-km) advance to the Union front, it was not until early on April 6 that his troops fell upon the enemy near Shiloh Church. Grant's position was unfortified, in spite of orders to the contrary from General Halleck, Union commander in the West. Having offensive plans of his own, Grant expected no attack, and consequently his irregularly placed divisions were thrown back in confusion at the Confederate assault. In the day's fighting the Confederates swept the field, but Johnston was killed. When Beauregard, who assumed command, ceased battle at nightfall, the Union forces had been pushed back over a mile from their first positions but, although hard-pressed, still held Pittsburg Landing, which the Confederates wanted to secure in order to cut off retreat. With 20,000 reinforcements from the division at Crump's Landing and the advance divisions of Buell's army, the Federals took the offensive on April 7. Beauregard, outnumbered and without fresh troops, resisted for about eight hours and then proceeded to withdraw on Corinth; the Union command did not make any effective pursuit. Corinth was abandoned to the Union forces one month later. Ultimately, Shiloh may be considered a Union victory because it led to later successful campaigns in the West. It was one of the bloodiest contests of the war, losses on each side reaching over 10,000, and, with the possible exception of Gettysburg, it has been the subject of more controversy than any other Civil War battle.

Shiloh National Military Park: see NATIONAL PARKS AND MONUMENTS (table).

Shiloni (shīlō'nī) or **Shilonites** (shīlō'nīts, shī'lōnīts): see SHELAH **1.** The term refers to inhabitants of Shiloh.

Shilshah (shĭl'shə), son of Zophah. 1 Chron. 7.37.

Shimada (shĭmä'dä), city (1970 pop. 66,489), Shizuoka prefecture, E central Honshu, Japan, on the Oi River. It is a distribution point for timber and rice and a center for chemical and mechanical industries.

Shimane (shĭmä'nä), prefecture (1970 pop. 773,575), SW Honshu, Japan, on the Sea of Japan. MATSUE (the capital), HAMADA, and Izumo are the most important cities. Stock raising, lumbering, and fishing are important activities. The Oki Islands are part of Shimane.

Shimea (shĭm'ēə). **1, 2** Levites. 1 Chron. 6.30,39. **3** See SHAMMUA **1. 4** See SHAMMAH **1.**

Shimeah (shĭm'ēə). **1** See SHAMMAH **1. 2** See SHIMEAM.

Shimeam (shĭm'ēəm), Gibeonite. 1 Chron. 9.38. Shimeah: 1 Chron. 8.32.

Shimeath (shĭm'ēăth), mother of Jozachar the murderer. 2 Kings 12.21.

Shimei (shĭm'ēī). **1** Benjamite who cursed David. 2 Sam. 16.5-14; 1 Kings 2.36-46. **2** Royal official. 1 Kings 1.8; 4.18. **3** Ancestor of Mordecai. Esther 2.5. **4** Gershonite family. 1 Chron. 23.7,9,10. Shimi: Ex. 6.17. **5** Brother of Zerubbabel. 1 Chron. 3.19. **6** Simeonite. 1 Chron. 4.26,27. **7** Reubenite. 1 Chron. 5.4. **8, 9** Levites. 1 Chron. 6.29,42. **10** Course of priests. 1 Chron. 25.17. **11** Keeper of vineyards. 1 Chron. 27.27. **12, 13** Levites contemporary with Hezekiah. 2 Chron. 29.14; 31.12. **14, 15, 16** Husbands of foreign wives. Ezra 10.23,33,38.

Shimeon (shĭm'ēŏn), Israelite who had a foreign wife. Ezra 10.31.

Shimhi (shĭm'hī), Benjamite. 1 Chron. 8.21.

Shimi (shī'mī), variant of SHIMEI **4.**

Shimizu (shĭmē'zōō), city (1970 pop. 234,966), Shizuoka prefecture, E central Honshu, Japan, on Suruga Bay. A port and fishing center, it exports tea, oranges, and canned food. Nearby is Miko-no-matsubara, a breakwater famed for its beauty.

Shimma: see SHAMMAH **1.**

Shimoda (shĭmō'dä), town (1970 pop. 66,489), Shizuoka prefecture, E central Honshu, Japan, at the south extremity of Izu peninsula, on Shimoda Bay. It is a fishing base and an important port for the peninsula. Under the U.S.-Japanese treaty of 1854, its port was to be opened to American trade, but its poor harbor rendered this impracticable. The first U.S. consulate, under Townsend Harris, was opened at Shimoda in 1856. The Gyokusenji Temple, where Harris resided (1856-57), is now a memorial.

Shimoga (shĭmō'gə), town (1971 pop. 102,703), Karnataka state, SW India, on the Tunga River. Shimoga is district headquarters for a region that produces teak, sandalwood, rosewood, and rice. The town was plundered by the Mahrattas in 1798 and occupied by the British in the early 19th cent. after the Mahratta wars.

Shimon (shī'mŏn), name in a genealogy of Judah. 1 Chron. 4.20.

Shimonoseki (shē'mōnōsä"kē), city (1970 pop. 258,422), Yamaguchi prefecture, extreme SW Honshu, Japan. An important port and fishing center on Shimonoseki Strait, it is opposite Kitakyushu, with which it is connected by a tunnel. Shimonoseki is a railroad and industrial center, with engineering works, shipyards, and metal and chemical plants. It is also a port, with ferry connections to Pusan, South Korea. In the city is Akamagu, a 12th-century shrine dedicated to Emperor Antoku and to the Taira clan, which was defeated at Shimonoseki by the Minamoto clan in the famous naval battle of Dannoura. In 1864 a fleet of U.S., British, French, and Dutch ships bombarded the port in retaliation for hostile acts of the Choshu clan. The Treaty of Shimonoseki, which ended the Sino-Japanese War, was negotiated and signed in 1895.

Shimonoseki, Treaty of, April 17, 1895, ending the First SINO-JAPANESE WAR. It was negotiated and signed by Ito Hirobumi for Japan and Li Hung-chang for China. Harsh terms were imposed on a badly defeated China. The treaty provided for the end of Chinese suzerainty over Korea, giving Korea at least nominal independence, and for the cession to Japan of Taiwan, the Pescadores islands, and Port Arthur and the Liaotung peninsula. Japan also imposed a large indemnity and forced China to open five new treaty ports. A week after the treaty was signed, however, Russia, France, and Germany together—in the so-called Triple Intervention—demanded that Japan renounce claims to Port Arthur and the Liaotung peninsula. Japan reluctantly agreed (Nov., 1895), but China was forced to pay an additional indemnity.

shimose (shəmō'sə), a high EXPLOSIVE containing PICRIC ACID.

Shimrath (shĭm'răth), descendant of Benjamin. 1 Chron. 8.21.

Shimri (shĭm'rī). **1** Descendant of Simeon. 1 Chron. 4.37. **2** Father of one of David's guard. 1 Chron. 11.45. **3** One who helped clean the Temple in Hezekiah's reign. 2 Chron. 29.13.

Shimrith (shĭm'rĭth), same as SHOMER **2.**

Shimrom (shĭm'rŏm) or **Shimron** (-rŏn). **1** Son of Issachar. Gen. 46.13; Num. 26.24; 1 Chron. 7.1. **2** Unlocated town of Zebulun. Joshua 11.1; 19.15. This may be the same as **Shimron-meron,** a place whose king Joshua defeated. Joshua 12.20.

Shimshai (shĭm'shī, shĭm'shāī), author of a letter to Artaxerxes that stopped the work on the Temple. Ezra 4.8,9,17,23.

Shinab (shī'năb), king of Admah. Gen. 14.2.

Shinano (shĭnä'nō), river, longest of Honshu, Japan, c.230 mi (370 km) long. It rises in the mountains of central Honshu and flows generally NE to the Sea of Japan at Niigata. It waters the fertile Niigata plain.

Shinar (shī'när), in the Bible, the whole or a part of Babylonia. Gen. 10.10; 11.2; 14.1; Isa. 11.11; Dan. 1.2; Zech. 5.11.

shiner: see MINNOW.

Shingishu: see SINUIJI, North Korea.

shingles: see HERPES ZOSTER.

Shinn, Everett, 1876-1953, American painter and magazine illustrator, b. Woodstown, N.J., studied at the Pennsylvania Academy of the Fine Arts. Moving to New York City, Shinn created a series of murals for Stanford WHITE that led to numerous commissions. He is best known for his street scenes and vignettes of theatrical life, such as *London Music Hall* (Metropolitan Mus.) or *Revue* (Whitney Mus., N.Y.). One of his plays, *Hazel Weston; or, More Sinned Against than Usual,* played in 7 languages for over 25 years. He was the youngest member of the EIGHT.

Shinto (shĭn'tō), ancient native religion of Japan, still practiced in a form modified by the influence of Buddhism and Confucianism. In its present form it is not so much a religion as a set of traditional rituals and customs involving pilgrimages to famous shrines and celebrating popular festivals. *Shinto,* a term of Chinese origin, is the equivalent of the Japanese *kami-no-michi,* "the way of the gods" or "the way of those above." The word *kami,* meaning "above" or "superior," is the name used to designate a great host of supernatural beings or deities. In general the kami are beneficent; many of them are felt to be responsible for the fertility of the crops. Shinto cannot be traced to its beginnings, because until the 5th cent. (when Chinese writing was introduced into Japan) the myths and rituals were transmitted orally. There are, however, three compilations in which much of the ancient belief and custom is gathered together. The mythical matter is contained chiefly in the *Kojiki* [records of ancient matters], prepared under imperial order and completed in A.D. 712, and the *Nihongi* [chronicles of Japan], completed in A.D. 720. Both were written in Chinese script. The *Yengishiki*, compiled in the 10th cent., is the first written record of ritual and prayers; the texts of prayers of earlier times are included. From those first Japanese accounts of the religion of days then already far past, it can be seen that a worship of the forces and forms of nature had grown into a certain stage of polytheism in which spiritual conceptions had only a small place. Nor was there any clear realization of a personal character in the beings held to be divine, and there were practically no images of the deities. There was no one deity supreme over all, but some gods were raised to higher ranks, and the one who held the most exalted position was the sun-goddess, known as the Ruler of Heaven. According to the mythology, kami first had their being on the Heavenly Plain, after heaven and earth had taken form out of original chaos. There were three kami at first. Others came after them. At length two, Izanagi and Izanami, a pair of creators, standing on the rainbow, "the bridge of heaven," and piercing with a jewel spear the surface of the mass of matter beneath, made an island to which they descended. They then produced the other islands of Japan and brought forth many gods and goddesses, among them the sun-goddess, Amaterasu-o-mi-kami, and her brother, the storm-god, Susa-no-wo, who in some ways seems to represent a principle of evil or disorder. His rough behavior made Amaterasu retire into a heavenly cave, withdrawing her radiance from the earth. Finally, enticed by the kami with music, dancing, offerings, and proffer of a mirror, she emerged and restored light to the world. The emperors of Japan are said to be descended from her in unbroken line beginning with the first, Jimmu, who ascended his throne in 660 B.C. The mirror bestowed upon him by his divine ancestress, it is claimed, is in her shrine (one of the great shrines of Ise at Uji-Yamada), where many pilgrims go to worship. Thus the emperor was looked upon as divine, even while living; by divine right he was the chief priest, and as such he presided over ceremonies of foremost importance. Aside from this, his religious responsibilities were delegated to others. A Shinto shrine, unaffected by other religious influences, is a simple unpainted wooden building, having some object within it which is believed to be the dwelling place of the kami. Before the shrine stands the detached portal called the torii. In many shrines Buddhist influences are seen and Buddhist priests serve. The worship under their direction is more elaborate than that of pure Shinto, which consists almost entirely in reciting prayers, dances by the priests, and the offering of food. Since Buddhism entered Japan in the 6th cent. A.D., there has been considerable syncretism between the two religions. A vigorous effort was made, beginning in the 17th cent., to revive the old ways and ideas, and after the restoration of imperial power in 1868, the ancient department of Shinto rites was reestablished. Reverence of ancestors and worship of the spirits of dead heroes as kami, originally introduced from China with Buddhism, is still an essential part of Shinto. In present-day Shinto there is no dogmatic system. Ceremonial purity is strongly insisted upon, and bodily cleanliness is an absolute necessity. In ancient times, wounds, sickness, and even death were considered states of pollution. There is no formulated code of morals; only the socially immoral have a need for prescribed ethics. In 1882 all Shinto organizations were divided into two groups, state shrines (supervised and partially supported by the government) and sectarian churches. The official cult became a powerful instrument in the hands of the militarists, who used it to glorify their policy of aggression. Shinto flourished even abroad wherever large Japanese communities existed, as in the United States and South America. The defeat of Japan in World War II brought about a collapse of state Shinto. In 1946 in a New Year's rescript, Emperor Hirohito destroyed its chief foundation by disavowing his divinity; in the same year Gen. Douglas MacArthur forbade the use of public funds to support Shinto. At the present time sectarian Shinto thrives in much the same form as before, although some of the newer sects stress world peace and brotherhood. See W. G. Aston, *Shinto* (1905, repr. 1968); D. C. Holtom, *Modern Japan and Shinto Nationalism* (rev. ed. 1947, repr. 1963); Aisaburo Akiyama, *Shinto and Its Architecture* (2d ed. 1956); Sokyo Ono, *Shinto: The Kami Way* (1962); F. H. Ross, *Shinto* (1965); Jean Herbert, *Shinto* (1966).

ship, large craft in which persons and goods may be conveyed on water. The term *boat* is sometimes employed when *ship* is meant, and there are some vessels that may be called by either name. Seagoing vessels large enough to be called ships were used in ancient times by the Egyptians, Cretans, Greeks, Phoenicians, Romans, and Chinese. Ancient ships were propelled by oars or by sails or by both. They were of different types for different functions. Heavy and slow ships transported grain. The trireme used by the Greeks and the Romans was the most famous warship of ancient times (see GALLEY). In the Middle Ages Viking ships, propelled by both oars and sails, carried Leif Ericsson to America; their structure is well known from such evidences as the Gokstad ship (unearthed in 1880), which is 80 ft (24.4 m) long, 16 ft 6 in. (5 m) wide, and 6 ft 10 in. (2.1 m) deep. The introduction of the mariner's compass and the transoceanic voyages of the Portuguese who rounded Africa and of Columbus and other explorers of the New World gave impetus to the building and navigation of ships. Many sturdy and refined types of wooden sailing vessels were developed. Men-of-war included the SHIP OF THE LINE, the FRIGATE, and the CORVETTE. By type of design, differing especially in such details as number and position of masts, with sails either square-rigged or fore-and-aft, ships were differentiated into such types as BRIG, CLIPPER, and SCHOONER. Building wooden ships became an important industry, especially in Britain and the United States. The success of Fulton's *Clermont* on the Hudson River (1807) prepared the way for the superseding of sailing ships by steamships (see STEAMSHIP), and later in the 19th cent. steel began to replace wood as material for shipbuilding. Steel ships are often much larger than wooden ships. The steam engine was followed by the steam TURBINE, which actuated the propeller directly or through gear mechanisms. Both methods of power production underwent many improvements through the years before the DIESEL ENGINE came (1902–3) into maritime use. In the 1950s nuclear marine engines were introduced into use (see NUCLEAR ENERGY). Modern freight ships are equipped with powerful machines for handling cargo; and, although the airplane has led to the demise of the great ocean liner, cruise ships continue to be built, providing the luxuries of the finest hotels. The pivotal vessels of modern warfare are the AIRCRAFT CARRIER and the SUBMARINE; other warships important in recent times include the BATTLESHIP, CRUISER, and DESTROYER. See S. R. H. Rogers, *Book of the Sailing Ship* (1931); H. I. Chapelle, *American Sailing Craft* (1936); W. H. Clark, *Ships and Sailors* (1938); C. E. Gibson, *The Story of Ships* (1949); Cecil Torr, *Ancient Ships* (1964); W. A. Baker, *From Paddle-Steamer to Nuclear Ship* (1966); A. K. Laing, *American Ships* (1971); *Jane's Fighting Ships* (pub. annually since 1897).

Shiphi (shĭ'fī), father of a Simeonite prince. 1 Chron. 4.37.

Shiphmite (shĭf'mīt), geographical epithet of David's officer, Zabdi. 1 Chron. 27.27. Some connect it with the town of SHEPHAM.

Shiphrah (shĭf'rə), midwife ordered to kill Hebrew boys. Ex. 1.15,16.

Shiphtan (shĭf'tăn), Ephraimite. Num. 34.24.

Shipka (shĭp'kä), pass through the Balkans, alt. c.4,370 ft (1,330 m), central Bulgaria. It is crossed by a highway. Gabrovo, north of the pass, was the scene of a Russo-Bulgarian victory over the Turks in 1878.

Shipley, urban district (1971 pop. 28,444), West Riding of Yorkshire, N England, on the Aire River. Of its varied industries, light engineering and the manufacture of woolens and worsteds are most important. Within the district is Saltaire, a model village founded by Sir Titus Salt in 1853 for the manufacture of alpaca. In 1974, Shipley became part of the new metropolitan county of West Yorkshire.

ship of the line, large, square-rigged warship, carrying from 70 to 140 guns on two or more completely armed gun decks. In the great naval wars of the 17th, 18th, and early 19th cent., ships of the line were the largest naval units employed. They passed from use with the advent of the IRONCLAD and the BATTLESHIP. One of the few remaining examples of a ship of the line is Lord Nelson's flagship, the H.M.S. *Victory*, which has been preserved at Portsmouth, England.

Shippen, William, Jr., 1736–1808, American surgeon, b. Philadelphia, M.D. Edinburgh, 1761. A pioneer lecturer on anatomy and midwifery, he was instrumental in the organization (1765) at the College of Philadelphia (later the Univ. of Pennsylvania) of the first medical school in the United States, where he served as professor of anatomy and surgery. The actual plans for the medical school were drawn up by John Morgan, but Shippen claimed that Morgan had taken over his idea, and a bitter rivalry grew up. Shippen succeeded Morgan as head of the army medical service; both men were court-martialed on charges arising from their feud and were acquitted. Shippen afterward resumed teaching at the medical school.

shipping, transportation of passengers and goods on waterways. From prehistoric times shipping has had a major influence on man's social development. Water routes, unlike roads, did not need building, and the difficulties and dangers were less than those offered by mountains, marshes, and enemy tribes. Therefore the first civilizations developed on navigable rivers or on the coasts of warm seas. Ancient peoples famous for their shipping enterprises include the Phoenicians, the Cretans, the Egyptians, the Greeks, and the Romans. The shipping routes of those highly civilized peoples were chiefly in the Mediterranean, but their voyages extended to India, along the Atlantic coast of Africa, and to Britain, where tin was secured. The goods shipped consisted largely of luxuries, including spices, perfumes, and such fine pottery as the famous Athenian ware; but shipments of grain became important as cities grew in size. The great modern merchant marine (a country's fleet of commercial ships) first appeared in the commercial revolution. Leaders in shipping included the Spanish, the Portuguese, and the Venetians. The activities of mariners of SW Europe included discovery and conquest in the New World. In the 13th and 14th cent. the HANSEATIC LEAGUE built up a great trading and fishing fleet, while the Italian city-republics developed marine insurance on modern lines. England's shipping industry was associated with colonization, with the development of manufacturing, and especially with leadership in the Industrial Revolution. The greatest competitors of the British were the French and the Dutch. Both were vanquished in war and strangled in peace by the British NAVIGATION ACTS. The introduction of slave labor into the American colonies made the slave trade one of the most profitable branches of shipping for two centuries. America's vast resources in timber provided an advantage in building wooden ships, and swift sailing vessels of American design, such as the schooner and the clipper, dominated shipping until the mid-19th cent. The introduction of steel steamships enabled Great Britain to reassume the chief place in shipbuilding and shipping. From about 1900 until World War I, Germany held second place in the world in both navy and merchant marine, and its challenge to Great Britain's domination of the sea was an important cause of the war. In the period between the two world wars the principal maritime nations were Great Britain and its dominions, the United States, Japan, Norway, Germany, Italy, the Netherlands, and France. The United States merchant marine steadily declined, and in order to stimulate shipbuilding the Merchant Marine Act of 1936 created the U.S. Maritime Commission. At the beginning of World War II in Europe, U.S. shipping, handicapped by the NEUTRALITY ACT, again declined. American vessels were diverted to trade outside the war zones and many were transferred to other flags, mainly the Panamanian. After the entry of the United States into the war (Dec., 1941), a huge shipbuilding program rapidly got under way, and standardized vessels were turned out by assembly-line methods. A brief period of United States dominance in world shipping followed the war. Subsequently, however, the U.S. merchant marine again declined steadily; as the expense of American labor and ship construction increased, the cost of operation went beyond competitive levels, despite the fact that the American shipping industry was receiving a large subsidy from the Federal government. Much of the cargo formerly carried in American vessels and in those of other major nations is now carried by so-called "flag of convenience" fleets. Such lines arose with the tendency of large shippers, especially those of Greece and the United States, to avoid the high taxes of their home countries by registering their ships in low-tax nations such as Liberia and Panama. The merchant tonnage of Liberia, for example, grew

MAJOR SHIPWRECKS SINCE 1850

Year	Name	Type of ship	Cause of disaster	Lives lost
1852	*Birkenhead*	troopship	wrecked	450
1865	*Sultana*	steamship	explosion	1,450
1873	*Atlantic*	steamship	wrecked	550
1878	*Princess Alice*	steamship	collision	700
1891	*Utopia*	steamship	collision	560
1894	*Norge*	steamship	wrecked	600
1898	*La Bourgogne*	steamship	collision	560
1898	*Cromartyshire*	sailing ship		
1904	*General Slocum*	steamship	fire	1,020
1912	*Titanic*	steamship	struck iceberg	1,500
1912	*Kichermary*	steamship	wrecked	1,000
1914	*Empress of Ireland*	steamship	collision	1,023
1914	*Storstad*	collier		
1916	*Hsin Yu*	steamship	wrecked	1,000
1921	*Hongkong*	steamship	foundered	1,000
1934	*Morro Castle*	steamship	fire	135
1948	*Kingya*	refugee ship	explosion	1,000
1954	*Toya Maru*	ferryboat	foundered	1,172
1955	*Novorossiisk*	battleship	explosion	1,500
1956	*Andrea Doria*	steamship	collision	51
1961	*Save*	passenger ship	ran aground	259
1963	*Thresher*	nuclear submarine	failed to surface	129
1966	*Heraklion*	ferryship	foundered	264
1967	*Forrestal*	aircraft carrier	explosion	134
1968	*Dumaguete*	ferryboat	foundered	400
1970	*Namyung-Ho*	ferryboat	capsized	261

from approximately zero in 1939 to over 25 million in the late 1960s, making Liberia one of the largest shipping nations in the world. See SHIP; MARITIME LAW. See James Hornell, *Water Transport: Origins and Early Evolution* (1946, repr. 1970); A. E. Branch, *Elements of Shipping* (2d ed. 1970).

Shipton, Mother, legendary English prophetess. She was first mentioned in an anonymous pamphlet, published in 1641, which described her as having prophesied various events of the reign of Henry VIII and later. She rapidly entered the folklore of English literature, her fame being increased by the great fire of London (1666), which she was also alleged to have predicted. A life by Richard Head was first published in 1667, and an anonymous pamphlet of 1686 purported to identify her as Ursula Shipton (1488–1561) of Knaresborough, Yorkshire. A new version of her life in 1862, with additional prophecies, was discovered to be a forgery.

shipworm or **teredo** (tĕrē'dō), marine BIVALVE mollusk of the family Teredinidae, specialized for boring in wood. A shipworm is not a worm, but a greatly elongated CLAM. Its two shells, enclosing only the front end of the body, function as a tool, rather than a protective covering; their ridged and roughened surfaces are used for boring. The burrow (lined with a calcareous coating produced by the clam's mantle) is begun when the animal is in its larval stage and is expanded as it grows. The common shipworm of the North Atlantic Ocean, *Teredo navalis,* may grow up to 2 ft (60 cm) long, although its shells remain only ½ in. (12 mm) long. Shipworms feed on wood particles and minute organisms. They do enormous damage to piers and ships, and although they are deterred by chemicals, control is still a problem. Shipworms are classified in the phylum MOLLUSCA, class Pelecypoda, order Eulamellibranchia, family Teredinidae.

shipwreck, complete or partial destruction of a vessel as a result of collision, fire, grounding, storm, explosion, or other mishap. In the ancient world sea travel was hazardous, but in modern times the number of shipwrecks due to nonhostile causes has steadily declined. Factors contributing to the decrease are improvements in ship construction, modern methods of navigation, efficient ship-to-ship and ship-to-shore communication, more accurate meteorological reports and storm warnings, and the use of radar equipment. The greater size and larger accommodations of present-day vessels, however, involve greater potential loss of life and cargo in each ship disaster. One of the most famous modern sea disasters was the sinking of the TITANIC in 1912.

Shiraz (shēräz'), city (1966 pop. 269,865), capital of Fars prov., SW Iran, at an altitude of c.5,200 ft (1,580 m). It is a commercial and industrial center and has long been known for its wines, carpets, and metalwork. Other manufactures include textiles, petrochemicals, cement, and sugar. An old settlement, Shiraz became an important commercial, military, and administrative center in the late 7th cent. In the 9th cent. two brothers of Imam Riza died in Shiraz; their tombs are still visited by pilgrims. From about the 10th cent. Shirazi traders were active along the E African coast. Tamerlane sacked the city in the late 14th cent., but later, under the Safavids, it was embellished with numerous new buildings. Under Karim Khan, the city served (1750–79) as capital of Persia; it declined after Karim's successor, Aga Muhammad Khan, moved the capital to Tehran. Hafiz and Sadi, two of Persia's greatest poets, are buried in garden-enclosed tombs in Shiraz. Pahlavi Univ. (founded 1945) and the Fars Museum are also in the city. Nearby are the ruins of PERSEPOLIS.

Shirbarghan (shērbär'gän), city (1967 pop. 50,440), N Afghanistan. It is a market for agricultural produce and Karakul lamb skins and is the site of an ancient citadel.

Shiré (shē'rā), river, c.250 mi (400 km) long, flowing from the southern end of Lake Nyasa, Malawi, SE Africa, to the Zambezi River in central Mozambique. It is navigable to Port Herald. The upper Shiré is being developed for irrigation and power production. Cotton is raised in the valley.

Shire horse, a breed of DRAFT HORSE native to central England. It is equal in weight to the BELGIAN HORSE and is usually slightly taller. Widely used as a war horse during the Middle Ages, it was well adapted to carry the excessive weight of armor worn by both horse and rider. The Shire was introduced to the United States in the late 1800s, but was never as popular as the CLYDESDALE or PERCHERON. It is similar in appearance to the former, with feathery fetlocks. It stands 17 hands (68 in./170 cm) high and normally exceeds 2,000 lb (900 kg).

Shirley or **Sherley, Sir Anthony,** 1565–1636?, English adventurer. He fought in the Netherlands (1586) under the earl of Leicester and in France (1591) under the earl of Essex, who became his patron. He was knighted by Henry IV of France but without the permission of Elizabeth I, who had him imprisoned. Released after relinquishing the honor, he was still generally known as Sir Anthony. He organized a buccaneering expedition in 1595, and his adventures in Jamaica and North America were related (1598) in Richard Hakluyt's collection of narratives of voyages. In 1598 he set out for Persia, where, falsely representing himself as an English envoy, he gained some trading privileges. Returning (1600) to Europe as the shah's envoy, he visited various European courts attempting to arrange alliances with Persia against the Turks. Although unsuccessful in this, he was favorably received at many courts. Holy Roman Emperor Rudolf II sent him (1605) on a mission to Morocco. He was made a count of the Holy Roman Empire and an admiral of the Spanish navy. After the failure (1609) of an expedition that he led for Spain against the Turks in the Mediterranean, Shirley lost favor at the Spanish court, although he received a pension. After 1611 he lived in Madrid in poverty. His account of his Persian travels was published in London in 1613. See Samuel Chew, *The Crescent and the Rose* (1937, repr. 1965) and D. W. Davies, *Elizabethans Errant* (1967).

Shirley, James, 1596–1666, English dramatist. Ordained in the Church of England, he later was converted to Roman Catholicism and became a schoolmaster. He resigned that position, however, soon after the success of his first play, *Love Tricks,* in 1625. Included among his more than 37 plays are the comedies *Hyde Park* (1632) and *The Lady of Pleasure* (1635); the tragedies *The Traitor* (1631) and *The Cardinal* (1641); and the masques *The Triumph of Peace* (1633) and *The Contention of Ajax and Ulysses* (1659). Shirley is best remembered for his witty, satiric comedies, which brilliantly and realistically portray London society.

Shirley, William, 1694–1771, colonial governor in British North America, b. England. He became a lawyer and in 1731 emigrated to Massachusetts. In 1741 he became governor of Massachusetts. He opposed the issuance of more paper money, and in the war with France he promoted the successful expedition (1745) against LOUISBURG. British specie payments for the expenses of that expedition helped redeem the paper money and stabilize the colony's currency. Shirley led (1755) an unsuccessful expedition against Canada in the French and Indian War and was briefly commander of British forces in America after the death (1755) of Gen. Edward Braddock. He was removed as governor in 1756 but cleared of charges of treason concerning the Canadian expedition. He served (1761–70) as governor of the Bahamas and retired to Roxbury, Mass. His correspondence was edited by C. H. Lincoln (1912). See biographies by G. A. Wood (1920) and J. A. Schutz (1961).

Shirpurla: see LAGASH.

Shisha (shī'shə), David's scribe: see SHAVSHA.

Shishak: see SHESHONK I.

Shitrai (shĭt'rāī, shĭtrā'ī), chief herdsman of David. 1 Chron. 27.29.

Shittim (shĭt'ĭm), last place in which the Israelites encamped before reaching the Holy Land. It was E of Jericho. Num. 25.1; Joshua 2.1; 3.1; Micah 6.5. Abel-shittim: Num. 33.49. The valley of Shittim of Joel 3.18 is not the same place.

shittim wood, wood of the shittah tree (Isa. 41.19), probably an ACACIA, from which the Ark of the Covenant and furniture of the Tabernacle were made (Ex. 25.10). The Revised Version of the Bible calls it acacia wood. It seems to have been held in high esteem (Ex. 25.5). The name shittim wood is also sometimes applied to two plants that are not acacias, the BUCKTHORN and the false buckthorn.

Shiva (shē'və), one of the greatest gods of HINDUISM, also called Mahadeva. The "horned god" and phallic worship of the INDUS VALLEY CIVILIZATION may have been a prototype of Shiva worship or Shaivism. Shaivism is mentioned as early as the Upanishads and the Mahabharata (500–200 B.C.). Shiva is identified with the fierce Vedic god Rudra and, in his terrible aspect, is the god of destruction and cosmic dissolution. He is commonly worshipped in the form of the *lingam,* or symbolic phallus. His other main forms are the great yogi, or ascetic, and Nataraja, Lord of the Cosmic Dance. As a yogi he is depicted as seated deep in meditation in the Himalayas, holding a trident, a snake coiled around his neck, his body smeared with ashes, and his hair long and matted. As Nataraja, he is shown four-armed, bearing various emblems, and dancing on one foot on a prostrate demon. Shiva's mount is the bull Nandi, and his consort is the goddess Uma, Parvati, Durga, or KALI.

Shively (shīv'lē), city (1970 pop. 19,150), Jefferson co., N Ky., adjacent to Louisville; settled c.1885, inc. 1938. It is mostly residential. Liquor distillation is the main industry.

Shiza (shī'zə), father of one of David's valiant men. 1 Chron. 11.42.

Shizuoka (shĭzōō'ôkä), city (1970 pop. 416,379), capital of Shizuoka prefecture, E central Honshu, Japan, on Suruga Bay. It is a port and communications center and is known for its tea, oranges, and lacquer ware. Long the eastern outpost for Tokyo, Shizuoka retains a castle of the last of the Tokugawa shoguns. A statue of Ieyasu, founder of the Tokugawa shogunate, stands in a Buddhist temple in the city. Shizuoka prefecture (1970 pop. 3,089,890), 3,000 sq mi (7,770 sq km), is the chief tea-producing area of Japan. In the prefecture is the celebrated volcano Fujiyama.

Shkhara (shŭk'hərä), peak, c.17,064 ft (5,201 m) high, in the Greater Caucasus, S European USSR, SW of Nalchik and on the border between the Georgian and Russian republics.

Shklovski, Victor Borisovich (vēk'tər bərē'səvĭch shklôf'skē), 1893–, Russian critic and writer. Shklovski was an exponent of the formalist school, which held that in literature only the form and structure of a work are important, not its content or the social conditions that produced it. After a period of opposing the Bolshevik government he spent two years abroad, chiefly in Berlin, where he wrote *A Sentimental Journey* (1923), an autobiography covering the years from 1917 to 1922. Among his critical works are *The Technique of the Writer's Craft* (1928) and works on Leo Tolstoy (1928), Mayakovsky (1940), and Dostoyevsky (1957). Shklovski also wrote numerous film scenarios.

Shklovsky, Iosif Samuilovich (yôs'ĭf səmōō'ēl'əvĭch shklôf'skē), 1916–, Soviet astronomer, grad. Univ. of Moscow (1938). He was head of the department of radio-astronomy at the Sternberg Astronomical Institute, Moscow, and professor of astronomy at the Univ. of Moscow. He showed, in 1946, that the radio wave radiations from the sun emanate from the ionized layers of its corona, and he developed a mathematical method for discriminating between thermal and nonthermal radio waves in the Milky Way. He is noted especially for his theory that cosmic rays reaching the earth originate in the Great Spiral Nebula of Andromeda, and he suggested that intelligent life may exist in the nebula. His proposal that one of the moons of Mars could be an artificial satellite made by a civilization that perished a billion years ago has not been widely accepted. His works include *Physics of the Solar Corona* (1966), *Intelligent Life in the Universe* (with Carl Sagan, 1968), and *Supernovae* (1969).

Shkodër (shkō'dər) or **Scutari** (sko͞o'tərē), Serbo-Croatian *Skadar*, anc. *Scodra*, city (1970 pop. 55,300), capital of Shkodër prov., NW Albania, at the outlet of Lake Scutari. It is located in a fertile agricultural area that produces a variety of crops. Shkodër is the industrial and cultural center of N Albania and has industries that manufacture cement, textiles, tobacco products, foodstuffs, and leather goods. It is also an important fishing center. An ancient Illyrian capital, Shkodër became (168 B.C.) a Roman colony, passed to Byzantium, and was conquered by the Serbs in the 7th cent. A.D. Until the fall of Serbia in the late 14th cent., Shkodër was the seat of the princes of Zeta (i.e., Montenegro), who pledged it to Venice in return for a subsidy in the war against Turkey. However, it was captured by Sultan Muhammad II in 1479. Shkodër, known under Turkish rule as Iskenderiye, was the seat of a pashalik. The pashas, often chosen from among Montenegrin renegades, fought for centuries against their Albanian neighbors. Montenegrin troops occupied (1913) Shkodër in the Balkan Wars, but the European powers assigned the city to newly independent Albania. There was fighting in the city during World War I. Shkodër was made a Roman Catholic archdiocese in 1867. The city has a large bazaar and is dominated by a citadel built by the Venetians. It has a Catholic cathedral and several mosques.

Shoa (shō'ə), people mentioned in Ezek. 23.23 in connection with Mesopotamian nations.

Shoa: see ETHIOPIA.

Shobab (shō'băb). **1** Son of David. 2 Sam. 5.14; 1 Chron. 3.5;14.4. **2** Descendant of Caleb. 1 Chron. 2.18.

Shobach (shō'băk), Syrian general defeated by David. 2 Sam. 10.16,18. Shophach: 1 Chron. 19.16,18.

Shobai (shō'bāī, shōbā'ī), family of temple doorkeepers. Ezra 2.42; Neh. 7.45.

Shobal (shō'băl), three descendants of Judah. Gen. 36.20,23,29; 1 Chron. 1.38,40; 2.50; 4.1,2. These may be one person.

Shobek (shō'bĕk), signer of the covenant. Neh. 10.24.

Shobi (shō'bī), Ammonite who was kind to David. 2 Sam. 17.27. See HANUN **1.**

Shocho or **Shochoh** (both: shō'kō): see SOCOH.

shock, any condition in which the CARDIOVASCULAR SYSTEM is unable to provide adequate circulation to the body tissues, also called circulatory failure or circulatory collapse. Shock results in the slowing of vital functions and in severe cases, if untreated, in death. It may be caused by inadequate pumping by the heart, by reduction of the blood volume due to dehydration or to loss of blood or plasma, or by reduced blood pressure resulting from dilation of the blood vessels. Inadequate pumping may occur as a result of various kinds of heart disease. Blood loss may result from injuries or from such internal conditions as bleeding ulcers. Burns produce extensive plasma loss from blood vessels into the burned area; crush injuries may result in loss of blood and plasma into the injured tissues. Dilation of blood vessels may be caused by injury to the nervous system, or by pain or emotional stress. FAINTING is a form of shock brought about by a sudden reduction of the blood supply to the brain. Symptoms of shock include weakness, pallor, cold and moist skin, and thirst. The arterial blood pressure is reduced, the pulse is weak and rapid, and the surface veins of the limbs may collapse. Emergency aid for shock victims includes maintaining a clear breathing passage, administering oxygen, controlling bleeding, and keeping the patient warm and in a supine position with legs elevated. Therapy may include blood or plasma transfusion to restore the normal circulation, as well as treatment of the underlying cause of shock. The term *shock* is also applied to a variety of other conditions such as ELECTRIC SHOCK, allergic shock (see ANAPHYLAXIS), and emotional shock. See FIRST AID.

shock absorber, device for reducing the effect of a sudden shock by the dissipation of the shock's energy. On an automobile, springs and shock absorbers are mounted between the wheels and the frame. When the wheels hit a hole or a raised spot on a road, the springs absorb the resultant shock by expanding and contracting. To prevent the springs from shaking the frame excessively, their motion is restrained by shock absorbers, which are also known by the more descriptive term dampers. The type of shock absorber found on automobiles is usually a hydraulic type that has a casing consisting of two tubes, one telescoping into the other. In order for a spring to expand and contract, it must pull apart and push together the ends of this shock absorber. But the ends offer so much resistance that the motion of the spring quickly dies out. The ends are connected to a piston in an oil-filled chamber in the shock absorber's inner tube. The piston can only move if it forces oil past it through valves. This arrangement creates a large resistance to any motion by the piston and consequently by the ends. On some automobiles a type of hydraulic suspension is used to function both as a spring and as a shock absorber. It comprises a sealed spherical container filled with equal volumes of hydraulic fluid and gas under pressure. The compression of the gas, which absorbs the shock, is supplied by the vehicle's engine. Shock absorbers are used on aircraft to ease the impact upon landing. Some machines are mounted on resilient materials composed, e.g., of cork or rubber. The materials act as shock absorbers, isolating the vibrations of the machine from the surrounding area.

shock therapy, in psychiatry, treatment of certain mental illnesses by means of chemical agents or electricity. The therapeutic possibilities of these treatments were discovered in the 1930s by Manfred Sakel, a Polish psychiatrist, using insulin; L. J. Meduna, an American psychiatrist, using Metrazol; and Ugo Cerletti and Lucio Bini, Italian psychiatrists, using electric shock. Injection of insulin causes coma; Metrazol and electric shock result in convulsions similar to those of epileptics. There is no general agreement as to the overall value of shock therapy or the way it works, although electric shock has had unquestionable success with involutional melancholia and other depressive disorders. Metrazol and insulin have accounted for a very limited number of remissions in cases of schizophrenia. Shock therapy is sometimes used to make the psychotic patient rational enough for psychotherapy. In recent years this practice has been largely replaced by the use of tranquilizers. See A. S. Hermreck and A. P. Thal, *The Adrenergic Drugs and Their Use in Shock Therapy* (1968); L. B. Kalinowsky and Hanns Hippius, *Pharmacological, Convulsive, and other Somatic Treatments in Psychiatry* (1969).

shock wave, wave formed of a zone of extremely high pressure within a fluid, especially the atmosphere, that propagates through the fluid at a speed in excess of the speed of sound. A shock wave is caused by the sudden, violent disturbance of a fluid, such as that created by a powerful explosion or by the supersonic flow of the fluid over a solid object. Propagating from the point of the disturbance, a shock wave carries energy and can have destructive effects as it impinges on solid objects. A shock wave decays rapidly with increasing distance from its point of origin, gradually changing into an ordinary sound wave. Continuous shock waves, such as those produced by supersonic aircraft, are of particular concern as they tend to recur along regular routes. Even after they have decayed into sound waves, thus losing their destructive force, they remain capable of creating noise levels harmful to human beings and animals.

Shoco (shō'kō), variant of SOCOH.

shoe, foot covering, usually of leather, consisting of a sole and a portion above the sole called an upper. In prehistoric times skins or hides were probably tied around the foot for protection and warmth. The sandal, probably the earliest form of shoe, was worn in Egypt, Greece, and Rome; an early form of the boot was also known in Greece and Rome. The characteristic shoe of the Middle Ages was the soft clinging moccasin, which extended to the ankle. It was highly decorated and was of velvet, cloth of gold, and, increasingly, of leather. By the 13th cent. the toe had become greatly elongated until a century later the point had to be held aloft by a chain attached to the knee. After 1377 wooden clogs, called poulaines or pattens, were introduced. A forerunner of the heeled shoe, they were fastened under the shoe (if not a part of the shoe itself) to protect it from mud or water. The chopine, an ornamental shoe with a very high sole, went to fantastic heights. After 1500, styles reversed themselves, and the width of the toe was exaggerated; two colors and slashing were often employed to complement the costume. The high heel came into fashion with Elizabeth's reign in the late 16th cent. and was worn by both men and women; the shoe was colorfully decorated with rosettes, lace, and embroidery. France introduced (c.1600) the high top boot which developed into the cavalier's boot with its wide, floppy top. The late 17th cent. saw the emergence of the square toe, high tongue, and buckles. Heels were lowered, becoming the French curved heel, until they disappeared (c.1780). With the new Empire styles, flat soft shoes with ribbon ties became the style for women, and military boots became the vogue for men. Guilds of shoemakers or *cobelers* existed in the Middle Ages; in the American colonies, the earliest known shoemaker was Thomas Beard, who arrived in Salem, Mass., in 1629. Early shoemakers worked at home, in small shops, or as itinerant workers who went to homes to make up the annual supply. Hand processes were used until c.1833; thereafter the rapid invention and development of machinery revolutionized the industry; today over 180 different kinds of machines are employed. As machinery became more specialized and the use of leather became primary, shoe styles and measurements became more refined and exact. From the high button shoe of the late 19th cent. to the low-cut pump of modern times (popular after 1920), the range of materials has increased, and styles are designed for every purpose and need. See R. Turner Wilcox, *The Mode in Footwear* (1948).

shoebill stork, common name for a large (up to 54 in./122 cm) tall, storklike bird, *Balaeniceps rex.* Also known as the whalehead, it is noted for its large head and unusually long and wide, many-colored bill, which ends in a hooked tip. It has broad wings and long, strong legs with large, unwebbed feet. A solitary, silent bird, the shoebill stork is native to the marshy banks of the papyrus swamps of the East African White Nile and its tributaries, where it feeds on a diet of frogs, small crocodiles, and especially lungfish and other mud puddle fish. It obtains this diet by probing the mud with its bootlike bill. Partially nocturnal, it tends to be sluggish but is nonetheless a strong flyer and soarer. In several respects, shoebills are similar to herons, e.g., they fly with their heads and necks folded back. A ground nester, the shoebill deposits its one or two chalky white eggs in a nest of grasses on a high, dry spot, where its downy young remain, helpless for some time after hatching. Shoebills are classified in the phylum CHORDATA, subphylum Vertebrata, class Aves, order Ciconiiformes, family Balaenicipitidae.

Shoemaker, Willie (William Lee Shoemaker), 1931–, American jockey, b. Fabens, Texas. Becoming a jockey at an early age, he won his first race when he was 18. Considered one of the greatest American jockeys, in 1974 after 25 years of racing he had won 6,633 victories, more than any other jockey. In 1972, he became the highest career stakes winner in racing.

shogun (shō'gŭn''), title of the feudal military dictators who from the 12th cent. to the 19th cent. were the actual rulers of Japan. The title itself, Sei-i-tai Shogun [barbarian-subduing generalissimo], dates back to 794 and originally meant commander of the imperial armies. The shogunate as a system of military government was established by YORITOMO after 1185 and was known as the Bakufu [literally, army headquarters]. The imperial court at Kyoto continued to exist, but effective power and actual administration were in the hands of the hereditary shoguns. The shogunate was held in turn by the Minamoto family and their successors, with their capital at Kamakura (1192–1333); the Ashikaga, with their capital at Kyoto (1338–1597); and the TOKUGAWA, with their capital at Yedo (Tokyo) after 1603. The overthrow of the shogun in 1867 brought the MEIJI RESTORATION and the beginning of modern Japan. See DAIMYO.

Shoham (shō'hăm), descendant of Merari. 1 Chron. 24.27.

Sholapur (shō'ləpo͝or, shōləpo͝or'), city (1971 pop. 398,122), Maharashtra state, W central India, on the Deccan plateau. Once a fortress town, Sholapur is now a district administrative center, a great textile-manufacturing city, and a market for oilseed and tobacco. It passed to the Moguls in 1668, to Hyderabad in 1723, to the Mahrattas in 1795, and to the British in 1818. A 14th-century Muslim fort is in the city.

Sholokhov, Mikhail Aleksandrovich (mēkhəyĕl' əlyĭksän'drəvĭch shô'ləkhôf), 1905–, Russian novelist. Sholokhov won international fame for an epic novel of his native land, *The Silent Don* (4 vol., 1928–40; tr. in 2 vol., *And Quiet Flows the Don*, 1934, and *The Don Flows Home to the Sea*, 1940). The work, which won a Stalin Prize in 1941, describes the effect of World War I, the revolution, and the civil war on the lives of the Don Cossacks. A propagandistic novel, *Virgin Soil Upturned*, deals with the collectivization of agriculture; it won a Lenin Prize in 1960. Its first volume is *Seeds of Tomorrow* (1932–33, tr. 1935), and the second is *Harvest on the Don* (1960, tr. 1961). His stories are collected in *Tales of the Don* (tr. 1962) and *One Man's Destiny* (tr. 1967). Sholokhov was awarded the 1965 Nobel Prize in Literature, being the first officially sanctioned Soviet laureate. See E. J. Simmons, *Russian Fiction and Soviet Ideology*; studies by D. H. Stewart (1967) and Michael Klimenko (1972).

Sholom Aleichem: see ALEICHEM, SHOLOM.

Shomer (shō'mər). **1** See SHAMER **2**. **2** Mother of one of the murderers of King Joash. 2 Kings 12.21. Shimrith: 2 Chron. 24.26.

shooting, firing with rifle, shotgun, pistol, or revolver at stationary or moving targets. The term *shooting* is also used in Great Britain to mean small-game HUNTING. In the 19th cent. the sport of rifle shooting became increasingly popular in England and in the United States, where the National Rifle Association (NRA) was formed (1871) to standardize the rules for rifle marksmanship. Matches were arranged and trophies offered. Pistol and revolver events were added in 1900. Shooting events have been included in the OLYMPIC GAMES since 1896. Among the Olympic events are pistol shooting at 50 m (164 ft), rifle shooting at 300 m (984 ft), trapshooting and skeet, and small-bore rifle shooting. NRA-sponsored tournaments are divided into sections for small-bore rifles, high-power rifles, pistols, and revolvers. In small-bore rifle shooting the targets range in distance from 50 ft to 200 yd (15.24–182.88 m), and in pistol and revolver shooting from 50 ft to 50 yd (15.24–45.72 m). For long-range rifle marksmanship, targets from 200 to 1,000 yd (182.88–914.4 m) are used. A shooting target is made of black-on-white cardboard and is composed of a bullseye (black) and several concentric circles. Competitors shoot from four positions with the rifle—prone, sitting, kneeling, and standing. Matches in which competing teams exchange scores by telegraphic and postal facilities are common. Trapshooting with shotguns began in England in the 19th cent. To simulate the flight of game birds, "clay pigeons" (originally made of clay but now molded of silt and pitch in the shape of saucers) are hurled from a mechanical contrivance (the trap). The distance between the shooter and his target varies from 16 to 25 yd (14.63–22.86 m); a 12-gauge gun is preferred. Trapshooting was adopted in the United States in the late 19th cent., and in 1900 the American Trapshooting Association was organized. Annual championship matches are held at Vandalia, Ohio. Skeet, in its early years called "round the clock" shooting, was devised (1910) by C. E. Davies of Andover, Mass. The name, chosen in a magazine contest, is an old Scandinavian form of the word *shoot*. Two trapshooting devices hurl "pigeons" at and over each other from 40 yd (36.58 m) apart. The marksman shoots at the moving target from different stations on the perimeter of a semicircle connecting the traps. Guns used are 12-, 16-, 20-, and 28-gauge and .410 bore. In skeet matches 25 "pigeons" are thrown, of which 8 are hurled in pairs. The United States and the Soviet Union excel in international shooting competition. See W. F. Roper, *Pistol and Revolver Shooting* (1945); M. M. Russell, *Skeet* (1954); C. E. Chapel, *Field, Skeet, and Trap Shooting* (rev. ed. 1962); Jack O'Connor, *Complete Book of Shooting* (1965); Jaroslav Lugs, *A History of Shooting* (1968).

shooting star, in astronomy: see METEOR.

shooting star, in botany: see PRIMROSE.

Shophach (shō'făk), variant of SHOBACH.

Shophan: see ATROTH.

Shore, Jane, d. 1527?, mistress of Edward IV of England. The wife of William Shore, a goldsmith, she became c.1470 mistress to Edward IV and exerted a great influence over the king. After Edward's death (1483) she became the mistress of Thomas Grey, 1st marquess of Dorset, and then of Lord Hastings. Probably only out of political motives, she was accused of sorcery (1483) by Richard III, placed in the Tower of London, and later forced to do public penance as a harlot. Her great beauty attracted the king's solicitor, Thomas Lynon, but their proposed marriage failed to come about, and Jane died in poverty. Her life was the subject of Nicholas Rowe's *Tragedy of Jane Shore* (1714). See C. J. S. Thompson, *The Witchery of Jane Shore* (1933).

shore: see COAST; BEACH.

shore bird, common name for members of the large order Charadriiformes, which includes birds found on coasts and beaches throughout the world. Included in this group are the AVOCET, CURLEW, OYSTER CATCHER, PHALAROPE, PLOVER, SANDPIPER, SNIPE, and STILT. The similarity and close relationship of these birds is illustrated by the surf birds, which are also called plover-billed turnstones and are considered by some to be intermediate between plovers and turnstones and by others to be most closely allied to the sandpipers. The godwits, which migrate from subarctic regions S to Africa and Australia, are related to the curlews but resemble the phalaropes in their breeding and nesting habits. Shore birds in general are shy, inconspicuously marked birds with long, slender bills for probing the sand or mud for food and relatively long, strong legs for wading and running. The order Charadriiformes is classified in the phylum CHORDATA, subphylum Vertebrata, class Aves.

Shoreview, residential village (1970 pop. 10,995), Ramsey co., SE Minn., a suburb of St. Paul; settled 1850, set off from Mounds View and inc. 1957. It has a number of arsenals that produce arms and ammunition. The village is built around seven beautiful lakes.

Shorewood, village (1970 pop. 15,576), Milwaukee co., SE Wis., between the Milwaukee River and Lake Michigan, a suburb of Milwaukee; settled c. 1835, inc. 1900. It is mostly residential.

shoring, placing of props or braces, called shores, against or beneath a structure for support. Shoring is often used to stabilize a building when it is to undergo structural modification or repair. Commonly made of timbers measuring 12 in. (30.5 cm) by 12 in., shores are placed in an inclined position, bearing against the external walls of the building. The upper ends, which are sometimes capped with steel, fit into niches cut in brickwork, and the lower ends rest on bases or platforms, frequently of steel plate. The application of wedges or steel jacks between the lower ends of the shores and the platforms shifts part of the weight of a building from its foundation to the shoring. Shores are frequently used as supplemental support for buildings damaged by fire or by underpinning failure. When employed horizontally, e.g., when a building is removed from between two others, the shores consist of wooden struts suitably braced and exerting pressure on wall plates in order to distribute the thrust over a wide area. Shoring is also used widely in shipbuilding to support hulls that are under construction. See Lazarus White and E. A. Prentis, *Underpinning: Its Practice and Applications* (1931, rev. ed. 1950).

short circuit, deflection of the current in an electric circuit whenever the resistance in its path is changed. In common usage the term is often used to indicate a broken ELECTRIC CIRCUIT, which occurs when an electric FUSE "blows out," when a CIRCUIT BREAKER is tripped, or when a connecting wire in the circuit is broken and current no longer passes through it.

shorthand, any brief, rapid system of writing that may be used in transcribing, or recording, the spoken word. Such systems, many having characters based on the letters of the alphabet, were used in ancient times; the shorthand of Tiro, Cicero's amanuensis, was used for centuries. Modern systems date from 1588, when Timothy Bright published his 500-odd symbols for words; a French system was developed by Jacques Cossard in 1651, a German one in 1679. In 1602, Rev. John Willis published the *Arte of Stenographie;* there followed dozens of systems before 1837, when the shorthand of Isaac PITMAN appeared. This, with improvements, is in wide use in English-speaking countries today; it is perhaps the most rapid shorthand system and is favored by many court and convention reporters. The Pitman system makes use of shading (a line heavily drawn has a meaning different from that of the same line lightly drawn) and of differences in slope and position on a given line; it is geometric in outline and is difficult to master, but makes possible very great speed. John Robert Gregg (1867–1948) in 1888 published a popular system of business shorthand in use today. Its outlines are curved and natural, resembling those of ordinary script; need for lifting the pen was eliminated as much as possible, so that a cursive motion is used; there is no shading, but variation in length of line indicates variation in meaning. The outlines were scientifically worked out for simplicity and writing ease. Other shorthand systems employ shortened forms of longhand, e.g., Speedwriting, used where legibility is the principal concern. On the Continent, F. X. Gabelsberger (Germany) and Émile Duployé (France) originated widely used systems; in South America and Canada, the Sloan-Duployan shorthand is favored. Rapid writing with shorthand machines has also developed. Use of keyboard machines such as the Stenotype or Stenograph machines is extensive in courts of law and other places where great speed, silence, and portability of equipment are essential in recording speech. See Hans Glatte, *Shorthand Systems of the World* (1959); L. A. Leslie, *The Story of Gregg Shorthand* (1964); J. R. Gregg, *Gregg Shorthand Dictionary* (1972).

Shorthorn cattle, breed of beef cattle developed from the native cattle of the Tees valley of Yorkshire and Durham counties in NE England; they were formerly called Durham cattle. The systematic breeding of Shorthorns was undertaken in the latter part of the 18th cent. They were first imported to the United States in 1783 and are now found in every part of the country. Shorthorns are the largest of the beef breeds, with compact, low-set, rectangular bodies. In color they vary from red to white or may be any combination of these colors, with a predominance of roan. Because of their strength and docility, Shorthorns occasionally have been used as draft animals. The Milking Shorthorn, developed in England from the Shorthorn, is now the most popular dual-purpose breed (dairy and beef) found in the N Central United States. The Polled (hornless) Shorthorns represent about one third of the beef Shorthorn cattle registered in the United States.

Short Parliament: see ENGLISH CIVIL WAR.

short story, brief prose fiction. The term covers a wide variety of narratives—from stories in which the main focus is on the course of events to studies of character, from the "short short" story to extended and complex narratives such as Thomas Mann's *Death in Venice*. Most often the short story is restricted in character and situation and is concerned with creating a single, dynamic effect. Its length usually falls between 2,000 and 10,000 words. Short stories date back to earliest times; they can be found in the Bible, in the *Gesta Romanorum* of the Middle Ages, in Boccaccio's *Decameron*, and in Chaucer's *Canterbury Tales*. The modern short story is said to have begun in the 19th cent. with the works of Edgar Allan Poe and Guy de Maupassant. Notable

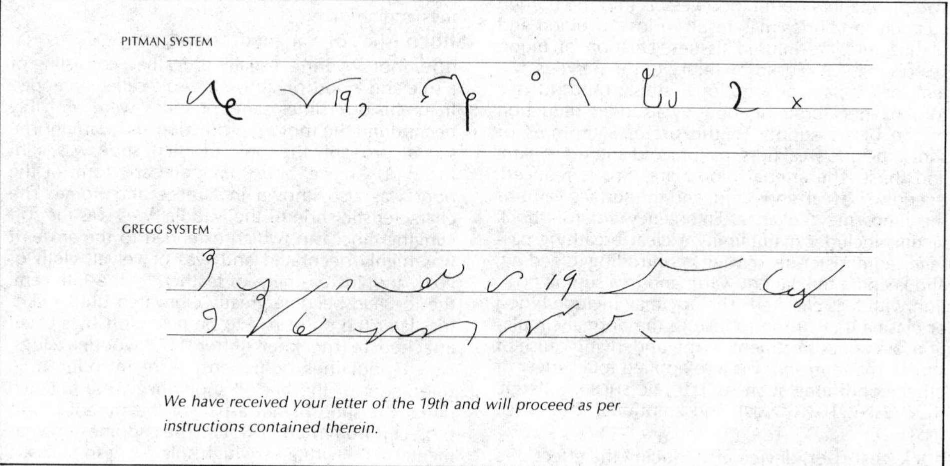
PITMAN SYSTEM
GREGG SYSTEM
We have received your letter of the 19th and will proceed as per instructions contained therein.

Shorthand systems

among the exponents of the form are Henry James, O. Henry, E. T. A. Hoffmann, Chekhov, Kafka, D. H. Lawrence, Katherine Mansfield, Sherwood Anderson, Ernest Hemingway, Katherine Anne Porter, John O'Hara, Flannery O'Connor, J. D. Salinger, and John Cheever. See studies by Gerald Levin, ed. (1967) and F. L. Ingram (1971).

short takeoff and landing aircraft (STOL), heavier-than-air craft, capable of rising from and descending to the ground with only a short length of runway, but incapable of doing so vertically. The precise definition of an STOL aircraft has not been universally agreed upon. However, it has been tentatively defined as an aircraft that upon taking off needs only 1,000 ft (305 m) of runway to clear a 50-ft (15-m) obstacle at the end of that distance and upon landing can clear the same obstacle and then land within 1,000 ft. Typically, STOL aircraft have large wings that are equipped with special aerodynamic devices such as slotted flaps, drooped leading edges, and auxiliary spoilers that augment lift, increase stability, and improve the effect of control surfaces. As the airfields from which STOL planes are expected to operate will be in confined areas, the ability to fly stably at low speeds, especially in turbulent air, is an important design requirement for them. See VERTICAL TAKEOFF AND LANDING AIRCRAFT.

short waves, radio waves whose frequencies range from about 3 to 25 megahertz (Mhz), corresponding roughly to the high-frequency band (see RADIO FREQUENCY). When they impinge on certain layers of the ionosphere, short waves are largely reflected back toward the earth. By one or more reflections between the earth and the ionosphere, a short-wave radio signal can be received at long distances from the transmitter.

Shoshannim and **Shoshannim-Eduth** (shōshăn'-ĭm-ē'dəth): see AIJELETH SHAHAR.

Shoshenk I: see SHESHONK I.

Shoshone Falls, 212 ft (65 m) high, flowing over a rim 900 ft (274 m) wide in the Snake River, S Idaho. Once a great spectacle, the falls have been reduced by irrigation projects upstream.

Shoshone Indians, North American Indians whose language belongs to the Shoshonean group of the Uto-Aztecan branch of the Aztec-Tanoan linguistic stock (see AMERICAN INDIAN LANGUAGES). In the early 19th cent. the Shoshone occupied SE California, NW Utah, SW Montana, W Wyoming, S Idaho, and NE Nevada. The Shoshone were historically divided into four groups: the COMANCHE of W Texas, a historically recent subdivision of the Wind River Shoshone of Wyoming; the Northern Shoshone of Idaho and Utah, who had horses and ranged across the Great Plains in search of buffalo; the western Shoshone, who did not use horses and subsisted mainly on nuts and other wild vegetation; and the Wind River Shoshone of Wyoming. Today the Shoshone live on reservations in California, Idaho, Nevada, Utah, and Wyoming; they number some 8,000. See V. C. Trenholm and Maurine Carley, *The Shoshonis, Sentinels of the Rockies* (1964); Edward Dorn, *The Shoshoneans* (1966); J. G. Jorgensen, *The Sun Dance Religion* (1972).

Shoshone project, NW Wyo., near the Mont. line and in the Shoshone River basin. Developed by the U.S. Bureau of Reclamation, it irrigates c.94,000 acres (38,000 hectares) and has four divisions. The project is supplied by a system of small diversion dams and canals and by Buffalo Bill Dam (325 ft/99 m high; completed 1910) on the Shoshone River. The Shoshone power plant (5,600 kw capacity; completed 1922) at Buffalo Bill Dam and the Heart Mt. power plant (5,000 kw; 1948) supply power for the project. The power system is integrated with the MISSOURI RIVER BASIN PROJECT. Cody and Powell, Wyo., are on the project.

Shostakovich, Dmitri (dyĭmē'trē shŏstŏkô'vĭch), 1906–, Russian composer, b. St. Petersburg. Shostakovich studied at the Leningrad Conservatory, 1919–25. The early success of his First Symphony (1925) was confirmed by two satirical works—an opera, *The Nose* (Leningrad, 1930; from a tale by Gogol), and a ballet the same year, *The Golden Age.* Shostakovich has sought Soviet approval and has survived the changing tides of opinion. Severely castigated after the public triumph of his opera *Lady Macbeth of the District of Mzensk* (1934), he was restored to favor with his Fifth Symphony (1937). His outstanding works include a piano concerto (1933), the Piano Quintet (1940), the Second String Quartet (1944), the Ninth Symphony (1945), and his piano preludes. See biography by V. I. Seroff and N. K. Shohat (1970); study by N. F. Kay (1971).

shotgun: see SMALL ARMS.

Shotwell, James Thomson, 1874–1965, Canadian-American historian, b. Strathroy, Ont. A teacher of history at Columbia from 1900 and professor from 1908 to 1942, Shotwell also worked tirelessly to promote international understanding. He was an active member of several national and international labor, peace, and historical conferences, including the Paris Peace Conference (1918–19) and the conference at San Francisco (1945). He was director of the division of economics and history (1942–49) and president (1949–50) of the Carnegie Endowment for International Peace and served as chairman (1932–43) of the American committee on International Intellectual Cooperation of the League of Nations. Among his many works are *An Introduction to the History of History* (1922; rev. ed. *The History of History,* Vol. I, 1939), *Plans and Protocols to End War* (1925), *War as an Instrument of National Policy* (1929), *The Origins of the International Labor Organization* (1934), *On the Rim of the Abyss* (1936), *The Great Decision* (1944), and *The Long Way to Freedom* (1960). Shotwell was also coauthor of several authoritative studies on international relations and editor of *Economic and Social History of the World War* (150 vol., 1919–29). See his autobiography (1961).

shovelhead shark: see HAMMERHEAD SHARK.

Shovell, Sir Clowdisley, or **Sir Cloudesley Shovel** (kloudz'lē shŭv'əl), 1650–1707, English admiral. In the War of the Grand Alliance he burned enemy ships at the battle of La Hogue in 1692 and was joint commander of the English fleet in 1693. In the War of the Spanish Succession he brought home the silver captured by Sir George ROOKE at Vigo (1702), helped him capture Gibraltar (1704), and assisted at the capture of Barcelona (1705). Returning from an abortive attack on Toulon in 1707, he was lost with 800 or 900 men when his ship was wrecked off the Scilly Islands.

showboat. In the early 19th cent. entertainment was brought by boat to the pioneers that settled along the western rivers (especially the Mississippi and Ohio) of the United States. At first companies only traveled by boat, performing on land. Later the boats themselves, first paddle boats and finally steamboats, were equipped with stages. Docking near a town, they would herald their arrival with trumpets and flags. The companies presented popular melodramas, with vaudeville performances, called olios, between the acts; by day, the boats often served as museums. With the coming of the Civil War, their popularity dwindled. Edna Ferber's novel *Show Boat* is an interesting description of the life of its people. See historical study by Philip Graham (1951, repr. 1970).

Shreveport (shrēv'pôrt), city (1970 pop. 182,064), seat of Caddo parish, NW La., on the Red River near the Texas and Ark. lines; inc. 1839. The second-largest city in the state, it is an oil and natural-gas center, with important metal, cotton, and lumber manufactures. Dairy goods, feed and grain, machinery, telephones, defense products, and chemicals are also made. The city was founded after the Red River there was laboriously cleared (1833–36) of logs and driftwood, rendering it navigable. It became the Confederate capital of Louisiana in 1863. The discovery of oil in 1906 provided the greatest impetus for Shreveport's growth. It is the seat of Centenary College of Louisiana, Louisiana State Univ. in Shreveport, the Louisiana State Univ. School of Medicine in Shreveport, two junior colleges, and the state fairgrounds. Of interest are the ruins of Confederate Fort Humbug, which was defended with fake cannons. Barksdale Air Force Base, headquarters of the 2d U.S. Air Force and a strategic command installation, is just across the river. Nearby is Cross Lake, with recreational facilities.

shrew, common name for the small, insectivorous mammals of the family Soricidae, related to the moles. Shrews include the smallest mammals; the smallest shrews are under 2 in. (5.1 cm) long, excluding the tail, and the largest are about 6 in. (15 cm) long. Light-boned and fragile, shrews have mouselike bodies and long, pointed snouts with tiny, sharp teeth. They are terrestrial and nocturnal, mostly living under vegetation; some occupy the burrows of other small animals. Their musky odor, produced by a pair of glands on their flanks, deters some of their potential predators. Extremely active and nervous, they have a higher metabolic rate than any other animal. The heart of the masked shrew, *Sorex cinereus,* beats 800 times a minute, considerably faster than that of the hummingbird. Shrews must eat incessantly in order to stay alive; most will starve to death if deprived of food for half a day. They eat anything available, but prefer small animals; they are economically important as destroyers of insects and slugs that harm crops. Shrews are easily startled and will jump, faint, or drop dead at a sudden noise. They are vicious fighters, killing and eating larger animals, such as mice, as well as other shrews. A belief that the shrew's bite is poisonous was dismissed for years as a folk tale, but has since been substantiated: the saliva of at least one species of shrew is lethal to mice and can cause considerable pain to humans. Shrews live about 15 months and reproduce rapidly, bearing up to four litters a year, with up to eight young in a litter. Shrews are found in Europe, Asia, North and Central America, and N South America. There are over 100 species, all rather similar, classified in about 20 genera. The subfamily of red-toothed shrews, with orange- or red-tipped teeth, includes both Old and New World species; the white-toothed shrews are confined to the Old World. The common shrews of the Northern Hemisphere belong to the red-toothed genus *Sorex,* with many species in North America and a few in Europe and Asia. The water shrew of Canada and N United States, *Sorex palustris,* is adapted to aquatic living and can actually walk on the surface of water for a short distance. There are other aquatic shrews, of several genera, in Europe and Asia. The giant water shrew of Africa is not a true shrew but an insectivore related to the TENREC. The elephant, or jumping, shrews of Africa are insectivores of the family Macroscelididae; they resemble miniature kangaroos with trunks. The Oriental tree shrew is an insectivore-like PRIMATE. True shrews are classified in the phylum CHORDATA, subphylum Vertebrata, class Mammalia, order Insectivora, family Soricidae.

Shrewsbury, Charles Talbot, duke of (shrōz'bərē, shrōōz'-), 1660–1718, English statesman. Brought up a Roman Catholic, he embraced Protestantism in 1679. A powerful Whig, he was one of the seven nobles who signed the invitation to William of Orange (later William III) to take the throne in 1688. After the Glorious Revolution, William made him (1689) secretary of state and privy councilor. He resigned in 1690, but William reappointed him in 1694 and made him duke of Shrewsbury. Despite persistent rumors of his correspondence with the Jacobites, it was against William's will that he resigned in 1699. Shrewsbury lived in Rome, uninvolved in politics, until 1706. On his return to England, he was won over by Robert Harley to the Tory cause, became lord chamberlain (1710), lord lieutenant of Ireland (1713), and lord treasurer (1714). He supported the Hanoverian succession and was briefly (1714–15) lord chamberlain under George I. See biographies by T. C. Nicholson, A. S. Turberville (1930), and D. H. Somerville (1962).

Shrewsbury, Elizabeth Talbot, countess of, 1520–1608, English noblewoman, known as Bess of Hardwick. At the age of 12 she married Robert Barlow, who died shortly afterward. She was married and widowed twice more, inheriting large estates, before she was married in 1568 to George Talbot, 6th earl of Shrewsbury. The marriage (1574) of her daughter Elizabeth to Charles Stuart, brother of Lord Darnley, angered Queen Elizabeth I because Stuart had a claim to the throne, and the countess was sent to the Tower of London for three months. The countess quarreled with her husband and accused (1584) him of a love affair with Mary Queen of Scots, whose custodian he was (1569–84), but the couple was nominally reconciled before his death (1590). She built a number of great mansions, including Hardwick Hall. See biography by E. Carleton Williams (1959).

Shrewsbury, John Talbot, 1st **earl of,** 1388?–1453, English soldier. As lieutenant of Ireland (1414–19, 1445–47) he quelled unrest in that country, but he achieved his greatest fame for his military daring in France during the latter years of the Hundred Years War. He was present at the siege of Orléans and was taken prisoner (1429) at Patay and held for four years. He was finally slain at Castillon.

Shrewsbury (shrōōz-'), municipal borough (1971 pop. 56,140), county town of Shropshire, W England, on the Severn River. Shrewsbury is a road and rail junction. There are varied manufactures, including diesel engines. It was an ancient Saxon and Norman stronghold. The earldom of Shrewsbury was an important marcher lordship (see WELSH MARCHES). There are ruins of an 11th-century castle and abbey and several old churches. The narrow streets are lined by many oak-timbered, black-and-white houses of the 15th, 16th, and 17th cent., and there is a fine public garden and park that adds to the city's beauty. In 1403, Henry IV defeated Henry Percy

(Hotspur) on a plain near Shrewsbury and had the body of the rebel displayed to the townspeople as proof. Shrewsbury School, a public school founded in 1552 by King Edward VI, overlooks the Severn. Sir Philip Sidney, Charles Darwin (who was born in Shrewsbury), and Fulke Greville studied there. In 1974, Shewsbury became part of the new nonmetropolitan county of Salop.

Shrewsbury, town (1970 pop. 19,196), Worcester co., central Mass.; inc. 1727. Plastic goods are manufactured there. Gen. Artemas Ward was born in Shrewsbury.

shrike or **butcher bird**, predatory songbird found in most parts of the world except Australia and South America. The plumage of the European and North American species is mostly gray, black, and white; the tail is long and rounded, and the wings are rather short. Some African species are brilliantly colored. The name butcher bird reflects its habit of impaling its prey—small birds and mammals and large insects—on a thorn or sharp twig before tearing it apart with its strong, tip-hooked beak. North American shrikes include the loggerhead, great gray or northern, and California shrikes. Shrikes are classified in the phylum CHORDATA, subphylum Vertebrata, class Aves, order Passeriformes, family Laniidae.

shrimp, small marine decapod CRUSTACEAN with 10 jointed legs on the thorax, well-developed swimmerets on the abdominal segments, and a body that is compressed laterally. Shrimp differ from their close relatives, the lobsters and crabs, in that they are primarily swimmers rather than crawlers. As with other crustaceans, the body is covered with a smooth exoskeleton that must be periodically shed and re-formed as the animal grows. However, the shrimp's exoskeleton tends to be thinner than that of most other crustaceans; it is grayish and almost transparent. In some areas of the United States the term prawn is loosely applied to any large shrimp. However, in Europe, only members of the genus *Crangon,* distinguished from other shrimp by a slender body and a depressed abdomen, are considered true shrimp, while decapod crustaceans having toothed beaks (rostrums), long antennae, slender legs, and laterally compressed abdomens are called prawns. Tropical shrimp have bizarre shapes and colors. One of the most unusual shrimp is the pistol shrimp, a burrow dweller whose third right appendage is adapted into a huge claw with a moveable finger that can be snapped shut with so much force that the resulting sound waves kill or stun nearby prey. Shrimp are widely distributed in temperate and tropical salt and fresh waters. They may grow as long as 9 in. (23 cm), but most are smaller. They swim forward by paddling their abdominal swimmerets and can move backward with swift strokes of their fanlike tails. The common commercial shrimp, of the genus *Peneus,* is found in coastal waters from Virginia south. Shrimp flesh, which turns pink and white when cooked, is by far the most popular crustacean food and forms the basis of an important industry with centers in all the Gulf states. Shrimp are caught in large baglike nets that are dragged over the ocean floor. The flesh is canned in large quantities; fresh shrimp is packed in ice for shipping, or frozen and packaged. Dried shrimp is exported to the Orient, although there are major shrimp fisheries there, especially in Japan. There are several other crustacean forms that are commonly called shrimp although they do not belong to the same order as the true shrimp, order Decapoda, which also includes the lobsters and crabs. The MANTIS SHRIMP, possessing strong grasping legs resembling those of a praying mantis, make up the order Stomatopoda. The tiny BRINE SHRIMP and fairy shrimp that seldom reach 1 in. (2.54 cm) in length belong to a completely separate subclass, Branchiopoda, order Anostraca. Two other branchiopods, tadpole shrimp and clam shrimp, are classified in the orders Notostraca and Diplostraca, respectively. Mysid shrimp are members of the order Mysidacea. True shrimp are classified in the phylum ARTHROPODA, class Crustacea, order Decapoda.

Shrine: see PILGRIM.

Shriver, Robert Sargent, 1915–, U.S. public official, b. Westminster, Md. A lawyer, he served in World War II and was (1945–46) an assistant editor of *Newsweek* magazine before joining the business enterprises of his future father-in-law, Joseph P. Kennedy. He participated in John F. Kennedy's successful presidential campaign, and in 1961 he was appointed the first director of the U.S. PEACE CORPS. An effective head of this organization, he was named (1964) director of the Office of Economic Opportunity (OEO) by President Lyndon B. Johnson and held both posts until 1966, when he resigned from the Peace Corps to devote himself to OEO. In 1968 he was appointed ambassador to France; he held that post until 1970. A Democrat, he became George McGovern's vice presidential running mate in 1972, after Thomas Eagleton withdrew from the Democratic ticket. McGovern and Shriver were defeated. See his *Point of the Lance* (1964); biography by R. A. Liston (1964).

Shropshire (shrŏp'shĭr, -shər), county (1971 pop. 336,934), 1,348 sq mi (3,491 sq km), W England. It is also sometimes called Salop. The county town is SHREWSBURY. The terrain to the north and east of the Severn, Shropshire's principal river, is level; toward the Welsh border and the south the land is hilly. The county is chiefly agricultural, but some coal is mined and there are metal products and food-processing industries. The ancient Watling Street and Offa's Dyke cross the county. In Anglo-Saxon times Shropshire was a part of the kingdom of MERCIA. After the Norman Conquest it became an important part of the WELSH MARCHES and was the scene of much border conflict recalled by the ruins of many medieval castles. There are also many very old monastic remains. The quiet beauty of the countryside is suggested in A. E. Housman's *Shropshire Lad.* In 1974, Shropshire became part of the new nonmetropolitan county of Salop.

Shropshire sheep, mutton breed developed from the native sheep of Shropshire and Staffordshire, England. As early as 1340 there was a grade of wool known as Shropshire, but the breed was not officially recognized until about the middle of the 19th cent. The Shropshire is of medium size, has a dark face, is prolific and fast growing, and produces a good grade of mutton and wool. Because of its adaptability, it has spread widely over the world. It is the most popular breed of English origin in the United States, to which its importation began c.1855.

Shrove Tuesday, day before ASH WEDNESDAY (the beginning of LENT). In the Latin countries it is the last day of the carnival, called by the French MARDI GRAS.

shrub, any woody, perennial, bushy plant that branches into several stems or trunks at the base and is smaller than a TREE. Shrubs are an important feature of permanent landscape planting, being used for formal decorative groups, hedges, screens, and background plantings, to which they contribute pattern, color, fragrance, or utility. In the natural style of landscape gardening they are simply allowed to grow untended, but in many gardens they are pruned in the spring or fall for greater shapeliness and to induce more compact growth. Many shrubs are beautiful even in winter because of their green foliage (as in the evergreen arborvitae and rhododendron) and decorative stem and branch forms and brightly colored fruits. Among the most frequently used shrubs in America are the lilac, mock orange, viburnum, forsythia, azalea, flowering shadbush, cotoneaster, and barberry. In arid, arctic, and other regions of extreme climatic conditions where trees do not thrive, shrubs often provide valuable forage for wildlife and livestock as well as wood for local construction and for fuel. Tree species may grow as shrubs under unfavorable environmental conditions, and the distinction between trees and shrubs becomes one of usage rather than of strictly botanical characteristics. See Donald Wyman, *Shrubs and Vines for American Gardens* (rev. ed. 1969).

Shua (sho͞o'ə). **1** Asherite woman. 1 Chron. 7.32. **2** Father of one of Judah's wives. Gen. 38.2.

Shuah (sho͞o'ə), son of Abraham. Gen. 25.2. Descendants are the Shuhites, an Arab tribe; Bildad the Shuhite was probably a member. Job 2.11.

Shual (sho͞o'əl), descendant of Asher. 1 Chron. 7.36.

Shubael (sho͞o'bāl, sho͞obā'əl), variant of SHEBUEL.

Shubert Brothers (sho͞o'bərt), theatrical managers and producers. The brothers were Sam S. (1876–1905), Jacob J. (1880–1963), and Lee (1883–1953). They began as managers of touring companies. In 1900 they became managers of the Herald Square Theatre, New York City, thereafter managing and building many theaters in New York and other U.S. cities. Known for their productions of operettas, they introduced many stars to the public and were the first to stage the modern revue. The Shuberts continually suffered financial losses in an effort to keep the New York theater alive and productive. From 1953 until his retirement (c.1959), Jacob was the sole head of Shubert Enterprises, with offices in the Shubert Theatre (opened 1913) off the famous Shubert Alley in New York City. See Jerry Stogg, *The Brothers Shubert* (1968).

Shubun (sho͞o'bo͝on'), fl. 1st half of 15th cent., Japanese painter and Zen Buddhist priest. He studied under Josetsu, and became the central figure in the renaissance in Japan of the Chinese style of ink painting. Shubun and Sesshu, who may have been his pupil, are regarded as the two greatest masters of ink painting of the Muromachi period. There are many landscape paintings in ink attributed to Shubun, which vary in quality and style. Examples are in the Fujiwara collection and the Seikado Foundation.

shuffleboard, sport in which players use cue sticks to push disks onto a scoring diagram at either end of a concrete or terrazzo court. The court is 52 ft (15.85 m) long and 6 ft (1.83 m) wide. The bases of the triangular scoring diagrams are parallel to and 8 ft (2.44 m) from the court's end lines. Each diagram is 9 ft (2.74 m) long and 6 ft (1.83 m) wide at the base. Lines parallel to the base divide each diagram into 7-, 8-, and 10-point sections. Extending 1.5 ft (45 cm) below the base is a penalty area worth minus ten points. Each player uses four disks, each of which is about 1 in. (2.54 cm) thick, 6 in. (15.24 cm) in diameter, and weighs a little less than a pound (.45 kg). Play can be for two (singles) or four (doubles), and a winning point total is usually set at 50, 75, or 100 points. Probably originating in 13th-century England, shuffleboard is similar to CURLING. It has long been a popular recreation for the elderly and for cruise-ship passengers. The modern version of the game was introduced (1913) to the United States by hotel proprietors in Daytona Beach, Fla. The National Shuffleboard Association was founded (1931) to devise uniform rules for the rapidly growing sport. It also sponsors national championships for men and women. See C. S. Haslam, *How-To Book of Shuffleboard* (2d. ed. 1965); O. C. Catan, *Secrets of Shuffleboard Strategy* (1967).

Shuham (sho͞o'hăm), son of Dan. Num. 26.42. Hushim: Gen. 46.23.

Shuhite (sho͞o'hīt), a patronymic: see SHUAH.

Shuji, Tsushima: see DAZAI, OSAMU.

Shulamite (sho͞o'ləmīt), female character of the Song of Solomon. Cant. 6.13. See SHUNEM.

Shultz, George Pratt, 1920–, U.S. economist and government official, b. New York City, grad. Princeton, 1942, Ph.D. Massachusetts Institute of Technology, 1949. He taught at the Massachusetts Institute of Technology (1946–57) before becoming (1957) professor of industrial relations in the Univ. of Chicago graduate school of business; he was dean of that school from 1962 to 1969. Shultz served as an economic consultant to the Eisenhower, Kennedy, and Johnson administrations, and in 1969 he became Secretary of Labor under President Richard Nixon. In 1970 he was appointed chairman of the new Office of Management and Budget, and in 1972 he was made Secretary of the Treasury, becoming also a special economic adviser to the President. Although an advocate of a free-market economy, Shultz nonetheless implemented Nixon's policy of wage and price controls. He resigned in May, 1974.

Shumathites (sho͞o'məthīts), family of Kirjathjearim. 1 Chron. 2.53.

Shumen (sho͞o'mĕn), city (1968 est. pop. 68,100), NE Bulgaria. It is a railway junction and a market for grains and other agricultural products. Brewing, canning, flour milling, motor vehicle assembling, and the manufacture of spare parts for automobiles and tractors are the chief industries. Founded in 927, the city was fortified under Turkish rule (15th–19th cent.) and was strategically important in the Russo-Turkish Wars of the 18th and 19th cent. It is also the site of the largest mosque (built 1649) in Bulgaria. Originally called Shumen or Shumla, the city was renamed (1950) Kolarovgrad in honor of Bulgarian Communist leader Kolarov, who was born there. The name was changed back to Shumen in 1965.

Shunem (sho͞o'nəm), town of Issachar, on the north side of the vale of Jezreel. The adjective SHULAMITE probably refers to it. Joshua 19.18; 1 Sam. 28.4. It is the present-day Sulam (Israel).

Shuni (sho͞o'nī), founder of a family of Gadites. Gen. 46.16; Num. 26.15.

Shunsho (Katsukawa Shunsho) (kätso͞o'käwä sho͞on'shō), 1726–92, Japanese painter and printmaker. A painter of the ukiyo-e style (see JAPANESE ART), in which costume design and color are executed with precision in an otherwise stylized setting, Shunsho specialized in portraits of Kabuki actors in their famous roles. Shunsho was noted for his ability to capture the actors' faces and to express their acting style pictorially.

Shupham (shōō'făm) or **Shuppim** (shŭp'ĭm), family of Benjamin. Num. 26.39; 1 Chron. 7.12,15; 26.16. Muppim: Gen. 46.21. Shephuphan: 1 Chron. 8.5.

Shur (shŭr), landmark of the Egyptian border N of the Red Sea, also called the Wilderness of Shur. It is associated with the wandering of Hagar and with the Exodus. Gen. 16.7; 20.1; 25.18; Ex. 15.22; 1 Sam. 15.7; 27.8.

Shuri, city: see RYUKYU ISLANDS.

Shushan (shōō'shăn): see SUSA.

Shushan-eduth (shōō'shăn-ē'dəth): see AIJELETH SHAHAR.

Shushtar (shōōshtär'), town (1966 pop. 24,000), Khuzistan prov., SW Iran, on the Karun River. It is an agricultural trade center and has long been known for its brocaded textiles and metalwork. Nearby are major petroleum fields. It was at Shushtar that Shapur I, after his great victory (A.D. 260) over Valerian at Édhessa, set his captives to work building vast hydraulic works, including a large dam across the Karun River. Later, under the Mongols (13th–14th cent.), Shushtar was a beautiful and prosperous town. It was captured by Tamerlane in 1393 and by Shah Ismail in 1508. After the 18th cent. it declined in importance. A serious outbreak of plague occurred there in 1876.

Shuster, George Nauman, 1894–, American educator, b. Lancaster, Wis., grad. Norte Dame (B.A., 1915; M.A., 1920) and Columbia (Ph.D, 1940). He was head of the department of English at Notre Dame (1920–24) and professor of English at St. Joseph's College for Women, Brooklyn, N.Y. (1924–35), and at Hunter College he was dean and acting president (1939–40) and president (1940–60). Upon retirement from Hunter he became assistant to the president of the Univ. of Notre Dame. His writings include *The Catholic Spirit in Modern English Literature* (1922), *The Germans* (1932), *The English Ode from Milton to Keats* (1940), *Education and Moral Wisdom* (1960), and *Catholic Education in a Changing World* (1968). See his autobiographical *The Ground I Walked on* (1961, 2d enl. ed. 1969).

Shuswap Indians (shōō'swŏp), North American Indians whose language belongs to the Salishan branch of the Algonquian-Wakashan linguistic stock (see AMERICAN INDIAN LANGUAGES). In the mid-19th cent. they lived in S British Columbia on the Fraser River and numbered some 7,000. The Shuswap are now on reservations in British Columbia.

Shute, Nevil (Nevil Shute Norway), 1899–1960, English novelist, b. Ealing, Middlesex, grad. Oxford, 1922. After serving in World War I, he was manager of a construction company until 1938. He fought also in World War II and emigrated to Australia in 1950. Shute wrote 26 novels, which, taken collectively, have sold more than the works of any other contemporary British writer. His novels are fast-paced and usually have moral themes. They include *Ordeal* (1939), *The Pied Piper* (1944), *On the Beach* (1957), and *Trustee from the Toolroom* (1960).

Shuthelah (shōō'thēlə), head of an Ephraimite family. Num. 26.35; 1 Chron. 7.20.

shuttle: see LOOM.

Shuvalov, Piotr Andreyevich, Count (pyô'tər əndrā'əvĭch shōōvä'ləf), 1827–89, Russian administrator and diplomat. An adviser to Czar Alexander II, he opposed the czar's reforms and headed (1866–73) the notorious third section, or political police, of the imperial chancellery. He also served as envoy (1873), then ambassador (1874–79), to Great Britain. In 1878, at the end of the Russo-Turkish War (1877–78), he negotiated to secure a treaty that would please Great Britain more than the Treaty of San Stefano, which had greatly enhanced Russian influence in SE Europe. His willingness to accommodate Great Britain led to the Congress of Berlin, which abrogated the territorial gains of the Treaty of San Stefano. The new territorial arrangements were unpopular in Russia, and Shuvalov was recalled.

Si, Hsi (both: sē), or **Si-kiang** (shē-jēäng), great river of S China, c.1,250 mi (2,010 km) long, rising in E Yünnan prov. and flowing generally E through Kwangsi and Kwangtung provs. to the South China Sea near Canton; the Kuei, Pei, and Tung rivers are its chief tributaries. The Si flows mainly through narrow, confined valleys. At the junction with the Pei, E of Canton, the Si forms the vast Canton River delta (2,890 sq mi/7,485 sq km), consisting of a maze of channels and canals. The densely populated delta is one of China's chief economic areas; agriculture (rice, sugarcane, fruit) predominates. One of China's principal inland waterways, the Si is navigable for large ships along most of its length.

Si, chemical symbol of the element SILICON.

SI: see INTERNATIONAL SYSTEM OF UNITS.

Sia (sī'ə) or **Siaha** (sī'əhə), family returned from the Exile. Ezra 2.44; Neh. 7.47.

sial: see CONTINENT.

sialic acid: see GLYCOPROTEIN.

Sialkot (syäl'kōt), city (1972 metropolitan area est. pop. 168,500), E Pakistan. It is a rail junction and a major trade and processing center. Manufactures include bicycles, surgical instruments, sporting goods, cutlery, rubber products, and ceramics. Textile weaving is also important. A fortress built in 1181 by Muhammad of Ghor and the mausoleum of Guru Nanak, founder of the Sikh religion, are in Sialkot. The city is also the birthplace of the philosopher-poet Muhammad Iqbal.

Siam: see THAILAND.

Siam, Gulf of, shallow arm of the South China Sea, c.500 mi (800 km) long and up to 350 mi (560 km) wide, separating the Malay Peninsula from E Thailand, Cambodia, and South Vietnam. Bangkok, the gulf's chief port, is at the mouth of the Chao Phraya River.

siamang: see GIBBON.

Siamese art and architecture. The earliest known art of Siam (Thailand) originated with the Mon people, who came from S Burma and invaded the Mekong valley between the 6th and 8th cent. Their Buddhist images reveal regional iconography as well as the influence of Indian models of the Gupta period. Instead of adhering to the Indian canon of proportions, however, they created somewhat larger, more individualized heads with carefully patterned curls. The Mon figurative conventions are preserved in two massive Buddha sculptures at Tham Rusi (6th–7th cent.). The Hindu sculpture of Siam, in its geometrical simplicity, reflected the Pallava style of SE India. In architecture the shape of the shikhara tower and the use of the protoma window also recall the Pallava style. With the Khmer invasion in the 10th cent., the Siamese assimilated characteristics of the art and architecture of Cambodia. Sculpture of this period combined Hinduism and Buddhism in fusing human and divine imagery in portraiture. A number of bronze sculptures and ritual utensils survive. The Khmer established a capital at Lopburi, where buildings, such as the Wat Mahadhatu, were derived from the temples at ANGKOR. Khmer style was retained long after the Khmer themselves were expelled by the Thai people in the 13th cent. The Thai formed a dynasty at Sukhothai and under them a distinctive decorative style emerged. A splendid head of Buddha in the Museum of Fine Arts, Boston, illustrates the tendency toward linear ornament. The treatment of the figure became increasingly decorated and at the same time less organic. The Thai excelled in ceramics, enhanced by Chinese glazing and brushwork techniques that were developed into a vital independent style. By the 15th cent., during the Ayutthaya period, artists in the south produced illuminated manuscripts, murals, and temple banners, whose development in style parallels that of bronze sculptures. Conventional sculptures were repeated on a vast scale, which caused a decline of aesthetic and technical quality. Ayutthaya was the Siamese capital from 1350 to 1767. The shrines built there were variations of the STUPA form, of round shape and with a series of receding rings that led up to a dome. The architecture bore a resemblance to types developed in Burma and Ceylon. In the 18th cent. Chinese building techniques became popular, and many curved-eave roofs appeared in Bangkok. Since the latter part of the 18th cent. Thai art has revealed Western influence and become highly decorative and superficial to appeal to the tourist trade. See R. S. Le May, *A Concise History of Buddhist Art in Siam* (1938); Theodore Bowie, ed., *The Arts of Thailand* (1960).

Siamese cat: see CAT.

Siamese fighting fish: see BETTA.

Siamese language: see THAI LANGUAGE.

Siamese twins, congenitally united organisms that are complete or nearly complete individuals. They develop from a single fertilized ovum that has divided imperfectly; complete division would produce identical twins, having the same sex and general characteristics. Siamese twins remain attached at the abdomen, chest, back, or top of the head, depending on where the division of the ovum has failed. In some instances the individuals are joined only by a band of musculofibrous tissue and can be separated surgically, but in other instances they share vital organs and separation may not be possible. Sometimes an ovum divides in such a way that an organism develops having one body and two heads, or one head and two sets of limbs; such organisms are known as monsters. Only rarely do Siamese twins survive birth. When they do, fatal illness in one dooms the other unless separation is possible. The name Siamese twins derives from the most famous of conjoined male twins, Chang and Eng, born in Siam of Chinese parents in 1811. They were exhibited in Barnum's circus for many years; although never separated, they married and fathered a total of 22 children. They died within 2 hours of each other in 1874. See MULTIPLE BIRTH.

Sian: see HSI-AN, China.

Siang, river, China: see HSIANG.

Siangtan: see HSIANG-T'AN, China.

Siauliai (shēou'lyī), Ger. *Schaulen*, Rus. *Shavli*, city (1969 est. pop. 88,000), W European USSR, in Lithuania. It is a rail hub and has railroad repair shops. Siauliai is also a major tanning, shoe-manufacturing, and flax-processing center. First known in the 15th cent., Siauliai belonged from 1589 until 1772 to the Polish crown. It passed to Russia in 1795 and to newly independent Lithuania in 1920. Siauliai was the site of a Lithuanian victory over the Livonian Knights in 1236; the German free corps was defeated there in 1919.

sib: see CLAN.

Sibawaihi (sēbäwĭhē), c. 760–793, Persian grammarian, considered the most important Arabic grammarian. His book *al-Kitah fi'l nahwi* is the first complete Arabic grammar, upon which all other Arabic grammars are based. It classified words according to function and established rules for vowel endings. The work is filled with quotations from poetry, prose, proverbs, and the Koran.

Sibbald's rorqual: see BLUE WHALE.

Sibbecai or **Sibbechai** (both: sĭb'əkī, -kā'ī), one of David's guard, noted for his fight with the Philistine giant. 2 Sam. 21.18; 1 Chron. 11.29; 20.4; 27.11. Mebunnai: 2 Sam. 23.27.

Sibboleth: see SHIBBOLETH.

Sibelius, Jean Julius Christian (zhän yōō'lyōōs krĭs'tyän sĭbā'lyōōs), 1865–1957, Finnish composer. Sibelius was a highly personal, romantic composer, yet at the same time he represents the culmination of nationalism in Finnish music. He studied in Berlin (1889) and with Karl Goldmark in Vienna (1890). Although Sibelius wrote chamber music, piano music, and violin music, he is best known for his orchestral works. These include tone poems on national subjects, such as *En Saga* (1892; rev. 1901) and *Finlandia* (1900); *The Swan of Tuonela* (1893; from the suite *Lemminkainen*); *Valse triste* (1903); a violin concerto (1903); and seven symphonies (1899, 1901, 1907, 1911, 1915, 1923, and 1924). His works express an intense, mystical love of nature, often conveying the brooding melancholy of his country's northern landscape. In his symphonies he adapted traditional form to his individual manner of building upon short motifs. These themes, while always original, have come to be regarded as folk music. In 1897 he was awarded a lifetime grant by the state which permitted him to devote his career to composing. See biographies by Karl Ekman (tr. 1938), E. Arnold (1941), Harold Johnson (1959), and R. Layton, *Sibelius* (1965) and *Sibelius and His World* (1970).

Šibenik (shēbĕ'nĭk), Ital. *Sebenico,* town (1971 pop. 78,600), W Yugoslavia, in Croatia, on the Adriatic Sea. It is a seaport and naval base on the Dalmatian coast. The city has aluminum, chemical, and textile industries. Founded in the 10th cent., Šibenik was an early residence of the kings of Croatia. It was captured by Venice in 1117, but was held by Hungary from 1351 to 1412, when it again passed to Venice. It passed (1797) to Austria, which held it until 1918. The city was incorporated into Yugoslavia in 1922. Šibenik's finest buildings date from the Venetian period, notably the Cathedral of St. Jacob (1431–55) and a town hall with a Renaissance loggia (built in 1542).

Siberia (sībēr'ēə), Rus. *Sibir,* vast geographical region of the Asian USSR. Although it has no official standing as a political or territorial division, it is generally understood to comprise the northern third of Asia, stretching from the Urals in the west to the mountain ranges of the Pacific Ocean watershed in the east and from the Laptev, Kara, and East Siberian seas (arms of the Arctic Ocean) in the north to the Kazakh steppes, the Altai and Sayan mountain systems, and the borders of the Mongolian People's Republic in the south. The Soviet Far East, which is commonly considered to be part of Siberia, is treated separately in Soviet regional schemes. For a discussion of that region, see SOVIET FAR EAST. Siberia covers c.2,900,000 sq mi (7,511,000 sq km) and has an estimated population (1970) of 29,820,000. Siberia's administrative units are the Yakut, Buryat, and Tuva autonomous republics, the Altai and Krasnoyarsk krays, and the Omsk, Novosibirsk, Tomsk, Kemerovo, Irkutsk, and Chita oblasts. Lying off Siberia in the Arctic Ocean are the New Siberian Islands, the Severnaya Zemlya Archipelago, and other islands. Siberia may be divided, from north to south, into the zones of vegetation that run across the entire USSR—the TUNDRAS (extending c.200 mi/320 km inland along the entire Arctic coast), the TAIGA, the mixed forest belt, and the steppe zone. Forests occupy about 40% of Siberia's land. Siberia is drained, from south to north, by the mighty Ob, Yenisei, and Lena rivers (and their tributaries), which also provide the only means of longitudinal transportation. These rivers empty northward into the Arctic Ocean. East-West transportation depends largely on the Trans-Siberian RR (which follows the steppe belt) and to an increasing extent on the Arctic sea route. Siberia is conventionally subdivided into the following four geomorphological areas: the West Siberian lowland; the Central Siberian plateaus, or uplands; the mountains of the south; and the northeast Siberian mountain systems. The lowland occupies the western third of Siberia; it stretches from the Urals to the Yenisei and is mainly a low-lying, often marshy, plain. It is drained by the Ob and Irtysh rivers, which are ice-free and navigable for about half the year. Situated far from vulnerable frontiers, SW Siberia contains about 60% of Siberia's population, one of the USSR's major industrial complexes, and such important Soviet cities as NOVOSIBIRSK (the leading industrial and scientific research center of Siberia), OMSK, TOMSK, TOBOLSK, BARNAUL, and NOVOKUZNETSK. The wooded steppe and fertile black earth of W Siberia favor agriculture and, especially in the BARABA STEPPE, dairying. Wheat is the principal crop; rye, oats, potatoes, sunflowers, flax, and sugar beets are also important. Butter is the major dairy product. The KUZNETSK BASIN, in W Siberia, is one of the world's richest coal regions and also has large iron deposits. It forms the basis for the region's iron, steel, and heavy metallurgical industries. Rich oil and natural gas fields have recently been discovered in the West Siberian lowlands, from which a network of pipelines now serves the European USSR. E Siberia, which is drained by the Lena, extends from the Yenisei to a huge mountain chain, an offshoot of the mountains of Central Asia, comprising (from southwest to northeast) the Yablonovy, Stanovoy, Verkhoyansk, Kolyma, and Cherskogo ranges. In the center of E Siberia rise the Central Siberian uplands, which are separated from the northeastern mountains by the plateaus along the Vitim and Aldan rivers. South of the uplands lies Lake Baykal, the world's deepest lake, surrounded by mountains. E Siberia's important cities include KRASNOYARSK, IRKUTSK, ULAN-UDE, Cheremkhovo, YAKUTSK, and CHITA; but most of the region is sparsely populated because of the extreme rigors of the climate and the difficulties of communication. VERKHOYANSK, where the lowest temperatures on earth have been recorded, has summer heats rising above 90°F (32°C). E Siberia is the USSR's leading producer of gold, diamonds, mica, and aluminum, and there are large reserves of iron ore, coal, graphite, and nonferrous metals. Exploitation of the region's rich waterpower resources began in the mid-1950s with the construction of two giant hydroelectric power stations on the Angara River at Irkutsk and Bratsk. Forestry, like mining, is a major economic activity in E Siberia. Agriculture (wheat and oats) is practiced in the south, and animal husbandry is prevalent among the indigenous Siberian peoples. Reindeer breeding, fishing, sealing, hunting, and fur processing are important occupations in the Arctic north. The great majority of the Siberian population is made up of Russians and Ukrainians. Non-Russian groups include Turkic-speaking nationalities in the YAKUT AUTONOMOUS SOVIET SOCIALIST REPUBLIC, the GORNO-ALTAI AUTONOMOUS OBLAST, the KHAKASS AUTONOMOUS OBLAST, the TUVA AUTONOMOUS SOVIET SOCIALIST REPUBLIC, and the Kemerovo oblast; Buryat-Mongols in the BURYAT AUTONOMOUS SOVIET SOCIALIST REPUBLIC; Finno-Ugric Ostyaks (Khanty) and Voguls (Mansi) in the KHANTY-MANSI NATIONAL OKRUG; Samoyedes (Nentsy) in the TAYMYR PENINSULA; and Tungus Evenki in the EVENKI NATIONAL OKRUG. The largely nomadic Mongol and Turkic herdsmen of S Siberia have mostly settled down to agriculture under the Soviet government. The indigenous peoples of central and N Siberia remain, for the most part, hunters and fishermen. The chief non-Christian religions in Siberia are Islam and Tibetan Buddhism in the south and primitive shamanism elsewhere.

History. Numerous remains indicate that Siberia has been inhabited from prehistoric times. In the historic period, S Siberia frequently served as the point of departure for several nomadic hordes, such as the Huns, the Mongols, and the Manchus, who within relatively short time spans conquered and lost immense empires. Among the political entities emerging after the breakup of the Mongol state of the Golden Horde in the mid-15th cent. was the Tatar khanate of Sibir. Although Russian traders from Novgorod crossed the Urals as early as the 13th cent. to trade in furs with native tribes, the Russian conquest of Siberia began much later. Czar Ivan IV's capture of the Kazan khanate in 1552 opened the way for Russian expansion into Siberia. In 1581 a band of Cossacks under YERMAK Timofeyev crossed the middle Urals and took the city of SIBIR (near modern Tobolsk), capital of the Sibir khanate, which gave its name to the entire vast region. Russia's conquest of the Tatar khanate was completed in 1598 (see TATARS), and during the 17th cent. all of W Siberia was annexed to Russia. The Cossacks rapidly penetrated eastward by land and on their riverboats, building a string of small fortresses and levying tribute for Moscow from the sparse population in the form of precious furs. By 1640 they had reached the Sea of Okhotsk, an arm of the Pacific Ocean, and soon afterward they collided with Chinese troops. By the Treaty of Nerchinsk (1689), Russia abandoned to China the region later known as the Far Eastern Territory, which was ceded to Russia only from 1858 to 1860. Meanwhile, Russian settlement of Siberia was spurred by groups of *zemleprokhodtsy* (literally, "crossers of land"), who came mostly from N European Russia and traversed the easy portages linking the east-west Siberian river systems to pioneer new forts and trading communities. A colony of the Russian Empire, Siberia was administered by a colonial office based first in Moscow and later (after its founding in 1703) in the new Russian capital of St. Petersburg (now Leningrad). Although military governors collected tribute, they interfered little with native Siberian customs and religions; while the smaller, weaker ethnic groups succumbed to Russian influence, larger tribes such as the Kazakhs and Yakuts thrived and reaped material benefits under Russian administration. Siberian furs constituted an important source of wealth for Russia and figured prominently in Russian trade with Western Europe. These furs, along with customs duties levied on all Siberian raw materials acquired by Russian entrepreneurs, more than reimbursed the state for the costs of its Siberian conquest and administration. With the decline of the fur trade in the early 18th cent., mining became the chief economic activity in Siberia. The state was the chief entrepreneur, but wealthy private families were also involved. Silver, lead, and copper mining began around 1700; gold mining did not develop until the 1830s. Forced labor in the mines, often using convicts, proved generally unproductive; the gold miners were usually free laborers. Siberian agriculture was stimulated in the late 16th and 17th cent. by the needs of the Russian military and administrative personnel stationed there. From the early 17th cent. Siberia was used as a penal colony and a place of exile for political prisoners; among the latter there emerged (especially after the exile of leaders of the Decembrist Conspiracy of 1825) a small but vocal Siberian intelligentsia, who agitated for an end of Siberia's colonial status. Meanwhile, Russian colonizers continued to push southward, establishing forts along the steppe to thwart nomadic raids. Newly emancipated (1861) Russian serfs were allowed to take free possession of Siberian land, but they received little state assistance and suffered intolerable hardships. Russian settlement of Siberia on a large scale began only with the construction (1892–1905) of the Trans-Siberian RR, after which the eastward migratory movement reached gigantic proportions. P. A. Stolypin, the interior minister under Nicholas II, made a special effort to reduce rural overpopulation in European Russia by encouraging Siberian colonization. Siberia's population doubled between 1914 and 1946. The railroad also enabled European Russia to obtain cheap grain from W Siberia and butter from the Baraba Steppe. The railroad's needs spurred the development of coal mining and the opening of repair shops. Before the Russian Revolution, however, Siberia contributed only a minute fraction of Russia's industrial output, mainly in the form of gold. Siberia played a key role in the Russian civil war of 1918–20 (see RUSSIAN REVOLUTION). An autonomous Siberian government formed in early 1918 was soon superseded by the regime of the counterrevolutionary Admiral A. V. KOLCHAK, who made his capital at Omsk. The White forces were aided by contingents of czarist political exiles and by the Czech Legion, a group of Austrian army deserters who had hoped to fight alongside the czarist army. In Aug., 1918, a U.S., British, French, and Japanese expeditionary force joined the anti-Bolshevik units in Siberia. The main purpose of this allied expedition was probably to prevent German use of Siberian resources in World War I. Most of Siberia was in White hands by late 1918, but Czar Nicholas II and his family were murdered by the Bolsheviks at Ekaterinburg (now Sverdlovsk) that year. Early in 1920, Admiral Kolchak's government collapsed, and he was executed. Under the Soviet government, Siberia, especially the Ural-Kuznetsk complex, underwent dramatic economic development. Under the First Five-Year Plan (1928–33), forced labor was instrumental in mining coal and building the iron and steel complex of the Kuznetsk Basin. In addition, part of the agricultural colonization of Siberia was carried out by the forced resettlement of large segments of the Russian rural population, notably the expropriated kulaks. Forced labor was also employed extensively in the E Siberian gold mines. Parts of the vast Siberian concentration and forced labor camp network established by Stalin may still exist. Siberia's economic development increased dramatically during World War II with the transfer of many industries from European USSR to the other side of the Urals, where they would be less vulnerable to German seizure. Siberian grain was essential in enabling the Soviet Union to resist the German wartime onslaught despite the loss of valuable agricultural areas in W USSR. Postwar industrialization of Siberia continued at a rapid pace, with special concentration on SW Siberia and the Lake Baykal region. Siberian agriculture, which suffered during the Stalinist collectivization campaign, was revived in the mid-1950s by Premier Khrushchev's "virgin lands" program, focusing on cultivation in the steppes of SW Siberia and N Kazakhstan. The Seven-Year Plan (1958–65) emphasized construction of large thermal and hydroelectric power plants in Siberia and elsewhere. International attention focused on Siberia in the late 1960s and early 1970s, when the Soviet government began seeking U.S., West European, and Japanese capital, credits, and technology for the joint development of Siberia's vast petroleum, natural gas, timber, and other resources. See Harmon Tupper, *To the Great Ocean: Siberia and the Trans-Siberian Railway* (1965); M. P. Griaznov, *Southern Siberia* (tr. 1969); Farley Mowat, *The Siberians* (1970); Paul Dibb, *Siberia and the Pacific: A Study of Economic Development and Trade Prospects* (1972); G. V. Lantzeff, *Siberia in the Seventeenth Century* (1943, repr. 1972); Walter Slipchenko, *Siberia 1971* (1972); Hugo Portisch, *Promise in the East: The New Siberia* (1973); L. I. Shinkarev, *The Land beyond the Mountains: Siberia and Its People Today* (1973).

Siberian husky, breed of medium-sized, muscular WORKING DOG whose origins date back thousands of years in Siberia. It stands from 20 to 23½ in. (50.8–59.7 cm) high at the shoulder and weighs from 35 to 60 lb (15.9–27.2 kg). Its weather-resistant double coat is composed of a dense, downy underlayer and a medium-length, very dense, soft outercoat. It may be any color, but it is usually black, white, tan, gray, or various combinations of these colors. Raised by the Eskimolike Churchis of NE Siberia to pull their sleds, the Siberian also acted as a guard to their homes and as a companion. Down through the centuries this service has created in the Siberian husky a strong sense of gentleness and devotion to man and his family. The Siberian has also been popular in dogsled racing. Among purebred dogs, the term *husky* is properly applied only to this breed, although it is often used of any mixed-breed arctic sled dog. See DOG.

Siberian Platform or **Angara Shield,** large, geologically stable area of Precambrian rocks, N Asia, comprising much of Siberia, USSR. It is bounded, in general, on the west by the Yenisei River, on the east by the Lena River, on the north by the Arctic Ocean, and on the south by the general latitude of Lake Baykal. Most of the region is covered by strata of lower Paleozoic sediments and it is thought that since the early Paleozoic era it has remained above the level of invading seas that flooded most continental land masses. Tundra and taiga cover the region, which also has a rich variety of minerals.

Sibir (sĭbēr'), former city, southeast of present-day Tobolsk, W Siberian USSR. Founded in the 11th or 12th cent., it became (early 16th cent.) the capital of the Tatar khanate of Sibir, which arose after the disintegration of the empire of the GOLDEN HORDE. The Cossack YERMAK took the city of Sibir in 1581, thus marking the start of Moscow's conquest of what is now Siberia. The city was abandoned after the founding of Tobolsk in 1587.

Sibiu (sēbyo͞o'), Ger. *Hermannstadt,* Hung. *Nagyszeben,* city (1970 est. pop. 120,000), central Rumania, at the foot of the Transylvanian Alps. There are mechanical engineering works and industries producing textiles, agricultural machinery, chemicals, and leather. The city is also a market for farm products and cattle. Founded in the 12th cent. by German colonists, Sibiu was destroyed by the Tatars in 1241. In the 14th cent. it became a leading administrative and commercial center of the German communities in Transylvania. It suffered greatly in the wars against the Turks and in the 17th cent. came under Austrian control. The city preserves much of its medieval character and has a considerable German minority, although many Germans were forced to leave after World War II. Long a cultural center of Transylvania, Sibiu has a state theater, a philharmonic orchestra, and the Bruhenthal museum. The city is an Orthodox metropolitan see and has two cathedrals.

Sibley, Henry Hastings, 1811–91, first governor of Minnesota, b. Detroit. After two years of law study, he was (1830–34) a clerk for the American Fur Company. He later became (1834) a partner and engaged in trading in the Wisconsin and Dakota territories. He was (1848) delegate to Congress from Wisconsin Territory and promoted (1849) the organization of Minnesota Territory. He was then its territorial delegate, and when it became (1858) a state, Sibley was (1858–60) its first governor. He commanded expeditions against the Sioux after the massacre of Minnesota settlers in 1862. See biographies by Nathaniel West (1889) and W. P. Shortridge (1922).

Sibmah (sĭb'mə), same as SHEBAM.

Sibraim (sĭ'brāĭm, sĭbrā'ĭm), unlocated landmark, extreme N Palestine. Ezek. 47.16.

sibyl (sĭb'ĭl), in classical mythology, prophetess. There were said to be as many as 10 sibyls, variously located and represented. The most famous was the Cumaean sibyl, described by Vergil in the *Aeneid.* When she offered Tarquin her prophetic writings, the so-called sibylline books, he refused to pay her high price. She kept burning the books until finally he bought the remaining three at the original price. Although the historical origins of the books are uncertain, they were actually kept at Rome in the Capitol and were consulted by the state in times of emergency. The books were destroyed in the burning of the Capitol in 83 B.C., but a new collection was made. This was burned in A.D. 405. The sibyls achieved a stature in Christian literature and art similar to that of the Old Testament prophets.

Sibylline Oracles: see PSEUDEPIGRAPHA.

Siccuth (sĭk'əth) or **Sakkuth** (säk'-), in Amos 5.26 RSV, a heathen god. Many texts regard this as a common noun; thus KJV translates it as "tabernacle."

Sichem (sĭk'əm), variant of SHECHEM.

Sicilian Vespers, in Italian history, name given the rebellion staged by the Sicilians against the Angevin French domination of Sicily; the rebellion broke out at Palermo at the start of Vespers on Easter Monday, March 30, 1282. The revolt quickly spread over the island; nearly all the French in Sicily were massacred. Although basically a move for Sicilian independence, the insurrection was instigated as part of a widespread conspiracy against the Angevin ruler of Naples and Sicily, King CHARLES I, who dreamed of establishing an Angevin empire in the East. Byzantine Emperor MICHAEL VIII financed the plot, hoping to preoccupy Charles and thus avert the Angevin's imminent invasion of the Byzantine Empire. JOHN OF PROCIDA, a loyal supporter of the Hohenstaufen, and King PETER III of Aragón, who claimed rule of the island as the husband of Constance, heiress of the Hohenstaufen claim there, also joined the intrigue. Peter accepted the throne offered by the Sicilians, and a 20-year war for possession of Sicily followed between the Angevin kings of Naples and the Aragonese kings of Sicily. The rising secured Sicilian independence for more than a century, with the house of Aragón keeping Sicily and the Angevin dynasty holding the S Italian mainland kingdom of Naples. The two territories were finally reunited (1442) under Alfonso V of Aragón. See study by Steven Runciman (1958).

Sicily (sĭs'ĭlē), Ital. *Sicilia,* region (1971 pop. 4,667,316), 9,925 sq mi (25,706 sq km), S Italy, mainly situated on the island of Sicily, which is bounded by the Mediterranean Sea on the west and south, by the Ionian Sea on the east, and by the Tyrrhenian Sea on the north, and which is separated from the Italian mainland by the narrow Strait of Messina. The region also includes the EGADI ISLANDS, the LIPARI ISLANDS, the Pelagie Islands (see LAMPEDUSA), PANTELLERIA island, and Ustica island. PALERMO is the capital of Sicily, which is divided into the provinces of Agrigento, Caltanisetta, Catania, Enna, Messina, Palermo, Ragusa, Syracuse, and Trapani (named for their capitals). The largest Mediterranean island, Sicily is triangular and formerly was sometimes called Trinacria [Gr.,=triangle]; capes Boeo (or Lilibeo), Passero, and Punta del Faro (or Peloro) are the vertices of the triangle. The island is almost entirely covered by hills and mountains (continuations of the Apennines); Mt. ETNA (10,700 ft/3,261 m), in the east, is the highest point. The only wide valley is the fertile plain of Catania in the east, mostly located along the lower Simeto River. There are also narrow coastal strips in the south and west, and a small fertile plain (the Conca d'Oro) near Palermo in the northwest. Sicily has long been noted for the fertility of its soil, its pleasant climate, and its natural beauties. However, agriculture, the chief economic activity, has long been hampered by absentee ownership, primitive methods of cultivation, and inadequate irrigation. Since the establishment (1950) of the *Cassa per il Mezzogiorno* (Southern Italy Development Fund) by the national government, there have been reforms in land ownership, additional tracts of land have been opened to cultivation, and the island's economy has been generally developed. Wheat, barley, maize, olives, citrus fruit, almonds, wine grapes, and some cotton are produced; cattle, mules, donkeys, and sheep are raised. There are important tuna and sardine fisheries. Sicily's manufactures include processed food, chemicals, fertilizers, textiles, ships, leather goods, forest products, and refined petroleum. There are major petroleum fields in the southeast, and large quantities of natural gas and sulfur are also produced. The chief ports of the island are Palermo, Catania, and Messina. Sicily has had a varied and colorful history. The first known inhabitants of the island were the Elymi, Sicani, and Siculi. Phoenicians later settled on the west coast, notably at Panormus (now Palermo); Carthaginians founded LILYBAEUM and Drepanum (now TRAPANI); and on the east and southeast coasts Greeks founded (8th–6th cent. B.C.) such cities as SYRACUSE, CATANIA, Zancle (now MESSINA), GELA, and SELINUS and settled in older towns like SEGESTA. The Greek cities flourished and in turn founded such cities as Acragas (now AGRIGENTO) and HIMERA. Their originally democratic governments were gradually replaced by tyrannies, particularly those of PHALARIS at Acragas and of GELON, HIERO I, and others at Syracuse. In the 5th cent. B.C., Syracuse gained hegemony over the other cities. Phoenician influence was reinvigorated by Carthaginian expansion; although HAMILCAR was repulsed at Himera in 480 B.C., later Carthaginian invaders gained control (by c.400 B.C.) of more than half of the island. Interlopers from mainland Greece seized the remainder, and Sicily became a battleground for rival empires. A century of antagonism between Greeks and Carthaginians was followed by strife between Romans and Carthaginians, which flared (264 B.C.) in the first of the PUNIC WARS. Rome was victorious by 241 B.C., and after the death (c.215) of HIERO II of Syracuse, virtually all of Sicily came under Rome. The Romans completed the enriching Hellenization of Sicilian culture. However, the resources of the island—known as the Breadbasket of Rome—were depleted by the Romans, who also founded the large estates (*latifundia*) that subsequently greatly hampered the economic development of Sicily. Roman rule was often corrupt, and corruption reached a peak under governor Caius VERRES (73–71 B.C.). Slave revolts (135–132 B.C. and 104–100 B.C.) were cruelly suppressed. Many remains of the Greek and Roman periods have been found on Sicily, especially at Agrigento, Syracuse, Segesta, and Selinunte. After the fall of Rome, Sicily passed from the Vandals (mid-5th cent. A.D.) to the Goths (493) and then to the Byzantines (535). The Arabs conquered the island in the 9th cent. after raiding it for two centuries. They promoted agriculture, commerce, and the arts and sciences. The Arabs were displaced by the Norman conquest of Sicily (1060–91), led by ROGER I. ROGER II became (1130) the first king of Sicily; he forced (1139) Pope Innocent II, who claimed suzerainty over Sicily, to invest him with the kingdom, which included the Norman holdings in S Italy. The brilliant court of Roger II did much to introduce Arabic learning to Western Europe. Roger's last direct descendant, CONSTANCE, married Holy Roman Emperor Henry VI; their son and heir, Holy Roman Emperor FREDERICK II, was more interested in the kingdom of Sicily (where he reigned as king from 1197 to 1250) than in the Holy Roman Empire. After Frederick's death and the failures of the last Hohenstaufen claimants (CONRAD IV, MANFRED, and CONRADIN), Pope Clement IV crowned (1266) CHARLES I (Charles of Anjou) king of Naples and Sicily as his vassal. The unpopular government of the French brought on the SICILIAN VESPERS revolt (1282) and the Sicilians chose PETER III of Aragón as king. The resulting war between the Angevin line and the Aragonese ended temporarily in 1302, with FREDERICK II (see also ARAGÓN, HOUSE OF) becoming king of Sicily and Charles II of Anjou keeping S Italy (see NAPLES, KINGDOM OF). In 1373, JOANNA I of Naples formally renounced Sicily. After the Sicilian branch of Aragón became extinct, Sicily reverted (1409) to the main branch. Under Aragonese rule local liberties were maintained, and the Sicilian national assembly enjoyed wide powers. With the accession of the house of Hapsburg to the Spanish throne (early 16th cent.), there was more centralization, and Spanish governors were sent to Sicily to tighten the imperial bonds. Corruption increased, and the island came under the control of a few powerful nobles and churchmen. In 1713 the Peace of Utrecht assigned Sicily to Savoy, which in 1720 exchanged it with Emperor Charles VI for Sardinia. However, as a result of the War of the POLISH SUCCESSION, both Sicily and Naples came under (1735) the rule of Don Carlos of Bourbon (later CHARLES III of Spain). The Bourbon kings resided at Naples, except in 1799 and from 1806 to 1815, when Naples was held by the French. The centralizing policies of the Bourbons were resisted by the Sicilian nobles, who welcomed British intervention (1811–14). Feudal privileges were formally renounced in 1812, but in practice they continued much longer. Naples and Sicily were merged, despite Sicilian protests, in 1816, when FERDINAND I styled himself officially king of the TWO SICILIES. The Sicilian spirit of independence gave rise to revolts in 1820 and 1848–49, which were mercilessly suppressed; the bombardments of Messina (1848) and of Palermo (1849) earned FERDINAND II the nickname "King Bomba." In 1860, GARIBALDI conquered the island, which then voted to join the kingdom of Sardinia. Even after the unification of Italy was completed, Sicily was neglected by the central government, and the basic economic and social problems of the island long remained unattended. In World War II a large-scale amphibious landing was carried out by the Allies from N African bases on July 9–10, 1943. After heavy fighting, the Allied conquest of Sicily was completed on Aug. 8, 1943. Sicily was given limited autonomy under the Italian constitution of 1947. There are universities at Catania, Messina, and Palermo. See *A History of Sicily*: vol. I by M. I. Finley (1968); vol. II and III by Denis Mack Smith (1968).

Sickert, Walter Richard, 1860–1942, English painter. After a brief career on the stage Sickert was apprenticed to Whistler and later worked with Degas. His preferred subjects were scenes of music halls and the London demimonde. Painting in deep, rich browns with vital, immediate brushwork, Sickert became celebrated for his personal and spontaneous works. He was a major link between French and English painting at the turn of the century. See his posthumously published writings, *A Free House* (1947); studies by Wendy Baron (1973) and Marjorie Lilly (1973).

Sickingen, Franz von (fränts fən zĭ'kĭngən), 1481–1523, German knight. Placed under the ban of the Holy Roman Empire because of his profitable forays along the Rhine, he served King Francis I of France and then made peace with Holy Roman Emperor Maximilian I, whose service he entered. His presence with an army near Frankfurt helped insure the election (1519) of Maximilian's grandson, Charles V, as Holy Roman emperor. Influenced by Ulrich von HUTTEN, Sickingen aided persecuted reformers like Johann REUCHLIN and Martin LUTHER. He led (1522) the knights of SW Germany in a war, sometimes called the Knights' War, against the ecclesiastical princes, aiming at the secularization of ecclesiastical lands. Unsuccessfully laying siege to Trier, he was again put under the imperial ban and was besieged at his castle of Landstuhl by the princes of Trier, Hesse, and the Palatinate. Forced to capitulate, he died of his wounds. His defeat symbolized the end of the power of German knighthood. He appears, much romanticized, in Goethe's drama *Götz von Berlichingen* and in Wilhelm Hauff's novel *Lichtenstein.*

sickle-cell anemia, inherited disorder of the blood in which a large proportion of the erythrocytes (red blood cells) assume distorted, sicklelike shapes. The disease is confined mainly to blacks, especially those of W African descent. There is no cure and most patients die in childhood of cerebral hemorrhage or shock. Painful hemolytic crises occur during the course of the disease and symptoms that accompany such crises—including fever, joint and abdominal pain, and jaundice—are usually treated with pain killers, although there has been experimentation with the use of urea and cyanate. The crises are caused by the sickling of the normally disc-shaped erythrocytes, a phenomenon that occurs naturally when the concentration of oxygen in the blood is low; however, the sickling of the erythrocytes of patients with the disease begins when the oxygen concentration is at normal levels for venous blood. In 1949, Linus Pauling discovered that a chemical abnormality of the hemoglobin molecule causes the erythrocytes to become misshapen. Sickle cells are fragile, subject to rupture, and tend to block the capillary beds in various organs. Under normal circumstances the sickling phenomenon occurs only in those patients who inherit the abnormal hemoglobin from both parents. This so-called homozygous form of the disease occurs in 1 in 500 American blacks. About 7% of American blacks are nonanemic carriers of the disease, i.e., they have inherited normal hemoglobin from one parent and hemoglobin-S (sickle-cell hemoglobin) from the other. Much lower-than-normal concentrations of oxygen are necessary to cause the erythrocytes of these so-called heterozygous carriers to sickle and most never exhibit symptoms of the disease. Interest in sickle-cell anemia in the United States increased in the early 1970s, and with the support of grants mainly from the Federal government, there occurred a significant upsurge in the amount of research conducted. Free tests for the sickle-cell trait are readily available in health centers throughout the United States.

Sickles, Daniel Edgar, 1819–1914, American politician, Union general in the Civil War, b. New York City. A lawyer, he became active in Democratic politics, serving in the New York legislature. He was a member of Congress from 1857 to 1861. In 1859 he was acquitted on grounds of temporary mental aberration of the murder of Philip Barton Key (Francis Scott Key's son), whom he shot in Washington because of Key's attentions to Sickles's wife. In the Civil War, Sickles fought in the Peninsular campaign (1862), at Chancellorsville (1863), and in the Gettysburg campaign, where he lost a leg. His severity as military commander in the Carolinas (1865–67) led President Andrew Johnson to transfer him to another command. He retired from the army in 1869 as a major general. He was later minister to Spain (1869–73), held various political offices in New York, and served again (1893–95) in Congress. See biographies by Edgcumb Pinchom (1945) and W. A. Swanberg (1956).

Sicyon (sĭsh'ēŏn, sĭs'-), ancient city of Greece, in the Peloponnesus, NW of Corinth and 2 mi (3.2 km) S of the Gulf of Corinth. Sicyon was founded by Argos and attained its greatest power under the tyrant CLEISTHENES in the 6th cent. B.C. Under the leadership of the general ARATUS, Sicyon joined (3d cent. B.C.) the Achaean League. With the destruction (146 B.C.) of Corinth by the Romans, Sicyon briefly regained power but subsequently declined. Sicyon was an important center of art. In the archaic period of Greek art (625–480 B.C.) it was famous for painting and pottery. In the 4th cent. B.C. the Sicyonic school of painting, founded by EUPOMPUS, produced such artists as Pamphilus and APELLES. See C. H. Skalet, *Ancient Sicyon* (1928).

Siddhartha: see BUDDHA.

Siddim, locale of the battle of the kings, said to mean the valley of the Dead Sea. Gen. 14.3.

Siddons, Sarah Kemble, 1755–1831, English actress. The most distinguished of the famous KEMBLE family, she had early theatrical experience in her father's traveling company, and at 18 she married William Siddons, an actor. Brought to the attention of David Garrick, she was engaged by him for a Drury Lane performance in 1775–76, which failed. In 1782, after appearances in the provinces had greatly increased her powers, she played Isabella in Southerne's *Fatal Marriage* at Drury Lane. Her success was instant and indisputable, and her fame grew in such roles as Queen Katharine, Desdemona, and as Volumnia to the Coriolanus of John Philip Kemble, her brother, with whom she often starred. In the role of Lady Macbeth, which she first played in 1785 and which was her farewell performance in 1812, she was unequaled. Siddons' warm, rich voice and majestic presence held audiences in awe, and though she shunned publicity, she won the praise of the poets and critics of her day. Her portrait was painted by Gainsborough and by Reynolds, the latter representing her as *The Tragic Muse.* Her statue, by Chantrey, is in Westminster Abbey. See her *Reminiscences, 1773–1785* (ed. by William Van Lennep, 1942); James Boaden, *Memoirs of Mrs. Siddons* (1827); biographies by Roger Manvell (1971) and Thomas Campbell (1839, repr. 1972).

sideband, any frequency component of a modulated carrier wave other than the frequency of the carrier wave itself, i.e., any frequency added to the carrier as a result of MODULATION; sidebands carry the actual information while the carrier contributes none at all. In theory, if a signal is to be received without distortion, the receiver must accept substantially all the sidebands; in practice, especially in FM, certain compromises must be made, but distortion can usually be kept acceptably low. See RADIO.

side-necked turtle, name for the long-necked TURTLE of the families Chelidae and Pelomedusidae, found only in the Southern Hemisphere. The neck in these two families is of a different structure from that of other turtles and is folded sideways under the shell for concealment instead of being pulled straight back. Members of the family Chelidae, sometimes called snake-necked turtles, are river turtles of South America and the Australia–New Guinea region. Several species have slender, elongated snouts. Among these is the matamata (*Chelys fimbriata*) of Brazil and N South America. The matamata is a weak-jawed turtle that lies in wait for its prey, chiefly fish, and sucks it up with the snout. Its shell has high bumps and is covered with moss and water plants, so that when motionless the turtle looks like a rock. The family Pelomedusidae includes two African genera, *Pelomedusa* and *Pelusios.* Members of the latter genus resemble the North American box turtles, with a hinged shell. A third genus, *Podocnemis,* is found in rivers of South America and Madagascar. Side-necked turtles are classified in the phylum CHORDATA, subphylum Vertebrata, class Reptilia, order Chelonia.

sidereal day: see SIDEREAL TIME.

sidereal period, in astronomy, length of time a body takes to complete an orbit relative to the fixed stars. See SIDEREAL TIME.

sidereal time (S.T.), TIME measured relative to the fixed stars; thus, the sidereal day is the period during which the earth completes one rotation on its axis so that some chosen star appears twice on the observer's CELESTIAL MERIDIAN. Because the earth moves in its orbit about the sun, the sidereal day is about 4 min shorter than the solar day (see MEAN SOLAR TIME). Thus, a given star will appear to rise 4 min earlier each night, so that different stars are visible at different times of the year. The local sidereal time of an observer is equal to the HOUR ANGLE of the vernal equinox.

sidereal year, time required for the earth to complete an orbit of the sun relative to the stars. The sidereal year is 365 days, 6 hr, 9 min, 9.5 sec of MEAN SOLAR TIME. It is 20 min longer than the TROPICAL YEAR because of the PRECESSION OF THE EQUINOXES; for this reason, the sidereal year does not stay in step with the seasons.

siderite (sĭd'ərīt) or **chalybite** (kăl'ĭbīt), a mineral, varying in color from brown, green, or gray to black and occurring in nature in massive and crystalline form. A carbonate of iron, $FeCO_3$, it serves as an iron ore, especially in the British Isles. It is widely distributed, being found also in the United States, Europe, South America, and Australia.

siderolite: see METEORITE.

siderotil: see FERROUS SULFATE.

sidewinder, common name for a RATTLESNAKE, *Crotalus cerastes,* found in the deserts of the SW United States. This 2-ft (60-cm), pale yellow and pink snake is named for its curious method of locomotion. It throws out successive loops at oblique angles, which gives it the appearance of moving sideways. This mode of progression, also evolved by certain African desert snakes, enables it to move over sand, which offers little traction. The sidewinder has prominent, erect scales above its eyes and is sometimes known as the horned rattlesnake. During the heat of the day it lies half buried in the sand; it hunts small animals in the evening. The sidewinder is classified in the phylum CHORDATA, subphylum Vertebrata, class Reptilia, order Squamata, family Crotalidae.

Sidgwick, Henry (sĭj'wĭk), 1838–1900, English philosopher. He studied at Trinity College, Cambridge, and taught moral philosophy there from 1869 until 1900. The basis of his thought was British utilitarianism. Analyzing the intuitionist and utilitarian arguments, he indicated their interrelationship by showing how the doctrine of common sense rests on the principles of utilitarianism. In *The Methods of Ethics* (1874) he differentiated between two ethical ideas of utilitarianism, one based on self-interest and the other on altruism. Sidgwick was active in the administrative affairs of the university, and he was interested in the advancement of woman's rights, aiding in the planning and founding of Newnham College for women. He was also a founder of the Society of Psychical Research. Other major published works are *Principles of Political Economy* (1883), *Philosophy: Its Scope and Relations* (1902), and *The Development of European Polity* (1903). See Alan Gould, *The Founders of Psychical Research* (1968); study by D. G. James (1970).

Sidi-bel-Abbès (sē"dē-bĕl-äbĕs'), city (1966 pop. 91,527), W central Algeria, on the Mekerra River. It is the commercial center of an important area of vineyards, market gardens, orchards, and grain fields. The city developed around a French camp built in 1843. Until 1962, Sidi-bel-Abbès was headquarters of the French Foreign Legion.

Siding Spring Observatory, astronomical OBSERVATORY located on Siding Spring Mountain, near Coonabarabran, at an altitude of nearly 4,000 ft (1,220 m) in the Warrumbungle Mts. of New South Wales, Australia. It is a field station for Mt. Stromlo Observatory and is operated by the Australian National Univ. The principal instrument is a 150-in. (381-cm) reflecting telescope, one of the largest in the world, which was jointly financed by the Australian and British governments. Other equipment includes 40-in. (102-cm) and 26-in. (66-cm) reflectors, a 48-in. (122-cm) Schmidt camera telescope similar to that at Palomar Observatory, and a 24-in. (61-cm) rotating telescope used for measuring the polarization of starlight.

Sidlaw Hills (sĭd'lô), range, E Scotland, between Strathmore and the Firth of Tay. It extends c.30 mi (50 km) NE from near Perth into Angus-shire. The highest hills, including Dunsinane, are more than 1,000 ft (305 m). Sheep are grazed there.

Sidmouth, Henry Addington, Viscount, 1757–1844, British statesman. He entered Parliament in 1784 and in 1789, through the sponsorship of William PITT, became speaker of the House of Commons. He subscribed to Pitt's policies in the French wars, and when Pitt resigned because of George III's refusal to approve Catholic Emancipation, Addington became (1801) prime minister. The chief event of his administration was the Treaty of Amiens (1802) with Napoleon I. On the renewal of war, his ineffectual ministry yielded (1804) to Pitt, upon whose tolerance it had depended. Addington was created Viscount Sidmouth in 1805. Since Sidmouth controlled nearly 50 votes in Parliament, his support remained valuable to the government, and he served as president of the council under Pitt (1805), Lord Grenville (1806–7), and Spencer Perceval (1812) and as home secretary under Lord Liverpool (1812–22). In the last position he incurred great odium for his part in the government's policy of repression—its strong measures against the LUDDITES, its periodic suspension of habeas corpus, and the PETERLOO MASSACRE. See biography by Philip Ziegler (1965).

Sidney or **Sydney, Algernon,** 1622–83, English politician; son of Robert Sidney, earl of Leicester. He served in the parliamentary forces during the English civil war and was a member (1652–53) of the council of state of the Commonwealth, but he opposed the dictatorial rule of Oliver Cromwell. Reappointed (1659) to the council of state, he was abroad at the time of the Restoration (1660) and remained there until 1677, when he returned to England to attend to personal affairs. He soon became associated with the opposition to Charles II, however, joining Lord William RUSSELL and others in negotiations with French agents and in vague plots for an insurrection, perhaps to place the duke of MONMOUTH on the throne. His implication in these conspiracies was discovered by the exposure of the RYE HOUSE PLOT. After a brutal and arbitrary trial by Judge Jeffreys, Sidney was convicted of treason and executed. His name was cleared in 1689. Sidney's liberal ideals were set forth in his *Discourses Concerning Government* (1698), a treatise that had great influence on 18th-century political thought, especially in the American colonies. See biography by A. C. Ewald (2 vol., 1873).

Sidney or **Sydney, Sir Philip,** 1554–86, English author and courtier. He was one of the leading members of Queen Elizabeth's court and a model of Renaissance chivalry. He served in several diplomatic missions on the Continent and in 1586 was fatally wounded at the battle of Zutphen. Sidney exerted a strong influence on English poetry as patron, critic, and example. His literary efforts circulated only in manuscript during his lifetime. *Arcadia* (1590), a series of verse idyls connected by prose narrative, was written for his sister Mary, countess of Pembroke. It is the earliest renowned pastoral in English literature. Sidney's prose criticism of the nature of poetry, written as a rebuttal to Stephen Gosson's *The School of Abuse*, appeared in two slightly different versions—*The Defense of Poesie* and *An Apology for Poetry* (both 1595). *Astrophel and Stella* (1591) is one of the great sonnet sequences in English and was inspired by his love for Penelope Devereux, later Lady Rich. Sidney, however, married Frances Walsingham in 1583. See his works ed. by A. Feuillerat (1962); *The Psalms of Sir Philip Sidney and the Countess of Pembroke* (ed. by J. C. A. Rathmell, 1963); biographies by M. W. Wallace (1915, repr. 1967); R. Howell (1968), and J. M. Osborn (1972); study by S. M. Cooper (1968).

Sidney, city (1970 pop. 16,332), seat of Shelby co., W central Ohio, on the Great Miami River, in a farm area; founded 1811, inc. 1834. Refrigerator parts and machine tools are produced there.

Sidon (sī'dən), ancient city, one of the great seaports of the Phoenicians, in present-day Lebanon. It is one of the oldest Phoenician cities and is mentioned in the TEL EL AMARNA letters c.1400 B.C. After the 2d millennium B.C., all Phoenicians were called Sidonians. It was always an important center for trade, particularly in a later period when it was known for its purple dyes and for glassware (glass blowing is said to have begun at Sidon). Sidon has been excavated, and the sarcophagus of Eshmunzar that was found preserves an inscription of 22 lines mentioning various deities such as Baal and Ashtoreth. Although eclipsed by its own colony, Tyre, Sidon continued to be a port of prominence under the Persians, in the Hellenistic world, and in the later Roman Empire. It is often mentioned in the Bible and sometimes appears as Zidon. Gen. 10.19; 1 Kings 16.31; Mat. 15.21; Acts 27.3. See study by F. C. Eiselen (1907, repr. 1966).

Sidonius, Apollinaris: see APOLLINARIS SIDONIUS.

Sidra, Gulf of (sĭd'rə), Arab. *Khalij Surt*, arm of the Mediterranean Sea, lying between Misratah and Benghazi, Libya.

Siebengebirge (zē'bəngəbĭr"gə) [Ger.,=seven mountains], small wooded range of the Rhenish Slate Mts., W West Germany. Of volcanic origin, it extends for c.10 mi (16 km) S of Bonn along the Rhine River and rises to 1,509 ft (460 m) in the Grosser Ölberg. One of the most scenic spots of the Rhineland, the entire range is a national park and particularly famous for the DRACHENFELS.

Siebold, Philipp Franz van (fē'lĭp fränts fen), 1796–1866, German naturalist and physician; son of A. E. von Siebold. He was noted for his studies of the natural history, ethnography, and language of Japan, a country then very little known. First there from 1823 to 1830 as a member of a scientific expedition sent by the Dutch East India Company, he served on a second visit (1859–62) as mediator between Japan and the European powers. Chief of his authoritative works is *Nippon: Archiv zur Beschreibung von Japan* (20 parts, 1832–54; new ed., 5 vol., 1930–31). See study by L. B. Holthuis and Tsune Sakai (1970).

siege, assault against a city or fortress with the purpose of capturing it. The history of siegecraft parallels the development of FORTIFICATION and, later, ARTILLERY. In early times battering rams and bores were employed to break down the walls and gates of a fortified place (see CASTLE). To protect the attackers from missiles, hot oil, and GREEK FIRE launched by the defenders, a "penthouse" shelter was constructed, usually from huge wicker shields covered with wood or hide (mantelets). Mounds and movable wooden towers were built by both besieger and besieged in a race to attain heights from which the adversary could be assailed. Engines of war, such as the CATAPULT, were brought into play by both sides to hurl stones, spears, pots of fire, and arrows. It was also ancient practice for the besiegers to build a wall (circumvallation) around their objective and a second wall (contravallation) around their own army as security against relieving forces. Mining was employed by the assailants from earliest times, and the besieged dug countermines in defense; such tactics greatly increased in effectiveness with the introduction of gunpowder. Artillery that could breach the strongest walls made ancient and medieval fortifications obsolete; sieges became a matter of employing heavy artillery to bombard an objective into submission while the besieged tried to destroy the attackers' artillery with counterfire from their own. The development of tanks, aircraft, and missiles in the 20th cent. has given the besieger a great advantage in firepower and mobility. It has also become possible, in effect, to besiege a whole country at one time through the use of air power. Some notable sieges of history include those of Syracuse (415–413 B.C.), Jerusalem (A.D. 70), Acre (1189–90), Constantinople (1453), Quebec (1759–60), Sevastopol (1854–55, 1941–42), Vicksburg (1863), Port Arthur (1904), Malta (1940–43), Leningrad (1941–43), and, more recently, Dienbienphu (1954) and Khe Sanh (1968). See Sir C. W. C. Oman, *Art of War in the Middle Ages* (2d ed. 1924, repr. 1959); Sidney Toy, *A History of Fortification from 3000 B.C. to A.D. 1700* (2d ed. 1966); Vezio Melegari, *The Great Military Sieges* (1972).

Siegen, Ludwig von (lo͝ot'vĭkh fən zē'gən), c.1609–1680, German engraver, b. Holland, educated in Germany. He is said to have invented (c.1640) the mezzotint process of engraving. Among his seven known plates are portraits of Amalia Elisabeth of Hesse and of William II, prince of Orange, and his wife, Mary. His new method of engraving, long a secret, was revealed to Prince Rupert of the Palatinate in 1654. Through him it was communicated to the English engravers. A collection of Siegen's work is in the British Museum.

Siegen, city (1970 pop. 57,302), North Rhine-Westphalia, W West Germany, on the Sieg River. Iron ore is mined nearby, and the city has iron foundries. Other manufactures include leather goods and machinery. Siegen was the residence of the princes of Nassau-Siegen from 1606 to 1743. The city was severely damaged in World War II. Noteworthy buildings include two castles and the Nikolaikirche, a 13th-century church. Peter Paul Rubens was born (1577) in Siegen.

Siegfried (sēg'frēd) or **Sigurd** (sĭg'ərd), great folk hero of early and medieval Germanic mythology. His legend, important in several Germanic epics, recounts his killing of the dragon Fafnir, his marriage to Gudrun (or Kriemhild), his love and betrayal of Brunhild, and his tragic death. See VOLSUNGASAGA; Niebelungenlied under NIBELUNGEN.

Siemens, Ernst Werner von (ĕrnst vĕr'nər fən zē'məns), 1816–92, German electrical engineer and inventor. He was a founder and director of Siemens and Halske, a firm that made electrical apparatus. He was co-inventor of an electroplating process (1841), and alone developed an electric dynamo. He laid the first telegraph line and built the first electric railway in Germany and, with his brother Sir William Siemens, developed (1866) a widely used process of steelmaking. The Siemens unit of electrical resistance was proposed by him. In 1884 he founded a research laboratory at Charlottenburg. See his *Personal Recollections* (1892, tr. 1893) and his *Scientific and Technical Papers* (2 vol., tr. 1892–95).

Siemens, Sir William, 1823–83, English electrical engineer, b. Germany; brother of Ernst Werner von Siemens. Originally his name was Carl Wilhelm Siemens. After visiting England to introduce his own and his brother Ernst's electroplating device he returned in 1844 and became (1859) a naturalized British subject. He was head of the English branch of the Siemens firm, which made telegraphic and other electrical apparatus and handled electrical engineering projects. Among his important inventions were a water meter (1851) and a device for reproducing printing that remained standard until the development of photography, and he was one of the first to apply (1883) electric power to railways. With his brother Frederick he developed an improved regenerative furnace that was later of great importance to a number of industries. The furnace was used by the Siemens brothers in improving the steel made by their process of manufacture; the process, and a variation of it introduced by Pierre Martin, came to be known as the open-hearth process. He was knighted in 1883.

Siemianowice Śląskie (shĕmyänôvē'tsĕ shlăN'-skyĕ), city (1970 pop. 67,278), S Poland. A center of the Katowice mining and industrial region, it has ironworks and steelworks and coal mines. Manufactures include machinery and metals. Its first coal mine was opened in 1797. The city has a 19th-century castle.

Siena (syĕ'nä), city (1971 pop. 65,347), capital of Siena prov., Tuscany, central Italy. Rich in art treasures and historic architecture, it is one of the most popular tourist centers in Italy. The city is also noted for its wine and for its marble, a rich orange with purple and black veinings. According to tradition, Siena was founded at the beginning of Roman times by Senus, the son of Remus. It became a free commune in the 12th cent. and, gradually extending its territory, developed into a wealthy republic. The city was characterized by continuous internal strife between popular and aristocratic factions. Despite frequent wars, particularly with Florence, Siena maintained its independence. After the rule of the Petrucci family (1487–1523), the Spanish and French struggled for control of the city, which fell after a siege (1554–55) to Emperor Charles V. Shortly thereafter it passed to Cosimo I de' Medici, duke of Tuscany. The local interpretation of the Gothic style produced fine works of architecture and sculpture, but the city's artistic fame is due mainly to the paintings of the Sienese school (13th–14th cent.), best represented in the works of Guido of Siena, Duccio di Buoninsegna, Simone Martini, and the two Lorenzetti. On the fan-shaped main square, the Piazza del Campo, are the imposing Gothic Palazzo Pubblico (1297–1310), containing works by Ambrogio Lorenzetti, Martini, and Guido of Siena; the slender Mangia tower (334 ft/102 m high); a 14th-century chapel; the Fonte Gaia (a copy of the 15th-century sculptured fountain by Jacopo della Quercia); and several medieval palaces. The Palio festival, a horse race first run in 1656, is held in the Piazza del Campo twice each summer. The city's cathedral (11th–14th cent.), a splendid example of Italian Gothic, has an elaborate striped facade of polychrome marble (mostly by Giovanni Pisano) and a pulpit (1265–68) by Nicolò Pisano. The adjoining Piccolomini library (1495) is adorned with ten famous frescoes by Pinturicchio (1509). Also of note in Siena are the Baptistery of San Giovanni, with a 15th-century font by Jacopo della Quercia; the rich art gallery (Pinacoteca); the Gothic St. Dominic's Church, with frescoes by Il Sodoma; and Piccolomini palace. The city has a university (founded in the 13th cent.) and an academy of music.

Sienkiewicz, Henryk (hĕn'rĭk shĕnkyĕ'vĕch), 1846–1916, Polish novelist and short-story writer. The best-known of Sienkiewicz's vivid historical novels is *Quo Vadis?* (1895, tr. 1896), concerning Christianity in the time of Nero. He glorified the Polish struggle for national existence in the popular trilogy *With Fire and Sword* (1883, tr. 1890), *The Deluge* (1886, tr. 1891), and *Pan Michael* (1887–88, tr. 1893). *Yanko the Musician* (1879, tr. 1893) is a collection of his short stories. He described his journey through the United States in a collection of letters, *Portrait of America* (tr. 1959). Sienkiewicz was awarded the 1905 Nobel Prize in Literature. His works brought him enormous international acclaim. See biography by Mieczyslaw Giergielewicz (1968).

sienna: see OCHER.

Sierra, Justo (ho͞o'stō syĕ'rä), 1848–1912, Mexican educator and historian. He entered the literary life as a romantic poet but later devoted himself wholeheartedly to founding schools, lecturing, and seeking in every way to quicken new intellectual life in Mexico. Sierra was to a large extent responsible for the intellectual renaissance in Mexico early in the 20th cent. He was minister of education under Porfirio Díaz and refounded the National Univ. of Mexico. His best-known work is a history of Mexico showing the growth of national feeling and culture, *La evolución política del pueblo mexicano* (1900–1902, tr. 1969). See study by R. W. Weatherhead (1966).

Sierra Club, national organization in the United States dedicated to the preservation and expansion of the world's parks, wildlife, and wilderness areas. Founded (1892) in California by a group led by the Scottish-American conservationist John MUIR, the Sierra Club is made up of more than 140,000 people devoted to the exploration, enjoyment, and protection of man's natural environment. The club was instrumental in helping to create the National Park Service and the National Forest Service, as well as in the formation of individual recreation areas, such as Olympic and Redwood national parks. The group has also led efforts to obtain new parklands in Alaska. Through a program of court litigation and congressional action, the Sierra Club has opposed strip mining, the use of DDT, offshore oil drilling, and most other forms of chemical or aesthetic pollution. The Sierra Club has also broadened its program to include activities dealing with the urban environment and overpopulation. Through its 34 regional offices the Sierra Club sponsors a series of nature outings, and its national office, located in San Francisco, publishes a monthly bulletin as well as numerous books about ecology and the environment.

Sierra Leone (sēĕr'ə lēō'nē, lēōn', sĕr'əlēōn), republic (1973 est. pop. 2,650,000), 27,699 sq mi (71,740 sq km), W Africa, bordered by the Atlantic Ocean in the west, by Guinea in the north and east, and by Liberia in the south. FREETOWN is the capital; other cities include Bo, Kenema, Kono Town, and Makeni. Sierra Leone's 350-mi (560-km) Atlantic coastline is

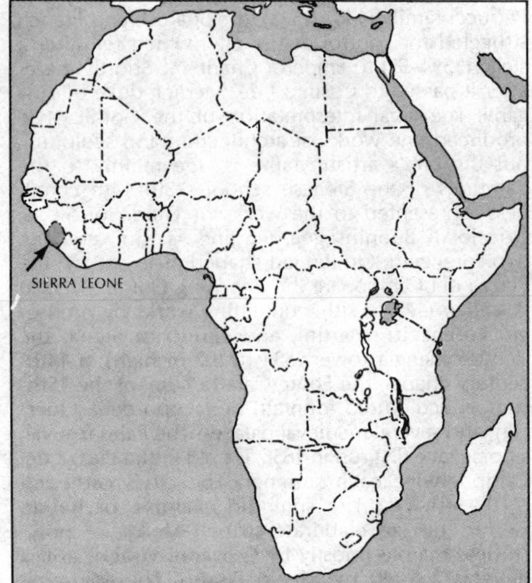

made up of a belt (average width 30 mi/50 km) of low-lying mangrove swamps, except for the mountainous Sierra Leone Peninsula (on which Freetown is situated). The coastline is broken by numerous estuaries and has some wide, sandy beaches. Behind the coastal belt is a wooded plateau (average elevation: 1,000 ft/300 m). The eastern half of the country is mostly mountainous and includes Sierra Leone's loftiest point (6,390 ft/1,948 m), located near the Guinea border. Several rivers, including the Great Scarcies (which makes up a section of the boundary with Guinea) and the Mano (which forms part of the border with Liberia), flow through the country to the Atlantic. The headwaters of the Niger River are situated in the mountains of the northeast. The great majority of the inhabitants of Sierra Leone are black Africans. The two main ethnic groups are the Mende (about 25% of the population), who speak a Mande language and live in the central and southern parts of the country, and the Temne (about 20% of the population), who speak a language closely related to Bantu and live in the north. Creoles, descendants of freed slaves from Nova Scotia and the West Indies, make up about 25% of the population in Freetown. There are also small numbers of Indians and Lebanese, who play a major role in the nation's commerce. English is the country's official language. The majority of the population follows traditional religious beliefs, but there are significant numbers of Muslims and Christians. Sierra Leone's economy is predominantly agricultural, with most of its workers engaged in subsistence farming, largely on small plots of land. The principal food crops are rice, cassava, maize, pulses, plantains, and tomatoes. The leading cash crops, most of which are exported, are palm kernels, piassava, cacao, coffee, kola nuts, groundnuts, and ginger. Large numbers of poultry, cattle, sheep, and goats are raised. The country has an important mining industry that is largely controlled by companies headquartered in Great Britain, Switzerland, and the United States. The main minerals extracted are diamonds, iron ore, bauxite, and titanium (ilmenite); together they account for about 80% of the country's exports by value. Diamonds are mainly found in E Sierra Leone, and iron ore is chiefly produced in the west central part of the country. In 1972 the third largest diamond ever found, the 969.8-carat "Star of Sierra Leone," was discovered in the country and subsequently sold to a U.S. jewelry firm. In 1974, Sierra Leone joined with six other nations to form the International Association of Producers of Bauxite, headquartered in Jamaica. The country's few manufactures include palm products, construction materials, refined petroleum, chemicals, lumber, and basic consumer goods such as processed food, beverages, clothing, footwear, furniture, and tobacco products. There is a growing fishing industry. Sierra Leone has limited rail and highway networks, which mostly serve the central and western parts of the country. Freetown has excellent port facilities; smaller ports are located at Bonthe (on Sherbro Island) and Pepel (near Freetown). The Great and Little Scarcies rivers are navigable by small craft for short distances. The cost of Sierra Leone's imports is usually slightly higher than its earnings from exports. The principal imports are machinery, manufactured consumer goods, foodstuffs, transportation equipment, and chemicals; the chief exports besides minerals are palm kernels, cacao, and coffee. In the 1960s a large percentage of the diamonds produced were smuggled out of the country, but smuggling was reduced sharply in the early 1970s. Sierra Leone's leading trade partners are Great Britain, Japan, the Netherlands, and the United States.

History. The Temne were living along the northern coast of present-day Sierra Leone when the first Portuguese navigators reached the region in 1460. The Portuguese landed on the Sierra Leone Peninsula, naming it [Sierra Leone = lion mountains] after the mountains located there. Beginning c.1500, European traders stopped regularly on the peninsula, exchanging cloth and metal goods for ivory, timber, and small numbers of black African slaves. Beginning in the mid-16th cent. Mande-speaking people migrated into Sierra Leone from present-day Liberia, and they eventually established the Mende states of Bullom, Loko, Boure, and Sherbro. In the early 17th cent. British traders became increasingly active along the Sierra Leone coast. In the early 18th cent. Fulani and Mande-speaking persons from the Fouta Jallon region of present-day Guinea converted numerous Temne of N Sierra Leone to Islam. Sierra Leone was a minor source of slaves during the 17th and 18th cent. for the transatlantic slave trade, exporting a maximum of about 2,000 persons annually. In 1772 slavery was abolished in England, largely as a result of the agitation of Granville Sharp, and after the American Revolutionary War (1775–83) attempts were made to resettle freed slaves in Africa. In 1787, 400 persons (including 330 blacks and 70 white prostitutes) arrived at the Sierra Leone Peninsula, bought land from local Temne leaders, and established the Province of Freedom near present-day Freetown. The settlement did not fare well, and most of the inhabitants died of disease in the first year. In 1790 a group of Temne destroyed what remained of the colony. A renewed attempt at settlement was made in 1792, when about 1,100 freed slaves (mostly from Nova Scotia) under the leadership of the abolitionist Thomas Clarkson landed on the peninsula and founded Freetown. The new colony was controlled by the Sierra Leone Company, which forcefully held off the Temne, who resented the presence of foreigners. In 1800 about 500 free blacks from Jamaica arrived in Freetown via Nova Scotia. The colony had little contact with the interior, and most of its members supported themselves by farming. In 1807, Great Britain outlawed the slave trade, and in early 1808 the British government took over Freetown from the financially troubled company, using it as a naval base for antislavery patrols. Between 1808 and 1864 approximately 50,000 liberated slaves were settled at Freetown. Protestant missionaries were active there, and in 1827 they founded Fourah Bay College (now part of the Univ. of Sierra Leone), where black Africans were educated. Most of the freedmen and their descendants, known as Creoles, were Christians. They became active as missionaries, traders, and civil servants along the Sierra Leone coast and on Sherbro Island as well as in other regions of coastal W Africa, especially among the Yoruba of present-day SW Nigeria. During the periods 1821 to 1827, 1843 to 1850, and 1866 to 1874, British holdings on the Gold Coast (present-day Ghana) were placed under the governor of Sierra Leone. In 1863 an advisory legislative council was established in Sierra Leone, but it was not until 1924 that black Africans sat on it and only in 1948 were they given a majority of seats. The British were reluctant to assume added responsibility by increasing the size of the colony, but in 1896 (near the end of the scramble for African territory among the European powers) the interior was proclaimed a British protectorate, mainly in order to forestall French ambitions in the region, and the Colony and Protectorate of Sierra Leone was established. The protectorate was ruled "indirectly" (i.e., through the rulers of the numerous small states, rather than by creating an entirely new administrative structure) and a hut tax was imposed in 1898 to pay for administrative costs. The black Africans protested the tax in a war (1898) led in the north by Bai Bureh (a Temne) and in the south by the Poro secret society; the British quickly emerged victorious and there were no further major armed protests. Under the British, little economic development was undertaken in the protectorate until the 1950s, although a railroad was built and the production for export of palm products and groundnuts was encouraged. In the 20th cent. the Creoles of the colony were largely excluded from higher government posts in favor of whites from Great Britain. The Creoles sought a larger voice in the affairs of Sierra Leone, and after World War II the British introduced changes designed to give the black Africans more political power. However, under the constitution of 1951, additional power was given to the black Africans on the basis of votes received in the colony and protectorate combined, in which the Creoles were a small minority. In the elections of 1951, the protectorate-based Sierra Leone Peoples party (SLPP), led by Dr. Milton Margai (a Mende), emerged victorious. During the 1950s, the black Africans were given more political responsibility, and educational opportunities were enlarged. In the economic sphere, mining (especially of diamonds and iron ore) increased greatly. On April 27, 1961, Sierra Leone became independent, with Margai as prime minister; he died in 1964 and was succeeded by his brother, Albert M. Margai. The prime minister was appointed by the governor general (a Sierra Leonian who represented the British monarch) and was responsible with his cabinet to the unicameral parliament (made up of 66 elected and 12 appointed members). General elections were held in March, 1967, amid protests over Albert Margai's intention of creating a one-party state; the chief opposition party was the All Peoples Congress party (APC), led by Siaka Stevens and based among the Temne. The results of the election were never announced, but Stevens formed (March 21) a government at the request of the governor general. However, a military coup led by Brigadier David Lansana in support of Margai ousted Stevens a few minutes after he took the oath of office. Amid rioting by supporters of Stevens, the Lansana government was toppled and replaced (March 23–24) by a National Reformation Council headed by Col. Andrew Juxom-Smith. In April, 1968, lower-level army personnel led a revolt that overthrew the NRC and returned the nation to parliamentary government, with Stevens as prime minister. The following years were marked by considerable unrest, caused by tribal and army disaffection with the central government. In March, 1971, after an abortive military coup, Stevens requested the presence of troops from Guinea to give his government support. On April 19, 1971, parliament declared Sierra Leone to be a republic; Stevens began a five-year term as president (the country's chief executive officer under the new constitution) and Sorie Ibrahim Koroma was appointed vice president and prime minister. The Guinean troops left Sierra Leone in early 1973, and parliamentary elections were held—again amid considerable unrest—in May, 1973. Charging harassment by Stevens's APC, the SLPP withdrew from the election and the APC emerged with 84 of the 85 elected parliamentary seats; one seat was held by an independent and 12 others were occupied by appointed tribal leaders. Thus, Sierra Leone became in fact, if not in law, a one-party state. See Christopher Fyfe, *A History of Sierra Leone* (1963) and *Sierra Leone Inheritance* (1964); J. H. Kopytoff, *A Preface to Modern Nigeria: The "Sierra Leonians" in Yoruba, 1830–1890* (1965); Martin Kilson, *Political Change in a West African State: A Study of the Modernization Process in Sierra Leone* (1966); R. G. Saylor, *The Economic System of Sierra Leone* (1967); John Cartwright, *Politics in Sierra Leone*, 1947–67 (1970); A. B. Sibthorpe, *The History of Sierra Leone* (4th ed. 1971).

Sierra Madre (sēēr'ə mä'drā), residential city (1970 pop. 12,140), Los Angeles co., S Calif., at the foot of Mt. Wilson; inc. 1907.

Sierra Madre (syā'rä mä'thrā), chief mountain system of Mexico, consisting of the Sierra Madre Oriental, the Sierra Madre Occidental, and the Sierra Madre del Sur and forming the dissected edges of the vast central Mexican plateau; a volcanic belt along the plateau's southern edge links the three sierras. Extending from northwest to southeast through Mexico from the U.S. border, the rugged Sierra Madres, 6,000–12,000 ft (1,829–3,658 m) high, with deep, steep-sided canyons (*barrancas*), have long been a barrier to east-west travel. The terrain ranges from permanently snow-covered peaks to hot, tropical valleys; and from the humid, thickly vegetated seaward slopes to the dry, largely barren interior-facing slopes. Agricultural products vary according to the climate. Lumbering is done in the N Sierra Madre Occidental. The Sierra Madres have a great wealth of minerals including iron ore, lead, silver, and gold. The mountains are sparsely populated, with settlement limited to mining towns and agricultural communities. The Sierra Madres hold good potential for hydroelectric-power development, and several stations have been built in the northern ranges. The **Sierra Madre Oriental** (ōryĕntăl′), beginning in barren hills S of the Rio Grande, runs for c.700 mi (1,130 km) roughly parallel to the coast of the Gulf of Mexico, ranging from 10 to 200 mi (16-320 km) inland. It reaches an elevation of 18,700 ft (5,700 m) in ORIZABA peak, which belongs also to the volcanic belt, Cordillera de Anáhuac. This belt, which divides Mexico in half at about lat. 19° N and includes the peaks POPOCATEPETL and IXTACIHUATL, on the other end joins the **Sierra Madre Occidental** (ōk″sēdĕntăl′). This range, paralleling the Pacific coast for c.1,000 mi (1,610 km), extends SE from Arizona. Its main escarpment is more abrupt than that of the eastern cordillera. From c.5,000 ft (1,520 m) in the north, elevations reach over 10,000 ft (3,048 m) in the south. The **Sierra Madre del Sur** (dĕl so͞or′) is a tumbled, broken mass of uptilted mountains that touch the Pacific coast but form into no clearly defined range. It spreads over S Mexico between the volcanic belt and the Isthmus of Tehuantepec and forms the natural harbor of Acapulco.

Sierra Maestra (syā′rä mää′strä), rugged mountain range, Oriente prov., SE Cuba, rising abruptly from the coast. Consisting of connecting ranges with local names, the Sierra Maestra is the highest system of Cuba. It is rich in minerals, especially copper, manganese, chromium, and iron. Pico Turquino (6,560 ft/1,999 m) is the highest point. In the 1950s Fidel Castro had his base of operations in the mountains.

Sierra Morena (syā′rä mōrā′nä), mountain range, SW Spain, extending c.375 mi (600 km) eastward along the southern edge of the Meseta (central plateau) from the Portuguese border to the Sierra de Alcaraz. Its highest peak is Bañuelo (c.4,340 ft/1,320 m). The range is rich in a great variety of minerals including copper, lead, and coal. The Sierra Morena is crossed by highways and railroads built to take the minerals out of the region. The Despeñaperros Pass is the main route through the mountains, linking Castile and Andalusia.

Sierra Nevada (syā′rä nāvä′thä), chief mountain range of S Spain, in Granada, running from east to west for c.60 mi (100 km), parallel to the Mediterranean Sea. The highest peak of the range and of Spain is Mulhacén (11,411 ft/3,478 m). Grapes, olives, and sugarcane are raised on the range's southern slopes.

Sierra Nevada (sēĕr′ə nəvä′də), mountain range, c.400 mi (640 km) long and from c.40 to 80 mi (60-130 km) wide, mostly in E Calif. It rises to 14,495 ft (4,418 m) in Mt. Whitney, the highest peak in the coterminous United States. The mountains extend NW from Tehachapi Pass near Bakersfield, Calif., to the gap S of Lassen Peak. A tilted fault-block in structure (the largest in the United States), the Sierra Nevada's eastern front rises sharply from the Great Basin, while its western slope descends gradually to the hills bordering the Central Valley of California. Heavy winter precipitation is economically important to the surrounding areas; snow-fed streams supply irrigation water to the Central Valley and to W Nevada and also generate hydroelectricity. High, rugged, and frequently snowbound in winter, the mountains are a formidable barrier to overland travel. Donner Pass (alt. 7,089 ft/2,161 m), the principal pass across the mountains, was used by thousands of California-bound gold-seekers and immigrants in the middle and late 1800s. The Sierra Nevada are known for their magnificent scenery (especially in the High Sierra S of Lake Tahoe and in Yosemite, Sequoia, and Kings Canyon national parks) and for their year-round resorts.

Sierra Nevada de Mérida (syā′rä nāvä′thä thā mā′rēthä), mountain range, NW Venezuela, a spur of the Andes extending c.200 mi (320 km) NE from the Colombian border to the Caribbean coastal range. From 30 to 50 mi (48-80 km) wide, it rises between the Orinoco llanos and Maracaibo lowlands to perpetually snow-capped peaks. Pico Bolívar (c.16,420 ft/5,000 m high) is the highest point in Venezuela. Coffee is raised in the Mérida.

Sierre (syĕr), Ger. *Siders,* town (1970 pop. 11,017), Valais canton, S Switzerland, on the Rhône River. A market town, it is the center of a rich horticultural region. There is a large aluminum plant nearby. Sierre has a 13th-century tower and a 16th-century castle. The poet Rilke lived there.

Sieyès, Emmanuel Joseph (ĕmänüĕl′ zhōzĕf′ syāĕs′), 1748-1836, French revolutionary and statesman. He was a clergyman before the Revolution and was known as Abbé Sieyès. His pamphlet *Qu'est-ce que le tiers état?* [What is the third estate?] (1789), attacking noble and clerical privileges, was immensely popular throughout France, and he was elected deputy from the third estate to the States-General of 1789. He edited the tennis court oath, which marked the formation of the national assembly, and participated in the writing of the Declaration of the Rights of Man and Citizen and the constitution of 1791 (see FRENCH REVOLUTION). He made his chief contributions in 1789-91 with the theory of national sovereignty and the distinction between active and passive citizens, which restricted the vote to men of property. As a member of the Convention he voted for the execution of King Louis XVI. His prudent silence enabled him to live through the Reign of Terror, and after the overthrow of Maximilien ROBESPIERRE on 9 Thermidor (1794), Sieyès again became active in the government. In 1799 he entered the DIRECTORY. Later that year he conspired with Napoleon Bonaparte (see NAPOLEON I) in the overthrow of the Directory by the coup d'etat of 18 Brumaire. Sieyès became, with Bonaparte and Roger Ducos, one of the three provisional consuls. His sketch for the constitution of the year VIII was, however, changed in decisive points by Bonaparte, and Sieyès and Ducos were replaced (Dec., 1799) as consuls. He became senator and senator of the empire and, after the Bourbon restoration, lived in exile (1816-30) in Brussels. The name also appears as Sieyes. See studies by J. H. Clapham (1912) and G. G. Van Deusen (1932, repr. 1969).

Sífnos (sĭf′nôs) or **Siphnos** (sĭf′nəs), island, c.32 sq mi (83 sq km), SE Greece, in the Aegean Sea; one of the Cyclades. It is a resort area and produces olive oil. In ancient times it had gold and silver mines.

Sifton, Sir Clifford, 1861-1929, Canadian political leader, b. Ontario. A lawyer in Manitoba, he sat (1888-96) in the provincial legislature and then served (1896-1911) in the Canadian House of Commons. As minister of the interior (1896-1905) in Wilfrid Laurier's cabinet he pursued a vigorous immigration policy, which brought to W Canada many settlers from the United States and Europe. Disagreement with Laurier over religious education in the schools in Alberta and Saskatchewan caused him to resign his ministry. In 1911 he withdrew from Parliament and from the Liberal party in opposition to Laurier's reciprocal trade policy. He was chairman of the Canadian conservation commission from 1909 to 1918. Sifton was knighted in 1915.

Sigebert I (sĭg′əbərt), d. 575, Frankish king of Austrasia (561-75), son of Clotaire I. He constantly feuded with his brother CHILPERIC I, who had inherited the western portion of the Frankish lands, which came to be known as Neustria. The hatred between the two was intensified after Chilperic murdered (567) his wife, Galswintha, who was the sister of Sigebert's wife, BRUNHILDA. When Chilperic attacked Austrasia in 573, a desire for vengeance made Sigebert vindictive, and in the fighting he overran Neustria. He was about to be proclaimed king of Neustria when he was assassinated by order of FREDEGUNDE, whom Chilperic had married after Galswintha's death.

Sigel, Franz (fränts sē′gəl), 1824-1902, Union general in the American Civil War, b. Sinsheim, Baden, Germany. An officer in the army of Baden, he was a leader (1848-49) of the Baden revolutionary forces. After Prussia suppressed them (1849), he fled to Switzerland and then to England. Emigrating to the United States in 1852, he lived first in New York City and then in St. Louis. There at the beginning of the Civil War he organized the 3d Missouri Volunteers. His command was routed at WILSON'S CREEK, but Sigel later distinguished himself in the campaign that rid Missouri of Confederate forces. He led a corps at the second battle of Bull Run (Aug., 1862). In 1864 he was given command of the Dept. of West Virginia, but after General Breckinridge defeated him at NEW MARKET (May), he was replaced by David Hunter. After the war Sigel moved (1867) to New York City, where he held several political offices and was an editor of German periodicals.

Siger de Brabant (sēzhā′ də bräbäN′), fl. 1260-77, French theologian, head of the movement known as Latin Averroism. At the Univ. of Paris he taught that the individual soul had no immortality and that only the universal "active intellect" was immortal. He maintained also that the world had existed from eternity. In an attempt to reconcile these beliefs with Christian faith, Siger adopted the Averroist notion of "double truth"—that something could be true in rational philosophy but false in religious belief. St. THOMAS AQUINAS vigorously attacked Siger's teachings, and the doctrines were condemned in Paris in and after 1270. Siger died in Italy. See Fernand van Steenberghen, *Aristotle in the West* (tr. 1956).

Sigerist, Henry Ernest (sĭg′ərĭst), 1891-1957, American medical historian and writer, b. Paris, M.D. Univ. of Zürich, 1917. He taught history of medicine at the universities of Zürich (1921-23) and Leipzig (1925-32) before coming to the United States. From 1932 to 1947 he was professor at and director of the institute of the history of medicine at Johns Hopkins. In 1947 he returned to Switzerland to work on a comprehensive multivolume history of medicine. His publications include *Man and Medicine* (1932), *Great Doctors* (1933), *Socialized Medicine in the Soviet Union* (1937), *Medicine and Human Welfare* (1941), *Civilization and Disease* (1943), and *A History of Medicine* (2 vol., 1951-61). See his autobiography ed. by his daughter, Nora Beeson.

sight: see VISION.

Sigillaria (sĭjĭlâr′ēə), genus of fossil club moss allied to LEPIDODENDRON, abundant in the Carboniferous period. The thick trunk was rarely branched and was covered for several feet from the top with erect leaves that were larger than those of *Lepidodendron;* the leaf scars were in vertical rows. The fossilized root stocks of *Sigillaria,* as of *Lepidodendron,* are known as stigmaria. Club mosses are classified in the division LYCOPODIOPHYTA.

Sigismund (sĭj′ĭsmənd, sĭg′-), 1368-1437, Holy Roman emperor (1433-37), German king (1410-37), king of Hungary (1387-1437) and of Bohemia (1419-37), elector of Brandenburg (1376-1415), son of Holy Roman Emperor Charles IV. Through his marriage to Mary, who became queen of Hungary in 1382, Sigismund acceded to the Hungarian throne. However, dynastic conflicts there prevented his coronation until 1387. In the interim Mary was deposed, and Charles II (CHARLES III, king of Naples) became king (1385). Following Charles's death (1386) Mary was restored, and Sigismund came to power. During this period the Ottomans (Turks) were advancing in Europe, and in 1395 they invaded Hungary. Sigismund led a general European crusade against them but was crushingly defeated in 1396 by Sultan BEYAZID I at Nikopol. Sigismund's absence and the death of Mary (1395) had weakened his hold on the Hungarian throne. In 1403 he put down a revolt in Hungary in support of Lancelot of Naples, the son of Charles II. After the death of the German king and uncrowned Holy Roman Emperor Rupert in 1410, both Sigismund and his cousin, Jobst of Moravia, claimed victory in the imperial elections. Since Sigismund's half brother WENCESLAUS, who had been deposed from the German throne in 1400, had never waived his title, there were, for a time, three rulers of Germany. The death of Jobst (1411) and the withdrawal of Wenceslaus left Sigismund sole king and Holy Roman emperor-elect. One of Sigismund's first tasks was to end the Great SCHISM in the church. He persuaded John XXIII (see COSSA, BALDASSARE), the strongest of the three schismatic popes, to summon a council at Constance (see CONSTANCE, COUNCIL OF). After three years of deliberation by the council, the schism was ended (1417). John HUSS, the Czech religious reformer, had attended the council with Sigismund's guarantee of safe-conduct, but, nevertheless, the council began heresy proceedings against him and condemned him to death. Sigismund signed his death sentence. The burning of Huss hastened the Reformation in Bohemia and earned Sigismund the lasting hatred of the Czechs. When Sigismund succeeded to the Bohemian throne on his brother Wenceslaus's death (1419), he was bitterly opposed. To secure an army against the rebellious Bohemians, Sigismund convinced Pope MARTIN V to proclaim (March, 1420) a crusade against the HUSSITES. He had himself crowned king of Bohemia at Prague but was defeated by the Hussites under John ZIZKA and withdrew. In 1421 a Czech assembly declared him deposed and shortly afterward the Hussites began their incursions into Germany (see HUSSITE WARS). Renewed attacks by the Turks occupied Sigismund in Hungary, while in Germany and Bohemia the Hussites continued to be victorious, defeating a new crusade (1431) against them. Negotiations to heal the breach in the church were held at the Council of Basel (see BASEL, COUNCIL OF) and resulted in compromise with the drafting of the Compactata. The religious agreement opened the way to Sigismund's acceptance as king by the Bohemians in 1436. Shortly afterward, Sigismund died. The last emperor of the Luxemburg dynasty, Sigismund arranged for the succession to his titles by his son-in-law, Albert of Austria (later King Albert II). Sigismund had earlier transferred Brandenburg to Frederick of Hohenzollern (FREDERICK I of Brandenburg). See Archibald Main, *The Emperor Sigismund* (1903).

Sigismund I, 1467-1548, king of Poland (1506-48), son of Casimir IV. Elected to succeed his brother, Alexander I, Sigismund faced the problem of consolidating his domestic power in order successfully to counter external threats to Poland. The enactment (1505) during Alexander's rule of the law *Nihil Novi,* which forbade the kings to enact laws without the consent of the diet, seriously handicapped Sigismund in his struggle with the magnates and nobles. Nevertheless, he established (1527) a regular army and a fiscal system to finance its maintenance. Intermittent war with Vasily III of Moscow began in 1507; in 1514 Smolensk fell to the Muscovite forces. In 1515 Sigismund entered an alliance with Holy Roman Emperor Maximilian I. Maximilian acknowledged the provisions of the Second Peace of TORUN, and Sigismund consented to the marriage of the children of his brother, ULADISLAUS II of Bohemia and Hungary, with the grandchildren of Maximilian. Through this double marriage contract Bohemia and Hungary passed to the house of Hapsburg on the death (1526) of Sigismund's nephew, Louis II. Sigismund's wars against the Teutonic Knights ended in 1525, when their grand master, ALBERT OF BRANDENBURG, having converted to Lutheranism, secularized the order and did homage to Sigismund, who invested him with the domains of the order as the first duke of Prussia. Sigismund sought peaceful relations with the khans of Crimea but was nonetheless involved in border warfare with them. Sigismund was a distinguished humanist; he and his second wife, Bona Sforza, daughter of Gian Galeazzo Sforza of Milan, were patrons of Renaissance culture, which began to flower in Poland during their reign. He was succeeded by his son, Sigismund II.

Sigismund II or **Sigismund Augustus,** 1520–72, king of Poland (1548–72). Crowned in 1530 to assure his succession, he assumed the royal functions at the death of his father, Sigismund I. By the Union of Lublin (1569) he transferred his hereditary grand duchy of LITHUANIA to the Polish crown, creating the unified Polish-Lithuanian state. His great diplomatic skill enabled him to conciliate the dissident elements both in Poland and among the Lithuanian magnates who opposed the fusion. Upon the dissolution (1561) of the Livonian Knights, Sigismund gained control over Courland, Latgale, and other parts of LIVONIA. Opposed in this claim by Holy Roman Emperor Ferdinand I, Sigismund granted (1562) the elector of Brandenburg hereditary succession in the duchy of Prussia in exchange for diplomatic support. The widened frontiers brought Sigismund into conflict with Ivan IV of Russia, who took (1563) Polotsk. The Polish Reformation reached its height during Sigismund's reign; in 1570 most of the Protestant sects formed a union to strengthen their cause. An open-minded, tolerant monarch and a loyal Roman Catholic, Sigismund sought peacefully to counteract the Reformation; he abolished (1562) ecclesiastic courts but introduced (1565) the Society of Jesus, which successfully preached the Catholic Reformation. The Renaissance flowered at this time (see also POLISH LITERATURE), and Sigismund himself was an accomplished humanist and theologian. The last of the JAGIELLO dynasty to rule Poland, Sigismund died childless. After an interregnum and the brief rule of Henry of Valois (later Henry III of France), Stephen Báthory was elected (1575) king.

Sigismund III, 1566–1632, king of Poland (1587–1632) and Sweden (1592–99). The son of John III of Sweden and Catherine, sister of Sigismund II of Poland, he united the VASA and JAGIELLO dynasties. He was a Roman Catholic; his marriage (1592) with Anne of Hapsburg linked him with the Catholic monarchs of Europe. A period of factional strife after the death (1586) of King Stephen Báthory was ended by the election of Sigismund as king of Poland, effected through the support of Jan ZAMOJSKI, who opposed the candidacy of Maximilian of Austria. In 1592, Sigismund inherited the Swedish throne from his father, but his reluctance to accept Protestantism as the state religion in Sweden involved him in conflict with the Swedes and with his uncle, who was regent (see CHARLES IX). Although finally crowned in 1594, Sigismund was defeated (1598) at Stangebro and was formally deposed by the Swedish diet in 1599. He retained his claims to Sweden and after 1600 fought intermittently with his uncle and later with his nephew, GUSTAVUS II, to whom he lost (1629) most of Livonia. Sigismund intervened in Russia, in the turmoil after the death of Boris Godunov, by sanctioning Polish support of the two pretenders who claimed to be DMITRI. Sigismund dreamed of conquering all of Russia. In 1610, taking advantage of chaos in that country, Sigismund continued his military conquest and took Moscow. His son Ladislaus was elected czar, but Sigismund desired the throne for himself. As a Catholic, he was opposed for religious as well as political reasons. In 1612 an improvised Russian army under Prince Pozharski expelled the Poles, and Michael Romanov was elected czar of Russia. Poland retained Smolensk and other border towns. Peace with Russia came only after Sigismund's death—in 1634, under Ladislaus IV, Sigismund's son and successor. Sigismund's pro-Catholic policy helped to effect the union (1596) of the Ruthenian Church in Poland-Lithuania with the Church of Rome. This period also saw the start of intermittent war with Turkey, lasting until Poland obtained a favorable treaty in 1621. Sigismund's use of Austrian aid to limit the powers of the diet and the dissatisfaction of the Protestants led to a rebellion (1606–7) under Nicholas Zebrzydowski, the palatine of Kraków. Although the rebels were defeated, their cause triumphed; no more attempts were made to change the constitution.

Sigismund Augustus: see SIGISMUND II.

Siglufjörður (sĭk'ləfyör"thər), town (1970 pop. 2,161), N Iceland, on the Greenland Sea. It is known as the capital of Iceland's herring industry.

sigma point, in astronomy: see EQUATORIAL COORDINATE SYSTEM.

Signac, Paul (pōl sĕnyäk'), 1863–1935, French neo-impressionist painter. First influenced by Monet, he was later associated with SEURAT in developing the divisionist technique. Interested in the science of color, he painted with a greater intensity and with broader strokes than Seurat. In such vigorous, colorful works as *Port of St. Tropez* (1916; Brooklyn Mus., New York City) Signac broke through the confines of neo-impressionist theory. He wrote a treatise, *D'Eugène Delacroix au néo-impressionisme* (1889), long considered the foremost work on the school. See study by his granddaughter, Françoise Cachin (tr. 1973).

signaling, transmission of information by visible or audible means. The fall of Troy was signaled to Greece by means of fires lighted on mountain tops. Primitive peoples in Africa and elsewhere have transmitted messages by drums, the tone and the rhythm determining the meaning. The American Indians employed smoke signals, and in the American Revolution the colonists used combinations of three articles—a barrel, a basket, and a flag placed in different positions atop a post. In the early days of railroading, men were posted at places where accidents might occur, e.g., at stations and tunnels, and signaled to the engineer by flag or lamp. Modern railroad signaling depends upon electrically operated indicators which constitute a SEMAPHORE system. The position of a movable arm swinging from a pivot indicates whether the train can go forward or must wait and whether it should go rapidly or slowly. In the interlocking and signaling system used at terminals, freight yards, sidings, and crossovers, coordination of movements of trains is achieved; when one unit is given clearance, all others that may possibly foul the section are signaled not to encroach or are barred from doing so by switching devices. In automatic block signaling the line is divided into blocks and each block is connected with its neighbors by electric circuits that pass either through wires alongside the line or through the rails. Thus, a signal, generally colored lights, indicates to the engineer whether or not the next block is clear. This block-signal system is responsible for the infrequency of rear-end collisions on railroads. Most electric trains, including subways, are fitted with automatic devices that turn the power off and the brakes on if the engineer ignores a stop signal. Railroads also use light signals to duplicate the positions of a semaphore arm. Brightly painted disks on swinging arms are sometimes used to convey information to approaching trains. The electricity or compressed air used for actuating a signal system automatically may be further controlled by a signalman in a tower or other control center of a railroad. In marine signaling, flags have been used for hundreds of years. The International Code of Signals was compiled by the British government in 1857 and, by international agreement, was amended to the present system in 1901. It utilizes a number of flags of various colors and forms; each flag represents a certain letter or number, and the flags are hoisted to convey a message to another vessel or to the shore. Blinker lights are much used by naval units. At night flash lamps using MORSE CODE or another code may be used for signaling. Fog signals are commonly used by vessels and lighthouses when visibility conditions make visual warnings ineffective. They include bells, gongs, horns, compressed-air or steam whistles, and sirens. International law requires seagoing vessels to possess and use fog signals in prescribed fashion. In modern times aerial and marine craft are commonly given directional data through radio beacon signals. Infrared radiation is used in devices for optical and sound signaling. Radio and telephone apparatus have largely superseded other means of communication in military use. See INFORMATION THEORY; CODE.

signature, in music: see MUSICAL NOTATION.

sign language, substitute for normal spoken language, not including letter-for-letter signaling. It is derived from the body movements and facial expressions that accompany speech. Sign languages include those of Trappist monks, who have a rule of silence, and Plains Indians, where speakers of mutually unintelligible languages communicated freely. Examples from the Plains Indian sign language are: for a lie, first two fingers of the right hand spread apart and extended from the lips (i.e., two tongues); a dog, same two fingers drawn across the breast (i.e., track of a travois); a horse, same two fingers astride the extended fingers of the left hand (i.e., something ridden). Australian aborigines and people of Sudan and the Sahara also have a complete sign language. Many languages have conventionalized body gestures elaborated to accompany or supplement speech, e.g., the Neapolitan gesture language. The widely used manual language of the deaf, or language of signs, was first systematized in the 18th

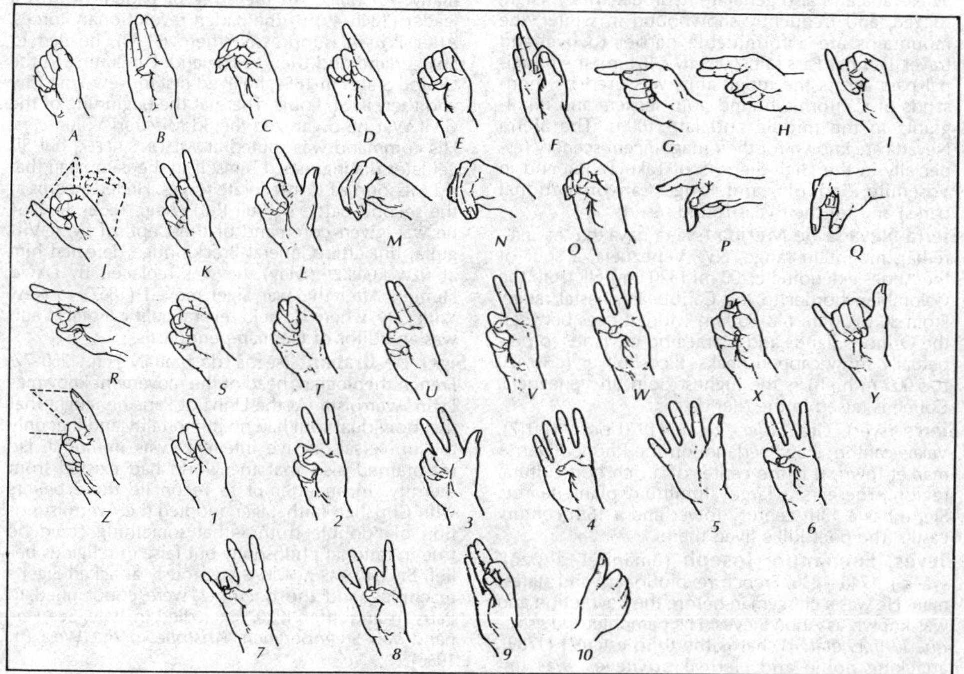

Manual alphabet

century by the French abbé Charles Michel de l'Épée. It was brought to the United States by T. H. Gallaudet. The language of signs is a conventional system of gestures of the hands and arms roughly suggestive of the form of thought they represent. A dictionary of signs has been compiled. Often the language of signs is taught along with lip-reading and with a manual alphabet, i.e., a method of forming the letters of the alphabet by fixed positions of the fingers in the air (see DEAFNESS). The American sign language developed for the deaf is currently being taught to chimpanzees at the University of Oklahoma and elsewhere, producing a major breakthrough in primate communication. See W. C. Stokoe, *Semiotics and Human Sign Languages* (1972); B. E. Babbini, *Manual Communication* (1973).

Signorelli, Luca (lo͞o'kä sĕnyōrĕl'lē), 1441?–1523, Italian painter of the Umbrian school, who probably studied with Piero della Francesca. He worked in Cortona, where some of his paintings have remained. Subsequently he worked in the Cathedral of Perugia, in Volterra, and at Monte Oliveto before undertaking (1499) the decoration of the Cappella Nuova in the Orvieto Cathedral. There he represented the apocalyptic series of the *Story of the Anti-Christ,* the *End of the World,* the *Resurrection of the Bodies, Paradise,* and the *Inferno,* as well as figurations from antique poems and the *Divine Comedy.* The infernal scenes are remarkable for their imaginative evocation of fiends and tortures of Hell. Michelangelo was influenced by his powerful treatment of anatomy and the vivid realism he used for dramatic ends. Signorelli's paintings in the Vatican, where he went in 1508, were later sacrificed to make way for some of Raphael's work. Examples of his work are in the National Gallery of Art, Washington, D.C.; the Metropolitan Museum; and the museums of Philadelphia, Kansas City, and Detroit.

Sigsbee, Charles Dwight, 1845–1923, American naval officer, b. Albany, N.Y. He saw service in the Gulf of Mexico in the Civil War, was subsequently stationed with the Asian squadron, taught at Annapolis, and served (1873–88) in the Hydrographic Office and the Coast Survey. There Sigsbee invented several marine instruments that revolutionized deep-sea exploration. He also made the first complete deep-water survey of the Gulf of Mexico. In 1897 he achieved the rank of captain and commanded the MAINE until it was destroyed in Havana harbor. He was commended for his conduct pending investigation of the incident. While in command of the *St. Paul* in the Spanish-American War, Sigsbee defeated the destroyer *Terror* and the cruiser *Isabella II.* Commissioned as rear admiral (1903), he commanded the Caribbean squadron and then a squadron of the Atlantic Fleet. He wrote *Deep-Sea Sounding and Dredging* (1880) and *The "Maine": an Account of Her Destruction in Havana Harbor* (1899).

Sigtuna (sĭg'tü"nä), town (1970 pop 3,648), Stockholm co., E Sweden, on Lake Skarven, near Stockholm. Founded c.1000, it was one of Sweden's earliest towns, its first capital, and a center of Christian missionary activity. Sweden's first coin was minted there and carried the motto "Situna Dei" (God's Sigtuna). The town was plundered and burned by Estonian pirates in 1187 and subsequently quickly declined. Today it is a popular tourist spot and an educational center.

Sigüenza y Góngora, Carlos de (kär'lōs thā sĕgwān'sä ē gōng'gōrä), 1645–1700, Mexican writer and humanist. The foremost intellectual figure of colonial Mexico, he wrote on mathematics, astronomy, history, geography, and other fields. His works include *Manifiesto filosófico contra los cometas* [philosophical treatise against comets] (1680) and *Infortunios de Alonso Ramírez* (1690; tr. *The Misadventures of Alonso Ramírez,* 1962), a forerunner of the novel in Latin America.

Siguiri (sēgē'rē), town (1961 est. pop. 12,000), NE Guinea, on the Niger River. It is the commercial center for a region where rice, millet, and cotton are grown. Alluvial gold is found in the area. The French established a post in Siguiri in 1886.

Sigurd: see SIEGFRIED.

Sigurðsson, Jón (yōn sĭ'khürthsōn), 1811–79, Icelandic statesman and historian. A student in Copenhagen from 1833, he developed an interest in Icelandic literature and history, on which he became the outstanding authority. He was active in many learned societies, which published his editions of the sagas and other literary works. As secretary (1840), later president (1851), of the Icelandic Literary Society, he directed the publication of monumental studies in Icelandic history and literature; he began the series *Diplomatarium Islandicum* in 1857. He served twice (1849–57, 1865–79) as president of the Althing, or parliament, but his journalistic activity was his great contribution to the Icelandic political revival. In 1841 he founded the periodical *Ny felagsrit,* the most influential Icelandic political journal, which endured until 1873. The constitution granted to Iceland in 1874 was largely the result of Sigurðsson's efforts, as was the grant of free trade (1854). During most of these years he lived in Copenhagen, the leader of a group of Icelandic writers, scholars, and diplomats.

Sihanouk, Norodom: see NORODOM SIHANOUK.

Sihanoukville: see KOMPONG SOM, Cambodia.

Sihon (sī'hən), king of the Amorites, who attacked Israel. He became a figure for the mighty fallen. Num. 21.21–30; Ps. 135.10,11.

Sihor (sī'hôr) or **Shihor** (shī'hôr), name for the river Nile or its east arm. 1 Chron. 13.5; Isa. 23.3; Jer. 2.18. In Joshua 13.3 a boundary of Canaan seems indicated.

Sihun: see SYR DARYA, river, USSR.

Sikang: see HSI-K'ANG, China.

Sikar (sē'kər), walled town (1971 pop. 70,983), Rajasthan state, NW India. Sikar, c.1,500 ft (460 m) above sea level, is a district administrative center and a market for grain and tobacco. The Harasmath temple was reputedly built c.1000 A.D.

Sikasso (sēkä'sō), town (1970 est. pop. 17,000), S Mali. It is the trade center for a region where peanuts, cotton, rice, fruit, and vegetables are grown. The town has cotton ginneries and rice mills. Sikasso was the large, fortified capital of a prosperous trading state that was founded in the 1870s. In the 1880s and 90s, Sikasso was attacked by the armies of the Muslim leader SAMORY. The French conquered Sikasso in 1898.

Sikeston (sĭks'tən), city (1970 pop. 14,699), New Madrid and Scott counties, SE Mo., in the Mississippi plain; inc. 1874. It is the shipping, marketing, and processing center of a cotton, soybean, and grain region.

Sikhote-Alin (sēkhətĕ-əlyĕn'yə), mountain range, c.625 mi (990 km) long, S Far Eastern USSR. It is composed of a series of ridges lying between the Sea of Japan and the Ussuri and Amur rivers. Its forests are a source of lumber, and there are deposits of coal, lead, zinc, silver, and tin.

Sikhs (sēks), religious community of N India, mainly in Punjab state, numbering some 6 million persons. The religion was founded by the mystic Nanak (c.1469–c.1539), the first guru [Hindi,=teacher]. In an attempt to reconcile Muslim and Hindu, he taught a monotheistic creed, the fundamental identity of all religions, and the realization of God through religious exercises and meditation. Nanak opposed idolatry and ritual and the maintenance of a priesthood and of the CASTE system. Angad (1504–52), the third guru, separated the ascetics *(udasis)* from the laity, eliminated most features of Hinduism, and introduced the Gurmukhi script. Under the fourth guru, Ram Das, AMRITSAR was founded as a sacred city. Arjun, the fifth guru, compiled the Adigranth, or first scripture of the community, containing many devotional poems that are still recited in the Golden Temple at Amritsar. By the mid-17th cent. the position of guru had become hereditary, and the Sikhs split into several divisions (sometimes antagonistic). Under succeeding gurus the Sikh community was gradually knit together and began to develop military power. AURANGZEB, the Mogul emperor, ordered the destruction of Sikh temples and seized and killed the ninth guru. Govind Singh (1666–1708), the tenth and last guru, hastened the militarization of the Sikhs as unreconcilable enemies of the Mogul empire and of Islam. Through a military baptism, after which the initiate took the surname Singh [lion], he created the military fraternity called the Khalsa, or "pure," whose ideal was the soldier-saint. He introduced the Sikh practices of wearing a turban, carrying a dagger, and never cutting the hair or beard. The Sikhs conquered most of the Punjab by the late 18th cent. and established a number of feudal states. Their greatest leader in the early 19th cent. was RANJIT SINGH, who conquered much territory and established a Sikh state in the Punjab. After his death, conflict with the British caused the SIKH WARS and the subjugation of the Punjab. Sikh soldiers formed a large element of the British armies in India. In 1947 in the partition of the Indian subcontinent, the Sikh territory in the Punjab was divided, despite Sikh protests. The militant Sikhs, supported by the Hindu Jats, fought with the Muslims of Punjab in a holy war that resulted in over a million casualties. Some 2.5 million Sikhs moved from West Punjab (which became part of Pakistan) into East Punjab (India) at this time. See Kushwant Singh, *A History of the Sikhs* (2 vol., 1963–66) and *The Sikhs Today* (rev. ed. 1964); Harbans Singh, *The Heritage of the Sikh* (1964); J. D. Cunningham, *A History of the Sikhs* (1966); Gopal Singh, *The Religion of the Sikhs* (1971).

Sikh Wars (1845–49), two conflicts preceding the British annexation of the Punjab. By a treaty with the British in 1809, the Sikh ruler of the Punjab, RANJIT SINGH, had accepted the Sutlej River as the southern boundary of his domain. After his death (1839) the Punjab fell into a state of disorder in which a succession of rulers were rapidly overthrown by the army. In 1845 the regent, Jhindan, who was both fearful of British intentions and anxious to distract the Sikh army, sent troops across the Sutlej (Dec. 11). The British, under Sir Hugh (later Viscount) Gouge, Sir Harry Smith, and others, won several preliminary victories and then decisively defeated the Sikhs at Aliwal (Jan. 28, 1846) and Sobraon (Feb. 10). They occupied Lahore on Feb. 20. By the Treaty of Lahore (March, 1846), the Sikhs were forced to cede Kashmir and to pay an indemnity of 55 million rupees. The British established a protectorate, which was resented. In April, 1848, a riot occurred, in which two British officers were killed. There was a general uprising, followed by a second war. A costly (for the British) battle at Chilianwalla (Jan. 13, 1849) was indecisive, but the British completely routed the Sikhs at Gujrat (Feb. 21). The Sikhs surrendered on March 12. Lord Dalhousie, the governor general, annexed all the Sikh territory on March 30. See B. J. Hasrat, *Anglo-Sikh Relations, 1799–1849* (1968).

Sikkim (sĭk'ĭm), constitutional monarchy (1971 pop. 204,760), 2,745 sq mi (7,110 sq km), S central Asia, in the E Himalayas; controlled by India. The capital and only town is Gangtok. Sikkim is bordered on the W by Nepal, on the N by the Tibet region of China, on the E by Bhutan, and on the S by India. Most of Sikkim is mountainous, and rivers, including the Tista, flow through deep valleys, intersecting the country and hindering travel. In the mountains are extensive forests and grazing land for sheep, goats, cattle, and yaks. Corn is the major crop of the tropical lowland valleys, and rice, millet, wheat, bar-

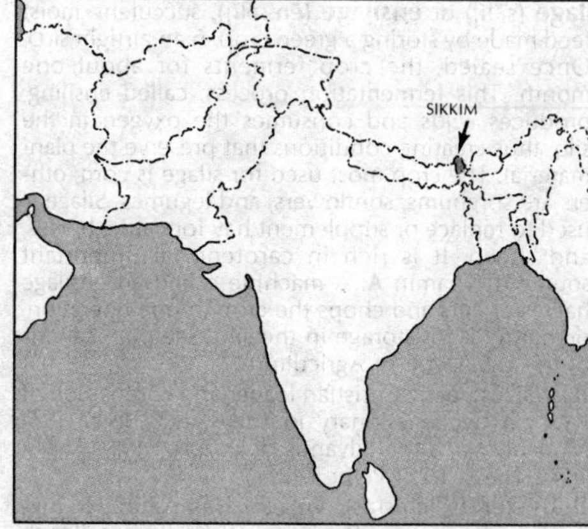

ley, legumes, fruits, and cardamom are also grown. Agriculture is chiefly for subsistence. Sikkim has some copper deposits, which are worked by primitive methods. There is a handicraft industry, and cotton weaving is common. Sikkim's people are predominantly of Nepalese extraction; the minority Bhotias (Tibetan in origin) and aboriginal Lepchas are mainly pastoral nomads. Although the Nepalese practice Hinduism, Buddhism is professed by the maharaja and the official class, and Sikkim is noted for its Buddhist monasteries. Tibeto-Burmese languages and dialects are spoken widely. In the 16th cent. Tibetans began to settle Sikkim, whose native Lepchas were probably converted to Buddhism by Tibetan lamas. In 1642 a Tibetan king, from whom the present chogyal claims descent, started a hereditary line of Sikkimese rulers. Gurkhas from Nepal invaded Sikkim several times in the 18th and 19th cent.; but the British, expanding their presence in India, forced the Gurkhas out of Sikkim (1814–16). Later (1835, 1849) the Sikkimese had to cede territory to the British, who assumed a protectorate; China, nominal suzerain of the area, finally recognized the protectorate in 1890, after a British victory over Tibet. British protection ended when India won independence in 1947, but political and social unrest in newly independent Sikkim led to a treaty (1950) by which the kingdom became an Indian protectorate. India directed defense and foreign relations and communications, while Sikkim retained internal autonomy. The Indians financed construction in Sikkim of strategic roads that traverse the mountain passes into Tibet. These and other roads, in addition to other social and economic modernization, helped Sikkim to overcome its long isolation from the outside world. In 1974, India virtually ended Sikkim's last vestiges of independence. Under a new constitution, accepted under pressure by the kingdom's chogyal, Kumar Palden Thondup Namgyal (reigned 1963–), and passed by India's parliament, Sikkim was made an associate state of India and the chogyal was reduced to a titular position; executive power was vested in a chief minister appointed by India who headed a five-member council of ministers.

Sikorski, Władysław (vlädĭ'släf sēkôr'skē), 1881–1943, Polish general and politician. He fought in World War I and later (1922–25) held various cabinet posts. Premier Pilsudski dismissed him from public service in 1928, but after the German conquest of Poland, Sikorski became (1939) premier of the Polish government in exile. He also was commander in chief of the Polish forces that continued to fight alongside the Allies in World War II. Sikorski restored (1941) diplomatic relations with the USSR, but after the KATYN incident relations were again broken off (1943). Sikorski was seeking to heal the breach when he was killed in an airplane crash near Gibraltar.

Sikorsky, Igor Ivanovich (sĭkôr'skē), 1889–1972, American aeronautical engineer, b. Kiev, Russia. He immigrated to the United States in 1919 and was naturalized in 1928. Sikorsky built and flew the first multimotored plane (1913) and established the world's endurance record for sustained flight in a helicopter of his own design (1941). He organized corporations to manufacture airplanes (in 1923, 1925, and 1928) and became engineering manager of the Vought-Sikorsky Aircraft Division of the United Aircraft Manufacturing Corp. He is best known for his work on the development of the helicopter. In 1968 he was awarded the National Medal of Science. See his *Story of the Winged-S* (rev. ed. 1967) and *Invisible Encounter* (1947); biography by R. M. Bartlett (1947).

Siksika Indians (sĭk'səkə): see BLACKFOOT INDIANS.

silage (sī'lĭj) or **ensilage** (ĕn'səlĭj), succulent, moist feed made by storing a green crop in an airtight SILO. Once sealed, the crop ferments for about one month. This fermentation process, called ensiling, produces acids and consumes the oxygen in the silo, thus creating conditions that preserve the plant material. The crop most used for silage is corn; others are sorghums, sunflowers, and legumes. Silage is used to replace or supplement hay for cattle, horses, and sheep. It is rich in carotene, an important source of vitamin A. A machine called an ensilage harvester cuts and chops the crop in one operation, preparing it for storage in the silo. See publications of the U.S. Dept. of Agriculture.

Silas (sī'ləs), early Christian leader and companion of Paul on two missionary journeys. Acts 15.22–18.5. Probably he is the Silvanus of 2 Cor. 1.19; 1 Thess. 1.1; 2 Thess. 1.1; 1 Peter 5.12.

Silchester (sĭl'chĭstər), village, Hampshire, S England. It is noted for the ruins of the Roman-British town Calleva Atrebatum. The outside walls (2,760 yd/2,524 m in circumference), forum, amphitheater, and entire plan of the city, including baths and several temples, were revealed through excavations beginning in the 1890s. Small articles were removed to Reading Museum.

silenus (sīlē'nəs), in Greek mythology, part bestial and part human creature of the forests and mountains. Part of Dionysus' entourage, the sileni are usually represented as aged satyrs—drunken, jolly, bald, fat, and bearded. According to some myths they were prophets; but according to others they were so perpetually stupefied with drink that they were unable to distinguish truth from falsehood. In some legends only one such creature appears, Silenus, described as the oldest of the satyrs, the son of Hermes or Pan. He was the companion, adviser, or tutor of Dionysus.

Silesia (sīlē'zhə, -shə, sī-), Czech *Slezsko,* Ger. *Schlesien,* Pol. *Śląsk,* region of E central Europe, extending along both banks of the Oder River and bounded in the south by the mountain ranges of the Sudetes—particularly the KRKONOŠE (Ger. *Riesengebirge*)—and the W Carpathians. Politically, almost all of Silesia is divided between Poland and Czechoslovakia. The Polish portion comprises most of the former Prussian provinces of Upper Silesia and Lower Silesia, both of which were transferred to Polish administration at the Potsdam Conference of 1945; the Polish portion also includes those parts of Upper Silesia that were ceded by Germany to Poland after World War I and part of the former Austrian principality of TESCHEN. A second, much smaller part of Silesia has belonged to Czechoslovakia since 1918. Except in the south, Silesia is largely an agricultural and forested lowland, drained by the Oder and its tributaries. WROCŁAW, LEGNICA, and Głogów are among the chief cities. Along the slopes of the Sudetes there are numerous small industrial centers with traditional textile and glass industries. Czech Silesia comprises the rich Karvinna coal basin. The most important part of Silesia is, however, its southern tip—Upper Silesia, in Poland. One of the largest industrial concentrations of Europe, it has extensive coal and lignite deposits and zinc, lead, iron, and other ores. The industrial area around KATOWICE comprises such important centers as BYTOM, GLIWICE, ZABRZE, and CZĘSTOCHOWA, and has iron and steel mills, coke ovens, and chemical plants. OPOLE, the former capital of Upper Silesia, is an important trade center.

Historic Silesia. Some historians maintain that the area was inhabited by the Silingae, a Vandal tribe, from the 3d cent. B.C. to the 3d cent. A.D. Slavic tribes settled here A.D. c.500, and Silesia was an integral part of Poland by the 11th cent. King Boleslaus III (reigned 1102–38), of the PIAST dynasty, divided Poland into four hereditary duchies (of which Silesia was one) for the benefit of his sons. After 1200 the duchy of Silesia fell apart into numerous minor principalities. The Silesian Piasts encouraged German colonization of their lands, the larger part of which became thoroughly Germanized, and in the early 14th cent. the Silesian princes accepted the king of Bohemia as their suzerain and thus became mediate princes of the Holy Roman Empire. During the Hussite Wars of the 15th cent. Silesia, with Moravia, was temporarily detached from the Bohemian crown and was ruled by Hungary. In 1490, however, both Silesia and Moravia reverted to Bohemia, with which they passed to the house of Hapsburg in 1526. Hapsburg rule and increasing Germanization loosened Silesia's historic ties with Poland. However, the ducal title, along with several fiefs, remained with the Silesian branch of the Piast dynasty until the extinction of the line in 1675. The margraviate of Jägerndorf was purchased in 1523 by a cadet branch of the Hohenzollern dynasty of Brandenburg, which later also claimed inheritance to other Silesian fiefs. Elector Joachim II of Brandenburg, moreover, concluded (1537) an alliance with the Piast duke, by which Brandenburg would inherit the Piast principalities if the Piast dynasty became extinct. This treaty was declared invalid by King Ferdinand I of Bohemia (later Emperor Ferdinand I). In 1621, John George of Jägerndorf, brother of the elector of Brandenburg, lost his fief for having supported Frederick the Winter King. The Thirty Years War (1618–48) brought untold misery to Silesia under successive Saxon, imperial, and Swedish occupation. It reverted to Austrian control at the Peace of Westphalia (1648). In 1675, on the death of the last Piast, Austria incorporated the Piast territories into the Bohemian crown domain. The Catholic Reformation had by then made great progress in Silesia, although Lutheranism was tolerated in Breslau (Wrocław) and certain other districts. It was on the very shaky dynastic grounds indicated above that Frederick II of Prussia, as heir of the house of Brandenburg, claimed a portion of Silesia in 1740 from Maria Theresa, who had just assumed the succession to Austria, Bohemia, and Hungary. His claim and his offer to assist Maria Theresa in the impending War of the Austrian Succession were rejected by the queen while Prussian troops were already invading Silesia. The Silesian Wars (1740–42 and 1744–45) were part of the general War of the AUSTRIAN SUCCESSION. By the Treaty of Berlin (1742), Maria Theresa ceded all of Silesia except Teschen and present Czech Silesia to Prussia; this cession was ratified by the Treaty of Dresden (1745). In the SEVEN YEARS WAR, Prussia retained Silesia.

Modern Silesia. During the Industrial Revolution of the late 18th and 19th cent. textile weaving and coal mining developed rapidly in Silesia, but industrialization brought great social tension. The Silesian weavers became dependent on entrepreneurs who farmed out work; working conditions and unemployment became intolerable, and outbreaks were frequent. Most coal mining was in the hands of private industry, which often mistreated the miners. Landholding conditions also were iniquitous, most of the land being held by owners of large estates. The resulting tensions assumed an ethnic character, since the upper and middle classes were predominantly German, while a large percentage of the workers were Polish. Though these conditions were gradually improved, Silesia even in the 20th cent. remained, despite its great productivity, a relatively backward area. After World War I the Treaty of Versailles (1919) provided for a plebiscite to determine if Upper Silesia was to remain German or to pass to Poland. The results of the plebiscite (1921) were favorable to Germany except in the easternmost part of Upper Silesia, where the Polish population predominated. After an armed rising of the Poles (1922) the League of Nations accepted a partition of the territory; the larger part of the industrial district, including Katowice, passed to Poland. The contested city and district of Teschen were partitioned in 1920 between Poland and Czechoslovakia (to the satisfaction of neither) by the conference of ambassadors. The political division of the Silesian industrial district was carried out so arbitrarily that the boundaries often cut through mines; some workers slept in one country and worked in another. As a result of the MUNICH PACT of 1938 most of Czech Silesia was partitioned between Germany and Poland, and after the German conquest of Poland in 1939 all Polish Silesia was annexed to Germany. After World War II the pre-1938 boundaries were restored, but all formerly Prussian Silesia E of the Lusatian Neisse was placed under Polish administration (a small section of Lower Silesia W of the Neisse was incorporated with the East German state of Saxony). The Allies also allowed the expulsion (in an "orderly and humane" manner) of the German population from Czech Silesia, Polish Silesia, and Polish-administered Silesia. The mass expulsion of Germans was, perforce, neither orderly nor humane; moreover, although the transfer of territories to Polish administration was made subject to revision in a final peace treaty with Germany, the Polish government treated all Silesia as integral Polish territory. West Germany finally relinquished all claims to the area under the terms of a nonaggression pact with Poland in 1972.

Silesius, Angelus: see ANGELUS SILESIUS.

Siles Zuazo, Hernán (ärnän' sē'läs swä'sō), 1914–, president of Bolivia (1956–60). The son of Hernando Siles Reyes (president of Bolivia, 1926–30) and an attorney, he was founder of the pro-miner National Revolutionary Movement (MNR) and a leader of the bloody revolt (April, 1952) that brought the MNR into power. He served as vice president (1952–56) under Victor PAZ ESTENSSORO and succeeded him as president in 1956. He continued the reform programs initiated by President Paz and launched, with some success, a campaign to cure the country's economic ills. He was succeeded by Paz, who was reelected in 1960. Although in exile after 1964, he remained politically active, emerging as leader of a faction of the MNR.

silhouette (sĭl"o͞oĕt'), outline image, especially a profile drawing solidly filled in or a cutout pasted against a lighter background. It was named for Étienne de Silhouette (1709–67), who was the finance minister to Louis XV; it is said that he was so noted for his stinginess that cheap articles, including portraits, were designated *à la Silhouette.* Drawings in silhouette became very popular in Europe during the last decades of the 18th cent. and replaced miniature paintings at French and German courts. In England and America profile portraitists proliferated in the 19th cent. and numerous magazine and book illustrators, e.g., Arthur Rackham, employed silhouettes, or, as they were called in England, shades. Their popularity was fostered by the interest in Lavater's science of physiognomy and by the strong interest in classical art, especially in Greek black-figure vase painting. Silhouette drawings decreased in popularity after the invention of the daguerreotype. See Alice V. Carrick, *A History of American Silhouettes* (1968); Norman Laliberté and Alex Mogelon, *Silhouettes, Shadows and Cutouts* (1968).

silica or **silicon dioxide,** chemical compound, SiO_2. It is insoluble in water, slightly soluble in alkalies, and soluble in dilute hydrofluoric acid. Pure silica is colorless to white. It occurs in several forms and is widely and abundantly distributed throughout the earth, both in the pure state and in SILICATES, e.g., in quartz (agate, amethyst, chalcedony, flint, jaspar, onyx, and rock crystal), opal, sand, sandstone, clay, granite, and many other rocks; in skeletal parts of various animals and plants, such as certain protozoa and DIATOMS; and in the stems and other tissue of higher plants. Silica has many important uses. It is used as a filler for paint and rubber; in making ordinary GLASS; in ceramics; in construction; and in the preparation of other substances, e.g., SILICON CARBIDE. Fused quartz is pure amorphous silica; it is used in special chemical and optical apparatus. Because it has a low thermal coefficient of expansion, it withstands sudden changes in temperature and can be used in parts that are subjected to wide ranges of heat and cold. Unlike ordinary glass, it does not absorb infrared and ultraviolet light.

silica gel, chemical compound. It is a colloidal form of SILICA, and usually resembles coarse white sand. It may be prepared by partial dehydration of *meta*silicic acid, H_2SiO_3. Because it has many tiny pores, it has great adsorptive power. It is used as a drying agent, as a catalyst or catalyst carrier, and in purifying various substances. Silica aerogel is fully dehydrated silica gel; it is very porous and is often used in insulation, e.g., for refrigerators.

silicate, chemical compound containing silicon, oxygen, and one or more metals, e.g., aluminum, barium, beryllium, calcium, iron, magnesium, manganese, potassium, sodium, or zirconium. Silicates may be considered chemically as salts of the various silicic acids. For a long time classified as ortho-, meta-, di-, or trisilicates according to the acid from which they are (theoretically) derived, they are now also classified by an X-ray diffraction method according to their crystalline structure. Silicates are widely distributed in nature, making up most of the earth's outer crust. Most of the common rock-forming minerals (e.g., QUARTZ, FELDSPAR, MICA, and PYROXENE) are silicates, as are ASBESTOS, BERYL, AQUAMARINE, EMERALD, SERPENTINE, and TALC. CLAY consists essentially of hydrous aluminum silicates mixed with other substances. GLASS is a mixture of silicates, as is WATER GLASS. See SODIUM SILICATE.

silicon, nonmetallic chemical element; symbol Si; at. no. 14; at. wt. 28.086; m.p. 1410°C; b.p. 2355°C; sp. gr. 2.33 at 25°C; valence usually +4. Silicon is the element directly below carbon and above germanium in group IVa of the PERIODIC TABLE. It is more metallic in its properties than carbon; in many ways it resembles germanium. Silicon has two allotropic forms, a brown amorphous form and a dark crystalline form. The crystalline form has a structure like diamond and the physical properties given above. Silicon forms compounds with metals (silicides) and with nonmetals. With carbon it forms SILICON CARBIDE; with oxygen a dioxide, SILICA; with oxygen and metals, SILICATES. With hydrogen it forms several hydrides or silanes, the simplest being monosilane, SiH_4, a colorless gas. It also forms compounds with the halogens, sulfur, and nitrogen and forms numerous organo-silicon compounds. Silicon is the second most abundant element of the earth's crust; it makes up about 28% of the crust by weight. Oxygen, most abundant, makes up about 47%. Aluminum, third in abundance, makes up about 8%. Silicon is widely distributed, occurring in silica and silicates, but never uncombined. Silicon is obtained commercially by heating sand and coke in an electric furnace. It is used in the steel industry in an alloy known as ferrosilicon, and also to form other alloys, such as those with aluminum, copper, and manganese; in these alloys it contributes hardness and corrosion resistance. A purified silicon is used in the preparation of SILICONES. Silicon of very high purity is prepared by thermal decomposition of silanes; it is used in transistors and other SEMICONDUCTOR devices. Silica is widely used in the production of GLASS. Silicates in the form of CLAY are used in pottery, brick, tile, and other ceramics. Silicon is found in many plants and animals; it is a major component of the test (cell wall) of diatoms. SILICOSIS is a lung disease caused by inhaling silica dust. Discovery of the element is usually credited to J. J. Berzelius, who in 1824 prepared fairly pure amorphous silicon.

silicon carbide, chemical compound, SiC, that forms extremely hard, dark, iridescent crystals that are insoluble in water and other common solvents. Widely used as an ABRASIVE, it is marketed under such familiar trade names as Carborundum and Crystolon. It is heat resistant, decomposing when heated to about 2700°C; it is used in refractory materials, e.g., rods, tubes, firebrick, and in special parts for nuclear reactors. Very pure silicon carbide is white or colorless; crystals of it are used in semiconductors for high-temperature applications. Silicon carbide fibers, added as reinforcement to plastics or light metals, impart increased strength and stiffness. Silicon carbide is prepared commercially by fusing sand and coke in an electric furnace at temperatures above 2200°C; a flux, e.g., sodium chloride, may be added to eliminate impurities. Silicon carbide was discovered (1891) by E. G. Acheson; early studies of it were made by Henri Moissan.

silicone, POLYMER in which atoms of silicon and oxygen alternate in a chain; various organic radicals, such as the methyl group, CH_3, are bound to the silicon atoms. Silicones, which are unusually stable at extreme temperatures (both high and low) may occur as liquids, rubbers, resins, or greases. Silicones are prepared from halides of organic silicon compounds by decomposition. Such compounds are chosen and used in mixtures that allow the desired molecular weight and degree of cross-linking to be obtained in the final polymer.

silicosis (sĭlĭkō'sĭs), occupational disease of the lungs caused by inhalation of free silica (quartz) dust over a prolonged period of time. Free silica is dispersed in the air and inhaled by workers engaged in the mining of lead, hard coal, and gold, in cutting sandstone and granite, in sandblasting, and in the manufacture of silica abrasives. The irritative action of the silica in the lung results in the formation of nodular lesions; these may coalesce and form massive areas of fibrous tissue. In advanced cases patients experience difficult breathing, coughing with sputum, chest pain, and a tendency to develop tuberculosis or repeated attacks of pneumonia. Once fibrosis has developed there is no cure, and treatment is directed at the management of symptoms. Preventive measures adopted in industries where the hazard of silicosis exists have greatly reduced its incidence.

Silistra (sĭlĭ'strä), town (1968 est. pop. 36,200), NE Bulgaria, a port on the Danube River bordering Rumania. Products include foodstuffs, ceramics, and furniture. The Roman Durostorum, it was founded in 29 B.C. and became an important town of Moesia. Its importance continued under Byzantine and Bulgar rule. After the Turkish conquest (1388) the town was strongly fortified. It was captured (1877) by the Russians and ceded to Bulgaria. Transferred to Rumania in 1913, it was returned to Bulgaria in 1940. There are several mosques and the ruins of an ancient fortress. The name is sometimes spelled Silistria.

silk, fine, horny, translucent, yellowish fiber produced by the silkworm in making its cocoon and covered with sericin, a protein. Many varieties of silk-spinning worms and insects are known, but the silkworm of commerce is the larva of the *Bombyx mori*, or mulberry silkworm, and other closely related moths. Sericulture (the culture of the silkworm) and the weaving of silk have been practiced in China from a remote period. Legend dates this back to 2640 B.C., to Empress Si Ling-chi, who not only encouraged the culture of the silkworm but also developed the process of reeling from the cocoon. This was a closely guarded secret for some 3,000 years. Silk seems to have been woven very early on the island of Kós, which Aristotle mentions, in a vague description of the silkworm, as the place where silk was "first spun," In the 1st and 2d cent. A.D. silk fabrics imported to Greece and Rome were sold for fabulous prices. Up to the 6th cent. raw silk was brought from China, but death was the penalty for exporting silkworm eggs. About A.D. 550 two former missionaries to China, incited by Emperor Justinian, succeeded (says Procopius) in smuggling to Constantinople, in a hollow staff, both the eggs of the silkworm and the seeds of the mulberry tree. Byzantium became famous for splendid silken textiles and embroideries, used throughout medieval Europe for royal and ecclesiastical costume and furnishing. In the 8th cent. the Moors began to carry the arts of silk culture and weaving across the northern coast of Africa and to Spain and Sicily, and in the 12th cent. Spain and Sicily were weaving silks of exquisite texture and design. Italy developed great weaving centers. Lucca, in N Italy, had established looms by the 13th cent., and in the 14th cent. the city became famous for its materials and designs. Florence and Venice followed and wove sumptuous fabrics and velvets enriched with gold thread. Genoa's velvets became well known. France established looms, and under Louis XIV's minister Jean Baptiste Colbert it set the fashion with its beautiful silks. Lyons in S France became an important weaving center. Early attempts were made in England under Henry VI to establish the silk industry, but it was not until the revocation of the Edict of Nantes, when many French refugee weavers fled to England, that the industry received a real impetus. The French settled in Canterbury, Norwich, and other places; but it was in Spitalfields, London, that the industry became important. Many attempts were made to establish sericulture in the American colonies: inducements such as land grants and bounties were offered, and many mulberry trees were planted. In 1759, Georgia sold more than 10,000 lb (4,535 kg) of cocoons in London. Pennsylvania had a silk industry, fostered by Benjamin Franklin, up to the Revolution. The high cost of labor seems to have been the main deterrent to the success of sericulture in America. Wild silk is the product of the tussah worm of India and China, which feeds on oaks. It is now semicultivated, as groves of dwarf trees are provided for its feeding. It spins a coarser, flatter, yellower filament than the *Bombyx mori*, and the color does not boil out with the gum. Tussah silk is a rough, durable, washable fabric known as shantung or pongee. In silk manufacture, the first operation is reeling. The cocoons, having been sorted for color and texture, are steamed or placed in warm water to soften the natural gum. They are then unwound; each cocoon may give from 2,000 to 3,000 ft (610-915 m) of filament, from 4 to 18 strands of which are reeled or twisted together to make an even thread strong enough to handle. This is called raw silk. Formerly a hand process, this work is now done in Europe and in some parts of the Orient in factories on simple machines called filatures. The next step, called throwing, is preparing the raw silk for the loom by twisting and doubling it to the required strength and thickness. This process also is now mostly done in large mills with specialized machinery. Silk, after throwing, has three forms—singles, which are untwisted, used for the warp of very delicate fabrics; tram, two or more singles, twisted and doubled, used for the weft of various fabrics; and organzine, made of singles twisted one way, then doubled and twisted in the opposite direction, used for the warp of heavy fabrics. For sewing and embroidery thread, more doubles and smoother twists are made. In modern factories spinning frames complete the preparation for the loom. The silk is boiled off in soapsuds to remove gum and prepare it for dyeing. For white and pale tints it must be bleached. Scouring or boiling causes loss of weight, sometimes made up by loading with metallic salts, as tin, which has an affinity for silk and can be absorbed to excess, causing weakening of the fiber. Dyeing may be done in the yarn or in the piece. Finishing processes are varying and important, as in making moires. WEAVING is done as with other textiles, but on more delicate and specialized looms. Fabrics made are plain weaves (taffeta, pongee), cords (faille, poplin), gauzes (net malines), pile fabrics (plush, velvet), crepes, satins, damask, ribbons, and brocade. Some of these weaves are ancient, developed on the shuttle looms of China and the handlooms of India, Greece, and Europe. In Europe and in the Orient the handloom is still used for the finest fabrics. Japan and China lead in the production of raw silk, with India, Italy, and France following. The United States is the largest importer. See Luce Boulnois, *The Silk Road* (tr. 1966).

Silkeborg (sĭl'kəbôr"), city (1970 com. pop. 43,125), Århus co., central Denmark, on the Gudenå River. It is a tourist and health resort surrounded by beautiful lakes and woods. Nearby is a memorial to the playwright Kaj Munk, who was murdered (1944) in Silkeborg by Nazi terrorists.

silk-screen printing, multiple PRINTING technique, also known as serigraphy, involving the use of stencils to transfer the design. Paint is applied to a silk or nylon screen and penetrates areas of the screen not blocked by the stencil. By using several stencils a number of colors may be employed in a single print. Silk-screen printing was developed as a commercial medium; it is used by modern artists, including Andy WARHOL, who have combined it with photographic processes.

silkweed: see MILKWEED.

silkworm, name for the LARVA of various species of moths, indigenous to Asia and Africa but now domesticated and raised for SILK production throughout most of the temperate zone. The culture of silkworms is called sericulture. The various species of silkworms raised today are distinguished by the quality of the silk they produce, the type of leaves on which they feed, and the number of breedings per year. The most widely raised type and the producer of the finest silk is the larva of *Bombyx mori*, of Asian origin. After centuries of domestication, *Bombyx mori* is no longer found anywhere in a natural state. The legs of the larvae have degenerated, and the adults do not fly. Hatched from eggs so small that about 35,000 of them weigh only an ounce, these silkworms are immediately quite active and feed voraciously on mulberry leaves. At the end of the larval stage (32 to 38 days after hatching) they are about 3 in. (7.5 cm) long. A mature larva attaches itself to a twig and, with a weaving motion of its head and a slow, circular motion of its body, begins to spin its cocoon (see PUPA). A moist substance, fibroin, is manufactured in two silk glands located on the underside of the larva's body; mixed with a small amount of wax, it is emitted from an orifice called the spinneret, in the lip of the larva. The fibroin dries quickly in the air, hardening into a half-mile-long thread of silk that makes up the cocoon. The adult moth, with a wingspread of 1.75 in. (4.5 cm), emerges from the cocoon in about two weeks. The moths mate and lay their eggs (several hundred from each female) within a week; the eggs hatch in about ten days. Only enough cocoons to ensure adequate reproduction are allowed to hatch; the rest are unwound after developing for a week, and the silk is processed. The giant silkworms used in some Oriental and South American sericulture are the larvae of the closely related saturnid moths (family Saturniidae). They include the tussah moth (*Antherala pernyi),* the producer of tussah silk. The ailanthus moth (*Samia walkeri*), a large, olive-green saturnid moth used in China to produce a coarse grade of silk, was imported to the United States along with its food plant, the Chinese ailanthus tree, as the basis of an industry that never materialized; the moth has been firmly established in the New York City area since 1861. Diseases of silkworms have occasioned important scientific work. When Pasteur saved the French silk industry from destruction by pébrine, a protozoan disease of insects, in the mid-18th cent., he also made an important contribution to the germ theory of disease. The common silkworm, *Bombyx mori,* is classified in the phylum ARTHROPODA, class Insecta, order Lepidoptera, family Bombycidae. See S. N. Chowdhury, *The Silkworm and Its Culture* (1967); P. A. Kovalev, *Silkworm Breeding Stocks* (1970).

silky terrier, breed of agile, spirited TOY DOG originated in Australia in the early 20th cent. It stands about 10 in. (25 cm) high at the shoulder and weighs from 8 to 10 lb (3.6–4.5 kg). Its silky, flat-lying hair is between 5 and 6 in. (12.7–15.2 cm) long and hangs straight down from the sides of the body. Its color is blue with tan markings on the face and legs and a silver or fawn topknot. The silky terrier resulted from crossings of Yorkshire terrier and Australian terrier. It has always been raised as a house pet and companion. See DOG.

Sill, Edward Rowland, 1841–87, American poet and educator, b. Windsor, Conn., grad. Yale, 1861. He was professor of English at the Univ. of California from 1874 to 1882. Of his slender output, only *The Hermitage and Other Poems* (1868) was published during his lifetime; after his death his collected prose (1900) and collected poems (1902) appeared. Best known of his lyrics are "The Fool's Prayer" and "Opportunity."

Sill, Fort: see FORT SILL.

Silla (sĭl'ə), locale at Jerusalem, possibly near Mt. Zion. 2 Kings 12.20.

Sillanpää, Frans Eemil (fräns ā'mĭl sĭl'länpä"), 1888–1964, Finnish novelist. As a young man Sillanpää studied natural science at Helsinki and came under the influence of an artistic circle that included the composer Sibelius. He soon won acclaim with his short stories and his first novel, *Life and Sun* (1916). *Meek Heritage* (1919, tr. 1938) won him recognition as Finland's foremost writer; it described the period of the Finnish civil war of 1918 with sympathy and realism. *Fallen Asleep while Young* (1931; tr. *The Maid Silja,* 1933) treats the conflicts of the same era caused by the disintegration of older values. His *People in a Summer Night* (1934, tr. 1966) concerns the mysteries of nature. Sillanpää was awarded the 1939 Nobel Prize in Literature.

Silliman, Benjamin, 1779–1864, American chemist, geologist, and physicist, b. Trumbull, Conn., grad. Yale, 1796. In 1802 he was appointed first professor of chemistry and natural history at Yale; he traveled abroad and then returned to teach at Yale until 1853. He was noted as a teacher, as a popular lecturer on scientific subjects, and as a founder and editor (1818–46) of the *American Journal of Science and Arts.* He was the first president of the Association of American Geologists, which became (1848) the American Association for the Advancement of Science, and a founding member of the National Academy of Sciences, and he helped to establish the medical school at Yale. His son, **Benjamin Silliman,** 1816–85, American chemist, b. New Haven, Conn., grad. Yale, 1837, was professor at Yale (1846–49) and then at the Univ. of Louisville (1849–54). In 1854 he returned to Yale, succeeding his father. The school of chemistry which he had established there (1847) later developed into the Sheffield Scientific School.

Sills, Beverly, 1929–, American coloratura soprano, b. Brooklyn, N.Y. as Belle Silverman. Her childhood career as a radio singer led to voice studies with Estelle Liebling. She toured extensively in the United States and Europe before making her debut with the New York City Opera singing Rosalinda in Johann Strauss's *Die Fledermaus* in 1955. She subsequently became the leading soprano with that company. In 1969 she made a triumphal debut at the La Scala Opera as Pamira in Rossini's *Siege of Corinth,* the role in which she was scheduled to make her Metropolitan Opera debut in April, 1975. Regarded as one of the great American sopranos, Sills is famous not only for her light coloratura voice but also for her considerable acting ability. She has appeared in such roles as Cleopatra in Handel's *Julius Caesar,* Elvira in Bellini's *I Puritani,* all four female roles in Offenbach's *Tales of Hoffmann,* and the title roles in Massenet's *Manon* and Donizetti's *Maria Stuarda, Anna Bolena,* and *Lucia di Lammermoor.*

silo, watertight and airtight structure for making and storing SILAGE. Silos vary in form from a covered pit, such as was used by the early Romans, to the modern storage tower, dating from the 19th cent. A silo may be made of wood, brick, reinforced concrete, metal, or tile blocks, and is sealed with earth, airproof paper, or plastic. Most of the more modern upright cylindrical silos are glass-lined and are considered the most efficient. Older or less expensive styles include the box silo, made of planks lined with heavy paper; the fence silo, with pickets arranged in a circle and lined with paper; the concrete-lined trench silo, into which dump trucks unload the chopped fodder; and the underground pit, built like a well or cistern.

Siloah (sīlō'ə), variant of SILOAM.

Siloam (sīlō'əm), pool, SE of Jerusalem, Palestine, in the Kidron valley, mentioned in the Old and New Testaments. It is connected with the Virgin's Pool by a winding rocky conduit 1,700 ft (518 m) long, in the southern end of which was discovered in 1880 an inscription in Hebrew; it dates from the time of Hezekiah and describes the cutting of the tunnel. Shiloah: Isa. 8.6. Siloah: Neh. 3.15. See Luke 13.4; John 9.7.

Silone, Ignazio (ēnyä'tsyō sēlō'nā), 1900–, Italian novelist and journalist, whose original name was Secondo Tranquilli. A Socialist and for a time a Communist, he has devoted his writings to attacking Fascism and promoting Socialism without sacrificing human and literary values to his thesis. He fled Italy in 1931, and, after living in Switzerland, he returned to his native country in 1944 to become editor of the newspaper *Avanti.* His novel *Fontamara* (1933, tr., 1934) was rewritten after World War II to reflect his matured political thought; an English translation of the second version appeared in 1960. Silone's other works include *Pane e vino* (1937, tr. *Bread and Wine,* 1962); *The School for Dictators* (tr. 1938); *The Living Thoughts of Mazzini* (tr. 1939); *Il seme sotto la neve* (1940; tr. *The Seed beneath the Snow,* 1942); *Emergency Exit* (1951, tr. 1968); and *The Story of a Humble Christian* (1968, tr. 1970). Silone contributed critical and political articles to various periodicals. See N. A. Scott, *Rehearsals of Discomposure* (1952).

silt, predominantly quartz mineral particles that are between sand size and clay size, i.e., between 1/16 and 1/256 mm (1/406–1/6502 in.) in diameter. Silt, like clay and sand, is a product of the weathering and decomposition of preexisting rock. Hardened silt forms a sedimentary rock called **siltstone,** which tends to deposit in thin layers sometimes referred to as flagstone because it is hard, durable, and flat, breaking into nearly rectangular slabs.

Silurian period (sĭlŏŏr'ēən, sī-) [from the Silures, ancient tribe of S Wales, where the period was first studied; named by the British geologist R. I. Murchison], third period of the PALEOZOIC ERA of geologic time (see GEOLOGIC ERAS, table). The continents in the Silurian period remained much as they had been in the preceding ORDOVICIAN PERIOD, approximately the same areas being subject to flooding by shallow seas. The transition between the Ordovician and Silurian rocks is not clearly marked in the United States. The Medina sandstone extending from New York to Alabama has been assigned to both periods but is generally considered to be Silurian. Three main series, based on the succession of strata in New York state, are usually distinguished—the lower Silurian (Medinan, or Alexandrian, series), the middle Silurian (Niagaran series), and the upper Silurian (Cayugan series). The early Silurian deposits in the east are commonly sandstone, shale, and conglomerate, comprising erosion products from high-standing mountains; in the west, marine limestone predominates. The great event of the Silurian period in North America was the flooding of the interior basin by warm waters originating in the arctic regions and the deposition of the Niagaran limestone, which can best be seen at Niagara Falls. The withdrawal of the Niagaran flood was apparently followed by desert conditions, under which the Salinan "red beds" of the Appalachian area and the salt deposits of New York, Michigan, Ontario, and Ohio were formed. Some areas were later reflooded, the Cobleskill and Rondout limestone of New York being deposited. The Silurian of the Far West is as yet not well established. In North America, the Silurian ended quietly; however, in the British Isles, Scandinavia, and France, as a result of the Caledonian disturbance, great mountains were thrust up. Economic resources of the Silurian strata, besides salt, are iron ore (near Birmingham, Ala.) and quartz sandstones, used in glass manufacture. Dominating the life of the Silurian were marine invertebrates, including crinoids and cystoids, mollusks (some of them the fiercest inhabitants of the sea), and eurypterids, invertebrates related to crabs and insects. The Niagaran limestone contains extensive coral reefs. Members of the trilobite family were still numerous; primitive fishes increased in number. Most notable in the Silurian fauna were scorpions, possibly the first animals to live on land and take their oxygen from the air.

Silva, Antonio José da (əntô'nyŏŏ zhŏŏzĕ' dä sēl'-və), 1705–39, Portuguese playwright, b. Rio de Janeiro, Brazil. He belonged to a family of "New Christians" (Jews forced to convert), suspected of remaining secretly loyal to Judaism. Silva practiced law in Portugal and wrote a number of vigorous, satiric plays. They are related to the commedia dell' arte but have more vitality than polish. Among them are *A vida do grande Dom Quixote* [the life of Don Quixote] (1733) and *Guerras do alecrim e da mangerona* [wars between the rosemary and the marjoram] (1737), considered Silva's best work. Brought before the Inquisition in 1737, he and his family were convicted of practicing Jewish rites, strangled, and burned at the stake.

Silva, José Asunción (hōsā' äsōōnsyōn' sĭl'vä), 1865–96, Colombian poet, one of the creators of MODERNISMO. Writing superbly under the inspiration of contemporary European poets, Silva finally gained a publisher in France, but his manuscript was lost in a shipwreck. His father died leaving tremendous debts, which Silva attempted to repay. After the tragic death of a beloved sister, he committed suicide at 31, leaving behind him poems marked by technical innovations, haunting musical tones, and a brooding spirit of pessimism. They had great influence on Rubén DARÍO and other *modernistas.* The best known are "Nocturno III," an elegy for his sister, "Crepusculo," and "El dia de difuntos" [the day of the dead].

Silvanus (sĭlvā'nəs), in the Bible, probably the same as SILAS.

Silvanus, in Roman religion, ancient pastoral deity, protector of uncultivated lands. It was also said that he was the guardian of field boundaries, flocks, and herds. Like the Greek Pan, with whom he was often identified, he could be dangerous as well as beneficent.

Silver, Abba Hillel, 1893–1963, American rabbi and Zionist leader, b. Lithuania. He was taken to the United States in 1902. Educated at the Univ. of Cincinnati (B.A., 1915) and Hebrew Union College, Cincinnati, he became rabbi of the The Temple, Cleveland, in 1917. He was cochairman of the American Zionist Emergency Council during World War II and chairman of the American section of the Jewish Agency for Palestine, and he thus played a part in the founding of the state of Israel. He was the author of several books, including *Democratic Impulse and Jewish History* (1928), *Vision and Victory* (1949), and *A History of Messianic Speculation in Israel* (1959). See his selected writings, ed. by Herbert Weiner (1967).

silver, metallic chemical element; symbol Ag [Lat. *argentum*]; at. no. 47; at. wt. 107.868; m.p. 961°C; b.p. 2212°C; sp. gr. 10.5 at 20°C; valence +1 or +2. Pure silver is nearly white, lustrous, soft, very ductile, malleable, and an excellent conductor of heat and electricity. In many of its properties it resembles copper and gold, the elements above and below it in group Ib of the PERIODIC TABLE. It is not a chemically active metal, being considerably below hydrogen in the electromotive series (see METAL). It is, however, attacked by nitric acid (forming the nitrate) and by hot concentrated sulfuric acid. Silver is almost always monovalent in its compounds, but an oxide, a fluoride, and a sulfide of divalent silver are known. It does not oxidize in air but reacts with the hydrogen sulfide present in the air, forming silver sulfide (tarnish). SILVER NITRATE is the most important compound. Silver chloride, bromide, and iodide are used in still PHOTOGRAPHY because of their sensitivity to light. Solutions of certain protein complexes containing silver are used as antiseptics. A mirror can be made by coating glass with metallic silver derived from the reaction of a solution of a silver ammonia complex with an organic reducing agent such as formaldehyde. Although silver can be found uncombined in nature, most silver used today is obtained from its ores. Among these the most important are argentite or silver glance (silver sulfide), which is found associated with other metal sulfides, e.g., galena; horn silver or cerargyrite (silver chloride); two ores composed of silver and antimony (in different proportions) called pyrargyrite (or ruby silver ore) and stephanite; and another ore composed of silver and arsenic sulfides called proustite. Mexico, the United States (Idaho, Montana, Arizona, Colorado, Utah, Nevada, California, New Mexico, and Texas), the USSR, Peru, Australia, and Canada are the leading producers. The metal is prepared in various ways depending upon the nature of its occurrence; the greatest quantity is obtained in connection with the refining of lead and copper. It is separated from lead by the Parkes process, which is based upon the fact that silver is soluble in molten zinc whereas lead is not. The CYANIDE PROCESS has largely replaced an AMALGAM process in which silver is dissolved in mercury. Some of the silver produced today is used, as in the past, in making coins (see COIN; MONEY; BIMETALLISM). Large quantities are used for silver utensils and jewelry, and in plating tableware electrolytically from a solution of sodium silver cyanide. Alloys of silver with copper, in which the copper adds hardness, are important. Coin silver is an alloy consisting of 90% silver and 10% copper. Sterling silver contains 92.5% silver and 7.5% copper. Silver alloys are used in dental amalgams and for electrical contacts. Silver was one of the first metals to be used by man (see SILVERWORK).

Silver Age: see AGE.

silver chloride, chemical compound, AgCl, a white cubic crystalline solid. It is nearly insoluble in water but is soluble in a water solution of ammonia, potassium cyanide, or sodium thiosulfate ("hypo"). On exposure to light it becomes a deep grayish blue due to its decomposition into metallic silver and atomic chlorine. This light-sensitive behavior is the basis of photographic processes (see PHOTOGRAPHY, STILL). Since silver bromide, AgBr, and silver iodide, AgI, react similarly, all three of these silver halide salts are used in making photographic films and plates. Both the bromide and iodide are less soluble in water and more sensitive to light than the chloride. The bromide forms light yellow cubic crystals; the iodide forms yellow hexagonal or yellow-orange cubic crystals, depending on the temperature. Besides use in photography, silver chloride is used in silver plating, and silver iodide is used for seeding clouds. The chloride, bromide, and iodide occur naturally as the minerals cerargyrite, bromyrite, and iodyrite, respectively. Silver fluoride, AgF, forms colorless cubic crystals; it is much more soluble in water than the other silver halides.

silvereye: see WHITE-EYE.

silverfish, common name for primitive, wingless INSECTS of the family Lepismatidae. The silverfish, which has two long antennae and three long tail bristles, is named for its covering of tiny, silvery scales. It develops directly in six or more molts into an adult about ½ in. (1.27 cm) long. It has chewing mouthparts set in a head cavity and eats starch from book bindings, wallpaper, and clothing. The silverfish is common indoors in cool, damp places such as basements. The firebrat, in the same taxonomic family, is found in warm places, e.g., near steampipes and boilers. Silverfish are classified in the phylum ARTHROPODA, class Insecta, order Thysanura, family Lepismatidae.

Silverius, Saint (sĭlvēr'ēəs), d. 537, pope (536–37), an Italian; successor of St. Agapetus I. The son of Pope Hormisdas, who had been married before taking orders, St. Silverius was elected pope at the instance of the Ostrogothic king, Theodahad, although VIGILIUS, as Agapetus' deacon, was the logical candidate. Failing to win Silverius over to MONOPHYSITISM, Empress THEODORA intrigued to make Vigilius pope. On a trumped-up charge of treason, Pope Silverius was sent into exile; Vigilius was declared pope, and Silverius died shortly afterward. He is believed to have been murdered. Feast: June 20.

Silverman, Joseph, 1860–1930, American rabbi, b. Cincinnati. He was rabbi at Dallas, Texas (1884–85), at Galveston (1885–88), and at the Temple Emanu-El, New York City (1888–1922). He was president (1900–1903) of the Central Conference of American Rabbis and was founder and president of the Emanu-El Brotherhood. He wrote *A Catechism on Judaism* (1886), made numerous contributions to periodicals, and was active in Zionist work.

silver nitrate (nī'trāt), chemical compound, $AgNO_3$, a colorless crystalline material that is very soluble in water. The most important compound of silver, it is used in the preparation of silver salts for PHOTOGRAPHY, in chemical analysis, in silver plating, in inks and hair dyes, and to silver mirrors. It is used in medicine in the treatment of eye infections and gonorrhea. Fused silver nitrate is also called lunar caustic. Taken internally silver nitrate is a poison. It is prepared by reaction of nitric acid with silver, and purified by recrystallization. It is darkened by sunlight or contact with organic matter such as the skin.

silverpoint, method of drawing whereby a silver-tipped instrument is dragged across paper prepared with ground bone dust and gum water and then tinted with a pigment. The procedure results in drawings of extraordinary delicacy. It was used extensively in Europe from the late Middle Ages to the early 16th cent. The silverpoint instrument was a silver thread encased in wood, similar in design to a modern lead pencil. Among the foremost practitioners of the medium were Leonardo da Vinci and Dürer.

silver poplar: see WILLOW.

Silver Purchase Act: see SHERMAN SILVER PURCHASE ACT.

silversides, common name for small shore fishes, belonging to the family Antherinidae, abundant in the warmer waters of the Atlantic and Pacific, and named for the silvery stripe on either side of the body. Silversides, known commercially as whitebait, eat insects and small crustaceans. The small (3 in./7.5 cm) tidewater silversides, *Menidia menidia,* is found along the Atlantic coast; the similar brook silversides is a freshwater species. Larger and better known is the California grunion (5–8 in./12.5–20 cm), which rides in on high tides to lay its eggs in the sand. Beached grunions are collected by hand in large quantities. Other Pacific silversides are the top smelts and jack smelts, important to California's smelt fisheries. The mullets (family Mugilidae), blunt-nosed warm-water fishes of both oceans, are closely related to the silversides. Small schools of mullets frequent shallow waters, feeding on aquatic plants and on mud, which is ground up in the gizzardlike stomach. The striped mullet, *Mugil cephalus,* is quite common, a bluish fish that attains a weight of 1 lb (0.45 kg). Mullets are good food fish and are preyed upon heavily by larger carnivorous fishes. Silversides and mullets are classified in the phylum CHORDATA, subphylum Vertebrata, class Osteichthyes, order Perciformes, families Antherinidae and Mugilidae, respectively.

Silver Spring, uninc. city (1970 pop. 77,496), Montgomery co., W central Md., a residential suburb of Washington, D.C. It has a large naval ordnance laboratory, several large research laboratories (for the development of missiles and of electronic and prosthetic equipment), and a plant making precision instruments.

Silver Springs, mineral spring, N central Fla., source of the Silver River. The spring, one of the world's largest and most famous, has a basin 80 ft (24 m) deep and 300 ft (91 m) wide. The water temperature is 72°F (22°C) throughout the year. The extreme clearness of the water, which makes it a favored site for underwater photography, is due to the filtration of rainwater through the porous soil and substrata. Silver Springs is a major tourist attraction; a great variety of aquatic life may be seen through glass-bottomed boats. The Spanish explorer Hernando De Soto was probably the first white man to visit the spring (1539). The town of Silver Springs is nearby.

silverwork includes ecclesiastical and domestic plate, flatware, jewelry, buttons, buckles, boxes, toilet articles, weapons, furniture, and horse trappings. It involves a variety of embellishments, such as chasing, repoussé, filigree, and inlaying, which have engaged the talents of skilled artisans since prehistoric times. That it was highly developed among the ancients is evidenced by treasures and funeral objects from Egyptian tombs; Minoan silver cups, seals, and ornaments of c.2000 B.C.; and silver vases and the inlays on bronze blades of Mycenae. Work attributed to the Phoenicians has been found in Greece, where early native examples are few. Roman silverwork displays rich, often high, reliefs. Byzantine silverwork and goldwork enriched churches and monasteries. Much Italian and French silverwork was melted down for reuse and thus lost. Early German Renaissance silverwork is less abundant than that of the 16th cent. from the two most prolific centers, Augsburg and Nuremberg, with their numerous Italian artisans. German characteristics prevail in Swiss silverwork, and the influence extended to Spain but was overbalanced by the presence of many Italian craftsmen there in the 15th cent. Spanish silver of the 16th cent. carries elaborate designs, and in the 17th cent. silversmiths added filigree and enamel to the decoration. A Spanish architectural style of the 16th cent. is called PLATERESQUE for its profusion of ornate motifs similar to the work of the silversmiths of that period. Much fine 17th- and 18th-century Dutch silver shows designs in the French taste. Poland and Russia produced ecclesiastical plate, domestic ware, and horse trappings. Silversmiths of Oriental countries have been expert from early times. The British Museum and the Victoria and Albert Museum contain representative pieces of superior workmanship, some from Persia, India, Tibet, and China. The Reformation brought destruction to ecclesiastical art of N Europe, and much plate was melted down in England during the Wars of the Roses so that little early English silver is extant. The HALLMARK came into use c.1300. Elizabethan pieces display German influence, and work of the period of Charles II is loaded with ornament. Cromwellian influence is reflected in English silverwork of extreme simplicity; French tendencies of the Louis XIV regime contributed great enrichment and were followed by the later rococo style; under Robert Adam's influence there was a classic reaction. SHEFFIELD PLATE was an innovation of the 18th cent.; since then plated ware has become the product of important industries in England and the United States. Silverwork is an important native craft in Mexico, among Indian tribes in the W United States, and in Peru, where the abundant metal is often used unalloyed. In the American colonies silversmithing proved so profitable that it attracted several hundred silverworkers. It was highly developed in New England, by such leaders as John Hull, Jeremiah Dummer, John Coney, and Paul Revere in Boston and Samuel Vernon in Newport, R.I., and in other American cities including Philadelphia and New York, where the Boelen family and Jacobus van der Spiegel were especially noted. Colonial silver, simple in design, is much sought by collectors. The modern revival of handwrought silver has been greatly influenced by the severe forms of Danish work. See S. B. Wyler, *The Book of Old Silver* (1937); G. B. Hughes and Therle Hughes, *Modern Silver Throughout the World* (1967) and *Three Centuries of English Domestic Silver* (1952, repr. 1968); Frank Davis, *French Silver, 1450–1825* (1970); and Graham Hood, *American Silver* (1971).

Silvester: see SYLVESTER.

Silvestre de Sacy: see SACY, ANTOINE ISAAC, BARON SILVESTRE DE.

silviculture: see FORESTRY.

Silvretta (sĭlvrĕt'ə, Ger. zĭlvrĕt'ä), mountain group of the Alps, in E Switzerland and SW Austria. Its highest peak, Piz Linard (11,185 ft/3,409 m) is in Switzerland; Piz Buin (10,869 ft/3,313 m) is the highest of the group in Austria. Extensive glaciers cover the slopes.

sima: see CONTINENT.

Simancas (sēmäng'käs), village, Valladolid prov., NW Spain, in León. The castle, an old fort rebuilt in the 15th cent., contains the Spanish national archives. Begun by Ferdinand V in Valladolid, the collection was transferred to Simancas in 1563 by Emperor Charles V and was much enriched by Philip II.

Simbirsk: see ULYANOVSK, USSR.

Simcoe, John Graves (sĭm'kō), 1752–1806, British army officer, first governor of Upper Canada (Ontario). He served with the British in the American Revolution. Upon the division of Quebec into the two Canadas, he was appointed (1791) lieutenant governor of Upper Canada. In 1792 he arrived at Niagara (which he called Newark), his temporary capital; he moved to York (now Toronto) in 1793. Zealous to make the province a strong colony, Simcoe encouraged immigration (particularly of the American Loyalists), fostered agricultural development, and urged the imperial government to establish a provincial college. He was sent (1796) to take part in the ineffective campaign in Haiti and then returned to England. See biographies by W. R. Ridell (1926), D. C. Scott (rev. ed. 1926), and Marcus Van Steen (1968).

Simcoe, town (1971 pop. 10,793), S Ont., Canada, on the Lynn River SW of Hamilton. It is a market center for a region producing fruit, vegetables, and tobacco. There are food-processing and canning plants in Simcoe.

Simcoe, Lake, 539 sq mi (1,396 sq km), S Ont., Canada, between Georgian Bay and Lake Ontario. Cook Bay, Kempenfelt Bay, and Lake Couchiching are arms of the lake. Lake Simcoe drains N through the Severn River to Georgian Bay and forms part of the Trent Canal system. Orillia, Barrie, and several small resorts are on the lake.

Simeon I, c.863–927, ruler (893–927) and later first czar of Bulgaria. He was placed on the throne by his father, BORIS I, who had returned from a monastery to depose his first son, Vladimir (reigned 889–93), for attempting to reintroduce paganism. Simeon, ambitious to conquer a vast empire, made duties levied on Bulgarian trade a pretext for attacking the Byzantine emperor Leo VI. Simeon defeated Leo but was defeated in turn by Leo's allies, the MAGYARS under Arpad. However, aided by the Pechenegs, he drove the Magyars into their present domain in Hungary. Simeon ravaged the Byzantine Empire, threatened Constantinople several times, and temporarily held Adrianople. He conquered most of Serbia and took (925) the title czar of the Bulgars and autocrat of the Greeks, which was approved (926) by Pope John X. Denying the supremacy of the patriarch at Constantinople, he raised the archbishop of Bulgaria to the rank of patriarch. At his capital, Preslav, Simeon held a court of unprecedented splendor. Under his rule the first Bulgarian empire attained its greatest power, and Church Slavonic literature reached its golden age. An able Greek scholar, Simeon fostered the translation of Greek works into Church Slavonic. During the reign of his son and successor, Peter, the empire was destroyed by internal dissension and foreign attacks.

Simeon II, 1937–, czar of Bulgaria (1943–46). He succeeded his father, Boris III, under a regency. After the occupation (1944) of Bulgaria by Russian forces he remained nominal ruler under a new council of regents. In 1946 a plebiscite abolished the monarchy, and he went into exile in Madrid.

Simeon or **Symeon** (both: sĭm'ēŏn). **1** Second son of Jacob and Leah and ancestor of the southernmost tribe of Israel. He and his tribe are seldom mentioned individually. Gen. 29.33; 34; 49.5–7; Joshua 19. **2** Name in the Gospel genealogy. Luke 3.30. **3** Devout man who blessed Jesus when He was presented in the Temple. He uttered NUNC DIMITTIS. Luke 2.21–34. **4 Simeon Niger,** early Christian, prominent in Antioch. Acts 13.1. In Acts 15.14 Simeon appears for the usual Simon, referring to St. Peter.

Simeon Stylites, Saint (stīlī'tēz) [Gr.,= of a pillar], d. 459?, Syrian hermit. He lived for more than 35 years on a small platform on top of a high pillar. He had many imitators (called stylites) and gained the reverence of the whole Christian world. Feast: Jan. 5.

Simferopol (sĕmfyĭrô'pəl), city (1970 pop. 250,000), capital of Crimean oblast, SE European USSR, in the Ukraine, on the Salgir River and on the Sevastopol-Kharkov rail line. It is a land and water transport hub and a commercial center in the heart of a truck-farming and fruit-growing region. Industries include food processing, wine making, fruit canning, and the manufacture of machinery, machine tools, power station equipment, and knitwear. Tourism is also economically important. Simferopol occupies the site of an ancient Scythian capital founded (3d cent. B.C.) by King Skilur as the fortress of Neapolis. Called Ak-Mechet under Tatar rule (15th–18th cent.), it was renamed Simferopol after its annexation to Russia in 1784. The city became the capital of the Crimean Tatar nationalist government in 1918 and of Gen. P. N. Wrangel's White government in 1920. It was the capital of the Crimean Autonomous SSR from 1921 until 1946. The old section of Simferopol has retained its Oriental appearance.

Sími (sē'mē) or **Syme** (sē'mē, sī'–), island (1971 pop. 2,489), 22 sq mi (57 sq km), SE Greece, in the Aegean Sea, one of the Dodecanese. The main town is Sími, located on the northeast shore. The monastery of Panormetes is on the island.

simile (sĭm'əlē) [Lat.,= likeness], in rhetoric, a figure of speech in which an object is explicitly compared to another object. Robert Burns's poem "A Red Red Rose" contains two straightforward similes:

My love is like a red, red rose
That's newly sprung in June:
My love is like the melody
That's sweetly played in tune.

The epic, or Homeric, simile is an elaborate, formal, and sustained simile derived from those of Homer.

Simi Valley (sē'mē, sĭm'ē), city (1970 pop. 56,464), Ventura co., S Calif., in an oil, farm, and livestock region; laid out 1887, inc. 1969. Campers, toothpaste tubes, plastic containers, sportswear, sewage units, and liquid oxygen are manufactured. Of interest are an historical park, Indian caves, and the old stagecoach road. A junior college is nearby.

Simkhovitch, Mary Kingsbury (sĭmkō'vĭch), 1867–1951, American social worker, b. Chestnut Hill, Mass., grad. Boston Univ., 1890. After several years of further study at Radcliffe, Columbia, and the Univ. of Berlin, she became active in settlement work and the study of social economy. In 1902 she and several others founded Greenwich House, in the Greenwich Village district of New York City. Greenwich House became famous for its activities in social service, music, and handicrafts (see SETTLEMENT HOUSE). She was its director from 1902 until 1946, when she retired to become director emeritus. Her writings include *Neighborhood* (1938), *Group Life* (1940), *Quicksand* (with Elizabeth Ogg, 1942), and her autobiography, *Here Is God's Plenty* (1949).

Simla (sĭm'lə), town (1971 pop. 55,326), capital of Himachal Pradesh state, NW India. It is situated on a forested ridge (c.7,100 ft/2,165 m high) in the W Himalayas. Simla is a summer resort and a large market for potatoes. It is also the headquarters of the Indian army.

Simmel, Georg (gā'ôrk zĭm'əl), 1858–1918, German philosopher and sociologist. At the universities of Berlin and Strasbourg he was an influential lecturer. Basing his social philosophy on a broad historical foundation, he did much to establish German sociology as an independent discipline. His chief works are *Soziologie* (1908) and *Lebensanschauung* [philosophy of life] (1918). See his *On Individuality and Social Forms: Selected Writings,* ed. and with an introd. by D. N. Levine (1971); essays by and about Simmel, edited by K. H. Wolff (1965); studies by N. J. Spykman (1925, repr. 1964) and L. A. Coser (1965).

Simmons College, at Boston, Mass.; primarily for women; chartered 1889, opened 1902; called Simmons Female Academy until 1915. Its program was among the first to offer women college-level instruction in liberal arts and professional studies.

Simms, William Gilmore, 1806–70, American novelist, b. Charleston, S.C. He wrote prolifically, both prose and poetry, but it is for his historical romances about his own state that he is remembered and often compared with James Fenimore Cooper. His tales of the Southern frontier include *Guy Rivers* (1834) and *Beauchampe* (1842; one part rewritten as *Charlemont,* 1856); those of colonial times are *The Yemassee* (1835) and *The Cassique of Kiawah* (1859); romances of Revolutionary times include a series—*The Partisan* (1835), *Mellichampe* (1836), and *Katharine Walton* (1851)—and *The Forayers* (1855) and its sequel, *Eutaw* (1856). He also wrote less successful novels of Spanish history. Besides continually writing fiction, he edited (1849–56) the *Southern Quarterly Review* and wrote local history and biographies of Francis Marion (1844), Nathanael Greene (1849), and others. His volumes of short stories are entitled *Carl Werner* (1838) and *The Wigwam and the Cabin* (two series, both 1845). His home and fortune were destroyed in the Civil War. See biographies by J. V. Ridgely (1962) and W. P. Trent (1968); studies by E. W. Parks (1961) and J. L. Wakelyn (1973).

Simnel, Lambert (sĭm'nəl), c.1475–1525, impostor and pretender to the English throne. Little is known of his early life, but before 1486 he caught the attention of an Oxford priest, Richard Simon or Symonds, who trained him to impersonate Richard, duke of York, younger son of Edward IV. The plan was changed, however, and in 1486 Simon took Simnel to Ireland, claiming that he was Edward, earl of Warwick. (Warwick, son of George, duke of Clarence, was at that time imprisoned in the Tower of London. He was executed in 1499.) A number of Yorkist adherents rallied to his cause, and in May, 1487, Simnel and his supporters, led by John de la Pole, earl of Lincoln (see under POLE, family), crossed to England and were defeated by the forces of Henry VII at the battle of Stoke (June, 1487). Simnel was taken prisoner but pardoned and supposedly was employed thereafter as a scullion in the royal kitchen.

Simoïs (sĭm'ōĭs), small river, NW Turkey, a tributary of the Scamander. It was the scene of many legendary events of Asia Minor, particularly during the siege of Troy.

Simon, Saint (sī'mən), one of the Twelve Disciples. In the Gospels he is called the Canaanite or Cananaean or Zelotes, synonymous terms referring probably to association with the fanatical sect of ZEALOTS (Mat. 10.4; Mark 3.18; Luke 6.15; Acts 1.13). Feast (with St. JUDE): Oct. 28.

Simon, in the Bible. **1** One of the MACCABEES. **2** or **Simon Peter:** see PETER, SAINT. **3** See SIMON, SAINT. **4** Kinsman of Jesus. Mat. 13.55; Mark 6.3. **5** Leper of Bethany in whose house a woman anointed Jesus' feet. He may have been the father of Lazarus. Mat. 26.6; Mark 14.3. **6** Pharisee in whose house Jesus was entertained. Luke 7.36–50. **7** Father of Judas Iscariot. John 6.71; 13.2,26. **8** See SIMON OF CYRENE. **9** Tanner of Joppa with whom Peter stayed. Acts 9.43. **10** See SIMON MAGUS.

Simon, Antoine (äNtwän' sēmôN'), 1736–94, French revolutionary, often called "the shoemaker," a member of the Commune of Paris. He and his wife guarded the dauphin, Louis XVIII, in prison. Their reputed brutality and coarseness made them infamous. A friend of Maximilien Robespierre and Jean Paul Marat, Simon was executed after the coup d'etat of 9 Thermidor.

Simon, John Allsebrook Simon, 1st Viscount, 1873–1954, British statesman and jurist. He was called to the bar in 1899 and entered the House of Commons as a Liberal in 1906. He became solicitor general (1910), attorney general (1913), and home secretary (1915), but he resigned (1916) because of his opposition to the introduction of conscription during World War I. He lost his seat in Parliament in 1918 but was returned again in 1922. In 1926 he was leading counsel for Newfoundland in the Labrador boundary settlement, and he served as chairman (1927–30) of the commission to study the operation of the Montagu-Chelmsford reforms of 1919 in India. In the National government he was foreign secretary (1931–35), home secretary (1935–37), and chancellor of the exchequer (1937–40). He gained a reputation as one of the most outspoken advocates of the appeasement policy toward Germany. Simon was created viscount in 1940 and held the position of lord chancellor from 1940 to 1945. See his memoirs (1952).

Simon, Jules (zhül sēmôN'), 1814–96, French statesman. His full name was Jules François Simon Suisse. He taught philosophy at the Sorbonne from 1839 to 1852, during which time he edited the works of several philosophers and wrote his *Histoire de l'école d'Alexandrie* (2 vol., 1844–45). He was elected (1848) to the national assembly and later entered the council of state. His republican opinions led to his retirement, and his subsequent refusal to swear allegiance to Louis Napoleon lost him his professorship (1852). Until 1863, Simon devoted himself to intellectual pursuits, writing *Natural Religion* (1856, tr. 1857), *La Liberté* (1859), and other works. Resuming political activity, he served as deputy (1863–75) and then was made senator for life. A member of the government of national defense after the French defeat at Sedan, he served (1870–73) as minister of education and proposed many educational reforms that helped to liberalize the secondary school system. Because of Simon's moderate republicanism President MACMAHON chose him as premier (1876–77) in preference to Léon Gambetta. As premier, Simon was involved in a governmental crisis in May, 1877; his refusal to accede to the president's demand for his resignation established the principle of parliamentary primacy and the responsibility of the premier to the legislature.

Simon, Neil (Marvin Neil Simon), 1927–, American playwright, b. New York City. His plays, nearly all of them successful, are comedies treating recognizable aspects of modern, middle-class life. Particularly adept at portraying the middle-aged, Simon builds up his characters through funny lines rather than plot. His plays include *Come Blow Your Horn* (1961), *Barefoot in the Park* (1963), *The Odd Couple* (1965), *Plaza Suite* (1968), *The Prisoner of Second Avenue* (1971), *The Good Doctor* (1973), and *God's Favorite* (1974).

Simon, Théodore: see BINET, ALFRED.

Simon, William Edward, 1927–, U.S. Secretary of the Treasury (1974–), b. Paterson, N.J. He served (1946–48) in the U.S. army in Japan and later became (1952) a Wall Street bond dealer. Recognized in the financial world as a leading expert on government bonds, Simon served (1972–74) as deputy secretary of the Treasury before succeeding George Schultz as Treasury Secretary. He also briefly directed (1973–74) the Federal Energy Office during the critical months of the Arab oil embargo.

Simone Martini: see MARTINI, SIMONE.

Simonides of Amorgos: see SEMONIDES OF AMORGOS.

Simonides of Ceos (sīmŏn'ĭdēz, sē'ŏs), c.556–468? B.C., Greek lyric poet, b. Ceos. At Athens for a time under the patronage of Hipparchus, he seems then to have gone to Thessaly, returning to Athens at the time of the Persian Wars. He was a friend of most prominent Athenians. After the wars he went (with his nephew Bacchylides) to the court of Hiero I of Syracuse, where he was a rival of Pindar. There are only fragments left of his work, but they contain some of the finest Greek poetry. He wrote, in an epigrammatic manner, verses of many kinds; some of these—encomia, epinicia, and dirges—he brought to a new perfection. Two of his finest epitaphs are on the fallen at Marathon and at Thermopylae.

Simon Magus (mā'gəs), Samaritan sorcerer who attempted to buy spiritual power from the apostles. From this comes the term SIMONY. Acts 8.9-24. He was said to have founded a Gnostic sect.

Simon of Cyrene (sīrē'nē), bystander made to carry Jesus' cross. He was probably an African Jew, and is identified as the father of Alexander and Rufus. Mat. 27.32; Mark 15.21; Luke 23.26.

Simonov, Konstantin Kirill Mikhailovich (kənstəntyēn' kĭrēl' mēkhī'ləvĭch sē'mənəf), 1915–, Russian writer. Simonov's sentimental and patriotic poems made him popular during World War II. His reports from the front were published in book form in *Stalingrad Fights On* (1942) and *No Quarter* (1943, tr. 1943). Simonov's novel of the defense of Stalingrad, *Days and Nights* (1945, tr. 1945), is a perceptive picture of wartime psychology; it was awarded a Stalin Prize. He also treated war themes in *Victims and Heroes* (tr. 1963) and in the novel *The Living and the Dead* (1960, tr. 1962). His works, acclaiming human courage without resorting to propaganda, were enormously popular in Russia and abroad.

Simon Peter: see PETER, ST.

Simons, Menno: see MENNO SIMONS.

Simons, Walter (väl'tər zē'môns), 1861-1937, German jurist and statesman. He served (1919) as commissioner general to the German delegation at Versailles, but resigned in opposition to the signing of the peace treaty. He later served as foreign minister (1920-21), president of the German supreme court (1922-29), and acting president of the republic (March-May, 1925). He later taught at the Univ. of Leipzig. An outstanding authority on international law, Simons wrote several works, notably *The Evolution of International Public Law in Europe since Grotius* (1931).

Simonstown (sī'mənztoun), town (1970 pop. 6,500), Cape Prov., SW South Africa, on False Bay, an arm of the Atlantic Ocean. It is a seaside resort and a station of the South African navy; industry centers around ship construction and repair. There is also a fishing industry, and fish oil is processed. Simonstown was founded by the Dutch in 1741 as a naval depot and named for Simon van der Stel, governor of Cape Colony from 1679 to 1697. In 1814 the town became the headquarters of the British South Atlantic squadron. In 1957 the base was turned over to South Africa, which allows Britain to continue using it. Simonstown took on renewed strategic importance as a result of the closing of the Suez Canal after the 1967 Arab-Israeli war and the resulting increase in naval traffic around Africa. The oldest English church (consecrated 1814; rebuilt 1834) in South Africa is in Simonstown.

simony (sĭm'ənē), in CANON LAW, buying or selling of any spiritual benefit for a temporal consideration. The name is derived from SIMON MAGUS, who tried to buy the gifts of the Holy Ghost from St. Peter (Acts 8). Simony is a very grave sin, and ecclesiastics who commit it may be excommunicated. The temporal price may be one of many kinds, e.g., money or high office. What is sold may be the performance of a sacrament or any other spiritual service; it is also simony to sell a benefice or endowment or other temporality to which anything spiritual is attached. Because of the frequency of simony at times in the history of the Roman Catholic Church, the legislation of the church is very strict; e.g., simony in the election of a pope invalidates the election (law of Julius II, 1503); no priest may ask for a baptismal fee in any way; and Mass stipends are fixed by the bishop and are governed by the expense of the Mass and the necessities of the priest. The sale of indulgences is prohibited in any form, and no blessed article may be sold as blessed. The prevalence of simony was most important in bringing about the reform of Hildebrand (who reigned as Pope Gregory VII) and the Catholic Reformation. The sale of indulgences was one of the great abuses in the church cited by Martin Luther.

simoom or **simoon:** see SANDSTORM.

simple harmonic motion: see HARMONIC MOTION.

Simplon (sĭm'plŏn), pass, 6,590 ft (2,009 m) high, in the Lepontine Alps, Valais canton, S Switzerland. It is crossed by the **Simplon Road** built (1800-1806) by Napoleon I. The Simplon Railway passes through **Simplon Tunnel I** and **II,** the longest (both 12.3 mi/19.8 km) in the world. Opened in 1906 and 1922, respectively, the tunnels cross the Swiss-Italian border from Brig to Isella. They have a maximum elevation of 2,313 ft (705 m).

Simpson, Sir George, 1792?-1860, governor of the Hudson's Bay Company in Canada (1821-56), b. Scotland. In 1820 he was sent by the Hudson's Bay Company to Canada, where he took charge of the important Athabaska fur district. Appointed (1821) governor of the northern department of the company (with which the North West Company was merged that year), he became governor of the northern department of the united company and later was made governor of Rupert's Land and general superintendent of the company in North America. Simpson encouraged exploration of his vast realm; his cousin Thomas Simpson explored the arctic coast, and he himself journeyed constantly (twice crossing the continent) from one wilderness trading post to another. His famous "overland" trip (1841-42) around the world, during which he crossed Siberia to St. Petersburg, is described in his *Narrative of an Overland Journey round the World* (1847). Simpson was knighted in 1841. His journal (1824-25), edited by Frederick Merk, was published as *Fur Trade and Empire* (1931). E. E. Rich edited his *Journal of Occurrences in the Athabasca Department* (1938) and *Part of a Dispatch . . . to the Hudson's Bay Company . . . 1829* (1947). See biography by A. S. Morton (1944).

Simpson, George Gaylord, 1902–, American paleontologist and zoologist, b. Chicago, Ph.D. Yale, 1926. He became assistant curator of vertebrate paleontology at the American Museum of Natural History in New York City in 1927. From fossil material gathered on trips to the W and SE United States and to Argentina, he discovered migratory and evolutionary patterns of the prehistoric fauna of the Americas. His deductions that species reached adaptive peaks and suffered accidental dispersal contributed greatly to the study of evolution. He served as professor of vertebrate paleontology at Columbia (1945-59) and at Harvard (1959-70). He has received many scientific awards. His works include *Tempo and Mode in Evolution* (1949), *The Major Features of Evolution* (1953); *The Geography of Evolution* (1965), and *Biology and Man* (1969).

Simpson, Sir James Young, 1811-70, Scottish physician, M.D. Univ. of Edinburgh, 1832. He became (1839) professor of medicine and midwifery at Edinburgh. For a while he employed ether anesthesia in childbirth, but soon abandoned its use in favor of chloroform, which he introduced as an anesthetic in 1847. Eminent as an obstetrician, he was also known as an archaeologist. See study by H. L. Gordon (1897).

Simpson, Louis, 1923–, American poet, b. Jamaica, grad. Columbia (B.S., 1948; Ph.D., 1959). Since 1959 he has taught at the Univ. of California at Berkeley. Using literary allusions and personal experience—often drawn from his childhood in Jamaica—Simpson writes finely crafted and witty poems. His volumes of poetry include *The Arrivisites: Poems 1940-1948* (1949), *A Dream of Governors* (1959), *At the End of the Open Road* (1963; Pulitzer Prize), and *North of Jamića* (1972).

Simpson, Matthew, 1811-84, American Methodist bishop, b. Cadiz, Ohio. In 1839 he became the first president of Indiana Asbury Univ. (now DePauw Univ.). He edited (1848-52) the *Western Christian Advocate* and was consecrated bishop in 1852. He used his oratorical skill on behalf of the Union in the Civil War and in eulogizing his friend, Abraham Lincoln, at Lincoln's burial services in Springfield, Ill. See E. M. Wood, *The Peerless Orator* (1909); R. D. Clark, *The Life of Matthew Simpson* (1956).

Simpson, Thomas, 1808-40, British arctic explorer, b. Scotland. He entered (1829) the service of the Hudson's Bay Company and was sent to Canada. Along with Peter Dease, the Canadian explorer, he traced (1836-39) the coast of the Arctic Ocean from the mouth of the Mackenzie River to Point Barrow and from the mouth of the Coppermine River to the Gulf of Boothia; he discovered Victoria Island. On the return from his final trip he went insane and was either killed, perhaps by members of his party, or committed suicide. He wrote *Narrative of the Discoveries on the North Coast of America* (1843).

Simpson, Wallis Warfield: see WINDSOR, WALLIS WARFIELD, DUCHESS OF.

Simri (sĭm'rī) [Heb., =SHIMRI], head of a Merarite family. 1 Chron. 26.10.

Sims, James Marion, 1813-83, American gynecologist, b. Lancaster co., S.C., M.D. Jefferson Medical College, Philadelphia, 1835. He practiced in Mt. Meigs, Ala. A surgeon of international repute, he introduced new operations and instruments (including a vaginal speculum) and wrote the important *Clinical Notes on Uterine Surgery* (1866). In 1855 he founded Woman's Hospital in New York City. See his autobiography (1884).

Sims, William Sowden, 1858-1936, American naval officer, b. Port Hope, Upper Canada (now Ontario), of American parents. After serving with the Atlantic and Pacific fleets, he was (1897-1900) naval attaché in Paris and St. Petersburg. While in Europe he sent numerous reports to the Navy Dept. urging the adoption of new ship designs and gunnery, and in 1902 he wrote to President Theodore Roosevelt criticizing the inefficiency of the navy. His letters had some effect and he was ordered to Washington, serving (1902-9) with the Bureau of Navigation and (1907-9) as naval aide to the President. After leading (1913-15) the Atlantic torpedo flotilla he was appointed (1917) rear admiral and president of the Naval War College. In World War I he commanded (1917-18) U.S. operations in European waters. He again became president of the Naval War College in 1919 and served there until 1922, when he retired. He was made full admiral by act of Congress in 1930. He wrote, with Burton J. Hendrick, *The Victory at Sea* (1920). See biography by E. E. Morison (1942, repr. 1968).

Simsbury, town (1970 pop. 17,475), Hartford co., N Conn.; inc. 1670. Detonating fuses and machinery are the chief manufactures. Cigar tobacco is grown nearby. The Westminster School and the Ethel Walker School are located in Simsbury, and Gifford Pinchot, the forester and public official, was born there.

Sin (sĭn), moon god of Semitic origin, worshiped in ancient Middle Eastern religions. One of the principal deities in the Babylonian and Assyrian pantheons, he was lord of the calendar and of wisdom. The chief centers of his worship were at Harran and at Ur, where he was known as Nanna.

Sin. **1** Wilderness through which the Israelites wandered when they came up out of Egypt. It is not the same as ZIN. Ex. 16.1; 17.1; Num. 33.11. **2** Same as PELUSIUM. Ezek. 30.15,16.

sin, in religion, unethical act. The term implies disobedience to a personal God, as in Judaism, Christianity, and Islam, and is not used so often in systems such as Buddhism where there is no personal divinity. In ancient Israel, besides personal sin there was national sin, usually idolatry; to regain God's favor the whole people had to be purified. Ex. 32-34. Crimes of a few might also be visited on all, but punishment of the criminals could avert this. Joshua 7. Apart from ORIGINAL SIN, Christianity and Islam have no developed idea of collective sin. As to what constitutes sin, Christian ideas differ. Some Christians divide human acts into good, indifferent, and bad; others regard all acts not positively good as necessarily sinful. Thus, some may think gambling is indifferent so long as no obligation is infringed, while others consider gambling wrong as such. The traditional view, presupposed by Christian asceticism, is that a major way to perfection lies in performing or in refraining from indifferent acts solely to please God. The theory that no act is really indifferent is common among conservative "evangelical" Protestants. For Christians, the effect of sin may be twofold, since a sin is at once a rebellion against the omnipotent Creator, risking punishment (even HELL), and a cruel offense against a Father and friend. The idea that sin is a grief to the loving Friend, shutting him out of one's life, was popularized in the Middle Ages, notably by the Cistercians in the 12th cent. and the Franciscans in the 13th. It is explicit in Western mysticism and in modern Roman Catholic teaching. Among Protestants it was typical of Martin Luther and John Wesley. In Western theology (particularly Roman Catholicism) sins are mortal if committed with knowing and deliberate intent in a serious matter; other sins are venial. Habitual sin is called vice. Roman Catholics are required to confess individually all mortal sins (see PENANCE). The seven deadly, or capital, sins are pride, covetousness, lust, anger, gluttony, envy, and sloth. The sins that cry out to heaven for vengeance are willful murder (Gen. 4.10), the sin of Sodom (Gen. 18.20,21), oppression of the poor (Ex. 2.23), and defrauding the laborer of his wages (James 5.4). The sin of the angels (specifically of SATAN) is pride.

The opposite of sin is VIRTUE, but in Christian practice the opposite of sin is GRACE, i.e., the merits of Christ's virtues given to man. See ATONEMENT; BAPTISM; ETHICS; PURGATORY.

Sinai (sī'nī), triangular peninsula, c.23,000 sq mi (59,570 sq km), NE Egypt. It is c.230 mi (370 km) long and 150 mi (240 km) wide and extends north into a broad isthmus linking Africa and Asia. Sinai is bounded on the E by the Gulf of Aqaba and on the W by the Gulf of Suez, which is linked to the Mediterranean Sea by the Suez Canal; the Negev desert is to the northeast. Level and sandy in the north, Sinai rises to the south in granitic ridges; Mt. Catherine (Arabic *Jabal Katrinah*), c.8,650 ft (2,640 m), is the highest peak. Sharm al-Sheikh, a strategic promontory overlooking the Strait of Tiran, is near the southern tip of Sinai, at the mouth of the Gulf of Aqaba. Sinai has a very hot and dry climate and is sparsely vegetated; abandoned watercourses indicate that the region was once humid. Limestone quarrying and oil drilling are the main economic activities; nomadic herding is practiced. Jabal Musa [Arabic,=mount of Moses], or Mt. Sinai, c.7,500 ft (2,290 m), is said to be the place where Moses received the Ten Commandments; however, some authorities suggest that the site could have been any one of several nearby peaks. On Jabal Musa is the famed Greek Orthodox monastery of St. Catherine, founded A.D. c.250; in 1844 the Codex Sinaiticus, one of the oldest manuscripts of the New Testament, was found there. (The manuscripts were purchased from the USSR by the British Museum in 1933, and by 1950, the 3,000 volumes were microfilmed.) In ancient times Sinai was ruled by the Arabs of Petra (Ex. 3.1; 19); however, for most of its history it was under the Egyptian kings, who worked its copper mines. Sinai was the scene of fighting during the Arab-Israeli Wars of 1956, 1967, and 1973. Israel occupied, then withdrew from, the peninsula in 1956. In 1967, Israel again drove the Egyptians from Sinai, establishing a defense line along the Suez Canal and capturing strategic outposts overlooking the Gulf of Aqaba. In the 1973 war, the Egyptian army crossed the Suez Canal and recaptured territory in the Sinai. Under the terms of an agreement reached in early 1974, Israeli forces withdrew further into Sinai, while United Nations units were positioned between the Israelis and the Egyptians, who continued to occupy a narrow strip of recaptured land on the east bank of the canal.

Sinaia (sēnī'ä), town (1966 pop. 11,976), S central Rumania, in Walachia, in the Transylvanian Alps. It is a health and winter sports resort and has heavy and light industries. Sinaia was the summer residence of the kings of Rumania until the abdication (1947) of King Michael. In the town are two former royal palaces (one of which, built in Renaissance style, contains an internationally famous art collection) as well as the royal hunting lodge, a 17th-century monastery, and a castle.

Sinai campaign: see ARAB-ISRAELI WARS.

Sinaloa (sēnälō'ä), state (1970 pop. 1,273,228), 22,582 sq mi (58,487 sq km), W Mexico, on the Gulf of California and the Pacific Ocean. CULIACÁN is the capital. A long, narrow territory lying between the ocean and mountain spurs of the Sierra Madre Occidental, Sinaloa has low, hot, humid plains and numerous marshes. The varying elevation, many rivers, and fertile valleys contribute to the variety of crops grown; Sinaloa is a leading national producer of rice, sugarcane, and cotton. The state's industry is mostly related to the processing of agricultural products. Fishing and livestock breeding are economically important. Although Sinaloa lies in a rich mining region, its gold, silver, and copper remain largely untapped. Forest products—fine woods and rubber—are also not widely exploited. The state has numerous mineral springs. Sinaloa's coast has many sheltered harbors, but only Mazatlán is a major port. Sinaloa was joined with Sonora during the Spanish period; it became a separate state in 1830.

Sinan (sēnän), Muslim architect, 1489?-1578?. He is regarded as the greatest of Islamic builders, his achievement lying in his solutions to spatial problems in cupola-topped structures. He was active during the reigns of Selim I, Sulayman I, and Selim II, and in 1539 he was named court architect. His masterpieces are the mosques of Sha Zade and Sulayman I, both at Constantinople (now İstanbul), and the mosque of Selim II at Adrianople. His autobiography lists more than 300 buildings of his design. See study by Arthur Stratton (1972).

Sinanthropus pekinensis (sənăn'thrəpəs pēkĭnĕn'səs): see HOMO ERECTUS.

Sinatra, Frank (Francis Albert Sinatra), 1915–, American singer and actor, b. Hoboken, N.J. During the late 1930s and early 1940s he sang with the Harry James and Tommy Dorsey bands, causing teenage girls to shriek and swoon over his romantic, casual renditions of such songs as "I'll Never Smile Again" and "This Love of Mine." He has also had a long-lived and successful movie career, appearing in such films as *On the Town* (1949), *From Here to Eternity* (1953, Academy Award), *Guys and Dolls* (1955), *Pal Joey* (1957), *The Manchurian Candidate* (1962), and *The Detective* (1968). Sinatra also directed and produced several films. He retired from show business in 1971 but returned in 1974 with a concert tour. See A. I. Lonstein, *The Compleat Sinatra* (1970); Gene Ringgold and Clifford McCarthy, *The Films of Frank Sinatra* (1971).

Sinclair, Sir John, 1754-1835, Scottish agricultural economist and statistician. He compiled *A Statistical Account of Scotland* (21 vol., 1791-99), giving information on farming and other industries, notes on natural history, and statistics on population. A member of Parliament (1780-1811), Sinclair also served as the first president of the newly established board of agriculture.

Sinclair, Upton, 1878-1968, American novelist and socialist, b. Baltimore, grad. College of the City of New York, 1897. He was one of the MUCKRAKERS, and an interest in social and industrial reform underlies most of his writing. *The Jungle* (1906), a brutally graphic novel of the Chicago stockyards, aroused great public indignation and led to reform of Federal food inspection laws. With the money from that novel, Sinclair established in 1906 his short-lived socialist community, Helicon Home Colony, at Englewood, N.J. Among Sinclair's other novels exposing social evils are *King Coal* (1917), *Oil!* (1927), *Boston* (on the Sacco-Vanzetti Case, 1928), and *Little Steel* (1938). In his social studies, such as *The Brass Check* (1919), on journalism, and *The Goose-Step* (1923), on education, he tried to uncover the harmful effects of capitalist economic pressure on institutions of learning and culture. An ardent socialist, Sinclair was in and out of the American Socialist party. In 1934 he was defeated as the Democratic candidate for governor of California. *World's End* (1940) is the first of a cycle of 11 novels that deal with world events since 1914 and feature the fictional Lanny Budd as hero; the third, *Dragon's Teeth* (1942), won a Pulitzer Prize. Many of Sinclair's more than 80 books have been widely translated, and he is one of the best-known American authors in Europe. See his autobiography (1962) and reminiscences, *American Outpost* (1932) and *My Lifetime in Letters* (1960). See study by Floyd Dell (1927, repr. 1970); bibliography by Ronald Gottesman (1973).

Sind (sĭnd), province (1969 est. pop. 11,100,000), c.50,000 sq mi (129,500 sq km), SE Pakistan, roughly coextensive with the lower Indus River valley and bounded by India on the east and south and by the Arabian Sea on the southwest. KARACHI is the capital. Despite some hilly and desert areas, it consists mainly of the alluvial plain and delta of the Indus River. Hot and arid, the region depends almost exclusively on irrigation for agriculture. Watered by the great SUKKUR and Kotri barrages, it supports wheat, rice, millet, cotton, oilseed, sugarcane, fruits, and some tobacco. There are also sheep and cattle breeding and poultry farming. Other resources include gypsum and iron ore. The great majority of the population engages in agriculture, but HYDERABAD is a leading Pakistani industrial center. The region is noted for handicrafts, especially lacquer ware, mirror embroidery, and tile work. Fishing is important in coastal areas. The chief language is Sindhi. Sind may have been the site of the subcontinent's earliest civilization (see INDUS VALLEY CIVILIZATION). The region was taken (5th cent. B.C.) by Darius I of Persia, invaded (325 B.C.) by Alexander the Great, annexed (c.3d cent. B.C.) by the MAURYA empire, overrun (165 B.C.) by the Huns, and ruled (1st-2d cent. A.D.) by the Kushan dynasty. The Arab invaders of Sind in 711 were the first permanent Muslim settlers on the subcontinent; Sind remained under direct or nominal Arab rule until the 11th cent., when it passed to the Muslim Turkic Ghaznivids. Arab religious, social, and cultural influences remain strong in present-day Sind. Although briefly incorporated into the Mogul empire by Akbar (who was born in Sind), the region remained for centuries under local Muslim dynasties. Emirs of Sind, chieftains of Baluch descent, held power in the late 18th and early 19th cent. until Sir Charles Napier, the British general, defeated them in 1843. The British made Karachi the capital and administered Sind as part of the Bombay presidency until 1937, when it became an autonomous province. After Pakistan became independent in 1947, Karachi was made the national capital, and Sind's capital was shifted to Hyderabad. From 1955 to 1970, Sind was part of West Pakistan prov.; it became a separate province again in 1970, with Karachi the capital.

Sindhi (sĭn'dē), language belonging to the Indic group of the Indo-Iranian subfamily of the Indo-European family of languages. See INDO-IRANIAN LANGUAGES.

Sinding, Christian (krĭs'tyän sĭn'dĭng), 1856-1941, Norwegian nationalist composer, studied at the Leipzig Conservatory. He is best remembered for his lyrical, romantic piano works, including the popular *Rustle of Spring.* He also wrote the opera *Der Heilige Berg* (*The Holy Mountain,* 1914), orchestral works, chamber music, and songs. His government granted him a yearly stipend from 1890 until his death. In 1921-22 he taught at the Eastman School of Music in Rochester, N.Y.

sine, in trigonometry, relation defined in a right triangle for one of the acute angles (A) as the ratio of the length of the side opposite that angle (a) to the length of the hypotenuse (c), or $\sin A=a/c$. The concept may be extended to any plane triangle, in which case the Law of Sines is found to hold; i.e., $a/\sin A=b/\sin B=c/\sin C$, where A, B, and C are the vertex angles and a, b, and c are the respective sides opposite them. In general, the sine function may be expressed as an infinite SERIES, $\sin x=x-x^3/3!+x^5/5!-x^7/7!+\cdots$, where $n!=1\cdot2\cdot3\cdots n$. See TRIGONOMETRY.

Singanallur (sĭng'gənəlo͝or), city (1971 pop. 113,397), Tamil Nadu state, S India. It is a suburb of Coimbatore and has developing industries.

Singapore (sĭng'gəpôr, sĭng'ə-, sĭng"gəpôr'), republic (1970 pop. 2,074,507), 225 sq mi (583 sq km), consisting of the island of Singapore (210 sq mi/544 sq km) and about 60 small adjacent islands, SE Asia, at the southern tip of the Malay Peninsula. Singapore city (1970 est. pop. 1,240,000), the capital, largest city, and chief port, is located on the southern shore of the island. The distinction between Singapore and Singapore city is disappearing, as the entire island becomes urbanized. Jurong Industrial Estate (c.20 sq mi/50 sq km), an industrial park built largely on reclaimed swampland, is in SW Singapore. Lying just north of the equator and located between the

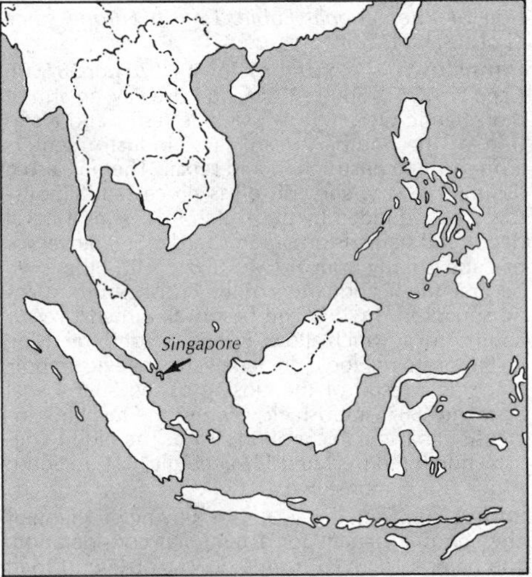

Indian Ocean and the South China Sea, Singapore is situated at the convergence of some of the world's major sea-lanes. It is separated from Indonesia to the south by the Singapore Strait and from Malaysia to the north by the Johore Strait. Singapore island is low lying and is composed of a granitic core (rising to 580 ft/177 m at Bukit Timah, the country's highest point) surrounded by sedimentary lowlands. The coast is broken by many inlets, and there are extensive mangrove swamps. Keppel Harbor, site of the port of Singapore, is a natural deepwater anchorage between Singapore and the islands of Brani and Blakang Mati. Singapore has a tropical rain-forest climate with uniformly high temperatures and rainfall throughout the year. The island was once covered by rain forest, which is now limited to the central portion and included in Bukit Timah Nature Reserve. Less than one fourth of Singapore's land is used for agriculture; tropical fruits and vegetables are intensively cultivated and poultry and hogs are raised. However, most of the cultivable land is given over to coconut and rubber plantations. Singapore is a major fishing center of SE Asia. There are no exploitable natural resources in the country. Its power is produced by thermoelectric plants. Singapore has a good road system, a railroad crosses the island, and a causeway carrying road and rail traffic links Singapore to the mainland. The population is about 76% Chinese; Malays and Indians constitute large minorities. Singapore is one of the world's most densely populated countries with about 9,200 people per sq mi (about 3,500 people per sq km). The country has a predominantly urban population, the only nonurban areas being in the northwestern and central portions of Singapore island and on the lesser islands. A massive urban renewal program, begun in the 1960s, has replaced some of Singapore's slums with modern housing units. As a result of family planning and a strict immigration policy, the birth rate had declined by the early 1970s to about 1.5%, down from 4.5% in the 1950s. Buddhism, Islam, Hinduism, and Christianity are the religions of Singapore. The country has four official languages—Malay, Chinese, Tamil, and English—and one of the highest literacy rates (a product of a fine uniform education system conducted in all the official languages). It also has one of the highest standards of living in Asia. The Univ. of Singapore, Nanyang Univ., and The Singapore Polytechnic are the leading educational institutions. Singapore's working force is employed primarily in the service industries, in manufacturing, and in commerce, with a very small proportion engaged in agriculture. Unemployment remains high, although a shift in educational priorities, a slower population growth rate, and a broader industrial base have decreased the number of unemployed. Singapore is one of the world's greatest commercial centers and has one of the world's largest and busiest ports. Commerce has historically been the chief source of income. For many years the largest importer in SE Asia, Singapore is a free port and an entrepôt that reexports more than half of what it imports, especially rubber, petroleum, textiles, timber, and tin. It also exports locally manufactured items such as electrical goods, petroleum products, and processed food, rubber, and tin. The country imports most of its food requirements. Singapore's chief trading partners are Malaysia and Japan. With more than 300 factories and deepwater wharves, the Jurong Industrial Estate is Singapore's principal industrial complex. The country has a number of large petroleum storing and refining facilities; and Keppel Harbor has container-handling facilities. Development of the former British naval base at Sembawang on the Johore Strait, now a commercial shipyard, has helped to enhance Singapore's status as a major center for shipbuilding and repairs. The country is governed by the constitution of 1966. It has a parliamentary form of government, with a president as head of state and a prime minister as head of government. There is a 65-seat unicameral Parliament whose members are popularly elected. The supreme court, the nation's highest judicial body, has seven members. The People's Action party (PAP) is the most important of Singapore's numerous political parties. It has been in power since 1959, despite two splits within the party in the early 1960s. Singapore was a trading center in the Srivijaya empire before it was destroyed in the 14th cent. by the Majapahit empire. It later became part of Johore (see JOHOR) in the Malacca Sultanate. The sparsely populated island was ceded (1819) to the British East India Company through the efforts of Sir T. Stamford RAFFLES; he founded the modern city of Singapore there that same year. In 1824, Singapore came under the complete control of the British and, although containing only a small fishing and trading village, quickly attracted Chinese and Malay merchants. The port grew rapidly, soon overshadowing Penang (see PINANG) and Malacca (see MELAKA) in importance. With them Singapore became part of the STRAITS SETTLEMENTS in 1826. The development of Malaya under British rule in the late 19th and early 20th cent. made Singapore one of the leading ports of the world for the export of tin and rubber. The construction of a railroad through the Malay Peninsula to Bangkok swelled Singapore's trade, and the building of airports made it more than ever a communication center. A naval base at Sembawang, begun in 1924, was completed in 1938; the island, sometimes called the Malta of the East, was reinforced in the early days of World War II. After the swift Japanese campaign in Malaya, however, Singapore was successfully attacked across the Johore Strait, and on Feb. 15, 1942, the British garrison surrendered; Singapore was reoccupied by the British in Sept., 1945. In 1946, Singapore, no longer a part of the Straits Settlements, was constituted, with Christmas Island and the Cocos-Keeling islands, a crown colony. Following a decade of Communist terrorism, Singapore, separated from Christmas Island and the Cocos-Keeling islands, became (June, 1959) a self-governing state. In the 1959 general elections the PAP won control of the government and continued in power after winning the 1963 elections. Under the policies of Prime Minister LEE KUAN YEW, Singapore's economic base was strengthened and a greater degree of social and cultural homogeneity was achieved. With the establishment of the Economic Development Board, the Development Bank of Singapore, and the International Trading Company in the 1960s, and the subsequent influx of foreign investments, Singapore's industrial base was diversified, expanded, and modernized. Following the 1962 referendum, Singapore merged (Aug., 1963) with Malaya, Sarawak, and Sabah to form the Federation of Malaysia. However, because of deep divisions over numerous issues, especially the racial antagonism between the Malays and the Chinese, Singapore was, by mutual agreement, separated from the federation in Aug., 1965, and became an independent republic. Singapore has remained in the Commonwealth of Nations and joined the United Nations in 1965. In the 1968 and 1972 general elections the PAP won every parliamentary seat, although the 1972 elections produced a larger opposition vote. See B. C. Maday et al., *Area Handbook for Malaysia and Singapore* (1966); Noel Barber, *A Sinister Twilight: The Fall of Singapore, 1942* (1968); H. C. Chan, *Singapore* (1971); R. G. Wilson, *The Future Role of Singapore* (1972).

Singapore Strait, channel, 65 mi (105 km) long and 10 mi (16.1 km) wide, between Singapore island and Kepulanan Riau, Indonesia. It links the Strait of Malacca with the South China Sea and is a major shipping route of SE Asia.

Singer, Isaac Bashevis (bäshĕv'ĭs), 1904–, American novelist and short-story writer, younger brother of I. J. Singer, b. Poland. He emigrated to the United States in 1935 and for a time worked in New York City as a journalist on the *Jewish Daily Forward.* In 1943 he became an American citizen. Singer writes in Yiddish and is widely regarded as the last, and perhaps the greatest, of the New York-based Yiddish school of writers. Like mainstream Yiddish fiction, his work is philosophical, but his style is uncharacteristically clean and objective. Singer is sensitive to psychological motivation, and many of his works treat the loneliness of old age and the sense of alienation produced in Jews by the dissolution of Jewish values and way of life through assimilation with the Gentile world. His novels include *The Family Moskat* (1950), *Satan in Goray* (1955), *The Manor* (1967), *The Estate* (1970), and *Enemies: A Love Story* (1972). Singer is also highly regarded for his short stories, which are imaginative, perceptive, and witty. Collections include *Gimpel the Fool and Other Stories* (1961), *The Spinoza of Market Street and Other Stories* (1961), and *A Crown of Feathers* (1973). He has also written many delightful books for children and several plays, notably *The Mirror,* (1973). Many of Singer's works have been translated into English. See studies by Marcia Allentuck (1969) and Irving Malin (1972).

Singer, Isaac Merritt, 1811–75, American inventor, b. Rensselaer co., N.Y. As a child he lived in Oswego, N.Y. He patented in 1851 a practical sewing machine that could do continuous stitching. Although he lost a suit for infringement brought by Elias Howe, his company was already so well established that it took the lead in a subsequent combination of manufactures and pooling of patents. Between 1851 and 1865 Singer patented 20 improvements, including the yielding presser foot and a continuous wheel feed.

Singer, Israel Joshua, 1893–1944, Polish-American novelist and playwright who wrote in Yiddish. Living variously in Poland and Russia, he earned a literary reputation in both countries. His collection of stories *Perl un Andere Dertzeylungen* (1922; tr. *Pearls,* 1923) was acclaimed by the New York publisher Abraham Cahan, who hired Singer as Polish correspondent to his Yiddish newspaper the *Jewish Daily Forward.* Singer's epic masterpiece *Di Bruder Ashkenazi* (tr. *The Brothers Ashkenazi,* 1936) details Jewish industrial development before World War I. Singer emigrated to the United States in 1934.

Singhalese (sĭng'gəlēz), language belonging to the Indic group of the Indo-Iranian subfamily of the Indo-European family of languages. An alternate spelling for Singhalese is Sinhalese. See INDO-IRANIAN LANGUAGES.

single tax, any levy that serves as the government's only source of revenue. Generally, however, it is understood to mean a tax derived from economic RENT and used as the sole source of public receipts. As such, it is based on the doctrine that land and the natural resources are the source of all wealth, and it corresponds substantially to the *impôt unique* of the 18th-century PHYSIOCRATS. Basic to the theory is the belief that the land and its wealth belong to all. The most effective advocate of the single tax was Henry GEORGE, who held that economic rent tends to enrich the owner at the expense of the community and is thus the cause of poverty; he believed that by appropriating all (or nearly all) economic rent governments could wipe out social distress and even acquire a surplus without recourse to any other taxes. George's theories have had some influence on land taxation in Britain, several of the former dominions, the W United States, and several European nations. See Henry George, *Progress and Poverty* (1879); H. G. Brown et al., *Land-Value Taxation Around the World* (1955).

Sing Sing: see OSSINING, N.Y.

Singspiel: see OPERA.

Sinha, Satyendra Prassano, 1st **Baron Sinha of Raipur** (sətĕn'drə prəsän'ô sĭn'hä), 1864–1928, Indian statesman. A successful lawyer, he was the first Indian to hold several important administrative positions under the British: advocate general of Bengal (1907), member of the governor general's executive council (1909), and provincial governor (1920). In 1919 he became undersecretary for India in the British government and played a key role in framing the Government of India Act (1919). He became governor of Bihar and Orissa in 1920, but poor health forced his resignation the next year. He was knighted in 1914 and raised to the peerage in 1919.

Sinhalese: see SINGHALESE.

Sinim (sī'nĭm), a remote people. Isa. 49.12. In RSV it is translated as Syene.

Sining: see HSI-NING, China.

Sinites (sī'nīts), Canaanite people of ancient Syria. Gen. 10.17; 1 Chron. 1.15.

Sinkao Shan, peak, Taiwan: see HSIN-KAO SHAN.

Sinkiang (sĭn'kyăng, shĭn'jēăng'), autonomous region (1968 est. pop. 8,000,000), c.660,000 sq mi (1,709,400 sq km), NW China. It is officially known as the Sinkiang Uigur Autonomous Region (Mandarin *Hsin-chiang-wei-wu-erh-tzu-chih-ch'ü*) and is also called Chinese Turkistan or Eastern Turkistan. The capital is WU-LU-MU-CH'I (Urumchi); other important cities are I-NING (Kuldja), KASHGAR, HO-T'IEN (Khotan), and A-K'O-SU (Aksu). Sinkiang [Chinese, = new frontier] shares a 1,800-mile (2,900-km) border with the USSR on the north and west, and is bordered by the Mongolian People's Republic on the east and by Kashmir and Tibet on the south. The great Altai, Tien Shan, and Kunlun mountain ranges enclose it on the north, west, and south, respectively; a barren plateau lies to the west. The rivers of Sinkiang, including the Tarim, the Yarkand, the Ili, the Ma-na-ssu, and the Ho-t'ien, rise in the mountains and flow from east to west. The level land, divided by the rugged Tien Shan in central Sinkiang, comprises the DZUNGARIA, a grazing region to the north, and the Tarim basin (Takla Makan), a vast desert to the south. Lop Nor (Lo-pu po), a largely dried up salt lake in the Tarim basin, is the site of the nuclear test explosions conducted by the Communist government. Sinkiang has a dry continental climate with great extremes of winter and summer temperature. Rainfall is scant, seldom exceeding 10 in. (30 cm) annually. The bulk of the population lives along the borders of the Dzungaria and the Tarim basin, where cotton and silk (both locally spun and woven) are produced and wheat, rice, millet, potatoes, kaoliang, sugarbeets, and fruit are grown. Turkic-speaking Uigurs (mainly Muslims), who comprise Sinkiang's majority ethnic group, have traditionally excelled in building the intricate systems of canals and wells that supply water to the fields. The Ma-na-ssu irrigation project in S Dzungaria is one of several extensive government attempts to expand the area under cultivation. In recent years extensive areas of grazing land have been converted to raising wheat. Large-scale animal husbandry remains important, however, and the number of livestock (sheep, goats, cattle, horses, and camels) is increasing. Many of the Kazakh and Mongol stockherders are still at least seminomadic. Sinkiang is now linked to the Chinese rail network by completion of a railroad from Lan-chou, Kansu, to Wu-lu-mu-ch'i (1963), but west and south of Wu-lu-mu-ch'i transportation is still mainly along two ancient roads; the north road, which skirts the southern edge of the Dzungaria and connects Wu-lu-mu-ch'i with the Soviet Turkistan-Siberia RR, and the south road, which encircles the Tarim basin. The camel remains an important means of transport, but the use of trucks is increasing. Sinkiang, although a predominantly agricultural and pastoral region, has rich mineral resources. The vast oil fields at Karamai (served by both highways and an airline) are among the largest in China, and there are extensive deposits of coal, silver, copper, lead, nitrates, gold, and zinc. Large uranium reserves have been reported. The central government has in recent years greatly increased Sinkiang's mineral productivity. New mines as well as associated industry, such as refineries, ironworks, steelworks, and chemical plants, have been established. Other industries include textile (the region produces large quantities of cotton and wool) and cement production and sugar refining. Sinkiang has had a turbulent history. It first passed under Chinese rule in the 1st cent. B.C., when the emperor Wu Ti sent a Chinese army to defeat the Huns and occupy the region. In the 2d cent. A.D., China lost Sinkiang to the Uzbek Confederation but reoccupied it in the mid-7th cent. It was conquered (8th cent.) by the Tibetans, overrun by the Uigurs, who established a kingdom there, and subsequently invaded (10th cent.) by the Arabs. Sinkiang passed to the Mongols in the 13th cent. An anarchic period followed until the Manchus established (1756) loose control. The subsequent relations between China and Sinkiang were marked by cultural and religious conflict, bloody rebellions, and tribal dissensions. In the 19th cent. this unrest was encouraged by Great Britain and czarist Russia to protect India and Siberia, respectively. Sinkiang became a Chinese province in 1881, but even as late as the establishment (1912) of the Chinese republic it remained more or less independent of the central government. Rebellions in 1936, 1937, and 1944 further eased Chinese rule. Late in 1949, Sinkiang capitulated to the Chinese Communists without a struggle. On the basis of the 1953 census which showed the Uigurs to comprise 74% of the population, Sinkiang prov. was reconstituted (1955) as the Sinkiang Uigur Autonomous Region. Autonomous districts were created as well for the Kazakh, Mongol, Hui, and Kirghiz minority groups. In the 1950s and 1960s the central government sent massive numbers of Chinese to Sinkiang to help develop water conservancy and mineral exploitation schemes. This has drastically altered the traditional population balance of the region and the Chinese are approaching numerical parity with the Uigurs. National defense has also been a consideration in the mass influx of Chinese, for the region is a strategic and sensitive one. In 1969 frontier incidents led to serious fighting between Soviet and Chinese forces along the Sinkiang-USSR border. Sinkiang Univ. is in Wu-lu-mu-ch'i.

sinking fund, sum set apart periodically from the income of a government or a business and allowed to accumulate in order ultimately to pay off a debt. A preferred investment for a sinking fund is the purchase of the government's or firm's bonds that are to be paid off. Usually the fund is administered by a trustee. See AMORTIZATION.

Sinn Fein (shĭn fān) [Irish,=we, ourselves], Irish nationalist movement. It had its roots in the Irish cultural revival at the end of the 19th cent. and the growing nationalist disenchantment with the constitutional HOME RULE movement. The founder of Sinn Fein was Arthur GRIFFITH, who in 1899 established the first of his patriotic journals, the *United Irishman*, in which he advocated complete national self-reliance. The movement was not, at first, an overtly political one, nor did it advocate violence. Its method was, rather, one of passive resistance to all things English and included an attempted revival of Irish Gaelic. In 1905, Sinn Fein was organized politically, but until the outbreak of World War I it gained little strength. The British suppression of the Easter Rebellion of 1916 greatly stimulated the growth of Sinn Fein. In 1917 many of its leaders, released from internment, met to reorganize under the leadership of Eamon DE VALERA. In the election of 1918, Sinn Fein put up a candidate for every Irish seat in the British Parliament and won 73 seats. The elected members declined to go to Westminster; they set up an Irish assembly in Dublin, called the DÁIL ÉIREANN, which declared Irish independence. The British attempted to suppress terrorists, led by Michael COLLINS, by a policy of counterterror and sent (1920) a body of military irregulars, popularly known as the Black and Tans, to reestablish order. The populace rallied to Sinn Fein. In 1921 the British government yielded and began negotiations to establish the Irish Free State. The partition provisions of the resulting treaty did not, however, satisfy the militant wing of Sinn Fein, represented by De Valera, and civil war ensued. Gradually most of the country became reconciled to the new government, and Sinn Fein virtually came to an end when De Valera withdrew from it in 1927 and entered the Dáil. In 1938 the few remaining intransigents merged with the IRISH REPUBLICAN ARMY (IRA). Officially outlawed since 1936, the IRA functions as a terrorist organization and has persistently advocated unification of Ireland by force. It recognizes its own political arm, still known as Sinn Fein, as the only lawful government of Ireland. See studies by R. M. Henry (1920, repr. 1970) and P. S. O'Hegarty (1924); M. F. Caulfield, *The Easter Rebellion* (1963); T. P. Coogan, *Ireland since the Rising* (1966).

Sino-Japanese War, First, 1894–95. China and Japan were rivals for control of Korea in the late 19th cent. The Li-Ito Convention of 1885 established Korea as a coprotectorate of China and Japan. Accordingly, when a Korean revolt erupted in 1894, both countries sent troops. However, after the insurrection had been suppressed, Japan refused to withdraw its troops and induced the Korean court to abrogate its agreement with China. The fighting that ensued between Chinese and Japanese forces ended with an easy victory for the better-equipped Japanese army. The Treaty of SHIMONOSEKI (1895) made Korea nominally independent and provided for the cession of Taiwan, the Pescadores, and the Liaotung peninsula by China to Japan. China also had to pay a large indemnity. Within a week of the treaty signing, however, the diplomatic intervention of Russia, France, and Germany forced Japan to return the Liaotung peninsula to China. Under a subsidiary commercial treaty (1896), China yielded to Japanese nationals the right to open factories and engage in manufacturing in the trade ports. This right was automatically extended to the Western maritime powers under the MOST-FAVORED-NATION CLAUSE. See Tatsuji Takeuchi, *War and Diplomacy in the Japanese Empire* (1935, repr. 1966); F. H. Conroy, *The Japanese Seizure of Korea, 1868–1910* (1960).

Sino-Japanese War, Second, 1937–45. Following the MANCHURIAN INCIDENT (Sept., 1931), the Japanese Kwantung army occupied Manchuria and established the puppet state of MANCHUKUO (Feb., 1932). Japan pressed China to recognize the independence of Manchukuo, suppress anti-Japanese activities, and form autonomous regional governments in N China. The Japanese were partially successful in 1933 and 1935 when they forced China to form two demilitarized autonomous zones bordering Manchuria. There was growing domestic opposition to the Nationalist government's policy of self-strengthening before counterattacking in N China and Manchuria. In Dec., 1936, Chiang Kai-shek was kidnapped at Kian by CHANG HSÜEH-LIANG and forced to agree to a united anti-Japanese front with the Communists as a condition for his release. The situation was tense, and in 1937 full war commenced. A clash (July, 1937) between soldiers of the Japanese garrison at Peking and Chinese forces at the Marco Polo Bridge was the pretext for Japanese occupation at Peking and Tientsin. Chiang Kai-shek refused to negotiate an end to hostilities on Japanese terms and placed crack troops outside the Japanese settlement at Shanghai. After a protracted struggle Shanghai and the national capital, Nanking, fell to the Japanese. The Chinese broke the Yellow River dikes (June, 1938) to slow the enemy advance. In late 1938, Hankow and Canton were taken. Japanese strategy was aimed at taking the cities, the roads, and the railroads, thereby gaining a net of control. Thus, although the Japanese by 1940 had swept over the eastern coastal area, guerrilla fighting still went on in the conquered regions. The Nationalist government, driven back to a temporary capital at Chungking, struggled on with little help from outside. Chinese resources were not adequate, and the supplies sent over the Burma Road were far from adequate. The Chinese cause continued to decline despite vast and bloody fighting. Dubious of China's ability to sustain a protracted war, WANG CHING-WEI broke with Chiang Kai-shek, and established a collaborationist regime at Nanking (1940). The Japanese bombing of Pearl Harbor brought the United States into the war and merged the Sino-Japanese War in World War II as China declared war on Japan, Germany, and Italy. American and British loans and supplies, the establishment of military air bases in China, and the aid of an increasing number of U.S. and British advisers helped to reinforce the relief of China as Japan diverted armies elsewhere. Nevertheless, China's military position continued to deteriorate until April, 1945. In May the Chinese launched a successful offensive at Chihkiang; this lasted until Japanese capitulation on Aug. 14. The Japanese troops in China formally surrendered Sept. 9, 1945. By the provisions of the Cairo Declaration, Manchuria, Taiwan, and the Pescadores were restored to China. The war sapped the Nationalist government's strength while allowing the Communists to gain control over large areas through organization of guerrilla units. Thus, it was an important factor in the eventual Communist defeat of the Nationalist forces in 1949. In its early stage, the war was often called the China Incident. See H. Feis, *The China Tangle* (1953); F. C. Jones, *Japan's New Order in East Asia* (1954); D. J. Lu, *From the Marco Polo Bridge to Pearl Harbor* (1961); J. H. Boyle, *China and Japan at War, 1937–1945* (1972).

Sinop (sēnōp'), anc. *Sinope*, town (1970 pop. 15,107), capital of Sinop prov., N Turkey, on the Black Sea. A small port, it has an excellent harbor but lacks adequate communications with the interior of Turkey. Ancient Sinop was founded by colonists from Miletus in the 8th cent. B.C., was rebuilt after its destruction (7th cent. B.C.) by the Cimmerians, rose to great commercial and political importance, and established numerous colonies on the Euxine shores. One of its chief exports was cinnabar, which derives its name from Sinop. The city fell (c.183 B.C.) to the kings of Pontus, whose capital it became. Sinop was then the most important port on the Black Sea. The Romans under Lucullus captured it from Mithridates VI in the Third Mithridatic War (74–63 B.C.) and made it a free city. Sinop was occupied and devastated by Pharnaces II but was restored by Julius Caesar. Under the Roman Empire the city again reached great prosperity, which continued under the Byzantine Empire. When the Byzantine Empire broke up in 1204, Sinop joined the Greek empire of Trebizond, but within a few years it was occupied by the Seljuk Turks, and its decline began. In 1853 a Russian naval squadron surprised a Turkish flotilla there and completely destroyed it. This event served to hasten the approaching Crimean War. Sinop was the birthplace of Diogenes.

Sino-Tibetan languages, family of languages spoken by approximately 900 million people in central and SE Asia. This linguistic family is second only to the Indo-European stock in the number of its speakers. It is usually said to have three subfamilies: Tibeto-Burman, CHINESE, and Tai or Thai. One school of thought, however, assigns the Tai and Chinese languages to a single subfamily called Sino-Siamese or Sinitic. The classification of a number of the languages suggested for the Sino-Tibetan family and its various subfamilies is still unresolved, and more work must be done before general agreement is reached. Some linguists have even proposed a relationship between Sino-Tibetan and the Athabascan group of North American Indian languages (to which Navaho and Apache belong). The Sino-Tibetan languages have in common several features, which are exhibited to a greater or lesser extent in the individual tongues. For example, they show a tendency to be monosyllabic and isolating and to use tones or musical pitch. In an isolating language the words do not change their form or show inflection. Because of the relative absence of inflection, word order is the key to expressing grammatical relationships. A monosyllabic language has a limited number of syllables since the sound combinations that are possible are also limited in number. Because there are so many words that sound alike, two words of similar meaning are often used together to make the sense clearer. Combinations of two or more monosyllabic words also increase the vocabulary. Classifiers, which vary according to the sense of the words with which they are used, aid in making root meanings clear. For instance, one classifier is employed with round articles, and another with items of clothing. The use of different tones for each monosyllable has two striking benefits. It increases the vocabulary by multiplying the number of possible monosyllables, and it also is helpful in distinguishing among homophones. The number of tones differs in each language; three tones are found in Burmese, five in Thai, four in Mandarin Chinese, and nine in Cantonese Chinese. The Tibeto-Burman languages include TIBETAN, BURMESE, and a number of other tongues, among which are the Bodo, Garo, and Lushai of Assam, the Kachin of Burma, and perhaps also the languages of the Chins and Nagas of Burma, the Karen tongues of Burma and Thailand, and the Lolo of SW China. Tibeto-Burman languages are likely to be tonal and have anywhere from two to six tones. They are less monosyllabic and isolating than the languages of the other Sino-Tibetan families. In fact, they tend to be somewhat agglutinative and exhibit some degree of inflection. In an agglutinative language, different linguistic elements, each of which exists separately and has a fixed meaning, are joined to form one word. Affixes added to an unchanged root serve as the usual method of indicating inflection in the Tibeto-Burman tongues. Chinese is the leading representative of the Sino-Tibetan family. It has a number of variants that are often called dialects and sometimes regarded as separate languages. Mandarin Chinese is the standard form of Chinese and is spoken in N and central China by about 655 million people. Other leading dialects of languages of the Chinese subfamily are Cantonese (spoken in Kwangtung and Kwangsi provinces and also frequently outside of mainland China), Wu (the tongue of Shanghai and Chekiang province), Hakka or Hakkha (current in Kwangtung and Kiangsi provinces), and Fukienese (found in Fukien province and many places outside of mainland China, such as the island of Taiwan, now the headquarters of Nationalist China). The Tai or Thai subfamily of Sino-Tibetan is made up of the THAI LANGUAGE (formerly called Siamese) of Thailand, the Lao tongue of Laos, the Shan language of Burma, possibly the Vietnamese tongue of North Vietnam and South Vietnam, and a number of others. The Miae and Yao of China are sometimes classified as Tai or Thai and sometimes as Tibeto-Burman. See also SOUTHEAST-ASIAN LANGUAGES. See Paul K. Benedict, *Sino-Tibetan: A Conspectus* (Princeton-Cambridge Studies in Chinese Linguistics Ser., No. 2; 1972); Robert Shafer, *Introduction to Sino-Tibetan* (1966–73).

sintering, process of forming objects from a metal powder by heating the powder at a temperature below its melting point. In the production of small metal objects it is often not practical to cast them. Through chemical or mechanical procedures a fine powder of the metal can be produced. When the powder is compacted into the desired shape and heated, i.e., sintered, for up to three hours, the particles composing the powder join together to form a single solid object.

Sint-Niklaas (sĭnt-nē'kläs), Fr. *Saint-Nicolas,* city (1970 pop. 49,214), East Flanders prov., N Belgium. It is the commercial, industrial, and transportation center of the Waas region, formerly a wasteland but now intensively cultivated.

Sintra: see CINTRA, Portugal.

Sint-Truiden (sĭnt-troi'dən), Fr. *Saint-Trond,* town (1970 pop. 21,473), Limburg prov., E Belgium. It is an industrial center and is noted for its cherries. Sint-Truiden developed around an abbey founded in the 7th cent. by St. Trudo. Of note are a 13th-century Beguinage church and the 15th-century Church of Notre Dame.

Sinuiju (sēn'o͞o'ē'jo͞o), Jap. *Shingishu,* city, W North Korea, on the Yellow Sea at the mouth of the Yalu River. A main northern gateway to Korea, it developed from a logging center into a port and rail terminus. A bridge (built 1910) over the Yalu connects it with NE China. In World War II it became an industrial center with manufactures of chemicals and aluminum. Power comes from the huge Supung Dam.

sinus, cavity or hollow space in the body, usually filled with air or blood. In humans the paranasal sinuses, mucus-lined cavities in the bones of the face, are connected by passageways to the nose and probably help to warm and moisten inhaled air. When drainage from them is blocked, as after a cold, these sinuses often become infected, a condition called sinusitis. The accumulation of pus results in pressure, headaches, pain, and general discomfort. In invertebrates one of the spaces among the muscles and viscera through which blood returns to the heart is also known as a sinus.

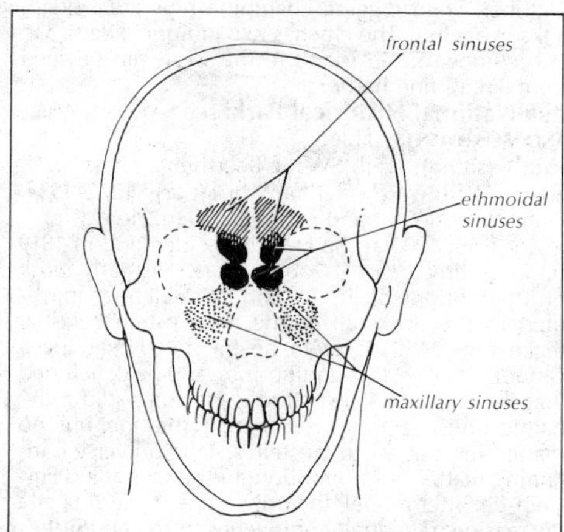

Sinuses of the face

Sinus Arabicus: see RED SEA.

Sinyang: see HSIN-YANG, China.

Sion (sī'ən), in the Bible. **1** Same as Mt. HERMON. **2** Variant of ZION.

Sion (syôN), Ger. *Sitten,* town (1970 pop. 21,925), capital of Valais canton, SW Switzerland, on the Rhône River. An ancient town, Sion is now a wine and horticultural market center. There are hydroelectric plants and coal mines nearby. Sion has been an episcopal see since the 6th cent. The town is rich in historic remains, among which are a 13th-century castle, a late Gothic cathedral, and a 17th-century town hall.

Siouan (so͞o'ən), branch of North American Indian languages belonging to the Hokan-Siouan linguistic family, or stock, of North and Central America (including Mexico). See AMERICAN INDIAN LANGUAGES.

Sioux City, city (1970 pop. 85,925), seat of Woodbury co., NW Iowa, at the junction of the Big Sioux and the Floyd rivers with the Missouri; inc. 1857. It is a shipping, trade, and industrial center for an extensive agricultural and livestock area (including nearby states). It has a huge, central livestock market, a leading hog market, meat-packing houses, and processing plants for popcorn and honey. Fertilizers, electric tools, radios, feed, and seed are also produced. Morningside College, Briar Cliff College, and an art center are there. Nearby are a state park and a monument commemorating the death and burial in 1804 of Sgt. Charles Floyd of the Lewis and Clark expedition.

Sioux Falls, city (1970 pop. 72,488), seat of Minnehaha co., SE S.Dak., on the Big Sioux River; settled 1856, inc. as a village 1877, as a city 1883. White settlers abandoned the site in 1862, because of Indian raids, but with the establishment (1865) of Fort Dakota it was resettled. Named for the falls on the Big Sioux River (which furnish power), Sioux Falls is the largest city in the state and the commercial, industrial, and shipping center of an extensive agricultural area. It has an important livestock market and there are meat processing plants. Sandstone ("Sioux Falls granite") is quarried nearby. Sioux Falls College, Augustana College, a museum, and a state penitentiary are in the city.

Sioux Indians or **Dakota Indians,** confederation of North American Indian tribes, the dominant group of the Hokan-Siouan linguistic stock, which is divided into several separate branches (see AMERICAN INDIAN LANGUAGES). The Sioux, or Dakota, consisted of seven tribes: Wahpekute, Mdewakanton, Wahpeton, Sisseton (who together formed the Santee or Eastern division), Yankton, Yanktonai, and Teton. The Sioux were first noted historically in the *Jesuit Relation* of 1640 when they were living in what is now Minnesota. Their traditions indicate that they had moved there some time before from the northeast. They were noted in 1678 by the French explorer Daniel Duluth and in 1680 by Father Louis Hennepin in the Mille Lacs region in Minnesota. Their migration had been in a southwesterly direction in the face of the hostile Ojibwa, who had been equipped with guns by Europeans. In the mid-18th cent., having driven the Cheyenne and Kiowa out of the Black Hills, the Sioux inhabited the N Great Plains and the western prairies—mainly in Wisconsin, Iowa, Minnesota, North and South Dakota, and up into the bordering provinces of Canada. They then numbered at least 30,000. The Teton Dakota, numbering some 15,000, was the most populous of the seven tribes, and the Oglala Sioux, the largest group of the Teton, numbered some 3,000. The Sioux had a typical Plains area culture, including buffalo hunting and the sun dance. In relations with the white settlers all the divisions of the Sioux have a similar history. The Sioux became friendly with the British after the fall of the French power and supported the British against the United States in the American Revolution and (with the exception of one chief, Tohami, also known as Rising Moose) in the War of 1812. The United States concluded treaties with the Sioux in 1815, 1825, and 1851. A portion of the Sioux under Little Crow rose in 1862 and massacred more than 800 settlers and soldiers in Minnesota; this revolt was suppressed but unrest continued. In 1867 a treaty was concluded by which the Sioux gave up a large section of territory and agreed to retire to a reservation in SW Dakota before 1876. The discovery of gold in the Black Hills and the subsequent rush of prospectors brought resistance under the leadership of such chiefs as SITTING BULL, RED CLOUD, Rain-in-the-Face, CRAZY HORSE, American Horse, and Gall. In this revolt occurred the famous last stand by Gen. George Armstrong CUSTER. The last major conflict fought by the Sioux was the battle of WOUNDED KNEE, Dec. 29, 1890, which resulted in the massacre of over 200 Indians. Today they live on reservations in Minnesota, Nebraska, North Dakota, South Dakota, and Montana; they number over 40,000. In Feb., 1973, about 200 Indian supporters, mostly Sioux, of the AMERICAN INDIAN MOVEMENT seized control of the hamlet of Wounded Knee, S.Dak., demanding U.S. Senate investigations of Indian conditions. The occupation lasted 70 days, during which about 300 persons were arrested by Federal agents. See R. H. Ruby, *The Oglala Sioux* (1955); G. E. Hyde, *A Sioux Chronicle* (1956); C. M. Oehler, *The Great Sioux Uprising* (1959); Kenneth Carley, *The Sioux Uprising of 1862* (1961); R. M. Utley, *The Last Days of the Sioux Nation* (1963); Royal Hassrick, *The Sioux* (1964); Ethel Nurge, ed., *The Modern Sioux* (1970); Robert Burnette, *The Tortured Americans* (1971).

Siphmoth (sĭf'mŏth), unidentified place, S Palestine, associated with David. 1 Sam. 30.28.

Siphnos, Greece: see SÍFNOS.

siphon (sī'fən, -fŏn), tube through which a liquid is lifted over an elevation by the pressure of the atmosphere and is then emptied at a lower level. To start the siphon, it must first be filled with the liquid before it is placed into position. The elevation over which a siphon will lift a liquid is limited by the atmospheric pressure. At sea level, water may be lifted c.34 ft (10.4 m). The siphon must discharge at a level lower than that of the liquid at the intake.

Sippai (sĭp'āī), variant of SAPH.

Sippar (sĭpär'), ancient city of N Babylonia, on the Euphrates in present Iraq, 20 mi (32 km) SW of Baghdad. It was one of the capitals of Sargon and had a great temple to the sungod Shamash. Excavations begun in 1882 have yielded thousands of inscribed clay tablets.

Siqueiros, David Alfaro (dävēth' älfä'rō sākā'rōs), 1896–1974, Mexican painter, b. Chihuahua. Siqueiros was among Mexico's most original and eminent painters. His career as an artist was always related to his vigorous socialist revolutionary activities. He enlisted in the Batallón Mamá ("Baby's Brigade") in the Carranza army and at 17 was a staff officer. As military attaché at the Mexican legation in Paris (1919–21), he came into contact with stimulating contemporary artistic movements. Upon his return to Mexico in 1922, he became a leader of the Syndicate of Technical Workers, Artists, and Sculptors and a founder of the magazine *Machete,* which expounded the principles of a new national "people's art." After frequent imprisonment for political activities and extensive travel abroad, Siqueiros served as an officer in the Spanish republican army (1938). His art is one of violent social protest expressed in dynamic, swirling brushwork, dramatic contrasts of light and shade, and heroic themes. Among his best-known works are murals at the National Preparatory School, Mexico City (1922–24), and at the Plaza Art Center, Los Angeles (1932; destroyed). His other major murals include the vast *Liberation of Chile,* at the Mexican school, Chillán, Chile (1942); *New Democracy,* at the National Institute of Fine Arts, Mexico City (1945); a series at the Polytechnic Institute, Mexico City (1952); and the culmination of his work, *The March of Humanity* (1968, Hotel de Mexico, Mexico City). See B. S. Myers, *Mexican Painting in Our Time* (1956).

Siquijor (sēkēhôr'), island (130 sq mi/337 sq km), one of the Visayan Islands, the Philippines, just off the southeast coast of Negros. It is primarily agricultural. The main town and chief seaport is also called Siquijor.

Sirach (sī'rək), father of the author of ECCLESIASTICUS.

Sirah (sī'rə), well, between Hebron and Jerusalem, where Abner was intercepted by Joab's emissaries. 2 Sam. 3.26.

Siren (sī'rən), in Greek mythology, one of three sea nymphs, usually represented with the head of a woman and the body of a bird. Daughters of PHORCUS or of ACHELOUS, the Sirens inhabited an island surrounded by dangerous rocks. They sang so enchantingly that all who heard were drawn near and shipwrecked. Jason and the Argonauts were saved from them by the music of Orpheus, whose songs were lovelier. Odysseus escaped them by having himself tied securely to a mast and by stopping the ears of his men.

siren: see SALAMANDER.

sirenian (sīrē'nēən) or **sea cow,** name for a large aquatic mammal of the order Sirenia. Living sirenians are the dugong and the manatee, both found in warm, shallow waters in sheltered regions, where they feed on seaweeds and sea grasses. Sirenians are the only marine mammals, outside of the WHALE order, that spend their entire lives in the water, and they are the only marine mammals that feed exclusively on vegetation. Their heavy, thickset bodies are fishlike in form, the tail ending in a horizontally flattened fin. There are no hind legs and the forelegs are modified into weak flippers. The gray skin is completely hairless, except for the bristles around the fleshy lips; the upper lip is cleft into two lobes, used for gathering food. The female has a pair of mammary glands on the chest, and holds the pup in her flippers while nursing. It has been speculated that the manatees, which nurse on the water's surface, are the source of mermaid legends. Manatees (genus *Trichechus*) are found on both sides of the tropical Atlantic Ocean. They are sluggish, largely nocturnal bottom feeders and consume up to 100 lb (45 kg) of vegetation daily. They must surface for air every 15 or 20 min. They are usually 7 to 12 ft (2.1–3.6 m) long and weigh about 500 lb (225 kg), although males sometimes grow much larger. Their paddlelike tail fin is nearly circular in shape. Both parents care for the young, one holding it while the other dives for food. The Florida manatee, *Trichechus manatus*, is found in offshore waters, bays, estuaries, and river mouths in Florida, Central America, and the West Indies. It is protected by law in Florida. A second species, *T. inunguis*, is found in rivers of NE South America, ascending the Amazon as far as Ecuador. The African manatee, *T. senegalensis*, lives in the coastal rivers and lagoons of W Africa. The dugong, *Dugong dugon*, is found in offshore waters of the Red Sea, Indian Ocean, and W South Pacific Ocean. More strictly marine than the manatee, it seldom enters rivers. Its tail fin is crescent-shaped and the male has long, tusklike incisor teeth. The male may reach a length of 12 ft (3.6 m) and weigh over 600 lb (270 kg). The dugongs' numbers have been depleted by hunting for flesh, hides, tusks, and oil. Steller's sea cow was a large northern species that formerly inhabited the Bering Straits. It reached a length of 30 ft (9 m), weighed up to 4 tons (2,400 kg), and was insulated by very thick blubber. When it was discovered by Bering in 1741, the population was very small; within 30 years it was exterminated by hunting. Although superficially they resemble whales, sirenians have evolved independently. They are descended from a primitive group of land mammals that also gave rise to the elephants. The living sirenians are classified in the phylum CHORDATA, subphylum Vertebrata, class Mammalia, order Sirenia, families Trichechidae and Dugongidae.

Siretul (sĭrĕ'to͞ol), Ukr. *Seret,* river, c.450 mi (720 km) long, rising in the Carpathian Mts., W Ukraine, USSR, and flowing SE through E Rumania to the Danube River at Galaţi. Its chief tributaries are the Bistriţa and Moldava rivers. Timber is floated on the river to Galaţi.

Sir George Williams University, at Montreal, Que., Canada; English language; founded 1929. It developed from the formal educational work of the Montreal Young Men's Christian Association, inaugurated in 1873. It has faculties of arts, science, commerce, engineering, and graduate studies.

Sirion (sĭr'ēŏn), Sidonian name of Mt. HERMON. Deut. 3.9; Ps. 29.6.

Siris, Greece: see SÉRRAI.

Sirius (sĭr'ēəs), or **Dog Star,** brightest star in the sky. It is located in the constellation CANIS MAJOR (1970 position R.A. $6^h43.8^m$, Dec. −16°41'); its Bayer designation is Alpha Canis Majoris. Sirius [Gr.,=scorching], having an apparent MAGNITUDE of −1.45, is exceeded in brightness only by the sun, the moon, and Venus and by Mars and Jupiter at their maximum brightness. A white, main-sequence star of SPECTRAL CLASS Al V, Sirius is about twice the size of the sun and about 20 times as luminous. It is also one of the nearest stars, lying at a distance of 8.7 light-years, so that it has been studied extensively. From an analysis of its motions, F. W. Bessel concluded (1844) that it had an unseen companion, which was later (1862) confirmed by observation. The companion, Sirius B, is a white-dwarf star and has also been the object of considerable study because it is the first white dwarf whose spectrum was found to exhibit a gravitational RED SHIFT as predicted by the general theory of RELATIVITY.

Sirmium (sûr'mēəm), ancient city of Pannonia. The site is near modern Sremska Mitrovica, Yugoslavia. Sirmium was unimportant until occupied late in the 1st cent. B.C. by the Romans in the conquest of Pannonia. It was prominent later, especially in the 3d and 4th cent. A.D., and the chief city of Lower Pannonia.

sirocco (sərŏk'ō) [Ital., from Arab. *sharq*=east], hot, dust-laden, dry, southerly wind originating in the N African desert (most commonly in the spring) and reaching Italy and nearby Mediterranean areas. The term more generally denotes any oppressive, warm, southerly or southeasterly wind in this region.

Síros (sē'rôs) or **Syros** (sī'rŏs), island (1971 pop. 18,642), 33 sq mi (85 sq km), SE Greece, in the Aegean Sea, one of the Cyclades. HERMOUPOLIS, or Síros, is the island's main town and port. Síros is the richest and most populous of the Cyclades. During the Greek War of Independence (1821–29) the island remained neutral and many Greeks took refuge on it. By the mid-19th cent. the island had considerable commercial importance. It is also known as Syra.

Síros, city, Greece: see HERMOUPOLIS.

sisal hemp (sī'səl, sĭs'əl, sēsäl') [from Sisal, former chief port of Yucatan], important cordage fiber obtained from the leaves of the sisal hemp plant, an extensively cultivated tropical agave of the family Amaryllidaceae. It is considered second to Manila hemp in strength and value and is used chiefly for cordage. About half the sisal produced is exported to the United States and Canada, where much of it is used as binding twine for grain-harvesting machines. True sisal (*Agave sisalana*), henequen (*Agave fourcroydes*), and many other similar fibers from the agave and closely related genera are often collectively called sisal hemp. Henequen [from the Mexican name; its fiber was used by the pre-Columbian Indians] is grown chiefly in Yucatan, and production of henequen twine is a major industry there. The false sisal of Florida (*A. decipiens*) produces an inferior fiber. Sisal hemp is classified in the division MAGNOLIOPHYTA, class Magnoliopsida, order Amaryllidales, family Amaryllidaceae.

Sisamai (sĭsăm'āī, sĭs"əmā'ī), descendant of Judah. 1 Chron. 2.40.

Sisera (sĭs'ərə). **1** Canaanite captain, defeated by Deborah and Barak and murdered by Jael. Judges 4.2. **2** Family in the return to Palestine. Ezra 2.53; Neh. 7.55.

Sisley, Alfred (älfrĕd' sĭs'lē, sēslā'), 1839–99, French impressionist landscape painter, b. Paris, of English parents. He studied under Corot, Gleyre, and Courbet. After 1871, Sisley lived modestly at Moret-sur-Loing and painted landscapes that reveal a wistful, lyrical sensibility. Influenced by Monet in his selection of colors, Sisley was less daring than Monet in his use of the "rainbow palette" and closer to the Barbizon tradition. He is well represented in many modern galleries. *Street in Moret* and *Sand Heaps* are in the Art Institute, Chicago.

Sismondi, Jean Charles Léonard Simonde de (zhäN shärl lāônär' sēmôNd' də sēsmôNdē'), 1773–1842, Swiss historian, economist, and critic. A member of the circle of Mme de Staël, he was a moderate liberal; his political views colored his writings. His celebrated *History of the Italian Republics in the Middle Ages* (16 vol., 1809–18; tr., abr. and rev., 1906) is marred by his Calvinist bias against the Roman Catholic Church, which he considered chiefly responsible for the loss of liberty in the Italian states. However, the work shows Sismondi to have been among the first historians to appreciate economic influence on cultural and political developments. Sismondi popularized the laissez-faire economics of Adam Smith in his *De la richesse commerciale* (1802). However, the social effects of the Industrial Revolution in England led him to become a critic of capitalism and a precursor of socialism in *Nouveaux Principes d'économie politique* (1819). In literary history, Sismondi's *De la littérature du Midi de l'Europe* (1813) helped found the romantic school of criticism. Sismondi considered literature a natural product of political and social institutions.

Sistan, region, Afghanistan and Iran: see SEISTAN.

sisterhood: see MONASTICISM.

Sisters of Charity, in the Roman Catholic Church, name of many independent communities of women. Most of them owe their origin to the institute of St. VINCENT DE PAUL, founded (1634) for works of mercy. The foundation of Mother Seton in America was affiliated to this. The Sisters of Charity are active in parochial schools, hospitals, orphanages, and colleges.

Sistine Chapel (sĭs'tēn) [for SIXTUS IV], private chapel of the popes in Rome, one of the principal glories of the Vatican. It was built (1473) under Pope Sixtus IV. Not especially remarkable for size or architecture, it is world famous for its decorations. There are fine varicolored marble floor mosaics, but the paintings on walls and ceiling make its renown unique. Frescoes by Perugino, Pinturicchio, Botticelli, Ghirlandaio, and other 15th-century painters decorate the side walls. They depict scenes from the lives of Moses and of Christ, symbolizing the reign of law and of grace, respectively. However, the greatest achievements in the chapel are the work of MICHELANGELO. Across the ceiling he painted the principal themes of the Bible. There are representations of the stages of creation, man's temptation and fall, Noah and the Deluge. Below these scenes are the statuesque figures of prophets and sibyls, with episodes from the Old Testament in the spandrels, all designed to prefigure the salvation of Christianity. The last great work to be executed in the chapel is Michelangelo's awesome *Last Judgment* on the altar wall. Another treasure of the chapel is its collection of illuminated music manuscripts in the archives of the choir.

Sisyphus (sĭs'ĭfəs), in Greek mythology, son of Aeolus and founder and king of Corinth. Renowned for his cunning, he was said to have outwitted even Death. For his disrespect to Zeus, he was condemned to eternal punishment in Tartarus, where he toiled vainly, trying to push a heavy rock to the top of a steep hill. Albert Camus' essay *The Myth of Sisyphus* is based on this legend.

Sitapur (sē'täpo͝or), town (1971 pop. 66,663), Uttar Pradesh state, N central India. The town is a market for grain, oilseed, and jute. The leather and plywood industries are important. Sitapur is a district administrative center and is on the route of the Bareilly-Lucknow railroad. The town passed under British control in 1856.

sitar (sĭtär'), fretted string instrument with a gourd-like body and a long neck, similar to the lute. It has from 3 to 7 gut strings, tuned in fourths or fifths (or both), and a lower course of 12 wire strings that vibrate sympathetically with the first set. It is played alone or in a small ensemble. Indigenous to India, the sitar was popularized in the West in the 1960s by the Indian virtuoso Ravi SHANKAR and is often used in rock music.

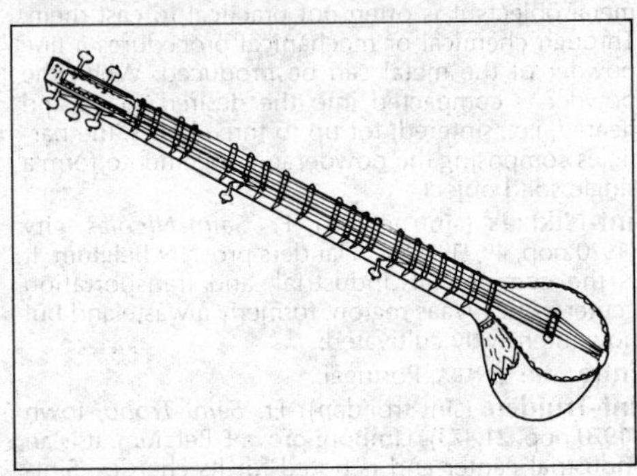

Sitar

sitatunga: see BUSHBUCK.

Sitka (sĭt'kə), city (1970 pop. 3,370), Sitka census div., SE Alaska, in the Alexander Archipelago, on Baranof Island; inc. 1971. Fishing, its first industry, remains important; salmon, halibut, red snapper, crab, herring, abalone, and clams are caught. There are also canning, lumbering, and pulp-processing enterprises. Sitka was founded (1799) by Aleksandr Baranov. Destroyed by Tlingit Indians in 1802, it was rebuilt and became the flourishing capital of Russian America. There, in 1867, the United States officially took possession of Alaska from Russia, and Sitka remained the capital until 1900. Points of interest include Sitka National Historical Park, scene of a decisive battle (1804) between the Russians and the Indians; the Russian Orthodox Cathedral of St. Michael (built 1844–48); and Castle Hill, site of the transfer of Alaska to the United States, which is commemorated by the annual Alaska Day Festival in October. State logging championships are held in Sitka every July. The city has two junior colleges. Mt. Edgecumbe, on an island to the west, can be seen from Sitka's fine harbor.

Sitka National Historical Park: see NATIONAL PARKS AND MONUMENTS, table.

Sitnah (sĭt'nə), well, SW of Beersheba. Gen. 26.21.

Sitter, Willem de (vĭl'əm də sĭt'ər), 1872–1934, Dutch astronomer and mathematician. He was professor from 1908 at the Univ. of Leiden and in 1919 became director of its observatory. His early work on the motions of Jupiter and its satellites contributed to the downfall of the pre-Einstein celestial mechanics. With Einstein he theorized that space cannot be in a stable equilibrium, and he concluded that the universe is expanding. He suggested a dynamic universe in which there is motion but no matter, in contrast to Einstein's static universe containing matter but no motion. In the combined Einstein-de Sitter model, the universe is expanding at a decreasing rate that approaches zero. De Sitter's works in English include *Kosmos* (1932) and *The Astronomical Aspect of the Theory of Relativity* (1933).

Sittingbourne and Milton (sĭt'ĭngbôrn), urban district (1971 pop. 30,861), Kent, SE England, on the ancient Watling Street and on the old route of pilgrimage to Canterbury. It is an agricultural market with paper, paint, and cement works.

Sitting Bull, c.1831-1890, Indian chief, Sioux leader in the battle of the Little Bighorn. He rose to prominence in the Sioux warfare against the whites and the resistance of the Indians under his command to forced settlement on a reservation led to a punitive expedition. In the course of the resistance occurred the Indian victory on the Little Bighorn, where George Armstrong CUSTER and his men were defeated and killed on June 25, 1876. Sitting Bull and some of his followers escaped to Canada, but returned (1881) on a promise of a pardon and were settled on a reservation. In 1885 he appeared in Buffalo Bill's Wild West Show, but his championship of the Indian cause was not at an end. He encouraged the Sioux to refuse to sell their lands, and he advocated the ghost dance religion. He was killed by Indian police on a charge of resisting arrest. He was buried in North Dakota, but in 1954 his remains were removed to South Dakota. See biographies by U. L. Burdick (1941), Stanley Vestal (rev. ed. 1957, repr. 1972), and A. B. Adams (1973).

Sittwe (sĭt'wē), city (1962 est. pop. 86,500), capital of Arakan division, W Burma, at the mouth of the Kaladan River and on the Bay of Bengal. It is an important port and rice-milling center. Originally a small fishing village, it became a port for the export of rice after the British occupied it in 1826. It was formerly called Akyab.

Sitwell, Dame Edith, 1887-1964, English poet and critic, **Sir Osbert Sitwell,** 1892-1969, English author, and **Sacheverell Sitwell** (səshĕv'ərəl), 1897-, English art critic. The Sitwell family is probably the most celebrated literary family of the 20th cent. All three Sitwells evidenced a lively interest in contemporary movements in music, art, and literature. Although all were noted for their frivolity, precocity, and sophistication, a somber despair with the modern world underlies many of their works. The Sitwells were the children of Sir George Sitwell, an antiquarian and genealogist, and they were reared on the family estate in Derbyshire. An angular, aristocratic woman, 6 ft (183 cm) tall, Edith Sitwell was famous for her eccentric appearance and her wit. Her poetry, strongly influenced by the French symbolists, ranges from the artificial and clever verse of her early years to the deeper and more religious poems of her maturity. Collections of her work include *Clowns' Houses* (1918), *Rustic Elegies* (1927), *Gold Coast Customs* (1929), *The Song of the Cold* (1948), *Façade, and Other Poems 1920-1935* (1950), *Gardeners and Astronomers* (1953), and *The Outcasts* (1962). Her *Collected Poems* appeared in 1954. *Façade*, characterized by ragtime rhythms and abstract word patterns, was set to music by William Walton and first read by her in 1922. Important among her critical works are *Poetry and Criticism* (1925), *Aspects of Modern Poetry* (1934), and *A Poet's Notebook* (1943), a collection of aphorisms on the art of poetry. Other prose works include *Alexander Pope* (1930); *The English Eccentrics* (1933); *I Live under a Black Sun* (1937), a novel about Jonathan Swift; and *Fanfare for Elizabeth* (1946) and *The Queens and the Hive* (1962), biographies of Queen Elizabeth I. In 1954 she was made dame of the British Empire. Sir Osbert Sitwell was the author of poems, short stories, novels, and memoirs. Most of his verse is light and satiric. His works include *Triple Fugue* (1924), short stories; *Before the Bombardment* (1926), a novel; *Collected Poems and Satires* (1931); *Selected Poems* (1943); *Four Songs of the Italian Earth* (1948); *Collected Stories* (1953); *The Four Continents* (1954), discursions on travel, art, and life; and *Tales My Father Taught Me* (1962). His five-volume reminiscences about his family are a delightful account of British society of the Edwardian era—*Left Hand, Right Hand* (1944), *The Scarlet Tree* (1946), *Great Morning* (1947), *Laughter in the Next Room* (1948), and *Noble Essences* (1950). Upon his father's death in 1943, he became 5th baronet. Sacheverell Sitwell is known for his art criticism—*Southern Baroque Art* (1924), *German Baroque Art* (1927), and *The Gothick North* (1929)—and for his poetry—*The Cyder Feast* (1927) and *Canons of Giant Art* (1933). He is also the author of biographies, *Mozart* (1932) and *Liszt* (rev. ed. 1955); essays and observations, *Conversation Pieces* (1936), *The Hunters and the Hunted* (1948), and *Cupid and the Jacaranda* (1952); and travel books, *Spain* (1950), *Denmark* (1956), and *Golden Wall and Mirador* (1961). See Dame Edith's autobiography, *Taken Care Of* (1964), selected letters (1970), study of her by G. Singleton (1960); R. Fulford, *Osbert Sitwell* (1951); J. Lehman, *A Nest of Tigers: The Sitwells in Their Times* (Am. ed. 1968).

Siva: see SHIVA.

Sivaji (sĭvä'jē), 1627-80, Indian ruler, leader of the MAHRATTAS. The son of a Mahratta chieftain, he was imbued from early childhood with hatred of the Mogul empire, which controlled most of India. From his capital at Poona he made guerrilla attacks on the Muslim kingdom of Bijapur and gradually carved out a considerable domain. In 1657 his troops were soundly beaten by the Mogul army, but the Moguls then withdrew, and Sivaji returned to raiding and several times defeated the Bijapur army. In 1664 he sacked the rich Mogul port of Surat and thus provoked an organized Mogul campaign against him. Defeated in 1665, Sivaji went (1666) to Agra to negotiate with Aurangzeb, the Mogul emperor, but was imprisoned. After a daring escape he returned to W India and undertook a series of raids that were not countered by the Moguls. By 1674 he was secure enough to crown himself king of the Mahratta empire, although fighting continued until his death. He is the modern Mahratta hero. See biographies by V. B. Kulkarni (1963) and K. L. Mahaley (1969); Jadunath Sarkar, *Shivaji and his Times* (5th ed. 1952).

Sivan (sēvän'), in the Jewish CALENDAR, the third month (or ninth month, depending upon the system of reckoning). Esther 8.9; Baruch 1.8.

Sivas (sĭväs'), city (1970 pop. 132,527), capital of Sivas prov., central Turkey, on the Kızıl Irmak. An important trade and manufacturing center, it has cement, textile, and rug factories. Iron ore is mined nearby. Known as Sebaste, Sebastia, or Cabira in ancient times, it was an important city of Asia Minor under the Romans, the Byzantines, and the Seljuk Turks. Part of the Seljuk empire of Rum in the late 12th cent., Sivas fell to the Mongols and later (15th cent.) to the Ottoman Turks. In 1919, Kemal Atatürk held an important nationalist congress there.

Sivash Sea (sēvăsh') or **Putrid Sea,** Rus. *Gniloye More,* salt lagoon, c.1,000 sq mi (2,590 sq km), SW European USSR, in the Ukraine, extending along the northeastern coast of the Crimea. It is separated—except at the Genichesk Strait—from the Sea of Azov by the Tongue of Arabat, a narrow sandspit c.70 mi (110 km) long; the Perekop Isthmus separates it from the Black Sea in the north. The sea is a complex system of shallow inlets, straits, and sand bars. The water, which has a salt content of up to 20%, has been the source of table salt and of several chemicals, including bromine.

Siwah or **Siwa** (both: sē'wä), oasis, c.35 sq mi (90 sq km), NW Egypt, in the Libyan (Western) Desert. Dates and tea are grown in the oasis, parts of which are c.200 ft (60 m) below sea level. Siwah was the seat of the temple and oracle of Zeus Amon (Zeus represented with the horns of Amon). Alexander the Great visited the oracle.

Siwalik Hills (sĭwä'lĭk), southernmost range of the Himalayas, S central Asia, extending c.1,050 mi (1,690 km) from SW Kashmir through N India into S Nepal paralleling the main range from a distance of c.90 mi (140 km). The highest point is 3,500 ft (1,067 m). The Siwalik Hills are noted for their vast vertebrate fossil beds.

Siward (syōō'ərd), d. 1055, earl of Northumbria. A Danish warrior, he probably came to England with King Canute. At the behest of King Harthacanute in 1041 he ravaged Worcestershire and perhaps murdered Eadwulf of Northumbria; thereafter he was himself earl of Northumbria. He supported EDWARD THE CONFESSOR against Earl Godwin in 1051 and in 1054 defeated MACBETH, king of Scotland, on behalf of Siward's nephew, later Malcolm III.

Six-Day War: see ARAB-ISRAELI WARS.

Six Dynasties, period of Chinese history between the fall of the Han dynasty (A.D. 220) and the establishment of the Sui dynasty (A.D. 581). It is named for the six successive dynasties that appeared in China during the period: the Wu (222-80), the Eastern Ch'in (317-419), the Liu-Sung (420-79), the Southern Ch'i (479-502), the Liang (502-57), and the Ch'en (557-89). Although a time of severe political disunion, the period of the Six Dynasties was marked by a number of advances, including the invention of gunpowder and the introduction of coal and tea.

Six Nations: see IROQUOIS CONFEDERACY.

Sixtus IV (sĭk'stəs), 1414-84, pope (1471-84), an Italian (b. near Savona) named Francesco della Rovere; successor of Paul II. He was made general of his order, the Franciscans, in 1464 and became (1467) a cardinal. Sixtus was expected to be a reformer, but he was too much embroiled in political difficulties. The struggle with the French monarchy over the control of the church in France was complicated by Louis XI's efforts to replace Ferdinand I of Naples with a Frenchman. A quarrel with Lorenzo de' MEDICI became critical after the PAZZI CONSPIRACY (1478), since an important instigator was Girolamo Riario, nephew of Sixtus, and the pope seems to have had prior knowledge of the plot. He waged war on Florence afterward. Though a reconciliation was made in 1479, Lorenzo joined Louis XI in threatening schism. Relations with Italian states other than Florence were also unhappy. Sixtus consented (1478) to the establishment of the Spanish INQUISITION and then found the Spanish ignoring his rebukes for illegal procedure and jurisdiction and his demands for moderation. He welcomed into the Papal States the Jews expelled from Spain. The behavior of his favored nephews was disgraceful; a happy exception was Giuliano della Rovere (later Pope Julius II). Sixtus was an excellent administrator of the city and did much to improve and beautify Rome. He was an important benefactor of the Vatican Library, and he founded the Sistine Chapel. He summoned Josquin Desprez to Rome and legislated for the improvement of church music. He was succeeded by Innocent VIII.

Sixtus V, 1521-90, pope (1585-90), an Italian (b. near Montalto) named Felice Peretti; successor of Gregory XIII. He entered the Franciscan order in early youth. After ordination (1547) he became a famous preacher and was patronized by zealous leaders of the Catholic Reformation, notably Cardinal Carafa (later Paul IV), Cardinal Ghislieri (later St. Pius V), St. Philip Neri, and St. Ignatius of Loyola. From 1556 to 1560 he was counselor to the Inquisition in Venice, but his ardor caused trouble and he was recalled. In 1565 he went to Spain to look into the alleged heresy of the archbishop of Toledo and so seriously fell out with his companion, Cardinal Buoncompagni (later Gregory XIII), that they became enemies for life. He was created cardinal (1570) by St. Pius V. As pope, Sixtus V set about bringing order to the Papal States, which were at the mercy of brigands, and his methods, if violent, were successful. He spent a vast amount of money on the city of Rome, rebuilding countless churches, beautifying streets, and erecting new buildings and monuments. Sixtus left a tremendous surplus in the treasury, but in doing so he nearly ruined commerce in the Papal States. He reorganized the pontifical administration and the sacred college, which he set at the number of 70. He gave his sanction to Philip II of Spain's attempt to invade and restore Catholicism to England, an endeavor that ended in the defeat of the Spanish Armada. Sixtus V is one of the great figures of the Catholic Reformation. He was succeeded by Urban VII.

Sixtus of Bourbon-Parma, Prince, 1886-1934, son of Robert, last duke of Parma. While serving as an officer in the Belgian army, he was the intermediary for his brother-in-law, Emperor CHARLES I of Austria-Hungary, in Charles's secret attempt to negotiate peace with the Allies in 1917. The effort came to nothing, but in April, 1918, the French government, in retaliation for attacks made by the Austrian foreign minister CZERNIN, published a letter written by Charles to Sixtus. The letter justified French claims to Alsace-Lorraine, and its publication caused acute embarrassment to the Austrian government.

Sjaelland (shĕ'län) or **Zealand** (zē'lənd), Ger. *Seeland,* island (1965 pop. 2,055,040), 2,709 sq mi (7,016 sq km), E Denmark, between the Kattegat and the Baltic Sea. Denmark's largest island, it is separated from Fyn by the Store Baelt and from Sweden by the Øresund. Sjaelland includes most of Copenhagen, the Danish capital, and the cities of Roskilde, Helsingør, Hillerød, Holbaek, Naestved, Køge, and Birkerød. The island is generally low-lying, rising to a maximum height of 413 ft (126 m) in the northeast, and has much fertile farmland. Wheat growing, dairy farming, cattle breeding, and fishing are important occupations. Sjaelland's northern shore is indented by the many-branched Isefjord.

Skadar: see SHKODËR, Albania.

Skagen (skä'gən), city (1970 com. pop. 13,512), Nordjylland co., N Denmark, a port on Skagens Odde peninsula (The Skaw) at the northern end of Jylland and on the Kattegat. It has fisheries, shipyards, and fish canneries and is a popular summer resort.

Skagerrak (skă'gərăk), strait, c.150 mi (240 km) long and 85 mi (140 km) wide, between Norway and Denmark, linking the North Sea and the Baltic Sea by way of the Kattegat. It is shallow on the Danish shore and deepens toward the Norwegian coast. For the battle of the Skagerrak, see JUTLAND, BATTLE OF.

Skagit (skăj'ĭt), river, c.150 mi (240 km) long, rising in the Cascade Range, British Columbia, and flowing SW through Wash. into Puget Sound. Gorge High Dam (with a 134,000 kw capacity), Diablo Dam (120,000 kw), and Ross Dam (360,000 kw) provide electricity for Seattle. The lakes formed behind the dams are in a 40-mi (64-km) stretch of river canyon that makes up Ross Lake National Recreation Area (see NATIONAL PARKS AND MONUMENTS, table). Ross Lake, 24 mi (39 km) long, extends to the Canadian border.

Skagway (skăg'wā"), city (1970 pop. 675), Skagway-Yakutat census div., SE Alaska, in the Panhandle, at the head of Lynn Canal; founded 1897. It is a port of entry; a trade and tourist center; the coastal terminus of the White Pass and Yukon Railway, which is in operation all year; and the northernmost terminal of the state ferry system from Prince Rupert, British Columbia. During the gold rush of 1897–98 it was a major disembarking point to the Klondike.

Skanderbeg: see SCANDERBEG.

Skåne (skō'nə) or **Scania** (skān'yə, –ēə), historic province of extreme S Sweden, now included in Malmöhus and Kristianstad counties. Skåne, the scene of many battles, was held by Denmark until 1658, when it was conquered by Charles X of Sweden. Of note are numerous prehistoric dolmens and tumuli and many medieval castles and manors.

Skara (skä'rä"), city (1970 pop. 10,284), Skaraborg co., S Sweden. Situated in a farming region, it has industries that manufacture metal goods and footwear. Dating from at least the 9th cent., Skara is one of Sweden's oldest cities; the country's first bishopric was established there in the 11th cent. The city has also been an educational center since 1641, when Sweden's earliest institutions of higher learning were founded there. Skara has an imposing cathedral (12th cent.; restored 1894).

Skara Brae (skâr'ə brā), Stone Age village, on Mainland in the Orkney Islands, N Scotland. Dating from c.2000 to 1500 B.C., the village was preserved under a sand dune until uncovered by a storm in 1851. It contains seven underground chambers furnished with stone dressers, tables, and beds. Skara Brae is considered an outstanding preserved Stone Age village.

skate, fish: see RAY.

skating, gliding along an ice surface on keellike runners known as ice skates. The earliest skates (c.9th cent.) were made of bone, which gave way to wood, probably in the 14th cent. These materials frequently proved fragile under strain, and wooden skates shod with iron came into use. Skates made entirely of iron were introduced in the 17th cent. Steel skates, with straps and clamps to fasten them to the shoes, were first made in the 1850s, and later came the skate permanently attached to the shoe. Skating has long been a means of travel in countries with long, cold winters, such as Norway, Sweden, Finland, Russia, and especially Holland. There are references to skating in English books as early as the 12th cent. By the 17th cent. skating was not only a means of travel but also a well-established sport. It was introduced early into America by European colonists and became a popular sport in the N United States and Canada. Skating, besides being an important form of winter recreation and the essential skill in the game of ice hockey (see HOCKEY, ICE) has developed as a sport for exhibition along two lines—speed skating and figure skating. In Europe many skating contests are held at St. Moritz, Oslo, Chamonix, Cortina, and Garmisch-Partenkirchen, while in North America, Montreal, Toronto, Lake Placid, Sun Valley, Colorado Springs, and Squaw Valley are well-known centers for skating events. There are also many indoor skating rinks, where ice is artificially produced. Since 1924 figure-skating contests for women and men, as well as 500-, 1,500-, 5,000-, and 10,000-meter speed-skating events, have become an important part of the Olympic winter games. Olympic speed-skating events, in which participants may reach speeds as high as 30 mi (48 km) per hr, are usually won by athletes from Scandinavia, the Soviet Union, or the United States. Figure skating, invented by Jackson Haines (1860s), an American, is generally considered one of the most beautiful and graceful events in all sport. Olympic figure skating is divided into compulsory and free skating sections. In the compulsory round, contestants are judged for the precision with which they execute specified patterns (e.g., the figure eight). In free skating, also known as ice dancing, skaters choreographically interpret music that they have chosen. Sonja HENIE did much to bring skating to wide public notice in the United States, and after she turned (1936) professional, the ice carnival became a favorite American amusement. The ice carnival has attracted other successful Olympic skaters, including Peggy Fleming and Dick Button. Considered one of the most outstanding men's figure skaters of all time, the latter won five straight world, seven consecutive U.S., and two Olympic championships before turning professional in 1952. In 1960 the National Ice Skating Hall of Fame was established at Newburgh, N.Y. See R. S. Ogilvie, *Basic Ice Skating Skills* (1968); Michael Kirby, *Ice Skating* (1971); John Wild, *Power Skating* (1971). **Roller skating,** gliding on a hard, smooth, durable surface on skates with rollers or wheels, in recent years has become a popular adult sport. Skates mounted on wooden rollers date from the 1860s, and soon wooden wheels replaced the rollers. The ball-bearing skate wheel was invented in the 1880s. The origin of roller skates is obscure (perhaps they were first used in Holland), but the sport became popular among children throughout the world. When figure skating and dance movements were adopted from ice skating, roller skating gained a large adult following. Numerous roller-skating rinks were built in the United States in the 20th cent., and several roller-skating tournaments are now held annually. Following World War II, a spectator sport called the roller derby gained prominence, due primarily to television. More a staged theatrical event than a sport, roller derby involves team competition on banked indoor tracks. See R. D. Martin, *Roller Skating* (1944); E. R. O'Neill, *Roller Skating* (1960).

Skaw, the, Denmark: see SKAGEN.

Skeat, Walter William, 1835–1912, English scholar and philologist. Skeat took holy orders in 1860, but illness cut short his church career. At Cambridge he served as a lecturer in mathematics (1864–71), began the study of Old English, and was professor of Anglo-Saxon (1878–1912). In 1873 he founded the English Dialect Society, which brought about the *English Dialect Dictionary*, edited by Joseph Wright (1896–1905). Skeat was the author of a number of textbooks, contributed freely to learned journals, and led the way in the study of English place names. Among the many works he edited are *Lancelot of the Laik* (1865), *Piers Plowman* (1867–85), John Barbour's *The Bruce* (4 parts, 1870–89), Ælfric's *Lives of Saints* (2 parts, 1881–1900), and a seven-volume edition of Chaucer (1894–97). His important work, *An Etymological Dictionary of the English Language* (1882), was a standard reference for many years.

Skeena (skē'nə), river, c.360 mi (580 km) long, rising in the Stikine Mts., W British Columbia, Canada, and flowing S and SW to the Pacific Ocean near Prince Rupert. It is navigable for c.100 mi (160 km) upstream. There are fish-processing plants near the mouth of the river. The Bulkley River is its chief tributary.

skeet: see SHOOTING.

skeleton, stiff supportive framework of the body. The two basic types found among animals are the exoskeleton and the endoskeleton. The shell of the clam is an exoskeleton composed primarily of cal-

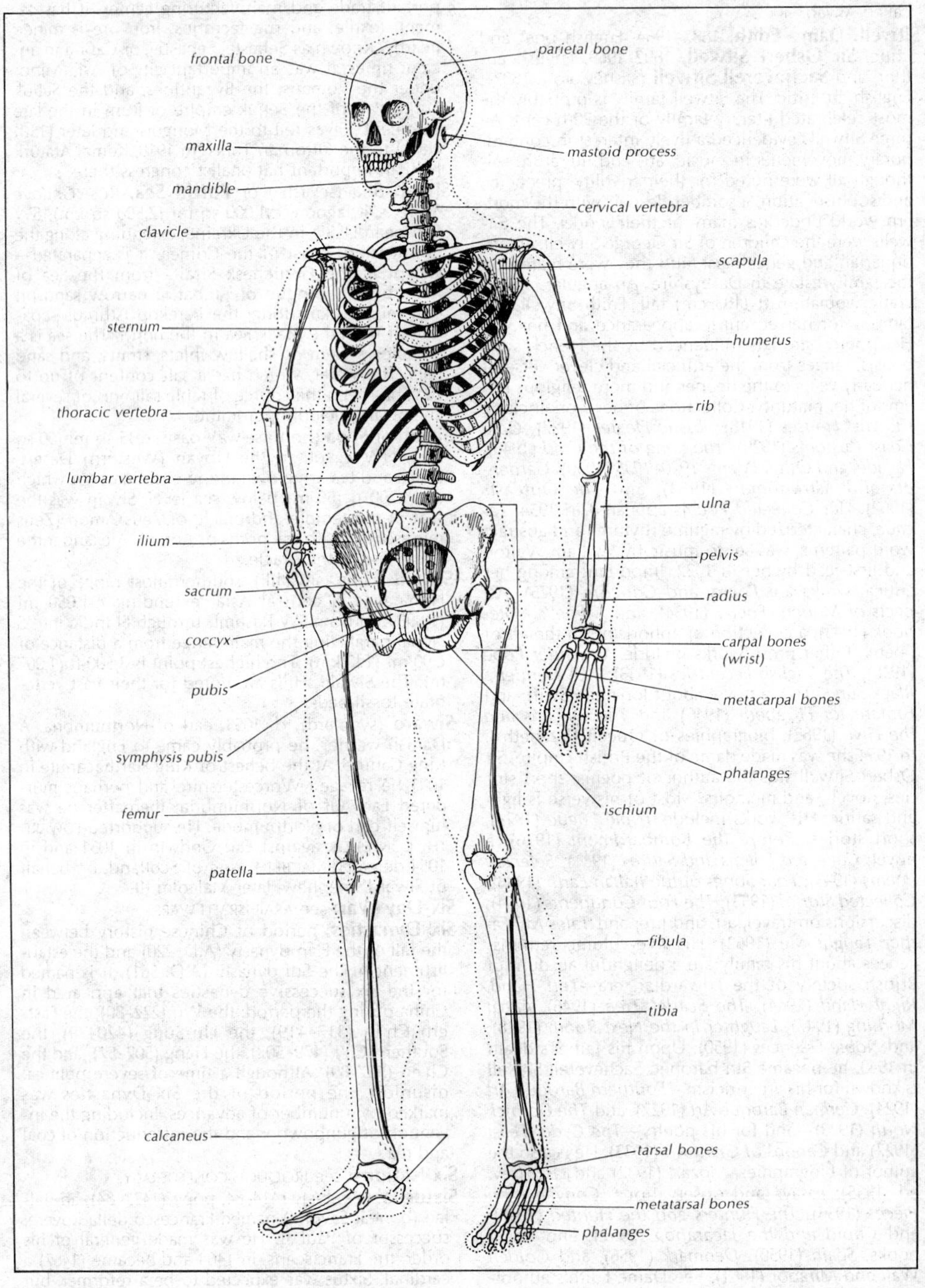

Human skeleton

cium carbonate. It provides formidable protection, but it is bulky and severely restrictive of movement. The smallest exoskeletons are found on microscopic animals such as diatoms and certain protozoans. Coral reefs are made up of the accumulated exoskeletons of the coral polyp. The firm, flexible, chitinous (horny) insect skeleton is a combination of protective armor and a framework for attachment of the muscles used in rapid movement. The disadvantage of an exoskeleton is that it is nonliving and must be shed periodically to allow for growth—a process limiting the maximum size of the organism. The endoskeleton, a framework of living material enclosed within the body, permits larger size coupled with freedom of movement and is characteristic of vertebrate animals. In certain fish it is made up entirely of CARTILAGE, but in most vertebrates it is a mixture of BONE and cartilage. The general arrangement of skeletal parts into SKULL, SPINAL COLUMN, and RIBS is the same in all vertebrates. In addition to its supportive function, the skeleton provides sites for the attachment of the muscles used in movement and shields vital organs such as the brain and lungs. The skeleton of birds is especially adapted for flight; the bones are modified into light, hollow tubes penetrated by air sacs. The human skeleton consists of 206 bones held together by flexible tissue consisting of cartilage and LIGAMENTS. It is composed of two basic parts, the axial and the appendicular skeletons. The axial skeleton includes the skull, jawbone, ribs, sternum, and spinal column. The appendicular skeleton is made up of the upper (shoulder or pectoral) and lower (pelvic) girdles (see PELVIS), and the bones of the arms and legs.

Skellefteå (shĕlĕf'təō"), city (1970 pop. 47,519), Västerbotten co., NE Sweden, on the Gulf of Bothnia at the mouth of the Skellefte älv River. The center of a rich mining region (copper, lead, gold, silver, and zinc), the city has several smelters and refineries. First chartered in 1621, it was rechartered in 1845, when its modern growth began. It has a large wooden city hall (19th cent.).

Skellefte älv (shĕlĕf'tə ĕlv), river, c.255 mi (410 km) long, rising in Norrbotten co., N Sweden, in the mountains along the Norwegian border. It flows SE through Uddjaur lake (30 mi/48 km long; 92 sq mi/238 sq km) to the Gulf of Bothnia at Skellefteå. The river traverses a rich copper- and gold-mining region near Boliden and Kristianstad; Könnskär is a smelting town near the mouth.

Skelligs, rocky islands, off SW Republic of Ireland, in Co. Kerry, comprising Lemon Rock, Little Skellig, and Great Skellig. Climbing the rocks to the peaks of Great Skellig was part of an ancient means of penance. The island has a lighthouse and ruins of a monastery.

Skelmersdale, new town (1971 pop. 26,681), Lancashire, NW England. Skelmersdale was designated one of the NEW TOWNS in 1961 to alleviate overpopulation in Liverpool and the N Merseyside area. Its population is expected to grow to 80,000. The area of the new town lies wholly within the area of the new urban district of Skelmersdale and Holland, created in 1968 chiefly from the former urban districts of Skelmersdale and Up Holland.

Skelton, John, 1460–1529, English poet and humanist. Tutor to Prince Henry (later Henry VIII), he later (c.1502) became rector of Diss, Norfolk. In 1512 he began to call himself royal orator, a position that may have been conferred by Henry VIII requiring that Skelton carry on some royal correspondence and write occasional official poems. He wrote a long allegorical poem, *The Garland of Laurel* (1523), but is remembered for his scathing and often obscene satires on the court, the clergy, and Cardinal Wolsey—*The Bowge of Court* (1499), *Speak, Parrot* (1521), *Colin Clout* (1522), and *Why Come Ye Not to Court?* (c.1522)—and the mock dirge "Philip Sparrow." Many of his works are written in verse forms he himself devised, called Skeltonics. They consist of short lines and insistent rhymes, sometimes repeated through several sets of couplets; they also employ alliteration. See Skelton's works (ed. by Rev. Alexander Dyce, 2 vol., 1843); studies by A. R. Heiserman (1961), S. E. Fish (1965), and Maurice Pollet (tr. 1971).

skepticism (skĕp'tĭsĭzəm) [from Gr.,=to reflect], philosophic position holding that the possibility of knowledge is limited either because of the limitations of the mind or because of the inaccessibility of its object. It is more loosely used to denote any questioning attitude. Extreme skepticism holds that no knowledge is possible, but this is logically untenable since the statement contradicts itself. The first important skeptical view was held by DEMOCRITUS, who saw sense perception as no certain guide to objective reality. The SOPHISTS were the earliest group of skeptics. PROTAGORAS taught the relativity of knowledge, and GORGIAS held that either nothing could be known, or if anything were known, it could not be communicated. PYRRHO later held a similarly extreme position, seeing reality as inaccessible. ARCESILAUS taught that certitude is impossible and only probable knowledge is attainable. In the Renaissance, skepticism is seen in the writings of Michel de MONTAIGNE, Pierre CHARRON, and Blaise PASCAL. For René DESCARTES skepticism was a methodology that allowed him to arrive at certain incontrovertible truths. At the end of the 18th cent. Pierre BAYLE skeptically challenged philosophical and theological theories. David HUME has a reputation as a modern skeptic, although skepticism is not characteristic of his thought. In his criticism of basic concepts he sharply limited man's supposed knowledge of substance, causality, and the self. The greatest of modern skeptics is Immanuel KANT, whose antinomies of reason demonstrate that certain problems are insoluble by reason. As a result, Kantian AGNOSTICISM is closely linked in basis with skepticism. The scientific method demands that all things assumed as facts be questioned and is, therefore, skeptical to a degree. However, the positivism of many scientists, whether latent or open, is incompatible with skepticism, for it accepts without question the assumption that material effect is impossible without material cause. See F. L. Baumer, *Religion and the Rise of Skepticism* (1960, repr. 1969); R. H. Popkin, *The History of Skepticism from Erasmus to Descartes* (rev. ed. 1968); C. L. Stough, *Greek Skepticism* (1969); K. E. Nielsen, *Skepticism* (1972).

sketch, a rapidly executed kind of pictorial note-taking. The sketch is not usually intended as an autonomous work of art although many have been considered masterpieces in their own right. Used extensively in the planning of large, complex projects, the sketch allows the artist to visualize quickly the bend of a knee or the sweep of an arm without having to experiment directly on the work itself. See CARTOON.

skiagraph: see X RAY.

Skiddaw (skĭd'ô), mountain, 3,054 ft (931 m) high, Cumbria, NW England, in the Lake District.

Skidmore, Owings and Merrill, American architectural firm founded in 1936 in New York City by Louis Skidmore (1897–1962), Nathaniel A. Owings (1903–), and John O. Merrill (1923–, now retired). The firm is among the principal popularizers of large glass-and-steel office buildings. An example is Lever House (1952), designed by Gordon Bunshaft, a partner in the firm, which reflects the influence of work by Mies Van der Rohe. This simple, elegant structure has been characteristic of the firm's architectural aesthetic since the 1950s and has been imitated in many countries. This style is a postwar manifestation of the INTERNATIONAL STYLE of the 1920s. Among the firm's most recent buildings are the U.S. Steel Building (1973) and the Ahnnenberg Tower of the Mount Sinai Hospital complex (1974).

Skidmore College, at Saratoga Springs, N.Y.; chartered and opened 1911 as Skidmore School of Arts (for women) through a gift from Lucy Skidmore Scribner; chartered as a college 1922. In 1972 the school was opened to male students.

Skien (shē'ən, shā'ən), city (1970 pop. 45,471), capital of Telemark co., SE Norway, a port on the Skienselva River and on the Telemark Canal. Manufactures include processed food, forest products, and footwear. Ibsen was born in Skien in 1828.

Skierniewice (skyĕrnyĕvē'tsĕ), town (1970 pop. 25,600), E central Poland. It is a railway junction and manufacturing center where metals, glass, and ceramics are produced. Chartered in 1463, it was a residence of the bishops of Gniezno (17th–18th cent.). Skierniewice has a 17th-century episcopal palace.

skiing, sport of sliding over snow on skis—long, narrow, flexible runners. Skis, made of highly polished wood, of metal, or even of plastic, average 6½ ft (about 2 m) in length, 3 in. (7.62 cm) in width, and ¾ in. (1.91 cm) in thickness under the foot. Novice skiers sometimes start with skis that are only about 3 ft (91 cm) long, and then gradually move up to the regular size skis. The binding, which attaches the boot to the ski, is made of metal or leather. To aid himself in accelerating, turning, and balancing, the skier uses a pair of poles, each of which has a leather wriststrap on the top, a sharp metal tip on the bottom, and a circular ring about 4 in. (10 cm) from the tip to prevent it from sinking into the snow. Although its origin is obscure, skiing is known to have been a vital means of transportation in Scandinavia for many centuries. Skis more than 4,000 years old have been discovered in parts of Scandinavia. They are thought to have been made from the smoothed-down bones of large animals. In the Middle Ages skiing was used by the Swedes in warfare, and its use as a military technique has continued and spread to other countries. Ski troops were widely used by the Finns in the Russo-Finnish War (1939–40). Skiing was introduced into Central Europe at the close of the 16th cent. It began as an organized sport in Norway in the last half of the 19th cent. and is now Norway's national sport. Competitive skiing comprises four events: the downhill (the most dangerous), a straight, steep descent in a race against time; the slalom (the most graceful), raced on a sharply twisting course marked off by flags; the ski jump (the most spectacular), in which each contestant leaps twice from specially prepared jump slopes, attempting to score the highest point total judged on distance and form; and the cross-country (the most grueling), over a long course (ranging from 10 to 50 km in Olympic games), in which the natural terrain and obstacles test the skier's stamina and maneuverability. The first two are referred to as the Alpine events, the last two as the Nordic events. Women compete only in downhill, cross-country, and slalom events. It is uncertain whether Americans learned skiing from the Indians or whether it was brought to America by Norwegian and Swedish immigrants in the mid-19th cent. At any rate, the first U.S. ski club was formed in 1872, and the National Ski Association was founded in 1904. Twenty years later (1924) the *Fédération Internationale de Ski* was founded, and skiing was added to the Winter Olympics program. Skiing (mainly downhill) has enjoyed a tremendous boom as a recreational sport since the 1930s, spurred by the Winter Olympics at Lake Placid, N.Y. (1932), and Squaw Valley, Calif. (1960), and by the development of ski tows and ski lifts. Skiers now reach the summit of a ski run in minutes, whereas formerly it took hours. Artificial snow-making machines and the construction of runs of varying levels of difficulty have also contributed to the sport's expansion. It is estimated that in 1920 no more than 4,000 Americans skied. By 1970 this number had increased a thousand-fold and was still growing by some 15% a year. WATER SKIING is a warm-weather sport in which a skier is towed through the water by a motor-propelled craft. See Marvin I. Clein and Joan Sanders, *Beginning Skiing* (1968); Robert Scharff et al., *Ski Magazine's Encyclopedia of Skiing* (1970); Mark Heller, *Ski* (1970); Art Broten, *Skiing* (1971).

Skikda (skēk'də), formerly **Philippeville** (fēlēpvēl'), city (1966 pop. 72,742), NE Algeria, a port on the Gulf of Stora of the Mediterranean Sea. It is the port for CONSTANTINE and handles mostly agricultural products. Skikda was founded by the French in 1838 on the site of a Carthaginian colony, Rusicada, which later flourished as a port under the Romans.

skimmer, common name for certain sea birds resembling the related tern. Skimmers (genus *Rhynchops*) have long, laterally compressed bills of which the lower mandible is one fourth longer than the movable upper mandible. This bill is adapted to their technique of skimming the water's surface to catch the shrimp and small fish that form their diet. Skimmers are gregarious and partly nocturnal; their sensitive eyes narrow to slits while they roost during the day. The black skimmer, *R. nigra,* (black back and white belly), the largest (20 in./50 cm) of the family and the only American member, is found on the Atlantic coast of North America and on both coasts of South America. Skimmers are classified in the phylum CHORDATA, subphylum Vertebrata, class Aves, order Charadriiformes, family Rhynchopidae.

skin, the flexible tissue (integument) enclosing the body of vertebrate animals. In humans and other mammals, the skin is a complex organ of numerous structures (sometimes called the integumentary system) serving vital protective and metabolic functions. It is composed of two main layers of cells: a thin outer layer, the epidermis, and a thicker inner layer, the dermis. Along the internal surface of the epidermis, young cells continuously multiply, pushing the older cells outward. At the outer surface the older cells flatten and overlap to form a tough membrane and gradually are shed as dead skin. HORNS, HOOFS, HAIR (fur), FEATHERS, and SCALES are evolutionary adaptations of the epidermis. Although the epidermis has no blood vessels, its deeper strata contain melanin, the pigment that gives color to the skin. The underlying dermis consists of connective tissue in which are embedded blood vessels, lymph channels, nerve endings, sweat glands, SEBACEOUS GLANDS, fat cells, hair follicles, and muscles. The nerve endings, called receptors, perform an impor-

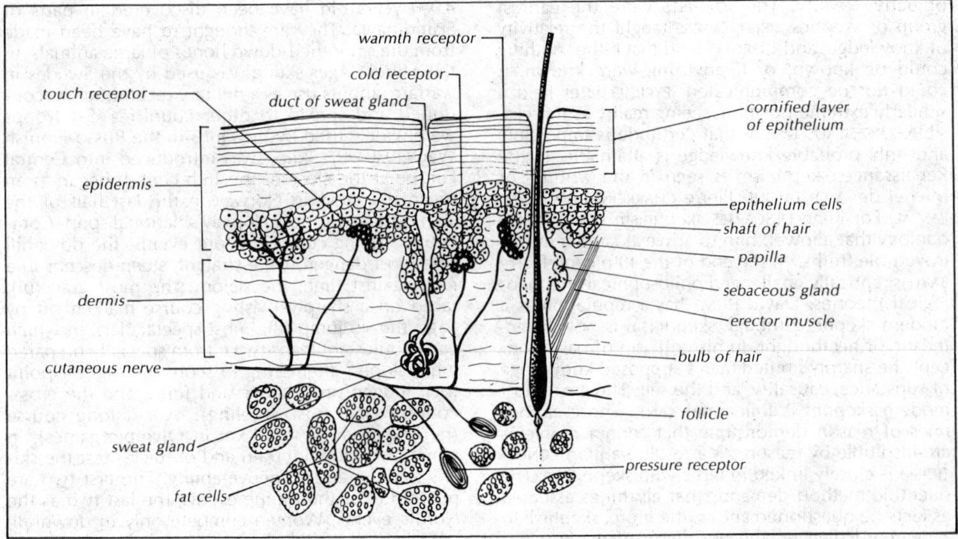

Cross section of skin

tant sensory function. They respond to various stimuli, including contact, heat, and cold. Response to cold activates the erector muscles, causing hair or fur to stand erect; fright also causes this reaction. From the outer surface of the dermis extend numerous projections (papillae) that fit into pits on the inner surface of the epidermis so that the two layers are firmly locked together. In humans, whorls on the fingers show where the epidermis falls between rows of papillae, making the patterns used in fingerprinting. The skin provides a barrier against invasion by outside organisms and protects underlying tissues and organs from abrasion and other injury, and its pigments shield the body from the dangerous ultraviolet rays in sunlight. It also waterproofs the body, preventing excessive loss or gain of bodily moisture. Human skin performs several functions that help maintain normal body temperature: its numerous sweat glands excrete waste products along with salt-laden moisture, the evaporation of which may account, in certain circumstances, for as much as 90% of the cooling of the body; its fat cells act as insulation against cold; and when the body is overheated, the skin's extensive small blood vessels carry warm blood near the surface where it is cooled. The skin is lubricated by its own oil glands, which keep both the outside layer of the epidermis and the hair from drying to brittleness. Human skin has remarkable self-healing properties, particularly when only the epidermis is damaged. Even when the injury damages the dermis, healing may still be complete if the wounded area is in a part of the body with a rich blood supply. Deeper wounds, penetrating to the underlying tissue, heal by scar formation. Scar tissue lacks the infection-resisting and metabolic functions of healthy skin; hence, sufficiently extensive skin loss by widespread burns or wounds may cause death.

skin diving, act of swimming freely under water. It is done with the aid of a face mask, swimming fins for the feet, and either a SNORKEL breathing tube or scuba [acronym for self-contained underwater breathing apparatus] gear. The fins increase the propulsion and agility of the swimmer. Skin diving is used in scientific, commercial, and military activities and in recent years has gained enormous popularity as a beach sport. Free underwater swimming is not new, and as long ago as the 8th cent. B.C. Greek divers, unconnected to the surface by air hoses or lines, collected sponges and mollusks in depths as great as 100 ft (30 m). The Greeks and Romans employed underwater warriors, trained to hold their breath for long periods of time, to sabotage enemy fleets. In the Pacific islands natives have long practiced skin diving and spear fishing. Many improvements in skin-diving equipment were made during World War II, and the so-called frogmen of the U.S. and British navies played a vital role in operations. An important development of this period was scuba diving with an Aqua-lung (see DIVING, DEEP-SEA). The scuba diver, with his greater mobility, has replaced in many areas of underwater activity the conventional sea diver who is encumbered by heavy equipment and limited by a lifeline and air hose. However, it is dangerous for a scuba diver to work below a 130-ft (40-m) depth, and although free dives have been made to more than 300 ft (91 m), conventional dress and equipment are generally used for deep descents. See Joe Strykowski, *Diving for Fun* (3d ed. 1971); Hans Hass, *Challenging the Deep* (tr. 1973).

Skinner, Burrhus Frederic, 1904–, American psychologist, b. Susquehanna, Pa. He received his Ph.D. from Harvard in 1931 and remained there as an instructor before moving to the Univ. of Minnesota (1937–45) and to Indiana Univ., where he was chairman of the psychology department (1945–48). He returned to Harvard in 1948, becoming the Edgar Pierce Professor of Psychology in 1958. Skinner is the leading exponent of the school of psychology known as BEHAVIORISM, which explains human behavior in terms of physiological responses of the organism to external stimuli. Like other behaviorists, he rejects the unobservable and concerns himself only with patterns of responses to rewards and stimuli. He has done extensive research with animals, notably rats and pigeons, and with electronic devices to support his theories. He has achieved examples of unusual learned behavior in animals by using the reward technique, applied also to human learning in another Skinner invention, the teaching machine. Such machines, and accompanying programmed instruction, have profoundly affected educational theories and methods in the United States. Skinner's more well-known published works include *The Behavior of Organisms* (1938), *Science and Human Behavior* (1953), *Verbal Behavior* (1957), *Walden Two* (1961), *Beyond Freedom and Dignity* (1971), and *About Behaviorism* (1974). See his *Cumulative Record* (3d ed. 1972); studies by R. I. Evans (1968) and Finley Carpenter (1974).

Skinner, Otis, 1858–1942, American actor, b. Cambridge, Mass. Skinner made his New York debut in 1879. After years as supporting player to Booth and Barrett, he toured with Augustin Daly and later with Modjeska. Enjoying a long and varied career, he won lasting fame in *Kismet* (1911). Skinner wrote extensively about the theater. *The Last Tragedian* (1939) contains his selections from Booth's correspondence. See his *Footlights and Spotlights* (1924, repr. 1972) and *Mad Folk of the Theatre* (1928). His daughter, **Cornelia Otis Skinner,** 1901–, American actress and author, b. Chicago, first appeared in her father's company in 1921. She has won fame for her one-woman shows and original monologues. She wrote *Our Hearts Were Young and Gay* (with Emily Kimbrough, 1942), the autobiographical *Family Circle* (1948), *Elegant Wits and Grand Horizontals* (1962), and *Madame Sarah* (1967), a biography of Bernhardt.

skipjack: see HERRING.

skipper: see BUTTERFLY.

Skíros (skē'rôs) or **Scyros** (sī'rəs), island (1971 pop. 2,352), c.80 sq mi (210 sq km), E Greece, in the Aegean Sea, largest of the N SPORADES. It is a summer resort noted for its fine beaches and grottoes. Skíros is also known for the furniture designed by local craftsmen. Wheat, figs, and olives are grown there; chromite and iron ore are mined; and fishing and sponge diving are important occupations. In ancient legend Thetis concealed her son Achilles on Skíros; Neoptolemus, son of Achilles by Deidamia, was reared on the island; and Theseus was killed by Lycomedes there. Skíros was conquered c.469 B.C. by Athenians led by Cimon. The English poet Rupert Brooke, who died (1915) during the Gallipoli campaign of World War I, is buried on Skíros.

Skive (skē'və), city (1970 com. pop. 25,530), Viborg co., N Denmark, on the Limfjord at the mouth of the Skive River. It is a commercial center and a tourist resort. Nearby is Spøttrup castle (14th cent.).

Skobelev, Mikhail Dmitreyevich (mēkhəyĕl' dəmē'trēəvĭch skô'bĭlyĭf), 1843–82, Russian general, one of the military commanders responsible for the Russian conquests in Turkistan. He took part in the expedition (1873) to Khiva and led the expedition to Kokand in 1875–76. He was appointed governor of the Khanate of Kokand, which the Russians renamed Fergana. Skobelev distinguished himself in the Russo-Turkish War of 1877–78, and in 1881 he led the spectacular march to Geok-Tepe, which completed the conquest of Russian Turkistan.

Skobelev: see FERGANA, USSR.

Skokie (skō'kē), village (1970 pop. 68,627), Cook co., NE Ill., an industrial suburb adjacent to Chicago; inc. 1888. Its many varied products include communications and electrical equipment and pharmaceuticals. Hebrew Theological College is there.

Skopje (skôp'yə) or **Skoplje** (skôp'əlyə), city (1971 pop. 387,889), capital of Yugoslav Macedonia, S Yugoslavia, on the Vardar River. It is an important transportation and trade center as well as an industrial hub where metals, textiles, and glass are produced. The city is also the see of an Orthodox Eastern metropolitan and the seat of a Macedonian university (founded 1946). Dating from Roman times, Skopje was captured by the Serbs in 1282 and was the scene (1346) of Stephen Dušan's coronation as czar of Serbia. It fell to the Turks in 1392 and until the fall of Constantinople (1453) was considered the second city of Turkey. Skopje was taken by the Serbs in the Balkan Wars of 1912–13 and was included in Yugoslavia in 1918. Among the many ancient landmarks of the city are the Stephen Dušan bridge across the Vardar (said to date from Roman times and rebuilt in the 15th cent.), the Turkish citadel, the fine Mosques of Mustafa Pasha and of Sultan Murad (both 15th cent.), and the Oriental bazaar. Much of the city had to be rebuilt after a disastrous earthquake in 1963.

Skoplje: see SKOPJE, Yugoslavia.

Skövde (sköv'də), city (1970 pop. 26,397), Skaraborg co., S Sweden, midway between lakes Vänern and Vättern. During the Middle Ages many pilgrims visited the shrine of St. Elin (Helen) of Skövde, a local woman canonized in 1164. Not far from the city is the Gothic church of the former Cistercian monastery of Varnhem, where several Swedish kings are buried.

Skram, Amalie (ämä'lēə skräm), 1847–1905, Norwegian writer. In Denmark, where she lived most of her life, Skram wrote *Constance Ring* (1885), her first major novel. It was followed by the series of novels entitled *Hellemyrsfolket* [the people of Hellemyr] (4 vol., 1887–98), the play *Agnete* (1893), and the collection of short stories *Julehelg* [Christmas] (1900). Skram's works, written in a naturalistic style and pessimistic in tone, are often concerned with the problems of women.

Skriabin, Aleksandr Nikolayevich: see SCRIABIN.

skua: see JAEGER.

skull, the skeletal structure of the head, composed of the facial and cranial bones. The skull houses and protects the brain and the chief sense organs; i.e.,

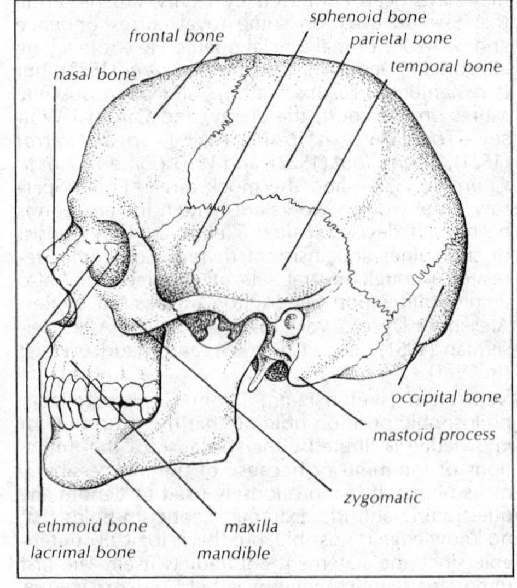

Bones of skull

the eyes, ears, nose, mouth, and tongue. In man, some 14 bones shape the face, most occurring in symmetrical pairs. They are the lacrimals at the inner sides of the eyes, the nasals and nasal conchae (nose), the palatines (palate), the zygomatics, or malars (cheeks), the vomer (nasal septum), the maxillae (upper jaw), and the mandible (lower jaw). The adult human cranium, or braincase, is formed of fused skull bones: the parietals, temporals, ethmoid, sphenoid, frontal, and occipital. These are separate plates of bone in the fetus, but by birth they have grown sufficiently for most of their edges to meet. The remaining separations are known as fontanels, the most prominent being the soft spot atop a newborn's head. By the age of two years, all the fontanels have been closed over by the growing cranial bones. However, the seams (sutures) between the bones do not completely knit until the age of 20. The occipital bone at the base of the skull forms a complex joint with the first vertebra (atlas) of the neck, permitting rotation and bending of the head (see SPINAL COLUMN). Study of the fossil skulls of man and of man's precursors has made important contributions to evolutionary theory and to the science of anthropology.

skunk, name for several related New World mammals of the WEASEL family, characterized by their conspicuous black and white markings and use of a strong, highly offensive odor for defense. The scent glands of skunks produce an oily, yellowish liquid, which the animal squirts with great force from vents under the tail; this produces a fine mist which, in addition to stinking, causes choking and tearing of the eyes. Skunks do not make use of this weapon unless severely provoked and then only after raising the tail in a warning display. Most animals quickly learn to recognize and avoid skunks, which are consequently quite fearless and move about openly. The two common skunks of the United States, the striped skunk and the spotted skunk, are nocturnal animals; their diets include rodents, insects, eggs, carrion, and vegetable matter. They live, often several individuals or families together, in dens made in abandoned burrows or buildings or in rock piles. Most familiar is the striped skunk, *Mephitis mephitis*, of the United States, N Mexico, and Canada S of Hudson Bay. It has thick black fur, usually with two white stripes on the back. It is 13 to 18 in. (33–46 cm) long, excluding the bushy tail (7–10 in./18–25 cm), and weighs 6 to 14 lb (2.7–6.4 kg). Because it destroys pests, it is protected in many states. In northern parts of their range the animals sleep through much of the winter, but they do not truly hibernate and may emerge during warm spells. The small, slender, spotted skunk, *Spilogale putorius*, has several irregular white stripes or lines of spots. It inhabits Mexico and the W, S, and central United States. Its combined head and body length is 9 to 13 in. (23–33 cm) and the tail is 4 to 9 in. (10–23 cm) long. This skunk balances on its front paws as part of its warning display. Central and South American skunks, species of the genus *Conepatus*, have white backs and tails and black underparts. Good diggers with large claws, they root in the ground for food. One species, the hognose skunk (*Conepatus leuconotus*), ranges as far north as the SW United States. Skunk fur, especially that of the striped skunk, is much used for coat trimmings. The animals are sometimes kept as pets, usually after having the scent glands removed. Skunks are classified in the phylum CHORDATA, subphylum Vertebrata, class Mammalia, order Carnivora, family Mustelidae.

skunk cabbage: see ARUM.

sky, apparent dome over the earth, background of the clouds, sun, moon, and stars. The blue color of the clear daytime sky results from the selective scattering of light rays by the minute particles of dust and vapor in the earth's ATMOSPHERE. The rays with longer wavelengths (the reds and yellows) pass through most readily, whereas the shorter rays (the blues) are scattered. An excess of dust, especially in large particles, causes scattering of many rays besides the blue, and the sky "fades" and becomes whitish or hazy. The sky thus is clearest in winter, in the morning, after a rain, over a mountain, or over the ocean. Leonardo da Vinci experimented with light and attempted an explanation of the sky's blue color. The work on light and its behavior by Sir Isaac Newton, Lord Rayleigh, and other physicists provided explanations of rainbows, sky color, mirages, and other atmospheric phenomena.

sky diving, sport of descending by parachute from an airplane or similar craft. Engaged in for both recreational and competitive purposes, sky diving involves three phases of activity: the free fall, the descent with open parachute, and the landing. In competitive sky diving, participants are judged according to their style in free fall and their accuracy in landing near a designated point. During the descent, divers can control the accuracy of their landing by manipulating the open parachute as a type of sail; skilled parachutists with good equipment can travel horizontally up to 10 mi (16 km) per hr during a normal fall. For reasons of safety, sky divers are required to open their parachutes at about 2,200 ft (670 m). Sky diving became a competitive sport after World War II. In 1951 the Fédération Aéronautique Internationale (founded 1905), the world organizing body for most aeronautic sports, sponsored the first world championship of sky diving. In the United States the U.S. Parachute Association (founded 1957) sponsors an annual national championship. See Ray Darby, *Space Age Sport* (1964).

Skye (skī), island (1971 pop. 7,372), 670 sq mi (1,735 sq km), one of the Inner Hebrides, Inverness-shire, NW Scotland. It has an irregular coastline, and many of its lochs are rimmed by lofty, sheer precipices. The Cuillin Hills rise to more than 3,000 ft (910 m). Only a small part of the island is arable. Sheep and cattle raising, crofting, wool weaving, whiskey distilling, and fishing are the chief industries; diatomite is mined in the northeastern region. The climate is mild, and Skye is a resort despite its heavy rainfall. Portree, on the east coast, is the leading town. Gaelic is spoken. At Dunvegan, on the west coast, is the castle of the Macleod clan. At the north end of the island are the ruins of Duntulm Castle, belonging to the rival clan, the Macdonalds. Skye has many associations with Prince Charles Edward Stuart, who took refuge there after his defeat at Culloden Moor in 1746. Flora Macdonald, who aided Charles's escape, is buried in Kilmuir, near Dunvegan.

Skye terrier, breed of sturdy, short-legged TERRIER developed in the northwestern islands of Scotland more than four centuries ago. It takes its name from the principal island in the group. The Skye terrier stands about 10 in. (25 cm) high at the shoulder and weighs about 25 lb (11 kg). Its double coat consists of a short, close-lying, woolly underlayer and a profuse, straight-hanging, flat topcoat about 5½ in. (14 cm) long. It may be black, blue, gray, fawn, or cream in color. Bred originally to hunt small game both on land and in the water, the Skye later became a favorite at the English court. Today it is raised as a pet. See DOG.

skylark, common name for a passerine songbird (*Alauda arvensis*) famous for the soaring, melodious flight of the courting male. Found in Europe (except in the Mediterranean area), it is 7¼ in. (18.2 cm) long, brown streaked with black above, and streaked buff-white below. Skylarks were a table delicacy in Europe. Attempts to introduce the bird into North America have failed, except on Vancouver Island. Skylarks are classified in the phylum CHORDATA, subphylum Vertebrata, class Aves, order Passeriformes, family Alaudidae.

skyscraper, modern building of great height, constructed on a steel skeleton. The form originated in the United States, and many mechanical and structural developments in the last quarter of the 19th cent. contributed to its evolution. In 1887 the first electric elevator was installed, and with the eventual perfecting of high-speed electric elevators skyscrapers were free to attain any desired height. The earliest tall buildings were of solid masonry construction, with the thick walls of the lower stories usurping a disproportionate amount of floor space. In order to permit thinner walls through the entire height of the building, architects began to use cast iron in conjunction with masonry. This was followed by cage construction, in which the iron frame supported the floors and the masonry walls bore their own weight. The next step was the invention of a system in which the metal framework would support not only the floors but also the walls. This innovation appeared in the Home Insurance Building in Chicago, designed in 1883 by William Le Baron Jenny—the first building in the world to employ steel skeleton construction and embody the general characteristics of a modern skyscraper. The subsequent erection in Chicago of a number of similar buildings made it the center of the early skyscraper industry. In the 1890s the steel frame was formed into a completely riveted skeleton bearing all the structural loads, with the exterior or thin curtain walls serving merely as an enclosing screen. In 1892 the New York Building Law made its first provisions for skeleton constructions. There followed a period of experimentation to devise efficient floor plans and aesthetically satisfying forms. In New York City the Flatiron Building was constructed in 1902, the Metropolitan Life Insurance Tower in 1909, and the Woolworth Building, 60 stories high, by Cass Gilbert, in 1913. The last, with Gothic ornamentation, exemplifies the general tendency at that time to adapt earlier architectural styles to modern construction. The radical innovator Louis Sullivan gave impulse to a new aesthetic for skyscrapers, emphasizing their underlying structure and fenestration. An excellent example is his design for the Carson, Pirie, Scott building (1899–1904) in Chicago. In 1916, New York City adopted the Building Zone Resolution, establishing legal control over the height and plan of buildings and over the factors relating to health, fire hazard, and assurance of adequate light and air to buildings and streets. Regulations regarding the setting back of exterior walls above a determined height gave rise to buildings whose stepped profiles characterize the contemporary American skyscraper. With the complex structural and planning problems solved, architects still seek solutions to the difficulties of integrating skyscrapers with community requirements of hygiene, transportation, and commercial interest. The proper placing and regulating of such structures has become of prime importance in modern CITY PLANNING. The tallest skyscraper now in use is the Sears Tower in Chicago; its 110 stories rise 1,454 ft (473 m) with an additional 350 ft (107 m) for the television antenna on top. Among the highest New York skyscrapers are the World Trade Center, which has two unstepped, rectangular towers of 110 stories, 1,350 ft (442 m) each; the Empire State, with 102 stories, 1,250 ft (412 m) high, or 1,472 ft (479 m) high including the television mast; Chrysler, with 77 stories, 1,046 ft (349 m) high; RCA in Rockefeller Center, with 70 stories, 850 ft (259 m) high; and 60 Wall Tower, with 67 stories, 950 ft (290 m) high. Of the above examples only Rockefeller Center was planned to achieve an overall unity of design. Plazas and open spaces were arranged so that light and air would not be blocked. In New York during the 1950s public plazas were incorporated into the designs of the Lever House by Gordon Bunshaft and the Seagram Building of Miës van der Rohe. These buildings are also examples of the effective use of vast expanses of glass in skyscrapers. See C. W. Condit, *The Rise of the Skyscraper* (1952); Earle Shultz, *Offices in the Sky* (1959); Hans Aregger, *Highrise Building and Urban Design* (tr. 1967).

skywriting, advertising medium in which aircraft spell out trade names and sales slogans in the sky by means of the controlled emission of thick smoke. The technique was first developed (1922) by J. C. Savage, a pioneer English aviator. Letters a mile high and a mile wide can be formed by the movements of specially built planes equipped with the smoke-emitting apparatus. Engine heat is used to turn specially treated paraffin oil into white smoke, which is discharged under pressure. The "writing" is done at heights of 10,000 to 17,000 ft (3,048–5,182 m) and is feasible only in cloudless skies in which there is no more than a moderate wind. Contracts are commonly made for skywriting over a designated place, e.g., a racetrack, fair, bathing beach, or carnival, and for a specified day and time. Skytyping, the name given to a more modern form of skywriting, involves the use of five to seven planes. They fly rigidly parallel and equidistant courses as nearly in perfect unison as possible. The message to be written is arranged on a master control panel, and as the planes fly abreast electronic signals cause the smoke-emission mechanism in each plane to release puffs of smoke accordingly.

Slade, Felix, 1790–1868, English art collector and philanthropist. He endowed the Slade professorships of fine arts at Oxford and Cambridge universities and at University College, London, which also received six Slade scholarships in art. His fine collections of glass, books, and engravings were given to the British Museum.

Sládek, Joseph Václav (yô'zĕf väts'läf slä'dĕk), 1845–1912, Czech poet and translator. He lived in the United States from 1868 to 1870. Sládek later taught English in Prague and translated much English and American poetry into Czech, including 32 of Shakespeare's plays. His own lyrics are highly personal and are written in the style of folk poetry. His verses are varied, including short, whimsical creations, poems of personal sorrow, and patriotic works. His major collections include *Básně* [poems] (1875) and *Sluncem a stínem* [in sun and shade] (1887).

slag: see METALLURGY.

Slagelse (slä'yəlsə), city (1970 com. pop. 32,332), Vestsjaelland co., S central Denmark. It is an industrial center and a rail junction. The city has an 11th-century church, and nearby is Traelleborg, a Viking fortress.

slaked lime: see CALCIUM HYDROXIDE.

slander: see LIBEL AND SLANDER.

slang, vernacular vocabulary not generally acceptable in formal usage. It is notable for its liveliness, humor, emphasis, brevity, novelty, and exaggeration. Most slang is faddish and ephemeral, but some words are retained for long periods and eventually become part of the standard language (e.g., phony, blizzard, movie). On the scale used to indicate a word's status in the language, slang ranks third behind standard and colloquial (or informal) and before cant. Slang often conveys an acerbic, even offensive, no-nonsense attitude and lends itself to poking fun at pretentiousness. Frequently grotesque and fantastic, it is usually spoken with intent to produce a startling or original effect. It is especially well developed in the speaking vocabularies of cultured, sophisticated, linguistically rich languages. Characteristically individual, slang often incorporates elements of the jargons of special-interest groups (e.g., professional, sport, regional, criminal, and drug subcultures). Slang is very old, and the reasons for its development have been much investigated. American slang has several distinct peculiarities: It contains more words of a regional nature and more foreign words than the slang of other countries; the vogue for a particular word or phrase is of shorter duration; and slang words and phrases evolve more quickly in the United States than elsewhere. The following list is a small sample of American slang descriptive of a broad range of subjects: of madness—bananas, bughouse, loony, screwy, nuts; of crime—heist, gat, heat, grifter; of women—chick, quail, tomato, frail, skirt; of drunken people—sloshed, plastered, ossified, stewed, looped, smashed; of drugs—speed, bummer, tripping, downer, freak-out; of caressing—spoon, neck, make out, pet; of states of mind—cool, uptight, wired, hip, mellow; of money—lettuce, dough, bread, bucks; the verb *to go*—scat, scram, split, skeedaddle, scoot, vamoose; miscellaneous phrases—not my *scene, get it together,* can you *dig where I'm at,* does his *number, do* her *thing,* what's his *story,* he *grooves on* it, I'm not *into* that. See H. L. Mencken, *The American Language* (3 vol., 1936–48); Harold Wentworth and Stuart Flexner, *Dictionary of American Slang* (1967); Eric Partridge, *A Dictionary of Slang and Unconventional English* (7th ed., 2 vol., 1970).

slash pine: see PINE.

slate, fine-grained ROCK formed when sedimentary rocks such as SHALE are metamorphosed by great pressure. Slate splits into perfectly cleaved, broad thin layers; this characteristically regular and planar cleavage is called slaty cleavage. In the formation of slate, pressure causes the flaky minerals within the sedimentary rock, such as mica, clay, and chlorite, to be reoriented; the flat faces of the minerals lie at right angles to the source of the pressure, and the planes of easy cleavage are also at right angles to the source of the pressure. The rock is not necessarily compressed in the same direction as the sedimentary layers were originally laid down, and because the compression crumples and deforms the original sedimentary layers, the planes of slaty cleavage usually cut through the old bedding planes. Slate is intermediate in hardness between mica SCHISTS and shale; the better grades are used for roofing. Its characteristic color is gray-blue. Slate is mined in Maine, Vermont, Pennsylvania, Georgia, Lake Superior, and the Rocky Mts.

Slater, Samuel, 1768–1835, American pioneer in the cotton textile industry, b. Derbyshire, England. As an apprentice and later a mill supervisor, he gained a thorough knowledge of all the cotton-manufacturing machinery then in use. Drawn by the bounties offered for the encouragement of the textile industry in America, he left England in disguise, since the emigration of textile workers was forbidden, and reached New York in 1789. In 1790 he went to Providence, R.I., where he met Moses BROWN and contracted to reproduce the complicated machinery for the firm of Almy and Brown, to which his name was soon added. This he accomplished by a remarkable feat of memory, because all attempts to obtain English models, by purchase or smuggling, had been futile. The first mill was replaced by another in 1793, at nearby Pawtucket. In 1798 he formed an additional partnership, with his relatives by marriage, called Samuel Slater and Company, and built another mill near Pawtucket, R.I. He later established mills at Slatersville (now in the town of North Smithfield), R.I., and elsewhere in New England, becoming very prosperous. He exercised strict but paternal supervision over his employees. See biographies by G. S. White (1836, repr. 1967) and E. H. Cameron (1960); W. R. Bagnall, *Samuel Slater and the Early Development of Cotton Manufacture in the United States* (1890).

Slatin, Rudolf Carl, Freiherr von (rōō'dôlf kärl frī'hĕr fən slä'tĭn), known as **Slatin Pasha** (pä'shä), 1857–1932, Austrian adventurer in British and Egyptian service. Called to Egypt by C. G. Gordon, Slatin became governor of Dara (1879) and governor general of Darfur (1881). In the Mahdist War he was forced to surrender (1883) to the Arab leader, the Mahdi Muhammad Ahmad; he was a prisoner until 1895, when he escaped to Cairo. After serving under Kitchener in the reconquest of the Sudan, he became inspector general of the Sudan (1900–1914). During World War I he headed the prisoners-of-war section of the Austrian Red Cross. He wrote *Fire and Sword in the Sudan* (tr. 1897) and was ennobled by the Austrian emperor in 1906. See biographies by Richard Hill (1965) and Gordon Brook-Shepherd (1973).

slaughterhouse: see ABATTOIR; MEAT-PACKING.

Slaughterhouse Cases, cases decided by the U.S. Supreme Court in 1873. In 1869 the Louisiana legislature granted a 25-year monopoly to a slaughterhouse concern in New Orleans for the stated purpose of protecting the people's health. Other slaughterhouse operators thus barred from their trade brought suit, principally on the ground that they had been deprived of their property without due process of law in violation of the FOURTEENTH AMENDMENT. The U.S. Supreme Court, with Justice Samuel F. Miller rendering the majority decision, decided against the slaughterhouse operators. It held that the Fourteenth Amendment had to be considered in connection with the original purpose of its framers, i.e., to guarantee the freedom of former Negro slaves. Although the amendment could not be construed to refer only to Negro slavery, its scope as originally planned did not include rights such as those in question. A distinction was drawn between citizenship of the United States and citizenship of a state, and it was held that the amendment did not intend to deprive the state of its legal jurisdiction over the civil rights of its citizens. The restraint placed by the Louisiana legislators on the slaughterhouse operators was declared not to deprive them of their property without due process. The decision was a conservative one, since it declared the police power of states intact and did not extend Federal power.

Slave, river, c.310 mi (500 km) long, S Mackenzie dist., Northwest Territories, Canada. It comprises the middle sections of the Mackenzie River system. The river channels the waters of Lake Athabasca and the Peace River into Great Slave Lake at Fort Resolution. It is navigable for steamers except for the rapids between Fort Fitzgerald and Fort Smith, where it breaks through the Cariboo Hills. There is a wagon road portage (16 mi/26 km long) around the rapids.

Slave Coast, name given by European traders to the coast bordering the Bight of Benin on the Gulf of Guinea, W Africa. It was the principal source of slaves from W Africa from the 16th cent. to the mid-19th cent.

Slave dynasty: see DELHI SULTANATE.

slavery, institution based on a relationship of dominance and submission, whereby one person owns another and can exact from that person labor or other services. Slavery has been found among many groups of low material culture, as in the Malay Peninsula and among some North American Indians; it also flourished in more highly developed societies, such as the Southern United States. Although it is commonly held that slavery was rare among primitive pastoral peoples and that it appeared in full form only with the development of an agricultural economy, there are numerous instances that contradict this belief. Domestic slavery and sometimes concubine slavery appeared among the nomadic Arabs, among North American Indians primarily devoted to hunting, and among the seafaring Vikings. Some ascribe the beginnings of slavery to war and the consequent subjection of one group by another. Slavery as a result of debt, however, existed in very early times, and some African peoples have had the custom of putting up wives and children as hostages for an obligation; if the obligation was unfulfilled, the hostages became permanent slaves.

Slavery in the Ancient World. The institution of slavery extends back beyond recorded history. References to it appear in the ancient Babylonian code of Hammurabi. Its form and nature varied greatly in ancient society. It seems to have been common in the Tigris-Euphrates civilizations and in ancient Persia. In ancient Egypt slave labor was used in building temples and pyramids. The institution was familiar to the ancient Hebrews, according to passages in the Bible. Slavery was an established institution in the Greece of Homer's time, and a large portion of the population of the Greek city-states in later days were of the servile class. There were domestic slaves, agricultural slaves, and artisans and workmen. In Greece, although not quite as commonly as in Asia Minor, there were also public slaves, for example, those belonging to the temples. In general it is thought that slaves in the Greek city-states were relatively well treated, and there were laws protecting them against excessive cruelty or abuse. However, the slaves were regarded as property and had no rights in courts of law. Slaves could obtain their freedom by buying it, by being granted it in the owner's will, or as a reward for outstanding service. Slavery in early Roman history seems to have been of the same type as in Greece, but by the 1st cent. B.C., as the Roman Empire continued to expand, a form of agricultural slavery called estate slavery was introduced on a wide scale; in this form agriculture was pursued by large numbers of slaves in an impersonal relationship with the landowner, who had practically absolute power over them. The increasing wealth of Rome led to an expansion in domestic slaves, and the servile class grew to great numbers. They were employed in the theater, in gladiatorial combats, and, to some extent, in prostitution. Most of the slaves were foreign, and some were highly educated and were employed as instructors. Having a large retinue of slaves became one of the prime marks of luxury, and exotic, especially Oriental, slaves were in great demand. As the number of conquered provinces grew, so did the slave supply. With this increased supply of slaves, manumission (emancipation from slavery) was common, and freedmen became a significant factor in the Roman social system. The slave had almost no legal status, although custom mitigated against extreme forms of brutality; the slave could testify against his master only in a very limited number of serious crimes (adultery, incest, and, later, lese majesty). As the Roman expansion abated, conditions of slavery improved somewhat.

Slavery after the Fall of the Roman Empire. The introduction of Christianity toward the end of the Roman Empire had no effect on the abolition of slavery, since the church at that time did not oppose the institution. However, a change in economic life set in and resulted in the gradual disappearance of the agricultural slaves, who became, for all practical purposes, one with the coloni (tenant farmers who were technically free but were in fact bound to the land by debts). This process helped prepare the way for an economy in which the agricultural slave became the serf. The semifreedom of serfdom was the dominant theme in the Middle Ages, although domestic slavery (and, to some extent, other forms) did not disappear. The church began to encourage manumission, while ignoring the fact that many slaves were attached to churchmen and church property. Sale into slavery continued to be an extreme punishment for serious crimes. Slavery flourished in the Byzantine Empire, and the pirates of the Mediterranean continued their custom of enslaving the victims of their raids. Islam, like Christianity, accepted slavery, and it became a standard institution in Muslim lands. One form of Muslim slavery was in the EUNUCH guardians of the harems; eunuchs had been widely known in Grecian, Roman, and especially Byzantine times, but it was among the Muslims and in the Orient that they were to survive longest. In Western Europe slavery had largely disappeared by the later Middle Ages, although it still remained in such manifestations as the use of slaves on galleys. In Russia slavery persisted longer than in Western Europe, and indeed the serfs were pushed into the classification of slavery by Peter the Great.

Modern Slavery. A revolution in the institution of slavery came in the 15th and 16th cent. The explorations of the African coast by Portuguese navigators resulted in the exploitation of the African as a slave, and for nearly five centuries the predations of slave raiders along the coasts of Africa were to be a lucrative and important business conducted with appalling brutality. The British, Dutch, French, Spanish, and Portuguese all engaged in the African slave trade. Although Africans were, as early as 1440, brought back to Portugal, and although subsequent importations were large enough to change distinctly the ethnography of that country, it was not in Europe that African slavery was to be most profitable and widespread, but in the Americas, where European exploitation began at the end of the 15th cent. The first people to be enslaved by the Spanish and Portuguese in the West Indies and Latin America were the native Indians, but, because the majority of Indian slaves either revolted or escaped, other forms of forced labor, akin to serfdom, were introduced (see REPARTIMIENTO and ENCOMIENDA). The resistance of the Indians to slavery only increased the demand for Africans to replace them. Africans proved to be profitable laborers in the Caribbean islands and the lowlands of the South American mainland. In the colder highlands Indian slavery or quasi-slavery continued; long after the introduction of the first Africans the paulistas (inhabitants of the city and state of São Paulo, Brazil) continued their slave raids against the Indians of the Brazilian hinterlands. But African slavery gradually became dominant. African slaves were introduced to the British settlements on the Atlantic coast with the arrival of the first shipload in Virginia in 1619. The raising of staple crops—coffee, tobacco, sugar, rice, and, much later, cotton—and the plantation economy made the importation of slaves from Africa particularly valuable in the Southern colonies of North America. The slave trade moved in a triangle; setting out from British ports, ships would transport various goods to the western coast of Africa, where they would be exchanged for slaves. The slaves were then brought to the West Indies or to the colonies of North or South America, where they were traded for agricultural staples for the return voyage back to England. Later, New England ports were included in this last leg. The number of slaves in the colonies increased until in some (notably French Saint-Domingue, the modern HAITI) they constituted a majority of the population.

The Antislavery movement. The growth of humanitarian feeling during the Age of Enlightenment in the 18th cent., the spread of the ideas of Jean Jacques Rousseau and others, and the increase of democratic sentiment led to a growing attack on the slave trade. The French Revolution had a great effect not only in the spread of agitation for human rights but more directly in the uprisings in Saint-Domingue and the establishment of Haitian independence. The movement for the abolition of slavery, despite the existence of pockets of antislavery sentiment, did not have much popular support in the United States during the 18th and the first half of the 19th cent. The slave trade was not prohibited until 20 years after the Constitution was ratified. British humanitarians who had incorporated the abolition of slavery into their conception of Christianity labored successfully to outlaw (1807) the British slave trade. These same men, especially William WILBERFORCE, Thomas CLARKSON, Zachary Macaulay, and Lord Brougham (Henry Peter BROUGHAM), continued to work for the abolition of slavery throughout the British Empire, which was finally effected with the Abolition Act of 1833. However, according to some writers, the British, in abolishing slavery, were primarily motivated by economic, not humanitarian, interests. These critics argued that, while the institution produced great wealth under the mercantilist system, it became unprofitable with the rise of industrial capitalism, which displaced mercantilism early in the 19th cent. At any rate, the abolition legislation of 1833 was followed by the gradual abolition of slavery in all lands under British control, principally by the device of invalidating the legality of slavery and removing its legal safeguards, usually by recompensing the owners. As the South American nations gained independence they broadened their democratic principles to include absolute prohibition of slavery (Argentina in 1813, Colombia in 1821, and Mexico in 1829). In the United States, slavery had proved unprofitable in the Northern states and by the early 19th cent. had disappeared. Its abolition had been hastened by the work of the Quakers, who, as in Great Britain, were staunchly opposed to slavery. In the South, however, slavery came to be an integral part of the plantation system (especially after the introduction of the cotton gin in 1793). While the institution of slavery tended in North America to reinforce feelings of racial superiority on the part of the whites, some writers have argued that the treatment of slaves there was more humane than it was in the Catholic or Latin countries. Others have countered that the opposite is true, i.e., that the clergy in the Latin countries took a greater interest in the welfare of the slaves; that there was less race prejudice among the Portuguese and Spanish; and, finally, that the Latin colonies were more closely tied to their colonizing countries in Europe, thus allowing more control over the plantation owners vis-à-vis the slaves. In the Northern United States, humanitarian principles led to the appearance of the ABOLITIONISTS. They knew little of the actual conditions in the South and were fighting not for economic reform but for idealistic principles. The abolitionists in general tended to regard slavery as an unmitigated evil. The small Northern farmer also feared slavery as a system of cheap labor against which it was difficult to compete. The South, eager to conserve the status quo, developed a bellicose defense of the system, which was hardened by such factors as the slave uprising led by Nat TURNER, the troubles over fugitive slaves, and the very active propaganda against the South. The question, involving the very existence of Southern society as then organized, was the dominant one in U.S. history from 1830 to 1860. The political expression of the struggle was largely an attempt on the part of the South to maintain legislative guarantees of the system against the efforts of the abolitionists. The chief question concerned the right of extension of slavery in the Western territories. This first became important in 1820 with the Missouri Compromise. Many leading statesmen of the time sought an answer: Henry CLAY, the great compromiser; Daniel WEBSTER; John C. CALHOUN; Stephen A. DOUGLAS, who proposed squatter sovereignty (see POPULAR SOVEREIGNTY) to decide the free or slave status of territories; and the uncompromising antislavery men, such as Charles SUMNER and William H. SEWARD. The great compromises—the MISSOURI COMPROMISE, the COMPROMISE OF 1850, and the KANSAS-NEBRASKA ACT—were ultimately ineffective. Sectional opposition, which involved even broader questions than slavery, including the constitutional issue of STATES' RIGHTS, grew more passionate as the two sections became more and more hostile. The OSTEND MANIFESTO and the proposed annexation of Cuba, the FUGITIVE SLAVE LAWS, the operations of the UNDERGROUND RAILROAD, the furor caused by the DRED SCOTT CASE, the WILMOT PROVISO—all heightened the tension. Sporadic armed conflict erupted in Kansas and in the Harpers Ferry raid of John BROWN. The struggle became more clearly defined as the Republican party was formed with a definite antislavery platform. In the victory of the Republican presidential candidate, Abraham Lincoln (1860), the South saw a threat to Southern institutions, and the Southern states in an effort to secure those institutions resorted to SECESSION and formed the Confederacy. The Civil War followed, and the victory of the North brought an end to slavery in the United States. Lincoln's EMANCIPATION PROCLAMATION (issued in 1863, it declared all slaves in the Southern secessionist states free) was followed by other legislation, especially the Thirteenth Amendment to the Constitution. In other countries emancipation of slaves was also a serious problem, but never to such an extent as in the United States, chiefly perhaps because the question of race prejudice was nowhere else so important. In BRAZIL the opposition of the planters to abolishing slavery was strong, and it was only after a series of rather ineffective measures that the slaves were emancipated in 1888. Opposition to that action helped to launch the revolution of 1889. In later years the slave trade was conducted on the east coast of Africa, the market being in Muslim lands. Most antislavery efforts during the 19th cent. were directed against slave trading. Great Britain had passed antislave-trade laws in 1807 and 1811; the British attempted to enlist other nations in an effort to stop the slave trade, and several treaties for such a purpose were signed in the 1840s. However the first important international agreement was not reached until the Berlin Conference in 1885, which bound the more important Muslim potentates to act against the slave traffic. This was supplemented by the even more significant Brussels Act of 1890, to which 18 states were signatory. The emperor of Abyssinia (Ethiopia) was unable to prevent traffic from that land to Arabia, and a rather brisk trade went on over the Red Sea. International scandals occurred from time to time with regard to forced labor; three notable ones concerned the Congo, LIBERIA, and the Putumayo region of Peru in the 1930s (Indian servitude). The League of Nations adopted the resolutions of the International Slavery Convention of 1926, which considered an advance over the Brussels Act of 1890; its main weakness was in not providing a permanent commission to oversee the total abolition of slavery. Slavery continued to exist in parts of Asia, the Middle East, and, despite increasingly successful efforts to abolish it, in various parts of Africa. The United Nations has continued the efforts of the League of Nations to achieve worldwide abolition of slavery. The Declaration of Human Rights, adopted by the General Assembly in 1948, contained a provision prohibiting slavery or trading in slaves. The Security Council in 1954 condemned systems of forced labor, particularly those employed as a means of political coercion. In 1956 a UN conference of plenipotentiaries adopted a convention on the abolition of slavery; an important aspect of the convention was the inclusion of other institutions similar to slavery as practices to be abolished. However a report prepared for the United Nations in 1966 charged that slavery still existed in parts of Africa and Asia. See W. E. B. Du Bois, *The Suppression of the African Slave-Trade to the United States of America, 1638-1870* (1896, repr. 1970); A. H. Abel, *The Slaveholding Indians* (3 vol., 1915-25, repr. 1970); Gustave Glotz, *Ancient Greece at Work: An Economic History of Greece from the Homeric Period to the Roman Conquest* (1926, repr. 1967); R. H. Barrow, *Slavery in the Roman Empire* (1928, repr. 1968); U. B. Phillips, *Life and Labor in the Old South* (1929, repr. 1963); W. L. Westermann, *Upon Slavery in Ptolemaic Egypt* (1929); M. W. Jernegan, *Laboring and Dependent Classes in Colonial America, 1607-1738* (1931, repr. 1965); W. L. Mathieson, *British Slavery and Its Abolition, 1823-1838* (1926, repr. 1967), *Great Britain and the Slave Trade, 1839-1865* (1929, repr. 1967), and *British Slave Emancipation, 1838-1849* (1932, repr. 1967); Elizabeth Donnan, ed., *Documents Illustrative of the History of the Slave Trade to America* (4 vol., 1930-35; repr. 1965); George MacMann, *Slavery through the Ages* (1938); Reginald Coupland, *The Exploitation of East Africa, 1856-1890: The Slave Trade and the Scramble* (1939, repr. 1968); I. E. Edwards, *Towards Emancipation: A Study in South African Slavery* (1942); Eric Williams, *Capitalism and Slavery* (1944, repr. 1964); Fisk Univ., Social Science Institute, *Unwritten History of Slavery: Autobiographical Account of Negro Ex-Slaves* (1945, repr. 1970); Gilberto Freyre, *The Masters and the Slaves: A Study in the Development of Brazilian Civilization* (tr. 1946; 2d ed. 1956, repr. 1963); Isaac Mendelsohn, *Slavery in the Ancient Near East* (1949); M. I. Rostovzeff, *The Social and Economic History of the Hellenistic World* (3 vol., 1941; repr. 1959) and *The Social and Economic History of the Roman Empire* (2 vol., 2d ed. 1957); C. W. W. Greenidge, *Slavery* (1958); M. I. Finley, ed., *Slavery in Classical Antiquity* (1960, repr. 1968); Sean O'Callaghan, *The Slave Trade Today* (1962); D. P. Mannix, *Black Cargoes: A History of the Atlantic Slave Trade, 1518-1865* (with Malcolm Cowley, 1962); Joel Williamson, *After Slavery* (1965); Mohamed Awad, *Report on Slavery* (1966); D. B. Davis, *The Problem of Slavery in Western Culture* (1966); Arthur Zilversmidt, *The First Emancipation: The Abolition of Slavery in the North* (1967); Allen Weinstein, ed., *American Negro Slavery: A Modern Reader* (1968); S. M. Elkins, *Slavery* (2d ed. 1968); Laura Foner and E. D. Genovese, ed., *Slavery in the New World* (1969); D. L. Robinson, *Slavery in the Structure of American Politics, 1765-1820* (1970); R. S. Starobin, *Industrial Slavery in the Old South* (1970); A. J. Lane, ed., *The Debate over Slavery* (1971); R. W. Winks, *Slavery: A Comparative Perspective* (1972); Robert Fogel and Stanley Engerman, *Time on the Cross: The Economics of American Negro Slavery* (1974); E. D. Genovese, *Roll Jordan Roll: The World the Slaves Made* (1974).

Slavic languages, also called Slavonic languages, a subfamily of the Indo-European family of languages. Because the Slavic group of languages seems to be closer to the Baltic group than to any other, some scholars combine the two in a Balto-Slavic subfamily of the Indo-European classification. All of the Slavic tongues are believed to have evolved from a single parent language, usually called Proto-Slavic, which, in turn, is thought to have split off much earlier (possibly c.2000 B.C.) from Proto-Indo-European, the original ancestor of the members of the Indo-European language family. Proto-Slavic was probably still common to all Slavs in the 1st cent. B.C., and possibly as late as the 8th or 9th cent. A.D., but by the 10th cent. A.D. the individual Slavic languages had begun to emerge. Today, for the most part, Slavic languages are spoken in E Europe and N Asia. The total number of people for whom a Slavic language is the mother tongue is estimated at more than 260 million; the great majority of them live in the USSR. The Slavic subfamily has three divisions: East Slavic, West Slavic, and South Slavic. Members of the East Slavic branch are Russian, or Great Russian; Ukrainian, also called Little Russian or Ruthenian; and Belorussian, or White Russian. Together they claim about 180 million speakers, almost all in the Soviet Union. The West Slavic branch includes Polish, Czech, Slovak, Lusatian, Kashubian, and the extinct Polabian. The living West Slavic languages can claim approximately 50 million speakers, chiefly in Poland and Czechoslovakia. The South Slavic tongues consist of Serbo-Croatian, Slovenian, Macedonian, and Bulgarian, together with the liturgical language known as Church Slavonic. The first four are native to some 25 million people, largely in Yugoslavia and Bulgaria. Grammatically the Slavic languages, with the exception of Bulgarian and Macedonian, have a highly developed inflection of the noun, with up to seven cases (nominative, genitive, dative, accusative, locative, instrumental, and vocative). The Slavic verb usually takes one of three simple tenses (past, present, and future), but it is further characterized by a complex feature called aspect, which can be either imperfective (showing continuous or repeated action) or perfective (denoting a completed action). Participles and gerunds are often employed where in English clauses would be used. The article is lacking in all Slavic languages except Bulgarian and Macedonian. Members of the Slavic subfamily are more conservative and thus closer to Proto-Indo-European than languages in the Germanic and Romance groups, as is witnessed by their preservation of seven of the eight cases for the noun that Proto-Indo-European possessed and by their continuation of aspects for the verb. The spoken Slavic tongues resemble one another more closely than do those of the Germanic and Romance groups; yet, although Slavic languages have much in common in basic vocabulary, grammar, and phonetic characteristics, they differ with regard to such features in many instances. One feature common to most of them is the relatively large number of consonant sounds, many of which have both palatal and nonpalatal forms. A striking instance showing divided usage is the varied position of the primary accent in the individual Slavic languages. For example, in Czech the stress falls on the initial syllable of a word and in Polish on the next-to-the-last syllable, whereas in Russian and Bulgarian the accent can fall on any syllable. It is in writing, perhaps, that the most dramatic difference occurs. Some Slavic languages (notably, Czech, Slovak, Slovenian, and Polish) are written in differing versions of the Roman alphabet because their speakers are predominantly Roman Catholic. Other Slavic languages (such as Russian, Ukrainian, Belorussian, Macedonian, and Bulgarian) use variations of the Cyrillic alphabet as a result of the influence of the Orthodox Eastern Church. The single language Serbo-Croatian is called Serbian when it is written by Serbs in the Cyrillic alphabet and Croatian when it is written by Croats in the Roman alphabet. The invention of the Cyrillic alphabet is ascribed traditionally to Cyril, a Greek missionary sent by Constantinople to the Slavic peoples in the 9th cent. A.D., although it may have been the work of his followers. The Cyrillic alphabet was augmented with signs based on the Greek alphabet, added to denote Slavic sounds not found in Greek. So far as is known, no writing in a Slavic language existed before the 9th cent. A.D.; the oldest Slavic texts to survive are in Old Church Slavonic and belong to the 10th and 11th cent. The vocabulary of the Slavic languages is substantially of Indo-European origin; there is an important Balto-Slavic element as well. Loan words or loan translations can be traced to the Iranian and Germanic groups and also to Greek, Latin, and Turkish. More recently, Italian and French have had some measure of influence. Slavic languages have also borrowed from each other. They tend, however, to translate and imitate foreign words rather than directly absorb them. See also the articles on many of the languages mentioned and INDO-EUROPEAN. See Roman Jakobson, *Slavic Languages* (2d ed. 1955); W. J. Entwistle and W. A. Morison, *Russian and the Slavonic Languages* (2d ed. 1964); R. G. de Bray, *Guide to Slavonic Languages* (rev. ed. 1969).

Slavic religion, pre-Christian religious practices among the Slavs of Eastern Europe. There is only fragmentary and scattered information about the myths and legends of the pagan Slavs, and it is not possible to trace the history of their religion or to reconstruct the whole Slavic pantheon. Nevertheless, there were certain common beliefs among most of the pre-Christian Slavs. It is generally thought that the earliest religious beliefs of the Slavs were based on the principle that the whole natural world is inhabited and directed by spirits or mysterious forces. Later, particularly in areas where the Slavs had a more organized cultural life and were integrated with foreign peoples, the spiritual beliefs became less rustic, and the vague spirits of nature were anthropomorphized into divinities with special powers and functions. The supreme god of the East and South Slavs was Perun, god of lightning and thunder. Because he controlled the elements of nature, his aid and protection were strongly evoked at seed time and harvest. Until the end of the 10th cent. an idol of Perun existed in Kiev. Svarog, a god known to most of the Slavic people, was regarded as the father of the chief Slavic deities. Among his sons were Dazhbog, god of the sun, and Svarazic, god of fire. Two important gods of Slavic religion were Byelobog (or Byelun) [the White God] and Chernobog [the Black God]. These two gods, who represented the opposing forces of good and evil, reflected the Slavic belief in the dualistic nature of the universe. Various myths and ritualistic data, however, reveal the cults of many other gods and lesser divinities, including the worship of earth goddesses. The Baltic Slavs had a particularly rich tradition and a highly organized religious life. Religious centers, with temples, oracles, and a hierarchy of priests were created under the influence of foreign religion, particularly Scandinavian. The gods of the Baltic Slavs were younger in origin than those of the other Slavs and were often created to serve political purposes. Possibly the most powerful cult of the Baltic Slavs was that of Radogost-Svarazic, whose worship held together many Obodrite tribes. When in the 12th cent. Retra fell, Arcona became the major political center, and its god Svantovit became the ruling Slavic god and the highest solar deity. With the coming of Christianity, the great divinities of the Slavs vanished in name, but many elements of pagan belief survived in popular tradition. Pagan rites became an integral part of the religious ceremonies of the Christian Slavs.

Slavkov u Brna, Czechoslovakia: see AUSTERLITZ.

Slavonia (slәvō'nēә), Serbo-Croatian *Slavonija,* historic region, N Yugoslavia, now part of Croatia. It is a fertile agricultural and forested lowland bounded, in part, by the Drava River in the north and the Sava River in the south. Wheat and corn are the major crops, and the leading industry is food processing. The population is largely Croatian and Serbian. OSIJEK is the chief city. The region was originally part of the Roman province of Pannonia. In the 7th cent. a Slavic state was established owing allegiance to the Avars. With Croatia, Slavonia was united with Hungary in 1102. It came under Turkish rule in the 16th cent. and was recovered by Hungary from the Turks through the Treaty of Karlowitz (1699). As a result of the Revolution of 1848, Hungary lost Slavonia, which was made an Austrian crownland, but in 1868, Slavonia was restored to the Hungarian crown; it was united with Croatia. It has been part of Yugoslavia since 1918.

Slavonic: see SLAVIC LANGUAGES.

Slavophiles and Westernizers, designation for two groups of intellectuals in mid-19th-century Russia that represented opposing schools of thought concerning the nature of Russian civilization. The differences between them, however, were not always clear cut. The Slavophiles held that Russian civilization was unique and superior to Western culture because it was based on such institutions as the Orthodox Eastern Church, the village community, or MIR, and the ancient popular assembly, the *zemsky sobor.* The Slavophiles supported autocracy and opposed political participation; however, they also favored emancipation of serfs and freedom of speech and press. The Slavophiles became increasingly nationalistic; many ardently supported PAN-SLAVISM after Russia's defeat in the Crimean War (1854–56). Prominent among them were Ivan Kireyevsky, Aleksey Khomiakov, and Konstantin and Ivan Aksakov. The Westernizers believed that Russia's development depended on the adoption of Western technology and liberal government. In their approach they were rationalistic and often agnostic rather than emotional and mystical. Some remained moderate liberals, while others became socialists and political radicals. The leading Westernizers included Piotr Y. CHAADAYEV, Aleksandr I. HERZEN, and Vissarion G. BELINSKY. See Nicholas Riasovsky, *Russia and the West in the Teaching of the Slavophiles* (1952); T. G. Masaryk, *The Spirit of Russia* (3 vol., rev. ed. 1967); P. K. Christoff, *Third Heart* (1970).

Slavs (slävz, slăvz), the largest ethnic and linguistic group of peoples in Europe belonging to the Indo-European linguistic family. It is estimated that the Slavs number over 230 million in the world. They are usually classified in three main divisions. The West Slavs include the Poles, the Czechs, the Slovaks, and the WENDS (also known as Lusatians) and other small groups in E Germany. The South Slavs include the Serbs, the Croats, the Slovenes, the Macedonians, the Montenegrins, the Bosnians, and the Bulgars. The East Slavs, the largest group, include the Great Russians, Ukrainians, and Belorussians (or White Russians). Religiously and culturally, the Slavs fall into two main groups—those traditionally associated with the Orthodox Eastern Church (the Great Russians, most of the Ukrainians, some of the Belorussians, the Bulgarians, the Serbs, and the Macedonians) and those historically affiliated with the Roman Catholic Church (the West Slavs, most of the Belorussians, some of the Ukrainians, and the Croats and Slovenes). The cleavage into Eastern Church and Western Church is symbolized by the use of the Cyrillic alphabet by the first group and of the Roman alphabet by the latter. Ethnically the Slavs possess little unity, for they have mixed for centuries with other peoples, including Turko-Tatars, Finnic peoples, Germans, Mongols, Greeks, and Illyrian tribes. The Bulgarians are not of Slavic origin. The obscure beginnings of the Slavs have given rise to several theories, all of which include as a possible place of origin the area of the Polesie marshes in Galicia. The ancestors of the Slavs were Neolithic tribes who occupied this territory a few centuries before the Christian era, and the similarities of these Proto-Slavs to the Proto-Balts has led to a theory of a Proto-Baltic Slav period (see BALTS). There was presumably no one Proto-Slavic language, but rather a blending of tribal dialects that emerged as differentiated Slavic languages; the Slavs' unifying medium is today chiefly that of language. The Slavs were probably dominated in succession by the Scythians and the Sarmatians (both Iranian tribes), by the Goths, by the Huns, and by the Avars, in whose westward expansion they shared and whose slaves they often were. By the 6th cent., Slavs had settled in Germany E of the Elbe River. In the Balkan Peninsula they invaded the Byzantine Empire in 576 and again in 746, and they settled in the country districts of Greece. A sedentary, agricultural people, the Slavs tended to adopt a loosely democratic organization. Primitive Slavic religion shows Iranian influence. The Slavs were animists; their supreme god was the god of lightning. In material culture, especially in military matters, the Slavs were greatly influenced by the Goths. In the 8th cent. Charlemagne temporarily subdued the Slavs E of the Elbe, and German eastward expansion, which permanently pushed the Slavs beyond the Oder River, came in the 12th cent. with Henry the Lion of Saxony, the Wendic Crusade, Albert the Bear of Brandenburg, and the Teutonic Knights. From the 12th cent. on, the area of the Bohemian and Polish states was greatly changed by German immigration. The Bohemian, Moravian, and Slovak tribes were converted (9th cent.) to Christianity by Saints CYRIL AND METHODIUS. A large Slavic empire emerged at that time under the leadership of MORAVIA, but it was soon destroyed by the Magyars. The duchies (later kingdoms) of POLAND and BOHEMIA, most powerful of the Western Slavic medieval states, cooperated in the 10th cent. to resist German conquest. In the south, BULGARIA, SERBIA, Bosnia, and CROATIA each reached a relatively high degree of political development before being absorbed (14th–15th cent.) by the Ottoman Empire. Most important was the East Slavic Kievan state, which rose in the 10th cent. and was destroyed by the Mongol invasion in the 13th cent. Thereafter the principalities of Galich-Volhynia and Moscow (see MOSCOW, GRAND DUCHY OF) became prominent. From the 17th cent. on PAN-SLAVISM increased and became to some extent a development in opposition to Pan-Germanism. The history of the West Slavs and the South Slavs during the past three centuries is dominated by their struggles for liberation from Turkish, German, and Magyar domination. The Slavs, however, have not been able to unify politically, mainly as the result of different national interests. See Konrad Jazdzewski, *Atlas to the Prehistory of the Slavs* (tr., 2 vols., 1948–49); J. S. Roucek, ed., *Slavonic Encyclopaedia* (4 vol., 1949, repr. 1969); Francis Dvornik, *The Slavs* (1956) and *The Slavs in European History and Civilization* (1962); S. H. Cross, *Slavic Civilization through the Ages* (1963); A. P. Vlasto, *The Entry of the Slavs into Christendom* (1970); M. A. Gimbutas, *The Slavs* (1971).

Slavyansk (slәvyänsk'), city (1970 pop. 124,000), S European USSR, in the Ukraine, in the Donets Basin. It is a railroad junction and has salt and soda works and machine and ceramic plants. Nearby is a health resort. Founded in 1676 as Tor, the city was renamed in the late 18th cent.

sled or **sledge,** vehicle that moves by sliding. Evidence indicates that the sled was used in the Neolithic period, before the invention of the wheel or the use of any draft animal except the dog. Probably it was first drawn by man. Whether the sled originated in the Old World or the New, or independently in each, is not known. Eskimos used a dogsled in pre-Columbian America. In ancient Egypt sleds were used to haul blocks of stone. The simplest form of the sled is a board turned up in front, as in the toboggan. Developments include the addition of runners, the coupling of two sleds in tandem (the bobsled), and the introduction of light and graceful horse-drawn passenger sleds. The sled is still commonly used in northern regions. See BOBSLEDDING; TOBOGGANING.

sleep, resting state in which an individual becomes relatively quiescent and relatively unaware of the environment. During sleep, which is in part a period of rest and relaxation, most physiological functions such as body temperature, blood pressure, and rate of breathing and heartbeat decrease. However, sleep is also a time of repair and growth, and some tissues, e.g., epithelium, proliferate more rapidly during sleep. Sleep occurs in cyclical patterns; in each cycle of 1½ to 2 hr the sleeper spends about three fourths of the time in so-called S sleep, characterized by large, slow delta brain waves (see ELECTROENCEPHALOGRAPHY). The second stage of sleep, called D sleep, is also called paradoxical sleep because, although the sleeper is deeply asleep, parts of the nervous system are very active and rapid eye movements occur; sleepers awakened during rapid-eye-movement (REM) sleep usually report that they have been dreaming. D sleep is common in mammals, but is not usually found in birds, reptiles, or fish. In humans dream deprivation or sleep deprivation results in changes in personality and perceptual and intellectual processes. There is evidence that emotional and environmental deprivation disrupts the sleep patterns of young children, which in turn inhibits the secretion of growth hormone, normally secreted maximally during sleep; many such severely deprived children are dwarfed. The amount of sleep needed depends on both the individual and the environment, i.e., worrying, critical individuals tend to need both more sleep and more dream sleep than easygoing ones, and stress and worry during the day result in an increase in paradoxical sleep. It has been hypothesized that while S sleep is physically restorative, D sleep is psychically restorative. D sleep is also believed to integrate new information into the brain and to reactivate the sleeping brain without waking the sleeper. There is evidence that the hypothalamus and thalamus of the brain initiate sleep and that part of the midbrain acts as an arousal system. The presence of certain amines, e.g., SEROTONIN, has been related to different stages of sleep and wakefulness; recently a PEPTIDE has been found that induces S sleep when injected into an awake animal. See also INSOMNIA.

Sleeping Bear Dunes National Lakeshore: see NATIONAL PARKS AND MONUMENTS (table).

sleeping pill: see BARBITURATE.

sleeping sickness: see ENCEPHALITIS; TRYPANOSOMIASIS.

sleepwalking or **somnambulism** (sŏmnăm'byo͞olĭzəm), dissociated state in which a person performs actions during sleep, characterized by partial consciousness and sleeptalking. It is similar to hypnosis in that somnambulistic episodes may not be remembered upon awakening. Psychiatrists believe that actions executed in this way are symbolic representations of unconscious wishes. Occurrence is most common in childhood and puberty and is considered a symptom of personality disturbance in adults.

sleet, precipitation of small, partially melted grains of ice. As raindrops fall from clouds, they pass through layers of air at different temperatures. If they pass through a layer with a temperature below the freezing point, they turn into sleet. Snowflakes that have melted by passing through a warm layer will turn into sleet if they then pass through a freezing layer. Sleet often falls together with snow and rain, and may deposit an icy coating on exposed surfaces. Sleet occurs only during the winter, while HAIL, a different form of icy precipitation, may fall at any time of the year.

Slevogt, Max (mäks slā'fôkht), 1868–1932, German painter. Slevogt, together with Max Liebermann and Lovis Corinth, was among the principal exponents of German impressionism and was influenced by Millet and Courbet. A prolific painter, he attempted to capture movement through broad, informal brush work. His portrait of the singer Francisco d'Andrade as Don Giovanni (1902) is in the Staatsgalerie, Stuttgart.

Slezak, Leo (slā'zäk), 1873–1946, Czech tenor, pupil of Jean de Reszke. After his debut as Lohengrin at Brno in 1896, he sang in Vienna, Berlin, and later at the Metropolitan Opera, New York City (1909–12). He was famous for his robust voice and physique, and he had a flamboyant sense of humor. See his memoirs (1928, tr. 1937); biography by his son, the actor Walter Slezak (1962).

Slick, Sam: see HALIBURTON, THOMAS CHANDLER.

Slidell, John (slīdĕl', slī'dəl), 1793–1871, American political leader and diplomat, b. New York City. He became a prominent lawyer and political figure in New Orleans and served as a Democrat in Congress (1843–45). In 1845, Slidell was appointed special U.S. envoy to Mexico to adjust the Texas boundary and to negotiate the purchase of California and New Mexico; the Mexican government, which had broken off diplomatic relations after the U.S. Congress had provided for the annexation of Texas, refused to receive him (see MEXICAN WAR). Senator from Louisiana (1853–61), he was influential in securing the nomination and election of James Buchanan to the presidency (1856) and was a power in the administration. Slidell joined the Confederate cause early in 1861. Appointed Confederate commissioner to France the same year, he figured with James M. Mason in the TRENT AFFAIR. Although cordially received in Paris, Slidell was unable to get official recognition or any material aid for the Confederacy from the French emperor, Napoleon III. After the Civil War, Slidell resided in France. See L. M. Sears, *John Slidell* (1925); Beckles Willson, *John Slidell and the Confederates in Paris* (1932, repr. 1970).

Slidell (slīdĕl'), city (1970 pop. 16,101), St. Tammany parish, SE La., near Lake Pontchartrain, there crossed by a bridge to New Orleans; inc. 1888. Originally a shipbuilding and brick-manufacturing town in a farm and timber region, it now serves primarily as a bedroom community for the aerospace industry that has developed (1960s) in the surrounding area.

slide rule, instrument for making numerical computations and readings, the results of which may be read easily and quickly after performing simple mechanical manipulations. Multiplication and division, finding of powers and roots, and other more complicated calculations may be performed with a slide rule. Based on John Napier's principle of the LOGARITHM, it came into use after Edmund Gunter created a logarithmic scale in 1620. Gunter's rule consisted of a straight line on which numbers were spaced at intervals proportional to their common logarithms. Using this scale, William Oughtred and Edmund Wingate developed independently (c.1630) the first slide rules. Amédée Mannheim, a French army officer, established the present form of the slide rule in 1850. This modern, 10-inch slide rule has three parts, the stock, the slide, and the cursor (indicator). The stock consists of two fixed parallel rules, each with a scale on its inner edge. The slide is a single rule, moving between them. It has two scales on its outer edge, each scale corresponding to the fixed scale to which it is adjacent. The cursor, a transparent square with a hair line, may be moved the length of the rule to aid in reading it. Many slide rules have additional scales, either on the same side or on the reverse side, that may be used to determine sines, tangents, logarithms, and other quantities. Other instruments, based on the same principle, by which more complicated calculations may be made, are the calculating circle and the calculating cylinder. Most manufacturers of slide rules publish manuals of instructions. See W. S. Mittelstadt, *Basic Slide Rule Operation* (2d ed. 1971).

Slieve Bloom (slēv), mountain range, 15 mi (24 km) long, central Republic of Ireland, on the border of Counties Laoighis and Offaly. The range, which rises to 1,733 ft (528 m) at Arderin, is the source of the Barrow River.

Slieve Donard, peak: see MOURNE MOUNTAINS, Northern Ireland.

Sligo (slī'gō), county (1971 pop. 50,236), 694 sq mi (1,797 sq km), N Republic of Ireland. The county town is SLIGO. The irregular coast line is deeply indented by Killala Bay and Sligo Bay. The interior is mountainous, with the Slieve Gamph, or Ox Mts., in the west and the Dartry range, rising to c.2,000 ft (610 m) in the northeast. Cattle raising (beef and dairy) is the chief occupation. The population is less than one third of what it was before the potato famine of the mid-19th cent. A round tower at Drumcliffe is what remains of a monastery founded by St. Columba in 575.

Sligo, urban district (1971 pop. 14,071), county town of Co. Sligo, N Republic of Ireland, at the mouth of the Garavogue River on Sligo Bay. It is a seaport and fishing center, with a woolen trade and other industries. There are remains of a Dominican monastery (Sligo Abbey), built in the 13th cent. by Maurice Fitzgerald, earl of Kildare. The abbey burned in 1414, was rebuilt, and again burned in 1641 when the town was sacked by the parliamentarians. Other interesting features are the Church of St. John and the Roman Catholic cathedral, college, and bishop's palace. W. B. Yeats was born in Sligo.

Slim, William Joseph Slim, 1st **Viscount,** 1891–1970, British field marshal. He saw service in several campaigns, notably Gallipoli and Mesopotamia, in World War I. After the war he joined the Indian army, rising in rank to brigadier in 1940. He commanded (1940) British forces in the Sudan and led (1941) a division in Iran and Iraq. He went (1942) to Burma as corps commander and led (1943–45) the 14th British Army in the reconquest of that country from the Japanese. He was made field marshal in 1949. He served as governor general of Australia from 1953 to 1960, when he was created viscount. See his *Unofficial History* (1959) and *Defeat into Victory* (rev. ed. 1961); G. C. Evans, *Slim as Military Commander* (1969).

slime mold or **slime fungus,** organism usually regarded as a fungus, although it shows equal affinity to the PROTOZOA. Slime molds have complex life cycles that may be divided into an animallike motile phase, in which growth and feeding occur, and a plantlike, immotile, reproductive phase. The motile phase is commonly found under rotting logs and damp leaves, where cellulose is abundant. It consists in some slime molds of solitary, amebalike cells, and in others of a multinucleate mass of protoplasm called a plasmodium, which creeps about by ameboid movement. Plasmodia often grow to a diameter of several inches and are frequently brightly colored. Slime molds of both types can ingest solid food particles; they feed on living microorganisms as well as decaying vegetation. Before entering the reproductive stage, a plasmodium moves to a drier, better-lit place, such as the top of a log. In the amebalike, or cellular, slime molds, many individual cells aggregate and flow together, forming a mass called a pseudoplasmodium that resembles a slug and crawls about before settling in a suitable location. In the reproductive stage the plasmodium or pseudoplasmodium is transformed, by migration of its cells, into one or more reproductive structures called fruiting bodies, each consisting of a stalk topped by a spore-producing capsule. Often highly colorful and ornate, the fruiting bodies resemble the reproductive structures of many other fungi. Eventually the resistant, cellulose-walled spores are released and dispersed; they germinate in wet places, releasing naked cells. In some slime molds the cells go through a flagellated swimming stage, followed by sexual fusions and cell divisions, but in all they ultimately become ameboid cells. In the case of the amebalike slime molds, this completes the life cycle; in slime molds of the plasmodium type, the ameboid cell grows and its nucleus divides repeatedly, resulting in the formation of a new plasmodium. Under adverse conditions a plasmodium may be transformed into a hard, dry, inactive mass called a sclerotium, which is resistant to desiccation and becomes a plasmodium again when favorable conditions return. There are about 400 known slime mold species, found in forests throughout the world. In a few species the plasmodium, under favorable conditions, may cover an area of several square feet. A slime mold is the cause of CLUBROOT, a disease of cabbage and related plants. Slime molds constitute the class Myxomycetes of the division FUNGI or, in some recent systems, a separate division, the Myxomycophyta.

slip, propagation by: see CUTTING.

Slipher, Vesto Melvin (slī'fər), 1875–1969, American astronomer, b. Mulberry, Ind., grad. Univ. of Indiana, 1901. From 1901 he was at Lowell Observatory, Flagstaff, Ariz., where he served as director from 1917 to 1954. He was head of the Lowell solar eclipse expeditions of 1918 and 1923. In 1919 he was awarded the Lalande Prize and the gold medal of the Paris Academy of Sciences. Much of his attention was devoted to the investigation of astronomical spectroscopy, and particular study was given to the rotations and atmospheres of planets and nebulas. He made discoveries regarding the rapid rotation of nebulas and the high velocities of star clusters. His brother, **Earl C. Slipher,** 1883–1964, was also an astronomer. He, too, worked at the Lowell Observatory and was an authority on the planet Mars.

slipped disc, rupture or herniation of an intervertebral disc. These discs separate and cushion the vertebrae, the segments of the SPINAL COLUMN. They are composed of an outer rim of fibrous connective tissue and a gelatin-like inner core. If the fibrous rim breaks the core may leak into the spinal canal, resulting in severe pain that is aggravated by bending, straining, or coughing. Material from the disc may press on spinal nerves and cause numbness or tingling, weakness, or paralysis in the area of the body enervated by those nerves. Slipped discs occur as a result of severe strain or without any apparent stress at all. They are most common in the lower back and neck. Treatment consists of bed rest, usually with a hard board placed beneath the mattress, local application of heat, and the administration of muscle relaxants to relieve spasms. If natural healing fails to occur surgery may be required to remove the disc, and the affected vertebrae fused to keep them from rubbing together.

slipperwort: see FIGWORT.

slipware, pottery decorated with various colors of slip, a thin mixture of clay and water. Slip may form a design on a contrasting background, or lines may be scratched through a coating of slip to show the color beneath, in the style called graffito. The decorated plates of the Pennsylvania Germans are good examples of slipware. Great beauty in decoration achieved through the use of slip may be seen on Greek pottery.

Sliven (slē'věn), city (1968 est. pop. 77,500), E central Bulgaria, at the foot of the Balkan Mts. A textile center, it also produces textile machinery, glass, electrical goods, wood and metal products, foodstuffs, and wine. Coal is mined nearby. Sliven is the seat of an Eastern Orthodox metropolitan. The city has long been strategically important because of its location at the entrance to Balkan passes. There are several churches and mosques and the ruins of a medieval fortress. Sliven is also known as Slivno.

slivovitz: see BRANDY.

Sloan, Alfred Pritchard, 1875–1966, American businessman and philanthropist, b. New Haven, Conn., grad. Massachusetts Institute of Technology, 1895. He began his career as a draftsman for the Hyatt Roller Bearing Company, becoming its president in 1901; under his leadership the income and assets of the company were greatly increased. He sold the company to General Motors in 1916 and later became its president. As head of General Motors, Sloan inaugurated "standard procedures" (i.e., rules to effect better management); he was chairman of the board from 1937 to 1956. His philanthropic interests extended to many institutions, including the Sloan-Kettering Institute for Cancer Research and the Sloan Foundation. He wrote *My Years with General Motors* (1964).

Sloan, John, 1871–1951, American painter and etcher, b. Lock Haven, Pa. He studied at the Pennsylvania Academy of the Fine Arts and worked for 12 years as an illustrator on the Philadelphia *Inquirer* and Philadelphia *Press.* In 1905 he went to New York City, where he worked as an illustrator. A member of the EIGHT, he was active in organizing the Society of Independent Artists and was its president from 1918. Long a popular teacher at the Art Students League of New York City, he was elected president in 1930. His scenes of city life and his nude studies are in leading museums throughout the United States. Characteristic are *McSorley's Bar* (Detroit Inst. of Arts); *Renganeschi's, Saturday Night* (Art Inst., Chicago); *Wake of the Ferry* (Phillips Memorial Gall., Washington, D.C.); and *Nude with Nine Apples* (Whitney Mus., New York City). Sloan's painting owes its distinction to a natural interest in human beings, whose life he portrayed with a directness often verging on satire. As an etcher he was equally gifted. See his *Gist of Art* (1939); his correspondence ed. by B. St. John (1965); prints by P. Morse (1969); biography by B. St. John (1971); studies by Lloyd Goodrich (1952), Van Wyck Brooks (1955), and D. W. Scott and E. J. Bullard (1971).

Sloan Foundation, fund established (1934) by automobile executive Alfred P. Sloan, Jr., as a philanthropic institution supporting research in various areas. In its early years it stressed support of U.S. economic education and research. After World War II its emphasis shifted to medical research, particularly cancer research. In the late 1960s its activities were expanded to include studies in current social problems, science, and technology. The foundation has been a major financial supporter of the Sloan-Kettering Institute for Cancer Research, established in 1945. It also conducts a scholarship program for minority students in management and medicine. In 1972 its endowment exceeded $367 million.

Sloat, John Drake, 1781–1867, American naval officer, b. near Goshen, N.Y. He entered the navy as a midshipman in 1800 and resigned after a year's service, but reentered for service in the War of 1812. He was aboard the *United States* when she captured the *Macedonian.* After the war he served against the pirates in the West Indies. He was commander of the Pacific squadron from 1844 to 1846, and in July, 1846, soon after war was declared against Mexico, he occupied Monterey, Calif., on the grounds that the British were about to do so. He also took San Francisco and held it until relieved by Robert F. Stockton. He retired in 1855, but was promoted to commodore (1862) and rear admiral (1866) on the retired list.

Slocum, Henry Warner (slō'kəm), b. 1826 or 1827, d. 1894, Union general in the American Civil War, b. Delphi, Onondaga co., N.Y. A West Point graduate, he resigned from the army in 1856 and practiced law in Syracuse, N.Y., until war broke out. Slocum, rising to a major generalcy of volunteers (1862), fought in all the Eastern campaigns through Gettysburg (1863), where he commanded the right wing. In 1864 he led the 20th Corps at the end of General Sherman's Atlanta campaign. His troops constituted Sherman's left wing in the march through Georgia and the Carolinas (1864-65). After the war, Slocum settled in Brooklyn, where he practiced law. He was a Democratic Representative in Congress (1869-73, 1883-85).

sloe, name applied to the BLACKTHORN and also to various American wild plums.

sloop, fore-and-aft-rigged, single-masted sailing vessel with a single headsail jib. A sloop differs from a CUTTER in that it has a jibstay—a support leading from the bow to the masthead on which the jib is set. A sloop of war was a small warship, variously rigged as a barque, brig, brigantine, or ship, that carried fewer than 18 guns in the British navy and fewer than 24 in the American navy. These vessels played an active role in the American Revolution and the French Revolutionary Wars. The sloop disappeared as a warship in the mid-19th cent., but during World War II the British revived the term to designate a small escort vessel armed with 4-in. (10.2-cm) guns and depth charges.

sloth (slōth, slôth), arboreal mammal found in Central and South America distantly related to armadillos and anteaters. Sloths live in tropical forests, where they sleep, eat, and travel through the trees suspended upside down, clinging to branches with the powerful curved claws of their forelimbs and hindlimbs. Algae that grow on the hair impart a greenish color to the coat so that it blends with the foliage. There is no tail. The three-toed sloth (*Bradypus*) is about the size of a house cat, with a dense, furry coat and yellowish face. It has three toes on the front feet and five on the hind feet. It feeds almost exclusively on the leaves, buds, and stems of *Cecropia*, a tropical relative of the mulberry. The somewhat larger two-toed sloth (*Choloepus*) has very long hair. It eats a less restricted vegetarian diet. Sloths move sluggishly but can strike swiftly and powerfully if attacked. Huge ground sloths (see MEGATHERIUM) are extinct forms. Sloths are classified in the phylum CHORDATA, subphylum Vertebrata, class Mammalia, order Edentata, family Bradypodidae.

Slough (slou), municipal borough (1971 pop. 86,757), Buckinghamshire, central England. After World War I, Slough underwent rapid industrial development, owing in part to its proximity to London. Slough was the home of the astronomer Sir William Herschel. In 1974, Slough became part of the new nonmetropolitan county of Berkshire.

Slovakia (slōvä'kēə, slōvä'kēə), Slovak *Slovensko* (slô'věnskô), constituent land (18,917 sq mi/48,995 sq km) of CZECHOSLOVAKIA. BRATISLAVA is the capital. Slovakia is bordered by Moravia in the west, by Austria in the southwest, by Hungary in the south, by the Ukraine in the east, and by Poland in the north. Most of Slovakia is traversed by the Carpathian Mts., including the Tatra and the Beskids. Gerlachovka (8,737 ft/2,663 m) in the High Tatra, is the highest peak. S Slovakia is a part of the Little Alföld, a plain. Its fertile soil is drained by the Danube and its tributaries, notably the Váh. The mountainous part of Slovakia has vast forests and pastures, used for intensive sheep grazing, and is rich in mineral resources, including high-grade iron ore, copper, mercury, gold, silver, lead, and lignite. There are also numerous mineral springs, notably at Piešt'any, and many popular resorts. Farms, vineyards, orchards, and pastures for stock form the basis of S Slovakia's economy. Slovakia has undergone considerable industrialization and urbanization since World War II; mining, shipbuilding, and agricultural and metal processing have become important industries. Major Slovakian cities include Bratislava and KOMARNO, which are the major Danubian ports; and KOŠICE, TRNAVA, and NITRA. The Slovaks comprise about 87% of the population; other groups include Hungarians (about 10%), Ukrainians, and Czechs. Roman Catholicism is the chief religion. Although the Slovaks and the Czechs are ethnically and linguistically related, they have been politically and culturally separate for 1,000 years.

The Slovaks in History. The area now constituting Slovakia was settled by Slavic tribes in the 5th-6th cent. A.D. In the 9th cent. Slovakia formed part of the great empire of MORAVIA, under whose rulers Christianity was introduced by Saints Cyril and Methodius. From the Magyar conquest of Slovakia early in the 10th cent. until 1918, Slovakia was generally under Hungarian rule. German and Jewish settlements in Slovakian cities date from the Middle Ages; most of the Slovaks remained peasants in the countryside, although some became burghers. Czech-Slovak contacts, broken after the demise of the Moravian empire, were restored by the 14th cent.; and the 15th-century HUSSITE movement in Bohemia enjoyed influence in Slovakia. After the Ottoman Turkish victory at MOHÁCS in 1526 over Louis II of Hungary and Bohemia, Slovakia, along with western Hungary, fell under Hapsburg rule. It thus escaped Turkish domination but became a stronghold of the great Hungarian nobles, who owned most of the land and treated the Slovaks with contempt. Slovakia, however, played an important political role, with Bratislava serving as the Hapsburg capital, until all of Hungary was finally freed from the Turks in the late 17th cent. Slovakia also enjoyed more religious toleration than much of the Hapsburg empire, and Protestantism thrived. In the 18th cent. MARIA THERESA and JOSEPH II pursued religious freedom and social reform in Slovakia but greatly intensified Germanization. This policy spurred a Slovak national revival, which grew steadily in the 19th cent. The Catholic clergy, which constituted the only sizable body of Slovak intellectuals, exercised the main leadership of the nationalist movement. L'udovít Štúr became the father of the modern Slovak literary language. During the anti-Hapsburg revolutions of 1848, Štúr joined Czech representatives in a Pan-Slav congress at Prague. Also in 1848, the Slovaks formulated a set of demands for increased political and linguistic rights. Some clashes between Slovaks and Hungarians occurred, and Magyarization lessened temporarily; but after the *Ausgleich* establishing the dual AUSTRO-HUNGARIAN MONARCHY in 1867, Magyarization again intensified, thus further heightening Slovak nationalism. Large-scale immigration (1900–1910) of the landless Slovak peasants to America gave the Slovak independence movement considerable support in the United States during World War I, during which the Slovaks and other nationalities of the Hapsburg empire agitated for freedom. The so-called Pittsburgh Declaration, signed by Czech and Slovak patriots in May, 1918, provided for a united Czechoslovak republic, in which Slovakia would retain broad autonomy, with its own governmental institutions and official language. On October 30 the Slovak National Council formally proclaimed independence from Hungary and incorporation into Czechoslovakia. The new republic's boundaries, established in 1920 by the Treaty of Trianon, encompassed areas where more than one million Hungarians lived. Hungary, meanwhile, continued to claim at least part of Slovakia, while a large Slovak People's party, led by Msgr Andrej Hlinka, accused the Czechoslovak government of denying Slovakia the autonomous rights promised. Indeed, from 1918 until 1938, Slovakia held the status of a simple province, although the Slovak language was official within its boundaries. The minority problem was complicated by religion: the majority of Slovaks were Catholic, while the Prague government was distinctly anticlerical. Monsignor Hlinka and his successor as leader of the Slovak People's party, Father Jozef Tiso, demanded full autonomy for Slovakia on a basis of complete equality for both Czechs and Slovaks. After the MUNICH PACT of 1938, Slovakia became an autonomous state within reorganized Czecho-Slovakia, with Father Tiso as Slovak premier. At the same time a large part of S Slovakia was ceded to Hungary and some northern districts to Poland. When the Prague government dismissed (March, 1939) Tiso as premier, he appealed to Adolf Hitler, who used this appeal as a pretext for making Bohemia, Moravia, and Silesia a German protectorate. Slovakia became a nominally independent state under German protection and Tiso's one-party rule. Tiso allowed German troops to occupy Slovakia in Aug., 1939, and entered World War II as Germany's ally. A pro-Allied Slovak underground movement gained strength, however, and powerfully aided the Soviet troops who drove the Germans out of Slovakia late in 1944. The Allied victory in 1945 restored Slovakia to its territorial status before the Munich Pact, and the constitution of 1948 recognized Slovakia as one of the constituent states of a reestablished Czechoslovakia; the other state was composed of Bohemia, Moravia, and Silesia. The constitution also established separate government organs for Slovakia. The accession in 1948 of a Communist government in Czechoslovakia revived the old antagonism between Czechs and Slovaks. The Catholic clergy in Slovakia, militantly opposed to Communism, was persecuted, and the autonomous Slovak government came entirely under the control of the Czechoslovak Communist party, which began to transfer authority from Bratislava to Prague. In 1960 a new constitution seriously curtailed Slovakia's autonomy. The liberal Communist regime of Alexander Dubček, which came into power in 1967, responded to Slovak discontent by promising federalization of the republic. Despite the invasion (1968) of Czechoslovakia by the Soviet Union, the new Socialist Federal Republic came into being on Jan. 1, 1969; the constituent Czech and Slovak republics received autonomy over local affairs, with the federal government responsible for foreign relations, defense, and finance. See Jozef Lettrich, *History of Modern Slovakia* (1955); G. L. Oddo, *Slovakia and its People* (1960); J. A. Mikuš, *Slovakia, a Political History: 1918–1950* (tr., rev. ed. 1963); R. W. Seton-Watson, *A History of the Czechs and Slovaks* (1943, repr. 1965); Eugen Steiner, *The Slovak Dilemma* (1973).

Slovak literature. The earliest documents written in the Slovak language date from the 15th cent. Following the Czech Hussite movement, many Czech cultural leaders emigrated (16th cent.) to Slovakia, and Czech was used in Protestant liturgical and secular writings, while Latin and later (17th cent.) Slovak was used by Slovak Catholics. The Slovak language was first codified by Anton Bernolák (1762–1813), but its final standardization was brought about by Ľudovít Štúr and his collaborators, who introduced the speech of central Slovakia as the basis for modern literary Slovak. A Slovak classicist, Ján Hollý (1785–1849), wrote epic ballads that glorified Slovak history, while Pan-Slavism found major expression in Ján Kollár's *Daughter of Slava* (1924) and in the scholarly works of Pavel Josef ŠAFAŘÍK. Slovak romantic poetry of the early 19th cent. is represented by the satirical writings of Samo Chalupka (1812–83), the epic ballads of Ján Botto (1829–81), the exquisite melancholy verses of Janko Kráľ (1822–76), and the philosophical lyric poetry of Andrej Sládkovič (1820–72), who also exerted a strong influence on the development of the Slovak national theater, established in 1841. The novels of Ján Kalincak (1822–71) contained perceptive descriptions of Slovak life. In the late 19th cent. Slovak literary life centered around the publication *Slovak Views.* A major writer of this period was Svetozár Hurban Vajanský (1847–1916), whose lyric poetry expressed his strong yearning for freedom and whose social novels helped initiate Slovak realism. Pavel Országh-Hviezdoslav (1849–1921) wrote lyric and epic poetry that remains the finest of Slovak verse. Realism in Slovak prose is represented by the works of Martin Kukučín (1860–1928), by the village novels of Elena Marothy-Soltesova (1855–1939), Timrava (pseud. of Božena Slančíkova, 1867–1939), and Josef Gregor Tajovsky (1874–1941), and by the dramas of Ferko Urbanek (1859–1934). In the 20th cent. Slovak verse found significant expression in the sensuous melodious poetry of Ján Smrek, the intellectual religious lyrics of Emil Boleslav Lukáč, and the patriotic humanitarian verse of Andrej Zarnov (pseud. of František Subik), who inspired a whole generation of Slovak writers. The patriotic poetry and prose of Martin Rázus was largely political, while the poet and novelist Janko Jesenky escaped the conventions of Slovak romanticism. Valentin Beniak and Ivan Krasko wrote original lyric verse, and Rudolf Dilong and Rudolf Fabry created surrealist poetry. The most prominent Slovak novelists of the 20th cent. are Josef Ciger Hronsky and Milo Urban. Writers of the Communist period in Slovakia include Laco Novomeský, Petr Karvas, Ladislav Mňačko, and Alfonz Bednár. See the anthologies, ed. by Mojmír Otruba and Zdeněk Pešat (tr. 1962) and by Paul Selver (tr. 1929, repr. 1969); Julius Noge, *An Outline of Slovakian Literature* (tr. 1968).

Slovenia (slōvē'nēə), Slovene *Slovenija,* constituent republic of Yugoslavia (1971 pop. 1,725,088), 7,817 sq mi (20,246 sq km), NW Yugoslavia. LJUBLJANA, the capital, and MARIBOR and CELJE are the chief cities. Most of Slovenia is situated in the Karst plateau and in the Julian Alps. The republic is drained by the Drava and Sava rivers. Although farming and livestock raising are the chief occupations, Slovenia is the most industrialized and urbanized of all the Yugoslav republics. Iron, steel, and aluminum are produced, and there are mineral resources of oil, coal, and mercury. The Slovenes, most of whom are Roman Catholic, have the highest per capita income of any of the Yugoslav people. Until 1918 the region was largely comprised in the Austrian crownlands of CARINTHIA, CARNIOLA, and STYRIA. In ancient times this region was inhabited by the Illyrian and Celtic tribes. In the 1st cent. B.C. they fell under the Roman provinces of Pannonia and Noricum. The region was settled in the 6th cent. A.D. by the South Slavs, who set up the early Slav state of Samo, which in 788 passed to the Franks. At the division of Charlemagne's empire (843) the region passed to the dukes of Bavaria. In 1335, Carinthia and Carniola passed to the Hapsburgs. From that time until 1918 Slovenia was part of Austria. In 1918, Slovenia was included in the kingdom of Serbs, Croats, and Slovenes (called Yugoslavia after 1929), and in 1919 Austria formally ceded the region by the Treaty of Saint-Germain. In World War II Slovenia was divided (1941) among Germany, Italy, and Hungary. After the war, Slovenia was made (1945) a constituent republic of Yugoslavia and received part of the former Italian region of Venezia Giulia.

Słowacki, Juliusz (yo͞ol'yo͞osh slôväts'kē), 1809–49, Polish writer, one of the foremost Polish romantic poets. A revolutionist, he joined the Polish expatriates in Paris and died there prematurely of tuberculosis. Słowacki was extremely conscious of the great literary traditions, and his works show the influence of other authors. His poetic tragedies deal with the conflict of good and evil, particularly in Polish history, and are reminiscent of the works of Shakespeare. Słowacki's *Balladina* (1834) and *Lilla Weneda* (1839) were drawn from early legends. His *Horsztynski* (1840) is known as the Polish *Hamlet. King Spirit* (1847), a philosophic poem influenced by Dante's *Divine Comedy*, reveals his later mystical tendencies and exemplifies his stylistic virtuosity. His epic of manners *Beniowski* (1841) brought the Don Juan theme to Polish literature. Słowacki is considered the national bard. See studies by Manfred Kridl (1958) and Stefan Treugutt (1959).

slug, name for a terrestrial GASTROPOD mollusk in which the characteristic molluscan shell is reduced to a thin plate embedded in the tissues. Like the terrestrial snails of the same order, slugs have a distinct head with a mouth, tentacles bearing eyes, and a lung for breathing air. They move on a muscular foot over a trail of slime which they secrete. Certain species, such as *Limax maximus*, have become serious pests in gardens and truck farms, particularly in the W United States. Gliding out to feed at night, they devour both the roots and aerial portions of plants with their rasplike radula. The SEA SLUGS (nudibranchs) and the sea hares are marine gastropods that feed mainly on small animal life. Terrestrial slugs are classified in the phylum MOLLUSCA, class Gastropoda, order Stylommatophora.

Sluis (slois), municipality, Zeeland prov., SW Netherlands, on the Scheldt estuary, near the Belgian border. Sluis was founded in the 13th cent. and later accorded trading privileges to the Hanseatic League. In 1340, Edward III of England defeated the fleet of Philip VI of France off Sluis in the first important engagement of the Hundred Years War. Sluis fell to the Spanish in 1587 and was recovered by the Dutch in 1604. It subsequently lost importance as a port. It is also known by its French name, L'Écluse. The Dutch name was formerly spelled Sluys.

slum clearance: see HOUSING; CITY PLANNING.

Słupsk (slo͞opsk), Ger. *Stolp*, city (1970 pop. 68,300), NW Poland. It is a rail junction and commercial center, with food-processing plants, breweries, distilleries, and industries manufacturing metals, building materials, farm machinery, furniture, and chemicals. Nearby are lignite mines. Chartered in 1310, Słupsk passed in 1648 from Poland to Brandenburg (after 1701 known as Prussia). It reverted to Poland in 1945. Landmarks include a 16th-century castle and 14th-century town gates.

Sluter, Claus (klous slü'tər), d. 1406, Flemish sculptor, probably of Dutch extraction, active in Burgundy. Under Philip the Bold of Burgundy he had charge of the sculptural works for the porch of the Chartreuse of Champmol, near Dijon; there stands his pedestal for a Calvary—the *Well of Moses*—with its strongly individualized figures of Moses, David, and the Prophets, a masterpiece of realism, dignity, and power. Another magnificent work at Dijon is the tomb of Philip the Bold, with a recumbent effigy upon the sarcophagus and 40 small alabaster figures of mourners set in niches in its sides. The tomb was finished by Claus de Werve, nephew and pupil of Sluter and also his assistant on the *Well of Moses.*

Sluys, Netherlands: see SLUIS.

Slye, Maud (slī), 1879–1954, American pathologist, b. Minneapolis, grad. Brown, 1899. At the Univ. of Chicago she taught pathology, becoming professor emeritus in 1945, and was a member (1911–43) of the staff of the Sprague Memorial Institute. Working on cancer, she produced susceptible and resistant strains of mice and suggested that cancer in humans might be eliminated by selective breeding if proper eugenic methods were adopted.

Sm, chemical symbol of the element SAMARIUM.

Small, Albion Woodbury, 1854–1926, American sociologist, b. Buckfield, Maine, grad. Colby College, 1876, and further educated in Germany. He was made president of Colby in 1889, but left it in 1892 to found at the Univ. of Chicago the first department of sociology in an American university. Small also established (1895) and edited the *American Journal of Sociology*, the first such journal in the United States. He did much to establish sociology as a valid field for academic study, and he occupied a leading place as a historian of sociological thought. *General Sociology* (1905) is the chief of his several works.

small arms, firearms designed primarily to be carried and fired by one man and, generally, held in the hands, as distinguished from heavy arms, or ARTILLERY. The first small arms came into general use at the end of the 14th cent. Initially they were nothing more than a small cannon held in the hands, fired by placing a lighted match at the touchhole; later a stock was added. The matchlock, the first real handgun, was fired by pulling a trigger that moved a lighted match to the touchhole; it was superseded by the wheel lock, which was fired by a spark-producing mechanism that ignited the gunpowder. By the end of the 16th cent. the wheel lock had been replaced by the flintlock, in which flint striking against steel produced a spark to fire the powder. Early matchlocks, wheel locks, and flintlocks bore many different names; common types included the musket, harquebus, and pistol. The musket was a heavy military firearm designed to be fired from the shoulder; the harquebus, a heavier weapon, was fired from a support. The pistol, in contrast, was designed to be held and fired with one hand. The rifle, invented in the 15th cent., is a firearm with a grooved, or rifled, bore that imparts a spinning motion to the bullet, giving it greater accuracy. (The principle of rifling the inner surface of the barrel is applied also to artillery.) Rifles first came into widespread practical use in E United States. The rifle used by German and Swiss colonists in Pennsylvania in the early 1730s may have been constructed in what is now Lancaster co. during the same decade; later called the Kentucky rifle, it had a long range and great accuracy but was very difficult to reload. Because of its slow rate of fire the rifle remained relatively unused as a military weapon in Europe, and until the middle of the 19th cent. the musket was the standard small arm. In the early 19th cent. firearms were revolutionized by the invention of the percussion-cap method of igniting gunpowder. The percussion cap was a small metal capsule, filled with fulminate of mercury that exploded when struck and fired the gun instantly; it soon replaced the flintlock as the major method of igniting gunpowder. Another important advance was the development of gas-expanding bullets, such as the minié bullet, in the 1840s. Such bullets could be dropped loosely down the barrel of a rifled gun, without the need of a mallet; when the powder ignited, the gases formed rushed into the bullet's hollow base and forced it to expand to fit the rifling of the barrel. In 1855 the United States adopted a new form of firearm called the rifled musket—a gun that looked like a musket, used the minié bullet, had a rifled barrel, was muzzle-loaded, and was fired by percussion caps. It was used by both sides in the U.S. Civil War. Thereafter all guns became rifled with the exception of the shotgun, a smoothbore firearm designed for short-range firing of either a single slug or a number of small shot. Shotguns are either double-barreled or single-barreled and can be single-shot or repeaters; they are used mainly for hunting. Although gunsmiths had experimented with breech-loading cannon and small arms almost since the invention of firearms, it was not until c.1870 that practical breech-loading firearms came into general use. By the 1880s magazine loading, smokeless powder, and the bolt action had also been developed in Europe and the United States and were in general use as military small arms. Although the earliest examples of the revolver date from the second half of the 16th cent., and a usable multi-firing weapon of the revolver type, called the "pepperbox," appeared in the first quarter of the 19th cent., it was not until Samuel COLT patented his revolving pistol that the revolver won a place as one of the world's standard small arms. Colt's weapon was a pistol with a revolving cylinder, capable of firing several shots without reloading. The revolver and the magazine-loading rifle were the standard small arms of the world in the last part of the 19th cent. until the invention of automatic firearms shortly before 1900. Automatic small arms were developed almost exclusively by inventors of American birth. A forerunner of the modern machine gun was built by R. J. GATLING during the Civil War. Later types of machine guns, which fired rifle bullets with great rapidity and whose firing mechanism worked by either the power of the gun's recoil or the force of the expanding gases, were developed by Hiram MAXIM, B. B. Hotchkiss, I. N. Lewis, and J. M. Browning. Machine guns were first used in the Franco-Prussian War, but did not reach their full development until the trench warfare of World War I. In the years just before and after World War I a host of automatic small arms were invented and developed. The automatic pistol to some extent replaced the revolver as the standard military side arm; the revolver, however, remained the weapon of most police forces in the United States even though it has less fire power and carries less ammunition than the automatic pistol. The submachine gun, which is a light, portable automatic weapon that can be fired from either the hip or the shoulder, was sometimes employed by the Germans and Italians during World War I. In the United States, J. T. Thompson, in cooperation with J. N. Blish, perfected (1920) one of the first notable submachine guns. The Thompson submachine gun (nicknamed "tommy gun" after its inventor) fires .45-caliber cartridges at a rate of 450 to 600 rounds per minute. It was used extensively in World War II as were more recently developed submachine guns such as the British Sten gun and the American weapon known as the M-3 or "grease gun" (because of its resemblance to the air-pressure devices used in automobile lubrication). Just before World War I the automatic rifle, sometimes known as the light machine gun or machine rifle, was developed; part rifle, part machine gun, it is mounted on a bipod, has a shoulder stock, and is magazine-fed. Outstanding types of this weapon are the British Bren gun and the American Browning Automatic Rifle (BAR). Although they work on the same principle as the machine gun, they carry far less ammunition, weigh only slightly more than a rifle, and are automatic or semiautomatic. The BAR was used by the U.S. army in both world wars and in the Korean war and is still used by some armies. During World War II the bolt-action rifle was supplemented by the semiautomatic Garand rifle—a self-loading, clip-fed, gas-operated shoulder weapon weighing just over 9 lb (4.1 kg) and firing .30-caliber ammunition. It was the standard service rifle of the U.S. army and marine corps during World War II and the Korean war. From the Garand rifles and other similar semiautomatic rifles, substitutes for the older automatic rifle were developed. After World War II, the United States and the Soviet Union adapted automatic rifles to the use of reduced-power bullets. The American M-16 rifle, which is widely used, can be fired accurately up to 500 yd (457 m) when hand-held and up to 800 yd (732 m) when mounted. See M. M. Johnson, Jr., and C. T. Haven, *Automatic Arms* (1941); W. Y. Carman, *A History of Firearms from Earliest Times to 1914* (1955); W. H. B. Smith and J. E. Smith, *Small Arms of the World: A Basic Manual of Military Small Arms* (9th ed., rev. 1969); A. J. Cormack, *Small Arms in Profile* (1972).

smallpox, acute, highly contagious disease causing a high fever and successive stages of severe skin eruptions. The disease occurs throughout the world where vaccination is not practiced and has occurred in epidemics throughout history. It is caused by a filterable virus that may be airborne or spread by direct contact. After an incubation period of about two weeks, fever, aching, and prostration occur, lasting two or three days. An eruption then appears and spreads over the entire body; the lesions become blisterlike and pustular within a week. The lesions then open and crust over, causing itching and pain. When the crusts fall off, usually in another one or two weeks, the extent of permanent damage to the skin (pockmarks) becomes evident. There is no specific treatment for smallpox; penicillin is administered to prevent secondary bacterial infection. Routine vaccination of children before they reach their first birthday has eliminated the scourge of smallpox in technically advanced countries. One of the projects of the World Health Organization has been to extend the benefits of vaccination to underdeveloped areas still without it. Edward Jenner demonstrated the practicability of vaccination with cowpox virus, which causes the production of antibodies that also protect the body against invasion by smallpox viruses.

smaltite (smôl'tīt), opaque tin-white to steel-gray mineral of the pyrite group, a compound of cobalt and arsenic. It occurs in massive form, occasionally in crystals (cubes) of the isometric system. It is an important ore of cobalt and is found in Saxony, Norway, Sweden, and Ontario.

Smart, Christopher, 1722–71, English poet. A graduate of Cambridge, he lived in London writing poems, editing a humorous magazine, and producing plays. His one great poem, *Song to David* (1763), an inspirational piece containing superb imagery, was written while he was confined in an asylum for a religious mania. See study by F. E. Anderson (1974).

smartweed: see BUCKWHEAT.

Smeaton, John (smē'tən), 1724–92, English civil engineer. He became an instrument maker, improved navigation instruments, and carried out many experiments on mechanical apparatus. Between 1750 and 1755 his interests turned increasingly to engineering, as evidenced by a number of papers read before the Royal Society during this period. He rebuilt (1756–59) the Eddystone lighthouse and worked on the Forth and Clyde Canal, Ramsgate Harbour and many important bridges. Within 10 years he became recognized as the first fully professional engineer of his time.

Smederevo (smĕ'dĕrĕvô), town (1971 pop. 90,739), E Yugoslavia, in Serbia, a port on the Danube River. Its industries include oil refining and steel manufacturing. Wine is produced in the surrounding region. Dating from Roman times, Smederevo was the capital of Serbia in the 15th cent. A fortress built in 1429 and taken by the Turks in 1456 still stands.

smell, sense that enables an organism to perceive and distinguish the odors of various substances. In man the organ of smell is situated in the mucous membrane of the upper portion of the nasal cavity. It is made up of the olfactory cells, which are actually nerve cells that function as receptors for the sense of smell. The free ends of the cells project outward from the epithelial tissue in the form of numerous hairlike processes (about 1,000 per olfactory cell). These fibers are buried in the mucus that coats the inner surface of the nasal cavity and are stimulated by various odors. Nerve fibers extend from the olfactory cells to an area of the brain called the olfactory bulb. Any disturbance of the nasal cavity, such as the common cold in which the olfactory hairs are covered with excess mucus or other material, interferes with the sense of smell. Most physiologists agree that although a substance must be volatile to be sniffed by the nose, it must subsequently be dissolved in the mucous lining of the nasal cavity to be smelled. It is also believed that there are only a few basic odors (perhaps about seven), and that all other odors are a combination of these. Attempts at classifying the so-called primary sensations of smell have not yet been successful. How the olfactory cells distinguish between even a limited number of basic odors is not yet known, although many believe that the sensation of smell is a response to differences in molecular structure of the smelled substances. The sense of smell is not as strongly developed in man as in many other vertebrates. To many invertebrates (especially insects) as well as many vertebrates, smell is important in obtaining food, in finding mating partners, and in recognizing other animals.

smelling salts: see AMMONIA.

smelt, common name for a small, slender fish of the family Osmeridae, closely allied to the grayling of the family Salmonidae (SALMON family). Most species are marine, but some ascend freshwater streams to spawn and others are landlocked in lakes. The American smelt (or icefish), *Osmerus mordax*, averages 10 in. (25 cm) in length and 1 lb (.45 kg) in weight. It is valued for its delicious, fragrant flesh, although its feeding habits are destructive and sometimes cannibalistic. The candlefish (or eulachon), a smelt found from Oregon to Alaska, is named for the fact that it is so fat at spawning time that when dried and strung on a wick it can be burned as a primitive candle. In Alaska and NE Asia are found the northwestern smelt (or rainbow herring) and the pond smelt. The top smelt, *Atherinops affinis*, and jack smelt are Pacific SILVERSIDES of the family Atherinidae, which belong to a different order. The deep-sea smelts, family Bathylagidae, are closely related to the true smelts. Deep-sea and true smelts are classified in the phylum CHORDATA, subphylum Vertebrata, class Osteichthyes, order Clupeiformes, families Bathylagidae and Osmeridae, respectively.

smelting, in metallurgy, any process of melting or fusion, especially to extract a metal from its ore. Smelting processes vary in detail depending on the nature of the ore and the metal involved, but they are typified in the use of the BLAST FURNACE and the REVERBERATORY FURNACE.

Smerdis (smûr'dĭs), d. c.528 B.C., second son of CYRUS THE GREAT, king of Persia. He is also called Bardiya. He was assassinated by his brother Cambyses II, who kept the murder a secret. Patizithes, the Magian custodian of Cambyses' palace, deposed Cambyses (who was campaigning in Egypt), put forward his own brother Guamata to impersonate Smerdis, and proclaimed him king. After a reign of seven months the false Smerdis was overthrown (521 B.C.) and slain. Darius I succeeded Guamata.

Smet, Pierre Jean de: see DE SMET, PIERRE JEAN.

Smetana, Bedřich (bĕ'dərzhĭkh smĕ'tänä), 1824–84, Czech composer, creator of a national style in Czech music. He studied in Pilsen and in Prague, where in 1849, with the encouragement of Liszt, he opened a music school. From 1856 to 1860 he was a conductor at Göteborg, Sweden. In 1861 he returned to Prague and took an active role in founding a national opera house. His first patriotic opera, *The Brandenburgers in Bohemia*, was produced there in 1866. In the same season his most famous work, *The Bartered Bride*, was staged. It presented a genial picture of village life in Bohemia and reflected the spirit of Czech folk music and dance. The opera was immensely successful, and Smetana was appointed chief conductor of the National Theater. He retained that post until 1874, when he became deaf. Afflicted by nervous disorder for many years, he died in an insane asylum. Smetana's other operas include *Dalibor* (1868), *The Kiss* (1876), *The Secret* (1878), and *Libuše* (1881). His symphonic poem *My Fatherland* (1879) contains the well-known section *Vltava* (*The Moldau*). Almost all his music is programmatic, even two string quartets, *From My Life* (1876, 1882), the earlier of which is one of his finest works. See biographies by B. Large (1970) and John Clapham (1972).

Smethwick: see WARLEY.

Smetona, Antanas (äntä'näs smĕ'tōnä), 1874–1944, Lithuanian dictator. A lawyer, he became a leader of the Lithuanian autonomists under the czarist regime. He was provisional president (1919–20) of Lithuania when it gained independence. After the military coup d'etat (Nov., 1926) against the Socialist government, Smetona was elected president with Augustin Voldemaras as premier. Parliamentary government was suspended, and in 1929, Smetona forced Voldemaras to resign and assumed full dictatorial power. He was reelected in 1931 and 1938. After Lithuania was incorporated (1940) into the USSR, Smetona fled to Germany and then (1941) to the United States, where he died.

Smibert or **Smybert, John** (both: smī'bərt), 1688–1751, American portrait painter, b. Scotland, the first skillful painter in New England. After his apprenticeship to an Edinburgh house painter, he went to London. There he studied art, made a trip to Italy, then returned to London, where he had small success. He emigrated (1729) to America with Dean (later Bishop) Berkeley, who had persuaded him to teach art at his college in Bermuda, though the plan did not materialize. After a stay in Newport, R.I., Smibert went to Boston. There in 1730 he assembled probably the first art show in America. He married an heiress, became a successful portrait painter, and won considerable social standing. Among his works are portraits of Judge Edmund Quincy (Mus. of Fine Arts, Boston) and Peter Faneuil (Mass. Historical Society, Boston). Harvard, Bowdoin, and other institutions house examples of his formal portraiture. Yale owns the first important portrait group painted in America, Smibert's *Bishop Berkeley and His Entourage* (1731), including a self-portrait. The artist's influence is evident in the work of such early Americans as Copley, Washington Allston, and John Trumbull. See study by Henry Foote (1950, repr. 1969).

Śmigły-Rydz, Edward: see RYDZ-ŚMIGŁY, EDWARD.

smilax, common name for a florists' plant of two separate genera (*Asparagus* and *Smilax*), both of the family Liliaceae (LILY family). The greenbriers, prickly vines often weedy in North America, belong to the same genus (*Smilax*) as the plants yielding sarsaparilla. Both genera are classified in the division MAGNOLIOPHYTA, class Liliatae, order Liliales, family Liliaceae.

Smillie, Robert (smī'lē), 1857–1940, British labor official, b. Belfast, Ireland, of Scottish parents. He was president of the Scottish Miners' Federation from 1894 to 1918 and from 1921 until his death, and as president (1912–21) of the Miners' Federation of Great Britain he led the coal miners' strike of 1912. For many years he advocated the nationalization of mines. He served as a Labour member of Parliament from 1923 to 1929. See his autobiography, *My Life for Labour* (1924).

Smirke, Sir Robert, 1781–1867, English architect, one of the most noted exponents of the CLASSIC REVIVAL. His best-known design is the main facade of the British Museum (1823–47). Other buildings in London are the General Post Office and the Royal College of Physicians. Smirke's influence resulted in a more accurate interpretation of Greek forms in the English work of the time. Upon his retirement (1847), his brother, **Sydney Smirke,** 1798–1877, took up the work at the British Museum, where he erected the western side of the quadrangle and the new reading room (1854–57). In 1857 he rebuilt the Carlton Club, London, on a design adopted from the Library of St. Mark's at Venice; he also built the exhibition galleries for the Royal Academy at Burlington House (1866).

Smith, Adam, 1723–90, Scottish economist, educated at Glasgow and Oxford. He became professor of moral philosophy at the Univ. of Glasgow in 1752, and while teaching there wrote his *Theory of Moral Sentiments* (1759), which gave him the beginnings of an international reputation. He traveled on the Continent from 1764 to 1766 as tutor to the duke of Buccleuch and while in France met some of the PHYSIOCRATS and began to write *An Inquiry into the Nature and Causes of the Wealth of Nations,* finally published in 1776. Smith postulated the theory of the division of labor and emphasized that value arises from the labor expended in the process of production. He was led by the rationalist current of the century, as well as by the more direct influence of Hume and others, to believe that in a laissez-faire economy the impulse of self-interest would bring about the public welfare; at the same time he was capable of appreciating that private groups such as manufacturers might at times oppose the public interest. Smith was opposed to monopolies and the concepts of mercantilism in general but admitted restrictions to free trade, such as the NAVIGATION ACTS, as sometimes necessary national economic weapons in the existing state of the world. Smith wrote before the Industrial Revolution was fully developed, and some of his theories were voided by its development, but as an analyst of institutions and an influence on later economists he has never been surpassed. His pragmatism, as well as the leaven of ethical content and social insight in his thought, differentiates him from the rigidity of David Ricardo and the school of early 19th-century utilitarianism. In 1778, Smith was appointed commissioner of customs for Scotland. His *Essays on Philosophical Subjects* (1795) appeared posthumously. See biography by John Rae (1895, repr. 1965); studies by Eli Ginzberg (1934, repr. 1964), T. D. Campbell (1971), and Samuel Hollander (1973).

Smith, Alfred Emanuel, 1873–1944, American political leader, b. New York City. Reared in poor surroundings, he took various jobs—including work in the Fulton fish market—to help support his family. In 1895, through the help of a Tammany district leader, he was appointed a clerk in the office of the county commissioner of jurors. As a member (1904–15) of the New York state assembly, he took a prominent role in state Democratic politics, became (1913) speaker of the assembly, and gained a reputation for progressive policies. He was (1915–17) sheriff of New York co. and then was elected (1917) president of the New York City board of aldermen. In 1918, Smith was elected governor of New York. He was defeated for reelection in 1920 but regained the office in 1922 and was reelected twice again (1924, 1926). He proved a forceful and well-liked governor and achieved the passage of much reform legislation. In 1928, Smith, helped by Franklin Delano Roosevelt, won the Democratic nomination for President, the first Roman Catholic to receive this recognition. After his defeat by Herbert Hoover, he retired to private life, becoming (1929) president of the firm that owned and operated the Empire State Building in New York City. He served (1932–34) as editor of the magazine *New Outlook.* He became a bitter opponent of President Roosevelt's New Deal policies and supported the Republican presidential candidates in 1936 and 1940. Smith was the author of *Up to Now* (1929). See biographies by Frank Graham (1945), E. S. Warner (1956), Oscar Handlin (1958), Matthew Josephson (1969), and Richard O'Connor (1970); F. D. Roosevelt, *The Happy Warrior* (1928).

Smith, Bessie, 1898?–1937, American singer, b. Chattanooga, Tenn. About 1910 Smith became the protégée of Gertrude (Ma) Rainey, one of the earliest blues singers. After working in traveling shows she went to New York City, where she made (1923–27) recordings, accompanied by such outstanding artists as Louis Armstrong, Fletcher Henderson, and James P. Johnson. She quickly became the favorite singer of the jazz public. The power and somber beauty of her voice, coupled with songs representing every variety of the blues, earned her the title "Empress of the Blues." Around 1928, changing popular taste and her growing alcoholism led to a decline in her popularity. Though she continued to tour, her last years were embittered. She died after an automobile accident while on tour in Mississippi. Many felt that immediate medical attention, which might have saved her life, was denied to her because she was black. This view is put forth in Edward Albee's play *The Death of Bessie Smith* (1960). Numerous critics regarded her as the greatest of all jazz artists, and her fame increased enormously after her death. See biography by Chris Albertson (1973).

Smith, David, 1906–65, American sculptor, b. Decatur, Ind., studied painting at the Art Students League, New York City, and with Jan Matulka. In the 1930s he began experimenting with sculpture. After 1935 he worked primarily in this medium. His mature works, in wrought iron and cut steel, exhibit fantastic imagery and constructivist diagramming of space. His open constructions, such as *Hudson River Landscape* (Ogunquit Mus., Maine), stress the play of sculptural silhouettes against directional lines. Other works include abstract variations of natural subjects, such as *Cockfight* (Whitney Mus., New York City), and open, totemlike forms that frequently incorporate miscellaneous "found" objects. See R. E. Kraus, *Terminal Ironworks: The Sculpture of David Smith* (1971).

Smith, Donald Alexander: see STRATHCONA AND MOUNT ROYAL, DONALD ALEXANDER SMITH, 1ST BARON.

Smith, Edmund Kirby, or **Edmund Kirby-Smith,** 1824–93, American soldier, Confederate general in the Civil War, b. St. Augustine, Fla. A West Point graduate, he was cited for gallantry in the Mexican War. A major when he resigned from the U.S. army (March, 1861) to fight for the Confederacy, he served in the Shenandoah under J. E. Johnston, and fought at BULL RUN (July). Smith led the Confederate advance into Kentucky and defeated a Union force at Richmond, Ky. (Aug., 1862). He ably commanded the isolated Trans-Mississippi Dept. (1863–65) and was promoted to general in Feb., 1864. The unsuccessful Red River campaign of Nathaniel P. Banks was directed against his forces. Smith was the last Confederate general to surrender (May 26, 1865). After the war he was chancellor of the Univ. of Nashville (now George Peabody College for Teachers) from 1870 to 1875 and professor at the Univ. of the South, Sewanee, Tenn., from 1875 to 1893. See biographies by A. H. Noll (1907) and J. H. Parks (1954); R. L. Kerby, *Kirby Smith's Confederacy* (1972).

Smith, Frederick Edwin: see BIRKENHEAD, FREDERICK EDWIN SMITH, 1ST EARL OF.

Smith, George, 1840–76, English Orientalist. His paper on the Chaldean account of the Deluge brought him wide fame and resulted in an excavation trip to Nineveh (1873), sponsored by the London *Daily Telegraph,* to locate missing fragments. While on another undertaking of excavation he died at Alep. His works include *Ancient History from the Monuments: Assyria* (1875) and *Ancient History from the Monuments: the History of Babylonia* (1877); *Assyrian Discoveries* (1875); and *The Chaldean Account of Genesis* (1876, new ed. 1880).

Smith, Sir George Adam, 1856–1942, Scottish biblical scholar and Hebraist, b. Calcutta, India. He was professor of Old Testament language, literature, and theology in the United Free Church College of Glasgow from 1892 to 1909 and thereafter, until 1935, principal and vice chancellor of the Univ. of Aberdeen. He frequently traveled and lectured in the United States. Smith was knighted in 1916. He is especially noted for his *Historical Geography of the Holy Land* (2d ed. 1894, repr. 1966 of 1932 ed.).

Smith, Gerrit, 1797–1874, American reformer, b. Utica, N.Y. He spent much of his fortune in various reforms, most notably abolition. He was an organizer of the Liberty party and was candidate for governor of New York in 1840. A Congressman in 1853, he resigned in 1854. He again ran for governor in 1858. He is thought to have aided John Brown in planning the Harpers Ferry raid. See biographies by O. B. Frothingham (1878, repr. 1969) and R. V. Harlow (1939, repr. 1972).

Smith, Gipsy, 1860–1947, English evangelist, originally named Rodney Smith, b. Wanstead. His father, a gypsy, was also an evangelist. When Rodney was still a youth he became a member of General Booth's Christian Mission of London, which later became the Salvation Army. However, his connection with the organization was severed in 1882. From 1883, Smith's evangelistic labors gradually extended throughout England and to Scotland, the United States, Australia, and South Africa. He was a special missioner (1897–1912) of the National Free Church Council and after World War I toured England for the Methodist Church. He wrote *Gipsy Smith: His Life and Work* (rev. ed. 1925). See David Lazell, *From the Forest I Came* (1970).

Smith, Goldwin, 1823–1910, English educator, historian, and journalist. Educated at Oxford, he took a prominent part in executing reforms at the university and became (1858) professor of modern history there. In many writings he expounded his ardently democratic, strongly anti-imperialistic, and antimilitaristic outlook. In 1868, Smith moved to the United States after accepting a position as professor of English literature and constitutional history at Cornell Univ. Although he retained the professorship until 1881, his removal to Canada (1870) prevented him from assuming fulltime duties at the university during most of his tenure. His journals, including the short-lived *Nation* and *Leader,* and his numerous studies in social science, literature, and religion earned him great respect in North America and Great Britain as an educator and a liberal social critic. See his reminiscences (1910) and correspondence (1913), both ed. by Arnold Haultain; biographies by Haultain (1913) and Elisabeth Wallace (1957).

Smith, Sir Harry George Wakelyn, 1787–1860, British general and administrator. He served in the Peninsular War and in the War of 1812 and was a brigade major at the battle of Waterloo. He commanded a division in the Kafir War (1834–36), in which he made his famous ride of 700 mi (1,130 km) from Capetown to Grahamstown in less than six days. He was governor of the newly annexed frontier territory, named Queen Adelaide prov., from 1835 until the annexation was repudiated by the British government in 1837. He was then transferred to India as deputy adjutant general. He distinguished himself in the Sikh Wars and was created baronet for the victory at Aliwal (1846). Returning to South Africa as governor of the Cape Colony (1847–52), he resumed his policy of expansion and carried on war with the Boers, accelerating their movement northward. See his autobiography (ed. by G. C. Moore Smith, 2 vol., 1901).

Smith, Henry John Stephen, 1826–83, British mathematician. He was a lecturer in mathematics (1850–73) and, from 1860 to 1883, Savilian professor of geometry at Oxford Univ. He is especially noted for his work on the theory of numbers and on elliptic functions. His scientific papers were collected and edited by J. W. L. Glaisher (1894).

Smith, Hoke, 1855–1931, American political leader, b. Newton, N.C. A successful lawyer in Atlanta, he acquired the Atlanta *Journal* in 1887. He served (1893–96) in President Cleveland's cabinet as Secretary of the Interior. He later was governor of Georgia (1907–9, 1911) and U.S. Senator (1911–21). As governor he vigorously supported railroad regulation, educational reform, and direct primary legislation. He won popularity among white Southerners by his anti-Negro policies and he helped disenfranchise Georgia blacks. After his defeat (1920) for reelection, he returned to the practice of law. See biography by D. W. Grantham, Jr. (1958, repr. 1967).

Smith, Holland McTyeire, 1882–1967, American general, b. Seale, Ala. He was commissioned in the marines in 1905 and served in France in World War I. In World War II, Smith pioneered in developing amphibious tactics. He commanded troops in actions in the Gilbert, Marshall, and Marianas islands and at Iwo Jima. He commanded the Fleet Marine Force in the Pacific (1944–45) and retired (1946) from the marines as a general. He wrote *Coral and Brass* (1949).

Smith, Horatio or **Horace,** 1779–1849, and **James Smith,** 1775–1839, English parodists, brothers. They wrote the famous *Rejected Addresses* (1812) which burlesqued such contemporary poets as Wordsworth, Scott, Coleridge, and Byron. James Smith, who produced the better pieces, never wrote anything of value afterward. Horatio Smith was the author of several novels, including *Brambletye House* (1826), an imitation of Scott. *Horace in London* (1813) was a collection of their early work.

Smith, Ian Douglas, 1919–, Rhodesian political leader. After serving in the British Royal Air Force in World War II, he entered (1948) the Southern Rhodesia legislative assembly. In 1953, when the Central African Federation was formed out of Southern Rhodesia (Rhodesia), Northern Rhodesia (Zambia), and Nyasaland (Malawi), Smith was elected to the federal Parliament. He served until 1961, when he helped found the Rhodesian Front party, a white supremacist organization that favored independence for Southern Rhodesia from Great Britain. In Dec., 1962, shortly before the breakup of the Central African Federation, the party's surprise electoral victory in Southern Rhodesia elevated Smith to the posts of deputy prime minister and minister of the treasury; he succeeded as prime minister of Rhodesia in April, 1964. He immediately suppressed black African nationalist activities and put down resulting riots with brutal police action. Negotiations with Great Britain for independence foundered on the issue of eventual African majority rule in Rhodesia, and Smith unilaterally declared (Nov., 1965) Rhodesian independence. Despite economic sanctions against Rhodesia by Great Britain and many other countries, Smith consolidated white rule and apartheid and, in 1970, declared Rhodesia a republic. His government won overwhelming victories in the elections of 1970 and 1974.

Smith, James, c.1719–1806, political leader in the American Revolution, signer of the Declaration of Independence, b. Ireland. He settled in Pennsylvania in his youth and practiced law at York. He served in provincial assemblies and conventions and advocated independence early. He was (1776–78) a member of the Continental Congress.

Smith, James, 1775–1839: see SMITH, HORATIO.

Smith, Jedediah Strong, 1799–1831, American explorer, one of the greatest of the MOUNTAIN MEN, b. near Binghamton, N.Y. He was a superb rifleman, dauntless in peril, and devoted to Bible reading. He seems to have arrived in St. Louis in 1822 and to have joined the expedition of William Ashley, an American fur trader, but little is known of that first expedition. However, Smith became prominent on the 1823 expedition. Early in 1824 he and Thomas Fitzpatrick took a party through South Pass and thus began the regular use of that route. Smith and a few men then headed north and along with Alexander Ross, a Canadian fur trader, went into present-day Montana and as far north as the present Canadian boundary before going back to Great Salt Lake. In 1825 he set out from Great Salt Lake on his most famous venture. Traveling southwest with a small band of men, he crossed the Colorado River and the Mojave Desert, arriving in San Diego, Calif., then part of Mexico. Leaving California, Smith and two of his men became the first white men to cross the Sierra Nevada and the Great Salt Desert from west to east. Smith and a party returned (1827) to California on the southwestern route, but on the way they were attacked by Mojave Indians; the survivors reached California and the men who had been left there. After trouble with Mexican authorities, Smith and his men went N toward the Columbia River. Only he and three others escaped an Indian attack and arrived at the Hudson's Bay Company post, Fort Vancouver, where John McLoughlin, a Canadian fur trader, befriended them. Smith's company—Smith, Jackson, and Sublette—was broken up in 1830, and the Rocky Mountain Fur Company was formed. Smith returned to St. Louis. In 1831 he set out with a company on the Santa Fe Trail and was killed along the Cimarron River by Comanche Indians. His extraordinarily wide travels opened not only the rich fur trapping and trading country but also trails and territory that were soon frequented by American pioneers going to California and the Pacific Northwest. His journal was edited by Maurice Sullivan (1934). See biography by Maurice Sullivan (1936, repr. 1972); study by J. G. Neihardt (1920, repr. 1970).

Smith, John, d. 1612, English nonconformist: see SMYTH, JOHN.

Smith, John, c.1580–1631, English colonist in America, b. Willoughby, Lincolnshire, England. A merchant's apprentice until his father's death in 1596, he thereafter lived an adventurous life, traveling, fighting in wars against the Turks in Transylvania and Hungary, and surviving a period of slavery in Turkey. His own account of these adventures has been doubted by some investigators but has been substantiated in a number of particulars. Returning to England, he invested in the new LONDON COMPANY and in 1606 sailed from London for America with Capt. Christopher NEWPORT. On arrival in Virginia, Smith was named a member of the governing council of the Jamestown settlement, although not permitted to serve immediately, and began his explorations of the surrounding territory. He established trade relations with the Indians, drew up a map of Virginia, and finally fell into the hands of the Indian chief POWHATAN. Although there is no definite proof of the famous incident of Smith's being saved from death by Powhatan's daughter, POCAHONTAS, it is considered quite probable that it happened. After his return (1608) to Jamestown, Smith's enemies arrested him, but he was saved from hanging by the arrival of Newport with new settlers. Smith then became president of the council and energetically resisted the company's peremptory demands that the colonists find gold. Maintaining his leadership despite opposition, he carried the colony through periods of intense suffering, hunger, and want (the "starving time"), remaining firm, tactful, and resourceful. Injured in an explosion, he returned to England in 1609. In 1614 he was sent to New England by a group of London merchants, and returned with a valuable cargo of fish and furs. He emphasized the importance of fishing and upheld the prospects for settlement in New England. On another voyage he was captured by pirates and then by the French, but eventually returned to England. He wrote *A True Relation of . . . Virginia* (1608), *A Map of Virginia* (1612), *A Description of New England* (1616), *New England's Trials* (1620, 2d ed. 1622), *The Generall Historie of Virginia, New-England, and the Summer Isles* (1624), *An Accidence; or, The Path-Way to Experience* (1626; enl. and repub. as *A Sea Grammer,* 1627), *The True Travels, Adventures, and Observations of Captaine John Smith* (1630), and *Advertisements for the Unexperienced Planters of New England, or Anywhere* (1631). See edition of his works by Edward Arber (1884; repr. and ed. by A. G. Bradley, 2 vol., 1910, repr. 1967); biographies by J. G. Fletcher (1928, repr. 1972), Bradford Smith (1953), P. L. Barbour (1964), N. B. Gerson (1966), and E. H. Emerson (1971).

Smith, Joseph, 1805–44, American Mormon leader, founder of the Church of Jesus Christ of the Latter-Day Saints, b. Sharon, Vt. When he was a boy his family moved to Palmyra, N.Y., where he experienced the poverty and hardships of life on a rough frontier. He had visions when he was still young and later recorded that he was first told in a vision in 1823 of the existence of secret records, but it was not until 1827 that the hiding place of the records was revealed to him. According to his account, in 1827 he unearthed golden tablets inscribed with sacred writings that he translated. Oliver Cowdery, Martin Harris, and others transcribed these records from his dictation, and the *Book of Mormon* was published in 1829. Further revelations led him to found a new religion after priesthood had been conferred upon him and Cowdery by an "angel." As prophet and seer he founded (1830) his church in Fayette, N.Y. (see LATTER-DAY SAINTS, CHURCH OF JESUS CHRIST OF; MORMONS). The hostility of his neighbors forced him to move his headquarters to Kirtland, Ohio, where with the help of Sidney Rigdon and others he embarked on extensive business affairs. The Panic of 1837 was one of the reasons for removal farther west to Missouri. There the industrious and self-contained members of his faith again ran into difficulties with their neighbors. Smith and others were arrested but escaped, and his faithful followers were driven from Missouri. Having obtained a favorable charter from Illinois, Smith founded the settlement of Nauvoo, which, thanks to the concerted efforts of the members of his church, was soon flourishing. Disaffection grew, however, and some of the dissident members founded a newspaper, the *Expositor,* in which they bitterly criticized him. He put down the opposition, thereby giving the hostile non-Mormons a pretext for attacking him. When in 1844 he announced himself as candidate for the presidency of the United States, his enemies set upon him. He and his brother Hyrum were arrested on charges of treason and conspiracy. They were lodged in the jail at Carthage, Ill., and there on June 27, 1844, they were murdered by a mob. The revelations experienced by Smith—including one enjoining plural marriage, which he obeyed by taking many wives and which later caused the Mormons much trouble—were the foundation stones of a faith that after his death grew to be one of the great religions of the United States. Because he was a highly controversial figure, the literature on him is also controversial. See biography by Lucy Smith (1908, repr. 1969); studies by Rudolph Etzenhouser (1894, repr. 1971), Fawn Brodie (2d ed. 1971), and R. L. Anderson (1971).

Smith, Kirby: see SMITH, EDMUND KIRBY.

Smith, Lillian, 1897–1966, American writer and social critic, b. Jasper, Fla. She was a social worker in Georgia for several years. Her bestselling novel *Strange Fruit* (1944) is set in the South and depicts the tragic love of a white boy for a black girl. Smith was active in the Congress of Racial Equality (CORE) but resigned when CORE supported the use of violence as a means to its ends. Her nonfiction works include *Killers of the Dream* (1949), *Now is the Time* (1955), and *Memory of a Large Christmas* (1962).

Smith, Logan Pearsall, 1865–1946, Anglo-American author, b. Millville, N.J. After 1888 he lived in England, studied at Oxford, and became a man of letters. His brief and exquisite essays were collected as *All Trivia* (1933). Other works include writings on the English language, a biography of Sir Henry Wotton (1907), *On Reading Shakespeare* (1933), *Reperusals and Re-collections* (1936), and *Milton and His Modern Critics* (1940). See his autobiography, *Unforgotten Years* (1939); Robert Gathorne-Hardy, *Recollections of Logan Pearsall Smith* (1949).

Smith, Maggie, 1934–, English actress. Smith first appeared on stage in *Twelfth Night* (1952). Her New York debut was in the revue *New Faces of 1956.* Adept at both comic and serious roles, Smith worked with the OLD VIC Company and the National Theatre, giving notable performances in *As You Like It, Richard II, The Rehearsal, Mary, Mary,* and *Private Lives.* Among her major films are *Othello* (1966), *Hot Millions* (1968), *The Prime of Miss Jean Brodie* (1969), for which she won an Academy Award, and *Travels with My Aunt* (1973).

Smith, Margaret Chase, 1897–, U.S. Senator from Maine (1949–73), b. Skowhegan, Maine. She taught school briefly and then worked (1919–28) on the Skowhegan weekly newspaper. In 1930 she married Clyde Smith, the publisher of the paper, and upon his election as U.S. Representative served in Washington as his secretary, researcher, and office manager. Active in Republican party politics, she was elected after the death of her husband in 1940 to finish his unexpired term and was then reelected four times. Maine's first congresswoman, she was elected U.S. Senator in 1948 and reelected in 1954, 1960, and 1966. She was unexpectedly defeated in the 1972 election by her Democratic opponent.

Smith, Oliver, 1918–, American producer and scene designer for theater, film, ballet, and opera, b. Wawpawn, Wis. With a background in painting, Smith created his first professional stage design for the ballet *Rodeo* (1942). Since then he has designed many Broadway shows, including *On the Town* (1945), *Brigadoon* (1946), *My Fair Lady* (1956), *Auntie Mame* (1956), *Becket* (1960), and *Hello, Dolly!* (1963). Smith's films include *Oklahoma!* (1955), *Guys and Dolls* (1955), and *Porgy and Bess* (1959). He is codirector of the American Ballet Theatre.

Smith, Preserved, 1880–1941, American historian, b. Cincinnati. He taught history at Williams, Amherst, and Harvard before becoming (1922) professor of history at Cornell Univ., where he remained until his death. He was an editor of the *Journal of Modern History* (1929–32) and of the *American Historical Review* (1936–41). Among his books are *The Life and Letters of Martin Luther* (1911; 2d ed. 1914), *The Age of the Reformation* (1920), *Erasmus* (1923), and *A History of Modern Culture* (2 vol., 1930–34).

Smith, Red, 1905–, American sportswriter, b. Green Bay, Wis., grad. Notre Dame, 1927; his original name was Walter Wellesley. After working on newspapers in St. Louis and Philadelphia, he began a syndicated column in the New York *Herald Tribune* in 1945. He joined the staff of the New York *Times* in 1972. Smith is widely regarded as one of the nation's most literate and amusing sportswriters. Among his books are *Out of the Red* (1950) and *Views of Sport* (1954).

Smith, Robert, 1757–1842, U.S. government official, b. Lancaster, Pa. Admitted to the bar in 1786, he practiced law in Baltimore before serving in the Maryland state senate (1793–95) and in the Baltimore city council (1798–1801). An ardent Republican, he was (1801–9) Secretary of the Navy under President Thomas Jefferson. Smith successfully maintained a blockading squadron in the Mediterranean during the war against the Barbary states. He also served (1809–11) as Secretary of State under President James Madison but resigned at Madison's request because of disagreements over policy toward Great Britain and France.

Smith, Samuel Francis, 1808–95, American Baptist clergyman and poet, b. Boston. He is remembered as the author of the national hymn "America," written while he was a student at Andover Theological Seminary. Among his many other hymns is "The Morning Light Is Breaking."

Smith, Seba, 1792–1868, American humorist, b. Buckfield, Maine. He founded the Portland *Courier* in 1829 and in it began (1830) a series of humorous letters on politics under the pen name Major Jack Downing. His use of comic rustic speech and satirical comments on various political issues made him outstanding in the development of American humor. He eventually settled in New York City, where he wrote for various magazines. His works include *Powhatan* (1841) and *Way Down East* (1853).

Smith, Stevie (Margaret Florence Smith), 1902–71, English poet and novelist, b. Hull, Yorkshire. She worked in a London publisher's office until 1953. Her poetry is witty and gay, but beneath its surface lies a deep acceptance of life as it is. Her works include the novels *Novel on Yellow Paper* (1936) and *Holiday* (1949) and the volumes of poetry *Not Waving But Drowning* (1957) and *Selected Poems* (1962).

Smith, Sydney, 1771–1845, English clergyman, writer, and wit, ordained in the Church of England in 1794. In 1798 he went as a tutor to Edinburgh, where he studied medicine, occasionally preached, and with Jeffrey and others founded (1802) the *Edinburgh Review.* His brilliant contributions were a strong factor in the periodical's success. Moving to London in 1803, Smith lectured on moral philosophy at the Royal Institution and became a well-known figure in literary society. His "Peter Plymley" letters (published anonymously in 1807–8) in defense of Catholic Emancipation were the first of his many appeals for religious toleration. In 1809 he moved to Yorkshire, where he had been given a living of £500 a year. There he also acted as magistrate and village doctor. He went to a parish in Somerset in 1829; in 1831 he was given a residentiary canonry at St. Paul's. Smith's religion was strong and of a practical nature. A lover of justice and truth, he was a life-long defender of the oppressed. His failure to rise higher in the church is attributed to his wide reputation as a master of wit and satire. He is placed among the premier English wits and has been compared to Swift and to Voltaire. See his works (4 vol., 1839–40); his letters (ed. by Nowell Smith, 2 vol., 1953); selections from his writings (ed. by W. H. Auden, 1956); memoir by his daughter, Lady Holland (2 vol., 1855); biographies by G. W. Russell (1905, repr. 1971), Hesketh Pearson (1934, repr. 1971), and G. W. Bullett (1951, repr. 1971).

Smith, Theobald, 1859–1934, American pathologist, b. Albany, N.Y., M.D. Albany Medical College, 1883. He was professor of bacteriology at Columbian (now George Washington) Univ. (1886–95) and of comparative pathology at Harvard (1896–1915) and served (1915–29) as director of the department of animal pathology at Rockefeller Institute (now Rockefeller Univ.). He demonstrated the etiology of Texas cattle fever, differentiated between human and bovine tubercle bacilli, and, in his work on immunity, noted the allergylike reaction later investigated by Richet.

Smith, Thomas, Captain, American painter, active in New England from 1675 to 1690. Smith introduced baroque painting techniques into American art. He made use of chiaroscuro technique to render solid forms and reveal his psychological insight. His best-known work is his *Self-Portrait* (c.1690; Worcester Art Mus., Mass.).

Smith, Tony, 1912–, American sculptor, b. South Orange, N.J. Formerly an architect associated with Frank Lloyd Wright, Smith applies architectural principles to his monumental black steel sculpture. Allied with the minimalist school (see MODERN ART), he works with simple geometrical modules combined on a three-dimensional grid, creating drama through simplicity and scale. His work is represented at the Museum of Modern Art, New York City. See study by L. R. Lippard (1972).

Smith, Walter Bedell, 1895–1961, U.S. general, b. Indianapolis, Ind. He enlisted (1910) in the Indiana National Guard, won a commission in the U.S. army (1918), and advanced to the rank of lieutenant general (1943). Secretary (1941–42) to the general staff, he became (1942) the U.S. secretary to the combined chiefs of staff, and as Dwight D. Eisenhower's chief of staff (1942–45) he signed the surrender terms with Italy (1943) and with Germany (1945). Smith served (1946–49) as ambassador to the USSR, director of the Central Intelligence Agency (1950–53), and Undersecretary of State (1953–54). He wrote *My Three Years in Moscow* (1950) and *Eisenhower's Six Great Decisions: Europe 1944–1945* (1956).

Smith, W. Eugene, 1918–, American photojournalist, b. Wichita, Kan. Smith is considered one of the principal masters of modern photojournalism. The distorted newspaper coverage of his father's suicide made him determined to seek absolute personal honesty in his own documentary work. After a short time on the staff of *Newsweek,* he freelanced for many leading magazines, including *Life, Collier's,* and *Harper's Bazaar,* and for the New York *Times.* He worked with miniature (35 mm) cameras and developed an innovative flash technique that enabled him to produce indoor photographs having the appearance of natural or lamp light. Smith's photographic record of events in the Pacific theater of World War II are ranked among the grimmest and most powerful visual indictments of war. Severely wounded in 1945, he was unable to work for two years. The first photograph he made upon recuperation (of his two children walking toward a sunlit area on a wooded path) was chosen as the final work in the "Family of Man" exhibition (Mus. of Modern Art, New York City; 1955). From 1947 to 1954 Smith worked full-time for *Life* creating a series of major photo essays, including "Trial by Jury" (1948), "Country Doctor" (1948), "Nurse Midwife" (1951), "The Reign of Chemistry" (1953), and "A Man of Mercy" (concerning Albert Schweitzer, 1954). With a Guggenheim Fellowship he created his celebrated "Pittsburgh" essay (1956). In 1963 Smith began an intensive photographic study of Japan. While documenting the maiming effects of mercury poisoning from factory pollution on the residents of the fishing village of Minamata (1971–73), he was brutally beaten; as a result he lost his sight temporarily in 1974. See *aperture* monograph, *W. Eugene Smith: His Photographs and Notes* (1969).

Smith, William, 1769–1839, English geologist. He made a systematic study of the geological strata of England and identified the fossils peculiar to each layer, thereby introducing the method of estimating, from the fossils present, the age of geological formations. His *Geological Map of England* (1815), one of the first of its kind, was followed by similar maps of English counties. Smith was known as a founder of English stratigraphic geology.

Smith, Sir William, 1813–93, English editor and lexicographer. He was editor of the *Quarterly Review* from 1867 until his death and also edited reference works esteemed for their accuracy and comprehensiveness. These included dictionaries of Greek and Roman antiquities (1842), biography and mythology (1844–49), and geography (1854–57) and a dictionary of the Bible (1860–63).

Smith, William Robertson, 1846–94, Scottish biblical scholar and Orientalist. He studied for the ministry of the Free Church of Scotland. From 1870 he was professor of Oriental languages and Old Testament exegesis at the Free Church College, Aberdeen. Certain articles on biblical subjects that he wrote for *The Encyclopaedia Britannica* (9th ed.) roused a storm in his church, and in 1881 he was removed from his professorship. This cause célèbre was an important factor in the modernizing of Scottish Presbyterian theology. He was soon made an editor of *The Encyclopaedia Britannica* and in 1887 became editor in chief. He was professor of Arabic at Cambridge (from 1883) and chief librarian there (1886). Among his works are *The Old Testament in the Jewish Church* (1881), *The Prophets of Israel* (1882), and *The Religion of the Semites* (1889). See biography by J. S. Black (1902).

Smith, Sir William Sidney, 1764–1840, British admiral. He was a distinguished commander in the French Revolutionary and Napoleonic Wars and is especially remembered for his defense of Acre against Napoleon in 1799.

Smith College, at Northampton, Mass.; undergraduate for women, graduate coeducational; chartered 1871, opened 1875 through a bequest of Sophia Smith. The first president, Laurenus Clark SEELYE, was influential in establishing high standards of scholarship. Smith is known for its junior-year-abroad program. It has a noted school of social work, and its art galleries are renowned for their collections of modern art. Its library has collections relating to music of the 16th and 17th cent., botany, and Jean Jacques Rousseau. The school participates in a cooperative program with Amherst, Hampshire College, Mount Holyoke College, and the Univ. of Massachusetts.

Smithfield, district of the City of London, England. Beginning in the 12th cent. it was used for fairs, markets, jousts, and executions. During the reign of Queen Mary I (1553–58) Protestants were executed there. London's central meat market is in Smithfield.

Smithfield, town (1970 pop. 13,468), Providence co., N R.I.; set off from Providence and inc. 1731. Long a textile town, it now has diversified industries. It was settled early in the 18th cent., mainly by Friends.

smithing: see FORGING.

Smithson, Robert, 1938–73, American sculptor, b. Passaic, N.J. After first making modular, serial sculpture, Smithson began to design EARTH WORKS in the 1960s. His major pieces associated with the earth works movement are *Spiral Jetty* (1970; Great Salt Lake, Utah) and *Broken Circle* and *Spiral Hill* (both 1971; in a quarry in Holland). His work is represented in the Whitney and Modern Art museums in New York City. He died in an airplane crash at 35.

Smithsonian Institution, research and education center, at Washington, D.C.; founded 1846 under terms of the will of James Smithson of London, who in 1829 bequeathed his fortune to the United States to create an establishment for the "increase and diffusion of knowledge among men." The institution began as a museum. Today it is a vast complex comprising the National Museum of Natural History, National Museum of History and Technology, National Air and Space Museum, National Zoological Park, Freer Gallery of Art, National Gallery of Art, National Collection of Fine Arts, National Portrait Gallery, Joseph H. Hirshhorn Museum and Sculpture Garden, John F. Kennedy Center for the Performing Arts, Smithsonian Astrophysical Observatory, Smithsonian Tropical Research Institute, Radiation Biology Laboratory, National Armed Forces Museum Advisory Board, Woodrow Wilson International Center for Scholars, Anacostia Neighborhood Museum, Cooper-Hewitt Museum of Decorative Arts and Design (in 1974 it was announced that the museum would be renamed the National Museum of Design), International Exchange Service, and the Science Information Exchange.

smog (smŏg) [from *sm*oke and f*og*], dense, visible AIR POLLUTION. Smog is commonly of two types. The gray smog of older industrial cities like London and New York derives from the massive combustion of coal and fuel oil in or near the city, releasing tons of ashes, soot, and sulfur compounds into the air. The brown smog characteristic of Los Angeles and Denver is caused by automobiles. Nitric oxide from automobile exhaust combines with oxygen in the air to form the brown gas nitrogen dioxide. Also, when hydrocarbons and nitrous oxides from auto emissions are exposed to sunlight, a photochemical reaction takes place that results in the formation of ozone and other irritating compounds. In some instances, atmospheric pollutants accumulate and become concentrated when air movement is stopped by a TEMPERATURE INVERSION: Usually the air is warmer at the earth's surface and colder above; in a temperature inversion a layer of warm air forms above and holds down a layer of cool air at the ground. Smog usually results in reduced visibility, irritation of the eyes and respiratory system, and damage to paint, metal, rubber, and other materials. Prolonged smogs (generally caused by temperature inversions) are often lethal to persons with respiratory ailments. As the result of an unremitting smog in 1948 in Donora, Pa., more than 5,000 persons were reported ill and the deaths of 20 persons were recorded. In London, smog accounted for the deaths of more than 4,000 persons in 1952 and 106 persons in 1962.

Smohalla (smōhăl'ə), c.1815–1907, American Indian prophet, chief of a small tribe (the Wanapun) of the Columbia River valley. He preached a religion based on a vision of returning to Indian modes of living. His followers, called the Dreamers, did not advocate force, but they caused some difficulty to the government in its policy of forcing Indians to settle on reservations. See Click Relander, *Drummers and Dreamers* (1956).

smoke, visible gaseous product of incomplete combustion. Smoke varies with its source, but it usually comprises hot gas and suspended particles of carbon and tarry substances, or soot. To reduce the amount of smoke entering the atmosphere, AIR POLLUTION laws generally require that power plants, factories, and other large combustion facilities burn anthracite (hard) coal, natural gas, or low-sulfur fuel oil rather than bituminous (soft) coal or high-sulfur fuel oil, and that smokestacks be equipped with scrubbers or other devices. Proper firing techniques and equipment can eliminate or greatly reduce the smoke produced by any fuel. Wood gives little smoke if burned when dry and if the fire is given a good supply of air. Where it is necessary to use soft coal because of its lower cost or because other fuel is not available, the grate and flue must be built to insure maximum combustion, the coal supply must be carefully regulated, and adequate air must be supplied. There are various ways of reducing the amount of smoke escaping into the air. Some methods utilize electricity or sound waves for precipitation of the suspended particles, others employ chemicals; the method using an electric current at high potential is perhaps best known. Smoke precipitates may yield valuable by-products; for example, fly ash can be used as a construction material. Among the evils of smoke are interference with sunlight, causing the most healthful rays of the sun to be filtered out and necessitating the use of artificial light; disfigurement of buildings, leaving deposits that are costly to remove and causing corrosion of stone and metalwork; destruction of plant life by shutting out sunlight and by clogging the stomata of leaves with oily deposits; and injury to the respiratory systems of humans and livestock. Tobacco smoke, in particular, is known to be related to cancer of the lungs. In addition to such damages, smoke also represents a waste of energy, as imperfect combustion dissipates potential heat into the atmosphere. Smoke particles and other air pollutants are often trapped in the atmosphere by a combination of environmental circumstances (see TEMPERATURE INVERSION), forming SMOG. Paris early passed stringent laws in an effort to preserve architectural and sculptural monuments, and most U.S. cities had smoke-nuisance laws before air pollution regulations were put into effect. Smoke-nuisance laws are difficult to enforce and often are not applicable to existing residential heating units, although these are often important contributors to pollution. In order to comply with Federal air pollution standards many cities have now adopted building codes that require minimally polluting heating units in new buildings and that forbid the use of incinerators.

smokeball: see PUFFBALL.

smokeless powder: see EXPLOSIVE.

smoking, inhalation and exhalation of the fumes of burning tobacco in cigarettes, cigars, and pipes. Some persons draw the smoke into their lungs; others do not. Smoking was probably first practiced by the Indians of the Western Hemisphere. Originally used in religious rituals, and in some instances for medicinal purposes, smoking and the use of tobacco eventually became a widespread practice. Tobacco was introduced into Europe in the 16th cent. by the explorers of the New World; however, many rulers of that time prohibited its use and penalized offenders. By the end of the 19th cent. mass production of cigarettes had begun, and the smoking of cigarettes became prevalent as the use of cigars and pipes declined. Despite controversy as to the effects of smoking and bans on smoking by certain religious groups, the use of tobacco continued to increase. Smoking is considered a health hazard because tobacco contains nicotine, a poisonous alkaloid, and other harmful substances such as carbon monoxide, acrolein, ammonia, prussic acid, and a number of aldehydes and tars. Several statistical studies made in the 1950s reported a higher death rate in specific age groups among smokers than among nonsmokers. However, many persons, including some physicians, believed the statistics were inconclusive. In 1964 definitive proof that cigarette smoking is a serious health hazard was contained in a report by the Surgeon General's Advisory Committee on Health, appointed by the U.S. Public Health Service. The committee drew evidence from a multitude of studies conducted over the previous 50 years. They concluded that a smoker has a significantly greater chance of contracting lung cancer than a nonsmoker, the rate varying according to factors such as the number of cigarettes smoked per day, the number of years the subject smoked, and the time in the person's life that he began smoking. Cigarette smoking was also found to be an important cause of bronchitis and, to a lesser extent, emphysema and other respiratory diseases. There was also found to be a definitive relationship between smoking and coronary artery disease. Pipe and cigar smokers, especially if they do not inhale, are not as prone to lung cancer as cigarette smokers, but they are more likely to develop cancer of the lip. Those who chew tobacco run a greater risk of developing cancer of the mouth. See also CIGAR AND CIGARETTE. See H. S. Diehl, *Tobacco and Your Health: The Smoking Controversy* (1969); W. L. Dunn, Jr., *Smoking Behavior: Motives and Incentives* (1973).

Smoky, river, c.250 mi (400 km) long, rising in Jasper National Park, W Alta., Canada, and flowing generally NE to the Peace River. It receives the Wapiti and Little Smoky rivers. It was discovered (1792) by Alexander Mackenzie.

Smoky Hill River, c.560 mi (900 km) long, rising on the Great Plains, E Colo., and flowing E across Kansas to join the Republican River and form the Kansas River at Junction City. The Saline River is its chief tributary. The Smoky Hill basin is included in the MISSOURI RIVER BASIN PROJECT. Kanopolis Dam (completed 1948) and Cedar Bluff Dam (1951) are used for irrigation and flood control.

Smoky Mountains: see GREAT SMOKY MOUNTAINS.

Smolensk (smōlĕnsk', smô-, Rus. sməlyĕnsk'), city (1970 pop. 211,000), capital of Smolensk oblast, W central European USSR, a port on the Dnepr River. It is an important rail junction, a distribution point for the region's agricultural products, and a commercial, cultural, and educational center. Smolensk is the head of navigation on the Dnepr. The city, a major linen producer, has one of the USSR's largest flax-processing mills. Other industries include metalworking, machine building, flour milling, food processing, and the manufacture of textiles. One of Russia's oldest cities, Smolensk derived its name from the resin [Rus.,=smola] extracted from the surrounding pine trees. The city was already a commercial center in the late 9th cent., when it was the capital of the Krivichi tribe and a fortress and settlement for traders and craftsmen. It then fell under Kiev's rule. Its control of the key portages between the Dnepr and Western Dvina rivers gave Smolensk its early strategic importance. It also lay astride the trade route from the Baltic to Constantinople; Smolensk was connected with the Black Sea by the Dnepr and with the Hanseatic cities of the Baltic Sea and with Moscow and Novgorod by some of the most important medieval trade links. The city declined in the 11th cent. but revived in the 12th cent. to become the capital of an independent Belorussian principality. Smolensk was sacked by the Mongols in 1238–40. The westward expansion of the grand duchy of Moscow made Smolensk a target of prolonged struggle between Moscow and Poland-Lithuania. It was captured by the Lithuanians in 1408, taken by the Russians in 1514, occupied by the Poles in 1611, and reconquered in 1654 by the Russians, to whom it passed by the Treaty of Andrusov (1667). Its location on the main route from Moscow to Warsaw made Smolensk a target for Napoleon I, who seized the city in Aug., 1812, after a brief but heroic resistance. Having burned Moscow, Napoleon retreated in November to Smolensk but was forced by the Russians under General Kutuzov to continue his retreat. The city, scene of some of World War II's heaviest fighting, was captured by the Germans in 1941 and retaken by Soviet troops in 1943. Virtually razed, Smolensk was rebuilt with its original pattern largely preserved. Historic buildings now restored include the famous kremlin and town walls (1596–1602), the Uspensky Cathedral (1677–79), several 12th-century churches, and monuments to Kutuzov and to the composer M. I. Glinka.

Smolenskin, Perez (pĕr'ĕts smōlĕn'skĭn), c.1840–1885, Russian novelist and essayist who wrote in Hebrew. He settled in Vienna and founded the Hebrew monthly journal *Ha-Shahar,* which he edited until his death. His articles favored increased contact with the West. After the Russian pogroms of 1880–81, however, he became a champion of ZIONISM. His best-known novel is probably *Am 'Olam* (1873).

Smollett, Tobias George (smŏl'ĭt), 1721–71, Scottish novelist. After studying at Glasgow he came to London in 1739. Failing to get his tragedy *The Regicide* produced, he shipped as a surgeon's mate in the British navy the following year. In 1744 he returned to London with his wife, a Jamaican heiress, practiced as a surgeon for a time, and then began an active literary career. His first three novels, *Roderick Random* (1748), *Peregrine Pickle* (1751), and *Ferdinand Count Fathom* (1753), are tough, coarse, episodic adventure stories, exposing a crude and brutal society. In 1755, Smollett translated Cervantes's *Don Quixote* into English. His novel *Sir Lancelot Greaves* (1760–62), which is based on *Don Quixote*, is considered his weakest work. Smollett achieved his greatest success with *Humphry Clinker* (1771), a comical but sympathetic story of a family's adventures through England and Scotland written in the form of letters. These novels, rich in character, incident, and realistic detail, were drawn largely from Smollett's own wide experience. His influence on later novelists, most notably Dickens, has been great. In addition to writing he had an active publishing career, editing periodicals, translating, and compiling. His other works include a popular *History of England* (1757), an entertaining but splenetic *Travels through France and Italy* (1766), and a brutal satire on public affairs, *The History and Adventures of an Atom* (1769). See his letters ed. by L. M. Knapp (1949, repr. 1970); biographies by L. M. Knapp (1949, repr. 1963) and D. J. W. Bruce (Am. ed. 1965); studies by R. Giddings (1968) and R. D. Spector (1968).

Smoot, Reed (smo͞ot), 1862–1941, U.S. Senator (1903–33), b. Salt Lake City, Utah. He became successful as a banker and was prominent in the affairs of the Church of the Latter-Day Saints. He was the first Mormon to be elected (1902) to the U.S. Senate. Efforts were made to bar him from his seat because he was a Mormon, but he was seated after a Senate investigation. Smoot, a conservative Republican, joined the "irreconcilables" in opposing the League of Nations and was one of the group that worked for Warren G. Harding's nomination (1920). In his later years in the Senate he was chairman of the finance committee; he helped write the HAWLEY-SMOOT TARIFF ACT (1930), which he cosponsored with Oregon Representative Willis C. Hawley.

smoothhound: see DOGFISH.

smuggling, illegal import or export of goods or persons liable to customs or to prohibition. Smuggling has been carried on in nearly all nations and has occasionally been adopted as an instrument of national policy, as by Great Britain against Spain and France in the 18th and 19th cent. and by the Western powers and later Japan against China. The restrictive economic policies of MERCANTILISM in the 17th and 18th cent. gave rise to smuggling in France, the Spanish colonies, and North America. British attempts to halt the practice by stringent enforcement of the NAVIGATION ACTS were a contributory cause of the American Revolution. Napoleon's decrees attempting to seal off the European continent from British commerce gave rise to widespread smuggling in the early 19th cent. Smuggling in England shifted from export, especially of wool, to the importation of luxury articles, such as silks and brandy, during the recurrent wars with France from 1689 to 1815. Britain, source of free-trade philosophy, has been more liberal in her antismuggling laws than others; and the practice was condoned in a famous passage by Adam SMITH. Smuggling into the United States revived on a large scale in the prohibition era and was carried on practically with impunity by boat from overseas and overland from Canada. Illegal entry of immigrants into the United States also presented a problem after the drastic curtailment of immigration at the end of World War I. Luxury articles and specifically prohibited goods such as narcotics are also smuggled. The U.S. coast guard has the suppression of smuggling as one of its chief activities. U.S. law declares the article smuggled to be forfeit and the smuggler, on conviction, liable to a fine of $5,000, or imprisonment, or both. Examples of the smuggling of persons contrary to law are the slave trade to the United States and Latin America following its outlawry by the great powers in the early 19th cent., the more recent slave trade in countries bordering the Red Sea, and the traffic in women for immoral purposes, contrary to international convention. The smuggling of illicit narcotics was a worldwide problem of the 1970s. See J. J. Farjeon, *The Compleat Smuggler* (1938); Neville Williams, *Contraband Cargoes* (1959); Timothy Green, *The Smugglers* (1969); Harold Waters, *Smugglers of Spirits* (1971).

smut, name for various DISEASES OF PLANTS caused by parasitic fungi of the order Ustilaginales that produce sootlike masses of spores on the host. The spore masses may break up into a dustlike powder readily scattered by wind (loose smuts) or remain more or less covered by a smooth membrane (covered or kernel smuts). Smuts lower the vitality of the host plant and often cause deformities. There is no alternation of hosts. Smuts are a most serious threat to cereal grain crops. Among those that cause severe annual losses to crops are corn smut, oat smut, bunt or stinking smut, and loose smut of wheat. Bunt is probably the most serious disease that attacks wheat at the young or seedling stage and spoils the grain. It has the odor of sour herring and is caused by either of two smut fungi. The fungus may be present on the wheat seed or in the soil in which the seed is sown, or it may be blown into a field by the wind. Control methods include treating the seeds (to which the spores of some smuts adhere) with organic mercury and sulfur dusts, rotating crops, and using smut-resistant varieties and strains. Smuts are classified in the division FUNGI, class Basidiomycetes, order Ustilaginales.

Smuts, Jan Christiaan (yän krĭs'tyän smŭts), 1870–1950, South African statesman and soldier, b. Cape prov. Of Boer stock, but a British subject by birth, he was educated at Victoria College (at Stellenbosch) and at Cambridge Univ., where he won highest honors in law. In 1895 he was admitted to the Cape Colony bar. When the Jameson Raid (see JAMESON, SIR LEANDER STARR) convinced him that Great Britain intended to conquer the South African Republic, he renounced his British citizenship and moved to the republic, where he became (1898) state attorney. In the SOUTH AFRICAN WAR, Smuts commanded (1901–2) Boer guerrilla forces in the Cape Colony. By 1904 he concluded that the cooperation of Boer and British elements was essential to the greatness of South Africa, and he joined with Louis BOTHA to achieve this alliance. Smuts was instrumental in the creation (1910) of the Union of South Africa (see SOUTH AFRICA, REPUBLIC OF). Smuts continuously held office in Botha's cabinet, serving as minister of defense (1910–19), of interior and mines (1910–12), and of finance (1912–13). His use of military force and of admittedly illegal deportations in breaking a miners' strike cost him the support of labor. Early in World War I, Smuts smashed a new Boer uprising, and in 1916 he served successfully as a general in South Africa's campaign against German East Africa. He was a member (1917–18) of the imperial war cabinet in London, and he signed the Treaty of Versailles. However, he protested that its terms would outrage Germany and prevent the harmonious world order that he believed could best be served by the League of Nations. Upon Botha's death (1919), Smuts headed the United South African (Unionist) party, and from 1919 to 1924 he was prime minister and minister for native affairs. Weakened by his frequent absences and another strike-breaking incident, his party lost the election of 1924 to a coalition of labor and anti-British nationalists. Smuts in retirement wrote *Holism and Evolution* (1926, 3d ed. 1936), in which he developed the view that evolution is a sequence of ever more comprehensive integrations; in the political sphere the British Empire and the developing world community provided the highest examples. Smuts was (1933–39) minister of justice in a coalition cabinet, but when Prime Minister HERTZOG opposed entering World War II, Smuts became prime minister. In 1941 he was created field marshal. He spent most of the war in London, where he had a high place in the British war councils, and he was very active in organizing the United Nations. In South Africa, however, Smuts's party lost the election of 1948 to the Nationalists. Smuts represented that portion of South African sentiment that stood for cooperation with the British Empire and that had somewhat less extreme racial views than the Nationalists. His speeches are collected in *Plans for a Better World* (1942). See Jean Van Der Poel, ed., *Selections from the Smuts Papers* (7 vol., 1966–73); biographies by F. S. Crafford (1943), René Kraus (1944), J. C. Smuts, his son (1952, repr. 1973), W. K. Hancock (2 vol., 1962–68), Joan Joseph (1969), and T. J. Haarhoff (1970); Basil Williams, *Botha, Smuts, and South Africa* (1946, repr. 1962).

Smybert, John: see SMIBERT, JOHN.

Smyrna: see IZMIR.

Smyrna, city (1970 pop. 19,157), Cobb co., NW Ga., a residential suburb of Atlanta; inc. 1872. Originally a religious camping ground, the city grew with the coming of the railroad. It has a bird sanctuary and is noted for its jonquils. The city was almost totally destroyed during the Civil War.

Smyth, Dame Ethel Mary (smĭth), 1858–1944, English composer, studied at the Leipzig Conservatory. Besides her many songs and chamber music she wrote operas, including *The Wreckers* (1906) and *The Boatswain's Mate* (1916), and a Mass in D (1893). In 1922 she was made Dame of the British Empire. Her autobiographical writings include *Impressions That Remain* (1919), *Streaks of Life* (1921), *As Time Went On* (1935), and *What Happened Next* (1940).

Smyth or **Smith, John,** c.1554–1612, English nonconformist clergyman and early believer in adult baptism. Influenced by the Brownists, he separated from the Church of England and became (1606) minister of an independent congregation at Gainsborough. Shortly thereafter he and his followers went to Holland to escape persecution. There, under Mennonite influence, he became convinced that the Scriptures did not authorize infant baptism; he baptized himself (for which he was called se-baptist, or self-baptizer) and some of his followers. Later he was excommunicated by his followers. He attempted to join the Mennonite church, was refused admission and died soon after. See biography in Smyth's works (ed. by W. T. Whitley, 1915); W. H. Burgess, *John Smith the Se-Baptist* (1911).

Smythson, Robert, 1536?–1614, English architect of the Elizabethan era. From 1568, Smythson was freemason to John Thynne in finishing (1567–75) the country house Longleat, Wiltshire. Striking in its symmetry, its outward-looking plan, and its numerous and large windows, it revealed a new concept of domestic design, showing admirably refined use of classical detail. His chief work was Wollaton Hall, Nottinghamshire (1580–88). Although he followed the pattern of Serlio and other continental architects, he was ingenious in his adaptations.

Sn, chemical symbol of the element TIN.

snail, name commonly used for a GASTROPOD mollusk with a spiral shell. Included in the thousands of species are terrestrial, freshwater, and marine forms. Some eat both plant and animal matter; others eat only one type of food. Respiration is carried on by gills in the aquatic species; terrestrial forms have a pulmonary sac, or lung, in the mantle cavity. A few terrestrial species have returned to the sea, and consequently must rise to the surface to breathe. Eyes are borne on stalks or tentacles. Many snails, including all land snails, are hermaphroditic, but the majority of the marine species have separate sexes. A snail secretes a slimy path over which it progresses slowly by rhythmic contractions of the muscular base, or foot. Marine and terrestrial snails are eaten in various parts of the world. Snails are considered a delicacy in Europe and were eaten by primitive man and raised for food by the Romans. Certain harmful freshwater species harbor flukes and other parasites that cause disease in humans. Although some land snails cause economic losses by destroying vegetation, even more harm is done to gardens by SLUGS. Snails are classified in the phylum MOLLUSCA, class Gastropoda.

Snake, river, 1,038 mi (1,670 km) long, NW United States, the chief tributary of the Columbia; once called the Lewis River. The Snake rises in NW Wyoming, in Yellowstone National Park, flows through Jackson Lake in Grand Teton National Park, then S and W into Idaho and northwest to its junction with the Henrys Fork River. The combined stream runs southwest, then northwest, crossing Idaho through the Snake River plain; there are several notable falls. The Snake makes a bend into Oregon and turns north to form the Idaho-Oregon and Idaho-Washington lines (receiving several tributaries, including the Boise and Salmon rivers), then turns at Lewiston, Idaho (at the mouth of the Clearwater River), and flows generally west to join the Columbia River near Pasco, Wash. Hell's Canyon is the greatest of the Snake's many gorges and one of the deepest in the world. Extending c.125 mi (200 km) N along the Oregon-Idaho line, it reaches a maximum depth of c.7,900 ft (2,410 m). The Snake was discovered by the Lewis and Clark expedition (1803–6) and was of major importance in U.S. expansion into the Pacific Northwest. It is a major source of electricity; numerous hydroelectric power plants have a total capacity of more than 7,100,000 kw. The upper and middle courses of the Snake and its tributaries are much used for irrigation by private projects (one of the most notable being at Twin Falls) and by projects of the U.S. Bureau of Reclamation, including the Minidoka project, the Boise project, the Palisades project, and the Owyhee project. Four navigation and hydroelectric power projects along the lower Snake provide slack water navigation from the mouth of the Snake 140 mi (225 km) upstream to Lewiston, Idaho. The projects are linked with the navigation system on the Columbia River, which extends 342 mi (550 km) to the Pacific Ocean from its confluence with the Snake.

snake, common name for an elongated, limbless reptile of the order Squamata, which also includes the lizards. Snakes constitute the suborder Serpentes (or Ophidia). In most snakes limbs are entirely lacking, but a few have traces of hind limbs. The skin, which is covered with horny scales, is shed, usually several times a year. The extremely long, narrow body is associated with distinctive internal features. The number of vertebrae is much larger than in most vertebrates, paired internal organs are arranged linearly rather than side by side, and only one lung is developed, except in members of the boa family, which have two lungs. The jaws of snakes are loosely jointed and extremely flexible. The pointed, backward-curved teeth are fused to the supporting bones of the head. There are no ears or movable eyelids. Snakes have good vision. They do not hear airborne sound waves, but can perceive low-frequency vibrations (100–700 Hz) transmitted from the ground to the bones of the skull. A chemosensory organ opens into the roof of the mouth; it receives stimuli from the forked tongue that constantly tastes the surroundings as the animal moves along. Snakes have no larynx or vocal chords, but are capable of producing a hissing sound. A snake moves by means of muscular contraction, which can produce several types of locomotion, the commonest types being undulation and straight-line movement. Straight-line movement is aided by the ventral plates, elongated scales on the abdomen that overlap with their open ends pointing toward the tail. These plates can be moved forward by means of muscles attached to the ribs. It is believed that snakes are descended from lizards, and that limblessness was an evolutionary advantage in the dense vegetation that formed their early environment. Most snakes live on the ground, but some are burrowers, arboreal, or aquatic; one group is exclusively marine. In temperate climates they hibernate. They are generally solitary in their habits, although they may congregate in places offering food or shelter, and large numbers may hibernate together. Snakes range in length from about 4 in. (10 cm) to over 30 ft (9 m). Most are protectively colored. Small snakes feed on insects and larger ones on proportionately larger animals. Their teeth are designed for catching and holding prey, but not for chewing. The construction of the jaws, the ribs, and the expandable skin enable them to swallow very large prey whole. Some snakes capture animals by pinning them to the ground; some—the constrictors—crush them by wrapping their bodies around them and squeezing; still others—the venomous snakes—inject poison into their victims. The poison, or VENOM, is produced by modified salivary glands from which it passes through either a groove or a hollow bore in the fangs, the enlarged, specialized teeth found in venomous snakes. A snake may bite a person when threatened or alarmed; if the snake is venomous the bite can sometimes prove fatal (see SNAKEBITE). Only by familiarity with the appearance of particular species, or by examination of the fangs, can the venomous snakes be distinguished from the harmless ones. Fertilization is internal in snakes; as in lizards, the males have paired copulatory organs, either of which may be used in mating. Females of some species can store sperm for several years to insure future fertilization. In most species the female lays eggs; in some the eggs are incubated and hatched within the mother's body; in a few there is true viviparity, or live birth, with the young nourished by means of a placenta rather than an egg. Some egg-laying snakes brood the eggs, but there is no parental care of the young. The approximately 2,700 snake species, of which about four-fifths are nonvenomous, are distributed throughout the temperate and tropical zones of the world (except in New Zealand, Ireland, and some isolated oceanic islands) and are found in greatest profusion in the tropics. About two-thirds of all snake species belong to the family Colubridae; most of these are nonvenomous. Among the harmless colubrid snakes of North America are the GARTER SNAKES (including the ribbon snake), the water snakes, the green, or grass, snakes, the BLACK SNAKES, the RACERS, the KING SNAKES (including the milk snake), and the bull, hognose, and rat snakes. The family Boidae (BOAS and PYTHONS) includes the world's largest snakes, the South American anaconda and the Oriental reticulated python, as well as the smaller boa constrictor and the tree and sand boas. Most poisonous New World snakes belong to the PIT VIPER family; these include the COPPERHEAD, WATER MOCCASIN, RATTLESNAKE, fer-de-lance, and BUSHMASTER. Venomous Old World snakes are the true VIPERS, including the adder and the ASP, and members of the cobra family, including the MAMBA of Africa and the krait of Asia. The poisonous CORAL SNAKES of the New World also belong to this family. The venomous sea snakes inhabit tropical oceans. Snakes are of major importance as pest controllers because of their extensive predation on destructive mammals such as rats and mice. Some, like the SEA SNAKES and pythons, are highly regarded as food in the Orient but, although most are probably edible, snakes are not widely used for meat. The skin is often used for belts, bags, and shoes. Venom is removed from snakes for use in treating certain diseases and to make antivenin for snakebites. Snakes are classified in the phylum CHORDATA, subphylum Vertebrata, class Reptilia, order Squamata, suborder Serpentes. See also SNAKE WORSHIP. See R. L. Ditmars, *Field Book of North American Snakes* (1939) and *Snakes of the World* (1931, repr. 1966); A. H. and

A. A. Wright, *A Handbook of Snakes of the United States and Canada* (2 vol., 1957); H. H. Harrison, *The World of the Snake* (1971); John Stidworthy, *Snakes of the World* (1971).

snake-bird: see DARTER.

snakebite, wound inflicted by the teeth of a snake. The bite of a nonvenomous snake is rarely serious. Venomous snakes have fangs, hollow teeth through which poison is injected into a victim. All types of snake venom contain a toxin that affects the nerves and tends to paralyze the victim. In addition, the venom of the coral snake, the cobra, and the South American rattlesnake contains constituents that damage blood cells and dissolve the linings of the blood vessels and the lymphatic vessels, causing severe or fatal internal hemorrhage and collapse. First aid for venomous snakebites consists of retarding the spread of the poison through the circulatory system by applying a constricting band or an ice pack, or by spraying ethyl chloride on the wound. It is essential that the patient avoid exertion and the taking of stimulants, as both increase the pulse rate. The constricting band should be applied above the swelling caused by the wound; it should be tight, but not tight enough to stop the pulsing of the blood. If only a few minutes have passed since the infliction of the bite, it is possible to remove much of the poison by suction (see FIRST AID). Antivenins, which counteract the toxins, are available for most types of snake venom. The two main groups of poisonous snakes in the United States are the coral snakes, which rarely attack humans unless provoked, and the pit vipers (copperhead, cottonmouth moccasin, the various rattlers), which require no provocation.

Snake Indians, name given by white settlers to certain North American Indian tribes, particularly in S Idaho, N Nevada, and N Utah. Other articles on these Indians appear under the SHOSHONE INDIANS, the BANNOCK INDIANS, and the PAIUTE INDIANS.

snake-necked turtle: see SIDE-NECKED TURTLE.

snakeroot, name for several plants, among them black snakeroot (see BUGBANE), button snakeroot or BLAZING STAR, senega snakeroot (see MILKWORT), and WHITE SNAKEROOT.

snake worship. The snake has been variously adored as a regenerative power, as a god of evil, as a god of good, as Christ (by the Gnostics), as a phallic deity, as a solar deity, and as a god of death. It has also served as the symbol of Satan and many deities, including Apollo and the Egyptian god Ra. Snake worship found expression in both the Toltec and Aztec periods of prehistoric Mexican civilization. In Aztec mythology a half-divine, half-human being descended to earth for a while as the great teacher of mankind; the Aztecs called him the "feathered serpent," the incarnation of the serpent sun. In Egypt, according to one authority, each temple had a reserved area where snakes were kept. In Greek religion the snake was frequently considered divine. Among the Greek Dionysian cults it signified wisdom and was a symbol of fertility. The Greek god most closely associated with snake worship is Apollo; the original name of Apollo's temple at Delphi was Pytho, after the snake PYTHON. In Rome during the period of the empire, a sacred snake was kept within the city and was attended by the vestal virgins; it was believed that if the snake refused to accept food from the hand of one of its attendants, the attendant was no longer a virgin, and she was promptly killed. The ancient Mesopotamians and Semites believed that the snake was immortal because it shed its skin and appeared in a fresh guise. The Indians, Burmese, and Siamese worshiped the snake as a demon who also had good aspects. Primitive Hindu snake cults were incorporated into the worship of Krishna and eventually into the worship of Vishnu. Buddhist legends relate that Buddha was given the true Buddhism by the "king of the serpents" (often seen as the cobra), and Buddhists also revere the regenerative powers the snake exhibits. In China the serpent, in the form of the dragon, figures as a fierce but protective divinity. Snake charming, not to be confused with snake worship, is the art of fascinating, capturing, and controlling serpents.

snapdragon: see FIGWORT.

snapper, name for members of the Lutianidae, a family of spiny-finned food and game fishes found chiefly in tropical coastal waters. Snappers are carnivorous, active, and voracious, with large mouths and sharp teeth. Most species travel in dense schools. Best known is the red snapper, an important food fish. It is abundant in the Gulf of Mexico and also frequents the Atlantic Coast north to Long Island. The red snapper grows to 3 ft (90 cm) in length, weights up to 35 lb (16 kg), and is a deep rose-red in color. Its flesh keeps well and is shipped in quantity to many parts of the United States. Other snappers are the Pensacola and Caribbean red snappers, the mangrove and dog snappers, the muttonfish, and the yellowtail. Snappers are classified in the phylum CHORDATA, subphylum Vertebrata, class Osteichthyes, order Charadriiformes, family Scolapacidae.

snapping turtle, large, aggressive New World freshwater TURTLE. The two snapping turtle species are the sole members of the family Chelydridae. Snapping turtles prefer quiet, muddy water. They spend most of their time submerged, surfacing periodically to breathe. They feed on fish and other aquatic animals as well as on vegetation and decaying matter; they are valuable scavengers. They have long necks, powerful jaws, and fierce dispositions, lunging at aggressors and biting them. The common snapping turtle, or snapper (*Chelydra serpentina*), is found from SE and S central Canada to NE South America. The adult is often over 18 in. (45 cm) long and weighs over 30 lb (14 kg); some specimens weigh twice as much. The alligator snapper (*Macrochelys temmincki*) is found in the SE United States and the Mississippi valley. One of the world's largest turtles, it may reach a length of 30 in. (75 cm) and weigh 200 lb (90 kg). It has a muscular, wormlike projection on the tongue, which it uses as a fishing lure as it lies concealed in the mud of a river bottom. Snapping turtles lay their eggs in the ground in early summer, often at some distance from water. The eggs, about 20 in a clutch, hatch after a 10-week incubation, and the young find their way to water. Snapping turtles are classified in the phylum CHORDATA, subphylum Vertebrata, class Reptilia, order Chelonia, family Chelydridae.

snapweed: see JEWELWEED.

snare drum, small DRUM having a drumhead at either end. One head is struck with wooden drumsticks, and on the other are stretched several strings, called snares, which cause a rattling against the head. The snare drum was used only in military bands until the 19th cent., when it became an orchestral instrument.

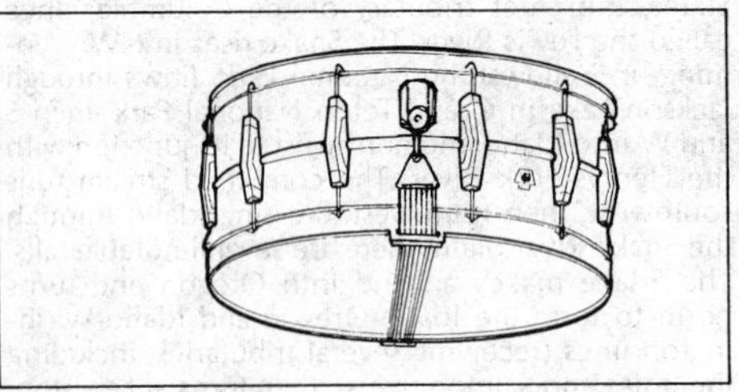

Snare drum

Snead, Samuel Jackson (Sam Snead) (snēd), 1912–, American golfer, b. Hot Springs, Va. An outstanding high school athlete, he turned to golf after injuring a hand as a football player. He attracted attention with several professional victories in 1937 and won his first major title, the Professional Golf Association (PGA) championship, in 1942. After serving in World War II, he returned to the game and won (1946) the British Open title. In 1949, Snead won the PGA and the Master's. He gained his third PGA in 1951 and added the Master's title in 1952 and 1954. Snead (teamed with Arnold Palmer in 1960 and with Jimmy Demaret in 1961) figured in two Canada Cup victories for the United States. In 1961 he gained the International championship. Snead, nicknamed "Slamming Sammy" because of his graceful but powerful tee shots, was one of the highest PGA money winners. He wrote *How to Play Golf* (1946).

sneeze, involuntary violent expiration of air through the nose and mouth. It results from stimulation of the nervous system in the nose, causing sudden contraction of the muscles of expiration. The stimulus may be provoked by any irritating factor in the nose—inflammation of the tissues as the result of a cold or infection, allergic irritants (HAY FEVER), or irritating substances such as snuff and dust. An occasional sneeze has no significance. Repeated sneezing indicates that some condition of the nose or in the immediate atmosphere requires attention.

sneeze gas, POISON GAS used in riot control and chemical warfare. It is highly irritating to the nose and throat; inhalation of the substance causes sneezing and coughing, but rarely causes permanent injury. Mixed with CN (common TEAR GAS, chloroacetophenone), it is used by police for dispersing crowds. Chemically, it is diphenylamine chloroarsine; sneeze gas is prepared by heating diphenylamine with arsenic trichloride.

sneezeweed, name for any plant of the genus *Helenium*, American meadow and field herbs of the family Compositae (COMPOSITE family), with daisylike heads of yellow (or occasionally purple) flowers. A few of the more attractive sneezeweeds are cultivated in gardens, such as varieties of *H. autumnale*, the most common species of E North America. The bitter sap of some sneezeweeds (e.g., *H. tenuifolium*, a Southern plant also called bitterweed) imparts a disagreeable flavor to the milk of cows that graze on them. Sneezeweeds are classified in the division MAGNOLIOPHYTA, class Magnoliopsida, order Asterales, family Compositae.

Snefru (snĕf'rōō), fl. c.2780 B.C., king of ancient Egypt, last king of the III dynasty; predecessor of Khufu. Snefru began commerce across the open sea with Phoenicia, for the cedar logs of Lebanon, and built ships nearly 170 ft (50 m) long for use on the Nile. He was successful against Nubia in the south and permanently established Egypt's power in the copper-producing Sinai peninsula. His tomb was the largest up to that time.

Snell, Peter George, 1938–, New Zealand athlete. While attending grammar school, Snell played rugby and cricket and was a champion tennis player and track star. In 1959 he won several New Zealand amateur athletic track championships. Snell broke a leg in early 1960 but quickly recovered, and in the Olympic Games at Rome in September he set an Olympic record of 1 min 46.3 sec for the 800-meter race. In Jan., 1962, at Wanganui, New Zealand, Snell ran a mile in 3 min 54.4 sec, a new world's record.

Snell or **Snellius, Willebrord** (vĭl'əbrôrt snĕl, snĕlēəs), 1591–1626, Dutch mathematician. He is generally credited with the discovery (1621) of the law of the refraction of light. In 1613 he became professor of mathematics at the Univ. of Leiden. His two chief works are *Eratosthenes Batavus* (1617) and *Cyclometricus* (1621).

Snelling, Fort: see FORT SNELLING.

Snellius, Willebrord: see SNELL, WILLEBRORD.

Snell's law: see REFRACTION.

snipe, common name for a shore bird of the family Scolopacidae (SANDPIPER family), native to the Old and New Worlds. The common, or Wilson's snipe (*Capella gallinago*), also called jacksnipe, is a game bird of marshes and meadows. It has an unusual courtship dance, circling and diving in the air. The mud snipe or woodcock (*Scolopax rusticola*) is a nocturnal woodland bird. The eastern dowitcher, *Limnodromus griseus*, also called the red-breasted, or robin, snipe, frequents mud flats and shores, as does the long-billed dowitcher of W North America and South America (rare on the Atlantic coast). The European common snipe, found also in Asia and Africa, is similar to the Wilson's snipe. Snipes are classified in the phylum CHORDATA, subphylum Vertebrata, class Aves, order Charadriiformes, family Scolopacidae.

Snodgrass, W.D. (William DeWitt Snodgrass), 1926–, American poet and translator, b. Wilkinsburg, Pa., grad. Univ. of Iowa, 1959. He has taught at various colleges and universities in the United States. Snodgrass is known for *Heart's Needle* (1959; Pulitzer Prize), a collection of poems about a father's love for his daughter. Although personal, the poems are universal in their treatment of the theme of separation. Snodgrass has also published several translations from the German, notably of works by Christian Morgenstern, and *In Radical Pursuit* (1975), a collection of essays.

Snøhetta, peak: see DOVREFJELL, Norway.

snook: see BASS, fish.

snoring, rough, vibratory sounds made in breathing during sleep or coma. The noisy breathing is the result of an open mouth and a relaxation of the palate; it is frequently induced by lying on one's back. Snoring may indicate some obstruction to nasal breathing such as enlarged adenoids; this is especially true in children. In some individuals it is merely a poor breathing habit and usually disappears when the person lies on his side.

snorkel, tube through which a submarine or diver can draw air while under water. When in use, the top of the snorkel tube extends above the water surface into the air. The first snorkels were probably devised in ancient times out of the hollow reeds that are common to many lakes and marsh areas. Since they are mentioned by Pliny the Elder, a Roman naturalist of the 1st cent. A.D., it is certain that such devices were in use during the early years of the Roman Empire. The first modern snorkel was devised by Leonardo da Vinci at the request of the Venetian senate. It consisted of a hollow breathing tube that was attached to a diver's helmet of leather. The present-day diver's snorkel is typically a J-shaped tube that is open at the top and has a mouthpiece at the other end. Usually no more than 2 ft (61 cm) long, the snorkel can only be used as a breathing device when a diver is swimming face down near the surface. At greater depths, the diver must hold his breath and keep his tongue over the mouthpiece to prevent water seepage. When the diver nears the surface, a strong exhalation will clear the tube of water so that breathing can begin again. A common type of toy snorkel used by many children is S-shaped, with a plastic ball or cork that automatically rises into the upper part of the tube to prevent water seepage in subsurface dives. Because the ball or cork often blocks the tube at the wrong time, however, this type of snorkel is not used by skilled divers. The extensible snorkel of the submarine is usually used while the ship is submerged at about periscope depth. The air it supplies is necessary for the operation of the vessel's diesel engines. A submarine snorkel is normally equipped with safety devices that prevent seepage even if the water level should rise above the tube. When the devices are in use, the engines operate with air from the interior of the vessel. The engines are, in turn, equipped with devices that halt their operation when the air pressure in the submarine falls below about 12 psi (82.74×10^3N per sq m). Engine exhaust is discharged through a pipe somewhat shorter than the snorkel.

Snorri Sturluson (snôr'rē stür'lüsôn) or **Sturleson** (-lĕsôn), 1178–1241, Icelandic chieftain, historian, critic, and saga teller, the leading figure in medieval Norse literature. He was the author of the invaluable *Prose Edda* (see EDDA),—a treatise on the art of poetry and a compendium of Norse mythology. His great saga the *Heimskringla* recounts the history of Norway to 1177; it combines traditional legend with substantial historical information and is of great literary merit. Snorri's sense of drama was outstanding, his mastery of form and method superb. Of an aristocratic family, Snorri acquired great wealth and became one of the most influential men in Iceland. Active in the politics of his day, he agreed to support the plan of Haakon IV for the annexation of Iceland to Norway, and thereafter he became increasingly entangled in intrigues and hostilities. In the struggle for control of Iceland he was killed by henchmen of his son-in-law, for political reasons as well as for reasons of inheritance.

snout beetle: see WEEVIL.

Snow, C. P. (Charles Percy Snow; Baron Snow of Leicester), 1905–, English author and physicist. Snow has had an active, varied career and has held several important positions in the British government. He served as technical director of the ministry of labor from 1940 to 1944; held the post of civil service commissioner from 1945 to 1960; and was parliamentary secretary to the minister of technology from 1964 to 1966. As a novelist, Snow is particularly noted for his series of 11 related novels known collectively as *Strangers and Brothers.* The series traces the career of Lewis Eliot from his boyhood in a provincial town, through law school, to years as a fellow at Cambridge, to an important government position; in many respects Eliot's career parallels that of Snow himself. Although the series has been called both a study of power and an analysis of the relationship between science and the community, it is also a perceptive and frequently moving delineation of the changes in English life during the 20th century. Among the novels in the series are *Strangers and Brothers* (1940), *The Masters* (1951), *The New Men* (1954), *The Affair* (1960), *Corridors of Power* (1964), and *Last Things* (1970). Snow is also the author of *The Search* (1934) and *In Their Wisdom* (1974), both novels; *Science and Government* (1961), a collection of essays concerning the vocation of the scientist; *A Variety of Men* (1967), biographical studies of several important men; and *Public Affairs* (1971), a collection of lectures about the benefits and dangers of technology. Snow was knighted in 1957 and created baron (life peer) in 1964. See studies by Jerome Thale (1964) and R. G. Davis (1965). His wife, **Pamela Hansford Johnson,** 1912–, is also a well-known writer. Her novels, usually character studies, are highly individualistic; they include *This Bed Thy Centre* (1935), *Too Dear for My Possessing* (1940), *The Survival of the Fittest* (1968), and *The Honours Board* (1971). She has also written *On Iniquity: Some Personal Reflections Arising out of the Moors Murder Trial* (1967) and the autobiographical *Important to Me* (1974). See study by Isabel Quigly (1968).

Snow, Lorenzo, 1814–1901, American Mormon leader, b. Mantua, Ohio, studied at Oberlin College. Entering the Mormon church (1836), Snow became an apostle in 1849. Upon his return from missionary work abroad, he settled in Utah, where, at Brigham, he established (1864) a mercantile and manufacturing cooperative. In 1889 he was made president of the Twelve Apostles and in 1898 president of the Mormon church. His works include an Italian translation of the *Book of Mormon* and *The Only Way to Be Saved* (1851). See biography by his sister, E. R. Smith (1884).

snow, precipitation formed by the sublimation of water vapor into solid crystals at temperatures below freezing. Sublimation resulting in the formation of snow takes place about a dust particle, as in the formation of raindrops. Snowflakes form symmetrical (hexagonal) crystals, sometimes matted together if they descend through air warmer than that of the cloud in which they originated. Apparently, no two snow crystals are alike; they differ from each other in size, lacy structure, and surface markings. Snowfall, reduced to its liquid equivalent, is usually included in statistics on rainfall; the factors determining snowfall are similar to those affecting rainfall.

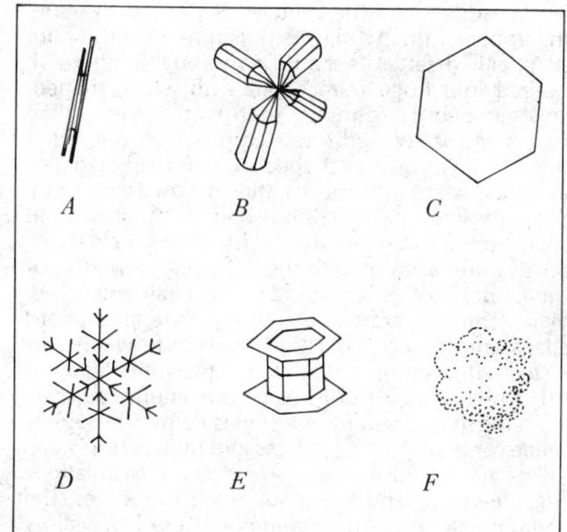

Snow occurs in many different forms. Among the various recognized classes of forms are (A) needles; (B) columns and groups of columns; (C) plates; (D) branched, or dendritic, plates; (E)combinations of plates and columns; and (F) irregular, lumpy particles called graupel.

On an average, 10 in. (25 cm) of snow is equivalent to 1 in. (2.5 cm) of rain. In the United States the average snowfall is about 28 in. (71 cm) per winter. Snow that piles up on slopes may suddenly slide downward in an AVALANCHE. A glacier consists of ice that was formed from compacted snow. Snow serves an an insulating blanket, lessening to some extent the extremes of temperature fluctuation to which the soil is subjected, but it also brings about a rapid cooling of the overlying atmosphere, giving rise to polar AIR MASSES. Snow lessens loss of water by dormant plants. The sudden melting of snow is a primary cause of floods. Snow necessitates the building of snowsheds over rail lines and highways in certain mountain localities where a heavy fall is likely to impede travel; the use of snowplows to clear sidewalks, streets, and roads; the use of snow fences to prevent drifting over roads; and the use of skis, snowshoes, toboggans, snowmobiles, and sleds for travel. It is a primary factor in the location of winter sports centers and so has great economic value to certain areas. In some ski resorts machines are used to make artificial snow. As in the case of rainfall, snowfall has been produced artificially by introducing dry-ice pellets into supercooled clouds, that is, clouds containing unfrozen water droplets at temperatures below freezing.

snowball: see HONEYSUCKLE.

snowberry, name for several shrubby plants bearing white berries, especially species of the genus *Symphoricarpos* which is classified in the division MAGNOLIOPHYTA, class Magnoliopsida, order Dipsacales, family Caprifoliaceae (HONEYSUCKLE family).

snowbird: see JUNCO.

Snowden, Philip Snowden, 1st Viscount (snō'dən), 1864–1937, British statesman. Born to poverty, he was a civil service clerk until crippled by a spinal ailment. Resigning in 1893, he began to work for the Independent Labour party (ILP). He was twice (1903–6, 1917–20) chairman of the party, but resigned in 1927 in favor of the Labour party proper as a protest against what he considered the revolutionary tendencies of the ILP. He belonged to the pacifist minority of the socialist group during World War I. Snowden served in the House of Commons from 1906 to 1918 and from 1922 until 1931. As an acknowledged specialist in finance, he became chancellor of the exchequer in the Labour ministries formed by Ramsay MacDonald in 1924 and 1929. He won popularity by his refusal to accept a reduction in the British share of German reparations in the Young Plan (1929). However, his rigidly orthodox financial measures, including the maintenance of free trade and balanced budgets, were insufficient to stem the growing economic depression. Snowden remained chancellor in the national government of 1931 and announced (1931) the suspension of the gold standard. Created Viscount Snowden of Ickornshaw in 1931, he served (1931–32) as lord privy seal but resigned when free trade was abandoned. See his autobiography (1934).

Snowdon, Welsh *Eryri,* highest mountain of Wales, 3,560 ft (1,085 m) high, Caernarvonshire, NW Wales. Its five peaks are separated by passes. There is a rack and pinion railway (opened 1896) from Llanberis to the summit. The Snowdon district, or Snowdonia, is noted for its scenic beauty; most of it is included in Snowdonia National Park (est. 1951). A nuclear power station (500,000-kw capacity; completed 1964) and a hydroelectric power project are in the region.

snowdrop: see AMARYLLIS.

snow line, altitude above which or latitude beyond which snow does not melt in summer (usually called the permanent snow line), or, in winter, the line to which snow extends at a given point in time. Factors affecting the location of the snow line are the quantity of snowfall, the steepness of the slope on which snow rests, the exposure of an area to the sun and prevailing winds, the type and velocity of the winds, and the presence or absence of large bodies of water. The level of the snow line is much lower in winter than in summer. It is also affected by distance from the equator, along which it is found at an altitude of c.3 mi (5 km); in polar regions it is at sea level.

snowmobile, vehicle designed to travel over snow, ice, and similar surfaces that offer limited traction and weight-supporting capability. As the performance of the vehicle depends to a large extent on keeping its weight as low as possible, there is no enclosure for the driver and passenger, who ride exposed, as on a motorcycle. Since the two-cycle internal-combustion engine and the Wankel engine are lighter for a given horsepower than a four-cycle engine, they are preferred for powering snowmobiles. The vehicle is supported and moved by one or two endless treads, similar to those used on military tanks and construction vehicles, except that they are of the lightest practicable weight. The driver steers by manipulating handlebars that control skilike devices on the front of the vehicle and by shifting his body weight.

snow-on-the-mountain: see SPURGE.

snow plant: see INDIAN PIPE.

snowshoe rabbit: see VARYING HARE.

snowshoes, footgear enabling the wearer to walk on soft snow without sinking. A snowshoe consists of a light frame of tough wood or aluminum, roughly the shape of a large tennis racket, which is strung with caribou skin or other material and is attached to the shoe in back of a central crossbar in the frame. A primitive form of snowshoe is that used by the Eskimo and North American Indians, but the designs differ considerably. The Eskimo use one shape that is triangular, about 18 in. (46 cm) in length, and another that is nearly circular. The Cree Indians, farther south, use a long narrow hunting shoe, about 6 ft (2 m) in length; in open country and for speed this type is the most suitable. The toes are slightly turned up to prevent catching if there is a crust on the snow. The shoes worn by lumbermen are about 3.5 ft (1 m) long and proportionately broad, while a tracker's shoe is at least 5 ft (1.5 m) long and very narrow. Manufactured snowshoes are often made with the moccasin attached. Snowshoe races are now popular at winter carnivals, and the sport is governed in the United States and Canada by the International Snow-Shoe Congress.

snowy heron: see EGRET.

Snowy Mountains, range of the Australian Alps, SE Australia. It is the site of the Snowy Mts. Hydroelectric Scheme, Australia's most extensive hydroelectric project. The scheme, begun in 1949, is designed to double Australia's power output and to quadruple the irrigated area of the Murray basin by 1980. A series of dams and tunnels will control the Tumut and Snowy-Murray river systems and will divert water from eastward-flowing streams back across the Great Dividing Range. Sixteen power stations will have a combined capacity of 4,000,000 kw.

snuff, preparation of pulverized tobacco used by sniffing it into the nostrils, chewing it, or placing it between the gums and the cheek. The blended tobacco from which it is made is often aged for two or three years, fermented at least twice, ground, and usually flavored and scented. In pre-Columbian times, snuff was used in the West Indies, in Mexico, and in parts of South America. Adoption of the practice in Europe was encouraged by belief in its medicinal virtue. From Europe the custom was carried to the Orient. The highest status of snuff taking was attained in the 18th cent., when it was practiced by both men and women. The richly ornamented snuffboxes of the time are now esteemed by collectors. A ritual of taking snuff developed, with prescribed ways of tapping and opening the box and offering it to others. Later the practice of dipping snuff into the mouth with a stick or brush, or of inserting it between the cheek and gums, largely replaced sniffing it into the nostrils.

Snyder, John Wesley, 1895–, U.S. Secretary of the Treasury (1946–53), b. Jonesboro, Ark. An executive in various Arkansas and Missouri banks, he became national bank receiver in the Office of the Comptroller of the Currency (1931–37). Later he served in the Reconstruction Finance Corporation (1937–45), became Federal loan administrator (1945), was head of the Office of War Mobilization and Reconversion (1945–46), and then was Secretary of the Treasury until the end of the Truman administration, when he resigned.

Snyder, city (1970 pop. 11,171), seat of Scurry co., NW Texas, in a prairie and mesquite region; inc. 1907. Oil production is the city's main industry; natural gas is also refined and processed. Ranching and farming are important, and cotton, grain, sorghum, wheat, fruits, and vegetables are the chief crops. Snyder grew as a cow town around a trading post established in 1876. A junior college is in the city.

Snyders, Frans (fräns snī'dərs), 1579–1657, most celebrated Flemish still-life and animal painter, b. Antwerp. He studied with Bruegel, the younger, and Hendrik van Balen but was principally influenced by Rubens. Snyders often collaborated with Rubens and Jordaens, sometimes painting the animals in their pictures, while they in turn did figures for some of his paintings of the hunt. The early work of Snyders was largely still life, but he is best known for his spirited animal compositions, primarily hunting scenes and struggles between wild animals. He painted many works for Philip III of Spain, a number of which are in the Prado. His paintings are fresh and luminous in color and strong in composition. His best-known works include *Stag Hunt* (The Hague); *Hippopotamus Hunt* (Rijks Mus.); *Lioness Attacking a Boar; Dogs in the Kitchen* (Louvre); *Lions Chasing a Deer* (Metropolitan Mus.); and *Boar Hunt* (Mus. of Fine Arts, Boston).

So, king of Egypt to whom Hoshea of Israel sent messengers. He is mentioned only in 2 Kings 17.4. Identification of So is difficult in the confused state of Egypt at that time.

Soane, Sir John (sōn), 1753–1837, English architect. After study with George Dance, the younger, he won a fellowship to Rome. He toured Italy and returned in 1780 to begin his practice in England. In 1788 he was chosen to succeed Sir Robert Taylor as architect for the Bank of England, his largest and most important work. Among other works are the Dulwich Picture Gallery, Pitzhanger Manor at Ealing, and his own residence at Lincoln's Inn Fields, now known as the Soane Museum, which he bequeathed as a museum for his collections. He devoted his later years to teaching architecture and delivering lectures. Although one of the leaders of the CLASSIC REVIVAL in England, he went beyond the mere imitation of classical models generally prevalent and evolved a highly individual style through an imaginative and flexible use of Greek and Roman motifs. He became a member of the Royal Academy of Arts in 1802 and was knighted in 1831. See study by John Summerson (1952).

soap. Ancient peoples are believed to have employed wood ashes and water for washing and to have relieved the resulting irritation with grease or oil. In the 1st cent. A.D., Pliny described a soap of tallow and wood ashes used by Germanic tribes to brighten their hair. A soap factory and bars of scented soap were excavated at Pompeii. Soap fell into disuse after the fall of Rome but was revived in Italy probably in the 8th cent. and reached France c.1200; Marseilles became noted as a soapmaking center. Although soap was known in England in the 14th cent., the first English patent to a soapmaker was issued in the 17th cent. The industry was handicapped in England from 1712 to 1853 by a heavy tax on soap. In the American colonies soap factories appeared at an early date, and many housewives made soap from waste fats and lye (obtained by leaching wood ashes). The manufacture of soap was stimulated by Chevreul's discovery of oleic and stearic acids in the early 19th cent. and by Leblanc's method (1791) of preparing soda from salt. Chemically, soaps are metallic salts of FATTY ACIDS. The manufacture of soap is based on a chemical reaction (saponification) in which an alkali acts upon a fat to form a metal salt (soap) and an alcohol (glycerol). A number of methods may be employed to make soap, but all are based on the same principle of operation. Fats and oils (often blended) are heated in a large vessel, then enough alkali to react with all the fat is stirred in. Salt is added, and the soap then forms a light curd that floats to the surface. Glycerol, a valuable by-product, can be distilled from the liquid residue. To produce a purer soap, the curds are washed with salt solution, water is later added, and the solution is allowed to settle; the upper of the two layers thus formed is the pure soap, called settled soap. It is thoroughly churned, poured into huge frames, cut with wires, shaped, and stamped. Hard-milled soap is run over chilled rollers and is scraped off as chips which are rolled into ribbons, cut, and shaped. Soap is marketed also as chips, flakes, and beads and in powdered form. Soap powders, as distinguished from powdered soap, contain builders that assist in rough cleaning. Soaps differ according to the lathering properties of the fat or oils and according to the alkali employed. When sodium hydroxide is used as the alkali, hard soaps are formed; potassium hydroxide yields soft soaps. Aluminum, calcium, magnesium, lead, or other metals are used in place of sodium or potassium for soaps used in industry as paint driers, ointments, and lubricating greases and in waterproofing. Fillers are added to many soaps to increase lathering, cleansing, and water-softening properties; the sodium salt of rosin is commonly used in yellow laundry soap to increase lathering. Soap substitutes include saponin-containing plants such as soapwort and shagbark and the modern soapless detergents (usually sulfonated alcohols), which may be used in hard water and even in salt water without forming curds. Soap cleanses by lowering the surface tension of water, by emulsifying grease, and by absorbing dirt into the foam.

soapbark tree: see SOAP PLANT.

soapberry, common name for the plant family Sapindaceae as well as a genus, *Sapindus,* in that family found in Asia and the Americas. The soapberry family includes the LITCHI. The soapberry is classified in the division MAGNOLIOPHYTA, class Magnoliopsida, order Sapindales.

soap plant, any of various plants having cleansing properties. A few are of commercial importance, but most soap plants are used locally, as in early times, for toilet and laundry purposes. The soapbark (now often included in hair tonics) and the soapberry have been particularly valued for shampooing, and the California soap plant, the soapbark, and the soapwort for washing delicate fabrics. Soap plants contain no alkali and are considered mild and beneficial for cleansing purposes, with the exception of the soapberry, which is thought to harm some textile materials. The lather-producing substance is saponin, often poisonous if taken internally. This poisonous quality was utilized by the Indians, who caught fish by first stupefying them with bits of the plants thrown into pools. There are many plants that are saponaceous, but only a few are known to contain appreciable amounts of saponin. The dried inner bark of the soapbark tree (*Quillaja saponaria*) of the rue family, native to the Andes, is collected also for commercial use in fire-extinguishing solutions and as an emulsifying agent for medicines and tars. New World and Old World species of soapberry (genus *Sapindus*) provide saponin from the fruits. Since antiquity, *S mukorossi* has been used in E Asia and the Himalayas as a detergent for shawls and silks and by jewelers for cleaning silver. The soapwort, or bouncing Bet (*Saponaria officinalis*), of the PINK family is the best-known soap plant in America; it is indigenous to W Asia and Europe but was cultivated in colonial gardens of North America and is now widely naturalized. The lather is obtained from all parts of the plant. This plant, a perennial herb, and related species sometimes called soapwort are also used medicinally. The California soap plant or soaproot (*Chlorogalum pomeridianum*) is collected in the W United States for its liliaceous bulb. Other soap plants used locally include an acacia (*Acacia concinna*), whose pods are used like the soapberry, and, among American plants, species of YUCCA and agave (see AMARYLLIS), the red buckeye (*Aesculus pavia*), the California pigweed (*Chenopodium californicum*), the senega snakeroot (*Polygala senega*), and species of *Zygadenus* and *Ceanothus.* The Spanish name *amole* is sometimes given to American soap plants, particularly those of the Southwest, where they are most abundant and are still in common use.

soapstone or **steatite** (stē'ətīt), metamorphic rock of which the characteristic and usually chief mineral is TALC, but which also contains varying parts of chlorite, mica, tremolite, quartz, magnetite, and iron compounds. It is gray to green in color, has a soapy feel, and is notable for its high degree of resistance to acids and heat. It is so soft that it can be easily cut with a knife or other sharp tool, making it a popular material for sculpting. The chief deposits of commercial importance are in the United States, Norway, and Canada. It is used in the manufacture of laboratory table tops, kitchen sinks, laundry tubs, furnace linings, and electrical apparatus.

soapwort, name for a SOAP PLANT of the PINK family.

Soares, Mario (mä'ryo͞o swä'rəsh), 1924–, Portuguese lawyer and politician. Educated at the Univ. of Lisbon and the Sorbonne, Soares rose to prominence as a socialist leader of the United Democratic Movement. A vocal critic of the Salazar regime and an advocate of democracy and economic development, he was imprisoned on numerous occasions. Exiled in 1968 and again in 1970, he returned from Paris in April, 1974, following the military coup that ousted the government of Premier Marcello Caetano. Shortly afterward Soares was appointed foreign minister for the new military junta.

soaring: see FLIGHT; GLIDER.

Sobat (sō'bät), river, c.200 mi (320 km) long, formed on the Ethiopia-Sudan border, E Africa, by the confluence of the Baro and Pibor rivers. It flows generally NW through SE Sudan, past Nasir, to the White Nile at Taufikia. It is navigable in the flood season.

Sobhuza II (sōbo͞o'zə), 1899–, king of Swaziland. He became paramount chief of the Swazi in 1921 and was officially recognized as king by Great Britain when Swaziland received (1967) the right to internal self-government. He continued to reign after Swaziland became independent in 1968. In 1973 he repealed the 1968 constitution and assumed supreme power.

Sobieski, John: see JOHN III, king of Poland.

socage: see TENURE.

soccer, outdoor ball and goal game, also called association football or simply football. The first recorded soccer game probably took place on a Shrove Tuesday in Derby, England, as part of a festival to celebrate the victory of English soldiers over a contingent of Roman troops (A.D. 217). By 1175 the annual Shrove Tuesday soccer game was a regular event. The sport remained popular for many centuries in England under the name football. But the advent of rugby (1823) as a variant led to confusion in names. The London Football Association was formed (1863) to further the game that emphasized only the kicking of the ball. The game became known as association football and then, through use of the abbreviation of *association,* as soccer. It gained tremendous popularity in Great Britain and was rapidly adopted by the continental countries, where it still generally goes under the name football. Played in more than 140 countries, soccer is unquestionably the most popular international sport, although it is a secondary sport in the United States because of the development of American football, a descendant of soccer and rugby. The U.S. Soccer Football Association (formed 1913) is the organizing body for both amateur and professional soccer in the United States. International competition is regulated by the Fédération Internationale de Football Association (founded 1940), which sponsors the quadrennial World Cup competition and whose membership is larger than that of the United Nations. Soccer has been an Olympic event since 1900. The game is played on a grassy field preferably measuring 120 yd by 75 yd (110 m by 70 m). Centered on each end line is a goal, 8 yd (7.3 m) wide by 8 ft (2.4 m) high, backed with netting. A soccer team consists of 11 men—a goalkeeper, two fullbacks, three halfbacks, and five forwards. No substitution is allowed, and play is continuous through two 45-min periods. Overtime is played in case of ties. The object of the game is to advance a round, inflated leather ball—about 28 in. (71 cm) in circumference—to the opponent's goal. The ball is kicked (often dribbled with short kicks) or may be advanced by other parts of the body such as the head and chest, but only the goalkeeper may use his hands. Each goal counts one point. Penalties meted out by a referee, who is assisted by linesmen, are various types of free kicks, depending on the infraction. Perhaps the greatest soccer player of all time is Brazil's Edson Arantes do Nascimento, better known as PELÉ, the most popular and highest paid athlete in the world. See Denzil Batchelor, *Soccer: A History of Association Football* (1954); Brian Glanville, *Soccer: A History of the Game, Its Players and Its Strategy* (1968); Ted Smits, *The Game of Soccer* (1968).

Sochi (sô'chē), city (1970 pop. 224,000), Krasnodar Kray, S European USSR, on the east shore of the Black Sea, in the foothills of the Caucasus. It is a port and subtropical resort, established as a spa in 1910. Sochi receives about 300,000 visitors yearly.

Socho or **Sochoh** (both: sō'kō), variants of SOCOH.

social contract, agreement or covenant by which men are said to have abandoned the "state of nature" to form the society in which they now live. The theory of such a contract, first formulated by the English philosophers Thomas Hobbes (in the *Leviathan,* 1651) and John Locke, assumes that men at first lived in a state of anarchy in which there was no society, no government, and no organized coercion of the individual by the group. Hobbes maintained that by the social contract men had surrendered their natural liberties in order to enjoy the order and safety of the organized state. Locke made the social contract the basis of his advocacy of popular sovereignty, the idea that the monarch or government must reflect the will of the people. Like Locke, the French philosopher Jean Jacques Rousseau, in *Le Contrat social* (1762), found the general will a means of establishing reciprocal rights and duties, privileges, and responsibilities as a basis of the state. Similar ideas were used as a justification for both the American and the French revolutions in the 18th cent. Thomas Jefferson held that the preservation of certain natural rights was an essential part of the social contract, and that "consent of the governed" was fundamental to any exercise of governmental power. Although historically important, the theory as a basis of society and the state has generally been discarded by modern social and political scientists. See Ernest Barker, *Social Contract* (1948, repr. 1962); J. W. Gough, *The Social Contract: A Critical Study of Its Development* (2d ed. 1957); Alfred Cobban, *Rousseau and the Modern State* (2d ed. 1964); L. G. Crocker, *Rousseau's Social Contract; an Interpretive Essay* (1968).

Social Credit, economic plan in Canada, based on the theories of Clifford Hugh DOUGLAS. The central idea is that the problems fundamental to economic depression are those of unequal distribution owing to lack of purchasing power. To solve these difficulties Douglas proposed a system of issuing to every citizen dividends, the amount of which would be determined by an estimate of the nation's real wealth; the establishment of a just price for all goods would be the result. The democracy of the process would be insured by a "union of electors." The program became highly influential in Alberta during the depression years, and the Social Credit party, led by William ABERHART, won a resounding victory in the provincial elections of 1935. The program included distribution of a social dividend of $25 a month, but it proved impossible to put this scheme into practice. Attempts to tax banks and to enter on currency schemes were disallowed by the confederation government (the constitution leaves monetary control with the confederation government) and declared unconstitutional by the courts. Nevertheless, the party remained in power in Alberta until defeated in 1971. In 1972 the party suffered a further reverse with the fall of its only other provincial government, in British Columbia. In the federal parliamentary elections of that year it won 15 seats. In the 1974 elections this number was reduced to 11, all of them from Quebec, where the party is known as Ralliement Créditiste. Although the party continues to announce its economic reforms, most of its political and social program is strongly conservative and traditional. See J. R. Mallory, *Social Credit and the Federal Power in Canada* (1960); Maurice Pinard, *The Rise of a Third Party* (1971); M. B. Stein, *The Dynamics of Right-Wing Protest* (1973).

Social Gospel, liberal movement within American Protestantism that attempted to apply biblical teachings to problems associated with industrialization. It took form during the latter half of the 19th cent. under the leadership of Washington GLADDEN and Walter RAUSCHENBUSCH, who feared the isolation of religion from the working class. They believed in social progress and the essential goodness of man. The views of the Social Gospel movement were given formal expression in 1908 when the Federal Council of the Churches of Christ in America adopted what was later called "the social creed of the churches." Advocated in the creed were the abolition of child labor, better working conditions for women, one day off during the week, and the right of every worker to a living wage. With the rise of the organized labor movement in the early 20th cent. the Social Gospel movement lost much of its appeal as an independent force. However, many of its ideals were later embodied in the New Deal legislation of the 1930s.

socialism, general term for the political and economic theory that advocates a system of collective or government ownership and management of the means of production and distribution of goods. Because of the collective nature of socialism, it is to be contrasted to the doctrine of the sanctity of private property that characterizes CAPITALISM. Where capitalism stresses competition and profit, socialism calls for cooperation and social service. In a broader sense, the term socialism is often used loosely to describe economic theories ranging from those that hold that only certain public utilities and natural resources should be owned by the state to those holding that the state should assume responsibility for all economic planning and direction. In the past 150 years there have been innumerable differing socialist programs. For this reason socialism as a doctrine is ill-defined, although its main purpose, the establishment of cooperation in place of competition among men, remains fixed.

The Early Theorists. Socialism arose in the late 18th and early 19th cent. as a reaction to the economic and social changes associated with the INDUSTRIAL REVOLUTION. While rapid wealth came to the factory owners, the workers became increasingly impoverished. They were underpaid and overworked and forced to live in slums. As this capitalist industrial system spread, reactions in the form of socialism increased proportionately. Although many thinkers in the past expressed ideas that were similar to later socialist thought, the first theorist who may properly be called socialist was François Noël BABEUF, who came to prominence during the French Revolution. Babeuf propounded the doctrine of class war between capital and labor later to be seen in Marxism. Socialist writers who followed him, however, were more moderate. Known as "utopian socialists" they included the comte de SAINT-SIMON, Charles FOURIER, and Robert OWEN. Saint-Simon proposed that production and distribution be carried out by the state. The leaders of society would be industrialists who would found a national community based upon cooperation and who would eliminate the poverty of the lowest classes. Fourier and Owen, though differing in many respects, both believed that social organization should be based on small local collective communities, rather than the large centralist state of Saint-Simon. All these men agreed, however, that there should be cooperation among all members of society and implicitly rejected any notions of class struggle. In the early 19th cent. numerous utopian COMMUNISTIC SETTLEMENTS founded on the principles of Fourier and Owen sprang up in Europe and the United States; NEW HARMONY and BROOK FARM were notable examples. Following the utopians came thinkers such as Louis BLANC who were more political in their socialist formulations. Blanc put forward a system of social workshops (1840) that would be controlled by the workers themselves with the support of the state. Capitalists would be welcome in this venture, and each person would receive goods in proportion to his needs. Blanc became a member of the French provisional government of 1848 and attempted to put some of his proposals into effect, but his efforts were sabotaged by his opponents. The anarchist Pierre Joseph PROUDHON and the insurrectionist Auguste BLANQUI were also influential socialist leaders of the early and mid-19th cent.

Marxism and Gradualism. In the 1840s the term *communism* came into use to denote loosely a militant leftist form of socialism; it was associated with the writings of Étienne CABET and his theories of common ownership. Karl MARX and Friedrich ENGELS later used it to describe the movement that advocated class struggle and revolution to establish a society of cooperation. In 1848, Marx and Engels wrote the famous *Communist Manifesto,* in which they set forth the principles of what Marx called "scientific socialism," arguing the historical inevitability of revolutionary conflict between capital and labor. In all of his works Marx attacked the socialists as being theoretical utopian dreamers who disregarded the absolute necessity of revolutionary struggle to implement their doctrines. In the atmosphere of disillusionment and bitterness that increasingly pervaded European socialism, MARXISM later became the theoretical basis for most socialist thought. But the failure of the REVOLUTIONS OF 1848 caused a decline in socialist action in the following two decades, and it was not until the late 1860s that socialism once more emerged as a powerful social force. Other varieties of socialism continued to exist along side Marxism, such as CHRISTIAN SOCIALISM, which was led in England by Frederick Denison MAURICE and Charles KINGSLEY and advocated the establishment of cooperative workshops based on Christian principles. Ferdinand LASSALLE, founder of the first workers' party in Germany (1863), stressed the possibility of achieving socialism through state action in individual nations, as opposed to the Marxian emphasis on international revolution and the disappearance of the state. Through the efforts of Wilhelm LIEBKNECHT and August BEBEL, the Lassallian group was brought into the mainstream of Marxian socialism. By the 1870s socialism was once more active. SOCIALIST PARTIES sprang up in many European countries, and they eventually formed the Second INTERNATIONAL. With the increasing improvement of labor conditions, however, and the apparent failure of the capitalist state to show signs of weakening, a major schism began to show itself within the movement. The issue was revolution. While nearly all socialists condemned the bourgeois capitalist state, a large number apparently felt it more expedient or more efficient to adapt to and reform the state structure, rather than overthrow it. Opposed to these gradualists were the orthodox Marxists and the advocates of ANARCHISM and SYNDICALISM, all of whom believed in the absolute necessity of violent struggle. In 1898, Eduard BERNSTEIN denied the inevitability of class conflict and called for a revision of Marxism that would allow an evolutionary socialism. This dichotomy between evolutionists and revolutionists affected the socialist movement throughout the world. In Germany, Bernstein's chief opponent, Karl KAUTSKY, held the Social Democratic party strictly, at least in theory, to orthodox Marxist principles. In other countries, however, revisionism made more progress. In Great Britain, for instance, where orthodox Marxism had never been a powerful force, the Fabian Society, founded in 1884, set forth basic principles of evolutionary socialism that later became the theoretical basis of the British LABOUR PARTY. The principles of William MORRIS, dictated by aesthetic and ethical aims, and the small but able group that forwarded GUILD SOCIALISM also had influence on British thought, but the Labour party, with its policy of gradualism, represented the mainstream of British socialism. In the United States, the ideological issue led to a split in the SOCIALIST LABOR PARTY, founded in 1876 under strong German influence, and the formation (1901) of the revisionist SOCIALIST PARTY, which soon became the largest socialist group. The most momentous split, however, took place in the Russian Social Democratic Labor party, which divided into the rival camps of BOLSHEVISM AND MENSHEVISM. Again, gradualism was the chief issue. It was the revolutionary opponents of gradualism, the Bolsheviks, who eventually seized power in the Russian Revolution of 1917 and became the Communist party of the USSR. World War I—and the question whether socialists should support their national governments in the war effort (most did)—had already badly divided the socialist movement; and the Russian Revolution split it irrevocably. The Russian Communists founded the COMINTERN in order to seize leadership of the international socialist movement and to foment world revolution, but most European Socialist parties, including the mainstream of the powerful German party (which despite its espousal of Marxist orthodoxy in the prewar years had been notably nonrevolutionary in practical politics), repudiated the Bolsheviks. Thereafter, revolutionary socialism, or COMMUNISM, and evolutionary, or democratic, socialism were two separate and frequently mutually antagonistic movements.

Democratic Socialism. Democratic socialism took firm root in European politics after the war, and socialist democratic parties were active and took part in government in Great Britain, Germany, Sweden, Belgium, Holland, and others. Socialism also became a powerful force in parts of Latin America, Asia, and Africa. To the Indian leader Jawaharlal NEHRU and other leaders of independence movements, it was attractive as an economic alternative to the private enterprise systems established by imperialist countries. After World War II, socialist parties came to power in many more nations throughout the world, and much formerly private industry was nationalized. Today in Africa and Asia where the workers are agrarian, not industrial, laborers, socialist programs stress land reform and other agrarian measures. In addition, these nations also emphasize government planning for rapid and efficient economic development. In Africa a central feature of socialism is the preservation of the values and institutions of a precolonial way of life, while at the same time modernizing through the centralized apparatus of the one-party state. See G. D. H. Cole, *A History of Socialist Thought* (5 vol., 1953–60); Joseph Schumpeter, *Capitalism, Socialism and Democracy* (3d ed. 1950, repr. 1962); Max Beer, *The General History of Socialism and Social Struggle* (1957); Harry W. Laidler, *History of Socialism* (1968); Massimo Salvadori, *Modern Socialism* (1968); George Lichtheim, *A Short History of Socialism* (1970); Michael Harrington, *Socialism* (1972).

Socialist Labor party, in the United States, begun in 1877 by New York City socialists. Its membership came largely from German-American workingmen. During the 1880s a national organization was established and the party concentrated, unsuccessfully, on electoral politics. The depression conditions of the 1890s brought it renewed strength, and, under the leadership of Daniel DE LEON, a Marxist revolutionary, it emphasized militant labor activities and organized (1896) its own union. After many members who opposed the leadership of De Leon withdrew (1899) and joined the less militant Social Democratic party (see SOCIALIST PARTY), the Socialist Labor party did not regain its previous importance.

Socialist parties, in European history, political organizations formed in the European countries to achieve the goals of SOCIALISM. In the late 19th cent. the gradual enfranchisement of the working classes gave great impetus to socialism and led to the formation of Socialist political parties in many countries. Most were directly influenced by the teachings of Karl MARX. At the same time labor unions (see UNION, LABOR) were formed to improve the worker's economic status. In the 1870s and 80s, Socialist parties were constituted in most European states, and in 1889 they joined in the formation of the Second INTERNATIONAL. Despite general similarities, the varying economic, social, and political conditions within countries gave a national character to the different socialist organizations. In France the political defeats experienced by socialists and other worker groups of the February Revolution (1848) and the Commune of Paris (1871) encouraged SYNDICALISM and the revolutionary doctrine of Louis Auguste BLANQUI. In Germany the state socialism of Ferdinand LASSALLE gained wide acceptance. (For more detailed historical sketches of the Socialist parties in France and Germany, see below.) In Russia agrarian socialist ideas evolved indigenously (as did ANARCHISM), finding expression in the Populist movement (see NARODNIKI) and in the works of Aleksandr Herzen, Mikhail Bakunin, and others. Georgi PLEKHANOV introduced Marxism to Russia. (For the subsequent history of political socialism in Russia, see SOCIALIST REVOLUTIONARY PARTY; BOLSHEVISM AND MENSHEVISM; COMMUNISM.) Socialism in Great Britain developed in close association with the trade union movement and obtained its ideological direction from the evolutionary socialists of the FABIAN SOCIETY rather than from Marxism (see LABOUR PARTY). The Socialist parties in the Scandinavian countries were also generally moderate, and in the 20th cent. they soon gained a prominent political role. All European Socialist parties were marked by schisms; the main issue dividing them was whether party members should cooperate with and participate in the bourgeois-dominated governments in order to achieve gradual reforms, or whether they should work extralegally to hasten what Marxism considered to be the inevitable proletarian revolution. Eduard BERNSTEIN, in Germany, was one of the first to deny (1898) some of Marx's doctrines and to argue for "revisionism," or basic deviation from Marxist theory. World War I brought the collapse of internationalism within the parties. Many socialists supported their national governments in prosecuting the war, and some accepted ministerial positions. Of those who opposed this policy the most notable were the Russian Bolsheviks, who in 1917 won control of their country in the Russian Revolution. After the war the left-wing socialists, who hoped for an extension of the Russian Revolution to other European countries, split off from the more moderate majority and formed Communist parties. The division was reflected in the formation of a Third (Communist) International to rival the Second International. In the interwar years most of the majority Socialist parties discarded their revolutionary ideology. Many of them participated in coalition governments with the bourgeois parties, and in Great Britain, Norway, Sweden, and Denmark they formed their own governments. However, the condition of being in either a coalition or a minority government prevented them from achieving any structural socialist changes, although some social reforms were enacted. Socialists were not able to counter the rise of fascism, and in Italy, Germany, and Spain the parties were suppressed. During World War II, socialists were prominent in the resistance movement in the countries occupied by Germany. In the postwar period the COLD WAR widened the gulf between the Socialist and Communist parties, and most Socialist parties moved even further away from Marxism. Substantial periods of power have, however, enabled them to forward their goals of a planned economy and a welfare state in many European countries; their position has been especially strong in the Scandinavian countries. See Max Beer, *General History of Socialism and Social Struggles* (1957); Carl Landauer, *European Socialism* (1959); G. D. H. Cole, *The Second International, 1889–1914* (1956), *Communism and Social Democracy, 1914–1931* (1958), and *Socialism and Fascism, 1931–1939* (1960).

In Germany. In 1875, at Gotha, the followers of Lassalle united with the Marxist group of Wilhelm LIEBKNECHT and August BEBEL to form the Socialist Labor party, later known as the Social Democratic party of Germany (Sozialdemokratische Partei Deutschlands, or SPD). Despite repressive laws the SPD grew rapidly and by 1912 was the largest single party in the Reichstag. In 1891 the Erfurt Program, adopted at a party congress in Erfurt, repudiated Lassalle's theories and placed the party on a strictly Marxist theoretical basis. Ideological debate shook the party throughout the 1890s. Bernstein led the revisionists in urging the SPD to alter its acceptance of the Marxist theories of inevitable revolution and the class struggle and to emphasize the forming of alliances with middle-class parties. Karl KAUTSKY was the leading supporter of Marxist orthodoxy, and his position was formally upheld by the party, but in practice revisionism prevailed. When World War I broke out (1914), the Social Democrats in the Reichstag voted for war credits, and in 1916 SPD deputies entered the government. Late in 1915 a group opposed to the continuation of the war broke off from the Majority Socialists and took (1917) the name Independent Socialists. They were led by Hugo HAASE. Another, more radical group also broke away; led by Karl LIEBKNECHT and Rosa LUXEMBURG, they called themselves the SPARTACUS PARTY. With the German revolution of Nov., 1918, an SPD government under Friedrich EBERT and Haase took control. The failure of the new government to forward any measure of socialization led to the almost immediate withdrawal of Haase and an ill-organized Spartacist revolt (Jan., 1919), which was brutally suppressed. Under the Weimar Republic the Social Democrats joined coalitions with other parties and succeeded in improving the condition of the working classes but were unable to counter the antidemocratic elements in Germany. With the rise of Adolf Hitler the SPD, which had been the best-organized Socialist party in Europe, was destroyed. After World War II the revived SPD in East Germany was forced to merge (1946) with the Communists in the Socialist Unity party. In West Germany, on the other hand, the SPD emerged immediately as the leading opposition party. It remained in that position until 1966, when it entered a "grand coalition" with the other major party, the Christian Democratic Union. In 1969 the SPD became the dominant party in a governing coalition with the small Free Democratic party. Led by Chancellor Willy BRANDT, this government pursued a policy of normalization of relations with the Soviet Union and its East European allies, including East Germany. In 1974, Brandt resigned as a result of a spy scandal and was succeeded as chancellor by Helmut SCHMIDT. See studies by A. J. Berlau (1949), C. E. Schorske (1955, repr. 1970), and D. A. Chalmers (1964).

In France. The French Socialist party, known as the SFIO from its official name *Section française de l'internationale ouvrière* [French section of the Worker's International], was formed in 1905 by a merger of various socialist groups that had long quarreled over tactics. Led by Jean JAURÈS and Jules GUESDE, the SFIO grew rapidly to become a major political force. In 1914 the party supported French participation in World War I, and members accepted ministerial posts. The duration of the war and the example of the Russian Revolution stimulated the growth of a pro-Bolshevik element in the SFIO. By 1920 the Communists held a majority in the party, and a split was unavoidable. The minority, led by Léon BLUM, reconstituted the SFIO. The party revived and in 1924 joined a coalition government with the Radical Socialist party (a non-Socialist group despite its name). In 1936, faced by economic depression, government corruption, and the rise of French fascism, the Socialists allied with the Communists and Radical Socialists to form the Popular Front. The alliance won the national elections and Blum was (1937–38) premier. In World War II the SFIO played a heroic role in the French Resistance. It emerged in 1945 as one of the strongest government parties. Flanked by the Communists on the left and the more conservative powers on the right, it gradually lost strength and numbers, although it frequently was the leading party in governing coalitions. The party split over the question of support for the Fifth Republic in 1958. There followed a succession of alliances among the various socialist groups, certain middle-of-the-road parties, and the Communist party in rather unsuccessful opposition to the ruling Gaullists. Reorganized in 1969 as the *Parti Socialiste*, the Socialists remain the largest non-Communist group opposing the Gaullist government. In 1974, the Socialist candidate François MITTERRAND, supported also by the Communists, was only narrowly defeated for the presidency by Gaullist Valéry Giscard d'Estaing. See H. G. Simmons, *French Socialists in Search of a Role* (1970).

Socialist party, in U.S. history, political party formed to promote public control of the means of production and distribution. In 1898 the Social Democratic party was formed by a group led by Eugene V. DEBS and Victor BERGER. Two years later, Debs ran for president with the support of the more moderate wing of the SOCIALIST LABOR PARTY, and in 1901 this group, led by Morris HILLQUIT, united with the Social Democratic party to form the Socialist party. The new party differed from the more radical Socialist Labor party in favoring an evolutionary, as opposed to revolutionary, socialism, and it soon outsized the older organization. The Socialist party did not show much electoral strength until 1910 and 1911, when its candidates won numerous state and local elections. In 1912, Debs received nearly 900,000 votes (6% of the votes cast) as the party's presidential candidate. The party reached its peak membership (nearly 120,000) in that year. Allan Benson ran for president in 1916, but his percentage of the national vote dropped to 3%. In 1917 the party opposed the American entry into World War I, with a small faction of dissenting prowar members seceding from the party. Debs and a number of others were arrested for their opposition to the war, although Debs ran for president in 1920 while imprisoned and received 920,000 votes. After serving part of his sentence he was later pardoned by President Harding. Following the Russian Revolution, a substantial group within the party advocated that the organization drop its evolutionary and reformist position and work instead for the immediate overthrow of the capitalist system. In 1919 this faction withdrew from the party, thereby substantially weakening it, and formed the COMMUNIST PARTY of the United States. In 1924 the Socialist party supported the Progressive party candidate for president, Robert LA FOLLETTE, but in 1928 it once again nominated its own candidate, Norman THOMAS, who ran in the following five presidential elections. The party lost much of its support during the 1930s when the NEW DEAL came into effect, implementing many programs that the Socialists had long demanded. Since then the party has all but disappeared. In the 1952 and 1956 presidential elections Darlington Hoppes ran as the Socialist candidate, receiving fewer than 2,500 votes in the latter election. Although other minor parties espousing socialism currently participate in national elections, the Socialist party decided in 1960 to withdraw from national politics and concentrate on education. In 1972 it changed its name to the Social Democratic party. See W. B. Hesseltine, *The Rise and Fall of Third Parties* (1948, repr. 1957); Ira Kipnis, *The American Socialist Movement* (1952, repr. 1972); David Shannon, *The Socialist Party of America* (1955, repr. 1967); Howard Nash, Jr., *Third Parties in American Politics*

(1959); James Weinstein, *The Decline of Socialism in America, 1912–1925* (1967).

socialist realism, Soviet artistic and literary directive. During the first Five-Year Plan (1928–32) there existed in the USSR a virtual literary dictatorship by the Russian Association of Proletarian Writers. Its leading critic, Leopold Averbakh, decreed the social, agricultural, and industrial themes deemed suitable for Soviet writers. In reaction against this, the role of literature and art was redefined in 1932 when the newly created Union of Soviet Writers proclaimed socialist realism as compulsory literary practice. As conceived by Stalin, Zhdanov, and Gorky, socialist realism prescribed a generally optimistic picture of socialist reality and of the development of the Communist revolution. Its purpose was education in the spirit of socialism. Its practice is marked by strict adherence to party doctrine and to conventional techniques of realism. Socialist realism has been widely condemned as stifling to artistic values. After the death of Stalin in 1953 some relaxation of strictures was evident, although socialist realism continued as the official doctrine. This approach to art and literature has also appeared in mainland Chinese literature. See study by Abram Tertz (tr. 1961); Marc Slonim, *Soviet Russian Literature* (rev. ed. 1967).

Socialist Revolutionary party, in Russian history, an agrarian party founded by various Populist groups in 1901. Its program, adopted in 1906, called for the overthrow of the autocracy, the establishment of a classless society, self-determination for national minorities, and socialization of the land, which was to be distributed among the peasants on the basis of need. Viktor CHERNOV was a party leader. A secret "combat organization" within the party arranged political assassinations, notably that of V. K. Plehve (1904) and Grand Duke Sergei (1905). Originally made up of students and intellectuals, the party later gained support from the peasantry. In 1917 some Socialist Revolutionaries participated in the Petrograd soviet and in the provisional government. The party won a majority in the short-lived constituent assembly (Jan., 1918), which was disbanded by the Bolsheviks. By 1922 the party was suppressed. See Oliver Radkey, *The Agrarian Foes of Bolshevism* (1958) and *The Sickle under the Hammer* (1963).

socialized medicine, publicly administered system of national health care. The term is used to describe programs that range from government operation of medical facilities to national health-insurance plans. Most European nations have legislated some form of socialized medicine. In 1948, Great Britain passed the National Health Service Act that provided free use of all medical services. The system was later amended so as to charge a small fee for the filling of prescriptions and the purchasing of eyeglasses and dentures; it is funded jointly by a health-insurance tax and by the national treasury. Doctors are salaried by the government and receive an additional allotment per patient and for the performance of special services. Sweden maintains a compulsory health-insurance plan that provides for income compensation, hospital treatment, most of the physician's fee, and part of the cost of medicines. Maternity benefits are provided for expectant women. In the Soviet Union, as in most Communist countries, medical care is provided and financed by the government. More than 70% of Israel's medical care is provided by the Histadrut, the national labor union. A number of private welfare organizations also provide care, and the armed forces maintain a number of military hospitals whose services are widely used since nearly all citizens of Israel are military veterans. The United States and Canada are the only major Western countries without extensive socialized medical care. However, the latter has recently established a federally sponsored system of medical insurance with voluntary participation on the part of each province. The United States has initiated Medicare, a Federally administered program for those over 65, and MEDICAID, a program of medical care for the poor that is Federally funded but administered by the individual states.

social psychology, study of the relationships between one individual and another, between an individual and a group, and between one group and another. Typical research subjects include the influence of social institutions on the development of the individual; the study of communication, leadership, cooperation, competition, and problem solving within groups; the nature and measurement of attitudes; and the study of imitation and suggestion and their effect upon fashions and fads. Social psychology developed from the work of Moritz Lazarus, Heymann Steinthal, and Wilhelm Wundt (folk psychology); of Gabriel de Tarde (imitation); and the general work of Sigmund Freud and William McDougall. The increasing use of BEHAVIORISM was followed by the application of GESTALT principles to social psychology. See David Krech, *Individual in Society* (1962); R. W. Brown, *Social Psychology* (1965); F. H. Allport, *Social Psychology* (1924, repr. 1967); Dorwin Cartwright and Alvin Zander, ed., *Group Dynamics* (3d ed. 1968); E. A. Ross, *Social Psychology, an Outline and Source Book* (1908, repr. 1974).

social science, term for any or all of the branches of study that deal with humans in their social relations. Often these studies are referred to in the plural as the social sciences. Although human social behavior has been studied since antiquity, the modern social sciences as disciplines rooted in the scientific method date only from the 18th cent. Enlightenment. Interest at first centered on ECONOMICS, but by the 19th cent. separate disciplines had been developed in ANTHROPOLOGY, POLITICAL SCIENCE, PSYCHOLOGY, and SOCIOLOGY. The 19th cent. was characterized by the development of wide-ranging theories (e.g., the work of Auguste Comte, Karl Marx, and Herbert Spencer). Developments in the 20th cent. have moved in these directions: the improvement and increased use of quantitative methods and statistical techniques; increased use of the empirical method, as opposed to general theorizing; and the direct practical application of social science knowledge. Despite the fact that social science knowledge has not reached the level of the natural or physical sciences, social science departments are now firmly established in universities, and social scientists are increasingly called upon to advise industries and governments for future planning. See Stuart Chase, *The Proper Study of Mankind* (2d rev. ed. 1962, repr. 1965); K. E. Boulding, *The Impact of the Social Sciences* (1966); George Homans, *The Nature of Social Science* (1967); B. F. Hoselitz, ed., *A Reader's Guide to the Social Sciences* (1970); C. M. White, *Sources of Information in the Social Sciences* (2d ed. 1973).

social security, public program providing for the economic security and welfare of individuals and their dependents. The programs classified under the term social security differ from one country to another, but all have in common that they are established by government legislation and provide some kind of cash payment to defray a loss or deficiency in income. A social security program was adopted first in Germany in the 1880s, when Chancellor Otto von Bismarck advocated social legislation not only in order to benefit the workers but also to forestall the program of the Socialists and gain the support of the workers for his own party. Compulsory sickness insurance, of which the worker contributed two thirds and the employer one third of the funds, was passed in Germany in 1883; compulsory old-age insurance (see PENSION), of which the employee, employer, and government shared the payment, was adopted in 1889; unemployment insurance legislation, however, was not passed until 1927. As economic insecurity among workers in the highly industrialized countries spread, an increasing number of social security programs were enacted. In Great Britain, the National Insurance Act, devised by David Lloyd George, was passed in 1911, and a compulsory unemployment insurance program as well as old-age insurance and sickness insurance programs were established. The unemployment insurance system excluded many workers, notably government employees, nurses, casual workers, and those who earned over £250 per annum. A survivors insurance program was adopted (1925); in 1942, Parliament was presented with a plan, by Sir William Henry BEVERIDGE, for a more expanded social security program, much of which was enacted after World War II. France adopted in 1905 a program of voluntary unemployment insurance and in 1928 made insurance plans for old age and sickness mandatory. Meanwhile, diverse social security programs were adopted throughout Europe, differing from country to country as to the kinds of insurance instituted, the categories of workers eligible, the proportions paid by employee, employer, and government, the conditions for receipt of benefits, the amounts of the benefits, and finally in the overall effects of the programs. In 1922, the Soviet Union adopted comprehensive social security plans as part of their socialist economy. One major difference between social security programs in socialist countries (e.g., China, Cuba, the Soviet Union) and nonsocialist countries is that in the former the insured person or employee makes no direct contribution toward the coverage. Chile became (1924) the first Latin American country to adopt a social security program. The United States did not have social security on a national level until 1935, when the Social Security Act was passed as part of President Franklin Delano Roosevelt's New Deal program. The act contained two social insurance programs: a Federal-state program of unemployment compensation and a Federal program of old-age retirement insurance. It also provided for Federal grants to assist the states with programs for the disabled, the aged, child welfare services, public health services, and vocational rehabilitation. It established a system of compulsory old-age insurance, paying benefits proportionate to prior earnings for persons over 65, with a reserve fund being accumulated through payroll taxes on employers and employees; the rate of the tax, which was originally set at 1%, was gradually increased, and by 1973 it was over 5%. The original Social Security Act of 1935 covered only workers in commercial and industrial occupations; but since then several major amendments have increased the categories of persons eligible for benefits. The amendment of 1939 provided for benefits to the dependents and survivors of workers; an amendment in 1950 broadened the coverage to include fulltime farm and domestic workers, many self-employed persons, employees of state and local governments, and employees of nonprofit organizations; later amendments extended coverage to members of the armed forces and to self-employed professionals; and a 1957 amendment provided cash benefits to insured workers 50 years of age and older who became permanently and totally disabled. The age of eligibility for retirement benefits has been lowered from 65 to 62, with somewhat lower benefits for persons retiring at age 62. In 1965, Congress enacted the Medicare program, providing medical benefits for persons over the age of 65, and an accompanying Medicaid program for the indigent. Social security retirement benefits were raised 10% in 1971 and 20% in 1972, the 1972 increase being accompanied by an amendment tying future increases to rises in the Consumer Price Index. This provision resulted in a 5.6% increase in 1973 and an 11% increase in two stages (March and June) in 1974. Administration of the Social Security Act, except unemployment insurance, is vested in the Social Security Administration of the U.S. Dept. of Health, Education, and Welfare. However, contributions are collected by the Internal Revenue Service, while the preparation of benefit checks and the management of trust funds are the responsibility of the Dept. of the Treasury. The unemployment insurance program is administered by the U.S. Dept. of Labor. See Otto Eckstein, ed., *Studies in the Economics of Income Maintenance* (1967); P. A. Brinker, *Economic Insecurity and Social Security* (1968); E. M. Kassalow, ed., *The Role of Social Security in Economic Development* (1968); Roy Lubove, *The Struggle for Social Security, 1900–1935* (1968); International Labor Office, *An Introduction to Social Security* (1970); Charles McKinley, *Launching Social Security* (1970); G. V. Rimlinger, *Welfare Policy and Industrialization in Europe, America, Russia* (1971); Philip Booth, *Social Security in America* (1973).

social settlement: see SETTLEMENT HOUSE.

Social War or **Marsic War** [Lat. *socii*=allies], 90 B.C.–88 B.C., struggle brought on by demands of the Italian allies for the privileges of Roman citizenship. The allies had fought on the side of Rome and had helped establish Roman hegemony, but they did not have the rights of the Romans and were subject to the autocratic decisions of Roman magistrates. The senate was greatly averse to sharing the rule, but Marcus Livius Drusus in 91 B.C. proposed laws granting the allies citizenship. He was murdered, and a coalition of the allies, chief among them the people called the Marsians, arose in desperation, waged war against Rome, and planned an Italian federation. Led by Quintus Pompaedius Silo and Caius Papius Mutilus, they gained some success but could not overcome the power of Rome. The Roman armies, even under MARIUS and SULLA, were unable to crush the revolt, which died down only after Lucius Julius Caesar secured passage of a law granting citizenship to allies who had not joined the revolt and to those who laid down their arms immediately. The allies were divided, and the revolt ceased. Citizenship was soon given not only to all of them but also to the people of Cisalpine Gaul.

social welfare or **public charity,** organized provision of educational, cultural, medical, and financial assistance to the needy. Among the Greeks and Romans public assistance was given chiefly to those holding full citizenship. It was early connected with religion, as among the Hebrews and, from them, among the Christians and later the Muslims. The

Christian Church was the main agency of social welfare in the Middle Ages, supplemented by the guilds. Later, national and local governmental agencies, as well as many private agencies, took over much of the charitable activity of the church. First of the extensive state efforts was the Elizabethan POOR LAW of 1601, which attempted to classify dependents and provide special treatment for each group on the local (parish) level. During the Industrial Revolution, many entrepreneurs believed that social welfare programs undertaken by the state violated the concepts of laissez faire, and therefore opposed such measures. Exceptions were such men as Robert OWEN, who believed that social welfare measures were essential but their implementation should be undertaken cooperatively rather than as a function of the state. The first modern government-supported social welfare program for broad groups of people, not just the poor, was undertaken by the German government in 1883. Legislation in that year provided for health insurance for workers, while subsequent legislation introduced compulsory accident insurance and retirement pensions. In the next 50 years, spurred by socialist theory and the increasing power of organized labor, state-supported social welfare programs grew rapidly, so that by the 1930s most of the world's industrial nations had some type of social welfare program. In the United States the Social Security Act of 1935 provided for Federally funded financial assistance to the elderly, the blind, and dependent children. Subsequent amendments broadened the act in terms of coverage provided and eligibility requirements; significant among such extensions was the provision for medical insurance to the aged (1960, amended 1965) under the so-called Medicare program. Of course, not all governments have equally extensive social welfare systems. Generally speaking, Great Britain and the Scandinavian countries, often termed "welfare states," have very wide-ranging social welfare legislation. Britain's National Health Service, for example, was established (1948) to provide free medical treatment to all. Private philanthropies and charitable organizations, however, continue to operate in these countries in many areas of public welfare. In Communist countries social welfare is administered exclusively by the state. In the United States public assistance has come more and more under state and Federal control, although private PHILANTHROPY still plays a major role. International relief bodies, such as the RED CROSS, and agencies of the United Nations, such as the World Health Organization (WHO) and the United Nations Children's Fund (UNICEF), provide social welfare services throughout the world, especially during times of distress and in poverty-stricken areas. Modern social welfare measures may include any of the following: the care of destitute adults; the treatment of the mentally ill; the rehabilitation of criminals; the care of destitute, neglected, and delinquent children; the care and relief of the sick or handicapped; the care and relief of needy families; and supervisory, educational, and constructive activity, especially for the young. See R. E. Asher, *United Nations and the Promotion of the General Welfare* (1957); Hertha Kraus, ed., *International Cooperation for Social Welfare* (1960); A. C. Marts, *Man's Concern for His Fellow-man* (1961); Samuel Mencher, *Poor Law to Poverty Program* (1967); J. F. Handler, *Reforming the Poor* (1972); E. W. Martin, *Comparative Development in Social Welfare* (1972); W. I. Trattner, *From Poor Law to Welfare State* (1974).

social work, organized effort to help individuals and families to adjust themselves to the community, as well as to adapt the community to the needs of such persons and families. Social work has grown by gradual steps out of the early efforts of churches and philanthropic groups to relieve the effects of poverty, to bring the comforts of religion to the poor, to promote temperance and encourage thrift, to care for children, the sick, and the aged, and to correct the delinquent. Orphanages and homes for the elderly were typical results of these activities. The word *charity* best describes the early activities, which were aimed at the piecemeal alleviation of particular maladjustments. In such charitable work the principal criterion in determining aid to families was worthiness, while the emphasis in later social work was on restoring individuals to normal life both for their own sake and for the sake of the community. The first attempts to solve the problem of poverty in a scientific way was made by P. G. F. Le Play, who in the 1850s made a detailed study of the budgets of hundreds of French workers' families. Forty years later Charles Booth made an investigation of wages and prices, working conditions, housing and health, standards of living, and leisure activities among the poor of London that revealed the extreme poverty of a third of the population. The social survey introduced by Booth became a method for determining the extent of social maladjustment, and through surveys in other cities in Europe and the United States a vast number of facts were accumulated, and methods were developed that provided the basis for modern social work. In 1874 the National Conference of Charities and Correction (now called the National Conference on Social Welfare) was organized in the United States; but public relief and private philanthropic effort remained largely matters of local and state concern until after 1930, when the Federal government entered the field of social work on a large scale to cope with the effects of the economic depression. Resources were made available, the number of social workers was greatly increased, and it became necessary to coordinate public and private activities. Modern social work employs three methods of assistance: case work, group work, and community organization. Case work is the method by which individual persons and families are assisted. The person in need of case work may be physically, mentally, or socially handicapped. Among those regarded as socially handicapped are: the unemployed, the homeless, members of broken families, alcoholics, drug addicts, and neglected or problem children. To determine the cause of maladjustment, the social worker must understand individual psychology as well as the sociology of the community. Physicians, psychiatrists, and other specialists may be required to help diagnose the difficulty. Social group work is exemplified by the social settlement, the supervised playground and gymnasium, and the classroom where handicrafts may be learned. The community may be called upon to provide the buildings and grounds for such activities; often the services of volunteers and of public groups are utilized; in recent years people living in poverty areas have been employed to work in and direct poverty projects in their own communities. Through community organization the welfare work of single agencies as well as of whole communities is directed, cooperation between public and private agencies is secured, and funds are raised and administered. The funds required by private agencies are often pooled in a COMMUNITY CHEST, from which each agency receives a share. Community welfare councils are organized to map programs of rehabilitation, to eliminate duplication of services, and to discover and meet overlooked needs. Social work has been steadily professionalized, and special graduate schools as well as departments in universities have been established to train the needed workers. By the early 1970s there were over 400 schools of social work in more than 50 countries. See A. E. Fink et al., *The Field of Social Work* (5th ed. 1968); W. A. Friedlander, *Introduction to Social Welfare* (3d ed. 1968); E. A. Ferguson, *Social Work: An Introduction* (2d ed. 1969); I. A. Spergel, *Community Problem Solving* (1969); R. E. Smith and Dorothy Zietz, *American Social Welfare Institutions* (1970); W. C. Richan and A. R. Mendelsohn, *Social Work* (1973).

societies, learned and literary, associations of individuals with a common professional interest, intended to promote learning. Many societies publish the proceedings of their meetings as well as journals, reports, and outstanding investigations by their members. They often award prizes, encourage or subsidize research, and maintain libraries. A forerunner of the modern society was the Museum, founded c.300 B.C. in Alexandria by Ptolemy I. The earliest important medieval society was established by Charlemagne under the guidance of Alcuin. Learned societies of the modern type originated in Italy as literary academies during the revival of classical learning. The shortlived Accademia Platonica, founded in the 15th cent. by Cosimo de' Medici, served as a model. The most widely known extant society of the early period is the Accademia della Crusca, founded (1582) in Florence and several times reorganized. The Accademia Secretorum Naturae (Naples, c.1560) is believed to have been the earliest scientific society. Outstanding among European societies are the FRENCH ACADEMY (1635), now a section of the INSTITUT DE FRANCE; the ROYAL SOCIETY (1662); the Prussian Academy of Sciences founded by Frederick I in 1700 as the Societas Regia Scientarum, and the Academy of Sciences founded at St. Petersburg in 1725. Many countries have national academies, and local and regional societies have flourished. Although many societies—e.g., the British Association for the Advancement of Science (1831), the American Association for the Advancement of Science (1847), the National Academy of Sciences (established in 1863 by the U.S. Congress), the AMERICAN PHILOSOPHICAL SOCIETY (incorporated under its present name in 1769), and the American Academy of Arts and Sciences (chartered in 1780 in Boston)—cover a broad field, the specialization of knowledge has resulted in the establishment of literary, historical, archaeological, and scientific societies covering very restricted fields. The specialization of fields and the geographical distribution of societies necessitate methods of coordination including informal cooperation and formal affiliations, as in the American Medical Association (1847), in which local medical organizations are represented. Among the newer learned societies are the American Studies Association (1951), the Royal Australian Academy (1952), and the Danish Academy (1960). See K. O. Murra, ed., *International Scientific Organizations* (1962); *Directory of Selected Scientific Institutions in the U.S.S.R.* (1963); *Scientific and Learned Societies of Great Britain* (61st ed. 1964).

Society Islands, island group (1970 pop. 105,328), South Pacific, a part of FRENCH POLYNESIA. The group comprises the Windward Islands and the Leeward Islands (total land area c.650 sq mi/1,680 sq km), two clusters of volcanic and coral islands lying in a 450-mi (724-km) chain. Only eight of the islands are inhabited. The Windward Islands include TAHITI, MOOREA, Mehetia, and Tetiaroa; the Leeward Islands include RAIATEA (largest island of the Leeward group), Huahine, BORA-BORA, Maupiti, Tahaa, Maiao, Mopihaa, Motu-iti, Scilly Island, and Bellingshausen Island. The islands are mountainous, and there are breadfruit, pandanus, and coconut trees; the limited fauna includes wild pigs, rats, and small lizards. The major products are copra, sugar, rum, mother-of-pearl, and vanilla. The Society Islands were discovered in 1767 by the English navigator Samuel Wallis, who claimed them for Great Britain. A year later, however, the French navigator Louis Antoine de BOUGAINVILLE established a French claim. They were named the Society Islands in 1769 by Capt. James COOK. The group became a protectorate of France in 1843 and a colony in 1880. In 1946 the Society Islands were made an overseas territory of France.

Socinianism (sōsĭ'nēənĭzəm), anti-Trinitarian religious movement organized in Poland in the 16th cent. by Faustus SOCINUS. Antecedents of the movement were such Italian humanist reformers as Bernardino Ochino, Georgio Blandrata, and Laelius SOCINUS, who fled to Poland from persecution first in Italy and then in Calvinist Switzerland. Michael SERVETUS appears to have influenced their anti-Trinitarian views. Socinianist reformers organized (1556) the Minor Reformed Church of Poland and established Rakow as an intellectual center. Faustus went to Poland in 1579 and became the movement's leader and principal theologian. Socinianism represented an extreme attempt to reconcile Christianity with humanism. The doctrine of the Holy Trinity was rejected, the Scriptures were considered authoritative but were interpreted in the light of the new rationalism, and the sacraments were viewed as spiritual symbols. The Nicene and Athanasian creeds were rejected and Jesus was held to be only the human instrument of divine mercy and the Holy Spirit merely the activity of God. Under Faustus the movement became known as the Polish Brethren, and communities were formed in imitation of the early Christian church. Its members refused to hold serfs or to participate in war. Never strong, the movement dissolved (c.1638) in the face of severe Roman Catholic persecution. Some of its members settled in Holland and there played a part in liberalizing Reformed doctrine. Faustus's teachings were compiled by disciples as the Racovian Catechism (1605). Socinianism is sometimes called Old Unitarianism and, erroneously, Polish Arianism. See Stanislaw Kot, *Socinianism in Poland* (tr. 1957).

Socinus, Faustus (fôs'təs sōsĭ'nəs) or **Fausto Sozzini** (fou'stō sōt-tsē'nē), 1539–1604, Italian religious reformer, founder of SOCINIANISM. Socinus left the Roman Catholic Church when, influenced by the writings of his uncle, Laelius Socinus, he came to deny the Trinity and other traditional doctrines. Faustus left Italy for Basel in 1575, and in 1579 he went to Poland, where he spent the remainder of his life. In Poland he gradually organized the anti-Trinitarian groups into the sect of Polish Brethren and thereby founded the movement known as Socinianism.

Socinus, Laelius (lē'lēəs) or **Lelio Sozzini** (lā'lyō), 1525–62, Italian religious reformer. After becoming interested in Protestantism, Socinus left Italy in 1544 for the Swiss cantons to escape the newly established Inquisition. He had been attracted by the writings of Martin Luther, and during his wide travels he met many leaders of the Reformation. In Switzerland, Heinrich Bullinger became his good friend. John Calvin, however, suspected Socinus of doctrinal differences, and to allay these suspicions Socinus signed a confession of faith in 1555. However, there seems reason to believe that the burning of the anti-Trinitarian SERVETUS in 1553 and Socinus's friendship with Bernardino Ochino had led him to entertain private anti-Trinitarian views. The writings of Socinus, left to his nephew Faustus, were used in the development of SOCINIANISM.

sociology, scientific study of human social behavior. As the study of humans in their collective aspect, sociology is concerned with all group activities—economic, social, political, and religious. Sociology tries to determine the laws governing human behavior in social contexts; it is distinguished as a general social science from the special social sciences, such as economics and political science, which confine themselves to a selected group of social facts or relations. Sociology investigates such areas as bureaucracy, community, deviant behavior, social change, social mobility, and social stratification. From the time of the Renaissance, political theorists and philosophers—e.g., Machiavelli, Vico, Hobbes, Locke, Montesquieu, and Rousseau—have treated political problems from a larger point of view that would at a later time be regarded as sociological. Thus Montesquieu regarded the political forms of different states as a consequence of the working of deep, underlying factors: climatic, geographic, economic, and psychological. In the 18th cent., Scottish thinkers made advanced inquiries into the nature of society; scholars like Adam Smith explored the economic causes of social organization and social change, while Adam Ferguson considered the noneconomic causes of social cohesion. But it was not until the 19th cent., when the concept of society was finally separated from that of the state, that sociology developed into an independent study. The term *sociology* was coined (1838) by Auguste COMTE. He attempted to analyze all aspects of cultural, political, and economic life and to identify the unifying principles of society at each stage of human social development. Herbert SPENCER applied the principles of Darwinian evolution to the development of human society in his *Principles of Sociology* (1876–96), and gave a further impetus to social studies. An important stimulus to sociological thought came from the work of Karl MARX, who emphasized the economic basis of the organization of society and its division into classes and saw in the class struggle the main agent of social progress. The founders of the modern study of sociology were Émile DURKHEIM and Max WEBER. Durkheim pioneered in the use of empirical evidence and statistical material in the study of society. Weber's major contribution was as a theorist, and his generalizations about social organization are still influential. He developed the use of the ideal type—a working model, based on the selective combination of certain elements of historical fact or current reality—as a tool of sociological analysis. In the United States the study of sociology was pioneered and developed by Lester Frank WARD and William Graham SUMNER. The most important theoretical sociology in the 20th cent. has moved in three directions: conflict theory, structural-functional theory, and symbolic interaction theory. Conflict theory draws heavily on the work of Karl Marx and assumes that social change can be explained in terms of underlying conflict; prominent conflict theorists included Ralf Dahrendorf and C. Wright Mills. Structural-functional theory, developed by Talcott PARSONS and advanced by Robert Merton, assumes that major social institutions function through a balancing process. Symbolic interaction, begun by George Herbert Mead and further developed by Herbert Blumer and others, focuses on the symbolic processes of communication. See P. A. Sorokin, *Contemporary Sociological Theories* (1928, repr. 1964); C. Wright Mills, ed., *Images of Man* (1960); R. E. L. Faris, ed., *Handbook of Modern Sociology* (1964); Robert Nisbet, *The Sociological Tradition* (1966); Nicklous Timasheff, *Sociological Theories* (3d ed. 1967); Robert Merton, *Social Theory and Social Structure* (enl. ed. 1968); G. D. Mitchell, *A Hundred Years of Sociology* (1968); Herbert Blumer, *Symbolic Interactionism* (1969); J. H. Abraham, *The Origins and Growth of Sociology* (1973); J. E. Goldthorpe, *An Introduction to Sociology* (1974).

Socoh (sō'kō). **1** Town, SW Palestine, SW of Bethlehem. Joshua 15.35. Shochoh: 1 Sam. 17.1. Shoco: 2 Chron. 11.7. Shocho: 2 Chron. 28.18. **2** Town, in the hill country of Judah, SW of Hebron. Joshua 15.48. **3** Town, central Palestine, NW of Samaria. 1 Kings 4.10.

Socotra (səkō'trə, sō-), island, 1,383 sq mi (3,582 sq km), Southern Yemen, at the mouth of the Gulf of Aden. The mountainous interior rises to c.5,000 ft (1,520 m). The island's inhabitants farm, fish, and herd; exports include dried fish, aloes, ghee, and pearls. Known to the ancient Greeks, Socotra shared the political fortunes of S Arabia, except for a brief Portuguese occupation in the early 1500s. The island was occupied by the East India Company in 1834, and in 1886 it became part of Britain's Aden protectorate and was used as a refueling station. In 1967, Socotra was joined to the newly formed nation of Southern Yemen.

Socrates (sŏk'rətēz), 469–399 B.C., Greek philosopher of Athens. Famous for his view of philosophy as a pursuit proper and necessary to all intelligent men, he is one of the great examples of a man who lived by his principles even though they ultimately cost him his life. Knowledge of the man and his teachings comes indirectly from certain dialogues of his disciple PLATO and from the *Memorabilia* of XENOPHON. In spite of conflicting interpretations of his teachings, the accounts of these two writers are largely supplementary. Socrates was the son of Sophroniscus, a sculptor. It is said that in early life he practiced his father's art. In middle life he married Xanthippe, who is legendary as a shrew although the stories have little basis in ascertainable fact. It is not certain who were Socrates' teachers in philosophy, but he seems to have been acquainted with the doctrines of PARMENIDES, HERACLITUS, ANAXAGORAS, and the atomists. He was widely known for his intellectual powers even before he was 40 when, according to Plato's report of Socrates speech in the *Apology*, the oracle at DELPHI pronounced him the wisest man in Greece. In that speech Socrates maintained that he was puzzled by this acclaim until he discovered that, while others professed knowledge without realizing their ignorance, he at least was aware of his own ignorance. He became convinced that his calling was to search for wisdom about right conduct by which he might guide the intellectual and moral improvement of the Athenians. Neglecting, therefore, his own affairs, he spent his time discussing virtue, justice, and piety wherever his fellow citizens congregated. Some felt that he also neglected public duty, for he never sought public office, although he was famous for his courage in the military campaigns in which he served. In his self-appointed task as gadfly to the Athenians, Socrates made numerous enemies. ARISTOPHANES burlesqued Socrates in his play *The Clouds* and attributed to him some of the faults of the Sophists (professional teachers of rhetoric). Although Socrates in fact baited the Sophists, his other critics seem to have held a view similar to that of Aristophanes. In 399 B.C. he was brought to trial for corrupting youth and for religious heresies. Obscure political issues surrounded the trial, but it seems that Socrates was being tried also as the friend and teacher of ALCIBIADES and CRITIAS, both of whom had betrayed Athens. The trial and death of Socrates, who was given poison hemlock to drink, are described in the *Apology*, the *Crito*, and the *Phaedo* of Plato with great dramatic power. Socrates' contributions to philosophy were a new method of approaching knowledge, a conception of the soul as the seat both of normal waking consciousness and of moral character, and a sense of the universe as purposively mind-ordered. The method, called DIALECTIC, consisted in examining statements by pursuing their implications, on the assumption that if a statement were true it could not lead to false consequences. The method may have been suggested by ZENO OF ELEA, but Socrates refined it and applied it to ethical problems. His doctrine of the soul led him to the belief that all virtues converge into one, which is the good, or knowledge of one's true self and purposes through the course of a lifetime. Knowledge in turn depends on the nature or essence of things as they really are, for the underlying forms of things are more real than their experienced exemplifications. This conception leads to a teleological view of the world that all the forms participate in and lead to the highest form, the form of the good. Plato later elaborated this doctrine as central to his own philosophy. Socrates' view is often described as holding virtue and knowledge to be identical, so that no man knowingly does wrong. Since virtue is identical with knowledge, it can be taught, but not as a professional specialty as the Sophists had pretended to teach it. However, Socrates himself gave no final answer to how virtue can be learned. See Eduard Zeller, *Socrates and the Socratic Schools* (tr. 1885, repr. 1962); A. E. Taylor, *Socrates* (1953); Norman Gulley, *The Philosophy of Socrates* (1968).

Socrates Scholasticus (skōlăs'tĭkəs), fl. 5th cent., Byzantine historian. His *Ecclesiastical History* (in Greek, 7 vol.) continues the work of Eusebius for the period from 305 to 439. The work is unusual for its objectivity, dependence on original primary sources (e.g., acts of councils, the chronicle of Constantinople, letters of kings and bishops), and impartial descriptions of heresies.

soda: see SODIUM CARBONATE.

soda ash: see SODIUM CARBONATE.

soda niter: see SODIUM NITRATE.

soda water, a solution of CARBON DIOXIDE in water.

Soddy, Frederick (sŏd'ē), 1877–1956, English chemist. He worked under Lord Rutherford at McGill Univ. and with Sir William Ramsay at the Univ. of London. After serving (1910–14) as lecturer in physical chemistry and radioactivity at the Univ. of Glasgow, he was professor of chemistry at the Univ. of Aberdeen (1914–19) and at Oxford (1919–36). He was especially noted for his research in radioactivity. With others he discovered a relationship between radioactive elements and the parent compound, which led to his theory of isotopes; for this work he won the 1921 Nobel Prize in Chemistry. His scientific books have become classics and include *The Interpretation of Radium* (1909, rev. ed. 1922), *Matter and Energy* (1912), *The Chemistry of the Radio-Elements* (2 parts, 1911–14), and *Atomic Transmutation* (1953). An advocate of technocracy and of the social credit movement, he wrote several books setting forth his political and economic views.

Söderberg, Hjalmar (yäl'mär sö'dərbĕr"yə), 1869–1941, Swedish writer. His lyrical but melancholic and disillusioned mood is reminiscent of Heinrich Heine. Söderberg's first novel, *Martin Birck's Youth* (1901, tr. 1930), is the story of a dreamer living a drab middle-class existence. His novels are unsurpassed at evoking Stockholm life at the turn of the century; major examples include *Doctor Glas* (1905) and *The Serious Game* (1912). His witty short stories, considered his finest work, mock complacency and deceit. A selection of stories has been translated by C. W. Stork (1935).

Söderblom, Nathan (nä'tän sö'dərblo͝om"), 1866–1931, Swedish churchman, primate of the Lutheran Church of Sweden, archbishop of Uppsala. He was professor of the history of religion and from 1914 to 1931 vice chancellor at the Univ. of Uppsala. Söderblom was a leader in the ECUMENICAL MOVEMENT for the unification of the Christian churches. For his labors for international peace he was awarded the 1930 Nobel Peace Prize. Among English translations of his works are *Christian Fellowship* (1923), *The Living God* (1933), and *The Nature of Revelation* (1934). See biographies by C. J. Curtis (1967) and B. G. Sundkler (1968).

Söderhamn (södərhä'mən), city (1970 pop. 12,467), Gävleborg co., E Sweden, a seaport on the Gulf of Bothnia; chartered 1620. It is a commercial and industrial center with sawmills and ironworks. Iron ore, forest products, and fish are exported.

Södertälje (södərtĕl'yə), city (1970 pop. 55,457), Stockholm co., E Sweden, on a narrow bay of Lake Mälaren, near Stockholm. It is an industrial center and a health resort. Manufactures include motor vehicles, machinery, tobacco products, and pharmaceuticals. Originally known as Tälje, it was a trade center during the Viking era (9th–11th cent.) and is one of Sweden's earliest cities. The **Södertälje Canal,** connecting Lake Mälaren and the Baltic Sea, was built in 1807–19 and was enlarged to accommodate bigger ships in 1917–24.

sod house, house with walls made of strips of sod laid horizontally in courses like bricks. Sod houses were common in the frontier days on the western plains of the United States, where wood and stone were scarce. The sod, turned by the plow and held together by roots, was lifted in strips and usually cut in 3-ft (1-m) lengths (sods). The walls were hewed smooth with a spade and were often plastered with clay and ashes. Sometimes roofs were of frame construction; usually they were thatched or covered with sods, which had to be replaced after heavy rains. Sod walls were fire- and windproof and good insulators, but they permitted only small window openings, were seldom entirely rainproof, and made the house dirty. Sods were also used to build fences, but after rain they became unsightly mounds of mud and tangled roots—probably the origin of the expression "homely as a mud fence." For other earth houses, see RAMMED EARTH. See Everett Dick, *The Sod-House Frontier* (1937).

Sodi (sō'dī), father of Gaddiel, a spy sent into Canaan. Num. 13.10.

sodium, a metallic chemical element; symbol Na [Lat. *natrium*]; at. no. 11; at. wt. 22.9898; m.p. 97.8°C; b.p. 892°C; sp. gr. 0.971 at 20°C; valence +1. Sodium is a soft, silver-white metal. Extremely reactive chemically, it is one of the ALKALI METALS in group Ia of the PERIODIC TABLE. Like potassium, which it closely resembles, it oxidizes rapidly in air; it also reacts violently with water, liberating hydrogen (which may ignite) and forming the hydroxide. It must be stored out of contact with air and water and should be handled carefully. Sodium combines directly with the halogens. The metal is usually prepared by electrolysis of the fused chloride (the Downs process); formerly, the chief method of preparation was by electrolysis of the fused hydroxide (the Castner process). Metallic sodium has limited use. It is used in sodium arc lamps for street lighting; pure or alloyed with potassium, it has found use as a heat-transfer liquid, e.g., in certain nuclear reactors. It is used principally in the manufacture of tetraethyl lead (a gasoline anti-knock compound) and of sodamide, $NaNH_2$, sodium cyanide, NaCN, sodium peroxide, Na_2O_2, and sodium hydride, NaH. Sodium compounds are extensively used in industry and for many nonindustrial purposes. Among the most important compounds are chloride (common salt, NaCl), bicarbonate (baking soda, $NaHCO_3$), carbonate (soda ash, or washing soda, Na_2CO_3), hydroxide (caustic soda, or lye, NaOH), nitrate (Chile saltpeter, $NaNO_3$), thiosulfate (hypo, $Na_2S_2O_3 \cdot 5H_2O$), phosphates, and BORAX ($Na_2B_4O_7 \cdot 10H_2O$). Sodium hydroxide is used wherever a cheap alkali is needed, for example, in making SOAP. Substances containing sodium impart a characteristic yellow color to a flame. Because of its activity sodium is not found uncombined in nature. It occurs abundantly and widely distributed in its compounds, which are present in rocks and soil, in the oceans, in salt lakes, in mineral waters, and in deposits in various parts of the world. Sodium compounds are found in the tissues of plants and animals. Sodium is an essential element in the diet, but some people must limit the amount of sodium in their food for medical reasons. Discovery of sodium is usually credited to Sir Humphry Davy, who prepared the metal from its hydroxide in 1807; its compounds have been known since antiquity.

sodium benzoate or **benzoate of soda,** chemical compound, $C_6H_5CO_2Na$, colorless or white crystalline, aromatic compound; the sodium salt of BENZOIC ACID. It is soluble in water and is used as a preservative in foods and beverages; because it is poisonous, the concentration is limited by law to one tenth of one percent.

sodium bicarbonate or **sodium hydrogen carbonate,** chemical compound, $NaHCO_3$, a white crystalline or granular powder, commonly known as bicarbonate of soda or baking soda. It is soluble in water and very slightly soluble in alcohol. It evolves carbon dioxide gas when heated above about 50°C, a property made use of in baking powder, of which it is a component. It is also decomposed by most acids; the acid is neutralized and carbon dioxide is given off. The major use of sodium bicarbonate is in foods, e.g., baked goods. It is used in effervescent "salts" and is sometimes used medically to correct excess stomach acidity. It is also used in several kinds of fire extinguishers. Although it is an intermediate product in the SOLVAY PROCESS for making SODIUM CARBONATE, it is more economical to prepare it from purified sodium carbonate than to purify the intermediate. Because the bicarbonate is less soluble than the carbonate, carbon dioxide gas is bubbled into a saturated solution of pure carbonate, and the bicarbonate precipitates out to be collected and dried.

sodium carbonate, chemical compound, Na_2CO_3, soluble in water and very slightly soluble in alcohol. Pure sodium carbonate is a white, odorless powder that absorbs moisture from the air, has an alkaline taste, and forms a strongly alkaline water solution. It is one of the most basic industrial chemicals. Sodium carbonate decahydrate, $Na_2CO_3 \cdot 10H_2O$, is a colorless, transparent crystalline compound commonly called sal soda or washing soda. Because seaweed ashes were an early source of sodium carbonate, it is often called soda ash or, simply, soda. The SOLVAY PROCESS provides most sodium carbonate for industrial use. It is found in large natural deposits and is mined in Wyoming; it is also recovered (with other chemicals) from lake brines in California. The principal uses of sodium carbonate are in the manufacture of GLASS and the production of chemicals. It is also used in processing wood pulp to make paper, in making SOAPS and detergents, in refining aluminum, in water softening, and in many other applications. The Leblanc process, the first successful commercial process for making soda, is no longer used in the United States but played a major role in the Industrial Revolution.

sodium chloride, NaCl, common salt. It is readily soluble in water and insoluble or only slightly soluble in most other liquids. It forms small, transparent, colorless to white cubic crystals. It is odorless but has a characteristic taste. It is an ionic compound, being made up of equal numbers of positively charged sodium and negatively charged chloride IONS. When it is melted or dissolved in water the ions can move about freely, so that dissolved or molten sodium chloride is a conductor of electricity; it can be decomposed into sodium and chlorine by passing an electrical current through it (see ELECTROLYSIS). Salt is important in many ways. It is an essential part of the diet of both men and animals, and is a part of most animal fluids, such as blood, sweat, and tears. It aids digestion by providing chlorine for hydrochloric acid, a small but essential part of human digestive fluid. Persons with hypertensive heart disease often must restrict the amount of salt in their diet. Salt is widely used as a seasoning for foods, and is used in curing meats and preserving fish and other foods. As a chemical it is used in making glass, pottery, textile dyes, and soap. It is used in large amounts to melt ice and snow on streets and highways. The major use of salt is as a raw material for the production of CHLORINE, SODIUM metal, and SODIUM HYDROXIDE; it is also used in large amounts in the SOLVAY PROCESS for making SODIUM CARBONATE. Nearly all chemical compounds that contain either sodium or chlorine are ultimately derived from salt. Salt is widely and abundantly distributed in nature. It makes up nearly 80% of the dissolved material in sea water, and is the greater part of dissolved matter in the Dead Sea, the Great Salt Lake, and in salt wells in various parts of the world. It is also widely distributed in solid form. The mineral halite is pure salt. Rock, or mineral, salt is usually less pure; it is found in large deposits in the United States, notably in New York, Michigan, Ohio, Kansas, Texas, and Louisiana, and also in Great Britain, France, West Germany, the Soviet Union, China, and India. Salt is mined from deposits or is obtained as a brine by introducing water into the deposits to dissolve the salt and then pumping the solution to the surface. Salt is also obtained by evaporation of sea water, usually in shallow basins warmed by sunlight; salt so obtained was formerly called bay salt, and is now often called solar salt. Most salt for table use is obtained from sea water; it is usually not pure sodium chloride, small amounts of other substances (e.g., magnesium carbonate, hydrated calcium silicate, or tricalcium phosphate) being added to it to prevent lumping. Iodized table salt usually contains small amounts of potassium iodide, sodium carbonate, and sodium thiosulfate. Manufacture and use of salt is one of the oldest chemical industries. Salt has been used as money. A high tax on salt was a contributing cause of the French Revolution. See G. L. Eskew, *Salt, the Fifth Element* (1948); D. W. Kaufmann, ed., *Sodium Chloride* (1968).

sodium hydrate: see SODIUM HYDROXIDE.

sodium hydrogen carbonate: see SODIUM BICARBONATE.

sodium hydroxide, chemical compound, NaOH, a white crystalline substance that readily absorbs carbon dioxide and moisture from the air. It is very soluble in water, alcohol, and glycerin. It is a CAUSTIC and a strong base (see ACIDS AND BASES). Commonly known as caustic soda, lye, or sodium hydrate, it is available commercially in various solid forms, e.g., pellets, sticks, or chips, and in water solutions of various concentrations; both solid and liquid forms vary in purity. The major use of sodium hydroxide is as a chemical and in the manufacture of other chemicals; because it is inexpensive, it is widely used wherever a strong base is needed. It is also used in producing rayon and other textiles, in making paper, in etching aluminum, in making soaps and detergents, and in a wide variety of other uses. The principal method for its manufacture is electrolytic dissociation of sodium chloride; chlorine gas is a coproduct. Small amounts of sodium hydroxide are produced by the soda-lime process in which a concentrated solution of sodium carbonate (soda) is reacted with calcium hydroxide (slaked lime); calcium carbonate precipitates, leaving a sodium hydroxide solution.

sodium nitrate, chemical compound, $NaNO_3$, a colorless, odorless, salty and bitter-tasting crystalline compound that closely resembles potassium nitrate (saltpeter or niter) in appearance and chemical properties. It is soluble in water, alcohol, and liquid ammonia. Sodium nitrate is also called soda niter or Chile saltpeter. It is found naturally in large deposits in arid regions of Chile, Peru, Argentina, and Bolivia as caliche, a crude, impure nitrate rock or gravel. Natural deposits are the major source of sodium nitrate; it is also obtained in small amounts as a by-product of chlorine production by the nitrosyl chloride process, in which sodium chloride (common salt) is reacted with nitric acid. Sodium nitrate is used in making potassium nitrate, fertilizers, and explosives. It was formerly an important raw material for the production of nitric acid.

sodium silicate, any one of several compounds containing sodium oxide, Na_2O, and SILICA, Si_2O, or a mixture of sodium silicates. Sodium *ortho*silicate is Na_4SiO_4 (or $2Na_2O \cdot SiO_2$); sodium *meta*silicate is Na_2SiO_3 (or $Na_2O \cdot SiO_2$); sodium *di*silicate is $Na_2Si_2O_5$ (or $Na_2O \cdot 2SiO_2$); sodium *tetra*silicate is $Na_2Si_4O_9$ (or $Na_2O \cdot 4SiO_2$). All these compounds are transparent, glassy or crystalline solids that have high melting points (above 800°C) and are water soluble. They are produced chiefly by fusing sand and sodium carbonate in various proportions. The product is commonly known as WATER GLASS. The greatest single use of sodium silicates is as a raw material for making SILICA GEL.

sodium sulfate, chemical compound, Na_2SO_4. It is a white, orthorhombic crystalline compound at ordinary temperatures; above 100°C it assumes a monoclinic structure, and above about 250°C it assumes a hexagonal structure. Sodium sulfate is soluble in cold water and very soluble in hot water. It forms two hydrates; the decahydrate is GLAUBER'S SALT. Anhydrous sodium sulfate is found in nature as the mineral thenardite. The major commercial source of sodium sulfate is salt cake, a by-product of the production of hydrochloric acid from sodium chloride (common salt) by treatment with sulfuric acid. It is obtained (with other chemicals) by evaporation of natural brines. It is also obtained as a by-product of viscose rayon manufacture and in several other, less important ways. The principal use of sodium sulfate is in processing wood pulp for making kraft paper. It is also used in glass manufacture, textile dyeing, and synthetic detergents.

sodium tetraborate decahydrate: see BORAX.

sodium thiosulfate, $Na_2S_2O_3$, colorless crystalline compound that is more familiar as the pentahydrate, $Na_2S_2O_3 \cdot 5H_2O$, an efflorescent, monoclinic crystalline substance also called sodium hyposulfite or "hypo." Sodium thiosulfate is readily soluble in water and is a mild reducing agent. Because it dissolves silver salts, its major use is in photography for developing film. It is also used in chrome-tanning leather and in chemical manufacture. Sodium thiosulfate is produced chiefly from liquid waste products of sodium sulfide or sulfur dye manufacture. It is also produced from sodium carbonate, sulfur dioxide, and sulfur by a process that involves several steps.

Sodom (sŏd'əm) or **Sodoma** (sŏd'ōmə), in the Bible, the principal of the Cities of the Plain (the others being Gomorrah, Admah, Zeboiim, and Zoar, which was spared) destroyed by fire from heaven because of their unnatural carnal wickedness. Gen. 10.19; 13; 14; 18; 19; Deut. 29.23; Amos 4.11; Mat. 10.15; Mark 6.11; Rom. 9.29; 2 Peter 2.6; Jude 7. The cities lay probably in the southern portion of the Dead Sea.

Sodoma, Il (ēl sô'dōmä), c.1477–1549, Sienese painter, whose real name was Giovanni Antonio Bazzi. Born in Vercelli, Piedmont, he came to Rome c.1508. Commissioned by Pope Julius II, he painted frescoes in the Camera della Segnatura in the Vatican. Raphael's frescoes afterward replaced most of his work there. For Agostino Chigi in the Farnesina Villa, Sodoma painted two frescoes, *The Marriage of Alexander* and *Alexander in the Tent of Darius.* In Siena and its vicinity he produced many works, executed in a saccharine style. Among these paintings are scenes from the life of St. Catherine (San Domenico) and from the life of St. Benedict (Monte Oliveto).

Soemba: see SUMBA, Indonesia.

Soembawa: see SUMBAWA, Indonesia.

Soerabaja: see SURABAJA, Indonesia.

Soerakarta: see SURAKARTA, Indonesia.

Soest (zōst), city (1970 pop. 37,675), North Rhine-Westphalia, W West Germany. It is a manufacturing city and an agricultural trade center. Known in the 7th cent., Soest is one of the oldest cities of Germany. It was the chief town of Westphalia in the Middle Ages and was a flourishing member of the

Hanseatic League. Until the mid-15th cent. Soest was included in the archbishopric of Cologne and was later in the county of Mark (under the duke of Cleves); but it enjoyed virtual independence under its charter. The city passed to Brandenburg in 1614. Soest was badly damaged in World War II. Its noteworthy buildings include the St. Patroklidom (12th cent.), a Romanesque cathedral; the Romanesque Nicholas Chapel (c.1150); the Wiesenkirche (14th-15th cent.), a lovely late Gothic church; and many medieval and Renaissance style houses. Much of the old city wall remains.

Sofia (sōfē'ə, sō'fēə), Bulg. *Sofiya*, city (1968 est. pop. 950,700), capital of Bulgaria, W central Bulgaria, on a high plain surrounded by the Balkan Mts. It is Bulgaria's chief industrial, transportation, and commercial center. Among the chief manufactures are engineering and metal products, machinery, textiles, rubber and leather goods, furniture, footwear, chemicals, and bricks and tiles. A Thracian settlement once occupied the site of Sofia. It was taken by the Romans in 29 A.D. and flourished, especially, under the Emperor Trajan, as Sardica. Destroyed by the Huns in 447, the city was rebuilt (6th cent.) by Byzantine emperor Justinian I and renamed Triaditsa by the Byzantines. It formed part of the first Bulgarian kingdom (809-1018), reverted to the Byzantines (1018-1186), and was included in the second Bulgarian kingdom (1186-1382). Known as Sredets under the Bulgars, it was renamed Sofia or Sophya in 1376. Sofia passed to the Ottomans in 1382 and became the residence of the Turkish governors of RUMELIA. Taken by the Russians in the Russo-Turkish War of 1877-78, it became (1879) the capital of newly independent Bulgaria. During World War II the Russians captured Sofia from the Germans (1944) and installed a Communist government. The city has a university (founded 1889) and numerous other educational and cultural facilities. It is the see of an Eastern Orthodox metropolitan and of a Roman Catholic bishop and also retains many old churches, mosques, and synagogues. Landmarks include the parliament building, the state opera house, the former royal palace, the Church of St. George (4th-5th cent.), the Church of St. Sofia (6th-7th cent.), the Banya Bashi mosque (1474), the mausoleum of Georgi Dimitrov, Bulgaria's first Communist party leader, and the Alexander Nevski Cathedral.

softball, variant of baseball played with a larger ball on a smaller field. Invented (1888) in Chicago as an indoor game, it was at various times called indoor baseball, mush ball, playground ball, kitten ball, and, because it was also played by women, ladies' baseball. The name softball was given to the game in 1926. A tournament (1933) at the Chicago World's Fair spurred interest in the game. The Amateur Softball Association of America (founded 1934) governs the game in the United States and sponsors annual sectional and world series championships. The International Softball Federation regulates rules of play in 42 countries, including the United States and Canada. Despite the name, the ball used is not soft. It is about 12 in. (30 cm) in circumference, which is 3 in. (8 cm) larger than a baseball. The softball infield is 60 sq ft (5.6 sq m), about 30 sq ft (3 sq m) smaller than a baseball infield. As in baseball, two teams of 9 players each compete (until 1946 softball teams included 10 players). Softball rules vary somewhat from those of baseball. Two major differences are that the ball must be pitched underhand—from 43 ft (13.1 m) as compared with 60.5 ft (18.4 m) in baseball—and that seven innings instead of nine constitute a regulation game. See A. T. Noren, *Softball* (3d ed. rev. 1966).

soft-coated wheaten terrier, breed of medium-sized dog developed and perfected in Ireland. It stands from 17 to 19 in. (43.1-48.3 cm) high at the shoulder and weighs from 30 to 45 lb (13.6-20.4 kg). Its abundant, soft, medium-length coat is silky and slightly wavy and may be any shade of wheat in color. Related to the Kerry blue and Irish terrier, the soft-coated wheaten has been raised for many years in its native land as a farm dog and vermin destroyer. In recent times it has begun to be popular as a pet in the United States, where it is exhibited in the miscellaneous class at dog shows sanctioned by the American Kennel Club. See DOG.

Sogdiana (sŏgdēā'nə), part of the ancient Persian Empire in central Asia between the Oxus and Jaxartes rivers, corresponding to the later emirate of Bukhara and region of Samarkand. It was a satrapy under Darius I and was later invaded by Alexander the Great.

Sognafjord or **Sogne Fjord** (both: sông'nəfyôr"), inlet of the Norwegian Sea, SW Norway, in Sogn og Fjordane co. Extending c.110 mi (180 km) inland and reaching a depth of c.4,000 ft (1,220 m), it is the longest and deepest fjord in Norway. It has several branches that cut into the Jotunheimen mts. and the Jostedalsbreen glacier. In some places the mountains drop a sheer 3,000 ft (910 m) to the water on both sides of the fjord. The beauty of the region has made it a popular tourist area, and there are many well-known resorts along the fjord.

Sogn og Fjordane (sông'nə ô fyôr'dänə), county (1972 est. pop. 102,000), c.7,150 sq mi (18,500 sq km), W Norway, bordering on the Atlantic Ocean in the west. Hermansverk is the capital. The county's coast is deeply indented by the Sognafjord in the south and by the Nordfjord in the north, between which is the Jostedalsbreen, continental Europe's largest icefield. Fishing and farming are the main occupations in Sogn og Fjordane.

Sogwali: see SEQUOYAH.

Sohag: see SAWHAJ, Egypt.

Soho (sōhō', sə-), district of Westminster, London, England, known for its continental restaurants. It is a center of the London motion picture industry. Once a fashionable quarter, it became popular among writers and artists in the 19th cent. Past residents of Soho include John Dryden, William Hazlitt, William Blake, Thomas De Quincey, and Ernest Dowson.

Soignies (swänyē'), Flemish *Zinnik*, town (1970 pop. 12,006), Hainaut prov., S Belgium. Paper is manufactured, and limestone is quarried nearby. Of note is the Church of St. Vincent (10th-12th cent.).

soil, surface layer of earth containing organic matter and capable of supporting vegetation. Soil may be from a few inches to several feet thick. It consists of fine rock material, disintegrated by geological changes such as glaciation and volcanic eruption; HUMUS, the organic remains of decomposed vegetation; air; and water. The inorganic fraction of soil consists of various sizes and shapes of rocks and minerals; in order of increasing size these are termed CLAY, SILT, SAND, GRAVEL, and STONE. Soils with large amounts of coarse sand, gravel, or stone have low capacity to retain plant nutrients, gases, and water, whereas soils with high clay content tend to retain these substances. The arrangement of soil particles is known as soil structure; in most soils, clay and organic particles combine to form aggregates in the shape of plates, blocks, prisms, or granules. The soil structure largely determines the pore space of the soil and its bulk density; these factors contribute to the air and water capacity of the soil and also affect plant growth. Organic matter consists of decomposed plant and animal material and living plant roots; soil microorganisms, also found in the organic portion of soil, are necessary to return to the soil nutrients bound up in plant and animal matter. Organic matter has colloidal properties, holding more nutrients, water, and gases than clay. The addition of organic matter is often needed to correct sticky or hard and lumpy soils. Soils can be divided into layers roughly parallel to the surface called horizons. The A horizon is the surface layer, containing most humus. The B layer beneath contains inorganic compounds formed from decomposition of organic material, a process known as mineralization; the material is brought to the B layer by the downward leaching action of water. The lowest soil layer, the C layer, represents the weathered mineral parent substance. Besides organic matter, soil is largely composed of elements and compounds of silicon, aluminum, iron, oxygen, and, in smaller quantities, calcium, magnesium, sodium, and potassium. Factors determining the nature of soil are vegetation type, climate, and parent rock material; geographic relief and the geological age of the developing soil are also factors. Acidic soils occur in humid regions because alkaline minerals are removed downward by leaching, whereas soil alkalinity occurs in regions of low rainfall because inadequate leaching results in a high surface concentration of alkaline salts. Geologically young soils reflect the parent material type more than older soils, which have been altered over time by climate and vegetation. Many systems of soil classification have been devised. The Russian system, from which most classification systems have been derived, is based on the distinctive horizons that comprise the soil profile. Soil fertility depends on various factors, including the texture of the soil, its chemical composition, its supply of water, and its temperature. The fertility of a given soil can be fairly accurately determined by testing samples. Often soils can be made more productive by the correct use of a FERTILIZER, such as MANURE; without the addition of organic matter soil is not capable of producing good crops indefinitely. The frequency and kind of cultivation also affect fertility (see COVER CROP; ROTATION OF CROPS). Soil acidity can be decreased, if necessary, by addition of calcium carbonate and can be increased by adding sulfuric acid. Soil deterioration caused by human mismanagement, e.g., by erosion and nutrient loss, is checked by methods of conservation. For advice and information on soils, consult state agricultural experiment stations and their publications. See T. L. Lyon and H. O. Buckman, *Nature and Properties of Soils* (6th ed. 1960); Martin Alexander, *Introduction to Soil Microbiology* (1961); R. B. Held and Marion Clawson, *Soil Conservation in Perspective* (1965); publications of the U.S. Soil Conservation Service.

soiling, agricultural practice of feeding green fodder to livestock in the barn or dry lot. It is followed in the United States mostly in the dairy industry in seasons when pastures are short, but in Europe more generally. For best results the crop must be cut daily. Among the crops used for soiling are clovers, alfalfa, cowpeas, soybeans, corn, and rye.

soilless gardening: see HYDROPONICS.

Soissons (swäsôN'), city (1968 pop. 27,641), Aisne dept., N France, on the Aisne River. It is an agricultural and industrial center. Soissons was an old Roman town and early episcopal see. Its strategic location has made it the scene of many battles throughout history. Clovis I defeated the Roman legions at Soissons in 486, and the city was the capital of several MEROVINGIAN kings (5th-7th cent.). Pepin the Short dethroned Childeric III there in 751; and Robert I, grandfather of Hugh Capet (see CAPETIANS), was killed in battle at Soissons in 923. Throughout the 19th and 20th cent. the city was the scene of warfare, culminating in the German invasion of 1940. Part of the Abbey of Saint-Jean-des-Vignes (where Thomas à Becket lived for several years) survives, as does the nearby Abbey of St. Médard, a burial place of Merovingian kings. The Gothic Cathedral of Saint-Gervais and Saint-Protais (12th-13th cent.) has stained-glass windows by Rubens.

Sojourner Truth: see TRUTH, SOJOURNER.

Soka (sō'kä), city (1970 pop. 123,269), Saitama prefecture, E central Honshu, Japan. It is a suburb of Tokyo.

Soka Gakkai (sō'kä gäk'kī) [Value Creation Society], Japan-based lay Buddhist group that is a theological offshoot of the Nichiren sect. Founded (1937) by Makiguchi Tsunesaburo, the militantly evangelistic movement claimed a membership of some 7 million households by 1970. The group was persecuted and forced to disband during World War II, but its Japanese membership expanded rapidly in the years following the war. Its simple doctrines of absolute faith and immediate worldly benefits appeal to the desire of many Japanese for traditional values in a rapidly changing world. At their meetings, adherents chant the secret prayer, or *daimoku, "namu Myoho rengekyo,"* which has been translated as "I am the Supreme Power." In addition to religious, educational, and cultural activities, the Soka Gakkai actively participates in Japanese politics. It first ran candidates for office in 1955, and by 1964 had organized its own party, Komeito, or the Clean Government party. The fourth largest political party in Japan, Komeito's platform is a unique blend of reformist socialism and traditional Buddhist conservativism. Since 1960 the Soka Gakkai has been led by Daisuku Ikeda, who has supported a program of international conversion; its adherents proselytize in major North American cities. Ikeda is the author of a variety of books, including *Essays on Life* (1970), *The Human Revolution* (7 vol., 1965-72), and *Dialogue on Life* (1973).

Sokoloff, Nicolai (nyĭkəlī' sŏ'kəlôf"), 1886-1965, American conductor and violinist, b. near Kiev, Russia. After studying at Yale and under Charles Martin Loeffler, he toured France and England as a violinist. He was the first conductor of the Cleveland Symphony Orchestra, 1918-32; directed the Federal Music Project, 1935-38; and conducted the Seattle Symphony Orchestra, 1938-40. Subsequently he directed the Musical Arts Society at La Jolla, Calif.

Sokolova, Lydia (sōkəlō'və), 1896-1974, English ballerina, b. Wanstead, as Hilda Munnings. Trained at Stedman's Academy in London, Sokolova joined the Diaghilev Ballets Russes in 1913 and became the company's principal character dancer until it disbanded in 1929. She then retired to teach and coach in England. See her memoirs, *Dancing for Diaghilev* (1961).

Sokolow, Nahum (nä'əm sō'kəlō), 1859-1936, Jewish writer and Zionist leader, b. Poland. He served (1906-9) as general secretary of the Zionist Organization editing its various publications. With Chaim Weizmann he participated in the London meetings during World War I that led to the Balfour Declaration and the Palestinian mandate. He succeeded Weizmann as president (1931–35) of the World Zionist Organization. Sokolow was an accomplished linguist. From 1873 he contributed articles to various Hebrew newspapers, and he wrote *History of Zionism, 1600–1918* (2 vol., 1919). See biography by Simcha Kling (1960).

Sokoto (sōkō'tō, sō'kətō), city (1969 est. pop. 104,000), NW Nigeria, on the Sokoto River. It is the commercial center for a wide region and a collection place for hides, skins, and groundnuts. Rice and tobacco are grown for local consumption. The city has cement, pottery, and leather tanning and dyeing industries. Sokoto was founded in 1809 by Usuman dan Fodio, the FULANI leader who established a large Muslim empire including most of N Nigeria. It became the capital of the empire and was built up in the 1820s by Muhammadu Bello, dan Fodio's son. In 1903, Sokoto fell to British forces under Frederick LUGARD. The tomb of dan Fodio and other shrines in the city have made it a place of pilgrimage for Muslims.

sol, in chemistry: see COLLOID.

Sol (sŏl), in Roman religion, sun god. An ancient god of Mesopotamian origin, he was introduced (c.220) into Roman religion as Sol Invictus by emperor Heliogabalus. His worship remained an important cult of Rome until the rise of Christianity.

solar cell, SEMICONDUCTOR devised to convert light to electric current. It is a specially constructed DIODE, usually made of silicon crystal. When light strikes the exposed active surface, it knocks electrons loose from their sites in the crystal. Some of the electrons have sufficient energy to cross the diode junction and, having done so, cannot return to positions on the other side of the junction without passing through an external circuit. Since the current obtained from these devices is small and the voltage is low, they must be connected in large series-parallel arrays if useful amounts of energy are to be converted. Practical devices of this kind are about 10% to 15% efficient and have been used to provide electric power for spacecraft. Devices using indium phosphide and gallium arsenide are in principle more efficient than silicon devices but are more costly to produce. For large-scale power conversion solar cells offer a number of practical problems; one of the most serious of these is the wide variation of output voltage and current accompanying changes in the amount of incident light.

solar constant, the average amount of radiant energy received by the earth's atmosphere from the sun; its value is about 2 calories per min incident on each square centimeter of the upper atmosphere. The actual value of the energy varies with several factors; the most important factor is the earth's distance from the sun, which changes because of the earth's elliptical orbit. For computing the value of the solar constant, the ASTRONOMICAL UNIT, or average earth-sun distance, is used.

solar energy, any form of ENERGY radiated by the SUN, including light, radio waves, and X rays. Solar energy is needed by green plants for the process of PHOTOSYNTHESIS, which is the ultimate source of all food. The energy in fossil fuels (e.g., coal and oil) and other organic fuels (e.g., wood) is derived from solar energy. Difficulties with these fuels have led to the invention of devices that directly convert solar energy into usable forms of energy, such as electricity. Solar batteries, which operate on the principle that light falling on photosensitive substances causes a flow of electricity, play an important part in astronautics but are too expensive to be in common use on the earth (see SOLAR CELL). Thermoelectric generators convert the heat generated by solar energy directly into electricity (see THERMOELECTRICITY). It has been suggested that electricity could be generated on a large scale by using the solar energy available in desert areas, e.g., SW United States, the Sahara, and central Australia. One proposal has been to place in these areas large numbers of solar batteries to generate electricity. Another proposal has been to place there specially coated pipes containing molten sodium and potassium that can trap the heat from sunlight falling on them. The heat would then be converted into electricity (see POWER, ELECTRIC). Heat from the sun is used in air-drying a variety of materials and in producing salt by the evaporation of sea water. Experimental solar heating systems can supply heat and hot water for domestic use; heat collected in special plates on the roof of a house is stored in rocks or water held in a large container. Such systems, however, usually require a conventional heater to supplement them. Solar stoves, which focus the sun's heat directly, are employed in regions where there is much perennial sunlight. See also ENERGY, SOURCES OF. See Farrington Daniels, *Direct Use of the Sun's Energy* (1964, repr. 1974).

solar plexus, dense cluster of nerve cells and supporting tissue, located behind the stomach in the region of the celiac artery just below the diaphragm. It is also known as the celiac plexus. Rich in ganglia and interconnected neurons, the solar plexus is the largest autonomic nerve center in the abdominal cavity (see NERVOUS SYSTEM). Through branches it controls many vital functions such as adrenal secretion and intestinal contraction. Popularly, the term "solar plexus" may refer to the pit of the stomach. A blow to that area, if it penetrates to the true solar plexus, not only causes great pain but may also temporarily halt visceral functioning.

solar system, the sun and the family of planets, natural SATELLITES, asteroids, meteoroids, and comets that are its captives. The motion of the planets was first described accurately by Johannes Kepler at the beginning of the 17th cent.; he showed that the planets move in nearly circular elliptical orbits. Isaac Newton later showed that the laws of planetary motion discovered by Kepler apply also to all other bodies in the solar system and are based on the force of GRAVITATION. The sun's gravitational pull is the dominant force in the solar system; the forces exerted by the other celestial bodies on one another produce small shifts and variations, called PERTURBATIONS, in their orbits. The SUN is by far the most massive part of the solar system, containing almost 99.9% of the system's total mass. The sun is a rather typical star, a luminous sphere of incandescent gas with a diameter of 864,000 mi (1.4 million km), about 109 times the diameter of the earth. Its mass is roughly 2 thousand trillion trillion tons (10^{30} kg), about 333,000 times the mass of the earth. The sun obtains its energy from nuclear reactions in its interior and supplies all the light and nearly all the heat in the solar system. The principal members of the sun's retinue are the nine major PLANETS; in order of increasing distance from the sun, they are Mercury, Venus, Earth, Mars, Jupiter, Saturn, Uranus, Neptune, and Pluto (see table). The three outermost planets were unknown in antiquity. Uranus was discovered in 1781 by William Herschel, who at first mistook it for a comet. Calculations based on perturbations in the orbit of Uranus led to the discovery of Neptune in 1846. The agreement between the observed and calculated positions of the new planet was justly regarded as a major confirmation of Newton's theory of gravitation. The outermost planet, Pluto, was discovered in 1930; the possibility of planets beyond Pluto remains open. The unit for measuring distance in the solar system is the ASTRONOMICAL UNIT (AU), the average distance between the earth and the sun. The distances of the planets from the sun range from 0.39 AU for Mercury to 39 AU for Pluto. All the planets orbit the sun in approximately the same plane (that of the ECLIPTIC) and move in the same direction—from west to east, or counterclockwise as viewed from above (north). A planet's year, or sidereal period, is the time required for it to complete one full circuit around the sun. Mercury's year is 88 earth days, while Pluto's year is 248 earth years. All the planets rotate about their own axes as they revolve around the sun; their periods of rotation vary from just under 10 hr for Jupiter to 243 earth days for Venus. The rotation of Venus is from east to west, an example of RETROGRADE MOTION. The equatorial planes of the planets are tilted to various degrees with respect to their orbital planes, giving rise to yearly seasons. The smallest tilt, that of Jupiter, is 3°, whereas that of Uranus is 98°, causing its axis of rotation to lie nearly in the plane of the planet's orbit. The tilt of the earth's equatorial plane is 23½°. The planets are grouped according to their physical properties. The inner planets (Mercury, Venus, Earth, and Mars) resemble the Earth and are therefore called the terrestrial planets. They are dense and small in size, with solid, rocky crusts and molten metallic interiors. Except for Mercury, they possess gaseous atmospheres from which lighter elements have escaped because of the low gravitational force. The Jovian planets (Jupiter, Saturn, Uranus, and Neptune) all resemble Jupiter; they have great volume and mass but relatively low density. Jupiter is heavier than all the other planets combined; it is 318 times as heavy as the earth and 1,300 times as large, making its density only about one fourth that of the earth. Saturn has a mass 95 times that of the earth and a density less than that of water. The atmospheres of the Jovian planets are very thick, merging imperceptibly with the bodies of the planets, and are rich in hydrogen, hydrogen compounds, and helium. Because of its size and apparent density, Pluto is sometimes classed with the terrestrial planets, but it is more properly considered a special case; its orbit crosses that of Neptune, indicating that it may be an escaped satellite of that planet. Most of the nine major planets have one or more satellites. Jupiter leads with 12 known satellites; the largest, GANYMEDE, is greater in size than the planet Mercury. The earth's moon is unusually large in relation to its planet. Other members of the solar system are the comets, asteroids, and meteoroids. COMETS are loose aggregates of small particles that move in highly elliptical orbits; many of these orbits are so elongated that they appear to have the shape of parabolas. As comets round the sun, tails of vaporized material millions of miles in length stream behind them. ASTEROIDS are the tens of thousands of minor planets that orbit in a belt between Mars and Jupiter. The largest of them, Ceres, is 470 mi (756 km) in diameter. The origin of asteroids is unclear; one theory claims they are fragments of a planet that occupied approximately their present position and met with some disaster in the remote past. Meteoroids, which are even smaller bodies scattered in orbits throughout the solar system, are countless in number. They are too tiny to observe except when they plunge into the earth's atmosphere and are seen as METEORS, or shooting stars.

Origin of the Solar System. Several theories of the origin of the solar system have been proposed since the turn of the 19th cent., but none has adequately withstood close scientific and mathematical analysis. Besides explaining the birth of the sun, planets, satellites, asteroids, and comets, such a theory must explain the chemical and physical differences of the planets and their orbital regularities, i.e., why they lie almost on the same plane and revolve in the same direction in nearly circular orbits; it must also account for the relative angular momentum of the sun and planets arising from their rotational and orbital motions. The nebular hypothesis, developed by Immanuel Kant and given scientific form by P. S.

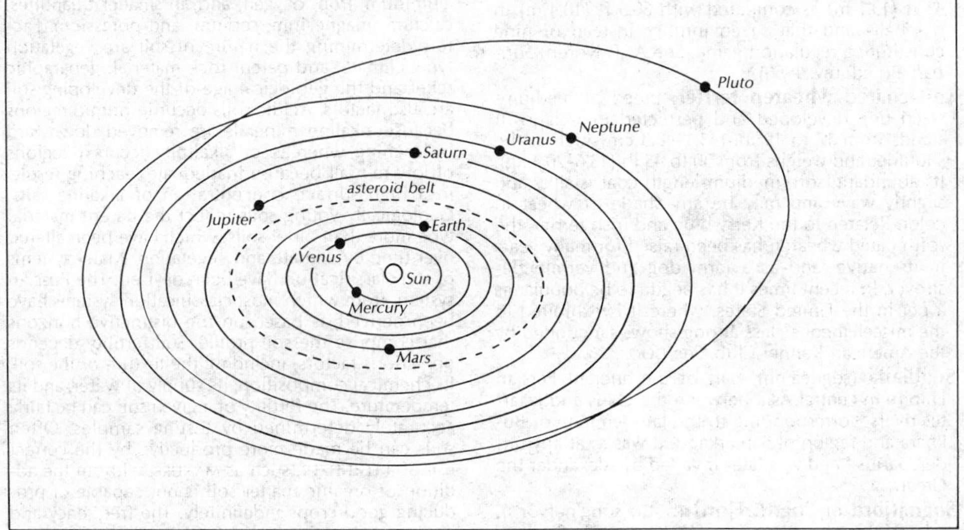

Solar system

Laplace at the end of the 18th cent., assumed that the solar system in its first state was a nebula, a hot, slowly rotating mass of rarefied matter, which gradually cooled and contracted. As the volume decreased, the rotation became more rapid, and this in turn gave the nebula a flattened, disklike shape. In time, when the centrifugal force at the equator of the nebula equaled the pull of gravity, a ring of gaseous matter became separated from the outer part of the disk. The process was repeated several times, until the diminished nebula at the center was surrounded by a series of rings. Out of the material of each ring a great ball of gases was formed, which by shrinking eventually became a planet. The mass at the center of the system condensed to form the sun. Many objections weaken this hypothesis, particularly the argument that the central mass, which became the sun, would have needed far more angular momentum than the rings in order to throw them off. In fact, because of their great mass and speed the Jovian planets carry about 98% of the angular momentum of the solar system, whereas the sun, although a thousand times the mass of Jupiter, rotates slowly and contributes less than 2%. Another objection is that the rings, instead of condensing into single planets, would tend to form swarms of small bodies similar to the asteroids or the rings of Saturn. Encounter or collision theories, in which a star passes close by or actually collides with the sun, try to explain the distribution of angular momentum. According to the planetesimal theory developed by T. C. Chamberlin and F. R. Moulton in the early part of the 20th cent., a star passed close enough to the sun to exert a strong attractive force upon the sun's fluid mass. Huge tides were raised on the surface; some of this erupted matter was torn free and, by a cross-pull from the star, was thrust into elliptical orbits around the sun. The smaller masses quickly cooled to become solid bodies, called planetesimals. As their orbits crossed, the larger bodies grew by absorbing the planetesimals, thus becoming planets. The theory explains the asteroid belt as a region in which no dominating body existed to bring the planetesimals together as a planet. The tidal theory, proposed by James Jeans and Harold Jeffreys in 1918, is a variation of the planetesimal concept; it suggests that a huge tidal wave, raised on the sun by a passing star, was drawn into a long filament and became detached from the principal mass. As the stream of gaseous material condensed, it separated into masses of various sizes, which, by further condensation, took the form of the planets. This theory did not completely satisfy the conditions of angular momentum, and Jeffreys later discarded it for one in which another star brushes the sun's surface, causing tidal waves and subsequent planet formation. Serious objections against the encounter theories remain. The angular momentum problem is not fully explained. In addition, the great unlikelihood of one star passing so close to another would indicate a rarity of planetary systems in the galaxy, but other evidence indicates that these systems are not so rare. Contemporary theories return to a form of the nebular hypothesis to explain the transfer of momentum from the central mass to the outer material. The nebula is seen as a dense nucleus, or protosun, surrounded by a thin shell of gaseous matter extending to the edges of the solar system. According to the theory of the protoplanets as developed by G. P. Kuiper, the nebula ceased to rotate uniformly and, under the influence of turbulence and tidal action, broke into whirlpools of gas, called protoplanets, within the rotating mass. In time the protoplanets condensed to form the planets. Although Kuiper's theory allows for the distribution of angular momentum, it does not explain adequately the chemical and physical differences of the planets. Using a chemical approach, H. C. Urey has given evidence that the terrestrial planets were formed at low temperatures, less than 2,200°F (1,200°C). He proposed that the temperatures were high enough to drive off most of the lighter substances, e.g., hydrogen and helium, but low enough to allow for the condensation of heavier substances, e.g., iron and silica, into solid particles, or planetesimals. Eventually, the planetesimals pulled together into protoplanets, the temperature increased, and the metals formed a molten core. At the distances of the Jovian planets the methane, water, and ammonia were frozen, preventing the earthy materials from condensing into small solids and resulting in the different composition of these planets and their great size and low density. See G. P. Kuiper, ed., *The Solar System* (4 vol., 1953–63); Thornton and L. W. Page, ed., *The Origin of the Solar System* (1966); F. L. Whipple, *Earth, Moon, and Planets* (3d ed. 1968); Patrick Moore, *The New Guide to the Planets* (1954, repr. 1971).

solar time, TIME defined by the position of the sun. The solar DAY is the time it takes for the sun to return to the same meridian in the sky. Local solar time is measured by a SUNDIAL. When the center of the sun is on an observer's meridian, the observer's local solar time is zero hours (noon). Because the earth moves with varying speed in its orbit at different times of the year and because the plane of the earth's equator is inclined to its orbital plane, the length of the solar day is different depending on the time of year. It is more convenient to define time in terms of the average of local solar time. Such time, called mean solar time, may be thought of as being measured relative to an imaginary sun (the mean sun) that lies in the earth's equatorial plane and about which the earth orbits with constant speed. Every mean solar day is of the same length. The difference between the local solar time and the mean solar time at a given location is known as the equation of time. Tables used by navigators list the equation of time for different times of year so that an observer can calculate his mean solar time from his local solar time (found by determining the sun's HOUR ANGLE). Mean solar time is the basis for CIVIL TIME and STANDARD TIME.

solar wind, stream of ionized hydrogen and helium that radiates outward from the sun at high speeds. The continuous expansion of the solar CORONA into the surrounding vacuum of space carries away from the sun about 1 million tons of gas per sec; this blows out like a wind through the solar system. During the days of quiet sunspot activity the wind at the sun has an approximate density of 1 billion atoms per cc, a velocity of a few hundred yards per sec, and a temperature of about 1 million degrees Fahrenheit. Near the earth it has a density ranging from 3 to 6 atoms per cc, a velocity of 450 mi (700 km) per sec, and a temperature of about 1300°F (700°C); during periods of greater sunspot activity it shows corresponding increases in density, velocity, and temperature. The wind is believed to extend out to between 100 and 200 AU (1 AU is the mean distance between the earth and the sun), far beyond Pluto (at 39 AU), where it is dispersed in the interstellar gases. Many effects result from the solar wind. The characteristic that a COMET tail always points away from the sun is explained by the pressure of the wind pushing it out. The intensity of the cosmic rays in the inner part of the solar system is reduced by the magnetic fields carried on the wind, which tend to deflect the rays, thus making it a kind of shield against that radiation. The interaction of the wind with the earth's magnetic field is responsible in part for such phenomena as auroras and geomagnetic storms.

solder (sŏd'ər), metal alloy used in the molten state as a metallic binder. The type of solder to be used is determined by the metals to be united. Soft solders are commonly composed of lead and tin and have low melting points. Hard solders (i.e., silver solders) have high melting points and are suited for use with ferrous and high-melting-point nonferrous alloys. Areas to be soldered are cleaned and coated with a flux (such as hydrochloric acid or borax) to prevent oxides from separating the solder from the surface. When brass is used in the solder or when brass surfaces are to be joined, the process is known as brazing, though the name is sometimes applied also to other hard soldering.

sole: see FLATFISH.

Solemn League and Covenant: see COVENANTERS.

solenodon (sōlē'nədŏn), insectivorous mammal, genus *Solenodon*, found in the West Indies. Related to moles, shrews, and hedgehogs, the solenodon resembles a rat with an elongated snout and coarse, shaggy fur. Its body is about 14 in. (36 cm) long, and its naked, scaly tail c.9 in. (23 cm) long. Solenodons are chiefly nocturnal; they eat insects, lizards, frogs, and other small animals, as well as carrion. Easily irritated, they fly into sudden rages, screaming and biting without provocation. There are two solenodon species. *S. cubanus*, found in the Bayama Mts. of Cuba, is rusty brown with black on its back and throat; *S. paradoxus*, found in Haiti, is darker brown with a yellowish face and a ruff of hair about the shoulders. Solenodons are slow breeders, bearing a single litter of one to three young each year. Their numbers have been greatly reduced since the introduction of predators such as the mongoose, the cat, and the dog, and they are now threatened with extinction. They are classified in the phylum CHORDATA, subphylum Vertebrata, class Mammalia, order Insectivora, family Solenodontidae.

solenoid (sō'lənoid"), device made of a long wire that has been wound many times into a tightly packed coil; it has the shape of a long cylinder. If current is sent through a solenoid made of insulated wire and having a length much greater than its diameter, a uniform magnetic field will be created inside the solenoid. This field can be intensified by inserting a ferromagnetic core into the solenoid. See ELECTROMAGNET; MAGNETISM.

Solent, The (sō'lənt), channel, c.30 mi (50 km) long and ¾ to 5 mi (1.2–8 km) wide, between the Isle of Wight and Hampshire, S England. It serves as an anchorage for ships entering Southampton Water. Yacht races are held there.

Soler, Antonio (äntō'nyō sōlār'), 1729–83, Spanish composer. Soler became a monk in 1752 and lived the remainder of his life in the Escorial monastery. He was a pupil of Domenico Scarlatti. His works include church music, quintets for organ or harpsichord and strings, harpsichord sonatas, and incidental music. Soler also wrote a treatise on music theory.

Soleri, Paolo, 1920–, Italian-American architect. Soleri's works have been influenced by both Frank Lloyd Wright, with whom he worked, and Antoni Gaudí. He has developed an architecture that expresses a functional and organic way of life. Soleri has produced extraordinary designs for vast, self-sufficient communities built in the desert. These, which he terms arcologies, are proposed alternatives and responses to the increased problems of overpopulation and urban decay; they express an almost utopian architectural vision. Soleri and his students and assistants are at present building an arcology, Arcosanti, near Scottsdale, Ariz. He is the author of *Arcology: The City in the Image of Man* (1969). See his *Sketchbooks* (1971).

Solesmes (sôlĕm'), village (1968 pop. 820), Sarthe dept., NW France. Its famous Benedictine Abbey de Saint-Pierre de Solesmes (founded 1010) was a pilgrimage site and led in the revival of the pure Gregorian chant (see PLAINSONG). The abbey church contains invaluable 15th- and 16th-century sculptures.

solfège (sôlfĕzh') [Fr.] or **solfeggio** (sōlfĕd'jō) [Ital.], in music, systems of vocal exercises employing the solmization syllables of Guido d'Arezzo, i.e., do, re, mi. Solfège has the dual purpose of vocalization and practice in sight reading. The term has often been used loosely to cover training in the various fundamentals of music.

Solferino (sōlfārē'nō), village (1971 pop. 1,811), Lombardy, N Italy, near Mantua. There, on June 24, 1859, the French and Sardinians fought a bloody battle with the Austrians (see RISORGIMENTO). Al-

MAJOR PLANETS OF THE SOLAR SYSTEM

Planet	Distance from the sun (AU)	Mass (earth = 1.0)	Period of revolution	Period of rotation	Number of known satellites
Mercury	.39	.06	88 days	59 days	0
Venus	.72	.82	225 days	243 days	0
Earth	1.0	1.0	365 days	24 hours	1
Mars	1.5	.11	687 days	25 hours	2
Jupiter	5.2	318	12 years	10 hours	12
Saturn	9.5	95	29 years	11 hours	10
Uranus	19	15	84 years	11 hours	5
Neptune	30	17	165 years	16 hours?	2
Pluto	39	.06?	248 years	6.4 days	0

though the battle resulted in no clear decision, the Austrians withdrew to their strategic fortresses. Napoleon III, shocked by the huge losses and aware of the difficulties of continuing the war, soon afterward met Emperor Francis Joseph of Austria at VILLAFRANCA DI VERONA, where a preliminary peace was arranged. By a coincidence, J. Henry DUNANT, the Swiss philanthropist, was present at the battle, which he described in *Un Souvenir de Solférino*. His experience in witnessing the battle later inspired him to promote the Red Cross (founded 1864).

Soli (sō'lī), ancient city of Cilicia, SW of Tarsus, in present-day Turkey. It was founded c.700 B.C. by colonists from Rhodes. An important port at the time of Alexander the Great, Soli was destroyed in the 1st cent. B.C. by Tigranes of Armenia. It was rebuilt by Pompey, who called it Pompeiopolis. The word *solecism* is derived from the corrupt dialect of Greek spoken by the people of Soli.

solicitor, in English law, person duly admitted to practice before the supreme court of judicature. He is the agent of the person whose suit he handles and is distinguished from a barrister, who argues the case before the judge (see ATTORNEY); the solicitor, however, has the right of audience in the minor courts. Before the Judicature Act of 1873, solicitors were officers of the courts of EQUITY only. An attorney could practice in cases at COMMON LAW, while a proctor had similar practice in the admiralty courts. The act of 1873 generally abolished this distinction; all such agents are now solicitors. They are officers of the court; they have a monopoly of certain legal business and are subject to court regulation. The training required of a solicitor, set by the Law Society (earlier called the Incorporated Law Society), includes several years of clerkship under a practicing solicitor and attendance at a law school.

solid, one of the three states in which MATTER occurs, i.e., that state, as distinguished from liquid and gas, in which a substance has both a definite shape and a definite volume. Solids resemble liquids in having a definite volume, but differ from both liquids and gases in having a definite shape. The molecules of a solid, like those of a liquid, are very close together, but whereas the molecules of a liquid are free to move around, those of a solid have less thermal energy and are held fixed in their places by INTERMOLECULAR FORCES. Their only movement is a vibration about a fixed position. A solid changes to a liquid when its temperature is raised to its MELTING POINT. A definite quantity of heat (called the heat of fusion) is needed to change each gram of the substance from solid to liquid. Some substances change directly from solid to gas without passing through the liquid state (see SUBLIMATION), but most change from solid to liquid before becoming gaseous. Solids are of various types. Metals, their alloys, some nonmetals, and ionic chemical compounds are crystalline in form. Some solids, e.g., chalk and clay, have no regular structure and are called amorphous. Substances such as pitch and resin are called semisolids; these are actually very viscid liquids, but their flow or change of shape is so slow at ordinary temperatures as to be scarcely discernible by the human eye (see VISCOSITY). Properties in which solids differ from one another include density, hardness, malleability, ductility, elasticity, brittleness, and tensile strength.

solid-state physics, study of the properties of bulk MATTER rather than those of the individual particles that compose it. Solid-state physics is concerned with the properties exhibited by atoms and molecules because of their association and regular, periodic arrangement in CRYSTALS. The descriptive side of the study of solids is CRYSTALLOGRAPHY. From a practical point of view, searches are made for new characteristics and behavior of various materials. The most spectacular discovery resulting from these searches has been the TRANSISTOR. From a theoretical point of view, attempts are made to predict and explain the nature of aggregates of atoms in terms of the basic laws of the QUANTUM THEORY and the well-understood properties of individual atoms. An important concern of solid-state physics is the mechanical and thermal behavior of solids; specific areas of study include the allowed vibration modes of crystals (see PHONON), the transmission of vibrational energy (thermal conductivity), the amount of energy that must be absorbed to produce a given change in temperature (SPECIFIC HEAT), and phase transitions such as the MELTING POINTS of crystals. Although the crystalline, mechanical, thermal, and optical properties of solids are of great interest, it is the electrical properties that most clearly demarcate the various types of materials and which exhibit the greatest diversity of behavior. The single most important electrical characteristic of a solid is its electrical conductivity (the ease with which electric currents flow through it). See CONDUCTION. Metals are highly conductive solids that offer little resistance to electric currents. Most solid nonmetals, on the other hand, are insulators (solids whose conductivity is nearly zero); they offer virtually infinite resistance to electric currents. A third class of solids possesses electrical conductivity that is neither very high nor very low; these solids are called SEMICONDUCTORS. A principal triumph of quantum mechanics in solid-state physics is the explanation of these extreme variations of electrical conductivity in terms of the atomic structure of the three types of solids.

solid waste, discarded materials other than fluids. Household, commercial, and industrial garbage, along with refuse from hospitals, schools, and other institutions, totals some 360 million tons annually in the United States. Nearly 200 million tons—more than 5 lb (11 kg) per person daily—are collected and disposed of by municipalities at a cost of $5 billion. In a typical year, municipal garbage includes 48 billion cans, 26 billion glass containers, 30 million tons of paper, 4 million tons of plastic; in addition enormous tonnages of food residues, offal, rubber, textiles, and sludge formed in sewage treatment are produced. More than 7 million motor vehicles are junked annually, and a like number of television sets. Because of population growth and trends toward disposable products, extensive prepackaging, and built-in obsolescence, the amount of solid waste increases each year. Moreover, the most common disposal methods pollute land, water, or air to some degree (see POLLUTION). Management of solid waste therefore presents an increasingly acute problem. About 65% of all municipal refuse is simply deposited in open dumps. This practice causes proliferation of rats, flies, and other vermin, encourages growth of disease-carrying organisms, contaminates surface and underground water, scars the land, and preempts open space. An alternative, accounting for 10% of collected refuse, is the sanitary landfill: waste is spread in thin layers, each tamped compactly and covered by a layer of earth. While more expensive than open dumping, the sanitary landfill eliminates health hazards and permits reclamation of the site for construction, recreation, or other purposes. The chief drawback is that feasible locations are relatively rare and costly, and that sites must be insulated from water resources to avoid polluting them (see WATER POLLUTION). Both open dump and sanitary landfill disposal depend on the natural degradability of wastes for an ultimate return to normal earth conditions. Decay, however, takes time; buried paper, for example, can persist as long as 60 years. Many plastics and synthetic textiles do not degrade at all. To reduce the bulk of solid waste, burning of paper, plastic, and other components is often resorted to either in open dumps or incinerators. Fly ash, noxious gases, and chemical contaminants can thus be released into the air (see AIR POLLUTION). However, new techniques for "scrubbing" pollutants from incinerator stacks are being developed. Incineration of typical garbage reduces its weight and volume by as much as 80%. The residue—chiefly aluminum cans, tinned-steel cans, and glass bottles—must then be disposed of. In theory these could be recycled into new metal and glass. To an extent such recycling is being done with aluminum and glass, but the tin coating of steel food cans interferes with recovery processes. Industry is working to eliminate the necessity for tin, and anticipates that in a few years possibly 50% of steel cans will be untinned. Salvaging of solid waste not only facilitates disposal; it conserves energy, cuts pollution, and preserves natural resources. To make cans from recovered aluminum, for example, requires 10% of the energy needed to make them from virgin ore. At the same time ore is saved, and pollutants released in mining and processing are avoided. Making steel bars from scrap requires 74% less energy and 50% less water, while reducing air-polluting emissions by 85% and mining wastes by 95%. A major difficulty in recycling is the need to separate eligible materials from other waste. For that reason most recycled waste is industrial waste, already separated and relatively clean. Thus incidental glass waste (cullet) in glass-producing plants accounts for about 15% of new glass production. Metal waste (scrap) incurred in metals manufacture accounts for some 20% of metals production. Discarded automobiles are another prime source of recycled metal. Nearly 20% of paper production consists of recycled paper; here a considerable portion of the recovered waste comes from domestic rather than industrial sources since it is practical for private citizens to separate newspapers and cardboard from other waste materials. One obstacle to recycling in the United States is that freight rates and depletion allowances tend to favor the use of virgin pulp and ore over paper waste and scrap. Another is that if wastes are to be recycled in significant quantity, new uses and markets must be developed. Crushed glass, for instance, might be substituted for gravel or sand in road surfacing and other construction applications. Currently less than 4% of municipal solid waste is recycled. About 1% is processed to form COMPOST, but it usually cannot compete in price with synthetic fertilizers. Similarly, sludge from treated sewage might be used for fertilizer, but it is less costly to dump it at sea or on open land (see SEWERAGE). Dumped sludge is killing off marine life and threatening beaches around the Eastern seaboard; elsewhere in the United States it is a growing nuisance. The Federal government now provides assistance to localities in developing new means of recovering materials and energy from solid waste, and encourages private industry to seek similar goals. One technique being tried involves intensified combustion of wastes to produce heat for generating power. A second promising approach is pyrolysis, the thermal decomposition of wastes in controlled amounts of oxygen to produce valuable petrochemicals; the residue is an inert char of little bulk. Wider application of such processes is being advocated not only to diminish pollution of the environment by solid waste, but to conserve natural resources. See ENVIRONMENTALISM.

Solihull (sōlĭhŭl'), county borough (1971 pop. 106,968), Warwickshire, central England, a mainly residential suburb of Birmingham. Automobiles, chemicals, and tools are made. Solihull became a county borough in 1964. The 13th-century Church of St. Alphege has a graceful 168-ft (51-m) spire in which 10 bells still chime the curfew every evening. There is a 16th-century boys school in Solihull. Packwood House (15th cent.) and Malvern House (18th cent.) are architecturally notable. In 1974, Solihull became part of the new metropolitan county of West Midlands.

soliloquy, the speech by a character in a literary composition, usually a play, delivered while the speaker is alone. In its most effective use it reveals to the audience or reader the innermost thoughts of the speaker, thus pointing up the drama of internal conflict, as in Richard III's opening speech, "Now is the winter of our discontent." The form was quite popular in Elizabethan drama, notably in the plays of Shakespeare. The soliloquy may also act simply as a vehicle for information about absent characters or events occurring at some other time or place. In the modern theater the soliloquy has tended to disappear completely, although experimentations in its use were attempted by such playwrights as Eugene O'Neill, who sought through the soliloquy to achieve a greater psychological realism. See MONOLOGUE.

Soliman. For Ottoman sultans thus named, see SULAYMAN.

Solimena, Francesco (fränchās'kō sōlēmä'nä), 1657–1717, Italian painter. Painting in the decorative tradition of the late baroque in Naples, Solimena was a technical virtuoso. His decorations for building interiors (e.g., Gesù Nuovo; 1725) are filled with twisting, dramatically foreshortened figures. Solimena was a teacher of international influence.

Solimões, river, Brazil: see AMAZON, river.

Solin, Yugoslavia: see SALONA.

Solingen (zō'lĭng-ən), city (1970 pop. 176,420), North Rhine-Westphalia, W West Germany, on the Wupper River opposite Remscheid. It is a major center of the West German cutlery industry. Solingen steel, used in making knives, scissors, razors, and surgical instruments, is world famous for its excellence. Solingen was chartered in 1374 and has been known for its fine blades since the Middle Ages. It belonged to the duchy of Berg until 1600 and passed to Prussia in 1815.

Solís, Juan Díaz de (hwän dē'äth dā sōlēs'), d. 1516, Spanish navigator. He first became prominent in the service of Portugal. Returning to Spain, he joined Vicente Yáñez (see under PINZÓN, MARTÍN) in a voyage (1508–9) of exploration to the coasts of Yucatán, Honduras, and Venezuela. In 1512, upon the death of Amerigo Vespucci, he was named pilot major. Solís was commissioned in 1514 to explore the coast of South America and seek a passage between the two seas. He sailed from Spain in Oct., 1515, and in Feb., 1516, entered the estuary of the Río de la Plata, which he called the Mar Dulce [fresh sea]. Landing on the coast of the present Uruguay, he and a small shore party were killed by Indians.

Solís y Rivadeneyra, Antonio de (äntō'nyō thā sōlēs' ē rē"vāthānä'rä), 1610–86, Spanish historian and dramatic poet. His intricate comic dramas were popular at court and the best are still performed. He is celebrated for his *Historia de la conquista de México* (1684), one of the finest prose works of the 17th century. It is not considered a great history, however, as it ignores the Aztec tragedy while glorifying Cortés.

solitaire or **patience,** any card game that can be played by one person. Solitaire is the American name; in England it is known as patience. There are probably more kinds of solitaire than all other card games together. The aim in most is to segregate the four suits, each in sequence, against the luck of the shuffle. The game is usually played with one or two decks. Cards are laid out on the table in an arrangement called the tableau. All the cards of a certain rank form the foundations on which the suits are built. Play proceeds either until the game is won (called "making" or "breaking" the game) or until further play is impossible. Although the names of games vary greatly, the most popular solitaires include Klondike (probably the best known), Canfield (named for Richard A. CANFIELD), accordion, spider, golf, and clock. In double solitaire, for two persons, each plays his own game of either Klondike or Canfield, but each can build on his opponent's (as well as his own) aces. The object is to play the greater number of cards to the center. See A. H. Morehead and Geoffrey Mott-Smith, *Complete Book of Solitaire and Patience Games* (1949, repr. 1973); G. F. Hervey, *Card Games for One* (1965).

Solkhat: see STARY KRYM, USSR.

Sollefteå (sôlĕf'təō"), city (1970 pop. 8,326), Västernorrland co., central Sweden, on the Ångermanälven River. It is a winter sports center and has a large military garrison. Sollefteå has been known since the 13th cent. and was chartered in 1917.

Solna (sōl'nä), city (1970 pop. 55,557), Stockholm co., E Sweden, an industrial suburb of Stockholm. Manufactures include machinery, electrical goods, paper, and chocolate. It is the seat of the Swedish motion picture industry and has numerous scientific institutes, including the Nobel Institute. There are also large hospitals; the War Academy (housed since 1792 in Karlsberg Castle, one of Solna's several castles); and the Rasunda sports stadium, where international soccer matches are played.

Solo: see SURAKARTA, Indonesia.

Sologub, Feodor (fyô'dər sələgo͞op'), pseud. of **Feodor Kuzmich Teternikov,** 1863–1927, Russian poet and prose writer. By profession a schoolteacher and as a poet one of the older symbolists, he began his literary career in 1896 with a volume of verse, a collection of tales, and a novel, *Bad Dreams,* which described the squalid existence of a schoolmaster. His masterpiece of fiction is the novel *The Little Demon* (1907, tr. 1916), in which the perverted schoolteacher Peredonov embodies senseless evil. Peredonovism became a common term in Russia to denote the moral corruption of petty officials. Two collections of Sologub's poetry notable for pessimism are *The Circle of Fire* (1908) and *Pearly Stars* (1913). Opposed to the Bolsheviks, Sologub wrote nothing after his wife's suicide, which followed government persecution in 1921.

Solo man: see NEANDERTHAL MAN.

Solomon, d. c.932 B.C., king of the ancient Hebrews (c.972–c.932 B.C.), son and successor of David. His mother was Bath-sheba. His accession probably took place c.970 B.C., when he was still quite young. The reign of Solomon was eminently peaceful, marked by foreign alliances, notably with Egypt and with Phoenicia (he was on especially good terms with Hiram of Tyre). To develop trade and commerce, he built numerous cities and constructed copper smelting furnaces in the Negev. As he grew older his despotism became worse. His exactions caused the alienation of N Israel, which led to the revolt of Jeroboam I. Solomon's wisdom is proverbial, and in the East he has been a popular subject of legend. He built the first Hebrew temple at Jerusalem, insuring the city the central position in Israel. The biblical account of Solomon is preserved, according to the critics, comparatively intact. Proverbs and Ecclesiastes were ascribed to him, and the SONG OF SOLOMON bears his name. WISDOM was also anciently ascribed to him. In the PSEUDEPIGRAPHA are the Psalms of Solomon. Solomon's name was at first Jedidiah. 2 Sam. 12.24,25; 1 Kings 1–11; 2 Chron. 1–9.

Solomon Islands, volcanic group (1970 est. pop. 240,000), c.15,500 sq mi (40,150 sq km), SW Pacific, E of New Guinea. The 900-mi (1,448-km) chain comprises the British Solomon Islands Protectorate (1970 pop. 161,524; c.11,500 sq mi/29,790 sq km) and the northernmost islands of BOUGAINVILLE and Buka, which belong to Papua New Guinea. The British islands include GUADALCANAL, Malaita, New Georgia, the Santa Cruz Islands, Choiseul, Ysabel (Santa Isabel), San Cristobal, and the Shortland Islands. They are administered by a high commissioner, who is assisted by a nominated executive council and a partially elected legislature. Under the provisions of the 1970 constitution, elected islanders were given a majority over the appointed British members of the legislature. Headquarters are at Honiara, on Guadalcanal. The Solomons are sparsely populated and are mountainous and heavily wooded. Economic development has been slow; the only significant export crops are copra and timber. There is very little manufacturing. The inhabitants of the Solomons are largely Melanesians, although some Polynesians live in the outlying atolls. A Spanish explorer, Álvaro de Mendeña de Neira, was the first European to visit the islands (1568), but his efforts to colonize them failed. European settlers and missionaries arrived throughout the 18th and 19th cent. In 1885 the German New Guinea Company established control over the N Solomons. The southern islands were placed under British protectorate in 1893; the eastern islands were added to the protectorate in 1898. In 1900, Germany transferred its islands (except Bougainville and Buka) to Great Britain in return for British withdrawal from Western Samoa. Bougainville and Buka were occupied by Australian forces during World War I and were placed under Australian mandate by the League of Nations in 1920. During World War II, Choiseul, New Georgia, Ysabel, and Guadalcanal were occupied by the Japanese (1942) but were liberated by U.S. forces (1943–44).

Solomon R. Guggenheim Museum, major gallery of modern art in New York City. Founded in 1939 as the Museum of Non-objective Art, the Guggenheim is best known for its remarkable circular building designed by Frank Lloyd Wright and completed in 1959. It holds major temporary exhibitions of the works of contemporary artists. Its permanent collection includes numerous works by Brancusi and Kandinsky.

Solomon's-seal, any plant of the genus *Polygonatum,* north-temperate perennial herbs of the family Liliaceae (LILY family). The hairy Solomon's-seal (*P. pubescens*) and the smooth Solomon's-seal (*P. biflorum*) are well-known wild flowers in most of North America. They characteristically have dark blue berries at each pair of leaf axils. The name has been attributed to leaf scars on the rhizome that resemble seals. Species of Solomon's-seal were formerly used in applications for the skin, and the roots and young shoots have been used for food. They are often grown in wild-flower gardens. False Solomon's-seal or wild spikenard (*Smilacina racemosa*), of the same family, is similar but has a cluster of red berries. It is unrelated to the true spikenards. Solomon's-seal is classified in the division MAGNOLIOPHYTA, class Liliatae, order Liliales, family Liliaceae.

Solon (sō'lən), c.639–c.559 B.C., Athenian statesman, lawgiver, and reformer. He was also a poet, and some of his patriotic verse in the Ionic dialect is extant. At some time (perhaps c.600 B.C.) he led the Athenians in the recapture of Salamis from the Megarians. He was elected chief ARCHON in 594 at a time of social, economic, and political stress in Athens. With most of the land and political power in the hands of the nobles, the peasants were rapidly losing not only their land but their freedom as well. Solon annulled all mortgages and debts, limited the amount of land anyone might add to his holdings, and outlawed all borrowing in which a person's liberty might be pledged. This last reform put an end to serfdom in Attica. Other economic reforms included a ban on the export of all agricultural products except olive oil and the granting of citizenship to immigrant craftsmen. Solon also made important constitutional changes. The assembly was opened to all freemen, the AREOPAGUS was continued with new powers, and the Council of Four Hundred was created to represent the propertied classes and to prepare the agenda for the popular assembly. Although there was opposition to Solon's reforms, they subsequently became the basis of the Athenian state. He also introduced a more humane law code to replace the code of DRACO.

Solon, city (1970 pop. 11,519), Cuyahoga co., NE Ohio, a suburb of Cleveland; founded 1820, inc. as a city 1960. Its manufactures include metal products, machinery, electrical equipment, tools, containers, and electronic components.

Solothurn (zō'lōto͝orn), Fr. *Soleure,* canton (1970 pop. 224,133), 306 sq mi (793 sq km), NW Switzerland. Very irregular in shape, Solothurn lies mostly in the Jura mts. Cereals are grown and cattle are raised in the fertile valley of the Aare River. The population is mainly German-speaking and Roman Catholic. Industry is largely concentrated in the towns of OLTEN and **Solothurn** (1970 pop. 17,708), the capital. Situated on the Aare, Solothurn was a Roman settlement called Salodurum. It had been a free town of the Holy Roman Empire since 1218 and was admitted to the Swiss Confederation in 1481. Until 1797, Solothurn was the residence of the French ambassadors to the Swiss diet and a center of cultural life. The town retains much of its historic character. It has old fortifications, a 13th-century clock tower, a 15th-century town hall, and the 18th-century Cathedral of St. Ursus and St. Victor, the see of the bishop of Basel and Lugano. Electrical equipment, watches, and metal goods are made in the town.

Solovetski Islands (sələvyĕt'skē), archipelago, c.150 sq mi (390 sq km), N European USSR, in the White Sea at the entrance of Onega Bay. A monastery, built in the first half of the 15th cent., is on the largest island. It was used as a military fortress against Sweden in the 16th and 17th cent., and the early settlement and economic development of the Karelo-Murmansk area was from there. From the reign of Ivan IV until 1956 the islands were a dreaded place of exile for criminals and for political and religious prisoners. Solovetski forced labor camps produced lumber, peat, and building stone.

Soloviev, Vladimir Sergeyevich (vlədyē'mĭr sĭrgā'əvĭch sələvyôf'), 1853–1900, Russian religious philosopher and poet; son of Sergei Mikhailovich Soloviev. Soloviev believed in the incarnation of divine wisdom in a being called Sophia, a concept that greatly influenced the young symbolist poets, especially Blok. He advocated a synthesis of Eastern and Western churches in *Russia and the Universal Church,* which he wrote in French in 1889 (tr. 1948). The imminent coming of the Antichrist was the theme of his *Three Conversations on War, Progress, and the End of History* (1899, tr. 1915). The best known of his mystical poems is *Three Meetings* (1899), which describes his visions of Sophia. Soloviev is also noted for political writings and literary criticism. See biography by Michel d'Herbigny (1918); studies by Egbert Munzer (1956) and P. M. Allen (1973).

Solow, Robert M., 1924–, American economist, b. Brooklyn, N.Y., grad. Harvard Univ. (B.A. 1947, M.A. 1949, Ph.D. 1951). He began teaching economics at the Massachusetts Institute of Technology in 1949. Solow also held several governmental positions, including those of senior economist for the Council of Economic Advisers (1961–62) and member of the President's Commission on Income Maintenance (1968–70). His scholarly works are in the fields of employment and growth policies, the theory of capital, and the use of linear programming techniques in solving economic problems.

solstice (sŏl'stĭs) [Lat.,=sun stands still], in astronomy, either of the two points on the ECLIPTIC that lie midway between the EQUINOXES (separated from them by an angular distance of 90°). At the solstices the sun's apparent position on the CELESTIAL SPHERE reaches its greatest distance above or below the celestial equator (see EQUATORIAL COORDINATE SYSTEM), about 23½° of arc. At the time of summer solstice, about June 22, the sun is directly overhead at noon at the Tropic of Cancer (see TROPICS). In the Northern Hemisphere the longest day and shortest night of the year occur on this date, marking the beginning of summer. At winter solstice, about Dec. 22, the sun is overhead at noon at the Tropic of Capricorn; this marks the beginning of winter in the Northern Hemisphere. For several days before and after each solstice the sun appears to stand still in the sky, i.e., its noontime elevation does not seem to change from day to day.

soluble glass: see WATER GLASS.

solution, in chemistry, homogeneous MIXTURE of two or more substances. The dissolving medium is called the SOLVENT, and the dissolved material is called the solute. In most common solutions, the solvent is a liquid, often water, and the solute may be a solid, gas, or liquid. For example, syrups are solutions of sugar, a solid, in water, a liquid; household ammonia is a solution of ammonia gas in water; and vinegar is a solution of acetic acid, a liquid, in water. When two liquids, e.g., water and ethanol, can be mixed in any proportions, the solvent is commonly considered to be the one present in greater proportion. Some ALLOYS are solutions of one solid in another, as are many rocks. A mixture of gases, such as air, is usually not thought of as a solution. A solution is distinct from a COLLOID or a SUSPENSION. The solute particles in a solution are generally of molecular size or smaller, much smaller than those in a colloid or a suspension. The solute particles cannot be observed even with an ultramicroscope. They do not settle out from the solvent on standing, and they cannot be separated from the solvent by physical means, such as filtration or centrifugation. On the other hand, a solution differs from a COMPOUND in that its components can occur in continuously varying proportions, within certain limits (although within a given solution they are present in the same proportions throughout the solution), while the components of a compound can

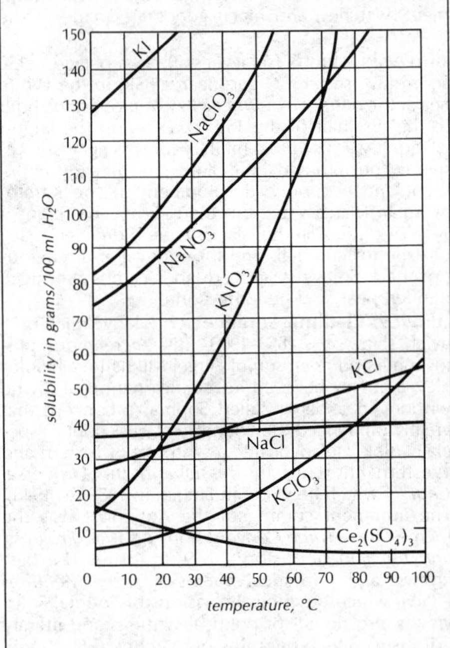

Solubility curves

occur only in certain fixed proportions. The proportion of solute to solvent in a given solution is expressed by the CONCENTRATION of the solution. Concentrations may be stated in a number of ways, such as giving the amount of solute contained in a given volume of solution or the amount dissolved in a given mass of solvent. A solution having a relatively high concentration is said to be concentrated, and a solution having a low concentration is said to be dilute. In many solutions the concentration has a maximum limit that depends on various factors, such as temperature, pressure, and the nature of the solvent. The maximum concentration is called the solubility of the solute under those conditions. When a solution contains the maximum amount of solute, it is said to be saturated; if it contains less than that amount, it is unsaturated. The most obvious factor affecting solubility is the nature of the solvent. Ordinary table salt (sodium chloride) is soluble in water, but only slightly soluble in ethanol, and insoluble in diethyl ether. Temperature is also important in determining solubility. Solids are usually more soluble at higher temperatures; more salt will dissolve in warm water than in an equal amount of cold water. Graphs showing the solubility of different solids as a function of temperature are called solubility curves and are very useful in chemical analysis. Solubility also depends on pressure, especially in the case of gases, which are more soluble at higher pressures. Under certain conditions a solution may be made to contain more solute than a saturated solution at the same temperature and pressure; such a solution is called supersaturated. If even a single crystal of undissolved solute is added to a supersaturated solution, all the excess solute above the normal solubility concentration will immediately crystallize out of the solution. The addition of some solutes to a solvent will raise the temperature of the solution, while others may lower the temperature and still others will have no noticeable effect. This behavior depends on the heat of solution of the solute in the given solvent. The heat of solution, i.e., the amount of heat given off or absorbed during the process of solution, is equal to the difference between the energy that must be supplied to break up the crystals of the solute and the energy that is released when the solute particles are taken into solution by the solvent (see ENTHALPY). If the heat of solution is negative (i.e., more energy is required to break up the crystal than is released in forming the solution), then the temperature will decrease; if the heat of solution is positive, the temperature will increase. The addition of solute also affects the boiling point, freezing point, and vapor pressure of the solution, in general raising the boiling point, depressing the freezing point, and lowering the vapor pressure (see RAOULT'S LAW). A number of substances (acids, bases, and salts) exhibit characteristic behavior in aqueous solution. These substances dissociate in water to form positive and negative IONS that enable the solution to conduct electricity. Such solutions are called electrolytic (see ELECTROLYTE).

Solutré-Pouilly (sôlütrā'-po͞oyē'), village (1968 pop. 378), Saône-et-Loire dept., E central France, in Burgundy. It is known for its white wines. It is the site of a rock shelter and burial place of prehistoric man (discovered 1867) and gives its name to the Solutrean phase of the PALEOLITHIC PERIOD.

Solvay, Ernest (ĕrnĕst' sôlvā'), 1838–1922, Belgian industrial chemist and philanthropist. He originated the SOLVAY PROCESS and established (1863) near Charleroi, Belgium, the first plant for making soda by this process; later, plants were set up in many countries. He founded at Brussels the Solvay institutes of physiology (1893) and sociology (1901) and made large gifts to European universities.

Solvay process [for Ernest Solvay], commercial process for the manufacture of sodium carbonate (washing soda). Ammonia and carbon dioxide are passed into a saturated sodium chloride solution to form soluble ammonium hydrogen carbonate, which reacts with the sodium chloride to form soluble ammonium chloride and a precipitate of sodium hydrogen carbonate (sodium bicarbonate) if the temperature is maintained below 15°C. The sodium hydrogen carbonate is filtered off and heated to produce sodium carbonate.

solvent, constituent of a solution that acts as a dissolving agent. In solutions of solids or gases in a liquid, the liquid is the solvent. In all other solutions (i.e., liquids in liquids or solids in solids) the constituent that is present in larger quantity is considered the solvent. The most familiar and widely used solvent is water. Other compounds valuable as solvents because they dissolve materials that are insoluble or nearly insoluble in water are acetone, alcohol, benzene (or benzol), benzine, carbon disulfide, carbon tetrachloride, chloroform, ether, ethyl acetate, furfural, gasoline, toluene, turpentine, and xylene (or xylol). Solvents are predominantly organic compounds. They may be divided into polar and nonpolar types. Polar solvents, of which water is an example, have molecules whose electric charges are unequally distributed, leaving one end of each molecule more positive than the other. Nonpolar solvents, of which carbon tetrachloride is an example, have molecules whose electric charges are equally distributed.

Solway Firth (sŏl'wā), arm of the Irish Sea, c.40 mi (60 km) long, separating NW England from SW Scotland. It receives the Esk, Annan, Nith, Urr, Eden, and Derwent rivers. Its salmon fisheries are important. Near Annan the firth is crossed by a railway bridge. There is a tidal bore on the firth. Hadrian's Wall terminated at Bowness, on the south shore.

Solyman. For Ottoman sultans thus named, see SULAYMAN.

Solzhenitsyn, Aleksandr Isayevich (əlyĭksän'dər ēsī'əvĭch sôl"zhənē't'sĭn), 1918–, Soviet writer. Solzhenitsyn was born in Kislovodsk and grew up in Rostov, where he studied mathematics at the university. During World War II he served in the Red Army, rising to the rank of artillery captain, and was decorated for bravery. In 1945, while still serving on the German front, he was arrested for criticizing Stalin in letters to a friend. In the Moscow prisons he was for the first time confronted with the tragic fates of other political prisoners. Sentenced to eight years in labor camps, he worked as a menial laborer and was stricken with cancer (from which he later recovered). After completing his prison sentence, Solzhenitsyn was exiled to Kazakhstan, but after Stalin's death in 1953 his position improved, and his citizenship was restored in 1956. His first novels describe the grimness of life in the vast labor-camp system. *One Day in the Life of Ivan Denisovich* was permitted publication in 1962 as a result of the personal intervention of Nikita Khrushchev, in an effort to encourage anti-Stalinist feeling. The book was hailed as an exposé of Stalinist methods, and it placed the author in the foremost ranks of Soviet writers. With Khrushchev's own deposition, Solzhenitsyn's succeeding works were banned and he was continually censured by the Soviet press. With subsequent novels—*The First Circle* (1964), detailing the lives of scientists forced to work in a Stalinist research center and *Cancer Ward* (1966), concerning the complex social microcosm within a government hospital—censorship tightened, and Solzhenitsyn was increasingly regarded as a dangerous and hostile critic of Soviet society. His books found publication and an enormous audience abroad, and in the USSR they were circulated in *samizdat* (self-publishing, underground) editions. Solzhenitsyn was expelled from the Union of Soviet Writers and prohibited from living in Moscow. In 1970 he was awarded the Nobel Prize for Literature, but government pressure, specifically the threat of not being allowed to return from Stockholm, compelled him to decline the prize. His next novel, *August 1914,* Part I (1972), is a compelling exposition of the internal strife in Russia leading to the Revolution of 1917. In 1974, fearing that he might soon be imprisoned again, Solzhenitsyn authorized the foreign publication of *The Gulag Archipelago,* a vast work which documents with personal interviews and reminiscences the operation of the oppressive Soviet totalitarian system from 1918 to 1956. Five sequels dealing with the repression of the Khrushchev and Brezhnev years remain unpublished. In Feb., 1974, Solzhenitsyn was arrested, formally accused of treason, stripped of his citizenship, and forcibly deported to the West. Proficient in German, he took up residence in Switzerland with his family, who were permitted to join him. In exile he was able to accept personally his Nobel Prize in Stockholm (1974). Solzhenitsyn is respected not only as a fearless novelist who, in convincing terms, describes techniques of terror and the resulting moral debasement, but also as a leader of a small but vociferous group of intellectual dissidents endeavoring to expose the nature of the Soviet system. See also his *Stories and Prose Poems* (tr. 1971); his plays, *The Love-Girl and the Innocent* (tr. 1969) and *Candle in the Wind* (tr. 1973); his *Nobel Lecture* (tr. 1972); his *Critical Essays and Documentary Materials* (1973); biographies by Hans Björkegren (tr. 1972), David Burg and George Feifer (1972), and Giovanni Grazzini (tr. 1973); studies by Abraham Rothberg (1971) and Christopher Moody (1973); bibliography ed. by D. M. Fiene (1973); Leopold Labedz, ed., *Solzhenitsyn: A Documentary Record* (1973).

soma (sō'mə), psychotropic plant, the juice of which was sometimes drunk as part of the Vedic sacrifice (see VEDA). Many hymns in the *Rig-Veda* are in praise of soma. In the late Vedic period substitutes for soma came to be used, and the original plant was lost. It has recently been identified with the fly agaric mushroom, *amanita muscaria,* used in Siberian shamanism. See R. G. Wasson, *Soma: Divine Mushroom of Immortality* (1971).

Somalia or **Somali:** see SOMALI DEMOCRATIC REPUBLIC.

Somali Democratic Republic (sōmä'lē) or **Somalia** (sōmä'leə), republic (1973 est. pop. 2,970,000), 246,200 sq mi (637,657 sq km), extreme E Africa, directly S of the Arabian Peninsula across the Gulf of Aden. MOGADISHO is the capital; other important cities are HARGHESSA, BERBERA (the main northern port), and KISMAYU (the principal port of the south).

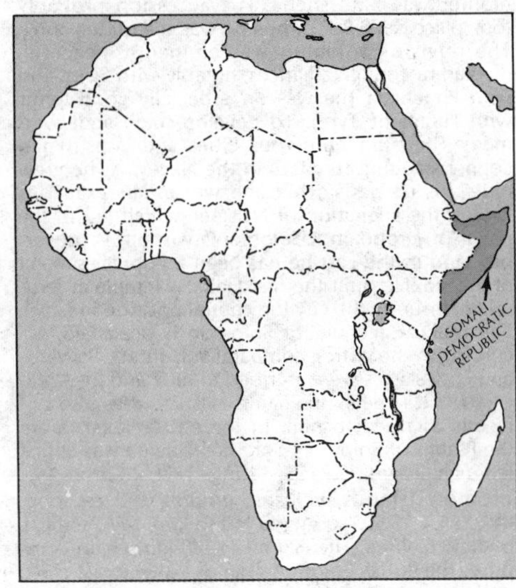

Somalia comprises almost the entire African coast of the Gulf of Aden and a longer stretch on the Indian Ocean. It is bounded on the NW by the French Territory of the Afars and the Issas, on the W by Ethiopia, on the SW by Kenya, and on the S and E by the Indian Ocean. Arid, semidesert conditions make the country relatively unproductive. In most areas, a barren coastal lowland (widest in the south) is abruptly succeeded by a rise to the great interior plateau, which is generally c.3,000 ft (910 m) high and stretches toward the northern and western highlands. The Juba and the Shebeli are the only important rivers. Somalia has no railroads. Pastoralism is the dominant mode of life; both nomadic and sedentary herding of camels, sheep, goats, and cattle are carried on. Live animals, hides, skins, and clarified butter (ghee) are exported. The major cash crop is bananas, which are grown on irrigated riverside plantations. Many of the plantations are Italian-owned, and Italy is the major market. Other crops include citrus fruits, peanuts, cotton, sorghum, and millet. Somalia's most valuable mineral resource is uranium. Raw material processing constitutes the bulk of Somalian industry, which includes meat and fish (notably tuna) canning, sugar refining, oilseed processing, leather tanning, and the production of cotton textiles, iron products, soap, shoes, and cement. More than 80% of the republic's population is made up of Somali, who speak a Cushitic language and are Sunni Muslims by faith. Islam is the state religion. Although Somali is the national tongue, Arabic, Italian, and English are used officially. There are Bantu-speaking tribes in the southwest and numerous Arabs in the coastal towns. Somalia also has Italian, Indian, and Pakistani minorities. Between the 7th and 10th cent., immigrant Muslim Arabs and Persians established trading posts along Somalia's Gulf of Aden and Indian Ocean coasts; Mogadisho began its existence as an Islamic trading station. During the 15th and 16th cent. Somali warriors regularly joined the armies of the Muslim sultanates in their battles with Christian Ethiopia. British, French, and Italian imperialism all played an active role in the region in the 19th cent. Great Britain's concern with the area was largely to safeguard trade links with its Aden colony (founded 1839), which depended especially on mutton from Somalia. The British opportunity came when Egyptian forces, having occupied much of the region in the 1870s, withdrew in 1884 to fight the Mahdi in Sudan. British penetration led to a series of agreements (1884–86) with local tribal chiefs, and in 1887, to the establishment of a protectorate. France first acquired a foothold in the area in the 1860s. An Anglo-French agreement of 1888 defined the boundary between the Somalian possessions of the two countries. Italy first asserted its authority in the area in 1889 by creating a small protectorate in the central zone, to which other concessions were later added in the south (territory ceded by the sultan of Zanzibar) and north. In 1925, Jubaland, or the Trans-Juba (E of the Juba River), was detached from Kenya to become the westernmost part of the Italian colony. In 1936, Italian Somaliland was combined with Somali-speaking districts of Ethiopia to form a province of the newly formed ITALIAN EAST AFRICA. During World War II, Italian forces invaded British Somaliland; but the British, operating from Kenya, retook the region in 1941 and went on to conquer Italian Somaliland. Britain ruled the combined regions until 1950, when Italian Somaliland became a United Nations trust territory under Italian control. In accordance with UN decisions, Italian Somaliland, renamed Somalia, was granted internal autonomy in 1956 and independence in 1960. Britain proclaimed the end of its protectorate in June, 1960, and on July 1, the legislatures of the two new states created the United Republic of Somalia. Pan-Somali sentiment had been disappointed, however, by Britain's return (1954) to Ethiopia of the Ogaden region, with its large Somali population. In the early years of independence the government was faced with a severely underdeveloped economy and with a strong demand for a "Greater Somalia" that would include the estimated 350,000 Somalis in adjacent areas of Kenya, French Somaliland (now the French Territory of the Afars and the Issas), and Ethiopia. The nomadic existence of many Somali herdsmen and the ill-defined frontiers worsened the irredentist problem. Hostilities between Somalia and Ethiopia erupted in 1964, and Kenya also became involved in the conflict, which continued until mediation by the Zambian president, Kenneth Kaunda, restored peace in 1967. Somalia's hope of incorporating French Somaliland was dashed in 1967 with a French-sponsored referendum in which the majority of the inhabitants rejected independence (a possible step toward union with Somalia) in favor of continued association with France. In 1969, President Abd-i-rashid Ali Shermarke was assassinated, and a few days later, the army and police staged a coup and imprisoned the prime minister. The new rulers, led by Maj. Gen. Muhammad Siyad Barrah, dissolved the national assembly, banned political parties, and established a supreme revolutionary council with the power to rule by decree pending adoption of a new constitution. The country's name was changed to Somali Democratic Republic. Somalia's territorial disputes with her neighbors, particularly Ethiopia, have continued to plague international relations in E Africa; the Organization of African Unity has attempted mediation. Somalia joined the Arab League in 1974. See Saadia Touval, *Somali Nationalism* (1963); I. M. Lewis, *The Modern History of Somaliland From Nation to State* (1965); R. L. Hess, *Italian Colonialism in Somalia* (1966); C. P. Potholm, *Four African Political Systems* (1970).

Somaliland, French: see AFARS AND THE ISSAS, FRENCH TERRITORY OF THE, Africa.

soman, colorless liquid used as a NERVE GAS. It boils at 167°C, evolving an odorless vapor. It is rapidly absorbed through the skin; death may result within 15 min of exposure. In nonfatal concentrations it is hazardous to the eyes. Soman is more powerful than tabun, acting faster and at lower concentrations. Chemically, soman is fluoromethylpinacolyloxyphosphine oxide.

somatotropin: see GROWTH HORMONE.

Sombart, Werner (vĕr'nər zôm'bärt), 1863–1941, German economist. In 1917 he became professor of economics at the Univ. of Berlin. Influenced by Marx's historical approach to economics, he produced several analyses of capitalism, including *Der moderne Kapitalismus* (Vol. I and II, 1902; Vol. III, 1928) and *Der Bourgeois* (1913, tr. *The Quintessence of Capitalism,* 1915). He later turned toward German romanticism, becoming eventually, in *Deutscher Sozialismus* (1934; tr. *A New Social Philosophy*, 1937), an exponent of the authoritarian state, accepting Nazism. See study by M. J. Plotnik (1937).

Somers, Sir George, 1554–1610, English naval commander. The leader of several successful privateering ventures against the Spanish, he was knighted in 1603. He was a founder (1606) of the LONDON COMPANY and set out with settlers for Virginia in 1609. They were shipwrecked and landed in the Bermudas, which Somers claimed for Britain. He continued to Virginia but returned to Bermuda (1610), where he died. Several versions of his shipwreck were written at the time, one of which is supposed to have inspired Shakespeare's *The Tempest.*

Somers, John Somers or **Sommers, Baron** (sŭm'-ərz), 1651–1716, English jurist and statesman. In the GLORIOUS REVOLUTION he secured Parliament's acceptance of the official statement that James II had "abdicated" the throne, and he presided over the framing of the Bill of Rights (1689). William III rewarded him with the office of solicitor general (1689), and he advanced to become attorney general (1692), lord keeper of the seal (1693), and lord chancellor (1697), taking the title Baron Somers of Evesham. He was politically influential throughout the reign of William, but was forced to resign as lord chancellor in 1700 after repeated attacks directed against him, in part for his support of the ventures of Capt. William KIDD. He was a leader of the Whig Junto under Queen Anne and supported the Act of Union with Scotland (1707). He was made (1708) president of the council, but he lost office (1710) when the Tories came to power. A friend of such writers as John Locke and Jonathan Swift, Somers himself wrote a number of political tracts. His valuable collection of papers and manuscripts was edited by Sir Walter Scott as the *Somers Tracts* (13 vol., 1809–15).

Somerset, Charles Seymour, 6th **duke of,** 1662–1748, English nobleman. He succeeded to the dukedom in 1678 and in 1682 married Elizabeth Percy, heiress of the enormously wealthy earl of Northumberland. An influential Whig, he supported William III in 1688 and became a favorite of Princess Anne. After Anne's accession (1702) to the throne, he received several honorary posts, and his wife was an intimate of the queen, despite Tory attempts to have her removed from the court. Known as "the proud duke," Somerset used his influence in favor of the succession of George I.

Somerset, Edmund Beaufort, 2d **duke of,** d. 1455, English statesman and general. He fought in France in the Hundred Years War, receiving his first command in 1431, recapturing Harfleur in 1440, and relieving Calais in 1442. For this last feat he was made (1442) earl of Dorset. In 1444 he succeeded his brother John as earl of Somerset. He became lieutenant of France in 1447 and was created duke of Somerset in 1448. After the war in France was resumed in 1449, Somerset's army was consistently defeated, and by 1453 all of England's French possessions except Calais had been lost. Since the murder (1450) of William de la Pole, 1st duke of Suffolk, Somerset had been the head of the court faction and was protected by HENRY VI against popular resentment and the attacks of the Yorkists. He was imprisoned by Richard, duke of YORK, during Henry's first period of insanity (1453–55) but returned to power when the king recovered. Somerset was killed at St. Albans in the first battle of the Wars of the Roses.

Somerset, Edward Seymour, duke of, 1506?–1552, protector of England. He served on various military and diplomatic missions for Henry VIII and, after the marriage of his sister Jane to the king, was created Viscount Beauchamp (1536) and earl of Hertford (1537). In 1544, as lieutenant general in the north, he invaded Scotland and captured and burned Edinburgh. He took part in the 1545 expedition against Boulogne and became captain general there in 1546. On the death (1547) of Henry VIII Seymour gained custody of the young heir, EDWARD VI (who was Seymour's nephew) and was named protector of the realm by the council of regency. Shortly thereafter he took the posts of lord treasurer and earl marshal and the title duke of Somerset. He managed to free himself from the restrictions of the council and wielded almost royal authority in effecting major Protestant reforms in the church and in relaxing such measures as the heresy and treason laws. He was ably seconded by Archbishop Thomas CRANMER, and their efforts resulted in the adoption of the first Book of Common Prayer, whose use was required by an Act of Uniformity in 1549. Meanwhile Somerset tried to enforce a marriage treaty arranged by Henry VIII between the young Edward VI and Mary Queen of Scots. He invaded Scotland, crushed his opponents at Pinkie (1547), and completely alienated the Scots when he laid waste to SE Scotland. The fall and execution (1549) of his brother, Baron SEYMOUR OF SUDELEY, lord high admiral, was a strong blow to the protector's authority and power, which was further undermined by his lenient enforcement of religious innovations, his unsuccessful attempts to prevent the enclosure of land, English setbacks in renewed war with France, and the poor condition of the exchequer. John Dudley, earl of Warwick (later duke of NORTHUMBERLAND) took advantage of these misfortunes, and, joining Thomas Wriothesley, earl of Southampton, and others, he deprived (1549) Somerset of the protectorate and imprisoned him in the Tower of London. Somerset was released in 1550, but a revival of his influence led Warwick to arrest (1551) him again. He was convicted (1552) on a charge of felony and beheaded. Though personally ambitious, Somerset was a man of firm beliefs and excellent military ability. See A. F. Pollard, *England under Protector Somerset* (1900, repr. 1966).

Somerset, Fitzroy James Henry: see RAGLAN, FITZROY JAMES HENRY SOMERSET, 1ST BARON.

Somerset, Robert Carr, earl of, 1587?–1645, Scottish favorite of James I of England. His family name also appears as Ker. He may have accompanied James to England as a page in 1603, but he appears to have spent some time in France before returning to the English court. He soon became close to James, was knighted (1607), and in 1609 he was granted lands that had been forfeited by Sir Walter Raleigh. He was created (1611) Viscount Rochester, served James as personal secretary, and became earl of Somerset in 1613. In the same year he married Frances Howard, the countess of Essex (who had her marriage to the 3d earl of Essex annulled in a sensational trial). In 1614, Somerset was made lord chamberlain. He became an important counselor to the king, but his jealous and arrogant nature alienated James's affections. On the discovery of the murder of his former friend, Sir Thomas OVERBURY, Somerset and his wife were tried and found guilty (1616) of perpetrating it, although Somerset's guilt was not definitely established. They were both pardoned but not released until 1622. See Philip Gibbs, *The King's Favourite* (1929); M. A. DeFord, *The Overbury Affair* (1960).

Somerset, William Seymour, 2d **duke of:** see HERTFORD, WILLIAM SEYMOUR, 1ST MARQUESS AND 2D EARL OF.

Somerset, county (1971 pop. 681,974), 1,613 sq mi (4,180 sq km), SW England, on the Bristol Channel.

The county town is TAUNTON. The terrain is level in the center, with the Mendip Hills to the east and Exmoor National Park and the Quantock Hills to the west. The principal rivers are the Bristol Avon, the Exe, and the Parrett and tributaries, whose fertile valleys are devoted to agriculture. Dairy farming (Cheddar cheese) and fruit growing are important, and much of the land is devoted to cattle grazing. Woolens, leather goods, and other products are manufactured. Coal and limestone are extracted. There are prehistoric remains at Cheddar and Glastonbury. At BATH, which reached its greatest importance as a fashionable watering place in the 18th cent., are located some of the most important Roman remains in Britain. As a resort town modern Bath is rivaled by WESTON-SUPER-MARE. In the early Middle Ages the region became a part of the Anglo-Saxon kingdom of Wessex. The county has associations with King Alfred and the legend of King Arthur, and Glastonbury is important in England's religious legend and history. The churches of the county are famous, notably the Cathedral of Bath and Wells. In 1974, Somerset was reorganized into a nonmetropolitan county.

Somerset. 1 City (1970 pop. 10,436), seat of Pulaski co., S Ky., in a farm, coal, and limestone area of the Cumberland foothills; inc. 1810. It has railroad shops and yards and diversified manufactures. A national cemetery is nearby. 2 Town (1970 pop. 18,088), Bristol co., SE Mass., on the Taunton River; settled 1677, set off from Swansea and inc. 1790. It has varied industries.

Somervile or **Somerville, William** (both: sŭm'ərvĭl), 1675–1742, English poet. His best-known work, *The Chase* (1734), a description of the art of hunting with hounds, reflects his life as a country squire.

Somerville, William: see SOMERVILE, WILLIAM.

Somerville. 1 City (1970 pop. 88,779), Middlesex co., E Mass., a residential and industrial suburb of Boston, on the Mystic River; settled 1630, set off from Charlestown 1842, inc. as a city 1872. Slaughtering and meat-packing are its leading industries. Historical attractions include the Old Powder House, used in the Revolution; Prospect Hill Tower, where General Putnam raised the first flag of the united colonies (1776) and which served as a prison camp in the Civil War; and Ploughed Hill, one of the fortified hills used in the siege of Boston (1775). 2 Residential borough (1970 pop. 13,652), seat of Somerset co., N central N.J., on the Raritan River; settled 1683, inc. as a borough 1909. It is a farm trade center. Electronic parts and pharmaceuticals are made there. Of interest are the Wallace House (residence of George Washington 1778–79), the old Dutch parsonage (1751; now a DAR museum), and the Duke estate (with gardens) on the river. A junior college is in the city.

Somme (sôm), department (1968 pop. 512,113), N France, in Picardy, on the English Channel. AMIENS is the capital.

Somme, river, c.150 mi (240 km) long, rising near Saint-Quentin, N France, and flowing generally NW past Amiens into the English Channel; connected by canal with the Scheldt and Oise rivers. Once an obstacle to east-west movement, the now reclaimed marshlands in the valley are noted for truck farming. During World War I heavy fighting took place there.

Sommer, William, 1867–1949, American painter and lithographer, b. Detroit. He was apprenticed as a lithographer and studied drawing with Julius Melchers in Detroit and drawing and painting in Munich. He settled near Cleveland. After years of painting part-time in addition to his work in lithography, he developed in the 1920s a highly personal style, which fused fine line and sensitive color into intense, evocative visions of rural scenes, children, and still lifes. Working chiefly in watercolor, he made portraits of children that are remarkable and highly original. Among his many works in the Cleveland Museum of Art are *The Pompous Boy, Pink Snow*, and *The Blue Vase.*

Sommerfeld, Arnold Johannes Wilhelm (är'nōlt yōhän'əs vĭl'hĕlm zôm'ərfĕlt), 1868–1951, German physicist and teacher. He received a Ph.D. at Königsburg Univ. in 1891 and was a professor of physics at the Univ. of Munich from 1906 to 1940. During his early years at Munich his research was devoted principally to a study of the wave character of X rays. In 1915, Sommerfeld made a major contribution to Niels Bohr's atomic theory by adducing elliptical paths for electrons. In 1916 he devised a formula for the structure of spectral lines and a general quantum theory of spectral lines. Applying quantum theory to the structure of metals, in 1927 he developed a theory of metallic electrons. His book *Atomblau und Spektrallinien,* published in 1919, became a standard in the field of theoretical spectroscopy. Sommerfeld was awarded the 1948 Oersted Medal in recognition of his service as an outstanding teacher.

somnambulism: see SLEEPWALKING.

Somoza, Anastasio (änästä'syō sōmō'sä), 1896–1956, president of Nicaragua (1937–47, 1950–56). After the end (1933) of U.S. military intervention in Nicaragua, he rose to power as head of the national guard. Though himself a member of the Liberal party, he engineered (1936) a successful coup against the incumbent Liberal regime. In 1937 he formally assumed the presidency. In 1947 he withdrew, but before a month had elapsed he ousted his successor and installed a puppet president. He was accused (1948) by Costa Rica of aiding a group of rebels bent on overthrowing the liberal regime in that country. The Organization of American States investigated the charges, ruled in favor of Costa Rica, and reprimanded Somoza. Undeterred, he had himself reelected in 1950 over the ineffectual opposition of Emiliano CHAMORRO and continued his dictatorial rule and provocations against Costa Rica. He maintained, however, very cordial relations with the United States. On Sept. 21, 1956, he was shot; eight days later he died. His son, Luis Somoza, succeeded him to the presidency.

Somoza Debayle, Anastasio (änästäs'yō sōmō'sä thăbī'lā), 1925–, president of Nicaragua (1967–72, 1974–). A younger son of the dictator Anastasio Somoza, he graduated from the U.S. military academy at West Point and, returning to Nicaragua, at the age of 21 assumed command of the national guard, a powerful position that he never relinquished. He was elected president in 1967 and, prohibited from immediately succeeding himself, resigned in 1972, nominally yielding power to a triumvirate until the 1974 presidential elections; however, as commander of the national guard, he continued to rule through the triumvirate. As president, he imposed austerity measures to counteract an economic recession and dealt strongly with student and university dissent.

Somoza Debayle, Luis (lōōēs'), 1922–67, president of Nicaragua (1957–63). The oldest son of the dictator Anastasio Somoza, he was educated in the United States. Returning to Nicaragua, he entered congress in 1950 and was president of the chamber of deputies when he became acting president (1956) and then president (1957) upon the assassination of his father. He liberalized his father's regime somewhat, instituted social reforms, and improved the economy, chiefly through diversification and foreign loans. He was a blunt anti-Communist. He pushed a reform law that prohibited his own reelection and prevented any member of his family from immediately succeeding him. After relinquishing the presidency to his chosen successor, René Schick Gutiérrez, he served in the senate. In 1967 he managed his brother's successful presidential campaign.

sonar (sō'när), device used under water for locating submerged objects and for submarine communication by means of sound waves. The term *sonar* is an acronym for *so*und *n*avigation *r*anging. The main component of sonar equipment is an electroacoustic transducer that is in direct contact with the water. It is suspended from the hull of a ship or on a cable from a low-flying helicopter. The transducer converts electric energy into acoustic energy (thus acting as a projector), much as does a loudspeaker, and converts acoustic energy into electric energy (serving as a hydrophone), as does a microphone. A pulse of electric energy vibrates the diaphragm of the projector, sending sound waves through the water. These waves are concentrated into a sound beam, which scans the water when the projector is rotated. After the sound wave is emitted, the projector is converted into a hydrophone and listens for an echo. The cycle is repeated periodically. A returning echo is converted into an electric current by the transducer and may be interpreted (for range, bearing, and the nature of the target) aurally or by a cathode-ray tube, as is done with radar signals. The various types of sonar in use can be put into three classes: direct listening, communications, and echo ranging. In direct listening, the object under observation generates the sounds that are received. In communications and echo ranging the sonar must generate its own signals. Sonar operates in the 10- to 50-kilocycle acoustical frequency range. It is used for communication between submerged submarines or between a submarine and a surface vessel, for locating mines and underwater hazards to navigation, and also as a fathometer, or depth finder. Sonar is widely used by commercial fishermen for locating shoals of fish. See J. W. Horton, *Fundamentals of Sonar* (1957); D. G. Tucker, *Underwater Observation Using Sonar* (1966).

sonata (sənä'tə), in music, type of instrumental composition that arose in Italy in the 17th cent. At first the term merely distinguished an instrumental piece from a piece with voice, which was called a cantata. Thus many early concertos, suites, and sets of variations were called sonatas. As the various instrumental forms acquired differentiated characteristics during the baroque period, the term began to identify two specific types: the *sonata de chiesa*, or church sonata, and the *sonata da camera*, or chamber sonata. Both were written most commonly for two melody instruments, usually violins or flutes, with a bass instrument and a keyboard instrument, both of which played the thorough bass (see FIGURED BASS). The *sonata da chiesa* was in four movements—slow, fast, slow, fast—and its contrapuntal style was largely derived from the CANZONE. The *sonata da camera* was basically a SUITE of dances, although nondance movements were added later. In the late 17th cent. these two types merged into the outstanding baroque chamber music form, the trio sonata. This form was brought to perfection in the works of Arcangelo Corelli and Evaristo dall' Abaco (1675–1742) and adopted in the sonatas of J. S. Bach and Handel. In the later 18th cent. sonatas for groups of instruments began to be designated string quartet and SYMPHONY, and the term *sonata* was limited to pieces for one keyboard instrument or for one solo instrument (e.g., violin) with keyboard accompaniment. The keyboard sonata was developed in the works of rococo Italian composers such as Galuppi, G. B. Sammartini (1698–1775), and P. D. Paradies (1710–92). This rococo sonata was more homophonic than the trio sonata, having one outstanding melodic line with accompanying harmonic background, such as the Alberti bass. In sonatas of this type, particularly those of C. P. E. Bach, an expressive quality and pianistic style were developed that influenced the classical sonata, perfected by Haydn, Mozart, and Beethoven. The classical sonata's movements are usually fast-slow-fast, and a minuet or scherzo is often inserted before the last movement. The first movement—and possibly one or more of the others—was in what is called **sonata form.** This is essentially a binary form, the first part being an exposition of two (or sometimes three) contrasted themes. The second part consists of a development of these themes and a recapitulation of the beginning exposition. Sonata form is employed in the string quartet, in the symphony, and to some extent in the concerto, as well as in the solo sonata. After the classical era the most significant development was the use of one thematic idea in all movements, in each of which the basic idea is transformed in mood and character. This type of sonata was fully realized in the Sonata in B Minor of Franz Liszt. See critical studies of the composers mentioned; W. S. Newman, *The Sonata in the Baroque Era* (3d ed. 1972), *The Sonata in the Classic Era* (2d ed. 1972), and *The Sonata Since Beethoven* (2d ed. 1972).

Sønderborg (sö'nərbôr), Ger. *Sonderburg,* city (1970 com. pop. 29,638), Sønderjylland co., S Denmark, on both sides of the Als Sund. The older section of the city is situated on Als Island and is connected by bridge with the newer quarter on Jylland. Sønderborg is a port, an industrial and commercial center, and a seaside resort. Manufactures include textiles, machinery, and beer. The city developed around a 13th-century castle and was part of the duchy of Schleswig. After his deposition, Christian II was held prisoner there from 1532 to 1549. Christian III (reigned 1534–59) created the duchy of Sønderborg for his younger son John, from which the branch of Schleswig-Holstein-Sønderborg-Glücksburg (which has occupied the Danish throne since 1863) is descended. The city was held by Prussia from 1864 to 1920.

Sonderbund (zôn'dərbōōnt) [Ger., = separate league], 1845–47, defensive league of seven Roman Catholic cantons of Switzerland; it was formed to protect Catholic interests and prevent the establishment of a more centralized Swiss government. The cantons were Lucerne, Fribourg, Valais, Uri, Schwyz, Unterwalden, and Zug. The rise of the Radical party in the majority of cantons had resulted in anti-Catholic measures such as the closing (1841) of all convents in Aargau. When Lucerne retaliated (1844) by recalling the Jesuits, armed bandits of Radicals invaded the canton. This action, combined with the Catholic cantons' opposition to the Radicals' program of a more unified federalization (which imperiled the position of the predominantly rural, reactionary, and sparsely populated Catholic cantons), provoked the seven cantons to form a defensive alliance (1845). The Radical majority in the federal diet declared the Sonderbund dissolved (1847) and shortly afterward sent an army, under Gen. Guillaume Henri Dufour, against the separatist forces. Lord Palmerston, the British foreign minister, helped prevent foreign intervention, and in an almost bloodless campaign the Sonderbund was defeated. The adoption (1848) of a federal constitution ended the virtual sovereignty of the individual cantons. The Society of Jesus was banned from Switzerland, and the establishment of new religious houses was forbidden.

Sondershausen (zôn″dərs-hou′zən), commune (1970 pop. 22,880), Erfurt district, SW East Germany, near the western foot of Kyffhäuser mt. It is an industrial city and a potash-mining center. Manufactures include textiles, clothing, and paper. Nearby are petroleum deposits. From the late 16th cent. until 1918 Sondershausen was the capital of the principality of Schwarzburg-Sondershausen. There is a notable palace (16th–18th cent.) in the city.

Sondrio (sōn′drēō), town (1971 pop. 22,734), capital of Sondrio prov., Lombardy, N Italy, on the Mallero River near its confluence with the Adda River. The chief town of the VALTELLINA, it is an agricultural market and an industrial and tourist center.

song, relatively brief, simple vocal composition, usually a setting of a poetic text for accompanied solo VOICE, believed to be the earliest musical form. The song literature of Western music embodies two broad classifications—FOLK SONG and art song. Apart from the recently discovered cuneiform tablet containing a song from the Middle East of the 2d millennium B.C., now thought to be the oldest notated music known, and apart from ancient Greek song (see GREEK MUSIC), the manuscripts of which are lost, the first outstanding examples of art song before the baroque period are those of the TROUBADOURS, TROUVÈRES, MINNESINGERS, and MEISTERSINGERS. The refined, lyrical *air de cour* of late 16th-century France, for one or more voices with lute accompaniment, provided the inspiration for the *ayre* composed by the early 17th-century English lutanists, among whom were John Dowland, Thomas Campion, and Thomas Morley. In the 14th and 16th cent., Italian composers contributed the polyphonic MADRIGAL, generally considered apart from art-song literature because of its complexity. The Italians centered their principal attention upon the development of the OPERA. The principle of accompanied monody, which originated in Italy and is inseparable from the early development of opera, also marked the beginning of modern accompanied song. A direct influence is shown in the German lied of the 17th cent., a monodic song with a basso continuo accompaniment. Outstanding among earlier examples are the *Arien* of Heinrich Albert (1604–51) and those of Adam Krieger (1634–66). The German romantic lieder of the 19th cent., in which the vocal line and the piano accompaniment are of equal musical significance, are considered to be among the finest of all art songs. The lied style was articulated by Schubert and developed further by Schumann, Brahms, and Hugo Wolf. Among the poets whose lyrics they used were Goethe, Chamisso, Eichendorff, Rüchert, Wilhelm Müller, Heine, and Mörike. Among modern German songs those of Hindemith and of Schoenberg are outstanding. Some of these require the technique of *Sprechstimme*, a pitched declamation that is a hybrid of song and speech. In France a renewed interest in song composition began in the 19th cent. with Berlioz and was continued in the works of Franck, Fauré, Debussy, Ravel, and Poulenc. The foremost Russian composers of the genre include Glinka, Rachmaninoff, Tchaikovsky, Gretchaninov, and Glière. The dramatic songs of Moussorgsky are particularly significant. In the United States the songs of Stephen Foster had such national appeal as to become incorporated into the folk tradition. Charles Ives brought a striking originality to the modern American art song. See also BIRDSONG. See AMERICAN NEGRO SPIRITUALS; BALLAD; CAROL; CHANTEY; HYMN; PLAINSONG. See Peter Warlock, *The English Ayre* (1926); W. T. Upton, *The Art-Song in America* (1930); Elisabeth Schumann, *German Song* (1948); Sergius Kagen, *Music for the Voice* (1949); Denis Stevens, ed., *A History of Song* (1960); Donald Ivey, *Song: Anatomy, Imagery, and Styles* (1970); H. T. Finck, *Songs and Song Writers* (1900, repr. 1973).

song, bird: see BIRDSONG.

Song Ba (sông bä), river, c.200 mi (320 km) long, rising in the Annamese Cordillera, central South Vietnam, and flowing S past An Tuc to Hau Bon, then SE past Son Hoa to the South China Sea at Tuy Hoa. Diverse tropical crops are grown along its lower course.

Song Dong Nai: see DONG NAI, river, South Vietnam.

Songhai or **Songhay** (both: sŏng′-gī′), largest of the ancient native empires of W Africa. The state was founded (c.700) by Berbers on the Middle Niger. The rulers accepted Islam c.1000. Its power was much increased by Sonni Ali (1464–92) who occupied Timbuktu in 1468. Songhai reached its greatest extent under Askia Muhammad I (c.1493–1528). He was deposed by his son, and in the subsequent conflicts among his successors the empire slowly began to decline. The breakup of the state was accelerated by a Moroccan invasion in 1591.

Song My: see MY LAI INCIDENT.

Song of Solomon, Song of Songs, or **Canticles,** book of the Old Testament, 22d in the order of the Authorized Version. Although traditionally ascribed to King Solomon, many scholars date it as late as the 3d cent. B.C. It is in form a collection of love poems. Its preservation in the Jewish and Christian canon is due not to its universally admitted poetic beauty, but to the acceptance of it as an allegory or parable of God's love for Israel, or for the church, or for the soul that loves Him. Famous among such interpretations are St. Bernard of Clairvaux's 86 sermons on the book (tr. 1895) and St. Francis of Sales's explanation (tr. 1908). See studies by G. T. Dickinson (1971) and Carlo Suares (1972).

sonic boom, SHOCK WAVE produced by an object moving through the air at supersonic speed, i.e., faster than the speed of sound. Since sound is a mechanical disturbance that propagates through the air, there is a limit to its speed. An object such as an airplane, moving through the air, generates sound.

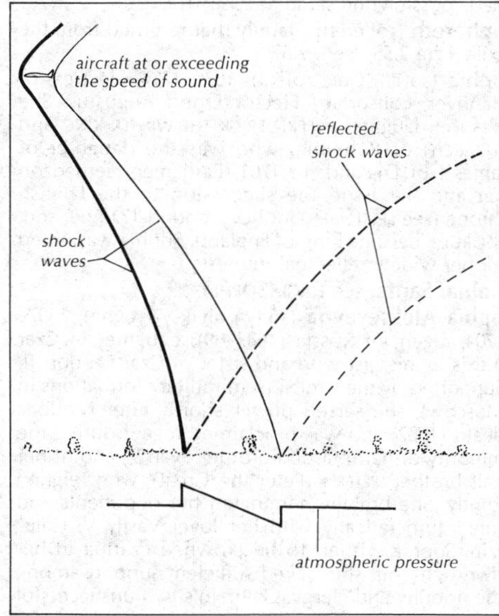

Sonic boom wave pattern from a supersonic aircraft and variation in pressure

When the speed of the object reaches or exceeds the speed of sound, the object catches up with its own noise; at higher speeds, it forces the sound ahead of itself faster than the noise would ordinarily travel. The piled-up sound takes the form of a violent shock wave called a sonic boom propagating behind the object. Sonic booms occasionally have mechanically destructive effects in addition to their role as noise pollutants.

Sonneberg (zôn′əbĕrgh″), city (1970 pop. 29,767), Suhl district, S East Germany; first mentioned 1317. It is the center of the Thuringian toy industry. Other products include clothing and cartons.

Sonneborn, Tracy Morton, 1905–, American geneticist, b. Baltimore, grad. Johns Hopkins Univ. (B.A., 1925; Ph.D., 1928). From 1930 to 1939 he taught and conducted research at Johns Hopkins Univ. He went to Indiana Univ. in 1939 and became (1943) professor of zoology. He is known for his studies of cytoplasmic inheritance in the paramecium, showing that certain hereditary characters can be transmitted from parents to offspring by means other than the genes.

Sonneck, Oscar George Theodore (sŭn′ĕk), 1873–1928, American musicologist, b. Jersey City, N.J., educated in Germany. As chief (1902–17) of the music division of the Library of Congress, he developed one of the outstanding music libraries of the world. He edited the *Musical Quarterly* from its founding in 1915 until his death, and he held a position at the music publishing house of G. Schirmer, Inc. His writings rank him as one of the foremost, as well as one of the first, American musicologists, particularly in the field of early American music. They include *A Bibliography of Early Secular American Music* (1905, rev. ed. 1945); *Early Concert-Life in America* (1907); *The Star-Spangled Banner* (1914); *Catalogue of Opera Librettos Printed before 1800* (2 vol., 1914); *Early Opera in America* (1915); and several works of Beethoven scholarship.

sonnet, poem of 14 lines, usually in iambic pentameter, restricted to a definite rhyme scheme. There are two prominent types: the Italian, or Petrarchan, sonnet, composed of an octave and a sestet (rhyming *abbaabba cdecde*), and the Elizabethan, or Shakespearean, sonnet, consisting of three quatrains and a couplet (rhyming *abab cdcd efef gg*). Variations of these schemes occur, notably the Spenserian sonnet, after Edmund Spenser (rhyming *abab bcbc cdcd ee*). The sonnet is generally believed to have developed from medieval songs. In Italy, where it was cultivated during the Renaissance, it achieved great expression in the work of PETRARCH, Dante, Tasso, and Michelangelo. The form was introduced into Spain by Almogáver, into Portugal by Camões, into France by Saint-Gelays and Marot, and into England by Wyatt and Surrey. The sonnet came into prominence in Germany during the romantic period in the work of Goethe, Schlegel, Heyse, and others. Innumerable sonnets and sonnet sequences appeared in Elizabethan England, notably by Sidney, Spenser, and Shakespeare. Around the time of Milton's great sonnets, the use of the form began to decrease, but with the advent of romanticism in the early 19th cent. the sonnet again achieved popularity in the poetry of Wordsworth and Keats. Poets such as Elizabeth Barrett Browning, the Rossettis, and George Meredith in the 19th cent. and Dylan Thomas and W. H. Auden in the 20th cent. also wrote sonnets. American poets noted for their sonnets include Longfellow, E. A. Robinson, Elinor Wylie, and Edna St. Vincent Millay.

Sonni Ali: see SONGHAI.

Sonnino, Sidney, Barone (bärō′nā sōn-nē′nō), 1847–1922, Italian foreign minister instrumental in Italy's entry into World War I. A member of the diplomatic corps (1867–73), he later became interested in social and economic problems, particularly in the conditions of the peasants, and founded an economic review, later converted into a political daily. Sonnino entered parliament in 1880 and as minister of finance (1893–96) under Crispi took drastic measures and succeeded in balancing the budget. He was twice premier (1906, 1909–10). As foreign minister during World War I, he negotiated (1915) the secret Treaty of London, by which Italy entered the war on the Allied side in exchange for promises of vast territorial gains. The opposition of President Wilson to the fulfillment of the secret treaty caused major difficulties at the Paris Peace Conference of 1919, where Sonnino represented Italy with Vittorio Emanuele ORLANDO. Sonnino retired from politics in 1919.

Sonora (sōnō′rä), state (1970 pop. 1,092,458), 70,484 sq mi (182,554 sq km), NW Mexico, on the Gulf of California, S of Arizona. HERMOSILLO is the capital. Sonora is mostly mountainous, with vast desert stretches; along the gulf are low, broad coastlands. Reclamation projects on the Yaqui, Sonora, Mayo, and other rivers have opened large areas to agriculture. The most extensively irrigated of all Mexican states, Sonora is a leading national producer of cotton and wheat; other cereals and vegetables are also grown. Agriculture is highly mechanized. Cattle raising and fishing are important, and large quantities of shrimp are exported to the United States. Gold, silver, copper, and other metals are mined in Sonora, but the state's forest wealth remains untapped. Power plants at Hermosillo and Guaymas have aided industrialization, and food processing and textile manufacture are major industries. Communications within the state are good. Nogales is the chief point of entry from the United States. Systematic Spanish exploration of Sonora, principally by Cristóbal de Oñate, began after Coronado's expedition in 1540. Spanish missionaries, notably Eusebio Francisco Kino, were active in colonizing the territory during the 17th cent. and in gaining some control over hostile Indian tribes. However, punitive expeditions were sent against the Yaqui Indians as late as the 20th cent. Originally part of Nueva Viscaya, which also included the present-day states of Chihuahua and Durango, Sonora was later united with

Sinaloa; they became separate states in 1830. Sonora played a key role in the Mexican revolution against Spain that began in 1910.

Sons of Liberty, secret organizations formed in the American colonies in protest against the Stamp Act (1765). They took their name from a phrase used by Isaac Barré in a speech against the Stamp Act in Parliament, and were organized by merchants, businessmen, lawyers, journalists, and others who would be most affected by the Stamp Act. The leaders included John Lamb and Alexander McDougall in New York, and Samuel Adams and James Otis in New England. The societies kept in touch with each other through committees of correspondence, supported the nonimportation agreement, forced the resignation of stamp distributors, and incited destruction of stamped paper and violence against British officials. They participated in calling the Continental Congress of 1774. In the Civil War, the KNIGHTS OF THE GOLDEN CIRCLE adopted (1864) the name Sons of Liberty.

Sons of the American Revolution, national patriotic organization, founded (1889) in New York City by a union of the Sons of Revolutionary Sires and certain members of the Society of the Sons of the Revolution. Membership is open to those whose ancestors saw active service in the Revolutionary forces. In 1906 it was incorporated nationally by congressional act. With a national office in Washington, D.C., the organization has about 20,000 members. A similar but unconnected organization is the Sons of the Revolution.

Sonsonate (sōnsōnä'tā), city (1968 est. pop. 31,000), SW El Salvador. It is the commercial center of one of the richest agricultural regions of El Salvador, where dairy products, coffee, sugar, tobacco, Peruvian balsam, and subsistence crops are produced. The city was founded in 1524 by the Spanish conquistador Pedro de Alvarado. Sonsonate has two beautiful churches and is a point of departure for excursions to the parks and resorts around nearby Izalco volcano. The neighboring village of Asunción Izalco has colorful fiestas.

Sontag, Henriette (hĕnrēĕt'ə zôn'täk), later **Contessa Rossi** (kôntĕs'sä rôs'sē), 1806–54, German operatic soprano, studied at the Prague Conservatory. In Vienna in 1823 she created the leading role in Weber's *Euryanthe* and in 1824 was soprano soloist in the premieres of Beethoven's Ninth Symphony and *Missa Solemnis.* She made triumphant debuts in Berlin (1825), Paris (1826), and London (1828). After her marriage to a Sardinian ambassador, Conte Rossi, she left the stage in 1830 at the height of her success. In 1849 she resumed her career and in 1852 sang in the United States. See biography by Frank Russell (1964).

Sontag, Susan (sŏn'täg), 1933–, American writer, b. New York City. She grew up in Arizona and California and studied philosophy at the University of Chicago. Regarded as a brilliant and original thinker, Sontag is known chiefly for her critical essays on avant-garde culture in the 1960s. Most of them were collected in *Against Interpretation* (1966), in which she popularized the word *camp,* referring to exaggerated reproductions of the style and emotions of pop culture. Her other works include short stories, novels such as *The Benefactor* (1963) and *Death Kit* (1967), and essays on radical politics, collected in *Styles of Radical Will* (1969). She has also written and directed motion pictures, including *Duet for Cannibals* (1969), *Brother Carl* (1971), and *Promised Lands* (1974). The screenplay for *Brother Carl* was published in 1974.

Soo Canals: see SAULTE SAINTE MARIE CANALS, United States and Canada.

Soochow: see SU-CHOU, China.

Soong (sŏŏng), Mandarin *Sung,* Chinese family, prominent in public affairs. **Soong Yao-ju,** or **Charles Jones Soong,** 1866–1918, graduated from Vanderbilt Univ. and, after returning to China (1886), was a Methodist missionary in Shanghai. He resigned from mission work in 1892 and thereafter was a successful merchant. **Soong Tzu-wen,** better known as **T. V. Soong,** 1894–1971, his most distinguished son, was educated at Harvard and later (1917–23) engaged in private business in China. He occupied several official positions in the Kuomintang government, including governor of the Central Bank of China and minister of finance (1928–31, 1932–33); minister of foreign affairs (1942–45); and president of the Executive Yuan (1945–47). He lived in the United States after 1949. The three daughters of Charles Jones Soong also became well known. **Soong Ai-ling,** 1890–, graduated from Wesleyan College in Macon, Ga. She married Hsiang-hsi K'UNG and engaged in child welfare work. **Soong Ch'ing-ling,** 1892–, also graduated from Wesleyan College. She early became prominent in revolutionary politics, and in 1914 she married SUN YAT-SEN in Japan. After Sun's death (1925) she became more active in Kuomintang affairs, gaining election (1926) to the central executive committee. After the party's expulsion (1927) of the Communists, however, she resigned and went abroad. With the outbreak (1937) of the Sino-Japanese War, she was reconciled with the Kuomintang and became (1939) a state councilor of the national government. She again left the government when a civil war broke out between the Kuomintang and the Communists in 1946. Since 1949 she has, under various titles, served as vice chairman of the government of the People's Republic of China. In 1951 she was awarded the Stalin Peace Prize, and in 1953 a collection of her writings, *Struggle for New China,* was published. **Soong Mei-ling,** c.1897–, graduated from Wellesley College. She married CHIANG KAI-SHEK in 1927. She was a member of the Legislative Yuan (1930–32) and secretary general of the Chinese Aeronautical Affairs Commission (1936–38). In 1945 she became a member of the central executive committee of the Kuomintang. Through numerous publications, radio broadcasts, and personal appearances, she sought to enlist American support for the Nationalists in their struggle with the Chinese Communists. See Emily Hahn, *The Soong Sisters* (1941, repr. 1970).

soot, black or dull brown deposit of fine powder resulting from incomplete combustion of fuel of high carbon content, e.g., coal, wood, and oil. It consists chiefly of amorphous carbon and tarry substances that cause it to adhere to surfaces. Soot obtained from coal also contains sulfur and ammonia. See CARBON BLACK.

Sopater (sŏp'ətər), companion of St. Paul. Acts 20.4. He is possibly the same as SOSIPATER.

Sophereth (sŏf'ērĕth), family that returned from the Exile. Ezra 2.55; Neh. 7.57.

Sophia (sōfī'ə, Ger. zōfē'ä), 1630–1714, electress of Hanover, consort of Elector Ernest Augustus. She was the daughter of FREDERICK THE WINTER KING and ELIZABETH of Bohemia, who was the daughter of James I of England. In 1701, Parliament settled on her and her issue the succession to the English throne (see SETTLEMENT, ACT OF), and in 1714 her son, GEORGE I, became king of England. Sophia was noted for her wide intellectual interests.

Sophia, Santa: see HAGIA SOPHIA.

Sophia Alekseyevna (sô'fyə əlyĭksyā'yəvnə), 1657–1704, regent of Russia (1682–89); daughter of Czar Alexis by his first wife and sister of Czar Feodor III. Supported by the streltsi (semimilitary formations in Moscow), she seized power shortly after Feodor's death (1682) and was proclaimed regent during the minority of her retarded brother, Ivan V, and of her half brother, PETER I (Peter the Great), who reigned jointly. She brutally eliminated her opponents and ruled autocratically with her lover Vasily V. Gallitzin. Sophia wished to be crowned czarina in her own right, but she lacked sufficient support among the nobility and clergy. Gallitzin's two unsuccessful campaigns against the khan of Crimea helped undermine Sophia's power. When it was rumored that she intended to kill Peter and proclaim herself sole ruler, Peter summoned the nobles and his loyal guards, overthrew the regency, deposed Ivan, exiled Gallitzin, and had Sophia confined in a convent. After an attempted revolt of the streltsi, Peter forced her (1689) to take the veil. See C. B. O'Brien, *Russia under Two Tsars, 1682–1689* (1952).

Sophia Charlotte (zōfē'ä shärlôt'ə), 1668–1705, first queen of Prussia, second wife of King FREDERICK I, daughter of Electress Sophia of Hanover, and sister of King George I of England. She was noted for her literary and philosophic interests and for her friendship with Gottfried Wilhelm von LEIBNIZ.

Sophia Dorothea (sōfī'ə dŏrəthē'ə), 1666–1726, electress of Hanover, wife of Elector George Louis (later King George I of England); sometimes called Sophia Dorothea of Celle. Married to George in 1682, she bore him two children: George, later George II of England, and Sophia Dorothea, who became the wife of Frederick William I of Prussia. In 1694 she was accused of having an affair with Count Philipp KÖNIGSMARK. Her presumed lover disappeared (probably murdered), and she herself was divorced and imprisoned for life. George I's harsh treatment of her was one major cause of the king's unpopularity in England.

Sophists (sŏf'ĭsts), originally, itinerant teachers in Greece (5th cent. B.C.) who provided education through lectures and in return received fees from their audiences. The term was given as a mark of respect. PROTAGORAS was perhaps the first to style himself a Sophist and to receive payment for his instruction. He and GORGIAS were respected thinkers, but others after them, notably Thrasymachus and Hippias, and many lesser figures, turned education into the development of skills useful to political careers. Hence, they cared little for the disciplined search for truth (dialectics), teaching in its place the art of persuasion (rhetoric). Although not properly speaking a philosophical school, they appear to have shared a basic SKEPTICISM regarding the possibility of knowing truth. The more notorious of them boasted of their ability to "make the worst appear the better reason." They were criticized by Plato and Aristotle for their emphasis on rhetoric rather than on pure knowledge and for their acceptance of money, a judgment that has passed into history and has given the term *sophist* its present meaning. George Grote's *History of Greece* (1846) was one of the first defenses of the Sophists. Modern studies have stressed the contributions of Protagoras and Gorgias to a theory of knowledge and to ethics. They are frequently cited today as forerunners of pragmatism. See W. K. C. Guthrie, *Sophists* (1971); Hermann Diels, ed., *The Older Sophists* (1972).

Sophocles (sŏf'əklēz), c.496 B.C.–406 B.C., Greek tragic poet, younger contemporary of AESCHYLUS and older contemporary of EURIPIDES, b. Colonus, near Athens. A man of wealth, charm, and genius, Sophocles was given posts of responsibility in peace and in war by the Athenians. He was a general and a priest; after his death he was worshiped as a hero. At the age of 16 he led the chorus in a paean on the victory of Salamis. He won his first dramatic triumph in 468, over Aeschylus, and thenceforth wrote copiously (he composed about 123 dramas), winning first place about 20 times and never falling lower than second. A definitive innovator in the drama, he added a third actor—thereby tremendously increasing the dramatic possibilities of the medium—increased the size of the chorus, abandoned the trilogy of plays for the self-contained tragedy, and introduced scene painting. Seven complete tragedies (difficult to date), part of a satyr play, and over 1,000 fragments survive. *Ajax* is perhaps the earliest tragedy; three actors are used but the form is handled imperfectly. In his other plays, whether with two or three actors, the dialogue is polished and smooth. *Antigone* (c.441) contains extraordinarily fine characterization. The most famous of his tragedies (cited by Aristotle as a perfect example of tragedy) is *Oedipus Rex* or *Oedipus Tyrannus* (c.429), in which the strength of Greek dramatic irony reaches an apex. The plot is based on the OEDIPUS legend. *Electra* (date uncertain), the *Trachiniae* (date uncertain; on the death of Hercules by the blood of Nessus), and *Philoctetes* (409) followed. *Oedipus at Colonus* was written shortly before Sophocles' death and was produced by his son in 401. A sequel to *Oedipus Rex,* it tells of the last days and death of Oedipus; it is a quiet, simple play. There is also extant about half of a satyr play (*Ichneutae* or *The Trackers,* written perhaps c.460) on Hermes' theft of Apollo's cattle. The characters in Sophocles are governed in their fate more by their own faults than by actions of the Aeschylean gods. Sophocles is supposed to have said that Aeschylus composed correctly without knowing it, Euripides portrayed men as they were, and he painted men as they ought to be. The translation by Richmond Lattimore and David Grene, *The Complete Greek Tragedies* (1959) is one of the many English translations of Sophocles. See studies by C. H. Whitman (1951), A. J. A. Waldcock (1966), D. Grene (1967), and T. B. L. Webster (1969).

Sophonias (sō"fənī'əs), Greek form of ZEPHANIAH.

Sophonisba (sōfənĭz'bə), fl. 3d cent. B.C., Carthaginian noblewoman, daughter of HASDRUBAL. She was the Carthaginian wife of Syphax of Numidia, who after the marriage fought for Carthage. When he was defeated (203 B.C.) by Masinissa and the Romans, Sophonisba took poison. According to an old version of the story—which is probably at least partially true—she was betrothed to Masinissa before her father married her to Syphax. After Syphax was slain, Masinissa married her, and to thwart the demand of the Romans to display her in their triumph, he sent her a bowl of poison to drink. This tragedy was the subject of plays by Alfieri, Trissino, Corneille, James Thomson, Voltaire, and others. The correct spelling of the name is Saphanba'al.

soporific (sŏp"ərĭf'ĭk) or **sleeping pill,** medication that depresses the central nervous system and induces sleep. See HYPNOTIC DRUGS; DEPRESSANT.

Sopot (sô'pôt), Ger. *Zoppot,* city (1970 pop. 47,600), N Poland, on the Baltic Sea and the Gulf of Danzig. A seaside resort and tourist center, it had a fashionable gambling casino before World War II. Sopot belonged to the city of Danzig (now Gdańsk) from 1283 to 1807. It passed to Prussia in 1814. Included in the Free City of Danzig in 1919, it was ceded to Poland in 1945. Sopot has schools of economics and music and several theaters.

soprano [Ital.,=above], female voice of highest pitch. The three basic types of solo soprano are coloratura, lyric, and dramatic. The coloratura has a great range and impressive vocal agility; the lyric soprano has a light, pretty voice; and the dramatic soprano has a sustained power suitable for operatic roles. The voices of boys who have not reached puberty are generally in the soprano range and replace women's voices in some church choirs. In the CASTRATO of the 18th cent. the quality of a boy's voice combined with the lung power of a man made for vocal powers of great brilliance (see EUNUCH). The highest-pitched member of various families of instruments is termed soprano, e.g., soprano saxophone.

Sopron (shô'prôn), Ger. *Ödenburg,* city (1970 pop. 47,100), NW Hungary, near the Austrian border. It is a commercial center and produces cotton textiles, woolens, and wines. There are also fruit-preserving and sugar-refining industries. Originally a Celtic settlement called Scarabantia, it became a military outpost under the Romans. Hungarians settling the area in the 10th and 11th cent. made the city an important fortress. Sopron was the site of the coronation of King (later emperor) Ferdinand III of Hungary and Bohemia in 1625 and a meeting place of the Hungarian Parliament in 1681. Part of the BURGENLAND, it was transferred to Austria after World War I but was returned to Hungary after a plebiscite (1921). Sopron is one of the oldest cultural centers in Hungary; it has a university, three 13th-century churches, and a 15th-century palace. Franz Liszt was born at nearby Dobojan.

Sorabji, Cornelia (sōräb'jē), c.1870–1954, Indian lawyer and author. She took a law degree at Oxford in 1893. She served (1904–23) as a special legal adviser to the Court of Wards of Bengal, Bihar, Orissa, and Assam; in this office, which was created through her efforts, she was responsible for the interests of women property holders who lived in purdah. In 1923 she was called to the English bar, but continued to practice in India. She was in favor of continued British rule, and in later years lived in London. Her writings include *Love and Life behind the Purdah* (1901), *Sun Babies* (1904; 2d series, 1909), *Indian Tales of the Great Ones* (1916), *The Purdahnashin* (1917), *Therefore* (1924), and *India Recalled* (1936). See her memoirs, *India Calling* (1934).

Soracte (sōrăk'tē), isolated mountain, 2,267 ft (691 m) high, in Latium, central Italy, N of Rome. It was celebrated in the poetry of Vergil and Horace. In ancient times it was crowned with a temple of Apollo; there is now a convent near the summit.

Soranus (sərā'nəs), fl. 1st–2d cent. A.D., Greek physician, probably b. Ephesus. He is believed to have practiced in Alexandria and in Rome and was an authority on obstetrics, gynecology, and pediatrics. His treatise *On Midwifery and the Diseases of Women* (tr. 1882) remained an influential work until the 16th cent.

Sorbonne (sôrbôn'), first endowed college in the Univ. of Paris, founded by Robert de Sorbon (1201–74), chaplain of Louis IX, and opened in 1253 for the purpose of providing quarters for theology students who were not friars. Gaining academic and theological distinction in the late Middle Ages and early modern times, the Sorbonne gained preponderance over its early mendicant college rivals, and Sorbonne doctors were frequently called upon to render opinions on important ecclesiastical and theological issues. In the 16th cent., because it became the place for the deliberations of the faculty of theology, this faculty came to be called the Sorbonne, although all its members did not belong to this college. In 1626 it was enlarged. After its suppression (1792) in the French Revolution, the Univ. of Paris took over (1808) the Sorbonne grounds, so that for the years between 1808 and 1885 the Sorbonne existed as the seat of the three faculties of theology and of the Académie de Paris. In 1885 a general council of faculties, presided over by the rector of the university, was created. Sorbonne is frequently used as a name for the Univ. of Paris.

Sorbs: see WENDS.

sorcery: see INCANTATION; MAGIC; SPELL; WITCHCRAFT.

Sordello (sōrdĕl'lō), c.1180–1269?, Italian troubadour. A life of brawling and intrigue took him to Provence, where he served at court. Like other Italian troubadours before him, he wrote in Provençal (see ITALIAN LITERATURE). His best-known poem, *Serventese* (1237), is a bitter lament on the death of his patron. Dante gave Sordello a patriot's status in *Purgatorio,* VI, 73. Robert Browning used him as the subject of a long poem, *Sordello* (1840).

Sorek (sō'rĕk), valley, SW Palestine, the home of Delilah. It is the modern Nahal Soreg (Israel), which enters the sea NW of Yibna. Judges 16.4.

Sorel, Agnès (änyĕs' sôrĕl'), c.1422–1450, mistress (1444–50) of Charles VII of France. She was the first mistress of a French king to be officially recognized as such. Witty and astute as well as beautiful, she wielded considerable influence over the king and his policies. After her death, the enemies of Jacques CŒUR, the financier, spread the rumor that he had had Agnès Sorel killed by poisoning.

Sorel, Albert (älbĕr'), 1842–1906, French historian. After a diplomatic career that gave him unique access to the archives of the foreign ministry, Sorel concentrated on diplomatic history. His monumental *Europe et la Révolution française* (8 vol., 1895–1904) surveyed the influence of the French Revolution in Europe. Applying to diplomatic history the Tocqueville thesis of essential continuity between the ancien régime and Revolutionary France, Sorel asserted that after the revolutionists began to claim France's "natural frontiers," continuous struggle with Europe, and especially England, was inevitable. The introductory section of this work has been translated as *Europe under the Old Regime* (1947).

Sorel, Georges (zhôrzh), 1847–1922, French social philosopher. He was an engineer by profession, but, becoming interested in social problems, he eventually resigned his position and devoted himself to study and writing. He found in the political and social life of bourgeois democracy the triumph of mediocrity and espoused various forms of socialism, chiefly revolutionary SYNDICALISM. In his best-known work, *Reflections on Violence* (1908, tr. 1912), which became the basic text of syndicalism, Sorel expounded his theory of "violence" as the creative power of the proletariat that could overcome "force," the coercive economic power of the bourgeoisie. He was not consistent in his political thought, however, and supported at various times such disparate alternatives to the existing order as extreme French monarchism and the Bolshevik Revolution. See study by R. D. Humphrey (1951, repr. 1971); I. L. Horowitz, *Radicalism and the Revolt Against Reason* (1968).

Sorel, city (1971 pop. 19,347), S Que., Canada, at the confluence of the St. Lawrence and Richelieu rivers. It is a grain-shipping center with an important shipbuilding industry. Iron and steel, metal products, textiles, and clothing are made in Sorel. The city is on the site of Fort Richelieu, built by Pierre de Saurel in 1665.

Sörensen, Sören Peter Lauritz (sö'rən pē'tər lou'rēts sö'rənsən), 1868–1939, Danish biochemist. In 1899 he received a Ph.D. degree in Copenhagen. Sörensen was director of chemistry at Carlsberg Laboratory and worked as a professor in Copenhagen. His work on hydrogen ion concentration led him to suggest that it be measured in a unit he called *p*H. Numerical values based on this unit, now universally in use, give an indication of the acidity of solutions. He also did pioneering research on amino acid synthesis and on the nature of enzyme reactions.

sore throat, streptococcal (strĕp"təkŏk'əl), infection and inflammation of the pharynx caused by certain streptococcal bacteria. These organisms are known as hemolytic streptococci because they secrete toxins that dissolve, or cause hemolysis of, red blood cells. Acute streptococcal sore throat is usually characterized by an extremely painful throat, enlarged tonsils, and sometimes gastrointestinal disturbances. SCARLET FEVER, which is caused by the same streptococcal bacteria, occurs when the microorganisms produce a toxin that, in sensitive individuals, causes appearance of a characteristic rash. Complications of streptococcal infection, which include RHEUMATIC FEVER and sometimes ARTHRITIS and NEPHRITIS, can be prevented by early, vigorous treatment with PENICILLIN or other suitable antibiotics.

sorghum, tall, coarse annual (*Sorghum vulgare*) of the family Gramineae (GRASS family), somewhat similar in appearance to corn (but having the grain in a panicle rather than an ear) and used for much the same purposes. Probably indigenous to Africa, it is one of the longest-cultivated plants of warm regions there and in Asia—especially in India, China, and Manchuria. Because of its extreme drought resistance (due to the unusually extensive branching root system) and its ability to withstand hotter climates than corn, sorghum has been introduced to the United States and other regions. Its innumerable varieties are generally classified as the sweet sorghums or sorgos, yielding sorghum syrups and MOLASSES from the cane juice; the broomcorns, yielding a fiber from the inflorescence that is used for making brooms; the grass sorghums (e.g., Sudan grass), used for pasture and hay; and the grain sorghums, e.g., durra, feterita, kaffir or kaffir corn, kaoliang, milo or milo maize, and shallu. The pulverized grain is used for stock and poultry feeds and, in the Old World, for human food. Sorghums also provide cover crops and green manures, grain substitutes for any industrial processes that employ corn, and fuel and weaving material from the stems. In the United States, sorghum is grown throughout the Great Plains area and in Arizona and California; about half the crop is used for forage and silage and half for feed grains. Only a small amount is grown for syrup, most of which is consumed locally. Johnson grass (*S. halapense*) is similar to Sudan grass but is a perennial. Native to the Mediterranean and naturalized in the United States, especially in the Southwest, it is a noxious weed in cultivated fields but is also used as a forage crop. Sorghum is classified in the division MAGNOLIOPHYTA, class Liliatae, order Cyperales, family Gramineae. See bulletins of the U.S. Dept. of Agriculture.

Soria (sōr'yä), town (1970 pop. 25,030), capital of Soria prov., N central Spain, in Old Castile, on the Duero River. It is the center of a pastoral region. The Church of San Pedro and the palace of the counts of Gómara are the chief landmarks. Nearby are the ruins of NUMANTIA.

Sorø (sô'rö), town (1970 com. pop. 13,930), Vestsjaelland co., E Denmark. It is a cultural and resort center. There is an academy founded by Christian IV in 1623 and other educational institutions established in the 19th cent.

Sorocaba (so͝oro͝okä'bə), city (1970 pop. 175,888), São Paulo state, S Brazil, on the Sorocaba River. It is a transportation hub and a manufacturing center where textiles, cement, vegetable oils, agricultural machinery, explosives, and food products are made. Natural resources in the municipal area include iron, gold, and silver. Sorocaba, established in 1661, was famous in the 19th cent. for its cattle fairs and iron foundry.

Sorokin, Pitirim Alexandrovitch (pĭtĭrēm' ăl"ĭgzăn'drəvĭch sōrō'kĭn), 1889–1968, Russian-American sociologist. Supporting himself as artisan and clerk, he was able to study at the Univ. of St. Petersburg and to teach sociology. Sorokin was imprisoned three times by the czarist regime; during the Russian Revolution he was a member of the Kerensky government. After the October Revolution he engaged in anti-Bolshevik activities and was condemned to death; the sentence was commuted to banishment. He emigrated (1923) to the United States and was naturalized in 1930. Sorokin was professor of sociology at the Univ. of Minnesota (1924–30) and at Harvard (1930–55). His writings cover the breadth of sociology; his controversial theories of social process and of the historical typology of cultures are expounded in *Social and Cultural Dynamics* (4 vol., 1937–41; rev. and abridged ed. 1957) and many other works. See his autobiography, *Leaves from a Russian Diary—and Thirty Years After* (enl. ed. 1950, repr. 1970); study by J. J. P. Maquet (1951, repr. 1973); F. R. Cowell, *Values in Human Society; the Contributions of P. A. Sorokin to Sociology* (1970).

Sorolla y Bastida, Joaquín (hwäkēn' sōrō'lyä ē bästē'thä), 1863–1923, Spanish painter, b. Valencia. He is noted for his large landscapes in full, glowing sunlight, painted in strong color and in a bold, fluent style. Sorolla's best-known works include *Beaching the Boat* (Hispanic Society, New York City) and *The Swimmers* (Metropolitan Mus.).

sororate: see MARRIAGE.

sorority: see FRATERNITY.

sorrel, name for several plants, particularly species of dock (see BUCKWHEAT) and OXALIS.

sorrel tree, common name for a variety of plants, including the Australian hibiscus, *Hibiscus heterophyllus,* of the MALLOW family. The staggerbush, *Lyoma mariana,* and the sourwood, *Oxydendron arboreum,* of the heath family, are also called sorrel tree.

Sorrento (sōr-rān'tō), town (1971 pop. 15,133), Campania, S Italy, on the Sorrento Peninsula, which separates the Bay of Naples from the Gulf of Salerno. Beautifully situated, it is a tourist center and a summer resort.

Sør-Trøndelag (sör'-trön'dəläg), county (1972 est. pop. 236,000), c.7,250 sq mi (18,800 sq km), central Norway, bordering on Sweden in the east. Trondheim is the capital. The county has productive farmland and extensive forests, and there are copper and pyrite mines at Røros and some industry centered at Trondheim.

SOS, code letters of the international distress signal. The signal is expressed in the Morse code as . . . — — — . . . (three dots, three dashes, three dots). This combination of letters was selected by the International Radiotelegraphic Convention at London in 1912. The letters (SOS) do not refer to any words but were selected because they are easy to transmit. The distress code by radiotelephony is MAY DAY, which corresponds to the French "m'aider." The signal PAN, not followed by a message, also has the same meaning.

Sosipater (sōsĭp'ətər), Christian at Corinth. Rom. 16.21. He is possibly the same as SOPATER.

Sosnowiec (sôsnô'vyĕts), Ger. *Sosnowitz,* city (1970 pop. 145,000), S Poland. A center of the Katowice mining and industrial region, it has coal mines and ironworks and steelworks as well as industries producing machinery, chemicals, and metals. Sosnowiec passed to Prussia in 1795, to Russia in 1815, and reverted to Poland in 1919. The city has a 17th-century castle.

Sosthenes (sŏs'thənēz). **1** Prominent Jew at Corinth, beaten by the crowd when Gallio refused to try Paul for heresy. Acts 18.17. **2** Early Christian. 1 Cor. 1.1.

Sotai (sō'tāī, sōtā'ī), family that returned from the Exile. Ezra 2.55; Neh. 7.57.

Soto, Hernando de: see DE SOTO, HERNANDO.

souari or **swarri nut,** name for tropical trees of the genus *Caryocar,* abundant in N South America. The fatty "nuts," botanically drupe fruits, somewhat resemble Brazil nuts but are much larger and richer in taste. The flesh surrounding the seeds is sometimes cooked as a vegetable or used as a meat condiment. The extracted oil (souari fat) is used in cooking and is exported commercially as a nondrying oil. Other names for the souari are piquia and paradise, butter, or guiana nut. It is also spelled suari or Sawarri.

Soubise, Benjamin de Rohan, seigneur de (bäNzhämăN' də rōăN' sānyûr' də sōōbēz'), 1583–1642, French Protestant general. He fought under Maurice of Nassau in the Netherlands and subsequently shared the leadership of the Huguenots with his brother, Henri, duc de ROHAN. He directed the defense of La Rochelle (1627–28) against Cardinal Richelieu's forces and after that city's fall retired to England.

Soufflot, Jacques Germain (zhäk zhĕrmăN' sōōflō'), 1709–80, French architect, noted chiefly as the designer of the Panthéon (see under PANTHEON) (1764–89) in Paris. He won the commission in an open competition. The building contains a remarkable masonry dome, and because of its classical features it is considered the forerunner of the eclecticism that prevailed in the architecture of the 19th cent. The dome was uncompleted at Soufflot's death, and the work was continued by others and completed by his pupil J. P. Rondelet. Soufflot's other works include the theater and the Hôtel-Dieu, Lyons, and the École de Droit, Paris.

Soufrière (sōōfrēēr'), dormant volcano, 4,813 ft (1,467 m) high, on Guadeloupe island, French West Indies. Called also La Grande Soufrière, it is the highest mountain in the Lesser Antilles. Some of its many craters emit sulfurous gases.

Soufrière, volcano, 4,048 ft (1,234 m) high, on St. Vincent island, British West Indies. On May 7, 1902, the day before the great eruption of PELÉE on Martinique island, Soufrière erupted, laying waste a third of St. Vincent, killing more than 1,000 people, and scattering a heavy fall of ash on Barbados island, c.75 mi (120 km) to the east.

soul, the vital, immaterial, life principle, generally conceived as existing within man and sometimes within all living things, inanimate objects, and the universe as a whole. Religion and philosophy have long been concerned with the nature of the soul in their attempts to understand existence and the meaning of life. In more primitive religions (forms of animism and spiritism), the soul is often conceived as controlling both motor and mental processes; death, the cessation of these processes, is thus viewed as caused by the departure of the soul. Pantheism denies the individuation of human souls, and materialism declares the soul nonexistent. One of the widespread concepts in religion is that of IMMORTALITY, which almost always postulates the existence of a soul that lives apart from the body after death. In early Hebrew thought, soul connoted the life principle, but in later times the concept of a soul independent of the body arose. The soul of the righteous was seen as achieving immortality, rejoining the resurrected body at the end of days. Similarly, in Islam, man's soul is, according to the Koran, the original spirit that God breathed into Adam. Its seat is the heart and it is endowed with two basic impulses—good and evil. After death the souls of the pious stay near Allah and will be reunited with their risen bodies on the Day of Judgment. In Eastern religions, which do not stress individual salvation, the emphasis is placed on transcendent principles embodied in a multiplicity of gods (see WORLD SOUL). The Hindu and Buddhist doctrines of reincarnation do not posit the existence of an individual soul, but rather stress the closeness of the human person, in successive transformations, to an overriding principle of virtue, piety, and peace. In Christianity the soul is all-important. However, because the Bible does not give a formal definition of the concept, Christian interpretations vary greatly. Under the influence of the Neoplatonists, the soul often came to be set over against the body in a dualistic concept that posited a God-given soul distinct from an inferior, earth-bound body. Scholasticism (specifically that of St. Thomas Aquinas) studied the soul in great elaboration, and the scholastic definition of the soul as "substantial form of the body" obviates many philosophical difficulties. The nature of man is involved in the whole consideration of the soul; hence the term "rational soul" for the distinctive soul of man. The soul of beasts is called the "animal soul," and that of plants the "vegetative soul." The scholastics considered the rational soul alone as immortal and capable of union with God. The origin of the soul has been a controversial question in Christian history. Two points of view may be distinguished: creationism, that God creates each individual soul in a special act of creation (at the time of conception according to some or that of birth according to others), and traducianism, that the parents in begetting the child beget the soul too. The creationist principle has been generally triumphant in Christianity. No distinction between the rational soul and others is made in many systems; such a distinction is quite impossible in most forms of REINCARNATION and of TRANSMIGRATION OF SOULS. The soul of humanity when such is conceived as existing is called the world soul or *anima mundi.* For many Western philosophers the term *soul* is synonymous with *mind* (e.g., René Descartes). Others, although asserting its undefinability, have seen it as a useful element in a system of ethics (e.g., Immanuel Kant). This undefinability has led yet others to reject the idea of a soul and to postulate ethical systems based upon a different conception of man's nature (e.g., William James).

Soulé, Pierre (pyĕr sōōlā'), 1801–70, American political leader and diplomat, b. Castillon, France. A lawyer, he was arrested and imprisoned for republican activities against the conservative government of the restored Bourbons, but he escaped and fled (1825) to the United States. He ultimately became a prominent citizen of New Orleans and a power in the Democratic party in Louisiana. Soulé served in the U.S. Senate in 1847 and from 1849 to 1853, when he resigned to become minister to Spain. Instructed to try to secure Cuba from Spain, he overreached himself, especially in drawing up, with James Buchanan and John Y. Mason, the notorious OSTEND MANIFESTO. After its repudiation by the United States, he resigned (Dec., 1854). In the Civil War he served (1863–64) in the Confederate government at Richmond in a minor capacity. See study by A. A. Ettinger (1932).

Soule (sōōl), small region, in Pyrénées-Atlantiques dept., SW France, bordering on Spain. Mauléon-Licharre is the traditional capital. An ancient province of the Basque country, it was annexed to the French crown lands in 1451.

Souli, Greece: see SULI.

Soulouque, Faustin Élie (fōstăN' ālē' sōōlōōk'), c.1785–1867, Negro emperor of Haiti (1849–59). An illiterate former slave, he became president in 1847 and then declared himself emperor as Faustin I. His reign was corrupt, sanguinary, and terror-ridden; his court was a caricature of Napoleon's. Although he failed in his attempt to conquer Santo Domingo, he held Haiti under stern control until overthrown by a revolution led by Nicholas Fabre GEFFRARD.

Soult, Nicolas Jean de Dieu (nēkôlä' zhäN də dyö sōōlt), 1769–1851, marshal of France. Having won distinction in the Napoleonic Wars, especially at the battle of Austerlitz, he was created (1808) duke of Dalmatia and was given command in the PENINSULAR WAR. After the restoration (1814) of the monarchy, King Louis XVIII made him minister of war, but he rejoined Napoleon I in the Hundred Days (1815). Exiled after the second restoration, he returned to France in 1819, was restored to his rank, and was made (1827) a peer by King Charles X. Under King Louis Philippe, Soult held several ministerial posts, including that of premier (1832–34, 1839–40, 1840–47). His last premiership was only nominal, since his cabinet was really dominated by François GUIZOT, who succeeded him.

Sound, the: see ØRESUND, Denmark and Sweden.

sound. When a body vibrates, or moves back and forth (see VIBRATION), the oscillation causes a periodic disturbance of the surrounding air or other medium that radiates outward in straight lines in the form of a pressure WAVE. The effect these waves produce upon the ear is perceived as sound. Sounds are generally audible to the human ear if their frequency (number of vibrations per second) lies between 20 and 20,000 vibrations per second, but the range varies considerably with the individual. Sound waves with frequencies less than those of audible waves are called subsonic; those with frequencies above the audible range are called ultrasonic (see ULTRASONICS). From the point of view of physics, sound is considered to be the waves of vibratory motion themselves, whether or not they are heard by the human ear. When a violin string vibrates upon being bowed or plucked, its movement in one direction pushes the molecules of the air before it, crowding them together in its path. When it moves back again past its original position and on to the other side, it leaves behind it a nearly empty space, i.e., a space with relatively few molecules in it. In the meantime, however, the molecules which were at first crowded together have transmitted some of their energy of motion to other molecules still farther on and are returning to fill again the space originally occupied and now left empty by the retreating violin string. In other words, the vibratory motion set up by the violin string causes alternately in a given space a crowding together of the molecules of air (a condensation) and a thinning out of the molecules (a rarefaction). Taken together a condensation and a rarefaction make up a sound wave; such a wave is called longitudinal, or compressional, because the vibratory motion is forward and backward along the direction that the wave is following. Because such a wave travels by disturbing the particles of a material medium, sound waves cannot travel through a vacuum. A sound wave is usually represented graphically by a wavy, horizontal line; the upper part of the wave (the crest) indicates a condensation and the lower part (the trough) indicates a rarefaction. This graph, however, is merely a representation and is not an actual picture of a wave. The length of a sound wave, or the wavelength, is measured as the distance from one point of greatest condensation to the next following it or from any point on one wave to the corresponding point on the next in a train of waves. The wavelength depends upon the velocity of sound in a given medium at a given temperature and upon the frequency of vibration. The wavelength of a sound can be determined by dividing the numerical value for the velocity of sound in the given medium at the given temperature by the frequency of vibration. For example, if the velocity of sound in air is 1,130 ft per second and the frequency of vibration is 256, then the wave length is approximately 4.4 ft. The velocity of sound is not constant, however, for it

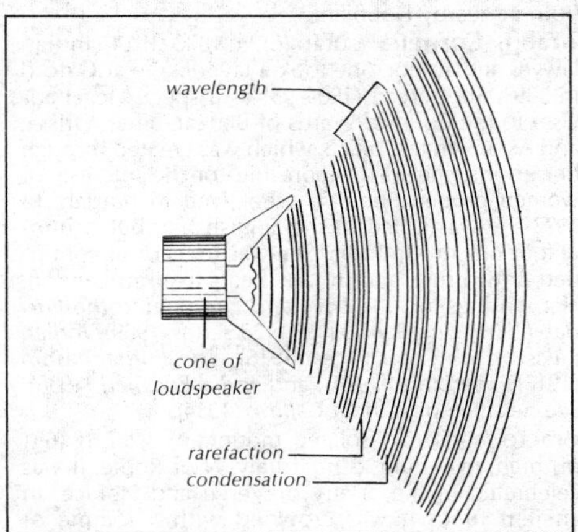

Sound waves: An air pressure wave radiating outward from a loudspeaker is perceived as sound.

varies in different media and in the same medium at different temperatures. For example, in air at 0°C. it is approximately 1,089 ft per second, but at 20°C. it is increased to about 1,130 ft per second, or an increase of about 2 ft per second for every centigrade degree rise in temperature. Sound travels more slowly in gases than in liquids, and more slowly in liquids than in solids. Since the ability to conduct sound is dependent on the density of the medium, solids are better conductors than liquids, liquids are better conductors than gases. Sound waves can be reflected, refracted (or bent), and absorbed as light waves can be. The reflection of sound waves can result in an ECHO—an important factor in the ACOUSTICS of theaters and auditoriums. A sound wave can be reinforced with waves from a body having the same frequency of vibration, but the combination of waves of different frequencies of vibration may produce so-called "beats" or pulsations or may result in other forms of INTERFERENCE. Musical sounds are distinguished from noises in that they are composed of regular, uniform vibrations, while noises are irregular and disordered vibrations. Composers, however, frequently use noises as well as musical sounds. One musical tone is distinguished from another on the basis of pitch, intensity, or loudness, and quality, or timbre. Pitch describes how high or low a tone is and depends upon the rapidity with which a sounding body vibrates, i.e., upon the frequency of vibration. The higher the frequency of vibration, the higher the tone; the pitch of a siren gets higher and higher as the frequency of vibration increases. The apparent change in the pitch of a sound as a source approaches or moves away from an observer is described by the DOPPLER EFFECT. The intensity or loudness of a sound depends upon the extent to which the sounding body vibrates, i.e., the amplitude of vibration. A sound is louder as the amplitude of vibration is greater, and the intensity decreases as the distance from the source increases. Loudness is measured in units called DECIBELS. The sound waves given off by different vibrating bodies differ in quality, or timbre. A note from a saxophone, for instance, differs from a note of the same pitch and intensity produced by a violin or a xylophone; similarly vibrating reeds, columns of air, and strings all differ. Quality is dependent on the number and relative intensity of overtones produced by the vibrating body (see HARMONIC), and these in turn depend upon the nature of the vibrating body. See Graham Chedd, *Sound* (1970).

sound barrier: see AERODYNAMICS.

sound recording, process of converting the acoustic energy of sound into some form in which it can be permanently stored and reproduced at any time. In 1855 inventor Leon Scott constructed a device called a phonautograph that recorded tracings of the vibrations of sound. Thomas Edison, starting about 1877, made great improvements in mechanical sound recording and was the first inventor to achieve the actually audible reproduction of recorded sound; the greatest advances, however, were made after the adoption in 1925 of electromechanical systems using electronic amplifiers (see RECORD PLAYER). Generally, in recording, the sound waves impinge on a microphone and are converted into an electrical signal that is recorded by a tape recorder. The tape can be edited if desired. When a commercial record is to be made, a disk of soft acetate composition coated on an aluminum base, called an original, is placed on a rotating turntable. The tape is played back and controls a stylus which cuts a spiral groove starting from the outer edge and moving to the inner of the original. For monophonic sound the stylus vibrates from side to side as it cuts the groove. For stereophonic sound the stylus vibrates vertically, as well as from side to side, recording one sound channel in the left wall of the groove and one in the right. In a series of steps the original is used to make a metal stamper that presses the groove into commercial records. In order to play a commercial record, a stylus, or needle, is placed in the disk's groove while it is in motion on a turntable. The vibrations of the stylus cause the transducer to which it is attached to produce a varying voltage. This voltage is amplified and fed into a loudspeaker. In magnetic tape systems the varying electrical voltage is converted in a small electromagnet, called a head, into a varying magnetic field that causes magnetic particles imbedded in the tape to become aligned in varying degrees as the tape passes through the magnetic field. On playback, the magnetic tape moves past the head, generating a varying voltage in the coil of the head, which is boosted in an amplifier and converted to sound by a loudspeaker. Motion picture sound tracks are called optical recordings. The sound to be recorded is converted into an electrical signal that is used to modulate the intensity of a beam of light. This modulated beam exposes a moving film to make a recording of the sound. Reproduction is effected by shining a steady beam of light through the developed film that is the sound track. As the film moves across the light beam, some of the light passes through it into a photocell, the amplified output of which activates a loudspeaker. See TAPE RECORDER. See H. M. Tremaine, *Audio Cyclopedia* (1969); H. F. Olson, *Modern Sound Reproduction* (1972).

soup, liquid food, in which different kinds of solid food have been cooked, e.g., meat, fish, fowl, vegetables, cereals, or fruit. Many soups are peculiar to certain localities, e.g., the pot-au-feu of France, the borscht of Russia, the mutton broth of Scotland, the minestrone of Italy, and the chowders of various seacoast places. Broth is a thin soup of meat or shellfish liquor, sometimes with cereals added, as in barley broth. Clear soups, made from a rich meat stock, include consommé (beef, veal, or fowl) and bouillon (beef or chicken). A clear soup with finely shredded vegetables added is a julienne soup. Thick soups include vegetable soups made with stock and vegetables (as in pot-au-feu) or with milk and flour (cream soups) or by cooking fish and vegetables in water as for a CHOWDER. A puree differs from a cream soup in that it is thickened with pulp, usually of a vegetable; sometimes, particularly when made with fish, it is called a bisque. Gumbo is either vegetable or meat soup thickened with okra. Stock, the basis of a great many soups, is made by placing lean meat, bones, fowl, fish, or vegetables in cold water, simmering in a covered pot, skimming, straining, and removing the fat. Bones supply marrow and gelatin. The bones of old animals are much richer in marrow and gelatin than those of young ones. Stock is either white or brown; for white, fowl or veal is used; for brown, beef and beef bones or beef combined with veal are used. Jellied soups, served as appetizers in hot weather, may be made from stock or from strained vegetable juices with the addition of gelatin. Gazpacho, the cold soup of Spain, is made of cucumbers, tomatoes, onions, peppers, and seasonings in a base of tomato juice. Soups vary widely as to dietary value. The clear, delicately seasoned ones are important as appetizers and appetite stimulants, while the more substantial ones, like chowders, form, with the addition of bread, a one-dish meal.

Soupault, Philippe (fēlēp' so͞opō'), 1897–, French poet, novelist, critic, and political activist. He took an active role in the dadaist movement and later founded the surrealist movement with André BRETON (see DADA; SURREALISM). After imprisonment by the Nazis in World War II, Soupault traveled to the United States but subsequently returned to France. His works include such volumes of poetry as *Aquarium* (1917) and *Rose des vents* [compass card] (1920) and the novel *Les Dernières Nuits de Paris* (1928; tr. *Last Nights of Paris,* 1929).

Souphanouvong, Prince (so͞ofä'no͞ovông"), 1902–, Laotian government official; half brother of Prince SOUVANNA PHOUMA. Of royal background, he was an active nationalist and fought the French as a member of the pro-Communist Pathet Lao. He formed the Nationalist party in 1950 and later served (1958) as a cabinet minister. Arrested in 1959, he escaped in 1960 to lead the Pathet Lao forces opposing the government and then was a Pathet Lao delegate to the Geneva conference on Laos (1961–62). In the coalition government that followed, he was vice premier and minister of economic planning. The coalition was short-lived, however, and he soon rejoined the Pathet Lao. In 1973 an agreement was reached with Souvanna Phouma ending the fighting between Pathet Lao and government troops. A new coalition government was formed (1974), in which Souphanouvong became president of the National Political Council, an advisory body.

sour gum: see BLACK GUM.

Souris (so͞or'ĭs), river, c.450 mi (720 km) long, rising in S Sask., Canada, and flowing southeast with a great loop into N. Dak. (passing Minot), then N and NE to the Assiniboine River in SW Man.

Souris East, town (1971 pop. 1,393), NE Prince Edward Island, Canada, on the Gulf of St. Lawrence. Settled in 1748 by Acadians, it is a fishing port.

Sousa, John Philip (so͞o'zə, -sə), 1854–1932, American bandmaster and composer, b. Washington, D.C. He studied violin and harmony in his native city and learned band instruments as an apprentice to the U.S. Marine Band, of which his father was a member. Early in his career he conducted theater orchestras, and he played in Offenbach's orchestra in its American tour (1876–77). Sousa was leader of the U.S. Marine Band from 1880 until 1892, when he formed his own band. With great success he toured the United States, Canada, Europe, and other parts of the world. He composed about 100 marches, many of which became immensely popular, including "Semper fidelis" (1888), "The Washington Post March" (1889), "The Stars and Stripes Forever" (1897), and "Hands across the Sea" (1899). He also wrote comic operas, such as *El capitan* (1896), *The Bride Elect* (1898), and *The Free Lance* (1906); and some orchestral music. In the development of the concert band he was the successor of Patrick S. Gilmore and did much to improve the instrumentation and quality of band music. See his autobiography, *Marching Along* (1928); biographies by A. M. Lingg (1954), K. Berger (1957), and P. E. Bierley (1973).

Sousa, Martim Afonso de (mərtēm' əfôn'zō dĭ sō'-zə), 1500?–1564, Portuguese colonial administrator. A military man, he was commissioned in 1530 to drive the French corsairs from the Brazilian coasts and to establish colonies. He succeeded in clearing the coasts, founded the colony of São Vicente, established sugarcane growing, and introduced other crops and cattle. He initiated the successful settlement and colonization of Brazil that was continued by Tomé de Sousa, Mem de SÁ, and the Jesuits Manuel de Nóbrega and José de ANCHIETA.

souslik: see GROUND SQUIRREL.

Sousse: see SUSAH, Tunisia.

South, Robert, 1634–1716, English clergyman. He was ordained in 1658. After the Restoration he was appointed public orator (1660) at Oxford Univ. and then a prebendary (1663) of Westminster, a canon (1670) of Christ Church, Oxford, and rector (1678) of Islip. In his vigorous defense of the Church of England, he firmly opposed both dissenters and Roman Catholics, and preached the divine right of kings. In 1693 he entered into a controversy with William Sherlock, publishing *Animadversions upon Dr. Sherlock's Book Entitled a Vindication of the Holy and Ever-Blessed Trinity* (1693). The king put an end to the disputation that followed. South is chiefly remembered for his pithy, vigorous sermons; his *Sermons Preached upon Several Occasions* (1679) has passed through a number of editions.

South, the, region of the United States embracing the southeastern and south-central parts of the country. It includes, at the most, 14 states—Maryland, Virginia, North Carolina, South Carolina, Georgia, Florida, Kentucky, Tennessee, Alabama, Mississippi, Arkansas, Louisiana, Oklahoma, and Texas. Traditionally, all states S of the MASON-DIXON LINE and the Ohio River (except West Virginia) make up the South, but to many the region is restricted to the 11 states S of the Potomac River that comprised the CONFEDERACY—those named above minus Maryland and Kentucky, border slave states which were held for the Union in the Civil War, and Oklahoma, which did not become a state until 1907. Missouri and Delaware were two other border slave states in which the Southern tradition was strong. The South has long been a section apart, even though it is not isolated by any formidable natural barriers and is itself divided into many distinctive regions: the coastal plains along the Atlantic Ocean and the Gulf of Mexico; the Piedmont; the ridges, valleys, and high mountains bordering the Piedmont, especially the Great Smoky Mts. in North Carolina and Tennessee; areas of bluegrass, black-soiled prairies, and clay hills west of the mountains; bluffs, flood plains, bayous, and delta lands along the Mississippi River; and W of the Mississippi, the interior plains, the Ozark Plateau, and large stretches of arid lands. The climate, however, is one unifying factor. Over the year the region has greater humidity, more sunshine, and less wind than other sections. Winters are neither long nor very cold, and no month averages below freezing; rainfall is heavy. The long, hot growing season (nine months at its peak along the Gulf) and the fertile soil (much of it overworked or ruined by erosion) make the South an agricultural region where such staples as tobacco, cotton (see BLACK BELT), corn, and, to a lesser extent, rice and sugarcane have long flourished; citrus fruits, livestock, and timber are also important. Petroleum and natural gas are the region's chief mineral resources. It now has diversified industries, and the tourist trade is important there. The chief cities of the South are Houston, Dallas, New Orleans, Atlanta, and Miami.

History. The basic agricultural economy of the Old South, which was determined by the climate and the soil, led to the introduction (1617) of the Negro as a source of cheap labor under the twin institutions of the plantation and SLAVERY. Slavery might well have expired had not the invention of the cotton gin (1793) given it a firmer hold, but even so there would have remained the problem of racial tension. The central theme in the history of the South—and as Rupert B. Vance says, "history, not geography, made the solid South"—is, the historian Ulrich B. Phillips concluded, "white supremacy," which, until the defeat of the South in the Civil War, was almost completely identified with the perpetuation of slavery. Although Southerners had taken care to have their "peculiar institution" protected by the Constitution of the United States, it was not until the period beginning with the MISSOURI COMPROMISE (1820-21) that the South definitely became "a conscious minority" in the nation. That event marked the rise of Southern sectionalism, rooted in the political doctrine of STATES' RIGHTS, with John C. CALHOUN as its greatest advocate. When differences with the North, especially over the issue of the extension of slavery into the Federal territories, ultimately appeared insoluble, the South turned (1860-61) the doctrine of states' rights into SECESSION (or independence), which in turn led inevitably to the CIVIL WAR. Most of the major battles and campaigns of the war were fought in the South, and by the end of the war, with slavery abolished and most of the area in ruins, the Old South had died. The period of RECONSTRUCTION following the war set the South's political and social attitude for years to come. During this difficult time radical Republicans, CARPETBAGGERS, Negroes, and SCALAWAGS ruled the South with the support of Federal troops. The white Southerners, objecting to this rule, resorted to terrorism and violence and, with the aid of such organizations as the KU KLUX KLAN, drove the Reconstruction governments from power. The breakdown of the plantation system during the Civil War gave rise to sharecropping, the tenant-farming system of agriculture that still exists in areas of the South. The last half of the 19th cent. saw the beginning of industrialization in the South, with the introduction of textile mills and various industries. The troubled economic and political life of the region in the years between 1880 and World War II was marked by the rise of the Farmers' Alliance, Populism, and Jim Crow laws and by the careers of such Southerners as Tom WATSON, Theodore BILBO, Benjamin TILLMAN, Huey LONG, Sam Rayburn, and Lyndon JOHNSON. Since World War II the South has been experiencing profound political, economic, and social change. Southern reaction to the policies of the New Deal, the Fair Deal, the New Frontier, and the Great Society caused the emergence of a genuine two-party system in certain states of the South and led conservative Southern Democrats into a close congressional liaison with Northern conservative Republicans. The influx of new industries into the region has made the economic life of the South more diversified and more similar to that of other sections of the United States. Of more importance, the Negro became unwilling to accept continued inequality. Aided by advocates of full civil rights for all citizens and supported by the Federal courts, the Southern Negro has made great progress in ending political inferiority and social segregation. The advocates of white supremacy resisted the change bitterly and sometimes violently (see INTEGRATION), but many Southerners have recognized the futility of resisting the inevitable and have realized that the South's failure to move toward a nationally acceptable solution of the race problem has been retarding the region. From William Byrd (1674-1744) to William Faulkner the South has always had a strong regional literature. Its principal subject has been the Civil War, reflected in song from Paul Hamilton Hayne to Allen Tate and in novels from Thomas Nelson Page to Margaret Mitchell. See works by Clement Eaton, H. W. Odum, U. B. Phillips, and C. Vann Woodward; W. J. Cash, *The Mind of the South* (1941); W. H. Stephenson and E. M. Coulter, ed., *A History of the South* (10 vol., 1947-73); V. O. Key, Jr., *Southern Politics in State and Nation* (1949); J. F. Hart, *The Southeastern United States* (1967); T. D. Clark, *The Emerging South* (1961, repr. 1968), and *The South Since Reconstruction* (1972); F. B. Simkins and C. P. Roland, *A History of the South* (4th ed. 1972).

South, University of the, called **Sewanee,** at Sewanee, Tenn., E of Winchester; Episcopal; coeducational; chartered 1858, opened 1868. It has a college of arts and sciences and a theological school. The university publishes the *Sewanee Review,* an influential literary magazine. See history by A. B. Chitty (1954).

South Africa, Republic of, Afrikaans *Republiek van Suid-Afrika,* republic (1970 pop. 21,448,172), 471,442 sq mi (1,221,037 sq km), S Africa, bordering on the Atlantic Ocean in the west, on South West Africa in the northwest, on Botswana and Rhodesia in the north, on Mozambique and Swaziland in the northeast, and on the Indian Ocean in the east and south. SOUTH WEST AFRICA (Namibia) is administered as an integral part of the country, and Lesotho is an independent enclave in the east. The administrative capital of South Africa is PRETORIA; the legislative capital is CAPE TOWN; the judicial capital is BLOEMFONTEIN. The republic is divided into four provinces: Cape of Good Hope (see CAPE PROVINCE), NATAL, ORANGE FREE STATE, and TRANSVAAL. In addition, under acts of Parliament (especially those of 1951, 1959, and 1971) about 14% of the country's land area was designated to be set aside for black Africans in ultimately independent territories ("Bantustans"). As of late 1974, nine such territories (Basotho-Qwaqwa, Bophuthatswana, Ciskei, Gazankulu, Kwazulu, Lebowa, South Ndebele, TRANSKEI, and Venda) were planned; all except Basotho-Qwaqwa, Kwazulu, and South Ndebele had been given limited internal self-government. South Africa has three main geographic regions: a great interior plateau; an escarpment of mountain ranges that rims the plateau on the east, south, and west; and a marginal area lying between the escarpment and the sea. Most of the plateau consists of highveld, rolling grassland situated at 4,000 to 6,000 ft (1,220-1,830 m). In addition, in the northeast are the WITWATERSRAND (a ridge of rock where gold has been mined since 1886), the Bushveld Basin (a zone of savanna situated at 2,000-3,000 ft/610-910 m), and the Limpopo River basin; in the north are the southern fringes of the Kalahari desert; and in the west is the semiarid Cape middleveld, which includes part of the Orange River and is situated at 2,500 to 4,000 ft (760-1,220 m). The escarpment reaches its greatest heights (10,000-11,000 ft/3,050-3,350 m) in the Drakensberg Mts. in the east. The marginal area varies in width between 35 and 150 mi (60-240 km) and most of it is bordered by a narrow, low-lying coastal strip. The region also includes considerable stretches of grassland in the east; mountains and the semiarid Great and Little Karroo tablelands in the south; and desert (a southern extension of the Namib desert) in the west. KRUGER NATIONAL PARK is in NE South Africa. According to the official classifications of the 1970 census, the population of South Africa is made up of 14,741,000 black Africans ("Bantus"); 3,751,000 whites; 2,019,000 people of mixed white, Malayan, and black African descent ("Coloureds"); and 620,000 Asians, most of whom are Hindus of Indian descent. The black Africans fall into 10 main groups, based on their first language: Zulu (4,026,000 members), Xhosa (3,930,000), Tswana (1,719,000), Sepedi or North Sotho (1,604,000), Seshoeshoe or South Sotho (1,453,000), Shangaan (737,000), Swazi (499,000), Venda (358,000), South Ndebele (233,000), and North Ndebele (182,000). Afrikaans is the first language of about 60% of the whites and about 90% of the Coloureds; English is the first language of most of the rest of the whites and Coloureds and of most of the Asians. Many of the black Africans also speak English or Afrikaans, which are both official languages of the country. About 2 million whites belong to the influential Dutch Reformed Church, and about 965,000 nonwhites are members of Dutch Reformed Mission Churches; about 1.5 million persons (of all ethnic backgrounds) belong to the Anglican church; about 1.5 million nonwhites and about 300,000 whites are Methodists; about 1.2 million persons (including about 500,000 black Africans) are Roman Catholic; and about 700,000 nonwhites and 40,000 whites are Lutherans. In addition, there are about 2,000 independent black African Christian groups with a total of about 2.5 million members. Until about 1870 the economy of the region was almost entirely based on agriculture. With the discovery (1867) of diamonds along the Vaal and Orange rivers, mining became the foundation for rapid economic development; this process was accelerated by the discovery (1886) of gold on the Witwatersrand. In the 20th cent. the country's economy was diversified, so that by 1945 manufacturing was the leading contributor to the annual national product. At the end of the 1960s, manufacturing contributed about 23% of the annual national product; trade and tourism about 14%; mining and quarrying about 12%; finance, insurance, and real estate about 10%; and agriculture, forestry, and fishing about 9.5%. However, within the money economy, about 37% of the work force was employed in agriculture and only about 29% in manufacturing (including construction); in addition, many nonwhites worked as subsistence farmers. The economy is controlled by whites, but nonwhites make up more than 75% of the work force. Many black Africans work as contract laborers for specified periods (usually 12 months) in factories and mines, and they live (apart from their families, which remain in rural areas) in special housing complexes. Roughly 500,000 black African migratory workers from Mozambique, Rhodesia, Lesotho, Malawi, and Botswana are employed

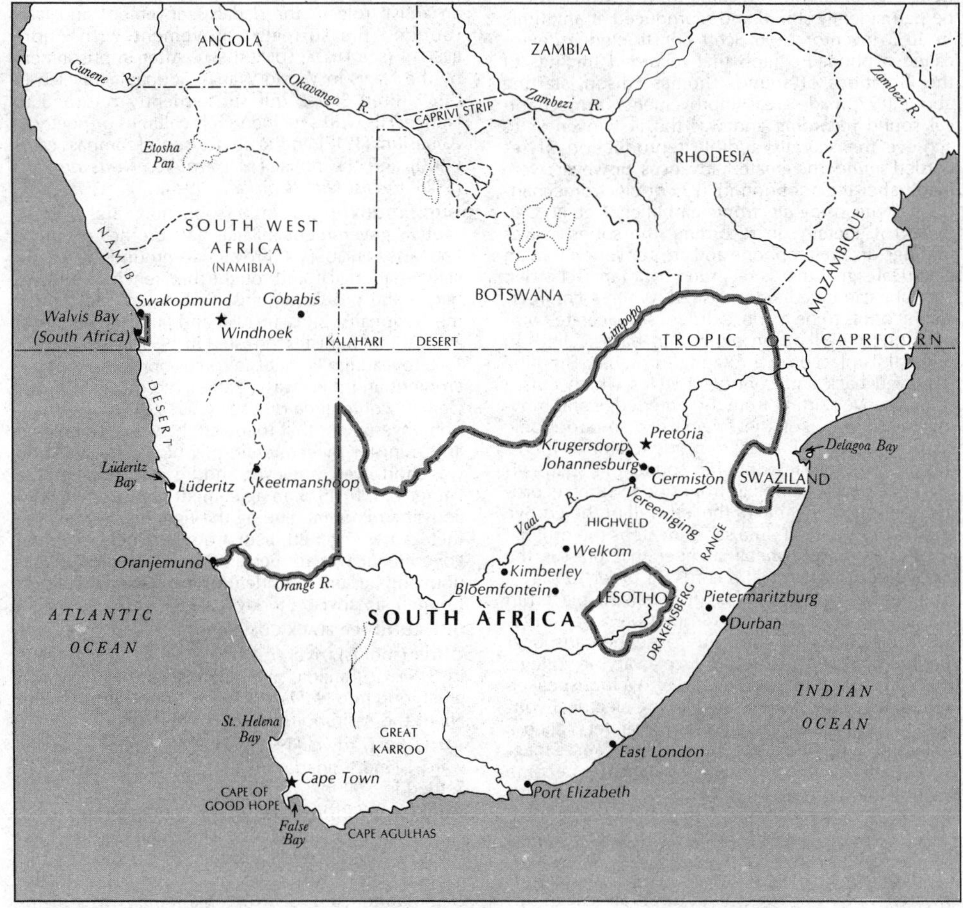

in South Africa, mainly in the gold mines. About 15% of the land in South Africa is arable. The chief crops grown are maize, wheat, oats, barley, sorghum, potatoes, groundnuts, deciduous and citrus fruit, cotton, tobacco, and sugarcane. In addition, large numbers of dairy and beef cattle, sheep, goats (including many Angora goats), and hogs are raised. The main industrial centers are JOHANNESBURG, Cape Town, PORT ELIZABETH, DURBAN, Pretoria, and GERMISTON. The principal manufactures are processed food, beverages (including wine), textiles, clothing, forest products, chemicals, iron and steel, metal products, machinery, and motor vehicles. The leading minerals extracted (in terms of value) are gold (South Africa produces about 67% of the annual world total), copper ore, coal, gem and industrial diamonds, asbestos, iron ore, platinum, chrome, antimony, and manganese. There is a large fishing industry, and much fishmeal is produced. The country has good road and rail networks; the chief seaports are Durban, Cape Town, Port Elizabeth, EAST LONDON, and Mosselbaai (Mossel Bay). The Orange River Project, a major hydroelectric and irrigation scheme, is under way (to be completed c.2000) in central South Africa. South Africa carries on a large-scale foreign trade, and the annual value of imports is usually considerably higher than the value of exports. However, the trade deficit is more than covered by foreign sales of gold. The main imports are machinery, transport equipment, manufactured consumer goods, chemicals, petroleum and petroleum products, industrial raw materials, and foodstuffs; the chief exports are manufactured goods, woolens, foodstuffs, and diamonds. The principal trade partners are Great Britain, the United States, West Germany, and Japan.

History. Little is known about the prehistory of South Africa, but remains of early man dating to the late Paleolithic period have been found in the country. By the first millennium A.D. the southern and central parts of the country were inhabited by KHOIKHOI (Hottentots) and small bands of SAN (Bushmen). By about 1500, Bantu-speaking black Africans moving southward from E central Africa, had reached the region between the Great Kei and the Great Fish rivers in SE South Africa. In 1488, Bartolomeu DIAS, a Portuguese navigator, became the first European to round the Cape of Good Hope (so-named by King John II of Portugal). The diaries of shipwrecked Portuguese sailors attest to a large Bantu-speaking population in present-day Natal by 1552. Although European seamen frequently passed by South Africa on their way to E Africa and India, and sometimes stopped for provisions or rest, no permanent European settlement was made until 1652, when Jan van Riebeeck and about 90 other persons set up a provisioning station for the Dutch East India Company at Table Bay on the Cape of Good Hope. Soon van Riebeeck began to trade with nearby Khoikhoi, gave Europeans lands to establish private farms, and brought in black Africans from W and E Africa, and Malayans, as slaves. By 1662, about 250 Europeans were living near the Cape and gradually they moved inland, founding STELLENBOSCH in 1679. In 1689 about 200 Huguenot refugees from Europe arrived; they established a wine industry and intermarried with the earlier Dutch settlers. By 1707 there were about 1,780 freeholders of European descent in South Africa, and they owned about 1,100 slaves. By the early 18th cent., most San had migrated into inaccessible parts of the country to avoid European domination; the more numerous Khoikhoi either remained near the Cape, where they became virtual serfs of the Europeans, or dispersed into the interior. A great smallpox outbreak in 1713 killed many Europeans and most of the Khoikhoi living near the Cape. During the 18th cent. interbreeding between Khoikhoi, slaves, and Europeans began to create what became later known as the Coloured population. At the same time white farmers (known as BOERS) began to TREK (journey) increasingly farther from the Cape in search of pasture and cropland. By 1750 some farmers had migrated to the region between the Gamtoos and Great Fish rivers, where they encountered the Xhosa. At first the whites and blacks engaged in friendly trade, but in 1779 the first of a long series of so-called Kaffir Wars (1789, 1799, 1812, 1819, 1834, 1846, 1850, 1877) broke out between them, primarily over land and cattle ownership. The whites sought to establish the Great Fish as the southern frontier of the Xhosa. During the French Revolutionary and Napoleonic Wars the British replaced the Dutch at the Cape from 1795 to 1803 and again from 1806 to 1814, when the territory was assigned to Great Britain by the Congress of Vienna. In 1820, 5,000 British settlers were given small farms near the Great Fish River. They were intended to form a barrier to the southern movement of the Xhosa, but most soon gave up farming and moved to nearby towns such as Port Elizabeth and GRAHAMSTOWN. They were the first large body of Europeans not to be assimilated into the Afrikaner culture that had developed in the 17th and 18th cent. Great Britain disaffected the Boers by remodeling the administration along British lines, by tending to call for better treatment of the Coloured and black Africans who worked for the Boers as servants or slaves, by granting (Ordinance 50, 1828) free nonwhites legal rights equal to those of the whites, and by restricting the acquisition of new land by the Boers. In 1833 slavery was abolished in the British Empire, and slaveowners in South Africa were given only slight compensation for their loss; in addition, the compensation proved difficult to obtain. Seeking freedom from the restrictions of British rule as well as new land, about 12,000 Boers left the Cape between 1835 and 1843 in what is known as the Great Trek. Led by Andries Potgieter, Gerit Marais, Piet Retief, and others, the Voortrekkers (as these Boers are known) migrated beyond the Orange River. Some remained in the highveld of the interior, forming isolated communities and small states. Retief led a large group eastward into Natal, where he and 70 other Boers were killed (Feb., 1838) at the hands of Dingaan, the Zulu chief. This massacre was avenged (Dec., 1838) by Andries PRETORIUS at the battle of Blood River, and the Boers proceeded to establish farms in Natal. However, most of them migrated back to the interior after Britain annexed Natal in 1843. In the 1850s the Boer republics of the Orange Free State and the Transvaal were established. In 1860 the first indentured laborers from India arrived in Natal to work on the sugar plantations, and by 1900 they outnumbered the whites there. Diamonds were discovered in 1867 along the Vaal and Orange rivers and in 1870 at what became (1871) KIMBERLEY; in 1886 gold was discovered on the Witwatersrand. These discoveries (especially that of gold) spurred great economic development in S Africa during 1870–1900; foreign trade increased dramatically, rail trackage expanded from c.70 mi (110 km) in 1870 to c.3,600 mi (5,790 km) in 1895, and the number of whites rose from about 300,000 in 1870 to about one million in 1900. At the same time there were complex political developments. In 1871 the British annexed the diamond-mining region (known as Griqualand West), despite the protests of the Orange Free State. Seeking to unite the various territories of S Africa, Britain annexed the Transvaal in 1877 but, after a revolt, restored its independence in 1881. In 1889, Cape Colony and the Orange Free State joined in a customs union, but the Transvaal (led by Paul KRUGER, known as Oom Paul) adamantly refused to take part. In 1890, Cecil J. RHODES, an ardent advocate of federation in S Africa, became prime minister of Cape Colony, and by 1894 he was encouraging the non-Afrikaner whites (known as the Uitlanders) in the Transvaal to overthrow Kruger. In Dec., 1895, Leander Starr JAMESON, a close associate of Rhodes, invaded the Transvaal with a small force, planning to assist a hoped-for Uitlander rising; however, the Uitlanders did not revolt, and Jameson was defeated by early Jan., 1896. Tension mounted in the following years as British Prime Minister Joseph Chamberlain and the British high commissioner in South Africa, Alfred MILNER, supported the Uitlanders against the dominant Afrikaners. In 1896, the Transvaal and the Orange Free State formed an alliance, and in 1899 they declared war on Great Britain. The SOUTH AFRICAN WAR (Boer War; 1899–1902) was won by the British. In 1910 the Union of South Africa, with dominion status, was established by the British; it included Cape of Good Hope, Natal, the Orange Free State, and the Transvaal as provinces. Under the Union's constitution, power was centralized; the Dutch language (and in 1925 Afrikaans) was given equal status with English, and each province retained its existing franchise qualifications (the Cape's were somewhat more generous to nonwhites). After elections in 1910, Louis BOTHA became the first prime minister; he headed the South African party, an amalgam of Afrikaner parties that advocated close cooperation between Afrikaners and persons of British descent. In 1912, J. B. M. HERTZOG founded the Afrikaner-oriented Nationalist party. By 1914, largely as a result of the efforts of Mohandas K. GANDHI, Indian immigration into South Africa had stopped, and the Indians living there were receiving somewhat better treatment. Botha led (1914) South Africa into World War I on the side of the Allies and quickly squashed a revolt by Afrikaners who opposed this alignment. In 1915, South African forces captured South West Africa from the Germans, and after the war the territory was placed under the Union as a League of Nations mandate. In 1919, Botha was succeeded as prime minister by his close associate J. C. SMUTS. In 1921–22 skilled white mine workers on the Witwatersrand, fearful of losing their jobs to lower-paid nonwhites, staged a major strike, which Smuts ended only with a use of force that cost about 230 lives. In 1924, Hertzog became prime minister and remained in office until 1939; from 1934 to 1939 he was supported by Smuts, with whom he formed the United South African National party. Hertzog led an Afrikaner cultural and economic revival; was influential in gaining additional British recognition of South African independence (through the Balfour Declaration of 1926 and the Statute of Westminster of 1931); took (Dec., 1932) South Africa off the gold standard, thus raising the price of gold and stimulating the gold-mining industry and the economy in general; curtailed the electoral power of nonwhites; and furthered the system of allocating "reserved" areas for black Africans as their permanent homes and at the same time regulating their movement in the remainder of the country. With the outbreak of World War II, the Smuts-Hertzog alliance disintegrated. Winning a crucial vote in parliament (Sept., 1939), Smuts became prime minister again and brought South Africa into the war on the British (Allied) side; Hertzog, who was not alarmed by Nazi German aggression and had little affection for Great Britain, went into opposition. South African troops made an important contribution to the Allied war effort, helping to end Italian control in Ethiopia and fighting with distinction in Italy and Madagascar. The Nationalist party won the 1948 elections, partly by criticizing the somewhat liberal policy toward nonwhites associated with Jan Hofmeyr, Smuts's close aid. D. F. Malan of the Nationalist party was prime minister from 1948 to 1954, and he was followed by J. G. Strijdom (1954–58), H. F. VERWOERD (1958–66), and B. J. VORSTER (1966–)—all members of the Nationalist party, which won succeeding general elections (1953, 1958, 1961, 1966, and 1970) by substantial margins. These governments greatly strengthened white control of the country. The policy of segregating whites and nonwhites, known as APARTHEID [Afrikaans,=apartness], in almost all social relations was further implemented by a varied series of laws that included additional curbs on free movement (partly through the use of passbooks, which most black Africans were required to carry) and the planned establishment of a number of independent homelands for black African ethnic groups. The black Africans had long protested their inferior treatment through organizations such as the African National Congress (ANC; founded 1912) and the Industrial and Commercial Workers Union of Africa (founded 1919 by Clements Kadalie). In the 1950s and early 60s there were various protests against the Nationalist party's policies, involving passive resistance and the burning of passbooks; in 1960 a peaceful protest against the pass laws organized by the Pan-Africanist Congress (an offshoot of the ANC) at Sharpville (near Johannesburg) ended when police opened fire, killing about 70 protesters and wounding about 190 others. In the 1960s most leaders (whites as well as blacks) of the opposition to apartheid were either in jail or were living in exile, and the government proceeded with its plans to segregate the black Africans on a more permanent basis. In 1961, South Africa left the British Commonwealth of Nations (whose members were strongly critical of South Africa's apartheid policies) and became a republic. The first president of the new republic was C. R. Swart; he was succeeded by T. E. Donges (1967–68) and J. J. Fouché (1968–). In the 1960s there were international attempts to wrest South West Africa from South Africa's control, but South Africa tenaciously maintained its hold on the territory. In 1966, Prime Minister Verwoerd was assassinated by a discontented white government employee. From the late 1960s, the Vorster government began to try to start a dialogue on racial and other matters with independent black African nations; these attempts met with little success, except for the establishment of diplomatic relations with Malawi and the adjacent nations of Lesotho, Botswana, and Swaziland, all of which were economically dependent on South Africa. South Africa was strongly opposed to the establishment of black rule in the white-dominated countries of Angola, Mozambique, and Rhodesia, and gave military assistance to the whites there. However, by late 1974, with independence for Angola and Mozambique under black rule imminent, South Africa, as one of the few remaining white-ruled nations of Africa, faced the prospect of further isolation from the international community. In the early 1970s increasing numbers of whites (especially students) protested apartheid, and the Nationalist party itself was divided, largely on questions of race relations, into the somewhat liberal *verligte* [Afrikaans,=enlightened] faction and the conservative *verkramte* [Afrikaans,=narrow-minded] group.

Government. Under the 1961 constitution as amended, South Africa has a bicameral Parliament made up of a Senate (54 members) and a House of Assembly (171 members). The country's chief executive and head of state is the president, elected to a normally nonrenewable 7-year term by an electoral college consisting of members of Parliament and presided over by the chief justice of South Africa or another judge designated by him. The usually nonpolitical president acts on the advice of the executive council or cabinet (led by the prime minister), which must have the support of a majority in the House. In practice, the prime minister is the country's leading executive and legislative figure. See C. W. de Kiewiet, *A History of South Africa* (1946); E. A. Walker, *A History of South Africa* (rev. ed. 1949); E. H. Brookes and J. B. Macaulay, *Civil Liberty in South Africa* (1959); Arthur Keppel-Jones, *South Africa: A Short History* (rev. ed. 1962); Edward Roux, *Time Longer than Rope* (1964); Pierre L. Van den Berghe, *South Africa: A Study in Conflict* (1965); W. H. Votcher, *White Laager: The Rise of Afrikaner Nationalism* (1965); H. D. Hobart, *The South African Economy* (1967); William R. Frye, *In Whitest Africa: The Dynamics of Apartheid* (1968); D. L. Niddrie, *South Africa: Nation or Nations?* (1968); Monica Wilson and Leonard Thompson, ed., *The Oxford History of South Africa:* Vol. I., *South Africa to 1870* (1969); Vol. II, *1870–1966* (1971); Albie Sachs, *Justice in South Africa* (1973).

South African literature. Populated by diverse ethnic and language groups, South Africa has a distinctive literature in Afrikaans (a vernacular derived from Dutch), English, and many African tribal languages. Because of its location, the country was long isolated from the world's intellectual crosscurrents. Its original Dutch settlers, the pioneers who farmed in remote areas, had little time and less use for reading. The Bible was virtually their sole available book, and it was used also as a textbook to teach reading. In time, Afrikaans evolved as the spoken tongue, but Dutch remained the official language in government and was compulsory in the schools. The pressure of nationalism led finally to the legal recognition of Afrikaans in 1925, and it replaced Dutch completely. There soon emerged several authors writing in Afrikaans. Notable among them was C. J. Langenhoven, who wrote novels and poems, translated the *Rubaiyat* of Omar Khayyam into Afrikaans, and wrote the words of the national anthem. His efforts led to the compilation of an Afrikaans dictionary. Other well-known Afrikaans writers were the poets Christian L. Leipoldt, Christiaan M. van der Heever, and Eugene Marais. A. A. Pienaar (1894–) under the pseudonym Sangiro wrote nature stories. Most versatile is Uys Krige (1910–), whose works include novels, short stories, poems, and plays, in both Afrikaans and English. Important poets who have written in Afrikaans include N. P. van Wyk Louw, Ingred Jonker (1936–65), and Adam Small (1936–). At first, the limited local market retarded the development of an indigenous English-language literature. Writers preferred to publish in Great Britain and the United States. With the growth of the publishing industry, an increasing population, and the spread of education, a vital literary community developed in the mid-20th cent. Best known among the English-language novelists are Olive Schreiner, author of *The Story of an African Farm* (1883); Sarah G. Millin, whose major work is *God's Stepchildren* (1924); James Percy Fitzpatrick, who wrote *Jock of the Bushveld* (1907); Alan Paton, whose novel *Cry, the Beloved Country* (1948) was widely acclaimed in America; and Elizabeth C. Webster, who won an English prize for *Ceremony of Innocence* (1949). Roy Campbell is known as a South African poet, although he lived in England after 1926. Besides numerous other works, Stuart Cloete wrote *Turning Wheels* (1939), a story of the Great Trek, which was made into a film in the United States. Most prolific among the writers of romanticized travel and historical works are Lawrence G. Green, who also wrote the autobiographical *Where Men Still Dream* (1945), and Thomas V. Bulpin, whose *Lost Trails of the Lowveld* (1956) received wide acclaim. Other internationally known works include H. V. Morton's *In Search of South Africa* (1948) and *Episode in the Transvaal* (1955) by Harry Bloom, who also wrote the book for the first all-African opera, *King Kong* (1958). Writers who gained prominence in the 1950s and 60s include Jack Cope, Nadine Gordimer, Frans Ventner, Bessie Head, Dan Jacobson, Peter Abrahams, Alex La Guma, Lewis Nkosi, Sonya Rollnick, Laurens Van Der Post, David Lytton, and Athol Fugard. Numerous works in the various native tongues have appeared since the 1940s; most of them are popular romantic or adventure stories. Among the serious works in English by African authors are *Down Second Avenue* (1959), an autobiographical account of life in one of Johannesburg's African townships, and *Voices in the Whirlwind* (1972), a collection of essays about South Africa, both by Ezekial Mphahlele. See AFRICAN NEGRO LITERATURE. See *South African Writing Today,* ed. by Nadine Gordimer and Lionel Abrahams (1967).

South African War or **Boer War,** 1899–1902, war of the South African Republic (Transvaal) and the Orange Free State against Great Britain. Beginning with the acquisition in 1814 of the Cape of Good Hope, Great Britain gradually increased its territorial possessions in S Africa and by the late 19th cent. held Natal, Basutoland, Swaziland, Rhodesia, Bechuanaland, and other Bantu lands. The Boers (Dutch), already settled in some of these areas, strongly resented British incursions. Resentment was especially marked in the Transvaal (headed by the strongly anti-British Paul Kruger), which had actually been annexed (1877–81) to Great Britain. Anti-British sentiment was further inflamed after the discovery (1886) of gold in the Witwatersrand brought a great influx of prospectors (mainly British) into the Transvaal. Soon almost all the newly established mines as well as much of the commerce passed into British hands. The Boer government, to protect itself from the growing number of foreigners, denied these *Uitlanders* [foreigners] citizenship and taxed them heavily, despite British objections. In 1895 the Jameson raid (see JAMESON, SIR LEANDER STARR), which Transvaalers considered an officially sponsored plot to seize their country, aggravated the situation, and in 1896 the Transvaal and the Orange Free State formed a military alliance to protect their independence. The British, after the appointment (1897) of Sir Alfred Milner as governor of their South African territories, determined upon a showdown in defense of what they considered their commercial rights. Troops were dispatched from Britain, and after Boer protestations were refused, the Transvaal and the Orange Free State declared war (Oct. 12, 1899). The Boer forces, well equipped by Germany, were larger than those immediately available to the British, and they scored impressive victories in the areas adjacent to the Boer territories. In the Cape Colony, Mafeking was captured and Kimberley besieged; in Natal, Ladysmith was placed under siege. Reinforcements under the command of Sir Redvers Buller were sent from Britain. His failure to dislodge the Boers led to his replacement by Frederick Sleigh Roberts, with Lord Kitchener as his chief of staff. They landed in 1900 with heavy reinforcements and soon won victories; Kimberley and Ladysmith were relieved, and General Cronje was forced to surrender. Roberts advanced into the Orange Free State, captured its capital, Bloemfontein, and occupied the entire territory by May. By the end of June, Mafeking had been relieved, the Transvaal invaded, and Johannesburg and Pretoria captured. The Boer states were formally annexed and Kruger, a fugitive in Europe, appealed in vain for help there. Roberts, believing the war to be over, left South Africa and delegated the mopping up to Kitchener. The Boers, however, continued an extensive and coordinated guerrilla warfare. Under their leaders, including Smuts, De Wet, and Botha, they disrupted communications, attacked outposts and, with their intimate knowledge of the countryside, eluded capture. Kitchener soon realized that final victory lay only in the systematic destruction of these guerrilla units. Boer women and children were herded into concentration camps (where many died), and chains of blockhouses were erected, so disposed as to cut off large areas. Dragnets of troops went through the guerrilla country section by section, and by 1902, the British force (about 350,000) had reduced to final submission the Boer troops (approximately 60,000). The Treaty of Vereeniging (May 31, 1902) ended hostilities. The Boers accepted British sovereignty in exchange for a promise of responsible government in the near future. Great Britain agreed to grant a £3 million indemnity for property destruction and promised not to assess taxes to cover the expenses of the war. Amnesty was granted to all who had not violated the rules of war and repatriation to those who accepted the British king. British loss of life was over 5,000; the Boers lost about 3,700 people. The war left much bitterness, which continued to affect the political life of the Union of South Africa (organized 1910). See Leopold Amery, ed., *The Times History of the War in South Africa* (7 vol., 1900–1909); Deneys Reitz, *Commando: A Boer Journal of the Boer War* (new ed. 1945, repr. 1970); Edgar Holt, *The Boer War* (1958); W. B. Pemberton, *Battles of the Boer War* (1964); T. C. Caldwell, ed., *The Anglo-Boer War* (1965); G. H. L. Le May, *British Supremacy in South Africa* (1965); J. M. Selby, *The Boer War* (1969).

South America, fourth largest continent (1971 est. pop. 195,000,000), c.6,880,000 sq mi (17,819,000 sq km), the southern of the two continents of the Western Hemisphere. It is divided politically into 11 independent countries—ARGENTINA, BOLIVIA, BRAZIL, CHILE, COLOMBIA, ECUADOR, GUYANA, PARAGUAY, PERU, URUGUAY, and VENEZUELA—and the colonies of SURINAM (Dutch) and FRENCH GUIANA. The continent extends c.4,750 mi (7,640 km) from Punta Gallinas, Colombia, in the north to Cape Horn, Chile, in the south. At its broadest point, near where it is crossed by the equator, the continent extends c.3,300 mi (5,300 km) from east to west. South America is connected to North America by the Isthmus of Panama; it is washed on the N by the Caribbean Sea, on the E by the Atlantic Ocean, and on the W by the Pacific Ocean. Topographically the continent is divided into three sections—the South American cordillera, the interior lowlands, and the continental shield. The continental shield, in the east, which is separated into two unequal sections (the Guiana Highlands and the Brazilian Highlands) by the Amazon geosyncline, contains the continent's oldest rocks. Geologic studies in South America have supported the theory of continental drift and have shown that until 135 million years ago South America was joined to Africa; a Brazil-Gabon link has been established on the basis of tectonic matching. Extending down the middle of the continent is a series of lowlands running southward from the llanos of the north, through the selva of the great Amazon basin and the Gran Chaco, to the Pampa of Argentina. Paralleling the Pacific shore is the great cordillera composed of the Andes ranges and high intermontane valleys and plateaus. The Andes rise to numerous snow-capped peaks; Mt. Aconcagua (22,835 ft/6,960 m) in Argentina is the highest point in the Western Hemisphere. The Andes region is seismically active and prone to earthquakes. Volcanoes are present but currently inactive. Patagonia, a windy, semiarid plateau region, lies to the E of the Andes in S Argentina. On the Pacific coast, the land between the Andes and the sea widens northward from the islands of S Chile. In N Chile lies the barren Desert of Atacama. There are few good natural harbors along the South American coast. The continent's great river systems empty into the Atlantic Ocean and the Caribbean Sea; from north to south they are the Magdalena, Orinoco, Amazon, and Paraguay-Paraná systems. Only short streams flow into the Pacific Ocean. Excluding Lake Maracaibo, which is actually an arm of the Caribbean Sea, Lake Titicaca, on the Peru-Bolivia border, is the largest of the continent's lakes. South America embraces every climatic zone—tropical rainy, desert, high alpine—and vegetation varies accordingly. European exploration and penetration of South America began at the beginning of the 16th cent. Under the Treaty of Tordesillas, Portugal claimed what is now Brazil, and Spanish claims were established throughout the rest of the continent with the exception of the Guianas. An Iberian culture and Roman Catholicism were early New World transplants—as were coffee, sugarcane, and wheat. Spain and Portugal maintained their colonies in South America until the first quarter of the 19th cent., when successful revolutions resulted in the creation of independent states. The subjugation of the indigenous Indian civilizations was a ruthless accompaniment to settlement efforts, particularly those of Spain. The Inca Empire, centered at Cuzco, Peru, was conquered (1531–35) by Francisco Pizarro; other Indian cultures quickly declined or retreated in the face of conquest, conversion attempts, and subjugation. Today Indians constitute a significant portion of the continent's Andean population, especially in Bolivia, Ecuador, Peru, and Paraguay. Elsewhere in South America the population is generally mestizo, although Argentina, Uruguay, S Brazil, and Chile have primarily European populations. There are sizable black populations in the Guianas, NE Brazil, Colombia, and Venezuela. Immigration since 1800 has brought European, Middle Eastern, and Asian (especially Japanese) peoples to the continent, particularly to Argentina and Brazil. The population of South America is growing at a faster rate than that of any other part of the world except Central America. Outside the cities the population density of the continent is very low, with vast portions of the interior virtually uninhabited; most of the people live within 200 mi (320 km) of the coast. With the post-World War II trend of rural-to-city migration, urban population growth is rapidly expanding. São Paulo, Brazil, whose metropolitan population exceeds 8,000,000, is the largest city of South America and the fastest growing city of its size in the world. With the exception of Brazil and Ecuador, the national capitals have the largest populations and are the economic, cultural, and political centers of the countries. Squatter settlements have multiplied outside of urban areas as the poor and unskilled flock to the cities; widespread unemployment is common. Since the 17th cent. the exploitation of the continent's resources and the development of its industries have been the result of foreign investment and initiative, especially that of Spain, Great Britain, and the United States. Without this foreign influence, the development of the region's natural resources and economy would have progressed more slowly. Since World War II, many of the nations of South America have sought greater economic independence. Foreign-owned companies have been nationalized, and raw materials, once almost exclusively exported to the highly industrialized nations, are now being used in local industries. An increasing number of South American industrial centers have developed heavy industries to supplement the light industries on which they had previously concentrated. An obstacle to industrial growth in South America is the scarcity of coal. The continent must therefore rely on its petroleum reserves, most notably in Venezuela and also in Argentina, Bolivia, Colombia, Ecuador, and Peru, as a source of fuel; the utilization of natural gas is limited by the remoteness of the fields from population centers, although steps have been taken to extend its use. Iron ore deposits are plentiful in the Guiana and Brazilian highlands, and copper is abundant in the central Andes mountain region of Chile and Peru. Other important mineral resources include tin in Bolivia, manganese in Brazil, and bauxite in Guyana. Although only a small portion of South American hydroelectric power potential has been harnessed, it produces most of the continent's electricity. The largest hydroelectric facilities are

The key to pronunciation appears on page xi.

found in Brazil. Three types of agriculture predominate in South America, and much of what is produced is used to supply local needs. A generally impoverished subsistence farming prevails in much of the continent, with about 50% of the people working only about 5% of the land. Dense forests, steep slopes, and unfavorable climatic conditions, along with crude agricultural methods, limit the amount of cultivable land. Commercial agriculture, especially the plantation type, fares better in terms of production because of the large scale and the opportunity to use modern, mechanized farming methods. Among the agricultural exports are coffee, bananas, sugarcane, tobacco, cacao, and grains. Livestock grazing is important in the grassland regions; Argentina and Uruguay export meat. In the interior of the continent hunting and gathering of forest products are the chief economic activities of the indigenous peoples. In the more accessible areas, forest products are removed for export. Fishing is especially important off the west coast of the continent. See C. H. Haring, *The Spanish Empire in America* (1947, repr. 1963); Germán Arciniegas, *Latin America: A Cultural History* (1968); Preston James, *Latin America* (4th ed. 1969); George Pendle, *South America* (2d ed. 1970); R. H. Whitbeck and F. E. Williams, *Economic Geography of South America* (3d ed. 1971); E. J. Goodman, *The Explorers of South America* (1972); K. E. Webb, *Geography of Latin America* (1972).

Southampton, Henry Wriothesley, 3d **earl of** (rŏt'slē), 1573–1624, English nobleman and patron of letters. He succeeded to his title in 1581, was educated at Cambridge, and gained favor at the court of Queen Elizabeth I. A generous patron of such writers as Barnabe Barnes, Thomas Nash, and John Florio, he is best known as the patron of William Shakespeare, who dedicated *Venus and Adonis* (1593) and *The Rape of Lucrece* (1594) to him. Some scholars have maintained that Southampton is the patron and friend described in Shakespeare's sonnets. A friend of Robert Devereux, 2d earl of ESSEX, Southampton accompanied him on military and naval expeditions in 1596 and 1597. His secret marriage (1598) to Elizabeth Vernon, one of Elizabeth's ladies in waiting, angered the queen greatly, and she never forgave him. Southampton accompanied Essex to Ireland in 1599 as general of the horse, but Elizabeth revoked his appointment. He was closely involved in Essex's rebellion (1601) and was sentenced to death, but this sentence was changed to life imprisonment. Upon the accession (1603) of James I, Southampton was released and restored to favor. He became interested in colonial explorations and was a member of the Virginia Company and of the British East India Company. Although his impetuosity involved him in a number of court brawls, Southampton became (1619) a privy councilor. He lost favor, however, because of his opposition to the 1st duke of Buckingham. In 1624 he volunteered, with his son James, to lead a troop of English volunteers to fight for the Netherlands against Spain. Shortly after arriving in the Netherlands, both Southampton and his son died of fever. See biography by A. L. Rowse (1965).

Southampton, Thomas Wriothesley, 1st **earl of,** c.1500–1550, lord chancellor of England. Appointed a clerk of the signet in 1530, he rose in the favor of Thomas Cromwell and Henry VIII, who granted him many of the lands of the dissolved monasteries. He was knighted in 1537 and became (1540) a principal secretary of state. For his efforts in negotiating an alliance with Holy Roman Emperor Charles V, he was created (1544) Baron Wriothesley and made lord chancellor—an office in which he became notorious for his severity. He was one of the executors of Henry VIII's will but acceded to the appointment of Edward Seymour, duke of SOMERSET, as protector. Somerset, however, though he gave Wriothesley the earldom of Southampton, dismissed (1547) him from the lord chancellorship on the ground that he had delegated his legal duties without consulting the council. Southampton's consequent grievance against Somerset led him to support John Dudley, earl of Warwick (later duke of Northumberland), in overthrowing the protector in 1549.

Southampton, Thomas Wriothesley, 4th **earl of,** 1607–67, English nobleman; son of the 3d earl. At first an opponent of the court party in the events leading up to the English civil war, he later joined the royalists and served Charles I as an intimate adviser. He negotiated for Charles with Parliament in 1643 and 1645. After the king's execution (1649) he retired. At the Restoration (1660), Southampton became lord high treasurer. He counseled leniency toward the regicides. He disapproved of the immorality and ostentation of Charles II and his court and soon retired from active politics.

Southampton, county borough (1971 pop. 214,826), Hampshire, S England, at the head of Southampton Water. Southampton is England's chief port for passenger ships. It is also important for commercial trade. Raw materials and foodstuffs are imported and manufactured goods exported. Southampton has large shipbuilding and yacht-building industries, aircraft and marine engine factories, and food-processing plants. There is a large oil refinery nearby at Fawley. Southampton is the site of the Roman Clausentum and of the Saxon Hamtune or Suth-Hamtun. Remains of the ancient town walls and reworked Norman structures may be seen. The Crusaders under Richard I, Henry V on his expedition to France (1415), and the Pilgrims all embarked from Southampton. Until the discovery (16th cent.) of a new trade route to India, Southampton had a lucrative trade in goods from the East with Venice. In the 18th cent. it was a fashionable spa. Trade with the United States, the construction of modern docks and the railroad to London (1840), and the coming of the steamboat all worked to convert the spa back into a commercial port. Southampton was one of Britain's chief military transport stations in both World Wars. The city suffered considerable damage in World War II, as a result of which there are new dock facilities and shopping districts. The city received a grant of county land after the war to accommodate its growing industrial population. Among its schools are the Univ. of Southampton and a teacher-training college.

Southampton Insurrection, slave uprising in Virginia (1831) led by Nat TURNER.

Southampton Island, c.15,700 sq mi (40,700 sq km), E Keewatin dist., Northwest Territories, Canada, at the entrance to Hudson Bay. It is separated from the mainland by Ross Welcome Sound and Frozen Strait. With lowlands in the west, the tundra-covered island rises to c.2,000 ft (610 m) in the east. Coral Harbour, a trading post and airfield, is at the head of South Bay.

South Arabia, Federation of, federation, 1963–67, S Arabian Peninsula, formed by the merger of the British colony of Aden with the Federation of the Emirates of the South, a British protectorate. The Federation of the Emirates of the South was formed (Feb., 1959) by the union of six emirates, sultanates, and sheikhdoms; by the end of 1960 there were 10 members. In Jan., 1963, the Aden colony joined the federation, which was then renamed the Federation of South Arabia. The British-sponsored federation met with considerable opposition from the people of Aden, who feared domination by the conservative tribal states. Two rival nationalist groups emerged in the aftermath of the federation—the National Liberation Front (NLF) and the Front for the Liberation of Occupied South Yemen (FLOSY). By late 1967 the NLF had become the dominant group and forced the collapse of the federal government. British forces were withdrawn in Nov., 1967, and Aden and South Arabia became the independent state of Southern Yemen (see YEMEN, SOUTHERN).

South Australia, state (1971 pop. 1,173,707), 380,070 sq mi (984,381 sq km), S central Australia. It is bounded on the S by the Indian Ocean. KANGAROO ISLAND and many smaller islands off the south coast are included in the state. ADELAIDE is the capital; other important cities are Salisbury, Elizabeth, WHYALLA, and Mt. Gambier. Two thirds of the state's population live in the Adelaide metropolitan area. Much of South Australia is wasteland—deserts, mountains, salt lakes, and swampland. The Musgrave Ranges are in the north, the Flinders Ranges in the east, and the Great Victoria Desert and the Nullarbor Plain in the west. The only important river is the Murray, in the extreme southeast. The heavily populated southeastern area has a mild and healthful climate, while the north is arid to semiarid. Agriculture, confined almost exclusively to the Murray River area, consists of the raising of barley and grapes (for wine and brandy) and of wheat, oats, and rye. Livestock are grazed in the northern plains. There are valuable mineral deposits in the state; iron ore, salt, and gypsum are mined, and coal and natural gas are exploited. Industry developed rapidly during and after World War II; the chief products are industrial metals and transportation equipment. South Australia's coastal areas were visited by the Dutch in 1627. The British explorer Matthew Flinders noted likely settlement sites in 1802. Prompted by the writings of Edward Gibbon Wakefield, a British colonial statesman, the English Parliament passed the South Australian Colonization Act in 1834, and in Dec., 1836, the first colonists arrived and proclaimed South Australia a colony. In South Australia, unlike Western Australia, convicts were not admitted as settlers. In 1901, South Australia was federated as a state of the commonwealth. Northern Territory, which had been included in the state in 1863, was transferred in 1911 to the commonwealth government. The government of South Australia consists of a premier, a cabinet, and a bicameral state parliament. The nominal chief executive is the governor, appointed by the British crown on advice of the cabinet.

South Bend, city (1970 pop. 125,580), seat of St. Joseph co., N Ind., on the great south bend of the St. Joseph River; inc. as a city 1865. It lies in a farming and mint-growing region. Its manufactures include automotive parts, paints, nonelectrical machinery, rubber, plastics, metal products, and farm equipment. The Studebaker corporation, founded there in 1852, was a major producer of automobiles in the 20th cent. until production ceased in 1963. Robert LaSalle, the French explorer, camped in the area while making a portage from the St. Joseph River to the Kankakee River in 1679. South Bend was settled c.1820 as a post of the AMERICAN FUR COMPANY on the site of a French mission and trading post. The old St. Joseph County Courthouse (1855) now houses a museum. A branch of Indiana Univ. is in South Bend.

Southbridge, town (1970 pop. 17,057), Worcester co., S Mass., on the Quinebaug River; settled 1730, inc. 1816. Textiles are produced there.

South Burlington, city (1970 pop. 10,032), Chittenden co., NW Vt., on Lake Champlain; inc. 1971. It is a resort with some light industry.

South Carolina, state (1970 pop. 2,590,516), 31,055 sq mi (80,432 sq km), SE United States, one of the Thirteen Colonies. COLUMBIA is the capital and the largest city; CHARLESTON, GREENVILLE, and SPARTANBURG are other major cities. Roughly triangular in shape, South Carolina is bounded on the N by North Carolina, on the SW by Georgia (with the Savannah River and its tributaries forming the state line), and on the SE by the Atlantic Ocean. The long coast, firm and even above Georgetown and lined with beautiful sand beaches, becomes generally marshy to the south and is sliced by a network of rivers and creeks, creating a maze of inlets and the famous SEA ISLANDS. The coastal climate is humid and subtropical, with long, hot summers and short, mild winters. In this area are found cypress swamps, moss-hung oaks, beautiful flowering gardens, antebellum plantations, and the quaint historic seaports of Georgetown, Beaufort, and Charleston, the latter a major tourist attraction and one of the chief ports of entry in the Southeast. The coastal plain is separated from the rolling Piedmont plateau of the upcountry by the fall line, which runs generally parallel to the coast, passing through Columbia. Inland, the climate is temperate, becoming progressively cooler as the altitude increases. In the extreme northwest are the Blue Ridge mts.; they occupy only c.500 sq mi (1,290 sq km) in the state, with Sassafras Mt. (3,560 ft/1,085 m) the highest point. Rainfall is abundant and well distributed throughout South Carolina. The Pee Dee, Santee, Edisto, and Savannah river systems drain the state, flowing from the highlands to the sea with increasing speed, creating rapids and waterfalls. This abundant source of hydroelectric power is one of South Carolina's most important natural resources. The older dams—the Saluda (with its reservoir, Lake Murray) and Buzzard Roost dams on the Saluda River, and the Santee and Pinoplis dams (with their reservoirs, Lake Marion

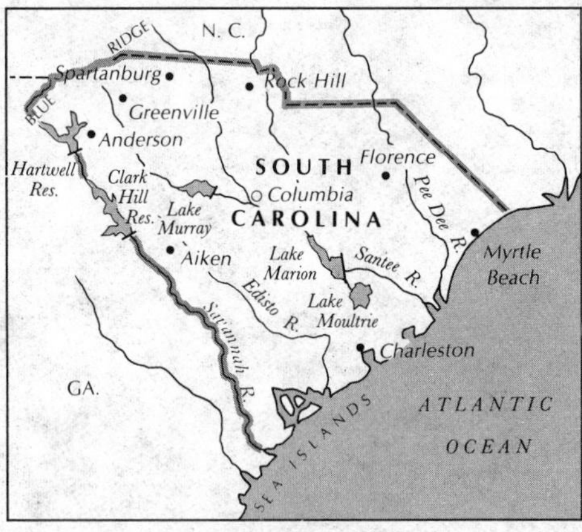

and Lake Moultrie) on the Santee River—have been supplemented by the Clark Hill and Hartwell dams on the Savannah River, part of a planned 11-dam project. A nuclear reactor power plant went into operation at Parr Shoals on the Broad River in 1963, the Trotter Shoals Dam on the Savannah was authorized in 1966, and in 1967 construction began on the Keeowee-Toxaway atomic power project near Greenville. This continuing power development is fueling the new industry that in recent decades has been compensating for the depletion of the quality of the soil, converting South Carolina's traditionally agrarian economy into a predominantly manufacturing one. The leading industries, nevertheless, are based largely on the state's agricultural products—the huge textile and clothing industries, centered in the Piedmont, being based on that region's cotton crop, and lumbering and related enterprises (such as the manufacture of pulp and paper) on the c.12,500,000 acres (5,058,750 hectares) of forestland that cover the state; the longleaf and loblolly pine are prevalent, and pine lumber is an important product. Other leading manufactures are chemicals, machinery, and foodstuffs. Perhaps the state's most impressive industrial installation is the Atomic Energy Commission's enormous Savannah River Atomic Energy Plant (mostly in Aiken co.), which produces plutonium and other nuclear materials. South Carolina has considerable mineral resources, but not all can be profitably mined, and their importance in the state's economy is not great. Principal minerals are nonmetallic—cement, stone, clays, and sand and gravel; South Carolina ranks second (1970) in the nation in vermiculite output and fourth in feldspar and mica. In agriculture, tobacco and soybeans have surpassed cotton as South Carolina's chief crops; the state ranks third (1972) in the nation in tobacco production. Cotton lint, corn, and cattle are economically important, and peanuts, pecans, sweet potatoes, and peaches (South Carolina is second in their production) are grown in abundance. Fishing is a major commercial enterprise; the chief catches are hard blue crabs and shrimps. Income from tourism is steadily increasing. Thousands of vacationers are attracted to famous Myrtle Beach and to the Sea Island resorts. The state's historical places of interest include Fort Sumter National Monument, Kings Mountain National Military Park, and Cowpens National Battlefield (see NATIONAL PARKS AND MONUMENTS, table). At an unknown coastal site in the region that is now the Carolinas, what may have been the first white settlement in North America was founded (1526; not permanent) by an expedition under the Spanish explorer Lucas Vásquez de Ayllón. Later Hernando De Soto penetrated (1540) the Savannah River region. The Frenchman Jean Ribaut established (1562) a short-lived Huguenot settlement on Parris Island in Port Royal Sound, but French colonizing ambitions were thoroughly thwarted by Pedro Menéndez de Avilés. Spanish missions soon extended N from Florida almost to the site of present-day Charleston, and they remained until the arrival of the English. Charles I asserted England's claim as early as 1629 by granting the territory from lat. 36°N to lat. 31°N (later named Carolina for Charles I) to Sir Robert Heath, but since no settlements were made Heath's charter was forfeited. In 1663, Charles II awarded the area to eight of his prominent supporters, the most active of whom was Anthony Ashley Cooper (Lord Ashley, later 1st earl of SHAFTESBURY). The northern and southern sections of Carolina developed separately. The first permanent colony was established in 1670 at Albemarle Point under William Sayle. To govern it, John Locke wrote (at Lord Ashley's behest) the Fundamental Constitutions (1669), which granted some popular rights but at the same time retained feudal privileges and limitations. The settlers refused to ratify it. Actual government consisted of a powerful council, of which half was appointed by the proprietors in England; a governor, also appointed by the proprietors; and a relatively weak assembly, elected by all freemen. In 1680 the colony moved across the river to Oyster Point, which was better suited for defense. There the colonists established their capital, called Charles Town (later Charleston), which was to become the chief center of culture and of wealth in the South. The 1680s saw the beginnings of prosperity. Wealthy colonists set up plantations worked by indentured servants and Negro and Indian slaves, while freemen (many of them former indentured servants) cultivated the 50 acres (20 hectares) granted them by the proprietors. On plantations and small farms alike, corn, livestock, and some cotton were raised at first, and tobacco was cultivated in plenitude. Rice, introduced c.1680, flourished in the marshy tidewater area and soon became the plantation staple. Forests yielded rich timber and naval stores. The fur trade (especially in deerskins) with the CREEK INDIANS and other friendly tribes prospered. But conflict with the Spanish and French increased, and the encroachment of the two countries dramatized the proprietors' lack of concern and their inability to defend the distant colony. Popular antagonism to proprietary rule was spurred by the parceling of much of the land into a few large grants, by the quitrent system, and most important by the issue of religion. Several religious groups had freely practiced their faith in the colony until the early 18th cent.; these included Anglicans, dissenters from Britain (see NONCONFORMISTS), and French Huguenots. In 1704 the Anglicans, without opposition from the proprietors, managed to deprive the other groups of their religious liberty, and it was not until the English government took action (1706) that religious toleration was restored. The colony was divided into North and South Carolina in 1713. In 1715–16 the settlers were attacked by the once friendly YAMASEE INDIANS, who had become resentful of exploitation by the Carolina traders. The uprising was finally quelled after much loss of life and property. These attacks further revealed the lack of protection afforded by the proprietors, and in 1719 the colonists rebelled and received royal protection. The crown sent Francis Nicholson as provincial royal governor in 1720, and South Carolina formally became a royal colony in 1729, when the proprietors finally accepted terms. Conditions were now in many respects improved. Pirates such as BLACKBEARD who had infested the coast had been hanged or dispersed. In addition the founding (1733) of Georgia to the south provided a buffer against the Spanish. Loss of territory and some of the colony's fur trade to Georgia was more than compensated for when indigo, supported by British bounty, became (1740s) the colony's second staple. To counterbalance the vast number of Negro slaves being imported for plantation labor, white immigration was encouraged. Germans and Swiss, arriving in the 1730s and 40s, and Scotch-Irish and other migrants from Virginia and Pennsylvania, arriving in the 60s, settled the colony's lower middle country and uplands. Regional antipathies were generated by economic and social differences; the small, self-sufficient farmer of the up-country, demanding courts, roads, and defense against outlaws and the CHEROKEE INDIANS, elicited little sympathy from the powerful plantation lords of lower Carolina. In the late 1760s discontent culminated in the formation of the REGULATOR MOVEMENT. Finally the legislature was impelled to grant certain up-country demands, including the establishment of courts in the region. South Carolina's long friendship with the mother country was reflected in trade benefits resulting from the NAVIGATION ACTS and in protection by the strong British navy. However, public sentiment in the colony was transformed by the STAMP ACT, the TOWNSHEND ACTS, and British political claims. South Carolinians—Christopher Gadsden, Henry Laurens, and Arthur Middleton—were leaders in the movement for independence, and in March, 1776, an independent government of South Carolina was set up with John Rutledge as president. In the American Revolution the British failed to take Charleston in June, 1776 (see FORT MOULTRIE), but Sir Henry Clinton successfully besieged the town in 1780. In the ensuing CAROLINA CAMPAIGN the British were ultimately forced to retreat, although they held Charleston until Dec., 1782. In 1786 the site of Columbia was chosen for the new capital; its central location mollified the up-country population. South Carolina ratified the Federal Constitution in May, 1788, and replaced the royal charter with a state charter in 1790. Complete religious liberty was established, and primogeniture was abolished, but property qualifications for voting and office holding ensured planter control of the legislature. The constitutional amendment known as the "compromise of 1808" somewhat alleviated the sectional antagonism by reapportioning representation. By this time, however, Eli Whitney's cotton gin had enabled cotton plantations to spread far into the upper regions; thus the planters continued to dominate state policies. In the late 1820s cotton from the fertile western states glutted the market, and prosperity declined in South Carolina. Discontent was aggravated by national tariff policies that were unfavorable to South Carolina's agrarian economy. In 1832 the state passed its NULLIFICATION act, declaring the tariff laws null and void and not binding upon South Carolina citizens. President Andrew Jackson acted firmly for the Union in this crisis, and in 1833 South Carolina repealed its act. Tariff reform that same year brought relief, but the possibility of secession had been broached and was subsequently renewed in reaction to abolitionist attacks and further economic grievances. John C. Calhoun, supported by Robert Y. Hayne, became the acknowledged leader of the whole South with his defense of the STATES' RIGHTS doctrine; his political philosophy was later to form the intellectual basis for the CONFEDERACY. Some of the state's apologists for slavery, notably Robert B. Rhett, equaled the most radical abolitionists in their zeal. After Lincoln's election South Carolina was the first state to secede (Dec. 20, 1860) from the Union. Gov. Francis W. Pickens immediately demanded all Federal property within the state, including FORT SUMTER, which was held by Union men under Major Robert Anderson. The firing on Sumter by Confederate batteries on April 12, 1861, precipitated the Civil War. In Nov., 1861, a Union naval force under Samuel F. Du Pont took the forts of Port Royal Sound, but Charleston's forts withstood severe bombardments in 1863, and the state was saved from heavy military action until early in 1865. Then Gen. William T. Sherman, commanding the army that had marched through Georgia, crossed the Savannah River and advanced north through the state. Because South Carolina was viewed as the birthplace of secession, it was difficult to restrain many of the Union soldiers, and the deliberate devastation, culminating in the burning of Columbia, was appalling. The RECONSTRUCTION period that followed the war was no less disastrous. South Carolina was selected for President Andrew Johnson's moderate program, but the program had only a brief trial before the radical Republicans took over. For a decade the state was ruled by CARPETBAGGERS and SCALAWAGS, with the support of Negro votes. The constitution of 1868, which established universal male suffrage and ended property qualifications for office holding, gained the state readmittance (June, 1868) to the Union. During the period from 1868 to 1874 accomplishments such as the building of schools and railroads were offset by waste and corruption in the state government and by high taxation. Many of these abuses were corrected by the honest administration of Gov. Daniel H. Chamberlain (1874–76). However, Chamberlain was the state's last Republican governor. The Democratic party regained vitality in 1876, and South Carolina's war hero, Wade Hampton, was selected as candidate for governor. The election of 1876 was marked by irregular practices on both sides, and although Hampton gained a majority, Chamberlain refused to accept defeat. Thus there existed two state governments until 1877, when President Rutherford B. Hayes removed all Federal troops from the South, and Chamberlain, bereft of the support which had made Republican rule possible, withdrew. Hampton attempted moderation on race issues, but, despite his efforts, by 1882 the vast majority of Negroes had lost the vote; white political supremacy was assured. The wartime destruction and the abolition of slavery had nearly ruined the state's basic agricultural economy. Although some vigorous planters and merchants managed to recoup their fortunes, farm tenancy (replacing the old plantation system) held most of the state's farmers in economic bondage. The Panic of 1873 was followed by two decades of agrarian hard times. The rice plantations, which had already begun to decline, were hardest hit. Popular discontent was not ameliorated until the election (1890) of Benjamin Tillman, leader of the up-country farmers, as governor. Tillmanites wrested control of the Democratic party from the conservative element (the tidewater "Bourbon aristocracy"), reapportioned taxes and representation, expanded public education, and established preliminary labor reform laws. Reflecting another aspect of Tillman's policies, the constitution of 1895 initiated "Jim Crow laws" and adopted voting qualifications that excluded virtually all Negroes from the crucial Democratic primaries. Renewed agrarian prosperity after 1900 was accompanied by political stagnation that lasted until the governorship (1914–18) of Richard I. Manning; progressive trends already evident in other parts of the country were now belatedly manifested in South Carolina in the passage of education and labor laws. Agriculture again suffered a setback in the 1920s. Contributing factors were the destruction of the Sea Islands cotton crop by the boll weevil and the erosion of the land as a result of long adherence to the one-crop system. Industry, especially the textile industry (which had been increasing in importance since the Civil War), also suffered in the Great Depression of the 1930s. New Deal legislation and the state road-building program provided South Carolina with some relief. During World War I the position of the Negro had been improved through war work and service in the armed forces; however, in the 1920s the renewed power of the Ku Klux Klan had again brought oppression, and Negro migration began on a scale sufficient to bring the whites into the majority in the state by 1930. World War II and the postwar period brought great changes. A state court decision in 1947 opened the Democratic primaries to the Negro vote. Under the governorship (1951–55) of the nationally prominent James F. Byrnes, the poll tax was abolished as a voting requirement, steps were taken to curb Ku Klux Klan activities, and the educational system was greatly expanded. Integration of the schools after the 1954 U.S. Supreme Court decision met considerable opposition, but in 1963 South Carolinians accepted token integration of Clemson College without incident, and desegregation began in the Charleston schools. By 1970 all of the public school districts were technically in compliance with Federal desegregation requirements. That year four Negroes were elected to the previously all-white state legislature. Politically, South Carolina has been strongly Democratic since the end of Reconstruction, although in the late 1960s and early 70s Republicans gained strength in both state and national elections; the state voted for Republican candidates for president in 1964, 1968, and 1972. The executive branch is headed by a governor elected for a four-year term and ineligible for reelection. All governors were Democratic from 1876 to 1975, when James B. Edwards, a Republican, took office. South Carolina's bicameral legislature has a senate with 46 members elected for four-year terms and a house of representatives with 124 members elected for two years; in 1973 only 24 of the 170 legislators were Republicans. The state sends 2 Senators and 6 Representatives to the U.S. Congress and has 8 electoral votes. In the early 1970s the state's 1895 constitution was extensively revised. Among South Carolina's institutions of higher education are The Citadel (The Military College of South Carolina), at Charleston; Clemson Univ., at Clemson; South Carolina State College, at Orangeburg; and the Univ. of South Carolina, at Columbia. See Edward McCrady, *The History of South Carolina in the Revolution* (2 vol., 1901–2); A. H. Hirsch, *The Huguenots of Colonial South Carolina* (1928); G. C. Williams, *A Social Interpretation of South Carolina* (1946); J. G. Barrett, *Sherman's March through the Carolinas* (1956); D. D. Wallace, *South Carolina: A Short History, 1520–1948* (1961); F. B. Simkins and R. H. Woody, *South Carolina during Reconstruction* (1932, repr. 1966); E. M. Lander, *A History of South Carolina, 1865–1960* (2d ed. 1970); T. T. Su, *The South Carolina Economy* (1970); P. M. Hamer, *The Secession Movement in South Carolina, 1847–1852* (1918, repr. 1971); E. B. Sloan, *Scenic South Carolina* (2d ed. 1971); Federal Writers' Project, *South Carolina, A Guide to the Palmetto State* (1941, repr. 1972).

South Carolina, University of, at Columbia; state supported; coeducational; chartered 1801, opened as a college 1805; became a university 1906. One of the earliest state-supported colleges, it has a library housing notable collections relating to Southern history. The university operates two-year branches at Allendale and Beaufort.

South Charleston, city (1970 pop. 16,333), Kanawha co., W W.Va., on the Kanawha River, in a highly industrialized area; settled 1782, inc. 1917. It is an important chemical-manufacturing center. Nearby are an Adena Indian Mound (opened 1856–57); Kanawha Airport; and a large electric power plant.

South China Sea, western arm of the Pacific Ocean, c.1,000,000 sq mi (2,590,000 sq km), between the SE Asian mainland and Taiwan, the Philippines, and Borneo. It is connected with the East China Sea by the Formosa Strait. The Gulf of Tonkin and the Gulf of Siam are its chief embayments. The southwestern part of the sea from the Gulf of Siam to the Java Sea is an enormous submerged plain called the Sunda Platform; water is generally shallow (less than 200 ft/61 m) throughout this vast area. In contrast, the northeastern part of the sea is a deep basin, reaching depths of up to c.18,000 ft (5,490 m). The Si, Red, Mekong, and Chao Phraya are the largest rivers flowing into the South China Sea. Many islands dot the sea, which is a region subject to violent typhoons.

Southcott, Joanna (south'kət), 1750–1814, English religious visionary. Uneducated, even illiterate, she spent her earlier years in domestic service. She began c.1792 to claim the gift of prophecy; her "revelations" attracted many followers. Later she announced that, as the woman in Revelation 12, she would be the mother of the coming Messiah. Soon after the time she had set for the birth of the "second Shiloh," she died of brain disease, at the age of 64. Her followers continued to study the 60 or more tracts and books of her writing; the sect never completely died out. She left a locked box with instructions that it be opened only in the presence of all the bishops at a time of national crisis. In 1928, a box alleged to be hers was opened when one bishop agreed to be present; it revealed nothing of interest. Among her books is *The Strange Effects of Faith* (2 vol., 1801–2). See G. R. Balleine, *Past Finding Out* (1956).

South Dakota (dəkō'tə), state (1970 pop. 666,257), 77,047 sq mi (199,552 sq km), N central United States, admitted to the Union in 1889 simultaneously with North Dakota (they are the 40th and 39th states). PIERRE is the capital; the largest cities are SIOUX FALLS, ABERDEEN, and RAPID CITY. South Dakota is bounded on the N by North Dakota; on the E by Minnesota (with the Minnesota River forming part of the boundary) and Iowa (from which it is separated by the Big Sioux River); on the S by Nebraska (with the Missouri River forming part of the boundary); and on the W by Wyoming and Montana. South Dakota shows some of the earliest geologic history of the continent in the rock formations of the ancient Black Hills and in the Badlands. At their extreme between the White River and the south fork of the Cheyenne, the Badlands display in their deeply eroded clay gullies not only colorful, fantastic shapes, but also a wealth of easily accessible marine and land fossils (the Badlands National Monument preserves the area for its startling scenery and geologic interest). The whole of South Dakota has a continental climate; summer brings a succession of

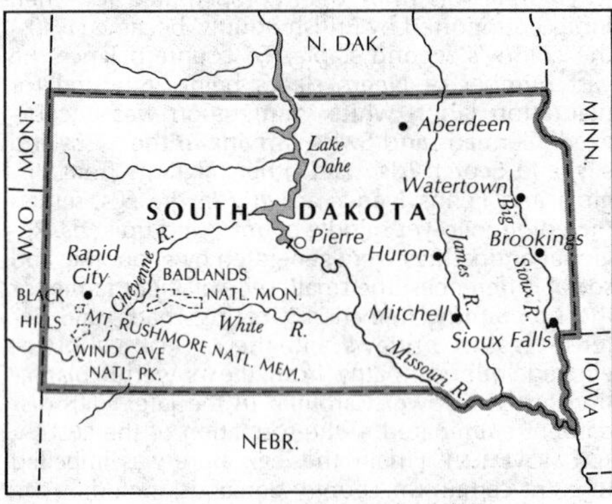

hot, cloudless days, and in the winter blizzards sweep across bare hillsides, filling the coulees with deep snow. The average annual rainfall is low, although variable across the state, and in years of drought summer winds blow away acres of top soil in "black blizzards." From east to west the state rises some 6,000 ft (1,829 m) to Harney Peak (7,242 ft/2,207 m) in the Black Hills, highest point in the United States E of the Rockies. Through the center of the state the Missouri River cuts a wide path southward; other principal rivers include the James and Big Sioux to the east, and the Cheyenne, Belle Fourche, the Moreau, the Grand River, and the White River to the west. Almost one third of the region W of the Missouri River, a semiarid, treeless plain, belongs to the Indians, most of whom live on reservations such as Cheyenne River, Pine Ridge, Rosebud, and Standing Rock. The remaining area is divided into large ranches; there cattle and sheep ranching provide the major source of income, with hay and wheat growing secondary. In the more productive region E of the Missouri, livestock and livestock products comprise the primary source of income. Wheat and corn are South Dakota's chief cash crops, but oats, flaxseed, soybeans, and barley are also grown. Although there is a certain amount of diversified industry in the main cities of Sioux Falls and Rapid City, meat packing and food processing constitute by far the major industries of the state. Gold is South Dakota's most important mineral, and the town of Lead in the Black Hills is the country's leading gold-mining center. In 1972 the state ranked second in the nation in gold production, second in beryllium concentrate, and second in tin concentrate. Stone, sand and gravel, and cement are also important minerals. At the time of the white man's arrival, South Dakota was inhabited by the agricultural Arikara and the nomadic Sioux (Dakota) Indians. By the 1830s the Sioux had driven the Arikara from the area. Part of the region that is now South Dakota was explored in the mid-18th cent. by sons of the sieur de la Vérendrye. The United States acquired the region as part of the LOUISIANA PURCHASE, and it was partially explored by Lewis and Clark in their Missouri River expedition of 1804–6. Later explorers became well acquainted with the warlike Sioux, who continued to dominate the region during the period of the fur trade down to the middle of the 19th cent. Individual traders from the time of Pierre Dorion in the late 18th cent. made the region their home, and the posts founded by Pierre Chouteau and the American Fur Company were the first bases for settlement. (Fort Pierre was established in 1817.) The introduction of the steamboat on the upper Missouri in 1831 brought renewed vigor to the fur trade, but it was not until land speculators and farmers moved westward from Minnesota and Iowa in the 1850s that any real settlement developed. Two land companies were established at Sioux Falls in 1856, and in 1859 Yankton, Bon Homme, and Vermillion were laid out. A treaty with the Sioux opened the land between the Big Sioux and the Missouri, and in 1861 Dakota Territory was set up, embracing not only present-day North Dakota and South Dakota but also E Wyoming and E Montana. Yankton was the capital. Settlers were discouraged by droughts, Indian raids, and plagues of locusts; however, by the time the railroad pushed to Yankton in 1872, the region had received the first of the European immigrants who later came in great numbers, contributing significant German, Scandinavian, and Russian elements to the Dakotas. Rumors of gold in the Black Hills, confirmed by a military expedition led by George A. Custer in 1874, excited national interest, and Americans began to pour into the area. However, much of the Black Hills region had been granted (1868) to the Sioux by treaty, and when the Indians refused to sell either mining rights or the reservation itself, warfare with the Sioux again broke out. The defeat (1876) of Custer and his men by Sitting Bull, Crazy Horse, and Gall in the battle of Little Bighorn (in what is now Montana) did not prevent the white man from gradually acquiring more and more Indian land, including the gold-lined Black Hills. The extinction of the buffalo herds as well as Sitting Bull's death (1890) at the hands of army-trained Indian police and the subsequent massacre of Big Foot's band at WOUNDED KNEE Creek were factors leading to the permanent end of Indian resistance in South Dakota. Tribal organization was weakened by the DAWES ACT of 1887 (although the Indian Reorganization Act of 1934 attempted to restore tribal ownership of repurchased lands, the younger generations have been moving to the cities in increasing numbers). During the 1870s the gold fever mounted; Deadwood had its day of gaudy glory, Wild Bill Hickok and Calamity Jane created frontier legends, and the town of Lead began its long, productive career. Although gold did not make the fortune of South Dakota, it laid the foundation by stimulating cattle ranching—herds of cattle were first brought to the grasslands of W South Dakota partly to supply food for the miners. Settlement in the east also increased, and the period from 1878 to 1886, following the resumption of railroad building after the financial depression earlier in the decade, was the time of the great Dakota land boom, when population increased threefold. Agitation for statehood developed; in 1888 the Republican party adopted the statehood movement as a campaign issue, and in 1889 Congress passed an enabling act. The Dakotas were divided; South Dakota became a state with Pierre as capital. Disasters, however, rocked its security. The unusually severe winter of 1886–87 had destroyed huge herds of cattle in the west, ruining the great bonanza ranches and promoting among the ranchers the trend—since dominant—of having smaller herds with provisions for winter shelter and feeding. Cattle grazed on public domain and were rounded up only for branding and shipment to market. Recurrent droughts added to the difficulties of the farmers, who sought relief in the cooperative ventures of the Farmers' Alliance and political action in the POPULIST PARTY, which won a resounding victory in 1896. Initiative and referendum were adopted (1898; South Dakota was the first state to adopt them) and other progressive measures of the day were enacted, but prosperity quickly returned South Dakota to political conservatism and the Republican party. The extension of railroads (particularly the Milwaukee, which was the only transcontinental line passing through South Dakota) encouraged further expansion of agriculture, but new droughts (especially that of 1910–11) brought a brief period of emigration. Many new farmsteads were abandoned, and a turn toward political radicalism developed. The Progressive party, led by Peter Norbeck (governor 1917–21) and operating as a branch of the Republican party, revived the attempts of Populist reform programs to regulate railroad rates and raise assessments of corporate property and entered in experiments in state ownership of business. New prosperity-depression cycles occurred after the boom of World War I. The combination of droughts and the Great Depression brought widespread calamities in the late 1920s and early 30s, and the state's population declined by 50,000 between 1930 and 1940. Vigorous measures of relief were instituted under the New Deal, and higher farm prices during World War II and the ensuing years brought a new era of hopefulness. Although South Dakotans had supported Franklin D. Roosevelt in his first two elections, they returned to the Republican party in 1940. In the 1950s the Democrats showed new strength. George McGovern was elected to the House in 1956 and to the Senate in 1962, 1968, and 1974. Richard F. Kneip, a Democrat, was elected governor in 1972 and was reelected in 1974. In the postwar period adoption of improved farming techniques resulted in a steady increase in agricultural and livestock production. This was accompanied, however, by the consolidation of small farms into large units and the displacement of many small farmers. Irrigation projects, extension of hydroelectric power, and protective measures against wind and water erosion have been forwarded to avoid the threat of new disasters. Under the Missouri River basin project four dams were built. The Belle Fourche, or Orman, Dam on the Belle Fourche River is another important irrigation source. But devastating floods occurred in 1969 and 1972. South Dakota is governed under the 1889 constitution. The legislature consists of 35 senators and 75 representatives, all elected for two-year terms. The governor is also elected for two years. The state chooses two U.S. Representatives and two Senators and has four electoral votes. Among the state's attractions are Wind Cave National Park, Jewel Cave National Monument, Badlands National Monument, and the famous mammoth carvings of the Mount Rushmore National Memorial (see NATIONAL PARKS AND MONUMENTS, table). Institutions of higher learning in South Dakota include Augustana College, at Sioux Falls; South Dakota School of Mines and Technology, at Rapid City; South Dakota State Univ., at Brookings; the Univ. of South Dakota, at Vermillion; and Northern State College, at Aberdeen. See Harold E. Briggs, *Frontiers of the Northwest* (1940); Federal Writers' Project, *South Dakota: A Guide to the State* (2d ed. 1952); Herbert S. Schell, *South Dakota: Its Beginnings and Growth* (1960) and *History of South Dakota* (1961); J. Leonard Jennewein and Jane Boorman, ed., *Dakota Panorama* (1961); H. S. Schell, *History of South Dakota* (1968).

South Dakota, University of, at Vermillion; state supported; coeducational; chartered 1862, opened 1882 as the Univ. of Dakota. In 1891 it was renamed the Univ. of South Dakota; in 1959 it became the State University of South Dakota; and in 1964 its present name was again adopted. There is a branch campus at Springfield.

South Dakota School of Mines and Technology, at Rapid City; state supported; coeducational; chartered 1885, opened 1887 as Dakota School of Mines, renamed 1943. Of note are the school of engineering and mining, the experiment station, and a geology museum.

South Dakota State University, at Brookings; land-grant support; coeducational; chartered 1883 as Dakota Agricultural College, opened 1884. In 1907 it became South Dakota State College of Agriculture and Mechanic Arts, and in 1964 its present name was adopted.

South Downs: see DOWNS, NORTH, chalk hills, England.

Southdown sheep, mutton breed of sheep originated on the South Downs of Sussex, England, and now raised throughout the world. It is a small sheep, the most thickset of all breeds, and it is valued for the meatiness of the lamb carcasses. The wool is of medium length and fine grade; it varies in color from gray to brown on the face and feet. The Southdown, one of the oldest English breeds, has been extensively used in improving other breeds; it was first imported to the United States in 1803 and has found acceptance in farm flock areas.

Southeast Asia, region of Asia (est. pop. 225,000,000), c.1,740,000 sq mi (4,506,600 sq km), bounded roughly by the Indian subcontinent on the west, China on the north, and the Pacific Ocean on the east. The name "Southeast Asia" came into popular use after World War II and has replaced such phrases as "Further India," "the East Indies," "Indo-China," and "the Malay Peninsula," which formerly designated all or part of the region. Southeast Asia includes the Indochina Peninsula, which juts into the South China Sea, the Malay Peninsula, and the Malaya Archipelago. The region has 10 independent countries: Burma, Thailand, Malaysia, Cambodia, Laos, North Vietnam, South Vietnam, the Philippines, Singapore, and Indonesia. It also includes Brunei, a British protectorate, and Portuguese Timor, an overseas territory of Portugal. Peninsular Southeast Asia is a rugged region traversed by many mountains and drained by great rivers such as the Salween, Irrawaddy, Chao Phraya, and Mekong. Insular Southeast Asia is made up of numerous volcanic and coral islands. Southeast Asia has a generally tropical rainy climate, with the exception of the northwestern part, which has a humid subtropical climate. The wet monsoon winds are vital for the economic well-being of the region. Tropical forests cover most of the area. Rice is the chief crop of the region; rubber, tea, spices, and coconuts are also important. The region has a great variety of minerals and produces most of the world's tin. Population is unevenly distributed, with the highest density in lowland areas. Most of the people live in small agrarian villages; the largest cities are Djakarta, Indonesia; Bangkok, Thailand; Singapore; Manila, Philippines; and Saigon, South Vietnam. There is a great diversity in culture, history, religion, and ethnic composition. Many different languages are spoken, such as those of the Tibeto-Burman, Mon-Khmer, and Malayo-Polynesian families. Religions include Buddhism, Islam, Roman Catholicism, and Confucianism. Animism is still widely practiced among the many primitive tribes of the region. Most of the influences that molded the societies of Southeast Asia predated European colonization, coming from early Indian and Chinese sources. Several great civilizations, including those of the Khmers and Malays, flourished there. In the late 15th cent., Islamic influences grew strong but were overshadowed by the arrival of the Europeans, who established their power throughout Southeast Asia; only Thailand remained free of colonial occupation. Because of Southeast Asia's strategic location between Japan and India, and the importance of shipping routes that traverse it, the region became the scene of battles between Allied and Japanese forces during World War II. Since the war the countries of Southeast Asia have reemerged as independent nations. They have been plagued by political turmoil, weak economies, ethnic strife, and social inequities. Throughout the 1960s and early 1970s there were open conflicts between Communist and non-Communist factions throughout most of the region, especially in Vietnam, Laos, and Cambodia (see VIETNAM WAR). See C. A. Fisher, *Southeast Asia* (2d ed. 1966); E. H. G. Dobby, *Southeast Asia* (10th ed. 1967); D. G. E. Hall, *A History of South East Asia* (3d ed. 1968); J. S. Bastin and H. J. Benda, *History of Modern Southeast Asia* (1968); Gunnar Myrdal, *Asian Drama* (3 vol., 1968); George Coedès, *The Making of Southeast Asia* (tr. 1969); Richard Allen, *Short Introduction to the History and Politics of Southeast Asia* (1970); D. W. Fryer, *Emerging Southeast Asia* (1970); D. J. Steinberg, ed., *In Search of Southeast Asia* (1971); Alice Taylor, ed., *Focus on Southeast Asia* (1972).

Southeast Asian languages, family of languages, sometimes also called Austroasiatic, spoken in SE Asia by about 45 million people. According to one school of thought, it has three subfamilies: the Mon-Khmer languages, the Munda languages, and the Annamese-Muong subfamily. As yet there is considerable evidence but no definite proof that all of these groups are derived from a single ancestor language, which is the essential requirement for classification in the same linguistic family. Languages of the Mon-Khmer subfamily are spoken by about 8 million people. Included in the Mon-Khmer subfamily are Cambodian (or Khmer), the official tongue of Cambodia and the language of 5 million people in that country; Mon (or Talaing), spoken by 300,000 people in Burma; and a number of other languages, such as Cham of Cambodia and South Vietnam, Semang and Sakai of the Malay Peninsula, Nicobarese of the Nicobar Islands, and Khasi of Assam in India. Grammatically, the Mon-Khmer languages make great use of affixes (or prefixes, infixes, and suffixes). They are agglutinative in that different linguistic elements, each of which exists separately and has a fixed meaning, are often joined to form one word. Cambodian and Mon have their own scripts, which are descended from alphabets of India. Both are written from left to right. The languages of the Munda subfamily are spoken in parts of N and central India by about 6 million people and comprise more than 20 tongues, the most important of which is Santali, with 3 million speakers in Orissa. The Munda languages use affixes extensively and are agglutinative. There are two genders for nouns in most of the Munda tongues, animate and inanimate. Most Munda languages also have three numbers, singular, dual, and plural. Suffixes and particles placed after the noun are used to express such features as number and possession, which are often indicated in Indo-European tongues by case inflection. The Annamese-Muong subfamily is composed of Muong, spoken by 200,000 people in Indochina, and Vietnamese (also called Annamese). The latter is the tongue of 31 million persons in North Vietnam and South Vietnam and is the official language in both countries. It is also spoken in Cambodia, Laos, and Thailand. Vietnamese is basically monosyllabic, but it has many words of two or more syllables. It is also tonal, with six tones that frequently help to distinguish homonyms. Vietnamese uses particles but has no prefixes and suffixes. Word order is very important for showing grammatical relationships since there is no inflection. The vocabulary has many loanwords from Chinese. An alphabet based on Roman letters and adapted for Vietnamese, as by adding diacriticals, is generally used today in place of the traditional Chinese-type writing of the past. The classification of Vietnamese is still disputed; some regard it as a Mon-Khmer tongue, others as a Tai (or Thai) language (see SINO-TIBETAN LANGUAGES), and still others as a language unrelated to any other known tongue. Clearly, more research is needed on the Southeast Asian languages before more definite conclusions can be drawn regarding their classification and other linguistic features. The use of the term *Southeast Asian languages* in this article is based on linguistic considerations; however, the term is also employed by some scholars in a geographical sense to include three distinct language families of the region, namely, MALAYO-POLYNESIAN LANGUAGES, Sino-Tibetan languages, and Mon-Khmer languages. A grouping together of the Malayo-Polynesian and Southeast Asian (or Austroasiatic) languages into a single Austric family has also been proposed on the basis of certain phonetic, lexical, and grammatical similarities, but this grouping has not yet been generally accepted. See Norman H. Zide, ed., *Studies in Comparative Austroasiatic Linguistics* (1966).

Southeast Asia Treaty Organization (SEATO), alliance organized (1954) under the Southeast Asia Collective Defense Treaty by representatives of Australia, France, Great Britain, New Zealand, Pakistan, the Philippines, Thailand, and the United States. Established under Western auspices after the French defeat and withdrawal from Indochina, SEATO was created to oppose further Communist gains in Southeast Asia. The treaty was supplemented by a Pacific Charter, affirming the rights of Asian and Pacific peoples to equality and self-determination and setting forth goals of economic, social, and cultural cooperation between the member countries. The civil and military organizations established under the treaty have their headquarters in Bangkok, Thailand. SEATO has no standing military force but relies on the forces of member nations; joint maneuvers are held annually. SEATO's principal role has been to sanction (since 1964) the U.S. presence in Vietnam, although France and Pakistan have withheld their support. The organization lost further international support when Great Britain announced (1968) a troop reduction in Southeast Asia. Pakistan officially withdrew from SEATO in 1972. By 1973, the future of the organization was in doubt, and New Zealand had called for a new alliance to supersede SEATO.

South El Monte, city (1970 pop. 13,443), Los Angeles co., S Calif., in the San Gabriel Valley; inc. 1958. Its manufactures include home furnishings, household appliances, building materials, and various farm implements.

Southend-on-Sea, county borough (1971 pop. 162,326), Essex, E England, at the mouth of the Thames River. It is a popular seaside resort. Its manufactures include aluminum foil, paint, electronic equipment, and pharmaceuticals. Yachting events are held annually. The borough has an important airport.

Southern Alps, mountain range, on South Island, New Zealand, paralleling the west coast. It rises to (12,349 ft/3,764 m) at Mt. Cook, New Zealand's highest peak. Extensively glaciated, the snow-capped range has many deep gorges; Tasman and Franz Josef glaciers are there.

Southern California, University of, at Los Angeles; coeducational; chartered and opened 1880. The university's facilities include von KleinSmid Center for International and Public Affairs and the Allan Hancock Foundation for Scientific Research, which conducts work in oceanography and marine biology. There is a noteworthy fine arts gallery and a library that houses outstanding collections in American literature and the biological sciences. The university maintains a medical school campus in downtown Los Angeles.

Southern Cross: see CRUX.

Southerne, Thomas (sŭth'ərn), 1660–1746, English dramatist, b. Ireland. Educated at Trinity College, Dublin, he moved to London where he pursued a career as a writer. He was a friend of Dryden and wrote prologues and epilogues for several of Dryden's plays. Southerne is chiefly remembered for his two sentimental tragedies, *The Fatal Marriage* (1694) and *Oroonoko* (1696), both based on novels by Aphra Behn. See study by J. W. Dodds (1933, repr. 1970).

Southern Illinois University, mainly at Carbondale; state supported; coeducational; est. 1869, opened 1874 as a normal school; renamed 1947. It has a branch campus at Edwardsville.

southern lights: see AURORA BOREALIS.

Southern Methodist University, at Dallas, Texas; coeducational; chartered 1911, opened by the Methodist Church. The school's facilities include the Graduate Research Center.

Southern Morocco: see MOROCCO.

Southern Pacific Company, transportation system chartered (1865) in California and later reincorporated in Kentucky (1885) and Delaware (1947). Small railroads—known collectively as the Southern Pacific—were built and merged after 1865 in S California to provide feeder lines to the Central Pacific RR and eventually to provide connections between San Francisco and New Orleans. The Southern Pacific RR survived the Panic of 1873 and inadequate financing, and in 1883, after the company had purchased several Texas railroads, Houston, Galveston, and New Orleans were reached. In 1884 the Southern Pacific and Central Pacific railroads—which were conceived and constructed as parts of one system—were combined under the leadership of Leland STANFORD and Collis P. HUNTINGTON as a unit of interdependent systems. Edward H. HARRIMAN gained control (1901) of the Southern Pacific after Huntington's death and expanded the lines. The Southern Pacific Company added several smaller railroads in the 20th cent. In 1923, after the U.S. Supreme Court had directed (1922) the company to separate the control of the Southern Pacific and Central Pacific railroads, the Interstate Commerce Commission allowed the Southern Pacific to lease the Central Pacific's facilities. The Southern Pacific soon gained control of several bus lines in the Far West and in 1938 took over the trucking service previously provided by the Pacific Motor Transport Company. At the end of World War II the company failed to resume operation of its steamship services from New York City and Baltimore to Galveston, thus abandoning a service that it had operated for over a half a century. Nevertheless, the Southern Pacific has continued a leader in the field of diversified transportation. In addition to its railroad holdings, the company owns pipelines and operates trucks on over 25,000 mi (40,734 km) of highway. See Stuart Daggett, *Chapters on the History of the Southern Pacific* (1922, repr. 1966); N. C. Wilson and F. J. Taylor, *Southern Pacific* (1952); G. L. Dunscomb, *A Century of Southern Pacific Steam Locomotives, 1862–1962* (1963).

Southern Rhodesia: see RHODESIA.

Southern Yemen: see YEMEN, SOUTHERN.

South Euclid (yo͞o'klĭd), city (1970 pop. 29,579), Cuyahoga co., NE Ohio, a suburb of Cleveland; inc. as a city 1940. It is mostly residential and is the site of Notre Dame College, a Roman Catholic school for women.

Southey, Robert (sou'thē, sŭth'ē), 1774–1843, English author. Primarily a poet, he was numbered among the so-called Lake poets. While at Oxford he formed (1794) a friendship with Coleridge and joined with him in a plan for an American utopia along the Susquehanna River that was never actualized. Southey married in 1795, made several trips to Portugal, and in 1803 settled with his wife and the Coleridges near Keswick in the Lake District. A prolific writer, he enjoyed great popularity and renown in his day and was made poet laureate in 1813. Today, however, his reputation as a poet rests upon his friendships with Coleridge and Wordsworth and a handful of short poems, notably "The Battle of Blenheim," "The Holly Tree," and the epic *Vision of Judgment* (1821). As a prose writer, however, his reputation has increased. Included among his prose works are biographies of Nelson (1813) and Wesley (1820), several histories, ecclesiastical writings, and translations from the French and Spanish. See his letters (ed. by Jack Simmons, 1951); study by Geoffrey Carnall (1960); Lionel Madden, ed., *Robert Southey: The Critical Heritage* (1972).

South Farmingdale, uninc. town (1970 pop. 20,464), Nassau co., SE N.Y., on Long Island.

Southfield, city (1970 pop. 69,285), Oakland co., SE Mich., a suburb of Detroit, on the Rouge River; laid out 1817, inc. as a city 1958. Many well-known companies have offices there. The city also has varied light manufacturing and a warehousing industry. Duns Scotus College, Lawrence Institute of Technology, and an extension center of Wayne State Univ. are there.

South Gate, city (1970 pop. 56,909), Los Angeles co., S Calif., an industrial suburb of Los Angeles; inc. 1923.

Southgate, city (1970 pop. 33,909), Wayne co., SE Mich., a residential suburb of Detroit; settled 1840–60, inc. 1958.

South Georgia, island, c.1,450 sq mi (3,760 sq km), S Atlantic Ocean, c.1,200 mi (1,930 km) E of Cape Horn. It is a dependency of the British colony of the FALKLAND ISLANDS and with the Falklands is claimed by Argentina. Capt. James Cook took possession of South Georgia in 1775. The island, located in the world's greatest whaling area, is a center for whalers. The population fluctuates seasonally.

South Glamorgan (gləmôr'gən), nonmetropolitan county, S Wales, created under the Local Government Act of 1972 (effective 1974). It comprises the county borough of CARDIFF and portions of the former counties of GLAMORGANSHIRE and MONMOUTHSHIRE.

South Hadley, residential town (1970 pop. 17,033), Hampshire co., W Mass., on the Connecticut River near the Holyoke Range; settled 1684, inc. 1775. Its paper industry dates from the early 19th cent. Today electronic equipment, machinery, metal stampings, and concrete products are also made. The first navigable canal in the United States began operation there in 1795. Mount Holyoke College is in South Hadley.

South Holland, Dutch *Zuidholland,* province (1971 pop. 2,991,700), c.1,085 sq mi (2,810 sq km), W Netherlands, bounded by the North Sea in the west. The Hague is the capital; other cities include Rotterdam, Dordrecht, Leiden, Delft, Schiedam, and Gouda. A fertile lowland, protected by dunes and dikes along the coast, its physical geography is similar to that of NORTH HOLLAND, with which it was united until 1840 as HOLLAND.

South Holland, village (1970 pop. 23,931), Cook co., NE Ill., a suburb of Chicago; settled 1846 by Dutch, inc. 1894.

South Houston, city (1970 pop. 11,527), Harris co., S Texas, an industrial suburb of Houston; inc. 1911.

South India, Church of, merger of six major Protestant denominations in India. The churches in the merger were four Anglican dioceses in India, Burma, and Ceylon (Sri Lanka); the Methodist Church of South India; and the South India United Church, which itself was formed in 1908 by a union of Congregationalists, Presbyterians, and Dutch Reformed groups, to which was added in 1919 the Basel Malabar Mission containing some Lutherans. Discussions concerning union began at a conference at Tranquebar in 1919, and in 1947, after India attained independence, the union was completed. The Church of South India has its own service book and communion service, both of which draw from several denominational sources. It is in limited communion with the Anglican Church and the Protestant Episcopal Church of the United States. The union, especially in its reconciliation of the Anglican doctrine of apostolic succession with the views of other denominations, is often cited as a landmark in the ECUMENICAL MOVEMENT. The Church of South India has 16 dioceses and a membership of about 1.1 million. See Bengt Sundkler, *Church of South India* (rev. ed. 1965); T. S. Garrett, *Liturgy of the Church of South India* (1958).

Southington (sŭth'ĭngtən), town (1970 pop. 30,946), Hartford co., central Conn.; settled 1696, inc. 1779. Manufacturing began in Southington in the 1770s, and its thriving machine tool industry was spurred by inventions made there before 1840. Chemicals, primary and fabricated metals, and electrical and transportation equipment are among the town's other manufactures.

South Island (1971 pop. 811,268), 58,093 sq mi (150,461 sq km), New Zealand. It is the larger but less populous of the two principal islands of the country. It is separated from North Island by Cook Strait and from Stewart Island by Foveaux Strait. The Clutha and the Waitaki are the largest rivers. The Southern Alps extend almost the entire length of the island. The Fiordland National Park includes a major portion of the southwest area. South Island's principal cities are CHRISTCHURCH, DUNEDIN, and INVERCARGILL. Grain, fruit, timber, and sheep are the leading products; some coal, gold, and oil is found there. The island has several large hydroelectric projects.

South Kensington Museum: see VICTORIA AND ALBERT MUSEUM.

South Kingstown (kĭng'stən, kĭngz'toun"), town (1970 pop. 16,913), seat of Washington co., S R.I.; settled 1641, inc. 1674 as Kingstown, divided into South Kingstown and North Kingstown 1723. Textiles are the chief product. South Kingstown includes the villages of Kingston, seat of the Univ. of Rhode Island, and Wakefield, birthplace (now a museum) of Oliver Hazard Perry. The Narragansett Indians made their last stand in KING PHILIP'S WAR at nearby Great Swamp, now a historical site called Great Swamp Reservation.

South Manchurian Railway, Japanese-developed enterprise, with a trackage of 701 mi (1128 km). The line from Ch'ang-ch'un to Port Arthur (Lü-shun), originally belonging to the Russian-built Chinese Eastern Railway, was part of Japan's indemnity in the Russo-Japanese War (1904–5). Japan later constructed a line to connect Mukden (Shen-yang) and Tan-tung. Other cities served by the railroad are Talien (Dairen), An-shan, and Fu-shun. The prosperity of Manchuria is in large part attributable to the linking by the railroad of the coastal ports and the hinterland. The **South Manchurian Railway Company,** formerly the largest economic enterprise in Manchuria and the main agency of Japanese penetration, was organized shortly after the Russo-Japanese War. It undertook construction of towns, harbor improvements, coal and iron mining, utility development, and agricultural experimentation. When the Manchurian warlord CHANG HSUEH-LIANG refused to halt construction of a competing Chinese railway network, the Japanese Kwantung army staged the MANCHURIAN INCIDENT (1931) and set up the state of Manchukuo (1932). At the end of World War II, China expropriated the company's property.

South Miami, city (1970 pop. 19,571), Dade co., SE Fla., a suburb of Miami; settled 1899, inc. 1926. Baked goods are produced there.

South Milwaukee, industrial city (1970 pop. 23,297), Milwaukee co., SE Wis., on Lake Michigan; settled 1835, inc. 1897. Excavating machinery, electrical transmission equipment, street lights, and leather products are among the many manufactures. The city is the site of an annual music festival.

South Orange, village (1970 pop. 16,971), Essex co., NE N.J., inc. 1869. It is mostly residential and is the home of Seton Hall Univ.

South Orkney Islands, group in the South Atlantic, c.850 mi (1,370 km) SE of Cape Horn. Discovered in 1821, they were claimed by the British and are included as dependencies of the colony of the FALKLAND ISLANDS. The Argentine government, which also claims them, maintains meteorological and wireless stations on Laurie Island.

South Ossetia: see OSSETIA, USSR.

South Pasadena (păs"ədē'nə), city (1970 pop. 22,979), Los Angeles co., S Calif., a suburb of Los Angeles; inc. 1888. It is chiefly residential, but there is some industry.

South Pass, broad, level valley (alt. c.7,550 ft/2,300 m), SW Wyo., cutting across the Rocky Mts. An important unit of the Oregon Trail, it served for many years as a gateway for immigration to the Far West. South Pass has been designated a national historic landmark.

South Plainfield, borough (1970 pop. 21,142), Middlesex co., NE N.J.; inc. 1926. It is the seat of several research and consulting firms and has plants making chemicals, electrical machinery, structural steel, gypsum products, and toys.

South Platte (plăt), river, c.450 mi (720 km) long, rising in the Rocky Mts. in many branches, which then join in central Colorado. It flows in a narrow canyon E and NE to Denver, then NE across the Great Plains to join the North Platte in central Nebraska, where it forms the Platte River. On the Great

Plains the river is broad and shallow and loses much water by evaporation. Grazing and irrigated agriculture are important there. The river basin has many private irrigation dams. The upper course of the South Platte is part of the Bureau of Reclamation's Colorado-Big Thompson project.

South Pole, southern end of the earth's axis, lat. 90° S and long. 0°. It is distinguished from the south MAGNETIC POLE. The South Pole was reached by Roald Amundsen, a Norwegian explorer, in 1911. See ANTARCTICA.

Southport, county borough (1971 pop. 84,349), Lancashire, NW England. A seaside resort with light industries, it has the Atkinson Art Gallery, several art and technical schools, and a fine boulevard—Lord Street. Flower shows and golf tournaments are held annually. In 1974, Southport became part of the new metropolitan county of Merseyside.

South Portland, city (1970 pop. 23,267), Cumberland co., SW Maine, on the Fore River and Casco Bay, part of the Portland metropolitan area; inc. 1898. Ships have been built there since the 17th cent. The industry has been particularly important since 1845 and expanded greatly during World War II. In addition to shipyards, the city has an industrial center with many varied light manufactures. The area was settled c.1633. Fort Preble was built there before the War of 1812. Portland Head Light, near the fort, is the oldest lighthouse (1791) on the Maine coast. The Univ. of Maine at Portland-Gorham is in nearby Gorham.

South River, borough (1970 pop. 15,428), Middlesex co., E N.J.; settled 1720, inc. 1898. Dress manufacturing is its major industry.

South Saint Paul, city (1970 pop. 25,016), Dakota co., SE Minn., a suburb of St. Paul, on the Mississippi River; inc. 1887. It is known for its stockyards and meat-packing industries and is the terminal marketing point for livestock producers in some 20 states. Its 75-acre (30-hectare) public livestock market on the banks of the Mississippi is one of the nation's largest. Building materials and sheet-metal and wood products are also made. The city was settled in 1853 on the site of an Indian village, and the first stockyard was opened in 1887.

South San Francisco, city (1970 pop. 46,646), San Mateo co., W Calif.; inc. 1908. South San Francisco has several industrial parks; its manufactures include steel, chemicals, metal products, paints, and processed foods. The city's founding and growth were spurred in the late 19th cent. by the cattle-ranching and meat-packing industries.

South Saskatchewan: see SASKATCHEWAN, river.

South Sea Bubble, popular name in England for the speculation in the South Sea Company, which failed disastrously in 1720. The company was formed in 1711 by Robert HARLEY, who needed allies to carry through the peace negotiations to end the War of the Spanish Succession. Holders of £9,000,000 worth of government bonds were allowed to exchange their bonds for stock (with 6% interest) in the new company, which was given a monopoly of British trade with the islands of the South Seas and South America. The monopoly was based on the expectation of securing extensive trading concessions from Spain in the peace treaty. These concessions barely materialized, however, so that the company had a very shaky commercial basis. Nonetheless, it was active financially, and in 1720 it proposed that it should assume responsibility for the entire national debt, again offering its own stock in exchange for government bonds, a transaction on which it expected to make a considerable profit. The government accepted this proposal, and the result was an incredible wave of speculation, which drove the price of the company's stock from £128½ in Jan., 1720, to £1000 in August. Many dishonest and imprudent speculative ventures sprang up in imitation. In Sept., 1720, the bubble burst. Banks failed when they could not collect loans on inflated stock, prices of stock fell, thousands were ruined (including many members of the government), and fraud in the South Sea Company was exposed. Robert WALPOLE became first lord of the treasury and chancellor of the exchequer and started a series of measures to restore the credit of the company and to reorganize it. The bursting of the bubble, which coincided with the similar collapse of the MISSISSIPPI SCHEME in France, ended the prevalent belief that prosperity could be achieved through unlimited expansion of credit. Legislation was enacted that forbade unincorporated joint stock enterprise. See studies by L. S. Benjamin (1921, repr. 1968), John Carswell (1960), and V. S. Cowles (1960).

South Seas, name given by early explorers to the whole of the Pacific Ocean. In recent times the name has been used to mean only the central Pacific, the S Pacific, and the SW Pacific. More particularly it is applied to the South Sea Islands (see OCEANIA) and the waters about them.

South Shetland Islands, barren, snow-covered archipelago off N Antarctic Peninsula, W Antarctica; Livingston and King George islands are the largest. The South Shetlands were bases for sealers in the 19th cent., whalers in the early 20th cent., and also for antarctic exploration; they now have scientific bases. The South Shetlands, discovered by the British mariner William Smith in 1819, are claimed by Great Britain, and are part of the British Antarctic Territories. Argentina and Chile challenge this claim.

South Shields, county borough (1971 pop. 100,513), Durham, NE England, at the mouth of the Tyne River. It is a significant port that exports coal and iron. Shipbuilding and marine engineering are the main industries, and chemicals and paints are made. Within the borough are large parks, and there are ruins of a Roman fort on Lawe Hill, above the Tyne. South Shields has a Marine and Technical College. The first unsinkable, self-righting lifeboat, designed by William Wouldhave, was launched at South Shields in 1790. In 1974, South Shields became part of the new metropolitan county of Tyne and Wear.

South Suburban, city (1971 pop. 273,762), West Bengal state, NE India. It is a suburb of Calcutta.

South Vietnam: see VIETNAM.

Southwark (sŭth'ərk, south'wərk), borough (1971 pop. 259,982) of Greater London, SE England, on the Thames River. The borough was created in 1965 by the amalgamation of the metropolitan boroughs of Bermondsey, Camberwell, and Southwark. Printing, engineering, and furniture manufacture are the main industries. Camberwell is mainly residential. The old Southwark area is situated at the convergence of roads to London. It had a number of famous inns, including the TABARD INN; the George Inn (17th cent.), now owned by the National Trust, is still in operation. The Bankside district of Southwark contains the GLOBE THEATER and other places associated with Shakespeare. It was also the location of the Clink Prison, once used for the detention of heretics. Dulwich College, in the Dulwich district of Camberwell, is a public school that opened in 1619. Camberwell has notable art galleries.

Southwell, Robert, 1561?-1595, English Jesuit poet, venerated by Roman Catholics as a martyr, b. Norfolk. He was brought up a Catholic and educated abroad, mainly at Douai. In 1580 he made his simple vows as a Jesuit, and in 1586 at his own request, desiring martyrdom as he said, he was sent to England with Father Garnett to minister to the oppressed Catholics. For six years he was active in the south of England as their pastor, but in 1592 he was arrested and imprisoned. After being tortured he was tried for treason, and on admitting his priesthood, he was hanged. His poetry is deeply religious, extolling the beauty and magnificence of the spiritual in contrast to the material. Southwell's major work is *St. Peter's Complaint* (1595), but he also wrote several fine short devotional poems, such as "The Burning Babe." See his complete poems (1872, repr. 1971); biography by C. Devlin (new ed. 1967).

Southwell (sŭth'əl, south'əl), rural district (1971 pop. 57,365), Nottinghamshire, central England. It includes the small civil parish of Southwell, which since 1884 has been the cathedral town of Nottinghamshire. Charles I surrendered to the Scottish commissioners at the King's Arms (now Saracen's Head) Inn in 1646. The present cathedral, begun c.1110, is on the site of a church said to have been founded in the 7th cent. by Paulinus.

South West Africa or **Namibia** (nămĭb'ēə), Afrik. *Suidwes-Afrika*, country (1970 pop. 746,328), c.318,000 sq mi (823,620 sq km), SW Africa, administered by the Republic of South Africa. It is bordered by Angola in the north, by Zambia in the northeast, by Botswana in the east, by South Africa in the southeast and south, and by the Atlantic Ocean in the west. The Orange River forms the southern boundary, and the Kunene, Okavango, and Zambezi rivers form parts of the northern and northeastern borders. The country includes the CAPRIVI STRIP in the northeast, and the South African enclave of WALVIS BAY in the west. The capital and largest city of South West Africa is WINDHOEK; other towns include KEETMANSHOOP, TSUMEB, LÜDERITZ, GOBABIS, and Otjiwarongo. The country has four main geographical regions: the arid and barren Namib Desert, which runs along the entire Atlantic coast with widths of from 50 to 80 mi (80–130 km); an extensive central plateau that averages c.3,600 ft (1,100 m) in elevation; the western fringes of the Kalahari Desert in the east; and an alluvial plain in the north that includes the Etosha Pan, a large salt marsh. The highest point is Brandberg Mt. (8,402 ft/2,561 m), situated in the western part of the central plateau. The country has an ethnically diverse population that includes the Bantu-speaking Ovambo, Okavango, and HERERO (together 441,000 persons); various Nama (see KHOIKHOI) groups (33,000); the distinctive Bergdama (65,000), whose origins are uncertain; Bushman, or SAN (22,000); and whites of South African, German, and British descent (together 91,000). English and Afrikaans are official languages. About half the population is Christian, and the rest, mostly black Africans, follow traditional beliefs. Because of inadequate rainfall, crops are not widely raised and pastoralism forms the backbone of the economy. Goats and sheep are raised mainly in the south, and cattle are herded chiefly in the north. Agricultural income is derived mainly from Karakul pelts, livestock, and dairy goods. The country's few manufactures are made up mostly of processed food. There is an extensive mining industry, run principally by foreign-owned companies. The chief minerals are diamonds, copper, lead, manganese ore, zinc concentrate, salt, amethyst, germanium, and vanadium. Fishing fleets operate in the Atlantic. The central part of the country is served by roads and rail lines

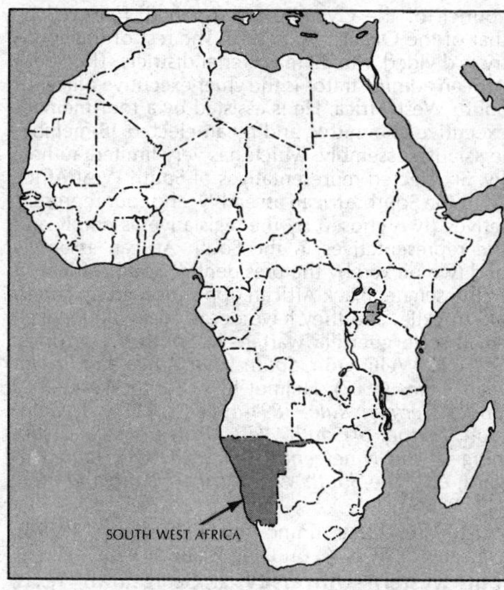

that are linked to the South African systems. The earliest inhabitants of South West Africa were San hunters and gatherers, who lived there as early as 2,000 years ago. By A.D. c.500, Nama herders had entered the region; they have left early records of their activities in the form of cave paintings. The Herero and Ovambo migrated into South West Africa from present-day Zaïre after about 1800. Diogo Cam and Bartolomeu Dias, both Portuguese navigators, landed on the coast in the early 15th cent. Portuguese and Dutch expeditions explored the coastal regions, and in the late 18th cent. Dutch and British captains laid claim to parts of the coast. These claims, however, were disallowed by their governments. In the 18th cent., English missionaries arrived, and they were followed by German missionaries in the 1840s. During the 1860s and the early 1880s, missionaries appealed in vain to Britain for protection from the effects of the endemic warfare among the black Africans. However, Britain did annex Walvis Bay in 1878. The Bremen trading firm of F. A. E. Lüderitz gained a cession of land at Angra Pequeña (now Lüderitz) in 1883, and in 1884 the German government under Otto von Bismarck proclaimed a protectorate over this area, to which the rest of South West Africa (Ger. *Süd-West Afrika*) was soon added. Conflicts between the indigenous population and the Europeans, mainly over control of land, led to outbreaks of violence in the 1890s and especially in the 1900s. In 1903 the Nama began a revolt, joined by the Herero in 1904. The Germans pursued an uncompromising military campaign that by 1908 had resulted in the death of about 54,000 Herero (out of a total Herero population of about 70,000), many of whom were driven into the Kalahari Desert, where they perished; 30,000 other black Africans also died in the revolt. In 1908 diamonds were discovered near Lüderitz, and a large influx of Europeans began. During World War I the country was occupied (1915) by South African forces, and after the war South Africa began (1920) to administer it as a C-type MANDATE under the League of Nations. In 1921-22 the Bondelzwarts, a small Nama group, revolted against South African rule, but they were crushed by South African forces employing air power. After the founding of the United Nations in 1945, South Africa, unlike the other League of Nations mandatories, refused to surrender its mandate and place South West Africa under the UN trusteeship system. In 1960, Ethiopia and Liberia (both of which had been members of the League) initiated proceedings in the International Court of Justice (The Hague) to have the mandate declared as being in force and to have South Africa charged with failing to fulfill the terms of the mandate. The court ruled in July, 1966, that Ethiopia and Liberia had not established a legal right or interest entitling them to bring the case. However, the UN General Assembly in Oct., 1966, passed a resolution terminating the mandate, and in 1968 it resolved that the country be known as Namibia. In June, 1971, the International Court of Justice reaffirmed the General Assembly's 1966 resolution and ruled that South Africa should immediately withdraw its administrators. However, the South African government has maintained that the United Nations has no authority over South West Africa, and it has proceeded with plans for establishing 10 African homelands (Bantustans) in the country and for tying it more closely to South Africa. The homeland areas are to be governed by elected legislative councils. In 1968, the legislative council of the Ovambo was opened, followed by that of the Okavango in 1970. The rest of the country is divided into 22 magisterial districts. The South African administrator is the chief executive officer of South West Africa. He is assisted by a four-member executive committee and by an elected 18-member legislative assembly, which has very limited authority. Six elected representatives of South West Africa sit in the South African assembly, and four representatives (two chosen by the legislative assembly and the representatives in the South African assembly and two picked by the president of South Africa) sit in the senate. Black African opposition groups operate in exile, and they have occasionally undertaken small-scale guerrilla warfare in South West Africa. See J. H. Wellington, *South West Africa and Its Human Issues* (1967); Helmut Bley, *South West Africa under German Rule, 1894-1914* (tr. 1971); I. Goldblatt, *History of South West Africa from the Beginning of the Nineteenth Century* (1971); John Dugard, ed., *The South West Africa/Namibia Dispute* (1973).

South Westbury, uninc. town (1970 pop. 10,978), Nassau co., SE N.Y., on Long Island.

Southwestern University, at Georgetown, Texas; coeducational; United Methodist; chartered 1840 as Ruterville College. The school merged with several other Methodist colleges to become a university in 1875.

South Windsor (wĭn'zər), town (1970 pop. 15,553), Hartford co., N Conn.; set off from Windsor 1845. Oliver Wolcott, a signer of the Declaration of Independence, was born there.

South Yorkshire, metropolitan county (1972 est. pop. 1,315,000), N central England, created under the Local Government Act of 1972 (effective 1974). It is subdivided into four metropolitan districts. South Yorkshire comprises the county boroughs of BARNSLEY, DONCASTER, ROTHERHAM, and SHEFFIELD, and parts of the former counties of NOTTINGHAMSHIRE and YORKSHIRE (West Riding).

Soutine, Chaïm (khī'yĭm so͞otĕn'), 1894-1943, French expressionist painter, b. Lithuania. He went to Paris in 1913 and joined the bohemian society of the SCHOOL OF PARIS. Soutine portrayed artist friends, hotel valets, choir boys, and cooks; he also painted still lifes and landscapes. His art was turbulent, slashing, and visceral. He depicted slaughterhouses and human corrosion and depravity, powerfully expressing a tortured sensibility. Characteristic is his *Page Boy at Maxim's* (Albright-Knox Art Gall., Buffalo), executed in brilliant color and heavy impasto. Soutine is represented in many leading collections including the Phillips Gallery, Washington, D.C., and the Art Institute, Chicago. The Barnes Foundation, Merion, Pa., owns 100 of his works. See catalog by M. Tuchman (1968); studies by M. Wheeler (1950), M. Castaing and J. Leymarie (1964), and A. Forge (1965).

Souvanna Phouma, Prince (so͞ovä'nä fo͞o'mä), 1901–, government official of Laos; half brother of Prince SOUPHANOUVONG. Of royal background, he was trained as an engineer; he served in the ministry of public works (1931-45) and became its head (1950-51). From 1950 he held a variety of key government posts, including the premiership (1951-54, 1956-58, and 1960). He led the neutralist government from 1960 to 1962, and after the Geneva conference on Laos he assumed (1962) the offices of prime minister and minister of defense in the short-lived coalition with the Communist Pathet Lao. Continuing as premier, he later took on additional cabinet posts. In 1973, despite right-wing opposition, he signed an agreement with the pro-Communist Pathet Lao in order to end fighting between government and Pathet Lao troops. In 1974 he formed a new coalition government with the Pathet Lao, in which his half brother Souphanouvong, leader of the Pathet Lao, was included.

sovereignty, supreme authority in a political community. The concept of sovereignty has had a long history of development, and it may be said that every political theorist since Plato has dealt with the notion in some manner, although not always explicitly. Jean BODIN was the first theorist to formulate a modern concept of sovereignty. In his *Six Bookes of a Commonweale* (1576) Bodin asserted that the prince, or the sovereign, has the power to declare law. Thomas HOBBES later furthered the concept of kingly sovereignty by stating that the king not only declares law but creates it; he thereby gave the sovereign both absolute moral and political power. Hobbes, like other social contract theorists, asserted that the king derives his power from a populace who have collectively given up their own former personal sovereignty and power and placed it irretrievably in the king. The concept of sovereignty was closely related to the growth of the modern nation-state, and today the term is used almost exclusively to describe the attributes of a state rather than a person. A sovereign state is often described as one that is free and independent. In its internal affairs it has undivided jurisdiction over all persons and property within its territory. It claims the right to regulate its economic life without regard for its neighbors and to increase armaments without limit. No other nation may rightfully interfere in its domestic affairs. In its external relations it claims the right to enforce its own conception of rights and to declare war. This description of a sovereign state is denied, however, by those who assert that international law is binding. Because states are limited by treaties and international obligations and are not legally permitted by the UNITED NATIONS Charter to commit aggression at will, they argue that the absolute freedom of a sovereign state is, and should be, a thing of the past. In current international practice this view is generally accepted. The United Nations is today considered the principal organ for restraining the exercise of sovereignty. See C. E. Merriam, *History of the Theory of Sovereignty since Rousseau* (1900, repr. 1968); H. J. Laski, *Studies in the Problem of Sovereignty* (1917, repr. 1968); Bertrand de Jouvenel, *Sovereignty* (tr. 1957); J. L. Brierly, *The Law of Nations* (6th ed. 1963); F. H. Hinsley, *Sovereignty* (1966).

Sovetsk (səvyĕtsk'), formerly **Tilsit** (tĭl'zĭt), town (1967 est. pop. 36,000), NW European USSR, on the Neman River at the mouth of the Tilse. It is a rail junction, a river port, and an industrial and commercial center in an agricultural area. Lumbering and woodworking are the chief industries; others include the production of machines, iron, cotton cloth, and Tilsit cheese. The town grew around a castle built in 1288 by the Teutonic Knights and was chartered in 1552. Napoleon I, having won the battle of Friedland, met Emperor Alexander I of Russia on June 25, 1807, on a raft in the Neman River off Tilsit. Their negotiations, joined later by King Frederick William III of Prussia, an ally of Russia, led to the treaties of Tilsit of July 7 and July 9, 1807. By the first treaty, France made peace with Russia, which recognized the grand duchy of Warsaw and which secretly promised to mediate between France and England; if England should reject mediation, Russia was to ally itself with France. At the same time, France gave Russia a free hand with regard to Finland, then a Swedish possession. The Russo-French alliance proved tenuous and collapsed altogether in 1812. In the second treaty, Napoleon drastically reduced Prussia, which lost all its territory west of the Elbe to France and most of its Polish provinces to the grand duchy of Warsaw. Danzig became a free city, the Prussian army was reduced to 42,000 men, several leading Prussian fortresses were to be garrisoned by French troops, and Prussia was to join in the Continental System against England. Prussia was thus reduced to virtual vassalage to France, from which it freed itself only in 1813. Tilsit was occupied by Soviet forces in World War II and was transferred, along with other sections of East Prussia, to the USSR at the Potsdam Conference of 1945.

soviet, primary unit in the political organization of the USSR. The term is the Russian word for council. In the modern political meaning of the word, the first soviets were revolutionary committees organized by the Russian socialists in the Revolution of 1905 among striking factory workers. When the RUSSIAN REVOLUTION broke out in 1917, workers', peasants', and soldiers' soviets sprang up all over Russia. They were led by a central executive committee, which was socialist in composition, but which included not only Bolsheviks, but also Mensheviks (see BOLSHEVISM and MENSHEVISM) and members of the Socialist Revolutionary party. At the first all-Russian soviet congress (June, 1917), the Socialist Revolutionaries had 285 deputies, the Mensheviks 248, and the Bolsheviks 105. The soviets rather than the provisional government represented the real power in Russia, and when the Bolsheviks under V. I. Lenin captured the most important soviets in Petrograd (Leningrad), in Moscow, and in the armed forces, their success was assured. The example was imitated by leftist revolutionists in other countries, notably in Germany and Hungary, where, from 1918 to 1920, workers', peasants', and soldiers' councils were formed with less success. A soviet republic in BAVARIA was shortlived, and the regime of Béla KUN in Hungary was put down by a counterrevolutionary army and by Rumanian intervention. Soviets in the Baltic republics met a similar fate. In Russia the soviets remained the basic political units, forming a hierarchy from rural councils to the Supreme Soviet, the highest legislative body in the USSR. Under the first Soviet constitution only the local soviets were elected by direct suffrage. The constitution of 1936 abolished the division of the electorate into occupational classes and instituted elections of all soviets by direct universal suffrage. The soviets, while forming the broadest base of governmental activity, are dominated by the parallel hierarchy of the Communist party.

Soviet Far East, region (1970 pop. 5,800,000), c.2,400,000 sq mi (6,216,000 sq km), encompassing the entire northeast coast of Asia and including the PRIMORSKY KRAY (Maritime Territory), KHABAROVSK KRAY, and Amur, Magadan, Kamchatka, and Sakhalin oblasts of the USSR. Although often considered a part of Siberia, the Soviet Far East is treated separately in USSR regional schemes. (For information on Siberia, see separate article.) The Soviet Far East is bounded on the NW by the Yakut Autonomous SSR, on the N by the East Siberian Sea, on the NE by the Bering Sea, on the SE by the Sea of Japan, on the S by China (Manchuria), and on the SW by the Yablonovy Mts. Other ranges in this mountainous area include the Stanovoy, Dzhugdzhur, and Kolyma. Arctic TUNDRA covers the far north of the region, and forest TAIGA occupies the central section. In the south are the fertile Amur and Ussuri river valleys, which support crops of wheat, oats, soybeans, and sugar beets. The Soviet Far East is virtually self-sufficient economically. Iron and steel manufacturing, oil refining, lumbering, and machine building are among the many industries that have developed in such important urban centers as VLADIVOSTOK, KOMSOMOLSK, KHABAROVSK, USSURIYSK, and Nikolayevsk. Large thermoelectric stations furnish industrial power. Coal is mined in the Buryea River basin and on SAKHALIN, whose northern half also contains major oil fields. The Kolyma gold fields constitute the chief source of Soviet gold, and there are rich deposits of iron ore, lignite, lead, zinc, and silver in the Soviet Far East. Fishing, fur hunting, and trapping are important occupations. Major means of transport in the region include the Trans-Siberian RR and the Amur River. More than 25 ethnic groups inhabit the Soviet Far East, among them Russians, Jews (see JEWISH AUTONOMOUS OBLAST), Koryaks, Tungus, Chukchi, and Kamchatkans. Russian colonization of the area began in the late 16th cent., when Cossacks built forts and settlements there; Russian fur traders arrived soon afterward. In 1856-57 the Russians took advantage of a weak Chinese empire to occupy all of the territory N of the Amur, and in 1860 they seized the land E of the Ussuri; the People's Republic of China has denounced the "unequal treaties" by which Russia sought to legitimize these conquests. In 1875 the Russians took Sakhalin (formerly under joint Russo-Japanese control) from Japan. With completion of the Trans-Siberian RR, Russian settlement of the Far East accelerated. Russia retained N Sakhalin under the Treaty of Portsmouth (1905), but Japan was awarded the rest of the island. After the Russian Revolution (1917), Japanese forces landed at Vladivostok and occupied large parts of the Russian territory. They were joined by a U.S., British, and French expeditionary force, which arrived in the apparent hope of preventing the German enemy from using the area's plentiful resources during World War I. The interventionist forces gave considerable support to the anti-Bolshevik units of Admiral KOLCHAK, which had occupied most of the region. By 1920, Communist units had defeated Kolchak's troops, and the Allies withdrew. However, the Japanese remained, and in 1920 the Far Eastern Republic was formed as a buffer state between Japan and the Soviet Union. In 1922, the Japanese forces withdrew, the republic was dissolved, and the area was incorporated into the USSR as an oblast. From 1926 to 1938 the whole area was called the Far Eastern Territory. In the settlement following World War II, the USSR acquired the southern half of Sakhalin and the Kuril Islands. The Japanese, however, have since disputed Soviet rights to part of the Kuril chain. In 1969, Sino-Soviet clashes erupted along the Amur and Ussuri frontiers between the countries. Subsequent negotiations bogged down, and both sides reinforced their military capabilities on the long borders. In the early 1970s the USSR began to give new Russian names to cities and physical features in the Soviet Far East with Chinese-sounding names. In response, China accused the USSR of "cartographic aggression," arguing that territory claimed by the Chinese has been shown on Soviet maps to belong to the USSR.

Sower or **Sauer, Christopher** (both: sō'ər, sou'-), 1693–1758, American printer, b. Germany. In 1724, Sower came to America where he worked first as a tailor and then as a farmer. He learned clockmaking and herbal medicine, and in 1738 he founded a printing shop in Germantown, Pa., using types imported from Germany. A book he printed in 1738 was the first German book printed in America. In the same year he established the first German periodical in America, at first a quarterly, later a monthly. In 1743 he printed a German Bible, the second Bible printed in America (the first was the Bible translated into "the Indian Language" in 1663 by John Eliot). His son **Christopher Sower,** 1721–84, established in Germantown the first type foundry in America in 1772. He printed the second Sower German Bible in 1763, the third in 1776. He was a bishop of the Baptist Dunker sect and attacked slavery from the pulpit and the family newspaper. Accused of treason, Sower suffered imprisonment, abuse, and confiscation of his property as a result of clearly stating his pacifist principles during the Revolution. See Felix Reichmann, *Christopher Sower, Sr., 1694–1758: An Annotated Bibliography* (1943).

Sowerby, Leo (sō'ərbē), 1895–1968, American composer and organist, b. Grand Rapids, Mich. Sowerby studied at the American Conservatory, Chicago, and with Percy Grainger. In 1921 an American Prix de Rome was created to enable him to study in Rome. In 1925 he became teacher of composition at the American Conservatory and in 1927 organist and choirmaster of St. James Episcopal Church, Chicago. A prolific composer, he wrote such important works as *A Set of Four* (1917), Symphony in B Minor (1927), and Symphony in F Sharp Minor (1940), for orchestra; a concerto (1938), for organ and orchestra; the oratorios *The Vision of Sir Launfal* (1925) and *The Canticle of the Sun* (1944); and Symphony in G (1932), for organ.

Soya Strait: see LA PÉROUSE STRAIT, Japan-USSR.

soybean, soya bean, or **soy pea,** leguminous plant (*Glycine max, G. soja, or Soja max*) of the family Leguminosae (PULSE family), native to tropical and warm temperate regions of the Orient, where it has been cultivated as a principal crop for at least 5,000 years. There are over 2,500 varieties in cultivation, producing beans of many sizes, shapes, and colors. As a crop, soybeans are high in yield and easy to harvest; they grow well wherever corn is cultivated. In the Orient they are used in a multitude of forms, e.g., as soybean sauce, meal, vegetable oil, vegetable cheese and milk, curds or cake, and as a coffee substitute. The green crop is used for forage and hay, and the cake as stock feed and as fertilizer. In the West these and many other products are produced from soybeans. Soybean oil is used commercially in the manufacture of glycerin, paints, soaps, linoleum, rubber substitutes, plastics, printing ink, and other products. Cultivation of the soybean, long confined chiefly to China and Manchuria, gradually spread to other countries. During World War II soybeans became important in both North America and Europe chiefly as substitutes for other protein foods and as a source of oil. In the United States they are now a leading crop, grown in some 100 varieties; large quantities are exported, chiefly to Japan. Soybeans are classified in the division MAGNOLIOPHYTA, class Magnoliopsida, order Rosales, family Leguminosae. See M. M. Lager, *The Useful Soybean* (1945); J. P. Houck et al., *Soybeans and Their Products* (1972).

Soyer, three brothers, American painters, emigrated with their family from Russia in 1912. Two were twins, **Raphael Soyer,** 1899–, and **Moses Soyer,** 1899–1974, b. Borisoglebsk. They settled in New York City making its inhabitants the chief subject of their paintings. They concentrated on the depiction of the natural attitudes, thoughts, and gestures of individuals in the performance of habitual tasks. Raphael's subdued, realistic style expresses an intimate sympathy for people, as in *Office Workers* (Whitney Mus., New York City) or in his portraits, e.g., *Mina* (Metropolitan Mus.). Moses' figures are usually presented in higher-keyed color or sharper contrasts of black and white, as in *The Old Worker* (Phillips Memorial Gall., Washington, D.C.). Their younger brother, **Isaac Soyer,** 1907–, b. Borisoglebsk, also specialized in everyday figure scenes. His *Employment Agency* (Whitney Mus., New York City) reveals the social realities of the depression years. The Soyers's concern with people and their environment places them within the tradition of American realism established by Winslow Homer, Thomas Eakins, and the EIGHT. See Raphael Soyer's memoirs, *Self-Revealment* (1969); biography by Lloyd Goodrich (1972); Sylvan Cole, Jr., ed., *Fifty Years of Printmaking* (1967); biography of Moses Soyer by Bernard Smith and Charlotte Willard (1944).

Soyer, Alexis Benoît (ālĕksē' bənwä' swäyā'), 1809–58, French chef and writer on gastronomy and dietary reform. After the Revolution of 1830 he went to London and was notable as chef (1837–50) of the Reform Club. In 1847 he was commissioned by the government to open kitchens in Dublin for the benefit of Irish sufferers from famine, and he was (1855–57) in the Crimea as a cooking adviser to the British army, which was suffering from poor diet. Soyer invented relishes and sauces, innumerable kitchen utensils, and several types of stove. His publications include *The Pantropheon; or, History of Food* (1853) and *A Shilling Cookery* (1854). See Helen Morris, *Portrait of a Chef* (1938).

Sozomen (sōzō'mĕn), 5th cent., Byzantine church historian, b. Gaza. A fuller form of his name is Salaminius Hermias Sozomenus. His *Ecclesiastical History* was written in 439–50. The nine extant books, written in an elegant Greek style, cover the years 324–425 and are primarily drawn from the history of SOCRATES SCHOLASTICUS, to which Sozomen added some new material. Sozomen's history continues that of EUSEBIUS OF CAESAREA.

Sozzini, Fausto, and **Lelio Sozzini:** see SOCINUS.

Spa, town (1970 pop. 9,504), Liège prov., E Belgium, in the Ardennes. Its therapeutic mineral springs and baths, frequented since the 16th cent., made it an internationally fashionable watering place, and its name became so well known that the word *spa* now designates any similar health resort. The town had its greatest vogue in the 18th and 19th cent. At the Spa Conference (1920) the Allies accepted a German scheme for paying reparations.

Spaak, Paul Henri (pôl äNrē' späk), 1899–1972, Belgian statesman and Socialist leader. He held various cabinet posts after 1935 and served almost continually as foreign minister from 1938 to 1949. A moderate Socialist, Spaak was three times premier (1938–39, 1946, 1947–49) in coalition governments. He was an opponent of the return of King Leopold III to Belgium. He was again foreign minister from 1954 to 1957, and he resumed that post from 1961 to 1966, serving also as vice premier (1961–65). Spaak acquired international stature as first president of the General Assembly of the United Nations (1946), chairman of the Council for European Recovery (1948–49), and secretary general of NATO (1957–61). In both national and international posts Spaak strove for the political and economic unification of Western Europe, and he was active in the creation of the EUROPEAN COMMUNITY.

space biology: see EXOBIOLOGY.

space exploration, the investigation of physical conditions in space and on stars, planets, and their moons through the use of artificial satellites, space probes, and manned spacecraft. Although studies from earth using optical and radio TELESCOPES had accumulated much data on the nature of celestial bodies, it was not until after World War II that the development of powerful ROCKETS made direct space exploration a technological possibility. The first artificial SATELLITE, Sputnik I, was launched by the USSR on Oct. 4, 1957, and spurred the dormant U.S. program into action, leading to international competition, popularly known as the "space race." Explorer I, the first American satellite, was launched on Jan. 31, 1958. Although earth-orbiting satellites have by far accounted for the great majority of launches in the space program, even more information on the moon, other planets, and the sun has been acquired by unmanned SPACE PROBES and manned spacecraft. In the decade following Sputnik I, the United States and the USSR between them launched about 50 unmanned space probes to explore the MOON. The first probes were intended either to pass very close to the moon (flyby) or to crash into it (hard landing). Later probes made soft landings with instruments intact and finally achieved stable orbits around the moon. Each of these four objectives required increasingly greater rocket power and more precise maneuvering; successive launches in the Soviet Luna series were the

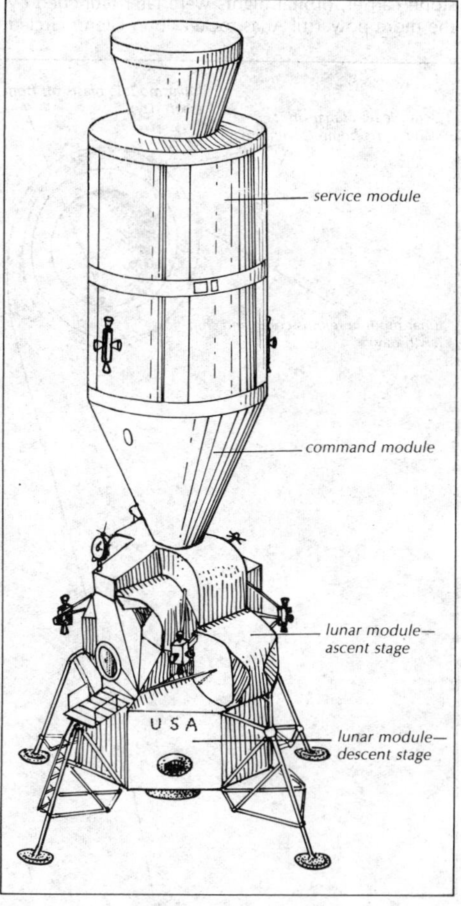

Moon mission assembly

first to accomplish each objective. Luna 2 made a hard lunar landing in Sept., 1959, and Luna 3 took pictures of the moon's far side as the probe flew by in Nov., 1959. Luna 9 soft-landed in Feb., 1966, and Luna 10 orbited the moon in April, 1966; both sent back many television pictures to earth. American successes generally lagged behind Soviet accomplishments by several months, but provided more detailed scientific information. In the U.S. program, the early Pioneer launches were largely failures, as were the first five launches in the Ranger series, which attempted semihard landings of rugged instruments. Subsequent Rangers carried only television cameras and impacted at full speed. Beginning in July, 1964, Rangers 7, 8, and 9 transmitted thousands of pictures, many taken at altitudes less than 1 mi just before impact and showing craters only a few feet in diameter. The Surveyor series was the American program for unmanned soft landings on the moon. Surveyor 1 touched down in June, 1966; in addition to television cameras, it carried instruments to measure soil strength and composition. The Surveyor program established that the moon's surface was solid enough to support a manned spacecraft. In August, 1966, the United States successfully launched the first Lunar Orbiter, which took pictures of both sides of the moon as well as the first pictures of the earth from the moon's vicinity. The Orbiter's primary mission was to locate suitable landing sites for Apollo, the manned-spacecraft program, but in the process it also discovered the lunar mascons, regions of mass concentration on the moon's surface. Between May, 1966, and Nov., 1968, the United States launched seven Surveyors and five Lunar Orbiters. The USSR launched four Lunas; it is believed that the Soviets intended a fifth Luna to make a soft landing, take rock samples, and return them to earth, but the mission, launched 33 days before Apollo 11, failed. A smaller Soviet program involved the Zond spacecraft; two Zonds circled the moon and returned to earth in what were believed to be unmanned tests for the Soyuz program. Manned spaceflight progressed from the simple to the complex, starting with suborbital flights; subsequent highlights included the launching of a single astronaut in orbit, several astronauts in a single capsule, rendezvous and docking of two spacecraft, lunar orbit, and finally the televised landing of man on the moon. The first man in earth orbit was a Soviet cosmonaut, Yuri Gagarin, in Vostok 1 on April 8, 1961. The American Mercury program began in 1960 with suborbital flights powered by the Redstone carrier; orbital flights were later launched by the more powerful Atlas rocket. John Glenn circled the earth three times in Feb., 1962, and a flight of 22 orbits was achieved by Mercury in May, 1963. In Oct., 1964, three Soviet cosmonauts were launched in a Voskhod spacecraft. During the second Voskhod flight in March, 1965, a cosmonaut left the capsule to make the first "walk in space." The first launch of the Gemini program, carrying two American astronauts, occurred a few days after the Soviet spacewalk. The United States made its first spacewalk during Gemini 4. Gemini 5 remained aloft for 120 orbits; Gemini 6 and 7 came within 1 ft (30 cm) of each other and flew in close formation for nearly 8 hr, thus demonstrating the feasibility of a space rendezvous and docking operation. The first actual docking of two craft in space was achieved in March, 1966, when Gemini 8 was attached to an unmanned vehicle. In Oct., 1967, two Soviet Cosmos spacecraft performed the first automatic, unmanned rendezvous and docking. Gemini and Voskhod were followed by the American Apollo and the Soviet Soyuz programs, respectively. In 1961, President Kennedy had committed the United States to the goal of landing men on the moon and bringing them safely back to earth by the end of the decade. The resulting Apollo program was the largest scientific and technological undertaking in history. The goal was spectacularly realized on July 20, 1969, when astronauts Neil A. Armstrong and Edwin E. ("Buzz") Aldrin, Jr., stepped out onto the moon, while a third astronaut, Michael Collins, orbited the moon in the command ship. In all, there were 17 Apollo missions and 6 lunar landings. The first 6 Apollo missions were unmanned checkouts of the complex equipment. Apollo 8 was the first to orbit both earth and moon. Apollo 11 was the first to land on the moon. Subsequent missions produced increasingly large amounts of scientific data, except the ill-fated Apollo 13, which was aborted although the astronauts returned safely. Apollo 15 marked the first use of the Lunar Rover, a jeeplike vehicle. Apollo moon flights were launched by the three-stage Saturn V rocket, which developed 7.5 million lb (3.4 million kg) of thrust at liftoff. At launch, the total assembly stood 363 ft (110 m) high and weighed more than 3,000 tons. The Apollo spacecraft itself weighed 44 tons and stood nearly 60 ft (20 m) high. It was composed of three sections: the command, service, and lunar modules. In earth orbit, the lunar module (LM) was freed from its protective compartment and docked to the nose of the command module. Once in lunar orbit, two astronauts transferred to the LM, which then detached from the command module and descended to the lunar surface. After lunar exploration, the descent stage of the LM remained on the moon, while the ascent stage was jettisoned after returning the astronauts to the command module. The service module was jettisoned just before reentering the earth's atmosphere. Thus, of the huge craft that left the earth, only the cone-shaped command module returned. The scientific mission of Apollo centered around an automated geophysical laboratory, ALSEP (Apollo Lunar Surface Experimental Package). Much was learned about the physical constitution and early history of the earth's only natural satellite, including information about magnetic fields, heat flow, volcanism, and seismic activity. The total lunar rock sample returned to earth weighed nearly 900 lb (400 kg). Until late 1969 it appeared that the USSR was also working toward a manned lunar landing. In Nov., 1968, a Soviet cosmonaut in Soyuz 3 participated in an automated rendezvous and manual approach sequence with the unmanned Soyuz 2. Soyuz 4 and 5 docked in space in Jan., 1969, and two cosmonauts transferred from Soyuz 5 to Soyuz 4; it was the first transfer of men in space from separately launched vehicles. After Apollo 11, however, the USSR apparently abandoned the goal of its own manned lunar exploration. In May, 1972, the United States and the USSR agreed on a plan to dock an Apollo and a Soyuz spacecraft while in earth orbit, the first international manned spaceflight. After the Apollo program, the United States continued manned space exploration with Skylab, an earth-orbiting space station that served as workshop and living quarters for three astronauts. The main capsule was launched by an unmanned booster; the crews arrived later in an Apollo-type craft that docked to the main capsule. Skylab had an operational lifetime of eight months, during which time three three-man crews remained in the space station for periods of about one month, two months, and three months, respectively. The first crew reached Skylab in May, 1972. The Skylab moved in a nearly circular orbit passing once every five days over every point on the earth's middle latitudes. Its interior volume, equal to that of a small house, offered comparative luxury to the occupants, including a large earth-viewing window. Skylab's scientific mission alternated between predominantly solar astrophysical research and study of the earth's natural resources; an overall objective was to evaluate man's response to prolonged conditions of weightlessness. The solar observatory contained eight high-resolution telescopes, each designed to study a different part of the SPECTRUM (e.g., visible, ultraviolet, X-ray, or infrared). Particular attention was given to the study of solar flares (see SUN). One telescope formed an image of the solar disk in a single red spectral line of hydrogen to show surface details more clearly. The earth applications, which involved remote sensing of natural resources, relied on visible and infrared light in a technique called multispectral scanning (see SPACE SCIENCE). The data collected helped scientists to forecast crop and timber yields, locate potentially productive land, detect insect infestation, map deserts, measure snow and ice cover, locate mineral de-

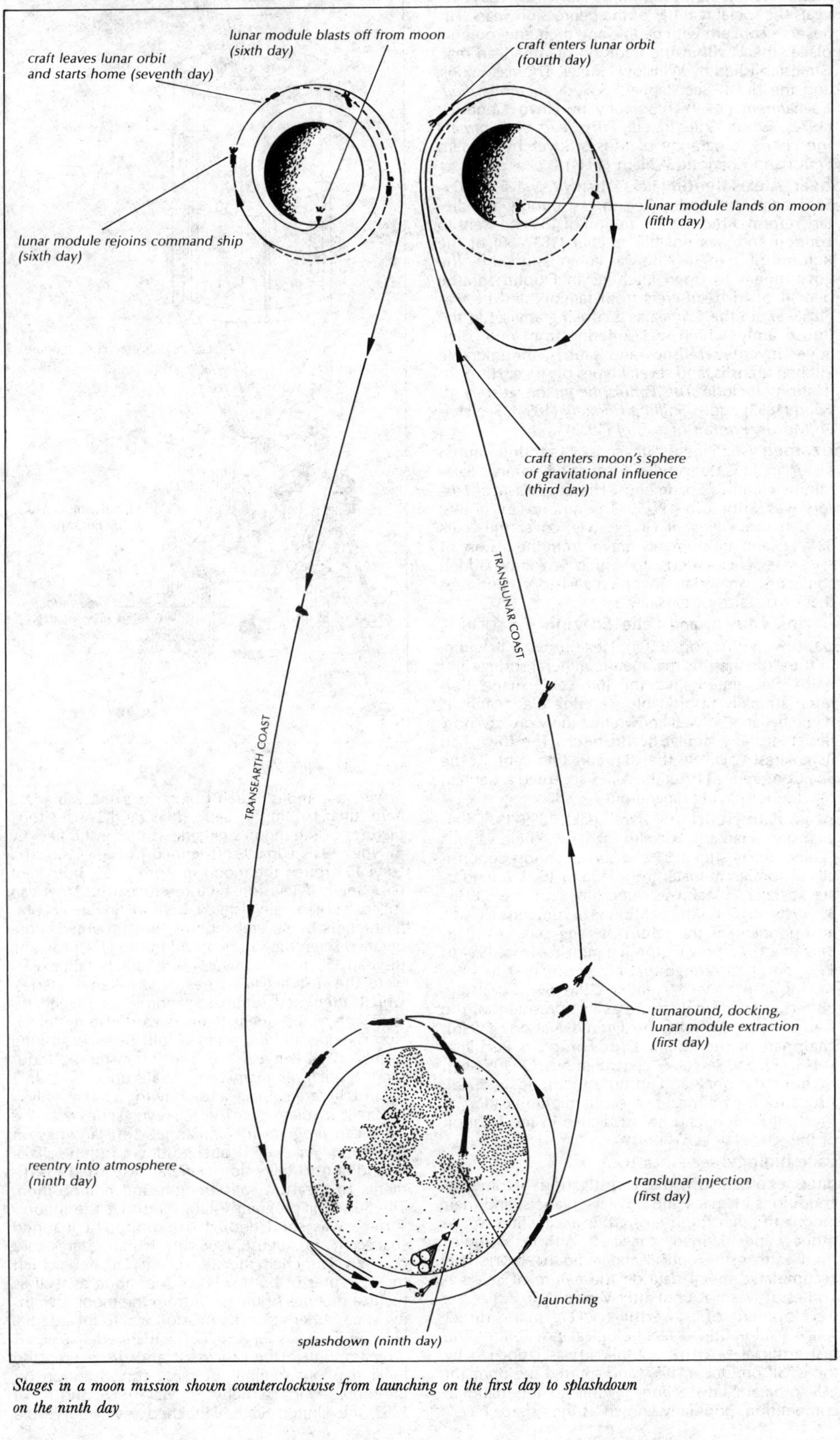

Stages in a moon mission shown counterclockwise from launching on the first day to splashdown on the ninth day

posits, trace marine and wildlife migrations, and detect the dispersal patterns of air and water pollution. In addition, radar studies yielded information about the surface roughness and electrical properties of the sea on a global basis. While the bulk of space exploration has been directed at the earth-moon system, important space probes have also been directed at other members of the solar system. The U.S. Mariner program studied Venus and Mars, the two planets closest to the earth. In 1962, Mariner 2 passed within 21,500 mi (37,600 km) of Venus; in 1965, Mariner 4 took the first close-up pictures of Mars; in 1967, Mariner 5 passed within 6,000 mi (10,200 km) of Venus, confirming earlier findings of a high surface temperature and a dense atmosphere rich in carbon dioxide; and in 1969, Mariners 6 and 7 also photographed Mars. The most surprising results of the Mars probes are those of Mariner 9, launched in 1971, which revealed that Mars is a geophysically evolving planet, with recent volcanism, mountains higher than those of earth, and signs of possible water erosion. In addition, close-range photographs revealed the irregular shape of Phobos, one of the tiny Martian moons. Another Mariner, launched in 1973, received a gravitational boost from Venus and went on to pass close to Mercury. Helios, a West German space probe launched by an American rocket, passed close to the sun, well inside Mercury's orbit. Exploration of Mars will continue with the Viking program of unmanned landings on the Martian surface. Two Viking spacecraft are scheduled to arrive on Mars in 1976. The primary mission is a search for life. Three mechanical arms will scoop up soil samples and automated tests will be conducted for photosynthesis, respiration, and metabolism by any microorganisms that may be present. A second pair of Vikings will be launched in 1979. In 1986, a surface roving vehicle will be landed on Mars, computer-programmed to ultimately operate independently of human control. Space probes have also been aimed at the outer planets, and more are projected. One such probe, Pioneer 10, passed through the asteroid belt in 1973, then became the first man-made object to escape the solar system. In 1974, Pioneer II photographed Jupiter's equatorial latitudes and its moons. Although plans were made to take advantage of a rare alignment of Jupiter, Saturn, Uranus, and Neptune, the schedule to visit all four planets with a single space probe between 1977 and 1986 was scrapped for budgetary reasons and replaced with a single Jupiter-Saturn project scheduled for 1977. The probe will pass Jupiter 18 months after launch and reach Saturn two years later, sending back data on the rings of Saturn and the nearly two dozen moons shared by the two giant planets. Manned space exploration will resume in 1978 with the Space Shuttle, designed to ferry men and equipment into orbit and back to earth. Its principal components are the Orbiter, which travels between earth and space, and the Space Tug, which remains in space. The Orbiter is a hypersonic delta-wing airplane about the size of a DC-9. Takeoff will be powered by three liquid-fuel engines fed from a drop tank and two solid-fuel engines. The solid fuel will burn out at an altitude of 26 mi (42 km) and the two engines will be recovered by parachute. Except for the drop tank, which is not recovered after being jettisoned in earth orbit, the same equipment may be reused for as many as 100 flights. By such economy, the cost of space exploration will be greatly reduced. The Orbiter's reentry into the earth's atmosphere will be unpowered, but the craft is capable of gliding 1,100 mi (1,800 km) to either side of its initial trajectory. The Orbiter can put its payload only in earth orbits below 600 mi (970 km). At first, every payload destined for higher altitudes will receive an extra boost from its own attached Centaur rocket. Later in the program, the Space Tug will be able to lift the Orbiter's payloads into higher orbit. (The Space Tug will remain in space indefinitely, refueling from the Orbiter.) Further plans for space exploration include a rendezvous with a comet in 1984 and with an asteroid in 1989. Both the moon and Mars have proved to be relatively active, evolving worlds, but it is hoped that comets and asteroids exist today just as they were formed 4.5 billion years ago, and thus are "fossils" of the creation of the solar system. See William Shelton, *American Space Exploration* (1967); L. P. Bloomfield, ed., *Outer Space* (rev. ed. 1968); Robert Marks, ed., *The New Dictionary and Handbook of Space* (1969); Wernher von Braun, *Space Frontier* (rev. ed. 1971); P. L. Smolders, *Soviets in Space* (tr. 1974).

space law, agreements governing the exploration and use of outer space. When space exploration began, a need was recognized for laws to govern this new activity. In 1963 the UN General Assembly unanimously passed a declaration of principles on space law. It stated that the exploration and use of outer space would be for the benefit and in the interest of all people; that the past practice of European explorers claiming land for their sovereigns would not be repeated; and that no country could claim sovereignty over a celestial body. The declaration also asserted that astronauts and launched objects would be returned promptly and safely if they landed in a foreign country, and that the nations that launched objects would be responsible for any resulting damages. A treaty embodying these principles and adding a prohibition on military use of outer space and a provision for inspection of installations made on celestial bodies was made in 1967. Both the United States and the Soviet Union signed. One of the major unresolved areas in space law is the lack of agreement on the boundary line between air space and outer space. Some favor a distance measure based on the composition of the atmosphere, while others favor a functional approach based on use; if commercial airlines were to use the space, for instance, it would be considered air space.

space medicine, study of the medical and biological effects of space travel on living organisms. The principal aim is to discover how well and for how long man can withstand the extreme conditions encountered in space, as well as how well he can readapt to the earth's environment after a space voyage. The medically significant aspects of space travel include WEIGHTLESSNESS, strong inertial forces experienced during lift-off, radiation exposure, absence of the earth's day-and-night cycle, and existence in a closed ecological environment. Less critical factors are the noise, vibration, and heat produced within the spacecraft. Of these conditions, weightlessness has the most drastic effects; moreover, it will be impossible to eliminate this aspect of space travel until large space stations are constructed that produce an artificial gravity by rotating. Because all life evolved under the constant influence of gravity, it was at first unknown what the effects of weightlessness would be even on the cellular level. It was feared that man in space might lose all coordination and become completely incapacitated. It was also thought that longer exposure to weightlessness might decrease the body's capacity to withstand any gravitational force at all, as a result of weakening of the heart, softening of bones, and deterioration of muscle tone. In the initial stages of manned space flight, weightlessness produced nausea, vomiting, sensory disorientation, and poor muscle coordination. Other effects were loss of weight, slight dehydration, and redistribution of body fluids. However, the eventual success of the manned space flight program has demonstrated that man can adapt to weightlessness for long periods with no significant loss of capacities. Inertial forces due to acceleration are experienced only during lift-off and recovery, but the consequences can be traumatic. The circulatory system is most strongly affected; deprivation of blood to the brain causes dimming of vision and even loss of consciousness. However, lying on a body-contoured couch, astronauts have survived inertial forces eight times stronger than normal gravity. In space the astronauts are exposed to ionizing radiation from particles trapped in the earth's magnetic field, from solar flares, and from the onboard nuclear reactors that help power the spacecraft. This radiation can produce deleterious effects, ranging from nausea and lowered blood count to genetic mutations and leukemia. However, protective shielding has proved adequate to reduce radiation exposure to acceptable levels. The absence of the earthly cycle of day and night during space travel produces subtle effects, both physiological and psychological. It is believed that all body rhythms, such as heart beat, respiration, and changes in body temperature, are regulated by biological clocks whose mechanism is still poorly understood. These rhythms are related to man's pattern of sleep and wakefulness, which in turn is based on the alternation of day and night. However, experience has shown that normal human behavior cycles can be maintained away from the earth by adherence to predetermined schedules. In the closed environment of the spacecraft care must be taken to prevent the buildup of toxic material to dangerous levels; this is accomplished by recycling waste material. The nature of the artificial atmosphere the astronaut breathes is an important biomedical consideration. Ideally, this atmosphere would be identical in composition and pressure to the earth's atmosphere. Any alteration involves the risk of decompression sickness. Despite this and other risks, it was deemed advisable for technical reasons to use a pure oxygen atmosphere at one third of the normal earth pressure during most phases of space travel. The largest body of useful medical data on the effects of prolonged space flight was obtained during the Skylab program of the early 1970s. Astronauts remained continuously in space for periods longer than two months. The loss of bone calcium was insignificant, work capacity was essentially unimpaired, appetite was good, and sleep came easily. However, it was found that the body loses between 6% and 20% of its red blood cells. This effect is still unexplained, but it causes no apparent disability and the blood returns to normal as the astronauts readjust to earth conditions. There have been many indirect benefits to medicine from space science. The need to maintain close watch over the physiological conditions of astronauts has spurred the development of improved means for electronically monitoring essential body functions. Studies of how man would walk in the moon's weak gravitational field has led to a deeper understanding of human locomotion. In the future, space medicine will examine the utility of anabiosis, or suspended animation, for prolonging man's ability to remain in space. Advances in this area may be useful in certain surgical procedures. See also SPACE SCIENCE.

space probe, unmanned space vehicle, usually carrying sophisticated instrumentation, designed to explore various aspects of the SOLAR SYSTEM (see SPACE EXPLORATION). Unlike an artificial satellite, which is placed in more or less permanent orbit around the earth, a space probe is launched with enough energy to escape the gravitational field of the earth and navigate between the planets. Radio-transmitted commands and on-board computers provide the means for mid-course corrections in the space probe's trajectory; some of the more advanced craft have executed complex maneuvers on command from earth when many millions of miles in space. Radio contact between the control station on earth and the space probe also provides a channel for transmitting data recorded by on-board instruments back to earth. Instruments carried by a space probe include radiometers, magnetometers, and television cameras sensitive to infrared, visible, and ultraviolet light; there are also special detectors for micrometeors, cosmic rays, and solar wind. A probe may be directed to orbit a planet, to soft-land instrument packages on a planetary surface, or to fly by as close as a few thousand miles from one or more planets. The particulars of trajectory and instrumentation of each space probe are tailored around the mission's scientific and technological objectives; the data provided by a single space probe may require months or even years of analysis. Much has been learned from probes about the origins, composition, and structure of various bodies in the solar system. Scientists trying to understand the earth's weather by constructing theoretical models of global weather systems make use of the knowledge that is gained concerning the atmospheres and meteorology of the planets. Because conditions on other planets are simpler than on earth, scientists can check each of their hypotheses separately in isolation from complicating factors. The Mariner and Pioneer series have been the most prominent space probes in the U.S. space program. Various Mariners have investigated Mars, Venus, and most recently, Mercury. (Contrary to expectations, Mercury was found to have both a magnetic field and an atmosphere.) Pioneer 10 explored Jupiter, discovering huge radiation belts surrounding that planet, went on to Saturn, and finally became the first man-made object to entirely escape the solar system as it voyaged off into interstellar space. Several Viking space probes are slated to soft-land on Mars in the late 1970s and conduct an automated search for life. Soviet space probes have included the Venera and Lunik series.

space science, body of scientific knowledge as it relates to SPACE EXPLORATION; it is sometimes also called astronautics. Space science draws on the conventional sciences of physics, chemistry, biology, and engineering, as well as requiring specific research of its own. The particular disciplines that are relevant depend on the type of mission being planned. There are four basic categories of space mission. The sounding ROCKET is restricted to suborbital flights with maximum altitude between 35 and 1,300 mi (55–2,100 km). Artificial SATELLITES orbit the earth at altitudes between one hundred and several thousand miles. Unmanned SPACE PROBES travel to the moon and planets. The final and most complex category is manned spaceflight, of which the Apollo moon landings and the Skylab space station are the outstanding examples. The problems that space science must deal with include prediction and control of trajectories and orbits, telecommunications between spacecraft and earth, rocket design and fabrication, and life-support systems for manned flight. The key contribution of physics is CELESTIAL MECHANICS, the laws that govern the motions of bodies moving under the influence of gravitation. By combining Newton's law of universal gravitation and his laws of motion, the path of a rocket in the earth's vicinity can be calculated. This path, known as the trajectory, is strictly determined by the initial thrust, the gravitational field of the earth, and the atmospheric drag encountered. Although the manner in which these factors interact is highly complex, it is possible to determine accurately in advance the trajectory of any rocket and even to alter its course by remote control. If a satellite or unpowered spacecraft is close to the earth, the effects of other heavenly bodies can be ignored and its orbit will be a CONIC SECTION: circular or elliptical for a satellite that remains in a closed orbit around the earth, and parabolic or hyperbolic for a spacecraft or space probe that escapes the earth's gravitational field into an open orbit. The criterion that separates the closed and open orbits is the ESCAPE VELOCITY, which for the earth is 7 mi (11.3 km) per sec. If the initial thrust provided by a rocket gives the object a speed greater than the escape velocity, it will move away from the earth in an open orbit; if the final velocity is smaller than the escape velocity, it will remain at finite distance from the earth in a closed orbit; if the final velocity is less than 5 mi (8 km) per sec, the flight will be suborbital and the object will follow an arc that returns it to earth. A satellite in orbit around the earth typically travels at a height of several hundred miles with a velocity of about 5 mi (8 km) per sec and a period of revolution of 90 min. For certain satellites, however—such as communications satellites—synchronous orbits are desirable; at a distance of 22,300 mi (35,900 km), a satellite's period is exactly 24 hours, so it appears to hover over the same point on the earth's surface. Circular orbits are usually the most desirable but are the hardest to achieve. If a satellite is launched eastward near the equator, it receives a boost from the earth's rotation, but the resulting orbit necessarily lies in the earth's equatorial plane. For some applications, polar orbits, which pass near both of the earth's poles, are preferred. In a polar orbit, a satellite will periodically pass directly over every point on the earth's surface. Translunar and interplanetary trajectories are highly complex, because no simplifying assumptions can be made; the gravitational influences of the sun, moon, and other planets must be considered. Such gravitational forces can be exploited advantageously; for example, in the slingshot effect, a space probe is accelerated as it swings past a planet on the correct trajectory. Landing on the earth or any planet with a significant atmosphere raises the problem of atmospheric friction, which can instantly burn up any spacecraft. In the manned space program, shielding that comes apart is used to absorb the frictional energy as the material of the shielding vaporizes. Also, a spacecraft enters the atmosphere at a shallow angle to avoid the friction produced by excessively high velocities. Long-range life support must be provided in manned spaceflight. This includes oxygen, food, and recycling of waste material. Shielding is also provided against encounters with micrometeorites and cosmic radiation that could damage the spacecraft or be a health hazard for its occupants. The spacesuit is a miniature life-support system for the individual astronaut; it provides sufficient oxygen at the correct pressure to sustain normal body functioning. In more advanced projects like Apollo and Skylab, a "shirt-sleeve" environment, in which the astronauts do not have to wear any life-support equipment, is provided in a large capsule. Spacecraft employ booster rockets for propulsion and small adjustable retro-rockets for changing the orientation of the craft. Rocket propulsion systems vary from the tiny Aerobee sounding rocket to the giant Saturn V used in the Apollo project. For interplanetary flights, propulsion by nuclear or solar energy may be possible. Also being considered are ion and photon engines, which very efficiently provide low thrust that can build up very high velocity during a long flight. Control over unmanned space probes and artificial satellites is maintained from the ground at control centers, where huge electronic computers analyze data and determine the exact moment when a change should be made. These instructions are relayed to the spacecraft by signals carried on certain radio frequencies. Instruments inside the craft also use radio signals to send data back to earth. Radio contact with spacecraft divides naturally into three categories: tracking, telemetry, and control. Tracking is the continuous reporting of a satellite's or space probe's position in space. Telemetry is the transmission of data back to earth by an on-board instrument (e.g., camera, Geiger counter, or magnetometer). Control includes the overall direction of a spacecraft to achieve the intended trajectory. Commands are specific control signals that order execution of a specific maneuver, such as turning on a camera or firing a retro-rocket. Without the development of modern electronics based on miniaturized transistor circuitry, space exploration would have been practically impossible. Unmanned space probes and satellites carry on-board computers of varying degrees of sophistication, and even on manned missions, maneuvering the spacecraft requires the rapid calculation and response available only through electronic logic devices. The instruments carried on spacecraft measure almost every conceivable physical parameter. Devices for measuring micrometeorite density, cosmic rays, magnetic fields, and solar wind were aboard even the early artificial satellites. Television cameras for both visible and infrared light are carried by most space probes. In addition, many spacecraft carry telescopes for different wavelengths of the spectrum, ranging from infrared to X rays and gamma rays. An important technique in space science is called multispectral scanning. Images are formed using only certain selected wavelengths; the data can be used to compile a single, detail color photograph, or can be studied separately. Certain space probes carry more specialized devices, such as ultraviolet spectrographs for studying stars, and coronographs and spectroheliographs for studying the sun. Space biology and space medicine study the reactions of human, animal, and plant life to the physical stresses encountered in space, such as weightlessness and radiation exposure. Attention is also given to the psychological effects on a group of men working together in confined quarters under demanding conditions. See Samuel Glasstone, *Sourcebook on the Space Sciences* (1965); W. M. Hunter, II, *Thrust into Space* (1966); A. C. Clarke, *The Promise of Space* (1968); R. C. Haymes, *Introduction to Space Science* (1971).

space-time, central concept in the theory of RELATIVITY that replaces the earlier concepts of space and TIME as separate absolute entities. In relativity one cannot uniquely distinguish space and time as elements in descriptions of events. Space and time are joined together in an intimate combination in which time becomes the "fourth dimension." The mathematical formulation of the theory by H. Lorentz (see LORENTZ CONTRACTION) preceded the interpretation by A. Einstein that space and time are not absolute. The abstract description of space-time was made by H. Minkowski. In space-time, events in the universe are described in terms of a four-dimensional continuum in which each observer locates an event by three spacelike coordinates (position) and one timelike coordinate. The choice of the timelike coordinate in space-time is not unique; hence, time is not absolute but is relative to the observer. A striking consequence is that simultaneity is no longer an intrinsic relation between two events; it exists only as a relation between two events and a particular observer. In general, events that are simultaneous for one observer will not be simultaneous for another observer. Other relativistic effects, such as the Lorentz contraction and time dilation, are due to the structure of space-time. See E. F. Taylor and J. A. Wheeler, *Spacetime Physics* (1966); N. D. Mermin, *Space and Time in Special Relativity* (1968).

space travel: see SPACE EXPLORATION; SPACE SCIENCE.

Spada, Lionello (lyōnĕl'lō spä'dä), 1576–1622, Italian painter, active mainly in Emilia. His signature was an *L* placed across a sword [Ital. *spada*=sword]. His work shows influence of the grand manner of the Carracci, as in *The Burning of Heretical Books* (San Domenico, Bologna), and of Caravaggio's naturalism, seen in dramatic religious and genre scenes such as *The Way to Calvary* (Parma). In his late works his manner became softer and warmer under Correggio's influence. An example is *The Marriage of St. Catherine* (Parma). Other works are in Reggio and Modena and in the Louvre.

spadefish: see BUTTERFLY FISH.

Spaeth, Sigmund (spāth), 1885–1965, American music critic and writer on music, b. Philadelphia. Spaeth was music editor of the New York *Evening Mail* (1914–18) and in 1919 was on the editorial staff of the New York *Times*. In 1937 he was appointed dean of the Wurlitzer School of Music. He is the compiler of several anthologies of sentimental songs. His books include *Music for Everybody* (1934), *A History of Popular Music in America* (1948), and *The Importance of Music* (1963).

spaghetti: see MACARONI.

Spagna, Lo (lō spä'nyä), c.1450–c.1528, Italian painter, b. Spain, whence his nickname. His real name was Giovanni di Pietro. His art belongs to the Umbrian school and reveals his indebtedness to Perugino and Pinturicchio and to Raphael in the Umbrian period. His works include frescoes and altarpieces in Assisi, *Virgin and Child* (Louvre), and *Madonna and Saints* and *Epiphany* (both: Vatican).

Spagnoletto, Lo: see RIBERA, JUSEPE.

Spahis (spä'hēz), mounted army corps under the Ottoman Empire (Turkey). Drawn from the Muslim population, the Spahis were organized on a basis of personal loyalty, and their officers held feudal fiefs. Mahmud II used the corps to destroy (1826) the JANISSARIES, and soon after he disbanded it. In the French army certain Algerian and Senegalese cavalry units, famed for their flashy dress uniforms, were also known as Spahis.

Spahn, Warren Edward, 1921–, American baseball player, b. Buffalo, N.Y. A spectacular pitcher in high school baseball, Spahn turned professional in 1939 and played in the minor leagues. In 1942 he joined the Boston Braves (later, the Milwaukee Braves) of the National League, but shortly thereafter he was called into service in World War II with the U.S. army; in Europe he won a battlefield commission. He returned to the Braves in 1945 and soon developed into one of the great pitchers of baseball. Before retiring at the age of 44, Spahn won a total of 363 games, a record for left-handed pitchers. He ranks fifth in total victories. In 1973 he was elected to the Baseball Hall of Fame.

Spain, Span. *España* (äspä'nyä), country (1970 pop. 33,823,918), 194,884 sq mi (504,750 sq km), including the Balearic and Canary islands, SW Europe. It consists of the Spanish mainland (190,190 sq mi/492,592 sq km), which occupies the major part of the Iberian Peninsula; of the BALEARIC ISLANDS in the Mediterranean Sea; and of the CANARY ISLANDS in the Atlantic Ocean. MADRID is the capital. The Spanish territories in Africa are SPANISH SAHARA and five enclaves in Morocco. Continental Spain extends from the Pyrenees, which separate it from France, and from the Bay of Biscay, an arm of the Atlantic Ocean, southward to the Strait of Gibraltar, which separates it from Africa. (GIBRALTAR itself is a British possession.) The eastern and southeastern coast of Spain, from the French border to the Strait of Gibraltar, is washed by the Mediterranean. In the west, Spain borders on the Atlantic Ocean both north and south of its frontier with Portugal. The small republic of Andorra is wedged between France and Spain in the Pyrenees. Administratively, Spain is divided into 50 provinces. However, the division into 15 geographic and historic regions, generally corresponding to the old Christian and Moorish kingdoms of Spain, has been maintained for most practical purposes. Spanish summers are generally warm, but winters vary sharply, being mild in coastal areas and colder inland. The center of Spain forms a vast plateau (Span. *Meseta Central*) extending from the Cantabrian Mts. in the north to the Sierra Morena in the south and from the Portuguese border in the west to the low ranges that separate the plateau from the Mediterranean coast in the east. It is traversed from west to east by mountain chains—notably the Sierra de Guadarrama—and the valleys of the Douro (Duero), the Tagus, and Guadiana rivers. Except for some fertile valleys and irrigated lands, the central plateau is arid and thinly populated; wheat growing, viniculture, and sheep raising are the principal economic activities. The plateau comprises CASTILE (Old and New), the heart of Spain, and in the west, LEÓN and ESTREMADURA. The chief cities are Madrid, BURGOS, VALLADOLID, and TOLEDO in Castile; LEÓN, ZAMORA, and SALAMANCA in León; and BADAJOZ in Estremadura. To the northeast of the central plateau is the broad valley of the Ebro, which traverses ARAGÓN and flows into the Mediterranean. Aragón has ZARAGOZA as its chief city; it is historically and geographically connected with CATALONIA, which occupies the Mediterranean coast from the French border to the mouth of the Ebro. BARCELONA, the chief Catalan city, is the largest port and the second largest city of Spain. The W Pyrenees and the northern coast, paralleled by the Cantabrian Mts., are occupied by NAVARRE, with the city of PAMPLONA; the BASQUE PROVINCES, with the ports of BILBAO and SAN SEBASTIÁN; SANTANDER; and ASTURIAS, with OVIEDO and the port of GIJÓN. The extreme northwestern section, occupied by GALICIA, has a deeply indented coast and the excellent ports of La CORUÑA, El FERROL, and VIGO. Along the eastern coast, S of Catalonia, extend the regions of VALENCIA and MURCIA, named after their chief cities. The Balearic Islands, with PALMA as their capital, are off the coast of Valencia. The southernmost part of Spain, S of the Sierra Morena, is ANDALUSIA; it is crossed by the fertile Guadalquivir valley. The chief cities of Andalusia are SEVILLE, CÓRDOBA, and GRANADA, the Mediterranean port of MÁLAGA, and the Atlantic port of CÁDIZ. The Sierra Nevada, rising from the Mediterranean coast, has the highest peak (Mulhacén, 11,411 ft/3,478 m) in continental Spain. Primarily an agricultural country, Spain produces large crops of wheat, potatoes, sugar beets, barley, tomatoes, olives, citrus fruit, grapes, and cork. The best-known wine regions are those of RIOJA, in the upper Ebro valley, and of MÁLAGA and JEREZ DE LA FRONTERA, in Andalusia. Agriculture is handicapped in many regions by an oppressive system of land tenure, by lack of mechanization, by insufficient irrigation, and by soil exhaustion and erosion. The major industries produce textiles, iron and steel, and chemicals. Industries are concentrated chiefly in the Madrid region; in Valladolid; in Catalonia, which has large textile manufactures; in Valencia; and in Asturias and the Basque Provinces, where the rich mineral resources of the Cantabrian Mts. (iron, coal, and zinc) are exploited. Copper is mined extensively at RÍO TINTO; other mineral resources include lead, silver, tin, and mercury. Petroleum is found near Burgos. Fishing, notably for sardines, tunny, cod, and anchovies, is an important source of livelihood for the coastal population, and fish canning is a major industry. Spain's greatest trade is with the United States, West Germany, France, and Great Britain. Among leading exports are fruit, wine, and other food products, ships and other transportation equipment, and chemicals; major imports include machinery, petroleum, and iron and steel. Tourism is Spain's greatest source of income. Formerly considered an extremely poor country, Spain has made great economic progress in recent years, but it is still the least prosperous nation in Western Europe. Overland communications are generally poor. Most Spanish railroads, unlike those of the rest of Western Europe, use broad-gauged tracks. The Spanish people, despite the strongly centralized government, display great regional diversity. Separatist tendencies remain particularly strong among the Catalans and the Basques. The Castilian dialect has become the standard Spanish language, but Catalan (akin to Provençal), Galician (akin to Portuguese), and Basque, unrelated to any other language, are still spoken and written extensively in their respective districts. The Roman Catholic Church is the established church in Spain. Illiteracy is high among the lower classes despite laws compelling elementary education. Among the 12 universities those of Navarre, Salamanca, Madrid, and Barcelona are the most important.

Government. Spain is governed under seven fundamental laws passed since 1938 and the organic law of 1966. Generalissimo Francisco Franco is the leader (caudillo), chief of state for life, commander in chief, and head of the Falange, the only legal party. Franco designated (1969) Prince Don Juan Carlos de Bourbon, grandson of Alfonso XIII, to succeed him upon his death; the prince will become king and chief of state. In a largely symbolic move, Franco relinquished (1973) the office of prime minister to Admiral Luis Carrero Blanco. Later that same year Carrero Blanco was assassinated by Basque separatists and was replaced by Carlos Arias Navarro. The Council of the Realm is an advisory body to the head of state. The legislature is the Cortes, whose members are chosen by the chief of state, the Falange, trade unions, and municipal and provisional councils; ministers of state and university rectors are ex officio members. The Cortes does little more than ratify executive decrees.

Spain before the Muslim Conquest. Civilization in Spain dates back to the Stone Age. The BASQUES may be descended from the prehistoric men whose art has been preserved in the caves at Altamira. They antedated the IBERIANS, who mixed with Celtic invaders at an early period. Because of its mineral and agricultural wealth and its position guarding the Strait of Gibraltar, Spain was known to the Mediterranean peoples from very early times. The Phoenicians passed through the strait and established (9th cent. B.C.) colonies in Andalusia, notably at Cádiz and Tartessus (possibly the biblical TARSHISH). Later the Carthaginians settled on the east coast and in the Balearic Islands, where Greek colonies also sprang up. In the 3d cent. B.C., the Carthaginians under HAMILCAR BARCA began to conquer most of the Iberian Peninsula and the Balearics and established CARTAGENA as capital. However, the Roman victory over Hannibal in the second of the PUNIC WARS (218–201 B.C.) resulted in the expulsion of the Carthaginians. The Romans conquered E and S Spain, but met strong resistance elsewhere, notably in the north. The fall (133 B.C.) of NUMANTIA marked the end of organized resistance, and by the 1st cent. A.D. Roman control was virtually complete. Except for the Basques, the Iberian population became thoroughly romanized, perhaps more so than any subject population. Roman rule brought political unity, law, and economic prosperity. Christianity was introduced early; St. Paul is supposed to have visited Spain, and St. James the Greater is its apostolic patron. Natives of Spain contributed increasingly to both pagan and Christian literature in Latin. Among them were Seneca, Martial, and Quintilian. In A.D. 409, Spain was overrun by the first wave of Germanic invaders, the Suevi and the VANDALS. They were followed by the VISIGOTHS, who forced the Vandals to emigrate into Africa and established (419) their kingdom in Spain and S Gaul, with Toulouse as capital. The victory (507) of the Franks under Clovis over ALARIC II at Vouillé resulted in the loss by the Visigoths of most of Gaul; in the Iberian Peninsula, Belisarius temporarily reconquered (554) S Spain for the Byzantine Empire; however, the Visigoths soon regained S Spain and in 585 also conquered the kingdom of the Suevi in Galicia. The Visigothic capital after the loss of Toulouse was at Toledo. The Germanic Visigoths, who adhered to Arianism until the late 6th cent., and the Catholic, romanized native population lived side by side under two separate codes of law (see GERMANIC LAWS); fusion of the two elements was

very slow. King RECCESWINTH imposed (c.654) a common law on all his subjects. His code remained the basis of medieval Spanish law. Learning was cultivated almost exclusively by the Roman Catholic clergy, among whom OROSIUS and St. Leander and his brother, St. ISIDORE OF SEVILLE, were outstanding. Byzantine cultural influence was strong, but was probably less important than that of the JEWS, who had settled in Spain in large numbers, and were persecuted after 600. Politically, the Visigothic kings were weak; the clergy, meeting in councils at Toledo, acquired secular power. Visigothic society was rent by a clash of Germanic, Hispano-Roman, and Jewish influences. When, in 711, a Muslim Berber army under TARIQ IBN ZIYAD crossed the Strait of Gibraltar into Spain, RODERICK, the last Visigothic king, was defeated, and his kingdom collapsed.

Muslim Spain and the Christian Reconquest. The MOORS, as the Berber conquerors were called, soon conquered the entire peninsula except for Asturias and the Basque country. Córdoba became the capital of the emir, who governed in the name of the Baghdad caliph. In 756, however, ABD AR-RAHMAN I, scion of the UMAYYAD dynasty, established an independent emirate. This Muslim state, which reached its greatest splendor under ABD AR-RAHMAN III, who set up the Western caliphate, or caliphate of Córdoba, included all but northernmost Spain. In the northeast, CHARLEMAGNE created (778) the Spanish March, out of which grew the county of Barcelona (i.e., Catalonia). In the W Pyrenees, the Basques held out against both Frankish and Moorish attacks and eventually united in the kingdom of Navarre. Asturias, the only remnant of Visigothic Spain, became the focus of the Christian reconquest. The rulers of Asturias, who were descended from the semilegendary PELAYO, conquered large territories in NW Spain and consolidated them with Asturias as the kingdom of León. Navarre, under a branch of the Asturian line, reached its greatest prominence under SANCHO III (1000–1035), who also controlled Aragón and Castile. His state split at his death into three kingdoms: Navarre, which soon lost its importance; Aragón, which united (1137) with Barcelona (see ARAGON, HOUSE OF); and Castile, which was eventually united with León (1230) under Ferdinand III and with Aragón (1479) under Isabella I and Ferdinand V. This long process of unification was accomplished by marriage and inheritance as well as by warfare among the Christian kings; it was accompanied by the expansion of the Christian kingdoms at the expense of the Moors. The Umayyad empire had broken up early in the 11th cent. into a number of petty kingdoms or emirates. The ABBADIDS of Córdoba were the most important of these dynasties. They called in the ALMORAVIDS from Africa to aid them against Alfonso VI of Castile. As a result, the Almoravids took over Moorish Spain, but they in turn were replaced (c.1174) by the ALMOHADS, another Berber dynasty. In the battle of Navas de Tolosa (1212), a turning point in Spanish history, the Almohads were defeated by Alfonso VIII of Castile, whose successors conquered most of Andalusia. Little more than the kingdom of Granada remained in Moorish hands; it held out until its conquest by Ferdinand and Isabella in 1492. Disunity among the Moors facilitated the Christian reconquest; however, the states of Christian Spain were also frequently engaged in bloody rivalry, and the Christian kings were in almost continuous conflict with the powerful nobles. Alliances between Muslim and Christian princes were not rare, and the Christian reconquest was a spasmodic, not a continuous, process. A major reason for the Christian victory was that Christian Spain was in a stage of dynamic expansion and religious enthusiasm while Moorish Spain, having attained a high degree of civilization and material prosperity, had lost its military vigor and religious zeal. In the Moorish cities Muslims, Jews, and Christians (see MOZARABS) lived side by side in relative harmony and mutual tolerance. Their excellent craftsmen and industries were famous throughout Europe, and their commerce prospered. Agriculture, helped by extensive irrigation systems, was more productive under the Moors than it has been ever since. To the Christian nobles of N Spain, particularly of Castile and León, the flourishing cities and countryside to the south were a constant temptation. The united state of Aragón and Catalonia, commercially more prosperous than the other Christian kingdoms, was less active in the reconquest and was more concerned with its Mediterranean empire—the Balearics (which for a time formed the separate kingdom of MAJORCA), Sardinia, Sicily, and Greece. Portugal also, after winning its independence in the 12th cent., developed as an Atlantic sea power and took part only in local campaigns against the Moors. It was thus under Castilian leadership that the reconquest was completed, and it was the Castilian nobility that formed the nucleus of the class of feudal magnates—the grandees—who were the ruling class of Spain for centuries after the reconquest. The fall of Granada (1492) made Ferdinand V (see FERDINAND II of Aragón) and ISABELLA I rulers of all Spain. In the same year, in their zeal to achieve religious unity, the Catholic rulers expelled the Jews from Spain. Until 1492 the Jews and the Muslims had been allowed to live in reconquered territory; attempts at conversion were made, but force was generally not used. The expulsion of the Jews deprived Spain of part of its most useful and active population. Many went to the Levant, to the Americas, and to the Netherlands, where their skills, capital, and commercial connections benefited their hosts. The Mudejares, as the Muslims in reconquered Spain were called, were not immediately expelled, but after an uprising they were forcibly converted (1502) to Christianity. Many of the MORISCOS [Christian Moors] secretly adhered to Islam. After many persecutions, they were finally expelled in 1609. The Jewish-Moorish legacy to Spain and to Western Europe is immense. Moorish architecture (see ISLAMIC ART AND ARCHITECTURE) has left a deep imprint on Spain; its most famous example is the ALHAMBRA of Granada. Arabic scholars such as AVERROËS and Jewish scholars such as MAIMONIDES had a major share in the development of Christian scholasticism. Material legacies of Moorish Spain included the great steel industry of Toledo, the silk industry of Granada, the leather industry of Córdoba, and the intensive plantations of olive and fruit trees. By fostering the exploitation of central Spain for sheep grazing, Ferdinand and Isabella unwittingly prepared the ruin of much land that had been fruitful under the Moors. The major economic revolution that occurred during their reign was, however, the discovery (1492) of America by Columbus. By the Treaty of TORDESILLAS (1494), Spain and Portugal divided the world into two spheres of influence. Almost all of South America, Central America, S North America, and the Philippines were added to the Spanish world empire in the 16th cent. Gold and silver, the primary objective of the conquistadores, flowed into Spain in fabulous quantities. Spain in the 16th cent. (the Golden Century) was the first power of the world, with an empire "on which the sun never set," with fleets on every sea, and with a brilliant cultural, artistic, and intellectual life. In the ITALIAN WARS (1494–1559), Spain triumphed over its chief rival, France, and added Naples (see NAPLES, KINGDOM OF) and the duchy of MILAN to its dependencies.

Golden Age and Decline. When Charles I (elected Holy Roman emperor in 1519 as CHARLES V), first of the HAPSBURG kings (who ruled Spain from 1516 to 1700), succeeded Ferdinand V, Spain was still divided into separate kingdoms and principalities, united chiefly in the person of a common ruler. Each kingdom had its separate CORTES and its own customary law. The cities, which had retained their individuality since Roman times, enjoyed great privileges and independence. Charles had to be acknowledged by each individual Cortes at his accession. Castile was nominally ruled jointly by Charles and his mother, JOANNA, until Joanna's death. The centralizing policies of Charles's predecessors had curtailed some of the local powers, particularly in Castile, but Charles's efforts to continue the centralizing process and his fiscal policies resulted in an uprising of the cities—the war of the COMUNIDADES—in 1520–21. The rising was suppressed, and its leader, PADILLA, was executed. By the time Charles abdicated (1556) in Spain in favor of his son PHILIP II, Spain was on its way to becoming a centralized and absolute monarchy. Under Philip II the process was continued, although Catalonia, Navarre, Aragón, Valencia, and the Basque Provinces still maintained a considerable degree of autonomy. During the 16th cent. the church enlarged its already dominant position in Spanish life. The Spanish INQUISITION, organized by Tomás de TORQUEMADA in the late 15th cent., reached its greatest power in the 16th cent. under Philip. At the same time the Catholic Reformation was advanced in Spain by St. IGNATIUS OF LOYOLA, St. Theresa of Ávila, and St. JOHN OF THE CROSS. With Spain, Philip had also inherited Sicily, Naples, Sardinia, Milan, Franche-Comté, the Netherlands, and all the Spanish colonies. His religious policies, fiscal demands, and high-handed rule precipitated the Dutch struggle for independence (see the NETHERLANDS). The northern provinces of the Netherlands shook off the Spanish yoke, but the southern provinces (see NETHERLANDS, AUSTRIAN AND SPANISH) were again subjugated. Spanish military power, which achieved its greatest successes against France, leading to the Treaty of CATEAU-CAMBRÉSIS (1559), and in the naval victory at LEPANTO over the Turks (1571), was on the decline. As the champion of Catholicism in Europe, Spain unsuccessfully intervened in the French Wars of Religion by sending an army to support the LEAGUE against Henry IV. The rivalry on the seas between Spain and England culminated in the attempted conquest of England by the Spanish ARMADA (1588); its complete failure at immense cost weakened Spain for a decade. Under Philip II's successors, PHILIP III and PHILIP IV, Spain was drawn into the THIRTY YEARS WAR (1618–48), prolonged by war with France until 1659. The peace treaties (see WESTPHALIA, PEACE OF; PYRENEES, PEACE OF THE) made France the leading power of continental Europe. The wars of Louis XIV of France (see DUTCH WARS 3; DEVOLUTION, WAR OF; GRAND ALLIANCE, WAR OF THE) cost Spain further territories and military prestige. PORTUGAL, united with Spain by Philip II in 1580, rebelled and regained its independence in 1640. In the same year a serious revolt began in Catalonia over the province's autonomous rights. In the end (1659) the Catalans retained most of their

RULERS OF SPAIN SINCE 1474 (*including dates of reign*)
Union of Castile and Aragón
Isabella I (of Castile), ruled jointly with Ferdinand II (of Aragón), 1474–1504 Ferdinand II, ruled jointly with Isabella I as Ferdinand V of Castile, 1474–1504; ruled Aragón only, 1504–16; ruled Castile as regent, 1506–16
Hapsburg Dynasty
Joanna (the Mad), daughter of Ferdinand and Isabella; ruled Castile only (jointly with Philip I in 1506), 1504–6 Philip I (the Handsome), son of Holy Roman Emperor Maximilian I; ruled Castile jointly with Joanna, 1506 Charles I (Holy Roman Emperor Charles V), son of Joanna and Philip, 1516–56 Philip II, son of Charles I, 1556–98 Philip III, son of Philip II, 1598–1621 Philip IV, son of Philip III, 1621–65 Charles II, son of Philip IV, 1665–1700
Bourbon Dynasty
Philip V, great-grandson of Philip IV, 1700–1746 Ferdinand VI, son of Philip V, 1746–59 Charles III, younger son of Philip V, 1759–88 Charles IV, second son of Charles III, 1788–1808 Ferdinand VII, son of Charles IV, 1808
French Intrusion
Joseph Bonaparte, 1808–13
Bourbon Restoration
Ferdinand VII, restored, 1813–33 Isabella II, daughter of Ferdinand VII, 1833–68
Elective Monarchy
Francisco Serrano Y Domínguez, regent, 1869–70 Amadeus, elected by a constituent assembly, 1870–73
First Republic
Estanislao Figueras, president, 1873 Francisco Pi y Margall, president, 1873 Nicolás Salmerón y Alonso, president, 1873 Emilio Castelar y Ripoll, prime minister, 1873–74
Bourbon Restoration
Alfonso XII, son of Isabella II, 1874–85 Alfonso XIII, son of Alfonso XII, 1886–1931
Second Republic
Niceta Alcalá Zamora, president, 1931–36 Manuel Azaña, president, 1936–39
Nationalist Government
Francisco Franco, chief of state, 1939–

privileges. The political weakness of Spain was complicated by the absence of a direct heir to CHARLES II, who succeeded Philip IV in 1665. The chief claimants to the succession were Louis XIV of France and Archduke Charles of Austria (later Holy Roman Emperor CHARLES VI). The pro-French party at the Spanish court ultimately won out when Charles II designated Louis XIV's grandson, Philip (later PHILIP V of Spain), as successor. The War of the SPANISH SUCCESSION (1701-14) broke out upon Charles's death. The Peace of Utrecht (see UTRECHT, PEACE OF) confirmed Philip V on the Spanish throne, but it transferred the Spanish Netherlands, Milan, Naples, and Sardinia to Austria and Sicily to Savoy. Another result of the war was that Catalonia, Valencia, and Aragón, which had opposed Philip, lost their political autonomy. Attempts to recover the lost possessions and to revive Spanish prestige were fostered by Philip's ambitious queen, ELIZABETH FARNESE, and his chief minister, ALBERONI; these attempts merely led (1718) to the formation of the QUADRUPLE ALLIANCE, which in 1720 imposed upon Spain a but slightly more favorable settlement in Italy. Spain under its BOURBON kings came increasingly under French influence after the FAMILY COMPACT of 1733 and its successors. With the support of France, Spain regained (1735) Naples and Sicily in the War of the POLISH SUCCESSION. These two kingdoms, however, were no longer administered by Spanish viceroys but were ruled independently by a cadet branch of the Spanish Bourbons. In the Treaty of Paris of 1763 (see under PARIS, TREATY OF), Spain lost FLORIDA to Britain but was compensated with LOUISIANA by France. In the American Revolution, Spain sided with the United States and France and recovered Florida in the Treaty of Paris of 1783. These, however, were short-lived successes. The economy of Spain had steadily deteriorated since the reign of Philip II. The influx of precious metal had long ceased, and little of it remained in Spain. The colonization of the vast Spanish Empire and the many costly wars had impoverished the country. Inflation led landowners to increase their holdings. The population had greatly increased and the peasants lived in misery, some of them on the inefficiently run estates of the grandees. The court and government had decayed in an atmosphere of bigotry, incompetence, and corruption. The church, exhausted by the struggle between the popes and the kings, had largely ceased its political role as a constructive force and was using its influence for the perpetuation of the existing order. The towering artistic and intellectual achievements of the 16th cent. had given way, by the mid-18th cent., to meaningless convention. Under Philip V's successors, FERDINAND VI and CHARLES III, the ministers ENSENADA and FLORIDABLANCA made basic reforms. Internal transportation was improved. Agricultural colonies were formed for better utilization of the land. The colonial trade was freed of centuries-old regulations and restrictions. Trade and commerce, especially in Cádiz and Barcelona, were stimulated. The Jesuits were expelled from Spain in 1767 as part of an effort to subordinate church to state. CHARLES IV, who succeeded Charles III, was an incompetent monarch, dominated by his wife, MARÍA LUISA, and their favorite, the able but unscrupulous GODOY. Drawn into the FRENCH REVOLUTIONARY WARS and the Wars of NAPOLEON I, Spain suffered its greatest humiliation in 1808 with the successive abdications of Charles and his son, FERDINAND VII, the installation of Joseph Bonaparte (see under BONAPARTE, family) on the Spanish throne, and the occupation of the country by French troops. However, the rigor and heroism displayed by the common people of Spain in their struggle against the conqueror (see PENINSULAR WAR) was an important factor in the eventual downfall of Napoleon. By 1814 the Spanish resistance forces and the British under Wellington had expelled the French, and Ferdinand VII was restored under a constitution drawn up in 1812 at Cádiz by the first national Cortes of Spain.

Monarchists and Republicans. The nationalist and liberal upsurge that swept over Spain and its overseas empire during the Peninsular War was focused, somewhat incomprehensibly, on the person of Ferdinand VII. After his restoration Ferdinand, through his reactionary measures, forced the forces that had placed him on the throne into opposition. At home, the liberal and radical groups attacked the very institution of the monarchy; overseas, they brought about the independence of the Latin American nations. By 1825 all Latin America except several territories in the West Indies had gained independence. In Spain itself, Ferdinand's refusal to honor the 1812 constitution led to the revolution of 1820, put down in 1823 by French troops acting for the Holy Alliance. Shortly before his death (1833), Ferdinand altered the law of succession in favor of his daughter, ISABELLA II, and to the detriment of his brother, Don CARLOS, Isabella succeeded under the regency of her mother, MARIA CHRISTINA, but her succession was contested by the CARLISTS in a bitter war that raged until 1839. Her turbulent reign (1833-68), which ended in abdication, was a series of uprisings, military coups d'etat, new constitutions, and dictatorships. Politics was largely a matter of personalities—among these ESPARTERO, NARVÁEZ, PRIM, and O'DONNELL were outstanding—but factions generally fell into three groups: the extreme reactionaries, who included the Carlists; the moderates and progressives, who theoretically favored a constitutional monarchy, but who tended to rule dictatorially when they came into power; and the republicans. The Catalan and Basque separatists favored whichever party happened to oppose the central government. After the abdication (1868) of Isabella, the Cortes set up a constitutional monarchy and chose AMADEUS, duke of Aosta, as king. Unable to obtain the cooperation of all factions, Amadeus abdicated in 1873. The short-lived first Spanish republic (1873-74) was torn by another Carlist War (1872-76) and by the cantonalist movement in the south, notably in Cartagena, which attempted to establish authorities independent of the central government. The Bourbon ALFONSO XII, son of Isabella, was placed on the throne by a coalition of moderate parties, and in 1876 a new constitution was adopted. By the end of the 19th cent. the Socialist and Anarcho-Syndicalist parties began to gain a wide following among the lower classes, particularly in industrial Catalonia, rural Andalusia, and in the mining districts of Asturias. Strikes and uprisings, usually suppressed with great brutality, became characteristic features of 20th-century Spain. As the church had become identified with the landowners, anticlerical feeling was violent among the revolutionary, and even among liberal, elements. The loss of most of the remainder of the Spanish Empire in the SPANISH-AMERICAN WAR (1898) prompted a period of self-examination that produced a cultural renaissance. Under Alfonso XIII (reigned 1886-1931), Spain remained neutral in World War I. But wartime trade had increased industrialists' profits. Great social and economic unrest marked the postwar period. Colonial rebellions in Morocco were a recurring problem. In 1923 a new outbreak in Catalonia was suppressed and resulted in the establishment of a military dictatorship under PRIMO DE RIVERA. Widespread opposition forced Primo de Rivera's resignation in 1930; in 1931, after a great republican victory in municipal elections, Alfonso XIII was deposed and the second republic established. Under the new president, the moderate liberal ALCALÁ ZAMORA, the regime instituted progressive reforms, including the distribution of church property, but met widespread opposition from rightist groups and also from the extreme left. There were serious separatist and Anarcho-Syndicalist uprisings in Catalonia. The government shifted to the right after the 1933 elections, and in 1934 a miners' uprising in the Asturias was put down with much bloodshed. The Popular Front (republicans, Socialists, Communists, and syndicalists) was victorious in the national elections of 1936. Before the government under Manuel AZAÑA had time to carry out its program, a military rebellion precipitated the great SPANISH CIVIL WAR of 1936-39. The Insurgents, who soon came under the leadership of Gen. Francisco FRANCO, embraced most conservative groups, notably the monarchists, the Carlists, most of the army officers, the clericalists, the landowners and industrialists, and the fascist FALANGE. Their forces received the immediate military aid of Germany and Italy. The Loyalists were supported by the Popular Front parties and by the nationalists in Catalonia and the Basque Provinces, which had at last been granted autonomy. Because of the nonintervention policy of Britain and France, the Loyalists received virtually no outside support except for an international brigade and some meager aid from the USSR. Despite military inferiority and bloody internal divisions, the Loyalists made a remarkably determined stand, particularly in central Spain. By the beginning of 1938, however, the territory held by the Loyalists had shrunk drastically, and with the fall (Jan., 1939) of Barcelona the war was almost over. Madrid surrendered in March, 1939. The Loyalist government and many thousands of refugees fled into France, and the government of Franco was soon recognized by all major powers except the USSR. A dictatorship was set up under Franco. The church was restored to its property and its favored position, although there was much friction between church and state. The Falange was made the sole legal party, and the leftist opposition was energetically suppressed. The Cortes and Catalan and Basque autonomy were abolished. Although it gave aid to the Axis, Spain remained a nonbelligerent in World War II. The Cortes was reestablished in 1942. The United Nations, refusing to recognize the constitutionality of the Franco regime, urged its members in 1946 to break diplomatic relations with Spain; this resolution was not rescinded until 1950. Spain entered the UN in 1955. An agreement with the United States in 1953 provided for U.S. bases in Spain and for economic and military aid. In 1956, Spanish Morocco became part of the independent state of Morocco; in 1968, Spanish Equatorial Guinea became independent; and in 1969 Ifni was ceded to Morocco. Spain has claimed sovereignty over Gibraltar, and in 1968 it closed the frontier with that British colony. The major problems of Spain remain the explosive political situation and the deep scars left by the civil war. Political unrest, partly over the problem of succession to the Franco regime, became increasingly evident in the 1950s, and at the start of the 60s the church, which had long been silent, began to voice some opposition to aspects of the dictatorship. In 1962 a series of strikes, beginning in the coal fields of Asturias, gave indication of widespread discontent. Student demonstrations also occurred. Basque separatism posed another serious problem for the regime. A new organic law (constitution) was announced by Franco in 1966. It separated the posts of head of government and chief of state, provided for direct election of about one quarter of the members of the Cortes, gave married women the vote, made religious freedom a legal right, and ended Falange control of labor unions. The forming of new political parties was still discouraged. Press censorship was ended in 1966, but strong guidelines remained. Economically, Spain progressed dramatically in the 1960s and early 70s; growth was particularly pronounced in the tourist, automobile, and construction industries. A standard historian of Spain is Rafael ALTAMIRA Y CREVEA. See also Salvador de Madariaga, *Spain* (new ed. 1958); Hugh Thomas, *The Spanish Civil War* (1961); Gerald Brenan, *The Spanish Labyrinth* (1962); R. B. Merriman, *The Rise of Spanish Empire* (4 vol., 1918-36; repr. 1962); Ruth Way and Margaret Simmons, *A Geography of Spain and Portugal* (1962); J. H. Elliott, *The Revolt of the Catalans* (1963) and *Imperial Spain* (1964); Richard Herr, *The Eighteenth-Century Revolution in Spain* (1958, repr. 1967); H. L. Livermore, *A History of Spain* (1968); Américo Castro, *The Spaniards: An Introduction to Their History* (tr. 1971); Ramón Menéndez Pidal, *The Cid and His Spain* (tr. 1934, repr. 1971); Gabriel Jackson, comp., *The Spanish Civil War* (1972); Max Gallo, *Spain under Franco* (1969, tr. 1974).

Spalatin, George (shpä'lätēn), 1484-1545, German Protestant reformer. His original name was Georg Burckhardt; he was called Spalatin after his birthplace, Spalt, near Nuremberg. An early friend of Martin Luther, Spalatin was devoted to the Lutheran cause, and as secretary and court preacher to Frederick III, elector of Saxony, he served as intermediary between Luther and Frederick—a factor important to the success of the Reformation. He wrote *Annales reformationis,* a record of events and rulers of the Reformation period. Many letters to him from Luther are extant.

Spalding, Albert (spôl'dĭng), 1888-1953, American violinist, b. Chicago, studied in Italy and France. He made his debuts in Paris in 1905 and in New York City in 1908 and won wide popularity on his extensive tours. See his autobiography, *Rise to Follow* (1943, repr. 1972).

Spallanzani, Lazzaro (läd'dzärō späl-läntsä'nē), 1729-99, Italian naturalist. He was professor at the universities of Modena (1763-69) and Pavia (from 1769). Spallanzani studied regeneration, fertilization, and the digestive action of saliva; using heat-sterilized cultures, he performed experiments that disproved J. T. Needham's theory of spontaneous generation.

Spandau (shpän'dou), district of West Berlin, Germany, at the confluence of the Havel and Spree rivers. It is a canal port and industrial center. Manufactures include steel and electrical equipment. Spandau was chartered as a town in 1232, and during 1560 to 1594 the electors of Brandenburg built a major fortress there on the Havel River. The fortress was occupied in the Thirty Years War by the Swedes (1631-34) and in the French Revolutionary Wars by the French (1806-13). It later became a dread political prison; several major Nazi war criminals were imprisoned there after the Nuremberg trials (1945–46). Spandau was incorporated into Berlin in 1920.

Spangenberg, August Gottlieb (ou'go͝ost gôt'lēp shpäng'ənbĕrk), 1704–92, a bishop of the MORAVIAN CHURCH and a founder of that church in America, b. Prussia. While at the Univ. of Jena, he met Graf von ZINZENDORF, and in 1730 he paid a visit to the Moravian colony, Herrnhut. In 1732, Spangenberg joined the theological faculty of the Univ. of Halle, but disagreement with the views of his superiors led to his dismissal. He became assistant to Zinzendorf and was sent by him on a mission to America in 1735. There, for a large portion of his life, Spangenberg was active in establishing settlements, churches, and schools in Georgia, Pennsylvania, and North Carolina. In 1744 he was made bishop. Zinzendorf died in 1760; two years later Spangenberg returned to Herrnhut, where he held a place of leadership among the Brethren. His *Idea Fidei Fratrum* (1779, tr. 1784) was adopted as the declaration of faith of the Moravian Church. Among his other writings is a biography of Zinzendorf.

spaniel: see SPORTING DOG; TOY DOG.

Spanish, river, c.150 mi (240 km) long, issuing from Spanish Lake, S Ont., Canada, NW of Sudbury, and flowing generally S through Biskotasi and Agnew lakes to Lake Huron opposite Manitoulin island. There are several hydroelectric stations on the river.

Spanish Africa, name for the Spanish possessions in Africa—CEUTA and MELILLA (enclaves in Morocco), the CANARY ISLANDS, and SPANISH SAHARA. Spain also formerly held IFNI (now part of Morocco) and EQUATORIAL GUINEA.

Spanish American literature. The history of Spanish American literature begins with the writings of the explorers, soldiers, and missionaries who participated in the conquest of the New World. Although they were not born in America, it is their writings, so thoroughly American in content, that form the literature of the early colonial period. Theirs were eyewitness accounts of the discovery, the conquest, the existing civilizations, and the natural wonders of the flora and fauna. These chronicles, letters, histories, religious pieces, and epic poems are the vibrant and fascinating expression of those who fought for church, crown, and gold. The letters of Christopher Columbus to Ferdinand V and Isabella I and those of Hernán Cortés, the conqueror of Mexico, to Charles V are among the classics of this period. Bernal DÍAZ DEL CASTILLO, one of the soldiers of Cortés, wrote a remarkable history of the conquest of Mexico, and the history by the Dominican friar Bartolomé de LAS CASAS of the destruction of the Indies made him the "apostle of the Indians" and the author of the "black legend" of Spain. In poetry there was the epic poem *La Araucana* (1569–89) by Alonso de ERCILLA Y ZÚÑIGA, a soldier who described the conflict between the Spaniards and the Araucanian Indians of Chile. The epic tradition was continued by Diego de HAJEDA and Bernardo de Balbuena. GARCILASO DE LA VEGA, the Inca, was among the first writers born in the New World to write about it. He wrote about the history of the Incas and of Peru. With the growth of Spanish colonial society in America, there was the concomitant growth of literary circles, especially in the viceregal capitals of Mexico City and Lima. The literature of that time was imitative of that which was in vogue in 17th-century Spain. Several notable figures were Juan RUIZ, the Mexican-born playwright, generally considered one of the great Spanish dramatists; JUANA INÉS DE LA CRUZ, Mexican nun, feminist, and intellectual, known for her lyric poetry, plays and prose; and the Peruvian Juan del Valle y Caviedes, known for his satiric poetry and sharp wit. The colonial period in Spanish American history and letters came to an end with the wars for independence in the early 19th cent. Prose writers and poets, imbued with the ideals of revolution and the nationalism of independence, expressed their thoughts in fiery prose and heroic verse. Simón Bolívar, the Liberator, is known for his analyses of the political scene as well as for his military exploits. The Mexican José Joaquín FERNÁNDEZ DE LIZARDI became famous as an ardent propagandist and pamphleteer. Basically a journalist, he is remembered as the author of the first Spanish American novel, *El Periquillo Sarniento* [the itching parrot] (1816), a work in the picaresque genre. José Joaquín Olmedo celebrated the victories of Bolívar in a heroic poem in the classical style entitled *La victoria de Junín: Canto a Bolívar* (1825). Andrés BELLO, the Venezuelan humanist, educator, and poet, also sang of America in his serene *Silva a la agricultura de la zona tórrida* [poem dedicated to the agriculture of the torrid zone] (1826). With political independence from Spain achieved, except in the island countries of the Caribbean, cultural independence swept the country, aided by the romantic tenets of freedom, emotional intensity, and individualism. For a while, classic forms coexisted with ROMANTICISM as in the poetry of José María HEREDIA of Cuba. His *En el teocalli de Cholula* [in the temple-pyramid of Cholula] (1820) is the first Spanish American romantic poem. Among the early romanticists were the young intellectuals who fled from the tyranny of Juan Manuel de Rosas in Argentina. Esteban ECHEVERRÍA expressed himself in the poetic narrative *La cautiva* [the captive] (1827). Domingo Faustino SARMIENTO, also of Argentina, was not only the leading exponent of romanticism but also a prolific writer and educator. His *Facundo* (1845), a study of personalism in politics, is among the classics of Spanish American letters. The emphasis on the national scene, so characteristic of romanticism, gave rise to the *gaucho* literature of Argentina and Uruguay, an indigenous literary genre. The GAUCHO, long the hero of popular tales and ballads, became the subject of some of the most original verse of the century in the poetry of Rafael Obligado, Estanislao del Campo, and in the classic *Martín Fierro* (1872–79) of José HERNÁNDEZ. The romanticist's interest in the search for his native roots can be seen in the epic poem *Tabaré* (1886) of Juan Zorrilla de San Martín, and in the historical anecdotes and sketches, the *Tradiciones peruanas* [Peruvian traditions] (1872–1910), of Ricardo PALMA. Several novels of the period reflect the various trends in letters. *Amalia* (1851–55), by José MÁRMOL, deals with life in Argentina under Juan Manuel de Rosas; *Martín Rivas* (1862), by Alberto BLEST GANA of Chile, depicts the life and customs of Chile; *María* (1867) is the tragic idyll of Jorge ISAACS of Colombia; and *Cumandá* (1871), by Ecuador's Juan León Mera, is a romantic portrayal of Indian life. This same period produced some of Spanish America's most notable essayists. Juan MONTALVO of Ecuador wielded his pen against the tyranny of García Moreno; Eugenio María de HOSTOS of Puerto Rico championed the cause of the independence and union of the islands of the Antilles; and Manuel GONZÁLEZ PRADA of Peru attacked the entire social and economic system of his country and spoke out in defense of the Indian. The writers of Spanish America in the last quarter of the 19th cent. broke with the nationalistic expression of the previous generation and immersed themselves in an artificial world. These were the *modernistas,* who believed in "art for art's sake" and were influenced by the French Parnassian and symbolist schools. They wrote on rare and exotic themes and experimented with language and meter. Those who initiated this literary movement, known as *modernismo,* were the Mexican Manuel GUTIÉRREZ NÁJERA, the Colombian José Asunción SILVA, and the Cubans Julián del CASAL and José MARTÍ, the latter known also for his struggle to gain Cuba's independence from Spain. The movement reached its peak with the publication of the Nicaraguan Rubén Darío's *Azul* [blue] (1888), which influenced writers throughout Spanish America. Among others there were Amado NERVO of Mexico, José Santos CHOCANO of Peru, Ricardo Jaimes Freyre of Bolivia, Guillermo VALENCIA of Colombia, Julio HERRERA Y REISSIG and José Enrique RODÓ of Uruguay, and Leopoldo LUGONES of Argentina. With the passing of modernism, poetry was influenced by many trends and movements. Three women poets, Alfonsina Storni, Juana de IBARBOUROU, and the Nobel Prize winner Gabriela MISTRAL, are known for their impassioned lyrics. Among the poets of the vanguard were Vicente HUIDOBRO of Chile, César VALLEJO of Peru, Jorge Luis BORGES of Argentina, and Chile's Pablo NERUDA, also a Nobel laureate. The prose writers turned their attention to social themes. The essay of the 20th cent., following a tradition perfected by Martí, González Prada, and Rodó, reached new heights of intensity in the writings of José VASCONCELOS of Mexico, known for his theories of race and culture as well as his participation in the Mexican Revolution of 1910 and in the educational reform of his country. The essay was cultivated in a more artistic and aesthetic form by the scholarly Alfonso REYES of Mexico and by Pedro Henríquez Ureña of the Dominican Republic. Later on Mariano Picón-Salas of Venezuela and Germán ARCINIEGAS of Colombia made the essay the vehicle of social, historical, and political ideas in Spanish America. Those who cultivated the novel and short story tended mainly toward social protest and probed the roots of injustice and oppression in humanity. The Mexican Revolution of 1910 produced a kind of sub-genre—the literature of the Mexican Revolution, generally first-hand accounts of every aspect of the revolution. The classic work of this genre is *Los de abajo* [the underdogs] (1915) by Mariano AZUELA. Other works of this type include *El áquila y la serpiente* [the eagle and the serpent] (1928) by Martín Luis GUZMÁN, and *El indio* [the indian] (1935) by Gregorio López y Fuentes. The Indian, the poor, the underdog of any sort now entered literature as an urgent social problem and not as an element of local color. Representative of this *indigenista* literature are *Raza de bronce* [bronze race] (1919), by the Bolivian Alcides ARGUEDAS, *El mundo es ancho y ajeno* [broad and alien is the world] (1941), by the Peruvian Ciro ALEGRÍA, and *Huasipungo* (1934), by the Ecuadorian Jorge ICAZA. The struggle between man and the forces of nature, whether on the plains, in the tropics, or in the cities, was a challenging subject for novels and short stories. The life of the gaucho on the Argentine pampas is depicted in the novel *El inglés de los güesos* [the Englishman with the bones] (1924), by Benito Lynch, and in *Don Segundo Sombra* (1926), by Ricardo GÜIRALDES. Life on the Venezuelan plains is portrayed in *Doña Bárbara* (1929), by Rómulo GALLEGOS. The tropics, replete with struggles of man against man as well as man against nature, are dramatically described in the short stories of the Uruguayan Horacio QUIROGA and in the novel *La vorágine* [the vortex] (1924), by Colombia's José Eustasio RIVERA. Urban society with its many social problems is the theme of the novels of Federico Gamboa of Mexico and Manuel Gálvez of Argentina and the short stories of Manuel Rojas of Chile. With the passage of time the novel and short story became removed from the geographical and social problems of Spanish America and became immersed in the universal currents of literature. There were the psychological novels of Chile's Eduardo BARRIOS and Argentina's Ernesto SÁBATO, the existential works of Argentina's Eduardo MALLEA, and the poetic novels of Mexico's Agustín YÁÑEZ. The contemporary scene in Spanish American letters is rich, especially in the novel and poetry. Both genres have received great critical acclaim outside of the Spanish-speaking world and have been translated into other languages. Guatemala's Nobel Prize-winning Miguel Angel ASTURIAS combined mythological and social themes in his *El señor presidente* [Mr. President] (1946) and *Mulata de tal* (1963). Cuba's Alejo CARPENTIER captured the world of magic and superstition in *El reino de este mundo* [the kingdom of this world] (1949), and Juan RULFO of Mexico recreated a poetic world of reality and fantasy in *Pedro Páramo* (1955). Jorge Luis Borges is noted for his brilliant style, which combines the philosophical, the real, and the fantastic; among his most famous works are his collections of short stories, including *Ficciones* [fictions] (1944) and *El aleph* (1949). Carlos FUENTES of Mexico is recognized among the contemporary novelists for *La región más transparente* [where the air is clear] (1958) and *La muerte de Artemio Cruz* [the death of Artemio Cruz] (1962). Also highly regarded are Mario VARGAS LLOSA of Peru for *La ciudad y los perros* [the city and the dogs] (1963) and *La casa verde* [the green house] (1968), Julio CORTÁZAR of Argentina for *Rayuela* [hopscotch] (1963) and Gabriel GARCÍA MÁRQUEZ of Colombia for *Cien años de soledad* [a hundred years of solitude] (1967). See also SPANISH LITERATURE; PORTUGUESE LITERATURE; BRAZILIAN LITERATURE. For anthologies in translation, see Germán Arciniegas, ed., *The Green Continent* (1944); Harriet de Onís, ed., *The Golden Land: An Anthology of Latin American Folklore in Literature* (1961); W. K. Jones, ed., *Spanish American Literature in Translation: A Selection of Poetry, Fiction and Drama Since 1888* (1963); Arturo Torres-Ríoseco, ed., *Short Stories of Latin America* (1963); Hortense Carpentier and Janet Brof, ed., *Doors and Mirrors: Fiction and Poetry from Spanish America, 1920–1970* (1972). For histories of Spanish American letters, see Arturo Torres-Ríoseco, *The Epic of Latin American Literature* (rev. ed. 1946, repr. 1959); W. R. Crawford, *A Century of Latin American Thought* (1961); Enrique Anderson Imbert, *Spanish-American Literature: A History* (2 vol., 2d ed. 1963); John Englekirk et al., *An Outline History of Spanish American Literature* (1965); Kessel Schwartz, *A New History of Spanish American Fiction* (1972).

Spanish-American War, 1898, brief conflict between Spain and the United States arising out of Spanish policies in Cuba. It was, to a large degree, brought about by the efforts of U.S. expansionists. Demands by Cuban patriots for independence from Spanish rule made U.S. intervention in Cuba a paramount issue in the relations between the United States and Spain from the 1870s to 1898. Sympathy for the Cuban insurgents ran high in America, especially after the savage TEN YEARS WAR (1868–78) and the unsuccessful revolt of 1895. After efforts to quell guerrilla activity had failed, the Spanish military commander, Valeriano WEYLER Y NICOLAU, instituted the *reconcentrado*, or concentration camp, system in 1896; Cuba's rural population was forcibly confined to centrally located garrison towns, where thousands died from disease, starvation, and exposure. Weyler's actions brought the rebels many new American sympathizers. These prorebel feelings were inflamed by the U.S. "yellow press," especially W. R. Hearst's New York *Journal* and Joseph Pulitzer's New York *World*, which distorted and slanted the news from Cuba. The U.S. government was also moved by the heavy losses of American investment in Cuba caused by the guerrilla warfare, an appreciation of the strategic importance of the island to Central America and a projected isthmian canal there, and a growing sense of U.S. power in the affairs of the Western Hemisphere. There was an unspoken threat of intervention, which grew sharper after the insurgents, refusing a Spanish offer of partial autonomy, determined to fight for full freedom. Although the majority of Americans, including President MCKINLEY, wished to avert war and hoped to settle the Cuban question by peaceful means, a series of incidents early in 1898 intensified U.S. feelings against Spain. The first of these was the publication by Hearst of a stolen letter (the de Lôme letter) that had been written by the Spanish minister at Washington, in which that incautious diplomat expressed contempt for McKinley. This was followed by the sinking of the U.S. battleship MAINE in Havana harbor on February 15, 1898, with a loss of 260 men. Although Spanish complicity was not proved, U.S. public opinion was aroused and war sentiment rose. The cause of the advocates of war was given further impetus as a result of eyewitness reports by members of the U.S. Congress on the effect of the *reconcentrado* policy in Cuba. In late March, McKinley proposed to Spain an armistice in Cuba. Meanwhile, however, under pressure from expansionists both in and out of Congress, he was won to the war cause. Although on April 10, 1898, McKinley was informed that the queen of Spain had ordered hostilities suspended, he barely referred to that fact when he addressed Congress on April 11. He asked for authority to intervene in Cuba. Congress responded by passing resolutions to demand Spanish withdrawal from Cuba and set terms for U.S. intervention; these included the Teller Amendment, which pledged that the United States would withdraw from the island when independence was assured. On April 22, Congress authorized the enlistment of volunteer troops, and a U.S. blockade of Spanish ports was instituted. On April 24, Spain declared war on the United States. The next day Congress retorted by declaring war on Spain, retroactive to April 21. The warfare that commenced was short and very one-sided. The first dramatic incident occurred on the other side of the world from Cuba. On May 1 a U.S. squadron under George DEWEY sailed into the harbor of Manila, Philippine Islands, and in a few hours thoroughly defeated the Spanish fleet there. Dewey's name was greeted across the United States with almost hysterical praise. On May 19, Admiral Pascual CERVERA Y TOPETE took the Spanish fleet into the harbor of Santiago de Cuba. Commodore W. S. SCHLEY established (May 28) a blockade of the harbor, in which Rear Admiral W. I. SAMPSON joined, taking command of the blockading fleet on June 1. When the Spanish fleet attempted to escape on July 3, it was destroyed. Meanwhile 17,000 more or less trained, poorly equipped, but enthusiastic U.S. troops under W. R. SHAFTER landed and undertook a campaign to capture Santiago. The Spanish forces were weak, but there was some heavy fighting (July 1) at El Caney and San Juan Hill, where the ROUGH RIDERS, under Leonard WOOD and Theodore ROOSEVELT, won their popular reputation. On July 17, Santiago surrendered. The war was, in effect, over. Troops sent under Nelson A. MILES to Puerto Rico were occupying that island when they received word that an armistice had been signed on Aug. 12. Dewey and Wesley Merritt led a successful land and sea assault and occupation of Manila on Aug. 13, after the armistice had been signed. Peace was arranged by the Treaty of Paris signed Dec. 10, 1898 (ratified by the U.S. Senate, Feb. 6, 1899). The Spanish Empire was practically dissolved. Cuba was freed, but under U.S. tutelage by terms of the Platt Amendment (see under PLATT, ORVILLE), with Spain assuming the Cuban debt. Puerto Rico and Guam were ceded to the United States as indemnity, and the Philippines were surrendered to the United States for a payment of $20 million. The United States emerged from the war with new international power. In both Latin America and the Far East it had established an imperial foothold. The war tied the United States more closely to the course of events in those areas. See A. T. Mahan, *Lessons of the War with Spain* (1900, repr. 1970); F. E. Chadwick, *Relations of the United States and Spain: Diplomacy* (1909, repr. 1968) and *Relations of the United States and Spain: The Spanish-American War* (1911, repr. 1968); Walter Millis, *The Martial Spirit* (1931); J. W. Pratt, *Expansionists of 1898* (1936, repr. 1959); F. B. Freidel, *The Splendid Little War* (1958); H. W. Morgan, *America's Road to Empire* (1965).

Spanish Armada: see ARMADA, SPANISH.

Spanish art and architecture. Open to a wide variety of cultural influences, the art and architecture of Spain have had an unusual and exciting heritage. Aside from important prehistoric remains, including cave paintings (see CAVE ART) at Altamira and at Cogul, near Lérida (see PALEOLITHIC ART), the earliest monuments date from the Roman occupation (3d cent. B.C.–5th cent. A.D.). Little remains of the works of the Visigothic period (6th–7th cent.), although crude classical motifs were used, especially in the decorative sculpture. Such monuments as the Church of San Juan de Baños in the province of Palencia (A.D. 661) suggest a possible Oriental influence in the use of a flattened horseshoe arch, which predates the full horseshoe arch introduced by the Moors (8th cent.) and extensively employed in the famous mosque at Córdoba (8th–10th cent.). In their palaces and mosques the Moors developed certain architectural features that have remained part of the Spanish tradition down to the present day. Moorish interiors, subdivided into isolated units, are cool and graceful and utilize intricate effects of light and shadow, as in the famous Court of the Lions in the ALHAMBRA (Granada). This tendency to enframe space is reflected in the enclosed choirs of almost all Spanish cathedrals and collegiate churches. Other Moorish elements, such as multifoil and intersecting arches, influenced the Christian buildings of medieval Spain, as did the Moorish love of reiteration and multiplicity of small motifs in luxuriant flat ornament (exemplified in the Alhambra). By 850 the Moors had conquered all Spain except the Asturias region. Characteristic of Asturian churches (9th cent.) is a basilican plan with square apses, rounded arches, and balustered windows. In Santa Maria de Naranco (mid-9th cent.) is found one of the earliest uses of barrel vaulting in the Middle Ages. The art and architecture of the Mozarabs (9th–11th cent.), combining Asturian and Moorish features, produced some of the most original and interesting European buildings of the time. During the Romanesque period (11th–12th cent.) Christian Spain in general exhibited characteristics common to the Romanesque style of Europe, but with traces of Oriental influence. The cathedral at Santiago de Compostela (11th–12th cent.) reveals striking analogies in both architecture and sculpture to Burgundian works. With the gradual unification of the Spanish kingdoms, there was increased prosperity and artistic activity during the Gothic period (13th–mid 16th cent.). Castilian architecture was basically French-inspired, although a distinctly native taste can be felt in the proportions and more ornate decorative features. Outstanding examples include the cathedrals of Burgos, Toledo, and León, the last being remarkable also for its stained glass. Catalan Gothic architecture, exemplified in the cathedrals at Barcelona and Palma de Majorca, made distinctive use of wide naves with two side aisles instead of the usual four; they have heavy interior buttresses and lateral chapels. At Gerona the aisles were suppressed altogether, so that the cathedral had one of the widest vaulted spans of medieval Europe. A pervasive element in Spanish architecture is the MUDÉJAR style, whose influence lasted well into the 18th cent. The favorite materials of the Mudéjar builders were brick, plaster, and wood, which they employed with singular versatility. Their decoration is distinguished by the use of the elaborate geometrical configurations and stylizations associated with most Islamic art. Gothic churches, particularly in the south, are frequently crowned by Mudéjar *artesonados*, or wooden roofs. Early Gothic sculpture was predominantly influenced by French models. In the 15th and early 16th cent. there were strong Flemish and German trends. RETABLES and choir stalls were elaborately sculptured and polychromed, the former being sometimes made of alabaster. Remarkable examples include those in the cathedrals of Tarragona, Seville, and Toledo. At the end of the 15th cent. Gil de Siloe executed the magnificent retable and royal monuments in the church of Miraflores (near Burgos), representative of a late Gothic realism. In painting of the 13th and 14th cent., there was a diffusion throughout Spain of the elegant and courtly style of French and Sienese artists, although strikingly expressive and original works of art were created by masters such as Ferrer Bassa and Luis Borassá. Extensive trade with the Netherlands in the 15th cent. encouraged the emergence of a Hispano-Flemish style, exemplified in the paintings of Jaume Huguet. A successful combination of Moorish and Flemish elements was developed in the works of the painter Fernando Gallego. In the 16th cent. Italian sculptors working in Spain, such as Jacopo Fiorentino, Domenico Fancelli, and Pietro Torrigiano, did much to popularize Renaissance motifs, which were combined with Gothic and Mudéjar in works of the PLATERESQUE style. An outstanding monument of the plateresque style is the cathedral of Granada by Diego Siloe. Its rotunda in particular, designed on the model of the Holy Sepulcher at Jerusalem, also reflects the humanistic aspirations of those architects who were classically inclined. Typical of the more ornamental plateresque are the facade of the Univ. of Salamanca (c.1520–30) and that of the Convent of San Marcos (León). A more developed High Renaissance style appears in such works as the unfinished palace of Charles V (Granada), designed by Pedro Machuca, and the ESCORIAL, designed by Juan Bautista de Toledo and finished by Juan de Herrera. Outstanding native sculptors, such as Alonso Berruguete, Juan de Juni, and Gregorio Fernández, were strongly influenced by the more tortuous creations of Donatello and Michelangelo. Italianate painters, such as Luis de Vargas and Luis de Morales, and, later, Juan de Juanes, developed eclectic and mannerist styles. It was only toward the end of the century that a genius appeared who truly incarnated the dark, mystical Spanish idiom—El Greco. With roots in the Byzantine and Venetian traditions, he translated aspects of Italian form in terms of his own highly spiritual, incandescent vision. The baroque period (17th–mid 18th cent.) was marked by decisive affirmation of native taste and individual genius in all the arts. Polychrome religious sculptures by Juan Martínez Montañés, Alonso Cano, and Pedro de Mena exemplify characteristic effects of extreme realism and an inward spirituality. Similarly in painting, sobriety of color and insistent naturalism, as well as dramatic contrasts of light and shade, were typical of such masters as Ribalta, Ribera, Navarrete, and Zurbarán, who are sometimes linked with Caravaggio and the Italians known for their dark palettes, termed *tenebrosi* [gloomy]. However, the outstanding master of the period was Velázquez, one of the greatest figures in the history of art. His paintings are admired as much for their display of technical virtuosity as for their profundity of characterization. The works of Murillo revealed a tendency to lyricism and decorative effects. In architecture an extreme reaction against the severity and restraint of Renaissance forms manifested itself in the Churrigueresque style, which was characterized by animation of surface, play of light and shade effects, and an exaggeration and sumptuousness of ornament (see under CHURRIGUERA). Examples of Churrigueresque architecture include the Transparente in Toledo cathedral and the sacristy of the Cartuja (Granada). The style was imported into the American colonies (see SPANISH COLONIAL ARCHITECTURE). Under the Bourbons there was strong reaction against the individualism and exuberance of late baroque art. The founding in 1752 of the first of the Spanish academies of art resulted in a wave of sterile academic neoclassicism that tended to discourage creativity in the arts for nearly two centuries. The great exception to the general decline was Francisco Goya, a frenzied spirit who detailed in his works the corruption and brutality of Spain. Among 19th-century painters, José de Madrazo y Agudo belonged with the school of Jacques-Louis David; Mariano Fortuny, with French romantic and historical painters. The foremost architect working in the neoclassical style was Juan de Villanueva. At the turn of the century the architect Antonio Gaudí designed a number of startling and enormously original structures in Barcelona, including the Expiatory Church of the Holy Family. The foremost of modern painters, Pablo Picasso, though born a Spaniard, is permanently associated with the SCHOOL OF PARIS, as are the cubist Juan Gris, the surrealists Joan Miró and Salvador Dali, and the sculptor Julio González. In the 1950s there was an outburst of ABSTRACT EXPRESSIONISM in Spain represented in the works of Antonio Tapies and Luis Sáez, among many others. In general, Spanish minor arts exhibited characteristics analogous to those of the major arts in the corresponding periods. Rich mineral resources in Spain and later in the colonies made for extensive development of wrought metalwork. Characteristically Spanish are luxuriantly decorated iron church screens or *rejas* (see REJERÍA). Moorish influence encouraged development of filigree and enamel as well as tooled leather. Flemish influence encouraged the establishment of tapestry works. In the 18th cent. Buen Retiro porcelains (named for the palace at Madrid) were among the finest ceramics produced in Europe. See articles on individual artists, e.g., GOYA. See George Kubler and Martin Soria, *Art and Architecture in Spain and Portugal and Their American Dominions* (1959); José Gudiol, *The Arts of Spain* (tr. 1964); Carmen Gomez-Moreno, *Spanish Painting: The Golden Century* (1965); C. R. Post, *A History of Spanish Painting* (14 vol. in 20, 1930–66); Bradley Smith, *Spain: A History in Art* (1966).

Spanish bayonet: see YUCCA.

Spanish civil war, 1936–39, conflict in which the conservative and traditionalist forces in Spain rose against and finally overthrew the second Spanish republic. The second republic, proclaimed after the fall of the monarchy in 1931, was at first dominated by middle-class liberals and moderate socialists, among them Niceto ALCALÁ ZAMORA, Francisco LARGO CABALLERO, and Manuel AZAÑA. They began an attack on the traditional privileged structure of Spanish society: Some large estates were redistributed; church and state were separated; and an antiwar, antimilitarist policy was proclaimed. With their interests and their ideals threatened, the landed aristocracy, the church, and a large military clique, as well as monarchists and CARLISTS, rallied against the government, as did the new fascist party, the FALANGE. The government's idealistic reforms failed to satisfy the left-wing radicals and did little to ameliorate the lot of the lower classes. The forces of the right gained a majority in the 1933 elections, and a series of weak coalition governments followed. Most of these were under the premiership of the moderate republican Alejandro LERROUX, but he was more or less dependent on the right wing and its leader José María GIL ROBLES. As a result many of the republican reforms were ignored or set aside. Left-wing strikes and risings buffeted the government while the political right, equally dissatisfied, increasingly resorted to plots and violence. When in 1936 the electoral victory of the Popular Front (composed of liberals, Socialists, and Communists) augured a renewal of leftist reforms, revolutionary sentiment on the right consolidated. In July, 1936, Gen. Francisco FRANCO led an army revolt in Morocco. Rightist groups rebelled in Spain, and the army officers led most of their forces into the revolutionary (Nationalist or insurgent) camp. In N Spain the revolutionists, under Gen. Emilio MOLA, quickly overran most of the conservative area that had favored the Carlists in the 19th cent. They also captured some key cities in the south. CATALONIA, where socialism and anarchism were strong, and which had been granted autonomy, remained republican (Loyalist). The Basques too sided with the republicans to protect their local liberties. This traditional Spanish separatism asserted itself particularly in republican territory and hindered effective military organization. By Nov., 1936, the Nationalists had Madrid under siege, but while the new republican government of Francisco Largo Caballero (to which the anarchists had been admitted) struggled to organize an effective army, the first incoming International Brigade helped the Loyalists to hold the city. The International Brigades, international groups of volunteers (largely Communist) that were organized in France, represented only a small part of the foreign participation in the war. From the first and throughout the war, Italy and Germany aided Franco with an abundance of planes, tanks, and other materials. Germany sent some 10,000 men, and Italy also sent large numbers of "volunteers," probably over 50,000. Great Britain and France, anxious to prevent a general European conflagration, proposed a nonintervention pact, which was signed in Aug., 1936, by 27 nations. The signatories included Italy, Germany, and the USSR, all of whom failed to heed their promises. The Spanish republic became dependent for supplies on the Soviet Union, which used its military aid to achieve its own political goals. As the war progressed the situation played into the hands of the extremists—the Falange and the Communists—who at the outset had been of negligible importance. The Loyalists ranks were riven by factional strife, which intensified as the Loyalist military position worsened; among its manifestations was the Communist suppression of the anarchists and of the Trotskyite Partido Obrero de Unificacion Marxista (POUM). On the Nationalist side internal conflict also existed, especially between the military and the fascists, but Franco was able to surmount it and consolidate his position. Gradually the Nationalists wore down republican strength. Bilbao, the last republican center in the north, fell in June, 1937, and in a series of attacks from March to June, 1938, the Nationalists cut the republican territory in two. Late in 1938, Franco mounted a major offensive against Catalonia, and Barcelona was taken in Jan., 1939. With the loss of Catalonia the republican cause had become hopeless. Republican efforts for a negotiated peace failed, and on March 27, 1939, the victorious Nationalists entered Madrid. Italy and Germany had recognized the Franco regime in 1936, Great Britain and France did so in Feb., 1939; international recognition of Franco's authoritarian government quickly followed. For Germany and Italy the Spanish civil war served as a testing ground for the blitzkrieg and other techniques to be used in World War II; for the European democracies it was another step on the road of appeasement; and for the politically conscious youth of the 1930s who joined the International Brigades, saving the Spanish republic was the idealistic cause of the era, a cause to which many gave their lives. For the Spanish people the civil war was an encounter whose huge toll of lives and material devastation were unparalleled in centuries of Spanish history. See George Orwell, *Homage to Catalonia* (1938, repr. 1969); Gerald Brenan, *The Spanish Labyrinth* (2d ed. 1950, repr. 1967); Hugh Thomas, *The Spanish Civil War* (1961); V. B. Johnston, *Legions of Babel; the International Brigades in the Spanish Civil War* (1968); Cecil Eby, *American Volunteers in the Spanish Civil War* (1969); Raymond Carr, ed., *The Republic and the Civil War in Spain* (1971); H. L. Matthews, *Half of Spain Died* (1973); Gabriel Jackson, *The Spanish Republic and the Civil War* (1965) and *A Concise History of the Spanish Civil War* (1974).

Spanish colonial art and architecture fl. 16th–early 19th cent. The art of the Spanish colonies followed the historical development of styles previously established in Spain, but developed original features in different regions. The main centers were in Peru and Mexico, where there were skilled native craftsmen and relatively strong political organization. The earliest buildings, constructed of impermanent materials, have disappeared, but by the end of the 16th cent. durable monumental architecture had been achieved. Most of the buildings of this time, including the cathedrals, were built for military purposes and were consequently massive and plain. This was a period of transition from Spanish Gothic to Spanish Renaissance, with many buildings reminiscent of the PLATERESQUE style, contrasting bare walls and ornamental doorways, and others of the austerity of the ESCORIAL. Although elaborate and intricate ornamentation was often employed, particularly in later times, a strong strain of simple, solid construction ran through the colonial period, as exemplified in the Spanish missions of California and the 18th-century Jesuit missions of Paraguay. The earliest cathedral in the New World, in Santo Domingo, Dominican Republic, (1512–41), has a plateresque portal on the west facade. In 16th-century Mexico the great builders were the Augustinian, Franciscan, and Dominican monastic orders. They introduced the open chapel, as in the monastery of San Francisco Tlalmanalco, which was built with only three walls in order to speed construction and to accommodate more people. The cathedrals of Puebla, Mérida, and Guadalajara were also begun in this period. During most of the 17th and 18th cent. the baroque style held sway, and in the 18th cent. the sumptuous Churrigueresque ornamentation (see under CHURRIGUERA) of Spain was exported to the colonies. In addition to employing the large forms and curving lines of the traditional European baroque, Spanish colonial buildings maintained the contrast between decorated and plain surfaces of the earlier period. A more conservative trend was manifested in Colombia, where churches and public buildings were simple and severe. Baroque features, combined with the inventiveness of native craftsmen, reached a climax in the cathedral in Mexico City. It has been called ultrabaroque because of its strong light-and-shade patterns, richly carved columns and entablatures, and violent alternations of curves and angles. In the late 1960s much of the cathedral was damaged by fire and had to undergo restoration. In the Puebla region glazed tiles were sometimes placed on the whole facade of a building, as in the Church of San Francisco Acatepec. Central American buildings were generally provincial versions of the Mexican, but in Guatemala structures were lower and of heavier proportions as a protection against earthquakes. Colonial artists, many of them native Indians, devoted themselves principally to the depiction of religious subjects from the New Testament. Indian sculptors, notably in Mexico, Guatemala, and Peru, but also in the Jesuit missions of Paraguay, developed a powerful folk art; polychromed wood, terra-cotta, and bas-relief work in the walls and columns of churches were widely used media. A favorite subject of sculptures was the agony of Christ; these figures, often given Indian features, are characterized by extraordinary pathos. In painting, the conceptions were frequently original and charged with remarkable intensity and piety. By 1600 numerous European artists had emigrated to the New World and contributed their talents, but the Indians, who had excelled at wall painting, books, and mosaics before the Conquest, were chiefly responsible for giving colonial art its unique flavor. (For the history of painting and sculpture in Middle America, see MEXICAN ART AND ARCHITECTURE). In the Andean region Flemish and Italian influences are evident in the great painting centers of Bogotá and Quito, but Cuzco was the main center of pictorial productivity, and here the contribution of the native Indian was of paramount importance. Native strains were also noticeable in the design of broadsides and *aleluyas* of the 18th and 19th cent; this art form, often called folk lithography, was common in Mexico and Venezuela and was often political in nature. In the architecture of the Andean region, as in Mexico, there was richness and inventiveness, but with some significant variations. One of the most important 16th-century buildings was the Church of San Francisco in Quito, Ecuador, in which Spanish and Italian styles were blended. In Peru architects preferred heavier and more massive forms. Huge curving forms projected over doors and windows in many buildings of Lima. Columns in Mexico were freely carved with great fantasy; in Peru they were heavy and often spiral. Peruvian wall surfaces were divided into a series of large compartments rather than covered with shallow carving as were those of Mexico. The Church of San Agustín (1720), with a statue in the central niche dominating the whole facade, illustrates a distinctive type developed in Lima. In S Peru and in Bolivia, Indian influence in ornamentation, in both technique and representation, pervaded the basic European architectural forms. On the facade of the Church of San Lorenzo (1728–44) in Potosí, richly decorated Indian figures function as CARYATIDS or spiral columns. In the last quarter of the 18th cent. a current of neoclassicism invaded Latin America along with the official academies, and the great days of Spanish colonial architecture were over. See George Kubler and Martin Soría, *Art and Architecture in Spain and Portugal and Their American Dominions* (1959); Bradley Smith, *Spain, A History in Art* (1971).

Spanish dagger: see YUCCA.

Spanish fly: see BLISTER BEETLE.

Spanish Guinea: see EQUATORIAL GUINEA.

Spanish language, member of the Romance group of the Italic subfamily of the Indo-European family of languages (see ROMANCE LANGUAGES). The official language of Spain and 18 Latin American nations, Spanish is spoken by about 145 million persons. It is the mother tongue of some 23 million people in Spain, where the language originated and whence it was later brought by Spanish explorers, colonists, and empire-builders to the Western Hemisphere and other parts of the world during the last few centuries. The importance of Spanish is indicated by the fact that it is one of the five official languages of the United Nations. Spanish is a descendant of the Vulgar Latin brought to the Iberian peninsula by the soldiers and colonists of ancient Rome (see LATIN LANGUAGE). Thus the Spanish vocabulary is basically of Latin origin, although it has been enriched by many loan words from other languages, especially Arabic, French, Italian, and various Indian languages of North, Central, and South America. The oldest extant written records of Spanish date from the middle of the 10th cent. A.D. There are a number of Spanish dialects; however, the Castilian dialect was already the accepted standard of the language by the middle of the 13th cent., largely owing to the political importance of Castile. There are several striking differences in pronunciation between Castilian and Latin American Spanish. In the former, *c* before *e* and *i*, and *z* before *a*, *o*, and *u*, are pronounced *th*, as in English *think*; in the latter, they are sounded as *s* in English *see*. Moreover, the alphabetical symbol *ll* in Castilian is pronounced as *lli* in English *billion*; but in Latin American Spanish, as *y* in English *you*. On the whole, however, the differences between the Spanish of Europe and of Latin America with reference to pronunciation, vocabulary, and grammar are relatively minor. A distinctive feature of Spanish is that there are two forms of the verb "to be": *estar*, which denotes a relatively temporary state, and *ser*, which denotes a relatively permanent condition and which is also used before a predicate noun. Reflexive verbs often perform the same function in Spanish that passive verbs do in English. Because the inflection of the Spanish verb indicates person very clearly, subject pronouns are not necessary. The Spanish language employs the Roman alphabet, to which the symbols *ch, ll, ñ*, and *rr* have been added. The tilde (˜) placed over the *n* (*ñ*) indicates the pronunciation *ni*, as in English *pinion*. The acute accent (´) is used to make clear which syllable of a word is to be stressed when the regular rules of stress are not followed. The acute accent is also employed to distinguish between homonyms, as in *sé* ("I know") and *se* ("self"). A peculiarity of Spanish is the use of an inverted question mark (¿) at the beginning of a question and of an inverted exclamation point (¡) at the beginning of an exclamation. The spelling of Spanish is a reliable guide to pronunciation, which follows regular rules. See W. J. Entwistle, *The Spanish Language, Together with Portuguese, Catalan and Basque* (2d ed. 1962); F. B. Agard, *Modern Approach to Spanish* (rev. ed. 1968); C. H. Stevenson, *The Spanish Language Today* (1970).

Spanish literature. Literature flourished on the Iberian Peninsula long before the evolution of the modern Spanish language. The Latin writers Seneca, Lucan, Martial, and Quintilian are among those who were born or who lived in Spain before the separation of the ROMANCE LANGUAGES. Twentieth-century research has uncovered texts of the 10th and 11th cent. written by Muslims and Jews living in Spain. The famous early classic of Spanish literature, the sober and unornamented epic poem *Cantar de Mío Cid* (12th cent.) deals with the life and deeds of the national hero, Rodrigo Díaz de Vivar, called the Cid Campeador. In the 13th cent. many other epic poems as well as the oldest popular lyrics appeared in the different provinces of the Iberian Peninsula. The first Spanish poet whose name is known is the priest Gonzalo de BERCEO. Under the patronage of King ALFONSO X (1221–84), himself a writer, Castilian prose was developed and many Oriental works were translated into Castilian. In the 14th cent. the most important writers were López de Ayala, whose poem *Rimado de palacio* satirized the customs of the age; Fernán Pérez de Guzmán, author of the historical *Generaciones y semblanzas;* the prince Don Juan Manuel, nephew of King Alfonso X, whose *Libro de los exemplos del conde Lucanor et de Patronio* was the first book of short stories in Spanish; and the satirical poet Juan RUIZ. During the reign of John II of Castile in the first half of the 15th cent., two important poets were Juan de MENA and the marqués de SANTILLANA, both of whom wrote under Italian influence. The Italian poetic forms were to be of great importance in aiding Spanish verse to grow beyond folk art and pseudo-Provençal, but they were not assimilated into Spanish letters for another century. The outstanding prose work of the period was the novel *La Celestina* (1499), attributed to Fernando de ROJAS. The first known novel of chivalry, AMADIS OF GAUL, was printed in Saragossa in 1508 and served as a model for the novels of chivalry that became (16th cent.) the most popular genre in Spain, together with the anonymous ballads (romances) that were sung and recited everywhere. Meanwhile the spirit of the Renaissance had been invading Spanish letters, and Spain had also become a dominant European power. In the reign of Emperor Charles V, the first picaresque novel, *Lazarillo de Tormes*, was published (1554); the identity of its author has remained a mystery. The latter part of the 16th cent. and most of the 17th was the great era of Spanish literature, known as the Golden Age. At the start of this period the poet GARCILASO DE LA VEGA, stimulated by the work of Juan BOSCÁN ALMOGÁVER, succeeded in mastering the meter and essence of Italian verse and in acclimating it to the Spanish spirit, thus revolutionizing Spanish poetry. The chief prose monument of the Golden Age, and one of the masterpieces of world literature, is the novel *Don Quixote de la Mancha* by Miguel de CERVANTES SAAVEDRA. The picaresque novel flourished; notable examples are those of Mateo ALEMÁN and Francisco de QUEVEDO Y VILLEGAS. Baltasar GRACIÁN was a leading didactic prose writer. The Golden Age also produced many superb playwrights. LOPE DE VEGA CARPIO, one of the most prolific authors of all time, wrote a multitude of dramas, comedies, and religious plays. TIRSO DE MOLINA, Guillén de CASTRO Y BELLVÍS, and Juan Ruiz de ALARCÓN Y MENDOZA were also outstanding playwrights. CALDERÓN DE LA BARCA was the last and probably the best dramatist of the epoch. To the Golden Age belong the great mystics St. THERESA of Ávila, author of an inspired spiritual autobiography, and her disciple St. JOHN OF THE CROSS, one of Spain's finest lyric poets. Fray Luis Ponce de LEÓN wrote exquisite pastorals and Fernando de HERRERA left stirring odes, but the most influential poet of the period was Luis de GÓNGORA Y ARGOTE, whose precious, ornate verse was the most extreme expression of the baroque in Spanish literature; a cultivated, affected style known as Gongorism dominated Spanish letters in the latter half of the 17th cent. In the 18th cent., French neoclassicism exerted a powerful—and inhibiting—influence on Spanish literature. The *Poética* of Ignacio de LUZÁN reflected the academic principles of the epoch. An important essayist was Benito Gerónimo FEYJÓO Y MONTENEGRO, a Benedictine who helped to usher the Enlightenment into Spain. Three authors stood out as notable exceptions in the midst of a general decline in literary creativity—Leandro FERNÁNDEZ DE MORATÍN, a writer of plays in the neoclassic vein; Ramón de la CRUZ, author of popular playlets called sainetes; and the poet Juan Meléndez Valdés. During the first years of the 19th cent. the rigors of the Napoleonic occupation virtually snuffed out intellectual creativity in Spain. Then in 1833, with the death of Ferdinand VII, romanticism swept the country like a grass fire; its ascendancy was dramatic but superficial. Much of the work of the leading romantic authors—Ángel de Saavedra, duque de RIVAS, José de ESPRONCEDA, and José ZORRILLA Y MORAL—echoed French and English models, but Mariano José de LARRA displayed originality in his admirable satirical sketches. Two gifted post-romantic poets were Rosalía de CASTRO (writing in Galician) and Gustavo Adolfo BÉCQUER. Larra's sketches were outstanding examples of *costumbrismo*—the literary depiction of local color, customs, and types—a genre that in Spain led to and was intimately associated with naturalism and realism. The towering figure of Benito PÉREZ GALDÓS dominated the realistic novel during the second half of the 19th cent., but Pedro Antonio de ALARCÓN, José María de Pereda, Armando PALACIO VALDÉS, Juan VALERA Y ALCALÁ GALIANO, and Emilia PARDO BAZÁN also wrote notable fiction. Realism continued to have leading exponents well into the 20th cent., notably Vicente BLASCO IBÁÑEZ, but at the turn of the century the intellectual and literary life of Spain underwent a deep transformation. With the loss of its colonial empire and the disastrous effects of the Carlist wars, Spain was economically and culturally bankrupt. The writers of the GENERATION OF '98, stimulated by French and German influences and by Rubén DARÍO and the MODERNISMO movement in Spanish America, set out to reevaluate and revitalize the cultural life of Spain. Ángel Ganivet, a precursor, had foreshadowed their work in his *Idearium español*. Miguel de UNAMUNO, as essayist, poet, novelist, and educator, emphasized the quixotic aspect of Spanish values and exerted great influence on Spanish youth. Azorín (see MARTÍNEZ RUIZ) created memorable impressionistic sketches. Ramón del VALLE INCLÁN brought a poetic sense of the fantastic and the bizarre to his novels and plays. Pío BAROJA Y NESSI infused his novels with a fierce independence of spirit that rejected all traditional values and sought to arouse people to action. The drama, whose only notable exponent in the late 19th cent. had been José ECHEGARAY, was revitalized by Jacinto GRAU, Gregorio MARTÍNEZ SIERRA, and especially by Jacinto BENAVENTE Y MARTÍNEZ. A major role in the Spanish cultural revival was played by the great educator Francisco GINER DE LOS RÍOS. After World War I the intellectual currents set in motion by the Generation of '98 merged with other forces in the European avant garde to create a mainstream that fertilized Spanish cultural life until the outbreak of the civil war. Criticism, which had flourished at the turn of the century under the erudite Marcelino MENÉNDEZ Y PELAYO, reached new heights in the works of the distinguished medievalist Ramón MENÉNDEZ PIDAL. The humorist Ramón GÓMEZ DE LA SERNA wrote his inimitable *greguerías*. It was in poetry, however, that Spanish literature produced its greatest achievements. The lyrics of Antonio MACHADO and of the great Juan Ramón JIMÉNEZ are among the finest in the language. José Moreno Villa, Rafael ALBERTI, Vicente ALEIXANDRE, Luis CERNUDA, Jorge GUILLÉN, Dámaso Alonso, and many others formed a brilliant constellation of poets, but the most engaging figure was that of the poet and dramatist Federico GARCÍA LORCA. Parallel to these developments in poetry was the work of one of Spain's most gifted essayists—José ORTEGA Y GASSET. The novelist Ramón PEREZ DE AYALA used his novels as a forum for intellectual discussion, whereas Gabriel Miró wrote novels that can be considered lyric prose poems, and Benjamín Jarnés produced surrealist novels. The novels of Ramón SENDER marked a return to social criticism. The Spanish civil war (1936–39) truncated the cultural evolution of the country. Many writers went into exile. Salinas, Guillén, Juan Larrea, and others distinguished themselves abroad. Among the novelists to emerge after the Spanish civil war were Camilo José CELA, Carman LAFORET, and José María Gironella. Salvador de MADARIAGA became known as a biographer and historian. In the 1950s and 60s a return to normality was noticeable. Scholarship again flourished, and much attention was paid to the Generation of '98 and to a reevaluation of earlier periods. Writers whose literary reputations have been established since World War II include the novelists Max AUB, Miguel DELIBES, Juan GOYTISOLO, Ana María MATUTE, and Rafael SÁNCHEZ FERLOSIO; the poets Manuel ALTOAGUIRRE and Gerardo DIEGO; and the playwrights Antonia BUERO VALLEJO, Alejandro CASONA, and Alfonso SASTRE. See also CATALAN LITERATURE; SPANISH AMERICAN LITERATURE. For anthologies in English translation see E. L. Turnbull, ed., *Ten Centuries of Spanish Poetry* (1955); Angel Flores, ed., *Masterpieces of the Spanish Golden Age* (1957); Seymour Resnick and Jeanne Pasmantier, *An Anthology of Spanish Literature in English Translation* (2 vol., 1958). For histories of Spanish letters see G. T. Northrup, *An Introduction to Spanish Literature* (3d ed. 1960); R. E. Chandler and Kessel Schwartz, *A New History of Spanish Literature* (1961); Gerald Brenan, *The Literature of the Spanish People* (2d ed. 1965); A. Díaz-Plaja, *A History of Spanish Literature* (1971).

Spanish Main, mainland of Spanish America, particularly the coast of South America from the isthmus of Panama to the mouth of the Orinoco River. Spanish treasure fleets, sailing home from the New World, passed through the Caribbean N of the Main and were attacked by English buccaneers, raiding from the islands and coast. Pirates congregated there until the 19th cent., and the words "Spanish Main" have become the symbol of piratic romance. See C. O. Saver, *The Early Spanish Main* (1966); A. O. Exquemelin, *The Buccaneers and Marooners of America* (1891, repr. 1971).

Spanish marriages: see ISABELLA II.

Spanish Morocco: see MOROCCO.

Spanish moss, fibrous grayish-green EPIPHYTE (*Tillandsia usneoides*) that hangs on trees of tropical America and the Southern states, also called Florida, southern, or long moss. It is not a true moss but a member of the pineapple family, and has inconspicuous flowers. It is used for stuffing furniture and as a packing material. Spanish moss is classified in the division MAGNOLIOPHYTA, class Liliatae, order Bromeliales, family Bromeliaceae.

Spanish needles: see BUR MARIGOLD.

Spanish Sahara, overseas province of Spain (1973 est. pop. 86,000), 102,703 sq mi (266,000 sq km), NW Africa, bordering on the Atlantic Ocean in the west, on Morocco in the north, on Algeria in the northeast, and on Mauritania in the east and south. The main towns are El Aaiún (the capital), Villa Cisneros, and Semara. The province is divided into two districts, Saguia el Hamra (in the north) and Río de Oro (in the south). Part of the Sahara, the province is

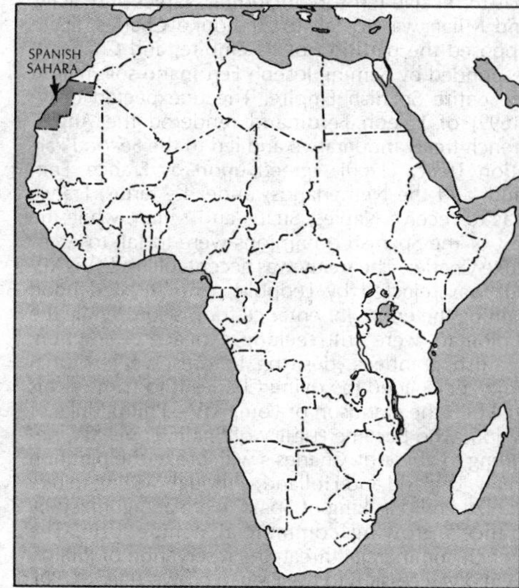

extremely arid and is almost entirely covered with stones, gravel, or sand. Rocky highlands in the east reach c.1,500 ft (460 m). The permanent population is made up of Arabs and Berbers (together about 55% of the total) and Spaniards (about half of whom are soldiers); during the rainy season some 50,000 pastoral nomads temporarily migrate into the province. The traditional economy is limited to the raising of goats, camels, and sheep, and the cultivation of date palms. There are coastal fisheries operated by persons from the nearby Canary Islands and by Spaniards. Large deposits of phosphates at Bu Craa (near El Aaiún) were first exploited by a Spanish-controlled firm in the early 1970s. Potash and iron deposits have been found but are not yet worked. There is a growing tourist industry. The province has a limited transportation network; the main seaports are Villa Cisneros and El Aaiún. Portuguese navigators reached Cape Bojador on the northern coast of present-day Spanish Sahara in 1434. However, there was little European contact with the region until the 19th cent. In 1884, Spain claimed a protectorate over the coast from Cape Bojador to Cap Blanc (at the present border with Mauritania). The boundaries of the protectorate were extended by Franco-Spanish agreements in 1900, 1904, and 1920. Semara was not captured until 1934, and the Spanish had only slight contact with the interior until the 1950s. In 1957 a rebel movement ousted the Spanish, who regained control of the region with French help in Feb., 1958. In April, 1958, Spain joined the previously separate districts of Saguia el Hamra and Río de Oro to form the province of Spanish Sahara. The province is headed by a governor general and has an advisory general assembly; three representatives sit in the Spanish Cortes. In the early 1970s dissident inhabitants of Spanish Sahara formed organizations seeking independence for the province. At the same time, neighboring nations (notably Mauritania, Morocco, and Algeria) pressured Spain to call a referendum on the area's future in accordance with UN resolutions. See René Pelissier, *Les Territoires Espagnols d'Afrique* (1963).

Spanish Succession, War of the, 1701–14, last of the general European wars caused by the efforts of King LOUIS XIV to extend French power. The precarious health of the childless King CHARLES II of Spain left the succession open to the claims of three principal pretenders—Louis XIV, in behalf of his eldest son, a grandson of King Philip IV of Spain through Philip's daughter, Marie Thérèse, to whom Louis XIV had been married; the electoral prince of Bavaria, Joseph Ferdinand, a great-grandson of Philip IV; and Holy Roman Emperor Leopold I, who had married a younger daughter of Philip IV, but claimed the succession in behalf of his son, Archduke Charles (later Holy Roman Emperor CHARLES VI), by a second marriage. England and Holland were opposed to the union of French and Spanish dominions, which would have made France the leading world power and diverted Spanish trade from England and Holland to France. On the other hand, England, Holland, and France were all opposed to Archduke Charles, because his accession would reunite the Spanish and Austrian branches of the Hapsburg family. Louis XIV, exhausted by the War of the Grand Alliance, sought a peaceful solution to the succession controversy and reached an agreement (1698) with King WILLIAM III of England. This First Partition Treaty designated Joseph Ferdinand as the principal heir; in compensation, the French dauphin was to receive territory including Naples and Sicily, and Milan was to fall to Archduke Charles. Spain opposed the partition of its empire, and Charles II responded by naming Joseph Ferdinand sole heir to the entire Spanish Empire. The unexpected death (1699) of Joseph Ferdinand rendered the Anglo-French treaty inoperative and led to the Second Partition Treaty (1700), agreed upon by France, England, and the Netherlands; under its terms, France was to receive Naples, Sicily, and Milan, while the rest of the Spanish dominions were to fall to Archduke Charles. The treaty was acceptable to Louis XIV but was rejected by Leopold, who insisted upon gaining the entire inheritance for his son. While the diplomats were still seeking a peaceful solution, Spanish grandees, desiring to preserve territorial unity, persuaded the dying Charles II to name as his sole heir the grandson of Louis XIV—Philip, duke of Anjou, who became PHILIP V of Spain. Louis XIV, deciding to abide by Charles's will, broke the partition treaty. England and Holland, although willing to recognize Philip as king of Spain, were antagonized by France's growing commercial competition. The French commercial threat, the reservation of Philip's right of succession to the French crown (Dec., 1700), and the French occupation of border fortresses between the Dutch and the Spanish Netherlands (Feb., 1701) led to an anti-French alliance among England, Leopold, and the Dutch. Hostilities between the French and the imperial forces began in Italy, where the imperial general, Prince EUGENE OF SAVOY, defeated Nicolas CATINAT and the duke of VILLEROI. The general war began in 1702, with England, Holland, and most of the German states opposing France, Spain, Bavaria, Portugal, and Savoy. The duke of MARLBOROUGH, though ill-supported by the Dutch, captured a number of places in the Low Countries (1702–3), while Eugene held his own against Villeroi and his successor, Louis Joseph, duc de VENDÔME. The duke of VILLARS, however, defeated Louis of Baden at Friedlingen (1702). The successes of the French in Alsace enabled them to menace Vienna (1703), but the opportunity was lost by dissension among their chiefs. In 1704, Marlborough succeeded in moving his troops from the Netherlands into Bavaria, where he joined Eugene and won the great victory of Blenheim over the French under the count of TALLARD (see BLENHEIM, BATTLE OF), and the French lost Bavaria. Meanwhile, Portugal and Savoy had changed sides (1703), and in 1704 the English captured Gibraltar. In 1705, Marlborough in the Netherlands and Eugene in Italy won moderate successes, although Vendôme defeated Eugene at Cassano. The year 1706 was marked by Eugene's victory at Turin, which resulted in French evacuation of N Italy, and by Marlborough's triumph at Ramillies (see RAMILLIES, BATTLE OF), which compelled the French to retreat in the Low Countries. In the same year, Louis XIV proposed peace to the Dutch, but English interference forced the continuance of the war. In 1707, Marlborough made little progress in the north and Eugene's expedition into Provence resulted only in the loss of 10,000 men; but in the following year Marlborough and Eugene won another great victory at Oudenarde, took Lille, and drove the French within their borders. Peace negotiations failed, and the allies won (1709) another success, though a costly one, at Malplaquet (see MALPLAQUET, BATTLE OF). Meanwhile the indecisive allied campaigns in Spain (1708–10) did little to weaken Philip V. The death (1711) of Holy Roman Emperor JOSEPH I, who had succeeded Leopold, and the accession of Charles VI led to the withdrawal of the English, who were as much opposed to the union of Spain and Austria as to that of Spain and France. Preliminary negotiations between England and France were pressed forward and a peace conference was opened (1712), followed shortly afterward by an Anglo-French armistice. In 1713, France, England, and Holland signed the Peace of Utrecht. Charles VI continued the war, although Eugene had been defeated (1712) at Denain and had been forced to retreat in the Spanish Netherlands. Seriously weakened by the defection of his allies, the emperor finally consented in 1714 to the treaties of Rastatt and of Baden, which complemented the general settlement (see UTRECHT, PEACE OF). With this settlement, the principle of a BALANCE OF POWER took precedence over dynastic or national rights in the negotiation of European affairs. The conflict in America corresponding to the period of the War of the Spanish Succession was known as Queen Anne's War (see FRENCH AND INDIAN WARS). See Frank Taylor, *The Wars of Marlborough, 1702–1709* (1921); J. B. Wolf, *The Emergence of the Great Powers, 1685–1715* (1951).

Spanish Town, city (1960 pop. 14,706), SE Jamaica, on the Cobre River. It is the commercial and processing center of a rich agricultural region, as well as the main rail and highway communications hub for traffic to and from Kingston (the capital) and other parts of Jamaica. Founded c.1525 and formerly called Villa de la Vega, Spanish Town was Jamaica's leading city from the destruction of Port Royal by earthquake in 1692 until Kingston became the capital in 1872.

spanworm: see INCHWORM.

spar. For dogtooth spar, see CALCITE; for fluorspar, see FLUORITE; for heavy spar, see BARITE; for satin spar, see CALCITE and GYPSUM. See also ICELAND SPAR and FELDSPAR.

Spargo, John (spär'gō), 1876–1966, American reformer and author, b. Cornwall, England. An early socialist, he was active in the Socialist party of the United States but resigned in 1917 because of its antiwar policy. With Samuel Gompers he organized (1917) the American Alliance for Labor and Democracy. He also founded a settlement house in Yonkers, N.Y. His many books include *The Bitter Cry of the Children* (1906), a biography of Karl Marx (1910), *Applied Socialism* (1912), *The Psychology of Bolshevism* (1919), and studies in Vermont history.

Spark, Muriel, 1918–, Scottish novelist. Her witty novels expose the petty, all too human foibles of her characters with merciless satire. She is a Roman Catholic, and she is interested in revealing the dark, terrifying, and unexplainable side of banal human experience. Spark's novels include *The Comforters* (1957), *Memento Mori* (1958), *The Bachelors* (1960), *The Girls of Slender Means* (1963), *The Mandelbaum Gate* (1965), *The Public Image* (1968), *The Driver's Seat* (1970), *Not to Disturb* (1972), and *The Abbess of Crewe* (1974). Her poems and short stories are compiled in *Collected Poems I* (1967) and *Collected Stories I* (1968). She has written critical studies of Mary Shelley (1951) and John Masefield (1953) and a biography of Emily Brontë (1953). Her short novel *The Prime of Miss Jean Brodie* (1961) was adapted for the stage by Jay Allen and produced successfully in London and New York City; it was also made into an acclaimed motion picture (1967). See studies by Derek Stanford (1963) and Karl Malkoff (1968).

spark, in electricity: see ARC.

spark chamber, in physics, device for recording the passage of ELEMENTARY PARTICLES produced by reactions in a PARTICLE ACCELERATOR. Particles pass through a stack of metal plates or wire grids that are maintained with high voltage between alternate layers. A high-pressure gas fills the gaps between the plates and is ionized along the path of the traversing charged particle. As a result, sparks jump between adjacent, oppositely charged plates and the trail of sparks left by the particle is seen as a series of dashes. The spark chamber has replaced the BUBBLE CHAMBER in certain applications. Although the particle paths are recorded more accurately in the bubble chamber, the bubble chamber indiscriminately records all events that occur in a comparatively long interval. The spark chamber operates much more rapidly and can be made highly selective by using auxiliary detectors to screen out unwanted events. Because of its selectivity, the spark chamber is most useful in searching for very rare events. Spark chambers can be highly automated, with data collected and stored electronically instead of photographically, as is necessary with the bubble chamber. The analysis of the data can then be accomplished by a high-speed computer, which may operate simultaneously with the experiment and thereby provide immediate evaluation of the quality of the data and allow optimum operating conditions to be maintained at all times.

spark plug: see IGNITION.

Sparks, Jared, 1789–1866, American historian and educator, b. Willington, Conn. He studied theology and was instructed in mathematics and natural philosophy at Harvard (1817–19). He was pastor of a Unitarian church in Baltimore (1819–23), founded and edited (1821–22) the *Unitarian Miscellany,* and was chaplain of the U.S. House of Representatives (1821–23). Returning to Boston, he bought and edited the *North American Review* (1824–30), of which he had previously (1817–18) served as editor, and founded and edited (1830) *The American Almanac and Repository of Useful Knowledge.* From 1838 to 1849 he was McLean professor of history at Harvard and then was president of the university (1849–53). His important collection of manuscripts is at Harvard. Among the many works he wrote or edited are *The Diplomatic Correspondence of the American Revolution* (12 vol., 1829–30), *The Life of Gouverneur Morris* (3 vol., 1832), *The Writings of George Washington* (12 vol., 1834–37), *The Library of American Biography* (25 vol., 1834–48), *The Works of Benjamin Franklin* (10 vol., 1836–40), and *Correspondence of the American Revolution* (4 vol., 1853). See biography by H. B. Adams (2 vol., 1893; repr. 1973).

Sparks, city (1970 pop. 24,187), Washoe co., W Nev., just E of Reno; inc. 1905. The Southern Pacific RR was the major employer until the dieselization of engines forced the closing (1957) of the railroad shops there. The city still has important railroad, distributing, and warehousing activities. Tourism is a major industry, and there is some light manufacturing. Points of interest include a planetarium and a monument honoring the Chinese who built the railroad in Sparks.

sparrow, common name of various small brown-and-gray perching birds. New World birds called sparrows are members of the FINCH family. They were named for their resemblance to the ENGLISH SPARROW and the European tree sparrow (members of the WEAVER BIRD family), both introduced in the

Americas. Members of both groups have stout, conical beaks adapted to seed eating. Among the many sparrows found in the United States are the song sparrow, the white-throated sparrow (or peabody bird), and the chipping, white-crowned, vesper, Lincoln's, fox, field, tree, and swamp sparrows. Sparrows are valuable to farmers in destroying weed seeds. Originally *sparrow* meant any small bird; the word appears in this sense in Greek mythology and in the Scriptures.

Spars [from the motto "Semper Paratus," Lat.,=always prepared], the women's reserve of the U.S. coast guard, created in Nov., 1942, to release men for sea duty. Wartime enlistment reached a peak of 10,000. The service was demobilized in 1946; but it was reactivated in 1965, and women were recruited for a variety of positions.

Sparta (spär'tə), city of ancient Greece, capital of Laconia, on the Eurotas (Evrótas) River in the Peloponnesus. The narrow, mountain-walled valley attracted invaders by its fertility, and the city-state of Sparta was created by invading Dorian Greeks, who later conquered the countryside of Laconia and Messenia (c.735–715 B.C.). The city was difficult to attack, and for a long time the Spartans had no city walls, trusting to the strength of their army for defense against invaders and against their own Laconian and Messenian subjects. Sparta became a strong city in Greece and in the 7th cent. B.C. enjoyed a period of wealth and culture, the time of the poets Tyrtaeus and Alcman. After 600 B.C., however, Sparta cultivated only the military arts, and the city became an armed camp, established (according to the official legend) by LYCURGUS, in reaction to a Messenian revolt (see MESSENIA). The ruling class, the Spartiates, gave themselves wholly to war. At birth a boy was inspected by the elders, and if he appeared too weakly for future military service, he was taken into the mountains and abandoned. If he was fit, he was taken from his mother at the age of seven to begin rigorous military training. He became a soldier at 20, a citizen at 30, and continued as a soldier until 60. Thus his entire life was spent under rigorous discipline. Spartiate women, under less severe discipline, were part of the soldierly society and were not secluded. The Spartiates were the only citizens and the only sharers in the allotment of lands and of the helots (serfs who were bound to the land). The helots farmed the land and paid part of the produce to their masters, the Spartiates. They could not be sold, but they had no legal or civil rights and were constantly watched by a sort of Spartiate secret police for fear of insurrection. In somewhat less stringent subjection were the perioeci, freemen who were permitted to carry on commerce and handicrafts, by which some of them prospered. The perioeci were entirely subordinate to the Spartiates. The government was headed by two hereditary kings furnished by two families; they were titular leaders in battle and in religion. Some of these kings were able (e.g., Cleomenes I, Leonidas, and Agis II), but they were held in check. There was a council of elders and a general assembly of citizens; but the real rulers were the board of five EPHORS, elected annually. The business of the state was conducted with secrecy (unlike the open forum methods of Athens), and every effort was made to keep the institutions unchanged. By the 6th cent. B.C., Sparta was the strongest Greek city. In the PERSIAN WARS, Sparta fought beside Athens, first at THERMOPYLAE (480), under Leonidas; later that year at Salamis; and in 479 at Plataea (won by PAUSANIAS). Before 500 B.C., Sparta had formed a confederacy of allies (the Peloponnesian League), which it dominated. Through the league and by direct methods Sparta was master of most of the Peloponnesus. After the Persian Wars rivalry with Athens sharpened, and Athens grew stronger. An earthquake at Sparta (464 B.C.), followed by a stubborn Messenian revolt, greatly weakened Sparta. In the end a contest with Athens came indirectly, provoked by Corinthian fears of Athenian imperialism. This was the great PELOPONNESIAN WAR (431–404 B.C.), which wrecked the Athenian empire. Soon afterward the dominant Spartans, led by AGESILAUS II, were involved in a war with Persia; then the Spartan envoy ANTALCIDAS concluded (386 B.C.) with Artaxerxes II a treaty by which Sparta surrendered the Greek cities of Asia Minor in return for withdrawal of Persian support from the Athenians, who were again at war with Sparta, and from the Athenians' allies, the Thebans. Thebes fought on and by the victory at Leuctra (371 B.C.) gained ascendancy in Greece. Sparta fell an easy prey to Macedonia and declined. In the 3d cent. B.C. there were determined but futile attempts by kings Agis IV (see under AGIS) and CLEOMENES III and by Nabis (d. 192 B.C.) to restore glory to Sparta by vigorous reforms. Under the Romans, Sparta prospered. It was devastated by the Goths in A.D. 395. The modern city of Sparta (now Spárti; 1971 pop. 10,549) dates only from the 19th cent. The ruins of old Sparta, including sanctuaries and a theater, are nearby. See Humfrey Michell, *Sparta* (1952, repr. 1964); G. L. Huxley, *Early Sparta* (1962, repr. 1970); A. H. M. Jones, *Sparta* (1967).

Spartacus (spär'təkəs), d. 71 B.C., leader in an ancient Italian slave revolt, b. Thrace. He broke out (73 B.C.) of a gladiators' school at Capua and fled to Mt. Vesuvius, where many fugitives joined him. Their army defeated several Roman forces and moved north, devastating S Italy and Campania; Spartacus' aim was a general escape from Italy, but his followers preferred plunder, and in 72 B.C. they were back in S Italy. They took Thurii and got through a cordon which Marcus Licinius Crassus stretched across the "toe" of Italy. Spartacus was killed in a battle with Crassus in Lucania. Pompey, back from Spain, helped annihilate the survivors. Of the captured slaves 6,000 were crucified along the Capua-Rome highway. After the death of Spartacus, 3,000 Roman prisoners were found unharmed in his camp. The revolt of Spartacus is also called the Third Servile War or the Gladiators' War. It served to caution the landowners against maltreatment of their slaves.

Spartacus party or **Spartacists,** radical group of German Socialists, formed c.March, 1916, and led by Karl LIEBKNECHT and Rosa LUXEMBURG. The name was derived from the pseudonym Spartacus used by Liebknecht in his pamphlets denouncing World War I, the government, and the majority section of the Social Democratic party; the name was used to typify the modern wage slave in revolt like the Roman gladiator. The Spartacists, demanding the establishment of a dictatorship of the proletariat by mass action, gathered followers among the workingmen. After the overthrow of the German emperor, William II (Nov., 1918), the Spartacists continued to oppose the government, then composed of Majority Socialists and Independent Socialists, and headed by President Friedrich EBERT. The Spartacists launched a press campaign against the government and engaged in sporadic acts of terrorism. At an organizational meeting (Dec. 29, 1918–Jan. 1, 1919), the Spartacists officially transformed themselves into the German Communist party, and on Jan. 5, 1919, a Communist revolt broke out in Berlin. A general strike was proclaimed (Jan. 6) and the rebels occupied a number of government buildings. Gustav NOSKE was sent to Berlin to put down the revolt. He marched on the occupied part of the city and by Jan. 13, had virtually defeated the Communists. Liebknecht and Luxemburg were arrested (Jan. 15) and brutally murdered.

Spartanburg, city (1970 pop. 44,546), seat of Spartanburg co., NW S.C., in the Piedmont near the N.C. line; inc. 1831. The metropolis of a large area of mill villages, the city is a noted textile center and an important commercial, transportation, and trade focus in an extensive cotton and farm-produce region. Textiles, machinery, ceramics, chemicals, plastic, rubber, and products of wood, metal, and paper are manufactured. A huge textile-research center is there. In the Revolutionary War, 11 major battles were fought in the area. The site was selected as the county seat in 1785. City and county were named for the "Spartan" regiment of Revolutionary troops recruited in the area. In the Civil War the city was a busy supply-manufacturing point. Spartanburg is the seat of Wofford College, Converse College, two junior colleges, a branch of the Univ. of South Carolina, and a state school for the deaf and blind (est. 1849). The city was the home of James F. Byrnes. Cowpens National Battlefield and a state park are nearby.

Spartivento, Cape (spärtēvĕn'tō), southeastern extremity of the "toe" of Italy, in Calabria, extending into the Ionian Sea. A lighthouse is there.

spasm, involuntary rigid muscle contraction, often persistent and often accompanied by pain. It usually has some underlying physical cause such as disease, strain, or injury to the muscle or nearby tissues, impairment of circulation, or a disturbance of body chemistry. The spasm may be confined to one group of muscles or it may be severe and fairly generalized, as in CONVULSIONS. Painless localized spasms are called tics. These purposeless movements, usually of some part of the face, may begin as purposeful movement in response to some stimulus but eventually are carried out automatically, apparently without reason. They may disappear spontaneously after a time, or may require the elimination of some physical or psychic cause.

Spassk-Ryazanski (späsk"-ryəzän'skē), city, E European USSR, a port on the Oka River. It is also a rail junction and has manufactures of machinery, clothing, leather, and starch. Across the river are the well-preserved ruins of Old Ryazan (Rus. *Staraya Ryazan*), which was founded in the 9th or 10th cent. and destroyed by the Mongols in 1237. Spassk-Ryazanski was chartered in 1778.

Spassky, Boris, 1937–, Soviet chess champion. A child prodigy, he became an international master at the age of 16 and in 1955, at age 18, he became an international grand master. Subsequently, in international matches his success was somewhat erratic, and in late 1960 Soviet officials removed Spassky temporarily from the international team. He continued to play in USSR championships, however, and subsequently twice won the right to challenge world champion Tigran Petrosian for the international title, defeating him in 1969. In 1972 he lost the title to U.S. grand master Bobby FISCHER.

spastic paralysis, form of paralysis in which the part of the NERVOUS SYSTEM that controls coordinated movement of the voluntary muscles is disabled. In spastic paralysis the nerves controlling muscle movement are hyperirritable and do not function in a coordinated manner, so that impulses from them cause spasmodic muscle contraction. Extreme spastic paralysis occurs after various kinds of brain damage, e.g., stroke (see APOPLEXY). Spinal cord injury, such as that produced by inflammatory diseases of nerve tissue, can injure motor neuron fibers in the spine and cause spastic paralysis. Congenital spastic paralysis, or CEREBRAL PALSY, is often a result of intrauterine disease or birth injury, or occasionally some inherited nervous system defect.

spatterdock: see WATER LILY.

spavin (spăv'ĭn), disease of horses affecting the hock joint. There are two types—bog spavin, in which the hock joint is distended as a result of the collection of synovial fluid; and bone spavin, the bony enlargement of the bones that constitute the hock joint. The latter is a form of arthritis and causes inflammation, swelling, and lameness. Spavin can be caused by faulty conformation, strain, or excessive concussion. Treatment consists of rest, corrective shoeing, the application of blistering ointment, and surgery.

spaying: see CASTRATION.

Speaker, Tris (Tristram Speaker), 1888–1958, American baseball player, b. Hubbard, Texas. He started (1906) in organized baseball as a left-handed pitcher for the Cleburne team of the North Texas League. He then became an outfielder with the Houston club and in 1907 was purchased by the Boston Red Sox of the American League. Traded to the Cleveland Indians of the American League in 1916, Speaker was (1919–26) player-manager of the club, leading the Indians to their first pennant and world championship in 1920. He played with the Washington Senators (1927) and the Philadelphia Athletics (1928). One of the outstanding batters in American League history (his major-league lifetime batting average was .344), he was also regarded as one of the best defensive outfielders in the league. In 1937 he was elected to the National Baseball Hall of Fame.

spear, primitive weapon consisting of a wooden shaft tipped with a sharp point, usually 8 to 9 ft (2.4–2.7 m) in length. The point was made first of flint, later of bronze, and ultimately of steel; the spear has been in use since prehistoric times, originally as a hand weapon and then as a missile. Spear-throwers, such as the ATLATL of the ancient Americas, are hooked sticks that are held in the hand in such a way as to increase the range and force with which a spear can be thrown. From the spears of antiquity the medieval lance and pike evolved. The pike is a long wooden shaft with a steel point that sometimes has a hook on one side. Longer by 2 or 3 ft (61–91 cm) than spears, lances were used by many European cavalry units as recently as the early 20th cent. In a few countries they are still borne in ceremonial military formations, sometimes with a small pennant near the point. Primitive peoples in remote areas still hunt and fight with spears, sometimes putting poison on the tips.

spearmint: see MINT.

Special Drawing Rights (SDRs), type of international monetary reserves established (1968) by the International Monetary Fund (IMF). Created in response to worries concerning the limitations of gold and dollars as the sole means of settling international accounts, SDRs are designed to augment international liquidity by supplementing gold and the standard reserve currencies. Also known as "paper gold," SDRs are assigned to the accounts of IMF members in proportion to their contributions to the fund. Each participating country agrees to accept them as exchangable for gold or reserve currencies in the settlement of international accounts. Deficit countries can use them to purchase stronger currencies, which then can be used to pay off balance of payments debts. The first installment of a proposed $9.5 billion of SDRs was put on international accounts in 1970, with the United States slated to receive about one fourth of the total allotment. Some economists hope that SDRs will eventually replace gold as the major international reserve.

species, in biology, a category of CLASSIFICATION, the original and still the basic unit in the demarcation of plant and animal types. The species marks the boundary between populations of organisms rather than between individuals. Because related species are not absolutely permanent (see EVOLUTION), a precise definition of the term is difficult. On the basis of genetics, scientists now include in a species all individuals that are potentially or actually capable of interbreeding and that share the same gene pool. The latter term refers to that collection of characteristics whose combination is unique in the species, although each individual of the group may not display every single one of the characteristics (see GENETICS). In the few cases where members of different species can interbreed, the offspring are usually sterile (e.g., the mule). Groups distinguished by lesser differences than those marking a species are called variously subspecies, varieties, races, or tribes.

specific gravity, ratio of the weight of a given volume of a substance to the weight of an equal volume of some reference substance, or, equivalently, the ratio of the masses of equal volumes of the two substances. Unlike DENSITY, which has units of mass per volume, specific gravity is a pure number, i.e., it has no associated unit of measure. If the densities of the substance of interest and the reference substance are known in the same units (e.g., both in g/cm^3 or lb/ft^3), then the specific gravity of the substance is equal to its density divided by that of the reference substance. Similarly, if the specific gravity of a substance is known and the density of the reference substance is known in some particular units, then the density of the substance of interest, in those units, is equal to the product of its specific gravity and the density of the reference substance. The most widely used reference substance for determining the specific gravities of solids and liquids is water. Because the density of water is very nearly 1 g/cm^3, the density of any substance in g/cm^3 is nearly the same numerically as its specific gravity relative to water. In the English system of units the density of water is about 62.4 lb/ft^3, so the near equality between specific gravity and density is not preserved in this system. Specific gravities of gases are often given with dry air as the reference substance. Because the densities of all substances vary with temperature and pressure, the temperature and (particularly for gases) the pressure for both the reference substance and the substance of interest are often included when precise values of specific gravities are given. A number of experimental methods for determining the specific gravities of solids, liquids, and gases have been devised. A solid is weighed first in air, then while immersed in water; the difference in the two weights, according to ARCHIMEDES' PRINCIPLE, is the weight of the water displaced by the volume of the solid. If the solid is less dense than water, some means must be adopted to fully submerge it, e.g., a system of pulleys or a sinker of known mass and volume. The specific gravity of the solid is the ratio of its weight in air to the difference between its weight in air and its weight immersed in water. Two methods are commonly used for determining the specific gravities of liquids. One method uses the HYDROMETER, an instrument that gives a specific gravity reading directly. A second method, called the bottle method, uses a "specific-gravity bottle," i.e., a flask made to hold a known volume of liquid at a specified temperature (usually 20°C). The bottle is weighed, filled with the liquid whose specific gravity is to be found, and weighed again. The difference in weights is divided by the weight of an equal volume of water to give the specific gravity of the liquid. For gases a method essentially the same as the bottle method for liquids is used. Specific gravities of gases are usually converted mathematically to their value at standard temperature and pressure (see separate article STP).

specific heat, ratio of the HEAT CAPACITY of a substance to the heat capacity of a reference substance, usually water. Heat capacity is the amount of HEAT needed to change the temperature of a unit mass 1°. The heat capacity of water is 1 calorie per gram per degree Celsius (1 cal/g-°C) or 1 British thermal unit per pound per degree Fahrenheit (1 Btu/lb-°F). Thus, the specific heat of some other substance relative to water will be numerically equal to its heat capacity; for this reason, "specific heat" is often used when the heat capacity actually is meant. Because the heat capacities of most substances vary with changes in temperature, the temperatures of both the specified substance and the reference substance must be known in order to give a precise value for the specific heat. The heat capacity of water at 15°C is a frequently used value. Like specific gravity, specific heat is a dimensionless quantity, i.e., a pure number having no unit of measurement associated with it.

spectacle bird: see WHITE-EYE.

Spectator, English daily periodical published jointly by Joseph ADDISON and Richard STEELE with occasional contributions from other writers. It succeeded the *Tatler,* a periodical begun by Steele on April 12, 1709, under the pseudonym Isaac Bickerstaff. The *Tatler* appeared twice weekly until it ended Jan. 2, 1711. The *Spectator* began March 1, 1711, appearing as a daily, and lasted until Dec. 6, 1712. Valuable as social history, the papers (dated from various London coffeehouses) provide an excellent commentary on the manners, morals, and literature of the day. The *Spectator* was supposedly written by members of a small club, representing figures of the British middle class: Sir Roger de Coverley (country gentry), Captain Sentry (military), Sir Andrew Freeport (commerce), Will Honeycomb (town), and Mr. Spectator himself. Addison joined Steele in writing the *Tatler* and continued his collaboration with him, writing about the same number of articles, in the *Spectator.* Both periodicals had a tremendous influence on public opinion and gave great impetus to the growth of journalism and periodical writing. The *Spectator,* which was succeeded by the *Guardian,* was revived for a time by Addison in 1714. See edition of the *Spectator* by Gregory Smith (1945); studies by G. S. Streatfeild (1923) and R. P. Bond (1971).

spectral class, in astronomy, a classification of the stars by their SPECTRUM and LUMINOSITY. In 1885, E. C. Pickering began the first extensive attempt to classify the stars spectroscopically. This work culminated in the publication of the *Henry Draper Catalogue* (1924), which lists the spectral classes of 255,000 stars. The stars are divided into 7 classes designated by the letters O, B, A, F, G, K, and M; the hottest stars (O and B) are blue-white in color, while the coolest (M) are red. Each of the letter classes has subdivisions indicated by numerals 0 through 9. Thus, a B0 is the hottest B-type star, B5 is halfway between types B and A, and B9 is only slightly hotter than type A. The accompanying table gives the characteristics of the seven principal types. To the seven main groups, four more groups have since been added.

CHARACTERISTICS OF SPECTRAL TYPES

Type	*Color*	*Temperature*	*Strong lines*
O	blue-white	35,000°C	ionized helium
B	blue-white	21,000°C	helium
A	white	10,000°C	hydrogen
F	creamy	7000°C	ionized calcium
G	yellow	6000°C	calcium
K	orange	4500°C	titanium oxide
M	red	3000°C	titanium oxide

R, N, and S are classes similar to the K and M types but denote somewhat different spectral characteristics; W indicates a Wolf-Rayet star, the hottest type of star that shines with a steady light. According to a system introduced by W. W. Morgan and others, a Roman numeral is added to the spectral class to specify the luminosity, or intrinsic intensity, of a star. A bright supergiant is Ia, a faint supergiant is Ib, a bright giant is II, a normal giant is III, a subgiant is IV, and a normal dwarf or main-sequence star is V. For example, Sirius is classed as A1 V, a main-sequence white star. Betelgeuse, M2 Ia, is a bright red supergiant. See also HERTZSPRUNG-RUSSELL DIAGRAM.

spectroheliograph, device for photographing the surface of the SUN in a single wavelength of light, usually one corresponding to a chief element contained in the sun, e.g., hydrogen or calcium; the resulting photograph is called a spectroheliogram. The spectroheliograph was invented in 1890 independently by G. Hale and by H. Deslandres and modernized (1932) by R. R. McMath to take motion pictures. In operation, the instrument is preset by means of a prism or grating and a narrow slit that passes only one wavelength of light to a photographic plate; the image of the sun is then moved slowly or stepwise across the entrance slit until the entire disk of the sun has been photographed. See SPECTRUM.

spectrophotometer, instrument for measuring and comparing the intensities of common spectral lines in the spectra of two different sources of light. See PHOTOMETRY; SPECTROSCOPE; SPECTRUM.

spectroscope, optical instrument for producing spectral lines and measuring their wave lengths and intensities, used in spectral analysis (see SPECTRUM). It commonly consists of three hollow tubes mounted horizontally on a disk that is supported by a vertical shaft. One of the hollow tubes, the collimator, has a slit at the outer end and a lens at the inner end that transforms the light entering through the slit into a thin beam of parallel rays. Another tube is a telescope to give the observer a clear view of the spectrum formed. The third tube contains a scale and is so constructed that this scale is transposed upon the image of the spectrum produced; direct measurement thus is made possible. At the center of the disk and between the three tubes is a PRISM or diffraction grating by means of which the light from the collimator is dispersed and directed into the telescope for observation. The **spectrograph** is based on the same principle as the spectroscope, but it has a camera in place of the telescope. In spectrographic analysis the spectrum of a substance is photographed and the densities of its spectral lines are measured with a densitometer. Since the photographic densities of the spectral lines are determined by the quantities of the elements in the substance, this method is useful in quantitative analysis. Spectrographs are designed for special applications to be used with emission or absorption spectra in the ultraviolet, visible, or infrared ranges. They are employed widely in research, in astronomy, and also in the metal, chemical, and food industries.

spectroscopic binary: see BINARY STAR.

spectrum, arrangement or display of LIGHT or other form of RADIATION separated according to wavelength, frequency, energy, or some other property. Dispersion, the separation of visible light into a spectrum, may be accomplished by means of a PRISM or a DIFFRACTION grating. Each different wavelength or frequency of visible light corresponds to a different COLOR, so that the spectrum appears as a band of colors ranging from violet at the short-wavelength (high-frequency) end of the spectrum through indigo, blue, green, yellow, and orange, to red at the long-wavelength (low-frequency) end of the spectrum. The spectrum formed from white light contains all colors, or frequencies, and is known as a continuous spectrum. Continuous spectra are produced by all incandescent solids and liquids, and by gases under high pressure. A gas under low pressure does not produce a continuous spectrum but instead produces a line spectrum, i.e., one composed of individual lines at specific frequencies characteristic of the gas, rather than a continuous band of all frequencies. If the gas is made incandescent by heat or an electric discharge, the resulting spectrum is a bright-line, or emission, spectrum, consisting of a series of bright lines against a dark background. A dark-line, or absorption, spectrum is the reverse of a bright-line spectrum; it is produced when white light containing all frequencies passes through a gas not hot enough to be incandescent. It consists of a series of dark lines superimposed on a continuous spectrum, each line corresponding to a frequency where a bright line would appear if the gas were incandescent. The Fraunhofer lines appearing in the spectrum of the sun are an example of a dark-line spectrum; they are caused by the absorption of certain frequencies of light by the cooler, outer layers of the solar atmosphere. Line spectra of either type are useful in chemical analy-

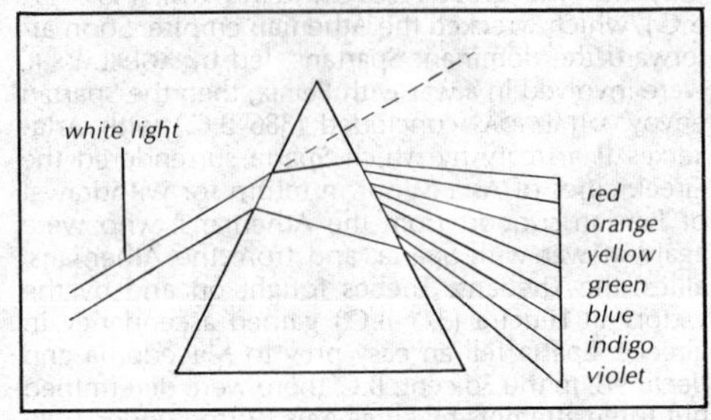

Dispersion of white light by a triangular prism

sis, since they reveal the presence of particular elements. The instrument used for studying line spectra is the SPECTROSCOPE. The explanation for exact spectral lines for each substance was provided by the QUANTUM THEORY. In his 1913 model of the hydrogen atom, Niels BOHR showed that the observed series of lines could be explained by assuming that electrons are restricted to atomic orbits in which their orbital angular MOMENTUM is an integral multiple of the quantity $h/2\pi$, where h is PLANCK'S CONSTANT. The integer multiple (e.g., 1, 2, 3 . . .) of $h/2\pi$ is usually called the quantum number and represented by the symbol n. When an electron changes from an orbit of higher energy (higher angular momentum) to one of lower energy, a PHOTON of light energy is emitted whose frequency ν is related to the energy difference ΔE by the equation $\nu = \Delta E/h$. For hydrogen, the frequencies of the spectral lines are given by $\nu = cR(1/n_f^2 - 1/n_i^2)$ where c is the speed of light, R is the RYDBERG CONSTANT, and n_f and n_i are the final and initial quantum numbers of the electron orbits (n_i is always greater than n_f). The series of spectral lines for which $n_f = 1$ is known as the Lyman series, that for $n_f = 2$ is the Balmer series, that for $n_f = 3$ is the Paschen series, that for $n_f = 4$ is the Brackett series, and that for $n_f = 5$ is the Pfund series. The Bohr theory was not as successful in explaining the spectra of other substances, but later developments of the quantum theory showed that all aspects of atomic and molecular spectra can be explained quantitatively in terms of energy transitions between different allowed quantum states. In addition to visible light, other types of ELECTROMAGNETIC RADIATION may be spread into a spectrum according to frequency or wavelength. Beams of charged particles can be separated into a spectrum according to mass in a mass spectrometer (see MASS SPECTROGRAPH). Physicists often find it useful to separate a beam of particles into a spectrum according to their energy.

speculation, practice of engaging in business in order to make quick profits from fluctuations in prices, as opposed to the practice of investing in a productive enterprise in order to share in its earnings. The term is sometimes applied to investment in a venture involving abnormal risks along with the chance to earn unusually large profits, but most speculation consists in the buying and selling of commodities and stocks and bonds with the object of taking advantage of rapid changes in price. While the investor seeks to protect his principal as it yields a moderate return, the speculator sacrifices the safety of his principal in hopes of receiving a large, rapid return. The practice is defended as tending to stabilize prices and guide investment; it is attacked as the mechanism of financial crisis and panic when prices decline rapidly and as an inflationary factor when a commodity is in shortage and speculation drives up its price. See MARGIN REQUIREMENT; PANIC. See Benjamin Graham, et al., *Security Analysis: Principles and Technique* (4th ed. 1962); C. P. Cowing, *Populists, Plungers, and Progressives* (1965); C. A. Dice, *The Stock Market* (4th ed. 1966).

Spee, Maximilian, Graf von (mäk"sēmē'lyän gräf fən shpā), 1861–1914, German admiral. At the start of World War I he commanded a squadron in the Far East. In Nov., 1914, he met and defeated the English commander Admiral Cradock off Coronel; however, he was defeated by Sir Frederick STURDEE near the Falkland Islands (Dec., 1914) and went down with his vessel. The incident became famous in German tradition. A German battleship was later named the Graf Spee. It sank many British cargo ships in the South Atlantic early in World War II before it was finally damaged heavily by three British cruisers in Dec., 1939, and scuttled by its crew.

speech: see LANGUAGE.

speech defect, any condition that interferes with the mental formation of words or their physical production. Speech defects in children generally become apparent in the early school years. Speech problems may arise from organic or functional abnormalities, but in practice the two are often hard to differentiate. Organic defects include deafness, CLEFT PALATE, dental abnormalities, and brain damage; most functional problems are basically psychological. Speech defects are generally categorized as disorders of sound production; disorders of voicing, e.g., loudness, pitch, and quality deviations; disorders of rhythm, such as stuttering and stammering; and disorders of language formulation and expression, including APHASIA, the inability to use words as symbols of ideas. Treatment of a speech defect may include correction of organic conditions, psychotherapy, and training in proper articulation; it is rarely limited to a single type of therapy.

Speed, John, 1552?–1629, English historian and cartographer. He abandoned his trade as a tailor to engage in mapmaking. Many of his maps of parts of England and Wales were published in *The Theatre of the Empire of Great Britain* (1611). His major work, *The History of Great Britain,* and his *Genealogies Recorded in Sacred Scripture* were published c.1611; they are based largely on earlier work.

speed, change in distance with respect to time. Speed is a scalar rather than a VECTOR quantity; i.e., the speed of a body tells one how fast the body is moving but not the direction of the motion. If during time t a body travels over a distance s, then the average speed of that body is equal to s/t. The speed and direction of a body's motion together determine the body's VELOCITY.

speedometer, instrument that indicates speed. A cable from an automotive speedometer is attached to the rear of the transmission of an automobile; the cable turns at a rate proportional to the speed of the car. In a very common type of speedometer the other end of the cable is attached to a simple magnetic device inside the speedometer. In response to the rotating cable, this device moves a needle along a calibrated dial to indicate the speed of the automobile. Another type of automobile speedometer uses centrifugal force and operates in a manner similar to a flyball GOVERNOR. The airplane speedometer is called an air-speed indicator. A dial that registers the speed in kilometers or miles per hour is actuated by the wind pressure in a tube located where it is not affected by the air stream from the engine. The speed of a watercraft is frequently determined by means of a patent or taffrail log. In this device a small propeller, which is towed astern, revolves as it moves through the water, activating a calibrated dial aboard the vessel. In another type of marine speedometer a tiny fin projects from the hull below the waterline. The resistance of the water to the passage of the fin is converted on a dial into terms of speed in knots.

Speedway, town (1970 pop. 15,056), Marion co., central Ind., just W of Indianapolis; inc. 1926. The Indianapolis Speedway is there.

speedwell: see FIGWORT.

Speer, Albert (äl'bĕrt shpār), 1905–, German architect and National Socialist (Nazi) leader. A member of the Nazi party from 1931, he became its official architect after Hitler came to power. His grandiose but coldly eclectic designs include the stadium at Nuremberg (1934). A highly efficient organizer, Speer became (1942) minister for armaments, succeeding the engineer Fritz Todt. In 1943 he also took over part of Hermann Goering's responsibilities as planner of the German war economy. From Todt, Speer inherited the *Organisation Todt* (OT), an organization using conscripted labor for the construction of strategic roads and defenses. Under Speer's direction, economic production reached its peak in 1944, despite Allied bombardment. In the last months of the war Speer did much to thwart Hitler's scorched-earth policy, which would have devastated Germany. Largely because of the OT's wide use of slave labor, Speer was sentenced (1946) to imprisonment for 20 years by the Nuremberg war-crimes tribunal. He was released from Spandau war crimes prison in 1966. See his memoirs, *Inside the Third Reich* (tr. 1970); biography by William Hamsher (1970).

Speke, John Hanning (spēk), 1827–64, English explorer in Africa. He joined Sir Richard Burton in his expeditions to Somaliland (1854) and to E central Africa (1857–59). Together they discovered (1858) Lake Tanganyika; then Speke continued alone and discovered Victoria Nyanza, which he believed to be a source of the Nile. In 1862 he returned to the lake and proved that the Victoria Nile issues from the north end over Ripon Falls. He wrote *Journal of the Discovery of the Source of the Nile* (1863). See biography by Alexander Maitland (1971).

speleology (spēlēŏl'əjē), systematic exploration of CAVES, popularly called spelunking. It includes the measuring and mapping of caves and reporting on the flora and fauna found in them. One application of speleology is the tracing of the movement of underground waters to prevent water pollution. See Roy Pinney, *The Complete Book of Cave Exploration* (1962); D. R. McClurg, *The Amateur's Guide to Caves and Caving* (1973); W. R. Halliday, *American Caves and Caving* (1974).

spell, word, formula, or INCANTATION believed to have magical powers. The spell can be used for evil or good ends; if evil, it is a technique of sorcery. Many authorities believe that the spell was the precursor of prayer. In Teutonic lore, the spell was a form of exercising occult power and was sometimes used to summon the spirits of departed heroes to give prophetic utterances. Once cast, the spell was supposed to remain in force until broken by a counterspell or exorcism.

Spellman, Francis Joseph, 1889–1967, American Roman Catholic prelate, cardinal of the Roman Catholic Church, b. Whitman, Mass. Educated at Fordham Univ. and the American College at Rome, he was ordained May 14, 1916. He was a parish priest in Roxbury, Mass., held various offices in the Boston archdiocese, and was the first American assistant to the papal secretariat of state in 1925. He was named (1932) auxiliary bishop of Boston and succeeded (1939) after the death of Cardinal Hayes to the archdiocese of New York. He was elevated to cardinal by Pope Pius XII in 1946. See biographies by R. I. Gannon (1962) and Warren Steibel (1966).

Spelman College: see ATLANTA UNIV. CENTER.

Spemann, Hans (häns shpä'män), 1869–1941, German embryologist. He was professor of zoology (1919–35) at the Univ. of Freiburg. By transplanting embryonic tissue to a new location or to another embryo, he investigated the agency that governs the growth and differentiation of cells. He received the 1935 Nobel Prize in Physiology and Medicine and described his research in *Embryonic Development and Induction* (1938).

Spenard, uninc. town (1970 pop. 18,089), Anchorage dist., S central Alaska, a suburb of Anchorage.

Spence, Thomas, 1750–1814, English agrarian socialist. A forerunner of the single taxers (see SINGLE TAX), he devised a scheme by which the parishes would assume ownership of the land and rent paid to the parish corporation would be the sole tax. He devoted much of his life to agitating for these principles and founded a society of Spenceans. He set forth his ideas in *The Real Rights of Man* (1775) and other pamphlets. See study by O. D. Rudkin (1927, repr. 1966).

Spencer, Anna Garlin, 1851–1931, American educator, feminist, and Unitarian minister, b. Attleboro, Mass. She married the Rev. William H. Spencer in 1878. She was a leader in the woman-suffrage and peace movements. Ordained in 1891, she held a pastorate in Providence, R.I. She was later associated with the New York Society for Ethical Culture (1903–9) and the New York School of Philanthropy (1903–13). Over a long period she was a popular lecturer and wrote on social problems, especially concerning women and family relations. Her writings include *Woman's Share in Social Culture* (1913) and *The Family and Its Members* (1922).

Spencer, George John Spencer, 2d **Earl,** 1758–1834, British public official. He was elected to the House of Commons in 1780 but in 1783 inherited the earldom. In 1794, William Pitt appointed him first lord of the admiralty. In his term of office the navy achieved the victories of St. Vincent and Camperdown, and Spencer was responsible for the selection of Horatio Nelson to command the fleet that won the famous battle of Aboukir (1798). He left office in 1801 but later served (1806–7) as home secretary. Afterward he devoted himself to literary and scientific pursuits. His son **John Charles Spencer,** 3d **Earl Spencer,** 1782–1845, better known as Viscount Althorp, was chancellor of the exchequer and leader of the House of Commons under the 2d Earl Grey. With Lord John Russell, he piloted the Reform Bill of 1832 through the Commons. He retired from politics when he succeeded (1834) to the earldom.

Spencer, Herbert, 1820–1903, English philosopher, b. Derby. He projected a vast 10-volume work, *Synthetic Philosophy,* in which all phenomena are interpreted according to the principle of evolutionary progress. Together with Charles Darwin and Thomas Huxley he was responsible for the acceptance of the theory of evolution. In *First Principles* (1862), the first of the projected volumes, Spencer distinguished phenomena from what he called the unknowable—an incomprehensible power or force from which everything derives. He limited knowledge to phenomena, i.e., the manifestations of the unknowable. He maintained that these manifestations proceed from their source according to a process of evolution. In *The Principles of Biology* (2 vol., 1864–67) and *The Principles of Psychology* (1855; rev. ed., 2 vol., 1870–72) Spencer gave a mechanistic explanation of how life has progressed by the continual adaptation of inner relations to outer ones. In *The Principles of Sociology* (3 vol., 1876–96) he analyzed the process by which the individual becomes differentiated from the group and gains increasing freedom. In *The Principles of Ethics* (2 vol., 1879–93) he developed a utilitarian system in which morality and survival are linked. Spencer's synthetic system had more popular appeal than scientific influence, but it served to bring the doctrines of evolution within the grasp of the general reading public and to establish sociology as a discipline. His *Autobiography* was published in 1904. See study by J. D. Peel (1971).

Spencer, Sir Stanley, 1891–1959, English painter. In his landscapes, portraits, and religious-allegorical themes, Spencer's paintings express a highly personal magic realism. His series of war murals in All Souls', Burghclere, Hampshire reflect the impact of his experiences in World War I. His other well-known paintings are the *Resurrection* (Tate Gall., London); *Jubilee Tree* (Art Gall. of Toronto); and *Christmas Stockings* (Mus. of Modern Art, New York City).

Spencer, city (1970 pop. 10,278), seat of Clay co., NW Iowa, on the Little Sioux River; inc. 1880. The city lies in a rich farm area. Beef is processed there. Work clothes, tools, prefabricated buildings, and beauty aids are among Spencer's manufactures. A famous county fair is held every September.

Spencer Gulf, inlet of the Indian Ocean, 200 mi (322 km) long and 80 mi (129 km) wide, SE South Australia state, Australia, between Eyre and Yorke peninsulas. The gulf is the major outlet for iron ore from Middleback Range. Whyalla, Port Pirie, and Port Augusta are on the gulf.

Spender, Stephen, 1909–, English poet and critic, educated at Oxford. His early poetry—like that of W. H. Auden, C. Day Lewis, and Louis MacNeice, with whom he became associated at Oxford—was inspired by social protest. His autobiography, *World within World* (1951), is a re-creation of much of the political and social atmosphere of the 1930s. His passionate and lyrical verse, filled with images of the modern industrial world, is collected in such volumes as *Twenty Poems* (1930), *The Still Centre* (1939), *Poems of Dedication* (1946), *The Edge of Being* (1949), *Collected Poems, 1928–1953* (1955), *Selected Poems* (1964), and *Generous Days* (1971). *The Destructive Element* (1935), *Forward from Liberalism* (1937), *The Creative Element* (1953), and *The Making of a Poem* (1955) contain literary and social criticism. His other works include short stories, the novel *The Backward Son* (1940), translations such as Schiller's *Mary Stuart* (1959), and sociological studies like *The Year of the Young Rebels* (1969), an analysis of the student rebellions of the late 1960s, and *Love-Hate Relations: English and American Sensibilities* (1974), about literary relations between Britain and the United States.

Spener, Philipp Jakob (fē'lĭp yä'kôp shpā'nər), 1635–1705, German theologian, founder of PIETISM. He was pastor of the Lutheran church at Frankfurt in 1670 when, to counteract the barren intellectualism of prevailing orthodoxy, he instituted meetings for fellowship and Bible study. These *Collegia Pietatis* led to a religious revival in many German states. His book, *Pia desideria* (1675), contained proposals for the reconstruction of the church. Spener became court chaplain at Dresden in 1686, but he aroused the opposition of the clergy and the elector and in 1691 accepted the rectorship at St. Nicholas, Berlin. Spener aided in the founding of the Univ. of Halle in 1694, and later, through the activities of his disciple August Hermann Francke, the city of Halle became a center of Pietism. The orthodox Lutheran clergy had continuously resented Spener's criticism and influence, and in 1695 the theological faculty at Wittenberg made formal charges against him. In spite of this opposition Spener's ideas spread to many congregations throughout Germany and in other parts of Europe.

Spengler, Oswald (spĕng'glər, Ger. ôs'vält shpĕng'glər), 1880–1936, German historian and philosopher. His studies covered many fields, among them mathematics, science, philosophy, history, and art. His major work, *The Decline of the West* (2 vol., 1918–22; tr. 1926–28), brought him worldwide fame. Spengler maintained that every culture passes a life cycle from youth through maturity and old age to death. Western culture, he believed, had proceeded through this same cycle and had entered the period of decline, from which there was no escape. Spengler upheld the ideal of obedience to the state and supported German hegemony in Europe. His refusal to support Nazi theories of racial superiority led to his ostracism after the Nazis came to power in 1933. See critical study by H. S. Hughes (1952).

Spenser, Edmund, 1552?–1599, English poet, b. London. He was the friend of men eminent in literature and at court, including Gabriel Harvey, Sir Philip Sidney, Sir Walter Raleigh, and Robert Sidney, earl of Leicester. After serving as secretary to the Bishop of Rochester, Spenser was appointed in 1580 secretary to Lord Grey, lord deputy of Ireland. Afterward Spenser lived in Ireland, holding minor civil offices and receiving the lands and castle of Kilcolman, Co. Cork. In 1589, under Raleigh's sponsorship, Spenser went to London, where he apparently sought court preferment and publication of the first three books of *The Faerie Queene*. After the Tyrone rebellion of 1598, in which Kilcolman Castle was burned, he returned to London, where he died in 1599. He is buried in Westminster Abbey. Recognized by his contemporaries as the foremost poet of his time, Spenser was not only a master of meter and language but a profound moral poet as well. Patterning his literary career after that of Vergil, Spenser first published 12 pastoral eclogues of *The Shepheardes Calender* (1579), which treat the shepherd as rustic priest and poet. His *Complaints* and *Daphnaida*, the latter an elegy on Douglas Howard, both appeared in 1591. In 1595 *Colin Clouts Come Home Againe*, a pastoral allegory dealing with Spenser's first London journey and the vices inherent in court life, and *Astrophel*, an elegy on Sir Philip Sidney, were published. In the same year *Amoretti*, Spenser's sonnet sequence commemorating his courtship of Elizabeth Boyle, and *Epithalamion*, a beautiful and complex wedding poem in honor of his marriage in 1594, were also published. *Fowre Hymnes*, which explains Spenser's Platonic and Christian views of love and beauty, and *Prothalamion* appeared in 1596. Also in 1596 the first six books of *The Faerie Queene*, Spenser's unfinished masterpiece, appeared. Although the poem is an epic, his method was to treat the moral virtues allegorically. The excellence of *The Faerie Queene* lies in the complexity and depth of Spenser's moral vision and in the Spenserian stanza (nine lines, eight of iambic pentameter followed by one of iambic hexameter, rhyming *ababbcbcc*), which Spenser invented for his masterpiece. Spenser's only extended prose work, *A View of the Present State of Ireland*, was first printed in 1633. See variorum edition of his works (ed. by E. Greenlaw and others, 1932–49), the three-volume edition of the poetical works (J. C. Smith and E. de Selincourt, 1909–10), and the four-volume edition of the minor works (W. L. Renwick, 1928–34). See biography by A. C. Judson (1945); studies by William Nelson (1963), W. L. Renwick (1925, repr. 1965), D. Cheney (1966), and Peter Bayley (1971); C. S. Lewis, *The Allegory of Love* (1936, repr. 1958) and F. Kermode, *Shakespeare, Spenser, Donne* (1971).

Speranski, Mikhail Mikhailovich (mēkhəyēl' mēkhī'ləvĭch spyĭrän'skē), 1772–1839, Russian public official, chief adviser to Czar Alexander I (1808–12). The son of a village priest, he rose as a civil servant, particularly after the accession of Alexander I. He proved an outstanding administrator, and in 1809 he drew up proposals for a constitution at Alexander's request. His plan called for some popular participation in legislation and for administrative reorganization of the country to provide limited local self-government; Alexander never adopted his proposals. Speranski did succeed in some reforms. He reorganized several ministries, emphasizing promotion on the basis of merit, and introduced a progressive income tax on the nobles. His proposals antagonized both nobles and bureaucrats, and shortly before the Napoleonic invasion of Russia they accused him of secret dealings with the French. Alexander exiled him in March, 1812. Speranski later returned to public service as governor of Penza (1816) and governor general of Siberia (1819). He went back to St. Petersburg in 1821 but never regained his influence with Alexander. Under Nicholas I he was responsible for the codification (1833) of Russian law. See biography by Marc Raeff (1957).

sperm or **spermatozoon** (spûr''mətəzō'ən, -zō'ŏn), in biology, the male gamete (sex cell), corresponding to the female OVUM in organisms that reproduce sexually. In higher animals the sperm is produced in the testis of the male; it is much smaller than the ovum and consists primarily of a head, whose nucleus bears the hereditary material (see CHROMOSOME) of the male parent, and a slender whiplike process (flagellum), which provides the motility necessary for FERTILIZATION in a fluid medium. In higher plants the sperm is contained in the POLLEN grain and is conveyed to the ovum by the pollen tube; in some lower plants (e.g., mosses and ferns) the sperm is actively motile.

spermaceti (spûr'məsē'tē), solid waxy substance, white, odorless, and tasteless, separated from the oils obtained from the sperm whale (see SPERM OIL) and other marine mammals. A mixture of esters of fatty acids, it is composed chiefly of cetyl palmitate. Spermaceti is insoluble in water and does not putrefy. It is used mostly in ointments and cosmetics and in fine candles and was widely employed formerly as the waterproofing medium for oilskins.

spermatozoon: see SPERM.

sperm oil, liquid wax obtained from the sperm whale, or cachalot, and related marine mammals. It flows readily, is clear, and varies in color from pale yellow to brownish yellow. Chemically it is not a true oil. It is secured from the blubber and from a huge cavity in the whale's head (this oil cavity helps the whale keep part of his head above water for breathing). A solid wax, SPERMACETI, is extracted from the oil by filtration and treatment with potassium hydroxide. The oil is an excellent lubricant, especially for watches and other delicate instruments, and is used as a dressing for leather, to protect plants from insects, in tempering steel, and in making soap.

sperm whale, largest of the toothed WHALES, *Physeter catodon*, found in the Atlantic and Pacific oceans. It is also called cachalot. Male sperm whales may grow to more than 70 ft (21 m) long and females to 30 ft (9 m). Most are dark blue-black all over; a few have white undersides. The large squarish head accounts for one third of the total length. The flippers are small and rounded, and there is a row of low humps toward the rear of the body; there is no dorsal fin. The sperm whale has a single nostril on the left side of its head, and the characteristic spout emerges diagonally. The lower jaw has a row of 20 to 30 teeth on either side; the toothless upper jaw has horny sheaths to receive the lower teeth. Sperm whales travel long distances, following the migrations of their prey. The adult females and the calves usually confine their movements to the latitudes between 40°N and 40°S of the equator. The range of adult males extends N to the Bering Sea and S to Antarctica; they join the females and young in the tropics during the breeding season. There are fewer males than females, and the animals are polygamous. The single calf, born after a gestation period of 12 months, is 12 to 14 ft (3.6–4.2 m) long at birth. Sperm whales feed chiefly on squid, octopus, and cuttlefish. A gray, cheeselike substance called AMBERGRIS, valuable as a perfume fixative, forms in the whale's intestine around the irritating, undigested beaks of squids. It is often expelled by vomiting and floats in chunks on the water. The head of the sperm whale may contain up to a ton of fine oil, known as SPERM OIL, and a wax called SPERMACETI. Sperm WHALING was the foundation of the economic expansion of New England in the 18th cent. The industries founded on ambergris, sperm oil, and spermaceti resulted in the slaughter of sperm whales almost to extinction. Hunting of this species has declined, and recently the species has somewhat increased in numbers. Sperm whales are among the most aggressive of whales; they battle 30-ft (9-m) giant squid to the death and have been known, when attacked, to sink a rowboat full of whalers. They are thought to live 80 to 100 years. The pygmy sperm whale, *Kogia breviceps*, of the same family, is similar to the cachalot in range and feeding habits. It is 9 to 13 ft (2.7–4 m) long, black above and gray below, with a sickle-shaped dorsal fin and has two teeth in its upper jaw. Sperm whales are classified in the phylum CHORDATA, subphylum Vertebrata, class Mammalia, order Cetacea, family Physeteridae.

Sperry, Elmer Ambrose, 1860–1930, American inventor, b. Cortland, N.Y. Although probably best known for his work on the gyroscope, he also invented the gyrocompass (1910), an extremely effective high-intensity searchlight, a new system of street lighting, and numerous electrical devices. He founded the American Institute of Electrical Engineers and the American Electrochemical Society. See study by T. P. Hughes (1971).

Speusippus (spyo͞osĭp'əs), fl. 347–339 B.C., Greek philosopher; disciple and nephew of Plato, whom he succeeded as head of the ACADEMY. Speusippus distinguished 10 grades of being, thereby prefiguring Neoplatonism. He held that the good is not the source of being but is its goal. One of his most significant ideas is that it is impossible to have satisfactory knowledge of anything without knowing all things besides. A portion of his writings on Pythagorean numbers has survived.

Spey (spā), river, c.105 mi (170 km) long, rising in the Mondhliath mts., NE Scotland, and flowing generally NE through the Moray Firth to the North Sea. The river is rapid and unnavigable. There are important salmon fisheries on the lower Spey. Water from the river is used in the manufacture of many of the famous Speyside whiskies.

Speyer, John of: see JOHN OF SPEYER.

Speyer (shpī'ər), city (1970 pop. 41,763), Rhineland-Palatinate, SW West Germany, on the Rhine River. The city, sometimes called Spires in English, is a river port and industrial center; manufactures include paper, chemicals, and textiles. There are also shipyards in the city. Speyer is a noted cultural and historical center of the Rhine plain. Its site was originally settled by the Celts and was known under the Romans as Augusta Nemetum and Noviomagus. The city was destroyed (c.450) by the Huns but was later rebuilt and became (7th cent.) an episcopal see; in 1146 the Second Crusade was preached at Speyer by St. Bernard of Clairvaux. It was made a free imperial city in 1294, but its bishops ruled substantial territories on both sides of the Rhine as princes of the Holy Roman Empire. Several imperial diets were held there, notably the diet of 1529 (see REFORMATION), at which Lutheran princes issued a strong protest against the anti-Lutheran measures of Emperor Charles V. The imperial chamber of justice (Ger. *Reichskammergericht*) was located at Speyer from 1526–27 to 1689; after the city had been devastated (1689) by the French during the War of the Grand Alliance, the chamber was moved to Wetzlar. Speyer, together with the territory of the bishops of Speyer W of the Rhine, was occupied by the French during the French Revolutionary Wars and formally ceded to France by the Treaty of Campo Formio (1797). The secularized bishopric E of the Rhine passed to Baden in 1803. Speyer and the episcopal lands W of the Rhine were subsequently given to Bavaria at the Congress of Vienna (1815); they were incorporated into the Rhenish Palatinate, of which Speyer was the capital until 1945. The city has retained parts of its medieval wall and gates. Its four-towered Imperial Cathedral (begun c.1030 by Konrad II, completed 1061; altered 1082–1125; restored several times thereafter), is one of the greatest Romanesque buildings in Germany and contains the tombs of eight emperors. The Historical Museum of the Palatinate, located at Speyer, has large collections of pre-Roman and Roman materials and includes a wine museum. An early center of printing, the city was the home of the 15th-century printers John of Speyer and his brother Wendelin.

Spezia, La (lä spĕt'syä), city (1971 pop. 124,863), capital of La Spezia prov., in Liguria, NW Italy, on the Gulf of La Spezia (an arm of the Ligurian Sea) and at the eastern end of the RIVIERA. It is the chief Italian naval station and arsenal and the seat of a school of navigation. The city is also a commercial port, with shipyards and industries producing steel and petroleum. Once a small fishing village, La Spezia has been fortified since the Middle Ages. It was badly damaged by Allied bombing in World War II. There is a notable cathedral (14th–16th cent.) in the city; nearby are the ruins of the important Roman town of Luna, which was destroyed in the Middle Ages. Along the picturesque Gulf of La Spezia there are several villages celebrated for their beauty, especially Portovenere, Lèrici, and San Terenzo.

sphagnum (sfăg'nəm) or **peat moss,** any species of the large and widely distributed genus *Sphagnum,* economically the most valuable MOSS. Sphagnums, the principal constituent of PEAT, typically grow as a floating mat on freshwater BOGS. Their leaflike appendages have many large cells with circular openings that enable them to absorb liquids readily; hence they are commercially important as packing material and absorbent dressings and for other uses. *Sphagnum* is classified in the division BRYOPHYTA, class Bryopsida.

sphalerite (sfăl'ərīt, sfā'-), mineral composed of zinc sulfide, usually containing some iron and a little cadmium. It occurs in crystals of the isometric system but more generally in cleavable, compact masses. It is transparent to translucent and varies greatly in color, iron-free specimens being pale yellow and those with iron being brown, red, black, or green. The most important source of ZINC, sphalerite is a widely distributed mineral that commonly occurs in association with galena. It is found in large deposits in many parts of the world.

sphenodon: see TUATARA.

sphere, in geometry, the three-dimensional analogue of a CIRCLE. The term is applied to the spherical surface, every point of which is the same distance (the radius) from a certain fixed point (the center), and also to the volume enclosed by such a surface. The curve formed by a plane cutting a sphere is a circle. If the plane goes through the center of the sphere, the circle is called a great circle of the sphere. It is the largest circle that can be drawn upon the sphere, and all great circles of the same or equal spheres are of equal size. The shortest distance between two points on a spherical surface, measured on the surface, is the distance along the great circle through those points. A plane cutting a sphere in a great circle divides the sphere into two equal segments called hemispheres. The diameter of a sphere is the diameter of one of its great circles. The formula for the area of the surface of a sphere is $S=4\pi r^2$, and for the volume it is $V=\frac{4}{3}\pi r^3$, where r is the radius of the sphere. Spherical geometry and spherical trigonometry are methods of determining magnitudes and figures on a spherical surface.

sphere of influence, term formerly applied to an area over which an outside power claims hegemony with the intention of subsequently gaining more definite control, as in COLONIZATION, or with the intention of securing an economic monopoly over the territory without assuming political control. A sphere of influence was usually claimed by an imperialistic nation over an underdeveloped or weak state that bordered an already existing colony. The expression came into common use with the colonial expansion of European powers in Africa during the late 19th cent. A sphere of influence was formalized by treaty, either between two colonizing nations who agreed not to interfere in one another's territory, or between the colonizing nation and a representative of the territory. Theoretically, the SOVEREIGNTY of a nation was not impaired by the establishment of a sphere of influence within its borders; in actuality, the interested power was able to exercise great authority in the territory it dominated, and if disorders occurred it was in a position to seize control. Thus the creation of spheres of influence was frequently the prelude to colonization or to the establishment of a PROTECTORATE. The term in this sense is no longer recognized in international law, however. Currently, it is used by the more powerful nations of the world to denote the exclusive or predominant interest they may have in certain areas of the globe, especially for the purposes of national SECURITY.

spherical aberration: see ABERRATION, in optics.

sphinx (sfĭngks), mythical beast of ancient Egypt, frequently symbolizing the pharaoh as an incarnation of the sun god Ra. The sphinx was represented in sculpture usually in a recumbent position with the head of a man and the body of a lion, although some were constructed with rams' heads and others with hawks' heads. Thousands of sphinxes were built in ancient Egypt; the most famous is the Great Sphinx at Al Jizah (formerly Gizeh), a colossal figure sculptured out of natural rock, near the pyramid of Khafre. Sphinxes, however, were not peculiar to Egypt; represented in various shapes and forms, they were common throughout the ancient Middle East and Greece. In Greek mythology and art the Sphinx was a winged monster with the head and breasts of a woman and the body of a lion. In the legend of OEDIPUS she acts as a destructive agent of the gods, posing the riddle of the three ages of man: "What walks on four feet in the morning, on two at noon, and on three in the evening?" She killed all who failed to answer her question until Oedipus solved the riddle by saying, "Man crawls on all fours as a baby, walks upright in the prime of life, and uses a staff in old age." The Sphinx then killed herself.

Spica (spī'kə), brightest star in the constellation VIRGO; Bayer designation Alpha Virginis; 1970 position R.A. $13^h23.6^m$, Dec. $-11°00'$. A bluish-white star of SPECTRAL CLASS B1 V, its apparent MAGNITUDE averages about 0.96, making it one of the 20 brightest stars in the sky. Because it is an eclipsing BINARY STAR, the magnitude ranges from 0.91 to 1.01 as the two components orbit about each other with a four-day period. Spica is at a distance of about 200 light-years. Its name is Latin for "ear of grain," referring to an ear of grain held by the figure traditionally associated with the constellation Virgo.

spice, aromatic vegetable product used as a flavoring or condiment. The term was formerly applied also to pungent or aromatic foods (e.g., gingerbread and currants), to ingredients of incense or perfume (e.g., myrrh), and to embalming agents. Modern usage tends to limit the term to flavorings used in food or drinks, although many spices have additional commercial uses, e.g., as ingredients of medicines, perfumes, incense, and soaps. Spices include stimulating condiments, e.g., pepper, mustard, and horseradish; aromatic spices, e.g., cloves, cinnamon, nutmeg, anise, and mace; and sweet herbs, e.g., thyme, marjoram, sage, and mint. Spices are taken from the part of the plant richest in flavor—bark, stem, flower bud, fruit, seed, or leaf. Although spices are very commonly used in the form of a powder, some are used as tinctures obtained by extracting essential oils, and many are used whole. Garlic, chives, caraway, mustard, and many herbs grow in temperate regions, and vanilla, allspice, and red pepper are indigenous to the West Indies and South America; most of the major spices, however, are produced in the East Indies, in tropical Asia, and in the Malay Archipelago. Spices from the Far East were in demand from ancient times; they were carried by caravan across China and India to ports of the Mediterranean Sea or the Persian Gulf and thence to the marketplaces of Athens, Rome, and other cities, where they were sold at exorbitant prices. Certain spices were used as media of exchange; Alaric I is said to have demanded pepper as part of the ransom for raising the siege of Rome in 408. In the early Middle Ages few spices reached the markets of Europe, but trade was slowly resumed in the 9th cent. and was later greatly stimulated by the Crusades. In Western Europe the desire for spices arose in part from the monotony of the diet and from poor facilities for the preservation of food, especially of meat. When overland trade routes from the Far East were cut off by the Mongols and Turks, the European demand for spices was a major factor in motivating a search for new trade routes around Africa and across the Atlantic and Pacific oceans. The high price obtainable for spices was partially responsible for the bitter rivalry of European powers for the control of spice-producing areas and of trade routes. Even after adequate supplies of spices were found and means of transportation made available, the cost long remained very high in Europe and in America. This was largely because of the expenses incident to attempts to retain monopoly of markets and to deliberately limit crops in order to secure high prices. Although spices today are still important in trade, their per capita use for flavoring food has declined in Western civilizations, and certain spices must compete with synthetic flavorings. The demand for spices has remained large in the Orient, where spices have a wider social and ceremonial significance than they ever obtained in the West. See J. W. Parry, *Spices* (2 vol., 1969); Frederic Rosengarten, Jr., *The Book of Spices* (rev. ed. 1973).

spicebush: see LAUREL.

Spice Islands: see MOLUCCAS, Indonesia.

spicule: see CHROMOSPHERE.

spider, organism, mostly terrestrial, of the class Arachnida with four pairs of legs and a two-part body consisting of a cephalothorax, or prosoma, and an unsegmented abdomen, or opisthosoma. The cephalothorax is covered by a shield, or carapace, and bears eight simple eyes. On the underside of the head (the cephalic part of the cephalothorax) are two pairs of appendages, the anterior pair called chelicerae and the second pair pedipalps, with which the spider captures and paralyzes its prey, injecting into it venom produced in the poison glands. The spider then liquefies the tissues of the prey with a digestive fluid and sucks this broth into its stomach where it may be stored in a digestive gland. Breathing is by means of tracheae (air tubes) or BOOK LUNGS, or both. Arachnid book lungs are similar to the gill books of HORSESHOE CRABS but are internal and adapted to a terrestrial habitat. Three pairs of spinnerets toward the tip of the abdomen produce protein-containing fluids that harden as they are drawn out to form silk threads. Several kinds of silk glands and spinnerets produce different kinds of silk used variously for constructing cocoons or egg sacs, spinning webs, and binding prey; other light strands are spun out for ballooning, or floating, the spiders, especially young ones, long distances on air currents. Man uses spider silk for the cross hairs in certain optical instruments. Spiders live chiefly on insects and other arthropods; some large spiders ensnare and kill small snakes, birds, and mammals. Many are cannibalistic; the female may eat the male when courtship and mating are completed. Young, growing spiders can regenerate missing legs and parts of legs. Several species of spiders have bites that are exceptionally painful, or even dangerous to man. Species of BLACK WIDOW spiders, which are found in the warmer parts of the world including the United States and S Canada, have a virulent neurotoxic venom. The bite venom of the brown recluse spider of SE and S central United

States decomposes tissue, resulting in slow healing and sometimes leaving a sunken scar as large as a quarter. Among the more interesting spiders are the TARANTULA; its relative the TRAP-DOOR SPIDER, which ambushes its prey from a silk-lined burrow covered by a hinged lid; the orb weavers, which spin beautiful circular webs; and the crab spider, jumping spider, and wolf spider, named for their habits. Spiders are classified in the phylum ARTHROPODA, class Arachnida, order Araneae. See J. H. Fabre, *The Life of the Spider* (tr., new ed. 1971); B. J. Kaston, *How to Know the Spiders* (2d ed. 1972); B. R. Headstrom, *Spiders of the United States* (1973).

spider-flower: see CAPER.

spiderhunter: see SUNBIRD.

spiderwort, common name for some members of the Commelinaceae, a family of tropical and subtropical succulent herbs found especially in Africa and the Americas. Species of the spiderworts (genus *Tradescantia*) and the dayflowers (genus *Commelina*) are indigenous to the United States, particularly in the Southeast. They are sometimes cultivated as ornamentals. The family is classified in the division MAGNOLIOPHYTA, class Liliatae, order Commelinales.

Spieghel, Hendrick Laurenszoon (hĕn'drək lou'rənszōn" spē'khəl), 1549–1612, Dutch poet. In his cycle of spiritual songs *Lieden Op't Vader Ons* (modern ed., 1957), he was among the first to successfully adapt the iambic rhythms of French Renaissance verse and melody to Dutch usage. He propounded the iambic principle in *Kort Begrijp des Redekavelings* (1585). Spieghel was a leader of the Amsterdam circle that preceded the Golden Age of Dutch literature, and as poet-philosopher he exerted an important influence on Pieter Corneliszoon Hooft.

Spielberg: see BRNO, Czechoslovakia.

Spielhagen, Friedrich (frē'drĭkh shpēl'hägən), 1829–1911, German novelist. His works, chiefly on social and political themes, include *Problematische Naturen* (1861, tr. *Problematic Characters,* 1869) and *Sturmflut* (1876, tr. *The Breaking of the Storm,* 1877). Also important are his theoretical works on the techniques of drama, the novel, and the epic.

spikenard (spīk'närd), name for several plants. The biblical spikenard, or nard, was a costly aromatic ointment, preserved in alabaster boxes, whose chief ingredient is believed to have been derived from *Nardostachys jatamansi,* a plant of the family Valerianaceae (VALERIAN family). Such was the precious box of ointment that Mary Magdalen broke over Jesus' feet. The American spikenard, or Indian root, is *Aralia racemosa,* of the family Araliaceae (GINSENG family). The fragrant rhizome of both of these plants is still sometimes used medicinally. The false Solomon's seal, of the family Liliaceae (LILY family), is sometimes called wild spikenard. Spikenards are all classified in the division MAGNOLIOPHYTA but differ in the classes, orders, and families to which they belong.

spinach, annual plant (*Spinacia oleracea*) of the family Chenopodiaceae (GOOSEFOOT family), probably of Persian origin and known to have been introduced into Europe in the 15th cent. It is valued as a vegetable for the high vitamin and iron content of its leaves, and numerous varieties of the species are cultivated. NEW ZEALAND SPINACH belongs to the family Azioaceae. Both families to which spinach plants belong are classified in the division MAGNOLIOPHYTA, class Magnoliopsida, order Caryophyllales.

spinal column, bony column forming the main structural support of the SKELETON of man and other vertebrates. It consists of segments (vertebrae) linked by flexible joints and held together by gelatinous disks of cartilage and by ligaments. In human beings, the spinal column of the child contains 33 vertebrae; the last 9 become fused into two immovable bones, the sacrum and the coccyx, forming the back of the PELVIS, so that in the adult there are 26 separate bony segments. The 24 movable vertebrae are the 7 cervical (neck), 12 dorsal (back of chest), and 5 lumbar (loin). Each vertebra has a somewhat cylindrical bony body (centrum), a number of winglike projections, and a bony arch. The bodies of the vertebrae form the strong but pliable supporting column of the skeleton. The arches are positioned so that the space they enclose is in effect a tube, the neural canal. It houses and protects the SPINAL CORD and within it the spinal fluid circulates. Ligaments and muscles are attached to various projections of the vertebrae. The 12 pairs of ribs that make up the front of the chest are linked to the dorsal vertebrae. The spine is subject to curvature, injury, infections, tumor formation, arthritic disorders, and puncture or slippage of the cartilage disks.

spinal cord, the part of the NERVOUS SYSTEM occupying the hollow interior (spinal canal) of the series of vertebrae that form the SPINAL COLUMN. Extending from the first lumbar vertebra to the medulla at the base of the BRAIN, the spinal cord of a human adult is about 18 in. (45 cm) long. Structurally the cord is a double-layered tube, butterfly-shaped in cross section. The outer layer consists of white matter, i.e., myelin-sheathed nerve fibers. These are bundled into specialized tracts that conduct impulses triggered by pressure, pain, heat, and other sensory stimuli or conduct motor impulses activating muscles and glands. The inner layer, or gray matter, is primarily composed of nerve cell bodies. Within the gray matter, running the length of the cord and extending into the brain, lies the central canal through which circulates the cerebrospinal fluid. Three protective membranes, the MENINGES, wrap the spinal cord and cover the brain. Connecting with the cord are 31 pairs of spinal nerves. These feed sensory impulses into the spinal cord, which in turn relays them to the brain. Conversely, motor impulses generated in the brain are relayed by the spinal cord to the spinal nerves, which pass the impulses to muscles and glands. The spinal cord mediates the reflex responses to some sensory impulses directly, i.e., without recourse to the brain, as when a person's leg is tapped producing the knee jerk reflex. Nerve fibers in the spinal cord usually do not regenerate if injured by accident or disease.

spinal puncture, surgical penetration of the spinal canal by a hollow needle introduced between two of the lumbar vertebrae. The arrangement permits injection of antibiotics or anesthetics (see ANESTHESIA) as well as dyes to facilitate X-ray studies. It also allows withdrawal of cerebrospinal fluid (CSF), the plasmalike liquid cushioning the brain and spinal cord, in which case the procedure is known as a spinal tap. Examination of the CSF is useful in diagnosing disease of the central NERVOUS SYSTEM. The fluid is first tested for pressure; a high reading may signal inflammation or tumor. If pressure is normal, a small sample can be taken. It is then analyzed for antibodies, white blood cells, cellular debris, bacteria, and other organisms. Unusual concentrations may indicate disorders such as spinal meningitis, polio, or cancer. The concentrations of protein, sugar, and other chemical components are also determined. Excessive protein may be a sign of spinal tuberculosis.

spinal tap: see SPINAL PUNCTURE.

spindle: see SPINNING.

spindle tree: see STAFF TREE.

spine: see SPINAL COLUMN.

spinel, magnesium aluminum oxide, $MgAl_2O_4$, a mineral crystallizing in the isometric system, usually as octahedrons. It occurs as an accessory mineral in basic igneous rocks, in aluminum-rich metamorphic rocks, and in contact-metamorphosed limestones. Common spinel usually ranges in color from dark green to brown or black, but transparent red, blue, and green varieties are found and are used as gemstones; Burma and Sri Lanka (Ceylon) are the principal producing countries. Much gem-quality spinel is now produced synthetically.

Spinello di Luca Spinelli (spēnĕl'lō dē lōō'kä spēnĕl'lē), c.1346–1410, Italian painter, usually called Spinello Aretino from his birthplace, Arezzo. He was a leading exponent of the late Giottesque style (see GIOTTO). He painted frescoes of the life of St. Benedict (Church of San Miniato, Florence), restored by a later painter, and the history of Pope Alexander III (Palazzo Pubblico, Siena). Several of his altarpieces are in the Academy, Florence; two paintings of the *Madonna and Child* are in the Fogg Museum, Cambridge; and *St. Mary Magdalen* is in the Metropolitan Museum.

spinet, musical instrument of the HARPSICHORD family. Although the terms *virginal* and *spinet,* interchangeable until the end of the 17th cent., were sometimes used indiscriminately to designate any harpsichord, they usually referred to small instruments having one keyboard, one string to each note, and the keys more or less perpendicular to the strings, similar to the clavichord. The first spinet, made in the 15th cent., may have been a clavichord to which a quill mechanism was added. In England in the 18th cent. the virginal was the instrument with a rectangular case, while the spinet had a triangular or wing-shaped case. Until the middle of the 18th cent. neither had legs attached. The Elizabethan virginalists, among them William Byrd, Thomas Morley, and Orlando Gibbons, were the composers of an important body of music, of which the outstanding collection is the *Fitzwilliam Virginal Book* (early 17th cent., publ. 1894–99).

Spingarn, Joel Elias (spĭn'gärn), 1875–1939, American educator and literary critic, b. New York City, grad. Columbia (B.A., 1895; Ph.D., 1899). He was professor (1899–1911) of comparative literature at Columbia, and a founder and member (1919–32) of the publishing firm of Harcourt, Brace and Company. His varied and detailed literary work includes *A History of Literary Criticism in the Renaissance* (1899), *The New Criticism* (1911), *Creative Criticism and Other Essays* (1931), and several books of poems. A prominent officer of the National Association for the Advancement of Colored People from 1913 to his death, he established in 1913 the Spingarn medal, awarded annually to a Negro for outstanding service to his race. See studies by Marshall van Deusen (1971) and B. Joyce Spingarn (1972).

spinning, the drawing out, twisting, and winding of fibers into a continuous thread or yarn. From antiquity until the Industrial Revolution, spinning was a household industry. The roughly carded fiber was at first held in one hand and drawn out and twisted by the other hand. The earliest tools were the distaff, a

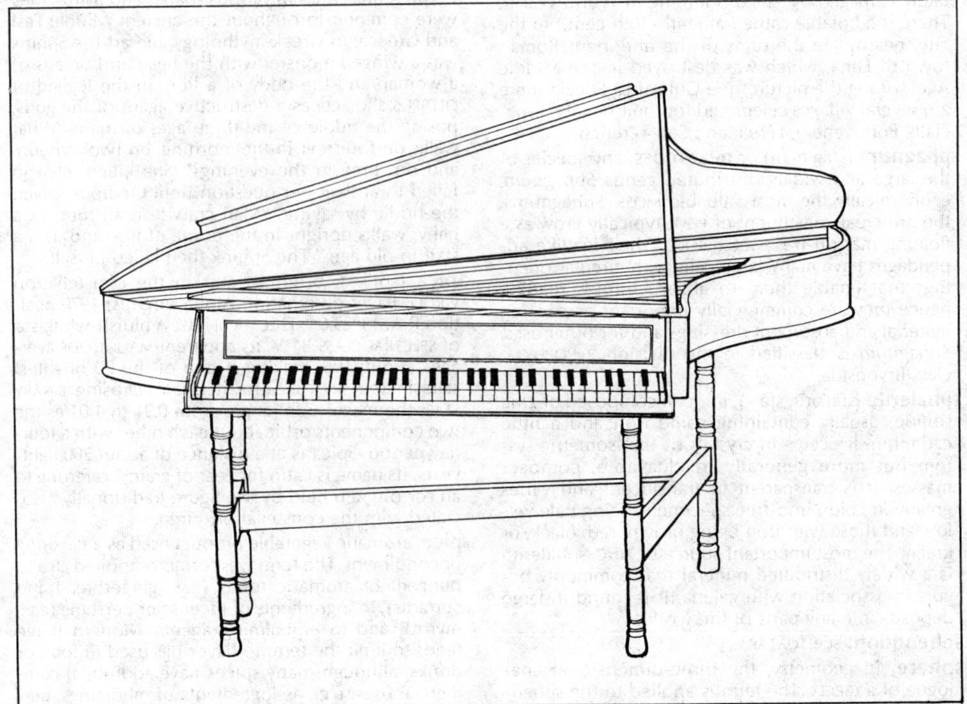
Spinet

stick on which the fiber was wrapped, and the spindle, a shorter, tapering stick notched at one end and weighted by the wharve or whorl (a disk of stone or clay). The spindle was twirled to twist the thread, which was then wound on it. With these simple tools were spun extremely fine yarns. In India the delicate threads for the famed Dacca muslin were produced by revolving needle-thin pieces of bamboo in a coconut shell. The primitive Gurkha wheel was used to spin coarse yarns. In Europe from the 14th to the 16th cent. the distaff and spindle were gradually superseded by the spinning wheel. It consisted of a spindle set in a frame and revolved by a driving belt passing over a wheel. The great, or wool, wheel, revolving the spindle directly, then by a pulley, twisted the thread; it was then stopped and revolved in the opposite direction to back off the spun yarn, which was then wound on the spindle. The flax, or Saxony, wheel—a more elaborate mechanism operated by a treadle—drew, twisted, and wound the yarn with a continuous motion suited to flax, wool, or cotton. In England improvements of the loom in the 18th cent., increasing the demand for yarn, stimulated inventions that revolutionized spinning. John Wyatt suggested the use of rollers to attenuate the yarn, a process patented in 1738 by his partner, Lewis Paul. James Hargreaves invented c.1765 the spinning jenny, a frame capable of spinning from 8 to 11 threads at once. The softly twisted yarns were not suitable for use as warp threads, but in 1769, Richard Arkwright brought out his frame, which by means of successive pairs of rollers, each revolving faster than the preceding pair, attenuated the yarn and twisted and wound it on bobbins in a continuous action. Operated at first by horse or mule power, later by water power, and still later by steam, spinning rapidly became a factory enterprise. In 1779, Samuel Crompton, combining the best features of the jenny and of Arkwright's frame, invented the mule spinning frame, forerunner of the modern self-acting mule. Because of its intermittent action, the mule is used for fine or delicate yarns. For the mass production of coarser yarns, the ring frame, an elaboration of Arkwright's machine invented by John Thorp c.1828, draws, twists, and winds the thread in one rapid, continuous operation.

Spinola, Ambrogio (ämbrô'jō spē'nōlä), 1569–1630, Spanish general, b. Italy, of a noble Genoese family. In 1602, Spinola entered Spanish service in the Netherlands. He took (1604) Ostend from Maurice of Nassau after a long siege and then carried the war into the northern provinces. Named commander in chief in the Netherlands by Philip II in 1605, Spinola negotiated the 12-year truce of 1609. Early in the Thirty Years War he led (1620) an army into the Palatinate against the Protestant Union; the following year he was created marqués de los Balbases by Philip IV. After the resumption (1621) of the fighting in the Netherlands, Spinola returned there and captured (1625) Breda. However, his conciliatory policy lost him the favor of Philip IV, who appointed him (1629) governor of Milan. Spinola died while trying to take Casale in the War of the Mantuan Succession.

Spínola, António Sebastião Ribeiro de (əntô'nyo͝o səbəstyouN' rēbĕ'ro͞o dĭ spē'no͝olə), 1910–, Portuguese army officer and political leader. Entering the Portuguese military academy in 1930, he later held a number of staff posts and then volunteered to serve in Angola to fight rebel forces there. From 1968 to 1972 he was commander in chief and governor of Portuguese Guinea and then served as deputy chief of staff of the Portuguese army. In Feb., 1974, he published *Portugal and the Future* in which he asserted that Portugal could not win a military victory in Africa. His book led to his dismissal from his army post in March. In April he led an army coup that ousted Premier Marcello CAETANO. Shortly afterward he became provisional president, welcoming liberals and socialists into the cabinet. After the withdrawal of the centrists from the cabinet in July, however, Spínola swore in a new cabinet, giving greater representation to the young military officers who had participated in the April coup. He initiated steps aimed at giving independence to Portugal's African colonies. He resigned on Sept. 30, 1974.

Spinone Italiano (spĭnō'nē ĭtălēä'nō, Ital. spēnô'nā ētälyä'nō), also called Italian pointer, breed of large, all-purpose hunting dog developed in the Piedmont district of NW Italy over three centuries ago. It stands from 20 to 26 in. (50.8–66.0 cm) high at the shoulder and weighs about 56 lb (25 kg). Its weather-resistant double coat consists of a smooth, dense underlayer and a short, hard, wiry topcoat. It may be solid white or white with light-brown or yellow patches. The Spinone is considered by many to be the best gundog of the various hunting breeds native to Italy. It is exhibited in the miscellaneous class at dog shows sanctioned by the American Kennel Club. See DOG.

Spinoza, Baruch or **Benedict** (spĭnō'zə), 1632–77, Dutch philosopher, b. Amsterdam. He belonged to the community of Jews from Spain and Portugal who had fled the Inquisition. Educated in the orthodox Jewish manner, he also studied Latin and the works of René Descartes, Thomas Hobbes, and other writers of the period, and also had a thorough grounding in scholastic theology and philosophy. His independence of thought led to his excommunication from the Jewish group in 1656; at about that time he abandoned the Hebrew form of his name, Baruch, for the Latin form, Benedict. Until about 1660 he lived in or near Amsterdam, and afterward lived in Rijnsburg, Voorburg, and The Hague. By trade a lens grinder of great skill, he lived modestly, devoting much of his time to the development of his philosophy. Spinoza became known in spite of his retiring mode of life; he had wide correspondence and was visited by other philosophers. In 1673 he was offered a professorship at Heidelberg, but he elected instead to retain his peaceful life and especially his independence of thought. He died of tuberculosis, a condition apparently aggravated by the glass dust from lens grinding. His major works, virtually all of which are available in translation, include a rewording (1663) of part of Descartes's work, *A Treatise on Religious and Political Philosophy* (1670, the only example of his own thought published in his lifetime), and his important *Ethics,* probably finished in 1665 but published posthumously (1677). His *Opera Posthuma* (1677) also include his *Political Treatise; Treatise on the Improvement of Understanding; Letters;* and his *Hebrew Grammar.* He began a translation of the Hebrew Bible and was one of the first to raise questions of higher criticism of the Bible. Spinoza's philosophy is deductive, rational, and monist. He shares with Descartes an intensely mathematical appreciation of the universe: Things make sense when understood in relation to a total structure; truth, like geometry, follows from first principles with a logic accessible and evident to man's mind. Unlike Descartes, Spinoza feels no discrepancy between the mind and the body, or between ideas and the physical universe. The two are merely different aspects of a single substance, which he calls alternately God and Nature. Just as the mind is not substantially alien to the body, so Nature is not the product or agency of a supernatural God. The universe is a single substance, capable of an infinity of attributes, but known through two of them: physical "extension" and "thought." God is not the creator of a Nature beyond himself; God is Nature in its fullness. Spinoza's rationalism, unlike that of later idealists, does not proceed at the expense of empirical observation; "adequate ideas" are a coherent logical association of physical experiences. When ideas are confused or contradictory it is not because they are false (in the sense of contrary to fact) but because they are incomplete or improperly related to the totality of experience. Spinoza's ethics proceed from a premise similar to that of Hobbes—that men call "good" whatever gives them pleasure—but they reach very different conclusions. Men, indeed all of Nature, share a common drive for self-preservation, the *conatus sese conservandi.* By this drive all men seek to maintain the power of their being, and in this sense virtue and power are one. But in Spinoza's system power is discovered to be a knowledge of necessity. A powerful, or virtuous, man acts because he understands why he must; other men act because they cannot help themselves. Freedom is to be guided by the law of one's own nature (which in Spinoza's rational universe is never at variance with the law of another nature); bondage consists in being moved by causes of which we are unaware because our ideas are confused. Spinoza's *conatus* is one predecessor of what Sigmund Freud termed *libido,* and, like Freud, Spinoza believed that to become aware of what moves us is no longer to fall victim to it. Another important feature of Spinoza's ethical system is his view of the intellect as active. He rejects the distinction between reason and will that assumes that ideas can be passively entertained. All thinking is action, and all action has its accompaniment in thought. What accounts for action is not an agency (the will) beyond the intellect, but ideas. Ideas are active and move us to act; an absence of action may be accounted an absence in insight: knowledge, virtue, and power are one. Politically, Spinoza and Hobbes again share assumptions about the social contract: Right derives from power, and the contract binds only as long as it is to one's advantage. The important difference between the two men is their understanding of the ends of the system: for Hobbes advantage lies in satisfying as many desires as possible, for Spinoza advantage lies in an escape from those desires through understanding. Put another way, Hobbes does not imagine a community of men whose desires can be consistently satisfied, so repression is always necessary; Spinoza can imagine such a community and such consistent satisfaction, so in his political and religious thought the notion of freedom, especially freedom of inquiry, is basic. Through Gotthold Lessing, Johann Gottfried von Herder, and Johann Wolfgang von Goethe, Spinoza influenced German idealism. During his lifetime and for a period afterward, however, his pantheism was regarded as blasphemous, which is one reason why most of his writing was published after his death. See Matthew Arnold, "Spinoza and the Bible," *Essays in Criticism* (first series, 1865, repr. 1968); A. O. Lovejoy, *The Dialectic of Breno and Spinoza* (1904); Leon Roth, *Spinoza, Descartes, and Maimonides* (1924, repr. 1954); H. A. Wolfson, *The Philosophy of Spinoza* (2 vol., 1934; repr. 1969); D. D. Runes, ed., *Spinoza Dictionary* (1951); G. H. R. Parkinson, *Spinoza's Theory of Knowledge* (1954, repr. 1964); Dan Levin, *Spinoza* (1970); T. C. Mark, *Spinoza's Theory of Truth* (1972); S. P. Kashap, ed., *Studies in Spinoza* (1973).

spiny anteater: see ECHIDNA.

spiraea (spīrē'ə), any plant of the genus *Spiraea,* Northern Hemisphere deciduous shrubs of the family Rosaceae (ROSE family). Most are indigenous to central and E Asia, whence come most of the popular ornamental species, e.g., the bridal wreath (*S. prunifolia*), native to Japan, and its similar hybrid *S. vanhouttei.* In these species the fragrant, spirelike flower clusters typical of the genus are borne on long, arching branches. Spiraeas native to North America include the hardhack, or steeplebush (*S. tomentosa*), a local source of astringent and tonic, and the meadowsweets (several species). The name meadowsweet is also applied to the related genus *Filipendula,* tall, hardy perennials (also often cultivated) formerly classified as *Spiraea* because of the similar showy blossoms. *Filipendula* includes the Eurasian dropwort (*F. hexapetala*), the queen of the meadow (*F. ulmaria*), now naturalized in the United States, and the North American queen of the prairie (*F. rubra*). Spiraeas are classified in the division MAGNOLIOPHYTA, class Magnoliopsida, order Rosales, family Rosaceae.

spiral nebula: see GALAXY.

spire, high, tapering structure crowning a tower and having a general pyramidal outline. The simplest spires were the steeply pitched timber roofs capping Romanesque towers and campaniles. In later Romanesque architecture the spire was commonly octagonal, topping a square tower. Transition between the two shapes was effected by filling each corner with a decorative pinnacle or a small turret. With Gothic development the spire became more elaborate. Generally the tower proper was capped by a parapet, behind which rose the stone spire, its edges finished with a molding and adorned with crockets. The corner pinnacles, with their niches, gables, and crockets, were often joined to the spire roof by flying arches. In France spires (called *flèches*) sometimes were placed over the two western towers of the cathedrals; at Chartres they are of two different periods, Romanesque and Gothic. In England the central tower of a cathedral often had a spire; at Lichfield one crowns each western tower as well. The ultimate elaboration in Gothic spires was attained with the addition of openwork tracery, as in the flamboyant example of Rouen (Tour de Beurre). The Germans, particularly, favored intricate openwork compositions, as at the cathedrals of Strasbourg (1015–1439) and Vienna (15th cent.). England in the late 17th cent. gave the spire new form in the numerous churches that Sir Christopher Wren built for London after the great fire. These were either the roof type, with richly curved baroque outlines, or cupola compositions with such classical features as columns and pediments. St. Martin's-in-the-Fields (1722–26), built by James Gibbs, illustrates the Georgian spire or steeple with its receding stages of classic architecture terminated by a steep pyramidal roof. It was an influential prototype for the slender, classical spires of American colonial churches.

spiritism or **spiritualism,** belief that the human personality continues to exist after death and can communicate with the living through the agency of a medium or psychic. The advocates of spiritism argue that death merely means a change of wavelength for those who die, and the medium is said to be able to receive radiations, frequencies, or vibrations that cannot be sensed by an ordinary person. Communication from the spirit world manifests itself in psychical phenomena (e.g., telepathy, clairvoyance, trance speaking, and apparitions) and in physical phenomena (e.g., levitation, automatic writing, and poltergeist and ectoplasmic activities). Ectoplasm is the mysterious visible substance in which the forces of the "other world" materialize. Closely related to the concept of the ectoplasm is the aura, a colored emanation that supposedly surrounds all individuals and that can be perceived by the medium. By noting variations in the hues of a person's aura, the medium is able to describe his personality, needs, and illnesses. The shriveling of the aura is considered a sign of impending death. In what is known as solar plexus voice mediumship, a spirit appears to speak through a medium's body. Modern spiritism in the United States dates from the activities of the Fox sisters (see FOX, MARGARET) in 1848. Such notable figures as Andrew Jackson Davis, Daniel Dunglas Home, Helena Petrovna Blavatsky, and Arthur Conan Doyle later became widely known spiritualists. The Society for Psychical Research has carried on investigations with some phenomena, mainly in connection with telepathy and apparitions, in hopes of finding scientific explanations for various spiritualistic occurrences (see PARAPSYCHOLOGY). See A. F. Schrenck von Notzing, *Phenomena of Materialization* (1920); Sir Arthur Conan Doyle, *History of Spiritualism* (1926); Sir Oliver Lodge, *Phantom Walls* (1930); S. E. White, *The Unobstructed Universe* (repr. 1959); G. K. Nelson, *Spiritualism and Society* (1969); Slater Brown, *The Heyday of Spiritualism* (1970).

spirit level, tool for determining whether a surface is horizontal. It consists essentially of a slightly bent transparent tube that is held in a frame. The tube contains some alcohol, ether, or similar fluid but is not entirely filled so that it also contains a small bubble. The position of the bubble within the tube indicates whether the instrument is horizontal. The spirit level used by carpenters and masons has two tubes at right angles to each other, so that the device registers a vertical as well as a horizontal position. The plumb line was used to determine vertical position from ancient times until the 19th cent. At that time the spirit level, which was invented in France during the 17th cent., came into general use and replaced the plumb line in some applications.

spirits of hartshorn: see AMMONIA.

spiritual: see AMERICAN NEGRO SPIRITUALS.

spiritualism: see SPIRITISM.

Spithead, eastern part of the channel between Hampshire, England, and the Isle of Wight. In 1797 a celebrated wartime mutiny occurred in the fleet stationed at Spithead: the crews sent the officers ashore, ran the ships by committee, and won their demands for better wages and working conditions.

Spitsbergen (spĭts'bərgən), formerly **Vestspitsbergen,** largest island (15,075 sq mi/39,044 sq km) of SVALBARD, a Norwegian possession in the Arctic Ocean. It rises to Newtontoppen mt. (c.5,650 ft/1,720 m), the highest point. It is indented by large bays including Isfjorden and Kongsfjorden. Spitsbergen contains the chief mining towns of Svalbard including Longyearbyen, the administrative center. The island served as the starting point for polar expeditions of Nils Nordenskjöld, Salomon Andrée, Roald Amundsen, Richard Byrd, Sir George Wilkins and others.

Spitteler, Carl Friedrich Georg (kärl frē'drĭkh gä'ôrkh shpĭt'ələr), 1845–1924, Swiss poet, whose pseudonym was Carl Felix Tandem. He was awarded the 1919 Nobel Prize in Literature. His chief works, imaginative and independent of the vogue for realism, include the epics *Prometheus und Epimetheus* (1881, tr. 1931) and *Olympischer Frühling* [Olympian spring] (2 vol., 1900–1906; revised version, 1910). The latter, set among the Greek gods, is an enormously original and complex allegory of the necessity for ethics in the modern world. A third epic, *Prometheus der Dulder* [suffering Prometheus] (1924), again stresses the role of ethics. Other works include novels, essays, and poems.

spittlebug: see FROGHOPPER.

Spitzweg, Karl (kärl shpĭts'vĕk), 1808–85, German genre painter and draftsman. Self-taught, he depicted the daily life of his native Munich in small, charming pictures in which realism, fancy, and humor are happily combined. Characteristic are *The Poor Poet, Two Hermits,* and *Scholar in the Attic.* He contributed many delightful drawings to the humorous periodical *Fliegende Blätter.*

spleen, soft, purplish-red organ that lies under the diaphragm on the left side of the abdominal cavity. The spleen acts as a filter against foreign organisms that infect the bloodstream, and it also filters out old red blood cells from the bloodstream and decomposes them. These functions are performed by phagocytic cells that are capable of engulfing and destroying bacteria, parasites, and debris. Certain white blood cells—the lymphocytes and monocytes—are formed in the spleen. Ordinarily, the spleen manufactures red blood cells only toward the end of fetal life, and after birth that function is taken over by the bone marrow. However, in cases of bone marrow breakdown, the spleen reverts to its fetal function. The spleen also acts as a blood reservoir; during stress or at other times when additional blood is needed, the spleen contracts, forcing stored blood into the circulation (see CIRCULATORY SYSTEM). It is possible to remove the spleen entirely, if necessary, without detriment to life, because other organs of the body are capable of performing all of its functions.

splint, rigid or flexible device for the immobilization of displaced or fractured parts of the body. Most commonly employed for fractures of bones, a splint may be a first-aid measure allowing the patient to be moved without displacing the injured part, or it may be a means of fixation to immobilize the bones until healing is complete. Any material that offers the degree of resistance required may be used for a temporary splint, e.g., cloth, gauze, paper (a magazine or folded newspaper), plaster, wood, or metal. A therapeutic splint should be applied only by a professional.

Split (splēt), Ital. *Spalato,* city (1971 pop. 183,912), W Yugoslavia, in Croatia, on the Dalmatian coast of the Adriatic Sea. It is a major seaport and a leading commercial center. Shipbuilding and the production of cement, chemicals, and textiles are the leading industries. The city's scenic location and historic monuments make it an important tourist and seaside resort. Split grew around the palace of Diocletian (who died there), built between 295 and 305. In the 7th cent. the inhabitants of nearby SALONA took refuge from the Avars in the palace, which became the nucleus of the city. Split soon was made an episcopal, later an archiepiscopal, see of the Roman Catholic Church and became a flourishing port of medieval Dalmatia. It passed to Venice in 1420, but the Treaty of Campo Formio (1797) gave it to Austria, to which it was restored (1815) after the Napoleonic Wars. It was included in Yugoslavia in 1918. The city has an archaeological museum, an oceanographic institute, and a teachers college. The palace of Diocletian is the most remarkable among the Roman remains in Split. Its other ancient buildings include the cathedral and the baptistery, both originally Roman temples; parts of its ancient walls and gates; and the town hall.

Splügen (shplü'gən), Ital. *Spluga,* pass, in the Rhaetian Alps, 6,946 ft (2,117 m) high, between Splügen, SE Switzerland, and Chiavenna, N Italy. Frequented since Roman times, it is crossed by the Splügen Road (built 1819–21), which passes above the Via Mala.

Spock, Benjamin McLane, 1903–, American author and pediatrician, b. New Haven, Conn., educ. Yale (B.A., 1925) and Columbia Univ. College of Physicians and Surgeons (M.D., 1929). In 1946, Dr. Spock published *The Common Sense Book of Baby and Child Care,* which has sold more copies than any other original title ever published in the United States. He was professor of child development at Western Reserve Univ. from 1955 until 1967, when he resigned in order to devote his full time to the campaign against the VIETNAM WAR. In 1972 he was the presidential candidate of the People's party, a coalition of pacifists and populists. Among his other writings are *A Baby's First Year* (1954), *Feeding Your Baby and Child* (1955), *Decent and Indecent* (1970), and *Raising Children in a Difficult Time* (1974). See biography by L. Z. Bloom (1972); Jessica Mitford, *The Trial of Dr. Spock* (1969).

Spode, Josiah, I, 1733–97, English potter. He founded a pottery firm in 1770 at Stoke-on-Trent in the Staffordshire pottery district. At first using Oriental designs, he developed a highly effective method of transfer printing with blue underglazes. He also experimented with a transparent but durable bone china, arriving at a formula that is still used. His son **Josiah Spode II,** 1754–1827, took over the pottery factory in 1797. He is credited with having introduced feldspar into Spode ware and for producing pottery of a high technical excellence. Under his direction the blue and white ware was noted for the novelty of its designs; these included genre scenes of an exotic character, such as tiger hunting in India. The firm is still in existence. See John Bedford, *Old Spode China* (1969); L. R. Whiter, *Spode: A History of the Family, Factory and Wares from 1733 to 1833* (1970).

Spofford, Ainsworth Rand (spŏf'ərd), 1825–1908, librarian of Congress of the United States, b. Belknap co., N.H. In 1861 he became chief assistant librarian of Congress and was appointed librarian by President Lincoln in 1864. He held the office until 1897, when he again became chief assistant librarian. Spofford was responsible for much of the growth and development of the library. He wrote many periodical articles on books and libraries and published or edited a number of books, including *A Book for All Readers* (3d ed. 1909), *The Library of Choice Literature* (10 vol., 1888); and the annual *American Almanac* (1878–89).

Spohr, Ludwig or **Louis** (lo͞ot'vĭkh shpōr, lo͞o'ē), 1784–1859, German composer, conductor, and violinist. After touring Europe extensively, he was (1822–57) court conductor in Kassel. His prolific output includes 11 operas, of which *Faust* (1816) and *Jessonda* (1823) are the most important; 9 symphonies, many of them programmatic; 15 violin concertos; numerous oratorios and other choral works; and a large quantity of chamber music. His music, which was influential in his day, shows a curious mixture of conservative and progressive tendencies. A mannered chromaticism, derived from Mozart, anticipated that of Wagner, whose works Spohr was one of the first to champion. As a violinist, Spohr developed a style which, through his teaching and his famous *Violinschule* (1831), became the basis for the German school of violin playing. See his autobiography (1845, tr. 1878).

spoiler: see AIRPLANE.

spoils system, in U.S. history, the practice of giving appointive offices to loyal members of the party in power. The name supposedly derived from a speech by Senator William Learned MARCY in which he stated, "to the victor belong the spoils." On a national scale, the spoils system was inaugurated with the development of two political parties, the Federalists and the Democratic Republicans, and was used by the earliest Presidents, particularly Thomas Jefferson. The system soon became entrenched in state politics and was practiced more extensively on a national scale during the administration of Andrew JACKSON, who declared (1829) that the Federal government would be bettered by having civil servants rotate in office. He replaced incumbent officeholders with members of his own party. Nevertheless, during Jackson's eight years in office not more than one fifth of officeholders were replaced. The dispensation of offices by strict party allegiance was followed in succeeding years and critical opposition grew. The corruption and inefficiency bred by the system reached staggering proportions in the administration of Ulysses S. Grant, and reaction against this helped bring about CIVIL SERVICE reform, which was inaugurated by creation of the Civil Service Commission in 1871. The spoils system has, however, continued for many Federal offices and is even more prevalent in state and local governments. See A. A. Hoogenboom, *Outlawing the Spoils* (1968).

Spokane (spōkăn'), city (1970 pop. 170,516), seat of Spokane co., E Wash., at the spectacular falls of the Spokane River; inc. 1881. It is a port of entry and the commercial, transportation, and industrial center of a productive region known as the "Inland Empire." The irrigated farms of the Columbia basin project contribute to the city's prosperity. The area has mineral deposits and cattle ranches and yields wheat, fruit, and other farm products. Spokane's diversified industries include lumbering, food processing and packing, aluminum smelting, metal refining, and the manufacture of paper, clay, and cement products. A trading fort was established there in 1810; settlement began in 1871. In 1889 a great fire destroyed most of the town, but it was rapidly rebuilt. Today Spokane is a focus of cultural and educational activities. It has a symphony orchestra, an art center, three museums, Roman Catholic and Episcopal cathedrals, and several fine parks. The city also has an international airport and is the seat of Gonzaga Univ., Whitworth College, Fort Wright College, and two junior colleges. A lilac festival is held every May. Numerous lakes in the vicinity provide recreational facilities. Fairchild Air Force Base is to the west.

Spokane, river, c.100 mi (160 km) long, rising in Coeur d'Alene Lake, N Idaho, and flowing through NE Washington to the Columbia River. Dams on the river include Nine Mile, Long Lake, and Little Falls. Farming, lumbering, and fishing are important in the valley.

Spokan Indians or **Spokane Indians** (both spōkăn'), North American Indians whose language belongs to the Salishan branch of the Algonquian-Wakashan linguistic stock (see AMERICAN INDIAN LANGUAGES). In the early 19th cent., according to Lewis and Clark, they lived in the vicinity of the Spokane River in NE Washington. They then numbered some 600. Today the Spokan live on a reservation in Washington; their number is still about 600. See R. H. Ruby and J. A. Brown, *The Spokan Indians, Children of the Sun* (1970).

Spoleto (spōlĕ'tō), city (1971 pop. 35,959), Umbria, central Italy. It is an industrial and tourist center. Manufactures include processed food, ceramics, and textiles. An Umbrian and later an Etruscan town, the city flourished after being taken (242 B.C.) by the Romans. It later became (c. A.D. 571) the seat of an important Lombard duchy that extended over much of Umbria, Marche, and the Abruzzi. The city was destroyed by Emperor Frederick I in 1155, but was rebuilt. Although Spoleto was included in Charlemagne's donation to the church (8th cent.), the dukes were named by the emperors until 1201, when Otto IV renounced the imperial rights. Soon afterward (1213) the duchy came under direct papal rule (to 1860). A local school of painting flourished in Spoleto in the 14th and 15th cent. In the city are ruins of a bridge, the arch of Drusus (A.D. 21), a theater, and an amphitheater, all dating from the Roman era. The 4th-century basilica of San Salvatore (renovated several times) is a remarkable example of early Christian architecture. The Cathedral of Santa Maria Assunta (begun by Frederick I) has frescoes by Filippo Lippi (who is buried in the cathedral) and Pinturicchio. "La Rocca," originally a castle (14th cent.), is now a penitentiary. The Festival of the Two Worlds, a major annual festival of the arts, was established (1958) mainly through the efforts of the composer Gian-Carlo Menotti.

Spoleto Festival, also called Festival of the Two Worlds, annual summer arts festival held in Spoleto, Italy. Founded by the composer Gian-Carlo MENOTTI and the conductor Thomas Schippers, the festival has been held annually since 1958. It features the works of young painters, sculptors, composers, and writers from all over the world and also presents young actors, singers, and musicians.

Sponde, Jean de (zhäN də spôNd), 1557–95, French poet and humanist. He held various posts in the court of Henry IV but died destitute because of his reckless nature. His *Sonnets of Love and Death* (1630, tr. 1962), considered his best work, abounds in antithesis and metaphor, foreshadowing the works of John DONNE. Sponde also published scholarly editions of Homer and Aristotle, *Homeri Poemarum Versio Latina* and *La Logique d'Aristotle.*

sponge, common name for members of the aquatic animal phylum PORIFERA, and for the dried, processed skeletons of certain species used to hold water. Over 4,500 living species are known; they are found throughout the world, especially in shallow temperate waters. All are marine except the members of a single freshwater family. Adult sponges are sessile, attaching themselves to rocks, coral, shells, and other substrates. They show so little movement that until the 18th cent. naturalists considered them plants. Most adults are colonial. Sexual reproduction gives rise to a free-swimming larva, which soon settles on a suitable substrate and develops into the adult form. Asexual reproduction also occurs. The individual sponge is saclike in construction; water is drawn into its central cavity through many tiny holes in the body wall and expelled through a large opening at the top of the body. Hard materials of various kinds, depending on the type of sponge, are imbedded in the body wall, forming a skeleton. A colony consists of a mass of many such individuals. Solitary sponges and colonies range in diameter from about ½ in. to 5 ft (1–150 cm) and vary greatly in shape. Some are branched, some more or less globular, and some are thin encrustations on rocks and pilings. Brilliantly colored sponges are common. Bath sponges are the skeletons of certain colonial sponges. These skeletons are composed of a fibrous meshwork of spongin, a material related to horn, and owe their absorbent properties to the fineness of the mesh. Sponges have been used to hold liquid since ancient times. The ancient Greeks used them for bathing and scrubbing, and Roman soldiers used them for drinking. Commercial sponges, species of the genera *Spongia* and *Hippospongia*, are harvested principally in the Mediterranean and Caribbean seas and off the Florida coast. They are brought up by divers in deep water, or raked in with long-handled forks in shallow water. They are left in water until the living tissue rots away; the skeletons are then cleaned and dried and sometimes bleached. Sponge fishing has declined in recent decades due to the use of synthetic sponges and to a decline in the population of commercially valuable natural sponges. The block-shaped sponges now commonly sold are the synthetic product. Dried natural sponges are light gray or brown and irregular in shape.

spontaneous combustion, phenomenon in which a substance unexpectedly bursts into flame without apparent cause. In ordinary COMBUSTION, a substance is deliberately heated to its ignition point to make it burn. Many substances undergo a slow oxidation that, like the rapid oxidation of burning, releases heat. If the heat so released cannot escape the substance, the temperature of the substance rises until ignition takes place. Spontaneous combustion often occurs in piles of oily rags, green hay, leaves, or coal; it can constitute a serious fire hazard.

Spontini, Gaspare (gäs'pärā spōntē'nē), 1774–1851, Italian opera composer. Spontini studied music in Naples. He went to Paris in 1803, won a prize from Napoleon for *La Vestale* (1807), and became court composer under Louis XVIII. In 1819 he was a leading musician at the court of Frederick William III of Prussia. Besides *La Vestale*, on which he worked for three years, Spontini had great successes with *Fernand Cortez* (1809), *Olympie* (1819, revised several times), and *Nurmahal* (1822). The pageantry and rich orchestration of his operas were greatly admired. In 1810, Spontini staged the first Paris performance of *Don Giovanni* in its original form.

spoon, implement with which to stir, serve, or eat, consisting of a shallow bowl with a rodlike, curved, or spatulate handle. Prehistoric peoples probably first used shells and later fashioned spoons of horn, wood, or flint. Wood, slate, and ivory examples from ancient Egypt have been preserved. Greek and Roman spoons of bronze and precious metals often had spike handles; Pompeian examples show decorative terminations in baluster and hind's-foot patterns. Spoons, often ornately decorated, have been used in religious rites since ancient times. The spoon used in England to anoint the monarch at his coronation dates from the 12th cent. Early medieval spoons were usually of horn, wood, or tin with knobs at the tip of the handles. Later spoons commonly terminated in effigies of the Madonna, saints, or apostles. Apostle spoons, relics of Tudor England, were commonly presented at christenings. During the Renaissance fig-shaped bowls were usual; pewter and brass were in common use, and silver was employed only for fine ware. The modern spoon with a spatulate handle dates from the 18th cent. Special sizes and styles of spoons are designed for soup, dessert, coffee, and tea, for serving, and for various other purposes.

spoonbill, common name for a large wading bird related to the ibis. It has a long bill with a tip like a flattened spoon, with which it captures small aquatic animals. The roseate spoonbill, *Ajaia ajaja*, its plumage rosy pink accented with carmine on the wings and tail, is found from the Gulf states S to Argentina and Chile. In the United States it was almost exterminated for its feathers. The common spoonbill of Europe, Asia, and Africa, *Platalea leucorodia*, is white and crested. Other species are found in Australia, Japan, and tropical Africa. The unrelated shoveler duck is sometimes called spoonbill, and there is a spoon-billed sandpiper. Spoonbills are classified in the phylum CHORDATA, subphylum Vertebrata, class Aves, order Ciconiiformes, family Threskiornithidae.

Sporades (spôr'ədēz, spŏr'–), islands, E and SE Greece, in the Aegean Sea. They have been grouped variously at different times. The Northern Sporades are generally understood to include Skíros, Skiathos, Skópelos, and some smaller islands off the coast of Évvoia and W Turkey. Límnos and Lesbos are sometimes also included. The Southern Sporades are generally understood to include Ikaría, Sámos, the Dodecanese, and sometimes Khíos. The main products of the Sporades are olive oil, wine, and citrus fruit.

spore, term applied both to a resistant or resting stage occurring among various unicellular organisms (especially bacteria) and to an asexual reproductive cell produced by many unicellular plants and animals and by all plants that undergo an alternation of generations. A spore is typically a mass of protoplasm containing a nucleus and surrounded by a cell wall; in resistant spores and in the resting stage of reproductive spores this wall becomes tough and waterproof, permitting the cell to survive unfavorable circumstances such as extremes of temperature and moisture. Many unicellular plants and animals reproduce both by the formation of spores and by simple cell division (mitosis), but may also produce dissimilar spores that conjugate to form a new individual. Yeasts, for instance, reproduce by forming both types of spores as well as by budding. Among the fungi some spores are thin-walled and germinate quickly; others are thick-walled resistant types. In multicellular plants the sporophyte generation produces (by meiosis) spores with half the normal number of chromosomes for the species; these grow directly into the gametophyte generation, which produces (by mitosis) male and female reproductive cells that when united give rise to a sporophyte (see REPRODUCTION).

sporophyte: see GAMETOPHYTE.

sporotrichosis: see FUNGUS INFECTION.

sport, in biology: see MUTATION.

sporting dog, classification used by breeders and kennel clubs to designate dogs bred for pointing, flushing, and retrieving game. These dogs hunt by air scent—as opposed to most hounds, which are ground scenters—and their quarry is primarily game birds. Included are the pointers, setters, retrievers, and spaniels. Pointers stand with nose and body rigidly still in front of their quarry, thus directing the hunter to its location. The setters were originally trained to set, or crouch, in front of game, the hunter then making the capture with a net. As bird shooting became popular, setters were trained to point. Retrievers find and return killed game to the hunter. Land spaniels spring, or flush, game, i.e., they startle a bird from its cover into flight. Water spaniels and many retrievers are especially equipped, as with a water-repellent coat and webbed feet, for retrieving downed waterfowl. The following 24 breeds are designated sporting dogs by the American Kennel Club: AMERICAN WATER SPANIEL, BRITTANY SPANIEL, CHESAPEAKE BAY RETRIEVER, CLUMBER SPANIEL, COCKER SPANIEL, CURLY-COATED RETRIEVER, ENGLISH COCKER SPANIEL, ENGLISH SETTER, ENGLISH SPRINGER SPANIEL, FIELD SPANIEL, FLAT-COATED RETRIEVER, GERMAN SHORTHAIRED POINTER, GERMAN WIREHAIRED POINTER, GOLDEN RETRIEVER, GORDON SETTER, IRISH SETTER, IRISH WATER SPANIEL, LABRADOR RETRIEVER, POINTER, SUSSEX SPANIEL, VIZSLA, WEIMARANER, WELSH SPRINGER SPANIEL, and WIREHAIRED POINTING GRIFFON. See DOG.

sports, athletic games or tests of skill undertaken primarily for the diversion of those who take part or those who observe them. The range, including both individual and competitive sports, is great. Usually, however, *sports* as a term is restricted to any play, pastime, exercise, game, or contest restricted by prescribed rules and performed under those rules indoors or outdoors, on an individual or a team basis, with or without competition, but requiring skill and physical prowess. Sports may be divided according to type (such as ball games), but the basis of enjoyment for all types is the same, whether one is taking part or merely a spectator. Track athletics are a matching of skill against time and space; sports such as hockey (see HOCKEY, FIELD; HOCKEY, ICE) depend on the stimulus of team competition, while ARCHERY is individual and as a sport a one-to-one competition. Some sports, such as HUNTING, FISHING, and SWIMMING, have their origins in man's primitive life, but as developed sports they have extreme sophistication in such things as highly developed sports guns, fly casting, and SKIN DIVING. The origins of most sports remain obscure. It is definitely known that BASKETBALL was invented in the United States in 1891 by James Naismith, but this is an exception. The origins of some sports, notably BASEBALL, are still the subject of much controversy. In ancient times the outstanding organized sports activities were the OLYMPIC GAMES. Several sports that developed in medieval Europe were organized by and for the royalty and nobility (e.g., COURT TENNIS), while other sports took root among the masses (see FOOTBALL). The disintegration of the feudal structure and the coming of the Industrial Revolution brought about profound changes in sports. While court tennis, archery, FALCONRY, and other pastimes of the nobility went into decline, CROQUET, BOXING, and SHOOTING increased in popularity. COCKFIGHTING, bare-fist boxing, and bull baiting, considered barbarous by many, were gradually banned by legislation, as the general desire to do away with crude brutalities in sports became more widespread. Equipment was standardized, local and national organizations were set up to govern the sports, and distinctions were made between AMATEUR and professional. In the late 19th cent.—when the Olympic games were revived—TENNIS, VOLLEYBALL, HANDBALL, BOWLING, RACQUETS, SQUASH RACQUETS, and SQUASH TENNIS came to the fore, while POLO was introduced from Asia to Europe. Sports that were traditionally played in various countries became, by legislative act or general acceptance, national sports—baseball in the United States, BULLFIGHTING in Spain and Mexico, CRICKET in England, and ice hockey in Canada. Moves were made to minimize the effects of gambling on sports, particularly in HORSE RACING. In the 20th cent., colleges led the way in emphasizing sports as an essential part of a person's education. ROWING, FENCING, TRACK AND FIELD ATHLETICS, and GYMNASTICS became popular participation sports on the campus as well as in the athletic club. College authorities, however, were soon subjected to severe criticism for commercializing spectator sports, especially football, and for the questionable amateur status of some of their athletes. Sports, participant and spectator, had a tremendous growth in the 20th cent. in those countries where a good percentage of the population had leisure time. They also took on an international flavor; aside from the world championships for individual sports, large-scale international meets, such as the PAN-AMERICAN GAMES and COMMONWEALTH GAMES, were inaugurated. International sports have also become instruments of political action. For example, Rhodesia was excluded from the 1972 Olympic games because of its separatist racial policies, and the visit of a U.S. table tennis team to Communist China was used to signal the start of improved Sino-American relations in the early 1970s. Several of the most popular spectator sports are today big businesses. In addition to the major sports mentioned here, this encyclopedia contains articles on many of the minor sports. For bibliography, see the individual articles; see also Walter Umminger, *Supermen, Heroes, and Gods* (tr. 1963); Frank G. Menke, *The Encyclopedia of Sports* (4th ed. 1969); Rudolph Brasch, *How Did Sports Begin?* (1970).

spot, fish: see CROAKER.

spots and stains: see STAIN REMOVAL.

Spotswood, Alexander, 1676–1740, colonial governor of Virginia, b. Tangier, Morocco. Appointed in 1710, he was officially lieutenant governor under the nominal governorship of George Hamilton, 1st earl of Orkney. One of the ablest of the royal governors, Spotswood encouraged settlement of the frontier by exempting the settlers from taxes and quitrents. His measures requiring the inspection of all tobacco intended for export or for use as legal tender (1713) and regulating trade with the Indians (1714) were unpopular, and upon petition by the assembly, the crown repealed them (1717). He also encountered difficulties in maintaining his right to appoint Anglican clergymen in the colony. In 1716, Spotswood led an expedition into the Shenandoah valley to hasten its settlement, and he negotiated a treaty (1722) with the Iroquois, by which they agreed to remain beyond the Potomac River and the Blue Ridge. At the end (1722) of his governorship, Spotswood remained in Virginia, having acquired a vast amount of land in Spotsylvania co., where he also had extensive iron interests. In 1730 he was made deputy postmaster general of the American colonies. See his *Official Letters* (ed. by R. A. Brock, 2 vol., 1882–85); biography by Leonidas Dodson (1932, repr. 1969).

Spotsylvania (spŏt″sĭlvā′nyə), rural county (1970 pop. 16,424), NE Va., formerly part of the estate of Alexander Spotswood, colonial governor of Virginia. It was the scene of several major engagements of the Civil War, including the battles of FREDERICKSBURG and CHANCELLORSVILLE and the battles of the Wilderness and Spotsylvania Courthouse in the WILDERNESS CAMPAIGN.

Spotted swine, breed that is predominantly black with many white spots. Except for its additional white coloring, it is much like the POLAND CHINA SWINE, which together with Gloucester Old Spot hogs forms the foundation stock of Spotted swine.

Spottiswoode, John (spŏt′ĭswo͝od), 1565–1639, Scottish prelate and church historian. Under James and Andrew Melville he studied for the ministry but later veered from strict Presbyterianism to the royal policy of Erastianism. James I named him archbishop of Glasgow in 1603, member of the privy council of Scotland in 1605, and archbishop of St. Andrews in 1615. As moderator of the general assembly (1618) of the church at Perth, Spottiswoode obtained its sanction of the king's plans for introducing episcopacy into Scotland, as embodied in the Articles of Perth. Charles I made him (1635) chancellor of Scotland, but Spottiswoode gradually lost his favor by trying to modify the monarch's plan of imposing the Anglican liturgy on the Scottish church. In 1638 he was deprived of his office, excommunicated, and deposed by the general assembly. He died in London. His *History of the Church of Scotland* (1655) has passed through several editions. Spottiswoode's name is also spelled Spottiswood and Spotswood.

Sprague, Frank Julian (sprāg), 1857–1934, American electrical engineer, b. Milford, Conn., grad. Annapolis, 1878. He was an assistant in 1883 to Thomas Edison and independently created a superior electric motor that was readily adaptable to industrial machinery. He also improved systems of electric energy and wheel suspension systems from which he developed the first electric street railway, installed at Richmond, Va., in 1887. He contributed greatly to the development of electric railways by inventing the multiple-unit system of automatic control, an automatic brake, and numerous other devices; he also developed the electric elevator.

Sprague, Oliver Mitchell Wentworth, 1873–1953, American economist, b. Somerville, Mass., Ph.D. Harvard, 1897. He taught (1904–5) at the Imperial Univ. of Tokyo and from 1908 to 1941 was assistant professor and later professor of banking and finance at Harvard. He served (1930–33) as economic adviser to the Bank of England and for a short time was one of the brain trust in the early New Deal. At other times he was consultant to the Reichsbank, the Bank of France, and the League of Nations. For a few months in 1933 he was executive assistant to the Secretary of the Treasury. His books include *Banking Reform in the United States* (1911) and *Recovery and Common Sense* (1934).

sprain, stretching or wrenching of the ligaments and tendons of a joint, often with rupture of the tissues but without dislocation. Sprains occur most commonly at the ankle, knee, or wrist joints, causing pain, swelling, and difficulty in moving the involved joint. Treatment consists of application of ice bags or cold compresses, elevation of the injured part, and strapping or bandaging to substitute for the support usually given by the ligaments. A severe ankle sprain may require a cast to immobilize the joint for healing. See FIRST AID.

Sprat, Thomas, 1635–1713, English author, bishop of Rochester and dean of Westminster. His poem on the death of Oliver Cromwell was published in Dryden's *Miscellany* (1659). Sprat is best-remembered for his *History of the Royal Society* (1667), of which he was one of the first members.

sprat: see HERRING.

spraying, horticultural practice of applying fungicides, insecticides, and herbicides, usually in solution, to plants. It may be accomplished by various means, e.g., the watering can, sprinkler attachment, spray gun, aerosol bomb, power spraying machine, or airplane. The spraying of powdered chemicals is called dusting. Spraying and dusting are chiefly preventive measures, but may also be used to check the spread of a pest among already infected plants. It is usually necessary for the spray to reach all exposed parts of the plant. The type of spray used and the timing of its application depend on the specific plant and its pest. Copper or sulfur compounds are common ingredients for a FUNGICIDE; nicotine, arsenic, or DDT for an INSECTICIDE. A criterion for any spray is that it does not injure the plant itself and that it is as specific as possible for the pest involved, i.e., that it inflict minimal damage to beneficial insects and to wildlife. The danger inherent in the use of poisonous sprays such as DDT cannot be overestimated, particularly in the case of those that are not eliminated or otherwise rendered ineffective (as by antitoxins) by the animals—including man—that feed on sprayed plants and insects, but accumulate in the tissues until a lethal concentration kills the animal or renders it unable to reproduce its kind. Spraying of selective herbicides is used in WEED control. See bulletins of the U.S. Dept. of Agriculture.

Spree (shprā), river, c.250 mi (400 km) long, rising in the Lausitz mts., SE East Germany, near the Czechoslovak border. It flows N past Cottbus, then NW through the Spree Forest, and from there it meanders east, north, and west before passing through Berlin to join the Havel River at Spandau. Navigable for c.110 mi (180 km), it is connected with the Oder River by the Oder-Spree Canal and with the Havel River by the Teltow Canal, which bypasses Berlin. The **Spree Forest** (Ger. *Spreewald*) in E East Germany, is a marshy region between Cottbus and Lübben, crisscrossed by small waterways that are the chief traffic lanes connecting the region's villages. Its population consists almost entirely of Slavic-speaking Wends, whose isolation has enabled them to keep their colorful traditions and local customs through the centuries. Eel fishing and truck farming are the chief economic activities there.

Sprengel, Christian Konrad (krĭs′tyän kôn′rät shprĕng′əl), 1750–1816, German botanist. Although director of a school at Spandau and tutor in Berlin, he devoted himself chiefly to the study of flowering plants. He pointed out (1793) the role of insects and of the wind in the cross-pollination of plants, but his observations were neglected until they were brought to public attention by Charles Darwin.

spring, in geology, natural flow of water from the ground or from rocks, representing an outlet for the water that has accumulated in permeable rock strata underground. Some of the water that falls as rain soaks into the soil and is drawn downward by gravity to a depth where all openings and pore spaces in the rock or soil have become completely saturated with water. This region is called the zone of saturation, and the water it holds, groundwater. The upper surface of the zone of saturation is called the water table. Above the water table lies the zone of aeration, where the pore spaces in the soil are quite dry and are filled with air. When the upper surface of the groundwater (water table) intersects a sloping land surface, a spring appears. The occurrence of springs is closely related to the geology of an area. If an impervious layer of rock, such as a clay deposit, underlies a layer of saturated soil or rock, then a line of springs will tend to appear on a slope where the clay layer outcrops. Igneous rocks are also impervious to water, yet they are often extensively fractured, and springs commonly appear where these fractures come to the surface. Fractures in limestone are often enlarged by the dissolving action of groundwater, forming small underground channels and caves. Where these channels outcrop, springs are likely to be found. Springs are common along major FAULTS because groundwater reaches the surface along the fault plane. Lines of springs help locate the position of faults such as the San Andreas of California. Springs can be a valuable water resource, and improvement in flow can often be accomplished simply by driving a pipe into the ground at the point where water seeps from the ground. Sometimes it is advisable to divert the spring water into a cistern or other storage reservoir from which the water can be pumped at will. When the water, because of the geological structure of the strata, issues under pressure, the spring is called artesian (see ARTESIAN WELL). Another type of spring is the GEYSER. Hot springs occur when the water issues from great depths or is heated by near-surface hot volcanic rock, as in Yellowstone National Park, Iceland, and New Zealand. Mineral springs are those with a high mineral content, usually silica or lime, dissolved from the rocks through which the water has passed (see MINERAL WATER). Many ancient city-states, such as Troy, had their sites determined by springs. Pioneer farmhouses often were located in the same way.

spring, in mechanics, any of several elastic devices used variously to store and to furnish energy, to absorb shock, to sustain the pressure between contacting surfaces, and to resist tensional or compressional stress. Springs are made of an elastic material, e.g., specially formulated steel alloys or certain types of rubber or plastic. A torsion spring that stores energy, e.g., for operating a watch, is a metal strip wound spirally around a fixed center from which it recedes constantly. For reducing concussion in some heavy trucks and railroad cars, helical, or coil, springs are used. Coil springs are commonly used for the same purpose in automobiles, as are leaf springs that consist of flat bars clamped together. These have been replaced in some vehicles by torsion bars that absorb stresses by twisting. The helical-coil compression spring provides the force to keep the operating surfaces together in the friction clutch (see TRANSMISSION). The extension spring is employed for the spring balance; the distance through which it is extended depends on the weight suspended from it. The disk spring, which consists of a laminated series of convex disks, is widely employed for heavy loads.

spring beauty: see PURSLANE.

springbok: see ANTELOPE.

Springdale, city (1970 pop. 16,783), Benton and Washington counties, NW Ark.; inc. 1878. The economy centers on poultry, eggs, and dairy products. There is also varied light manufacturing. The surrounding Ozark Mts. draw many tourists. An annual rodeo is held in the city.

Springer Mountain, 3,820 ft (1,164 m) high, N Ga. It is the southernmost peak of the Blue Ridge mts. and the southern terminus of the APPALACHIAN TRAIL.

springer spaniel: see ENGLISH SPRINGER SPANIEL; WELSH SPRINGER SPANIEL.

Springfield. 1 City (1970 pop. 91,753), state capital and seat of Sangamon co., central Ill., on the Sangamon River; settled 1818, inc. as a city 1840. In a rich agricultural and coal region, it is a governmental, commercial, medical, and insurance center, with varied manufactures. Abraham Lincoln, who was instrumental in having Springfield made the state capital in 1839, lived and practiced law there from 1837 to 1861. He is buried nearby, with his wife and three of their children, in a tomb and monument designed by L. G. Mead and dedicated in 1874. Lincoln's home is preserved as a shrine. Other places of interest include the capitol (1867-87), built in the style of Renaissance architecture; the old capitol (1837), where Lincoln made his "House Divided" speech and which now contains the state historical library; several Lincoln museums, including the Depot Museum, where Lincoln made his farewell address (1861); the governor's mansion (1853-57); the state art gallery; and the state fairgrounds. Vachel Lindsay was born there, and his house is now a museum. Springfield is the seat of Concordia Theological Seminary and two junior colleges. Nearby are New Salem (now a state park), Camp Butler National Cemetery, and Lake Springfield. See P. M. Angle, *"Here I Have Lived": A History of Lincoln's Springfield* (1935); F. S. Barringer, *Historic Houses of Springfield* (1966). **2** Industrial city (1970 pop. 163,905), seat of Hampden co., SW Mass., on the Connecticut River; inc. 1641. A port of entry, the city has insurance, chemical, plastic, metallurgical, paper, and printing industries. It was settled (1636) by Puritans under William Pynchon, and was one of the scenes in Shays's Rebellion (1786-87) and a station on the Underground Railroad. The U.S. Armory, which operated there from 1794 to 1966, was famous for the development of the Springfield and the Garand army rifles; it now contains an arms museum. The first American-made projection planetarium was designed and built (1937) by Frank Korkosz for the city's science museum, which also contains an aquarium. Saint-Gaudens's *Puritan* is in Merrick Park. Also in the city are Forest Park (which has a zoo) and several additional museums. The city is the seat of American International College, Springfield College (with a basketball hall of fame tracing the game's development since its invention there in 1891 by Dr. James Naismith), Western New England College, and a technical college. The city has a symphony orchestra. **3** City (1970 pop. 120,096), seat of Greene co., SW Mo., in a resort area of the Ozarks; inc. 1846. It is the industrial, trade, and shipping center of a rich area producing dairy products, livestock, poultry, grains, and fruits. The city has railroad shops, flour mills, food-processing plants, and factories making clothing, furniture, typewriters, adhesives, truck trailers, and rubber and paper products. Springfield is the seat of Drury College, Southwest Missouri State College, and Evangel College. It has an art museum and a symphony orchestra. Nearby are a national cemetery, the battlefield (1861) of WILSON'S CREEK, and the Mark Twain National Forest. **4** City (1970 pop. 81,941), seat of Clark co., W central Ohio, on the Mad River; settled 1799, inc. as a city 1850. A manufacturing center in a rich farm area, it is especially known for its production of farm machinery. The city grew with the building of the National Road (1838), the arrival of the railroads (mid-1800s), and the establishment of farm-machinery plants (late 1800s). Wittenberg Univ. is there. Nearby is George Rogers Clark Park. **5** City (1970 pop. 27,047), Lane co., W central Oregon, between the McKenzie and Willamette rivers; inc. 1885. In a rich dairy, livestock, and farm region, and near the forested foothills of the Cascade Range, it has important lumbering and forest-product industries. Foods and chemicals are also produced. The McKenzie River recreational area is nearby. **6** Industrial town (1970 pop. 10,063), Windsor co., SE Vt., on the Cascades of the Black River, in a fruit- and dairy-farming area; settled c.1772. James Hartness, an inventor, manufacturer, and political leader, helped found the machine-tool industry, which is still the town's largest. **7** Uninc. town (1970 pop. 11,613), Fairfax co., NE Va., a suburb of Washington, D.C.

springfish: see CAVE FISH.

Springhill, town (1971 pop. 5,262), N N.S., Canada. Located in a region of mixed farming and lumbering, it was formerly an active coal-mining center.

spring peeper: see TREE FROG.

Springs, city (1970 pop. 99,047), Transvaal, NE South Africa. It is the industrial center of a gold- and uranium-mining area. Manufactures include processed metals, chemicals, paper, glass, machine tools, bicycles, and printed materials. Springs began to develop after the start (1885) of coal mining nearby.

springtail, common name for any of the minute, primitive wingless INSECTS of the order Collembola. The springtail is named for a springlike mechanism on the underside of the abdomen. When at rest, the organ is folded forward and held in place under tension by a clasping structure; when the mechanism is released, the insect is able to jump a distance many times its own length. Of cosmopolitan distribution, springtails may be found in moist, dark places, on the surface of freshwater or tidal pools, and even on snow. They feed on decaying vegetation, algae, pollen, and other materials. Springtails are classified in the phylum ARTHROPODA, class Insecta, order Collembola.

Spring Valley. 1 Uninc. community (1970 pop. 29,742), within the confines of San Diego, San Diego co., SW Calif., on Sweetwater Lake. It is residential, with some light industry. The Bancroft Ranch House Museum (1856) is a national historic landmark. **2** Residential village (1970 pop. 18,112), Rockland co., SE N.Y., near the N.J. line; inc. 1902. It is a summer resort.

Spruance, Raymond Ames (spro͞o'əns), 1886-1969, American admiral, b. Baltimore, Md. Commissioned in the navy in 1908, he reached the rank of rear admiral in 1939. In World War II he distinguished himself at the battle of Midway (1942) and became chief of staff to Admiral Chester W. Nimitz. As head of the fleet in the central Pacific (later the 5th Fleet), he commanded (1943-44) the forces that invaded the Gilbert and Marshall Islands and was made a full admiral. He was (1945-46) commander in chief of the Pacific Fleet and retired from the navy in 1948. He served as ambassador to the Philippines (1952-55). See biography by T. B. Buell (1974).

spruce, any plant of the genus *Picea*, evergreen trees or shrubs of the family Pinaceae (PINE family) widely distributed in the Northern Hemisphere. The needles are angular in cross section, rather than flattened as in the related hemlocks and firs. The Norway spruce (*P. abies*), an important timber tree of Europe, is one of the most commonly cultivated evergreens. The Siberian spruce (*P. obovata*) grows in coniferous forests (taiga) of Russia and Siberia, the Oriental spruce (*P. orientalis*) is a major species of S Europe, and the yeddo spruce (*P. jezoensis*) of Manchuria and Japan is sometimes dwarfed and potted (see DWARF TREE). North American spruces used for timber are the red spruce (*P. rubens*), white spruce (*P. glauca*), and black spruce (*P. mariana*) of the East; the Engelmann spruce (*P. engelmanii*) of the Rocky Mountain forests; and the Sitka spruce (*P. sitchensis*) of the Pacific forest belt. Numerous spruces are cultivated as ornamentals; the most popular North American garden spruce is the frosty- or silvery-blue-needled Colorado blue spruce (*P. pungens*). Commercially, spruces are of particular value as the major source of pulpwood for the manufacture of paper. Wood of the various species is usually light, soft, and straight-grained and has been used for interior and exterior construction work, boats, airplanes, and woodenware. The bark is sometimes used for tanning, and some species yield a gum resin. Spruce beer has been made from the young shoots of the red spruce and the black spruce. The Indians in the West have used spruce gum for calking, the inner bark for food, and strips of spruce for weaving watertight mats and baskets. The Douglas spruce, or Douglas fir, is of the same family but is not a spruce. Spruce is classified in the division PINOPHYTA, class Pinopsida, order Coniferales, family Pinaceae.

sprue, chronic disorder of the small intestine caused by impaired absorption of fat and other nutrients. Two forms of the disease exist. Tropical sprue is mainly an adult disease; nontropical sprue, also called celiac disease, is primarily a disease of young children and usually begins between the ages of 6 and 18 months. Tropical sprue is apparently a deficiency state that responds to folic acid therapy, whereas celiac disease is a condition resulting from a special sensitivity to the proteins of wheat or rye (gluten); it disappears if gluten is eliminated from the diet. The symptoms of both types of sprue are generally the same: diarrhea with bulky, frothy, foul-smelling stools containing large amounts of fatty acids and soaps, and later weight loss, anemia, and other symptoms related to malabsorption of vitamins. X-ray examination of the small intestine revealing dilation, segmentation, and other typical changes is used in diagnosis.

Spühler, Willy (vĭl'ē shpü'lər), 1902–, Swiss political leader and economist. He held several government economic posts and served (1938-59) in the federal assembly. In 1959 he became a member of the federal council, the Swiss executive branch, and served as minister of transport, communications, and power (1959-65) and as minister of foreign affairs (1966-70). He served two one-year terms (1963, 1968) as president of Switzerland.

spurge (spûrj), common name for members of the Euphorbiaceae, a family of herbs, shrubs, and trees of greatly varied structure and almost cosmopolitan distribution, although most species are tropical. In the United States the family is most common in the Southeast. The spurges are of great economic importance as a source of food, drugs, rubber, and other products. The sap of most species is a milky latex, and the source of a very large part of the world's natural RUBBER is the latex of the PARÁ RUBBER TREE. Ceara rubber (from *Manihot glazioviana*) and several other latexes also come from plants of the spurge family. The tropical American *Manihot* genus includes the CASSAVA, the source of tapioca and the most important tropical root crop next to the sweet potato. Other valuable commercial products of this family are CASTOR OIL and TUNG OIL, expressed from the seeds of *Ricinus communis* and *Aleurites fordii* respectively. The castor oil plant, native to tropical Africa, where it grows as a tree, is now widespread and is sometimes cultivated in temperate regions as an annual ornamental. The tung tree, indigenous to E Asia and Malaysia, is the only important plant of the spurge family cultivated commercially in the United States. The candlenut tree (*A. moluccana*) and the Japanese wood oil tree (*A. cordata*), of the same genus as the tung tree, also yield oils, as does the Chinese tallow tree (*Sapium*

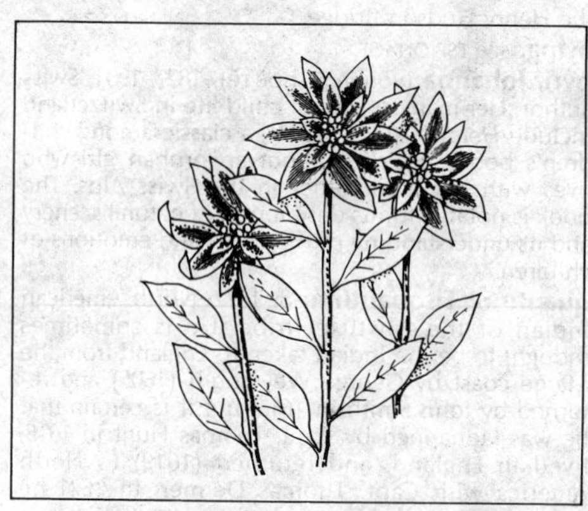

Snow-on-the-mountain, Euphorbia marginata

sebiferum), a source of grease for candles and soap. Many plants of the spurge family have reduced fleshy leaves, in particular the vast *Euphorbia* genus of approximately 1,600 subtropical and warm-temperate species. These cactuslike plants, comprising most of the species commonly called spurge, have spiny, jointed stems and are among the most common Old World desert succulents. The euphorbias and the cacti illustrate the biological phenomenon of convergent evolution, in which unrelated groups of organisms, subject to the same environmental factors, gradually develop similar structures. The euphorbias, which also bear latex, exhibit another family trait: "naked flowers" (i.e., flowers lacking petals and sometimes sepals) that are enclosed in a bract envelope, from which they emerge during the flowering period to permit pollination. Many species are cultivated for their brilliant, showy bracts as well as for their frequently colorful foliage. These include snow-on-the-mountain (*E. marginata*), native to the United States; the cypress spurge (*E. cyparissias*), a favored cemetery plant that was introduced from Europe and naturalized; the scarlet-bracted greenhouse plant crown-of-thorns (*E. splendens*), native to Madagascar; and the poinsettia (for J. R. Poinsett), an ornamental shrub native to Central America. The poinsettia, whose several species are sometimes considered a separate genus (*Poinsettia*), is a popular Christmas decoration with its large rosettes of usually bright-red bracts. Various spurges provide medicines, dyes, oils, and other products; primitive peoples utilized the poisonous saps of other spurges on arrow tips and to poison fish. The presence of poisonous substances in many euphorbias and in a number of other spurges has led these to be classed as noxious pests, especially when they grow as weeds on livestock ranges. Species of *Sapium* and *Sebastiana* are the source of the curious Mexican jumping beans; the seeds of these shrubs often contain moth larvae whose activity causes the "bean" to tumble. Spurge is classified in the division MAGNOLIOPHYTA, class Magnoliopsida, order Euphorbiales, family Euphorbiaceae.

Spurgeon, Charles Haddon, 1834–92, English Baptist preacher. He joined the Baptist communion in 1850. In 1852, at age 18, he took charge of a small congregation at Waterbeach, Cambridgeshire, and, at 20, went to London as pastor of the New Park St. Chapel. His immediate popularity made necessary larger buildings for his audiences, until the huge Metropolitan Tabernacle, erected for his use, was opened in 1861. Around this developed a pastors' college, an orphanage, and missions. Spurgeon's sermons, published weekly from 1854, were collected in 50 volumes. A strict Calvinist, he opposed the doctrine of baptismal regeneration, which caused his withdrawal in 1864 from the Evangelical Alliance. He separated (1887) from the Baptist Union because he believed that modern biblical criticism was threatening orthodoxy. Among his numerous publications are *John Ploughman's Talks* (1869) and *The Treasury of David* (7 vol., 1870–85). His autobiography (4 vol., 1897–1900), compiled by his wife from his diary and letters, was edited and condensed (1946) by D. O. Fuller. See biography by E. W. Bacon (1968).

spurry: see PINK.

Spurs, Battle of the: see BATTLE OF THE SPURS.

Sputnik: see SATELLITE, ARTIFICIAL; SPACE EXPLORATION.

Spuyten Duyvil Creek (spī'tən dī'vəl), tidal channel, now a ship canal, c.1 mi (1.6 km) long, SE N.Y., in New York City. It separates the northern tip of Manhattan island from the mainland and connects the Hudson and the Harlem rivers. It is crossed by the Henry Hudson Bridge.

spying: see ESPIONAGE.

Spyri, Johanna (yōhän'ä shpē'rē), 1827–1901, Swiss author. Her many stories of child life in Switzerland include *Heidi* (1880; tr. 1884), a classic among children's books. *Heidi* is about an orphan girl who lives with her grandfather in the Swiss Alps. The book is notable for its description of natural scenery and its understanding of the views and emotions of children.

Squanto or **Tisquantum,** d. 1622, North American Indian of the Pawtuxet tribe. He is sometimes thought to be the Indian taken to England from the Maine coast by George Weymouth (1605) and returned by John Smith in 1615, but it is certain that he was kidnapped by Capt. Thomas Hunt in 1615, lived in England, and returned (1619) to North America with Capt. Thomas Dermer. In 1621 he acted as interpreter in concluding a treaty between the Pilgrim settlers and Massasoit. Squanto became friendly with the Plymouth colonists, aiding them particularly in their planting and fishing. While acting as guide and interpreter on William Bradford's expedition around Cape Cod, he contracted smallpox and died.

Squarcione, Francesco (fränchā'skō skwärchō'nā), 1397–1468, Italian painter; teacher of Mantegna. According to tradition he was a tailor and embroiderer who turned to painting c.1429 and established a school of painting in Padua. Only two signed works of his exist, *Madonna with Child* (Berlin) and an altarpiece in five sections (Padua).

square, closed plane figure bounded by four straight line segments of equal length and meeting at right angles. The points of intersection of the lines, or sides, are called vertices. The diagonals of a square are the two lines joining opposite vertices; they are of equal length and are the perpendicular bisectors of one another. The perimeter of a square is the sum of the lengths of its sides, or $P=4s$, where s is the length of a side. The area enclosed by a square is $A=s^2$. The square is one of the commonest geometric figures and has long had various symbolic meanings in religion and art.

square, magic: see MAGIC SQUARE.

square root: see ROOT, in mathematics.

squaring the circle: see GEOMETRIC PROBLEMS OF ANTIQUITY.

squash: see GOURD; PUMPKIN.

squash bug, name for a true BUG, *Anasa tristis*, found throughout the United States and S Canada. It damages squash, pumpkin, and related plants by sucking the juices from leaves and stems. The adult is dark brown and measures about ⅔ in. (8 mm) long. The eggs are laid in the late spring and hatch in two weeks. The green larvae, or nymphs, soon turn brown or gray. Birds feed on both nymphs and adults, but the most effective natural enemy is the larva of a TACHINID FLY, which develops within the body of an adult or larval squash bug, feeding on and eventually killing the host. The squash bug is classified in the phylum ARTHROPODA, class Insecta, order Hemiptera, family Coreidae.

squash racquets, game played on a four-walled court, 16 ft (4.88 m) high by 18½ ft (5.64 m) wide by 32 ft (9.75 m) long. The back wall, shorter than the front wall, usually measures 9 ft (2.74 m). A horizontal service line 6½ ft (1.98 m) high is painted on the front wall, while a floor service line is marked off 10 ft (3.05 m) from, and parallel to, the back wall. The court is divided into two service zones by a line running midway between, and parallel to, the side walls. The inflated, black, hard rubber ball (1 ¾ in./ 3.18 cm in diameter) has a relatively "dead" bounce, and hard running and agility are required of the squash racquets player. From a back corner of the court he serves the ball with a racket that is no more than 27 in. (68.58 cm) long, round headed, and gut-strung. The ball must hit the front wall above the service line (with caroms off the side walls permitted) without bounding on the floor and must hit on the opposite service floor. Returning the ball before it hits the floor is permitted (even on the service return), and a point is scored when either player fails to return the ball before it touches the floor twice. As in tennis, two serves are allowed a player. The game may be played by partners. In match play, usually 15 points win a game and two out of three games win a match. Squash racquets probably originated in the late 19th cent. from the older game of RACQUETS and in the 20th cent. met with increasing popularity—especially in American colleges and universities. The U.S. Squash Racquets Association and the U.S. Women's Squash Racquets Association conduct annual national championships. See Peter Wood, *The Book of Squash* (1972).

squash tennis, game played on a four-walled court, similar in dimensions to the court on which SQUASH RACQUETS is played. The two games, however, differ in equipment, rules, and play. The squash tennis ball, the size of a lawn tennis ball, is larger and livelier than the squash racquets ball, and the squash tennis racket is the shape of a tennis racket but is smaller. The rules differ especially concerning the service; e.g., in squash tennis a ball may not carom off the side walls before hitting the front wall on the service, the service must bounce in front of the floor service line, volleying (i.e., returning the ball before it hits the floor) is forbidden in returning the service, and only the server may score a point. Squash tennis developed during the 1880s when some Americans began to play squash racquets with a modified tennis ball in order to speed up play. See Allison Danzig, *The Racquet Game* (1930).

squatter sovereignty: see POPULAR SOVEREIGNTY.

Squaw Valley, valley, NE Calif., in the Sierra Nevada Mts., NW of Lake Tahoe. A well-known ski resort, it was the site of the 1960 Winter Olympics. Ski lifts and trails are on Squaw Peak (8,960 ft/2,731 m high).

squawweed: see GROUNDSEL.

squeteague: see CROAKER.

squid, carnivorous marine CEPHALOPOD mollusk. The squid is one of the most highly developed invertebrates, well adapted to its active, predatory life. The characteristic molluscan shell is reduced to a horny plate shaped like a quill pen and buried under the mantle. The mantle, the chief swimming organ of the animal, is modified into lengthwise fins along the posterior end of the body and projects forward like a collar around the head. As the mantle relaxes and contracts, the squid swims forward, upward, and downward. Water is expelled in jets from the muscular funnel located just below the head, propelling the squid backward in abrupt jetlike motions. Two of the ten sucker-bearing arms (used to steer in swimming) are tentacles that can seize prey, which is then cut into pieces by the animal's strong beaklike jaws. The squid breathes through gills, and may emit a cloud of inky material from its ink sac when in danger. The circulatory and nervous systems are highly developed. The eye of the squid is remarkably similar to that of man—an example of convergent evolution, as there is no common ancestor. Squids are also distinguished by internal cartilaginous supports. Some deep-sea forms have luminescent organs. The common squid is found from Maine to the Carolinas, often moving in shoals. In the United States tons of squid are used for fish bait, particularly by the cod fisheries in New England. Squid is a favorite food in the Orient and in the Mediterranean area. Species range in size from about 2 in. (5 cm) to the proportions of the giant squid, *Architeuthis*, the largest of all invertebrates, which may grow to 50 ft (15.2 m). Squids are classified in the phylum MOLLUSCA, class Cephalopoda, order Teuthoidea.

Squier, Ephraim George, 1821–88, American archaeologist and journalist, b. Bethlehem, Albany co., N.Y. He is noted for his study of the prehistoric MOUND BUILDERS of the Mississippi and Ohio valleys. His works include *Ancient Monuments of the Mississippi Valley* (1848) and *Aboriginal Monuments of the State of New York* (1851).

squill, common name for two genera of Old World bulbous plants of the family Liliaceae (LILY family). The horticulturists' squill is any plant of the genus *Scilla*, mostly spring-blooming low herbs with commonly deep blue but also white, rose, or purplish flowers borne along a leafless stem; the leaves are usually narrow. Species of *Scilla* are naturalized and used in rock gardens and borders; of these, the Siberian squill (*S. sibirica*) has long been a rock-garden favorite. The wood, or wild, hyacinth, called also bluebell or harebell (*S. nonscripta*), is the common squill. The pharmacists' squill, or sea onion (*Urginea maritima*), produces whitish or rose flowers in the autumn before it produces leaves. Its bulbs, collected chiefly from the Mediterranean region, are sold as white or red squill—the white is an official drug used as a diuretic, stimulant, and expectorant; the red is used mostly as a rat poison. Squill is classified in the division MAGNOLIOPHYTA, class Liliatae, order Liliales, family Liliaceae.

squinch, in architecture, a piece of construction used for filling in the upper angles of a square room so as to form a proper base to receive an octagonal or spherical dome. It was the primitive solution of this problem, the perfected one being eventually provided by the pendentive. Squinches may be formed by masonry built out from the angle in corbeled courses, by filling the corner with a vise placed diagonally, or by building an arch or a number of corbeled arches diagonally across the corner. In Islamic architecture, especially in Persia, where it may have been invented, the squinch took the form of a succession of corbeled stalactites. Some early examples of the squinch can be seen in Roman domical buildings of the 3d cent. It was also commonly used in the early churches of Europe and the East.

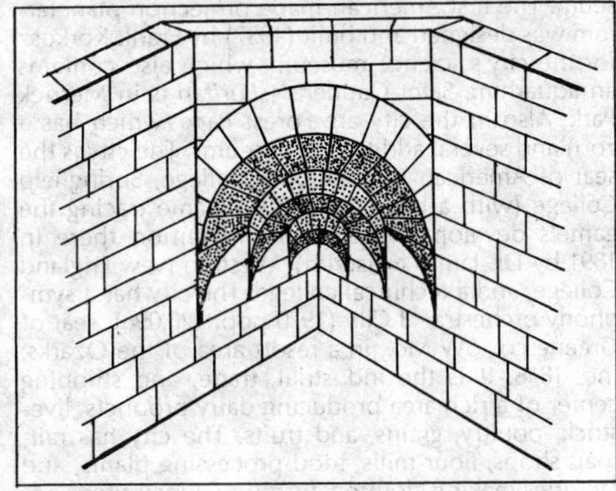

Squinch

squint: see STRABISMUS.

squirrel, name for small or medium-sized RODENTS of the family Sciuridae, found throughout the world except in Australia, Madagascar, and the polar regions; it is applied especially to the tree-living species. Tree squirrels range from the size of a mouse to the size of a house cat and vary greatly in color; some Asian tree squirrels are brilliantly patterned. The so-called typical tree squirrels are members of the genus *Sciurus*, with about 40 species distributed throughout forested regions of Eurasia and the Americas. These are day-active animals with slender bodies, sleek, thick fur, and bushy tails. Their coats are black, gray, brown, or reddish above and light-colored below. Light, swift, and agile, tree squirrels leap from branch to branch and scurry up and down trees using their sharp claws to dig into the trunk; they always descend head first. The tail is used as a rudder when the animal leaps and as a parachute when it drops. They have excellent sight, including good color vision. The handlike forepaws are used for holding food. Tree squirrels make nests in holes in trees or on branches. They spend much time on the ground, foraging for fruit, nuts, and insects; they also sometimes eat eggs, young birds, and smaller mammals. Members of many species store food for the winter in holes or buried in the ground; they locate these stores by means of smell. They do not hibernate. *Sciurus* species include the Eurasian red squirrel, *S. vulgaris*, and the North American gray squirrels, fox squirrel, and tufted-eared squirrels. Gray squirrels have tails about as long as the combined head and body length. The eastern gray squirrel, *S. carolinensis*, common in the eastern half of the United States and extreme southern Canada, is up to 20 in. (51 cm) in total length, 5 in. (13 cm) high at the shoulder, and weighs 1 to 1½ lb (450–700 grams). It has been introduced in Europe. The western gray squirrel, *S. griseus*, of the U.S. West Coast, is slightly larger. The fox squirrel, *S. niger*, is the largest North American squirrel, reaching 29 in. (74 cm) in total length; its head is somewhat square. It displays great variation in its fur color but is commonly light brown. It is found in the eastern half of the United States, excluding the extreme northeast. Although its numbers have been greatly diminished by hunting and clearing, it is still common in some areas. It has also been introduced in city parks in western states. The tufted-eared squirrels, also called tassel-eared, or Abert, squirrels, are very distinctive, with tall plumes of hair on their ears. They inhabit yellow pine forests of the Colorado Plateau. One variety, the Kaibab squirrel, is found only on the northern rim of the Grand Canyon. North American red squirrels, also known as pine squirrels and chickarees, are species of the genus *Tamiasciurus*. They are small and noisy, about 12 in. (30 cm) long and 3½ in. (9 cm) high, weighing 5 to 10 oz (140–280 grams). They are found in the pine forests of Alaska, Canada, and the N and W United States. Other genera of arboreal squirrels are found mostly in Africa, S and SE Asia, and Central and South America. In addition to the tree squirrels, the family includes the GROUND SQUIRREL, CHIPMUNK, MARMOT, WOODCHUCK, PRAIRIE DOG, and FLYING SQUIRREL. Squirrels are classified in the phylum CHORDATA, subphylum Vertebrata, class Mammalia, order Rodentia, family Sciuridae. See Dorcas MacClintock, *Squirrels of North America* (1970).

squirrel corn: see FUMITORY.

squirting cucumber: see GOURD.

Sr, chemical symbol of the element STRONTIUM.

Sremski Karlovci: see KARLOWITZ, TREATY OF.

Sri Aurobindo: see GHOSE, AUROBINDO.

Sri Lanka (srē läng'kə) [Sinhala, = resplendent land], formerly **Ceylon,** ancient *Taprobane*, island (1970 pop. 12,514,000), 25,332 sq mi (65,610 sq km), in the Indian Ocean, just SE of India. It is an independent republic within the Commonwealth of Nations. The capital is COLOMBO. The pearshaped island is 140 mi (225 km) across at its widest point and 270 mi (435 km) long. The narrow northern end is almost linked to SE India by Adam's Bridge, a chain of shoals that, although partly submerged, present an obstacle to

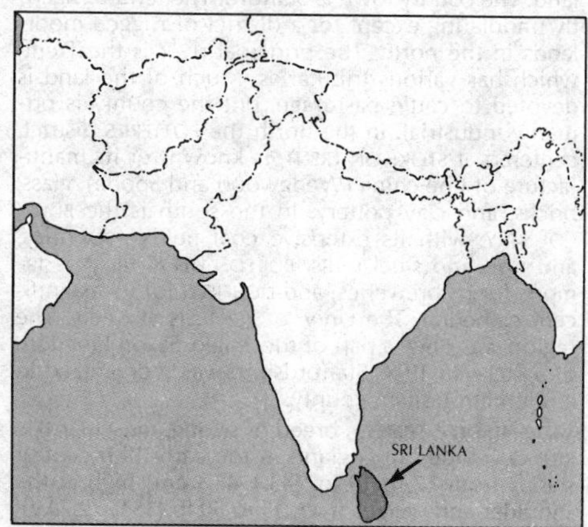

navigation. About four fifths of the island is flat or gently rolling; mountains in the south central area include Adam's Peak (7,360 ft/2,243 m) and rise to Pidurutalagal (8,291 ft/2,527 m), the highest point on the island. Sri Lanka has a generally uniform subtropical climate; the average lowland temperature is 80°F (27°C), but humidity is high. Rainfall, largely carried by monsoons, is adequate for agriculture, except in the north. The country's economy is agricultural, emphasis being on export crops; tea, rubber, and coconut (all plantation grown) comprise 90% of the island's exports. Cocoa, coffee, cinnamon, cardamom, pepper, cloves, nutmegs, citronella, and tobacco are also exported. Rice, fruit, and vegetables are grown for local consumption. Sri Lanka leads the world (1970) in the production of amorphous graphite, its principal mineral industry. Also mined are precious and semiprecious gems, mineral sands, clays, and limestones. Substantial deposits of iron ore have not yet been exploited. The island's swift rivers have considerable hydroelectric potential, which is being developed. Industry is centered chiefly around the processing of agricultural products, especially the money crops—tea, rubber, and coconut. A great variety of consumer goods are also manufactured. Although coastal lagoons provide many sheltered harbors, only S Sri Lanka lies on the main world shipping routes; the port of Colombo, on which most of the country's railroads and, to some extent, its road system converge, handles most of the foreign trade. Other important cities are Dehiwala-Mount Lavinia, KANDY, GALLE, and Jaffna. The population of Sri Lanka is composed mainly (about 69%) of Sinhalese, who are Hinayana Buddhists; Hindu Tamils make up a large minority (about 23%), and there are smaller groups of Muslim Moors, Burghers (descendants of Dutch and Portuguese colonists), and Eurasians. The official language is Sinhala; Tamil is a secondary language, and English is widely spoken. Education is free, through the university level; the literacy rate is about 80%. The most ancient of the inhabitants were probably the ancestors of the Veddas, an aboriginal people (numbering about 3,000) now living in remote mountain areas. They were conquered in the 6th cent. B.C. by the Sinhalese, who were originally from N India; the *Ramaya*, the ancient Hindu epic, probably reflects this conquest. The Sri Lanka chronicle *Mahavamsa* relates the arrival of Vijaya, the first Sinhalese king, in 483 B.C. The Sinhalese settled in the north and developed an elaborate irrigation system. They founded their capital at ANURADHAPURA, which, after the introduction of Buddhism from India in the 3d cent. B.C., became one of the chief world centers of that religion; a cutting of the pipal tree under which Buddha attained enlightenment at Bodh Gaya was planted there. The Temple of the Tooth at Kandy as well as the Dalada Maligawa are sacred Buddhist temples. Buddhism stimulated the fine arts in Sri Lanka, its classical period being from the 4th to the 6th cent. The proximity of Sri Lanka to S India resulted in many Tamil invasions. The CHOLA of S India conquered Anuradhapura in the early 11th cent. and made POLLONARRUA their capital. The Sinhalese soon regained power, but in the 12th cent. a Tamil kingdom arose in the north, and the Sinhalese were driven to the southwest. Arab traders, drawn by the island's spices, arrived in the 12th and 13th cent.; their descendants are the Muslim Moors. The Portuguese conquered the coastal areas in the early 16th cent. and introduced the Roman Catholic religion. By the mid-17th cent. the Dutch had taken over the Portuguese possessions and the rich spice trade. In 1795 the Dutch possessions were occupied by the British, who made the island a crown colony in 1798. In 1815 the island was brought under one rule for the first time when the central area, previously under the rule of Kandy, was conquered. Under the British, tea, coffee, and rubber plantations were developed, and schools, including a university, were opened. A movement for independence arose during World War I. The constitution of 1931 granted universal adult suffrage to the inhabitants; but demands for independence continued, and in 1946 a more liberal constitution was enacted. Full independence was finally granted to the island on Feb. 4, 1948, with dominion status in the British Commonwealth. In 1950 delegates of eight countries of the British Commonwealth met in Colombo and adopted the Colombo Plan for economic aid to S and SE Asia. Riots in 1958 between Sinhalese and the Tamil minority over demands by the Tamils for official recognition of their language and the establishment of a separate Tamil state under a federal system resulted in severe loss of life. In Sept., 1959, Prime Minister S. W. R. D. Bandaranaike was assassinated, and in 1960 his widow, Sirimavo BANDARANAIKE, became prime minister. The Federal party of the Tamils was outlawed in 1961, following new disorders. Certain Western business facilities were nationalized (1962), and the country became involved in disputes with the United States and Great Britain over compensation. The radical policies of Mrs. Bandaranaike aroused opposition, and the elections in 1965 gave a parliamentary plurality to the more moderate socialist party of Dudley Senanayake, who became prime minister with a multiparty coalition. Under Senanayake, closer relations with the West were established and compromise arrangements were made for recompensing nationalized companies. However, economic problems and severe inflation continued, aggravated by a burgeoning population (between 1946 and 1970 the population almost doubled). In 1970, Mrs. Bandaranaike and her three-party anticapitalist coalition won a landslide victory, following considerable preelection violence. She launched social welfare programs, including rice subsidies and free hospitalization, but failed to satisfy the extreme left, which, under the Marxist People's Liberation Front, attempted to overthrow the government in an armed rebellion (April–May, 1971). With Soviet, British, and Indian aid, the rebellion was quelled after heavy fighting. In 1972 the country adopted a new constitution, declared itself a republic while retaining membership in the Commonwealth of Nations, and changed its name to Sri Lanka. In the early 1970s the government was confronted with a severe economic crisis as the country's food supplies and foreign exchange reserves dwindled in the face of rising inflation, high unemployment, a huge trade deficit, and the traditional policy of extensive social-welfare programs. See M. R. Singer, *The Emerging Elite: A Study of Political Leadership in Ceylon* (1964); L. A. Mills, *Ceylon Under British Rule, 1795–1932* (1965); E. F. Ludowyk, *The Story of Ceylon* (2d ed. 1967); N. E. Weerasooria, *Ceylon and Her People* (4 vol., 1970–71); Roloff Beny, *Island Ceylon* (1971); H. N. Karunatilake, *Economic Development in Ceylon* (1971); R. F. Nyrop et al., *Area Handbook for Ceylon* (1971); M. D. Raghavan, *Tamil Culture in Ceylon* (1971); L. M. Jacob, *Sri Lanka: From Dominion to Republic* (1973); Geoffrey Powell, *The Kandyan Wars: The British Army in Ceylon*, 1803–1818 (1973).

Srinagar (srēnŭ'gər) or **Serinagar** (sərēnŭ'-), city (1971 pop. 403,612), historic capital of Kashmir, on the Jhelum River. Situated in the Vale of Kashmir, Srinagar is one of the most famed and beautiful summer resorts of the East. Seven wooden bridges cross the Jhelum and connect the sections of the city lying on either side of the river. There are many canals, and transportation is chiefly by boat. Houseboats on the canals serve as vacation hotels. In place of the hand-woven shawls (cashmeres) for which the city was famed, machine-made silks, woolens, and carpets are now manufactured. Other products include plywood and cement. The city was founded in the 6th cent., and the 7th-century Sankaracharya temple may be the oldest of the city's many historic remains. There is a 16th-century fort built by Akbar. Extensive Buddhist ruins are near the city. In 1948, Srinagar became the capital of the Indian sector of the disputed state of Jammu and Kashmir. Jammu and Kashmir Univ. is in the city.

Srirangam (srērŭng'gəm), town (1971 pop. 51,066), Tamil Nadu state, SE India, on an island in the Cauvery River. It is noted for a group of temples to Vishnu (built c.1600), which attract many Hindu pilgrims. Srirangam is also a market for grain, sugarcane, and pepper.

Srirangapatna (srērəng-gəpŭt'nə), town (1971 pop. 14,153), Karnataka state, S India, on an island in the Cauvery River. There are Hindu monuments, some built in the 13th cent. Most of the large buildings date from the 17th and 18th cent. when the city was the capital of Mysore. The greatest builder was Tippoo Sahib, who left a large mosque, a summer palace, and a mausoleum, where he and his father, Hyder Ali, are buried. The importance of Srirangapatna declined after its capture (1799) by the British in a battle in which Tippoo was killed.

SST: see AIRPLANE.

Ssu-ma Ch'ien (sŏŏ'mä chyĕn), 145?–90? B.C., Chinese historian; sometimes called the Father of Chinese History. He succeeded his father, Ssu-ma T'an, as grand historian (an office then dealing with astronomy and the calendar) at the court of the Early HAN emperor Wu. There he took up a project on history planned by his father and extended it into a history of China and of all regions and peoples known at that time. Incurring the emperor's displeasure, he suffered the punishment of castration. Rejecting the alternative of suicide, he chose to complete this work, the *Shih chi* [records of the historian]. In 130 chapters, including basic annals of dynasties or rulers, chronological tables, treatises, hereditary houses, and accounts of famous men and foreign lands and peoples, it has served as a model for subsequent Chinese dynastic histories. Its wide range, many-faceted characterizations, and vivid dialogue have won it the admiration of Oriental readers for 2,000 years. See *Records of the Grand Historian of China*, tr. by Burton Watson (2 vol., 1961, repr. 1969); study by Burton Watson (1958).

Ssu-ma Kuang (sōō-mä kwäng), 1018–86, Chinese statesman and historian of the Sung dynasty. He was a member (with Ou-yang Hsiu and SU TUNG-P'O) of the conservative bureacratic party that successfully opposed the reforms of WANG AN-SHIH. He edited *The Comprehensive Mirror for Aid in Government,* a gigantic history of the period from 403 B.C. to A.D. 959. The 12th cent. philosopher CHU HSI abridged and reworked the materials in Ssu-ma Kuang's work to produce the *Outline and Details of the Comprehensive Mirror.* These two works were the chief introductions to history for students in traditional China.

Stabat Mater Dolorosa (stä'bät mä'tĕr dō''lōrō'sä) [Latin,=the sorrowful mother was standing], 13th-century hymn of the Roman Church attributed to Jacopone da Todi. A prayer meditating on the sorrows of the Virgin Mary in her station at the Cross, it was the liturgical sequence for the Seven Sorrows of the Virgin (Sept. 15 and the Friday before Palm Sunday). It is no longer used on the Friday before Palm Sunday and is optional on Sept. 15, but it continues to be sung at nonliturgical Lenten services. It was not admitted as a liturgical sequence until 1727, and musical settings are more numerous after that date. Among composers who have used the text are Josquin Desprez, Palestrina, Pergolesi, Haydn, Schubert, and Rossini.

Stabiae: see CASTELLAMMARE DI STABIA, Italy.

stabile (stā'bēl), an abstract construction that is completely stationary. The form was pioneered by Alexander CALDER, and examples were termed *stabiles* to distinguish them from MOBILES, their moving counterparts, also invented by Calder.

stability: see EQUILIBRIUM.

stabilizer: see AIRPLANE.

Stabroek: see GEORGETOWN, Guyana.

Stachys (stā'kĭs), Christian at Rome. Rom. 16.9.

Stadion, Johann Philipp, Graf von (yō'hän fē'lĭp gräf fən shtä'dēōn), 1763–1824, Austrian politician. A diplomat, he was made (1805) foreign minister and campaigned for a German uprising under Austrian leadership against Napoleon. His program was acclaimed by German patriots, but after the Austrian defeats of 1809 he was replaced by Metternich. Stadion continued to act as an adviser and from 1816 served as finance minister.

stadium (stā'dēəm), racecourse in Greek cities where footraces and other athletic contests took place. The name is the Latin form of the Greek word for a standard of length and originally referred merely to the measured length of the course. Usually the stadiums were U-shaped, the curve being opposite the starting point. Natural slopes were used when possible to support the seats. The stadiums at Athens, Olympia, Delphi, and Epidaurus are among the best-known examples. The courses were generally 606 ft 9 in. long (600 Greek ft, or 185 m), although the length varied according to the local variations of the measuring unit. A similar plan was used for the hippodrome, the course where horses raced. The stadium at Athens, which was completely restored to serve for the first modern Olympic games in 1896, dates from 330 B.C. The great modern revival of interest in athletic contests has produced structures designed for various sports that seat many thousands of spectators. Although many are called stadiums, they are only slightly derivative from those of the Greeks and in most features resemble rather the Roman circuses and amphitheaters. In the United States stadiums have greatly increased in number and perfection since 1914. Their forms vary, being rectangular with curved corners, elliptical, or U-shaped. The modern stadium generally is designed for such sports as football, baseball, and track racing. The stadiums erected in European cities for Olympic games have usually been retained as permanent structures. For the 1960 Olympics in Rome, Pier Luigi NERVI designed two remarkable reinforced-concrete arenas spanned by delicately ribbed roofs. Among American stadiums with large seating capacities are Philadelphia Municipal Stadium (built for the Sesquicentennial Exposition), 105,000; Soldier Field, in Grant Park, Chicago, 85,000; Yale Bowl, New Haven, 75,000; the old Yankee Stadium, New York City, 70,000; and the Rose Bowl at Pasadena, Calif., more than 100,000. Some capacity estimates vary, as the source may include temporary seating and standing room. A recent innovation in stadium design is exemplified by the Harris County Domed Stadium, or "Astrodome," in Houston, Texas. Seating 60,000, the steel-supported structure incorporating 4,596 transparent plastic skylights was the first covered, temperature-controlled arena, and is the basis for many such designs subsequently developed throughout the United States.

Staël, Germaine de (zhĕrmĕn' də stäl), 1766–1817, French-Swiss woman of letters, whose full name was Anne Louise Germaine Necker, baronne de Staël-Holstein. Born in Paris, the daughter of Jacques and Suzanne Necker, she early absorbed the intellectual and political atmosphere of her mother's salon. In 1786 she married Baron Staël-Holstein, a Swedish diplomat. Though moderately sympathizing with the French Revolution, she left France in 1792. Returning to Paris under the Directory, she made her salon a powerful political and intellectual center. She separated, amicably, from her husband and became intimately associated with Benjamin Constant. Her love life remained, to the end, both complicated and unconventional. In 1803 her spirited opposition to Bonaparte caused her exile from Paris. Mme de Staël retired to her estate at Coppet, on the Lake of Geneva, where she attracted a brilliant circle. Already the author of a successful novel, *Delphine* (1802), and of a study of the influence of social conditions on literature (*De la littérature considérée dans ses rapports avec les institutions sociales,* 1800), she was inspired by a trip to Italy to write the novel *Corinne* (1807). Her principal work, *De l'Allemagne* (1810), was the result of a tour through Germany. Napoleon, who resented the book as an invidious comparison between German and French culture and mores, ordered the destruction of the entire first edition (1811) on the ground that it was "un-French." Threatened by Napoleon's police, Mme de Staël fled to Russia and England; in 1815 she returned to Coppet. Republished, *De l'Allemagne* tremendously influenced European thought and letters, which became imbued with Mme de Staël's enthusiasm for German romanticism. Among her other works are *Considérations sur les principaux événements de la Révolution française* (1818) and the autobiographical *Dix Années d'exile* (1818). There are English translations of most of her works. See her correspondence (tr. 1970); her memoirs (new ed. 1968); biography by C. Herold (1964); and M. Levaillant, *The Passionate Exiles* (1958, repr. 1971).

Staël, Nicholas de (nēkôlä' də stäl), 1914–55, French painter, b. St. Petersburg, Russia. Reared in Brussels, he traveled extensively before settling in France in 1940. De Staël evolved c.1942 a highly abstract style, developing a rich color fabric combined with strong elements of tension. His later works became gradually more representational. His artistic reputation was firmly established by the time of his suicide in 1955. See study by Denys Sutton (tr. 1959).

staff, in musical notation, a group of horizontal lines upon and between which notes are written so as to determine their pitch. In early attempts at the notation of plainsong, a single line was drawn, with neumes placed above and below it, giving a rough idea of the relative pitches of the tones. Guido d'Arezzo, in the 11th cent., used several lines and put letters on certain of them to indicate their pitch, thus foreshadowing the use of the clef (see MUSICAL NOTATION). Four-line staffs proved adequate for plainsong notation and are still employed for that purpose. In 16th-century keyboard music, staffs of six or seven lines were often employed, but later the five-line staff, with ledger lines for pitches outside the range provided for by the staff, became conventional.

Staffa (stăf'ə), uninhabited island, ¾ mi (1.2 km) long and ¼ mi (.4 km) wide, Argyllshire, NW Scotland, one of the Inner Hebrides, near Mull. Famous for FINGAL'S CAVE, Staffa has numerous other caves, and sea cliffs that reach 135 ft (41 m).

Stafford, Edward, 3d **duke of Buckingham,** 1478–1521, English nobleman; son of Henry Stafford, 2d duke of Buckingham. The attainder (1483) of his father was reversed on the accession (1485) of Henry VII, and after Henry VIII came to the throne (1509), he was made lord high constable, lord high steward, and a privy councilor. However, although Buckingham appeared to be high in the favor of Henry VIII, the king was both jealous and suspicious of him because of his wealth, his lands, and his descent; on the paternal side he was a descendant of Thomas of Woodstock, son of Edward III, and his mother was a sister of Edward IV's queen. He came to represent those nobles who resented the power of Cardinal Wolsey and their own exclusion from high offices. In 1521, Buckingham was arrested and tried on trumped-up charges that he had countenanced prophecies of his own succession to the throne and had expressed his intention to murder the king. He was executed.

Stafford, Henry, 2d **duke of Buckingham,** 1454?–1483, English nobleman. He was the grandson of Humphrey Stafford, the 1st duke, whom he succeeded in 1460. He passed the death sentence on George, duke of Clarence, in 1478, but it was not until the death (1483) of Edward IV that Buckingham achieved political prominence. Though married to a sister of Edward's widow, Elizabeth Woodville, he joined Richard of Gloucester (later RICHARD III) in taking custody of the young EDWARD V from the queen mother and figured largely in the political plot by which Richard seized the throne. He was given enormous power, especially in W England and Wales, but soon, for reasons not clear, he rebelled against Richard, intending to place Henry Tudor (later Henry VII) on the throne. His army, gathered in the west, was prevented from advancing by floods of the Wye and Severn rivers and soon dispersed. He went into hiding, was betrayed by one of his retainers, tried as a traitor, and beheaded. It has been suggested that, as constable of the Tower of London, Buckingham, rather than Richard III, was responsible for the murder of the princes in the Tower.

Stafford, Humphrey, 1st **duke of Buckingham,** 1402–60, English nobleman. He succeeded his father as earl of Stafford in 1403. He inherited the title of earl of Buckingham through his mother, Anne, countess of Buckingham, who was a daughter of Thomas of Woodstock, duke of Gloucester (son of Edward III). He served in France in the Hundred Years War as soldier and administrator. Made duke in 1444, he was later granted some of the estates of Humphrey, duke of Gloucester, whose policies he had opposed. In the Wars of the Roses he supported the Lancastrians and was killed at the battle of Northampton.

Stafford, Jean, 1915–, American writer, b. Covina, Calif., grad. Univ. of Colorado, 1936. Her literary reputation rests primarily on her exquisitely wrought short stories. Both these and her novels focus on lonely, isolated characters, usually adolescents, whom she depicts with gentle irony. Her works include the novels *Boston Adventure* (1944), *The Mountain Lion* (1948), and *The Catherine Wheel* (1952) and her *Collected Stories* (1969; Pulitzer Prize). She was married to Robert LOWELL.

Stafford, municipal borough (1971 pop. 54,890), county town of Staffordshire, W central England, on the Sow River, above its junction with the Trent. The chief industry is the manufacture of electrical goods, locomotives, and engines; other products are concrete, shoes and shoe-repairing machinery, and salt. The town has several half-timbered houses and two old churches that were restored by Sir George Gilbert Scott. Izaak Walton was born in Stafford, and his cottage at Shallowford nearby is now a museum. Richard Sheridan represented Stafford in Parliament from 1780 to 1806.

Staffordshire (stăf'ərdshĭr), county (1971 pop. 1,856,890), 1,157 sq mi (2,997 sq km), W central England. The county town is Stafford. The terrain is gently undulating except for a district of rugged moorlands in the north. The principal river is the Trent, which has various tributaries. Much of the land is devoted to cattle pasturage, but the county is primarily industrial. In the north the POTTERIES district, centered at STOKE-ON-TRENT, is known for its manufacture of fine china (Wedgwood and Spode), glass, bricks, and clay pottery. In the south is the BLACK COUNTRY, with its extensive coal fields, foundries, and iron and steel mills. BURTON UPON TRENT is famous for its breweries, and LICHFIELD for its magnificent cathedral. The Univ. of Keele is at Keele. The region was once a part of the Anglo-Saxon kingdom of MERCIA. In 1974, Staffordshire was reorganized as a nonmetropolitan county.

Staffordshire terrier, breed of strong, muscular TERRIER developed in England in the early 19th cent. It stands from 17 to 19 in. (43.1–48.3 cm) high at the shoulder and weighs from 35 to 50 lb (15.9–22.7 kg). Its short, close-lying, stiff coat is glossy and may be any color or combination of colors except solid white. As the popularity of bullbaiting and bearbaiting began to decline and the matching of dog against dog became more the fashion, British breeders crossed bulldogs with a now extinct black-and-tan terrier to produce the smaller, more agile pit dog necessary for this sort of contest. The result was the Staffordshire terrier. In recent times the Staffordshire has been raised as a pet and watchdog. See DOG.

Staffordshire ware, various products of the POTTERIES district, one of the most famous areas in England for the production of pottery. Late 17th-century SLIPWARE such as that attributed to Thomas Tofts shows a naïveté and liveliness that make its examples among the most desired objects of ceramics collectors. STONEWARE also was produced in the late 17th cent. and attained high quality. A white salt-glazed ware appeared in the first half of the 18th cent. Enamel glazes on top of salt glazing allowed for increasing richness. The end of the 18th cent. saw the advent of PORCELAIN manufacture. Among the famous Staffordshire potters were Josiah WEDGWOOD, Thomas MINTON, and Josiah SPODE.

staff tree, common name for some members of the Celastraceae, a family of trees and shrubs (many of them climbing forms), widely distributed except in arctic regions. These plants typically bear small greenish flowers and have seeds with brightly colored (often orange or scarlet) coats that are exposed when the matured seed pod splits open. Their fruit and brilliant autumn foliage make many species popular as ornamentals. The spindle trees (genus *Euonymus*) include the wahoo, or burning bush (*E. atropurpureas*), and the strawberry bush (*E. americanus*), both of E North America, and a Western species (*E. occidentalis*) that is also sometimes called wahoo. The wood of a related European bush (*E. europaea*) is used for the manufacture of spindles and other small objects. The Mediterranean plant *Catha edulis* is the source of Khat tea, a popular Arabian beverage. Several members of the family are valued for their medicinal bark as well as for decoration, e.g., the wahoo and the staff trees of the genus *Celastrus*. (*C. scandens* is the climbing BITTERSWEET of North America.) Staff trees are classified in the division MAGNOLIOPHYTA, class Magnoliopsida, order Celastrales, family Celastraceae.

stagecoach, heavy, closed vehicle on wheels, usually drawn by horses, formerly used to transport passengers and goods overland. Throughout the Middle Ages and until about the end of the 18th cent., the condition of roads in Europe discouraged the use of wheeled vehicles, and travel by land was regularly on horseback. In America until the end of the 18th cent. the traveler often had to make his way on horseback or on foot over an Indian trail. Slow and clumsy stagecoaches were operated irregularly in England and America from the early 18th cent. Stagecoaches first made their 400-mi (643-km) journey between London and Edinburgh in 1785, the time required being 10 days in summer and 12 days in winter. In the same year a stagecoach connection was established between New York City and Albany. Improved roads had made the stagecoach possible, and in turn the stagecoach encouraged the improvement of roads. Stagecoaches varied in design. Typically they were drawn by four or six horses, which were changed at the stages, or stations, along the route, the coach traveling about 12 to 18 hr a day and covering c.40 mi (60 km) a day in summer and 25 mi (40 km) in winter. Breeds of coach horses, e.g., the Cleveland bay and the German coach horse, were developed for strength and speed. The coach had room for eight to fourteen passengers, besides baggage, mail, and the driver. Two of the passengers rode in the seat with the driver; each of the other seats had room for three passengers. To diminish jolting, the body of the coach was supported by two leather straps (the "thorough braces"). The fare varied with time and place, averaging in America about five cents a mile. Competition from mail coaches, established in England in 1784, brought improvements in the comfort, speed, and schedules of stagecoaches, but the great period of the coaches ended in the early 19th cent. as railroads were built.

stage lighting and **stage setting:** see SCENE DESIGN AND STAGE LIGHTING.

Stagg, Amos Alonzo, 1862–1965, American football coach, b. West Orange, N.J., grad. Yale, 1888. He played end on the Yale football team and began his career as a coach (1889–91) at Springfield (Mass.) College. In 1892 he became athletic director at the Univ. of Chicago, coaching football there until 1933. In these 41 years he five times (1899, 1905, 1908, 1913, and 1924) coached undefeated teams. An authority on football, Stagg served (1904–32) on the football rules committee. Because of his age, he was compelled to resign his post at the Univ. of Chicago, but the "grand old man of football" later coached (1933–46) at the College of the Pacific and was (1947–52) assistant coach to his son at Susquehanna Univ. He collaborated in writing several books on football and is credited with the invention of numerous innovations in football play.

Stahl, Georg Ernst (gā'ôrkh ĕrnst shtäl), 1660–1734, German physician and chemist. He taught (1694–1716) at the Univ. of Halle, then went to Berlin as court physician. He is known for his promotion of the phlogiston theory of combustion and for his theory—developed in his *Theoria medica vera* (1707)—that the soul controls the function and structure of the body.

Stahlberg, Kaarlo Juho (kär'lō yo͞o'hō stäl'bĕrg), 1865–1952, first president of independent Finland (1919–25). A professor of law (1908–18) at the Univ. of Helsinki, he was president of the Finnish diet at the start of World War I and an opponent of Russian oppression in Finland. After serving as president of Finland, he was narrowly defeated in the elections of 1931 and 1937.

stained glass, in general, windows made of colored glass. To a large extent, the name is a misnomer, for staining is only one of the methods of coloring employed, and the best medieval glass made little use of it. Colored glass as window decoration is of great antiquity in the Far East. Muslim designers fitted small pieces of it into intricate window traceries of stone, wood, or plaster, and this type of window mosaic is still in use. Colored glass was used in windows of Christian churches as early as the 5th cent., and pictorial glass as early as the 10th cent. With the development of medieval architecture, stained glass assumed a structural and symbolic importance. As the Romanesque massiveness of the wall was eliminated, the use of glass was expanded. It was integrated with the lofty vertical elements of Gothic architecture, thus providing greater illumination. Symbolically, it was regarded as a manifestation of divine light. In these transparent mosaics, biblical history and church dogmas were portrayed with great effectiveness. Resplendent in its material and spiritual richness, stained glass became one of the most beautiful forms of medieval artistic expression. The early glaziers followed a sketched cartoon for their window design. They used a red-hot iron for cutting the glass to the required pieces, afterward firing in the kiln those which had received painted lines and shadings. The pieces were then fitted into the channeled lead strips, the leads soldered together at junction points, and the whole installed in a bracing framework of iron called the armature. The lead strips were adjusted to the articulation of the design and formed an integral part of it. The coloring of glass was achieved in the melting pot, where metallic oxides were fused with the glass. The metallic ores, although at first crude and limited, produced admirable color variations; the glass, available only in small pieces, gave thereby a jewel-like quality to the colors; the pieces, by their uneven surfaces and varying thicknesses, gave the advantage of irregular and scintillating refractions of light. With improved glassmaking many of these assets vanished. By the 16th cent. the material was smoother and in larger pieces; toward the middle of this century the use of enamel paints permitted the designs to be entirely painted on the glass and then fired. Only fragments remain of glass from the 11th cent. The period of greatest achievement in the art extended from 1150 to 1250. Some examples from the 12th cent. can be seen in the windows of Saint-Denis (Paris), Chartres, and Le Mans in France, as well as at Canterbury and at York Minster in England. The windows of this period were characterized by rich dark colors, single figures, and scrollwork. A recurrent design, that of the JESSE tree, continued in use until the 16th cent. By the beginning of the 13th cent. figures were abundantly used in scenes, being enclosed in geometrical medallions, such as circles, lozenges, or quatrefoils. A window was composed of many of these medallions. Color became more detailed and varied, and the prevailing scheme of red, blue, green, and purple, with small amounts of white, created tense and vibrant harmonies. In France the cathedral at Chartres is an unrivaled treasury of 13th-century glass; Sainte-Chapelle, Paris, is a triumph of architecture in which the walls present an illusion of being made entirely of fragile, exquisite stained glass. In England there are outstanding windows at York, Lincoln, and Salisbury. In the 14th cent. medallion compositions were replaced by a single figure framed in canopied shrines. Many windows showed clear areas designed in GRISAILLE. In the 15th cent. glass artists achieved a silvery tone by the use of large proportions of white glass, and their figures of saints and apostles were surmounted by elaborate canopies. In the 16th cent. the designers emulated the purely pictorial effects of Renaissance oil painting, with complicated perspectives, large scale, and realistic detail. Nineteenth-century romanticism and the Gothic revival brought fresh study and emulation of stained glass as well as of other medieval arts. The arts and crafts movement under William MORRIS was especially productive. A great contribution to American stained glass was made by John LA FARGE and Louis Comfort Tiffany. In modern art the medium has been used with great effectiveness by Rouault, Matisse, and Chagall. See also GLASS and ROSE WINDOW. See E. L. Armitage, *Stained Glass: History, Technology and Practice* (1959); J. Baker, *English Stained Glass* (1960); E. von Witzleben, *Stained Glass in French Cathedrals* (1968).

Stainer, Sir John (stā'nər), 1840–1901, English composer and organist, grad. Oxford. He was organist and choirmaster at St. Paul's Cathedral (1872–88), and he wrote music for the church service, cantatas, and two oratorios, one of which, *The Crucifixion* (1887), is still often performed.

Staines, urban district (1971 pop. 56,386), Surrey, SE England, on the Thames River. On the edge of Greater London, Staines is residential. There is some industry there, including the manufacture of diesel engines.

stainless steel: see STEEL.

stain removal, process of removing spots from fabrics. Prompt treatment may often prevent stains from penetrating fibers and may make the use of strong chemicals unnecessary. Certain fresh stains, especially grease spots, can be removed by applying an adsorbent, e.g., fuller's earth, chalk, whiting, or corn meal. Many spots can be removed from fabric that water does not injure by placing the fabric on a blotter or absorbent cloth, then sponging it with a damp cloth. Certain stains are removed only by the application of chemicals, which should be first tested on an inconspicuous part of the fabric to be sure they do not damage it. It should be borne in mind that many chemical cleaning fluids are toxic, and some have explosive vapors as well. Thus good ventilation is always necessary. In rubbing spots, it is best to use a clean cloth and work toward the center of the spot using a circular motion. Solvents used for removing spots include alcohol, benzene, gasoline, naphtha, turpentine, and carbon tetrachloride. Carbon tetrachloride, however, is dangerously toxic and is readily absorbed through the skin. The chief solvents used commercially include Stoddard's solution (a petroleum product), perchlorethylene, and trichlorethylene. Bleaches include hydrogen peroxide (a mild agent that may be used on many colored fabrics), commercial chlorine bleaches (not advisable for silk or wool), Javelle water, oxalic acid, and potassium permanganate (this sometimes leaves a brownish spot that can be removed with lemon juice, oxalic acid, or hydrogen peroxide; it is not safe for use on rayon). Bleaches are often applied with a medicine dropper to fabric stretched over a bowl of steaming water. See Ibert Mellan and Eleanor Mellan, *Removing Spots and Stains* (1959); A. C. Moore, *How to Clean Everything* (rev. ed. 1968).

Stair, James Dalrymple, 1st **Viscount** (dălrĭm'pəl, dăl'rĭmpəl), 1619–95, Scottish jurist. A student and then a regent of the Univ. of Glasgow, he was admitted to the bar in 1648. He supported the exiled Charles II and refused to swear allegiance to the Commonwealth, but he was nevertheless appointed (1657) a judge. After the Restoration he was prominent until his sympathy with the Covenanters at the time of the Scottish Test Act caused him to lose (1681) his appointment as judge. He then finished his *Institutions of the Law of Scotland* (1681), a great treatise on Scottish law. His exile in the Netherlands ended when he came (1688) to Great Britain with William III, who made him lord advocate and raised him to the peerage.

Stair, John Dalrymple, 1st **earl of,** 1648–1707, Scottish statesman; son of Viscount Stair. He served under James II, but sponsored the accession (1688) of William III in the Scottish Parliament and became (1691) that monarch's joint secretary of state for Scotland. His political skill and eloquence enabled him to dominate the Scottish Parliament. For his authorization of the massacre at GLENCOE (1692) he was forced to resign (1695). He reentered Parliament in 1700 and became a privy councilor (1702) and earl of Stair (1703). He actively promoted the union of Scotland and England.

Stair, John Dalrymple, 2d **earl of,** 1673–1747, Scottish general and diplomat; son of the 1st earl of Stair. He began a military career in the Netherlands, but on his father's death returned home and was elected (1707) one of 16 Scottish representative peers in the newly united Parliament of Great Britain. Becoming an assistant to the 1st duke of MARLBOROUGH in Flanders, he was sent (1709) as envoy to Augustus II of Poland. For his military achievements he was made (1710) general, but he fell from royal favor along with his friend Marlborough. At the accession of George I, Stair was sent as envoy to Paris, where from 1715 to 1720 his network of spies effectively thwarted the intrigues of the Jacobites. He was vice admiral of Scotland (1720–33) but lost the office because of his opposition to Robert Walpole's Excise Bill (1733). After Walpole fell from office in 1742, the earl was created field marshal and commanded the so-called pragmatic army in Flanders and Germany.

Staked Plain: see LLANO ESTACADO.

Stakhanovism (stăkä'nəvĭzm, stə–), movement begun (1935) in the Soviet Union aimed at increasing industrial production by the use of efficient working techniques. It was named for Aleksey Grigorevich Stakhanov, a coal miner in the Donets Basin, whose team increased its daily output sevenfold by organizing a more efficient division of labor system. The Soviet government, eager to ensure the success of the Five-Year Plan, encouraged the Stakhanov movement by offering higher pay and other privileges. In many cases the emphasis on speed resulted in poor quality. Stakhanovism was widely criticized outside the Soviet Union as another form of the speed-up system and was fought by labor unions in other countries. After World War II the Stakhanov movement gradually lapsed.

Stakhr, Iran: see ISTAKHR.

stalactite (stəlăk'tīt) and **stalagmite** (stəlăg'mīt), mineral forms often found in caves; sometimes collectively called dripstone. A stalactite is an icicle-shaped mass of calcite attached to the roof of a limestone cavern. Ground water trickling through cracks in the roofs of such caverns contains dissolved calcium bicarbonate. When a drop of water comes in contact with the air of the cavern, some of the calcium bicarbonate is transformed into calcium carbonate, which is precipitated out of the water solution and forms a ring of calcite on the roof of the cavern. By repetition of this process the length and thickness of the stalactite is increased. A stalagmite is a cone of calcite rising from the floor of a cavern. Stalagmites and stalactites are often found in pairs, the stalagmite being formed as a result of further evaporation and precipitation from solution after the trickle of water falls from the stalactite. Stalactites and stalagmites often meet each other to form solid pillars. Curtains of dripstone sometimes form when water drips from the ceiling of a cave along joint planes. Since stalactites, stalagmites, and curtains of dripstone form only in the presence of air, their existence in a cave indicates that the cave was above the water table while the dripstone was forming. The many colors often seen in these formations are caused by the presence of impurities. Celebrated caverns that owe much of their beauty to their stalactites and stalagmites are Mammoth Cave, Ky.; the Luray Caverns, Va.; and the Carlsbad Caverns, N.Mex. Onyx marble (Mexican onyx, Egyptian alabaster, or Oriental alabaster), used as a decorative stone, is derived from stalagmites and stalactites, as well as from similar deposits.

stalactite ornament, type of ornament characteristic of Islamic architecture. Generally executed in wood or in plaster over a wood or brick base, it consists of little vertical polygonal or curved niches rising and projecting in rows above one another in such a way as to create a general prismatic, corbeled form. Ingenious and intricate compositions of these elements are possible, and such purely geometric decoration was particularly acceptable to the Muslims in view of the Koran's prohibition of the use of natural forms. The primary use of stalactites was to form pendentives in the corners of a square room to receive the base of a circular dome, though this use was relatively infrequent in the Spanish Muslim style. Absent from the earlier Muslim buildings, they came into general use everywhere early in the 12th cent., forming cornices and the caps of posts and columns, decorating the heads of niches, and supporting the projecting balconies of minarets. In the interior of the Alhambra at Granada, Spain (13th–14th cent.), stalactites appear in particularly beautiful arrangements, especially in the decoration of arches and in the fantastic honeycombed ceiling vaults.

stalagmite: see STALACTITE AND STALAGMITE.

Stalin, Joseph Vissarionovich (stä'lĭn, Rus. vĭsəryô'nəvĭch stä'lyĭn), 1879–1953, Soviet Communist leader and head of the USSR from the death of V. I. LENIN (1924) until his own death, b. Gori, Georgia (now Georgian SSR). His real name was Dzhugashvili (also spelled Dzugashvili or Djugashvili); he adopted the name Stalin ("man of steel") about 1913. The son of a shoemaker, Stalin studied (1894–99) for the priesthood at the theological seminary at Tiflis, but was expelled. While still a divinity student, he became a convert to Marxism and joined the Social Democratic party in the Caucasus. He became a disciple of Lenin after the split (1903) of the party into factions of BOLSHEVISM AND MENSHEVISM. Stalin attended party congresses abroad (at Stockholm in 1906 and at London in 1907), but unlike Lenin, Leon TROTSKY, and other revolutionists he did not choose prolonged exile abroad. Under the alias of Koba, taken from the name of a famous Georgian outlaw, he remained in the Caucasus. He was especially active in the party press. Between 1902 and 1913 he was arrested five times and each time escaped. In 1911 he left the Caucasus for St. Petersburg, where in 1912 he became one of the first editors of *Pravda* [truth], then a small paper devoted to doctrinal disputes, later the official daily of the Communist party of the USSR. Stalin was arrested in 1913 and was exiled for life to N Siberia, where he remained until an amnesty was granted after the February Revolution of 1917. Back in St. Petersburg (by then, renamed Petrograd), he edited *Pravda* jointly with Lev KAMENEV.

The Making of Power. After the October Revolution of 1917, Stalin entered the Soviet cabinet as people's commissar for nationalities. From this position of great power over the non-Russian peoples of the country and from his membership in the central committee of the Bolshevik party (to which he had been elected in 1912), Stalin began to emerge as a leader of the new regime. During the civil war from 1918 to 1920 he played an important administrative role on the military fronts and in the capital. He was elected (1922) general secretary of the central committee of the party, enabling him to control the rank-and-file members and to build an apparatus loyal to him. Stalin's significance in the revolutionary movement and his relation to Lenin have been subjects of great controversy. Later Soviet writers portrayed Stalin as Lenin's closest aide both before and after the revolution. Stalin's enemies, notably Trotsky, claimed that Stalin's role in the movement was negligible. In reality, Stalin was one of many revolutionaries. He was highly regarded by Lenin as an administrator but not as a theoretician or leader. Toward the end of his illness, which began in 1922, Lenin wrote a testament in which he strongly criticized Stalin's arbitrary conduct as general secretary and recommended that he be removed. However, he died before any action could be taken, and the testament was suppressed. On Lenin's death, Stalin, Kamenev, and Grigori ZINOVIEV formed a triumvirate of successors allied against Trotsky, who was a strong contender to replace Lenin. After Trotsky was ousted (1925) as commissar of war, Stalin, now allied with Nikolai BUKHARIN, turned on Kamenev and Zinoviev. In a desperate attempt to counter Stalin's power, Zinoviev and Kamenev joined forces with Trotsky. Their efforts failed and they were forced to resign from the central committee of the Communist party. Stalin subsequently broke with Bukharin and engineered his fall from power. A primary issue around which these party struggles centered was the course of the Russian economy. The right wing, led by Bukharin, favored granting concessions to the peasantry and continuing Lenin's NEW ECONOMIC POLICY (NEP). The left, represented by Kamenev and Zinoviev, wished to proceed with industrialization on a large scale at the expense of the peasant. Stalin's position wavered, depending on the political situation, and the NEP continued until 1928 with considerable success. Then Stalin reversed this policy and inaugurated collectivization of agriculture and the FIVE-YEAR PLAN. Ruthless measures were taken against the kulaks, the farmers who had risen to prosperity under the NEP.

The Ruler. Stalin maintained that his program of consolidating "socialism in one country" (i.e., Russia), although demanding immense sacrifice and discipline, would render the USSR immune to attacks by capitalist nations and would demonstrate the superiority of the socialist system. He thus repudiated, for the time being, the role of Russia as torchbearer of world revolution. The political and cultural aims of Stalin's regime were to identify the totalitarian rule of the Communist party with stability and legitimacy. The basic Marxist tenet of the ultimate "withering away" of the state was all but repudiated. Instead the state was glorified. The shift to the right was equally manifest in the reorganization of the armed forces along disciplinarian lines reminiscent of the reign of Czar Nicholas I; in the official return to conservative divorce and abortion laws; in the gradual replacement of intransigent measures against the Russian Orthodox Church by a policy that made the church an instrument of the state; in the abandonment of experimental education in favor of rigid instruction; in the insistence on political criteria in the arts; and, most important, in the rebirth of nationalism and the mounting distrust of the West and of internationalism. This process was accompanied by repressive measures and terror, which reached their height in the political purges of the 1930s. Stalin made his dictatorship absolute by liquidating all opposition within the party. The purge was touched off by the murder (1934) of S. M. KIROV, Stalin's lieutenant, which led to prosecutions for an alleged plot—vast, Trotsky-inspired, and aided by Nazi Germany—to overthrow Stalin's government. In the purge trials many old Bolsheviks, including Kamenev, Zinoviev, Aleksey RYKOV, and Bukharin, were accused, pleaded guilty, and were executed. The purge extended even to the head of the SECRET POLICE, G. G. Yagoda, and to some of the highest army officers, notably Marshal Tukhachevski. The terror reached its height under the *Yezhovshchina,* the period (1937–38) when N. I. Yezhov directed the secret police. As the purges drew to a close (1939), the efforts of the secret police were concentrated on eliminating those elements of the population that might be disloyal in case of war. In internal policy, Stalin promulgated a new constitution in 1936 (see UNION OF SOVIET SOCIALIST REPUBLICS). Although it contained symbols of democratic institutions, effective political power was reserved to the Communist party as the vanguard of the working people. Although it reaffirmed the Soviet principle of autonomy for the various nationalities, the constitution in effect made it impossible for republics or other national groups to secede from the union.

Wartime Leader. Until 1934, Stalin pursued the policy, initiated by the Treaty of Rapallo (see RAPALLO, TREATY OF), of friendship with Germany. After Adolf Hitler had become (1933) chancellor of Germany, Stalin strove for international acceptance and cooperation, joining (1934) the League of Nations and attempting a rapprochement with Great Britain and France. The failure of such a rapprochement and the growing danger of war led Stalin to conciliate Hitler. The nonaggression pact with Germany (Aug., 1939) was designed to keep the USSR out of World War II. The territorial concessions and strategic advantages granted the Soviet Union by Germany at the expense of other East European nations contributed to Stalin's underestimation of the German threat. The Nazi invasion of Russia on June 22, 1941, took Stalin—who in May had taken over the premiership from V. M. Molotov—by surprise; it temporarily paralyzed his leadership and nearly led to the collapse of the Soviet army. The extent to which Stalin as a military leader subsequently contributed to Soviet victory has been fiercely debated among Soviet and Western authors; his forceful leadership was probably a greater asset than his military capability. He directed the war effort from the Kremlin, where he remained when the rest of the government was evacuated. He was voted the rank of marshal of the Soviet Union (1943) and of generalissimo (1945). At the TEHERAN CONFERENCE (1943) and the YALTA CONFERENCE (1945) with Franklin Delano Roosevelt and Winston Churchill and at the POTSDAM CONFERENCE (1945), Stalin proved an astute diplomat. His diplomatic skill led to the recognition by the Western powers of a Soviet sphere of influence in Eastern Europe. Having further strengthened his personal power in the course of World War II, Stalin used it ruthlessly to consolidate his control within the Soviet Union and the emerging Soviet empire against what he perceived as renewed capitalist threats. Always suspicious of Communist movements outside his control, he tried unsuccessfully to dissuade the Chinese Communists from taking power after World War II and broke with Josip Broz TITO in 1948 over the question of Yugoslavia's independent Communist policies. Stalin's paranoia during the last years of his life led to increased repression and persecution of his closest collaborators, reminiscent of the purges of the 1930s. His public appearances, which had always been rare, became even less frequent in the late 1940s and early 50s. His remoteness only stimulated the public worship bestowed upon him, which verged on apotheosis. Little is known of Stalin's private life except that he married twice and that both wives died (the second, Nadezhda Sergeyevna Alliluyeva, by suicide in 1932). Yakov, his son by his first wife, died in Nazi captivity. He had a son and a daughter by his second wife. His son, Vasily, was an officer in the Soviet air force before his death in 1962. His daughter, Svetlana Alliluyeva, defected to the United States in 1967.

Death and Denunciation. Stalin died March 5, 1953, of a cerebral hemorrhage. His body was entombed next to Lenin's in the mausoleum on Red Square in

Moscow. At the 20th All-Union Party Congress in 1956, Nikita Khrushchev and other Soviet leaders attacked the cult of Stalin, confirming many accusations long current outside the USSR. They did not repudiate Stalin's economic policies, but accused him of tyranny and terror, falsification of history, and self-glorification. In 1961 the 22d Party Congress voted to remove Stalin's body from the Lenin mausoleum; he was then interred in the heroes' cemetery near the Kremlin wall. Khrushchev's successor as first secretary (now general secretary) of the Communist party, Leonid Brezhnev—fearful that continued criticism of Stalinism might adversely affect the Soviet system as a whole—undertook a partial rehabilitation of Stalin, particularly as an economic and military leader. In 1970 a granite bust of Stalin was erected above his tomb. The term *Stalinist,* first used to distinguish Stalin's policies from those of Trotsky and others, came to mean a brand of Communism that was both national and repressive. Since Stalin's death the tyrannical implications of the term have become predominant. Stalin's writings form no cohesive body of political theory, although he claimed to represent the pure interpretation of Leninism and Marxism. Among his writings translated into English are *Leninism* (tr., 2 vol., 1928-33), *Problems of Leninism* (tr. 1934), *The Great Patriotic War of the Soviet Union* (tr. 1945), Stalin's *Works* (tr. 1952-55), and other collections of speeches, articles, and reports. There are numerous biographies of Stalin, some adulatory, such as that of Henri Barbusse (tr. 1935), some clearly prejudiced against him, such as that by Leon Trotsky (tr. 1946, rev. ed. 1967). See Boris Souvarine, *Stalin: A Critical Survey of Bolshevism* (tr. 1939, repr. 1972); B. D. Wolfe, *Three Who Made a Revolution* (1948); G. F. Kennan, *Russia and the West under Lenin and Stalin* (1961); Milovan Djilas, *Conversations with Stalin* (tr. 1962); M. D. Shulman, *Stalin's Foreign Policy Reappraised* (1963); Robert V. Daniels, ed., *The Stalin Revolution* (1965); Isaac Deutscher, *Stalin: A Political Biography* (2d ed. 1966); E. E. Smith, *The Young Stalin* (1967); Robert Conquest, *The Great Terror* (1968); Seweryn Bialer, ed., *Stalin and His Generals* (1969); R. A. Medvedev, *Let History Judge* (tr. 1971); Ronald Hingley, *Joseph Stalin: Man and Legend* (1973); A. B. Ulam, *Stalin: The Man and His Era* (1973); R. C. Tucker, *Stalin as Revolutionary, 1879-1929* (1973).

Stalin: see VARNA, Bulgaria.

Stalinabad: see DUSHANBE, USSR.

Stalingrad: see VOLGOGRAD, USSR.

Stalino: see DONETSK, USSR.

Stalinogorsk: see NOVOMOSKOVSK, USSR.

Stalinsk: see NOVOKUZNETSK, USSR.

stall, small division of a larger space, sometimes partly partitioned. The term is used for a booth for display and selling at an exhibition, for a compartment in a stable or kennel, or, in England, for the forward seats in a theater orchestra. In a church or cathedral the stalls are the fixed seats built in rows along the sides of the CHANCEL and used by the clergy and choir. They formed part of the church furniture at an early period when the officiating clergy had increased in number. At first movable seats, they later became an architectural feature. The choir stalls may be arranged in a single tier or in several tiers, one behind another. The prayer rest for each stall is formed by the back of the one preceding it. Each seat folds back to give space for kneeling or standing, and the miserere or projecting corbel upon its under surface then furnishes a rest for the priest in the long periods of standing. In the medieval stalls the miserere was carved with scenes from everyday life or with fabulous animal forms, called MISERICORDS. From the 14th cent. onward the stalls became objects of the woodcarver's limitless skill, with high, traceried backs and sculptured arms. The uppermost tier was often crowned by high gables or by canopies of richest tabernacle work, supported on colonnettes and terminating in spires. The magnificent stalls (c.1530) in St. George's Chapel, Windsor, assigned to the use of the Knights of the Garter, are of this kind. See M. D. Anderson, *Misericords* (1954).

Stamboliski, Aleksandr: see STAMBULISKI, ALEXANDER.

Stambul: see ISTANBUL, Turkey.

Stambuliski, Alexander, Bulgarian *Aleksandr Stamboliski* (both: älĕksän'dər stämbōlē'skē), 1879-1923, Bulgarian politician. He was a leader of the Peasants' party and by 1911 had become head of the opposition to Czar Ferdinand of Bulgaria. He was jailed (1915-18) for opposing the entry of Bulgaria into World War I on the side of the Central Powers. When he was released he proclaimed a republic, but the movement was defeated. After Ferdinand's deposition and the accession of Boris III, Stambuliski became premier (1919) and virtual dictator (1920). Supported by his peasant Orange Guard, he used his powers to carry out agrarian reforms and founded the Green Peasant International. He sought to carry out the provisions of the Treaty of Neuilly, which he had helped to negotiate in 1919. In 1923 a coup d'etat, supported by army officers and Macedonian nationalists led by Alexander TSANKOV, overthrew his government, and Stambuliski was killed.

Stambulov, Stefan (stĕ'fän stämbŏŏ'lôf), 1854-95, Bulgarian politician. Protesting Turkish rule in Bulgaria, he led the unsuccessful revolt of 1876, which was ruthlessly suppressed by the Turks in the "Bulgarian atrocities." Stambulov fought (1877-78) on the side of the Russians in the Russo-Turkish War and after the creation of the Bulgarian state became parliamentary leader of the National Liberal party. He opposed the group of officers that deposed Prince Alexander in 1886 and organized a counterrevolution that placed Ferdinand of Saxe-Coburg-Gotha on the throne in 1887. Ferdinand made him premier, and Stambulov wielded dictatorial power. He consolidated Bulgarian independence but did not secure Ferdinand's recognition by European powers. After having resigned in 1894, he was fatally wounded (1895) by an assassin.

stamen, one of the four basic parts of a FLOWER. The stamen (microsporophyll), is often called the flower's male reproductive organ. It is typically located between the central pistil and the surrounding petals. A stamen consists of a slender stalk (the filament) tipped by a usually bilobed sac (the anther) in which microspores develop as POLLEN grains. The number of stamens is a factor in classifying plant families, e.g., there are 5 (or multiples of 5) in the rose family and 10 in the pulse family. In most flowers the stamens are constructed so as to promote cross-pollination and to avoid self-pollination; e.g., they may be longer than the pistil or may be so placed in relation to the pistil (as in the mountain laurel and the lady's-slipper) as to prevent the pollinating insect from transferring the pollen of a flower to its own pistil. There may be differing maturation times for the stigma of the pistil and for the anther. In some plants there are some flowers (staminate) that bear stamens and no pistil and others (pistillate) that have a pistil and no stamens; these flowers may be borne on the same or on separate plants of the same species. In some highly developed flowers, especially double ones, and in some horticultural varieties (e.g., the geranium) the stamen may be modified into a sterile petallike organ.

Stamford, municipal borough (1971 pop. 14,485), in the Parts of Kesteven, Lincolnshire, E central England, on the Welland River. It is a market town. Products include diesel engines and electrical equipment, bricks, and tiles. It is the supposed site of a defeat of the Picts and Scots by the Saxons in 449 and was one of the Five Boroughs of the Danes. Stamford is noted for its architecture. Notable are part of an ancient Benedictine priory; a gate of Brasenose College (founded by a group from Oxford in 1333, when Stamford was famous as a seat of learning); several almshouses; and many 17th- and 18th-century buildings of Lincolnshire limestone. Nearby is Burghley House (16th cent.), home of Lord Burghley, the Elizabethan statesman, whose family, the Cecils, were prominent in Stamford's history.

Stamford, city (1970 pop. 108,798), Fairfield co., SW Conn., on Long Island Sound; settled 1641, inc. 1893 as a city within the town of Stamford (the two were consolidated in 1949). Office equipment, postage meters, bearings, chemicals, and cosmetics are among the manufactures. Numerous corporations have their headquarters there. The city is also a residential community for many New York City commuters. Cummings Park is on the sound. The sanctuary of the First Presbyterian Church was designed by Wallace K. Harrison and built (1958) in the shape of a whale. The Stamford Museum has a nature center and an observatory. A branch of the Univ. of Connecticut is in the city.

Stamitz, Johann (yō'hän shtä'mĭts), 1717-57, Bohemian-German composer. Stamitz came to Mannheim in 1741 and became concertmaster of the Mannheim orchestra in 1745. He made it the best in Europe. Stamitz wrote more than 70 symphonies, a dozen violin concertos, concertos for various other instruments, and chamber music. In developing the form of the sonata movement with two contrasting subjects and increasing the complexity of the bass part, Stamitz crucially influenced the course of symphonic writing. His most prominent son was **Karl Stamitz,** 1745-1801, a musician and composer. Karl was taught music by his father and F. X. Richter. He was a violin and viola d'amore virtuoso and wrote music of all kinds in the galant style (a light, gay style used for short movements of the classicial suite).

stammering: see STUTTERING.

Stamos, Theodoros (stăm'ōs), 1920-, American painter, b. New York City. Allied with the New York school of the 1960s (see MODERN ART), Stamos draws much of his inspiration from the mysticism of the Far East. He often creates a grainy, atmospheric surface with muted colors and calligraphic configurations in works that express the mysterious and insubstantial. His work is represented in New York City at the Whitney Museum and the Museum of Modern Art.

Stamp, Josiah Charles, 1st **Baron Stamp of Shortlands,** 1880-1941, English economist and financier. Active in many national and international economic commissions, he had an important part in the framing of the Dawes and Young plans for German reparations and was economic adviser to the British government after 1939. He was raised to the peerage in 1938. His books include *Fundamental Principles of Taxation in the Light of Modern Developments* (1921, rev. ed. 1936), *Financial Aftermath of the War* (1930), and *Christianity and Economics* (1939).

stamp: see POSTAGE STAMP; SEAL.

Stampa, Gaspara (gä'spärä stäm'pä), c.1523-1554, Italian poet. Plunged at an early age into the dissipated life of Venetian society, she became renowned for her brilliance and beauty. Her verse, which recounts an unhappy love affair, reflects her feelings of passionate tenderness and anguish.

Stamp Act, 1765, revenue law passed by the British Parliament during the ministry of George Grenville. The first direct tax to be levied on the American colonies, it required that all newspapers, pamphlets, legal documents, commercial bills, advertisements, and other papers issued in the colonies bear a stamp. The revenue obtained from the sale of stamps was designated for colonial defense; while the means of raising revenue was novel, the application of such revenue to defense continued existing British policy. The act was vehemently denounced in the colonies by those it most affected: businessmen, merchants, journalists, lawyers, and other powerful persons. Among these were Samuel ADAMS, Christopher Gadsden, Patrick Henry, John Dickinson, John Lamb, Joseph Warren, and Paul Revere. Associations known as the Sons of Liberty were formed to organize opposition to the Stamp Act. Merchants boycotted English goods; stamp distributors were forced to resign and stamps were destroyed; and the Massachusetts legislature, at the suggestion of James OTIS, issued a call for a general congress to find means of resisting the law. The **Stamp Act Congress,** which met in Oct., 1765, in New York City, included delegates from New York, New Jersey, Rhode Island, Massachusetts, Pennsylvania, Delaware, South Carolina, Maryland, and Connecticut. The congress adopted the Declaration of Rights and Grievances; it declared that freeborn Englishmen could not be taxed without their consent, and, since the colonists were not represented in Parliament, any tax imposed on them without the consent of their colonial legislatures was unconstitutional. Faced with a loss of trade, Parliament repealed the Stamp Act in 1766. See E. S. and H. M. Morgan, *The Stamp Act Crisis* (rev. ed. 1963).

stamp tax, method of collecting duties on certain transactions by means of a validating stamp attached to the taxable instrument, which may be a judicial act, a commercial document, a transfer of property, or law proceedings. Such a stamp is to be distinguished from a postage stamp, which is not a duty but a simple method of paying the government for a service rendered. Stamp taxes, apparently originating in the Netherlands, were introduced into England in 1694 and extended to the American colonies in 1765. Colonial opposition to stamp taxes contributed to the hostility against England that eventually resulted in the American Revolution. In the United States, stamp taxes, applying not only to legal and commercial acts but also to goods, were used to finance the Civil War and the Spanish-American War. Today the Federal government imposes stamp taxes on the issue and transfer of stocks and bonds, on deeds, and on playing cards. See John Due, *Government Finance* (4th ed. 1968); J. W. Pyke, ed., *An Alphabetical Guide to Stamp Duties* (1968).

Standardbred horse or **trotter,** American breed of LIGHT HORSE developed especially for harness, or sulky, racing. Of THOROUGHBRED ancestry, it is similar in appearance to a thoroughbred but has shorter legs. The breed is characterized by great stamina and its ability to trot or pace at extreme speeds without breaking into a running gallop. Sulky racing originated in the United States on the dirt roads of the early 19th cent., but it has since spread, as has the horse which made it possible, to Europe, Australia, Japan, and New Zealand. Standardbreds are any color, usually chestnut, black, or brown; they average 15 hands (60 in./160 cm) in height and weigh near 1,000 lb (450 kg).

standard of living, level of consumption to which an individual, group, or nation is accustomed. The evaluation of a standard of living is relative, depending upon the judgment of the observer as to what constitutes a high or a low scale. A relative index to the standard of living of a certain economic group can be gathered from a comparison of the cost of living and the wage scale or personal income. The elements that make up a standard of living include not only the material articles of consumption but also the number of dependents in a family, the environment, the educational opportunities, and the amount spent for health, recreation, and social services. Unemployment, low wages, crowded living conditions, and physical calamities, such as drought, flood, or war, may bring a drop in the standard of living, and, conversely, an increase in social benefits and higher wages may bring about a rise. The standard of living varies from nation to nation, and international comparisons are generally made by comparing the gross national product or per capita income of two or more countries. Nations enjoying a high standard of living include the United States, Canada, Switzerland, Great Britain, Australia, Sweden, and Denmark. In the United States, as in most Western nations, the standard of living has shown a steady trend upward. See J. S. Bain, *Pricing, Distribution, and Employment* (rev. ed. 1953); F. J. Bayliss, *The Standard of Living* (1969).

standard schnauzer: see SCHNAUZER.

standard temperature and pressure: see STP.

standard time, CIVIL TIME used within a given time zone. The earth is divided into 24 time zones, each of which is about 15° of longitude wide and corresponds to one hour of time. Standard time is based on GREENWICH MEAN TIME.

standing stones: see MEGALITHIC MONUMENTS.

Standish, Miles or **Myles,** c.1584–1656, American colonist, b. England. After serving as a soldier for a number of years, Standish accompanied the PILGRIMS to America on the *Mayflower* (1620) and was recognized at once as the military leader of PLYMOUTH COLONY. He was probably not a Puritan. He saved the colony from the Indians several times, most notably in 1623 when he defeated Indians threatening an attack on the settlement at Weymouth. In 1625 he was sent to England as a colonial agent particularly concerned with the colony's debt to its merchant backers in London. Back in Massachusetts, in 1628 he arrested Thomas MORTON of Merry Mount. Standish was treasurer of the colony (1644–49), held other posts, and was a founder of Duxbury, Mass. Henry W. Longfellow's *The Courtship of Miles Standish* and James R. Lowell's *Interview with Miles Standish* are wholly fictional. See biographies by J. S. C. Abbott (1872) and T. C. Porteus (1920).

standpatters, in U.S. history, term used early in the 20th cent. to designate conservatives in the Republican party as against the INSURGENTS or progressive Republicans. The term is said to have originated in Mark Hanna's remark concerning an election—all that was necessary for Republican success was, in poker parlance, to "stand pat."

standpipe, tank or pipe for holding water in an elevated position to create pressure in a water supply system. For a tall building, where the pressure from the mains at street level is insufficient to raise the water to the upper floors, water is pumped up to the standpipe and fed by gravity into the system.

Standwells, The, American puppet repertory theater, also known as The Little Players, established in 1960. The players are Isabelle Standwell and her brother Sicnarf, Mlle Garonce, Jonathan Smythe, and Elsie Lump. They all sing, play piano, and perform in a variety of roles by such dramatists as Shakespeare, Wilde, Chekov, and Molnár. They also appear in operetta and hold musical evenings at home performing works ranging from lieder to ragtime. The Standwell puppets are manipulated by Francis J. Peschka, who is aided by W. Gordon Murdock. All voices are by Mr. Peschka. The Standwells have appeared on nationwide television and have a regular annual season in New York City.

Stanfield, Clarkson, 1793–1867, English marine and landscape painter. He was first a sailor, then a scenery painter. Later he became known for his paintings of dramatic marine scenes. He is well represented at the Victoria and Albert Museum; his *Entrance to the Zuyder Zee* and *Lake Como* are in the Tate Gallery, London.

Stanfield, Robert Lorne, 1914–, Canadian political leader. A lawyer, he became (1948) leader of the Progressive Conservative party in Nova Scotia, entered the provincial legislature (1949), and served (1956–67) as Nova Scotia's prime minister. During his ministry he concentrated on the province's industrial development. After he was chosen his party's national leader (1967), he resigned as prime minister and entered the House of Commons, where he became leader of the opposition the same year. After losing to Pierre Elliott Trudeau in the 1974 elections, he stepped down as head of his party.

Stanford, Sir Charles Villiers, 1852–1924, English composer and teacher, b. Dublin, studied at Queens' College, Cambridge, and with Carl Reinecke in Leipzig. He was organist (1873–92) at Trinity College, Cambridge. In 1883 he became professor of music at the Royal College of Music, and in 1887 at Cambridge; he held both positions until his death. Stanford conducted (1885–1902) the Bach Choir of London and (from 1897) the Leeds Philharmonic Society. He was knighted in 1901. His compositions include seven operas, of which the comic opera *Shamus O'Brien* (1896) was most popular; seven symphonies; choral works; and chamber music. He edited and arranged collections of Irish songs and wrote a textbook of composition and several autobiographical works. See biography by H. P. Greene (1935).

Stanford, Leland, 1824–93, American railroad builder, politician, and philanthropist, b. Watervliet, N.Y. After practicing law in Wisconsin, he went (1852) to California, where he became a successful merchant. As Republican governor (1861–63), he helped hold California in the Union. He was one of the four founders of the Central Pacific RR, of which he was the president until his death, and he personally served as superintendent during part of its construction. He was also president (1885–90) of the Southern Pacific RR. From 1885 to his death he was a U.S. Senator. He founded and endowed STANFORD UNIVERSITY as a memorial to his son, Leland Stanford, Jr. His wife, **Jane Lathrop Stanford,** 1825–1905, b. Albany, N.Y., shared in founding the university and continued to aid it after her husband's death. See biographies by G. T. Clark (1931) and N. E. Tutorow (1970); Oscar Lewis, *The Big Four* (1938); Bertha Berner, *Mrs. Leland Stanford* (1935).

Stanford University, mainly at Palo Alto, Calif.; coeducational; chartered 1885; opened 1891 as Leland Stanford Junior Univ. (still the legal name). David Starr JORDAN was its first president. Stanford has extensive research facilities in many fields, e.g., a food research institute and large physics laboratories. There are excellent libraries, and its several museums include outstanding ones of zoology and entomology. The HOOVER INSTITUTION ON WAR, REVOLUTION, AND PEACE is located on the Palo Alto campus. Stanford has overseas campuses in Austria, England, West Germany, Italy, and Japan. See J. P. Mitchell, *Stanford University, 1916–1941* (1958).

Stanhope, Charles Stanhope, 3d **Earl** (stăn'əp), 1753–1816, British politician and inventor; grandson of the 1st earl. He was a friend of the younger William Pitt and married (1774) Pitt's sister, Hester. Sitting in the House of Commons (1780–86) before he succeeded to the peerage, he opposed the war with the American colonies and supported parliamentary reform and other measures advocated by Pitt. Stanhope became estranged from Pitt after the outbreak of the French Revolution, opposing the British government's repressive policies at home and its policy of intervention abroad. A vigorous supporter of the French republican ideal, he became known as "Citizen" Stanhope and absented himself from the House of Lords (1795–1800). His indefatigable scientific experiments produced a fireproof stucco, calculating machines, lenses, and, most important, machines for printing and stereotyping. Others, less successful, included experiments on steam navigation. The Stanhope lens and the Stanhope press are named for him. Lady Hester Stanhope was his daughter. See biography by G. P. Gooch (1914).

Stanhope, Lady Hester Lucy, 1776–1839, English traveler. She was private secretary and hostess for her uncle, William Pitt. Leaving England in 1810, she traveled in the Levant, adopting Eastern male dress and a religion that was a composite of Christianity and Islam. She finally settled among the Druses of the Lebanon Mts. in an abandoned convent that she rebuilt and fortified. The half-civilized tribes regarded her as a prophetess, as, in time, she came to regard herself; she incited them to resist an Egyptian invasion (1831) of Syria. European travelers, including A. M. L. de Lamartine and A. W. Kinglake, wrote accounts of their visits to her. Her personal physician, C. L. Meryon, recorded her life in *Memoirs of the Lady Hester Stanhope* (3 vol., 1845) and in *Travels of Lady Hester Stanhope* (3 vol., 1846). See biography by Doris Leslie (1972).

Stanhope, James Stanhope, 1st **Earl,** 1673–1721, English general and statesman. During the War of the Spanish Succession he participated in the capture (1705) of Barcelona, was appointed (1706) minister to Spain, and in 1708 became commander in chief of the British forces there. He soon captured Minorca, taking Port Mahon and making it a winter base for the British fleet. He won the battles of Almenara and Saragossa (1710) but lost his army to the French at Brihuega (1710) and was himself imprisoned for a year in Spain. On the accession (1714) in England of George I, Stanhope became a secretary of state. Devoting himself primarily to foreign affairs, he concluded a complex series of treaties, including the Triple Alliance (1717) with France and the Dutch. As chief minister (1717–18) he carried through the plans originated by Robert WALPOLE to fund the national debt and repealed (1718) the Occasional Conformity and Schism acts against dissenters. Becoming secretary of state again (1718), Stanhope negotiated the QUADRUPLE ALLIANCE of 1718 against Spain and formed (1719) a Baltic coalition to resist Russian expansion. His masterful diplomacy greatly strengthened Great Britain's position in Europe. He was created Earl Stanhope in 1718.

Stanhope, Philip Dormer: see CHESTERFIELD, PHILIP DORMER STANHOPE, 4TH EARL OF.

Stanhope, Philip Henry Stanhope, 5th **Earl,** 1805–75, English historian. He was undersecretary for foreign affairs (1834–35) in Sir Robert Peel's first ministry and secretary of the board of control (1845–46). He favored repeal of the corn laws and secured passage of the Copyright Act of 1842. Stanhope founded (1859) the National Portrait Gallery and was prime mover in organizing (1869) the Historical Manuscripts Commission. He wrote standard histories of the reign of Queen Anne (1870) and of the period from 1713 to 1783 (7 vol., 1836–54; repr. 1968).

Stanislaus I, 1677–1766, king of Poland (1704–1709, 1733–35) and duke of Lorraine (1735–66). He was born Stanislaus Leszczynski. Early in the NORTHERN WAR (1700–1721), Charles XII of Sweden overran Poland and expelled King AUGUSTUS II. In 1704, Charles secured the election of Leszczynski, a Polish nobleman. The majority of Poles remained loyal to Augustus, and Stanislaus, entirely dependent on Swedish arms, went into exile when Charles was routed (1709) at Poltava by Peter I of Russia. Stanislaus settled in France, emerging from oblivion when his daughter, MARIE LESZCZYNSKA, married (1725) Louis XV of France. On the death (1733) of Augustus II, Stanislaus returned to Poland and was again elected king. Under Russian pressure, a minority of the Polish diet chose instead AUGUSTUS III, precipitating the War of the POLISH SUCCESSION. Stanislaus, besieged at Danzig, received only moral support from France, while his rival was backed by Holy Roman Emperor Charles VI and had full military aid from Russia. Stanislaus was obliged to flee from Danzig in 1734, and in 1735 he accepted the terms of the preliminary Treaty of Vienna. He kept the royal title but renounced his actual rights in favor of Augustus III. In exchange, he received Lorraine and Bar, with the provision that they were to pass directly to the French crown upon his death. The former duke of Lorraine (later Holy Roman Emperor Francis I) was compensated with the promise of Tuscany. Stanislaus, an enlightened, humane, and cultured man, held a small but distinguished court at Lunéville. He contributed to the embellishment of NANCY, where the celebrated Place Stanislas still exhibits his generosity and good taste. Through his thought and writings he continued to influence Polish political ideas, and despite his concern with Polish affairs he ably administered Lorraine. He corresponded with the finest thinkers of his time, notably with Jean Jacques Rousseau, who on his request drafted a new constitution for Poland.

Stanislaus II, 1732–98, last king of Poland (1764–95). He was born Stanislaus Augustus Poniatowski. His mother was a member of the powerful CZARTORYSKI family, which furthered Stanislaus's career. He was

(1756–58) Polish ambassador to St. Petersburg, where he became a lover of Czarina Catherine II. Catherine, with Frederick II of Prussia, secured Stanislaus's election to the Polish throne after the death of Augustus III. Russian influence thus became paramount in Poland; the Russian ambassador at Warsaw virtually ruled the land. In 1768 anti-Russian members of the Polish nobility united (see BAR, CONFEDERATION OF) and in 1770 declared Stanislaus deposed. The rebellion was crushed by the Russians, and in 1772, Russia, Prussia, and Austria took vast territories from Poland in the first Polish partition (see POLAND, PARTITIONS OF). Although Stanislaus largely owed his throne to foreign powers, he sincerely sought to bulwark the decaying Polish state by internal reforms. In 1773 a national commission began the complete reorganization of Polish education. In 1791 the diet adopted the May Constitution, which abolished the *liberum veto,* a procedure that enabled a deputy to dissolve the diet and annul its previous decisions; strengthened the central administration; and opened public offices to the burgher class. The peasants' lot was ameliorated; serfdom, however, was not abolished. The throne, after the death of Stanislaus, was to be hereditary in the electoral branch of the house of Saxony. Russia, seeing its hold on Poland threatened, fostered the creation (1792) of the Confederation of Targovica, which sought to restore the old constitution. Russian troops, soon joined by Prussian forces, again invaded Poland. Stanislaus halted military resistance and, seeking a reconciliation with Russia, joined the Confederation of Targovica. The second Polish partition (1793) was the result. It left a truncated kingdom and made Stanislaus a vassal of Russia. The national uprising of 1794, led by KOSCIUSKO, was defeated by Russian and Prussian troops, and in 1795 the third partition completed the liquidation of Poland. Stanislaus, who had taken no firm stand in 1794, abdicated at Grodno and went to live in Russia. Although weak in politics, he was a generous patron of art, science, and—especially—literature. See A. N. Bain, *The Last King of Poland and His Contemporaries* (1909).

Stanislav: see IVANO-FRANKOVSK, USSR.

Stanislavsky, Constantin (kənstəntyēn' stənyĭsläf'skē), 1863–1938, Russian theatrical director, teacher, and actor, whose original name was Constantin Sergeyevich Alekseyev. He was cofounder with Vladimir Nemirovich-Danchenko of the MOSCOW ART THEATRE in 1898. As a director, he stressed ensemble acting as well as complete coordination of all phases of production. His outstanding productions included many of the plays of Chekhov, in which he emphasized the emotional truth of characters rather than the exterior truth of historical period. Striving to eliminate artificial and mechanical techniques in acting, Stanislavsky stressed the importance of the actor's inner identification with the character and the actor's natural use of body and voice. A tireless seeker after perfection, Stanislavsky was profoundly self-critical; his rare ability to extract the significant from his own experience was of enormous value to his students. His training, now termed the Stanislavsky method, had a vast influence on modern schools of acting. In New York City the celebrated Actors' Studio adapted many of his ideas to their use. Stanislavsky's *An Actor Prepares* (tr. 1936), *Building a Character* (tr. 1950), and *Creating a Role* (tr. 1961) contain the concepts upon which much current training in acting is based. See his autobiographical *My Life in Art* (tr. 1924); biography by David Magarshack (1951); Christine Edwards, *The Stanislavsky Heritage* (1965); Sonia Moore, *Training an Actor* (1968); Nikolai Gorchakov, *Stanislavsky Directs* (1968, repr. 1974).

Stanley, Arthur Penrhyn, 1815–81, English clergyman and author. As a student at Rugby he was influenced by the liberal views of Thomas ARNOLD. In 1838 he was elected a fellow of University College, Oxford. He became tutor and select preacher at Oxford and a recognized leader of Broad Church theology. He was strongly opposed to the agitation in the university against R. D. Hampden, although he urged leniency toward the Tractarians who were attacking Hampden (see OXFORD MOVEMENT). Stanley was made canon of Canterbury (1851), regius professor of ecclesiastical history at Oxford (1856), and canon of Christ Church (1858). Installed as dean of Westminster in 1864, he strove for the adoption of Broad Church policies. His inclusion of Christian ministers of all faiths among speakers from his pulpit and especially an invitation to some nonconformists to partake in the Holy Communion brought him into disfavor in circles of strict conformity. His voluminous writings include several volumes of ecclesiastical history, *The Life and Correspondence of Dr. Arnold* (1844), *Historical Memorials of Canterbury* (1855), and *Historical Memorials of Westminster Abbey* (1868). See R. E. Prothero and G. G. Bradley, *The Life and Correspondence of Arthur Penrhyn Stanley* (1893); A. V. Baillie and Hector Bolitho, *A Victorian Dean* (1930).

Stanley, Edward George Geoffrey Smith: see DERBY, EDWARD GEORGE GEOFFREY SMITH STANLEY, 14TH EARL OF.

Stanley, Edward Henry: see DERBY, EDWARD HENRY STANLEY, 15TH EARL OF.

Stanley, Sir Henry Morton, 1841–1904, Anglo-American journalist and empire builder, b. Denbigh, Wales. Originally named John Rowlands, he took the name of his adoptive father in New Orleans, where Stanley went in 1857. After fighting on both sides in the American Civil War, he drifted into journalism. His coverage of Lord Napier's Abyssinian campaign in 1868 for the New York *Herald* won him journalistic fame, and the *Herald* commissioned him to go to Africa to find David LIVINGSTONE. Stanley located the great explorer on Lake Tanganyika on Nov. 10, 1871, addressing him with the famous words, "Dr. Livingstone, I presume?" Failing to persuade Livingstone to leave Africa, Stanley returned to England with the news of his discovery. He found a mixed reception in England, where Livingstone's backers criticized Stanley's efforts and methods. Nevertheless, Stanley led a second expedition (1874–77), sponsored by newspapers, to further Livingstone's explorations. He followed the Congo River from its source to the sea, but he found the British uninterested in developing the region. Stanley then accepted the invitation of LEOPOLD II of Belgium to head another expedition. During this third journey (1879–84) he helped to organize the future Independent State of the Congo. At the Berlin Conference (1884–85; see BERLIN, CONFERENCE OF) he was instrumental in obtaining American support for Leopold's Congo venture. His last African journey (1887–89), to find EMIN PASHA, helped to put Uganda into the British sphere of influence. A naturalized U.S. citizen, Stanley again became a British subject in 1892, sat in Parliament (1895–1900), and was knighted (1899). Published accounts of his adventures include *How I Found Livingstone* (1872), *Through the Dark Continent* (2 vol., 1878), *In Darkest Africa* (2 vol., 1890), and *The Exploration Diaries of H. M. Stanley* (ed. by Richard Stanley and Alan Neame, 1961). See his *Autobiography,* ed. by his wife, Dorothy Stanley (1909, repr. 1969); Roger Jones, *The Rescue of Emin Pasha* (1973).

Stanley, James: see DERBY, JAMES STANLEY, 7TH EARL OF.

Stanley, Thomas: see DERBY, THOMAS STANLEY, 1ST EARL OF.

Stanley, town (1970 est. pop. 1,080), capital of the FALKLAND ISLANDS, S Atlantic Ocean, on East Falkland island. It is the main port and trading center of the islands. The name is sometimes written as Port Stanley.

Stanley Cup: see HOCKEY, ICE.

Stanley Falls, seven cataracts on the Lualaba River, extending c.60 mi (100 km) between Kisangani and Ubundu, N central Zaïre, central Africa. The falls have a drop of c.200 ft (60 m) and are circumvented by a short railroad. They are named for Henry Stanley, the explorer.

Stanley Pool, lakelike expansion of the Congo River, c.320 sq mi (830 sq km), along the Zaïre-Congo Republic border, W central Africa, c.350 mi (560 km) from the Congo's mouth. It is 22 mi (35 km) long and 14 mi (23 km) wide. Bamu Island (c.70 sq mi/180 sq km) is at its western end. Kinshasa and Brazzaville are important ports on its shores. In Zaïre it is known as Malebo Pool.

Stanley Steamer: see AUTOMOBILE.

Stanleyville, Zaïre: see KISANGANI.

stannic: a chemical compound containing TIN in the +4 valence state.

stannous: a chemical compound containing TIN in the +2 valence state.

Stanovoy Range (stənəvoi'), mountain range, c.450 mi (720 km) long, Far Eastern USSR, extending E from the Olekma River; it rises to c.8,150 ft (2,480 m) at Golets Skalisty. It forms part of the border between the Yakut Autonomous Republic and the Amur oblast. The range is continued by the Dzhugdzhur Range, which swings north parallel to the Sea of Okhotsk. The system forms the watershed between the Lena and Amur river basins.

Stans, Maurice Hubert, 1908–, U.S. government official, b. Shakopee, Minn. He worked as an accountant for many years before serving in the Eisenhower administration as Deputy Postmaster General (1955–57), deputy budget director (1957–58), and director of the budget (1958–61). Stans later became (1969) Secretary of Commerce under President Richard M. Nixon, but resigned (1971) to work as finance chairman for Nixon's reelection campaign. As a result of his activities in this post, he was indicted (1973) for perjury and conspiracy to obstruct justice and defraud the government, but he was acquitted (1974) of all charges.

Stanton, Edwin McMasters, 1814–69, American statesman, b. Steubenville, Ohio. He was admitted to the Ohio bar in 1836 and began to practice law in Cadiz. As his reputation grew, he moved first to Steubenville (1839), then to Pittsburgh (1847), and finally to Washington, D.C. (1856), becoming ever more prominent in his profession. In Dec., 1860, Stanton, a Democrat but a strong Unionist, succeeded Jeremiah S. BLACK as U.S. Attorney General in President Buchanan's cabinet. Later, he became legal adviser to Abraham Lincoln's Secretary of War, Simon Cameron. Appointed to take Cameron's place in Jan., 1862, he proved to be an extremely forceful and able Secretary of War. Contracts ceased to be opportunities for graft; the railroads were placed under military control; and Union generals in the field were supplied with necessary men and matériel. One of the leading radicals in the Lincoln administration, Stanton worked closely with the radicals in Congress and used his influence with Lincoln to advance their program. Deeply grieved by Lincoln's death, he arranged for a swift trial of the alleged conspirators by a military court. Stanton remained in President Andrew Johnson's cabinet, but serious differences over Reconstruction policy led Johnson to demand (Aug., 1867) his resignation. When he refused to resign, Johnson suspended him, first appointing Ulysses S. GRANT as secretary ad interim and then appointing Lorenzo Thomas as permanent Secretary of War. Stanton, however, barricaded himself in his office, and the radicals in Congress, claiming that Johnson's actions violated the Tenure of Office Act, initiated impeachment proceedings against him. When Johnson was acquitted (May, 1868), Stanton resigned. He died shortly after President Grant appointed him to the U.S. Supreme Court. See biographies by Fletcher Pratt (1953, repr. 1970) and B. P. Thomas and H. M. Hyman (1962).

Stanton, Elizabeth Cady, 1815–1902, American reformer, a leader of the woman suffrage movement, b. Johnstown, N.Y. She was educated at the Troy Female Seminary (now Emma Willard School) in Troy, N.Y. In 1840 she married Henry Brewster Stanton, a journalist and abolitionist, and attended with him the international slavery convention in London. The woman delegates were excluded from the floor of the convention; the indignation this aroused in Elizabeth Stanton and Lucretia Mott was an important factor in their efforts to organize women to win greater equality. With several others they called the first woman's rights convention in the United States in 1848 at Seneca Falls, N.Y. Stanton insisted that a suffrage clause be included in the bill of rights for women that was drawn up at the convention. From 1852, despite occasional disagreements, she was intimately associated with Susan B. ANTHONY in leading the woman's movement. She was president of the National Woman Suffrage Association (1869–90) and of the National American Woman Suffrage Association (1890–92). With Anthony as publisher she and Parker Pillsbury edited (1868–70) the *Revolution,* a militant feminist magazine. Elizabeth Stanton was a brilliant orator and an able journalist, and as a writer and lecturer she strove for legal, political, and industrial equality of women and for liberal divorce laws. She compiled with Susan B. Anthony and Matilda Joslyn Gage the first three volumes of *History of Woman Suffrage* (1881–86) and wrote *Eighty Years and More* (1898). See *Elizabeth Cady Stanton as Revealed in Her Letters, Diary and Reminiscences* (ed. by Theodore Stanton and Harriot Stanton Blatch, 1922); biography by W. E. Wise (1960).

Stanton, residential city (1970 pop. 18,149), Orange co., SW Calif.; inc. 1956.

Stanwix, Fort: see FORT STANWIX.

staphylococcus (stăf"ələkŏk'əs), any of the pathogenic BACTERIA, parasitic to man, that belong to the genus *Staphylococcus.* The spherical bacterial cells (cocci) typically occur in irregular clusters [Gr. *staphyle*=bunch of grapes]. The term *staphylococcus* is also commonly used for the cluster arrangement itself and, broadly, for any bacteria with such a growth pattern. The pigments produced by staphylococci are the basis of the names given to the various strains—those with colors ranging from orange to yellow are designated *S. aureus;* white strains are known as *S. albus.* Staphylococci cause abscesses, boils, and other infections of the skin, such as IMPETIGO. They can also produce infection in any organ of the body (e.g., staphylococcal pneumonia of the lungs). The most common form of FOOD POISONING is brought on by staphylococcus-contaminated food. The staphylococcus organisms also elaborate toxins and enzymes that can destroy both red and white blood cells. Unlike some other types of bacteria, staphylococci are generally partly or wholly resistant to antibiotic action; this raises serious problems in the treatment and control of staphylococcus infections (see DRUG RESISTANCE). Some synthetic penicillins developed for the purpose of staphylococcus control are thought to be effective against the previously resistant strains.

Staple, Merchants of the: see MERCHANTS OF THE STAPLE.

Stapleton, Maureen, 1925–, American actress, b. Troy, N.Y. Stapleton's first major stage success was in *The Rose Tattoo* (1951). Best-known for intelligent character roles, she has appeared on Broadway in *Orpheus Descending* (1957), *Toys in the Attic* (1960), *The Gingerbread Lady* (1970), and *The Country Girl* (1973). Her few films include *Lonelyhearts* (1959), *A View from the Bridge* (1962), and, repeating her stage performance, *Plaza Suite* (1972).

star, hot incandescent sphere of gas, held together by its own GRAVITATION, and emitting light and other forms of ELECTROMAGNETIC RADIATION whose ultimate source is NUCLEAR ENERGY. The universe contains billions of galaxies, and each GALAXY contains billions of stars. The stars visible to the unaided eye are all in our own galaxy, the MILKY WAY. The visible stars are divided into six classes according to apparent brightness; the brightest are first MAGNITUDE and the faintest are sixth magnitude. The stars differ in apparent brightness because they lie at different distances from us and vary in actual or intrinsic brightness. Stars are not spread uniformly through a galaxy. They are frequently bunched together in STAR CLUSTERS of as many as 100,000 stars. Many stars that appear as single points of light in even the most powerful telescopes are actually systems of two or more stars orbiting one another, bound together by their mutual gravitational attraction. The BINARY STARS are most common among these multiple star systems. In ancient times, the stars were believed to be motionless; their fixed patterns in the sky were designated as the constellations. It is now known that the stars move through space, although their motion is too small to be detected during a human lifetime without exacting measurements. From the observed PROPER MOTION (change in apparent position on the CELESTIAL SPHERE), distance of the star from the earth, and RADIAL VELOCITY (motion along the line of sight), the true velocity of a star through space can be determined. Stars differ widely in MASS, size, TEMPERATURE, and total energy output, or LUMINOSITY. The SUN, a typical star, has a mass of about 2×10^{33} grams, a radius of about 7×10^{10} cm, a surface temperature of about 6000°C, and a luminosity of about 4×10^{33} erg/sec. About 90% of all stars have masses between one tenth and 50 times that of the sun. Other stellar quantities vary over a much larger range. The most luminous stars (excluding SUPERNOVAS) are about a million times more powerful than the sun, while the least luminous are only one hundredth as powerful. VARIABLE STARS do not shine steadily but fluctuate in either a regular or irregular fashion; the supernova, or exploding star, is the most spectacular variable star. RED GIANTS, the largest stars, are hundreds of times greater in size than the sun; if one were placed at the sun's position, it would engulf Mars. At the opposite extreme, WHITE DWARFS are no larger than the earth, and NEUTRON STARS are only a few kilometers in radius. Light received from a star consists of a SPECTRUM of wavelengths; the hotter the star, the shorter the wavelength at which the light is most intense. The color of a star is closely related to its surface temperature. Red stars have surface temperatures around 3000°C and blue-white stars have surface temperatures above 20,000°C (see SPECTRAL CLASS). The theory of STELLAR STRUCTURE applies the laws of physics to calculation of the equilibrium configurations of stars. According to this theory, the mass and chemical composition of a star determine all its other characteristics. Because most stars are more than 90% hydrogen, variations in chemical composition are small and have a small effect. Variation in mass is the main factor; a doubling in mass increases the luminosity more than 10 times. For a star to be stable, the compressive force of gravitation must be exactly balanced by the tendency of the gas to expand. Thus, the size and temperature of a star are important, interrelated factors. Despite the tremendous pressure generated by the massive layers above it, the central region, or core, of a star remains gaseous. This is possible because the core has a temperature of millions of degrees. At this temperature, nuclear energy is released by the fusion of hydrogen to form helium; the principle is the same as that of the hydrogen bomb. By the time nuclear energy reaches the surface of the star, it has been largely converted into visible light with a spectrum characteristic of a very hot body (see BLACK BODY). The theory of STELLAR EVOLUTION states that a star must change as it consumes its hydrogen in the nuclear reactions that power it. Ultimately each star must die, possibly in a supernova explosion, when all its nuclear fuel is exhausted. The heavy atoms created in the late stages of stellar evolution (see NUCLEOSYNTHESIS) are spewed out to become part of the interstellar matter from which new stars are continuously formed.

Stara Planina, mountains: see BALKANS, Bulgaria.

Staraya Russa (stä'rīə ro͞o'sə), city (1970 pop. 35,000), W European USSR, near Lake Ilmen. It is a health resort with salt springs and mud baths. It is one of the oldest Russian settlements and was known to exist in 1167. The city was formerly a center for mining and processing salt.

Stara Zagora (stä'rä zä'gôrä), city (1968 est. pop. 103,900), central Bulgaria. It is a railway center and the market for a fertile farm area. The city's industries produce tobacco, textiles, foodstuff, beverages, agricultural machinery, furniture, and electrical and leather goods. Stara Zagora is the seat of an Orthodox Eastern bishopric. A Thracian settlement, it was known as Augusta Trajana under Roman rule. It was captured by the Turks in 1370 and renamed Eski-Zagra or Yeski-Zagra, from which its present name is derived. The city was destroyed in the Russo-Turkish War of 1877–78 and rebuilt along modern lines.

starch, white, odorless, tasteless, carbohydrate powder. It plays a vital role in the biochemistry of both plants and animals and has important commercial uses. In green plants starch is produced by PHOTOSYNTHESIS; it is one of the chief forms in which plants store food. It is stored most abundantly in tubers (e.g., the white potato), roots (e.g., the sweet potato), seeds, and fruits; it appears in the form of grains that differ in size, shape, and markings in various plants. The plant source can usually be identified by microscopic examination of the starch grains. Starch obtained by animals from plants is stored in the animal body in the form of GLYCOGEN. Digestive processes in both plants and animals convert starch to GLUCOSE, a source of energy. Starch is one of the major nutrients in the human diet. Its presence in foods and other substances can be detected by the blue-black color produced when iodine solution is added to a sample of the material to be tested. By treatment with hot water, starch granules have been shown to consist of at least two components, known as amylopectin and amylose. Amylopectin is a branched glucose polymer; amylose is a linear glucose polymer. Commercially starch is prepared chiefly from corn and potatoes. Starch is widely used for sizing paper and textiles, for stiffening laundered fabrics, in the manufacture of food products, and in making DEXTRIN. In addition to its other uses, CORNSTARCH is a source of corn syrup, of which large quantities are used in making table syrup, preserves, ice cream, and other confections. Corn sugar (glucose) is also derived from cornstarch. See also ARROWROOT.

Star Chamber, ancient meeting place of the king of England's councilors in the palace of Westminster in London, so called from stars painted on the ceiling. The court of the Star Chamber developed from the judicial proceedings traditionally carried out by the king and his council. In the 15th cent., under the Lancastrian and Yorkist kings, the role of the council as an equity and prerogative court increased, and it extended its jurisdiction over criminal matters. Faster and less rigid than the common law courts and with its jurisdiction extended by the Tudors, Star Chamber became increasingly the object of opposition from the common lawyers in Parliament. The traditional hostility between equity and common law was aggravated by the use made of Star Chamber by the Stuarts as a vehicle for exercising the royal prerogative, particularly over church matters, in defiance of Parliament. It was abolished by the Long Parliament in 1641. In its later period the court was so hated that *Star Chamber* became a byword for unfair judicial proceedings. The court's harshness, however, has been exaggerated.

star cluster, a group of stars near each other in space and resembling each other in certain characteristics that suggest a common origin for the group. Stars in the same cluster move at the same rate and in the same direction. Two types of clusters can be distinguished—open clusters, also called galactic clusters because of their wide distribution in our GALAXY (the Milky Way), and globular clusters. More than one thousand open clusters have been catalogued in the Milky Way, most of which are found in the spiral arms of the galaxy at a distance of 1,600 to 6,500 light-years from the sun. Typically, an open cluster contains from a few dozen to a thousand loosely scattered stars and exists in a region rich in gas and dust. Among those which can be detected with the unaided eye are the HYADES cluster in the constellation Taurus, the Coma Berenices cluster, the PLEIADES cluster, and the PRAESEPE cluster. Globular clusters are spherical aggregates of thousands or millions of densely concentrated stars. Rather than lying on the galactic plane, these clusters are members of the outer halo, moving around the nucleus in highly inclined orbits. Because of their distribution throughout the galaxy, they provide an outline of its shape. Over 100 globular clusters in the Milky Way are known, but astronomers suggest that several hundred others may be obscured from sight by the main bulk of the galaxy and by interstellar dust clouds. Visible to the unaided eye are Omega Centauri and 47 Tucanae, both in the southern skies. Originally mistaken as stars, they are 2 of the nearest globular clusters at about 20,000 light-years from the sun.

starfish: see SEA STAR.

Stargard: see SZCZECINSKI, Poland.

stargazer, common name for any of several species of marine fishes of the family Uranoscopidae, found in southern waters, and having the mouth, nostrils, and eyes set high in the head. Stargazers lie buried in the sand, waiting for their prey of small crustaceans. Some species have electrical cells, developed from the optic nerve, capable of inflicting strong shocks. A closely related family (Dactyloscopidae) comprises the sand stargazers, which have eyes also set high in the head. They are found in the Atlantic Ocean in both the Northern and Southern Hemispheres. Stargazers of both families are classified in the phylum CHORDATA, subphylum Vertebrata, class Osteichthyes, order Perciformes, families Uranoscopidae and Dactyloscopidae.

Starhemberg, Ernst Rüdiger, Graf von (ĕrnst rü'dĭgər gräf fən shtä'rəmbĕrk"), 1638–1701, Austrian field marshal. He served against the Turks in Hungary under Montecucculi and was made (1680) military commander of Vienna. From July to Sept., 1683, he held Vienna with a small garrison against a large Turkish army under the grand vizier Kara MUSTAFA. Vienna was about to succumb to the siege, which had reduced it to starvation, when it was relieved by an army under John III of Poland and Charles V of Lorraine. As a reward for his heroic role Starhemberg was made a field marshal and minister of state. In 1691 he became president of the war council. His cousin **Guidobald, Graf von Starhemberg** (gwē'dōbält"), 1657–1737, also took part in the defense of Vienna. He was made field marshal and served with distinction in the War of the Spanish Succession.

Starhemberg, Ernst Rüdiger von, 1899–1956, Austrian politician, a descendant of the 17th-century general of the same name. He took part in Hitler's "beer-hall putsch" of 1923 (see HITLER, ADOLF) but later opposed Hitler and became (1930) leader of the Heimwehr, an Austrian fascistic militia. He supported DOLLFUSS in 1932, his aim being an Austrian system of fascism. After helping to suppress the Social Democrats in Feb., 1934, he became vice chancellor and later was also minister of security in the Schuschnigg cabinet. He was forced to resign in 1936, and the Heimwehr was dissolved. During World War II, Starhemberg served for a time in the British and the Free French air forces. He lived in Argentina from 1942 to 1955, when he returned to Austria. See his memoirs, *Between Hitler and Mussolini* (1942).

Starhemberg, Guidobald, Graf von: see STARHEMBERG, ERNST RÜDIGER, GRAF VON (1638–1701).

stariny: see BYLINY.

Stark, Harold Raynsford, 1880–1972, American admiral, b. Wilkes-Barre, Pa. A graduate of the U.S. Naval Academy at Annapolis, he was commissioned (1905) an ensign in the navy. After service in World War I, he filled several important naval administrative posts. In 1939, Stark was made admiral and appointed chief of naval operations. Removed (1942) from this position after the attack on Pearl Harbor, he commanded (1942–45) U.S. naval forces in Europe in World War II and retired from active duty in 1946. Although the final years of his career were clouded by the Pearl Harbor disaster, Stark was absolved of any responsibility by presidential and congressional investigating committees.

Stark, John, 1728–1822, American Revolutionary soldier, b. Londonderry, N.H. He fought in the French and Indian Wars. At the start of the Revolution he distinguished himself at Bunker Hill, and he served in the Quebec campaign and with George Washington at Princeton and Trenton (1776–77). He went home in 1777, disgruntled over some promotions, but later in the year took the field as a commander of the New Hampshire militia in the Saratoga campaign. When General Burgoyne sent a detachment to take the colonial stores at Bennington (now in Vermont), Stark met and repulsed it. The battle of Bennington contributed to Burgoyne's discomfiture at Saratoga. For this service Stark received appointment as brigadier general from the Congress. See biography by H. P. Moore (1949).

Starkville, city (1970 pop. 11,369), seat of Oktibbeha co., E Miss., in a livestock, dairy, and farm area; inc. 1837. Textiles and clothing, milk products, and clocks are made. Mississippi State Univ. is nearby.

Starling, Ernest Henry, 1866–1927, English physiologist, b. India. He was professor (1899–1923) at University College, London. He was an authority on heart action and circulation. With Sir William M. Bayliss he introduced the concept of hormones and studied intestinal movement, describing (1899) peristalsis as a ganglionic reflex. His many works include *Principles of Human Physiology* (1912; 14th ed. with Sir Charles A. Evans, 1968). See study by C. B. Chapman (1962).

starling, any of a group of originally Old World birds that have become distributed worldwide. Starlings were brought to New York in 1890; since then the common starling (*Sturnus vulgaris*) has spread throughout North America. They often collect in loud, noisy flocks. Starlings destroy some insects, but they are generally considered a nuisance since they drive away smaller, desirable birds. They have iridescent, blackish plumage and a long bill which is yellow in spring and summer. They mimic bird songs and other sounds. Starlings are classified in the phylum CHORDATA, subphylum Vertebrata, class Aves, order Passeriformes, family Sturnidae.

Star of Bethlehem, name for the star in the east that, as related in the Gospel, led the Wise Men to Bethlehem (Mat. 2.1–10). According to astronomers the appearance of the star may have been caused by the conjunction of the planets Jupiter, Saturn, and Mars, or by a nova or a comet.

star-of-Bethlehem, in botany, low, spring-blooming bulbous plant (*Ornithogalum umbellatum*) of the family Liliaceae (LILY family), native to the Mediterranean region but naturalized in North America and cultivated in gardens. The plant has rather stiff, grasslike leaves and a cluster of white star-shaped flowers marked on the back with green. It spreads easily and tends to become weedy. Although the plant is poisonous, the bulbs have been prepared and used as food in the Old World. The flower has been associated with the star that guided the Wise Men to the manger. Star-of-Bethlehem is classified in the division MAGNOLIOPHYTA, class Liliatae, order Liliales, family Liliaceae.

Starr, Belle, 1848?–89, American outlaw, b. near Carthage, Mo. Her original name was Myra Belle Shirley; her father was a farmer and then operated a tavern in Carthage, where she spent her childhood. The Shirleys later (1864) moved to Dallas, Texas. Soon Belle met Cole Younger and had a child by him. Subsequently she met the gang headed by Jesse James, the rest of the Younger gang, and other outlaws, one of whom, Jim Reed, she married. After his death she married (1880) Sam Starr, an Indian, and went to live in the Indian Territory in Oklahoma. Her home there became a retreat for outlaws, for whom she operated mainly as a "fixer" with the legal authorities. In 1883 she was convicted of horse-stealing and briefly imprisoned. Belle Starr's reputation as a notorious horse thief and murderess was greatly magnified in the book *Bella Starr, the Bandit Queen; or, the Female Jesse James* (1889), by Richard K. Fox. It was written after she was shot to death by an unknown person. See biographies by Burton Rascoe (1941), E. P. Hicks (1963), and C. W. Breiham (1970).

Starrett, Paul (stăr'ĭt), 1866–1957, American builder, b. Lawrence, Kansas. After serving (1903–22) as president of the George A. Fuller Company in Chicago, he opened and headed the construction firm of Starrett Brothers, Inc., in New York City. Starrett was responsible for the erection of the Flatiron Building, the Empire State Building, the Pennsylvania RR station, and the Plaza, Biltmore, and Commodore hotels, all in New York. The Bellevue-Stratford Hotel in Philadelphia and the Lincoln Memorial in Washington were erected by the Fuller Company under his direction. See his autobiography, *Changing the Skyline* (1938).

star route, in the U.S. postal service, a surface route to post offices not accessible by railroad or steamboat. Private contracts to carry the mail over these routes are made with bonded bidders. The star route was so named because asterisks designate such routes in postal publications. In the days when star routes by stage or rider were important, particularly in the West, the law permitted easy readjustment of the contracts because of shifting population. In April, 1881, President Garfield dismissed a Second Assistant Postmaster General who was suspected of having fraudulently increased the compensation of numerous star-route contractors. The frauds, amounting to nearly half a million dollars, hastened civil service reform.

Star-spangled Banner, The, American national anthem, beginning, "O say can you see by the dawn's early light." The words were written by Francis Scott Key, a young Washington attorney who, during the War of 1812, sailed to the British fleet to obtain the release of a captured American. Key was detained by the British and was forced to witness from his ship the bombardment of Fort McHenry during the night of Sept. 13–14, 1814. Defended under the command of Major George Armistead, the fort withstood the attack, and the sight of the American flag still floating at dawn inspired Key's verses, which were written on the way ashore in the morning. After circulating as a handbill, the lyrics were published in a Baltimore newspaper on Sept. 20, 1814. The tune was taken from the popular English song "To Anacreon in Heaven." Although the army and the navy had for some years regarded "The Star-spangled Banner" as the national anthem, its designation as such first became official by executive order of President Wilson in 1916. This order was confirmed by act of Congress in 1931. See Victor Weybright, *The Star-spangled Banner* (1935).

starvation, condition in which deprivation of food has forced the body to feed on itself. The fat and carbohydrate reserves are used up first; then the body protein is converted into energy. The resulting loss of weight is unevenly distributed. First to be lost are fat deposits and large quantities of water. The liver, spleen, and muscle tissue then suffer the greatest loss of weight. The heart and brain show little loss proportionately. The starving person becomes weak and lethargic. Body temperature, pulse rate, blood pressure, and basal metabolism continue to fall as starvation progresses, and death eventually ensues.

Starved Rock, cliff, 140 ft (43 m) high, overlooking the Illinois River between La Salle and Ottawa, N Ill. It was visited by the French explorers Louis Jolliet and Father Marquette in 1673 and by Robert La Salle and Henri de Tonti in 1679; Tonti and La Salle built (1680–83) Fort St. Louis there. Legend says that in the 18th cent. the Ottawa Indians drove a band of Illinois Indians onto the cliff, where they died of thirst and starvation. In the early 19th cent. brigands and outlaws found refuge nearby in canyons and caves that were included in Starved Rock State Park (est. 1912). Starved Rock has been designated a national historic landmark.

Stary Krym (stä'rē krĭm) [Rus.,=Old Crimea], city, SE European USSR, in the Ukraine, on the Crimean peninsula. Known as Surkhat or Solkhat from the 13th to the 15th cent., it was the residence of the vice regents of the khans of the Golden Horde. It was a major caravan center on the route to the ancient Russian duchies, the Volga region, and Central Asia. The original capital (called Krym) of the Crimean khans in the 14th to 15th cent., it declined when the capital was transferred to Bakchisaray. Mosques (14th cent.), the ruins of a caravanserai (14th cent.), and ruins of an old fortress (15th cent.) remain today.

Stas, Jean Servais (zhäN' sĕrvā' stäs), 1813–91, Belgian chemist. He was assistant to J. B. A. Dumas and professor (1840–65) at the École royale militaire, Brussels. He is noted for his accurate determinations of atomic weights.

Stassen, Harold Edward (stăs'ən), 1907–, American public official and university president, b. West St. Paul, Minn. He was, at the age of 31, elected governor of Minnesota in 1938 and was twice (1940, 1942) reelected. In World War II, Stassen resigned (1943) as governor to enter the navy. He was a delegate (1945) to the San Francisco Conference called to create the United Nations, and in 1948 he was an unsuccessful candidate for the Republican presidential nomination. From 1949 to 1953, Stassen was president of the Univ. of Pennsylvania. During the Eisenhower administration he served as Mutual Security Administrator (1953), director of the Foreign Operations Administration (1953–55), and special presidential adviser on disarmament (1955–58). Stassen was again an unsuccessful candidate for the Republican presidential nomination in 1964 and 1968.

Stassfurt (shtäs'fŏŏrt), city (1970 pop. 25,695), Magdeburg district, W East Germany. It is a center of one of the world's great potash-mining regions. Manufactures of the city include chemicals, foodstuffs, furniture, and electronic equipment.

state: see GOVERNMENT.

State, United States Department of, executive department of the Federal government responsible for the determination and execution, under the President's direction, of American foreign policy. The first governmental body in America to deal with foreign affairs was the Committee of Secret Correspondence—a committee of five instituted (1775) by the Continental Congress and headed by Benjamin Franklin. In 1777 it was redesignated the Committee of Foreign Affairs, but this body after a time became so ineffective that it ceased to have jurisdiction. This committee was superseded in 1781 by the Dept. of Foreign Affairs, which, operating under the Articles of Confederation, also became ineffective. After the new government was organized under the Constitution of the United States, an act was passed (July, 1789) creating a new Dept. of Foreign Affairs. The organization of this department proved wholly inadequate, and in Sept., 1789, the Dept. of State was established with added functions. Besides being charged with foreign negotiations and correspondence, the department was given sundry duties such as keeping the Great Seal of the United States and receiving the bills and resolutions of Congress. The Dept. of State is the oldest of the Federal departments, and thus the Secretary of State, at the head of the department, is the first ranking cabinet officer. Thomas Jefferson, the first Secretary of State (1790–93), quickly brought prestige to the department, which was soon given added responsibilities—supervision of the U.S. Mint, the issuing of patents and to some extent copyrights, and the printing of the U.S. census. The responsibilities of the mint were transferred (1795) to the U.S. Treasury Dept., and other miscellaneous functions were taken away in the middle of the 19th cent. After 1849 many of the domestic responsibilities of the Dept. of State were transferred to the U.S. Dept. of the Interior. The affairs of the territories were supervised by the department until 1873, when they were given to the Dept. of the Interior. In the field of foreign affairs, the department did not expand much in the 18th cent. but thereafter grew in ever-widening circles. Under the direction of Secretary John Quincy Adams (1817–25) the organization of the department was clarified and improved, but the first major reorganization was effected by Secretary Louis McLane (1833–34) and Secretary John Forsyth (1834–41). Later, salaries were generally increased, more personnel added to meet the growing needs, and the position of First Assistant Secretary of State was created (1853). Three additional assistant secretaryships were later created in the department, and in 1919 the office of Under Secretary of State was established. In 1855, Congress passed a law formulating grades, posts, and salaries in both the diplomatic and the consular service attached to the department, and 50 years later diplomatic and consular positions, except for the posts of ambassador and minister, were put on a civil service basis. Largely through the efforts of Hamilton FISH (1808–93), who headed the department from 1869 to 1877, a sweeping reorganization of the Dept. of State was effected in 1870. To meet the demands of an economy-minded Congress, Fish made 31 officials the nucleus of the department and divided its activities among nine bureaus and two agencies. The First Diplomatic Bureau was set up to supervise correspondence with European and Far Eastern countries, and the Second Diplomatic Bureau was given jurisdiction over American diplomacy in Latin America, the Middle East, and Africa. The consular activities were similarly organized in 1870. Very few changes occurred in the department's organization in the later years of the 19th cent., but when the United States became a world power after the end of the Spanish-American War, there was a distinct need to adjust the department's facilities. Several important steps were taken during the secretaryships of John Hay (1898–1905) and Elihu Root (1905–9), but it was not until 1909, in the administration of Philander C. Knox, that the department was reorganized with the essentials of its present-day structure. Several new posts, notably those of counselor and resident diplomatic officer, were set up, the duties assigned to the Assistant Secretaries of State were altered, and foreign policy and relations were reorganized along new geographical divisions—Western European, Middle Eastern, Far Eastern, and Latin American. Before and during World War I, several new responsibilities were assumed during the tenures of William Jennings Bryan (1913–15) and Robert Lansing (1915–20). The Rogers Act of 1924 abolished the separate diplomatic and consular bureaus in favor of the Division of Foreign Service Information, and under the administrations of Frank B. Kellogg (1925–29) and Henry L. Stimson (1929–33) other new agencies were created. In 1931 the office of the solicitor—given charge through the years of such matters as extradition, naturalization, expatriation, passport problems, neutrality, and extraterritoriality—were superseded by the office of legal adviser. During the long administration (1933–44) of Cordell Hull a variety of changes was effected, at first to meet the needs of recovery from economic depression, but later to face the rising tide of World War II. In 1938 the Division of Cultural Relations—soon to undergo several changes—was begun to stimulate cooperation with other nations through the various media of mass communication; the same year the Division of International Communication was started to meet problems concerned with worldwide telecommunications. Two reorganizations within the Dept. of State occurred in 1943 and 1944, and with the close of the war the department's machinery was geared to dispense information to foreign nations (e.g., the radio program "The Voice of America"), to establish strict secrecy concerning its operations, to integrate foreign policy with the economic-aid programs, and to bring about effective liaison between the United States and the United Nations. In 1949 the Hoover Commission (Commission on Organization of the Executive Branch of the Government) criticized the fact that the Dept. of State and the Foreign Service were manned by a distinct and non-interchangeable corps of employees and urged amalgamation of the personnel of the two bodies. Opposition to this, especially from the Foreign Service, which considered itself an elite corps, was partly resolved in 1954, when a committee headed by Henry M. Wriston, president of Brown Univ., recommended integration rather than amalgamation of the personnel. The Foreign Service was greatly enlarged, and as a result it lost its semiautonomous position and was brought securely under the authority of the Secretary of State. In 1961 the AGENCY FOR INTERNATIONAL DEVELOPMENT and the PEACE CORPS were created as agencies within the Dept. of State. The Peace Corps was later removed from the department when it was merged (1971) with other volunteer service agencies. Today the Secretary of State, aided by an Under Secretary, an Under Secretary for Political Affairs, and 12 Assistant Secretaries, is charged not only with determining foreign policy and executing the manifold functions of the Dept. of State but also with supervising and coordinating the activities of more than 100 embassies, numerous consulates, and special missions. The function of determining foreign policy assigned to the Secretary of State, is, of course, limited by the role that the President takes in foreign affairs. In terms of policy formulation the Dept. suffered a decline in the 20th cent., especially after the administration of Franklin Delano Roosevelt, who was often said to be "his own Secretary of State." John Foster Dulles (1953–59) and Henry M. Kissinger (1973–) were, however, particularly strong secretaries. See James L. McCamy, *The Administration of American Foreign Affairs* (1950); D. K. Price, ed., *The Secretary of State* (1960, repr. 1970); Alexander De Conde, *The American Secretary of State: an Interpretation* (1962); Smith Simpson, *Anatomy of the State Department* (1967); J. P. Leacacos, *Fires in the In-Basket* (1968).

State College, borough (1970 pop. 33,778), Centre co., central Pa.; settled 1859, inc. 1896. State College is mostly residential; nearby is the Pennsylvania State Univ.

state flowers. Each state of the United States has designated, usually by legislative action, one flower as its floral emblem. No flower has been chosen as emblematic of the United States. The floral emblem of the District of Columbia is the American Beauty rose; the state flowers are: Alabama, camellia; Alaska, forget-me-not; Arizonia, saguaro cactus blossom; Arkansas, apple blossom; California, golden poppy; Colorado, mountain columbine; Connecticut, mountain laurel; Delaware, peach blossom; Florida, orange blossom; Georgia, Cherokee rose; Hawaii, red hibiscus; Idaho, syringa; Illinois, violet; Indiana, peony; Iowa, wild rose; Kansas, sunflower; Kentucky, goldenrod; Louisiana, magnolia; Maine, pine cone and tassel; Maryland, black-eyed Susan; Massachusetts, Mayflower; Michigan, apple blossom; Minnesota, lady-slipper; Mississippi, magnolia; Missouri, hawthorn; Montana, bitterroot; Nebraska, goldenrod; Nevada, sagebrush; New Hampshire, purple lilac; New Jersey, violet; New Mexico, yucca; New York, rose; North Carolina, dogwood; North Dakota, prairie rose; Ohio, red carnation; Oklahoma, mistletoe; Oregon, Oregon grape; Pennsylvania, mountain laurel; Rhode Island, violet; South Carolina, yellow jasmine; South Dakota, pasqueflower; Tennessee, iris; Texas, bluebonnet; Utah, sego lily; Vermont, red clover; Virginia, dogwood; Washington, coast rhododendron; West Virginia, rhododendron; Wisconsin, violet; Wyoming, Indian paintbrush.

Staten Island (1970 pop. 295,443), c.60 sq mi (160 sq km), SE N.Y., in New York Bay, SW of Manhattan, forming Richmond co. of New York state and Staten Island borough of New York City. It is separated from New Jersey by Kill Van Kull and Arthur Kill, which are crossed by bridges. Ferries connect the island with Manhattan, and the Verrazano-Narrows Bridge links it with Brooklyn. The hills of NE Staten Island rise to 410 ft (125 m) at Todt Hill, the highest point along the Atlantic coast S of Maine. Since the completion of the Verrazano-Narrows Bridge (1964), Staten Island has had an influx of new residents and industries and has lost much of its semirural character. The industrial area of Staten Island is located in the north, where docks line the northern and eastern shores. The availability of open space has made the island the site of large container-handling facilities. Centers of trade include St. George (the borough hall) and Port Richmond. Beaches and parks, including part of Gateway National Recreation Area, are found along the southeastern coast. The island was visited by Henry Hudson in 1609 and was called Staaten Eylandet by the Dutch. Hostile Indians drove off the first white settlers, but by 1661 a permanent settlement had been founded. Among the extant buildings of the 17th, 18th, and 19th cent. is the Billopp, or Conference, House (built before 1688), in which an unsuccessful Revolutionary War peace conference was held in 1776. The Richmondtown Restoration, an example of 18th and 19th cent. life on the island, includes Voorlezer's House (built c.1695). Other points of interest include several old churches, Sailor's Snug Harbor, the Garibaldi Memorial, Fort Wadsworth, and the Staten Island Zoo. Wagner College, Richmond College and Staten Island Community College (both part of the City Univ. of New York), and a branch of St. John's Univ. are on Staten Island.

Statesboro, city (1970 pop. 14,616), seat of Bulloch co., E Ga.; founded 1803, inc. 1902. It has a large tobacco market, an iron foundry, and textile, meatpacking, and lumbering industries. Georgia Southern College is there.

States-General or **Estates-General,** diet or national assembly in which the chief estates (see ESTATE) of the nation—usually clergy, nobles, and towns (or commons)—were represented as separate bodies. The name survives in the Netherlands, where the two houses of parliament are known as States-General; however, only the name has been preserved there, for the lower house represents the entire nation by direct election, and the upper house represents the provincial estates, which are also elected democratically. Like the English PARLIAMENT, the States-General of France and other European assemblies had their origin in the king's council, or curia regis. The CORTES of the Spanish kingdoms, the DIET of the Holy Roman Empire, and the diets of Bohemia, Hungary, Poland, and the Scandinavian countries all originated as royal councils and all represented, in varying degrees, the principal estates of the realm. They are generally said to have grown out of the earlier Germanic assemblies. Whatever their origin, they developed along entirely different lines in the various countries, and by the 16th cent. there was little or no resemblance between the English Parliament, the States-General of France, and the States-General of the United Provinces of the Netherlands.

The States-General of France. The French States-General owes its fame less to its importance than to the mode of its creation and the manner of its demise. The first French assembly known by that name was summoned in 1302 at Paris, by King PHILIP IV, in order to obtain national approval for his anticlerical policy. Philip may be said to have created the body only in the sense that he assembled a larger and more regular council than had before been assembled. From 1302 to 1797 its constitution retained the same division into the first, second, and third estates, i.e., the clergy, nobles, and commons. Its powers, never clearly defined, tended to vary inversely with those of the royal authority. The States-General of 1302 and 1308 dutifully approved, respectively, Philip's measures against Pope BONIFACE VIII and those against the KNIGHTS TEMPLARS; that of 1314 granted the king subsidies, but the grant was more or less nominal, with the king dictating his orders. The French States-General never obtained the financial control that made the English Parliament a powerful institution. It did not always meet as a single body, but often convened separately as the States-General of Langue d'Oïl (N France) and the States-General of Langue d'Oc (S France). The more important of these, the States-General of Langue d'Oïl made a strong bid for power in 1355–57, during the captivity of King John II in England. Under the leadership of Étienne MARCEL it forced the dauphin (later King Charles V) to promulgate the *Grande Ordonnance*, which would have greatly expanded its financial and administrative powers and made it the virtual legislature of France. The dauphin, however, revoked his concessions almost as soon as he had made them and called a rival assembly at Compiègne. Although later States-General often opposed the king and even won temporary concessions, the continuous consolidation of the royal power prevented the emergence of a truly parliamentary body. The States-General regained some importance in the chaotic period of the Wars of Religion (16th cent.). However, the opposing factions used it merely as an instrument for their own aims. The States-General of Paris of 1614 accomplished nothing, and the estates were not convoked again until 1789. Under the guidance of the chief ministers of state, Cardinals Richelieu and Mazarin, and under the firm hand of King Louis XIV, royal absolutism reached its apex in the 17th cent. The only serious check to the royal power was the Parlement of Paris (see PARLEMENT), which was a judicial rather than a representative body. Provincial estates, however, continued to function in the so-called *pays d'états*, i.e., the provinces of Brittany, Flanders, Artois, Lorraine, Alsace, Burgundy, Franche-Comté, Dauphiné, Provence, Languedoc, Béarn and Navarre, and several others. The major part of France, however, was more directly subject to the central administration. When in 1788 the Assembly of Notables (a meeting of the chief nobles, clerics, and magistrates) failed to solve the financial crisis of the French government, King Louis XVI ordered elections for the States-General as his last resort. Although no official pronouncement indicated that the assembly was to act as a truly deliberative body, its convocation was thus interpreted by the third estate and by the liberals among the nobility and clergy, who hoped to introduce English parliamentary government into France. At the same time, the government ordered the compilation of lists of grievances in the various provinces; these were to serve as a basis for discussing the necessary reforms. The preparation of the lists contributed to the impression that a general reform was impending and that the States-General was to act as a national assembly representing the sovereign will of the people. On May 5, 1789, the States-General assembled at Versailles. Almost immediately the crucial issue of voting procedure came under debate. If the three estates adhered to tradition and voted as separate bodies, the third estate was bound to be continually outvoted. If voting was by head, the third estate (whose deputies equaled in number those of the combined clergy and nobility) was bound to win on most points, for many clerics and nobles sympathized with its aspirations. In June, 1789, the third estate, joined by a number of deputies from the clergy, forced the issue and declared itself the National Assembly. With this act of defiance the FRENCH REVOLUTION may be said to have begun; and with Louis XVI's recognition of the fait accompli, the States-General ceased to exist. See Georges M. Picot, *Histoire des États Generaux* (5 vol., 2d ed. 1888, repr. 1969).

states of matter, forms of MATTER differing in several properties because of differences in the motions and forces of the molecules (or atoms or ions) of which they are composed. The states of matter are also known as phases of matter or states of aggregation. There are three commonly recognized states of matter: SOLID, LIQUID, and GAS. The molecules of a solid are limited to vibration about a fixed position. This restriction gives a solid both a definite volume and a definite shape. As energy in the form of HEAT is added to a solid, its molecules begin to vibrate more rapidly until they break out of their fixed positions and the solid becomes a liquid. The change from solid to liquid is called melting and occurs at a definite temperature, the MELTING POINT. The molecules of a liquid are free to move throughout the liquid but are held from escaping from the liquid by intermolecular forces (see ADHESION AND COHESION). This gives a liquid a definite volume but no definite shape. As more heat is added to the liquid, some molecules gain enough energy to break away completely from the liquid and escape into the surrounding space (see EVAPORATION). Finally a temperature is reached at which molecules throughout the liquid are becoming energetic enough to escape and bubbles of vapor form and rise to the surface. The change of the liquid to a vapor, or gas, in this manner is called boiling and occurs at the BOILING POINT. The molecules of a gas are free to move in every possible way; a gas has neither a definite shape nor a definite volume but expands to fill any container in which it is placed. In addition to these three states of matter, scientists also distinguish a fourth state—PLASMA. A plasma is formed by adding still more heat to the molecules of a gas. Eventually a point is reached where the molecules are moving so rapidly that the molecules become torn apart into their component atoms and individual electrons are pulled away from the atoms. This very hot mixture of negatively charged electrons and positively charged ions has properties distinct from those of the other states of matter.

States of the Church: see PAPAL STATES.

states' rights, in U.S. history, doctrine based on the Tenth Amendment to the Constitution, which states, "The powers not delegated to the United States by the Constitution, nor prohibited by it to the States, are reserved to the States respectively, or to the people." Immediately after the adoption of the Constitution, controversy arose as to how to interpret the enumerated powers granted the Federal government. Alexander HAMILTON and the FEDERALIST PARTY favored a broad interpretation, which meant a strong central government deriving its authority from implied as well as express powers contained in the Constitution. Thomas Jefferson and his followers, "strict constructionists," insisted that all powers not specifically granted the Federal government be reserved to the states. The KENTUCKY AND VIRGINIA RESOLUTIONS, written by Jefferson and James Madison, represent the first formulation of the doctrine of states' rights. The second important manifestation of states' rights occurred in New England among the Federalists in opposition, curiously enough, to Jefferson. His party, while in power, brought about (1803) the Louisiana Purchase, passed the Embargo Act of 1807 and other nonintercourse measures, and later declared war against Great Britain. All of these actions met with resistance in New England, and the War of 1812 finally led to the calling of the HARTFORD CONVENTION of 1814–15 in which New Englanders officially expressed their hostility to the Federal government. The fight over the constitutionality of the Bank of the United States made the central states—Pennsylvania, Maryland, and Ohio in particular—the next defenders of states' rights. The points at issue here were settled in MCCULLOCH VS. MARYLAND by decision of the U.S. Supreme Court, dominated by John MARSHALL, whose broad interpretation of the Constitution laid the foundations of strong central government. The doctrine was revived in the conflict between the Federal government and Georgia as to which had jurisdiction over Indian tribes within Georgia's boundaries, and Georgia for a time defied the Federal administration. Even more acute was the situation that developed in South Carolina in opposition to the tariff acts of 1828 and 1832, when, under the leadership of John C. CALHOUN, South Carolina passed its ordinance of NULLIFICATION. Calhoun's doctrine of absolute state sovereignty was the most extreme of states' rights theories. Although proslavery forces were usually identified with a strong states' rights position, the legislature of Wisconsin adopted (1859) resolutions defending state sovereignty after the Supreme Court overruled the Wisconsin courts and upheld the conviction of an abolitionist editor for violating the fugitive slave law. Ultimately the proslavery states used states' rights doctrines to justify their SECESSION. Eleven Southern states seceded in 1860–61 and formed the CONFEDERACY, in which, fittingly, the doctrine of states' rights was upheld by such governors as Joseph E. BROWN and Zebulon B. VANCE. This undoubtedly contributed to the Confederate defeat in the Civil War, just as the disposition of some of the Thirteen Colonies to act in complete independence of the Continental Congress had hampered the American Revolution. Although the Union victory in the Civil War definitively ended the possibility of nullification and secession, the states' rights doctrine did not die. In the second half of the 20th cent. it was vigorously revived by Southern opponents of the Federal civil rights program. In the presidential election of 1948, a Southern states' rights party (the Dixiecrats) was organized with J. Strom THURMOND of South Carolina as its candidate, and it carried four Southern states. The desegregation controversy of the 1950s, 60s, and 70s engendered many states' rights statements by Southern political leaders such as Gov. George C. WALLACE of Alabama. In 1962, Federal troops were used at the Univ. of Mississippi to enforce a Federal court ruling that ordered the admission of a Negro student to the university. Although the doctrine of states' rights is usually associated with the Southern wing of the Democratic party, it is not exclusive to any particular section or political party. The vast increase in the powers of the Federal government at the expense of the states, resulting from the incapacity of the states to deal with the complex problems of modern industrial civilization, has led to renewed interest in states' rights. See C. E. Merriam, *A History of American Political Theories* (1903, repr. 1968); Charles Warren, *The Supreme Court and Sovereign States* (1924); F. L. Owsley, *State Rights in the Confederacy* (1925, repr. 1961); E. S. Corwin, *Commerce Power Versus States' Rights* (1936, rev. ed. 1962); A. T. Mason, *The States Rights Debate* (2d ed. 1972).

Statesville, city (1970 pop. 19,996), seat of Iredell co., W central N.C., on a plateau in the Blue Ridge foothills; founded 1789, inc. 1847. It is a commercial and industrial center with several furniture factories. Textiles and related products are among the other manufactures. A junior college is there, and nearby is the site of Fort Dobbs (1755).

static, electrical NOISE in radio reception, especially noise that originates outside of a transmitter and receiver, e.g., in the atmosphere or in man-made devices. In general, a frequency MODULATION (FM) radio receiver is less susceptible to such noise than one using amplitude modulation (AM). Many receivers are equipped with devices, such as automatic limiting and silencing circuits, to lessen the effect of such noise on reception.

statics, branch of MECHANICS concerned with the maintenance of equilibrium in bodies by the interaction of forces upon them (see FORCE). It incorporates the study of the center of gravity (see CENTER OF MASS) and the MOMENT of inertia. In a state of equilibrium all the forces acting on a body are exactly counterbalanced by equal and opposite forces, thus keeping the body at rest. The principles of statics are widely applied in the design and construction of buildings and machinery.

statistics, science of collecting and classifying a group of facts according to their relative number and determining certain values that represent characteristics of the group. The most familiar statistical measure is the arithmetic MEAN, which is an average value for a group of numerical observations. A second important statistic or statistical measure is the standard deviation, which is a measure of how much the individual observations are scattered about the mean. The chi-square test is a method of determining the odds for or against a given deviation from expected statistical distribution. Other statistics indicate other characteristics of the group of observations. In addition to the problem of computing certain statistics for a particular group of observations, there is the problem of sampling. This is an attempt to determine for what larger group (called the population) of individuals or characteristics the statistics for this particular group (called the sample) would be a representative figure and how representative a figure it would be for a given larger group. This second problem of sampling can be solved only by resorting to the theory of PROBABILITY and higher mathematics. In most applications of statistics to scientific and social research, insurance, and finance, the statistician is interested not only in the characteristics of the sample but also in those of some much larger population. Consequently, the theory of sampling is the most important part of statistical theory. See William Mendenhall and R. L. Schaeffer, *Mathematical Statistics with Applications* (1972).

Statius, Publius Papinius (pŭb'lēəs pəpĭn'ēəs stā'shəs), A.D. c.40–A.D. c.96, Latin poet, b. Naples. A favorite of Emperor Domitian, he won the poetry prize at an annual festival under Domitian's auspices but later was an unsuccessful competitor at the Capitoline contest in Rome. His surviving works are two epics in the manner of Vergil—the *Thebaid,* on the SEVEN AGAINST THEBES, and the *Achilleid* (incomplete), on the early life of Achilles—and the *Silvae,* a collection of hasty but pleasing poems. Statius was much esteemed in his own time and through the Middle Ages.

stator: see GENERATOR; MOTOR, ELECTRIC.

Statue of Liberty National Monument: see LIBERTY, STATUE OF.

statute, in law, a formal, written enactment by the authorized powers of a state. The term is usually not applied to a written CONSTITUTION but is restricted to the enactments of a legislature. Statute law is to be distinguished chiefly from COMMON LAW, which may be defined as the body of legal rules derived from judicial decisions and custom. On most of the European continent all (or nearly all) the law is statutory and each field is subsumed by a CODE. In England and the United States, however, common law retains great importance, but with the expansion of government regulation there has been an immense growth in the statute law of those countries. In order to guide the courts many important statutes contain (usually in a preamble) a statement of the abuses that the legislation is intended to cure or of the general legislative intent. Great care must be taken in drafting statutes, since the usual (but not invariable) practice of the courts is to interpret the provisions in an extremely literal sense. Statutes are classified in various ways. Public statutes (e.g., those establishing crimes) are universal in application, while private statutes (e.g., one compensating a named person for injury) are limited. Public statutes may be local, i.e., affecting only part of the area over which the legislature has authority, or general. Statutes that explain or clarify previous enactments or rules of common law are sometimes called declaratory statutes.

Statute of Frauds: see FRAUDS, STATUTE OF.

Staubbach, waterfall: see LAUTERBRUNNEN, Switzerland.

Staunton (stăn'tən), city (1970 pop. 24,504), seat of Augusta co., W central Va., in the Shenandoah Valley; settled 1732, inc. as a city 1871. It is a trade and industrial center in a rich farm area known especially for its poultry, livestock, and apples. Other products include clothing, furniture, safety razors, and soft drinks. The city manager form of government originated in Staunton in 1908. In the city are Woodrow Wilson's birthplace, dedicated as a national shrine in 1941; Staunton Military Academy; Mary Baldwin College; a state hospital; a state school for the deaf and blind; a national cemetery; and many old houses.

Stavanger (stävăng'ər), city (1970 pop. 81,847), capital of Rogaland co., SW Norway, a port on the Stavangerfjord (an arm of the Boknfjord). It is an important commercial and industrial center where ships are built and fish processed. Founded in the 8th cent., Stavanger was an episcopal see from c.1125 to 1682. In World War II the city was occupied by the Germans on April 9, 1940. Of interest is the well-preserved stone Cathedral of St. Swithin (12th cent.). The city also has a museum with notable ethnological, ornithological, and archeological collections. The 12th-century Utstein monastery is nearby.

Stavelot (stävlō'), Flemish *Stablo,* town (1970 pop. 4,723), Liège prov., E Belgium, in the Ardennes. It developed around a Benedictine abbey founded c.650. The abbots were later princes of the Holy Roman Empire until their land was secularized in the French Revolutionary Wars. Until 1815 the principality included the Malmédy region, which then passed to Prussia, while Stavelot passed to the Netherlands and later to Belgium. In World War II, the Germans captured Stavelot early (Dec., 1944) in the BATTLE OF THE BULGE and massacred a number of U.S. prisoners of war held nearby.

Stavisky Affair (stävēskē'), financial and political scandal that shook France in 1934. Serge Alexandre Stavisky, a swindler associated with the municipal pawnshop of Bayonne, sold huge quantities of worthless bonds. Despite a shady past he had connections with many persons in responsible positions. Faced with exposure in Dec., 1933, he fled but was discovered by the police at Chamonix (Jan., 1934); he either committed suicide or was murdered by the police. Extremists, particularly of the right, accused the Radical Socialist government of Camille CHAUTEMPS of corrupt deals with Stavisky and forced its resignation. The rightists further alleged that Stavisky had been murdered to protect influential persons connected with him. Édouard DALADIER, the new premier, used force to repress bloody riots staged (Feb. 6–7, 1934) in Paris by extremists (chiefly royalists), but he too had to resign. He was replaced by Gaston Doumergue and a national unity cabinet. After a long trial (1935–36) of 20 defendants, none of them politically important, 11 of the accused, including Stavisky's widow, were acquitted. Some of the politicians so wildly accused of corruption—notably Chautemps—were later cleared. The affair had the unfortunate effect of discrediting not only the Radical Socialist party but also parliamentary democracy in general. See Alexander Werth, *France in Ferment* (1935, repr. 1968).

stavkirke (stäf'kēr"kə) [Nor.], medieval wooden church building of Scandinavian countries. Of hundreds erected in the 11th, 12th, and 13th cent., only a score survive, and these are all in Norway. Their architecture is unique; upturned dragon heads terminate gables; elaborate wood carvings illustrate saga myths as well as biblical stories; pagodalike shingled roofs, small surrounding cloisters, and leper windows (small openings through a chancel arch or wall) are other features. Architectural inspiration was probably drawn from the pagan temples that were being demolished at the time the *stavkirker* were being erected. Examples are Hitterdal in Telemark, Fantoft near Bergen, and Borgund near Sogne Fjord.

Stavropol (stä'vrəpəl), city (1970 pop. 198,00), capital of Stavropol Kray, S European USSR, on the Stavropol Plateau. It has machine-tool, wool, leather, and food-processing industries. There are natural gas fields in the area. Founded in 1777 as a Russian fortress, it was an important base for the subsequent Russian conquest of the Caucasus.

Stavropol Kray or **Stavropol Territory,** administrative division (1970 pop. 2,306,000), 31,120 sq mi (80,601 sq km), S European USSR, in the North Caucasus, the northern foothills of the main Caucasian range, and the dry steppes to the northeast. The central part of the territory occupies the Stavropol Plateau, a hilly region (rising to c.2,730 ft/830 m) drained by the Kuma and Kuban rivers. In the north is the Manych Depression. There are oil and natural gas deposits. The once drought-ridden territory has been irrigated since 1945. Winter wheat, corn, sunflowers, and cotton are grown; along the Kuma River grapes, other fruits, and vegetables are also cultivated. Sheep raising is an important occupation. The Pyatigorsk region has numerous mineral spas and is a major resort area. The chief towns are Stavropol, the capital; Pyatigorsk; Kislovodsk; and Cherkessk. The Karachay-Cherkess Autonomous Oblast is in the territory. The population is for the most part Russian and Ukrainian; minority groups are Circassians, Karachay, and Nogay Tatar herdsmen. The territory was first organized in 1924, when it was called North Caucasus Territory. It was renamed Ordzhonikidze Territory in 1937 and was given its present name in 1943.

Stead, Christina, 1902–, British novelist, b. Sydney, Australia. She worked in the United States in the 1940s and subsequently emigrated to England. Her novels are written in unsentimental prose and treat the problem of evil, particularly the destruction wrought by human obsessions. In addition to *The Man Who Loved Children* (1940), her masterpiece, her novels include *Seven Poor Men of Sydney* (1934), *For Love Alone* (1944), and *The Puzzleheaded Girl: 4 Novellas* (1967).

Stead, William Thomas (stĕd), 1849–1912, English journalist. From 1883 to 1889 he edited the *Pall Mall Gazette* and in 1890 founded the *Review of Reviews*, establishing similar publications in the United States (1891) and Australia (1892). He pioneered in modern journalistic methods in England, was an advocate of reform in the British navy, and championed child welfare and social legislation. In later years he was deeply interested in psychical research. He lost his life on the *Titanic*. Among his numerous works are *If Christ Came to Chicago* (1893), *The Americanization of the World* (1902), and *Peers or People* (1907). See biography by Frederick Whyte (1925).

steady-state theory: see COSMOLOGY.

steamboat: see STEAMSHIP.

steam engine, machine for converting heat energy into mechanical energy using steam as a medium, or working fluid. When water is converted into steam it expands, its volume increasing about 1,600 times. The force produced by the conversion is the basis of all steam engines. Steam engines operate by having superheated steam force a piston to reciprocate, or move back and forth, in a cylinder. The piston is attached by a connecting rod to a crankshaft that converts the back and forth motion of the piston to rotary motion for driving machinery. A flywheel attached to the crankshaft makes the rotary motion smooth and steady. The typical steam engine has an inlet valve at each end of the cylinder. Steam is admitted through one inlet valve, forcing the piston to move to the other end of the cylinder. This steam then exits through an exhaust valve. Steam from the other inlet valve then pushes the piston back to its original position, and the cycle starts again. In a single-cylinder steam engine the exhaust steam is usually expelled directly into the atmosphere. A compounded steam engine has several cylinders, which the steam passes through successively until, leaving the last cylinder, it is condensed into water and returned to the boiler. From the Greek inventor Heron of Alexandria to the Englishmen Thomas Newcomen and John Cawley, many persons contributed to the work of harnessing steam. However, James Watt's steam engine, patented in 1769, provided the first practical solution. Earlier engines depended on atmospheric pressure to push the piston into the cylinder, where a vacuum was created by sudden cooling of its steam content. Watt's use of a separate condenser resulted in a 75% saving in fuel. It also made possible the use of steam pressure to move the piston in both directions. Watt's continuing efforts produced a governor, a mercury steam gauge, and a crank-flywheel mechanism, all of which prepared the steam engine for a major role in the Industrial Revolution. Sailing vessels gave way to steamboats, and stagecoaches yielded to railroad trains as the steam engine was perfected. Transmitted by belts, ropes, shafts, pulleys, and gears, the energy from steam engines drove machines in factories and mills. Now, however, steam engines have been replaced in most applications by more economical and efficient devices, e.g., the steam TURBINE, the electric motor, the internal-combustion engine, and the diesel engine. They are still sufficiently economical to be used in industries where steam is necessary for some purpose in addition to that of driving an engine. See C. W. Pursell, *Early Stationary Steam Engines in America* (1969); Eric Robinson, *James Watt and the Steam Revolution* (1969); see also bibliography under LOCOMOTIVE.

steamship, watercraft propelled by a steam engine or a steam turbine. Marquis Claude de Jouffroy d'Abbans is generally credited with the first experimentally successful application of steam power to navigation; in 1783 his *Pyroscaphe* ran against the current of the Saone River for 15 min, although the boiler could not generate enough steam for extended operations. In 1787 a steamboat built by James Rumsey of Maryland was demonstrated on the Potomac River; propelled by a stream of water forced out of the stern by steam pressure, the vessel attained a speed of 4 mi (6.4 km) per hr. Rumsey received a grant to navigate the waters of New York, Maryland, and Virginia. In 1790, John Fitch, who had previously built several successful steamboats, one of which operated in 1787, built a vessel capable of 8 mi (12.9 km) per hr. It plied between Philadelphia and Burlington. Other early American steamboat inventors were Samuel Morey, Nathan Read, and John Stevens. In 1807, Robert Fulton launched the *Clermont*, 150 ft (46 m) long, 13 ft (4 m) wide, and 9 ft (2.7 m) in depth. She ran from New York City to Albany (150 mi/241 km) in 32 hr and made the return trip in 30 hr. On the other side of the Atlantic, Henry Bell launched (1812) the *Comet;* its trips around Scotland gave impetus to commercial steam navigation in the area. The first ocean crossing by a steam-propelled vessel was in 1819, when the *Savannah* voyaged from Savannah, Ga., to Liverpool in 29 days, 11 hr. She was a full-rigged sailing ship fitted with engines and side paddlewheels; during the crossing the engines were in use for about 85 hr. The first crossing under steam power alone was made in 1838, when two British steamship companies sent rival ships to New York within a few days of each other; the *Great Western* made the trip in 15 days, arriving a few hours after the *Sirius*, which had left England 4 days before her. The first seagoing vessel to be fitted with a screw propeller was the *Archimedes* (1840); the *Great Britain* (1845) was the first large iron steamship driven by a screw propeller to cross the Atlantic. By the late 1850s the screw propeller was conceded to be superior to paddlewheels, and the steamship began to supplant the sailing ship. In 1881 the *Servia*, a merchant steamer capable of crossing the Atlantic in 7 days, was the first vessel to be constructed of steel. Seven years later the *Philadelphia*, the first twin-screw steamship, was built at Glasgow. Great liners propelled by engines of 28,000 or more horsepower were soon plying the Atlantic on regular schedules. Sir Charles A. Parsons and C. G. P. de Laval developed the steam turbine during the 1880s. The *Turbinia*, the first vessel to be driven by a turbine, was first seen in 1897, and within 10 years several turbine-driven liners were in the Atlantic service. After that the steam turbine virtually eliminated the older reciprocating steam engine on major vessels; modern leviathans of the sea such as the *Queen Mary* (launched 1934), the *Queen* Elizabeth (1938), and the *United States* (1951) were turbine-powered steamships, as are most of the larger present-day passenger vessels, most of the larger cargo ships, and many warships. The diesel engine, developed in the first decade of the 20th cent., provides certain advantages over steam propulsion but has not yet replaced it; steam-turbine installations are thought to require less maintenance work and to be generally more reliable. A recent development in turbine-steam power has been the introduction of turbo-electric drive, a power plant in which electrical machinery converts steam energy into rotational power for turning the propeller shafts. The world's first nuclear-powered steamship, the *Savannah* (launched 1958) proved to be safe but not commercially feasible; it was laid up (1972) by the U.S. government. See P. J. Cowan, *A Short History of Naval and Marine Engineering* (1938); J. T. Flexner, *Steamboats Come True* (1944); Lamont Buchanan, *Ships of Steam* (1956); J. H. Morrison, *History of American Steam Navigation* (1958); K. T. Rowland, *Steam at Sea* (1970).

stearin (stēr'ĭn), fat that is the TRIGLYCERIDE of stearic acid, $CH_3(CH_2)_{16}CO_2H$, i.e., the tristearate ester of glycerol. It is a white crystalline solid at ordinary temperatures and is insoluble in water and very slightly soluble in alcohol. It is found (often mixed with PALMITIN) in many hard fats and oils, e.g., in tallow, suet, butterfat, cottonseed oil, and olive oil. It is used in making soap and candles.

steatite: see SOAPSTONE.

Stedman, Edmund Clarence, 1833–1908, American banker, poet, and critic, b. Hartford, Conn., attended Yale. A successful Wall St. broker, he was

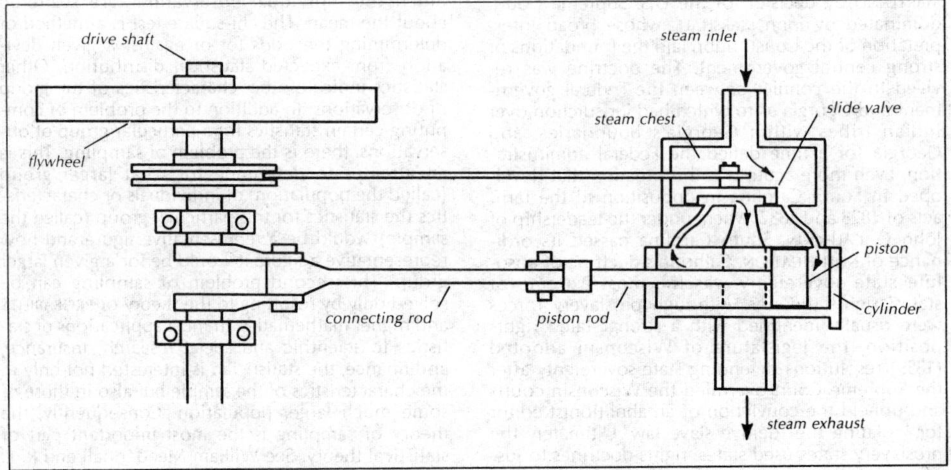

Steam engine

also one of the leading poets of his time although his somewhat derivative poetry, similar to Tennyson's in style, is little read today. As critic he wrote his most significant works, *Victorian Poets* (1876) and *The Poets of America* (1885); he compiled the excellent collections *A Victorian Anthology* (1895) and *An American Anthology* (1900). See his *Poems* (1908); biography by Laura Stedman and G. M. Gould (1910).

steel, alloy of iron, carbon, and small proportions of other elements. Iron contains impurities in the form of silicon, phosphorus, sulfur, and manganese; steelmaking involves the removal of these impurities, known as slag, and the addition of desirable alloying elements. Steel was first made by cementation, a process of heating bars of iron with charcoal in a closed furnace for a long period so that the surface of the iron acquired a high carbon content. The iron bars were then fused together, yielding a metal harder and stronger than either of the pieces of iron but lacking uniformity in these qualities. The crucible method, originally developed to remove the slag from cementation steel, consists in melting iron and other substances together in a fire-clay and graphite crucible. The purity of the final product depends on the raw materials used. One of the costlier steelmaking processes, the crucible method is employed only for making special steels. The famous blades of Damascus and of Toledo, Spain, were made by the cementation and crucible techniques. The BESSEMER PROCESS, the open-hearth process, and the BASIC OXYGEN PROCESS are more widely used in steelmaking. The open-hearth uses a type of furnace called a regenerative furnace; instead of a firebox at one end and a flue at the other, it has devices at each end for the intake and outflow of both fuel and air. The air is preheated by a system of current reversals that causes very high temperatures. This process, developed c.1866 by Sir William Siemens, uses iron ore and pig iron. In a variation of the process developed by Siemens with Pierre Martin, scrap steel replaces the ore and accomplishes the refinement. The difficulty of procuring ore free from sulfur and phosphorus, as required by the Siemens open-hearth method, resulted in greater use of the Siemens-Martin process. In the Linz-Donawitz process, or basic oxygen process, developed in the 1950s, the design of the furnace is changed, and oxygen added to the air intake permits more rapid refining of the charge (material in the furnace). The electric furnace is another modern development; it provides a means of making large quantities of high-grade steel, with the advantages of positive temperature control, freedom from contamination of the product by the fuel, and simultaneous deoxidation and desulfurization actions. Steel is shaped for commercial use in rolling mills, where successive passages of the red-hot ingot between variously shaped rollers give it the desired form. Pittsburgh, one of the world's great steel centers, built its first rolling mill in 1811; Bessemer steel rails were rolled in Chicago as early as 1865. Steel is often classified by its carbon content: A high-carbon steel is serviceable for dies and cutting tools because of its great hardness and brittleness; low- or medium-carbon steel is used for sheeting and structural forms because of its susceptibility to welding and tooling. Alloy steels, now most widely used, contain one or more other elements to give them special qualities. Aluminum steel is smooth and has a high tensile strength. Chromium steel finds wide use in automobile and airplane parts on account of its hardness, strength, and elasticity, as does the chromium-vanadium variety. Nickel steel is the most widely used of the alloys; it is nonmagnetic and has the tensile properties of high-carbon steel without the brittleness. Nickel-chromium steel possesses a shock resistant quality that makes it suitable for armor plate. Wolfram (tungsten), molybdenum, and high-manganese steel are other alloys. Stainless steel, which was developed in England, has a high tensile strength and resists abrasion and corrosion because of its high chromium content. See R. M. Brick, *Structure and Properties of Alloys* (1965); Kenneth Warren, *The American Steel Industry, 1850–1970* (1973).

Steele, Joel Dorman, 1836–86, American educator and textbook writer, b. Lima, N.Y., grad. Genesee College (now Syracuse Univ.), 1858. While serving as principal of the Elmira (N.Y.) Free Academy (1866–72), he wrote (1867) *Fourteen Weeks in Chemistry,* the first of a series of science texts that did much to popularize the subject. In collaboration with his wife, Esther Baker Steele, he also wrote a number of unusually successful history texts, including *Barnes' Brief History of the United States* (1871). See biography by A. C. Palmer (1900).

Steele, Sir Richard, 1672–1729, English essayist and playwright, b. Dublin. After studying at Charterhouse and Oxford, he entered the army in 1694 and rose to the rank of captain by 1700. His first book, a moral tract entitled *The Christian Hero,* appeared in 1701. The same year saw a production of his first play, *The Funeral,* a sentimental comedy, which he followed with two more comedies, *The Lying Lover* (1703) and *The Tender Husband* (1705). In 1722 he produced his last and most important play, *The Conscious Lovers.* A year after the death of his first wife in 1706, he married Mary Scurlock, the "dear Prue" of his famous letters. Steele, however, was not made for a domestic life, and much of his time was spent carousing with his companions. He held several minor government positions before beginning his famous periodical, the *Tatler* (1709–11), the writing of which was soon joined by his close friend Joseph ADDISON. This was followed by the SPECTATOR (1711–12), the *Guardian* (1713), and later periodicals of lesser importance. The partnership of Steele and Addison was one of the most successful in the history of English letters. Although they differed greatly in temperament, their aims and tastes were in the main united. They were Whig partisans, and sympathetic with the moral attitude of the rapidly growing middle class. Although Steele's prose lacks the polished grace of Addison's, his writing reflects his charm, spontaneity, wit, and imagination. In 1713, Steele carried on a celebrated political controversy with Swift, the chief Tory spokesman, in the course of which he wrote his pamphlet *The Crisis.* He became a Whig member of Parliament in 1713, was expelled by his political enemies the following year, but returned under the Hanoverians, and was knighted in 1715. His opposition to the Peerage Bill in his weekly, the *Plebeian* (1719), involved him in a quarrel with Addison, and Steele's attempt at reconciliation was frustrated by his friend's death. He founded the first theatrical paper, the *Theater,* in 1720. His improvidence and free-living finally caught up with him, and debts forced his retirement to Wales in 1724, where he spent his remaining years in obscurity. See his plays edited by G. A. Aitken (1894, repr. 1968); *The Spectator,* complete ed. by D. F. Bond (1966); his correspondence (1941, repr. 1971); biographies by G. A. Aitkin (1889, repr. 1968) and C. Winton (2 vol., 1964 and 1970).

Steele, Wilbur Daniel, 1886–1970, American author, b. Greensboro, N.C., grad. Univ. of Denver, 1907. He studied art in Boston, Paris, and New York City. He was particularly noted for his short stories, which are set in American locations and are often highly dramatic. Collections of his stories include *The Man Who Saw through Heaven* (1927), *Best Stories* (1946), and *Full Cargo* (1951). He also wrote novels, including *Taboo* (1925), *That Girl from Memphis* (1945), and *Their Town* (1952).

Steele, Mount, 16,644 ft (5,073 m) high, in the St. Elias Mts., SW Yukon Territory, Canada, in Kluane National Park near the Alaska line; one of Canada's tallest peaks.

steel engraving: see ENGRAVING.

steel wool, abrasive material composed of long steel fibers of varying degrees of fineness that are matted together. The coarser grades are used to remove paint and other finishes, the finer grades for polishing or smoothing a finished surface. Steel wool is much used in kitchens for cleaning and polishing metals, especially aluminum utensils.

steelyard: see BALANCE.

Steelyard, Merchants of the, German hanse, or merchants guild, residing at the Steelyard on the Thames near the present Ironbridge Wharf at London, England. The merchants of the HANSEATIC LEAGUE in London were licensed (1157) by King Henry II. These merchants, of the hanse of Cologne, were free from all London tolls and customs and could trade at fairs throughout England. The merchants of Lübeck and Hamburg, chartered in 1266 by King Henry III, coalesced with the Cologne association in 1282 to become the most powerful Hanseatic colony in London, with houses at many other English ports. Despite the privileges acquired from the English crown, the powerful German merchants refused to grant reciprocal trading rights to English merchants. In 1474, despite English hostility against alien traders, King Edward IV reconfirmed their privileges in payment for the German merchants' support during the Wars of the Roses in England; they also received property rights to the Steelyard. The Steelyard, also known as German House, was a walled community with its own warehouses, weighhouse, church, offices, and residential quarters; German merchants had occupied it since 1320. English merchants, organized after 1370, exerted great pressure on the monarchs to revoke Hanseatic privileges. In 1597, Queen Elizabeth I issued an edict expelling the German merchants from England, and in 1598 the Steelyard was closed.

Steen, Jan (yän stān), 1626–79, Dutch genre painter, b. Leiden. He studied in Utrecht and in Haarlem under Van Ostade and Van Goyen, whose daughter he married. His huge production of paintings, numbering nearly 900, reveal the influence of most of the major Dutch masters except Rembrandt, but retain a distinct and individual style. His painting offers a composite picture of the social life of his day, often tending toward the humorous or moralistic. His favorite themes were scenes of revelry and feasting. He was a superb draftsman and portraitist, and despite his love of the incidental, he handled his large groups of figures effectively and spontaneously. Among his many notable works are *The Feast of St. Nicolas* and *The Prince's Birthday* (Rijks Mus.); *The Menagerie* and *The Painter's Family* (The Hague); and *Skittle Players* (National Gall., London). The Metropolitan and Brooklyn museums and the Art Institute of Chicago have examples of his work.

Steenkerque (stānkĕrk'), Flemish *Steenkerke,* village, Hainaut prov., S Belgium, near Mons. There, in 1692, the French under Marshal François Henri de Luxembourg defeated William III of England in the War of the Grand Alliance.

steeplebush: see SPIRAEA.

Steep Rock Lake, 4 mi (6.4 km) long and 3 mi (4.8 km) wide, SW Ont., Canada, W of Lac des Mille Lacs. It is the site of important iron ore mining. Part of the lake was drained to facilitate the mining, and the flow of the Seine River was diverted.

Steer, Philip Wilson, 1860–1942, English landscape painter. Steer worked largely in the tradition of French impressionist painting and was considered the greatest English landscape painter of his day. He brought to his subjects a considerable understanding of pattern, color, space, and especially light effects. Examples of his work are *Chepstow Castle, Music Room* (Tate Gall., London) and a self-portrait (Uffizi). The Tate Gallery owns many of his works.

steering system, in automobiles, steering wheel, gears, linkages, and other components used to control the direction of a vehicle's motion. Because of friction between the front tires and the road, especially in parking, effort is required to turn the steering wheel. To lessen the effort required, the wheel is connected through a system of gears to components that position the front tires. The gears give the driver a mechanical advantage, i.e., they multiply the force he applies, but they also increase the distance through which he must turn the wheel in order to turn the tires a given amount. Various types of gear assemblies, none with any decisive advantages over the others, are used, although some manufacturers prefer a rack-and-pinion system. In faster, heavier cars the amount of force required to turn the tires can be very great. Many of these cars use a power steering system. The system contains a hydraulic booster, which operates when the engine is running and supplies most of the necessary force when the driver turns the wheel. When a vehicle turns at a rate exactly proportional to the rate at which the steering wheel is turned, it is said to have neutral steering; if it turns at a slower rate it is said to understeer; if it turns faster it is said to oversteer. While any vehicle can react in any of these ways under extreme conditions, most automobiles are built to understeer. Racing vehicles are often designed for neutral steering; few vehicles are built to oversteer, since this is considered hazardous by many authorities. As a safety feature in many modern cars the column on which the steering wheel is mounted will collapse if the driver is thrown against the wheel in a collision.

Stefan, Josef (yō'zĕf shtĕf'än), 1835–93, Austrian physicist. At the Univ. of Vienna he became a professor of physics and later director of the Physical Institute. From his observations on the relationship between radiant heat emitted by a body and its temperature, Stefan concluded that the total radiation of a body was proportional to the fourth power of its absolute temperature. One of his students, Austrian physicist Ludwig Boltzmann, later derived the same relationship from a thermodynamic viewpoint. This principle, called the Stefan-Boltzmann law, played an important part in considerations leading to Max Planck's quantum theory.

Stefansson, Vilhjalmur (vĭl'hyoulmər stĕf'ənsən), 1879–1962, Arctic explorer, b. Canada, of Icelandic parents, educated at the Univ. of North Dakota, the State Univ. of Iowa, and Harvard. He led several expeditions of exploration and of ethnological and archaeological investigation in the arctic regions. For supplies he relied heavily on local resources, and he adopted the Eskimo way of living, thus successfully demonstrating his theory that the rigors of existence in the Arctic are much reduced by the use of such techniques. He made two expeditions (1906-7, 1908-12) to the delta of the Mackenzie River. Later he undertook (1913-18) the most prolonged polar exploration in history by remaining N of the Arctic Circle for an unbroken period of more than five years while exploring the Canadian and Alaskan sectors of the arctic regions. In 1952, Stefansson Island, at the tip of Victoria Island, was named for him. He was the curator of the Stefansson Collection at Dartmouth College, to which he gave his library of polar material. His many books include *My Life with the Eskimo* (1913), *The Friendly Arctic* (1915, new enl. ed. 1943), *Iceland* (1939), *Greenland* (1942), and *Northwest to Fortune* (1958). He edited *Great Adventures and Explorations* (1947).

Steffen, Albert (äl'bĕrt shtĕf'ən), 1884-1963, Swiss novelist, poet, and playwright, who wrote in German. His works are colored with Christian symbolism and are specifically concerned with the martyrdom and redemption of Christ. To Steffen the solution to social ills lay in the emulation by all men of Christ's life. The mystical novel *Sucher nach sich selbst* [seeker after himself] (1931) expresses his religious outlook. With the death of Rudolf STEINER in 1905, Steffen became the leader of Steiner's mystical anthroposophy movement. His works in English translation include *Death Experience of Manes* (tr. 1970) and *Hiram and Solomon* (tr. 1971).

Steffens, Lincoln (Joseph Lincoln Steffens), 1866-1936, American editor and author, b. San Francisco, grad. Univ. of California, 1889, and studied three years in Europe. Steffens became one of the leading MUCKRAKERS, and while he held (1902-11) successive editorial positions on *McClure's*, the *American*, and *Everybody's* magazines he wrote sensational articles exposing municipal corruption; they were later collected in *The Shame of the Cities* (1904), *The Struggle for Self-Government* (1906), *Upbuilders* (1909), and other volumes. His autobiography (1931) contains not only personal reminiscences but also valuable information on the leftist movements of his era. See his *Lincoln Steffens Speaking* (1936) and his letters (ed. by Ella Winters and Granville Hicks, 2 vol., 1938); biography by Justin Kaplan (1974).

Stegosaurus (stĕgəsôr'əs) [Gr.,=roof lizard], quadruped vegetarian DINOSAUR of the Jurassic period. About 20 ft (6 m) long and weighing about 10 tons, it had short forelegs, two rows of upright bony plates on the back, and 4 long bony spikes on the tail. The brain weighed about 2½ oz (71 grams). Complete skeletons were found in the Jurassic beds of Colorado and Wyoming. The *Stegosaurus* is classified in the phylum CHORDATA, subphylum Vertebrata, class Reptilia, order Ornithischia.

Steichen, Edward (stī'kən), 1879-1973, American photographer, b. Luxembourg, reared in Hancock, Mich. Steichen is credited with the transformation of photography into an art form. At 16, while apprenticed as a lithographer, he taught himself photography and painted in his spare time. Studying art in Paris, he sought painterly effects in his photography, becoming an enormously successful portrait photographer. In New York City he was associated with Alfred STIEGLITZ in the founding of the "291" and Photo-Secession galleries. At "291" he brought works by Cézanne, Rodin, Picasso, and Matisse to American attention. Back in Paris, Steichen made botanical experiments, a lifelong passion; he was later to win added renown as a crossbreeder of flowers. During World War I Steichen was instrumental in the development of aerial photography. Fascinated by the technical potential of the medium, he produced pictures remarkable for their clarity, detail, and expressive use of light. From 1923 to 1938 he worked as a portrait and fashion photographer for the Condé Nast publications and opened a commercial studio. At this time he made superb photomurals, including those of the George Washington Bridge. During World War II, Steichen was placed in command of naval combat photography. He was director of the department of photography of the Museum of Modern Art (1947-62). In this capacity he organized the *Family of Man* exhibition (1955) to "mirror the essential oneness of mankind"; it is considered the greatest photographic exposition ever mounted. During his time at the museum, Steichen had virtually abandoned his own work; but in his last years he filmed the effect of the passing seasons on a flowering shadblow tree. Steichen's creative imagination and his extraordinarily powerful imagery forged for him and for his medium an honored place among the fine arts. See his *Life in Photography* (1963); Carl Sandburg (his brother-in-law) et al., *Steichen the Photographer* (1961).

Stein, Clarence, 1882-, American architect, b. New York City. Stein is noted for his design for Temple Emmanuel and other religious buildings in New York City. He was also a pioneer in the development of tract housing. Stein's conservative style is marked by emphasis on walls and the minimal use of ornamentation. Among his suburban projects are Greenbelt, Md., a planned town which provided middle-income families with efficient units; Hillside Homes in the Bronx, New York City (1960s); and Harbor Hill project in Los Angeles co., Calif. Stein is the author of *Toward New Towns for America* (1951).

Stein, Gertrude, 1874-1946, American author and patron of the arts, b. Allegheny (now part of Pittsburgh, Pa.). A celebrated personality, she encouraged, aided, and influenced--through her patronage as well as through her writing—many literary and artistic figures. After attending (1893-97) Radcliffe, where she was a student of William JAMES, she began premedical work at Johns Hopkins. In 1902, relinquishing her studies, she went abroad and from 1903 until her death lived chiefly in Paris. For many years her secretary and constant companion was Alice B. Toklas. In Paris, Stein became interested in modern art movements; she encouraged and purchased the work of many new painters, including Picasso and Matisse. During the 1920s she was the leader of a cultural salon, which included such writers as Hemingway, Sherwood Anderson, and F. Scott Fitzgerald, all of whose works she influenced. It was she who first coined the phrase "lost generation" for those post-World War I expatriates. During World War II she remained in France, and after the war her Paris home became a meeting place for American soldiers. Stein's own innovative writing emphasizes the sounds and rhythms rather than the sense of words. By departing from conventional meaning, grammar, and syntax, she attempted to capture "moments of consciousness," independent of time and memory. Her first published and perhaps best-known work is *Three Lives* (1909), short stories in which she explored the mental processes of three women. But her most characteristic and probably most difficult narrative is *The Making of Americans* (1925). The famous *Autobiography of Alice B. Toklas* (1933) is her own autobiographical work presented as that of her secretary-companion. Stein's critical essays were published as *Composition as Explanation* (1926), *How to Write* (1931), *Narration* (1935), and *Lectures in America* (1935). Her many other works include the volume of poetry *Tender Buttons* (1914), a series of "cubist" verbal portraits; *Four Saints in Three Acts* (1934), an opera with music by Virgil Thomson; *Wars I Have Seen* (1945), some personal observations; and *Brewsie and Willie* (1946), about American soldiers in France. See studies by J. M. Brinnin (1959), Allegra Stewart (1967), Richard Bridgman (1970), Donald Sutherland (1951, repr. 1972), and James B. Mellow (1974).

Stein, Karl, Freiherr vom und zum (kärl frī'hĕr fəm ŏŏnt tsŏŏm shtīn), 1757-1831, Prussian statesman and reformer. Rising through the Prussian bureaucracy, he became minister of commerce (1804-7) but was dismissed by King Frederick William III for his attempts to increase the power of the heads of the ministries. He was recalled (1807) as chief minister after Prussia's defeat by the French only to be dismissed again (1808) on pressure by NAPOLEON I. An exile in Russia, Stein helped to bring about the Russo-Prussian alliance of 1813 and returned to prominence as chief administrator of the reconquered and newly conquered Prussian provinces, following the Wars of Liberation against Napoleon. His hopes for a united Germany were disappointed at the Congress of Vienna, and his role after 1815, when Prussia turned to reaction, was not prominent. Few men have achieved as many radical and successful reforms in so peaceful a manner and in such difficult circumstances as did Baron Stein. His chief reforms were carried out in 1807-8, when Prussia was a defeated nation and a virtual dependency of France. They were continued by K. A. von HARDENBERG after Stein's exile, and they were forwarded by such men as Gerhard von SCHARNHORST in the military field and Wilhelm von HUMBOLDT in the educational system. Before Stein's reforms Prussia was still a semifeudal state. Stein caused the king to abolish serfdom and the estate system by the Edict of 1807. The law ended the restrictions against the sale to burghers of land owned by nobles; those restrictions had had disastrous effects on Prussian economy, for the nobles lacked the capital to till their land properly. The edict also opened all trades and professions to all classes. Stein instituted local self-government in towns, cities, and provinces. His administration transformed Prussia into a modern state and enabled it to play its leading role in the eventual unification of Germany. Stein was also responsible for the publication, beginning in 1826, of the *Monumenta Germaniae Historica,* which became the model for editions of national historical documents. See biography by Sir John R. Seeley (3 vol., 1878, repr. 1968); G. S. Ford, *Stein and the Era of Reform in Prussia* (1922, repr. 1965); R. C. Raack, *The Fall of Stein* (1965).

Stein, Lorenz von (lō'rĕnts fən shtīn), 1815-90, German economist and sociologist. He studied jurisprudence at the Univ. of Kiel and at Paris and taught (1846-51) at the Univ. of Kiel, but his advocacy of independence for his native Schleswig caused his dismissal. From 1855 until his death he taught at the Univ. of Vienna. He influenced the practice of public finance but is perhaps best known for his sociological ideas, set forth in the third edition of his history of the social movement in France (3 vol., 1850, tr. 1964). He outlined an economic interpretation of history that included concepts of the proletariat and of class struggle. Despite a similarity of these ideas with those of Marxism, the extent of Stein's influence on Karl Marx is uncertain.

Steinamanger: see SZOMBATHELY, Hungary.

Steinbeck, John, 1902-68, American writer, b. Salinas, Calif., studied at Stanford. He is probably best remembered for his strong sociological novel *The Grapes of Wrath,* considered one of the great American novels of the 20th cent. Steinbeck's early novels—*Cup of Gold* (1929), *The Pastures of Heaven* (1932), and *To a God Unknown* (1933)—attracted little critical attention, but *Tortilla Flat* (1935), an affectionate yet realistic novel about the lovable, exotic, Spanish-speaking poor of Monterey, was enthusiastically received. A compassionate understanding of the world's disinherited was to be Steinbeck's hallmark. The novel *In Dubious Battle* (1936) defends striking migrant agricultural workers in the California fields. In the novella *Of Mice and Men* (1937; later made into a play), Steinbeck again presents migrant workers, but this time in terms of human worth and integrity—a theme he also used in *The Moon Is Down* (1942; later made into a play), about Norwegian resistance to the Nazis. *The Grapes of Wrath* (1939; Pulitzer Prize), while treating the plight of dispossessed Dust Bowl farmers during the 1930s, presents a universal picture of victims of disaster. Steinbeck's depiction of the westward migration of the Joad family, and their subsequent struggles in the exploitative agricultural industry of California, is realistic and moving, and he endows his humble characters with nobility. Steinbeck's other works are diverse, ranging from the literal account of a voyage, *The Sea of Cortez* (1941; written with the marine biologist E. F. Ricketts); to a parable, *The Pearl* (1948); to a playful French folk piece, *The Short Reign of Pippin IV* (1957). Love of his native land shines through the exquisitely nostalgic story "The Red Pony" in *The Long Valley* (1938). The somewhat sentimental attitude of *Tortilla Flat* appears again in *Cannery Row* (1945), *The Wayward Bus* (1947), and *Sweet Thursday* (1954). More ambitious are the novels *East of Eden* (1952), a family chronicle with the Cain and Abel theme, and *Winter of Our Discontent* (1961), about a suburbanite's moral conflict. Steinbeck also wrote notable nonfiction, particularly *The Log from the Sea of Cortez* (1951) and *A Russian Journal* (1948), and the screenplays for the motion pictures *The Forgotten Village* (1941) and *Viva Zapata!* (1952). *Travels with Charley in Search of America* appeared in 1962 and *America and Americans* in 1966. Steinbeck was awarded the 1962 Nobel Prize in Literature. See biography by Joseph Fontenrose (1963); studies by Peter Lisca (1958), Joseph Fontenrose, ed. (1967), H. T. Moore (2d ed. 1968), and R. M. Davis, ed. (1972).

steinbok: see ANTELOPE.

Steinem, Gloria (stīn'əm), 1936-, American journalist and feminist, b. Toledo, Ohio, grad. Smith, 1956. Steinem gained prominence as an articulate spokeswoman for women's rights both in lectures and in television appearances. In 1971 she helped found the National Women's Political Caucus and the Women's Active Alliance. She is also a founder and editor of *Ms.*, a magazine for women.

Steiner, Jakob (yä'kôp shtī'nər), 1796-1863, Swiss mathematician. He was largely self-taught and was professor of geometry at the Univ. of Berlin from 1834. A pioneer in the development of synthetic, or pure, geometry (i.e., deduced by axiomatic methods, as Euclid's geometry), particularly projective geometry, he was considered by many the greatest geometer since Apollonius of Perga and exerted an important influence on his students, who included Bernhard Riemann.

Steiner, Rudolf (rōō'dôlf shtīn'ər), 1861–1925, German occultist and social philosopher. He was a leader in the founding of the German Theosophic Association (see THEOSOPHY). In time he abandoned theosophy and developed a distinctive philosophy which he called anthroposophy; this philosophy attempts to explain the world in terms of man's spiritual nature, or thinking independent of the senses. Translations of his works include *Investigations in Occultism* (1920) and *Philosophy of Spiritual Activity* (1922). He also wrote many works on Goethe. See his autobiography (rev. tr. 1951, repr. 1970).

Steinitz, Wilhelm (vĭl'hĕlm shtī'nĭts), 1836–1900, German chess player. In 1886 he won a match from Adolph Anderssen, the leading player after Paul Morphy's retirement, and became world champion, although the title did not officially exist. Until 1892, when he lost to Harry Nelson Pillsbury, he defeated all the leading players. In 1894 he lost the world championship to Emanuel Lasker. The closed position, characterized by fixed pawns on both sides and the establishment of lasting positional values, was Steinitz's forte. He edited (1885–91) the *International Chess Magazine* in New York City and wrote *The Modern Chess Instructor* (2 vol., 1889–95). See study by R. G. Thimann (1968).

Steinmetz, Charles Proteus (stīn'mĕts), 1865–1923, American electrical engineer, b. Breslau, Germany, studied at the Univ. of Breslau. Forced to flee Germany because of his socialist activities, he came to the United States in 1889. Rudolf Eickemeyer, who had just begun to build electrical apparatus in his factory in Yonkers, N.Y., gave him his start in electrical engineering research. When the General Electric Company bought out Eickemeyer in 1892, Steinmetz joined the new owners. He discovered the law of hysteresis, which made it possible to reduce the loss of efficiency in electrical apparatus resulting from alternating magnetism; developed a practical method of making calculations of alternating current, thus revolutionizing electrical engineering; and did valuable research on transient electrical phenomena (lightning). He built a generator that produced artificial lightning. Professor (1902–23) at Union College, Schenectady, N.Y., Steinmetz wrote many scientific papers and a number of standard texts. He remained a socialist and was president of the Schenectady board of education (1912–23) and of the common council (1916–23). See biographies by J. W. Hammond (1924) and J. N. Leonard (1929).

Stelazine (stĕl'əzēn"), drug used to treat mental disorders. See PHENOTHIAZINE.

stele (stē'lē), slab of stone or terra-cotta, usually oblong, set up in a vertical position, for votive or memorial purposes. Upon the slabs were carved inscriptions accompanied by ornamental designs or reliefs of particular significance. Stelae were often used as commemorative stones in ancient Egypt and as boundary markers in Mesopotamia. The marble funerary stelae of Greece, especially of Athens, are among the most beautiful monuments of classical art. Likenesses of the dead were sculptured in relief and painted upon them. Stelae of great age are found in China and among the ruins of the Mayan culture in Mexico and Central America.

Stella, Frank, 1936–, American painter, b. Malden, Mass. Stella exhibits in his works the precision and rationality that characterize the New York school of the 1960s (see MODERN ART). He uses concentric angular stripes to emphasize the shape of his large canvases. His innovative use of irregularly shaped canvas first appeared in his metallic series in 1960. Later examples of his work stress color in decorative curved motifs. The Whitney Museum, New York City, has several of his paintings. See study by William Rubin (1970).

Stella, Joseph, 1877–1946, American painter, b. Italy, emigrated to the United States in 1896. He studied at the Art Students League of New York City with William Chase and later in Italy and Paris. He is best known for his cubist- and futurist-inspired paintings executed in the years around 1920. These works strikingly expressed the vibrancy and dynamism of life in New York City. The best known of this group is "The Bridge," from the series *New York Interpreted* (Newark Mus., N.J.). He later turned to more mystical subjects, in paintings notable for their strong color and incisive realism. See biography by I. B. Jaffe (1970).

stellar evolution, life history of a STAR, beginning with its condensation out of the interstellar gas (see INTERSTELLAR MATTER) and ending, sometimes catastrophically, when the star has exhausted its nuclear fuel or can no longer adjust itself to a stable configuration. Because a star's total energy reserve is finite, a star shining today cannot continue to produce its present luminosity steadily into the indefinite future, nor can it have done so from the indefinite past. Thus, stellar evolution is a necessary consequence of the physical theory of STELLAR STRUCTURE, which requires that the luminosity, temperature, and size of a star must change as its chemical composition changes because of thermonuclear reactions. Because the computed lifetimes of stars range from millions to billions of years, one cannot follow an individual star through its life history observationally, or even observe significant changes in the whole span of human history, except from the violent events of nova and SUPERNOVA explosions. However, new stars are continually being formed and hence stars of all ages exist at the present epoch; examples of the various stages of stellar evolution can be found in different stars. The age of a star is not a directly observable characteristic but must be inferred from the very evolutionary theory one is trying to validate. Confidence in this circular reasoning results from its self-consistency and its ability to draw together into a unified COSMOLOGY a wide variety of observational data on individual stars, clusters of stars, and galaxies. The initial phase of stellar evolution is contraction of the protostar from the interstellar gas, which consists of mostly hydrogen, some helium, and traces of heavier elements. In this stage, which typically lasts millions of years, half the gravitational potential energy released by the collapsing protostar is radiated away and half goes into increasing the temperature of the forming star. Eventually the temperature becomes high enough for thermonuclear reactions to begin; in these reactions, loosely called "hydrogen burning," four hydrogen nuclei are fused to form a helium nucleus (see NUCLEOSYNTHESIS). This point in time is conventionally called age zero. The star then settles into a long "middle age" during which it shines steadily as it converts its hydrogen supply into helium. For stars of a given chemical composition, the mass alone determines the luminosity, surface temperature, and size of the star. The luminosity increases very sharply with an increase in the mass; doubling the mass (which is proportional to the energy supply) increases the luminosity (which is proportional to the rate of using energy) more than 10 times. Hence the more massive and luminous a star is, the faster it depletes its hydrogen and the faster it evolves. Because the middle age of a star is the longest period in stellar evolution, one would expect most of the observed stars to be at this stage and to show a strong correlation of luminosity with color (color is a measure of stellar temperature). This prediction is confirmed by plotting stars on a HERTZSPRUNG-RUSSELL DIAGRAM, in which the majority of stars fall along a diagonal line called the main sequence. The main sequence is most heavily populated at the low luminosity end; these are the stars that evolve most slowly and so remain longest on the main sequence. As a star's hydrogen is converted into helium, its chemical composition becomes inhomogeneous: helium-rich in the core, where the nuclear reactions occur, and more nearly pure hydrogen in the surrounding envelope. The hydrogen near the center of the core is consumed first. As this is depleted, the site of the nuclear reactions moves out from the center of the core and fusion occurs in successive concentric shells. Finally fusion occurs only in a thin, outer shell of the core, the only place where both the hydrogen content and the temperature are high enough to sustain the reactions. As its helium content builds up, the core contracts and releases gravitational energy, which heats up the core and actually increases the rates of the nuclear reactions. Thus the rate of hydrogen consumption rises as the hydrogen is used up. To accommodate the higher luminosity resulting from the increased reaction rates, the envelope must expand to allow an increased flow of energy to the surface of the star. As the outer regions of the star expand, they cool. The star now consists of a dense, helium-rich core surrounded by a huge, tenuous envelope of relatively cool gas; the star has become a RED GIANT. Eventually, the contracting stellar core will reach temperatures in excess of 100 million degrees Kelvin. At this point, helium burning sets in. With the ignition of that process, the expansion of the envelope is halted and then reversed; the star retreats from the red giant phase, shrinking in size and luminosity, and reapproaches the main sequence. The exact course of evolution is uncertain, but as the star recrosses the main sequence, it will probably become unstable. The star may eject some of its mass or become an exploding nova or supernova star; at the very least, it will become a pulsating variable star, possibly a CEPHEID VARIABLE. In the later stages of evolution, further contraction and elevation of temperature open up new thermonuclear reactions. It is believed that all the heavier elements in the universe were synthesized in the interiors of stars by a variety of intricate nuclear reactions, many involving neutron absorption. As a result of the nuclear reactions, the chemical composition of the late-stage star becomes highly inhomogeneous; its structure is fractionated into a number of concentric shells consisting of different elements around an

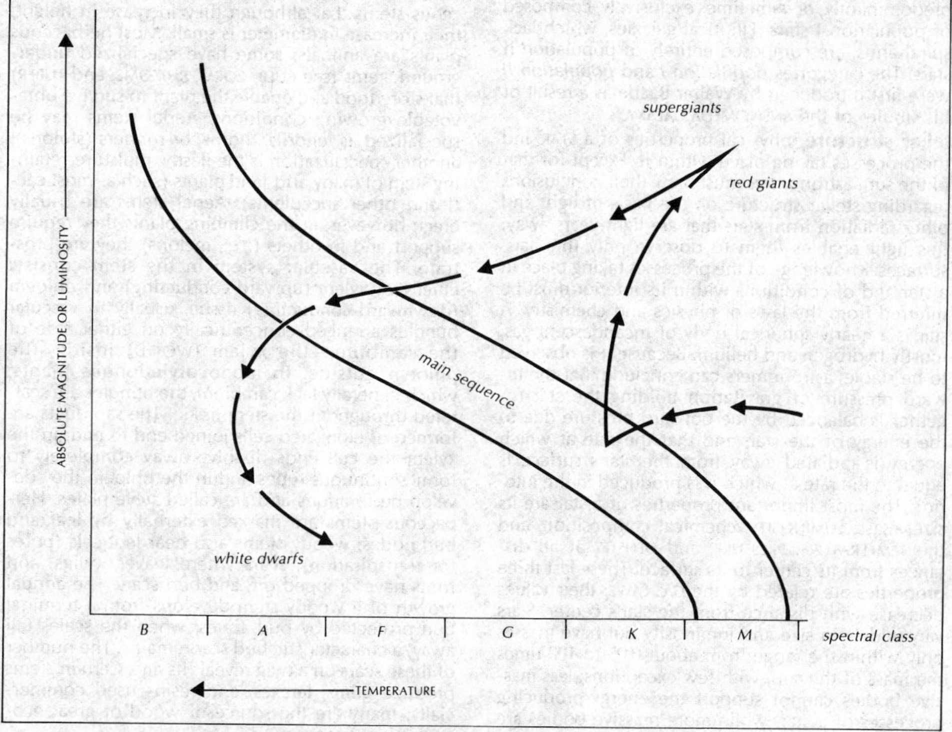

The above Hertzsprung-Russell (H-R) diagram shows the track of stellar evolution for a typical star. After spending much of its life evolving toward or along the main sequence, the star becomes a red giant star and finally shrinks to the white dwarf stage before burning out.

iron core. The final outcome of stellar evolution depends critically on the remaining mass of the old star. If the mass is not very much greater than the sun's mass (the Chandrasekhar mass limit), the star will become a WHITE DWARF, glowing feebly for billions of years by gravitational contraction until it becomes a black dwarf, a totally dead star. If the star is too massive to become a stable white dwarf, contraction will continue until the temperature reaches about five billion degrees Kelvin. At this temperature the iron nuclei in the core begin to absorb electrons; this creates neutron-rich ISOTOPES and simultaneously deprives the core of its pressure. With further collapse and increase in density, the core becomes a special kind of rigid solid. At still higher density, the solid "evaporates" as the nuclei break up into free neutrons. The resulting neutron fluid forms the core of a new astrophysical body, called a NEUTRON STAR. The "winking stars" known as PULSARS are now believed to be rotating neutron stars. If the stellar mass is too great to be stable even as a neutron star, complete GRAVITATIONAL COLLAPSE will ensue.

stellar populations, two broadly contrasting distributions of star types that are characteristic of different parts of a GALAXY. Population I stars are young, recently formed stars, whereas population II stars are old and highly evolved. Population II stars are formed early in the history of the galaxy from pure hydrogen with a possible admixture of primordial helium. Because massive blue-white giants burn their nuclear fuel quickly and therefore have lifetimes of only a few million years, no stars of this type are found in population II. The most luminous population II stars are red giants. Population I stars, of which the sun is typical, are young stars that still lie mostly on the main sequence of the HERTZSPRUNG-RUSSELL DIAGRAM. The most luminous population I stars are blue giants. Because they are second-generation stars formed from the debris of exploded population II stars, population I stars have a considerable content of heavy elements that were created by NUCLEOSYNTHESIS in the interiors of the earlier stars. Population I and population II stars are both found in the spiral galaxies. Population I stars are located in the disk singly and in galactic, or open, STAR CLUSTERS. They are particularly concentrated in the interstellar dust of the spiral arms, where new stars are continually being formed. The very brightest population I stars are not distributed at random, but are grouped in loose associations of several hundred stars that partake in the general galactic rotation and are believed to have a common origin. Population II stars are found both in the spiral arms and in the gas-free and dust-free regions of the spiral galaxies, i.e., the nucleus and the corona of high-velocity stars and globular clusters that surround the disk of the galaxy. Irregular galaxies are predominantly, or sometimes exclusively, composed of population I stars. Elliptical galaxies, which lack spiral arms, are composed entirely of population II stars. The categories *population I* and *population II* were first introduced by Walter Baade as a result of his studies of the ANDROMEDA GALAXY.

stellar structure, physical properties of a STAR and the processes taking place within it. Except for that of the sun, astronomers must draw their conclusions regarding stellar structure on the basis of light and other radiation from stars that are light-years away; this light enables them to observe only the stars' surfaces. Knowledge of the processes taking place in a star and of conditions within its interior must be inferred from the laws of physics and chemistry. A star is a nearly spherical body of incandescent gas, mostly hydrogen and helium. Because it is observed to be stable, astronomers can conclude that the inward pressure of gravitation holding the star together is balanced by the outward pressure due to the energy of the star, and that the rate at which energy is radiated away from the star's surface is equal to the rate at which it is produced in the interior. The most important properties of a star are its size, mass, LUMINOSITY, chemical composition, and the TEMPERATURE, PRESSURE, and DENSITY at all distances from its center to its surface. These last three properties are related by the GAS LAWS; their values decrease with distance from the star's center. Stars vary widely in size and luminosity but have masses only within the range from about 0.05 to 100 times the mass of the sun, with few exceptions; less massive bodies cannot support the energy-producing processes of a star, while more massive bodies are generally unstable. An ordinary star has surface temperatures of thousands of degrees, implying central temperatures of millions of degrees. The central pressure and density will also be extremely high, but the temperature is such that the material will still remain in the gaseous state. At these temperatures, energy is produced by thermonuclear fusion (see NUCLEAR ENERGY), in which two or more nuclei are fused to form a single heavier nucleus. As such fusion processes proceed within the star, its chemical composition necessarily changes, with heavier elements increasing at the expense of lighter elements (see NUCLEOSYNTHESIS). The mass and chemical composition of the star together determine all of its other properties, e.g., size, luminosity, and temperature. Astronomers can determine the temperature and chemical composition of the star's surface from analysis of the SPECTRUM of light from the star. Such a spectrum consists of a continuous BLACK-BODY spectrum produced by complex conditions within the star and superimposed on this a series of dark lines due to absorption of energy by the cooler stellar atmosphere. From such observations much is learned about the other properties and conditions within the star and thus about its stage of STELLAR EVOLUTION.

Stellenbosch (stĕl'anbo͝osh, -bŏs), city (1970 pop. 29,666), Cape Prov., SW South Africa, in the Eerste River valley. It is a wine-making and fruit-growing center. Other industries include sawmilling and the manufacture of bricks and tiles. Stellenbosch, founded in 1680 by Gov. Simon van der Stel, is the oldest European town in South Africa after Cape Town. The Univ. of Stellenbosch, a theological seminary, a technical college, and a teachers college are in the city. Stellenbosch Museum includes exhibits of Dutch and Boer artifacts.

Steller's sea cow: see SIRENIAN.

stellite, alloy consisting chiefly of cobalt, with chromium and tungsten. Stellite is used mainly for high-speed cutting tools because of its ability to retain its hardness and strength when hot. The alloy is highly resistant to corrosion and is suitable for instruments where the reflecting power of polished surfaces must be good. It is also used for machine parts and cutlery.

Stelvio Pass (stĕl'vyō), alt. 9,048 ft (2,758 m), in the central Alps, N Italy, near the Swiss and Austrian borders. It is crossed by the highest road in the Alps, connecting the Valtellina with the upper Adige River valley. The road, extending c.30 mi (50 km) from Bormio to Trafoi, was begun in 1820 by the Austrians.

stem, supporting structure of a plant, serving also to conduct and to store food materials. The stems of herbaceous and of woody plants differ: those of herbaceous plants are usually green and pliant and are covered by a thin epidermis instead of by the bark of woody plants. There is relatively more pith in herbaceous stems and the CAMBIUM, which increases the diameter of woody stems, is usually almost inactive; it is therefore characteristic of herbaceous stems that although they increase in height, their increase in diameter is small. Most herbaceous plants are annuals; some have specialized underground stems (see BULB, CORM, RHIZOME, and TUBER) that store food and enable the plant to survive unfavorable growing conditions. Aerial stems may be specialized as tendrils, thorns, or runners (stolons); another specialization is the fleshy, moisture-retaining stem of many arid-land plants (such as most cacti and other succulents). Aerial stems are usually erect; however, in the climbing plants they require support and in others (e.g., melons) they are prostrate. The vascular system in the stem consists chiefly of xylem (upward-conducting) and phloem (downward-conducting) tissue, usually in vascular bundles arranged concentrically on either side of the cambium—the xylem (WOOD) inside, the phloem outside. In monocotyledonous plants, which generally lack cambium, the bundles are scattered throughout the stem tissue. The sap ducts are formed of elongated cells joined end to end; in the xylem the cell ends dissolve away completely to form continuous tubes and in the phloem they develop perforations and are called sieve plates. Herbaceous stems are marked externally by leaf and bud nodes; woody stems also bear lenticels (pores for transpiration), scars where leaves, twigs, and fruits have dropped off, and bud scars. The annual growth of a woody stem develops from a terminal bud protected by bud scales; when the scales fall away, a characteristic bud scar remains. The number of these scars on a twig reveals its age. Certain stems produce gums, latexes, and resins used commercially; many are the source of wood of great economic importance.

Stenbock, Count Magnus (măng'nəs stān'bôk), 1665–1717, Swedish field marshal. One of the ablest lieutenants of Charles XII in the Northern War, he helped defeat (1700) Peter I of Russia at Narva and crushed (1710) a Danish expedition at Hälsingborg. Invading Holstein in 1713, he was outnumbered and was forced to surrender in the same year. He died in Danish captivity.

stencil, cutout device of oiled or shellacked tough and resistant paper, thin metal, or other material used in applying paint, dye, or ink to reproduce its design or lettering upon a surface. Designing an art stencil differs from ordinary drawing, since the design itself must be cut away, and ties must be arranged to hold the background together and to give definition to the pattern, somewhat in the manner of lines in mosaic or leaded glass. In a repeating border or design, registers are cut to coincide with some small detail or dot to enable the user to place the stencil accurately for each repetition. It is held securely upon the surface, while the stencil brush (with square-cut stiff bristles) is manipulated to work the medium over it (in a circular movement for fabrics) until every detail is evenly colored. The technique has been employed since ancient times for the decoration of walls and ceilings, pottery, furniture, textiles, leather, and small objects. It is also used in mimeographing, addressing, and lettering cases or cartons for shipping. The Chinese and Japanese employ a tough mulberry paper, making intricate stencils that are collected for their beauty. The silk-screen stencil, an innovation in SILK-SCREEN PRINTING, is used for posters, wallpapers and textiles. In handwork, silk fabric is stretched on a frame and then coated with glue or other impervious material; a stencil paste, rubbed on with a squeegee, passes through the uncoated portions. The method has been adapted by artists to make prints known as serigraphs. See C. Rubi, *Cut Paper, Silhouettes and Stencils: An Instruction Book* (1970).

Stendal (shtĕn'däl), city (1970 pop. 36,478), Magdeburg district, W East Germany, on the Uchte River. It is a major rail junction and has sugar refineries, metalworks, food canneries, and chemical factories. Stendal was founded in 1151 by Albert the Bear. From 1258 to 1309 it was the seat of the elder line of the Ascanian margraves of Brandenburg. The city joined the Hanseatic League c.1350. Among the numerous noteworthy structures of Stendal are the basilica (founded 1188), the city gates (13th–15th cent.), and the city hall (15th cent.). Johann Winckelmann, the archaeologist and historian, was born (1717) there, and Marie Henri Beyle (1783–1842), the French author, took his pen name (Stendhal) from the city.

Stendhal (stăNdäl'), pseud. of **Marie Henri Beyle** (mărē äNrē' bĕl), 1783–1842, French writer, recognized as one of the great French novelists. He grew up in Grenoble hating his father and the Jesuit, Royalist atmosphere in his home, and he went to Paris at his earliest opportunity. There influential relatives obtained a place for him at the ministry of war. In 1800 he became a dragoon in Napoleon's army, and the invasion of Italy took him to Milan. By 1802 he was back in Paris, where he pursued the amorous adventures that continued to interest him all his life. He read widely and kept notes and journals, which have been published. He again served with Napoleon's army in the disastrous Russian campaign (1812). After Napoleon's fall in 1814, Stendhal went to Milan, remaining there until 1820. There he began his literary career. In *Vie de Haydn, de Mozart, et de Métastase* (1814) and in *Rome, Naples, et Florence en 1817* (1817), he borrowed facts freely from other writers, but the point of view and wit were his own. His books were better known in England than in France, and from c.1817 he wrote for British journals. In this period, when he was suffering from his most genuine and most unhappy love affair, he wrote *De l'amour* (1822), a psychological analysis of love that predates Freud. Stendhal's first novel, *Armance* (1827), was scorned by the critics. In 1831 appeared the first of his two great novels, *Le Rouge et le Noir* (tr. *The Red and the Black*). The *Red* in the title symbolizes the army and liberalism, and the *Black* the reactionary clergy. It is, baldly, the story of a sensitive but calculating youth, Julien Sorel, who pursues his ambitions by seduction and is eventually guillotined for shooting his mistress. Its sympathetic and acute character analysis and its picture of the period make it one of the world's great novels. After the accession (1830) of Louis Philippe, Stendhal was appointed consul at Trieste, but because Metternich objected to his books and liberal ideas, he was shifted to Civitavecchia in 1831. He wrote constantly there, although he did not publish; among the works of that period are *Souvenirs d'égotisme* and *La Vie d'Henri Brulard,* both autobiographical, and *Lucien Leuwen,* a novel. During a three-year leave of absence (1836-39), which he spent in Paris or in traveling about France, he wrote what many consider his greatest novel, *La Chartreuse de Parme* (1839, tr. *The Charterhouse of Parma*). Its plot is from the Renaissance, but it is set in Italy of the 1830s. Its hero, Fabrizio del Dongo, like Julien Sorel, possesses a special egoism (termed Beylism by Stendhal) that derives its great energy from passion, has its own moral code, and consists of unswerving pursuit of happiness in the form of love or power. Stendhal returned to Paris a few months before he died. Nearly 50 years after his death, his unprinted works were discovered and published. See translations of his autobiographical works, *The Life of Henri Brulard* (1939), *Memoirs of Egotism* (1949), and *The Private Diaries of Stendhal* (1954).

Stengel, Casey (Charles Dillon Stengel), 1891-, American baseball player and manager, b. Kansas City, Mo. Stengel began playing professional baseball in 1910, and from 1912 to 1925 he played with the Brooklyn, Pittsburgh, Philadelphia, New York, and Boston clubs of the National League. Here he compiled a lifetime major-league batting average of .284. After 1925 he managed baseball teams in the American Association and the Pacific Coast League. In 1949 he became manager of the New York Yankees of the American League, and under his astute leadership the Yankees won ten pennants (1949-53, 1955-58, and 1960) and seven world championships. Stengel holds a spectacular major-league record for managing his team to five consecutive pennants and five consecutive world championships. A colorful figure, especially noted for his conversational ability, Stengel managed the New York Mets of the National League from 1962 through 1965. Stengel was elected to the Baseball Hall of Fame in 1966. See his autobiography (1961); biography by Joseph Durso (1967).

Stenness, Loch of (stĕnĕs'), lake on Mainland island, off N Scotland. An isthmus between Harray and Stenness lochs holds the Standing Stones of Stenness, two rings of flat tablets dating from c.2000 B.C. One had 12 stones, of which 2 remain standing. The larger, the Ring of Brogar, probably had 60 stones, of which 20 remain standing.

Steno, Nicolaus (nĭkəlā'əs stē'nō), Latinized form of **Niels Stenson** (nēls stăn'sən), 1638-86, Danish anatomist, geologist, and Roman Catholic prelate. He lived principally in Copenhagen, Paris, and Florence. He investigated the heart, brain, muscles, and glands and discovered (1661) the excretory duct (duct of Steno) of the parotid gland (one of the pairs of salivary glands). He pointed out the true origin of geological strata and of fossils and recorded his studies of crystallization. He was converted from Lutheranism to Roman Catholicism in 1667, became a priest in 1675, and vicar apostolic in N Europe in 1677. In his devotion to missionary work he virtually abandoned science. His *Earliest Geological Treatise* (1667) was translated and edited by Axel Garboe (1960). See biography by Raffaello Cioni (tr. 1962).

stenography: see SHORTHAND.

Stensen, Niels: see STENO, NICOLAUS.

Stepanakert (styĭpän''əkyĕrt'), city (1970 pop. 30,000), capital of Nagorno-Karabakh Autonomous Oblast, Azerbaijan Republic, S European USSR. Silk, wine, and food are processed in the city. Stepanakert became a town in the 1920s.

Stephanas (stĕf'ənəs), Corinthian Christian, companion of Paul. 1 Cor. 1.16; 16.15-17.

Stephansson, Stephan Guðmunðsson (stĕf'än gü̇th'münths-sŏn stĕf'äns-sŏn), 1853-1927, Icelandic novelist and poet. In 1873, Stephansson emigrated to Canada, where he farmed for a living and wrote prolifically. His collected poems were published in five volumes, including *Kolbeinslag* [lay of Kolbein] (1914) and *Vígslóði* [on the warpath] (1920). The novel series *Bréf og ritgerðir* (4 vol., 1938-48) reflects his concern for injustice and his liberal political philosophy. Stephansson is noted for his superb use of the Icelandic language.

Stephanus, family of printers: see ESTIENNE.

Stephen, Saint, d. A.D. 36?, first Christian martyr, stoned at Jerusalem. He was one of the seven deacons. Accused of blasphemy, he was brought before the Sanhedrin in Jerusalem. His speech defending his beliefs further enraged his accusers, who were Hellenistic Jews, and he was taken out and stoned to death. His teachings showed the growing differences between Judaism and the Jewish-Christian community in Jerusalem. Acts 6; 7. Feasts: Martyrdom on Dec. 26; Finding of St. Stephen's Body (415) on Aug. 3.

Stephen, Saint, or **Stephen I,** 975-1038, duke (997-1001) and first king (1001-38) of Hungary, called the Apostle of Hungary. The Hungarian state may be said to date from his reign. Because he continued the Christianization policy of his father, Duke Geza, and followed a pro-German policy, he had to put down revolts by pagan nobles. Married to a German princess, Stephen favored German immigration and modeled his administration on that of the German kings. He divided Hungary into counties, governed by royal officials, to prevent abuses by the nobles. His crown, sent to him by Pope Sylvester II, remained through the centuries the sacred symbol of Hungarian national existence. He is the spiritual patron of Hungary. Feast: Sept. 2 (in Hungary, Aug. 20).

Stephen II, d. 757, pope (752-57), successor of Pope St. Zacharias. When Rome was threatened by the Lombard king Aistulf, Stephen went to Gaul and appealed to Pepin the Short for help. He became the first pope to cross the Alps. Pepin responded and defeated (754 and 756) Aistulf and restored the lost papal territories. Pepin rejected the demands of the Byzantine emperor for the return of the exarchate Ravenna, which claimed temporal sovereignty over Rome. Instead, Pepin, in the so-called Act of Donation, ceded all the territories of the duchy of Rome to the papacy, thus laying the basis for the Papal States. In 755, Stephen renewed the coronation of Pepin and gave him and his two sons the title Patrician of the Romans (*Patricius Romanorum*). He was succeeded by Paul I. Another Stephen II, elected pope in 752 but who died before his coronation, was officially dropped from the list of popes in 1959.

Stephen, 1097?-1154, king of England (1135-54). The son of Stephen, count of Blois and Chartres, and Adela, daughter of William I of England, he was brought up by his uncle, Henry I of England, who presented him with estates in England and France and arranged his marriage to Matilda, daughter and heiress of Eustace III, count of Boulogne. Stephen was among the English nobles who in 1127, and again in 1131 and 1133, swore fealty to Henry's daughter, MATILDA, as Henry's successor to the throne. On Henry's death (1135), however, Stephen hastened to London, secured support, and was proclaimed king. He secured papal ratification, but his attempt to build up support by unprecedented concessions to the church and barons seriously weakened his authority, and his reign was one long struggle to retain his throne. In 1138, Matilda's half brother Robert, earl of GLOUCESTER, renounced his allegiance to Stephen, and David I of Scotland invaded England. Stephen defeated the Scots in the Battle of the Standard (although the ensuing treaty was entirely favorable to Scotland) and managed to wage an effective campaign against the insurrection in S and W England. However, in 1139 he made a fatal blunder in arresting his justiciar, Roger, bishop of Salisbury, and the latter's nephews, the bishops of Lincoln and Ely. This step not only threw the royal administration into confusion but alienated the church. Within a month Matilda had landed in England, and a long era of internal strife began. While besieging Lincoln Castle in 1141, Stephen was captured, and Matilda reigned for a short time. Her arrogance, however, soon cost her many supporters, and after Robert's capture later in the year she was forced to exchange Stephen for him. Stephen regained his throne and drove Matilda back into the western counties (1142). Virtual anarchy followed for five years; W and central England were devastated, while in France Matilda's husband, GEOFFREY IV of Anjou, conquered Normandy. In 1147, however, Robert died, and Matilda soon (1148) left England. In 1149, Henry of Anjou (later Henry II), Matilda's son, crossed to England and attempted unsuccessfully to further his mother's (and his own) cause. Stephen had again offended the clergy by quarreling with Theobald, archbishop of Canterbury, and the clerics refused to confirm his son, Eustace IV, count of Boulogne, as successor to the throne. When Eustace died (1153), Stephen bowed to the inevitable and concluded a treaty by which Henry was named as his heir. Stephen was a courageous soldier and a generous man, but he had neither the ability nor the strength of character necessary to deal with the turmoil of his reign. See biographies by R. H. C. Davies (1967) and J. T. Appleby (1969).

Stephen I, king of Hungary: see STEPHEN, SAINT (975-1038).

Stephen V, 1239-72, king of Hungary (1270-72), son and successor of Bela IV. As a child he was named duke of Transylvania, and in 1259 he was made duke of Styria. After the loss (1260) of Styria to Ottocar II of Bohemia, Stephen returned to Transylvania and married a Cuman princess. He rebelled against his father and in 1262 forced him to share the kingdom. After invading (1268) Bulgaria, Stephen took the title king of Bulgaria. He secured alliances by marrying his children into the ruling families of Naples, Byzantium, and other powers, and in 1271 he repulsed an invasion by Ottocar. He was succeeded by his son, Ladislaus IV.

Stephen, George: see MOUNT STEPHEN, GEORGE STEPHEN, 1ST BARON.

Stephen, Sir James, 1789-1859, British colonial administrator; father of Leslie and James Fitzjames Stephen. He served (1825-35) as permanent counsel to the colonial office and Board of Trade and drafted the bill (1833) for the abolition of the slave trade. As assistant undersecretary (1834-36) and undersecretary (1836-47) for the colonies, he was the effective director of British colonial policy. He promoted the extension of self-government to the colonies and rejected the "systematic colonization" schemes of Edward Gibbon WAKEFIELD, fearing oppression of the native populations. See study by Paul Knaplund (1953).

Stephen, Sir James Fitzjames, 1829-94, English jurist and journalist; brother of Sir Leslie Stephen. He was educated at Eton and Cambridge and was admitted to the bar in 1854. After 1855 he wrote many articles on ethics, literature, and current topics for periodicals, and he was (1865-70) an important contributor to the *Pall Mall Gazette*. The study of jurisprudence, however, was his chief interest. He wrote *A General View of the Criminal Law* (1863) to expose certain legal anomalies. He served (1869-72) as the legal member of the viceroy's council in India, preparing a draft codification (later adopted) of the law relating to contracts, crime, and evidence. Parliament, however, never enacted his proposed codification of English criminal law. Stephen contrasted what he considered the efficient British rule of India with the inept government at home, and in *Liberty, Equality, Fraternity* (1873) he deplored the extension of democracy in place of a more autocratic government. Stephen was (1879-91) a criminal court judge. He was made a baronet in 1891. His most famous work is his *History of the Criminal Law of England* (1883). See biography by his brother Leslie Stephen (1895, repr. 1972); Harold Potter, *Historical Introduction to English Law and its Institutions* (4th ed. 1958).

Stephen, Sir Leslie, 1832-1904, English author and critic. The first serious critic of the novel, he was also editor of the great *Dictionary of National Biography*. In 1859 he was ordained a minister. As a tutor at Cambridge his philosophical readings led him to skepticism, and later he relinquished his holy orders. He wrote several essays defending his agnostic position, notably *Essays on Free Thinking and Plain Speaking* (1873). He moved from Cambridge to London in 1864 and three years later married Harriet Marian, younger daughter of Thackeray. Some of the essays and sketches Stephen wrote for various periodicals were collected in *Hours in a Library* (1874-79). From 1871 to 1882 he was editor of *Cornhill Magazine;* during this time he encouraged such authors as Thomas Hardy, Robert Louis Stevenson, and Henry James. He was editor of the *Dictionary of National Biography* from its beginning in 1882 until 1891. Throughout his life Stephen was a prominent athlete and mountaineer. He wrote numerous articles on the subject of mountain climbing, many of which were collected in *The Playground of Europe* (1871). His major works include *History of English Thought in the Eighteenth Century* (1876); biographies of Johnson (1878), Pope (1880), Swift (1882), George Eliot (1902), and Hobbes (1904), all written for the "English Men of Letters" series; *Science of Ethics* (1882), which attempted to combine ethics with Darwin's theory of evolution; *Studies of a Biographer* (1898-1902); and *The English Utilitarians* (1900). Virginia Woolf was his youngest daughter by his second wife, Julia Jackson. See biography by F. W. Maitland (1906, repr. 1968); studies by N. G. Annan (1951) and D. D. Zink (1972).

Stephen Báthory (bä'tôrĭ), Pol. *Stefan Batory,* 1533-86, king of Poland (1575-86), prince of Transylvania (1571-75), son of Stephen BÁTHORY (1477-1534). He was elected to succeed John II as prince of Transylvania. In Poland, he was elected by a majority to succeed Henry of Valois, who had left Poland in 1574 to rule France as Henry III. A minority voted for Holy Roman Emperor Maximilian II, who died before he could make good his claim. As had been stipulated by the Polish diet, Stephen married Anna, daughter of Sigismund II, the last Jagiello king of Poland. To his brother, Christopher Báthory, he gave

Transylvania. With his chancellor, Jan ZAMOJSKI, Stephen fought several successful campaigns against Ivan IV of Russia in the lengthy war for the succession to LIVONIA. Peace was made in 1582 through papal mediation, and Poland retained Polotsk and its part of Livonia. Toward the end of his reign Stephen Báthory planned a Christian alliance against the Turks. He also schemed to make Russia a vassal state of Poland—a project that he considered a necessary step for his anti-Turkish crusade. He supported the Society of Jesus in Poland in an attempt to foster the Catholic Reform, and he effected useful judiciary reforms. After his death Sigismund III, a Swedish nephew of Sigismund II, was elected king.

Stephen Dušan or **Dushan** (both: stĕ'făn do͞o'-shän), c.1308–1355, king (1331–46) and czar (1346–55) of Serbia, son of Stephen Uros III. He is also known as Stephen Uros IV. He was proclaimed king after rebelling against his father, whom he then imprisoned. He reduced Bulgaria to dependency, gained the support of the prince of Walachia, and, taking advantage of the war between the rival Byzantine emperors, JOHN V and JOHN VI, conquered Macedonia (except Thessaloníki), Thessaly, and Epirus. After raising the archbishop of Serbia to the rank of patriarch, with his seat at Peč, he had himself crowned (1346), at Skopje, "czar and autocrat of the Serbs, Greeks, Bulgarians, and Albanians" by the patriarch of Peč and by the Bulgarian patriarch of Trnovo. He introduced Byzantine titles and ceremony into his court and drew up (1349–54) a law code for his empire. He later was involved in indecisive warfare against Bosnia and Louis I of Hungary, but in 1355, on the news of the fall of Emperor John VI, he decided to march on Constantinople. He died of fever en route. Stephen Dušan was one of the great conquerors in European history. Under his rule Serbia attained its greatest extent and glory. However, his empire lacked unity and fell apart soon after his death.

Stephen Dushan: see STEPHEN DUŠAN.

Stephen Harding, Saint, d. 1134, English monastic reformer. He entered the abbey at Sherborne in his youth; later (c.1077) he went to the Molesme abbey (near Chatillon-sur-Seine) in Burgundy. In 1098 he joined his abbot, St. Robert (d. 1111), in founding at Cîteaux a new abbey, where the Rule of St. Benedict might be observed in primitive rigor. Stephen was abbot there from c.1109 and from his abbacy date the CISTERCIANS; the spirit and organization of that order reflect St. Stephen's ideas. These are embodied in the Chart of Charity (c.1119); this, the main Cistercian constitutional paper, is a landmark in the course of Western monasticism. He supported with paternal affection the work of St. BERNARD OF CLAIRVAUX. Feast: April 17; among Cistercians, July 16. See Father Raymond, *Saga of Cîteaux*: *First Epoch* (3d ed., 1945).

Stephens, Alexander Hamilton, 1812–83, American political leader, Confederate vice president (1861–65), b. Taliaferro co. (then part of Wilkes co.), Ga. He was admitted to the bar in 1834, served six terms in the Georgia legislature, and was a Whig (later a Democratic) Representative in Congress from 1843 to 1859. Stephens, together with Howell Cobb and Robert Toombs, was influential in Georgia's acceptance of the Compromise of 1850, and with them he organized in the state the short-lived Constitutional Union party. He voted against secession in the Georgia convention of 1861, but accepted his state's decision and was a delegate to the convention in Montgomery, where the Confederacy was born. As vice president, Stephens consistently opposed the policies of Jefferson DAVIS, objecting notably to conscription and to suspension of the writ of habeas corpus. An early advocate of peace, he was one of three Confederate commissioners to the HAMPTON ROADS PEACE CONFERENCE. After the Civil War, Stephens was arrested and interned for several months in Fort Warren, Boston. After his release, he was elected (1866) to the U.S. Senate but was not allowed to take his seat. He then applied himself to the writing of *Constitutional View of the Late War between the States* (2 vol., 1868–70), considered the ablest defense of the right of secession. He served again in Congress from 1873 to 1882, when he was elected governor of Georgia. See biographies by Louis Pendleton (1908) and Rudolph von Abele (1946, repr. 1971).

Stephens, James, 1882–1950, Irish poet and fiction writer, b. Dublin. One of the leading figures of the IRISH LITERARY RENAISSANCE, Stephens is best known for his fanciful and highly colored prose writings—*The Crock of Gold* (1912), *The Demi-Gods* (1914), *Irish Fairy Tales* (1920), *Deirdre* (1923), and *In the Land of Youth* (1924). In these works and others he made vivacious use of Irish legend and folklore. His first volume of poetry, *Insurrections*, appeared in 1909. Later volumes include *Songs from the Clay* (1915) and *Kings and the Moon* (1938). Possessed of a superb speaking voice, he gave many recitations of his poetry and, in later years, lectured on the radio. See *A James Stephens Reader* (ed. by Lloyd Frankenberg, 1962).

Stephens, John Lloyd, 1805–52, American author and traveler, b. Shrewsbury, N.J., grad. Columbia, 1822. His travels (1834–36) in Europe, the Middle East, and Central America provided the material for a number of studies. By far the best are *Incidents of Travel in Egypt, Arabia, Petraea, and the Holy Land* (1837) and *Incidents of Travel in Greece, Turkey, Russia, and Poland* (1838). The last seven years of his life were devoted to planning the Panama RR. See V. W. von Hagen, *Maya Explorer*, Ann Sutton and Myron Sutton, *Among the Maya Ruins* (1967).

Stephens College, at Columbia, Mo.; primarily for women; chartered and opened 1833 as Columbia Female Academy, called Stephens Female College 1870–1917. It was certified as a junior college in 1913 and became a four-year college in 1927.

Stephenson, George, 1781–1848, English engineer, noted as a locomotive builder. He learned to read and write in night school at the age of 18, while working in a colliery. He constructed (1814) a traveling engine, or locomotive, to haul coal from mines and in 1815 built the first locomotive to use the steam blast. He also devised (c.1815) a miner's safety lamp at about the same time as did Sir Humphry Davy, whose lamp was adopted in 1816; it embodied some features of the Davy lamp and is considered by some to have antedated Davy's invention. His locomotive the *Rocket* bested the others in a contest in 1829 and was used on the Liverpool-Manchester Railway. He became engineer for several of the railroads that rapidly grew up and was consulted in the building of railroads and bridges in England and in other countries. His son **Robert Stephenson,** 1803–59, and a nephew, **George Robert Stephenson,** 1819–1905, were also railroad engineers, and both designed numerous bridges. See L. T. Rolt, *The Railway Revolution*: *George and Robert Stephenson* (1962); R. M. Robbins, *George and Robert Stephenson* (1966).

Stephen the Great, d.1504, prince of Moldavia (1457–1504). A great military and political leader, Stephen consolidated princely authority, furthered economic prosperity, and reorganized the army, thus creating a powerful Moldavian state that hindered the Ottoman advance. Although helped to the throne by Vlad the Impaler, prince of Walachia, Stephen attacked and defeated Vlad in 1462. Moldavia was prey to the expansionist interests of Hungary, Poland, and Turkey, and, in 1467, Stephen repelled an attack by King Matthias Corvinus of Hungary. To prevent the Turks from using Walachia as a base of operations, he invaded Walachia and replaced Vlad's pro-Turkish successor with his own candidate. Stephen continued to repulse Turkish attacks, winning decisively at Vaslui in 1475. Nevertheless, the Moldavian position grew increasingly weak as other countries, particularly Poland and Hungary, failed to aid Stephen. It was probably on Stephen's deathbed advice that his son and successor, Bogdan, purchased (1513) the continued existence of Moldavia by paying tribute to the sultan.

Stepinac, Aloysius (stĕp'ĭnäts), 1898–1960, Yugoslav prelate, cardinal of the Roman Catholic Church, b. Croatia. In 1937 he was made archbishop of Zagreb. After the German invasion of Yugoslavia in World War II, he became a member of the council of state of the puppet state of Croatia, set up by the terrorist Ustachi organization. Convicted (1946) of collaboration, he was released in 1951 but was ordered to remain in Krasic, the city of his birth. The controversy over the Yugoslav treatment of Stepinac served to widen the rift between the Tito government and the Vatican. Stepinac was elevated to cardinal in 1953.

Stepney: see TOWER HAMLETS.

Stepniak, S. (styĭpnyäk'), 1852–95, Russian revolutionary and writer, whose real name was Sergei Mikhailovich Kravchinski. He fled Russia in 1878 after taking part in the assassination of the czarist chief of police. His first book, *Underground Russia* (1882, tr. 1888) was written in Italian and consisted of profiles of Russian revolutionaries. He is best known for his novel *The Career of a Nihilist*; or, *Andrei Kozhukhov* (1889), which he wrote in English. He was killed in London by a train.

steppe (stĕp), temperate grassland of Eurasia, consisting of level, generally treeless plains. It extends over the lower regions of the Danube and in a broad belt over S and SE European USSR and Central Asian USSR, stretching E to the Altai and S to the Transbaykal and Manchurian plains. The term is sometimes applied to the corresponding temperate grasslands of Hungary (PUSZTA), the PRAIRIES of the United States, the PAMPAS of South America, and the high veld of South Africa; it is sometimes also applied to the semiarid regions on the fringe of the hot deserts. The steppe consists of three vegetation zones with significant differences in climate—the wooded, or forest, steppe; the tillable steppe, or prairie; and the nontillable steppe. The wooded steppe has deciduous trees and the heaviest annual rainfall, over 16 in. (41 cm). The tillable steppe has black earth and an annual rainfall of between 10 and 15 in. (25–38 cm). The nontillable steppe is a semidesert, found especially around the Caspian Sea, with an annual rainfall of less than 10 in. (25 cm). There is some grazing, and its soils are relatively fertile under irrigation. Although the tillable steppe was originally grassland used almost exclusively for grazing, it is now almost entirely under cultivation. Some of the world's most productive agricultural areas, such as the Ukraine and the U.S. wheat belt, are situated on the tillable steppe.

sterculia (stərkyo͞o'lēə), common name for some members of the Sterculiaceae, a family of herbs, shrubs, and trees of tropical and subtropical regions. The most important members of the family are the CACAO, source of cocoa and chocolate, and the COLA, the seeds of which are used commercially in soft drinks and medicines. Karaya, or Indian gum, from S. *urens*, is an inexpensive substitute for tragacanth. The family also includes several species cultivated as ornamentals, e.g., the flannel bush in the United States, the kurrajong in Australia, and the Chinese parasol tree. Sterculia is classified in the division MAGNOLIOPHYTA, class Magnoliopsida, order Malvales.

stereochemistry, study of the three-dimensional configuration of the atoms that make up a molecule and the ways in which this arrangement affects the physical and chemical properties of the molecule. It is a third aspect of CHEMICAL ANALYSIS, the first being the determination of which atoms are present in a molecule and the second being the determination of the interconnections between those atoms by CHEMICAL BONDS. Central to stereochemistry is the concept of isomerism. ISOMERS are sets of chemical compounds having identical atomic composition but different structural properties. With geometric isomers, the differences arise from the atoms being bonded in different sequences or patterns. An example is *ortho-* and *para*-chlorobenzene; the former has chlorine atoms replacing adjacent carbon atoms in a benzene ring while the latter has chlorine atoms replacing opposing carbon atoms. Optical isomers are pairs of molecules that differ in the same way that a lefthand and righthand screw differ; i.e., they are mirror images of each other. Such molecules with a "handedness" typically rotate the plane of polarization of light that passes through them, but in opposite directions. The sugars glucose and dextrose are a pair of optical isomers; glucose rotates the plane of polarization to the left and dextrose to the right. Stereochemistry is particularly important in biochemistry and molecular biology.

stereoisomer: see STEREOCHEMISTRY; ISOMER.

stereophonic sound, sound recorded simultaneously through two or more electronic channels having microphones placed in different positions relative to the sound source. The recorded sound is played back through loudspeakers placed more or less as the recording microphones were placed. The recorded sound does not seem to emanate from a point source, but instead the voices or instruments composing the sound seem to be spread out as they would be naturally. Thus, some of the ambience of the recording hall is recreated. In quadraphonic reproduction, i.e., reproduction through four channels, hall ambience is particularly enhanced. See RECORD PLAYER; SOUND RECORDING.

stereopticon (stĕrēŏp'tĭkən), optical projection instrument making multiple use of the magic lantern. The magic lantern uses lenses to throw on a screen a magnified image from a transparent slide or from an opaque object such as a photograph or the page of a book. The stereopticon combines two or three magic lanterns to focus, in the same area of light on the screen or wall, dissolving views or combinations of images.

stereoscope (stĕr'ēəskōp"), optical instrument that presents to a viewer two slightly differing pictures, one to each eye, to give the effect of depth. In normal vision the two eyes, being a certain distance apart, see slightly different aspects of a scene. The impression of depth is obtained when the brain combines the images. A single photograph shows no more than what one eye would see. In a stereoscope two photographs, taken from positions related approximately as the positions of a person's two eyes, are placed side by side. When a person observes these photographs, his brain combines the separate images from each eye into a single three-dimensional one. Scientists, among them the English physicist Sir Charles Wheatstone in 1838, constructed stereoscopes for use with drawings, but suitable views were not generally available until the development of photography. In 1849, Sir David Brewster, a Scottish physicist, improved the stereoscope and invented the double camera for taking stereoscopic views. Oliver Wendell Holmes invented the kind of stereoscope that, together with a collection of stereoscopic views, became a popular instrument of home entertainment in the United States until the advent of the home phonograph and the radio. The principle of the stereoscope is applied in binocular field glasses and binocular microscopes.

stereotype (stĕr'ēətīp"), plate from which printing is done, made by casting metal in a mold, usually of paper pulp. The process was patented in 1725 by the Scottish inventor William Ged. Firmin Didot improved the process, named it, and extended its use. Cylinder presses, by which newspapers are printed, use curved stereotype plates that fit the cylinders. For other applications, stereotype has largely been replaced by ELECTROTYPE.

sterility, inability to reproduce. Malfunctioning of the male sex gland (testes) usually results in the production of defective sperm or a decreased number of sperm, causing sterility. In the female, malfunctioning of the sex glands (ovaries) disturbs ovulation. Structural deformity may interrupt the functioning of the sex glands (e.g., when the tubes that form the passageway for sperm in the male, or ova in the female, are blocked, fertilization cannot take place). Disease is another cause of glandular malfunctioning; metabolic diseases sometimes cause imbalances in the hormones that control the activities of the sex glands, and infectious diseases of the reproductive organs, e.g., syphilis, may result in temporary or permanent sterility. In addition, psychological factors often require consideration when the cause of sterility is sought.

Sterling. 1 City (1970 pop. 10,636), seat of Logan co., NE Colo., on the South Platte River; inc. 1884. It is the trading center of an agricultural area. An oil boom occurred there in the 1950s. A junior college is in the city. **2** City (1970 pop. 16,113), Whiteside co., NW Ill., on the Rock River opposite Rock Falls; inc. 1841. It is an industrial center in a farm region. Steel products, farm equipment, and construction hardware are among its manufactures.

Sterlitamak (styĭrlyĕtəmäk'), city (1970 pop. 185,000), Bashkir Autonomous Republic, E European USSR, on the Belaya River. It is a port and the center of a chemical complex. Milling and construction equipment and food products are also made. Founded in the second half of the 18th cent., Sterlitamak became a trading and transit point for the products of European Russia. It was the capital of Bashkiria from 1920 to 1922.

Stern, Isaac, 1920–, American violinist, b. Soviet Union. Brought to the United States as an infant, Stern began piano lessons at the age of six and violin lessons at eight. He studied at the San Francisco Conservatory and made his debut at 11 with the San Francisco Symphony Orchestra. After his New York debut in 1937 at Town Hall, Stern made extensive and brilliantly successful world tours. He is considered one of the leading contemporary virtuosos.

Stern, Otto (stûrn, Ger. ô'tō shtĕrn), 1888–1969, American physicist, b. Germany, Ph.D. Univ. of Breslau, 1912. After resigning from his post at the Univ. of Hamburg in 1933, he became professor of physics at the Carnegie Institute of Technology and later professor emeritus at the Univ. of California, Berkeley. Stern was an outstanding experimental physicist; his contributions included development of the molecular-beam method, discovery of the quantization of space (with Gerlach, 1922), measurement of atomic magnetic moments, demonstration of the wave nature of atoms and molecules, and discovery of the proton's magnetic moment. He was awarded the 1943 Nobel Prize in Physics.

Sternberg, George Miller, 1838–1915, pioneer American bacteriologist, b. Hartwick Seminary, N.Y., M.D. College of Physicians and Surgeons, 1860. He was assistant surgeon in the U.S. army during the Civil War and became surgeon general in 1893. He discovered the diplococcus bacterium of pneumonia at the same time as Pasteur and contributed valuable work on typhoid and yellow fever. His works include *Textbook of Bacteriology* (1895) and *Infection and Immunity* (1903).

Sterne, Laurence (stûrn), 1713–68, English author, b. Ireland. Educated at Cambridge, he entered the Anglican church and was given the living of Sutton-in-the-Forest, Yorkshire, in 1738, where he remained until 1759. He came to London the following year and was a great social success. Unhappily married, he was involved with various women during his lifetime, most notably Mrs. Eliza Draper, for whom he wrote the *Journal to Eliza* (1767). He led a somewhat dissolute life and much of the time was plagued by ill health, dying finally of tuberculosis. In 1760 the first volume of his masterpiece *Tristram Shandy* appeared. Although it was denounced on moral and literary grounds by Dr. Johnson, Horace Walpole, and others, the book was a popular success and eight subsequent volumes followed (1761–67). As a result of his travels to the Continent (1762–66) he wrote, but left unfinished, *A Sentimental Journey* (1768). He also published in his lifetime several volumes of sermons. One of the most entertaining and original literary works in English, *Tristram Shandy* is, in a sense, a parody of a novel. It is a hodgepodge of character sketches, blank pages, dramatic action, transposed chapters, and various digressions. Sterne constantly obtrudes himself into the novel and is by turns witty, satiric, sentimental, knowledgeable, and obscene. Beneath this apparent chaos, however, is a structure based on the association of ideas. In *Tristram Shandy* Sterne enlarged the scope of the novel from the mere recording of external incidents to the depiction of a complex of internal impressions, thoughts, and feelings. See the Shakespeare Head Press edition of his works (7 vol., 1926–27); his letters (ed. by L. P. Curtis, 1935); his memoirs ed. by D. Grant (1950); biographies by W. L. Cross (3d rev. ed. 1967), W. B. Piper (1965), and David Thomsen (1973); studies by L. C. Hartley (1966), J. M. Stedmond (1967), and J. Traugott, comp. (1968).

Sternheim, Carl (kärl shtĕrn'hīm), 1878–1943, German dramatist. In his successful comedy *Die Hose* (1911, tr. *A Pair of Drawers,* 1927) and in his later works he satirized as corrupt the manners, morals, and beliefs of bourgeois society. Other works include the plays *Bürger Schippel* (1913) and *Die Marquise von Arcis* (1919, tr. *The Mask of Virtue,* 1935); the novel *Fairfax* (1921, tr. 1923), which satirized American life; and stories and critical essays. Sternheim's work had an influence on German expressionism. In the Nazi era he lived in Switzerland.

sternum: see RIB.

steroids, class of organic compounds having a particular molecular ring structure called the cyclopentanoperhydro-phenanthrene ring system. Steroids differ from one another only in the structure of various side chains and additional rings. Many steroids are biologically active HORMONES that control a number of the body's metabolic processes. The group includes the male sex hormone TESTOSTERONE, the female sex hormones ESTROGEN and PROGESTERONE, hormones of the adrenal cortex including CORTISONE, corticosterone, and ALDOSTERONE, several forms of vitamin D, digitalis, and CHOLESTEROL, and the bile acids. Steroids are found in plants and invertebrates as well as in higher animals. The medicinal uses of steroids include the treatment of arthritis and skin ailments, specific replacement therapy, and the treatment of several types of cancer.

Stesichorus (stēsĭk'ərəs), fl. c.600 B.C., Greek lyric poet. He lived at Himera and seems to have been originally named Tisias or Teisias. Legend says he invented the choral "heroic hymn" and added the epode to the Greek strophe and antistrophe, thenceforth much used (e.g., by the tragedians and by Pindar and Ibycus). Fragments of his verse have survived.

Stesimbrotus (stĕs"ĭmbrō'təs), fl. 5th cent. B.C., Greek biographer, b. Thasos. He wrote biographical studies of Pericles, Themistocles, and Thucydides, son of Melesias. In addition he wrote books on Homer and on Samothracian religious mysteries.

stethoscope (stĕth'əskōp") [Gr.,=chest viewer], instrument that enables the physican to hear the sounds made by the heart, the lungs, and various other organs. The earliest stethoscope, devised by the French physician R. T. H. Laënnec in the early 19th cent., consisted of a slender wooden tube about 1 ft (30 cm) long, one end of which had a broad flange, or bell-shaped opening. When this opening was placed against the chest of the patient, the physician, by placing his ear against the opposite opening, could hear the sounds of breathing and of heart action. The stethoscope changed little until the beginning of the 20th cent. when the binaural instrument was developed by G. P. Cammann, a New York physician. It consisted of two earpieces with flexible rubber tubing connecting them to the two-branched metal chest cone. Thus the sounds could be heard with both ears, and the instrument's flexibility permitted the physician to listen to various areas without changing his position. Stethoscopy (also called auscultation), used together with percussion (light tapping of the chest), is a fundamental diagnostic measure in medical practice. The qualities of the sounds emitted by the lungs and heart denote the health or abnormality of these organs. Many diseases of the heart and lungs, and sometimes of the stomach, blood vessels, and intestines, can be recognized early by skillful use of the stethoscope. An electronic stethoscope makes it possible for several clinicians to listen at the same time to the sounds emitted by a particular organ.

Stetson, John Batterson, 1830–1906, American hat manufacturer, b. Orange, N.J. Stetson, who had learned hatmaking, traveled to the West in the 1860s to improve his health. He returned to Philadelphia and began manufacturing hats suited to the needs of the Western cowboy. These hats, known as Stetsons, soon became the popular headgear of the West. The John B. Stetson Company, formed in 1885, became, under his direction, one of the largest hat firms in the world. He donated generously to De Land Univ. (at De Land, Fla.), which was renamed (1889) John B. Stetson Univ.

Stettin: see SZCZECIN, Poland.

Stettinius, Edward Reilly, Jr. (stətin'eəs), 1900–1949, American statesman and industrialist, b. Chicago. He held (1926–34) several executive posts in the General Motors Corp., and in 1938 he became chairman of the board of the U.S. Steel Corp. He resigned (1940) as a business executive to join the National Defense Advisory Commission. After serving as priorities director in the Office of Production Management and as lend-lease administrator (1941–43), he was (1943–44) Undersecretary of State and presided at the Dumbarton Oaks Conference (1944). Succeeding (Nov., 1944) Cordell Hull as Secretary of State, Stettinius attended the Yalta Conference and was chairman of the U.S. delegation to the San Francisco Conference. He resigned (June, 1945) his cabi-

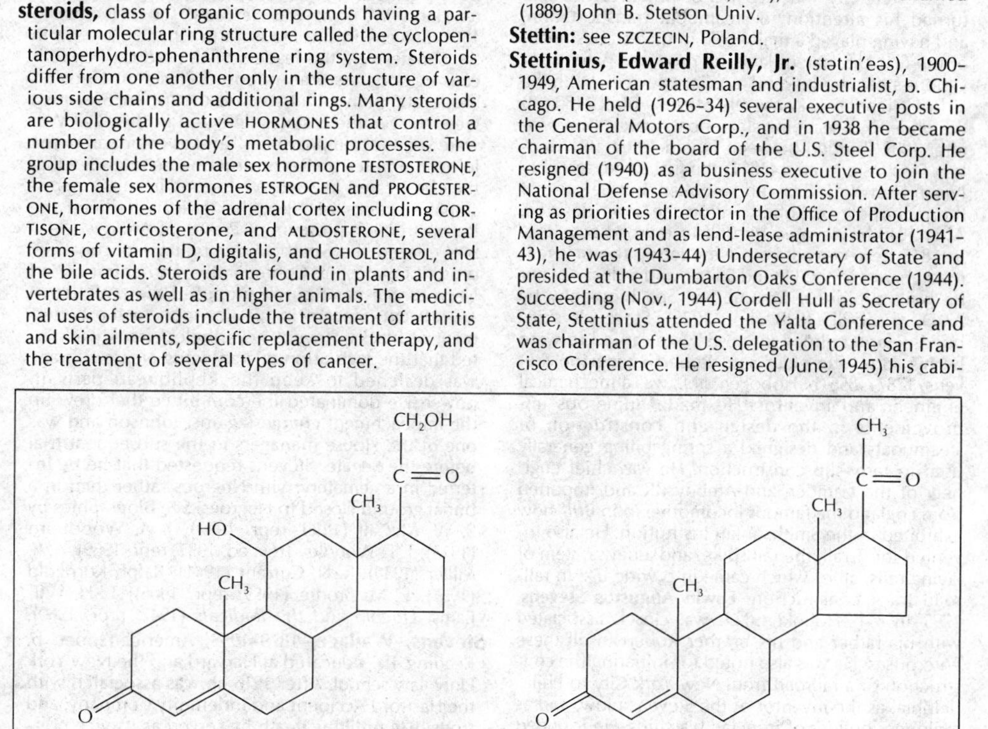

corticosterone

progesterone

Two examples of steroids

net post and served (1945–46) as U.S. representative to the United Nations. He wrote *Roosevelt and the Russians* (1949). See study by R. L. Walker (1965).

Steuben, Friedrich Wilhelm, Baron von (styōō'-bən, Ger. frē'drĭkh vĭl'hĕlm bärōn' fən shtoi'bən), 1730–94, Prussian army officer, general in the American Revolution, b. Magdeburg. He served in the Seven Years War and was a general staff officer. In 1762 he became an aide to Frederick the Great. Later, he was court chamberlain for the prince of Hohenzollern-Hechingen. After leaving the prince's service he met (1777) Benjamin Franklin in Paris and was given letters of introduction to George Washington. Arriving in America, Steuben served with Washington at Valley Forge in the winter of 1778 as acting inspector general of the army. He undertook the training of the Continental army, molding it into a powerful striking force. Congress made him inspector general in May, 1778. The effect of Steuben's training was seen at the battle of Monmouth (June, 1778), when American forces who had begun the retreat under orders from Charles Lee rallied against the British on Washington's arrival. Steuben commanded in the trenches at Yorktown. He was later granted a pension by Congress and large tracts of land by various states. See biographies by J. B. Doyle (1913, repr. 1970) and J. M. Palmer (1937, repr. 1966).

Steubenville (stōō'bənvĭl, styōō'–), city (1970 pop. 30,771), seat of Jefferson co., E central Ohio, on the Ohio River; laid out c.1797, inc. as a city 1851. The city's major industry is the production of steel. Bituminous coal is also mined. Of interest is the birthplace of Edwin M. Stanton. The College of Steubenville and a technical school are there.

Stevenage, urban district (1971 pop. 66,918), Hertfordshire, E central England. Stevenage was the first new town to be designated under the New Towns Act of 1946, a program to decentralize population and industry. The town has been planned to accommodate a population of 80,000. Manufactures include photographic apparatus, aircraft equipment, and electronic equipment. The old town, probably of Saxon origin, was an important stop for stagecoaches; several inns remain from that era.

Stevens, family of U.S. inventors. **John Stevens,** 1749–1838, b. New York City, was graduated from King's College (now Columbia Univ.) in 1768. He studied law (1768–71) and soon joined his father, a wealthy landowner and merchant, in New Jersey politics. During the American Revolution he served as treasurer of New Jersey and later (1782–83) was surveyor general of the state. In 1784 he bought an extensive tract of land in what is now Hoboken, N.J., and, when his father died in 1792, he inherited a large estate. By the late 1780s, however, he had turned his attention to steamboat transportation, and having played a major role in the establishment of the first U.S. patent laws, he procured patents for various steam boilers and auxiliary devices. With the aid of Nicholas J. Roosevelt, Stevens built (1806–8) the *Phoenix,* a seagoing steamboat, which, however, after 1809 shuttled between Philadelphia and Trenton. Stevens operated (1811) the first steam ferry between New York City and Hoboken, but because of the monopoly of Robert Fulton, he soon desisted. After 1810 he devoted himself to railroad activities. In 1815 he received from New Jersey the first railroad charter in the United States, and a decade later he built a pioneer locomotive. See biography by A. D. Turnbull (1928, repr. 1973). Stevens's shipbuilding and railroad interests were carried forward by his sons. The elder son, **Robert Livingston Stevens,** 1787–1856, b. Hoboken, N.J., was a mechanical engineer and inventor. He made numerous improvements in the design and construction of steamboats and designed a spring piling generally used in ferry-slip construction. He was chief engineer of the Camden and Amboy RR and imported from England the famous locomotive *John Bull,* now exhibited in the Smithsonian Institution. He also invented the T rail, the rail spike, and a new system of laying rails, all of which came into wide use in railroad track construction. **Edwin Augustus Stevens,** 1795–1868, b. Hoboken, N.J., was closely associated with his father and his brother Robert in all these enterprises. He was also noted for initiating the construction of a railroad from New York City to Philadelphia, as the inventor of the Stevens plow, and as a pioneer builder of ironclad warships. He founded the STEVENS INSTITUTE OF TECHNOLOGY.

Stevens, Abel, 1815–97, American clergyman, Methodist historian, b. Philadelphia, studied at Wesleyan Univ. He became (1834) a member of the New England Methodist Conference and filled pastorates in Boston, Providence, and New York. His works include *The History of the Religious Movement of the Eighteenth Century Called Methodism* (3 vol., 1858–61), *The History of the Methodist Episcopal Church in the United States* (4 vol., 1864–67), and *A Compendious History of American Methodism* (1867).

Stevens, Alfred Émile, 1823–1906, Belgian portrait and genre painter. He often lived in Paris and exhibited there regularly. His chief subjects, painted with admirable technique and color, were society women, fashionable Parisian interiors, and marine scenes. His *Japanese Robe* is in the Metropolitan Museum, and he is well represented in museums in Brussels and Marseilles. He is the author of *Impressions sur la peinture* (1886).

Stevens, Henry, 1819–86, American bookdealer and bibliographer, b. Barnet, Vt. After attending college and law school, Stevens went to Europe as agent for several important libraries of the United States and remained in England to collect Americana for the British Museum. While there he made catalogues of the museum's collections on the United States, Mexico, and Canada and lists of its famous Bibles.

Stevens, Siaka Probyn (sēä'kä prō'bĭn), 1905–, president of Sierra Leone (1971–). A mine worker, he became involved in union activities and later served (1951–57) in the legislative council. Appointed (1967) prime minister, he was briefly exiled but returned as prime minister (1968–71). In 1971 he assumed the office of president.

Stevens, Thaddeus, 1792–1868, U.S. Representative from Pennsylvania (1849–53, 1859–68), b. Danville, Vt. He taught in an academy at York, Pa., studied law, and was admitted to the bar in Maryland. He practiced law in Gettysburg (1816–42) and then in Lancaster, Pa. He also entered the iron business. Stevens first achieved political prominence as an Anti-Mason, and from 1833 to 1841 he served in the Pennsylvania legislature. An aggressive, uncompromising man possessing a formidable, sardonic wit, he helped defeat a bill abolishing the state's public school system and was a vigorous proponent of a protective tariff. In his first two terms in Congress, Stevens was a Whig but also a forthright abolitionist, and he quit in disgust at his party's moderate stand on the slavery issue. A leading organizer of the Republican party in Pennsylvania, he returned to Congress in 1859. As chairman of the House Committee on Ways and Means, he was a powerful figure throughout the Civil War. Stevens secured huge appropriations for the Union forces and succeeded in having paper money authorized as legal tender. His hatred of the South has been attributed by some to the destruction of his ironworks near Chambersburg in the Confederate invasion of 1863, but it seems also to have had basis in principle. After Henry W. DAVIS was defeated for reelection in 1864, Stevens in the House and Charles SUMNER in the Senate were the leaders of the radical Republicans in Congress who opposed President Lincoln's moderate plan of RECONSTRUCTION. In Stevens's view, the Southern states defeated in the Civil War were "conquered provinces" and as chairman of the joint committee on Reconstruction he intended that they be treated as such. Victorious in the congressional elections of 1866, the radicals nullified the Reconstruction program of President Andrew JOHNSON, placed the South under military occupation, proscribed most ex-Confederates, and enfranchised Negroes. Stevens himself proposed the FOURTEENTH AMENDMENT. Sincere in his devotion to the betterment of blacks, Stevens nevertheless frankly admitted that the legislation guaranteeing Negro suffrage was designed to keep the Republican party in power. He dominated the committee that drew up the impeachment charges against Johnson and was one of the House managers in the subsequent trial before the Senate. Stevens requested that he be interred in a cemetery with Negroes rather than in a burial ground closed to Negroes. See biographies by S. W. McCall (1899, repr. 1972), J. A. Woodburn (1913), T. F. Woodley (rev. ed. 1937, repr. 1969), A. B. Miller (1939), R. N. Current (1941), Ralph Korngold (1955), F. M. Brodie (1959, repr. 1966); T. H. Williams, *Lincoln and the Radicals* (1942, repr. 1960).

Stevens, Wallace, 1879–1955, American poet, b. Reading, Pa., educated at Harvard and the New York Univ. law school. After 1916 he was associated with the Hartford Accident and Indemnity Company, and from 1934 until his death he served as its vice president. A master of exquisite verse, Stevens was specifically concerned with creating some shape of order in the "slovenly wilderness" of chaos. These ideas are expressed in his earliest volume, *Harmonium* (1923), to which belongs the best known of his poems, "Sunday Morning." His ideas are developed in the subsequent volumes *Ideas of Order* (1936); *The Man with the Blue Guitar* (1937); *Parts of the World* (1942); *Transport to Summer* (1947), which includes the long poem "Notes toward a Supreme Fiction," in which Stevens elaborates on the poet's role in creating the fictions necessary to transform and harmonize the world; *The Auroras of Autumn* (1950); *The Necessary Angel,* essays (1951); *Collected Poems* (1954; Pulitzer Prize); and *Opus Posthumous* (1957). See his letters, ed. by Holly Stevens (1966); biographies by F. A. Doggett (1966) and S. F. Morse (1970); studies by W. A. Burney (1968), A. W. Litz (1972), A. K. Morris (1974), and Lucy Beckett (1974).

Stevens Institute of Technology, at Hoboken, N.J.; coeducational; chartered 1870, opened 1871 through a bequest from Edwin Augustus Stevens. It granted the first U.S. mechanical engineering degrees.

Stevenson, Adlai Ewing, 1835–1914, Vice President of the United States (1893–97), b. Christian co., Ky. He practiced law at Bloomington, Ill., and was twice (1874, 1878) elected to the U.S. Congress as a Democrat. He was First Assistant Postmaster General during Grover Cleveland's first term (1885–89) and Vice President during his second. In 1900, Stevenson again ran for Vice President on the Democratic ticket, this time with William Jennings Bryan. After losing this election he later ran (1908) for governor of Illinois but was defeated.

Stevenson, Adlai Ewing, 1900–1965, American statesman, b. Los Angeles; grandson of Adlai Ewing Stevenson (1835–1914). A graduate (1922) of Princeton, he received his law degree from Northwestern Univ., was admitted (1926) to the bar, and practiced law in Chicago. He entered government service as special counsel to the Agricultural Adjustment Administration (1933–34) and later served as assistant general counsel to the Federal Alcohol Bureau (1934) and as an assistant to the U.S. Secretary of the Navy (1941–44). In 1945 he became special assistant to Secretary of State Stettinius and attended the San Francisco Conference that founded the United Nations. He was a member of the U.S. mission to the UN General Assembly in 1946 and 1947. In 1949, Stevenson was elected Democratic governor of Illinois by an unprecedented majority; his record of reforms in office brought him national prominence, and he was drafted (1952) to be the Democratic presidential candidate. Despite an eloquent campaign, he was decisively defeated by Dwight D. Eisenhower. In 1956, Stevenson campaigned actively and successfully for renomination but was defeated by Eisenhower by an even greater margin. In 1960 he was a more reluctant contender for the Democratic nomination, which he lost to John F. Kennedy. In 1961, President Kennedy appointed him U.S. Ambassador to the United Nations, with cabinet rank. He held this position until his death. Despite his electoral defeats, Stevenson won enormous respect and admiration as an eloquent spokesman for liberal reform and for internationalism. His oldest son, Adlai Ewing Stevenson 3d, was elected U.S. Senator from Illinois in 1970. Stevenson's works include *A Call to Greatness* (1954), *Friends and Enemies* (1959), and *Putting First Things First* (1960). His papers are being edited by Walker Johnson (4 vol., 1972–). See biographies by K. S. Davis (1957, repr. 1967), S. G. Brown (1961), H. J. Muller (1967), and Bert Cochran (1969).

Stevenson, Burton Egbert, 1872–1962, American author, compiler and librarian, b. Chillicothe, Ohio, studied (1890–93) at Princeton. He was founder (1918) of the American Library in Paris and director (1918–20, 1925–30). Besides his well-known compilations, which include the *Home Book of Verse* (1912; many later editions) and the *Home Book of Quotations* (1934, rev. 1946), he wrote travel books, children's books, novels, and mystery stories.

Stevenson, Robert Louis, 1850–94, Scottish novelist, poet, and essayist, b. Edinburgh. Handicapped from youth by delicate health, he struggled all his life against tuberculosis. He studied law and was admitted to the bar in 1875, but he never practiced. At an early age he had begun to write, and gradually he devoted himself to literature. The essays that later were published as *Virginibus Puerisque* (1881) and *Familiar Studies of Men and Books* (1882) began to appear in the *Cornhill Magazine* in 1876; he was soon contributing to periodicals such famous stories as "A Lodging for the Night" and "The Sire de Malétroit's Door" and the tales later published as *New Arabian Nights* (1882). *An Inland Voyage* (1878), an account of a canoe trip in Belgium and France, was his first published book. In 1880, Stevenson married Frances Osbourne, an American divorcée 10 years his senior. With W. E. HENLEY he wrote four plays, only moderately successful. His first popular books were *Treasure Island* (1883), a swashbuckling adventure story of a search for Captain Kidd's buried treasure, and the fantasy *Prince Otto* (1885). *A Child's Garden of Verses* appeared in 1885, and in 1886 came two of his best-known works, *Kidnapped*, an adventure tale noted for its Scottish setting, and *The Strange Case of Dr. Jekyll and Mr. Hyde*, a science fiction thriller with moral overtones. Constantly in search of climates favorable to his health, Stevenson went in 1887 to Saranac Lake in New York, where he began *The Master of Ballantrae* (1889). In 1889 he and his family set out for the South Seas, settling on Samoa, where Stevenson gained influence over the natives, who knew him as Tusitala (teller of tales). At his estate there ("Vailima") he collaborated with his stepson, Lloyd Osbourne, on the novels *The Wrong Box* (1889), *The Wrecker* (1892), and *The Ebb Tide* (1894), and wrote and planned numerous tales and essays. He died in Samoa and, by his own request, was buried high on Mt. Vaea "under the wide and starry sky," which he described in his famous poem "Requiem." Among his other published works are *Travels with a Donkey in the Cévennes* (1879); *The Merry Men* (1887); *The Black Arrow* (1888), a novel; *A Footnote to History* (1893), a defense of Father DAMIEN; and a novel, *The Weir of Hermiston* (1896), which, although uncompleted, contains some of Stevenson's finest writing. Stevenson's reputation suffered severely after his death—he was considered an overly mannered writer of children's stories. However, by the mid-20th cent. he was regarded as a writer of power and originality with a strong moral vision. See biographies by J. C. Furnas (1962), Graham Balfour (2 vol., 1901; repr. 1968), and R. O. Masson (1914, repr. 1973); studies by Robert Kiely (1964) and E. M. Eigner (1966).

Stevens Point, city (1970 pop. 23,479), seat of Portage co., central Wis., on the Wisconsin and Plover rivers; inc. 1858. The major industries are insurance and the manufacture of paper and furniture. The Univ. of Wisconsin at Stevens Point is in the city.

Stevin, Simon (sē'môn stəvīn'), 1548–1620, Dutch engineer and mathematician. His experiments in hydrostatics showed that the pressure exerted by a liquid is dependent only on its vertical height and not on the shape of the liquid's container, and demonstrated the principle of the hydraulic press. He probably anticipated Galileo's experiments with falling bodies. Stevin is also credited with the introduction of decimals into common usage.

Steward, Julian Haynes, 1902–72, American anthropologist, b. Washington, D.C., grad. Cornell Univ., 1925, Ph.D. Univ. of California, 1929. He taught at the Univ. of Michigan (1928–30), Columbia (1946–52), and the Univ. of Illinois (1952–), as well as other universities. At the Smithsonian Institution he was anthropologist (1935–43) in the Bureau of American Ethnology, edited for the bureau the monumental *Handbook of South American Indians* (7 vol., 1946–59), and was director (1943–46) of the Institute of Social Anthropology. He became one of the foremost exponents of cultural evolution in the United States, and he made important contributions to the study of social organization and to North American ethnography. His writings include *South American Culture* (1949), *Area Research, Theory and Practice* (1950), and *Theory of Culture Change* (1955).

Stewart, alternate form of the name STUART.

Stewart, Alexander Turney, 1803–76, American merchant, b. Lisburn, Co. Antrim, Ireland. Arriving in New York c.1820, he started in business in 1823 by selling Irish laces. In 1846 he established a wholesale and retail dry goods business, which, by 1850, was the largest in the city; his new store (later sold to John Wanamaker), opened in 1862, was the largest retail store in the world. Owner of hotels and other enterprises in New York City, he maintained a controlling interest in mills in New England, New York, and New Jersey and built the planned community of Garden City, Long Island. He was appointed U.S. Secretary of the Treasury by President Ulysses S. Grant in 1869 but was prevented by law from taking office because of his business connections. His mansion on Fifth Ave. was regarded as one of the finest in America.

Stewart, Charles, 1778–1869, American naval officer, b. Philadelphia. He was commissioned a lieutenant in 1798 after having served in the merchant marine and was a brilliant commander of the CONSTITUTION in the War of 1812. After a long and varied career Stewart was promoted to rear admiral on the retired list in 1862.

Stewart, Dugald, 1753–1828, Scottish philosopher. He studied at the Univ. of Edinburgh, later becoming professor of mathematics (1775–85) and of moral philosophy (1785–1810). After retiring he devoted himself to writing. A student of Thomas REID and strongly influenced by him, Stewart is credited with aiding in the forming of the Scottish school of philosophy. His work was largely an exposition of Reid's philosophy, accepting the existence of the external world and applying the principle of common sense to the problems of philosophy. An eloquent lecturer and a brilliant writer, he is noted for these abilities rather than for any original philosophical development. Among his works are *Outlines of Moral Philosophy* (1793), *Elements of the Philosophy of the Human Mind* (3 vol., 1792–1827), and *Philosophical Essays* (1810). See his collected works ed. by Sir William Hamilton (1854–58), with a biography by John Vietch.

Stewart, Jackie (John Young Stewart), 1939–, Scottish automobile race driver. He began racing in 1961 and by 1973 had won 27 world championship Grand Prix victories. A dominant force in the sport, he won three world formula one championships before retiring in late 1973. See his autobiography, *Faster* (1972).

Stewart, James, 1908–, American actor, b. Indiana, Pa. As a leading man in American movies he is famous for his slow drawl and shy, homespun charm. His many films include *Mr. Smith Goes to Washington* (1939), *Destry Rides Again* (1939), *The Philadelphia Story* (1940), *Winchester 73* (1950), *Broken Arrow* (1950), *Harvey* (1950), *Rear Window* (1954), *The Spirit of St. Louis* (1957), *Vertigo* (1958), *Anatomy of a Murder* (1959), *The Flight of the Phoenix* (1965), and *Firecreek* (1967). He also starred in two television series.

Stewart, John Innes Mackintosh: see INNES, MICHAEL.

Stewart, Potter, 1915–, Associate Justice of the U.S. Supreme Court (1958–), b. Jackson, Mich. After receiving (1941) his law degree from Yale, he was admitted to the Ohio bar. He later practiced law in Cincinnati. A U.S. Circuit Court judge from 1954 to 1958, he was appointed by President Eisenhower to replace Harold H. Burton on the Supreme Court. An advocate of the careful exercise of judicial review, Stewart limited his decisions to narrow questions of law and rarely ruled on broad constitutional issues.

Stewart, William Morris, 1827–1909, American lawyer and political leader, b. Wayne co., N.Y. After migrating to California in 1850 he engaged in mining and held several state elective offices. He moved to Nevada, where his knowledge of mining law made him prominent, and upon Nevada's admission to the Union (1864) he became one of its first two senators. He served until 1875 and again from 1887 until 1905, when he retired. A strong supporter of the remonetization of silver, his political allegiance alternated between the Silver party and the Republican party. He wrote the Fifteenth Amendment to the Constitution in the form that was finally passed, was one of the first legislators to urge reclamation of land by irrigation, and played an important part in the passage of the National Mining Laws of 1866 and 1872. See G. R. Brown, ed., *Reminiscences of William Morris Stewart* (1908).

Stewart, river, 331 mi (533 km) long, rising in the Mackenzie Mts., central Yukon Territory, Canada, and flowing generally W to the Yukon River S of Dawson. The river is navigable for most of its length and is a transportation route for lead ore from its upper reaches. It was discovered (1850) by Robert Campbell of the Hudson's Bay Company.

Stewart Island, volcanic island (1966 pop. 329), 670 sq mi (1,735 sq km), S New Zealand, 20 mi (32 km) S of South Island across Foveaux Strait. A mountainous and scenic island, it is a summer resort. Frozen fish and granite are exported. It was discovered in 1808 by the British, who bought it in 1864 from the Maori natives, who call it Rakiura. Oban is the chief town.

Steyn, Martinus Theunis (märtē'nəs tö'nĭs stīn), 1857–1916, last president (1896–1900) of the Orange Free State, educated in the Netherlands and in England. He was admitted to the bar in 1882 and served as a judge. As president he made an alliance with the Transvaal. He led troops against British forces in the South African War, and he participated in the peace conference.

Steyr (shtī'ər), city (1971 pop. 40,600), Upper Austria prov., central Austria, on the Enns and Steyr rivers. It has been an ironworking center since the Middle Ages. Among Steyr's numerous well-preserved historic buildings are Lamberg castle (10th cent.; rebuilt in the 18th cent.) and a Gothic parish church of the 15th–16th cent.

stibnite (stĭb'nīt), antimony sulfide, Sb_2S_3, a mineral, silvery gray in color, with a metallic luster. It crystallizes in the orthorhombic system. Found in many parts of the world, it is the most important ore of antimony. It is commonly deposited by alkaline waters and occurs in association with quartz, calcite, sulfides of the base metals, arsenic, gold, and silver. Known in ancient times, stibnite was used in powdered form by women to darken their eyebrows and eyelashes. Antimony is used in alloys for type metal, storage batteries, pewter, babbitt, and antifriction metal for bearings. Its compounds find use in explosives, matches, and fireworks, in vulcanizing rubber, and in medicine as an emetic.

stick insect: see WALKING STICK.

stickleback, common name for members of the family Gasterosteidae, small fishes, widely distributed in both fresh and salt waters of the Northern Hemisphere. Sticklebacks range from 1½ to 4 in. (3.7–10 cm) in length and lack true scales; they are equipped with short, strong spines in front of the dorsal and on the ventral fins, the number varying with the species. These are used as offensive and defensive weapons, often against other sticklebacks during the breeding season, when the male is brightly colored and pugnacious. Each male constructs a roofed nest by gluing together bits of vegetation with a sticky secretion from glands near the kidneys. Under his persuasion, several females deposit eggs in the nest, which he guards jealously until well after the young hatch. Sticklebacks feed on smaller invertebrates and on the fry and eggs of other fish. Best known are the common stickleback, *Eucalia inconstaus*, a coastal species, and the brook stickleback, a smaller freshwater variety. Sticklebacks are classified in the phylum CHORDATA, subphylum Vertebrata, class Osteichthyes, order Gasterosteiformes, family Gasterosteidae.

stick-tight, name sometimes used for species of BEGGARWEED and of BUR MARIGOLD of the order Rosales, family Leguminosae, and the order Asterales, family Compositae, respectively.

Stiegel, Henry William (stē'gəl), 1729–85, American iron and glass manufacturer, b. Germany. He emigrated to America, arriving in Philadelphia (1750). In 1758 he purchased his father-in-law's ironworks near Brickerville, Pa., where he manufactured iron stoves, developing the template type that served as a standard for many generations. About 1760, Stiegel laid out a town in Lancaster Co., Pa., which he named Manheim. In 1763 he brought glassworkers from England and built a plant at Manheim that was probably the first manufactory of flint glass in America. He is best known for the famous Stiegel glass, which he manufactured in colors ranging from light green to deep emerald, wine, amethyst, and blue, in the form of bottles, decanters, drinking glasses, and other wares. See F. W. Hunter, *Stiegel Glass* (1950).

Stieglitz, Alfred (stēg'lĭts), 1864–1946, American photographer, editor, and art exhibitor, b. Hoboken, N.J. More than any other person Stieglitz compelled the recognition of photography as a fine art. In 1881 he went to Berlin to study engineering but soon devoted himself to photography. In 1890 he returned to the United States and for three years helped to direct the Heliochrome Engraving Company. He then edited a series of photography magazines, the *American Amateur Photographer* (1892–96), *Camera Notes* (1897–1902), and *Camera Work* (1902–17), the organ of the photo-secessionists. In 1905 he established the famous gallery "291" at 291 Fifth Ave., New York City, for the exhibition of photography as a fine art. Soon the gallery broadened its scope to include the works of the modern French art movement and introduced to the United States the work of Cézanne, Picasso, Braque, Brancusi, and many others. It also made known the work of such American artists as John Marin, Charles Demuth, Max Weber, and Georgia O'KEEFFE. Stieglitz married O'Keeffe in 1924. From 1917 to 1925 he produced his major works: the extraordinary portraits of O'Keeffe, studies of New York, and the great cloud series through which he developed his concept of photographic "equivalents." This concept greatly influenced photographic aesthetics. He then opened the Intimate Gallery (1925–30) and An American Place (1930–46), which continued the work of "291." Through his own superb photographic work and his generous championship of others, he promoted the symbolic and spiritually significant in American art, as opposed to the merely technically proficient. See

America and Alfred Stieglitz (ed. by W. D. Frank et al., 1934); biographies by Doris Bry (1965) and Dorothy Norman (1973).

Stieler, Adolf (ä'dôlf shtē'lər), 1775–1836, German cartographer. He worked most of his life in the Justus Perthes Geographical Institution, Gotha, which published his general atlas (1817–22; 10th ed. tr. 1934–39).

Stifter, Adalbert (ä'dälbĕrt shtĭf'tər), 1805–68, Austrian writer, b. Bohemia. Learned in law, mathematics, and science and accomplished as an artist, he was a tutor to important families, and later, a school inspector. His tales of the Bohemian Forest were widely read in his time and are still acclaimed for their sensitive descriptions of nature and of a simple and beautiful harmony between nature and man. Many of his tales were collected in *Studien* (6 vol., 1844–50). His late novels, *Der Nachsommer* (1857) and *Witiko* (3 vol., 1865–67), are considered diffuse. See biography by Margaret Gump (1973).

Stigand (stĭg'ənd), d. 1072, English prelate. He held simultaneously the sees of Winchester and Canterbury (from 1052). He received his pallium from the antipope Benedict X, and never submitted to the legitimate popes during the schism of this period. He was an opportunist, useful to Edward the Confessor (he negotiated the peace between Edward and Earl Godwin in 1052). Stigand welcomed William I and continued in his offices until a papal commission under Alexander II replaced him (1070) with Lanfranc.

stigma: see PISTIL.

stigmaria: see LEPIDODENDRON.

stigmata (stĭg'mətə, stĭgmăt'ə) [plural of *stigma*, from Gr.,=brand], wounds or marks on a person resembling the five wounds received by Jesus Christ at the crucifixion. Some 300 cases of stigmatization have been fully tested, nearly all of them being women. St. Francis of Assisi was the first known stigmatic. According to contemporary biographers, he had in his later life wounds in his hands, his feet, and his sides, which bled profusely and were intensely painful. St. Catherine of Siena reputedly bore invisible stigmata, which became visible after her death. The Roman Catholic Church investigates every such instance but avoids any pronouncement on their nature or cause. Modern stigmatics (including in the 20th cent. Therese Neumann and the Capuchin Padre Pio) have been examined by medical authorities. Scientists are inclined to believe that the stigmata are connected with nervous or cataleptic hysteria. See Herbert Thurston, *The Physical Phenomena of Mysticism* (1952); René Biot, *The Enigma of the Stigmata* (tr. 1962).

Stijl, de (də stīl) [Dutch,=the style], Dutch nonfigurative art movement, also called neoplasticism. In 1917 a group of artists, architects, and poets was organized under the name *de Stijl*, and a journal of the same name was initiated. The leaders of the movement were the artists Theo van DOESBURG and Piet MONDRIAN. They advocated a purification of art, eliminating subject matter in favor of vertical and horizontal elements, and the use of primary colors and noncolors. Their austerity of expression influenced architects, principally J. J. P. OUD and Gerrit RIETVELD. The movement lasted until 1931; in architecture a few *de Stijl* principles are still applied. See study by H. L. C. Jaffé (1968).

Stikine (stĭkēn'), river, 335 mi (539 km) long, rising in the Stikine Mts., NW British Columbia, Canada. It flows in an arc west and southwest, crossing SE Alaska, to the Pacific Ocean N of Wrangell Island. It is navigable for c.130 mi (210 km) upstream. It has cut deep gorges in the Coast Mts. The Stikine was one of the routes during the Klondike gold rush (1897–98). It is now a chief route to the Cassiar mining region of N British Columbia. The river is a noted salmon stream.

Stikine Mountains, range of the Rocky Mts., NW British Columbia, Canada, extending c.250 mi (400 km) northwest-southeast and rising to 8,200 ft (2,500 m) in Mt. Witt. The Stikine, Skeena, and Finlay rivers rise there.

Stiklestad (stĭ'kləstä"), village, Nord-Trøndelag co., central Norway, on the Trondheimsfjord. In a battle there in 1030, Olaf II (St. Olaf) was slain in an attempt to regain the crown of Norway.

Stiles, Ezra, 1727–95, American theologian and educator, b. North Haven, Conn., grad. Yale, 1746. He studied theology, was ordained in 1749, and tutored (1749–55) at Yale. Resigning from the ministry, he studied law and practiced in New Haven from 1753 to 1755, when he returned to the ministry for 22 years. He was pastor at Newport, R.I., and Portsmouth, N.H., and from 1778 until his death was president of Yale. While holding his pastorates, he studied science and European and Oriental languages and literature and corresponded with many scholars. At Yale he also was professor of ecclesiastical history and divinity and lectured on philosophy and astronomy. Stiles encouraged the sciences at Yale. Using equipment donated to the college by Benjamin Franklin, he conducted the first electrical experiments in New England. His more important writings are *History of Three of the Judges of King Charles I* (1794), *Literary Diary* (ed. by F. B. Dexter, 1901), *Extracts from the Itineraries and Other Miscellanies, 1755–1794* (ed. by F. B. Dexter, 1916), and his *Letters and Papers* (ed. by I. M. Calder, 1933). See biographies by his son-in-law, Abiel Holmes (1798), and E. S. Morgan (1962); Francis Parsons, *Six Men of Yale* (1939).

Stilicho, Flavius (flā'vēəs stĭ'lĭkō), d. 408, Roman general, a Vandal. He was the chief general of THEODOSIUS I, whose niece he married. By order of Theodosius, he served after Theodosius' death (395) as the regent for HONORIUS in the West. In 395 he was summoned from Italy to defend the Eastern Empire against the Visigoths under ALARIC I; but after his arrival in Greece he withdrew without fighting, under orders from ARCADIUS, who was influenced by his enemy and rival, RUFINUS. In 397 he returned and drove Alaric into the mountains but permitted him to escape. His position was strengthened by the marriage of his daughter to Honorius. He was responsible for putting down a revolt (397) in Africa. Subsequently he campaigned in Rhaetia against the Vandals and other barbarians (401–2), fought Alaric at Pollentia (402) and at Verona (403), and crushed Radagaisus near Fiesole (405). In 408, Honorius, influenced by an ambitious favorite, had Stilicho arrested and executed for high treason. Stilicho did not resist, although it was in his power to do so. Rumor accused him of planning the assassination of Rufinus, of plotting to make his son emperor, of making secret agreements with Alaric, and of inviting (406) the barbarians into Gaul; but evidence to support the charges is lacking. Stilicho is highly regarded in the verse of the poet, CLAUDIAN. He is generally regarded as a great statesman and general of the late empire.

Still, Andrew Taylor, 1828–1917, founder of OSTEOPATHY, b. Jonesboro, Va. He evolved the theory that all diseases and physical disorders ultimately derived from dislocations (which he called subluxations) of the vertebrae and that specific manipulations and massage—not drugs—could remedy any illness. In 1892 he founded a school of osteopathy in Kirksville, Mo. He wrote numerous works advancing his theories; his lengthy, colorfully illustrated autobiograhy (1897, rev. ed. 1908) includes descriptions of various cures.

Still, Clyfford, 1904–, American painter, b. Grandin, N. Dak. Still is a pioneer in the use of the mural-sized canvas. He paints vast, thick curtains of intense color, jaggedly torn to reveal other equally intense color areas. His work combines the gesture of ABSTRACT EXPRESSIONISM with a reliance on the sensations of pure color typical of POST-PAINTERLY ABSTRACTION. Still's work is represented in the Museum of Modern Art, New York City.

Still, William Grant, 1893–, American composer, b. Woodville, Miss. Still is of American Indian, Negro, and European ancestry. He studied music at Oberlin, with Chadwick at the New England Conservatory, and with Edgar Varèse. Much of his music reflects his Negro heritage. Among his works are three ballets, two symphonies, and three operas. His opera *Troubled Island* (1938) is set to a libretto by Langston Hughes.

still, term applied to the apparatus used in DISTILLATION, referring either to the flask in which a liquid to be distilled is evaporated, or to other pieces of equipment, or to the entire apparatus.

Stillingfleet, Edward, 1635–99, English prelate and author. A fellow of St. John's College, Cambridge, he became (1657) rector of Sutton, Bedfordshire. In 1661 he published *Irenicum*, a treatise on church government that sought to establish a compromise between episcopacy and the Presbyterian polity. In 1663 he issued *Origines Sacrae* and in 1664 *A Rational Account of the Grounds of the Protestant Religion*. In 1677 he became archdeacon of London and in 1678 dean of St. Paul's Cathedral, London. He was consecrated (1689) bishop of Worcester. Among his later works are *Origines Britannicae; or, Antiquities of the British Church* (1685) and *The Bishop of Worcester's Answer to Mr. Locke's Letter* (1697), in which he criticized John Locke for undermining the Trinity. An edition of his works, with a life by Richard Bentley, was published in six volumes in 1710.

still life, a pictorial representation of inanimate objects. The term derives from the 17th-century Dutch *still-leven*, meaning a motionless natural object or objects. Until the Renaissance, elements of still life, often imbued with symbolic or ritual significance, appeared as subordinate subject matter in religious or allegorical paintings. Hellenistic frescoes and mosaics from Pergamon, Alexandria, Rome, and Pompeii included depictions of plants and food in which a trompe l'oeil ILLUSIONISM was often stressed. In early Christian and Byzantine religious paintings still life elements were handled in a schematized and symbolic fashion until the end of the Middle Ages. Franco-Flemish paintings of the late Gothic era revealed close observation of natural details, as seen in much of the period's manuscript ILLUMINATION. At the beginning of the Italian Renaissance such detail was handled far more formally and was utterly dominated by the religious theme of the work, as in the paintings of Giotto. By the 15th cent. still life objects were used to enhance the illusion of scientific PERSPECTIVE, a subject of passionate study in the new humanism. At that time still life became a separate genre in Italy; it was used to great effect by masters of MARQUETRY. However, it was in the religious works of Northern European masters that the revival of the study of nature was most completely revealed. The van Eycks, van der Weyden, van der Goes, and Robert Campin, to name but a few, observed carefully and recorded exactly objects of everyday use and subjects from nature. They incorporated these into religious works, giving them more and more importance until the still life elements appeared in the foreground and diminished the religious, or landscape subject, as in the works of Aertsen and Beuckelaer. Specialists in the handling of specific textures or effects such as glass, fur, plants, and the translucence of grapes came into being. Where Italian artists had communication with Northern masters, their works reflected the Northern interest in still life subjects. The direction of this influence was reversed by the time of Caravaggio. Specialty pictures were the first major separate still lifes. These included works on the *vanitas vanitatum* theme featuring skull, hourglass, candle, book, and flowers in their iconography, as well as the banquet pieces that had become popular with collectors of 1600. Still life was developed as a separate genre primarily in the Netherlands in the works of Jan Bruegel, Rubens, Snyders, and Rembrandt. In France still life was used in the 17th cent. primarily for trompe l'oeil exercises and not significantly elevated until it received brilliant handling by Chardin in the 18th cent. French 19th-century masters, including Courbet and Cézanne, adopted still life wholeheartedly, giving it status equal to that of their other subjects. The cubist artists, Picasso, Braque, and Gris, painted still life subjects predominantly. In the United States, Harnett and Peto used still life in order to display brilliant trompe l'oeil techniques. In the 20th cent. both American and European artists' most characteristic subject matter was still life. The artists in many schools of abstract painting, beginning with Cézanne and continuing to the present day, foresook the objective representation of still life and developed myriad varieties of treatment of the subject, concentrating on color, form, and composition. Occasionally they painted other subjects, applying to these their still life stylistic techniques. The painters of the POP ART movement and their followers frequently criticized contemporary social values using, almost exclusively, still life subject matter. They chose objects of popular culture relevant to their thesis such as soup cans and comic strips. In the Far East still life subjects were depicted as early as the 11th cent. Chinese works were distinguished by brilliant brushwork and rapid execution. Objects were frequently endowed with symbolic import in both Chinese works and the Japanese compositions often derived from them. The importance of illusionistic representation of the object was minimized in Far Eastern Art, and in general its treatment of still life does not correspond with that of Western art. See Charles Sterling, *Still Life Painting* (rev. ed., tr. 1959); W. H. Gerdts and Russell Burke, *American Still-Life Painting* (1971).

Stillwater. **1** City (1970 pop. 10,191), seat of Washington co., E Minn., on the St. Croix River; inc. 1854. Shoes and clothing are among its manufactures. Stillwater was an early lumber center and a busy river town. A convention there drew up (1848) the petition to Congress for Minnesota's territorial organization. Stillwater has a historic museum and many old homes. **2** City (1970 pop. 31,126), seat of

Payne co., N central Okla.; inc. 1899. It is the seat of Oklahoma State Univ., which was established during the first year of settlement and was responsible for the city's growth. Stillwater is also the market and processing center of a farm and livestock area, with flour mills, meat-packing houses, and dairy plants. Oil and gas wells are in the area. Several lakes are nearby.

stilt, common name for some members of the family Recurvirostridae, shore birds including the AVOCET. Stilts, as their name implies, have the longest legs of any bird except the flamingo. They frequent open marshes and shallow water, wading with long strides and probing the mud for food with their long, thin bills. They are also good swimmers and fliers. Their floating nests are anchored along the edges of quiet pools. The common black-necked, or pied, stilt, *Himantopus mexicanus*, an elegant bird with a black back and white belly, is cosmopolitan in temperate and tropical regions. The banded stilt, *Cladorhyncus leucocephalus*, is found in Australia and Tasmania. Stilts are classified in the phylum CHORDATA, subphylum Vertebrata, class Aves, order Charadriiformes, family Recurvirostridae.

Stilton cheese, semihard, unpressed rennet cheese, veined, when well matured, by a blue-green penicillium mold. Stilton cheese was formerly distributed from Stilton, Huntingdonshire, England. The term is now restricted to cheese made chiefly in the counties of Leicester, Derby, and Nottingham.

Stilwell, Joseph Warren, 1883–1946, American general, b. Palatka, Fla. Commissioned in the army in 1904, he fought in World War I and later served for 13 years in China. In Feb., 1942, he went back to China, where he became (March, 1942) Chiang Kai-shek's chief of staff and commander of U.S. troops in the China-Burma-India area. Defeated in Burma by the Japanese troops, he retreated (May, 1942) through the jungles to India, where he built up forces for the successful counterattack (1943–44) in Burma. In Oct., 1944, Stilwell was recalled to the United States because of friction with Chiang. He became (Jan., 1945) chief of Army Ground Forces and commanded the U.S. 10th Army on Okinawa in the final months of the war. A frequently tactless but astute general, he was known as Vinegar Joe. His experiences in the Far East are recorded in the *Stilwell Papers* (ed. by T. H. White, 1948; repr. 1972). See study by Barbara Tuchman (1972).

Stimson, Henry Lewis, 1867–1950, American statesman, b. New York City. A graduate of Yale and of Harvard, he became associated with Elihu Root in law practice in New York City. Stimson was (1906–9) U.S. attorney for the southern district of New York state, and in 1910 he ran unsuccessfully for governor of New York on the Republican ticket. He was (1911–13) Secretary of War under President Taft and in World War I served as colonel of the 31st Field Artillery. In 1927, President Coolidge sent him to Nicaragua to negotiate an end to the civil strife in that country. His success in that mission led to his appointment (1927) as governor general of the Philippines, where, although he opposed Philippine independence, he softened the harsh policies of his predecessor, Gen. Leonard Wood. As Secretary of State (1929–33) in President Hoover's administration, Stimson was chairman of the American delegation to the London Naval Conference (1930-31) and of the delegation to the Geneva Disarmament Conference (1932). After the Japanese invasion of Manchuria, he issued (1932) a declaration that the United States would not recognize any situation or treaty that might impair U.S. treaty rights or that was brought about by means contrary to the Kellogg-Briand Pact (i.e., by aggression); this policy came to be known as the Stimson Doctrine. In 1933, Stimson resumed law practice, but he retained his interest in international affairs, advocating a firm attitude toward the Axis Powers. When President Franklin Delano Roosevelt appointed him Secretary of War in 1940, Stimson was read out of the Republican party. Despite his age, he served with energy throughout World War II, retiring in Sept., 1945. He wrote *American Policy in Nicaragua* (1927) and *The Far Eastern Crisis* (1936). See his autobiography, *On Active Service in Peace and War* (1948, repr. 1971); biographies by R. N. Current (1954, repr. 1970) and E. E. Morrison (1960, repr. 1964).

stimulant, any substance that causes an increase in activity in various parts of the NERVOUS SYSTEM or directly increases muscle activity. Cerebral, or psychic, stimulants act on the central nervous system and provide a temporary sense of alertness and well-being, as well as relief from fatigue. Drugs such as CAFFEINE and the AMPHETAMINES belong in this category, and several groups of drugs chemically similar to ANTIHISTAMINES and PHENOTHIAZINES also act as mild psychic stimulants (see PSYCHOPHARMACOLOGY). Cocaine, besides its effects as a local anesthetic, also stimulates the central nervous system, producing excitement and erratic behavior. The PSYCHOTOMIMETIC DRUGS, or hallucinogens, are also central nervous system stimulants. A second class of stimulants, that affect the medulla and spinal cord, include derivatives of niacinamide (nicotinic acid amide) and other chemically diverse compounds; they are sometimes used to speed the return to wakefulness after ANESTHESIA or to counteract barbiturate poisoning. Ammonia, in smelling salts, is also a medullary stimulant; the alkaloid strychnine is a spinal cord stimulant. Other substances act mainly on the autonomic nervous system. Drugs that stimulate the parasympathetic portion of the autonomic nervous system, such as PILOCARPINE, physostigmine, and NEOSTIGMINE, cause contracted pupils, salivation and sweating, slowed heartbeat, and lowered blood pressure. Drugs such as norepinephrine, EPINEPHRINE, and other CATECHOLAMINES and synthetic analogs stimulate the sympathetic portion of the autonomic nervous system, resulting in dilated pupils, rapid heartbeat, and increased blood pressure. Because the sympathetic and parasympathetic systems have opposing physiological effects, stimulation of one system amounts to depression of the other. Some of the alkaloids from the ERGOT fungus act by direct stimulation of smooth muscle, inducing contractions in uterine and intestinal muscle.

sting, in zoology, organ found in bees, many wasps, some ants, and in scorpions and sting rays, used defensively as well as to kill or paralyze prey. In the bee and the wasp the VENOM is produced by glands associated with the ovipositor (egg-laying organ) of the female. As symptoms differ, it is assumed that the venom of each species of insect probably has slightly different chemical properties. The bee's "acid gland" produces histamine and proteinlike substances that are extremely dangerous to persons with specific allergies to them. Adrenalin injections may be lifesaving in such cases. In the honeybee the sting is a minute needle with tiny serrated edges, the teeth of which point backward. This makes it hard for the insect to pull the organ loose and often results in the fatal loss of the sting, the poison gland, and part of the intestine. Hornets, yellow jackets, and other wasps have sharp, smooth stings that can be used repeatedly. A few ants produce formic acid as a venom. The scorpion kills its prey with poison injected by a curved spine at the tip of its tail; the wound is painful to human adults and may be fatal to children. Strictly speaking, spiders bite rather than sting, since they inject their venom by means of fanglike cheliceras. Coelenterates, e.g., the hydra, jellyfish, and certain corals, are equipped with stinging capsules (nematocysts) consisting of a trigger mechanism that, when stimulated, raises the hydrostatic pressure of the cell so that hollow venom-bearing threads are ejected with enough force to pierce the prey. The larger coelenterates, e.g., the Portuguese man-of-war and *Cyanea*, are dangerous to man. The stingrays, or stingarees, have long whip-like tails bearing one to three sharply toothed, bony, poisonous stingers capable of inflicting painful wounds.

stingray: see RAY.

stinkbug, member of a large, widely distributed family of true BUGS with flattened, shield-shaped bodies. Most are ¼ to ½ in. (6–12 mm) long. Those species whose hard upper covering, or scutellum, covers most of the abdomen are known as shield bugs. An unpleasant-smelling secretion is emitted from two glands on the thorax and remains on whatever the bugs visit. Most stinkbugs suck plant juices; some feed on other insects. Certain species, such as the brightly colored harlequin bug, are destructive to garden crops. Many stinkbugs are protectively colored in brown or green; a black species is common on blackberries and raspberries. The eggs are usually shaped like squat barrels with hinged lids and are glued upright in double rows to the leaf surface. The young mature in five nymphal stages (see INSECT). Stinkbugs of several species are used as human food in Mexico, India, and Africa. There are over 5,000 species, with several hundred in North America. Stinkbugs are classified in the phylum ARTHROPODA, class Insecta, order Hemiptera, family Pentatomidae.

Stinnes, Hugo (hōō'gō shtĭn'əs), 1870–1924, German industrialist. The son of a Westphalian mine owner, he founded his own company in 1892 and rapidly expanded his interests to build a huge "vertical trust" controlling mines, foundries, shipping, paper mills, and other industries. He owned vast tracts of land in South America, including the largest oil concession in Argentina. He controlled part of the press and exercised financial power through his banks. World War I helped to expand his enterprises; after the war, Stinnes took advantage of the German currency inflation to buy up businesses with worthless money. A founder of the German People's party, he was (1920–24) a member of the Reichstag.

Štip (shtēp), town (1971 pop. 40,766), SE Yugoslavia, in Macedonia. It is a processing center for opium poppies and has mineral waters. Štip was an important center of the medieval Serbian and Bulgarian empires. The town has preserved a 14th-century monastery and the ruins of its old castle.

Stirbei, Barbu: see under BIBESCU, family.

Stirling, Lord: see ALEXANDER, WILLIAM.

Stirling, James Hutchison, 1820–1909, Scottish philosopher. His most influential works are *The Secret of Hegel* (1865) and *Text Book to Kant* (1881), in which Stirling attempts to connect closely the theories of Kant and Hegel. See biography by A. H. Stirling (1912).

Stirling, William Alexander, earl of, 1567?–1640, Scottish poet. He was tutor of Prince Henry of Scotland and came to England on the accession of James I. The holder of various government offices, he was made Viscount Stirling in 1630 and earl of Stirling in 1633. His work includes *Aurora* (1604), love sonnets; *An Encouragement to Colonies* (1624); and *Four Monarchicke Tragedies* (1664–67), on Croesus, Darius, Alexander, and Julius Caesar. See his poetical works (ed. by L. E. Kastner and H. B. Charlton, 1921–29); biography by T. H. McGrail (1940).

Stirling, burgh (1971 pop. 29,769), county town of Stirlingshire, central Scotland, on the Forth River. The center of a large farm district, it has stock markets and light industries. There are coal fields nearby. Stirling is strategically located. Stirling Castle, on a hill above the burgh, long rivaled Edinburgh as a royal residence. A mighty fortress 420 ft (128 m) above the Forth, it overlooks several famous battlefields, including Stirling Bridge, where Sir William Wallace routed an English army in 1297, and BANNOCKBURN. The castle may have been built in the 12th cent.; it was the birthplace of James II and (probably) James III and James IV. Many assemblies were held in the castle's Parliament House, built by James III. Other points of interest are the Church of the Holy Rude (13th cent.), where Mary Stuart and James IV were crowned as infants, and monuments to Sir William Wallace and Robert I.

Stirlingshire (stûr'lĭngshĭr), county (1971 pop. 208,956), 451 sq mi (1,168 sq km), central Scotland. The county town is STIRLING. The region has a varied terrain of farmlands, peat bogs, pasture, and moorland, embracing parts of both the Highlands (in the west) and the Lowlands (in the east). The chief river is the Forth, which forms most of the northern boundary. Loch Lomond is on the western border. FALKIRK is the industrial center of the county; GRANGEMOUTH is the chief port. Formerly coal mining (in the southeast) was significant. Many important battles have been fought in Stirlingshire—Stirling Bridge (1297), the first battle of Falkirk (1298), BANNOCKBURN (1314), Kilsyth (1645), and the second battle of Falkirk (1746). The Roman Wall of Antoninus crossed the county. Under the Local Government Act of 1973, Stirlingshire was divided between the Central and Strathclyde regions.

stirrup, foot support for the rider of a horse in mounting and while riding. It is a ring with a horizontal bar to receive the foot and is attached by a strap to the saddle. To avoid the danger of having a foot caught in a stirrup if the rider is thrown, large stirrups are often used; one of the uses of the stirrup cover or stirrup hood is to prevent the foot from entering too far and getting caught; the same purpose is served by the high heels of the cowboy's boots. There is some evidence that stirrups were used in Assyria c.850 B.C. and in China as early as the Han dynasty, 202 B.C.–A.D. 220. Stirrups are not known to have been used in Europe before the raids of the Huns under Attila in the mid-5th cent.; probably they had their origin in central Asia.

Stjernstedt, Marika (märē'kä shĕrn'stĕt), 1875–1954, Swedish novelist. Stjernstedt's works reflect her distinguished family heritage as well as her liberal social and political interests. Her skill in narrative is revealed in the novels *Resning i målet* [higher aims] (1925), one of several of her works describing the life of the independent single woman, and *Spegling i en skärva* [images in a broken glass] (1936), concerning Russian aristocrats at the time of the Revolution of 1917.

stoa (stō'ə), in ancient Greek architecture, an extended, roofed, colonnade on a street or square. Early examples consisted of a simple open-fronted shed or porch with a roof sloping from the back wall to the row of columns along the front. Later stoas were often immense, running to two stories, each with a colonnade of a different order and having a ridged roof supported on internal colonnades; rows of shops or offices lined the back wall, which was sometimes decorated with paintings. Such stoas surrounded the agora or market place of every large city and were used for public meetings. The Stoa Poecile on the north side of the agora of Athens was the favorite meeting place of the philosopher ZENO OF CITIUM; hence his followers are called Stoics and his system STOICISM.

stoat (stōt), European name for the short-tailed WEASEL, *Mustela erminea*, also called ERMINE when in its white winter phase.

Stobaeus, Joannes (jōăn'ēz stōbē'əs), fl. 5th cent.? A.D., Greek anthologist. He made a large collection of excerpts from poets and prose writers on a variety of subjects, originally for the education of his son. The collection is valuable because it preserves fragments from many since lost works of early Greek authors. It came to be divided into two parts, called *Eclogues* and *Anthology*.

Stock, Frederick (Friedrich Wilhelm August Stock) (stŏk), 1872–1942, German-American conductor and composer. He came to the United States in 1895 as a violist in the Chicago Orchestra and became (1901) assistant conductor. As permanent conductor from 1905 until his death, Stock was responsible for the many premieres of new works. His own compositions include songs, orchestral works, and chamber music.

stock, in botany, common name for any species of the genus *Matthiola*, for *Malcomia maritima* (Virginia stock), and for the wallflower, all belonging to the family Cruciferae (MUSTARD family), and for a carnation of the family Caryophyllaceae (PINK family). Most are herbs indigenous to the Mediterranean region and to S Africa. A few are widely cultivated, both in greenhouses and in gardens, for the fragrant blossoms—usually purplish in the wild but of various colors in horticultural types. The evening stock, or perfume plant (*Matthiola bicornis*), is night-blooming; the Brampton stock, or gillyflower (*M. incana*), has an early blooming variety (*annua*), known as ten-weeks-stock or cut-and-come-again, which is sometimes grown as a house plant. The name *gillyflower* is also used for the Virginia stock, the wallflower, and for the carnation of the PINK family. Stock is classified in the division MAGNOLIOPHYTA, class Magnoliopsida, order Capparales, family Cruciferae; and order Caryophyllaceae, family Caryophyllaceae.

stock, in finance, instrument certifying to shares in the ownership of a corporation. Bonds are similar evidences of shares in a loan to a corporation. Stock yields no dividends until claims of bondholders have been met. Preferred stock is entitled to dividends of a specified percentage per annum before common stock is entitled to any dividends; the common stock is then usually entitled to the rest of the profits. In case of liquidation of the company, holders of bonds and preferred stock take precedence over holders of common stock in the division of assets. Holders of common stock usually have voting rights in the management of the corporation; bondholders and, usually, holders of preferred stock have no voting rights. Since the value of common stock depends largely on its earnings, it is often issued with no par value. Public demand for securities and the need of corporations for ready capital have led to the development of stock exchanges in most of the major cities of the world (see STOCK EXCHANGE). On the New York Stock Exchange, over 1,400 companies offer securities to investors.

stock, in horticulture: see GRAFTING.

Stockbridge, town (1970 pop. 2,312), Berkshire co., W Mass., on the Housatonic River, in the Berkshire mts.; inc. 1739. It is a summer resort center, and its proximity to ski areas attracts winter visitors as well. Stockbridge was founded (1734) by John Sergeant as a mission for the Muhhekanuk Indians; the mission house, restored as a museum, was built in 1739. Jonathan Edwards taught there (1750–57). The Berkshire Playhouse, a leading summer theater; a large art colony; and several galleries and museums are there. The annual Berkshire Festival is held at Tanglewood, a former estate largely in the town of Stockbridge although near the center of Lenox. Also of interest are the studio of sculptor Daniel Chester French; Indian burial grounds; the children's bell tower; a large green garden center nearby; and the Old Corner House (18th cent.; restored), which contains many Norman Rockwell paintings. The Boston Symphony Orchestra maintains a music school in Stockbridge.

Stockbridge Indians, North American Indians of the Algonquian-Wakashan linguistic stock (see AMERICAN INDIAN LANGUAGES). In the early 17th cent. they were known as the Housatonic Indians and were part of the Mahican confederacy. They then occupied part of the valley of the Housatonic River in SW Massachusetts. Their principal village, Westenhuck, was for a long time the Mahican capital after the removal of the council fire from Schodac. In 1734, John Sergeant began missionary work among them, and two years later the Indians were moved to a tract reserved for them by the colonial government. After the village of Stockbridge was established, they became known as the Stockbridge Indians. They suffered terribly in the French and Indian War, at the close of which they numbered 200. Accepting an invitation from the Oneida, the remnants of the Stockbridge moved to New York, where they established New Stockbridge. In 1833 they moved to a reservation at Green Bay, Wis., where they joined the Munsee. In 1850 most of them moved to a reservation in Shawano co., Wis., where today they number about 450.

stock exchange, organized market for the trading of stocks and bonds (see BOND; STOCK). Such markets were originally open to all, but at present only members of the owning association may buy and sell directly. Members buy and sell for themselves or for others, charging commissions. A stock may be bought or sold only if it is listed on an exchange, and it may not be listed unless it meets certain requirements set by the exchange's board of governors. There are stock exchanges in all important financial centers of the world; the New York Stock Exchange (founded 1790) is the largest in the United States. Stock exchanges play an important part in the machinery of corporate capitalism. By providing a centralized, ready market for the exchange of securities, they greatly facilitate the financing of business through flotation of stocks and bonds. But speculation and gambling in stocks can sometimes accentuate the instability of an economy. The interstate sale of securities and certain practices of stock exchanges in the United States are regulated by Federal laws administered by the SECURITIES AND EXCHANGE COMMISSION. In Europe a stock exchange is called a bourse. See BROKER; MARGIN REQUIREMENT. See Raymond Vernon, *Regulation of Stock Exchange Members* (1941, repr. 1972); G. L. Leffler, *The Stock Market* (3d ed. 1963); C. A. Dice and W. J. Eitelman, *Stock Market* (4th ed. 1966).

Stockhausen, Karlheinz (kärl'hīnts shtōk'houzən), 1928–, German composer, music theorist, and teacher; his first name is also spelled Karl Heinz. He studied composition with Frank Martin in Cologne (1950–51) and with Olivier Messiaen and Darius Milhaud in Paris (1951–53). Stockhausen is ranked with the most inventive of the avant-garde composers. He often employs SERIAL MUSIC techniques in his works, and he is a major proponent of ELECTRONIC MUSIC. Often using complicated contrapuntal systems, Stockhausen's compositions are characterized by much emphasis on free rhythms, tonal repetition, dissonance, and percussive effects. He is an adherent of ALEATORY MUSIC and allows performers to determine certain aspects of a performance; that is, they can improvise, begin and end at different points, and decide at what speed to sing and play. Stockhausen's unique approach is well-illustrated by his composition *Gruppen* [groups] (1959); in this piece three separate orchestras, each with its own conductor, play simultaneously; sometimes their music coincides; sometimes they play against one another; sometimes they play antiphonally. Among Stockhausen's other compositions are *Kreuzspiel* (1948); *Kontrapunkte No. 1* (1953), for 10 instruments; *Kontakte* (1959), for electronic music; and *Stimmung* (American premiere, 1971), for voices.

Stockholm (stŏk'hôlm''), city (1970 pop. 746,560), capital of Sweden and of Stockholm co., E Sweden, situated where Lake Mälaren flows into the Baltic Sea. It is Sweden's largest city and its economic, transportation, administrative, and cultural center. Manufactures include machinery, textiles, clothing, communications equipment, motor vehicles, rubber, processed food, printed materials, porcelain, and liquor. The city also has a large port and an important shipbuilding industry. It is the seat of Sweden's principal stock exchange. Founded in the mid-13th cent. on the site of a fishing village, Stockholm became an important trade center, dominated by the Hanseatic League (especially Lübeck). In 1520, Christian II of Denmark and Norway proclaimed himself also king of Sweden at Stockholm; a large number of Swedish nobles had gathered to attend the coronation and Christian instigated the massacre of about 100 of the anti-Danish nobility. The Stockholm massacre led to the successful uprising of Swedes under Gustavus Vasa, who became king of Sweden as Gustavus I (1523–60). Gustavus made Stockholm the center of his kingdom and ended the privileges there of the Hanseatic merchants. Stockholm was made the official capital of Sweden in 1634, about the same time that it became a European intellectual center under Queen Christina, who attracted men like the philosopher Descartes to her court. Stockholm's modern industrial development dates from the mid-19th cent.; it grew from a city of about 100,000 inhabitants in 1850 to one of about 300,000 in 1900. Architecturally, modern Stockholm is one of the finest cities in the world, with broad streets, many parks, and well-planned housing projects. Often called the "Venice of the North," it is built on several peninsulas and islands (including Städsholmen, Riddarholmen, Kungsholmen, and Södermalm islands). Its large bodies of water contribute to a feeling of spaciousness in the city. Stockholm's most famous landmark is probably the new city hall (1911–23), which faces Lake Mälaren; designed by the Swedish architect Ragnar Östberg, it is an impressive modern interpretation of the characteristic Scandinavian Renaissance style. Also well-known are the large residential districts of cooperative houses that have helped make Stockholm a virtually slumless city. On Städsholmen, which has retained much of its medieval character, are the Church of St. Nicholas or Storkyrka [great church], dating from the 13th cent.; the Church of St. Gertrude, or the German Church, originally built for the Hanseatic merchants; and several old Hanseatic houses. Also on the island are the Great Square, where the Stockholm massacre began; the Riddarhuset [assembly hall of the nobility], a 17th-century structure in the Dutch Renaissance style and with heroic statues; Tessin Palace (18th cent.); and the Royal Palace, built (1754) in Italian Renaissance style. Stockholm is the seat of a university (founded 1877), a technical university, a school of economics, and royal academies of music, science, art, and medicine. A Nobel institute is also located there, and each year the Nobel prizes (except the Nobel Peace Prize) are awarded in the city. Also of note are the opera house (opened 1898); the Royal Dramatic Theatre (opened 1908); numerous museums, including the large Skansen open-air museum; and a zoological garden. Stockholm has a lively musical, theatrical, and literary life. The 1912 Olympic games were held there.

stocking: see HOSE.

Stockmar, Christian Friedrich, Baron von (krĭs'tyän frē'drĭk bärōn' fŭn shtōk'mär), 1787–1863, Anglo-Belgian diplomat and courtier, b. Coburg, Germany. A physician, Stockmar became (1816) adviser of Prince Leopold of Saxe-Coburg, who in 1831 became King LEOPOLD I of the Belgians. At Leopold's request Stockmar, created baron in 1831, became (1837) an unofficial adviser to Leopold's niece, Queen VICTORIA of England. Wielding an increasing influence over the young queen, he was instrumental in bringing about the marriage (1840) of Victoria to Leopold's nephew, Prince ALBERT. His influence still continued after Albert's arrival, and he was regarded as something of a mystery man. In 1848, Stockmar represented Saxe-Coburg-Gotha at the Frankfurt Parliament, but he returned to England occasionally and continued his role as unofficial adviser to Victoria and Albert.

Stockport, county borough (1971 pop. 139,633), partly in Cheshire, partly in Lancashire, W central England, on the slopes of a narrow valley at the head of the Mersey River. The ravine is crossed by a high railroad viaduct built in the 19th cent. Engineering and cotton textiles are the largest industries; chemicals, hats, chocolate, and metal products are also produced. There is a 14th-century church and a grammar school founded in the 15th cent. Vernon Park has a museum. Richard Cobden represented Stockport in Parliament from 1841 to 1847. In 1974, Stockport became part of the new metropolitan county of Greater Manchester.

Stockton, Francis Richard (Frank R. Stockton), 1834–1902, American humorist and story writer, b. Philadelphia. He wrote several children's books including *Ting-a-Ling* (1870) and *The Floating Prince and Other Fairy Tales* (1881). Most notable among his many humorous books for adults were *Rudder Grange* (1879) and its sequels, *The Rudder Grangers Abroad* (1891) and *Pomona's Travels* (1894), and the famous title story of *The Lady or the Tiger?* (1884). His works were collected in 23 volumes (1899–1904).

Stockton, Richard, 1730–81, political leader in the American Revolution, signer of the Declaration of Independence, b. near Princeton, N.J. A successful lawyer in New Jersey, he tried to find means of reconciliation in the conflict between England and the American colonies. However, after his election (1776) to the Continental Congress he sought independence. Stockton was captured by the British while on an inspection tour, and although he was soon released, the effects of harsh treatment as a prisoner eventually brought about his death.

Stockton, Robert Field, 1795–1866, American naval officer, b. Princeton, N.J. He left the College of New Jersey (now Princeton) to enter the U.S. Navy at 16 and served in the War of 1812 and in the subsequent campaigns against the Barbary pirates. He negotiated (1821) a territorial concession on the west coast of Africa for the American Colonization Society; the region later became Liberia. While on leave (1828–38) he became interested in the Delaware and Raritan Canal and was a major figure in its construction. In the Mexican War he commanded the Pacific squadron, took Los Angeles and San Diego, and proclaimed (1846) himself governor of the newly organized civil government of California. He later (1847) installed John C. Frémont as civil governor. He left the navy in 1850. As U.S. Senator from New Jersey (1851–53), he introduced a bill to stop flogging in the navy. Stockton resigned in 1853 to become the first president of the Delaware and Raritan Canal Company, a position he held until his death.

Stockton, city (1970 pop. 109,963), seat of San Joaquin co., central Calif., on the San Joaquin River; inc. 1850. It is an inland seaport located at the head of the San Joaquin delta; its harbor has been developed to accommodate oceangoing vessels. It is also a railroad center and a processing and distributing point for farm products from the San Joaquin valley. It has many canneries. Farm machinery, building materials, and boats are also made. The city was an outfitting center in the gold-rush days. It has a historical museum, an art gallery, and an impressive civic auditorium. The Univ. of the Pacific, a junior college, a state mental hospital, and two army depots are there. A U.S. navy communications station is on a nearby island.

Stockton-on-Tees, England: see TEESIDE.

Stoicism (stō'ĭsĭzəm), school of philosophy founded by ZENO OF CITIUM (in Cyprus) c.300 B.C. The first Stoics were so called because they met in the Stoa Poecile [Gr.,=painted porch], at Athens, a colonnade near the Agora, to hear their master Zeno lecture. He had studied with Crates the Cynic, and his own teaching included the Cynic adaptation of the Socratic ideals of virtue, endurance, and self-sufficiency. He added to them the explanation of the physical universe given by Heraclitus and something of the logic of Aristotle. The development and organization of Zeno's doctrines into a great system of metaphysics was the work of Chrysippus (c.280–207 B.C.), successor to Cleanthes. Among the acknowledged leaders of the Stoics in the following period was Panaetius of Rhodes, who in the 2d cent. B.C. introduced Stoicism into Rome. He and his pupil Posidonius sought to lessen the attacks of critics by mingling with the Stoic doctrines some of Plato's psychological views. Cicero, a pupil of Posidonius, was indebted to a work of Panaetius for the basis of his own treatise *De officiis*. The Romans, who had received Stoicism more cordially than they did any other Greek philosophy, can claim the third period as their own. To it belong the philosophers SENECA and EPICTETUS of Phrygia and the emperor MARCUS AURELIUS. Stoicism, with its roots in earlier doctrines and theories of man and the universe, built up an ideal virtuous, wise man. Regarding philosophy as divided into physics, logic, and ethics, Zeno in his plan made of the physics and logic a foundation to serve as the best support he could contrive for the ethical portion of his system. His logic was based upon Aristotle's *Organon*, but he held that all knowledge is ultimately founded on sense perception. The physical theory underlying Stoicism is materialistic. All that has reality is material. Force, which is the shaping principle, is joined with matter. This universal working force, God, pervades all and becomes the reason and soul in the animate creation. The ethical creed of the Stoics accepted virtue as the highest good in life. "To live consistently with nature" was a familiar maxim among them. Human conduct should be brought into agreement with the law of nature. Only by putting aside passion, unjust thoughts, and indulgence and by performing duty with the right disposition can man attain true freedom and rule as lord over his own life. The writings of Epictetus best set forth the ethical truths of Stoicism. See Ludwig Edelstein, *The Meaning of Stoicism* (1966); J. M. Rist, *Stoic Philosophy* (1969); A. A. Long, ed., *Problems in Stoicism* (1971).

Stoke-on-Trent, county borough (1971 pop. 265,153), Staffordshire, W central England. The borough forms the bulk of the area known as the POTTERIES. Situated in a coal field, it is the center of the Staffordshire pottery-making industry. Coal is mined, and brick, tile, chemicals, and tires are manufactured. The Trent to Mersey Canal (opened 1777), which passes through the borough, aided the growth of the pottery industry in the 18th cent. Stoke-on-Trent has several museums and pottery collections; Josiah Wedgwood, Josiah Spode, and Thomas and Herbert Minton have been among the famous potters from the area. North Staffordshire Technical College and the British Ceramic Research Laboratories are there. The writer Arnold Bennett was born in Stoke-on-Trent and is buried there.

Stoker, Bram (Abraham Stoker), 1847–1912, English novelist, b. Ireland. He is best remembered as the author of *Dracula* (1897), a horror story recounting the adventures of the vampire Count Dracula. The fame of the leading character was furthered by popular stage and film adaptations of the novel. Stoker's other novels include *The Jewel of Seven Stars* (1904). For 27 years he was manager for the actor Sir Henry Irving. See R. T. McNally and Radu Florescu, *In Search of Dracula* (1972).

Stokes, Sir George Gabriel, 1819–1903, British mathematician and physicist, b. Ireland, studied at Cambridge. From 1849 he was a professor of mathematics at Cambridge; he served as secretary (1854–85) and as president (1885–92) of the Royal Society. His researches, done in many fields, developed the modern theory of viscous fluids, revealed the nature of fluorescence, and helped to establish the composition of chlorophyll. The important work he did on the undulatory theory of light led to publication of his *Dynamical Theory of Diffraction* (1849). His other publications include *Light* (1884) and *Natural Theology* (1891).

Stokowski, Leopold (stəkŏf'skē), 1882–, American conductor, b. London. Stokowski studied in England and at the Paris Conservatory. He was organist and choirmaster at St. Bartholomew's Church, New York City (1905–8), and was conductor of the Cincinnati Symphony (1909–12). As conductor of the Philadelphia Orchestra (1912–36) he became known for brilliant interpretation and performance; he introduced unknown contemporary works and, with his own controversial transcriptions, popularized much of Bach's music. Stokowski continued to conduct for part of each season until 1941. In 1940 he organized the All-American Youth Orchestra. He was coconductor, with Toscanini, of the NBC Symphony Orchestra (1942–43). Stokowski was musical supervisor of Walt Disney's film *Fantasia* (1940), in which he also appeared. He has been conductor of many renowned orchestras for brief periods. Stokowski was influential in the improvement of music-recording techniques. In 1962 he founded the American Symphony Orchestra, New York City, a forum for young performers. His first wife was the pianist and teacher Olga Samaroff. See his *Music for All of Us* (1943).

STOL aircraft: see SHORT TAKEOFF AND LANDING AIRCRAFT.

Stolberg (shtôl'bĕrkh"), city (1970 pop. 39,632), North Rhine-Westphalia, W West Germany; chartered 1856. It is a center of the West German brass industry, which was started (c.1600) there by Protestant settlers from nearby Aachen. Other manufactures include chemicals, pharmaceuticals, and glass.

stolen goods. The chief legal problem connected with stolen goods is that of TITLE. A thief cannot acquire title to goods that he has stolen, and therefore he cannot transfer title even by sale to an innocent purchaser. Hence the rightful owner of the goods may take them without compensation from anyone who has their possession. The innocent purchaser, however, may sue the seller of the goods (even if he is the thief) for breach of his implied warranty of good title. These rules invariably apply to goods procured by larceny; in certain jurisdictions they obtain also when goods are acquired by embezzlement. The law respecting the sale of a stolen negotiable instrument differs somewhat. There, if the owner is a bona fide purchaser for value, he takes an absolute title. To be such a purchaser he must pay for the instrument with some thing of value (usually money) and must not be aware of anything suspicious in the ownership. The person from whom the instrument was stolen may recover it (without payment) from a holder who is not a bona fide purchaser for value. Such a holder—e.g., one who received the instrument as a gift—may sue the prior endorsers of the instrument for breaching their implied warranty of good title unless they had protected themselves in writing, using the words "without recourse." The person who knowingly receives stolen goods to make a profit—the fence—is guilty of a felony in most jurisdictions. At common law, however, the fence was an ACCESSORY after the fact and hence merely committed a misdemeanor. That the accused knew the goods were stolen usually must be proved from circumstances and his previous conduct. Thus, if he has frequently been in possession of recently stolen goods, there is a strong probability of his guilty knowledge.

Stolp: see SŁUPSK, Poland.

Stolypin, Piotr Arkadevich (pyô'tər ərkä'dyĭvĭch stəlĭ'pĭn), 1862–1911, Russian premier and minister of the interior (1906–11) for Czar Nicholas II. He sought to fight the revolutionary movement with both severe repression and social reform. He instituted a regime of courts-martial to suppress revolutionary terrorism and peasant disorders, and hundreds were executed in 1906 and 1907. To stem peasant unrest Stolypin attempted to create a class of peasant landowners that would be conservative and loyal to the czar. The roots of unrest lay partly in the Edict of Emancipation of 1861 (see EMANCIPATION, EDICT OF), which had given land to the village communes, instead of individually to the newly freed serfs. The commune usually distributed scattered strips to provide families with generally equal allotments. Stolypin's land reforms of 1906 gave the peasant communes the right to dissolve themselves, entitled each peasant to own and consolidate the strips given him by the commune, and provided financial aid to peasants who wished to buy more land. The land reform was designed to transform the peasants gradually into landowners without hurting the interests of the large landowners. At the same time it enabled peasants to seek industrial employment in the cities if they wished to leave the land. It was opposed by the leftist majority in the first DUMA, which favored extensive expropriation of the land. The first and second Dumas were dissolved, and Stolypin made sure of a conservative majority in the third Duma by altering (1907) the election laws. Some of Stolypin's measures were opposed by the Socialists and liberals, others by the extreme reactionaries. His agrarian reform came too late to conciliate the peasantry as a body. When the Russian Revolution of 1917 broke out, the number of small holdings had increased, but not sufficiently to create a conservative peasant class. His attempt to extend the government's policy of Russification to Finland, where he restricted (1910) the authority of the diet, met with wide opposition. While his secret police continued their repressive activities, the government took no action against the anti-Jewish pogroms organized by extreme reactionary societies. Stolypin was assassinated by a revolutionary terrorist who was also a police agent.

stomach, saclike dilation in the gastrointestinal tract between the ESOPHAGUS and the INTESTINES, forming an organ of digestion. The stomach is present in virtually all vertebrate animals and in many invertebrates. In RUMINANTS such as the cow, the stomach is divided into four separate chambers. One of these, called the rumen, breaks down complex plant materials, particularly cellulose. In birds the stomach forms a thick-walled gizzard that is capable of grinding food. The human stomach is a muscular, elastic, pear-shaped bag, lying crosswise in the abdominal cavity beneath the diaphragm. It is capable of gross alterations in size and shape, depending on the position of the body and the amount of food inside. The stomach is about 12 in. (30.5 cm) long and is 6 in. (15.2 cm) wide at its widest point. Its capacity is about 1 qt (0.94 liters) in the adult. Food enters the stomach from the esophagus, through a ring of muscles known as the cardiac sphincter that normally prevents food from passing back to the esophagus. The other end of the stomach empties into the first section of the small intestine, or duodenum; the pyloric sphincter, which separates the two, remains closed until the food in the stomach has been modified and is in suitable condition to pass into the small intestine. The wall of the stomach is composed of four layers: an outer fibrous membrane called the serosa, a three-ply layer of muscle, a submucous layer, and, forming the stomach lining, a mucous layer called the gastric mucosa. The surface of the mucosa is honeycombed with over 35,000 gastric glands and is folded into numerous ridges that almost disappear when the stomach is distended with food. The muscular action of the stomach and the digestive action of the GASTRIC JUICE convert food in the stomach into a semiliquid state (chyme). See also DIGESTIVE SYSTEM.

Stone, Barton Warren, 1772–1844, American clergyman of Kentucky. With four other ministers he withdrew from the Presbyterian Church and in 1804 began to form new churches whose members called themselves simply CHRISTIANS. Through his acquaintance with Alexander CAMPBELL he sought to merge (1832) the Christians with the Disciples of Christ. See C. C. Ware, *Barton Warren Stone, Pathfinder of Christian Union* (1932).

Stone, Edward Durell, 1902–, American architect, b. Fayetteville, Ark. Stone's first major work, designed in the starkly functional International style in collaboration with Philip L. Goodwin, was the Museum of Modern Art, New York City (1937–39). Stone won renown for his design of the U.S. embassy at New Delhi (1958). In this building he introduced traditional Muslim motifs, including lacy grille patterns. Stone subsequently applied grillwork to many of his buildings, including the U.S. pavilion for the Brussels World's Fair (1958) and the Huntington Hartford Museum (1962; now the New York Cultural Center), New York City. Among his later works are the Amarillo Fine Arts Museum (1969); the Univ. of Alabama law school (1970); the John F. Kennedy Center for the Performing Arts (1971), Washington D.C.; and the Community Hospital of Monterey Peninsula, Carmel, Calif. See his autobiography (1962) and *Recent and Future Architecture* (1967).

Stone, Harlan Fiske, 1872–1946, American jurist, 12th Chief Justice of the United States (1941–46), b. Chesterfield, N.H. A graduate (1898) of Columbia Univ. law school, he was admitted (1899) to the bar, practiced law in New York City, and lectured at the Columbia law school, where he became professor (1902) and dean (1910). He resigned his deanship in 1923 and, as U.S. Attorney General (1924–25) under President Coolidge, helped to restore faith in the Dept. of Justice after the Teapot Dome scandals. Appointed (1925) Associate Justice of the Supreme Court, he established a reputation for his vigorous minority opinions, especially those in which he defended the social and economic welfare legislation of the New Deal against the conservative majority. Stone saw many of his minority opinions later accepted as majority decisions. He succeeded Charles Evans Hughes as Chief Justice. *Public Control of Business* (1940) is a selection of Stone's opinions as Associate Justice. See biography by A. T. Mason (1956, repr. 1968) and study by S. J. Konefsky (1946, repr. 1971).

Stone, Lucy, 1818–93, reformer and leader in the woman's rights movement, b. near West Brookfield, Mass., grad. Oberlin, 1847. In 1847 she gave her first lecture on woman's rights, and the following year she was engaged by the Anti-Slavery Society as one of their regular lecturers. As a speaker she had great eloquence and was often able to sway an unruly and antagonistic audience. She married Henry Brown BLACKWELL in 1855 but continued, as a matter of principle, to use her own name and was known as Mrs. Stone. In 1870 she founded the *Woman's Journal,* which was for nearly 50 years the official organ of the National American Woman Suffrage Association. After her death it was edited by her daughter, Alice Stone Blackwell. In 1921 the Lucy Stone League was formed to continue the battle for women's rights. See biographies by her daughter (1930, repr. 1971) and E. R. Hays (1961).

Stone, Melville Elijah, 1848–1929, American journalist, b. Hudson, Ill.; brother of Ormond Stone. With others he founded in 1876 the first Chicago penny paper, the *Daily News,* and in 1881 the *Morning News* (later the *Record*). Stone became general manager of the reorganized Associated Press in 1893, and under his direction it became one of the great news agencies. He retired in 1921. See his *Fifty Years a Journalist* (1921, repr. 1970).

Stone, Nicholas, 1586–1647, English sculptor and mason, b. Devonshire. He rose to a position of highest importance as a decorative sculptor, working after designs by Inigo Jones. His independent productions include the gate at St. Mary's, Oxford, and numerous tombs, such as that of the Viscount Dorchester, Westminster Abbey. His notebook and account book are preserved in the Soane Museum, London, and give much information about his trade. He also wrote a work on fortifications (1645).

Stone, Thomas, 1743–87, political leader in the American Revolution, signer of the Declaration of Independence, b. Charles co., Md. A lawyer, he was (1775–78) a delegate to the Continental Congress, where he served on the committee that framed the Articles of Confederation. Later, he again served briefly in Congress.

stone, in weights and measures: see ENGLISH UNITS OF MEASUREMENT.

Stone Age: see PALEOLITHIC PERIOD; MESOLITHIC PERIOD; NEOLITHIC PERIOD.

stonecat: see CATFISH.

stonecrop, common name for members of the Crassulaceae (also called orpine, or hen-and-chickens, family), a family of succulent, fleshy herbs and shrubs mostly inhabiting arid regions in many parts of the world. Among the larger genera are the S African genus *Crassula* and the genus *Sedum* with many species native to the United States, most abundantly in the West and Southwest. Members of this family are popular garden, rock-garden, and cemetery plants, e.g., frogplant, live-forever, garden orpine, houseleek, hen-and-chickens, and gold moss. These common names are not consistent: in usage the same name is often applied to different species, and different names to a single botanical species. The family is classified in the division MAGNOLIOPHYTA, class Magnoliopsida, order Rosales.

stone curlew: see THICK-KNEE.

stonefly, any insect of the order Plecoptera. North American species, of which there are more than 200, are yellowish, greenish, or brownish in the adult stage and have transparent wings, usually two pairs, but seldom fly. The eggs are deposited in the water; the abundant aquatic nymphs are found under stones, hence their name. Since the gills are poorly developed, the nymphs are confined to well-aerated waters, such as fast streams, where they form one of the most important food supplies for fresh-water fishes. One to three years may be required to reach the adult stage. Fishermen refer to adult stoneflies as browns and imitate their shape in lures. Stoneflies are classified in the phylum ARTHROPODA, class Insecta, order Plecoptera.

Stoneham (stōn'əm), town (1970 pop. 20,725), Middlesex co., NE Mass., a suburb of Boston; settled 1645, set off from Charlestown and inc. 1725. Although chiefly residential, it has a long-standing shoe industry and other varied manufactures.

Stonehaven, burgh (1971 pop. 4,729), county town of Kincardineshire, E Scotland, on the North Sea. A resort town, its products include whiskey and leather and woolen goods. Fishing is carried on. Nearby are the notable ruins of Dunnottar Castle. The castle, on a nearly impregnable cliff 160 ft (49 m) high, was first built in the 7th cent.

Stonehenge (stōn'hĕnj"), group of standing stones on Salisbury Plain, Wiltshire, S England. Preeminent among MEGALITHIC MONUMENTS in the British Isles, it is similar to an older and larger monument at AVEBURY. The great prehistoric structure is enclosed within a circular ditch 300 ft (91 m) in diameter, with a bank on the inner side, and is approached by a broad roadway called the Avenue. Within the circular trench the stones are arranged in four series: the outermost is a circle of sandstones about 13.5 ft (4.1 m) high connected by lintels; the second is a circle of bluestone MENHIRS; the third is horseshoe shaped; the innermost is ovoid. Within the ovoid lies the Altar Stone. The Heelstone is a great upright stone in the Avenue, northeast of the circle. It was at one time widely believed that Stonehenge was a druid temple, but this is contradicted by the fact that the druids probably did not arrive in Britain until c.250 B.C. Most archaeologists agree, however, that Stonehenge served some sort of religious function. In 1963, the British astronomer Gerald Hawkins theorized that Stonehenge was used as a huge astronomical instrument that could accurately measure solar and lunar movements as well as eclipses. Hawkins used a computer to test his calculations and found definite correlations between his figures and the solar and lunar positions in 1500 B.C. Some archaeologists object to Hawkins's theory on the basis that it requires too much sophistication in the accumulation and passing on of data for the Bronze Age culture that existed in England during the 16th cent. B.C. See G. S. Hawkins, *Stonehenge Decoded* (1965); Harry Harrison and L. E. Stover, *Stonehenge* (1972).

Stoneman, George, 1822–94, Union general in the American Civil War, b. Busti, N.Y. As commander of Fort Brown, Texas, in Feb., 1861, he refused to obey the order of General Twiggs to surrender to Texas authorities, but evacuated the fort and sailed for the North with part of his command. He was made a brigadier general of volunteers in Aug., 1861, was chief of cavalry in General McClellan's Peninsular campaign (1862), and commanded an infantry corps at Fredericksburg. In 1863, Stoneman made a spectacular but unsuccessful raid to General Lee's rear just before the battle of Chancellorsville. In the Atlanta campaign (1864) he commanded the cavalry of the Army of the Ohio. While making a raid on Andersonville, Ga., he was captured. Exchanged after a three-month imprisonment, he resumed cavalry operations in E Tennessee, W Virginia, and W North Carolina. He retired from the army in 1871 and moved to California. He served as governor of California from 1883 to 1887. See I. W. Van Noppen, *Stoneman's Last Raid* (1961).

stone marten: see MARTEN.

Stone Mountain Memorial, memorial to the Confederacy, consisting of the equestrian figures of Robert E. Lee, Stonewall Jackson, and Jefferson Davis carved on the northern face of Stone Mt., a granite dome 650 ft high (198 m) in NW Ga., NE of Atlanta. The memorial was commissioned by the Daughters of the Confederacy in 1916 and was designed and partially executed by Gutzon Borglum. In 1924, however, Borglum resigned and destroyed his models over a disagreement with the memorial's sponsors. Sculptor Augustus Lukeman took charge of the project in 1925 and abandoned the original design. Work stopped in 1930 and was not resumed until 1963, when the state of Georgia purchased the mountain and established a state park. Walter Hahock completed the sculpture, which was dedicated in 1970.

stones, precious: see GEM.

Stones River National Battlefield: see NATIONAL PARKS AND MONUMENTS (table).

stoneware, hard POTTERY made from siliceous paste, fired at high temperature to vitrify (make glassy) the body. Stoneware is heavier and more opaque than porcelain and differs from terra-cotta in being nonporous and nonabsorbent. The usual color of fired stoneware tends toward gray, though there may be a wide range of color, depending on the clay. It has been produced in China since ancient times and is the forerunner of Chinese porcelain. It is difficult to distinguish between early porcelaneous stoneware and true porcelain. During the Ming dynasty (1368–1644) a porcelainlike stoneware was developed with remarkable red and green glazes. In the 16th cent. it was extensively manufactured in Yi-hsing in Kiangsu prov., which is notable for its unusual teapots of red, buff, or gray and glazed or enameled stoneware. In Europe stoneware was manufactured in the 12th cent. in Germany, especially in the north and on the lower Rhine. Early salt-glazed wares have been found at Aachen and Cologne; these grayish, blue, and brown wares were exported in quantity to the Lowlands and England. Dutch, Flemish, and German potteries of the late 14th cent. made a distinctive stoneware, known as Cologne ware or *grès de Flandres,* with stamped or profusely modeled decoration; most of the examples exhibit a lead glaze, though a cream-colored variety was usually left unglazed. In the 1670s, John Dwight started to make stoneware jugs and mugs in England and climaxed his work with remarkable figurines and portrait busts of porcelaneous stoneware. By the turn of the century a white salt-glazed ware was being widely produced in Staffordshire. In the last quarter of the 18th cent. Josiah WEDGWOOD invented and developed two stonewares that are still justly prized: basalt ware and jasper ware. Stoneware remains one of the most common forms of ceramics and is often employed in commercial and industrial products. See PORCELAIN.

stonework, term applied to various types of work—that of the lapidary who shapes, cuts, and polishes gemstones or engraves them for seals and ornaments; of the jeweler or craftsman who mounts or encrusts them in gold, silver, or other metal; of the stonemason who executes the plan of architect or engineer for wall, pier, vault, bridge, or dam; of the carver who chisels bas-relief, intaglio, or freestanding figure, using a pointing machine for accuracy; and of the printer at his imposing stone. The term *stonework* is most frequently used to refer to the craft of masonry, as old as civilization and still widely used. Of Roman masonry buildings, some aqueducts, arches, basilicas, and baths still remain. Masonry is classified according to finish, rubble being of rough-quarried or field stone and ashlar of dressed stone. It may be laid without mortar (and is then called dry, or Cyclopean) or with mortar to bind the stones closely together, the outside finish of such joints being called pointing. Stonemasonry may be of hard materials, such as granite, bluestone, or marble, requiring full finish before laying, or of softer varieties, such as brownstone, laid with rough exterior, the decoration being carved afterward. The pyramids (see PYRAMID) and the SPHINX of Egypt are among the world's greatest masterpieces of stonework.

stonewort: see CHLOROPHYTA.

Stoney Creek, town (1971 pop. 8,380), SE Ont., Canada. It is a suburb of HAMILTON and was the site of an American defeat (1813) in the War of 1812.

Stonington (stōn'ĭngtən), town (1970 pop. 15,940), New London co., extreme SE Conn., on a peninsula jutting into Long Island Sound; settled 1649 from Plymouth, inc. 1662. Fishing, boatbuilding, and the manufacture of precision tools and textiles are the leading industries. Stonington was once an important shipbuilding and whaling center, and many houses built by sea captains still remain. Whistler lived there. The town includes the village of Mystic and several shore resorts.

stop: see PUNCTUATION.

stope, underground mine opening, room, or cavern, normally of high vertical extent, from which ore is removed.

Stopes, Marie Carmichael (stōps), 1880-1958, English paleobotanist and eugenicist, b. Edinburgh, D.Sc. Univ. of London, Ph.D. Univ. of Munich. She lectured on paleobotany at the universities of London and Manchester. In 1921, with Humphrey Verdon Roe, her second husband, she founded the first birth-control clinic in the British Empire. Her activities in this field gave impetus to similar movements elsewhere. Her many works include books on eugenics, birth control, and paleobotany. See biographies by Aylmer Maude (1933) and Keith Briant (1962).

Stoph, Willi (vĭl'ē shtôf), 1914-, East German political leader. A member of the German Communist party from 1931, he helped build the East German Socialist Unity (Communist) party after World War II. In 1953 he was named to the party's politburo. Stoph served (1952-55) as minister of internal affairs and minister for national defense (1956-60), in which capacity he developed the East German army. Deputy chairman of the council of ministers (1954-64), he became chairman, or prime minister, in 1964. In March, 1970, he met with West German Chancellor Willy Brandt and initiated negotiations for a nonaggression treaty and the normalization of relations; it was the first meeting between leaders of East and West Germany. He was replaced (1974) as prime minister by Horst Sindermann and given the ceremonial position of chairman of the Council of State.

storage battery: see BATTERY, ELECTRIC.

storage tube, ELECTRON TUBE used for storing information. The information can be introduced in the form of an electric or other signal, and later read out, electrically or in some other form. A television camera tube is a form of storage tube as well as a transducer, since the patterns of light form accumulations of electric charge on the tube's photosensitive surface that remain stored on the surface until read out by an electron beam. In another type of storage tube, known as a display storage tube, an image formed on the phosphor-coated surface by an impinging electron beam persists until erased. The pattern of electric charges introduced into the tube during a "write" cycle modulates the electron beam that is swept across the surface, thus producing the image. Certain tubes of this type are designed for particular purposes, as for displaying alphabetic characters and numerals. Increasingly, display storage tubes are being replaced by ordinary cathode-ray tubes connected to computerlike devices that continually refresh the displayed image. Some types of tubes designed for computer storage are being replaced by solid-state devices. Certain semiconductor devices even show promise as replacements for television camera tubes.

storax (stôr'ăks) or **styrax** (stī'raks), balsam resin from the trunk of the *Liquidambar orientalis,* a plant of the WITCH HAZEL family, found in Asia Minor. Purified storax is a dark brown, viscous liquid with a strong aromatic odor and taste. It is used in medicine and perfumes.

store, commonly a shop or stall for the retail sale of commodities, but also a place where wholesale supplies are kept, exhibited, or sold. Retailing—the sale of merchandise to the consumer—is one of the oldest businesses in the world. It was even practiced in prehistoric times, and it has been the custom of all primitive peoples. The earliest form of retail merchandising was probably the exchange of food and weapons; later came traders and peddlers, and by 3000 B.C. shops had become common. During the Greek and Roman period, stores, including many specialty shops, developed in the form of open booths, attracting large and cosmopolitan crowds. After the decline of the Roman Empire, merchants resorted to the older practice of barter in designated marketplaces, but by the 14th cent. retail trade had again assumed importance. Merchants, who in early times were viewed with suspicion, rose in the social scale. Small stores, each carrying its special line of goods, reached their peak in the 18th cent. The wholesale business developed, and traveling salesmen and standard prices came into general use. In America the general store preceded the single-line store and is still common in a few small rural communities. In the late 19th cent. the department store came into being—a large-scale general store or a combination of single-line stores in which each line of merchandise is operated as a separate department. Such stores provide the convenience of easy accessibility to a large variety of goods, all displayed in one location. Modern department stores have been vital to the development of many suburban shopping malls, huge retail developments that contain a wide variety of stores and services, as well as ample automobile parking space. Retail concerns that do business principally through the mails are called mail-order houses. In the United States the two oldest and largest are Montgomery Ward (founded 1872) and Sears, Roebuck, and Company (founded 1886); both have warehouses, showrooms, and retail stores in many urban communities, but sell their goods to rural residents by means of free annual catalogs. Chain stores, though known in earlier times, first developed their modern form in 1859, when the Great Atlantic and Pacific Tea Company (A&P) standardized the quality and price of all merchandise sold in their stores. Through central management, quantity purchasing, the elimination of middlemen, standardization of business methods, and limited individual service, the chains are able to sell their goods well below prices charged by independent stores. Most common among chain stores are five-and-ten-cent stores (e.g., F. W. Woolworth Company), bakeries, tobacco stores, drugstores, groceries, and department stores. Chain stores now dominate the retail trade business, and since the independent retailer finds it difficult to match the prices of the chain stores, considerable antagonism has developed. Some independent grocers have combined to form voluntary chains purchasing their supplies from a single wholesaler in order to obtain chain-store discounts. Several states have imposed FAIR-TRADE LAWS to limit the power of chain stores; such statutes have been upheld by the Supreme Court. Consumers' cooperative stores (see COOPERATIVE MOVEMENT) have been established in Europe and America; such stores are profit-sharing organizations, which benefit the consumer by eliminating the cost of middlemen. See C. H. McGregor, *Retail Management Problems of Small and Medium Size Stores* (3d ed. 1962); G. M. Lebhar, *Chain Stores in America, 1859-1959* (3d ed. 1963).

Store Baelt (stô'rə bĕlt) and **Lille Baelt** (lĭl'ə) [Great Belt and Little Belt], two shallow straits, S Denmark, connecting the Kattegat with the Baltic Sea. The Store Baelt, c.40 mi (60 km) long and from 10 to 20 mi (16-32 km) wide, separates Sjaelland and Fyn islands. The Lille Baelt, c.30 mi (50 km) long and from .5 to 18 mi (.8-29 km) wide, between Fyn and Jutland, is crossed by a road and railroad bridge.

Storey, David, 1933-, English novelist and playwright, b. Wakefield, Yorkshire. From the experience of playing professional rugby came his first novel, *This Sporting Life* (1960), about the brutalization of a man who has no choice other than to play football. His best-known play, *Home* (1971), set in an old people's asylum, also treats the theme of dehumanization. Storey's other works include the novels *Pasmore* (1974) and *A Temporary Life* (1974), and the plays *The Restoration of Arthur Middleton* (1966), *The Contractor* (1971), and *The Changing Room* (1972).

Storey, Moorfield, 1845-1929, American lawyer, b. Roxbury, Mass., grad. Harvard, 1866. He attended Harvard law school and was admitted (1869) to the bar. He was (1867-69) secretary to Charles Sumner and thereafter practiced law in Boston. Noted for his reform leanings, he fought political corruption, opposed American colonial expansion, and sought the advancement of Negroes and Indians in the United States. He was president of the National Association for the Advancement of Colored People from 1910 until his death. His writings include a biography of Charles Sumner (1900, repr. 1970) and *Problems of Today* (1920). See biography by M. A. De Wolfe Howe (1932); study by W. B. Hixson (1972).

Storfjord (stôr'fyôr''), deep inlet of the Norwegian Sea, c.70 mi (110 km) long, Møre og Romsdal co., SW Norway. A scenic area with sheer cliffs and high waterfalls, Storfjord branches into several fjords, the most famous of which is Geirangerfjord. Cruise ships call regularly every summer. Some of the farms on its cliffs are accessible only by ladder.

stork, common name for members of a family of long-legged wading birds. The storks are related to the herons and ibises, and are found in most of the warmer parts of the world. Storks have long, broad, powerful wings; in flight they flap their wings or soar with their legs dangling and their long necks bent back in an S shape. They feed on fish, reptiles, amphibians, mollusks, and insects, which they catch with quick thrusts of their long, heavy bills. Having no syrinx muscles, storks are mute—though they produce a clattering noise by snapping their bills. The only storks found in the Americas are the American wood stork, previously known as the wood ibis, a white bird about 4 ft (122 cm) long with a glossy greenish-black tail, found in temperate and tropical regions; and the jabiru, of the tropics, with a white-and-black body and naked black head. In Europe the white stork, *Ciconia ciconia,* (c.40 in./100 cm long, with red bill and legs) is regarded as a good omen, particularly of fertility, and is encouraged to build its platform nest on housetops. It is common from Holland to the Balkans. The black stork of Eurasia, *C. nigra,* is smaller and wilder. Largest of the family are the saddle-billed stork of Africa and the adjutant storks of S Asia and tropical Africa, so named (despite their untidy head feathers) for their upright military bearing. One Indian species, called also marabou, has soft tail feathers used in millinery and once popular for making feather boas. Adjutant storks are valued and protected as scavengers. Storks are classified in the phylum CHORDATA, subphylum Vertebrata, class Aves, order Ciconiiformes, family Ciconiidae.

Storm, Theodor (tā'ōdôr shtôrm), 1817-88, German poet and novelist, b. Schleswig-Holstein. From 1843 to 1853 he practiced law in his native Husum, but he was exiled (1853-64) by Denmark for irredentism. After Schleswig-Holstein became Prussian he served the government as a judge, retiring in 1880 to Hademarschen, where his country place became a literary mecca. His view that literature should stem from true emotion is reflected in his lyric poetry. Many of his earlier poems, stories, and novellas relate the rustic joys of his native province; the popular story *Immensee* (1852) is marked by nostalgic lyricism. Later works, melancholy and realistic, show a marked change in tone, and *Der Schimmelreiter* (1888; tr. *The Rider of the White Horse,* 1915) exemplifies the full development of a stern yet noble sense of tragedy. Among his many other works is *Aquis Submersus* (1877, tr. 1910), a historical novella. See biography by A. T. Alt (1973); study by C. A. Bernd (rev. ed. 1966).

storm, disturbance of the ordinary conditions of the atmosphere attended by wind, rain, snow, sleet, hail, or thunder and lightning. Types of storms include the extratropical CYCLONE, the common, large-scale storm of temperate latitudes; the tropical cyclone, or HURRICANE, which is somewhat smaller in area than the former and accompanied by high winds and heavy rains; the TORNADO, or "twister," a small but intense storm with very high winds, usually of limited duration; and the THUNDERSTORM, local in nature and accompanied by brief but heavy rain showers and often by hail. The term *storm* is also applied to blizzards, sandstorms, and dust storms, in which high wind is the dominant meteorological element. A storm surge is a type of TIDAL WAVE.

Storm and Stress: see STURM UND DRANG.

Storm King, mountain, 1,355 ft (413 m) high, SE N.Y., on the west shore of the Hudson River near West Point. It is included in the Palisades Interstate Park.

storm petrel: see PETREL.

Storrs, Richard Salter, 1821-1900, American Congregational minister, b. Braintree, Mass. From 1846 he was pastor of the Church of the Pilgrims, Brooklyn, N.Y. From 1848 to 1861 he was an editor of the *Independent,* of which he was a founder. Storrs was noted for his eloquence in the pulpit and on the lecture platform.

Storrs (stôrz), community (1970 pop. 10,691), a part of the town of Mansfield, Tolland co., NE Conn. It is the seat of the Univ. of Connecticut.

Storting (stôr'tĭng), national parliament of Norway, dating from 1814. Its members are elected by direct universal suffrage for a four-year term, and representation is proportional. The Storting elects one fourth of its members to form the Lagting, or upper house, the remainder constituting the Odelsting or lower house, in which all bills must originate. Ministers may attend the Storting but may not vote.

Story, Joseph, 1779–1845, American jurist, Associate Justice of the Supreme Court (1811–45), b. Marblehead, Mass. Admitted to the Massachusetts bar in 1801, he practiced law in Salem and was several times elected to the Massachusetts legislature. He served briefly in Congress in 1808–9. Story's legal scholarship quickly earned him great prominence, and in 1811 (at the age of 32) he was appointed by President Madison to the U.S. Supreme Court, the youngest person ever to hold that position. In the early period of his judicial tenure, as part of his duties on the Supreme Court, he was also a circuit justice in New England. His decisions helped frame U.S. admiralty and prize law. Story's judicial views nearly always agreed with those of John MARSHALL; this was not the case with Marshall's successor, Roger B. Taney. One of the most important opinions Story wrote for the Supreme Court was *Martin* vs. *Hunter's Lessee* (1816); it established the power of the court to review issues of constitutional law raised in state cases. Story expressed his strong antislavery sentiments in several judgments that ordered the repatriation to Africa of Negroes brought into U.S. ports by slavers. In 1829, Story became the first Dane professor of law at Harvard. For the remainder of his life he sat on the Supreme Court, taught at Harvard, and, in connection with his teaching, wrote many legal works, systematic summaries of bodies of case law (mostly British), so treated as to elucidate the legal and philosophical bases. Story's texts must be ranked with James Kent's *Commentaries on the American Law* as formative influences on American jurisprudence and legal education. They include commentaries on bailments (1832), the U.S. Constitution (3 vol., 1833), conflict of laws (1834), equity jurisprudence (2 vol., 1836), equity pleading (1838), agency (1839), partnership (1841), bills of exchange (1843), and promissory notes (1845). All his books appeared in several editions; that on equity jurisprudence (14th ed. 1918) perhaps retained its utility longest. See *Life and Letters of Joseph Story,* ed. by his son, W. W. Story (1851); M. D. Schwartz and J. C. Hogan, ed., *Joseph Story: A Collection of Writings by and about an Eminent American Jurist* (1959); studies by G. T. Dunne (1971) and James McClellan (1971).

Story, William Wetmore, 1819–95, American sculptor and writer, b. Salem, Mass.; son of Supreme Court Justice Joseph Story. In the late 1840s he published two legal treatises and a volume of poetry. Chosen in 1847 to make a statue of his father (Mt. Auburn Chapel, Cambridge, Mass.), he went to Italy to study sculpture. From 1856 he lived in Rome, devoting his time to sculpture. His brilliant personal gifts made his studio a social and artistic center; the Brownings and Nathaniel Hawthorne, who lavishly praised Story's *Cleopatra,* were among his friends. His sculptures, which were highly admired in their time, comprise draped classic figures of women and somewhat stiff, incisive portrait statues of eminent contemporaries. His works include *Semiramis, Medea,* and *Salome* (Metropolitan Mus.), and *Chief Justice Marshall* and *Professor Henry* (Washington, D.C.). Among his books are *Roba di Roma* (1862), a collection of essays, and *Graffiti d'Italia* (1868), containing his most sustained poetry. See Henry James, *William Wetmore Story and His Friends* (1903).

Stoss, Veit (fĭt shtôs), c.1445–1533, German sculptor. He worked in Kraków (1477–86, 1488–96) and Nuremberg, his birthplace. The great carved wooden high altar in St. Mary's, Kraków, is a significant early work. His stone tomb of King Casimir IV is also in Kraków. The *Annunciation* carved in wood (1517–19), his most famous work, is in the Church of St. Lawrence, Nuremberg. His art is characterized by an expressive realism, angular poses and drapery, precise technique, and tightly packed composition, typical of late German Gothic work. His later style shows greater breadth in the treatment of drapery and poses.

Stoughton, William (stō'tən), 1631–1701, American colonial statesman. He was probably born in England but studied at Harvard (grad. 1650) before attending New College, Oxford (M.A., 1653). At the Restoration (1660) he was ejected from his fellowship at Oxford. He returned (1662) to Massachusetts Bay colony, where he became active in public life, serving as colonial assistant (1671–86). Between 1677 and 1679 he represented the colony in England in regard to the claims of the heirs of John MASON (1586–1635) and Sir Ferdinando GORGES. Stoughton was a member of the council of Gov. Edmund ANDROS but eventually joined the opposition. From 1692 to his death he was lieutenant governor of the colony, and for about five years of that time he served as acting governor. He presided with great severity at the Salem witchcraft trials (1692). Stoughton was one of the major early benefactors of Harvard College; Stoughton Hall was named for him.

Stoughton (stō'tən), town (1970 pop. 23,459), Norfolk co., E Mass.; founded 1637, inc. 1726. Shoes, woolen textiles, and electrical equipment are among its manufactures.

Stourbridge (sto͝or'brĭj, stour'–), municipal borough (1971 pop. 54,331), Worcestershire, W central England. In the 16th cent. Stourbridge's famous glass-making industry was established. Other products are chains, tools, and heating apparatus. In 1974, Stourbridge became part of the new nonmetropolitan county of Hereford and Worcester.

Stout, Rex, 1886–, American novelist, b. Noblesville, Ind. He served in the navy and worked in New York City as founder and director of the Vanguard Press. His best-known works are nearly 70 mystery stories featuring Nero Wolfe, a large gourmet detective who solves crimes from the safety of his study. Collections of his Nero Wolfe novels include *Homicide Trinity* (1962), *Royal Flush* (1965), *Three Aces* (1971), and *Please Pass the Guilt* (1973). Stout's *Nero Wolfe Cookbook* appeared in 1973. See study by W. S. Baring-Gould (1969).

stout, alcoholic beverage: see BEER.

stove, device used for HEATING or for cooking food. As early as Roman times stoves made of clay, tile, or earthenware were in use in central and N Europe. A cast-iron stove made in China before 200 A.D. has been found, but it was not until late in the 15th cent. that cast-iron stoves were first made in Europe. These consisted of plates that were grooved to fit together in the shape of a box. Probably the earliest of this type were earthenware stoves enclosed in iron castings decorated with biblical scenes and armorial and arabesque designs. They often bore inscriptions in Norse, German, Dutch, French, or sometimes Latin, and some were dated. Many were highly artistic specimens of handicraft. A typical early iron stove is the wall-jamb, or five-plate, stove, which was fueled from an adjoining room. Some exquisitely colored and glazed tile stoves, dating from the 16th and 17th cent., show traces of Moorish influence. Early Swiss stoves of clay or brick, without chimneys, were built against the outer house wall, with an opening to the outside through which they were fueled and through which the smoke could escape. Scarcity of fuel made an economical heat-retaining device necessary, and these primitive stoves, built of clay, brick, tile, or plastered masonry, became common in the Scandinavian countries, Holland, Germany, and N France. In Russia large brick stoves formed a partition between two rooms. Because of the very long flue, which wound back and forth inside the structure, these could be heated for some hours with a small amount of light fuel. Dutch, Swedish, and German settlers of the American colonies, especially those of Delaware, Pennsylvania, and New Jersey, brought with them five-plate stoves or molds for casting them. Iron founding began c.1724 in America, and old forges or foundries have left records of five-plate stoves sold in 1728 as Dutch stoves or, less commonly, carved stoves. These continued to be made until Revolutionary times, when they were superseded by the English, or 10-plate, stove, which stood free of the wall and had a draft or fuel door. These 10-plate devices could cook and warm at the same time and replaced, in part, the large masonry baking oven, usually built outside the house. The stove was regarded as a cooking device supplementary to the fireplace, near which it stood; its stovepipe led into the fireplace chimney. It was not until about the middle of the 19th cent., when the coal-burning range with removable lids came into general use, that the fireplace was finally supplanted as the chief cooking agency. For heating, the Franklin stove, invented in 1743, was the lineal descendant of the fireplace, being at first only a portable downdraft iron fireplace that could be set into, or before, the chimney. It was soon elaborated into what was known as the Pennsylvania fireplace, with a grate and sliding doors. In common use for a period after the Revolution, it was followed by a variety of heaters burning wood and coal. The base burner, or magazine coal heater, was widely used before the general adoption of central heating. Since gas and electricity have become generally available, the wood-burning or coal-burning range has been largely superseded by a wide variety of cooking apparatus, using natural or manufactured gas, oil, acetylene, gasoline, or electricity as fuel. In areas of the world where there is abundant sunshine, solar stoves are becoming increasingly popular. Their heat is supplied by the sun's rays, which are focused by means of a concave reflector. The microwave oven uses radiowaves of high frequency to cook foods very quickly without heating the oven itself. It is used mainly in commercial establishments where speed is an advantage.

Stow, John, 1525?–1605, English chronicler and antiquarian. He was a tailor in his youth, but after 1560 he came under the patronage of Archbishop Mathew Parker, whose Society of Antiquaries he joined, and began collecting historical documents and manuscripts. His edition of Chaucer appeared in 1561, and in 1565 he produced a *Summarie of Englyshe Chronicles.* His work was periodically examined by the government, as he was suspected of Roman Catholic inclinations. His *Chronicles of England* (1580) was first called *Annales of England* (its best-known title) in the edition of 1592. He produced editions of the work of Holinshed and other English chroniclers. In 1598 there appeared his *Survey of London,* an immensely valuable account of the city in Elizabethan times. John Strype issued a new edition in 1720 (repr. 1971). Stow is one of the most trustworthy of 16th-century chroniclers.

Stow (stō), city (1970 pop. 19,847), Summit co., NE Ohio, a suburb of Akron; settled 1802, inc. as a city 1960. Chiefly residential, it has some industry, including automobile assembly.

Stowe, Calvin Ellis (stō), 1802–86, American educator, b. Natick, Mass., grad. Bowdoin College, 1824, and Andover Theological Seminary, 1828; husband of Harriet Beecher Stowe. He was professor of Greek (1831–33) at Dartmouth and of sacred literature (1833–50) at Lane Theological Seminary, Cincinnati, of which Lyman Beecher was president. He married Harriet Beecher in 1836. He was also professor of religion (1850–52) at Bowdoin and of sacred literature (1852–64) at Andover Theological Seminary. While in Cincinnati, Stowe became interested in the improvement of the public elementary schools; the College of Teachers in Cincinnati was founded in 1833 largely through his efforts. His writings include *Introduction to the Criticism and Interpretation of the Bible* (1835), *Report on Elementary Instruction in Europe* (1837), and *The Origin and History of the Books of the Bible* (1867).

Stowe, Harriet Beecher, 1811–96, American novelist and humanitarian, b. Litchfield, Conn. With her novel *Uncle Tom's Cabin,* she helped to stir the conscience of Americans concerning slavery and thereby influenced the course of American history. The daughter of Lyman Beecher, pastor of the Congregational Church in Litchfield, and the sister of Henry Ward Beecher, Harriet grew up in an atmosphere of rigid New England Puritanism and, like all the Beechers, early developed an interest in theology and in schemes for improving humanity. In 1824 she went to Hartford, at first to study, later to teach in her sister Catherine's school. When her father became head of Lane Theological Seminary in Cincinnati, she moved to that city with him, and there began teaching again and writing. In 1836 she married Professor Calvin Ellis Stowe. Cincinnati, a border city, was torn with abolitionist conflicts. Harriet's brothers were violently opposed to slavery, and she had seen its effects in Kentucky and had aided a runaway slave, but it was not until the Fugitive Slave Act (1850) that she was moved to write on the subject. *Uncle Tom's Cabin* (1852), first published serially in an abolitionist paper, the *National Era* (1851–52), was not intended as abolitionist propaganda, nor was it directed against the South, although slaveholders condemned the book as unfair; indeed, it presented some of the favorable aspects of slavery, but it also crystallized the sentiments of the North. In one year over 300,000 copies were sold, and the dramatization by G. L. Aiken had a long run. The book was translated into many foreign languages, and when Mrs. Stowe visited Europe in 1853 numerous honors were bestowed on her. Her second novel of slavery, *Dred* (1856), while better constructed and more accurate, failed to recapture the warm characterization of the first. During the 1850s she worked vigorously for the antislavery effort, although she never allied herself with the abolitionists, whom she considered extremists. After the Civil War she bought a plantation to help the emancipated Negroes, but the venture was a failure. The mother of six children, she was constantly harassed by financial worries, for despite the great popularity of her books her earnings were never large, and she and her husband were unbusinesslike and overly generous. Interested in other reform movements, such as temperance and woman suffrage, she also wrote religious poems and articles for religious magazines and housekeeping manuals. Her works are generally given to sermonizing, but in *The Minister's Wooing* (1859) and *Old Town Folks* (1869) she catches the New England of her childhood. A prolific writer whose works fill 16 volumes, she was chiefly popular because she so aptly expressed the sentiments of the 19th-century middle class. See her life and letters, ed. by Annie Fields (1897, repr. 1970); biographies by her son, Charles Edward Stowe (1889, repr. 1967), and Forrest Wilson (1941); study by A. C. Crozier (1969).

Stowe (stō), resort town (1970 pop. 2,388), Lamoille co., N central Vt.; settled 1794, inc. 1896. It is surrounded by mountains, including Mt. Mansfield, Vermont's highest. Stowe is one of New England's largest ski resort areas. In addition to tourism and a thriving trade in antiques, dairying and farming are carried on in Stowe, and wood products and maple sugar are made. The area has many scenic attractions, and there are several state forests and a state park nearby.

STP or **standard temperature and pressure,** standard conditions for measurement of the properties of matter. The standard temperature is the freezing point of pure water, 0°C or 273.15°K. The standard pressure is the pressure exerted by a column of mercury (symbol Hg) 760 mm high, often designated 760 mm Hg. This pressure is also called one atmosphere and is equal to 1.01325×10^6 dynes per sq cm, or approximately 14.7 lb per sq in. The density (mass per volume) of a gas is usually reported as its value at STP. Properties that cannot be measured at STP are measured under other conditions; usually the values obtained are then mathematically extrapolated to their values at STP.

strabismus (strəbĭz'məs), inability of the eyes to focus together because of an imbalance in the muscles that control EYE movement; also called squint. It is a consequence of weakness or uneven development of one or more of the six small muscles that surround the eye. One or both eyes may be affected. Horizontal strabismus is caused when the eyes do not move together laterally; this condition is known as cross-eye if the eye turns inward or walleye if the eye turns outward. Vertical strabismus results when the eye rolls upward or downward in its socket. There is also torsional strabismus in which the eyes do not rotate together about their optical axes. Strabismo is usually present at birth and becomes apparent early in infancy, but it may also result from illness or injury. Because the condition results in perception of a double image, there is a tendency to use only one eye. It is important that treatment be started as soon as possible to prevent loss of sight in the unused eye. Corrective therapy includes exercise that strengthens eye muscles and prescription of corrective lenses. Sometimes a patch is placed alternately on each eye so that neither is allowed to become completely unused. If necessary, the eye muscles may be shortened or lengthened surgically.

Strabo (strā'bō), b. c.63 B.C., d. after A.D. 21, Greek geographer, historian, and philosopher, b. Amasya, Pontus. He studied in Asia Minor, Greece, Rome, and Alexandria and traveled in Europe, N Africa, and W Asia. Primarily a historian, he wrote a group of historical sketches (47 books) quoted by later authors but almost entirely lost. His *Geographia,* written subsequently, is based on his own observations and on the works of his predecessors, including Homer, Eratosthenes, Polybius, and Posidonius; it contains historical material as well as descriptions of places and peoples and is a rich source of ancient knowledge of the world. Its value is uneven, in great part because Strabo attributed to Homer an accurate knowledge of places and peoples mentioned in his epics and because he virtually disregarded Herodotus' information, which was often firsthand. The *Geographia* (extant except for part of the 7th book) is divided into 17 books: 2 introductory (largely a discussion of the definition and scope of geography), 8 on Europe, 6 on Asia, and one on Africa, mainly Egypt. Although a Latin translation appeared in 1472, the first printed edition in the original Greek was the Aldine (1516). There are numerous modern editions and translations into several languages. See the Loeb Classical Library edition, *The Geography of Strabo* (ed. by H. L. Jones, 8 vol., 1917–32), with an introduction on Strabo's life and works.

Strachan, John (strôn), 1778–1867, Canadian Anglican prelate, b. Scotland. As a member of the executive council of Upper Canada (1815–36) and of the legislative council (1820–41), he was an influential leader on the Conservative side. In 1839 he became the first Anglican bishop of Toronto. Strachan worked earnestly for education, but always firmly advocated control by the Anglican church of all institutions of learning. In the long struggle to settle the matter of the CLERGY RESERVES, he unequivocally maintained that the Anglican church had the sole claim to their use. See biography by Sylvia Boorman (1969); studies by J. L. Henderson (1969) and David Flint (1971).

Strachey, John (Evelyn John St. Loe Strachey)(strā'chē; ēv'lĭn, sənt lo͞o), 1901–63, British politician and writer; son of John St. Loe Strachey. He served as a Labour member of Parliament from 1929 to 1931, but he withdrew from the Labour party in 1931 and joined Oswald MOSLEY in forming the more radical New Party. While Mosley moved to the right, however, Strachey became a Marxist theorist. *The Coming Struggle for Power* (1932), his best-known work, was followed by other books on political and economic theory—*The Nature of Capitalist Crisis* (1935), *The Theory and Practice of Socialism* (1936), and *A Programme for Progress* (1939). Having rejoined (1943) the Labour party, he was returned to Parliament again in 1945. From 1946 to 1950 he served as food minister; from 1950 to 1951 he was secretary for war. His later writings include *Contemporary Capitalism* (1956), *End of Empire* (1959), and *The Strangled Cry and Other Unparliamentary Papers* (1962). See biography by Hugh Thomas (1973).

Strachey, Lytton (Giles Lytton Strachey), 1880–1932, English biographer and critic, educated at Cambridge. He was one of the leading members of the BLOOMSBURY GROUP. Strachey is credited with having revolutionized the art of writing biography. In reaction to the copious dull scholarship and the lengthy panegyrics of the 19th cent., he determined to write biographies that were swift, selective, critical, witty, and artistic. His work includes *Eminent Victorians* (1918), a volume of short biographical studies; *Queen Victoria* (1921), his masterpiece; *Elizabeth and Essex* (1928); and *Portraits in Miniature* (1931). As a critic, Strachey was the author of such works as *Landmarks in French Literature* (1912), a study of the classical spirit, and *Books and Characters* (1922). See biography by Michael Holroyd (2 vol., 1968).

Strachey, William, 1572–1621, English colonial historian; educated at Cambridge. In 1609 he sailed to Virginia with Sir Thomas GATES. A storm wrecked his ship in the Bermudas, and the party remained there for nearly a year. A letter written by Strachey describing this experience was supposedly seen by Shakespeare and served as inspiration for his *Tempest.* When Strachey arrived (1610) at the colony he was made secretary and wrote, for the Virginia Company, a report of conditions under the title *Historie of Travaile into Virginia Britannia* (pub. by the Hakluyt Society, 1849 and 1951). His writings are prime sources for the early history of Virginia. See biography by S. G. Culliford (1965).

Stradella, Alessandro (älĕs-sän'drō strädĕl'lä), 1642?–1682, Italian composer of operas, cantatas, oratorios, and instrumental music. Few facts but many legends exist concerning his life; he is said to have been assassinated at the behest of a Venetian nobleman with whose mistress Stradella had eloped. His life is the subject of several operas, one by Friedrich von Flotow (1844). Stradella's music is generally lighthearted and melodious. He helped to develop the structural form and expressive power of the aria and to increase the use of contrapuntal techniques in opera. Handel was influenced by his oratorios and even borrowed some of his musical ideas.

Stradivari, Antonio (äntô'nyō strädĕvä'rē), or **Antonius Stradivarius** (ăntō'nēəs strădĭvâr'ēəs), 1644–1737, Italian violin maker of Cremona; pupil of Niccolò Amati. He was apprenticed to Amati c.1658 and may have remained with him until Amati's death in 1684. Stradivari's earliest extant label is dated 1666 and his last 1737. His finest instruments were made after 1700. Careful research by the Hill brothers of London revealed that he produced at least 1,116 instruments, of which 540 violins, 12 violas, and 50 cellos were known to them. He also made viols, guitars, and mandolins. His workmanship brought the violin to perfection, and later craftsmen have tried to imitate his instruments. He was recognized in his time, and his commissions included those from James II of England and Charles III of Spain. Two of his sons, Francesco Stradivari (1671–1743) and Omobono Stradivari (1679–1742), worked with him and continued the craft after his death, producing a number of fine instruments. See biographies by W. Henley (1961) and W. H. Hill (1963).

Strafford, Thomas Wentworth, 1st **earl of,** 1593–1641, English statesman. Regularly elected to Parliament from 1614 on, he became one of the critics of George Villiers, 1st duke of Buckingham, and of the war with Spain. CHARLES I made him sheriff of Yorkshire in order to exclude him from the Parliament of 1626, but Wentworth continued his opposition and was imprisoned (1627) for refusing to pay the forced loan. In the Parliament of 1628 he advocated a moderate version of the Petition of Right, but when Sir John Eliot and Sir Edward Coke succeeded in carrying their more severe form of the petition, he lost influence. At this point Charles sought his adherence by creating him baron and viscount and president of the council of the north (1628), and Wentworth realigned himself as a firm supporter of royal prerogative. With William LAUD, Wentworth evolved the policy known as "Thorough" to achieve an absolutist but just and efficient regime. As lord deputy of Ireland (1632–40) he systematically applied this policy. He cleared the sea of pirates, bolstered trade and industry (always with an eye to England's interest), began a reorganization of the church in Ireland, and enforced reforms in financial administration that doubled the state's revenue. However, his methods were ruthlessly despotic, and he aroused even more fear and hatred. After Charles I's humiliation by the Scots in the first Bishops' War, Wentworth was recalled (1639) to England to become the king's chief adviser. Created earl of Strafford in 1640, he obtained money from the Irish Parliament to raise Irish troops to fight the Scots, but he was unable to get a similar grant of supplies from the Short Parliament (summoned on his advice) in England. An English army of sorts was mustered and placed under Strafford's command, but it was easily defeated by the Scots in a second war. When the Long Parliament assembled (1640), it declared that Strafford had intended to use Irish troops against the king's English opponents (although in fact the Irish army had never materialized). Impeachment proceedings were begun, but Strafford defended himself so ably that the opposition changed its tactics and introduced a bill of attainder against him. The bill was finally passed in the panic following the discovery of the so-called army plot, by which the king had hoped to rescue Strafford and dissolve the Parliament. Charles after long hesitation signed the bill, and Strafford was beheaded. See biographies by H. D. Traill (1889, repr. 1970), W. A. Burghclere (1931), and C. V. Wedgwood (1961); H. F. Kearney, *Strafford in Ireland* (1959).

strain: see STRENGTH OF MATERIALS.

Straits: see DARDANELLES; BOSPORUS.

Straits of Mackinac Bridge: see MACKINAC.

Straits Settlements, collective name for certain former British colonies in Southeast Asia. The three British East India Company territories of PINANG, SINGAPORE, and Malacca (see MELAKA) were given a unified administration in 1826 and called the Straits Settlements. The company was dissolved in 1858 and the territories were placed under the jurisdiction of the India Office. In 1867 the Straits Settlements became a crown colony administered by the Colonial Office. LABUAN, which had been made a dependency of Singapore in 1906, was constituted a fourth Settlement in 1912. (The Cocos or Keeling Islands and Christmas Island had been made dependencies of Singapore in 1883 and 1903, respectively.) The Straits Settlement crown colony was dissolved in 1946; Singapore with its dependencies became a separate crown colony, and Pinang and Malacca were included in the Malayan Union, which became the Federation of Malaya in 1948. See MALAYSIA, FEDERATION OF.

Stralsund (shtrăl'zo͝ont"), city (1970 pop. 71,551), Rostock district, N East Germany, on the Strelasund (an inlet of the Baltic Sea), opposite Rügen Island. It is an industrial center and seaport, with shipyards. Manufactures include metal goods, furniture, refined sugar and other processed food, and beer. Founded in 1209, Stralsund became (late 13th cent.) a leading member of the HANSEATIC LEAGUE. The Treaty of Stralsund (1370) between Denmark and the league was signed there. Stralsund was a chief city of POMERANIA, but was virtually independent of the dukes of Pomerania. In the Thirty Years War, Stralsund withstood (1628) a siege by Wallenstein. It was aided by Danish, then by Swedish, troops, and at the Peace of Westphalia (1648) it passed to Sweden. The city was taken by the French in 1807 and passed to Denmark by the Treaty of Kiel (1814) and to Prussia at the Congress of Vienna (1814–15). It was heavily damaged in World War II. Noteworthy buildings include the Church of St. Nicholas (13th–14th cent.), the city hall (13th–14th cent.), and several medieval gates. The chemist K. W. Scheele was born (1742) there.

stramonium: see JIMSON WEED.

Strand, Paul, 1890–, American photographer, b. New York City. Strand studied under Lewis HINE, who introduced him to Alfred STIEGLITZ. At Stieglitz's famed "291" gallery, Strand had his first one-man exhibition (1916); the last two issues of Stieglitz's *Camera Work* (1917) were devoted to Strand's photography. His principal early subjects were Manhattan life and 20th-century machinery. In the 1920s he made his exquisitely composed landscape and nature photographs. Strand made documentary films in Mexico, the USSR, and the United States. His superb portraits of regions are reproduced in *Time in New England* (1950), *Un Paese* (1954), *Tir A'Mhurain* (1968, on the Hebrides), and *Living Egypt* (1969). See his *Retrospective Monograph* (2 vol., 1972).

Strand, street in London, England, roughly parallel with the Thames River, running from the Temple to Trafalgar Square. It is a street of law courts, hotels, theaters, and office buildings and is the main artery between the City and the West End.

strand wolf: see HYENA.

Strang, James Jesse (străng), 1813–56, American Mormon leader, b. Cayuga co., N.Y. A lawyer and teacher, he migrated in 1843 to Wisconsin, was converted to Mormonism, and at the death of Joseph Smith (1844) claimed the succession, saying that he had had a vision in which God had proclaimed him prophet. Excommunicated, Strang organized a colony in Walworth co., Wis., calling it Voree. Many Mormons unwilling to accept the leadership of Brigham Young were attracted to Strang's colony. In 1846 a conference of the Mormon church proclaimed Strang prophet and first president. Aware of the difficulty of founding his ideal community in a Gentile neighborhood, he sought a more suitable site. In 1847 he selected Beaver Island in Lake Michigan, then sparsely peopled by trappers and fishermen. There he established a colony, driving out other settlers and setting up a despotic rule. The inhabitants of the mainland were violently opposed to the Mormon colony, and public opinion finally forced the Federal government to bring numerous charges against Strang, but he successfully defended himself. His power over the Mormons increased; in 1850 he was crowned King James, and he was later elected to the Michigan house of representatives. His harsh rule had made him bitter enemies, however, and in 1856 he was assassinated. The colony was soon dispersed and the land and property seized by inhabitants of the mainland. See his diary (ed. by M. M. Strang, 1961); biographies by D. C. Fitzpatrick (1970) and R. P. Weeks (1971).

Strange, Sir Robert, 1721–92, English engraver. The outstanding historical engraver of his day, he became a member of the academies of Rome, Florence, Bologna, and France and was the only English engraver whose portrait was painted on the ceiling of the Vatican print room. His most distinguished works are Van Dyck's *Charles I with His Horse* and *Charles I in His Robes.* For his engraving of West's *Apotheosis of the Royal Children* he was knighted in 1787.

Strangford Lough (străng'fərd lŏkh), inlet of the Irish Sea, 17 mi (27 km) long and 4 mi (6.4 km) wide, Co. Down, E Northern Ireland, entered through a 5-mi (8-km) strait. One of the largest of the inlet's many small islands is Mahee island, which is the site of ancient monastic ruins.

strangler fig, common name for several plant species, including the golden FIG, *Ficus aurea,* of the SE United States. The name strangler fig is also used for several vines that grow on other plants, especially the pitch apple, *Clusia rosea,* a tropical American tree that when young grows over other trees like a vine and strangles them.

Strängnäs (strĕng'nĕs"), city (1970 pop. 16,132), Södermanland co., E Sweden, on Strängnäsfjärden, an arm of Lake Mälaren. Manufactures include medical supplies and pharmaceuticals. Known in the 11th cent. as a pagan site for human sacrifices, it became (c.1120) the seat of a Christian bishop. The city has a famous cathedral (begun in the mid-13th cent.), where several Swedish kings are buried. Gustavus Vasa was elected (1523) king of Sweden there.

Stranraer (strənrär', străn–), burgh (1971 pop. 9,853), Wigtownshire, SW Scotland, at the head of Loch Ryan. A fishing port, it has a prosperous trade with Northern Ireland. Food-processing industries are there. Viscount Dundee occupied the 15th-century castle while suppressing Covenanters in Galloway in 1682. Northwest Castle was the home of the explorer Sir John Ross.

Straparola, Giovanni Francesco (jōvän'nē fränchās'kō sträpärô'lä), d. c.1557, Italian writer. His lyric verse was not of lasting merit, but he excelled as a storyteller. He was perhaps the first to use popular folklore as a basis for fiction. His *Piacevoli notti* (2 vol., 1550–55; tr. *Nights of Straparola,* 1894) was enormously successful; it mixed such folk stories as *Beauty and the Beast* with ridiculous tales, supernatural narratives, and topical jokes, all recounted in a pointed and earthy manner. His influence on the fairy-tale genre was great.

Strasberg, Lee, 1901–, American theatrical director, teacher, and actor, b. Austria. Strasberg emigrated to New York City in 1909. He was a cofounder in 1931 of the GROUP THEATRE. There until 1937, he initiated training in the Stanislavsky acting method. Among the world's foremost teachers of acting, Strasberg has been closely associated with The Actors' Studio in New York and became its director in 1950. He made his movie debut in *The Godfather Part II* (1974). See *Strasberg at the Actors Studio,* ed. by R. H. Hethmon (1965).

Strasbourg (sträzbo͝or'), Ger. *Strassburg,* city (1968 pop. 254,038), capital of Bas-Rhin dept., NE France, on the Ill River near its junction with the Rhine. It is the intellectual and commercial capital of ALSACE. The city's chief industries are metal casting, machine and tool construction, oil and gas refining, and boatbuilding. Strasbourg's goose-liver pâté is famous. Iron, potassium, gasoline, and numerous industrial products are shipped through Strasbourg's great port on the Rhine. The city has an important nuclear research center. In Roman times Strasbourg was called Argentoratum and was an important city in the province of Upper Germany. It became an episcopal see in the 4th cent. Occupied and destroyed by the Huns in the 5th cent., the city was rebuilt and called Strateburgum [city of roadways]. After becoming part of the Holy Roman Empire in 923, Strasbourg, with the surrounding rural area, came under the temporal rule of its bishops. Its location at the crossroads of Flanders, Italy, France, and central Europe made it an increasingly important commercial center. In 1262, after some struggles with the bishops, the burghers secured the status of a free imperial city for the city proper. An upheaval in 1332 established a corporate government in which the guilds played a leading role. In Strasbourg medieval German literature reached its height in Gottfried von Strassburg. There also Johann Gutenberg's printing press may have been invented (15th cent.). Strasbourg accepted the Reformation in the 1520s under the leadership of Martin Bucer, and the city became an important Protestant center. The Univ. of Strasbourg, founded in the 16th cent. as a Protestant university, numbered Goethe and Metternich among its students. The city's prosperity began to decline in the early 17th cent. and was severely damaged by the Thirty Years War (1618–48). In 1681, Louis XIV seized Strasbourg, which was confirmed in French possession by the Treaty of RYSWICK (1697). The persecutions of French Protestants after 1685 were not carried into Strasbourg, which raised little objection to the annexation. The city enthusiastically supported the French Revolution and thereafter increasingly adopted French customs and speech. Strasbourg, bombarded by the Prussians during the FRANCO-PRUSSIAN WAR, was ceded to Germany by the Treaty of Frankfurt (1871). It was recovered by France in 1919, following World War I. The city was occupied by the Germans and severely damaged in World War II. Most historical monuments, however, were saved. Chief among these is the Roman Catholic cathedral, begun in 1015 and completed in 1439, a masterpiece of Rhenish architecture, with a famous astronomic clock installed in 1574. In 1949, Strasbourg became the seat of the Council of Europe. Since its return from Germany, the city has been expanding toward the east and south; in 1967 some 30 neighboring towns were absorbed into a new Community of Strasbourg, thus giving the city's metropolitan area a population in excess of 400,000.

Strasbourg, Oath of, 842, oath sworn by Charles the Bald (later Holy Roman Emperor CHARLES II) and LOUIS THE GERMAN in solemnizing their alliance against their brother, Emperor LOTHAIR I. The chief political result of this alliance was the Treaty of Verdun (843; see VERDUN, TREATY OF). Each brother made his oath in the language of the other's followers, so that it might be understood. The version used by Louis is often considered the oldest known specimen of French.

Strassburg: see STRASBOURG.

Strasser, Gregor (grä'gōr shträs'ər), 1892–1934, German political leader. A pharmacist, he joined the National Socialist (Nazi) party in its infancy and participated in Adolf Hitler's abortive coup in 1923. After Hitler's imprisonment, he briefly led the party. As the leader of the wing of the party that emphasized a socially radical program, Strasser soon came into conflict with Hitler. In 1932 he was placed in charge of party organization, but Hitler, fearful of an alliance between Strasser and the German Chancellor Kurt von Schleicher, soon outmaneuvered Strasser and forced him to resign his party membership. In 1934, Strasser was murdered during Hitler's purge of political rivals.

strategy and tactics, in warfare, relative terms referring, respectively, to large-scale and small-scale planning to achieve military success. Strategy may be defined as the general scheme of the conduct of a war, tactics as the planning of means to achieve strategic objectives. But many other definitions have been put forth. In the original Greek and in its literal sense, *strategy* means generalship, but as warfare expanded in scope the term gained broader meaning. Karl von CLAUSEWITZ, the great German philosopher of war, described strategy as the planning of a whole campaign and tactics as the planning of a single battle. In Clausewitz's theory all military strategy is part of the larger political pattern, and all the nation's resources are to be subordinated to the task of attaining the political objective of the war; to this concerted effort he gave the name "grand strategy." Antoine H. JOMINI, an influential French theoretician and general, regarded strategy as the art of moving forces to the field of battle and tactics as the conduct of forces in battle. Another school views strategy as a means of bringing the enemy to battle and tactics as the means of defeating him in battle. Despite the dearth of source material concerning the conduct of his campaigns, Cyrus the Great has come to occupy an important place in military history as the first accomplished strategist. However, the towering figure in early military science was ALEXANDER THE GREAT, who destroyed the Persian Empire built by Cyrus. He recognized for the first time the importance of maintaining reserves, pursuing the enemy, building up supplies (stockpiling), and making use of elaborate scouting (intelligence). In the Punic Wars (between Rome and Carthage), HANNIBAL emerged as the outstanding field commander. His famous victory at Cannae (216 B.C.), over the Roman armies of Aemilius Paullus and Terentius Varro, became a classic example of battlefield tactics. Hannibal's reputation is based on his skill as a tactician, since faulty strategy was subsequently his undoing. Scipio Africanus Major, his victorious opponent and a great strategist, is less noted than the defeated Hannibal. The study of military theory captured the imagination of the later Byzantine emperors, who hoped to restore the glory of the Roman Empire. They analyzed the operations of the Roman legions and reduced the studies to what may be called the foundations of military science. *Strategicon* (c.578), compiled by Emperor Maurice, and *Tactics* (c.900), issued by Emperor Leo VI (Leo the Wise), are exhaustive treatises on the subject. In the West during the Middle Ages military science declined, although siege craft (see SIEGE) was much studied. The Crusaders conducted themselves in total ignorance and conspicuous violation of the most elementary principles of military functioning. The use of strategy and tactics in the West was revived by John ZIZKA, the leader of the Czech Hussites, in the early 15th cent. He adopted the wagon-fort as a unit of tactics, made artillery a maneuverable arm, and was the first commander to employ cavalry, infantry, and artillery in efficient tactical combination. Zizka also espoused the principle that mobility is a better protection than armor. In the 17th and 18th cent. professional armies proved costly to build up and maintain, and military strategists employed a cautious approach with minimal risk of bloodshed. Even so aggressive a commander as Frederick the Great was inhibited by fear of a bloody defeat; nevertheless, his wars left Prussia exhausted. It was NAPOLEON I who, despite his mistakes, revolutionized the strategy and tactics of his time. Aided by a mass army, he made great use of the powerful shock attack, carefully planned in advance. He also introduced the loose formation, divisional organization, and the use of light, long-range artillery. Clausewitz's *On War* (1832) was an outgrowth of his studies of Napoleonic campaigns; it demonstrated the importance of destroying the enemy on the battlefield and underplayed the importance of the geometrical organization of troops in the field. Jomini's classic *Précis de l'art de la guerre* (1836), also influenced by a study of Napoleon's campaigns, had a different emphasis. Jomini stressed occupation of enemy territory through carefully planned geometric maneuvers. His work had important influence on strategic practice, but the main line of strategic theory followed Clausewitz and culminated in the work of the Prussian-German school of H. K. von MOLTKE and Alfred von Schlieffen. The first modern total war, fought with mass armies and modern firearms, was the U.S. Civil War. Beginning as a contest between armies, it grew into a conflict between two societies; before its termination almost the entire resources of both North and South were being used in the war effort. Union military leaders such as Ulysses S. Grant and William T. Sherman saw that in order to defeat the armed forces of the Confederacy the Union had to destroy the will and the means of the people of the South to continue the war. Thus the Union army waged campaigns such as Sherman's famous march through Georgia, in which his forces destroyed virtually everything in their path. The formal maneuvers advocated by Jomini proved impractical because of the increased effectiveness of small arms in the Civil War, and by the war's end both sides were making use of trench warfare. The lessons of the U.S. Civil War were little noticed in Europe, where strategy and tactics continued to be thought of in terms of mid-19th-century practice. The introduction in World War I of rapid-fire SMALL ARMS (such as the machine gun) and rapid-fire ARTILLERY led to a strategic and tactical stalemate. It was a war characterized by TRENCH WARFARE and by bloody frontal attacks, which were stopped at great cost to the attackers by massed small arms and artillery fire. Although a victory was finally obtained by the allies via the strategy and tactics of attrition, it was clearly a Pyrrhic one that necessitated new breakthroughs in strategy and tactics. In an effort to break the stalemate, both sides had turned to new technical devices such as the TANK, the AIRPLANE, and POISON GAS. The importance of the tank was stressed in theories of MECHANIZED WARFARE, formulated in the 1920s and 30s in the writings of B. H. LIDDELL HART and Charles DE GAULLE and in *Lectures on F.S.R. III* (1932), by J. F. C. FULLER, that proved to be prophetic when the Nazi blitzkrieg marked World War II as a war of mobility, characterized by vast movements of mechanized armies. The introduction of aircraft in World War I gave rise to theories of AIR POWER that have dominated strategic and tactical thinking ever since. The basis of air power was set down by such men as Giulio DOUHET, H. M. TRENCHARD, and William MITCHELL, who believed that future wars would be won by aircraft. Their theory of strategic bombardment called for aerial attacks on the enemy centers of population and industrial production to destroy through bombardment the enemy's will and ability to continue fighting. In World War II that strategy was carried out in massive form by the British and U.S. air forces in attacks on Germany and Japan. It was found, however, that aerial bombardment did not entirely destroy the enemy's will and means to continue, and in order to win the war the Allies had to conduct a number of campaigns with ground forces and, in the case of Germany, occupy the enemy's homeland. The introduction and development of nuclear weapons and the GUIDED MISSILE has not changed the basic strategic theory of air power, but those new weapons nevertheless have revolutionized air power itself. The replacement of high-explosive bombs by nuclear bombs and the change from propeller-driven manned aircraft to rocket-driven guided missiles means that a force armed with these weapons can destroy any target on earth. During the 1950s, with the development of nuclear weapons, a policy of reliance upon "massive retaliation," i.e., massive attack against any nation committing an act of aggression, was formulated by the United States, Great Britain, and the Soviet Union. In the early 1960s the inability of this tactic to combat GUERRILLA WARFARE and internal subversion gave rise to a greater stress on nonnuclear weapons and introduced a greater tactical and strategic flexibility. Naval strategy and tactics have had a development similar to and, in many respects, parallel with that of land and air strategy and tactics. In the earliest naval battles—the Athenian wars of the 5th cent. B.C.—vessels were used to ram enemy ships, and the crews attacked each other with swords, spears, and oars. These methods were supported by boarding enemy craft, either to complete the destruction of ship and crew or to capture them as booty and prisoners. Most of the engines of war developed for ground warfare ultimately came into use on ships. Catapults, blowers of GREEK FIRE, and flaming arrows were a few of the early shipboard weapons. With the introduction of artillery the method of closing with an enemy vessel and boarding it was replaced by that of forcing enemy vessels into submission by gunfire. The Spanish Armada in 1588 was vanquished when its pike-armed marines could not be brought into action against English vessels, which, instead of closing with the Spanish ships and boarding them, stood off and bombarded them with gunfire. From the introduction of cannon in the great naval wars of the 17th, 18th, and early 19th cent., naval tactics remained much the same until the advent of the steam-driven steel warship. Not until Alfred T. MAHAN wrote *The Influence of Sea Power upon History* in the last decade of the 19th cent. was the central theme of naval strategy formulated. The main strategy of sea power was defined as "command of the sea," i.e., the ability to deny use of the sea as a means of transportation to an enemy and at the same time protect one's own merchant shipping from attack. Despite the introduction of new weapons such as steam warships, armored ships, heavy ordnance, submarines, and aircraft, "command of the sea" remained a fundamental objective of naval strategy. Another important naval strategy is "overseas presence," i.e., the visible display of sea power as a deterrent to intervention by opposing powers in key areas of international tension. The development of air power has led to a host of changes including the emergence of aircraft carriers and naval air fleets and the development of submarine-based retaliatory missile forces. The employment of land-based and carrier-based aircraft during World War II showed that command of the seas rested in great part on control of the air above it. The submarine, introduced in World War I, greatly changed naval strategy and led to the development of many new weapons and tactics. In both world wars the submarine was employed mainly as a commerce destroyer and as such could not by itself gain command of the sea. However, the use of long-range guided missiles on nuclear-powered submarines in the 1960s transformed the submarine into a major weapon of strategic bombardment. Nuclear-powered submarines carrying guided missiles are almost invulnerable to attack. It is evident that the introduction of guided missiles and nuclear weapons to warfare at the end of World War II, combined with the development of the guided missile and other technological advances, has revolutionized military strategy and tactics. Military strategy on the highest level has become national strategy, involving complex assessments of technological resources and national priorities. At the same time, however, the Korean and Vietnam wars have been limited wars, calling for types of strategy and tactics in many ways continuous with the past. See T. H. Wintringham, *The Story of Weapons and Tactics* (1943); A. H. Burne, *Strategy as Exemplified in the Second World War* (1946); E. J. Kingston-McCloughry, *War in Three Dimensions* (1950); Bernard Brodie, *Guide to Naval Strategy* (rev. ed. 1959) and *Strategy in the Missile Age* (1959); B. H. Liddell Hart, *Strategy* (2d ed. 1967); H. W. Baldwin, *Strategy for Tomorrow* (1970); see also bibliographies under AIR POWER; GUERRILLA WARFARE; FORTIFICATION; AIR FORCES; NAVY; articles on military strategists mentioned.

Stratford, John de, d. 1348, English ecclesiastic, archbishop of Canterbury, 1333–48. A doctor of civil and canon law, he was a legal adviser to the court of Edward II and several times an emissary to France and the Vatican. He played a passive role in the overthrow (1327) of Edward, and although nominally a member of the council that ruled on behalf of the young Edward III, he did not support the dominant faction under Roger de Mortimer. When Edward seized power for himself (1330), however, Stratford became the king's chief adviser. He was chancellor for most of the following decade and was made archbishop of Canterbury (1333). He went on embassies to France both with and for Edward and headed the council in his absence. He resigned as chancellor in 1340 under charges of mismanagement of supplies for the French wars. Although he and the king were formally reconciled, Stratford exerted no further political influence.

Stratford, city (1971 pop. 24,508), S Ont., Canada, on the Avon River, SW of Toronto. It is an industrial center, with plants manufacturing textiles, furniture, automobile parts, and rubber and leather products. Food products from the surrounding farm area are processed there. The city is the home of the noted Stratford Shakespearean Festival (started 1953).

Stratford, town (1970 pop. 49,775), Fairfield co., SW Conn., at the mouth of the Housatonic River on Long Island Sound; inc. 1639. Aircraft engines, helicopters, machinery, hardware items, and asbestos products are among its many manufactures. The American Shakespeare Festival Theater and Academy opened there in 1955. The David Judson house (1723) has been restored and is maintained as an historical preserve.

Stratford, home of the Lee family, overlooking the Potomac River, E Va., SE of Fredericksburg. A national shrine dedicated in 1935, the site was purchased in 1716 by Thomas Lee, who built the mansion Stratford Hall in 1729–30. It was the birthplace of Richard Henry Lee and Francis L. Lee, the home of Henry Lee, and the birthplace of his son Robert E. Lee. At the shrine the activities of an antebellum plantation are carried on—spinning, weaving, curing hams, and grinding meal.

Stratford de Redcliffe, Stratford Canning, Viscount, 1786–1880, British diplomat. He entered (1807) the foreign office under the aegis of his cousin, George Canning. Sent (1808) to Turkey, he negotiated the Treaty of Bucharest (1812) between Turkey and Russia. He served in Switzerland (1814–18), at the Congress of Vienna, and in Washington (1819–23), where he negotiated concerning disputes arising from the War of 1812. In Turkey again (1825–29, 1831), he helped settle the frontier problem with Greece. After a period in Parliament he returned (1842) to Turkey, remaining with interruptions until 1858. Stratford exercised enormous influence over Sultan ABD AL-MAJID, but the documentary evidence does not support the belief of his contemporaries that he encouraged Turkish intransigence in the face of Russian demands in 1853 and thus brought on the CRIMEAN WAR. He appears rather to have counseled moderation and attempted to avert the war. He was created a viscount in 1852. See his *Eastern Question* (1881); biography by E. F. Malcolm-Smith (1933); study by L. G. Byrne (1971).

Stratford-upon-Avon, municipal borough (1971 pop. 19,449), Warwickshire, central England, on the Avon River. A market town with light industries including brewing, canning, and the manufacture of aluminum goods, Stratford owes its great fame to its associations with William SHAKESPEARE. A gabled building on Henley St., believed to be the poet's birthplace, is open to the public. The site of the home he purchased in 1597, and where he died in 1616, is marked (the building having been torn down in 1759). His grave is beside that of his wife, Anne Hathaway (whose home, "Anne Hathaway's Cottage," is near Stratford), in the fine old Church of the Holy Trinity. This church has a bust and memorial to the poet and a stained-glass window (given by Americans in 1885) depicting Shakespeare's "seven ages of man." The town's principal memorial is a theater, where annual Shakespeare festivals are held. The first theater, built in the late 19th cent., was destroyed by fire in 1926, but the attached gallery, library, and museum were saved. The new theater was dedicated in 1932. Most of the structures and places in Stratford connected with the life of Shakespeare were acquired by the nation in the 19th cent. Edward VI's Grammar School, which Shakespeare may have attended, is also now national property. Shakespeare scholars from all over the world attend the Shakespeare Institute of the Univ. of Birmingham. In 1964 the Shakespeare Centre, also for scholars, was erected on Henley St.

Strathclyde (străth"klīd') [Gaelic,=Clyde valley], one of several early medieval Celtic or Welsh kingdoms in present-day S Scotland and N England. Strathclyde was in SW Scotland. To the east was the kingdom of Manaw Gododdin and to the south, Rheged. Little is known of the history of Strathclyde and the other Welsh (Cumbrian) kingdoms. The origin of Strathclyde is uncertain, but there is evidence that the kingdom had been consolidated by the middle of the 5th cent. In 945, King Edmund of England defeated Strathclyde and awarded it to King Malcolm of Scotland; however, Scotland did not permanently absorb the kingdom until the 11th cent. The reason for the disappearance of the ancient British language and culture in the kingdoms is not definitely known. DUMBARTON was the principal town in Strathclyde. See John Rhys, *Celtic Britain* (1882); F. M. Stenton, *Anglo-Saxon England* (1947); P. H. Blair, *An Introduction to Anglo-Saxon England* (1962).

Strathclyde, University of, at Glasgow, Scotland; founded 1796 as Anderson's Institution. In 1886 its name was changed to Glasgow and West of Scotland Technical College, and in 1956 it became known as Royal College of Science and Technology. It was affiliated with the Univ. of Glasgow from 1913 until 1964, when it received its charter as a university and assumed its present name. It has schools of mathematics and physics, chemical and material sciences, mechanical and chemical engineering and naval architecture, civil and mining engineering and applied geology, electrical and electronic engineering, architecture, building science and planning, pharmaceutical sciences, biological sciences, arts and social studies, and business administration. The Centre for Industrial Innovation, the David Livingstone Institute of Overseas Development Studies, and the Scottish Universities Research and Reactor Centre are affiliated.

Strathcona and Mount Royal, Donald Alexander Smith, 1st **Baron** (străthkō'nə), 1820–1914, Canadian fur trader, financier, and railroad builder, b. Scotland. Coming to Canada in 1838, he was hired by the Hudson's Bay Company, of which he later was governor (1889–1914). Smith's skill in finance was early apparent. He came into public notice in 1869 when he was sent by the government to deal with Louis RIEL, leader of the Red River Rebellion. From 1871 to 1880 and from 1887 to 1896 Smith sat in the dominion Parliament. His break with John Macdonald at the height of the PACIFIC SCANDAL (1873) was in part responsible for the downfall of Macdonald's administration. With associates he gained control of the Great Northern lines in 1878 and later was a leading force in the company that completed (1885) the Canadian Pacific Railway. In 1886 he was knighted, and while serving (1896–1914) as Canadian high commissioner in England he was created baron (1897). Out of the great fortune that he amassed, he gave large sums to charitable and educational enterprises. A highly controversial figure, Strathcona was characterized by his enemies as a conniving self-seeker and by his admirers as a vigorous empire builder. See biography by John Macnaughton (1926).

Strathmore (străthmôr'), valley, c.55 mi (90 km) long and 5 to 10 mi (8–16 km) wide, in Tayside region, E central Scotland, running from northeast to southwest between the Grampians and the Sidlaw Hills. It has some of Scotland's best farm-land, producing oats, barley, and hay. The name is sometimes applied to the depression across central Scotland (c.100 mi/160 km long) formed by a great fault in the earth's crust.

stratification (Lat.,=made in layers), layered structure formed by the deposition of sedimentary ROCKS. Changes between strata are interpreted as the result of fluctuations in the intensity and persistence of the depositional agent, e.g., currents, wind, or waves, or in changes in the source of the sediment. Changes in the mineral composition between two adjacent layers will often result in two layers of distinctly different color. Changes in the texture of the sedimentary particles from one layer to another (as from sand to gravel) result in the development of prominent stratification. In shales, stratification can be seen by the tendency of the rock to split into thin flakes, caused by the parallel arrangement of the tiny clay mineral fragments. Initially, most sediments are deposited with essentially horizontal stratification, although the layers may later be tilted or folded by internal earth forces. Persistent, regular stratification is a reflection of the persistence and regularity of the depositional agent. Agents such as broad ocean or atmospheric currents tend to produce widespread and uniform strata, whereas currents that operate over limited areas and show evidence of turbulence, such as stream currents or irregular wind patterns, form irregular strata.

stratigraphy, branch of geology specifically concerned with the arrangement of layered rocks (see STRATIFICATION). Stratigraphy is based on the law of superposition, which states that in a normal sequence of rock layers the youngest is on top and the oldest on the bottom. Local sequences are studied, and after considering such factors as the average rate of deposition of the different rocks, their composition, the width and extent of the strata, the fossils contained, and the periods of uplift and erosion, the geological history of the sequence is reconstructed. These sequences are then correlated to those of similar age in other regions with the ultimate aim of establishing a consistent geochronology for the entire earth. In areas where the strata have undergone folding, faulting, and erosion, stratigraphic techniques are used to determine their correct sequence. The fossil has hitherto been the most important means of correlation because, as a result of EVOLUTION, rock strata of approximately equal age exhibit similar flora and fauna. Dating and correlation of stratified rocks by means of fossils is called stratigraphic paleontology. See also DATING. See C. O. Dunbar and John Rogers, *Principles of Stratigraphy* (1957); Bernhard Kummel, *History of the Earth* (1961); E. W. Spencer, *Basic Concepts of Historical Geology* (1962); R. K. Matthews, *Dynamic Stratigraphy* (1974).

stratocumulus: see CLOUD.

stratosphere (străt'əsfēr), second lowest layer of the earth's ATMOSPHERE. The level from which it extends outward varies with latitude; it begins c.5½ mi (9 km) above the poles, c.6 or 7 mi (c.10 or 11 km) in the middle latitudes, and c.10 mi (16 km) at the equator, and extends outward c.20 mi (32 km). It is a zone of dry, thin air, cold and clear, whose horizontal temperature gradient, in its lower level, is the reverse of that near the earth's surface. In polar regions the temperature is −40°F to −50°F (−40°C to −46°C), but near the equator it ranges from −80°F to below −100°F (−62°C to below −74°C); in the middle latitudes it remains steady at about −67°F (−55°C). The stratified variations in temperature were deduced from the behavior of sound waves transmitted through the atmosphere, which travel faster in warm air than in cold air. Within the stratosphere at altitudes of 12 to 30 mi (19–48 km) is the ozone layer. Its capacity to intercept most of the sun's ultraviolet rays is fundamental to the maintenance of life on the earth. Without this filtering effect, the sun's full radiation would destroy animal tissue, but sufficient ultraviolet radiation reaches the earth to support the activation of vitamin D in humans. Elevated temperatures found in the ozone layer result from its absorption of radiant energy. Balloons carrying electronic equipment are launched to ascertain conditions in the stratosphere.

stratus: see CLOUD.

Straubing (shtrou'bĭng), city (1970 pop. 37,531), Bavaria, SE West Germany, on the Danube (Donau) River. It is an agricultural market of Lower Bavaria and an industrial center. Manufactures include machinery, precision instruments, textiles, and beer. Originally a Roman camp, Straubing later became (1353) the capital of the duchy of Bavaria-Straubing, which was ruled by a branch of the Wittelsbach family. Noteworthy buildings include the Peterskirche, a 12th-century Romanesque church; the Gothic Church of St. Jacob (15th–16th cent.); and the Gothic city hall (1382).

Straus (strous), family of American merchants, public officials, and philanthropists. **Isidor Straus,** 1845–1912, b. Rhenish Bavaria, emigrated (1854) with his brothers to the United States in order to join their father, Lazarus Straus, who had already settled in Talbotton, Ga. The family moved (1865) to New York City, and there Isidor took a large part in forming and directing the importing firm of L. Straus & Sons. Isidor, with his brother Nathan, became associated with R. H. Macy & Company in 1874, became a partner in 1888, and by 1896 had acquired ownership of the firm. As a Representative (1894–95) in the U.S. Congress, Isidor aided in drafting nonprotectionist tariff legislation. He later devoted his attention to philanthropy and reform. He and his wife were lost when the *Titanic* sank. His brother **Nathan Straus,** 1848–1931, b. Rhenish Bavaria, joined Isidor in business but was especially outstanding for his philanthropy. He established pasteurization stations to supply sanitary milk to the poor, made his milk stations relief depots in the Panic of 1893, and was a leader in the field of child health. He was a prominent Zionist leader and contributed generously to the general improvement of conditions in Palestine. Another brother, **Oscar Solomon Straus,** 1850–1926, b. Rhenish Bavaria, grad. Columbia (B.A., 1871; LL.B., 1873), was a diplomat and author. He practiced law in New York City until 1881 and then went into business with his brothers. He was minister to Turkey (1887–89) under President Grover Cleveland and again (1898–1900) under William McKinley and was ambassador to Turkey (1909–10) under William H. Taft. He was appointed (1902) to the Permanent Court of Arbitration (the Hague Tribunal) and was (1906–9) Secretary of Commerce and Labor under Theodore Roosevelt. He was candidate for governor of New York on the Progressive party ticket in 1912. He wrote several books, including *Roger Williams* (1894), *The American Spirit* (1913), and *Under Four Administrations* (1922). A son of Isidor Straus, **Jesse Isidor Straus,** 1872–1936, b. New York City, grad. Harvard, 1893, became president of R. H. Macy & Company in 1919 and served (1933–36) as ambassador to France. **Nathan Straus,** 1889–1961, b. New York City, son of the elder Nathan Straus, was a journalist and public official. He served (1921–26) in the New York state legislature and headed (1937–42) the U.S. Housing Authority. He wrote *Seven Myths of Housing* (1944) and *Two Thirds of a Nation* (1952).

Straus, Oscar (ôs'kär shtrous), 1870–1954, Austrian composer; studied in Vienna and with Max Bruch in Berlin. After a brief career as conductor he turned entirely to composition. His operas and instrumental works are eclipsed by his successful operettas, particularly *A Waltz Dream* (1907) and *The Chocolate Soldier* (1908; based on G. B. Shaw's *Arms and the Man*). During the early 1930s Straus wrote scores for films in Hollywood. In 1939 he became a French citizen, and in 1940 he moved to the United States.

Strauss (strous, Ger. shtrous), family of Viennese musicians. **Johann Strauss,** 1804–49, learned to play the violin against his parents' wishes. In 1823 he joined the dance orchestra of Josef Lanner (1801–43), whom he later rivaled. In 1826 Strauss organized his own orchestra. His waltzes won him fame that was extended over all Europe when he toured Austria (1833) and played in Berlin (1834) and in Paris and London (1837–38). His son, **Johann Strauss,** 1825–99, followed a musical career against his father's wishes. In 1844 he formed an orchestra that was immediately successful and became the rival of his father's. After the elder Johann's death, the son combined the two orchestras. He composed more than 400 waltzes, on which his fame largely rests and which include the enormously popular *Blue Danube* (1866) and *Tales from the Vienna Woods* (1868). With these he brought the Viennese waltz to a height of musical artistry, endowing it with new melodic, rhythmic, and orchestral richness. He also composed a number of operettas of which *Die Fledermaus* [the bat] (1873) and *Der Zigeunerbaron* (*The Gypsy Baron,* 1885) are outstanding. His other works for the stage were hampered by their inadequate librettos and a lack of dramatic interest. Two of his brothers, **Josef Strauss,** 1827–70, and **Eduard Strauss,** 1835–1916, were also successful composers and conductors. See biography of Johann (father and son) by H. Fantel (1972). See also biographies of the Strauss family, by Jerome Pastene (1951, repr. 1971) and Joseph Wechsberg (1973).

Strauss, David Friedrich (dä'vēt frē'drĭkh shtrous), 1808–74, German theologian and philosopher. In Berlin he studied (1831–32) Hegelian philosophy. As tutor at Tübingen he lectured on Hegel, modern philosophy, and Plato. His *Das Leben Jesu* (2 vol., 1835–36) aroused much interest because it applied the "myth theory" to the life of Jesus, treated the Gospel narrative like any other historical work, and denied all supernatural elements in the Gospels. It was translated into English in 1846 by George Eliot. In 1839, Strauss was appointed to a post at the Univ. of Zürich, but public opposition prevented him from taking it. His other theological writings include *Die Christliche Glaubenslehre* (2 vol., 1840–41) and *Der alte und der neue Glaube* (1872; tr. *The Old Faith and the New,* 1873). His writings mark a turning point in the critical study of the life of Jesus. Strauss was also the author of critical biographies of Ulrich von Hutten (3 vol., 1858–60) and Hermann Samuel Reimarus (1862). See study by Horton Harris (1974).

Strauss, Eduard: see STRAUSS, family.

Strauss, Emil (āmēl' shtrous), 1866–1960, German novelist. His writings exemplify the transition from naturalism to impressionism by containing elements of both. His novel *Freund Hein* (1902) rapidly gained fame for its portrayal of a tyrannical German secondary school. In it, as in his plays, in the short stories of *Hans und Grete* (1909), and in such novels as *Kreuzungen* (1904), he exalted the virtues of experience and of free moral and creative development. *Vaterland* (1923) and later works stress patriotism above personal happiness.

Strauss, Franz Josef (fräns yō'zĕf), 1915–, West German political figure, leader of the Christian Social Union. He became prominent in the Bavarian Christian Social Union (the Bavarian wing of the Christian Democratic Union) after World War II. Elected to the Bundestag in 1949, he became (1956) minister of defense of the Federal Republic of Germany (West Germany) in the coalition government of Christian Democratic chancellor Konrad Adenauer. In 1962, Strauss was widely attacked for his role in the government raids on the offices of the opposition news magazine *Der Spiegel* and arrests of the magazine's personnel. As a result of the *Der Spiegel* affair Adenauer was forced to form a new cabinet from which Strauss was excluded. He later served (Dec., 1966-Oct., 1969) as finance minister in the government of Christian Democratic chancellor Kurt Kiesinger. He opposed the 1973 treaty normalizing relations between East and West Germany on the grounds that it violated the constitutional provision requiring the government to seek reunification.

Strauss, Johann: see STRAUSS, family.

Strauss, Josef: see STRAUSS, family.

Strauss, Lewis Lichtenstein (strôz), 1896-1974, American financier, chairman of the Atomic Energy Commission (1953-58), b. Charleston, W.Va. In World War I he served under Herbert Hoover on the Belgian Relief Commission and the Allied Supreme Economic Council. He was a special assistant to Secretary of the Navy James Forrestal in World War II, rising to the rank of rear admiral. Associated with Kuhn, Loeb & Company from 1919, as a partner after 1929, he resigned in 1946. Strauss was a member of the Atomic Energy Commission from 1946 to 1950 and returned as its chairman in 1953. His service on the AEC was marked by several controversies, including one with the atomic physicist J. Robert Oppenheimer, who had opposed development of the hydrogen bomb, a project Strauss strongly advocated. His term as AEC chairman ended in June, 1958, and President Dwight D. Eisenhower appointed him (Nov., 1958) Secretary of Commerce. Strauss held this office until June, 1959, when the Senate, in a close vote, refused to confirm the appointment. See his memoirs, *Men and Decisions* (ed. by C. C. Rogers, 1962).

Strauss, Richard (rĭkh'ärt shtrous), 1864-1949, German composer. Strauss brought to a culmination the development of the 19th-century symphonic poem; he was a leading composer of romantic opera in the early 20th cent. Son of a celebrated horn player, he had extensive musical instruction and began composing as a child of six. His first major work, the symphony in D minor, was first performed in 1880. Strauss's early works, in classical forms, brought him instant acclaim. He succeeded Hans von Bülow as conductor at Meiningen (1885-86) and later as conductor of the Berlin Philharmonic concerts (1894-95). His friendship with the poet Alexander Ritter influenced him to adopt the romantic aesthetic philosophy and style of Liszt and Wagner. A group of songs, the symphonic fantasy *Aus Italien* (1886), and the symphonic poems *Don Juan* (1888) and *Death and Transfiguration* (1889) were the first works composed in his new romantic manner. These and the works that followed established him as a master of highly evocative, original, and richly orchestrated program music. These works—including *Till Eulenspiegels lustige Streiche* (1895); *Thus Spake Zarathustra* (1895), after Nietzsche; *Don Quixote* (1898), a tone poem in the form of variations with a cello solo; and *A Hero's Life* (1898)—were violently lauded and damned as the very essence of musical modernism. Strauss gained wide renown for his operas including *Salomé* (1905), after Oscar Wilde's play; the brilliantly dramatic *Electra* (1909); the delightful comedy *Der Rosenkavalier* (1911); *Ariadne auf Naxos* (1912); and *Die Frau ohne Schatten* (1919). He wrote all but the first of these, as well as *Die aegyptische Helena* (1928) and *Arabella* (1933), in collaboration with the poet Hugo von Hofmannsthal. After Hofmannsthal died (1929) Strauss's librettists were Stefan Zweig for *Die schweigsame Frau* (1935) and Josef Gregor for *Friedenstag* (1938), *Daphne* (1938), and *Die Liebe der Danaë* (1938-40). Strauss's operas, carrying the Wagnerian leitmotif concept to its fullest development, went beyond Wagner in intensity of drama and psychological treatment of character motivation. The operas display his music at its most sensuous and passionate. From 1919 until 1924 Strauss was codirector of the Vienna State Opera. During this period he made extended tours abroad, including his second one to the United States (1922). Strauss served briefly as head of musical affairs (Reichsmusikkammer president) under the Nazis; he was officially exonerated of collaboration in 1948. Among Strauss's last major works are the sorrowful *Metamorphosen* (1946), for string instruments, and two pieces for voice and orchestra, *Drei Gesänge* and *Im Abendrot* (both 1948), considered the final musical expression of dying German romanticism. See his correspondence ed. by Rollo Myers (1968); biographies by Norman Del Mar (1962), William S. Mann (1964), and Alan Jefferson (1963 and 1971).

Stravinsky, Igor Fedorovich (ē'gər fyô'dərô"vyĭch strəvĭn'skē), 1882-1971, Russian-American composer. Considered by many the greatest and most versatile composer of the 20th cent., Stravinsky helped to revolutionize modern music. His father, an actor and singer in St. Petersburg, had him educated for the law. Music was only an avocation for Stravinsky until his meeting in 1902 with Rimsky-Korsakov, with whom he studied formally from 1907 to 1908. Stravinsky's First Symphony in E Flat Major (1907) is pervaded by the influence of Rimsky-Korsakov's nationalistic style. The work of Stravinsky interested the ballet impressario Sergei Diaghilev, and Stravinsky's first strikingly original compositions—*L'Oiseau de Feu* (*The Firebird,* 1910) and *Petrouchka* (1911)—were written for Diaghilev's Ballets Russes in Paris. In the ballet *Le Sacre du printemps* (*The Rite of Spring,* 1913) he departed radically from musical tradition by using irregular, primitive rhythms and harsh dissonances. The audience at the premiere of the ballet reacted with riotous disfavor. However, in the following year the work was performed by a symphony orchestra, and it was recognized as a landmark and masterpiece of modern music. At the beginning of World War I, Stravinsky moved to Switzerland, where he composed several works based on Russian themes, including the ballet *Les Noces* (*The Wedding,* 1923). Influenced by 18th-century music, he embarked on an austere, neoclassical style in such works as the poetic dance-drama *Histoire du Soldat* (*The Soldier's Tale,* 1918), the opera-oratorio *Oedipus Rex* (1927; text by Jean Cocteau after Sophocles), and the choral composition *Symphonie de psaumes* (*Symphony of Psalms,* 1930). In the 1930s, Stravinsky toured throughout Europe and the United States as a pianist and conductor of his own works. He became a French citizen in 1934, but three years later he moved to the United States, becoming an American citizen in 1945. Compositions of the 1940s include such diverse works as the *Ebony Concerto* (1946) for clarinet and swing band; the Third Symphony (1946) in three movements; the ballet *Orpheus* (1947); and a mass (1948) for voices and double wind quintet. After composing the opera *The Rake's Progress* (1951; inspired by Hogarth's engravings, with libretto by W. H. Auden and Chester Kallman), Stravinsky turned to experiments with serial techniques (see SERIAL MUSIC). In *Cantata* (1952) the new technique was evident, and in the chamber piece *Septuor* (1953) he made the full transition to serialism. He continued to compose in this exacting style in the abstract ballet *Agon* (1957) and in *Threni* (1958), a work for voices and orchestra. His creative originality was undiminished in his late works, which display remarkable freshness, meticulous craftsmanship, and an experimental quality. Stravinsky's influence on 20th-century music is immeasurable. He revitalized the rhythms of European music and achieved entirely new sonorities and blends of orchestral colors. A series of lectures he delivered at Harvard Univ. were published as *Poétique musicale* (1942, tr. *Poetics of Music,* 1948). See his autobiography *Chronicles of My Life* (1935, tr. 1936); his *Memories and Commentaries* (1960), *Expositions and Developments* (1962), and *Dialogues and a Diary* (1963), all three written with Robert Craft. See also biographies by R. Siohan (1965), A. Dobrin (1970), P. Horgan (1972), R. Craft (1972), and L. Libman (1972).

straw, dried stalks of threshed grains, especially wheat, barley, oats, and rye. It has been used from antiquity for bedding, covering floors, and thatching roofs, as fodder and litter for animals, and in weaving such articles as mats, screens, baskets, ornaments and hangings, hats, sandals, fans, and armor. Straw hats are woven in one piece or made from braids sewn together. Braids have been made in Europe from medieval times and probably originated in Tuscany, Italy. They are usually made from straw selected for color, length, and lightness and are grown under special conditions of soil and climate. Fine braids, such as leghorn, are commonly of wheat stalks, often cut before they are fully ripe. Hats made of other fibers, such as the leaf fiber of the screw pine used for Panama hats, are also known as straw hats. Straw was once widely used as a packing material and in the manufacture of strawboard (a cheap cardboard) and, in combination with less brittle materials, of paper.

strawberry, any plant of the genus *Fragaria* of the family Rosaceae (ROSE family), low herbaceous perennials with edible red fruits, native to temperate regions. The European everbearing strawberry (*F. vesca*) is the only species that does not put out the stolons typical of this easily propagated genus. It has been cultivated sporadically since pre-Christian times but intensively only since the 15th cent. The common strawberry, grown in many varieties in both Europe and America, is *F. chiloensis,* believed to be indigenous to Chile and to the mountains of W North America. It has probably hybridized to some extent with the wild strawberry (*F. virginiana*) of E North America. Both species were introduced to Europe by New World explorers; the large French industry grew from a single common strawberry plant. In the United States the many growing regions harvest their crops in different seasons, from winter (Florida) to late spring (chiefly Michigan, Oregon, and Washington). Strawberries are sold fresh, frozen, or in preserves and are used in confectionery and for flavoring. Strawberries are classified in the division MAGNOLIOPHYTA, class Magnoliopsida, order Rosales, family Rosaceae. See G. M. Darron, *The Strawberry* (1966).

strawberry geranium: see SAXIFRAGE.

Strawberry Hill Press: see WALPOLE, HORACE.

Strawberry valley project, N central Utah, developed by the U.S. Bureau of Reclamation for irrigating lands S of Utah Lake; constructed 1906-13. The water of Strawberry River (a tributary of the Duchesne River in the Green River system) and its tributaries is carried by a tunnel through the Wasatch Range to a tributary of the Spanish Fork and is used for lands (c.50,000 acres/20,230 hectares) in the vicinity of Salem, Spanish Fork, Springville, Payson, and Santaquin. The project is supplemented by the Central Utah project.

strawflower, garden annual (*Helichrysum bracteatum*) of the family Compositae (COMPOSITE family), a favorite as an EVERLASTING, but also grown for its fresh flowers. The plant is native to Australia. The flower heads are made up of papery petallike parts and are of various colors. Other everlastings and the bellwort (*Uvularia*) are sometimes called strawflower. Strawflowers are classified in the division MAGNOLIOPHYTA, class Magnoliopsida, order Asterales, family Compositae.

Strawson, Peter Frederick, 1919-, British philosopher, grad. Oxford. An influential spokesman for so-called ordinary language philosophy, he began teaching at Oxford in 1947 and in 1968 became Waynflete professor of metaphysics. In an early article, "On Referring" (*Mind,* 1950), he disputed Bertrand Russell's theory of definite descriptions, drawing a distinction between referring to an entity and asserting its existence. He also disputed, on linguistic grounds, the correspondence theory of truth, maintaining that a "fact" is not something that corresponds to a true statement, but something stated; facts are not something to which statements refer, rather "facts are what statements (when true) state." In his first book, *Introduction to Logical Theory* (1952), Strawson studied the relationship between common language and the language of formal logic. Later his concern shifted to what he calls descriptive metaphysics, a description of the actual structure of our thought about the world. His development of and work in this area revived interest in metaphysics as a respectable philosophic enterprise. Strawson's other works include *Individuals* (2d ed. 1965), *The Bounds of Sense* (1966), *Logico-Linguistic Papers* (1971), and *Freedom and Restraint* (1974).

stream, general term applied to all bodies of water flowing in channels regardless of their size. See RIVER; FLOOD; OXBOW LAKE.

streamline, path of a fluid flowing steadily and without appreciable turbulence. A body is said to be streamlined if its shape offers the least possible resistance to a current of air, water, or other fluid. The current that a streamlined body breaks simply reunites in its wake, as contrasted with the retarding eddies and turbulence created by the partial vacuum in the wake of a nonstreamlined body. The streamline design is typically a long ellipse tapering to a point in the direction of flow; it is illustrated in the cross section of an airplane wing and in the bodies of fishes and birds. Vehicles such as automobiles, aircraft, railroad cars, and boats are designed to provide maximum streamline.

stream of consciousness, in literature, technique that records the multifarious thoughts and feelings of a character without regard to logical argument or narrative sequence. The writer attempts by the stream of consciousness to reflect all the forces, external and internal, influencing the psychology of a character at a single moment. The technique was first employed by Édouard Dujardin (1861-1949) in his novel *Les Lauriers sont coupés* (1888) and was subsequently used by such notable writers as James Joyce, Virginia Woolf, and William Faulkner. The phrase "stream of consciousness" to indicate the flow of inner experience was first used by William James in *Principles of Psychology* (1890). See study by M. J. Friedman (1955).

Streamwood, village (1970 pop. 18,176), Cook co., NE Ill.; inc. 1957.

Streator (strē'tər), city (1970 pop. 15,600), La Salle and Livingston counties, N central Ill., on the Vermillion River; inc. 1882. It is an industrial center in an area of clay and shale deposits. Coal, discovered in the early 1860s, was the principal source of livelihood until the deposits were exhausted (c.1900). Several state parks are in the area.

Street, George Edmund, 1824-81, English architect. One of the foremost champions of the Gothic revival, he did much church work, including St. Mary Magdalene, Paddington, London; St. James the Less, Westminster; St. Paul's American Church in Rome; and restorations to the Bristol Cathedral and to Christchurch, Dublin. His most notable work, the Royal Courts of Justice (1874-82) in London, was the last great attempt to apply the Gothic revival to a public building. The results of his study of medieval Gothic buildings in England and on the Continent were published in *The Brick and Marble Architecture of North Italy in the Middle Ages* (1855) and *Some Account of Gothic Architecture of Spain* (1865). He was buried in Westminster Abbey.

streetcar, small, self-propelled railroad car, similar to the type used in rapid transit systems, that operates on tracks running through city streets and is used to carry passengers. Most often cars of this type are powered by electricity supplied through an underground third rail or an overhead wire. A device called a trolley that is connected to the streetcar's electrical system makes rolling or sliding contact with the rail or wire, hence the name trolley car often is applied to such vehicles. Streetcars are sometimes powered by diesel or other internal-combustion engines, generally in suburban or rural areas, where the distances to be covered make the cost of electrification prohibitive. The first streetcars, which were drawn by horses, were introduced in New York City during the 1830s. The first electric streetcar system for urban passenger service in the United States was introduced in Cleveland during the 1880s. The use of streetcars expanded in the United States until World War I. Since then they have been replaced for the most part by buses, although they remain in considerable use throughout the rest of the world.

street cries. The imaginative, musical cries of ragpickers, scissors grinders, menders, and vendors of various sorts form a distinctive type of folk song. Literary records of them date from the Middle Ages in both France and England. A given cry might change remarkably little over the years: one English cry of 1393 was used until the end of the 18th cent. The use of both texts and melodies in polyphonic songs was fashionable in the 16th cent. Authentic street cries have often been combined ingeniously in concert works. The London cry "Who'll buy my sweet lavender?" provided a theme for Vaughan Williams's *London Symphony,* while Charpentier made effective use of Parisian cries in his opera *Louise.* Few cries survive in the 20th cent., an exception being several that are extant in the S United States, especially those of fish vendors and flower sellers. Gershwin introduced the cry of the strawberry vendor into his opera *Porgy and Bess.* The street criers themselves were rendered by a number of 18th-century printmakers, including Wheatley and Laroon. See Sir Frederick Bridge, *The Old Cryes of London* (1921); Raphael Nelson, *Cries and Criers of Old London* (1942).

Strehlenau, Nikolaus Niembsch Edler von: see LENAU, NIKOLAUS.

Streicher, Julius (yo͞o'lyo͞os shtrī'khər), 1885-1946, German National Socialist (Nazi) leader. An early party member, originally a schoolteacher, he aired his sadistic and anti-Semitic mania in his periodical, *Der Stürmer.* Streicher was also the host of the yearly Nazi party congresses at Nuremberg and, after 1933, was gauleiter (district leader) of Franconia. He was convicted at the Nuremberg war crimes trial and was hanged.

Streisand, Barbra, 1942-, American singer and actress, b. New York City. Streisand first gained critical and public acclaim for her portrayal of Fanny Brice in the Broadway show *Funny Girl* (1964). She won an Academy Award for her performance in the film version (1968). Noted for her strong, clear soprano voice and her dynamic presence, she made numerous popular recordings. Her other films include *Hello, Dolly* (1969), *The Owl and the Pussy Cat* (1970), *What's Up, Doc?* (1972), and *The Way We Were* (1973).

Strelitz: see NEUSTRELITZ, East Germany.

strength of materials, measurement in engineering of the capacity of metal, wood, concrete, and other materials to withstand stress and strain. Stress is the internal force exerted by one part of an elastic body upon the adjoining part, and strain is the deformation or change in dimension occasioned by stress. When a body is subjected to pull, it is said to be under tension, or tensional stress, and when it is being pushed, i.e., is supporting a weight, it is under compression, or compressive stress. Shear, or shearing stress, results when a force tends to make part of the body or one side of a plane slide past the other. Torsion, or torsional stress, occurs when external forces tend to twist a body around an axis. Materials are considered to be elastic in relation to an applied stress if the strain disappears after the force is removed. The elastic limit is the maximum stress a material can sustain and still return to its original form. According to Hooke's law, the stress created in an elastic material is proportional to strain, within the elastic limit (see ELASTICITY). In calculating the dimensions of materials required for specific application, the engineer uses working stresses that are ultimate strengths, or elastic limits, divided by a quantity called factor of safety. In laboratories materials are frequently "tested to destruction." They are deliberately overloaded with the particular force that acts against the property or strength to be measured. Changes in form are measured to the millionth of an inch. Static tests are conducted to determine a material's elastic limit, ductility, hardness, reaction to temperature change, and other qualities. Dynamic tests are those in which the material is exposed to a combination of expected operating circumstances including impact (e.g., a shell against a steel tank), vibration, cyclic stress, fluctuating loads, and fatigue. Polarized light, X rays, ultrasonic waves, and microscopic examination are some of the means of testing materials. See H. E. Parker, *Simplified Mechanics and Strength of Materials* (rev. ed. 1961); Alfred Jensen, *Statics and Strength of Materials* (2d ed. 1967); Stephen Timoshenko and D. H. Young, *Elements of Strength of Materials* (5th ed. 1968).

streptococcus (strĕp"təkŏk'əs), any of a group of gram-positive bacteria of the genus *Streptococcus,* some of which cause disease in man and some of which are important in fermentation. Streptococci are spherical in shape and divide by fission, but they remain connected and so grow in beadlike chains. Strains of streptococci have been classified according to their ability to produce fermentation and their action on blood growth media. The viridans, or green-colony, type, often cause disease of the teeth, ears, and sinuses. Hemolytic streptococci produce hemolysins, proteins that destroy red blood cells; they also produce toxic substances that affect white blood cells and the clotting properties of blood. Hemolytic streptococci of a particular strain (group A) cause a wide variety of diseases, including some pneumonias, erysipelas (a generalized body infection), mastoiditis, osteomyelitis, and puerperal fever. Scarlet fever is also a streptococcal, or strep, infection; the rash is a response to a TOXIN produced by the bacteria that cause streptococcal sore throat. RHEUMATIC FEVER results from initial infection by the group-A strain of hemolytic streptococci: Proteins of the streptococcal cells stimulate antibody formation by the body (see IMMUNITY) and these antistreptococcal antibodies are believed to react with and damage many tissues of the body, especially heart muscle. Sulfa drugs, penicillin, and many other antibiotic drugs are effective in treating streptococcal infections. Lactic streptococci are used in starter cultures in the production of fermented dairy products, e.g., buttermilk and cheese.

Streptomyces (strĕp"təmī'sēz), bacterial genus of the order Actinomycetales, members of which resemble fungi in their branching filamentous structure. Various species produce such antibiotics as streptomycin and various TETRACYCLINES.

streptomycin (strĕp"tōmī'sĭn), ANTIBIOTIC produced by soil bacteria of the genus *Streptomyces* and active against both gram-positive and gram-negative bacteria (see GRAM'S STAIN), including species resistant to other antibiotics, e.g., some streptococci, penicillin-resistant staphylococci, and bacteria of the genera *Proteus* and *Pseudomonas.* Originally isolated by Selman A. Waksman and Albert Schatz in 1947, streptomycin is effective against tubercle bacilli and is a mainstay of tuberculosis therapy. Because streptomycin-resistant tubercle bacilli emerge during treatment, the antibiotic is usually used in combination with one or more of the drugs ISONIAZID, ethambutol, and aminosalicylic acid. Streptomycin acts by inhibiting protein synthesis and damaging cell membranes in susceptible microorganisms. Possible side effects include injury to the kidneys and nerve damage that can result in dizziness and deafness.

Stresa (strā'zä), town (1971 pop. 5,168), Piedmont, N Italy, on the western shore of Lake Maggiore. Its lovely gardens and villas and the scenic Borromean Islands nearby have made it one of the most popular resorts in the Italian lake country. In 1932 a conference of 15 European nations on economic collaboration was held at Stresa. At another conference held (1935) in Stresa, Great Britain, France, and Italy made (but never implemented) a decision to maintain a common posture toward Germany, which had begun to rearm in violation of the Treaty of Versailles.

Stresemann, Gustav (go͞os'täf shtrā'zəmän), 1878-1929, German statesman. A founder (1902) and director (until 1918) of the Association of Saxon Industrialists, Stresemann entered the Reichstag in 1907 as a deputy of the National Liberal party and represented the interests of big business. During World War I, he supported the monarchy and an annexationist policy, but after the proclamation of a German republic in 1918 he founded the conservative German People's party and turned to a conciliatory policy in harmony with the weak position of his country. As chancellor (1923) and as foreign minister from 1923 until his death, he made it his task to reconcile the former enemy nations to Germany, to remove the harsh clauses of the Treaty of Versailles, and to regain for Germany a respected place in the world. His policy, although it alienated from him the nationalist and monarchist elements in Germany, was remarkably successful. Although he knew of efforts by Hans von SEECKT to evade the disarmament clauses of the Treaty of Versailles, he won the confidence of the Allies. He ended (1923) the passive resistance in the RUHR district against French and Belgian occupation and obtained the evacuation of the Ruhr in 1924; he accepted the DAWES PLAN (1924) and the YOUNG PLAN (1929) for reparations; he raised the hope for peace by his part in the LOCARNO PACT (1925); he renewed (1926) the Rapallo treaty with the USSR; and he had Germany admitted (1926) into the League of Nations with the rank of a great power. His harmonious relation with Aristide BRIAND became one of personal friendship. In 1928, Stresemann signed the KELLOGG-BRIAND PACT. Soon after obtaining his last success, the evacuation of the Rhineland, Stresemann died of the consequences of overwork. His death was, prophetically, considered a calamity by all but the extremist elements in Germany. Stresemann shared the 1926 Nobel Peace Prize with Briand. See his *Essays and Speeches* (tr. 1930, repr. 1968); Eric Sutton, ed., *Gustav Stresemann: His Diaries, Letters, and Papers* (3 vol., 1935-40); studies by H. L. Bretton (1953), H. A. Turner (1963), Donald Warren (1964), F. E. Hirsch (1964); and C. M. Kimmich (1968).

stress: see STRENGTH OF MATERIALS.

Stretford, municipal borough (1971 pop. 54,011), Lancashire, NW England. Contiguous with Manchester and Salford, it has a large dock area and varied manufactures. In 1974, Stretford became part of the new metropolitan county of Greater Manchester.

Streuvels, Stijn (stīn strö'vəls), pseud. of **Frank Lateur** (frängk lätör'), 1871-1969, Flemish novelist and short-story writer; nephew of Guido Gezelle. Streuvels's works are realistic, moving portrayals of everyday life. His early novels show the influence of Russian fatalism; *De Vlaschaard* (1907), his masterpiece, strikes a more optimistic note. The short-story collection *The Path of Life* (1899, tr. 1915), the novels *Old Jan* (1902, tr. 1936) and *Werkmenschen* (1927), and an autobiography (1966) are among his other works.

Streymoy (strām'oi") or **Strømø** (ström'ö"), island (1966 pop. 14,078), 144 sq mi (373 sq km), Denmark, the largest of the FAEROE ISLANDS. Tórshavn is the main town.

Strickland, Agnes, 1796-1874, English historian. With the collaboration of her sister Elizabeth she wrote children's books and *The Lives of the Queens of England* (12 vol., 1840-48), *Letters of Mary, Queen of Scots* (1843), and *The Lives of the Queens of Scotland* (1850-59). See biography by U. B. Pope-Hennessy (1940).

Strickland, William, 1788-1854, American architect of the classic revival, b. Navesink, New Jersey. He studied under B. H. Latrobe. In his buildings Strickland sought to reconcile the proportions of ancient architecture with modern utilitarian needs. He worked mostly in Philadelphia, where in 1818 he won the competition for the Second Bank of the United States (later the customhouse, now a historical site) and superintended its construction (1819–24). His most distinctive building is the Merchants' Exchange (1832–34), a significant work in the classical style. In 1828 he restored the steeple of Independence Hall. A late work was the state capitol at Nashville, Tenn. His book *Reports on Canals, Railways, Roads, and Other Subjects* (1826) shows his engraving and engineering capacities. See study by Agnes Gilchrist (1950).

strike, concentrated work stoppage by a group of employees, the chief weapon of organized labor. A suspension of work on the employer's part is called a LOCKOUT. Work stoppages in North America date from colonial times, but organized strikes—collective action by large numbers of employees within one industry or firm to gain definite ends—began in the 1870s. The first nationwide strike occurred in 1877, when railroad workers struck in the middle of an economic depression. With the advent, in the 1880s, of such labor organizations as the Knights of Labor and the American Federation of Labor, strikes became more frequent. Strikes usually result from conflict of interests between the employer and employees who seek higher wages (or in times of depression try to stop wage decreases), shorter hours, better working conditions, union recognition, or improved fringe benefits. Another cause of strikes has been the introduction of automation without monetary or other forms of compensation for workers; examples are the typesetters' strikes that stopped production of newspapers in Cleveland, Ohio (1962–63), New York City (1962–63, 1965), Los Angeles (1968), and Detroit (1968). Employers may attempt to continue operation without the striking employees, and in such cases violence may occur. Violence, long a feature of U.S. labor history, often resulted from the use of armed guards (hired by the employer) or of police or state militia against pickets (see PICKETING) or for the protection of strikebreakers. A notorious example of the importation of strikebreakers was in the HOMESTEAD STRIKE of 1892. The first use of the INJUNCTION against strikers was during the PULLMAN STRIKE in 1894. During the middle and late 1930s workers in the mass-production industries (especially in the automobile industry) perfected the technique of the sit-down, later declared illegal, which was designed to prevent strikebreaking because the workers remained on the premises while refusing to work. Some of the more important industry-wide strikes in the United States have been those waged by the railroad employees in 1877 and 1894, by the United Mine Workers in 1902 and 1946–47, by the steel workers in 1919, 1937, 1952, and 1959, and by the auto workers in 1937 and 1946. Important local strikes have included those of the WESTERN FEDERATION OF MINERS in the early years of the 20th century and of the teamsters in Minneapolis in 1934. Another cause of strikes has been the jurisdictional dispute to determine which union should be the bargaining agent for the employees. After the separation of the Congress of Industrial Organizations from the American Federation of Labor in 1935 (see AMERICAN FEDERATION OF LABOR AND CONGRESS OF INDUSTRIAL ORGANIZATIONS), such strikes were numerous until they were forbidden by the Taft-Hartley Labor Act in 1947. Generally the tendency in the United States after World War II was toward fewer strikes and more government mediation and intervention. The 1960s and 70s witnessed an increasing number of strikes by public employees, notably teachers, municipal workers, policemen, and firemen. Strikes have been frequent in all industrialized countries where labor has the right to freedom of action. In Great Britain, where the Industrial Revolution occurred first, strikes of various sorts took place during the 19th cent.; these include the antimachine riots of the Luddites and the political demonstrations of the Chartists. Among other notable strikes are the successful work stoppage in 1889 by the London dock workers and the bitter and unsuccessful strikes by coal miners in 1898 and 1926, the latter leading to a GENERAL STRIKE. The general strike, more successful in countries where labor unions are more closely linked to political parties than in the United States, has nevertheless also been attempted in cities there. Work stoppages have also occurred under authoritarian regimes (which often legally forbid strikes) as protests against both economic and political disabilities. Strikes against foreign owners of mines and oil fields have occurred at various times in Mexico, Bolivia, Chile, Venezuela, and Iran. The strike has also been used as a political weapon in the movements for independence in Asia and Africa. See Florence Peterson, *Strikes in the United States, 1880–1936* (1937, repr. 1972); F. R. Dulles, *Labor in America* (1966); T. R. Brooks, *Toil and Trouble* (1971); H. H. Hart, *The Strike* (1971); Jeremy Brecher, *Strike!* (1972); W. H. Hutt, *The Strike-Threat System* (1973).

Strimón: see STRUMA, river, Bulgaria and Greece.

Strindberg, Johan August (strĭnd'bərg, Swed. yōō'hän ou'gəst strĭnd'bĕr"yə), 1849–1912, Swedish dramatist and novelist. He was the greatest master of the Swedish language and an innovator in dramatic and literary styles. Strindberg was the unwanted fourth child of a once well-to-do father and a mother who had come to his father's house as a servant. He studied intermittently at the Univ. of Uppsala but poverty forced him to leave without a degree, taking work as a tutor, journalist, and librarian. His first mature drama, *Master Olaf* (written c.1873), showed the influence of Ibsen and Shakespeare; it represented the personality of the author in three characters. The play was refused production until 1881 because of its realistic portrayal of national figures and its unprecedented use of prose for dramatic tragedy. But with the novel *The Red Room* (1879), in which he satirized hypocrisy and injustice in Swedish life, Strindberg achieved renown. *The Red Room,* which helped initiate Swedish realism, revealed Strindberg's remarkable style, brilliantly visual and precisely suited to his ideas. He developed it more fully in the next decade, pouring forth an impressive assortment of novels, plays, stories, histories, and poems. His life was complicated by an unsuccessful suit brought against him for blasphemy as a result of his stories in *Married* (2 vol., 1884–85), which derogated women and denounced conventional religious practices. Although this conflict stirred a persecution complex in Strindberg, he remained, for a time, prolific and creative. His bitter and revealing autobiography *Tjänstekvinnans son* (tr. *Son of a Servant,* 1913) appeared in 1886. In the late 1880s he began to experiment with free verse and created the great dramas *The Father* (1887), *Miss Julie* (1888), and *Creditors* (1888). These plays follow naturalism in their emphasis on the pathological and in their realism, but they depart from its objective, documentary techniques to achieve a subjective and emotional tone. *The Father* vividly expresses Strindberg's view of the war between the sexes, in which he saw man as victimized by woman. *Miss Julie* is a psychological study of the seduction of an upper-class woman by an insensitive chauffeur. These works show the influence of the ideas of Zola and Nietzsche. In 1891 the first of Strindberg's three wretched marriages ended in divorce, and his second marriage and separation soon followed. He was precipitated into his "inferno crisis" (1894–96), in which he explored the occult and entertained the delusion that he was persecuted by creatures from another world, an experience later described in *Inferno* (1897). His inner turmoil subsided somewhat as he adopted Swedenborgian mysticism, and he entered a new period of creativity. In 1901 he married the actress Harriet Bosse; they parted in 1904 and, as with his previous marriages, he lost custody of their offspring. In his dramas of this period Strindberg began to experiment with visual effects and other aspects of dramatic form, initiating changes that still remain living influences in the modern theater. Expressionist dream sequences and symbolism were combined with realism and with religious mysticism. Major works in this vein are *The Dream Play* (1902), *To Damascus* (3 parts, 1898–1904), and *The Ghost Sonata* (1907); in all there prevails some compassion for man's discordant existence, accompanied by varying degrees of pessimism. Strindberg also wrote many historical dramas, including the outstanding *Gustav Vasa* (1899). His last play, *The Great Highway* (1909), was a symbolic study of his own life. Many of his works have been translated into English. See his *Open Letters to the Intimate Theatre* (1966) and his letters (1939, repr. 1959); biography by M. Lamm (tr. 1971); studies by W. G. Johnson (1963) and E. O. Johannesson (1968).

stringed instrument, any musical instrument whose tone is produced by vibrating strings. Those whose strings are plucked with the finger or a plectrum include the BALALAIKA, BANJO, GUITAR, HARP, LUTE, MANDOLIN, and ZITHER; those plucked by means of a keyboard include the HARPSICHORD and SPINET. Those played with the bow are principally of the VIOL and VIOLIN families. Instruments whose strings are struck include the DULCIMER and several keyboard instruments, among them the PIANO and CLAVICHORD.

strip cropping, practice of growing field crops in narrow strips either at right angles to the direction of the prevailing wind, or following the natural contours of the terrain to prevent wind and water erosion of the soil.

strip mining: see COAL MINING.

stroboscope (strŏb'əskōp), optical instrument for making a moving object appear to be slowed down or stationary. This effect is created by interrupting the observer's view so that the object is seen only at regularly spaced intervals rather than continuously. In its simplest form the stroboscope is a rotating disk; along its edge are evenly spaced holes through which the moving object is observed. If the object's motion is cyclic, the speed of the disk can be synchronized with it so that the object always appears in the same position when viewed through one of the holes. During the time that a solid area is blocking the line of sight, the persistence of vision enables the eye to retain the image previously seen, while the object moves to the same or a similar position by the time the next hole is in front of the eye. The effect is thus one of a stationary object. If the stroboscope is not quite synchronized with the object's motion, the object will appear to move slowly either backward or forward, depending upon whether the stroboscope's rotation is too fast or too slow. For more accurate observation a flashing light (stroboscopic light) is used instead of a disk. A stroboscopic light can also be used to study motion that is not cyclic, e.g., a speeding bullet, when used in conjunction with a camera; the resulting photograph shows a series of still images whose separations are proportional to the object's speed. The stroboscope has various uses in scientific research, teaching, and industry, where it is used to study stresses on parts of machines while in motion.

Stroessner, Alfredo (älfrā'thō shtrös'nər), 1912–, president of Paraguay (1954–). Of a German Paraguayan family, he was commissioned an army officer in 1932 and fought with distinction in the Chaco War (1932–35). He became commander in chief of the armed forces in 1951 and in 1954 engineered the coup that toppled the Federico Chávez regime and set the stage for his own election as president that same year. Retaining command of the armed forces, he suppressed all opposition; he was "reelected" in 1958, 1963, 1968, and 1973. His long rule brought order and monetary stability. With foreign aid, he launched a development program, emphasizing the building of schools, roads, bridges, and power facilities. In the 1960s he began to permit some political dissent and the formation of opposition parties, which gained some representation in congress, but his rule remained essentially totalitarian.

stroke: see APOPLEXY.

Stromboli, island, Italy: see LIPARI ISLANDS.

Stromness, burgh, county town of Orkney, on Mainland island, N Scotland. It has a harbor with shipyards and docks. Eggs are exported. In the 18th and 19th cent. Stromness was a whaling center and a port of call for the Hudson's Bay Company. There is a famous museum of Orkney antiquities.

Strømø: see STREYMOY, Faeroe Islands, Denmark.

Strong, William Duncan, 1899–1962, American anthropologist, b. Portland, Oregon, grad. Univ. of California (B.A., 1923; Ph.D., 1926). He served as curator at the Chicago Field Museum (1926–29) and as senior anthropologist at the Bureau of American Ethnology (1931–37) and taught at the Univ. of Nebraska (1929–31) and at Columbia (1937–62). A pioneer in the stratigraphic analysis of archaeological deposits, he conducted research projects in Labrador, the Great Plains, Honduras, and Peru. His writings include *An Introduction to Nebraska Archeology* (1935), *Cultural Resemblances in Nuclear America* (1951), and *Cultural Stratigraphy in the Viru Valley, Northern Peru* (with Clifford Evans, 1952).

Strongbow, Richard: see PEMBROKE, RICHARD DE CLARE, 2D EARL OF.

Strongsville, city (1970 pop. 15,182), Cuyahoga co., NE Ohio, a residential suburb of Cleveland; settled 1816, inc. 1927. It has a text-book publishing company, a research laboratory, and some light manufacturing.

strontium (strŏn'shēəm) [from *Strontian,* a Scottish town], a metallic chemical element; symbol Sr; at. no. 38; at. wt. 87.62; m.p. 769°C; b.p. 1384°C; sp. gr. 2.6 at 20°C; valence +2. Strontium is a soft, silver-yellow metal with three allotropic crystalline forms (see ALLOTROPY). It is an ALKALINE-EARTH METAL; in its physical and chemical properties it resembles calcium and barium, the elements above and below it in group IIa of the PERIODIC TABLE. Since strontium reacts vigorously with water and quickly tarnishes in air, it must be stored out of contact with air and water. Among its compounds are the oxide strontia, SrO; peroxide, SrO_2; hydroxide, $Sr(OH)_2$; nitrate, $Sr(NO_3)_2$; the carbonate strontianite, $SrCO_3$; the sulfate celestite, $SrSO_4$; carbide, SrC_2; and halides, $SrBr_2$, $SrCl_2$, SrF_2, and SrI_2. CELESTITE and strontianite are the chief ores of strontium. The metal may be prepared by electrolysis of fused strontium chloride; small amounts of the metal are used in semiconductor devices. Although strontium has uses similar to those of calcium and barium, it is rarely employed, because of its higher cost. Principal uses of strontium compounds are in pyrotechnics (chiefly the nitrate) and in greases (the hydroxide). In fireworks and signal flares strontium compounds add a bright red or crimson color to the flame. Naturally occurring strontium is a mixture of four stable isotopes. Twelve unstable isotopes exist; the most stable of these is the radioactive isotope strontium-90 (half-life 28.1 years), which is the chief immediate hazard in FALLOUT. As a result of atmospheric nuclear tests, strontium-90 is dispersed in varying concentrations throughout the earth's atmosphere and soil. Because of its chemical similarity to calcium, it is readily taken up in the tissues of plants and animals; it may enter the human food supply, mainly in milk. It is particularly dangerous for growing children as it is easily deposited in the bones and is believed to induce bone cancer and leukemia. Strontium-90 also has some uses in luminous signs and in nuclear batteries. Strontium was first recognized as distinct from barium in 1790 by A. Crawford in a sample of its carbonate from a mine near Strontian, Scotland; his finding was later confirmed by T. C. Hope, M. H. Klaproth, and others. It was first isolated by electrolysis in 1808 by Humphry Davy.

Strozzi (strôt'tsē), noble Florentine family. It grew rich through commerce and took an active part in the government of the city after the 13th cent. Later the Strozzi strongly opposed the Medici rule of Florence. Among the Strozzi, there were several eminent soldiers, scholars, and men of letters. At an early date the family divided into several branches. **Palla Strozzi,** c.1373-1462, a politician and ardent humanist, furthered Greek studies in Florence and Padua. **Filippo Strozzi,** 1428-91, was banished by the Medici, gained wealth and influence in Naples, and after his return to Florence began to build the celebrated Strozzi Palace. His son **Filippo Strozzi,** 1489-1538, married a granddaughter of Lorenzo de' Medici; he was first friendly to the Medici, then became a staunch opponent. He led Florentine exiles against Cosimo I de' Medici, was captured, and died in prison. His son **Leone Strozzi,** 1515-54, first entered the Order of Malta and later became an admiral in the French service. He distinguished himself in wars against Spain and England. Another son of Filippo, **Piero Strozzi,** d. 1558, a violent enemy of the Medici, fought for the French in the Italian Wars and was made a marshal of France. He took part in the French siege of Calais (1557). **Filippo Strozzi,** 1541-82, was also in the French service. He was captured and killed by the Spanish in a naval battle off the Azores.

Strozzi, Bernardo (bĕrnär'dō), 1581-1644, Italian painter, b. Genoa. He is considered one of the greatest of the generation of early 17th-century Italian painters who made the transition from the mannerist to the baroque style. In 1598, Strozzi became a Capuchin monk, thus earning the names "Il Cappucino" and later "Il Prete Genovese." Strozzi was influenced by the work of Rubens, who in 1607 was in Genoa. Strozzi's own influence on the painting of Genoa was very great. His early works were marked by strong chiaroscuro (high-contrast) effects, as in his *St. Augustine Washing Christ's Feet* (Genoa). But his palette had begun to lighten when he went to Venice in 1630. He became one of the artists who rekindled the spirit of great painting in Venice. Examples of Strozzi's work are in the major European museums and in Baltimore, Cleveland, and the Metropolitan Museum.

structural formula: see FORMULA.

Struensee, Johann Friedrich (yō'hän frē'drĭkh shtrōō'ənzā, strōō'-), 1737-72, Danish politician, b. Germany. As physician to CHRISTIAN VII he gained complete mastery over the insane king and became the favorite of the young queen, Caroline Matilda. With her support he became (1771) minister of state, was created a count, and suppressed the privy council, which had limited the royal power. A virtual dictator, he accomplished industrial, commercial, and educational reforms; he attempted to free Denmark from Russian influence and to improve the condition of the peasantry. However, his ruthless methods provoked the enmity of the nobles, who terrorized the king into arresting him. He was accused of adultery with the queen and was executed.

Struma (strōō'mä), Gr. *Strimón,* river, 216 mi (348 km) long, rising in the mountains of W Bulgaria and flowing S, through NE Greece, to the Aegean Sea.

Strumica (strōō'mĭtsä), town (1971 pop. 76,964), SE Yugoslavia, in Macedonia. It is an agricultural center. Strumica, an ancient town, was long under Turkish rule; it was ceded to Bulgaria in 1913 and to Yugoslavia in 1919. Landmarks include the ruins of a castle built by the Roman Emperor Tiberius and remains of a castle that belonged to the 14th-century Serbian hero Marko Kraljevich.

Struthers (strŭth'ərz), city (1970 pop. 15,343), Mahoning co., NE Ohio, an industrial suburb of Youngstown, on the Mahoning River; founded 1800, inc. 1922. It is an iron and steel center.

Struve (shtrōō'və), family of astronomers. **Friedrich Georg Wilhelm von Struve,** 1793-1864, was born in Germany but later lived in Russia. While director (1817-39) of Dorpat Observatory he wrote *Stellarum Duplicum et Multiplicum* (1837), which proved that double stars are not exceptional and that star systems are governed by the laws of gravity. He made substantial contributions to the study of galactic structure and also engaged in notable geodetic operations such as the triangulation of Livonia and the measurement of an arc of the meridian. In 1839 he became director of the new Pulkovo Observatory and was one of the first three astronomers who almost simultaneously obtained an approximate stellar parallax. His son, **Otto Wilhelm von Struve,** 1819-1905, succeeded him as director (1862-89) of the Pulkovo Observatory. He discovered about 500 double stars and a satellite of Uranus, estimated the sun's velocity, made micrometrical measurements of Saturn's ring system, and studied nebulae and comets. **Otto Struve,** 1897-1963, grandson of Otto Wilhelm, was born in Russia and came to the United States in 1921 (he was naturalized in 1927). He received his Ph.D. (1923) from the Univ. of Chicago; in 1921 he joined the staff of its Yerkes Observatory. From 1932 to 1947 he was professor of astrophysics at the Univ. of Chicago and director of Yerkes Observatory and of McDonald Observatory (of the universities of Texas and Chicago). He served from 1950 to 1959 as professor of astrophysics at the Univ. of California and as director of its Leuschner Observatory; in 1960 he became director of the National Radio Astronomy Observatory at Green Bank, W.Va. He made many important studies of radial velocity, interstellar matter, and stellar evolution.

Stry (strē), Pol. *Stryj,* city (1967 est. pop. 46,000), SW European USSR, in the Ukraine, on the Stry River (a tributary of the Dnestr) and in the Carpathian foothills. It is a major rail junction and a center of the Drogobych oil region. Industries include lumbering and woodworking, railroad car repairing, flour milling, and the production of machinery and machine tools. An old Ukrainian settlement, Stry was chartered in 1431. It became a flourishing trade center from the 15th to 16th cent. but declined in the 17th cent. Stry passed to Austria in 1772, to Poland in 1919, and to Ukraine in 1939.

strychnine (strĭk'nīn), bitter alkaloid drug derived from the seeds of a tree, *Strychnos nux-vomica,* native to Sri Lanka, Australia, and India. It has been used as a rat poison for five centuries, and rat biscuits still remain a cause of accidental poisoning in humans. Strychnine is a potent stimulant of the spinal cord; it also increases the secretion of gastric juices and heightens sensory awareness. Strychnine poisoning is characterized by violent convulsions. It is treated by keeping the victim absolutely quiet and administering barbiturate sedatives and artificial respiration. See FIRST AID.

Strype, John (strīp), 1643-1737, English ecclesiastical historian and biographer. A graduate of Cambridge, he took holy orders. Much of his early life was spent in collecting old charters, letters, and various documents, mostly of the Tudor period. Later he used these in his cumbersome but valuable works. These include the *Annals of the Reformation* (2 parts, 1708-9) and biographies of Thomas Cranmer (2 parts, 1694), John Aylmer (1701), Sir John Cheke (1705), Edmund Grindal (1710), Matthew Parker (1711), and John Whitgift (2 parts, 1717-18). See biography by A. P. Wire (1902).

Stuart or **Stewart,** royal family that ruled Scotland and England. The Stuart lineage began in a family of hereditary stewards of Scotland, the earliest of whom was Walter (d. 1177), grandson of a Norman adventurer. Several early Stuarts were regents of Scotland, and after Robert, seventh in the hereditary line of stewards, became king as ROBERT II (1371), the crown remained in the family succession. The marriage of JAMES IV of Scotland to Margaret Tudor, daughter of Henry VII of England, made his granddaughter MARY QUEEN OF SCOTS a claimant to the English throne. Mary's claim was recognized when her son, James VI of Scotland, became JAMES I of England in 1603. CHARLES I, son of James I, was beheaded (1649) at the end of the English civil war, but after the interregnum of the Commonwealth and the Protectorate, his son CHARLES II was restored to the throne in 1660. With the deposition (1688) of Charles II's brother and successor, JAMES II, the crown passed to James's daughter MARY II and her husband, William III, and after them to ANNE, also daughter of James II. In the reign of Anne, the last of the Stuarts to rule England, the crowns of Scotland and England, united personally by the Stuarts, were permanently joined by the Act of Union (1707). After the death of Anne the crown passed (by the Act of SETTLEMENT, 1701) to George I of the house of Hanover, son of the Electress Sophia, who was the granddaughter of James I of England; thus the Hanoverians also had a Stuart claim. The parliamentary rule of succession was adopted because the claim to the throne of the Roman Catholic James II and his descendants, James Francis Edward Stuart (the Old Pretender), Charles Edward Stuart (the Young Pretender), and Henry Stuart (Cardinal York), was upheld by the JACOBITES. After 1807 this claim passed to the descendants of Henrietta, daughter of Charles I, through her grandson, King Charles Emmanuel III of Sardinia, to the 20th-century Prince Rupert of Bavaria. *Stuart,* the French form of the name, was popularized by Mary Queen of Scots. See Gordon Donaldson, *Scottish Kings* (1967); A. C. Addington, *The Royal House of Stuart* (2 vol., 1969-71); Eric Linklater, *The Royal House* (1970).

Stuart or **Stewart, Alexander, duke of Albany,** 1454?-1485, Scottish nobleman; second son of James II of Scotland. He was captured (1463) by the English while he was at sea en route to the Low Countries, but was soon released. He became high admiral of Scotland, warden of the marches, and lieutenant of the kingdom. In 1479, however, his brother JAMES III, suspecting Albany of plotting against the throne, had him imprisoned. Albany escaped to France and thence went to England, where he concluded (1481) a treaty with Edward IV, by which the English king agreed to recognize Albany as king of Scotland if the latter became his vassal. An English army invaded Scotland (1482), but Albany was persuaded by some of the Scottish nobles to renounce his pretensions to the throne in return for the restoration of his estates. He was briefly reconciled with James, but in 1483 he was sentenced to death and fled to England. After raiding Scotland in 1484, he went to France, where he was accidentally killed in a tournament.

Stuart or **Stewart, Alexander, earl of Buchan** (bŭkh'an, bŭk'-), 1343?-1405?, Scottish nobleman; fourth son of Robert II. He held various offices under the crown and was made lord of Badenoch in 1371 and earl of Buchan in 1382. In 1389 he was censured by the church for repudiating his wife. In his rage against the bishops he burned the town of Forres and the cathedral at Elgin (1390). For this violence he was excommunicated (but later absolved) and popularly called the Wolf of Badenoch.

Stuart or **Stewart, Arabella,** 1575-1615, cousin of James I of England (James VI of Scotland). She was the daughter of Charles Stuart, earl of Lennox, younger brother of Lord DARNLEY, and her descent from Henry VIII's sister MARGARET TUDOR placed her next after James in the line of succession to Elizabeth I of England. Many argued that her title was preferable to that of James because she was born on English soil. Her marriage was prevented in Elizabeth's reign, but after James's accession (1603) to the English throne, Arabella secretly married (1610) William Seymour (later marquess of HERTFORD), who was also of royal descent. They were arrested and imprisoned but escaped; however Arabella was recaptured (1611) and died in the Tower of London. See biographies by Phyllis Handover (1957) and Ian McInnes (1968).

Stuart or **Stewart, Charles Edward,** 1720-88, claimant to the English throne, b. Rome. First son of James Francis Edward STUART (the Old Pretender), he was known as Bonnie Prince Charlie and as the Young Pretender. When the failures and irregular life of the Old Pretender had alienated his followers, Charles

Edward, a charming young man, magnanimous and brave, became the hope of the JACOBITES. He led them in the rising of 1745, but all his enthusiasm could not avert the defeat at Culloden Moor in 1746. Charles fled to a Highland refuge, then escaped abroad with the aid of Flora MACDONALD. He was expelled from France after the Treaty of Aix-la-Chapelle (1748) and roamed about Europe, a broken drunkard. After his father's death (1766) he lived in Rome as the self-styled count of Albany and in 1772 married Princess Louise of Stolberg-Gedern (see ALBANY, LOUISA, COUNTESS OF). They separated in 1780, and Charles Edward was attended in his later years by his illegitimate daughter, Charlotte. He died in Rome. There is much English and Scottish poetry and romantic literature about Bonnie Prince Charlie. See biographies by Peter De Polnay (1952), Moray McLaren (1972), David Daiches (1973), and Margaret Forster (1974); see also bibliography under JACOBITES.

Stuart or **Stewart, David, duke of Rothesay** (rŏth'sē), 1378?-1402, Scottish prince; son and heir apparent of Robert III. On his father's accession (1390) to the throne, David became earl of Carrick and in 1398 duke of Rothesay. In 1399 he was made lieutenant of the kingdom by his invalid father and given sovereign powers for a three-year term, thus displacing the regency of his uncle Robert STUART, 1st duke of Albany. In 1402, at the end of Rothesay's tenure of office, Albany and Archibald Douglas, 4th earl of Douglas, had him arrested and imprisoned. He died, under questionable circumstances, in their custody.

Stuart or **Stewart, Esmé,** 1st **duke of Lennox** (ĕz'mē), 1542?-1583, Scottish nobleman; cousin to James VI of Scotland (later JAMES I of England). Born and reared in France, he succeeded his father as seigneur d'Aubigny in 1567. In 1579 he was sent to Scotland by the Guise family to restore French influence and weaken Protestantism. He soon won the friendship of the young King James, was admitted to the council, and was created successively earl (1580) and duke (1581) of Lennox. Although Lennox publicly proclaimed his conversion to Protestantism in 1580, he was suspected (with reason) of complicity in a projected Spanish invasion of England to release Mary Queen of Scots. This, with Lennox's part in the arrest and execution (1581) of the earl of Morton, led to the Protestant nobles' seizure of James in the raid of Ruthven (1582). Against both his own and the king's wishes, Lennox was forced to leave Scotland. He died shortly thereafter.

Stuart or **Stewart, Frances Teresa, duchess of Richmond and Lennox:** see RICHMOND AND LENNOX, FRANCES TERESA STUART OR STEWART, DUCHESS OF.

Stuart, Gilbert, 1755-1828, American portrait painter, b. North Kingstown, R.I., best known for his portraits of George Washington. Having shown an early talent for drawing, he became the pupil of Cosmo Alexander, a Scottish painter who was visiting America. He went with him to Edinburgh but returned to America after Alexander's death in 1773. When the Revolution threatened, he sailed to London. He became a protégé of Benjamin West, remaining with him for nearly five years. During this period he exhibited frequently at the Royal Academy of Arts and won renown by his *Portrait of a Gentleman Skating.* Although he was then eminently successful, his extravagant mode of living kept him in constant debt. In 1787 he moved to Dublin. He returned to America, first settling in Philadelphia and later permanently in Boston, where he became the most celebrated portrait painter of his day. He painted three portraits of Washington from life. His first, the so-called Vaughan type (1795), is a bust with the right side of the face shown; there are at least 15 replicas in existence. The second, the Lansdowne type (1796), painted for the marquess of Lansdowne, is a full-length study of the President; the original is in the Pennsylvania Academy of the Fine Arts. The third, unfinished, the Athenaeum Head (Mus. of Fine Arts, Boston), was commissioned (c.1796) by Martha Washington. The artist kept the original version while she had to remain content with one of the 75 replicas. This portrait has been immortalized by the engraving on the U.S. one-dollar bill. Stuart's elegant and brilliant style, partially modeled after Reynolds and Gainsborough, is seen at its best in such portraits as those of Mrs. Richard Yates (National Gall. of Art, Washington, D.C.), Josef and Matilda de Jaudenes y Nebot (Metropolitan Mus.), and John Adams (N.Y. Historical Society). The greater part of his works are in collections in Boston, New York City, and Philadelphia. See biographies by Charles Mount (1964) and John Morgan (1939, repr. 1969).

Stuart or **Stewart, Henry:** see DARNLEY, HENRY STUART, LORD.

Stuart or **Stewart, Henry Benedict Maria Clement,** known as **Cardinal York,** 1725-1807, claimant to the English throne, b. Rome. Second son of James Francis Edward STUART (the Old Pretender), he was the Jacobite duke of York until the death (1788) of his brother Charles Edward STUART (the Young Pretender), when he became royal claimant as Henry IX. He was the last of the direct male line of James II and the last pretender to press a claim to the throne (see STUART, family). He was in France in 1745, ready to help in the Scottish Jacobite rebellion, and on his return to Italy was made (1747) a cardinal of the Roman Catholic Church. In 1761 he was also made bishop of Frascati, where he lived and worked for years. His villa was sacked by the French in 1799, and he fled eventually to Venice. George III of England granted him a pension, and in gratitude Cardinal York bequeathed to George IV (then prince of Wales) the crown jewels of the Stuarts. See biographies by Alice Shield (1908) and Brian Fothergill (1958).

Stuart or **Stewart, James, earl of Arran** (âr'ən), d. 1595, Scottish nobleman. He spent his early years as a soldier of fortune fighting in the Dutch revolt against Spain, returned to Scotland in 1597, and ingratiated himself at the court of the young James VI (later JAMES I of England). As a reward for his services in accusing the earl of Morton of the murder of Lord Darnley, Stuart was made a member of the council and granted (1381) the earldom of Arran, then in the possession of the insane James HAMILTON, 3d earl of Arran. The king's arrest by the Protestant lords in the raid of Ruthven (1582) led to Arran's imprisonment. After the king's escape (1583), however, he was released and appointed lord chancellor. Arran set out to crush his opponents in Scotland, driving the Protestant lords into exile and seizing their lands. He and James also determined to overthrow Presbyterianism, and in 1584 Parliament passed an act requiring the church to acknowledge the king as its head. Arran's reckless use of power soon alienated his few supporters in Scotland, while his agent in England treacherously undermined the good relations that he had established initially with Elizabeth I. In 1585 the English queen accused Arran of the murder of Lord Francis Russell in a border fray. James was compelled to imprison Arran. After the return in force of the banished Protestant lords, Arran himself was banished (1586). He later returned to live in Scotland as Capt. James Stuart and intrigued unsuccessfully to return to power. He was slain in 1595 by Sir James Douglas, nephew of the earl of Morton, in revenge for Arran's part in the death of Morton.

Stuart or **Stewart, James:** see MURRAY, JAMES STUART, 1ST EARL OF.

Stuart, James, 1713-88, English architect, archaeologist, and painter. After working his way to Rome in 1742, Stuart accompanied Nicholas Revett on an archaeological expedition to Naples. Under the auspices of the Society of Dilettanti of London, they also went to Greece. In Athens (1751) they made accurate measurements of the ruins, particularly those of the Acropolis, and published their findings in *The Antiquities of Athens,* the first volume of which appeared in 1762. Its excellent illustrations depicted for the first time the great achievements of Greek architecture. Their work aroused wide attention and acted as a prime influence in the CLASSIC REVIVAL.

Stuart, James Ewell Brown (Jeb Stuart), 1833-64, Confederate cavalry commander in the American Civil War, b. Patrick co., Va. Most of his U.S. army service was with the 1st Cavalry in Kansas. On Virginia's secession, Stuart resigned (May, 1861) and became a captain of cavalry in the Confederate army. He distinguished himself at the first battle of Bull Run (July, 1861) and in September was made a brigadier general. In June, 1862, he conducted the first of his celebrated cavalry raids, making a complete circuit of General McClellan's army on the Virginia peninsula, noting the Union positions. General Lee used this information to advantage in the Peninsular campaign. Stuart was promoted to major general in July and given command of all the cavalry of the Army of Northern Virginia. After another bold and successful raid (Aug., 1862), this time to John Pope's rear, he covered the last stage of Stonewall Jackson's flanking movement before the second battle of Bull Run (Aug., 1862). He was actively engaged in that battle and in the subsequent Antietam campaign. Again in Oct., 1862, Stuart rode around the Union Army ranging as far as S Pennsylvania and capturing 1,200 horses. He made effective use of his famous horse artillery in the battle of Fredericksburg (Dec., 1862). In the battle of CHANCELLORSVILLE, he moved with Stonewall Jackson in the brilliant flank attack. When both Jackson and A. P. Hill were wounded, Stuart took command. In June, 1863, he fought his greatest cavalry battle at BRANDY STATION. For knowledge of the enemy Lee depended on Stuart, who, he said, never brought him a piece of false information. But in the GETTYSBURG CAMPAIGN, Stuart was absent from the army on a raid, and Lee was not apprised soon enough of the Union concentration N of the Potomac. On May 11, 1864, his corps, now decreased in size and deficient in equipment, met a force of Union cavalry at Yellow Tavern, and Jeb Stuart was mortally wounded. Not since the death of Stonewall Jackson had the South sustained so great a personal loss. His rollicking, infectious gaiety and hard fighting were sorely missed in the gloomy last days of Lee's army. See biographies by J. W. Thomason, Jr. (1934, repr. 1971) and Burke Davis (1957); W. W. Blackford, *War Years with Jeb Stuart* (1945).

Stuart or **Stewart, James Francis Edward,** 1688-1766, claimant to the English throne, son of JAMES II and MARY OF MODENA; called the Old Pretender. His birth, at which time it was rumored that he was not the son of the royal couple, helped to precipitate the GLORIOUS REVOLUTION of 1688. He was brought up in France and on his father's death (1701) was recognized there as James III of England. In England, however, the Act of Settlement (1701) had excluded the male line of Stuarts from the succession, and in 1702 he was attainted. His restoration to the English throne was the object of numerous plots and rebellions by the JACOBITES. After an abortive invasion of Scotland in 1708, James served in the French army at Oudenarde and Malplaquet, but in the Treaty of Utrecht (1713) Louis XIV recognized the succession of the house of Hanover to the English throne, and James was forced to leave France. His hopes of succeeding Queen Anne were dashed by the peaceful succession (1714) of the Hanoverian George I. An uprising in his favor (1715), led by the 6th earl of MAR, brought him to Scotland, but on the failure of the movement, James retired to France and finally to Rome. In 1719, James married Maria Clementina Sobieski, a Polish princess commonly called Princess Clementina. He did not take part in the Jacobite uprising of 1745, led by his son, Charles Edward STUART, the Young Pretender. See biographies by Alice Shield and Andrew Lang (1907), A. N. Tayler and H. A. H. Tayler (1934), and Bryan Bevan (1967); see also bibliography under JACOBITES.

Stuart or **Stewart, John, duke of Albany** (ôl'bənē), 1481-1536, regent of Scotland; son of Alexander Stuart, duke of Albany, and grandson of James II of Scotland. He was brought up on his estates in France by his mother, Anne de la Tour d'Auvergne, and always considered himself French. Shortly after the death (1513) of James IV, the Scottish nobles asked Albany, as heir presumptive, to assume the government for the infant JAMES V, but Albany's own lack of enthusiasm and the influence of Henry VIII of England prevented his departure from France until 1515. Upon arrival in Scotland, he assumed the regency forfeited by MARGARET TUDOR (the queen dowager and sister of Henry VIII) as a result of her marriage to Archibald DOUGLAS, 6th earl of Angus. Albany gained possession of Margaret's children and crushed a rebellion led by Lord Home, Angus, and James HAMILTON, 1st earl of Arran. Margaret fled to England and accused Albany of poisoning her infant son, the earl of Ross. Henry VIII's request to the Scottish Parliament for Albany's dismissal was emphatically refused, the duke being declared (1516) heir to the Scottish throne. Since conditions in Scotland seemed fairly stable, Albany returned (1517) temporarily to France, where he negotiated the Treaty of Rouen (renewing the alliance between France and Scotland and providing for the marriage of James V to a French princess) and promoted the interests of Scottish merchants. By a secret agreement between France and England, Albany was prevented from returning to Scotland until 1521. Margaret, who had broken with Angus, enlisted Albany's aid in securing a divorce, and false rumors (possibly started by Cardinal Wolsey) were circulated of their intimacy and projected marriage. Henry again demanded the dismissal of Albany, and, when the Scots refused, English forces raided (1522) the Scottish border. Albany led an army toward Carlisle, but the Scots refused to fight outside their own country, and the force disbanded. Albany returned to France, and Margaret in his absence used her influence in the interests of England. Albany returned in 1523 with French troops and gold, but a subsequent lack of military success on the border destroyed his prestige. While on a visit to France in 1524, Albany's regency was annulled, and he never returned to Scotland. He later served (1525) with the French army in Italy and was French ambassador to Rome (1530–33).

Stuart, John: see BUTE, JOHN STUART, 3D EARL OF.

Stuart or **Stewart, John,** 4th **earl of Atholl** (ăth'əl), d. 1579, Scottish nobleman. He succeeded his father to the earldom in 1542. A supporter of MARY OF GUISE, in 1559 he voted in Parliament against the Protestant confession of faith and expressed his adherence to Catholicism. He became a member of the council of MARY QUEEN OF SCOTS in 1561 and after her marriage to Lord Darnley was one of her chief counselors. However, after Darnley's murder and the rise of James Hepburn, earl of Bothwell, to power, Atholl joined the Protestant lords against Mary. He became a member of the council of regency for James VI, but his sympathies gradually switched back to the queen, and he joined the opposition to the king's party. He was unsuccessful in preventing the election of James Douglas, 4th earl of MORTON, to the regency in 1572. In 1574 proceedings were taken against Atholl as a Roman Catholic, and he probably recanted. With Colin Campbell, 6th earl of Argyll, he succeeded in ousting Morton as regent (1578). The three were uneasily reconciled the following year, shortly before Atholl's death, which was possibly from poisoning by Morton.

Stuart, John McDouall, 1815–66, Scottish explorer in Australia. He emigrated (1838) to S Australia; there, as a draftsman, he joined Charles Sturt's expedition (1844–45) to central Australia. Between 1858 and 1862 he led six expeditions from Adelaide and proved that there was much habitable country in areas about which discouraging reports had come from Sturt and other explorers. He was the first (1860) to reach the center of Australia; he climbed and named Mt. Sturt (later renamed Stuart). From 1860 he tried to cross the continent, and eventually he achieved his objective by reaching Van Diemen Gulf in 1862. See biographies by M. S. Webster (1959) and Ian Mudie (1968).

Stuart or **Stewart, Ludovick,** 2d **duke of Lennox** and **duke of Richmond,** 1574–1624, Scottish nobleman; son of Esmé Stuart, 1st duke of Lennox, and cousin of James VI of Scotland (James I of England). He succeeded to the dukedom of Lennox in 1583 and soon gained the favor of the king. He was named president of the council during James's absence in 1588. Despite his opposition to Ludovick's marriage to Lady Jane Ruthven, the king appointed him (1591) lord high admiral. Lennox accompanied James to England in 1603 and was appointed to the English privy council. He served as ambassador to Paris (1604–5) and was appointed high commissioner to the Scottish Parliament (1607). In 1623 he was created duke of Richmond. He left no children and was succeeded as duke of Lennox by his brother, Esmé.

Stuart or **Stewart, Mary:** see MARY QUEEN OF SCOTS.

Stuart or **Stewart, Matthew:** see LENNOX, MATTHEW STUART OR STEWART, 4TH EARL OF.

Stuart or **Stewart, Robert,** 1st **duke of Albany,** 1340?–1420, regent of Scotland; third son of Robert II. As earl of Fife and Monteith, he held commands under his father and more than once raided England, leading the invasion of 1388. Because of his father's old age he was given the power of government in 1389; he continued it during the reign of ROBERT III, his infirm brother. Made duke of Albany in 1398, in 1399 he was forced to give up the regency to his nephew, David STUART, duke of Rothesay. Rothesay died (1402) in the custody of Albany and Archibald Douglas, 4th earl of Douglas, both of whom were officially declared guiltless of his death. Albany became governor or warden again and continued in that position after Robert III's death because the new king, JAMES I, was a prisoner in England. During Albany's rule the struggle with England went on and the Scottish alliance with France was continued. At home he allowed the nobles much power, but put down (1411) a rebellion of Donald MacDonald, lord of the Isles. Apparently Albany tried to make his sovereignty hereditary in all but name, and he was succeeded as regent by his son Murdoch, 2d duke of Albany. The latter proved a weak ruler, however, and was executed (1425) after James I's return to Scotland.

Stuart, Robert, 1785–1843, American explorer, b. Scotland. He emigrated (1807) to Canada and became a fur trader. He joined in John Jacob Astor's Astoria venture, and in 1812 he led the overland party east. This party was the first known to have used the South Pass and to have followed the main route of the Oregon Trail. Later, as a partner in the American Fur Company, he directed trade around Mackinac, and he also did much for the development of Michigan. See P. A. Rollins, ed., *The Discovery of the Oregon Trail* (1935, repr. 1972); K. A. Spaulding, ed., *On the Oregon Trail* (1953).

Stuart: see ALICE SPRINGS, Australia.

Stubbs, George, 1724–1806, English painter of horses and etcher. Self-taught, Stubbs was interested in comparative anatomy and published his *Anatomy of the Horse* (1766), which is still admired for accuracy and elegance. It gained him a first-rate career as a painter of horse portraits and family groups with carriages. His *Phaeton and Pair* (National Gall., London) is well known. He painted several rural scenes and made many sporting etchings. See study by B. Taylor (1971).

Stubbs, William, 1825–1901, English historian, educated at Oxford. Ordained in 1850, he was a professor of modern history at Oxford until in 1884 he was made bishop of Chester. Stubbs's critical studies of source materials transformed the study of medieval history. His *Constitutional History of England* (3 vol., 1874–78) and *Select Charters* (1870, 9th ed. rev. by H. W. Davis, 1913) remain standard textbooks. Stubbs also edited many texts for the "Rolls Series" of medieval English chronicles.

stucco (stŭk'ō), in architecture, a term loosely applied to various kinds of plasterwork, both exterior and interior. It now commonly refers to a plaster or cement used for the external coating of buildings, most frequently employed in Mediterranean countries. It usually consists of a mixture of cement or lime and sand, applied in one or more coats over a rough masonry or frame structure; the finish is either troweled, floated, or rough textured. The finish called roughcast or rock cast, formerly common in England and the United States, consists of small gravel or other pebbles mixed with wet plaster and thrown or dashed forcibly against a freshly plastered wall. In Italy a form of decoration known as GRAFFITO is often applied to a stucco wall. In ancient Greece a form of stucco was often used over coarse stonework to give a fine surface suitable for receiving detail. The Romans employed stucco similarly on external surfaces and, with notable success, as an interior finish; for indoor work they used a mixture of plaster of Paris or powdered marble, capable of receiving a high finish. The term *stucco* is also applied to various forms of interior decoration in relief that more properly would be classified as PLASTERING.

Stuck, Hudson, 1863–1920, American missionary and explorer, b. London, England. He emigrated to the United States in 1885, graduated from the Univ. of the South (1892), and was dean (1894–1904) of the Protestant Episcopal cathedral at Dallas, Texas. In 1905 he became archdeacon of the Yukon and spent the remainder of his life in Alaska. With three companions he accomplished the first ascent (1913) of Mt. McKinley, and he traveled extensively in N Alaska. Alaskan geography and Eskimo customs are accurately described in his books, some of which are: *The Ascent of Denali (Mount McKinley)* (1914), *Ten Thousand Miles with a Dog Sled* (1914), *Voyages on the Yukon and Its Tributaries* (1917), and *A Winter Circuit of Our Arctic Coast* (1920).

Stucley or **Stukely, Thomas** (both: styo͞o'klē), 1525?–1578, English adventurer. He was rumored to be an illegitimate son of Henry VIII. He was in the service of Edward Seymour, duke of Somerset, and fled to France after Somerset's fall (1549). There he gained the favor of Henry II of France, who sent him (1552) on a mission to England. Stucley betrayed the projected French invasion of Calais but was imprisoned. Released in 1553, he joined the army of Emmanuel Philibert, duke of Savoy, in Flanders and took part in the battle of Saint-Quentin (1557). In 1563 Stucley organized a privateering expedition with Jean RIBAUT under the cover of helping to colonize Florida and with surreptitious aid from Queen Elizabeth I. The resulting complaints of foreign nations caused Elizabeth to arrest him in 1565, but he was immediately pardoned. Stucley then went to serve in Ireland and in 1566 purchased the title of marshal of Ireland. Elizabeth, who distrusted him, refused to recognize this title, and in 1569 he was accused of treason. Stucley fled (1570) to Spain, where he was received at court, knighted, and recognized as duke of Ireland. He planned a Spanish invasion of Ireland but fell from favor at Madrid. His conduct at the battle of Lepanto (1571), where he commanded three ships, brought Stucley back into favor with the Spanish, and he continued plotting against England. In 1577 he received aid from Pope Gregory XIII for an invasion of Ireland. He set sail, but at Lisbon was persuaded to join the Portuguese expedition of King Sebastian against Morocco and was killed at the battle of Alcazarquivir. His adventures have been the subject of ballads and plays. See biography by John Izon (1956).

student movements, designation given to the ideas and activities of student groups involved in social protest. Historically, student movements have been in existence almost as long as universities themselves. As early as the 4th cent., students were engaged in violent protests against professors with unpopular political views. St. Augustine, for example, left his teaching post in Carthage because of such activity. During the Middle Ages, the universities of Paris and Bologna were often the scene of violent confrontations between townsmen and students. The coming of the modern era saw an increase in student activism. Students played an important role in almost every one of the major revolutions of the 19th and 20th cent. In the United States, student unrest, although common during the colonial period, did not take on political overtones until the American Revolution. Following the Revolution, relative peace prevailed on U.S. campuses. Toward the end of the 19th cent., however, the new theories of socialism and communism being advanced in Europe took hold among many American students. The Intercollegiate Socialist Society was formed (1905) to advance the ideas of Marxism. Socialist activity and student protest, however, subsided during and shortly after World War I, only to come back again during the Great Depression. After another period of quiescence, student activism again became prominent in the United States during the 1960s. Spurred on by the civil rights movement and by growing activity against the Vietnam War, groups such as the Student Nonviolent Coordinating Committee and Students for a Democratic Society rose to prominence. A number of student strikes and violent confrontations occurred on various American campuses. Most notable among these were protests at the Univ. of California's Berkeley campus (1964) and at Columbia (1968) and a nationwide student strike at approximately 200 campuses in 1970. During this same period, Europe and Japan were also the scene of violent student protests. The largest of these was a nationwide strike of French students and workers (May–June, 1968). See Lewis S. Feuer, *Conflict of Generations* (1969); Elvin Abeles, *The Student and the University* (1969); William W. Brickman and Stanley Lehrer, ed., *Conflict and Change: The Response to Student Hyperactivism* (1970); Seymour M. Lipset and Gerald M. Schaflander, *Passion and Politics* (1971).

Stuhlweissenburg: see SZÉKESFÉHERVÁR, Hungary.

Stumpf, Carl (kärl shto͝ompf), 1848–1936, German psychologist, philosopher, and writer on the psychology of music. He was a professor at Berlin from 1894 to 1921. Interested in philosophy and music, Stumpf widened the study of psychology by creating a psychology of sound (*Tonpsychologie,* 2 vol., 1883–90) and by founding an institute to advance the phonographic method for the comparative study of primitive music. In 1901 he wrote a study of Siamese music. He founded the Berlin Association for Child Psychology, wrote on the evolution concept and on Spinoza, and developed original theories of space perception and sensation. See his *Senses and Sensibility* (1928).

stupa (sto͞o'pə) [Sanskrit, = mound], Buddhist monument of tumulus, or mound, form containing relics. The words *tope* and *dagoba* are synonymous, though the latter refers properly only to a Singhalese Buddhist stupa. The stupa is probably derived from a pre-Buddhist burial mound. The oldest known prototypes (c.700 B.C.) are the enormous mounds of earth at Lauriya Nandangarh in NE India. They were the burial places of royalty. Embedded in the center of these mounds were wood masts that probably carried the umbrellas that served as a sign of royalty and authority. Later the Buddhists used a mast or pole to symbolize the tree or axis of the universe. The Emperor ASOKA was the first to encourage the building of stupas. The earliest mound forms that can properly be termed stupas are those at Sanchi and Bharhut (see INDIAN ART AND ARCHITECTURE). They are hemispherical masses of earth raised on a base and faced with brick or stone. The structure was surrounded by a processional path, the whole being enclosed by a stone railing and topped by a balcony. Though in its development the stupa often became elaborate and complex, in its purest form the plan consisted of a circle within a square. The architectural elements both in plan and in mass represent the parts of the Buddhist universe. Many of the most significant monuments of the Buddhist world are stupas and are to be found in every country in which Buddhism was practiced. Some examples are the Thuparama dagoba of 244 B.C. in Ceylon (now Sri Lanka), Borobudur in Java (8th or 9th cent. A.D.), and the Mingalazedi stupa in Burma (A.D. 1274).

Sturbridge, town (1970 pop. 4,878), Worcester co., S Mass.; inc. 1738. Tourism is its major industry; Old Sturbridge Village, a model of an early American village, draws year-round visitors. Tools and dies are also manufactured. See Samuel Chamberlain, *A Tour of Old Sturbridge Village* (rev. ed. 1965).

Sturdee, Sir Frederick Charles Doveton (stûr'dē), 1859–1925, British admiral. He entered the navy in 1871 and rose to become (1914) chief of war staff at the admiralty on the outbreak of World War I. In Dec., 1914, he decisively defeated the German squadron under Graf von SPEE at the battle of the Falkland Islands, for which he was made a baronet (1916). Sturdee commanded a squadron at the battle of Jutland (1916), became an admiral in 1917, and was made admiral of the fleet in 1921.

Sturdza, Dimitrie A.: see STURZA, DIMITRIE A.

Sture (stü'rə), noble family that played a leading role in Sweden in the 15th and 16th cent. **Sten Sture,** the elder, c.1440–1503, was chosen regent in 1470. In the battle of Brunkeberg (1471) he defeated a Danish force sent by King CHRISTIAN I. The victory gave hope for permanent Swedish independence, but in 1497 Sture was forced to resign, and union with Denmark was recognized (see KALMAR UNION). In 1501 he again became regent. He took an active part in founding (1477) the Univ. of Uppsala. A member of a Danish Sture family, **Svante Sture,** d. 1512, succeeded him as regent. His rule was a period of continual warfare. His son and successor as regent was **Sten Sture,** the younger, c.1492–1520. He vigorously asserted the principle of the superiority of the state over the church, notably by securing (1517) from the Riksdag the deposition of Archbishop Gustaf Trolle, a member of a rival family. He refused to recognize Christian II of Denmark as king of Sweden. Christian sent a force to relieve the archbishop, who was besieged in his castle, but Sture defeated the Danish army and imprisoned Trolle. Warfare continued, and Sture was killed in battle shortly before Stockholm fell to Christian. As regents, the Stures paved the way for Swedish independence, attained under GUSTAVUS I.

sturgeon, primitive fish of the northern regions of Europe, Asia, and North America. Unlike evolutionarily advanced fishes, it has a fine-grained hide, with very reduced scalation, a mostly cartilaginous skeleton, upturned tail fins, and a mouth set well back on the underside of the head. It also has widely separated rows of heavy guard scales, four barbels or feelers that hang below the head and help to locate food, and a gas bladder from which isinglass is made. Some species are marine, e.g., the Atlantic sturgeon *Acipenser oxyrhyncus,* some ascend rivers to spawn, and some (the largest of inland fish) are found in landlocked waters. Sturgeons feed by sucking in their food—e.g., crayfish, snails, larvae, and small fishes—from the water bottom through their small, toothless, fleshy-lipped mouths. The largest species is the Russian sturgeon, or beluga (*A. huso*), of the Caspian and Black seas and the Sea of Azov; it reaches a length of 13 ft (396 cm) and a weight of up to a ton (454 kg). The Pacific sturgeon (*A. transmontanus*) may weigh over half a ton (227 kg) and attain a length of 12 ft (366 cm). The green sturgeon is a smaller Pacific variety, and the common sturgeon is found in coastal waters and rivers of Europe and E North America. Other American species are the rock, or lake, sturgeon (*A. fulvescens*) of the Great Lakes and the Mississippi valley and the shovelnosed sturgeon, or hackleback (*Scaphirhynchus platorynchus;* 3 ft/91 cm), also of the Mississippi valley. Although sturgeon flesh is coarse, smoked sturgeon is considered a delicacy in many areas and sturgeon eggs are the source of the better grades of CAVIAR, often in combination with eggs of the PADDLEFISH, a close relative. Sturgeons are classified in the phylum CHORDATA, subphylum Vertebrata, class Osteichthyes, order Acipenseriformes, family Acipenseridae.

Sturgis, Russell (stûr'jĭs), 1836–1909, American architect and writer, b. Baltimore co., Md., grad. College of the City of New York, 1856. He practiced architecture until 1880; the buildings he designed include the Flower Hospital in New York City and a chapel and several dormitories at Yale Univ. A leading authority on the history of architecture and art, Sturgis published many articles and gave lectures at universities and museums. He was first president (1895–97) of the Fine Arts Federation and president (1889–93) of the Architectural League of New York. His writings include *European Architecture* (1896), *A Dictionary of Architecture and Building* (3 vol., 1901–2), *How to Judge Architecture* (1903), *A Study of the Artist's Way of Working in the Various Handicrafts and Arts of Design* (1905), and *History of Architecture* (4 vol., 1906–15; Vol. III–IV completed after his death by A. L. Frothingham, Jr.).

Stürgkh, Karl, Graf von (kärl gräf fən shtürk), 1859–1916, prime minister of Austria (1911–16). During World War I he governed without the unruly parliament and was strongly opposed by liberals and radicals. He was assassinated by Friedrich Adler, an Austrian socialist.

Sturluson or **Sturleson, Snorri:** see SNORRI STURLUSON.

Sturm, Johannes (yōhä'nəs shtŏŏrm), 1507–89, German scholar and educator. He founded (1537) and directed for more than 40 years the Strasbourg Gymnasium. His system of graded readings and classes shaped the course of studies of European secondary schools. He wrote a number of Latin textbooks. The most important of his works on education was his *Book on the Right Method of Founding Schools for Literary Education* (1537).

Stürmer, Boris Vladimirovich (bərēs' vlədyē'mĭrəvĭch shtyŏŏr'mĭr), 1848–1917, Russian public official. He became premier early in 1916 and shortly afterward replaced Sazonov as foreign minister. Linked with Rasputin and with the Germanophile element in the court, he was violently attacked in the Duma and was obliged to resign in Nov., 1916. He was arrested after the February Revolution of 1917 and died in prison.

Sturm und Drang (shtŏŏrm ŏŏnt dräng) or **Storm and Stress,** movement in German literature that flourished from c.1770 to c.1784. It takes its name from a play by F. M. von Klinger, *Die Wirrwarr; oder, Sturm und Drang* (1776). The ideas of Jean Jacques Rousseau were a major stimulus of the movement, but it evolved more immediately from the influence of Herder, Lessing, and others. With Sturm und Drang, German authors became cultural leaders of Europe, writing literature that was revolutionary in its stress on subjectivity and on the unease of man in contemporary society. The movement was distinguished also by the intensity with which it developed the theme of youthful genius in rebellion against accepted standards, by its enthusiasm for nature, and by its rejection of the rules of 18th-century neoclassical style. The great figure of the movement was Goethe, who wrote its first major drama, *Götz von Berlichingen* (1773), and its most sensational and representative novel, *The Sorrows of Young Werther* (1774). Other writers of importance were Klopstock, J. M. R. Lenz, and Friedrich Müller. The last major figure was Schiller, whose *Die Räuber* and other early plays were also a prelude to romanticism. See studies by R. Pascal (1953, repr. 1967) and M. O. Kirsten (1969).

Štursa, Jan (yän shtŏŏr'sä), 1880–1925, Czech sculptor. His early work shows the influence of Rodin. Among his works are *The Melancholy Girl, Primavera, Eve,* and a monument to Hana Kvapilova, a Czech actress.

Sturt, Charles (stûrt), 1795–1869, English explorer and administrator in Australia, b. India. In 1827 he arrived in Sydney with a detachment of the British army. While in command of an expedition (1828–29) to find the source of the Macquarie, he discovered (1828) the Darling River. On a second journey (1829) he explored the Murrumbidgee and found its junction with the Murray, which he followed by boat to its mouth in Lake Alexandrina. He resigned (1833) his commission because of impaired eyesight and settled in Australia. In 1844 he continued his exploration of the river system of S Australia, traveling up the Murray and Darling rivers and penetrating (1845) almost to the center of the continent. He was colonial treasurer (1845) and colonial secretary (1849–51). In 1853 he returned to England. He wrote *Two Expeditions into the Interior of Southern Australia* (1833) and *Narrative of an Expedition into Central Australia* (1849, repr. 1969). See biographies by George Farwell (1963) and Michael Langley (1969).

Sturza or **Sturdza, Dimitrie A.** (both: dēmē'trēyĕ stŏŏr'dzə), 1833–1914, Rumanian statesman, of a prominent Moldavian family. With Ion Bratianu and Constantin Rosetti he helped bring about the abdication of Prince Alexander John Cuza in 1886 and established Carol I as his successor. After Bratianu's death (1891), Sturza was the recognized head of the National-Liberal party. Between 1895 and 1909, he was often premier of Rumania and forwarded the economic and intellectual progress of his nation. As secretary of the Rumanian Academy of Sciences he edited a collection of Rumanian historical sources (10 vol., 1889–1909).

Sturzo, Luigi (lŏŏē'jē stŏŏr'tsō), 1871–1959, Italian priest and political leader. He taught philosophy and sociology at a seminary in his native Sicily. In 1919 he founded the Popular (Roman Catholic) party and became its political secretary. In the elections of Nov., 1919, the new party secured about one fifth of the seats in parliament and became an important force in Italian politics. After the rise of Fascism in Italy Sturzo was forced to live in exile, first in England and later in the United States; his party was officially banned. It was revived, however, after Benito Mussolini's downfall and renamed the Christian Democratic party. Sturzo returned to Italy after World War II and in 1952 was made a senator for life.

stuttering or **stammering,** speech disorder marked by hesitation and inability to enunciate consonants without spasmodic repetition. Known technically as dysphemia, it is generally attributed to an underlying personality disorder. About half of all those who have speech and voice defects suffer from stuttering or stammering (the terms are used interchangeably). In 65% of stuttering cases there is a family history of the disorder, thus suggesting a hereditary predisposition. In many instances the speech disturbance appears to be precipitated by such situations as a change of surroundings, the advent of a younger child in the family, or, most frequently, by a family environment in which parents are overly concerned with childhood speech interruptions, which occur normally. Negative reactions to the stuttering frequently create feelings of inadequacy and anxiety in the stutterer, which, in turn, intensify the condition. Treatment of young children who stutter is directed toward the parents, who are urged to help their children develop positive attitudes about themselves and their speech. Older stutterers are taught to understand what processes interfere with fluent speech and to speak without the disruptions that are caused by tension. Psychiatric treatment and GROUP PSYCHOTHERAPY have been helpful in a number of cases. See H. R. Beech and Fay Fransella, *Research and Experiment in Stuttering* (1968); E. J. Brutten and O. J. Shoemaker, *The Modification of Stuttering* (1968); Charles Van Riper, *The Nature of Stuttering* (1971) and *The Treatment of Stuttering* (1973).

Stuttgart (shtŏŏt'gärt), city (1970 pop. 633,158), capital of Baden-Württemberg, SW West Germany, on the Neckar River. It is a major transportation point

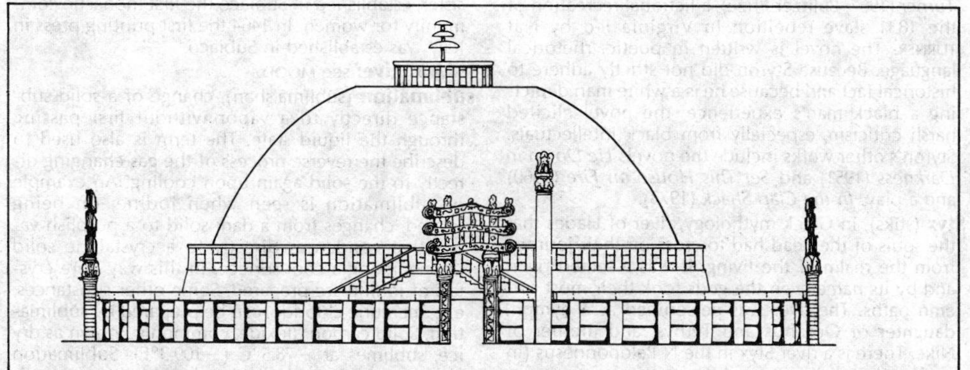

Stupa

and a sizable industrial center. Manufactures include electrical and photographic equipment, optical goods, textiles, clothing, printed materials, beverages (including wine and beer), pianos, and motor vehicles. It is also a tourist center and is the site of industrial fairs. Stuttgart was chartered in the 13th cent. In 1320 it became a residence of the counts (later dukes, from 1806 kings) of Württemberg, who made it their capital at the end of the 15th cent. The city expanded rapidly in the 19th and 20th cent. as its industrial plant grew. After World War I it became famous for the innovative architecture of its numerous modern buildings. Noteworthy are the housing developments in the outer residential districts, where contemporary theories of home building were applied on a large scale. The center of the city, which formed its oldest part, was almost totally destroyed in World War II. After 1945 many old buildings were restored and striking modern structures (such as the city hall and the concert hall) were erected. Other points of interest in the city include the Stiftskirche, a 12th-century church (redone in the 15th cent.); the rococo Solitude Palace (1763–67); the New Palace (1746–1807; now an administrative center); Rosenstein Palace (1824–29; now housing a museum of natural history); and the main railroad station (1914–27). The city has several other museums, a university, and an academy of fine arts. Friedrich von Schiller studied medicine in Stuttgart from 1773 to 1780.

Stuttgart (stŭt'gärt, -gərt), city (1970 pop. 10,477), a seat of Arkansas co., E central Ark.; inc. 1889. It is a trade and processing center of a rice-growing area that is also noted for its duck hunting. Shoes are manufactured in the city. A U.S. fish-farming experimental station is there, and a national wildlife region is nearby.

Stuttgart Ballet, the first major German ballet company. The company, housed in the Württemberg Staatstheater, rose rapidly to fame in the 1960s under the direction of John Cranko (1927–73), who left his position as staff choreographer of Great Britain's Royal Ballet to direct the company in 1961. He recruited spirited young dancers from around the world, staging colorful full-length "story" ballets. These included *Romeo and Juliet, Eugene Onegin, The Taming of the Shrew,* and *Carmen.* The company performs throughout Germany and on extensive tours abroad.

Stuyvesant, Peter (stī'vəsənt), c.1610–1672, Dutch director general of New Netherland. He served as governor of Curacao and lost a leg in an expedition against St. Martin before succeeding Willem KIEFT in New Netherland. On his arrival (1647) in New Amsterdam (later New York City), he immediately informed the colonists of his autocratic intentions. He set up a board of nine men to advise him but dissolved it (1651) when they asked for redress of their grievances in a remonstrance to the Dutch government. As a result of this petition, however, Holland granted (1653) municipal government to New Amsterdam. Nevertheless, Stuyvesant continued his harsh rule and was intolerant of religious dissenters, especially Quakers. While he lost territory to Connecticut (1650), he expanded the colony by conquering NEW SWEDEN (1655). Overwhelmed by a surprise English attack, Stuyvesant surrendered New Netherland to England in 1664. He spent the rest of his life on his Manhattan farm and was buried there under his chapel, now the site of a church, St. Mark's-in-the-Bouwerie. See Ellis L. Raesly, *Portrait of New Netherland* (1945, repr. 1965); H. H. Kessler and Eugene Rachlis, *Peter Stuyvesant and His New York* (1959).

sty, acute localized infection of one or more of the glands of the eyelid, with pain, swelling, and redness of the lid margin, usually caused by a staphylococcus infection. An external sty usually releases its pus and disappears in a day or so. Hot or cold compresses and antibiotic ointments are used to treat sties. Recurring sties are usually due to uncorrected refractive errors, poor general health, or infection elsewhere in the body. If a sty does not disappear in a few days, a physician should be consulted.

style: see PISTIL.

style, in literature, the mysterious yet recognizable result of a successful blending of form with content. Generally speaking, all the arts reflect one of two stylistic tendencies: the classical or the romantic. When applied to literature the first term suggests objective presentation, formal structure, and clear yet ceremonious language, and the second indicates subjective presentation, organic structure, and obscure, effusive, or everyday language. Stylistically, Milton's *Paradise Lost* is classical, whereas Shakespeare's *King Lear* tends toward the romantic (see CLASSICISM; ROMANTICISM). But style is also the badge of individuality that distinguishes a good writer from a poor or mediocre writer. A good poet's sense of style will ensure that the words and lines of his verse cannot be deleted or rearranged without ruining, or at least weakening, the poem as a whole. Keats's sense of style made him change Stanza 30 of "The Eve of St. Agnes" from "she slept" to "she slept an azure-lidded sleep." At the same time, a style that is overblown attracts the attention of parodists. In *The Canterbury Tales* Chaucer mimics the medieval romances in "The Tale of Sir Thopas"; Shakespeare parodies tragic diction in the "Pyramus and Thisbe" passage in *A Midsummer Night's Dream;* Robert Benchley's version of Dickens's *Christmas Carol* ends with a revised utterance from Tiny Tim, "God help us, every one." Commentaries on style abound. The most famous are themselves models of what they instruct. Among these are Horace's *Ars Poetica* (c.13 B.C.); Quintilian's *Institutio oratoria;* Boileau's *Art poetique* (1674) and Alexander Pope's *Essay on Criticism* (1711), both verse imitations of Horace; Buffon's *Discours sur le style* (1753), a work all the more remarkable for being written by a naturalist; and William Strunk and E. B. White's *Elements of Style* (1959), a charming yet practical primer for the would-be writer.

style, in printing, arbitrary rule or collection of rules governing the practice of a printer or a publisher in doubtful or disputed matters to obtain consistency. Correct spelling is a matter of literacy, but a rule prescribing the use of one of two correct spellings is a matter of style. The stylebook of a printer or a publisher is a collection of rules governing office usage in matters of style. It is not a substitute for grammars and reference works. Frequently used stylebooks are *A Manual of Style,* published by the Univ. of Chicago Press, the *Style Manual of the United States Government Printing Office,* and Skillin and Gay's *Words into Type.*

stylites: see SIMEON STYLITES.

stylus: see PEN.

Stymphalian birds (stĭmfā'lēən), in Greek mythology, dangerous man-eating birds that infested the woods around Lake Stymphalus in Arcadia. As his fifth labor, Hercules frightened the birds into the air with a huge rattle and then killed them.

styrax: see STORAX.

Styria (stĭr'ēə), Ger. *Steiermark* (shtī'ərmärk), province (1971 pop. 1,191,000), 6,324 sq mi (16,379 sq km), central and SE Austria. Graz is the capital. Bordering on Yugoslavia in the south, Styria is predominately mountainous, with many forests, pastures, and meadowlands. The province is drained by the Mur, Enns, and Raab rivers. It is the chief Austrian mining district (iron ore, lignite, and magnesite) and has a well-developed metals industry, particularly in the north, near the Erzberg. Cattle, horses, and poultry are raised, and forestry is an important occupation. There are many Alpine resorts. Styria was originally settled by Celts and later was part of Roman Noricum and Pannonia. It was made a duchy in 1180 and in 1192 passed to the Austrian house of Babenberg. Ottocar II of Bohemia successfully contested it with Bela IV of Hungary, but in 1278, at the battle of Marchfeld, Ottocar was defeated and killed by the forces of Rudolf I of Hapsburg. Rudolf declared (1282) Styria, Austria, and Carniola hereditary Hapsburg possessions. By the Treaty of Saint-Germain (1919) Styria's southern portion was ceded to Yugoslavia.

styrofoam: see POLYSTYRENE.

Styron, William, 1925–, American novelist, b. Newport News, Va., grad. Duke, 1947. He is best known for his controversial novel *The Confessions of Nat Turner* (1967; Pulitzer Prize), a fictional recreation of the 1831 slave rebellion in Virginia led by Nat TURNER. The novel is written in poetic, rhetorical language. Because Styron did not strictly adhere to historical fact and because he is a white man depicting a black man's experience, the novel elicited harsh criticism, especially from black intellectuals. Styron's other works include the novels *Lie Down in Darkness* (1951) and *Set This House on Fire* (1960) and a play, *In the Clap Shack* (1973).

Styx (stĭks), in Greek mythology, river of Hades that the souls of the dead had to cross on their journey from the realm of the living. It was a sacred river, and by its name even the gods took their most solemn oaths. The river was personified as a nymph, daughter of Oceanus and Tethys, and mother of Nike. There is a river Styx in the N Peloponnesus (in ancient Arcadia).

Suah (syo͞o'ə), Asherite. 1 Chron. 7.36.

Suardi, Bartolomeo: see BRAMANTINO.

Suárez, Francisco (fränthēs'kō swä'rāth), 1548–1617, Spanish Jesuit philosopher, b. Granada. He studied at Salamanca and was ordained in 1572. He taught successively at Ávila, Segovia, Valladolid, Rome, Alcalá, and Salamanca, and in 1597 was appointed to the Univ. of Coimbra, Portugal (then under Spanish dominion). He may be called the last of the scholastic philosophers (see SCHOLASTICISM). His system is mild and characteristic of the Jesuit theologians. His "congruism" is a middle course between the teachings of Luis MOLINA and the Dominican predestinarian teachings. Suárez taught that one may hold the same doctrine by science and faith. His teaching on the divine right of kings that earthly power is properly held by the body of men and that kingly power is derived from them so enraged James I of England that the king had Suárez's *De defensione fidei* burned by the hangman. This political doctrine, based on the Roman Catholic doctrine of the equality before God of all men, is a basis of subsequent Catholic teachings on democracy. Suárez was highly esteemed by Grotius and his followers. In his *Tractatus de legibus* he made an important distinction between natural law and international law, which he saw as based on custom. See Joseph H. Fichter, *Man of Spain* (1940); H. Lacarte, *The Nature of Canon Law according to Suarez* (1964).

Subbi: see MANDAEANS.

subconscious: see UNCONSCIOUS.

subduction zone, large-scaled feature in the earth's crust where, according to the PLATE TECTONICS theory of crustal evolution, masses of oceanic crust are forced downward into the earth's MANTLE along the leading edges of converging crustal slabs. Subduction zones are usually marked by deep ocean trenches, located seaward of arc-shaped volcanic island chains. Here the rigid oceanic crust is thrust downward into the hot, plastic ASTHENOSPHERE below the adjacent crustal plate. A pattern of earthquakes of shallow, intermediate, and deep focus occurs within the descending plate, which is steeply inclined (30°–60°) toward the continent behind the trench. This earthquake pattern enables geophysicists to trace the descending plate to depths of 600 to 700 km (370–440 mi), where temperatures are thought to be between 1000°C and 2000°C (1800°–3600°F). As the oceanic plate descends into the asthenosphere, friction between the two plates probably causes partial melting of the descending plate and the water-saturated sediments on its upper surface, forming a magma of andesitic composition that rises along fractures. If the overlying crustal plate is oceanic, the magma may erupt to form volcanic island arcs, such as Japan or the Aleutians. On the other hand, if the overlying plate is continental, a line of batholiths and volcanoes may be created as in the Coast Ranges of Canada and the W United States or the Andes of South America. The cessation of earthquake activity beyond 700-km (440-mi) depths is thought to be due to a complete loss of rigidity of the descending slab as it melts or alters to become part of the mantle. See CONTINENT; CONTINENTAL DRIFT; OCEAN; SEA-FLOOR SPREADING.

Subiaco (so͞obyä'kō), town (1971 pop. 8,365), Latium, central Italy, in the Apennines, at the confluence of the Aniene and the Acquaviva rivers. It is an agricultural, industrial, and tourist center. Manufactures include paper and optical equipment. St. Benedict of Nursia retired to Subiaco c.497 and lived there with his disciples until 529, when he moved to Monte Casino. The Benedictine abbey, which grew out of the 12 monastic communities founded there by the saint, rose to great wealth and political power in the Middle Ages. St. Scholastica, St. Benedict's sister, established in Subiaco the first monastic community for women. In 1464 the first printing press in Italy was established in Subiaco.

subjunctive: see MOOD.

sublimation (sŭblĭmā'shən), change of a solid substance directly to a vapor without first passing through the liquid state. The term is also used to describe the reverse process of the gas changing directly to the solid again upon cooling. An example of sublimation is seen when iodine, on being heated, changes from a dark solid to a purplish vapor that condenses directly to a crystalline solid upon striking a cool surface. In this way pure crystals of iodine are prepared. Some other substances, e.g., mercuric chloride, can be prepared by sublimation. Solid carbon dioxide, commonly known as dry ice, sublimes at −78.5°C (−109.3°F). Sublimation also occurs when air saturated with water vapor is suddenly cooled below the freezing point of water.

Frost and snowflakes are thus formed by water changing directly from the gaseous to the solid state.

sublimation, in psychology: see DEFENSE MECHANISM; PSYCHOANALYSIS.

subliminal perception: see PERCEPTION.

submarine, naval craft capable of operating for an extended period of time under water. The first practical submarine is generally conceded to have been built (c.1620) by Cornelis Jocobszoon DREBBEL. It consisted of a rowboat completely covered with leather and propelled by 12 oarsmen, the oars protruding through flexible leather seals on either side of the boat. Drebbel's method of renewing the air in the submerged craft with oxygen enabled the vessel to remain under water for as long as 15 hr. The first submarine used in combat was invented by the American David Bushnell in 1776. This vessel was a small, egg-shaped craft constructed of wood and was operated by one man who turned a propeller. The vessel was submerged by admitting water, and it was surfaced by forcing out the water with a hand pump. An attempt to blow up a British warship in New York harbor by boring a hole in its hull and placing a charge to be ignited by a time fuse failed because the boring tool, operated from inside the submarine, could not penetrate the copper sheathing of the warship. Many of Bushnell's principles were later used by Robert Fulton for the construction of his *Nautilus,* a submarine successfully operated (1800–1801) on the Seine River and at Le Havre. On one occasion the inventor remained submerged for 6 hr, receiving air through a tube extending up through the water. Later Fulton devised and used a spherical tank of compressed air to replenish the air in the submarine. This device, horizontal rudders, the screw to keep water out during submerged operation, and other features of Fulton's submersible vessel made it a forerunner of the modern submarine. In the American Civil War the Confederates used several submersible craft, all named *David,* fitted with a mine at the end of a spar that protruded from the bow. In 1864 one of these craft destroyed a Union vessel in Charleston harbor but was itself lost with its crew. The development of the modern submarine in the United States was advanced considerably by the work of John Holland and Simon Lake. One of Holland's submarines was propelled on the surface by a gasoline engine and when submerged by electric motors powered by storage batteries. The craft was 54 ft (16 m) long and had a speed of 6 knots and a crew of six. In 1900 it became the U.S. navy's first submarine. Holland's efforts were especially important in the development of submergence by water ballast and of horizontal rudders for diving. Lake's *Argonaut,* built in 1897, became the first submarine to navigate extensively in the open sea when it made (1898) a trip through heavy storms from Norfolk, Va., to New York City. However, the *Argonaut* was not accepted by the U.S. navy, and it was not until several European governments had made use of Lake's talents that the U.S. government employed him. In 1912, E-boats, the first U.S. diesel-engine submarines, appeared. They were 135 ft (41 m) long, housed 23 men, and were the first to cross the Atlantic. Development continued until World War I, when submarines were for the first time used extensively by both sides. The Germans used 200-ton submarines (U-boats), and later they employed 21,000-ton craft armed with as many as 19 torpedoes. To halt the heavy destruction of shipping by these U-boats the Allied powers resorted to depth charges, Q-ships (armed vessels disguised as merchantmen), and the use of escorted convoys. With improvements these methods also served in World War II. A typical U.S. navy submarine in World War II consisted of a 300-ft (91-m) craft of 1,450 tons displacement. A crew of 55 operated diesel engines (while surfaced) for a speed of 17 knots, electric motors (while submerged) for a speed of 8 knots. The ship was armed with one 3-in. (7.6-cm) dual-purpose gun, several light automatic weapons, and 10 21-in. (53-cm) torpedo tubes. In World War II the Allies and neutrals lost some 4,770 ships to submarines, and U.S. submarines had sunk some 550 Japanese ships by 1944. Aircraft aided by radar were extensively used by the Allies for hunting and attacking submarines and were a major factor in destroying Germany's U-boats. A periscope is an integral part of every submarine. It extends up through the water and by a mirror arrangement provides the observer below with a view of the surface of the sea. Similar in appearance but totally different in purpose is the snorkel apparatus first employed by the Germans and now in general use. It admits air but not water, and by supplying a flow of fresh air and a means of egress for foul air makes it possible for a submarine to remain submerged for as much as nine tenths of a voyage. With the advent of atomic power, the submarine underwent major changes in propulsion and striking power. In the nuclear-powered submarine an atomic reactor generates heat that drives a high-speed turbine engine. The first nuclear-powered submarine was the U.S.S. *Nautilus,* completed in 1954. Atomic submarines, with underwater speeds of above 20 knots, can remain submerged for almost unlimited periods of time and have circumnavigated the globe without surfacing. In 1960 the U.S.S. *George Washington* was the first submarine to fire a guided missile from a submerged position. The development of atomic submarines capable of launching missiles without surfacing has greatly altered the role of the submarine; its primary mission is no longer the destruction of ships but the firing of missiles at land targets deep inside an enemy's borders. See *Jane's Fighting Ships* (pub. annually since 1897); Bernard Brodie, *Sea Power in the Machine Age* (1943, repr. 1969); F. W. Lipscomb, *The British Submarine* (1954); Harald Busch, *U-Boats at War* (1955, repr. 1967); E. L. Beach, *Submarine* (1959); A. R. Hezlet, *The Submarine and Sea Power* (1967); E. P. Stafford, *The Far and the Deep* (1967).

submersible, small, mobile undersea research vessel capable of functioning in the ocean depths. Development of a great variety of submersibles during the later 1950s and 1960s came about as a result of improved technology and in response to a demonstrated need for the capability to send man into the ocean depths to make direct observations and measurements, to recover lost equipment, and for possible rescue activity. Submersibles are constructed in a variety of sizes and shapes and are designed to perform different and often highly specialized tasks. All contain a crew compartment within a pressure hull, life support systems, power sources, and sensors (lights, cameras, sonar hydrophones). Some also have mechanical arms (manipulators) that enable the crew to collect samples and perform other modest tasks outside the vessel. Most modern submersibles are descendants of the first diving sphere (bathysphere), developed in the 1930s, and the more mobile submarine, which cannot operate at great depths. The inherent danger in a bathysphere was its inability to surface on its own accord, being raised and lowered by a winch system on a surface vessel. In 1954 one of the first types of submersible, the bathyscaphe, was designed and successfully tested by the Belgian scientist Auguste Piccard to overcome this problem and to provide limited maneuverability. A bathyscaphe is in effect an underwater balloon. The cabin is suspended beneath a large flotation chamber that contains gasoline and iron pellets. Submersion is accomplished by release of some gasoline, rendering the craft heavier than water. To rise, some of the iron-shot ballast is released. A second model of the bathyscaphe, called the Trieste II, carried two men to a record-breaking depth of 35,800 ft (10,900 m) at the bottom of the Mariana trench in 1960. One of the most impressive submersibles is the Aluminaut, constructed of high strength aluminum alloys and able to operate at 15,000 ft (4,570 m) carrying a crew of six. The Alvin, operated by Woods Hole Oceanographic Institution, is capable of diving to depths of 6,000 ft (1,800 m) and, like the Aluminaut, is equipped with mechanical arms. In 1974 the Alvin and two French submersibles, the Archimède and Cyana, were used in a joint French-American venture, project FAMOUS (for French-American Mid-Ocean Undersea Study), to learn more about SEA FLOOR SPREADING.

Subotica (so͞o"bô'tĭtsä), Ger. *Maria Theresiopel* or *Theresiopel,* Hung. *Szabadka,* city (1971 pop. 146,755), N Yugoslavia, in the Vojvodina region of Serbia. An important railway junction and an industrial center, it has factories that produce foodstuffs, textiles, chemicals, electrical products, and agricultural machinery. Originally a Roman outpost, Subotica became a royal free city of Hungary until its transfer to Yugoslavia by the Treaty of Trianon (1920).

subpoena (səpē'nə) [Lat.,=under penalty], in law, an order to a witness to appear before a court. A special type of subpoena is needed to compel the production of documents. Failure to obey a subpoena constitutes CONTEMPT of court.

subsidence, lowering of a portion of the earth's crust, usually resulting from readjustments in the interior of the earth. The subsidence of land areas accessible to the ocean results in submergence by shallow seas. Land subsidence can occur through the removal of underground solid or fluid matter. For example, withdrawal of oil from the field at Long Beach, California, beginning in 1936 resulted in subsidence at rates ranging from 0.5 to 2.0 ft (0.15–0.61 m) per yr in the center of the field. By 1962 the center of the oil field had subsided slightly over 27 ft (8.5 m). Because some of the land had sunk to below sea level, dikes and levees were built to preserve the land area. This subsidence was caused by the removal of fluid from the pore spaces in the underground rock, allowing the grains to pack more closely together. Remedial measures were taken to halt the subsidence by pumping salt water back into the reservoir layers, thus replenishing the fluid lost. Similarly, withdrawal of ground water through well pumping has resulted in subsidence in Mexico City, Houston, Texas, and elsewhere. Subsidence is also caused by the collapse of mines and caverns and by surface pressures, such as those caused by glacial ice. Charles Darwin suggested that CORAL atoll formation is caused by the subsidence of oceanic crust under volcanic islands.

subsidy, financial assistance granted by a government or philanthropic foundation to a person or association for the purpose of promoting an enterprise considered beneficial to the public. They are most important as grants to private corporations for performing some public service, such as to shipping companies and airlines for carrying the mails, or to railroads for maintaining passenger service. Technically the subsidy is merely the amount paid the company over and above its legitimate charge for services, and it is granted to provide the company enough revenue to assure its remaining in operation and to enable it to give regular public service. The United States also grants subsidies to shipping lines in order to maintain the competitive position of American vessels in overseas trade and to ensure that a national merchant marine will be available in case of war. American cities have frequently subsidized transit companies to induce them to provide public transportation facilities for the community. Other commonly subsidized enterprises include agriculture, business expansion, and housing and regional development. Very similar to a subsidy is a BOUNTY, except that it usually takes the form of a per unit premium or reward for a service already performed. Today, medical and educational institutions are among the largest recipients of subsidies (see FOUNDATION). Subsidies have also been granted by one country to another country to aid it in prosecuting a war, to gain its goodwill, or to help stabilize its economy. A different kind of subsidy was used in England in the later Middle Ages, when Parliament granted funds to the king to augment or replace customs and other taxes collected by royal prerogative; such early subsidies later became the means by which the power of taxation was taken from the king and lodged in Parliament. At first a nationwide levy, it became (in the reign of Charles II) a land tax levied annually without the intervention of a parliamentary vote. Such a subsidy has been used in many other states, but was never so important as in England. In France the king was able to retain his control and acquire financial powers that made him independent of any subsidy granted by the States-General.

subspecies, also called *race,* a genetically distinct geographical subunit of a SPECIES. See also CLASSIFICATION.

substance, in philosophy, term used to denote the changeless substratum presumed in some philosophies to be present in all being. Aristotle defined substance as that which possesses attributes but is itself the attribute of nothing. Less precise usage identifies substance with being and essence. The quest of philosophers for the ultimate identity of reality led some to define substance as one (see MONISM). Frequently the monist has identified substance with God, an absolute existing within itself and creating all other forms (Spinoza). DUALISM generally considers both mind and matter as independent substances, not as attributes of a more fundamental substance (Descartes). The pluralist may believe that the world consists of many separate realities (Aristotle) or of a multiplicity of self-contained forces (Leibniz). Others have defined substance as material (Hobbes) or mental (Lotze), as static (Parmenides) or dynamic (Heraclitus), as knowable (Aristotle) or unknowable (Hume). Philosophy since Hume has largely discarded the concept of substance for that of force (Spencer) or process (Whitehead). See A. L. Hammond, *Ideas About Substance* (1969).

subtraction, fundamental operation of arithmetic; the inverse of addition. If *a* and *b* are real numbers (see NUMBER), then the number $a-b$ is that number (called the difference) which when added to *b* (the subtractor) equals *a* (the subtrahend). In terms of addition the symbol $-b$ is called the additive inverse of *b* with the property that the sum of a number and its inverse equals 0, or $b+(-b)=0$. The subtraction of *b* from *a* is the same as the addition of *a* and the inverse of *b*, or $a-b=a+(-b)$; e.g., when $a=10$ and $b=5$, then $10-5=10+(-5)$.

subtreasury. After President Andrew JACKSON vetoed (July 10, 1832) the bill to recharter the Second BANK OF THE UNITED STATES, the deposits were removed and placed in state banks that came to be called Jackson's "pets." This process was accomplished by the President only with great difficulty, for there was grave doubt as to its constitutionality (see MCLANE, LOUIS; DUANE, WILLIAM JOHN; TANEY, ROGER BROOKE). The situation remained somewhat in suspension and debate until a subtreasury system, as such, was established (July 4, 1840) with the act to set up the INDEPENDENT TREASURY SYSTEM. This act, never strictly carried out, was repealed (Aug. 13, 1841) by the Whigs. In 1846 the Independent Treasury was finally and rigidly established and with it the subtreasury system. Public funds were not to be deposited in any bank but either kept in coin in the Treasury or subtreasuries or retained by the public officers receiving them until paid out on proper authority. No banknotes were to be received in payments to the government. The subtreasuries were maintained, chiefly through political influence, until the passage of the General Appropriation Act (May 29, 1920) and the transfer of their functions to the Treasury, the mints and assay offices, and the Federal reserve banks, which was completed in 1921.

subway: see RAPID TRANSIT.

succession: see ECOLOGY.

succession, apostolic: see APOSTOLIC SUCCESSION.

succinic acid: see CITRIC ACID CYCLE.

succory: see CHICORY.

Succoth (sŭk'ŏth). **1** City, Palestine, E of the Jordan, by the Jabbok River, where Jacob paused on his return to his native land. Through it Gideon passed in pursuit of the Midianites. It is the modern Tell Deir Alla (Jordan). Gen. 33.17; Joshua 13.27; Judges 8.5,6, 8,14,15,16; 1 Kings 7.46. Valley of Succoth: Ps. 60.6. **2** Place, Egypt, where the Israelites made their first camp on their exodus. Ex. 12.37; 13.20; Num. 33.5.

Succoth-benoth (sŭk'ŏth-bē'nŏth), deity worshiped by Babylonian captives in Samaria. 2 Kings 17.30.

succubus: see INCUBUS.

succulent (sŭk'yələnt), any fleshy plant that belongs to one of many diverse families, among them species of cactus, aloe, stonecrop, houseleek, agave, and yucca. Most succulents are indigenous to arid or semiarid regions, and their succulence is simply an evolutionary adaptation to the extreme heat and dryness of the environment. Typically the plants have greatly reduced leaves with a hard and heavily cutinized outer surface which minimizes evaporation from the inner, juicy tissue that can retain and store water over long periods. Many are grown horticulturally for their interesting and often grotesque forms, e.g., the ice plant; a few have very attractive flowers. See Hermann Jacobsen, *A Handbook of Succulent Plants* (3 vol., 1973).

Suceava (so͞ochä'vä), town (1970 est. pop. 45,000), NE Rumania, in Bukovina, on the Suceava River. It is a commercial center and has industries that manufacture food products, leather, textiles, and cellulose. Suceava was the capital of Moldavia from 1388 to 1565, when it was succeeded by Iasi. A historic shrine with many churches (notably the 16th-century St. George Church, a famous pilgrimage center), the town is also the seat of an Orthodox metropolitan. Nearby is the renowned 17th-century Dragomirna monastery.

Suchathites (syo͞o'kəthīts), family of scribes. 1 Chron. 2.55.

Su-chou, Soochow (so͞o-chou, so͞o-jō), or **Wuhsien** (wo͞o'shēēn'), city (1970 est. pop. 1,300,000), SE Kiangsu prov., E central China, on the Grand Canal near Tai Lake. Su-chou, famous for its silks since the Sung dynasty, is still a silk center; it also has cotton and embroidery manufactures and an important food-processing industry. On the city's outskirts are a small integrated steel complex and plants making chemicals, paper, machine tools, and motor vehicles. Su-chou was capital of the Wu kingdom in the 5th cent. B.C., from whence it derives the name Wuhsien; it was renamed Su-chou in the 6th cent. A.D. The city was almost destroyed in the Taiping Rebellion but was quickly rebuilt. In 1896 it became a treaty port. It was occupied by the Japanese in World War II, and in 1949 it passed to the Chinese Communists. Su-chou is famous for its beauty, with many canals crossed by arched bridges, and lovely gardens. A nine-storied pagoda there (c.250 ft/80 m high) may be the tallest in China. A technical college is in the city.

Süchow: see HSÜ-CHOU, China.

sucker, common name for members of the family Catostomidae, freshwater fish related to the MINNOW and CATFISH families and like them possessing an intricate set of bones forming a highly sensitive hearing apparatus. Suckers range in size from 6 in. (15 cm) to 3 ft (90 cm). They have fleshy, sucking mouths and are sluggish bottom feeders, eating small aquatic animals and plants. The white, or common, sucker, found throughout North America, is an important food fish with firm, sweet (though bony) flesh. Buffalo fish are large suckers whose coarse, bony, nutritious flesh is also much used as food in the central states. The bigmouth buffalo fish reaches 4 ft (120 cm) in length and 65 lb (29 kg) in weight, the smallmouth buffalo fish sometimes attains 20 lb (9 kg), and the black, or mongrel, buffalo fish is intermediate in size. Other suckers are known as red horses, carp suckers, and freshwater mullets. Suckers are classified in the phylum CHORDATA, subphylum Vertebrata, class Osteichthyes, order Mormyriformes, family Catostomidae.

suckerfish: see REMORA.

Suckert, Curzio: see MALAPARTE.

Suckling, Sir John, 1609-42, one of the English CAVALIER POETS. He was educated at Cambridge and Gray's Inn. An accomplished gallant, he was given to all the extravagances of the court of Charles I. He was a prolific lover, a sparkling wit, and an excessive gamester. The antiquary John Aubrey credits him with having invented the game of cribbage. Subjected to a humiliating defeat in Charles I's Scottish campaign of 1639, he was said to be more fit for the boudoir than the battlefield. An ardent royalist, he took part in the plot to rescue (1641) Thomas Wentworth, 1st earl of Strafford, from the Tower of London and to secure aid for Charles from the French. On the failure of these endeavors Suckling fled to France, where, it is conjectured, being unable to face poverty, he was driven to suicide. After his death appeared *Fragmenta Aurea* (1646), a collection of poems, plays, letters, and tracts, including the essay "An Account of Religion by Reason." Today he is best known for the poem "Ballad Upon a Wedding" and the lyrics "Why so pale and wan, fond lover?" and "Out upon it, I have loved three whole days together." See his works ed. by T. Clayton and L. A. Beaurline (1971).

Sucre, Antonio José de (äntô'nyō hōsā' thā so͞o'-krā), 1795–1830, South American revolutionist, b. Cumaná, Venezuela. He joined (1811) the forces fighting for independence from Spain and rose to be the chief lieutenant of Simón BOLÍVAR. After Colombia had been liberated from the Spanish, Bolívar sent Sucre to the Quito region (now Ecuador), where he won (1822) the brilliant victory of PICHINCHA. Accompanying Bolívar to Peru, he distinguished himself in the revolutionary victory of Junín (Aug., 1824). Bolívar was absent and Sucre was the chief commander when the battle of Ayacucho was fought (Dec., 1824). Sucre's military genius was splendidly displayed in this victory, which assured the independence of South America. The terms he granted to the defeated were generous, and Sucre was known for his kindness as well as his honesty and self-effacing modesty. It was against his own will that he became president of the newly created state of Bolivia, and he was not happy in the post. Despite the conciliatory spirit of his rule, an attempt was made on his life. In 1828 he resigned and returned to Quito. A few months later he led the forces that repelled a Peruvian invasion. He was elected president of the constitutional convention which met in 1830 in an effort to prevent Bolívar's large republic of Colombia from disintegrating. Sucre's efforts to prevent Venezuela from seceding and becoming a separate state failed. In June, 1830, when he was riding back from the congress to his home in Quito, he was waylaid by unknown men in a wild mountainous region and killed.

Sucre, city (1969 est. pop. 47,800), S central Bolivia, constitutional capital of Bolivia and capital of Chuquisaca dept. Since 1898, La Paz has been the administrative capital of Bolivia. Sucre was founded in 1538 and called La Plata; the city was also called Chuquisaca and Charcas. It was given its present name in 1839 in honor of the revolutionary leader Antonio José de Sucre. The city lies in a mountain valley on the eastern slope of the Andes at an altitude of c.8,500 ft (2,590 m). The climate is moderate. Sucre is a major agricultural center and supplies the mining communities of the barren altiplano. It also has an oil refinery. The city is the seat of the archbishopric, the supreme court, and the national university, San Francisco Xavier, which was founded c.1625 and specializes in law. The revolt against Spanish rule began in Sucre in 1809.

sucrose (so͞o'krōs), commonest of the sugars, a white, crystalline solid disaccharide (see CARBOHYDRATE) with a sweet taste, melting and decomposing at 186°C to form caramel. It is known commonly as cane sugar, beet sugar, or maple sugar, depending upon its natural source. It has the same empirical formula ($C_{12}H_{22}O_{11}$) as lactose and maltose but differs from both in structure (see ISOMER). Hydrolysis of sucrose yields D-glucose and D-fructose; the process is called inversion and the sugar mixture produced is known as invert sugar because, although sucrose itself rotates plane-polarized light to the right, the mixture "inverts" this light by rotating it to the left. Sucrose is obtained from the "juice" of sugarcane or the sugar beet and from the sap of the sugar maple. The cane or beets are crushed, and the juice, after treatment with lime to neutralize acids, is evaporated in vacuum pans that permit the process to be carried out at relatively low temperatures. The brownish liquid obtained, called molasses, evaporates further, leaving the sugar, brownish in color, which is dissolved in water, treated with animal charcoal to remove the color resulting from the presence of impurities, and recrystallized.

Sudak (so͞odäk'), town, SE European USSR, in the Ukraine, on the Crimean peninsula. It is a resort on the Black Sea. Its major industries are rose oil processing and the production of fine quality wines and champagnes. Founded as a Greek settlement in the 3d cent. A.D., the town passed to Novgorod around 800. From the 9th to 11th cent., the port played an important role in trade with Byzantium and the Mediterranean area. In the 13th cent., Marco Polo passed through the town, and the Venetians established a community there. After repeated Tatar attacks (1289, 1322, 1327), Sudak passed to Genoa and was fortified; but it declined steadily under the Genoese and the Crimean Tatars, to whom it passed in 1475. Russia acquired Sudak in 1783 with the rest of the Crimea.

Sudan (so͞odăn'), officially Democratic Republic of the Sudan, republic (1973 est. pop. 16,700,000), 967,494 sq mi (2,505,813 sq km), NE Africa, bordering on Egypt in the north, on the Red Sea in the northeast, on Ethiopia in the east, on Kenya, Uganda, and Zaïre in the south, on the Central African Republic and Chad in the west, and on Libya in the northwest. KHARTOUM is the capital. The main geographical feature of Sudan, Africa's largest country, is the

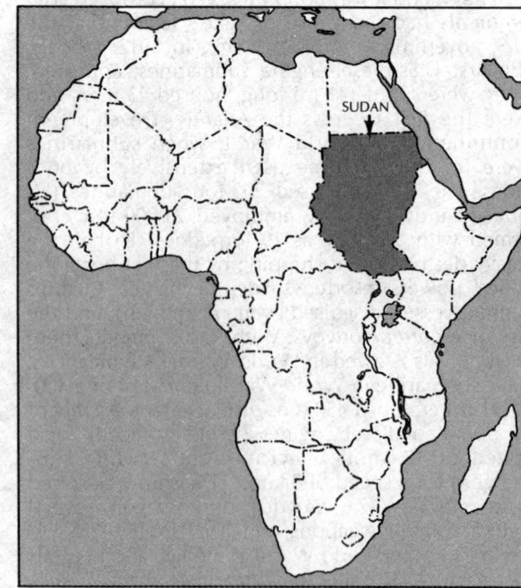

Nile River, which, with its tributaries (including the Atbara, Blue Nile, and White Nile rivers), traverses the eastern part of the country from south to north. The Nile system provides irrigation for strips of agricultural settlement for much of its course in Sudan and also for the AL JAZIRAH (Gazira) plain, situated between the White Nile and the Blue Nile, just south of their confluence at Khartoum. In the extreme north, the Nile broadens into Lake Nasser, formed by the Aswan High Dam in Egypt. Much of the rest of the country is made up of an undulating plateau (1,000-2,000 ft/305-610 m high), which rises to higher levels in the mountains located in the northeast near the Red Sea, as well as in the central, western, and extreme southern portions of the country. The highest point in the Sudan is Kinyeti (10,456 ft/3,187 m), in the southeast. Rainfall diminishes from south to north in Sudan; thus, the south is characterized by swampland (the SUDD region) and rain forest, the center by savanna and grassland, and the north by desert and semidesert. The inhabitants of Sudan are divided into three main groups: the northerners, about 39% of the population according to the most recent census (1956); the southerners, about 30%; and the westerners, about 13%. The northerners, who inhabit the country roughly north of 12°N lat. and mainly near the Nile, are Muslim (mostly of the Sunni branch), speak Arabic (the country's official language), and follow Arab cultural patterns (although only relatively few are descended from the Arabs who immigrated into the region during the 13th-19th cent.). The westerners, so called because they immigrated (mostly in the 20th cent.) from W Africa, are also Muslim, live mostly in the central part of the Sudan, and work as farmers or agricultural laborers. The southerners largely follow traditional religious beliefs, although some are Christian; they practice shifting cultivation or are pastoralists, and most speak Nilotic languages. The leading ethnic groups in the south are the Dinka, Nuer, Shilluk, Bari, and Azande. The great majority of the country's population live in villages or small towns; the only sizable cities are PORT SUDAN, WAD MADANI, AL UBAYYID, and the conurbation of Khartoum, OMDURMAN, and KHARTOUM NORTH. The desert and semidesert of the north are largely uninhabited. Sudan is an overwhelmingly agricultural country; much of the farming is of a subsistence kind and is carried out largely outside the money economy. Within the money economy, agriculture, in the later 1960s, contributed about 34% of the annual national product, industry only about 11%. The government plays a major role in planning the economy. The leading farm crops are cotton (predominantly of the long-staple variety), durra and other millets, groundnuts, sesame, dates, plantains, sugarcane, and coffee. Large numbers of cattle, sheep, goats, and camels are raised. A variety of forest products are produced, by far the most important being gum arabic, with Sudan accounting for about 90% of total world production. In the south, fish caught in the Nile system are an important dietary staple. The leading products of the country's small mining industry are chromite; copper, manganese, and iron ores; salt; and gold. Manufacturing is mostly related to basic consumer needs; the chief products include processed food, beverages, textiles and clothing, footwear, and cement. The main source of energy is hydroelectric power. The country has a very limited transportation network. Foreign trade is largely conducted via Port Sudan, located on the Red Sea. Chief among the annual imports, the value of which is usually slightly higher than that of exports, are machinery, transport equipment, textiles, petroleum products, and iron and steel; the principal exports are ginned cotton, gum arabic, sesame, and groundnuts. The leading trade partners are Great Britain, India, West Germany, Japan, and the USSR. Educational facilities being very limited, in the early 1970s only about 19% of the population 10 years or older was literate. The main institutions of higher education are the Univ. of Khartoum and the Khartoum branch of the Univ. of Cairo.

History. Northeast Sudan, called NUBIA in ancient times, was colonized (c.2000 B.C.) by Egypt as far as the 4th cataract of the Nile (near modern Karima). From the 8th cent. B.C. to the 4th cent. A.D. this region was ruled by the CUSH kingdom, centered first at NAPATA (near the 4th cataract) and after c.600 B.C. at MEROË (between the 5th and 6th cataracts). From c.750 to c.650 B.C., Cush conquered and ruled Egypt. Meroë was a center of trade and ironworking, and from there iron technology probably spread to other parts of Africa. Most of the inhabitants of Nubia were converted to Coptic Christianity in the 6th cent. A.D., and by the 8th cent. two states flourished in the area. These states long resisted invasions from Egypt, which had been converted to Islam in the 7th cent.; however, from the 13th to the 15th cent. the region was increasingly infiltrated by peoples from the north; the states collapsed, and Nubia was converted to Islam. The southern part of modern Sudan remained pagan. Much of the north was ruled by the Muslim state of Funj from the 16th cent. until 1821, when it was conquered by armies sent by Muhammad Ali of Egypt. The Egyptians founded (1823) Khartoum as their headquarters and developed Sudan's trade in ivory and slaves. Ismail Pasha (in office 1863-79) tried to extend Egyptian influence further south in Sudan, ostensibly to end the slave trade. This campaign, which was headed first by Sir Samuel Baker and then by Charles GORDON, provoked a complex revolt (1881) by the MAHDI, who sought to end Egyptian influence and to purify Islam in Sudan. The Mahdists defeated Anglo-Egyptian punitive expeditions, and Britain and Egypt decided to abandon Sudan. Gordon, sent to evacuate the British and Egyptian troops, was defeated and killed by the Mahdists at Khartoum in early 1885. The Mahdi died in the same year, but his successor, the Khalifa Abdallahi, continued to build up the theocratic Mahdist state. In the 1890s the British decided to gain control of Sudan, and, in a series of campaigns between 1896 and 1898, an Anglo-Egyptian force under Herbert (later Lord) KITCHENER destroyed the power of the Mahdists. Agreements in 1899 (reaffirmed by the Anglo-Egyptian treaty of 1936) established the condominium government of the Anglo-Egyptian Sudan. Under the condominium, Sudan was administered by a governor general, appointed by Egypt with the consent of Great Britain; in practice, however, the British controlled the government of Sudan. The Sudanese continued to oppose colonial rule, and the Egyptians resented their subordinate role to the British. In 1924 the British instituted a policy of isolating southern Sudan by administering it separately from the north. An advisory council for northern Sudan was established in 1943, and in 1948 a predominantly elective legislative assembly for the whole territory was set up. In the 1948 elections, the Independence Front, which favored the creation of an independent republic, gained a majority over the National Front, which sought union with Egypt. After the 1952 revolution in Egypt, Britain and Egypt agreed to prepare Sudan for independence in 1956. In 1955 southerners, fearing that the new nation would be dominated by the Muslim north, began a revolt that lasted 17 years. Nevertheless, Sudan achieved independence as a parliamentary republic in 1956, as planned. In 1958, Gen. Ibrahim Abboud led a military coup that ended the parliamentary system. Unable to improve the country's weak economy or to end the southern revolt, Abboud in 1964 agreed to the reestablishment of civilian government. The new regime also had little success in coping with the country's problems, and, in 1969, Col. Jaafar al-Numeiry staged a successful coup. He established a leftist government and banned all political parties; numerous industries and banks were subsequently nationalized. In July, 1971, a Communist-led coup attempt was defeated by al-Numeiry. The bloody civil war, which had resulted in the death in battle and by starvation and disease of about 1.5 million southerners, was ended by an agreement between the government and the Southern-Sudan Liberation Front (whose military arm was known as Anya Nya) signed (Feb., 1972) at Addis Ababa; under the agreement the southern Sudan received considerable autonomy. Also in 1972, the Sudanese Socialist Union, the country's only political organization, held its first congress, and a "people's assembly" was elected to draw up a new constitution for the country. In 1973 a constitution calling for one-party parliamentary government and granting much autonomy to the south was adopted. In March, 1973, Palestinian guerrillas belonging to the black September group kidnapped three foreign diplomats (including the U.S. ambassador to Sudan, Cleo A. Noel, Jr.) in Khartoum; the Palestinians unsuccessfully demanded the release of fellow guerrillas imprisoned in Jordan and Israel and of Sirhan B. Sirhan, the convicted assassin of U.S. Senator Robert Kennedy. They killed the diplomats shortly before surrendering (March 4) to Sudanese authorities. See Mandour el Mahdi, *A Short History of the Sudan* (1965); Fritz Hintze and Ursula Frintze, *Civilizations of the Old Sudan* (tr. 1968); Tore Nordenstam, *Sudanese Ethics* (1968); A. S. Kanya-Forstner, *The Conquest of the Western Sudan* (1969); P. M. Holt, *A Modern History of the Sudan* (1962) and *The Mahdist State in the Sudan, 1881-1898* (2d ed. 1970); Gabriel Warburg, *The Sudan under Wingate* (1971); D. M. Wai, ed., *The Southern Sudan: The Problem of National Integration* (1973).

Sudanese Republic: see MALI.

Sudan grass: see SORGHUM.

Sudbury, city (1971 pop. 90,535), central Ont., Canada. It is the center of Canada's largest mining region, which produces much of the world's nickel and large quantities of copper, platinum, gold, silver, and sulfur. Laurentian Univ. (1960) is there.

Sudbury, town (1970 pop. 13,506), Middlesex co., E Mass.; inc. 1639. Electrical and electronic equipment is manufactured. The tavern (built 1686; restored) that was the scene of Longfellow's *Tales of a Wayside Inn* is there.

Sudd (so͝od), swampy region, c.200 mi (320 km) long, and c.150 mi (240 km) wide, S Republic of the Sudan, E central Africa. It is fed by the Bahr al-Jebel, the Bahr al-Ghazal, and the Bahr al-Arab, headwaters of the Nile. Thick aquatic vegetation (sudd) disperses the river water into numerous channels. About half the water is lost through evaporation and absorption before leaving the Sudd. The vegetation hinders navigation and long barred attempts to trace the Nile to its source. An Egyptian expedition first succeeded in crossing the Sudd in 1840. It took much effort to clear (1899-1903) a channel for regular navigation, and constant maintenance is necessary to keep it open. Indigenous tribes live on level grassy plains between the channels.

Sudermann, Hermann (hĕr'män zo͞o'dərmän), 1857-1928, German dramatist and novelist. His play *Die Ehre* (1889; tr. *Honor,* 1906) was one of the first successes of the burgeoning German naturalist movement. Sudermann's works became immensely popular, particularly the psychological novel *Frau Sorge* (1887; tr. *Dame Care,* 1891) and the play *Heimat* (1893; tr. *Magda,* 1896), a vehicle for Sarah Bernhardt and for Mrs. Patrick Campbell. His finest drama is probably *Fritzchen,* one of the three one-act plays published in *Morituri* (1897); it portrays the harshness of the Prussian officer code. Many of Sudermann's plays and such novels as *Es war* (1894) and *Das hohe Lied* (1908; tr. *The Song of Songs,* 1909) effectively bare the crudity and immorality of the Prussian aristocracy and the corruption of Berlin society.

Sudetes (so͞odē'tēz), Czech *Sudety,* Ger. *Sudeten,* mountain range, along the border of Czechoslovakia and Poland, extending c.185 mi (300 km) between the Elbe and Oder rivers. It is continued on the W by the Erzgebirge and on the E by the Carpathians. The Sudetes are divided into several groups. Farthest west, bordering on SE East Germany, are the Lusatian (Pol. *Luzické*) Mts; along the border with SW Poland are, from west to east, the Isergebirge, the Krkonoše (Ger. *Riesengebirge*), the Adlergebirge, and the Jeseniky mts. The mineral deposits of the Sudetes include coal, lignite, iron, nickel, copper, silver, graphite, kaolin, and pyrites. Industry flourishes on both slopes of the Sudetes; lumber products, glass and porcelain, paper, and textiles are the chief products. Home industries have long held an important place in the Sudetes. There are also numerous mineral springs and resorts. The region was largely German-speaking until 1945. However, the term "Sudete Germans" designated all the German-speaking population in the regions of Czechoslovakia bordering on Germany. The Sudetenland, home of these Germans for centuries, has always been a part of Bohemia. The Sudete German party, founded by Konrad Henlein in 1934, was an offshoot of the German National Socialist party. In 1938 the party became Hitler's chief instrument in the events leading to the MUNICH PACT and the annexation of the Sudetenland to Germany. The districts were recovered by Czechoslovakia in 1945, and most of the German population was expelled.

Sue, Eugène (özhĕn' sü), 1804-57, French novelist, whose name was originally Marie Joseph Sue. A surgeon in the French navy, he went into exile when Napoleon III came to power. Sue's popular and sensational tales of the Parisian underworld and slum life embraced humanitarian and reform ideals. Among them are *Les Mystères de Paris* (pub. serially, 1842-43; tr. *The Mysteries of Paris,* 1844) and *Le Juif errant* (1844-45; tr. *The Wandering Jew,* 1845).

Suess, Eduard (ä'do͞oärt züs), 1831-1914, Austrian geologist, b. London. He was a professor (1857-1901) at the Univ. of Vienna and served for more than 20 years in the Austrian parliament. He was an authority on structural geology, especially of mountains, and postulated the existence of the giant land mass Gondwanaland (see CONTINENTAL DRIFT). His great work was *Das Antlitz der Erde* (5 vol., 1883-1901; tr. *The Face of the Earth,* 1904-24).

Suetonius (Caius Suetonius Tranquillus) (swētō'nēəs), A.D. c.69-A.D. c.140, Roman biographer. Little is known about his life except that he was briefly the private secretary of Emperor Hadrian. His *De vita Caesarum* [concerning the lives of the Caesars] survives almost in full; it was translated into English by Robert Graves as *The Twelve Caesars* (1957).

There are also fragments of a much larger collection of biographies, *De viris illustribus* [concerning illustrious men]. He gathered together all sorts of anecdotes, and the resultant biographies are lively and informative. Suetonius was taken as a model by many later biographers.

Suetonius Paulinus: see PAULINUS.

Suez (so͞oĕz'), city (1970 est. pop. 315,000), NE Egypt, at the northern end of the Gulf of Suez and at the southern terminus of the Suez Canal. An important port with extensive facilities, it is also a refueling station, a holding area for ships entering the canal, and a center for the storage and refining of oil. Petroleum products, paper, and fertilizers are major manufactures. Suez is linked by rail with Ismailia and Cairo; oil is conveyed by pipelines to Cairo. The city is also a departure point for pilgrims on their way to Mecca. Although the site of the city was occupied in antiquity, Suez was little more than a small village throughout most of its history. In the 16th cent. it became a naval and trading station under the Ottoman Turks. After the completion (1869) of the Suez Canal the city became a major port. Its economy suffered during the periods that the canal was closed following the Arab-Israeli Wars. During the 1973 war the city was damaged, and parts of it were occupied by Israeli forces.

Suez Canal, Arab. *Qanat as Suways,* waterway of Egypt extending from Port Said to Port Tawfiq (near Suez) and connecting the Mediterranean Sea with the Gulf of Suez and thence with the Red Sea. The canal is somewhat more than 100 mi (160 km) long. Proceeding S from Port Said, it runs in an almost undeviating straight line to Lake Timsah. From there a cutting leads to the Bitter Lakes (now one body of water), and a final cutting then reaches the Gulf of Suez. The canal has no locks and can accommodate ships of almost any draft. The desirability of a water connection between the Mediterranean and the Red Sea was long appreciated in antiquity. A canal was built in the 20th or 19th cent. B.C. to Lake Timsah (then the northern end of the Red Sea). When the Red Sea receded, Xerxes I had the canal extended. It was restored several times (notably by Ptolemy II and Trajan) until the 8th cent. A.D., when it was closed and fell into disrepair. The modern canal was planned by the French engineer Ferdinand de Lesseps, who also supervised construction (1859-69). Great Britain, which had opposed the construction of the canal, became the largest shareholder in 1875 by purchasing the interest of the Egyptian khedive. The Convention of Constantinople signed in 1888 by all major European powers of the time declared the canal neutral and guaranteed free passage to all in time of peace and war. Great Britain was the guarantor of the neutrality of the canal; management was placed in the hands of the Suez Canal Company. Under the Anglo-Egyptian treaty of 1936, which made Egypt virtually independent, Britain reserved rights for the protection of the canal, but after World War II, Egypt pressed for evacuation of British troops from the area. Egypt in 1951 repudiated the 1936 treaty, and anti-British rioting and some clashes on the border of the zone erupted. In 1954, Britain agreed to withdraw, and in June, 1956, the British completed their evacuation of armed forces from Egypt and the canal zone. After Great Britain and the United States withdrew their pledges of financial support to help Egypt build the Aswan High Dam (see under ASWAN), Egyptian President Gamal Abdal NASSER nationalized (July, 1956) the Suez Canal and set up the Egyptian Canal Authority to replace the existing privately owned company. In August, British oil and embassy officials were expelled from the country. On Oct. 29, 1956, Israel, having been denied passage through the canal since 1950 and having suffered repeated border raids from Egypt, invaded Egyptian territory. Within a few days France and Great Britain sent armed forces to retake the Suez Canal. Intervention by the United Nations brought an armistice in early November, and a UN emergency force replaced the British and French troops. The canal, blocked for more than six months because of damage and sunken ships, was cleared with UN help and reopened in April, 1957. Egypt agreed to pay, in six annual installments, approximately $81 million to shareholders of the nationalized Suez Canal Company; final payment was made on Jan. 1, 1963. Despite UN efforts to guarantee the free passage of vessels through the canal, Egypt prevented Israeli ships from using the waterway. The canal was closed by Egypt during the Arab-Israeli War of 1967, after which it formed part of the boundary between Egypt and the Israeli-occupied Sinai peninsula. Egypt lost considerable revenue (in 1966 receipts totaled some $260 million) as a result of the closing of the canal, but friendly Arab countries agreed to subsidize the Egyptian economy with contributions roughly equaling the former income from the canal. After the Suez Canal was closed, many ships (especially tankers) were built that were too large for the canal, and alternate sea routes were used increasingly in world trade. In Oct., 1973, Egyptian troops crossed the canal and breached the Israeli lines. In the ensuing conflict a complex military situation evolved, with Egyptians retrieving land on the east bank of the canal while Israeli units established a salient on the west bank. In early 1974, Egypt and Israel signed an agreement providing for a disengagement of military forces and for a withdrawal of Israeli troops into the Sinai. With both banks of the canal again in Egyptian hands, the government of Egypt, with the assistance of the U.S. navy, began clearing the canal of the mines and wreckage left from the 1967 war; however, by Jan., 1975, the canal had not yet been reopened. See D. A. Farnie, *East and West of Suez: The Suez Canal in History, 1854–1956* (1969); Kenneth Love, *Suez, the Twice-Fought War* (1969); A. G. Mezerik, ed., *The Suez Canal 1956 Crisis-1967 War* (1969); H. J. Schonfield, *The Suez Canal in Peace and War, 1869–1969* (rev. ed. 1969); C. W. Hallberg, *The Suez Canal* (1931, repr. 1972).

suffocation: see ASPHYXIA.

Suffolk, dukes and earls of: see POLE, family.

Suffolk, Charles Brandon, 1st duke of (sŭf'ək), d. 1545, English nobleman. A member of the court of Henry VIII, he received many preferments. He was created (1513) Viscount Lisle on his betrothal to his ward, Elizabeth Grey, Viscountess Lisle (in her own right), but the title was canceled when Elizabeth, on coming of age, refused to marry him. He was created duke of Suffolk in 1514, perhaps to aid him in his suit of Margaret of Austria, regent of the Netherlands. In 1515, while on an embassy to the new king of France, Francis I, Suffolk married MARY OF ENGLAND, widow of Louis XII of France and sister of Henry VIII. This ambitious marriage, complicated by the fact that one of Brandon's two former wives was still living, angered Henry considerably, and it was only by the payment of jewels and large sums of money that the couple regained favor. Suffolk accompanied Henry to the Field of the Cloth of Gold (1520) and led an invading army into France (1523). He supported the king's divorce from Katharine of Aragón, received confiscated monastery lands, led troops against the rebels in the Pilgrimage of Grace (1536), and led an invasion of France (1544).

Suffolk, Henry Grey, duke of, d. 1554, English nobleman. He became 3d marquess of Dorset on his father's death (1530), and in 1534 he married Frances, daughter of Charles Brandon, duke of Suffolk, and Mary of England (sister of Henry VIII). During Henry's reign he was active at court. Upon the accession (1547) of Edward VI, Grey at first supported the protectorship of the duke of Somerset but soon shifted his allegiance to John Dudley, earl of Warwick (later duke of NORTHUMBERLAND). He received favors at court and was created (1551) duke of Suffolk through his wife's claim. Lady Jane GREY was his daughter, and, upon the death (1553) of Edward, Suffolk joined Northumberland's plot to place her on the throne. However, when the plot failed, he deserted her cause and proclaimed Mary I queen. He was pardoned, largely because of his wife's friendship with Mary, but in 1554 he joined the rebellion of Sir Thomas WYATT and was soon captured, convicted of treason, and executed.

Suffolk, Thomas Howard, 1st earl of, 1561–1626, English nobleman; son of the 4th duke of Norfolk. He was attainted at the time of his father's execution (1572), but his rights were restored in 1584. He volunteered for naval duty against the Spanish Armada (1588), was knighted at sea, and rose quickly to high rank. Howard led the squadron that attacked the Spanish treasure fleet off the Azores in 1591 and shared command of the expedition against Cádiz in 1596. He was created Baron Howard de Walden in 1597. Upon the accession (1603) of James I, he was created earl of Suffolk and later held a number of official posts. In 1614 he became lord high treasurer. His daughter, Frances Howard, and her husband, Robert Carr, earl of SOMERSET, were tried and convicted (1616) of the murder of Sir Thomas Overbury. Suffolk himself was accused (1618) of embezzlement and fraud as treasurer. He was tried (1619), convicted, and heavily fined. Although both he and his wife, who was thought to have influenced him, were soon released, he did not regain prominence.

Suffolk, county, E central England, divided since 1888 for administrative purposes into **East Suffolk** (1971 pop. 380,524), 870 sq mi (2,253 sq km) and **West Suffolk** (1971 pop. 164,201), 611 sq mi (1,582 sq km). The county town is IPSWICH, East Suffolk. BURY ST. EDMUNDS is the administrative center of West Suffolk. Suffolk is bordered on the N by the Ouse and Waveney rivers and on the S by the Stour River. The terrain is low and undulating, and the region, mainly agricultural, is one of the chief producers of grain and sugar beets in England. Breeds of horses, hogs, sheep, and cattle have been developed, and stock and poultry raising are important occupations. Along the coast (especially at LOWESTOFT) fishing is important. Industries include milling, malting, and the making of farm machinery, fertilizers, and processed foods. Suffolk and Norfolk formed the Kingdom of the Iceni, whose Queen Boadicea led a revolt (A.D. 60) against the Romans. In Anglo-Saxon times Suffolk was part of the kingdom of EAST ANGLIA, inhabited by the "south folk" of that kingdom, whence its name. In the Middle Ages Suffolk was the center of a large wool industry. In 1974, East Suffolk and West Suffolk were joined together as the new nonmetropolitan county of Suffolk.

Suffolk sheep, relatively large breed, developed in England, well-known for its high quality meat. Considered to be a recent introduction to the United States, the breed has many desirable qualities and is becoming widely accepted there. Suffolks have bare heads, black faces, and bare black legs but no horns. They breed aggressively and have upstanding carriage, an active nature, the capacity for rapid growth, and a good mutton build; they are, however, relatively light fleece producers. Suffolk rams are widely used with ewes of other breeds to produce crossbred lambs for slaughter.

suffrage: see BALLOT; ELECTION; FRANCHISE; VOTING; WOMAN SUFFRAGE.

Suffren de Saint-Tropez, Pierre André de (pyĕr äNdrā' də süfrĕn' də săN-trôpā'), 1726–88, French admiral. He participated in naval warfare in the War of the Austrian Succession and in the Seven Years War. In 1779 he was sent with the comte d'ESTAING to aid the American Revolutionaries, and two years later he began his famous cruise to the East Indies. He attacked the English at the Cape Verde Islands, saved the Dutch colony at Capetown from English capture, and then began his campaign against the British navy in India under Sir Edward Hughes. Suffren seriously impeded British operations, fighting five major battles in 1782–83. Each ended in a virtual draw, which was a considerable achievement for the French against the British fleet of that day.

Sufism (so͞o'fĭzəm), Muslim philosophical and literary movement. The Sufis included the greatest of the Persian poets—Abu Said ibn Abi al-Khair, Farid ad-Din Attar, Hafiz, Jami, Omar Khayyam, and Jalal ad-Din Rumi. The highly developed symbolism of the soul's union with God is expressed in exquisite lyric style. Sufism, which emerged among the Shiites in the late 10th and early 11th cent., was, however, a broad philosophy, not simply a literary movement. It borrowed ideas from Neoplatonism, Buddhism, and Christianity. The semimonastic order arose with variant ideas and practices. Some members stressed ascetic practices, some stressed quietism. All were united in emphasis on the immediate personal union of the soul with God. In some variations the beliefs of Sufism verge sharply toward pantheism, thus almost leaving Islam altogether. The movement was strongest in Persia, and its greatest purely philosophical exponent was GHAZALI, AL-. A great many of the modern dervish orders also profess Sufism. See Idries Shah, *The Sufis* (1964) and *The Way of the Sufi* (1968); A. J. Arberry, *Sufism* (1970); Leonard Lewin, ed., *The Diffusion of Sufi Ideas in the West* (1972).

sugar, compound of carbon, hydrogen, and oxygen belonging to a class of substances called CARBOHYDRATES. Sugars fall into three groups: the monosaccharides, disaccharides, and trisaccharides. The monosaccharides are the simple sugars; they include FRUCTOSE and GLUCOSE. The disaccharides are formed by the union of two monosaccharides with the loss of one molecule of water. Disaccharides include LACTOSE, MALTOSE, and SUCROSE. Less well known are the trisaccharides; raffinose is a trisaccharide present in cottonseed and in sugar beets. The letter D- or L- written before the name of a sugar indicates the position of a certain hydroxyl group in the molecule and signifies that the sugar is a member of the D- or L- family of sugars; the D- sugars are related to D-glyceraldehyde (or D-glyceric aldehyde) and the L-sugars to L-glyceraldehyde.

sugar beet, variety of BEET used commercially as a source of sugar.

sugarcane, tall tropical perennials (species of *Saccharum,* chiefly *S. officinarum*) of the family Gramineae (GRASS family), probably cultivated in their native Asia from prehistoric times. Sugarcane somewhat resembles corn and sorghum, with a large terminal panicle and a noded stalk. In biblical times one of the only sweetenings in the world was honey. It was not until the Middle Ages that the "Indian honey-bearing reed" was introduced to the Middle East and became accessible to Europe, where sugar was sold from druggists' shelves as a costly medicinal or luxury. Later, sugarcane plants were introduced by Spanish and Portuguese explorers of the 15th and 16th cent. throughout the Old and New World tropics, and the large cane industry rapidly took shape. Today sugarcane and the sugar beet (see BEET), a temperate plant developed as a commercial sugar source c.1800, are the only two major economic sources of SUGAR. Cuba and India together produce over one third of the world's tropical sugar, cane sugar. Cane is harvested by cutting down the plant stalks, which are then pressed several times to extract the juice. The juice is concentrated by evaporation into dark, sticky sugar, often sold locally. Refined sugar, less nourishing as food, is obtained by precipitating out the non-sugar components. Almost pure SUCROSE, it is the main commercial product. By-products obtained from sugarcane include MOLASSES, RUM, alcohol, fuel, livestock feed, and from the stalk residue, paper and wallboard. Sugarcane is classified in the division MAGNOLIOPHYTA, class Liliatae, order Cyperales, family Gramineae. See Andrew Van Hook, *Sugar, Its Production, Technology, and Uses* (1949); A. C. Barnes, *The Sugar Cane* (2d ed. 1973).

sugar maple: see MAPLE.

sugar of lead: see LEAD ACETATE.

Suger (süzhĕr'), 1081–1151, French cleric and statesman, abbot of Saint-Denis from 1122, minister of kings Louis VI and Louis VII. He was noted for his financial ability and his talent for conciliation. In 1147, Louis VII left on crusade and appointed a council of regency, of which Suger was the leading member. During his administration (1147–49) Suger succeeded in maintaining peace at home and in raising funds to meet the king's expenses. He liberated the abbey at Saint-Denis from the tribute formerly paid to robber barons, recovered alienated properties, built a new church, and enriched it with works of art. At the same time he introduced a more severe discipline. He wrote a life of Louis VI, fragments of a life of Louis VII, and an account of his renovation of Saint-Denis (tr. 1946).

Suharto (so͝ohär'tō), 1921–, president of Indonesia. A veteran of the war for independence (1945–49) against the Dutch, he rose to army chief of staff in 1965 and supreme commander in 1968. He opposed the pro-Chinese policies of President SUKARNO and crushed a Communist coup d'etat in 1965. Suharto assumed key civilian cabinet offices in 1966, became acting president in 1967, and was elected president in 1968. He was reelected in 1973. His policies gradually retrieved Indonesia from the economic morass into which it had fallen under Sukarno. See biography by O. G. Roeder (2d ed. 1970).

Suhl (zo͞ol), city (1970 pop. 31,445), capital of Suhl district, SW East Germany. It is an industrial city manufacturing precision instruments, chemicals, toys, porcelain, and motor vehicles. First mentioned in the 13th cent., Suhl was a noted center of the German arms industry in the Thirty Years War (1618–48).

Sui (swē), dynasty of China that ruled from 581 to 618. From his capital at Ch'angan, and later at Anyang, Yang Chien (541–604), the first Sui emperor (he had been a Northern Chou official who usurped the throne), ruled an empire extending from the Great Wall to Annam. Yang Chien reunited China after 400 years of division. Chinese arms were extended into Central Asia and north to Mongolia. The Sui armies used nomadic cavalry tactics to conquer large areas, and they built canals to ensure strategic mobility. They made the Grand Canal into a trunk system connecting the Wei, Fen, Yellow, Hwai, and Yangtze rivers. Buddhism and Taoism were favored. Yang Chien's son, Yang Kuang, following his father's example of usurpation, killed him, and then carried on his work. The Great Wall was refortified at great cost in human life, and Ch'angan, Loyang, and Yangchow were beautified. Faced with internal rebellion, Yang Kuang ended his campaigns to conquer Korea (612–14). After his defeat by the Eastern Turks (615), he fled to S China, where he was assassinated (618). The succeeding T'ANG dynasty was established with the aid of the Eastern Turks.

suicide [Lat.,=self-killing], the taking of one's own life in a deliberate manner. Putting oneself to death may be obligatory or voluntary. In the first case, suicide is prescribed by custom or enjoined by the authorities, usually as an alternative to death at the hands of others. In the second case, it is thought to be committed for personal motives; depending on the time and place, it may be regarded as a heroic deed or condemned by religious and civil authorities. Compulsory suicide may be performed out of loyalty to a dead master or spouse. Examples of this are suttee in India and the similar behavior expected of the dead emperor's favorite courtiers in ancient China. Such practices, now largely extinct, undoubtedly derived from the ancient and widespread custom of immolating servants and wives on the grave of a chief or noble (see FUNERAL CUSTOMS). Self-murder may also be enjoined for the welfare of the group, as among those primitive peoples where the elderly who could no longer contribute to their own subsistence asked to be put to death or undertook the task themselves. Finally, suicide may be offered to a favored few as an alternative to execution, as among the feudal Japanese gentry (see HARA-KIRI), the Greeks (see SOCRATES), and the Roman nobility. Self-killing may be practiced by peoples lacking a codified law, an example of which were the Trobriand Islanders, who hurled themselves ceremonially from the tops of palm trees after a serious public loss of face. There the line between social pressure and personal motivation begins to blur. Self-immolations based on a traditional concept of honor are usually sanctioned by the society in which they occur. In less traditionalistic societies, where customs lose sway and individualism prevails, the causes of suicide are more difficult to establish. The problem has been approached from two different angles: the sociological, which stresses social pressures and the importance of social integration, and the psychoanalytic, which centers on the driving force of guilt and anxiety and the inverting of aggressive impulses. Studies reveal that inner tendencies to self-destruction are fostered or inhibited by various external factors. Recent studies have done much to dispel some of the myths surrounding suicide, such as the belief that suicidal tendencies are inherited; that suicidal tendencies cannot be reversed; that persons who announce their intention to commit suicide will not carry out the threat; and that suicide occurs more frequently among the wealthy. Self-killing is expressly condemned by Judaism, Christianity, and Islam, and attempts are punishable by law in certain countries. It was classified as a felony in 11th-century England because the self-murderer was considered to have broken his bond of fealty, and his property was forfeited to the king. Suicides could not be buried in consecrated ground, but were interred on public highways with a stake driven through the heart; this practice was observed as late as 1823. In 1961, Great Britain abolished criminal penalties for attempting to commit suicide. By the early 1970s only 9 U.S. states still listed suicide as a crime; however, 18 states have laws against helping someone to commit suicide. See Emile Durkheim, *Suicide* (1897, tr. 1951); Ruth Cavan, *Suicide* (1928, repr. 1965); Edward Stengel, *Suicide and Attempted Suicide* (1965); Jack Douglas, *The Social Meanings of Suicide* (1967); Edwin Shneidman, ed., *Essays in Self-Destruction* (1967); M. L. Farber, *The Theory of Suicide* (1968); E. A. Grollman, *Suicide* (1970); A. Alvarez, *The Savage God* (1972); Jacques Choron, *Suicide* (1972); David Lester, *Why People Kill Themselves* (1972).

Suidas (syo͞o'ĭdəs), title of a Greek lexicon-encyclopedia. The name is also applied to its compiler, who seems to have lived in the 10th cent. A.D. Included in the lexicon are texts from classical Greek works and the commentaries. Though mostly derived from late and corrupt sources, the *Suidas* preserves much information about Greek literature that would otherwise be lost.

Suifu: see I-PIN, China.

Suir (sho͝or), river, 85 mi (137 km) long, rising on Devilsbit Mt., central Republic of Ireland. It flows south through a fertile agricultural region, then east past Clonmel and Waterford to the Barrow River, with which it forms Waterford Harbour. It receives the Aherlow River.

suit, in law: see PROCEDURE.

suite (swēt), in music, instrumental form derived from dance and consisting of a series of movements usually in the same key but contrasting in rhythm and mood. The principle of the suite can be seen in the playing together of two dances in contrasting meters, e.g., pavan and galliard or *passamezzo-saltarello* in the 16th cent. The early 17th-century English composers William Byrd, John Bull, and Orlando Gibbons published small groups of dances, with several movements written for the virginals. In France and Italy there developed sophisticated techniques for linking dances together, which were adopted by German musicians in the early 17th cent. As the connection with actual dancing disappeared, the baroque suite evolved. In France stylized dances were collected into *ordres* such as those of François COUPERIN, while in Italy nondance movements were introduced into the developing *sonata da camera* (see SONATA). In Germany the suites of Johann Jakob Froberger established the basic group of movements as allemande, courante, and sarabande, with a gigue often played between the last two. The gigue was later the final movement of four. The late baroque suite, e.g., the partitas of J. S. Bach, frequently has an introductory movement and one or more of several simpler dances—minuet, bourrée, gavotte, passepied, and others—added to the basic group. Suites for orchestra, including Bach's, were sometimes called *ouvertures.* In the classical period the SERENADE was a kind of suite. Mozart wrote several of this sort for orchestra. The 19th-century suite became a collection of pieces drawn from incidental music for plays or from the score of a ballet, e.g., Grieg's *Peer Gynt Suite* and Tchaikovsky's *Nutcracker Suite.*

Suitland, uninc. city (1970 pop. 30,355 including Silver Hill), Prince Georges co., central Md., a suburb of Washington, D.C. It is the seat of the U.S. Bureau of the Census and of the U.S. navy hydrographic office. Nearby are the Washington National, Cedar Hill, and Lincoln Memorial cemeteries.

Suitland Parkway: see NATIONAL PARKS AND MONUMENTS (table).

Suiyuan (swē'yüän'), Mandarin *Sui-yuan,* former province (c.126,000 sq mi/326,340 sq km), N China. The capital was Kweisui (Hu-ho-hao-t'e). The region of Suiyuan, part of Inner Mongolia, is chiefly a high arid plateau; it comprises the Ordos desert region in the southwest, grazing areas in the north, and a fertile belt along the Huang Ho (Yellow River), which crosses Suiyuan from west to east. Livestock raising and the growing of grains, chiefly wheat, support most of the people. Several roads and a railroad to Peking provide communications with E China. Suiyuan was overrun (1937) by the Japanese, who included it in Menchiang (Mongol Border Land). In 1954 it was made part of the Inner Mongolian Autonomous Region.

Suk, Josef (yô'zĕf so͝ok), 1874–1935, Czech composer and violinist, grad. Prague Conservatory, 1891; pupil and son-in-law of Dvořák. While still at the Prague Conservatory, he and three of his fellow students founded the Bohemian String Quartet, of which Suk was second violinist. Though his early works were influenced by Brahms and Dvořák, he developed in his later works a chromatic polyphony approaching atonality. His second symphony, *Asrael* (1907), expresses his grief at the deaths of Dvořák and of his wife, Dvořák's daughter. Suk joined the faculty of the Prague Conservatory in 1922 and later became its rector.

Sukarno (so͞okär'nō), 1901–70, Indonesian statesman, first president of the republic of Indonesia. A leader of the radical nationalist movement founded in 1927, he was jailed and exiled by the Dutch at various times in the 1930s. During World War II, Sukarno cooperated with the Japanese when Indonesia was occupied by them, while still continuing his agitation for Indonesian independence. After the war he and Mohammad HATTA played a crucial part in the establishment (Aug., 1945) of the republic of Indonesia. In the 1950s, Sukarno attempted to consolidate his multi-island nation. He established (1956) a "guided democracy," with a cabinet that represented all political parties. Regional and factional problems, however, led him, in July, 1959, to dissolve the constituent assembly and assume full dictatorial powers. In 1962, Sukarno ordered sporadic raids on Dutch New Guinea, intensifying a conflict that resulted in UN intervention; his action, however, brought Dutch New Guinea under Indonesian administration in May, 1963. Sukarno, who proclaimed himself president for life in 1963, increased his country's ties to Communist China in the late 1950s and 60s and admitted increasing numbers of Communists and pro-Communists to his government. In 1963 he announced his opposition to the British-sponsored Federation of Malaysia and withdrew (1965) Indonesia from the United Nations after Malaysia took its seat on the Security Council. An attempted Communist coup d'etat late in 1965 led to a military takeover in Indonesia by General

Suharto, who replaced Sukarno as effective ruler of Indonesia. In 1966, Sukarno was stripped of his title of president for life. He remained under house arrest until his death. See biography by J. D. Legge (1972); Tarzie Vittachi, *The Fall of Sukarno* (1967); Bernhard Dahim, *Sukarno and the Struggle for Indonesian Independence* (tr. 1969).

Sukhona (so͝okhô'nə), river, c.350 mi (560 km) long, N European USSR. It flows from Kubeno Lake NE into the Yug River at Veliki Ustyug to form the Northern Dvina River.

Sukhumi (so͝okho͞o'mē), city (1970 pop. 102,000), capital of the Abkhaz Autonomous Republic, SE European USSR, in Georgia, on the Black Sea. It is a port, a rail junction, and a major subtropical resort, whose sulfur baths have been frequented since Roman times. The city has several institutes affiliated with the Georgian Academy of Sciences. The Greek colony of Dioscurias was founded on the site of the city in the 6th cent. B.C. It was known as Sebastopolis under Rome and Byzantium. Russia acquired it in 1810 as the Turkish fortress of Sukhum-Kale. The **Sukhumi Military Road** crosses the Caucasus at the Klukhori Pass (9,235 ft/2,815 m) and continues SW to Sukhumi. It is c.120 mi (190 km) long.

Sukkertoppen (so͞o'kərtô"pən), town (1969 pop. 2,600), in Sukkertoppen dist. (1969 pop. 2,676), W Greenland. The town is a fishing center with modern canneries.

Sukkiim (sŭk'ēĭm), nation, presumably African, which contributed to the army of Pharaoh Shishak (see SHESHONK I) in invading Palestine. 2 Chron. 12.3.

Sukkoth: see TABERNACLES, FEAST OF.

Sukkur (so͝ok'ko͝or), city (1972 metropolitan area pop. 143,000), SE Pakistan, on the Indus River. It is an important commercial and industrial city and a center for trade with Afghanistan. Its industries produce cotton and silk textiles, hosiery, and foodstuffs. Handloom weaving is also important. Modern Sukkur was built by the British general Sir Charles Napier in the 1840s. The city has a college. **Sukkur Barrage,** a dam across the Indus, controls one of the largest irrigation systems in the world. It was built from 1923 to 1932, is c.5,000 ft (1,520 m) long, and waters more than 5 million acres (2,023,000 hectares).

Sulaimaniyah (so͞o"lämän'ēə), town (1965 pop. 86,877), NE Iraq. The town is a trade center and tourist resort. Inhabited by Kurds, it is known as a center of Kurdish nationalism. It was founded in 1789.

Sulaiman Mountains (so͞olīmän'), range, extending c.250 mi (400 km) from north to south along the western edge of the Indus River valley, central Pakistan. The twin peaks of Takht-i-Sulaiman [Persian, = throne of Solomon], 11,295 ft (3,443 m) and 11,085 ft (3,379 m) high, at the northern end of the range, are the highest points. A Muslim shrine there attracts many pilgrims.

Sulawesi: see CELEBES, Indonesia.

Sulayman I (so͞olämän', sūlī-) or **Sulayman the Magnificent,** 1494–1566, Ottoman sultan (1520–66), son and successor of Selim I. He is sometimes erroneously called Sulayman II. Under him the Ottoman Empire (Turkey) reached the height of its power and prestige. He continued his father's conquests in the Balkans and the Mediterranean, conquering Belgrade in 1521, expelling the Knights Hospitalers from Rhodes in 1522, and inflicting a crushing defeat on the Hungarians at MOHÁCS in 1526. He unsuccessfully besieged Vienna in 1529 and supported John Zapolya (John I of Hungary) against Ferdinand of Hungary and Bohemia (later Holy Roman Emperor FERDINAND I). John's death in 1540 and the accession of JOHN II were pretexts for the outright annexation of Hungary (except for Transylvania and the section held by Ferdinand) to the Ottoman Empire. In 1536, Sulayman entered a formal alliance with Francis I of France against the house of HAPSBURG; this alliance remained the basis of Turkish foreign policy for more than three centuries. Although Sulayman's vassal BARBAROSSA made the Turkish fleet the terror of the Mediterranean, Sulayman was, on the whole, unsuccessful in his naval warfare against Holy Roman Emperor Charles V and against Venice. He lost Tunis to Charles in 1535 and failed to take Malta in 1565. Sulayman undertook several successful campaigns against Persia. An Ottoman naval expedition to the Red Sea resulted in the conquest of the Arabian coastlands. Having resumed (1566) warfare in Hungary, Sulayman died during the siege of Szigetvar. The later years of Sulayman's reign had been marred by family disputes over the succession. His favorite wife, Roxelana (or Khurema) intrigued against his eldest son, Mustafa, on behalf of her two sons, Selim and Beyazid. Mustafa built up his own faction, which seemed a threat to Sulayman. In 1553, Sulayman had him executed. Upon Roxelana's death, Selim and Beyazid quarreled. Beyazid rose in revolt, met defeat, and fled to Persia. The shah of Persia was induced to return him for a large sum, and Beyazid was executed. Selim succeeded Sulayman as Selim II. Sulayman's grand viziers, notably İbrahim (who held office from 1523 until he was executed in 1536), Rustem, and Sokolli, were capable administrators and contributed to the greatness of his reign. In his government Sulayman was distinguished for his justice. His military, educational, and legal reforms earned him the name Sulayman the Lawgiver among Muslims. He was fond of pomp and splendor and was a lavish patron of the arts and of literature. Sinan, the greatest Turkish architect, worked under his orders (see ISLAMIC ART AND ARCHITECTURE). See biography by Harold Lamb (1951); studies by A. H. Lybyer (1913, repr. 1966) and R. B. Merriman (1966).

Sulayman II, 1642–91, Ottoman sultan (1687–91), brother and successor of Muhammad IV to the throne of the Ottoman Empire (Turkey). His grand vizier (chief executive officer), Mustafa KÖPRÜLÜ, was at first successful in taking the offensive against the Austrians, but Köprülü was killed shortly after Sulayman's death, in the battle of SLANKAMEN (1691). Sulayman was succeeded by his brother, Ahmed II.

Sulayman the Magnificent: see SULAYMAN I.

Suleiman. For Ottoman sultans thus named, see SULAYMAN.

Süleyman. For Ottoman sultans thus named, see SULAYMAN.

sulfa drug, any of a class of synthetic chemical substances derived from sulfanilamide, or para-aminobenzenesulfonamide. Sulfa drugs are used to treat bacterial infections, although they have largely been replaced for this purpose by ANTIBIOTICS; some are also used in the treatment of diabetes (see ORINASE). Because sulfa drugs were first used to elucidate ways in which substances can interfere with the metabolism of invading microorganisms, they are of historical interest. The parent compound, para-aminobenzenesulfonamide, was synthesized in 1908 by Paul Gelmo, an Austrian industrial chemist. In 1932 the German chemist Gerhard Domagk discovered that the dye Prontosil had antagonistic properties against a wide range of bacteria, and in 1935 it was found that the sulfanilamide portion of the Prontosil molecule was responsible for its antibacterial effect. In 1940 it was shown that sulfanilamide inhibited the action of the physiological substance para-aminobenzoic acid, which bacteria need to synthesize folic acid. The idea that the two substances were antagonists led to a theory of the mechanism of action of drugs: Many chemotherapeutic substances compete with structurally similar substances that are necessary to the metabolism of invading microorganisms. Since sulfanilamide first came into use, more than 150 different derivatives have appeared on the market, chemically modified to achieve more effective antibacterial activity, wider spectrum of microorganisms affected, or more prolonged action. Because of their low cost they are still used in many parts of the world. However, resistance to sulfa drugs has emerged among many microorganisms, especially streptococci, meningococci, and shigella, making them less effective than formerly (see DRUG RESISTANCE). The substances are still used to treat some urinary tract infections, leprosy, and in combination with other drugs, fungal diseases such as toxoplasmosis.

sulfate, chemical compound containing the sulfate (SO_4) RADICAL. Sulfates are salts or esters of SULFURIC ACID, H_2SO_4, formed by replacing one or both of the hydrogens with a metal (e.g., sodium) or a radical (e.g., ammonium or ethyl). Sulfates in which both hydrogens are replaced are called normal sulfates; sulfates in which only one hydrogen is replaced are called hydrogen sulfates, acid sulfates, or bisulfates. Most metal sulfates are readily soluble in water, but calcium and mercuric sulfates are only slightly soluble, while barium, lead, strontium, and mercurous sulfates are insoluble. In chemical analysis, the sulfate ION, SO_4^{-2}, is usually detected by adding barium chloride solution; the white barium sulfate precipitate that forms is insoluble in hydrochloric acid. Sulfates are widely distributed in nature. Barium sulfate occurs as BARITE; calcium sulfate is found as GYPSUM, ALABASTER, and SELENITE; EPSOM SALTS is magnesium sulfate; SODIUM SULFATE occurs as its decahydrate, GLAUBER'S SALT; and strontium sulfate occurs as CELESTITE. Some sulfates were formerly known as vitriols; blue vitriol is CUPRIC SULFATE, green vitriol is FERROUS SULFATE, and white vitriol is ZINC SULFATE. ALUMS are double sulfates, containing two different metals and two sulfate radicals. Organic sulfates are esters. They can be formed by reacting an alcohol with cold sulfuric acid. They are also formed by the reaction of sulfuric acid with a double bond in an alkene; the product is called an alkyl hydrogen sulfate. An alkyl hydrogen sulfate can be broken down to an alcohol and sulfuric acid by heating it with water (HYDROLYSIS); this reaction is often used to synthesize alcohols.

sulfide, chemical compound containing sulfur and one other element or sulfur and a RADICAL. Sulfides may be salts or esters of HYDROGEN SULFIDE, H_2S, or may be formed directly, e.g., by heating a metal with sulfur. Hydrosulfides are formed when only one of the hydrogens in hydrogen sulfide is replaced with a metal or radical. Soluble metal sulfides are used in preparing dyes, in leather tanning, as depilatory compounds, and as pesticides. Sulfides of antimony, copper, lead, mercury, silver, and zinc are important as ores; the ores are often roasted, yielding SULFUR DIOXIDE and an oxide of the metal. PYRITE is iron disulfide; tarnish on silver is mostly silver sulfide. In chemical analysis, hydrogen sulfide is often used to precipitate from a solution of metal salts certain metal sulfides that have characteristic colors and solubilities. CARBON DISULFIDE is an important solvent for organic compounds.

sulfiram, antialcoholic drug marketed under the trade name ANTABUSE.

sulfonic acid (səlfŏn'ĭk), organic compound containing the FUNCTIONAL GROUP RSO_2OH, which consists of a sulfur atom, S, bonded to a carbon atom that may be part of a large aliphatic or aromatic HYDROCARBON, *R*, and also bonded to three oxygen atoms, O, one of which has a hydrogen atom, H, attached to it. The hydrogen atom makes the compound acidic, much as the hydrogen of a CARBOXYLIC ACID makes it acidic (see ACIDS AND BASES). However, while carboxylic acids are weak (with dissociation constants of about 10^{-5}), sulfonic acids are considered strong acids (with dissociation constants of about 10^{-2}). Because sulfonic acids are so acidic, they generally exist as their SALTS and thus tend to be quite soluble in water. Sulfonic acid groups are often introduced into organic molecules such as dyes to stabilize them for use in aqueous dye baths. Sulfonic acid groups also improve the washfastness of wool and silk dyes by enabling the dye to bind more tightly to the fabric. The most important use of sulfonic acid salts (sulfonates) is in the detergent industry. Sodium salts of long-chain aliphatic or aromatic sulfonic acids are used as detergents. Unlike ordinary SOAPS, which contain carboxylic acid salts, soaps containing sulfonates do not form a scum in hard water because the calcium and magnesium ions present in the hard water do not form insoluble precipitates with sulfonates as they do with carboxylates. Some sulfonic acid derivatives, e.g., the sulfa drugs, are important as antibiotics.

sulfur or **sulphur** (sŭl'fər), nonmetallic chemical element; symbol S; atomic number 16; atomic weight 32.064; melting point 112.8°C (rhombic), 119.0°C (monoclinic), about 120°C (amorphous); boiling point 444.6°C; specific gravity at 20°C, 2.07 (rhombic), 1.957 (monoclinic), 1.92 (amorphous); valence −2, +4, or +6. Sulfur is found in group VIa of the PERIODIC TABLE. It exhibits ALLOTROPY. Solid sulfur occurs principally in three forms, all of which are brittle, yellow in color, odorless, tasteless, and insoluble in water. Two of these solid forms are crystalline, composed of molecules containing eight sulfur atoms and having molecular weight 256.512 amu. Rhombic sulfur has orthorhombic crystalline structure and is stable below 95.5°C; most sulfur is in this form. The monoclinic, or prismatic, form has long, needlelike, nearly transparent crystals; it is stable between 95.5°C and its melting point, but re-

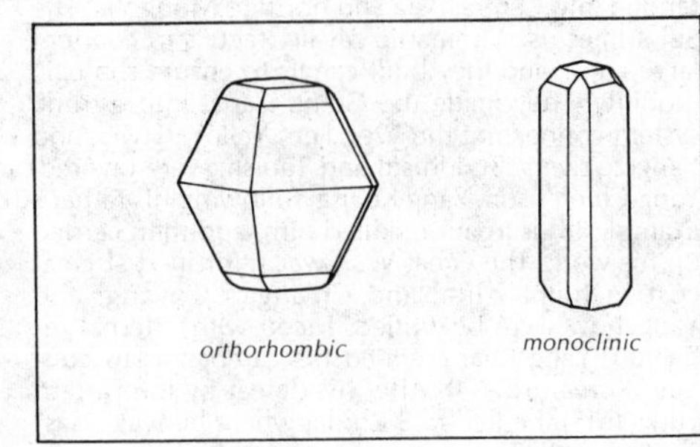

Sulfur crystals

verts to the rhombic form on standing at room temperature. Amorphous sulfur is a dark, noncrystalline, gumlike substance. It is often thought to be a supercooled liquid; it is formed by rapidly cooling molten sulfur, e.g., by pouring it into cold water. It slowly reverts to the rhombic form on standing. The crystalline forms are readily soluble in carbon disulfide, but the amorphous form is not. Many other forms of sulfur exist. Liquid sulfur is unusual in that its viscosity increases as it is heated. This property is thought to be due to the formation of long polymeric chains of sulfur molecules. Sulfur is a chemically active element and forms many compounds, both by itself (SULFIDES) and in combination with other elements. It is part of many organic compounds, e.g., mercaptans (thiols) and thio compounds. It burns in air with a blue flame, forming sulfur dioxide, SO_2. Sulfur is widely distributed in nature. It is found in many minerals and ores, e.g., iron pyrites, galena, cinnabar, zinc blende, gypsum, barite, and epsom salts and in mineral springs and other waters. It is found uncombined in some volcanic regions and in large underground deposits in Sicily and in the United States in Texas and Louisiana. Sulfur often occurs with coal, petroleum, and natural gas and has been found in meteorites. It is found in plants and animals, being an element of most proteins and protoplasm. Sulfur is produced chiefly by the FRASCH PROCESS, although it is also produced by the Sicilian method and by other methods. In the Sicilian method the sulfur-bearing ores are piled in a mound and ignited. The heat produced by the burning melts some of the sulfur, which is collected and cast. This sulfur is impure and is usually purified by sublimation. Sulfur is also recovered from natural gas, coal, crude oil, and other sources, e.g., the flue dusts and gases from the refining of metal sulfide ores. Elemental sulfur is obtained in several forms, including flowers of sulfur, a fine crystalline powder, and roll sulfur (cast cakes or sticks). It is used in black GUNPOWDER, matches, and fireworks; in the VULCANIZATION of rubber; as a fungicide and insecticide; and in the treatment of certain skin diseases. The principal use of sulfur is in the preparation of its compounds. The most important sulfur compound is SULFURIC ACID. Other important compounds include sulfur dioxide, used as a bleaching agent, disinfectant, and refrigerant; sodium bisulfite, used in paper manufacture; carbon disulfide, an important organic solvent; hydrogen sulfide, sulfur trioxide, and thionyl chloride, used as reagents in chemistry; the numerous SULFATE compounds; and sulfa drugs. Sulfur was known to the ancients; it is the brimstone of the Bible. It was first recognized as an element in 1777 by A. L. Lavoisier.

sulfur dioxide, chemical compound, SO_2, a colorless gas with a pungent, suffocating odor. It is readily soluble in cold water, sparingly soluble in hot water, and soluble in alcohol, acetic acid, and sulfuric acid. It is corrosive to organic materials and dissolves in water to form sulfurous acid, H_2SO_3. Sulfur dioxide is used in bleaching and in chemical manufacture and as a refrigerant and a food preservative, e.g., for fumigating fruit. It may be produced by reaction of sulfur with oxygen, e.g., by burning sulfur in air, and it is often produced during the roasting of sulfide ores, e.g., in zinc smelting. Sulfur dioxide is a dangerous air pollutant because of its corrosive properties; it irritates the eyes, nose, and lungs. It is produced by combustion of coal, fuel oil, and gasoline, since these fuels contain sulfur. The sulfur content of a fuel can be reduced by refining, so that less sulfur dioxide is emitted when the fuel is burned.

sulfuric acid, chemical compound, H_2SO_4, colorless, odorless, extremely corrosive, oily liquid. It is sometimes called oil of vitriol. When heated, the pure 100% acid loses sulfur trioxide gas, SO_3, until a constant-boiling solution, or azeotrope, containing about 98.5% H_2SO_4 is formed at 337°C. Concentrated sulfuric acid is a weak acid (see ACIDS AND BASES) and a poor ELECTROLYTE because relatively little of it is dissociated into ions at room temperature. When cold it does not react readily with such common metals as iron or copper. When hot it is an oxidizing agent, the sulfur in it being reduced; sulfur dioxide gas may be released. Hot concentrated sulfuric acid reacts with most metals and with several nonmetals, e.g., sulfur and carbon. Because the concentrated acid has a fairly high boiling point, it can be used to release more volatile acids from their salts, e.g., when sodium chloride (NaCl), or common salt, is heated with concentrated sulfuric acid, hydrogen chloride gas, HCl, is evolved. Concentrated sulfuric acid has a very strong affinity for water. It is sometimes used as a drying agent and can be used to dehydrate (chemically remove water from) many compounds, e.g., carbohydrates. It reacts with the sugar sucrose, $C_{12}H_{22}O_{11}$, removing eleven molecules of water, H_2O, from each molecule of sucrose and leaving a brittle spongy black mass of carbon and diluted sulfuric acid. The acid reacts similarly with skin, cellulose, and other plant and animal matter. When the concentrated acid mixes with water, large amounts of heat are released. To dilute the acid, the acid should be added slowly to cold water with constant stirring to limit the buildup of heat. If water is added to the concentrated acid, enough heat can be released at once to boil the water and spatter the acid. Sulfuric acid reacts with water to form hydrates with distinct properties. Sulfuric acid is a strong acid and a good electrolyte when diluted; it is highly ionized, much of the heat released in dilution coming from hydration of the hydrogen IONS. The dilute acid has most of the properties of common strong acids. It turns blue litmus red and has a sour taste. It reacts with many metals (e.g., with zinc), releasing hydrogen gas, H_2, and forming the SULFATE of the metal. It reacts with most hydroxides and oxides, with some carbonates and sulfides, and with some salts. Since it is dibasic (i.e., it has two replaceable hydrogen atoms in each molecule), it forms both normal sulfates (with both hydrogens replaced, e.g., sodium sulfate, Na_2SO_4) and acid sulfates, also called bisulfates or hydrogen sulfates (with only one hydrogen replaced, e.g., sodium bisulfate, $NaHSO_4$). Sulfuric acid is one of the most important industrial chemicals. More of it is made each year than is made of any other manufactured chemical; nearly 30 million tons of it were produced in the United States in 1970. It has widely varied uses and plays some part in the production of nearly all manufactured goods. The major use of sulfuric acid is in the production of fertilizers e.g., superphosphate of lime and ammonium sulfate. It is widely used in the manufacture of chemicals, e.g., in making hydrochloric acid, nitric acid, sulfate salts, synthetic detergents, dyes and pigments, explosives, and drugs. It is used in petroleum refining to wash impurities out of gasoline and other refinery products. Sulfuric acid is used in processing metals, e.g., in pickling (cleaning) iron and steel before plating them with tin or zinc. Rayon is made with sulfuric acid. It serves as the electrolyte in the lead-acid storage battery commonly used in motor vehicles (acid for this use, containing about 33% H_2SO_4 and with specific gravity about 1.25, is often called battery acid). There are two major processes (lead chamber and contact) for production of sulfuric acid, and it is available commercially in a number of grades and concentrations. The lead chamber process, the older of the two processes, is used to produce much of the acid used to make fertilizers; it produces a relatively dilute acid (62%-78% H_2SO_4). The contact process produces a purer, more concentrated acid but requires purer raw materials and the use of expensive catalysts. In both processes SULFUR DIOXIDE is oxidized and dissolved in water. The sulfur dioxide is obtained by burning sulfur, by burning pyrites (iron sulfides), by roasting nonferrous sulfide ores preparatory to smelting, or by burning hydrogen sulfide gas. Some sulfuric acid is also made from ferrous sulfate waste solutions from pickling iron and steel and from waste acid sludge from oil refineries. In the lead chamber process hot sulfur dioxide gas enters the bottom of a reactor called a Glover tower where it is washed with nitrous vitriol (sulfuric acid with nitric oxide, NO, and nitrogen dioxide, NO_2, dissolved in it) and mixed with nitric oxide and nitrogen dioxide gases; some of the sulfur dioxide is oxidized to sulfur trioxide and dissolved in the acid wash to form tower acid or Glover acid (about 78% H_2SO_4). From the Glover tower a mixture of gases (including sulfur dioxide and trioxide, nitrogen oxides, nitrogen, oxygen, and steam) is transferred to a lead-lined chamber where it is reacted with more water. The chamber may be a large, boxlike room or an enclosure in the form of a truncated cone. Sulfuric acid is formed by a complex series of reactions; it condenses on the walls and collects on the floor of the chamber. There may be from three to twelve chambers in a series; the gases pass through each in succession. The acid produced in the chambers, often called chamber acid or fertilizer acid, contains 62% to 68% H_2SO_4. After the gases have passed through the chambers they are passed into a reactor called the Gay-Lussac tower where they are washed with cooled concentrated acid (from the Glover tower); the nitrogen oxides and unreacted sulfur dioxide dissolve in the acid to form the nitrous vitriol used in the Glover tower. Remaining waste gases are usually discharged into the atmosphere. In the contact process, purified sulfur dioxide and air are mixed, heated to about 450°C, and passed over a catalyst; the sulfur dioxide is oxidized to sulfur trioxide. The catalyst is usually platinum on a silica or asbestos carrier or vanadium pentoxide on a silica carrier. The sulfur trioxide is cooled and passed through two towers. In the first tower it is washed with oleum (fuming sulfuric acid, 100% sulfuric acid with sulfur trioxide dissolved in it). In the second tower it is washed with 97% sulfuric acid; 98% sulfuric acid is usually produced in this tower. Waste gases are usually discharged into the atmosphere. Acid of any desired concentration may be produced by mixing or diluting the products of this process. Although sulfuric acid is now one of the most widely used chemicals, it was probably little known before the 16th cent. It was prepared by Johann Van Helmont (c.1600) by destructive distillation of green vitriol (ferrous sulfate) and by burning sulfur. The first major industrial demand for sulfuric acid was the Leblanc process for making sodium carbonate (developed c.1790). Sulfuric acid was produced at Nordhausen from green vitriol but was expensive. A process for its synthesis by burning sulfur with saltpeter (potassium nitrate) was first used by Johann Glauber in the 17th cent. and developed commercially by Joshua Ward in England c.1740. It was soon superseded by the lead chamber process, invented by John Roebuck in 1746 and since improved by many others. The contact process was originally developed c.1830 by Peregrine Phillips in England; it was little used until a need for concentrated acid arose, particularly for the manufacture of synthetic organic dyes.

Suli or **Souli** (both: so͞o'lyē), small mountainous district, N Greece, in Epirus. Its inhabitants, the Suliotes, who lived in fortlike villages in the mountains, remained independent during most of the occupation of Greece by the Ottoman Turks. They fought successfully (1790–1802) against Ali Pasha, the Turkish governor of Ioánnina. In 1803, however, Ali Pasha massacred many of them after concluding a false truce. The Suliotes were again decimated in a new rebellion in 1820, when many fled to the Ionian Islands.

Sulitjelma (so͞olētyĕl'mä), town, Nordland co., E Norway, at the foot of the Sulitjelma Mts., near the Swedish border. It has been a mining and smelting center since the end of the 19th cent.; much copper and zinc is shipped to Bodø for export. Sulitjelma's wild beauty has made it a popular tourist center.

Sulla, Lucius Cornelius (lo͞o'shəs kôrnē'lyəs sŭl'ə), 138 B.C.–78 B.C., Roman general. His name is also spelled Sylla. At the height of his career he assumed the name Felix. He served under MARIUS in Africa and became consul in 88 B.C., when Mithradates VI of Pontus was overrunning Roman territory. Sulla and Marius both wanted the command against Mithradates—Marius as a popular leader, Sulla as a senatorial favorite. Sulla got the office by marching (88 B.C.) his soldiers on Rome. By 85 B.C. he had driven Mithradates' armies back to Asia; Sulla's exploits had included a bloody sack of Athens (86 B.C.). After Marius' death in 86 B.C., his party (led by CINNA) sent another army to Greece, designed to supplant Sulla's, but the other Marian commander, Fimbria, fought independently. Mithradates was defeated (84 B.C.); then Sulla defeated Fimbria. Sulla came back to Italy (83 B.C.) with 40,000 men. The ensuing civil war lasted about a year in Italy (SERTORIUS continued it in Spain); Sulla's chief opponent was Cneius Papirius CARBO. The war ended just after the battle of the Colline Gate, a last desperate foray by Marians from Samnium; Sulla captured and massacred 8,000 prisoners. He had himself named dictator (82 B.C.) and began the systematic butchery of his enemies; this proscription, done with public lists, soon surpassed all Roman precedents. As the murders were legalized, the property of the victims, naturally including many very rich men, went to Sulla's friends. The dictator reorganized the government with measures, suggested by the METELLUS faction, which would remove any popular check on the senate. Sulla also founded a number of colonies for his veterans. In 79 B.C. he retired. His so-called reforms did not last. Sulla's dictatorship was notorious for its cruelty and lack of legality. See biography by G. P. Baker (1927, repr. 1967); A. H. Beesly, *The Gracchi, Marius, and Sulla* (1898).

Sullivan, Anne: see MACY, ANNE S.

Sullivan, Sir Arthur Seymour, 1842–1900, English composer, famous for a series of brilliant comic operas written in collaboration with the librettist W. S. GILBERT. As a boy he sang in the choir of the Chapel Royal. He was the first holder of the Mendelssohn scholarship at the Royal Academy of Music, entitling him to study at the Leipzig Conservatory, where he composed the incidental music to Shakespeare's *Tempest*, produced in 1862. Sullivan became organist at St. Michael's, London, in 1861 and professor of composition at the Royal Academy of Music in 1866. His first comic opera, *Cox and Box*, appeared in 1867. In 1871 he began his long and successful collaboration with Gilbert. Their first important satirical operetta, *Trial by Jury* (1875), was followed by even greater triumphs, such as *H. M. S. Pinafore* (1878), *The Pirates of Penzance* (1879), *Patience* (1881), *Iolanthe* (1882), *Princess Ida* (1884), *The Mikado* (1885), *Ruddigore* (1887), *The Yeoman of the Guard* (1888), and *The Gondoliers* (1889). These were produced by Richard D'Oyly Carte, who in 1881 built the Savoy Theater in London expressly for the production of works by Gilbert and Sullivan. Sullivan brought to Gilbert's witty lyrics a wealth of melodic invention and orchestral ingenuity, creating light operas that have charmed audiences for many generations. Despite the success of the comic operas, Sullivan felt that his best work was his serious music, chiefly his oratorios—which include *Kenilworth* (1864), *The Prodigal Son* (1869), *The Light of the World* (1873), and *The Golden Legend* (1886)—and his serious opera *Ivanhoe* (1891). He composed many songs, among which "The Lost Chord" (1878) became very popular; hymns, including "Onward, Christian Soldiers" (1871); anthems; ballets; and dramatic music. He was also noted as a conductor. In addition to performances of the operettas, he conducted the London Philharmonic Orchestra, 1885–87, and the Leeds Festivals, 1880–98. When the National Training School for Music was organized (1876), he became its principal, remaining in that position until 1881. Although he and Gilbert were ideally suited as collaborators, their different temperaments caused quarrels and eventual separation in about 1896. See biography by Herbert Sullivan and Sir Newman Flower (2d ed. 1952); Gervase Hughes, *The Music of Arthur Sullivan* (1960, repr. 1973).

Sullivan, Harry Stack, 1892–1949, American psychiatrist, b. Norwich, N.Y., M.D. Chicago College of Medicine and Surgery, 1917. He later taught at the Univ. of Maryland and at Georgetown Univ. Sullivan believed that to understand mental disorders psychoanalysis, although essentially valid, needed to be supplemented by a thorough-going study of the impact of cultural forces upon the personality. In his dual role as head of the William Alanson White Foundation (1934–43) and of the Washington School of Psychiatry (1936–47), he had the collaboration of like-minded psychologists and sociologists in bringing this view to public and professional attention. Sullivan also contributed significantly to the understanding of schizophrenia and obsessional states. A number of his papers published originally in the periodical *Psychiatry*, of which he was an editor, were gathered together to make up *Conceptions of Modern Psychiatry* (1940). See his *Interpersonal Theory of Psychiatry* (ed. by H. S. Perry and M. L. Gawel, 1953); study by Patrick Mullahy (1970).

Sullivan, John, 1740–95, American Revolutionary general, b. Somersworth, N.H. He was a lawyer and a delegate (1774–75, 1780–81) to the Continental Congress but is better remembered as a military leader. He served at the siege of Boston, and in 1776, while fighting under George Washington at the battle of Long Island, he was captured by the British. He was exchanged in time to fight at Trenton and Princeton and later at Brandywine and Germantown. In 1778 he was sent to cooperate with the French fleet in an attack on Newport. The fleet was forced to withdraw, however, and the attack had to be given up. The next year, with Gen. James CLINTON, he conducted a retaliatory campaign against the Iroquois and Loyalists on the New York frontier. The Indians and Loyalists were defeated in the battle of Newtown (near Elmira), and much of the Iroquois country was laid waste. Sullivan was later elected chief executive (1786, 1787, 1789) of New Hampshire. He also helped to put down Shays's Rebellion and was influential in getting the Constitution ratified. See biographies by T. C. Amory (1868, repr. 1968) and C. P. Whittemore (1961).

Sullivan, John Lawrence, 1858–1918, American boxer, b. Roxbury, Mass. After gaining a local reputation in amateur boxing, the Boston Strong Boy, as Sullivan came to be called, toured New England cities and after 1878 boxed professionally. Sullivan, with a devastating right-handed punch, was successful from the start and in 1882 won the bare-knuckles heavyweight championship by knocking out Paddy Ryan in nine rounds in Mississippi City, Miss. The "Great John L." met all comers. Sullivan's prowess in the ring and his swashbuckling personality won him many friends and made him the idol of American sports fans. He fought and won the last bare-knuckles championship bout (1889) by subduing Jake Kilrain in 75 rounds at Richburg, Miss. Fighting with gloves under the Queensberry rules for BOXING, Sullivan was defeated (1892) by James J. Corbett in New Orleans. He retired from the ring in 1896, still in possession of the bare-knuckles crown. In 1905, Sullivan, dramatically renouncing his old way of life, became a temperance advocate. See biographies of D. B. Chidsey (1942) and Nat Fleischer (1951).

Sullivan, Louis Henry, 1856–1924, American architect, b. Boston, studied at the Massachusetts Institute of Technology and the École des Beaux-Arts, Paris. He was of great importance in the evolution of modern architecture in the United States. His dominating principle, demonstrated in his writings and in his executed buildings, was that outward form should faithfully express the function beneath. This doctrine, the accepted and guiding one of modern architecture throughout the world, gained for Sullivan, however, few contemporary adherents. In the face of the powerful revival of traditional classicism led by C. F. McKim in the final years of the 19th cent., little interest was focused on Sullivan's plea for the establishment of an architecture that should be functional and also truly American. Sullivan was employed in the Chicago office of William Le Baron Jenney, designer of the first steel-skeleton skyscraper, and later entered the office of Dankmar Adler, where he became chief draftsman and in 1880 was made a member of the firm. Adler and Sullivan rapidly became prominent. In Sullivan's Wainwright Building in St. Louis (1890) a tall steel-frame building was so designed as not to belie the structural skeleton. His Transportation Building at the World's Columbian Exposition, Chicago (1893), shared nothing of the traditional classicism dominating the rest of the fair, and has become renowned for its originality and for heralding a new viewpoint. Sullivan in 1901 began to advocate a more imaginative as well as functional expression of architecture in his essays, collected as *Kindergarten Chats* (1918; ed. by Isabella Athey, 1947). Sullivan's works all bore his stamp in the highly individual ornament that he had built up into a complete style, now identified with his name. The *Autobiography of an Idea* (1924), which he wrote in his last years, contains the philosophy of his life and work. His executed designs include the Auditorium Building, the Gage Building, the Stock Exchange Building, and the structure that now houses the Carson Pirie Scott department store, all in Chicago; the Guaranty Building, Buffalo, N.Y.; a series of small banks; and a number of memorials, including the Getty Tomb in Chicago. Sullivan's pupils and followers include Claude Bragdon and Frank Lloyd Wright. See biography by H. Morrison (1935, repr. 1971); studies by A. Bush-Brown (1960) and M. D. Kaufman (1969); Frank Lloyd Wright, *Genius and the Mobocracy* (1949, repr. 1972).

Sullivan, Robert Baldwin, 1802–53, Canadian politician and judge, b. Ireland. He emigrated to Canada in 1819, became a lawyer, and was elected mayor of Toronto (1835). He became a member of the executive council of Upper Canada in 1836 and in 1839 a member of the legislative council. Sullivan played a prominent role in effecting the union of Upper Canada and Lower Canada. After the Act of Union (1840) he became a member and then president of the legislative council of Canada. Although a Conservative, he sided with the Reform party in its struggle for responsible government and resigned (1843) in opposition to Sir Charles METCALFE's reactionary policy.

Sully, Maurice de (mōrēs' də sülē'), c.1100–1196, French bishop. After studying theology in Paris he was named (1160) bishop of that city. While serving in this position he instigated the building of the Cathedral of Notre-Dame de Paris.

Sully, Maximilien de Béthune, duc de (mäksēmēlyăN' də bātün' dük də), 1560–1641, French statesman. Born and reared a Protestant, he fought in the Wars of Religion under the Huguenot leader Henry of Navarre (later King Henry IV of France). Before 1606 he was known as baron de Rosny. Appointed to the finance commission in 1596, he became sole superintendent of finances in 1598. To restore the finances, which King Henry III's extravagance and the Wars of Religion had plunged into disorder, he canceled portions of the public debt, recovered alienated sources of revenue, instituted an annual tax on officeholders, and strictly controlled all expenditures. As a result, there was a large surplus in the treasury at the end of Henry's reign. Sully restored French prosperity by encouraging agriculture and public works; he set about building a network of roads and canals. He was Henry IV's closest adviser and had gained his personal friendship; after Henry's assassination (1610), he resigned his office (1611). Besides being an admirable administrator, Sully was a man of remarkable vision, as is shown in his Great Design, a plan for a federation of all Christian nations, which appeared in his memoirs (1638); he attributed the plan to Henry IV. See E. C. Lodge, *Sully, Colbert, and Turgot* (1931, repr. 1970); David Buisseret, *Sully and the Growth of Centralized Government in France* (1968).

Sully, Thomas, 1783–1872, American painter, b. England. Having come to the United States as a child, he first studied with his brother Lawrence, a miniaturist, and later for a brief time with Gilbert Stuart. During a year (1809–10) in England he came under the influence of Benjamin West and Sir Thomas Lawrence. In 1810 he settled in Philadelphia, where he quickly became the leading portrait painter. On a second trip to England he was commissioned to paint the young Queen Victoria. Known chiefly as a portraitist, Sully also painted noteworthy historical compositions, such as *Washington's Passage of the Delaware* (Mus. of Fine Arts, Boston). His elegant and romantic portraits are to be found in many collections. Typical of his works are *Mother and Son* and a sketch of Queen Victoria (both: Metropolitan Mus.) and portraits of Fanny Kemble (Pa. Acad. of the Fine Arts), Andrew Jackson (National Gall. of Art, Washington, D.C.), and Presidents Jefferson and Monroe (U.S. Military Acad., West Point, N.Y.). He wrote a treatise on painting, *Hints to Young Portrait Painters* (1873, repr. 1965). See studies by C. H. Hart (1909) and Thomas Biddle and Mantle Fielding (1921).

Sully-Prudhomme, René François Armand (rənā' fräNswä' ärmäN' sülē'-prüdôm'), 1839–1907, French poet associated with the PARNASSIANS. His early poetry, including *Stances et poèmes* (1865), *Les Épreuves* (1866), *Les Solitudes* (1869), and *Les Vaines Tendresses* (1875), was subjective and melancholy. His major works are two long philosophical poems, *La Justice* (1878) and *Le Bonheur* [happiness] (1888), which treat abstract, humanitarian themes. His prose, also philosophical, includes *Que sais-je?* [what do I know?] (1896). In 1901 he was awarded the first Nobel Prize in literature.

Sulmona (so͝olmô'nä), town (1971 pop. 20,548), Abruzzi, central Italy, on the Gizio River. A commercial and industrial center, it lies in a small, fertile plain enclosed by Apennine peaks. Of note are the Palazzo dell'Annunziata (15th–16th cent.), the Gothic Napoli gate, and the Cathedral of San Panfilo.

sulphate: see SULFATE.

sulphide: see SULFIDE.

Sulphur, city (1970 pop. 13,551), Calcasieu parish, SW La.; inc. 1914. It is a trade center for an area producing rice, natural gas, timber, and oil. Its industry centers chiefly around petroleum products, chemicals, and related enterprises. The city was named for a now abandoned sulfur dome. In 1924 oil was discovered nearby. An annual state high-school championship rodeo is held in Sulphur.

sulphur: see SULFUR.

sulphur-bottom whale: see BLUE WHALE.

sulphuric acid: see SULFURIC ACID.

Sulphur Island: see IWO JIMA.

Sulphur Springs, city (1970 pop. 10,642), seat of Hopkins co., NE Texas, in a dairy area; inc. 1859. Milk and milk products are produced there. A trading post was established on the site in 1845. Sulphur Springs grew as a cotton and farm-produce market. It became county seat in 1871.

Sultan Husayn (so͞oltän' ho͞osän'), d. 1729, Safavid shah of Persia (1694–1722). A weak and superstitious man, Shah Sultan Husayn was surrounded by astrologers and fanatics and was able to offer little opposition to the uprising of the Afghans. He gave up his throne, and the bloody rule of Mahmud followed. Persian administration was restored only later by Nadir Shah.

Sulu Archipelago (so͞o'lo͞o), island group (1970 pop. 427,386), 1,086 sq mi (2,813 sq km), the Philippines, SW of Mindanao. Lying between the Celebes and Sulu seas, it includes over 400 volcanic islands and coral islets extending almost to Borneo. Basilan is the largest island, Jolo the most important. Fishing is the major source of livelihood; the Sulu Sea supplies a large proportion of the nation's commercial catch. The archipelago is also the prime source for pearls, marine turtles, seashells, and sea cucumbers. Tawi-Tawi has one of the best fleet anchorages in the world. The islands are heavily forested, but local farming is nonetheless carried on and meets the needs of the people. Large quantities of manioc (a root staple) are grown. The inhabitants are Moros, a Malayan people who were converted when Islam spread from Malaya and Borneo in the 14th and 15th cent. Formerly notorious as pirates, the Muslim Moros resisted Spanish rule until the 19th cent. The Moro sultanate (est. in the 16th cent.) passed to U.S. control in 1899 and continued to flourish under a mutually advantageous treaty with the United States. In 1940 the sultanate was abolished and Sulu became part of the Philippine Commonwealth.

Sulzbach (zōōlts'bäkh), city (1970 pop. 22,974), Saarland, SW West Germany; chartered 1946. It is an industrial center of the Saar coal basin.

Sulzberger, Arthur Hays, 1891–1968, American newspaper publisher, b. New York City. He joined the New York *Times* in 1918 and assisted his father-in-law, the publisher Adolph S. OCHS, succeeding Ochs upon his death in 1935. Retaining the paper's outstanding news coverage, Sulzberger broadened its use of background reporting, pictures, and feature articles. He supervised the development of facsimile transmission for photographs and built the *Times* radio station, WQXR, into a leading vehicle for news and music. Under Sulzberger the *Times* began to publish editions in Paris and Los Angeles with remote-control typesetting machines. In 1961 he turned the management of the paper over to his son-in-law, Orvil E. Dryfoos, although he remained chairman of the board. See G. Berger, *The Story of The New York Times* (1951, repr. 1970).

sumac or **sumach** (shōō'măk, sōō'-), common name for some members of the Anacardiaceae, a family of trees and shrubs native chiefly to the tropics but ranging into north temperate regions and characterized by resinous, often acrid, sap. The sap of certain of these plants—especially POISON IVY and related species of the New World genus *Toxicodendron*—contains an essential oil that is a toxic skin irritant. In these and other species the sap is also a major source of tannin, e.g., the QUEBRACHO tree of Paraguay, the LACQUER tree of SE Asia, and the TEREBINTH or turpentine tree and the MASTIC trees of the Mediterranean area. The PISTACHIO, CASHEW, and MANGO provide important foods both for local consumption and for trade. The resin content is responsible for the acid taste of mango and cashew fruits

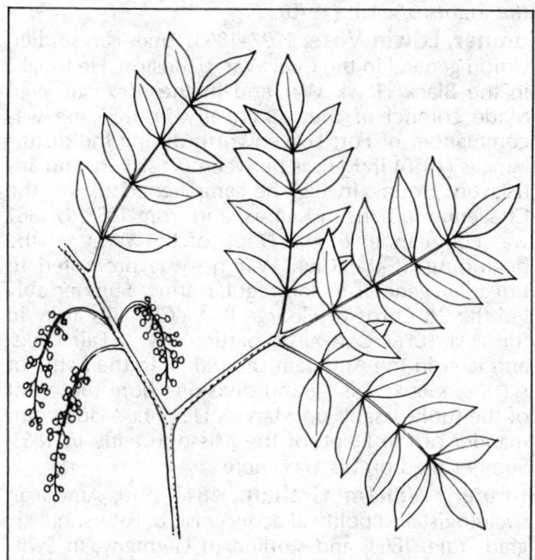

Poison sumac, Rhus vernix

and for the oil (sometimes extracted) in pistachio and cashew nuts. The true sumacs belong to the genus *Rhus;* some botanists include the poison ivy, poison oak, and poison sumac in that genus. Several species of sumacs are native to North America, usually in dry areas, and are noted for their brilliant autumn coloration. The common staghorn sumac (*R. typhira*) of the Eastern states is one of the species whose fruit is used in wine making and for medicinal purposes. Most of the sumacs contain tannin, and some—e.g., the Sicilian sumac (*R. coriaria*) of S Europe—are cultivated for this product. Sumacs are also cultivated as ornamentals, e.g., the smoke tree (*Cotinus coggygria*) of S Eurasia, whose bark is sometimes used for a dye, and the pepper tree, or Peruvian mastic (*Schinus molle*), of the American tropics. The latter, with its drooping branches and red fruits, is a favorite avenue ornamental in S California; however, it is highly susceptible to black scale, a disease destructive to fruit trees, and hence must be destroyed in areas where there are citrus groves. Sumac is classified in the division MAGNOLIOPHYTA, class Magnoliopsida, order Sapindales, family Anacardiaceae.

Sumarokov, Aleksandr Petrovich (əlyĭksän'dər pĕtrô'vĭch sōōmərô'kəf), 1718–77, Russian dramatist and poet. Sumarokov wrote fables, satires, lyrics, and comic odes in the classical style. His *Khorev* (1747) and *Tresotinius* (1750) were respectively the first classical tragedy and comedy in Russian. Enormously prolific, he is considered the first professional man of letters in Russian literature.

Sumatra (sōōmä'trə), island (1971 est. pop. 20,800,000), c.183,000 sq mi (473,970 sq km), Indonesia, in the Indian Ocean along the equator, S and W of the Malay Peninsula (from which it is separated by the Strait of Malacca) and NW of Java (across the narrow Sunda Strait). The westernmost and second largest island of Indonesia, Sumatra is c.1,110 mi (1,790 km) long and c.270 mi (435 km) wide and is fringed with smaller islands off its western and eastern coasts. The Barisan, a volcanic mountain range, traverses its length, reaching 12,467 ft (3,800 m) at Mt. Kerintji. Rising in the Barisan range are several large rivers, including the Hari, Indragiri, and Musi; some rivers are being developed for hydroelectric power. In the north is Lake Toba, a great salt lake. Because of the hot, moist climate and the heavy rainfall, the vegetation is luxuriant, and much of the eastern half of the island is swampland. The interior is covered largely by impenetrable rain forests. Among the animals are elephants, clouded leopards, tapirs, tigers, Malayan bears, and snakes. Sumatra has great natural wealth; about 70% of the country's income is produced there. The island has some of Indonesia's richest oil fields, its finest coalfields, and deposits of gold and silver. Its offshore islands are known for their tin and bauxite. Most of the country's rubber is grown in Sumatra; pepper, coffee, tea, sugarcane, and oil palms are also grown on plantations. The Deli region around Medan is famous for its tobacco. Rice, corn, and root crops are raised for local consumption. Timber cut includes camphor and ebony. Sumatra is a sparsely settled island, with principal centers at Medan and Palembang; also important are Djambi and Padang. The four largest ethnic groups are the Atjehnese, Batak, Menangkabu, and coastal Malays. In the interior highlands are found the Gajo-Alas and the Rejang-Lampoeng groups. Islam is the predominant religion, though there are many Christians among the Batak and the Gajo-Alas. Chinese, Arabs, and Indians live on the coasts, and some 15 different languages are spoken on the island. Sumatra had early contact with the Hindu civilization, and by the 7th cent. A.D. the powerful Hindu-Sumatran kingdom of Sri Vijaya (with its capital near Palembang) flourished under the house of Sailendra. The kingdom extended its control over a large part of Indonesia and also over the Malay Peninsula. By the 14th cent., Sumatran supremacy had waned, and the island fell under the Javanese kingdom of Majapahit. The Arabs, who may have first arrived as early as the 10th cent., established the sultanate of Achin, which reached its height in the 17th cent. and controlled most of the island. The first European to visit Sumatra was Marco Polo, who was there for a brief period c.1292. Following the Portuguese, who came in 1509, the Dutch arrived in 1596 and gradually gained control of all the native states including Achin. The British had brief control over parts of the island in the late 18th and early 19th cent. The Achinese (now more commonly the Atjehnese) launched a rebellion in 1873 and were not subdued by the Dutch until 1904. In World War II, Japanese troops landed (Feb., 1942) in Sumatra and occupied it throughout the war. After independence was granted (1949), all of Sumatra was included in the new republic of Indonesia. Since then there has been much tribal agitation and repeated demands for local autonomy. The Atjehnese have waged occasional guerrilla warfare against the government, and in 1958 a full-scale rebellion was launched by dissident army officers. It spread to other islands before being quelled by the government. Sumatra now comprises eight provinces. There are state universities in Djambi, Medan, Padang, Pakanbaru, and Palembang. See study by E. M. Loeb (1935, repr. 1973).

Sumava: see BOHEMIAN FOREST.

Sumba or **Soemba** (both: sōōm'bä), island (1961 pop. 251,126), 4,305 sq mi (11,150 sq km), Indonesia, one of the Lesser Sundas, in the Indian Ocean, S of Flores across Sumba Strait. The chief town and port is Waingapu. The island is noted for horse breeding. Formerly Sumba was known as Sandalwood Island because of its large exports (17th–19th cent.) of sandalwood. The island was first visited by Europeans in 1522 and passed to the direct control of the Dutch in 1866.

Sumbawa or **Soembawa** (both: sōōmbä'wä), island (1961 pop. 407,596), 5,964 sq mi (15,447 sq km), Indonesia, one of the Lesser Sundas, between the Flores Sea and the Indian Ocean. Bima, with an excellent harbor, is the port for Raba, the chief town. Sumbawa is mountainous, rising to c.9,350 ft (2,850 m); there are many volcanic peaks. The soil is fertile, and tropical fruit and rice are produced. Cattle raising is important.

Sumer (sōō'mər) and **Sumerian civilization** (sōōmĕr'ēən). The term *Sumer* is used today to designate the southern part of ancient MESOPOTAMIA. From the earliest date of which there is any record, S Mesopotamia was occupied by a people speaking a non-Semitic language, known as Sumerians. The questions concerning their origin cannot be answered with certainty. Some evidence suggests that they may have come as conquerors from the East (possibly from Iran or India). At any rate, as modern excavations have shown, there was in the 5th millennium B.C. a prehistoric village culture in the area. By 3000 B.C. a flourishing urban civilization existed. Sumerian civilization was predominantly agricultural and had a well-organized communal life. The Sumerians were adept at building canals and at developing effective systems of irrigation. Excavated objects such as pottery, jewelry, and weapons show that they were also skilled in the use of such metals as copper, gold, and silver and had developed by 3000 B.C. fine artistry as well as considerable technological knowledge. The Sumerians are credited with inventing the CUNEIFORM system of writing. Between the years 3000 and 2340 the kings of important Sumerian cities, such as KISH, ERECH, and UR, were able from time to time to extend their control over large areas, forming various dynasties. However, Mesopotamia was also the home of a group of people speaking Semitic languages and with a culture different from that of the Sumerians (see SEMITE). From the earliest times the Semites were in contact with Sumerian culture, and the increasing Semitic strength, which was already present in the north, culminated in the establishment (c.2340) of the Akkadian dynasty by SARGON, who for the first time imposed a wide imperial organization over the whole of Mesopotamia. This conquest gave impetus to the blending, already long in progress, of Sumerian and Semitic cultures. After the collapse of AKKAD (c.2180) under the pressure of invading barbarians from the northeast, peace and civilization were maintained only in LAGASH, under Gudea. However, the Sumerians were able to recover their political prestige and had a final revival under the third dynasty of Ur (c.2060). After this dynasty fell (c.1950) to the W Amorities and the Guti, a tribe from ELAM, the Sumerians were never again able to gain a political hegemony. With the rise of HAMMURABI, the control of the country passed to Babylonia, and the Sumerians, as a nation, disappeared. See C. L. Woolley, *The Sumerians* (1928, repr. 1971); C. J. Gadd, *History and Monuments of Ur* (1929); T. B. Jones, comp., *The Sumerian Problem* (1969); S. N. Kramer, *The Sumerians: Their History, Culture, and Character* (1971) and *Sumerian Mythology* (1973).

Sumerian and Babylonian art. The peoples of MESOPOTAMIA had an artistic tradition of remarkable antiquity, variety, and richness. The art of the Sumerian civilization, as revealed by excavations at UR, BABYLON, ERECH, MARI, KISH, and LAGASH, among other cities, was one of enormous power and originality that influenced all of the major cultures of ancient western Asia. Their techniques and motifs were made widely available by means of CUNEIFORM writing, which they invented before 3000 B.C. Poor in the raw materials of art, the Sumerians traded crops from their fertile soil for the metal, stone, and wood that they required. Clay was their most abundant native material, and its qualities determined their style of baked-mud building and the nature of their fine-textured pottery. Sumerian craftsmanship was of marked excellence from very early times. A vase in alabaster from Erech (c.3500 B.C.; Iraq Mus., Baghdad) shows a detailed ceremonial procession of men and animals to the fertility goddess Inanna, carved in four bands on an elegant vase shape. A major peak of artistic achievement is represented by a female head, called *Lady of Warka* (Erech) from about 3200 B.C. (Iraq Mus.). It is carved in white marble with simplicity and subtlety. The vast royal cemetery at Ur has yielded many masterpieces of

Sumerian work. Outstanding among these are a wooden harp detailed with gold and mosaic inlay picturing mythological scenes on the soundbox, surmounted by a black-bearded golden head of a bull (c.2650 B.C.; Univ. of Pennsylvania, Philadelphia); a gaming board of wood inlaid with bone, lapis lazuli, shell, and stone, mounted in bitumin (c.2700 B.C.; British Mus.); a ritual offering stand in the shape of a ram, made of silver, lapis lazuli, and mussel shells, rearing on his hind legs to eat from a tree of gold; and a splendid gold helmet fashioned from a single sheet of metal and beaten into the form of a head of wavy hair with a chignon at the back (c.2500 B.C.; Baghdad). At Lagash a strongly modeled head of stone (c.2500 B.C.) portrays a Sumerian man, clearly representing the structural type of the race. Its large and widely spaced features set on a heavy round skull are revealed in bas-relief and inlay work of the period. Examples of the famous votive stone sculptures of Sumer discovered at Tell Asmar represent tall, long-haired, bearded figures with huge, staring eyes and long, pleated skirts, standing rigidly with hands folded above the waist. Some are portrayed kneeling. The ZIGGURAT temple form was the most striking architectural achievement of the Sumerians. One ziggurat at Erech extended over an area of half a million square feet (46,500 sq m); it was set upon a mound, and the platform built to support its crowning shrine was 40 feet (12 m) high. Among other Sumerian arts, one of the most sophisticated was the cylinder seal, a small carved cylinder of stone or metal that, when rolled over seals of moist clay, would leave the reverse image of its carving in relief as an identifying mark or signature. Used to mark documents and property, the cylinders were worn on a wristband or necklace during their owners' lifetime and were buried with them. A great many examples survive, bearing primarily scenes of religious ritual, often portraying the legendary hero GILGAMESH. With the ascent to power of SARGON of AKKAD, Sumerian art reached new heights of expression, particularly in sculpture. The greatest known examples reflecting that splendor include a bronze head thought to be a portrait of Sargon himself (from Nineveh, c.2300 B.C.; Iraq Mus., Baghdad), from which the gemstone eyes have been stolen, and the stele of Naram-sin, a triumphal relief showing the deified grandson of Sargon in battle (2261–24 B.C.; Louvre). The Akkadians spread cuneiform writing throughout the Near East, and even after the destruction of Sargon's empire by invasions from the east in the latter part of the 3d millennium B.C., Sumerian artistic techniques and styles exerted profound influence on contemporary and later cultures. The city of Lagash survived the invasions and was beautified by its governor Gudea with numerous works of art. These were carved of dark, hard diorite; many represented the dignified and serene seated figure of Gudea himself. Although most are small in stature, they convey a sense of grandeur and monumentality. After the invasions the glory of Sumer was revived from 2200 to 2100 B.C. During this period the great ziggurat of the moon god at Ur was built. Invasions of Semitic peoples from what are now Iran and Syria ended the last Sumerian golden age. The site of Mari has yielded the most complete archaeological evidence of Sumerian civilization during that transitional time. The great Mari royal palace with its labyrinthine corridors, frescoed walls, royal residential rooms, courts and temple buildings, and scribal school containing more than 25,000 cuneiform tablets, reveal the brilliance of a vanished world. In the 18th cent. B.C., Babylonia under HAMMURABI rose to power and dominated Mesopotamia. A diorite head, wide-eyed, bearded, and hatted, found at Susa (1792–50 B.C.; Louvre), is generally taken to be a portrait of Hammurabi. The surface is carved to show the marks of aging on a sensitive face. A sculpture from Mari of a fertility goddess (Aleppo Mus.), holding a vase from which water flows down her skirt, further attests to the genius of Babylonian sculptors. The great basalt stele found in Susa upon which Hammurabi's immortal code of law is inscribed bears a relief at the top showing the king himself before the sun god who commands him to set down the law for his people (c.1750 B.C.; Louvre). Hammurabi is also represented kneeling in prayer in a sculpture in the round that is colored green and on which the hands and face have been gilded (from Larsa; Louvre). A number of terra-cotta plaques of this period (several examples: Louvre) depict scenes of Babylonian daily life, including agricultural pursuits and crafts such as carpentry. Babylonia was also a glassmaking center, but far less glass than sculpture has survived its destructive climate. After Hammurabi's death Mesopotamia was torn for centuries by foreign invasions. For a time the Assyrian warrior people held sway and established some cultural coherence (see ASSYRIAN ART). One of their kings, SENNACHERIB, razed the city of Babylon. Babylonia was not to be reborn until NEBUCHADNEZZAR divided the Assyrian lands with the Medes in 612 B.C. Under his rule the Babylonians developed to perfection one of their most striking arts: the great polychrome-glazed brick walls modeled in relief, the foremost example of which is the Ishtar gates of Babylon. These, produced for Nebuchadnezzar, contain 575 reliefs of lions, dragons, and bulls of superb workmanship (6th cent. B.C.; one lion exhibited at the Metropolitan Mus.). The king's palace, with its courtyard and hanging (balconied) gardens (constructed more than a century before Nebuchadnezzar came to power), the Ishtar gates, and the royal processional road made Babylon a city of unrivalled magnificence in its time. Its artisans were able to draw upon materials and styles from an area bounded only by Egypt and India. The new splendor was short-lived; less than a century later Babylonia fell prey to more invasions, and the Persians, Greeks, and Romans ruled in succession. The great Mesopotamian civilizations eventually crumbled and were forgotten until archaeologists of the 19th cent. A.D. began to bring to light something of their history and appearance. See also HITTITE ART; PHOENICIAN ART. See C. L. Woolley, *Ur Excavations* (1956) and *The Art of the Middle East* (1960); Seton Lloyd, *Art of the Ancient Near East* (1961); Henri Frankfort, *Cylinder Seals* (1965); H. W. F. Saggs, *The Greatness That Was Babylon* (1966).

Sumer Is Icumen In (so͞om'ər ĭs ēko͞o'mən ĭn) [M.E.,=summer has (literally: is) come in], an English rota or round. It is the earliest extant example of canon, of six part music, and of ground bass. Four tenor voices are in canon and two bass voices sing the pes, or ground, also in canon. The secular text is in Wessex dialect, and in the same manuscript source, from Reading Abbey in England, is a Latin text to adapt the tune for church use. The manuscript was discovered in 1709 in the same folio with a calendar made at Reading between 1239 and 1260. Although the early date of the piece has been questioned because it is so different from other works of the period, paleographic and linguistic evidence tends to support the original assumption that it was written in the 13th cent. It is generally credited to the monk John of Fornsete, who kept the records of Reading Abbey and in whose handwriting it seems to have been written.

Sumgait (so͞omgēt'), city (1970 pop. 124,000), Azerbaijan Republic, S European USSR, on the Caspian Sea at the mouth of the Sumgait River. It is a major industrial center of Azerbaijan with a pipe-rolling mill and aluminum and synthetic rubber factories. It was founded in 1948.

Summerhill, radical progressive school in Leiston, Suffolk, England, and the educational movement based on principles developed at the school. The school was founded (1924) by A. S. Neill, who headed the institution until his death in 1973. It has about 50 students between the ages of 4 and 16. The main principle behind the operation of the school is freedom. There is no compulsory attendance at classes, and most administrative questions are decided by the students themselves. Critics of Summerhill charge that its students lack moral education and training in social responsibility. A number of schools based on similar principles, in both Britain and the United States, describe themselves as Summerhill schools. See A. S. Neill, *Summerhill: A Radical Approach to Child Rearing* (1960); John Walmsley, *Neill & Summerhill: A Man and His Work* (1969); Harold H. Hart, ed., *Summerhill: For & Against* (1970).

Summerside, town (1971 pop. 9,439), SW Prince Edward Island, Canada, on Bedeque Bay, an arm of Northumberland Strait. It is a tourist center and port. Potatoes, dairy products, and oysters are produced in the region. There is an experimental fur farm in the town.

Summit. 1 Village (1970 pop. 11,569), Cook co., NE Ill., a suburb of Chicago; inc. 1890. It has a huge freight train terminal and one of the world's largest grain-milling plants. **2** City (1970 pop. 23,620), Union co., NE N.J., a residential suburb of the New York City–N New Jersey metropolitan area; settled c.1720, set off from Springfield and New Providence and inc. 1869. Pharmaceuticals are made, and several major companies have research facilities there. Situated on a ridge of Watchung Mt., it was the site of an important American lookout post during the Revolutionary War.

summons: see PROCEDURE.

Sumner, Charles, 1811–74, U.S. Senator from Massachusetts (1851–74), b. Boston. He attended (1831–33) and was later a lecturer at Harvard law school, was admitted (1834) to the bar, and practiced in Boston. He spent the years 1837 to 1840 in Europe. Later he became involved in several reform movements, including antislavery, and in 1851 a combination of Free-Soilers and Democrats sent him to the Senate. An aggressive abolitionist, Sumner attacked the fugitive slave laws, denounced the Kansas-Nebraska Act of 1854, and on May 19–20, 1856, delivered his notable antislavery speech called "The Crime against Kansas." A master of invective, he singled out as his special victim Senator Andrew Pickens Butler of South Carolina, who was not there to reply. Two days later he was assaulted in the Senate chamber by Preston S. BROOKS, Butler's nephew. It took Sumner more than three years to recover from the attack, but Massachusetts reelected him, and he resumed his seat in Dec., 1859. He had been important in organizing the new Republican party and in 1861 was made chairman of the Senate foreign relations committee. In the TRENT AFFAIR he favored the release of the captured Confederate commissioners. Sumner highly approved Lincoln's Emancipation Proclamation; indeed he had been impatient at the long delay. Sumner in the Senate and Thaddeus STEVENS in the House led the radical Republicans in their RECONSTRUCTION program for the South. He held that the Southern states had "committed suicide" by their secession and thus had lost any rights under the Constitution. Reconstruction he considered the function of Congress alone and he was most active in trying to secure the conviction of President Andrew Johnson on the impeachment charges. During the administration of Ulysses S. Grant, Sumner's excessive demands regarding Civil War claims against Great Britain hampered the administration's negotiations with that country. His relationship with Grant deteriorated further when Sumner denounced Grant's questionable scheme to annex Santo Domingo; this led to his removal (March, 1871) from the chairmanship of the committee on foreign relations. Humiliated, Sumner helped organize (1872) the short-lived LIBERAL REPUBLICAN PARTY. Sumner wrote and spoke widely, and there are two editions of his works (15 vol., 1870–83; 20 vol., 1900). See E. L. Pierce, *Memoir and Letters of Charles Sumner* (4 vol., 1877–93); David Donald, *Charles Sumner and the Coming of the Civil War* (1960, repr. 1970) and *Charles Sumner and the Rights of Man* (1970).

Sumner, Edwin Vose, 1797–1863, American soldier, Union general in the Civil War, b. Boston. He fought in the Black Hawk War and in the Mexican War. Made colonel of the 1st Cavalry in 1855, he was commander of Fort Leavenworth during the disturbances (1856) in Kansas between proslavery and antislavery groups. In 1857 he campaigned against the Cheyenne Indians in Kansas, and from 1858 to 1861 was commander of the Dept. of the West. At the beginning of the Civil War he was promoted to brigadier general in the regular army. Sumner ably led the 2d Corps of George B. McClellan's army in the PENINSULAR CAMPAIGN, particularly at Fair Oaks, and later in the Antietam campaign. In the battle of FREDERICKSBURG his "grand division" bore the brunt of the futile assault on Marye's Heights. Made commander of the Dept. of the Missouri early in 1863, Sumner died on his way there.

Sumner, William Graham, 1840–1910, American sociologist and political economist, b. Paterson, N.J., grad. Yale, 1863, and studied in Germany, in Switzerland, and at Oxford. He was ordained an Episcopal minister and from 1872 was professor of political and social science at Yale. In economics he advocated a policy of extreme LAISSEZ-FAIRE, violently opposing any government measures that he thought interfered with the natural economics of trade. As a sociologist he did valuable work in charting the course of human customs—FOLKWAYS and MORES. He concluded that the power of these forces, developed in the course of human evolution, rendered useless any attempts at social reform. He also originated the concept of ethnocentrism, a term now commonly used, to designate attitudes of superiority about one's own group in comparison with others. His major work was *Folkways* (1907). The monumental *Science of Society* by Sumner and Albert G. Keller, a colleague, was not completed and published until 1927 (4 vol.; Vol. IV by Sumner, Keller, and M. R. Davie). See H. E. Starr, *William Graham Sumner* (1925); A. G. Keller, *Reminiscences (Mainly Personal) of William Graham Sumner* (1933); W. G.

Green, *Sumner Today* (1940, repr. 1971); R. G. McCloskey, *American Conservatism in the Age of Enterprise* (1951, repr. 1964); M. R. Davie, *William Graham Sumner* (1963).

sumo: see WRESTLING.

sumptuary laws (sŭmp'cho͞oĕ"rē), regulations based on social, religious, or moral grounds directed against overindulgence of luxury in diet and drink and extravagance in dress and mode of living. Such laws existed in ancient Greece and Rome, and in Japan they were applied to the peasant and commercial classes until the mid-19th cent. In the 14th and 15th cent. several statutes were passed in England that regulated ornateness of dress and the people's diet. These regulations varied according to the rank of the person, peasants being subject to rules different from those of the gentry. The main purpose of the legislation was to mark class distinctions clearly and to prevent any person from assuming the appearance of a superior class. See F. E. Baldwin, *Sumptuary Legislation and Personal Regulation in England* (1926).

Sumter, Thomas, 1734–1832, American Revolutionary officer, b. near Charlottesville, Va. He served with Edward Braddock (1755) and John Forbes (1758) in their expeditions against Fort Duquesne in the French and Indian War, and later he fought against the Cherokee. He settled (1765) in South Carolina. Like Francis Marion, he formed (1780) a guerrilla band in the Revolution and harassed the British in the Carolinas. He and the British leader, Banastre Tarleton, struck at each other through 1780. The "gamecock of the Revolution," as Sumter was called, was successful at Hanging Rock, barely escaped with his life at Fishing Creek, was repulsed in a raid on the British post at Rocky Mount, but won again at Blackstock. After the war, he was U.S. Representative (1789–93, 1797–1801), Senator (1801–10), and minister to Brazil (1810–11). Fort Sumter in Charleston harbor is named for him. See biographies by A. K. Gregorie (1931) and R. D. Bass (1961).

Sumter, city (1970 pop. 24,555), seat of Sumter co., central S.C.; founded 1785, inc. 1845. It is the trade, processing, and shipping center of an important lumber, livestock, and farm region. Textile products, furniture, electric storage batteries, frozen foods, medical supplies, fabricated steel, and paints and varnishes are made there. Of interest are the tombs of Revolutionary War hero Gen. Thomas Sumter and Joel Poinsett, for whom the poinsettia is named. Swan Lake Iris gardens attract many visitors, and there is a U.S. tree nursery. Morris College and a junior-college branch of Clemson Univ. are in Sumter. Shaw Air Force Base, headquarters of the 9th U.S. Air Force, is to the west. Poinsett State Park is in the area.

Sumter, Fort: see FORT SUMTER.

Sun, river, c.130 mi (210 km) long, rising in the Rocky Mts., NW Mont., and flowing generally E to the Missouri River at Great Falls. The Sun River project of the U.S. Bureau of Reclamation utilizes the Sun and its tributaries to irrigate c.92,000 acres (37,230 hectares); Gibson Dam (completed 1929) is the project's largest dam.

sun, intensely hot, self-luminous body of gases at the center of the SOLAR SYSTEM. The sun is actually a star of about medium size; it appears larger than the other stars because of its relative nearness to the earth. Its gravitational attraction maintains the planets, comets, and other bodies of the solar system in their orbits. Without the heat and light of the sun, life as we know it could not exist on the earth. Since solar energy is used by green plants in the process of photosynthesis, the sun is the ultimate source of the energy stored in food and coal. Solar heating sets up convection currents, and thus is the source of the energy of moving air. Falling rain also owes its energy to the sun because of the relation of solar radiation to the water cycle. The earth's distance from the sun varies from 91,377,000 mi (147,053,000 km) at perihelion to 94,537,000 mi (152,138,000 km) at aphelion (see APSIS). The mean distance is c.92,960,000 mi (149,591,000 km); this is taken as the ASTRONOMICAL UNIT of distance used for measuring distances within the solar system. The sun is approximately 865,400 mi (2,240,000 km) in diameter, and its volume is about 1,300,000 times that of the earth. Its mass is almost 700 times the total mass of all the bodies in the solar system and 332,000 times that of the earth. The sun's surface gravity is almost 28 times that of the earth; i.e., a body on the surface of the sun would weigh about 28 times its weight on earth. The density of the material composing the sun is about one fourth that of the earth; compared with water, the sun's average density is 1.41. At its center, the sun has a density of over 100 times that of water, a temperature of 10 to 20 million degrees Celsius, and a pressure of over 1 billion atmospheres. Observations of sunspots and studies of the solar spectrum indicate that the sun rotates on its axis from east to west; because of its gaseous nature its rate of rotation varies somewhat with latitude, the speed being greatest (a period of almost 25 days) in the equatorial region and least at the poles (a period of about 35 days). The axis of the sun is inclined at an angle of about 7° to the plane of the ECLIPTIC. The bright surface of the sun is called the PHOTOSPHERE. Its temperature is about 6000°C. The photosphere appears darker near the edge (limb) of the sun's disk because of greater absorption of light by the sun's atmosphere in this area; this phenomenon is called limb darkening. During an eclipse of the sun the CHROMOSPHERE and the CORONA (the outer layers of the sun's atmosphere) are observed. By means of the spectroscope much has been learned about the composition of the sun. There are numerous dark lines of varying widths in the solar SPECTRUM. These were first intensively studied by Joseph Fraunhofer and are commonly known by his name. From a study of the lines the chemical composition of the sun is determined on the basis of the discovery by Kirchhoff that the dark lines correspond in position to the bright lines characteristic of the spectra produced by elements in the laboratory. The darkness of the lines in the sun's spectrum is attributed to the presence of a slightly cooler layer of gases above the photosphere, known as the reversing layer, which absorbs selectively the light of the photosphere and thus causes dark lines instead of bright ones to be observed through the spectroscope. By comparison of the sun's spectrum with laboratory spectra of incandescent elements, more than two thirds of the elements known on earth have been identified in the sun's atmosphere. Beyond the red portion of the visible solar spectrum is the infrared spectrum; for the study of these heat rays S. P. Langley invented the bolometer, a highly sensitive electrical device for measuring temperature. Solar heat and energy are measured by an instrument called the pyrheliometer. Other instruments devised especially for the study of the sun are the CORONAGRAPH and the SPECTROHELIOGRAPH. These instruments have revealed a number of interesting phenomena occurring during the periods of solar activity associated with SUNSPOTS, e.g., faculae, plages (flocculi), prominences, and flares. Also of interest is the high-speed, tenuous extension of the corona known as the SOLAR WIND. The source of the sun's energy has long been a subject of investigation. The vast and continual production of solar energy cannot be attributed merely to combustion, to the gradual cooling of a hot body, to the fall of meteorites into the sun, or to gradual shrinkage with transformation of potential energy into heat (a theory proposed by Helmholtz). The theory of relatively with its implication of the equivalence of mass and energy led to the assumption that energy stored in the atoms constituting the sun's gases is constantly being released by conversion of some of the masses of the atom's nuclei during nuclear transmutations (see NUCLEAR ENERGY). H. A. Bethe proposed a cycle of nuclear reactions known as the carbon cycle, or CNO bi-cycle, to account for the nuclear changes. In this cycle carbon acts much as a catalyst, while hydrogen is transformed by a series of reactions into helium and large amounts of high-energy gamma radiation are released. It is now thought that the so-called proton-proton process is a more important energy source; this process begins with the collision of two protons and ends with the production of helium, while gamma radiation is released throughout. See NUCLEOSYNTHESIS; STELLAR EVOLUTION. See George Gamow, *The Birth and Death of the Sun* (1960); Giorgio Abetti, *The Sun* (tr., 2d ed., 1963); M. A. Ellison, *The Sun and its Influence* (3d ed. 1968); George Abell, *Exploration of the Universe* (2d ed. 1969); W. M. Baxter, *The Sun and the Amateur Astronomer* (rev. ed. 1973).

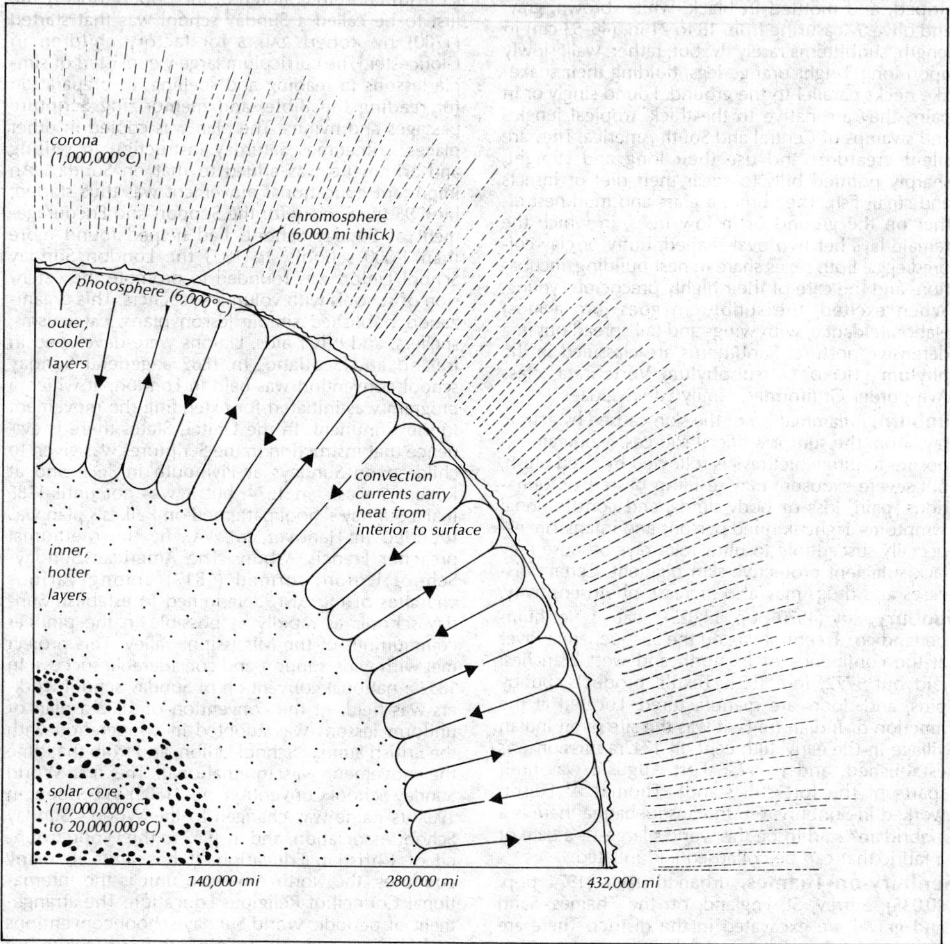

Structure of the sun

Sunay, Cevdet (jĕvdĕt' so͞onī'), 1900–, Turkish political leader and army officer, president of Turkey (1966–73). Educated at military schools, he served in World War I and the subsequent nationalist revolt. Rising through the ranks to become a full general in 1959, he held important military posts, was made commander in chief of the land forces in 1960, and then chief of staff. In 1966 he succeeded the ailing Cemal Gürsel as president of Turkey. He maintained his office despite increasing terrorist activity, student riots, and threatened coups. When his term expired in 1973 he was made a permanent senator.

sunbird, common name for tropical, Old World birds, including more than one hundred species in the family Nectariniidae. Like the unrelated New

World hummingbirds, to which sunbirds are often compared, sunbirds have long and slender, highly curved bills, tube-shaped tongues, and feed primarily on nectar and small insects. However, they perch when feeding rather than hovering as the hummingbirds do. They are typically small birds, with the largest, the great sunbird (*Dreptes thomensis*) reaching a maximum length of 8½ in. (22 cm), and are native to forest and brush throughout Africa, Asia, and the South Pacific. Some common species are the variable sunbird (*Cinnyris venustus*), the purple sunbird (*Nectarinia asiatica*), and the golden-winged sunbird (*N. reichenowi*). The males of most species are brightly colored, with metallic, sometimes velvety, plumage. Out of breeding season, the males tend to take on the duller female plumage. Sunbirds may change their feeding grounds during the nonbreeding season but are not particularly migratory. They are not very gregarious, and males tend to be aggressive, especially during breeding season. Sunbirds build a characteristic purselike, hanging nest, into which the female deposits her two, rarely three, white or pale blue, variously spotted or striped eggs. Two unrelated Madagascan species in the genus *Neodrepenis* are known as false sunbirds, and are easily confused with the sunbirds, which they resemble in habits, habitat, diet, and somewhat in appearance. They are, however, slenderer and shorter-legged, with more markedly down-curved bills. The related spider hunters, of the genus *Arachnothera,* are members of the true sunbird family and are found in the Orient. They lack the metallic coloration of their sunbird relatives, and the sexes are more alike, both being dull greens, browns, or yellows. Spider hunters (e.g., the little spider hunter, *A. longirostris*) feed largely on insects and spiders. Their singular cup-shaped nest is built on the bottom of a broad leaf and attached firmly by cobwebs and plant fibers, which the bird sews and knots together. Both sexes build the nest and share incubation of the two to three eggs laid per clutch. Sunbirds and their relatives are classified in the phylum CHORDATA, subphylum Vertebrata, class Aves, order Passeriformes, family Nectariniidae.

sunbittern, common name for a graceful, stout-bodied, bitternlike bird, *Eurypyga helias.* It is named for its wing markings, an orange-chestnut shield set in an orange-buff circle, which looks like a setting sun. The rest of its plumage is intricately barred, striped, and mottled in black, white, brown, gray, and olive. Measuring from 18 to 21 in. (46–53 cm) in length, sunbitterns rarely fly, but, rather, walk slowly upon long, bright orange legs, holding their snakelike necks parallel to the ground. Found singly or in pairs, they are native to the thick, tropical jungles and swamps of Central and South America. They are silent creatures and use their long and straight, sharply pointed bills to spear their diet of insects and small fish. They build a grass and mud nest either on the ground or in low trees, in which the female lays her two oval-shaped, buffy or clay-colored eggs. Both sexes share in nest building, incubation, and the care of their highly precocious young. When excited, the sunbittern goes into a most elaborate dance, with wings and tail spread out in a defensive posture. Sunbitterns are classified in the phylum CHORDATA, subphylum Vertebrata, class Aves, order Gruiformes, family Eurypygidae.

sunburn, inflammation of the skin caused by actinic rays from the sun or artificial sources. Moderate exposure to ultraviolet rays is followed by a red blush, but severe exposure may result in blisterlike formations, pain, loss of body fluids, and constitutional symptoms. Light-skinned persons and infants are especially susceptible to ultraviolet rays because they lack sufficient protective skin pigment. Certain diseases and drugs may also increase photosensitivity.

Sunbury, city (1970 pop. 13,025), seat of Northumberland co., E central Pa., on the Susquehanna River at the confluence of its north and west branches; laid out 1772, inc. 1921. Textile products, bobby pins, and doors are manufactured. Located at the junction of Indian trails, it was the site of an Indian village in the early 18th cent. In 1742 a mission was established, and in 1756 Fort Augusta was built (parts of the fort still stand). Thomas A. Edison worked in Sunbury. On the Susquehanna there is a "fabridam" said to be the world's largest—a dam of a fabric that can be collapsed and inflated.

Sunbury-on-Thames, urban district (1971 pop. 40,035), Surrey, SE England, on the Thames. Sand and gravel are excavated in the district. There are motion-picture studios in Sunbury-on-Thames. The community of Shepperton has preserved a village center from the 17th–18th cent. The novelist Thomas Love Peacock lived in the district and is buried in Shepperton.

Sunchon (so͞on'chŭn'), city (1970 est. pop. 91,000), SW South Korea. It is a railroad junction and an agricultural center.

Sunda Islands (sŭn'də), Indonesia, between the South China Sea and the Indian Ocean, comprising the western part of the Malay Archipelago. It includes two main groups: the Greater Sunda Islands, to which belong the largest islands of Borneo, Sumatra, Java, and Celebes; and the Lesser Sundas, which lie E of Java and include Sumbawa, Flores, Timor, and Sumba (the largest islands). Bali and Lombok, although smaller, are the most important. The Lesser Sundas were renamed Nusatenggara [southeastern islands] in 1954. Sunda Strait, 20 to 65 mi (32–100 km) wide, is between Java and Sumatra and connects the Java Sea with the Indian Ocean.

sun dance, ceremony typical of the Plains Indians of North America. The ceremony was performed in the summer and usually lasted eight days. Some of the ceremony was secret. Smoking, fasting, and other rites were part of the ceremony. Penance through self-torture was the main object of the ceremony. Among some Indians, a bison skull was pulled around the lodge by means of a thong and peg inserted through the skin of the participant's chest. The missionaries and the government discouraged the ceremony to such an extent that the rites are now almost forgotten and the true meaning has been lost.

Sunday, Billy (William Ashley Sunday), 1863–1935, American evangelist, b. Ames, Iowa. He was a professional baseball player from 1883 to 1890 and worked for the Young Men's Christian Association in Chicago from 1891 to 1895. In 1896 he became an evangelist, drawing large crowds to his revivals. He was ordained in 1903 in the Presbyterian ministry. See biographies by Melton Wright (1951), W. G. McLoughlin, Jr. (1955), and Thomas Lee (1961).

Sunday: see SABBATH; WEEK.

Sunday school, institution for instruction in religion and morals, usually conducted in churches as part of the church organization but sometimes maintained by other religious or philanthropic bodies. In England during the 18th cent., occasional efforts were made by charitable individuals to provide some education in religious matters as well as secular instruction to children of the poor. Probably the first to be called a Sunday school was that started (1780) by Robert RAIKES for factory children in Gloucester. The curriculum largely consisted of simple lessons in reading and spelling, in preparation for reading the Bible, and memorizing Scripture passages and hymns. The plan was copied in other places; sometimes Saturday instruction in writing and arithmetic was added to that on Sunday. An important educational movement was thus started; by 1795 the Society for the Support and Encouragement of Sunday Schools had helped found more than 1,000 schools. In 1803 the London Sunday School Union was founded to promote the extension of schools with voluntary teachers. This organization published simple lesson plans, catechisms, spellers, and other aids. Unions were developed in Ireland and Scotland. In 1862 a general Sunday school convention was held in London, at which a program was initiated for extending the movement to the Continent. In the United States there is evidence that instruction in the Scriptures was given to children on Sundays at Plymouth in 1669 and at Roxbury, Mass., in 1674, but it was not until 1786 that a Sunday school patterned on Raikes's plan was founded in Hanover co., Va., by the Methodist preacher Francis Asbury. The American Sunday-School Union, formed (1817) among various churches of the East, determined to establish Sunday schools as rapidly as possible in the pioneer communities of the Mississippi valley. This project met with wide support and considerable success. In 1832 a national convention of Sunday school workers was held. At the convention of 1872 a plan of uniform lessons was adopted in cooperation with the British Sunday School Union, and from that time the movement was international. The first World Sunday School Convention met (1889) in London; in 1907 its name was changed to the World's Sunday School Association, and in 1947 to the World Council of Christian Education. It has units in many countries; the North American unit is the International Council of Religious Education. The arrangement of periodic world Sunday school conventions and aid in leadership training and curriculum are among the chief concerns of the council. See Rachel Swann, *The Small Church and Christian Education* (1961); E. W. Rice, *The Sunday School Movement, 1780–1917* (1917, repr. 1971); R. W. Lynn, *The Big Little School* (1971).

Sundbyberg (sŭnd"bübĕr'yə), city (1970 pop. 28,016), Stockholm co., E Sweden, an industrial suburb of Stockholm; founded 1877. Manufactures include chemicals, paper, chocolate, and cables.

Sunderland, Charles Spencer, 3d earl of, 1674–1722, English statesman; son of the 2d earl. His marriage (1700) to a daughter of the 1st duke of Marlborough brought him a secretaryship of state (1706), and he was powerful in the Whig junto that controlled affairs from 1708 to 1710. He fell with the Whigs in 1710. After the accession (1714) of George I, he was at first given minor offices, but through intrigue he secured the dismissal of Viscount TOWNSHEND and Robert WALPOLE and became a secretary of state (1717) and first lord of the treasury (1718), sharing leadership with the 1st Earl STANHOPE. He was so involved with the development of the SOUTH SEA BUBBLE that its collapse forced him out of office in 1721. He was an important collector of books and manuscripts.

Sunderland, Robert Spencer, 2d earl of, 1641–1702, English statesman. He succeeded to the earldom in 1643. During the reign of Charles II he served on various diplomatic missions and in 1679 was made a secretary of state. His support of the bill to exclude the duke of York (later James II) from the succession resulted in his dismissal (1681), but he quickly regained his position through the influence of the king's mistress, the duchess of Portsmouth. Under James II he gained favor by urging severe repression of the rebellion of the duke of Monmouth and by his support for the abolition of the religious tests. He was made lord president of the council (1685), and by intrigue he supplanted the earl of Rochester as chief minister. In 1688 he declared himself a Roman Catholic, but he soon argued with James on religious policy and was dismissed. He fled to Holland, convinced William of Orange (later William III) that he had supported his interests, and, after William's accession to the English throne, was allowed to return (1691) to England. He renounced his Catholicism and became an influential adviser of William. It was Sunderland who persuaded the king to abandon a mixed ministry and employ only Whigs—a significant (if unintentional) step in English constitutional development. He was appointed lord chamberlain in 1697 but was forced out of office by a distrustful Parliament. See biography by J. P. Kenyon (1958).

Sunderland, county borough (1971 pop. 216,892), Durham, NE England, at the mouth of the Wear River. Sunderland was established as a shipbuilding center and coal-shipping port in the 14th cent. Today it exports iron and steel and manufactured goods, and imports raw materials. Shipbuilding is still an important industry, as are engineering, coal mining, and the manufacture of aircraft components, electrical goods, glass, clothes, chemicals, and pottery. A great Benedictine abbey, at which BEDE studied, was founded there in 674. It was destroyed by the Danes, and its remains are incorporated in the Church of St. Peter. Educational and cultural facilities include Sunderland Polytechnic College, Sunderland College for teacher training, and art museums. The borough includes the seaside resorts of Roker and Seaburn. In 1974, Sunderland became part of the new metropolitan county of Tyne and Wear.

sundew: see VENUS'S-FLYTRAP.

sundial, instrument that indicates the time of day by the shadow, cast on a surface marked to show hours or fractions of hours, of an object on which the sun's rays fall. Although any object whose shadow is used to determine time is called a gnomon, the term is usually applied to a style, pin, metal plate, or other shadow-casting object that is an integral part of a sundial. Forerunners of the sundial include poles or upright stones used as gnomons; pyramids and obelisks were so used in Egypt. Both stationary and portable sundials were probably developed in Egypt or in Mesopotamia. The earliest extant sundial, an Egyptian instrument of c.1500 B.C., is a flat stone on which is fixed an L-shaped bar whose short vertical limb casts a shadow measured by markings on the longer horizontal limb. The sundial was greatly improved (c.1st cent. A.D.) by setting the gnomon parallel to the earth's axis of rotation so that the apparent east-to-west motion of the sun governs the swing of the shadow. The development of trigonometry permitted precise calculations for the marking of dials and stimulated the advance of gnomonics (dial marking). Although watches and clocks came into popular use in the 18th cent., sundials were long employed for setting and checking them. The heliochronometer, a highly accurate instrument in which the shadow is cast by a fine wire, was used until c.1900 to set the watches of French railwaymen. Solar (or apparent) time indicated by sundials and clock (or mean) time are different and must be correlated by the use of tables showing daily variations in sun time. A correction must also be made for the difference in longitude between the position of a sundial and the standard time meridian of a given locality. Although sundials are still used in many areas, including Japan and China, they are regarded today chiefly as adornments. The largest sundial in the world, constructed c.1724 in Jaipur, India, covers almost one acre (.4 hectare) and has a gnomon over 100 ft (30 m) high surmounted by an observatory. Notable collections of sundials are at the Adler Planetarium, the Metropolitan Museum of Art, and the Harvard College Observatory. See F. W. Cousins, *Sundials* (1969); R. R. J. Rohr, *Sundials* (tr. 1970).

Sundsvall (sŭnts'väl''), city (1970 pop. 60,562), Västernorrland co., E Sweden, a major seaport on the Sundsvallfjärden, an arm of the Gulf of Bothnia. Manufactures include cellulose, metal goods, aluminum, and dairy products. Sundsvall was chartered in 1621. Its main industrial growth dates from the late 19th cent., when it also suffered (1888) a destructive fire.

sunfish, common name for members of the family Centrachidae, comprising numerous species of spiny-finned, freshwater fishes with deep, laterally flattened bodies found in temperate North America. All members of the family, which includes the black basses (genus *Micropterus*) and the crappies (genus *Pomoxis*), prefer fertile lakes with firm bottoms and build nests, which the males guard pugnaciously. The sunfishes, or breams, genus *Lepomis*, are smaller (¼ lb/.14 kg average) members indigenous to E North America but successfully introduced in the West. Common eastern varieties are the rock bass, the bluegill and green sunfishes, and the long-eared and common, or pumpkinseed, sunfishes, brilliantly colored with bright orange bellies. The redear and warmouth sunfishes are found in the Mississippi basin; the spotted sunfish, or stumpknocker, is a denizen of the South. The Sacramento perch is the only native western sunfish. The black basses, the most important and valuable of American freshwater game fishes, are longer bodied and larger (averaging 2–3 lb/.9–1.4 kg); they include the largemouth and smallmouth black basses and the spotted bass. The crappies are the largest sunfishes, attaining a length of 1 ft (2.5 cm) and a weight of 2 lb (.9 kg). There are two species, the white crappie (*P. annularis*) and the black crappie or calico bass (*P. nigro-maculatus*). The pigmy sunfishes, rarely over 1½ in. (3.8 cm) long, bear an uncertain relationship to the family and are classed separately. The totally unrelated ocean sunfish, or headfish, *Mola mola*, of the family Molidae, is allied to the PUFFER. Sunfishes are classified in the phylum CHORDATA, subphylum Vertebrata, class Osteichthyes, order Perciformes, family Centrachidae.

sunflower, any plant of the genus *Helianthus* of the family Compositae (COMPOSITE family), annual or perennial herbs native to the New World and common throughout the United States. In cultivation, the flower heads, commonly having yellow rays, sometimes reach 1 ft (30 cm) in diameter. The common sunflower (*H. annuus*) is an annual, native from Minnesota to Texas and California and perhaps also in Central and South America. The Indians cultivated the plant and found many uses for it: the nutritious seeds were eaten raw, made into a meal, or used as a source of hair oil; a yellow dye was obtained from the flower heads, and a fiber from the stalks; the roots of certain other species were eaten. Today the common sunflower is widely cultivated; it is particularly valued in the Soviet Union, where the seeds are made into bread. The seeds are almost universally used as a poultry food and as the source of an oil utilized for such purposes as cooking and soapmaking; the oil cake is fed to stock. The flowers are used for the production of nectar, and the leaves have been used for fodder. The common sunflower is the state flower of Kansas, and a sunflower is regarded as the floral emblem of Peru, where it was revered by the ancient sun worshipers. Several other species are in cultivation—some are garden flowers; the JERUSALEM ARTICHOKE is a food plant. Other plants are sometimes called sunflower. Sunflowers are classified in the division MAGNOLIOPHYTA, class Magnoliopsida, order Asterales, family Compositae.

Sung (so͝ong), dynasty of China that ruled 960–1279. The first emperor, CHAO K'UANG-YIN, consolidated several warring states and established a domain that, at its maximum, extended from the Great Wall in the north to Hainan island in the south. Even at its height, however, the Sung was not the military power that the T'ang had once been. Fear of a return to the warlordism that had ultimately destroyed the T'ang led the Sung government to a jealous move of overcentralizing military authority, hampering frontier generals. Hard pressed by the Jurchen and the Mongols, the Sung paid tribute to avert invasion. Despite its relative military weakness compared to the northern nomads, domestically the Sung created an autocratic state ruled by an elite civil service administration. Bureaucratic factionalism (see WANG AN-SHIH) arose replacing the military and aristocratic power struggles that had plagued earlier dynasties. Frequent policy shifts and purges of leadership resulted. The Sung dynasty was a period of great social and intellectual change. Literacy increased as a result of the spread of printing, and more men competed for office in the examination system. Confucian philosophy, revived and broadened by CHU HSI and others, triumphed over Buddhism and Taoism. Many new cities were built, the cultivation of tea and cotton became widespread, and gun powder was used for the first time. Internal trade was facilitated by building canals. There was much overseas commerce, especially with India and Persia, and voyages were made safer by advances in naval architecture and by the use of the magnetic compass. In the early, relatively stable period of the dynasty many scholarly works were produced, including encyclopedia compilations, critical histories, and scientific treatises. The main literary forms were the drama (however, no plays have survived without later alterations) and the picaresque novel (most notably *All Men Are Brothers*). The fine arts (except sculpture) flourished, and connoisseurs consider Sung landscapes the greatest achievement in Chinese painting. In 1126 the Jurchen seized the Yellow River valley including the capital at Kaifeng. The dynasty reestablished itself in central and S China, ruling from Hangchow until the Mongols conquered (1273–79) the entire country and established the Yuan dynasty. For a panoramic description of urban life in the last decades of the Sung, see Jacques Gernet, *Daily Life in China on the Eve of the Mongol Invasion, 1250–1276* (tr. 1970). See studies by Wolfram Eberhard (1965) and J. T. C. Liu (1969).

Sungari (so͝ong'gərē', so͞on'gä'rē'), Mandarin *Sunghwa,* river of NE China, c.1,150 mi (1,850 km) long, rising in the Ch'ang-pai mts., Kirin prov., and flowing generally north, through Heilungkiang prov., to the Amur River on the China-USSR border. It is the northernmost river system in China and forms a main gateway to the S Manchurian plain. The Sungari, which passes the cities of Kirin and Harbin, is navigable for most of its length, and it is an important trade artery in a rich agricultural region. Fengman Dam (completed 1946) was built by the Japanese above Kirin and forms a huge reservoir.

Sungaria: see DZUNGARIA, China.

Sung Chiao-jen (so͝ong jēou-jŭn), 1882–1913, Chinese revolutionary and political leader. He was a founding member (1905) and a leading activist in the Revolutionary Alliance (see SUN YAT-SEN), an organization dedicated to overthrowing the Manchu dynasty in favor of a republic. After the republican revolution of 1911, Sung guided the Revolutionary Alliance into a merger with several parliamentary parties to form the KUOMINTANG, or Nationalist party. The parliamentary majority achieved by the Kuomintang in the elections of 1912–13 was largely due to Sung's superb organizing ability. He advocated a party cabinet to check the power of the first president, YUAN SHIH-K'AI. Sung was assassinated, allegedly at the instigation of Yuan.

Sungkiang (so͝ong'gyäng', -jēäng'), Mandarin *Sungchiang,* former province (c.32,000 sq mi/82,880 sq km), NE China. Mutankiang (Mu-tan-chiang) was the capital. It was one of nine provinces created in Manchuria by the Chinese Nationalist government after World War II. Since the Nationalists never gained effective control of Manchuria, the province existed only on paper. It was bordered on the E by the USSR, and along part of the southern border ran the Nonni (Nen Chiang) and Sungari rivers. In 1954, Sungkiang became part of Heilungkiang prov.

sun god: see SUN WORSHIP.

sun grebe, common name for a tropical, mainly aquatic bird of the family Heliornithidae. Sun grebes, also called finfoots, are remarkable for their colorful, puffy-toed, webbed feet, which may serve as lures for fish and other aquatic animals. They are good divers and hunt, either swimming partially submerged or from low perches. Their diet consists mainly of small aquatic animals, but they are also known to eat some plant matter. They have elongate bodies, about 12 to 20 in. (30.5–51 cm) long, and necks with long and pointed, grebelike bills. However, they are not related to the true grebe. Shy and solitary creatures, sun grebes are found singly or in pairs, typically in the vicinity of densely wooded pools and streams, and little is known of their habits. Once widely distributed, they are now limited to three species. The largest of these is the Asian sun grebe (*Heliopais personata*) measuring up to 20 in. (51 cm) in length, and found from Bengal to Malaya and Sumatra. Its body is olive-brown above, with a black head and throat, a yellow bill, and bright green legs with white stripes. At 16 in. (41 cm), the African finfoot (*Podica senegalis*) is dark brown with black and white spots above, a white belly, and bright red feet and legs. It is thought to be more of a climber than the other species. Only a third to a quarter as bulky as the Asian sun grebe and measuring less than 12 in. (30 cm) in length is the American sun grebe (*Heliornis fulica*) of South and Central America. Its plumage is colored similarly to that of the Asian sun grebe, but it is scarlet-billed with yellow, black-striped legs. All three species are marked by a white band running from eye to neck. Sun grebes build their nests from grass and reed, on platforms away from water. The female lays from two to five white, red-and-buff streaked eggs per clutch. Sun grebes are classified in the phylum CHORDATA, subphylum Vertebrata, class Aves, order Gruiformes, family Heliornithidae.

suni: see ANTELOPE.

Sunni (so͝o'nī) [Arab. *Sunna,*=tradition], in ISLAM, adherents of the chief branch of the Muslims, called traditionalist or orthodox. The Sunni comprise about 85% of all Muslims. They differ from the SHIITES, the other major division of Islam, in accepting as authoritative the traditions (Sunna) of Muhammad and in approving the historic order of succession of the first four successors of Muhammad. The Shiites maintain that the fourth of them, ALI, should have been the first. Claims to sovereign political rights in later times have been based on one side or the other of this dispute. Most of the Muslims of Turkey, the Middle East, Afghanistan, and Africa are Sunni. Differences in ritual and law divide the Sunni into the four orthodox rites, the Hanafites, the Malikites, the Shafites, and the Hanbalites.

Sunnyvale, city (1970 pop. 95,408), Santa Clara co., W Calif., near San Francisco; settled 1849, inc. 1912. Its manufactures include electronic and electrical equipment, food products, pharmaceuticals, and paper products. Moffet Field Naval Air Station is in Sunnyvale.

Sunset Crater National Monument: see NATIONAL PARKS AND MONUMENTS (table).

sunspots, dark, usually irregularly shaped spots on the sun's surface that are actually solar magnetic storms. Since the introduction of the telescope c.1610 they have been objects of study. The temperature of the spots is lower than that of the surrounding photosphere; thus the spots are, by contrast, darker. All but the smallest show a dark central portion (the umbra) with a lighter outer area (the penumbra). Studies of the spectra of sunspots show evidence of the ZEEMAN EFFECT, thus indicating the presence of a large magnetic field. In addition, measurements of the DOPPLER EFFECT in the spectral lines show that there is a vortex motion in sunspots similar to that of a tornado on earth. The lower temperature of the gases constituting a sunspot results from the lower pressure due to the spinning magnetic field. Sunspots appear usually only between latitudes from 5° to 35° north and south of the sun's equator. Sunspots are not permanent since the sun's surface is gaseous. Because the sun rotates on its axis, a sunspot cannot be observed continuously for more than about two weeks. Since about the middle of the 19th cent. it has been recognized that periods of great sunspot activity come in cycles. An 11-year cycle from one period of maximum activity to the next is usually observed. However, a period during which most sunspots have one magnetic polarity is followed by another period during which most have the opposite magnetic polarity; thus, the cycle may actually cover 22 years. During each 11-year period sunspots appear first at higher latitudes and later at latitudes closer to the solar equator as the cycle progresses. The spots often form in pairs or groups, with a large, long-lived leader spot matched with one or more smaller spots of opposite magnetic polarity. A number of phenomena are associated with sunspots. Periods in which an increase of sunspots is observed are called active periods; the terms "active sun" and "quiet sun" refer to periods of greater or lesser sunspot activity. During periods of sunspot activity various disturbances are produced on earth—these include magnetic storms, interference with radio reception, and disturbances of the magnetic compass.

sunstroke: see HEATSTROKE.

Sun-tzu (so͞on-dzo͞o), fl. c.6th cent. B.C., Chinese general and military theorist. Sun-tzu lived during a period of expanding interstate feudal conflict. His sophisticated treatise on strategy, tactics, logistics, and espionage, known as *The Art of War,* deeply influenced traditional Chinese military science. See *The Art of War* (tr. by S. B. Griffith, 1969).

Sun Valley, mountain resort city (1970 pop. 180), alt. c.6,000 ft (1,830 m), Blaine co., S central Idaho; inc. 1967. It is a popular year-round resort with both winter and summer sports. It was founded as a ski resort in 1936 by W. Averell Harriman (then chairman of the board of the Union Pacific RR) after an extensive search for an ideal site. The railroad purchased 4,300 acres (1,740 hectares) near the declining mining village of Ketchum and built the resort as a means of attracting more passenger traffic to the West. In 1964 it was sold to a land development corporation, and in 1967 Bill Janss, a former Olympic skier, became sole owner. The Hemingway Memorial, on a bluff overlooking a swift-flowing trout stream, was dedicated in 1966.

sun worship. Deification and adoration of the sun occurred primarily in agrarian societies. When man became a farmer, and thus dependent upon daily and seasonal changes of weather, he often turned to worship the great force that regulated these changes—the light and heat of the sun. The worship of the sun, although not peculiar to any one time or place, received its greatest prominence in ancient Egypt. There, the daily birth, journey, and death of the sun was the dominating feature of life. One of the most important gods of Egyptian religion was Ra, the sun-god, who was considered the first king of Egypt. The pharaoh, said to be the son of Ra, was the sun-god's representative on earth. In later Egyptian religion, under the rule of Ikhnaton, the sun-god Aton gained complete supremacy in what was Egypt's only monotheistic period. In Mesopotamia, where sun worship was also very important, the sun-god Shamash was a major deity and was equated with justice. In Greece there were two sun deities, Apollo and Helios, although there was no institutionalized form of sun worship. The influence of the sun in religious belief also appears in Zoroastrianism, Mithraism, Roman religion, Hinduism, Buddhism, and among the Druids of England, the Aztecs of Mexico, and many American Indians.

Sunwui: see HSIN-HUI, China.

sunyata (sho͞on'yətə) [Skt.,=emptiness], one of the main tenets of Mahayana BUDDHISM, first presented by the Perfection of Wisdom (*Prajna-paramita*) scriptures (1st cent. B.C. on) and later systematized by the MADHYAMIKA school. Early Buddhist schools of ABHIDHARMA, or scholastic metaphysics, analyzed reality into ultimate entities, or DHARMAS, arising and ceasing in irreducible moments in time. The Mahayanists reacted against this realistic pluralism by stating that all *dharmas* are "empty," without self-nature (*svabhava*) or essence. This was a radical restatement of the central Buddhist teaching of non-self (*anatman*). It was declared that not only ordinary objects, but the Buddha, NIRVANA, and also emptiness itself are all "empty." The teaching attempts to eradicate mental attachment and the perception of duality, which, since it is a basis for aversion to bondage in birth-and-death (*samsara*) and desire for nirvana, may obstruct the *bodhisattva's* compassionate vow to save all beings before entering nirvana himself. Wisdom (*prajna*), or direct insight into emptiness, is the sixth perfection (*paramita*) of a *bodhisattva*. It is stressed by both Buddhist writers and Western scholars that emptiness is not an entity nor a metaphysical or cosmological absolute, nor is it nothingness or annihilation. "Empty" things are neither existent or nonexistent, and their true nature is thus called not only emptiness but also suchness (*tathata*). See Edward Conze, *Buddhist Wisdom Books* (1958). F. J. Streng, *Emptiness* (1967).

Sun Yat-sen (so͝on yät-sĕn), Mandarin *Sun Wen,* 1866–1925, Chinese revolutionary. He was born near Canton of a farm-owning family. He attended (1879-82) an Anglican boys school in Honolulu, where he came under Western influence, particularly that of Christianity. In 1892 he received a diploma from a Hong Kong medical school, and he subsequently practiced medicine in that city. Thereafter all his activities were devoted to overthrowing the Ch'ing dynasty and establishing a stable Chinese republic. He fled China in 1895, after an abortive revolt, and then toured the world several times to enlist the aid of overseas Chinese in financing his activities. In that period he made an intensive study of Western political and social theory and was deeply impressed with the writings of Karl Marx and Henry George. Sun organized (1905) a revolutionary league, the T'ung Meng Hui, in Japan and gradually perfected his political conceptions, which were based on the Three People's Principles: nationalism, democracy, and the people's livelihood. Revolution erupted in China, and Sun was elected provisional president of the Chinese republic in Dec., 1911, but two months later he resigned in favor of YÜAN SHIH-K'AI. Later, when Sung Chiao-jen transformed the T'ung Meng Hui into a federated political party called the KUOMINTANG, Sun served as its director. Meanwhile, opposition developed to Yüan's dictatorial methods; in 1913 Sun led an unsuccessful revolt against Yüan, and he was forced to seek asylum in Japan, where he reorganized the Kuomintang. He returned to China in 1917, and in 1921 he was elected president of a self-proclaimed national government at Canton in S China. To develop the military power needed for the NORTHERN EXPEDITION against the militarists at Peking, he established the Whampoa Military Academy, with CHIANG KAI-SHEK as its commandant and with such party leaders as WANG CHING-WEI and HU HAN-MIN as political instructors. In 1924, to hasten the conquest of China, he began a policy of active cooperation with the Chinese Communists and he accepted the help of the USSR in reorganizing the Kuomintang. After his death, when the Communists and the Kuomintang split (1927), each group claimed to be his true heirs. The official veneration of Sun's memory (especially in the Kuomintang) was a virtual cult, which centered around his tomb in Nanking. His widow, the former Soong Ch'ing-ling (see SOONG, family), whom he married in 1914, rose to a high position in the government of Communist China. He wrote *San Min Chu I* (tr. 1928), *Memoirs of a Chinese Revolutionary* (1927, repr. 1970), and *Fundamentals of National Reconstruction* (tr. 1953). See biographies by Lyon Sharman (1934) and B. D. Martin (1952); L. S. Hsu, *Sun Yat-sen, His Political and Social Ideals: A Sourcebook* (1933); S. C. Leng and N. D. Palmer, *Sun Yat-sen and Communism* (1960); H. Z. Schiffrin, *Sun Yat-sen and the Origins of the Chinese Revolution* (1970).

superconductivity, abnormally high electrical conductivity of certain substances when they are cooled to temperatures near absolute zero. The property is displayed by some metals, including zinc, magnesium, lead, gray tin, aluminum, mercury, and cadmium. Other metals, such as molybdenum, may exhibit superconductivity after high purification. Alloys (e.g., two parts of gold to one part of bismuth) and such compounds as tungsten carbide and lead sulfide may also be superconductors. Thin films of normal metals and superconductors that are brought into contact can form superconductive electronic devices, which replace transistors in some applications. An interesting aspect of the phenomenon is the continued flow of current in a superconducting circuit after the source of current has been shut off: for example, if a lead ring is immersed in liquid helium, an electric current that is induced magnetically will continue to flow after the removal of the magnetic field. Powerful electromagnets, which, once energized, retain magnetism virtually indefinitely, have been developed using several superconductors. The phenomenon of superconductivity was discovered in 1911 by Kamerlingh Onnes. The 1972 Nobel prize in physics was awarded to J. Bardeen, L. Cooper, and S. Schrieffer for their BCS theory of superconductivity. This quantum mechanical theory proposes that at very low temperatures electrons in an electric current move in pairs. Such pairing enables them to move through a crystal lattice without having their motion disrupted by collisions with the lattice.

superego: see PSYCHOANALYSIS.

superfluidity, tendency of liquid helium below a temperature of 2.19°K to flow freely, even upward, with little apparent friction. Helium becomes a liquid when it is cooled to 4.2°K. Special methods are needed to cool a substance below this temperature, which is very near absolute zero (see KELVIN TEMPERATURE SCALE; LOW-TEMPERATURE PHYSICS). When the temperature reaches 2.19°K, the properties of liquid helium change abruptly, so much so that ordinary helium is known as helium I and helium below this temperature is known as helium II. The transition temperature between helium I and helium II is known as the lambda point because a graph of certain properties of helium takes a sharp turn at this temperature and resembles the Greek letter lambda (Λ). Liquid helium II flows easily through capillary tubes that resist the flow of ordinary fluids (see CAPILLARITY) and a DEWAR FLASK filled with helium II from a larger container will empty itself back into the original container because the liquid helium flows spontaneously in an invisible film over the surface of the flask. The behavior of helium II can be partially understood in terms of certain quantum effects (see QUANTUM THEORY). Helium stays a liquid down to absolute zero because its zero-point energy is such that it cannot become a solid without giving up an amount of energy that is less than that allowed by the quantum theory. Similarly, quantum restrictions keep helium II from behaving like a normal fluid because the energy interactions associated with friction and viscosity in normal fluid flow involve amounts not possible for helium II.

supergiant star: see RED GIANT.

superheterodyne: see RADIO.

Superior, city (1970 pop. 32,237), seat of Douglas co., NW Wis., on Superior Bay of Lake Superior, at the mouths of the St. Louis and the Nemadji rivers; inc. 1883. It is a railroad center and port of entry. Its superb natural harbor, shared with Duluth, Minn., has some of the nation's largest coal and ore docks. In tonnage handled it is second only to Chicago on the Great Lakes and ranks high among the ports in the nation. Superior has shipyards, huge grain elevators, an oil refinery, and a large dairy products industry. The area was visited by the French explorers Radisson (1661) and Duluth (1679). The city grew after iron ore was discovered (1880s) in the Gogebic range. The Univ. of Wisconsin at Superior is there.

Superior, Lake, largest freshwater lake in the world, 31,820 sq mi (82,414 sq km), 350 mi (563 km) long and 160 mi (257 km) at its greatest width, bordered on the W by NE Minnesota, on the N and E by Ontario, Canada, and on the S by NW Michigan and NW Wisconsin; largest, highest, and deepest of the GREAT LAKES, having a surface elevation of 602 ft (183 m) and a maximum depth of 1,302 ft (397 m). Lake Superior drains into Lake Huron through the St. Marys River and receives the waters of many short, swift-flowing streams including the Nipigon, Kaministikwia, St. Louis, and Pigeon rivers. The largest islands are Isle Royale, Isle St. Ignace, and Simpson and Michipicoten islands. The shoreline is irregular (with many large bays, inlets, and peninsulas) and in places is high and rocky. The waters of Lake Superior are generally purer than those of the lower lakes and are only locally polluted; a U.S.-Canadian pact (1972) seeks to prevent further pollution and to maintain and improve the water's quality. Commercial and sport fishing are important. Lake Superior is part of the Great Lakes–St. Lawrence Seaway system, and it is reached by oceangoing and lake vessels through the Sault Ste Marie canals, which bypass rapids in the St. Marys River. The principal cargoes are grain from the Canadian prairies and iron ore and pellets obtained from the Mesabi Range and other nearby areas. The lake does not freeze completely, but ice impedes navigation from mid-December to the end of March at the lake's outlet and from early December to the end of April in harbors on the south shore. Fog and rough water are hazards. The chief Canadian urban areas on the lake are Michipicoten and Thunder Bay. The principal cities on the more populated U.S. shore are Marquette, Superior, Ashland, and Duluth. Recreational facilities are found on Isle Royale (part of a U.S. national park), in Pukaskwa National Park (Ontario), and at state and provincial parks on the lake's shores and islands; the U.S. Apostle Islands and Pictured Rocks national lakeshores are there. Étienne Brulé, the French explorer, probably discovered the lake in 1616; Pierre Radisson and the sieur des Groseilliers visited it in 1659-60; Father Allouez established (1665) a mission near Ashland; and the sieur Duluth visited the lake in 1678-79. See Charles Steinhacker, *Superior* (1970); bibliography by Water Resources Scientific Information Center (1972).

superior planet, planet whose orbit lies outside that of the earth. The superior planets are Mars, Jupiter, Saturn, Uranus, Neptune, and Pluto.

supernova, exploding star that suddenly increases its energy output as much as a billionfold and then slowly fades to less than its original brightness. At peak intensity, it can outshine the entire galaxy in which it occurs. Novas are less spectacular and more common; they increase in brightness only by a few thousand times, and dozens occur in our galaxy every year. Only 50 supernovas have been observed in recorded history; of these, only 3 have occurred in our galaxy; the "guest star" in Taurus described by Chinese astronomers in 1054; Tycho's star in Cassiopeia, observed by Tycho Brahe in 1572; and Kepler's supernova, which occurred in 1604. In 1885 the first extragalactic supernova was discovered telescopically in the ANDROMEDA GALAXY. The causes of supernovas have been studied extensively. It is believed that supernovas represent a catastrophic stage of STELLAR EVOLUTION that occurs for all but the least massive stars. The star has exhausted its nuclear energy and begins to contract. The collapse of the inner core sends out a shock wave that reverses the initial contraction of the outer layers and violently ejects them from the star. As much as 10% of the star is flung out into space at speeds exceeding 8,000 km per sec. The theory of stellar structure predicts that the heavy elements are created in the interior of the star by nuclear reactions. The spewing forth of matter from a supernova distributes the heavy elements in the INTERSTELLAR MATTER, where metal-rich stars can then condense. After the supernova explosion, there remains a small, hot core surrounded by an incandescent expanding cloud, such as that seen in the CRAB NEBULA.

superphosphate or **superphosphate of lime,** compound produced by treating rock phosphate with sulfuric acid or phosphoric acid, or a mixture of the two; it is the principal carrier of phosphate, the form of phosphorus usable by plants, in fertilizers. Ordinary superphosphate contains about 20% available phosphate; double superphosphate (also called treble superphosphate) contains 40%–50% available phosphate.

supersonic speed: see AERODYNAMICS.

supersonic transport: see AIRPLANE.

superstition, an irrational belief or practice resulting from ignorance or fear of the unknown. The validity of superstitions is based on belief in the power of magic and witchcraft and in such invisible forces as spirits and demons. A common superstition in the Middle Ages was that the devil could enter a person during that unguarded moment when that person was sneezing; this could be avoided if anyone present immediately appealed to the name of God. The tradition of saying "God bless you" when someone sneezes still remains today.

Supervielle, Jules (zhül süpĕrvyĕl'), 1884–1960, French author, b. Uruguay. His life was divided between Montevideo, where he was born, and Paris, where he was educated. The freshness and originality of his works are often attributed to his South American background. His stories treat grand subjects with everyday simplicity, making much use of fantasy, allegory, and myth. Among his works are the novels *L'Homme de la pampa* (1923) and *Le Survivant* (1928); volumes of short stories including *L'Enfant de la haute mer* (1931) and *Le Petit Bos* (1942); plays such as *Bolivar* (1936); and volumes of poetry including *Poemes de la France malheureuse* (1941). See his *Selected Writings* (tr. 1967).

Supilo, Frano (frä'nō sŏŏpē'lō), 1870–1917, Croatian journalist and politician. A member of the Hungarian parliament, Supilo led Croatian opposition to Magyar domination before World War I. A member of the Yugoslav Committee established in London during the war, he toured the Allied capitals promoting his conception of a South Slavic state. Before his death he approved the Pact of Corfu (1917), which laid the basis for the state of Yugoslavia.

Suppé, Franz von (fränts fən zŏŏp'ā), 1819–95, Austrian composer, b. Split, Dalmatia. His operettas were among the best by Viennese composers and rivaled Offenbach's in popularity. He wrote many works including *Poet and Peasant* (1846), the overture of which has remained popular. His *Light Cavalry Overture* is frequently performed.

supply and demand, in classical economics, factors that are said to determine price and that, widely interpreted, may be thought of as the forces guiding economic life in an economy based on private property. Supply refers to the varying amounts of a good that producers will supply at different prices; in general, a higher price yields a greater supply. Demand refers to the quantity of a good that is demanded by consumers at any given price. According to the law of demand, demand decreases as the price rises. In a perfectly competitive economy, the combination of the upward-sloping supply curve and the downward-sloping demand curve yields a supply and demand schedule that, at the intersection of the two curves, reveals the equilibrium price of an item. In reality, however, monopoly elements, government regulation, and many other factors combine to limit the effect of supply and demand, even in capitalist economies. See P. B. Trescott, *The Logic of the Price System* (1970); R. B. Ekelund, *The Evolution of Modern Demand Theory* (1972).

suprarenal gland: see ADRENAL GLAND.

suprematism, Russian art movement founded (1913) by Casimir Malevich in Moscow, parallel to CONSTRUCTIVISM. Malevich drew Alexander Rodchenko and El Lissitsky (1890–1947) to his revolutionary, nonobjective art. In Malevich's words, suprematism sought "to liberate art from the ballast of the representational world." It consisted of geometrical shapes flatly painted on the pure canvas surface. Malevich's white square on a white ground (Mus. of Modern Art, New York City) embodied the movement's principles. Suprematism, through its dissemination by the BAUHAUS, deeply influenced the development of modern European art, architecture, and industrial design.

Supreme Court, United States, highest court of the United States, established by Article 3 of the Constitution of the United States. Section 1 of Article 3 provides for vesting the judicial power of the United States in one supreme court and in such inferior courts as Congress establishes. Furthermore all Federal judges retain their office during "good behavior" (only in one instance—that of Justice Samuel CHASE in 1805—were impeachment proceedings ever brought against a member of the Supreme Court). A judge's compensation may not be reduced during his term of office. Section 2 defines the scope of U.S. judicial power and establishes the jurisdiction of the Supreme Court. The judicial power extends to all cases arising under the Constitution, laws, and treaties of the United States; to cases concerning foreign diplomats and admiralty practice; and to diversity cases (those between citizens of different states) and cases in which the United States or a state is a party (however, the Eleventh Amendment, adopted in 1798, forbids Federal cognizance of cases brought against a state by citizens of another state or by citizens of a foreign state). The cases in which the Supreme Court has original jurisdiction—i.e., where another court need not first consider the controversy—are those in which diplomats or a state is a party; even here, it has been held, inferior courts may enjoy concomitant jurisdiction. In all other Federal cases the Supreme Court exercises appellate jurisdiction, but subject to all limitations and regulations made by Congress. Members of the court are appointed by the President with the advice and consent of the Senate. The size of the Supreme Court is not prescribed by the Constitution; it is set by statute. The court began in 1789 with 6 members and was increased to 7 in 1807, to 9 in 1837, and to 10 in 1863. In 1866 the membership was reduced to 8 to prevent President Andrew Johnson from filling any vacancies. Since 1869 the court has comprised 9 members. By early 1975, a total of 101 men had sat on the bench. Four had served both as Associate Justice and as Chief Justice; they were John RUTLEDGE (appointed Chief Justice in 1795 but never confirmed by the Senate), Edward D. WHITE (appointed to the court in 1894 and Chief Justice from 1910 to 1921), Charles Evans HUGHES (an Associate Justice from 1910 to 1916, he served as Chief Justice from 1930 to 1941), and Harlan F. STONE (appointed to the court in 1925 and Chief Justice from 1941 to 1946). There are regularly two annual terms of court, one in October and one in March. Five justices constitute a quorum to hear a case, and decision is rendered by majority vote. In the event of a tie the previous judgment is affirmed. Under the Judiciary Law as amended in 1934, cases are usually brought to the court by appeal or by writ of certiorari. The appeal procedure is used when the highest state court has declared that a U.S. statute is unconstitutional or that a state statute does not violate the U.S. Constitution, laws, or treaties. If a lower Federal court rules that a U.S. statute is unconstitutional, the government may prosecute an immediate appeal. Certiorari is granted at the court's discretion, with most applications refused. It may be used to review the constitutional decisions of state courts of last resort and Federal decisions on any important matter, especially when the inferior courts are in disagreement. The Supreme Court has basically a dual function. On the one hand it must interpret and expound all congressional enactments brought before it in proper cases; in this respect its role parallels that of the state courts of final resort in making the decisive interpretation of state law. On the other hand the Supreme Court has power (superseding that of all other courts) to examine Federal and state statutes and executive actions to determine whether they conform to the U.S. Constitution. When the court rules against the constitutionality of a statute or an executive action, its decision can be overcome only if the Constitution is amended or if the court later overrules itself or modifies its previous opinion. Thus, in the U.S. governmental system the Supreme Court potentially wields the highest power. The decisions, of course, are not confined to the specific cases but also are intended to guide legislatures and the executive authority; thereby they mold the development of law. In no other country does the highest court possess such far-reaching power, for all other national legislatures may enact statutes without fear that the judiciary will refuse to enforce them on the grounds of unconstitutionality. The Supreme Court, however, has found many constitutional limitations on its powers and has voluntarily adopted others so as not to interfere unduly with the other branches of government or with the states. Thus, the court long eschewed political disputes, i.e., issues that are considered to be policy matters of legislative or executive authorities. However, in 1962 the court, over protests that it was entering a "political thicket," ruled in BAKER VS. CARR that the legislatures of several states must correct the imbalance in representation between rural and urban areas. The court refuses to confine in any way the power of the President over foreign affairs. Self-imposed restraints include consideration of a constitutional issue only if the case cannot be considered on other grounds and the formulation of constitutional decisions in the narrowest terms. The court prefers even a strained interpretation of a statute if it may thereby be found constitutional. The history of the Supreme Court reflects the development of the U.S. economy, the alteration of political views, and the evolution of the Federal structure. In its earliest years the court had little business to transact. Much of the justices' time was consumed in appearing on the Federal courts of appeal in the judicial circuits assigned to them. This obligation of circuit riding was later to interfere seriously with the performance of the court's more important business. For the most part the full bench—sitting first in New York City, then in Philadelphia, finally in Washington—was a court of last resort in admiralty cases and in cases arising out of diversity of citizenship. The court somewhat later decided (in 1842 in *Swift* vs. *Tyson*) that in diversity suits it would follow not state law but a presumed Federal common law. The status of the Supreme Court was somewhat uncertain until the tenure (1801–35) of John Marshall, the "great Chief Justice." Marshall, a strong Federalist, in MARBURY VS. MADISON established the principle of judicial review, i.e., the right of all courts to refuse the enforcement of unconstitutional enactments of Congress. The same power in regard to state laws was asserted in the opinion of MARTIN VS. HUNTER'S LESSEE (1816) delivered by Justice Joseph STORY. In other opinions, Marshall further strengthened the Federalist position as against those who espoused STATES' RIGHTS. This is seen notably in MCCULLOCH VS. MARYLAND (1819), which, by holding the creation of the second National Bank a legitimate power of Congress, gave judicial sanction to Alexander Hamilton's loose interpretation of the Constitution and broadened the powers of the Federal government over matters of decisive economic importance; and in GIBBONS VS. OGDEN (1824), which confirmed the power of Congress to regulate commerce. Also of sweeping importance was Marshall's decision in the DARTMOUTH COLLEGE CASE (1819), which protected the contract clause of the Constitution from impairment by state legislatures. Marshall's successor as Chief Justice, Roger B. Taney, instead of continuing a strong policy of building Federal strength, abandoned some of the strong nationalism of Marshall and the court recognized to some extent the extreme states' rights position advocated by John C. Calhoun and others. However, in the DRED SCOTT CASE, Taney made what many persons considered an unwarranted limitation of Federal authority in forbidding Congress to prohibit slavery in the territories. So violent was the reaction of antislavery forces to the decision that in the North the prestige of the court declined greatly. The low point in the judiciary's estate came during the Civil War when Taney's challenge of President Lincoln's power to suspend habeas corpus was ignored by the President and denounced by the Northern press (see MERRYMAN, EX PARTE). The end of the Civil War to 1937 encompasses the second great period in the history of the court. After the adoption (1868) of the FOURTEENTH AMENDMENT the character of litigation before the court was altered, and there were many cases alleging that state legislation took liberty or property without due process of law or denied equal protection of the laws. In the late 19th cent. the flood of litigation arising from a wide variety of causes was delaying the disposition of cases up to three years. Relief was imperative, and finally, in 1891, Congress created the circuit courts of appeals to give a final hearing to most appeals and excused the justices from riding circuit (however, each justice still heads one or more circuits). In the early 20th cent. the court to many seemed highly conservative in its views. It showed in general a rigid adherence to *stare decisis* (the rule that precedents are to be followed), a tendency to prevent the states from adopting laws that restricted business in its employment practices and other activities, and little disposition to restrain the states from restricting civil liberties. In the Insular Cases (1901), arising out of questions concerning the status of peoples in the territories acquired as a result of the Spanish American War, the court asserted that the civil rights guaranteed by the Constitution did not automatically apply to the people of an annexed territory, i.e., the Constitution did not follow the flag. In one notable case, *Muller* vs. *Oregon* (1908), the court departed from its conservative stand to uphold a state law limiting the maximum working hours of women. The case was unique in that Louis D. BRANDEIS, counsel for the state, and later to become a distinguished member of the court, eschewed the traditional legal arguments and showed with overwhelming evidence from physicians, factory inspectors, and social workers that the number of hours women worked affected their health and morale. A third great period of constitutional history began after President Franklin Delano Roosevelt came to office and Congress passed economic legislation of a far-reaching and novel character. Soon the new laws were attacked on various constitutional grounds, e.g., that they were unwarranted delegations of legislative power to the President and interfered in the exclusive power of the states over intrastate commerce. From 1935 to 1937 the court struck down such major pieces of New Deal legislation as the National Industrial Recovery Act (in the Schechter Poultry Case), the Agricultural Adjustment Act, and the Bituminous Coal Act. Some of the laws were condemned by five-to-four decisions. Unalterably in the conservative camp were Pierce Butler, James McReynolds, George Sutherland, and Willis Van Devanter. The liberals (and supporters for the most part of New Deal legislation) were Benjamin N. Cardozo, Brandeis, and Harlan F. Stone. In the center were Chief Justice Hughes and Owen J. Roberts. Roosevelt, who had not appointed a single justice, was determined to change the composition of the court and proposed (Feb., 1937) a measure designed to displace the "nine old men" and to infuse the bench with "new blood" of his choosing. His plan—which even his opponents conceded was probably constitutional—was to provide retirement at full pay for all members of the court over 70; if a justice refused to retire, an "assistant" with full voting rights was to be appointed. In no case might there be more than 15 justices. The majority in Congress, which characterized the scheme as "packing the court," prevented it from ever coming up for a vote, and it was abandoned in July. In April, however, Hughes and Roberts joined the liberal group, thus giving the New Deal a precarious majority of one. By five-to-four votes the National Labor Relations Act and the Social Security Act were upheld. The majority justified these and other decisions by pointing out that the scope of Federal legislation had to expand because the growing interdependence of the country made local economic legislation of little value. The court also enunciated the novel view that in acting under the "general welfare" clause of Article 1, Section 8, of the Constitution, Congress was not limited to carrying out its express powers as listed in Article 1 but might pursue any objective. Congress was thus given a vast new range of legislative power free of Supreme Court censure. In 1938 the court took another revolutionary step in overruling *Swift* vs. *Tyson*. The doctrine of a Federal common law was repudiated, and in handling diversity suits the Federal courts were directed to use state law. While in this case the Supreme Court limited the scope of Federal activity, it took certain steps in the opposite direction. In the conflict of laws (juristic relations between states) it announced many new principles, and it forbade even limited state taxation of Federal facilities but offered Congress fairly wide scope to tax various state-supported activities. The court of the 1940s, with seven appointments by Roosevelt, was not more unified than its predecessor of the 30s. On the contrary, the percentage of dissents and of special opinions was greater than at any previous time. There was less public concern, however, since the court did not invalidate major legislation, while the diverse views of its members on technical subjects—antitrust and patent law, conflict of laws, taxation—mainly concerned lawyers and business. In the 1950s the court found itself more and more concerned with the constitutional rights of the individual. Freedom of speech and other civil liberty issues were repeatedly brought before the court during this period of concern over internal subversion. Similarly, Congressional interrogation practices, state sedition laws, and other questionable methods used by the authorities in uncovering Communists in and out of government came under severe scrutiny near the end of the decade. The court's willingness to hold the constitutional guarantees of free speech and due process as above the alleged needs of internal security brought strong criticism from conservative jurists and led to attempts in Congress to curb the court's jurisdiction. By the late 1950s a fairly clear division on civil liberties had been established on the court. One wing, often called the judicial pacifists, seemed to feel with its leader, Felix FRANKFURTER, that legislation and inquiries concerning internal security should be given the benefit of doubt despite infringements of personal liberty. The court should avoid the role of policy making. The judicial activist wing led by Justices Hugo L. BLACK and William O. DOUGLAS felt that the freedoms guaranteed by the Bill of Rights are absolute and should be considered beyond the power of Congress or the executive to modify. This group argued that it was the duty of the court to shape the law to meet the needs of its own generation. However, in civil rights litigation the court closed ranks in 1954,

SUPREME COURT JUSTICES (*including dates on bench*)

Chief Justices	
John Jay, 1789–95	Edward D. White, 1910–21
John Rutledge, 1795	William H. Taft, 1921–30
Oliver Ellsworth, 1796–1800	Charles E. Hughes, 1930–41
John Marshall, 1801–35	Harlan F. Stone, 1941–46
Roger B. Taney, 1836–64	Fred M. Vinson, 1946–53
Salmon P. Chase, 1864–73	Earl Warren, 1953–69
Morrison R. Waite, 1874–88	Warren E. Burger, 1969–
Melville W. Fuller, 1888–1910	

Associate Justices	
John Rutledge, 1789–91	Henry B. Brown, 1891–1906
William Cushing, 1789–1810	George Shiras, Jr., 1892–1903
James Wilson, 1789–98	Howell E. Jackson, 1893–95
John Blair, 1789–96	Edward D. White, 1894–1910
Robert H. Harrison, 1789–90	Rufus W. Peckham, 1896–1909
James Iredell, 1790–99	Joseph McKenna, 1898–1925
Thomas Johnson, 1791–93	Oliver W. Holmes, 1902–32
William Paterson, 1793–1806	William R. Day, 1903–22
Samuel Chase, 1796–1811	William H. Moody, 1906–10
Bushrod Washington, 1798–1829	Horace H. Lurton, 1910–14
Alfred Moore, 1799–1804	Charles E. Hughes, 1910–16
William Johnson, 1804–34	Willis Van Devanter, 1911–37
Henry Brockholst Livingston, 1806–23	Joseph R. Lamar, 1911–16
Thomas Todd, 1807–26	Mahlon Pitney, 1912–22
Gabriel Duval, 1811–36	James C. McReynolds, 1914–41
Joseph Storey, 1811–45	Louis D. Brandeis, 1916–39
Smith Thompson, 1823–43	John H. Clarke, 1916–22
Robert Trimble, 1826–28	George Sutherland, 1922–38
John McLean, 1829–61	Pierce Butler, 1923–39
Henry Baldwin, 1830–44	Edward T. Sanford, 1923–30
James M. Wayne, 1835–67	Harlan F. Stone, 1925–41
Philip P. Barbour, 1836–41	Owen J. Roberts, 1930–45
John Catron, 1837–65	Benjamin N. Cardozo, 1932–38
John McKinley, 1837–52	Hugo Black, 1937–71
Peter V. Daniel, 1841–60	Stanley F. Reed, 1938–57
Samuel Nelson, 1845–72	Felix Frankfurter, 1939–62
Levi Woodbury, 1845–51	William O. Douglas, 1939–
Robert C. Grier, 1846–70	Frank Murphy, 1940–49
Benjamin R. Curtis, 1851–57	James F. Byrnes, 1941–42
John A. Campbell, 1853–61	Robert H. Jackson, 1941–54
Nathan Clifford, 1858–81	Wiley B. Rutledge, 1943–49
Noah H. Swayne, 1862–81	Harold H. Burton, 1945–58
Samuel F. Miller, 1862–90	Thomas C. Clark, 1949–67
David Davis, 1862–77	Sherman Minton, 1949–56
Stephen J. Field, 1863–97	John M. Harlan, 1955–71
William Strong, 1870–80	William J. Brennan, Jr., 1956–
Joseph P. Bradley, 1870–92	Charles E. Whittaker, 1957–62
Ward Hunt, 1873–82	Potter Stewart, 1958–
John M. Harlan, 1877–1911	Byron R. White, 1962–
William B. Woods, 1881–87	Arthur J. Goldberg, 1962–65
Stanley Matthews, 1881–89	Abe Fortas, 1965–69
Horace Gray, 1882–1902	Thurgood Marshall, 1967–
Samuel Blatchford, 1882–93	Harry A. Blackmun, 1970–
Lucius G. C. Lamar, 1888–93	Lewis F. Powell, Jr., 1971–
David J. Brewer, 1890–1910	William H. Rehnquist, 1971–

under Chief Justice Earl Warren, to order the desegregation of Southern public schools by a unanimous vote (see INTEGRATION; BROWN VS. BOARD OF EDUCATION OF TOPEKA, KANSAS). In the 1960s the court expanded the protection given individuals accused of crimes, especially in the areas of search and seizures (MAPP VS. OHIO), confessions (MIRANDA VS. ARIZONA), and the right to an attorney (GIDEON VS. WAINWRIGHT). In 1967, President Lyndon B. Johnson appointed the first black, Thurgood MARSHALL, to the court. In his first term in office President Richard M. Nixon was able to greatly affect the outlook of the court by appointing a Chief Justice, Warren Burger, and three Associate Justices, Harry BLACKMUN, Lewis POWELL, and William REHNQUIST. Byron WHITE, appointed by John F. Kennedy, often voted with the four to cut back the scope of the Warren court on criminal and other holdings. Emphasizing private property and freedom from government interference, the court held that a private club with a state liquor license could refuse to serve guests because of their race and that a private shopping center could selectively ban political pickets. But the opinions were not always examples of conservatism and judicial restraint. The death penalty as applied was declared unconstitutional in *Furman* vs. *Georgia* on the grounds that it constituted cruel and unusual punishment in violation of the Eighth Amendment to the U.S. Constitution. A woman's right to an abortion during the early stages of pregnancy was recognized in *Roe* vs. *Wade.* At the beginning of 1975, the other members of the court were Justice Douglas, appointed by President Roosevelt, and Justices William Brennan and Potter Stewart appointed by President Eisenhower.

Bibliography. Scholarly studies include Felix Frankfurter and J. M. Landis, *The Business of the Supreme Court* (1928, repr. 1972); Charles Warren, *Congress, the Constitution and the Supreme Court* (1925, repr. 1968) and *The Supreme Court in United States History* (rev. ed. 1926, 2 vol.; repr. 1960); C. G. Haines, *The American Doctrine of Judicial Supremacy* (2d ed. 1932, repr. 1973); L. B. Boudin, *Government by Judiciary* (2 vol., 1932; repr. 1969); C. P. Curtis, *Lions under the Throne* (1947); E. N. Cahn, ed., *Supreme Court and Supreme Law* (1954, repr. 1968); A. M. Bickel, ed., *The Unpublished Opinions of Mr. Justice Brandeis* (1957, repr. 1967); Bernard Schwartz, *The Supreme Court: Constitutional Revolution in Retrospect* (1957); C. G. Haines and F. H. Sherwood, *The Role of the Supreme Court in American Government and Politics* (1957, repr. 1973); R. G. McCloskey, *The American Supreme Court* (1960); P. A. Freund, *The Supreme Court of the United States: Its Business, Purpose, and Performance* (1961, repr. 1972); L. I. Salomon, ed., *The Supreme Court* (1961); W. F. Murphy, *Congress and the Court* (1962); A. M. Bickel, *The Least Dangerous Branch* (1962); Wallace Mendelson, *Justices Black and Frankfurter: Conflict in the Court* (2d ed. 1966); L. H. Pollak, *The Constitution and the Supreme Court* (2 vol., 1966); Archibald Cox, *The Warren Court* (1968); A. T. Mason, *The Supreme Court from Taft to Warren* (rev. ed. 1968); Leon Friedman, ed., *The Justices of the United States Supreme Court, 1789–1969* (1969); C. B. Swisher, *Historic Decisions of the Supreme Court* (2d ed. 1969); W. F. Swindler, *Court and Constitution in the Twentieth Century* (2 vol., 1969–1970); A. M. Bickel, *The Supreme Court and the Idea of Progress* (1970); R. J. Steamer, *The Supreme Court in Crisis* (1971).

Supung (so͞o'po͝ong), dam on the Yalu River, on the border between North Korea and Liaoning prov., NE China. One of the largest dams in Asia (525 ft/160 m high and 2,800 ft/853 m long), it was built by the Japanese occupation forces in 1941. Its enormous supply of hydroelectric power is now shared by nearby North Korean and Chinese industrial areas.

Sur, Lebanon: see TYRE.

Sura (so͞orä'), river, c.540 mi (870 km) long, rising E of Penza, S central European USSR. It flows generally north to empty into the Volga River. It is navigable for about 100 mi (160 km) upstream.

Surabaja or **Soerabaja** (both: so͞orəbī'ə, Du. so͞oräbä'yä), city (1971 est. pop. 1,273,000), capital of East Java prov., NE Java, Indonesia, on the Kali Mas River just above its mouth at the western end of Madura Strait. Chief rival of Djakarta in size and commercial and industrial importance, Surabaja is the country's second largest city and its major naval base, with a huge shipyard, a naval college, and numerous specialized naval schools. An industrial center, it has railroad shops, an automobile assembly plant, and an oil refinery. Manufactures include textiles, glass, fertilizer, shoes, tobacco products, machinery, metal products, processed foods, tools, and cement. North of the city proper is its port, Tanjungperak, which ships sugar, rubber, coffee, and spices. Early in World War II, Surabaja was occupied by the Japanese. Although damaged during the postwar struggle for Indonesian independence, it has been rebuilt. It is the seat of a superior court and of Airlangga Univ. and an institute of technology.

Surakarta or **Soerakarta** (both: so͞oräkär'ta), city (1961 pop. 367,626), on central Java, Indonesia, on the Solo River. Connected by rail with Surabaja and Djakarta, it is a trade center for an area producing tobacco, rice, and sugar. Manufactures include textiles, leather work, machinery, metal products, furniture, and cigarettes, but Surakarta is particularly noted for its batik cloth and goldwork. It is also a cultural center, featuring gamelan music and wayang, or shadow plays. Surakarta's outstanding feature is the vast, walled palace of the sultan, virtually a city in itself. The European section of the city, which contains a Dutch fort built in 1799, resembles an old Dutch town. Surakarta is the seat of a private university and an extension facility of Islamic Univ. of Indonesia. The city is commonly called Solo.

Surat (so͞o'rət, so͞orät'), city (1971 pop. 471,815), Gujarat state, W central India, on the Gulf of Cambay. British and Dutch trading posts were established there in the early 17th cent. Surat became one of India's most populous cities and busiest ports during the 17th cent.; but in 1664, at the height of its opulence, it was sacked by the Mahrattas and declined in importance. Today the city is a district administrative center, a small port, and a railroad junction. There are textile mills, cotton gins, and engineering works. Sandalwood and ivory carvings are made. Surat is also the educational and cultural center of S Gujarat.

Suresnes (sürĕn'), city (1968 pop. 41,263), Hauts-de-Seine dept., N central France, a residential and industrial suburb of Paris. Its manufactures include automobiles, aeronautic equipment, pharmaceuticals, and metal pipes. In 1593 a conference in Suresnes between Catholics and Protestants led to the adoption of Catholicism by Henry IV. In one section of the city is Mt. Valérien, which has a commanding view of the Parisian countryside and a fort that has been crucial in the defense of Paris.

surf: see WAVE, in oceanography; BEACH.

surface chemistry, study of chemical reactions in which the reactants are first adsorbed onto a surface medium (see ADSORPTION) that then acts as a CATALYST for the reaction; after the reaction the products are desorbed and the surface is left unchanged. Since the entire reaction takes place on the surface, the amount of surface area of catalyst per unit weight determines the effectiveness of the surface in the reaction. Some silica surfaces have over 200 square meters of surface area per gram. An example of a surface reaction is the reaction of an unsaturated organic molecule with hydrogen on finely divided platinum or with bromine on finely divided silica. ENZYME reactions can, in principle, also be considered surface reactions, since the reaction takes place on the enzyme surface after the enzyme has bound the reactants; however, usually only heterogeneous (two-phase) reactions are considered true surface reactions, while enzyme reactions are homogeneous (one-phase) systems.

surface tension, tendency of liquids to reduce their exposed surface to the smallest possible area. A drop of water, for example, tends to assume the shape of a sphere. The phenomenon is attributed to cohesion, the attractive forces acting between the molecules of the liquid (see ADHESION AND COHESION). The molecules within the liquid are attracted equally from all sides, but those near the surface experience unequal attractions and thus are drawn toward the center of the liquid mass by this net force. The surface then appears to act like an extremely thin membrane, and the small volume of water that makes up a drop assumes the shape of a sphere, held constant when an equilibrium between the internal pressure and that due to surface tension is reached. Because of surface tension, various small insects are able to skate across the surface of a pond, objects of greater density than water can be made to float, and molten lead when dropped into a cool liquid forms suddenly into shot. See CAPILLARITY.

surf bird: see SHORE BIRD.

surf fish: see SURFPERCH.

surfing, sport of gliding toward the shore on a breaking wave. It is done on a balsa, polyurethane, or fiber glass board that may weigh up to 40 lb (18.1 kg) and may be anywhere from 4 to 12 ft (122–366 cm) long and 1 to 2 ft (30.5–61 cm) wide. Larger boards have a small stabilizing fin, or skeg, in the rear. The surfer begins at the point where the waves begin to form; facing shore, he paddles toward the beach with an oncoming wave. When the wave catches the board, the surfer stands up and glides along the crest of the wave until it breaks. Although the origins of surfing are obscure, it is clear that it developed in Hawaii, where it was popular during the 19th cent. It spread to the California coast during the 1920s and became very popular with American youth in the 60s. It is now practiced in many other Pacific nations, including Australia and Peru. The mecca of the sport remains Hawaii, where the international surfing championships are held annually at Makaha beach. See Midget Farrelly, *The Surfing Life* (1967).

surfperch, any member of the family Embiotocidae, a large family of spiny-finned, carnivorous fishes of the perch order. Also known as seaperches and surf fish, most surfperches are found off sandy shores of the North American Pacific Coast. Two species are found off Japan and Korea, and one, the Tule perch, is found in freshwater in the Sacramento River of California. Surfperches, unlike most other marine fishes, bear live young. The various species grow to average lengths of 6 to 18 in. (15–45 cm); most are richly colored. They are classified in the phylum CHORDATA, subphylum Vertebrata, class Osteichthyes, order Perciformes, family Embiotocidae.

surgery, branch of MEDICINE concerned with the diagnosis and treatment of injuries and pathological conditions requiring manual or instrumental operative procedures. In prehistoric times sharpened flints and other sharp-edged devices were used to perform various surgical operations. Such operations included trephining (removing circular pieces of the skull to relieve pressure caused by injury or often in the belief that the evil spirit thought to be causing a disorder would thereby be released), bloodletting, opening abscesses, and scarifying the flesh. Circumcision and other ritualistic operations were later performed with similar instruments. There are indications that in Neolithic times saws of stone and bone were used to perform amputations. Nearly all major operations were performed by the ancient Hindus nearly a thousand years before the advent of Greek medicine. Knowledge of the use of soporific potions to alleviate suffering can be traced to remote antiquity. The early Greeks and Romans practiced surgery with great skill and with such cleanliness that infection of surgical and other wounds was relatively uncommon. Their cleanliness and their use of boiled water or wine for irrigating wounds was probably suggested by Hippocrates, a competent surgeon and diagnostician of that time. Other notable early surgeons were Erasistratus and Herophilus of the medical school at Alexandria, and Galen, whose numerous treatises were long influential. The surgical and sanitary techniques employed by the Greeks and Romans were lost with the decline of their civilizations. During the Middle Ages in Europe there was a marked regression in surgical knowledge, and postoperative infection was common. A schism between the physician and the surgeon developed, and surgical practice fell into the hands of the unskilled and uneducated. The barber-surgeon, who performed the usual functions of a barber as well as surgical operations, became a common figure, especially in England and France. Guilds of barber-surgeons were organized in England, and they gradually gained status. It was not until the 18th cent., however, that surgery began to reach a professional level. There were, nevertheless, notable figures in early surgery, among them Guy de Chauliac in the 14th cent. and in the 16th cent. Ambroise Paré. With the introduction of antiseptic methods surgery entered its modern phase. Louis Pasteur established the fact that microbes are responsible for infection and disease. Sir Joseph Lister studied Pasteur's work and attributed surgical infection to the same cause; in the 1860s he introduced the use of carbolic acid as a cleansing and disinfecting agent, and his results in reducing infection were dramatic. It was found later that the carbolic acid spray that Lister used to cleanse the air about the patient was unnecessary, but the ANTISEPTIC treatment of instruments and other articles in contact with the patient continued until antisepsis was gradually replaced by the aseptic methods employed in modern hospitals. Before the discovery of antisepsis by Lister, about 80% of surgical patients contracted gangrene. Ernst von Bergmann is credited with introducing steam sterilization under pressure for treating instruments and all other medical equipment used for a surgical patient. In the late 19th cent. rubber gloves that could, like the instruments, be sterilized came into use and thus prevented infection through the hands of the surgeon. The development of methods of ANESTHESIA, especially the discovery, in the 1840s, of the value of ether, has been of immeasurable value. In the 20th cent. surgery has benefited from an improved understanding of the causes of shock and its treatment; knowledge of blood group typing and transfusion techniques; understanding of blood clotting and the use of ANTICOAGULANTS; and the development of ANTIBIOTICS, to control infection, and other forms of CHEMOTHERAPY. Surgical instruments have developed along with modern technology and are now sophisticated, meticulously designed devices. Electrically powered surgical instruments are invaluable for CAUTERY, and for separating hard tissues such as bone with minimal damage. Surgical stapling instruments, first developed in the Soviet Union, can join blood vessels or other tissues in less than half the time required by hand stitching. With the development of X-ray techniques and fluoroscopy, surgery gained valuable instruments of diagnosis. More recently, the cryogenic, or supercooled, probe has been used in the removal of cataracts and in other delicate operations. Ultrasonic probes, using very high frequency sound waves, are used to break up kidney stones, and are employed in brain and inner ear operations, which require great precision and control. They are also used to scan the pregnant uterus, a process that, unlike X-ray scanning, does not endanger the fetus. The medical laser, which produces amplified monochromatic light waves in a very narrowly focused beam, has become a useful tool in eye surgery. The heart-lung machine has made open-heart surgery possible. Cold surgery, by which the body is cooled to temperatures as low as 86°F (30°C) to lower the rate of metabolism and thus reduce the need for oxygen, has made long operations, especially those involving TRANSPLANTATION, possible. Recent surgical advances include transplant procedures involving the liver, lungs, pancreas, bone marrow, and most successfully, the kidney. The first human heart transplant was performed in 1967 by South African surgeon Christian Barnard. Usefulness of the technique is currently limited by the fact that physicians are still unable to successfully halt the body's rejection of foreign tissue. New orthopedic surgical techniques have been introduced, including the use of cementing substances to unite bones destroyed by tumor. Interest in the Chinese use of ACUPUNCTURE to replace anesthesia in some surgical operations has grown, partly as a result of increased contact between the United States and mainland China. See A. S. Earle, ed., *Surgery in America* (1965); F. F. Cartwright, *The Development of Modern Surgery* (1967); R. H. Meade, *An Introduction to the History of General Surgery* (1968); R. G. Richardson, *Surgery: Old and New Frontiers* (1968).

suricate: see MONGOOSE.

Surinam (sŏŏrĭnäm′, -năm′), Du. *Suriname,* also known as Dutch Guiana or Netherlands Guiana (1971 pop. 384,900), 63,037 sq mi (163,266 sq km), part of the kingdom of the Netherlands, NE South America, on the Atlantic Ocean. Part of the GUIANA region, it is separated from Brazil on the S by the Tumuc-Humac Mts., from Guyana on the W by the Courantyne River, and from French Guiana on the E by the Maroni River. The capital is PARAMARIBO, which is situated on the Suriname River. The population is mixed, with Creoles, Asian Indians, and Indonesians forming the largest groups. Dutch is the official language, although many others are spoken. Surinam is internally self-governing and has a parliamentary form of government. It is one of the world's great producers of bauxite, most of which is shipped to the United States. Other exports are rice, citrus fruits, bananas, and shrimps. Rice is the chief subsistence crop; sugarcane, coffee, and coconuts are also cultivated. The leading industries process bauxite, foodstuffs, and timber. Although the first Dutch expeditions to the region took place in 1597–98, the first colony, on Essequibo Island in present-day Guyana, was not founded until 1616. To exploit the territory the Dutch West India Company was founded in 1621. The Dutch hold on the east coast was interrupted by English and French attacks and by a slave insurrection (1762–63). The Treaty of Breda gave all the English territory in Guiana to the Dutch, but in 1815 the Congress of Vienna awarded the area of Guyana to Britain while reaffirming the Dutch hold on Surinam. The Dutch granted Surinam a parliament in 1866. In 1954, Surinam officially became an internally autonomous part of the kingdom of the Netherlands. In May, 1974, the Dutch agreed to grant Surinam full independence by the end of 1975. See P. H. Hess, *Netherlands America* (1943); W. N. Van de Poll, *Surinam, the Country and Its People* (tr. 1951); International Bank for Reconstruction and Development, *Surinam: Recommendations for a Ten-Year Development Program* (1952); M. J. Herskovits and F. J. Herskovits, *Suriname Folklore* (1937, repr. 1969).

Surma (sûr′mə, sŏŏr′mä), river, 320 mi (515 km) long, rising in the Manipur hills, NE India, and flowing generally SW through the Surma valley, where the river is dispersed into numerous streams; rejoined at the western end of the valley, the Surma joins the Meghna River in NE Bangladesh. The alluvial valley, astride the India-Bangladesh border, is fertile; rice, tea, and oilseed are the chief crops.

Surratt, Mary Eugenia (sərăt′), 1820–65, alleged conspirator in the assassination of Abraham Lincoln, hanged on July 7, 1865. A widow (her maiden name was Jenkins) who had moved from Surrattsville (now Clinton), Md., to Washington, D.C., she kept the boardinghouse where John Wilkes BOOTH hatched his unsuccessful plot to abduct the President and his successful assassination plan. After Lincoln's assassination eight alleged accomplices in Booth's crime were tried (May 10–June 29, 1865) before a special military tribunal. Hanged with Mary Surratt and unquestionably guilty were Lewis Thornton Powell (or Payne), David E. Herold, and George A. Atzerodt. Samuel Arnold and Michael O'Laughlin, Confederate ex-soldiers from Maryland who had taken part in the attempted abduction but not in the assassination, were sentenced to life imprisonment, as was Dr. Samuel A. Mudd, who had set Booth's broken leg. Edward Spangler, a stagehand at Ford's Theater, charged with abetting Booth's escape, was given six years. Mary Surratt's son, who had participated in the abduction plot, was tried (June 10–Aug. 10, 1867) before a civil court. Although the jury stood eight to four for acquittal, he was not released from prison until June, 1868. The hanging of his mother is generally considered to have been a gross miscarriage of justice. The prosecution, headed by Judge Advocate General Joseph HOLT, never established that Mary Surratt even knew (although she might have known) of the abduction plot, and it now seems certain that she was not a party to the assassination plans. Booth's diary and other evidence that might have cast doubt on the prosecution's case were suppressed by the government, and it is generally believed that some of the testimony against Mary Surratt was false. She has appealed to many writers and is the subject of several dramas, such as John Patrick's *Story of Mary Surratt* (1947). See D. M. De Witt, *The Judicial Murder of Mary E. Surratt* (1895, repr. 1970); Helen Jones Campbell, *The Case for Mrs. Surratt* (1943); G. W. Moore, *The Case of Mrs. Surratt* (1954).

surrealism (sərē′əlĭzəm), literary and art movement influenced by Freudianism and dedicated to the expression of imagination as revealed in dreams, free of the conscious control of reason and free of convention. The movement was founded (1924) in Paris by André Breton, with his *Manifeste du surréalisme,* but its ancestry is traced to the French poets Baudelaire, Rimbaud, Apollinaire, and to the Italian painter, Giorgio de Chirico. Many of its adherents had belonged to the DADA movement. In literature, surrealism was confined almost exclusively to France. Surrealist writers were interested in the associations and implications of words rather than their literal meanings; their works are thus extraordinarily difficult to read. Among the leading surrealist writers were Louis Aragon, Paul Eluard, Robert DESNOS, and Jean COCTEAU, the last noted particularly for his surreal films. In art the movement became dominant in the 1920s and 30s and was internationally practiced with many and varied forms of expression. Salvador Dali and Yves Tanguy used dreamlike perception of space and dream-inspired symbols such as melting watches and huge metronomes. Max Ernst and René Magritte constructed fantastic imagery from startling combinations of incongruous elements of reality painted with photographic attention to detail. These artists have been labeled as verists because their paintings involve transformations of the real world. "Absolute" surrealism depends upon images derived from psychic automatism, the subconscious, or spontaneous thought. Works by Joan Miró and André Masson are in this vein. The movement survived but was greatly diminished after World War II. See André Breton, *Manifestoes of Surrealism* (tr. 1969); Lucy Lippard, ed., *Surrealists on Art* (1970); studies by Patrick Waldberg (1966), Maurice Nadeau (tr. 1967), W. S. Rubin (1969), Sarane Alexandrian (1970), and H. S. Gershman (1969, repr. 1974).

Surrey, Henry Howard, earl of, 1517?–1547, English poet; son of Thomas Howard, 3d duke of Norfolk. His irascibility and continuous vaunting of his descent from Edward I resulted in his imprisonment on several occasions. Eventually he was convicted of treason on a trumped-up charge and executed. He introduced blank verse to English in translating two books of Vergil's *Aeneid.* Along with his friend Sir Thomas Wyatt, he popularized the Petrarchan sonnet form in English. He was the only poet mentioned on the title page of the well-known miscellany (1557) of Richard TOTTEL.

Surrey, county (1971 pop. 999,588), 653 sq mi (1,691 sq km), SE England. The county town is GUILDFORD. The North Downs cross the county from east to west. To the north the land slopes gently downward to the Thames, into which flow the Wey and the Mole, Surrey's principal streams. The southern slopes of the Downs are more rugged. Surrey is one of the "Home Counties" around London; there are still attractive woodland areas to the south. About one quarter of the total area is devoted to agriculture. There is dairy farming, market gardening, and wheat and oats cultivation. Manufactures include radio and radar equipment and aircraft. The town of EPSOM AND EWELL is known for its horse racing, and KEW GARDENS for the Royal Botanic Gardens. On RUNNYMEDE King John signed the Magna Carta in 1215. In Anglo-Saxon times Surrey was variously under the dominion of Mercia and Wessex and was overrun in the 9th cent. by the Danes. In 1974, Surrey was reorganized as a nonmetropolitan county; a small area in the southeast was assigned to the new nonmetropolitan county of West Sussex.

Surtees, Robert Smith (sûr′tēz), 1803–64, English novelist. He created John Jorrocks, the sporting grocer, who appears in *Jorrocks' Jaunts and Jollities* (1838), a series of humorous sketches first published in the *New Sporting Magazine,* which Surtees had helped to found in 1831. The novel *Handley Cross* (1843) continued the career of Jorrocks. Surtees's other novels include *Hawbuck Grange* (1847), *Hillingdon Hall* (1845), *Mr. Sponge's Sporting Tour* (1853), *Ask Mamma* (1858), *Plain or Ringlets?* (1860), and *Mr. Facey Romford's Hounds* (1865). Surtees knew English hunting life well, and his books have a tone of lusty humor and hearty satire. Many of his sketches were enhanced by the spirited illustrations of John Leech. See *Hunting Scenes from Surtees* (comp. by Lionel Gough, 1953).

Surtsey, volcanic island, c.1.25 sq mi (3.2 sq km), S of Iceland in Vestmannaeyjar (Westman Islands). The island was formed by the eruption (Nov., 1963) of Sutur, an underwater volcano named for a giant of Icelandic legend. For four months the fissure, estimated to be c.1,500 ft (460 m) long, emitted explosions of ash, cinders, and pumice in a column rising more than 1,000 ft (305 m). Lava flowed from April, 1964, to May, 1965, forming a shell that guaranteed the existence of the island. Scientists have been able to study the formation of tornadoes, waterspouts, hail, and lightning—all manifestations of the volcano itself—as well as the first evidence of life on the new island. Surtsey was designated a nature reserve in 1965.

surveying, method and technology of determining accurately points and lines of direction (bearings) on the earth's surface and preparing from them maps or plans. Boundaries, areas, elevations, construction lines, and geographical or artificial features are determined by the measurement of horizontal and vertical distances and angles and by computations based on geometry and trigonometry. Hydrographic surveying deals with bodies of water and coast lines, is recorded on charts, and shows such features as bottom contours, channels, buoys, and shoals. Land surveying includes both geodetic surveying, used for large areas and taking into account the curvature of the earth's surface (see GEODESY), and plane surveying, which deals with areas sufficiently small that the earth's curvature is negligible and can be disregarded. Plane surveying dates from ancient times and was highly developed in Egypt. It played an important role in American history in marking boundaries for settlements; surveying was a profession of distinction—both Washington and Jefferson worked for a time as surveyors. Branches of surveying are named according to their purpose, e.g., topographic surveying, used to determine relief (see CONTOUR), route surveying, mine surveying, construction surveying; or according to the method used, e.g., transit surveying, plane-table surveying, photogrammetic surveying (securing data by photographs). Surveys based on photographs are especially useful in rugged or inaccessible country and for reconnaissance surveys for construction, mapping, or military purposes. In air photographs, errors resulting from tilt of the airplane or arising from distortion of ground relief may be corrected in part by checking against control points fixed by ground surveys and by taking overlapping photographs and matching and assembling the relatively undistorted central portions into a mosaic. These are usually examined stereoscopically. In surveying, measurements may be made directly, electronically, by the use of optical instruments, by computations from known lines and angles, or by combination methods. Instruments used for direct linear measurements include the Gunter's chain (known also as the surveyor's chain), which is 66 ft (20 m) long and divided into 100 links; the engineer's chain, 100 ft (30 m) long and also consisting of 100 links; the tape, usually of steel, which has largely superseded chains; and the rod. Tapes and rods made of Invar metal (an alloy of steel and nickel) are used for very precise work because of their low coefficient of thermal expansion. In many situations electronic instruments, such as the geodimeter, which uses light waves, and the tellurometer, which uses microwaves, provide a more convenient and more accurate means of determining distance than do tapes and rods. The height of points in relation to a datum line (usually mean sea level) is measured with a leveling instrument consisting of a telescope fitted with a spirit level and usually mounted on a tripod. It is used in conjunction with a leveling rod placed at the point to be measured and sighted through the telescope. The transit is used to measure vertical and horizontal angles and may be used also for leveling; its chief elements are a telescope that can be rotated (transited) about a horizontal and about a vertical axis, spirit levels, and graduated circles supplemented by vernier scales. Known also as a transit theodolite, or transit compass, the transit is a modification of the theodolite, an instrument that, in its original form, could not be rotated in a vertical axis. A plane table consists of a drawing board fixed on a tripod and equipped with an alidade (a rule combined with a telescope); it is used for direct plotting of data on a chart and is suitable for rapid work not requiring a high degree of precision. The stadia method of measuring distance, a rapid system useful in surveying inaccessible terrain and in checking more precise measurements, consists in observing through a telescope equipped with two horizontal cross hairs or wires (stadia hairs) the interval delimited by the hairs on a calibrated stadia rod; the interval depends on the distance between the rod and the telescope. See M. V. Smirnoff, *Measurements for Engineering and Other Surveying* (1961); W. N. Thomas, *Surveying* (5th ed. 1961); J. A. Sandover, *Plane Surveying* (1961); R. E. Davis and J. W. Kelly, *Elementary Plane Surveying* (4th ed. 1967); W. H. Rayner and M. O. Schmidt, *Fundamentals of Surveying* (5th ed. 1969); R. F. Spier, *Surveying and Mapping* (1970).

Susa (so͞o'zə, -sə), ancient city, capital of ELAM. The site is 15 mi (23 km) SW of modern Dizful, Iran. It is the biblical Shushan (Neh. 1.1; Esther 1.2; Dan. 8.2), and its inhabitants were called Susanchites. From the 4th millennium B.C., Elam was under the cultural influence of Mesopotamia. Excavations at Susa uncovered the stele of Naram-sin and the code of Hammurabi, which were among the many art objects carried off by the Elamites from Babylonia. Destroyed in the 7th cent. B.C. by Assurbanipal, Susa was revived in the empire of the Achaemenid rulers of Persia. Darius I and Artaxerxes I built magnificent winter palaces in the city. Susa was later thoroughly Hellenized and continued prominent in the Roman Empire.

Susah (so͞o'sä) or **Sousse** (so͞os), ancient *Hadrumetum*, city (1966 pop. 58,161), NE Tunisia, on the Gulf of Hammamet, an arm of the Mediterranean Sea. It is a fishing port and export point for olive oil. The city was founded c.9th cent. B.C. by the Phoenicians. It was destroyed (A.D. 434) by the Vandals and rebuilt by Justinian. Susah was briefly held by Roger II of Sicily (c.1150). Ancient remains include Christian catacombs.

Susak: see RIJEKA, Yugoslavia.

Susanchites (so͞o'zənkīts), inhabitants of SUSA in Elam. Ezra 4.9.

Susanna. 1 Heroine of a story told in Dan. 13, a chapter placed in the Apocrypha in the Authorized Version (see DANIEL). Two elders attempt to seduce Susanna and are repulsed; they accuse her of illicit relations with a young man, but she is saved from punishment by young Daniel, who traps the false accusers in discrepancies in their testimony. Susanna has been a favorite subject of Christian iconography. **2** Woman who ministered to Jesus. Luke 8.3.

Susi (so͞o'sī), father of Gaddi, a spy sent into Canaan by Moses. Num. 13.11.

Susiana: see ELAM.

Suslov, Mikhail Andreyevich (mēkhəyēl' əndrā'yəvĭch so͞oslôf'), 1902–, Soviet politician and ideologist. A Communist party member since 1921, he rose to prominence in the party hierarchy in the late 1930s and early 1940s. In 1941 he was named to the party's central committee. He rapidly gained distinction as a leading party theoretician, noted for his condemnation of deviations from Soviet policy, particularly for his anti-Yugoslav propaganda in 1948. In 1955 he became a member of the presidium (later politburo) of the central committee. A shrewd political maneuverer, he supported Nikita Khrushchev's bid for power in 1957 and was probably influential in his downfall in 1964.

Suso, Heinrich (hīn'rĭkh zo͞o'zō), c.1295–1366, German mystic, a Dominican friar. While studying at Cologne he came under the influence of Meister ECKHART, whose writings he defended against charges of heresy. He became a popular preacher and was associated with Johannes TAULER. At first harshly ascetic, he gradually emphasized detachment rather than mortification as central in the Christian discipline. His mysticism was expressed in terms of the contemporary literary romantic cult of the minnesingers. This gave him the epithet Sweet Suso. His writings include *Das Büchlein der ewigen Weisheit* [the little book of eternal wisdom], an autobiography and a guide to beginners in the spiritual life; *Das Minnebüchlein* [the little book of love]; a scholarly defense of Eckhart and an attack on the BEGHARDS and Brethren of the Free Spirit; and miscellaneous sermons. He was beatified in 1831. His autobiography is not of certain authenticity; it purports to be made from notes taken from his oral accounts and then edited by him. See T. F. Knox, *The Life of Blessed Heinrich Suso by Himself* (1913); J. M. Clark, *The Great German Mystics* (1949, repr. 1970).

suspension, in automobiles, system of springs used to suspend the frame, body, engine, and power train above the wheels. Its principal purpose is to lessen the jarring of the automobile that is caused by irregularities in the roads traveled. Since the wheels of an automobile accelerate, stop, and steer it, the suspension must also serve to keep the wheels in close contact with the road surface at all times. The types of springs used in suspensions include leaf springs, coil springs, torsion bars, and air springs. There have been many refinements in modern suspensions. On most vehicles the front wheels are suspended independently, i.e., the front axle has been eliminated. Certain vehicles also have the rear wheels suspended independently. Hydraulic SHOCK ABSORBERS have been included to prevent the springs from shaking the automobile excessively after a jolt. An elaborate system of mechanical linkages is often included to position the mass of the vehicle accurately with respect to its wheels during accelerating, braking, and steering.

suspension, in chemistry, mixture of two substances, one of which is finely divided and dispersed in the other. Common suspensions include sand in water, fine soot or dust in air, and droplets of oil in air. A suspension is different from a COLLOID or SOLUTION. Particles in a suspension are larger than those in colloids or solutions; they are visible under a microscope, and some can be seen with the naked eye. Particles in a suspension precipitate if the suspension is allowed to stand undisturbed.

suspension bridge: see BRIDGE.

Susquehanna (səskwĭhăn'ə), river, 444 mi (715 km) long, rising in Otsego Lake, central N.Y., and zigzagging SE and SW through E central Pa. to Chesapeake Bay near Havre de Grace, Md. The bay is the drowned lower course of the river. The West Branch (c.160 mi/260 km long), which rises in the Allegheny Mts., W Pa., and follows a circuitous course eastward to Sunbury, Pa., is the river's chief tributary. The Susquehanna River traverses an anthracite coal region, and there are many mining and industrial cities on its banks, including Binghamton and Owego, N.Y., and Pittston, Wilkes-Barre, and Harrisburg, Pa. The shallow, swift-flowing river is unsuited for navigation. There are several hydroelectric power plants on the Susquehanna; the Conowingo plant in Maryland is one of the largest non-Federal power stations in the nation. The Susquehanna and its tributaries have extensive flood control works. However in June, 1972, the river, swollen by the torrential rains of Hurricane Agnes, breached 40-ft (12-m) dikes in places and flooded most of the basin, causing one of the greatest flood disasters in the history of the United States.

Susquehanna Company, land company formed (1753) in Connecticut for the purpose of developing the WYOMING VALLEY in Pennsylvania. A tract of land was purchased from the Indians in 1754, and preparations were made for development. Aid was sought in England and Eliphalet DYER was sent in an unsuccessful attempt to secure confirmation of the land grant. Colonization from Connecticut was first attempted in 1762–63, but it was 1769 before any definite settlement was made. Soon the settlers were embroiled in troubles with the rival settlers from Pennsylvania, leading to the Pennamite Wars, in which Zebulon BUTLER led the Connecticut forces.

Süss, Hans: see KULMBACH, HANS VON.

Sussex, Thomas Radcliffe, 3d **earl of,** 1526?–1583, English nobleman. Styled Viscount Fitzwalter after his father became (1542) the 2d earl of Sussex, he served in the army in France and on diplomatic missions abroad. In 1554 he was made Baron Fitzwalter, and in 1557 he succeeded his father as earl of Sussex. He served as lord deputy of Ireland under Mary I (1556–58) and again (1559–64) under Elizabeth I, who gave him the title of lord lieutenant. Sussex was a vigorous general, although he never succeeded in subduing Shane O'NEILL, and it was during his administration that English influence was first extended outside the Pale. Sussex's desire for Elizabeth to marry outside England brought him into sharp conflict with the earl of Leicester. His attempts to negotiate a marriage between the queen and Archduke Charles of Austria, brother of Holy Roman Emperor Maximilian II, collapsed in 1567. In 1568, Sussex became lord lieutenant of the north, and he aided in the suppression of the revolt (1569–70) of the earls of Northumberland and Westmorland. He became lord chamberlain in 1572.

Sussex, county, SE England, since 1888 divided for administrative purposes into East Sussex (1971 pop. 750,312), 829 sq mi (2,147 sq km), and West Sussex (1971 pop. 491,020), 633 sq mi (1,639 sq km). The county town is LEWES; CHICHESTER is the administrative center for West Sussex. The South Downs, low, rolling hills that cross the county from east to west and terminate at Beachy Head on the English Channel coast, are Sussex's most notable geographical feature. The principal streams are the Arun, the Ouse, the Rother, and the Adur. The long coast line along the Channel is famous for its resorts, such as BRIGHTON and EASTBOURNE. Sussex is almost exclusively an agricultural region devoted to dairy farming, wheat growing, and market gardening. It has many residential suburbs of London. The old kingdom of the South Saxons (Sussex) was founded by King Ælle in the late 5th cent. Later the region was incorporated into Wessex. William I (William the Conqueror) landed at Pevensey in 1066 and defeated Harold's Saxons at HASTINGS. In 1974, East Sussex and West Sussex were reorganized as nonmetropolitan counties.

Sussex, kingdom of, one of the Anglo-Saxon heptarchy (seven kingdoms) in England, located S of the

Weald. It was settled in the late 5th cent. (according to tradition in 477) by Saxons under Ælle, who defeated the Celts in several battles and established toward the close of the century a brief military supremacy. Little is known of its history for almost two centuries. The South Saxons remained heathen until St. Wilfrid, bishop of York, led (681–86) the Christian conversion of the people. Conquered (685–88) by Cædwalla of WESSEX, Sussex remained subject to his successor, Ine (688–726). By 771, Offa of MERCIA had conquered all the petty kingdoms including Sussex into which the South Saxons were divided, and they remained under Mercia until they joined other eastern states in submitting to Egbert of Wessex in 825.

Sussex spaniel, breed of short, stocky SPORTING DOG developed in England in the late 18th and early 19th cent. It stands about 15 in. (38 cm) high at the shoulder and weighs between 35 and 45 lb (15.9–20.4 kg). Its medium-length coat, which is golden liver in color, is flat or slightly wavy and forms fringes, or feathers, on the ears, chest, underside, and stern. The tail is docked to approximately 6 in. (15 cm). Originally used to hunt in areas of abundant upland game, it could not compete with the faster field dogs when introduced into areas where game was less dense. It has therefore become more popular as a bench competitor and pet. See DOG.

Sutherland, George, 1862–1942, Associate Justice of the U.S. Supreme Court (1922–38), b. Buckinghamshire, England. He was taken (1864) by his family to Springville, Utah. After studying law at the Univ. of Michigan, he was admitted (1883) to the bar, practiced law in Utah, and was (1896–1900) a member of the state senate. Sutherland became important in Republican party politics and served in the House of Representatives (1901–2) and then in the Senate (1905–17). As Associate Justice of the Supreme Court, Sutherland was known as a staunch conservative. He is the author of *Constitutional Power and World Affairs* (1919). See biography by J. F. Paschal (1951, repr. 1969).

Sutherland, Graham, 1903–, English painter. Sutherland began his career as a painter at 35 and gained international acclaim with his paintings of war devastation. Among his major religious works are a tapestry for Coventry Cathedral and a series of paintings entitled *Thorns.* Realistically painted in sharp, cruel forms, they are symbolic of the Passion. See studies by Edward Sackville-West (1955) and Douglas Cooper (1962).

Sutherland, Joan, 1926–, Australian soprano. Sutherland studied at the Sydney Conservatory, where she made her debut in Eugene Goossen's *Judith* in 1950. Since 1952 she has been a leading singer at the Royal Opera House Covent Garden in London. She sang for the first time at La Scala in Milan in 1961 and made her Metropolitan Opera debut the same year. Sutherland is considered unsurpassed in the bel canto repertory among contemporary singers. She is particularly celebrated for her singing of the title role in Donizetti's *Lucia di Lammermoor.* She frequently performs with her husband, Richard Bonynge, conducting. See biographies by R. R. Braddon (1962) and Edward Greenfield (1973).

Sutherland Falls, waterfall, 1,904 ft (580 m) high, between Lake Quill and Arthur River, SW South Island, New Zealand. It is the world's fifth-highest waterfall. It is a major tourist attraction in Fjordland National Park.

Sutherlandshire (suth'ərləndshĭr) or **Sutherland,** county (1971 pop. 13,053), 2,028 sq mi (5,253 sq km), N Scotland. Dornoch is the county town; Golspie is the administrative center. Except for the coastal area at Dornoch Firth, the terrain is mountainous with many rivers and lochs. Cape Wrath is the northwest extremity of the county and of the Scottish mainland. The county is famous for its spectacular scenery. The interior, almost uninhabited, is covered with peat moors (used for rough grazing) and deer forests; less than 2% of the land is arable. Herring and salmon fishing is important. Gaelic is spoken in parts of the county. Under the Local Government Act of 1973, Sutherlandshire became part of the Highland region.

Sutlej (sŭt'lĕj), longest of the five rivers of the PUNJAB, c.900 mi (1,450 km) long, rising in the Kailas Range, SW Tibet (China), and flowing generally west, meandering through the Himalayas in India, then onto the Punjab plain where it receives the Beas River and forms part of the India-Pakistan border; continuing into Pakistan, it is joined by the Chenab River (which received the Jhelum and Ravi rivers). The combined stream, the Panjnad, channels the collected waters of all five rivers of the Punjab into the Indus River. The Sutlej is extensively used for irrigation; many large canals branch from it. Bhakra Dam in Punjab state, N India, one of the highest dams in the world (750 ft/229 m), impounds water for irrigation and power production (450,000-kw capacity). Until the Sikh Wars in the 1840s, the Sutlej was the border between the Sikh and British spheres of influence.

Sutra: see SANSKRIT LITERATURE.

suttee (sŭ"tē', sŭ'tē") [Skt. *sati,* = faithful wife], former Indian funeral practice in which the widow immolated herself on her husband's funeral pyre. The practice of killing a favorite wife on her husband's grave has been found in many parts of the world; it was followed by such peoples as the Thracians, the Scythians, the ancient Egyptians, the Scandinavians, the Chinese, and peoples of Oceania and Africa. Suttee was probably taken over by Hinduism from a more ancient source. Its stated purpose was to expiate the sins of both husband and wife and to ensure the couple's reunion beyond the grave, but it was encouraged by the low regard in which widows were held. The practice was not universal throughout Hindu history. It was abolished by law in British India in 1829, but isolated cases of voluntary suttee have occurred into the 20th cent. See also FUNERAL CUSTOMS and SUICIDE. See E. J. Thompson, *Suttee* (1928).

Sutter, John Augustus, 1803–80, American pioneer, b. Kandern, Baden, of Swiss parents. His original name was Johann August Suter. He emigrated to the United States in 1834, went to St. Louis, then to Santa Fe. Fired with a desire to go to the Pacific coast, he went to the Oregon country and entered the coast trade in the Northwest, going to the Hawaiian Islands, to Sitka, Alaska, and finally (1839) to California. He settled in the Sacramento valley and obtained large grants of land from the Mexican governor of California. There he established his colony, known as New Helvetia, and built Sutter's Fort (see SACRAMENTO). Rich and powerful, Sutter helped many newcomers to California. In 1848, James W. MARSHALL found gold while building a sawmill on Sutter's land. The news spread, and gold-mad crowds poured across the continent in the rush of '49. They killed Sutter's cattle and swarmed over his lands hunting for gold. He struggled against them in vain, and moved E to Pennsylvania, a ruined man, in 1873. He had earlier been granted a pension from California, and to the end he hoped that the U.S. Congress would reimburse him for his losses. Original materials are to be found in Erwin Gudde, *Sutter's Own Story* (1936), in Sutter's *New Helvetia Diary* (1939), and in his *Statement regarding Early California Experiences* (ed. by Allan Ottley, 1943). See biographies by Julian Dana (1934), J. P. Zollinger (1939, repr. 1967), M. K. Wilbur (1949), and R. H. Dillon (1967); Oscar Lewis, *Sutter's Fort* (1966).

Suttner, Bertha (Gräfin Kinsky), Freifrau von (bĕr'tä, grāf'ĭn kĭns'kē, frī'frou fən zōōt'nər), 1843–1914, Austrian novelist, known chiefly as an ardent pacifist. Her pacifist novel *Die Waffen nieder* (1889, tr. *Lay Down Your Arms,* 1892) had great social impact. Through her subsequent friendship with Alfred Nobel, she influenced him to establish the Nobel Prizes. She was the first woman awarded (1905) the Nobel Peace Prize. See her *Memoirs* (1909, tr. 1910); biography by Beatrix Kempf (tr. 1973).

Sutton, borough (1971 pop. 168,775) of Greater London, SE England. Sutton was created in 1965 by the merger of the municipal boroughs of Sutton and Cheam and of Beddington and Wallington with the urban district of Carshalton. It is mainly residential, but plastics, chemicals, radio components, and paper goods are produced. The areas of present-day Sutton were all mentioned in the Domesday Book. All Saints Church in Carshalton (12th cent.) and Beddington Church (14th cent.) are notable.

Sutton Coldfield, municipal borough (1971 pop. 83,130), Warwickshire, central England, residential suburb of Birmingham. There is a metal products industry. Sutton Park (2,400 acres/971 hectares) is a public recreation ground. The moated New Hall dates partly from the 13th cent. There is a large television transmitting station. In 1974, Sutton Coldfield became part of the new metropolitan county of West Midlands.

Sutton Hoo (sŭt'ən hōō), archaeological site near Woodbridge, East Suffolk, E England, containing 11 barrows. Excavations here in 1938–39 revealed remains of a Saxon ship (c.660), which with its gold and silver treasures is now in the British Museum. The absence of a body and of personal objects in the ship has led archaeologists to conclude that the site was a cenotaph rather than a grave.

Sutton-in-Ashfield, urban district (1971 pop. 40,725), Nottinghamshire, central England. There are lace and hosiery factories, coal mines, and other industries. The Church of St. Mary Magdalene dates partly from the 12th and 14th cent.

Su Tung-po (sōō dōōng-pô) or **Su T'ung-po** (tōōng-pô), 1036–1101, Chinese poet. He was also called Su Shih. Born in present-day Szechwan prov., he was one of a literary family. Su occupied many official posts, rising to president of the board of rites (which regulated imperial ceremonies and worship). He designed the parks surrounding Lake Si in Hangchow. His satiric verses and opposition to official policies frequently lost him his official status. Su's poetry and art were inspired by Taoism and Buddhism, although his political views were founded in Confucian philosophy. Su is generally considered the greatest poet of the Sung dynasty. His work frequently expresses regret for the evanescence of beauty and the limited span of life. Su is noted for his *fu,* satiric poems which approach free verse, and for letters and essays. See translations by Burton Watson (1965); Lin Yutang, *The Gay Genius: The Life and Times of Su Tungpo* (1947).

Suva (sōō'vä), city (1971 est. pop. 63,200), capital of FIJI, on the southeastern coast of VITI LEVU island, S Pacific. It is a major shipping and commercial center of the S Pacific. Coconut oil and soap are manufactured; sugar, copra, gold, and tropical fruits are exported. The Central Medical School is in the city. Suva became the capital of Fiji in 1882. During World War II it was an important Allied airbase.

Suvero, Mark di (dē sōō'vərō), 1933–, American sculptor, b. Shanghai. Di Suvero's major works are constructions of huge, weathered timbers, tires, chains, and rope. They are remarkable for their large scale, their composition from common materials, and the effect of motion that they produce. Di Suvero's work is represented in the Art Institute of Chicago; the Wadsworth Atheneum, Hartford, Conn.; and the Whitney Museum, New York City.

Suvorov, Aleksandr Vasilyevich (əlyĭksän' dər vəsē'lyəvĭch sōōvô'rəf), 1729–1800, Russian field marshal. Suvorov entered the army as a youth and rose rapidly through the ranks. He fought in the Russo-Turkish War of 1768–74, helped suppress the peasant rebellion led by Pugachev in 1775, and was created count for his victories in the Russo-Turkish War of 1787–92, notably at Focsani, Rimnik, and at Izmail in Bessarabia. In 1794, Suvorov commanded the Russian army that suppressed the Polish revolt after the second partition of Poland by Russia and Prussia. In a swift campaign, culminating in the battle of Praga and the capture of Warsaw, he crushed Polish resistance. Suvorov's reputation reached its peak in the FRENCH REVOLUTIONARY WARS of 1798–99, in which he commanded Austro-Russian forces against the armies of the French Republic. Sent to oust the French from Italy, he defeated them at Cassano, took Milan and Turin, and routed the French on the Trebbia and at Novi. Having driven the French out of N Italy, Suvorov planned to march on Paris, but instead was ordered to Switzerland over the St. Gotthard Pass to join the forces of General Korsakov and Austrian Archduke Charles and to drive the French out of Switzerland. Before Suvorov could join Korsakov, Archduke Charles and his Austrian forces had been ordered back to the Rhine. Korsakov's troops, greatly outnumbered, were defeated by the French commander MASSÉNA at Zurich (Sept., 1799). Suvorov was still struggling through the almost impassable Alpine mountain paths when news of Korsakov's disaster reached him. Harassed by the French, he succeeded in leading his half-starved and ragged troops to Lindau. He refused to participate in further action with the Austrians, and shortly afterward Russia withdrew from the war. For his exploits in Italy he was created Prince Italiski. Idolized by his men, Suvorov demanded discipline and sacrifice, but his willingness to let his soldiers plunder conquered territory gave Russian troops a bad reputation throughout Europe. One of the great generals of modern times, Suvorov was never defeated in battle; he ascribed his success to the principle of "intuition, rapidity, impact."

Suwannee (swô'nē, swä'–), river, c.240 mi (390 km) long, rising in Okefenokee Swamp, SE Ga., and winding generally S through N Fla. to the Gulf of Mexico; it is dredged to accommodate shallow-draft vessels for 135 mi (217 km) upstream. Its name was used by chance in Stephen Foster's famous song "Old Folks at Home" or "Swanee River."

Suwon (sōō'wŭn'), city (1970 est. pop. 171,000), capital of Kyonggi prov., NW South Korea. It is an important communications point and a local agricultural center. Suwon has large silk and rayon textile mills.

Suzdal (so͞oz'dəl), city, central European USSR, near Moscow. Founded c.1024 as a fortress town, it developed from the 11th to 12th cent. as an important city of the grand duchy of Vladimir-Suzdal (see VLADIMIR) and a political and religious center of NE Russia. In the early 13th cent. it became the capital of the Suzdal principality, but it was destroyed by the Tatars in 1238 and never recovered its importance. In 1451, Suzdal passed to the grand duchy of Moscow. Landmarks include an ancient kremlin with a cathedral and a monastery, a 17th-century bell tower, and bishops' palaces from the 15th to 18th cent.

Suzor-Côté, Marc Aurèle de Foy (märk ôrĕl' də fwä süzôr'-kōtā'), 1869–1937, Canadian painter and sculptor, b. Quebec prov. He studied in Paris in the 1890s, then returned to paint Canadian genre scenes in an impressionist style. He was also skillful as a sculptor, as shown in the bronze group, *Caughnawaga Women* (Vancouver Art Gall.).

Suzuka (so͞ozo͞o'kä), city (1970 pop. 131,185), Mie prefecture, central Honshu, Japan. It is a manufacturing center with chemical, mechanical, and textile industries.

Suzuki, Daisetz Teitaro (dī'sĕts tätä'rō so͞ozo͞o'kē), 1870–1966, Japanese Buddhist scholar, educated at Tokyo Univ. After studying (1897–1909) in the United States, he became a lecturer at Tokyo Univ.; he later taught at leading universities in Japan, Europe, and the United States. One of the greatest authorities on Buddhism, he is known for his introduction of Zen Buddhism to the West. Among his many works are *Essays in Zen Buddhism* (3 vol., 1927–33), *The Training of the Buddhist Monk* (1934), *Zen Buddhism and Its Influence on Japanese Culture* (1938, rev. ed. 1959), *An Introduction to Zen Buddhism* (1949), and *Mysticism: Christian and Buddhist* (1957). See also his *Outlines of Mahayana Buddhism* (1963) and *Shin Buddhism* (1970).

Suzuki, Kantaro (käntärō'), 1867–1948, Japanese admiral. He served briefly as prime minister from April, 1945, until Aug. 15, the day after the announcement of Japan's surrender in the last days of World War II. He favored the acceptance of unconditional surrender with the understanding that it did not alter the position of the emperor. Opposed by the military, which wished to negotiate a more favorable settlement, Suzuki called two imperial conferences at which the emperor (see HIROHITO) ordered his ministers to capitulate.

Svalbard (sväl'bärd), archipelago (23,958 sq mi/62,051 sq km), a possession of Norway, located in the Arctic Ocean, c.400 mi (640 km) N of the Norwegian mainland and between lat. 74°N and 81°N. The population in 1972 was 4,225. The main islands of the group are Spitsbergen (formerly Vestspitsbergen), Nordaustlandet, Edgeøya, Barentsøya, and Prins Karls Forland; surrounding islands include Hopen, Kong Karls Land, Kvitøya, and Bjørnøya (Bear Island). The islands form plateaus intersected by deep fjords, of which Isfjorden is the largest. Spitsbergen, the largest island, contains the highest mountain of the group (Newtontoppen, c.5,650 ft/1,720 m) and the principal settlements of Longyearbyen (the administrative center), Ny-Alesund, Barentsburg, and Grumantbyen. Spitsbergen has served as the base for many polar expeditions. The warm North Atlantic Drift makes navigation possible for more than half the year along the western coasts. Ice fields and glaciers cover more than 60% of the area, but some 130 species of arctic vegetation flourish near the coast and on patches of interior tundra. Waterfowl abound, but land game has been rendered nearly extinct by hunting and is now protected. Although there is some sealing, whaling, and fishing, the chief wealth of the islands is derived from their mineral resources, most notably coal; deposits of asbestos, copper, gypsum, iron, marble, zinc, and phosphate also exist. Discovered (1194) by the Vikings, the islands were forgotten until their rediscovery (1596) by William Barentz, the Dutch navigator. For a decade after Henry Hudson reported (1607) good whaling there, English and Dutch whalers quarreled over the territory; in 1618 they compromised, the Dutch limiting their operations to the northern part, leaving the rest to the English, the French, and the Hanseatic League. The Danes at the same time claimed the islands as part of Greenland. After the decline of whaling, the group became (18th cent.) a hunting ground for Russian and Scandinavian fur traders. In the late 19th cent., the islands were mapped by many notable explorers, and important coal deposits were discovered. For a half century after the discovery of coal, Norway, Russia, and Sweden negotiated for the islands. By a treaty signed at Paris in 1920 and subsequently ratified by the other claimants, they were awarded to Norway who took formal possession of them in 1925. The treaty prohibited military installations on the islands and ensured recognition of claims of other countries to parts of the coal fields. In World War II, Svalbard was raided (Aug., 1941) by an Allied party that evacuated the civilian population to England and rendered the mines inoperable. A German garrison was expelled in 1942 by a small Norwegian force. In Sept., 1943, the German battleships *Tirpitz* and *Scharnhorst*, with 10 destroyers, completed the devastation of the mines and mining installations by bombarding the islands. In 1944 the USSR—which had not signed the 1920 treaty but which had later adhered to it—was refused a request to share with Norway in the administration and defense of Svalbard. After the war the mining settlements were rebuilt. Coal mining concessions operated by the USSR since the 1920s account for about one third of the coal shipped from Svalbard.

Svanetia (svänē'shə), mountainous region, S European USSR, in Georgia, on the southern slopes of the Greater Caucasus. It is very difficult of access, and its inhabitants, the Svans, have been little touched by modern civilization. They speak a South Caucasian language, like the Georgians. The Svanetian Range, a spur of the central Greater Caucasus, extends c.50 mi (80 km) west from the main range near the Dykh-Tau and rises to 13,110 ft (3,996 m).

Svealand or **Svearike:** see SWEDEN.

Svedberg, Theodor or **The** (tā'ōdôr svād'běryə, tā), 1884–1971, Swedish chemist. He was professor of physical chemistry from 1912 to 1949 at the Univ. of Uppsala. For his fundamental research on colloid chemistry he received the 1926 Nobel Prize in Chemistry. Svedberg studied especially the giant protein molecules, evolving for this work an ultracentrifuge. He wrote *Colloid Chemistry* (1924, 2d ed. 1928) and was (with K. O. Pedersen) coauthor of *The Ultracentrifuge* (1940).

Svein: see SWEYN.

Svendborg (svĕn'bôr), city (1970 com. pop. 35,809), Fyn co., S Denmark, a seaport on the Svendborg Sund (an arm of the Lille Baelt); founded c.1200.

Sverdlovsk (svyĭrdlôfsk'), city (1970 pop. 1,026,000), capital of Sverdlovsk oblast, E European USSR, in the eastern foothills of the central Urals, on the Iset River. One of the largest cities of the Urals, it is an air and rail junction (a western terminus of the Trans-Siberian RR) and a leading industrial, scientific, and cultural center. Sverdlovsk is among the USSR's leading producers of heavy machinery. Other industries include metallurgy, gem cutting, and the manufacture of chemicals, pharmaceuticals, building materials, and electrical apparatus. Nearby are gold and copper mines. Sverdlovsk began as a fort and metallurgical factory built in 1721 on the site of an earlier settlement. In 1723 the city was named Ekaterinburg in honor of Peter I's wife, who became Empress Catherine I. The first ironworks were established in 1726, and the city developed steadily as an administrative center for the mining towns of the Urals and Siberia. Its importance was enhanced by the building of the Great Siberian Highway through the city in 1783, but even more so by the construction of the Trans-Siberian RR in the 19th cent. Czar Nicholas and his family were imprisoned and shot by the Bolsheviks at Ekaterinburg in 1918. The city was renamed in 1924 for the Communist leader Y. M. Sverdlov. The transfer of much Soviet industry from European USSR to the less vulnerable Urals during World War II further stimulated the growth of Sverdlovsk. The city's educational and cultural institutions include the Urals branch of the Soviet Academy of Sciences, several mining schools, and a meteorological observatory.

Sverdrup, Johan (yōhän'), 1816–92, Norwegian prime minister. As a member of the Storting (1851–84) and as prime minister (1884–89) he successfully advocated parliamentary government with ministerial responsibility, trial by jury, and the political and social advancement of the farmers. His party, the Left, founded in 1869, united the various opposition groups into a single powerful majority. In 1880, Sverdrup's bill for seating the governmental ministers in the Storting was vetoed by King Oscar II of Sweden and Norway. A constitutional struggle resulted over the relative powers held by the king, the ministers, and the Storting. In 1884 the opposition succeeded in having the Conservative cabinet impeached by a special tribunal. Sverdrup became premier, and the cabinet was seated in the Storting, a move that ultimately made the ministers responsible to the Storting. He failed, however, to satisfy the extremist wing of his party and resigned in 1889.

Sverdrup, Otto (ô'tō), 1855–1930, Norwegian arctic explorer. A companion of Fridtjof Nansen on the voyage across Greenland in 1888 and on Nansen's later (1893–96) polar expedition, Sverdrup was leader of an arctic expedition (1898–1902) that attempted to reach the North Pole by way of Smith Sound but failed because of ice in Kennedy Channel. However, valuable topographical observations were made in N Greenland; the unknown western part of Ellesmere Island was explored and charted, and Axel Heiberg Island and other areas were discovered. His *New Land* (tr. 1904) described this expedition. His later arctic expeditions included a voyage to the Kara Sea in 1920 and a searching trip for the Italian explorer Umberto Nobile's *Italia* in 1928.

Sverdrup Islands: see QUEEN ELIZABETH ISLANDS.

Sverre (svĕ'rə), d. 1202, king of Norway (1184–1202). He claimed to be the illegitimate son of King Sigurd; the question of his paternity is still disputed. He spent his childhood in the Faeroe Islands, was educated for the priesthood, and went to Norway in 1176. The Birkebeiner faction, which opposed Erling Skakke and his son, the puppet king Magnus, adopted the cause of Sverre. The party took (1177) Trondheim, and a bitter civil war began. Sverre secured control of Norway in 1178, but Magnus with foreign aid continued to attack Sverre until Magnus's death in battle (1184). Civil war continued. From 1196 to 1201 the Baglar, an aristocratic and clerical faction, fought vigorously against the Birkebeiners, but it was defeated. The victory of the faction of the common people led to the destruction of aristocratic power and increased royal control. Sverre quarreled with the Archbishop of Trondheim, who refused to crown him and fled (1190) the country. As a result the king was excommunicated by Pope Innocent III. Sverre was succeeded by his son Haakon III. See biography by G. M. Gathorne-Hardy (1956).

Svevo, Italo (ē'tälō zvā'vō), 1861–1928, Italian novelist, whose real name was Ettore Schmitz. A businessman of Trieste, he wrote several works of fiction, which remained practically unknown until discovered by James Joyce. His fiction is psychological and introspective, his characters mainly narcissistic, and his style witty. His best-known work is *La coscienza di Zeno* (1923, tr. *The Confessions of Zeno*, 1930); also translated is *Una burla riuscita* (1928, tr. *The Hoax*, 1929).

Sviatoslav (svyä'təsləv), d. 972, duke of Kiev (945–72), son of IGOR and of St. Olga. His mother acted as regent for him until c.962, when he came of age. During his reign, which was spent in conquests, he created an empire that stretched from the Volga to the Danube. By 965 he had defeated the Volga Bulgars and the Khazars, thus bringing under Kievan control the entire area of the Volga River. Then, as an ally of the Byzantine Empire, which was at war with the Bulgars, Sviatoslav defeated the Bulgars of the Danube (968) and further extended Kievan control in the Balkans. He was forced to give up the Balkan lands (971), however, in a war with the Byzantine emperor John I. On his way back to Kiev, Sviatoslav was slain by the PECHENEGS (or Patzinaks).

Svinhufvud, Pehr Evind (pār ā'vĭnd svēn'ho͞o"vəd, svĭn'ho͞ovo͞od), 1861–1944, president of Finland (1931–37). A judge under the Russian czarist regime in Finland, he played a major part in the movement for Finnish independence and was banished (1914–17) to Siberia. On his return he headed the provisional government and proclaimed (Dec., 1917) the independence of Finland. In alliance with Germany, he directed the war (1918) against the Finnish Bolsheviks, who were aided by the Soviet Union. Svinhufvud became premier in 1930 and in 1931 succeeded K. J. Stahlberg as president of Finland. He took strong measures against the Communists and also suppressed the Fascist movement known as the Lapua, which had helped him to office. In 1937 he was succeeded as president by Kyosti Kallio, of the Agrarian party. Svinhufvud went into retirement, emerging briefly in 1940 to aid in negotiating the Finnish-German treaty.

Svir (svēr), river, c.140 mi (230 km) long, NW European USSR, flowing W from Lake Onega into Lake Ladoga. It is part of the VOLGA-BALTIC WATERWAY. There are hydroelectric stations at Svirstroy and Podporozhye.

Svishtov (svēshtôf'), town (1968 est. pop. 22,500), N Bulgaria, a port on the Danube River. It is an agricultural center. With a history dating to Roman times, it became, under Turkish rule (15th–19th cent.), an important commercial and military center known as Sistova. The city has a 19th-century cathedral, a university, and an archaeological museum.

Svoboda, Ludvík (lo͝od'vĕk svô'bôdä), 1895–, Czechoslovak general and political leader. Svoboda served in the Czech Legion in World War I and became an officer (1922) in the army of the newly founded Czechoslovak republic. He was forced to flee (1939) to the USSR when the Germans entered Prague. In World War II he organized and led a Czech army unit that fought (1941–45) under the Soviet high command. After the war Svoboda was (1949–50) Czechoslovak minister of defense. Regarded as a national hero, he emerged from retirement in 1968 to serve as president of Czechoslovakia after the resignation of Antonín NOVOTNÝ. He continued in this largely ceremonial post after the liberal regime was suppressed by the USSR (Aug., 1968).

Svolvaer (svōl'vĕr), town, Nordland co., W Norway, on Austvågøya island. It is the administrative center of the Lofoten island group and has fisheries.

Swabia (swā'bēə), Ger. *Schwaben,* historic region, mainly in S Baden-Württemberg and SW Bavaria, SW West Germany. It is bounded in the east by Upper Bavaria, in the west by France, and in the south by Switzerland and Austria. It includes the former Prussian province of Hohenzollern. The main physical features of Swabia are the BLACK FOREST; the valley of the upper Danube River, which rises there; the Swabian Jura, a mountain range that extends parallel to and N of the Danube; and the valley of the upper Neckar River. The Rhine and the Lake of Constance (sometimes called the Swabian Sea) form the western and southern borders. The easternmost section of Swabia is part of the Danubian plateau of Bavaria and is a Bavarian province (c.3,940 sq mi/10,205 sq km), with Augsburg as capital. Stuttgart, the capital of Baden-Württemberg, is the chief city of W Swabia. Swabia is predominantly made up of agricultural or forested country and is famous for the loveliness of its landscape. Farming, forestry, and livestock raising are major occupations. Industrial products include textiles, machinery, chemicals, and metal goods. Swabia is rich in history and is a treasury of German architecture. Settled in the 3d cent. by the Germanic Suebi and ALEMANNI during the great migrations, the region was also known as Alamannia until the 11th cent. It became one of the five basic or stem duchies of medieval Germany in the 9th cent., when it far exceeded its present boundaries, including also Alsace and Switzerland E of the Reuss River. In 1079 the duchy was bestowed on the house of HOHENSTAUFEN, which in 1138 also obtained the imperial dignity. On the extinction (1268) of the dynasty, Swabia broke up into small temporal and ecclesiastic lordships and lost its political identity. Territories in Alsace, S Baden, and Switzerland had already passed under the control of the house of Hapsburg. The Swiss part became independent in 1291 and the Hapsburg territories in Alsace passed to France in 1648, but Breisgau and the other Hapsburg domains in S Baden remained Austrian until 1803–6, except from 1469 to 1477, when they were ruled by Charles the Bold of Burgundy. The rest of Swabia was held in large part by the counts (later dukes) of Württemberg, by the margraves of Baden-Durlach, by the landgraves of Fürstenberg, by the princes of Hohenzollern, by the bishops of Strasbourg, Constance, and Augsburg, by several powerful abbeys, and by a multitude of petty princes, counts, and knights. The numerous and prosperous towns of Swabia were not slow in taking advantage of the political divisions of the feudal lords. Most of them had obtained the status of free imperial cities (i.e., virtually independent republics) by 1300. Among them were Augsburg, Ulm, Schwäbisch Gmünd, Reutlingen, and Ravensburg. Their wealth, due mainly to commerce and industry, made them the most powerful element of the country, and they made their superior power felt by forming a series of leagues, starting in 1331. The SWABIAN LEAGUE of 1376–89 successfully opposed Emperor Charles IV but was eventually defeated by the count of Württemberg. The most important Swabian League was that of 1488–1534. The chief Swabian cities accepted the Reformation in the 16th cent., but the countryside has remained divided between Catholics and Protestants to the present day. With the commercial revolution of the 15th and 16th cent. the Swabian cities temporarily lost most of their importance. In the 19th cent. some (especially Stuttgart) revived as industrial centers. When the Holy Roman Empire was organized in circles in the 16th cent., the Swabian Circle, similar in extent to the present region, was created. At the diet of Regensburg of 1801–3, which acted largely under the influence of Napoleon I, many of the small ecclesiastic and feudal holdings were taken over by Baden, Württemberg, and Bavaria. The Alemannic, or Swabian, dialects of the various regions of Swabia (in its largest sense) remain linguistically closely related.

Swabian League, association of Swabian cities and other powers in SW Germany for the protection of trade and for regional peace. The Swabian League of 1488–1534 is the best known of the long series dating from the 14th cent. Supported by the Holy Roman emperor as an instrument of imperial power, it comprised more than 26 cities and many nobles, knights, and prelates. The league had a court, a powerful army, and a formal constitution (renewed in 1496, 1500, 1512, and 1522). It backed the election (1519) of Holy Roman Emperor Charles V, and it used its military power to expel Duke Ulrich I from WÜRTTEMBERG. The league played a leading role in putting down the knights' revolt led by Franz von SICKINGEN, and it helped defeat the peasants in the PEASANTS' WAR. The dissolution (1534) of the league resulted from the opposition of interests between its feudal members and its cities and from the religious split caused by the Reformation. Many Protestant members in 1531 joined the SCHMALKALDIC LEAGUE. Later attempts by Charles V to restore the Swabian League failed.

Swahili (swähē'lē) [Arab.,=coast people], name for some of the inhabitants of the Kenya, Tanzania, Somali, and Mozambique coasts, Zanzibar, and E Zaïre. Descendants of black Africans and Arab traders (who came to the E African coast about A.D. 500), the Swahili do not form a cohesive ethnic group but are loosely united by common economic pursuits (especially trade), by cultural traditions, and particularly by the use of the SWAHILI LANGUAGE.

Swahili language, member of the Bantu group of African languages (see AFRICAN LANGUAGES and BANTU LANGUAGES). Swahili is spoken by 11 million people, chiefly in Tanzania, Kenya, Zaïre, Burundi, and Uganda, and serves as a lingua franca for additional millions in E Africa, including Europeans, Arabs, and Indians as well as Negro Africans. It is also now the official language of Kenya and Tanzania and has the largest number of speakers of the Bantu group of languages. Although grammatically a Bantu tongue, Swahili has been greatly influenced by Arabic, from which it has borrowed many words. It is the vehicle of a noteworthy literature that goes back to the beginning of the 18th cent. and is written in a form of the Arabic alphabet. In the second half of the 19th cent., missionaries introduced the Roman alphabet for recording Swahili. Since then writing has flourished, and some native authors of distinction have appeared. See Edgar C. Polomé, *Swahili Language Handbook* (1967).

Swains Island, island (1970 pop. 74), 1 sq mi (2.59 sq km), district of AMERICAN SAMOA, c.200 mi (320 km) N of TUTUILA. It is a ring of sand and coral with luxuriant vegetation. Swains Island has been privately owned by the same family for more than 100 years. Local government was ordered for the indigenous residents by the U.S. government in 1954. The island sends one nonvoting member to the territorial legislature.

swallow, common name for small perching birds of almost worldwide distribution. There are about 100 species of swallows, including the martins, which belong to the same family. Swallows have long, narrow wings, forked tails, and weak feet. They are extremely graceful in flight, making abrupt changes in speed and direction as they feed on the wing, catching insects in their wide mouths. Their plumage is blue or black with a metallic sheen, generally darker above than below. They nest in flocks in barns, sheds, chimneys, or other secluded places. The common American barn swallow, *Hirundo rustica,* is steel-blue above and pinkish beneath, with a rusty forehead and deeply forked tail. The purple martin, *Progne subis,* is deep violet with black wings and tail. Other American swallows, all with shallowly forked tails, are the cliff, or eave, swallow (*Petrochelidon pyrrhonota*), which builds jug-shaped nests of mud and clay lined with grass and feathers; the bank swallow or sand martin, which burrows into shore banks to nest; and the tree (*Iridoprocne bicolor*) and rough-winged (*Stelgidopteryx ruficollis*) swallows. The so-called chimney swallow is a SWIFT. Swallows are classified in the phylum CHORDATA, subphylum Vertebrata, class Aves, order Passeriformes, family Hirundinidae.

Swammerdam, Jan (yän svä'mərdäm), 1637–80, Dutch naturalist. He was a pioneer in the use of the microscope. Before he turned to religious contemplation his chief interest was the study of invertebrates. He investigated the life histories of frogs and of numerous insects, which he classified on the basis of their metamorphic development. He also made valuable observations on human anatomy and was probably the first to detect red blood cells (1658). A composite collection of his descriptions and of his accurate and exquisitely executed drawings was published posthumously (2 vol., 1737–38) and appeared in English as *The Book of Nature* (1758). He was an early and influential proponent of the theory of EVOLUTION, in opposition to the current belief in spontaneous generation.

swamp, shallow body of water in a low-lying, poorly drained depression, usually containing abundant plant growth dominated by trees, such as cypress, and high shrubs. Swamps develop in moist climates, generally in such places as low-lying coastal plains, flood plains of rivers, and old lake basins or in areas where normal drainage has been disrupted by glacial deposits. In the United States, swamps cover approximately 100,000 sq mi (260,000 sq km), most of them occurring as small swamps in northeastern states that were covered with glaciers in the past. The most extensive swamps are found along the Atlantic and Gulf coastal plains, notable examples being the EVERGLADES of S Florida, DISMAL SWAMP of Virginia, and OKEFENOKEE SWAMP of Georgia and N Florida. Because the bottom of a swamp is at or below the water table, swamps serve to channel runoff into the groundwater supply, thus helping to stabilize the water table. During periods of very heavy rains, a swamp can act as a natural flood control device, as excess runoff can be temporarily stored in its basin. Swamp vegetation varies with climate. Grasses, rushes, and sphagnum moss predominate in temperate climates; cypress and mangrove predominate in more tropical regions. Lush vegetation provides great protection for nesting waterfowl and fish as well as a hospitable habitat for many types of small mammal such as beaver and otter. Swamps that are drained make excellent agricultural land because of the high organic content of the bottom sediments. In addition, rising land values and demand have encouraged the drainage of many swamplands, such as coastal Florida, for home development. However, a problem associated with recently drained swamps is oxidation of the thick peat deposits forming the soil, which can result in subsidence of the land and such problems as cracked walls, broken underground pipes, and buckled roadways. The increased use of drained swampland for urban construction, with its associated acres of blacktop paving and storm sewers, results in greater runoff and increases the probability of flooding and pollution in these regions. Swamp drainage also destroys the nesting areas of many wildlife species. Thus, environmentalists have urged, with increasing success, the slowing down of swamp drainage. There are a variety of local terms for swamps, including BOG, *marsh, fen,* and *moor.* However, *bog* usually refers to a swampy depression with a thick mat of living and dead organic matter floating on the water surface and a low level of oxygen in the water below. *Marsh* implies a large area of wet land where the dominant vegetation consists of low-lying grasses, rushes, and sedges.

Swampscott (swŏmp'skət), town (1970 pop. 13,578), Essex co., E Mass., a resort on Massachusetts Bay; settled 1629, set off from Lynn and inc. 1852. It has a fishing industry. The Mary Baker Eddy house is preserved.

Swan, Sir Joseph Wilson, 1828–1914, English chemist and physicist. He made an incandescent lamp using a carbon filament (1860), 20 years before Edison's lamp. Noted for important contributions to photography as well, he devised the first commercially practical process for carbon printing, introduced the dry plate, and invented bromide paper. Swan also experimented with the production of man-made fibers. He was knighted in 1904.

swan, common name for a large aquatic bird of both hemispheres, related to ducks and geese. It has a long, gracefully curved neck and an extremely long, convoluted trachea which makes possible its far-carrying calls. The orange-billed white trumpeter swan, *Cygnus buccinator,* seen in parks, is the mute swan, of Old World origin. It breeds in the wild state in parts of Europe, Asia, and the United States. During the breeding season it has a trumpetlike note, softer in the tame birds. The whistling swan migrates from the arctic to Mexico. Conservation measures saved the almost extinct trumpeter swan of North America, the largest species. Wild species in Europe include the whooper (or whooping) and the Bewick swans. The black swan, *Chenopis atrata,* is native to Australia, and the black-necked swan, *Cygnus melancoriphus,* to South America. The black swan has been domesticated. Swans are classified in the phylum CHORDATA, subphylum Vertebrata, class Aves, order Anseriformes, family Anatidae. See study by Peter Scott and the Wildfowl Trust (1972).

Swanee, river: see SUWANNEE.

Swanscombe man: see MAN, PREHISTORIC.

Swansea (swŏn'zē, -sē) or **Abertawe** (ăbərtou'ē), county borough (1971 pop. 172,566), Glamorganshire, S Wales, on Swansea Bay at the mouth of the Tawe River. It is a metallurgical center; steel and tinplate are the most important products. There are sheet-metal mills, foundries, and smelting works. Other industries are engineering, shipbuilding, oil refining (at the suburb Llandarcy), and the export of anthracite. Crude oil, metals, timber, grain, and rubber are imported. Swansea ware, of rich blue coloring with decorative painting, was made at the Swansea potteries in the first half of the 19th cent. The Royal Institution of South Wales, the University College of Swansea, and a medieval castle on the site of a ruined Norman castle are points of special interest. In 1974, Swansea became part of the new nonmetropolitan county of West Glamorgan.

Swansea (swŏn'zē), town (1970 pop. 12,640), Bristol co., SE Mass., a suburb of Fall River, on an inlet of Mount Hope Bay; founded 1667, inc. 1785. Once a vast farmland, it is now chiefly residential. Cloth is manufactured. Many of its inhabitants were massacred in King Philip's War (1675), but the town was later rebuilt and prospered.

Swanson, Claude Augustus, 1862-1939, American politician, b. Pittsylvania co., Va. He practiced law in Chatham, Va., and after serving (1893-1905) in the U.S. House of Representatives he was (1906-10) governor of Virginia. In the U.S. Senate (1910-33), Swanson became recognized as one of the foremost authorities on naval and foreign affairs in the United States; he was a delegate to the London Naval Conference in 1931 and the Geneva Disarmament Conference in 1932. As U.S. Secretary of the Navy (1933-39), Swanson directed a vast naval expansion program.

Swanson, Gloria, 1899-, American movie actress, b. Chicago. Swanson began her career in films in 1913, later working for Mack Sennett. From 1920 until 1932 she produced her own films. Her first sound film was *The Trespasser* (1929). Noted in silent films for her worldly glamour, she made a successful comeback in *Sunset Boulevard* (1950), portraying an aging movie queen. Since then she has worked to find and preserve silent films. Swanson appeared on Broadway in *Butterflies Are Free* in 1971.

Swanson, Howard, 1909-, American composer, b. Atlanta. Swanson, a Negro, worked during his childhood on the railroad. He studied at the Cleveland Institute of Music and in Paris with Nadia Boulanger. For a time he earned a living working for the Internal Revenue Service. Among his compositions are two symphonies, two piano concertos, *Night Music* for chamber orchestra, a *Short Symphony,* and songs, five of which are settings of poems by Langston Hughes.

Swarthmore College, at Swarthmore, Pa.; coeducational; founded 1864 by the Society of Friends. It maintains a cooperative program with Bryn Mawr, Haverford College, and the Univ. of Pennsylvania.

Swasey, Ambrose, 1846-1937, American engineer and manufacturer, b. Exeter, N.H. While an apprentice toolmaker in Exeter, he met Worcester Reed Warner, a fellow apprentice. The two men later worked in a machine shop in Hartford, Conn., and in 1880 went to Chicago, where they established a machine-tool factory. The firm moved (c.1881) to Cleveland and was incorporated (1900) as the Warner and Swasey Company. The firm produced an epicycloidal milling machine; an accurate dividing machine; a gear-cutting machine; and the Swasey range and position finder, adopted by the U.S. government. However, the firm is known especially for the manufacture of telescope mountings, notably the mountings of the 40-in. (100-cm) refracting telescope at Yerkes Observatory and of the 36-in. (91-cm) refractor at Lick Observatory.

Swat (swät), largest and most important of the princely states that still remain intact in the North-West Frontier Province, Pakistan. Saidu is the capital. The largely inaccessible region is reached through mountain passes from the south. Swat is famous for its beautiful forests and gardens and has a noted wood-carving industry. Fruit and honey are also important products, and curtains and woolen blankets are made by cottage industries. There is a college. Archaeological evidence indicates that Swat's history dates back to at least the 3d cent. B.C. Long a stronghold of Buddhism, it has several Buddhist stupas.

Swatow: see SHAN-T'OU, China.

Swaziland (swä'zēlănd), kingdom (1972 est. pop. 442,000), 6,705 sq mi (17,366 sq km), SE Africa. The capital is MBABANE. Swaziland is bordered on the S, W, and N by the Republic of South Africa and on the E by Mozambique. The country is mountainous, with steplike plateaus descending from the highveld (3,500-5,000 ft/1,067-1,524 m) in the W through the middleveld (1,500-3,000 ft/457-914 m) and the lowveld (500-1,500 ft/152-457 m), then rising to the rolling plateau of the Lebombo Mts. Swaziland is cut by four major river systems, which have vast hydroelectric potential and are increasingly used for irrigation. The country has excellent agricultural and ranching land. Sugarcane, citrus fruits, rice, cotton, maize, sorghum, tobacco, and peanuts are the principal crops. Cattle, a major export, and goats are raised in large numbers. About 56% of the land is held by the Swazi and the rest mainly by South Africans and Europeans. The forests of the highveld yield wood pulp and timber. Swaziland's mineral resources include iron ore—most of which is shipped to Japan via Mozambique—asbestos, coal, tin, and

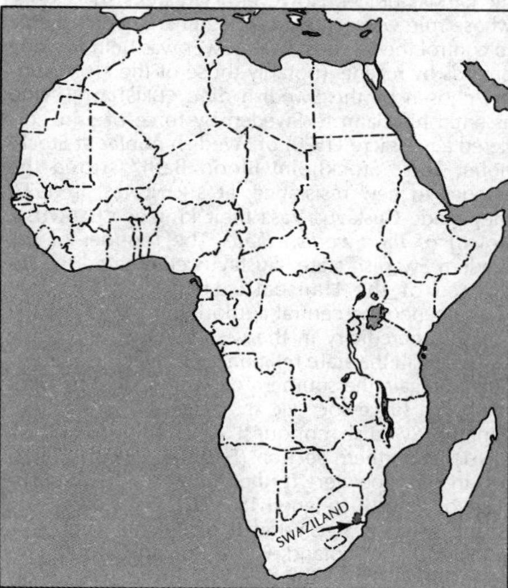

barite. Many Swazis are employed in South Africa's mines. Industry in Swaziland consists chiefly of food processing and the manufacture of light consumer goods. Tourism is being encouraged. Swaziland's major trading partners are Great Britain and South Africa. The unit of currency is the South African rand. Swaziland, Lesotho, and Botswana form a customs and monetary unit with South Africa. English is the official language, but the bulk of the population speaks SiSwati, a Zulu dialect. About 40% of the people practice traditional religions; most of the rest are Christians. The Swazi probably moved southward into the Mozambique area in the 16th cent. Fleeing Zulu attacks in the early 19th cent., they arrived in present-day Swaziland. During the 1800s, Europeans entered the area to seek concessions, and in 1888 the Swazi king granted them self-government. In 1903, Swaziland became a High Commission Territory ruled by a British commissioner. Limited self-government was not granted until 1963, and four years later Swaziland became a kingdom under a new constitution. On Sept. 6, 1968, Swaziland achieved complete independence but retained membership in the Commonwealth of Nations. The king is the head of state. Until 1973, when King Sobhuza II (reigned 1921-) abrogated the constitution and assumed personal power, the monarch administered through a cabinet and a prime minister chosen by parliament. Partly elected and partly appointed by the king, parliament consisted of a senate and a house of assembly. The king's party, the Imbokodvo National Movement, was the country's dominant political force. Parliament could not legislate on questions regulated by Swazi law or custom unless authorized by the Swazi National Council, an advisory body consisting of the king, the queen mother, and all adult male Swazis. The Swazi people continue to find a common cause in resistance to incorporation into South Africa, which is favored by the country's Afrikaner minority. See Hilda Kuper, *The Swazi: A South African Kingdom* (1963); Christian P. Potholm, *Swaziland: The Dynamics of Political Modernization* (1972).

swearing, in law: see OATH.

sweat or **perspiration,** fluid secreted by the sweat glands of mammalian skin and containing water, salts, and waste products of body metabolism such as urea. The dissolved solid content of sweat is only one eighth that of an equal volume of urine, the body's main vehicle of salt excretion; however, excessive sweating may produce severe salt loss (see HEAT EXHAUSTION). Human sweat glands are of two types, eccrine and apocrine. The eccrine glands, found everywhere on the body surface, are vital to the regulation of body temperature. Evaporation of the sweat secreted by the eccrines cools the body, dissipating the heat generated by metabolic processes. The release of such sweat is usually imperceptible; yet even in cool weather an individual will lose from 1 pt to 3 qt of fluid per day. Only when environmental conditions are especially hot or humid, or during periods of exercise or emotional stress, does the output of sweat exceed the rate of evaporation, so that noticeable beads of moisture appear on the skin. When such conditions are extreme, the body may lose up to 20 qt of fluid per day. Production of sweat is controlled by the temperature-regulating center of the hypothalamus. The apocrine glands, which occur only in the armpits and about the ears, nipples, navel, and anogenital region, are scent glands. They function in response to stress or sexual stimulation, playing no part in temperature regulation. The apocrines exude a sticky fluid quite different from the watery sweat of the eccrines. Apocrine fluid is rich in organic substances that are odorless when fresh but are quickly degraded by bacteria on the skin to produce characteristic odors. Copious sweating in the armpits comes not from the apocrines but from the eccrines interspersed among them.

sweating system, method of exploiting labor by supplying materials to workers and paying by the piece (see PIECEWORK) for work done on those materials in the workers' homes or in small workshops (sweatshops). The system (sometimes known as the cottage industry) evolved especially in those industries that did not require expensive machinery, as in making garments. Employees were typically found among women, children, the elderly, and invalids. The worst aspects associated with this system were long hours (sometimes 15-18 hr a day), very low wages, and unsanitary conditions. The term has also been applied to the subcontracting of work to a middleman who has the work done in his home by persons hired by him. In Great Britain the system first appeared early in the 19th cent. and was not prohibited by law until 1909. In the United States it began in the Civil War period, when the wives and children of soldiers were employed in making uniforms. Before the Industrial Revolution household industries had been customary but were quite different in nature: the household supplied its own materials, marketed the finished product in the neighborhood, and combined its industry with subsistence farming. With the introduction of standardization in industry, the advantages of the low cost of production in the sweating system have lessened. See Beatrice Webb, *How Best to Do Away with the Sweating System* (1892); J. R. Commons, *Trade Unionism and Labor Problems* (1905, repr. 1967).

swede: see TURNIP.

Sweden, Swed. *Sverige,* constitutional monarchy (1973 est. pop. 8,200,000), 173,648 sq mi (449,750 sq km), N Europe, occupying the eastern part of the Scandinavian peninsula and bordering on Norway in the west, on Finland in the northeast, on the Gulf of Bothnia in the east, on the Baltic Sea in the south, and on the Øresund (The Sound), the Kattegat, and the Skagerrak in the southwest. The country includes several islands, notably GOTLAND and ÖLAND, in the Baltic. STOCKHOLM is the capital and largest city of Sweden, which is divided into 24 counties (*län*). Sweden falls into two main geographical regions: the north (Norrland), comprising about two thirds of the country, which is mountainous (except for a narrow strip of lowland along the Gulf of Bothnia); and the south (Svealand and Götaland), which is mostly low-lying and where most of the population lives. About 55% of Sweden's land area is forested and only about 8% is arable. The country has several large rivers, which generally flow in a southeastward direction; these include the Götaälv, the Dalälven, the Indalsälven, the Angermanälven, the Umeälv, the Skellefteälv, the Luleälv, and the Torneälv. There are also a number of large lakes, including lakes Vänern, Vättern, Mälaren, Storsjön, Hjälmaren, Siljan, and Uddjaur. The highest point in Sweden is Kebnekaise (6,965 ft/2,123 m), located in the Kölen (Kjölen) mts. in LAPLAND. The great majority of the population speaks Swedish and is descended from Scandinavian tribes (see GERMANS); there are small Finnish and Lapp-speaking minorities. Virtually all Swedes belong to the Lutheran church, whose metropolitan see is UPPSALA. Sweden is a highly industrialized country and has one of the highest living standards in the world. Since 1940 there has been a great movement of workers from farms to cities; nevertheless, agricultural output has increased considerably with the application of scientific farming methods. At the start of the 1970s manufacturing contributed about 32% of the annual national income and agriculture about 4%. Farming

is concentrated in the southern part of the country; the leading commodities produced are dairy goods, grain (including fodder crops), sugar beets, and potatoes. Large numbers of poultry, hogs, and cattle are raised. Sweden is one of the world's leading producers of iron ore; important mines are at KIRUNA, Gällivare, and Grängesberg. Copper, lead, and zinc ores and pyrite are also extracted in sizable quantities. The country's chief industrial centers are Stockholm, GÖTEBORG, MALMÖ, Uppsala, VÄSTERÅS, HÄLSINGBORG, and NORRKÖPING. The leading manufactures include iron and steel, metal goods, machinery, forest products, construction materials, textiles, clothing, processed food, refined petroleum, motor vehicles, and ships. Sweden is known for its decorative art, its folk art, its fine glassware (made especially at ORREFORS), and its high-quality steel cutlery and blades. Much hydroelectric power is generated. The country's beautiful scenery and handsome towns and cities attract large numbers of tourists. Sweden carries on a large foreign trade, and the value of imports usually slightly exceeds the value of exports. The main imports are machinery, transport equipment, food, petroleum and petroleum products, and chemicals; the chief exports are machinery, ships, forest products, iron ore, and iron and steel. The principal trade partners are West Germany, Great Britain, Denmark, Norway, and the United States. Sweden is a member of the European Free Trade Association, and in 1972 it signed an industrial free trade agreement with the European Common Market. The educational and cultural level in Sweden is high, and the school system is outstanding. There are universities at Göteborg, Karlstad, Linköping, Lund, Örebro, Stockholm, Umeå, Uppsala, and Växjö. The Nobel Prizes (except the Peace Prize) are awarded annually in Sweden. Social welfare legislation has long been advanced and comprehensive; it provides for universal pension systems (for old age, disability, and survivors) and also for maternity benefits, workmen's compensation insurance, sickness insurance, and allowances for all children.

Origins of Sweden. In early historic times, Svealand was inhabited by the Svear (mentioned as the Suiones by Tacitus in the late 1st cent. A.D.). They engaged in wars with their southern neighbors, who inhabited Götaland and who according to an unproved tradition were the ancestors of the Goths. By the 6th cent. A.D. the Svear had conquered the Gotar, with whom they merged. The early Swedes were combined and confused with other Scandinavians (e.g., the piratical VIKINGS and NORSEMEN). The Swedes alone, known as VARANGIANS in Russia, extended (10th cent.) their influence to the Black Sea. The Swedish kings warred for centuries with their Danish and Norwegian neighbors. St. Ansgar introduced Christianity c.829, but paganism was fully eradicated only in the 12th cent. by ERIC IX, who also conquered Finland. The royal authority was weakened before the 13th cent. by the rise of an independent feudal class. The Swedish cities also began to acquire wide rights at that time and were strongly influenced by German merchants of the HANSEATIC LEAGUE, active especially at VISBY. In 1319, Sweden and Norway were united under MAGNUS VII, and in 1397 Queen MARGARET effected the personal union of Sweden, Norway, and Denmark through the KALMAR UNION. However, Margaret's successors, whose rule was centered in Denmark, were unable to control the Swedes. Real power was held for long periods by regents (notably those of the STURE family) chosen by the Swedish diet. CHRISTIAN II, who asserted his claim to Sweden by force of arms, ordered a massacre (1520) of Swedish nobles at Stockholm. This "Stockholm Blood Bath" stirred the Swedes to new resistance; at STRÄNGNÄS, in 1523, they made Gustavus Vasa their king as GUSTAVUS I.

Growth of the Swedish State. The founder of the modern Swedish state, Gustavus eliminated the influence of the Hanseatic League in Sweden, strengthened the central authority, made (1544) the kingship hereditary in the VASA dynasty, and made Lutheranism the state religion. However, he was unable to regain the southern provinces, held by Denmark. His successor, ERIC XIV (reigned 1560–68), began the Swedish conquest of LIVONIA by taking (1561) its northern section (Estonia). Swedish interests in E Europe were further enhanced by the marriage of John III (reigned 1569–92), Eric's successor, to the sister of Sigismund II of Poland. Their son, SIGISMUND III of Poland, was a Roman Catholic; his accession (1592) to the Swedish throne was deeply resented by the Protestant Swedes. He was deposed in 1599, and his uncle became regent and then king of Sweden as CHARLES IX (reigned 1607–11). Charles's son, GUSTAVUS II (Gustavus Adolphus; reigned 1611–32), made Sweden a great European power. Through a war with Russia, he acquired (1617) Ingermanland and Karelia; from Poland he took nearly all of Livonia. By his victories at Breitenfeld (1631) and Lützen (1632) in the THIRTY YEARS WAR, Gustavus made Sweden the dominant Protestant power of continental Europe. Axel OXENSTIERNA, appointed chancellor by Gustavus in 1612, was highly influential during Gustavus's reign and the first half of the reign of Queen CHRISTINA (1632–54). In the 17th cent. Swedish colonial aspirations in North America (see NEW SWEDEN) proved short-lived. The Peace of Westphalia (1648; see WESTPHALIA, PEACE OF), which ended the Thirty Years War, gave W POMERANIA, WISMAR, and the archbishopric of BREMEN to Sweden, making the Swedish kings princes of the Holy Roman Empire. CHARLES X, who became king on the abdication (1654) of Christina, successfully led wars against Poland and Denmark. The southern provinces of Sweden were definitively recovered from Denmark in 1660. Under CHARLES XI (reigned 1660–97), Sweden became an absolute monarchy, and the great nobles lost their independence. In the NORTHERN WAR (1700–21), which broke out shortly after the accession of CHARLES XII (reigned 1697–1718), Sweden was crushed after gaining its greatest military triumphs (e.g., at NARVA and in Livonia). Under the treaties of Stockholm (1720) and Nystad (1721), Sweden ceded the archbishopric of Bremen to Hanover, part of Pomerania to Prussia, and Livonia, Ingermanland, and Karelia to Russia. Internally, Sweden was torn in the 18th cent. by political intrigue and civil discord. Ulrica Eleonora (d.1741) succeeded her brother, Charles XII, in 1718, but abdicated (1720) in favor of her husband, Frederick I (d. 1751), a prince of Hesse-Kassel. The constitution of 1720 gave increased powers to the Riksdag (diet) and the political scene was dominated (1738–65) by the faction known as the Hats, who favored an aggressive anti-Russian policy in alliance with France and who represented the nobility and the bureaucracy. They were successfully challenged in 1765 by the Caps, who sought peaceful relations with Russia and who represented the lesser estates. In 1751 the house of Oldenburg-Holstein-Gottorp gained the Swedish throne when Adolphus Frederick became king. His son, GUSTAVUS III (reigned 1771–92), restored absolutism in 1772 but was later assassinated by a conspiracy of nobles. GUSTAVUS IV (reigned 1792–1809), a despotic ruler, involved Sweden in war with Napoleon I and then (1806–9) with Russia. A coup d'etat (1809) placed his uncle, CHARLES XIII, on the throne, and later in the same year Sweden was forced to cede Finland to Russia. A constitutional monarchy was established by the constitution of 1809, which, although modified considerably (e.g., in 1866 and 1969), remained in effect until Jan. 1, 1975. From 1810, Swedish affairs were in the hands of Charles's adopted heir, Marshal Bernadotte (later CHARLES XIV). Sweden again joined the allies against Napoleon in 1813; this was the last war in which Sweden has participated. The Congress of Vienna compensated (1814) Sweden for its loss of Pomerania and Finland with NORWAY, which remained a separate kingdom in personal union with Sweden until 1905.

Sweden since 1814. The history of 19th-century Sweden, under Charles XIV (reigned 1818–44), OSCAR I (1844–59), CHARLES XV (1859–72), and OSCAR II (1872–1907), was one of progressive liberalization in government and of industrial development. Freedom of the press (1844) and internal free trade (1864) were established, and the suffrage bill of 1865 enfranchised the middle class. The accelerated industrial development of the late 19th cent. was accompanied by the rise of the Social Democratic party, which dominated Swedish politics after 1920. From 1870 to 1914 about 1.5 million Swedes emigrated to the United States, mostly to the Midwest. Relations with Norway were strained throughout the 19th cent., and in 1905 the union of Norway and Sweden was peacefully terminated. Under GUSTAVUS V (reigned 1907–50), Sweden averted involvement in World War I and II, making armed neutrality the basis of its foreign policy, and, except for the early 1920s and early 1930s, enjoyed economic prosperity. Universal taxpayer suffrage was introduced in 1907, and in 1910 a workmen's compensation insurance law began the long series of Swedish welfare legislation. Sweden entered the United Nations in 1946, and Dag Hammerskjöld, a Swedish diplomat, was secretary-general of the organization from 1953 until his death in 1961. In 1950, GUSTAVUS VI ascended the throne; he was succeeded in 1973 by CHARLES XVI GUSTAVUS. Sweden refused to join the North Atlantic Treaty Organization (NATO) in 1949 in order not to compromise its neutrality, and for similar reasons withdrew its application for full membership in the European Economic Community (Common Market) in 1971. The Social Democrats, led by Tage Erlander from 1946 to 1969 and thereafter by Olof Palme, controlled the government after 1945, usually at the head of coalition governments. Considerable new social welfare legislation was passed, but from the mid-1960s Swedish economic growth slowed, and there were sizable increases in unemployment and in the rate of inflation in the early 1970s. Elections in 1973 left the Riksdag deadlocked, with both the Social Democrats (and their Communist allies) and the more conservative opposition having an equal number of members. However, Palme continued as prime minister, at the head of a revised cabinet.

Government. Under the constitution of 1975, which replaced that of 1809, the king is head of state but has little power. Legislative power is vested in the unicameral Riksdag, made up of 349 members elected by a system of proportional representation to three-year terms. The country's executive is the cabinet, headed by the prime minister, which must have the confidence of the Riksdag. Public administration is to a large extent decentralized, so that elected county and municipal governments play a major role in running the country. See Ingvar Andersson, *A History of Sweden* (tr. 1968); Kurt Samuelsson, *From Great Power to Welfare State* (1968); R. N. Bain, *Charles XII and the Collapse of the Swedish Empire, 1682–1719* (1895, repr. 1969); J. B. Board, *The Government and Politics of Sweden* (1970); C. J. Hallendorf and Adolf Schüch, *History of Sweden* (1929, repr. 1970); R. F. Tomasson, *Sweden: Proto-*

type of Modern Society (1970); M. D. Hancock, *Sweden: The Politics of Post Industrial Change* (1972); Vilhelm Moberg, *A History of the Swedish People* (2 vol., tr. 1972 and 1974); Irene Scobbie, *Sweden* (1972); Wilfrid Fleisher, *Sweden, The Welfare State* (1956, repr. 1973).

Swedenborg, Emanuel (swēd'ənbôrg; āmä'nōōĕl svä"dənbŏrk'), 1688–1772, Swedish scientist, religious teacher, and mystic. His religious system, sometimes called Swedenborgianism, is largely incorporated in the Church of the NEW JERUSALEM, founded some years after his death. His father was Bishop Swedberg, professor at Uppsala Univ. The name became Swedenborg when the family was ennobled (1719). Emanuel traveled extensively and was made (1716) assessor of the Royal College of Mines; his engineering skill made him widely known. He took active part in the proceedings of the house of nobles, where he showed himself an ardent reformer. A series of scientific works by him began to appear in 1734. The first, *Principia*, was an attempt to trace the system of the world philosophically. He studied almost every field of scientific investigation and wrote copiously, anticipating in many instances later discoveries and inventions. His studies of man in works on the animal kingdom, the human brain, and psychology were published before 1747, when he resigned his post and gave himself to the contemplation of spiritual matters, especially to the work of making clear to mankind the true inner doctrines of the divine Word as he claimed that they were revealed to him by direct insight into the spiritual world after "heaven was opened" to him in 1745. Visions and communication with spirits and angels helped prepare him to set forth the teachings of what he termed the New Church, the inauguration of which he believed to have taken place in 1757 with the second coming of Christ. He claimed to have received from the Lord himself the true sense of the Scriptures. His expositions of Genesis and Exodus were published as *Arcana Coelestia* (1749–56). Of the many works that followed, a number have been published in English, among them *Heaven and Hell; Divine Love and Wisdom; True Christian Religion*, stating fully his system of doctrine; and the *Apocalypse Revealed*. His writings have been translated into numerous other languages. It was not Swedenborg's intention to establish a new sect. In his mind the New Church might include members of any Christian churches. The latter part of his life he spent partly in London, partly in Amsterdam and Stockholm. In 1810 a society was founded for publishing Swedenborg's works in English. In Stockholm lithographed facsimiles of his manuscripts were issued in 1869–70, and an 18-volume edition of his writings was published between 1901 and 1916. See R. F. Tafel, ed., *Documents Concerning Swedenborg* (1857–77); biographies by George Trobridge (4th ed. 1968) and C. S. Sigstedt (1971); studies by H. A. Keller (1927, repr. 1972), J. H. Spalding (1957), and Inge Jonsson (tr. 1971).

Swedish language, member of the North Germanic, or Scandinavian, group of the Germanic subfamily of the INDO-EUROPEAN family of languages. It is the official language of Sweden and one of the official languages of Finland, and it is spoken by about 9 million people: 7,500,000 in Sweden, 500,000 in Finland and Estonia, and 1 million in the United States and Canada. A descendant of Old Norse (see GERMANIC LANGUAGES; NORSE), the Swedish language falls into two major periods historically: Old Swedish, the early form of the language (usually dated from the 9th cent. to the early 16th cent.), and New Swedish, the modern form of the language (since the early 16th cent.). The Swedish language underwent many changes during the Middle Ages but began to be standardized in the 16th cent. as a result of such events as the throwing off of Danish domination, the Reformation, and the translation of the Bible into Swedish. In 1786 the Swedish Academy was established to oversee the development of the language. Swedish absorbed a number of words from Low German in the Middle Ages, from High German in the 16th and 17th cent., from French in the 18th cent., and from English in the 20th cent. On the whole, Swedish grammar is simple. The noun has only the singular, possessive, and plural forms. There are two genders for nouns, a nonneuter (or common) class and a neuter class. The former includes masculine, feminine, and common nouns; the latter, nouns for such categories as countries and substances and also many abstract nouns. Swedish is noted for its musical quality. This results partly from the use of pitch accents, which sometimes serve to differentiate the meanings of homonyms. There is considerable difference between the spoken and written forms of Swedish. For example, a number of inflections used in literary Swedish are not employed in the spoken language. Until the early 13th cent., RUNES were used for recording Swedish, but thereafter (as Christianity took hold in Scandinavia) they began to be replaced by the Roman alphabet, to which three symbols, *å*, *ä*, and *ö*, have been added. See Gösta Bergman, *A Short History of the Swedish Language* (tr. 1947); Immanuel Björkhagen, *Modern Swedish Grammar* (9th ed. 1962).

Swedish literature. Literature in the Swedish language may have flourished in early medieval times, but few written traces remain. Historical chronicles, religious writings, and ballads and verse in Swedish are extant from the 12th cent. The earliest major religious writer was St. BRIDGET OF SWEDEN (c.1300–1373). As Danish influence grew after the Kalmar Union (1397), there was a period of literary decline. Of note in the 15th cent. were the poems of Bishop Thomas of Strängnäs (d. 1443) in praise of liberty. The Reformation (16th cent.) conferred a somber spirit upon Sweden, and few secular works were written. The theological and historical works of Olaus Petri (1493–1552) are notable for beginning the linguistic transition to modern Swedish. Petri also assisted in the great Swedish translation of the Bible (1540–41), a project directed by his brother Laurentius Petri (1499–1573). Sweden's emergence by 1648 as a great power was not accompanied by comparable literary splendor, but under Queen Christina continental influence helped to bring about a literary renaissance. Georg Stiernhielm (1598–1672) wrote verse that was sophisticated both in form and in content, combining classical idealism with a Gothic strain. The folk songs in medieval style of Lasse Lucidor (1638–74) and the baroque rhymes of Gunno Dahlstjerna were outstanding among poetical works. Ideas of the Enlightenment, introduced by Olof von DALIN in the 1730s, spread steadily, and great mystical intellectualism was set forth in the numerous works of Emanuel SWEDENBORG. The greatest Swedish poet of the age, Carl Michael BELLMAN, wrote superb verse inspired by traditional Swedish songs. In the reign of GUSTAVUS III, founder of the Swedish Academy in 1786, the important court circle of writers included the eminent poet and critic Johan Henrik Kellgren. The great scientist Carolus LINNAEUS made enormously influential contributions to Swedish literature. Classical standards were upheld by the academy, but the sentimentality of Rousseau and other European writers, strongly defended by Thomas Thorild (1759–1808), began in the late 18th cent. to permeate the middle classes. When romanticism flowered in the golden age of Swedish poetry (c.1820–1840), the movement became Germanic in character and conservative in tone; many of its themes were taken from folk culture. Historical and folk interests are typified by the work of A. A. AFZELIUS. Three of the finest romantic poets were Erik GEIJER, Per Atterbom, and Esaias TEGNÉR. The tales of C. J. L. ALMQUIST show the development of Swedish prose and also serve to divide the declining romantic movement from the literary ferment of the 1840s. By mid-century a mild utilitarianism and social criticism, modeled along English lines, was prevalent in Swedish literature and journalism. Fredrika BREMER gained international renown as a reporter and activist for women's rights. The major spokesman for an idealistic vision was the philosopher Abraham RYDBERG. The first appearance of true realism, influenced by the great dramatist August STRINDBERG, proved short-lived; the talents of the realists of Young Sweden, among them Gustaf af GEIJERSTAM, did not overshadow a movement toward creative individualism. Verner von HEIDENSTAM was the great exponent of personal expression, and the poet Gustaf FRÖDING and the novelist Selma LAGERLÖF followed equally personal paths. In the early 20th cent. the plays and novels of Hjalmar SÖDERBERG presaged a renewed emphasis on restraint and realism. Proletarian themes were developed after World War I by Vilhelm MOBERG, Ludvig Nordström, and Martin Koch. The Nobel laureate Pär LAGERKVIST, considered the greatest Swedish writer of the 20th cent., developed and sustained Swedish expressionism, as did the novelist Hjalmar BERGMAN and the poet Birger Sjöberg. Modernism, with its emphasis on experimental form, was a strong trend in the 1920s; a group of young writers, influenced by Hemingway, concerned themselves with labor themes and were collectively termed "The Young Five." These were Artur Lundkvist, Harry MARTINSON, Gustav Sandgren, Erik Asklund, and Josef Kjellgren. A number of fine writers emerged both before and after World War II, including the novelist Eyvind JOHNSON (who shared the 1974 Nobel Prize in literature with Harry Martinson), Ivar Lo-Johansson, and Agnes von KRUSENSTIERNA. None, however, approached the stature of Lagerkvist, who has remained the giant of Swedish literature. See Alrik Gustafson, *Six Scandinavian Novelists* (1940) and *A History of Swedish Literature* (1961); collections of poetry ed. by C. W. Stork (1930) and R. J. McClean (1968).

Sweelinck, Jan Pieterszoon (yän pē'tərsōn swā'lĭngk), 1562–1621, Dutch organist and composer, called the "maker of German organists" because the succession of his pupils descended directly to J. S. Bach and Handel. In his organ fugues he was the first to give an independent part to the pedals.

sweepstakes, contest or race, usually a horse race, on which a lottery is run. Prizes are awarded to the holders of winning tickets. In the case of a horse race, the draw is made from the names of all the horses entered in the race and vast numbers of blanks. Thus most ticket holders draw blanks, while only a few draw the name of a horse. In some sweepstakes, prizes are awarded to persons holding tickets bearing the name of horses that win, place, and show, while in others prizes are given also to those whose tickets bear the names of all the horses that started in the race. In still another form of sweepstakes, the tickets sold bear numbers, some of which are to be assigned to the horses that will run in the race. The term *sweepstakes* may also refer to the total amount of money contributed. The Irish Hospitals Sweepstakes is probably the most popular in existence today. Because of a scandal over the Louisiana State lottery, the U.S. Congress in 1890 passed a law making it illegal in the United States to import, to send through the mails, or to ship in interstate commerce any sweepstakes tickets. In 1963 a legal state sweepstakes lottery was initiated in New Hampshire to provide funds for state education. Other states soon followed with similar lotteries.

Sweet, Henry, 1845–1912, English philologist and phonetician. An authority on Anglo-Saxon and the history of the English language, Sweet was also a pioneer in modern scientific phonetics. His *History of English Sounds* (1874) was a landmark in that study. In 1901 he was made a reader in phonetics at Oxford. Among his other writings are *A Handbook of Phonetics* (1877), *A New English Grammar* (2 parts, 1892–95), *The History of Language* (1900), *The Sounds of English* (1908), and works on Anglo-Saxon, Middle English, and Icelandic. Sweet was the model for Professor Higgins in G. B. Shaw's play *Pygmalion*.

sweetbread. The thymus gland (known as throat sweetbread) and the pancreas (stomach sweetbread), especially of the calf and lamb (although beef sweetbreads are sometimes eaten), are considered delicacies and are rich in mineral elements and vitamins. The pancreas is generally preferred to the thymus. Sweetbreads are highly perishable and, immediately after removal from refrigeration, should be soaked and parboiled, then creamed, curried, braised, or otherwise prepared for serving.

sweetbriar: see SWEETBRIER.

Sweet Briar College, at Sweet Briar, Va., NE of Lynchburg; for women; chartered 1901, opened 1906.

sweetbrier, sweetbriar, or **eglantine** (ĕg'ləntīn, -tēn) [O. Fr. from Lat.,=needle], wild ROSE of Europe (*Rosa eglanteria*), cultivated and now naturalized in the United States. The bush has fragrant foliage, and in the spring it has pink blossoms (usually single), which are followed by rose hips sometimes used in preserves. Sweetbrier is classified in the division MAGNOLIOPHYTA, class Magnoliopsida, order Rosales, family Rosaceae.

sweet cicely (sĭs'əlē), name for the European herb *Myrrhis odorata* and for closely related American and Asian plants of the genus *Osmorhiza*, all of the family Umbelliferae (CARROT family). Both sweet cicely plants are fragrant perennials having aromatic, licorice-flavored roots, once considered medicinal. They resemble the poison and water hemlocks but are usually distinguishable by their elongated, rather than rounded, seedlike fruits. The European sweet cicely, sometimes called myrrh, was formerly used for salads and greens, and an oil to polish oak was extracted from the seeds. Sweet cicely is classified in the division MAGNOLIOPHYTA, class Magnoliopsida, order Umbellales, family Umbelliferae.

sweet clover or **melilot** (mĕl'əlŏt), Eurasian and North African leguminous herbs of the genus *Melilotus* of the family Leguminosae (PULSE family). Sweet clovers, now widely naturalized in North America, are used as forage, cover, and soiling crops. Attractive to bees for their fragrant blossoms, they are also honey plants. *Melilotus* is a different genus from that of the true clovers. Sweet clover is classified in the division MAGNOLIOPHYTA, class Magnoliopsida, order Rosales, family Leguminosae.

sweet fern, common name for several plants belonging to different botanical divisions. One is a shrub of the family Myricaceae (BAYBERRY family) in the division MAGNOLIOPHYTA; others are plants of the genus *Dryopteris* in the division POLYPODIOPHYTA (FERNS).

sweet flag: see ARUM.

sweet gale: see BAYBERRY.

sweet gum: see WITCH HAZEL.

sweet pea, annual climbing plant (*Lathyrus odoratus*) of the family Leguminosae (PULSE family), a legume native to S Europe but, since its introduction to horticulture c.1700, widely cultivated for its fragrant flowers. There are three main types: dwarf, summer flowering (garden sweet peas), and winter flowering (florists' sweet peas). As cut flowers, sweet peas are one of the more important of florists' plants and are available in a wide range of shades. The vines climb by tendrils and require support. The sweet pea is also a honey plant and the source of an essential oil used in perfumery, although today this oil is more often made synthetically. The green PEA and CHICK-PEA are related but of separate genera. The term *pea* is sometimes used generally for a seed in the pod of any leguminous plant. Sweet peas are classified in the division MAGNOLIOPHYTA, class Magnoliopsida, order Rosales, family Leguminosae.

sweet potato, trailing perennial plant (*Ipomoea batatas*) of the family Convolvulaceae (MORNING GLORY family), native to the New World tropics. Cultivated from ancient times by the Aztecs for its edible tubers, it was introduced into Europe in the 16th cent. and later spread to Asia. It is now the most important of tropical root crops and is grown in many varieties (differentiated by their leaf shapes). In the United States it is cultivated chiefly in the South, though a few hardy varieties are grown as far north as Massachusetts. Sweet potatoes are used mostly for human consumption but are sometimes fed to swine. They yield starch, flour, glucose, and alcohol and are especially rich in vitamin A. The sweet potato is sometimes confused with the YAM, which belongs to another family. Sweet potatoes are classified in the division MAGNOLIOPHYTA, class Magnoliopsida, order Polemoniales, family Convolvulaceae.

Sweetwater, city (1970 pop. 12,020), seat of Nolan co., W Texas; inc. 1884. It is a rail shipping point for cattle ranches in a mesquite and scrub oak region.

sweet William: see PINK.

swell: see WAVE, in oceanography.

Sweyn (swān), c.960–1014, king of Denmark (986–1014), son of Harold Bluetooth. Although baptized, he reverted to paganism and rebelled against his father, who was killed in battle. Sweyn was expelled shortly after his accession by the Swedish king Eric the Victorious, but his subsequent marriage to Eric's widow led to his restoration to the Danish throne and to an alliance with Sweden. At the battle of Svolder (1000) the Swedes and Danes defeated and killed King Olaf I of Norway and divided his kingdom. Sweyn had previously invaded England and exacted DANEGELD from King ÆTHELRED. He invaded England again in 1003–4 and in 1013, when the English finally submitted and accepted him as king. He died before his coronation. His son CANUTE succeeded him in England (1014) and Denmark (1018). The name also appears as Svein.

Sweynheym, Conrad (kôn'rät svīn'hīm), fl. 15th cent., early printer. Originally from near Mainz, Germany, Sweynheym with Arnold Pannartz established (c.1464) in the monastery of Subiaco the first known printing press in Italy. Sweynheym and Pannartz first used Greek type there in 1465. They moved to Rome in 1467. Their typefaces, though not truly roman, had capitals that were distinctly roman.

Świdnica (shvēdnē'tsä), Ger. *Schweidnitz,* town (1970 pop. 47,452), SW Poland. It has textile mills, sugar refineries, and various manufactures. An early residence of the Piast dukes of Silesia, Świdnica and the surrounding principality came to the Bohemian crown in 1368 and were ceded to Prussia in 1745.

Swift, Jonathan, 1667–1745, English author, b. Dublin. Since his father, an Englishman who had settled in Ireland, died before his birth and his mother deserted him for some time, Swift was dependent upon an uncle for his education. He was sent first to Kilkenny School and then to Trinity College, Dublin, where he managed, in spite of his rebellious behavior, to obtain a degree. In 1689 he became secretary to Sir William Temple at Moor Park, Surrey, where he formed his lifelong attachment to Esther Johnson, the "Stella" of his famous journal. Disappointed of church preferment in England, Swift returned to Ireland, where he was ordained an Anglican priest and in 1695 was given the small prebend of Kilroot. Unable to make a success there, he returned to Moor Park the following year, remaining until Temple's death in 1699. During this period he wrote *The Battle of the Books,* in which he defended Temple's contention that the ancients were superior to the moderns in literature and learning, and *A Tale of a Tub,* a satire on religious excesses. These works were not published, however, until 1704. Again disappointment with his advancement sent him back to Ireland, where he was given the living of Laracor. In the course of numerous visits to London he became friendly with Addison and Steele and active in Whig politics. His Whig sympathies were severed, however, when that party demonstrated its unfriendliness to the Anglican Church. In 1708 he began a series of pamphlets on ecclesiastical issues with his ironic *Argument against Abolishing Christianity.* He joined the Tories in 1710, edited the *Tory Examiner* for a year, and wrote various political pamphlets, notably *The Conduct of the Allies* (1711), *Remarks on the Barrier Treaty* (1712), and *The Public Spirit of the Whigs* (1714), in reply to Steele's *Crisis.* In 1713 he joined Pope, Arbuthnot, Gay, and others in forming the celebrated SCRIBLERUS CLUB. About this time Swift became involved with another woman, Esther Vanhomrigh, the "Vanessa" of his poem *Cadenus and Vanessa.* The intensity of his relationship with her, as with Stella, is questionable, but Vanessa died a few weeks after his final rupture with her in 1723. Swift became a national hero of the Irish with his *Drapier Letters* (1724) and his bitterly ironical pamphlet *A Modest Proposal* (1729), which propounds that the children of the poor be sold as food for the tables of the rich. His satirical masterpiece *Gulliver's Travels* appeared in 1726. Written in four parts, it describes the travels of Lemuel Gulliver to Lilliput, a land inhabited by tiny people whose diminutive size renders all their pompous activities absurd; to Brobdingnag, a land populated by giants who are amused when Gulliver tells them about the glories of England; to Laputa and its neighbor Lagado, peopled by quack philosophers and scientists; and to the land of the Houhynhnms, where horses behave with reason and men, called Yahoos, behave as beasts. Ironically, this ruthless satire of human follies subsequently was turned into an expurgated story for children. In his last years Swift was paralyzed and afflicted with a brain disorder, and by 1742 he was declared unsound of mind. He was buried in St. Patrick's, Dublin, beside Stella. See his prose (ed. by H. Davis, 14 vol., 1939; repr. 1964–68); his poetry (ed. by H. Davis, 3 vol., 2d ed. 1958), *The Portable Swift,* ed. by C. Van Doren (new ed. 1968); his correspondence (ed. by H. Williams, 5 vol., 1963); biographies by C. Van Doren (1930, repr. 1964), J. M. Murray (1954), and I. Ephrenpreis (Vol. I, 1962; Vol. II, 1967); studies by R. Quintana (1936, repr. 1965; and 1955, repr. 1962), R. Hunting (1966), N. F. Dennis (1964, repr. 1967), and D. Donoghue (1969).

swift, common name for small, swallowlike birds related to the hummingbird and found all over the world, chiefly in the tropics. They range in size from 6 to 12 in. (15–30 cm) in length. Swifts have long wings and small feet and can perch only on vertical surfaces. They scoop up insects in their wide mouths while on the wing. Swifts are the most rapid fliers known among living creatures. In the United States the common eastern species is the chimney swift, *Chaetura pelagica,* miscalled chimney swallow. Its spiny tail acts as a prop when it clings to the chimneys in which it builds its nest of twigs, cemented with saliva. In the W United States are the black, Vaux's, and white-throated swifts. Some Oriental swifts make their entire nest of a salivary secretion; these are the nests that are used to make bird's-nest soup. The common European swift is sometimes called hawk swallow. Other species include the brown-throated spinetail swift (*C. gigantea)* of India and the Philippines; the scissor-tailed swift (*Panyptila sancti-Hieronymi)* of Guatemala; the white-rumped swift (*Apus caffer)* of Africa; and the palm swift (*Cypsiurus parvus)* of SE Asia. True swifts vary greatly in their nesting habits, some being cliff breeders, some using palm leaves for building their nests, and others nesting in chimneys. Found in a separate family of the same order are the crested swifts, which are restricted to SE Asia. These birds roost in trees and inhabit the open woodlands. They feed on insects, caught on the wing. Crested swifts build tiny nests, about the size of a silver dollar, on tree branches. They deposit a single gray-blue egg, which is glued to the center of the nest. Swifts are classified in the phylum CHORDATA, subphylum Vertebrata, class Aves, order Apodiformes, families Apodidae (swifts) and Hemiprocnidae (crested swifts).

Swift Current, city (1971 pop. 15,415), SW Sask., Canada, on Swift Current Creek. It is a distributing and processing center for a farm and oil region. Other industries are helium extraction and the manufacture of farm machinery and plastic goods. There is a government experimental farm nearby.

Swilly, Lough (lŏkh swĭl'ē), inlet of the Atlantic Ocean, c.25 mi (40 km) long, Co. Donegal, NW Republic of Ireland. It is narrow and irregular in shape, with numerous islands. There is a lighthouse at Fanad Point. The resort town of Buncrana is on the eastern shore. On the lough, Wolfe Tone, an Irish revolutionary, was captured (1798) in an ill-fated insurrection against English rule.

swim bladder, large, thin-walled sac in some fishes that may function in several ways, e.g., as a buoyant float, a sound producer and receptor, and a respiratory organ. The swim bladder, or air bladder, is located in the dorsal portion of the body cavity and is filled with gases. When gas is added to the swim bladder, by diffusion through the blood vessels in the bladder walls, the fish becomes less dense overall; when gas is removed the fish becomes more dense. The addition and removal of gases is a mechanism by which the density of the fish can be made equal to that of the surrounding water at a given depth. The swim bladder produces sound by vibrating; these sounds are probably used in courtship. The organ also amplifies water-borne sounds and thus is an aid to hearing. In most fish the swim bladder has no connection to the digestive tract, but in some, such as the lungfish, there is a connecting tube leading to the pharynx, indicating that the organ may aid in respiration.

swimming, self-propulsion through water, usually as a competitive sport or recreation. One of man's oldest activities, it probably dates back to prehistoric times. It is mentioned in many of the classics in connection with heroic acts or religious rites. The first book on the methods of swimming was Nicolas Wynman's *Dialogue Concerning the Art of Swimming* (1538). Swimming calls more muscles into play with exact coordination than most other sports, and its high repetition of movement makes it extremely beneficial to the cardiovascular system. Swimming strokes should be accomplished with the least possible resistance to water; there should be a minimum of splashing so that the forward motion is smooth and not jerky. The stroke most commonly used to attain speed in swimming is the crawl stroke, standardized in Australia (hence sometimes called the Australian crawl) and perfected in the United States. In the crawl the body is prone; alternating overarm strokes and the flutter kick are used, and the head alternates from side to side at water level. The trudgen stroke (named for the man whose speed in using it made it famous), popular in Spain, Latin America, and then England, also involves alternate overarm strokes from a prone position, but a scissors kick is used and the head remains on one side. The backstroke is done in a supine position and in racing requires alternate over-the-head strokes and a flutter kick. For endurance swimming, the backstroke involves alternation of the frog kick with simultaneous strokes of the arms, which are extended at shoulder level and moved in an arc toward the hips. The sidestroke, a relaxing movement, entails a forward underwater stroke with the body on one side and a scissors kick. The breaststroke can also be a restful stroke and is accomplished in a prone position; frog kicking alternates with a simultaneous movement of the arms from a point in front of the head to shoulder level. The most difficult and exhausting stroke is the butterfly. Second only to the crawl in speed, the butterfly is done in a prone position and employs the dolphin kick with a windmill-like double arm movement. It is mastered by only the best swimmers. The dog paddle, a very simple stroke that takes its name from the way a dog swims, is done by reaching forward with the arms underwater and by a modified flutter kick. In free-style swimming any stroke may be used, but the crawl, considered the speediest, is most favored. No matter what the stroke, however, the breathing should be easy and natural, since the specific gravity of the human body, although it varies with the individual, is almost always such that the body floats if the lungs are functioning normally. In races, facility in diving from a firm surface is essential. Swimming, a universal practice that claims many participants in all sections of the world, became organized as an amateur sport in the late 19th cent. in several countries. Its popularity increased with the development and improvement of the swimming pool, and at the first modern Olympic Games (1896) swimming became part of the meet. Olympic swimming meets for women were included in 1912. Today Olympic swimming events comprise 100-, 400-, 800-, and 1,500-meter freestyle races; 400- and 800-meter freestyle relay races; the 400-meter medley (mixed stroke) relay; 100- and 200-meter backstroke, breaststroke, and butterfly races; 200- and 400-meter individual medley races; springboard and high diving events (see DIVING, SPRINGBOARD AND PLATFORM); and WATER POLO. The United States and (to a lesser extent) Australia excel in Olympic and other international swim meets. Among the more successful American Olympic swimmers have been John Weissmuller, Buster Crabbe, Esther Williams, Don Schollander, and Mark Spitz. Spitz's domination of the 1972 Olympics was remarkable. He won four individual and three team gold medals to set an Olympic record of seven. His time of 51.22 sec for the 100-meter freestyle event made Spitz the fastest swimmer in history. For many decades swimming the English Channel has been highly publicized. The first successful attempt was made (1875) by Matthew Webb of England, and Gertrude Ederle of the United States was the first woman to perform (1926) this feat. See D. A. Armbruster et al., *Swimming and Diving* (5th ed. 1968); François Oppenheim, *The History of Swimming* (1970); Pat Besford, *Encyclopaedia of Swimming* (1971).

Świna (shvē'nä) or **Swine** (svē'nə), channel, 13 mi (21 km) long, NW Poland, leading from the Stettiner Haff (Pol. *Zalew Szczeciński*) to the Baltic Sea. It passes between the islands of Wollin and Usedom. Świnoujście, on Usedom, lies at its mouth.

Swinburne, Algernon Charles, 1837–1909, English poet and critic. His poetry is noted for its vitality and for the music of its language. After attending Eton (1849–53) and Oxford (1856–60) he settled in London on an allowance from his father. His first published volume, containing two blank verse plays entitled *The Queen Mother* and *Rosamond* (1860), attracted little attention, but *Atalanta in Calydon* (1865), a poetic drama modeled on Greek tragedy, brought him fame. In 1866 he published *Poems and Ballads.* The poems in this volume were savagely attacked for their sensuality and anti-Christian sentiments, but almost as excessively praised in other quarters for their technical facility and infusion of new energy into Victorian poetry. The poet's enthusiasm for the dreams for Italian unification of Giuseppe MAZZINI (whom he met in 1867) found expression in *A Song of Italy* (1867) and *Songs before Sunrise* (1871). Swinburne had certain masochistic tendencies that, combined with his chronic epilepsy and his alcoholism, seriously undermined his health. By 1878 he was near death. He was restored to health under the supervision of Theodore WATTS-DUNTON, with whom he lived after 1879. For the final 30 years of his life he lived a closely supervised and highly ordered existence. Swinburne is equally famous as a poet and as a critic. Although many of his lyrics are weakened by verbosity and excessive use of stylistic devices, these flaws do not obscure the vigor and music in such pieces as the choruses from *Atalanta,* "The Garden of Proserpine," "The Triumph of Time," "A Forsaken Garden," "Ave atque vale" (an elegy on Baudelaire), and "Hertha." Swinburne also wrote three closet dramas on Mary Queen of Scots—*Chastelard* (1865), *Bothwell* (1874), and *Mary Stuart* (1881). His long poem *Tristram of Lyonesse* (1882) presents an intensely passionate vision of the medieval legend. Swinburne's critical work is marred by exaggerated vituperation and praise, digressiveness, and a flamboyant style, but he performed useful services in stimulating just appreciation of older English dramatists and of William Blake. See his complete works (ed. by Edmund Gosse and T. J. Wise, 20 vol., 1925–27; repr. 1968); his letters (ed. by C. Y. Lang, 6 vol., 1959–62); biographies by Georges Lafourcade (1932, repr. 1967), J. O. Fuller (1971), Mollie Panter-Downes (1971), and Philip Henderson (1974); studies by S. C. Chew (1929, repr. 1966), Edward Thomas (1912, repr. 1970), and C. K. Hyder, ed. (1970).

Swindon, municipal borough (1971 pop. 90,830), Wiltshire, S central England. Swindon was a small village until 1841, when the Great Western RR opened its locomotive and car works there. Since then, with government support, it has become the largest and most highly industrialized town in Wiltshire.

swine, name for any of the cloven-hoofed mammals of the family Suidae, native to the Old World. A swine has a rather long, mobile snout, a heavy, relatively short-legged body, a thick, bristly hide, and a small tail. The name swine is applied especially to domestic animals, which are also known as hogs. Sometimes these are called pigs, a term which in the United States is more correctly reserved for the young animals. Wild boar is a name for the common wild swine, *Sus scrofa,* of Eurasia and N Africa. Boar is a term for a male domestic swine suitable for breeding. There are no true swine native to the New World, although a similar, related animal, the PECCARY, is found in Central and South America. The wild hogs found in the mountains of SE United States are descendants of the European wild boar, introduced by sportsmen for hunting. The wild boar may reach a height of 3 ft (90 cm) and a length of 5 ft (150 cm). It has 9-in. (30-cm) tusks and a fierce disposition. It was formerly common in the forests of Europe and was a favorite game of sportsmen. It is now rare in Europe, but it is still common in parts of Asia. The wild boar was domesticated in N Europe c.1500 B.C., and it is believed that the modern domesticated hogs are descended chiefly from this European boar, with some admixture of *Sus indica,* a smaller Asiatic species domesticated in China c.3000 B.C. Hogs were introduced into America by Spanish explorers in the 16th cent. and were early shipped to the American colonies from England. Swine are valuable for their flesh, prepared as ham, bacon, and pork, and for their fat (lard); they also provide many other products, e.g., leather for gloves, footballs, and numerous other articles and bristles for brushes. When raising swine it is important that the animals have clean, well-ventilated barns and pens and that they be exposed to some sunlight and allowed to exercise by grazing in pastures. Hogs will eat almost any food. Considered especially good for fattening hogs is a diet of corn and alfalfa supplemented by a protein food in the form of shorts or middlings. Peanuts, soybeans, barley, and wheat also furnish good feed; milk is much used in dairying regions. Hogs are raised in nearly all parts of the United States, but the corn belt of the Midwest is the chief hog-raising area. Hogs are commonly grouped as meat-type, lard-type, or bacon-type hogs. Meat-type breeds include the Hereford and BERKSHIRE. Lard-type breeds include the POLAND CHINA, DUROC, and SPOTTED SWINE. Bacon-type swine are fed on little corn and chiefly on such foods as alfalfa, barley, and skim milk. They are the chief type raised in Canada. Breeds include the Tamworth, Yorkshire, and AMERICAN LANDRACE. Hogs are probably susceptible to a greater number of diseases than any other domestic animal, and many of their ills are transmissible to man. Among them are brucellosis, trichinosis, and cysticercosis. The last two are supposedly the basis of the first food-sanitation codes. Swine are classified in the phylum CHORDATA, subphylum Vertebrata, class Mammalia, order Artiodactyla, family Suidae. See C. W. Towne and E. N. Wentworth, *Pigs from Cave to Corn Belt* (1950); J. L. Krider and W. E. Carroll, *Swine Production* (4th ed., 1971).

swine fever: see HOG CHOLERA.

Swinemünde: see ŚWINOUJŚCIE, Poland.

swing music: see JAZZ.

Swinnerton, Frank, 1884–, English novelist and critic, b. Wood Green, Middlesex. In addition to serving variously as an editor and a drama critic he has written over 30 novels. His novels are old-fashioned, exhibiting the eager secularism and sensuality of the early 20th cent. They include *Nocturne* (1917), *A Month in Gordon Square* (1953), and *Nor All Thy Tears* (1972). He has also written *George Gissing* (1912) and *R. L. Stevenson* (1914).

Świnoujście (shfēnôo͞o'ēshchě), Ger. *Swinemünde,* town (1970 pop. 27,900), NW Poland, on the island of Usedom, at the mouth of the Świna River. It is the outer port for Szczecin and a fishing center and seaside resort. Chartered in 1765, the town became part of the Prussian province of Pomerania; it passed to Poland in 1945. During World War II the town was a German naval base.

Swinton and Pendlebury, municipal borough (1971 pop. 40,124), Lancashire, NW England. The borough has coal mines, cotton mills, and factories for pottery and storage batteries. In 1974, Swinton and Pendlebury became part of the new metropolitan county of Greater Manchester.

Swiss chard: see BEET.

Swiss Confederation: see SWITZERLAND.

Swiss Guards, Swiss mercenaries who fought in various European armies from the 15th cent. until the 19th cent. These mercenaries, who were not volunteers, were put at the disposal of foreign powers by treaties (called capitulations) between the Swiss diet, the separate cantons, and the foreign power concerned, in return for money payments. As a result of the traditional alliance between Switzerland and France—dating from the Everlasting Peace of 1516—the Swiss mercenaries played their most important role in the military history of France. Francis I used some 120,000 Swiss levies in his wars, and in the battle of Pavia (1525) his personal guard, the Hundred Swiss, was slain before Francis was captured by the Spanish. Under Louis XIV, the Swiss troops were organized in two categories: the king's military household and the ordinary Swiss regiments. The most famous episode in the history of the Swiss Guards was their defense (Aug. 10, 1792) of the Tuileries palace in Paris in the French Revolution. Some 500 men of the regiment were massacred by the invading mob. Their heroic stand is commemorated by the *Lion of Lucerne,* the impressive monument by Thorvaldsen at Lucerne, Switzerland. The French revolutionists abolished Swiss troops, but Napoleon I obtained (1803) several Swiss regiments, which were virtually annihilated in the Russian campaign of 1812. Swiss troops were used in the Bourbon restoration, and many of them were massacred in the July Revolution of 1830, after which they were permanently abolished. The Swiss constitution of 1874 forbade all military capitulations and recruitment of Swiss by foreign powers, although volunteering in foreign armies continued until absolutely prohibited in 1927. An exception to the ruling of 1874 is the Swiss Guard of the Vatican, founded in 1505 by Pope Julius II, which is the personal guard of the pope. Recruited from the Catholic cantons of central Switzerland, the Swiss Guard at the Vatican is garbed in colorful costume of Renaissance design.

Swiss literature. The literature of Switzerland is written in German, French, Italian, and ROMANSH, with German predominating. The extensive literature in Romansh dialect is little known outside Switzerland. During the Middle Ages the larger monasteries, notably St. Gall, were known as cultural centers. Among the monks of considerable literary achievements were NOTKER BALBULUS, NOTKER LABEO, Ulrich BONER, and several of the monks called EKKEHARD. These men wrote mainly in Middle High German, but at the same time High German and Swiss regional dialects came into literary use. Religious writing was established by the great reformer, ZWINGLI, as well as by Calvin, who lived in Geneva for a time. Later writers in this tradition were, in the 19th cent., Jeremias GOTTHELF, often considered the greatest Swiss writer, and, in the 20th cent., the priest and novelist Heinrich Federer (1866–1928) and Albert Steffen, leader of the anthroposophical movement. The celebrated French writers Jean-Jacques Rousseau and Germaine de Staël were born in Switzerland. Other writers in French include the literary critics Louis de Muralt (1665–1743), H. F. AMIEL, and Édouard ROD, and the novelist C. F. RAMUZ. The chief Swiss writers in Italian were Stefans Franscini (1726–1857) and Pietro Peri (1794–1869). Heinrich PESTALOZZI and Gottfried KELLER were among major innovators in education as well as outstanding literary figures. Swiss books for children, notably *The Swiss Family Robinson,* by J. D. Wyss, and *Heidi,* by Johanna Spyri, have become worldwide classics. In the 18th cent. major Swiss authors included the historian Johann Zschokke, the poet and scientist Albrecht von Haller, and the poet and painter Salomon Gessner. Leading figures of the 19th cent. were the novelist C. F. MEYER, the historian Jacob BURCKHARDT, the critic Johann BODMER, and the art historian Heinrich WÖLFFLIN. The poet C. F. G. SPITTELER won the Nobel Prize in literature in 1919. Jakob Schaffner (1875–1944), Friedrich DÜRRENMATT, and Max FRISCH have also gained international renown in the 20th cent. See Alex Natan, ed., *Swiss Men of Letters* (1970); Walter Sorell, *The Swiss* (1972).

Swissvale, borough (1970 pop. 13,819), Allegheny co., SW Pa., an industrial suburb of Pittsburgh; settled c.1760, inc. 1898.

switch, electrical device having two states, on, or closed, and off, or open, and, ideally, having the property that when closed it offers a zero IMPEDANCE to a current and when open it offers infinite impedance to a current. No practical switch is this perfect, but the impedance of a closed switch can be reduced to a few thousandths of an ohm and that of an open switch can be made many millions of ohms. Mechanical switches, which operate by moving contacts together and apart, are often classified by the number of connections they can make or break at once and the number of closed positions in which they can be placed. A single-pole double-throw switch can be placed in either of two closed positions, making one connection in each position. A double-pole single-throw switch can open or close two connections at once. For many operations, as in digital computers, the operation of mechanical switches is too slow. When faster switching is required, transistors or vacuum tubes are used, operated in such a way that they conduct either heavily or very little. See RELAY.

Swithin or **Swithun, Saint** (both: swĭth'ən), fl. 860, English bishop of Winchester. He was buried, according to his wishes, outside his church, but his relics were later removed to the new cathedral. According to tradition, if it rains on his feast day, July 15, the anniversary of the removal, it will rain daily thereafter for 40 days; if it is fair on St. Swithin's Day, it will not rain for 40 days.

Switzerland (swĭt'sərlənd), Fr. *Suisse,* Ger. *Schweiz,* Ital. *Svizzera,* also called the **Swiss Confederation,** republic (1970 pop. 6,269,783), 15,941 sq mi (41,287 sq km), central Europe. The federal capital is Bern; other large cities are Zürich, Basel, and Geneva. Switzerland borders on France in the west and southwest, with the Jura mts. and the Lake of Geneva (traversed by the Rhône River) forming the frontier; in the north it is separated from West Germany by the Rhine River and the Lake of Constance; its eastern neighbors are Austria and Liechtenstein; in the southeast and south it is divided from Italy by the Alpine crests, the Lake of Lugano, and Lago Maggiore. Between the Jura and the Central Alps, which occupy the southern section (more than half) of the country, there is a long, narrow plateau, crossed by the Aare River and containing the lakes of Neuchâtel and Zürich. Alpine communications are assured by numerous PASSES and by railroad tunnels, notably the Lötschberg, St. Gotthard, and Simplon. Although poor in natural resources except water power, Switzerland has attained prosperity through the export of its manufactures and through its technological achievements. The industries, employing almost half of the labor force (a significant

minority of whom are non-Swiss), are mainly in the north; the chief manufactures are textiles, chemicals, machinery, instruments, watches and watch movements (in which Switzerland leads the world), jewelry, and foodstuffs (notably chocolate). The major source of power is hydroelectricity; the railroads, more than half of which are government-owned, use electric power on all main lines. In the alpine regions there is much dairying, with cheese the principal export. The agricultural yield of fruits, vegetables, and grains is supplemented by imports; other main imports are machinery, motor vehicles, and iron and steel. The main trading partners are West Germany, France, Italy, the United States, and Great Britain. Imports exceed exports, but Switzerland is favored by the huge profits of its tourist industry; each year several million people visit its alpine resorts. The stability of Swiss politics and of the Swiss currency (the Swiss franc is backed by a large gold reserve) has, moreover, made Switzerland a world banking center. Switzerland consists of 22 cantons, or rather of 25 federated states of which 19 are called cantons and 6 are called half cantons. The cantons are ZÜRICH, BERN, LUCERNE, URI, SCHWYZ, GLARUS, ZUG, FRIBOURG, SOLOTHURN, SCHAFFHAUSEN, SAINT GALL, the GRISONS, AARGAU, THURGAU, TICINO, VAUD, VALAIS, NEUCHÂTEL, and GENEVA. Of the half cantons, Obwalden and Nidwalden together form UNTERWALDEN, Basel-Land and Basel-Stadt form BASEL, and Ausser-Rhoden and Inner-Rhoden form APPENZELL. The federal constitution (1874) assigns specified functions, notably communications, foreign relations, and tariffs, to the confederation, leaving the cantons sovereign in other respects. There is universal male suffrage; women were granted (by a referendum in 1971) the vote in federal elections and may vote in most cantonal and local elections. A council of states (two members from each canton, one from each half canton) and a 200-member national council (whose members are directly elected every four years) together form the federal assembly. The chief executive, or federal council, is composed of seven members (elected for four years by the federal assembly) and includes the president of the confederation (elected by the federal assembly annually). The three largest parties are the Radical, Social Democratic, and Christian Democratic. Switzerland frequently employs the referendum as well as the popular initiative to achieve political change. The constitution provides for religious equality, compulsory education, and universal military training. Cantonal constitutions differ widely. In Unterwalden, Clarus, and Appenzell the entire male electorate legislates directly in yearly outdoor meetings called *Landsgemeinden;* elsewhere a unicameral legislative council and an elected executive council are common. German, French, Italian, and Romansh (a Rhaeto-Roman dialect spoken in parts of the Grisons) are the national languages of Switzerland. German dialects (Schwyzerdütsch) are spoken by about 65% of the inhabitants; French, spoken by about 18%, predominates in the southwest; Italian, spoken by about 12%, is the language of Ticino, in the south. The few Romansh-speakers (less than 1%) are in the southeast. Approximately 48% of the population is Protestant and 49% Roman Catholic. There are universities at Lausanne, Geneva, Bern, Basel, Zürich, St. Gall, Neuchâtel, and Fribourg.

Emergence of the Swiss Nation. In 58 B.C. the Helvetii who inhabited the country (see HELVETIA) were conquered by the Romans. Invaded (5th cent. A.D.) by the Alemanni and by the Burgundii, the area passed to the Franks in the 6th cent. Divided (9th cent.) between SWABIA and Transjurane BURGUNDY, it was united (1033) under the Holy Roman Empire. The expanding feudal houses, notably ZÄHRINGEN and Kyburg, were supplanted (13th cent.) by the houses of HAPSBURG and of SAVOY. Hapsburg encroachments on the privileges of the three localities of Uri, Schwyz, and Unterwalden resulted in the conclusion (1291) of a defensive league among them. The legendary hero of this event is William TELL. The league triumphed at Morgarten (1315) and, joined by Lucerne, Zürich, Zug, Glarus, and Bern, decisively defeated the Hapsburgs at SEMPACH (1386) and Näfels (1388). In the 15th cent. the Swiss league rose to the first rank as a military power. The conquest of Aargau, Thurgau, and the valleys of Ticino, which were ruled as subject territories until 1798, was followed by Swiss victories over CHARLES THE BOLD of Burgundy (1476–77) and over Emperor Maximilian I, who in 1499 granted Switzerland virtual independence. By 1513, the admission to the confederation of Fribourg, Solothurn, Basel, Schaffhausen, and Appenzell had raised the number of cantons to 13, and this number was maintained until 1798. The conquest by Bern of Vaud from Savoy (1536), and close alliances with the Grisons, Geneva, St. Gall, and other towns and regions, further increased the Swiss orbit, but Switzerland's importance as a European power was broken in 1515 when the French defeated the Swiss at MARIGNANO (see also ITALIAN WARS). A "perpetual alliance" with France (1516) and neutrality became the basis of Swiss policy. Swiss mercenaries, however, continued to serve abroad for three centuries (see SWISS GUARDS). The cantons, loosely bound by a federal diet and by individual treaties and often torn by internal feuds, were seriously split by the REFORMATION, preached by ZWINGLI at Zürich and by CALVIN at Geneva. The Catholics, led by the FOUR FOREST CANTONS, defeated the Protestants in battle; the Treaty of Kappel (1531) preserved Catholicism in Lucerne, Uri, Schwyz, Unterwalden, Zug, Fribourg, and Solothurn. National unity almost disappeared for more than two centuries, but religious divisions did not prevent the Swiss (except the Grisons) from remaining neutral throughout the Thirty Years War. Switzerland was an island of prosperity when, in 1648, at the end of the war, its formal independence was recognized in the Peace of Westphalia.

Internal Conflict and Consolidation. In the following century and a half, government in many cantons became the exclusive business of a small oligarchy. While Switzerland became insignificant politically in the 18th cent., its wealth steadily increased, and its scientists and writers (von Haller, von Mühler, Pestalozzi, Rousseau) made it an intellectual center. The Swiss oligarchies strongly opposed the French Revolution. Invading French armies established the HELVETIC REPUBLIC (1798–1803) and in 1799 clashed with Austrian and Russian forces. Napoleon's Act of Mediation (1803) partially restored the old confederation, and, at the Congress of Vienna, the Pact of Restoration (1815) substantially reestablished the old regime, except that the confirmation of nine new cantons brought the total to its present number. By the Treaty of Paris (1815), Swiss neutrality was guaranteed for all time. A subsequent economic depression, which caused large-scale emigration to North and South America, and generally reactionary rule contributed to widely successful demands for revision of the cantonal constitutions and the rise of the Radical party, which favored greater centralization. Opposition to centralization centered in the Catholic rural cantons, which in 1845 formed the SONDERBUND, a defensive alliance. After a brief and almost bloodless civil war (1847) the victorious Radicals transformed the confederation into one federal state under a new constitution adopted in 1848 (and recast in 1874). National unity grew, and much socialist legislation (such as railroad nationalization and social insurance) was enacted as the country developed economically and industrially. Armed neutrality was maintained throughout World Wars I and II. Switzerland was a member of the League of Nations and participates in many activities of the United Nations; the UN Charter, however, makes Swiss membership in that body impossible without some modification of the strict Swiss interpretation of neutrality. In 1959, Switzerland became a member of the European Free Trade Association, and in 1972 it signed an industrial free-trade agreement with the European Common Market. In the 1950s, French-speaking inhabitants of the Jura region of Bern canton unsuccessfully demanded, with some violence, the creation of a Jura canton. However, in a plebiscite in 1974 about half the Jura region voted to establish a separate canton, a development made possible by amendments to the Bern Constitution. See Edgar Bonjour et al., *Short History of Switzerland* (2d ed. 1955); Hans Kohn, *Nationalism and Liberty: The Swiss Example* (1956); Allen Young, *Swiss Neutrality in the Cold War* (1962); William Martin, *Switzerland, from Roman Times to the Present* (tr. of 6th ed., 1971); Max Iklé, *Switzerland: An International Banking and Finance Center* (tr. 1972); Walter Sorell, *The Swiss: A Cultural Panorama of Switzerland* (1972); Armin Gretler and P. E. Mandl, *Values, Trends and Alternatives in Swiss Society* (1973).

sword, weapon of offense and defense in personal combat, consisting of a blade with a sharp point and one or two cutting edges, set in a hilt with a handle protected by a metal case or cross guard. The sword was developed from the dagger at the beginning of the Bronze Age. It was not, however, until the more durable iron sword was introduced in the early Iron Age that the sword became an effective weapon. Greek and Roman swords were very short, with pointed ends, and had two cutting edges. Medieval knights used two types of swords: a short sword with a pointed end that was used with one hand and a heavy two-handed sword with a rounded end. During the Middle Ages the best blades were those made by the Arabs in Damascus and those made in Toledo. Swords were widely used in the Middle and Far East as well as in Europe. The scimitar, used by the Persians and Arabs, is a curved steel sword. One of the best known of the Oriental swords is the Japanese SAMURAI sword that consists of a curved single-edged tempered steel blade set in a long handle. As a highly personal weapon the sword attained symbolic importance; surrendering one's sword became a token of submission, and the custom of taking an officer's sword away from him and breaking the blade when he was dismissed from the service in disgrace arose because a sword is the mark of an officer and a gentleman. During the Crusades and later, the sword, because of its shape, frequently was used to symbolize the Cross. The sword is now obsolete as a weapon and is carried in some military units for decorative purposes in times of peace. Special types of swords are the rapier, the épée, and the saber. See FENCING.

swordfish, large food and game fish, *Xiphias gladius,* of the warmer Atlantic and Pacific waters, related to the sailfish. It is named for its sharp, broad, elongated upper jaw, which it uses to flail and pierce its prey of smaller fish, rising beneath a school to kill and then devour. Swordfish breed as far N as Nova Scotia; they are often seen basking on the water's surface, and their fins are sometimes mistaken for those of sharks. They may reach 15 ft (457 cm) and 1,000 lb (450 kg); however, specimens half this size are considered large. Swordfish are harpooned commercially; their liver oil is rich in vitamins. Swordfish are classified in the phylum CHORDATA, subphylum Vertebrata, class Osteichthyes, order Perciformes, family Xiphiidae.

Sybaris (sĭb'ərĭs), ancient city of Magna Graecia, S Italy, in Bruttium, on the Gulf of Tarentum (now Taranto). It was founded in 720 B.C. by Achaeans and people from Argolis, the Troezenians. It became a wealthy Greek city, and its inhabitants were reputed to live voluptuous lives, hence the word *sybaritic.* The Troezenians, ejected by the Achaeans, obtained the help of neighboring Crotona and destroyed the city in 510 B.C. Thurii was supposedly built on the site. See J. S. Callaway, *Sybaris* (1950); O. H. Bullitt, *Search for Sybaris* (1969).

Sybel, Heinrich von (hīn'rĭkh fən zē'bəl), 1817–95, German historian. He studied under Ranke at the Univ. of Berlin, but later abandoned the Rankean striving for objective history; he began to take an active part in politics and promoted the nationalist and Protestant causes in his speeches and writings. In 1859, Sybel founded the *Historische Zeitschrift.* After 1875 he was director of the Prussian state archives, which he used extensively for his chief work, *Founding of the German Empire by William I* (tr., 7 vol., 1890–98). His other works include a history of the revolutionary period from 1789 to 1800, part of which was translated as *History of the French Revolution* (4 vol., 1867–79).

sycamore: see PLANE TREE.

Sychar (sī'kər), unidentified city, central Samaria, near Jacob's well where Jesus talked with the Samaritan woman. John 4.5.

Sychem (sī'kəm), variant of SHECHEM.

Sydenham, Charles Edward Poulett Thomson, Baron (sĭd'ənəm), 1799–1841, British statesman. Entering Parliament (1826) as a Liberal with the aid of Jeremy Bentham, he became a proponent of free trade and financial reform. He was a leader of the colonial reformers, a group that promoted liberalized but permanent imperial ties. He supported the views of Edward Gibbon WAKEFIELD on systematic colonization. He was made president of the Board of Trade in 1834, and in 1839 he was appointed governor general of Canada. There, in accordance with the policy of his predecessor, the 1st earl of DURHAM, he successfully carried through the union of Upper and Lower Canada, accomplished by the Act of Union (1840). He was raised to the peerage in 1840.

Sydenham, Thomas, 1624–89, English physician, called "the English Hippocrates." He studied at Oxford and Montpellier, and practiced in London. His conceptions of the causes and treatments of epidemics and his classic descriptions of gout, smallpox, malaria, scarlet fever, hysteria, and chorea established him as a founder of modern clinical medicine and epidemiology. He advocated direct observation instead of theorizing to determine the nature of disease and introduced the use of such drugs as cinchona bark (containing quinine) in treating malaria, and laudanum in treating other disorders. See studies by J. F. Payne (1900) and David Riesman (1926); Kenneth Dewhurst, *Dr. Thomas Sydenham, 1624–1689: His Life and Original Writings* (1966).

Sydenham's chorea: see CHOREA.

Sydney, Algernon: see SIDNEY, ALGERNON.

Sydney, Sir Philip: see SIDNEY, SIR PHILIP.

Sydney, city (1971 pop. 61,940; urban agglomeration pop. 2,717,069), capital of New South Wales, SE Australia, surrounding Port Jackson inlet on the Pacific Ocean. Sydney is Australia's largest city, chief port, and main cultural and industrial center. Its main exports are wool, wheat, flour, sheepskins, and meat; the chief imports are petroleum, coal, timber, and sugar. Sydney has shipyards, oil refineries, textile mills, brass foundries, and automobile, electronics, and chemical plants. The city was founded in 1788 as the first penal settlement of Australia. Its name was taken from a cave named for Captain Cook's patron, Viscount Sydney. In World War II the city was an Allied military base. Two notable bridges cross Port Jackson inlet: the Sydney Harbour Bridge (1932) and the Gladesville Bridge (1964). In the city are the Univ. of Sydney (1850), Macquarie Univ. (1964), and the Univ. of New South Wales (1949). Sydney is the seat of Roman Catholic and Anglican archbishops. Among its museums are the National Gallery of Art and the Australian Museum (natural history). The modernistic Sydney Opera House complex was largely designed by Joern Utzon, the Danish winner of an international competition; it opened in 1974.

Sydney, city (1971 pop. 33,230), Cape Breton Island, N.S., Canada, on the northeast coast at the head of the South Arm of Sydney Harbour. It is the port and the commercial, trade, and industrial center of an important coal-mining area. The city has steel mills and plants manufacturing wood, food products, and chemicals. Sydney was founded (1783) by UNITED EMPIRE LOYALISTS and was the capital (1784–1820) of Cape Breton prov. St. George's Church (1786) is one of the oldest Anglican churches in Canada.

Sydney Mines, town (1971 pop. 8,991), Cape Breton Island, N.S., Canada, on Sydney Harbour. It is a coal-mining center, coal having been mined in the area since 1784. There are steel mills, foundries, and machine shops. The town is the terminus of a transatlantic cable.

Syene: see ASWAN, Egypt.

syenite (sī'ənīt), coarse-grained igneous ROCK, similar in appearance and composition to granite. Unlike granite, it contains little or no quartz. The chief minerals in syenite are the feldspars, with mica, hornblende, and pyroxene. Varieties are distinguished (according to the ferromagnesian minerals contained) as augite syenite, hornblende syenite, mica syenite, and nepheline syenite. Syenites are comparatively rare rocks, being found chiefly in a few areas of the United States and Germany. They are occasionally substituted for granites as building stones.

Syktyvkar (sĭktĭfkär'), city (1970 pop. 125,000), capital of Komi Autonomous Republic, NW European USSR, a port on the Sysola River near its entry into the Vychegda. Lumbering and the manufacture of wood products are the chief industries. Near Syktyvkar, on the Vychegda, is one of the USSR's largest woodworking complexes. A settlement existed on the site of Syktyvkar by the late 16th cent. During the 17th and 18th cent. there was a flourishing grain and fur trade. The city, a center of Russian colonization in the late 18th and early 19th cent., was called Ust-Sysolsk until 1930.

Sylacauga (sĭləkô'gə), city (1970 pop. 12,255), Talladega co., central Ala.; inc. 1839. It is a processing center for a cotton, livestock, and timber area. Built upon a solid bed of cream-white marble, it has three quarries. In addition to marble, which has been produced there since 1840, textiles, clothing, metal goods, and dairy products are made. Iron ore is also found in the area. Nearby are Talladega National Forest and Flagg Mountain, which was a signal relay station during the Civil War.

Sylhet (sĭlhĕt'), town (1961 est. pop. 37,740), E Bangladesh, on the Surma River. It is the administrative center for a district of rice and tea cultivation and extensive limestone quarrying. Sylhet, which has tea factories and a noted cane industry, is also a center of Islamic culture and the site of several tombs of Muslim holy men. In the city are three colleges affiliated with the Univ. of Dacca.

Sylla, Lucius Cornelius: see SULLA.

syllogism, a mode of argument that forms the core of the body of Western logical thought. Aristotle defined syllogistic logic, and his formulations were thought to be the final word in logic; they underwent only minor revisions in the subsequent 2,200 years. Every syllogism is a sequence of three propositions such that the first two imply the third, the conclusion. There are three basic types of syllogism: hypothetical, disjunctive, and categorical. The hypothetical syllogism, *modus ponens,* has as its first premise a conditional hypothesis: *If p then q;* it continues: *p,* therefore *q.* The disjunctive syllogism, *modus tollens,* has as first premise a statement of alternatives: *Either p or q;* it continues: not *q,* therefore *p.* The categorical syllogism comprises three categorical propositions, statements of the form *all x are y, no x is y, some x is y,* or *some x is not y.* A categorical syllogism contains precisely three terms: the major term, which is the predicate of the conclusion; the minor term, the subject of the conclusion; and the middle term, which appears in both premises but not in the conclusion. Thus: *All philosophers are men* (middle term); *all men are mortal;* therefore, *All philosophers* (minor term) *are mortal* (major term). The premises containing the major and minor terms are named the major and minor premises, respectively. Aristotle noted five basic rules governing the validity of categorical syllogisms: The middle term must be distributed at least once (a term is said to be distributed when it refers to all members of the denoted class, as in *all x are y* and *no x is y*); a term distributed in the conclusion must be distributed in the premise in which it occurs; two negative premises imply no valid conclusion; if one premise is negative, then the conclusion must be negative; and two affirmatives imply an affirmative. John Venn, an English logician, in 1880 introduced a device for analyzing categorical syllogisms, known as the Venn diagram. Three overlapping circles are drawn to represent the classes denoted by the three terms. Universal propositions (*all x are y, no x is y*) are indicated by shading the sections of the circles representing the excluded classes. Particular propositions (*some x is y, some x is not y*) are indicated by placing some mark, usually an "X," in the section of the circle representing the class whose members are specified. The conclusion may then be read directly from the diagram. Thus:

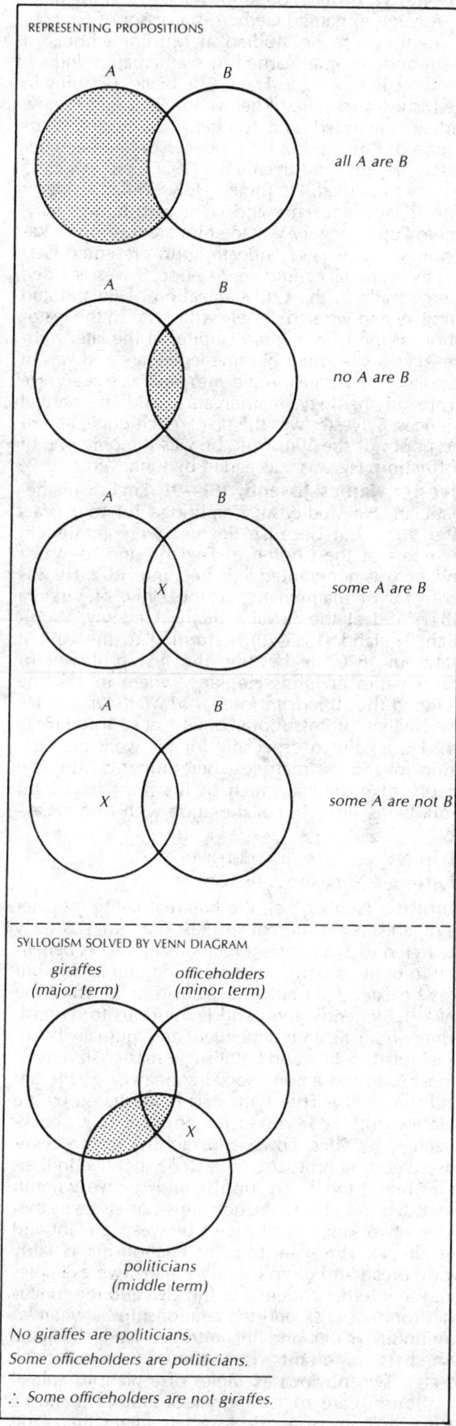

Categorical syllogism: Venn diagram

Sylt (zĭlt), island (1967 est. pop. 23,000), 36 sq mi (93 sq km), Schleswig-Holstein, N West Germany, in the North Sea. It is the largest of the North FRISIAN ISLANDS and is connected by a dam with the mainland; the two main towns are Westerland, a popular seaside resort, and Kampen. Except in its cultivated western tip, the island is covered by dunes and heath land; fishing, agriculture, and tourism are the chief industries. Sylt was fortified in the 1930s and during World War II was one of the earliest air targets of the Allies.

Sylva, Carmen: see ELIZABETH, queen of Rumania.

Sylvania (sĭlvān'yə), city (1970 pop. 12,031), Lucas co., NW Ohio, a suburb of Toledo at the Mich. line; inc. 1867. It is chiefly residential, but building materials are made. A junior college is there.

Sylvester I, Saint, pope (314–35), a Roman; successor of St. Miltiades (St. Melchiades). He was pope under the reign of Emperor Constantine I, who built for him the Lateran and other churches. St. Sylvester sent legates to the First Council of Nicaea and took strong interest in the controversy over ARIANISM. The spurious Donation of Constantine (see CONSTANTINE, DONATION OF) was supposedly given to St. Sylvester. The name is also spelled Silvester. He was succeeded by St. Marcus. Feast: Dec. 31.

Sylvester II, d. 1003, pope (999–1003), a Frenchman (b. Auvergne) named Gerbert; successor of Gregory V. In his youth he studied at Muslim schools in Spain and became learned in mathematics and astronomy. Returning to France, he began teaching in the bishop's school at Rheims. In 991, Gerbert, now widely celebrated as a teacher, was elected archbishop of Rheims; but his predecessor had been deposed illegally, and eventually (995) Gerbert's election was nullified. He joined Holy Roman Emperor Otto III as his teacher and went with him to Italy, where Pope Gregory V made him archbishop of Ravenna. Upon Gregory's death, Otto presented Gerbert as his papal candidate. As pope, Sylvester aided energetically in the Christianization of Poland and Hungary and worked closely with Otto in the restoration of the Holy Roman Empire. In the later Middle Ages his learning became legendary and was in popular belief transformed into skill at sorcery. He wrote on theology, mathematics, and the natural sciences. Sylvester was the first French pope, and of the popes of the 10th cent. he was the only one of distinction. He was succeeded by John XVII.

Sylvester, James Joseph, 1814–97, English mathematician. He studied at Cambridge for four years after 1831, but because degrees were limited to members of the Church of England and he was a Jew, he was not granted a degree until 1872. He was professor of mathematics at the Univ. of Virginia (1841) and at the Royal Military Academy, Woolwich, England (1855–70). Returning to the United States in 1876, he became the first professor of mathematics at Johns Hopkins, where in 1878 he founded the *American Journal of Mathematics.* He was Savilian professor of geometry at Oxford (1883–94). He is known especially for his work on algebraic invariants, matrices, determinants, and the theory of numbers, much of his most important work being done in collaboration with Arthur Cayley.

sylvinite: see POTASSIUM CHLORIDE.

sylvite: see POTASSIUM CHLORIDE.

symbiosis (sĭmbēō'sĭs), the habitual living together of organisms of different species. The term is usually restricted to a dependent relationship that is beneficial to both participants (also called mutualism) but may be extended to include parasitism, in which the PARASITE depends upon and is injurious to its host; commensalism, an independent and mutually beneficial relationship; and helotism, a master-slave relationship found among social animals (e.g., the ant and the APHID). True symbiosis is illustrated by the relationship of herbivorous animals (e.g., cockroaches, termites, cows, and rabbits) to the cellulose-digesting protozoa or bacteria that live in their intestines; neither organism could survive without the other. Symbiotic relationships can also exist between two kinds of plants or between a plant and an animal. The plant-to-plant relationship is fairly widespread and often useful to man. Two examples are the interdependence of the alga and the fungus that form a LICHEN and the relationship between leguminous plants and the nitrogen-fixing bacteria, which is important in agriculture (see NITROGEN CYCLE). Two obvious examples of a plant-to-animal relationship are YUCCA and yucca moth, FIG and fig wasp; in both cases the insect fertilizes the plant, and the plant supplies food for the larvae of the insect.

symbol, sign representing something that has an independent existence. The most important use of symbols is in LANGUAGE. To say so, however, does not solve the perennial philosophical questions as to the nature of the linguistic sign. The question remains whether the word *chair* stands for any chair, for a particular chair, or for the idea of a chair. This is the problem of nominalism and realism. A secondary linguistic symbolism is WRITING. Another, still connected with language, appears in systems of LOGIC and MATHEMATICS (see also NUMBER). Modern science has in its development profited from the conciseness provided by many symbols. In chemical symbols, for example, each ELEMENT is represented by one or two letters (e.g., carbon, C; zinc, Zn). Some symbols are derived from non-English names, e.g., Ag for silver (Latin *argentum*). A chemical FORMULA is written in chemical symbols. In art a distinction of terms is introduced that modifies the term *symbol.* Although the drawings at Altamira are considered symbolic in one sense (i.e., a drawn reindeer is the symbol for a live reindeer), they are said not to be symbols in another more common sense, since the artist represented a reindeer by copying its appearance. If he had drawn two horns and considered that to represent a reindeer adequately, the two horns might be said to be a symbol for a reindeer. Such symbolism is all-pervasive in every kind of art, especially because it lends itself to rapid, comprehensive, and compact use. Religious symbolism is best known in its more ancient form from the discoveries of archaeologists; this is especially important in the study of EGYPTIAN RELIGION, in which the symbol of the god often appeared more frequently than the likeness of the god himself. GREEK RELIGION, on the contrary, seemed to eliminate symbols of gods in favor of actual images. In Judaism and Christianity religious symbolism is important, notably in the prophetic passages in the Bible and in the uses of public worship (see, for example, CANDLE; INCENSE; LITURGY; SACRAMENT; see also ICONOGRAPHY). Modern patriotism, particularly in the United States, has found a revered symbol in the FLAG, which began, like all HERALDRY, as a means of recognition. Trade symbols are sometimes quite widespread; although the wooden Indian signifying the tobacco shop has disappeared, barber poles are still very common. The investigations of Sir James FRAZER in comparative religion and those of Sigmund FREUD in psychology, extreme though they may be, have shown that human beings tend always to use a wide symbolism, even in thinking itself, to cover ideas they avoid out of fear, propriety, or some other motive.

symbolic logic or **mathematical logic,** formalized system of deductive logic, employing abstract symbols for the various aspects of natural language. Symbolic logic draws on the concepts and techniques of mathematics, notably SET theory, and in turn has contributed to the development of the foundations of mathematics. Symbolic logic dates from the work of Augustus De Morgan and George Boole in the mid-19th cent. and was further developed by W. S. Jevons, C. S. Peirce, Ernst Schröder, Gottlob Frege, Giuseppe Peano, Bertrand Russell, A. N. Whitehead, David Hilbert, and others. The first part of symbolic logic is known as truth-functional analysis, the propositional calculus, or the sentential calculus; it deals with statements that can be assigned truth values (true or false). Combinations of these statements are called truth functions, and their truth values can be determined from the truth values of their components. The basic connectives in truth-functional analysis are usually negation, conjunction, and alternation. The negation of a statement is false if the original statement is true and true if the original statement is false; negation corresponds to "it is not the case that," or simply "not" in ordinary language. The conjunction of two statements is true only if both are true; it is false in all other instances. Conjunction corresponds to "and" in ordinary language. The alternation, or disjunction, of two statements is false only if both are false and is true in all other instances; alternation corresponds to the nonexclusive sense of "or" in ordinary language (Lat. *vel*), as opposed to the exclusive "either . . . or . . . but not both" (Lat. *aut*). Other connectives commonly used in truth-functional analysis are the conditional and the biconditional. The conditional, or implication, corresponds to "if . . . then" or "implies" in ordinary language, but only in a weak sense. The conditional is false only if the antecedent is true and the consequent is false; it is true in all other instances. This kind of implication, in which the connection between the antecedent and the consequent is merely formal, is known as material implication. The biconditional, or double implication, is the equivalence relation and is true only if the two statements have the same truth value, either true or false. In any truth function one may substitute an equivalent expression for all or any part of the function. The validity of arguments may be analyzed by assigning all possible combinations of truth values to the component statements; such an array of truth values is called a truth table. There are many valid argument forms, however, that cannot be analyzed by truth-functional methods, e.g., the classic SYLLOGISM: "All men are mortal. Socrates is a man. Therefore Socrates is mortal." The syllogism and many other more complicated arguments are the subject of the predicate calculus, or quantification theory, which is based on the calculus of classes. The predicate calculus of monadic (one-variable) predicates, also called uniform quantification theory, has been shown to be complete and has a decision procedure, analogous to truth tables for truth-functional analysis, whereby the validity or invalidity of any statement can be determined. The general predicate calculus, or quantification theory, was also shown to be complete by Kurt Gödel, but Alonso Church subsequently proved (1936) that it has no possible decision procedure. Symbolic logic has been extended to a description and analysis of the foundations of mathematics, particularly number theory. Gödel also made (1931) the surprising discovery that number theory cannot be complete, i.e., that no matter what axioms are chosen as a basis for number theory, there will always be some true statements that cannot be deducted from them, although they can be proved within the larger context of symbolic logic. Since many branches of mathematics are ultimately based on number theory, this result has been interpreted by some as affirming that mathematics is an open, creative discipline whose possibilities cannot be delineated. The work of Gödel, Church, and others has led to the development of proof theory, or metamathematics, which deals with the nature of mathematics itself. See David Hilbert and Wilhelm Ackermann, *Principles of Mathematical Logic* (tr. of 2d ed. 1950); W. V. Quine, *Mathematical Logic* (1968) and *Methods of Logic* (3d ed. 1972).

symbolists, in literature, a school originating in France toward the end of the 19th cent. in reaction to the naturalism and realism of the period. Designed to convey impressions by suggestion rather than by direct statement, symbolism found its first expression in poetry but was later extended to the other arts. The early symbolists experimented with form, revolting against the rigidity of the PARNASSIANS with a FREE VERSE that has outlived the movement itself. The precursors of the school, all influenced by Baudelaire, included Verlaine, Mallarmé, and Rimbaud. They were accused of writing with a decadent morbidity, partly as the result of their utilization of imagination as a reality. The movement was continued in poetry by Laforgue, Moréas, and Régnier; in drama by Maeterlinck; in criticism by Remy de Gourmont; and in music by Debussy. Among the later symbolists were Claudel, Valéry, Jammes, and the critic Camille Mauclair. The influence of the French symbolists not only gave rise to similar schools in England, Germany, and other countries, but also may be traced in the development of the IMAGISTS and DECADENTS; it is likewise evident in the work of Arthur Symons, T. S. Eliot, Marcel Proust, James Joyce, Gertrude Stein, Eugene O'Neill, Hart Crane, Wallace Stevens, Dylan Thomas, William Faulkner, and e e cummings. See C. M. Bowra, *The Heritage of Symbolism* (1943); Anna Balakian, *The Symbolist Movement* (1967); W. K. Cornell, *The Symbolist Movement* (1970).

Syme, Greece: see SÍMI.

Symeon: see SIMEON.

Symington, William Stuart, 1901–, U.S. Senator (1953–), b. Amherst, Mass. He interrupted a successful business career in 1941 to accept a War Department assignment involving a study of airplane armament in England. After serving (1945–46) as administrator of the Surplus Property Administration he was appointed (Sept., 1947) by President Harry S. Truman to be the first Secretary of the Air Force. He advocated a greatly increased air force as necessary for national defense, and when appropriations for his department were reduced he resigned (April, 1950) in protest. After serving (1951–52) as administrator of the Reconstruction Finance Corporation, Symington, a Democrat, was elected in 1952 as U.S. Senator for Missouri. In his early years in the Senate, he was mainly preoccupied with the question of national defense and warned the nation of the danger of the Soviet lead in the missile race. Symington was easily reelected to the Senate in 1958, 1964, and 1970; in 1960 he was an unsuccessful candidate for the Democratic presidential nomination. See biography by P. I. Wellman (1960).

Symmachus, Quintus Aurelius (sĭm'əkəs), c.345–c.405, Roman government official and orator. Educated in Gaul, he held several official positions, including the consulship in 391. He is best known for his report to the emperor VALENTINIAN II in 384 in which he argued for the retention of the old Roman religion in official state functions. His eloquent defense of ancient religious customs in the face of the inroads made by Christianity was successfully opposed by St. AMBROSE. His official correspondence was later collected by his son.

symmetry, generally speaking, a balance or correspondence between various parts of an object; the term *symmetry* is used both in the arts and in the sciences. In art and design, it is often used in a somewhat loose sense, to mean a kind of balance in which the corresponding parts are not necessarily alike but only similar. A symmetrical design should produce a pleasing effect; if there is too close a correspondence, the effect may be monotonous. Ancient Greek architecture is particularly distinguished for its symmetry. In modern art, the Dutch artist M. C. Escher achieved a number of striking effects in his works exploring mathematical symmetry. A mathematical operation, or transformation, that results in the same figure as the original figure (or its mirror image) is called a symmetry operation. Such operations include reflection, rotation, double reflection, and translation. The set of all operations on a given figure that leave the figure unchanged constitutes the symmetry GROUP for that figure. The symmetry groups of three-dimensional figures are of special interest because of their application in fields such as crystallography (see CRYSTAL). In general, a symmetry operation on a figure is defined with respect to a given point (center of symmetry), line (axis of symmetry), or plane (plane of symmetry). In biology, symmetry is studied in the correspondences between different parts of a given organism, as between the left and right halves of the human body or between the various segments of a starfish (see SYMMETRY, BIOLOGICAL). In physics, basic symmetries in nature underlie the various CONSERVATION LAWS. For example, the symmetry of space and time with respect to translation and rotation means that a given experiment should yield the same results regardless of where it is performed, what direction the equipment is pointing in, or when it is performed. These three symmetries can be shown to imply the laws of conservation of linear momentum, angular momentum, and energy, respectively. See Hermann Weyl, *Symmetry* (1952); J. E. Brigham, tr., *The Graphic Work of M. C. Escher* (rev. ed. 1967); H. S. M. Coxeter, *Introduction to Geometry* (2d ed. 1969).

symmetry, biological, similarity or balance between parts of an object so that when a straight cut is made through a point or along a line, equal, mirror-image halves are formed. Symmetry in body shapes is related to the life styles of organisms. Asymmetry, or the absence of symmetry, most often occurs in sessile organisms or in slow-moving forms such as *Amoeba.* Most other organisms can generally be classified in three groups with respect to symmetry type. In spherical, or point, symmetry, any straight cut through the central point of a sphere divides it into mirror-image halves. Point symmetry, often called universal symmetry by biologists, is seen in some floating animals with radiating parts, such as the single-celled protozoans of the order Radiolaria. Radial, or line, symmetry, as exemplified by a cone or a disk that is symmetrical about a central axis, is especially suitable for sessile or floating animals. Most radially symmetrical animals are symmetrical about an axis extending from the center of the oral surface, which contains the mouth, to the center of the opposite, or aboral, end. Radial symmetry is seen in sessile organisms such as the sea anemone, floating organisms such as jellyfish, and slow-moving organisms such as sea stars, or starfish. Many jellyfish have four radial canals and are said to have tetramerous radial symmetry; sea stars, with five arms, have pentamerous radial symmetry. Many flowers, such as dandelions and daffodils, are radially symmetrical. Nonradial parts, such as the slit-shaped gullets of sea anemones, are often present in otherwise radial animals. In plane, or bilateral, symmetry, one particular plane, termed the sagittal plane, divides the body into two equal halves, usually right and left halves that are mirror images of each other. Flowers such as orchids and sweet peas are bilaterally symmetrical. Bilateral symmetry is most suitable for actively moving organisms, as it permits streamlining, and is the most common symmetry among animals. In animals this symmetry type also favors the formation of main nerve centers and special sense organs and contributes to cephalization, or the evolutionary development of a head.

Symonds, John Addington (sĭm'ŭnz), 1840-93, English author. Educated at Harrow and Oxford, constant ill-health exiled him for the greater part of his life to Italy and Switzerland. His many writings include travel books, *Sketches in Italy and Greece* (1874) and *Italian Byways* (1883); literary essays, *Introduction to the Study of Dante* (1872) and *Studies of Greek Poets* (1873-76); biographies of Shelley (1878), Sir Philip Sidney (1886), Ben Jonson (1886), and Michelangelo (1893); a masterly translation of the autobiography of Benvenuto Cellini (1888); and several volumes of verse, notably *Many Moods* (1878) and *Animi Figura* (1882). Symonds's major work, *The Renaissance in Italy* (7 vol., 1875-86), is a classic collection of sketches in cultural history. See biography by Phyllis Grosskurth (1964); study by Van Wyck Brooks (1914, repr. 1970).

Symons, Arthur (sĭm'ənz), 1865-1945, English poet and critic. A leader of the SYMBOLISTS in England, Symons interpreted French decadent poetry to the English through translations, criticism, and his own imitative poems. He was editor of the *Savoy* (1896) until a period of insanity, movingly described in his *Confessions* (1930), incapacitated him from 1908 to 1910. After that time he was forced to live very quietly. His chief critical work is *The Symbolist Movement in Literature* (1899); others are *The Romantic Movement in English Poetry* (1909) and studies of Baudelaire, Blake, and Rossetti. His poetry includes *Days and Nights* (1889), *Poems* (1902), and *Love's Cruelty* (1923). See biography by Roger Lhombreaud (1963); studies by T. E. Welby (1925) and J. M. Munro (1969).

sympathetic nervous system: see NERVOUS SYSTEM.

sympathomimetic drug (sĭmpăth"ōmĭmĕt'ĭk), any of a group of substances whose actions resemble the response of stimulated sympathetic nerves (see NERVOUS SYSTEM). These drugs include EPINEPHRINE and other CATECHOLAMINES that are naturally produced in the body, and chemically similar substances such as EPHEDRINE. Sympathomimetic drugs excite the central nervous system and heart and affect the diameter of blood vessels. They are used as decongestants and to alleviate bronchial ASTHMA. Because they inhibit the production of the body substance HISTAMINE, they are prescribed for allergic conditions along with ANTIHISTAMINES.

symphonic poem, type of orchestral composition created by Liszt, also called tone poem. Discarding classical principles of form, it begins with a poetic or other literary inspiration. Although it is usually considered PROGRAM MUSIC, no literal following of a program was intended by Liszt. His *Tasso* and *Hamlet* are compositions of this sort. Although the symphonic poem better expressed the spirit of romanticism than did the symphony, it did not supersede the symphony; many composers, e.g., Tchaikovsky, Saint-Saëns, Sibelius, Franck, and Dvořák, wrote in both forms. In the symphonic poems of Smetana and Sibelius an element of nationalism is added. Influenced by Alexander Ritter's tone poems, Richard Strauss carried the programmatic possibilities to an extreme of realism, in contrast to the impressionistic tone poems of Debussy, which are closer to the Lisztian concept.

symphony [Gr.,=sounding together], a SONATA for orchestra. The Italian operatic overture, called sinfonia, was standardized by Alessandro Scarlatti at the end of the 17th cent. into three sections, the first and last being fast and the middle one slower in tempo. Since these sinfonie had little musical connection with the operas they preceded, they could be played alone in concert. It became customary in the early 18th cent. to write independent orchestral pieces in the same style, which were the first real symphonies. G. B. Sammartini (1698-1775) wrote a number of works that influenced and partially defined symphonic form and style. Johann Stamitz (1717-57), who was leader of the Mannheim group of composers, was one of the first to add a second lyrical theme in the first movement and to expand the symphony's three movements to four. Other important contributions to the development of the symphony were made by C. P. E. Bach, Johann Christian Bach, J. G. Graun, and F. J. Gossec. It was Haydn and Mozart, however, who synthesized the techniques of all preceding schools into the Viennese classical symphony. This consisted of four movements—the first, a fast sonata movement; the second, a slow movement; the third, a dance, usually a minuet; and the fourth, a fast finale, usually a rondo and frequently a combination of sonata form and rondo. Beethoven expanded the dimensions of this form and intensified the element of personal expression far beyond the styles of Haydn and Mozart. He also initiated the use of a chorus in the symphony. After Beethoven the classical ideal was continued in the symphonies of Schubert, Mendelssohn, and Schumann, although the classical elements are often overshadowed by romantic traits—repetition in place of actual thematic development, profusion of themes rather than severely limited thematic material, and concern for mood and atmosphere in orchestral color and tone painting. Berlioz adapted the symphonic style and form to program music in his *Symphonie fantastique,* a procedure that was transformed by Liszt into the SYMPHONIC POEM and brought to its height by Richard Strauss. Brahms, reacting strongly to the romantic orchestral style, revived the classical model as defined by Beethoven. Although his harmony, melodic formulas, and use of orchestral color are romantic, Brahms's formal designs and developmental procedures are classical. Bruckner combined classical formal outlines with the chromatic harmonies and extended melodic structures of the Wagnerian style, and his symphonies influenced those of Mahler in their huge orchestral dimensions. Other important romantic symphonists were Dvořák and Tchaikovsky in the 19th cent. and Sibelius in the 20th cent. The symphony has been treated with unprecedented freedom by contemporary composers, as illustrated by Stravinsky's Symphony of Psalms, Bloch's *Israel,* which includes voices, von Webern's Symphony for nine solo instruments, Hindemith's Symphony for Concert Band, and Roy Harris's Folksong Symphony and Symphony for Voices. Other important American symphonists are Aaron Copland, Virgil Thomson, Walter Piston, Roger Sessions, Henry Cowell, Randall Thompson, and Howard Hanson. See Robert Simpson, ed., *The Symphony* (2 vol., 1972); D. F. Tovey, *Essays in Musical Analysis: Symphonies* (1935, repr. 1972); Roland Nadeau, *The Symphony* (rev. ed. 1974).

Symplegades (sĭmplĕg'ədēz), in Greek mythology, two floating cliffs that swung together and crushed anything going between them until Jason's ship, the *Argo,* passed safely through them. They remained still forever after, forming the entrance to the Black Sea.

synagogue (sĭn'əgŏg) [from Gr.,=assembly], Jews' place of assembly for worship, education, and communal affairs. The institution of the synagogue probably dates to the Babylonian exile of the 6th cent. B.C. The returnees appear to have brought back with them the basic structure that was to develop by the 1st cent. A.D. into the well-defined institution around which the religious, intellectual, and communal life of the Jews in the Holy Land and the Diaspora was to be centered from this earliest period to the present. The destruction of the Temple (A.D. 70) and the dispersion over the following centuries increased the synagogue's importance. Services in the synagogue were conducted in a simpler manner than in the Temple. There was no officially appointed priest, the services being conducted by a chazan (reader). The role the synagogue played in preserving Judaism intact through the centuries cannot be overestimated, nor can its influence as an intellectual and cultural force. The subsequent partial assimilation of the Jews, the widening of their intellectual and cultural interests, and particularly the reform movement have now restricted its use to almost purely religious purposes, although among the Orthodox Jews of Eastern Europe and the Orient its scope has not diminished. In more recent times the synagogue has again taken on its former functions as a social and communal center. In the United States, the national synagogue associations, the Union of Orthodox Jewish Congregations, the United Synagogue of America (Conservative), and the Union of American Hebrew Congregations (Reform) are organized in the Synagogue Council of America. The oldest synagogue in the United States (1763) is at Newport, R.I. See Uri Kaploun, ed., *The Synagogue* (1973); Azriel Eisenberg, *The Synagogue through the Ages* (1974).

synapse (sĭn'ăps), junction of nerve cells. A nerve impulse reaches the synapse through the axon, or transmitting end, of a nerve cell, or neuron. Most axons have terminal knobs that respond to the impulse by releasing a chemical substance. Crossing a gap of less than a millionth of an inch known as the synaptic cleft, the substance contacts the adjacent nerve cell or its branch receptor sites, called dendrites. The substance, according to its chemistry, either excites or inhibits the recipient cell and thereby relays or damps the impulse. If sufficiently excited, this second cell in turn transmits the impulse, typically to a muscle, gland, or another synapse. ACETYL-

CHOLINE is recognized as an exciting substance, although there are probably others. Inhibiting substances have not yet been positively identified.

synapsis: see CROSSING OVER.

synchrocyclotron: see PARTICLE ACCELERATOR.

synchrotron: see PARTICLE ACCELERATOR.

synchrotron radiation, in physics, ELECTROMAGNETIC RADIATION emitted by high-speed electrons spiraling along the lines of force of a magnetic field (see MAGNETISM). Depending on the electron's energy and the strength of the magnetic field, the maximum intensity will occur as radio waves, visible light, or X rays. The emission is a consequence of the constant acceleration experienced by the electrons as they move in nearly circular orbits; according to Maxwell's equations, all accelerated charged particles emit electromagnetic radiation. Although predicted much earlier, synchrotron radiation was first observed as a glow associated with protons orbiting in high-energy PARTICLE ACCELERATORS, such as the synchrotron. In astronomy, synchrotron radiation has been suggested as the mechanism for producing strong celestial radio sources like the CRAB NEBULA (see RADIO ASTRONOMY).

Syncom: see COMMUNICATIONS SATELLITE.

syncopation (sĭng″kəpā′shən, sĭn″-) [New Gr.,=cut off], in music, the accentuation of a beat that normally would be weak according to the rhythmic division of the measure. Although the normally strong beat is not usually effaced by the process, there are occasions (e.g., the second theme in the final movement of Schumann's Piano Concerto in A Minor) when the natural rhythmic structure is entirely altered, the syncopation being so elaborate and persistent that the actual metrical structure is obliterated aurally. Occasional syncopation is present in music of all types and in all periods. It predominates, however, in African music and therefore in the music of Negroes of the United States through whom it became the principal element in ragtime (see JAZZ).

syndicalism (sĭn′dĭkəlĭzəm), political and economic doctrine that advocates control of the means and processes of production by organized bodies of workers. Like anarchists, syndicalists believe that any form of state is an instrument of oppression and that the state should be abolished. Viewing the trade union as the essential unit of production, they believe that it should be the basic organizational unit of society. To achieve their aims, syndicalists advocate direct industrial action, e.g., the GENERAL STRIKE, SABOTAGE, slowdowns, and other means of disrupting the existing system of production. They eschew political action as both corruptive and self-defeating. The writings of Pierre Joseph PROUDHON, with his attacks on property, and of Georges SOREL, who espoused violence, have influenced syndicalist doctrine. Syndicalism, like ANARCHISM, has flourished largely in Latin countries, especially in France, where trade unionism was for years strongly influenced by syndicalist programs. Syndicalism began a steady decline after World War I as a result of competition from Communist unions, government suppression, and internal splits between the revolutionary anarcho-syndicalists and moderate reformers. In the United States the chief organization of the syndicalist type was the INDUSTRIAL WORKERS OF THE WORLD, which flourished early in the 20th cent. but was virtually extinguished after World War I. See F. F. Ridley, *Revolutionary Syndicalism in France* (1970).

synecdoche (sĭnĕk′dəkē), figure of speech, a species of METAPHOR, in which a part of a person or thing is used to designate the whole—thus, "The house was built by 40 hands" for "The house was built by 20 men." See METONYMY.

Synge, John Millington (sĭng), 1871–1909, Irish poet and dramatist, b. near Dublin, of Protestant parents. He was an important figure in the IRISH LITERARY RENAISSANCE. As a young man he studied music in Germany and later lived in Paris, where he wrote literary criticism. In Paris he met his compatriot William Butler Yeats, who persuaded Synge to live for a while in the Aran Islands and then return to Dublin and devote himself to creative work. All of Synge's plays reflect his experiences in the Aran Islands. Intense and poetic in style, his works depict the bleak and tragic lives of Irish peasants and fisherfolk. His first two one-act plays, *In the Shadow of the Glen* (1903), a comedy, and *Riders to the Sea* (1904), considered one of the finest tragedies ever written, were presented by the Irish National Theatre Society. In 1904 this group, with Synge, Yeats, and Lady Gregory as codirectors, organized the famous ABBEY THEATRE. Two of Synge's comedies, *The Well of the Saints* (1905) and *The Playboy of the Western World* (1907), were presented by the Abbey players. The latter play created a furor of resentment among Irish patriots stung by Synge's bitter humor. His later works were *The Tinker's Wedding,* published in 1908 but not produced for fear of further riots, and *Deirdre of the Sorrows,* a tragedy unfinished at the time of his death but presented by the Abbey players in 1910. *The Aran Islands* (1907) is Synge's journal of his stay on the islands. See biographies by D. H. Greene and E. M. Stephens (1959) and Donna Gerstenberger (1964); studies by Daniel Corkery (1931, repr. 1965), Maurice Bourgeois (1913, repr. 1969), W. B. Yeats (1911, repr. 1971), and Robin Skelton (1971).

synodic period (sĭnŏd′ĭk), in astronomy, length of time during which a body in the solar system makes one ORBIT of the sun relative to the earth, i.e., returns to the same ELONGATION. Because the earth moves in its own orbit, the synodic period differs from the sidereal period, which is measured relative to the stars. The synodic period of the moon, which is called the lunar month, or lunation, is 29½ days long; it is longer than the sidereal month. The moon is full when it is at OPPOSITION. One sidereal month later it will not yet be full, since it must travel further in its orbit around the earth to reach the point of opposition, which has moved relative to the stars because of the earth's motion. Since the calendar month is not equal to the lunar month, the full moon does not occur on the same day every month. The length of time between recurrences of the full moon on the same date is 235 lunar months, or 19 years. This period, called the Metonic cycle, was discovered by the Greek astronomer Meton in 433 B.C. It is used in determining the date of Easter in the Gregorian CALENDAR and was used in placing the intercalary month in the ancient Greek calendar. For the INFERIOR PLANETS the synodic period is longer than the sidereal period, but for the SUPERIOR PLANETS it is shorter; for Pluto the synodic period is slightly more than one year, while its sidereal period is nearly 250 years.

synonym (sĭn′ənĭm) [Gr.,=having the same name], word having a meaning that is the same as or very similar to the meaning of another word of the same language. Some are alike in some meanings only, as *live* and *dwell.* As a language develops, words that once were synonyms tend to become restricted so that eventually they differ in meaning or in usage (e.g., *prostitute* and *strumpet,* in which the latter is now confined to literary use). Words taken into English from French and Latin have created many synonyms, e.g., *wax* (taken from Old English), *increase* (taken from Old French), and *augment* (taken from Latin). The classic English synonym collections are George Crabb's *Synonymes* and P. M. Roget's *Thesaurus.*

Synoptic Gospels (sĭnŏp′tĭk) [Gr. *synopsis*=view together], the first three GOSPELS (MATTHEW, MARK, and LUKE), considered as a unit. They bear greater similarity to each other than any of them does to JOHN, which differs also from them in purpose. The question of the relations between the three is called the Synoptic problem. Most Protestant and some Roman Catholic scholars agree that Matthew and Luke were written later than Mark, which they followed closely. Matthew then divided Mark into five portions and used them in order, separating them by other material. Luke divided the book only in two, nine chapters (9.51–18.14) being inserted between. Mark, however, only accounts for half of the other two Gospels. Matthew and Luke each have about 100 verses in common, most of them sayings (notably the BEATITUDES); to explain this agreement, scholars assume that there was a primitive document, which they call Q. It consisted largely of sayings of Jesus and was circulated in forms varying from place to place. Matthew and Luke are said to have used different versions of Q. This leaves a good third each in Matthew and Luke that cannot be explained by a common origin; there is no one widely accepted theory on the source or sources for these portions. The traditional Roman Catholic view is that Matthew (in an Aramaic version) preceded Mark and Luke, but that Matthew's Greek translation of his Aramaic Gospel may have come after Mark and Luke. See R. K. Bultmann, *The History of the Synoptic Tradition* (tr. rev. ed. 1968); R. C. Briggs, *Interpreting the Gospels* (1969).

synovial fluid: see JOINT.

syntax: see GRAMMAR.

synthesizer, musical: see ELECTRONIC MUSIC.

synthetic elements, in chemistry, radioactive elements that were not discovered occurring in nature but as artificially produced isotopes. They are TECHNETIUM (at. no. 43), PROMETHIUM (at. no. 61), ASTATINE (at. no. 85), FRANCIUM (at. no. 87), and the TRANSURANIUM ELEMENTS. Some of these elements have since been shown to exist in minute amounts in nature, usually as short-lived members of natural radioactive decay series (see RADIOACTIVITY).

synthetic fur: see FUR.

synthetic rubber: see RUBBER.

synthetic textile fibers have revolutionized the textile industry. Such artificial fibers are usually long-chain polymers, produced industrially by the condensation of many small units. ORLON is the trade name for a polyacrylonitrile fiber made from natural gas, oxygen, and nitrogen. It combines bulk with light weight and is resistant to acids and sun damage. It is much used for sweaters and other clothing. DACRON is the trade name for a polyester fiber of great strength and wrinkle resistance. It is often blended with other fabrics. Vinyl fibers, such as SARAN, are used for screening and heavy-duty upholstery. See also FIBER GLASS; NYLON; RAYON.

Syntyche (sĭn′tĭkē), Philippian Christian in disharmony with EUODIAS. Philip. 4.2.

syphilis (sĭf′əlĭs), contagious disease, the most serious of the VENEREAL DISEASES, caused by a spirochete, *Treponema pallidum* (described by F. R. Schaudinn and Eric Hoffmann in 1905). Syphilis first appeared in Spain among sailors who had returned from the New World in 1493. It was carried into Italy by the armies of Charles VIII of France and spread throughout Europe, being known variously as Neapolitan disease and French pox. The most prevalent mode of transmission is by sexual contact; infection by other means is possible, but its occurrence depends upon an open wound or lesion to permit invasion of the organisms. Transmission may also occur through infected blood or plasma and from an infected mother to her fetus. The development of syphilis occurs in three stages. The primary stage is the appearance of a chancre at the site of infection about three or four weeks after contact, with enlargement of the regional lymph nodes. There are no other symptoms. The secondary stage usually begins with a generalized eruption of the skin and mucous membranes; there may be inflammatory involvement of the eyes, bones, liver, heart, or central nervous system. Tests of the blood serum give proof of infection; many states require such tests before issuing marriage licenses. The tertiary stage is characterized by skin lesions that tend to be chronic and destructive, by tumors in the subcutaneous tissues and in the internal organs, severe damage to the heart and aorta, and progressive central nervous system involvement including locomotor ataxia, degeneration of the optic nerves with possible blindness, and insanity. Until the advent of penicillin during the 1940s, specific and protracted treatment for syphilis was with arsenic, mercury, and bismuth. Present-day therapy is with penicillin for all stages and types of syphilis. The early stage of the disease, and in most cases the secondary stage also, can be cured with penicillin. Even central nervous system syphilis may be cured by penicillin if damage to the nerve tissue has not begun. The incidence of syphilis and other venereal diseases in the United States has been rising, especially among teenagers and homosexuals, causing renewed concern among public health officials.

Syra, Greece: see SÍROS.

Syracuse (sĭr′əkyo͞os, -kyo͞oz), Ital. *Siracusa,* city (1971 pop. 108,685), capital of Syracuse prov., SE Sicily, Italy, on the Ionian Sea. It is a port and a food-processing and tourist center. The old town, on the small island of Ortygia, is connected by a bridge with the mainland, where the more modern districts are situated. Founded (734 B.C.) by Greek colonists from Corinth, Syracuse grew rapidly and soon founded colonies of its own. Its democratic government was suppressed by GELON, tyrant of Gela, who took possession of the city in 485 B.C. Under his rule, marked by a great victory (480 B.C.) over Carthage at Himera, Syracuse took the lead among the Greek cities of Sicily. Gelon's successor, Hiero I, made it one of the great centers of Greek culture; the poet Pindar and the dramatist Aeschylus lived at his court. Soon after Hiero's death a democracy was again established; it lasted from 466 B.C. to 406 B.C. During this period Syracuse extended its control over E Sicily and defeated an Athenian expedition (begun in 415 B.C. by Alcibiades) in a great land and sea battle (414 B.C.). In 406 B.C., DIONYSIUS THE ELDER became tyrant. Under his long rule Syracuse reached the high point of its power and territorial expansion. After the death of Dionysius there followed a period of bitter internal struggle in which DIONYSIUS THE

YOUNGER, DION OF SYRACUSE, and TIMOLEON were the chief protagonists. There were several decades of democratic government until tyranny was reestablished by Agathocles and HIERO II (4th–3d cent. B.C.). Hiero's reign was relatively peaceful and prosperous, but after his death Syracuse suffered catastrophically when it abandoned its traditional ally Rome in favor of Carthage, in the second of the PUNIC WARS. After a long siege by the Roman consul Marcellus, the city fell in 212 B.C. and was sacked; Syracuse thence was reduced to the status of a provincial town. The period from Dionysius the Elder to 212 B.C. was brilliant in terms of culture. The philosopher Plato visited Syracuse several times, and the poet Theocritus probably lived at the court of Hiero II. The mathematician and physicist Archimedes, born (287 B.C.) in Syracuse, directed the defense of the city against the Romans and was killed during the sack of the city. Syracuse suffered another major setback in the late 9th cent. A.D., when it was badly damaged by Arab conquerors. It was captured by the Normans in 1085. Numerous remains testify to the city's past greatness. On Ortygia are the cathedral, built (7th cent. A.D.) on the remains of a Greek temple, with 12 Doric columns; the remarkable archaeological museum; the fountain of Arethusa; ruins of a temple of Apollo; and a castle built (13th cent. A.D.) by emperor Frederick II. Among the remains on the mainland are a large, well-preserved Greek theater (5th cent. B.C.), still used for performances of classical works; a Roman amphitheater (2d cent. A.D.); the large Greek fortress of Euralus; and the extensive Catacombs of St. John (5th–6th cent. A.D.).

Syracuse (sĭr'əkyōōs, sĕr'–), city (1970 pop. 197,297), seat of Onondaga co., central N.Y., on Onondaga Lake and the Barge Canal; settled c.1788, inc. as a city 1848. It is a port of entry, and its many manufactures include air conditioners, electrical and electronic equipment, automobile and aircraft parts, soda ash, chinaware, shoes, and typewriters. Salt springs were discovered there in 1654. Saltmaking, the city's chief industry from its settlement until after the Civil War, declined under competition. However, favorable location on the Erie Canal (opened there in 1819) and on railroads stimulated industrial development. The city is the seat of Syracuse Univ., Le Moyne College, the State Univ. Upstate Medical Center, and two junior colleges. Cultural facilities include the Everson Museum of Fine Arts, the Syracuse Symphony, and the Syracuse Repertory Theater. Of interest are a salt museum and an Erie Canal museum. An annual state fair has been held there since 1841. Nearby is Hancock International Airport and the Onondaga Indian Reservation. Many recreational lakes and streams are in the area.

Syracuse University, mainly at Syracuse, N.Y.; coeducational; chartered 1870, opened 1871. Syracuse, which consists of 19 schools and colleges, is noted for its research programs in government and industry. The university library houses fine collections in Russian history, literature, and European history. The State University of New York College of Environmental Science and Forestry is there. A branch (Utica College) is at Utica, N.Y. See W. F. Galpin, *Syracuse University* (3 vol., 1952–62); A. N. Charters, *The Hill and the Valley: The Story of University College at Syracuse University* (1972).

Syr Darya (sēr däryä'), ancient *Jaxartes* or *Yaxartes*, Pers. *Sihun*, river, c.1,380 mi (2,220 km) long, Central Asian USSR. One of the principal rivers of central Asia, it is formed in the FERGANA VALLEY, E Uzbekistan, by the junction of the Naryn and Kara Darya rivers, which rise in the Tien Shan mts. It flows W through Tadzhikistan, then NW through Uzbekistan and Kazakhstan, past Kzyl-Orda, and into the northern end of the Aral Sea; Kazalinsk is at the head of the delta. Its shallowness makes it unfit for navigation, but its waters are used for irrigating the important cotton-growing areas along its course and for hydroelectric power. The Syr Darya forms the northern and eastern limits of the Kyzyl Kum desert. It is paralleled in its lower course by the Trans-Caspian RR. Alexander the Great in his conquest of Persia reached the river c.329 B.C. and may have founded the chief city on its course—Leninabad (formerly Khodzhent)—on the site of an older city.

Syria (sēr'ēə), officially Syrian Arab Republic, republic (1970 pop. 6,292,000), 71,467 sq mi (185,100 sq km), W Asia, bordering on Lebanon and the Mediterranean Sea in the west, on Turkey in the northwest and north, on Iraq in the east and south, and on Jordan and Israel in the southwest. DAMASCUS is the country's capital and its largest city; others include ALEPPO, HIMS, HAMAH, LATAKIA, DAYR AZ ZAWR, and Al Hasakah. The country is divided into 13 governorates. Syria falls into two main geographical regions, a western region and a much larger eastern region. The western region, which includes about two thirds of the country's population, can be subdivided into four parallel north-south zones. In the far west is a narrow, discontinuous lowland strip along the Mediterranean. It is bordered, and partly cut, by the Jabal an Nusayriyah, a mountain range (average elevation: 4,000 ft/1,220 m; highest point: 5,123 ft/1,561 m) that is crossed by deep valleys. In the east the Jabal an Nusayriyah drops sharply to the Great Rift Valley, which continues southward into Africa and which in Syria contains the Orontes River. East of the rift are mountain ranges, including the Anti-Lebanon Mts. (which include Mount Hermon, 9,232 ft/2,814 m, Syria's loftiest point) and scattered ranges in NW Syria. Within these ranges are several fertile basins, including ones occupied by Damascus and Aleppo. The eastern region is made up of a plateau (average elevation: 2,000 ft/610 m), which is in large part bisected by a series of ranges that fan out northeastward from the Anti-Lebanon Mts. In the south are the Jabal ad Duruz Mts., from which the plain of HAWRAN extends westward to the Sea of Galilee. Other mountains are located in the north. Much of the southern section of the plateau forms part of the Syrian Desert; otherwise, the plateau is largely covered with steppe. There are irrigated, cultivated areas along the Euphrates River in the east, whose basin makes up part

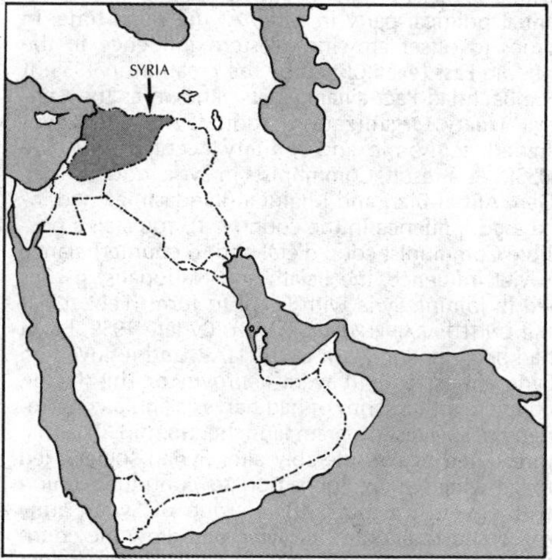

of the Fertile Crescent, as does the Mediterranean coast of Syria. Most Syrians are of Arab descent and speak Arabic, the country's official language. The chief minorities are the Kurds (numbering about 250,000) and the Turkomans (30,000), most of whom live in the north; the Armenians (130,000), many of whom live in Aleppo; and the Circassians (25,000), most of whom live in and near Qunaytirah in the southwest. About 75% of the country's inhabitants are Muslim, mostly of the Sunni sect. There are also significant numbers of Shiite Muslims, especially the Alawi (410,000), who live in the Jabal an Nusayriyah. The DRUSES (120,000), whose religion combines Muslim and Christian elements, live in the south, principally in the Jabal ad Duruz. Approximately 15% of the people are Christian; the largest Christian groups are the Greek Orthodox, the Armenian Orthodox, and the Syrian Orthodox. Syria was an overwhelmingly agricultural country until the mid-1940s, when planned large-scale industrialization began. In the early 1970s agriculture was still the mainstay of the economy, employing about 50% of the work force and contributing about 27% of the annual national product. However, industry's role was steadily increasing, and, with construction, it contributed about 20% of the annual national product. The state plays a major role in the country's economy, particularly in industry and commerce. About one third of Syria's land area is estimated to be arable, but only about one seventh is actually cultivated. The best farmland is located along the coast and in the Jabal an Nusayriyah, around Aleppo, in the region between Hama and Hims, in the Damascus area, and in the land between the Euphrates and Khabur rivers, which is known as Al Jazirah [Arabic, = the island]. The principal crops produced in the country are wheat, barley, cotton, grapes, tomatoes, sugar beets, olives, citrus fruit, lentils, onions, tobacco, and potatoes. Large numbers of poultry, sheep, goats, and cattle are raised. Damascus, Aleppo, and Hims are the chief industrial centers. The main manufactures are refined petroleum, cement, textiles, processed food, beverages, chemicals, cigarettes, soap, and glass. Handicraftsmen make articles of silk, leather, and glass. The principal minerals extracted are petroleum, found mainly at Qarah Shuk (Karachuk) in the extreme northeast; natural gas, found mainly in the Al Jazirah region; phosphates; and salt. Petroleum pipelines from Iraq and Jordan cross Syria, and there is also a pipeline from Qarah Shuk to the Mediterranean coast. Syria's limited transportation network serves mainly the western part of the country. Latakia is the leading seaport. The annual value of Syria's imports is usually considerably greater than the value of its exports. The principal imports are foodstuffs, machinery, iron and steel, textiles, petroleum and petroleum products, and motor vehicles; the chief exports are raw cotton and cotton textiles, wool, cereals, and live animals. The leading trade partners are Italy, the USSR, Lebanon, and West Germany.

History. Until the 20th cent. the term *Syria* generally denoted those lands of the Levant, or eastern littoral of the Mediterranean, that correspond to modern Syria and Lebanon, most of Israel and Jordan, W Iraq, and N Saudi Arabia. Three geographical factors have played major parts in determining the history of Syria—its location on the trade and military routes between the Mediterranean and Mesopotamia; its topography, which made political unity difficult to attain; and the encroaching desert, from which many of its inhabitants and cultural movements have come. Syria has always been an object of conquest, and it has been held by foreign powers during much of its history. One of the earliest settlements was probably at Ugarit. The AMORITES, coming c.2100 B.C. from the Arabian peninsula, were the first important Semitic people to settle in the region, and they established many small states. From the 15th to the 13th cent. B.C. the area probably was part of the empire of the HITTITES, although it came under Egyptian rule for long periods during that time. The first great indigenous culture was that of PHOENICIA (located mostly in present-day Lebanon), which flourished after 1250 B.C. in a group of trading cities along the coast. In the 10th cent. B.C. two Hebrew kingdoms were organized in PALESTINE (see also JEWS). Syria suffered (11th–6th cent. B.C.) long invasions and intermittent control by the empire of ASSYRIA. Babylonian conquerors also found success in Syria, and Egypt constantly sought to reestablish its position there. The Syrians were subjected to massacres, plundering, and forced deportations. Under the Persian Empire, with its efficient administrative system, Syria's standard of living improved (6th–4th cent. B.C.). Alexander the Great conquered Syria between 333 and 331 B.C., and his short-lived empire was followed by that of the Seleucidae (see SELEUCUS I), who are usually called kings of Syria, although they did not always have a secure grip on much of Syria and had many other possessions. Their control of Syria was constantly threatened by Egypt, which was ruled by the Ptolemies. The Egyptians usually held the south until Antiochus III conquered (early 2d cent. B.C.) the region, which was generally called Coele Syria, a name which had been vaguely applied to all of W Syria. The Seleucidae founded cities and military colonies and introduced Hellenistic civilization to Syria. Syria long showed the revivifying effects of this new culture. Many of the cities became cultural centers, but the change did not reach the lower levels of the population. When invasions began again, first by the Armenians under Tigranes and then by the Parthians—both in the 1st cent. B.C.—the Hellenistic sheen was soon dulled. The Romans under Pompey conquered the region by 63 B.C., but they continued to fight the Parthians there, and the Syrians benefitted little from the Roman presence. There were many changes in administration, and Rome drew from Syria numerous soldiers and slaves. The old pagan gods of Syria were also taken up by the Romans. More significant for the future of Syria, Christianity was started in Palestine and soon exerted some influence over all of Syria; St. Paul was converted from Judaism to Christianity on the road to Damascus. In central Syria, PALMYRA was allowed to grow (3d cent. A.D.) to considerable power as an autonomous state, but it was conquered by the Romans when it threatened their ascendancy. After the division of Rome into the Eastern and Western empires in the 4th cent., Syria came under Byzantine rule. In the 5th and 6th cent. MONOPHYSITISM, a Christian heresy with political overtones, gained many adherents in Syria. Byzantine control there was seriously weakened by the 7th cent. Between 633 and 640, Muslim Arabs conquered Syria, and most Syrians were converted to Islam. Damascus was the usual capital of the UMAYYAD caliph (661–750) and enjoyed a period of great splendor. The Umayyads were forcibly displaced by the Abbasids, whose residence was in Iraq, thus ending Syria's dominant position in the Islamic world. At the same time the ties between Muslim Syria and the predominantly Christian southwest (later Lebanon) began to loosen. However, groups of Christians remained in the Muslim areas, and they generally rendered aid to the Christians who came to Syria on CRUSADES (11th–14th cent.). By the late 11th cent. the Seljuk Turks had captured most of Syria, and the Christians fought against them as well as against SALADIN, who triumphed (late 12th cent.) over both the Christians and his fellow Muslims. After Saladin's death (1193), Syria fell into disunity, and in the mid-13th cent. it was overrun by the Mongols under HULAGU KHAN, who destroyed (1260) much of Aleppo and Damascus, massacring about 50,000 inhabitants of Aleppo. The Mongols were defeated later in 1260 by Baybars, the Mameluke ruler of Egypt. The MAMELUKES held control of Syria for most of the time until 1516, when the Ottoman Empire annexed the area. The Mameluke period was largely a time of economic stagnation and political unrest. In 1401 the Mongol conqueror TAMERLANE sacked Aleppo and Damascus. For most of the four centuries of Ottoman control, Syria's economy continued to be weak, and its politics remained fragmented. From the later 16th cent., government in Syria was not directly controlled by the Ottomans but was in the hands of several Syrian families who often fought each other. From the late 18th cent. the European powers took an increasing interest in Syrian affairs, the British as friends of the Druses, the Russians as protectors of the Orthodox Christians, and the French as allies of the Roman Catholics (especially the Maronites). In 1798–99, Napoleon I of France invaded Egypt and also briefly held parts of the Syrian coast. In 1832–33, IBRAHIM PASHA, the son of Muhammad Ali of Egypt, annexed Syria to Egypt. Egypt held Syria until 1840, when the European powers (particularly Great Britain) forced its return to the Ottomans; during this time Syria's economy was revived and numerous schools were established. During the rest of the 19th cent. the Syrian economy was modernized somewhat and educational opportunities were increased; however, conditions were far from good, and growing resentment of Ottoman rule developed among the Syrians. After bloody fighting between Christians and Druses, Lebanon (largely inhabited by Christians) was given considerable autonomy in 1860. During World War I the British encouraged Syrian nationalists to fight against the Ottoman Empire. The ambitions of the nationalists were thwarted in the peace settlement, which gave (1920) France a League of Nations mandate over the Levant States (roughly present-day Syria and Lebanon). From this time the term *Syria* referred approximately to its present territorial extent. France divided Syria into three administrative districts on the theory that political decentralization would safeguard the rights of minorities. The Arab nationalists angrily asserted that decentralization was also a means of maintaining French control by a divide-and-rule policy. The French made some concessions after serious disturbances in 1925, which included a rebellion by the Druses and the French bombardment of Damascus. Lebanon was made a completely separate state in 1926, and after long negotiations a treaty was signed (1936) giving Syria a large measure of autonomy. Nationalist agitation for complete independence continued and grew increasingly bitter when France failed to ratify the 1936 treaty. Anti-French feeling ran particularly high after the troubles that resulted in the cession of the sanjak of Alexandretta (see ALEXANDRETTA, SANJAK OF) to Turkey, completed in 1939. In the same year the French suspended the Syrian constitution, and in World War II they garrisoned Syria with a large number of troops, most of whom, after the fall of France in June, 1940, declared loyalty to the Vichy government. Relations with Great Britain deteriorated, and when it was discovered that Syrian airfields had been used by German planes en route to Iraq, British and Free French forces invaded and occupied Syria in June, 1941. In accordance with previous promises, the French proclaimed the creation of an independent Syrian republic in Sept., 1941, and an independent Lebanese republic in Nov., 1941. In 1943, Shukri al-Kuwatli was elected president of Syria, and on Jan. 1., 1944, the country achieved complete independence. However, the continued presence of French troops in Syria caused increasing friction and bloodshed, as well as severely straining Anglo-French relations. It was not until April, 1946, that all foreign troops were withdrawn from the country. In 1945, Syria had become a charter member of the United Nations. Independent Syria has been characterized chiefly by economic growth and diversification, by political instability, and by conflict with Israel (see ARAB-ISRAELI WARS). A member of the Arab League, Syria joined other Arab states in the unsuccessful war (1948–49) against Israel. The defeat at the hands of Israel, coupled with serious internal divisions resulting from disagreements over whether to unite with Iraq (and thus form a "Greater Syria"), undermined confidence in parliamentary government and led to a series of three coups d'etat in 1949. Lt. Col. Adib al-Shishakli led the third coup (Dec., 1949), and he governed the country until 1954. A new constitution providing for parliamentary government was promulgated in 1950, but it was suspended in late 1951. From then until 1954, al-Shishakli ruled (with the support of the military) as a virtual dictator. In 1953 he issued a new constitution establishing a presidential form of government and was elected president. Opposition to al-Shishakli's one-man rule and controversy over whether Syria should align itself with Egypt (as al-Shishakli favored) or with Iraq led to his downfall in early 1954 and the reinstitution of the 1950 constitution. After elections in late 1954 a coalition government uniting the People's, National, and Ba'ath parties and headed by Sabri al-Asali of the National party was established; al-Kuwatli was elected president. In the following years the Ba'ath party, which combined Arab nationalism with a socialist program, emerged as the most influential political party in Syria. At the same time, in order to offset growing Western influence in the Middle East (exemplified by the creation in 1955 of the Baghdad Pact alliance, later known as the Central Treaty Organization), both Syria and Egypt signed economic and military accords with the USSR. As a result, Communists in Syria, notably Maj. Gen. Afif al-Bizri and Khalid al-Baqdash, gained increased influence in the country. To forestall a possible Communist coup d'etat and to counterbalance Soviet influence, the Ba'ath and Nationalist parties led in joining Syria with Egypt to form (Feb., 1958) the UNITED ARAB REPUBLIC (UAR). By late 1959, Egypt had become dominant in the UAR, and it governed Syria almost as if it were a province. This factor, coupled with a series of bad harvests and a comprehensive socialist program launched in mid-1961 that threatened to considerably alter Syrian society, led to growing Syrian opposition to continued union with Egypt. In Sept., 1961, a group of Syrian army officers seized control of Syria, withdrew the country from the UAR, and established the independent Syrian Arab Republic. Elections for a constituent assembly were held in late 1961, and the People's, Nationalist, and Ba'ath parties reemerged as the leading parties. The assembly chose Maruf al-Dawalibi as prime minister and Nazim al-Qudsi as president of the country; both were conservatives and members of the People's party. In early 1962 a military coup d'etat ended this arrangement, and in late 1962 the 1950 constitution was reinstated. However, national politics remained confused. In 1963 another coup d'etat brought a joint Ba'ath-military government to power. This regime was headed, at different times, by Salah al-Din al-Bitar, a moderate leader of the Ba'ath party, and by Gen. Amin al-Hafiz, and it nationalized much of the economy and redistributed land to the peasants. At the same time a cleavage in the Ba'ath party between moderate and radical elements was growing. In early 1966 the radicals staged a successful coup d'etat and installed Yusseff Zayen as prime minister and Nureddin al-Attassi as president. The new government strengthened Syria's ties with Egypt and the USSR. There were several border incidents with Israel between 1962 and 1966, and renewed Syrian-Israeli tension was a major reason for the outbreak of the Arab-Israeli War of June, 1967. During the war Israel captured the Golan Heights (stretching about 12 mi/19 km into Syria northeast of the Sea of Galilee), and it held onto this territory after a cease-fire went into effect. After the war Syria maintained an uncompromising attitude toward Israel, and there were numerous border incidents. In 1968–69 the Ba'ath party was again torn by factional strife, and it divided into the "progressives" (led by al-Attassi), who were doctrinaire Marxists favoring state control of the economy and close cooperation with the USSR, and the pragmatic "nationalists" (headed by Gen. Hafez al-Assad), who emphasized the need to defeat Israel, to improve relations with other Arab states, and to lessen Syria's economic and military dependence on the USSR. Al-Assad attempted without success to take over the government in early 1969, but in Nov., 1970, he successfully ousted al-Attassi. In early 1971, al-Assad was overwhelmingly elected to a 7-year term as president (the most important government post in the country), and Gen. Abdul Rahman Khleyfawi became prime minister. Later in 1971, Syria, Libya, and Egypt agreed to unite loosely in the Federation of Arab Republics. Syria continued to be on good terms with the USSR, which equipped the Syrian army with modern weapons. In early 1973 a new constitution was approved, and the Ba'ath party won 70% of the seats in elections in May for the 186-member People's Council. Al-Assad generally allowed a freer expression of political views than his predecessor. In July–Aug., 1973, about 42 army officers (all Sunni Muslims) were executed after allegedly plotting to assassinate al-Assad, who, they claimed, showed undue favoritism to his fellow Alawi Muslims in the army. In Oct., 1973, the fourth Arab-Israeli War erupted; after initial Syrian advances in the Golan Heights, Israel gained the offensive and pushed into Syria a few miles beyond the Golan Heights region. Syria (like Israel) accepted the UN Security Council cease-fire resolution of Oct. 25, 1973, but fighting continued into 1974. In May, 1974, largely through the mediation of U.S. Secretary of State Henry Kissinger, Syria and Israel signed an agreement in Geneva that ended the fighting. Under the terms of the accord, Israel pulled back to the 1967 cease-fire line and also returned the city of Qunaytirah (Kuneitra) to Syria; prisoners of war were returned to their respective countries; a buffer zone in the Golan Heights patrolled by UN troops was established; and al-Assad promised to try to prevent guerrilla incursions into Israel from Syria. In June, 1974, U.S. President Richard M. Nixon visited Syria, which appeared willing to establish closer ties (especially in economic matters) with Western countries. See Patrick Seale, *The Struggle for Syria: A Study of Post-War Arab Politics, 1945–1958* (1965); Giorgio Buccellati, *Cities and Nations of Ancient Syria* (1967); M. S. Drower, *Syria c.1550–1400 B.C.* (2 vol., 1970); R. F. Nyrop et al., *Area Handbook for Syria* (1971); S. H. Longrigg, *Syria and Lebanon under French Mandate* (1958, repr. 1972); Tabitha Petran, *Syria* (1972); Itamar Rabinovich, *Syria under the Ba'ath, 1963–1966* (1972).

Syriac (sĕr'ēăk"), late dialect of ARAMAIC, which is a Northwest Semitic language (see HAMITO-SEMITIC LANGUAGES). The early Christians of Mesopotamia and Syria gave the Greek name *Syriac* to the Aramaic dialect they spoke when the term *Aramaic* acquired the meaning of "pagan" or "heathen." The oldest Syriac script, which dates back to the 1st cent. A.D., evolved from the Aramaic alphabet. Syriac began to yield to Arabic after the coming of Islam in the 7th cent. A.D. Today it survives as the tongue of probably fewer than 200,000 people in the Middle East. However, it is also used as a liturgical language of the Syrian Church.

Syrian Desert, Arabic *Badiyat Ash Sham,* arid wasteland, SW Asia, between the cultivated lands along the E Mediterranean coast and the fertile Euphrates River valley. It extends N from the Arabian Desert in Saudi Arabia and comprises W Iraq, E Jordan, and SE Syria. The famous Arabian horses are raised along the edges of the desert, which in the north is crossed by oil pipelines and by a motor route from Damascus to Baghdad. Several nomadic tribes inhabit the desert. Palmyra and other oases served as staging posts on ancient Mediterranean-Mesopotamian trade routes.

syringa: see SAXIFRAGE. For the genus *Syringa,* see LILAC.

syrinx: see PANPIPES.

Syros, Greece: see SÍROS.

systematics: see CLASSIFICATION.

System International (SI): see INTERNATIONAL SYSTEM OF UNITS.

Syzran (sĭ'zrănyə), city (1970 pop. 173,000), S central European USSR, on the Volga River near its junction with the Syzran. The city is a major river port and rail center. Manufactures include hydroturbines and combines, and there are large oil refineries and tanneries. Oil, asphalt, limestone, and slate are extracted in the area. Syzran was founded as a Russian military settlement in 1683 and was an important grain market from the mid-19th cent. until the 1920s.

syzygy (sĭz'əjē), in astronomy, alignment of three bodies of the solar system along a straight or nearly straight line. A planet is in syzygy with the earth and sun when it is in OPPOSITION or CONJUNCTION, i.e., when its ELONGATION is 180° or 0°. The moon is in syzygy with the earth and sun when it is new or full.

Szatmar, Peace of: see RÁKÓCZY.

Szatmarnemeti or **Szatmar:** see SATU-MARE.

Száva, river: see SAVA, river, Yugoslavia.

Szczecin (shchĕ'tsĕn), Ger. *Stettin,* city (1970 pop. 337,204), NW Poland, formerly capital of the Prussian province of Pomerania, on the Oder near its influx into the Zalew Szczeciński (Stettiner Haff). A major Baltic port, Szczecin is also an industrial center with shipyards, ironworks, coke works, and industries producing chemicals, metals, and foodstuffs. Świnoujście (Ger. *Swinemünde)* is its outer port. A fortress and the largest Pomeranian town as early as the 12th cent., it was until 1637 the residence of the dukes of Pomerania and was an important member (from the 13th cent.) of the Hanseatic League. At the Peace of Westphalia (1648) it passed, with Hither POMERANIA, to Sweden, but at the end of the Northern War, Sweden ceded it (1720) to Prussia. Szczecin had a French garrison (1806-13) during the Napoleonic Wars. The construction (1914) of a canal to Berlin greatly enhanced the city as a commercial port, and its present harbor installations are very extensive. During World War II the city suffered heavy damage from repeated bombings. Although four fifths of Szczecin, including the old section, are on the left (western) bank of the Oder, the Potsdam agreement of 1945 transferring Pomerania E of the Oder to Polish administration was interpreted to include the city in the transfer. The German population was expelled and replaced by Poles.

Szczeciński (shchĕtsĕn'skē), Ger. *Stargard,* town (1970 pop. 44,500), NW Poland. It is a rail junction and has metalworking and chemical industries. Chartered in the 13th cent., the town later joined the Hanseatic League. It was the capital of Farther Pomerania, with which it passed to Brandenburg in 1648. The town, which was virtually obliterated during World War II, remained in German hands until its incorporation into Poland in 1945.

Sze, Sao-ke Alfred (sou-kē zē, so͞o), Mandarin *Shih Chao-Chi,* 1877-1958, Chinese diplomat, grad. Cornell. He was (1914-21, 1929-32) Chinese minister to Great Britain and represented (1921-28, 1933-37) China in the United States. He served China as a delegate to the Paris Peace Conference (1919) and was chief delegate to the Washington Conference (1921-22) and the League of Nations (1931). He was senior advisor to the Chinese delegation at the UN Charter conference at San Francisco in 1945.

Szechenyi, Count Stephen (sā'chĕnyē), Hung. *Széchenyi István,* 1791-1860, Hungarian politician. Influenced by his studies in England, he championed the modernization of Hungarian economic, social, and intellectual life and was the leader of the moderate liberal group in the Hungarian diet. His political and economic essays stimulated the development of liberal thought in Hungary. He was (1848) minister of transportation in the first revolutionary government of Hungary, but he resigned when an open break with Austria impended, and he opposed the nationalism of Louis KOSSUTH. In 1859, Szechenyi wrote a satire against the absolute rule of the Austrian minister Bach, incurring serious difficulties with the authorities. Szechenyi, who had suffered a mental breakdown once before, committed suicide.

Szechwan (sĕ'chwän', sŭ'-), Mandarin *Ssu-ch'uan* [four rivers], province (1968 est. pop. 70,000,000), c.220,000 sq mi (569,800 sq km), SW China. The capital is CH'ENG-TU. A naturally isolated region completely surrounded by mountains, Szechwan is accessible to the rest of China by the Yangtze River, which flows through the south and receives several large tributaries, notably the Min, the To, and the Chia-ling. The spectacular gorges found along the eastern part of the Yangtze's course through Szechwan make it difficult to navigate to Chungking, the chief provincial port. Transportation, formerly limited to the turbulent rivers, has been greatly expanded in the 1960s and 70s; railroads now connect Ch'eng-tu with Chungking and Szechwan with Shensi and Yünnan provs. A highway to Lhasa links the province with Tibet. Central Szechwan is generally a rough plateau that is called the Red Basin because of its red sandstone formation. The basin includes the fertile, densely populated Chengtu Plain (c.1,700 sq mi/4,400 sq km), the only large, level area in the province; however, extensive terracing adds much cultivated land, and with a hot, humid climate, adequate rainfall, effective irrigation systems, and fertile soil, two harvests a year are usual. Szechwan, the "rice bowl" of China, is the country's leading rice producer and ranks second in the production of sugarcane. Potatoes, citrus fruits, wheat, corn, sugar beets, sweet potatoes, and beans are also grown. Szechwan is a major cotton producer; other economic crops include ramie (in which the province ranks second in production), hemp, medicinal herbs, tea, and oilseed. About 20% of the province is forested, and tung oil is a major export. Silk, grown on both mulberry and oak trees, is still produced; Szechwan was once famous for its Shu brocades and Pa satins. In the western areas (formerly Sikang prov.), there is much grazing land, and the province's cattle population is said to be the largest in the country. Other livestock raised are yaks, horses, sheep, goats, and pigs, whose bristles are a Chinese export. Salt has been mined since ancient times; other mineral resources include oil, natural gas, coal, iron, copper, lead, zinc, asbestos, and mercury. Industry is centered in Ch'eng-tu, Chungking, Nei-chiang, I-pin, Wan-hsien, and Nan-ch'ung. Szechwan has often been an independent kingdom. It was early a center of Thai culture; its Indian influence came in via the Burma-Yünnan trade route. The Chinese Communists controlled much of N Szechwan in the early 1930s, and the province served as a refuge during the LONG MARCH. In the Second Sino-Japanese War (1937-45), Szechwan was the temporary center of Nationalist China. In 1955 the area of Sikang prov. E of the Yangtze was added to it, nearly doubling the area of Szechwan. The province has many ethnic groups; there are three large minority autonomous regions. Szechwan Univ. is in Ch'eng-tu.

Szeged (sĕ'gĕd), city (1970 pop. 118,490), S Hungary, at the confluence of the Tisza and Maros rivers. It is a river port, a railroad hub, and an agricultural center. Food processing, flour milling, boatbuilding, and the production of textiles, leather footwear, and tobacco are among the city's industries. Szeged is the seat of a Roman Catholic bishopric. It has a university (founded 1921), a medical school, and a large library. The first national assembly of the Magyar tribes under their chief, Arpad, met (9th or 10th cent.) in the city, which became a military stronghold and trade center of the Arpad kings. Szeged was sacked by the Tatars and the Turks and was ruled by the latter from 1542 to 1686. The city was partly destroyed by a flood in 1879 and was rebuilt in modern style. Among its landmarks are a 13th-century Romanesque tower and the 16th-century Mathias church.

Székely (sā'kəlē), ethnic group of TRANSYLVANIA and of present-day Rumania. They number c.400,000 and are recognized by the Rumanian government as a distinct minority group. Except in a few isolated communities, however, where the ancient customs of the Székely have survived, there is little difference between Székely and Magyars. The Székely (also known as Szeklers or Siculi) came into Transylvania either with or before the MAGYARS. Their organization was of the Turkic type, and they are probably of Turkic (possibly Avar) stock. By the 11th cent., however, they had adopted Magyar speech. They later formed one of three privileged nations of Transylvania (the others were the Magyars and the Saxons). With their own military and civil organization, they enjoyed autonomy under the Hungarian crown and were, without exception, regarded as of noble birth; they were exempt from taxation. In the 16th cent. the majority of the Székely accepted Calvinism as their religion, while some became Unitarians or remained Roman Catholics. Their privileges declined in the 18th cent. under the rule of Maria Theresa and Joseph II. The Austrian attempt to impress the Székely into service as a border militia met with widespread resistance. In 1763 a large number of Székely who sought to escape the Austrian recruiting agents were massacred at Madefalva. Many subsequently emigrated to Bukovina and Moldavia. The last remnants of Székely autonomy were suppressed by Austria after the Revolution of 1848.

Székesfehérvár (sā'kĕshfĕ"hârvär), Ger. *Stuhlweissenburg,* city (1970 pop. 72,940), W central Hungary. It is a county administrative center, a road and rail junction, and an industrial center, with industries producing aluminum, machinery, chemicals, and leather. Dating from Roman times and known until the middle 16th cent. as Alba Regia, it was (1027-1527) the coronation and burial place of Hungary's kings. An important fortress town, Székesfehérvár was destroyed during the Turkish occupation of Hungary (1543-1688) and rebuilt in the 18th cent. It is the seat of a Roman Catholic bishop and has two palaces, several churches, and a museum containing Roman antiquities. The city was heavily damaged during World War II.

Szell, George (sĕl), 1897-1970, American conductor and pianist, b. Budapest. He moved with his family to Vienna during his childhood and started his piano training at an early age. At the age of 11 he played his own Rondo for piano and orchestra with the Vienna Symphony Orchestra. He studied at the State Academy of Music in Vienna and in Leipzig. Deciding on a career as a conductor, Szell assisted Richard Strauss at the Berlin State Opera, then held conducting posts in Strasbourg (1917), Prague (1919-21), Darmstadt (1922), and Düsseldorf (1922-24). He was the chief conductor of the Berlin State Opera from 1924 to 1930. Szell made his American debut (1930) with the St. Louis Symphony Orchestra. From 1930 to 1936 he was again in Prague as conductor of the German Opera, after which he directed (1937-39) the Scottish Symphony in Glasgow. Szell then returned to the United States, where he taught at the New School for Social Research and at the Mannes School of Music in New York City and was principal conductor at the Metropolitan Opera (1942-46). In 1946 he became a U.S. citizen. From that year until his death he was musical director of the Cleveland Orchestra, which, under his leadership, became one of the world's finest orchestras. He took leave to conduct the Concertgebouw Orchestra of Amsterdam, and returned (1963) to the United States as guest conductor of the New York Philharmonic-Symphony Orchestra, for which he also acted as interim conductor during the period from 1969 to 1970. Szell's interpretations were marked by clarity and objective adherence to the composer's intentions.

Széll, Kálmán (käl'män sāl), 1845-1915, Hungarian premier (1899-1903). A close associate of DEAK, he was a deputy from 1867, minister of finance (1875-78), and then premier.

Szentgotthard (sĕnt'gôt'härd), town (1970 pop. 8,195), W Hungary, on the Rába River near the Austrian border. In 1664, Montecucculi defeated the Turks at Szentgotthard. The town is also known as St. Gotthard.

Szent-Gyorgyi, Albert von (äl'bĕrt fən sĕnt"-dyör-dyĭ), 1893-, American biochemist, b. Hungary, M.D. Univ. of Budapest, 1917; Ph.D. Cambridge, 1927. After teaching at the universities of Szeged and Budapest, he came to the United States in 1947 and assumed the post of director of research at the Institute of Muscle Research, Marine Biological Laboratories, Woods Hole, Mass. He was naturalized in 1955. He received the 1937 Nobel Prize in Physiology and Medicine for his studies of biological oxidations and for discovering ascorbic acid in adrenal glands. His later researches were chiefly on muscle chemistry. His writings include *On Oxidation, Fermentation, Vitamins, Health, and Disease* (1939), *Chemistry of Muscular Contraction* (1947, rev. ed. 1951), *Bioenergetics* (1957), and *Introduction to a Submolecular Biology* (1960).

Szigeti, Joseph (sĕgĕt'ē, Hung. sĭ'gĕtĭ), 1892-1973, Hungarian-American violinist. After his debut at 13, Szigeti made his first European tour in 1912. Thereafter he achieved worldwide recognition for his musicianship and his interest in the music of contemporary composers. Szigeti made his American debut in 1925. He made more than 100 recordings; in 1960 he retired. See his memoirs, *With Strings Attached* (1947).

Szigetköz, island, Hungary: see under SCHÜTT, GREAT.

Szigetvár (sĭ'gĕtvär), town (1970 pop. 10,409), SW Hungary. A medieval fortress, it was defended in 1566 by Nicholas Zrinyi against the Ottoman sultan Sulayman I, who died during the siege. Zrinyi was killed during a sortie, and the fortress eventually fell to the Turks. A mosque originally built for Sultan Sulayman I is now a church.

Szilard, Leo (sĭ'lärd), 1898-1964, American nuclear physicist and biophysicist, born in Hungary. He was educated at the Budapest Institute of Technology and the Univ. of Berlin, receiving a doctorate from the latter in 1922. Working at the Univ. of Chicago with Enrico Fermi, he developed the first self-sustained nuclear reactor based on uranium fission. Szilard was one of the first to realize that nuclear chain reactions could be used in bombs and was instrumental in urging the U.S. government to prepare the first atomic bomb, but he later actively protested nuclear warfare and supported the use of nuclear energy for peaceful purposes.

Szold, Henrietta (zōld), 1860-1945, American Jewish leader, b. Baltimore. After graduating from high school in 1877 she taught (1878-92) in private schools, organizing many Americanization classes for immigrants. From 1892 to 1916 she was a member of the editorial staff of the Jewish Publication Society of America. In 1909 she visited Palestine, and her concern over the inadequate medical service in that country led her to devote her life to the cause of ZIONISM. In 1912 she founded the Zionist women's organization HADASSAH, of which she was president from 1912 to 1926. After 1920 she lived in Palestine, directing the organization's medical service and relief work. She is particularly esteemed for her leadership (1933–45) of the Youth Aliyah, an organization which rehabilitated thousands of children. She translated works from French, German, and Hebrew, including *The Legends of the Jews,* by Louis Ginzberg (tr., 7 vol., 1909–38), and *The Ethics of Judaism,* by Moritz Lazarus (tr., 2 vol., 1900). See biographies by Marvin Lowenthal (1942), Rose Zeitlin (1952), and Irving Fineman (1960).

Szolnok (sôl'nôk), city (1970 pop. 61,418), E central Hungary, at the confluence of the Tisza and Zagyva rivers. It is a river port and a road and rail junction. Manufactures include chemicals, cellulose, footwear, and furniture. An old settlement, Szolnok was a flourishing salt-trading center from the onset of Arpad rule (late 9th cent.) until the 19th cent. The city also gained historical importance as a fortress disputed between the Magyars and the Turks. Szolnok has a large Franciscan convent, a college of engineering, and an artists' colony, founded in the 19th cent. Nearby are medicinal baths.

Szombathely (sôm'bŏt-hā''), Ger. *Steinamanger,* city (1970 pop. 64,745), W Hungary, near the Austrian border. An important railway junction, it produces agricultural machinery, textiles, and shoes and is also a market for local farm products. Szombathely has been an episcopal see since the 17th cent and has a women's college. The city was founded in 48 A.D. by the Roman emperor Claudius and called Sabaria. Septimius SEVERUS was proclaimed (193) emperor there, and St. Martin of Tours was born (c.316) in the city. Szombathely was destroyed (5th cent.) by the Huns but was rebuilt. The city has an 18th-century cathedral, a 17th-century Dominican church, and an episcopal palace with a museum of antiquities. Ruins of a triumphal arch, an amphitheater, and an aqueduct have been excavated nearby.

Szondi test: see PSYCHOLOGICAL TESTS.

szonolmokite: see FERROUS SULFATE.

Szymanowski, Karol (kä'rôl shĭmänôf'skē), 1882–1937, Polish composer; studied in Berlin and Warsaw. His early works show marked German, French, and Russian influences, but in his later compositions he developed a distinctive, national style. Yet his music was not readily accepted in Poland. He was a founder of Young Poland in Music, an association of composers. His works include nine preludes for piano (1906); *Love Songs of Hafiz* (1911–14), for voice and instruments; *Mythes* (1915), a set of three pieces for violin and piano which includes *The Fountain of Arethusa;* two operas, *Hagith* (written 1912; produced 1922) and *King Roger* (Warsaw, 1926); the ballet *Harnasie* (1935); and three symphonies; orchestral and chamber music; songs; and liturgical music.

T

T, 20th letter of the ALPHABET. It corresponds to the Greek tau. It represents the unvoiced dental or, as in English, the alveolar stop. The diagraph *th* represents the characteristic English interdental fricative, voiced in *this,* voiceless in *thing.* For modern misapprehensions concerning older signs for the fricative, see the letter Y.

Ta, chemical symbol of the element TANTALUM.

Taaffe, Eduard, Graf von (ä'do͞oärt gräf fən tä'fə), 1833–95, Austrian premier (1868–70, 1879–93), of Irish descent. A childhood friend of Emperor Francis Joseph, he was twice premier. Taaffe sought by a series of compromises to cope with the tempestuous crises brought about by the conflict of nationalities within the Austro-Hungarian Empire. He relied on an alliance of Slav and German conservatives against a liberal and nationalist German opposition. In 1879 he sought to conciliate the Czechs by granting limited recognition to Czech as a national language in Bohemia and Moravia. His efforts to reconcile the nationalities brought 14 years of relative calm and prosperity. However, he antagonized the liberal "Young Czechs," who were rapidly gaining the upper hand in Bohemia, and other nationalities were only partly satisfied. Taaffe was forced to resign by a coalition of widely opposed interests when he presented an electoral reform bill granting a general and equal franchise.

Taal, Lake (tä–äl'), 94 sq mi (243 sq km), SW Luzon, the Philippines, S of Manila. One of the most picturesque places in the country, it contains Volcano Island, with Mt. Taal, an active volcano, rising to 984 ft (300 m). Its eruption in 1911 caused much destruction. The last major eruption occurred in 1968.

Taanach (tā'ənăk, tā'năk), royal city of Canaan, central Palestine, the modern Tell Ti'innik (Jordan), SE of Megiddo. Sisera was defeated here by Deborah and Barak. Joshua 12.21; 17.11; Judges 1.27; 5.19; 1 Kings 4.12; 1 Chron. 7.29. Tanach: Joshua 21.25. Remains dating from about the 26th cent. B.C. were excavated (1901–4) here.

Taanath-shiloh (tā'ənăth"–shī'lō), unlocated town, E central Palestine. Joshua 16.6.

Tabard Inn (tăb'ərd), in Southwark borough, Greater London, England. The inn, demolished in the 19th cent., was mentioned by Geoffrey Chaucer in the Prologue of the *Canterbury Tales* as the starting point of Chaucer's pilgrims.

Tabari (Abu Jafar Muhammad ibn Jarir at-Tabari) (täbä'rē), c.839–c.923, Arab historian and commentator. The name Tabari was given him because he was born in Tabaristan, Persia. He traveled widely in Syria and Egypt, setting finally in Baghdad. He was admired for his erudition, his memory, and his industry. He wrote two great works, a commentary on the Koran and *Annals of the Apostles and the Kings.* The commentary became a standard from which later commentators drew. The annals are an attempt at recounting universal history from the creation to 915. Condensed from an even longer work, they are not a continuous narrative but contain differing versions of the same story and are thus a prime collection of Arabic sources. Tabari also taught law.

Tabasco (täbäs'kō), state (1970 pop. 766,346), 9,783 sq mi (25,338 sq km), E Mexico, on the Gulf of Campeche. VILLAHERMOSA is the capital. Tabasco (an Indian name meaning "damp earth") is predominantly a densely forested tropical plain broken by numerous rivers, swamps, and lagoons. The climate is sultry, and rainfall in some areas exceeds 200 in. (508 cm) annually. Although Tabasco has modern roads and railways, rivers (especially the Grijalva and the Usumacinta) constitute the chief mode of transportation. Tropical agriculture (bananas, cacao, sugarcane, hardwoods, and fruits) and cattle raising are the leading economic activities, but rich oil fields discovered along the coast have brought sweeping economic and social changes to Tabasco. The area, first explored by the Spanish in 1518, was conquered in 1530 by Francisco de Montejo. During the 17th and early 18th cent., Tabasco was contested between Spain and England. From 1921 to 1935 it was the virtual fiefdom of the caudillo Tomás Garrido Canabal.

Tabb, John Banister, 1845–1909, American poet, b. Amelia co., Va. He was converted to Roman Catholicism in 1872 and entered the priesthood in 1884. His poems on nature and religion are simple and polished and, at their best, reminiscent of the 17th-century English devotional poets. Among the published volumes are *Poems* (1894) and *The Rosary in Rhyme* (1904).

Tabbaoth (tăb'āŏth, təbā'ŏth), family returned from exile. Ezra 2.43; Neh. 7.46.

Tabbath (tăb'ăth), unlocated place, NW Palestine. Judges 7.22.

tabby cat: see CAT.

Tabeal (tā'bēəl, təbē'əl), father of the proposed usurper of Ahaz's throne. Isa. 7.6.

Tabeel (tā'bēĕl, təbē'ĕl), Persian official in Samaria. Ezra 4.7.

Taber (tā'bər), town (1971 pop. 4,765), S Alta., Canada, NE of Lethbridge. The area is irrigated for crop and livestock raising. The town has a sugar beet refinery and a vegetable cannery. Coal, oil, and natural gas are found nearby.

Taberah (tăb'ērə), camp in the wanderings, in the SE Sinai peninsula. Num. 11.3; Deut. 9.22.

Tabernacle (tăb'ərnăk"əl), in the Bible, the portable holy place of the Jews during their wanderings in the wilderness. It was apparently a tent to house the Ark of the Covenant when that was set down. It was considered in a sense the dwelling of God Himself. It was set up in the center of the camp at every halt. For the directions for the making of the Tabernacle and its appointments, see Ex. 25–27; 29.30–44; 30; 31; 33.7, 8, 9, 10; 35–40. The Tabernacle was finally placed at Shiloh. Joshua 18.51. The term is applied also to the small receptacle, used in the Roman Catholic Church, in which the Host in the ciborium is reserved on the altar. These tabernacles are often elaborately worked, especially the doors. They are usually cubical in shape.

Tabernacles, Feast of, one of the oldest and most joyous of Jewish holidays, called in the Bible the Feast of Ingathering and today often called by its Hebrew name, Sukkoth [Heb.,=booth]. The holiday begins on the 15th day of Tishri, the seventh month in the Jewish calendar, and lasts for nine days (eight days in Israel), ending in another holiday, Simhath Torah [Heb.,=rejoicing of the law], of medieval origin. The Feast of Tabernacles, which marked the closing of the harvest season for the Jews of ancient Palestine, is today celebrated by the taking of all meals in a lightly constructed booth covered with thatch in memory of the wanderings in the wilderness. The palm branch (lulab) and citrus fruit (ethrog) procession performed in conjunction with prayers of the Feast of Tabernacles possibly goes back to the harvest festival associated with the holiday. Ex. 23.16; Lev. 23.33–44; Num. 29.12–40; Ezek. 45.25. See Hayyim Schauss, *Guide to Jewish Holy Days* (1938, repr. 1970); Philip Goodman, *The Sukkot and Simhat Torah Anthology* (1974).

Tabitha (tăb'ĭthə), same as DORCAS.

tablature (tăb'ləcho͝or), in music, name for various systems of MUSICAL NOTATION in use in the 15th, 16th, and 17th cent. for keyboard and lute music. German keyboard tablatures before 1550 used a mixed system employing letters for the lower parts and staff notation for the upper parts. Later, letters were employed exclusively. Above the letters were symbols indicating the duration of the tones. In Spanish keyboard tablatures there is a line to represent each voice of the music, with a number representing the scale degree of the tone. Lute tablatures have lines representing the strings of the lute. Spanish and Italian lute tablatures used numbers to indicate the position for stopping the string. The French system, which superseded all others in the 17th cent., used letters for this purpose. A German system also existed, more complicated than these. Tablatures are used today to notate music for guitar and ukulele. These have vertical lines representing strings of the instrument, horizontal lines for the frets, and dots to show the position of the fingers. See Willi Apel, *The Notation of Polyphonic Music, 900–1600* (4th ed., 1953).

table, article of furniture employed for household or ecclesiastical purposes. Elaborately decorated tables of wood or metal were known in ancient Egypt and Assyria, and the Greeks used small tables of low construction to be placed beside a couch. During the Roman Empire massive rectangular pieces were developed, which were made of marble and supported by carved end slabs as well as square or circular forms of bronze supported on a pedestal or on legs often representing wild beasts, sphinxes, or other figures. Although small tables of various shapes, some covered with precious metals, were used during the Middle Ages, the most common form was the long trestle table that was disassembled and removed after meals. Tables of the Italian and Spanish Renaissance were rectangular with end supports braced by stretchers; they often had an arcade of columns through the center. The magnificent Farnese table of marble inlay, attributed to Vignola (Metropolitan Museum of Art), is a notable piece from this period. Tables of the Elizabethan Age were supported on bulbous legs and included the draw table, forerunner of the extension dining table. By the end of the 17th cent. the console, the gateleg, and a variety of occasional tables had come into use. Striking tables of modern workmanship include elegant, simple designs in glass and chromium or stainless steel, and in a great variety of unvarnished woods. Tables vary in size with their purpose from the smallest candlestand to the great banquet table. They are named according to the place for which they are intended (center, library, side, sofa, tavern), their use (tea, china, drawing, writing, sewing, billiard, dining), their form (folding, console, extension, parson's trestle or sawhorse, piecrust, gateleg, butterfly, drop-leaf, tilt-top, nest), period or style (Gothic, Queen Anne, Empire), or the names of designers who created distinctive types (Adam, Chippendale, Hepplewhite, Sheraton, or Phyfe).

Table Bay, inlet of the Atlantic Ocean, 6 mi (9.7 km) wide, lying off W Cape Prov., Republic of South Africa. Table Mt. overlooks the bay, which was discovered in the late 15th cent. by Portuguese voyagers to India. The shore of Table Bay was settled by the Dutch in 1652, with the founding of Cape Town. The open anchorage is protected by large breakwaters.

Table Mountain, 3,567 ft (1,087 m) high, W Cape Prov., Republic of South Africa. It overlooks Cape Town and Table Bay. The summit is flat, and the dense white mist that often covers it is called the "tablecloth." A cableway (built 1929) carries visitors to the summit.

table tennis, game played, usually indoors, by two or four players; it is more or less a miniature form of lawn TENNIS. It is also called Ping-Pong, after the trade name for a kind of table tennis. The regulation game is played on a table that measures 9 ft by 5 ft (2.74 m by 1.52 m) and stands 2.5 ft (76.2 cm) from the floor. A transverse net 6 in. (15.24 cm) high divides the surface, which is generally dark in color, edged with light stripes, and halved longitudinally (for doubles play) by another light stripe. The celluloid ball is hollow, seamless, and about 1.5 in. (3.81 cm) in diameter, with a weight of .1 oz (2.8 grams); the racket is a wooden paddle with a handle 3 in. (7.62 cm) long and a round blade about 6.5 in. (16.5 cm) long, often covered with rubber or sandpaper. In the service (unlike tennis) the ball must bounce once before clearing the net and again bounce once on the near surface. After the service (only one is allowed, not two as in tennis), the returns should go over the net without bouncing on the near surface. A point is scored when a service goes foul or when a player fails to return the ball properly. Each player in turn serves consecutively five times until the winning score of 21 is reached. (If the score is tied at 20-all, play must continue until a 2-point margin is earned.) In doubles matches partners rotate in units of five consecutive services, and the server must deliver the ball into the diagonally opposite box. Table tennis probably originated in the late 19th cent. First popular in England, it spread to several European countries and to the United States in the early 20th cent. The International Table Tennis Federation was founded (1926) to standardize the rules and equipment of the game. It also sponsors team and individual world championships every two years. The group is composed of over 70 national governing bodies, including the U.S. Table Tennis Association (founded 1933). Primarily a recreational sport in the United States, table tennis is a major competitive sport in the Orient and parts of Europe. In 1971 the sport achieved a great measure of publicity when, while touring Japan, a U.S. table tennis team was invited to play in Communist China, thereby initiating the first officially sanctioned Chinese-American cultural exchange in almost twenty years. See Dick Miles, *The Game of Table Tennis* (1968).

taboo or **tabu** (both: tăbo͞o', tə-), prohibition of an act or the use of an object or word under pain of punishment. Originally a Polynesian word, *taboo* can apply to the sacred or consecrated or to the dangerous, unclean, and forbidden. A taboo can be placed on an object, person, place, or word that is believed to have inherent power above the ordinary. This power, called mana, can only be approached by special priests. To give distinction to special moments in the life cycle, taboos are often declared at births, deaths, initiations, and marriages. Taboos are commonly placed on a clan's ancestral guardian, called the TOTEM. The breaking of a taboo usually requires extermination of the offender or some sort of ceremonial purification in order to remove the taint from the community. Often the mana of a taboo is so great that the offender will suffer punishment, even death, merely through fear of its powers. See J. G. Frazer, *Taboo and the Perils of the Soul* (3d ed. 1955); Sigmund Freud, *Totem and Taboo* (1960, orig. 1918); Mary Douglas, *Purity and Danger* (1970).

Tabor, Horace Austin Warner (tā'bər), 1830–99, American prospector, known as Silver Dollar Tabor, b. Holland, Vt. From the Matchless Mine at Leadville, Colo., he gained tremendous wealth by mining silver, and he spent money lavishly in Leadville and Denver. He became (1878) the first mayor of Leadville, served (1878–83) as lieutenant governor of Colorado, and sat in the U.S. Senate for about one month to complete an unexpired term (1883). He lost most of his fortune and at his death begged his second wife, **Elizabeth McCourt Tabor,** 1862–1935, known as Baby Doe, to hold the Matchless Mine, which he believed would again yield wealth. She was found frozen to death in a shack near the mine, where she had lived alone for many years. Douglas Moore's opera *The Ballad of Baby Doe* (1956) portrays the love affair of Tabor and Baby Doe. See G. L. Hall, *The Two Lives of Baby Doe* (1962); D. A. Smith, *Horace Tabor: His Life and the Legend* (1973).

Tabor, in the Bible. **1** Mt. TABOR. **2** Levitical city. 1 Chron. 6.77. **3** Oak (AV mistranslates "plain"), near Bethel, on Saul's way home after his anointing. 1 Sam. 10.3. **4** Unidentified place. Judges 8.18.

Tábor (tä'bôr), city (1970 pop. 22,236), W Czechoslovakia, in Bohemia. Machinery, machine tools, electrical equipment, and textiles are the chief manufactures. The city was founded in 1420 by John Žižka on a hill near the castle where John Huss had retired in 1412. Named after Mt. Tabor in Palestine, it became the stronghold of the Taborites, the extreme wing of the Hussites. Tábor retains the round tower of a 13th-century castle, many old houses, and a 16th-century town hall with a large collection of Hussite relics.

Tabor, Mount, 1,929 ft (588 m) high, N Israel, in Galilee. Ruins of an ancient stronghold crown its summit; on its slopes Barak assembled the army that defeated Sisera (Joshua 19.22; Judges 4; Jer. 46.18). Many Christians believe it was the scene of Jesus' transfiguration.

Tabora (täbō'rä), city (1967 pop. 21,012), capital of Tabora region, W central Tanzania. It is a trade and transportation center, connected by rail with Dar es Salaam on the Indian Ocean, Kigoma-Ujiji on Lake Tanganyika, and Mwanza on Lake Victoria. Peanuts, cotton, cattle, and other agricultural commodities are shipped. Tabora was founded in 1852 by Arab traders from the Indian Ocean coast and was located at the junction of important caravan routes. It was captured in 1891 by the Germans and became a center of administration of German East Africa.

Taborites: see HUSSITES.

Tabrimon (tăb'rĭmən), father of King Benhadad. 1 Kings 15.18.

Tabriz (täbrēz'), city (1971 est. pop. 420,000), capital of East Azerbaijan prov., NW Iran, on the Aji Chai (Talkheh) River, in the foothills of Mt. Sahand, at an elevation of c.4,600 ft (1,400 m). The fourth largest city in Iran, it is a summer resort and a commercial, industrial, and transportation center. Its manufactures include carpets, textiles, food products, shoes, and soap. There is also an extensive bazaar. Historically, much of the city's importance has resulted from its strategic position for trade to the north (now the Soviet Union) and to the west (now Turkey). Tabriz, then known as Tauris, was (3d cent. A.D.) the capital of Armenia under King Tiridates III. It was sacked by the Oghuz Turks c.1029, but by 1054, when it was captured by the Seljuk Turks, Tabriz had recovered and was a provincial capital. In 1295, Ghazan Khan, the Mongol ruler of Persia, made it the chief administrative center of an empire stretching from Egypt to the Oxus River and from the Caucasus to the Indian Ocean. Under his rule new walls were built around the city, and numerous public buildings, educational facilities, and caravansaries were erected. Tabriz was captured by Tamerlane in the late 14th cent., and Shah Ismail made it the capital of his empire from 1501 until his defeat (1514) by the Ottoman Turks. The Ottomans occupied Tabriz on a number of occasions thereafter, including the whole period from 1585 to 1603. Nevertheless, by the 17th cent. it was a major commercial center, carrying on trade with Turkey, Russia, central Asia, and India. Later, the city was again occupied (1724–30) by the Ottomans, and it was held by Russia in 1827–28. Tabriz played an important part in the Persian constitutional movement at the beginning of the 20th cent. After World War II it was the scene of a revolution led by the leftist Tudeh party, and a Tudeh regime, which had the support of the Soviet Union, held power for a few months in 1946. The city has often been devastated by earthquakes (e.g., in 858, 1041, and 1721) and has few historical remains; of these, the most important are the beautiful Blue Mosque (15th cent.) and the Ark, or Ali Shah, Mosque (14th cent.), whose walls are 85 ft (25.9 m) high. Tabriz is the site of a university (founded 1946) and contains the Azerbaijan Museum.

tabu: see TABOO.

tabun (tä'bən), liquid chemical compound used as a NERVE GAS. It boils at 240°C with some decomposition. The liquid is colorless to brownish; its vapors have a fruity odor similar to that of bitter almonds. The liquid is absorbed through the skin, but the vapor is not. Although tabun is destroyed by its reaction with bleaching powder, the poisonous gas cyanogen chloride is produced. Chemically, tabun is cyanodimethylaminoethoxyphosphine oxide.

tacamahac: see BALM OF GILEAD.

Tacaná (täkänä'), volcano, 13,333 ft (4,064 m) high, on the Mexico-Guatemala boundary; second highest peak in Central America. Major eruptions occurred in 1855 and 1878.

Tacca, Pietro (pyā'trō täk'kä), 1577–1644, Italian sculptor. A pupil of Giovanni BOLOGNA, Tacca adopted the tortuous poses of MANNERISM and combined them in his bronzes with a classical naturalism. Tacca's works (e.g., the equestrian portrait of Philip IV of Spain, Madrid) form a link between mannerist and baroque sculpture.

Taché, Sir Étienne Paschal (ātyĕn' päskäl' tăshā'), 1795–1865, Canadian statesman, b. Quebec prov. He fought with the British in the War of 1812 and then became a doctor. He entered (1848) cabinet-level politics as commissioner of public works in the Baldwin-La Fontaine administration. He was receiver general in several administrations from 1849 to 1857. In 1856 he became joint premier with John A. MACDONALD, but he retired in 1857. He was called from retirement to again become joint premier in 1864 in the second Taché-Macdonald administration. He presided over the Quebec conference (1864) on confederation, but he died before confederation was achieved. He was knighted in 1858.

T'a-ch'eng (tä-chŭng) or **Chuguchak** (cho͞ogo͞ochäk'), town, N Sinkiang Uigur Autonomous Region, China, in the Dzungarian basin, bordering on the USSR. Long a major center for trade with the USSR, it is an agricultural hub and has a lumbering industry. Iron deposits are in the area. The town is sometimes called Tarbagatai.

Tachikawa (tächē'käwə), city (1970 pop. 117,057), Tokyo Metropolis, E central Honshu, Japan. It is an industrial suburb of Tokyo.

tachinid fly (tăk'ənĭd), common name for any of the FLIES of the family Tachinidae, which parasitize caterpillars, beetles, grasshoppers, and other insects. Tachinid flies are generally small (about the size of houseflies), often bristly, and sometimes brilliantly colored. There are nearly 1300 North American species. The female typically lays her white oval eggs on the skin of the host insect, though the eggs of some species are inserted in the host's body, and the eggs of others are left in the host's environment, as for example on leaves, where the host will ingest them. The larvae feed on the host tissues, causing death. Tachinid flies are widely used as a means of biological control of insect pests. Some tachinid flies are themselves parasitized by certain WASPS (see ICHNEUMON FLY). Tachinid flies are classified in the phylum ARTHROPODA, class Insecta, order Diptera, family Tachinidae.

Tachmonite (tăk'mōnīt, tăkmō'-): see HACHMONI.

tachometer (tăkŏm'ətər), instrument that indicates the speed, usually in revolutions per minute, at which an engine shaft is rotating. Some tachometers, especially those used in automobiles, are similar in construction and operation to automotive SPEEDOMETERS. Other types, often connected directly to the shaft whose speed they indicate, are small electric generators whose output voltage is proportional to speed. This voltage is applied to a voltmeter whose dial is calibrated in speed units. Another type, used only with engines having an ignition system, operates by counting the pulsations of current or voltage in the ignition system, the number of these being proportional to the speed of the shaft.

tachycardia: see ARRHYTHMIA.

tachyon (tăk'ēŏn"), hypothetical ELEMENTARY PARTICLE that travels only at speeds exceeding that of light. According to the theory of RELATIVITY, the speed of light is the limiting velocity for all ordinary material particles. Particles having nonzero rest mass can approach, but not reach, the speed of light, since their mass would become infinite at that speed. On the other hand, particles with zero rest mass, such as the PHOTON and the NEUTRINO, must always travel at the speed of light; they cannot be brought to rest or even slowed down. Theorists have argued that since nothing in principle prohibits the existence of a third class of particles that travel only at speeds exceeding that of light, such particles, called tachyons [Gr. *tachys,* = swift] may quite possibly exist. In the terminology of the theory, the particles that travel only at the speed of light are called luxons, and those that travel at lesser speeds are called tardyons. Like the original theory of relativity, the theory of tachyons has several aspects that appear to contradict common sense but that are fully self-consistent. For example, a tachyon must have an imaginary (in the mathematical sense) rest mass, or proper mass, and it must travel faster rather than slow down when it loses energy.

Tacitus (Marcus Claudius Tacitus) (tăs'ĭtəs), d. 276, Roman emperor (275–76). An elderly senator with a reputation for honesty and vigor, he was chosen by the senate to succeed the murdered AURELIAN. He failed to restore the glory of the senate, and after reigning only a few months he died when on campaign in Asia. He was almost certainly murdered. Probus succeeded him.

Tacitus (Cornelius Tacitus), A.D. c.55–A.D. c.117, Roman historian. Little is known for certain of his life. He was a friend of Pliny the Younger and married the daughter of Cneius Julius Agricola. In A.D. 97 he was appointed substitute consul under Nerva, and later he was proconsul of Asia. The first of his works was the *Dialogus* [dialogue], a discussion of oratory in the style of Cicero, demonstrating to some degree why Tacitus was celebrated as an eloquent speaker; this work was long disputed, but his authorship is now generally accepted. Tacitus then wrote a biography of Agricola, expressing his admiration for his father-in-law as a good and able man. Perhaps the most widely known of his works is the small treatise *De origine et situ Germanorum* [concerning the origin and location of the Germans], commonly called the *Germania* or *Germany.* It supplies (along with the earlier account of Julius Caesar) the principal written material on the Germanic tribes. Archaeology bears out the accuracy of Tacitus, but the work is not objective; it is a picture of the simple Germans glorified by comparison with the corruption and luxurious immorality of the Romans. This moral purpose and severe criticism of contemporary Rome, fallen from the virtuous vigor of the old republic, also underlies his two long works, commonly called in English the *Histories* (of which four books and part of a fifth survive) and the *Annals* (of which twelve books—Books I-VI, XI-XVI—survive). The extant books of the *Histories* cover only the reign of Galba (A.D. 68-69) and the beginning (to A.D. 70) of the reign of Vespasian but give a thorough view of Roman life—persons, places, and events. The surviving books of the *Annals* tell of the reign of Tiberius, of the last years of Claudius, and of the first years of Nero. The account contains incisive character sketches, ironic passages, and eloquent moral conclusions. The declamatory writing of the *Dialogus* is replaced in the historical works by a polished and highly individual style, marked by a wide range of vocabulary, intricate and startling syntax, and a consistent nobility of tone. See his complete works (tr. by Moses Hadas, 1942); studies by C. W. Mendell (1957, repr. 1970), Donald Dudley (1969), and Ronald Syme (1958, 2 vol., 1970).

Tacloban (täklō'bän), city (1970 pop. 76,531), capital of Leyte prov., NE Leyte, the Philippines, on an inlet of Leyte Gulf. It is a port and trade center. Tacloban was the first landing place (Oct., 1944) for U.S. troops in the World War II campaign that liberated the Philippines from the Japanese; a monument there commemorates the event. The city is the seat of Divine Word Univ. and the Leyte Institute of Technology.

Tacna-Arica Controversy (täk'nə-ərē'kə), 1883–1929, dispute between Chile and Peru. It arose from provisions of the Treaty of Ancón (1883), which ended the War of the Pacific (see PACIFIC, WAR OF THE). Victorious Chile was ceded the southern provinces of Peru, Tacna and Arica, but only for 10 years; a plebiscite was then to determine the ownership. The plebiscite was not held because negotiations between the countries failed. Chile in 1909 began colonizing the two provinces—a course that led in 1911 to a diplomatic break between Peru and Chile. The United States watched with concern while relations grew worse. In 1922 representatives of Chile and Peru, meeting in Washington, agreed upon arbitration by the President of the United States. Calvin Coolidge in 1925 sent as plebiscitary commissioner Gen. John J. Pershing, who was replaced (1926) by Gen. William Lassiter. Neither commissioner achieved anything of note, but at the suggestion of Frank B. Kellogg, diplomatic relations between Peru and Chile were resumed in 1928. The next year President Herbert Hoover made a proposal accepted by both Peru and Chile. It provided that Chile should retain Arica but return Tacna to Peru; construct a free port for Peru at Arica, with port and rail installations; transfer all state-owned real estate and buildings in Tacna to Peru; and pay an indemnity of $6 million. See W. J. Dennis, ed., *Documentary History of the Tacna-Arica Dispute* (Univ. of Iowa Studies in Social Sciences, 1927, repr. 1971); *Tacna and Arica: An Account of the Chile-Peru Boundary Dispute and of the Arbitrations by the United States* (1931).

taco (tä'kō) [Mex. Sp.,=snack], food composed of a tortilla (round, thin piece of bread made from corn meal) filled with either beans, chicken, or beef. On top of this tomatoes, peppers, onions, lettuce, cheese, or avocado slices may be heaped. The filling is then covered with a highly spiced chili sauce. Originally made in Mexico, tacos have gained great popularity in the United States.

Tacoma (təkō'mə), city (1970 pop. 154,581), seat of Pierce co., W Wash., on Commencement Bay and Puget Sound at the mouth of the Puyallup River; inc. 1884. It is a major seaport and railroad terminus and one of the chief industrial cities in the Northwest. Once known as the lumber capital of America, it is still an important center for forest-products industries. It has railroad shops and plants that manufacture chemicals and electro-chemical products, explosives, paints, bleaches, fertilizers, heavy cranes and machines, adhesives, minerals, metals and alloys, furniture, boats, clothing, and food products. The huge Tacoma smelter, with a smokestack taller than the Washington Monument, is a tourist attraction. Other points of interest include the nation's tallest totem pole, built by Alaskan Indians in 1903; and Point Defiance Park, containing a zoo, an aquarium, a children's fantasy-land park, a forestry museum, and a reconstruction of Fort Nisqually (1833). The fort's original grainery, built in 1843, still stands. The city is the seat of the Univ. of Puget Sound, Pacific Lutheran Univ., two junior colleges, and the state historical society museum. It has an arboretum and a number of art galleries. Beautifully situated between bay and mountains, in sight of Mt. Rainier, Tacoma is the gateway to several national parks and scenic wonders. The Tacoma Narrows suspension bridge links the city with the Olympic Peninsula; it replaced "Galloping Gertie," which collapsed (1940) in a windstorm only four months after it had opened. McChord Air Force Base, Fort Lewis (a major army training center), and the state national guard headquarters are nearby. A daffodil festival is held in Tacoma every April.

Taconic Mountains (təkŏn'ĭk), range of the Appalachian Mts., extending c.150 mi (240 km) north-south between the Green Mts. and the Hudson Valley along parts of New York's border with Vermont, Massachusetts, and Connecticut. Mt. Equinox (3,816 ft/1,163 m) is the highest point. The Taconics, among the oldest mountains in North America, have been worn low by millions of years of erosion. The Berkshire Hills, W Mass., are part of the range. Taconic State Park along the N.Y.-Mass. and N.Y.-Conn. borders is a popular recreational area.

taconite, low-grade iron ore, a flintlike rock usually containing less than 30% iron. Resistant to drilling and to the extraction of its contained metal, the rock was long considered worthless. Experiments begun in 1912 by the American scientist Edward W. Davis and continued by him for nearly 40 years produced the pelletizing method for upgrading the ore. The development of the jet piercer (a high-temperature flame thrower) provided penetration speeds of up to 40 ft (12 m) an hour for blasting holes in the rock. In 1956 exploitation of the vast reserves of taconite in the Mesabi range of Minnesota was begun by some of the largest steel companies in the United States.

tactics: see STRATEGY AND TACTICS.

Tadema, Alma: see ALMA-TADEMA, SIR LAWRENCE.

Tadjiks: see TADZHIK SOVIET SOCIALIST REPUBLIC.

Tadmor, ancient city: see PALMYRA.

Tadoussac (tăd'o͞osăk), village (1971 est. pop. 1,000), S Que., Canada, at the confluence of the Saguenay and the St. Lawrence rivers. It is a summer resort in a dairying and lumbering region. The site was visited by Jacques Cartier in 1535. An attempt (1600–1601) to establish a French colony there failed, but Tadoussac later became the site of the oldest Christian mission in Canada and an important French furtrading post.

tadpole, larval, aquatic stage of any of the AMPHIBIAN animals. After hatching from the egg, the tadpole, sometimes called a polliwog, is gill-breathing and legless and propels itself by means of a tail. During the period of metamorphosis it develops the lungs, legs, and other organs of the adult and, in the frog and the toad, loses the tail.

tadpole shrimp: see SHRIMP.

Tadzhik Soviet Socialist Republic (täjĭk', -jēk', Rus. təjĭk') or **Tadzhikistan** (təjĭkĭstăn', -stän', täjĭ-, Rus. təjĭkĭstän'), constituent republic (1970 pop. 2,900,000), 55,251 sq mi (143,100 sq km), Central Asian USSR. DUSHANBE is the capital; other important cities are LENINABAD, Ura-Tyube, and Kurgan-Tyube. Tadzhikistan borders on China in the east, Afghanistan in the south, the Kirghiz SSR in the north, and the Uzbek SSR in the west and northwest. Parts of the Pamir and Trans-Alai mt. systems are in the east, and the republic contains the highest and third highest peaks of the USSR, Mt. Communism (24,590 ft/7,495 m) and Lenin Peak (23,405 ft/7,134 m). The southeast is occupied by an arid plateau c.12,000 to 15,000 ft (3,660–4,570 m) high. The only extensive low districts are the Tadzhik section of the Fergana Valley in the north and the hot, dry Gissar and Vakhsh valleys in the southwest. The Amu Darya, Syr Darya, and Zeravshan are the chief rivers and are used for irrigation. Additional dams and irrigation projects, notably the Great Gissar Canal, have opened almost 1,000,000 acres (400,000 hectares) of land to cultivation. Most of the population is concentrated in the narrow, deep intermontane valleys. The easternmost section of the republic constitutes the GORNO-BADAKHSHAN AUTONOMOUS OBLAST. Tadzhikistan's economy is based mostly on agriculture, livestock raising, mining, and raw material processing. The lowlands specialize in the cultivation of long-staple cotton, wheat, barley, fruit (including wine grapes), and mulberry trees (for silk). Karakul sheep, dairy cattle, and yaks are raised. The republic's mountains yield coal, antimony, gold, salt, fluorspar, and numerous other minerals. Mineral springs provide the basis for numerous health resorts. Cotton ginning, silk spinning, fruit canning, winemaking, carpet weaving, metalworking, machine building, and the manufacture of cotton, silk, and woolen textiles and leather goods are the leading industries. Tadzhikistan ranks among the top Soviet republics in hydroelectric resources. About 53% of the population is composed of Tadzhiks (also spelled Tadjiks or Tajiks); the rest are mainly Uzbeks (18%), Russians (13%), Tatars, Kirghiz, and Ukrainians. The Tadzhiks are an Iranian people of the Sunni Muslim religion. They are probably descended from the inhabitants of ancient Sogdiana. By the 9th and 10th cent., the Tadzhiks had achieved much success in fruit growing, cattle raising, and the development of handicrafts and trade. The Tadzhik territory was conquered by the Mongols in the 13th cent. In the 16th cent., it became part of the khanate of Bukhara. By the mid-19th cent., the Tadzhiks were divided among several internally weak khanates. Russia took control of the Tadzhik lands in the 1880s and 90s, but the Tadzhiks remained split among several administrative-political entities, and their territories were economically backward and were exploited for their raw materials. In the aftermath of the 1917 Russian Revolution, the Tadzhiks rebelled against Russian rule; the Red Army did not establish control over them until 1921. Tadzhikistan was made an autonomous republic within Uzbekistan in 1924; in 1929 it became a constituent republic of the USSR.

Taegu (tī'go͞o'), Jap. *Taiku*, city (1970 est. pop. 1,083,000), S South Korea, on the Kum River. It is a railroad junction, a major industrial center, and a primary collection and distribution point for an extensive agricultural and mining region. Taegu has important textile industries. The Naktong River basin supplies raw materials for industry. During the Korean War the city formed a major bastion in the United Nations perimeter defense of the Pusan beachhead, and in Aug., 1950, it became the temporary capital of Korea. Its name also appears as Taeku, Taiku, and Taikyu.

Taejon (tī'jŭn'), city (1970 est. pop. 415,000), capital of South Chungchong prov., central South Korea. It is a railroad hub and agricultural center, with rice mills, silk and textile factories, and food-processing plants.

taffeta, cloth, originally silk but now also made of synthetic fibers, supposed to have originated in Persia. The name, derived from Persian, means "twisted woven." Taffeta is in the same class and demand as satin made of silk. The cloth is made of a plain or tabby weave, and the textures vary considerably. In addition there are two types of silk taffeta. Piece-dyed taffeta is often used in linings and is quite soft. Yarn-dyed taffeta is much stiffer and is often used in evening dresses. Taffeta is also used in ribbons, umbrellas, and some electrical insulation.

Tafilelt (täfē'lĕlt) or **Tafilet** (–lĕt), oasis in the Sahara, SE Morocco, c.530 sq mi (1,370 sq km). It has date groves and small trading settlements. After c.760 it was an independent kingdom for nearly two centuries, growing rich on the caravan trade with lands south of the Sahara. Sijilmasa (now in ruins) was the chief trade center and the capital of the kingdom. Since the Middle Ages the region has been noted for its dates and leather. It was the original seat of the ruling dynasty of Morocco, which came to power in the late 17th cent.

Taft, Lorado (lərā'dō), 1860–1936, American sculptor, lecturer, and writer on art, b. Elmwood, Ill., studied at the École des Beaux-Arts. In 1886 he became instructor at the Art Institute of Chicago, exerting a strong influence over the young sculptors of the West. Through his lectures and writings he spread a knowledge of art and aesthetics. After creating decorative sculptures for the Horticultural Building of the World's Columbian Exposition, Chicago, 1893, he produced portrait work, military monuments, and groups such as *Solitude of the Soul* and *The Blind* (Art Inst., Chicago). Large memorials and fountains occupied his later years, among them the colossal *Black Hawk* overlooking Rock River, Ill.; the Washington monument, Seattle, Wash.; Columbus Memorial Fountain, Washington, D.C.; and *Fountain of the Great Lakes* and *Fountain of Time,* Chicago. His principal literary works are *The History of American Sculpture* (1903) and *Recent Tendencies in Sculpture* (1921).

Taft, Robert Alphonso, 1889–1953, American politician, b. Cincinnati, Ohio; son of William Howard Taft. He practiced law in Ohio and served (1921–26, 1931–32) in the state legislature. Elected to the U.S. Senate in 1938, Taft quickly became the acknowledged leader of conservative Republicans. He attacked President Franklin Delano Roosevelt and the New Deal for the expansion of Federal power at the expense of state and local government and vigorously urged economy in government and restoration of balanced budgets. A leading advocate of isolationism before World War II, he later backed U.S. participation in the United Nations. In 1947 he helped write the TAFT-HARTLEY LABOR ACT. Taft strongly opposed postwar Democratic policies, particularly in foreign affairs. He voted against ratification of the North Atlantic Treaty Organization, changed his position on the United Nations, condemned the Korean policy of the Truman administration, opposed its China policy, and objected to Secretary of State Dean Acheson. Known to friends and enemies alike as "Mr. Republican," Taft was a leading contender for the Republican presidential nomination in 1952 but lost to Dwight D. Eisenhower. After Eisenhower's election, Taft became Senate majority leader and a friend and influential adviser of Eisenhower in his first months as President. He acted as an important bridge between the Eastern and Midwestern factions of his party. Taft's *Foreign Policy for Americans* appeared in 1951. See biography by J. T. Patterson (1972); study by Russell Kirk and James McClelland (1967). His son **Robert Alphonso Taft, Jr.,** 1917–, b. Cincinnati, served as Republican in the Ohio legislature (1955–62) and in the U.S. House of Representatives (1963–64, 1967–70), before being elected (1970) to the U.S. Senate.

Taft, William Howard, 1857–1930, 27th President of the United States (1909–13) and 10th Chief Justice of the United States (1921–30), b. Cincinnati. After graduating (1878) from Yale, he attended Cincinnati Law School. He received his law degree in 1880. He became a Cincinnati lawyer and soon had political posts as assistant prosecuting attorney for Hamilton co. (1881–83), assistant county solicitor (1885–87), and judge of the superior court of Ohio (1887–90). He became nationally prominent as a figure in Republican politics in 1890, when President Benjamin Harrison chose him as U.S. Solicitor General. After service as a federal circuit judge (1892–1900) and as dean of the Cincinnati law school (1898–1900), he was appointed (1900) head of the commission sent to organize civil government in the Philippines, and he was named first civil governor of the Philippine Islands; he did much to better relations between Filipinos and Americans. In 1904 his friend President Theodore Roosevelt appointed Taft Secretary of War. Taft became a close adviser of the President and was prominent in Latin American affairs, conducting the delicate negotiations attending U.S. intervention in Cuba in 1906. Roosevelt chose Taft as his successor, and the Republican party named him as presidential candidate in the election of 1908, in which he defeated William Jennings Bryan. He was expected to continue Roosevelt's policies, and to a large extent he did. Trusts were vigorously prosecuted under the SHERMAN ANTITRUST ACT; the Interstate Commerce Commission was strengthened by the Mann-Elkins Act (1910); and Taft's Latin American policy, known as "dollar diplomacy," was to an extent only an enlargement of Roosevelt's Panama policy and the Roosevelt Corollary to the MONROE DOCTRINE. The emphasis in all these policies had, however, changed. In Latin America, for instance, the accent was on protection of property and interests of Americans abroad rather than on national interest. Members of the Republican party who favored progressive policies were increasingly restive, and the INSURGENTS movement grew strong. The administration made positive achievements in the inauguration of the postal savings bank (1910) and the parcel-post system (1912), and the creation of the Dept. of Labor (1911). Nevertheless, Taft was generally at odds with the progressive elements in his party: he failed to support the Insurgents' attempt to oust the dictatorial speaker of the House of Representatives, Joseph Cannon; he favored the PAYNE-ALDRICH TARIFF, a high-tariff measure that was denounced by progressive Republicans; and he supported Richard BALLINGER against Gifford PINCHOT in the Ballinger-Pinchot controversy. Meanwhile, Taft's relations with Roosevelt deteriorated, and the former President joined the opposition to Taft. In 1912, Roosevelt fought vigorously for the Republican presidential nomination. When he failed and Taft got the nomination, Roosevelt headed the PROGRESSIVE PARTY and ran in the election as the Progressive (popularly called the Bull Moose) candidate. The Republican vote was split, and the Democratic candidate, Woodrow Wilson, won. Taft retired from public life and taught law (1912–21) at Yale. He was cochairman (1918–19) of the War Labor Conference in World War I. In 1921, President Harding appointed him Chief Justice. His chief contribution to the Supreme Court was his administrative efficiency. His writings include *The United States and Peace* (1914) and *Our Chief Magistrate and His Powers* (1916). See *Taft and Roosevelt: The Intimate Letters of Archie Butt* (1930, repr. 1971); biographies by H. S. Duffy (1930) and H. F. Pringle (1939, repr. 1964); A. T. Mason, *William Howard Taft, Chief Justice* (1965); P. E. Coletta, *The Presidency of William Howard Taft* (1973).

Taft-Hartley Labor Act, 1947, passed by the U.S. Congress, officially known as the Labor-Management Relations Act. Sponsored by Senator Robert Alphonso Taft and Representative Fred Allan Hartley, the act qualified or amended much of the National Labor Relations (Wagner) Act of 1935, the Federal law regulating labor relations of enterprises engaged in interstate commerce, and it nullified parts of the Federal Anti-Injunction (Norris-LaGuardia) Act of 1932. The act established control of labor disputes on a new basis by enlarging the NATIONAL LABOR RELATIONS BOARD and providing that the union or the employer must, before terminating a collective-bargaining agreement, serve notice on the other party and on a government mediation service. The government was empowered to obtain an 80-day injunction against any strike that it deemed a peril to national health or safety. The act also prohibited jurisdictional strikes (dispute between two unions over which should act as the bargaining agent for the employees) and secondary boycotts (boycott against an already organized company doing business with another company that a union is trying to organize), declared that it did not extend protection to workers on wildcat strikes, outlawed the closed shop, and permitted the union shop only on a vote of a majority of the employees. Most of the collective-bargaining provisions were retained, with the extra provision that a union before using the facilities of the National Labor Relations Board must file with the U.S. Dept. of Labor financial reports and affidavits that union officers are not Communists. The act also forbade unions to contribute to political campaigns. Although President Truman vetoed the act, it was passed over his veto. Federal courts have upheld major provisions of the act with the exception of the clauses about political expenditures. Attempts to repeal it have been unsuccessful, but the LANDRUM-GRIFFIN ACT (1959) amended some features of the Taft-Hartley Labor Act.

Tagalog (təgä'ləg, tägä'lŏg) or **Tagal** (tägäl'), dominant people of Luzon, the Philippines, and the second largest ethnolinguistic group in the Philippines. They number about 4 million. Most of the population is Christian. Tagalog, a Malayo-Polynesian language that had a written standard form before the coming of the Spanish, is by law the national language of the Philippines.

Tagalog language: see MALAYO-POLYNESIAN LANGUAGES.

Taganrog (təgənrôk'), city (1970 pop. 254,000), S European USSR, on the Gulf of Taganrog, an arm of the Sea of Azov. It is a port, exporting mainly grains and coal. Iron and steel milling, metallurgy, ship repairing, leather working, commercial fishing, agricultural processing, and the manufacture of heavy machinery and furniture are the city's major industries. A Pisan colony on the site was destroyed by the Mongols in the 13th cent.; Turks later settled there. In 1698, Peter the Great founded Taganrog as a fortress and naval base. The Turks recaptured it twice (1712 and 1739), but it was taken by the Russians in 1769 and definitively ceded by Turkey in the Treaty of Kuchuk Kainarji (1774). Superseded by Odessa in the late 19th cent. as a major grain exporter, Taganrog retained importance as a military and naval base and a manufacturing city. Landmarks include the imperial palace (now an historical museum) in which Czar Alexander I reportedly died and a memorial museum at the home of the writer Anton Chekhov, who was born in Taganrog.

Taggard, Genevieve, 1894–1948, American poet, b. Waitsburg, Wash. Her early years were spent in Hawaii. She returned to the United States in 1914, graduated from the Univ. of California in 1919, and taught English at several women's colleges. Her poetry ranges from the deeply personal poems of her early career to her later verse of social commentary. Among her volumes of poetry are *For Eager Lovers* (1922), *Hawaiian Hilltop* (1923), *Calling Western Union* (1936), *Long View* (1942), and *Collected Poems: 1918–1938* (1938). She compiled several anthologies, including a collection of metaphysical verse.

Taglioni, Maria, 1804–84, Italian ballerina, b. Stockholm. Taglioni is considered the first and foremost ballerina of the romantic period. She made her debut in Vienna in 1822 in a ballet created for her by her father, the Italian choreographer Filippo Taglioni. Although she danced with the Paris Opéra from 1827, she did not achieve success until 1832, when she interpreted the title role of her father's new work, *La Sylphide,* which all Europe acclaimed. Taglioni's ethereal style and high elevations and leaps greatly influenced the development of ballet. She danced with the St. Petersburg Imperial Theatre from 1837 through 1839. Having retired in 1848, she was forced by bankruptcy to teach dance in Paris and London in her last years.

Tagore, Sir Rabindranath (rəbĭn'drənät təgôr', täkŏŏr'), 1861–1941, Indian author and guru, b. Calcutta. Tagore came of a wealthy Bengali family. He went abroad in 1877 to study law in England but soon returned to India. For a time he managed his father's estates and became involved with the Indian nationalist movement, writing propaganda. His characteristic later style combines natural descriptions with religious and philosophical speculation. Tagore drew on all the classical literature of India, especially the ancient Sanskrit scriptures and the writings of Kalidasa. His prodigious output includes approximately 50 dramas, 100 books of verse (much of which he set to music), 40 volumes of novels and shorter fiction, and books of essays and philosophy. Tagore, in his devotion to peace, denounced nationalism and violence. He sought to instill in men a sense of their unity; he was severely critical of the Indian caste system. His most important philosophical work is *Sadhana: The Realization of Life* (1913), which echoes the fundamental ideas inherent in sacred Hindu writings. His dramas are filled with lyricism and philosophy, while his poems deal with amorous, mystical, and fabulous themes. In India his appeal was nearly universal. A man of striking appearance, Tagore came to be regarded with the reverence due an ancient teacher. He wrote in Bengali but translated much of his work into English. It attracted attention in the West, and he was awarded the 1913 Nobel Prize in Literature, especially for his collection of poetry, *Gitanjali* (1912). Tagore's best-known novels and poetry include *The Gardener* (1913), *The Crescent Moon* (1913), *Songs of Kabir* (1915), *Cycle of Spring* (1917), *Fireflies* (1928), and *Sheaves* (1932). Among his plays are *The Post Office* (1914), *Chitra* (1917), and *Red Oleanders* (1924). Philosophical works include *Personality* (1917), *Nationalism* (1917), *The Home and the World* (1919), *The Religion of Man* (1931), and *Man* (1932). In 1915, Tagore was knighted. His travels and lectures took him around the world. He was impressed with the capacity of the West for accomplishing its practical goals, but he deprecated what he considered its spiritual emptiness and waste. In 1922, Santiniketan (abode of peace), the school he had founded at Bolpur in 1901, was expanded into the internationally attended Visva-Bharati Univ. The curriculum stressed social reform, international unity, and rural reconstruction. See his collected poems and plays (1951); his memoirs (1917); biography by Krishna Kripalani (1962); studies by S. K. Ghose (1961) and B. C. Chakravarty (1971); Amiya Chakravarty, ed., *A Tagore Reader* (1961).

tagua (tä'gwä), fruit of the ivory-nut palm (*Phytelephas macrocarpa*), which flourishes in tropical America from Paraguay to Panama. The female palms bear burrlike fruits, each containing several seeds about the size of hen's eggs. These are the ivory nuts, white or cream in color and very hard. Known in the trade also as vegetable ivory, the substance is used as a substitute for ivory and has long been carved into curios for tourists. Its commercial value originated in the mid-19th cent. when African ivory began to grow scarce. Tagua became a commodity of considerable importance, great quantities being exported to the United States and Europe for the manufacture of buttons and other small articles. Today, however, it is largely supplanted by less expensive synthetic materials. Tagua is classified in the division MAGNOLIOPHYTA, class Liliatae, order Arecales, family Palmae.

Tagus (tā'gəs), Span. *Tajo,* Port. *Tejo,* river, c.585 mi (940 km) long, rising in the Sierra de Gúdar, E Spain, and draining the central part of the Iberian Peninsula. It is usually described as the peninsula's longest river although some estimate it to be slightly shorter than the Ebro River. The Tagus flows northwest through the mountains, past Teruel, then north across the Meseta of central Spain, past Toledo, to form part of the Spanish-Portuguese border. Entering Portugal, it flows southwest, past Santarém and into the Atlantic Ocean at Lisbon. The estuary of the Tagus (12 mi/19 km long) is one of Europe's finest harbors; Salazar Bridge, one of the longest suspension bridges in Europe, spans the estuary. The Tagus is navigable for c.80 mi (130 km) upstream. Its lower and upper courses pass through deep gorges and are broken by waterfalls. The river has great hydroelectric-power potential. The middle Tagus flows through a fertile section of the Meseta and is used for irrigation. The chief tributaries of the Tagus are the Alagón and Jarama rivers.

Tahan (tā'hăn), descendant of Ephraim. Num. 26.35; 1 Chron. 7.25.

Tahapanes, ancient city: see TAHPANHES.

Taharka (təhär'kə) or **Tirhakah** (tĕr'əkə, tērhä'kə), d. 663 B.C., king of ancient Egypt, last ruler of the XXV dynasty; son of Piankhi. Before he was king, he led the Egyptians against Sennacherib, who disastrously defeated him. Seizing (688 B.C.) the throne by force, Taharka established a residence at Tanis. In 671 he lost Memphis and Lower Egypt to the Assyrians under ESAR HADON. On the withdrawal of the Assyrians, Taharka again entered Lower Egypt, only to be expelled (667) by ASSURBANIPAL. He restored the temples at Napata. Taharka is mentioned in the Bible (2 Kings 19.9; Isa. 37.9).

Tahath (tä'hăth). **1** Ancestor of Samuel. 1 Chron. 6.24. **2, 3** Two Ephraimites. 1 Chron. 7.20. **4** Unlocated desert resting place of the Jews. Num. 33.26.

Tahiti (tähē'tē), island (1970 est. pop. 84,552), South Pacific, in the Windward group of the SOCIETY ISLANDS, FRENCH POLYNESIA. The capital is PAPEETE. The classic island paradise of the South Seas, Tahiti is the largest (402 sq mi/1,041 sq km) and most important of the French islands. The peninsula of Taiarapu, which forms E Tahiti, is joined to the western part of the island by the Isthmus of Taravao. Tahiti is mountainous, with four prominent peaks, the highest of which is Mt. Orohena (7,618 ft/2,322 m). The chief products are tropical fruits, copra, vanilla, and sugarcane; there are pearl fisheries off the coast. The inhabitants of Tahiti are mostly Polynesian, but there is a large Chinese minority. The island was settled by Polynesians in the 14th cent; the first European to discover Tahiti was the English navigator Samuel Wallis, and later visits (1769, 1773, 1777) were made by Capt. James COOK, and by the *Bounty* under Lt. William BLIGH (1788). English and French missionaries arrived in the latter part of the 18th cent. In 1843 the Tahitian queen Pomare IV was forced to agree to the establishment of a French protectorate. After her death (1877) and the subsequent abdication (1880) of her son Pomare V, France made Tahiti a colony. During World War II the Tahitians voted (1940) to support the Free French; in 1946 all the indigenous inhabitants became French citizens. Paul GAUGUIN did many of his paintings in Tahiti, and Robert Louis STEVENSON spent some time there. Tahiti was formerly called Otaheite and King George III Island.

Tahmasp (tä'mäsp), 1514–76, shah of Persia (1524–76), son and successor of ISMAIL and the second of the Safavid dynasty. He successfully repulsed persistent invasions by the Uzbeks. Sulayman I also invaded Persia, continuing the wars between Ottomans and Persians commenced by Selim I. One stage of these wars ended with a peace treaty in 1555. In 1561 an Englishman, Anthony Jenkinson, succeeded in establishing a trade route to Central Asia and Persia across Russia. Continual warfare during the reign of Tahmasp helped bring about internal decline.

Tahmasp Kuli Khan: see NADIR SHAH.

Tahoe, Lake (tä'hō, tā'-), 193 sq mi (500 sq km), on the Calif.-Nev. line. Fed by many streams, the lake occupies a basin in the Sierra Nevada; it is drained by the Truckee River. Lake Tahoe lies 6,228 ft (1,898 m) above sea level, but its depth (1,645 ft/501 m) prevents it from freezing. The lake, discovered in 1844 by U.S. explorer John Frémont, is noted for its clearness and is a year-round resort.

Tahoua (tou'ä), town (1970 est. pop. 20,335), SW Niger. Still a largely traditional town, it is a farming community and trade center frequented by TUAREG and FULANI pastoral nomads. Gypsum and phosphates are mined. A teacher-training school is in Tahoua.

Tahpanhes (tä'pənhēz), **Tahapanes** (tāhăp'ənēz), or **Tehaphnehes** (tēhăf'nĭhēz), ancient city, NE Egypt, on Lake Manzala. The site is now on the Suez Canal. Herodotus states that the city (called by the Greeks Daphnae) had a garrison of Psamtik's troops and, in the early 5th cent. B.C., a Persian garrison. It was superseded as a port by Naucratis. A colony of Jews settled there in the 6th cent. B.C., and the city is mentioned in the Bible (Jer. 2.16; 43.7; 46.14; Ezek. 30.18).

Tahpenes (tä'pēnēz''), queen of a Pharaoh. 1 Kings 11.19,20.

Tahquamenon (təkwä'mənən, -mənŏn''), river, c.80 mi (130 km) long, rising in the E Upper Peninsula, N Mich., and flowing E and NE to Whitefish Bay of Lake Superior. It was once a well-known logging river. It is noted for its waterfalls and is celebrated in Longfellow's *Hiawatha.*

Tahrea (tərē'ə), descendant of Saul. 1 Chron. 9.41. Tarea: 1 Chron. 8.35.

Tahtim-hodshi (tä'tĭm-hŏd'shī), region, E of the Jordan, mentioned in the textually difficult account of the census of David. 2 Sam. 24.6.

Tai, peak: see T'AI-SHAN, China.

T'ai or **Tai** (tī), lake, c.1,300 sq mi (3,370 sq km), on the border between Kiangsu prov. and Chekiang prov., E China; second largest freshwater lake in China. Dotted with islands, it is one of China's most scenic areas. The lake basin is one of the richest agricultural regions in China; rice, wheat, and cotton are grown. The lake is linked to the Grand Canal.

T'ai-chung or **Taichung** (both: tī-jo͝ong), city (1969 pop. 428,426), W central Taiwan. Situated in an area where rice, sugarcane, and bananas are grown, T'aichung is a central distributing and processing center for these products. The city has textile, machine-building, food-processing, and chemical industries. A noted educational and cultural center, it is the home of the Chinese National Palace Museum and the Chinese National Central Museum. A fine park and several scenic spots are in the city.

Taif (tīf), city (1963 est. pop. 54,000), W Saudi Arabia, in the Hejaz. It is c.5,000 ft (1,520 m) above sea level. Taif is revered by Muslims for the tomb of Abdullah ibn Abbas, a cousin of the Prophet Muhammad, and for the graves of two infant sons of the Prophet. It is also a summer resort.

taiga (tī'gə), northern coniferous-forest belt of Eurasia, bordered on the north by the treeless tundra and on the south by the steppe. This vast belt, comprising about one third of the forest land of the world, extends south from the tundra to about lat. 62°N in Norway, Sweden, and Finland, but dips still farther south to about lat. 53°N in the Urals. It extends through northern European USSR across the Ural Mountains and over most of Siberia. It has a continental climate, with long, severe winters of 6 or 7 months. Thawing occurs during late April or early May, and the growing season is short. The mean average summer temperatures are fairly high, but there are night frosts. Podzols are the soils of this zone. Only the hardier cereals and roots, such as barley, oats, and potatoes, can be cultivated. The principal species of trees are cedar, pine, spruce, larch, birch, and aspen. The taiga has many swampy areas formed during the spring.

Taiku or **Taikyu:** see TAEGU, Korea.

tail assembly: see AIRPLANE.

taille: see TALLAGE.

Taillefer (tīəfĕr'), fl. 1066, Norman warrior and trouvère. According to medieval chronicles and evidence in the Bayeux Tapestry, he led the Norman army at Hastings into battle, singing of ROLAND at Roncesvalles; he was killed in the conflict.

Taimyra: see TAYMYRA, river, USSR.

Taimyr Peninsula: see TAYMYR PENINSULA, USSR.

T'ai-nan or **Tainan** (both: tī-nän), city (1969 pop. 461,838), W central Taiwan, on the Taiwan (Formosa) Strait. The third largest city of Taiwan, it has industries producing metals, textiles, machinery, and processed foods. It is also a center for the marketing and processing of sugarcane, rice, peanuts, and salt, and there is an important fishing industry. Settled in 1590, T'ai-nan is the oldest city of Taiwan. It was taken over by the Dutch and used as their headquarters from 1624 to 1662. It then became the island's capital under KOXINGA and his son. Called Taiwan or Taiwanfu, it remained the political center of the island until the transfer of government to Taipei in 1885, when the city was renamed T'ai-nan. A cultural center, it has many temples, the shrine of Koxinga, and a modern college of engineering.

Tainaron, Cape, Greece: see MATAPAN, CAPE.

Taine, Hippolyte Adolphe (tān, Fr. ēpôlēt' ädôlf' tĕn), 1828–93, French critic and historian. A brilliant student, he gained recognition with the publication of his doctoral thesis, *Essai sur les fables de La Fontaine* (1853). His deterministic theories, which held that man was the product of heredity, historical conditioning, and environment, became the theoretical basis for the naturalistic school. His best-known works are *Histoire de la littérature anglaise* (1864; tr. *History of English Literature,* 1871–72); *De l'intelligence* (1870; tr. *On Intelligence,* 1871); and *Les Origines de la France contemporaine* (6 vol., 1876–93; tr. *The Origins of Contemporary France,* 6 vol., 1876–94). By his studies of the *ancien régime,* the French Revolution, and contemporary France he spread the idea of history as being concerned with the whole social life of any nation. In 1864 he began a 20-year career as professor of aesthetics and art history at the École des Beaux-Arts. Taine and his contemporary Ernest Renan were the most influential intellectual figures of their period. Although Taine has been attacked for sacrificing truth to his passion for formula and system, his learning, industry, and breadth of interest inspired scholars and critics of his time and later; his socio-historical method of analysis had considerable influence on philosophy, aesthetics, literary criticism, and the social sciences. See study by Leo Weinstein (1972); S. J. Kahn, *Science and Aesthetic Judgment* (1953).

Taipei (tīpā') or **Taipeh,** city (1969 pop. 1,712,108), N Taiwan, capital of Taiwan and provisional capital of the Republic of China. Taiwan's largest city, it is the administrative, cultural, and industrial center of the island. The major industries produce wood and paper products, textiles, metals, machinery, chemicals, food products, and fertilizers. Founded in the 18th cent. by immigrants from Fukien prov. on the China mainland, Taipei began its modern development only after 1885, when it replaced T'ai-nan as the capital of Taiwan prov. It continued to serve as a political center and underwent considerable enlargement and modernization under Japanese rule (1895–1945). In 1949, when the Communists forced the government of Chiang Kai-shek to flee from the mainland of China, Taipei became the headquarters of the Nationalists. In 1967 the city became a special municipality with a status equal to that of a province. It is administered by a governor appointed by the central government and a council of 48 members. Two universities are in Taipei.

Taiping (tīpĭng'), city, Perak, Malaysia, central Malay Peninsula. Once the leading tin-mining center of Malaya, it has been supplanted by the Kinta Valley. The city is picturesquely situated at the foot of Maxwell's Hill (alt. c.4,000 ft/1,220 m), a noted hill station and holiday resort.

Taiping Rebellion, 1850–64, revolt against the Ch'ing (Manchu) dynasty of China. It was led by Hung Hsiu-ch'üan, a visionary from Kwangtung who evolved a political creed including derived elements of Protestantism. His object was to found a new dynasty, the Taiping [great peace]. Strong discontent with the Chinese government brought him many adherents, especially among the poorer classes, and the movement spread with great violence through the eastern valley of the Yangtze River. The rebels captured Nanking in 1853 and made it their capital. The Western powers, who at first sympathized with the movement, soon realized that the Ch'ing dynasty might collapse and with it foreign trade. They offered military help, and Frederick T. Ward and later Charles George ("Chinese") GORDON, a British soldier, led the Ever-Victorious Army, which protected Shanghai from the Taipings. The Taipings, weakened by strategic blunders and internal dissension, were finally defeated by new provincial armies led by Tseng Kuo-fan and Li Hung-chang. See J. M. Callery and Melchior Yvan, *History of the Insurrection in China* (tr. 1853, repr. 1969); W. J. Hail, *Tseng Kuo-fan and the Taiping Rebellion* (1927, repr. 1964); E. P. Boardman, *Christian Influence upon the Ideology of the Taiping Rebellion, 1851–1864* (1952); F. H. Michael, *The Taiping Rebellion* (3 vol., 1966–71).

Taisha (tī'shō), 1879–1926, reign name of emperor of Japan (1912–26). His given name was Yoshihito. The son of Mutsuhito, the Emperor MEIJI, he succeeded to the throne in 1912, but was later declared mentally incompetent; his son HIROHITO was made regent in 1921.

Taisha, town, Shimane prefecture, SW Honshu, Japan, on the Sea of Japan. It is a religious center, famous as the site of the ancient Izumo shrine. The shrine, said to be the oldest in Japan, is splendidly situated among majestic pines. Together with its many secondary buildings it was rebuilt in 1874. Traditionally all the Shinto gods convene there each October. The town also has a 6th-century Buddhist temple.

T'ai-shan (tī-shän) or **Tai** (tī), peak, 5,069 ft (1,545 m) high, W Shantung prov., E China. Located in the homeland of Confucius, it is China's most sacred mountain. In ancient times it was believed that T'ai-shan controlled man's fate on earth. The peak is revered by Buddhists and Taoists and has long been the goal of pilgrimages; it has many temples and shrines. T'ai-shan is also called Tung Yo [eastern peak].

Tait, Archibald Campbell, 1811–82, British churchman, archbishop of Canterbury, b. Edinburgh. He grew up a Presbyterian, but he early decided to enter the ministry of the Church of England. In 1834 he was elected a fellow of Balliol College, Oxford; in 1836 he was ordained an Anglican priest. The OXFORD MOVEMENT never won his favor, and when

Tract 90 appeared (1841) he was one of the "Four Tutors" who issued a formal protest. Tait succeeded Thomas Arnold as headmaster at Rugby in 1842. He became dean of Carlisle (1849), then bishop of London (1856), where his open-air preaching increased his fame. In 1868 he was named archbishop of Canterbury. He sympathized with Broad Church views, although he joined in the censure of *Essays and Reviews* (1860). An antiritualist, he was one of the creators of the Public Worship Regulation Act (1874), but its final form was more severe than he intended. See biography by R. T. Davidson and D. Benham (2 vol., 1891); study by P. T. Marsh (1969).

Tait, Peter Guthrie, 1831–1901, Scottish physicist and mathematician. He was professor of natural philosophy at Edinburgh from 1860 and conducted important investigations in thermodynamics and the kinetic theory of gases. His early work in mathematics was mainly concerned with quaternions. His writings include *Treatise on Natural Philosophy* (with Lord Kelvin, 1867) and *Scientific Papers* (2 vol., 1898–1900).

T'ai-tung or **Taitung** (both: tī-do͝ong), city (1969 est. pop. 46,000), W Taiwan. Rice, sugarcane, and peanuts are the major crops marketed and processed in T'ai-tung. The lack of a good harbor and harbor facilities has greatly retarded industrial progress and development of local natural resources.

Taiwan (tī'wän'), Portuguese *Formosa,* island (1971 est. pop. 14,810,929), 13,885 sq mi (35,961 sq km), in the Pacific Ocean, separated from the mainland of S China by the 100-mile-wide (161-km) Formosa Strait. Together with many nearby islets, including the Pescadores and the island groups of Quemoy and Ma-tsu, it forms the seat of the Republic of China. The provisional capital is TAIPEI; Nanking, on mainland China, is regarded as the official capital of the republic. Other major cities include KAOH-SIUNG, T'AI-NAN, T'AI-CHUNG, and CHI-LUNG. The heavily forested hills and mountains of central and E Taiwan reach their summit at Hsin-kao Shan (13,113 ft/3,997 m high); there are about 70 peaks exceeding 10,000 ft (3,048 m). This mountainous area produces some minerals, chiefly gold, silver, copper, and coal, but

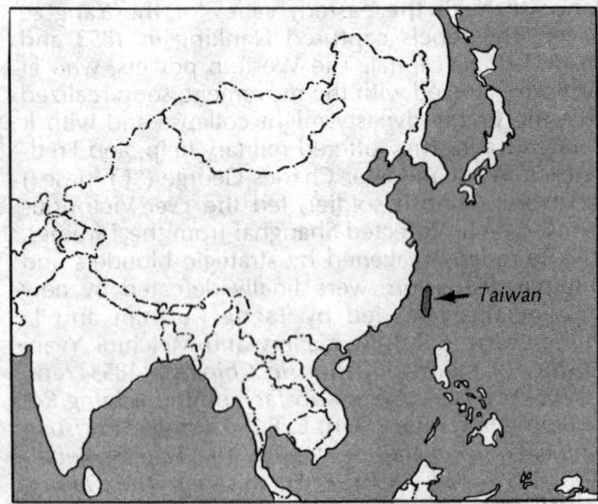

its main resources are forest products, including valuable hardwoods and natural camphor. The broad coastal plain in the west supports most of the island's population and is the chief agricultural zone. Typhoons are common. Taiwan, with a semitropical climate and rainfall ranging from moderate to heavy, produces abundant food crops. Rice is the chief crop, followed by sugarcane; sweet potatoes, potatoes, bananas, peanuts, citrus fruits, pineapples, and tea are also important. The island has a sizable fishing fleet. Industry, once concerned mainly with rice and sugar milling, has diversified to include food processing and the production of textiles and chemicals. The manufacture of consumer goods, especially electrical appliances, has also become increasingly significant. Most industries are privately run, but the government operates those considered essential to national defense, such as steel. Railroad and bus lines are also government operated. Taiwan trades chiefly with the United States and Japan. Major exports are textiles, clothing, fruits, and vegetables; imports include nonelectrical and electrical machinery and transportation equipment. The overwhelming majority of the people are Chinese; they generally speak the Fukienese (Amoy) and Hakka dialects. There are also Malayan aborigines living in the mountainous interior. Numerous religions are practiced on Taiwan, including Taoism, Buddhism, Confucianism, Shamanism, and Christianity. Elementary education is compulsory, and educational facilities were greatly improved in the 1950s and 1960s. The earliest Chinese settlements on Taiwan began in the 7th cent., chiefly from the mainland provinces of Fukien and Kwangtung. The island was reached in 1590 by the Portuguese, who named it Formosa [=beautiful]. In 1624 the Dutch founded forts in the south at present T'ai-nan, while the Spanish established bases in the north. The Dutch, however, succeeded in expelling the Spaniards in 1641 and assumed control of the entire island. They in turn were forced to abandon Taiwan in 1662, when Koxinga, a general of the Ming dynasty of China who had to flee from the Manchus, seized the island and established an independent kingdom. However, the island fell to the Manchus in 1683. Chinese immigration increased, and the aboriginal population was gradually pushed into the interior. Japan, attracted by the island's strategic and economic importance, acquired Taiwan by the Treaty of Shimonoseki (1895) after the First SINO-JAPANESE WAR. Japan exploited the island for the benefit of the Japanese home economy and tried to establish Japanese as the language of the island. The island was scarcely used, however, for Japanese colonization. Under Japan, Taiwan's economy was modernized and industrialized, railroads were built, and the large cities expanded. During World War II, Taiwan was heavily bombed by U.S. planes. In accordance with the Cairo declaration of 1943 and the Potsdam Conference of 1945, Taiwan was returned to China as a province after the war. In 1949, as the Chinese Communists gained complete control of the mainland, the Nationalist government of Chiang Kai-shek and the remnants of his army took refuge on the island. The Chinese Communists planned an invasion of Taiwan in 1950, but it was thwarted when President Truman ordered the U.S. 7th Fleet to patrol Formosa Strait. Japan renounced all claims to Taiwan and the Pescadores in the peace treaty of 1951, but Taiwan's territorial status remained a major issue among the great powers. In 1953, President Eisenhower announced the lifting of the blockade of Taiwan by the U.S. navy. In 1955, following repeated attacks by the People's Republic of China against the Nationalist-held islands of Quemoy and Ma-tsu, the United States entered into a mutual security treaty with the Nationalists in which the United States promised to defend Taiwan from outside attack. In 1958 there was continuous, intensive shelling of Quemoy and Ma-tsu, and an invasion was again threatened. Communist China reiterated its demands to the island, but the United States reasserted its determination to defend Taiwan, although it stressed that there was no commitment to help the Nationalist government return to the mainland. By the spring of 1959 bombardment of the islands had diminished, but no agreement had been reached. The Nationalist army, trained and equipped by the United States, now numbers about 600,000, and there is also a navy and a modern air force. In support of Chiang's repeated declaration to free China from the Communists, Taiwan has served as a base for espionage and guerrilla forays into the Chinese mainland and for reconnaissance flights over Communist China. Internally, the Nationalist government implemented land reforms, which improved the lot of the peasants by allowing tenants to purchase their own land; much of it was bought by the government from big landlords and sold to tenant farmers under lenient terms. With U.S. economic aid, Taiwan enjoyed spectacular economic growth after 1950. The aid program was so successful that it was terminated after 1965. Taiwan's government is based on the constitution of 1946, which was drawn up to govern the whole of China. An elected national assembly of 1,488 members chooses the president and vice-president and is empowered to amend the constitution. The government is made up of five yuan, or branches: the Executive yuan, where most political power rests, is similar to a cabinet and is headed by the president; the Legislative yuan, which is elected, has 493 members and handles all legislation; the Judicial yuan is appointed by the president and serves as the highest judicial authority; the Control yuan is in charge of censorship; and the Examination yuan supervises examinations for government positions. The dominant political party is the Kuomintang (Nationalist party). Two other political parties exist, but neither has participated in local elections in Taiwan. Chiang Kai-shek, elected to his fifth 6-year term as president in 1972, is also the leader of the Kuomintang. Chiang's son, Chiang Ching-kuo, serves as deputy premier and carries out some of the presidential duties of his father. Taiwan's internal affairs are controlled by an elected provincial assembly and a governor appointed by the national president. Although friction between the island Chinese, who make up about 80% of the population, and those who came from the mainland has lessened, it still remains a problem. Chiang's regime has been criticized for dictatorial methods, and between a native Taiwanese movement for independence and the continuing threat from Communist China, the position of the Nationalist government was far from secure in the 1960s and 70s. China's seat in the United Nations was taken away from the Republic of China and given to the People's Republic in 1971. Taiwan's international position continued to weaken in the early 1970s as the United States sought to improve relations with the People's Republic of China and as more large countries, such as Canada and Japan, moved to recognize the mainland government. See F. H. Chaffee et al., *Area Handbook for the Republic of China* (1969); L. H. Gordon, ed., *Taiwan* (1970); W. M. Bueler, *U.S. China Policy and the Problem of Taiwan* (1971); G. W. Barclay, *Colonial Development and Population in Taiwan* (1954, repr. 1972); Hungdah Chiu, ed., *China and the Question of Taiwan* (1973).

T'ai-yüan or **Taiyüan** (both: tī-yüän), city (1970 est. pop. 2,725,000), capital of Shansi prov., N China, on the Fen River, in one of the world's richest coal and iron areas. It is a mining and smelting center with a large iron and steel complex and plants making heavy machinery, chemicals, plastics, fertilizer, cement, paper products, and processed foods. T'ai-yüan is connected by rail with Peking. An ancient walled city, it fell to the Communists in 1949 after a siege in which thousands starved. Shansi Medical College is in the city. T'ai-yüan was formerly called Yangku.

Taizz (tă-ĭz'), city (1970 est. pop. 80,000), S Yemen, in the interior highlands. It is an agricultural marketing center and the focus of trade routes. Taizz was the administrative capital of Yemen from 1948 to 1962.

Tajiks: see TADZHIK SOVIET SOCIALIST REPUBLIC.

Tajimi (tä"jē'mē), city (1970 pop. 63,522), Gifu prefecture, central Honshu, Japan. It is the country's leading center for the production of ceramics.

Tajín: see PAPANTLA, Mexico.

Taj Mahal (täzh məhäl', täj məhŭl'), mausoleum, Agra, Uttar Pradesh state, N India, on the Jumna River. It is considered one of the most beautiful buildings in the world and the finest example of the late style of Indian Muslim architecture. The Mogul emperor Shah Jahan ordered it built after the death (1629) of his favorite wife, Mumtaz Mahal. The building, which was begun in 1630 and completed in 1648, was designed by a Turkish architect. The Taj Mahal is in a walled garden adorned with fountains and marble pavements. The building is reflected in an oblong pool, and dark cypresses surround it on three sides. It rises from a platform 313 ft (95 m) on a side, bearing a white marble minaret at each corner; the enclosure, 186 ft (57 m) on a side, has truncated corners and a high portal on each side. The white marble exterior is inlaid with semiprecious stones arranged in Arabic inscriptions (designed by a Persian calligrapher), floral designs, and arabesques, and the salient features of the interior are accented with agate, jasper, and colored marbles. The roofing dome, on the inside, is 80 ft (24.4 m) high and 50 ft (15.2 m) in diameter; outside, it forms a bulb, which tapers to a spire topped by a crescent. The tomb chamber, with its two sarcophagi, is an octagonal room in the center of the edifice (the royal couple, however, are buried in a vault beneath the floor). The chamber is softly illuminated by the light that passes through double screens of intricately carved marble set high in the walls. The building is in a perfect state of preservation.

Tajo, river: see TAGUS.

Tajrish (täjrēsh'), city (1966 pop. 157,486), Tehran prov., N Iran, a suburb of Tehran. It is a summer resort.

Tajumulco (tähōōmōōl'kō), inactive volcano, 13,816 ft (4,211 m) high, W Guatemala. It is the highest mountain in Central America.

Takada (tä"kä'dä), city (1970 pop. 75,053), Niigata prefecture, W central Honshu, Japan. It is an agriculture market, ski resort, and center for chemical industries.

Takahashi, Korekiyo (kōrā'kēō tä"kähä'shē), 1854–1936, Japanese statesman and financier. Long an official of the Yokohama Specie Bank, he became its president in 1906, and from 1911 to 1913 he was president of the Bank of Japan. In 1921, after the assassination of Hara Kei, he became prime minister and head of the Seiyukai party, but his cabinet fell in 1922. He was one of Japan's greatest finance ministers, serving in that capacity in 1913–14, 1918–22,

1927, and 1931-36. An advocate of sound government finance, supported by the business interests, he opposed army demands for larger military appropriations and warned against inflation and overexpansion of the national debt. He was assassinated by army extremists in the unsuccessful military coup of Feb. 26, 1936.

Takamatsu (täkä'mätsōō), city (1970 pop. 274,331), capital of Kagawa prefecture, NE Shikoku, Japan, a port on the Inland Sea. It is the chief communications point between Shikoku and Honshu islands. Lacquer ware and paper products are manufactured in the city. Takamatsu was the seat of the Matsudaira family during the feudal period. Ritsurin Park, on the site of a 14th-century castle, has noted landscape gardens.

Takamine, Jokichi (jō'kēchē täkä'mīnā"), 1854-1922, Japanese chemist. He served (1881-84) as chemist in the employ of the Japanese government and (1887) organized a fertilizer manufacturing company. In 1890 he settled in the United States, where he did research in applied chemistry. He isolated adrenaline (1901) and Taka-Diastase (an enzyme of rice malt). He also devised methods of using the diastase as a starch digestant in manufacturing.

Takaoka (täkä'ôkä), city (1970 pop. 159,664), Toyama prefecture, W central Honshu, Japan, on the Sho River. It is a center for mechanical, textile, and paper industries.

Takarazuka (täkä"rä'zōōkä), city (1970 pop. 127,129), Hyogo prefecture, SW Honshu, Japan. It is a suburb and a resort serving the Osaka-Kobe areas.

Takasago (täkäsä'gō), city (1970 pop. 68,900), Hyogo prefecture, SW Honshu, Japan. It is an industrial center.

Takasaki (täkäsä'kē), city (1970 pop. 193,073), Gumma prefecture, central Honshu, Japan. A transportation and industrial center, with flour mills, silk textile factories, and food-processing plants, it is known chiefly for its statue (130 ft/40 m high) of Kannon, goddess of mercy.

Takayama (täkä'yämə), city (1970 pop. 56,459), Gifu prefecture, W central Honshu, Japan, on the Jinzu River. A former castle town from the Edo era, it is now an agricultural market and handicrafts center.

Takemitsu, Toru (tō'rōō täkä'mītsōō), 1930–, Japanese composer. Takemitsu organized an avant-garde group in Tokyo in 1951. He has combined serial methods with traditional Japanese music. His best-known work is the *Requiem* (1958) for strings. His other works include piano, chamber, and orchestral music.

Takht-i-Sulaiman, peaks: see SULAIMAN MOUNTAINS.

takin (təkēn'), hoofed mammal, *Budorcas toxicolor,* found in Asia, most closely related to the muskox. The takin is oxlike in build and may reach a shoulder height of 3½ ft (107 cm). It has a large head with a broad blunt muzzle; both sexes have high-set, outward-curving horns. Takins are found in the wooded mountains and valleys of W China and in the Himalayas. Although ungainly in their movements they are agile climbers. Powerful animals, they are especially fierce when cornered or wounded. They feed on a wide variety of plant life. Members of the western race are dull yellow-brown in color, but members of the races found in China are bright yellow with areas of black. The golden takin of Shensi prov. is a metallic gold with black hindparts. Takins are classified in the phylum CHORDATA, subphylum Vertebrata, class Mammalia, order Artiodactyla, family Bovidae.

Takla Makan (tä'klä mäkän'), Mandarin *Ta-k'e-la-ma,* vast sandy desert, c.125,000 sq mi (323,750 sq km), central Sinkiang Uigur Autonomous Region, NW China, between the Kunlun mts. on the south and the Tien Shan mts. and Tarim River on the north; occupies most of the Tarim basin. The Takla Makan is a bleak and uninhabited region, rimmed by many oases linked by caravan routes. Numerous mountain streams disappear into the desert, which is traversed by the channel of the Ho-t'ien (Khotan), an intermittent stream. The chief towns and oases are Yarkand and Ho-t'ien. The earliest Chinese contacts with the West were made along the Takla Makan oases.

Takoma Park (təkō'mə), city (1970 pop. 18,455), Montgomery and Prince Georges counties, W central Md., a residential suburb of Washington, D.C.; inc. 1890. It is the seat of Columbia Union College and a junior college. Also there are a publishing company and the headquarters for the Potomac Conference of the Seventh Day Adventist Church.

Takoradi: see SEKONDI-TAKORADI, Ghana.

Talass Ala-Tau, mountains, Asia: see ALA-TAU.

Talavera de la Reina (tälävä'rä thā lä rā'nä), town (1970 pop. 45,327), Toledo prov., central Spain, in New Castile, on the Tagus River. It is in an agricultural region and is known for its fine ceramics industry. At Talavera, in 1809, in the Peninsular War, the English and Spanish under Wellesley defeated the French under Joseph Bonaparte. After the battle Wellesley was made Viscount Wellington. The historian Juan de Mariana was born in the town.

Talbot, Richard: see TYRCONNEL, RICHARD TALBOT, DUKE AND EARL OF.

Talbot, Thomas, 1771-1853, Canadian colonist, b. Ireland. He was a soldier and first came to Canada in 1790. In 1800 he left the army and obtained a grant of 5,000 acres (2,023 hectares) on the north shore of Lake Erie. He subsequently developed an arrangement whereby he received additional grants as more immigrants settled on his land. He founded (1802) Port Talbot and 27 other townships along the lake's shore. The eccentric Talbot governed in dictatorial style for nearly 50 years. See F. C. Hamil, *Lake Erie Baron: The Story of Colonel Thomas Talbot* (1955).

Talbot, William Henry Fox, 1800-1877, English inventor of photographic processes (see PHOTOGRAPHY, STILL). A man of enormously versatile intelligence, he invented the "photogenic drawing" process in 1834. From 1841 on he patented his numerous processes for making negatives and positive prints, called calotypes and later talbotypes. His patents threatened to impede the technical progress of the medium and Talbot was forced to release his processes. His relationships with other early photographers and photographic inventors were very bitter. Talbot wrote *The Pencil of Nature* (1844), one of the first books illustrated with photographs. Interested also in archaeology, he was one of the first to decipher the cuneiform inscriptions at Nineveh. See study by André Jammes (1974).

talc, mineral ranging in color from white through various shades of gray and green to the red and brown of impure specimens, translucent to opaque, and having a greasy, soapy feel. It is a hydrous silicate of magnesium, $Mg_3Si_4O_{10}(OH)_2$, and usually contains small quantities of nickel, iron, and aluminum as impurities. It occurs commonly in folia (thin layers), but is also found in coarsely granular, finely granular, or cryptocrystalline masses. SOAPSTONE, or steatite, is a massive, granular form of talc. French chalk is a fine-grained variety. Talc is usually associated with chlorite schists, serpentine, dolomite, and other metamorphic rocks; it is apparently a secondary mineral formed by the alteration of other magnesium silicates. There are important deposits of talc in Austria, Italy, France, and Canada and in the United States in California, North Carolina, Texas, Georgia, and Montana. Talc is used in making paper (as a filler), paints, face and talcum powder, soap, fireproof roofing, foundry facings, lubricants, linoleum and oilcloth, electrical insulation, and pottery.

Talca (täl'kä), city (1970 pop. 102,522), capital of Talca prov., S central Chile, in the central valley of Chile between Santiago and Concepción. Agriculture (especially wheat) is important in the region, which is also Chile's greatest wine-producing area. Talca is one of the largest manufacturing centers in Chile, with distilleries, foundries, a tannery, and factories making matches, shoes, tobacco products, paper, and flour. Founded in 1692, Talca was prominent during colonial times. It was leveled by an earthquake in 1928. At Talca on Feb. 12, 1818, Bernardo O'HIGGINS formally proclaimed Chile's independence.

Talcahuano (tälkäwä'nō), city (1970 pop. 150,011), S central Chile, a port on the Pacific Ocean. On the best harbor along the Chilean coast, Talcahuano is an important naval base. It has a large fishing industry, and fish are canned and exported. It also has extensive dry-dock facilities, metallurgical plants, and petroleum refineries, and it handles the exporting of the agricultural products of the interior. Anchored in Talcahuano's harbor is the Peruvian warship *Huascar,* whose capture decisively established Chilean naval supremacy during the War of the Pacific (1879).

Ta-li (dä-lē'), city, W central Yünnan, on the west shore of Ta-li lake. It has long been famous for its Ta-li marble, which is still being produced.

Ta-lien or **Talien** (both: dä-lyĕn), Rus. *Dalny,* Jap. *Dairen,* city (1970 est. pop. 4,000,000), S Liaoning prov., China, on the Liao-tung peninsula in the Bay of Korea. It has been combined with Lü-shun (Port Arthur) into the joint municipality of LÜ-TA. With a huge, well-protected harbor, modern freight-handling facilities, and fine rail connections, Ta-lien is the chief commercial port of Manchuria. It is also a major industrial center with large shipyards, fisheries, an oil refinery, textile mills, chemical and fertilizer plants, and factories making locomotives, rolling stock, and electrical equipment. Ta-lien has two sections: a former Japanese district and a Chinese residential area. The city first became important when Russia occupied it as part of the Liao-tung leasehold (1898). Under the Russians the city was developed as the southern terminus of the South Manchurian RR and as the chief ice-free port on the route to Vladivostok. When the Japanese acquired the territory in 1905 (thereafter known as the Kwantung leasehold), Ta-lien was enlarged and modernized. In 1945, Russia occupied Ta-lien and received a free lease from Nationalist China on half the city's port facilities. This arrangement was continued under the Communist government, and a joint Sino-Soviet company was set up to develop shipping. Russian troops remained there until 1955. Ta-lien is the seat of a technical university, a medical college, and several specialized schools.

Taliesin or **Taliessin** (both: tălēĕs'ĭn), 6th cent.?, Welsh bard, whose *Book of Taliesin* is one of the great Welsh poetic works. The book exists only in a 13th-century form, but tradition puts Taliesin in the 6th cent., as a contemporary of the battles his poems celebrate. One theory about Taliesin is that he was an ancient Celtic mythical character, about whose name have collected a series of traditional poems.

talipes: see CLUBFOOT.

talisman: see AMULET.

Talitha cumi (tăl'ĭthə kyōō'mī) [Aramaic,=maiden, arise], in Mark 5.41, the words said by Jesus to the daughter of the ruler of the synagogue as he raised her from the dead. The words are left, and a translation is given, in all the European versions of this Gospel.

Talladega (tălədē'gə), city (1970 pop. 17,662), seat of Talladega co., NE central Ala., in the Blue Ridge foothills; inc. 1835. Textiles and clothing are its chief products; sawmill machinery and iron castings are also made. In Nov., 1813, Andrew Jackson defeated the Creek Indians at this Indian border town. It is the seat of Talladega College and the state institute for the deaf and blind. There are many antebellum homes in the city.

tallage (tăl'ĭj), Fr. *taille,* a type of feudal tax. In its origins tallage is not clearly distinguishable from AIDS, and in Germany it never developed beyond an occasional "voluntary" gift from vassal to lord. The French taille, which became widespread and varied according to local custom, was generally a tax levied by the king or lord on his subjects or on the lands or other property they held. In the 15th cent. the taille became a royal tax from which the nobility was exempt, and other privileged groups, including the clergy and the bourgeoisie, later managed to gain exemption. Thus the main burden of the taille, which had become the most important direct tax, fell upon the peasantry and was lifted only by the French Revolution. The English tax known as tallage, introduced by the Norman kings as a partial substitute for the DANEGELD, was levied by the kings and lords on their demesne lands (see DEMESNE); under Richard I and John it became a common source of royal revenue. Included within the royal demesne were the chartered towns, which resisted the collection of tallage. London especially protested the tax, and the legality of the tallage collection in that city is a much-disputed historical problem. In 1297 a petition of Edward I prohibited tallage collection without the assent of barons, knights, and burgesses; however, this was not a statute, and the king did not cede his right to tallage. In 1312, London again resisted a tallage; in 1332 Parliament protested imposition of a tallage; and in 1340 Edward III, in return for a subsidy, made an agreement often interpreted as a promise not to collect tallage but apparently only a pledge not to violate old custom. As other means of raising money grew common, tallage disappeared in the reign of Edward III.

Tallahassee (tăləhăs'ē), city (1970 pop. 72,586), state capital and seat of Leon co., NW Fla.; inc. 1825. The state government, Florida State Univ., and Florida Agricultural and Mechanical Univ. are major sources of employment. Lumber and wood products are manufactured, and food is processed. The city is in a hilly agricultural area known for its lakes, springs, forests, and picturesque gardens. When De Soto arrived there in 1539, he found a flourishing settlement of Apalachee Indians. Spanish missionaries and settlers followed, but the Indian village remained the major settlement until Tallahassee was founded (1824) as the capital of the Florida Territory. The ordinance of secession was adopted there in 1861. The city successfully resisted Union attempts to capture it; a nearby state monument marks the site of the battle of Natural Bridge (March, 1865), where Tallahassee cadets helped repel a Federal attack. The city still retains its antebellum charm, and many old homes are preserved. The capitol (1845; remodeled 1901) contains the state library. The graves of Prince Achille Murat and his wife are there. Nearby are Apalachicola National Forest; First Christmas State Park, where De Soto's expedition celebrated its first Christmas in the new world; and Wakulla Springs.

Tallapoosa, river, 268 mi (431 km) long, rising in NW Ga. and flowing SW through E Ala.; joins the Coosa River near Montgomery, Ala., to form the Alabama River. Martin Dam (154,000-kw capacity) impounds Lake Martin, with an area of 63 sq mi (163 sq km).

Tallard or **Tallart, Camille, marquis de la Baume-d'Hostun, baron d'Arlanc, comte de** (kämē'yə märkē' də lä bōm''-dôstōN' bärôN' därläNk' kôNt də tälär'), 1652–1728, French diplomat, marshal of France. He negotiated the partition treaties of 1698 and 1700 that preceded the War of the Spanish Succession (see SPANISH SUCCESSION, WAR OF THE). Although victorious at Speyer (1703), he was defeated and taken prisoner at Blenheim (1704). He served as minister of state in 1726.

Tallchief, Maria, 1925–, American ballerina, b. Fairfax, Okla. Tallchief, of Osage Indian descent, was trained both as a pianist and as a dancer. Choosing ballet, she studied under Bronislava NIJINSKA, Ernest Belcher, and George BALANCHINE, whom she later married. She performed with the Ballet Russe de Monte Carlo from 1942 to 1947, when she joined the Ballet Society (later the New York City Ballet). Through her 18 years as that company's prima ballerina and through her tours and television appearances with the American Ballet Theatre and other companies in the 1960s, Tallchief contributed greatly to the fame and prestige of American ballet. Her younger sister, **Marjorie Tallchief** (1927–), b. Denver Colo., was première danseuse with the Paris Opéra Ballet from 1957 to 1962. She also performed with many other companies, retiring in 1966.

Tallemant des Réaux, Gédéon (zhädāôN' tälə-mäN' dā rāō'), 1619–92, French writer. His one great work is a series of brief anecdotal portraits of persons prominent in the Paris of his day, written after 1657 but not published until 1834. They present a vivid, faithful, and acute picture of the society of the period. The *Historiettes* have appeared in English as *Miniature Portraits* (1926).

Talleyrand or **Talleyrand-Périgord, Charles Maurice de** (tăl'ērănd'', Fr. shärl mōrēs' də tälārăN'-pārēgôr'), 1754–1838, French statesman and diplomat. Born into the high nobility, he was early destined for the Roman Catholic Church because of a childhood accident that left him partially lame. Despite his notorious impiety, he was made (1789) bishop of Autun by King Louis XVI. A representative of the clergy in the States-General of 1789, he sided with the revolutionists. He proposed the appropriation of church lands by the state, endorsed the civil constitution of the clergy, and was excommunicated (1791) by the pope, after consecrating two "constitutional" bishops. In 1792 he was sent by the National Assembly on a mission to London to secure Great Britain's neutrality, but the radical turn of the French Revolution nullified his success. A lifelong advocate of constitutional monarchy and peace, Talleyrand sought refuge in England in Sept., 1792, following the fall of the monarchy. In 1794 he went to the United States, where he stayed until after the establishment (Nov., 1795) of the Directory in France, when he returned (Sept., 1796) to Paris. Made foreign minister in 1797, he hitched his career to the rising fortune of Napoleon Bonaparte. His part in the XYZ AFFAIR and his endorsement of Napoleon's plan for seizing Egypt in 1798 had unfortunate consequences for France. In July, 1799, he resigned his post, only to resume it after helping Napoleon gain power under the CONSULATE (Nov., 1799). He helped to bring about the Concordat of 1801 with the Vatican, shortly after which the ban of excommunication against him was lifted (1802). The following year he was appointed to the lucrative position of grand chamberlain under Napoleon, now emperor, who in 1806 created him prince of Benevento. Napoleon tended more and more to ignore Talleyrand's cautious advice, and the split between the two widened as Talleyrand tried unsuccessfully to restrain Napoleon's ambitions. Despite the accusations of Talleyrand's enemies (especially Joseph Fouché), he apparently played only a passive role in the abduction of the duke of ENGHIEN. Napoleon's moves to gain Spain triggered Talleyrand's resignation (1807), although he remained in the imperial council and continued as grand chamberlain until early 1809. Ironically, Talleyrand was assigned the distasteful duty of keeping the three Spanish princes seized at Bayonne captive in his château. Convinced of the necessity of a strong Austria to maintain European stability, Talleyrand, who accompanied Napoleon to the Congress of Erfurt (1808), secretly worked in Austria's rather than Napoleon's interest by persuading the Russian Czar Alexander I to oppose Napoleon's designs against Austria. He also had a hand in bringing about Napoleon's marriage to Marie Louise, daughter of the Austrian emperor, Francis I, in 1810. Napoleon's attack on Russia (1812) completed Talleyrand's alienation from the French emperor. When the allies entered Paris in 1814, Talleyrand persuaded them to restore the Bourbons in the person of LOUIS XVIII, who made him foreign minister. He negotiated the first Treaty of Paris of May, 1814, by which France, despite the defeat, was granted the French borders of 1792. He represented France at the Congress of Vienna (see VIENNA, CONGRESS OF) of 1814–15, where he scored his greatest diplomatic triumphs. Winning the European powers to his principle of "legitimacy," namely, the restoration of Europe to its prerevolutionary status, and shrewdly exploiting the dissension among the allies, he succeeded in taking part in the negotiations on equal terms with the principal victorious powers. He remained in Vienna during the Hundred Days but resigned in Sept., 1815, shortly after the second Bourbon Restoration—according to his memoirs because of his opposition to the second Treaty of Paris of Nov., 1815, but in all probability because of pressure from the ultraroyalist chamber on Louis XVIII to dismiss him. In 1830, Louis Philippe, whom he had helped to power, offered him the portfolio of foreign affairs, but Talleyrand preferred to serve as ambassador to London. He resigned in 1834, after having achieved the recognition of Belgium (1831) and signed the QUADRUPLE ALLIANCE of 1834. The prototype of the witty, cynical diplomat, Talleyrand has been either exalted as the savior of Europe in 1815 or damned as an opportunist or even a traitor. His corruption was undeniable, and his pliability enabled him to hold power under the ancien régime, the Revolution, Napoleon, the Restoration, and the July Monarchy. Yet Talleyrand was a good European, and his policy was aimed consistently—and often courageously—at the peace and stability of Europe as a whole. See his memoirs (1891–92; tr., 5 vol., 1891–92). The standard biography is by Georges Lacour-Gayet (4 vol., 1928–30, in French). See also biographies by Duff Cooper (1932, repr. 1958), Émile Dard (tr. 1937), C. C. Brinton (1936, repr. 1963), J. F. Bernard (1973), and Jean Orieux (tr. 1974).

Tallien, Jean Lambert (zhäN läNbĕr' tälyăN'), 1767–1820, French revolutionary. A law clerk and later a printer, he became known through his Jacobin journal, *Ami des citoyens.* A leader in the attack (Aug., 1792) on the Tuileries, he became secretary of the Commune of Paris and sent circulars to the departments, urging the spread of the September massacres. In the Convention and the Committee of General Security he aided in overthrowing the Girondists; sent to Bordeaux in Sept., 1793, he used extreme methods to spread the Reign of Terror. Recalled to Paris in May, 1794, he was given the charge of many important prisoners, and fell in love with one of them, Theresa Cabarrus, whom he married (see TALLIEN, THERESA CABARRUS). Denounced (June 12) by Maximilien Robespierre, Tallien began the attack on Robespierre in the coup d'etat of 9 Thermidor. A leader of the Thermidorian reaction, he thereafter lost importance. He accompanied (1798) Napoleon Bonaparte to Egypt, was captured by the English and lived briefly in England before returning (1802) to France and comparative obscurity.

Tallien, Thérésa Cabarrus (tārāzä' käbärüs'), 1773–1835, French political figure, of Spanish parentage. The divorced wife of a marquis de Fontenay, she became intimate with the revolutionary Jean Lambert Tallien, whom she married (1794) and whose policies she influenced strongly. She was nicknamed Notre Dame de Thermidor in allusion to her husband's part in the coup d'etat of 9 Thermidor (1794). Her salon was famous, and she originated the neo-Greek feminine styles of the Directoire period. Having divorced Tallien in 1802, she married the banker Caraman, who was later created prince de Chimay.

Tallinn (tä'lĭn), Ger. *Reval,* city (1970 pop. 363,000), capital of the Estonian Soviet Socialist Republic, NW European USSR, on the Gulf of Finland, opposite Helsinki. It is a major Baltic port, a rail and highway junction, and an industrial center. Tallinn has extensive military and naval installations. Industries include shipbuilding, metalworking, food and fish processing, and the manufacture of machinery, electrical and radio apparatus, oil field equipment, cables, and building materials. The city contains the Estonian Academy of Sciences and many other educational and cultural institutions. Tallinn was first mentioned by the Arabian geographer Idrisi in 1154. It was destroyed in 1219 by Waldemar II of Denmark, who built a fortress on the site. The city's name comes from the Estonian words *Taani linn* ("Danish castle"). A member of the Hanseatic League from 1285, Tallinn was sold (1346) with the rest of Estonia by Waldemar IV to the Livonian Knights. Upon the dissolution of the Livonian Order in 1561, it passed to Sweden. Captured by Peter I in 1710 during the Northern War, Tallinn was formally ceded to Russia by the Treaty of Nystad in 1721. It underwent development as a port for Russia's Baltic fleet and in 1870 was linked by rail with St. Petersburg (now Leningrad). Tallinn became the capital of independent Estonia in 1919 and of the Estonian SSR in 1940. It suffered considerable damage during the German occupation in World War II. The historical center of Tallinn consists of an upper town, on a steep hill topped by a medieval cathedral, and an adjoining lower town dating from Hanseatic times. The picturesque lower town is surrounded by a medieval wall with massive round towers. Its landmarks include the 13th-century Danish Toompea Castle (rebuilt in 1935 as a government building), the 13th-century Gothic Church of St. Olai, and the 14th-century city hall.

Tallis or **Tallys, Thomas,** c.1510–1585, English composer. In 1575 a royal license for the exclusive printing of music and music paper was granted to William Byrd and Tallis, and in the same year they published their *Cantiones Sacrae,* containing 18 Latin motets by Byrd and 16 by Tallis. The two men also shared the post of organist of the Chapel Royal. Although Tallis wrote a few madrigals and some instrumental music, he is remembered almost entirely for his hymn tunes, services, and anthems.

tallit (tälēt'), four-cornered, fringed shawl worn by Jewish males during the morning prayers. It is donned before putting on the PHYLACTERIES, except on Yom Kippur when it is worn all through the day (phylacteries are not worn on this day). The Reform movement, however, requires that only those officiating at the service wear the tallit, leaving it as an optional practice for the congregants. Woven into the white garment is a blue fringe (tzitzit), worn in fulfillment of the biblical commandment (Num. 15.37–41). To be distinguished from this tallit, known as the Tallit Gadol [large tallit] is the Tallit Katan [small tallit], which is worn under the outer garments throughout the day. This practice is less widely observed.

Tallmadge, Benjamin (tăl'mĭj), 1754–1835, American Revolutionary soldier, b. Brookhaven, N.Y. Joining a Connecticut regiment, he served throughout the Revolution, fighting at Brandywine, Germantown, and Monmouth. In 1780 he commanded in the successful attack against Fort St. George and in the destruction of British supplies on Long Island. A confidential agent (1778–83), he corresponded with George Washington and had custody of Major John André until André's execution. After the war Tallmadge retired to Litchfield, Conn., became a merchant, and sat (1801–17) in the U.S. House of Representatives as a Federalist. See *Memoir of Colonel Benjamin Tallmadge, Prepared by Himself* (1858; repr. and ed. by H. P. Johnston, 1904); biography by C. S. Hall (1943).

Tallmadge, city (1970 pop. 15,274), Summit co., NE Ohio, an industrial suburb of Akron; settled 1807, inc. 1950.

tallow, solid fat extracted from the tissues and fatty deposits of animals, especially from suet (the fat of cattle and sheep). Pure tallow is white, odorless and tasteless; it consists chiefly of TRIGLYCERIDES of stearic, palmitic, and oleic acids. It is usually obtained commercially by heating suet under pressure in closed vessels. Tallow is used to make soap and candles. It was formerly in common use as a lubricant.

tallow tree: see SPURGE.

tall tale, extravagantly and humorously exaggerated story of the backwoods exploits of an American frontiersman. Originating in the 1820s, the genre remained popular well into the 20th cent. One of the earliest heroes of this type of folklore, Colonel Davy Crockett of Tennessee, boasted:

> I'm that same David Crockett, fresh from
> the backwoods, half-horse, half-alligator,
> a little touched with the snapping turtle;
> can wade the Mississippi, leap the Ohio,
> ride a streak of lightning, slip without
> a scratch down a honey locust, can whip
> my weight in wildcats . . .

These bold deeds were made famous throughout the West by Crockett's *Autobiography* (1834) and by his *Almanacs* (1835-56). Crockett also popularized the deeds of the gigantic Mike Fink, "King of the Mississippi Keelboatmen," who was said to have once slain with a single shot both a deer and an Indian who was pursuing it. From Canada came the tales of the hero of the lumberjacks, Paul Bunyan, whose Blue Ox "Babe" was "forty-two ax handles and a plug of chewing tobacco between the eyes." The cowboys' hero was Pecos Bill, who "taught the bronco how to buck," and the Southern Negroes told tales of John Henry, the railroader and steamboat roustabout who once won a contest against a steam drill.

Tallys, Thomas: see TALLIS, THOMAS.

Talma, François Joseph (fräNswä' zhôzĕf' tälmä'), 1763-1826, French actor. The greatest tragedian of his time, he broke with past traditions and foreshadowed the great romanticists. He continued Lekain's reforms in costuming and speaking technique. In 1787 he made his debut at the Comédie Française in Voltaire's *Mahomet* and in 1789 gained fame in Chenier's Revolutionary play, *Charles IX*. Siding with the Revolution, Talma left the Comédie Française and set up his own theater, called the Théâtre de la République, which was eventually united (1799) with the Comédie by Napoleon. See biography by H. F. Collins (1964).

Talmadge, Eugene, 1884-1946, governor of Georgia (1933-37, 1941-43), b. Forsyth, Ga. He practiced law at McRae, Ga., and later was (1927-33) state commissioner of agriculture. In his second term as governor (1935-37), his staff was forbidden by Harry Hopkins to disburse Federal relief funds; and Talmadge became violently opposed to the New Deal. Twice defeated (1936, 1938) for the Democratic nomination for the U.S. Senate, he won the governorship again in 1940. His dismissal (1941) of several educators in the state university system who had advocated racial equality in the schools aroused much resentment, and in 1942 he lost the Democratic gubernatorial nomination. Talmadge, however, had strong support among the rural counties and became governor-elect again in 1946. He died before taking office. His son, **Herman Talmadge,** 1913-, b. McRae, Ga., practiced law for a time with his father. He won a special Democratic primary for governor in 1947 and was reelected in 1950. He was elected to the U.S. Senate in 1956 and reelected in 1962, 1968, and 1974. A Southern Democrat, he was one of the members of the Senate Select Committee on Presidential Campaign Activities, which investigated (1973-74) the Watergate affair.

Talmage, Thomas De Witt (tăl'mĭj), 1832-1902, American Presbyterian clergyman, b. near Bound Brook, N.J., grad. New Brunswick Theological Seminary (1856). His work in Brooklyn, N.Y., began in 1869 in the Central Presbyterian Church. The Tabernacle, built in 1870 to accommodate the great audiences attracted by his sensational style of preaching, was burned in 1872, as were two other large buildings erected by his congregation during the next 20 years. Between 1873 and 1902 Talmage edited in turn the *Christian at Work*, the *Advance*, *Frank Leslie's Sunday Magazine*, and the *Christian Herald*. He made popular lecture tours in the United States and England.

Talmai (tăl'mī). **1** King of Geshur and grandfather of Absalom, who took refuge with him. 2 Sam. 3.3; 13.37,38. **2** One of the three sons of ANAK.

Talmon (tăl'mŏn), family of temple doorkeepers. 1 Chron. 9.17; Ezra 2.42; Neh. 7.45. The Talmon of Neh. 12.25 is probably the same as TELEM **1.**

Talmud (tăl'məd) [Aramaic from Heb.,=learning], vast compilation of the Oral Law of the Jews, with rabbinical elucidations, elaborations, and commentaries, in contradistinction to the Scriptures or Written Laws. The Talmud is the accepted authority for Orthodox Jews everywhere. Its two divisions are the MISHNA or text of the Oral Law (in Hebrew) and the Gemara (in Aramaic), a sort of commentary on the Mishna, which it supplements. The Mishna is divided into six Orders (Sedarim) and comprises 63 tractates (Massektoth), only 36½ of which have a Gemara. The present Mishna was compiled almost entirely by Judah I (ha-Nasi), who collected and codified the legal material that had accumulated through the exposition of the Law by the Scribes (Soferim), particularly Hillel and Shammai, and its elaboration by the TANNAIM of the 1st and 2d cent. A.D., particularly Akiba ben Joseph. The Gemara developed out of the interpretations of the Mishna by the AMORAIM. These scholars were led by their love of hairsplitting arguments into so many extraneous channels that the work became in addition a veritable treasury of information and comment on such subjects as astronomy, geography, historical gossip, domestic relations, and folklore. The legal sections of the Talmud are known as the HALAKAH; the poetical digressions, illustrating the application of religious and ethical principles through parables, legends, allegories, tales, and anecdotes, constitute the Aggada. In the Middle Ages there arose a vast literature of commentaries on the Gemara—commentaries on those commentaries—and responsa (questions and answers); Rashi was one of the commentators. Both the Palestinian and Babylonian schools produced Talmuds, known respectively as the Talmud Yerushalmi (compiled c.5th cent. A.D.) and the Talmud Babli (c.6th cent. A.D.). The text of the first was not well preserved, and the Babylonian Talmud became the authoritative work. It is three times the length of the Palestinian version. In the Middle Ages thousands of Talmud manuscripts were destroyed by the Christians. The term Talmud is sometimes used to refer to the Gemara alone. See H. L. Strack, *Introduction to the Talmud and Midrash* (1931, repr. 1969); *The Babylonian Talmud* (34 vol., 1935-48); Abraham Cohen, *Everyman's Talmud* (1949); Judah Goldin, *The Living Talmud* (1957, repr. 1964); Jacob Neuser, *Invitation to the Talmud* (1973).

Talon, Jean Baptiste (zhäN bätēst' tälôN'), 1625?-1694, intendant of New France, b. France. He entered French administrative service c.1653. In his short tenure (1665-68, 1670-72) as intendant of New France he accomplished much. He encouraged agriculture, sent prospectors to hunt for minerals and to explore little-known territory, made energetic efforts to introduce brewing, lumbering, and shipbuilding industries, planned for trade with the West Indies and France, and encouraged immigration so vigorously that the population almost doubled during his tenure. After his return to France in 1672, he became a royal secretary. See Thomas Chapais, *The Great Intendant* (1914).

talus (tā'ləs), deposit of rock fragments detached from cliffs or mountain slopes by WEATHERING and piled up at their bases. A talus is a common geologic feature in regions of high cliffs. The angle of slope of a talus is rarely greater than 40° The constant weathering to which a talus is subjected, which breaks the rock fragments into finer pieces, and the impact of new material being added from above give the base of the talus a tendency to creep and slide. The term *talus* is often used to refer to the fragments themselves.

Tamah (tā'mə), family returned from exile. Neh. 7.55. Thamah: Ezra 2.53.

Tamale (təmä'lē), town (1970 pop. 81,612), capital of the Northern Region, N Ghana. It is a road junction and agricultural trade center. There are several schools in the town.

tamale, Mexican food of which the chief ingredients are corn meal, minced meat, chilies, and seasonings. It is usually wrapped in cornhusks and steamed.

Tamalpais, Mount (tăm'əlpīəs''), peak, 2,604 ft (794 m) high, W Calif., across the Golden Gate from San Francisco. The mountain is a game preserve and a resort. The city of Mill Valley and Muir Woods National Monument, a redwood grove, lie at its base.

Taman Peninsula (təmän'), c.20 mi (30 km) long and 8 mi (12.9 km) wide, Krasnodar Kray, SE European USSR, projecting westward between the Sea of Azov and the Black Sea. It is separated from the Crimea by the Kerch Strait. There are small mud volcanoes and gas and petroleum deposits. In the 6th cent. B.C., the Greeks established several colonies here. The modern Taman, a small port, became, in the 10th cent. A.D., a feudal center which was converted (13th cent.) into a fortress by the Genoese. Taman became a Turkish fortress in 1482 and was ceded to Russia in 1774.

Tamar (tā'mär). **1** Mother of Judah's twin sons Pharez and Zerah. Gen. 38; Ruth 4.12; 1 Chron. 2.4. Thamar: Mat. 1.3. **2** Daughter of David and Maachah. She was the victim of her half brother Amnon's passion. 2 Sam. 13. **3** Daughter of Absalom. 2 Sam. 14.27. **4** Unlocated boundary site, S Palestine. Ezek. 47.19; 48.28. Tadmor: 1 Kings 9.18.

tamarack: see LARCH.

tamarin: see MARMOSET.

tamarind (tăm'ərĭnd), tropical ornamental evergreen tree (*Tamarindus indica*) of the family Leguminosae (PULSE family), native to Africa and probably to Asia. The fruit, a brown pod from 3 to 8 in. (8-20 cm) long, has been an article of commerce since medieval times. Within the pod is a juicy, acid pulp used as an ingredient in chutneys and curries and in medicines and for preserving fish. A refreshing drink is made by adding sugar and water to the pulp. A dye is obtained from the leaves. The tamarind is grown in the West Indies and Florida especially as a flavoring for guava jellies. Tamarind is classified in the division MAGNOLIOPHYTA, class Magnoliopsida, order Rosales, family Leguminosae.

tamarisk (tăm'ərĭsk), shrub or small tree of the genus *Tamarix*, native chiefly to the Mediterranean area and to central Asia. The plants are often heathlike and thrive in arid and coastal regions. Several species are cultivated as ornamentals for their feathery foliage and pink or white blossoms, e.g., *T. gallica*, which is now naturalized in suitable habitats in the S United States. *T. mannifera* produces the MANNA of the Bedouins, a white substance exuded through insect punctures. *T. articulata* furnishes a superior purplish tanning material used by the Arabs. Tamarisks are classified in the division MAGNOLIOPHYTA, class Magnoliopsida, order Violales, family Tamaricaceae.

tamarou: see BUFFALO.

Tamatave (tämätäv'), city (1970 est. pop. 57,000), NE Malagasy Republic, on Madagascar. Situated on the Indian Ocean, it is the nation's chief port and is connected by rail with Tananarive. Tamatave exports sugar, coffee, cloves, and rice. Food processing is the chief industry. The town was founded in the 18th cent. around a European trading post. After its capture (1817) by Radama I, it became the chief port of his kingdom. Tamatave was occupied repeatedly by the French, and it was the base for their conquest (1894) of the interior. Severely damaged (1927) by a storm, the city was subsequently rebuilt.

Tamaulipas (tämoulē'päs), state (1970 pop. 1,438,-350), 30,734 sq mi (79,601 sq km), NE Mexico, on the Gulf of Mexico. VICTORIA is the capital. The central and western parts of the state are in the mountains of the Sierra Madre Oriental. In the north and south are arable plains, particularly in the long panhandle beginning at Nuevo Laredo and following the Rio Grande opposite Texas to Matamoros. The coast is low, sandy, fringed with lagoons, and (except for Matamoros and Tampico) virtually uninhabited. The extreme southwestern mining area borders on the vast semiarid basins of central Mexico. Except in the elevated interior, the climate is hot and humid. The state's greatest source of wealth is petroleum and its by-products, but agriculture and cattle raising are also important. Tamaulipas is a leading national producer of sugarcane and cotton; cereals, tobacco, and corn are other major crops, and citrus fruits are cultivated around Victoria. The state's industries include vegetable-oil extraction, flour milling, and the manufacture of chemicals and soap. Some hides are exported. Tourism is economically important. First explored by the Spanish in 1519, the territory, inhabited by Tamaulipan Indians, was conquered and then abandoned. Colonization began in 1747, and independence was won from Spain in 1824. Franciscan missions flourished in the 18th cent.

Tamayo, Rufino (ro͞ofē'nō tämä'yō), 1899-, Mexican painter, b. Oaxaca. Considered one of the leading painters in Mexico, Tamayo first gained his reputation in the United States and in Europe before he was acclaimed in his native land. Less interested than Rivera or Siqueiros in an art of social message, Tamayo concentrated more on the formal and decorative elements of painting. Strong influences from cubism and fauvism are apparent in Tamayo's work, as well as elements from Mexican folklore. Characteristic examples are *Women of Tehuantepec* (1939; Albright-Knox Art Gallery, Buffalo), and his murals at Smith College, Northampton, Mass. (1943), which are brilliantly colored and whimsically drawn. His work of the 1950s produced a powerful strain of ABSTRACT EXPRESSIONISM. See study by R. J. Goldwater (1947); B. S. Myers, *Mexican Painting in Our Time* (1956).

Tamayo y Baus, Manuel (mänwĕl' tämä'yō ē bous), 1829-98, Spanish dramatist. Born into a family of actors, Tamayo became one of the most popular and versatile Spanish playwrights of the 19th cent. Among his many successful plays are the historical *Locura de amor* [the madness of love] (1855) and his tragic masterpiece, *Un drama nuevo* (1867; tr. *A New Drama,* 1915). In his contemporary thesis dramas he wrote of social problems. See biography by G. C. Flynn (1973).

tambourine (tăm″bərēn′), musical instrument of the percussion family, having a narrow circular frame and a single parchment drumhead, with metal plates or jingles set in the frame. The ancient Romans used

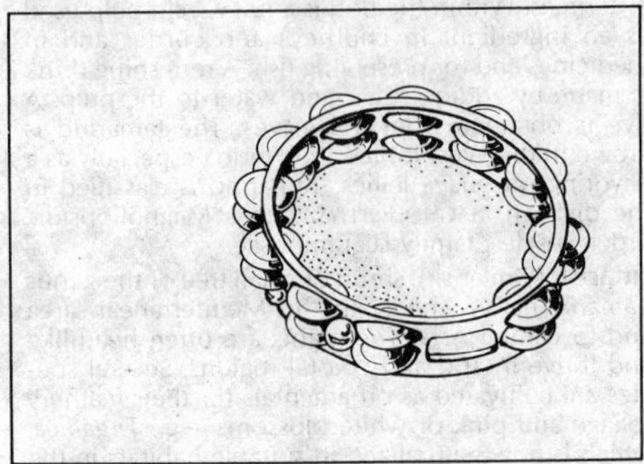

Tambourine

it, and in the Middle Ages and the Renaissance it was used by traveling musicians and entertainers. In the 19th cent. it became a military-band instrument, appearing later and very occasionally in the orchestra. The timbrel or tabret of the Bible was probably similar to the tambourine.

Tambov (təmbôf′), city (1970 pop. 230,000), capital of Tambov oblast, S central European USSR. A rail junction and manufacturing center, it produces machine tools, instruments, and chemicals. Founded in 1636 as an outpost against the Crimean Tatars, Tambov became (18th cent.) an administrative center. The poet Derzhavin was governor there from 1786 to 1788.

Tamerlane (tăm′ərlăn) or **Timur** (tĭmo͝or′), c.1336–1405, Mongol conqueror, b. Kesh, near Samarkand. He is also called Timur Leng [Timur the lame]. He was the son of a tribal leader, and he claimed (apparently for the first time in 1370) to be a descendant of Jenghiz Khan. With an army composed of Turks and Turkic-speaking Mongols, remnants of the empire of the MONGOLS, Tamerlane spent his early military career in subduing his rivals in what is now Soviet Turkistan; by 1369 he firmly controlled

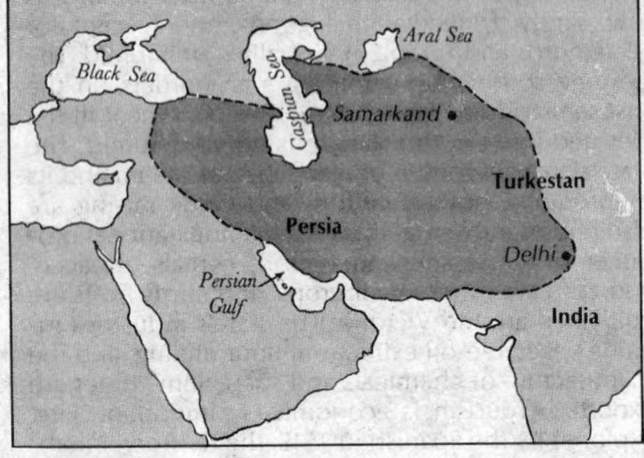

Empire of Tamerlane (1405)

the entire area from his capital at SAMARKAND. Campaigns against Persia occupied him until 1387. By that time he had in his possession the lands stretching E from the Euphrates River. He advanced (1392) across the Euphrates, conquered the territory between the Caspian and Black seas, and invaded several of the Russian states. By weakening the Crimean Tatars he helped clear the way for the conquests of the grand duchy of Moscow. Tamerlane abandoned some of his Russian conquests to return to Samarkand and invade (1398) India along the route of the Indus River. He took Delhi and brought the DELHI SULTANATE to an end, but he withdrew with little addition to his domain. In 1400, Tamerlane ravaged Georgia and proceeded to the Levant, where he took Aleppo and Baghdad. His next war was fought in Asia Minor against the Ottoman Turks, and in 1402, at Angora, he captured their sultan, Beyazid I, who, contrary to popular belief, was well treated. Tamerlane died while planning an invasion of China. His tomb at Samarkand was long known to archaeologists, but it is only recently that his skeleton, buried in a deep crypt, was found. Tamerlane's reputation is that of a cruel conqueror. After capturing certain cities he slaughtered thousands of the defenders (perhaps 80,000 at Delhi) and built pyramids of their skulls. Although a Muslim, he was scarcely more merciful to those of his own faith than to infidels. His positive achievements were the encouragement of art, literature, and science and the construction of vast public works. He had little hope that his vast conquests would remain intact, and before his death he arranged for them to be divided among his sons. The TIMURIDS are the line of rulers descended from him. Christopher Marlowe's play *Tamburlaine* luridly recounts his conquests. See biographies by Harold Lamb (1928) and Hilda Hookham (1962); J. H. Sanders, tr., *Tamerlane* (tr. of late 14th-century Arabic work by Ahmed Ibn Arabshah, 1936).

Tamesis: see THAMES, river, England.

Tamil (tăm′ĭl), Dravidian language of India. See DRAVIDIAN LANGUAGES.

Tamil Nadu (tăm′əl nä′do͞o), formerly **Madras,** state (1971 pop. 41,103,125), 50,180 sq mi (129,966 sq km), SE India, on the Bay of Bengal. On a low-lying plain bounded by the Eastern Ghats in the north, the state has large fertile areas along the Coromandel Coast. Agriculture is the chief occupation, with rice, cotton, tea, tobacco, groundnuts, and millet as the principal crops. The main industries are food processing and the manufacture of cotton and silk cloth; "bleeding Madras," a uniquely dyed cloth, is the most famous product. Building materials and vehicles are also manufactured. There are irrigation canals and hydroelectric stations along the Cauvery River; the only other large river is the Godavari. An extensive rail network linking the coastal cities with inland areas facilitates an important overseas trade. Most of the population is of Dravidian stock, speaks Tamil, and practices Hinduism. An ancient center of Dravidian culture, the region has the finest remaining examples of southern Indian art and architecture. Tamil Nadu was the seat of the CHOLA empire (10th–13th cent.). Muslims swept away the Hindu Vijayanagar kingdom in the 16th cent. and controlled the area for about a century. The Portuguese established trading posts in the 16th cent., followed by the Dutch, French, and British in the early 17th cent. After a sharp struggle (1741–63) with the French and with Haidar Ali and Tippoo Sahib, the British emerged victorious. Under Great Britain, the Madras state was considerably enlarged, but in 1953 its Telugu-speaking areas were transferred to Andhra Pradesh, and in 1956 the Kannada-speaking areas were transferred to Mysore (now Karnataka), and the Malayalam areas to Kerala. Those transfers reduced the state's area by half. In 1969 the name of the state was changed from Madras to Tamil Nadu. It is governed by a chief minister and cabinet responsible to a bicameral legislature with one elected house and by a governor appointed by the president of India.

Tammany (tăm′ənē), popular name for the Democratic political machine in Manhattan. After the American Revolution several patriotic societies sprang up to promote various political causes and economic interests. Among these were the Tammany societies, founded in New York, Philadelphia, and other cities. The societies took the name of a Delaware Indian chief, Tamanend, who is said to have welcomed William Penn and to have signed with him the Treaty of Shakamaxon. The Tammany Society, or Columbian Order of New York City, the only Tammany society to have a long life, was formed c.1786 and was incorporated in 1789. Divided into 13 tribes, corresponding to the 13 states, it had as its motto "Freedom Our Rock"; its rites and ceremonials were based on pseudo-Indian forms, and the titles of its officials were also pseudo-Indian. Although its activities were at first mostly social, ceremonial, and patriotic, the society gradually became the principal upholder of Jeffersonian politics in New York City. After 1798, Tammany came under the control of Aaron BURR. While Tammany was fighting the political forces of De Witt Clinton, it consolidated its position in the city. Tammany backed Andrew Jackson for President, and after his victories in 1828 and 1832 it became a dominant force, fighting for democratic suffrage and the abolition of imprisonment for debt in New York state. Although it stood for reforms on behalf of the common man, it was nonetheless increasingly controlled by men of the privileged classes. The hostility of workingmen toward this "aristocratic" control promoted splits within the Democratic party in the city and state, such as the revolt of the LOCOFOCOS in the 1830s and the contest between the BARNBURNERS and the HUNKERS in the late 1840s. Tammany meanwhile triumphed over the Know-Nothing movement and the local Whig party alike and steadily gained strength by bringing newly arrived immigrants into its fold. The immigrants were helped to obtain jobs, then quickly naturalized and persuaded to vote for their benefactors. Because of the willingness of Tammany to provide them with food, clothing, and fuel in emergencies and to aid those who ran afoul of the law, these new Americans became devoted to the organization and were willing to overlook the fraudulent election practices, the graft, the corruption, and the other abuses that often characterized Tammany administrations. Flagrant abuses during the reign of William M. TWEED led to reforms instituted (1872) by Samuel J. TILDEN. However, Tammany returned to power under John KELLY, and the boss system (see BOSSISM) became firmly entrenched in New York City. Corruption under Richard CROKER provoked new investigations, such as that initiated by Charles PARKHURST, and when Seth LOW became (1901) mayor, Tammany was eclipsed for a time. Charles MURPHY succeeded Croker as boss. His reign was interrupted by the brief administration of John P. Mitchel, who, like Gov. William Sulzer, was a Democrat but an opponent of Tammany. Alfred E. SMITH, a protégé of Murphy, became strong enough to create a so-called "new" Tammany, in which he was an important figure. Corruption in city politics continued, however, and investigations, including that headed by Samuel SEABURY (1930–31), of the city magistrates' courts completely discredited Tammany Hall and ultimately brought about the resignation (1932) of Mayor James J. WALKER. Tammany suffered a telling defeat in the election of 1932 and did not regain its former strength in succeeding elections. The organization declined greatly during the administrations of Fiorello LaGuardia, 1933–45. The decline was accelerated by woman's suffrage, immigration restriction, and the social programs of the New Deal, which weakened voters' dependence on the machine. After World War II, Tammany revived considerably under the leadership of Carmine De Sapio, who successfully promoted the nomination and election of Robert F. Wagner, Jr., as mayor in 1953, and of W. A. Harriman as governor in 1954. De Sapio's leadership, however, came under increasing attack from reformers in the Democratic party. In 1961, Wagner was elected for a third term as the leader of a movement against boss rule, and De Sapio was ousted from his position as Tammany chief by the reform forces. Later attempts (1962–65) by De Sapio to regain power failed, and during the mayoralty of John V. Lindsay (1966–73), Tammany passed out of existence as a political machine. See Gustavus Myers, *The History of Tammany Hall* (1901; 2d ed. rev. and enl., 1917, repr. 1973); M. R. Werner, *Tammany Hall* (1932, repr. 1968); Alfred Connable and Edward Silberfarb, *Tigers of Tammany* (1967); Jerome Mushkat, *Tammany* (1971).

Tammerfors, Finland: see TAMPERE.

Tammuz (tä′məz), ancient nature deity worshiped in Babylonia. A god of agriculture and flocks, he personified the creative powers of spring. He was loved by the fertility goddess ISHTAR, who, according to one legend was so grief-stricken at his death, that she contrived to enter the underworld to get him back. According to another legend, she killed him and later restored him to life. These legends and his festival, commemorating the yearly death and rebirth of vegetation, corresponded to the festivals of the Phoenician and Greek ADONIS and of the Phrygian ATTIS. The Summerian name of Tammuz was Dumuzi. In the Bible his disappearance is mourned by the women of Jerusalem (Ezek. 8.14).

Tampa (tăm′pə), city (1970 pop. 277,767), seat of Hillsborough co., W Fla., a port of entry with an impressive harbor on Tampa Bay; inc. 1855. The third largest city in the state, Tampa is a popular resort, a processing and shipping hub for the products of the area, a phosphate-mining center, and a large port with phosphate docks and elevators. It has a shrimp fleet, citrus-packing houses, huge breweries, and a noted cigar industry. The bay was visited by Pánfilo de Narváez in 1528, and in 1539 De Soto rescued the sole survivor of that expedition. He negotiated (on the present site of the Univ. of Tampa) a peace treaty with the Indians, but the Indians remained so hostile that for almost 200 years Europeans avoided the area. The first white settlement began in 1823, and U.S. Fort Brooke was built in 1824; the town grew around the fort. In the Civil War, it was taken (May, 1864) by Union troops. Tampa's real development began with the growth of a fishing industry, the discovery of phosphate in 1883, and the construction of railroads and the introduction of cigar making in the late 1880s. (Ybor

City is the headquarters of the cigar industry and the center of Tampa's Hispanic population.) During the Spanish-American War, Tampa was a military base; Theodore Roosevelt trained his Rough Riders there. In 1953, Tampa's suburbs were consolidated with the city, almost doubling the population. The city extends down a peninsula, with Old Tampa Bay on the west, Tampa Bay to the south, and Hillsborough Bay on the east. MacDill Air Force Base is situated at the tip of the peninsula. Three long bridges link Tampa with Clearwater and St. Petersburg, on the Pinellas peninsula. The city is the seat of the Univ. of Tampa (a magnificent example of Moorish architecture, originally built as a huge hotel), the Univ. of South Florida, and a junior college. It has a veterans hospital and an international airport. Its many points of interest include colorful Ybor City, an African zoo and tropical garden, a cigar museum, a museum of science and natural history, the county historical museum, several children's amusement parks, and two racetracks. A state fair is held there, and the legend of José Gasparilla, an alleged pirate, is celebrated annually by a mock invasion of the city.

Tampa Bay, inlet of the Gulf of Mexico, 25 mi (40 km) long and 7 to 12 mi (11.3–19 km) wide, W Fla., separated from the Gulf by numerous small islands; it receives the Hillsborough River. St. Petersburg is on the western neck, Old Tampa Bay, and Tampa is on Hillsborough Bay, the eastern neck. Tampa Bay has dredged shipping channels. Spanish explorers Pánfilo de Narváez (1529) and Hernando De Soto (1539) landed at Tampa Bay.

Tampere (täm'pĕrä), Swed. *Tammerfors,* city (1970 pop. 157,697), Häme prov., SW Finland, on the banks of the rapids between lakes Näsijärvi and Pyhäjärvi. It is the second-largest city in Finland and a leading textile center of N Europe. There are also locomotive works and other industries. The city, an important trade center since the 11th cent., was chartered in 1775. In 1918 the White forces defeated the Finnish Bolsheviks at Tampere. The city has notable artworks and an unusual open-air theater.

Tampico (tämpē'kō), city (1970 pop. 196,147), Tamaulipas state, E Mexico, on the Pánuco River, a few miles inland from the Gulf of Mexico. Rivaling Veracruz as Mexico's most important seaport, Tampico has one of the nation's largest fishing industries (oyster and shrimp) and a considerable export trade in cattle, hides, and other agricultural products. In pre-Columbian times, Tampico was the site of the Huastec kingdom, which later became a tributary of the Aztec Empire. Spanish settlement dates back to the founding of a Franciscan mission there in the 1530s. Tampico was occupied by a U.S. force during the Mexican War and by French troops in 1862, during the French intervention. With the discovery of oil (c.1900) by English and American geologists, rapid development of petroleum industries began; before Mexico expropriated foreign-owned property, about one third of Tampico's landowners were Americans. The city boomed while much of the rest of Mexico was in revolutionary turmoil. Tampico, the seat of a state university and an episcopal see, is an active cultural center.

Tampico hemp, fiber of various tropical American plants, among them the agave (see AMARYLLIS).

Tamworth (tăm'wərth), city (1971 pop. 24,076), New South Wales, E Australia. It is an agricultural center and a transportation junction.

Tamworth, municipal borough (1971 pop. 40,245), Staffordshire, W central England. Its products include clothing, textiles, aluminum ware, paper, bricks, tiles, and agricultural machinery. Tamworth was burned by the Danes in the 9th cent. and rebuilt by Queen Æthelflæd in the 10th cent. The Church of St. Editha, built in the 8th cent. and rebuilt in 1345, has an unusual double spiral staircase. Sir Robert Peel, a member of Parliament for Tamworth, issued a set of principles in 1834 known as the Tamworth Manifesto. The town gives its name to a widely known breed of hog.

Tana (tä'nä), river, c.500 mi (800 km) long, rising near Mt. Kenya, central Kenya, E Africa, and flowing E then S across Kenya to the Indian Ocean. There are hydroelectric plants and irrigation projects in the Tana basin. The river is noted for the herds of elephants found along its middle course.

Tana (tä'nä) or **Tsana** (tsä'nä), largest lake of Ethiopia, c.1,400 sq mi (3,630 sq km), S of Gondar. It is fed by more than 60 streams, one of which is regarded as the source of the Blue Nile.

Tanabe (tä''nä'bā), city (1970 pop. 63,368), Wakayama prefecture, SW Honshu, Japan, on Tanabe Bay. It is a commercial and fishing port with a marine product processing industry.

Tanach (tä'năk), variant of TAANACH.

Tanaelv (tä'näĕlv''), Finn. *Tenojoki,* river, 205 mi (330 km) long, rising in Finnmark co., N Norway, and flowing NE to Tanafjord, NE Norway. It forms part of the Norway-Finland border. The river is noted for its salmon.

tanager (tăn'əjər), any of the small, migratory perching birds of the family Thraupidae, chiefly of the tropical New World. Only five species migrate to North America; of these the scarlet tanager (*Piranga olivacea*) has the widest range in the United States. It is about 7 in. (18 cm) long. As in most tanagers, only the male has brilliant plumage; it is scarlet with black wings, tail, and beak. The song of the scarlet tanager is less melodious than that of the rosy-red summer tanager (*P. rubra*) of the South. The male western, or Louisiana, tanager (*P. ludoviciana*) is yellow, black, and red. Females of these species are olive green above and yellow below. Tanagers are classified in the phylum CHORDATA, subphylum Vertebrata, class Aves, order Passeriformes, family Thraupidae.

Tanaïs: see DON, river, USSR; AZOV, city.

Tanaka, Giichi (gē-ē'chē tä'näkä), 1863–1929, Japanese statesman and general. He is famous as the alleged author of the so-called Tanaka Memorial (1927), purporting to set forth Japan's plans for foreign conquest. Although proven to be a forgery, its similarity in part to the subsequent course of Japanese military expansion convinced many of its authenticity. He was war minister (1918–21, 1923–24) and backed the Siberian expedition. He became president of the Seiyukai party in 1925. As prime minister and foreign minister (1927–29) he pursued an aggressive policy in China, including military intervention in Shantung in an unsuccessful attempt to prevent Chiang Kai-shek from unifying China. At home, his cabinet suppressed radicals and manipulated an election. Although it failed to win a majority, it remained in office. The downfall of Tanaka was hastened by his failure to control army extremists who assassinated the Manchurian warlord CHANG TSO-LIN, and by the charge that signing the KELLOGG-BRIAND PACT "in the name of the people" infringed the sovereignty of the emperor.

Tanaka, Kakuei (käkōō'ā tänä'kä), 1918–, Japanese political leader and prime minister (1972–74). Born to a poor rural family, he moved to Tokyo at the age of 15 and by 1937 had established his own construction firm. He prospered greatly during World War II and gained election to the lower house of the Diet, where he served from 1947. A member of Japan's dominant Liberal-Democratic party, he was twice (1965–66, 1968–71) its secretary general. Tanaka was also minister of finance (1962–65) and minister of international trade and industry (1971–72) before succeeding Eisaku Sato as prime minister. He was more colorful and somewhat more reformist than most of postwar Japan's other Liberal-Democratic prime ministers. Shortly after his election he journeyed to the People's Republic of China, where he signed an agreement to establish diplomatic relations between Japan and the Peking regime. He left office in Dec., 1974, as a result of alleged financial malfeasance.

Tanana (tăn'ənô), river, 600 mi (966 km) long, rising in W Yukon Territory near the Alaskan border and flowing NW across Alaska to the Yukon River; navigable for small boats to Fairbanks, the largest city on the river. The Tanana valley, near Fairbanks, is central Alaska's chief farming area; grains and vegetables are grown. The Tanana, discovered by Russian traders c.1860, became an important route to the Yukon goldfields in 1898. A section of the Alaska Highway runs parallel to the river.

Tananarive (tänänärēv'), city (1971 est. pop. 351,262), capital of the Malagasy Republic and its Tananarive prov., on the island of Madagascar. Tananarive is the largest city in the Malagasy Republic and is its administrative, communications, and economic center. It is the trade center for a productive agricultural region, whose main crop is rice. Railroads connect Tananarive with Tamatave, the country's chief port, and Antsirabe. Its manufactures include food products (especially meat), beverages, cigarettes, and textiles. Tananarive was founded c.1625 as a walled citadel. In 1797 it was made the fixed residence of the Merina rulers. The conquests of the Merina king Radama I (reigned 1810–28) made Tananarive the capital of almost all Madagascar. The city was captured by the French in 1895 and incorporated into their Madagascar protectorate. Today Tananarive is a modern city, built on the slopes of a ridge that rises to c.4,700 ft (1,430 m). At the top of the ridge is the former Merina royal residence; below, in descending order, are the administrative and financial areas and the commercial quarter. The Univ. of Madagascar and the Collège Rural d'Ambatobe are there as well as a Pasteur Institute and an astronomical observatory. The city is also spelled Antananarivo.

Tanaquil: see TARQUIN.

Tancred (Tancred of Lecce) (tăng'krĭd; lĕ'chā), b. 1130 or 1134, d. 1194, king of Sicily (1190–94), illegitimate son of Roger of Apulia and grandson of Roger II of Sicily. On the death of his cousin, William II of Sicily, Tancred was crowned (1190) king. The Sicilian crown was, however, claimed by CONSTANCE, who was William's aunt. Her husband, Holy Roman Emperor HENRY VI, made an unsuccessful expedition against Tancred in 1191 and, soon after Tancred's death, deposed (1194) Tancred's infant son, William III.

Tancred, 1076–1112, Crusader. He became a Crusader in 1096 with his uncle BOHEMOND I. After distinguishing himself at Nicaea, he struck out into Cilicia and besieged Tarsus, but was deprived of the city, after its fall, by Baldwin (BALDWIN I of Jerusalem) and was forced to rejoin the main army. He took part in the captures of Antioch (1098), Jerusalem (1099), and Haifa (1100) and was for a short time prince of Galilee, with his capital at Tiberias. While acting ((1100–1103) as regent of Antioch for Bohemond, he recaptured Laodicea and other towns and imprisoned RAYMOND IV of Toulouse. In 1104, after the capture of BALDWIN II of Jerusalem by the Muslims, he took over the government of Edessa and, after the departure of Bohemond for the West, the government of Antioch. He subsequently made extensive conquests in Cilicia and N Syria. Although Bohemond submitted (1108) to Byzantine Emperor ALEXIUS I, Tancred refused to surrender his conquests or to do the emperor homage.

Tandil (tändēl'), city (1970 pop. 76,933), Buenos Aires prov., E Argentina. Founded in 1823 as Fuerte Independencia, it was a military outpost against raiding Indians. Tandil is today an attractive resort city. Some of Argentina's best granite is quarried in the surrounding hills.

Tandy, James Napper, 1740–1803, Irish revolutionary. Originally a small tradesman in Dublin, he gained attention by his attacks on municipal corruption and his proposal to boycott English goods as a reprisal for the restrictions placed on Irish commerce. He joined the Irish volunteer army (see IRELAND), and he aided Theodore Wolfe Tone in founding (1791) the Dublin branch of the United Irish Society (see UNITED IRISHMEN). When faced with a sedition charge in 1793, Tandy fled to the United States and then to France (1798), where he was given the title of general. He landed (1798) in Ireland, but when he discovered that the French expedition of General Humbert to aid the Irish rebellion had failed, he fled to Hamburg, where he was arrested. He was returned to Ireland (1800), sentenced to execution, but reprieved through French influence. He died in France. His fame is perpetuated in the Irish ballad "The Wearing of the Green."

Tanega-shima (tänä'gä-shĭmä), island, 176 sq mi (456 sq km), off S Kyushu, Japan. Fishing and farming are important there. It is the site of a space satellite tracking station. Mendez Pinto, a Portuguese voyager on his way to China, landed (1543) there and introduced firearms to Japan. The name of the island came to mean "firearms" to the Japanese.

Taneiev, Sergei Ivanovich (syĭrgā' ēvä'nəvĭch tənyä'əf), 1856–1915, Russian composer and teacher. He studied at the Moscow Conservatory under Nicholas Rubinstein and Tchaikovsky, succeeding the latter as professor of harmony and orchestration in 1878; he served as director of the conservatory from 1885 to 1889 and taught composition there from 1889 to 1906. Taneiev composed an opera on Aeschylus' *Orestes* (1895), cantatas, symphonies, chamber music, and songs. A highly intellectual musician, he wrote several theoretical treatises. In his teaching, he guided a whole generation of composers including Scriabin, Rachmaninov, and Glière.

Taney, Roger Brooke (tô'nē), 1777–1864, American jurist, fifth Chief Justice of the United States (1836–64), b. Calvert co., Md., grad. Dickinson College, 1795. Taney was born of a wealthy slave-owning family of tobacco farmers. He was admitted to the bar in 1799 and as a Federalist served (1799–1800) one term in the Maryland house of delegates. He temporarily broke with the Federalist leadership over the party's opposition to the War of 1812, but he gained control of the Federalists in Maryland and in 1816 was elected to a five-year term in the state senate. Having built up a large practice, he moved (1823) from Frederick to Baltimore. In 1824 he permanently abandoned the Federalists to support Andrew Jackson. President JACKSON appointed (1831) Taney to the post of Attorney General to assist in the struggle with the BANK OF THE UNITED STATES. Taney wrote much of Jackson's message vetoing (1832) the act that rechartered the bank, and, when Louis McLane and William J. DUANE refused to withdraw Federal funds from the bank, Taney was appointed (1833) Secretary of the Treasury and effected the withdrawal. The Senate was incensed and refused in 1835 to ratify Taney's nomination as an Associate Justice of the Supreme Court, but the following year, somewhat changed in membership, the Senate ratified his appointment as Chief Justice. In the CHARLES RIVER BRIDGE CASE (1837) Taney declared that a state charter of a private business conferred only privileges expressly granted and that any ambiguity must be decided in favor of the state. His opinion outraged conservatives, who were opposed to any modification of the view that charters issued by states are inviolable, a view established by Taney's predecessor, John MARSHALL, in the DARTMOUTH COLLEGE CASE (1819). Taney felt that the POLICE POWER of a state entitled it to make reasonable regulatory laws even if they appeared to override provisions of the U.S. Constitution; thus, he held that, although Congress alone had the power to regulate interstate commerce, a state might exclude a corporation organized elsewhere. In sustaining FUGITIVE SLAVE LAWS, however, Taney denied to free states the power of refusing obedience to Federal statutes requiring the surrender of escaped slaves. Taney's support of the slavery laws was most clearly expressed in the DRED SCOTT CASE (1857). Here he held that slaves (and even the free descendants of slaves) were not citizens and might not sue in the Federal courts and that Congress could not forbid slavery in the territories of the United States. Opposition to the second holding was furiously expressed by the Republicans, and when Lincoln became President he considered Taney an arch foe. In the Civil War, Taney in vain ruled against Lincoln's suspension of the writ of habeas corpus (see MERRYMAN, EX PARTE). There was much antipathy to Taney at his death, but there has been a gradual increase in appreciation of his contributions to constitutional law; today he is looked upon as a great jurist. See biographies by B. C. Steiner (1922, repr. 1970), C. B. Swisher (1935, repr. 1961), and Walker Lewis (1965); R. K. Newmyer, *The Supreme Court under Marshall and Taney* (1969).

T'ang (täng), dynasty of China that ruled from 618 to 907. It was founded by Li Yuan and his son Li Shihmin, with the aid of Turkish allies. The early strength of the T'ang was built directly upon the excellent system of communications and administration established by the Sui. At first the neighboring peoples, nomadic and civilized, were held in check, and by the mid-7th cent. the T'ang occupied or controlled large portions of Korea, Manchuria, Mongolia, Tibet, and Turkistan. A tremendous cultural efflorescence (which powerfully influenced Japan and Annam) accompanied this territorial expansion. Sculpture flourished (T'ang horses are especially noted and the painting (of which few examples have survived) was considered superior. In literature poetry was the most highly developed form; Po Chu-I, Tu Fu, and Li Po were the most distinguished poets. The classics of Confucianism were closely studied and provided the basis for the civil service examinations (see CHINESE EXAMINATION SYSTEM). Although religious toleration was usually practiced, foreign cults were sometimes proscribed, and on several occasions Buddhist monasteries were dissolved, at great profit to the state treasury. The high-water mark of territorial expansion and political unity was reached during the reign of Emperor Hsuan Tsung (712-56). Defeat by the Arabs at the Talas River in W Turkistan (751) checked T'ang ambitions in the west, and the costly struggle against the An Lu-shan rebellion (755-63) finally exhausted the empire. Warlord governors turned many provinces into autonomous personal satrapies. The vigor of the early T'ang administration quickly declined, and control over border regions was lost, especially to the Uigurs, who became dominant in Mongolia. In the 9th cent. local maladministration became widespread, and revolts broke out in the south and in Tibet. After the T'ang collapse there was great disorder until the establishment of the Sung dynasty in 960. See Woodbridge Bingham, *The Founding of the T'ang Dynasty* (1941, repr. 1970); E. O. Reischauer, *Ennin's Travels in T'ang China* (1955); E. G. Pulleyblank, *The Background of the Rebellion of An Lu-shan* (1955); A. F. Wright and P. C. Twitchett, ed., *Perspectives on the T'ang* (1973).

tang: see BUTTERFLY FISH.

Tanga (täng'gə, -gä), city (1967 pop. 61,058), capital of Tanga prov., NE Tanzania, a port on the Indian Ocean. It is a commercial, industrial, and transportation center, connected by rail with the interior of Tanzania. Exports include sisal, tea, and coffee. Among its manufactures are rolled steel, plywood, clothing, and twine. Tanga was founded in the early 19th cent. as a base for caravans into the interior of E Africa.

Tanganyika: see TANZANIA, UNITED REPUBLIC OF.

Tanganyika, Lake, second largest lake of Africa, c.12,700 sq mi (32,890 sq km), E central Africa on the borders of Tanzania, Zaïre, Zambia, and Burundi. It is c.420 mi (680 km) long and up to 45 mi (72 km) wide. The lake lies in the Great Rift Valley (alt. 2,534 ft/772 m) and is the world's second deepest (c.4,700 ft/1,430 m) freshwater lake. Part of the lake's overflow eventually reaches the Atlantic Ocean by way of the Lukuga River. Lake Tanganyika has important fisheries. Steamer service connects the chief lakeside cities. John Speke and Sir Richard Burton, the British explorers, were the first (1858) Europeans to see the lake; David Livingstone and Henry M. Stanley explored (1871) the region. During World War I there were several small naval engagements between the British and the Germans on the lake.

Tange, Kenzo (kĕn'zō täng'ē), 1913–, Japanese architect. The Hiroshima Peace Center (1949), for which Tange designed three buildings, won him international fame. He is a leading creator of shell structures and has planned many throughout Japan. In his design for the Shizuoka convention hall, Ehima (1953–54), a hyperbolic paraboloidal system was used to span a distance of 375 ft (114 m). Tange's later works, such as the Kagawa prefectural office (1955–58), are notable for restraint of design and the employment of the traditional Japanese aesthetic in modern technical terms. His plan for the National Indoor Stadium at Yoyogi for the 1964 Tokyo Olympics is a striking example of suspension roofing. His recent works include the Japan Olivetti Technical Center. See studies by Robin Boyd (1962) and Udo Kultermann, ed. (1970).

tangelo: see ORANGE.

tangent, in mathematics. **1** In geometry, the tangent to a CIRCLE or sphere is a straight line that intersects the circle or sphere in one and only one point. For other curves and surfaces the tangent line at a given point P is defined as the limiting position, if such a LIMIT exists, of a secant line through P and another point P' on the curve or surface as P' is allowed to approach P. The tangent plane to a surface at a point is the plane in which every line in the plane that passes through the point is a tangent line to the surface at that point. The study of tangent lines and planes usually requires the concepts of the CALCULUS and is included within the scope of DIFFERENTIAL GEOMETRY. **2** In trigonometry, the tangent function is a relation defined in a right triangle for either of the acute angles (A) as the ratio of the length of the side opposite that angle (a) to the length of the adjacent side (b), that is, $\tan A = a/b$. This concept may be extended to any plane triangle, in which case the Law of Tangents would hold: $(a-b)/(a+b) = [\tan \frac{1}{2}(A-B)]/[\tan \frac{1}{2}(A+B)]$, where A and B are vertex angles and a and b the lengths of the sides opposite them. In general, the tangent function $\tan x$ may be expressed as an infinite SERIES, $\tan x = x + x^3/3 + 2x^5/15 + 17x^7/315 + 62x^9/2{,}835 + \ldots$, where x^2 must be less than $\pi^2/4$. See TRIGONOMETRY.

tangerine: see ORANGE.

Tangier (tănjēr'), ancient *Tingis,* city (1971 est. pop. 215,502), N Morocco, on the Strait of Gibraltar. The city is almost wholly without manufacturing industries, but the port is active. The walled Moorish town adjoins a modern European garden suburb. Tangier was probably founded by the Phoenicians. It was a free city under the Romans and the chief port and commercial center of Morocco until the founding (808) of Fez. It was captured from the Moors by the Portuguese in 1471 and was transferred to England as part of the dowry that Catherine of Braganza brought to Charles II. The English abandoned the city to the Moroccans in 1684. By the mid-19th cent. it had become the diplomatic center of Morocco. When the rest of the country was divided between Spanish and French protectorates in 1912, the status of Tangier remained vague. Finally, in 1923–24, an international zone administered by France, Spain, and Britain (Italy joined in 1928), was set up. The city was included in the zone as a duty-free port. During World War II, Spain controlled the zone. In 1945 it was returned to international control by agreement of Britain, France, the United States, and the USSR. Tangier remained under international control until 1956 when it was returned to Morocco. While it was an international port, the city was the base of operations for many Mediterranean smugglers.

Tangier, town (1970 pop. 814), E Va., on Tangier Island, in S Chesapeake Bay; inc. 1915. The island was discovered by Capt. John Smith in 1608, and in 1620 settlers arrived from Cornwall, England. Fishing is the only industry. Isolated from the mainland, the people of Tangier developed a distinct culture.

T'ang-ku-la Shan-Mo (täng-kōō-lä shän-mô) or **Tangla** (täng'lä, däng'lä), mountain range, southeast extension of the Karakorum range, in the central Tibetan plateau, on the Tibet-Tsinghai province border, W China; rises to about 20,000 ft (6,100 m). It is the watershed for the Salween and Mekong rivers. T'ang-ku-la Shan-k'ou (Tang Pass), alt. 16,760 ft (5,108 m), is on the main route connecting Tibet with the rest of China.

Tangla, mountain range: see T'ANG-KU-LA SHAN-MO, China.

Tanglewood: see BERKSHIRE FESTIVAL.

T'ang-shan or **Tangshan** (both: täng-shän), city (1970 est. pop. 1,200,000), NE Hopeh prov., China. A coal-mining center in the Kailan basin, T'ang-shan is also a major industrial hub with iron and steel works. Machinery, motor vehicles, chemicals, textiles, glass, petroleum products, and cement are also manufactured.

Tanguy, Yves (ēv täNgē'), 1900–1955, French surrealist painter. At first a merchant seaman, he saw a picture by Chirico in 1923 and instantly decided to take up painting. He created vast imaginary dream landscapes, in which float strange, often amorphous, objects and personages—all meticulously painted. His spontaneous, subconscious imagery remained curiously static throughout his career. Tanguy moved to the United States in 1939. A number of his paintings are in the Museum of Modern Art, New York City. See monograph by J. T. Soby (1955).

Tanhumeth (tănhyōō'məth), father of the captain Seraiah. 2 Kings 25.23; Jer. 40.8.

Tanimbar Islands (tănĭm'bär, tə-) or **Tenimbar Islands** (tĕnĭm'bär, tə-), group of about 30 islands (1965 est. pop. 50,000), c.2,100 sq mi (5,440 sq km), E Indonesia, in the Banda Sea, between the Aru Islands and Timor, in the Moluccas. The largest of the group is Jamdena. Saumlaki is the chief town. Important products are copra, tortoise shell, and trepang. The group is also called Timorlaut.

Tanis (tā'nĭs), ancient city of Egypt, in the eastern delta of the Nile. It is identified with the Hyksos capital, Avaris (XII dynasty). It was a significant city in the XIX dynasty and was capital of the XXI (Tanite) dynasty. On the Asian frontier, Tanis was important strategically and commercially until threatened inundation by Lake Manzala caused it to be abandoned after the 6th cent. A.D. for the city of Tennis. Excavations, first begun in 1860, revealed inscriptions, several temples and statues, and a royal necropolis. Tanis is the biblical Zoan (Num. 13.22; Ps. 78; Isa. 19; Ezek. 30.14). It may also be the biblical Raamses (Ex. 12.37).

Tanizaki, Junichiro (jōōnē'chērō tänē'zäkē), 1886–1965, Japanese writer. A prolific writer whose popularity extended through the reigns of three emperors, Tanizaki is perhaps best known for *Sasameyuki* (tr. *The Makioka Sisters,* 1957). It was the first major Japanese work of the post-World War II period; it is a detailed account of an Osaka family that embraces a tradition-bound way of life. Tanizaki's other novels include a modern version of *The Tale of Genji, Some Prefer Nettles* (tr. 1955), and *The Key* (tr. 1961). Many of his works carry an implied condemnation of excessive interest in Western things. See his *Seven Japanese Tales* (tr. 1963) and *Diary of a Mad Old Man* (tr. 1965).

Tanjore, India: see THANJAVUR.

tank, military, armored vehicle having caterpillar traction and armed with machine guns, cannon, rockets, or flame throwers. The tank, together with the airplane, opened up modern warfare, which had been immobilized and stalemated by the use of rifled guns (see MECHANIZED WARFARE). It was developed by the British and first employed in World War I in the battle of Flers-Courcellette, on the Somme, in Sept., 1916. In the beginning it was used incorrectly and seemed a failure, but in Nov., 1917, the tank achieved a major success at Cambrai, where 300 British tanks made a dawn attack on a 6-

mi (9.7-km) front and shattered the German defenses. Before World War II tanks and tank tactics were greatly improved, and in the first campaign of that war the German army, exploying large numbers of tanks, overran Poland in less than a month. Whole divisions and corps of tanks were soon formed on both sides, and in mass tank battles on the plains of Europe and N Africa the tide often swung toward the side with the best tanks. The Allies developed a number of specialized vehicles such as amphibious tanks and tanks to clear paths through mine fields. As tank design progressed, better antitank weapons were developed, such as bazookas, armor-piercing shells, recoilless rifles, and antitank missiles, as well as planes armed with rockets and bombs. Since World War II the basic features of tanks and tank tactics have remained unchanged, but there have been refinements. The MBT-70, a large battle tank jointly developed in the late 1960s by the United States and Germany, features a number of innovations in arrangement and armament, including a laser rangefinder, a stabilization device for moving fire, and a computer system for fire control and navigation. Tanks are vulnerable to many weapons but remain indispensable because of their mobility and versatile weaponry. See B. H. Liddell Hart, *The Tanks* (1959); Kenneth Mocksey and J. H. Batchelor, *Tank: A History of the Armoured Fighting Vehicle* (1970); Douglas Orgill, *The Tank* (1970).

Tannaim (tänäˈīm) [plural of Aramaic *tanna,* = one who studies or teaches], Jewish sages of the period from HILLEL to the compilation of the MISHNA. They functioned as both scholars and teachers, educating those in the synagogues as well as in the academies. Their opinions are found either in the Mishna or as collected in the TOSEFTA. After the fall of Jerusalem and the destruction of the Temple (A.D. 70), JOHANAN BEN ZAKKAI reconstituted the academy at Jabneh (see JAMNIA), where the work of the Tannaim flourished. AKIBA BEN JOSEPH was among their disciples. The defeat and expulsion of the Jews from Judaea to Galilee by the Romans in A.D. 135 caused a precarious situation that made it ever clearer that a compilation of the opinions of the scholars was necessary to prevent further erosion of the Jewish community and its way of life. This was undertaken by JUDAH I (ha-Nasi) as general editor, working with a staff of the most prominent scholars of his day; the result of their labors was the final codification of the Mishna. The Tannaim were succeeded by the AMORAIM. See H. L. Strack, *Introduction to the Talmud and Midrash* (1931, repr. 1969).

Tannenbaum, Frank, 1893–1969, American historian, b. Austria. He received his Ph.D. from the Brookings School of Economics in 1927. After an early career as a labor leader, journalist, and economic adviser, he became an expert in institutional history and made notable studies of labor, slavery, and the penal system. He is known chiefly, however, as an expert on Latin America. His work in the 1930s as an adviser to the Mexican government led to his book *Peace by Revolution: An Interpretation of Mexico* (1933). He played a key role in the development of the Farm Security Bill during the New Deal and in the creation of the university seminars at Columbia. He was professor of Latin American history at Columbia from 1935 until his retirement in 1962. His major works include *Slave and Citizen* (1947), *Mexico: The Struggle for Peace and Bread* (1950), *A Philosophy of Labor* (1951), and *Ten Keys to Latin America* (1962).

Tannenberg (täˈnənbĕrkʺ), Pol. *Stębark,* village, NE Poland, near Olsztyn. Formerly in East Prussia, it was transferred (1945) by the Potsdam Conference to Polish administration. Two important battles were fought there. In the first, fought in 1410 between Tannenberg and the nearby village of Grünwald, Polish and Lithuanian forces under Ladislaus II (Ladislaus Jagiello) halted the eastward expansion of the Teutonic Knights. The second and better-known battle occurred during World War I (Aug. 27–30, 1914). Russian armies under generals Samsonov and Rennenkampf had invaded East Prussia from the south and east, respectively. German strategy was to surround Samsonov's forces; 90,000 Russian prisoners were taken, and Samsonov committed suicide. Rennenkampf, whose unwillingness to aid Samsonov greatly facilitated the German victory, was defeated soon afterward in the battle of the Masurian Lakes. The Russian advance into East Prussia, though ill-fated, relieved considerably the German pressure against the West during the first critical weeks of the war. The battle of Tannenberg is a central event in Aleksandr Solzhenitsyn's novel *August 1914* (1972).

Tanner, Henry Ossawa, 1859–1937, American painter, b. Pittsburgh; son of a bishop of the African Methodist Episcopal Church. He studied with Eakins in Philadelphia and in Paris. Tanner made many trips to Palestine to obtain background for his religious paintings. His work is naturalistic, and the religious subjects especially are strongly rendered. Among his paintings are *Christ and Nicodemus* (Pa. Acad. of the Fine Arts); *Two Disciples at the Tomb* (Art Inst., Chicago); *The Banjo Lesson* (Hampton Inst., Hampton, Va.).

Tannhäuser (tänˈhoizər), 13th cent., German MINNESINGER, whose adventurous wanderings became the subject of legend. A few of his own lyrics are extant, including *Buszlied* (*Song of Repentance*). They indicate that he served several noble patrons and probably was a Crusader. In a 16th-century ballad, Tannhäuser escapes the snares of Venus with the help of Our Lady, but is refused papal absolution until the budding of his staff indicates divine grace. This story and that of his participation in a singing contest at the Wartburg are the materials for Wagner's opera *Tannhäuser* (1843–44). The story also figures in Swinburne's poem "Laus Veneris."

tannin, tannic acid, or **gallotannic acid,** astringent vegetable product found in a wide variety of plants. Sources include the bark of oak, hemlock, chestnut, and mangrove; the leaves of certain sumacs; and plant galls. Tannin is also present in tea, coffee, and walnuts. A solution of tannic acid is obtained from one of these natural sources by extraction with hot water; in particular, gallotannic acid is obtained from plant gall. Tannin varies somewhat in composition, having the approximate empirical formula $C_{76}H_{52}O_{46}$. Tannic acid is a colorless to pale yellow solid; it is believed to be a glucoside in which each of the five hydroxyl groups of the glucose molecule is esterified with a molecule of digallic acid. Tannin is used in tanning animal skins to make leather; it transforms certain proteins of animal tissue into compounds that resist decomposition. It is also used in manufacturing inks, as a mordant in dyeing, and in medicine as an astringent and for treatment of burns.

tanning, process by which skins and hides are converted into LEATHER. Vegetable tanning, a method requiring more than a month even with modern machinery and tanning liquors, employs tannin; its use is shown in Egyptian tomb paintings dating from 3000 B.C. Mineral tanning includes tawing, or alum tanning, another ancient method, and chrome tanning, the process most common today, based on the use of chrome salts and requiring only a few hours. Known as early as 1856, chrome tanning was first patented in the United States by Augustus Schultz in 1884. In oil tanning, or chamoising, the pelts are treated with fats and hung to dry; the leather is commonly napped on both sides and is very absorbent. The most recently developed tanning process employs artificial agents (syntans). Most heavy leathers, such as sole leather, are vegetable tanned; many light leathers are chrome tanned. The Indians of North America used the chamois method, employing the fat, livers, and brains of animals. Indian-tanned white buckskin was highly esteemed, especially for clothing, both by Indians and by colonial pioneers. In the tanyards of European settlers tanners used oak and hemlock bark; gallnuts; the wood, nuts, and leaves of the chestnut tree; and the leaves of sumac.

Tannu-Tuva: see TUVA AUTONOMOUS SOVIET SOCIALIST REPUBLIC.

tanrec: see TENREC.

tansy (tănˈzē), perennial herb (*Tanacetum vulgare*) of the family Compositae (COMPOSITE family), native to Europe but naturalized in North America. It was long cultivated for its ornamental foliage and clusters of yellow, buttonlike flowers; it was often used in old-fashioned dishes, such as tansy cakes and puddings, which were eaten in the spring, especially at Easter time, either in memory of the bitter herbs of the Jewish Passover or as a sort of tonic after the Lenten season. Tansy tea was formerly a household medicine and is still used as an anthelmintic and in the treatment of external bruises and inflammations. Tansy is classified in the division MAGNOLIOPHYTA, class Magnoliopsida, order Asterales, family Compositae.

Tanta (tänˈtä), city (1970 est. pop. 254,000), capital of Gharbiyah governorate, N Egypt, in the Nile River delta. It is a cotton-ginning center and the main railroad hub of the delta. Three annual festivals are held in Tanta in honor of Ahmad al-Badawi, a revered Muslim figure of the 13th cent., who is buried in a mosque in the city. A branch of Al Azhar Univ. (Cairo) is in Tanta.

tantalum (tănˈtələm) [from Tantalus], metallic chemical element; symbol Ta; at. no. 73; at. wt. 180.948; m.p. about 3000°C; b.p. about 5400°C; sp. gr. 16.65 at 20°C; valence +2, +3, +4, or +5. Tantalum is a rare, hard, blue-gray metal with a body-centered cubic crystalline structure. Its chemical characteristics resemble those of niobium, the element above it in group Vb of the PERIODIC TABLE. Pure tantalum is extremely ductile and can be drawn into a very thin wire. It is malleable and highly resistant to common acids and to corrosion at temperatures below about 150°C. Tantalum is obtained chiefly from the mineral tantalite, although it also occurs in euxenite, samarskite, and some other rare minerals. The major source of tantalum ore is Africa, although some is mined in Canada. Tantalum is almost always found in association with niobium; separation of the two metals is difficult. Major uses of tantalum include electrolytic capacitors, chemical equipment, and parts for vacuum furnaces, aircraft, and missiles. Tantalum was used in the filaments of electric light bulbs and electronic tubes but has been largely replaced by tungsten for these uses. It is often alloyed with other metals; it imparts strength, ductility, corrosion resistance, and a high melting point. Because it is unaffected by body fluids and causes no adverse tissue reactions, it is used in dental and surgical instruments and prostheses. Useful tantalum compounds include the carbide TaC_2, an abrasive that is almost as hard as diamond; and the oxide Ta_2O_5, used in making special highly refractive glass. Tantalum was discovered in 1802 by A. G. Ekeberg but for some time was confused with niobium.

Tantalus (tănˈtələs), in Greek mythology, king of Sipylos, son of Zeus and father of Pelops and Niobe. He was admitted to the society of the gods, but his abominable behavior aroused their anger, and Zeus condemned him to suffer eternally at Tartarus. One legend says that he had divulged divine secrets and stolen the gods' sacred food. Another tells that he had murdered his son Pelops and served his body to the gods to test their omniscience. As punishment he was condemned to hang from the bough of a fruit tree over a pool of water. When he bent to drink, the water would recede; when he reached for a fruit, the wind would blow it from his reach. A further account of his punishment tells of a great stone hanging over his head threatening to fall. The word *tantalize* originated from his name.

Tantra (tŭnˈtrə), in both Hinduism and Buddhism, esoteric tradition of ritual and YOGA. It is known for the elaborate use of MANTRA, or mystical words, and MANDALA, or sacred diagrams; the importance of female deities, or SHAKTI; the ritual use of wine, meat, and sexual intercourse; and cremation-ground practices such as meditation on corpses. Tantric meditation aims at the identification of the devotee's entire being, both mental and physical, with the chosen deity by means of both internal meditation and outer ritual. In Hindu Tantra, practice is graded into three types, corresponding to three classes of devotees: the animal, i.e., those in whom the guna, or quality, of tamas (darkness) predominates; the heroic, those in whom the guna of rajas (activity) predominates; and the divine, those in whom sattva (light) predominates (see INDIAN PHILOSOPHY). The practice of the heroic devotee includes the actual use of the five elements, called the five *m*'s: fish (*matsya*), meat (*mamsa*), wine (*madya*), aphrodisiac cereals (*mudra*), and sexual intercourse (*maithuna*). The animal devotee, not yet ready for the heroic practice, performs the rituals with material symbols, while the divine devotee is adept at the purely internal and symbolic performance of the ritual. The object of the ritual, attainable only by the divine devotee, is to awaken *kundalini* energy, which is identified with Shakti, and merge with the Godhead. In the Buddhist Tantra, or Vajrayana, in contrast to the Hindu, the female principle of "wisdom" (*prajna*) is static, whereas the male, or "means" (*upaya*), is active. In Buddhism, rituals that break the basic moral precepts have for the most part been dropped, but the complex meditation practices have been retained. See Aghenanda Bharati, *The Tantric Tradition* (1965).

Tantum ergo, hymn: see PANGE LINGUA.

Tan-tung (dän-dŏŏng) or **Antung** (änˈtŏŏngʹ), city (1970 est. pop. 450,000), SE Liaoning prov., China, at the mouth of the Yalu River, opposite Korea. It is a port, connected by rail with Shen-yang (Mukden) and with Sinuiju in North Korea. The Supung Dam on the Yalu supplies power for the city's industries, many of which are newly developed. Manufactures include paper, oakleaf silk, medicines, machinery, precision instruments, cement, and processed fish and other marine products. Tan-tung was opened as a treaty port in 1907.

Tanzania, United Republic of (tăn″zənē′ə, -zăn′-ēə, Swahili tän-zä nē′ä), republic (1970 est. pop. 13,273,000), 364,898 sq mi (945,087 km), E Africa, formed in 1964 by the union of the republics of Tanganyika and Zanzibar. For a description of the island of Zanzibar, and its history until 1964, see ZANZIBAR. Mainland Tanzania is bordered on the S by Mozambique, Malawi, and Zambia; on the W by Zaïre, Burundi, and Rwanda; on the N by Uganda and Kenya; and on the E by the Indian Ocean. Lake Nyasa forms part of the southern boundary, Lake Tanganyika part of the western boundary, and Victoria Nyanza part of the northern boundary. DAR-ES-SALAAM is the capital and largest city of the republic; other major towns on the mainland include Arusha, Dodoma, Iringa, Kigoma-Ujiji, Morogoro, Moshi, Mtwara-Mikindani, Mwanza, Tabora, and Tanga. The mainland is divided into 18 administrative regions. Tanzania falls into three major geographical zones—a narrow lowland coastal strip along the Indian Ocean; a vast interior plateau; and a number of scattered mountainous regions. The coastal zone (10–40 mi/16–60 km wide) receives considerable rainfall and has much fertile soil. The plateau (average elevation: 3,500–4,500 ft/1,070–1,370 m) extends over most of the interior and is cut in two places by branches of the Great Rift Valley. The western branch contains Lake Tanganyika (which includes

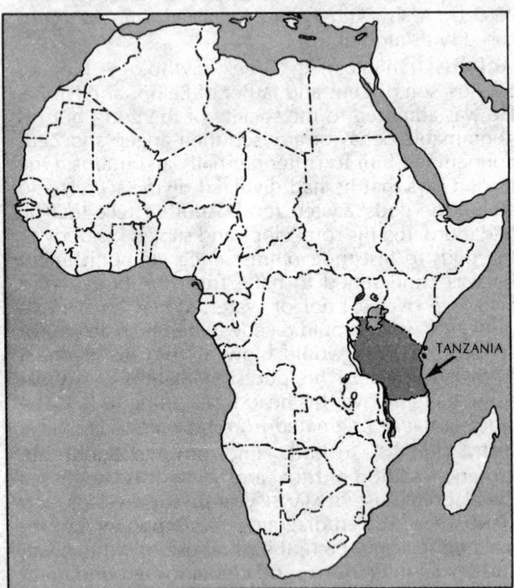

the lowest point in Africa) and the eastern branch runs through central Tanzania about 500 ft (150 m) below the level of the plateau; the two branches merge just north of Lake Nyasa. The plateau receives little rainfall, but in most parts there is enough to support agriculture. The Serengeti National Park, a large wildlife reserve, is east of Victoria Nyanza, and Lake Rukwa is in the southwest. The mountainous regions include Mt. Meru (14,979 ft/4,566 m) and Mt. Kilimanjaro (19,340 ft/5,895 m, the highest point in Africa) in the northeast; the Usambara, Nguru, and Uluguru mts. in the east; the Livingstone Mts. and the Kipengere Range near Lake Nyasa in the south; and the Ufipi Highlands in the southwest. Tanzania's few rivers include the Pangani, the Rufiji, and the Ruvuma (which forms part of the border with Mozambique), all of which flow into the Indian Ocean, and the Malagrasi River, which flows into Lake Tanganyika. Virtually all of Tanzania's inhabitants are black Africans, the great majority of whom speak Bantu languages. There are about 95,000 inhabitants of Indian descent and about 25,000 persons of Arab descent (with little or no black African admixture). The Bantu-speaking peoples include the Sukuma (the republic's largest ethnic group), Bena, Chagga, Gogo, Ha, Haya, Hehe, Luguru, Makua, Makonde, Ngoni, Nyakyusa, Nyamwezi, and Nyaturu. In addition, the Masai speak a Nilotic language; the Hadza speak a language related to San; the Sandawe speak a language akin to Khoikhoi; and the Iraqw speak a Cushitic language. Swahili is the republic's official language. About 45% of the people follow traditional religious beliefs; about 30% are Muslim; and about 25% are Christian (mostly Roman Catholic). The economy of Tanzania is overwhelmingly agricultural, with most workers engaged in subsistence farming. The principal crops are cassava, millet, sorghum, wheat, yams, rice, maize, plantains, and pulses. The chief cash crops are sisal, cotton, coffee, cashew nuts, sugarcane, tea, tobacco, and pyrethrum; these commodities account for the bulk of the exports originating on the mainland. In addition, large numbers of cattle, sheep, and goats are raised. Manufactures are largely limited to processed agricultural goods, beverages, and basic consumer items. Also, refined petroleum, aluminum goods, and construction materials (especially cement) are produced, and motor vehicles are assembled. Tanzania ranks among the world's 10 leading producers of diamonds; other minerals extracted in significant quantities include gold, salt, tin, and mica. Immense deposits of coal and iron ore have been found near Lake Nyasa, but, because of their inaccessibility, they have not been exploited as yet on a large scale. Tanzania's road and rail networks serve mainly the coastal, central, and north-central parts of the country. The main rail lines run from Dar-es-Salaam to Kigoma-Ujiji (on Lake Tanganyika) and from Tanga to Moshi and Arusha. The Tan-Zam railroad between Dar-es-Salaam and Zambia, built with the aid of the People's Republic of China, was scheduled for completion in 1976. The value of Tanzania's exports is usually somewhat higher than the value of its imports. The exports are made up of agricultural goods and diamonds. The principal imports are manufactured consumer goods, machinery, transportation equipment, foodstuffs, refined petroleum, and chemicals. The leading trade partners are Great Britain, the People's Republic of China, Kenya, Uganda, Zambia, and the United States. Tanzania is a member of the East African Community.

History. In 1959, Dr. L. S. B. Leakey, a British anthropologist, discovered at Olduvai Gorge in NE Tanzania the fossilized remains of what he called *Homo habilis,* who lived about 1.75 million years ago and was a direct ancestor of modern man (*Homo sapiens*). Tanzania was later the site of Paleolithic cultures. By the beginning of the first millennium A.D. scattered parts of the country, including the coast, were thinly populated. At this time overseas trade seems to have been carried out between the coast and NE Africa, SW Asia, and India. By about A.D. 900 traders from SW Asia and India had settled on the coast, exchanging cloth, beads, and metal goods for ivory. They also exported small numbers of black Africans as slaves. By this time there were also commercial contacts with China, directly and via Sri Vijaya (see under INDONESIA) and India. By about 1200, Kilwa Kisiwani (situated on an island) was a major trade center, handling gold exported from Sofala (on the coast of modern Mozambique) as well as goods (including ivory, beeswax, and animal skins) from the near interior of Tanzania. By about 1000 the migration of Bantu-speaking black Africans into the interior of Tanzania from the west and the south was well under way, and the population there had been greatly increased. The Bantu were organized in relatively small political units. In 1498, Vasco da Gama, the Portuguese explorer, became the first European to visit the Tanzanian coast; in 1502, on his second visit there, he made Kilwa tributary. In 1505, Kilwa was sacked by Francisco d'Almeida, another Portuguese explorer, and by 1506 Portugal controlled most of the coast of E Africa. The Portuguese did not cooperate with the local people, and their impact was mostly negative—trade was disrupted, towns declined, and people migrated from the region. However, Kilwa's trade seems to have grown as a result of contact with the Portuguese. Toward the end of the 16th cent., the Zimba, a warlike black African group from SE Africa, moved rapidly up the coast, causing considerable damage; in 1587 they sacked Kilwa and killed about 3,000 persons (roughly 40% of its inhabitants). In 1698 the Portuguese were expelled from the E African coast (except for a brief return in 1725) with the help of Arabs from Oman. In the early 18th cent., the Omanis showed some interest in the commerce of E Africa, and this increased after the Bu Said dynasty replaced the Yarubi rulers in 1741. Oman's commercial activity was centered on Zanzibar (and, to a lesser extent, at Mombasa), from where it controlled the overseas trade of E Africa. By the early 19th cent. numerous towns on the Tanzanian coast had been founded or revived; these included Tanga, Pangani, Bagamoyo, Kilwa Kivinje (situated on the mainland near Kilwa Kisiwani), Lindi, and Mikandani. Sayyid Said, the great Bu Saidi ruler, took a great interest in E Africa and in 1841 permanently moved his capital from Muscat, in Oman, to Zanzibar. He brought with him many Arabs, who settled in the mainland towns as well as on Zanzibar. As a result, the Swahili language (a blend of Bantu grammar and a mostly Arabic vocabulary) and culture gained new adherents. About the same time, new caravan routes into the far interior were opened up; the three main lines went from Kilwa and Lindi to the Lake Nyasa region; from Bagamoyo and Mbwamaji (near present-day Dar-es-Salaam) to Tabora, where one branch continued W to Ujiji (and on into modern Zaïre) and another went N to the Victoria Nyanza region; and from Pangani and Tanga northwest into modern Kenya via Mt. Kilimanjaro. The caravans following the southern route obtained mainly slaves and ivory; along the more northerly routes ivory was the chief commodity purchased. In the middle third of the 19th cent. several European missionaries and explorers (including J. L. Krapf, Richard Burton, John Hanning Speke, J. A. Grant, and David Livingstone) visited various parts of Tanzania, notably Mt. Kilimanjaro, Tabora, Victoria Nyanza, and Lake Nyasa. From the 1860s to the early 1880s Mirambo, a Nyamwezi, headed a large state that controlled much of the caravan trade of central and N Tanzania. About the same time Tippu Tib, a Zanzibari, organized large caravans that passed through Tanzania to present-day Zambia and Zaïre, where ivory and slaves were obtained. As the scramble for African territory among the European powers intensified in the 1880s, Carl Peters and other members of the Society for German Colonization signed treaties with black Africans (1884–85) in the hinterland of the Tanzanian coast. By an agreement with Great Britain in 1886, Germany established a vague sphere of influence over mainland Tanzania, except for a narrow strip of land along the coast that remained under the suzerainty of the sultan of Zanzibar, who leased it to the Germans. The German East Africa Company (founded 1887) governed the territory, called GERMAN EAST AFRICA. The company's aggressive conduct resulted in a major resistance movement along the coast by black Africans, Arabs, and Swahilis (whose main leaders were Abushiri and Bwana Heri) that was only defeated with the help of the German government. A second Anglo-German agreement (1890) added Rwanda, Burundi, and other regions to German East Africa. Because the company had proved to be an ineffective ruler, the German government in 1891 took over the country (which by then included the coast) and declared it a protectorate. However, it was not until 1898, with the death of the Hehe ruler, Mkwawa, who strongly opposed European rule, that the Germans succeeded in controlling the country. During the period 1905 to 1907 the transtribal, quasi-religious Maji Maji revolt against German rule engulfed most of SE Tanzania; about 75,000 black Africans lost their lives as a result of German military campaigns and lack of food. Under the Germans, several new crops (including sisal, cotton, and plantation-grown rubber) were introduced; the production and sale of other commodities (notably coffee, copra, sesame, and groundnuts) was encouraged, and railroads were built to Kigoma on Lake Tanganyika and to Moshi. In addition, many new Christian missions, which included rudimentary schools for the Africans, were established. During World War I, British and South African troops occupied (1916) most of German East Africa. In the postwar period the League of Nations made Tanganyika a British mandate, and RUANDA-URUNDI (later Rwanda and Burundi), a Belgian mandate; the Portuguese gained control of some land in the southeast. The British, especially during the administration (1925–31) of Gov. Sir Donald Cameron, attempted to rule "indirectly" through existing African leaders. However, unlike N Nigeria, where the policy of indirect rule was first developed (see Frederick LUGARD), Tanganyika had few indigenous large-scale political units. Therefore, African leaders had to be established in newly defined constituencies. The effect of British policy, as a result, was to alter considerably the patterns of African life in Tanganyika. After a slow start, the British developed the territory's economy largely along the lines established by the Germans. Increasing numbers of Africans worked for a wage on plantations, especially after 1945, when economic growth began to accelerate. Also after 1945 black Africans gradually gained more seats on the territory's legislative council (which had been established in 1926). In 1954, Julius NYERERE and Oscar Kambona transformed the Tanganyika African Association (founded in 1929) into the more politically oriented Tanganyika African National Union (TANU). TANU easily won the general elections of 1958–60, and when Tanganyika became independent on Dec. 9, 1961, Nyerere became its first prime minister. In Dec., 1962, Tanganyika became a republic within the British Commonwealth of Nations, and Nyerere was made president. On April 27, 1964, shortly after a leftist revolution in newly independent Zanzibar, Tanganyika and Zanzibar merged to form one republic, which was named Tanzania in Oct., 1964. Nyerere became Tanzania's first president and Abeid Amani Karume, the chairman of the Zanzibar Revolutionary Council, its first vice president. Nyerere was overwhelmingly reelected president in 1965 and 1970. Although formally united with the mainland, Zanzibar followed an independent course in many respects, especially economic. Karume, the leader of the dominant Afro-Shirazi party, headed the Zanzibar government until 1972, when he was assassinated. He was succeeded by Aboud Jumbe. In Feb., 1967, Nyerere issued the Arusha Declaration, a major policy statement that called for "egalitarianism" and self-reliance. The government was to be decentralized to avoid the concentration of power in an individual or national institution, and government officials were not to receive unnecessary privileges or to be paid large salaries; major economic institutions such as banks and large industries were to be nationalized; the development of the rural areas was to be given equal emphasis with the development of the cities; and the country was to develop principally by using its own resources and not to become dependent on loans and other aid from foreign countries or industrial firms. Nyerere put some of the declaration's principles into practice, but it was not clear whether or not power in Tanzania was in fact being decentralized. TANU was the mainland's sole legal political party, and it was tightly controlled by Nyerere. In the early 1970s there was tension (and occasional border clashes) between Tanzania and Uganda, caused mainly by Nyerere's continued support of Uganda's ousted president, A. Milton Obote. However, in 1973, Nyerere and Gen. Idi Amin, Uganda's new head of state, signed an agreement that appeared to end the hostility. Tanzania supported various movements against white-minority rule in S Africa, and several of these organizations had offices in Dar es Salaam.

Government. Under the 1965 constitution as amended, Tanzania's head of state and chief executive is the president, who is nominated to a five-year term by a conference of delegates of TANU (the only legal political party on the mainland) and the Afro-Shirazi party (the sole legal party in Zanzibar) and then either confirmed or rejected in a national plebiscite. The president is assisted by a cabinet, which includes the country's first vice president (a Zanzibari) and a prime minister (who is also the second vice president). The republic's legislative body is the national assembly, which is made up of 204 members (serving five-year terms), of whom 120 are popularly elected. About 55 members represent Zanzibar. All bills passed by the assembly must be approved by the president before they become law. The government of Zanzibar is headed by the president, who is also the chairman of the Revolutionary Council, Zanzibar's legislative body. See Norman R. Bennett, *Studies in East African History* (1963) and *Mirambo of Tanzania, 1840–1884* (1971); Roland Oliver and Gervase Mathew, ed., *History of East Africa,* Vol. I (1963); V. T. Harlow and E. M. Chilver, ed., *History of East Africa,* Vol. II (1965); Ralph A. Austen, *Northwest Tanzania under German and British Rule: Colonial Policy and Tribal Politics, 1889–1939* (1968); John Iliffe, *Tanganyika under German Rule, 1905–12* (1969); I. N. Kinambo and A. J. Temu, eds., *A History of Tanzania* (1969); Henry Bienen, *Tanzania: Party Transformation and Economic Development* (2d ed. 1970); R. F. Hopkins, *Political Roles in a New State* (1971); J. C. Hatch, *Tanzania: A Profile* (1972); C. R. Ingle, *From Village to State in Tanzania* (1972).

tanzanite (tănzăn'īt), beautiful gemstone discovered in 1967 in the Umba Valley near the Usambara Mts. in Tanzania, a precious variety of the mineral zoisite, a calcium aluminum silicate. Zoisite is a common rock-forming mineral and is usually white to gray in color. Tanzanite occurs as orthorhombic crystals, which may be colorless, yellow-green, brown, or blue to violet when found; when these crystals are heated to 300–400°C, many of them turn sapphire blue, which is the preferred color for gemstones. The blue color is attributed to the presence of small amounts of vanadium.

Taoism (dou'ĭzəm, tou'-, tä'ōĭzəm), philosophy and religion of China. The philosophical system chiefly derives from the book *Tao-te-ching,* traditionally ascribed to LAO-TZE but probably written in the mid-3d cent. B.C. The *Tao,* in the broadest sense, is the way the universe functions, the path [Chin. *tao*=path] taken by natural events. It is characterized by spontaneous creativity and by regular alternations of phenomena (such as day following night) that proceed without effort. Effortless action may be illustrated by the conduct of water, which unresistingly accepts the lowest level and yet wears away the hardest substance. Man, following the *Tao,* must abjure all striving. His ideal state of being, fully attainable by mystical contemplation alone, is freedom from desire and simplicity compared to that of an infant or an "uncarved block." The political doctrines developed by the Taoists reflect their quietistic philosophy. The duty of a ruler is to protect his people from experiencing material wants or strong passions and to impose a minimum of government. The social virtues expounded by CONFUCIUS were condemned as symptoms of excessive government and disregard of effortless action. Second only to Lao-tze as an exponent of philosophical Taoism was CHUANG-TZE, the author of brilliant satirical essays. Later Taoism emphasized the techniques [Chin. *te*=power] for realizing the effects supposed to flow from the *Tao,* especially long life and physical immortality. The search for the elixir of life and the philosopher's stone led to much study of ALCHEMY. By the 5th cent. A.D., Taoism was a fully developed religious system with many features adopted from Mahayana BUDDHISM. It offered emotional religious satisfactions for those who found the largely ethical system of Confucianism inadequate. Taoism developed a large pantheon (probably incorporating many local gods), monastic orders, and lay masters. In the 8th cent. there was founded a secular hierarchy, headed by the T'ien Shih [master of heaven]; he claimed succession from Chang Tao-lin, an alchemist of the 2d cent. who was reputed to have discovered the drug of immortality after receiving magical power from Lao-tze. Chinese literature, painting, and calligraphy were greatly influenced by Taoist ideals. Taoism is still practiced to some degree in modern China. Heading the commonly worshiped deities is the Jade Emperor. Directly under him, ruling from Mt. Tai, is the Emperor of the Eastern Mountain, who weighs merits and faults and assigns reward and punishment in this and future existences. Throughout its history Taoism has provided the basis for many Chinese secret societies, and in the 1950s, after the establishment of the Communist regime, Taoism was officially proscribed. See Arthur Waley, *The Way and Its Power* (1935); Holmes Welch, *The Parting of the Way* (rev. ed. 1966); William McNaughton, ed., *The Taoist View* (1971); Yen Lü, *The Secret of the Golden Flower,* ed. by Richard Wilhelm (rev. ed. 1972).

Taormina (täōrmē'nä), town (1971 pop. 9,113), E Sicily, Italy, overlooking the Ionian Sea and at the foot of Mt. Etna. It commands a magificent view and is a world-famous winter resort celebrated for its pleasant climate, natural beauties, and ancient ruins. Known in the 8th cent. B.C. and refounded by Carthaginians in the 4th cent. B.C., Taormina later flourished under the Greeks and then under the Romans. It was taken by the Arabs (early 10th cent.), fell to the Normans (late 11th cent.), and declined after the 15th cent. Of note are the foundations of several Greek temples and a Greek amphitheater (357 ft/109 m in diameter), rebuilt by the Romans, which is the second largest in Sicily. Nearby are ruins of a Roman theater, baths, and reservoirs. Among the many fine Arabic palaces, the Palazzo Corvala (14th cent.) is especially notable. The Convent of San Domenico, with its cloister, is now a fashionable hotel.

Taos (tous), town (1970 pop. 2,475), alt. c.7,000 ft (2,130 m), seat of Taos co., N N.Mex., between the Rio Grande and the Sangre de Cristo Mts.; founded c.1615, inc. 1934. In a region of great beauty and variety, Taos developed as an art colony (principally after 1898) and attracted many painters and writers, notably John Marin and D. H. Lawrence. Today there are artists' organizations and galleries, including the Harwood Foundation (gallery, studios, and school; owned by the Univ. of New Mexico). The town was founded in the early 17th cent. by Spaniards, and its official name is Don Fernando de Taos. For many years Taos was an important Indian and Spanish trading point. It was the center of the Pueblo revolt (1680) and of an anti-American revolt (1847). Places of interest include Kit Carson's house (1825) and grave and the colorful town plaza. The headquarters for Carson National Forest are there, and just south of the town is the adobe farming village of Ranchos de Taos, with the old St. Francis of Assisi Mission (present building dating from 1772). See Mabel Luhan, *Taos and Its Artists* (1947); Eric Sloane, *Return to Taos* (1960); Blanche Grant, *When Old Trails Were New* (1934, repr. 1963).

Taos, pueblo (1970 pop. 1,030), Taos co., N N.Mex., on a branch of the Rio Grande. The inhabitants, Pueblo Indians of the Tanoan linguistic family, raise grain and livestock. In the early 17th cent. Taos became the seat of the Spanish mission of San Gerónimo, but in the Pueblo revolt of 1680 the Indians, led by Popé, destroyed the mission. Taos resisted reconquest by the Spanish until 1696. A second revolt occurred in 1847, when the Indians, incited by Mexicans, killed Gov. Charles Bent. The ancient Pueblo communal dwellings in Taos are considered architectural masterpieces.

T'ao-yuan or **Taoyuan** (both: tou-yüän), city, N Taiwan. Situated in a rich agricultural area, it is a market center for local produce.

Tapachula (täpächo͞o'lä), city (1970 pop. 108,464) Chiapas state, SE Mexico, at the foot of the Chiapas highlands and near the Guatemala border. It is the commercial center of a coffee-growing region and an important transportation link between Mexico and Central America. Ceramics and leather goods are produced by local artisans.

tapa cloth: see BARK CLOTH.

Tapajós (täpäzhôs'), river, c.600 mi (970 km) long, formed at the border of Mato Grosso, Pará, and Amazonas states, central Brazil, by the confluence of the Juruena and Teles Pirez rivers. It flows NE across W Pará into the Amazon River at Santarém. There are many falls and rapids on the river above Itaituba, the head of navigation and an important river port at the junction with the Trans-Amazon Highway.

tape recorder, device for recording information on strips of plastic or paper tape that are coated with fine particles of a magnetic substance, usually an oxide of iron, cobalt, or chromium. The information to be recorded is picked up by the tape recorder through various devices. For example, in an audio tape recorder the MICROPHONE picks up information

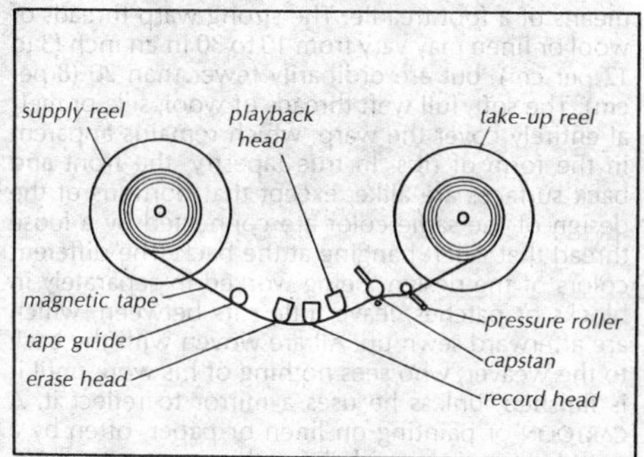

Magnetic tape-recording system

in the form of sound. In all cases the information, once picked up, is transformed into an electric current. The intensity and direction of the current vary according to the information received. The current is fed to a TRANSDUCER in the recording head of the tape recorder, which converts it into corresponding magnetic flux variations that magnetize the particles on the tape. A type of tape recorder is used in electronic computing and data-processing systems for the storage and input of information. See SOUND RECORDING; TELEVISION.

tapestry, hand-woven fabric of plain weave made without shuttle or drawboy, the design of weft threads being threaded into the warp with fingers or a bobbin. The name has been extended to cover a variety of heavy materials, such as imitation tapestries woven on Jacquard looms, tapestry carpets, and upholstery and drapery stuffs. True tapestries include various primitive textiles woven on the rudest of early looms, as well as the famous pictorial hangings of the Middle Ages. Antique specimens include a few surviving from Egypt of 1500 B.C. and Coptic tapestries made from the 4th to 8th cent. A.D. The Incas of Peru produced beautiful specimens, some of which date back to the pre-Columbian era. Ancient Chinese tapestries, *k'o ssu,* were made of light, thin silks, often interwoven with gold thread. Allusions in early Greek poetry and paintings on Greek vases show that tapestry weaving was an important household industry. The history of tapestry weaving is continuous. In the 5th cent. and in the centuries immediately after, monasteries and convents were the centers of the craft. Woolen tapestries appeared early in Europe. A few fragments woven in this material in the 10th or 11th cent. are still preserved. At Arras, early in the 14th cent., the first great French weaving was done, in wool. Soon Brussels achieved prominence and remained important through the 17th cent., until the rise of the GOBELINS works at Paris. By the 15th cent., tapestry weaving had reached a high degree of perfection, and from this century date many great Gothic sets rich with gold thread. A fine specimen is the set of *Burgundian Sacraments;* a late 15th-century example of a verdure background is the *Lady and the Unicorn* set (Musée de Cluny). An example of the Renaissance period is the widely acclaimed set, the *Acts of the Apostles,* from the cartoons of Raphael. Fine weaving was done at Beauvais in the mid-17th cent. Weavers at Aubusson, France, began in the 16th cent. to make an inferior textile that was gradually improved. The baroque style dominated the 17th cent.; the rococo and classical styles appeared in the 18th cent. Fine examples were woven from the cartoons of François Boucher, who worked both for the Beauvais and the Gobelins looms. In England much tapestry, known as Arras, was used before any was manufactured there. In the 16th cent. William Sheldon set up works in Warwickshire. An establishment in imitation of the Gobelins was opened at Mortlake in 1619 and employed Flemish weavers. In 1881, William Morris began weaving at Merton; his friend Edward Burne-Jones designed some of Morris's series. In 1893 tapestry looms were set up in New York City. Some interesting 20th-century tapestries have been woven in France from cartoons by Rouault, Braque, Lurçat, Picasso, and Calder. Important public collections in the United States are those in the Metropolitan Museum (including the magnificent *Hunt of the Unicorn* series at the Cloisters) and in the Museum of Fine Arts, Boston. The techniques for high- and low-warp work (*haute-lisse* and *basse-lisse*) differ; both were used in the 14th cent. In a high-warp loom the threads are stretched vertically in front of the weaver, and the *lisses* or loops which raise the alternate threads to make the shed are lifted by hand; in low-warp work, the warp threads are horizontal, and the *lisses* are moved by means of a foot treadle. The strong warp threads of wool or linen may vary from 10 to 30 in an inch (3 to 12 per cm), but are ordinarily fewer than 20 (8 per cm). The soft, full weft threads of wool, silk, or metal entirely cover the warp, which remains apparent in the form of ribs. In true tapestry, the front and back surfaces are alike, except that portions of the design of the same color are connected by a loose thread that is left hanging at the back. The different colors of the design, being worked in separately in blocks or patches, leave little slits between, which are afterward sewn up. All are woven with the back to the weaver, who sees nothing of his work until it is finished, unless he uses a mirror to reflect it. A CARTOON or painting on linen or paper, often by a noted artist, is provided for the weaver to copy. Themes for medieval hangings were drawn from ancient legends, mythology, allegory, history, religion, chivalry, and sport. The so-called BAYEUX TAPESTRY was actually embroidered. See Phyllis Ackerman, *Tapestry, the Mirror of Civilization* (1933); Madeleine Jarry, *World Tapestry* (1969).

tapeworm, name for the parasitic flatworms forming the class Cestoda. All tapeworms spend the adult phase of their lives as parasites in the gut of a vertebrate animal (called the primary host). Most tapeworms spend part of their life cycle in the tissues of one or more other animals (called intermediate hosts), which may be vertebrates or arthropods. An adult tapeworm consists of a knoblike head, or scolex, equipped with hooks for attaching to the intestinal wall of the host (which may be a human), a neck region, and a series of flat, rectangular body segments, or proglottids, generated by the neck. The chain of proglottids may reach a length of 15 or 20 ft (4.6–6.1 m). Terminal proglottids break off and are excreted in the feces of the host, but new ones are constantly formed at the anterior end of the worm. As long as the scolex and neck are intact the worm is alive and capable of growth. A rudimentary nervous system and excretory system run the length of the worm, through the proglottids. However, there is no digestive tract; the worm absorbs the host's digested food through its cuticle, or outer covering. Each proglottid contains a complete set of male and female reproductive organs that produce the sex cells. Fertilization is internal; in most species cross fertilization between two adjacent worms is necessary, but in a few species self-fertilization may occur between two proglottids of the same worm, or within the same proglottid. In some species the fertilized eggs are shed continuously and leave the host's body in the feces; in others the fertilized eggs are stored until the proglottid is filled with them and the entire proglottid is then shed. The eggs develop into embryos with a hard outer shell; these do not hatch until they are eaten by a suitable intermediate host. In the case of the human tapeworm most common in the United States (the beef tapeworm, *Taenia saginata*) the usual intermediate host is a cow, which ingests the proglottid while drinking or grazing. The round-bodied embryos, equipped with sharp hooks, hatch and bore through the cow's intestinal wall into the blood stream, where they are carried to the muscles. Here each embryo encloses itself in a cyst, or bladder; at this stage it is called a bladder worm. During the bladder worm stage the embryo develops into a miniature scolex; it remains encysted until the muscle is eaten by a primary host, in this case a human. If the scolex has not been killed by sufficient cooking of the meat, it sheds its covering and attaches to the intestinal wall, where it begins producing proglottids. A human tapeworm common in Mexico, the pork tapeworm (*T. solium*), has a similar life cycle, with a pig as the usual intermediate host. The fish tapeworm, *Diphyllobothrium latum,* transmitted to humans from fish, especially pike, is common in the Orient and in Canada and the northern lake regions of the United States. This tapeworm has a more elaborate life cycle, involving both a fish and a crustacean as intermediate hosts. The dwarf tapeworm, *Hymenolepsis nana,* is transmitted through fecal contamination and is common in children in the SE United States. Intestinal tapeworm infestation frequently occurs without symptoms; occasionally there is abdominal discomfort, diarrhea, constipation, or weight loss. The presence of tapeworm proglottids in clothing, bedding, or feces is the usual sign of infestation. Treatment is with quinacrine hydrochloride (Atabrine) or niclosamide, which kill the worm. The most serious tapeworm infestation in humans is caused by the ingestion of *T. solanum* eggs through fecal contamination, which results in the person serving as the intermediate, rather than the primary, host. The embryos migrate throughout the body, producing serious illness if they lodge in the central nervous system. There are several tapeworms for whom man is the usual intermediate host: Among these, the dog tapeworm, *Echinococcus granulosis,* spends its adult phase in the intestines of dogs and its embryos encyst in various internal organs of humans, commonly in the liver. The cysts produced by these embryos are of a type called hydatid cysts, and the infestation of the liver is called hydatid disease. Human tapeworm infestations are most common in regions where there is fecal contamination of soil and water and where meat and fish are eaten raw or lightly cooked. Tapeworms are classified in the phylum PLATYHELMINTHES, class Cestoda.

Taphath (tā'făth), Solomon's daughter who married one of his officers. 1 Kings 4.11.

tapioca (tăpēō'kə), widely used starchy food, obtained from the fleshy root of the bitter CASSAVA. Tapioca is sold in flake or flour form and as the pellet pearl tapioca. Tapioca flour is widely used in place of wheat flour in regions where it is grown, e.g., South and Central America, Africa, the West Indies, and parts of India. When cooked it becomes transparent and increases in size. It is used to thicken puddings and soups.

tapir (tā'pər), nocturnal, herbivorous mammal, genus *Tapirus,* of the jungles of Central and South America and SE Asia. The tapir is somewhat piglike in appearance; however, it is not related to the pig, but to the horse and the hippopotamus, with which it forms the order of odd-toed hoofed mammals. The body of the tapir is rounded and covered with sparse fur. Its snout is long and flexible. The legs are short and end in broad feet with hoofed toes; there are four toes on the front feet and five on the hind feet. Tapirs live in dense forest, browsing by night on leaves and twigs. Usually found near water, they swim well and drink a great deal. They often take to water when threatened and can crash through thick underbrush with great speed. The Asian tapir, *Tapirus indicus,* of Malaya and Sumatra, is black with a white saddle extending over the rump. The adult is about 3 ft (90 cm) high at the shoulder and 6 to 8 ft (180–240 cm) long; it weighs about 400 lb (180 kg). There are three New World species. The South American tapir, *T. terrestris,* inhabits marshy lowlands from Colombia to N Argentina. The adult, similar in size to the Asian species, is a uniform dark brown, but the young is conspicuously striped and spotted. The Central American tapir, *T. bairdi,* is similarly colored but almost as large as a donkey. It is found in undisturbed rain forests from S Mexico to NW South America; because of the continuous elimination of this habitat the existence of this species is threatened. The mountain tapir, *T. pinchaque,* is found at high altitudes in the Andes Mts. and has thick, black fur. Tapirs were widely distributed in tropical regions until the Pleistocene epoch, when most species became extinct. They are classified in the phylum CHORDATA, subphylum Vertebrata, class Mammalia, order Perissodactyla, family Tapiridae.

Tappan, Arthur (tăp'ən), 1786–1865, American abolitionist, b. Northampton, Mass. He made a fortune in the dry-goods business in New York City and with his brother and partner Lewis Tappan gave generously of his time and money to various causes, especially to the antislavery movement. He contributed to the establishment of Kenyon and Oberlin colleges in Ohio, was elected (1833) the first president of the American Anti-Slavery Society, and, after splitting with William Lloyd Garrison, helped organize (1840) and became president of the American and Foreign Anti-Slavery Society. See biography by Lewis Tappan (1870).

Tappan, Lewis, 1788–1873, American abolitionist, b. Northampton, Mass. He became a partner in his brother Arthur's New York mercantile house in 1828 and in 1841 founded the first agency for rating commercial credit in the United States. Lewis held important offices in several antislavery societies and was a delegate to the World Anti-Slavery Convention in London in 1843. He retired from business in 1849 to devote himself exclusively to humanitarian work, mostly for the Negro cause. He wrote a biography of his brother (1870). See study by Bertram Wyatt-Brown (1968).

Tappuah (tăpyōō'ə). **1** Son of Hebron and eponym of BETH-TAPPUAH. 1 Chron. 2.43. **2** Border town of Manasseh, probably c.5 mi (8.1 km) NW of Shiloh. Joshua 16.8; 17.8. En-tappuah: Joshua 17.7. **3** Unidentified town, perhaps the same as Beth-tappuah or as **2.** Joshua 12.17. See also TIPHSAH.

tar: see TAR AND PITCH.

Tara (târ'ə), village, Co. Meath, E Republic of Ireland. The Hill of Tara (507 ft/155 m high) was the seat of the high kings of Ireland from ancient times until the 6th cent. and may have been the site of religious ceremonies in prehistoric times. A statue of St. Patrick, who preached there, is supposed to mark the location of the Lia Fail, the Coronation Stone of the ancient high kings (see under CORONATION). There are six raths (earthwork enclosures), the largest of which is 850 ft (259 m) in diameter. The hill was the scene of the defeat of the Danes in 980 and the Irish insurgents in 1798, and of a mass meeting in 1843 addressed by Daniel O'Connell; hence its importance as a symbol of Irish nationalism.

Tarabulus: see TRIPOLI, Lebanon.

Tarah (tā'rə), unlocated desert resting place. Num. 33.27.

Tarahumara Indians (tärăōōmä'rä), Indian tribe of N Mexico, mostly in Chihuahua state. About 50,000 members strong, they live for the most part in the barren wilderness of the Sierra Madre Occidental, subsisting largely on hunting and on rudimentary agriculture. They are renowned for their ability to run down deer and horses, but are known chiefly for their religious practices, in which consumption of the peyote cactus figures prominently. The visions and ecstasies produced by mescalin, the active ingredient of this plant, are the culmination of Tarahumara ceremonies. The Mexican poet Alfonso Reyes dedicated to the Tarahumara one of his finest works, *Yerbas del Tarahumara* (1934; tr. *Tarahumara Herbs,* 1958). See Wendell C. Bennett and Robert M. Zingg, *The Tarahumara* (1935); C. W. Pennington, *The Tarahumar of Mexico* (1963, repr. 1969).

Taralah (târ'ələ, tərā'lə), unidentified town, N of Jerusalem. Joshua 18.27.

tar and pitch, viscous, dark-brown to black substances obtained by the destructive distillation of coal, wood, petroleum, peat, and certain other organic materials. The heating or partial burning of wood to make charcoal yields tar as a by-product and is an ancient method for the production of both tar and pitch. COAL TAR is a residue in the manufacture of coal gas and coke. By the application of heat, tar is separated into several materials, one of which is pitch. The terms *tar* and *pitch* are loosely applied to the many varieties of the two substances, sometimes interchangeably. For example, asphalt, which is naturally occurring pitch, is called mineral tar and mineral pitch. Tar is more or less fluid, depending upon its origin and the temperature to which it is exposed. Pitch tends to be more solid. When ships were made of wood, tar had numerous uses, and an available supply of tar was an important factor in maritime growth. Tar made vessels watertight and protected their ropes from deterioration. All but small quantities of the tar now produced is fractionally distilled to yield naphtha, creosote, carbolic oil, and other equally important crude products. Among the substances produced by refining the various crude materials are benzene, toluene, cresol, and phenol. Tar from pine wood is used in making soap and medicinal preparations. Pitch is used in the manufacture of roofing paper, in varnishes, as a lubricant, and as a binder for coal dust in the making of briquettes used as fuel. Coal-tar derivatives are used in the manufacture of dyes, cosmetics, and synthetic flavoring extracts.

tarantella (târ'əntĕl'ə), Neapolitan folk dance that first appeared in Taranto, Italy, in the 17th cent. It had rapid 6-8 meter with an increasing tempo and was thought to cure the bite of the tarantula, which supposedly caused the disease tarantism. Chopin, Liszt, Weber, and others used the dance in the form of a *perpetuum mobile.*

Taranto (tä'räntō), Lat. *Tarentum,* city (1971 pop. 222,826), capital of Taranto prov., Apulia, S Italy, on the Gulf of Taranto, an arm of the Ionian Sea. Taranto is, after La Spezia, the chief military port of Italy, and it is also an agricultural, industrial, and fishing center. Manufactures include chemicals, machinery, and ships. Founded by colonists from Sparta in the 8th cent. B.C., Taranto was a town of MAGNA GRAECIA and was powerful enough to resist the Romans until 272 B.C. It was destroyed (927) by the Arabs but was later rebuilt by the Byzantines. As a part of the kingdom of Naples the city was strongly fortified and was held as a principality by various lords. Its harbor, protected by the Italian fleet, was bombed several times in World War II. Of note in Taranto are the cathedral (11th-12th cent., with a baroque facade), a castle (originally Byzantine, rebuilt in 1480), and the national museum (with a fine collection of Greek pottery).

tarantula (tərăn'chələ), name applied chiefly to several species of the large, hairy SPIDERS of the families Theraphosidae and Dipluridae of N, central, and S America. The body of a tarantula may be as much as 3 in. (7.6 cm) long and, with legs extended, as much as 10 in. (25.4 cm) across. The N American tarantula, *Dugesiella hentzi,* has a leg spread of up to 6 in. (15.2 cm) and is common in parts of the SW United States. The largest tarantulas may kill small vertebrates, but their usual food is other arthropods. The bite of a tarantula may be painful but is not usually dangerous to humans. Some Asian spiders are also called tarantulas, and there is a tailless whip scorpion genus *Tarantula.* Originally the name was applied to a spider of the wolf spider family, *Lycosa tarentula,* of S Europe, whose bite was supposed to cause tarantism, a nervous condition characterized by hysteria; the best cure was believed to be strenuous and prolonged dancing of the tarantella. Spider families are classified in the phylum ARTHROPODA, class Arachnida, order Araneae.

Tarascan (tərä'skən), Indian people of the state of Michoacán, Mexico. Their language has no known relation to other languages. The ancient Tarascan people had a sophisticated political system, and ruins of their settlements date from 500 B.C. They had a rather highly developed civilization by the time the Spanish arrived. The Aztecs were unable to conquer the Tarascan warriors, and the Spanish had difficulty in subjugating them. On the shore of Lake PÁTZCUARO was their capital and chief stronghold, Tzintzuntzan [place of the hummingbirds]. In the chapel of the present village of Tzintzuntzan is Titian's *Entombment,* presented to the Tarascan by Charles V. Peculiar to their culture were T-shaped tombs, rising in terraces and faced with stone slabs without mortar. When the Spanish arrived, the Tarascan were skilled in weaving and famous for their feathered mosaics made from hummingbird plumage. The Tarascan still are noted for weaving, embroidery, and especially lacquerware, and their music has had an important influence on the folk music of Mexico. They work today as craftsmen, farmers, and as migrant workers in the United States. There are some 60,000 speakers of the Tarascan language in Michoacán. See R. A. M. van Zantwijk, *Servants of the Saints* (1967); Maurice Boyd, *Tarascan Myths and Legends* (1969).

Tarawa (tərä'wə, tăr'əwä), atoll (1968 pop. 12,642), capital of the British colony of the GILBERT AND ELLICE ISLANDS, central Pacific. Tarawa is the chief commercial center of the group and a port of entry through which copra, pearl shell, and phosphates are exported. It is the site of a government hospital and a leper station. During World War II the colony headquarters were moved there from OCEAN ISLAND. Tarawa was occupied by the Japanese (1941-43) and fell to U.S. Marines after a bitter and bloody battle. The population is mainly Micronesian.

Tarawera Mountain (tä"räwâr'ə), volcanic peak, 3,646 ft (1,111 m) high, on North Island, New Zealand, in the Hot Springs District. Its eruption in 1886 destroyed Lake Rotomahana, which contained unusual terraces formed by silica deposits.

Tarbagatai: see T'A-CH'ENG, China.

Tarbell, Ida Minerva, 1857-1944, American author, b. Erie co., Pa., grad. Allegheny College (B.A., 1880; M.A., 1883). One of the leading MUCKRAKERS, she is remembered for her investigations of industry published in *McClure's* magazine. Some of them were collected in her *History of the Standard Oil Company* (1904). She also wrote *Life of Abraham Lincoln* (1900), other books on Lincoln, and biographies of Elbert H. Gary (1925) and Owen D. Young (1932). Her economic studies culminated in *The Nationalizing of Business, 1878-1898* (1936). See her autobiography, *All in the Day's Work* (1939).

Tarbes (tärb), city (1968 pop. 59,432), capital of Hautes-Pyrénées dept., SW France, on the Adour River. It is an industrial, commercial, and tourist center in a cattle- and horse-raising area. In addition to the traditional forging and leather industries, there are machinery and electrical-equipment manufactures. The city was called Bigorra in Roman times and was later the capital of the earldom of Bigorre. In the 6th cent. it became an episcopal see. Invaded and destroyed many times in the course of its history, Tarbes was joined to the French crown in the 16th cent. In the city are the Cathedral of Notre-Dame-de-la-Sède (13th-15th cent.), the churches of St. Jean and St. Thérèse (13th cent.), and the base of a tower of an old castle built by the counts of Bigorre. Théophile Gautier and Marshal Ferdinand Foch were born in Tarbes.

Tarde, Gabriel de (gäbrēĕl' də tärd), 1843-1904, French sociologist and criminologist. During his years of public service as a magistrate, he became interested in the psychosocial bases of crime. In *Penal Philosophy* (1890, tr. 1912) and other early works he criticized the concept of the atavistic criminal as developed by Cesare LOMBROSO. Later he formulated a general social theory, distinguishing between inventive and imitative persons. Among his works are *On Communication and Social Influence* (tr. 1969) and *The Laws of Imitation* (1890, tr. 1903).

Tardenoisian: see MESOLITHIC PERIOD.

Tardieu, André (äNdrā' tärdyö'), 1876-1945, French statesman and journalist. He became (1905) chief political editor of the *Temps,* was elected (1914) a deputy, and was named minister (1919-20) of the liberated regions (Alsace and Lorraine) after World War I. As French plenipotentiary at the Paris Peace Conference (1919), he took an important part in negotiations leading to the Treaty of Versailles. Between 1926 and 1934 he held several cabinet posts and was three times premier (1929-30, 1930, 1932). A conservative and a nationalist, Tardieu championed the French demand for security from German aggression. He resigned as deputy in 1936 and agitated for vigorous action against German aggression and for a strong government. Although Tardieu never retained office long, he endured as a power behind the scenes and greatly influenced the policies of the rightist parties. He also wrote many political works. See Rudolph Binion, *Defeated Leaders* (1960).

tare (târ), name sometimes used as a synonym for any VETCH, most frequently for the common vetch. The tare of the Scriptures, a weed of grainfields and considered a seed of evil, is thought to have been the unrelated darnel (see RYE GRASS).

Tarea (tərē'ə), variant of TAHREA.

Tarentum: see TARANTO, Italy.

Targum (tär'gəm) [Aramaic,=translation], Aramaic paraphrase of the Old Testament. When Aramaic replaced the Hebrew tongue among the Jews of Palestine and Babylon, interpreters were called to translate and explain the scriptural passages that were read aloud during synagogue services. The oral Aramaic paraphrases were, in the course of time, put down in writing under the name Targum. One of the best-known Targums extant is the Targum Onkelos (see ONKELOS). The Targum is printed in the margin of corresponding parts of the Bible. A complete manuscript of a Palestinian Targum, the first of its kind, was found in 1956.

Tarifa (tärē'fä), town (1970 pop. 15,833), Cádiz prov., S Spain, in Andalusia. A minor seaport on the Strait of Gibraltar, it is the southernmost city of the European mainland. It was founded by the Greeks and later became the first Roman colony in Spain. The Berber leader Tarik captured it in 711. Tarifa is named after Tarif, another Berber chief.

tariff, tax on imported and, more rarely, exported goods. It is also called a customs duty. Tariffs may be distinguished from other taxes in that their predominant purpose is not financial but economic—not to increase a nation's revenue but to protect domestic industries from foreign competition. For that reason, protective tariffs, as they are often called, are opposed by advocates of FREE TRADE. Tariffs have been used by governments since ancient times, although they were originally meant to be sources of revenue rather than instruments of state economic policy. Such early customs duties consisted of payments for the use of trade and transportation facilities, including ports, markets, streets, and bridges. By the 17th cent., however, they came to be levied only at the boundary of a country and usually only on imports. At the same time, European powers established special low tariff rates for trade with their possessions; such systems of colonial preference formed the basis of the trading patterns that developed in the 17th and 18th cent. (see MERCANTILISM and NAVIGATION ACTS). Although the free trade movement in the early 19th cent. discouraged the use of tariffs, a new system of trade relations known as imperial preference developed in the late 19th cent. Great Britain and France, in particular, used preferential tariffs to organize the flow of foodstuffs and raw materials from their colonial dependencies and to regulate the export of domestic manufactured products into those areas. Other European nations retaliated by raising their tariffs, and a period of relatively high protective tariffs lasting through the Great Depression followed. Since World War II the trend has been away from tariffs and in favor of freer trade. Through instruments such as the MOST-FAVORED-NATION CLAUSE and the RECIPROCAL TRADE AGREEMENT, two nations may agree to lower their respective tariff barriers. More comprehensive agreements, such as the European Common Market and other customs unions, lower or even eliminate tariffs among large groups of nations. Finally, the General Agreement on Tariffs and Trade (GATT) has sponsored a number of initiatives since the 1950s that have been responsible for lowering the customs duties of most major trading nations. The United States has participated in the movement toward freer trade by gradually lowering its customs duties from the high rates of the Hawley-Smoot Tariff Act (1930) and by playing an instrumental role in many GATT tariff initiatives, especially the Dillon (1962) and Kennedy (1967) rounds of multilateral tariff reductions. Those customs duties that are still imposed are usually either one of two types—specific duty, a tax levied on the quantity, whether by weight, size, or number, of the goods; or ad valorem duty, a percentage of the foreign or domestic price. The ad valorem duty is generally considered to be preferable but more difficult to levy, requiring complex procedures to determine the value of goods. Specific duties are best applied for protectionist purposes, since their size varies inversely with the prices of imports. For example, an import taxed at $5 per ton, and costing $100 per ton, has an effective duty of 5%. However, if its price drops to $80 per ton—a threat to domestic producers—the good will have an effective duty of more than 6%. Certain tariffs are also designed to offset DUMPING. See also PROTECTION. See Jagdish Bhagwati, *Trade, Tariffs, and Growth* (1969); T. B. Curtis, *The Kennedy Round and the Future of American Trade* (1971); H. G. Johnson, *Aspects of the Theory of Tariffs* (1971); G. C. Reeves, *Tariff Preferences for Developing Countries* (1971).

Tariff Commission, United States, independent agency of the U.S. government established in 1916; it is charged with serving the President and Congress as an advisory, fact-finding agency on tariff, commercial-policy, and foreign-trade problems. Earlier tariff agencies had a definite policy of PROTECTION; the 1916 commission was considered the first truly unbiased agency and as such was empowered to suggest to the President such adjustments of rates as its investigations might prove to be desirable. The commission not only advises on the possible effects of pending trade agreements or tariff legislation, but under the Trade Expansion Act of 1962 it investigates alleged damage to a domestic industry of trade agreements in effect. Upon a finding of damage, the President may grant tariff relief or other aid to that industry. If the Secretary of the Treasury determines that a foreign nation or industry is DUMPING a class of imported merchandise, and the commission determines that such sales adversely affect a domestic industry, the Secretary can impose a "dumping duty" on such imports. The U.S. Tariff Commission consists of six members appointed by the President and confirmed by the Senate for terms of six years.

Tarija (tärē'hä), city (1969 est. pop. 23,300), alt. 6,421 ft (1,957 m), capital of Tarija dept., S Bolivia. Tarija lies in a fertile valley in the eastern watershed of the Andes near the oil fields of the Chaco. Lack of communications has retarded commercial growth, but the rich soil and moderate climate have made Tarija famous for vineyards and orchards that grow olives, pears, peaches, and apples. The city was founded in 1574.

Tarik ibn Ziyad (tä'rĭk), fl. 711, Berber leader of the Muslim invaders of Spain. When the heirs of the Visigothic king, Witiza, requested help from the Moors of N Africa against the usurper RODERICK, Tarik, with his Moorish army, crossed (711) from Africa to Gibraltar (originally named for him, in Arabic, Jebel-al-Tarik; i.e., Tarik's mountain). Tarik defeated Roderick in the same year in the battle of Guadalete, but he did not restore Witiza's heirs. Instead, he sent for African reinforcements and conquered most of the Iberian Peninsula within a few years. Thus began the Moorish domination of Spain, which was not fully ended until 1492.

Tarim (dārēm'), Mandarin *Ta-yen*, chief river of Sinkiang Uigur Autonomous Region, NW China, c.1,300 mi (2,090 km) long, formed by the union of the Kashgar and the Yarkand rivers at the western end of the Takla Makan desert, and flowing generally east, along the northern edge of the desert, to Lo-pu po (Lop Nor), a salt lake. Yarkand is the region's largest city. The river, which is silt-laden, gives its name to the arid Tarim basin, a great depression, c.800 mi (1,290 km) long and 400 mi (640 km) wide, surrounded by the lofty Tien Shan, Kunlun, and Pamir mountains; the Takla Makan occupies most of the basin. About 75% of Sinkiang's population live in the basin's oases. China's nuclear testing center is located at the eastern end of the Tarim basin, near Lo-pu po. The important Silk Road between China and Europe passed through the basin.

Tarkington, Booth (Newton Booth Tarkington), 1869–1946, American author, b. Indianapolis. His most characteristic and popular works were his genial novels of life in small Middle Western towns, including *The Gentleman from Indiana* (1899), *The Conquest of Canaan* (1905), and the trilogy *Growth* (1927), made up of *Turmoil* (1915), *The Magnificent Ambersons* (1918; Pulitzer Prize), and *The Midlander* (1923). *Alice Adams* (1921; Pulitzer Prize), considered by some his best novel, tells of the frustrated ambitions of a romantic lower-middle-class girl. He wrote several amusing novels of boyhood and adolescence, the most notable being *Penrod* (1914) and *Seventeen* (1916). His plays include a dramatization of his own historical romance *Monsieur Beaucaire* (1901) and *Clarence* (1921). See his reminiscences, *The World Does Move* (1928); biography by J. L. Woodress (1955, repr. 1969); study by K. J. Fennimore (1974).

Tarkwa (tär kwä'), town (1970 pop. 13,545), S Ghana. It is an administrative and commercial center and the headquarters of the State Gold Mining Corporation. Gold ore is mined nearby, and gold is extracted in Tarkwa, which also has a glass factory. Tarkwa School of Mines (1953) is in the town. One of the world's largest manganese mines is located nearby, in Nsuta.

Tarleton, Sir Banastre (bă'nəstər tärl'tən), 1754–1833, British army officer in the American Revolution. He arrived (1775) in America with General Cornwallis and was a member of the patrol that captured Gen. Charles Lee at Basking Ridge, N.J. He served with William Howe at Brandywine, Germantown, and Philadelphia. Tarleton went to Carolina as leader of a mixed force of cavalry and infantry and distinguished himself at Charleston and in the CAROLINA CAMPAIGN before he was overwhelmed by Daniel Morgan at Cowpens. After the battle of Guilford Courthouse, he retreated into Virginia and was active in the YORKTOWN CAMPAIGN. Tarleton returned (1782) to England and served (1790–1806, 1807–12) in Parliament. He wrote *A History of the Campaigns of 1780 and 1781 in the Southern Provinces of North America* (1787). See R. D. Bass, *The Green Dragon* (1957).

Tarlton, Richard, d. 1588, Elizabethan actor and clown. One of the Queen's Men, he gained fame for his improvised jests, jigs, and doggerel. A collection of anecdotes, *Tarlton's Jests* (pub. 1592?–1611?), is attributed to him. He is thought to have been the model for the jester Yorick described in *Hamlet*.

Tarn (tärn), department (1968 pop. 332,011), S France, in Languedoc. ALBI is the capital.

Tarn, river, c.235 mi (380 km) long, rising in the Cévennes mts., S France, and flowing southwest before emptying into the Garonne River. Deep gorges and canyons formed by the river are tourist attractions.

Tarn-et-Garonne (tärn-ā-gärôn'), department (1968 pop. 175,800), SW France. MONTAUBAN is the capital.

Tarnopol: see TERNOPOL, USSR.

Tarnów (tär' no͞of), city (1970 pop. 85,514), SE Poland. It is a railway junction and a leading center for the manufacture of basic chemicals and fertilizers. Settled by the 12th cent., Tarnów was chartered in 1330. It passed to Austria in 1772 and reverted to Poland after World War I. Its most notable landmark is the Gothic cathedral (built c.1393), which contains tombs that are regarded as among Poland's finest Renaissance treasures.

Tarnowskie Góry (tärnôf'skyĕ go͞o'rĭ), town (1970 pop. 34,300), S Poland. It is an industrial center where machinery, mining and railway equipment, and chemicals are produced. Nearby are coal, zinc, and lead mines. Chartered in 1526, the town passed from Germany to Poland after World War I.

taro: see ARUM.

tarots (târ'ōz), playing cards that are used mainly for fortunetelling, sometimes called "the book of divination of the gypsies." It is generally believed that the cards were introduced into Western Europe by the gypsies in the mid-15th cent. There is much conjecture about their origin. The pack of 78 cards is divided into the minor arcana, or 56 pictorial cards that roughly resemble the modern deck of 52 cards: wands (clubs), cups (hearts), swords (spades), and pentacles (diamonds). Each of the four suits comprises 14 cards, 10 numbered from ace to 10 and 4 court cards—king, queen, knight, and page. The 22 additional pictorial cards, called the major arcana, are numbered from zero to 21. The pictures on the 78 cards are allegorical, representing forces of nature and the virtues or vices of man. Interpretations and ways of determining the meanings of the cards vary greatly. See Eden Gray, *A Complete Guide to the Tarot* (1971); Alfred Douglas, *The Tarot* (1972).

tarpan: see PRZEWALSKI'S HORSE.

Tarpeia (tärpē'yə), in Roman legend, a Roman woman who betrayed her city to the Sabines for what they wore on their left arms (their gold bracelets). As they entered Rome they crushed her under a mound of shields, which they also wore on their left arms. The Tarpeian rock at Rome, from which criminals were thrown to death, bears her name.

Tarpelites (tär'pēlīts), people of Samaria. Ezra 4.9.

tarpon (tär'pŏn), common name for members of the family Elopidae, large herringlike game fish of the warm seas of the Western Hemisphere, ranging occasionally from Long Island to Brazil and to the west coast of Africa and entering freshwater streams freely. Their heavy, silvery scales, sometimes used as ornaments, give them the name silver king. Tarpons average 6 ft (183 cm) in length and 150 lb (67.5 kg) in weight, although some may be over 8 ft (244 cm) long and weigh more than 300 lb (135 kg). Active and predacious, they prey on schools of small fry. They are favorites of deep-sea fishermen, particularly *Tarpon atlanticus,* found in the warmer parts of the Atlantic Ocean. Tarpons are classified in the phylum CHORDATA, subphylum Vertebrata, class Osteichthyes, order Clupeiformes, family Elopidae.

Tarquin (tär'kwĭn) [Etruscan,=lord], in Roman tradition, an Etruscan family that ruled Rome. According to the historian Livy, when the rule of the Bacchiadae in Corinth was overthrown (c.657 B.C.) by the tyrant Cypselus, Demaratus, a Corinthian noble, migrated to Tarquinii, Etruria, where he married into one of the leading Etruscan families and had two sons, Aruns and Lucumo. Lucumo married Tanaquil, a daughter of the Etruscan aristocracy and a prophetess of high repute. At her urging he went to Rome, became a citizen, and took the name **Lucius Tarquinius Priscus**. He rose to high position, and on the death of ANCUS MARTIUS (c.616 B.C.) he either seized the Roman throne or was elected to it by a coalition of Etruscan families. Priscus fought successfully against the Sabines and subjugated all Latium to Rome. He is credited with the building of the first Circus Maximus and the Forum. During his reign Etruscan influences appeared in Roman politics, religion, and art. After a reign of 38 years he was assassinated by the sons of Ancus Martius, who were involved in a patrician plot attempting to limit the kingship to a religious role only. Through the influence of Priscus' wife, Tanaquil, the plot was halted and the kingship passed to Servius Tullius, Priscus' son-in-law. After a reign of 44 years, Tullius was murdered by Priscus' son **Lucius Tarquinius Superbus** (Tarquin the Proud), who thereupon seized the throne. Under his rule Etruscan influence was at its height, and the power of the monarchy was absolute. Despised by the people for his tyranny, he sought to win favor by successful wars but was deposed (510 B.C.) by the senate. The romantic reason traditionally given for the deposition of Tarquin was the rape of Lucretia (see LUCRECE) by his son **Sextus Tarquinius**. After the subsequent suicide of Lucretia, her husband, **Lucius Tarquinius Collatinus**, and the Brutus family (to which Lucretia belonged) raised a rebellion. Lucius Junius Brutus and Collatinus were elected consuls, and Tarquin fled north and appealed to Etruria to restore him to his throne. An army under LARS PORSENA marched against the Romans, and Rome (contrary to Roman historical accounts) was forced to surrender and to yield a large amount of territory. The two sons of Lucius Junius Brutus (see under BRUTUS), in opposition to the policy of their father, headed a conspiracy within Rome to restore Tarquin, but it failed. Porsena did not restore the Tarquin monarchy, and although Rome was seriously weakened, Etruscan supremacy there was at an end. While scholars have tended to reject the entire Tarquin legend, some have recently begun to accept a tentative and modified account of the story. The history of the Tarquins was probably distorted by anti-Etruscan propaganda among the Romans, who resented the Etruscan overlords dominant in Rome from the 8th to the 6th cent. B.C.

Tarquinii (tärkwĭn'ēī), ancient city of Etruria, central Italy, NW of Rome. The head of the Etruscan League, it was defeated in wars with Rome in the 4th cent. B.C. In the 3d cent. B.C. it lost its independence. Tarquinii continued to exist far into the Christian era and was sacked by the Arabs. After the 9th cent. A.D. it was superseded by nearby Corneto, which is now called Tarquinia and has a museum with Etruscan antiquities. Much knowledge of Etruscan life has been gained from paintings on the walls of tombs in the necropolis of Tarquinii.

tarragon (târ'əgŏn), perennial aromatic Old World herb (*Artemisia dracunculus*) of the family Compositae (COMPOSITE family), of the same genus as wormwood and sagebrush. It has long been cultivated in Europe and W Asia for its leaves, used for flavoring vinegar, salads, sauces, soups, and pickles. Its essential oil, sometimes called estragon, is occasionally used in perfume or, in the Old World, medicinally to stimulate appetite or as a diuretic. Tarragon is classified in the division MAGNOLIOPHYTA, class Magnoliopsida, order Asterales, family Compositae.

Tarragona (tärägō'nä), city (1970 pop. 78,238), capital of Tarragona prov., NE Spain, in Catalonia, on the Mediterranean Sea at the mouth of the Francolí River. A port and commercial center, it has a large wine export. An Iberian town, ancient Tarraco was captured (218 B.C.) by the Romans in the Second Punic War, and was fortified by them against Carthage. Augustus made it the capital of the vast Spanish province of Tarraconensis. It became a flourishing commercial center; among the important Roman remains are ruins of its ancient walls and a well-preserved aqueduct. Having fallen to the Visigoths (5th cent.) and to the Moors (8th cent.), Tarragona was recovered in the early 12th cent. for Christian Spain, but it declined when its trade was captured by Barcelona and Valencia. The city was one of the last (1939) to be captured by General Franco during the civil war. The construction of a modern port has given it new importance. Besides its Roman ruins, Tarragona has remnants of pre-Roman walls. The imposing Romanesque-Gothic cathedral has one of the finest cloisters (13th cent.) in Spain. Near the cathedral are the archiepiscopal palace and the archaeological museum. The Carthusian monks expelled (1903) from the Grande Chartreuse in France settled in the city and continue to produce their famous liqueur. There is a pontifical university in Tarragona.

Tarrasa (tärä'sä), town (1970 pop. 138,697), Barcelona prov., NE Spain, in Catalonia. It is an industrial town, long famous for its woolen textiles. The town dates back to Roman days. It has a textile school and a textile museum.

Tarrytown (târ'ētoun), village (1970 pop. 11,115), Westchester co., SE N.Y., a residential suburb of New York City, on the E bank of the Hudson opposite Nyack; settled in the 17th cent. by Dutch, inc. 1870. Precision instruments are manufactured, and there are industrial research centers and an automobile assembly plant in the village. Tarrytown is the eastern terminus of the Tappan Zee Bridge and the seat of Marymount College. Of interest are Sunnyside, the home of Washington Irving; Sleepy Hollow cemetery; Philipseburg Manor, an estate including a Dutch farmhouse (c.1683) and a restored operating gristmill; and Lyndhurst (1838), a Gothic Revival mansion once owned by Jay Gould overlooking the Hudson.

Tarshish (tär'shĭsh). **1** Eponym of a country distant from Palestine. It is traditional to identify the country Tarshish with Spain, especially with the region and city of Tartessus, a Phoenician settlement of S Spain. Some scholars suggest that the biblical "ships of Tarshish" were cargo ships that served metal-manufacturing centers on the Mediterranean coast. Gen. 10.4; 1 Chron. 1.7; Ps 48.7; Jonah 1.3. Tharshish: 1 Kings 22.48. **2** Counselor of Ahasuerus. Esther 1.14. **3** Benjamite. 1 Chron. 7.10.

tarsia: see INTARSIA.

tarsier (tär'sēər), small, nocturnal, forest-dwelling primate, genus *Tarsien.* The three species are found, respectively, in the Philippines, in Sumatra and Borneo, and in the Celebes. Tarsiers are about 6 in. (15 cm) long with a 10 in. (25 cm) tail, and weigh about 6 oz (170 g). The body is covered with soft, dense, brown fur; the tail is naked. Enormous round eyes are set close together in a flat face; the small, round skull bears large, naked ears. Tarsiers' legs are specialized for jumping and end in long, thin digits bearing adhesive pads. They spend most of the time in trees and feed on insects and some vegetable matter. Their habits are not well known. Tarsiers are an ancient group and are quite distinct anatomically from other primates, although superficially they resemble the lorises and lemurs. They are classified in the phylum CHORDATA, subphylum Vertebrata, class Mammalia, order Primates, family Tarsiidae.

Tarski, Alfred (tär'skē), 1902–, Polish-American mathematician and philosopher, Ph.D. Univ. of Warsaw, 1924. He lectured at Warsaw until 1939, emigrated to the United States, and then taught at the Univ. of California, Berkeley (1942–68). Tarski made extensive, basic contributions to the field of metamathematics, a branch of mathematical logic. His most important contribution to logic is the semantic method, a method that allows a more exacting study of formal scientific languages. His work is characterized by a basic acceptance and free use of the assumptions of set theory. For this reason he is regarded by some as a nominalist. His publications include *A Decision Method for Elementary Algebra and Geometry* (1948, rev. ed. 1957) and *Undecidable Theories* (with others, 1953; repr. 1968).

Tarsus (tär'səs, Turk. tärsōōs'), city (1970 pop. 78,033), S Turkey, in Cilicia, on the Tarsus (anc. Cydnus) River, near the Mediterranean Sea. It is an agricultural trade center; copper, zinc, chromium, and coal are mined in the region. Ancient Tarsus, first mentioned in the 8th cent. B.C., was the capital of Cilicia and one of the most important cities of Asia Minor. It reached the height of its prosperity and cultural achievement under Roman rule. The city was destroyed by the Arabs c.660 A.D. and was rebuilt by them in the 780s. It was captured by the Ottoman Turks in 1515. The apostle Paul was born there.

Tartaglia, Niccolò (nēk-kōlô' tärtä'lyä), c.1500–1577, Italian engineer and mathematician. Largely self-educated, he taught mathematics at Verona, Brescia, and Venice. A pioneer in applying mathematics to artillery, he recorded his results in *Della nova scientia* (1537). He developed a solution for cubic equations that Geronimo Cardano (with his pupil Ludovico Ferrari) completed and published in his *Ars magna* (1545), thereby precipitating a bitter dispute; Tartaglia published his version as *Quesiti et invenzioni diverse* (1546). He wrote also a treatise on pure and applied mathematics, *General trattato di numeri et misure* (6 parts, 1556–60) and made Italian translations of works of Euclid and Archimedes.

Tartak (tär'tăk), heathen god. 2 Kings 17.31.

Tartan (tär'tăn), official title of two Assyrians sent to Hezekiah by Sennacherib and Sargon. 2 Kings 18.17; Isa. 20.1.

tartan: see PLAID.

tartar or **argol** (är'gəl), impure potassium hydrogen tartrate deposited as a crust in fermenting vessels during wine making. When purified, it yields CREAM OF TARTAR. Tartar is the chief natural source of TARTARIC ACID.

tartar, dental, precipitate of saliva that accumulates around TEETH at the gum line. Composed primarily of calcium salts, tartar forms as a hard brownish substance that irritates gums and causes them to recede. Inflammation of this tissue may lead to the recession and infection of the bones in which teeth are imbedded and result in the loosening and loss of teeth. As symptoms may not become apparent until serious damage has occurred, periodic dental visits for the removal of tartar are recommended.

tartar emetic, poisonous, odorless, transparent rhombic crystals or white powder with a metallic, sweetish taste. Chemically, it is potassium antimony tartrate, $KSbC_4H_4O_7 \cdot \frac{1}{2}H_2O$. It is used as a mordant in dyeing. Medically, it was formerly used as an emetic and expectorant, to produce sweating, and in the treatment of several diseases, but had frequent toxic side effects.

tartaric acid, $HO_2CCHOHCHOHCO_2H$, white crystalline dicarboxylic acid. It occurs as three distinct ISOMERS, the *dextro-, levo-,* and *meso-* forms. The *dextro-* and *levo-* forms are optically active; the *meso-* form is optically inactive, as is racemic acid, a mixture of equal parts of the *dextro-* and *levo-*forms. Tartaric acid is found in many plants, e.g., grapes; this natural acid is chiefly the dextrorotatory *d*-tartaric acid, called also *d*-2,3-dihydroxysuccinic acid or L-2,3-dihydroxybutanedioic acid. This form can be partially converted to the others by heating it with an aqueous alkali, e.g., potassium hydroxide. Tartaric acids can be synthesized from maleic acids or FUMARIC ACIDS by reaction with aqueous potassium permanganate. The various isomeric forms differ in such physical properties as boiling point. Tartaric acid is used chiefly in the form of its salts, e.g., CREAM OF TARTAR and ROCHELLE SALT.

Tartars: see TATARS.

Tartarus, in Greek mythology, lowest region of the underworld. The wicked (e.g., SISYPHUS, TANTALUS, and IXION) were sent to Tartarus as punishment for their sins.

Tartini, Giuseppe (jōōzĕp'pā tärtē'nē), 1692–1770, Italian violinist, the greatest violin master of his day. In 1728 he founded at Padua a school of the violin that became known throughout Europe. Tartini altered the shape of the bow, revised bowing technique, and was probably the first to discover the difference tone (see TONE), which became a means of securing just intonation. He wrote a number of theoretical works and composed an estimated 150 violin concertos, many trios, and about 200 sonatas, among which *The Devil's Trill,* supposedly played to him by the devil in a dream, is the most famous.

Tartu (tär'tōō), Ger. and Swed. *Dorpat,* city (1969 est. pop. 87,000), W European USSR, in Estonia, a port on the Ema River. The second largest city of Estonia, it is an important industrial and cultural center and a rail junction. Food processing, metalworking, printing and publishing, lumbering, and the production of textiles, leather footwear, and agricultural machinery are the leading industries. Tartu's university was founded in 1632 by Gustavus II of Sweden, suppressed in 1656, and reopened in 1802. The city was founded in 1030 as Yurev by Yaroslav the Wise of Kiev. Named Dorpat after its capture by the Livonian Knights in 1224, it developed as a trade center of the Hanseatic League. After the dissolution (1561) of the Livonian Order, the city was contested by Poland, Sweden, and Russia. Gustavus II secured its formal cession in 1629 after a Polish-Swedish war. Captured by Peter I in 1704, during the Northern War, it was ceded to Russia by the Treaty of Nystad in 1721. The name Yurev was revived in 1893, only to be changed (1918) to Tartu when Estonia became independent. In 1920, Soviet peace treaties with Estonia and Finland were signed in the city. Tartu is built around a hill topped by an old fortified castle and a restored 13th-century cathedral (the site of the present university library). The rest of the city dates mostly from the 18th and 19th cent.

Tartus (tärtōōs'), town, W Syria, a port on the Mediterranean Sea. Olive oil is pressed, and petroleum, phosphates, and agricultural produce are shipped. Tartus occupies the ancient site of Antaradus. In A.D. 346 it was rebuilt by Constantine and came to be known, for a time, as Constantia. The town was in Byzantine hands from 968 until 1099, when it was occupied by Crusaders, who also held the town from 1102 to 1291 and renamed it Tartosa. It became famous for the manufacture of camlets, heavy cloths made from camel or goat hair. In 1183 the Knights Templars moved there and fortified the harbor. Tartus is the site of the earliest chapel dedicated to Mary; a cathedral was built around the chapel in the 12th–13th cent.

tarweed, any of several related resinous herbs (chiefly species of *Hemizonia* and *Madia*) of the family Compositae (COMPOSITE family), having strongly scented and sticky herbage. Most North American species are found in fields and on dry hillsides of the Southwest and the Pacific region. They bear daisylike heads of yellow or cream-colored flowers. The heads of the common tarweed (*M. elegans,* also called common madia) are marked with an inner red ring and, like those of other *Madia* species, open in the evening and close before noon. Similar related Western plants are the rosinweeds (*Calycademia*) and the gumweeds, or sticky-heads (*Grindelia*). Several gumweed species have become established in the East, where they are sometimes called tarweeds. The dried herbage of some gumweeds, containing resinous substances and essential oils, has been used in domestic remedies for treating burns and ivy poisoning. Tarweeds are classified in the division MAGNOLIOPHYTA, class Magnoliopsida, order Asterales, family Compositae.

Taschereau, Elzéar Alexandre (ĕlzäär' älĕksäN'drə tăshərō'), 1820–98, Canadian Roman Catholic cardinal, b. Quebec prov. He served the Quebec seminary for nearly 30 years, as professor, director, and superior. In 1871 he was made archbishop of Quebec; in 1886 he was created cardinal, the first Canadian to be so honored.

Taschereau, Sir Henri Elzéar, 1836–1911, Canadian jurist, b. Quebec prov., nephew of Elzéar Alexandre Cardinal Taschereau. He was a judge of the Supreme Court of Canada (1878) and was later chief justice (1902–6). He was knighted in 1902. His cousin, **Sir Henri Thomas Taschereau,** 1841–1909, was also a jurist. He was a judge of the superior court of Quebec (1878–1907) and chief justice of King's Bench in Quebec (1907–9). He was knighted in 1908. Sir Henri Thomas Taschereau's brother, **Louis Alexandre Taschereau,** 1867–1952, was minister of public works and labor in Quebec prov., attorney general, and prime minister of the province (1920–36). Louis's son, Robert, a jurist, served as chief justice of Canada in 1963–67.

Tashi Lumpo or **Tashi Lhümpo** (tä'shē lōōm'pō) [Tibetan,=mount of blessing], lamasery, SE Tibet, just outside Shigatse. Founded in the 15th cent., it is one of the best known and largest lamaseries in Tibet. Its grand lama, known as the Panchen Lama, or Tashi Lama, has, since the 17th cent., been second in rank only to the Dalai Lama. Before the Communist Chinese occupied Tibet in 1951 there were about 4,000 priests and monks at Tashi Lumpo. In 1959 the Dalai Lama fled to India, and the Chinese Communists installed the Panchen Lama in his place.

Tashkent (tăshkĕnt', täsh-, Rus. təshkyĕnt'), city (1970 pop. 1,385,000), capital of Tashkent oblast and of the Uzbek Soviet Socialist Republic, Central Asian USSR, in the foothills of the Tien Shan mts. The largest and one of the oldest cities of Central Asia, it is the economic heart of the region. It is also a major cultural center, a rail and highway junction, and an important air terminal. The city lies in a great oasis along the Chirchik River and on the Trans-Caspian RR. There is extensive trade in grain and raw cotton. Tashkent has one of the largest cotton textile mills in Asia. Other industries include railroad workshops, food- and tobacco-processing plants, and factories that manufacture machinery, electrical equipment, chemicals, pharmaceuticals, paper, furniture, pottery, hosiery, and perfume. Among the city's educational and cultural facilities are the Central Asian state university and the Uzbek Academy of Sciences. Tashkent is also a military center. The modern Russian section of the city coexists with the old Oriental quarter (partly reconstructed by the Soviet government), with its narrow, twisting streets, numerous mosques, and bazaar. The Tashkent oasis produces cotton and fruit. Irrigation canals on the Chirchik River supply power for several hydroelectric plants. First mentioned in the 1st cent. B.C., Tashkent came under Arabic rule in the 7th cent. A.D. and passed to the Turkish shahs of KHOREZM in the 12th cent. It developed as a commercial center on the historic trade route from Samarkand to Peking. Tashkent was captured in the 13th cent. by JENGHIZ KAHN and in the 14th cent. by TAMERLANE. With the breakup of the Timurid empire of Tamerlane's successors, the city passed to the khanate of Kokand. Captured by Russian forces in 1865, Tashkent became (1867) the administrative seat of Russian Turkistan. It remained active in the caravan trade between Central Asia and W Russia and gained new prosperity with the construction (1898) of the Trans-Caspian RR. From 1918 to 1924, Tashkent was the capital of the Turkistan Autonomous SSR, and in 1930 it replaced Samarkand as capital of the Uzbek SSR. A major earthquake in 1966 heavily damaged the city. Tashkent was also the site in 1966 of a meeting between Soviet Premier Kosygin, Indian Prime Minister Shastri, and Pakistani President Ayub Khan that represented a Soviet effort to mediate the Kashmir dispute. One of the ten most populous cities in the USSR, Tashkent has a population that is more than half Russian, with the rest mainly Uzbek.

Tashkent, Declaration of: see INDIA-PAKISTAN WARS.

Tashkurgan or **Tash-Kurgan** (täsh'ko͝orgän″), town (1967 pop. 30,000), N Afghanistan. It has extensive fruit orchards and is a market for wool and sheep.

Tasman, Abel Janszoon (ä'bəl yän'sōn tä'smän), 1603?–1659, Dutch navigator. In the service of the Dutch East India Company from c.1632 to 1653, he made several trading and exploring voyages in the Pacific and Indian oceans. On a voyage (1639–42) in the N Pacific he visited the Philippines and Taiwan, followed the coast of Japan, and discovered several small islands. In 1642 he sailed from Batavia in command of the *Heemskerck* and the *Zeehaen*. On that voyage he discovered Tasmania (which he named Van Diemen's Land) and New Zealand, touched the Tonga islands, and returned (1643) to Batavia, having circumnavigated Australia and thus demonstrated that no connection exists between it and a polar continent. In 1644 he was dispatched to discover the relationship between New Guinea, Tasmania, and the known port of Australia; he established the continuity of land from the Gulf of Carpentaria to the northwest coast of Australia at the Tropic of Capricorn. See biography by Andrew Sharp (1968).

Tasman Glacier, largest glacier of New Zealand, 18 mi (29 km) long and from 1 to 2 mi (1.6-3.2 km) wide, on South Island, in the Southern Alps. It flows SE to the Tasman River. Ski meets are held there.

Tasmania (tăzmā'nēə), island state (1970 est. pop. 392,500), 26,383 sq mi (68,332 sq km), SE Commonwealth of Australia. It is separated from Australia by the Bass Strait and lies 150 mi (240 km) south of the state of Victoria. Tasmania includes many offshore islands, among which are Bruny, the Hunter Islands, the FURNEAUX GROUP, King Island, and Macquarie Island. The Indian Ocean is to the west and the Pacific Ocean to the east. HOBART is the state capital. The only other city with a population of more than 50,000 is LAUNCESTON. Tasmania is geologically similar to the Australian continent. The climate is equable and the rainfall moderate. The island is mountainous and partly forested; Legge Tor (5,160 ft/1,573 m) is the highest peak. Great Lake in the interior is the largest lake and the reservoir of an important hydroelectric plant. The rapid development of hydroelectric power in Tasmania is eliminating an obstacle to industrialization. The state's major manufactures are metals and metal products and textiles. Agriculture is confined almost exclusively to small farms. The raising of sheep for wool in the east and dairy farming in the northwest are also important. The mining of copper, zinc, tin, lead, and iron has increased in recent years. The island was discovered in 1642 by the Dutch navigator Abel Tasman, who named it Van Diemen's Land. Capt. James Cook visited the island in 1777 and, in 1803, Great Britain took possession and established a penal colony. Governed by New South Wales until 1825, Tasmania was then constituted as a separate colony. The transportation of convicts ended in 1853 as a result of local opposition. In the 1850s the British established constitutional self-government in the colony. In 1901, Tasmania was federated as a state in the Commonwealth of Australia. The nominal head of the state government is the governor, appointed by the British crown on advice of the cabinet; however, actual executive powers are exercised by the premier and the cabinet, who are responsible to the bicameral state parliament.

Tasmanian devil, extremely voracious MARSUPIAL, or pouched mammal, of the DASYURE family, now found only on the island of Tasmania. The Tasmanian devil, *Sarcophilus harrisi*, formerly found also in Australia, is about 2 ft (60 cm) long, excluding the 12-in. (30-cm) tail. It has a large head, with powerful jaws, and weak hindquarters. Its blackish fur is marked with white patches on the throat, on each side, and on the rump. Its expression appears evil, and it has a fierce snarl. It is very strong for its size and preys on animals larger than itself, such as small kangaroos, as well as on rodents, lizards, and other small animals. It lives in burrows in rocky areas. Like the related THYLACINE, or Tasmanian wolf, the Tasmanian devil has been relentlessly hunted because of its inroads on domestic livestock and poultry; however, it survives in fair numbers in remote areas of the island. It is classified in the phylum CHORDATA, subphylum Vertebrata, class Mammalia, order Marsupialia, family Dasyuridae.

Tasmanian tiger or **Tasmanian wolf:** see THYLACINE.

Tasman Sea, arm of the S Pacific Ocean between Australia and New Zealand; named for Dutch explorer Abel Tasman. Sydney, Australia, is the largest city on the sea.

Tassie, James, 1735–99, Scottish gem engraver and modeler. At first a stonemason, he went to Dublin, where he assisted the gem engraver Dr. Henry Quin. With him Tassie invented an especially hard and fine-textured white enamel for making replicas of gems. In 1766 he went to London, where he duplicated famous gem collections, notably many thousands of specimens for Catherine the Great. R. E. Raspe prepared a catalog of Tassie's work in 1791. Working often for Wedgwood, he made the first plaster cast of the Portland vase. Many of his portrait medallions are in the Scottish National Portrait Gallery, Edinburgh.

Tasso, Torquato (tōrkwä'tō täs'sō), 1544–95, Italian poet, one of the foremost writers and a tragic figure of the Renaissance. Educated in Naples by Jesuits, he later studied law and philosophy (1560–62) at the Univ. of Padua. *Rinaldo* (1562), his first narrative work, brought him fame when he was 18; after completing his studies at the Univ. of Bologna, he received an invitation (1565) to join the brilliant court of the Este at Ferrara, where he remained for many years. There he wrote the charming pastoral play *Aminta* (completed 1573) and the first version (completed 1575) of his masterpiece, *Jerusalem Delivered* (Ital. *Gerusalemme liberata*), an epic of the exploits of Godfrey of Boulogne during the First Crusade. A victim of his own religious scruples, he submitted the epic to church authorities, whose judgment was unduly severe. He began the difficult task of revising it to suit his critics and assuage his own doubts. In 1575 he suffered a blow on the head from an irate court attaché and for the rest of his life was afflicted with recurring insanity in the form of persecution mania. He was confined, first in a convent, then intermittently from 1579 to 1587 in a hospital while controversy concerning his work continued. During his frequent lucid periods he wrote prolifically and revised his poem beyond all recognition. Fortunately, copies of the earlier version were published without his permission. In his last years he left the asylum to live with the Gonzagas in Mantua, and then wandered restlessly throughout Italy. He died at a convent in Rome, his sanity regained, shortly before he was to have been crowned poet laureate. Tasso's *Jerusalem Delivered* was lauded both as the embodiment of lyric sentiment and as the greatest poem of the Catholic Reformation. The religious motif is strong, the subplots of love and adventure are well developed, and chivalric exploits are recounted in a majestic classical style. The work had enormous influence on Milton. The legend of Tasso's doomed love for Leonora d'Este was immortalized in works by Byron, Goethe, and others and made Tasso a romantic hero. There are several good translations of Tasso's works. See studies by C. P. Brand (1965) and R. Cody (1969).

Tassoni, Alessandro (älĕs-sän'drō täs-sô'nē), 1565–1635, Italian poet. He spent much of his life in the service of Charles Emmanuel I of Savoy and Francesco I of Modena. His sharp letter (1602) of defense against accusations by the Italian Inquisition revealed him as a polemist of high order, as did his *Manifesto* (written 1627, pub. 1856), a bizarre and violent attack on the House of Savoy. Tassoni is best known for the mock-heroic poem *Secchia rapita* [the rape of the bucket] (1622), which ridicules the war between Bologna and Modena.

taste, response to chemical stimulation that enables an organism to detect flavors. In man and most vertebrate animals, taste is produced by the stimulation by various substances of the taste buds on the mucous membrane of the TONGUE. A taste bud consists of about 20 long, slender cells; a tiny hair projects from each cell to the surface of the tongue through a tiny pore. The taste cells contain the endings of nerve filaments that convey impulses to the taste center in the brain. Only four fundamental tastes, or a combination of these, can be detected by the buds: sweet, sour, salt, and bitter. Only the buds most sensitive to salty flavor are scattered evenly over the tongue. Sweet-sensitive taste buds are concentrated on the tip of the tongue, sour flavors are detected at the sides of the tongue, and bitter flavors at the back. The close relationship of taste to SMELL gives the impression that a greater variety of tastes exists. This is also why an impairment of smell, as during a cold, may impart the feeling that the sense of taste is diminished.

Tata (tä'tä), Parsi family of Indian industrialists, centered at Bombay. The Tata enterprises, which encompass vast holdings in iron and steel, power utilities, and textiles, were founded by Jamshed Tata (1839–1904), who accumulated a fortune from his textile mill at Nagpur. At Jamshedpur (named for the founder) his successors built (1911) the first steel mill in India. Eventually it became the largest in the British Empire. The family has contributed funds to the Institute of Science at Bangalore, beautified and developed the city of Bombay, and supported the economic growth of independent India.

Tatar Autonomous Soviet Socialist Republic (tä'tər, Rus. tətär'), autonomous republic (1970 pop. 3,131,000), 26,255 sq mi (68,000 sq km), E European USSR, in the middle Volga and lower Kama river valleys. KAZAN is the capital; other important cities are Almetevsk, LENINOGORSK, and Bugulma. The republic is a leading Soviet oil and natural gas producer and the starting point for the Friendship pipeline to Eastern Europe. There are also important deposits of brown coal, limestone, gypsum, dolomite, and marl. Lumbering and food, leather, and fur processing are major Tatar industries. Manufactures include machinery, chemicals, and pharmaceuticals. The low, rolling plain that makes up most of the republic's territory yields fodder crops, wheat and other cereals, sugar beets, sunflowers, and flax. The Volga, Kama, Belaya, and Vyatka rivers are important for both transportation and irrigation. There are several hydroelectric stations. Turco-Tatars make up around 50% of the population, and most live in rural areas. Russians, generally urban, constitute some 40%, and there are Chuvash, Udmurt, Mari, and Mordvinian minorities. Islam of the Sunnite branch is the chief religion. Bulgars dominated the region from the 8th to 13th cent., when it was conquered by the Mongols of the Golden Horde; their Tatar descendants, in turn, gradually replaced or absorbed the Bulgar population. Russian colonization followed the capture (1552) by Czar Ivan IV of the khanate of Kazan, the most powerful of the Tatar states emerging from the empire of the Golden Horde. The Tatar ASSR was organized in 1920 as one of the first autonomous areas established by the Soviet government.

Tatars (tä'tərz) or **Tartars** (tär'tərz), Turkic-speaking peoples living in the Soviet Union. They number about 6 million and are largely Sunni Muslims. The name is derived from Tata or Dada, a Mongolian tribe that inhabited present NE Mongolia in the 5th cent. First used to describe the peoples that overran parts of Asia and Europe under Mongol leadership in the 13th cent., it was later extended to include almost any Oriental nomadic invader. Before the 1920s, Russians used the name Tatar to designate the Azerbaijani Turks and several tribes of the Caucasus. The original Tatars probably came from E central Asia or central Siberia; unlike the MONGOLS, they spoke a Turkic language and were possibly akin to the CUMANS or Kipchaks and the PECHENEGS. However, after the conquests of the Mongol JENGHIZ KHAN, the Mongol and Turkic elements merged, and the invaders became known in Europe as Tatars. The Mongol invasion led by BATU KHAN into Hungary and Germany in 1241 is also known as the Tatar invasion. After the wave of invasion receded eastward, the Tatars continued to dominate nearly all of RUSSIA, the UKRAINE, and SIBERIA. They were originally nomads, moving across the vast Asiatic and Russian steppes with their families and their herds of cattle and sheep. Because of the gorgeous tents of Batu Khan, his followers were known as the GOLDEN HORDE. The empire of the Golden Horde—also known as the Kipchak khanate—controlled most of Russia either directly or through exacting tribute from the Russian princes. The Golden Horde adopted Islam as its religion in the 14th cent. Internal divisions, the expansion of Moscow, the invasion by TAMERLANE, and the appearance of the Ottoman Turks contributed to the disintegration of the Tatar empire in the late 15th cent. The independent khanates of KAZAN, ASTRAKHAN, SIBIR, and CRIMEA emerged. In the 16th cent. Russia conquered the khanates of Kazan, Astrakhan, and Sibir (Siberia); the khans of Crimea became (1478) vassals of the Ottoman Empire. Nevertheless Siberia long continued to be known as Tartary and the Crimean domains as Little Tartary. The Crimean Tatars continued to harass the Ukraine and Poland and to exact tribute from the czars of Russia; they raided Moscow in 1572. The majority of the Tatars in Russia had by that time reached a relatively high degree of civilization. They were generally settled, were skillful in agriculture and crafts, and had great centers of Muslim learning. Only minorities, such as the Nogais, who were subject to the Crimean khans, remained nomadic. Tatar political leaders, administrators, and traders had a great influence on Russian history. Many Russian noble families were of partly Tatar origin. The social and military organization of the Muscovite state was influenced by the institutions of the Tatars, and many Russian customs are traceable to them. In 1783 the last Tatar state, Crimea, was annexed to Russia. The Nogais were gradually pushed eastward into the Caucasus by the Russian settlers. The Crimean Tatars themselves—except for the large numbers that emigrated to Turkey at the time of the Russian conquest of Crimea and after the Crimean War—remained in the Crimea until World War II and formed the basis of the Crimean Autonomous SSR, founded in 1921. It was dissolved in 1945, and all Crimean Tatars (about 200,000 in 1939) were exiled to Uzbekistan and Kazakhstan for alleged collaboration with the Germans. In 1956 they regained civil rights but were no longer recognized as a people. The majority of Kazan Tatars live in the Volga region and the Urals. They predominate in the Tatar Autonomous SSR and the Bashkir Autonomous SSR, but they also live elsewhere in the Soviet Union. The Volga Tatars are the most industrially advanced of the Turkic-speaking peoples of the USSR. The so-called Siberian Tatars, numbering fewer than 100,000, live in small groups scattered over West Siberia. See B. S. Izhbolden, *Essays on Tatar History* (1963).

Tatar Strait, narrow body of water, c.350 mi (560 km) long and from 5 to 80 mi (8–129 km) wide, S Far Eastern USSR, between the island of Sakhalin and the Asian mainland. It connects the Sea of Japan, in the south, with the Sea of Okhotsk, in the north. Sovyetskaya Gavan is a fishing port and naval base on the strait. Pipelines across the strait link Sakhalin's oil fields with mainland refineries.

Tate, Allen (John Orley Allen Tate), 1899–, American poet and critic, b. Winchester, Ky., grad. Vanderbilt Univ., 1922. He was one of the founders and editors of the *Fugitive* (1922–25), a magazine that represented the Southern agrarian literary group of social and political conservatives. Among his early publications were interpretive biographies of Stonewall Jackson (1928) and Jefferson Davis (1929), and a novel, *The Fathers* (1938). He taught English literature at several colleges, was the resident fellow of poetry at Princeton (1939–42), held the chair of poetry at the Library of Congress (1934–44), edited the *Sewanee Review* (1944–46), and was an editor of books (1946–48); from 1951 to 1968 he taught English literature at the Univ. of Minnesota. The main body of his work is poetry and literary criticism. His critical writings, direct and perceptive, include *Reactionary Essays on Poetry and Ideas* (1936), *On the Limits of Poetry* (1948), and *The Man of Letters in the Modern World* (1955). His poems, filled with bitter and original imagery, exhibit an unusual skill with form; they reveal Tate's intense feeling for history and for man's estrangedness in the world. Among his most famous poems are "Ode to the Confederate Dead," "The Mediterranean," and "The Buried Lake." See his collected *Poems* (1960), *Swimmers and Other Selected Poems* (1971), and *Essays of Four Decades* (1969); studies by W. B. Arnold (1955) and R. K. Meiners (1963).

Tate, Nahum (nā'həm), 1652–1715, English poet and dramatist, b. Dublin. He wrote several popular adaptations of Shakespeare, the most famous being his *King Lear* (1681), in which he omitted the part of the fool and had Cordelia survive to marry Edgar. With Dryden he wrote the second part of *Absalom and Achitophel* (1682). In 1692 he became poet laureate. His metrical version of the *Psalms* (1696), written with Nicholas Brady, is generally regarded as tedious and verbose. He was the target of an attack by Pope in *The Dunciad.* See study by Christopher Spencer (1972).

Tatebayashi (tätābä'yäshē), city (1970 pop. 61,130), Gumma prefecture, central Honshu, Japan, on the Tone River. It is a manufacturing center with mechanical and textile industries.

Tate Gallery, Millbank, London, originally the National Gallery of British Art. The building (on the former site of Millbank Prison), with a collection of 65 modern British paintings, was given by Sir Henry Tate and was opened in 1897. It was extended by another gift of Tate's in 1899, and in 1910 the Turner wing was completed, the gift of Sir Joseph Duveen. A gallery of modern foreign art was added in 1916, and three new galleries for foreign art and one for the works of John Singer Sargent were opened in 1926. The museum was damaged in World War II but reopened in 1949. See J. K. M. Rothenstein, *The Tate Gallery* (1958).

Tati (tä'tē), region, c.2,070 sq mi (5,360 sq km), NE Botswana. Nickel, copper, asbestos, and manganese are mined in the region. Tati was a source of gold for centuries; mining ceased there in the early 1960s.

Tatian (tā'shən), 2d cent., Christian apologist. Probably born in Syria, he was a pupil of JUSTIN MARTYR. After his master's death, he left Christianity, becoming an Encratitic Gnostic—i.e., he regarded all matter as evil and denied the salvation of Adam. While a Christian, he wrote *Oratio ad Graecos* [address to the Greeks] (152–55), a defense of Christianity bolstered by a bitter attack on Greek arts, philosophers, and institutions, and the *Diatessaron,* a harmony of the four Gospels that was long the only life of Christ available in Syria.

Tatler: see SPECTATOR.

Tatnai (tăt'nāī), Persian governor of the province W of the Euphrates at the time of Zerubbabel. He opposed the rebuilding of the Temple. Ezra 5.3,6; 6.6,13.

Tatra (tä'trə) or **Tatras** (-trəz), Pol. and Slovak *Tatry,* highest group of the Carpathian mountain system, in E central Europe. The High Tatra (Slovak *Vysoké Tatry,* Pol. *Tatry Wysokie*) extends c.40 mi (60 km) along the Polish-Czechoslovak border; its highest peak, Gerlachovka (8,711 ft/2,655 m) is in NE Czechoslovakia. The Low Tatra, Slovak *Nízké Tatry,* lies entirely in Czechoslovakia; it rises to 6,702 ft (2,043 m) in the Ďumbier. The extensively glaciated mountains have numerous lakes, moraines, and hanging valleys. Tatra National Park (est. 1948) extends on both sides of the international border. The region's scenic beauty and excellent ski slopes have made it a year-round resort area. Vysoké Tatry, in Czechoslovakia, and Zakopane, Poland, are the chief resort centers.

Tatti, Jacopo: see SANSOVINO, JACOPO.

tattoo, in its specific sense, the marking of the skin with punctures accentuated by pigment. The word originates from the Tahitian word *tattau* [to mark]. The term is often extended to scarification, which consists of skin incisions into which irritants may be rubbed to produce a raised scar. Tattooing is done in modern times with an electric needle. Puncture tattoo reached its most elaborate and artistic development among the Maori of New Zealand and among the Japanese, who perfected the use of color. It was introduced into Europe by seamen. The Old Testament enjoins the Israelites against the practice, it was forbidden by Muhammad, and a Roman Catholic council condemned it in 787. In modern Western cultures it has been alternately regarded as a somewhat vulgar practice and as a sign of high fashion. Tattooing has been banned in some areas for health reasons; unclean needles can result in hepatitis. It has been used for practical purposes, such as the identification of criminals and political prisoners; in medicine, it may be used to remove birthmarks by injecting a pigment of the color of the natural skin. Tattoos may be removed by a slow process. For the significance of tattooing and scarification, see BODY-MARKING. See Albert Parry, *Tattoo* (1933, repr. 1971); Hanns Ebensten, *Pierced Hearts and True Love* (1953).

Tatum, Art (tā'təm), 1910–1956, American jazz pianist, b. Toledo, Ohio. Born with cataracts in both eyes, Tatum remained virtually blind for life. He read music in Braille, but his sensitive ear for music made reading almost unnecessary. Tatum, an unmatched piano virtuoso, could span 12 white notes with one hand. A brilliant improviser, he developed a style characterized by complex musical embroidery, such as rapid runs.

Tatum, Edward Lawrie, 1909–, American geneticist, b. Boulder, Colo., grad. Univ. of Wisconsin (B.A., 1931; M.S., 1932; Ph.D., 1935). From 1937 to 1945 he taught at Stanford and from 1945 to 1948 at Yale. Returning to Stanford in 1948 he became (1956) head of the department of biochemistry. He left Stanford in 1957 to become a member of the Rockefeller Institute for Medical Research, New York City. He shared with G. W. Beadle and Joshua Lederberg the 1958 Nobel Prize in Physiology and Medicine for work with Beadle establishing that genes in bread mold transmit hereditary characters by controlling specific chemical reactions.

Ta-t'ung or **Tatung** (both: dä'to͝ong), city (1970 est. pop. 300,000), N Shansi prov., China. It is an important industrial and railway center in a region of great coal deposits. A major, highly mechanized coal mine is there. Manufactures include locomotives, motor vehicles, textiles, and cement. As P'ing-ch'ang, the city was (5th–6th cent.) the capital of the T'o-pa Wei kingdom. Nearby limestone grottoes at Yung-kan contain Buddhist art from the 5th and 6th cent.

Tauber, Richard (tou'bər), 1891–1948, Austrian tenor. He made his debut (1913) in Chemnitz, Germany, as Tamino in Mozart's *Magic Flute.* Later he sang in opera and concert all over Europe and made his American debut in 1931. Although he was noted for his operatic roles and as a lieder singer, Tauber was best known for his work in operettas, particularly those of Lehar; in 1946 he appeared in New York City in *Yours Is My Heart,* an adaptation of Lehar's *Land of Smiles.* In 1938 he fled Austria, becoming a British subject in 1940.

Tauler, Johannes (yōhän'əs tou'lər), c.1300–1361, German mystic. He was a Dominican. He met Meister ECKHART, either at Strasbourg or in Cologne, where he went to study, and he was one of Eckhart's disciples. He also knew Heinrich SUSO. When the churches of Strasbourg were closed by the bishop of Strasbourg because of a serious quarrel between Pope John XXII and Emperor Louis IV, Tauler went to Basel (1338–39), where he became closely associated with the leaders of the Friends of God, a popular mystical movement that spread Eckhart's teachings. He was one of the greatest of medieval preachers, and his sermons were widely disseminated. They are intellectual appeals to practice detachment from the world and to abandon oneself to the Holy Spirit; they abound in striking analogies and keen observations. In spite of their orthodox and scholastic Catholicism, they have been much admired by Protestants. Collections of Tauler's work often include sermons falsely attributed to him. See his life and sermons, ed. by Susannah Winkworth (1962); study by S. E. Ozment (1969); J. M. Clark, *The Great German Mystics* (1949, repr. 1970).

Taunton (tôn'tən, tän'-), municipal borough (1971 pop. 37,373), county town of Somerset, SW England, on the Trove River. Its industries include the manufacture of textiles, shirts, gloves, and precision instruments. Taunton is also a market and railroad junction. There are three well-known schools for boys: King's College (1293), Queen's College (1843), and Taunton School (1847). In 1685, after Monmouth's Rebellion, Baron JEFFREYS OF WEM held the Bloody Assizes in Taunton.

Taunton (tăn'tən, tŏn-), industrial city (1970 pop. 43,756), a seat of Bristol co., SE Mass., on the Taunton River; settled 1638, inc. as a city 1864. Silverware, jewelry, and clothing are among its manufactures. The city was an ironworking center from 1656 to 1876.

Taunus (tou'no͞os), range of the Rhenish Slate Mts., W West Germany, extending c.50 mi (80 km) NE from the Rhine River, N of Mainz. It rises to 2,887 ft (880 m) in the Grosser Feldberg. The Taunus is covered by forests. Its southern slopes, the Rheingau region, have famous vineyards, notably at Rüdesheim, Johannisberg, Biebrich, and Kastel. Wiesbaden, Bad Nauheim, and Bad Homburg are the best known of the many mineral spas in the Taunus. There are many ruins of medieval castles and Roman fortifications.

Taupo, Lake (tou'pō), largest lake of New Zealand, 234 sq mi (606 sq km) and 552 ft (168 m) deep, on central North Island. Fed by more than 20 streams, the lake is drained by the Waikato River. Lake Taupo, located in the Hot Springs District, is surrounded by volcanoes. It is known for rainbow trout.

Taurage (tourägä'), Ger. *Tauroggen,* town (1967 est. pop. 17,000), W European USSR, in Lithuania, on the Yura River. It is a rail terminus and has meat-processing and vegetable-drying industries. Furniture, tiles, and tobacco pipes are produced. Dating from the 13th cent., Taurage belonged to Prussia from 1691 to 1793, when it passed to Russia. It was incorporated into independent Lithuania in 1920. The city is known historically as the site of the signing of the Convention of Tauroggen in Dec., 1812, between Russia and the Prussian general YORCK VON WARTENBURG. Acting on his own authority, Yorck, whose troops constituted a contingent of Napoleon I's defeated *Grande Armée,* declared his corps neutral and thus permitted the Russians to continue their pursuit of the French. This step prepared the alliance of Prussia, Great Britain, and Russia against Napoleon.

Tauranga, city (1971 pop. 28,188), N central North Island, New Zealand, on the Bay of Plenty. It is the leading New Zealand port for overseas trade. Wood products are the largest exports and fertilizers the largest imports.

Tauriscus: see FARNESE BULL.

Tauroggen, Convention of: see TAURAGE, USSR.

Taurus (tôr'əs), Turkish *Toros* (tôrōs'), mountain chain, S Turkey, extending c.350 mi (560 km) roughly parallel to the Mediterranean coast of S Asia Minor. It forms the southern border of the Anatolian plateau. Its northeastern extension across the Seyhan River is called the Anti-Taurus. The highest peak of the Taurus proper is the Ala Dağ (12,251 ft/3,734 m), at its eastern end. Erciyas Dağı (anc. *Mount Argaeus*), reaching 12,848 ft (3,916 m), is sometimes considered part of the Taurus although it rises in central Anatolia, in an outlier of the Taurus proper. The Amanos Mts., along the eastern shore of the Gulf of İskenderun, are also considered an offshoot of the main Taurus. The Taurus is crossed by five major passes; the CILICIAN GATES, N of Tarsus, is the best known. The mountains have long been a barrier to movement between the Anatolian basin and the Levant. The range has important chromium deposits and other minerals (notably copper, silver, lignite, zinc, iron, and arsenic). The Anti-Taurus are well-wooded.

Taurus [Lat.,= the bull], in astronomy, CONSTELLATION NW of Orion and lying on the ECLIPTIC (the sun's apparent path through the heavens) between Gemini and Aries; it is one of the constellations of the ZODIAC. Taurus is traditionally depicted as the forepart of a bull, in reference to the Greek legend in which Zeus either assumed the form of a bull himself or sent the bull to carry Europa over the sea to Crete. The constellation contains the bright stars Elnath (Beta Tauri) and ALDEBARAN (Alpha Tauri), long used in navigation. A line extended through and slightly up from Orion's belt will strike Aldebaran. Two notable star clusters, the PLEIADES and the HYADES, are found in Taurus, which also includes a number of double stars (observable with small telescopes) and the CRAB NEBULA (M1). Taurus reaches its highest point in the evening sky in January.

tautog: see WRASSE.

tautomer (tô'təmər), one of two or more structural ISOMERS that exist in equilibrium and are readily converted from one isomeric form to another. Of the various types of tautomerism that are possible, two are commonly observed. In keto-enol tautomerism a simultaneous shift of electrons and a hydrogen atom occurs; it was first observed by K. Meyer in the ethyl ester of 3-oxobutanoic acid (ethyl acetoacetate), which occurs naturally as a mixture of the two forms. Ring-chain tautomerism, first recognized by Emil Fischer, is exhibited by glucose. It arises as a result of the aldehyde group (—CHO) in a sugar chain molecule reacting with one of the hydroxy groups (—OH) in the same molecule to give it a cyclic (ring-shaped) form.

Tavastehus, Finland: see HÄMEENLINNA.

tavern: see INN.

Taverner, John, c.1495–1545, English organist and composer. He was choirmaster at Oxford from 1526 to 1530. His small body of work—eight masses, 28 motets, and three secular songs—may be considered the high point of development of early Tudor music. After 1530, Taverner seems to have abandoned music and to have spent his remaining years in zealous persecution of the Catholics, serving as an agent of Thomas Cromwell in the destruction of monasteries throughout England.

Tavernier, Jean Baptiste (zhäN bätēst' tävĕrnyā'), 1605–89, French traveler in Asia. He undertook six voyages, which took him as far as the East Indies and Java, and he acquired a fortune in the trade of precious stones. Ennobled (1669) by Louis XIV, he took the title baron d'Aubonne after an estate he bought near Geneva. A Protestant, he left France after the revocation (1685) of the Edict of Nantes and died on a seventh journey, which was to take him to the Orient by way of Russia. His *Six Voyages en Turquie, en Perse et aux Indes* (1676–77) contains a wealth of information and has been frequently reprinted. It has been translated into English by Valentine Ball as *Travels in India* (2d ed., 2 vol., 1925).

Tawney, Richard Henry (tô'nē), 1880–1962, British economic historian, b. Calcutta. He was professor at the Univ. of London from 1931 to 1949. A leading socialist, Tawney helped to formulate the economic and ethical views of the British Labour party through his many essays and books, and he participated in numerous government bodies concerned with education, trade, and industry. As a scholar Tawney was a foremost expert on early modern capitalism. His works, objective and masterly, include the classic *The Agrarian Problem in the 16th Century* (1912), which describes the creation of capitalistic modes of production, of an enclosure movement, and of a vigorous rising gentry in rural England. *Religion and the Rise of Capitalism* (1926) examines the relationship between the Protestant ethic and early capitalism. Among his other significant volumes are *The Acquisitive Society* (1920), *Equality* (1931, 4th ed. 1952), and *Land and Labour in China* (1932). See Ross Terrill, *R. H. Tawney and His Times* (1973).

taxa: see TAXON.

taxation, system used by governments to obtain money from people and organizations. The revenue collected is used by the government to support itself and to provide public services. Aside from being relatively permanent, taxation is compulsory and does not guarantee a direct relationship between the amount contributed by a citizen and the extent of governmental services provided to him. An enforced levy to meet an emergency (e.g., CAPITAL LEVY) is distinguished from taxation as not being part of a long-term system; fees for special services, such as postage, are not taxes. A government may secure its revenue without taxation, as from natural resources, manufactured products, or services. Taxes are sometimes resisted when those who must pay them consider them too onerous or unfair; such resistance was one of the causes of the American Revolution. Ease of collection is considered a merit in a tax, and ability to pay is one test of the amount that an individual should contribute. Such a progressive levy is the U.S. INHERITANCE TAX. A general property tax formerly met requirements in the United States satisfactorily (see LAND TAX); but as property increasingly assumed forms that escaped taxation, the burden on farms, once the usual form of property, became more than they could carry. A regressive levy, such as a general sales tax, tends to disregard ability to pay; a poor man may require as much salt, for example, as a rich man. A tax on luxuries is free in part from such an objection, although a luxury to one person may be a necessity to another. A modern variation of the sales tax is the VALUE-ADDED TAX. TARIFF duties have occasioned great debates on PROTECTION and FREE TRADE. Increasing use has been made of the graduated INCOME TAX. Excise taxes, as on tobacco and alcoholic beverages, encounter little resistance; when too high, however, they may encourage bootlegging. A SINGLE TAX on land is advocated by the followers of Henry GEORGE. Increases or decreases in taxes or changes in the types of taxes levied are often used to regulate a nation's economy. See Dick Netzer, *Economics of the Property Tax* (1966); J. F. Due, *Government Finance* (4th ed. 1968); C. S. Shoup, *Public Finance* (1969); H. M. Groves, *Financing Government* (7th ed. 1973).

Taxco (täs'kō), town (1970 pop. 64,368), Guerrero state, S Mexico. Founded in 1529 as a silver-mining community, Taxco was also an important stop between Mexico City and Acapulco in Spanish colonial trade with the Philippines. It achieved real prominence as a mining center under José de la Borda, who after 1717 constructed roads and built the superb colonial church. Clinging to the side of a mountain, Taxco is a splendid example of the Spanish colonial town, with steep, cobbled streets, overhanging grilled balconies, red-tile roofs, and fine glazed tiles set in white or pastel adobe walls. Modern buildings are prohibited, and colonial monuments are protected by the Mexican government. A famous center of silver smithing, Taxco attracts artists, writers, and tourists. The full name of the city is Taxco de Alarcón.

taxidermy (tăk'sĭdûr"mē), process of skinning, preserving, and mounting vertebrate animals so that they still appear lifelike. The fur or feathers are cleaned, and the skin, treated with a cleansing and preserving preparation, is mounted on a man-made skeleton. At first, taxidermy was used for the preservation of skins, hunting trophies, and travel souvenirs. Animals were literally stuffed; they were hung downward and filled with straw. Today, taxidermy is employed mainly by museums of science. Carl E. Akeley devised a method of mounting that is now standard. The true contours of the specimen are preserved by making a clay model, exactly duplicating the animal's muscle structure, over an armature that includes the original skeleton or parts of it. A plaster mold is then made, from which is produced a light, durable frame that holds the skin in position. Synthetic materials, especially celluloids, are now often used to reproduce the true color and translucence of such specimens as reptiles and fishes.

Taxila (tăk'sĭlŭ), archaeological site of three successive cities, near Rawalpindi, Pakistan. There between the 7th cent. B.C. and the 7th cent. A.D. was a flourishing city, famous as an ancient seat of learning. It was occupied (326 B.C.) by Alexander the Great, became prosperous under the empire of Asoka, and was overrun (c.1st–2d cent. A.D.) by the Kushans. It was a center of Buddhist studies and was visited in the 7th cent. by HSÜAN-TSANG. There are remains of Buddhist stupas and monasteries as well as sculpture of the Gandharan school of art.

taxis (tăk'sĭs), movement of animals either toward or away from a stimulus, such as light (phototaxis), heat (thermotaxis), chemicals (chemotaxis), gravity (geotaxis), and touch (thigmotaxis). The turning movements of plants in response to stimuli are called TROPISMS.

taxiway: see AIRPORT.

taxon (pl. taxa), in biology, a term used to denote any group or rank in the CLASSIFICATION of organisms, e.g., class, order, family.

taxonomy: see CLASSIFICATION.

Tay (tā), longest river of Scotland, 118 mi (190 km) long. It rises on Ben Lui in the Grampians as the Fillan and flows NE into Loch Dochart, whence it is called the Dochart until it enters Loch Tay, 14½ mi (23 km) long and 1 mi (1.6 km) wide. Turning SE at the junction with the Tummel River, its chief tributary, the Tay enters the North Sea through the Firth of Tay (25 mi/40 km long). Its drainage area includes most of Perthshire and parts of Angus and Argyllshire. The river has important salmon fisheries. Tay Bridge crosses the firth at Dundee. The original bridge collapsed (Dec. 28, 1879) during a storm, with the loss of 90 lives, and was rebuilt between 1883 and 1888.

Tayeh: see HUANG-SHIH, China.

Taygetus (tāĭ'jətəs), mountain range of the Peloponnesus, S Greece, extending c.65 mi (100 km) north from the southern end of Cape Matapan. It rises to c.7,900 ft (2,410 m) at Mt. Hagios Ilias (Mt. St. Elias) SW of Sparta.

Taylor, Alan John Percivale, 1906–, English historian, primarily interested in diplomatic and Central European history. He was educated at Oxford and became a fellow of Magdalen College in 1938. His *Habsburg Monarchy, 1809–1914* (new ed. 1948) is an excellent survey. His best-known works, contentious interpretations of the origin of modern wars, include an exoneration of Otto von Bismarck in *Bismarck, the Man and the Statesman* (1955); an indictment of German responsibility for World War I in *The Struggle for Mastery in Europe, 1848–1918* (1954); and a condemnation of French and English isolationism and vacillation in *The Origins of the Second World War* (1961).

Taylor, Bayard, 1825–78, American journalist and author, b. Kennett Square, Pa. His romantic verse in *Ximena . . . and Other Poems* (1844) secured him a long-standing assignment as correspondent for the New York *Tribune*. His trips to California, Mexico, Europe, Africa, and the Far East provided him with material for lectures, novels, and travel books. His contemporaries found these fascinating, but their popularity did not last. Perhaps the best of his poetry is in *Poems of the Orient* (1854) and in his verse drama *Prince Deukalion* (1878). His most ambitious work was his metrical translation into English (1870–71) of Goethe's *Faust*, which earned him appointment as U.S. minister to Germany in 1878. He died in Berlin.

Taylor, Brook, 1685–1731, English mathematician. He originated Taylor's theorem, a formula important in differential calculus, which relates a function to its derivatives by means of a power series. This theorem was set forth in his *Methodus incrementorum directa et inversa* (1715), which gave the first published treatment of the calculus of finite differences. His *Linear Perspective* (1715) expounded the principle of vanishing points and was of value to artists. His solution of the problem of the center of oscillation led to a translation into mathematical terms of the mechanical principles governing the vibration of a string.

Taylor, Deems (Joseph Deems Taylor), 1885–1966, American composer and music critic, b. New York City, grad. New York Univ., 1906. After other journalistic posts he was music critic (1921–25) of the New York *World* and editor (1927–29) of the magazine *Musical America*. In 1933 he was appointed music consultant for the Columbia Broadcasting System and later was a commentator (1936–43) for the New York Philharmonic broadcasts. His first widely recognized composition was the orchestral suite *Through the Looking Glass* (1919, rev. 1922). Two of his operas were commissioned by the Metropolitan Opera Company—*The King's Henchman* (1927), with libretto by Edna St. Vincent Millay, and *Peter Ibbetson* (1931), based on George Du Maurier's novel. Taylor composed several other orchestral works and incidental music for a number of plays. He appeared as commentator in Walt Disney's motion picture *Fantasia* (1940). His books include *Of Men and Music* (1937), *The Well-Tempered Listener* (1940), *Music to My Ears* (1949), and *Some Enchanted Evenings* (1953).

Taylor, Edward, c.1642–1729, American poet and clergyman, b. England, widely considered America's foremost colonial poet. He emigrated to America in 1668. After his graduation from Harvard in 1671 he became Congregational minister for the new frontier town of Westfield, Mass., a post he held until his death. An ardent Puritan, Taylor was completely in accord with the grim Calvinistic beliefs of his time. His best poems, "God's Determinations" and "Preparatory Meditations," show a strong similarity to the English devotional METAPHYSICAL POETS. Since he did not publish his poems in his lifetime, and he forbade his heirs to publish them, his poetry remained in manuscript until 1937. In 1939, T. H. Johnson published a selection of his poems. The most recent edition of Taylor's works was edited by D. E. Stanford in 1960. See studies by N. S. Grabo (1962), D. Stanford (1965), and W. J. Scheik (1974).

Taylor, Edward Thompson, 1793–1871, American Methodist missionary preacher among seamen, known as Father Taylor, b. Richmond, Va. He was licensed in 1814 to preach and ordained in 1819 in the Methodist ministry. In 1830 he became the missionary in charge of the Seamen's Bethel in Boston. He had spent much of his early life at sea, and his knowledge of nautical matters helped in his work among sailors; he was widely known and much loved. Walt Whitman wrote an article about him, and the sermon of Father Mapple in Melville's *Moby-Dick* reflects Taylor's speech and manner. He is mentioned in Dickens's *American Notes*, in Emerson's journals, and by other writers of the period.

Taylor, Elizabeth, 1932–, Anglo-American film actress, b. London. Regarded as one of the world's most beautiful women, Taylor is effective in dramatic roles, particularly as worldly or shrewish women. Her films include *National Velvet* (1944), *A Place in the Sun* (1951), *Cat on a Hot Tin Roof* (1958), *Butterfield 8* (1960), *Cleopatra* (1962), *Who's Afraid of Virginia Woolf?* (1966), and *Nightwatch* (1973). Taylor has been married five times; her fifth husband was Richard BURTON.

Taylor, Francis Henry, 1903–57, American museum director, b. Philadelphia, studied throughout Europe. He began his museum career as assistant curator (1927–28) and then curator of medieval art (1928–31) of the Philadelphia Museum of Art. As director of the Worcester (Mass.) Art Museum (1931–40; 1955–57) he did much to stimulate public interest in the museum. As director of the Metropolitan Museum (1940–55) he developed his theory of the museum as an institution of active public service, not simply a repository of art. His writings include *Babel's Tower* (1945); *The Taste of Angels* (1948), a history of art collecting; *Fifty Centuries of Art* (1954); and *Pierpont Morgan as Collector and Patron* (1957).

Taylor, Frederick Winslow, 1856–1915, American industrial engineer, b. Germantown, Pa., grad. Stevens Institute of Technology, 1883. He was called the father of scientific management. His management methods for shops, offices, and industrial plants were successfully introduced in many industries, notably steel mills. He was the author of *The Principles of Scientific Management* (1911), *Shop Management* (1911), *Concrete Costs* (with S. E. Thompson, 1912), and *Scientific Management* (ed. by C. B. Thompson, 1914). See the memorial volume ed. by the Taylor Society, New York (1920, repr. 1972); Sudhir Kakar, *Frederick Taylor: A Study in Personality and Innovation* (1970).

Taylor, George, 1716–81, political leader in the American Revolution, signer of the Declaration of Independence, b. Ireland. He settled in Pennsylvania (1736), where he became a manufacturer of iron. Taylor was a member of the Pennsylvania assembly, a county judge, an officer of the Pennsylvania militia, and a delegate to the Continental Congress (1776–77).

Taylor, Henry Osborn, 1856–1941, American historian and legal scholar, b. New York City. His lifework was the study of ancient and medieval civilizations. Among his books are *Ancient Ideals* (1896); his masterpiece, *The Medieval Mind* (1911); *Thought and Expression in the Sixteenth Century* (2d ed. 1930); and *A Historian's Creed* (1939).

Taylor, Isaac, 1829–1901, English clergyman, antiquarian, and author, chiefly noted for researches in philology. In 1885, Taylor became canon of York. His inclination towards controversy led to the writing of several theological pamphlets, among them *The Liturgy and the Dissenters* (1860). His study of Islam resulted in *Leaves from an Egyptian Notebook* (1888). Early philological investigations were incorporated in *Words and Places* (1864); *Etruscan Researches* (1874); and *Greeks and Goths* (1879), dealing with the origin of the RUNES. His most celebrated work, *The Alphabet*, was published in 1883. Taylor's *Origin of the Aryans* (1890) challenged the theory of Max Müller, then generally accepted, that central Asia was the cradle of the Indo-European peoples.

Taylor, Jeremy, 1613–67, English bishop and theological and devotional writer. He was distinguished as a preacher and as the author of some of the most noted religious works in English. After completing his studies at Cambridge and taking (1633) holy orders, he was nominated (1635) by Archbishop Laud to a fellowship at All Souls College, Oxford. He became chaplain to Laud and rector (1638) of Uppingham, Rutlandshire, but as a chaplain in ordinary to Charles I, Taylor left his country church to serve the king at the outbreak (1642) of the civil war. In a royalist defeat (1645) before Cardigan Castle, in Wales, he was briefly imprisoned. In 1645 he became principal of a school in Caermarthenshire, Wales, and served as private chaplain to the 2d earl of Carbery, at whose home, Golden Grove, Taylor wrote some of his most distinguished works. His period of greatest literary production was between 1646 and 1660. *The Liberty of Prophesying* (1647) was a noteworthy call for toleration. His *Great Exemplar . . . the Life and Death of Jesus Christ* (1649) was followed by other books of devotion—*Holy Living* (1650), *Holy Dying* (1651), *The Golden Grove* (1655), and *The Worthy Communicant* (1660). His learned *Ductor Dubitantium; or, The Rule of Conscience* (1660) was dedicated to Charles II. After the Restoration (1660) he was given the bishopric of Down and Connor, in Ireland, and appointed vice-chancellor of Trinity College, Dublin. At Dromore, which was added to his see, Taylor built (1661) the church in which he is buried. His tenure (1660–67) as bishop was a period of turbulent dispute with the Presbyterian ministers who refused to acknowledge episcopal jurisdiction. Taylor has been called the Shakespeare and the Spenser of the pulpit. A number of his sermons were published; many critics consider that in them his mastery of fine metaphor and his poetic imagination are best revealed. Taylor's *Whole Works* (ed. with an admirable biography by Reginald Heber, 15 vol., 1822) was edited and revised by C. P. Eden (10 vol., 1847–52). *The Golden Grove*, with selected passages from Taylor's sermons and writings, was edited in 1930 by Logan Pearsall Smith and contains a bibliography of Taylor's works by Robert Gathorne-Hardy. See biographies by Edmund Gosse (1904, repr. 1968) and C. J. Stranks (1952); studies by H. T. Hughes (1960) and F. L. Huntley (1970).

Taylor, John, 1578?–1653, English writer. He was a boatman on the Thames and hence is often called the Water Poet. A traveler throughout England and the Continent, he recorded his observations in both poetry and prose. See his works (5 vol., 1870–78); study by Wallace Notestein (1956).

Taylor, John, 1753–1824, American political philosopher. Known as John Taylor of Caroline, he was born in Virginia, probably in Caroline co., where he later lived at "Hazlewood." Orphaned at 10, he was adopted by his maternal uncle, Edmund Pendleton, who sent him to the College of William and Mary and under whom he studied law. Taylor fought in the American Revolution, rising to the rank of major, and was a member of the Virginia house of delegates (1779–81, 1783–85, 1796–1800) and of the U.S. Senate (1792–94, 1803, 1822–24). The STATES' RIGHTS doctrine (see KENTUCKY AND VIRGINIA RESOLUTIONS) was introduced in the Virginia house by Taylor, who became a leading publicist of Jeffersonian democracy. Although a strict constructionist, he defended the constitutionality of the Louisiana Purchase in *A Defense of the Measures of the Administration of Thomas Jefferson* (1804). In Thomas Jefferson's second term Taylor was a leader of the Quids, who, disliking James Madison, supported James Monroe for President, but he became a peacemaker between the factions. His greatest work, *An Inquiry into the Principles and Policy of the Government of the United States* (1814), was an attack on the growing power of finance capitalism and its harmful effects on agriculture and democracy. In *Construction Construed and Constitutions Vindicated* (1820), *Tyranny Unmasked* (1822), and *New Views of the Constitution* (1823), he opposed John Marshall and the growing power of the Federal government. An agrarian liberal, he was much concerned with the economic and political well-being of the farmer, and his *Arator* (1813) was one of the first analytical treatises on American agriculture and its problems. He is best known, however, as one of the first formulators of the states' rights doctrine. See biography by Henry Simms (1932); study by E. T. Mudge (1939, repr. 1968).

Taylor, John, 1808–87, American leader of the Mormon church, b. England. He emigrated in 1832 to Canada, where he was converted (1836) to the Mormon faith. He moved to the United States and became (1838) an apostle in the Mormon church. He was also active in missionary work in Europe. While a newspaper editor (1842–46) at Nauvoo, Ill., he was wounded by the mob that assassinated Joseph Smith in Carthage. In the controversy over Smith's successor, Taylor supported Brigham Young and assisted in the Utah colonization. In Utah he served in the territorial legislature (1857–76) and as probate judge (1868–70). After the death of Young, he became acting president (1877) and official president (1880) of the Mormon church. From 1884 until his death he directed the affairs of the church while in hiding to avoid arrest for polygamy.

Taylor, Laurette, 1884–1946, American actress, b. New York City as Helen Laurette Cooney. Taylor worked for many years in vaudeville and in stock companies before her first major success in *Alias Jimmy Valentine* (1910). She played in *Peg O' My Heart* (1912), her outstanding early triumph. In 1945, after an absence of several years, she returned to the stage to enormous acclaim as Amanda in *The Glass Menagerie*. Taylor was married to the playwright John Manners. See biography by Marguerite Courtney (1955).

Taylor, Maxwell Davenport, 1901–, U.S. general, b. Keytesville, Mo., grad. West Point, 1922. In World War II he served in Europe as chief of staff and artillery commander of the 82d Airborne Division and then as commander of the 101st Airborne Division. He was superintendent of West Point (1945–49), chief of staff of American forces in Europe (1949), and U.S. commander in Berlin (1949–51). He was appointed commander of the 8th Army in Korea (1953), commander of all U.S. forces in the Far East (1954), and then supreme commander of the UN forces in Korea (April, 1955). From 1955 to 1959 he served as army chief of staff, and he argued for an expanded, flexible army capable of fighting a limited war. When the Eisenhower administration disregarded his arguments, he resigned; he outlined his views in *An Uncertain Trumpet* (1959). In 1961, President John F. Kennedy appointed Taylor to the newly established post of military representative to the President, and in 1962 he became chairman of the joint chiefs of staff. He served until 1964, when President Lyndon B. Johnson named him ambassador to South Vietnam. While in that post he urged greater U.S. participation in the VIETNAM WAR. After resigning (1965) as ambassador he was, until 1970, a presidential consultant. He wrote *Responsibility and Response* (1967) and *Swords and Plowshares* (1972), a memoir.

Taylor, Myron Charles, 1874–1959, American industrialist and diplomat, b. Lyons, N.Y. He practiced law and then ran a group of textile mills in New England. In 1932 he succeeded J. P. Morgan, Jr., as chairman of the board of the U.S. Steel Corp. In 1937, after meetings with John L. Lewis, then president of the Committee for Industrial Organization, Taylor brought his board to agree to collective bargaining with the Steel Workers Organizing Committee, thus averting a serious strike. He retired from business in 1938 and served on several diplomatic and charitable committees. Taylor was (1939–50) the President's personal diplomatic representative to the Vatican. He retained the rank of ambassador until 1953 and served on several special missions.

Taylor, Paul, 1930–, American modern dance choreographer, b. Pittsburgh, Pa. Taylor was training as an artist before he received scholarships to study dance. He made his debut with the Merce Cunningham company in 1953 and in the same year performed his first dance composition. From 1955 to 1961 he won acclaim both as leading soloist with the Martha Graham company and as creator of avant-garde dances for his own company, which he formed in 1954. His innovations included performing to the sound of heartbeats and telephone time signals (see MODERN DANCE). Since 1961 he has devoted himself to choreography for his company much of which is often considered less radical than his earlier work.

Taylor, Richard, 1826-79, Confederate general in the American Civil War, b. near Louisville, Ky.; son of Zachary Taylor. A Louisiana planter, he attained some political prominence and was a member of the Louisiana secession convention. In the Civil War he was made a brigadier general (Oct., 1861) and fought under Thomas J. (Stonewall) Jackson in the Shenandoah Valley and in the Seven Days battles of the Peninsular campaign. He was made commander in Louisiana in 1862. His victory at SABINE CROSSROADS (April 8, 1864), although followed by a repulse at Pleasant Hill the next day, induced Gen. Nathaniel P. BANKS to abandon his Red River expedition. In Aug., 1864, Taylor was promoted to lieutenant general and made commander in the lower South. The collapse of the Confederate armies in the East led him to surrender in May, 1865. In 1879 he wrote *Destruction and Reconstruction* (ed. by R. B. Harwell, 1955).

Taylor, Robert Love, 1850-1912, governor of Tennessee (1887-91, 1897-99), b. Carter co., Tenn. A lawyer, he was a Democrat in Congress (1879-81) and in 1886 defeated his brother Alfred Alexander Taylor (1848-1931), a Republican, for the governorship. As governor he conciliated between the old-line states' rights Democrats, the rising industrialist class, and the forces of agrarian unrest that had brought him to power. He was a U.S. Senator (1907-12) and, beloved by the common people, a popular lecturer. See D. M. Robison, *Bob Taylor and the Agrarian Revolt in Tennessee* (1935).

Taylor, Tom, 1817-80, English dramatist and editor. His most famous play is *Our American Cousin* (1858), performed at Ford's Theater in Washington, D. C., when Lincoln was assassinated. Of his more than 100 plays, others are *The Ticket-of-Leave Man* (1863) and, written with his friend Charles Reade, *Masks and Faces* (1852). He edited B. R. Haydon's autobiography (1853, new ed. 1926) and was editor of *Punch* from 1874 to 1880. See Winton Tolles, *Tom Taylor and the Victorian Drama* (1940).

Taylor, Zachary (zăk'ərē), 1784-1850, 12th President of the United States (1849-50), b. Orange co., Va. He was raised in Kentucky. Taylor joined the army in 1808, became a captain in 1810, and was promoted to major for his defense of Fort Harrison (1812) in the War of 1812. Continuing his army career, he became a colonel (1832) and served in the Black Hawk War and in the campaigns against the Seminole Indians in Florida, winning the nickname of "Old Rough and Ready." Sent to the Southwest to command the army at the Texas border, Taylor began (1845) to prepare for hostilities with Mexico regarding the annexation of Texas. He pushed into the disputed territory S of the Nueces River and, in the MEXICAN WAR, defeated the Mexicans at PALO ALTO and RESACA DE LA PALMA, drove them across the Rio Grande, and took Matamoros. Later he forced the surrender of the Mexican stronghold at Monterrey. In 1847 he won the decisive battle of BUENA VISTA in the face of great odds. A popular hero, Taylor was nominated for President on the Whig ticket, was elected, and assumed office in 1849. His nonpartisan tendencies were changed under the influence of Senator William H. Seward, and Taylor was soon a strong supporter of Whig policy. As President, he supported the Wilmot Proviso, which excluded slavery from all the territory acquired as a result of the Mexican War. He favored the rapid admission of both California and New Mexico to the Union and the strict limitation of the Texas boundary claims. His free-soil views put him in opposition to the measures that were to become the COMPROMISE of 1850. After charges of corruption were lodged against members of his cabinet, he determined on a reorganization, but he was stricken with cholera morbus and died on July 9, 1850. He was succeeded by Millard Fillmore. See biographies by Holman Hamilton (2 vol., 1941 and 1951; repr. 1966), Brainerd Dyer (1946, repr. 1967), and S. B. McKinley and Silas Bent (1946); E. J. Nichols, *Zach Taylor's Little Army* (1963).

Taylor, city (1970 pop. 70,020), Wayne co., SE Mich., a suburb of Detroit adjacent to Dearborn; founded 1847 as a township, inc. as a city 1968. A small rural village until World War II, it grew from c.5,000 to its present size in two decades. Its growth has been commercial as well as residential, and its manufactures include tools and machines.

Taylorville, city (1970 pop. 10,927), seat of Christian co., central Ill., in a farm and coal area; inc. 1882. Soybeans are processed, coal is mined, and farm and coal equipment and paper, plastic, and metal products are made.

Tayma (tä'mä), large oasis, SW Saudi Arabia. Cuneiform inscriptions possibly dating from the 6th cent. B.C. have been recovered from Tayma. In ancient Arabic tradition the oasis was noted as a prosperous Jewish colony, rich in water wells and handsome buildings. It is mentioned several times in the Bible (Job 6.19; Isa. 21.14; Jer. 25.23). The biblical eponym is apparently Tema, one of the sons of Ishmael (Gen. 25.15; 1 Chron. 1.30).

Taymyra or **Taimyra** (both: tīmē'rə), river, c.400 mi (640 km) long, rising in the center of the Taymyr Peninsula, N Siberian USSR. It flows NE through Lake Taymyr (c.2,700 sq mi/6,990 sq km) and into the Taymyr Gulf of the Kara Sea. Taymyr Island is near its mouth. There are coal deposits near Lake Taymyr.

Taymyr Peninsula or **Taimyr Peninsula** (both: tīmĭr'), northernmost projection of Siberia, N central Siberian USSR, between the estuaries of the Yenisei and Khatanga rivers and extending into the Arctic Ocean. Cape Chelyuskin at the tip of the peninsula is the northernmost point of the Asian mainland. The peninsula, covered mostly with tundra and drained by the Taymyra River, forms most of the Taymyr National Okrug.

Tay Ninh (tā nĭn), city, South Vietnam, NW of Saigon. It is the center of the Cao Dai, a politically active religious group that was suppressed by South Vietnamese forces after an armed insurrection in 1955. The Cao Dai are still active but are no longer a political threat to the South Vietnam central government. Of interest is the Cao Dai cathedral, which has a blend of Christian, Islam, and Buddhist architectural features. The city has a large Khmer population.

Tazoult (täzült'), formerly **Lambèse** (läNbĕz'), town (1966 pop. 6,000), NE Algeria. It is noted for the ruins of a Roman town (Lambaesis) founded in the 2d cent. under Emperor Hadrian as the encampment of the third Augustan Legion and destroyed in the 5th cent. The ruins consist of barracks, baths, offices, and an amphitheater. The town lost its importance from the time of the Byzantine Empire. The modern village has a famous penitentiary.

Tb, chemical symbol of the element TERBIUM.

Tbilisi (təbĭl'ēsē, ətbĭlyē'sē) or **Tiflis** (tĭf'lĭs, Rus. tĭflyēs'), city (1970 pop. 889,000), capital of the Georgian Soviet Socialist Republic, SE European USSR, on the Kura River and the Transcaucasian RR and at the southern end of the Georgian Military Road. Located in a mountain-ringed basin, Tbilisi is the economic, administrative, and cultural heartland of Transcaucasia. It is also a major transportation center. Industries include filmmaking, printing and publishing, machine building, food processing, tanning, silk weaving, and the production of machine tools, electrical equipment, locomotives, and plastics. Orchards and vineyards surround the city. The region's mineral springs provide the basis for numerous health resorts. Tbilisi is one of the USSR's oldest cities. Archaeological evidence indicates that the site was settled as early as the 4th cent. B.C. The Persian military governor of Georgia built a fortress on the hill of Tbilisi in the 4th cent. A.D., and in the 5th cent. the capital of the old Georgian kingdom was transferred there from Mtskheta. In the 6th cent., Tbilisi became the seat of the Iberian dynasty. The city lay along the natural trade route between the Caspian and Black seas but was also astride one of the world's great crossroads of invasion and migration. Tbilisi was a stronghold of Muslim power and a commercial center from the 8th to 11th cent.; during this period Arabs, Khazars, Seljuks, and Ottoman Turks successively ruled the city. From 1096 to 1225 it flourished as the capital of an independent Georgian state. It was ruled from the 13th to 18th cent. by Mongols, Iranians, and Turks before coming under Russian control in 1800-1801. It became the seat of the czarist government in the Caucasus but also developed as a revolutionary center from the second half of the 19th cent. and played a leading role in the Revolution of 1905. Tbilisi was the capital of the anti-Bolshevik Transcaucasian Federation (1917-18), of independent Georgia (1918-20), and of the Transcaucasian Socialist Federated Soviet Republic (1922-36). Georgia was made a separate constituent republic in 1936, with Tbilisi as its capital. The city rises in terraces from both banks of the Kura. In the old section are medieval buildings and courtyards, narrow streets, overhanging balconies, and the famous hot sulfur springs. The rest of the city has been extensively modernized. Landmarks include the remains of the Zion Cathedral (6th cent.; rebuilt 16th-18th cent.), the Anchiskhat Basilica (6th-7th cent.), and the Metekhi castle and church (1278-89). A funicular railway runs to Mt. David. Tbilisi's educational and cultural facilities include the Georgian State Univ. (1918), the Georgian Academy of Art (1922), and the Academy of Science (1941). Stalin studied at the city's Orthodox seminary and worked with Bolshevik underground groups in Tbilisi.

Tc, chemical symbol of the element TECHNETIUM.

Tch-. For Russian names beginning thus and not listed here, see CH—; e.g., for Tchekhoff, see CHEKHOV; for Tchicherin, see CHICHERIN.

Tchaikovsky, Peter Ilyich (ĭlyēch' chĭkôf'skē), 1840-93, Russian composer. Variant spellings of his name include Tschaikovsky and Chaikovsky. He is a towering figure in Russian music and one of the most popular composers in history. The son of a mining inspector, Tchaikovsky studied music as a child. At 19 he became a government clerk and at 21 entered the St. Petersburg Conservatory, where he studied composition with Anton Rubinstein. He graduated in 1865 and taught theory and composition at Nicholas Rubinstein's Moscow Conservatory from 1865 to 1878. An annuity from his wealthy patroness, Mme von Meck (whom he never met though he corresponded with her for 14 years and dedicated his Fourth Symphony to her in 1878), made it possible for him to devote himself entirely to composition. Tchaikovsky wrote nine operas, four concertos, six symphonies, a great number of songs and short piano pieces, three ballets, three string quartets, suites and symphonic poems, and numerous other works. His compositions sustained him throughout his continuous battle with his own nature. In 1877 Tchaikovsky made a disastrous marriage in order to defeat the torment of his homosexuality and to deny the spreading rumors of it. His work was again his consolation when Mme van Meck terminated her friendship and support without apparent reason. Tchaikovsky was opposed to the aims of the Russian nationalist composers and used Western European forms and idioms, although his work instinctively reflects the Russian temperament. His orchestration is rich, and his music is melodious, intensely emotional, and often melancholy. Most successful are his orchestral works, notably his last three symphonies; the fantasies *Romeo and Juliet* (1869, rev. 1870 and 1879) and *Francesca da Rimini* (1876); *Marche slave* (1876); the Manfred Symphony (1885); the ballets *Swan Lake* (1876), *The Sleeping Beauty* (1889), and *The Nutcracker* (1892; also arranged as a suite for orchestra); and the Piano Concerto in B Flat Minor (1875) and the Violin Concerto in D (1878). Of his operas, notable are *Vakula, the Smith* (1876); *Eugene Onegin* (1879) and *The Queen of Spades* (1890), both from stories by Pushkin; and *The Maid of Orleans* (1881). None of the operas, however, achieved the popularity of his symphonies, ballets, and concertos. He toured Europe as a conductor and conducted his *Marche solennelle* at the opening concert in Carnegie Hall, New York City, in 1891. A few days after he conducted the première of his Sixth Symphony, or *Symphonie pathétique,* he died of cholera. In Russia his most gifted followers were Rachmaninov and Arenski. His influence has been great in Russia during the Soviet era, as well as in England and the United States. See his life and letters by his brother Modeste, ed. by Rosa Newmarch (2 vol., 1905, repr. 1970); diaries, ed. by Wladimir Lakond (tr. 1945); biographies by Herbert Weinstock (1943) and Lawrence and Elisabeth Hanson (1966); studies by G. E. H. Abraham, ed. (1946, repr. 1969), J. H. Warrack (1969) and Edward Garden (1973).

Tchelitchew, Pavel (pä'vĕl chālē'chĕf), 1898-1957, Russian-American painter. His first commissions, ballet designs, were given him while he was living in Berlin (1921-23), whence he had fled from the Russian Revolution. Moving to Paris (1923), he became associated with Diaghilev. In 1926 he developed his technique of multiple images on a single canvas, which he later combined with triple perspective. Experimenting thus with juxtaposed objects, he sought to recreate the motion of the body. These interior landscapes resulted in complex and fantastic compositions. The best-known work in this manner is *Hide and Seek* (Mus. of Modern Art, New York City). He was also a portraitist, Edith Sitwell being among his sitters. See biography by Parker Tyler (1967); study by J. T. Soby (1942, repr. 1972).

Tchernaiev or **Chernyaiev, Mikhail Grigoryevich** (mēkhəyēl' grĭgôr'yəvĭch chĭrnyī'əf), 1828-98, Russian general and Pan-Slavist. Sent on a minor mission to central Asia in 1864, he exceeded his instructions and conquered (1865) Tashkent, principal city of the Muslim khanate of Kokand. His action precipitated further Russian expansion in central Asia. Because of his adventurous deeds, however, he was forced to retire from the army. As the owner of a periodical, he was an ardent exponent of Pan-Slavism. When Serbia went to the aid of Balkan rebels against Turkey (1876), he offered his services to the Serbs and was given command of Serbian forces, but was defeated. From 1882 to 1884 he was governor general of Russian Turkistan.

Tchernihovsky, Saul (chərnəhôf'skē), 1875–1943, Russian poet who wrote in Hebrew. He was a practicing physician. His sonnets and idylls eschew the didacticism of typical Hebrew poetry and show a pantheistic outlook, derived from the Greek classics, which he admired and translated into Hebrew.

Tczew (chĕf), Ger. *Dirschau,* town (1970 pop. 40,794), N Poland, a port on the Vistula River. It is a rail junction, with railroad workshops and industries producing river boats, farm machinery, construction materials, and enamelware. Chartered in 1260, Tczew became part of Poland in the late 13th cent. but was held by the TEUTONIC KNIGHTS from 1308 to 1466, when it reverted to Poland. It passed to Russia in 1772 and was not reincorporated into Poland until 1919.

TDP (thymidine diphosphate): see THYMINE.

Te, chemical symbol of the element TELLURIUM.

tea, tree or bush, its leaves, and the beverage made from the leaves. The plant (*Thea sinensis, Camellia thea,* or *C. sinensis*) is an evergreen related to the camellia and indigenous to Assam (India) and probably to parts of China and Japan. In its native state it grows to a height of about 30 ft (9.1 m), but in cultivation it is pruned to from 3 to 5 ft (91–152 cm). The lanceolate leaves are dark green; the blossom is cream-colored and fragrant. Tea was cultivated in China in prehistoric times and was probably first used as a vegetable relish (as it was in the American colonies and still is in some parts of the Orient) and medicinally. By the 8th cent. cultivation had begun on a commercial scale in China and shortly thereafter in Japan. The tea ceremony of Japan was introduced from China in the 15th cent. by Buddhists as a semireligious social custom. Tea was first imported into Europe by the Dutch East India Company in the early 17th cent., and its subsequent popularity played an important part in opening the Orient to Occidental commerce. Until 1834 the British East India Company held a monopoly on imports to Great Britain, trading by direct and indirect routes exclusively with China. Only after this monopoly was broken did other tea-producing areas develop as major exporters—chiefly India, Ceylon (Sri Lanka), Indonesia, Japan, and Formosa (Taiwan). Today the United Kingdom consumes nearly one third of the approximately one million tons of tea produced annually throughout the world. Other leading importers are Australia, Canada, the USSR, and the Netherlands; the United States also is a large importer, although coffee was given impetus as a more popular beverage by the Boston Tea Party. Tea culture requires a protected, well-drained habitat in a warm climate with ample rainfall. The leaves are picked by hand, principally during flushes (periods of active growth), the most desirable being those near the growing tip. They are prepared by withering, rolling, and firing (i.e., heating). Black teas (e.g., pekoes, souchongs, and congous) differ from green teas (e.g., imperials, gunpowders, and hysons) in having been fermented before firing; oolongs, intermediate in color and flavor, are partially fermented. Green teas are produced chiefly in China and Japan; black teas in China, Java, India, and Ceylon; and oolongs in Formosa. China, where the plant is traditionally grown in family plots, remains the largest tea grower of the world; elsewhere tea is usually grown on plantations. Although much black tea is now produced in Brazil and elsewhere in South America, cultivation in North America has been found impractical because of the shortage of cheap labor. The many kinds of tea are usually named for their color and grade (the best teas using only the two terminal leaves) or for their district of origin, e.g., Darjeeling and Lapsang. Brick tea is made from tea dust or inferior tea pressed into blocks. The flavor of tea is due to volatile oils, its stimulating properties to CAFFEINE, and its astringency to the tannin content (reduced in black teas by the fermentation process). Teas are sometimes scented by exposure to fragrant flowers, e.g., jasmine. Today tea is used by more people and in greater quantity than any beverage except water. In all parts of the world tealike beverages (sometimes called tisanes) are made from the leaves or flowers of a wide variety of other plants, often for their medicinal properties. Tea is classified in the division MAGNOLIOPHYTA, class Magnoliopsida, order Theales, family Theaceae. See C. R. Harler, *Tea Manufacture* (1963) and *Tea Growing* (1966); Jamie Shalleck, *Tea* (1972).

Teach, Edward: see BLACKBEARD.

teachers colleges: see TEACHER TRAINING.

teacher training, professional preparation of teachers, usually through formal course work and practice teaching. Specific training for teachers was originated in France (1685) by St. JOHN BAPTIST DE LA SALLE. Teacher training spread rapidly in Europe as a result of the work of August Hermann FRANCKE and Johann PESTALOZZI and through the influence of the MONITORIAL SYSTEM. From Europe the monitorial training method spread to the United States (c.1810). Prior to that time, especially during the colonial period, the only requirements for teaching in the lower schools were a modicum of learning and a willingness to work in what was then an ill-paid, low-prestige occupation. By the 1820s and 30s, however, teacher training became common in the academies, the equivalent of today's secondary schools. The nation's first private normal school, a two-year post-high school training institute for elementary school teachers, was opened by Samuel R. Hall (1823); the first state-supported normal school was created by Massachusetts (1839). With the assistance of Henry Barnard and Horace Mann, the number of normal schools in the United States increased rapidly during the latter half of the 19th cent. Their sole purpose, however, continued to be professional instruction of elementary school teachers; to meet this goal an especially strong emphasis was placed on the psychology of child development. Training for secondary school teaching was largely a function of liberal arts colleges that had introduced pedagogical courses into their curriculums, but the need for greater numbers of teachers at the turn of the century led the normal schools to expand into four-year degree-granting teachers colleges. By the 1920s and 30s these teachers colleges, generally supported by the public, were training substantial numbers of the nation's public school teachers. Since 1940, however, the character of the teachers colleges has undergone considerable change. Increasingly they have lost their identity as single-purpose institutions and have become liberal arts colleges offering a broad general education in addition to the specialized courses in pedagogy. John DEWEY, who formulated basic concepts of teaching methods, profoundly influenced the development of teacher training in the 20th cent. Certification requirements for teaching have advanced with educational opportunity, although they vary from state to state. The trend in certification has been toward requiring more complete training, with practice teaching and extensive graduate work for specialized positions. In many states extension or summer graduate work is required of teachers or is made a prerequisite for advancement. The first graduate program in education was established at New York University (1887). In the following year the teacher-training school that is presently known as Teachers College, Columbia Univ., was founded. Since the establishment of those two institutions, graduate study in education has expanded rapidly. A number of graduate professional degrees are now offered, including the Master of Arts in Teaching and the Doctor of Education. While the professional requirements for teaching in the United States have in the past stressed method and psychology, increasing emphasis is now being placed on subject matter specialization; European countries have generally stressed scholarship. The success of teacher training for elementary and secondary education has led some college administrations to consider requiring such training for college teaching also. See EDUCATION; PROGRESSIVE EDUCATION; VOCATIONAL EDUCATION; PROGRAMMED INSTRUCTION. See W. S. Monroe, *Teaching-Learning Theory and Teacher Education* (1952); M. L. Borrowman, *The Liberal and Technical in Teacher Education* (1956); J. B. Conant, *The Education of American Teachers* (1963); Lawrence K. Levan et al., *Teacher Education* (1967); Edmund J. King, *The Education of Teachers* (1970).

teaching machines: see PROGRAMMED INSTRUCTION.

teak, tall deciduous tree (*Tectona grandis*) of the family Verbenaceae (VERVAIN family), native to India and Malaysia but now widely cultivated in other tropical areas. Teakwood is moderately hard, easily worked, and extremely durable; beams said to be over 1,000 years old are still functional. The wood contains an essential oil that resists the action of water and prevents the rusting of iron. The heartwood is resistant to termites. Teak is superior to all other woods for shipbuilding and is also used for furniture, flooring, and general construction. Several other similar woods from unrelated trees are sometimes also called teak. Teak (*Tectona grandis*) is classified in the division MAGNOLIOPHYTA, class Magnoliopsida, order Famiales, family Verbenaceae.

teal: see DUCK.

Teamsters union, U.S. labor union formed in 1903 by the amalgamation of the Team Drivers International Union and the Teamsters National Union. Its full name is the International Brotherhood of Teamsters, Chauffeurs, Warehousemen, and Helpers of America, the majority of its members being truck drivers. The strongest centers of unionized teamsters at the turn of the century were in Chicago, New York City, Boston, and St. Louis. Chicago had about half the membership and was the scene of an unsuccessful strike against Montgomery Ward & Co. in 1905; it resulted in a decline in union membership. In 1907, Daniel J. Tobin, a Boston teamster unconnected with the strike, became president. He held the position until 1952, and his policy of avoiding sympathetic action on behalf of other unions and zealously guarding the expenditure of union funds helped the union to grow. The growth continued after 1933, when the teamsters undertook the organization of the rapidly growing long-distance trucking industry. By threatening to stop deliveries to and from employers who refused to come to terms, the Teamsters were able to gain contracts not only in trucking but in related enterprises. By 1940 the Teamsters was the single largest union in the country, a position it has since maintained. In the early 1940s, Tobin successfully withstood a threat to his leadership from a Minneapolis local led by the Dunne brothers and Farrell Dobbs. During the presidencies of Tobin's two immediate successors, Dave BECK and James R. HOFFA, charges of corruption were levied against the union. The revelations of a Senate investigating committee led the American Federation of Labor and Congress of Industrial Organizations (AFL-CIO) to expel the Teamsters in 1957 and they remain so today. Beck was sent to prison the following year for larceny and income tax dodging. The evasiveness of Beck and Hoffa before various Senate committees was an important factor in the passage (1959) of the LANDRUM-GRIFFIN ACT. Opposition within the union to Hoffa forced him to accept a three-man monitorship over his presidency until 1961, but that did not seriously impair his power. Hoffa himself was sent to prison in 1967; he retained the presidency of the union, however, until 1971, when he resigned and was succeeded by Frank E. Fitzsimmons. Under conditions of parole, Hoffa was barred from holding union office until 1980, but sued in 1974 to have this restriction lifted on the grounds that a deal had been worked out whereby Fitzsimmons would support President Nixon's reelection in return for the assurance that Hoffa would not be able to challenge Fitzsimmons's presidency. In recent years the Teamsters have followed a course somewhat independent of the rest of organized labor, e.g., Fitzsimmons refused (1972) to resign from the Wage and Price Commission although the other labor representatives did so. In addition, the Teamsters were the only major union to support President Nixon's reelection bid in 1972. See R. D. Leiter, *The Teamsters Union* (1957); Sam Romer, *The International Brotherhood of Teamsters* (1962); Donald Garnel, *The Rise of Teamster Power in the West* (1972).

Teaneck (tē'nĕk), residential suburban township (1970 pop. 42,355), Bergen co., NE N.J., near the Hackensack River; settled in the early 1600s, inc. 1895. Porcelain, bulbs and fuses, food seasonings, and textile looms are among its manufactures. Teaneck developed rapidly after the construction of the George Washington Bridge (1931). Fairleigh Dickinson Univ. has a campus there. The city has several 18th-century homes.

Teapot Dome, in U.S. history, oil reserve scandal that began during the administration of President HARDING. In 1921, by executive order of the President, control of naval oil reserves at Teapot Dome, Wyo., and at Elk Hills, Calif., was transferred from the Navy Dept. to the Dept. of the Interior. The oil reserves had been set aside for the navy by President Wilson. In 1922, Albert B. FALL, U.S. Secretary of the Interior, leased, without competitive bidding, the Teapot Dome fields to Harry F. Sinclair, an oil operator, and the field at Elk Hills, Calif., to Edward L. Doheny. These transactions became (1922–23) the subject of a Senate investigation conducted by Sen. Thomas J. WALSH. It was found that in 1921, Doheny had lent Fall $100,000, interest-free, and that upon

Fall's retirement as Secretary of the Interior (March, 1923) Sinclair also "loaned" him a large amount of money. The investigation led to criminal prosecutions. Fall was indicted for conspiracy and for accepting bribes. Convicted of the latter charge, he was sentenced to a year in prison and fined $100,000. In another trial for bribery Doheny and Sinclair were acquitted, although Sinclair was subsequently sentenced to prison for contempt of the Senate and for employing detectives to shadow members of the jury in his case. The oil fields were restored to the U.S. government through a Supreme Court decision in 1927. See M. R. Werner and John Starr, *Teapot Dome* (1959); Burl Noggle, *Teapot Dome* (1962).

tear gas, gas that causes temporary blindness through the excessive flow of tears resulting from irritation of the eyes. The gas is used in CHEMICAL WARFARE and as a means for dispersing mobs. Compounds that cause lacrimation (watering of the eyes) include bromoacetone, benzyl bromide, chloroacetophenone, ethyl iodoacetate, chloropicrin bromobenzyl cyanide, and bromine-substituted xylenes. In warfare a lacrimating compound in liquid form is placed in bombs, shells, or grenades; when the device explodes, the liquid is dispersed as an aerosol.

tears, watery secretion of the lacrimal gland, which is located at the outer corner of the eye socket immediately above the eyeball. Tearing, or lacrimation, is a continuous and largely involuntary process stimulated by the autonomic nervous system. Fluid is secreted into the lacrimal lake, the area between the eyeball and the upper eyelid, and spread across the surface of the eye by blinking. Tears serve to bathe and lubricate the cornea, the sensitive outer covering of the eyeball. Typically, the fluid either evaporates or is drained off through tiny canals at the inner corner of the eye, but in times of excessive tearing the apparatus is overwhelmed and tears overflow the eyes.

Teasdale, Sara (tēz'dāl), 1884–1933, American poet, b. St. Louis. She wrote several volumes of delicate and highly personal lyrics, including *Helen of Troy and Other Poems* (1911), *Rivers to the Sea* (1915), *Flame and Shadow* (1920), and *Strange Victory* (1933). An extraordinarily sensitive, almost reclusive, woman, Teasdale ended her life by suicide at the age of 48.

teasel, common name for some members of the Dipsacaceae, a family of chiefly Old World herbs found mostly in the Mediterranean and Balkan areas but ranging to India and to S Africa. Species of *Dipsacus* and *Scabiosa* have become widely naturalized in America. *Scabiosa*, commonly called sweet scabious, mourning bride, or pincushion flower (for its head of small, lacy flowers) includes several ornamentals and was formerly used as a remedy for the itch (scabies). Fuller's teasel (*D. fullonum*) is a noxious biennial weed whose heads of small flowers bear sharp prongs still sometimes used in the textile industry for teasing or raising the nap on wool. Teasels are often used in EVERLASTING bouquets. Teasels are classified in the division MAGNOLIOPHYTA, class Magnoliopsida, order Dipsacales.

Tebah (tē'bə), son of Nahor, eponym of Tibhath. Gen. 22.24.

Tebaldi, Renata (rānä'tä täbäl'dē), 1922–, Italian lyric soprano. She received early musical training at home and at the Boito Conservatory, Parma. In 1944 she made her professional debut and in 1946 sang at the reopening of La Scala in Milan. She has been a member of the Metropolitan Opera since 1955. Tebaldi has sung and recorded in many countries and has been particularly acclaimed for her interpretations of the title roles in *Tosca, Aïda,* and *Madame Butterfly.* See biography by V. I. Seroff (1970).

Tebaliah (tĕb"əlī'ə), doorkeeper. 1 Chron. 26.11.

Tebessa (təbĕs'ə), Fr. *Tébessa*, ancient *Theveste*, town (1966 pop. 46,148), NE Algeria, in the Atlas Mts. The town is an important agricultural market and is noted for its silk embroidery and carpets. The surrounding area is an important phosphate- and iron-mining region. Extensive ancient remains include the Roman Arch of Caracalla, a Christian basilica (c.4th cent. A.D.), and restored Byzantine walls and temples.

Teche, Bayou (bī'ō tĕsh, bī'o͞o), 125 mi (201 km) long, S La., formed by tributary bayous and flowing SE to the Atchafalaya River near Morgan City. Navigable for more than 100 mi (161 km), it flows through a fertile sugarcane area. Bayou Teche was the setting for Longfellow's *Evangeline*.

technetium (tĕknē'shēəm) [Gr. *technetos*=artificial], artificially produced radioactive chemical element; symbol Tc; at. no. 43; mass no. of most stable isotope 97; m.p. about 2200°C; b.p. about 5030°C; sp. gr. 11.5 (calculated); valence +4, +6, or +7. Technetium is a radioactive silver-gray metal. In some of its chemical properties it resembles rhenium, the element below it in group VIIb of the PERIODIC TABLE. It tarnishes slowly when exposed to moist air. Although it is not attacked by hydrochloric acid, it dissolves in concentrated sulfuric or nitric acid and in aqua regia. The pure metal may be prepared by chemical reduction of certain of its compounds with hydrogen gas. Potassium technetate, $KTcO_4$, has found some use in alloys with iron and steel; the addition of a small amount renders the alloy highly resistant to corrosion. This use is limited by the radioactivity of the element. The most stable isotope, technetium-97, has a half-life of 2.6 million years; most of the other 15 known isotopes are much less stable. Technetium-95m is a gamma ray emitter with a half-life of 61 days that is sometimes used in radioactive tracer studies. Technetium was once very rare and expensive but is now obtained in quantity from nuclear reactor fission products. Although the spectra of some stars show that they contain technetium, the naturally occurring element has not been found on earth. It is called technetium because it was the first element to be prepared synthetically. Its existence was predicted from the periodic table. Discovery of the element in nature was erroneously claimed in 1925 by the German chemists I. W. and W. K. Noddack, who called it masurium. The element was discovered in 1937 by C. Perrier and E.G. Segrè of Italy in a sample of molybdenum that was bombarded with deuterons in a cyclotron at the Univ. of California at Berkeley and sent to them by E. O. Lawrence.

Tecumseh (tĭkŭm'sē), 1768?–1813, chief of the SHAWNEE INDIANS, b. probably in Clark co., Ohio. Among his people he became distinguished for his prowess in battle, but he opposed the practice of torturing prisoners. When the United States refused to recognize his principle that all Indian land was the common possession of all the Indians and that land could not rightly be ceded by, or purchased from, an individual tribe, Tecumseh set out to bind together the Indians of the Old Northwest, the South, and the eastern Mississippi valley. His plan failed with the defeat of his brother, the SHAWNEE PROPHET, at TIPPECANOE (1811). Though Tippecanoe was, properly speaking, a drawn battle, it marked the collapse of the Indian military movement. In the War of 1812, Tecumseh allied himself with the British and was made a brigadier general. He led a large force of Indians in the siege of Fort Meigs, covered Gen. Henry Procter's retreat after the American victory on Lake Erie, and lost his life in the battle of the Thames (see THAMES, BATTLE OF THE), in which Gen. William Henry HARRISON overwhelmed Procter and his Indian allies. Tecumseh had great ability as an organizer and a leader and is considered one of the outstanding Indians in American history. See biographies by Benjamin Drake (1841, repr. 1969), J. M. Oskison (1938), and Glenn Tucker (1956, repr. 1973); C. F. Klinck, *Tecumseh: Fact and Fiction in Early Records* (1961); A. W. Eckert, *The Frontiersmen* (1967).

Tedder, Arthur William Tedder, 1st **Baron,** 1890–1967, British air marshal. He saw service in the infantry and the Royal Flying Corps in World War I. After 1919 he held important positions in the Royal Air Force and the air ministry. Tedder was sent to the Middle East in 1940 and, as air chief there (1941–43), helped sweep the Germans from Tunisia. In 1943 he held a Mediterranean command and later that year was appointed deputy supreme commander of the Allied invasion forces. Raised to the peerage in 1946, he served as air chief of staff (1946–50) and in 1950 became chancellor of Cambridge Univ. See his memoirs, *With Prejudice* (1966).

Te Deum laudamus (tē dē'əm lôdā'məs, tā dā'o͝om loudä'mo͞os) [Latin,=we praise Thee, O God], ancient hymn of the Western Church beginning, "We praise Thee, O God, we acknowledge Thee to be the Lord." Legend ascribes it to an ecstatic outburst of St. Ambrose when he baptized St. Augustine. It is now widely attributed to Bishop Nicetas of Dacia (c.335–414). Some scholars believe it to be a composite of Greek sources from the 5th cent. or earlier. It is sung at morning prayer in Anglican churches and at matins in the Roman office; it is the chief hymn of rejoicing in the Roman Catholic Church.

Tedzhen, river: see HARI RUD.

Tees, river, c.70 mi (110 km) long, rising on Cross Fell in the Pennines, N England, and flowing generally E between Durham and North Yorkshire and through Cleveland to the North Sea. Its upper valley is picturesque; the falls of Caldron Snout and High Force are notable. The lower reaches pass through Teeside, a major industrial region. The river is navigable through a dredged channel to Stockton-on-Tees.

Teeside, county borough (1971 pop. 395,477), Durham and North Riding of Yorkshire, NE England at the mouth of the Tees River. Teeside was created in 1968 by the merger of the county borough of Middlesbrough; the municipal boroughs of Stockton-on-Tees, Thornaby-on-Tees, and Redcar (except for a very small part); most of the urban districts of Billingham and Eston; smaller portions of the urban districts of Guisborough, Saltburn, and Marske-by-the-Sea; and parts of the rural districts of Stockton and Stokesley. Boulby Cliff, the highest cliff on the English coastline, is within its borders. Iron ore and coal are mined in the surrounding area. There are iron and steel works, shipbuilding and repair yards, and chemical plants that are among the largest in England and produce items ranging from explosives to synthetic fabrics. Iron ore from Middlesbrough was used in several bridges in other parts of the world. Before iron was discovered there in 1831, Middlesbrough was a coal port. Stockton-on-Tees developed industrially after the opening of the Stockton and Darlington Railway (the first important railroad in Great Britain) in 1825. It has large iron works and is also a market for cattle and agricultural produce. Thomas Sheraton, the furniture designer, was born there. Redcar, a former fishing village, is now a seaside resort. In 1974, Teeside became part of the new nonmetropolitan county of Cleveland. The name is also spelled Teesside.

teeth, hard, calcified structures embedded in the bone of the jaws that perform the function of mastication. Man and most other mammals have a temporary set of teeth, the deciduous, or milk, teeth; in human beings they usually develop between the 6th and 30th months. These number 20 in all: 2 central incisors, 2 lateral incisors, 2 canines, and 4 premolars in each jaw. At about six years of age the preliminary teeth begin to be shed as the permanent set

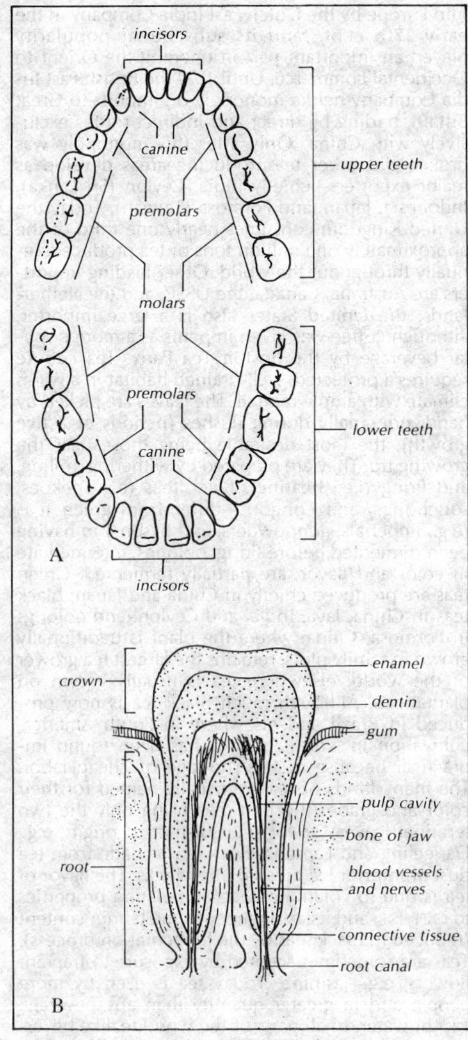

A. *Upper and lower teeth of an adult*

B. *Cross section of a molar*

replaces them. The last of the permanent teeth (wisdom teeth) may not appear until the 25th year and in some persons do not erupt at all. The permanent teeth number 32 in all: 4 incisors, 2 canines, 4 bicuspids, and 4 (or 6, if wisdom teeth develop) molars in each jaw. A tooth consists of a crown, the portion visible in the mouth, and one or more roots embedded in a gum socket. The portion of the gum that surrounds the root, called the periodontal membrane, cushions the tooth in its bony socket. The jawbone serves as a firm anchor for the root. The center of the crown is filled with soft pulpy tissue containing blood vessels and nerves; this tissue extends to the tip of the root by means of a canal. Surrounding the pulp and making up the greater bulk of the tooth is a hard bony substance, dentin. The root portion has an overlayer of cementum, while the crown portion has an additional layer of enamel, the hardest substance in the body. Proper diet is necessary for the development and maintenance of sound teeth, especially sufficient calcium, phosphorus, and vitamins D and C. The most common disorder that affects the teeth is dental caries (tooth decay). A widely accepted explanation of the process of tooth decay is that salivary bacteria convert carbohydrate particles in the mouth into lactic acid, which attacks the enamel, dentin, and, if left untreated, the pulp of the teeth. Regular cleansing and semiannual dental examinations are important in preventing dental caries and gum disorders. There is recent evidence that fluorides help prevent cavities in children. See DENTITION.

Teflon, trade name for a solid, chemically inert POLYMER. It is produced by the free-radical polymerization of tetrafluoroethylene, $F_2C{=}CF_2$. Teflon is stable up to temperatures around 300°C (572°F). It is used in electrical insulation and gaskets and in the preparation of low-adhesion surfaces, e.g., in cooking utensils.

Tegea (tē'jēə), ancient city of Greece, SE Arcadia, in the Peloponnesus. From the middle of the 6th cent. B.C. until the Spartan defeat at the battle of Leuctra (371 B.C.), it was dominated by Sparta. In 362 B.C. Tegea allied with its rival, Mantinea, against Sparta, but later it again opposed Mantinea. At Tegea there are remains of the temple of Athena Alea, which was rebuilt (c.370–355 B.C.). Scopas was the architect and sculptor.

Tegnér, Esaias (ĕsī'äs tĕng-nâr'), 1782–1846, Swedish poet, bishop of Växjö. Tegnér was the most popular of the Swedish romantic poets. An optimistic nationalist and liberal in his youth, he later became melancholy and conservative and was subject to periods of madness. His militant anti-Russian *Svea* (1811) and *Axel* (1821, tr. 1870) were followed by his great *Frithjof's Saga* (1825), which is based on collections of Scandinavian sagas and is considered the masterpiece of the Swedish Gothic tradition. Tegnér's sermons and speeches are classics of the Swedish language.

Tegucigalpa (tāgōōsēgäl'pä), city (1969 est. pop. 218,510), capital and largest city of Honduras, in a small valley in the mountains of S central Honduras. Textiles, sugar, and cigarettes are produced in the city. Old Tegucigalpa, built on a steep hill and never destroyed by earthquake, retains many quaint colonial aspects, with narrow streets and sidewalks, overhanging balconies, and stair-stepped streets. Across the Choluteca River lies Comayagüela, the more modern section. Founded late in the 16th cent., Tegucigalpa was a colonial center of silver and gold mining. With independence from Spain (1821), it became the stronghold of the liberals under MORAZÁN. The city vied with Comayagua as the republic's capital, not securing the title permanently until 1880. Its university was founded in 1895. The city is unusual for a capital in that it is not served by a railroad.

Tehama, region of the Arabian Peninsula: see TIHAMAH.

Tehaphnehes, ancient city: see TAHPANHES.

Teheran, Iran: see TEHRAN.

Teheran Conference, Nov. 28–Dec. 1, 1943, meeting of President Franklin Delano Roosevelt, Prime Minister Winston Churchill, and Premier Joseph Stalin at Teheran (Tehran), Iran. The conference was held to strengthen the cooperation of the United States, Great Britain, and the USSR in World War II. It followed the CAIRO CONFERENCE with Chiang Kai-Shek and was the first three-power war conference attended by Stalin. Agreement was reached on the scope and timing of operations against Germany, including plans for the Allied invasion of France. Stalin reaffirmed his pledge to commit Soviet forces against Japan after the defeat of Germany. The final communiqué also stressed the need for cooperation through the United Nations in meeting the problems of peace. A separate protocol pledged the three powers to maintain the independence of Iran.

Tehinnah (tēhĭn'ə), founder of the city of Nahash. 1 Chron. 4.12.

Tehran or **Teheran,** city (1966 pop. 2,719,730), capital of Iran and Tehran prov., N Iran, near Mt. Damavand. It is Iran's largest city and its administrative, commercial, and industrial center. Manufactures include textiles, sugar, and cement; motor vehicles are assembled. The city has a large bazaar and is a leading center for the sale and export of carpets. It is served by rail lines, roads, and an international airport. Tehran was long overshadowed by nearby RAGES, but in the 13th cent., when the latter was destroyed by the Mongols, many of its inhabitants migrated to Tehran. It served as the occasional residence of the Safavid rulers in the 17th cent. and became the capital of Persia in 1788. Tehran was renovated by Fath Ali Shah (reigned 1797–1834) and by Nasir ad-Din Shah (reigned 1848–96). Under Reza Shah Pahlevi (reigned 1925–41) the city was much modernized. During World War II, when the Allies occupied (1941) Iran, British and Soviet troops entered Tehran's suburbs. The city was the site of the TEHERAN CONFERENCE (1943), which brought together President Roosevelt, Prime Minister Churchill, and Premier Stalin. The center of the city is the large Maidan-i Sipah Square, south of which is the Gulistan Square with its royal throne hall and its museum containing the Peacock Throne, brought to Persia from Delhi, India, by Nadir Shah in 1739. Tehran's importance and population grew greatly in the 20th cent., and today it is one of the major cities of the Middle East. It is the site of the National Univ. (1960), the Univ. of Tehran (1934), a university of technology, a college of fine arts, a military academy, several Muslim religious schools, and other educational institutions. An ethnological museum and an archaeological museum are there.

Tehuantepec (tāwäntāpĕk'), town (1970 pop. 67,520), Oaxaca state, S Mexico, on a wide bend of the Tehuantepec River not far from the Gulf of Tehuantepec, an arm of the Pacific. The town is on the Isthmus of Tehuantepec. The climate is hot and humid. The population is largely Zapotec, and the society is matriarchal. Tehuantepec, the commercial and social rival of JUCHITÁN, is celebrated for its beautiful, industrious, and strikingly clothed women (called *tehuanas*), who travel by train from Veracruz to Tapachula to sell or barter the products of the region.

Tehuantepec, Isthmus of, c.125 mi (200 km) wide at its narrowest, S Mexico, between the Gulf of Campeche and the Gulf of Tehuantepec. It is mostly a rolling, tropical lowland with the lowest pass elevation at 754 ft (230 m) above sea level. Building of an interoceanic canal there was long considered, but estimated costs proved prohibitive. A transisthmian railroad between Coatzacoalcos and Salina Cruz was opened in 1907.

Teignmouth (tĭn'məth), urban district (1971 pop. 12,554), Devonshire, SW England, at the mouth of the Teign River on the English Channel. Teignmouth is a seaport and resort. The harbor, important in the Middle Ages, is now used chiefly by yachtsmen and fishermen.

Teilhard de Chardin, Pierre (pyĕr tāyär' də shärdăN'), 1881–1955, French paleontologist and philosopher. He entered (1899) the Jesuit order, was ordained (1911), and received a doctorate in paleontology from the Sorbonne (1922). He lectured (1920–23) at the Institut Catholique in Paris. After visiting China (1923–24), he resumed teaching at the Institut, but in 1926 he was forced by his superiors to abandon teaching and return to China because of his controversial attempts to reconcile the traditional view of original sin with his concept of evolution; at that time it was also decided that his publications should be limited to purely scientific material, a limitation that continued throughout his lifetime. Shortly after his return to China, Teilhard was named adviser to the National Geological Survey, and in that capacity he collaborated on research that resulted in the discovery (1929) of Peking man (see HOMO ERECTUS). While in China (1926–46) he also completed the manuscript of *The Phenomenon of Man* (published posthumously, 1955; tr. 1959), in which he outlined his concept of cosmic evolution and his conviction that belief in evolution does not entail a rejection of Christianity. Evolution he saw to be a process involving all matter, not just biological material, the cosmos undergoing successively more complex changes that would lead ultimately to "Omega Point," which has been variously interpreted as the integration of all personal consciousness and as the second coming of Christ. Teilhard's ardent evolutionism earned him the distrust of his religious superiors, while his religious mysticism made scientific circles suspicious; but despite much opposition—or perhaps because of it—there was an unusually broad popular response to his work after its posthumous publication. The interest may be explained by his boldly anthropocentric, and somewhat mystical, understanding of the cosmos: man for him is the axis of the cosmic flow, the key of the universe. Teilhard de Chardin's other works (all published posthumously) include *Letters from a Traveller* (1956, tr. 1962), *The Divine Milieu* (1957, tr. 1960),*The Future of Man* (1959, tr. 1964), *Human Energy* (1962, tr. 1969), *Activation of Energy* (1963, tr. 1971), and *Hymn of the Universe* (1964, tr. 1965). See biographies by Claude Cuénot (tr. 1965) and Robert Speaight (1968); studies by M. H. Murray (1966); Robert Faricy (1967); R. G. North (1967); Bernard Delfgaauw (1969); Philip Hefner(1970); H. J. Birx (1972); collection of studies ed. by Anthony Hanson (1970).

Teixeira, Pedro (pĕ'drōō tā'shārə), d. 1640, Portuguese explorer, one of the early voyagers on the Amazon. He commanded the expedition sent by the governor of Maranhão up the Amazon in the autumn of 1637. He reached the upper Amazon early in 1638, discovering the Rio Negro, and in July he met an expedition under Pedro de Costa Favilla on the Napo. Later he reached Quito, then returned down the Amazon. He was accompanied on this return journey by the Jesuit priest Cristóbal de ACUÑA, who wrote an account of the voyage. He claimed the Napo for Portugal, at that time united with Spain through the king, Philip IV of Spain (Philip III of Portugal).

Tejend, river: see HARI RUD.

Tejo, river: see TAGUS.

Tekakwitha, Catherine: see CATHERINE TEKAKWITHA.

Tekirdağ (tĕkĕr'dä), city (1970 pop. 33,112), capital of Tekirdağ prov., NW Turkey, on the Sea of Marmara. It is a small port and an agricultural trade center. It was known in ancient times as Bisanthe and as Rhaedestus and later as Rodosto. Founded by Greek colonists from Sámos, it later became an important city of the Thracian kingdom. It was conquered by the Ottoman Turks c.1360. The name was officially changed to Tekirdağ in 1923.

Tekoa or **Tekoah** (both: tēkō'ə), ancient town, S Palestine, S of Bethlehem. It is on the edge of a desolate country; to the east the land drops off precipitously to the Dead Sea. The wilderness of Tekoa was the home of Amos. See 2 Sam. 14.2; 23.26; 1 Chron. 2.24; 4.5; 2 Chron. 11.6; Neh. 3.5,27; Jer. 6.1; Amos 1.1.

tektite (tĕktīt), naturally occurring, silica-rich (65%–80% SiO_2) glass resembling obsidian. Although tektites were originally thought to be glassy meteorites, they have not been seen to fall, and their identification as meteorites is now disputed. They appear as rounded or elongated objects ranging from a fraction of an ounce to several pounds in weight and are normally jet black in reflected light. They are found in limited areas on the earth's surface (in contrast to meteorites, which show a random distribution over the whole earth). Tektites are usually given a name derived from the region in which they are found: moldavites (from the Moldau River in Czechoslovakia), bediasites (from the territory of the Bedias Indians in Texas), indochinites, philippinites, australites, javanites, and Ivory Coast tektites are the principal groups. Their peculiar composition and their restricted geographic distribution gave rise to the theory of a lunar origin, i.e., that they were splashes of molten lunar rock caused by a meteorite impact; however, the composition of moon rocks does not resemble tektites, and the lunar-origin theory, for the most part, has been abandoned. Another theory suggests their origin to be through the fusion and ejection of terrestrial material by the impact of giant meteorites or comets on the earth; the moldavites and the Ivory Coast tektites have been linked with such impacts, but the source of the remaining tektite groups is still uncertain.

Tela (tā'lä), town, NW Honduras, on the Caribbean Sea. It is a port and commercial center and the headquarters for a large area of banana plantations.

Tel-abib (tĕl-ā'bĭb), unidentified city of Mesopotamia, where Ezekiel preached. Ezek. 3.15.

Telah (tē'lə), ancestor of Joshua, 1 Chron. 7.25.

Telaim (tĕl′āĭm, tĕlā′ĭm), place, S Palestine, where Saul's army gathered. It is identical with TELEM **2.** 1 Sam. 15.4.

Telamon (tĕl′əmŏn), in Greek mythology, son of Aeacus and father of Ajax. He and Peleus killed their half-brother Phocus and were banished from Aegina. Telamon fled to Salamis, where he became king. For his aid to Hercules against Laomedon, Hercules rewarded him with Laomedon's daughter, Hesione, who bore him Teucer.

Telassar (tĕlăs′ər), region, Assyria, probably in the hill country N of the Euphrates River. Isa. 37.12. Thelasar: 2 Kings 19.12.

Telavi (tyĭlä′vē), city, SE European USSR, in Georgia. It is the center of the Kakhetian wine district and has food-processing and silk-spinning industries. Founded in 893, Telavi was the capital of Kakhetia until the 17th cent. There are ruins of its medieval fortifications.

Tel Aviv-Jaffa (tĕl əvēv′-jä′fə, -yä′fä), city (1972 pop. 362,900), W central Israel, on the Mediterranean Sea. It is Israel's largest city and its commercial, financial, communications, and cultural center. Construction is the main industry; textiles, clothing, and processed food are the chief manufactures, and pharmaceuticals, electrical appliances, printed materials, and chemicals are also produced. The city is a tourist resort with wide, attractive beaches. Tel Aviv was founded in 1909 by Jews from Jaffa who wished to build a modern suburb. The population grew dramatically in the late 1920s, again after Hitler came to power (1933) in Germany, and after World War II. When the state of Israel was proclaimed on May 14, 1948, Tel Aviv was briefly the capital; in 1949 the government was transferred to Jerusalem. In 1950, Tel Aviv and Jaffa were merged. Tel Aviv Univ., the Afro-Asian Institute for Labor Studies and Cooperation, the Israel Philharmonic Orchestra, and Habimah (the Israel National Theatre), Haaretz Museum, and Tel Aviv Museum are in the city. The home of H. N. Bialik, the national poet, is preserved as a library and memorial.

Telegonus (təlĕg′ənəs): see CIRCE.

telegraph, term originally applied to any device or system for distant communication by means of visible or audible signals, now commonly restricted to electrically operated devices. Attempts at long distance communication date back thousands of years (see SIGNALING). As electricity came into greater use, various practical and experimental methods of signaling were tried. A method that has come into general use throughout most of the world is based in large part on the work of Samuel F. B. Morse. In Morse telegraphy, an electric circuit is set up customarily by using only a single overhead wire and employing the earth as the other conductor to complete the circuit. An electromagnet in the receiver is activated by alternately making and breaking the circuit. Reception by sound, with the MORSE CODE signals received as audible clicks, is a swift and reliable method of signaling. The first permanently successful telegraphic CABLE crossing the Atlantic Ocean was laid in 1866. In 1872, J. B. Stearns of Massachusetts devised a method for "duplex" telegraphy, enabling two messages to be sent over the same wire at the same time. In 1874, Thomas A. Edison invented the "quadruplex" method for the simultaneous transmission of four messages over the same wire. In addition to wires and cables, telegraph messages are now sent by such means as radio waves, microwaves, and communications satellites (see SATELLITES, ARTIFICIAL). Telegraph instruments have been devised by which messages are transmitted and received in printed form. In this method, as the message is typed on an instrument resembling a typewriter, it is automatically coded and transmitted as a series of pulses. At the receiving station the pulses are decoded by a similar instrument and the message is automatically typed. Using telegraph lines, FACSIMILE machines are able to transmit and reproduce photographs and drawings. See J. W. Freebody, *Telegraphy* (1959); E. H. Jolley, *Introduction to Telephony and Telegraphy* (1970).

Teleki, Count Paul (tĕ′lĕkĭ), 1879–1941, Hungarian premier (1920–21, 1939–41), geographer, and political writer. He studied law, political science, and geography at the Univ. of Budapest, where he later held a chair in geography. A member of the Hungarian parliament from 1905, he was the official geographic expert in the Hungarian delegation at the Paris Peace Conference (1919–20) and was foreign minister in the counterrevolutionary government at Szeged. Appointed (1920) premier by Admiral Horthy, he secured the ratification of the Treaty of Trianon by the Hungarian parliament. He retired from politics in 1921 and was replaced as premier by Stephen Bethlen. Called again to the premiership in 1939, he signed (1940) the Berlin Pact (see AXIS) and concluded a mutual-assistance treaty with Yugoslavia. When, early in 1941, it became evident that Hungary would be forced by Germany to invade Yugoslavia, Teleki committed suicide. Teleki's best-known work is *The Evolution of Hungary and Its Place in European History* (1923, in English).

Tel el Amarna or **Tell el Amarna** (tĕl ĕl ämär′nä), ancient locality, Egypt, near the Nile and c.60 mi (100 km) N of Asyut. Ikhnaton's capital, Akhetaton, was in Tel el Amarna. About 400 tablets with inscriptions in Akkadian cuneiform were found there in 1887. They constitute correspondence between Amenhotep III and Ikhnaton and the governors of the cities in Palestine and Syria, and they shed much light on ancient Egypt and the Middle East. The tablets are mostly in the Berlin, British, and Cairo museums; the Metropolitan Museum, New York City, has two. All were translated into English by Samuel A. B. Mercer. See studies by James Baikie (1926), J. D. S. Pendlebury (1935), C. F. Pfeiffer (1963), and E. F. Campbell, Jr. (1964).

Telem (tē′lĕm). **1** Gatekeeper who had married a foreigner. Ezra 10.24. The Talmon of Neh. 12.25 is probably the same. **2** Unidentified place, S Palestine. Joshua 15.24.

Telemachus (təlĕm′əkəs): see ODYSSEUS.

Telemann, Georg Philipp (gā′ôrk fē′lĭp tĕl′əmän), 1681–1767, German composer. From 1721 until his death he was director of music for the five major churches in Hamburg. Extremely prolific, he composed over 600 overtures, 40 operas, 12 complete services for the year, and other works in practically every form. Although he was highly regarded in his day, his reputation later declined because he was not an innovator; by the mid-20th cent., however, his critical reputation was again on the rise. Telemann is a major representative of the Hamburg school of the early 18th cent. A mixture of counterpoint and Italian operatic air forms his style. One of his best-known works is the oratorio entitled *Der Tag des Gerichts* [the day of judgment] (1762).

Telemark (tĕ′ləmärk), county (1972 est. pop. 158,000), 5,915 sq mi (15,320 sq km), SE Norway, bordering on the Skagerrak in the east. Skien (the capital), Porsgrunn, Kragerø, and Notodden are the chief towns. The county includes the Hardangervidda plateau in the northwest and the Tokke River, and it is noted for its lakes, mountain scenery, and handicrafts. Farming, mining, and the manufacture of forest products, chemicals, and porcelain are the main occupations. Much hydroelectric power is produced in Telemark. It was there that skiing as a sport first became popular (late 19th cent.).

teleology (tĕl″ēŏl′əjē, tē″lē-), in philosophy, term applied to any system attempting to explain a series of events in terms of ends, goals, or purposes. It is opposed to mechanism, the theory that all events may be explained by mechanical principles of causation. Aristotle argued that all nature reflects the purposes of an immanent final cause. Frequently, teleologists have identified purpose in the universe with God's will. The teleological argument for the existence of God holds that order in the world could not be accidental and that since there is design there must be a designer. A more recent evolutionary view finds purpose in the higher levels of organic life but holds that it is not necessarily based in any transcendent being. See Pierre Lecomte du Noüy, *Human Destiny* (1947, repr. 1956); H. C. Sandbeck, *Nature and Destiny* (1960); P. C. Gasson, *Theory of Design* (1973).

telepathy, apparent communication between two persons without recourse to the senses. The word was formulated in 1882 by Frederic William Henry Myers, English poet, essayist, and a leading founder of the Society for Psychical Research in London. Telepathy experiments have been conducted in Europe, the Soviet Union, and the United States. See PARAPSYCHOLOGY.

telephone, device for communicating sound, especially speech, by means of wires in an electrical circuit. The telephones now in general use are developments of the device invented by Alexander Graham Bell and patented by him in 1876 and 1877. Although Bell is recognized as the inventor, his telephone was preceded by many attempts to produce such an instrument. The principles on which it is based, and effective model instruments, were developed by different men at so nearly the same time that there are disputes about priority. While earlier telephones were incapable of providing satisfactory transmission of speech, Bell's instrument employed an electric current of fluctuating intensity and frequency that varied in accordance with sound waves. A thin plate of soft iron, called the diaphragm, vibrated to sound waves just as does the tympanum, or eardrum, of the human ear. The vibrations disturbed the magnetic field of a bar magnet placed near the diaphragm, and this disturbance induced an electric current in a thin copper wire wound about the magnet. That current when transmitted to a distant identical instrument caused the diaphragm in it to vibrate in response to the fluctuations induced in the nearby magnetic field. Bell's instrument was thus both transmitter and receiver; the user alternately spoke into and listened to it. The first notable improvement of the Bell telephone differentiated the transmitting instrument from the receiving instrument. The new transmitter abandoned the use of the bar magnet, derived its current from batteries, and was called a MICROPHONE. Many other inventions have improved the telephone and microphone and have adapted them to new uses. Largely because of the development of SEMICONDUCTOR technology, problems attendant upon long-distance and intercity telephone service have been met with increasing success. The telephone lines used include the ordinary open wire lines, lead-sheathed CABLES consisting of many lines, and coaxial cables. Coaxial cables are placed underground, but other cables may be either overhead or underground. Transmission of telephone messages over long distances is often accomplished by means of radio and microwave transmissions. In some cases microwaves are sent to an orbiting communications satellite (see SATELLITE, ARTIFICIAL) from which they are relayed back to a distant point on the earth. See T. B. Costain, *Chord of Steel: The Story of the Invention of the Telephone* (1960); E. H. Jolley, *Introduction to Telephony and Telegraphy* (1970).

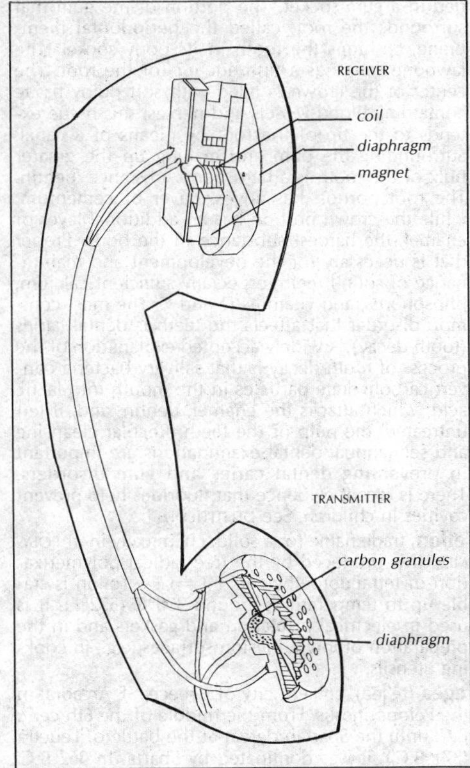

Hand telephone

telescope, system of lenses, mirrors, or both, used to gather light from a distant object and form a real optical image of it. This image can be magnified for visual inspection or photographed directly. There are three major types of telescope, classified according to the element that gathers and focuses the incoming light. In the refracting telescope, or refractor, light is bent, or refracted, as it passes through an objective lens. The objective lens is convex, i.e., thicker at the middle than the edges. Parallel light passing through the lens is refracted so that it converges to a point behind the lens, called the focus. The distance from the lens to the focus is called the focal length. In a reflecting telescope, or reflector, light is reflected by a concave mirror and brought to a focus in front of the mirror. If parallel light rays are to be reflected so that they converge to a single point, the mirror must be paraboloid in shape. A glass disk is ground to this shape and then coated with a thin layer of silver or aluminum to make it highly reflecting. The third type of telescope, the catadioptric system, focuses light by a combination of lenses and mirrors. The properties of the image are similar, whether formed by lenses or mirrors. The real image produced by a telescope is inverted; i.e., up and down are reversed, as are left and right. In a terrestrial refracting telescope, used to view objects on the earth, an additional lens is used to invert the image a second time, so that objects appear as they do when viewed with the unaided eye; in an astronomical telescope, image inversion is unimportant and no lens is used to invert the image a second time. The angular size of an object as seen from the position of the telescope may be expressed in degrees or in radians (1 radian = about 57°). The angle in radians subtended by the object is given by the ratio of the object's diameter to its distance from the telescope. The size of the object's image is the product of this and the focal length of the image-forming lens or mirror. For example, the moon subtends an angle of ½°, or roughly 1/100 radian; a telescope with a focal length of 60 in. (152 cm) would produce an image of the moon 0.6 in. (1.52 cm) in diameter. The brightness of the image depends on the total light gathered and hence is proportional to the area of the objective or the square of the diameter of the telescope (see LIGHT-GATHERING POWER). The resolution of the telescope is a measure of how sharply defined the details of the image are. The laws of diffraction make a certain amount of blurring unavoidable, because of the wave nature of light. If two stars are very close, a given telescope may not be able to separate them into two distinct points. The smallest angular separation that can be unambiguously distinguished is called the resolving power of the telescope and is proportional to the ratio of the wavelength of light being observed to the diameter of the telescope. Thus, the larger the diameter, the smaller the minimum angle and the higher the resolving power. The magnification, or power, of the telescope is relevant only when an eyepiece, or ocular, is used to magnify the image for visual inspection. The angular size of the virtual image seen by the observer will be larger than the actual angular size of the object. The ratio of these two sizes is the magnifying power and is equal to the ratio of the focal lengths of the objective and ocular. Any desired magnification can be obtained with a given telescope by the use of an appropriate ocular, but beyond a point determined by the resolving power, no further details are revealed at higher power. In addition to diffraction, other defects limit the performance of real optical systems. The most serious of these for lenses is chromatic ABERRATION. Other defects include coma, astigmatism, distortion, and curvature of field. In general, it is easier to eliminate these faults in the reflector than in the refractor. However, the prime focus of the reflector is inside the main tube of the telescope and thus the image cannot be observed there without blocking part of the incoming light. A variety of schemes are employed to divert the image to a more convenient location. The simplest of these, constituting the Newtonian reflector, is the placement of a flat secondary mirror in the path of the converging light just before the prime focus. The small secondary mirror, which blocks a negligible portion of the primary mirror, is tilted at an angle of 45° in order to reflect the convergent light at right angles and bring it to a focus outside the telescope tube. In the Cassegrain system, the secondary mirror is convex and reflects the convergent light directly back along the axis of the telescope through a hole in the center of the primary mirror. By causing light to traverse a longer path, the effective focal length is increased and a larger image is formed. The Gregorian system is similar to the Cassegrain, except that the secondary mirror is concave. The Coudé system uses both a convex secondary mirror and one or more diagonal flat mirrors to produce a focus outside the tube. The secondaries are arranged so that the position of the focus remains stationary as the telescope rotates, allowing the use of image-recording and analyzing devices that would be too heavy to mount directly on a moving telescope. The Schmidt camera telescope, invented in 1930 by Bernard Schmidt, is a catadioptric system used principally for wide-angle photography of star fields. The primary mirror is spherical instead of paraboloidal, which requires a special correcting lens to be used on the front of the tube. The Maksutov telescope, invented by D. D. Maksutov in 1941, is similar in design and purpose to the Schmidt telescope but has a spherical meniscus in place of the correcting plate of the Schmidt. Equal in importance to the mirrors and lenses constituting the optics of a telescope is the mounting of the telescope. The mounting must be massive, in order to minimize mechanical vibration that would blur the image, especially at high magnification or during long-exposure photography. At the same time, motion of the telescope must be precise and smooth. To allow the telescope to be pointed in any direction in the sky, the mounting must provide rotation about two perpendicular axes. In the altazimuth mounting, one axis points to the zenith and allows rotation along the horizon and the other allows changes in altitude, or distance above the horizon. This mounting is used principally for terrestrial telescopes. It is not practical for astronomical telescopes because rotation about both axes is required to follow a star in its apparent motion arising from the earth's rotation. Most astronomical telescopes use the equatorial mounting, in which one axis points at the celestial pole and hence is parallel to the earth's axis. Rotation about this axis allows changes in right ascension or celestial longitude; rotation about a second axis allows changes in declination or celestial latitude. To compensate for the earth's rotation it is only necessary to turn the polar axis east to west at the rate of one rotation per sidereal day. This motion of the telescope is generally provided by a clock drive mechanism. The first practical telescopes were produced at the beginning of the 17th cent. By 1610, Galileo had made extensive astronomical use of the simple refractor. The best telescopes of this period had very long focal lengths to minimize the chromatic aberration inherent in the single-element objective. The multielement objective, invented in 1733, allowed the construction of telescopes of large aperture. The art of building refracting telescopes reached a zenith in the 19th cent. The largest refractor in existence, with an objective lens 40 in. (102 cm) in diameter, is located at the Yerkes Observatory in Williams Bay, Wis. A 36-in. (91-cm) refractor is located at the Lick Observatory in California and a 33-in. (84-cm) refractor is located at Meudon, France. These giant telescopes represent the practical limit on the size of a refractor. Because a lens can be supported only at its edge, the weight of the lens itself produces unavoidable distortion in the shape. Because a mirror can be supported from behind, it can be much more massive without incurring distortion, and mirrors many feet in diameter have been constructed. The first reflecting telescope, built by Isaac Newton in 1672, had a mirror made of a metal alloy. When techniques for depositing metal films on glass surfaces were developed, reflecting telescopes became comparable in precision to refractors. An important advantage of the reflecting telescope is the absence of chromatic aberration. Because only one surface must be ground to an exact shape, the reflector is also easier to manufacture. A number of very large reflectors have been constructed, including those at Zelenchukskaya, USSR (with a diameter of 236 in./6 m), the HALE OBSERVATORIES at Mt. Palomar, Calif. (200 in./5 m) and Mt. Wilson, Calif. (100 in./2.5 m), the CERRO-TOLOLO INTER-AMERICAN OBSERVATORY, Chile, and the KITT PEAK NATIONAL OBSERVATORY, Ariz. (158 in./4 m each), the EUROPEAN SOUTHERN OBSERVATORY, Chile (142 in./3.6 m), MOUNT STROMLO OBSERVATORY, Australia (150 in./3.8 m), LICK OBSERVATORY, Calif. (120 in./3 m), and MCDONALD OBSERVATORY, Texas (107 in./2.7 m). Large Schmidt telescopes are at Palomar, SIDING SPRING OBSERVATORY, Australia, and the European Southern Observatory. A novel approach to the problems of building a large reflector is the multiple-mirror telescope at the MOUNT HOPKINS OBSERVATORY, Ariz., consisting of six 72-in. (1.8-m) telescopes on a common mounting and having a light-gathering power equal to that of a 176-in. (4.5-m) reflector of conventional design. See G. P. Kuiper and B. M. Middlehurst, ed., *Telescopes* (1960); H. E. Paul, *Telescopes for Skygazing* (2d ed. 1966); M. F. Riemer, *The Telescope and the World of Astronomy* (3d ed. 1967).

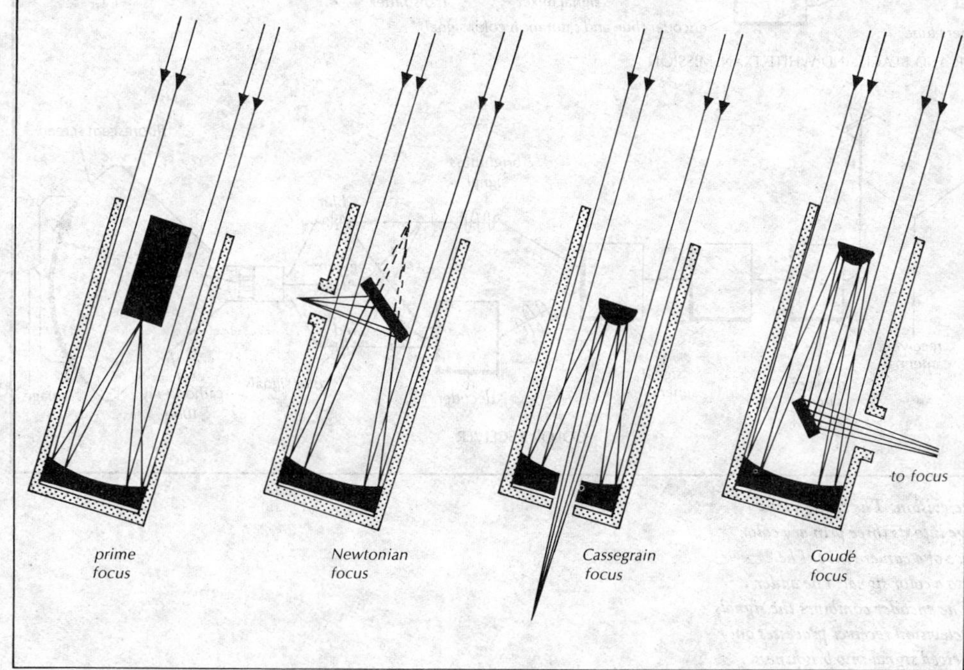

Mirror arrangements for a reflecting telescope

Telesio, Bernardino (bĕrnärdē'nō tālā'zyō), 1509–88, Italian philosopher, one of the leaders in the attack on that part of Aristotelian philosophy that had furnished the foundation for scholasticism. With Bruno and Campanella, he opened the way to a new naturalism, deemphasizing theories of metaphysics and urging the importance of scientific knowledge based upon experience and experiment. He was born into a noble family and studied first with a scholarly uncle in Milan. Further study followed at Rome and in Padua. At Naples he lectured and afterward established his Academia Cosentina in the interest of more scientific methods of thought. While he produced many works on science and philosophy, the outstanding achievement is his *De natura rerum juxta propria principia* [on the nature of things according to their own principles] (1565–86, new ed. 1910–23). In this he regarded matter as a positive reality that has no need to look outside itself for its sufficient explanation. Out of two opposing fundamental forces (the dry-warm and the moist-cold) in conflict, he sought to produce the reason for all forms of life, great and small. These principles, unscientific by modern standards, were derived from early Greek naturalistic philosophy.

teletypewriter: see TYPEWRITER.

television, transmission and reception of still or moving images by means of electrical signals, especially by means of ELECTROMAGNETIC RADIATION using the techniques of RADIO. The idea of "seeing by telegraph" engrossed many inventors after the discovery in 1873 of variation in the electrical conductivity of selenium when exposed to light. Selenium cells were used in early television devices; the results were unsatisfactory, however, chiefly because the response of selenium to light-intensity variations was not rapid enough. Moreover, until the development of the ELECTRON TUBE there was no way of sufficiently amplifying the weak output signals. These limitations precluded the success of a television method for which Paul Nipkow in Germany received (1884) a patent; his system employed selenium and a scanning disk and embodied the essential features of later successful devices. A scanning disk has a single row of holes arranged so that they spiral inward toward the center from a point near the edge. The disk revolves in front of a light-sensitive plate on which a lens forms an image; each hole passes across, or "scans," a narrow, ring-shaped area of the image. Thus the holes trace contiguous concentric rings, so that in one revolution of the disk the entire plate is scanned. When the light-sensitive cell is connected in an electric circuit, the variations in light cause corresponding fluctuations in the electric current. The image can be reproduced by a receiver whose luminous area is scanned by a similar disk synchronized with the disk of the transmitter. Although selenium cells proved inadequate, the development of the phototube (see PHOTOELECTRIC CELL) made the mechanical disk-scanning method practicable. In 1926, J. L. Baird in England and C. F. Jenkins in the United States successfully demonstrated television systems using mechanical scanning disks. These were soon superseded, however, by electronic scanning methods; a television system employing electronic scanning was patented by V. K. Zworykin in 1928. The 1930s saw the laboratory perfection of television equipment that began to reach the market in 1945 after World War II. In the ensuing years television has become a major industry, especially in the industrialized nations, and a major medium of communication and source of home entertainment. Television is put to varied use in industry, e.g., for surveillance in places inaccessible to or dangerous for human beings; in science, e.g., in tissue microscopy (see MICROSCOPE); and in education. Zworykin's iconoscope (1923) had been one of the successful camera tubes in wide use. Its functioning involves many fundamental principles common to all television image pickup devices. The face of the iconoscope consists of a thin sheet of mica upon which thousands of microscopic globules of a photosensitive silver-cesium compound have been deposited. Backed with a metallic conductor, this expanse of mica becomes a mosaic of tiny photoelectric cells and condensers. The differing light intensities of various points of a scene cause the cells of the mosaic to emit varying quantities of electrons. The cells are left with positive charges in strengths proportionate to the electrons lost. An electron gun, or "scanner," passes its beam across the cells. As it does so, the charge is released, causing an electrical signal to appear on the back of the mosaic, which is connected externally to an amplifier. The strength of the signal is proportional to the amount of charge released. Processes in which the size of the signal from any cell depends on the charge built up on the cell during the time the electron beam was scanning all the other cells are said to be based on the storage principle. This gives the iconoscope a much greater efficiency than nonstorage devices such as the mechanical disk scanner. The orthicon and image orthicon tubes are similar to the iconoscope in mode of operation but are improvements upon it. The Vidicon is a pickup tube in which the photoemissive mosaic of the iconoscope or orthicon is replaced by a photoconductive layer, resulting in increased efficiency. The dissector tube, developed by P. T. Farnsworth, is a nonstorage device, but has certain advantages as long as the illumination is adequate. The scanning process, which is the essence of television accomplishment, operates as do the eyes in reading a page of printed matter, i.e., line by line. A complex circuit of horizontal and vertical deflection coils controls this movement and causes the electronic beam to scan the back of the mosaic in a 525-line zigzag 30 times each second. Because of persistence of vision only about 30 pictures need be transmitted each second to give the effect of motion. The development of "interlinear scanning" results in alternate lines being scanned each 1/60 sec, the remaining lines being covered in the next 1/60 sec. The two principal means of recording television programs for future use are video tape recording and kinescope. Video tape recording is similar to conventional tape recording (see TAPE RECORDER) except that because of the wide frequency range—4.2 megahertz (MHz)—occupied by a video signal, the effective speed at which the tape passes the head is kept very high. The sound is recorded along with the video signal on the same tape. Kinescope is a method in which programs are recorded on motion-picture film. If appropriate changes are made in the signal-carrying circuitry, a kinescope can be played back from a developed negative as well as from a positive. In recent years video tape systems that make compromises in picture quality in order to achieve reduced cost have become available, potentially for home use. Several systems for recording television programs on disks have also been recently developed. In one system the information is read from the disk by a laser beam. When a television program is broadcast, either "live" or from a recording, the varying electrical signals are then amplified and used to modulate a carrier wave (see MODULATION); the modulated carrier is usually fed to an antenna, where it is converted to electromagnetic waves and broadcast over a large region. The waves are sensed by antennas connected to television receivers. Here the image is reconstructed essentially by reversing the pickup operation. The final image is displayed on the face of a CATHODE-RAY TUBE, where an electron beam scans the fluorescent face, called the "screen," line for line with the pickup scanning. The fluorescent deposit on the tube's inside face glows when hit by the electrons, and the visual image is reproduced. Often a thin film of aluminum is deposited over the fluorescent screen to enhance the image. Other devices in the receiver establish the crucial synchronization, the demodulation (separation of the information signal from the carrier wave), and the filtering or other counteraction of undesirable visual and audio effects. In the United States the Federal Communications Commission (FCC) has assigned 12 television channels between 54 and 216 MHz in the very-high-frequency (VHF) range, and 70 channels between 470 and 890 MHz in the ultra-high-frequency (UHF) range (see RADIO FREQUENCY). At these frequencies radio waves propagate in almost straight lines from the transmitting antenna. For broadcasting over large areas, the earth's curvature necessitates either cable connections or relay stations. Cable television has come into increasing use because of the improved reception of signals it provides. Many cables to individual receivers can be run from a single, community antenna. Relay stations can be in the form of towers, hovering aircraft, or communications satellites. The first transatlantic television broadcast was accomplished by such a satellite, called Telstar, on July 10, 1962. Several systems of color television have been developed. In one of these a motor-driven disk with segments in three primary colors, red, blue, and

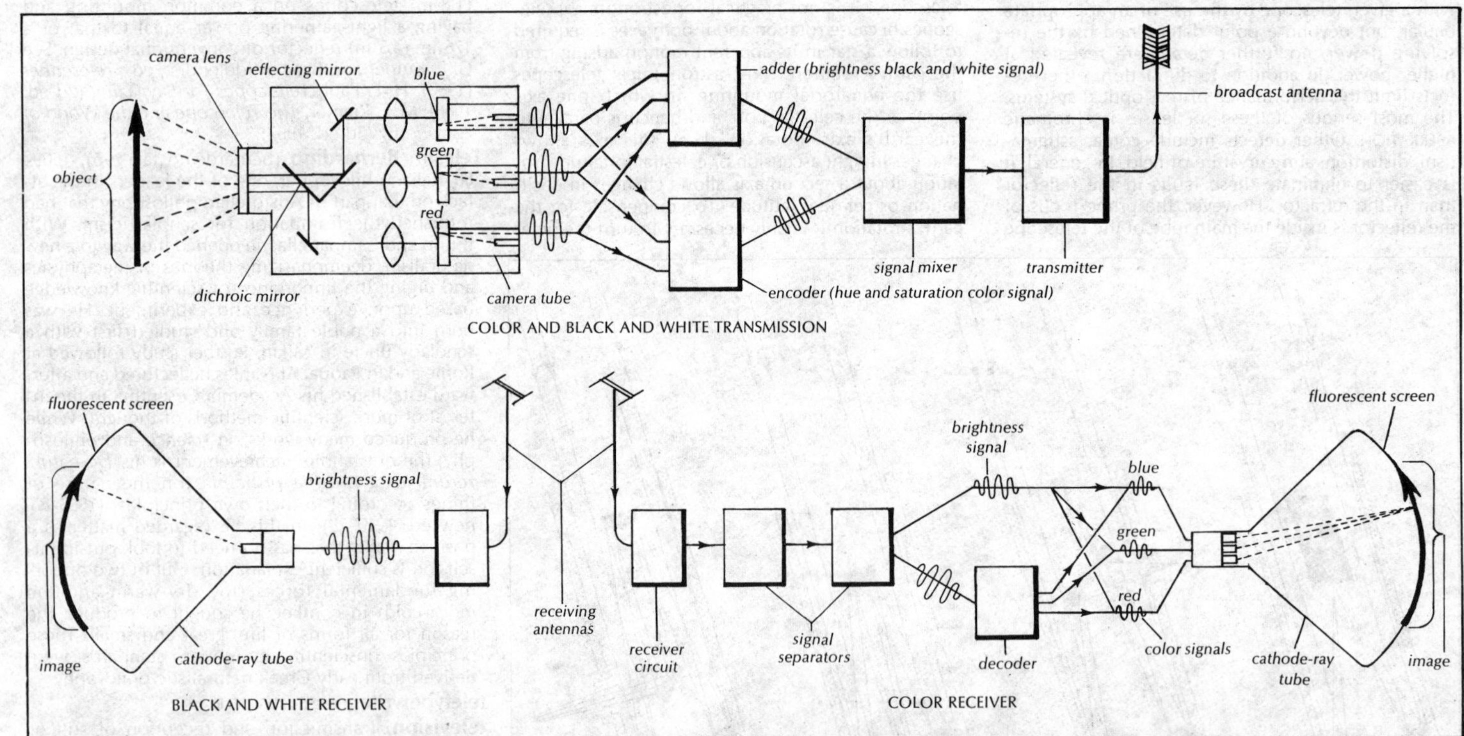

Video transmission and reception of color and black and white television: The camera lens focuses collected light rays into mirrors, which separate the image into its three primary color component images. Each color component is focused onto the face of a camera tube. The scanning beam of each tube converts the primary color image into a color signal. The adder combines the three color signals to make the brightness signal. The encoder combines the signals to transmit hue and saturation information. A black and white television receiver processes only the brightness signal. A color television receiver separates the received signal into brightness and hue and saturation components, which are recombined to produce primary color signals for the picture tube.

green, rotates behind the camera lens, filtering the light from the subject so that the colors pass through in succession. The receiving unit of this system forms monochrome (black-and-white) images through the usual cathode-ray tube, but a color wheel, identical with that affixed to the camera and synchronized with it, transforms the images back to their original appearance. This method is said to be "field-sequential" because the monochrome image is "painted" first in one color, then another, and finally in the third, in rapid enough succession so that the individual colors are blended by the retentive capacities of the eye, giving the viewer the impression of a full colored image. This system, developed by the Columbia Broadcasting System (CBS), was established in 1950 as standard for the United States by the FCC. However, it was not "compatible," i.e., from the same signal a good picture could not be obtained on standard black-and-white sets, so it found scant public acceptance. Another color television system, called "field-simultaneous," uses a separate television system for each of the three colors; but because this system requires a larger channel bandwidth than the others, it has not been received favorably. In a third system, the "line-sequential" system, red, green, and blue lines are scanned alternately. Although this system can be made compatible, it has a number of disadvantages. A fourth system, a simultaneous compatible system, was developed by the Radio Corporation of America (RCA). In 1953 the FCC reversed its 1950 ruling and revised the standards for acceptable color television systems. The RCA system met the new standards (the CBS system did not) and has been well received by the public. This system is based on an "element-sequential" system. Light from the subject is broken up into its three color components, which are simultaneously scanned by three pickups. However, the signals corresponding to the red, green, and blue portions of each scanned element are transmitted in sequence so that the required 4.1-MHz bandwidth can be used. In the receiver the signals are brought together again. The elements, or dots, on the picture tube screen are each subdivided into areas of red, green, and blue phosphor. In the tube, called a Tricolor Kinescope, beams from three electron guns, modulated by the three color signals, scan the elements together in such a way that the beam from the gun using a given color signal strikes the phosphor of the same color. Provision is made electronically for forming proper half-tones in black-and-white receivers. See D. G. Fink and D. M. Lutyens, *The Physics of Television* (1960); W. P. Dizard, *Television: A World View* (1966); M. S. Kiver, *Television Simplified* (7th ed. 1973).

television microscope: see MICROSCOPE.

Telford, Thomas, 1757–1834, Scottish civil engineer. He greatly improved road building in England and Scotland. He introduced the use of a base of large stones surfaced with compacted layers of small stones. His engineering works include harbors and docks at Aberdeen, Dundee, and London, many notable bridges, including those across the Tay River and the Menai Strait, and an aqueduct across the Dee; he was engineer in chief of the Caledonian Canal. He is buried in Westminster Abbey.

Telford, new town (1971 pop. 75,579), Shropshire, W England. It was originally designated a NEW TOWN in 1963 as Dawley but was enlarged and renamed in 1968. The purpose of Telford is to alleviate overpopulation in Birmingham and the BLACK COUNTRY; the planned population is 220,000. Telford's industries include engineering, quarrying, brickmaking, coal mining, iron founding, and brewing. In 1974, Telford became part of the new nonmetropolitan county of Salop.

Tel-haresha (tĕl-hərē'shə) or **Tel-harsa** (-här'sə), unlocated Babylonian town. Ezra 2.59; Neh. 7.61.

Tell, William, legendary Swiss patriot. According to legend, Tell was a native of Uri, one of the forest cantons in Switzerland. Gessler, the Austrian bailiff of the canton, decreed that Swiss citizens must remove their hats before his hat, which he had posted on top of a stake in the canton's largest town. Tell refused and as punishment was ordered to shoot an apple off his small son's head. Although he succeeded in doing so, he was held prisoner by Gessler when he revealed that had he failed he planned to kill Gessler with an arrow he had hidden on his person. Tell later escaped and eventually shot Gessler from ambush at Küssnacht, thus setting off the revolt that ousted the bailiff on Jan. 1, 1308. While there is no valid proof of Tell's existence, the legend represents a distorted account of actual events that resulted (1291) in the formation of the Everlasting League between the cantons of SCHWYZ, URI, and UNTERWALDEN. Schiller's popular drama *Wilhelm Tell* is based on the legend; Rossini's opera *William Tell* is based on Schiller's drama.

Tell el Amarna, Egypt: see TEL EL AMARNA.

Teller, Edward, 1908–, American physicist, b. Hungary, Ph.D. Univ. of Leipzig, 1930. He came to the United States in 1935 and was naturalized in 1941. From 1935 to 1941 he was professor of physics at George Washington Univ. and during World War II worked on atomic bomb research at Columbia Univ. in a group headed by Enrico Fermi. Later he was (1946–52) professor of physics at the Univ. of Chicago. He was also associated (1949–51) with the thermonuclear research program of the Los Alamos National Laboratory. From 1952, Teller was professor of physics at the Univ. of California and director of the Livermore division of its radiation laboratory. In 1960 he resigned from his laboratory post to devote his time to teaching and research. Teller was instrumental in making possible the first successful U.S. hydrogen bomb explosion, Nov. 1, 1952. For his contributions to the development, use, and control of nuclear energy, Teller received the 1962 Enrico Fermi Award. His writings include *The Legacy of Hiroshima* (with Allen Brown; 1962) and *The Constructive Uses of Nuclear Explosives* (with others, 1968).

Teller, Henry Moore, 1830–1914, American statesman, b. Allegany co., N.Y. A lawyer, he practiced in Colorado after 1861. He commanded a militia district in the Civil War period. When Colorado became (1876) a state, Teller was elected U.S. Senator as a Republican. He resigned in 1882 to become Secretary of the Interior under President Arthur. Teller returned (1885) to the Senate and was reelected in 1891. As the leader of a group of silver Republicans, Teller supported William J. Bryan, Democratic and Populist candidate for President in 1896, and was returned to the Senate as an independent silver Republican. In 1902, he was elected on the Democratic ticket. In 1898, he secured the adoption of the Teller Resolution to the declaration of war against Spain, which pledged the United States to an independent Cuba. See biography by Elmer Ellis (1941).

Téllez, Gabriel: see TIRSO DE MOLINA.

Telloh: see LAGASH.

tellurium (tĕlo͝or'ēəm) [Lat.,=earth], semimetallic chemical element; symbol Te; at. no. 52; at. wt. 127.60; m.p. 450°C; b.p. 990°C; sp. gr. 6.24 at 20°C; valence −2, +4, or +6. Tellurium is a lustrous, brittle, crystalline, silver-white metalloid. A powdery brown form of the element is also known. Tellurium forms many compounds corresponding to those of sulfur and selenium, the elements above it in group VIa of the PERIODIC TABLE. The dioxide, TeO_2, is formed when the element is burned in air. Tellurium forms two weak acids and a number of halogen compounds. With hydrogen and with some metals it forms tellurides. Tellurium and its compounds are probably poisonous. Tellurium is occasionally found uncombined in nature but is more often found combined with metals, as in the minerals calaverite (gold telluride) and sylvanite (silver-gold telluride). Tellurium is recovered as a by-product of the electrolytic refining of blister copper. It is used as an additive to steel and is often alloyed with aluminum, copper, lead, or tin. It is used in vulcanizing rubber, as a coloring agent in glass and ceramics, and in catalysts for petroleum cracking. Tellurium is a semiconductor material and is slightly photosensitive. It is used with bismuth in thermoelectric devices. Tellurium was discovered in 1782 by Franz Muller von Reichenstein. It was named by M. H. Klaproth, who isolated it in 1798.

tellurometer: see SURVEYING.

Tellus (tĕl'əs), in Roman religion, earth goddess; also called Terra Mater. As a goddess of fertility, she was worshiped at festivals held in January (in conjunction with Ceres) and in April. Tellus was identified with the Greek Gaea.

Tel-melah (tĕl-mē'lə), unlocated Babylonian town. Ezra 2.59; Neh. 7.61.

Telpos-Iz (tyĭlpôs'-ēs), peak 5,304 ft (1,617 m) high, NE European USSR, in the N Urals. It was thought to be the highest in the Urals until the discovery of Naroda peak.

Telstar: see COMMUNICATIONS SATELLITE.

Telugu (tĕl'əgo͞o'), Dravidian language of India: see DRAVIDIAN LANGUAGES.

Tema: see TAYMA, Saudi Arabia.

Tema (tāmə), city (1970 pop. 60,767), SE Ghana, on the Gulf of Guinea. With the opening of an artificial harbor in 1961, Tema developed from a small fishing village to become Ghana's leading seaport and an industrial center. Most of the country's chief export, cacao, is shipped from Tema. Manufactures include aluminum, steel, refined petroleum, soap, processed fish, chocolate, textiles, cement, and chemicals.

Teman (tē'mən), grandson of Esau and eponym of a tribe living in Edom, SE of the Dead Sea. A member of the tribe was known as a Temani or a Temanite. Gen. 36.11, 15,34,42; 1 Chron. 1.36,53; Job 2.11; Jer. 49.7,20; Ezek. 25.13; Amos 1.12; Obad. 9; Hab. 3.3.

Temeni (tĕm'ĕnī, tēmē'nī, tē'mĕnī), son of Ashur and Naarah. 1 Chron. 4.6.

Temesvar, Banat of: see BANAT.

Temirtau or **Temir-Tau** (both: tyĭmĕr-tou'), city (1970 pop. 167,000), Central Asian USSR, in Kazakhstan, on the Nura River. It is a major industrial center, with large iron and steel plants and synthetic rubber and metal factories. Temirtau is also the site of the Samarkand reservoir and a large thermoelectric plant.

Temiscaming (təmĭs'kəmĭng) or **Témiscamingue** (tāmĭskämăNg') or **Timiskaming** (tĭmĭs'kəmĭng), town (1966 pop. 2,769), SW Que., Canada, at the south end of Lake Timiscaming, NE of North Bay. Gold, silver, cobalt, and arsenic are mined in the region.

Temiscaming, Lake, Fr. *Témiscamingue*, an expansion of the Ottawa River, 121 sq mi (313 sq km), SW Que., Canada, extending 62 mi (100 km) SE from New Liskeard to Temiscaming. The surrounding area is rich in minerals.

Témiscamingue, Que., Canada: see TEMISCAMING.

Tempe (tĕm'pē), city (1970 pop. 63,550), Maricopa co., S Ariz., in the Salt River valley; inc. 1894. It is a health resort, an agricultural center, and the seat of Arizona State Univ. Indian ruins are nearby, and across the Salt River is Papago State Park.

Tempe, Vale of, Gr. *Témbi*, valley, c.5 mi (8 km) long, E central Greece, NE Thessaly, between Mt. Olympus and Mt. Óssa. Traversed by the Piniós River, the valley is famous for its rugged grandeur. Its beauty was celebrated by ancient poets, as by Vergil in the *Georgics*. The Vale of Tempe was sacred to Apollo, and laurel for the wreaths of victors of the Pythian games was gathered there. Strategically important as a route into central Greece, the valley was fortified by the Romans and the Byzantines. Among the ruins is a temple of Apollo.

Tempelhof (tĕm'pəlhôf), district, E West Berlin. A workers' residential quarter and a film production center, it became part of the U.S. occupation sector after 1945. The district includes Tempelhof Field, West Berlin's chief airport. During the Soviet blockade (June, 1948–May, 1949) of the western sectors of Berlin, Tempelhof Field was the main terminal of the U.S. airlift and was considerably enlarged. It now contains an impressive monument (built 1951) commemorating the U.S. and British airmen who died during the airlift.

tempera (tĕm'pərə), painting method in which finely ground pigment is mixed with a solidifying base such as albumen, fig sap, or thin glue. When used in mural painting it is also known as *fresco secco* (dry FRESCO) to distinguish it from the *buon fresco* (true fresco) applied to damp walls. The name *distemper* is given to the method when a glue base is involved. When used on wood panels, as it most frequently was for altarpieces and other easel pictures, it was applied on a gesso underpainting that was smooth, very white and brilliant. Tempera's particular advantage is that clear, pure colors are produced, which are not so subject to oxidation as are oils. However, tempera does not lend itself to the expression of nuances of color and atmosphere. Well known from antiquity, tempera was the exclusive panel medium in the Middle Ages and the early Renaissance, and in Italy it was not supplanted by oil until c.1500. In the north oil superseded tempera about a century earlier. Tempera was also much used in combination with oils. In modern times there has been a revival of tempera painting. Böcklin and Hodler in the 19th cent. experimented with it, and some 20th-century American artists, notably Ben Shahn and Andrew Wyeth, have renewed an interest in the old medium. Pigment mixed with egg yolk applied to a sized panel is the common preparation. In industrial art, notably for posters, a simplified distemper is often used. An excellent account of the early Renaissance use of tempera is found in Cennino Cennini's *Treatise on Painting* (c.1437, tr. 1933). See D. V. Thompson, *The Practice of Tempera Painting* (1936); P. Albenda, *Creative Painting with Tempera* (1970).

temperament, in music, the altering of certain intervals from their acoustically correct values to provide a system of tuning whereby any instrument may be played in all keys. The system has been in general, although not universal, use in Western music since the 18th cent. Pythagoras set down the frequency ratios of the pure or acoustically correct intervals (see INTERVAL), namely 2:1 for the octave, 3:2 for the pure fifth, and 5:4 for the pure third. If a set of resonators is tuned to a cycle of pure fifths, e.g., tuning C to 256 vibrations per second, G a pure fifth higher, and so on, it will be found upon reaching B sharp, which is the same note as C on the modern piano, that it is slightly higher than C. A similar downward cycle will yield a B flat, for example, which is lower than A sharp, although one note suffices for both on the piano. By tuning to a fifth which is slightly flat, one arrives at equal temperament (see TUNING SYSTEMS).

temperance movements, organized efforts to induce people to abstain—partially or completely—from drinking alcoholic beverages. Such movements occurred in ancient times, but ceased until the wide use of distilled liquors in the modern period resulted in increasing drunkenness. The stirrings of temperance activity began in the 19th cent. in the United States, Great Britain, and the countries of N Europe, where drinking had greatly increased. Relying on personal appeal, such individuals as Father Theobald MATHEW in Ireland and Great Britain and John Bartholomew Gough in the United States secured temperance pledges by preaching that moral degradation, ill health, poverty, and crime were the results of alcoholism. In 1808 a temperance group was formed in Saratoga, N.Y., and in the next few decades societies sprang up in other states and in the British Isles, Norway, and Sweden. International cooperation was begun in the latter half of the 19th cent., one of the most effective groups being the WOMAN'S CHRISTIAN TEMPERANCE UNION (WCTU) founded in 1874 in the United States. The WCTU and the strong ANTI-SALOON LEAGUE (founded in 1895 and now known as the American Council on Alcohol Problems) wielded significant political power in the United States and, turning from moral appeals for moderation and abstinence, demanded government control of liquor. Backed by church groups and some industrialists, they influenced the passage of many LIQUOR LAWS and eventually succeeded in securing Federal PROHIBITION (1919–33). Among the outstanding women temperance workers of the period were Frances Elizabeth WILLARD, Susan B. ANTHONY, and Carry NATION. Among the effects of temperance agitation were the stimulation of interest in the scientific study of ALCOHOLISM, general instruction in the schools on the effects of alcohol, and provision of reasonable government regulation. See J. A. Krout, *The Origins of Prohibition* (1925); Herbert Asbury, *The Great Illusion* (1950); J. R. Gusfield, *Symbolic Crusade: Status Politics and the American Temperance Movement* (1963); J. H. Bechtel, *Temperance Selections* (1893, repr. 1970).

temperature, measure of the relative warmth or coolness of an object. Temperature is measured by means of a THERMOMETER or other instrument having a scale calibrated in units called degrees. The size of a degree depends on the particular temperature scale being used. A temperature scale is determined by choosing two reference temperatures and dividing the temperature difference between these two points into a certain number of degrees. The two reference temperatures used for most common scales are the MELTING POINT of ice and the BOILING POINT of water. On the CELSIUS TEMPERATURE SCALE, or centigrade scale, the melting point is taken as 0°C and the boiling point as 100°C, and the difference between them is divided into 100 degrees. On the FAHRENHEIT TEMPERATURE SCALE, the melting point is taken as 32°F and the boiling point as 212°F, with the difference between them equal to 180 degrees. The Réaumur scale, used in some parts of Europe, also sets the melting point at zero, but it has an 80-degree temperature difference between 0°R and the boiling point at 80°R. The temperature of a substance does not measure its heat content but rather the average kinetic energy of its molecules resulting from their motions. A one-pound block of iron and a two-pound block of iron at the same temperature do not have the same heat content. Because they are at the same temperature the average kinetic energy of the molecules is the same; however, the two-pound block has more molecules than the one-pound block and thus has greater heat energy. A temperature scale can be defined theoretically for which zero degree corresponds to zero average kinetic energy. Such a scale is known as an absolute temperature scale. The KELVIN TEMPERATURE SCALE is an absolute scale having degrees the same size as those

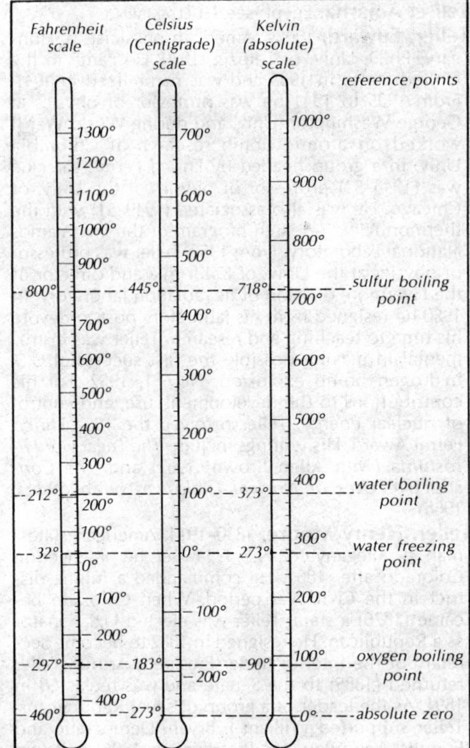

Temperature scales

of the Celsius scale (see GAS LAWS). The relationship between absolute temperature and average molecular kinetic energy is one result of the KINETIC-MOLECULAR THEORY OF GASES. See HEAT; THERMODYNAMICS.

temperature, body: see BODY TEMPERATURE; FEVER.

temperature-humidity index: see HUMIDITY.

temperature inversion, condition in which the temperature of the atmosphere increases with altitude in contrast to the normal decrease with altitude. When temperature inversion occurs, cold air underlies warmer air at higher altitudes. Temperature inversion may occur during the passage of a cold front or result from the invasion of sea air by a cooler onshore breeze. Overnight radiative cooling of surface air often results in a nocturnal temperature inversion that is dissipated after sunrise by the warming of air near the ground. A more long-lived temperature inversion accompanies the dynamics of the large high-pressure systems depicted on weather maps. Descending currents of air near the center of the high-pressure system produce a warming (by adiabatic compression), causing air at middle altitudes to become warmer than the surface air. Rising currents of cool air lose their buoyancy and are thereby inhibited from rising further when they reach the warmer, less dense air in the upper layers of a temperature inversion. During a temperature inversion air pollution released into the atmosphere's lowest layer is trapped there and can be removed only by strong horizontal winds. Because high-pressure systems often combine temperature inversion conditions and low wind speeds, their long residency over an industrial area usually results in episodes of severe smog.

tempering, process involving slow and moderate heating to increase the hardness and toughness of metals that have undergone previous heat treatment. Metals are usually hardened (see HARDENING) by being heated to high temperatures and quenched rapidly. This treatment causes brittleness, which is reduced by tempering. Steel is notably responsive to tempering, and makers of tools, weapons, armor, and other articles of steel have long had great skill in the process. Tempering is not necessary for such products as razors and files, in which hardness is sought but brittleness is not a serious disadvantage. Other products, e.g., swords and saws, require tempering for toughness. In the handicraft process of tempering, the condition of the steel during heating is judged by its color, caused by an oxide film. A desired hardness can be achieved by plunging the steel into a bath when it has cooled to the right shade of yellow or brown or blue. To secure a bath of the right temperature, various liquids are used, e.g., pure water, salt water, oil, and molten metal. The process of softening steel that is harder than desired is called annealing. In modern mass production the processes of tempering are guided by scientific tests in place of the craftsman's skill. Comparable to tempering is the process of hastening the cooling of a casting to increase the hardness of the part so "chilled."

Templars: see KNIGHTS TEMPLARS.

Temple, Frederick, 1821–1902, Anglican prelate, archbishop of Canterbury, b. Santa Maura, one of the Ionian Islands. A fellow of Balliol College, Oxford, he was ordained a priest in 1847. He was an advocate of educational reform and schooling for the poor, and from 1848 to 1857 he worked in the Government Education Dept. He was appointed headmaster of Rugby in 1857. An essay published in the controversial *Essays and Reviews* (1860) awakened suspicions that Temple leaned toward radicalism. When Gladstone nominated him (1869) to the bishopric of Exeter there was much protest. However, he was consecrated in that year and in 1885 was made bishop of London. In his later years he was often in conflict with the High Church party. In 1896 he was created archbishop of Canterbury, and a year later he and the archbishop of York issued the official rebuttal to the papal encyclical that denied the validity of Anglican orders. His works include *The Relations Between Religion and Science* (1885). See *Memoirs of Archbishop Temple by Seven Friends* (ed. E. G. Sandford, 2 vol., 1906).

Temple, Richard Grenville-Temple, Earl, 1711–79, British statesman; elder brother of George GRENVILLE and brother-in-law of William Pitt, 1st earl of CHATHAM. He succeeded to his mother's peerage in 1752. He was closer to Pitt than to his brother and, as first lord of the admiralty (1756–57) in the Pitt-Devonshire ministry and lord privy seal (1757–61) under Pitt and the duke of Newcastle, gave strong backing to Pitt's war policy. He also joined Pitt in vigorous opposition to Grenville's ministry (1763–65), financing John WILKES in his attacks upon the government. However, when Pitt (by then Lord Chatham) formed another ministry in 1766, Temple quarreled with him and allied himself with Grenville. After Grenville's death (1770) he was reconciled with Chatham.

Temple, Sir William, 1628–99, English diplomat and author. He was married in 1655 to Dorothy OSBORNE. They settled in Ireland, and in 1661 Temple entered the Irish Parliament. He moved (1663) to England, served on various diplomatic missions, and was made a baronet (1666). In 1668 he negotiated with great skill and speed a triple alliance with the Netherlands and Sweden to check the power of France. He became (1668) ambassador to The Hague but was secretly recalled (1670) after CHARLES II had concluded the secret Treaty of Dover with Louis XIV. He was reappointed (1674) at the conclusion of the unpopular English-Dutch war, and negotiated the marriage (1677) of William of Orange to Princess Mary of England. Temple several times refused to become secretary of state, but he did promote a reorganization (1679) of the privy council. After this proved a failure, he retired (1681) to his estate, Moor Park, in Surrey, and devoted his time to writing. He produced a number of political works and essays. Jonathan SWIFT, who was Temple's secretary for various periods in the 1690s, helped prepare his letters (1700–1703) and memoirs for publication (parts of both had earlier unauthorized publication). Temple's essay, *Of Ancient and Modern Learning* (1690), precipitated the famous "ancients versus moderns" controversy, which caused Swift to write *The Battle of the Books* (1697). Temple's style in his personal essays was long considered a model of balanced and polished prose. See his life and works (1814); biographies by Homer Woodbridge (1940, repr. 1966) and R. C. Steensma (1970).

Temple, William, 1881–1944, archbishop of York (1929–42) and archbishop of Canterbury (1942–44); son of Frederick Temple. At Balliol College, Oxford, he became (1904) president of the Oxford Union. He was fellow and lecturer in philosophy (1904–10) at Queen's College, Oxford, and in 1909 was ordained priest. Temple served as headmaster (1910–14) of Repton School and as rector (1914–17) of St. James's, Piccadilly. He joined the Life and Liberty Movement, which strove for an autonomous Church of England; the goal was achieved in part by the Enabling Act of 1919. He was canon (1919–21) of Westminster and bishop (1921–29) of Manchester. He was made archbishop of York in 1929, and in 1942 he became archbishop of Canterbury. Keenly interested in social and economic reform, he was a friend of labor and the first president (1908–24) of the Workers' Educational Association. His leadership in the movement to form a world council of churches was outstanding. Among his numerous publications are *Christianity and the State* (1928), *Nature, Man, and God* (1934), and *The Church Looks Forward* (1944). See F. A. Iremonger, *William Temple, Archbishop of Canterbury* (1948, abr. 1963); J. F. Fletcher, *William Temple, Twentieth Century Christian* (1963); A. M. Ramsey, *An Era in Anglican Theology* (1960).

Temple, city (1970 pop. 33,431), Bell co., central Texas; inc. 1882. In a rich blackland region, Temple has grain and textile mills, railroad shops, and plants making a wide variety of products. Several state and Federal agencies have agricultural research centers there. The city has three private hospitals, a veterans' hospital, and a junior college. U.S. Fort Hood is in the area.

temple, edifice or sometimes merely an enclosed area dedicated to the worship of a deity and the enshrinement of holy objects connected with such worship. The temple has been employed in most of the world's religions. Although remains of Egyptian temples of c.2000 B.C. show well-defined architectural forms, it seems likely that temples were hewed in living rock at a still earlier age: the cave temples of Egypt, India, China, and the Mediterranean basin may be viewed as later developments of such primitive shrines. In Egypt in the New Empire impressive rock temples were hewed from cliffsides, the finest being the great temple of ABU-SIMBEL constructed by Ramses II. In the developed structural temples of Egypt a doorway, flanked by moumental towers or pylons, led to an unroofed open court, generally surrounded on three sides by a colonnaded passage. Beyond the court lay the majestic hypostyle hall and a variety of chambers preceding and surrounding the holy of holies. From the temple entrance to this innermost sanctuary the various units diminished progressively in size and height, while the direct outside light was also reduced. The typical temple later accumulated additional pylons, courts, and rooms, the entire group being enclosed by a massive wall. Only monarchs and priests had access to the chambers beyond the hypostyle hall. The New Empire was the most active period of temple construction, although the grandest temple, that of Amon at Al Karnak, was begun much earlier. In the ancient Babylonian and Assyrian periods of W Asia the temple, or ZIGGURAT, was a square pyramidal structure about 300 ft (90 m) high built up in successive, inclined terraces, sometimes as many as seven; with accessory buildings it was enclosed by walls. At its summit was a chamber that served both as a shrine and for astronomical observations. Glazed colored bricks faced the walls. The temple of Solomon at Jerusalem, the only known monumental structure of the ancient Hebrews, consisted, according to biblical descriptions, of entrance pylons, courts, and a naos giving entrance to the holy of holies, which housed the Ark of the Covenant. Its several destructions and reconstructions (one by Herod in 20 B.C.) have rendered unrecognizable any remains of the original edifice. The workmanship, characteristically Phoenician, was of stone, timber, and metal. The temple of Herod, to which Jesus went, was destroyed A.D. 70; its ruins have symbolized to the Jews their dispersion. The Dorian immigration (before 1000 B.C.) was a prelude to the building of Greek temples, at first made of timber and sun-dried brick. The superb stone and marble buildings on a defined floor plan were achieved in the middle of the 6th cent. B.C., although the most perfect examples, like the PARTHENON (5th cent. B.C.), came later. The Greek temple customarily stood in a temenos, or sacred enclosure, along with accessory shrines, colonnades, and buildings housing the temple treasures. It was built not as a place for assembled worship but as the dwelling for the deity, his colossal sculptured representation being placed in a large rectangular chamber, or naos, and illuminated by the daylight entering through the tall entrance portal. In larger temples, to support the roof lintels, two interior rows of columns divided the naos into nave and side aisles. The Roman temple, while based upon the Greek type, retained elements from Etruscan architecture, as in its deep front portico and its elevation upon a high base, or podium, whose wings extended forward to flank the broad entrance steps. The Maison Carrée at Nîmes, France (1st cent. B.C.), the best-preserved Roman temple, is the common pseudoperipteral type, with engaged columns or pilasters attached to its walls. Unlike the long narrow Greek naos, the Roman cella was nearly square in plan. Of the polygonal and circular temples the circular Pantheon at Rome (2d cent. A.D.) (see under PANTHEON) with its magnificent dome is the most remarkable. Many temples, particularly those of the Eastern colonies, as at Baalbek in Syria, had magnificent settings of entrance courts enclosed by colonnades. In India the most ancient remaining temples are the rock-hewed monuments of the Buddhist period (c.255 B.C.–A.D. c.300); important groups exist in W India, E of Bombay. The typical interior is a vast cave divided by lavishly sculptured rock piers into nave and aisles; the sculptured facade, hewed from the cliff face, has a single huge opening to admit light. The principal Indian temples are gradual accretions around a sacred site, forming a religious center comprising shrines, cells for priests, and accommodations for pilgrims. The expression of symbolism is of paramount importance in both structure and ornaments. In China the characteristic temple differs from the form of a dwelling only in its size and richness. Besides the temple a Buddhist monastery includes a relic shrine, a pagoda, a library, and quarters for the monks. In Japan the temple harmonizes with the picturesque landscape in which it is set, with architectural emphasis upon an unsymmetrical grouping of torii (sacred gateways), shrines, pagodas, and terraces. See GREEK ARCHITECTURE; ROMAN ARCHITECTURE; INDIAN ART AND ARCHITECTURE; CHINESE ARCHITECTURE; JAPANESE ARCHITECTURE; PRE-COLUMBIAN ART AND ARCHITECTURE.

Temple, the, district of the City of London, England. The name refers to two of the four INNS OF COURT, the Middle Temple and the Inner Temple. The Temple was originally the English seat of the famous order of Knights Templars. The Inner Temple hall and library and the Temple Church—a Norman round church dedicated in 1185—have been restored in their original styles following severe damage in World War II. The Temple Bar is the gate built by Sir Christopher Wren c.1672 on the site of the bar or chain that marked one of the entrances to the City of London. The Bar was removed in 1878 and is now in Theobalds Park near Waltham; there is a monument on the old London site, at the junction of Fleet St. and the Strand. Here the lord mayor officially receives personages from outside the City. In the 17th and 18th cent. heads of traitors were displayed there.

Temple City, residential suburban city (1970 pop. 31,040), Los Angeles co., S Calif.; settled 1827, inc. 1960. It has light manufacturing and service businesses.

Temple of Heaven: see CHINESE ARCHITECTURE.

Temple University, mainly in Philadelphia, Pa.; coeducational; opened 1884 by Russell H. CONWELL, chartered 1888 as a college, became a university 1907. In 1965 the university became a state-related institution. It has a well-known medical school and technical institute. There is a two-year branch campus at Ambler.

Templewood, Samuel John Gurney Hoare, 1st Viscount, 1880–1959, British statesman. He entered parliament as Conservative in 1910, served (1922–24, 1924–29) as secretary of state for air, and in 1931 became secretary of state for India. He piloted through Parliament the Government of India Act (1935), providing limited home rule for India. Appointed foreign secretary in 1935, Hoare was faced with the task of forestalling the Italian conquest of Ethiopia. He made a speech before the League of Nations in favor of collective security, but later he and Pierre LAVAL of France secretly agreed (Dec., 1935) on a plan of settlement by which a large portion of Ethiopia would have been surrendered to Italian control. The plan, when leaked to the press, raised a storm of protest in Great Britain, and Hoare resigned. He was henceforth labelled as an appeaser. Hoare reentered (1936) the cabinet as first lord of the admiralty and was home secretary from 1937 to 1939. He was made secretary for air (1940) and served as special ambassador to Spain (1940–44), with the task of keeping that country neutral in World War II. He was raised to the peerage in 1944. His numerous writings include *Nine Troubled Years* (1954).

tempo [Ital.,=time], in music, the speed of a composition. The composer's intentions as to tempo are conventionally indicated by a set of Italian terms, of which the principal ones are *presto* (very fast), *vivace* (lively), *allegro* (fast), *moderato* (moderate), *cantabile* (singingly), *andante* (moderate, literally a "walking" tempo), *adagio* (slow), *lento* (slower than *adagio*), and *largo* (very slow); *accelerando* (increasing the speed) and *ritardando* (slowing down) are directions to alter the tempo momentarily and are canceled by a *tempo*. Since Beethoven's time many composers have given metronomic indications, which, despite their seeming infallibility, are often misleading, and tempo remains a point of subjective interpretation. Acoustical factors influence the choice of a tempo but account less for the divergence between different performances than does the performer's interpretation of the work.

Temposil (tĕm'pəsĭl), trade name for an antialcoholic drug. See ANTABUSE.

Temuco (tāmo͞o'kō), city (1970 pop. 146,039), capital of Cautin prov., S central Chile, on the Cautin River. It is a commercial city dealing in livestock and in the agricultural produce of the region. Temuco, founded in 1881, was the point from which the colonization of S Chile was begun, chiefly by German immigrants. The region was occupied by Araucanian Indians; on a hill near Temuco, the treaty ending the last serious Araucanian uprising was signed (1881). Indians still constitute an important and colorful element in the life of Temuco, which has an Araucanian museum.

Ten, Council of, in the republic of VENICE, a special tribunal created (1310) to avert plots and crimes against the state. It was a direct result of the unsuccessful Tiepolo conspiracy against the Venetian oligarchy. In 1335 the body was given permanent status. It consisted actually of 17 members—the doge, 10 members chosen by the grand council, and 6 elected by the lesser council. After 1539 three members served as inquisitors of state and investigated, by means of a secret police, all criminal, moral, religious, and political offenses. The inquisitors reported their findings to the Ten, who rendered an irrevocable verdict. As the power of the Council of Ten expanded, it came to control foreign relations and financial matters. In 1582 the conservative nobles attempted to reduce its authority but failed; the Ten remained the most important governing body of the state until the fall (1797) of the republic. Although the mystery that veiled its operations gave it an aura of tyrannical despotism, it was in general an efficient and highly effective body.

Tenafly (tĕn'əflī), residential suburban borough (1970 pop. 14,827), Bergen co., NE N.J., on the Hudson River; settled 1640, inc. 1894.

Tenali (tānä'lē), city (1971 pop. 102,703), Andhra Pradesh state, SE India, on the Krishna River delta. It is a market for rice paddy.

Tenasserim (tĕnăs'ərĭm), division (1969 est. pop. 1,856,000), 21,297 sq mi (55,159 sq km), extreme S Burma. MOULMEIN, the capital, and Tavoy and Mergui are the chief towns. A narrow strip of coast between Thailand on the east and the Andaman Sea on the west, Tenasserim extends south for c.600 mi (970 km) from the Gulf of Martaban to the Isthmus of Kra and includes many offshore islands. The rainfall is heavy (about 200 in./508 cm a year); rice, vegetables, coconuts, and rubber are grown. Tin and tungsten are extracted, and teak is cut. The people speak a distinct dialect of Burmese, and their culture shows many Siamese and Malay influences. Tenasserim was long subject in turn to Siam and Burma, but remained in Burmese hands when the long wars of the Thai and Burmese ended late in the 18th cent. As a result the first Anglo-Burmese War (1824–26), Tenasserim passed under British rule.

Ten Commandments or **Decalogue** (dĕk'-) [Gr.,=ten words], in the Bible, the summary of divine law given by God to Moses on Mt. Sinai. They have a paramount place in the ethical system in Judaism, Christianity, and Islam. In the Authorized Version the commandments are stated in Ex. 20.2–17 and in Deut. 5.6–21. The Decalogue is in fact divisible into 12 commandments, since the first of the 10 actually consists of three passages. However, two traditions divide them in differing enumerations. For the Orthodox Eastern and most Protestants the command to worship no gods before God is the first; the prohibition of graven images, the second. Following the more ancient Jewish tradition, the Roman Catholics and Lutherans combine these two as the first. Thus, the third to the ninth commandments in one system correspond to the second to the eighth in the other. Again following Jewish tradition, for Roman Catholics and Lutherans, the ninth forbids coveting one's neighbor's wife, the tenth his property. Other Protestants and the Orthodox combine these two as the tenth.

Tenda or **Tende:** see BRIGUE AND TENDE.

tendon, tough cord composed of closely packed white fibers of connective tissue that serves to attach muscle to bone. Sometimes when the muscle involved is thin and wide, the tendon is not a cord but a thin sheet known as an aponeurosis. The purpose of the tendon in attaching muscle to bone is to enable the power of a muscle to be transferred over a distance. For example, when one wants to move a finger, specific muscles in the forearm contract and pull on ligaments that in turn pull the finger bones to produce the desired action.

tendrec: see TENREC.

tendril, slender, sensitive structure of many climbing plants that by a response to contact (see AUXIN) supports the plant. Tendrils are modified stems, leaves, or leaf parts. Most young tendrils revolve slowly in their natural growth, as do the growing tips of roots and shoots; the tendrils of different plant varieties may have a consistent tendency to clockwise or to counterclockwise spiraling. The most common kind of tendril (pea, grape) coils around a slender support and then contracts spirally, becoming springy and drawing the plant to the support. The disk-tipped tendril (Virginia creeper, Boston ivy) adheres firmly to brick, stone, or wood, after which it too contracts. For other means of climbing in plants, see CLIMBING PLANT.

Tenebrae (tĕn'ĕbrā) [Lat.,=darkness], in the Roman Catholic Church, ceremony performed on the Wednesday and following evenings of HOLY WEEK. As the choir chants, a number of candles set on a hearse (a kind of candelabrum) are put out one by one until only one remains. The last candle is hidden behind the altar, and in the darkness a noise is made, symbolizing the convulsion of Nature at the Crucifixion. The single lighted candle is then replaced on the hearse. The traditional plainsong for the ceremony is much esteemed.

Tenedos, Turkey: see BOZCAADA.

tenement house: see APARTMENT HOUSE; HOUSE; HOUSING.

Tenerani, Pietro (pyĕ'trō tänärä'nē), c.1789–1869, Italian sculptor. He studied with both Canova and Thorvaldsen. Of his many works on classical and Christian subjects, the best known include *Psyche with Pandora's Box, Cupid and Venus,* and *Deposition from the Cross,* a large relief in the Lateran, Rome. He made the tomb of Pius VIII in St. Peter's, Rome, and a statue of Bolívar for Colombia.

Teneriffe or **Tenerife** (both: tĕn'ərĭf, tĕnərēf', Span. tānārē'fā), island (1970 pop. 500,381), 795 sq mi (2,059 sq km), in the Atlantic off NW Africa, the largest of the CANARY ISLANDS, Spain. A scenic island, it is dominated by Mt. Teide, a snow-capped volcanic peak (12,198 ft/3,718 m). Santa Cruz, capital of Santa Cruz de Tenerife prov., is on the island.

Teng Hsiao-p'ing (tŭng shēou-pĭng, dŭng), 1904–, Chinese Communist political leader. Following work and study in France and in the Soviet Union, Teng returned to China to serve as a Communist political officer (1926–27) in the NORTHERN EXPEDITION. From 1929 to 1949 he was a Red Army political officer, and after the Communist victory he became a top official in SW China. Teng was transferred (1952) to Peking, where he rose quickly in the party central hierarchy. In 1956 he became party general secretary, and was elevated to membership on the politburo standing committee, the party's supreme decision-making body. During the next decade Teng was deeply involved in relations with foreign Communist parties, and was a central figure in the growing Sino-Soviet dispute over the direction of the international Communist movement. He was attacked in the Red Guard press during the Cultural Revolution (1966–69), and was purged from power in 1967. He was rehabilitated in 1973.

Teniers, David (tənĕrz', tĕn'yərz, Flemish tĕnērs'), the elder, 1582–1649, Flemish painter. He spent many years in Rome. Works attributed to him have often been confused with the early work of his famous son and pupil. **David Teniers,** the younger, 1610–90, noted Flemish genre painter, worked with his father in Antwerp. His early works show the influence of Bruegel, the elder, his father-in-law. A protégé of Rubens, Teniers became court painter to the governor of the Netherlands and also worked for Philip IV of Spain. Heavily commissioned, he painted a prodigious number of small, very finished pictures. His favorite subjects were quiet scenes from peasant life. His subtle color and brilliant technique are unexcelled among the genre painters of his period. Among his well-known pictures are several versions of *Flemish Kermess* in the museums of Antwerp and Vienna and a version of *The Alchemist* in The Hague. The National Gallery, London, and the Prado have many examples of his work.

Tenimbar Islands: see TANIMBAR ISLANDS, Indonesia.

Tenison, Thomas (tĕn'ĭsən), 1636–1715, English churchman, archbishop of Canterbury (1695–1715). In 1680 he became rector of St. Martin's-in-the-Fields, London; there he came into prominence as a preacher and as an author, and he founded a free library. He was consecrated bishop of Lincoln in 1691 and was named archbishop of Canterbury in 1695. He administered to both William and Mary at their deathbeds but was not popular with Queen Anne. He had Low Church views and supported the Hanoverian succession. He was a founder (1701) of the Society for the Propagation of the Gospel and wrote books on Thomas Hobbes (1670) and Francis Bacon (1679).

Tennant, Smithson, 1761–1815, English chemist. In 1796 he proved, by burning a diamond, that the diamond consists solely of carbon. In 1804 he announced his discovery of osmium and iridium.

Tennent, Gilbert, 1703–64, American Presbyterian clergyman, leading preacher of the GREAT AWAKENING, b. Ireland; son of William Tennent. He moved with his parents to Pennsylvania c.1718. Installed as pastor at New Brunswick, N.J., in 1726, he soon became the leader of a revival movement among the Presbyterians in New Jersey, New York, and Pennsylvania. A friend of George WHITEFIELD, Tennent made (1740–41) an evangelistic tour in New England. Opposition to the revival from conservatives in the Presbyterian Church led to a schism (1741–58). Tennent led the "New Side" but later used his influence to heal the breach. He was interested in the College of New Jersey (now Princeton Univ.) and in 1753 he went to Great Britain with Samuel DAVIES to secure funds for the college.

Tennent, William, 1673–1745, American Presbyterian clergyman and educator, b. Ireland, grad. Univ. of Edinburgh, 1695. He was ordained in the Church of Ireland in 1706. He emigrated to America c.1718; in 1726 he was called to a pastorate in Neshaminy, Pa., where he stayed the remainder of his life. Here, in a log cabin, Tennent established a school that became famous as the Log College. He filled his pupils with evangelical zeal, and a number became revivalist preachers in the GREAT AWAKENING. The educational influence of the Log College was of importance since many of its graduates founded schools along the frontier. Princeton Univ. is regarded as a successor to the Log College. See Thomas Murphy, *The Presbytery of the Log College* (1889); Archibald Alexander, *The Log College* (1968).

Tennessee (tĕn'əsē", tĕn"əsē'), state (1970 pop. 3,924,164), 42,244 sq mi (109,412 sq km), S central United States, admitted 1796 as the 16th state (slaveholding). NASHVILLE is the capital and the second largest city. The largest city is MEMPHIS. The state is bounded on the N by Kentucky and Virginia; on the E by North Carolina; on the S by Georgia, Alabama, and Mississippi; and on the W by the Mississippi River, which separates it from Missouri and Arkansas. Although Tennessee is now primarily industrial, with 54% of its population in urban areas, many Tennesseans still derive their livelihood from the land of the state's three sharply defined regions: E Tennessee, Middle Tennessee, and W Tennessee. In E Tennessee the Great Smoky Mts., Cumberland Plateau, and the narrow river valleys and heavily forested foothills generally restrict farming there to the subsistence level; but this region has two of the state's most industrialized cities, Chattanooga (fourth largest) and Knoxville (third largest). Middle Tennessee is hemmed in by the Tennessee River, which flows SW through E Tennessee into N Alabama, looping back up into W Tennessee in its circuitous route to the Ohio. Gently rolling, fertile, bluegrass country, it is ideal for livestock raising and dairy farming. Middle Tennessee is still noted for its fine horses and mules, e.g., the Tennessee walking horse. W Tennessee, with its rich river-bottom lands on which most of the state's cotton is grown, lies between the Tennessee and the Mississippi rivers. The average rainfall ranges from 40 to 50 in. (101.6–127 cm), and the climate is generally mild, with the rigors of a northern winter usually affecting only the most mountainous parts of E Tennessee. The state's leading crops are tobacco, soybeans, hay, and cotton; cattle and dairy products are also principal farm commodities. Tennessee's leading mineral, in dollar value, is stone; zinc ranks second (Tennessee leads the nation in its production), followed by cement and coal. Tennessee is also the nation's largest producer of pyrites and is third in the production of phosphate rock. Industry is being continually diversified; the state's leading manufactures are chemicals and related products, foods, textiles and apparel, electrical machinery, primary metals, and stone, clay, and glass items. Aluminum production has been important since World War I, and more recently a missile industry has been developed in Bristol. Tourism is increasing. Many beautiful lakes have been built by the Tennessee Valley Authority (TVA) and the Army Corps of Engineers; 26 large ones are publicly owned. The TVA has also developed the Land Between the Lakes, an enormous Kentucky-Tennessee recreation area. Twenty-three state parks, covering some 132,000 acres (53,420 hectares) and parts of the Great Smoky Mountains National Park, Cherokee National Forest, and Cumberland Gap National Historical Park are in Tennessee. Sportsmen and visitors are attracted to Reelfoot Lake, originally formed by an earthquake; stumps and other remains of a once dense forest, together with the lotus bed covering the shallow waters, give the lake an eerie beauty. Tennessee has long been known as the national center of folk music. It also has many sites of historic interest, including the Hermitage, home of Andrew Jackson; the Andrew Johnson National Historic Site; the Fort Donelson and Shiloh national military parks; and Stones River National Battlefield. Part of the Chickamauga and Chattanooga National Military Park is also in Tennessee (see NATIONAL PARKS AND MONUMENTS, table). The Natchez Trace National Parkway generally follows the old Natchez Trace, and W Tennessee abounds in artifacts of the MOUND BUILDERS. Cherokee, Chickasaw, Shawnee, and Creek Indians were in the region when it was first visited by a European expedition under De Soto in 1540. French explorers came down the Mississippi River, claiming both sides for France, and c.1682 La Salle built Fort Prudhomme, possibly on the site of present-day Memphis. The French established additional trading posts in the area, but they suffered continual harassment from the Chickasaw Indians. Meanwhile, English fur traders and long hunters (frontiersmen who spent long periods hunting in this area) came over the mountains from the Carolinas and Virginia, prevailed over the Cherokee Indians, and made ineffectual the French claims to the area, which in any event was lost (1763) by the French as a result of the French and Indian Wars. In that fighting, British regulars and South Carolina militiamen had established (1756) Fort Loudoun on the Little Tennessee River, only to have their garrison massacred by the Cherokee in 1760. The first permanent settlement was made (1769) in the Watauga River valley of E Tennessee by Virginians; they were soon joined by North Carolinians, including perhaps a few refugees of the Regulator movement. In 1772 these hardy settlers living beyond the frontier formed the WATAUGA

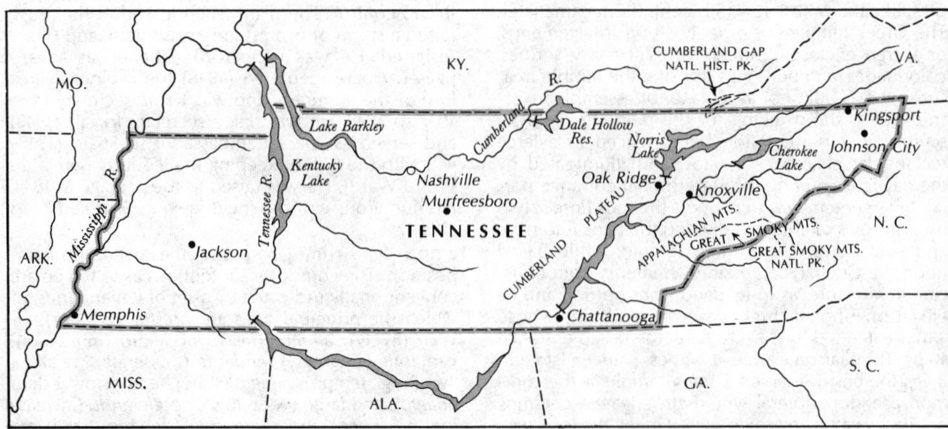

ASSOCIATION, the first attempt at government in Tennessee, and in 1777, at their request, North Carolina organized those settlements into Washington co.; Jonesboro, the county seat and oldest town in Tennessee, was founded two years later. In 1777 the Cherokee ceded a large area of land to Virginia and North Carolina, but one element of the tribe (the Chickamauga) refused to recognize the treaty and, joined by other Indians and by renegade whites, warred against the new settlements. In the American Revolution, John Sevier was among the notable Tennesseans who served with distinction. When, after the war, North Carolina ceded its western lands to the Federal government, the E Tennessee settlers, incensed at being transferred without their consent, formed a short-lived independent government (1784–88) under John Sevier (see FRANKLIN, STATE OF). The cession was reenacted in 1789, and in 1790 the Federal government created the Territory of the United States South of the River Ohio (Southwest Territory), with William Blount as governor. This act disposed of various schemes to place the area under the control of Spanish Louisiana, and, in 1796, Tennessee, with substantially its present boundaries, was admitted to the Union, with its capital at Knoxville. It was the first state to be carved out of national territory. Tennessee's constitution, which provided for universal manhood suffrage (that is, to include free Negroes), was described by Thomas Jefferson as "the least imperfect and most republican" of any state. Armed with land grants awarded for service in the American Revolution, veterans and speculators (who had acquired the grants from veterans, sometimes fraudulently) swarmed in from the Carolinas, Virginia, Pennsylvania, and even from New England via such overland routes as the Wilderness Road and Cumberland Gap. Others poled keelboats from the Ohio up the Cumberland and Tennessee rivers. For the most part a rough and ready people, numbering over 100,000 by 1800, the settlers were nevertheless strongly influenced by the Great Revival, a wave of religious hysteria which swept the state in that year. The virtues and vices of their strongly egalitarian society were exemplified by Andrew Jackson, who was prominent in the faction-ridden politics of Tennessee. By the time Jackson became (1829) President, the state was prospering. The first steamboat had reached Nashville in 1819, the year in which Memphis, soon to become the metropolis of a fast-growing cotton kingdom, was platted. Internal improvements—canals and then railroads—were pushed, and a new, smaller wave of immigrants (predominantly Irish and German) arrived after the Cherokee and the Chickasaw were banished West in the late 1830s. Insatiable land hunger, the spirit of adventure, and personal considerations carried many white Tennesseans beyond the state; among them were Gov. Samuel Houston and David Crockett, both of whom had been conspicuous in the fight for Texan independence. A decade later the response of Tennessee for volunteers in the Mexican War was so overwhelming that it has since been known as the "volunteer state." Tennessee's James K. Polk, a Jackson protégé, was the President of the United States during that war. Although Negro slaves were numerous in W Tennessee, and to a lesser extent in Middle Tennessee, and free Negroes were subjected to a series of discriminatory regulations, the state was pro-Union; it voted in the presidential election of 1860 for its own John Bell, candidate of the moderate CONSTITUTIONAL UNION PARTY. Secession was rejected in a popular referendum on Feb. 9, 1861. However, after the firing on Fort Sumter and Lincoln's call for troops, the pro-Confederate element, led by Gov. Isham G. Harris, canvassed the state, and on June 8, 1861, a second referendum approved secession by a two-thirds majority. The one third opposed represented mainly E Tennessee, where slavery was a negligible factor and where Andrew Johnson (then U.S. Senator) and William G. Brownlow had strengthened the natural Union loyalties of the people. In the Civil War, Tennessee was, after Virginia, the biggest and bloodiest battleground. The rivers served as Union invasion routes. Nashville was occupied by Gen. D. C. Buell in Feb., 1862, after the victories of Gen. Ulysses S. Grant on the lower Tennessee and Cumberland rivers (see FORT HENRY and FORT DONELSON). In April one of the bloodiest battles of the war was fought near the Mississippi state line (see SHILOH, BATTLE OF), and Memphis fell to a Union fleet in June. Confederate Gen. Braxton Bragg, defeated at Perryville, Ky., in Oct., 1862, retreated further in Jan., 1863, after the battle of MURFREESBORO, and Grant, successful in the VICKSBURG CAMPAIGN, completely routed him (Nov., 1863) in the CHATTANOOGA CAMPAIGN. The Confederates did manage to hold on to Knoxville until Sept., 1863, and their cavalry, particularly the forces of Gen. N. B. Forrest and Gen. J. H. Morgan, remained active. An army under Gen. J. B. Hood made a last desperate attempt to regain the state late in 1864 but was defeated at FRANKLIN (Nov. 30) and annihilated at Nashville (Dec. 15–16) by Federals under G. H. Thomas. The Union military government which had been set up under Andrew Johnson in 1862 was succeeded in April, 1865, by a civil government headed by Brownlow. An amendment to the state constitution of 1834 freed the slaves, and, with ex-Confederates disfranchised and radical Republicans in control, the state was readmitted to the Union in March, 1866. As the first Southern state to be readmitted, Tennessee was spared the worst aspects of Congressional RECONSTRUCTION, but the postwar years were nonetheless bitter. That effective instrument for reestablishing "white supremacy" in the South, the KU KLUX KLAN, was founded (1866) in Tennessee, at Pulaski. The situation improved after Brownlow left (1869) the governorship for the U.S. Senate, to which the state also returned (1875) Andrew Johnson in vindication of his record as Lincoln's successor in the presidency. Brownlow's successor, Gov. De Witt C. Senter, although nominally a Republican, encouraged the calling of a new state constitutional convention. In 1870 it drew up a constitution rejecting the reforms of the radical Republicans; Negro suffrage was limited by means of the poll tax, and former Confederates were reenfranchised. Economically, the farm-tenancy system, which had replaced the plantation system, brought much misery; industry, however, made advances after the war. The iron and steelworks of E Tennessee were unable to meet the competition of Birmingham, Ala., but coal mining continued, and textile production increased. The use of convict labor in the mines precipitated the state's first major labor disturbance (1891–92), but not until 1936 was the convict-leasing system abolished. A statewide prohibition bill (not repealed until 1939) was passed over a governor's veto in 1909, and the affair so divided the Democratic party that in 1910 a Republican was elected governor for the first time since 1880. In World War I the thousands of Tennessean volunteers in the U.S. armed forces included Sgt. Alvin C. York, who became one of the nation's most highly publicized heroes. In 1925 the state attracted international attention with the famous SCOPES TRIAL at Dayton, and the fact that the state law banning the teaching of evolution was not repealed until 1967 indicates the strong hold that Protestant fundamentalism had on the people; in 1973 a bill prohibiting the teaching of evolution as a fact was passed. One of the most important events in Tennessee since the Civil War was the establishment of the TVA. Although opposed by private power companies, the TVA succeeded in providing hydroelectric power cheaply and in abundance, bringing modern comforts to thousands. Over the years it has expanded and been supplemented by other projects for water-resources development. Most important, TVA was chiefly responsible for the basic change in the state's economy from agriculture to industry and for the significant growth and diversification of industry, especially during and after World War II. TVA has also come to be associated with atomic energy, for it provides the power for OAK RIDGE, one of the sources of production of the constituents for the first atomic bombs. The 1954 Supreme Court decision outlawing racial segregation in the public schools had far-reaching consequences for Tennessee. Despite rioting, notably at Clinton, and other instances of violence and lawlessness, considerable progress in INTEGRATION has been made. Tennessee has had three constitutions: the first was drafted in 1796, the second in 1834, and the present constitution dates from 1870. It has been amended three times: in 1953, when, among other things, the poll tax was repealed and home rule was established for cities, and in 1960 and 1965, when further provisions were adopted to modernize the state government. Tennessee's executive branch is headed by a governor, elected for a four-year term and not permitted to succeed himself. The state's bicameral legislature has a senate, with 33 members elected for four-year terms, and a house, with 99 members elected for two-year terms. The state elects two Senators and eight Representatives to the U.S. Congress and has 10 electoral votes. Democrats have played an overwhelmingly dominant role in Tennessee politics since the Civil War, although E Tennessee is largely Republican and the state is gradually increasing its Republican vote in national elections. In 1974, Ray Blanton, a Democrat, was elected governor. Among the state's many institutions of higher learning are the Univ. of Tennessee, chiefly at Knoxville; East Tennessee State Univ., at Johnson City; Fisk Univ. and Vanderbilt Univ., at Nashville; Memphis State Univ., at Memphis; Tennessee Technological Univ., at Cookeville; and the Univ. of the South, at Sewanee. See P. M. Hamer, ed., *Tennessee: A History, 1673–1932* (4 vol., 1933); W. H. Combs, *Tennessee: A Political Study* (1940); Tennessee Historical Society, *Tennessee Old and New: Sesquicentennial Edition, 1796–1946* (2 vol., 1946); P. E. Isaac, *Prohibition and Politics* (1965); J. W. Patton, *Unionism and Reconstruction in Tennessee, 1860–1869* (1934, repr. 1966); T. P. Abernethy, *From Frontier to Plantation in Tennessee* (1932, repr. 1967); S. J. Folmsbee et al., *History of Tennessee* (1961, repr. 1969); Joe Clark, *Tennessee Hill Folk* (1972); Federal Writers' Project, *Tennessee: A Guide to the State* (1939, repr. 1972).

Tennessee, river, c.650 mi (1,050 km) long, the principal tributary of the Ohio River. It is formed by the confluence of the Holston and French Broad rivers near Knoxville, Tenn., and follows a U-shaped course to enter the Ohio River at Paducah, Ky. Its drainage basin covers c.41,000 sq mi (106,200 sq km) and includes parts of seven states. Navigation was long impeded by variations in channel depths and by rapids, such as Muscle Shoals. However, the TENNESSEE VALLEY AUTHORITY (est. 1933) has converted the river into a chain of lakes held back by nine major dams (Kentucky, Pickwick Landing, Wilson, Wheeler, Guntersville, Nickajack, Chickamauga, Watts Bar, and Fort Loudoun). As a result of these improvements river traffic has increased; flooding has been controlled; a water-oriented recreations industry has been established; and electric power generated at the dams has attracted new industries to the region. A canal, scheduled for completion in the 1980s, will link the Tennessee River with the Gulf of Mexico by way of the Tombigee River. During the Civil War, the Tennessee River was an excellent approach for a Union invasion of the South, and several great battles were fought there (see FORT HENRY; SHILOH, BATTLE OF; CHATTANOOGA CAMPAIGN).

Tennessee, University of, mainly at Knoxville; land-grant and state supported; coeducational; chartered 1794, opened 1795 as Blount College, closed 1807–20; became Univ. of Tennessee 1879. There is a branch at Chattanooga, and at Memphis are the school of medicine and related schools. The graduate school of social work is at Nashville, and the campus at Martin is primarily for agriculture, education, and home economics. There is an extensive library system and a noteworthy museum of natural history. The university maintains agricultural experiment stations throughout the state.

Tennessee Valley Authority (TVA), independent U.S. government corporate agency, created in 1933 by act of Congress; it is responsible for the integrated development of the Tennessee River basin. The history of TVA began in the early 1920s, when Senator George William NORRIS sponsored a plan to have the government take over and operate Wilson Dam and other installations that had been built by the government for national defense purposes during World War I at MUSCLE SHOALS, Ala. However, legislation to this effect was vetoed in 1928 and in 1931 by Presidents Calvin Coolidge and Herbert Hoover. The 1933 TVA Act, redrafted by President Franklin Delano Roosevelt, went far beyond the earlier proposals and launched the Federal government into a vast scheme of regional planning and development—an undertaking that became the model for similar river projects. The TVA concept was a dramatic experiment in that it was the first time that a single agency was directed to address itself to the total resource development needs of a major region. TVA was instructed to take on the problems presented by devastating floods, badly eroded lands, a deficient economy, and a steady outmigration—all in one unified development effort. The act provided for the integrated development of the whole Tennessee River basin—an area of about 41,000 sq mi (106,200 sq km), with a present-day population of nearly 3,900,000. TVA is governed by a three-person board of directors. The fact that its main offices are located in the region, rather than in Washington, D.C., makes TVA unique among Federal agencies. It is this location that allows the agency to maintain a close working relationship with the people of the region, a valuable asset in carrying out its programs. Throughout the history of TVA, opponents of the authority have argued that it is too costly and that government should not compete with private enterprise. In 1959, Congress authorized TVA to issue bonds and notes to be used in financing needed additions to power system capacity; it also established a more specific schedule of repayments and dividends to the U.S. Treasury on appropriations previously used in building the power system. The power system is now self-financing, and has paid back about $1 billion into the U.S. Treasury. Other TVA resource development programs continue to be financed largely from Federal appropriations, except that sales of experimental fertilizer materials are used in financing production of these materials. The most noteworthy feature of TVA is the system of multipurpose dams and reservoirs that have contributed greatly to the economic life of the area. There are 42 dams in the system, including some owned by the Aluminum Company of America and operated by TVA. The agency also markets power from eight hydroelectric plants along the nearby Cumberland River and its tributaries. The hydroelectric system had an installed capacity in excess of 4 million kw in the early 1970s. To meet the growing demand for power over and above the hydroelectric capacity of the system, TVA began in 1940 to construct steam-generating facilities. By the 1970s over 80% of the installed capacity of the TVA system was provided by its coal-burning steam plants; in the early 1970s the major plants had an installed capacity that totaled more than 15 million kw. In addition, the steadily mounting power demands turned TVA toward nuclear energy. In the early 1970s the agency had under construction Browns Ferry, Sequoyah, and Watts Bar nuclear plants, with a combined planned capacity of nearly 8.5 million kw. The electric power from all sources is allocated with a view to promoting the widest possible use of electricity throughout the area—with local municipalities, state and Federal agencies, and farmer cooperatives receiving priority over private utility companies and industrial establishments. The availability of this low-cost electricity has attracted large numbers of businesses and industries to the area. A 630-mi (1,014-km) navigation channel extends from the mouth of the Tennessee River to Knoxville, Tenn. It has been responsible for an enormous increase in river traffic, chiefly in coal, construction material, grain, petroleum, chemical, and forest products. The chemical works at the town of Muscle Shoals produce experimental fertilizers, which are supplied to colleges and demonstration farms for experimental purposes. Other TVA activities, carried out in cooperation with local authorities, include land conservation; tree planting; malaria control; the development of fish, wildlife, and mineral resources; social and educational programs; and the establishment of recreational facilities along the banks of its reservoirs. By the 1960s many of the problems faced by TVA in its early years had been overcome. Per capita income in the region had greatly increased, and there was an end to the rapid outmigration of the past. However, TVA continues to seek ways of making the largely rural parts of the area an attractive alternative to overcrowded cities. In the late 1960s and early 70s TVA began to place greater emphasis on environmental protection, as industrialization and rising living standards resulted in increasingly urgent demands on the environment. In the conflict between economic and environmental objectives, TVA sought a suitable balance in carrying out its operations, particularly its power program. Despite TVA's environmental protection efforts, the agency came under criticism from a number of sources, principally environmental groups. One of the most controversial issues involved construction of the Tellico Dam and Reservoir on the Little Tennessee River. See P. J. Hubbard, *Origins of the TVA* (1961, repr. 1968); John Moore, ed., *The Economic Impact of TVA* (1967); Thomas McGraw, *TVA and the Power Fight, 1933–1939* (1971); Marguerite Owen, *The Tennessee Valley Authority* (1973).

Tenniel, Sir John (tĕn'yəl), 1820–1914, English caricaturist and illustrator. He became well known for his original and good-humored political cartoons in *Punch*, with which he was associated from 1851 to 1901. Tenniel is also known for his illustrations of Thomas Moore's *Lalla Rookh; Aesop's Fables; The Ingoldsby Legends;* and, above all, Lewis Carroll's *Alice in Wonderland* and *Through the Looking Glass.* See study by F. Sarzano (1948).

tennis, game played indoors or outdoors by two players (singles) or four players (doubles) on a level court. Lawn tennis was originally played only on grass courts, and most major tennis matches are still played on grass, natural or artificial. But since grass courts are expensive to maintain (for the most part only private clubs have them), they are not so numerous as the outdoor courts of clay or asphalt that the general tennis-playing public uses. Play on one type of court naturally differs somewhat from that on another type (e.g., the ball bounces more quickly on clay), but the rules of the game are the same for all kinds of courts. In singles play the court measures 78 ft by 27 ft (23.8 m by 8.2 m), and in doubles play it is 4.5 ft (1.4 m) wider on either side. The court is divided in half by a net 3 ft (91 cm) high (roughly, the length plus the width of a racket) in the middle and 3.5 ft (1.1 m) high at the end posts. On either side of the net lie the forecourts, each of which comprises two adjacent service courts of equal size measuring 21 ft by 13.5 ft (6.4 m by 4.1 m). Behind each pair of forecourts lies a backcourt that is 18 ft (5.5 m) long and terminates in a base line parallel to the net. The 4½-foot-wide (1.4-m) alleys, which flank either side of the court perpendicular to the net, are used only in doubles play. Tennis play is directed toward hitting the inflated rubber, felt-covered, unstitched ball (about the size of a baseball) with the tennis racket—oval headed, usually 27 in. (68.58 cm) long, the hitting surface strung with resilient fiber—into the opponent's court out of his reach or so that he returns the ball out of bounds or into the net. One player serves an entire game and is given two service tries each time the ball is put in play. He serves the ball diagonally from behind the base line so that it bounces into the opposite serving court beyond the net. A let ball, which caroms off the top of the net into the proper service court, warrants another try (not counting as a faulty service). A foot fault (commonly, stepping on or over the base line on the serve) is penalized by forfeiture of the service try. Service is alternately from right- and left-hand courts. After the first game, the players change sides; thereafter, they change every two games. Once the serve is completed, the ball may be hit into any part of the opponent's court until a point is scored. A point may be won by either the server or the receiver, and points are scored in the progression 15, 30, 40, and game. The term *love* in tennis scoring means 0. When the game goes to deuce (tied at 40-40) the first player to go two points ahead takes the game. The first player to win six games takes the set, provided his opponent has won no more than four games. Traditionally, after the players were tied at five games all, the first to go two games ahead won the set. However, in 1970 the United States Lawn Tennis Association (USLTA, founded 1881), U.S. tennis's national governing body, initiated the sudden-death tie-breaker game. By that rule, if a set is tied at six games all, a special game of nine points is played. The winner of that game wins the set. The tie-breaker rule, with modifications, was later adopted by other national tennis federations, including the British. The best two out of three sets wins a match in women's play; the best three out of five sets wins a match in men's play. The plays of the game are called by an umpire, and in important matches a net umpire, a referee, foot fault judges, and linesmen often assist. Unlike most other sports, lawn tennis has an origin that can be marked with precision. It was invented (1873) by an Englishman, Major Walter C. Wingfield, and first played at a garden party in Wales during the same year. Called "Sphairistiké" [Gr., = ball playing] by its inventor, the early game was played on an hourglass-shaped court, widest at the baselines and narrowest at the net. In creating the new sport, Major Wingfield borrowed heavily from the older games of SQUASH RACQUETS and COURT TENNIS, and probably even from the Indian game of BADMINTON. Lawn tennis caught on quickly in Great Britain, and soon the All England Croquet Club at Wimbledon held the first world tennis championship (1877). Restricted to male players only, that event became the famous Wimbledon Tournament for the British National Championship, the most prestigious event in tennis. In 1884 a women's championship was inaugurated at Wimbledon. Soon the game became popular in many parts of the British Empire, especially in Australia. Tennis spread to the United States by way of Bermuda. While vacationing there, Mary Ewing Outerbridge of New York was introduced (1874) to the game by an army friend of Major Wingfield. She returned to the United States with a net, balls, and rackets, and with the help of her brother set up a tennis court in Staten Island, N.Y. Another court was built in Nahant, Mass., and the sport spread quickly throughout the country. The first National Championship, for men only, was held (1881) at Newport, R.I. A women's championship was begun six years later, and in 1915 the National Championship was moved to its present site at the West Side Tennis Club in Forest Hills, N.Y. In 1900 the international team competition known as the Davis Cup tournament was initiated. Along with the Wightman Cup (begun 1923), an annual tournament between British and American women's teams, the Davis Cup helped to focus international attention on tennis. Meanwhile, the construction of tennis courts on school and community playgrounds helped to make the sport available to all classes of the population. Professional tennis in the United States began with the establishment (1927) of the United States Professional Lawn Tennis Association. After the professional game showed itself to be highly profitable, a number of amateur players joined the tour. One of the first to do so was William TILDEN, perhaps the greatest player in the history of tennis. Before this great amateur turned pro (1931), he won a total of seven United States singles championships and three Wimbledon championships. The continued defection of amateur players into the professional ranks was one of the factors that led amateur tennis's world governing body, the International Lawn Tennis Federation (ILTF, founded 1913), to open its tournaments to both professionals and amateurs in 1968. For many years the major ILTF-sponsored tournaments, including Wimbledon and the U.S. National Championship, were restricted to amateurs. With the advent of open tennis, however, the world's great professionals were allowed to compete in those important events. The Davis Cup competition, however, remained an amateurs-only tournament. From its earliest days tennis was played by both men and women; most of the major tournaments have male and female divisions, and mixed doubles is a common form of play. It was not until 1971, however, that the establishment of a women-only professional tour gave female pros financial parity with their male counterparts. In the same year Billie Jean King, a tennis pro, became the first woman athlete in any sport to earn more than $100,000 in one year. International tennis, both amateur and professional, has been dominated by the United States and Australia since World War II. Among the many great players in the history of tennis, there are only four—Don Budge and Rod Laver among men, Maureen Connolly and Margaret Court among women—who have won the "grand slam" (the national championships of the United States, Great Britain, Australia, and France). Other great figures in the history of tennis include Dwight Davis, James Dwight, Althea Gibson, Pancho Gonzales, Jack Kramer, Suzanne Lenglen, Helen Roark, Richard Sears, and Hazel Hotchkiss Wightman. The USLTA maintains a tennis Hall of Fame at Newport, R.I. See Peter Everett and Virginia Skillman, *Beginning Tennis* (1962); Will Grimsley, *Tennis, Its History, People and Events* (1971); United States Lawn Tennis Association, *Official Encyclopedia of Tennis* (1972).

Tennyson, Alfred Tennyson, 1st **Baron** (tĕn'ĭsən), 1809–92, English poet. The most famous poet of the Victorian age, he was a profound spokesman for the ideas and values of his times. He was the son of an intelligent but unstable clergyman in Lincolnshire. His early literary attempts included a play, *The Devil and the Lady,* composed at 14, and poems written with his brothers Frederick and Charles but entitled *Poems by Two Brothers* (1827). In his three years at Cambridge, Tennyson wrote a prize-winning poem, *Timbuctoo* (1829), and *Poems, Chiefly Lyrical* (1830) and began his close friendship with Arthur Henry Hallam, son of the historian Henry Hallam. Upon the death of his father in 1831, Tennyson became responsible for the family and its precarious finances. His volume *Poems* (1832) included some of his most famous pieces, such as "The Lotus-Eaters," "A Dream of Fair Women," "Œnone," and "The Lady of Shalott." In 1833, Tennyson was overwhelmed by the sudden death of Hallam. His next published work, *Poems* (1842), expressed his philosophic doubts in a materialistic, increasingly scientific age and his longing for a sustaining faith. The new poems included "Locksley Hall," "Ulysses," "Morte d'Arthur," and "Break, Break, Break." With this book he was acclaimed a great poet, and in addition, in 1845, he was given a government pension of £200 yearly. *The Princess* (1847) was followed in 1850 by the masterful *In Memoriam,* an elegy sequence that records Tennyson's years of doubt and despair after Hallam's death and culminates in an affirmation of immortality. The same year saw his appointment as poet laureate and his marriage to Emily Sellwood, whom he had courted since 1836 but had been unable to marry because of his precarious financial position. Occasional poems, such as the "Ode on the Death of the Duke of Wellington" (1852) and "The Charge of the Light Brigade" (1855), were part of his duties as laureate. The first group of *Idylls of the King* appeared in 1859; it was expanded in 1869, again in 1872, and in 1885 Tennyson added the final poem. He arranged the 12 poems chronologically in 1888 to constitute a somber ethical epic of the glory and the downfall of King Arthur. In the Arthurian legend, Tennyson projected his vision of the hollowness of his own civilization. Included among his other works are *Maud* (1855), a "monodrama"; *Enoch Arden* (1864); several poetic dramas, most notably *Becket* (1879; produced 1893); *Ballads and Other Poems* (1880); and *Demeter and Other Poems* (1889), which contained "Crossing the Bar." Tennyson passed his last years in comfort. In 1883 he was created a peer and occupied a seat in the House of Lords; he was a popular as well as critical success and was venerated by the general public. Ignored early in the 20th cent., Tennyson has since been recognized as a great poet, notable for his mastery of technique, his superb use of sensuous language, and his profundity of thought. There are several good editions of his works. See biographies by his son Hallam Tennyson (4 vol., 1897), his grandson Charles Tennyson (1949, repr. 1968), and H. L. Fausset (1923, repr. 1968); studies by J. H. Buckley (1960), Christopher Ricks (1972), and D. J. Palmer, ed. (1973).

Tenochtitlán (tänōchtētlän'), ancient city in the central valley of Mexico. The capital of the AZTEC, it was founded (A.D. c.1345) on a marshy island in Lake Texcoco. It was a flourishing city (with an estimated population of between 200,000 and 300,000), connected with the mainland by three great causeways. These ran along massive dike constructions erected to prevent the salty floodwaters of the eastern lake from mingling with the fresh water surrounding the island city. The dikes thereby protected the unique system of lake agriculture known as chinampas. Canals within the chinampas served to convey traffic throughout the city, including to and from the bustling, highly organized market at Tlatelolco. The ceremonial precinct contained many structures, including a great pyramid sacred to the Aztec war god HUITZILOPOCHTLI. It was to Tenochtitlán and the court of Montezuma that Hernán Cortés came, and it was from Tenochtitlán that the Spanish fled on the night of June 30, 1520, under heavy Aztec attack—the so-called *noche triste.* Cortés returned in 1521, took the city after a three-month siege, razed it, and captured the ruler, CUAUHTÉMOC, successor to Montezuma. The Spaniard founded present-day Mexico City on the ruins. See studies in the *Handbook of Middle American Indians,* ed. by Robert Wauchope (13 vol., 1964–73); M. P. Weaver, *The Aztecs, Maya, and Their Predecessors* (1972).

Tenojoki, river: see TANAELV, Norway-Finland.

tenor, highest natural male VOICE. In medieval polyphony, tenor was the name given to the voice that had the cantus firmus, a preexisting melody, often a fragment of plainsong, to which other voices in counterpoint were added. The cantus was arranged in notes of long duration, hence the term *tenor,* from the Latin *tenere,* to hold. In about the 12th cent., when this practice arose, the various parts in polyphonic music were roughly equal in range, and it was some centuries later that tenor came to denote a voice of any certain range. The male alto range is termed COUNTERTENOR. In certain families of instruments the member whose register corresponds to that of the tenor voice is called tenor, e.g., tenor horn and tenor trombone.

Tenos, Greece: see TÍNOS.

tenpins: see BOWLING.

tenrec (tĕn'rĕk), any of the small insectivorous mammals of the family Tenrecidae, also called tendrecs or tanrecs. These animals are found on the island of Madagascar. In that closed environment they have evolved diverse forms, filling various ecological niches occupied by other small mammals elsewhere. There are about 30 tenrec species, classified in 10 genera. The common tenrec, *Tenrec ecaudatus,* is one of the world's largest insectivores. It is tailless, with a body length of 12 to 16 in. (30–41 cm). Its coat is a yellow-brown mixture of hair, bristles, and spines. The hedgehog tenrec, *Setifer setosus,* resembles a true hedgehog. The short-haired rice tenrecs, genus *Oryzorictes,* are molelike animals whose tunneling causes much damage in rice fields. The long-tailed tenrec, *Microgale longicaudata,* is mouselike in size and appearance, with a tail two and a half times its body length, and it is able to jump. The water tenrec, *Linmogale mergulus,* is a rat-sized aquatic animal with webbed feet and a keeled tail. All tenrecs are nocturnal, most hibernate in the winter, and many are dormant in hot weather. They live on a diet of small animals, chiefly worms and insects. Females have as many as twenty-two teats and give birth to litters of fifteen to twenty young. The giant water shrews of the central African forest belong to the family Potamogalidae, sometimes considered a subfamily of the Tenrecidae. These animals are otterlike in appearance and way of life, with fine fur and a laterally compressed tail. Other animals called water shrews are members of the true SHREW family. Tenrecs are classified in the phylum CHORDATA, subphylum Vertebrata, class Mammalia, order Insectivora, family Tenrecidae.

tense [O.Fr., from Lat., = time], in the GRAMMAR of many languages, the category of verb forms referring to the time of an action. In Latin INFLECTION the tenses are usually sets of personal verb forms and are themselves members of MOODS. English tenses are classified as simple (e.g., *look* and *looked*) or compound (e.g., *have looked, am looking,* and *will look*). A tenselike distinction found in many languages (e.g., Russian and Hebrew) is that of aspect, by which verbs refer not to the time but to the completeness of the action; thus, *he is dead* might be translated by a verb in a perfective aspect, and *he is dying* by the same verb in an imperfective aspect. Some terms borrowed from Greek grammar into English suggest aspectlike differences of meaning; these are imperfect (translating *I was reading when . . .*), perfect (*I've read the book*), aorist (*I read it last year*), and pluperfect (*I had read it already*).

Tenskwautawa: see SHAWNEE PROPHET.

tensor, in mathematics, quantity that depends linearly on several VECTOR variables and that varies covariantly with respect to some variables and contravariantly with respect to others when the coordinate axes are rotated (see CARTESIAN COORDINATES). Tensors appear throughout mathematics, though they were first treated systematically in the CALCULUS of differential forms and in DIFFERENTIAL GEOMETRY. They play an important role in mathematical physics, particularly in the theory of RELATIVITY. Tensors are also important in the theory of elasticity, where they are used to describe stress and strain. The study of tensors was formerly known as the absolute differential calculus but is now called simply tensor analysis. See A. J. McConnell, *Applications of Tensor Analysis* (1957).

tent, portable shelter of canvas, skins, felt, matting, or other material usually supported by poles and used chiefly by nomads, hunters, and campers. Tents have been used by pastoral peoples since ancient times and are mentioned in the Old Testament and in Homer. Persian tents, usually circular, were early noted for rich hangings and rugs. Army tents developed by ancient peoples include the small, skin-covered tents of the Greeks and the Roman tents of canvas supported by two upright poles and a ridgepole. Medieval military tents were round or oval and were often lavishly hung with silks or furs. Army tents were widely used in Europe in the 17th and 18th cent. but are now employed chiefly for training purposes. Modern types include bell tents with a central pole; the A tents with sides sloping from a ridgepole; and the marquee, a large field tent, used for mess or hospital shelters. The yurt, a circular, felt-covered structure of latticework surmounted by curved poles fitted at the top into a ring forming a smoke hole, has long been used by nomads of the Asian steppes. Desert tribesmen of W Asia and North Africa generally use a ridgepole tent. One of the simplest tent forms is the windbreak, mainly used in Patagonia. See also TEPEE.

tent caterpillar, common name for the larvae of the members of a family of moths (Lasiocampidae), easily recognized by the large silk tents, or webs, that the larvae construct during the spring in the crotches of trees, particularly apple and cherry trees. Tent caterpillars are hairy and usually brightly colored, with blue and yellow spots. Periodically they become serious orchard pests and occur in large enough numbers to defoliate whole trees and damage the fruit. Many larvae live gregariously within the tent, which they use for shelter during the night and in rainy weather. During the day, the larvae leave the tent and feed on the leaves in nearby branches. The best known tent maker is the eastern tent caterpillar, *Malacosoma americanum.* Other species of *Malacosoma* occur both in E and W North America and have been known to defoliate large areas by attacking a variety of forest and shade trees. Not all species build tents; despite the name forest tent caterpillar, *M. disstria,* at times an extremely destructive pest that migrates by the millions to new food plants, never weaves a tent. The tent caterpillar pupates within the oval white cocoon it spins, and the adult emerges during midsummer as a reddish brown or gray, medium-sized, stout-bodied, hairy moth with feathery antennae. After mating, the adult deposits several hundred eggs, covered by a thick, foamy brown crust, in bands around the twigs of the host tree. The eggs overwinter until the early spring when they hatch. Larvae from several egg masses congregate near a fork in a limb and form the tent by crawling about, leaving silk behind. Removing egg masses during the winter or removing tents in the early spring and soaking them in kerosene or burning them, are the most effective means of control. Tent caterpillars are classified in the phylum ARTHROPODA, class Insecta, order Lepidoptera, superfamily Bombycoidea, family Lasiocampidae.

Ten Thousand, March of the: see XENOPHON.

Ten Thousand Islands, group of small islands in the Gulf of Mexico, off SW Fla., covered with mangrove forests and surrounded by clam beds. Most of the islands are in Everglades National Park.

Ten Thousand Smokes, Valley of: see KATMAI NATIONAL MONUMENT.

ten tribes: see LOST TRIBES.

tenure, in education, a guarantee of the permanence of a college or university teacher's position, awarded upon successful completion of a probationary period, usually seven years. Tenure is designed to make a teaching career more attractive by providing job security; by protecting the teacher's position, tenure also tends to enforce ACADEMIC FREEDOM. Those who argue against the institution of tenure claim that the security it provides often results in a lessening of the diligence and efforts of some teachers, that it sometimes provides permanent positions for incompetent teachers, and that it tends to close off opportunities for younger teachers. A tenured teacher may be dismissed for adequate cause, provided that the cause is established in proceedings with all the precautions of due process. Financial exigencies of an institution may also be recognized as justification for terminating appointments of tenured teachers.

tenure, in law, manner in which property in land is held. The nature of tenure has long been of great importance, both in law and in the broader economic and political context. Tenure has varied greatly from feudal to modern times; although the patterns of transition have been many, the essential nature of the problem and its legal complexities can be seen in the development of tenure in English law.

Tenure in Feudal Law. The term *tenure* may refer to landholding of any type; it usually implies, however, that the landholder does not have absolute possession but derives his right from some other person. This meaning of the word originates from its sense in feudalism; so used, tenure is the antithesis of ALOD, absolute ownership without obligation to others. The modern Anglo-American law of land developed out of the institutions of English feudalism established after the Norman Conquest (1066). Theoretically, the king was the ultimate owner of all the land; in practice, however, certain land was held according to earlier custom. Those who were feudal tenants always held land of another (the lord or landlord) to whom obligations were owed. The tenant's type of tenure essentially established his social status; the term *estate* (deriving from status) thus came to be applied to the various types of tenure. The early tenures were classified basically as free or unfree. Unfree, or servile, tenure was generally that of the VILLEIN, who performed menial services and was a tenant at the will of the lord (see MANORIAL SYSTEM). Tenancy by custom eventually became a permanent right in the property when such tenures were recorded in the copy rolls (parchment records) of the manorial court, and the villein became a copyhold tenant. The various types of free tenure are sometimes described as means for ensuring performance of all the services required by the state. Military needs were guaranteed by knight tenure (see KNIGHT, **2**). Spiritual welfare was provided for by frankalmoign tenure, i.e., granting lands in charity to religious bodies. SERJEANTY tenure furnished the king with needed officials and with personal services. Finally, the vital cultivation of the land was accomplished by socage tenure wherever villeinage was not in use. Socage tenure is especially important because it is the basis of all modern estates, while the other classes of tenure have all disappeared. The socage tenant, or socager, held his land in return for performing duties to the lord. These incidents of socage were essentially like the AIDS and SCUTAGE exacted of knights; like those, they were also eventually commutated into fixed money payments. In the development of the law of land perhaps the most important incident was the fine for alienation. This was the payment of a sum to the lord for permission to alien (or alienate) the estate, i.e., to grant it (sell or make a gift of it) to another. The right of free alienation, a cornerstone of modern property law, was partly guaranteed in 1290 by the statute *Quia emptores,* which abolished the fine. However, freedom to dispose of land by will on the tenant's death was not established until passage of the Statute of Wills (1540). In inheritance of land PRIMOGENITURE was usually observed; different local customs, notably BOROUGH-ENGLISH and GAVELKIND, were, however, also observed. If the tenant had no heir the estate went back to the lord; such reversion was called escheat. Socage tenure eventually developed many varieties, commonly called fees. (The word *fee* stems directly from *fief* and ultimately from *feud,* both terms of feudal law.) Fees are divided into freehold and nonfreehold. The freehold fees are fee simple, fee tail, and life fee. A fee simple is essentially absolute ownership of land; it includes, therefore, complete freedom of alienation and (since 1540) of devising (bestowing by will). An estate in fee tail was one bestowed as a gift to the donee and to his issue (children) or a class (male or female) of his issue. Read literally, the terms of the grant prevented alienation of the land out of the prescribed line of succession. A life fee or a life estate was one that would endure for the lifetime of the grantee and after his death would go to some other person. The life tenant had no power of alienation. Nonfreehold estates include estates for years, periodic estates, estates at will, and estates at sufferance. An estate for years is one that will expire at the end of a fixed period. A periodic estate is one for a set term, which is automatically renewed if neither party takes steps to terminate it. Most modern leases of real property and buildings establish periodic estates. A tenancy at will is one that may be terminated by the tenant or the landlord; it is generally interpreted by a court as being implied from the facts. An estate at sufferance arises when a tenant continues to occupy the land after his right to occupancy has expired; the tenancy subsists only so long as the landlord does not object. The struggle over whether land should be freely alienable dominated English land law; it was resolved by the 18th cent. when the alienation of land could no longer be restricted beyond a limited period. The ultimate effect of this tendency was to assimilate the law of real PROPERTY in most important respects to that governing personal property. At the time of the American colonization this development to free alienation was already well advanced; hence, few of the typically feudal features of land law were adopted in America. Today some of the states provide that landownership shall be in free and common socage and others that it shall be alodial. In practice there is little difference. See Frederick Pollock, *The Land Laws* (3d ed. 1896); William S. Holdsworth, *An Historical Introduction to the Land Law* (1927); C. J. Moynihan, *Introduction to the Law of Real Property* (1962).

Land Tenure as a Modern Problem. In modern times land tenure has been a vexing economic and political issue throughout the world; it has given impetus to nationalism and to revolution, especially in largely agrarian Asia, Africa, and Latin America. In the 19th and 20th cent. there has been wide demand for small farmer ownership and for secure tenure for tenants. The end of feudalism and of serfdom in Europe and elsewhere left small holders in an insecure position. After the French Revolution, security of tenure was provided for French cultivators, but elsewhere in Europe, where servile obligations were generally abolished by 1860, most of the land was possessed by nobles and other wealthy classes; tenant cultivators were subject to high rents, easy ejection, and no allowance for improvements. Thus there arose the demand for peasant proprietorship through the purchase or appropriation of land by the government, which would then resell small parcels to the peasantry on easy terms. Also, agitation began for legislation favorable to tenants regarding rent, sale, lease, land improvement, and absentee landlordism. Since the late 19th cent. such programs have been established in most countries of Europe, Ireland (see IRISH LAND QUESTION) and the Scandinavian countries being among the first. Most recently in Europe, especially where the long establishment of secure tenure has led to minute subdivision, government activity has tended to favor some consolidation of holdings, as in the Netherlands. In the 19th cent. the spacious lands of Australia, Canada, and the United States enabled the governments of those countries to grant substantial holdings cheaply to farmers, who thus became owners rather than tenants. However, problems did develop, notably in the struggle of the sheep or cattle ranchers, who desired secure tenure for the vast lands they required, against the small farmers, who in turn wanted the right to settle and own parts of these tracts. These difficulties, particularly prominent in Australia, were resolved in the several nations by the early 20th cent., generally in favor of the small farmers. Legislation was also passed in the 20th cent. to provide secure tenure and easy farm purchase for the body of tenants who had by this time emerged. The fundamental purchase enactment in the United States was the Bankhead-Jones Farm Tenant Act (1937). In Latin America, the tenure problem remains widespread, and in many countries a few owners still hold most of the land, while the majority of the cultivators are squatters.

Customary Tenure in Slow Transition: Africa and Asia. Characteristically, under customary tenures the rights of peasant transfer remain limited, obligations for the payment of rent are often imposed upon the cultivating community as a whole, and debts are hereditary from generation to generation. Such conditions still prevail in much of Africa and Asia. In the Middle East, tenure was long dominated by customary and feudal characteristics and also by religious considerations. Under Muslim rule the state theoretically owned all land, and rent and other tenure conditions were different for Muslims and non-Muslims. A wide variety of tenures grew up, including free usage of land for religious purposes and unrestricted ownership. These have had counterparts in Europe under customary tenures. Large-scale reform and redistribution of land was begun in Egypt by the laws of 1952, and Turkey passed reforms in 1945, but in much of the region customary and semifeudal land tenures prevail. British reforms in India also illustrate some of the complex problems of replacing customary tenures with a contractual system. In contrast to native systems, the British introduced easy transfer of agricultural holdings and allowed foreclosure of property for debt. Consequently the commercially knowledgeable class, the moneylenders, were able to gain many holdings because the poor and inexperienced peasantry contracted unrepayable debts. Where permanently low rents were established in India, landholders sublet at outrageous prices when land values rose. Similar problems have arisen elsewhere in the transformation from customary to contractual tenures. In those Asian countries where American influence became strong, tenure reform has usually taken place, as in Japan (1946) and Korea (1948). There and elsewhere, experience has shown that without accompanying reforms of agricultural credit, education, and taxation, enabling peasant proprietors to discharge contractual obligations, tenure reforms are only partly successful. The Communist government of the Soviet Union long vacillated, for economic and political reasons, between collectivization of land (see COLLECTIVE FARM) and allowing a substantial number of private holdings. The same situation has existed under other Communist governments, including that of China. See E. H. Tuma, *Twenty-Six Centuries of Agrarian Reform* (1965).

Tenure of Office Act, in U.S. history, measure passed on March 2, 1867, by Congress over the veto of President Andrew JOHNSON; it forbade the President to remove any Federal officeholder appointed by and with the advice and consent of the Senate without the further approval of the Senate. It also provided that members of the President's cabinet should hold office for the full term of the President who appointed them and one month thereafter, subject to removal by the Senate. With this measure the radical Republicans in Congress hoped to assure the continuance in office of Secretary of War Edwin M. STANTON and thus prevent any interference with the military occupation of the South in their RECONSTRUCTION plan. In order to bring about a court test of the constitutionality of the act, Johnson dismissed Stanton, but the Supreme Court, intimidated by the radicals, refused to pass on the case. Gen. Ulysses S. GRANT, whom Johnson appointed Secretary ad interim, turned the office back to Stanton when the Senate refused to approve his dismissal. Johnson then appointed Gen. Lorenzo Thomas Secretary of War, but Stanton, barricading himself in the department, refused to yield. Johnson's alleged violation of the Tenure of Office Act was the principal charge in the impeachment proceedings against him. When this move failed (May, 1868), Stanton finally gave up. The act, considerably modified in Grant's administration, was in large part repealed in 1887, and in 1926 the Supreme Court declared its principles unconstitutional.

Ten Years War, 1868–78, struggle for Cuban independence from Spain. Discontent was caused in Cuba by excessive taxation, trade restrictions, and virtual exclusion of native Cubans from governmental posts. Disaffection grew until 1868, when Carlos Manuel de CÉSPEDES and other patriots raised the standard of revolt. On April 20, 1869, the revolutionary republic of Cuba was established, with BAYAMO as provisional capital. The capital was burned later in the year, and the republican government was forced to change its seat frequently. The warfare was purely guerrilla fighting without major battles, but it raged furiously in the eastern provinces. Chief field commanders were Máximo GOMEZ Y BÁEZ, Antonio Maceo, and Calixto García y Iñiguez; late in the war the government was headed by Tomás ESTRADA PALMA. Under orders of the Spanish commandant, Gen. Valeriano WEYLER Y NICOLAU carried out bloody and ruthless reprisals against the patriots. The Cubans retaliated by attacking all upholders of the Spanish cause. U.S. sympathy for the rebels was intensified by the destruction of U.S. property in Cuba, while the activities of American mercenaries and soldiers of fortune aroused the indignation of Spain. In 1873 the VIRGINIUS affair brought Spanish-American relations to a crisis. The war dragged on without decisive incident. When internal affairs in Spain settled somewhat, greater attention was given the war in Cuba. General MARTÍNEZ DE CAMPOS managed to conclude the Treaty of Zanjón, which nominally granted reforms and gave the Cubans governmental representation; the promises were not kept, and conditions did not improve. The costly and bitter war was seemingly without result, but actually it foreshadowed the Cuban war of independence that broke out in 1895 and the subsequent Spanish-American War.

teosinte: see CORN, in botany.

Teotihuacán (tāōtēwäkän'), ancient commercial and religious center in the central valley of Mexico, c.30 mi (48 km) NE of Mexico City. Once thought to be the great religious center of the TOLTEC, it is now held to be the relic of an earlier civilization. Teotihuacán is the largest (c.7 sq mi/18.1 sq km) and most impressive urban site of ancient America. The Pyramid of the Sun, the tallest in Mexico, is 216 ft (65 m) high and covers approximately 10 acres (4 hectares) at the base; it dominates the symmetrical ground plan laid out in grid fashion along major thoroughfares, including the city's central axis—the Street of the Dead. Other buildings along this axis include the Pyramid of the Moon; the Citadel containing the Temple of Quetzalcoatl, so called because of its carvings of feathered serpents; the Temple of Agriculture; and the Quetzalpapalotl Palace. The earliest cultural horizon at Teotihuacán dates to c.100 B.C. The culture flourished from about A.D. 300 to 900, undergoing tremendous expansion. Excavations have revealed large chambered structures resembling communal dwellings. The people of Teotihuacán brought sculpture, the art of carving exquisitely stylized stone masks, ceramic manufacture and decoration, and mural painting on walls to a high degree of refinement. The designs show a strong concern for cosmological matters, indicating the existence of a complex religious system. Recent archaeological work at the site, as well as elsewhere in Mexico, has revealed that Teotihuacán was a commercial as well as a religious center. Craft specialization is evident in various parts of the city, and Teotihuacán influence is seen in such far-off places as the Guatemala highlands, the Maya lowlands, and the valley of Oaxaca. One portion of the city seems to have been colonized by a group from Oaxaca who retained their ethnic identity. The political organization of Teotihuacán and its sphere of influence are unknown. See R. F. Millon et al., ed., *Pyramid of the Sun at Teotihuacán* (1965) and *Urbanization at Teotihuacán* (1973).

tepee or **tipi** (both: tē'pē), typical dwelling of North American Indians living on the Great Plains. It was usually made by arranging tent poles into a conical frame and spreading skins, usually buffalo hide, tightly over it. An aperture was generally left at the top for smoke. The tepee was sometimes very elaborately decorated. It was highly mobile and provided a strong shelter against the weather; it was thus an ideal dwelling for the nomadic Plains area tribes such as the Sioux and the Blackfoot. Because of the adaptability of the tepee to prairie life, Gen. Henry Sibley used it as a model for the tent that bears his name. See Reginald Laubin and Gladys Laubin, *The Indian Tipi* (1957, repr. 1971).

Tepe Gawra (tĕ'pĕ gourä') [Kurdish, = great mound], locality in N Iraq, 15 mi (24 km) NE of Mosul. In 1927 the archaeologist Ephraim Speiser discovered it to be the site of ancient settlements. The excavations were directed by Speiser and Charles Bache over a 12-year period. In all, 24 levels and sublevels were unearthed; they date from the 5th millennium B.C. to the 2d millennium B.C. The levels are numbered from top to bottom. The upper levels were not very distinctive; they show a type of civilization less advanced than that found in the lower levels. In the lower levels the chronological sequence of the Tell Halaf (c.5000 B.C.), Al' Ubaid (c.4100–3500 B.C.), and Jemdet Nasr (3500–3000 B.C.) periods is well represented (see MESOPOTAMIA). The number of architectural remains from these early periods at Tepe Gawra makes it one of the most important sites of N Mesopotamia. The three monumental temple remains on an acropolis of the 13th level represent the finest architecture at the site. See E. A. Speiser *et al., Excavations at Tepe Gawra* (2 vol, 1935–50).

tephillin: see PHYLACTERIES.

Tepic (tāpēk'), city (1970 pop. 117,331), capital of Nayarit state, W Mexico, on the Tepic River. A commercial center on the coastal line of the Mexican National Railways and on a major highway, Tepic lies in a prosperous maize, sugarcane, and cattle-raising area. The city has sugar mills and textile factories. Wild mountain scenery surrounds Tepic, which, despite modernization, retains some of its colonial charm.

Tepl, Johannes von: see JOHANNES VON SAAZ.

Teplice (tĕ'plĭtsĕ) or **Teplice-Šanov** (-shä'nôf), Ger. *Teplitz-Schönau,* city (1970 pop. 51,374), NW Czechoslovakia, in Bohemia, in the Erzgebirge ("ore mountains") and near the East German border. It is a road and rail hub and an industrial center in the heart of a lignite-mining area. In addition to coal the city produces machinery, glassware, ceramics, metal goods, chemicals, textiles, and foodstuffs. Teplice is also a famous resort and spa, whose hot mineral springs were known prior to Roman times. A historic encounter between Beethoven and Goethe took place in the city in 1812. Industrialization dates from the late 19th cent., when large lignite deposits were discovered nearby. German forces held the city from 1938 to 1945, after which it was returned to Czechoslovakia and the German population was expelled. Teplice has a noted medieval castle.

tequila: see MESCAL.

Terah (tē'rə), father of Abraham. Gen. 11.24; Joshua 24.2. Thara: Luke 3.34.

Teramo (tĕ'rämō), city (1971 pop. 47,878), capital of Teramo prov., Abruzzi, central Italy. It is an agricultural and industrial center. Manufactures include textiles and processed food. Of pre-Roman origin, Teramo was included in the medieval duchy of Spoleto and, from 1814 to 1860, in the kingdom of Naples. Of note is the Romanesque cathedral (restored in the 14th cent.).

teraphim (tĕr'əfĭm), biblical term of uncertain origin referring either to household idols or to idols used in the local sanctuaries for purposes of divination. Concerning their form not much is known, except that they were sometimes of a man's size and sometimes small enough to be carried by hand. Judges 17.3–5; 18.17,18,20. See also Gen. 31.30; 1 Sam. 15.22; 19.13,16; 2 Kings 23.24.

terbium (tûr'bēəm) [from *Ytterby,* a village in Sweden], metallic chemical element; symbol Tb; at. no. 65; at. wt. 158.925; m.p. about 1360°C; b.p. about 3000°C; sp. gr. about 8.25; valence +3 or +4. Terbium is a soft, malleable, ductile, silver-gray metal. It is one of the RARE-EARTH METALS of the LANTHANIDE SERIES in group IIIb of the PERIODIC TABLE. It does not tarnish rapidly in air. Its oxide, terbia, Tb_2O_3, is white; its peroxide, Tb_4O_7, is dark brown to black. Most of the salts are colorless or white and all contain trivalent terbium. The element and its compounds have limited commercial importance; some minor uses are in lasers, semiconductor devices, and phosphors for color television picture tubes. Terbium is found in gadolinite, cerite, and other rare-earth minerals and is recovered from euxenite, monazite, and zenotime. It is difficult to separate it from the other rare-earth metals; several methods are used. The pure metal may be produced by chemical reduction of the halide with calcium. The element was discovered in 1843 by C. G. Mosander as its oxide, which he called erbia. The element has been known as terbium since 1877.

Ter Borch or **Terborch, Gerard** (gä'rärt tərbôrkh'), 1617–81, Dutch genre and portrait painter. He studied with his father and traveled throughout Europe, showing extraordinary precocity in his early work. In 1648 he attended the congress at Münster and painted portraits of the delegates that he incorporated in his celebrated group, *The Peace of Münster* (National Gall., London). Soon after, he was invited to Spain, where he worked for Philip IV. He returned to Holland in 1650, portraying the life and customs of the wealthy burgher class with rare distinction. His tiny portraits and interiors are painted with elegance, serenity, and a technique of consummate craftsmanship. Among his most famous pictures are *Self-Portrait* and *The Toilet* (The Hague), and *The Guitar Lesson* (National Gall., London). Ter Borch is also represented in the National Gallery of Art, Washington, D.C., the Metropolitan Museum, the Art Institute of Chicago, and the Frick Collection, New York City.

Terbrugghen, Hendrick (hĕn'drĭk tĕrbro͝og'hən), 1588–1629, Dutch painter, a leading member of the Utrecht school. He was a pupil of the history painter Bloemaert before living (c.1604–14) in Italy. *Crowning of Thorns* (1620; Copenhagen) is his first known dated work. Like his contemporaries Honthorst and Baburen, he was largely influenced by Caravaggio, although an awareness of Dürer and Lucas van Leyden recurs throughout his work. His intimate and restrained genre compositions foreshadow in coloring the work of Vermeer. Many of Terbrugghen's paintings are nighttime genre scenes. His work is represented in the major European museums. Typical examples are his *St. Sebastian* (Allen Mus., Oberlin, Ohio), *Old Man Writing* (Smith College Mus., Northampton, Mass.), and *Crucifixion* (1620s; Metropolitan Mus.). See monograph by Benedict Nicolson (1958).

Terceira (tĕrsā'rə), island (1960 pop. 72,485), 153 sq mi (396 sq km), in the N Atlantic, one of the central AZORES, Portugal. The chief town is Angra do Heroísmo, which gives its name to the district. Grains, cattle, and embroidery are exported. There is a U.S. air base there.

terebinth (tĕr'əbĭnth) or **turpentine tree,** small deciduous tree (*Pistacia terebinthus*) of the family Anacardiaceae (SUMAC family), native to the Mediterranean region. It yielded probably the earliest-known form of turpentine, said to have been used in medicine by the ancient Greeks. The yield of the terebinth is now called Chian, Scio, or Cyprian turpentine. The terebinth is classified in the division MAGNOLIOPHYTA, class Magnoliopsida, order Lapindales, family Anacardiaceae.

teredo: see SHIPWORM.

Terek (tyĕ'rĭk), river, c.370 mi (600 km) long, S European USSR, rising in the Caucasus, in Georgia, in glaciers W of Mt. Kazbek. It flows N through the Daryal gorge past Ordzhonikidze, then E past Grozny and NE into the Caspian Sea. Below Kizlyar it forms a swampy delta c.60 mi (100 km) wide. In its lower course the Terek is used for irrigation. The upper valley is paralleled by the Georgian Military Road.

Terence (Publius Terentius Afer) (tĕr'əns), b. c.185 or c.195 B.C., d. c.159 B.C., Roman writer of comedies, b. Carthage. As a boy he was a slave of Terentius Lucanus, a Roman senator, who brought him to Rome, educated him, and gave him his freedom. Six comedies by him survive—*Andria, Heautontimorumenos, Eunuchus, Phormio, Adelphi,* and *Hecyra.* All are adapted (with considerable liberty) from Greek plays by Menander and others. The writing is polished and urbane, the humor broad, and the characters realistic. See G. E. Duckworth, *The Complete Roman Drama* (1942); study by Gilbert Norwood (1923, repr. 1965).

Terengganu or **Trengganu** (both: trəng-gä'no͞o, trĕng-), state (1971 pop. 405,751), c.5,000 sq mi (12,950 sq km), Malaysia, central Malay Peninsula, on the South China Sea. The capital is KUALA TERENGGANU. The state has a large iron mine. Rice and rubber are grown, and fish are caught. The population is mainly Malay. Before the 19th cent. Terengganu was the vassal state of the powers that in turn dominated the Malay Peninsula. The influence of Siam upon Terengganu grew during the 19th cent., although the sultan of Terengganu maintained his independence. According to the terms of the Anglo-Siamese treaty of 1909, Terengganu became a British protectorate. Until the establishment of the Federation of Malaya (1948), it was classed as one of the Unfederated Malay States. See MALAYSIA, FEDERATION OF.

Teresa, Saint: see THERESA, SAINT.

Teresh (tē'rĕsh), conspirator with Bigthan. Esther 2.21.

Teresina (tārāzē'nä), city (1970 pop. 220,520), capital of Piauí state, NE Brazil, on the Parnaíba River. It is the main commercial and agricultural distribution center in the Parnaíba valley; cattle, hides and skins, rice, maize, cotton, and manioc are shipped through the city. Its industries produce textiles, sugar, soap, and lumber. Teresina was a planned city formally established in 1852 and named for Brazilian Empress Teresa Cristina Maria.

Tereus (tĕr'ēəs): see PHILOMELA AND PROCNE.

Terman, Lewis Madison (tûr'mən), 1877–1956, American psychologist, b. Johnson co., Ind., grad. Indiana Univ., 1902, Ph.D. Clark Univ., 1905. He joined the faculty of Stanford in 1910 and was chairman of the psychology department from 1922 to 1942, when he retired. In World War I he served as a major and helped to deal with psychological testing. He is best known for his application of intelligence tests to schoolchildren, and for his chief work, the Stanford Revision of the Binet-Simon Intelligence Tests (1916; with Maud A. Merrill, 2d rev., 1937; 3d rev. 1960). He also wrote *The Intelligence of School Children* (1919), *Genetic Studies of Genius* (with others, 3 vol., 1925–30), and *Sex and Personality* (with C. M. Cox, 1936, repr. 1968).

Termez (tyĭrmyĕs'), city (1970 pop. 35,000), capital of Surkhan-Darya oblast, Central Asian USSR, in Uzbekistan, a port on the Amu Darya River, near the Afghanistan border. It is the center of an agricultural region and has cotton and food processing and brick and tile industries. The temperature rises as high as 122°F (50°C) in Termez, one of the hottest cities in the USSR. Part of the Bactrian kingdom in the 1st cent. B.C., Termez later developed as a river port and feudal trade center. Remains of a 9th-century mausoleum and relics of iron, ceramics, and Buddhist pottery have been unearthed there.

Terminus (tûr'mĭnəs), in ancient Rome, both the boundary markers between properties and the name of the god who watched over boundaries. Property lines were of great importance, particularly to farmers, and boundary stones were laid in a solemn ceremony. The rites of the Terminalia, held on Feb. 23, reinforced the sanctity of these markers. Terminus was often merged with Jupiter as Jupiter Terminus.

termite or **white ant,** common name for a soft-bodied, social insect of the order Isoptera. Termites are easily distinguished from ants by comparison of the base of the abdomen, which is broadly joined to the thorax in termites; in ants, there is only a slender connection (petiole) joining these segments. In addition, the antennae of termites are beadlike or threadlike, while ant antennae are elbowed. Termites have chewing mouthparts. They feed chiefly on wood, from which they obtain cellulose. In primitive species cellulose is converted into various sugars by specialized gut protozoans and in the more highly evolved termites by specialized bacteria living symbiotically in the termite's digestive tract. Termites undergo gradual metamorphosis (see INSECT). The nearly 2,000 species are mostly tropical, and some build huge mounds to house their colonies. These mounds, up to 40 ft (122 m) high, are a characteristic feature of the landscape in parts of Africa and Australia. Termite colonies are composed of three castes; the reproductives (kings and queens), the soldiers, and the workers. The kings and queens are sexually mature termites, with compound eyes and fully developed wings. These reproductives are produced in large numbers during certain seasons and leave the colony in a swarm. They are poor fliers, and most are eaten by birds and other animals. When the surviving termites settle their wings break off along a weakened seam at the base. They then form pairs, each of which establishes a new colony. A couple excavates a chamber in wood or soil, in which they mate; they remain permanently paired and the queen eventually produces as many as 30,000 eggs per day. Two or three weeks after mating, the young nymphs hatch and are fed on liquid secreted by the parents and on fecal wastes, from which they obtain the protozoan or bacterial symbionts essential for life. The caste into which the young termite, or nymph, develops is dependent upon the amount of growth-inhibiting substance (a pheromone) passed to it during feeding and grooming. The pheromone is secreted by the reproductives and, when present in a high enough concentration, prevents the development of nymphs into reproductives. As more workers and soldiers are added, since they do not produce pheromone, its concentration in the colony is correspondingly decreased. Therefore when the colony reaches a certain size, some of the nymphs begin to develop into reproductives, which then produce pheromones. This phenomenon also occurs if the original reproductives die. The increase in the pheromone level prevents the maturation of additional nymphs into reproductives; these remaining nymphs then become workers. A large colony may have several pairs of reproductives. In a similar way, the appearance of soldiers appears to inhibit the production of more soldiers. In some families of termites, no workers develop, and the nymphs perform worker functions, which include feeding the royal couple, the soldiers, and the very young nymphs; caring for the eggs; grooming the queen; constructing and repairing the nest; and foraging for food. The workers and soldiers lack wings and compound eyes. The soldiers have heads as large as the rest of the body and equipped with strong mandibles used in defense of the colony. They attack any intruders to the colony and stand guard at the entrances, in some species closing the entrances by putting their heads in the holes. Soldiers of certain species squirt a sticky, poisonous secretion at enemies. There are two major groups of termites, the wood dwellers and the soil dwellers. The latter causes over $250 million loss per year in the United States alone. The Formosan termite, a more aggressive species than the U.S. species, was discovered in the United States in 1965 along the Gulf and Atlantic port cities. Soil dwellers attack only wood that is in contact with the ground or close enough to be reached through enclosed earthen runways, which are connected to the termite's underground galleries. Treatment of soil, use of treated wood, or shielding with metal and concrete are among the methods used to prevent entry of termites into buildings. Drywood termites do not require as high a humidity as do soil dwellers and will attack trees, fence posts, stumps, and wooden buildings. For information on prevention and control of termites, see publications of the U.S. Dept. of Agriculture or State Extension Service. Termites are classified in the phylum ARTHROPODA, class Insecta, order Isoptera. See Kumar Krishna and F. M. Weesner, ed., *Biology of Termites* (2 vol., 1969–70); P. E. Howse, *Termites: A Study in Social Behavior* (1970).

Termonde: see DENDERMONDE, Belgium.

tern, common name for a sea bird of the Old and New Worlds, smaller than the related GULL. Because of their graceful flight and their long pointed wings and forked tails, some terns are called sea swallows. They plunge headlong into the water to catch small fish. The arctic tern migrates from the arctic to the antarctic. American terns include the common, least, Forster's, noddy, sooty, roseate, and royal terns, all of the genus *Sterna*. Terns are classified in the phylum CHORDATA, subphylum Vertebrata, class Aves, order Charadriiformes, family Laridae.

Ternate (tĕrnä'tā), volcanic island (c.40 sq mi/100 sq km), E Indonesia, in the Molucca Sea, one of the Moluccas. It is heavily forested and mountainous, rising to c.5,600 ft (1,710 m). The principal town, also called Ternate, is an important transit port for New Guinea and Halmahera; exports include spices and copra. Despite its relatively small size, the island was for centuries a major spice center and one of the most important islands of the Moluccas. Ruled by a powerful sultan, it became an important Muslim center in the 15th cent. The Portuguese built a fort there in 1522. They were expelled during a native revolt in 1574. The sultan granted the spice concession to the Dutch in 1607. Popular revolts were suppressed by the Dutch in 1650 and 1683, after which the Dutch were in complete control.

Terni (tär'nē), city (1971 pop. 106,982), capital of Terni prov., Umbria region, central Italy, on the Nera River. Manufactures of this industrial center include iron and steel, munitions, textiles, machinery, and chemicals. Hydroelectric power is generated at nearby waterfalls (including the famous Cascata delle Marmore). The falls were formed in 272 B.C., when the Romans connected the Velino River with the Nera. Terni was an ancient Umbrian town and passed to the papacy in the 14th cent. The ruins of a Roman town are nearby, at Carsulae. The historian Tacitus was born (A.D. 55) in Terni.

Ternopol (tyĭrnô'pəl), Ukr. *Ternopil,* Pol. *Tarnopol,* city (1970 pop. 85,000), capital of Ternopol oblast, SW European USSR, in the Ukraine, on the Seret River, a tributary of the Dnestr. It is an important rail junction and highway hub. Industries include food processing and the manufacture of machinery, building materials, electrical apparatus, clothing, leather products, footwear, and porcelain. Founded by the princes of Galicia in 1540 as a castle, Ternopol was fortified and developed as a trade center. It declined after passing to Austria in 1772 but revived in the 19th cent. with the coming of the railroad. The city became part of Poland in 1919 and of the Ukraine in 1939.

Terpander (tûrpăn'dər), fl. c.675 B.C., musician of Lesbos, one of the earliest founders of Greek classical music. Upon somewhat doubtful evidence, Terpander is credited with having completed the octave and adding the sixth and seventh strings to the kithara. He was also known as a poet, teacher, and composer.

Terpsichore (tərpsĭk'ərē): see MUSES.

Terra, Gabriel (gäbrēēl' tĕ'rä), 1873–1942, president of Uruguay (1931–38). In his early career a member of the Colorado party under the leadership of BATLLE Y ORDÓÑEZ, Terra served in several political and diplomatic posts. He suspended congress in 1933, disbanded the council of administration (a body created by the constitution of 1919 as a check on executive power), and abolished the constitution. After a new constitution, promulgated in 1934, restored presidential authority, Terra was reelected and ruled largely by dictatorial decree. He suppressed a serious revolt in 1935. During his administration, however, the socialization of the republic, begun by Batlle, was continued. He was succeeded by an elected president, Alfredo Baldomir.

terra-cotta (tĕr'ə kŏt'ə) [Ital.,=baked earth], form of hard-baked pottery, widely used in the decorative arts, especially as an architectural material, either in its natural red-brown color, or painted, or with a baked glaze. Its prevalence as a medium of artistic expression since the earliest periods of history is indicated by statuettes and vases from predynastic Egypt, polychrome tiles from Assyria and Persia, vases and figures from various Central American pre-Columbian sites, and Chinese vases dating probably from 3000 B.C. Terra-cotta first gained importance as an architectural material in classical Greece, where, beginning about the 7th cent. B.C., temples and other structures were often enriched with roof tiles, metopes, acroteria, and various other modeled and painted ornamental features of terra-cotta. Similar roof tiles and ornaments are found in Etruscan and Roman work. However, the golden age of terra-cotta was the Renaissance; it was widely used in N Italy and in N Germany, which have a scarcity of good building stone. The towns of Lombardy, Emilia, and Venetia are rich in brick buildings (e.g., the Certosa di Pavia, begun 1396) that are decorated with a profusion of molded terra-cotta detail, such as cornices, string courses, window frames, and other exterior ornament. Similarly, the 14th- and 15th-century brick Gothic buildings of N Germany, especially of the district around Brandenburg, had lavish displays of molded terra-cotta. The delicate tracery and other Gothic details of the Church of St. Catherine at Brandenburg (1400) testify to the high technical skill of the craftsmen of that period. As the Renaissance progressed in Italy, terra-cotta was established not only as an architectural but as a sculptural material, used with consummate skill by Della QUERCIA. In its decorative application, it reached distinction in the 15th cent. when the DELLA ROBBIA family developed their characteristic and celebrated polychrome enameled terra-cotta reliefs. In addition to magnificent doorway tympana and decorative medallions, especially the series of Madonna compositions, they used terra-cotta for tombs, fountains, and altars. The material was favored for *bozzetti*, or sculptors' sketches, as well as for large pieces. From Italy terra-cotta work spread to other countries, largely through the activities of migrant Italian artisans. The Château Madrid, now destroyed, designed by Girolamo della Robbia and built for Francis I, was richly decorated with terra-cotta details. The art was introduced (c.1510) into Tudor England, probably by the Florentine sculptor Torrigiano. In the districts of SE England, where good stone is lacking, important country mansions (such as Layer Marney and Sutton Place) had ornamental detail of molded terra-cotta; on Hampton Court, Wolsey employed Italian workmen, who produced portrait medallions and other decorations of merit. The use of terra-cotta in England ceased, in general, when, after the death of Henry VIII, the Italian artists returned home. The figurines of the 18th-century French sculptors Pigalle, Houdon, and Clodion are outstanding examples of terra-cotta sketches. In modern times terra-cotta has been used in the Victorian Gothic revival, notably by Alfred WATERHOUSE, and has received widespread application in the United States as an exterior covering for the skeleton steel structure. It was used with consummate skill by Louis Sullivan for decorative stringcourses on many of his buildings. Modern sculptors who have made notable terra-cotta works include Maillol, Despiau, Epstein, and Picasso. Terra-cotta has often been molded into the forms of the classical and other styles, with textures closely simulating various kinds of stone. However, it has been most successfully used not imitatively but on its own merits as a lightweight, nonbearing material, perfectly adapted to the task of sheathing a steel frame. Hollow blocks or tile of rough terra-cotta are used extensively as a structural material for walls and partitions, for floor arches, and for fireproofing. In modern practice terra-cotta is manufactured from carefully selected clays, which, combined with water and vitrifying ingredients, are put through a pug mill or other device to reduce the mass to homogeneity. In cakes of convenient size the clay passes to the molding room. Individual pieces are modeled by hand; in the case of repetitive pieces, the clay is pressed into plaster molds to form a shell. The molded pieces are finished by hand and then are ready for baking in a kiln or reverberatory furnace. See I. C. Hill, *Decorated Architectural Terracottas* (1929); Felicity Nicholson, *Greek, Etruscan and Roman Pottery* (1965); Alexander von Wuthenau, *Art of Terracotta Pottery in Pre-Columbian Central and South America* (1969).

terrain-clearance indicator: see ALTIMETER.

Terra Mater: see TELLUS.

Terramycin (tĕr''əmī'sĭn), trade name for oxytetracycline, a broad spectrum ANTIBIOTIC. See TETRACYCLINE.

Terranova di Sicilia: see GELA, Italy.

Terra Nova National Park, 153 sq mi (396 sq km), E N.F., Canada, on Bonavista Bay; est. 1957. It is a rugged, deeply indented coastal area with forests and bogs.

terrapin (tĕr'əpĭn), name for several edible TURTLES of fresh or brackish water.

terrarium, a miniature garden in an artificial environment, in which small plants and animals may be kept as ornament or for educational purposes. Fish bowls, small fish tanks, large bottles, and carboys are often employed as containers for terrariums; such vessels permit the necessary entrance of light for photosynthesis by the plants, and are suitable for display. The most important aspect of a terrarium is its relatively high humidity, maintained either by using a container with only a small aperture or by keeping the container covered. The humid atmosphere enables mosses and other sensitive woodland plants to flourish.

Terre Haute (tĕr'ə hōt, tĕr'ē hŭt), city (1970 pop. 70,335), seat of Vigo co., W Ind., on the Wabash River; inc. 1816. The commercial and trade center of a farming and coal-mining region, its many products include food items, phonograph records, aluminum and steel products, and farm and communications equipment. Founded (1811) as Fort Harrison, it grew as a river town. Eugene Debs and Theodore Dreiser were born there, and a park is dedicated to the memory of the songwriter Paul Dresser (Dreiser's brother). Points of interest include the Debs home, the Early Wheels Museum, an art gallery, and a historical museum. Terre Haute is the seat of Indiana State Univ., the Rose-Hulman Institute of Technology, and a vocational technical institute. Nearby are St. Mary-of-the-Woods College and a Federal penitentiary. The city has a large stadium.

Terrell (tĕr'əl), city (1970 pop. 14,182), Kaufman co., N Texas; inc. 1883. Cattle are raised on the surrounding rich blackland prairies. The state mental hospital in Terrell is the largest source of employment in the city. There are also small manufacturing plants. A junior college is in the city.

terrestrial planet, the earth or a planet that resembles the earth in its physical characteristics. The terrestrial planets in the solar system are the EARTH, MERCURY, VENUS, and MARS; PLUTO is sometimes also classified as a terrestrial planet. These planets are approximately the same size, with the earth the largest. They are considerably denser than the JOVIAN PLANETS, ranging from a specific gravity of 4 for Mars to 5.5 for the earth. Because they spin less rapidly than the Jovian planets, the terrestrial planets are less flattened at their poles.

terrier, classification used by breeders and kennel clubs to designate dogs originally bred to start small game and vermin from their burrows or, in the case of several breeds in this group, to go to earth and kill their prey. Today these dogs are raised chiefly as pets. The following 20 terrier breeds are registered with the American Kennel Club: AIREDALE TERRIER, AUSTRALIAN TERRIER; BEDLINGTON TERRIER; BORDER TERRIER; BULL TERRIER; CAIRN TERRIER; DANDIE DINMONT TER-

RIER; FOX TERRIER; IRISH TERRIER; KERRY BLUE TERRIER; LAKELAND TERRIER; MANCHESTER TERRIER; SCHNAUZER (miniature); NORWICH TERRIER; SCOTTISH TERRIER; SEALYHAM TERRIER; SKYE TERRIER; STAFFORDSHIRE TERRIER; WELSH TERRIER; and WEST HIGHLAND WHITE TERRIER. See DOG.

territorial waters: see WATERS, TERRITORIAL.

territory, in U.S. history, a portion of the national domain that is given limited self-government, usually in preparation for statehood. Territorial governments have been similar in form to those of the states, but have been subject to greater authority of the Federal government. The ORDINANCE OF 1787, adopted by the Congress of the Confederation of the United States to create the NORTHWEST TERRITORY, furnished the basis upon which territorial governments were later organized under the Constitution of the United States. The LOUISIANA PURCHASE of 1803 raised the problem of the relationship of the United States to newly acquired domains—a subject treated vaguely in the Constitution of the United States. The Supreme Court, however, established the right of Congress to set up territorial governments and to admit territories to the Union. With the rapid westward expansion of the United States in the 19th cent., and the acquisition of large portions of land through treaty, purchase, and war, Congress shaped territorial boundaries and prescribed government. Territorial governments usually have consisted of a governor, a bicameral legislature, a secretary to keep records, and a system of courts. A territory may be admitted to the Union as a state after its officers petition Congress for an enabling act, establish a constitution, and meet certain requirements (often regarding population) as set forth by the U.S. Congress. Congress itself may initiate such action. Except for the Thirteen Colonies and California, Kentucky, Maine, Texas, Vermont, and West Virginia, all the states went through a territorial stage before they were admitted to the Union. The affairs of territories were under the Dept. of State until 1873, when their supervision was given to the Dept. of the Interior. Present U.S. territories include the Virgin Islands, Guam, and American Samoa. In Canada and Australia a similarly organized portion of the country not yet formed as part of the dominion is known as a territory.

Terror, Reign of: see REIGN OF TERROR.

Terry, Alfred Howe, 1827-90, American general, b. Hartford, Conn. A lawyer, he led a regiment of Connecticut volunteers at the first battle of Bull Run in the Civil War. Made a brigadier general of volunteers in 1862, he took part in various operations along the S Atlantic coast in 1862-63. For his capture of FORT FISHER in Jan., 1865, he was promoted to major general of volunteers and made a brigadier general in the regular army. In 1876 he directed the campaign against the Sioux and personally led the column converging on the Indians from Dakota. The cavalry under Gen. George CUSTER, massacred at the Little Bighorn, included part of Terry's force. He was promoted to major general in 1886 and retired in 1888.

Terry, Dame Ellen Alicia, 1848-1928, English actress. Of a prominent theatrical family, she made her debut at eight as Mamillius in Charles Kean's production of *The Winter's Tale.* She played juvenile roles until her unsuccessful marriage, at 16, to G. F. WATTS, the painter. She retired from the stage for six years, during which time she had two children, Edith Craig and Edward Gordon CRAIG, by E. W. Godwin. In 1878 she joined Sir Henry IRVING at the Lyceum Theatre as his leading lady. With him she toured the United States, later under the management of Charles FROHMAN. After 1902 she left Irving to manage the Imperial Theatre, where her son, Edward, designed the sets. She also lectured on Shakespeare in England and in the United States. An actress of charm, beauty and joyousness, she was admired in such roles as Portia, Olivia, and especially Beatrice. Her jubilee was celebrated in 1906, and in 1925 she was made Dame of the British Empire. See her memoirs, ed. by Edith Craig and Christopher St. John (1908, repr. 1969); her correspondence with G. B. Shaw, ed. by Christopher St. John (1931, repr. 1949); biographies by E. G. Craig (1932), Roger Manvell (1968), and Constance Fecher (1971).

Terry, Sir Richard Runciman, 1865-1938, English organist and musicologist. He was organist and choir director (1901-24) of Westminster Cathedral. Terry studied and made collections of early English church music and edited the *Westminster Hymnal* (1912), the official hymnal for Roman Catholic use in England. He is author of *Catholic Church Music* (1907) and *The Music of the Roman Rite* (1931).

Tersanctus: see SANCTUS.

Terschelling (tərskĕl'ĭng), island, c.40 sq mi (100 sq km), Friesland prov., N Netherlands, in the North Sea, one of the West Frisian Islands. West-Terschelling (1970 pop. 4,294) is the main town. Farming and fishing are pursued on the island, which is a popular summer resort.

Terskei Ala-Tau, mountains, Asia: see ALA-TAU.

tertiary (tûr'shēârē), in the Roman Catholic Church, member of a third order. The third orders are chiefly annexes of the FRIARS—Franciscans (the most numerous), Dominicans, and Carmelites. They have rules reflecting the spirit of the corresponding order but adapted to life in the world; hence, the offices to be read are short and the fasts are mild. The promises made on joining are not vows; their purpose is the sanctification of the members. Secular members of third orders (i.e., those who live in the world) may be priests or laymen; there are also tertiaries who live in communities, the regular tertiaries. The name tertiary recalls their origin among the Franciscans, for St. Francis founded his order for laymen only after he had instituted his order for men (the friars) and after St. Clare had founded the nuns (second order, the Poor Clares). See MONASTICISM.

Tertiary period (tûr'shēĕr"ē), name for the major portion of the CENOZOIC ERA, the most recent of the geologic eras (see GEOLOGIC ERAS, table). The name *Tertiary* was first applied about the middle of the 18th cent. to a layer of deposits, largely unconsolidated sediments, geologically younger than, and overlying, certain other deposits then known as Primary and Secondary. Later (c.1830) a fourth division, the Quaternary, was added. Although these divisions of the earth's crust seemed adequate for the region to which the designations were originally applied (parts of the Alps and plains of Italy), when the same system was later extended to other parts of Europe and to America it proved to be inapplicable. It was realized that one scheme of classification could not be applied universally, since all mountain ranges were not of the same age and did not have the same history. The names *Primary* and *Secondary* were generally abandoned, but *Tertiary* and *Quaternary* were firmly entrenched in geologic literature and are still used. Many authorities recommend that the use of *Tertiary* and *Quaternary* also be abandoned. The main divisions of the Tertiary are the PALEOCENE, EOCENE, OLIGOCENE, MIOCENE, and PLIOCENE EPOCHS. Sometimes the Paleocene is included in the Eocene. At the beginning of the Tertiary, the outlines of the North American continent were very similar to those of today; by the close of the period, Europe also had emerged substantially in its present form. Marine submergences in Europe were moderately extensive, but in North America they never went beyond the Atlantic, Gulf, and Pacific coasts and the lower Mississippi valley. These inundations took place chiefly in the Eocene, Oligocene, and Miocene epochs, the continents being generally emergent in the Pliocene epoch. The Tertiary formations of either unconsolidated sediments or quite soft rocks are widespread. Throughout the Tertiary there was extensive mountain making. The previously existing mountain ranges of North America were again elevated, the Alps, Pyrenees, Carpathians, and other ranges were formed in Europe, and in Asia the Himalayas arose. Widespread volcanic activity was prevalent. At the beginning of the period the mammals replaced the reptiles as the dominant animals; each epoch was marked by striking developments in mammalian life. Modern types of birds, reptiles, amphibians, fishes, and invertebrates either were already numerous at the beginning of the period or appeared early in its history.

Tertius (tûr'shəs), amanuensis of the epistle to the Romans. Rom. 16.22.

Tertullian (Quintus Septimus Florens Tertullianus) (tûrtŭl'yən), c.160-c.230, Roman theologian and Christian apologist, b. Carthage. He was the son of a centurion and was well educated, especially in law. Converted to Christianity c.197, he became the most formidable defender of the faith in his day. His Latin is vigorous and effective and reflects his juridical training. Sentences of his that have become proverbial are "The blood of martyrs is the seed of the church," and "It is certain because it is impossible" (often quoted incorrectly as "I believe it because it is impossible"). Some of Tertullian's opinions differed from the main stream of Christian thought, particularly his more rigorous view of sin and its forgiveness. After long defending the Montanists (see MONTANISM), he left the church (213) to join them; he later established his own sect, known as Tertullianists. Tertullian's most important writings are *Apologeticus, Ad Nationes,* and *De Praescriptione.* See studies by B. B. Warfield (1930), T. D. Barnes (1971), and R. D. Sider (1971).

Tertullus (tərtŭl'əs), accuser of Paul before Felix. Acts 24.1,2.

Teruel (tĕrwĕl'), town (1970 pop. 21,638), capital of Teruel prov., E central Spain, in Aragón, at the confluence of the Guadalaviar and Alfambra rivers. The city is an agricultural trade center; the province has iron and coal mines and sulfur, zinc, and manganese deposits. The center of bitter fighting in the Spanish civil war of 1936-39, it was largely destroyed, but has since been rebuilt. There are a Renaissance cathedral, a Gothic church, and an imposing two-storied aqueduct (16th cent.). The "lovers of Teruel" (13th cent.) are buried in the San Pedro cloisters.

Teschen (tĕ'shən), Czech *Těšín,* Pol. *Cieszyn,* former principality (c.850 sq mi/2,200 sq km), now divided between Czechoslovakia and Poland. Teschen was its chief town. A part of Silesia, the principality was under Bohemia from 1292 to 1625, when it came under Hapsburg rule. It remained part of Austria until 1918. Its important coal mines (the Karviná basin) and iron deposits and its strategic concentration of several major rail lines made it an object of dispute between Poland and Czechoslovakia, each of which claimed Teschen on ethnic grounds. After World War I the Conference of Ambassadors, a body formed to help implement the Versailles Treaty, divided (1920) Teschen, giving the western section, including the Karviná basin, to Czechoslovakia and the eastern agricultural section to Poland. The town of Teschen also was divided into a Polish section, Cieszyn, and a Czech section, Ceský Těšín. Poland, however, continued to claim the Czech section and seized it (Oct., 1938) after the Munich Pact. During World War II the entire region was annexed to Germany, but in 1945 the status quo as of 1920 was restored despite Polish claims.

Tesla, Nikola (tĕs'lə), 1856-1943, American electrician and inventor, b. Croatia (then in Austria-Hungary). He emigrated to the United States in 1884, worked for a short period for Edison, and became a naturalized American citizen. A pioneer in the field of high-tension electricity, he made many discoveries and inventions of great value to the development of radio transmission and to the field of electricity. These include a system of arc lighting, the Tesla induction motor and system of alternating-current transmission, the Tesla coil, generators of high-frequency currents, a transformer to increase oscillating currents to high potentials, a system of wireless communication, and a system of transmitting electric power without wires. He designed the great power system at Niagara Falls, N.Y. See biographies by H. B. Walters (1961) and J. J. O'Neill (1968).

Teslin Lake (tĕs'lĭn, tĕz-), narrow lake, 80 mi (129 km) long, NW British Columbia and S Yukon Territory, Canada, SE of Whitehorse. It receives the Nisutlin River and is drained by the Teslin River, one of the headwaters of the Yukon River.

tessera: see MOSAIC.

Tessin: see TICINO, Switzerland.

Test Act, 1673, English statute that excluded from public office (both military and civil) all those who refused to take the oaths of allegiance and supremacy, who refused to receive the communion according to the rites of the Church of England, or who refused to renounce belief in the Roman Catholic doctrine of transubstantiation. Although directed primarily against Roman Catholics, it also excluded Protestant nonconformists. In 1678 it was extended to members of Parliament. The law was modified by the Act of Toleration of 1689, which enabled most non-Catholics to qualify. However, some Protestants did not conform and were disqualified from office until the repeal of the act at the time of CATHOLIC EMANCIPATION. See PENAL LAWS.

testament: see NEW TESTAMENT; OLD TESTAMENT; WILL.

test-ban treaty, nuclear: see DISARMAMENT, NUCLEAR.

testis (tĕs'tĭs) or **testicle** (tĕs'tĭkəl), one of a pair of glands that produce the male reproductive cells, or SPERM. In fetal life the testes develop in the abdomen, then descend into an external sac, the scrotum. A testis is composed of about 800 coiled seminiferous tubules whose linings contain cells that develop into sperm. These tubules merge into a larger tube called the epididymis that leads out of the testis into the vas deferens. Between the seminiferous tubules there is interstitial tissue that secretes the male sex hormone TESTOSTERONE, which stimulates the development of the male reproductive system and secondary sex characteristics. Sometimes the testes do not descend normally before or shortly after birth and remain in the abdomen or groin. Such a condition requires medical attention or the gland will eventually become sterile. See also REPRODUCTIVE SYSTEM.

testosterone (tĕstŏs'tərōn), principal androgen, or male sex HORMONE. One of the group of compounds known as STEROIDS, testosterone is secreted by the testes (see TESTIS) but is also synthesized in small quantities in the OVARIES, cortices of the ADRENAL GLANDS, and placenta, usually from CHOLESTEROL.

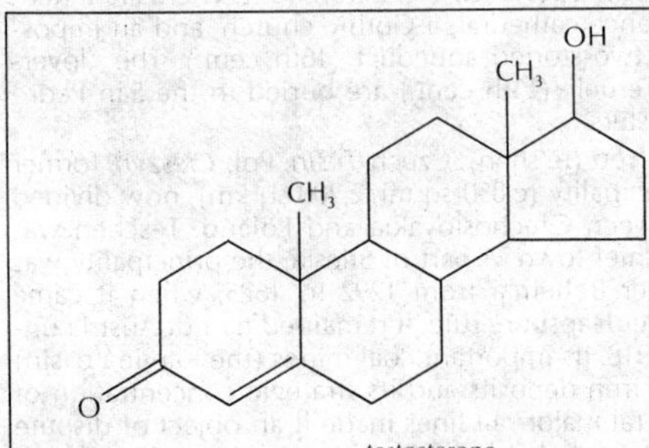

OH
CH_3
CH_3
O
testosterone

Testosterone is necessary in the fetus for the development of male external genitalia; increased levels of testosterone at puberty are responsible for further growth of male genitalia and for the development and maintenance of male secondary sex characteristics such as facial hair and voice changes. Testosterone also stimulates protein synthesis and accounts for the greater muscular development of the male (see METABOLISM). Chief medical uses of androgens include replacement therapy in testosterone-deficient males and therapy for carcinoma (cancer) of the breast.

tetanus (tĕt'nəs, -ənəs) or **lockjaw,** acute infectious disease of the central nervous system caused by the toxins of *Clostridium tetani.* The organism has a widespread distribution and is common in the digestive tracts of animals and humans; however, the toxin is destroyed by intestinal enzymes. Infection with the tetanus bacillus may follow any type of injury, whether incurred indoors or out, including nail puncture wounds, insect bites, splinter injuries, gunshot wounds, blank-cartridge or other burns, lacerations, and fractures. Deep puncture wounds are most dangerous, since the bacillus thrives in an anaerobic environment. The tetanus toxin, one of the most potent poisons known, acts on the motor nerves and causes muscle spasm at the site of infection and in other areas of the body. The most frequent symptom is stiffness of the jaw (lockjaw) and facial muscles. Severe convulsions may ensue. The mortality rate is very high, especially in the very young and the aged; overall it is about 40%. Treatment with tetanus antitoxin should be started promptly in patients who are not sensitive to horse serum. Otherwise human immune globulin must be given. However, it is preferable to prevent the disease by active immunization (including booster shots) with tetanus toxoid.

tetany (tĕt'ənē), condition of mineral imbalance in the body that results in severe muscle spasms. Tetany occurs when the concentration of calcium ions (Ca^{++}) in extracellular fluids such as plasma falls below normal. The nervous system becomes increasingly excitable, and nerves discharge spontaneously, sending impulses to skeletal muscles and causing spasmodic contractions. Mild tetany is characterized by tingling in the fingers, toes, and lips; acute tetany, consisting of severe muscular contractions, tremors, and cramps, can result in death. Abnormally low extracellular calcium ion concentration can result from failure of the PARATHYROID GLANDS to release parathyroid hormone, the substance responsible for the regulation of calcium concentration in the body; a deficiency in vitamin D, which facilitates calcium ion absorption from the gastrointestinal tract; or alkalosis, an excessively alkaline state of body fluids resulting from persistent vomiting, rapid breathing, or excess activity of the hormone ALDOSTERONE (see ACIDOSIS). Most forms of tetany can be treated with calcium, vitamin D, and a controlled diet. Muscle tetany is also caused by the pathogenic bacterium *Clostridium tetani* in the disease TETANUS.

Tete (tā'tə, tā'tā), town (1960 pop. 38,962), capital of Tete district, W central Mozambique, on the Zambezi River. It is a trade center; coal mines are at nearby Vila Moatize. Founded by the Portuguese in 1531, Tete long served as headquarters for traders, slave-raiders, and gold prospectors. Of note is the cathedral, built in 1563.

Teternikov, Feodor Kuzmich: see SOLOGUB, FEODOR.

Tethys (tē'thĭs), in astronomy, one of the 10 known moons, or natural satellites, of SATURN.

Tethys, in Greek religion, a Titan, daughter of Gaea and Uranus. She was the wife of the seagod Oceanus and the mother of the Oceanids.

Teton (tē'tŏn'). **1** River, 143 mi (230 km) long, rising in several branches in the Rocky Mts., NW Mont., and flowing E to the Marias River. Bynum Reservoir, on a tributary, is a unit in the irrigation system of the Teton. **2** River, c.60 mi (100 km) long, rising in W Wyoming, in forks which unite in SE Idaho. The Teton flows N and W to Henrys Fork River, near Rexburg, Idaho. In its early course it runs through Teton Basin, formerly Pierre's Hole, famous haunt of trappers; a battle with the Gros Ventres Indians was fought (1832) there.

Teton Indians: see SIOUX INDIANS.

Teton Range, part of the Rocky Mts., NW Wyo. and SE Idaho, just S of Yellowstone National Park. The highest peaks are within Grand Teton National Park, with Grand Teton (13,747 ft/4,190 m) the highest peak in the range. Teton Pass (8,431 ft/2,570 m) and Phillips Pass (10,700 ft/3,261 m) are just south of the park. The Teton Range includes part of Targhee National Forest. The first white man to see (c.1807) the range is said to have been John Colter, the American fur trapper. In 1811 the Astorians, led by Wilson Price Hunt, crossed Teton Pass. Fur trappers and traders (the mountain men) frequented the mountains in the first half of the 19th cent.

tetra: see CHARACIN.

tetrachloromethane: see CARBON TETRACHLORIDE.

tetracycline (tĕ"trəsī'klēn), any of a group of antibiotics produced by bacteria of the genus *Streptomyces.* They are effective against a wide range of Gram positive and Gram negative bacteria, interfering with protein synthesis in these microorganisms (see GRAM'S STAIN). Tetracycline is used to treat rickettsial bacterial infections such as Rocky Mountain spotted fever, some eye, respiratory, intestinal, and urinary infections, some kinds of acne, and some diseases where the infecting microorganism is resistant to PENICILLIN (see DRUG RESISTANCE). Tetracycline may cause permanent discoloration of developing teeth, and it is not given to pregnant and lactating women and growing children. Because of the development of strains of microorganisms resistant to the tetracyclines, these antibiotics have lost some of their usefulness. Aureomycin is a trade name for the derivative chlortetracycline, and Terramycin is a trade name for oxytetracycline.

tetraethyl lead (tĕt"rəĕth'əl), $(C_2H_5)_4Pb$, viscous, colorless, poisonous liquid. It is an organometallic compound prepared by reacting ethyl chloride with a sodium-lead alloy. When added to gasoline, it improves the combustion characteristics (see OCTANE NUMBER). When tetraethyl lead burns in an engine, lead oxide is formed. Ethylene dibromide is usually also added to the gasoline; on burning, the resulting mixture forms products that react with the lead oxide to form lead bromide, a volatile compound that escapes from the engine with other exhausted products. Because the lead bromide is poisonous, lead-free gasolines are preferred.

tetrahedron: see POLYHEDRON.

tetrahydrofolic acid: see COENZYME.

tetrahydrofuran: see FURFURAL.

Tetrazzini, Luisa (lwĕ'zä täträt-tsē'nē), 1871–1940, Italian coloratura soprano. She made her debut in Florence in 1895. After appearances in Spain, Portugal, Russia, and Latin America, she made her debut in the United States at San Francisco in 1904 and her London debut in 1907. She sang with the Manhattan Opera Company (1908–10), afterward appearing with the Metropolitan Opera Company (1911–12) and the Chicago Opera Company. She continued her concert career until 1931. Her sensational success was due to her brilliant high tones and her agility in coloratura work. She wrote two books, *My Life of Song* (1921) and *How to Sing* (1923).

tetrode: see GRID.

tetroon: see WEATHER BALLOON.

Tetschen: see DĚČIN, Czechoslovakia.

Tetuán (tātwän'), city (1970 est. pop. 125,000), N Morocco. The city has some light industry and is an export point for livestock and agricultural products. Its old casbah and mosques are tourist attractions. Tetuán was founded in the 14th cent. on the site of an earlier town at the foot of a high hill a short distance from the Mediterranean Sea. Castilians destroyed it c.1400 because it was a base for pirates. Muslim refugees from Spain refounded (1492) the city, and its flourishing handicrafts owe much to them. Tetuán was captured by the Spanish in 1860 and was reoccupied by them in 1913. It was the capital of Spanish Morocco from 1913 to 1956.

Tetzel, Johann (yō'hän tĕt'səl), c.1465–1519, German preacher, b. Pirna (in present-day East Germany). He joined the Dominicans. He became a well-known preacher and was made inquisitor general of Poland at the instance of CAJETAN. In 1503 he preached an INDULGENCE mission for the Teutonic Knights and in 1506 another along the Rhine. In 1517 his promotion of the indulgence for the erection of St. Peter's Church aroused the indignation of Martin LUTHER, whose theses were in part promoted by Tetzel's preaching. In 1518, Tetzel replied to Luther's theses, and their dispute became famous throughout Germany. Tetzel soon retired in bad health to his monastery at Leipzig, where he was overwhelmed by the attacks of his enemies and the censures of the papal legate. Tetzel has been greatly overrated in importance. He had no thought of personal gain from his preaching of the indulgence. His teaching on indulgences was not in accord with the doctrine of the church; the sine qua non in gaining an indulgence is to feel contrition for all sins, but Tetzel did not require that for indulgences gained on behalf of the dead, only for those gained for oneself.

Teucer (tyōō'sər), in Greek mythology. **1** Ancestor and king of the Trojans, who are also called the Teucri. He was the father-in-law of Dardanus. **2** Son of Telamon and Hesione. He was the greatest archer in the Trojan War and a faithful comrade of his half brother, the Telamonian Ajax. When he returned home he was banished by his father, who mistakenly thought that Teucer was responsible for the death of Ajax. Teucer went to Cyprus, where he founded the town of Salamis and ruled as king.

Teutoburg Forest, Ger. *Teutoburger Wald,* hilly range, in N central West Germany, stretching roughly between Osnabrück and Paderborn. It is forested, and it rises to 1,465 ft (447 m) S of Detmold. Near Detmold is a monument (the *Hermannsdenkmal*) commemorating the victory (A.D. 9) of the Germans under Arminius (or Hermann, in modern German) over the Roman legions under Varus. The war (late 8th cent.) between Charlemagne and the Saxon Widukind took place in this region.

Teutones or **Teutons:** see GERMANS.

Teutonic Knights or **Teutonic Order** (tōōtŏn'ĭk), German military religious order founded (1190–91) during the siege of Acre in the Third Crusade. It was originally known as the Order of the Knights of the Hospital of St. Mary of the Teutons in Jerusalem. The order was one of nobles, and the knights took the monastic vows of poverty, chastity, and obedience. Under Hermann von SALZA, its grand master in the early 13th cent., the order moved to E Europe and rose to prominence. After a brief period (1221–25) in Transylvania, where it fought for King Andrew II of Hungary against the CUMANS, the order responded to a call (1226) of the Polish Duke Conrad of Masovia for a crusade against the heathen Prussians. Holy Roman Emperor Frederick II granted (1226) it vast privileges, and Conrad invested it with the lands the order had conquered from the pagans. However, Hermann von Salza placed (1234) his conquests under papal suzerainty and set about to organize them as a separate German state. The Poles were long unsuccessful in asserting their claim to suzerainty over the order. After some 50 years of successful campaigning the knights had subdued PRUSSIA (i.e., the lands later known as East Prussia and West Prussia) and founded numerous towns and fortresses. The expansion of the LIVONIAN BROTHERS OF THE SWORD took place further east; they were united with the Teutonic Order from 1237 to 1525. The Prussians, who had repeatedly risen in revolt, were either exterminated (13th cent.) or reduced to serfdom, and German emigrants arrived to settle the land. The order was strongly centralized, and its administration and colonization laid the foundation of the Prussian state. The knights administered their lands from Marienburg, but they granted considerable freedom to the cities, many of which joined the HANSEATIC LEAGUE. In 1263 the pope allowed the knights to engage in trading, a privilege that they increasingly abused. Their seizure (1308–9) of Pomerelia (see POMERANIA) from Brandenburg brought on intermittent warfare with Poland, which claimed the province. In 1410 the Poles and Lithuanians routed the order at TANNENBERG; successive warfare with Poles ensued and by the second Treaty of Torun (1466) the knights were forced to cede West Prussia and Pomerelia to Poland, retaining only East Prussia as a Polish fief. Their capital was transferred to Königsberg in East Prussia. The fatal blow to the order was delivered in 1525 by its own grand master, ALBERT OF BRANDENBURG, who accepted the Reformation, declared Prussia a secular duchy, and was invested as duke by Sigismund I of Poland. Stripped of all importance, the Teutonic Order continued in Catholic Germany until its remaining possessions were secularized in 1809. It was later revived in Austria, but merely as an honorary body. The habit of the order was a white robe with a black cross.

Teutonic religion: see GERMANIC RELIGION.

Teūtonĭcus: see NOTKER LABEO.

Tevere, river: see TIBER.

Tewfik Pasha (Muhammad Tewfik) (toufĕk'pāshä'), 1852-92, khedive of Egypt (1879-92). He acceded to office when his father, Ismail Pasha, was deposed. In 1880, Tewfik accepted joint French-British control over the nation's finances. This act provoked a nationalist uprising that forced Tewfik to appoint a cabinet hostile to the European powers. The British and the French, however, quickly compelled the cabinet to resign. Later, in 1882, Great Britain, alarmed by renewed agitation, bombarded Alexandria and landed troops. France had refused to support this action and ended participation in Egyptian affairs, thus leaving Great Britain in sole control. Tewfik, who was generally Western in his outlook, devoted much attention to educational and legal reforms. He was succeeded as khedive by his son ABBAS II.

Tewkesbury (tyo͞oks'bərē), municipal borough (1971 pop. 8,742), Gloucestershire, W central England, on the Avon River near its junction with the Severn. Once noted for mustard production, it now has minor manufactures. The site was occupied c.715 by a monastery, refounded in the 12th cent.; it became one of the richest and most widely renowned Benedictine abbeys in England. The church, completed in 1123, is an impressive ruin, with a noteworthy west front. At "Bloody Meadow," south of the town, Edward IV in 1471 defeated the Lancastrians in the Wars of the Roses.

Tewksbury, town (1970 pop. 22,755), Middlesex co., NE Mass.; settled 1637, set off from Billerica and inc. 1734. It was the site of an Indian colony. Now a residential area, it has some light manufacturing. A state hospital is there.

Texarkana (tĕk"särkăn'ə), city (1970 pop.: in Texas, 30,497; in Ark., 21,682), Bowie co. (Texas) and seat of Miller co. (Ark.), on the Texas-Ark. line; inc. 1880. The state line runs through the center of the post office. Texarkana is a transportation and trade center for a large agricultural and pine forest area. Its many industries include cotton processing, lumbering and woodworking, and the manufacture of tires, clay products, rock wool, mobile homes, furniture, and garments. The U.S. army has a huge arsenal and depot there, and the city has a junior college. Nearby Spring Lake Park is the site where DeSoto camped c.1541, leaving a mutinous follower hanging from an oak tree. Lake Texarkana, a large reservoir to the southwest, serves as a resort area.

Texas (tĕk'səs), state (1970 pop. 11,196,730), 267,339 sq mi (692,408 sq km), including 4,369 sq mi (11,316 sq km) of water surface, SW United States, admitted to the Union in 1845 as the 28th state. AUSTIN is the capital; HOUSTON, DALLAS, and SAN ANTONIO are the largest cities. The second largest state in the Union, Texas is roughly spade-shaped. Its Panhandle projects N into Oklahoma, with New Mexico on the west. Below the Panhandle, Texas continues its western border with New Mexico but has a southwest shoulder that thrusts W between New Mexico and Mexico. The state is bounded on the SW and S by Mexico (the Rio Grande marks the entire international boundary), on the SE by the Gulf of Mexico, and on the E by Louisiana (the Sabine River forms much of the line). In the extreme northeast, Texas has a short border with Arkansas, and to the north, the Red River marks the boundary with Oklahoma W to the Panhandle. The vast expanse of Texas contains great regional differences (the distance from Beaumont to El Paso is greater than that from New York to Chicago). East Texas—the land between the Sabine and Trinity rivers—is Southern in character, with pine-covered hills, cypress swamps, and remnants of the great cotton plantations founded before the Civil War. Cotton farming has been supplemented by diversified agriculture, including rice cultivation; almost all of the state's huge rice crop comes from E Texas, and the industrial cities of BEAUMONT and PORT ARTHUR are surrounded by rice fields. The inland pines still supply a lumbering industry; HUNTSVILLE, LUFKIN, and NACOGDOCHES are important lumber towns. The real wealth of E Texas, however, comes from the immense, rich oil fields discovered in the 1920s. LONGVIEW, once one of the nation's big sawmill towns, is now an oil center, and TYLER is the headquarters of the East Texas Oil Field. Oil is also the principal economic support of Beaumont and Port Arthur and the basis for much of the heavy industry that crowds the Gulf Coast. The industrial heart of the coastal area is Houston, the largest city in the South and Southwest and the sixth largest in the nation. Houston's development was spearheaded by the digging (1912-14) of a ship canal to the Gulf of Mexico, and the city today is the nation's third largest port in tonnage handled. Other Gulf ports are GALVESTON, TEXAS CITY, Brazosport (formerly Freeport), PORT LAVACA, CORPUS CHRISTI, and BROWNSVILLE. The low Gulf Coastal Plains, perpetually wet with heavy rains in the east, grow drier in the south and become semiarid as they near the Rio Grande. The S Gulf Coast is a popular tourist area, and some of the ports, such as Galveston and Corpus Christi, have economies dependent on both heavy industry and tourism. Brownsville, the southernmost Texas city and the terminus of the Intracoastal Waterway, is also the shipping center for the intensively farmed and irrigated section along the lower Rio Grande, where citrus fruits and winter vegetables are grown. The long stretch of plain along the Rio Grande valley is largely given over to cattle ranching; in this area ranches average c.9,000 acres (3,640 hectares) in size. Texas has c.1,000 mi (1,610 km) of border with Mexico, and many S and W Texas towns have a colorful Mexican flavor. Some towns are bilingual, and in some areas persons of Mexican descent make up as much as 80% of the population. LAREDO is the most important gateway to Mexico, with an excellent highway to Mexico City and a thriving over-the-border commerce. The first region to be farmed when Americans came to Texas in the 1820s was the bottoms of the lower Brazos and the Colorado, but not until settlers moved into the rolling blackland prairies of central and N central Texas was the agricultural wealth of the area realized. The heart of this region is the trading and shipping center of WACO; at the southwest extremity is San Antonio, the commercial center of a wide cotton, grain, and cattle country. To the north, Dallas and its neighboring city of FORT WORTH are the focus of one of the most rapidly developing industrial sections of the country. Their oil refining, grain milling, and cotton and food processing have been supplemented since World War II by huge aircraft-manufacturing and electronics industries. The Balcones Escarpment marks the western margin of the Gulf Coastal Plain; in central Texas the line is visible in a series of waterfalls and rough, tree-covered hills. To the west lie the south central plains and the Edwards Plateau; they are essentially extensions of the Great Plains but are sharply divided from the high, windswept, and canyon-cut Llano Estacado (Staked Plains) in the W Panhandle by the erosive division of the Cap Rock Escarpment. No traces of the subtropical lushness of the Gulf Coastal Plain are found in these regions; the climate is strictly continental, with occasional blizzards blowing across the flat land in winter. The Red River area, including the farming and oil center of WICHITA FALLS, can have extreme cold in winter, though without the severity that is intermittently experienced in the commercial center of the Panhandle, AMARILLO, or in the dry-farming area around LUBBOCK. Cattle ranching, which began in the late 1870s (settlers were slow in coming to the High Plains), still persists, and huge ranches vie with extensive wheat and cotton farms for domination of the treeless land. Oil and grain, however, have revolutionized the economy of this section of the state, and industry has grown. All of W Texas (that part of the state west of long. 100°W) is semiarid. South of the Panhandle lie the rolling plains around ABILENE, a region cultivated in cotton, sorghum, and wheat, and the site of newer oil fields discovered in the 1940s. The dry fields of W Texas are still given over to ranching, except for small irrigated areas that can be farmed. SAN ANGELO serves as the commercial center of this area. The land beyond the Pecos River, rising to the mountains with high, sweeping plains and rough uplands, offers the finest scenery of Texas. There are found the Davis Mts. and Guadalupe Peak, the highest point (8,751 ft/2,667 m) in the state. The wilderness of the Big Bend of the Rio Grande is typical of the barrenness of most of this area, where water and people are almost equally scarce. El Paso, a thriving city of diverse industries and an important center of trade with Mexico, is a population oasis in that desolate region. In the state

The key to pronunciation appears on page xi.

as a whole, mineral resources compete with industry for primary economic importance. Texas is the wealthiest mineral producer in the nation; its chief minerals are oil, natural gas, and natural gas liquids. Texas is the nation's leading petroleum state, normally producing one third of the country's petroleum and containing one half of its known reserves. Texas also ranks first in the production of natural gas, natural gas liquids, asphalt, and pyrites. It is second in helium, magnesium compounds (from salt water), salt, sulfur, sodium sulfate, clays, and gypsum; third in cement; and fourth in lime and talc. Chemicals and chemical products are the state's chief manufactures (19 out of the 20 largest U.S. chemical companies are based there), followed by petroleum, food and food products, transportation equipment, machinery, and primary and fabricated metals. Agriculturally, Texas is one of the most important states in the country. It has more farms, farmland, cattle, sheep, and lambs than any other state, and it is the nation's leading producer of cotton and cottonseed. Principal crops are cotton lint, sorghum grain, hay, and rice; the greatest farm income is derived from cattle, sorghum grain, cotton lint, and dairy products. Swine, wool, and mohair are also important. Texas is second among the states in the production of carrots, onions, spinach, watermelons, and honeydew melons. Citrus fruits, wheat, pecans, oats, and barley are also grown in abundance. Texas is a leading commercial fishing state; the value of its fish catch in 1972 was exceeded only by that of California. Principal catches are shrimp, oysters, and menhaden. The region that is now Texas was early known to the Spanish, who were, however, slow to settle there. Cabeza de Vaca, shipwrecked off the coast in 1528, wandered through the area in the 1530s, and Coronado probably crossed the northwest section in 1541. De Soto died before reaching Texas, but his men continued west, crossing the Red River in 1542. The first Spanish settlement was made (1682) at Ysleta on the site of El Paso by refugees from present New Mexico after the Pueblo revolt of 1680. Several missions were established in the area; but the Comanche, the Apache, and other Indian tribes were unfriendly, and the settlements did not flourish. A French expedition led by La Salle penetrated E Texas in 1685 after failing to locate the mouth of the Mississippi. This incursion, though brief, stirred the Spanish to establish missions to hold the area. The first mission, founded in 1690 near the Neches, was named Francisco de los Tejas after the so-called *tejas* [friends] Indians. However, the tribes proved to be hostile, and the missionaries withdrew (1693). New attempts at settlement were prompted by the French threat from Louisiana, and missions, sometimes protected by presidios, were established at San Antonio (1718), Goliad (1749), Nacogdoches (permanently, 1779), and elsewhere. A few scattered Spanish colonists also settled at Laredo and along the lower Rio Grande. The transfer of Louisiana from France to Spain in 1762 removed the French threat but brought a new fear of British incursion from the north. The decaying missions in the east were therefore abandoned while the northern frontier and Gulf settlements were strengthened. In general, Spanish attempts to gain wealth from the wild region and to convert the Indians were unsuccessful, and in most places occupation was desultory. By the early 19th cent. Americans were covetously eyeing Texas, especially after the Louisiana Purchase (1803) had extended the U.S. border to that fertile wilderness. Attempts to free Texas from Spanish rule were made in the filibustering expeditions of the adventurers Gutiérrez and Magee (1812–13) and James Long (1819). In 1821, Moses Austin secured a colonization grant from the Spanish authorities in San Antonio. He died from the rigors of his return trip from that distant outpost; however, his son, Stephen F. Austin, had the grant confirmed and in Dec., 1821, led 300 families across the Sabine to the region between the Brazos and Colorado rivers, where they established the first American settlement in Texas. These hardworking farmers, who built crude cabins and cleared and plowed the wilderness while fighting off wild animals and Indians, were the spearhead of the American colonization, and Austin is justly called the father of Texas. The newly independent government of Mexico, pleased with Austin's prospering colony, readily offered grants to other American empresarios and even huge land tracts to individual settlers. Americans from all over the Union, but particularly from the South, poured into Texas, and within a decade considerable settlements had been established at Brazoria, Washington-on-the-Brazos, San Felipe de Austin, Anahuac, and Gonzales. The Americans easily avoided Mexican requirements that all settlers be Roman Catholic, but conflict with Mexican settlers over land titles resulted in the FREDONIAN REBELLION (1826–27). By 1830 the Americans outnumbered the Mexican settlers by more than three to one and had formed their own compact society. The Mexican government became understandably alarmed. Its sporadic attempts to tighten control over Texas had been hampered by its own political instability, but in 1830 measures were taken to stop the influx of Americans. Troops were sent to police the border, close the seaports, occupy the towns, and levy taxes on imported goods. The troops were withdrawn in 1832, when Mexico was again in political upheaval, but the Texans, alarmed and hoping to achieve a greater measure of self-government, petitioned Mexico for separate statehood (Texas was then part of Coahuila). When Austin presented the petition in Mexico City, Antonio López de Santa Anna had become military dictator. Austin was arrested and imprisoned for eighteen months, and Texas was regarrisoned. The Texas Revolution broke out (1835) in Gonzales when the Mexicans attempted to disarm the Americans and were routed. The American settlers then drove all the Mexican troops from Texas, overwhelming each command in surprise attacks. At a convention called at Washington-on-the-Brazos, Texas declared its independence (March 2, 1836). A constitution was adopted and David Burnet was named interim president. The arrival of Santa Anna with a large army to crush the rebellion resulted in the heroic and tragic defense of the ALAMO and massacre of several hundred Texans captured at GOLIAD. Santa Anna then divided his huge force to cover as much territory as possible, cutting a wide swath of destruction as terrified settlers fled for Louisiana in what became known as the "Runaway Scrape." The small Texas army, commanded by Samuel Houston, protected their rear, retreating strategically until Houston finally maneuvered Santa Anna into a cul-de-sac formed by heavy rains and flooding bayous, near the site of present-day Houston. In the battle of SAN JACINTO (April 21, 1836), Houston surprised the larger Mexican force during its afternoon siesta and scored a resounding victory. Santa Anna was captured and compelled to recognize the independence of Texas. Texans sought annexation to the United States, but antislavery forces in the United States vehemently opposed the admission of another slave state, and Texas remained an independent republic under its Lone Star flag for almost 10 years. The Texas constitution was closely modeled after that of the United States, but slaveholding was expressly recognized. Houston, the hero of the Revolution, was the leading figure of the Republic, serving twice as president. Under President Mirabeau Lamar large tracts of land were granted as endowments for educational institutions, and Austin was made (1839) the new capital of the republic. Despite the efforts of presidents Houston and Anson Jones, a combination of factors—confusion in the land system, low credit abroad, and the expense of maintaining the Texas Rangers and protecting Texas from marauding Mexican forces—contributed to impoverishing the republic and increasing the urgency for its annexation to the United States. Southerners pressed hard for the admission of Texas, the intrigues of British and French diplomats in Texas aroused U.S. concern, and expansionist policies began to gain popular support. President Tyler narrowly pushed the admission of Texas through Congress shortly before the expiration of his term; Texas formally accepted annexation in July, 1845. This act was the immediate cause of the MEXICAN WAR. After Gen. Zachary Taylor defeated the Mexicans at PALO ALTO and RESACA DE LA PALMA, the Mexican forces retreated back across the Rio Grande. During the pre-Civil War period settlers, attracted by cheap land, poured into Texas. Although open range cattle ranching was beginning to spread rapidly, cotton was the state's chief crop. The planter class, with its slaveholding interests, was strong and carried the state for the Confederacy, despite the opposition of Sam Houston and his followers. During the Civil War, Texas was the only Confederate state not overrun by Union troops. Remaining relatively prosperous, it liberally contributed men and provisions to the Southern cause. Reconstruction brought great lawlessness, aggravated by the appearance of roving desperadoes. Radical Republicans, CARPETBAGGERS, and SCALAWAGS controlled the government for several years, during which time they managed to lay the foundations for better road and school systems. Texas was readmitted to the Union in March, 1870, after ratifying the Thirteenth, Fourteenth, and Fifteenth amendments. Although Texas was not as racially embittered as the Deep South, the KU KLUX KLAN and its methods flourished for a time as a means of opposing the policies of the radical Republicans. RECONSTRUCTION in Texas ended in 1874 when the Democrats took control of the government (a control that they have never lost). The following decade was politically conservative, highlighted by the passage of the constitution of 1876, which, although frequently amended, remains the basic law of the state. As in the rest of the South, the war and Reconstruction had resulted in the breakdown of the plantation system and the rise of tenant farming. This did not, however, have as marked an effect as elsewhere, partly because much of the land was still unsettled, more perhaps because the Texas tradition is only partly Southern. In the decades following the war the Western element in Texas was strengthened as stock raising became a dominant strain in Texas life. This was the era of the buffalo hunter and of the last of the Indian uprisings. From the open range and then from great fenced ranches Texas cowboys drove herds of longhorn cattle over trails such as the Chisholm Trail to the railheads in Kansas, and even farther to the grasslands of Montana. Even today the symbols of Texas are more the "ten-gallon" hat, the cattle brand, and spurs and saddles than any reminiscence of the Old South. As railroads advanced across the state during the 1870s, farmlands were increasingly settled, and the small farmers (the "nesters") came into violent conflict with the ranchers, a conflict which was not resolved until the governorship of John Ireland. Many European immigrants—especially Germans and Bohemians (Czechs)—took part in the peopling of the plains (they continued to come in the 20th cent., when many Mexicans entered). Agrarian discontent saw the rise of the GREENBACK PARTY, and during the 1880s demands for economic reform and limitation of the railroads' vast land domains were championed by the Farmers' Alliance and Gov. James S. Hogg. However, antitrust legislation was insufficient to curb the power of big business, and the transformation of Texas into a partly urban and industrial society was greatly hastened by the uncovering of the state's tremendous oil deposits. The discovery in 1901 of the spectacular Spindletop oil field near Beaumont dwarfed previous findings in Texas, but Spindletop itself was later surpassed as oil was discovered in nearly every part of Texas. Texas industry developed rapidly during the first years of the 20th cent., but conditions worsened for the tenant farmers, who by 1910 made up the majority of cultivators. Discontented tenants were largely responsible for the election of James Ferguson as governor. World War I had a somewhat liberating effect on Texas Negroes, but the reappearance of the Ku Klux Klan after the war helped to enforce "white supremacy." The economic boom of the 1920s was accompanied by further industrialization. The Great Depression of the 1930s, while severe, was less serious than in most states; the chemical and oil industries in particular continued to grow (the East Texas Oil Field was discovered in 1930). The significance of the petrochemical and natural gas industries increased during World War II, when the aircraft industry also rose to prominence and the establishment of military bases throughout Texas greatly contributed to the state's economy. Postwar years brought continued prosperity and industrial expansion, although in the 1950s the state experienced the worst drought in its history and had its share of destructive hurricanes and flooding. Many projects for increased flood control, improved irrigation, and power supply have been undertaken in Texas; notable among these are Denison Dam, forming Lake Texoma (shared between Texas and Oklahoma); Lewisville Dam and its reservoir, supplying Fort Worth and Dallas; Lake Texarkana on the Sulphur River; and Falcon Dam and its reservoir on the Rio Grande. The Amistad Dam on the Rio Grande, serving both the United States and Mexico, was completed in 1969. There are several other dams on the Brazos and its tributaries. In 1965, Congress authorized the Trinity River project to connect Dallas with the Gulf of Mexico. Texas has made considerable progress in desegregating its schools since the 1954 Supreme Court decision on school integration, and the number of black voters has increased by more than 25% since the 1965 voting rights law. Politically, Texas continues to be strongly Democratic, although in a special election in 1961, John G. Tower became the first Republican since Reconstruction to win election to the U.S. Senate; he was reelected in 1966 and in 1972. Texas politics have contributed such outstanding national figures as Sam Rayburn, longtime Speaker of the U.S. House of Representatives, and Lyndon B. Johnson, who became (1963) President after the assassination of John F. Kennedy in Dallas and was reelected to the Presidency in 1964. The state's present constitution was adopted in 1876, replacing the "carpetbag" constitution of 1869. The state's executive branch is headed by a governor elected for a four-year term (before 1974 the governor's term was two years). All Texas governors have been Democrats since 1874. In 1972, Dolph Briscoe, a rancher and oil man, was elected governor; he was reelected in 1974. The state's bicameral legislature has a senate with 31 members elected for four-year terms and a house with 150 representatives elected for two years. The state elects 2 Senators and 24 Representatives to the U.S. Congress and has 26 electoral votes. Among the many institutions of higher learning in Texas are the Univ. of Texas, mainly at Austin, but with large branches at Arlington and El Paso; Baylor Univ., at Waco; East Texas State Univ., at Commerce; North Texas State Univ., at Denton; Rice Univ., at Houston; Southern Methodist Univ., at Dallas; Texas Arts and Industries Univ., at Kingsville; Texas Agricultural and Mechanical Univ., at College Station; Texas Christian Univ., at Fort Worth; and Texas Southern Univ. and the Univ. of Houston, both at Houston. The Lyndon B. Johnson Space Center is also in Houston. Other places of interest in the state include Big Bend National Park, Guadalupe Mts. National Park, Amistad National Recreation Area, Padre Island National Seashore, San Jose Mission National Historic Site (see NATIONAL PARKS AND MONUMENTS, table), and Aransas National Wildlife Refuge, winter home of the whooping crane. The classic history of Texas is that by Henderson Yoakum (1856); the old history of John Henry Brown (2 vol., 1892–93) as well as his *Indian Wars and Pioneers of Texas* (1896?) are still read. See C. W. Ramsdell, *Reconstruction in Texas* (1910); W. C. Binkley, *The Texas Revolution* (1952); W. C. Nunn, *Texas under the Carpetbaggers* (1962); E. C. Barker, *Mexico and Texas* (1928, repr. 1965); K. W. Wheeler, *To Wear a City's Crown: The Beginnings of Urban Growth in Texas, 1836–1865* (1968); Federal Writers' Project, *Texas: A Guide to the Lone Star State* (rev. ed. 1969); R. N. Richardson et al., *Texas, the Lone Star State* (3d ed. 1970); S. V. Connor, *Texas, A History* (1971); J. H. Smith, *The Annexation of Texas* (1911, repr. 1971); John Bainbridge, *The Super-Americans* (1972); Clifton McCleskey and T. C. Sinclair, *The Government and Politics of Texas* (4th ed. 1972); William Seale, *Texas in Our Time: A History of Texas in the Twentieth Century* (1972); see also *Texas Almanac* (latest edition).

Texas, University of, mainly at Austin; coeducational; state supported; chartered 1881, opened 1883. A medical branch is at Galveston and a dental branch at Houston. The Health Science Center, which includes Southwestern Medical School, is at Dallas. The university operates a branch (formerly Texas Western College) at El Paso and one at Arlington. The library has noted collections in the fields of literature and history. The Lyndon Baines Johnson Presidential Library (dedicated 1971) and the Lyndon Baines Johnson School of Public Affairs are located on the Austin campus.

Texas Agricultural and Mechanical University, at College Station; land-grant and state supported; coeducational; chartered 1871, opened 1876. The school gained university status in 1963. The university's facilities include a maritime academy and a forestry service as well as an agricultural and mechanical college at Prairie View.

Texas Christian University, at Fort Worth; coeducational; Disciples of Christ; opened 1873 at Thorp Spring, chartered 1874 as AddRan Male and Female College. It assumed its present name in 1902 and moved to Forth Worth in 1910. The university is affiliated with Jarvis Christian College. Its notable programs include a graduate seminary and a ranch training program (est. 1956) for practical instruction in ranch management. The university library houses a noted collection relating to English and American literature.

Texas City, city (1970 pop. 38,908), Galveston co., S Texas, on Galveston Bay, opposite the city of Galveston; inc. 1911. It is an industrial city and port with giant oil refineries, petrochemical plants, a huge tin smelter, and factories making fertilizer, valves, and pipes. Its industries were expanded during World War II. In April, 1947, a series of blasts and fires were set off by the explosion of a nitrate-laden ship. Over 500 lives were lost, several thousand people were injured, and property worth millions of dollars was destroyed; however, industrial facilities were rapidly restored and increased. Hurricanes in 1900, 1915, 1943, and 1961 also caused severe damage. A junior college is there.

Texas Rangers, mounted fighting force organized (1835) during the Texas Revolution. During the republic they became established as the guardians of the Texas frontier, particularly against American Indians. The Texas Rangers at first consisted of three companies of 25 men each. Said to "ride like Mexicans, shoot like Tennesseeans, and fight like the very devil," the rangers were unique as a police force in that they never drilled, were not required to salute officers, and wore neither uniforms nor any standard gear except the six-shooter. In their first decade of operation, the rangers effectively quelled lawlessness in Texas on frequent occasions, and in the Mexican War (1846–48) they served as scouts and guerrilla fighters, gaining a wide reputation for valor and effectiveness. In the late 1850s the rangers fought vicious battles with the Comanche, and in the Civil War, Terry's Texas Rangers gained renown. In the Reconstruction era the Texas Rangers were engaged to control outlaws, feuding groups, and Mexican marauders and were responsible for keeping law and order along the Rio Grande. In 1874 the Texas Rangers were organized for the first time on a permanent basis in two battalions; one was assigned to arbitrate range wars on the frontier, and the other was sent to control cattle rustling on the Texas-Mexico border. The heyday of the great cattle business, with its feuds and shootings, its outlaws and rustlers, was also the heyday of the Texas Rangers. In the 20th cent. the police responsibilities of the rangers, around whom much lore had built up, decreased, and by 1935 their numbers had diminished considerably. By act (1935) of the Texas legislature, the rangers were merged with the state highway patrol under the jurisdiction of the state department of public safety. In 1967 rangers were sent into Starr co. to maintain order during a strike by farm workers. In the aftermath, widespread charges of brutality and strikebreaking were leveled against the rangers. See W. P. Webb, *The Texas Rangers* (2d ed. 1965).

Texas Tech University, at Lubbock; coeducational; state supported; chartered 1923, opened 1925.

Texcoco, Lake: see MEXICO, city; TENOCHTITLÁN.

Texel (tĕk'səl, tĕ'səl), island (1970 pop. 11,394), 71 sq mi (184 sq km), North Holland prov., NW Netherlands, in the North Sea, the largest and southernmost of the West Frisian Islands. It is a popular summer resort and has grazing land on which sheep are raised. The island is also a breeding ground for sea birds.

Texoma, Lake: see DENISON DAM.

textiles, all fabrics made by weaving, felting, knitting, braiding, or netting, from the various textile fibers (see FIBER). Yarn, fabrics, and tools for spinning and weaving have been found among the earliest relics of human habitations. Linen fabrics dating from 5000 B.C. have been found in Egypt. Woolen textiles from the early Bronze Age in Scandinavia and Switzerland have been discovered. Cotton has been spun and woven in India since 3000 B.C., and silk has been woven in China since at least 1000 B.C. About the 4th cent. A.D., Constantinople began to weave the raw silk imported from China. A century later silk culture spread to the Western countries, and textile making developed rapidly. By the 14th cent. splendid fabrics were being woven on the hand looms of the Mediterranean countries in practically all the basic structures known to modern craftsmen, and there has been no change in fundamental processes since that time, although methods and equipment have been radically altered. Textiles are classified according to their component fibers into silk, wool, linen, cotton, such synthetic fibers as rayon, nylon, and polyesters, and some inorganic fibers, as cloth of gold, glass fiber, and asbestos cloth. They are also classified as to their structure or weave, according to the manner in which warp and weft cross each other in the loom (see LOOM; WEAVING). Value or quality in textiles depends on several factors, such as the quality of the raw material used and the character of the yarn spun from the fibers, whether clean, smooth, fine, or coarse and whether hard, soft, or medium twisted. Density of weave and finishing processes are also important elements in determining the quality of fabrics. TAPESTRY, sometimes classed as embroidery, is a modified form of plain cloth weaving. The weaving of CARPET and rugs is a special branch of the textile industry. Other specially prepared fabrics not woven are felt and bark (or tapa) cloth, which are beaten or matted together, and a few in which a single thread is looped or plaited, as in crotchet and netting work and various laces. Most textiles are now produced in factories, with highly specialized power looms, but many of the finest velvets, brocades, and table linens are still made by hand. **Textile printing,** the various processes by which fabrics are printed in colored design, is an ancient art. Although the time and place of origin are uncertain, examples of Greek fabrics from the 4th cent. B.C. have been found. India exported block prints to the Mediterranean region in the 5th cent. B.C., and Indian chintz was imported into Europe during the Renaissance and widely imitated. France became a leading center and was noted especially for the toile de Jouy manufactured at Jouy from 1760 to 1811. Early forms of textile printing are stencil work, highly developed by Japanese artists, and block printing. In the latter method a block of wood, copper, or other material bearing a design in intaglio with the dye paste applied to the surface is pressed on the fabric and struck with a mallet. A separate block is used for each color, and pitch pins at the corners guide the placing of the blocks to assure accurate repeating of the pattern. In cylinder or roller printing, developed c.1785, the fabric is carried on a rotating central cylinder and pressed by a series of rollers each bearing one color. The design is engraved on the copper rollers by hand or machine pressure or etched by pantograph or photoengraving methods; the color paste is applied to the rollers through feed rollers rotating in a color box, the color being scraped off the smooth portion of the rollers with knives. More recent printing processes include screen printing, a hand method especially suitable for large patterns with soft outlines, in which screens, one for each color, are placed on the fabric and the color paste pressed through by a wooden squeegee; spray printing, in which a spray gun forces the color through a screen; and electrocoating, used to apply a patterned pile. Color may be applied by the various processes directly; by the discharge method, which uses chemicals to destroy a portion of a previously dyed ground; or by the resist, or reserve, method, which prevents the development of a subsequently applied color to a portion of the fabric treated with a chemical or with a mechanical resist. See E. R. Kaswell, *Handbook of Industrial Textiles* (1963); M. P. Johnston, *Design on Fabrics* (1967); A. T. C. Robinson, *Woven Cloth Construction* (1967); E. E. Stout, *Introduction to Textiles,* (3d ed. 1970).

Tezcatlipoca (tĕskätlĕpō'kä), ancient deity of the TOLTEC in Mexico. Identified with the night sky, the moon, and the stars, and associated with the forces of evil and destruction, Tezcatlipoca shared dominion over humanity with QUETZALCOATL, the god of light and good. Of the various legends surrounding their continual feud, one of the most important tells of Quetzalcoatl's expulsion from TULA, the Toltec capital.

T group: see GROUP PSYCHOTHERAPY.

Th, chemical symbol of the element THORIUM.

Thackeray, William Makepeace (thăk'ərē), 1811–63, English novelist, b. Calcutta, India. He is important not only as a great novelist but also as a brilliant satirist. In 1830, Thackeray left Cambridge without a degree and later entered the Middle Temple to study law. In 1833 he became editor of a periodical, the *National Standard,* but the following year he settled in Paris to study art. There he met Isabella Shawe, whom he married in 1836. He returned to England in 1837, supporting himself and his wife by literary hack work and by illustrating. Three years later his wife became hopelessly insane; she was cared for by a family in Essex and survived her husband by 30 years. Thackeray sent his two young daughters to live with his parents in Paris, lived himself the life of a clubman in London, and worked assiduously to support his family. Throughout the 1830s and '40s, his novels appeared serially together with miscellaneous writings in several magazines. His "Yellowplush Correspondence," in which a footman assumes the role of social and literary critic of the times, appeared (1837–38) in *Fraser's.* As a contributor to *Punch* he often parodied the false romantic sentiment pervading the fiction of his day. In 1848, Thackeray achieved widespread popularity with his humorous *Book of Snobs* and the same year rose to major rank among English novelists with *Vanity Fair,* a satirical panorama of upper-middle-class London life and manners at the beginning of the 19th cent. The novel contains many fascinating characters, particularly Becky Sharp, who, although clever and unscrupulous, is also extremely appealing. His reputation increased in 1850 with the completion of the partly autobiographical novel *Pen-*

dennis. In 1851 he delivered a series of lectures, *English Humorists of the Eighteenth Century,* which he repeated in a tour of the United States in 1852-53. In 1852 his novel of 18th-century life, *Henry Esmond,* appeared. *The Newcomes,* in which some of the characters of *Pendennis* reappear, came out serially in 1853-55. In 1855-56 he delivered another series of lectures in the United States entitled *The Four Georges* (pub. 1860). His next novel, *The Virginians* (1857-59), is a continuation of the Esmond story. In 1860 Thackeray became editor of the newly founded *Cornhill Magazine,* in which his last novels appeared—*Lovel the Widower* (1860), *The Adventures of Philip* (1861-62), and the unfinished historical romance, *Denis Duval* (1864). Thackeray's eldest daughter, Lady Anne RITCHIE, was also an author; his younger daughter Harriet married Sir Leslie STEPHEN. See his complete works (26 vol., 1910-11); his letters (ed. by G. N. Ray, 4 vol., 1945-46); G. N. Ray, *Thackeray* (2 vol., 1955 and 1958, repr. 1972) and *The Buried Life* (1952, repr. 1974).

Thaddaeus (thădē'əs), apostle: see JUDE, ST.

Thaddeus Kosciuszko National Memorial: see NATIONAL PARKS AND MONUMENTS, table.

Thahash (thā'hăsh), son of Nahor. Gen. 22.24.

Thailand (tī'lănd, -lənd), Thai *Prathet Thai* [land of the free], formerly Siam, constitutional monarchy (1970 pop. 34,152,000), 198,455 sq mi (514,000 sq km), Southeast Asia. BANGKOK is the capital. Occupying a central position on the Southeast Asia peninsula, Thailand is bordered by Burma on the west and northwest, by Laos on the north and east (the Mekong River forms much of the line), by Cambodia on the southeast, and by the Gulf of Siam and Malaysia on the south. A southward extension into the Malay Peninsula gives Thailand a long coastline on the Gulf of Siam and on the Andaman Sea. The heart of the country, the fertile and thickly populated central plain, is virtually one vast rice paddy,

entirely flat and rarely more than a few feet above sea level. It is watered by the Chao Phraya and lesser rivers and is elaborately veined by a system of canals (called klongs) for irrigation and drainage. Bangkok and AYUTTHAYA, the old capital, are in that basin. The north is mountainous, with peaks rising to c.8,500 ft (2,590 m); mountains stretch south along the boundary with Burma on the west. Extensive forests in the north yield teak, which is cut, hauled to the rivers by elephants (for which Thailand is famous), and floated to market. Although the population in the north is relatively sparse, rice is intensively cultivated in the river valleys, and the country's second largest city, CHIANGMAI, is in that area. Most of NE and E Thailand is occupied by the Korat (Khorat) plateau, which is cut off from the rest of the country by highlands and the Phetchabun mts. It is a hilly, dry, and generally poor region, where livestock raising is dominant. Chief towns are NAKHON RATCHASIMA (Korat), Udon Thani, and Ubon Ratchathani. Peninsular Thailand in the south (which includes PHUKET and other offshore islands) is largely mountainous and covered with jungles. It is the principal source of the rubber and tin that rank Thailand third (1970) in world production of both. Chief towns of the peninsula are Ban Hat Yai and Songkhla, the second largest port of the country. Thailand has a tropical and monsoonal climate. The economy is heavily agricultural, with rice by far the leading crop and the major factor in a normally favorable trade balance; Thailand is second only to the United States in the amount of rice exported. Other commercial crops include rubber, corn, kenaf, jute, tapioca, cotton, tobacco, kapok, and sugarcane. Thailand's teak, once a major export, still supplies a large share of the world market. Marine and freshwater fisheries are important; fish provide most of the protein in the diet, and some of the deep-sea catches (mackerel, shark, shrimp, crab) are now being exported. Tin, by far the most valuable mineral, is a major export item. Tungsten, lead, zinc, and antimony are also mined for export. Iron ore, gold, precious and semiprecious stones, salt, lignite, petroleum, asphaltic sand, and glass sand are exploited on a smaller scale. Thailand has substantial hydroelectric potential, which is being developed; projects have been constructed on the Ping, Mekong, Phong, and Songkhram rivers. Industry is minor and is centered chiefly in the processing of agricultural products; rice milling is by far the most important, followed by sugar producing, textile spinning and weaving, and the processing of rubber, tobacco, and forest products. Lumbering is concentrated in the north. A major tin smelter is on Phuket island. The country also has a small steel mill, an oil refinery, and vehicle and machine assembly plants. Small factories, many of which are in the Bangkok area, manufacture building materials, glass, pharmaceuticals, and various consumer goods. Handicraft production (Thailand is especially famous for its nielloware) exceeds total factory output and has a ready market in the tourist trade. Tourism is an important source of foreign exchange; Bangkok is now a key point on round-the-world air routes. It is the political, commercial, cultural, and transportation center of the country, with the only port that can accommodate oceangoing vessels. Thailand's railroads originate in Bangkok and extend to Chiangmai, the Korat plateau, and to Cambodia, Laos, and Malaysia. A corresponding network of paved highways has recently been constructed. Thailand's inland waterways—a complex, interconnected system of rivers, streams, and canals—have been important arteries since ancient times; barges and boats still carry well over half the cargo moved in the central plain. Local trade is chiefly in the hands of the large Chinese minority (about 3,000,000), and as a consequence there is tension between Thais and Chinese. Other substantial minorities include the Muslim Malays (about 1,000,000), concentrated in the southern peninsula; the hill tribes of the north (about 250,000); the Khmers, or Cambodians (about 200,000), who are found in the southeast and on the Cambodian border; and the Vietnamese (about 50,000), chiefly recent refugees who live along the Mekong River. While the ethnic minorities generally speak their own languages, Thai (linguistically related to Chinese) is the official tongue; English predominates among the Western languages. Hinayana Buddhism is the state religion; more than 93% of the people are Buddhists. Like other countries of Southeast Asia, Thailand in prehistoric times was peopled through successive migrations from central Asia into territory already inhabited by primitive Negrito tribes. Although a few Thai tribes (ethnically related to the Shan of Burma and the Lao of Laos) migrated to the northern hill country of Thailand, the main body of Thais remained in Yünnan, China, where by A.D. 650 they had organized the independent kingdom of Nanchao. By 1000, however, the Chinese had overrun Nanchao and made it a tributary state. With the destruction of the kingdom of Nanchao by the Mongols under Kublai Khan in 1253, the slow infiltration of Thailand from the north turned into a mass migration. By that time the KHMER EMPIRE was well established in the Chao Phraya valley and on the Korat plateau. The Thais captured the Khmer town of Sukhothai, in N central Thailand, and a new Thai nation, with its capital at Sukhothai, soon developed. During this period (c.1260-1350), King Rama Kamheng, whose 40-year reign began c.1275, borrowed from the Khmers of Cambodia the alphabet which the Thais still use. He extended Sukhothai power southward to the sea and down the Malay Peninsula, and contact was made with the ancient civilization of India. After the death of Rama Kamheng, Sukhothai declined and was absorbed by Rama Tibodi, prince of Utong, who established (c.1350) a new capital at Ayutthaya. The kings of Ayutthaya consolidated their power in S Siam and the Malay Peninsula, then launched a long series of indecisive wars against the Lao state of Chiang Mai and against Cambodia, which did not end until the 19th cent. The 16th cent. saw the beginnings of warfare with the Burmese; in 1568 the Burmese captured Ayutthaya and dominated the country until c.1583, when King Naresuan (1555-1605) drove the Burmese from Siam. He captured Tenasserim and Tavoy in S Burma and the major port of Mergui. Siam's relations with the West commenced after 1511, when Portuguese traders and missionaries began to arrive; adroit diplomacy, developed during this time, enabled Siam to remain independent of European colonization, the only country in Southeast Asia able to do so. In the early 17th cent. the Dutch and British broke Portugal's monopoly. Siam became, so far as Europe was concerned, the most consequential kingdom in Southeast Asia, and the brilliance of its court under King Narai (reigned 1657-88) was proverbial. The French, aided by the Greek adventurer Constantine Phaulkon, who had risen to power at the Siamese court, launched a bid for dominance in Siam that provoked an antiforeign coup d'etat (1688). Phaulkon was executed, and Siam was closed to most foreigners for over a century. In 1767 the Burmese, after several attempts, finally destroyed Ayutthaya. Gen. Phya Tak, or Taksin, however, quickly rallied the Thai forces, and within a decade he drove (c.1777) the Burmese from the country and established his capital at Thon Buri. His successor, General Chakkri (reigned 1782-1809), later known as Rama I, moved the capital from Thon Buri across the river to Bangkok and founded the Chakkri dynasty, thereafter the ruling house of Siam. In the 19th cent. the authority of Bangkok was at last established over N Siam, and relations with the West were resumed; Siam signed commercial treaties with Great Britain (1826) and the United States (1833). The independence of the kingdom was threatened, however, when Great Britain extended her sway to Malaya and Burma, and France carved out an empire in Indochina. By opening their posts to European trade, by bringing in Western advisers, by strengthening the central administration as against the hereditary provincial chieftains, and by playing off British against French interests, the Siamese managed to stay free. Even so, the establishment of Siam's boundaries meant the surrender of its claims to Laos (1893) and parts of Cambodia (1907) and of its suzerainty over Kedah, Perlis, Kelantan, and Terengganu (1909), on the Malay Peninsula. The Westernization of Siam took place under an absolute monarchy and was chiefly the work of Mongkut (reigned 1851-68), or Rama IV, and his son Chulalongkorn (reigned 1868-1910), or Rama V. Siam became a constitutional monarchy in 1932, when a bloodless coup d'etat forced Prajadhipok (reigned 1925-35), Rama VII, to grant a constitution. The two young leaders of the coup, Pibul Songgram and Pridi Phanomyang, both educated in Europe and influenced by Western ideas, came to dominate Thai politics in the ensuing years. In 1934 the first general elections were held; a year later Prajadhipok abdicated, and a council of regency chose Ananda (reigned 1935-46) as Rama VIII. Pibul Songgram, a militarist, became premier in 1938. He changed the country's name to Thailand and instituted a program of expansion. Taking advantage of the French defeat (1940) in World War II, he renewed Thai claims in Cambodia and Laos. Japanese "mediation" resulted (1941) in territorial concessions to Thailand. In Dec., 1941, Pibul, despite the objections of Pridi Phanomyang, permitted the Japanese to enter Thailand, and in 1942 the government, under Japanese pressure, declared war on Great Britain and the United States. With the help of the United States, Pridi formed a militant anti-Japanese underground. In 1943, Japan "granted" to Thailand territory in N Malaya and in the Shan states of Burma, but after the war Thailand was forced to return these territories and those acquired in 1941 to French and British control. Pridi Phanomyang became premier in the postwar government, while Pibul was briefly jailed as a war criminal. Pridi restored the name Siam as a repudiation of Pibul's policies. Inflation, corruption in government, and the mysterious death (1946) of King Ananda all contributed to the overthrow (1947) of Pridi's government by Pibul. Pridi fled the country and in 1954 appeared in Peking as the professed leader of the Communist "Free Thai" movement, allegedly representing numerous Thais still in Yünnan, China. Under Pibul's military dictatorship, the name Thailand was again adopted; Thailand signed (1950) a technical and economic aid agreement with the United States and sent troops in support of the United Nations action in Korea. Thailand has received huge military grants from the United States and is the seat (since 1954) of the Southeast Asia Treaty Organization. The country, increasingly apprehensive over its proximity to Communist China, has remained consistently pro-Western in international outlook. The present king is Bhumibol Adulyadej (Rama IX; crowned in 1950 after a four-year regency). In 1957 a military coup led by Field Marshal Sarit Thanarat finally overthrew Pibul Songgram, making Gen. Thanom Kittikachorn premier. In 1958, however, with the stated purpose of combating Communism, Sarit deposed his own premier, suspended the constitution, and declared martial law. King Bhumibol Adulyadej proclaimed an interim constitution in 1959 and named Sarit premier. When Sarit died in 1963, Thanom Kittikachorn was returned to power. A new constitution was finally promulgated in 1968. Under Sarit and Thanom the country's economy in the 1960s continued to boom; spurred by a favorable export market and considerable U.S. aid, it expanded at a rate of 7.5% per year. Thailand strongly supported the U.S. policy in South Vietnam, providing bases for U.S. troops and airfields for strikes against the North Vietnamese; thousands of Thai troops were sent in support of South Vietnam. The nation's foreign policy was closely geared to the U.S. presence in Southeast Asia and its economy became increasingly dependent upon U.S. military spending and subsidies. Economic reversals came in 1970 when the international demand for rice dropped substantially (due in part to improved farming techniques in other countries) and the prices of tin and rubber fell; Thailand for the first time since 1933 suffered a trade deficit. In addition, the security of the country appeared threatened by the spread of the Vietnam War into Cambodia and Laos and by growing insurgencies, chiefly Communist led, in three separate areas within Thailand itself: in the south, where Malaysian Communists were using Thailand as a staging base for operations in Malaysia; in the north, where Communists trained in North Vietnam were believed to be organizing the hill peoples; and, most significantly, in the economically backward northeastern provinces, where a discontented minority had been active since the mid-1950s. The increasing economic and security problems prompted a coup in Nov., 1971, by Premier Thanom Kittikachorn and three military aides, in which they abolished the constitution and the parliament and imposed military rule. In 1972 this new military junta launched a major four-month operation against the insurgents, but achieved few concrete results. Guerrilla raids against both Thai government forces and U.S. air bases continued. Economic conditions improved throughout 1972 as large numbers of U.S. military personnel were transferred from South Vietnam to bases in Thailand; by June of that year there were more U.S. forces in Thailand than in South Vietnam. In Oct., 1973, the military regime of Thanom was toppled after a week of student demonstrations and violence in Bangkok. King Bhumibol Adulyadej appointed Sanya Thammasak as Thanom's successor, giving Thailand its first civilian premier in twenty years. The new premier promised to complete a constitution and to hold general elections. In May, 1974, citing the heavy burden of the office and the sharp criticism directed against the government, Sanya resigned but was soon persuaded to form a new government. In June he was sworn in as the head of a revamped, all-civilian cabinet. A new constitution was promulgated in Oct., 1974. Despite its new economic problems, Thailand continues to have one of the highest standards of living in SE Asia. Institutions of higher learning include five universities in Bangkok, one in Chiangmai, and some eighteen technical colleges throughout the country. See D. A. Wilson, *Politics in Thailand* (1962) and *The United States and the Future of Thailand* (1970); A. A. Rozenthal, *Finance and Development in Thailand* (1970); J. R. Basche, *Thailand* (1971); J. W. Henderson et al., *Area Handbook for Thailand* (3d rev. ed. 1971); Joyce Nakahara and R. A. Witton, *Development and Conflict in Thailand* (1971); Rong Syamananda, *A History of Thailand* (1971); Sir John Bowring, *The Kingdom and People of Siam* (2 vol., 1857; repr. 1972); W. A. Wood, *A History of Siam from the Earliest Times to the Year A.D. 1781* (rev. ed. 1933, repr. 1972); K. P. Landon, *The Chinese in Thailand* (1941, repr. 1973).

Thai language (tī), formerly Siamese, member of the Tai or Thai subfamily of the Sino-Tibetan family of languages (see SINO-TIBETAN LANGUAGES). The official language of Thailand, Thai is spoken by approximately 24 million people in Thailand, Vietnam, and the Yünnan province of China. It has several dialects. Although most of the words are monosyllables, a number of them are polysyllabic. Because there is no inflection, word order is important for showing grammatical relationships. The Thai language is also tonal, and the tones serve to distinguish meanings of words otherwise pronounced alike. There are five tones: high, middle, low, rising, and falling. Over the centuries Thai has borrowed many words from Chinese, Khmer, Pali, Sanskrit, and, more recently, from European languages such as French and English. The Thai language has its own alphabet, which ultimately goes back to a script of S India and which was adopted in the 13th cent. A.D. Thai is written from left to right. See E. M. Anthony et al., *Foundations of Thai* (1968); Udom Warotamasikkhadit, *Thai Syntax: An Outline* (1972); M. R. Haas and H. R. Subhanka, *Spoken Thai* (1973).

Thaïs (thā'ĭs), fl. 4th cent. B.C., Athenian courtesan. At best semihistoric, she is said to have been the mistress of Alexander the Great and later the mistress of the king of Egypt. A legend, which is probably false, says that she persuaded Alexander to burn Persepolis, the seat of the Persian kings.

Thaïs, fl. 4th cent. A.D., legendary Alexandrian courtesan. She was a beautiful, wealthy, and licentious woman who was converted to a life of Christian piety and penitence. Her conversion is often attributed to St. Paphnutius. Although the story of Thaïs probably has no basis in fact, it supplied a framework for a novel by Anatole France, about which Jules Massenet composed his opera *Thaïs*.

thalamus (thăl'əməs), mass of nerve cells centrally located in the BRAIN just below the cerebrum and resembling a large egg in size and shape. The thalamus is a routing station for all incoming sensory impulses except those of smell, transmitting them to higher (cerebral) nerve centers. In addition, it connects various brain centers with others. Thus the thalamus is a major integrative complex, enabling sensory stimuli to evoke appropriate physical reactions as well as to affect emotions. With the HYPOTHALAMUS, the thalamus establishes levels of sleep and wakefulness. It is also vital to the neural feedback system controlling brain wave rhythms.

thalassemia: see ANEMIA.

Thales (thā'lēz), c.636–c.546 B.C., pre-Socratic Greek philosopher of Miletus and reputed founder of the Milesian school of philosophy. He is the first recorded Western philosopher. Thales taught that everything in nature is composed of one basic stuff, which he thought to be water. Prior to Thales, mythology had been used to explain the nature of the physical world; the significance of Thales thus lies not in his answer but in his approach. Although he apparently wrote nothing, he is believed to have introduced geometry into Greece and to have been a capable astronomer. It is said he predicted an eclipse of the sun in 585 B.C. Thales studied practical as well as speculative problems and was acknowledged one of the Seven Wise Men of Greece for his exhortation to unity among the Ionian Greeks. See G. S. Kirk and J. E. Raven, *The Presocratic Philosophers* (1957).

Thalia (thəlī'ə, thā'lēə): see MUSES and GRACES.

thalidomide (thəlĭd'əmīd''), sleep-inducing drug found to produce skeletal defects in developing fetuses. The drug was marketed in Europe, especially in West Germany and Britain, from 1957 to 1961, and was thought to be so safe that it was sold without prescription. In 1961 an extremely high incidence of European babies born with malformed, shortened limbs was correlated with use of thalidomide by women in their first trimester of pregnancy. Before it was recalled from use thalidomide had caused the malformation of about 8,000 children throughout the world.

thallium (thăl'ēəm), metallic chemical element; symbol Tl; at. no. 81; at. wt. 204.37; m.p. 303.5°C; b.p. about 1460°C; sp. gr. 11.85 at 20°C; valence +1 or +3. Thallium is a soft, malleable, lustrous silver-gray metal with a hexagonal close-packed crystalline structure. A member of group IIIa of the PERIODIC TABLE, it resembles aluminum in its chemical properties. In its physical properties it resembles lead. It forms univalent compounds similar to those of the alkali metals. It tarnishes rapidly in dry air, forming a heavy oxide coating; in moist air or water the hydroxide is formed. It dissolves in nitric or sulfuric acid. Thallium is widely distributed in nature, but the only minerals rich in the element are crooksite and lorandite. It is also found in copper pyrites and lead and zinc ores; it is recovered during the processing of these ores, the method of recovery depending on the source. Thallium is used in low-melting alloys with other metals and in compounds. Both the metal and its compounds are very poisonous. The sulfide is used as a rat poison and the sulfate as an insecticide. The oxide is used in special highly refractive optical glass. Several compounds are used in photoelectric cells and infrared detectors. Discovered spectroscopically in 1861 by Sir William Crookes, it was isolated independently by Crookes and C. A. Lamy in 1862.

thallophyte, common name for members of the Thallophyta (or Thallobionta), a taxonomic group composed of the various divisions of the lower plants, e.g., the BACTERIA, ALGAE, and FUNGI. Although the divisions within the Thallophyta are very diverse, they are united in their common lack of a clear-cut or conspicuous alternation of generations, i.e., an alternation between a haploid phase and a diploid phase (see GAMETOPHYTE; REPRODUCTION). Thallophytes also lack an organized plant body (stem, root, and leaf) and consist instead of one cell or a mass of cells called a thallus. EMBRYOPHYTES, which have a clear alternation of generations, include the higher plant divisions of the plant kingdom, i.e., the mosses, ferns and fern allies, gymnosperms, and angiosperms.

Thamah (thā'mə), variant of TAMAH.

Thamar (thā'mär), variant of TAMAR **1.**

Thames (tĕmz), river, c.160 mi (260 km) long, rising NW of Woodstock, S Ont., Canada, and flowing SW past London and Chatham to Lake St. Clair. It is navigable to Chatham, near which was fought (1813) the battle of the Thames (see THAMES, BATTLE OF THE) in the War of 1812.

Thames, Rom. *Tamesis,* principal river of England, c.210 mi (340 km) long. It rises in four headstreams (the Thames or Isis, Churn, Coln, and Leach) in the Cotswold Hills, E Gloucestershire, and flows generally eastward across S England and through London to the North Sea at The Nore. In its upper course—around and above Oxford—it is often called Isis. The Thames drains c.5,250 sq mi (13,600 sq km); its tributaries include the Windrush, Cherwell, Thame, Kennet, Wey, Mole, Lea, Roding, and Medway. It is joined by canals (including the Oxford, Thames and Severn, and Grand Junction) that cover a wide area. The river is navigable by barges to Lechlade, below which there are a number of locks. The Thames is tidal to Teddington; there is a 23-ft (7-m) difference between low and high tide at London Bridge. The part of the stream near London Bridge is known as the Pool. The main part of the port of London stretches from London Bridge to Blackwall. The Thames Conservancy Board was established in 1857; the docks and the tidal part of the river below Teddington have been administered by the Port of London Authority since 1908. Part of the river is of great beauty, is much used for boating, and is still popular for fishing. The upper valley of the Thames is a broad, flat basin of alluvial clay soil, through which the river winds and turns constantly in all directions. At Goring Gap the valley narrows, separating the Chiltern Hills from the Berkshire Downs. The lower valley forms a second broad basin through which the Thames also meanders. The land around the river was formerly marshy, and the ancient roads were far from the river banks. In the Middle Ages the valley was very prosperous, with many famous religious houses and several large towns, including Reading and Windsor. Between Oxford and London, the valley is predominantly agricultural, with scattered villages; Reading is the only industrial town there. The Greater London conurbation along the river's lower course is one of the most important industrial regions of Great Britain. Among the many interesting archaeological discoveries made in the valley are fossils of seashells and a human skull from the Paleolithic period. In London the river is crossed by 27 bridges, including the new London Bridge, Westminster Bridge, Waterloo Bridge, and Tower Bridge. There are two main tunnels under the river in London, and one between Dartford and Purfleet, as well as several footpaths and 5 railroad tunnels.

Thames (thāmz, tĕmz), river, c.15 mi (25 km) long, formed by the confluence of the Yantic and Shetucket rivers at Norwich, E Conn., and flowing south to Long Island Sound at New London. Primarily a tidal estuary, it is New London's harbor and the site of the U.S. Coast Guard Academy and a U.S. navy submarine base. Since 1878 it has been the scene of Yale-Harvard rowing contests.

Thames, battle of the, engagement fought on the Thames River near Chatham, Ont. (Oct. 5, 1813), in the War of 1812. Gen. William H. HARRISON led an

American force of about 3,000 against a British army of approximately 400 regulars commanded by Gen. Henry A. Procter, reinforced by 1,000 Indians under TECUMSEH. After the British were driven from Detroit, Harrison followed their retreating army into Ontario and up the Thames River until General Procter was forced to give battle. A cavalry charge broke the British ranks, and the Indians offered the only real resistance. Tecumseh was slain in battle, thus completely destroying the Indian confederacy he had raised against the United States. By the battle of the Thames, U.S. control in the Northwest was restored.

Thanet, Isle of (thăn'ĭt), former island forming the NE portion of Kent, SE England, bounded by the North Sea and branches of the Stour River. The isle was occupied by the Romans, who had a fort guarding the Wantsum, the channel that once separated the isle from the mainland. Silting and land reclamation have since joined the isle to the mainland. The surface is generally low, but cliffs form part of the shores. Most of the towns, which include Ramsgate, Margate, and Broadstairs, are seaside resorts.

Thanh Hoa (tän wä), city, E central North Vietnam, near the mouth of the Song Ma River, in a cotton-growing area. It is on the highway and railroad from Hanoi south to the demarcation line. Iron and phosphate are mined, and building materials are manufactured. Antimony and chromite deposits have also been found in the vicinity.

Thanjavur (tənjä'vo͝or), formerly **Tanjore** (tănjôr'), city (1971 pop. 140,470), Tamil Nadu state, SE India. It is a district administrative headquarters and a rice-milling center on the Cauvery River delta, known as the "rice bowl" of India. Thanjavur is also a center of craftsmanship noted especially for its silks and bronze ware and is a leading S Indian music and dance center. Among the city's many Hindu temples, the most famous is the Brahadeswara temple, one of the greatest examples of Dravidian architecture, which dates to the 11th cent., when Thanjavur was capital of the Hindu CHOLA kingdom. The city passed under British rule in 1799.

Thanksgiving Day, national holiday in the United States commemorating the harvest reaped by the Plymouth Colony in 1621, after a winter of great starvation and privation. In that year Gov. William Bradford proclaimed a day of thanksgiving, and the feast was shared by all the colonists and the neighboring Indians. Although similar observances were held locally, they were sporadic and at no set time. After the American Revolution the first national Thanksgiving Day, proclaimed by George Washington, was Nov. 26, 1789. Abraham Lincoln, urged by Sarah J. Hale, revived the custom in 1863, appointing as the date the last Thursday of November. In 1939, 1940, and 1941 Franklin D. Roosevelt proclaimed Thanksgiving the third Thursday in November. When a contradiction arose between Roosevelt's proclamation and some of those of state governors, Congress passed a joint resolution in 1941 decreeing that Thanksgiving should fall on the fourth Thursday of November. The day is observed by church services and family reunions; the customary turkey dinner is a reminder of the four wild turkeys served at the Pilgrims' first thanksgiving feast.

Thanom Kittikachorn (tä'no͞om kĭt''əkəchôrn'), 1911-, Thai political leader. He entered the army in 1929 and rose to command a division by 1950. After supporting a coup d'etat in 1957 by Sarit Thanarat, he served (1957-63) as defense minister and was (1958-59) also briefly prime minister. On Sarit's death in 1963, Thanom succeeded him as prime minister. A staunch anti-Communist, he supported U.S. policy in Southeast Asia. In 1971, Thanom increased his powers through a military takeover of the government. Protests against the abolition of constitutional government and Thanom's personal aggrandizement finally forced his resignation in 1973.

Thant, U (o͞o thänt), 1909-74, Burmese diplomat, secretary general of the United Nations (1962-72). Educated at University College, Rangoon, he later held positions in education, the press, and broadcasting. He was with the Burmese ministry of information (1949-57) and served as chairman of the Burmese delegation to the United Nations from 1947. In 1953 he was appointed Burma's permanent representative to the United Nations. He succeeded Dag Hammarskjöld as acting secretary general of the United Nations in 1961 and was elected secretary general in 1962. In the early years of his tenure, he was deeply involved in the settlement of major international disputes, including the transfer of Irian Barat (West New Guinea) to Indonesia (1962); the removal of Soviet missiles from Cuba (1962); the resolution of the civil war in the Republic of the Congo (now Zaïre) in 1963; the establishment of a peace-keeping force on Cyprus (1964); and the achievement of a cease-fire in the 1965 India-Pakistan War. Elected to a second term in 1966, U Thant had less success in dealing with the major crises of this later period, which included the Vietnam War, the Middle East crisis, and another India-Pakistan War (1971), among others. This declining role in international peace-keeping was offset by a greatly increased UN involvement in the economic and social development of the Third World countries, which by that time made up a large majority of the United Nations. U Thant was never able to solve the chronic problem of financing UN operations. In 1972, after declining another term, he was succeeded as secretary general by Kurt Waldheim. He is the author of several books, including *Cities and Their Stories* (1930), *The League of Nations School Book* (1932), *Towards a New Education* (1946), and a *History of Postwar Burma* (3 vol., 1961). See a selection of his writings and speeches in *Portfolio for Peace* (1968); study by June Bingham (1966).

Thapsacus (thăp'səkəs), ancient city, N central Syria, on the Euphrates. It was at a ford in the river, which was the chief crossing for many hundreds of miles and was used by various conquerors, including Alexander the Great. It is the Tiphsah of 1 Kings 4.24.

Thapsus (thăp'səs), ancient N African seaport, c.100 mi (161 km) SE of Carthage in what is now Tunisia. The last stronghold of Pompey's party, the town was besieged in 46 B.C. by Julius Caesar. There Metellus Pius SCIPIO and the Numidians under JUBA I offered battle, but were defeated, with a tremendous loss of men. Their defeat marked the end of opposition to Caesar in Africa.

Thara (thā'rə), variant of TERAH.

Thar Desert (tär, tûr) or **Great Indian Desert,** extensive arid region, c.500 mi (800 km) long and c.250 mi (400 km) wide, S Asia, in NW India and E Pakistan, between the Indus and Sutlej river valleys on the west and the Aravalli Range on the east. Largely a desolate region of shifting sand dunes and scrub vegetation, it receives an annual average rainfall of less than 10 in. (25.4 cm). The sparsely populated region has a pastoral economy; irrigation has reclaimed some land for agriculture along the northern and western edges. In May, 1974, India exploded its first nuclear device in the desert in Rajasthan state.

Tharshish (thär'shĭsh). **1** Benjamite. 1 Chron. 7.10. **2** Variant of TARSHISH **1**.

Thásos (thā'sŏs), island (1971 pop. 13,316), c.170 sq mi (440 sq km), NE Greece, in the Aegean Sea. Timber, olive oil, honey, wine, and lead-zinc ores are its chief products; stock raising and fishing are important occupations. In legend its earliest colonists were led by Thasus, son of Poseidon, for whom the island was named. It was famous in ancient times for its gold mines, which were exploited by the Phoenicians. The island was colonized c.708 B.C. by persons from Páros, among whom was the poet Archilochus. In the 5th cent. B.C. it was subdued by Persia and then fell to Athens. A revolt against Athens was put down by Cimon in 463 B.C. The Ottoman Turks held Thásos almost continuously from the mid-15th cent. A.D. until 1912, when it passed to Greece.

Thatch, Edward: see BLACKBEARD.

Thaulow, Fritz (tou'lō), 1847-1906, Norwegian landscape painter. He studied in Paris. Influenced by impressionism, he painted canals, riverbanks, and snow scenes. Thaulow is represented in various Swedish galleries and in the museums of Baltimore, Chicago, Pittsburgh, San Francisco, and Worcester, Mass.

Thayendanegea: see BRANT, JOSEPH.

Thayer, Abbott Handerson (thâr), 1849-1921, American painter, b. Boston, studied in Paris with Gérôme and at the École des Beaux-Arts. Known as a painter of animals and of landscapes, he was also noted for his idealized figures of women, among these *The Virgin* (Freer Gall. of Art, Washington, D.C.), *Caritas* (Mus. of Fine Arts, Boston), and *Young Woman* (Metropolitan Mus.). He also worked in portraiture. With his son Gerald Thayer, he wrote *Protective Coloration of the Animal Kingdom* (1909), which was used in camouflaging in World War I. See study by N. C. White (1951).

Thayer, Eli, 1819-99, American abolitionist, b. Medon, Mass. He was a Free-Soiler in the Massachusetts legislature (1853-54), organized the New England EMIGRANT AID COMPANY for sending antislavery settlers to Kansas, and was a Republican member of the House of Representatives (1857-61). He wrote *A History of the Kansas Crusade* (1889).

Thayer, Sylvanus, 1785-1872, American soldier and educator, b. Braintree, Mass., grad. Dartmouth, 1807, and West Point, 1808. During the War of 1812 he served as an engineer, and afterward he was sent to Europe to study military schools and fortifications. From 1817 to 1833 he served as superintendent at West Point, which he so thoroughly reorganized, placing it on a sound basis, that he is known as the "father of the Military Academy." He endowed an academy at Braintree and established and endowed (1867) the Thayer School of Civil Engineering at Dartmouth.

theater, building in which dramatic performances take place. In its broadest sense theater can be defined as including everything connected with dramatic art—the play itself, the stage with its scenery and lighting, makeup, costumes, acting, and actors. Theater in ancient Greece developed from the ceremonial worship of the god Dionysus (in which the death and rebirth of the god were celebrated) and was communal in nature. The focal point of the structure in which the ceremony took place was a level, circular space at the foot of a hill. Around this

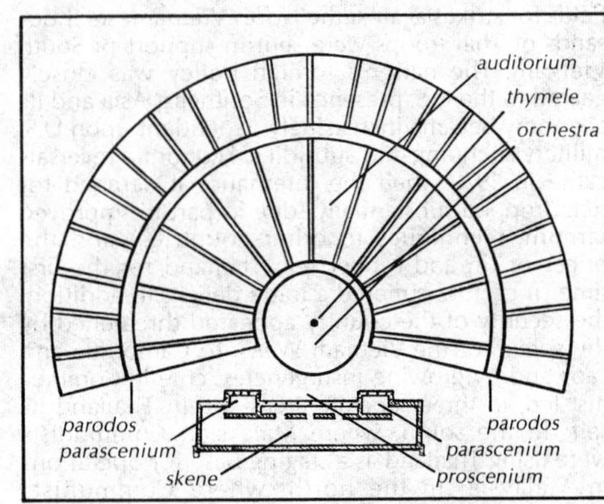

Plan of Greek amphitheater

space, called the *orchēstra,* an auditorium rose in a large semicircle. Behind the *orchēstra* was the *skēne,* a building where the actors could change costume. Between the *skēne* and the *orchēstra* was a space called the *proskenion,* which later developed into the stage. The original religious nature of Greek drama made audiences particularly receptive to the cosmic themes presented in classical TRAGEDY. Greek actors performed in masks and stylized costumes (see MASK). The CHORUS remained in the *orchēstra* throughout the play, performing intricate dances and chants while commenting on the dramatic action taking place on the *proskenion.* The date at which the *proskenion* became a raised stage is uncertain, but it had definitely achieved this status by the Hellenistic period (3d-1st cent. B.C.). The years from the decline of classical Greece through the Hellenistic period to the Roman era saw the erosion of serious drama and a corresponding increase in the architectural grandeur of theaters. As the religious and thus the choral element diminished, the *skēne* became an elaborate structure and the *orchēstra* was increasingly reduced in size. In Rome, for the first time, theaters were enclosed within a single wall, making them architectural units. The Roman *skēne* (in Latin the *scaenae frons*) was frequently monumental in scale. Roman audiences never evinced an interest in serious drama but accepted romantic COMEDY as long as it included an element of FARCE. By the Empire period, Roman theater had degenerated into brutal and obscene spectacle, and it was finally banned by the Christian

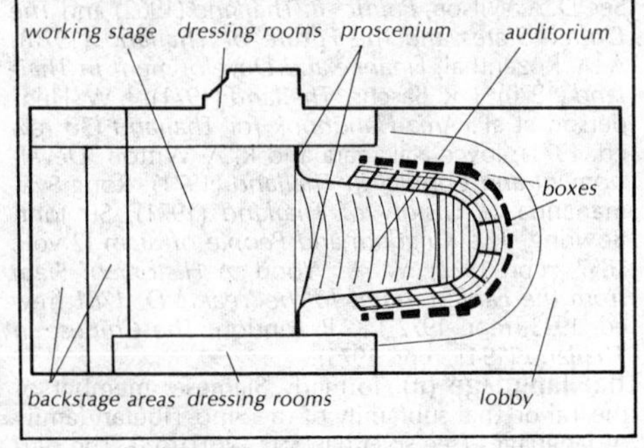

Proscenium theater

church. While Greek actors were highly respected, their Roman counterparts were originally slaves. Although the position of Roman actors had improved by the 1st cent. B.C. (as evidenced by the career of Quintus ROSCIUS), later Christian antipathy to the stage led to the view of the actor as a social outcast. Until the 10th cent., theatrical performances were restricted to traveling acrobats, jugglers, mimes, and the like. Popular types of traveling theater, performed on plain wooden platforms, also existed throughout the Greek and Roman periods. Native farce and BURLESQUE probably flourished before Aristophanes; it certainly did by the 3d cent. B.C. in the Greek *phylakes* and the Roman *fabula Atellana.* In the 9th cent. drama returned to the Western world in the form of mystery and miracle plays, which were performed in churches (see MIRACLE PLAY). Usually stories from the Bible, such plays were first acted by priests, their stage consisting of different platform sets arranged in rows along the side of the nave of the church. One effect of the church setting was to create a close relationship between audience and performer. Later these plays were moved out of the church into the street, where the platform sets were arranged around an area in which the audience could stand or move from place to place in a prescribed order. Acting took place either on the platforms, in front of them, or between them, depending on the need. The platforms were often elaborate in their decoration and stage machinery. With the shift to the streets, acting was transferred from the priesthood to the amateurs of the guilds or professional players. After the advent of the Renaissance in Italy, there were various attempts to construct theaters on Roman models, the culmination of this movement being the Teatro Olimpico (1580–84) at Vicenza, designed by Andrea PALLADIO. However, the development of the theater form that was to dominate until the 20th cent. began with the Teatro Farnese (1618) at Parma, designed by Gian-Battista Aleotti. Of primary importance was Aleotti's use of the proscenium arch creating the picture-frame stage. Italians also introduced painted perspective scenery, first outlined in the treatise *Architettura* (1537–45) of Sebastiano SERLIO. While these developments were taking place in an academic and aristocratic milieu, the COMMEDIA DELL'ARTE was carrying on a popular theater of improvisation, which did much toward developing professional acting as opposed to courtly amateurism. In England and Spain, theories of theater construction were less tied to classical example than in Italy. The Spanish theater developed in the *corral,* or courtyard, of various large buildings, where plays were originally performed, while the innyard served as a similar model in England. These theaters offered greater flexibility of movement than did the Italian. The Elizabethan audience in England included all levels of society, and professional actors were treated with relative respect. In 17th-century Europe the trend in theater production was increasingly toward more elaborate machinery and scenery with less and less concern for the drama itself. This trend is illustrated by the triumph of opera in Italy and Spain and, later, by the popularity of the exuberant baroque architecture and scene design of the BIBIENA family throughout 18th-century Europe. In 17th-century England the designs of Inigo JONES revealed Italian influence in their use of perspective scenery and the proscenium arch. Before the closing of the theaters by the Puritans in 1642, English audiences had become overwhelmingly aristocratic, a tendency that continued in the Restoration period. However, English theater never indulged in the architectural extravaganzas that proliferated on the continent. The development of a middle-class audience in 18th-century France and England created a desire for more realistic settings and acting. Although some attempts were made in the 18th cent. (notably by David GARRICK in England and Adrienne LECOUVREUR in France) to combat the artificial, rhetorical style of acting then popular, it was not until the late 19th cent. that histrionic techniques finally vanished. Of great importance in the emergence of realistic acting was Constantin STANISLAVSKI, cofounder of the MOSCOW ART THEATRE, who stressed the actor's absolute identification with the character he portrays. Similarly, realism in scenery and costumes was not popular until well into the 19th cent. The creation of realistic effects was facilitated by the introduction of gas lights in the early 19th cent. and of electricity later in the century. Electric lighting was, however, also used for antirealistic effects by such scene designers as Adolphe APPIA and Edward Gordon CRAIG. The introduction of gas lighting made it possible to dim the auditorium lights, a practice that tended to make the audience more separate from the stage. Richard WAGNER, in his opera theater at Bayreuth, attempted further to isolate

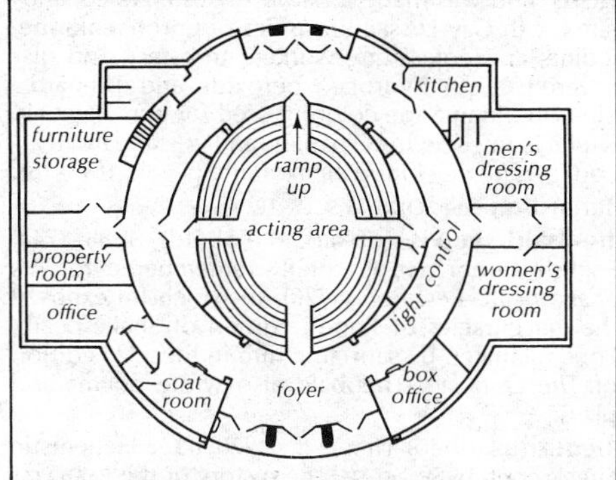

Theater-in-the-round.

the audience by means of a gap of darkness between a double proscenium arch. While most commercial theaters today still use the proscenium arch stage, there has been much experimental work to restore a vital relationship between audience and stage. By the late 19th cent., theater was dominated by commercial playhouses in large cities, particularly in England and the United States. But in the late 19th and early 20th cent. several independent theaters, more interested in art than in making money, came into being, including the THÉÂTRE LIBRE in Paris (1887), the Freie Bühne in Berlin (1889), the Independent Theatre Society in London (1891), the Moscow Art Theatre in Russia (1891), and the PROVINCETOWN PLAYERS (1915) in the United States. Concurrently, antirealistic expressionist and symbolic movements in theater were developing, such as Vsevolod MEYERHOLD'S constructivism, the "theater of cruelty" of Antonin ARTAUD, and the "epic theater" of Bertolt BRECHT. There was also a growing interest in the oriental theater, which seemed attractive to many because of its relatively bare stage, symbolic stage properties, and stylized, nonrealistic acting (see ORIENTAL DRAMA). Theatrical developments since World War II, especially in noncommercial theater, have brought the stage more in contact with the audience. Theater-in-the-round became popular at American universities in the 1930s, and in the 1950s and 60s many "music tents" featuring theater-in-the-round sprang up in American cities. Experimental relationships between audience and acting space have also been constructed. Such groups as the Living Theater of Julian BECK and Judith Malina produced orgiastic revelries in which audience and actors mingled, thus removing completely traditional barriers between them. For further information see separate articles on DRAMA, WESTERN; ACTING; DIRECTING; and SCENE DESIGN AND STAGE LIGHTING. See also articles on theaters and theater groups: AMERICAN NATIONAL THEATER AND ACADEMY (ANTA); ASSOCIATION OF PRODUCING ARTISTS-PHOENIX (APA-PHOENIX); COMÉDIE FRANÇAISE; DEUTSCHES THEATER; DRURY LANE; FEDERAL THEATRE; GLOBE THEATRE; GROUP THEATRE; HABIMA THEATER; HÔTEL DE BOURGOGNE; MEININGEN PLAYERS; NATIONAL THEATRE OF GREAT BRITAIN; OLD VIC; ROYAL SHAKESPEARE COMPANY; and THEATRE GUILD. See the general theater histories by O. G. Brockett (1968), Bamber Gascoigne (1968), George Freedley and J. A. Reeves (3d ed. 1968), and Sheldon Cheney (3d ed. 1972); Alec Clunes, *The British Theatre* (1964); Edward Csato, *The Polish Theatre* (tr. 1965); Allardyce Nicoll, *Development of the Theatre* (5th ed. 1967) and *English Drama 1900–1930* (1972); Howard Taubman, *The Making of the American Theatre* (rev. ed. 1967); O. G. Brockett, *Perspectives on Contemporary Theatre* (1971).

theater-in-the-round: see THEATER.

theater of the absurd: see DRAMA, WESTERN.

Theatines: see CAJETAN, SAINT.

Théâtre Français: see COMÉDIE FRANÇAISE.

Theatre Guild, organization formed in 1919 by members of the Washington Square Players (formed 1914), New York City, and financed at first by Otto H. Kahn and later largely by subscription. The group opened with Benavente's *Bonds of Interest,* and in 1925 it opened the theater which it had built on 52d St. Its efforts to present a program of cultural plays, both American and foreign, met with continuous success, and in 1927 it began to present plays in other theaters in New York and elsewhere. Shaw and O'Neill were among the dramatists who received the Guild's support. The Guild aided in the development of musical theater, producing *Porgy and Bess* and bringing together Richard Rodgers and Oscar Hammerstein II to collaborate on *Oklahoma!* From 1945 to 1963 the "Theatre Guild on the Air" brought first-rate drama to radio and television audiences.

Théâtre Libre (tāät'rə lēb'rə), French theatrical company founded in Paris in 1887 by André ANTOINE. Inspired by the work of the MEININGEN PLAYERS, Antoine's theater became a showcase for naturalist drama. Plays of Zola, Becque, Brieux, and of contemporary German, Scandinavian, and Russian masters were produced. The Théâtre Libre became a model for experimental theaters throughout Europe and the United States. See S. M. Waxman, *Antoine and the Théâtre-Libre* (1926).

Thebes (thēbz), city of ancient Egypt. Al Uqsur (see UQSUR, AL) and Al Karnak (see KARNAK, AL) now occupy parts of its site. The city developed at a very early date from a number of small villages, particularly one around modern Al Uqsur (then called Epet), but remained relatively obscure until the rise of the Theban family that established the XI dynasty (c.2134 B.C.). The city rapidly became prominent as the royal residence and as a seat of the worship of the god AMON. At Thebes, also, was the necropolis in the Valley of the Tombs where the kings and nobles were entombed in great splendor in crypts cut into the cliffs on the west bank of the Nile. The city's greatest period was that of the empire, during which it served as a reservoir for the immense wealth that poured in from the conquered countries. As the empire began to decay and the locus of power to shift to the Nile delta, Thebes went into decline. For a time in the 11th cent. B.C., it was a separate political entity under sacerdotal rule. Thebes was sacked by the Assyrians in 661 B.C., an event referred to in the Bible (Nah. 3.8–10), where the city is called No [city]. The Romans sacked it in 29 B.C., and by 20 B.C. a Greek visitor to the site reported only a few scattered villages. The temples and tombs that have survived, including the tomb of TUTANKHAMEN, are among the most splendid in the world, and the site of the ancient city has been the scene of much important archaeological work. See H. E. Winlock, *The Rise and Fall of the Middle Kingdom in Thebes* (1947) and C. F. Nims, *Thebes of the Pharaohs* (1965).

Thebes, chief city of Boeotia, in ancient Greece. It was originally a Mycenaean city. Thebes is rich in associations with Greek legend and religion (see OEDIPUS; the SEVEN AGAINST THEBES; EPIGONI). Sometime before 1000 B.C., Thebes was settled by Boeotians and rapidly replaced Orchomenus as the region's leading city. At the end of the 6th cent. B.C. it began its struggle with Athens to maintain its position in Boeotia and in Greece. In the Persian Wars, Thebes, motivated by hostility to Athens, sided (480–479 B.C.) with the Persians. When the Persians were defeated, Thebes was punished, and only the intervention of Sparta, which saw in the city a balance to the power of Athens, saved it from destruction. Thebes supported Sparta against Athens in the Peloponnesian War but, fearing Spartan territorial ambitions, withdrew this support and joined (394 B.C.) the confederation against Sparta. Sparta was able to place (382 B.C.) a garrison in Thebes, but the city was freed by one of its great generals, Pelopidas, three years later. This freedom was insured (371 B.C.) by the Spartan defeat at Leuctra by the Theban Epaminondas. Thebes joined Athens against Philip II of Macedon and shared in the defeat at Chaeronea (338 B.C.). A revolt at Thebes caused Alexander the Great to attack and destroy (336 B.C.) the city. Cassander rebuilt Thebes c.315 B.C., but it never regained its former greatness. The modern Thívai occupies the site of the Theban acropolis, part of which still survives. There are also remains of the prehistoric city and the temple of Ismenian Apollo.

Thebez (thē'bēz), fortified town where Abimelech was killed, NE of Shechem. It is the modern Tubas (Jordan). Judges 9.50; 2 Sam. 11.21.

The Dalles (dălz), city (1970 pop. 10,423), seat of Wasco co., N Oregon, on the Columbia River; inc. 1857. It is a busy inland port; ships passing through the locks at Bonneville Dam (c.50 mi/80 km downstream) can tie up at The Dalles and proceed upstream through the locks of The Dalles Dam. A processing and shipping point in an area producing sweet cherries, wheat, and beef, the city has a flour mill, fruit-processing plants, and an aluminum-reduction plant. Mobile homes are also made. The Lewis and Clark expedition camped there in 1805, and later the site became the terminus of the Oregon Trail. A Methodist mission was founded there in 1838 and abandoned after an Indian massacre in 1847. It was replaced by a fort around which a settlement grew up c.1852; the fort is preserved as a museum. A gorge and rapids (from which its French name "Le Dalle"—the trough—derives) once rendered the river unnavigable at this point, but they were bypassed by a canal with several locks built (1908-15) from The Dalles to Celilo. In 1957 the gorge and rapids, as well as the canal, were inundated by the reservoir formed by The Dalles Dam, c.3 mi (5 km) above the city. A state hospital and training center are in The Dalles. The Winquatt Museum has a collection of artifacts and rock carvings of prehistoric Indians.

The Dalles Dam, 260 ft (79 m) high and 8,875 ft (2,705 m) long, on the Columbia River between Oregon and Wash., NE of The Dalles, Oregon; built 1952-57 by the U.S. Corps of Engineers. The dam, a major link in the development of the Columbia basin, provides hydroelectric power (ultimate capacity 1,806,800 kw) and improves navigation. Located at the head of the slackwater pool created by Bonneville Dam, it impounds a reservoir that provides ship passage 25 mi (40 km) upstream to John Day Dam. Fishways permit salmon and other migratory fish to pass the dam.

Theia (thē'ə): see HYPERION and TITAN.

Theiler, Max (mäks tī'lər), 1899-1972, South African-American research physician, b. Pretoria, educated at the Univ. of Cape Town, St. Thomas's Hospital (London), and the London School of Tropical Medicine. Theiler's research on yellow fever, begun while he was connected with the department of tropical medicine of Harvard Medical School (1922-30), was continued at the Rockefeller Foundation, of which he became a staff member in 1930. He became known for his researches on yellow fever, encephalomyelitis, and other viruses associated with the tropics. For his work in developing a vaccine for yellow fever he was awarded the 1951 Nobel Prize in Physiology and Medicine.

theism (thē'ĭzəm), in theology and philosophy, the belief in a personal God. It is opposed to atheism and agnosticism and is to be distinguished from PANTHEISM and deism (see DEISTS). Theism is distinguished from pantheism in that, while it holds to the IMMANENCE of God, it refuses to identify God and the universe. Theism differs from the deism of the 18th-century thinkers in that it rejects the deists' insistence on the purely transcendent nature of God, holding that God is at once immanent and transcendent. Theism has been traditionally supported by a number of arguments. For a summary of those arguments, see GOD.

Theiss, river: see TISZA.

Thelasar (thēlā'sər), variant of TELASSAR.

The Mar-A-Lago National Historic Site: see NATIONAL PARKS AND MONUMENTS (table).

thematic apperception test: see PSYCHOLOGICAL TESTS.

Themis (thē'mĭs), in Greek religion, a Titan. Sometimes identified as an earth goddess, she was more commonly a goddess of law, order, and justice. She was the mother by Zeus of the Horae (the Seasons) and the Moerae (the Fates). It was also said that she was the mother of Prometheus by Iapetus.

Themistocles (thəmĭs'təklēz), c.525-c.460 B.C., Athenian statesman and naval commander. He was elected one of the three ARCHONS in 493 B.C. In succeeding years many of his rivals were eliminated by OSTRACISM and he became the chief figure of Athenian politics. He persuaded the Athenians to build up their navy, foreseeing that the Persians, defeated at Marathon, would send another and stronger force against Greece (see PERSIAN WARS). Xerxes invaded Greece in 480, and military defense of Athens was impossible; Themistocles evacuated the city. Although the Greek fleet was entrusted to a Spartan, Themistocles determined its strategy, thus bringing about the decisive victory of Salamis (480) and the retreat of Xerxes to Persia. A copy of Themistocles' decree to evacuate Athens was discovered at Troezen in 1959; the document indicates that the evacuation, as well as the battle of Salamis, was not hastily planned but was a measure carefully conceived months before to trap the Persians at Salamis. Despite Themistocles' prominence, in 479 the chief commands went to his rivals, who had previously been recalled from exile to fight the Persians. Themistocles devoted himself to strengthening the navy and the fortifications, especially those of Piraeus. About 471, after his opponents came to power, he was exiled. Ultimately he lived in Persia, where King Artaxerxes made generous provision for him.

Thénard, Louis Jacques (lwē zhäk tānär'), 1777-1857, French chemist. He became professor at the Collège de France (1802), dean of the Faculty of Sciences, Paris (1821), chancellor of the Univ. of Paris (1832), and was made a baron in 1825. He collaborated with Gay-Lussac in studies of boron, chlorine, iodine, and potassium, worked on esters, and discovered (1799) hydrogen peroxide and Thénard's blue, an ultramarine coloring used for porcelain. He wrote many scientific papers and a standard textbook, *Traité de chimie élémentaire* (4 vol., 1813-16).

thenardite: see SODIUM SULFATE.

Theobald, Lewis (tĭb'əld, thē'ōbôld), 1688-1744, English author. He is chiefly remembered for his *Shakespeare Restored* (1726), in which he exposed the inaccuracies of Pope's edition of Shakespeare. Pope retaliated by satirizing him in the 1728 edition of *The Dunciad.* Theobald also wrote poems and plays.

Theocritus (thēŏk'rĭtəs), fl. c.270 B.C., Hellenistic Greek poet, b. Syracuse. The history of the PASTORAL begins with him, and in him the form seems to have reached its height. His poetic style is finished and at times artificial, but the bucolic characters in his idyls seem alive. Theocritus has been widely imitated (e.g., by such poets as Vergil and Spenser).

theodolite (thēŏd'əlīt"), optical instrument used for a number of purposes in surveying, navigation, and meteorology, such as visual tracking of WEATHER BALLOONS. It is similar in construction to a surveyor's transit, consisting of a telescope fitted with a spirit level and mounted on a tripod so that it is free to rotate about its vertical and horizontal axes. (Sometimes two or more telescopes of different magnifications are used.) Graduated scales are used to measure the amount of rotation about the axes. Measurements of the altitude and azimuth of the balloon at precise time intervals are used to compute the estimated wind velocity of the atmosphere through which the balloon is passing.

Theodora (thēədôr'ə), d. 548, Byzantine empress. Information about her early career comes from the often-questionable source, the *Secret History* of PROCOPIUS. It appears that she was the daughter of an animal trainer in the circus, and that she was an actress and prostitute before her marriage (523) to JUSTINIAN I, who, on his accession in 527, made her joint ruler of the empire. A stronger person than her husband, she helped save the throne through her energetic action in the Nika riot (532; see BLUES AND GREENS). In her youth Theodora came under the influence of the Monophysite sect; Justinian's efforts to reconcile the Monophysites to orthodoxy were probably inspired by her. She is represented in the mosaics of the church of San Vitale, in Ravenna. See Charles Diehl, *Byzantine Portraits* (1906, tr. 1927).

Theodore I (Theodore Lascaris), d. 1222, Byzantine emperor of Nicaea (1204-22), son-in-law of the Byzantine emperor Alexius III. He escaped from Constantinople after it was captured (1204) by the Latins of the Fourth Crusade and founded a Byzantine state at Nicaea (see NICAEA, EMPIRE OF). Uniting nearly all of W Asia Minor except the Turkish sultanate of Iconium, he kept his state intact against Henry of Flanders, Latin emperor of Constantinople, and against the Seljuk Turks. He was succeeded by his son-in-law, John III.

Theodore II (Theodore Lascaris), 1222-58, Byzantine emperor of Nicaea (1254-58), son and successor of John III. He fought the Bulgarians and temporarily regained parts of Thrace. He made Nicaea a cultural center. His son, John IV, succeeded him.

Theodore II, 1818-68, emperor of Ethiopia (1855-68), originally named Kasa or Lij Kasa. He was a commoner and a bold and clever warrior. He seized control of his native province, Kawara (in NW Ethiopia), in 1842 and steadily fought his way to the throne. At first he attempted to abolish slavery and to encourage trade. In his last years, however, he became unrestrainedly cruel. In 1868, embroiled in a dispute with Great Britain over his imprisonment of British subjects, he committed suicide after being defeated by a British rescue force under Robert C. Napier.

Theodore. For Russian rulers thus named, see FEODOR.

Theodore of Mopsuestia (mŏp"syŏŏĕs'chə), c.350-428, Syrian Christian theologian, bishop of Mopsuestia (from 392). Together with his lifelong friend, St. JOHN CHRYSOSTOM, he studied at the school of Antioch, adopted its exegetical methods, and became a diligent writer and preacher. His commentaries on the various books of the Bible were historical and rationalistic; he was one of the first Christians to consider the Song of Songs a marriage poem rather than an allegory, and he was opposed to a Messianic interpretation of the Psalms. Many of his theological treatises are lost or fragmentary. He seems to have been influenced by dynamistic MONARCHIANISM to emphasize the manhood of Christ; he said that Christ progressively received the Logos and the Holy Ghost and that the union became complete only at the Ascension and was never essential and hypostatic. Much of his work was orthodox, and he was considered orthodox for many years, although his pupil Nestorius directly derived his heresy from Theodore (see NESTORIANISM), and the Pelagians (see PELAGIANISM) drew from his works. He was condemned in 544 in the Three Chapters of Justinian (see MONOPHYSITISM). Pope VIGILIUS, under pressure, reluctantly concurred.

Theodore of Studium, Saint (stōō'dēəm), 759-826, Byzantine Greek monastic reformer, also called St. Theodore the Studite. As an abbot he was early exiled for opposing the marriage of Emperor Constantine VI to his mistress Theodota. In 799 he entered the Studium monastery, which he reformed and made the model monastery of the Byzantine rite. He was exiled again (809-11) after long quarrels with Nicephorus I. When Leo V began his iconoclastic campaign, St. Theodore boldly opposed him and was exiled once more (814). He never returned to his monastery. His influence was critical in the history of the BASILIAN MONKS. His writings deal with the monastic life and with iconoclasm. St. Theodore wrote many hymns, and his letters are extant. See Alice Gardner, *Theodore of Studium* (1905, repr. 1974). Feast: Nov. 11.

Theodore Roosevelt Birthplace National Historic Site: see NATIONAL PARKS AND MONUMENTS (table).

Theodore Roosevelt Inaugural National Historic Site: see NATIONAL PARKS AND MONUMENTS (table).

Theodore Roosevelt Island: see NATIONAL PARKS AND MONUMENTS (table).

Theodore Roosevelt National Memorial Park, 70,436 acres (28,505 hectares), W N.Dak., in the Badlands and on the Little Missouri River; est. 1947. There are three units—the North Unit, the Elkhorn Ranch Unit, and the South Unit. Roosevelt first came to the area in 1883 to hunt bison and other big game. In 1884 he established the Elkhorn Ranch, and for several years after that he returned to the ranch for short periods. The ranch house and other buildings have been accurately reproduced in a diorama. The landscape of the park is marked by tablelands, buttes, canyons, and rugged hills; animal life is diverse. Among the attractions are a coal vein that has been burning since 1951 and petrified forests.

Theodoret (thēŏd'ərĕt), c.393-c.458, Syrian churchman and theologian. He was a monk of Apamaea and a lifelong friend of Nestorius. In 423 he went unwillingly to be bishop of Cyrus, Syria, where he furthered the work of the church in a difficult see. At the time of the controversy over NESTORIANISM, Theodoret felt that Nestorius was misunderstood. As a result, he had a bitter controversy with St. CYRIL of Alexandria. At the Council of Ephesus (431), Theodoret voted to depose Cyril. In 449 the Robber Synod of Ephesus led by EUTYCHES declared Theodoret deposed, but Pope Leo I invalidated this decree. At the Council of Chalcedon (451), Theodoret reluctantly joined in the condemnation of Nestorianism, still holding that it misrepresented his friend. His writings against St. Cyril were condemned in Justinian's Three Chapters (see MONOPHYSITISM), but the church has never condemned him. A theologian of the Antiochene school, he was much less extreme than his tutor, THEODORE OF MOPSUESTIA. Some of his writings are translated in *A Select Library of Nicene and Post-Nicene Fathers.*

Theodoric I (thēŏd'ərĭk) or **Thierry I** (tĕrē', tēĕr'ē), d. 534, Frankish ruler, son of CLOVIS I. On his father's death (511) he shared equally with his brothers, Clodomer, CHILDEBERT I, and CLOTAIRE I, in the division of the Frankish kingdom. His capital was at Rheims. With Clotaire he subjugated the Thuringians. He was succeeded by his son Theodebert I, who was king (534-48) of the West Frankish kingdom of Austrasia, and by his grandson, the last member of Theodoric's line, Theodebald (reigned 548-55).

Theodoric the Great, c.454-526, king of the OSTROGOTHS and conqueror of Italy, b. Pannonia. He spent part of his youth as a hostage in Constantinople. Elected king in 471 after his father's death, he became involved in intrigues in which he was by turns the ally and the enemy of Byzantine emperor ZENO. In 483 he was appointed imperial master of soldiers and in 484 was consul. It was probably to be rid of him that Zeno commissioned him to lead a campaign against ODOACER in Italy. Theodoric with his Gothic army entered Italy in 488. He won battles at the Isonzo (489), at Milan (489), and at the Adda (490) and besieged and took Ravenna (493). Shortly after Odoacer's surrender Theodoric murdered him. Theodoric was now master in Italy; because of his great power he was able to avoid Byzantine supervision and thus was more than a mere official. His title was that of patrician. His long rule in Italy was most beneficent; he respected Roman institutions, preserved Roman laws, and appointed Romans to civil offices, at the same time retaining a Gothic army and settling Goths on the land. He improved the harbors and repaired the roads and public buildings. He allied himself by marriage with Clovis the Frank (Clovis I) and with the kings of the Visigoths, Vandals, and Burgundians. However, Clovis's ambition to rule all the Goths brought Theodoric into intermittent warfare with the Franks; between 506 and 523 Theodoric was several times successful in forestalling Frankish hegemony. An Arian, Theodoric was impartial in religious matters. The end of his reign was clouded by a quarrel with his Roman subjects and Pope John I over the edicts of Emperor Justin I against Arianism, and also by the hasty execution of the Roman statesman BOETHIUS, whom he accused of treason. Theodoric is the prototype for Dietrich von Bern in the German epic poem *Nibelungenlied.* His tomb is one of the finest monuments of Ravenna. He was succeeded by his grandson Athalaric, under the regency of Theodoric's daughter Amalasuntha. See Thomas Hodgkin, *Theodoric the Goth* (1891); J. B. Bury, *The Invasion of Europe by the Barbarians* (1928, repr. 1963).

Theodosia: see FEODOSIYA, USSR.

Theodosian Code (thē″ədō′shən), Latin *Codex Theodosianus,* Roman legal code, issued in 438 by THEODOSIUS II, emperor of the East. It was at once adopted by Valentinian III, emperor of the West. The code was intended to reduce and systematize the complex mass of law that had been issued since the reign of Constantine I. To a large extent it was based upon two private compilations, the Gregorian (*Codex Gregorianus*) and the Hermogenian (*Codex Hermogenianus*). The Theodosian Code was used in shaping the CORPUS JURIS CIVILIS.

Theodosiopolis: see ERZURUM.

Theodosius I or **Theodosius the Great,** 346?–395, Roman emperor of the East (379–95) and emperor of the West (392–95), son of THEODOSIUS, the general of Valentinian I. He became (375) military governor of Moesia, but following the execution (376) of his father he retired to Spain. He remained there until Emperor GRATIAN chose him to rule the East after the defeat and death (378) of Valens in the battle of Adrianople. Theodosius, whom Gratian made coaugustus in 379, took up arms against the VISIGOTHS, who were plundering the Balkan Peninsula. By 381 he had achieved an advantageous peace, permitting the Ostrogoths to settle in Pannonia and the Visigoths in N Thrace. In return he secured their services as soldiers, and soon Gothic influence predominated in the army. In 383, Gratian was murdered; Theodosius was forced to recognize the usurper, MAXIMUS, as emperor in the West outside Italy, where Gratian's brother and legal successor, VALENTINIAN II, held authority. When Maximus seized Italy, Theodosius attacked him, put him to death (388), and restored Valentinian. But Valentinian's Frankish general, Arbogast, assumed the power in Gaul, and in 392, Valentinian, who had sought to recover Gaul, was strangled, perhaps on the order of Arbogast, who installed the puppet emperor Eugenius. Theodosius again went to Italy. In 394 he met a large army commanded by Arbogast and Eugenius and consisting mostly of pagan barbarians. Defeated on the first day of battle, he refused to retreat, and on the following day, with the battle cry "Where is the God of Theodosius," won a resounding victory. Eugenius and Arbogast were slain. Having previously named his son Arcadius as his coemperor in the East, he now proclaimed his younger son, Honorius, as his coemperor in the West. Theodosius died the following year, and the Roman Empire remained divided into West and East. The reign of Theodosius is most notable for its prominence in the history of the Christian Church. Baptized in 380, Theodosius soon afterward issued an edict condemning ARIANISM and making belief in the Trinity the test of orthodoxy; subsequent edicts practically extinguished Arianism and paganism within the empire. Under his direction the First Council of Constantinople (see CONSTANTINOPLE, FIRST COUNCIL OF) was convened. The most eminent church figure of his reign was Saint AMBROSE, bishop of Milan. When Theodosius ordered a massacre in Salonica to punish the citizens for a rebellion against the garrison, he had to humble himself in the cathedral of Milan before Ambrose lifted his excommunication. See study by N. Q. King (1960).

Theodosius II, 401–50, Roman emperor of the East (408–50), son and successor of Arcadius. He preferred the study of theology and astronomy to public affairs, which he left to the guidance of his sister, PULCHERIA—and, at times, to that of his wife EUDOCIA. The chief political events of his reign were the establishment (425) of VALENTINIAN III as emperor in the West, the raids into the empire by the Huns under ATTILA, and the conferences held with Attila in regard to the ever-increasing tribute he demanded. In 431, Theodosius summoned the Council of Ephesus, which condemned NESTORIANISM, and in 449 he convoked and upheld the Robber Synod, which declared the orthodoxy of Eutychianism (see EUTYCHES). Among his other activities were the founding (425) of the higher school (or university) of Constantinople and the publication (438) of the THEODOSIAN CODE. His brother-in-law, Marcian, succeeded him.

Theodosius, d. 376, Roman general under VALENTINIAN I. He defeated (368–69) the Picts and Scots in Britain and the Alemanni in Gaul (369). He suppressed (372–74) a Berber uprising in N Africa, but was executed at Carthage by Valentinian's successor Gratian on unknown charges. His son became emperor as Theodosius I.

Theodosius the Great: see THEODOSIUS I.

Theodotians, small heretical sect, formed c.190 by Theodotus, a Byzantine. It lasted until the end of the 4th cent. The Theodotians taught that Jesus was a man, who became the Christ only after his baptism (a concept basic both to MONARCHIANISM and to ADOPTIONISM).

Théodule: see MATTERHORN, peak, Switzerland.

Theognis (thēŏg′nĭs), fl. 6th cent. B.C., Greek didactic poet of Megara. An aristocrat with fierce partisan feelings, he wrote for his young friend Cyrnus a series of elegies, often passionate in hate and in love, counseling moderation, faithfulness, and duty. Among the 1,400 surviving lines attributed to him are some known to be by other writers.

theology (thēŏl′əjē), in Christianity, the systematic study of the nature of God and His relationship with man and with the world. Although other religions may be said to have theologies, this is a matter of controversy within, for instance, JUDAISM (which holds that God is unknowable). This article will therefore confine itself to Christian theology. The development of theology in Christendom arose from the need for educated Christians of the ancient world to express their ideas in terminology familiar in current thought. Hence arose the close relation of Christian theology with Greek philosophy formulated by the Greek and Latin FATHERS OF THE CHURCH. St. AUGUSTINE, a Latin Father and one of the greatest of theologians, introduced and standardized in his writings what became the official theology of the church. The great theological problems of ancient times were the relation of Jesus with God and with man, and the relation of God with man. The struggle over ARIANISM (on the nature of Jesus) was probably the most serious theological quarrel Christianity has known, and the problem of GRACE has not ceased to arouse theologians. The thought of NEOPLATONISM has some connection with Christian theology, especially in the early Middle Ages. In reaction to it SCHOLASTICISM arose to vindicate reason and to criticize the whole theological system. Scholasticism differentiated carefully between theology and philosophy by confining theology to the field of the systematization and investigation of revealed truths; in this distinction philosophy is to proceed always from reason and does not investigate the truths that transcend reason. The distinction is maintained explicitly by Roman Catholic thinkers and implicitly by conservative Protestants. According to this differentiation CALVINISM and LUTHERANISM are theologies, not philosophies. As a result of the 18th-century Enlightenment, especially the work of Immanuel Kant, a new rational theology arose in the 19th cent. This must be carefully distinguished from the "rationalism" of scholasticism, because 19th-century rational theology assumes as axiomatic the ability of reason to criticize adequately every truth. The theological school of Tübingen was the center for the extreme "rationalistic theologians," and there the "higher criticism" of the Bible, which revolutionized much of Protestant thought, was brought to its first fruition. The most profound of 19th-century Protestant German theologians, and perhaps the most influential of the new rationalists, was Friedrich SCHLEIERMACHER. The new rationalistic theology developed very rapidly, and hardly any two theologians of it agree in detail; there are various systems of MODERNISM. In more recent times there has also arisen an existentialist theology, represented by the work of Paul TILLICH and Reinhold NIEBUHR. It stresses that man, however endowed with reason, must ultimately rely on the goodness of God. Rudolf BULTMANN further introduced the notion of "demythologizing" the New Testament in order to arrive at the essential message contained within it.

Theophilus (thēŏf′ĭləs), person to whom St. Luke's Gospel and the Acts of the Apostles are addressed. Luke 1.3; Acts 1.1.

Theophrastus (thē″ōfrăs′təs) [Gr.,=divinely speaking], c.372–c.287 B.C., Greek philosopher, Aristotle's successor as head of the PERIPATETICS. The school flourished under his leadership. He wrote on many subjects, but his works on plants are perhaps the most important of his technical writings. His *Characters,* a series of sketches of various ethical types, provides a valuable picture of his time. It anticipates such studies as those by Sir Thomas Overbury, John Earle, and La Bruyère.

Theopompus (thē″ōpŏm′pəs), fl. 4th cent. B.C., Greek historian and rhetorician, b. Chios. He studied with the orator ISOCRATES and became a friend of both Philip and Alexander of Macedon. His pro-Macedonian sympathies often caused trouble with his fellow Greeks. He wrote the *Hellenica,* a history of Greece from 411 B.C. to 394 B.C., and the *Philippica,* a discursive chronicle of Philip's life.

theorbo (thēôr′bō), large LUTE of the baroque period. It had an extra set of bass strings, not stopped on a fingerboard as the regular set are but plucked as open strings. These made it more suitable for playing baroque music than was the lute. It originated in the 16th cent. and survived until the end of the 18th cent. Its name was also spelled theorbe, theorboe, or tiorba.

Theorell, Axel Hugo Teodor, 1903–, Swedish biochemist, M.D. Caroline Institute, Stockholm, 1930. The results of an illness caused him to abandon his career as a physician, and he began to teach at the Univ. of Uppsala. He became (1937) professor of biochemistry and later head of the department at the Nobel medical institute, Stockholm. He was awarded the 1955 Nobel Prize in Physiology and Medicine for his discoveries concerning oxidation enzymes. Theorell was also the first to produce a pure form of myoglobin, the red-colored protein of muscles.

theorem, in mathematics and logic, statement in words or symbols that can be established by means of deductive logic; it differs from an AXIOM in that a PROOF is required for its acceptance. A lemma is a theorem that is demonstrated as an intermediate step in the proof of another, more basic theorem. A corollary is a theorem that follows as a direct consequence of another theorem or an axiom. There are many famous theorems in mathematics, often known by the name of their discoverer, e.g., the Pythagorean Theorem, concerning right triangles. One of the most famous unsolved problems of number theory is the proof of Fermat's Last Theorem: that 2 is the largest integer n for which the equation $x^n + y^n = z^n$ holds true, where x, y, and z are also integers.

theory, in music, discipline involving the construction of a cognitive system to be used as a tool for comprehending musical compositions. The discipline is subdivided into what can be called speculative and analytic theory. Speculative theory engages in reconciling with music certain philosophical observations of man and nature. It can be prescriptive when it imposes these extramusical contentions to establish an aesthetic norm. Music theory tended toward this aspect until the 20th cent. An example is the attempt to assert the superiority of tonal music over other systems by reference to the relationship of the triad to the natural overtone series. Analytic theory, on the other hand, undertakes detailed study of individual pieces. Analyses of compositions of a particular genre are synthesized into a general system, or reference, against which the individuality of these pieces can be perceived. In more general usage the term *theory* is used to include the study of acoustics, harmony, and ear training. In ancient Greece music theory was mainly concerned with describing different scales (modes) and their emotional character. This theory was transmitted, largely erroneously, to medieval Europe by the Roman philosopher BOETHIUS in his *De musica* (6th cent. A.D.). Medieval European theory dealt with notation, modal and rhythmic systems, and the relation of music to Christianity. Gioseffo Zarlino (1515–90) was the first to consider the triad as a compositional reference. In the 18th cent. Jean Philippe RAMEAU further codified the major-minor system and the concept of tonal center. The writings of Heinrich SCHENKER are among the most important in the sphere of tonal theory. Major contemporary theorists are Paul Hindemith, who propounded the idea of non-triadic pitch centrality, and Milton BABBITT, who has published revealing explications of twelve-tone music.

theosophy (thēŏs'əfē) [Gr.,=divine wisdom], philosophical system having affinities with MYSTICISM and claiming insight into the nature of God and the world through direct knowledge, philosophical speculation, or some physical process. This system of thought differs from many other philosophical positions in that it begins with an assumption of the absolute reality of the essence of God, from which it deduces the essentially spiritual nature of the universe. Other assumptions frequently found in theosophical doctrine are that God is the transcendent source of all being and all good; that evil exists in the world because of man's desire for finite goods and may be overcome by complete absorption in the infinite; and that sacred writings and doctrines are interpreted through allegory. This is the position of much speculative mysticism. However, mysticism generally confines itself to the soul's relation to God, while the theosophist uses his theories to formulate a complete philosophy of man and nature. The Neoplatonists, the Gnostics, and the Cabalists are generally considered types of theosophists. PARACELSUS is an example of the Renaissance philosopher who combined scientific ideas with theosophical speculation. More recent theosophists include Jakob BOEHME, F. W. J. Schelling, and Emanuel Swedenborg. Boehme, regarded as the father of modern theosophy, developed a complete theosophical system attempting to reconcile the existence of an all-powerful and all-good God with the presence of evil in the world. The philosophy and theology of the Orient, especially of India, contain a vast body of theosophical doctrine. Vedic, Buddhist, and Brahmanical literature are all charged with a mystical idea of a universal, eternal principle, basic to all life (see HINDUISM and BUDDHISM). Unity of living may be achieved by man through proper attitudes and exercises. Modern theosophy draws much of its vocabulary from Indian sources. The universe is viewed as existing on seven different levels, and human action is graded according to those levels, ranging from gross physical life to the complete perfection of the Universal Self. The latent spiritual power of man, realized in great spiritual leaders (such as the mahatmas), is considered almost boundless. To gain real spiritual knowledge and power the soul must pass through several existences (see TRANSMIGRATION OF SOULS) and gain much occult knowledge (stored in the soul, not the mind). The Theosophical Society, with which theosophy is now generally identified, was founded in 1875 by Helena Petrovna BLAVATSKY; associated with her were H. S. Olcott and W. Q. JUDGE. In 1895 Judge was the leader of a secession movement, and further divisions and schisms subsequently took place. The objects of the society are to form the nucleus of a universal brotherhood of humanity; to give encouragement to the study of comparative religions, philosophies, and sciences; and to carry on investigations of the laws of nature and of man's latent powers. An active exponent of theosophy in Europe, America, and the East was Annie BESANT, who added many works to the literature on the subject. Among other authoritative writings are those of Blavatsky, including *The Secret Doctrine* (1888, repr. 1964) and *Key to Theosophy* (1931, rev. ed. 1969). See also G. N. Drinkwater, *Theosophy and the Western Mysteries* (1944); C. W. Leadbeater, *Textbook of Theosophy* (10th ed. 1967).

Theotocopoulos, Domenicos: see GRECO, EL.

The Pas (päz, pä), town (1971 pop. 6,062), W Man., Canada, on the Saskatchewan River. Founded as a fur-trading post, it became in 1920 the starting point and headquarters of the Hudson Bay Railway to Churchill and an outfitting point for prospecting and mining expeditions into the northern mineral belt of Manitoba and Saskatchewan. In 1967 the provincial government began the development of a forest products industry in the area.

Thera, Greece: see THÍRA.

Theramenes (thərăm'ənēz), c.455–404? B.C., Athenian statesman. He helped to establish (411 B.C.) the oligarchical Four Hundred but was later active in overthrowing them. He fought in the Peloponnesian War, notably in the battle of Cyzicus (now in Turkey) and in the capture of Byzantium. In the great battle of Arginusae (406), where he commanded one ship, several Athenian ships were destroyed; Theramenes failed to rescue his men, but he was exonerated. Sent (404) to negotiate peace with Sparta, he was accused of treachery because of his deliberate waste of three months in discussion while Athens was under siege. He was elected one of the THIRTY TYRANTS. CRITIAS denounced him and caused him to be put to death. There was a great difference of opinion among the Greeks about Theramenes' motives in his frequent political shifts and his delay in negotiating.

Therapeutae (thĕrəpyo͞o'tē) [Gr.,=worshipers], Jewish monastic order living on the shore of Lake Mareotis, Egypt, about the 1st cent. A.D. They led an ascetic life devoted to solitary prayer and study of the scriptures, gathering on the sabbath for study and a communal meal. They may have a connection with the Essenes, although evidence is scanty. The only ancient source to mention them is Philo's *De vita contemplativa.*

therapy group: see GROUP PSYCHOTHERAPY.

Theravada Buddhism: see BUDDHISM.

Theresa or **Teresa, Saint** (Theresa of Ávila) (both: tĭrē'sə, -zə), 1515–82, Spanish Carmelite nun, Doctor of the Church, one of the principal saints of the Roman Catholic Church, one of the greatest mystics, and a leading figure in the Catholic Reformation. Her original name was Teresa de Cepeda y Ahumada, and her name in religion was Theresa of Jesus. She came of a well-to-do noble family. She entered the Carmelite order (possibly in 1536), suffered a serious illness, went through an arid period, and underwent (c.1555) a "second conversion," after which she experienced inner visions and went far in the path of mysticism. She had entertained a desire to found a house of reformed Carmelites (the Discalced, or Barefoot, Carmelites, living in strict observance of the rule) long before she had the opportunity in 1562 to found the Convent of St. Joseph in Ávila. Other foundations were made, and in the busy years that followed she traveled much to the various houses. She also founded convents of friars, having as her collaborator another great mystic, St. John of the Cross. One of the most remarkable women of all time, St. Theresa combined intense practicality with the most rarefied spirituality. Astute, shrewd, sometimes blunt, she yet kept the simplicity of water (water was one of her favorite metaphors) and had the same life-giving effect on those around her. She was an excellent and tireless manager. Her personal charm and tact helped her and the reform in the long years of persecution—mostly at the hands of the unreformed clergy—and she triumphed in the end. The Discalced Carmelites were finally separated from the older order. The reawakening of religious fervor that she brought about in Spain was astonishing. Her abounding energy and her good nature communicated themselves to her associates, who worked as if inspired. Soon after her death the movement spread beyond Spain and across Christendom, having a profound effect on the Catholic Reformation. She brought mysticism and its fruits to the common man. Feast: Oct. 15. *Literary Works.* The writings of St. Theresa have gained a steadily widening audience from the 16th cent. to the present. They are celebrated as literary masterpieces; their theological importance was underscored in 1970 when Pope Paul VI named St. Theresa a Doctor of the Church, the first woman so honored. The Castilian in which St. Theresa wrote stems from common speech, and the imagery is rich but simple. Candor and overflowing spiritual strength lend a greater beauty to the sometimes terse, sometimes discursive expressions. Her works, like herself, were dominated by love of God and characterized by humor, intelligence, and common sense. They are great literature but are far more important as founts of modern mysticism. The *Life* (written 1562–65) is a spiritual autobiography written for her confessors and containing not only the record of her progress in mysticism but also short treatises on prayer and vision; editions usually include the supplementary *Relations,* short pieces written for the same purpose as the *Life.* Her *Way of Perfection* was written after 1565 to supply her nuns worthy instruction on prayer; it is still found very useful by the religious and by laymen. In *Interior Castle* (written in 1577) she gives a glowing and powerful picture of the contemplative life; it is considered by many even finer than the *Life.* The *Foundations* (written 1573–82) is an account of the launching of her order. Her letters—brisk, vigorous, full of wisdom and humor—are much loved. She also wrote shorter pieces—*Exclamations of the Soul to God* (1569), rhapsodic meditations; a commentary on the mystic significance of the Song of Solomon; the *Constitutions,* for the Discalced Carmelite nuns; and *Method for the Visitation of Convents of Discalced Nuns.* She also wrote poems, many not rising above the level of serviceable verse. There have been several translations of her writings, the most recent by E. Allison Peers (3 vol., 1957). See biographies by H. A. Hatzfeld (1969) and E. A. Peers (1945, repr. 1973); studies by E. W. T. Dickens (1963) and R. T. Petersson (1970).

Theresa or **Teresa, Saint** (Theresa of Lisieux), 1873–97, French Carmelite nun, one of the most widely loved saints of the Roman Catholic Church, b. Alençon. Her original name was Thérèse Martin, and her name in religion was Theresa of the Child Jesus. The youngest of five daughters of a watchmaker, she became, as proclaimed by Pope Pius XI, "the greatest saint of modern times." At the age of 15 she was permitted to follow two of her sisters into the Carmelite convent at Lisieux. There she spent the remaining nine years of her life and died of tuberculosis. Many miracles are attributed to her, but perhaps the greatest miracle connected with her is that she became known at all. A simple nun in an obscure convent, she was remarkable only for her goodness. The holiness of her life so impressed her superior that Theresa was asked to write her spiritual autobiography. This has become one of the most widely read religious autobiographies. It is filled, as are her letters, with her message of seeking good with childlike simplicity. She exemplified the "little way"—achieving goodness by performing the humblest task and carrying out the most trivial action. St. Theresa was known as the Little Flower of Jesus. She was canonized in 1925, just 28 years after her death, and Lisieux has become a major place of pilgrimage. There are churches dedicated to St. Theresa throughout the Roman Catholic world, and meditations from her writings are read by many of the devout with the frequency of a manual of prayer. She is often represented in art with an armful of roses, because of her cryptic promise: "After my death, I will let fall a shower of roses." She is the patron of aviators and foreign missionaries. Feast: Sept. 30. See her autobiography (tr. 1958); biography by B. Ulanov (1965).

Therma, ancient Greece: see THESSALONÍKI.

thermae: see BATHS.

thermal capacity: see HEAT CAPACITY.

thermal pollution: see WATER POLLUTION.

thermal unit: see BRITISH THERMAL UNIT.

Thermidor (thûr'mĭdôr, Fr. tĕrmēdôr'), 11th month of the FRENCH REVOLUTIONARY CALENDAR. The coup d'etat of 9 Thermidor (July 27, 1794) marked the downfall of ROBESPIERRE and the end of the REIGN OF TERROR. The men who came into power were members of the old bourgeoisie and the newly rich who had profited from speculation and inflation. Extravagance in dress and manner prevailed. The JACOBINS were suppressed, but the royalists did not gain power. The Thermidorians removed economic controls, thus unleashing inflation, and established some freedom of worship. The principal figures in the so-called Thermidorian reaction were BARRAS, CAMBACÉRÈS, SIEYES, and TALLIEN. The period ended with the establishment of the DIRECTORY (1795). See Albert Mathiez, *The Thermidorian Reaction* (1929, tr. 1930).

thermionic emission (thûrm''īŏn'ĭk), emission of ELECTRONS or IONS by substances that are highly heated, the charged particles being called thermions. The number of thermions emitted increases rapidly as the temperature of the substance rises. The heated material may be in the form of a metal filament or of some compound that coats and is heated by the filament. If the heated body carries a positive or negative charge, the thermions will be of the same charge. At temperatures below red heat (see BLACK BODY), thermionic emission from uncharged bodies is chiefly positive; at higher temperatures it is negative. The effect was discovered by Thomas A. Edison in 1883 when he was working on filaments for the electric light. Thermionic emission finds important practical application in electronics, especially in the ELECTRON TUBE, since it is the mechanism by which electrons are emitted from the cathode.

thermite [from *Thermit,* a trade name], mixture of powdered or granular aluminum metal and powdered iron oxide. When ignited it gives off large amounts of heat. In wartime it has been used in incendiary bombs. A method for WELDING using thermite (invented by Dr. Hans Goldschmidt, a German chemist) is variously called the Goldschmidt process, the thermit process, or the aluminothermic process; it is used in welding large parts, e.g., castings, shafts, pipes, and steel rails. In the process the thermite, contained in a crucible, is ignited, e.g., by a strip of burning magnesium ribbon. The aluminum reduces the iron oxide to molten iron and forms a slag of aluminum oxide on its surface. The reaction is very exothermic; temperatures above 2500°C (4500°F) are often reached. Typically, the molten iron is poured into the joint to be welded, providing both heat for fusion and filler metal. Excess metal may be removed when the weld cools. Because thermite reacts with explosive violence once ignited, it cannot be heated as a mass to its kindling temperature (about 1550°C/2800°F); Goldschmidt was first to find a method for igniting thermite without explosion. He used a similar method to prepare various metals, e.g., chromium, manganese, and uranium, from their oxides.

thermocouple: see THERMOMETER; THERMOELECTRICITY.

thermodynamics, branch of science concerned with the nature of HEAT and its conversion to mechanical, electric, and chemical ENERGY. Historically, it grew out of efforts to construct more efficient heat engines—devices for extracting useful work from expanding hot gases. Toward the middle of the 19th cent. heat was recognized as a form of energy associated with the motion of the molecules of a body (see KINETIC-MOLECULAR THEORY OF GASES). Speaking more strictly, heat refers only to energy that is being transferred from one body to another. The total energy a body contains as a result of the positions and motions of its molecules is called its internal energy; in general, a body's TEMPERATURE is a direct measure of its internal energy. All bodies can increase their internal energies by absorbing heat (see HEAT CAPACITY). However, mechanical work done on a body can also increase its internal energy; e.g., the internal energy of a gas increases when the gas is compressed. Conversely, internal energy can be converted into mechanical energy; e.g., when a gas expands it does work on the external environment. In general, the change in a body's internal energy is equal to the heat absorbed from the environment minus the work done on the environment. This statement constitutes the first law of thermodynamics, which is a general form of the law of conservation of energy (see CONSERVATION LAWS). In thermodynamics, one usually considers both the thermodynamic system and its environment. The environment often contains one or more idealized heat reservoirs—heat sources with infinite heat capacity enabling them to give up or absorb heat without changing their temperature. (An ocean or other large body of water approximates a heat reservoir.) A typical thermodynamic system is a definite quantity of gas enclosed in a cylinder with a sliding piston that allows the volume to vary. In general, a thermodynamic system is defined by its temperature, volume, pressure, and chemical composition. A system is in equilibrium when these variables have the same value at all points. A mathematical statement that links the variables to show their interdependence is called an equation of state; the GAS LAWS are simple examples of such equations. Equations of state take on their simplest form when the KELVIN TEMPERATURE SCALE is used; on this scale 0° corresponds to the lowest temperature theoretically possible. When the external conditions are altered, a thermodynamic system will respond by changing its state; the temperature, volume, pressure, and chemical composition will adjust to a new equilibrium. The most important kinds of changes are adiabatic and isothermal changes. An adiabatic change is one that occurs without any flow of heat. The system is thermally insulated from the environment, and the first law of thermodynamics requires that the work done by or on the system be equal to the loss or gain of the system's internal energy. An isothermal change occurs when the system is in contact with a heat reservoir, so that the system remains at the temperature of the reservoir. In the isothermal process, heat flows from the reservoir if the system is expanding and into the reservoir if the system is being compressed. For an ideal gas the internal energy depends only on the temperature; hence the internal energy remains constant during an isothermal change, and the heat absorbed from or by the reservoir is equal to the work done on or by the environment. A cyclic process is one that returns the system, but not the environment, to its original state. A closed cycle consisting of two isothermal and two adiabatic transformations is called a Carnot cycle after the French physicist Sadi Carnot, who first discussed the implications of such cycles. During the Carnot cycle occurring in the operation of a heat engine, a definite quantity of heat is absorbed from a reservoir at high temperature; part of this heat is converted into useful work, but the balance is expelled into a low-temperature reservoir and thus "wasted." The greater the temperature difference between the two reservoirs, which in a steam engine are represented by the boiler and the condenser, the greater the fraction of absorbed heat that is converted into useful work. It is, however, theoretically impossible to convert all the heat extracted from the reservoir into useful work. In general it is impossible to perform a transformation whose only final result is to convert into useful work heat extracted from a source that is at the same temperature throughout. This statement is Lord Kelvin's version of the second law of thermodynamics. Another version of this law, formulated by R. J. E. Clausius, states that a transformation is impossible whose only final result is to transfer heat from a body at a given temperature to a body at higher temperature; in other words, the spontaneous flow of heat from hot to cold bodies is reversible only with the expenditure of mechanical or other nonthermal energy. These two versions of the second law of thermodynamics can be shown to be entirely equivalent. The second law is expressed mathematically in terms of the concept of ENTROPY. When a body absorbs an amount of heat Q from a reservoir at temperature T, the body gains and the reservoir loses an amount of entropy $S=Q/T$. Thus, in a reversible adiabatic process (no heat change) there is no change in the total entropy. If an amount of heat Q flows from a hot to a cold body, the total entropy increases; because $S=Q/T$ is larger for smaller values of T, the cold body gains more entropy than the hot body loses. The statement that heat never flows from a cold to a hot body can be generalized by saying that in no spontaneous process does the total entropy decrease. In all real physical processes entropy increases; in ideal reversible processes entropy remains constant. Thus, in the Carnot cycle, which is reversible, there is no change in the total entropy. The engine itself experiences no net change in entropy because it is returned to its original state at the end of the cycle. The entropy gained by the low temperature reservoir is equal to the entropy lost by the high temperature reservoir. However, according to the formula $S=Q/T$, less heat need be expelled into the low temperature reservoir than is extracted from the high temperature reservoir for equal and opposite changes in entropy. In the Carnot cycle this difference in heat appears as useful mechanical work. A postulate related to but independent of the second law is that it is impossible to cool a body to absolute zero by any finite process. Although one can approach absolute zero as closely as one desires, one cannot actually reach this limit. The third law of thermodynamics, formulated by Walter Nernst and also known as the Nernst heat theorem, states that if one could reach absolute zero, all bodies would have the same entropy. In other words, a body at absolute zero could exist in only one possible state, which would possess a definite energy, called the zero-point energy. This state is defined as having zero entropy. See Enrico Fermi, *Thermodynamics* (1937); F. W. Sears, *Thermodynamics, the Kinetic Theory of Gases, and Statistical Mechanics* (2d ed. 1953); M. W. Zemansky, *Heat and Thermodynamics* (5th ed. 1968).

thermoelectricity, direct conversion of heat into electric energy, or vice versa. The term is generally restricted to the irreversible conversion of electricity into heat described by the English physicist James P. Joule and to three reversible effects named for Seebeck, Peltier, and Thomson, their respective discoverers. According to Joule's law, a conductor carrying a current generates heat at a rate proportional to the product of the resistance (R) of the conductor and the square of the current (I). The German physicist Thomas J. Seebeck discovered in the 1820s that if a closed loop is formed by joining the ends of two strips of dissimilar metals and the two junctions of the metals are at different temperatures, an electromotive force, or voltage, arises that is proportional to the temperature difference between the junctions. A circuit of this type is called a thermocouple; a number of thermocouples connected in series is called a thermopile. In 1834 the French physicist Jean C. A. Peltier discovered an effect inverse to the Seebeck effect: If a current passes through a thermocouple, the temperature of one junction increases and the temperature of the other decreases, so that heat is transferred from one junction to the other. The rate of heat transfer is proportional to the current and the direction of transfer is reversed if the current is reversed. The Scottish scientist William Thomson (later Lord Kelvin) discovered in 1854 that if a temperature difference exists between any two points of a current-carrying conductor, heat is either evolved or absorbed depending upon the material. (This heat is not the same as Joule heat, or I^2R heat, which is always evolved.) If heat is absorbed by such a circuit, then heat may be evolved if the direction either of the current or of the temperature gradient is reversed. It can be shown that the Seebeck effect is a result of the combined Peltier and Thomson effects. Magnetic fields have been shown to influence all these effects. Many devices based on thermoelectric effects are used to measure temperature, transfer heat, or generate electricity.

thermography (thûr″mŏg′rəfē), contact photocopying process that produces a direct positive image and in which infrared rays are used to expose the copy paper. In a specially designed machine the original is placed in contact with a copy paper containing a heat-sensitive substance. As the infrared rays produced in the machine impinge on the dark or printed regions of the original, the heat generated is transferred to the adjoining areas of the sensitive paper. These areas become dark as well, creating an image of the original. As infrared rays are difficult to focus, the image formed is lacking in sharpness, resolution, and detail. The copies remain sensitive to heat, so that they may darken further with age. The advantages of this process are that it is low in cost and fast and can be performed with simple equipment.

thermohaline circulation: see OCEAN.

thermometer, instrument for measuring TEMPERATURE. Galileo and Sanctorius devised thermometers consisting essentially of a bulb with a tubular projection, the open end of which was immersed in a liquid. Heating or cooling the bulb affected the height of the column of liquid in the tube, on which a scale was marked. Over a century later appeared the three thermometers now most widely used—the Fahrenheit, the centigrade (Celsius), and the Réaumur (used to some extent in parts of Europe). The first, invented by Fahrenheit c.1714 in Danzig, initiated the use of mercury as a heat-measuring medium; the thermometer of Réaumur, invented c.1730, used alcohol; the Celsius, invented by Anders Celsius at Uppsala (probably 1742) is now most used in laboratory work. The clinical thermometer is a small tubular instrument of rather thick glass. It consists essentially of a small vacuum tube of uniform bore closed at one end and connected at the other with a mercury chamber (either a bulb or a short tube of larger bore). A Celsius or a Fahrenheit scale (or both) is etched on the front of the thermometer; opposite this the glass is milky or semiopaque, to facilitate reading the temperature. When heat is applied, the mercury expands and rises from the chamber past a narrowed point and up the small tube. This narrowed point prevents the mercury from sinking back until shaking forces it down. A thermocouple can be used as a thermometer for measuring temperatures outside the range of liquid-in-glass thermometers. It is based on the thermoelectric effect occurring when the two junctions of a closed loop made of two different metals are at different temperatures (see THERMOELECTRICITY).

thermonuclear energy: see NUCLEAR ENERGY.

thermopile: see THERMOELECTRICITY.

Thermopylae (thərmŏp′ĭlē) [Gr.,=hot gates, from hot mineral springs nearby], pass, E central Greece, SE of Lamía, between the cliffs of Mt. Oeta and the Malic Gulf. Silt accumulation has gradually widened the pass. In ancient times it was used as an entrance into Greece from the north. There in 480 B.C., Leonidas with his Spartans and their allies lost a heroic battle to the Persians under Xerxes (see PERSIAN WARS). At the pass in 279 B.C., the Greeks held back the Gauls under Brennus, who ultimately broke through, and in 191 B.C., Antiochus III of Syria was defeated there by the Romans.

thermosphere: see ATMOSPHERE.

thermostat, automatic device that regulates temperature in an enclosed area by controlling heating or refrigerating systems. It is commonly connected to one of these systems, turning it on or off in order to maintain a predetermined temperature. Its operating principle is based on the fact that one of its components expands or contracts significantly during a temperature change. This expansion or contraction actuates a control on a furnace, cooling system, or piece of machinery. The thermostat sometimes uses mercury, which expands when heated and rises in a glass tube until, at a predetermined point, it touches an electrical contact to complete a circuit and thereby actuate a control; conversely, during a lowering of temperature the mercury descends in the tube and breaks the circuit. The thermostat often uses a bimetallic strip, which is made of two thin metallic pieces of different composition that are bonded together. As the temperature of the strip changes, the two pieces change length at different rates, forcing the strip to bend. This bending causes the strip to make or break a circuit.

Thersander (thərsăn'dər), in Greek legend, son of Polynices. He avenged his father's death in the expedition of the EPIGONI and was made king of Thebes.

Thersites (thərsī'tēz), in Greek legend, member of the Greek army in the Trojan War. He was famous for his ugliness, his unpleasant temper, and his love of argument. When he mocked Achilles for mourning the dead Amazon queen Penthesilea, Achilles killed him.

Theseus (thē'syo͞os, -sēəs), in Greek mythology, hero of Athens; son of either King Aegeus or Poseidon. Before Aegeus left Troezen he placed his sword and sandals beneath a huge rock and told his wife Aethra that when their son, Theseus, could lift the rock he was to bring the gifts to his kingdom in Athens. At the age of 16 Theseus lifted the rock and began his journey, during which he freed the countryside of various monsters and villains (e.g., PROCRUSTES). When Theseus arrived at Athens, Medea, then wife of Aegeus, tried to kill him. Aegeus, however, recognized the sword and sandals, saved Theseus, and exiled Medea. Theseus subsequently had numerous adventures. His most famous exploit was against the Minotaur of King Minos of Crete. Theseus insisted on being one of the seven youths and seven maidens of Athens to be sacrificed to the monster as an annual tribute. He promised his father that if he were successful in killing the Minotaur he would on his return voyage replace his ship's black sails with white ones. Ariadne, daughter of King Minos, fell in love with Theseus and gave him a magic ball of thread to be dropped at the entrance of the LABYRINTH; it led Theseus to the Minotaur, which he killed, and he then followed the unwound thread back to the entrance. He left Crete with Ariadne but abandoned her at Naxos. When Theseus reached home he forgot to raise white sails. Aegeus saw black sails, and, thinking his son dead, the grief-stricken father threw himself into the sea, thereafter called the Aegean. As king of Athens, Theseus instituted several reforms, most notably the federalization of the scattered Attic communities. He journeyed to the land of the Amazons, where he abducted Antiope, who bore him HIPPOLYTUS. A vengeful Amazon army invaded Athens, but Theseus defeated it. Some say Antiope died fighting beside him in the battle; others claim that Theseus killed her when she objected to his marriage to PHAEDRA. For helping PIRITHOÜS to carry off Persephone, Theseus was imprisoned in Hades until Hercules rescued him. Upon his return to Athens, he found his once great kingdom a turmoil of corruption and rebellion. He regretfully sailed away and came to rest at Skyros, where he was treacherously murdered by King Lycomedes. Although Theseus is generally thought of as legendary, the Athenians believed he had been one of their early kings. See A. G. Ward, et al., *The Quest for Theseus* (1970).

Thespiae (thĕs'pē-ē"), ancient city of Greece, in S Boeotia, near Mt. Helicon (now Elikón) and SW of Thebes. The Thespians fought (479 B.C.) against the Persians at Thermopylae and Plataea. They joined (after 382 B.C.) the Spartans against their rivals, the Thebans. The famous statue of Eros by Praxiteles was a showpiece of Thespiae.

Thespis (thĕs'pĭs), fl. 534 B.C., of Icaria in Attica. In Greek tradition, he was the inventor of tragedy. Almost nothing is known of his life or works. He is supposed to have modified the dithyramb (which had been, in effect, exchanges between the leader and the chorus) by introducing an actor separate from the chorus. This actor was called the *hypocrite* or "responder." Thus there developed a spoken dialogue.

Thessalonians (thĕs"əlō'nēənz), two epistles of the New Testament, the 13th and 14th books in the usual order. They were written by St. PAUL from Corinth, A.D. c.52, addressed to the newly founded church at Thessalonica (Thessaloníki). First Thessalonians opens with a reminiscence of the founding of the Christian church there, all in a rather congratulatory tone. The second part (4–5) is taken up with advice on moral behavior and correction of one doctrinal point on which apparently Paul's converts had gone astray, the imminence and manner of the general resurrection. Second Thessalonians, a shorter letter written soon after, is stronger in condemning false notions that the Second Coming is at hand; in an apocalyptic passage St. Paul gives the signs that will precede the Judgment (2.1–12). This epistle includes an exhortation to work and a condemnation of idleness (3.6–12). Some scholars question the authenticity of the apocalyptic passage.

Thessaloníki (thĕ"sälōnē'kē) or **Salonica** (sălənē'-kə, səlŏn'ĭkə), city (1971 pop. 345,799), capital of Thessaloníki prefecture, N Greece, in Macedonia; on the Gulf of Thessaloníki, an inlet of the Aegean Sea, at the neck of the Khalkidhikí Peninsula. It is the second-largest city in Greece, a major modern port, and an industrial and commercial center. Exports from the port (opened in 1901) include grain, food products, tobacco, manganese and chrome ores, and hides. The city's industries produce textiles, machinery, metal goods, flour, cement, and explosives. Thessaloníki is also a transportation hub. It is the site of an annual trade fair. An old city, rich in history, Thessaloníki was founded (c.315 B.C.) by Cassander, king of Macedon, on or near the site of the ancient town of Therma, and was named for his wife. The city was located on the Via Egnatia, an important Roman road that linked Byzantium to Durrës (Dyrrhachium) on the Adriatic. It flourished after 146 B.C. as the capital of the Roman province of Macedon. Thessaloníki had from early times a sizeable Jewish colony, and it was an early Christian diocese. To the infant church there, St. Paul addressed his two epistles to the THESSALONIANS. Under the Byzantine Empire Thessaloníki was second only to Constantinople. The massacre (A.D. 390) of the rebellious citizens of Thessaloníki by order of Theodosius I led to the emperor's temporary excommunication. The city was occupied by the Saracens in 904 and by the Normans of Sicily in 1185. When in 1204 the leaders of the Fourth Crusade created a Latin empire (see CONSTANTINOPLE, LATIN EMPIRE OF), the kingdom of Thessaloníki, comprising most of N and central Greece, was its largest fief. It was given by Baldwin I to his rival Boniface, marquis of Montferrat, but it was seized (c.1222) by the Greek ruler of Epirus, who had himself proclaimed emperor. The kingdom of Thessaloníki fell into anarchy in the struggle between the Greek rulers of Epirus and the Greek emperors of Nicaea. In 1246 the city fell to the Nicaeans, who in 1261 restored it to the Byzantine Empire. Thessaloníki was conquered by the Ottoman Sultan Murad I in 1387, was restored to the Byzantine Empire c.1405, was bought by Venice in 1423, and was reconquered by the Ottoman Turks (under Murad II) in 1430. Thessaloníki remained in Ottoman hands until it was conquered by Greece in 1912 during the Balkan Wars. The city was the birthplace of Kemal Atatürk, the founder of modern Turkey, and was the headquarters of the Young Turk movement in the early 20th cent. In World War I the Allies landed (1915) at Thessaloníki, thus beginning the Thessaloníki campaigns, and in 1916 Venizelos established his pro-Allied provisional government of Greece there. A great fire in 1917 destroyed much of the city. Thessaloníki suffered considerable damage in World War II, and its large (c.50,000) Jewish population, which had been greatly increased in the late 15th and early 16th cent. by an influx of Jews from Spain, was nearly liquidated by the Germans. Although largely rebuilt in modern style, Thessaloníki still retains its famous white Byzantine walls, the 15th-century White Tower, and a Venetian citadel. The city is famous for its many fine churches, notably those of Hagia Sophia (modeled after its namesake in Istanbul and including fine mosaics), of St. George, and of St. Demetrius. The ruins of the triumphal arch of Emperor Constantine are there. The city is also known as Thessalonike, Thessalonica, Salonika, and Saloniki.

Thessaly (thĕs'əlē), largest ancient region of Greece in N central Greece. It corresponded roughly to the present-day nomes of Lárisa and Tríkkala, which form part of the modern region known as Thessaly. Ancient Thessaly was almost completely walled in by mountains, including Pindus, Ossa, and Othrys (now Othrís), and the plains were extremely fertile. Civilization dates from prehistoric times. Before 1000 B.C. a tribe called the Thessalians entered the area from the northwest. The chief Thessalian cities, Larissa (now Lárisa), Crannon, and Pherae, were oligarchical. The great families were the Aleuadae (at Larissa) and the Scopadae (at Crannon). The Thessalians were powerful in the 6th cent. B.C., partly through their control of the Amphictyonic League. Conflict between the oligarchies, however, contributed to Thessaly's decline. Jason, the tyrant of Pherae, succeeded (374 B.C.) in uniting Thessaly, which again became a force in Greece, but it did not remain powerful for long and was subjugated (344 B.C.) by Philip II of Macedon. Under the Roman emperors Thessaly was joined to Macedonia, but after the death of Constantine the Great it became a separate province. It passed (1355) to the Turks and was ceded to Greece in 1881. See A. J. B. Wace, *Prehistoric Thessaly* (1912); H. D. Hansen, *Early Civilization in Thessaly* (1933); and H. D. Westlake, *Thessaly in the Fourth Century B.C.* (1935).

Thetford Mines, city (1971 pop. 22,003), S Que., Canada, NE of Sherbrooke and S of Quebec. The city, developed after the discovery (1876) of large asbestos deposits, is located in one of the world's largest asbestos-producing regions. Chromium and feldspar are also mined.

Thetis (thē'tĭs), in Greek mythology, a nereid, mother of Achilles. She was loved by both Zeus and Poseidon, but because of a prophecy that her son would be greater than his father, the gods gave her in marriage to a mortal, Peleus. According to one legend, Thetis burned alive her first six sons and sent their immortal spirits to Olympus. Peleus, however, snatched the seventh, Achilles, from the fire and sent him to be raised by the centaur Chiron. See PARIS, in Greek mythology.

Theudas (thyo͞o'dăs), leader of insurgents mentioned by Gamaliel. Acts 5.36. Nothing is known of him; he is not the magician Theudas mentioned by Josephus.

Theus, Jeremiah (tho͞os, tois), c.1719–1744, American portrait painter, b. Switzerland. He emigrated to South Carolina as a child. By 1740, according to newspaper notices, he was painting portraits and teaching art in Charleston. His portraits were good likenesses. The Brooklyn Museum has a portrait of Elizabeth Rothmaler. See study by Margaret Middleton (1953).

Theveste: see TEBESSA, Algeria.

The Village, city (1970 pop. 13,695), Oklahoma co., central Okla., a residential suburb of Oklahoma City.

thiamine: see COENZYME; VITAMIN.

thiamine pyrophosphate: see COENZYME; VITAMIN.

Thibault, Jacques Anatole: see FRANCE, ANATOLE.

Thibaut IV (tēbō'), 1201–53, French trouvère, count of Champagne. He became Thibaut I, king of Navarre, in 1234, succeeding his uncle Sancho VII. He was defeated while leading a Crusade (1239), but he returned to become a poet and composer of first rank. Some of his songs and courtly verses are addressed to Blanche of Castile, regent of France.

Thibodaux (tĭb'ədō), city (1970 pop. 15,028), seat of Lafourche parish, SE La., on Bayou Lafourche; inc. 1838. It is the commercial center of an oil, sugarcane, and farm area in the bayou country. Petrochemicals are manufactured, and the area to the south attracts many fishermen and shellfish gatherers. Nearby is the home (built 1790) of Chief Justice Edward Douglass White, now a state memorial park. Among the many antebellum plantation houses in the area is "Rienzi," which was built in 1796. Nicholls State Univ. is there. Annual Mardi Gras celebrations attract visitors.

thick-knee, common name for terrestrial, Old World birds in the family Burhinidae. The name derives from the bird's thickened tarsal joints. Thick-knees are shy, solitary birds. They are rapid runners with long legs and partially webbed feet, which lack a hind toe. The wings may be long and pointed, or short and rounded, according to species. Generally they fly fast and low but only for short distances. In body length, thick-knees range from 14 to 20 in. (36–51 cm). Members of the genus *Burhinus* are among the smaller species. Their straight, stout bills are shorter than their heads. Thick-knees of the genus *Orthorhamphus* have massive bills considerably larger than their heads, while those of the genus *Esacus* are compressed and slightly upturned. Thick-knees are widely distributed throughout a range of temperate and tropical habitats including shore, scrub, desert, and savanna, but typically in somewhat open country. Their colorations vary with their backgrounds, usually dull gray-brown with darker streaks. They are nocturnal birds, with large, owl-like eyes. Their diet consists of a wide range of animals and plants, including insects, small mammals, seeds, and, occasionally, other birds. Their alternate name of stone curlew probably derives from their habit of laying their large eggs directly on bare, stony ground. The eggs range in color from cream to brown, with various darker markings according to local soil colors. Both sexes participate in incubation, and the highly precocious chicks are able to leave the nest almost immediately upon hatching. Thick-knees are classified in the phylum CHORDATA, subphylum Vertebrata, class Aves, order Charadriiformes, family Burhinidae.

Thierry I: see THEODORIC I.

Thierry, Augustin (ōgüstăN′ tyĕrē′), 1795–1856, French historian. His vivid literary style, romantic treatment of events, and use of contemporary documents helped to create interest in historical studies in the early 19th cent. His two most famous works, *Histoire de la conquête de l'Angleterre par les Normands* (3 vol., 1825; tr. *History of the Conquest of England by the Normans*, 3 vol., 1825) and *Récits des temps mérovingiens* (2 vol., 1840; tr. *Narratives of the Merovingian Era*, 1845), were great popular successes; however, they lacked exact scholarship and advanced conclusions based on dubious premises. See R. N. Smithson, *The Evolution of the Historical Method of Augustin Thierry* (1970).

Thiers, Adolphe (ädôlf′ tyĕr), 1797–1877, French statesman, journalist, and historian. After studying law at Aix-en-Provence, he went (1821) to Paris and joined the group of writers that attacked the reactionary government of King CHARLES X. Thiers reflected the views of the upper bourgeoisie. His *History of the French Revolution* (10 vol., 1823–27; tr., 5 vol., 1895) illustrated his moderate liberal views. With F. A. M. MIGNET and others he started (1830) the journal *National*, which had an important part in bringing about the JULY REVOLUTION of 1830. He held ministerial posts under LOUIS PHILIPPE, whose candidacy as king of the French he had promoted. As minister of the interior, he brutally suppressed the workers' insurrection of April, 1834, in Paris and Lyons. Thiers was premier in 1836, but his projected intervention against the CARLISTS in Spain caused his dismissal. In 1840 he again headed a cabinet, but his aggressive foreign policy—this time he sought to intervene in favor of MUHAMMAD ALI in Egypt, thus bringing France to the brink of war with Great Britain—once again lacked royal support and brought about his fall. He became a liberal opponent of the July Monarchy and again turned to writing, beginning his *History of the Consulate and the Empire* (20 vol., 1845–62; tr. 1845–62). In the midst of the FEBRUARY REVOLUTION of 1848, Louis Philippe again appointed him premier, but both king and premier were swept aside by the revolutionary tide. Elected (1848) to the constituent assembly, Thiers was a leader of the right-wing liberals and bitterly opposed the socialists. He supported Louis Napoleon Bonaparte (later Emperor NAPOLEON III) for president of the French republic, but his opposition to Bonaparte's coup d'etat in Dec., 1851, led to his arrest and exile. He was allowed to return not long afterward, but for ten years he remained out of government affairs. In 1863 he was elected to the legislature, where he opposed the emperor and helped to bring about reforms. Although he had previously favored an aggressive foreign policy, Thiers spoke out (1870) against involvement in the FRANCO-PRUSSIAN WAR. Vindicated by the disastrous defeat of France, he was chosen chief executive of the provisional government at Bordeaux in 1871. He negotiated the preliminary Peace of Versailles with Otto von Bismarck and ordered his troops to suppress the Commune of Paris of 1871—an order carried out with ferocious severity. In Aug., 1871, his title became president of the republic. Credit for France's quick payment of its war indemnity to Germany and for the consequent evacuation (1873) of France by German troops belongs largely to Thiers's efficient economic policy. However, his insistence upon a conservative republic alienated both the monarchist majority and the left-wing minority in the national assembly, and in 1873 he was forced to resign. In the elections of 1877 he helped to restore republican unity and bring about the election of a republican legislature. Although immensely popular in their time, Thiers's historical works are today generally regarded as superficial and inaccurate eulogies of the French Revolution and of Napoleon, written from the bourgeois point of view. See his memoirs (1903, tr. 1915); J. M. S. Allison, *Thiers and the French Monarchy* (1926, repr. 1968) and *Monsieur Thiers* (1932).

Thiès (tyĕs), city (1970 est. pop. 91,000), W Senegal, on the Dakar-Niger RR. It is the trade center for a farming region where groundnuts, cassava, and livestock are raised. Manufactures include construction materials, wood furniture and plywood, and textiles. Aluminum phosphate is mined nearby and processed in Thiès. The city was captured in 1862 by the French, who established a military post there in 1864.

Thiess, Frank (frängk tēs), 1890–, German novelist, b. Livonia. Thiess's many novels, noted for psychological insight, trace the changes in 20th-century German society. Among them are *The Devil's Shadow* (1924, tr. 1928), *Gateway to Life* (1926, tr. 1927), and *Gäa* (1957). See his autobiographical *Verbrannte Erde* (1963).

Thieu, Nguyen Van (nəwĭn′ vän tē′o͞o, tyo͞o), 1923–, president of the Republic of (South) Vietnam (1967–). After World War II he joined the Viet Minh, Ho Chi Minh's national liberation organization, but he later left it because of its Communist policies. He rose rapidly in the South Vietnamese army, becoming a division commander in the war against the Viet Cong and Communist North Vietnam. In 1963 he helped lead the coup d'etat that overthrew President Diem. Together with Nguyen Cao KY, Thieu was a leading force in a succession of South Vietnamese governments from 1963 to 1967. He was elected president in 1967 and retained office in a controversial election in 1971. His dictatorial domestic policies and his refusal to accept a political settlement of the war with North Vietnam (see VIETNAM WAR) brought criticism from many nations, but the United States continued to support him.

thimbleweed, name for several plants, especially an ANEMONE.

Thimbu: see BHUTAN.

Thimnathah (thĭm′nəthə): see TIMNAH **3.**

thin film circuits: see MICROELECTRONICS.

Thingvallavatn (thĕng′gvät″lävä″tən), Icelandic *Þingvallavatn*, lake, c.35 sq mi (90 sq km), SW Iceland, E of Reykjavík. It is Iceland's largest lake. On its north shore is historic Thingvellir.

Thingvellir (thĕng′gvĕt″lĭr), Icelandic *Þingvellir*, a wide lava plain, since 1928 a national park, the ancient place of assembly of the Icelandic ALTHING, which met there from 930 to 1798. It is located c.30 mi (50 km) NE of Reykjavík, on the north shore of Thingvallavatn.

thiol: see MERCAPTAN.

Thionville (tyôNvĕl′), Ger. *Diedenhofen*, town (1968 pop. 38,469), Moselle dept., NE France, in Lorraine. It is a center for metallurgical and chemical industries. The town was a favorite of Charlemagne. In the testament of Thionville (806) Charlemagne divided his kingdom among his sons. After being captured by the Prussians in 1870, the town remained German until 1919.

Thíra or **Thera** (both: thĕr′ə), volcanic island (1971 pop. 6,196), c.30 sq mi (80 sq km), SE Greece, in the Aegean Sea; one of the Cyclades. It is noted for its wine. Pumice stone and powdered tufa are exported. According to tradition, the island was first settled by Phoenicians and later by Laconians under the leader Thera. In 631 B.C. colonists from the island founded Cyrene in N Africa. From the Middle Ages until the 20th cent. Thíra was known as Santorin, for St. Irene, the protector of the island.

third market, over-the-counter trading of stocks and bonds that are also listed on formal exchanges. Large institutional securities holders engage in third market operations to avoid high commission fees on the regulated exchanges. Third market sales of securities listed on the New York Stock Exchange amount to almost 5% of the Exchange's volume.

Third Republic: see FRANCE.

Third World, technologically less advanced nations of Asia, Africa, and Latin America, generally characterized as, in addition to being poor in money income, poorly fed and largely agrarian. The nations also tend to have a high rate of illiteracy and disease, rapidly growing populations, and new, relatively inexperienced, and often unstable governments. Until recently most of the Third World was dominated by Western nations through some form of colonialism. The term "Third World" is intended to distinguish these nations from two groups of technologically advanced nations, one—the so-called Western nations—largely influenced by the United States and the other—the Soviet bloc—by the Soviet Union. Communist China, which used to be classified as a Third World country, might now more accurately be described as a fourth power in the balance of nations. See A. F. Noqueira, *The Third World* (1967); Peter Worsley, *The Third World* (2d ed. 1967); A. R. Kasdan, *The Third World: A New Focus for Development* (1973).

Thirlmere, lake, c.3 mi (5 km) long, in the Lake District, NW England, near Keswick. In 1894, through the construction of a high dam (which raised the water level c.50 ft/15 m) and an aqueduct c.100 mi (160 km) long, it became a source of water supply for Manchester.

Thirlwall, Connop (kŏn′əp thûrl′wôl), 1797–1875, English historian. He was bishop of St. David's, Wales, from 1840. His chief work is his *History of Greece* (8 vol., 1835–44); it was the first truly scholarly survey of Greece in any language. As a historian, Thirlwall was fair and judicious, his scholarship impeccable, and his knowledge of sources unexcelled. See biography by J. C. Thirlwall, Jr. (1936).

thirst, sensation that indicates the body's need for water. Dry or salty food and dry, dusty air may induce such a sensation by depleting moisture in the mucous membranes of the mouth and throat. Relief may be obtained by moistening the mucous membranes with a small amount of water. Relief is only temporary, however, if thirst is due to a generalized depletion of water in the system. About three fourths of the body is composed of fluids, and the average adult requires 2½ qt (2.4 liters) of fluid per day, supplied by water, other beverages, and foods. Depriving the body of water for any length of time interferes with its metabolism and functions, causing dehydration, which is eventually fatal. The unnatural thirst that accompanies fever, diabetes, and other disorders is caused by a rapid reduction of the body fluids.

Thirteen Colonies, the, term used for the colonies of British North America that joined together in the American Revolution against the mother country, adopted the Declaration of Independence in 1776, and became the Unites States. They were New Hampshire, Massachusetts, Rhode Island, Connecticut, New York, New Jersey, Pennsylvania, Delaware, Maryland, Virginia, North Carolina, South Carolina, and Georgia. They are also called the Thirteen Original States.

Thirty-nine Articles: see CREED **5.**

Thirty Tyrants, oligarchy of ancient Athens (404–403 B.C.). It was created by LYSANDER under Spartan auspices after the Peloponnesian War. CRITIAS and THERAMENES were prominent members. It was overthrown at Piraeus (now Piraiévs) by THRASYBULUS.

Thirty Years War, 1618–48, general European war fought mainly in Germany. There were many issues, territorial, dynastic, and religious. The extent of religious motives is debated, but cannot be dismissed, particularly in explaining individual behavior. Throughout the war there were shifting alliances and local peace treaties. The war as a whole may be considered a struggle of German Protestant princes and foreign powers (France, Sweden, Denmark, England, the United Provinces) against the unity and power of the Holy Roman Empire as represented by the Hapsburgs, allied with the Catholic princes, and against the Hapsburgs themselves. The war began with the resistance and eventual revolt of Protestant nobles in Bohemia, which was under Hapsburg domination, against the Catholic king Ferdinand (later Holy Roman Emperor FERDINAND II). It spread through Europe because of the constitutional frailty of the Holy Roman Empire, the inability of the German states to act in concert, and the ambitions of other European powers.

The Bohemian Period. The revolt began in Prague, where two royal officers were hurled from a window by Protestant members of the Bohemian diet—the so-called Defenestration of Prague (May, 1618). Ferdinand was declared deposed and the Bohemian throne was offered to Frederick V, the elector palatine. Revolt also appeared in other Hapsburg dominions, especially under Gabriel BETHLEN in Transylvania. Duke MAXIMILIAN I of Bavaria, with the army of the Catholic League under TILLY, helped the imperial forces defeat the Bohemians at the White Mt. near Prague (Nov., 1620). JOHN GEORGE of Saxony, a leading German Protestant prince, supported Ferdinand. Frederick, ever afterward called the Winter King, had lost his brief hold on Bohemia. The war continued in the Palatinate, and severe repression began in Bohemia.

The Palatinate Period. MANSFELD and CHRISTIAN OF BRUNSWICK led the revolutionary forces in the PALATINATE. Frederick expected aid from his father-in-law, James I of England, but got no effectual help. The Palatinate was taken by Tilly; he won at Wimpfen and Höchst (1622). Frederick's lands were confiscated by the emperor, and the Upper Palatinate and the electorate were conferred on Maximilian of Bavaria. The imperialist victory at Stadtlohn (1623) practically ended one phase of the war.

The Danish Period. The new phase saw the German war expanded into an international conflict. Christian IV of Denmark came into the fighting, principally because of his fear of the rise of Hapsburg power in N Germany; he openly avowed religious motives but hoped also to enlarge his German possessions. England and the United Provinces gave a subsidy to aid the opponents of the Hapsburgs, and England sent a few thousand soldiers. Christian IV advanced into Germany. The emperor's cause was advanced by the work of WALLENSTEIN, who gathered an effective army and defeated Mansfeld at Dessau (1626). A little later the Danish king was soundly defeated by Tilly at Lutter. The imperial armies swept through most of Germany. Wallenstein went into Jutland and vanquished the Danes but failed before Stralsund (1628). In 1629, Denmark, by the Treaty of Lübeck, withdrew from the war and surrendered the N German bishoprics. The Edict of Restitution (1629), issued by Ferdinand II, attempted to enforce the ecclesiastical reservation of the Peace of Augsburg and declared void Protestant titles to lands secularized after 1552; its full application would have had a disastrous effect on German Protestantism and naturally aroused the Protestant states to determined, if at first latent, hostility.

The Swedish Period. GUSTAVUS II (Gustavus Adolphus) of Sweden now came into the war. His territorial ambitions had embroiled him in wars with Poland, and he feared that Ferdinand's maritime designs might threaten Sweden's mastery of the Baltic. Moved also by his Protestantism, he declared against the emperor and was supported by an understanding with Catholic France, then under the leadership of Cardinal Richelieu. Swedish troops marched into Germany. Meanwhile Ferdinand had been prevailed upon (1630) to dismiss Wallenstein, who had powerful enemies in the empire. Tilly now headed the imperial forces. He was able to take the city of Magdeburg while the Protestant princes hesitated to join the Swedes. Only John George of Saxony, vascillating in his support between Tilly and the Swedish king, joined Gustavus Adolphus, who offered him better terms. The combined forces crushed Tilly at Breitenfeld (1631), thus winning N Germany. Gustavus Adolphus triumphantly advanced and Tilly was defeated and fatally wounded in the battle of the Lech (1632). Wallenstein, recalled with some pleading by the emperor, took the field. He defeated the Saxon forces and later met the Swedish forces at Lützen (Nov., 1632); there the imperialists were defeated, but Gustavus Adolphus was killed and the anti-Hapsburg troops were disorganized. Wallenstein after his great defeat remained inactive and entered into long negotiations with the enemy. Meanwhile the able anti-imperialist general, BERNHARD OF SAXE-WEIMAR, stormed Regensburg (1633). Wallenstein was murdered in 1634 by imperialist conspirators. Soon afterward the imperial forces under GALLAS defeated Bernhard at Nördlingen (Feb., 1634). Germany was in economic ruin, her fields devastated and bloodsoaked. There was strong feeling in Germany against the foreign soldiers that overran the land. A general desire for peace led to the Peace of Prague (1635). This agreement drastically modified the Edict of Restitution, thus helping to reconcile Catholic and Protestant. It was accepted by almost all the German princes and free cities. A united imperial army was to move against the Swedish troops in Germany. A general peace seemed to be forthcoming, but Richelieu was unwilling to see the Hapsburgs retain power.

The Franco-Swedish Period. France entered openly into the war in 1635. OXENSTIERNA, the Swedish chancellor, anxious to preserve Sweden's hold in Germany, supported Richelieu. The final stage of the Thirty Years War began. The war now occupied most of Europe, with fighting in the Low Countries, where the United Provinces and France opposed Spain; in Italy, where France and Spain struggled for power; in France; in Germany; in the Iberian peninsula, where Portugal revolted against, and France attacked, Spain; and in the North, where Denmark opposed Sweden. The Austrian forces went into France and achieved some success, but this was temporary. For the most part this period of the war was disastrous for the empire. Bernhard of Saxe-Weimar and the Swedish general, Baner, were victorious in Germany. In 1636, Baner won a notable victory at Wittstock. Bernhard conducted a series of brilliant campaigns, culminating in the capture of Breisach (1638). Bernhard died in 1639, Baner in 1641. Meanwhile Emperor Ferdinand II was succeeded by Ferdinand III (1637). In 1642, Richelieu died; his successor, Cardinal MAZARIN, continued the established French policy. Germany was exhausted. Peace negotiations were begun before 1640, but the intricate diplomacy proceeded slowly and haltingly. Meanwhile the empire was reduced by the armies of the Swedish TORSTENSSON, Louis II de Condé, and Turenne. Torstensson defeated the imperialists at Breitenfeld (1642), defeated Gallas after going north to subdue Danish opposition, then won a climactic victory over Hatzfeldt at Jankau (1645). Meanwhile Condé had destroyed the flower of the Spanish infantry at Rocroi (1643); in 1645 he and Turenne (after a severe defeat) were victorious near Nördlingen. Austria had been stripped of all conquests and her enemies were at the very door of Vienna. Austria's strongest ally, Bavaria, was overrun. The Swede Wrangel and the Frenchman Turenne were carrying on a successful campaign when the long-delayed peace was obtained (see WESTPHALIA, PEACE OF).

The Aftermath. The general results of the war may be said to have been a tremendous decrease in German population; devastation of German agriculture; ruin of German commerce and industry; the break-up of the Holy Roman Empire, which was a mere shell in the succeeding centuries; and the decline of Hapsburg greatness. The war ended the era of conflicts inspired by religious passion, and the Peace of Westphalia was an important step toward religious toleration. The incredible sufferings of the German peasantry were remembered for centuries. The political settlements of the peace were to the disadvantage of Germany as well as the Hapsburgs. The estrangement of N Germany from Austria, then begun, was to continue for more than two centuries. Many of the songs and writings of the war have been collected. See studies by S. R. Gardiner (1874, repr. 1968); C. R. L. Fletcher (1903, repr. 1963); C. V. Wedgwood (1962); S. H. Steinberg (1966); Georges Pages (tr. 1970); and J. V. Polisensky (tr. 1971).

Thisbe: see PYRAMUS AND THISBE.

Thisbe, town whence Tobit was carried, N of Jerusalem. Tobit 1.2.

thistle, popular name for many spiny and usually weedy plants, but especially applied to members of the family Compositae (COMPOSITE family) that have spiny leaves and often showy heads of purple, rose, white, or yellow flowers followed by thistledown seeds (a favorite food of the goldfinch). The Scotch thistle (variously identified, but most often as *Onopordum acanthium*, now cultivated as an ornamental) is the badge of the Scottish Order of the Thistle and the national emblem of Scotland. It is said that the presence of a band of Danish invaders was betrayed by the howl of one of its members who stepped on a Scotch thistle. The blessed thistle, or St.-Benedict's-thistle (*Cnicus benedictus,* the *Carduus benedictus* of Shakespeare's *Much Ado about Nothing,* iii:4) was at one time a heal-all and is still sometimes used medicinally. The common, or bull, thistle (*Cirsium lanceolatum*) and the pasture thistle (*Cirsium odoratum*) are attractive weeds not to be confused with the so-called Canada thistle (*Cirsium arvense*), naturalized from Europe, which has a creeping rootstock and has probably been more legislated against than any other weed because of its very persistent nature (it is an offense in most states to allow the seeds to mature). A few thistles are cultivated in gardens, e.g., the large-flowered globe thistles, species of the Old World genus *Echinops.* The Russian thistle is a TUMBLEWEED. Thistle is classified in the division MAGNOLIOPHYTA, class Magnoliopsida, order Asterales, family Compositae.

Thistlewood, Arthur, 1770–1820, British conspirator. He acquired revolutionary views while traveling in France and America and, after his return to England, joined the revolutionary Spencean Society (see SPENCE, THOMAS) in London. In 1816 he organized a public meeting at Spa Fields, at which a revolution was to be started. However, the meeting was easily dispersed, and Thistlewood was arrested and narrowly escaped conviction for treason. A year later he was imprisoned for challenging Lord Sidmouth, the home secretary, to a duel. Upon his release (1819) Thistlewood, dissatisfied with the milder efforts of his colleagues, plotted the assassination of cabinet members at a cabinet dinner. The government, apprised of the conspiracy, surprised the plotters at their arsenal in a Cato Street loft. Thistlewood was subsequently convicted of treason and executed for his part in what is known as the Cato Street Conspiracy.

Thívai: see THEBES, Greece.

Thjórsá (thyōrs'ou''), Icelandic *Þjórsá,* longest river of Iceland, c.150 mi (240 km) long. It rises on the eastern slopes of the Hofsjökull and flows SW to the Atlantic Ocean.

Thököly, Imre (ĭm'rĕ tö'kölyə), 1656–1705, Hungarian rebel, of a noble family of N Hungary. His father, Stephen Thököly, took an important part in the unsuccessful conspiracy of Francis I RÁKÓCZY and Peter ZRINYI against Holy Roman Emperor LEOPOLD I and died (1670) while defending his castle against imperial troops. Thököly fled to Poland. The severe reprisals meted out by the Austrian governor of Hungary led to a general uprising, supported after 1674 by Louis XIV of France. Thököly took command (1678) of the rebel army and in 1680 made a truce with Leopold. The emperor restored (1681) religious and political freedom in Hungary, but Thököly rejected his concessions as insufficient and began to plot with Turkey to make himself master of his country. In 1682 he married Helen Zrinyi, daughter of Peter Zrinyi and widow of Francis I Rákóczy, and late in the same year he was recognized by Sultan Muhammad IV as "king of Upper Hungary" under Turkish suzerainty. It was largely at his instigation that the sultan undertook his expedition against Vienna, and in 1683 Thököly joined the Turkish forces under Kara MUSTAFA in the siege of that city. The Turks blamed their rout on Thököly and imprisoned him briefly (1686) at Adrianople, but in 1690 they appointed him prince of Transylvania. He was driven out (1691) of Transylvania by the imperial force under Louis of Baden. The Treaty of Karlowitz (1699), by which the whole of Hungary passed to Leopold, also stipulated that Thököly was to be interned by the Turks in Asia Minor. He spent the remainder of his life near Constantinople. The name is also spelled Tokoly.

Thoma, Hans (häns tō'mä), 1839–1924, German painter and lithographer. He was influenced by Courbet. His later, individual style, modeled on that of old German woodcuts, shows rich coloring and depth of imaginative feeling. In 1899 he became director of the Karlsruhe Gallery and professor of the academy. The Metropolitan Museum has his painting *At Lake Garda.*

Thoma, Ludwig (lo͞ot'vĭkh), 1867–1921, German novelist, dramatist, and poet. Thoma's satiric representation of Bavarian rural and small-town life won him wide acclaim. The serious peasant novels *Andreas Vöst* (1905), *Der Wittiber* (1911), and *Der Ruepp* (1922), as well as his humorous collections *Assessor Karlchen* (1900), *Lausbubengeschichten* [rascal stories] (1904), and *Tante Frieda* [Aunt Frieda] (1906), are characterized by authenticity of regional language and life. Thoma's dramas, including *Die Medaille* [the medal] (1901), *Das Säuglingsheim* [the orphanage] (1913), and especially *Moral* (1908), reflect elements of folk theater.

Thomas, Saint, one of the Twelve Disciples, called Didymus. He refused to believe in the resurrection until he saw Jesus' wounds; hence the expression "doubting Thomas." John 11.16; 14.5; 20.24–29; 21.2. By universal tradition he is said to have gone as missionary to Parthia or India. The Syriac-rite Christians of Malabar in India, whose church was established by the 3d cent., claim St. Thomas as their founder. Among the PSEUDEPIGRAPHA are a Gospel of Thomas and Acts of Thomas. Feast: Dec. 21.

Thomas, Albert (älbĕr' tômä'), 1878–1932, French statesman and Socialist leader. He worked with Jean Jaurès on the journal *Humanité* and was active in socialist politics. In 1910 he was elected to the chamber of deputies, and during World War I he held cabinet positions, serving notably as minister of munitions. He was director (1919–32) of the International Labor Bureau of the League of Nations. Among his several books are *Le Syndicalisme allemand* (1903) and *Le 2d Empire* (1907). See study by E. J. Phelan (1949).

Thomas, Ambroise (äNbrwäz' tōmä'), 1811–96, French operatic composer, studied at the Paris Conservatory, receiving the Prix de Rome in 1832. He later taught composition there and became its director in 1871. Thomas wrote cantatas, a number of ballets, and 20 operas, of which *Le Caïd* (1849, a satire on Italian opera), *Mignon* (1866), and *Hamlet* (1868) were the most successful.

Thomas, Cyrus, 1825–1910, American anthropologist and entomologist, b. Kingsport, Tenn. He was a lawyer, then a minister (1865–69) of the Evangelical Lutheran Church. He was associated with the U.S. Geological and Geographical Survey of the Territories from 1869 to 1873. As state entomologist of Illinois (1874–76) and a member of the U.S. Entomological Commission (1876–77), he helped bring under control the insect plague that was retarding the agriculture of the border states. In 1882 he left natural science for social science, becoming archaeologist to the newly established U.S. Bureau of Ethnology, where he served until his death. Besides numerous articles on entomology and archaeology, he wrote *Introduction to the Study of North American Archaeology* (1898) and *The Indians of North America in Historic Times* (1903).

Thomas, David Alfred: see RHONDDA, DAVID ALFRED THOMAS, 1ST VISCOUNT.

Thomas, Dylan (dĭl'ən), 1914–53, Welsh poet, b. Swansea. An extraordinarily individualistic writer, Thomas is ranked among the great 20th-century poets. He grew up in Swansea, the son of a teacher, but left school at 17 to become a journalist. His *Eighteen Poems,* published in 1934, created controversy but won him immediate fame, which grew with the publication of *Twenty-five Poems* (1936), *The Map of Love* (1939; containing poetry and surrealistic prose), *The World I Breathe* (1939; also containing some prose), *Deaths and Entrances* (1946), and *In Country Sleep and Other Poems* (1952). The prose Thomas published is fragmented into stories and sketches, many autobiographical or pseudo-autobiographical, all touched with fantasy; they are collected in *Portrait of the Artist as a Young Dog* (1940), *Adventures in the Skin Trade* (1955), and *Quite Early One Morning* (1955). He had a remarkable speaking voice, flexible and resonant, and his radio readings over the BBC were popular. In addition he wrote for the radio *A Child's Christmas in Wales* (published 1954) and his striking dramatic work, *Under Milk Wood* (published 1954), which records life and love and introspection in a small Welsh town. Thomas greatly enjoyed his success but lived recklessly and drank heavily. His third highly popular tour of the United States ended in his death, which was brought on by alcoholism. Thomas's themes are traditional—love, death, mutability—and over the years he seemed to pass from religious doubt to joyous faith in God. His complex imagery is based on many sources, including Welsh legend, Christian symbolism, witchcraft, astronomy, and Freudian psychology, and the private myth he created makes his early poetry hard to understand. Yet his sure mastery of sound (perhaps related to his fine voice), his warm humor, and his robust love of life attract the reader instantaneously. The autobiography of Thomas's wife, Caitlin Thomas, *Leftover Life to Kill* (1957), and the account of the Thomases' tours by J. M. Brinnin, *Dylan Thomas in America* (1955), vividly describe his last years. See his *Collected Poems* (1953); his letters, ed. by Constantine FitzGibbon (1967); his notebooks, ed. by Ralph Maud (1967); biographies by Constantine FitzGibbon (1965) and John Ackerman (1965); studies by W. Y. Tindall (1962), W. T. Moynihan (1966), and Rushworth Kidder (1973).

Thomas, Edward, 1878–1917, English poet. He began his literary career writing essays, travel books, and critical studies. His friendship with Robert Frost, which began in 1912, turned him to writing poetry, primarily on nature themes. His first volume of verse, *Six Poems* (1916), mostly pastoral verse, was published shortly before he was killed in World War I. See his collected poems (1920, rev. ed. 1936); biography by R. P. Eckert (1937); studies by William Cooke (1970) and Henry Coombes (1956, repr. 1973).

Thomas, George Henry, 1816–70, Union general in the American Civil War, b. Southampton co., Va. He served in the Seminole War and in the Mexican War. Later he taught at West Point and served in Texas. As a brigadier general of volunteers, he was sent to Kentucky, where he defeated the Confederates at Mill Springs (Jan., 1862). Thomas served under General Buell at Shiloh, Corinth, and Perryville. In the Chattanooga campaign, his stand on Sept. 20, 1863, which saved the Union army from complete rout, won for him the sobriquet "Rock of Chickamauga." Appointed brigadier general in the regular army, he succeeded General Rosecrans in command of the Army of the Cumberland (Oct., 1863) and served under Ulysses S. Grant around Chattanooga and under General Sherman in the Atlanta campaign. With the fall of Atlanta (Sept., 1864), Grant ordered Thomas to pursue the army of General HOOD into Tennessee. Although accused by Grant of moving too slowly, and threatened with the loss of his command, Thomas waited and finally defeated Hood at Nashville (Dec., 1864). This victory brought him a promotion to major general in the regular army. After the war he held various commands. At the time of his death he was commander of the Military Division of the Pacific. See biographies by F. F. McKinney (1961) and W. D. Thomas (1964).

Thomas, Isaiah, 1749–1831, American patriot and printer, from Worcester, Mass. Thomas printed outspoken Whig editorials in the *Massachusetts Spy,* a newspaper that he helped to found. He fought at the battles of Lexington and Concord and after the Revolution settled in Worcester as a printer. He published in 1783 *A Specimen of Isaiah Thomas's Printing Types,* valued as evidence of the printing equipment of a leading American printer of the time. His other ventures included the *Massachusetts Magazine* (1789–95) and a folio Bible (1791). In 1810 he published the *History of Printing in America,* compiling during his research one of the most important collections of early American newspapers and pamphlets. He also founded and endowed the American Antiquarian Society of Worcester.

Thomas, James Henry, 1874–1949, British statesman and labor leader. A railroad worker, he held various offices in the Amalgamated Society of Railway Servants and was a leader of the railway strike of 1911. He helped organize (1913) the National Union of Railwaymen (NUR) of which he became general secretary in 1917. During the general strike (1926) he worked for conciliation. Thomas was colonial secretary in the 1924 Labour government and in 1929 was made lord privy seal and special minister for employment. He became dominion secretary in 1930 and retained that position in Ramsay MacDonald's National government (1931–35). As a result he was expelled from the Labour party and the NUR. Thomas was colonial secretary (1935–36) but was forced to resign after leaking budget secrets. See biography by Gregory Blaxland (1964).

Thomas, John Charles, 1891–1960, American baritone, b. Meyersdale, Pa., studied at the Peabody Conservatory, Baltimore. After a successful career in musical comedy he made his operatic debut in Washington, D.C., in 1924 and later sang with the Royal Opera, Brussels. He made his debut at the Metropolitan Opera House in 1934 in Verdi's *La Traviata,* joining the company in 1935. Well-known as a concert and radio singer, he also appeared in motion pictures.

Thomas, Martha Carey, 1857–1935, American educator and feminist, b. Baltimore, grad. Cornell Univ., 1877, studied at Johns Hopkins Univ. and at Leipzig, the Sorbonne, and Zurich (Ph.D., 1882). In 1884 she was appointed to organize Bryn Mawr College for women, serving as dean and professor of English until 1894 and as president from 1894 to 1922. She also established the summer school for women in industry at Bryn Mawr in 1921. A leader in the woman-suffrage movement, she was president of the National Collegiate Equal Suffrage League from 1906 to 1913. Her works include *The Higher Education of Women* (1900). See biography by Edith Finch (1947).

Thomas, Norman Mattoon, 1884–1968, American socialist leader, b. Marion, Ohio. A graduate of Princeton (1905) and Union Theological Seminary (1911), he served as pastor of several Presbyterian churches and did settlement work in New York City until 1918. (He formally left the ministry in 1931.) In World War I he became a pacifist and joined (1918) the Socialist party. He founded (1918) *The World Tomorrow,* was (1921–22) an associate editor of the *Nation,* and became (1922) codirector of the League for Industrial Democracy. He was also active in setting up the American Civil Liberties Union. Thomas unsuccessfully sought election as governor of New York (1924, 1938) and as mayor of New York City (1925, 1929). After the death (1926) of Eugene Debs he assumed leadership of the Socialist party and was repeatedly (1928, 1932, 1936, 1940, 1944, 1948) the party's candidate for President. He polled his highest vote, about 880,000, in 1932. An advocate of evolutionary socialism, Thomas was a constant critic of the American economic system and of both major parties; he strongly opposed American entry in World War II while bitterly denouncing both fascism and Soviet Communism. After the war he lectured and wrote extensively on the need for world disarmament and the easing of cold war tensions. In 1955 he resigned his official posts in the Socialist party, but he remained its chief spokesman until shortly before his death. His works include *The Conscientious Objector in America* (1923), *Socialism of Our Time* (1929), *Human Exploitation* (1934), *Appeal to the Nations* (1947), *Socialist's Faith* (1951), *The Test of Freedom* (1954), *The Prerequisite for Peace* (1959), *Great Dissenters* (1961), and *Socialism Reexamined* (1963). See biographies by M. B. Seidler (2d ed. 1967), Harry Fleischman (1964, repr. 1969), and B. K. Johnpoll (1970).

Thomas, Seth, 1785–1859, American clock manufacturer, b. Wolcott, Conn. In 1812 he sold his partnership in a clock business established by Eli Terry and set up a factory to make metal-movement clocks at Plymouth Hollow, Conn. (renamed Thomaston in his honor c.1860). He also built and operated a mill to roll brass and make wire for his clock factory. The business was continued and expanded by his son, Seth Thomas (1816–88), and the clocks they manufactured became known throughout the world.

Thomas à Becket, Saint or **Saint Thomas Becket,** 1118–70, English martyr, archbishop of Canterbury, b. London. He is called St. Thomas of Canterbury and occasionally St. Thomas of London. He came from a middle-class Norman family and was well educated, completing his studies at the Univ. of Paris. He entered (c. 1142) the household of Theobald, archbishop of Canterbury, in whose service he performed several delicate missions. Theobald apparently sent him to Bologna and to Auxerre to study law. In 1154 he was ordained deacon and appointed archdeacon of Canterbury. In the same year the young HENRY II, acting on the advice of Theobald, appointed him chancellor. Theobald and the clerical party expected Becket to represent their interests at court, but the chancellor, who rapidly became an intimate friend of the king, devoted himself largely to secular affairs. He lived in magnificence, took an unclerical part on the battlefield in the Toulouse campaign (1159) and, when a clash of interests arose between church and state, usually supported the king. It is not surprising, therefore, that when Theobald died (1161), Henry, who hoped to curb the growth of church power, nominated his friend to succeed to the archbishopric. Becket himself, foreseeing the conflict that lay ahead, was reluctant to accept, but the king insisted, and, in 1162, Becket was ordained priest and consecrated archbishop of Canterbury. Apparently determined to play this role as conscientiously as he had played that of chancellor, the new archbishop immediately changed his way of life. He abandoned his worldliness for a life of extreme asceticism, angered the king by resigning the chancellorship, and began to work exclusively for the interests of the church. He soon came into conflict with Henry, and as the tension between the two men mounted, the series of minor disputes developed into a major quarrel. Matters came to a head over the question of punishing "criminous clerks." At the Council of Westminster (1163), Henry claimed that such clerics, once tried and convicted in the ecclesiastical courts, should be punished by the secular authorities. Becket rejected this claim and also persuaded the other bishops to attach the qualification "saving our order" to their assent to the king's demand that they swear obedience to the (unspecified) "ancient customs" of the realm. Under pressure from the pope, Becket subsequently withdrew this reservation. The following year Henry codified these customs (including his claim concerning the "criminous clerks") in the Constitutions of Clarendon (see CLARENDON, CONSTITUTIONS OF) and Becket, although he refused to sign them, did give his verbal assent. The Constitutions of Clarendon were, for the most part, an accurate statement of the customs governing relations between church and state in the reign of Henry's grandfather, Henry I. Several of the practices were, however, contrary to canon law, and the pope now refused to approve them. This stiffened Becket's resolution, and he publicly indicated that he had perjured himself at Clarendon. In Oct., 1164, the archbishop was summoned to the Council of Northampton to stand trial for allegedly misappropriating funds while he was chancellor. There in a stormy meeting he openly breached two clauses of the constitutions, by denying the jurisdiction of the council over himself and by appealing to the pope. He fled the country immediately after. In exile for the next six years, Becket did not receive the active support from Pope ALEXANDER III for which he had hoped; the pope was too enmeshed in difficulties of his own to alienate the English king further. The quarrel dragged on, and both sides took extreme stands. Finally in 1170 a sort of reconciliation was arranged, but under circumstances that boded ill. In June, 1170, Henry had his eldest son crowned by the archbishop of York, in direct violation of custom and of a papal ban. Becket reacted by threatening, with papal support, to place England under an interdict. Under this threat the king hastily made his peace with his erstwhile friend. The peace did not last long, however. Before returning to England in Dec., 1170, Becket released papal letters suspending the bishops who had taken part in the coronation. He followed this, after his arrival, by excommunicating them. These actions infuriated the king, who, in his rage, uttered his fateful plea to be rid of the archbishop. Four knights of his household acted on his words. They hurried to Canterbury, where, on Dec. 29, 1170, they murdered Becket in the cathedral itself. Thomas à Becket's death shocked the whole of the Christian world, and his tomb in Canterbury became an immediate shrine. He was canonized in 1173, and in the following year Henry was forced by the weight of public revulsion to do penance at the saint's tomb. The popularity of the cult of St. Thomas continued through the Middle Ages; Canterbury's preeminence as a place of pilgrimage (immortalized in Chaucer's *Canterbury Tales*) continued until the shrine was destroyed, probably along with the martyr's remains, under Henry VIII in 1538. Feast: Dec. 29. T. S. Eliot's *Murder in the Cathedral* is a poetic dramatization of St. Thomas's martyrdom, and the saint's career is the subject of Jean Anouilh's play *Becket*. See J. C. Robertson, *Materials for the History of Thomas Becket* (7 vol., 1875–85, repr. 1965); biographies and studies by David Knowles (1951 and 1971), A. L. Duggan (1952, repr. 1966), Richard Winston (1967), and Beryl Smalley (1973); Z. N. Brooke, *The English Church and the Papacy From the Conquest to the Reign of John* (1931, repr. 1968).

Thomas à Kempis (kĕm'pĭs), b. 1379 or 1380, d. 1471, German monk, traditional author of *The Imitation of Christ*, b. Kempen, Germany. He was schooled at Deventer, in the Netherlands, the center of the Brothers of the Common Life founded by Gerard GROOTE. He joined the Augustinian canons (1399) and was ordained a priest (c.1413). His convent was Mt. St. Agnes, near Zwolle, in the Netherlands. Thomas worked principally at copying and writing. A number of his treatises on the monastic life and little devotional essays have been translated into English. The great devotional work *The Imitation of Christ* (c.1427) has traditionally been ascribed to him, although some scholars have contested his authorship. See IMITATION OF CHRIST, THE.

Thomas Aquinas, Saint (əkwī'nəs) [Lat.,=from Aquino], 1225–74, Italian philosopher and theologian, Doctor of the Church, known as the Angelic Doctor, b. Rocca Secca (near Naples). He is the greatest figure of SCHOLASTICISM, one of the principal saints of the Roman Catholic Church, and founder of the system declared by Pope Leo XIII (in the encyclical *Aeterni Patris*, 1879) to be the official Catholic philosophy. He came of the ruling family of Aquino, was educated as a child at Monte Cassino, and later studied at Naples. To his family's disappointment he entered (1244) the new Dominican order. In 1245 he began to study in Paris with Albertus Magnus, whose favorite pupil he became, and in 1248 he accompanied Albertus to Cologne. From there, Thomas went again (1252) to Paris, where he gained a great reputation and became professor of theology. He was leader of the friars in the controversy that occurred when the seculars sought to limit the friars' privileges at the university. After 1259 he spent several years in Italy as professor and adviser at the papal court. His return to Paris (1269) was probably precipitated by the furor over SIGER DE BRABANT and his Averroistic reading of Aristotle. The doctrinal struggle with Siger resulted in victory for Thomas and the triumph of his position. In 1272 he left Paris for Naples to organize a house of studies. Two years later when he and his constant companion, Brother Reginald, were at Fossanuova, on the way to the Council of Lyons, where he was to be a papal consultant, St. Thomas died. St. Thomas's classic nickname was the Dumb Ox, because he was slow in manner and quite stout. He was, however, a brilliant lecturer and a clear, sharp thinker, as his works show—not only in their rigid application of reason, but also in their Latin diction, which is admirably exact and simple. His spiritual character is manifest in the humility and charity of his conduct and the use to which he put his theories in his devotional works, notably in the Mass and office for the feast of Corpus Christi (June 21), which he wrote at Urban IV's request (1264). The four hymns of this Mass and office, *Laude Sion Salvatorem*, PANGE LINGUA, *Sacris solemniis*, and *Verbum supernum* (ending with *O Salutaris Hostia*), are classed among the greatest of Christian hymns. No single work of St. Thomas can be said fully to reveal his philosophy. His works may be classified according to their form and purpose. The principal ones are *Commentary in the Sentences* (a series of public lectures; 1254–56), his earliest great work; seven *quaestiones disputatae* (public debates; 1256–72); philosophical commentaries on Aristotle's *Physics, Metaphysics, De anima, Ethics*, part of the *De interpretatione*, and the *Posterior Analytics;* treatises on many subjects, including the *Summa contra Gentiles* (1258–60); and, most important of all, *Summa theologica* (1267–73), an incomplete but systematic exposition of theology on philosophical principles. St. Thomas's philosophy is avowedly Aristotelian; the methods and distinctions of Aristotle are adapted to revelation. The 13th cent. was a critical period in Christian thought, which was torn between the claims of the Averroists and the extreme Augustinians. Thomas opposed both schools, the Averroists led by Siger de Brabant who would separate faith and truth absolutely and the Augustinians who would make truth a matter of faith. St. Thomas held that reason and faith constitute two harmonious realms in which the truths of faith complement those of reason; both are gifts of God, but reason has an autonomy of its own. Thus he vindicated the rights of reason against the fearful who wished to suppress Aristotle as the father of Averroës and heresy. The first principle of philosophy according to St. Thomas is the affirmation of being. From this he proceeded to a consideration of the manner in which the intellect achieves knowledge. For man, all knowledge begins by way of the senses, which are the medium through which he grasps the intelligible world, the universal. According to the position of Thomas, which is known as moderate REALISM, the form or the universal may be said to exist in three ways: in God, in things, and in the mind (see UNIVERSALS). It is by the knowledge of things that we come to know of God's existence. In the natural order what God is can be known only by analogy and negation. Thomas's conviction that the existence of God can be discovered by reason is shown by his proofs of the existence of God. His analysis of that which is proceeds by way of the Aristotelian concepts of potency and act, matter and form, being and essence. A thing that requires completion by another is said to be in potency to that other; the realization of potency is called actuality. The universe is conceived of as a series of things arranged in an ascending order or potency, an act at once crowned and created by God, who alone is pure act. God is changeless because change means passage from potency to act, and so He is without beginning and end, since these demand change. Matter and form are necessary to the understanding of change, for change requires the union of that which becomes and that which it becomes. Matter is the first and form the second. All physical things are composed of matter and form. The difference between a thing as form, or character, and the actual existence of it is denoted by the terms *essence* and *being*. It is only in God that there is no distinction between the two. Both pairs—matter and form, essence and being—are special cases of potency and act. The system of St. Thomas rests upon these three distinctions. Being may also be characterized according to modes. Modes do not add anything to the idea of being but are ways of making explicit what is implicit in it. In one sense, mode means the division of being into categories. In another sense, it expresses certain distinctions of being as it is common to all kinds. In this sense, modes are known as transcendentals; along with being, these are principally unity, truth, and goodness. These terms are convertible one to another. Since the opposite of being does not exist and since the good is identical with being, it is obvious that for St. Thomas evil is but the absence of good. For a long time Thomas was either ignored or misunderstood by even the greatest philosophers, but his teachings ultimately triumphed. That they are official in the Roman Catholic Church does not mean that Catholics may not adhere to other philosophies, notably the Scotist teachings, developed from the doctrines of Duns Scotus. St. Thomas's magnificent synthesis is now recognized generally as one of the greatest works of human thought. His wide-embracing philosophy is applied to every realm of human life. Thomism is a complete structure in itself, not simply a collection of theories. The terms *New Thomism, neo-Thomism,* and NEO-SCHOLASTICISM are used for a school of philosophy of the 20th cent. The Catholic leaders of this school were Étienne Gilson and Jacques Maritain, who sought to apply Thomistic principles to modern economic, political, and social conditions. Non-Catholics also have adapted Thomistic principles to modern life; a leader among them is Mortimer Adler. In art St. Thomas is usually associated with a sacramental cup (representing his devotion to the sacrament) or a dove (representing the inspiration of the Holy Ghost) or depicted with a sun on his breast. He was canonized in 1323 and was proclaimed a Doctor of the Church in 1567. His tomb is in the Basilica of St. Sernin at Toulouse. Feast: March 7. His works have all been translated, the more important ones in various versions. Volumes of selections of his works are also available. See Étienne Gilson, *The Christian Philosophy of St. Thomas Aquinas* (1956); Jacques Maritain, *St. Thomas Aquinas* (rev. ed. 1958); Josef Pieper, *Guide to Thomas Aquinas* (tr. 1962); M. D. Chenu, *Toward Understanding St. Thomas* (1964); James A. Weisheipl, *Friar Thomas D'Aquino* (1974).

Thomasius, Christian (krĭs'tyän tōmä'zyōōs), 1655–1728, German jurist and philosopher. A lawyer, he lectured on natural law at Leipzig; he broke with the traditional custom of lecturing in Latin and from 1687 taught in German. This and other liberal stands forced him to move to Halle in 1690, where he helped establish (1694) the Univ. of Halle, in which he became a professor. In the practical philosophy of Thomasius every question was considered without prejudice and submitted to the judgment of common sense. He was a reformer who sought to liberate politics from religious domination, and within religion he strove for freedom and toleration. He was influential in pointing the way to the philosophy of the ENLIGHTENMENT. His chief work is *Institutionum jurisprudentiae divinae* (1688).

Thomas Jefferson Memorial, monument, 18 acres (7 hectares), in East Potomac Park, on the Tidal Basin, Washington, D.C.; authorized by Congress 1934, built 1938–43, dedicated 1943. The white marble building, designed by John Russell Pope, is a circular structure with a domed ceiling, surrounded by 26 columns. Inside is a 19-ft (5.8-m) statue of Jefferson by the sculptor Rudulph Evans.

Thomas More, Saint: see MORE, SIR THOMAS.

Thomas of Canterbury, Saint: see THOMAS À BECKET, SAINT.

Thomas of Celano (chālä'nō), fl. 13th cent., Italian Franciscan friar. One of the first companions of St. FRANCIS, he wrote the two principal lives of St. Francis, one for Gregory IX and the other for the minister general of the order. He was an early Franciscan missionary to Germany. He probably composed the sequence DIES IRAE and its celebrated plain song.

Thomas of Erceldoune (ûr'səldōōn''), fl. 1220?–1297?, Scottish seer and poet, also known as Thomas the Rhymer and Thomas Learmont. Evidence of his existence is founded on the mention of his name in documents of the 13th cent. Soon after his death his reputation as a prophet became proverbial. His reputed sayings were consulted as late as the Jacobite risings of 1715 and 1745. He supposedly predicted the battle of Bannockburn and the accession of James VI to the English throne. The poetical romance of Thomas and the Elf-Queen, attributed to him but actually composed about 1400, describes the events surrounding his receipt of the gift of prophecy.

Thomaston (tŏm'əstən), city (1970 pop. 10,024), seat of Upson co., W central Ga., near the Flint River; inc. 1857. It is a textile center with textile mills (the first was established in 1833) and plants where textile products are made. Of interest are an old covered bridge and a number of historic homes.

Thomasville. **1** City (1970 pop. 18,155), seat of Thomas co., SW Ga., near the Fla. line; inc. 1831. It is a farm trade center, with a large fresh vegetable market. Industries include meat-packing, baking, printing, and lumbering. The city has a mild climate and is a winter resort, with excellent hunting and fishing in the area. More than 25,000 rose bushes line the city streets, and an annual rose festival is held there. In Thomasville are a state mental hospital and two museums. **2** Industrial city (1970 pop. 15,230), Davidson co., central N.C., in the Piedmont; inc. 1854. It has cotton mills and textile, garment, and furniture industries.

Thompson, Benjamin: see RUMFORD, BENJAMIN THOMPSON, COUNT.

Thompson, Daniel Pierce, 1795–1868, American novelist, b. Charlestown, Mass. He wrote adventure novels, many of which deal with life in Vermont. His most famous work is *The Green Mountain Boys* (1839).

Thompson, David, 1770–1857, Canadian geographer, fur trader, and explorer, b. London, England. In 1784 he came to Fort Churchill, Canada, as an apprentice of the Hudson's Bay Company, and until 1797 he was a fur trader of Hudson Bay and in the Athabasca country to the west. Although he had little scientific training, he developed great skill in geodetic and astronomical observations, and after 1797, when he joined the North West Company, he methodically located points in W Canada and made surveys of astonishing exactitude. In 1797–98 he traveled far S to the Mandan villages on the Missouri and then surveyed the headwaters of the Mississippi River. His most notable exploring expeditions were those across the Rocky Mts. and on the Columbia River. In 1807 he was the first white man to cross the Howse Pass to the source of the Columbia River and travel its length; he then explored the Kootenai, Pend Oreille, and Clark Fork river basins. In 1810, prevented by the Piegan Indians from using Howse Pass, he went north to the head of the Athabasca River and across the mountains and explored all of the Columbia River system. He then went to Montreal, where he made (1812-14) a large and invaluable map of W Canada for the North West Company, long the best map of the region. Thompson, however, received little open recognition except an appointment (1816-26) to the commission for surveying the U.S.-Canadian boundary. It was not until the 20th cent. that his importance as a geographer was recognized. See his narrative (ed. by J. B. Tyrrell, 1916); biography by J. K. Smith (1971); study by Rowland Bond (1972).

Thompson, Ernest Seton: see SETON, ERNEST THOMPSON.

Thompson, Francis, 1859-1907, English poet. His poetry, usually on religious subjects, is noted for its brilliant imagery and sonorous language. He was educated for the Roman Catholic priesthood at Ushaw College but in 1877 entered Owens College, Manchester, to study medicine. Relinquishing his medical studies in 1885, he went to London where he lived a destitute life, suffering from ill health, poverty, and opium addiction. In 1888 he sent a manuscript to Wilfrid Meynell who, with his wife Alice MEYNELL, edited the Catholic periodical *Merry England.* They recognized Thompson's poetic ability and took him under their care. *Poems* (1893), which attracted much attention, contained "The Hound of Heaven," Thompson's chief and best-known work, describing the poet's futile flight from God. Two more volumes appeared, *Sister Songs* (1895) and *New Poems* (1897), both supplemented by the publication of a few more poems after his death. Thompson spent the years from 1893 to 1897 in a monastery in Wales. Although Thompson is considered an important English poet, his verse has frequently been criticized for its verbosity and lack of originality in thought. Thompson also wrote a number of essays, including a study of Shelley (1909). See his *Literary Criticisms* (ed. by T. L. Connolly, 1948); biographies by Everard Meynell (1913, repr. 1971), and P. van K. Thomson (1961, repr. 1972); studies by J. C. Reid (1959) and R. L. Mégroz (1927, repr. 1971).

Thompson, Jacob, 1810-85, U.S. Representative (1839-51) and Secretary of the Interior (1857-61), b. Caswell co., N.C. Thompson was a prosperous lawyer and prominent Democrat of Oxford, Miss. He was a member of President Buchanan's cabinet until the Fort Sumter crisis, and Mississippi's secession led him to resign in Jan., 1861. In the Civil War he served in the Confederate army, and in 1864 he became a Confederate agent in Canada. There he tried unsuccessfully to persuade Copperhead elements in the North to take up arms against the Union. Falsely accused of complicity in President Lincoln's assassination, he fled to Europe, where he remained for several years, and later lived in Memphis.

Thompson, Sir John Sparrow David, 1844-94, Canadian political leader, b. Nova Scotia. He was elected (1877) to the provincial assembly, was briefly provincial prime minister, and then was made a justice of the supreme court of Nova Scotia. In 1885, Sir John Macdonald appointed him minister of justice for Canada. In that post Thompson skillfully defended the government's position in the debates on the execution (1885) of Louis Riel and on the Jesuit Estates Act (1888). In 1892 he became prime minister of Canada. He died suddenly in England, shortly after having been sworn in as privy councilor. He was knighted in 1888.

Thompson, Joseph Parrish, 1819-79, American Congregational clergyman, b. Philadelphia, grad. Yale, 1838. He was pastor of the Broadway Tabernacle, New York City, from 1845 to 1871. He was a founder of the *New Englander* (1843) and one of the founders of the *Independent* (1848), both of which were periodicals.

Thompson, Mortimer Neal: see THOMSON, MORTIMER NEAL.

Thompson, Stith, 1885-, American educator and folklorist, b. Bloomfield, Ky. Thompson is best known for his pioneering works in the field of folklore: *The Types of the Folktale* (1928), which describes the major varieties and refers to printed examples in American and European archives, and the monumental and innovative *Motif-Index of Folk Literature* (6 vol., 1932-36), a brilliant classification system using the smallest identifiable narrative elements in an enormous variety of folktales, ballads, myths, fables, romances, etc. This index is an encyclopedia, dictionary, and bibliography in one and is still a chief reference tool. Thompson taught at Indiana Univ. from 1921 to 1955, writing and editing several books on English literature and language, including *A New Handbook of English* (1936, with Malcolm McLeod). His other well-known folklore studies include *Tales of North American Indians* (1929), *The Folktale* (1946), *Narrative Motif-Analysis as a Folklore Method* (1955), *Types of Indic Oral Tales* (1960, with W. E. Roberts), and *One Hundred Favorite Folktales* (1968).

Thompson, William Boyce, 1869-1930, American financier, b. Virginia City, Mont. He operated silver and copper mines in Montana and Arizona before moving to New York City. He was (1914-19) a director of the Federal reserve bank of New York and was twice (1916, 1920) a delegate to the Republican national convention. In World War I, he helped finance and accompanied (1917-18) a Red Cross mission to Russia. He contributed money to the government of Aleksandr Kerensky and, after the Bolsheviks seized power, advocated U.S. recognition of the Soviet government. In 1919, he founded the Boyce Thompson Institute for Plant Research in Yonkers, N.Y. See Hermann Hagedorn, *The Magnate* (1935).

Thompson, William Hale, 1869-1944, American politician, b. Boston. His family moved to Chicago when he was nine years old, and there he later entered politics as an alderman (1900-1902). He became commissioner of Cook co. (1902-4) and served (1915-23, 1927-31) three terms as mayor of Chicago. A flamboyant figure, he attracted much attention during the 1927 mayoralty campaign by his tirades against England. As mayor he was criticized for his failure to take effective action against the gangs led by Al Capone and others. In 1936 he ran for governor of Illinois but was defeated. See Lloyd Wendt and Herman Kogan, *Big Bill of Chicago* (1953).

Thompson, William T., 1812-82, American humorist and editor, b. Ravenna, Ohio. He was founder and editor of the Savannah *Morning News,* which became one of the most prominent newspapers in Georgia. In his editorials he often defended slavery. He is remembered for his use of dialect in short stories about life among the Georgia Crackers. They are collected in several volumes, including *Major Jones's Courtship* (1843) and *Chronicles of Pineville* (1845).

Thompson, city (1971 pop. 19,001), central Man., Canada, on the Burntwood River. A mining town, it developed after large nickel deposits were discovered in the area in 1956.

Thompson, river, 304 mi (489 km) long, formed by the junction of the North Thompson and the South Thompson rivers at Kamloops, S British Columbia, and flowing W and S to the Fraser River at Lytton. The North Thompson is usually considered part of the main stream. The river was discovered (1808) by Simon Fraser and named by him for David Thompson, a fellow explorer.

Thomsen, Vilhelm (vĭl'hĕlm tŏm'sĕn), 1842-1927, Danish philologist. For many years Thomsen was professor of comparative philology at the Univ. of Copenhagen, where he did important work in Indo-European linguistics. His best-known work was the decipherment of the bilingual Turkic-Chinese inscription found on the Orkhon River in Mongolia. The inscription, published in 1894, is in the most ancient form of Turkish yet found.

Thomson, Charles, 1729-1824, political leader in the American Revolution, b. Co. Londonderry, Ireland. Emigrating to America in 1739, he later taught school and became a merchant. His pre-Revolutionary activities led John Adams to call him "the Sam Adams of Philadelphia." As secretary of the Continental Congress (1774-89), Thomson kept careful records of all proceedings and full notes of the debates. He was the moving spirit in the committee that obtained the design for the Great Seal of the United States. He wrote *An Enquiry into the Causes of the Alienation of the Delaware and Shawanese Indians from the British Interest* (1759), translated the Septuagint and the New Testament (4 vol., 1808), and published *A Synopsis of the Four Evangelists* (1815). See biography by L. R. Harley (1900).

Thomson, Charles Edward Poulett: see SYDENHAM, CHARLES EDWARD POULETT THOMSON, BARON.

Thomson, Sir Charles Wyville, 1830-82, Scottish naturalist, noted as a marine biologist and deep-sea explorer. He participated in three deep-sea dredging expeditions (1868-70) and obtained evidence that animal life abounded in depths previously believed to be azoic; he recorded the results of his studies in *The Depths of the Sea* (1873), a classic in oceanography. He was director of the scientific work of the *Challenger* expedition (1872-76) and on his return was knighted and appointed director of a commission to distribute and study the collections of the expedition and to publish its results. He wrote an account of the cruise, *The Voyage of the "Challenger"* (1877). Thomson taught at several universities and was professor of natural history at the Univ. of Edinburgh from 1870.

Thomson, Sir George Paget, 1892-, English physicist; son of Sir Joseph John Thomson. He was professor of natural philosophy at the Univ. of Aberdeen (1922-30) and from 1930 to 1952 was professor of physics at Imperial College, Univ. of London. In 1952, he became master of Corpus Christi College, Cambridge. He shared with C. J. Davisson the 1937 Nobel Prize in Physics for their simultaneous, independent discovery of diffraction phenomena in the electron. In 1943 he was knighted. His works include *The Atom* (1930, 6th ed. 1962), *The Wave Mechanics of Free Electrons* (1930), *Theory and Practice of Electron Diffraction* (with William Cochrane, 1939), and *The Inspiration of Science* (1961).

Thomson, James, 1700-1748, Scottish poet. Educated at Edinburgh, he went to London, took a post as tutor, and became acquainted with such literary celebrities as Gay, Arbuthnot, and Pope. His most famous poem, *The Seasons,* was published in four parts, beginning with "Winter" (1726), which achieved an immediate success. "Summer" (1727) was followed by "Spring" (1728) and then "Autumn" in the first collected edition (1730); a revised edition appeared in 1744. In *The Seasons,* Thomson's faithful, sensitive descriptions of external nature were a direct challenge to the urban and artificial school of Pope and influenced the forerunners of romanticism, such as Gray and Cowper. His other important poems are *Liberty* (1735-36), a tribute to Britain, and *The Castle of Indolence* (1748), written in imitation of Spenser and reflecting the poet's delight in idleness. Thomson also wrote a series of tragedies along classical lines, with a strong political flavor. The most notable were *Sophonisba* (1730); *Edward and Eleanora* (1739), which was banned for political reasons; and *Tancred and Sigismunda* (1745). In 1740 he collaborated with his friend David Mallet on a masque, *Alfred,* which contains his famous ode "Rule Britannia." See his poetical works (ed. by J. L. Robertson, 1908, repr. 1965); biography by Douglas Grant (1951); studies by Ralph Cohen (1963 and 1970).

Thomson, James, 1834-82, Scottish poet and essayist. He is remembered for his darkly pessimistic poem *The City of Dreadful Night.* He was raised in an orphan asylum and became (1851) an army teacher at Ballincollig, Ireland. In 1862 he was dismissed from the service for a very minor offense, became a clerk in London, and contributed (using the signature B.V.) to the *National Reformer,* the magazine of his friend Charles Bradlaugh. Thomson's life in London was lonely and impoverished, aggravated by insomnia, his own incredibly melancholic disposition, and periodic bouts with alcoholism. His greatest poetical work, *The City of Dreadful Night* (1880, first published in the *National Reformer,* 1874), gives brilliant, haunting expression to his despair. The poem "Sunday up the River" (first published in *Fraser's Magazine,* 1869) is an example of his lyric gift. *Vane's Story* (1880) and *A Voice from the Nile* (1884) are later collections of his poems. Thomson also wrote many essays and criticisms. His collected poems appeared in 1895 and a volume of prose in 1896. See biography by H. S. Salt (rev. ed. 1914); study by I. B. Walker (1950).

Thomson, Sir John Arthur, 1861-1933, Scottish naturalist and writer. From 1899 to 1930 he was Regius professor of natural history at the Univ. of Aberdeen. In 1924 he lectured at Union Theological Seminary, New York City, and at Yale. He was knighted in 1930. He wrote about zoology, concentrating on the alcyonarians (subclass of marine coelenterates, including the soft corals), but he is especially remembered for his many popular works on science and on the reconciliation of science and religion. His works, scholarly in content and of good literary style, include *What is Man?* (1923), *Science and Religion* (1925), and *Modern Science* (1929). He edited *The Outline of Science* (4 vol., 1922; repr. 1937).

Thomson, Joseph, 1858-95, Scottish explorer in Africa. At the Univ. of Edinburgh he studied geology and botany. On his first expedition (1879) he reached Lake Tanganyika and then explored the relationships of the lakes in the Great Rift Valley to the drainage system of Africa. On another trip (1882–83) he traveled through Kenya and Uganda and climbed Kilimanjaro. Thomson explored (1885) present-day N Nigeria and forestalled German designs on the area by concluding many treaties with native chiefs on behalf of Great Britain. His last expedition (1890) was in SE Africa; he explored the Zambezi River and obtained extensive concessions for the British South Africa Company. His books include *To the Central African Lakes and Back* (2 vol., 1881) and *Through Masai Land* (rev. ed. 1887). See biography by James B. Thomson (1896); R. I. Rotberg, *Joseph Thomson and the Exploration of Africa* (1971).

Thomson, Sir Joseph John, 1856–1940, English physicist. From 1884 to 1919 he was Cavendish professor of experimental physics at Cambridge. J. J. Thomson was one of the founders of modern physics. Winner of the 1906 Nobel Prize in Physics for his study of conduction of electricity through gases, he is known also for his discovery (1897) of the electron and his investigation of its charge and mass, his development of the mathematical theory of electricity and magnetism, and his work with "positive rays" (positive ion beams), which led to a means of separating atoms and molecules according to their atomic weights. His work with F. W. Aston gave evidence of the existence of isotopes of neon; Aston was later able to show that most chemical elements have two or more different isotopes. In addition to his own research, Thomson made a significant contribution during his long tenure as director of the Cavendish Laboratory in making it a leading center for atomic research where many important developments in modern physics occurred. He was knighted (1908), served (1915–20) as president of the Royal Society, and was master of Trinity College, Cambridge, from 1918 until his death. He is buried in Westminster Abbey. His works include *Elements of the Mathematical Theory of Electricity and Magnetism* (1895, 5th ed. 1921), *Conduction of Electricity through Gases* (1903; 3d ed., with George Paget Thomson, 2 vol., 1928–33), and an autobiography, *Recollections and Reflections* (1936). See biography by R. J. Rayleigh (1942); Sir George Paget Thomson, *J. J. Thomson and the Cavendish Laboratory in His Day* (1965).

Thomson or **Thompson, Mortimer Neal,** 1831–75, American journalist and humorist who used the pseudonym Q. K. Philander Doesticks, P.B., b. Riga, N.Y. He joined the staff of the New York *Tribune* in 1855. His contributions in verse and prose, especially those against slavery, attracted wide attention. During the Civil War he served as a war correspondent for the *Tribune* and also as chaplain to a Union regiment. His best-known works include *Doesticks: What He Says* (1855) and a parody of Hiawatha, *Pluri-bus-tah* (1856).

Thomson, Tom, 1877–1917, Canadian painter of typically Canadian outdoor scenes, b. Ontario. Thomson was self-taught. Most of the year he served as a guide at Algonquin Provincial Park, in order to support himself as a painter. His love of the outdoors was reflected in bold, vibrantly colored landscapes, such as *A Northern Lake* (National Gall., Ottawa). Thomson was mysteriously drowned in the summer of 1917.

Thomson, Virgil, 1896–, American composer, critic, and organist, b. Kansas City, Mo. Thomson studied in Paris with Nadia Boulanger. Until about 1926 he wrote in a dissonant, neoclassic style, but after his *Sonata da chiesa* (1926) he began to employ a highly simplified style that shows the influence of Erik Satie. He wrote two operas, *Four Saints in Three Acts* (1928) and *The Mother of Us All* (1947), for librettos by Gertrude Stein; music for films including *The River* (1937) and *Louisiana Story* (1948); the ballet *Filling Station* (1937); an opera, *Lord Byron* (1972); and numerous works for organ, piano, and chamber ensembles. Thomson was music critic for the New York *Herald Tribune* from 1940 until 1954. His books include *The State of Music* (1939), *The Musical Scene* (1945), *The Art of Judging Music* (1948), and *American Music Since 1910* (1971). See his autobiography (1966); study by Kathleen O. Hoover and John Cage (1959).

Thomson, William: see KELVIN, WILLIAM THOMSON, 1ST BARON.

Thomson effect: see THERMOELECTRICITY.

Thon Buri (tŭn bŏŏr'ē), city (1970 pop. 919,000), central Thailand, on the west bank of the Chao Phraya River across from Bangkok. Part of metropolitan Bangkok, Thon Buri is a center of rice milling, sawmilling, and light manufacturing industries. It was capital of Siam from 1767 to 1782. The most famous landmark is the Wat Arun temple.

Thor (thôr), Germanic **Donar** (dō'när), Norse god of thunder. An ancient and highly revered divinity, Thor was the patron and protector of peasants and warriors. As a god of might and war he was represented as extremely powerful and fearless, occasionally slow-witted, armed with a magical hammer (which returned to him when he threw it), iron gloves, and a belt of strength. Being a god of the people he was also associated with marriage, with the hearth, and with agriculture. According to one legend he was the son of WODEN. Thor was identified with the Roman god Jupiter, and among Germanic peoples Jove's day became Thor's day (Thursday).

thorax, body division found in certain animals. In man and other mammals it lies between the neck and abdomen and is also called the chest. The skeletal frame of the thorax is formed by the sternum (breastbone) and ribs in front and the dorsal vertebrae in back. Within the thoracic cavity are the heart, lungs, and esophagus. The chest and abdominal cavities are separated by a muscular structure, the diaphragm. In insects and other arthropods the thorax is a body division consisting of several segments lying between the head and abdomen, to which are attached legs or other appendages.

Thorazine, trade name for CHLORPROMAZINE. See also PSYCHOPHARMACOLOGY; PHENOTHIAZINE.

Thorbecke, Jan Rudolf (yän rōō'dôlf tôr'bĕkə), 1798–1872, Dutch statesman. An eminent jurist and the leading liberal politician of his day, he was one of the men appointed in 1848 by King William II to revise the constitution. Thorbecke was largely responsible for the final revision, which increased the power of the States-General and reduced that of the king. He served (1849–52) as the first constitutional premier of the Netherlands and was twice more premier (1862–66, 1871–72). He gave Catholics equal rights with Protestants, extended the electorate, removed trade restrictions, and initiated projects for the construction of canals for reclaiming land from the sea.

Thoreau, Henry David (thôr'ō, thərō'), 1817–62, American author and naturalist, b. Concord, Mass.; grad. Harvard, 1837. Thoreau is considered one of the most influential figures in American thought and literature. A supreme individualist, he championed the human spirit against materialism and social conformity. His most famous book, *Walden* (1854), is an eloquent account of his experiment in near-solitary living in close harmony with nature; it is also an expression of his transcendentalist philosophy. Thoreau grew up in Concord and attended Harvard, where he was known as a serious though unconventional scholar. During his Harvard years he was exposed to the writings of Ralph Waldo Emerson, who later became his chief mentor and friend. After graduation, Thoreau worked for a time in his father's pencil shop and taught at a grammar school, but in 1841 he was invited to live in the Emerson household, where he remained intermittently until 1843. He served as handyman and assistant to Emerson, helping to edit and contributing poetry and prose to the transcendentalist magazine, *The Dial* (see TRANSCENDENTALISM). In 1845, Thoreau built himself a small cabin on the shore of Walden Pond, near Concord; there he remained for more than two years, "living deep and sucking out all the marrow of life." Wishing to lead a life free of materialistic pursuits, he supported himself by growing vegetables and by surveying and doing odd jobs in the nearby village. He devoted most of his time to observing nature, reading, and writing, and he kept a detailed journal of his observations, activities, and thoughts. It was from this journal that he later distilled *Walden*. The journal, begun in 1837, was also the source of his first book, *A Week on the Concord and Merrimack Rivers* (1849), as well as of his posthumously published *Excursions* (1863), *The Maine Woods* (1864), *Cape Cod* (1865), and *A Yankee in Canada* (1866). One of Thoreau's most important works, the essay "Civil Disobedience" (1849), grew out of an overnight stay in prison as a result of his conscientious refusal to pay a poll tax that supported the Mexican War, which to Thoreau represented an effort to extend slavery. Thoreau's advocacy of civil disobedience as a means for the individual to protest those actions of his government that he considers unjust has had a wide-ranging impact—on the British Labour movement, the passive resistance independence movement led by Gandhi in India, and the nonviolent civil rights movement led by Martin Luther King in the United States. Thoreau is also significant as a naturalist who emphasized the dynamic ecology of the natural world. Above all, Thoreau's quiet, one-man revolution in living at Walden has become a symbol of man's willed integrity, his inner freedom, and his ability to build his own life. Thoreau's writings, including his journals, were published in 20 volumes in 1906. See his collected poems, ed. by Carl Bode (rev. ed. 1964); his letters, ed. by Carl Bode and Walter Harding (1958, repr. 1974); biographies by H. S. Canby (1939, repr. 1965), Walter Harding (1965), and J. W. Krutch (1948, repr. 1973); studies by C. R. Anderson (1968), Sherman Paul (1972), and W. J. Wolf (1974); collections of critical essays, ed. by W. R. Harding (1960) and Sherman Paul (1962).

Thorez, Maurice (mōrēs' tôrĕz'), 1900–1964, French Communist leader. The son of a coal miner, Thorez himself worked in the mines. He early joined the Socialist party and in 1920 became one of the original members of the French Communist party. Largely self-taught, Thorez rose in the ranks and became party secretary in 1930 and a leader of the Communists in the chamber of deputies, to which he was elected in 1932. Conscripted when World War II broke out, Thorez deserted and went to Moscow. Although sentenced in absentia, he was amnestied (1944) after the liberation of France and was reelected a deputy. Under his leadership the Communists became the largest single party in the elections of 1945 and 1946. Thorez was vice premier in 1946–47 but afterward returned to the opposition. His position in national politics was subsequently weakened—particularly after the revelations of Stalinist atrocities, since Thorez had been associated with the Soviet leader. See his early autobiography (tr. 1938).

Thorfinn Karlsefni (thôr'fĭn kärl'sĕvnē), fl. 1002–15, Icelandic leader of an attempt to colonize North America. He appeared in Greenland in 1002 and married Gudrid, widow of one of the sons of Eric the Red. He set out c.1010 with an expedition consisting of three ships and 160 men to settle in VINLAND, which Leif Ericsson had discovered a few years before. There are two sources for this event, the "Saga of Eric the Red" in the collection of sagas known as *Hauksbok*, and a narrative interpolated in the "Saga of Olaf Tryggvason" in the *Flateyjarbok*. According to the former, which has been favored by most scholars, the expedition came first to a region they called Helluland. Then they passed on to a wooded country which they named Markland, sailed by sandy, desolate beaches called Furdustrands, and settled for the winter in a bay called Straumfjord. Still seeking the land of grapes, they proceeded southward the next spring until they reached a place called Hop. There they found vines, and there they settled for the next winter, selecting a spot up a river that widened into a lake. Several encounters with the natives, however, in which two of their number were killed, induced them to abandon Hop in the spring and return to Straumfjord, where they spent the third winter. One of the ships, commanded by Thorhall, had deserted the first year after a disagreement and had met disaster in Ireland. With the prospect of attack, plus growing dissension, it was decided to abandon the whole attempt. Returning by Markland, Thorfinn's ship reached Greenland safely; the other was wrecked in the Irish Sea and part of its crew saved. Much effort has been spent in attempts to identify the lands visited by Thorfinn and to discover his wintering sites, but no theory has won general acceptance. Places from Labrador to New England have been suggested, but such identifications are little more than guesses. There is also divergence on the dates assigned to Thorfinn's expedition. See bibliography under LEIF ERICSSON and VINLAND.

thorium (thôr'ēəm) [from *Thor*], radioactive chemical element; symbol Th; at. no. 90; mass no. of most stable isotope 232; m.p. about 1750°C; b.p. about 4000°C; sp. gr. 11.7 at 20°C; valence +4. Thorium is a soft, ductile, lustrous, silver-white, radioactive metal. At ordinary temperatures it has a face-centered cubic crystalline structure. It is a member of the ACTINIDE SERIES in group IIIb of the PERIODIC TABLE and is sometimes classed as one of the RARE-EARTH METALS. When pure, the metal is stable and resists oxidation, but it is usually contaminated with small amounts of the oxide, which cause it to tarnish rapidly. It reacts slowly with water and is attacked only by hydrochloric acid among the common acids. The finely divided metal readily ignites when heated, burning with a brilliant white flame; the oxide formed has the highest melting point of all oxides. Thorium forms numerous compounds with other elements. It is widely distributed in small amounts, e.g., in the minerals thorite (thorium silicate, $ThSiO_4$) and thorianite (mixed thorium and uranium oxides). A chief source of thorium is monazite sands obtained from India, Canada, and Brazil. Vast deposits of low-grade thorium ore in New Hampshire are a potential source. Thorium metal is isolated with difficulty; it is obtained from certain of its compounds by electrolysis or by chemical reduction. Thorium is used in magnesium alloys and in tungsten filaments for light bulbs and electronic tubes. The most important thorium compound is the oxide (thoria, ThO_2), which is the major incandescent component of the WELSBACH MANTLE; it is also used in crucibles, in special highly refractive optical glass, and in catalysts for several industrially important chemical reactions. Important uses of the element result from its natural radioactivity. There are 12 known radioactive isotopes. The most stable is thorium-232 (half-life 1.41×10^{10} years); it is the major component of naturally occurring thorium, which has atomic weight 232.038 atomic mass units. Thorium-232 undergoes natural disintegration and eventually is converted through a 10-step chain of isotopes to lead-208, a stable isotope; alpha and beta particles are emitted during this decay. One intermediate product is the gas RADON-220, also called thorium emanation or thoron. Thorium and its decay products are sometimes used in radiotherapy. Although thorium-232 is not itself a nuclear reactor fuel since it will not sustain a chain reaction, it is expected to become increasingly important for conversion into the fissionable fuel uranium-233. Thorium-232 can react with a thermal (slow) neutron to form thorium-233, emitting a gamma ray. Thorium-233 decays (half-life about 22 min) to protactinium-233, emitting a beta particle. The protactinium-233 decays (half-life about 27 days) with another beta particle emission to uranium-233. Fission of the uranium-233 can provide neutrons to start the cycle again. This cycle of reactions is known as the thorium cycle. Nuclear reactors that use a cycle like this to produce fuel are called BREEDER REACTORS. Thorium was discovered in 1828 by J. J. Berzelius but had few uses until the invention of the Welsbach mantle in 1885.

Thorn: see TORUŃ, Poland.

thorn, sharp-pointed projection on some plants, usually protective in function. Botanically, thorns are distinguished as modified stems (as in the honey locust and hawthorn) from spines, which are modified leaves (as in the barberry), and from prickles, which are epidermal outgrowths of the bark (as in the rose and blackberry). Cacti have both thorns and spines. Thorns have become symbolic of pain, adversity, and sorrow.

Thorndike, Edward Lee (thôrn'dīk), 1874–1949, American educator and psychologist, b. Williamsburg, Mass., grad. Wesleyan Univ., 1895, and Harvard, 1896, Ph.D. Columbia, 1898. Appointed instructor in genetic psychology at Teachers College, Columbia, in 1899, he served there until 1940 (as professor from 1904 and as director of the division of psychology of the Institute of Educational Research from 1922). His great contributions to educational psychology were largely in the methods he devised to test and measure children's intelligence and their ability to learn. He conducted studies in animal psychology and the psychology of learning, and compiled dictionaries for children (1935) and for young adults (1941). The great number of his writings includes *Educational Psychology* (1903), *Mental and Social Measurements* (1904), *Animal Intelligence* (1911), *A Teacher's Word Book* (1921), *Your City* (1939), and *Human Nature and the Social Order* (1940). See biography by G. M. Joncich (1968).

Thorndike, Lynn, 1882–1965, American historian, b. Lynn, Mass. He taught history at Northwestern Univ. (1907–9), at Western Reserve Univ. (1909–24), and at Columbia (1924–50). Among his books on magic and science in the Middle Ages are *A History of Magic and Experimental Science* (8 vol., 1923–58) and *Science and Thought in the Fifteenth Century* (1929). Thorndike also wrote *The History of Medieval Europe* (1917, 3d ed. 1949), widely used in American colleges, and *University Records and Life in the Middle Ages* (1944).

Thorndike, Dame Sybil, 1882–, English actress. Thorndike made her debut with the Ben Greet Players and toured the United States with them (1904–7). She worked with the Old Vic (1914–18) in Shakespearean repertory and thereafter played hundreds of classic roles. Thorndike was acclaimed for her performances in Euripides' *Medea* and *The Trojan Women* and in several of Shaw's works. She was made Dame of the British Empire in 1931. In 1969, Thorndike performed at the opening of the London theater named for her. See biographies by her brother, Russell Thorndike (2d ed. 1950), by her son, John Casson (1972), and by Elizabeth Sprigge (1971).

Thornhill, Sir James, 1676–1734, English decorative artist. George I made him court painter and later knighted him. He executed decorations in Hampton Court and the cupola of St. Paul's, London; the hall of Greenwich Hospital, Chatham, England; the great hall of Blenheim Palace; and various chapels at Oxford, where he also painted altarpieces for All Souls and Queen's colleges. As a teacher, he found a rare pupil in HOGARTH, who became his son-in-law. The limited number of Thornhill's etchings includes *Adam and Eve.*

Thornton, Matthew, 1714–1803, political leader in the American Revolution, signer of the Declaration of Independence, b. Ireland. Taken to America as a child, he studied medicine and in 1740 began practice at Londonderry, N.H. He served as an army surgeon in the French and Indian Wars and held political posts in New Hampshire before and after his term in the Continental Congress (1776–77).

Thornton, William, 1759–1828, American architect, b. Tortola, British Virgin Islands, of English Quaker parents. He studied (1781–84) medicine at Edinburgh but received his medical degree (1784) at the Univ. of Aberdeen. He traveled widely and studied architectural forms. In 1787 he emigrated to the United States and became a citizen in 1788. His plan for the Library Company in Philadelphia won a competition in 1789. Through Trumbull, the painter, he gained permission to submit a plan for the proposed Capitol at Washington in an official competition opened in 1792. Thornton's designs, submitted in 1793, were approved by President Washington, and their execution was entrusted to the supervision of E. S. HALLET and James Hoban. In 1794, however, Thornton himself, being appointed a commissioner of the District of Columbia, became supervisor and remained in charge until 1802. Despite important changes and additions, especially by LATROBE and Bullfinch, much of the design of the facade of the central portion of the Capitol is his. In Washington he also designed a number of residences, including the Tayloe house, known as the Octagon, later the headquarters of the American Institute of Architects. Thornton was the first to hold the post of clerk in charge of the Patent Office, and he served as commissioner of patents from 1802 until his death.

Thornton, city (1970 pop. 13,326), Adams co., NE Colo., a residential suburb of Denver; inc. 1956.

Thóroddsen, Jón (yōn tō'rôtsĕn), 1818–68, Icelandic novelist and poet. He studied law in Copenhagen intermittently from 1841 to 1850, fought in the Danish army, and after his return to Iceland was prefect of various districts until his death. Although he contributed to political and literary periodicals and wrote idyllic poetry, his chief importance was as a novelist. His *Lad and Lass* (1850, tr. 1890) was the first published novel in Icelandic. In a vigorous, concise style, showing the influence of the sagas, he depicted rural life in Iceland and created lively, highly individual characters. In his last novel, *Man and Wife* (1876), there is much folklore and superstition.

Thorold (thôr'ōld, -əld, thûr'-), town (1971 pop. 15,065), S Ont., Canada, on the Welland Ship Canal. It is a suburb of St. Catharines.

thoron: see RADON; THORIUM.

thorough bass: see FIGURED BASS.

Thoroughbred horse, breed of LIGHT HORSE more properly known as the English running horse. As its name implies, it was the first pedigreed, or "thorough bred" horse. It originated in England from a cross between an ARABIAN HORSE and a Turkish horse and has since been exported around the world. Fastest of all horses, it can maintain a speed of 45 mi (72 km) per hr for a distance of more than a mile (1.6 km). Taking into consideration both speed and endurance, it is considered by some to be the swiftest creature in existence. The Thoroughbred has held undisputed reign as king of horseracing and is also preeminent in the hunt, the steeplechase, and polo. Its temperament is racy and nervous. Thoroughbreds average over 16 hands (64 in./160 cm) in height, weigh around 1,100 lb (500 kg), and have a leggy appearance. They may be any color but usually have white markings.

thoroughwort: see BONESET.

Thorpe, Jim (James Thorpe), 1888–1953, American athlete, b. near Prague, Okla. Thorpe was probably the greatest all-round male athlete the United States has ever produced. His mother, a Sac Indian, named him Bright Path, and in 1907 he entered the Carlisle Indian School at Carlisle, Pa. He joined (1908) the Carlisle football team, coached by Glenn ("Pop") Warner, and in 1911–12 Thorpe, playing left halfback, led Carlisle in startling upsets over such highly rated teams as Harvard, Army, and the Univ. of Pennsylvania. In 1912, Thorpe took part in the Olympic games held at Stockholm, Sweden, and performed magnificently. He won the broad jump and the 200-meter and 1,500-meter runs of the pentathlon; won the shot put, the 1,500-meter run, and the hurdle race of the decathlon; and was the runner-up in the other events of the pentathlon and decathlon. In 1913, however, Thorpe surrendered his awards, at the request of the Amateur Athletic Union and the insistence of Glenn Warner, to the Olympic headquarters in Switzerland; it was discovered that Thorpe had played (1909–10) semiprofessional baseball with the Rocky Mount, N.C., team of the North Carolina Eastern League. In 1919, Thorpe played briefly with the New York Giants baseball team. He afterwards played professional football with the Canton (Ohio) Bulldogs and other teams and later became supervisor of recreation for the Chicago parks. Jim Thorpe, Pa., is named in his honor. With T. F. Collison, he wrote *Jim Thorpe's History of the Olympics* (1932). See biography by Gene Schoor (1951).

Thorshavn: see TÓRSHAVN, Faeroe Islands.

Thorvaldsen or **Thorwaldsen, Albert Bertel** (both: äl'bĕrt bĕr'təl tôr'välsən), 1770–1844, Danish sculptor, b. Copenhagen. In 1797 he went to Rome, where he shared with Canova the leadership of the neoclassicists. His adherence to Greek art is shown in his *Jason* (1802–3), one of his many classical subjects, rendered with an intellectual coolness and a respect for antique prototypes. For Prince Louis of Bavaria he made restorations of the ancient Aeginetan marbles. In 1819 he designed the famous *Lion of Lucerne,* carved from the native rock at Lucerne by his pupils—a memorial to the devotion of the Swiss Guard in the French Revolution. The works he executed for Copenhagen were chiefly the figural decorations for the Church of Our Lady, completed with the help of his numerous assistants. The *Christ* from this project is especially notable. Among Thorvaldsen's historical portrait sculptures are that of Pope Pius VII (St. Peter's, Rome) and *Conradin, Last of the Hohenstaufen* (Naples). The Thorvaldsen Museum, Copenhagen, contains in originals and models a large group of the sculptor's work, together with his collection of antiquities, paintings, and books. Many of the American sculptors of the period studied with Thorvaldsen.

Thoth (thŏth, tōt), in Egyptian religion, god of wisdom and magic. A patron of learning and of the arts, he was credited with many inventions, including writing, geometry, and astronomy. Perhaps originally a moon god, Thoth was also a messenger and scribe for the gods. He was identified by the Greeks with Hermes and as such was specifically named Hermes Trismegistus (see HERMETIC BOOKS). He was variously represented as an ibis, as an ibis-headed man, or as a baboon.

Thothmes: see THUTMOSE.

Thou, Jacques Auguste de (zhäk ôgüst' də to͞o), 1553–1617, French historian and magistrate. As a member of the Parlement of Paris, Thou rendered outstanding service to Henry IV. The first volumes of his great *History of His Own Times* (1604–8, in Latin), covering the Wars of Religion of the 16th cent., aroused Roman Catholic opposition because of his strictures against the Catholic League and his Gallican leanings. The complete work was published at Geneva in 1620 (tr., 2 vol., 1724–34). See study of his works by Samuel Kinser (1966). His son, **François Auguste de Thou,** 1607–42, played a minor role in the conspiracy of his friend CINQ MARS, but was executed for failing to reveal it to the authorities.

thought reading: see PARAPSYCHOLOGY; TELEPATHY.

Thousand and One Nights or **Arabian Nights,** a series of anonymous Oriental stories in Arabic, considered as an entity to be among the classics of world literature. The cohesive plot device concerns the efforts of Scheherezade, or Sheherazade, to keep her husband, Schariar, legendary king of Samarkand, from killing her by entertaining him with a tale a night for 1,001 nights. The best known of these stories are those of Ali Baba, Sinbad the Sailor, and Aladdin. Although many of the stories are set in India, their origins are unknown and have been the subject of intensive scholarly investigation. The present form of the *Thousand and One Nights* is completely Muslim in spirit and is thought to be native to Persia or one of the Arabic-speaking countries. The first European edition was a free translation by Abbé Antoine Galland into French (1704–17). Most subsequent French, German, and English versions lean heavily upon Galland. Among the English translations are the expurgated edition of E. W. Lane (1840), with excellent and copious notes; the unexpurgated edition by Sir Richard Burton in 16 volumes (1885–88); that of John Payne in 9 volumes (1882–84); and Powys Mathers's translation from the French text of J. C. Mardrus (rev. ed., 4 vol., 1937). See Joseph Campbell, ed., *The Portable Arabian Nights* (1952); A. J. Arberry, *Scheherezade* (1955).

Thousand Islands, a group of more than 1,800 islands and 3,000 shoals in the St. Lawrence River, E of Lake Ontario, N N.Y. and S Ont., stretching c.50 mi (80 km) along the U.S.-Canada line. Most of the islands are in Canada; Wolfe Island, Ont. (48 sq mi/124 sq km), is the largest. The islands are part of a belt of metamorphic rock connecting the Adirondack Mts. and the Canadian Shield; they were formed at the end of the Ice Age, when the St. Lawrence River became the chief outlet of the Great Lakes. The forested region is a popular summer resort; many of the islands are privately owned. There are numerous parks on the islands, including Canada's St. Lawrence Islands National Park. The five-span Thousand Islands Bridge and highway (7 mi/11 km long; opened 1938) between the New York and Ontario mainlands crosses several islands and channels.

Thousand Oaks, residential city (1970 pop. 35,873), Ventura co., S Calif., in a farm area; inc. 1964. It has some light manufacturing. Formerly known generally as the Conejo Valley, it became a stagecoach stop in 1874. California Lutheran College is there, and Oxnard Air Force Base is nearby.

Thrace (thrās), region, SE Europe, occupying the southeastern tip of the Balkan Peninsula and comprising NE Greece, S Bulgaria, and European Turkey. Its boundaries have varied in different periods. It is washed by the Black Sea in the northeast and by the Sea of Marmara and the Aegean Sea in the south. The Rhodope mts. separate Greek from Bulgarian Thrace, and the Maritsa River (called the Évros in Greece) separates Greek from Turkish Thrace. The chief cities are İstanbul, Edirne (formerly Adrianople), and Gallipoli (all in Turkey); İstanbul (Constantinople) is generally considered a separate entity. With the exception of the mountainous Bulgarian section, Thrace is mainly agricultural, producing tobacco, wheat, silk, cotton, olive oil, and fruit. Coal, chromium, and wolfram are mined. At the dawn of history the ancient Thracians—a group of tribes speaking an Indo-European language—extended as far west as the Adriatic Sea, but they were pushed eastward (c.1300 B.C.) by the Illyrians, and in the 5th cent. B.C. they lost their land W of the Struma (Strimón) River to Macedon. In the north, however, Thrace at that period still extended to the Danube. Unlike the Macedonians, the Thracians did not absorb Greek culture, and their tribes formed separate petty kingdoms. The Thracian Bronze Age was similar to that of Mycenaean Greece, and the Thracians had developed high forms of music and poetry, but their savage warfare led the Greeks to consider them barbarians. Many Greek colonies—e.g., Byzantium on the Hellespont and Tomi (modern Constanţa) on the Black Sea—were founded in Thrace by c.600 B.C. The Greeks exploited Thracian gold and silver mines, and they recruited Thracians for their infantry. Thrace was reduced to vassalage by Persia from c.512 B.C. to 479 B.C., and Persian customs were introduced. Thrace was united as a kingdom under the chieftain Sitalces, who aided Athens during the Peloponnesian War, but after his death (428 B.C.) the state again broke up. By 342 B.C. all Thrace was held by Philip II of Macedon, and after 323 B.C. most of the country was in the hands of Lysimachus. It fell apart once more after Lysimachus' death (281 B.C.), and it was conquered by the Romans late in the 1st cent. B.C. Emperor Claudius created (A.D. 46) the province of Thrace, comprising the territory S of the Balkans; the remainder was incorporated into Moesia. The chief centers of Roman Thrace were Sardica (modern Sofia), Philippopolis (Plovdiv), and Adrianople (Edirne). The region benefited greatly from Roman rule, but from the barbarian invasions of the 3d cent. A.D. until modern times it was almost continuously a battleground. The northern section passed (7th cent.) to the Bulgarians; the southern section remained in the Byzantine Empire, but it was largely conquered (13th cent.) by the second Bulgarian empire after a brief period under the Latin Empire of Constantinople. In 1361 the Ottoman Turks took Adrianople, and in 1453, after the fall of Constantinople, all of Thrace fell to the Turks. In 1878, N Thrace was made into the province of Eastern RUMELIA; after the annexation (1885) of Eastern Rumelia by Bulgaria (which had gained independence in 1878), the political meaning of the term *Thrace* became restricted to its southernmost part, which was still in Turkish hands. The terms *Eastern Thrace* and *Western Thrace* were used for the territories E and W of the Maritsa River. In the first of the BALKAN WARS (1912–13) Turkey ceded to Bulgaria all Western Thrace and the inland half of Eastern Thrace, including Adrianople, but after its defeat in the Second Balkan War (1913), Bulgaria retroceded all Thrace E of the Maritsa to Turkey. After World War I, Bulgaria ceded the southern part of its share of Thrace to Greece by the Treaty of Neuilly (1919), thus losing its only outlet to the Aegean. By the Treaty of Sèvres (1920) Greece also obtained most of Eastern Thrace except the zone of the Straits and Constantinople; the treaty, however, was superseded by the Treaty of Lausanne (1923), which restored to Turkey all Thrace E of the Maritsa. As a result of subsequent population movements, the ethnic composition of the various parts of Thrace now corresponds largely to the national divisions. The Greek-Bulgarian frontier of 1919 and the Turkish-Greek frontier of 1923 were left unchanged after World War II, during which Bulgaria had occupied (1941–44) Greek Thrace. The Greek-Bulgarian boundary remains a point of dispute between the two countries.

Thrale, Hester Lynch, later **Mrs. Piozzi** (pēŏz'ē, pēôt'sē), 1741–1821, Englishwoman, noted for her friendship with Samuel Johnson. Daughter of John Salusbury, she married in 1763 Henry Thrale, a wealthy brewer, whose home at Streatham became a second home to Johnson from 1765 until 1780. Mrs. Thrale's second marriage in 1784 to Gabriel Piozzi, an Italian music master, estranged her from Johnson. She later published *Anecdotes of the Late Samuel Johnson* (1786) and his correspondence with her (1788). See her diary, *Thraliana* (ed. by K. C. Balderston, 1942).

Thrasea Paetus (Publius Clodius Thrasea Paetus) (thrăsē'ə pē'təs), d. A.D. 66, Roman senator and Stoic philosopher. He criticized Nero, who commanded the senate to condemn him to death. When he heard the news, he committed suicide by cutting open the veins in his arm.

thrasher: see MIMIC THRUSH.

thrashing: see THRESHING.

Thrasybulus (thrăs"əbyōō'ləs), d. c.389 B.C., Athenian statesman. A strong supporter of the democratic and anti-Spartan party, he successfully opposed (411 B.C.) the oligarchical Four Hundred and later had ALCIBIADES recalled. In the Peloponnesian War he fought at Cyzicus (410; now in Turkey) and Arginusae (406). Banished by the THIRTY TYRANTS, he obtained the help of exiles in Thebes, marched with his force from Phyle to Piraeus, and overthrew (403) the Thirty. He was leading a campaign in a new war against Sparta when the excesses of his troops so outraged the citizens of Aspendus (now in Turkey) that they murdered him.

thread, a fine twist of fibrous material, distinguished from YARN in general by being smoother, stronger, and more pliable; it is also better suited to sewing, embroidery, and lacemaking. Sewing or spool COTTON is made by twisting several fine strands into three-cord or six-cord thread, the latter being three two-ply strands twisted together. The size is controlled by the twisting process. The fine linen thread used in making expensive laces is spun by hand and is very costly. Synthetic threads, such as nylon, are most often used for heavy-duty sewing in carpets, shoes, and heavy canvases. Many ordinary sewing threads now contain some proportion of synthetic fiber.

threat, in law, declaration of intent to injure another by doing an unlawful act, with a view to restraining his freedom of action. A threat is distinguishable from an ASSAULT, for an assault requires some physical act that appears likely to eventuate in violence, whereas a threat may consist of words only or an act that is not violent, e.g., unlawful prosecution. Threats made to obtain money or property wrongfully are crimes (see BLACKMAIL and EXTORTION), and under some statutes, the mere sending of nonextortionate letters that announce an intent to injure the person or property of another is criminal. Any contract concluded while one party is deprived of his freedom of will by a threat (see DURESS) is invalid and may be set aside.

Three Emperors' League, informal alliance among Austria-Hungary, Germany, and Russia, announced officially in 1872 on the occasion of the meeting of emperors Francis Joseph, William I, and Alexander II. The chief architects of the alliance were Julius Andrássy, Otto von Bismarck, and Prince Gorchakov. The aims of the league were to preserve the social order of the conservative powers of Europe and to keep the peace between Austria-Hungary and Russia. The Russo-Turkish War of 1877–78 shook the alliance (see BERLIN, CONGRESS OF). Although the agreement was secretly renewed in 1881, it was disrupted again in 1885 as a result of the Balkan flareup. However, it remained in force until 1887, when it was eclipsed by the German-Austrian alliance of 1879, which after the adherence of Italy (1882) became the Triple Alliance. From 1887 to 1890 all that remained of the Three Emperors' League was a Russo-German reinsurance treaty. The German chancellor Graf von Caprivi refused to renew even this in 1890, thus opening the way for the Franco-Russian rapprochement and the creation of the Triple Entente (see TRIPLE ALLIANCE AND TRIPLE ENTENTE).

Three Holy Children, the three men cast by Nebuchadnezzar into the fiery furnace and delivered by an angel. Their names are Abed-nego, Shadrach, and Meshach, in Babylonian; Azariah, Hananiah, and Mishael, in Hebrew; and Azarias, Ananias, and Misael, in Greek. Dan. 1.7; 3. The Song of the Three Holy Children is one of the portions of DANIEL that appears in the Greek texts but not in the Hebrew-Aramaic versions. Hence it is relegated in the Authorized Version to the Apocrypha; in the Western canon it is numbered 3.24–90. It recounts the actions of the three men in the furnace, first a prayer by Azarias for the victory of God, then a hymn by all three in praise of God (3.52–90); the portion from verse 57 is called Benedicite.

Three Kingdoms, period of Chinese history from 220 to 265, after the collapse of the Han dynasty. The period takes its name from the three states into which China was divided. Wei occupied the north and included most of Korea. South of Wei were Shu in the west and Wu in the east. Each of the states steadily expanded, especially Shu, which moved into modern Yünnan and Burma. Wei, however, later steadily increased its strength and crushed Shu in 264. When a usurper seized the Wei throne in 265 and founded the TSIN dynasty, the Three Kingdoms period officially came to an end. Disorders during the Three Kingdoms period included not only warfare between the Chinese states but also incursions into the north by the Hsiung-nu (Huns). The era is fondly regarded in China as exemplifying the highest ideals of chivalry and has been depicted in the adventurous novel *San Kuo Chih Yen I* [romance of the three kingdoms]. The disorder and disunity of the time caused the eclipse of Confucianism, but opened Chinese culture to new influences, such as native Taoism and Indian Buddhism. From India also came many advances in scientific learning. As knowledge of the outside world grew, maps were improved and a grid system of coordinates was invented. Art was predominantly Buddhist in inspiration and showed many central Asiatic traits.

Three Kings: see WISE MEN OF THE EAST.

Three Pagodas Pass, mountain pass, alt. 925 ft (282 m), at the southern end of the Dawna Range, on the Burma-Thailand border. It has long been the chief route between SE Burma and the Chao Phraya valley of Thailand.

Three Rivers, Que., Canada: see TROIS RIVIERES.

Three Taverns: see TRES TABERNAE.

threonine (thrē'ənēn), organic compound, one of the 22 α-AMINO ACIDS commonly found in animal proteins. Only the L-stereoisomer appears in mammalian protein. It is one of several essential amino acids needed in the diet; human beings cannot synthesize it from simpler metabolites. Young adults need about 14 mg of this amino acid per day per kilogram (6 mg per lb) of body weight. Although threonine participates in many reactions in bacteria, including the biosynthesis of vitamin B_{12} and ISOLEU-

CH_3
HCOH
H_2N—C—C(=O)OH
H

threonine

CINE, its metabolic role in higher animals, including man, remains obscure. It is known only as a constituent of proteins, and even in that form it is relatively unreactive. In spite of the fact that its side chain has a hydroxyl group similar to that of SERINE, there is no indication that it participates in the catalytic functions of any enzyme. Threonine was isolated from the protein fibrin in 1935 and synthesized in the same year.

thresher shark, long-tailed, warm-water shark, genus *Alopias.* The upper fork of its tail is slender and sickle-shaped and is about equal in length to the rest of the body. This shark uses its tail to herd the small schooling fish on which it feeds; the tail is flailed from side to side, sweeping the prey in front of the shark. It also slaps the water with its tail to frighten the fish. Threshers are found chiefly in offshore, tropical waters, but are also known in temperate regions. The common thresher, *A. vulpinus,* is widely distributed throughout the Atlantic and the E Pacific; it is common off the New England coast in summer and is fished commercially on the S California coast. It may reach a length of 20 ft (6.2 m) and weigh 1,000 lb (450 kg). A second species, *A. pelagicus,* is found in the W Pacific. The big-eyed thresher, *A. superciliosus,* is a deep-sea fish of the tropical and subtropical Atlantic. It is smaller than the common thresher, but its eyes may measure 4 in. (10 cm) in diameter. Thresher sharks are classified in the phylum CHORDATA, subphylum Vertebrata, class Chondrichthyes, order Selachii, family Alopiidae.

threshing or **thrashing,** separation of grain from the stalk on which it grows and from the chaff or pod that covers it. The first known method was by striking the reaped ears of grain with a flail. In another early method horses or oxen trod out the grain from stalks spread on a threshing floor. In both cases the straw was raked away and then the mixture of grain and chaff was winnowed, i.e., tossed into or poured through a current of air so that the light chaff was blown away from the heavier grain. In 1784 a Scotsman, Andrew Meikle, devised a threshing machine. Sheaves of grain were fed into a revolving cylinder armed with wooden beaters. Another toothed drum raked away the loose straw and pushed the remaining chaff and grain through a sieve onto a series of rollers that further separated the chaff from the grain in preparation for winnowing. The principle of Meikle's machine has been retained in all threshing machines up to and including the modern self-propelled COMBINES. See Michael Partridge, *Farm Tools through the Ages* (1973).

thrift: see LEADWORT.

thrips, minute, agile insect of the order Thysanoptera. Thrips have piercing-and-sucking mouthparts and cup-shaped feet from which bladderlike adhesive organs may be extended. Some species are wingless, but many have four narrow, featherlike wings fringed with hairs. METAMORPHOSIS is gradual, and some thrips frequently reproduce by PARTHENOGENESIS. A few species prey on mites and small insects; others, e.g., the onion, pear, greenhouse, and grass thrips, feed on the foliage and flowers of plants to which they may transmit virus diseases. Thrips are classified in the phylum ARTHROPODA, class Insecta, order Thysanoptera.

Throckmorton or **Throgmorton, Francis,** 1554–84, English conspirator; nephew of Sir Nicholas Throckmorton. A Roman Catholic, he began (1580) a tour of Europe, spent largely in discussing cooperative measures between French and English Catholics. In 1583 he returned to England and organized means of communication between the imprisoned Mary Queen of Scots and the French and Spanish courts. His activities aroused suspicion, and he was arrested (1583). A search of his house revealed a list of English Catholics willing to assist a rebellion against Queen Elizabeth I and other incriminating documents. Throckmorton was tortured and confessed. Although he later retracted his confession, he was convicted and executed.

Throckmorton or **Throgmorton, Sir Nicholas,** 1515–71, English diplomat. A relative of Catherine Parr, the last wife of Henry VIII, he became a staunch Protestant and gained the favor of the young Edward VI, who knighted him in 1547. He supported, for a time, the claims of Lady Jane GREY to the throne, and in 1554 he was tried for complicity in the rebellion of Sir Thomas WYATT. Although acquitted, he was kept in the Tower until 1555. Upon Elizabeth I's accession (1558) he was made ambassador to France, where he championed the cause of the Huguenots. While in France he negotiated with MARY QUEEN OF SCOTS and, despite religious differences, became her personal friend. In 1565, Throckmorton was sent to Scotland to attempt to prevent Mary's marriage to Lord Darnley, and in 1567 he tried to secure the release of the imprisoned Scottish queen. A supporter of the proposed match between the duke of Norfolk and Mary, he came under Elizabeth's suspicions. He was imprisoned in 1569 for his supposed complicity in the rebellion of the northern English Roman Catholics, but he was soon released. Throckmorton's daughter Elizabeth married Sir Walter Raleigh.

Throgmorton, Francis: see THROCKMORTON, FRANCIS.

Throgmorton, Sir Nicholas: see THROCKMORTON, SIR NICHOLAS.

thrombin: see BLOOD CLOTTING.

thrombocyte: see BLOOD CLOTTING.

thrombophlebitis: see PHLEBITIS.

thromboplastin: see BLOOD CLOTTING.

thrombosis (thrŏmbō'sĭs), obstruction of an artery or vein by a blood clot (thrombus). Arterial thrombosis is generally more serious because the supply of oxygen and nutrition to an area of the body is halted. Thrombosis of one of the arteries leading to the heart (heart attack) or of the brain (stroke) can result in death and, in a vessel of the extremities, may be followed by gangrene. Acute arterial thrombosis often results from the deposition of atherosclerotic material in the wall of an artery, which gradually narrows the channel, precipitating clot formation. A thrombus that breaks off and circulates through the blood stream is called an EMBOLUS.

throne, chair of state or the seat of a high dignitary. The throne was at first a stool or bench and later became an ornate armchair, usually raised on a dais and surmounted by a canopy. Often lavishly decorated, thrones have been made of a variety of materials, including wood, stone, ivory, and precious metals. Ancient Greek thrones were simple in form, with rectangular or curving legs and rosette adornments; they were adapted by the Etruscans, who made them more comfortable, and also by the Romans, who made them more ornate. The thrones of the East were usually more elaborate and fantastic in conception than those of Europe. In ancient times the Indian throne was a combined throne-altar, serving both a royal and a religious purpose. Thrones of the Renaissance in Europe were heavily ornamented with precious stones. Napoleon's throne was a gilded chair displaying eagles, lions, and other symbols. The throne of Great Britain is an oak chair in the House of Lords. At St. Peter's in Rome is the bronze papal throne designed by Bernini. The cathedra is the throne of a bishop in his cathedral church.

thrush, bird, common name for members of the Turdidae, a large family of birds found in most parts of the world and noted for their beautiful song. The majority are modestly colored, with spotted underparts, in either the young or the adult stage, although some have bright plumage. Among these are the American robin, *Turdus migratorius,* largest of the thrushes, and the Eastern bluebird, *Sialia sialis,* bright blue with a red breast. Other thrushes found in North America are the wood, olive-backed, and gray-cheeked thrushes, the solitaire, and the veery, or Wilson's, thrush. The hermit thrush, a shy forest dweller, is the finest singer. The European "blackbird," the nightingale, the missel thrush, the stonechat, and the wheatear are thrushes. Thrushes are classified in the phylum CHORDATA, subphylum Vertebrata, class Aves, order Passeriformes, family Turdidae.

thrush, in medicine, infection caused by the fungus *Candida albicans,* manifested by white, slightly raised patches on the mucous membrane of the tongue, mouth, and throat. The mucous membrane beneath the patches is usually raw and bleeding. The overgrowth of this fungus results when the balance in the normal oral microbe population is disturbed by malnutrition or disease. It occurs most frequently in infants and in adults suffering from chronic illnesses. Treatment includes rest, a nutritious diet, and applications of gentian violet and an antifungal antibiotic.

Thucydides (thōōsĭd'ĭdēz), c.460–c.400 B.C., Greek historian of Athens, one of the greatest of ancient historians. His family was partly Thracian. As a general in the PELOPONNESIAN WAR he failed (424 B.C.) to prevent the surrender of the city of Amphipolis to the Spartan commander Brasidas and was exiled until the end of the war. He thus had opportunity to acquaint himself with both the Athenians and the Spartans and to acquire firsthand information for his one work, the incomplete *History of the Peloponnesian War.* It covered the period from 431 to 411 and marked the beginning of a new style of history by reason of its generic character. Preeminently a military history, chronicling events by the seasons, it completely avoids any reference to social conditions or state policy, unless they have to deal with the progress of the war, and interprets the succession of events in view of the general nature and behavior of man rather than as the result of a fate outside man's influence. The outstanding feature of his writing, which is marked by accuracy and a studied impartiality, is his speeches; these he puts into the mouths of important persons to display their motives and beliefs about war. The most splendid of these is Pericles' funeral oration. Thucydides' account of the plague, through which he lived, displays his clinical and descriptive attitude and is a standard of its type. The classic English translation of the *History* is that of Thomas Hobbes (1629; ed. by David Grene, 1959); modern translations include those by Richard Crawley (1910, repr. 1952), Rex Warner (1954), and R. W. Livingstone (1960). See studies by J. H. Finley (1942, repr. 1967), G. B. Grundy (2d ed. 1948), Sir F. E. Adcock (1963), H. D. Westlake (1968), and A. G. Woodhead (1970); A. W. Gomme, *A Historical Commentary on Thucydides* (4 vol., 1945–70).

Thugga: see DOUGGA, Tunisia.

Thugs (thŭgz), former Indian religious sect of murderers and robbers, also called Phansigars [stranglers]. Membership was primarily hereditary and included both Hindus and Muslims, but all were devotees of the Hindu goddess KALI and committed their murders as sacrifices to her. A pickax (representing the tooth of Kali, which she was said to have bestowed upon the organization) was consecrated after the victim's grave had been dug with it. For most of the year Thugs followed ordinary occupations, but in the autumn they went about in bands, disguised as merchants or religious mendicants. When they encountered wealthy travelers, they would ingratiate themselves and await an opportunity to kill. The murder was effected by strangling the victim with a scarf reserved for the purpose. Women and members of certain low castes, such as sweepers, washermen, and musicians, were usually exempted from attack. The Thugs, whose activities are known as far back as the 13th cent., were protected by their strong organization and by local officials with whom they would divide the spoils. Early in the period of British rule in India the decision was made to destroy the Thugs. Sir William Sleeman accomplished the repression (1829–48) by mass arrests and executions. See G. L. Bruce, *The Stranglers* (1969).

Thule (thōō'lē), name given by the ancients to the most northerly land of Europe. It was an island discovered and described (c.310 B.C.) by the Greek navigator Pytheas and variously identified with Iceland, Norway, and the Shetland Islands. The phrase "Ultima Thule" is used figuratively to denote the most distant goal of human endeavor or a land remote beyond all reckoning.

Thule (thōō'lē, tōō'-), town in Thule dist. (1969 pop. 718), NW Greenland, NW of Cape York. It was founded (1910) by Knud Rasmussen, the Danish arctic explorer, in the Etah Eskimo area. It is a trading post and has a hospital and a radio and meteorological station. In World War II the United States built a military base at Thule. By agreement with Denmark, the base was greatly expanded after 1951 and is now the most important U.S. defense area in Greenland. It is also a base for Danish and U.S. scientific operations on the ice cap and on Peary Land.

thulium (thōō'lēəm) [from *Thule,* an ancient name for Scandinavia], metallic chemical element; symbol Tm; at. no. 69; at. wt. 168.934; m.p. 1545°C; b.p. 1727°C; sp. gr. 9.3; valence +3. Thulium is a soft, malleable, ductile, lustrous silver-white metal. It is one of the RARE-EARTH METALS of the LANTHANIDE SERIES in group IIIb of the PERIODIC TABLE. It does not tarnish rapidly in dry air but should be protected from moisture. It forms compounds with oxygen and the halogens, most of which are light green. The oxide, Tm_2O_3, is called thulia. Thulium is the least abundant of the rare-earth metals. It is found in the minerals gadolinite and euxenite and in monazite, the chief commercial source. The metal can be obtained by chemical reduction of its compounds. The pure metal and compounds have few commercial uses, but they are often used without purification in combination with the other rare-earth metals and compounds, e.g., in lighter flints and carbon electrodes for arc lighting. Although the only naturally occurring isotope (thulium-169) is stable, there are 15 unstable isotopes. Thulium-170 (half-life about 129 days), prepared by irradiating thulium-169 in a nuclear reactor, emits X rays; it is used in portable X-ray sources. Thulium was discovered in 1879 by P. T. Cleve.

Thummim: see URIM AND THUMMIM.

Thun (to͞on), city (1970 pop. 36,523), Bern canton, central Switzerland, on the Aare River, where it flows out of the Lake of Thun. Metal products, watches, and clothing are made there. Of interest are two castles, the 16th-century town hall, and the historical museum. The **Lake of Thun,** c.20 sq mi (52 sq km), is picturesquely situated at the foot of the Bernese Alps.

thunder, sound produced when a flash of lightning passes through air, heating the adjacent air and causing it to expand rapidly. A short flash of lightning creates a relatively short crash of thunder. Rolling thunder occurs either when there is a long flash of lightning generating thunder over a great distance or when clouds, mountains, differing layers of air, or other obstructions cause echoes and reverberations. Since sound travels about 1 mi in 5 sec, the distance between a lightning flash and an observer may be reckoned by counting the seconds between the sight of the flash and the sound of the thunder. Some lightning is so far distant from an observer that no thunder is heard, even though the lightning is seen. See THUNDERSTORM.

Thunder Bay, city (1971 pop. 108,411), SW Ont., Canada, on Thunder Bay inlet of Lake Superior. The city was created in 1970 by the amalgamation of the twin cities of Fort William and Port Arthur and two adjoining townships. It is one of Canada's major ports, shipping wheat, lumber, coal, and iron ore. The city has shipyards, grain elevators, lumber and pulp and paper mills, and an oil refinery. Manufactures include structural steel, transportation equipment, and chemical products. Port Arthur, originally a military post, was founded in the late 19th cent. Fort William was built by the North West Company in 1801 to serve as its western headquarters. It was the site of a fur-trading post built in 1679 and of Fort Kaministikwia, built by the French in 1717 and later abandoned. Kakabeka Falls, nearby, is a source of water power. Lakehead Univ. was founded in Port Arthur in 1957.

thunderstorm, violent, local atmospheric disturbance accompanied by LIGHTNING, THUNDER, and heavy rain, often by strong gusts of wind, and sometimes by HAIL. The typical thunderstorm caused by convection occurs on a hot summer afternoon when the sun's warmth has heated a large body of moist air near the ground. This air rises and is cooled by expansion. The cooling condenses the water vapor present in the air, forming a cumulus CLOUD. If the process continues and is violent, the cloud becomes immense; the summit often attains a height of 4 mi (6.5 km) above the base, and the top spreads out in the shape of an anvil as the transition to a cumulonimbus cloud takes place. The turbulent air currents within the cloud cause a continual breaking up and reuniting of the raindrops, building up strong electrical charges that result in lightning; it is these violent currents that also cause the formation of hail. As the storm approaches a given area, the gentle flow of warm air that has been feeding the cloud gives way to a strong, chilly gust of wind from the opposite direction, blowing outward from the base of the cloud. The rain begins with an intensity that gradually diminishes as the storm passes. Thunderstorms occurring at night are caused by the cooling of the upper layers of air by radiation, resulting in atmospheric instability. Another cause of thunderstorms is the approach of a cold air mass that advances as a wedge near the ground, forcing the warmer air in its path to rise. Even a forest fire or a volcanic eruption may create a condition of instability conducive to thunderstorm formation. The general direction of thunderstorms in the United States is from west to east, and the path, which broadens as the storm proceeds across the country, is usually relatively short—100 mi (160 km) or less. Thunderstorms occur most frequently over land areas in the equatorial zone (some localities have as many as 200 a year) and very seldom in the polar regions. In the United States they are most frequent along the E Gulf Coast (averaging more than 70 a year) and least frequent on the Pacific coast (less than 4 a year).

Thurber, James, 1894–1961, American humorist, b. Columbus, Ohio, studied at Ohio State Univ. After working on various newspapers he served on the staff of the *New Yorker* from 1927 to 1933 and was later a principal contributor, considerably influencing the tone of that magazine through his various drawings, stories, and anecdotes of his misadventures. Beneath the vague outlines of Thurber's cartoons and the wistful and ironic improbabilities of his writings, there is a deep psychological insight that sets him apart from most 20th-century humorists. With E. B. White he wrote and illustrated *Is Sex Necessary?* (1929), a satire on books of popular psychoanalysis. *The Male Animal* (1940), a play he wrote with Elliott Nugent, satirizes collegiate life. Collections of his drawings and writings include *The Owl in the Attic* (1931), *The Seal in the Bedroom* (1932), *My Life and Hard Times* (1933), *Fables for Our Time* (1940), *The Thurber Carnival* (1945), *Thurber Country* (1953), *Thurber's Dogs* (1955), *The Wonderful O* (1957), and *Credos and Curios* (1962). Among his other works are *The Thirteen Clocks* (1950), a children's book, and *The Years with Ross* (1959), a memoir of his days with the *New Yorker.* Thurber's later career was hampered by his growing blindness. See biographies by R. E. Morsberger (1964) and C. S. Holmes (1972); study by R. C. Tobias (1970).

Thurgau (to͞or'gou), canton (1970 pop. 182,835), 388 sq mi (1,005 sq km), NE Switzerland. Bordered in the north by the Lake of Constance and watered by the Thur River, Thurgau is a fertile and cultivated region. Cereals and fruit are grown, cattle are raised, and wine is produced. It has several industrial towns, notably Arbon and FRAUENFELD, the capital of the canton. The population is mainly Protestant and German-speaking. Thurgau was acquired (1264) by the Hapsburgs and was conquered (1460) by the Swiss cantons; it was ruled by the cantons until 1798, when the French invaded Switzerland. In 1803 it became a canton of Switzerland.

Thurii (thyo͞o'rēī), ancient city of Magna Graecia, S Italy, in Bruttium, on the Gulf of Tarentum (now Taranto). It was founded by Pericles in 443 B.C. to replace ruined Sybaris. New Greek colonists came, among them the city planner Hippodamus and possibly Herodotus and Lysias. Thurii became an ally of Rome and was pillaged (204 B.C.) by Hannibal. Rome revived (193 B.C.) the colony, but it did not thrive.

Thuringia (tho͞orĭn'jə), Ger. *Thüringen,* former state, c.6,000 sq mi (15,540 sq km), central Germany, located in what is now SW East Germany. As constituted in 1946 under Soviet military occupation, Thuringia consisted of the prewar state of Thuringia (c.4,540 sq mi/11,760 sq km), with the addition of former Prussian enclaves and border areas, notably Erfurt and Mühlhausen. Weimar (the capital), Jena, Gotha, Eisenach, Gera, Altenburg, Erfurt, Mühlhausen, and Suhl were the chief cities. In 1952 the state was abolished as an administrative unit. The region of Thuringia extends to the foot of the Harz mts. in the north and is crossed by the Thuringian Forest, Ger. *Thüringer Wald,* which stretches from the Werra River in the west to the Thüringer Saale River in the southeast and rises to an altitude of 3,222 ft (982 m) in the Grosser Beerberg. The ancient Thuringians, a Germanic tribe occupying central Germany between the Elbe and the Danube, were conquered by the Franks during the 6th cent. A.D. and were converted (8th cent.) to Christianity by St. Boniface. Charlemagne made Thuringia a march (frontier country) against the Slavs in the 9th cent., but it passed under the control of the Saxon dukes in the 10th cent. In the 11th cent. the landgraves of Thuringia, with their seat at the celebrated WARTBURG, emerged as princes of the Holy Roman Empire and ruled over much of the territory that is modern Thuringia. When Landgrave Louis IV died (1227) on a Crusade, Louis's widow, St. ELIZABETH of Hungary, was expelled by his brother and successor, Henry Raspe, who later was antiking to Conrad IV. Although the succession to Thuringia was long contested after Henry's death in 1247, the major part eventually fell to the house of WETTIN, i.e., to the margraves of Meissen, who in 1423 became electors of Saxony. The division (1485) of the Wettin lands left most of the Thuringian territories in the hands of the Ernestine branch of the family, which also received the electoral title. When Elector JOHN FREDERICK I was deprived of his lands in 1547, the Ernestine branch lost the electoral title and all their lands save Thuringia to the Albertine branch. Thuringia was split, under the Ernestines, into several duchies (see SAXE-ALTENBURG; SAXE-COBURG; SAXE-GOTHA; SAXE-MEININGEN; SAXE-WEIMAR). Principalities situated in Thuringia but not ruled by any of the branches of the Ernestine line were those of Reuss and Schwarzburg. Thuringia in the 16th cent. had been a center of the Lutheran Reformation, and its population remained thoroughly Protestant. Among the Ernestine duchies (which underwent several redivisions in the 17th, 18th, and 19th cent.) the most important, both politically and culturally, was SAXE-WEIMAR-EISENACH. All the Thuringian territories except Saxe-Meiningen sided with Prussia in the Austro-Prussian War of 1866. The Thuringian states had been members of the German Confederation from 1815; they joined the North German Confederation in 1866 and the German Empire in 1871. Their rulers were expelled in 1918, and in 1920 the state of Thuringia was founded under the Weimar Republic by the union of Saxe-Coburg-Gotha (without the city of Coburg, which went to Bavaria), Saxe-Weimar-Eisenach, Saxe-Altenburg, Saxe-Meiningen, the two sister principalities of Reuss, and the two sister principalities of Schwarzburg.

Thurloe, John, 1616–68, English politician. A lawyer, he became (1652) secretary to the council of state of the Commonwealth. He was given charge of the intelligence department (1653), which included foreign and domestic espionage, and the post office (1655). Through the post office Thurloe was able to intercept information of plots against the government. He entered Parliament in 1654, and supported the succession of Richard Cromwell (1658). He was deprived of office (1659) after the fall of the Protectorate, and was arrested for high treason after the Restoration (1660). He was not tried, and was released on the condition that his services be available to the Restoration government. Thurloe then retired from public life, but remained a valuable authority on foreign affairs and was often consulted by the king's ministers and diplomats. His vast correspondence, an important authority for the history of the Protectorate, is preserved in the Bodleian Library, Oxford, and in the British Museum. Part of it was published in 1742 by Thomas Birch.

Thurlow, Edward Thurlow, 1st Baron, 1731–1806, lord chancellor of England. Called to the bar in 1754, he enjoyed considerable success in legal practice. He was made a king's counsel in 1762 and entered Parliament in 1765. He was appointed solicitor general (1770) and attorney general (1771). His support of the policies of George III and Lord North with respect to the American colonies brought him a peerage and the lord chancellorship (1778). He held the latter office until Charles James Fox insisted upon his dismissal in 1783. William Pitt reappointed him in 1783, and he retained office until 1792. Then his opposition to Pitt's sinking fund and his intrigues against the ministry caused Pitt to demand his retirement. He had presided ably over the first part of the trial of Warren Hastings. Thurlow consistently opposed parliamentary reform, abolition of the slave trade, and other reforms. His manner inspired Charles James Fox's remark, "No man ever was so wise as Thurlow looks." See biography by Robert Gore-Brown (1953).

Thurmond, James Strom (thûr'mənd), 1902–, U.S. political leader, b. Edgeville, S.C. He read law while teaching (1923–29) in South Carolina schools and was admitted to the bar in 1930. Thurmond was elected (1933) to the state senate and became (1938) a circuit-court judge. After serving in World War II, he was elected (1946) governor of South Carolina. In 1948, Thurmond was chosen presidential candidate by the States' Rights Democrats, Southerners who bolted the Democratic party in opposition to President Harry S. Truman's civil-rights program; he won 39 electoral votes. In 1954 he was a successful write-in candidate as U.S. Senator. He was reelected in 1960, 1966, and 1972. A conservative, Thurmond switched from the Democratic to the Republican party in 1964.

Thurrock, urban district (1971 pop. 124,682), Essex, SE England, on the Thames River. With an area of 68 sq mi (176 sq km), Thurrock is the largest urban district in England. It includes Tilbury, which has large docks that are part of the Port of London. Among Thurrock's industries, located along the Thames, are oil refining and the manufacture of soap, margarine, paper board, cement, and shoes. Queen Elizabeth I reviewed the troops at Tilbury Fort in 1588 at the time of the Spanish Armada.

Thursday: see WEEK.

Thursday Island (1971 pop. 2,215), Queensland, NE Australia, N of Cape York Peninsula, in Torres Strait. It is the administrative center of the Torres Strait Islands.

Thurston, Lorrin Andrews, 1858–1931, lawyer and newspaper publisher. He was the son of missionaries in Hawaii. Favoring U.S. annexation of Hawaii, he was one of the leaders of the revolution (1893) that overthrew Queen Liliuokalani. Thurston drafted the constitution for the provisional Hawaiian government and headed the commission to Washington that negotiated for annexation. He helped draft the constitution of the Hawaiian Republic, and after annexation retired to private life. As principal owner and editor of the *Honolulu Advertiser,* he was a promoter of the tourist and pineapple industries.

Thutmose I (thŭt'mōz, tŭt'-) or **Thothmes I** (thŏth'mēz, tōt'mēs), d. 1495 B.C., king of ancient Egypt, third ruler of the XVIII dynasty; successor of Amenhotep I. He became king c.1525. In a great campaign he subjugated the valley of the NILE up to the Third Cataract (below the present Dongola). Syria occupied his attention, and he at least temporarily subdued the country as far as the Euphrates River. His son and successor, **Thutmose II,** reigned from c.1495 to 1490 B.C. Unlike HATSHEPSUT, his half-sister whom he married, Thutmose II did not have a royal mother. Before long Hatshepsut gained equal power and relegated him to the background, calling herself "king." At the death of Thutmose II, Hatshepsut became regent for **Thutmose III**, his son by a minor queen. She relegated Thutmose III to an inferior position for 22 years while she ruled Egypt. At her death (1468), he emerged as the sole ruler of Egypt and as a great conqueror. Almost immediately he advanced into Syria, where an Asiatic alliance against Egypt waited to oppose him. He was victor at MEGIDDO and consolidated all Syria, except Phoenicia, in his empire. In successive campaigns he reduced every ruler N of the Euphrates to the status of autonomous tributary and eventually conquered even powerful Kadesh and Mitanni, a kingdom E of the Euphrates River. His empire (the zenith of the New Empire), extending from the Third Cataract to the Euphrates, was used to enrich Egypt with wealth and man power. He built temples up and down the Nile and founded the wealth of the priesthood of Amon, to which he belonged. Thutmose died (1436), after having made his son Amenhotep II coregent, and was buried in the Valley of the Tombs at Thebes. His mummy is now at Cairo. **Thutmose IV** (reigned c.1406–1398 B.C.), son and successor of Amenhotep II, also invaded Asia and Nubia; he formed alliances with independent kings neighboring his Syrian tributaries and married a princess of Mitanni, who was mother of his son and successor, Amenhotep III.

Thwaites, Reuben Gold, 1853–1913, American historian, b. Dorchester, Mass. He was managing editor of the *Wisconsin State Journal* and later superintendent of the Wisconsin Historical Society. He was deeply interested in the history of the Old Northwest, and he and a staff of assistants edited some of the most valuable early accounts of Western history in *The Jesuits Relations* (73 vol., 1896–1901; repr. 1954) and *Early Western Travels, 1748–1846* (33 vol., 1904–7). He also edited many other early accounts in separate issues and wrote biographies (e.g., of Marquette) and special studies (e.g., of the Black Hawk War) related to the Old Northwest. He also contributed *France in America* to the "American Nation" series and wrote a secondary school history of the United States.

Thwing, Charles Franklin (twĭng), 1853–1937, American educator and Congregational clergyman, b. New Sharon, Maine, grad. Harvard, 1876, and Andover Theological Seminary, 1879. Until 1890 he served parishes in Cambridge, Mass., and Minneapolis. He was president of Western Reserve Univ. (now Case Western Reserve Univ.) and of Adelbert College (the men's college of that university) from 1890 to his retirement in 1921 and a trustee of the Carnegie Foundation after 1905. He wrote many books on religion and education, including *The College President* (1926), *Education and Religion* (1929), and *The American College and University* (1935).

Thyatira (thī"ətī'rə), ancient city of Lydia, now Akhisar, Turkey. It was one of the Seven Churches in Asia and was known for its purple dye (Acts 16.14).

Thyestes (thīĕs'tēz): see ATREUS.

thylacine (thī'ləsīn") or **Tasmanian wolf,** carnivorous MARSUPIAL, or pouched mammal, of Tasmania. The thylacine is often cited as an example of convergent evolution: It is superficially quite similar to a wolf or dog, although it has evolved entirely independently of these animals. About the size of a collie, it has a long tail and a wolflike head with short ears and strong jaws and teeth. Its coat is brownish with a series of black stripes across the back; it is also known as the Tasmanian tiger. A nocturnal hunter, the thylacine preys on animals up to the size of small kangaroos. The female gives birth to very undeveloped young, which are then carried in a pouch surrounding the teats. Thylacines have been hunted nearly to extinction because of their attacks on sheep and poultry; a few individuals are believed to survive in wild areas of W Tasmania. They are classified in the phylum CHORDATA, subphylum Vertebrata, class Mammalia, order Marsupialia, family Dasyuridae.

thyme (tīm), any species of the genus *Thymus,* aromatic herbs or shrubby plants of the family Labiatae (MINT family). The common thyme, which is used as a seasoning herb and yields a medicinal essential oil containing thymol, is the Old World *T. vulgaris,* an erect plant with grayish branches. It is cultivated mainly in Spain and in France. The wild or creeping thyme, or mother-of-thyme (*T. serpyllum*), also used medicinally, is an Old World evergreen naturalized in North America and popular as a ground cover, edging, and rock plant. This was the wild thyme mentioned in Shakespeare's *Midsummer Night's Dream.* The Greeks used thyme as a temple incense, and it has been prized since ancient times as a honey plant. Thyme is classified in the division MAGNOLIOPHYTA, class Magnoliopsida, order Lamiales, family Labiatae.

thymine (thī'mēn), organic base of the PYRIMIDINE family. Thymine was the first pyrimidine to be purified from a natural source, having been isolated from calf thymus and beef spleen in 1893–4. The accepted structure of the thymine molecule was published in 1900; this structure was confirmed when several investigators reported the synthesis of the compound during the period 1901 to 1910. Combined with the sugar deoxyribose in a glycosidic linkage, thymine forms a derivative called thymidine (a nucleoside), which in turn can be phosphorylated with from one to three phosphoric acid groups, yielding respectively the three NUCLEOTIDES TMP (thymidine monophosphate), TDP (thymidine diphosphate), and TTP (thymidine triphosphate). The analogous nucleosides and nucleotides formed from thymine and ribose occur only very rarely in living systems; such is not the case with the other pyrimidines. The nucleotide derivatives of thymine do not exhibit as much activity as COENZYMES, although TTP can readily donate one of its phosphate groups to adenosine diphosphate (ADP) to form ADENOSINE TRIPHOSPHATE (ATP), an extremely important intermediate in the transfer of chemical energy in living systems. Since the thymine nucleotides contain only deoxyribose and not ribose, TTP is the source of thymidine only in deoxyribonucleic acid (DNA); there is no thymine in ribonucleic acid (RNA). Thymidine is significant because of its involvement in the biosynthesis of DNA and in the preservation and transfer of genetic information. See NUCLEIC ACID.

thymus gland (thī'məs), mass of glandular tissue located in the neck or chest of most vertebrate animals. In humans the thymus is a soft, flattened, pinkish-gray organ located in the upper chest under the breastbone. It is relatively large in the newborn infant (about the size of the baby's fist) and continues to grow throughout childhood up to the age of puberty when it weighs about 1.2 oz (35 grams). Then it gradually decreases in size until it is hard to distinguish from the surrounding tissue. The functions of the thymus were not well understood until the early 1960s, when its role in the development of the body's system of immunity was discovered. Beginning during fetal development, the thymus processes many of the body's lymphocytes, which migrate throughout the body via the bloodstream, seeding lymph nodes and other lymphatic tissue. These lymphocytes, along with antibody-forming cells (plasma cells), are essential in protecting the body against invasions by foreign organisms (see IMMUNITY). If the thymus fails to develop or is removed early in fetal life, no immune system develops. Normally, by the time the infant is a few months old, the immune system is sufficiently developed to function throughout life. However, further growth and development of lymphoid tissue is still dependent on intervention of the thymus. It is believed that, after the initial seeding process, a hormonal substance is released by the thymus that stimulates further growth of lymphoidal tissue, although such a substance has not yet been isolated.

thyratron (thī'rətrŏn"), gas-filled triode ELECTRON TUBE that does not conduct an electric current until a certain critical voltage is applied to its grid; the voltage ionizes the gas in the tube, allowing a current between the anode and cathode. Once the current is established, the grid voltage has essentially no effect; the tube continues to conduct as long as the current through it remains above a certain critical value. The thyratron is no longer widely used, having been replaced in most of its applications by other devices.

thyroid gland, endocrine gland, situated in the neck, that regulates the body's metabolic rate. It consists of two lobes connected by a narrow segment called the isthmus. The lobes lie on either side of the trachea, the isthmus in front of it. Thyroid tissue is composed of millions of tiny saclike follicles, which store thyroid hormone in the form of thyroglobulin, an iodine compound. Thyroglobulin is the chief component of the jellylike substance, called colloid, that is secreted by the follicles. When it is secreted into the bloodstream, thyroglobulin is converted into THYROXINE and small quantities of the other closely related thyroid hormones. The amount of thyroxine production (and therefore the metabolic rate) is dependent on a sufficient intake of iodine and on stimulation by thyrotropic hormone

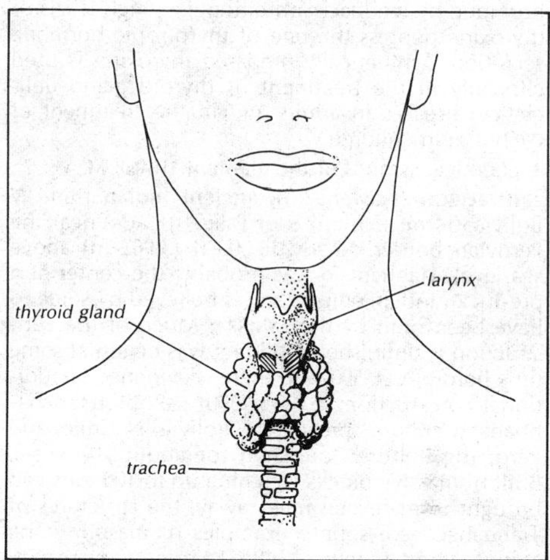

Thyroid gland

from the PITUITARY GLAND. Metabolic disorders result when the thyroid secretes too little or too much thyroxine. A deficiency of thyroxine secretion (hypothyroidism) occurs when insufficient iodine is taken in with the diet, a condition prevalent in certain areas of the world, particularly those remote from salt water, e.g., certain areas in the central United States. The result of such a deficiency is usually goiter, or enlargement of the thyroid. Endemic goiter has been virtually eliminated by the widespread use of iodized salt. Hypothyroidism that results from glandular malfunction is known as myxedema in the adult and CRETINISM in infancy and childhood. Treatment is by administration of thyroxine. Excessive secretion of thyroxine, or hyperthyroidism, causes an increased metabolic rate, loss of weight despite good appetite, protrusion of the eyeballs, rapid pulse, and irritability. The condition, also known as Graves' disease, may be accompanied by enlargement of the thyroid. Treatment is by administration of thiouracil, a chemical that inhibits thyroxine formation, by surgical removal of part of the gland, or by administration of radioactive iodine, which destroys over-functioning thyroid tissue. See also ENDOCRINE SYSTEM.

thyroid stimulating hormone (TSH): see THYROTROPIN.

thyrotropin (thī" rătrō'pĭn), HORMONE released by the anterior PITUITARY GLAND that stimulates the THYROID GLAND to release THYROXINE. The release of thyrotropin is in turn triggered by the action of thyrotropin-releasing factor (TRF), a substance found in the hypothalamus of the brain. TRF, once released from the hypothalamus, travels in the blood stream to the anterior pituitary, where, by means that are not clearly understood, it causes the release of thyrotropin. This latter substance, a glycoprotein (see PROTEIN), is carried to the thyroid gland by the blood and there stimulates the uptake of iodine, the conversion of diiodotyrosine to thyroxine, and the secretion of thyroid hormones into the blood stream. Thyroxine inhibits the further release of thyrotropin, some evidence suggests, by interfering in some way with the action of TRF; thus the levels of thyroid hormones are regulated. If not enough iodine is available in the diet, then not enough thyroxine will be made to shut off the release of thyrotropin. Prolonged stimulation of the thyroid by thyrotropin results in an abnormal enlargement of the gland, known as goiter. Thyrotropin is also known as thyrotropic hormone and thyroid stimulating hormone (TSH).

thyroxine (thīrŏk'sēn), substance secreted by the THYROID GLAND. A hormone, thyroxine is formed from the amino acid TYROSINE and iodine. Complexed to a protein, it is stored in thyroid cells; it is released into the bloodstream complexed to another protein, plasma globulin. Thyroxine increases the number and activity of mitochondria in cells, although the exact mechanism by which it exerts its principal effect, i.e., increasing the basal metabolic rate, is not known. Effects include an increased rate of carbohydrate metabolism and an increase in the rate of protein synthesis and breakdown. The hormone, which excites the nervous system and causes increased activity of the ENDOCRINE SYSTEM, remains active in the body for more than a month. Thyroxine activity is controlled by THYROTROPIC HORMONE, a substance released from the PITUITARY GLAND. Conversely, thyroxine regulates the effect of thyrotropic hormone by feedback inhibition, i.e., high levels of thyroxine depress the rate of thyrotropic hormone secretion. Synthetically prepared thyroxine is used clinically in the treatment of thyroid gland deficiency diseases in adults and in the treatment of CRETINISM in children.

Ti, chemical symbol of the element TITANIUM.

Tiahuanaco (tyäwänä'kō), ancient Indian ruin, W Bolivia, 34 mi (55 km) S of Lake TITICACA, near the Peruvian border. Nearly 13,000 ft (3,962 m) above sea level, Tiahuanaco was probably the center of a pre-Incan Indian empire and is believed by some to have been built by the AYMARA. Much of the construction is unfinished. Building was begun at some time before A.D. 500, and there is evidence of additional construction (c.1100–1300). About 1000, Tiahuanaco culture spread to E Bolivia, N Chile, and Peru; the culture flourished for about 200 years. Built of massive blocks weighing up to 100 tons and brought from several miles away, the structures of Tiahuanaco are superb examples of masonry. The stones, fitted together without mortar, were cut, squared, dressed, and notched with a precision equaled in no other aboriginal South American civilization, not even the Inca. Construction is largely of the platform or monolithic type decorated by conventional incised carving or heads in low relief. The creators of Tiahuanaco also excelled at ceramics; Tiahuanaco painted pottery is one of the great achievements of pre-Columbian art. See Arthur Posnansky, *Tiahuanacu: the Cradle of American Man* (4 vol., 1945–1958); J. Alden Mason, *The Ancient Civilizations of Peru* (1957).

tiang: see DAMALISK.

Tiaret (tyärā'), city (1966 pop. 37,059), NW Algeria, capital of Tiaret dept. Since Roman times it has been the center of a prosperous agricultural area. It was completely rebuilt after its capture by the French in 1843.

Tibaldi, Pellegrino (päl-lāgrē'nō tēbäl'dē), 1527–96, Italian Baroque painter and architect, whose real name was Pellegrino di Tibaldo de' Pellegrini. He studied in Bologna, and his early painting of the *Marriage of St. Catherine* attests the influence of Bagnacavallo, who may have been his first master. A trip to Rome in 1547, however, afforded Tibaldi a study of Michelangelo's art that was decisive for the formation of his style. He returned to Bologna in 1550 to supervise the completion of Cardinal Poggio's palace (now the Univ. of Bologna). He decorated the interior with scenes from the *Odyssey*, using illusionistically painted architecture as a framework. Later he executed decorative frescoes in the Ferretti Palace, Ancona. After 1565 he devoted himself principally to architecture. Under the patronage of Charles Borromeo, he was named architect of the city of Milan and was involved in the construction of the cathedral. He designed the courtyard of the archiepiscopal palace (1564–70) and the churches of San Fedele (1569–79) and San Sebastiano (1577) in Milan. Philip II summoned him to Spain, where he worked (1588–96) on frescoes at the Escorial. He returned to Milan in 1596 and continued work on the cathedral until his death.

Tibbett, Lawrence (tĭb'ĭt), 1896–1960, American baritone, b. Bakersfield, Calif. He made his debut at the Metropolitan Opera House in 1923. After a successful appearance as Ford in Verdi's *Falstaff*, he was given leading roles and became especially noted for those he created in American operas, including Louis Gruenberg's *Emperor Jones* (1933) and the operas of Deems Taylor. He was outstanding in the revival (1932) of Verdi's *Simon Boccanegra*. Beginning with *The Rogue Song* (1930) he appeared in a number of motion pictures and was long popular as a radio singer. In 1936 he helped found the American Guild of Musical Artists, of which he became president.

Tiber (tī'bər), Ital. *Tevere*, Latin *Tiberis*, river, 251 mi (404 km) long, rising in the Etruscan Apennines, central Italy. It flows generally S across Tuscany, Umbria, and N Latium, then SW through Rome to empty into the Tyrrhenian Sea by two mouths. It is connected with the Arno River by the Chiana Canal, an important route between Rome and Florence. The upper Tiber and its chief tributaries, the Nera and Aniene rivers, are used to generate electricity. Subject to floods, the banks of the Tiber, especially in Rome, are diked. The silt-laden Tiber continues to extend its delta westward. Ostia Antica, the site of Ostia, the coastal port of ancient Rome, now lies 4 mi (6 km) from the sea. Most of the marshland in the delta has been reclaimed for agriculture.

Tiberias (tībēr'ēəs), town (1972 pop. 23,800), NE Israel, on the Sea of Galilee, 682 ft (208 m) below sea level. It is a trade center for agricultural settlements, a resort and spa noted for its thermal springs, and a lake port. There are machine shops, fisheries, and sausage, candy, and box factories in Tiberias. Named for Emperor Tiberius, the town was built (A.D. c.20) by Herod Antipas; there are ruins of the baths he built. After the destruction of Jerusalem, Tiberias became (2d cent.) a center of Jewish learning; the Sanhedrin convened in the town, and parts of the Mishna and Jerusalem Talmud were edited there. Tiberias was captured by the Arabs in 637, taken by the Crusaders in the 11th cent., recaptured by Saladin in 1187, and occupied by Egypt in 1247. It became part of the OTTOMAN EMPIRE in the 16th cent. Rebuilt and fortified in the 18th cent. by Dahir al-Umar, the local Ottoman ruler, Tiberias resumed its position as a center of Jewish scholarship. In 1922 it joined Palestine. Maimonides (1135–1204), the Jewish philosopher and physician, is buried in Tiberias. Arabic forms of the name are Tabariya and Tubariya.

Tiberias, Lake: see GALILEE, SEA OF.

Tiberius (Tiberius Julius Caesar Augustus) (tībēr'ēəs), 42 B.C.–A.D. 37, second Roman emperor (A.D. 14–A.D. 37). He was the son of Tiberius Claudius Nero and LIVIA DRUSILLA and was originally named Tiberius Claudius Nero. He campaigned (20 B.C.) in Armenia, became (19 B.C.) governor of Transalpine Gaul, and aided (12 B.C.) his brother DRUSUS on the Rhine and the Danube. AUGUSTUS, his stepfather, compelled him (12 B.C.) to divorce his wife, Vipsania Agrippina, and to marry Julia, the widow of Agrippa and daughter of Augustus. After the death of Drusus (9 B.C.) he campaigned in Germany, and following a second consulship (7 B.C.) he retired to Rhodes for seven years. On his return he was adopted as heir of the emperor and was sent (A.D. 4) into Germany. Five years later he subjugated Illyricum. Tiberius succeeded without difficulty on the death of Augustus in A.D. 14. He spent his efforts in continuing the policies of Augustus, with one exception; he drastically cut luxury expenses, including public shows. By so doing and by reforming the tax situation in the provinces he greatly improved the financial state of the government and made himself extremely unpopular in Rome. For years SEJANUS was his chief aid and confidant. Tiberius retired to Capri in A.D. 26 and ruled thereafter by correspondence. He grew suspicious of intrigues and in A.D. 31 had Sejanus killed. Modern historians have been inclined to treat his administration more favorably than did Roman historians. He is the Tiberius of Luke 3.1. He was succeeded by Caligula. See studies by F. B. Marsh (1931) and Robin Seager (1972).

Tibesti Massif: see SAHARA.

Tibet (tĭbĕt'), Mandarin *Hsi Tsang Syi Dzang*, autonomous region (1968 est. pop. 1,400,000), c.471,700 sq mi (1,221,700 sq km), SW China. The capital is LHASA. A Chinese autonomous region since 1951 and formerly a Chinese protectorate, Tibet is bordered on the SE by Burma, on the S by India, Bhutan, Sikkim, and Nepal, on the W by India and Kashmir, and on the N and E by Chinese provinces. Almost completely surrounded by mountain ranges (including the Himalayas in the south and the Kunlun in the north), Tibet is largely a plateau averaging c.16,000 ft (4,880 m) in height. Many of the mightiest rivers of E Asia, especially the Yangtze, the Mekong, and the Salween, rise in Tibet; the most important is the navigable Tsangpo (the Brahmaputra), which follows an easterly course through S Tibet. North of the Tsangpo are many salt lakes, the largest being Na-mu Hu (Tengri Nor) in the east. In this land of scant rainfall and a short growing season, the only extensive agricultural region is the Tsangpo valley, where barley, wheat, potatoes, millet, and turnips are grown. In this valley are nearly all the large cities, including Lhasa, JIH-K'A-TSE (Shigatse), and Chiang-tzu (Gyangtse). Most other areas of Tibet are suited only for grazing; yaks, which can withstand the intense cold, are the principal domestic animals, and there are also large herds of goats and sheep. Much of the population is engaged in a pastoral life, but the advances made by irrigation and the growing of forage crops is decreasing the amount of nomadism. Stockbreeding cooperatives have been organized. In addition to vast salt reserves, Tibet has large deposits of gold, copper, and radioactive ores, but mining was long prohibited for religious reasons. Traditionally, goods for trade, particularly foreign trade, were carried by pack trains (yaks, mules, and horses) across the windswept plateau and over difficult mountain passes. In exchange for hides, wool, and salt there were imports of tea and silk from China and of manufactured goods from India. Motor roads now connect Lhasa with Ch'ang-tu (Chamdo) in E Tibet and with Jih-k'a-tse and Chiang-tzu in the Tsangpo area and link Ka-erh (Gartok) in W Tibet to the northern regions. A major highway runs from Tibet to Ch'eng-tu, in Szechwan prov., providing a link to the great Chinese cities in the east; Tibet is also connected by highway with Sinkiang and Tsinghai provs. in W China. The inhabitants of Tibet are of Mongolian stock and speak a Tibeto-Burman language. Before the unsuccessful revolt of 1959 (see below), many of the dwellers of the cities were Lamaist monks, who may have comprised as much as one sixth of the country's male population. The chief figures of Lamaism (see TIBETAN BUDDHISM), the Dalai Lama and the Panchen Lama (or Tashi Lama, for the lamastery at Tashi Lumpo), were at least the nominal heads of the Tibetan government. In general, administration was equally divided between lamas and laymen belonging to the feudal aristocracy. Over the centuries the Tsangpo valley was the focus of ancient trade routes from India, China, and central Asia. Tibet emerged from an obscure history to flourish in the 7th cent. A.D. as an independent kingdom with its capital at Lhasa. The Chinese first established relations with Tibet during the T'ang dynasty (618–906), and there were frequent wars of conquest. The Tibetan kingdom was associated with early Mahayana Buddhism, which the scholar Padmasambhava fashioned (8th cent.) into Lamaism. Toward the end of the 12th cent. many Indian Buddhists, fleeing before the Muslim invasion, went to Tibet. In the 13th cent. Tibet fell under Mongol influence, which was to last until the 18th cent. In 1270, Kublai Khan, emperor of China, was converted to Lamaism by the abbot of the Sakya lamasery; the abbot returned to Tibet to found the Sakya dynasty (1270–1340) and to become the first priest-king of Tibet. In 1720, the Manchu dynasty replaced Mongol rule in Tibet. China thereafter claimed suzerainty, often merely nominal. During the 18th cent., British authorities in India attempted to establish relations with Lhasa, but the Gurkha invasion of 1788 and the subsequent Gurkha war (1792) with Tibet brought an abrupt end to the rapprochement. Jesuits and Capuchins had visited Tibet in the 17th and 18th cent., but throughout the 19th cent. Tibet maintained its traditional seclusion. Meanwhile, Ladakh, long part of Tibet, was lost to the rulers of Kashmir, and Sikkim was detached (1890) by Britain. In 1893, Britain succeeded in obtaining a trading post at Ya-tung, but continued Tibetan interference led to the military expedition (1904) of Sir Francis YOUNGHUSBAND to Lhasa, which enforced the granting of trade posts at Ya-tung, Chiang-tzu, and Ka-erh. Subsequently, Britain recognized (1906, 1907) China's suzerainty over Tibet. However, the Tibetans were able, with the overthrow of the Manchu dynasty in China, to expel (1912) the Chinese in Tibet and reassert their independence. At a conference (1913–14) of British, Tibetans, and Chinese at Simla, India, Tibet was tentatively confirmed under Chinese suzerainty and divided into an inner Tibet, to be incorporated into China, and an outer autonomous Tibet. The Simla agreement was, however, never ratified by the Chinese, who continued to claim all of Tibet as a "special territory." After the death (1933) of the 13th Dalai Lama, Tibet gradually drifted back into the Chinese orbit. The 14th Dalai Lama, who was born in China, was installed in 1939–40 and assumed full powers (1950) after a ten-year regency. The succession of the 10th Panchen Lama, with rival candidates supported by Tibet and China, was one of the excuses for the Chinese invasion (Oct., 1950) of Tibet. By a Tibetan-Chinese agreement (May, 1951), Tibet became a "national autonomous region" of China under the traditional rule of the Dalai Lama, but under the actual control of a Chinese Communist Commission. The Communist government introduced far-reaching land reforms and sharply curtailed the power of the monastic orders. After 1956 scattered uprisings occurred throughout the country, but a full-scale revolt broke out in March, 1959, prompted in part by fears for the personal safety of the Dalai Lama. The Chinese suppressed the rebellion, but the Dalai Lama was able to escape to India, where he eventually established headquarters in exile. The Panchen Lama, who had accepted Chinese sponsorship, acceded to the spiritual leadership of Tibet. The Chinese adopted brutal repressive measures against the Tibetans, provoking charges from the Dalai Lama of genocide. Landholdings were seized, the lamaseries were virtually emptied, and thousands of monks were forced to find other work. The Panchen Lama was deposed in 1964 after making statements supporting the Dalai Lama; he was replaced by a secular Tibetan leader. In 1962, China launched attacks along the Indian-Tibetan border to consolidate territories it claimed had been wrongly given to India by the British McMahon Commission in 1914. Following a ceasefire, Chinese troops withdrew behind the disputed line in the east, but continued to occupy part of Ladakh in Kashmir. Some of the border areas are still in dispute. In 1965 the Tibetan Autonomous Region was formally established. See H. E. Richardson, *A Short History of Tibet* (1962), W. D. Shakabpa, *Tibet: A Political History* (1967), Giuseppe Tucci, *Tibet, Land of Snows* (tr. 1967), D. L. Snellgrove and Hugh Richardson, *A Cultural History of Tibet* (1968), Noël Barber, *From the Land of Lost Content: The Dalai Lama's Fight for Tibet* (1970), John MacGregor, *Tibet: A Chronicle of Exploration* (1970), R. A. Stein, *Tibetan Civilization* (tr., rev. ed. 1972), Michel Peissel, *The Secret War in Tibet* (1973).

Tibetan art and architecture have been almost entirely religious in character (see TIBETAN BUDDHISM). The art of Tibetan Lamaism retains strong elements drawn from the forms of both Hinduism and Buddhism in India and was later influenced by the arts of Nepal and China. In architecture, the chorten, or Tibetan STUPA, was derived from Indian prototypes and was composed of one or more square bases, a square balcony, a bulbous dome, and a mast upholding umbrellas, surmounted by a flame finial. Tibet is famed for its gigantic monastery-cities, which house thousands of monks. The one at Tashi Lumpo, built in the 15th cent., is the headquarters for the Tashi Lama. A labyrinthian complex, it is composed of long streets of cells, which surround courtyards. At the center is a shrine. The 17th-century monastery at Lhasa includes the Potala palace, residence of the Dalai Lama, and a series of monastic skyscrapers that echo the forms of the surrounding mountain peaks. Tibetan sculpture, often in the form of gilt bronze statuettes, consists of slim, elegant figures with heart-shaped heads, resembling the Indian Pala or Nepalese figures and frequently ornamented with elaborate jewels. Tibetan paintings appear most frequently in the form of tankas, or temple banners, usually in brilliant colors on cotton or silk. The central figures of tankas may follow Nepalese or Indian types, but their decorative details, such as cloud scrolls, flowers, and architectural motifs, are often of Chinese origin. It is difficult to date these paintings, since the text, canons of proportion, and technical rules for making them have been almost unvaried for centuries. The symbolism is highly complex. Strongly schematized paintings portray ritual diagrams, scenes of the pantheon of divinities, and the wheel of life. There are representations of Buddha in his myriad aspects and saints such as Padmasambhava or Atisa (Tsong-Kha-pa). There are also images of ferocious deities, accompanied by their female counterparts. Among the most famous of these are the dragon-headed Sridevi (Lhamo) and Yamantaka, with a bull's head. Religious significance is invested in eight glorious emblems, e.g., the white parasol, two fishes, the lotus, and the seashell, and countless symbols of tantric and nontantric origin. Tantric manifestations are generally fierce and include such objects as the ax, elephant goad, skullcap, skull drum, and ornaments made of human bones. Fine examples of Tibetan art may be seen at the British Museum; Musée Guimet, Paris; the Museum of Fine Arts, Boston; the City Art Museum of St. Louis; the Newark (N.J.) Museum; and the Jacques Marchais Center of Tibetan Arts, Staten Island, New York City. See A. B. Griswold et al., *The Art of Burma, Korea, Tibet* (1964); A. K. Gordon, *Tibetan Religious Art* (2d ed. 1964) and *The Iconography of Tibetan Lamaism* (rev. ed. 1967).

Tibetan Buddhism, form of BUDDHISM prevailing in Tibet, Bhutan, Sikkim, Mongolia, and parts of Siberia and SW China. It is sometimes called Lamaism, from the name of the Tibetan monks, the *lamas* [superior ones]. The religion is derived from the Indian Mahayana form of Buddhism, but much of its ritual is based on the esoteric mysticism of TANTRA and on the ancient shamanism and sorcery of Bon, a primitive animistic religion of Tibet. It is also called Tantrayana [tantra vehicle] or Vajrayana [vehicle of the thunderbolt]. The traditional account of its origin is that Buddhism was introduced into Tibet by a Nepali and a Chinese princess, devout Buddhists, who became (7th cent. A.D.) the wives of the Tibetan king Srongtsen Gampo. The new religion was actually established, however, by one of the successors of that king when he called from India the monk Padmasambhava, who founded (c.750) a Buddhist monastery near Lhasa. Buddhist writings were later translated from Sanskrit in two sections: the *Kanjur* [translated word], a collection of sacred texts, and the *Tanjur* [translated treatises], a collection of commentaries (see BUDDHIST LITERATURE). The early lamas and their successors, constituting the so-called Red Hat sects, rapidly built up power. The Bon shamans, however, fought back successfully, and for over a century the new faith was suppressed. In 1042 a reformer, Atisa (982–1054), a monk from India, arrived in Tibet, unified the priesthood, improved the moral tone by enforcing monastic rules, and tried to eliminate any vestiges of Bon ritual from the religion. He was the founder of the Kadampa sect. Another sect, the Kargyupa, was founded by the translator Marpa (1012–97) and his famous disciple MILAREPA. In the 13th cent. Kublai Khan, after his conversion, bestowed temporal rule upon the abbots of the Sas-Kya monastery, who subsequently ruled W Tibet from c.1270 to 1340. Their years of political control, marked by corruption and venality, generated much public cynicism. Finally, a great reformer, the lama Tsong-kha-pa (d. 1419), reorganized the orders, strengthened monastic discipline, introduced a rigid rule of celibacy, and prescribed rigorous routines for meetings, confessions, and retreats. This reform movement called itself the Gelukpa [virtuous] sect and is generally known as the Yellow Hat sect. Soon Yellow Hat influence spread to Mongolia, and in 1641 a ruling Mongol prince bestowed temporal and spiritual control of all Tibet upon the fifth grand lama of the order, whose title was Ta-lai or Dalai [ocean-wide] Lama. The Dalai Lama was proclaimed a divine reincarnation of the Bodhisattva Avalokitesvara, ancestor of the Tibetan people, and was installed in the Potala (palace) in Lhasa. He soon became the temporal leader of Tibet, while spiritual supremacy resided with the chief abbot of the powerful Tashi Lumpo monastery near Shigatse, who is known as the Tashi or Panchen Lama. The Panchen Lama is a reincarnation of Amitabha, the Buddha of Light. The succession to grand lama, either Dalai or Panchen, depends upon direct reincarnation. Upon the death of either, his spirit is believed to pass into the body of some infant just born. An exacting series of tests and divinations determine the proper boy, who is then carefully trained for his great responsibility. The monastic orders include abbots, ordained religious mendicants, novices (candidates), and neophytes (children on probation). The standing of nuns is inferior. The most dedicated Tibetan Buddhists seek NIRVANA, but for the common people the religion retains shamanistic elements. A protective formula of esoteric significance, *Om mani padme hum* [Om, the jewel in the lotus], is repeated endlessly; it is inscribed on rocks and walls, tallied on prayer wheels, and displayed on banners and streamers. The worship also includes reciting prayers and intoning hymns, often to the sound of great horns and drums. In addition to a large pantheon of spirits, ghouls, and genii, many Buddhas and *bodhisattvas* (future Buddhas) are worshiped along with their ferocious consorts, or Taras. The 14th Dalai Lama was installed in 1940 and the 9th Panchen Lama in 1944. In 1959, following the Tibetan revolt against the Chinese, the Dalai Lama went into exile in India, and the Chinese installed the Panchen Lama in his place as ruler. Until the Chinese repression of Buddhism in Tibet in the 1960s, nearly a fifth of the population resided in lamaseries. See Charles Bell, *The Religion of Tibet* (1931, repr. 1968); L. A. Waddell, *Buddhism of Tibet* (2d ed. 1939, repr. 1973); W. Y. Evans-Wentz, *Tibetan Yoga and Secret Doctrine* (1935, repr. 1958); P. H. Pott, *God and Demon in Buddhism* (1962).

Tibetan language, member of the Tibeto-Burman subfamily of the Sino-Tibetan family of languages (see SINO-TIBETAN LANGUAGES). It is spoken by 1.5 million people in Tibet and probably by 5 million more in the Tsinghai and Kansu provinces of mainland China and in Bhutan, Nepal, Sikkim, and part of Kashmir. There are a number of dialects. Tibetan tends to be monosyllabic and to lack inflection. Word order is, therefore, very important. Tibetan is also tonal, having six tones in all: short high, long high, short low, long low, high falling, and low falling. A system of writing that is a syllabary was devised for Tibetan in the 7th cent. A.D. and is derived ultimately from the northern Gupta alphabet of India, which, in turn, is a descendant of a Semitic script. Tibetan is written from left to right. See Hans N. von Koerber, *Morphology of the Tibetan Language* (c.1935); S. C. Das, *An Introduction to the Grammar of the Tibetan Language* (repr. 1972); G. N. Roerich and L. P. Lhalungpa, *Textbook of Colloquial Tibetan* (2nd rev. ed. 1973).

Tibetan terrier, breed of medium-sized dog originating in Tibet probably several thousand years ago. It stands from 14 to 16 in. (35.6–40.6 cm) high at the shoulder and weighs from 15 to 30 lb (6.8–13.6 kg). Its double coat consists of a soft, woolly underlayer and a profuse, finely textured, straight topcoat with hair falling over the eyes and forming a beard on the lower jaw. It may be solid white, cream, gray, smoke, black, or gold in color, or any of these in parti-color or tricolor patterns. Introduced into the United States in 1956, the Tibetan terrier is exhibited in the miscellaneous class at dog shows sanctioned by the American Kennel Club. See DOG.

Tibeto-Burman languages, subfamily of the Sino-Tibetan family of languages. See SINO-TIBETAN LANGUAGES; BURMESE; TIBETAN LANGUAGE.

Tibhath (tĭb'hăth), unidentified Syrian city. 1 Chron. 18.8. Betah: 2 Sam. 8.8. See TEBAH.

tibia: see LEG.

Tibni (tĭb'nī), unsuccessful contender with OMRI **1** for the throne of Israel after the death of Zimri. 1 Kings 16.21,22.

Tibullus (Albius Tibullus) (tĭbŭl'əs), c.48 B.C.–19 B.C., Roman elegiac poet, b. Pedum, near Praeneste. Probably of the equestrian order, he was a friend of Messala, whom he accompanied on campaign. A master of the Latin love elegy, Tibullus wrote two books of verse (concerned, respectively, with "Delia" and "Nemesis"—names symbolic of his loves) that were published during his lifetime; some doubtfully attributed posthumous pieces plus works by other poets constitute a third book.

Tibur: see TIVOLI, Italy.

tic: see SPASM.

Tichborne Case (tĭch'bôrn), in English law, a celebrated imposture trial, the longest in British history. In 1854, Roger Tichborne, heir to the Tichborne baronetcy and estates in Hampshire, England, was lost at sea when his ship disappeared after sailing from Brazil. His mother, Lady Tichborne, refused to accept his death and advertised widely for news of his whereabouts. In 1865, a man in Australia presented himself as Roger Tichborne. When he arrived (1866) in England, Lady Tichborne acknowledged him as her son, although other members of the family expressed doubts. The claimant initiated an ejection suit (1871–72) against Roger's nephew, who had succeeded to the baronetcy and the estates. The jury declared him an impostor, and he was identified as Arthur Orton, the son of a butcher from Wapping. He was then tried and convicted (1873–74) on two counts of perjury. After serving 10 years of a 14-year sentence, Orton was released and later published a confession. Still later, he denied the confession. See Lord Maugham, *The Tichborne Case* (1936); Douglas Woodruff, *The Tichborne Claimant* (1957).

Ticino (tēchē'nō), Fr. and Ger. *Tessin*, canton (1970 pop. 245,458), 1,086 sq mi (2,813 sq km), S Switzerland, on the southern slope of the central Alps, bordering on Italy. BELLINZONA is the capital. Largely a mountainous region, Ticino embraces the Ticino River valley and part of Lago Maggiore and of the Lake of Lugano. Although it has a pastoral economy, wine is widely produced in the valleys and corn and tobacco are cultivated. Industry, mainly in the south, produces metal goods and chemicals; there is an extensive hydroelectric system along the Ticino River. Ticino is noted for its resorts, particularly LOCARNO and LUGANO. The population is mostly Roman Catholic and Italian-speaking. A part of Transpadane Gaul under the Roman Empire, Ticino later shared the history of Lombardy until the Swiss confederates captured it (15th–16th cent.) from the duchy of Milan. It was ruled until 1798 by Schwyz and Uri cantons and became a Swiss canton in 1803.

Ticino, Lat. *Ticinus,* river, 154 mi (248 km) long, rising in Ticino canton, S Switzerland, and flowing generally S through Lago Maggiore into N Italy, joining the Po River below Pavia. In Switzerland, the Ticino is used to generate electricity. It provides irrigation in Italy; the important Cavour irrigation canal branches from the river. The Ticino River was the scene (218 B.C.) of Hannibal's victory over Scipio in the Second Punic War.

tick: see MITE.

Tickell, Thomas (tĭk'əl), 1686–1740, English poet and translator. A contributor of verse to the *Spectator,* he was a friend of Addison, for whom he wrote a fine elegy (1721). His translation of the first book of the *Iliad,* appearing simultaneously with Pope's (1715), caused a quarrel between Pope and Addison, who praised Tickell's work. See biography by R. E. Tickell (1931).

Ticknor, George (tĭk'nər), 1791–1871, American author and teacher, b. Boston, grad. Dartmouth, 1807. In 1815 he went to Germany to study at the Univ. of Göttingen. While abroad he was appointed Smith professor of French and Spanish languages and literatures at Harvard. After completing his European studies, he assumed his post at Harvard (1819). While he was there he improved elementary instruction in languages and introduced German methods of study. He resigned in 1835 to go abroad and collect more material for his great *History of Spanish Literature* (1849). His impressive collection of Spanish materials was left to the Boston Public Library, which he had helped to found.

Ticknor, William Davis, 1810–64, American publisher. John Reed and James T. FIELDS became Ticknor's partners in Boston, and their firm is best known as Ticknor and Fields. They published the works of many of the famous Americans of the day, including Longfellow, Lowell, and O. W. Holmes, and their offices were the meeting place of literary men. From 1854 to 1864 the firm published the *Atlantic Monthly* and the *North American Review.* Ticknor was the first American publisher to pay foreign authors for the rights to their works.

tickseed, name sometimes used for the BUR MARIGOLD, COREOPSIS, tick trefoil or BEGGARWEED, and other bur-producing weeds.

Ticonderoga (tī"kŏndərō'gə), resort village (1970 pop. 3,268), Essex co., NE N.Y., on a neck of land between lakes George and Champlain; settled in the 17th cent., inc. 1889. The falls of Lake George furnish power for its paper mill. At Ticonderoga and nearby Crown Point several battles of the French and Indian War took place. Fort Carillon, built there by the French in 1755, was successfully defended by Montcalm against James Abercromby in 1758, but it fell to Jeffrey Amherst in 1759, when it was renamed Fort Ticonderoga. It was captured (May 10, 1775) by a detachment of Green Mountain Boys under Ethan Allen and troops commanded by Benedict Arnold. In the Saratoga campaign it was abandoned (1777) without a fight by Arthur St. Clair to John Burgoyne. The British gave up the fort after the campaign but reoccupied it for a short time in 1780. The fort was restored as a museum in 1909. The headquarters of the New York State Historical Association is at Ticonderoga; the building is a reproduction of John Hancock's house and contains collections of historical material and paintings. A ferry crosses Lake Champlain to Shoreham, Vt.

Tidal (tī'dəl): see CHEDORLAOMER.

tidal theory: see SOLAR SYSTEM.

tidal wave, term properly applied to the crest of the tide as it moves around the earth. In popular usage it is applied to any destructive wave or to high water not related to tidal phenomena. These latter tidal waves are of two types: TSUNAMIS and storm surges. Storm surges are floods of ocean or lake water that occur chiefly in areas subject to tropical storms and bordering on shallow waters. In Galveston, Texas, in 1900 a wind velocity of more than 100 mi (160 km) per hr, combined with a very low barometric pressure, caused tides 15 ft (5 m) above normal that flooded coastal areas, resulting in the loss of thousands of lives and extensive property damage. See EARTHQUAKE.

tide, alternate rise and fall of SEA LEVEL in oceans and other large bodies of water. These changes are caused by the gravitational attraction of the moon and, to a lesser extent, of the sun for the earth. More generally, tides are the deformations of celestial bodies from a perfectly spherical shape that result from disruptive stresses created by their mutual GRAVITATION. Tides are raised in the earth's solid crust and atmosphere as well as in the oceans. Every body in the universe has some tidal effect, however small, on every other body. This effect is directly proportional to the mass of the body causing the tide but inversely proportional to the cube of the distance between the bodies. As a consequence, the nearby moon is about 2.17 times as effective as the more massive sun in raising tides on the earth. If the moon attracted every point within the earth with equal force, there would be no tides. But according to Newton's law of gravitation, the gravitational force decreases as the distance increases. Hence the force exerted by the moon is greater on the side of the earth facing the moon than on the opposite side, and the difference in the lunar force at various points on the earth's surface produces the tides. Although the sun exerts a much greater total force on the earth than does the moon, the solar force varies less from place to place on the earth's surface. Thus the moon's proximity explains its dominant role in creating tides. At any given time, there are two high tides on the earth, the direct tide on the side facing the moon and the indirect tide on the opposite side. The direct tide is easily understood as a bulge produced by the moon pulling the earth's water toward it, but the indirect tide is somewhat puzzling. The simplest explanation is that the moon's pull on the center of the earth is greater than on the water on the side of the earth opposite the moon. Hence, the earth is lifted away from the water most distant from the moon, producing a second bulge. Another way of viewing the tide is as the longest possible ocean wave, one which stretches all the way around the earth. The tide regarded as a wave is sometimes referred to as a TIDAL WAVE, although this term is more properly applied to the shock wave propagated by an underwater earthquake. To avoid confusion, such shock waves are now called TSUNAMIS, their Japanese name. As the earth rotates on its axis, the location of the two diametrically opposed tidal bulges varies on the earth's surface. The earth's rotation and the moon's revolution, which have the same direction, bring each point on the earth opposite the moon once every 24 hr and 50 min. Therefore, the average interval between direct and indirect high tides is about 12 hr and 25 min. In certain shallow seas and narrow estuaries, the tides differ from this simple pattern. For example, in certain regions one of the two daily tides is appreciably higher than the other, the interval between successive tides is unequal, or there is only one high tide per day. The range of the tides is the difference in sea level between high and low tides. Spring tide, having the maximum range, occurs during the full and new phases of the moon. At these times in the lunar cycle, the moon, earth, and sun are along a straight line, a condition known as syzygy. Neap tide, having the minimum range, occurs during the moon's first and last quarters, when the moon, earth, and sun form a right angle. The typical tidal range in the open ocean is only 2 ft (0.61 m) but is much greater near the coast. The world's widest tidal range occurs in the Bay of Fundy, in E Canada, where the sea level changes by 40 ft (12 m) during the day. As the tides change, currents must flow to redistribute the ocean's water. Near the coast, the direction of the current changes every 6¼ hr from toward the shore (flood current) to away from the shore (ebb current). In the open ocean, the tidal currents are rotary, shifting through all directions of the compass in a period matching that of the local tide. When tidal currents flow into the mouth of a river, they must speed up. In extreme cases, the tidal rise advances up the river as a solid wall of water often several feet high. This rare phenomenon is called a tidal BORE. Detailed prediction of ocean tides from theories of classical mechanics and hydrodynamics has not been successful, largely because of complications introduced by the irregular shape of the ocean basin and coastline. Useful results are obtained empirically by analyzing records of previous tides at a particular location to predict future tides. The importance of tides for maritime activities has prompted the compilation of tide tables for harbors; these give the time and height of high water and low water based on past observations corrected for the varying positions of celestial bodies. Numerous schemes have been proposed to harness the tides as a practical source of power, but none as yet has proved widely feasible. See Albert Defant, *Ebb and Flow: The Tides of Earth, Air and Water* (tr. 1958); E. P. Clancy, *The Tides* (1968).

tidewater, in U.S. history, that part of the Atlantic coastal plain between the shoreline and the farthest upstream points in rivers reached by oceanic tides. In many cases the fall line is given as the western boundary. The tidewater, or seaboard, with its good harbors readily accessible to the ocean, was settled first by European colonists. Later the Southern tidewater became the region of the large plantations and of the important commercial towns.

Tieck, Ludwig (lo͞ot'vĭkh tēk), 1773–1853, German writer. In his youth he led the transition from STURM UND DRANG to romanticism, writing with W. H. Wackenroder *Phantasien über die Kanst* (1799), essays on aesthetics, and *Franz Sternbalds Wanderungen* (1798), one of the first German romantic novels. His fairy tales and folk tales, notably *Der blonde Eckbert* (1796) and *Volksmärchen* (1797), illustrate the romantic refinement of these genres. *Kaiser Octavianus* (1804), a poetic drama, is an allegory of the rise of Christianity; it exemplifies the romantic glorification of the Middle Ages. Other works include *Der Aufruhr in den Cevennen* (1826), a fine example of romantic historical fiction, and *Phantasus* (3 vol., 1812–16; tr. *Tales from the Phantasus,* 1845), a collection of stories. Tieck also translated *Don Quixote* and completed, with his daughter Dorothea and her husband, Graf von Baudissin, the translations of Shakespeare begun by A. W. von Schlegel. See study by J. Trainer (1964).

tie-dyeing, dyeing method used by hand-loom weavers of ancient times. It became popular during the craft revival of the 1960s. The fabric to be colored is tied or knotted at intervals before being placed in the dye; the knotted areas remain untouched by the dye and create random patterns frequently resulting in a sunburst effect. Tie-dyeing is currently popular for the decoration of wall hangings and casual apparel. See Sara Néa, *Tie-Dye* (1972).

Tiele, Cornelis Petrus (kôrnā'lĭs pā'trəs tē'lə), 1830–1902, Dutch theologian and author of a number of valuable works on the history of religion. Important is his *Outlines of the History of Religion* (1876, tr. 1877).

T'ien-ching: see TIENTSIN, China.

Tienen or **Thienen** (both: tē'nən), Fr. *Tirlemont,* town (1970 pop. 24,134), Brabant prov., central Belgium. It is a commercial and industrial center, with a major beet sugar refining industry. Tienen has suffered numerous sieges in its history. In 1831 the last fighting in the struggle for Belgian independence took place there. Of note is the Church of Notre Dame du Lac (1296).

Tien Shan (tēĕn shän) [Chin.,=celestial mountains], mountain system of central Asia, extending c.1,500 mi (2,410 km) from the Pamir mts., USSR, NE through Sinkiang Uigur Autonomous Region, NW China, to the China-Mongolia border; Pobeda Peak (24,406 ft/7,439 m), on the USSR-China line, is the highest point. The E Tien Shan are relatively low parallel ranges that divide the Dzungaria and Tarim basins; the W Tien Shan separate into numerous complex branches. Some of the Ala-Tau ranges are extensions of the Tien Shan. Because of the dry climate, the Tien Shan's snow line is generally above 11,000 ft (3,350 m). The Syr Darya, Chu, and Ili are the largest of many rivers that rise in the system. Issyk-Kul, W Tien Shan, is one of the world's largest mountain lakes. Coal, iron, lead, and zinc are mined in the region; grains are the predominant crop in the valleys. China and the USSR are linked by several passes, notably the Terek Pass (alt. 12,730 ft/3,880 m) on the route connecting Kashgar and Samarkand.

Tientsin or **T'ien-ching** (both: tĭn"tsĭn', tēn"-, tyĕn"-, tĭn"sĭn'), city (1970 est. pop. 4,500,000), NE China. It is in east central Hopeh prov. but is politically independent of the province, being administered directly by the central government. The third largest city in China, Tientsin is a port at the confluence of the Hai River (c.30 mi/50 km from its mouth) with the Grand Canal. Although the harbor is poor, Tientsin is a leading international port of China and the collection and distribution center for the N China plain. It is connected by rail with much of China. The city is an important manufacturing center, with iron and steel works, textile mills (cotton, woolen, and hemp), machine shops, a chemical industry based on salt, flour mills and other food-processing establishments, paper mills, and plants making heavy machinery, automobiles, precision instruments, cement, fertilizer, rubber products, and woolen carpets. Strategically located on the overland route to Manchuria, Tientsin has been a frequent military objective since its rise to importance in the late 18th cent. Agreements exacted from China by the British and French in 1860 made Tientsin a treaty port and conceded parts of the city for foreign settlements and garrisons. In the Boxer Rebellion (1900) there was a joint foreign occupation, and the walls were razed by the Europeans. With the abolition of the last foreign concessions in 1946, Tientsin was completely restored to Chinese sovereignty. The city has an astronomical observatory and is the seat of Hopeh Univ., Nankai Univ., Tientsin Univ., a medical college, and a music conservatory.

Tiepolo, Giovanni Battista (jōvän'nē bät-tē'stä tyĕ'pōlō), 1696–1770, Italian painter, b. Venice. He was the most important Venetian painter and decorator of the 18th cent. His frescoes in the Labia Palace and the doge's palace won him international fame. In 1750, Tiepolo was summoned to Würzburg, where he decorated the palace of the archbishop with frescoes illustrating the life of Emperor Frederick I and with altarpieces depicting the *Ascension of the Virgin* and *Fall of the Angels*. In 1762 he went to Madrid, where he passed the remainder of his life and decorated the royal palace with frescoes representing *Spain and Her Provinces* and the *Apotheosis of Spain*. In oil he was also prolific. Tiepolo's works are in many European and American galleries. Among them are *The Crucifixion* (City Art Mus., St. Louis); *The Apotheosis of Aeneas* (Mus. of Fine Arts, Boston); and two allegorical pictures (Metropolitan Mus.). The National Gallery, Washington, D.C., has several pictures. As pure virtuosity, the art of Tiepolo is unsurpassed. Lightness and clarity of color, superb draftsmanship, and scintillating brushwork mark his style. Particularly in his fresco decorations, in which he sent foreshortened deities floating on clouds through sunny skies, his mastery and audacity are amazing. It is an art derived from Veronese, but it is less concerned with solid structure and shows more surface brilliance. Two of Tiepolo's sons, Giandomenico and Lorenzo, continued his tradition. Tiepolo was famous also as a draftsman and etcher. Technically, Goya learned much from him. See catalog of works (ed. by G. Knox, 1960); studies by A. Morassi (1955), P. Ancona (1956), V. Crivellaro (1962), and A. Rizzi (1972).

Tierra del Fuego (tyĕ'rä dĕl fwā'gō), [Span.=land of fire], archipelago, 28,476 sq mi (73,753 sq km), off S South America, separated from the mainland by the Strait of Magellan. It consists of one large island (sometimes called simply Tierra del Fuego), five medium-sized islands, and numerous small islands, islets, and rocks separated by many inlets and channels. The Andes extend through the western part, and the plateau of PATAGONIA continues into the eastern section. The coastal plains are bleak, with frequent high winds and much rainfall, while the inland areas and the mountains are often very cold. Tierra del Fuego is divided into two sections, the eastern part belonging to Argentina (the territory of Tierra del Fuego) and the larger western part to Chile (a part of Magallanes prov.). The economy is based on the raising of sheep and the exploitation of petroleum. Tierra del Fuego was discovered by Magellan in 1520 but was not well surveyed until the early 19th cent. The introduction of sheep farming and the discovery of gold in the 1880s led to European, Argentine, and Chilean immigration. The aboriginal peoples of Tierra del Fuego (the Onas, Alakalufs, and Yahgans) were gradually killed off by disease.

Tiffany, Charles Lewis (tĭf'ənē), 1812–1902, American merchant, b. Killingly, Conn. He founded the famous jewelry firm of Tiffany and Company, New York City. His improvements in styles of silverware won wide recognition, and when in 1851 he introduced the English standard of sterling silver, the leading silversmiths in the United States followed his example. Much of his later life was devoted to studying and encouraging the fine arts.

Tiffany, Louis Comfort, 1848–1933, American artist, decorative designer, and art patron, b. New York City; son of Charles Lewis Tiffany. He studied painting with Inness and in Paris and painted oils and watercolors in Europe and Morocco. Later he established the interior-decorating firm in New York City which came to be known as Tiffany Studios. The firm specialized in *favrile* glass work, characterized by iridescent colors and natural forms in the ART NOUVEAU style. This work ranged from lamps and vases to stained-glass windows and a huge glass curtain for the national theater in Mexico City. His lamps became enormously popular in the 1960s and were widely imitated. In 1919, Tiffany established the Louis Comfort Tiffany Foundation, which presently provides study and travel grants for art students. Tiffany is represented in the Metropolitan Museum by a painting, *Snake Charmer at Tangiers*, in the Museum of Modern Art (New York City) by several glass pieces, and most completely in the Neustadt Museum of Tiffany Art (New York City). See Egon Neustadt's *The Lamps of Tiffany* (1971).

Tiffin, city (1970 pop. 21,596), seat of Seneca co., N central Ohio, on the scenic Sandusky River in a farm area; inc. 1835. Radiators, china, glassware, heavy machinery, machine parts, wire and cable, and electrical equipment are made. Heidelberg College, Tiffin Univ. (a business school), and a state hospital are there.

Tiflis: see TBILISI, USSR.

Tifton, city (1970 pop. 12,179), seat of Tift co., S central Ga.; inc. 1890. Tobacco, cotton, and truck crops are marketed, meat is packed, and textiles and clothing, lumber, and plastics are produced. A state junior college and a state agricultural-experiment station are there. Of interest is an eternal-flame memorial for the war dead.

tiger, large carnivore of the CAT family, *Panthera leo*, found in the forests of Asia. Its coat is orange-yellow with numerous prominent black stripes. Black and albino specimens are sometimes found. The tiger has no mane comparable to that of a LION, although it may have a ruff around the sides of the head. Tigers and lions are quite similar anatomically and can be interbred, but some tigers, notably those of the Siberian race, are much larger than any lion. Male tigers are generally about 8 to 10 ft (2.4–3 m) long, including the 3-ft (1.8-m) tail. The Siberian tiger may be 13 ft (4 m) long, including the tail, and weigh 650 lb (290 kg). Tigers are found in a variety of climates, from N China and Siberia to the jungles of Indonesia and W to Iran and the Caucasus mts. They are solitary animals and usually hunt at night. Their vision and sense of smell are poor, and they rely strongly on hearing in hunting, which they do very stealthily and silently. They kill a variety of animals, including deer, antelope, wild pigs, and cattle. Tigers try to remain out of sight and hearing of their enemies, especially man; they prefer fleeing to fighting. They can be killed by wild dogs, elephants, and water buffalos. Man-eating tigers are usually individuals who are too old or sick to capture wild animals. Tigers are good swimmers and enjoy bathing, especially in hot weather, which appears to make them quite uncomfortable. They are poor climbers, taking to trees only in emergencies. The Indian, or Bengal, tiger is the most numerous. Tigers are classified in the phylum CHORDATA, subphylum Vertebrata, class Mammalia, order Carnivora, family Felidae.

tiger lily: see LILY.

tigernut, nearly cosmopolitan perennial (*Cyperus esculentum*) of the family Cyperaceae (SEDGE family) of the same genus as the papyrus plant. The tigernut has been cultivated since early times (chiefly in S Europe and W Africa) for its small, tuberous rhizomes, which are eaten raw or roasted, used for hog feed, and pressed for the juice to make a beverage. A nondrying oil (usually called chufa) is also obtained from the rhizome. In W Africa the plant often grows in great concentration and is gathered from the wild. In the S United States it is sometimes a troublesome weed in planted fields. Other names are earth almond and yellow nut grass. The tigernut is classified in the division MAGNOLIOPHYTA, class Liliatae, order Cyperales, family Cyperaceae.

Tiglathpileser I (tĭg"lăthpīlē'zər), d. c.1074 B.C., king of ancient Assyria. An able administrator, he was especially renowned for his military ability and invaded Asia Minor, N Syria, Armenia, and Babylonia. He rebuilt temples and palaces and recorded that he repaired all the irrigation works throughout the land.

Tiglathpileser III, d. 728 B.C., king of ancient Assyria. He seems to have usurped the throne in 745 B.C. He bore the alternative name of Pul, by which he was known in biblical history (2 Kings 15.19). He subdued the Aramaean tribes in Babylonia, and his general Ashur-danani campaigned against the Medes and fought as far as the Caspian Sea. The king defeated Urartu and became master of Syria. Appealed to by Ahaz, king of Judah, for assistance against Pekah of Israel and Resin of Damascus, he responded by defeating Ahaz's enemies and capturing Damascus. A revolt in Babylonia was crushed by Tiglathpileser, who became king of Babylon in name as well as in deed. He proved himself a great administrator and is considered one of the most remarkable figures in Assyrian history. In the Bible he is sometimes erroneously referred to as Tilgath-pilneser. See 2 Kings 15.29; 16.7,10; 1 Chron. 5.6,26; 2 Chron. 28.20.

Tigranes (tīgrā'nēz), c.140 B.C.–55 B.C., king of Armenia (c.96 B.C.–55 B.C.), called also Tigranes I and Tigranes the Great. By an alliance with his father-in-law, MITHRADATES VI of Pontus, he was able to extend his conquests across Asia Minor. He founded Tigranocerta (the modern Siirt, Turkey) as the capital of his large empire, but he and Mithradates were at war with Rome, and in 69 B.C. LUCULLUS captured Tigranocerta. POMPEY with the aid of Tigranes' son vanquished Tigranes, who lost all his conquests and had to pay tribute to Rome.

Tigre (tē'grā), city (1970 pop. 152,335), Buenos Aires prov., E Argentina. A railroad terminus and river port, Tigre is a market for the fruit grown in the surrounding area. The city has sawmills and shipyards, as well as a naval museum.

Tigré: see ETHIOPIA.

Tigris (tī'grĭs), river of SW Asia, c.1,150 mi (1,850 km) long, rising in the Taurus mts., E Turkey, and flowing SE through Iraq to join the Euphrates River, with which it forms the Shatt al Arab. The Tigris is called the Hiddekil in the Bible (Gen. 2.14; Dan. 10.4). It flows swiftly and receives many tributaries, including the Diyala, originating in the Zagros mts., and the Great and Little Zab. The lower Tigris is connected to the Euphrates by semipermanent natural channels and by ancient canals. Dams across the river divert water for irrigation. The Tigris is subject to sudden, devastating floods, and the Wadi Ath Tharthar Scheme, Iraq's largest flood-control project, protects Baghdad and vicinity from floods in addition to irrigating c.770,000 acres (311,600 hectares) of land. The Tigris is navigable to Baghdad for shallow-draft vessels; above Baghdad, rafts carry much of the trade to Mosul. Its importance as a trade artery has declined with improved road and rail connections. Basra, at the junction of the Tigris and Euphrates, is Iraq's chief port. In antiquity, some of the great cities of Mesopotamia, including Nineveh, Ctesiphon, and Seleucia, stood on the banks of the Tigris, and the river served as an important transportation route. The Tigris flood plain was cultivated by irrigation from the earliest times; the Sumerians dug a canal from the Tigris to Lagash c.2400 B.C.

Tihama, region of the Arabian Peninsula: see TIHAMAH.

Tihamah, Tihama, or **Tehama** (all: tĭhä'mə), narrow, extremely arid lowland region along the west coast of the Arabian Peninsula, extending c.1,300 mi (2,090 km) from the Gulf of Aqaba S to the Bab el Mandeb straits. Some agriculture is practiced on oases, and several deep inlets, called sharms, provide excellent anchorages along the coast.

Tihwa: see WU-LU-MU-CH'I, China.

Tijou, Jean (zhäN tēzhōō'), fl. 1689–c.1711, French designer of ironwork, known exclusively by his works in England. He arrived in England c.1689 when William and Mary, his lifelong patrons, began their reign. The purely French Renaissance type of design that he introduced greatly influenced English smithcraft and was perpetuated by his apprenticed artisans and by his *New Book of Drawings* (1693). His notable gates and railings adorn the grounds of Hampton Court Palace (1689–1700), and he fashioned the screens and grilles of St. Paul's Cathedral for Sir Christopher Wren. His cathedral irons show a characteristically lavish use of rosettes, figures, and embossed leafage, which marked the high point of English wrought ironwork.

Tijuana (tēhwä'nä), city (1970 pop. 335,125), Baja California state, NW Mexico, just south of the U.S. border. It is a gaudy border resort, noted for its racetracks and bullfights. An irrigated agricultural area surrounds the city. During the prohibition era Tijuana gained fame as a wide-open town. It expanded considerably in the wake of a booming tourist trade after World War II.

Tikal (tēkäl'), ruined city of the Classic Period of the MAYA, N central Petén, Guatemala. The largest and possibly the oldest of the Maya cities, Tikal consists of nine groups of courts and plazas built on hilly land above surrounding swamps (which may have been lakes in former times) and interconnected by bridges and causeways. The main civic and religious center of the city covers about 500 acres (200 hectares). Temples and palaces rise above the plazas. The design of the buildings is for the most part monumental and static and utilizes harmonious combinations of solid masses. The tallest structure, a temple, is 229 ft (70 m) high. With a backdrop of lush tropical vegetation the abandoned city is an impressive sight.

Tikvah (tĭk'və) or **Tikvath** (-văth). **1** Huldah's father-in-law. 2 Kings 22.14; 2 Chron. 34.22. **2** Jahaziah's father. Ezra 10.15.

Tilak, Bal Gangadhar (bäl gŭng'gədär tē'läk), 1856–1920, Indian nationalist leader. Although a Brahman by birth, he grew up in humble circumstances in Maharashtra. Tilak eventually turned to teaching and journalism in Poona, and in his newspapers, the Marathi-language *Kesari* [lion] and the English-language *Mahratta,* he set forth his nationalist ideals. He sought a Hindu revival based on Mahratta traditions and complete independence [swaraj] from Britain. After the Indian National Congress was founded (1885), Tilak became the acknowledged leader of the extreme wing. He fought the moderate measures of Gopal Krishna GOKHALE and advocated passive resistance to British rule; he was arrested (1897) by the British and imprisoned for 18 months. In 1907 a split took place in the Congress, and Tilak led his extremist wing out of the party. The next year he was again imprisoned, this time for six years. After his release he reentered the Congress and managed to win the support of Muslims (who had earlier been repelled by his aggressive Hinduism) in the Lucknow Pact (1916) between the Congress and the Muslim League. Unlike Mohandas Gandhi, he welcomed the Montagu-Chelmsford Report (1918), which conceded a substantial measure of self-rule. See biographies by T. V. Parvate (1959) and Ram Gopal (1965); S. A. Wolpert, *Tilak and Gokhale* (1962).

tilapia (təlä'pēə), any member of the genus *Tilapia,* spiny-finned freshwater fishes of the family Cichlidae, native chiefly to Africa and the Middle East. Tilapias incubate their eggs orally; one or both parents carry them in their mouths until (and for a short period after) the young hatch. A species of E and S Africa, *Tilapia mossambica,* has been successfully transplanted to parts of the Far East and South America, providing a cheap and rapidly breeding source of protein. Tilapia is classified in the phylum CHORDATA, subphylum Vertebrata, class Osteichthyes, order Perciformes, family Cichlidae.

Tilburg (tĭl'bərg), city (1971 pop. 153,734), North Brabant prov., S Netherlands, near the Belgian border. Manufactures include textiles, textile machinery, dyes, and leather. Its main industrial growth began in the late 19th cent. It is the site of the Catholic School of Economics. The present-day town hall was used in the first half of the 19th cent. as a royal residence by King William II of the Netherlands.

Tilbury (tĭl'bərē), part of the urban district of THURROCK, Essex, E England. Tilbury Fort originated under Henry VIII; it was rebuilt and strengthened in the 17th cent. Queen Elizabeth I, in 1588, reviewed royal troops there when the Spanish Armada threatened England. The Tilbury docks, begun in 1882, are included in the Port of London.

Tilden, Samuel Jones, 1814–86, American political figure, Democratic presidential candidate in 1876, b. New Lebanon, N.Y. Admitted to the bar in 1841, Tilden was an eminently successful lawyer, with many railroad companies as clients. He became a strong partisan of Martin Van Buren and the BARNBURNERS in New York Democratic politics. Unlike other Free-Soil Democrats of the 1850s, he did not join the new Republican party and later disapproved of the Civil War. As state Democratic chairman after 1866 he sought reform and gathered much of the evidence of corruption that broke the notorious Tweed Ring (see TWEED, WILLIAM MARCY). Elected governor of New York (1874), he further enhanced his reputation for reform by his successful attack on the corrupt "Canal ring," which made illegal profits on repair and extension of the state canal system. Tilden thus became the outstanding Democrat in the nation, and in 1876 his party nominated him for President. Rutherford B. HAYES was his Republican opponent. The campaign resulted in the most famous election dispute in American history. Tilden received a majority of the popular vote, but there were double and conflicting returns of electoral votes from Florida, Louisiana, and South Carolina and a contest over one Oregon elector. To settle the unusual question, not covered by the Constitution, Congress created an electoral commission of five Senators, five Representatives, and five Supreme Court Justices. Eight were Republicans and seven were Democrats, as plans for one independent failed. The commission, by partisan division, awarded (March 2, 1877) Hayes all the disputed votes, making his total a majority of one (185 to 184). Tilden discouraged further contest. He left a large sum toward establishing a free public library in New York City, and in 1895 this trust was joined with the Astor and Lenox libraries to form the New York Public Library. See biographies by John Bigelow (1895) and A. C. Flick (1939, repr. 1963); P. L. Haworth, *The Hayes-Tilden Disputed Presidential Election of 1876* (1906, new ed. 1927, repr. 1966).

Tilden, William Tatem II, 1893–1953, American tennis player, b. Philadelphia. He developed into a brilliant, versatile tennis player, and from 1913 he won several doubles titles in the United States. He became one of the foremost tennis players of the world by winning the U.S. singles championship seven times (1920–25, 1929) and the British singles crown three times (1920–21, 1930) while taking several other national tennis crowns throughout the world. "Big Bill," as he was called, was the leading member of the American team that won the Davis Cup and was chiefly responsible for U.S. retention of the cup until 1926. After turning professional in 1931, Tilden won the professional singles championship in 1931 and 1935. In 1945, at the age of 52, Tilden, along with Vincent Richards, won the professional doubles championship. He wrote numerous books on tennis. *Aces, Places, and Faults* (1938) and *My Story* (1948) are autobiographical.

tile, one of the ceramic products used in building, to which group brick and TERRA-COTTA also belong. The term designates the finished baked CLAY—the material of a wide variety of units used in architecture and engineering, such as wall slabs or blocks, floor pavings, coverings for roofs, and drainage pipes. In these products the distinction between terra-cotta and tile is often vague, and any small flat slab of ceramic material used for the veneering of wall, floor, or other surfaces is also called a tile. Tile-making evolved from primitive pottery manufacture. The earliest architectural sites give evidence of the use of tiles. As soon as the art of glazing was discovered, it became possible to use the thin slabs of hard-burnt clay, decorated in colors, as a decorative adjunct to architecture. This aesthetic use of tiles as a facing for walls distinguishes them from other ceramic products, such as brick, terra-cotta, and roofing units, which are essentially structural. Colored glazed tiles dated from 4700 B.C. have been found in Egypt. However, for lack of fuel, the Egyptians produced no extensive architectural ceramics. It was in Mesopotamia that ancient ceramics were perfected. Large wall surfaces were faced with bas-relief decorations executed in enameled tiles resembling modern bricks in shape, most notably at the palace at Khorsabad (722–705 B.C.) in Assyria, near ancient Nineveh, and the Ishtar Gate (c.7th cent. B.C.) in Babylon. From these regions ancient Persia acquired ceramic techniques for the fine bas-reliefs of animals and archers in the palaces of Susa and Persepolis (5th cent. B.C.). The Persians remain masters of tile decoration. Unsurpassed masterpieces of tile design were produced from the 12th to the 16th cent. Examples are the 15th-century Blue Mosque at Tabriz and numerous structures at Esfahan and Shiraz. The earliest tile sewer pipes are those excavated at Crete (c.1800 B.C.). The Greeks also employed tile drains and conduits and tiles for roofing. Their architectural ceramics were mostly confined to cornices and cornice adornments and are customarily classed as terra-cotta. The Romans made wide use of floor tiles of various shapes and of floor mosaics, as well as a variety of wall tiles, including a type similar to modern hollow tiles, which were used in bathing establishments for the passage of warm air and smoke and as insulation. But their tiles received no colored and glazed decoration. The Muslim peoples brought tile to its greatest splendor as a decorative medium, and in the countries that came under their influence the tradition of a brilliant ceramic art is still active. Developed to the highest opulence of color ornament and surface, tiles peculiarly suited the Eastern love of decoration, and Muslim architecture is distinguished by the lavish tile incrustations upon the exterior surfaces of walls, domes, and minarets, as well as in rooms, mosques, and patios. In Spain ceramics, firmly established by the 11th cent., became an integral element of architectural decoration, chiefly for floors and wainscots, their richness exemplified in the Alhambra at Granada. From Spain the art was transmitted not only to Italy and Holland and from there to England, but also into Mexico by the Spanish conquerors. The Spaniards in Mexico developed a distinctive style in the 16th to 18th cent., especially applied in the external decoration of domes. At Delft, Holland, tile manufacturing began early in the 16th cent., and by 1670 numbers of factories were making the celebrated blue-and-white Delft tiles, which enjoyed great popularity in N Europe and were exported to the American colonies for fireplace facings. In Holland tiles were used to cover large wall spaces in rooms, often being arranged to form complete pictorial murals. In Germany, Austria, and Switzerland tiles were used to cover heating stoves as early as the Gothic period and into the 19th cent., and numbers of these, decorated and beautifully executed, still remain. In modern times the vastly increased use for tiles, as in bathrooms, kitchens, and swimming pools and in industrial buildings, has created an extensive tile industry. Great technical advances have been made in composition and manufacture. Commercial tiles are made by machine processes, the clay being dried and ground to a powder and then packed into steel dies, submitted to heavy pressure, and completely solidified into cubes of glasslike appearance. There has also been a revival in the use of handmade tiles for interior decoration of homes. See A. A. J. Berendsen, *Tiles: A General History* (1967); and C. H. de Jongé, *Dutch Tiles* (1971).

tilefish, common name for a superior and brilliantly colored food fish of temperate and tropical waters, marked by fleshy flaps on the top of the head and at the corners of the mouth. It is a bottom feeder reaching 3 ft (91 cm) in length and 35 lb (15.8 kg) in weight. Since it thrives only at depths of 50 to 100 fathoms (300–600 ft/91–182 m) and temperatures of about 50° F (10°C), it is thought that the curious and dramatic fluctuations in its abundance are caused by shifting currents of varying temperatures. The common Atlantic tilefish is *Lopholatilus chamaeleonticeps.* Tilefishes are classified in the phylum CHORDATA, subphylum Vertebrata, class Osteichthyes, order Perciformes, family Branchiostegidae.

till: see DRIFT.

Tillamook Indians, North American Indians whose language belongs to the Salishan branch of the Algonquian-Wakashan linguistic stock (see AMERICAN INDIAN LANGUAGES). In the early 19th cent. they lived on Tillamook Bay in NW Oregon. They then numbered some 2,200 and were the most powerful tribe on the Oregon coast. By 1849, however, they had been reduced to some 200.

Tillett, Benjamin (tĭl'ĭt), 1860–1943, English labor organizer, b. Bristol, England. With Tom Mann and John Burns, he led the dock strike of 1889, the first big step toward industrial unionism in Great Britain. Tillett helped found several labor organizations, including the Dockers' Union and the General Federation of Trade Unions. He was a Labour party member of Parliament (1917–24, 1929–31). He wrote *Trade Unions and Socialism* (1894) and *Memories and Reflections* (1931).

Till Eulenspiegel: see EULENSPIEGEL, TILL.

Tilley, Sir Samuel Leonard, 1818–96, Canadian political leader, b. New Brunswick. He was active in provincial politics and led the government from 1861 to 1865. An advocate of a united Canada, he was an important figure at the conferences (1864) to discuss confederation and at the Westminster Conference, which drafted the provisions of the British North America Act (1867). He served in the first administration of John Macdonald as minister of customs (1867–73) and then of finance (1873). As minister of finance (1878–85) in the second Macdonald government, he formulated the protective tariff plan known as the National Policy. He was knighted in 1879.

Tillich, Paul Johannes (tĭl'ĭk), 1886–1965, American philosopher and theologian, b. Germany, educated at the universities of Berlin, Tübingen, Halle, and Breslau. In 1912 he was ordained a minister of the Evangelical Lutheran Church. He taught theology at the universities of Berlin, Marburg, Dresden, and Leipzig and philosophy at the Univ. of Frankfurt until he was dismissed in 1933 because of his opposition to the Nazi regime. In the same year, at the invitation of Reinhold Niebuhr, he went to the United States and joined the faculty of Union Theological Seminary. In 1954 he became a professor at Harvard; in 1962 he became Nuveen professor of theology at the Univ. of Chicago. His theological system embraced the concept of "the Protestant Principle," according to which every Yes must have its corresponding No, and no human truth is ultimate. Faith, to Tillich, was "ultimate concern," and God was "the God above God," the "Ground of Being," or "Being-Itself." "New Being," rather than "salvation," should be the human goal. Tillich incorporated depth psychology and existentialist philosophy into his system and considered them essential elaborations of Christian doctrine. He aimed at a correlation of the questions arising out of the human condition and the divine answers drawn from the symbolism of Christian revelation. The great questions, in his classification, dealt with being, existence, and life. His writings include *The Interpretation of History* (tr. 1936), *The Protestant Era* (tr. 1948), *The Shaking of the Foundations* (1948), *Sys-*

tematic Theology, (3 vol., 1951–63), *The Courage to Be* (1952), *Love, Power, and Justice* (1954), *Biblical Religion and the Search for Ultimate Reality* (1955), *The New Being* (1955), *Dynamics of Faith* (1957), *Christianity and the Encounter of the World Religions* (1963), *My Search for Absolutes* (1967), *My Travel Diary: 1936*, ed. by J. C. Brauer (1970), and *A History of Christian Thought*, ed. by C. E. Braaten (1972). See the reminiscences by his wife, Hanna (1973) and Rollo May (1973); C. J. Armbruster, *The Vision of Paul Tillich* (1967); J. R. Lyons, ed., *The Intellectual Legacy of Paul Tillich* (1969); L. F. Wheat, *Paul Tillich's Dialectical Humanism* (1970).

Tillman, Benjamin Ryan, 1847–1918, U.S. Senator from South Carolina (1895–1918), b. Edgefield co., S.C. A farmer, he became the leader of the backcountry whites in South Carolina and fostered their discontent with the ruling tidewater aristocracy. Supported by the Farmers' Alliance, he was elected governor in 1890 and served two terms (1890–94). His victory meant the downfall of Wade HAMPTON (1818–1902). Tillman greatly advanced agricultural education (Clemson and Winthrop colleges were opened) and railroad regulation. He was responsible for the adoption of the dispensary law, whereby the state controlled the sale of liquor. He dominated the state constitutional convention of 1895, which adopted rules virtually disfranchising South Carolina blacks. Tillman defended the use of force to prevent Negroes from voting. Many of his measures reflected the influence of Populism. In 1894, Tillman was elected Democratic U.S. Senator. In the Senate he was the champion of the Southern farmer and allied himself with the Populists against the currency program of President CLEVELAND. He vigorously attacked Cleveland in the Democratic convention of 1896 and gave support to William Jennings Bryan and free silver. He earned the nickname Pitchfork Ben when he threatened to stick his pitchfork into Cleveland. Although Tillman was at odds with President Theodore Roosevelt, he helped secure passage of the Hepburn rate bill for railroads. In general he supported Woodrow Wilson's administration, particularly Josephus Daniels's naval expansion program. See biography by F. B. Simkins (1944, repr. 1964); F. B. Simkins, *The Tillman Movement in South Carolina* (1926, repr. 1964).

Tillotson, John, 1630–94, English prelate, archbishop of Canterbury (1691–94). He was ordained in 1661. At the Savoy Conference (1661) he was present as an auditor on the side of the Presbyterians, but upon the passing of the Act of Uniformity (1662) he yielded to its requirements. In 1663 he became rector of Kedington, Suffolk, and in 1664 preacher at Lincoln's Inn. In 1670 he was made a prebendary of Canterbury, and in 1672 dean. He was chaplain to Charles II and was admitted to the special favor of William and Mary. He became (1689) dean of St. Paul's and was persuaded in 1691 to accept the archbishopric of Canterbury, left vacant when the nonjuror William Sancroft was deposed. A biography by Thomas Birch accompanied Tillotson's collected *Works* (3 vol., 1752).

Tilly, Johannes Tserklaes, count of (yōhän'əs tsĕrkläs' tĭl'ē), 1559–1632, general in Bavarian and later imperial service during the THIRTY YEARS WAR. A younger son of a noble family of Brabant, he served under Duke Alessandro FARNESE and against the Turks before entering the service of Duke MAXIMILIAN I of Bavaria, founder of the Catholic League. After the outbreak of the Thirty Years War, he commanded the army of the Catholic League, which with the imperial army put down the Bohemian Protestant forces at the White Mt. (1620). In the next phase of the war, centering about the Palatinate, Tilly was chief commander against Ernst von MANSFELD, CHRISTIAN OF BRUNSWICK, and others. He lost to Mansfeld (April, 1622), but won at Wimpfen (May) and Höchst (June) and also at Stadtlohn (1623). After King Christian IV of Denmark entered the war (1625) Tilly and Albrecht von WALLENSTEIN were the chief generals to oppose him. In 1626, aided by some of Wallenstein's troops, Tilly was victorious at Lutter. When Wallenstein was removed from command of the imperial army in 1630, Tilly was given command of that army also, but against Gustavus II (Gustavus Adolphus) of Sweden he was unsuccessful. On May 20, 1631, Tilly and Count Pappenheim stormed Magdeburg. Tilly's troops massacred the populace and sacked the city, although he tried to check the violence. Later in 1631, Tilly was thoroughly defeated by Gustavus Adolphus at Breitenfeld. The next year he was again defeated by Gustavus Adolphus at the crossing of the Lech, where Tilly was mortally wounded.

Tilon (tī'lŏn), descendant of Judah. 1 Chron. 4.20.

Tilsit: see SOVETSK, USSR.

Tilsit, Treaties of: see SOVETSK.

Tilton, Theodore, 1835–1907, American journalist, b. New York City. After working for the New York *Observer* he was (1863–71) editor in chief of the *Independent*, a Congregationalist weekly. He later managed (1872–74) his own weekly, the *Golden Age*. A popular lyceum speaker, Tilton supported various social reforms such as woman suffrage. He and his wife were active parishioners of Henry Ward BEECHER, whom Tilton sued (1874) for alleged adultery with Mrs. Tilton. The suit lasted for months and ended in the jury's disagreement over a verdict. In 1883, Tilton went to Europe, where he lived for the remainder of his life. His publications include a romantic novel, *Tempest Tossed* (1873), and several volumes of poetry. See Robert Shaplen, *Free Love and Heavenly Sinners* (1954).

Timaeus (tīmē'əs), c.356–c.260 B.C., Greek historian of Tauromenium (now Taormina), Sicily. Son of the tyrant of the city, he was banished by Agathocles either in 317 or 312 B.C. and lived for 50 years in Athens, where he wrote a history of his native land. This history, now lost except for fragments which have survived as quotations in other works, covered the period from earliest times to the events of his own lifetime. The work, though severely criticized by Polybius, was important in that it standardized the various accounts of Sicilian history. See study by T. S. Brown (1958).

Timaeus (tīmē'əs), in the Bible, father of BARTIMAEUS.

Timan (tyĕmän'), mountain ridge, c.350 mi (560 km) long, Komi Autonomous Republic, NE European USSR. The low Timan ridge divides the extensive Dvina-Pechora lowland into the E Pechora River basin and the western plain, watered by the Northern Dvina River. The ridge extends from the upper Vychegda River NNW to Chesha Bay and continues on Kanin Peninsula. It rises to 1,520 ft (463 m).

Timanthes (tĭmăn'thēz), fl. c.400 B.C., Greek painter of Sicyon, a contemporary of Parrhasius and Zeuxis. His masterpiece, *Sacrifice of Iphigenia*, was considered one of the great ancient paintings. His work is known through the writings of Pliny, who speaks of his skill in depicting emotions.

Timaru (tĭm'ərōō), city (1971 pop. 28,326), central South Island, New Zealand, on the Pacific Ocean. Frozen meats and other products are exported from the man-made harbor. Fresh fruit is the leading import. There are light industries in the city.

timber: see LUMBER; WOOD.

timberline, elevation above which trees cannot grow. Its location is influenced by the various factors that determine temperature, including latitude, prevailing wind directions, and exposure to sunlight. In general, the timberline is highest in the tropics and descends in elevation toward the polar regions; in the north it intersects the land surface approximately at the Arctic Circle. For example, the timberline is at about 2,500 ft (750 m) on Mt. McKinley, Alaska; 6,500 ft (1,950 m) on Mt. Shasta, Calif.; and 11,500 ft (3,450 m) in the San Francisco Mts., Ariz. These figures represent elevations on the sunny side of the mountains; the timberline is lower on the shaded sides. The timberline is roughly marked by the location of the 50°F (10°C) isotherm (see ISOPLETH) during the warmest month.

timbrel: see TAMBOURINE.

Timbuktu (tĭm"bŭktōō', tĭmbŭk'tōō), city (1970 est. pop. 10,000), central Mali, near the Niger River. Connected with the Niger by a series of canals, Timbuktu is served by the small river port of Kabara. Its salt trade and handicraft industries make it an important meeting place for the nomadic people of the Sahara. Timbuktu was founded (11th cent.) by the Tuareg as a seasonal camp. By the 14th cent., when it was part of the Mali empire, it had become one of the major commercial centers of the W Sudan region, famous for its gold trade. Under the Songhai empire (15th and 16th cent.) the city was a great Muslim educational center, with more than 100 Koranic schools and a university centered at the Sankoré mosque. Timbuktu was sacked in 1593 by invaders from Morocco and never again recovered its leading position. It was repeatedly conquered by neighboring peoples until it was captured (1894) by the French.

time, sequential arrangement of all events, or the interval between two events in such a sequence. The concept of time may be discussed on several different levels: psychological, philosophical, physical, and biological. As a practical matter, clocks and CALENDARS regulate everyday life. Yet at the most primitive level, man's awareness of time is simply his ability to distinguish which of any two events is earlier and which later, combined with his consciousness of an instantaneous present that is continually being transformed into a remembered past as it is replaced with an anticipated future. From these common human experiences evolved the view that time has an independent existence apart from physical reality. The belief in time as an absolute has a long tradition in philosophy and science. It still underlies the common sense notion of time. Isaac Newton, in formulating the basic concepts of classical physics, compared absolute time to a stream flowing at a uniform rate of its own accord. In everyday life, we likewise regard each instant of time as somehow possessing a unique existence apart from any particular observer or system of timekeeping. Inherent in the concept of absolute time is the assumption that the simultaneity of two given events is also absolute. In other words, if two events are simultaneous for one observer, they are simultaneous for all observers. Developments of modern physics have forced a modification of this view. As Albert Einstein demonstrated in his theory of RELATIVITY, when two observers are in relative motion, they will necessarily arrange events in a somewhat different time sequence. As a result, events that are simultaneous in one observer's time sequence will not be simultaneous in some other observer's sequence. In the theory of relativity, the intuitive notion of time as an independent entity is replaced by the concept that space and time are intertwined and inseparable aspects of a four-dimensional universe, which is given the name SPACE-TIME. One of the most curious aspects of the new theory is that all events appear to take place at a slower rate in a moving system when judged by a viewer in a stationary system. For example, a moving clock will appear to run slower than a stationary clock of identical construction. This effect, known as time dilation, depends on the relative velocities of the two clocks and is significant only for speeds comparable to the speed of light. Time dilation has been confirmed by observing the decay of rapidly moving subatomic particles that spontaneously decay into other particles. Stated naively, particles in motion decay more slowly than stationary particles. Another aspect of time relevant to physics is how one can distinguish the forward direction in time. This problem is apart from one's purely subjective awareness of time moving from past into future. According to classical physics, if all particles in a simple system are instantaneously reversed in their velocities, the system will proceed to retrace its entire past history. This property of the laws of classical physics is called time reversal invariance (see SYMMETRY); it means that when all microscopic motions of individual particles are precisely defined, there is no fundamental distinction between forward and backward in time. If the motions of very large collections of particles are treated statistically as in THERMODYNAMICS, then the forward direction of time is distinguished by the increase of ENTROPY, or disorder, in the system. However, recent discoveries in particle physics have shown that time reversal invariance is not valid even on the microscopic scale for certain phenomena governed by the so-called weak force of nuclear physics. In the life sciences, evidence has been found that many living organisms incorporate biological clocks that govern the rhythms of their behavior (see RHYTHM, BIOLOGICAL). Animals and even plants often exhibit a circadian (approximately daily) cycle in, for instance, temperature and metabolic rate that may have a genetic basis. Efforts to localize time sense in specialized areas within the brain have been largely unsuccessful. In man, the time sense may be connected to certain electrical rhythms in the brain, the most prominent of which is known as the alpha rhythm at about ten cycles per second. Apart from purely scientific questions, the accurate measurement of time by establishing accurate time standards poses difficult technological problems. In pre-history, man recognized the alternation of day and night, the phases of the moon, and the succession of the seasons; from these cycles, he developed the day, month, and year as the corresponding units of time. With the development of primitive CLOCKS and systematic astronomical observations, the day was divided into hours, minutes, and seconds. Any measurement of time is ultimately based on counting the cycles of some regularly recurring phenomenon and accurately measuring fractions of a cycle. The earth rotates on its axis at a very nearly constant rate, and the angular positions of celestial bodies can be determined with great precision. Therefore, astronomical observations provide an almost ideal method of measuring time. The true period of rotation of the earth, that with respect to the fixed stars, defines the sidereal day, which is the basis of SIDEREAL TIME. All sidereal days are equal. The period of rotation of the earth with respect to the sun (i.e., the interval between successive high noons) is the solar day, which is the basis for SOLAR TIME. Because of the earth's motion in its orbit around the sun, the sun appears to move eastward against the fixed stars and the earth must make slightly more than one complete rotation to bring the sun back to the observer's meridian. (The meridian is the great circle on the celestial sphere running through the north celestial pole and the observer's zenith; the passage of the sun across the meridian marks high noon.) But the earth's orbital motion is not uniform and the plane of the orbit is inclined to the celestial equator by 23½°. Hence the eastward motion of the sun against the stars is not uniform and the length of the true solar day varies seasonally, but on the average is four minutes longer than the sidereal day. True solar time, as measured by a sundial, does not move at a constant rate. Therefore the mean solar day, with a length equal to the annual average of the actual solar day, was introduced as the basis of mean solar time. Mean solar time does move at a constant rate and is the basis for civilian time kept by clocks. Actually, the earth's rotation is being slightly braked by tidal and other effects so that even mean solar time is not strictly uniform. The law of gravitation allows prediction of the moon's position in its orbit at a given time; inversely, the exact position of the moon provides a kind of clock that is not running down. Time calculated from the moon's position is called EPHEMERIS TIME and moves at a truly uniform rate. The accumulated difference between mean solar and ephemeris time since 1900 amounts to more than half a minute. However, the ultimate standard for time is provided by the natural frequencies of vibration of atoms and molecules. Atomic clocks, based on MASERS and LASERS, lose only about one second over periods of thousands of years. See STANDARD TIME. See Stephen V. Toulmin and J. Goodfield, *Discovery of Time* (1965); T. Gold and D. L. Schumacher, eds., *Nature of Time* (1967).

time, in music: see TEMPO; METER; RHYTHM; SYNCOPATION; METRONOME and MUSICAL NOTATION.

time-division: see MULTIPLEXING.

Times Square, in New York City. Formed by the intersection of Broadway, Seventh Ave., and 42d St., this famous square was named for the building there that formerly belonged to the New York *Times.* The building, located in the center of the square, is still famous for its band of electric lights that transmit up-to-the-minute news. Times Square and the adjacent area form the most concentrated entertainment district in the nation. Located in the area are several legitimate theaters and numerous motion picture houses as well as a vast array of shops, newsstands, bars, restaurants, and tawdry amusement centers. Broadway at Times Square, jammed with noisy traffic and illuminated at night by a profusion of enormous electrical signs, is known as the "Great White Way." On New Year's Eve close to a million people congregate there to celebrate the arrival of the new year.

Timgad (tĭm'găd), ancient *Thamugadi,* ruined city, Algeria, S of Constantine. It is sometimes called the Pompeii of North Africa because of the extensive remains of the Roman city founded here by Trajan in A.D. 100. This city was destroyed by Berbers in the 7th cent. and was unknown until excavations were begun in 1881. Its Roman ruins, which include a triumphal arch, public baths, a theater, a library, and a forum, are the best preserved and most extensive in Africa.

Timiskaming, Que., Canada: see TEMISCAMING.

Timişoara (tēmēshwä'rä), Hung. *Temesvár,* city (1970 est. pop. 193,000), W Rumania, in the BANAT, on the Beja Canal. The chief city of the former Banat of Temesvar, it is a railroad hub and an industrial center, with engineering works, plants processing food and tobacco, and factories manufacturing textiles, machinery, and chemicals. Timişoara is a Roman Catholic and an Orthodox episcopal see and has a university (founded 1945) and other institutions of higher education. It was an ancient Roman settlement and came under Magyar domination in 896 and was annexed to Hungary in 1010. An important frontier fortress, Timişoara was held by the Turks from 1552 until its liberation in 1716 by Eugene of Savoy. The Treaty of Passarowitz (1718) formally restored it to Austria-Hungary. It passed to Rumania by the Treaty of Trianon (1920). The inner city is surrounded by boulevards, which have replaced the former ramparts. The Roman Catholic and Orthodox cathedrals, the city hall, and other important buildings date from the 18th cent. A regional museum is housed in the 14th-15th-century Hunyadi castle.

Timmermans, Felix (fä'lĭks tĭm'ərmäns), 1886–1947, Flemish novelist. Among his most successful works are *Pallieter* (1916, tr. 1924), the story of a lusty Fleming of gigantic appetites, and *Pieter Breughel* (1928, tr. *Droll Peter,* 1930), a novel about the elder Pieter Bruegel.

Timmins, town (1971 pop. 28,542), central Ont., Canada, on the Mattagami River. Timmins is the commercial center of the rich Porcupine gold-mining district, where gold was first discovered in 1909. Silver, copper, lead, and zinc are also mined. The town has breweries and pulp, paper, and lumber mills.

Timna or **Timnah** (both: tĭm'nə). **1** Concubine of Esau's son Eliphaz. Gen. 36.12. **2** Daughter of Seir. Gen. 36.22; 1 Chron. 1.39. She may be the same as **1.** **3** Duke of Edom. Gen. 36.40; 1 Chron. 1.51.

Timnah (tĭm'nə) or **Timnath** (tĭm'năth) **1** Hill town, S Palestine. Joshua 15.57. **2** Place associated with Judah. Gen. 38.12. It may be the same as **1** or **3.** **3** Town associated with Samson's "Timnite" wife and also with Ahaz. Joshua 15.10; Judges 14.1,2,5; 15.6. Thimnathah: Joshua 19.43; 2 Chron. 28.18.

Timnath-heres (tĭm'năth-hē'rēs) or **Timnath-sereh** (-sē'rĕ), city, central Palestine, where Joshua was buried. Joshua 19.50; 24.30; Judges 2.9.

Timoleon (tĭmō'lēən), d. after 337 B.C., Greek statesman and general, noted as the scourge of tyrants. A Corinthian, he went (344) with a small army to Syracuse in answer to the appeal of the Syracusans to their mother city, Corinth, for aid against DIONYSIUS THE YOUNGER. Timoleon fought against Dionysius, as well as against Hicetas, tyrant of Leontini, who hoped to usurp Dionysius's power, and against Hicetas's Carthaginian allies. He drove Dionysius and Hicetas from Syracuse, set up a democratic government, and brought new Greek colonists. He defeated (341) a large Carthaginian force, but made peace (c.338) with Carthage. He also ousted (337) the tyrants from the other Sicilian cities before retiring from public life as a result of failing eyesight.

Timon (tī'mən), one of the seven deacons. Acts. 6.5.

Timon of Phlius (flī'əs), c.320–c.230 B.C., Greek skeptic philosopher, chief disciple of PYRRHO. Timon denied the possibility of certain knowledge and, like his master, taught that the philosopher can achieve peace of mind only by suspension of judgment and indifference to externals. After Timon's death the skeptics lost their separate identity and became absorbed into the Academy. Only fragments of his work have survived.

Timor (tē'môr) [Malay,=east], island (c.13,200 sq mi/34,200 sq km), largest and easternmost of the Lesser Sundas, belonging in part to Indonesia and in part to Portugal. Portuguese Timor (1970 pop. 610,541) comprises the eastern half of the island and the small enclave of Oe-Cusse (or Okusi Ambeno) in the Indonesian section; the capital and chief port is Dili. Indonesian Timor comprises the western half of the island; with adjacent islands, it forms the province of East Nusa Tenggara. A state university is in Kupang, the capital of the province. The island is long, narrow, and almost wholly mountainous. Rice, coconuts, and coffee are grown, sandalwood is cut, and stretches of grassland support cattle. The natives, who are of Malay and Papuan stock, are predominantly Christian. The Portuguese were the first Europeans to establish themselves in Timor; their claim to the island was disputed by the Dutch, who arrived in 1613. By a treaty of 1859, modified in 1893 and finally made effective in 1914, the border between the Dutch and Portuguese territories was settled. In World War II, Timor was occupied (early 1942) by the Japanese. With the creation of the Republic of Indonesia in 1950, Dutch Timor became Indonesian territory.

Timorlaut: see TANIMBAR ISLANDS, Indonesia.

Timoshenko, Semyon Konstantinovich (sĭmyôn kənstəntyē'nəvĭch tyēməshĕn'kə), 1895–1970, Russian marshal. He served in the civil war of 1918–20 as a cavalry commander and subsequently rose in the Soviet army. He commanded the Russian troops in their final victorious offensive in the Finnish-Russian War (1940). In May, 1940, he succeeded General VOROSHILOV as commissar for defense and held that position until it was assumed by Joseph Stalin in July, 1941. Having replaced Marshal BUDENNY on the southern front, he recaptured (Nov., 1941) Rostov from the Germans and helped to relieve Moscow. Later he commanded on the northwest front (1942), in the Caucasus (1943), and in Bessarabia (1944). After the war, he served as chief of the Belorussian military.

Timotheus: see TIMOTHY, SAINT.

Timotheus (tĭmō'thēəs), c.450–c.357 B.C., Greek poet and musician of Miletus. An innovator in music, he added a string to the kithara. Fragments of his dithyrambs and nomes remain. Euripides wrote the prologue for his *Persae,* a lyric nome.

Timotheus, fl. 4th cent. B.C., Greek sculptor of Athens, recorded as one of the sculptors who worked with Scopas on the Mausoleum at Halicarnassus. About 375 B.C., according to an inscription, he furnished models for sculptures on the temple of Asclepius at Epidaurus and executed acroteria (decorative figures placed above the pediments) for this building.

Timothy, Saint, d. c.100, early Christian, for whom two books of the New Testament are named. The son of a Greek father and a Jewish mother, he was the friend and companion of St. Paul. He became first bishop of Ephesus and, according to tradition, was martyred there. He is also called Timotheus. Feast: Jan. 24. Acts 16.1–3; Rom. 16.21; 1 Cor. 4.17; 2 Cor 1.1; Philip. 2.19; 1 Thes. 3.2; 2 Thes. 1.1; Philemon 1; Heb. 13.23.

Timothy, two epistles of the New Testament, the 15th and 16th books in the usual order. With TITUS they make up the Pastoral Epistles, in which Timothy or Titus is addressed by St. Paul, with advice on governing his church. The authorship and destination of all three are much questioned by scholars, who put the composition of the letters late in the 1st cent. A.D., although seeing in each portions by St. Paul. First Timothy, after an introduction (1), treats lengthily public prayer (2) and the qualifications of the clergy (3). Then come many details of advice, including admonitions on personal life (4.6–16) and the behavior of widows (5.1–16) and of the clergy (5.17–25). Second Timothy is much more a personal letter. The emphasis is on courage and fidelity (1.6–2.26); there are warnings of suffering to come and allusions to Paul's own trials (3.1–4.8). Paul speaks of his impending death (4.6–8, 16–18). The Pastoral Epistles are valuable for the light they shed on early church organization.

timothy or **herd's-grass,** perennial plant (*Phleum pratense*) of the family Gramineae (GRASS family), native to Europe and W Asia and now the most widely cultivated hay grass of North America. Adaptable to cool, moist climates, where it is sometimes grown in mixtures (especially with red clover), it is a late grass—usually sown in the fall—and can be stored after cutting. It is not used for permanent pastures because it cannot survive continuous grazing. Timothy production has decreased with the replacement of the horse by mechanized equipment. Timothy is classified in the division MAGNOLIOPHYTA, class Liliatae, order Cyperales, family Gramineae.

timpani: see KETTLEDRUM.

Timpanogos Cave National Monument: see NATIONAL PARKS AND MONUMENTS (table).

Timrod, Henry, 1828–67, American poet, b. Charleston, S.C., studied at the Univ. of Georgia. He was known as "the laureate of the Confederacy." Timrod became editor of the Columbia *South Carolinian* in 1864, but, ruined by the war, he died in poverty of tuberculosis, having published only one volume of poems (1860). His works were posthumously edited (1873) by his friend P. H. Hayne. Timrod's finest poems are his "Ode to the Confederate Dead at Magnolia Cemetery," "The Cotton Boll," "Carolina," and "Ethnogenesis." See the memorial edition of his *Poems* (1899) and critical editions of his *Last Years* (ed. by J. B. Hubbell, 1941), *Uncollected Poems* (ed. by G. A. Cardwell, Jr., 1942), and *Essays* (ed. by E. W. Parker, 1942). See also studies by E. W. Parks (1964) and H. T. Thompson (1928, repr. 1971).

Timur: see TAMERLANE.

Timurids (tĭmo͝or'ĭdz), dynasty founded by TAMERLANE (or Timur). After the death of Tamerlane (1405) there was a struggle for power over his empire, which then extended from the Euphrates River to the Jaxartes (Syr Darya) and Indus rivers. The western empire, which included Tabriz and Baghdad, lasted only a few years because of internal wars. The so-called Black Sheep Turkoman horde brought it to an end when they took (1410) Baghdad. Shah Rukh, Tamerlane's son, ruled (1409–46) the eastern empire, including Khorasan and Transoxiana (region E of the Amu Darya, or Oxus, River). He fought the Black

Sheep and succeeded in recapturing Tabriz and much of W Persia. His domain was the focal point of trade between the East and the West, and it attained a spectacular prosperity. Because all the Persian cities were desolated by previous wars, the seat of Persian culture was now in Samarkand and Herat; these cities became the center of the Timurid renaissance. This cultural rebirth had a double character; on one hand, there was a renewal of Persian civilization and art (distinguished by extensive adaptations from the Chinese), and on the other, an original national literature in the Turk-Jagatai language, which borrowed from Persian sources. Shah Rukh was succeeded by his son, Ulugh Beg (ruled 1447–49). He had earlier been (1409–47) viceroy of Transoxiana. He constructed many public buildings and was a patron of Persian art and literature; he made Samarkand a center of Muslim civilization. After his succession (ruled 1447–49) to the throne the Timurid empire fell into anarchy; the Turkoman horde known as the White Sheep conquered much territory, while the Uzbeks looted Samarkand. Petty princes took over the rule, and local dynasties sprang up. One of these princes, and the last of the Timurids, was BABUR.

tin, metallic chemical element; symbol Sn [from Lat. *stannum*]; at. no. 50; at. wt. 118.69; m.p. 231.89°C; b.p. about 2270°C; sp. gr. 5.75 (gray), 7.3 (white); valence +2 or +4. Tin exhibits ALLOTROPY; above 13.2°C it is a lustrous, silver-white, highly crystalline metal with tetragonal structure. A brittle form with orthorhombic structure may exist above 161°C. Below 13.2°C pure tin tends to become a gray powder, a change commonly designated "tin pest" or "tin disease." Tin is very soft (only slightly harder than lead) and malleable; it can be rolled, pressed, or hammered into extremely thin sheets (tin foil). When iron or steel is dipped into molten tin, a layer of tin is deposited on the surface. A tin coating may also be applied by electroplating, which uses less tin. The tin serves to prevent rusting, since it is barely affected by moisture. The tin plate used in tin cans is iron or steel sheet coated with tin. A tin coating is used to protect copper and other metals. Tin is a component of antifriction metal, bell metal, britannia metal, bronze, gunmetal, pewter, solder, and other alloys. Tin forms stannous compounds, in which it has valence +2, and stannic compounds, in which it has valence +4, as well as stannites, stannates, and other complex salts. Industrially useful compounds of tin include stannous chloride, important as a reducing agent, as a mordant in dyeing, and for weighting silk; stannic chloride, for the last two purposes and to stabilize perfume and color in soap; stannic oxide, for the preparation of white porcelain enamelware; and sodium stannite, a reducing agent. Stannous fluoride is added to toothpastes and water supplies to prevent tooth decay. Tin forms a number of toxic organometallic compounds that are used as fungicides, catalysts, and for other uses. Tin very rarely occurs uncombined in nature; the dioxide, which occurs as cassiterite, or tinstone, is the only ore of commercial importance. It is obtained chiefly from Bolivia, Indonesia, the Malay Peninsula, Zaïre, and Nigeria. The tin mines of Cornwall, England, were formerly the principal source. The metal is prepared from cassiterite by heating in the reverberatory furnace. The ore from the mines is first given special treatment, and the "concentrates" thus obtained are mixed with coal in the furnaces. Tin was known and used by man at least as early as the Bronze Age. The metal and its compounds were known and used by the alchemists. In 1673, Robert Boyle published a description of experiments on the oxidation (calcination) of tin. The metal was recognized as an element by Lavoisier.

tinamou (tĭn'əmo͞o), common name for a South American game bird related to the ostrich. It is protectively colored in browns and grays. The females are the aggressors in courtship, and the males incubate the colorful eggs and rear the young. Their flesh is delicious; attempts have been made to introduce them in North America. Although similar in appearance to partridges, tinamous are not related to them. Tinamous are classified in the phylum CHORDATA, subphylum Vertebrata, class Aves, order Tinamiformes, family Tinamidae.

Tinbergen, Jan (yän tĭn'bĕr"gən), 1903–, Dutch economist, co-winner with Ragnar FRISCH of the first Nobel Memorial Prize in economics (1969). A graduate of Leiden Univ. (1929), he worked (1929–45) with the Dutch government's Central Bureau of Statistics, and was briefly an advisor to the League of Nations (1936–38). He also served (1945–55) as director of the Dutch central planning bureau. Since 1933 he has been a professor at the Netherlands School of Economics in Rotterdam. His publications include *Economic Policy: Principles and Design* (1956), *Shaping the World Economy* (1963), and *Development Planning* (1967).

Tinbergen, Nikolaas, 1907–, British zoologist, b. Netherlands. He received his Ph.D. in 1932 from the Univ. of Leiden, where he became professor of zoology in 1947. In 1949 he joined the faculty of Oxford Univ. For his work in reviving and developing the biological science of animal behavior, Tinbergen was awarded the 1973 Nobel Prize in Medicine and Physiology. His first independent work concerned the landmark orientation of homing wasps. After collaborating with the Austrian ethologist Konrad Lorenz, he was invited to found a school of animal behavior at the Univ. of Leiden. Studies of the display behavior of certain species revealed that such displays result from a state of conflict between opposite motivations ("fight or flee"). Further work clarified the evolutionary origins of many social signals and their subsequent ritualization. Tinbergen emphasized the mutual interaction between predator and prey and, as scientific advisor to the Serengeti Research Institute in Tanzania, applied this approach to African plains game. His best known book is *The Herring Gull's World* (1953, rev. ed. 1961). He was named a fellow of the Royal Society in 1962 and a foreign fellow of the Netherlands Academy of Sciences in 1964.

Tindal, Matthew (tĭn'dəl), c.1655–1733, English deist. For a short time in the reign of James II he was a Roman Catholic, but in 1688 he returned to the Church of England. The first of his published writings to excite attention was *The Rights of the Christian Church Asserted* (1706), a defense of Erastianism; it was proscribed by Parliament. His *Defence of the Rights of the Christian Church* (1709) reiterated his position and was similarly condemned. Tindal's *Christianity as Old as the Creation* (1730), in which he set forth his rationalistic views, has been called the bible of deism. See Leslie Stephen, *History of English Thought in the Eighteenth Century* (3d ed. 1902).

Tindal or **Tindale, William:** see TYNDALE, WILLIAM.

Tinguely, Jean (zhäN tăNglē'), 1925–, Swiss artist. Tinguely is best known for his "metamechanics," electromechanical sculptures that perform tasks such as painting or playing music. Most celebrated of these works is *Homage to New York* (1959), a machine that destroyed itself when set into motion.

Tinian (tĭnēăn', tēnēăn'), island (1970 pop. 710), 39 sq mi (101 sq km), W Pacific, one of the MARIANAS ISLANDS in the U.S. Trust Territory of the PACIFIC ISLANDS. The island lies immediately SW of Saipan. The inhabitants are of mixed Micronesian, Filipino, and Spanish descent. Tinian's once large phosphate deposits have been depleted. Vegetable gardening is now the main occupation, but attempts have been made to raise large numbers of cattle. In World War II Tinian was taken (1944) by U.S. forces and made into an important military base for attacks on the Japanese mainland. The planes that dropped atomic bombs on Hiroshima and Nagasaki were flown from Tinian.

Tinicum Island (tĭn'ĭkəm), area in the Delaware River, SW of Philadelphia, separated from the mainland by creeks and marshes. Site of the first European settlement in Pennsylvania, it was the capital of NEW SWEDEN from 1643 to 1655.

Tinley Park, village (1970 pop. 12,382), Cook and Will counties, NE Ill., a residential suburb of Chicago; inc. 1892. A state mental hospital is there.

Tinnevelly, India: see TIRUNELVELI.

Tinnis, medieval city of Egypt, on an island in Lake Manzala, SW of modern Port Said. Tinnis, founded when TANIS was abandoned, was also spelled Tennis. The city was a port and center of commerce of some importance and was particularly notable for its fine textiles (much prized throughout the Muslim world).

Tínos or **Tenos** (both: tē'nôs), island (1971 pop. 8,232), 79 sq mi (204 sq km), SE Greece, in the Aegean Sea; one of the Cyclades. Wine, figs, wheat, and silk are produced on Tínos, and green marble is quarried. The island was a colony of Venice from 1390 to 1715, when it was captured by the Ottoman Turks. Tínos (1971 pop. 3,509), the main town, is the site of a church containing an icon of the Virgin Mary that attracts many pilgrims.

tinstone: see TIN.

Tintagel (tĭntă'jəl), village, Cornwall, SW England. It is S of Tintagel Head, a promontory connected to the mainland by a narrow, rocky neck of land. The ruined Tintagel Castle, which extends from the promontory across the isthmus, was built in the 12th cent. on the site of a Celtic monastery. The site is the reputed birthplace of King Arthur. In the area of the village are several other old structures.

Tintern Abbey, ruins of an abbey, Monmouthshire, W. England, near Chepstow. It was founded for Cistercians in 1131 by Walter de Clare and now consists mainly of 13th- and 14-century English work. It is the subject of a poem by Wordsworth.

Tintoretto (tēntōrĕt'tō), 1518–94, Venetian painter, whose real name was Jacopo Robusti. He was called Il Tintoretto [little dyer] from his father's trade. According to tradition, he studied for a brief time under Titian, but the precocity of the young painter is said to have aroused the jealousy of the master. Certainly his fiery temper and furtive business tactics caused him unpopularity among Venetian artists. It is rather difficult to verify his earlier paintings, as Tintoretto was able to assimilate styles with amazing ease. His early works are still confused with those of Bonifazio Veronese, Paris Bordone, and Andrea Schiavone. He copied drawings by Michelangelo and may even have met him on a supposed trip to Rome (c.1545). It is said that he aspired to combine the drawing of Michelangelo with the color of Titian. One of his early pictures, *Apollo and Marsyas,* was painted for the writer Pietro Aretino. Aretino praised it highly, commenting on the rapidity of execution. This mode of impulsive expression was current in Venice and became one of the characteristics of Tintoretto's art. In 1548 he painted the *Miracle of St. Mark* (Academy, Venice) for the Scuola di San Marco, a picture that attracted much attention. Although there are some Michelangelesque elements in the treatment of the figures, an independent spirit was emerging. He began to develop startling lighting effects and a highly dramatic rendering of narrative. These qualities are also evident in other works of the same period, such as the *Washing of Feet* (Escorial) and *Last Supper* (San Marcuola, Venice). In the next decade, Tintoretto tended more in the direction of mannerism. He introduced a flickering light, contorted figures, and irrational spatial elements into such pictures as *Presentation of the Virgin, Golden Calf,* and *Last Judgment* (all in the Madonna dell' Orto, Venice). He achieved an almost ghostly effect by funneling perspective into a long, narrow lane. This technique was used in the scenes from the life of St. Mark executed (1562–66) for the Scuola di San Marco (now in the Academy, Venice, and the Brera, Milan). In 1564 he began his great cycle of paintings in the Scuola di San Rocco, which he worked on intermittently until c.1587. The series includes an enormous *Crucifixion,* the glorification of the lives of the Venetian saints, and scenes from the Passion. Remarkable for their freedom of execution, these paintings are also noted for their startling changes in viewpoint, frenetic movement, and mystic conception. An incredibly versatile artist, Tintoretto painted many scenes for the ducal palace, varying from erotic mythological pictures such as *Bacchus and Ariadne, The Three Graces,* and *Minerva and Mars,* to historical themes such as *The Venetian Ambassadors before Frederick Barbarossa, The Battle of Zara,* and the gigantic *Paradise.* Many of his other works in the ducal palace were destroyed in the fire of 1577. The last phase of his art was of a highly visionary nature. He painted still more freely and obtained almost phosphorescent lighting effects in the *Last Supper* and *Entombment* (San Giorgio Maggiore, Venice). Three of his children, Domenico, Marco, and Marieta, became painters and assisted him. Tintoretto is considered one of the greatest painters in the Venetian tradition. His works in American collections include the *Baptism of Clorinda* (Art Inst., Chicago); *Miracle of the Loaves and Fishes* and *Finding of Moses* (Metropolitan Mus.); *Portrait of a Lady with her Daughter* (Walters Art Gall., Baltimore); *Portrait of Alexander Farnese* (Mus. of Fine Arts, Boston); a portrait of a Venetian senator (Frick Coll., New York City); and six paintings in the National Gallery of Art, Washington, D.C. See studies by Hans Tietze (1948) and Eric Newton (1952).

Tionontati Indians: see TOBACCO NATION.

Tiphsah (tĭf'sə). **1** See THAPSACUS. **2** Unidentified place, perhaps the same as one of the places named TAPPUAH. 2 Kings 15.16.

tipi: see TEPEE.

Tippecanoe (tĭp"əkəno͞o'), river, c.170 mi (270 km) long, rising in the lake district of NE Ind. and flowing SW to the Wabash River, near Lafayette. U.S. Gen. William Henry Harrison fought the Shawnee

Indians in the Battle of Tippecanoe, Nov. 7, 1811, on the site of the present-day town of Battle Ground, Ind. The Indians, urged on by their chief, Tecumseh, and by the British, had become incensed at the continued U.S. advance into their territory. At the time of Harrison's expedition, Tecumseh was away and his brother, the Shawnee Prophet, led the Indians. They attacked U.S. forces at dawn but were repelled; their village was subsequently razed by Harrison's men. Claimed as a U.S. victory, the battle was at best indecisive; the power of the Indians was broken, however, despite the subsequent American retreat.

Tipperary (tĭp″ərâr′ē), county (1971 pop. 123,196), 1,643 sq mi (4,255 sq km), S central Republic of Ireland. The county town is TIPPERARY. Administratively, the county is divided into North Riding (its administrative center at NENAGH) and South Riding (its administrative center at CLONMEL). The region is part of the central plain of Ireland, but the terrain is diversified by several mountain ranges: the Knockmealdown, the Galtee, the Arra, and the Silvermine. The southern portion of the county is drained by the Suir River; the northern by tributaries of the Shannon, which widens into Lough Derg on the northern border. There is much fertile land, especially in the region known as the Golden Vale, one of the richest agricultural areas in Ireland. Dairy farming and cattle raising are most important. Other industries are slate quarrying and the manufacture of meal and flour. The county was long under the domination of the powerful Butler family (the earls of Ormonde). Tipperary is rich in antiquarian remains, particularly in the vicinity of CASHEL.

Tipperary, urban district (1971 pop. 4,592), county town of Co. Tipperary, S central Republic of Ireland. The center of a rich agricultural region, it is a farm market. Linoleum, mineral water, condensed milk, and gloves are produced. There are ruins of a 13th-century Augustinian abbey.

Tippett, Sir Michael, 1905–, English composer, b. London. Tippett studied at the Royal College of Music. During World War II he was imprisoned as a conscientious objector; his strongly held social and political views are sometimes reflected in his work. Tippett has utilized British folk and American jazz and Negro elements in some of his music. He was knighted in 1966. His compositions include a concerto for double string orchestra (1939); the oratorio *A Child of Our Time* (1944); three symphonies (1945, 1958, 1973); and the operas *Midsummer Marriage* (1952), *King Priam* (1962), and *The Knot Garden* (1970).

Tippoo Sahib (tĭp′o͞o sä′hĭb), 1749–99, Indian ruler, sultan of Mysore (1782–99); son and successor of HAIDAR ALI. He fought in his father's campaigns against the Mahrattas and the British but, after his succession, made peace with the British in 1784. His invasion (1789) of Travancore, a state under British protection, provoked war anew, and in 1792 he was defeated by a force under Lord Cornwallis composed of British, Mahratta, and Hyderabad troops. He was forced to cede territory. In 1798, Tippoo formed a vague alliance with the French, which gave the British governor general Lord Wellesley a pretext to invade Mysore in alliance with the nizam of Hyderabad. Tippoo was killed (May, 1799) defending his magnificent capital at SRIRANGAPATNA. His kingdom was divided among the victors. His name also appears as Tipu Sahib or Tipu Sultan. See Mohibbul Hasan Khan, *History of Tipu Sultan* (1951); biography by D. M. Forrest (1970).

Tiptoft, John: see WORCESTER, JOHN TIPTOFT, EARL OF.

Tipu Sahib or **Tipu Sultan:** see TIPPOO SAHIB.

Tiradentes (tērəthĕn′təs), 1748–92, Brazilian patriot. His real name was José Joaquim da Silva Xavier. He gained his nickname, which means "tooth-puller," working as a healer in his youth. He later became an army officer. In the late 1780s he joined and soon became the leader of the *Inconfidência Mineira,* a movement against Portuguese rule and for revolutionary democracy in Brazil that was inspired by the American Revolution and was based in Vila Rica (now Ouro Prêto). In 1789 the movement was betrayed and its leaders were imprisoned. They were freed and exiled in 1792 with the exception of Tiradentes, who was executed in Rio de Janeiro.

Tiran, Straits of: see AQABA, GULF OF.

Tirana: see TIRANË, Albania.

Tiranë (tērä′nə) or **Tirana** (tērä′nä), city (1970 pop. 171,300), capital of Albania and of Tiranë prov., central Albania, on the Ishm River. It is the largest city and the chief industrial and cultural center of the country. Tiranë is located on a fertile plain that yields a variety of agricultural products. Its manufactures include textiles, metal products, footwear, agricultural machinery, and foodstuffs. Lignite is mined nearby. A railroad and highway link Tiranë with the port city of Durrës, its chief outlet. The V. I. Lenin hydroelectric plant supplies the city with power. Tiranë was founded in the early 17th cent. by the Turkish general Sulayman Pasha, who is buried there. It was originally named Teheran, for a Turkish victory in Persia. The larger part of Tiranë was built after 1920, when it was selected as the capital of Albania. A new residential quarter was built under Italian rule (1939–43), and an industrial sector was developed after World War II. The center of the city is Scanderbeg Square, with the government buildings and the 18th-century mosque of Etchem Bey. The bazaar and the mosque of Sulayman Pasha are nearby. The city has a university (founded 1957) and the institute of sciences of Albania. On Jan. 11, 1946, the Communist government of Enver Hoxha was proclaimed there.

Tirano (tērä′nō), town (1971 pop. 8,516), Lombardy, N Italy, on the Adda River, in the VALTELLINA, near the Swiss border. It is an agricultural and silk market. Nearby is the Church of the Madonna di Tirano (1503), a popular place of pilgrimage. The Bernina railroad, the highest in the Alps, runs from Tirano to St. Moritz, Switzerland.

Tiras (tī′rəs), Japheth's son. Gen. 10.2; 1 Chron. 1.5.

Tiraspol (tyĕrŭ′spôl), city (1970 pop. 105,000), SW European USSR, in Moldavia on the Dnestr River. It is a major agricultural processing center. Tiraspol was founded (1792) as a Russian fortress on the site of a Moldavian settlement. It was (1924–40) the capital of the Moldavian Autonomous Republic, which was later included in the Ukrainian Soviet Socialist Republic.

Tirathites (tī′rəthīts), family of scribes living at Jabez. 1 Chron. 2.55.

tire, device made of rubber and fabric and attached to the outer rim of a vehicle wheel. Solid rubber tires were in limited use before 1850; they are still used in some special applications, e.g., for industrial trucks in factories. The pneumatic rubber tire uses rubber and enclosed air to reduce vibration and improve traction. It was first patented by Robert W. Thomson, a Scottish civil engineer; however, it was not a commercial success until the Scottish inventor John Dunlop patented a pneumatic bicycle tire in 1888 and started a tire company. The main parts of a modern pneumatic tire are its body, tread and sidewalls, and beads. The body is made of layers of rubberized fabric, called plies, that give the tire strength and flexibility. The fabric is made of rayon, nylon, or polyester cord. Covering the plies are sidewalls and tread of chemically treated rubber. The sidewalls form the outer walls of the tire. The tread is a thick hoop of rubber that comes into direct contact with road surfaces. To improve its traction, the tread is grooved and often has protruding metal studs for use on ice and snow. Imbedded in the two inner edges of the tire are steel hoops, called beads, that hold the tire to the wheel rim. In the older type of pneumatic tire air is sealed in an inner tube of butyl rubber beneath the body. In a tubeless tire the seal between the beads and the wheel rim is airtight and the underside of the tire body is coated with butyl rubber to keep the air from escaping. In a bias-ply tire the cords in a single ply run diagonally from the beads on one inner rim to the beads on the other. However the orientation of the cords is reversed from ply to ply so that the cords crisscross each other. In a radial-ply tire the cords in every ply run perpendicularly from the beads on one inner rim to the beads on the other, and there is a rigid belt between the tread and the plies. This construction provides longer tread wear but a rougher ride. In a belted-bias ply tire the cords in the plies are aligned as in a bias-ply tire, but a rigid belt is added. This tire has longer tread life than a bias-ply tire and provides a more comfortable ride than does a radial-ply tire. Most tires are of the balloon type, with a large cross section and thin sidewalls. Their large size permits a low inflation pressure, and the increased tread area gives better traction and braking qualities. Excessive tire wear is caused by faulty inflation or wheel alignment, sudden braking, and high speed.

Tirebolu (tĭrē′bōlo͞o), anc. *Tripolis,* town (1970 pop. 6,108), N Turkey, a port on the Black Sea. Its exports include copper, manganese, and zinc. The remains of a Byzantine fortress are there.

Tiresias (tīrē′shəs, -sēəs), in Greek mythology, a blind soothsayer who appears in many legends. According to one myth, when he saw Athena bathing she blinded him, but by way of compensation granted him prophetic powers. Another story is that Hera blinded him for disparaging her sex when he claimed that women enjoyed love more than men; Zeus then recompensed him with long life and the power of prophecy.

Tîrgovişte (tûr″gôvēsh′tē), town (1970 est. pop. 33,000), S central Rumania, in Walachia, in a petroleum-producing region. Oil refining and the manufacture of oil-field equipment are the chief industries. Tîrgovişte was the administrative, political, and cultural center of Walachia from 1383 until 1698, when the capital was moved to Bucharest. It was destroyed by the Turks in 1737. The town is now the seat of an Orthodox bishopric. Many tourists are attracted by Tîrgovişte's historic buildings, including a remarkable 16th-century cathedral with nine towers, a 15th-century monastery, and the ruins of a 14th-century castle.

Tîrgu-Mureş (tûr′go͞o-mo͞o′rĕsh), Hung. *Maros Vásárhely,* city (1970 est. pop. 98,000), central Rumania, chief city of the Magyar Autonomous Region, in Transylvania, on the Mureşul River. It is a major industrial center, with sugar refineries, distilleries, and industries manufacturing food products, chemicals, fertilizers, machinery, and furniture. Tîrgu-Mureş is also a market for agricultural products. There are pedagogical and medical-pharmaceutical institutes in the city. Dating from the 12th cent., Tîrgu-Mureş was the scene (1704) of the proclamation of Francis II Rakoczy as "ruling prince" of Hungary. The city remained part of Hungary until 1918, when Rumania acquired Transylvania; more than half the population of Tîrgu-Mureş is Hungarian. Most of the city was rebuilt after a great fire in 1876, but surviving buildings include the 17th-century citadel, several old churches, and the baroque mansions once owned by the Teleki and Banffy families, magnates of Hungary. The 18th-century Telekiana library has valuable manuscripts, and the imposing, modern "cultural palace" contains an art gallery, an ethnographic museum, a library, and a conservatory of music.

Tirhakah: see TAHARKA.

Tirhanah (tûr′hənə), son of Caleb. 1 Chron. 2.48.

Tiria (tĭr′ēə), descendant of Judah. 1 Chron. 4.16.

Tirich Mir, peak: see HINDU KUSH.

Tiridates (tĭr″ĭdā′tēz), d. 211 B.C., king of Parthia (c.248–211 B.C.), 2d ruler of the Arsacid dynasty (see under ARSACES). He absorbed Hyrcania and, with the ruler of Bactria, successfully resisted the attacks of Seleucus II of Syria.

Tiridates, fl. A.D. c.63, king of Armenia. He was put on the throne by his brother Vologeses I, king of Parthia, and he was driven from it when the Romans under Corbulo won (A.D. 59) the Parthian campaign. Later he went to Rome and had his crown restored (A.D. 66?) by Nero.

Tirlemont: see TIENEN, Belgium.

Tirnovo: see TRNOVO, Bulgaria.

Tirpitz, Alfred von (äl′frāt fən tĭr′pĭts), 1849–1930, German admiral. His influence on German naval policy began with his study of the recently invented torpedo and his consequent appointment (1871) as chief of the torpedo division of the navy ministry. Appointed secretary of state for naval affairs in 1897, he began to build a powerful battle fleet. The expansion of the German fleet contributed to Anglo-German enmity. Upon the outbreak of World War I, Tirpitz began the construction of submarines and advocated unrestricted submarine warfare to destroy Allied commerce. He retired in 1916 in protest against Chancellor Bethmann-Hollweg's opposition to his submarine policy. Tirpitz returned to active political life as the member of a nationalist group in the Reichstag (1924–28). See his memoirs (tr. 1919).

Tirshatha (tĭr′shəthə), Persian title of a governor. Ezra 2.63; Neh. 7.65–70; 8.9; 10.1.

Tirso de Molina (tĕr′sō dā mōlē′nä), pseud. of **Fray Gabriel Téllez** (gäbrēĕl′ tĕl′yĕth), 1584?–1648, outstanding dramatist of the Spanish Golden Age, b. Madrid. His fame rests on *El burlador de Sevilla* (1630; tr. *The Love Rogue,* 1924), the earliest known literary version of the Don Juan legend. Among the 300 or 400 plays by Tirso de Molina are *El vergonzoso en palacio* [the bashful man at the palace], *La prudencia en la mujer* [prudence in a woman], *El condenado por desconfiado* (tr. *The Saint and the Sinner,* 1954), *Marta la piadosa* [pious Martha], and *El castigo del pensé que* (tr. by James Shirley as *The Opportunity,* 1640). He also wrote short novels, included in his prose collection *Los cigarrales de Toledo* (1621). He joined the Mercederian monks in 1601 and wrote a history of the order (1637–39). His dramas, influenced by Lope de Vega, excel in wit and sympathetic characterization. See studies by A. H. Bushee (1939) and I. L. McClelland (1948).

Tiruchirapalli (tĭr″o͝ochĭrəpŭl'lē) or **Trichinopoly** (trĭchĭnŏ'pəlē), city (1971 pop. 306,247), Tamil Nadu state, SE India, on the Cauvery River. It is a district administrative center and an important educational, religious, and commercial city known for its gold and silver filigree work and brassware. Tobacco is marketed, and there are railway and cement industries. The city's chief landmark is the shrine of Srirangam, an elaborately carved monument to the Hindu god Siva, at the base of a 270-ft (82-m) rock. Another temple stands at the top of the rock.

Tirunelveli (tĭro͞onĕl'vĕlē), town (1971 pop. 108,509), Tamil Nadu state, SE India. Now an agricultural trading center with a sugar refinery, it was once an imperial city of the CHOLA kingdom (c.900–1200). St. Francis Xavier conducted missionary activity in the area (c.1545).

Tiruppur (tĭ'ro͝opo͞or), city (1971 pop. 113,171), Tamil Nadu state, S India. Located in the Eastern Ghats valley, Tiruppur is a commercial center with cotton spinning and weaving industries.

Tiryns (tĭ'rĭnz), ancient city of Greece, in the NE Peloponnesus, 2.5 mi (4 km) N of Nauplia (now Návplion) and near Argos. The site seems to have been inhabited since the 3d millennium B.C. It was a city of splendor from c.1600 to c.1100 B.C. Excavations begun by Heinrich Schliemann and Wilhelm Dörpfeld in 1884–85 revealed not only extensive pre-Homeric palaces of the Mycenaean period but also remains going far back in prehistory. The old city was prominent in Greek legend.

Tirzah (tûr'zə). **1** Daughter and coheiress of Zelophehad. Num. 27.1–11. **2** City, Palestine, capital of the northern kingdom from the reign of Jeroboam I to Omri. Joshua 12.24; 1 Kings 14.17; 15.21; 16.

Tisa, river: see TISZA.

Tischbein, Johann Heinrich Wilhelm (yō'hän hīn'rĭkh vĭl'hĕlm tĭsh'bīn), 1751–1829, German classical painter and etcher. He was a popular portrait painter of the German royalty. He also executed several portraits of Goethe (e.g., *Goethe in the Roman Campagna,* 1786, Goethemuseum, Frankfurt). Tischbein worked for a time in Naples, making engravings from Greek vases. Many of his etchings are illustrations for the works of Homer.

Tischendorf, Lobegott Friedrich Konstantin von (lō'bəgôt frē'drĭkh kôn'stäntēn fən tĭsh'əndôrf), 1815–74, German biblical critic. In 1844 he discovered in the monastery of St. Catherine on Mt. Sinai a few pages of one of the oldest Greek manuscripts of the Bible, and in 1859, with the cooperation of the Russian government, he obtained the remainder of the manuscript, the Codex Sinaiticus, of which a facsimile was published at St. Petersburg in 1862. He made several critical editions of the Bible, his eighth edition of the New Testament (3 vol., 1869–94) being the most important.

Tiselius, Arne (är'nə tēsā'lyəs), 1902–71, Swedish biochemist. He received the 1948 Nobel Prize in Chemistry for developing new methods of separating and detecting colloids. One system (electrophoresis) employs an electrical apparatus (Tiselius apparatus) for the separation of heavy molecules in solution; the other is a method of adsorption analysis that permits the differentiation and separation of substances, e.g., proteins, sugars, salts, and acids. Tiselius isolated the virus of mouse paralysis and developed synthetic blood plasma. In 1925 he joined the faculty of the Univ. of Uppsala; he did research at the Institute for Advanced Studies at Princeton in 1934–35 and at the Rockefeller Institute, New York City, in 1939.

Tishbite, epithet of Elijah, referring to Tishbe, his place of origin or his family. 1 Kings 17.1.

Tisi, Benvenuto: see GAROFALO, IL.

Tisiphone (tĭsĭf'ənē): see FURIES.

Tisquantum: see SQUANTO.

Tissaphernes (tĭs″əfûr'nēz), d. 395 B.C., Persian satrap of coastal Asia Minor (c.413–395 B.C.). He was encouraged by Alcibiades (412) to intervene in the Peloponnesian War in support of Sparta. Out of favor with CYRUS THE YOUNGER, he rebuilt his fortunes by siding with Artaxerxes II and helping him to defeat Cyrus in the battle of CUNAXA (401). He pursued the retreating Greek allies (the Ten Thousand) and treacherously murdered CLEARCHUS and four other Greek leaders (see ANABASIS and XENOPHON). Tissaphernes and Pharnabazus were the chief figures in Artaxerxes' reign. After Tissaphernes asserted supremacy over the Ionian cities, he was involved in war with the Spartans, and AGESILAUS II defeated him in 395. He was removed from office and assassinated.

Tissot, James Joseph Jacques (zhāmz zhôzĕf' zhäk tēsō'), 1836–1902, French painter and etcher. After participating in the Franco-Prussian War he stayed for 10 years in London, where he was highly esteemed. In 1882 he went to Palestine and devoted his life to a series of watercolor drawings illustrating the Bible. Many of these are in the Brooklyn Museum. See study by James Laver (1936).

tissue, in biology, aggregation of cells that are similar in form and function and the intercellular substances produced by them. The fundamental tissues in animals are epithelial, nerve, connective, and muscle tissue; blood and lymph are commonly classed separately as vascular tissue. In the higher plants, there are four main types of tissue: (1) meristematic tissue (apical meristem and cambium), composed of cells that grow, divide, and differentiate into all the other cell types; (2) protective tissue (epidermis and cork), composed of thick-walled cells that cover roots, stem, and leaves; (3) fundamental tissues, consisting of cells that make up the bulk of the plant body, including parenchyma (thin-walled cells used for food storage), collenchyma (moderately thick-walled cells used for strength), and sclerenchyma (heavily thick-walled cells used for support in stems and roots); and (4) vascular tissue (xylem and phloem), specialized cells used for conduction. Organs are usually composed of several tissues. In many diseases there are apparent changes in tissue (see PATHOLOGY). HISTOLOGY is the study of the structure of tissues.

Tisza, Kálmán (käl'män tĭ'sŏ), 1830–1902, Hungarian premier (1875–90), of an old Calvinist family. He entered politics in the Hungarian revolution of March, 1848. Elected (1861) to the Hungarian parliament, he led the radical group that later opposed the *Ausgleich* [compromise] of 1867, which created the AUSTRO-HUNGARIAN MONARCHY. He was influential in maintaining Austro-Hungarian neutrality in the Franco-Prussian War. Having become (1875) premier of Hungary, he reversed his stand on the *Ausgleich* and formed the Liberal party, which dominated Hungarian politics during the following decades. His close support of the policies of Julius Andrássy, the Austro-Hungarian foreign minister, enabled Tisza to make Hungary an equal partner in the Dual Monarchy. During his 15-year premiership, Tisza rehabilitated Hungarian finances, introduced compulsory education, and strengthened the economic ties with Austria. He tried to absorb the Slavic and Rumanian minorities into a Magyar culture and nation.

Tisza, Count Stephen, 1861–1918, Hungarian premier (1903–5, 1913–17); son of Kálmán Tisza. He believed in strong personal government and sought to make Hungary a forceful partner in the Austro-Hungarian Monarchy. He took repressive measures against the Serbian and Rumanian minorities of Hungary, seeking to block their secessionist tendencies. Tisza strongly opposed the aggressive policy of Count Berchtold, the Austro-Hungarian foreign minister at the outbreak (1914) of World War I, but at last consented to declaring war on Serbia after being assured that no Serbian territory was to be annexed. Tisza's influence waned after the death of Emperor Francis Joseph and the accession of Charles I. His ministry fell in 1917, and Tisza took a military command on the Italian front. He was assassinated at Budapest by soldiers who believed him a chief instigator of the war.

Tisza (tĭs'ə), Serbo-Croatian *Tisa* (tē'sä), Rus. *Tissa* or *Tisa* (both: tĭs'ə), Ger. *Theiss* (tīs), river, c.600 mi (970 km) long, formed by two headstreams in the Carpathians, W Ukraine, W USSR. It flows generally S across E Hungary, past Szolnok and Szeged, into N Yugoslavia, where it enters the Danube River E of Novi Sad. The Körös and Mureşul rivers are its chief tributaries. There are hydroelectric facilities on the river in Hungary. The Tisza is navigable for small craft to Szolnok and is also used to float timber.

Titan (tī'tən), in astronomy, largest of the 10 known moons, or natural satellites, of SATURN and the only satellite in the solar system known to have its own atmosphere.

Titan, in Greek religion, one of 12 primeval deities. The female Titan is also called Titaness. The Titans—six sons and six daughters—were the children of Uranus and Gaea. They were Cronus, Iapetus, Hyperion, Oceanus, Coeus, Creus, Theia, Rhea, Mnemosyne, Phoebe, Tethys, and Themis. The name Titan was sometimes applied also to their descendants, such as Prometheus, Atlas, Hecate, Selene, and Helios. The Titans, led by Cronus, deposed their father and ruled the universe. They were in turn overthrown by the Olympians, led by Zeus, in the battle called the Titanomachy. Zeus freed from Tartarus the Cyclopes and the hundred-handed giants, the Hecatoncheires, to aid him in the war. The Cyclopes forged Hades' helmet of darkness, Poseidon's trident, and Zeus' thunderbolts. With these weapons Zeus and his brothers were able to defeat the Titans. After the struggle Zeus sent Cronus to rule the Isle of the Blessed and condemned Atlas to bear the sky on his shoulders. Prometheus (and, in some myths, Oceanus and Themis), because he sided with Zeus, was allowed to remain on Olympus, but all the other Titans were condemned to Tartarus.

Titania (tĭtā'nēə), in astronomy, largest of the five known moons, or natural satellites, of URANUS.

Titanic (tītăn'ĭk), British liner that sank on the night of April 14–15, 1912, after crashing into an iceberg in the N Atlantic S of Newfoundland. More than 1,500 lives were lost. The *Titanic,* thought to be the fastest ship afloat and almost unsinkable, was on her maiden voyage and carried many notables among the more than 2,200 persons aboard. These circumstances made the loss seem the more appalling to the public in England and the United States. Official and other investigations revealed that messages of warning had been sent but had either not been received by the commanding officers or had been ignored by them. The ship had continued at full speed even after the warnings were sent. She did not carry sufficient lifeboats, and many of the lifeboats were launched with only a few of the seats occupied. Other vessels in the vicinity were unable to reach the *Titanic* before she sank; one, only 10 mi (16 km) away, did not respond because her wireless operator had retired for the evening. The disaster did have some good effects in bringing about measures to promote safety at sea, particularly the establishment of a patrol to make known the location of icebergs and stringent regulations about the proper number and proper equipment of lifeboats to be carried by vessels. The catastrophe inspired a large literature. See Walter Lord, *A Night to Remember* (1959); Lawrence Beesley, *The Loss of the S.S. Titanic* (1912, repr. 1973); Archibald Gracie, *The Truth about the Titanic* (1913, repr. 1973).

titanium (tĭtā'nēəm, tī-) [from *Titan*], metallic chemical element; symbol Ti; at. no. 22; at. wt. 47.90; m.p. 1675°C; b.p. 3260°C; sp. gr. 4.54 at 20°C; valence +2, +3, or +4. Titanium is a lustrous silver-white metal that exhibits ALLOTROPY; below about 880°C it has a hexagonal crystalline structure, but above that temperature it changes to a cubic crystalline structure. The metal is strong and has low density; it is ductile when pure and malleable when heated. Its chemical properties resemble those of zirconium, the element below it in group IVb of the PERIODIC TABLE. When heated, it ignites and burns in air. It is the only element that burns in nitrogen. It is very corrosion resistant and is unattacked by most acids, by moist chlorine gas, or by common salt solutions. Several of its compounds are commercially important. Pure crystalline titanium dioxide (titania) is used as a gemstone. The dioxide is also widely used as a paint pigment, especially for exterior paints. Titanates are formed from the dioxide, which is weakly acidic. An interesting example is barium titanate, which is piezoelectric and can be used as a transducer for the interconversion of sound and electricity. Titanium tetrachloride, a liquid, fumes in moist air; it is used for smoke screens and in skywriting. It is also an important catalyst in the polymerization of olefins. Titanium esters, formed by the reaction of the tetrachloride with alcohols, are used as waterproofing agents on fabrics. Titanic sulfate is used as a textile mordant. Titanium metal and its alloys are light in weight and have very high tensile strength, even at high temperatures. These metals are utilized in aircraft and spacecraft construction and in naval ships, guided missiles, and lightweight armor plate for tanks. Titanium compounds are widely distributed in nature. Rutile, the native dioxide, and ilmenite, which contains, besides titanium, iron and oxygen, are its chief sources. The metal cannot be produced by reduction of the dioxide, because titanium reacts with both oxygen and nitrogen at high temperatures. One method used consists in passing chlorine over ilmenite or rutile, heated to redness with carbon. Titanium tetrachloride, which is formed, is condensed, purified by fractional distillation, and then reduced with molten magnesium at 800°C in an atmosphere of argon. Titanium is present in the sun and certain other stars, in meteorites, and on the moon. Titanium dioxide causes the star effect in certain sapphires and rubies. The element was discovered (1791) by William Gregor and rediscovered (1795) by M. H. Klaproth, who gave it its present name.

Titanomachy: see TITAN.

Titchener, Edward Bradford (tĭch'ənər), 1867–1927, American psychologist, b. Chichester, England, grad. Oxford, 1890. He studied in Leipzig (Ph.D. 1892) under Wundt (whose *Principles of Physiological Psychology* he translated), and in 1892 he became head of the new psychological laboratory at Cornell, where he was research professor from 1910. His works include *Experimental Psychology* (2 vol., 1901–5), *Lectures on the Elementary Psychology of Feeling and Attention* (1908), and *Systematic Psychology* (1929).

Tithonus (tĭthō'nəs), in Greek mythology, prince of Troy; son of Laomedon. He was loved by the dawn goddess, Eos, who bore him Memnon. When Eos begged Zeus to bestow immortality upon Tithonus, she forgot to ask the god to grant her lover eternal youth; so Tithonus grew older and older until Eos, out of pity, changed him into a grasshopper.

titi: see MONKEY.

Titian (tĭsh'ən), c.1490–1576, Venetian painter, whose name was Tiziano Vecellio, b. Pieve di Cadore in the Dolomites. Of the very first rank among the artists of the Renaissance, Titian had an immense influence on succeeding generations of painters, especially in his use of color. He studied painting in the shop of Gentile and Giovanni Bellini. He also worked with Giorgione in 1508 on frescoes (now nearly obliterated) for the facade of the Fondaco dei Tedeschi in Venice. In 1511 he executed frescoes of the miracles of St. Anthony for the Scuola del Santo, Padua. After the deaths of Giorgione and of Giovanni Bellini, Titian was established as the finest painter in Venice. In 1518 he completed the celebrated altarpiece of the *Assumption of the Virgin* (Church of Santa Maria Gloriosa dei Frari, Venice). During the rest of his career rulers throughout Europe showered him with commissions and honors. His work was eagerly sought by the ducal families of Ferrara, Mantua, and Urbino. Emperor Charles V made him a Count Palatine. Philip II of Spain was also an enthusiastic patron. In 1545, Titian went to Rome, where he was quartered in the Belvedere of the Vatican. He painted the striking, though unfinished, portrait of Pope Paul III with his grandsons Ottavio (the second Duke of Parma) and Cardinal Alessandro Farnese (Pinacoteca, Naples). For Cardinal Farnese he painted a *Danaë* (Naples), of which he was later to make several versions. Titian came into contact with Michelangelo and shared his interest in ancient monuments. Returning to Venice, he was invited in 1548 to Augsburg by Charles V. There he executed many portraits of dignitaries and probably, during the course of his conversations with the emperor, conceived the idea of the magnificent *La Gloria* (1554, Prado), in which Charles and his deceased wife are presented to the Holy Trinity. In 1553, Titian began work on a cycle of mythological pictures for Philip II which included *Diana and Callisto* and *Diana Surprised by Acteon* (both 1559; National Gall., Edinburgh); the *Rape of Europa* (1559; Gardner Mus., Boston); and *Perseus and Andromeda* (c.1555; Wallace Coll., London). Also for Philip II he executed a large number of religious works intended for the Monastery of San Lorenzo del Escorial. Among these were *Adam and Eve* (c.1570; Prado) and the *Martyrdom of St. Lawrence* (1564–67; Escorial). After 1552, Titian remained in Venice, living in princely splendor and surrounded by friends who included the writer Pietro Aretino and the architect Jacopo Sansovino. Throughout his long and prolific career, he explored many pictorial problems. Titian was particularly famous for his innovations in the handling of color, a major preoccupation of the Venetian School. His work may be divided into three phases. The first is marked by the strong influence of Giovanni Bellini and Giorgione, exemplified in the so-called *Sacred and Profane Love* (c.1513; Borghese Gall., Rome) and in the *Madonna of the Cherries* (c.1515; Vienna). The attribution of certain works such as the *Fête Champêtre* (Louvre) is still a matter of controversy. During the second phase (c.1518–1550) there is a full development of the dramatic monumentality characteristic of High Renaissance painting. Typical of this phase are the *Pesaro Altarpiece* (1519–26; Church of Santa Maria Gloriosa dei Frari, Venice), the *Presentation of the Virgin* (1534–38; Academy, Venice), and the *Christ Crowned with Thorns* (c.1542; Louvre). Titian also achieved a greater sumptuousness of color and an evocation of sensuous joy in such pictures as the *Worship of Venus* (1519; Prado), *Bacchus and Ariadne* (1523; National Gall., London), and the *Venus of Urbino* (1537; Uffizi). Many of Titian's most famous portraits were painted during this period, including *La Bella* (1537), *Ippolito Rinaldo* (c.1545; both: Pitti Palace), and the equestrian portrait of *Charles V at the Battle of Mühlberg* (1548; Prado). In Titian's last phase there is an intensification of emotional expression. A deeply personal and mystical spirit becomes visible in a new looseness of brush stroke and subtlety of color. A climactic example is his last painting, the *Pietà* (Academy, Venice), intended for the artist's own tomb and finished by Palma Giovane. Rubens, Velázquez, and countless other painters studied and valued his work. Although most of Titian's paintings are in Europe, examples may be seen in American collections, including the Gardner Museum and the Museum of Fine Arts, Boston; the Metropolitan Museum and the Frick Collection, New York City; the National Gallery of Art, Washington, D.C.; and the Detroit and Kansas City museums. See studies by Erwin Panofsky (1969) and H. E. Wethey (2 vol., 1970, 1972).

Titicaca (tētēkä'kä), lake, c.3,200 sq mi (8,290 sq km), 110 mi (177 km) long, and c.900 ft (270 m) deep, in the Andes mts., on the Bolivia-Peru border; largest freshwater lake in South America and the world's highest large lake (c.12,500 ft/3,810 m above sea level). The lake is divided into two basins by the Strait of Tiquina. Fed by many short mountain streams, the lake is drained by the Desaguadero River to Lake Poopó. A center of Indian life from pre-Incan times, the shores of Titicaca, presently crowded with Indian villages and terraced fields, are a major source of subsistence crops for the largely barren highland region. The almost constant temperature of the water (51°F/11°C) modifies the climate and makes possible the growing of maize and wheat at so high an altitude. Indian balsas, small flat-bottomed reed boats with reed sails, dot the lake and are used for commerce and fishing. Steamer service connects the lake ports of Guaqui, Bolivia, and Puno, Peru. Near the lake's southern shore is the pre-Incan ruin TIAHUANACO. In the lake are the islands of Titicaca and Coati, the legendary birthplace of the Incas, that contain ruins of past civilizations.

title, in law, the means by which the owner has just and legal possession of his or her property. It is distinct from the document (e.g., a deed) that is evidence of the title. Title can be lost or acquired only by the methods established by law, that is, by inheritance or by purchase. Several persons may have different titles to the same property. While one holds a legal title (a claim to the land that is recognized by a court), another may hold an equitable title (the right to have the legal title transferred to him if certain conditions are met). This occurs if there is a MORTGAGE on the land. If a person holds land free of all encumbrances he may claim to have perfect title. When property is purchased, a title search is made to make certain that the seller is the legitimate owner of the title he is selling; the resulting document is an ABSTRACT OF TITLE.

titles, terms used to designate degrees of sovereignty, nobility, and honor. The highest-ranking title, that of emperor, derived from the Latin *imperator*, was originally a military title; the leader of a victorious army was saluted *imperator* by his soldiers. It was assumed by Augustus Caesar and the sovereigns of the Roman and Byzantine empires who followed him. The title received its modern meaning when it was conferred on Charlemagne in 800, and it was revived when Otto I was crowned (962) Holy Roman emperor. In Russia it was used from the time of Peter I until the dissolution of imperial Russia. It has also been the equivalent of the titles of the sovereigns of China, Japan, Persia, the Ottoman Empire, Ethiopia, and India. Napoleon assumed the title of emperor of the French in 1804, and Queen Victoria was proclaimed empress of India in 1877. *Caesar*, the cognomen of Julius Caesar, was adopted by Augustus (44 B.C.), and his successors as emperor took the name until Hadrian, who designated *Caesar* as the title of the heir apparent; the imperial use of *Caesar* was continued with the German *Kaiser* and the Russian *czar*. Continental titles of nobility have evolved since the time of feudalism, when knights came to be regarded as noble and titles became hereditary. Under the Holy Roman Empire a complex nobility, not confined to the territories of the empire, developed; titles were conferred upon many persons outside the imperial boundaries. Most modern titles of nobility in the Western world descended from these (see the accompanying table for masculine and feminine forms of equivalent titles in Western Europe). The title *count* [Fr. *comte*, Ger. *Graf*, Ital. *conte*] comes from the Latin *comes*, a noble attached to a kingly court and serving as an adviser to the king. The title *Graf* was taken over by the Holy Roman Empire from Carolingian and Merovingian terms for a noble appointed by the king and having military and legal authority over a certain territory. The creation of border territories (see MARCH) gave rise to the title of *Markgraf* (in English, *margrave*); the corresponding French title is *marquis*, from which the English title *marquess* is derived. A *Landgraf* (in English, *landgrave*) was a count whose territory included a number of fiefs. There was also the title of *Pfalzgraf* (*count palatine*; see PALATINATE). *Herzog* (*duke*) was a title denoting sovereignty over a large territory such as Bavaria or Saxony. After 1806 the title *Grossherzog* (*grand duke*) was also used. The title *Fürst* (*prince*) was below that of *duke*; there existed also the title *Prinz*, which was a courtesy title extended to various persons, notably the sons of a duke or king. Titles in descending order below emperor and king were *Herzog; Pfalzgraf, Markgraf,* and *Landgraf*, all of about equal rank; *Graf; Baron, Freiherr* or *Freier* (all *baron* in English); and *Ritter* (*knight*). The prefix *Reichs-* before any of these titles meant that the holder held the title directly from the emperor, i.e., he was not the vassal of any other lord. At the dissolution of the Holy Roman Empire, the German and Austrian nobility retained the titles they had held under the empire. In addition, the male members of the Austrian imperial family were called *archdukes*, i.e., dukes of the blood royal. This corresponded to the title of *grand duke* in the Russian

HEREDITARY WESTERN EUROPEAN TITLES OF NOBILITY

ENGLISH		GERMAN		FRENCH		ITALIAN		SPANISH	
Masculine	*Feminine*	*Masculine*	*Feminine*	*Masculine*	*Feminine*	*Masculine*	*Feminine*	*Masculine*	*Feminine*
duke	duchess	Herzog	Herzogin	duc	duchesse	duca	duchesa	duque	duquesa
—	—	Prinz Fürst	Prinzessin Fürstin	prince	princesse	principe	principessa	príncipe	princípesa
marquess	marchioness	Pfalzgraf Markgraf Landgraf	Pfalzgräfin Markgräfin Landgräfin	marquis	marquise	marchese	marchesa	marqués	marquesa
earl	countess	Graf	Gräfin	comte	comtesse	conte	contessa	conde	condesa
viscount	viscountess	—	—	vicomte	vicomtesse	visconte	viscontessa	visconde	viscondesa
baron	baroness	Baron Freiherr Freier	Baronin Freiherrin Freierin	baron	baronne	barone	baronessa	barón	baronesa

imperial family and to *infante* in Spain. French titles of nobility in descending order are *duc; prince* (only a prince of the blood royal was above a duke; an ordinary prince was often the son of a duke and was below a duke), *marquis, comte, vicomte, baron, seigneur* or *sire*, and *chevalier* (*knight*). The heir to the throne was called the DAUPHIN. Members of the French nobility have no privileges at all, but they retain their titles under the law. Titles in England are, in descending order, *prince, duke, marquess, earl, viscount, baron, baronet*, and *knight*. All have evolved since the Norman Conquest except *earl*, which is a title of the same descent as the continental titles translated as *count*. The title of *earl* was long the highest-ranking hereditary title under that of *king*, and English earls under the Norman kings enjoyed great power. The title of *duke* was in use on the Continent long before its introduction into England by Edward III, who created his son, the Black Prince, duke of Cornwall, a title now belonging automatically to the sovereign's eldest son from his birth. The Norman kings were themselves dukes of Normandy, a very high-ranking title, and may have been reluctant to confer similar titles upon their subjects. Originally, in fact, the only English dukes were dukes of the blood royal, and the sons of the sovereign are generally created dukes soon after coming of age. The title of *marquess* came into English use in 1385 as a title between those of *earl* and *duke*. The title of *viscount*, formerly that of a county sheriff, became a degree of honor and was made hereditary in the reign of Henry VI. *Baron*, originally a title denoting the chief tenants of the land, who were subject to summons to the king's court, is the most general title of nobility; since 1387 the title has usually been created by a legal notice (generally by letters patent, but occasionally by writ of summons), and it has nothing to do with land tenure. The existing baronetage (below the peerage) dates from 1611, when James I revived the title. The title of *baronet* is not in the peerage but is heritable; that of KNIGHT is a title of honor rather than nobility. The title of *prince of Wales*, at first the only prince in England, is reserved for the eldest son of the sovereign, although not invariably conferred upon him. In the reign of James I, all the sons of the sovereign came to be called *prince*. Queen Victoria extended the title, along with that of *princess*, to the royal grandchildren who are children of sons. During the later Middle Ages life peerages (i.e., nonhereditary titles) were sometimes given as a further honor to one already holding a title. Legislation in 1887 conferred life peerages on all present and former lords of appeal. The Life Peerages Act of 1958 allowed for the creation of life peerages, with the right to sit and vote in the House of Lords, for both men and women. Since 1964 life peerages have been the only kind conferred. In Italy, titles of nobility, in descending order, are *duca, principe, marchese, conte, visconte*, and *barone*. In Spain they are *duque, principe, marqués, conde, visconde*, and *barón*.

Non-Western Titles. In the Muslim world the temporal successors of Muhammad received the title *caliph* (literally, "successor"). Later titles for Muslim rulers were *emir* and *sultan*. Other Muslim titles include *sherif*, a hereditary title; *pasha* and *bey*, originally military titles but later given as a civilian nonhereditary honor; and *sheikh*, a title of respect variously given to tribal chiefs, heads of religious orders and colleges, and town mayors. Titles in India derive from three sources—Hindu, Muslim, and European—and illustrate the rather tumultuous history of the subcontinent. *Raja* (ruler or king; *maharaja* means "great king"), *rani* (queen), and *rajput* (king's son, or prince) are of Hindu origin. *Nawab* is a Muslim title of Hindustani derivation for a nobleman, while *nizam* is of Arabic origin. Imperial China made use of over 600 titles beginning with *Huang Ti* (emperor), *Huang How* (empress), *Huang T'ai How* (dowager empress), and so on. Titles of the hereditary imperial nobility conferred on members of the imperial house were of 12 degrees, or lines of descent. These titles were also conferred on the princes and rulers of the Mongol tribes. They were hereditary for a period up to 26 generations. Lesser hereditary ranks of nobility and honorary titles were derived from the feudal order that existed in the 6th cent. B.C. Although they loosely resembled the European scheme—*Kung, How, Peh, Tsze*, and *Nan*, corresponding to *duke, marquis, earl, viscount*, and *baron*, they were not aristocratic titles in the European sense, as they were granted purely for military services. Titles of honor known as *Feng Tseng* were conferred as rewards for service or great merit. The Japanese emperor is sometimes called the *Mikado*, but this is a term used exclusively by Europeans, except for its use in Japanese poetry. The Japanese call him the *Tenshi* (Son of Heaven), *Tenno* (Heavenly King), *Arehito Tenno* (God Walking Among Men), *Kamigoichinin* (Upper Exalted Foremost Being), *Aramikami* (Incarnate God), and other titles that reflect the traditional belief in his divinity. Through much of Japanese history, the real power rested in the SHOGUN, the commander of the imperial armies. The great feudal vassals were the DAIMYOS, who led retinues of SAMURAI, members of the knightly class. The shogunate came to an end in 1868, giving the real power to the emperor. In 1884, with the feudal order disbanded and all loyalty pledged to the emperor, the holders of ancient titles were given new designations based upon the European system of baron, count, marquess, and so on. See W. F. Mayers, *The Chinese Government* (3d ed. 1897, repr. 1966); James McMillan, *The Honours Game* (1969); L. G. Pine, *The Story of Titles* (1969).

titmouse, common name for members of the Paridae, a family of passerine birds, which includes the tits, titmice, and chickadees. They are small, active birds with short, pointed bills and strong legs. Their soft, thick plumage is colored in grays and browns, occasionally highlighted by black and white or blue and yellow. Titmice are found chiefly in the Northern Hemisphere and also in Asia and Africa. They are adaptable and can be taught to perform tricks. In the wild, titmice travel in mixed flocks with nuthatches, creepers, kinglets, and woodpeckers, feeding mostly on small insects but also on seeds, fruits, and berries. Typical of the family are the blackcapped chickadee, *Parus atricapillus*, of the NE United States, the nearly identical Carolina chickadee of the South, and the similar willow tit of Europe and the British Isles. Some titmice have crests, e.g., the crested tit of Eurasia and the tufted titmouse, *Lophophanes bicolor*, a mouse-gray bird with rust side patches common in the E United States. These typical titmice nest in tree cavities; the long-tailed tits weave complex bag nests. To this group belongs the Javanese pygmy tit (3 in./7.5 cm long, most of it tail); the bush tits of the American West are closely related. A third group, the penduline tits, are named for their hanging bag nests; the only American species is the western verdin. Titmice are classified in the phylum CHORDATA, subphylum Vertebrata, class Aves, order Passeriformes, family Paridae.

Tito, Josip Broz (yô'sĭp brôz tē'tō), 1892–, Yugoslav Communist leader, marshal of Yugoslavia. He was originally Josip Broz, the son of a blacksmith in a Croatian village. He fought in Russia with the Austro-Hungarian army in World War I and was captured by the Russians. He served with distinction in the Red Army during the Russian civil war of 1918 to 1920. Several years later Broz returned to Croatia and, as a metalworker, was a prominent union organizer. He was (1929–34) imprisoned as a political agitator. In 1937 the Comintern assigned to him the reorganization of the Yugoslav Communist party, and in 1941 he emerged as a leader of Yugoslav partisan resistance forces after the defeat and occupation of Yugoslavia by the Axis Powers. It was then that he adopted the name Tito. Although the core of his partisan army was Communist, Tito's rapidly growing forces included many non-Communists. Despite the opposition of the Yugoslav government in exile, which supported the Serbian resistance leader Draža MIHAJLOVIĆ, Tito's army and its successes soon eclipsed Mihajlović and his chetniks. Among the causes of his success were his swift guerrilla tactics, his own magnetic personality, and the appeal of his political program—a federated Yugoslavia—to the non-Serbian elements of the population. Although they cooperated at first, Tito and Mihajlović soon clashed. By 1943, Tito headed a large army and controlled a sizable part of Yugoslavia, centered in Bosnia. Tito was supported from the first by the USSR, but in 1944 he also received the full support of Britain and the United States. In Nov., 1944, after the liberation of Belgrade, he negotiated a merger of the royal Yugoslav government and his own council of national liberation, and in March, 1945, he became head of the new federal Yugoslav government. Already the virtual dictator of Yugoslavia, he won a major electoral victory in Nov., 1945, at the head of the Communist-dominated National Liberation Front, whose candidates were the only ones permitted to run in the election. With the opposition abstaining, Tito won almost 80% of the total electorate. King Peter II was deposed, and a republic was proclaimed (see YUGOSLAVIA). As premier and minister of defense from 1945, Marshal Tito ruled Yugoslavia dictatorially. He suppressed internal opposition by such measures as the execution of Mihajlović and the jailing (1946) of Archbishop Stepinac of Zagreb, and he nationalized Yugoslav industry and undertook a planned economy. He did not attempt to collectivize the land of the Yugoslav small farmers, but he forced them, under severe penalties, to furnish large quotas of their produce to the state. Although Yugoslavia was closely associated with the USSR and was a leading member of the COMINFORM, Tito often pursued independent policies and did not hesitate to curtail the activities of Russian agents. In 1948 the Cominform accused Tito of having deviated from the correct Communist line. Tito denied the charges but refused to submit to the Cominform, from which Yugoslavia was expelled. Having already transformed Yugoslavia into an armed camp, built up a highly efficient secret police, and purged dissident elements in the Communist party, Tito succeeded in maintaining his position despite the hostility of the USSR and his neighbors. Although he accepted loans from the Western powers, he initially did not alter his internal program. In later years, however, he relaxed many of the regime's strict controls, particularly those affecting the small farmers. As a result, Yugoslavia became the most liberal Communist country of Europe. On close terms with President Nasser of Egypt and Prime Minister Jawaharlal Nehru of India, Tito unsuccessfully tried to develop common policies among nonaligned nations. Relations with the USSR were alternately friendly and hostile. In 1968, together with the Rumanian party chief, Nicolae Ceauçescu, Tito led the opposition to the Soviet intervention in Czechoslovakia. Tito was repeatedly reelected president from his first term in 1953, and in 1963 his term was made unlimited. In an effort to provide for succession to the leadership after his death, Tito established (1971) a 22-member collective presidency composed of the presidents of the 6 republican and 2 autonomous provincial assemblies and 14 members chosen from the republican and provincial assemblies for 5-year terms; in July, 1971, Tito was elected chairman of the new presidency. In the early 1970s he was under increasing pressure from nationalist forces within Yugoslavia, especially Croatian secessionists who threatened to break up the federation. Following their repression, Tito tightened control of intellectual life. See *The Essential Tito*, ed. by H. M. Christman (1970); the official biography by Vladimir Dedijer (1953, repr. 1972); other biographies by Fitzroy Maclean (1957) and Phyllis Auty (1970); W. R. Roberts, *Tito, Mihailović, and the Allies* (1973).

Titograd (tē'tōgräd), formerly *Podgorica*, town (1971 pop. 98,743), capital of Montenegro, S Yugoslavia, at the confluence of the Ribnica and Morača rivers. A commercial center, it has industries producing furniture, tobacco, and foodstuffs. An ancient town, it was the capital of Serbia in the 11th cent. and was known as Ribnica until the 13th cent. It was ruled by the Turks from the mid-15th cent. until 1878, when it was transferred to Montenegro.

Titov Veles (tē'tôf vě'lěs), town (1971 pop. 60,842), SE Yugoslavia, in Macedonia, on the Vardar River. It is a road and rail junction and the market center for an agricultural and silk-producing region. An ancient town, Titov Veles has Roman and medieval ruins.

titration (tītrā'shən), gradual addition of an acidic SOLUTION to a basic solution or vice versa (see ACIDS AND BASES); titrations are used to determine the CONCENTRATION of acids or bases in solution. For example, a given volume of a solution of unknown acidity may be titrated with a base of known concentration until complete NEUTRALIZATION has occurred. This point is called the equivalence point and is generally determined by observing a color change in an added indicator such as phenolphthalein. From the volume and concentration of added base and the volume of acid solution, the unknown concentration of the solution before titration can be determined. Titrations can also be used to determine the number of acidic or basic groups in an unknown compound. A specific weight of the compound is titrated with a known concentration of acid or base until the equivalence point has been reached. From the volume and concentration of added acid or base and the initial weight of the compound, the EQUIVALENT WEIGHT, and thus the number of acidic or basic groups, can be computed. Instead of adding an indicator to observe the equivalence point, one can construct a graph on which the *p*H (see separate article) at regular intervals is plotted along one axis and the number of moles of added acid or base at these intervals along the other axis; such a plot is called a titration curve and is usually sigmoid (*S*-shaped), with the inflection point, where the curve changes direction, corresponding to the equivalence point. From the *p*H at the equivalence point, the dissociation constant of the acidic or basic group can be determined (see CHEMICAL EQUILIBRIUM). If a compound contains several different acidic or basic groups, the titration curve will show several sigmoid-shaped curves like steps and the dissociation constant of each group can be obtained from the *p*H at its corresponding equivalence point.

Tittoni, Tommaso (tōm-mä'zō tēt-tô'nē), 1855–1931, Italian statesman. As minister of foreign affairs (1903–5, 1906–9), he sought closer ties with the Western powers, while remaining within the framework of the Triple Alliance with Germany and Austria-Hungary. He also tried to improve the position of Italy in the Balkans. He was ambassador to France (1910–16), foreign minister (1919–20), and president of the senate (1920–29). A Fascist sympathizer, he was named by Mussolini president of the Italian Academy (1929–30). He wrote several books on political economy.

Titulescu, Nicholas (tētōōlĕ'skōō), 1882?–1941, Rumanian statesman. A professor of law at Bucharest University, he was finance minister (1917, 1920–21) and served as foreign minister from 1927 to 1928 and from 1932 to 1936. Titulescu was one of the chief figures in the League of Nations, serving (1930, 1931) as president of the General Assembly. A champion of the French-sponsored policy of collective security, he was an architect of the LITTLE ENTENTE and later of the BALKAN ENTENTE (1934). He was detested by the fascist Iron Guard and by other extreme reactionary elements in his country; his resignation was forced in 1936. Shortly afterwards he settled in France, where he died.

Titus (Titus Flavius Sabinus Vespasianus) (tī'təs), A.D. 39–A.D. 81, Roman emperor (A.D. 79–A.D. 81). Son of Emperor Vespasian, Titus was closely associated with his father in military campaigns, and after A.D. 71 he acted as coruler with the emperor. He served in Britain and in Germany and captured and destroyed Jerusalem in A.D. 70. On succeeding his father he pursued a policy of conciliation and sought popular favor. A benevolent ruler, he stopped prosecutions for treason and was lavish with gifts to his subjects, a practice that caused financial difficulties for his successor. He completed the Colosseum and built a luxurious bath. During his reign there occurred two disasters—a great fire in Rome and the eruption of Vesuvius, which buried Pompeii and Herculaneum. On both occasions Titus was active in lending aid to the distressed. Although Titus was not friendly with his brother and successor, DOMITIAN, there is no reason to believe the rumor that it was Domitian who arranged his death. The **Arch of Titus,** now restored and standing outside the ancient entrance to the Palatine, was erected by Domitian to commemorate Titus' conquest of Jerusalem. See B. W. Henderson, *Five Roman Emperors* (1927).

Titus, early Christian, a missionary and friend of St. Paul. According to later tradition he was a bishop in Crete. 2 Cor. 2.13; 7.6,7; 8.16–24; Gal. 2.3; 2 Tim. 4.10.

Titus, epistle of the New Testament, the 17th book in the usual order. With First and Second TIMOTHY, it makes up the Pastoral Epistles, purportedly written by St. Paul and dealing with matters of church government. Titus resembles First Timothy in detail, being made up of points of regulation in governing the church. There are two notable passages on Christian motives (2.11–15; 3.4–7).

Titus, Arch of: see TITUS, Roman emperor.

Titus Justus, in the Bible: see JUSTUS **2**.

Titusville (tī'təsvĭl), city (1970 pop. 30,515), seat of Brevard co., E Fla., on Indian River (a lagoon); inc. 1886. It is a regional trade center. The construction in the 1950s of the space center on nearby Cape Canaveral brought much activity to the area and caused the city's population to increase tenfold in less than a decade.

Tiumen: see TYUMEN, USSR.

Tiverton (tĭv'ərtən), rural town (1970 pop. 12,559), Newport co., SE R.I., between the Sakonnet River and the Mass. line; settled 1680, included in Massachusetts until 1746, inc. 1747. Tiverton is a summer resort center in a farm area, and there are oyster fisheries. A bridge completed in 1956 connects the town to Portsmouth. The Revolutionary Fort Barton was near Tiverton village.

Tivoli (tē'vōlē), Lat. *Tibur*, city (1971 pop. 41,733), in Latium, central Italy, on the Aniene River. The city is beautifully situated on a terrace dominating nearby Rome and the plain to the sea. It is celebrated for the waterfalls formed there by the Aniene and for the VILLA D'ESTE. An old settlement, Tivoli was conquered by Rome in the 4th cent. B.C. and became a favorite summer resort under the Empire. There are ruins of several Roman villas, notably that of Emperor Hadrian, and the well-preserved Temple of Vesta, which is now a church. The city also has a cathedral (12th cent; rebuilt 17th–18th cent.), with a fine Romanesque campanile.

Tiw (tē'ōō), Norse **Tyr** (tür), ancient Germanic god. Originally a highly revered sky god, he was later worshiped as a god of war and of athletic events. He was identified with the Roman war god Mars, and among Germanic peoples Mars' day became Tiw's day (Tuesday).

Tiy (tē), fl. 1385 B.C., queen of ancient Egypt, wife of AMENHOTEP III (XVIII dynasty). Of humble origin, she was remarkable for her influence in state affairs in the reigns of her husband and of IKHNATON, her son. The occurrence of her name with that of Amenhotep III shows an official recognition of the queen that was most unusual for Egypt.

Tiy, fl. 1167 B.C., queen of ancient Egypt, wife of RAMSES III (XX dynasty). To gain the throne for her son, Pentewere, she led a palace conspiracy to displace her aging husband. At the last minute the plot was discovered, and 32 important courtiers were executed for complicity.

Tizard, Sir Henry Thomas, 1885–1959, English physical chemist and scientific adviser. He was educated at Westminster school and Magdalen College, Oxford, from which he received honors in natural science in 1908. During the years from the late 1920s to 1942, Tizard became an outstanding authority on aeronautics and championed the development of radar. His 1940 mission to Washington gave impetus to cooperation between scientists and the military in the United States. His own research concerned chemical indicators and aerodynamics, and his work on aircraft fuels led to the common use of octane ratings.

Tiziano Vecellio: see TITIAN.

Tizi Ouzou (tēzē' ōōzōō'), city (1966 pop. 25,852), capital of Tizi Ouzou dept., N Algeria. It is the administrative and commercial center of an agricultural region where figs and olives are grown.

Tizite (tī'zīt), epithet of unknown meaning given Joha, one of David's mighty men. 1 Chron. 11.45.

Tjirebon (chĕrĭbŏn'), city (1961 pop. 158,299) and seaport, N Java, Indonesia, on the Java Sea. Crops grown in the fertile coastal plain include sugar and rice. The city has diversified manufactures and is the seat of a private university. It was formerly the capital of a sultanate that was abolished after 1815. SW of Tjirebon is the resort village of Linggajati, where in 1946 was drafted the short-lived Dutch-Indonesian agreement for the establishment of the United States of Indonesia under the Dutch crown. The name was formerly spelled Cheribon.

Tl, chemical symbol of the element THALLIUM.

Tlalnepantla (tlälnāpän'tlä), city (1970 pop. 373,657), Mexico state, S central Mexico, on the Tlalnepantla River. It is a communications and industrial center that owes its importance largely to its proximity to Mexico City. Smelting, metalworking, machine-building, and chemical manufacturing are the chief industries. There are important archaeological ruins nearby.

Tlaquepaque (tläkāpä'kā), city (1970 pop. 108,119), Jalisco state, SW Mexico, in the Guadalajara valley. Its folklore and local artisanry, as well as its proximity to Guadalajara, make Tlaquepaque a popular tourist spot.

Tlaxcala (tläskä'lä), state (1970 pop. 418,334), 1,555 sq mi (4,027 sq km), E central Mexico. Tlaxcala is the capital. It is the smallest and one of the most densely populated Mexican states. The western part lies within Mexico's central plateau; the remainder, however, is extremely mountainous, with a temperate to cold climate. Maguey, cereals, and subsistence crops are grown in the valleys. In the mountains are the sources of the Río Balsas. The Tlaxcaltec Indians were never subjugated by the Aztecs, despite encirclement by their tributary tribes. Defeated by Cortés after fierce resistance, the Tlaxcaltecs later became valuable Spanish allies against the Aztecs.

Tlaxcala, city (1970 pop. 21,424), capital of Tlaxcala state, E central Mexico. It is the site of the oldest church in America, founded (1521) by the Spanish explorer Cortés. Nearby is a famous Mexican shrine, the Santuario y Colegiata de Ocotlán.

Tlemcen (tlĕmsĕn'), city (1966 pop. 87,210), NW Algeria, capital of Tlemcen dept. Its location on a crossroads between the Mediterranean coast and the Sahara and between Algeria and Morocco has made it a commercial center since ancient times. Its prime importance was as a trade center during the Middle Ages. It flourished (13th–15th cent.) as the capital of a Muslim Berber dynasty, which ruled over much of what is now Algeria. Tlemcen has numerous splendid mosques and retains the atmosphere of medieval Muslim life. It still exports the carpets, woolens, and leather goods for which it has long been noted.

Tlingit Indians (tlĭng'gĭt), group of related North American Indian tribes, speaking a language that forms a branch of the Nadene linguistic stock (see AMERICAN INDIAN LANGUAGES). The 14 divisions of the Tlingit may reflect a former era when they were entirely independent tribes. Important among the divisions are the Chilkat, the Yakutat, the Stikine, the Sitka, the Auk, and the Huna. In 1741, when visited by Aleksei Chirikov and Vitus Bering, the Tlingit Indians lived in SE Alaska, along the coast and on the islands that fringe the coast about Sitka, S to Prince of Wales Island and N to the Copper River. The Russians built (1799) a fort near the site of Sitka, but the Indians rebelled and drove them out. Aleksandr BARANOV, however, later captured the fort, killing many Indians. He established a trading post there, which grew into Sitka. There was constant trouble between the Tlingit and the Russians. The Tlingit numbered more than 5,800 in 1835, but today, on reservations in British Columbia and Alaska, they number some 1,600. Tlingit culture, like the Haida and the Tsimshian, was typical of the Northwest Coast area. The name is also spelled Tlinget, Tlinkit, and Tlinket. See Livingston Jones, *A Study of the Tlingets of Alaska* (1914, repr. 1970); T. M. Durlach, *The Relationship Systems of the Tlingit, Haida, and Tsimshian* (1928, repr. 1974); R. L. Olsen, *Social Structure and Social Life of the Tlingit in Alaska* (1967); Frederica De Laguna, *Under Mount Saint Elias* (1972).

Tm, chemical symbol for the element THULIUM.

TMP (thymidine monophosphate): see THYMINE.

TNT: see TRINITROTOLUENE.

toad, name applied to certain members of the AMPHIBIAN order Anura, which also includes the FROG. Although there is no clear-cut distinction between toads and frogs, the name *toad* commonly refers to those species that have relatively short legs, stout bodies, and thick skins, and are less aquatic as adults than the long-legged, slender-bodied frogs. Sometimes the term is restricted to the so-called true toads, members of the family Bufonidae. These are characterized by warty skins and prominent parotid glands behind the eyes and as a group are the most terrestrial of the order. In most the feet are only slightly webbed. They range in length from about 1 to 7 in. (2.5–18 cm). Most species belong to the genus *Bufo;* members of these species spend much of the time on land, generally near water. They generally live in cool, moist places and absorb moisture through the skin. The white fluid that they exude through the skin, as well as from the parotid glands, is very poisonous and causes intense burning if it comes in contact with the eyes or mouth; however, contrary to an old belief, it does not cause warts. Toads, like frogs, move on land by jumping and feed on insects and grubs. Also like frogs, they usually lay their eggs in water in strands of jelly. Fertilization is external. The egg hatches into a TADPOLE, a gilled, aquatic, larval toad that undergoes metamorphosis into the adult. There are about a dozen *Bufo* species in the United States, among them the common American toad (*Bufo americanus),* Fowlers toad (*B. fowleri),* of the E United States, and the red-spotted toad (*B. punctatus),* of the Southwest. The spadefoot toads, burrowing toads of the family Pelobatidae, are represented in the United States by several species of the genus *Scaphiopus.* Toads are classified in the phylum CHORDATA, subphylum Vertebrata, class Amphibia, order Anura.

toadfish, common name for the sluggish, bottom-feeding fishes of the genus *Opsanus,* found in the shallow waters from New Jersey to the Caribbean. Toadfishes feed almost entirely on crustaceans and small fishes. The head of a toadfish is broad and flat, with barbels and fleshy fringes, sharp gill covers, and spiny protrusions on the cheeks; the mouth is enormous and has many sharp teeth. The scaleless, slimy body tapers to a slender tail. Toadfishes grow to 1 ft (30 cm) in length. The eggs, sometimes laid in empty shells or tin cans, are guarded viciously by the male. The midshipmen (*Porichthys* species) of the same family are deepwater fishes of the Atlantic and Pacific oceans, with many small luminescent organs on the underside of the body. Other members of the family are found in tropical waters and have venomous spines. Toadfishes and their relatives are classified in the phylum CHORDATA, subphylum Vertebrata, class Osteichthyes, order Batrachoidiformes, family Batrachoididae.

toadflax: see FIGWORT.

toadstool: see MUSHROOM.

Toah (tō'ə), variant reading for NAHATH **3.**

Tob (tŏb) or **Ishtob** (ĭsh'-), petty Aramaean state, probably NE of Palestine. Judges 11.3,5; 2 Sam. 10.6,8.

Toba (tō'bä), largest lake of Indonesia, 448 sq mi (1,160 sq km), N Sumatra. It is drained by the Asahan River. In the lake is Samosir, a large island (205 sq mi/531 sq km) that is linked to the mainland by an isthmus.

tobacco, name for any plant of the genus *Nicotiana* of the Solanaceae family (NIGHSHADE family) and for the product manufactured from its leaf and used in the CIGAR AND CIGARETTE, SNUFF, and pipe and chewing tobacco. The chief commercial species, *N. tabacum,* is believed native to tropical America, like most NICOTIANA plants, but has been so long cultivated that it is no longer known in the wild. *N. rustica,* a mild-flavored, fast-burning species, was the tobacco originally raised in Virginia, but it is now grown chiefly in Turkey and the Levant; *N. persica,* a slow-burning tobacco suitable for the hookah, or water pipe, is grown in the Orient. The tobacco plant is a coarse, large-leaved perennial, usually cultivated as an annual, grown from seed in cold frames or hotbeds and then transplanted to the field. Tobacco requires a warm climate and rich, well-drained soil. The characteristics of many of the named grades depend upon the regional environmental conditions and cultivation techniques. Tobacco leaves are picked as they mature or they are harvested all together with the stalk. They are cured, fermented, and aged to develop aroma and reduce the harsh, rank odor and taste of fresh leaves. Fire-curing, dating from pre-Columbian times, is done by drying the leaves in smoke; in air-curing, the leaves are hung in well-ventilated structures; in flue-curing, used for over half the total crop, the leaves are dried by radiant heat from flues or pipes connected with a furnace. The cured tobacco is graded, bunched, and stacked in piles called bulks or in closed containers for active fermentation and aging. Most commercial tobaccos are blends of several types, and flavorings (e.g., maple and other sugars, rum, and coumarin) are also often added. The United States produces an average annual yield of almost one billion tons (about one fourth of world production), of which about one third is exported; it imports tobacco for special purposes, e.g., Oriental cigarette leaf for blending, Puerto Rican tobacco for cigar filler, and cigar-wrapper leaf from Sumatra and Java. In the United States about 60% of the crop is grown in North Carolina and Kentucky. China, India, Pakistan, the USSR, and the Philippines are the other chief producing countries, and Great Britain and N Europe are the major importers. The use of tobacco originated among aborigines in the Western Hemisphere in pre-Columbian times. Tobacco was introduced into Spain and Portugal in the mid-16th cent., initially for its supposed virtues as a panacea. It spread to other European countries, then to Asia and Africa, where its use became general in the 17th cent. The first tobacco to reach England was probably a crop harvested in Virginia, where John ROLFE experimented with Spanish types of tobacco seed and introduced tobacco as a crop as early as 1612. By 1619 tobacco had become a leading export of Virginia, where it was later used as a basis of currency. The alkaloid NICOTINE is the most characteristic constituent of tobacco and is responsible for its narcotic and soothing qualities. The possible harmful effects of the nicotine, tarry compounds, and carbon monoxide in tobacco smoke vary with the individual's tolerance. The tobacco plant is susceptible to numerous bacterial, fungus, and virus diseases (e.g., the tobacco mosaic virus) and is attacked by several species of worms, beetles, and moths. Tobacco is classified in the division MAGNOLIOPHYTA, class Magnoliopsida, order Polemoniales, family Solanaceae. See Raymond Jahn, ed., *Tobacco Dictionary* (1954); J. C. Robert, *The Story of Tobacco in America* (1967); E. R. Billings, *Tobacco* (1875, repr. 1973).

Tobacco Nation, North American Indians of the Iroquoian branch of the Hokan-Siouan linguistic stock (see AMERICAN INDIAN LANGUAGES), called also the Tionontati. In 1616, when visited by the French, they were living S of Nottawasaga Bay, in Ontario. The French called them the Tobacco Nation because the Indians had large fields of tobacco. After the dispersion (1648–49) of the Huron Indians by the Iroquois, many of the Huron refugees fled to the Tobacco Nation. This brought the wrath of the Iroquois upon the Tobacco Nation, and in 1649 the Iroquois attacked. The remnants of the Tobacco Nation, with the Huron, were forced to flee to a region SW of Lake Superior. About 1670 the two tribes were at Mackinac; soon after they assimilated into one tribe, known to history as the Wyandot.

Tob-adonijah (tŏb-ădōnī'jə), Levite. 2 Chron. 17.8.

Tobago: see TRINIDAD AND TOBAGO.

Tobata: see KITAKYUSHU, Japan.

Tobey, Mark, 1890–, American painter, b. Centerville, Wis. An extensive traveler, Tobey visited China and Japan in 1934. He then developed his celebrated "white writing," in which he attempted to symbolize the human spirit by applying principles of Eastern calligraphy to the rhythms of Western civilization. An exciting sense of motion and lyric treatment of light and color are revealed in his *San Francisco Street* (1941; Detroit Inst. of Arts) and *Fountains of Europe* (1955; Mus. of Fine Arts, Boston). In 1923, Tobey settled at the NW United States; much of his work is exhibited at the Seattle Art Museum. *Transit* (1948; Metropolitan Mus.) is characteristic of the Oriental influence in Tobey's art. See catalog by William Seitz (1962).

Tobiah (tōbī'ə). **1** Ammonite opposed to Nehemiah. Neh. 2.10,19; 4.3; 6.17,19; 13.4,7,8. **2** Family returned from exile. Ezra 2.60; Neh. 7.62.

Tobias: see TOBIT.

Tobijah (tōbī'jə). **1** Teacher of the Law. 2 Chron. 17.8. **2** Emissary to Jerusalem from the Jews in Babylon. Zech. 6.10.

Tobit (tō'bĭt) or **Tobias** (-bī'əs) [Gr. from Heb. *Tobijah*], biblical book placed after Nehemiah in the Western canon, but not included in the Hebrew Bible and placed in the Apocrypha in the Authorized Version. It tells of Tobit (Tobias in the Vulgate), a devout Jew in exile, and of his son Tobias. Despite his many good works, Tobit is mysteriously blinded and begs God to take his life. At the same time in Ecbatana one Sara, who is afflicted by a demon (Asmodeus) who has killed her seven husbands on their wedding day, also asks God for death. God hears both prayers and sends the archangel Raphael to help. Sent by his father on business to a distant city, the young Tobias and his dog are guided by Raphael (in the form of a young man) to the house of Sara. There Tobias marries Sara and, following Raphael's instructions, exorcises the devil. They return to his home, and the young man cures his father's blindness. The book ends with a prophecy by the father of the restoration of Jerusalem. The story inculcates ideals of benevolence, marriage, and prayer. The easy style and the homely realism of the book have made it a favorite. The ancient texts are of great diversity; hence the various English versions differ materially in detail. The original language of the book is not known; it probably must be dated before 200 B.C. The young Tobias and his dog with the angel have been a favorite subject of Christian iconography. For bibliography, see APOCRYPHA.

tobogganing, sport of coasting down snowy hillsides or chutes on a toboggan, a flat-bottomed vehicle made of hard wood. The toboggan, often measuring 3 ft by 8 ft (91 cm by 2.4 m), is curled up at the front end to allow it to slide over irregularities of surface. The bottom is waxed, and sometimes very low, broad steel runners are added to facilitate speed. The toboggan is a development of the simple bark-and-skin runnerless sled of the American Indians. Steering is accomplished by shifting weight and the use of trailing feet. At winter sports resorts special iced slides or chutes are constructed with elevated sides to eliminate the need for steering. Tobogganing is the forerunner of BOBSLEDDING.

Tobol (təbôl'), river, c.1,050 mi (1,690 km) long, rising in the Mugodzhar Hills, NE Kazakhstan, Central Asian USSR. It flows NE past Kustanay, into the Russian Republic, and past Kurgan to join the Irtysh River at Tobolsk. It is navigable in its lower course.

Tobolsk (təbôlsk'), city (1967 est. pop. 47,000), W Siberian USSR, a port on the Irtysh River near its confluence with the Tobol. Industries include shipbuilding; woodworking; fish, fur, leather, and flax processing; meat packing; and furniture and carpet making. Founded in 1587 by Cossacks on the site of a Tatar village, Tobolsk was one of Russian Siberia's first towns. It was moved to its present site in 1610. The city was the administrative seat of W Siberia from 1708 until 1824, when Omsk replaced it. The main Siberian highway went through Tobolsk in the 18th cent., but the city declined when the Trans-Siberian RR was built (1890s) far to the south. Emperor Nicholas II and his family were exiled there (1917–18) before being taken to Ekaterinburg (now Sverdlovsk) and executed.

Toboso, El (ĕl tōbō'sō), town (1970 pop. 2,889), Toledo prov., central Spain, in New Castile. It is an agricultural center of La Mancha. Contrary to widespread opinion, El Toboso was not the residence of Dulcinea del Toboso in Cervantes's *Don Quixote.* It was, rather, her birthplace.

Tobruk (tōbrŏŏk'), Arab. *Tubruq,* city (1970 est. pop. 28,000), NE Libya, a port on the Mediterranean Sea. It was a fiercely contested objective in World War II (see NORTH AFRICA, CAMPAIGNS IN). Tobruk was first taken by the British on Jan. 22, 1941. When the Germans under Erwin Rommel drove the British out of Libya (March–April, 1941), the Australian garrison at Tobruk was isolated. However, the Australians were provisioned by sea and withstood repeated German attacks. British Field Marshal Claude Auchinleck's drive late in 1941 relieved the siege (Dec. 10). During Rommel's second offensive (begun May 26, 1942), Tobruk fell (June 21) after a one-day assault. The city was retaken by the British on Nov. 30, 1942.

toby jug (tō'bē), small pottery pitcher or mug modeled in the form of a jolly, stout man wearing a cocked hat, a corner of which serves as pourer. The jug is also called fillpot, both names taken from Toby Fillpot, inebriate character in the 18th-century song *Little Brown Jug.* Popular in England and America of that day, the toby jug has become a collector's piece.

Tocantins (tŏŏkəntēns'), river, 1,640 mi (2,639 km) long, formed in S central Goiás state, Brazil, by the confluence of two headstreams. It flows N to the Pará River, the southern distributary of the Amazon, SW of Belém. It is only partly navigable because of rapids. There are diamond washes near Carolina. The main tributary is the ARAGUAIA.

toccata (təkä'tə, tō-) [Ital.,=touched], type of musical composition. Early examples were written for various instruments, but the best-known form of toccata originated about the beginning of the 17th cent. Free in form, it was one of the first attempts at idiomatic writing for keyboard instruments, in contrast to the strictly contrapuntal pieces of the Renaissance. The toccata was usually rhapsodic, often interspersing rapid passages of brilliant figuration with fugal sections. Andrea Gabrieli, Frescobaldi, Sweelinck, Froberger, Buxtehude, and Bach were outstanding masters of the toccata style. Schumann wrote a toccata for piano in sonata form. As a brilliant showpiece the toccata persists today in organ composition.

Tochen (tō'kĕn), unidentified town, S Palestine. 1 Chron. 4.32.

Tochigi (tō'chĭgē), prefecture (1970 pop. 1,580,021), central Honshu, Japan. UTSUNOMIYA (the capital), KANUMA, and Sano are the chief cities. Its many fertile river plains yield rice, wheat, and tobacco. Silk is produced there. In the mountainous area of W Tochigi is Nikko National Park.

tocopherol: see VITAMIN.

Tocqueville, Alexis de (ălĕksēs də tôkvēl'), 1805–59, French politician and writer. He was prominent in politics, particularly just before and just after the Revolution of 1848, and was minister of foreign affairs briefly in 1849. His observations made during a government mission to the United States to study the penal system resulted in *De la démocratie en Amérique* (2 vol., 1835; tr. *Democracy in America,* 4 vol., 1835–40), one of the classics of political literature. A liberal whose deepest commitment was to human freedom, Tocqueville believed that political democracy and social equality would, inevitably, replace the aristocratic institutions of Europe. He analyzed the American attempt to have both liberty and equality in terms of what lessons Europe could learn from American successes and failures. Tocqueville's other important works are *L'Ancien Régime et la révolution* (1856; tr. 1856), which stressed the continuance after the French Revolution of many trends that had begun before, and his *Recollections* (1893; tr. by Alexander Teixeira de Mattos, 1896; complete ed. by J. P. Mayer, 1949). There are numerous English editions of his works, correspondence, and travel notebooks. See biography by J. P. Mayer (tr. 1960, repr. 1966); studies by G. W. Pierson (1938, repr. 1969), Jack Lively (1962), Richard Herr (1962), E. T. Gargan (1965), Marvin Zetterbaum (1967), and S. I. Drescher (1968).

Todd, Mabel Loomis, 1858–1932, American author, b. Cambridge, Mass. A friend of Emily DICKINSON, she edited and deciphered much of the Dickinson material in *Poems* (with T. W. Higginson, Ser. 1 and Ser. 2, 1890–91), *Letters of Emily Dickinson* (2 vol., 1894), and *Poems* (Ser. 3, 1896). Todd also wrote poetry and a textbook, *Total Eclipses of the Sun* (1894).

toddy, sweetened mixture of spirits, water, and flavoring ingredients such as cloves, usually served hot; in certain tropical countries it is served cold. It is said to have originated as a fermented beverage made from the flower buds of the palm.

Todi, Jacopone da: see JACOPONE DA TODI.

Todi (tô'dē), town (1971 pop. 17,251), Umbria, central Italy, on a hill in the Apennines and on the Tiber River. It is an agricultural and industrial center. The picturesque town has important Etruscan remains and Roman ruins. Noteworthy buildings include the Gothic Priors' Palace, the Gothic Palace of the Captain of the People, the Church of San Fortunato (1292–1460), and the cathedral (16th–17th cent.).

Todleben, Eduard Ivanovich: see TOTLEBEN.

Todos os Santos Bay (tô'thōozōō sän'tōōs) [Port.,=all-saints bay], inlet of the Atlantic Ocean, 25 mi (40 km) long and 20 mi (32 km) wide, E Bahia, Brazil. It receives the Paraguaçu River. Brazil's first oilfield (1939) is located N of Salvador, the bay's chief city. Itaparica, a large island at the mouth of the bay, has saltworks and oilfields. The fertile Reconcavo lowland surrounds the bay; subsistence crops, sugarcane, cotton, and tobacco are raised there. Todos os Santos Bay was discovered in 1501 by Amerigo Vespucci.

Todt Hill, N.Y.: see STATEN ISLAND.

tody (tō'dē), common name for small (3–4 in./9–10 cm) West Indian birds of the family Todidae, comprising the single genus *Todus*. Bright green above with red throats, they are forest birds called robins by Jamaicans, although not related to the robin. They are typically divided into four lowland species, one each on the islands of Jamaica (*T. todus*), Puerto Rico, Cuba, and Hispaniola. A fifth mountain species is found also on Hispaniola. The lowland species are distinguished chiefly by call and breast coloration, and it has been suggested that they might be best considered as geographic races in a single species. The narrow-billed tody (*T. angustirostrus*) differs from the others in preferring high, humid forests. Tody bills are typically broad and flattened, with serrated edges and stiff, whiskerlike rictal bristles. Typically observed perched in pairs on branches, todies wait until they spy prey, then quickly fly off to catch an insect on the wing or a small lizard on the ground. In flight, their wings make a loud, whirring noise which the birds can control and which is often associated with the mating season. Todies nest in narrow ground tunnels, laying two to three, rarely four, white eggs per clutch. The nestlings are born gray-throated but soon molt to red. In Haiti, tody eggs are eaten. Todies are classified in the phylum CHORDATA, subphylum Vertebrata, class Aves, order Coraciiformes, family Todidae.

Togarmah (tōgär'mə), unidentified region, possibly SW Armenia. Gen. 10.3; 1 Chron. 1.6; Ezek. 27.14; 38.6.

Toggenburg (tôg'ənbōōrkh), region in the Thur valley, St. Gall canton, NE Switzerland. Dairying, livestock breeding, and textile production are its main industries, and tourism is significant. After the death (1436) of the last count of Toggenburg the territory was claimed by Zürich, and a civil war between Zürich and the rest of the Swiss Confederation resulted (1443–50); Zürich was defeated. The territory was purchased (1468) from the confederation by the abbot of St. Gall. In 1712 the quarrels between the abbot and the Protestant communities of the Toggenburg served as a pretext for the **War of the Toggenburg,** between the Catholic and the Protestant cantons of the Swiss Confederation. The Catholics, numerically weaker, were quickly defeated, and religious equality was established. In 1803 the region became part of St. Gall canton.

Toggenburg goat: see GOAT.

Togliatti, Palmiro (pälmē'rō tōlyät'tē), 1893–1964, Italian Communist leader. A lawyer, he helped found the Italian Communist party in 1921. He lived in Moscow for many years after the Fascist takeover. Under the pseudonym Ercole Ercoli he wrote and worked for the Comintern. He was chief of the Comintern in Spain during the civil war there. Returning from Moscow to Italy in 1944, he became the leader of the Italian Communist party. As a leading anti-Fascist, Togliatti held cabinet posts in coalition governments in 1944–45, but later led the Communist opposition. A liberal Communist, he advocated greater independence of national Communist parties from Russian control. Although he followed a moderate line, he never openly broke with Moscow or disagreed radically on basic policy issues.

Togo, Heihachiro (hā'hächĭrō' tō'gō), 1846–1934, Japanese admiral, Japan's greatest naval hero. He studied naval science in England (1871–78), gained international recognition for his service in the First Sino-Japanese War, and contributed greatly to the development of Japanese sea power. In the Russo-Japanese War he defeated the Russian fleet at Port Arthur in 1904 and destroyed the Russian Baltic fleet in 1905 at the battle of Tsushima. This historic battle broke Russian strength in the Far East. Later he was chief of the naval general staff and a member of the supreme war council. See Edwin A. Falk, *Togo and the Rise of Japanese Sea Power* (1936); Georges Blond, *Admiral Togo* (tr. 1960).

Togo, republic (1973 est. pop. 2,075,000), 21,622 sq mi (56,000 sq km), W Africa, bordering on the Gulf of Guinea in the south, on Ghana in the west, on Upper Volta in the north, and on Dahomey in the east. LOMÉ is the country's capital and its largest city; other cities include Sokodé, Palimé, Anécho, and Atakpamé. Togo is made up of five parallel geographic regions running from east to west. In the extreme south is a narrow sandy coastal strip (c.30 mi/50 km long), which is fringed by lagoons and creeks. A region (c.50 mi/80 km wide) of fertile clay soils lies north of the coast. The third region is made up of the clay-covered Mono Tableland, which reaches an altitude of c.1,500 ft (460 m) and is drained by the Mono River. North of the tableland is a mountainous area comprising the Togo mts. and the Atakora mts. and including Mt. Agou (c.3,940 ft/1,200 m), Togo's loftiest point. The fifth region, in

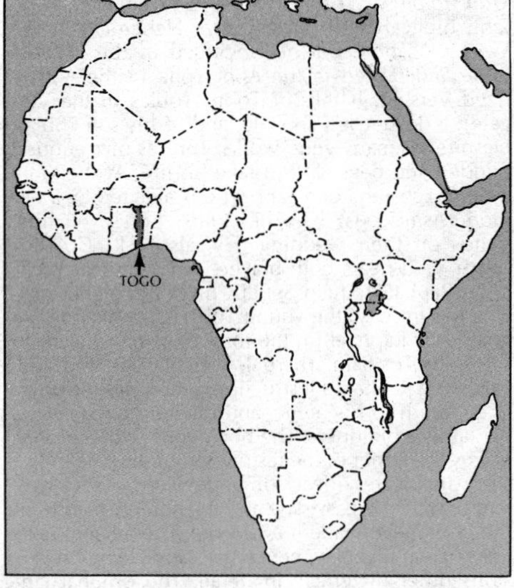

the extreme north, is the rolling sandstone Oti Plateau. The country is almost entirely covered with savanna, which has somewhat thicker vegetation in the south and somewhat thinner vegetation in the far north. The inhabitants of Togo are black Africans. The principal ethnic groups are the EWE, who live in the south, and various Voltaic-speaking peoples in the north. The majority of the inhabitants follow traditional African religious beliefs, but about 25% are Christian (mostly Roman Catholic) and about 8% are Muslim. French is the country's official language. The majority of Togo's workers are engaged in agriculture, but since the early 1960s mining has played an increasingly important role in the country's economy. The principal food crops are manioc, millet, maize, rice, pulses, and sweet potatoes. The leading cash crops are coffee, cacao, and palm crops, which are raised mainly on plantations in the south; in addition, cotton and groundnuts are grown in the north. Large numbers of sheep, goats, hogs, and cattle are raised. Major deposits of phosphates at Akoumapé (in the southeast) began to be worked on a large scale in 1963; in 1971, Togo was the world's seventh leading producer of phosphate ores. Small quantities of chromite, bauxite, limestone, and iron ore are also mined in Togo, and marble is quarried. The country's few manufactures consist mainly of basic consumer goods such as foodstuffs, beverages, clothing, footwear, and furniture. Processed phosphates and handicrafts are also important. Togo's limited road and rail transportation facilities are concentrated in the central and southern parts of the country; Lomé is the main port. The cost of Togo's imports is usually much higher than its earnings from export sales. The main imports are machinery, manufactured consumer goods, foodstuffs, and petroleum products; the leading exports are phosphates, cacao, coffee, palm products, and groundnuts. The principal trade partners are France, the Netherlands, and West Germany. For the history of Togo before it became independent on April 27, 1960, see TOGOLAND. At the time of independence, Sylvanus Olympio, the head of the Committee of Togolese Unity, was the country's prime minister, and when Togo adopted a presidential form of government in 1961, he became its first president. Until 1966 there were tense relations with neighboring Ghana, led by Kwame Nkrumah, who sought to merge Togo with Ghana—a plan that Togo strongly resisted. A major internal problem was the inability to find employment for most of the 600 men who had served in the French army and then had returned to Togo in the early 1960s. Some of these men took part in a successful coup d'etat on Jan. 13, 1963, during which Olympio was assassinated. Nicolas Grunitzky, Olympio's brother-in-law and an important political figure in the 1950s who had gone into exile (1958) in Dahomey, returned to Togo and became president. Grunitzky, leader of the Democratic Union of Togolese Populations, unsuccessfully attempted to unify the country by including several political parties in his government. On Jan. 13, 1967, he was toppled in a bloodless army coup led by Lt. Col. Ghansimgbe Eyadema, who became president in April, 1967, after an interlude of conciliar government. Eyadema was confirmed overwhelmingly as president in elections in 1972. Togo has maintained close relations with France and has received considerable economic aid from that country and from West Germany. See H. W. Debrunner, *A Church between Colonial Powers: A Study of the Church in Togo* (tr. 1965); Robert Cornevin, *Histoire du Togo* (3d ed. 1969, in French).

Togoland (tō'gōlănd") or **Togo** (tō'gō), historic region (c.33,500 sq mi/86,800 sq km), W Africa, bordering on the Gulf of Guinea in the south. The western section of Togoland is now part of GHANA, and the eastern portion constitutes the Republic of TOGO. The inhabitants of the region are black Africans, principally the EWE in the south and various Voltaic-speaking ethnic groups in the north. From the 17th cent. until the early 19th cent. the ASHANTI (situated in present-day Ghana) raided Togoland for slaves, who were then sold to European traders at the coast. European penetration of the region began in the 1840s with the arrival of German missionaries and German merchants who bought palm products. In 1884, Gustav NACHTIGAL signed treaties with several coastal rulers, and a German protectorate over S Togoland was recognized by the Conference of Berlin (1884–85). German military expeditions gained control of N Togoland during the 1890s, and the protectorate's boundaries were further delimited in treaties with France (1897) and Great Britain (1904). Germany instituted much economic development, building roads and railroads, constructing a good port at LOMÉ, and encouraging the production of palm products, rubber, cotton, and cacao. However, German levies of direct taxes and forced labor aroused resentment among the Togolese. In Aug., 1914, British and French forces easily captured Togoland from the Germans in the first Allied victory of World War I. In 1922, the League of Nations divided the region into two mandates, one French and the other British, and in 1946 the mandates became trust territories of the United Nations. French Togoland was administered as a separate unit (except between 1934 and 1937, when it was joined with Dahomey), and in 1960 it became independent as the Republic of Togo. British Togoland, made up of W Togoland, was administered as part of the British Gold Coast colony and protectorate and in 1957 became part of the independent state of Ghana. See Robert Cornevin, *Histoire du Togo* (3d ed. 1969, in French).

Tohu (tō'hyōō), variant reading for NAHATH **3.**

Toi (tō'ī), king of Hamath, father of JORAM **3.** 2 Sam. 8.10. Tou: 1 Chron. 18.9.

Tojo, Hideki (hēdā'kē tō'jō), 1884–1948, Japanese general and statesman. He became prime minister after he forced Konoye's resignation in Oct., 1941. His accession marked the final triumph of the military party which advocated war with the United States and Great Britain. As the most powerful leader in the government during World War II, he approved the attack on Pearl Harbor and pushed the Japanese offensive in China, SE Asia, and the Pacific. His military coordination with Nazi Germany was weakened by mutual mistrust and divergent Russian policies. At home, the Japanese government asserted totalitarian control. Tojo resigned in July, 1944, after the loss of Saipan in the Marianas. In April, 1945, he recommended that the war be fought to a finish. He attempted suicide in Sept., 1945, but he was arrested by the Allies as a war criminal, tried, convicted, and executed. See biography by Courtney Browne (1967); R. J. C. Butow, *Tojo and the Coming of the War* (1961).

Tokaj (tô'koi), town, NE Hungary, on the Tisza and Bodrog rivers. The grapes for the noted Tokay wine are grown in the surrounding region, where wine has been produced since the 12th cent.

Tokat (tōkät'), city (1970 pop. 44,825), capital of Tokat prov., N central Turkey. It is a copper-refining center and an agricultural market. An important town in Roman times, it declined under the Byzantines but revived after its capture by the Ottoman Turks in 1402.

tokay: see GECKO.

Tokay (tōkā'), fine, sweet, golden wine made without fortification. It is produced near Tokaj, Hungary. The very rare Imperial Tokay is made from juice oozed from overripe grapes without artificial pressure.

Tokelau (tōkəlou') or **Union Islands,** island group (1970 pop. 1,687), c.6 sq mi (16 sq km), South Pacific, a territory of New Zealand. It is composed of three atolls, Atafu, Nukunono, and Fakaofo. The chief export is copra. The Tokelau Islands administration is located in Apia, Western Samoa, and the New Zealand High Commissioner to Western Samoa is also the administrator of the group. Apia is the Tokelau's port of entry. Discovered by the British in 1765, the group was made a British protectorate in 1889 and was included (1916–25) in the Gilbert and Ellice Islands colony. From 1926 to 1948 the islands were under the Western Samoa mandate of New Zealand, and in 1949 the Tokelaus became part of New Zealand.

Tokio: see TOKYO, Japan.

Tokoly, Imre: see THÖKÖLY, IMRE.

Tokorozawa (tōkō"rō'zäwä), city (1970 pop. 136,611), Saitama prefecture, central Honshu, Japan. It is a suburb of Tokyo and an agricultural market for locally grown green tea.

Tokugawa (tō"kōōgä'wä), family that held the shogunate (see SHOGUN) and controlled Japan from 1603 to 1867. Founded by Ieyasu, the Tokugawa regime was a centralized feudalism. The Tokugawa themselves held approximately one fourth of the country in strategically located parcels, which they governed directly through a feudal bureaucracy. The *daimyo* [barons] owed allegiance to the Tokugawa but were permitted to rule their own domains. Care was taken to see that none of them became strong enough to challenge the Tokugawa. They were required to maintain residence at the shogun's capital, in Edo (Tokyo), and to leave hostages there during their absence. Travel was closely regulated, and officials called *metsuke* [censors] acted as a sort of secret police. Important economic and social changes occurred during the Tokugawa period. Improved farming methods and the growing of cash crops stimulated agricultural productivity; Osaka and Edo became centers of expanded interregional trade; urban life became more sophisticated; and literacy spread to almost half of the male population. Despite its efficient organization, the Tokugawa regime collapsed before a combination of internal and external forces in 1867, and the Meiji Restoration came about.

Tokushima (tōkōō'shĭmä), city (1970 pop. 223,331), capital of Tokushima prefecture, E Shikoku, Japan. It is a port and a center for the manufacture of cotton fabrics and wood products. Tokushima prefecture (1970 pop. 791,111), 1,600 sq mi (4,144 sq km), a mountainous region, rises to 6,414 ft (1,955 m) at Mt. Tsurugi. There are many farms, and raw silk, charcoal, fish, and salt are produced.

Tokyo (tō'kēō), city (1973 est. pop. 8,583,000), capital of Japan and of Tokyo prefecture, E central Honshu, at the head of Tokyo Bay. Greater Tokyo, the world's most populous city, consists of an urban area divided into 23 wards, a county area with farms and mountain villages, and the Izu Islands stretching to the S of Tokyo Bay. It is the administrative, financial, educational, and cultural center of Japan and a major industrial hub surrounded by numerous suburban manufacturing complexes. The city, which lies on the Kanto plain, is intersected by the Sumida River and has an extensive network of canals. YOKOHAMA is its seaport, but there is a large man-made port at the mouth of the Sumida, through which such items as iron, steel, machinery, and chemicals are exported. The deepening of Tokyo's harbor and the development of storage facilities have gradually lessened the city's dependence on Yokohama. The world's first public monorail line runs between downtown Tokyo and nearby Haneda international airport. The city's transportation system also includes "bullet trains" that travel at more than 300 mi (480 km) per hour between Tokyo and Osaka. Among the diverse industries of Tokyo are machine building, metalworking, printing and publishing, food processing, oil refining, and the manufacture of electronic apparatus, transport equipment, automobiles, steel, chemicals, cameras and optical goods, furniture, leather products, textiles, and a wide variety of consumer items. Tokyo prefecture is governed by a popularly elected governor and assembly. The wards and other subsidiary units of the city have their own assemblies. Archaeological evidence indicates that the site of Tokyo was inhabited by Stone Age tribes. The present city was founded in the 12th cent. as the village of Edo (also Yedo or Yeddo) [estuary]. A local warlord, Edo Taro Shigenada (whose family, according to tradition, probably took the name Edo from their place of residence) built a fort there. In 1456–57 Ota Dokan, ruler of the Kanto region under the Japanese shogunate, constructed a castle at Edo. The castle passed in 1590 to Ieyasu Tokugawa, founder of the Tokugawa line of shoguns, who made Edo the capital of a province and, after formally assuming the title of shogun in 1603, the capital of the shogunate. The imperial capital, however, remained at Kyoto. In Tokugawa times, the shogun's palace, encircled by the residences of the daimyos [feudal barons], samurai, and merchants, dominated the city's life. The urban population was increased by the shogun's retainers and by the large retinues of the daimyos, who were obliged to divide their time between their regional power centers and the capital. Although the city prospered as a commercial and cultural center, it later declined as the shogunate weakened. On April 11, 1868, the last Tokugawa shogun surrendered Edo Castle to the imperial forces. The emperor, restored to power, made Edo his capital, renaming the city Tokyo [eastern capital] as distinguished from Kyoto, then called Saikyo [western capital]. The castle then became the royal palace. The 1923 earthquake and fire destroyed nearly half the densely populated city and took more than 150,000 lives. The rebuilt city included wide streets, designed to serve as firebreaks. Heavy Allied bombing during World War II devastated half of Tokyo, destroyed or damaged many famous landmarks, and ruined nearly all of the city's industrial plant. The Meiji shrine (still the most popular in Japan), which was dedicated to Emperor Meiji and his consort, was badly damaged but has been restored. Left entirely intact were the imperial palace grounds and the surrounding area where the embassies, the diet building, and the newest office buildings stand; this area is the administrative center of the city. Tokyo's famed landmarks include the Hie Shrine; the temples of Sengakuji, Gokokuji, and Sensoji; and the Korakuen, a 17th-century landscape garden. The Ginza is Tokyo's shopping and entertainment center; the Marunouchi quarter is the business center. Tokyo Tower, reputedly the highest (1,092 ft/333 m) steel-supported structure of its type in the world, was built in 1958. One of the world's foremost educational centers, Tokyo has about 100 universities and colleges, including Keio-Gijuku Univ. (est. 1867); Tokyo Univ., formerly Tokyo Imperial Univ. (1869); Rikkyo or St. Paul's Univ. (1883); Waseda Univ. (1882); and Tokyo Women's College (1900). There are numerous museums and more than 200 parks and gardens. Frequent rebuilding in the wake of disasters has made Tokyo one of the most modern cities on the globe. Tokyo was the site of the 1964 summer Olympic games. See James Kirkup, *Tokyo* (1966); Atsushi Atzumi, *Tokyo* (1972).

Tola (tō'lə). **1** Son of Issachar. Gen. 46.13. **2** Judge of Israel. Judges 10.1,2.

Tolad (tō'ləd), same as ELTOLAD.

Toland, John (tō'lənd), 1670–1722, British deist, b. Ireland. Brought up a Roman Catholic, Toland became a Protestant at 16. He studied at Glasgow, Edinburgh, and Leiden and after 1694 lived at Oxford for several years. In 1696 he published *Christianity not Mysterious,* in which he tried to reconcile the scriptural claims of Christianity with the epistemology of John LOCKE. He asserted that neither God nor his revelation is above the comprehension of human reason. The book was widely attacked, and it was burned in Ireland in 1697. Toland's next work (1698) was a biography of John Milton, which also caused a scandal; it contained a passage that was believed to cast doubt on the authenticity of the New Testament. His *Anglia Libera* (1701), in support of the Act of Settlement (see SETTLEMENT, ACT OF), brought him favor from the court of Hanover, where he was received by the Electress Sophia. To her daughter, Sophia Charlotte, he addressed his *Letters to Serena* (1704), in which he argues that motion is an intrinsic quality of matter, thus repudiating the Cartesian conception. In his *Pantheisticon* (1720) he develops the pantheistic ideas implicit in the *Letters.* He is believed to have been the first to use the term pantheism.

Tolbert, William Richard, Jr. (tŏl'bərt), 1913–, president of Liberia. He worked in the treasury (1935–43) and then served in the house of representatives (1943–51) before he assumed the office of vice president (1951–71). Upon the death (1971) of William Tubman, Tolbert became president.

Tolbukhin (tôlbōō'khĭn), city (1968 est. pop. 238,300), NE Bulgaria, a commercial and cultural center of the DOBRUJA region. Foodstuffs, cotton textiles, metal goods, and farm machinery are produced. The city was formerly called Dobrich and, during its occupation by Rumania (1913–40), Bazargic. It was officially renamed in 1949 to honor Soviet marshal Tolbukhin, who liberated it in 1944.

tolbutamide (tŏlbyōōt'əmīd"): see ORINASE.

Toldy, Ferencz (fĕ'rĕnts tôl'dĭ), 1805–75, father of Hungarian literary history. Toldy edited various literary journals and founded (1842) *Nemzeti Könyvtár* [national library] to produce the critical edition of Hungary's classic poets. He also wrote two histories of Hungarian literature (1851, 1864–65), a Hungarian grammar (1866), and a manual of Magyar poetry (1876).

Toledo, Francisco de (fränthē'skō thā tōlā'thō), 1515?–84, Spanish viceroy of Peru (1569–81). He came from one of the noblest families of Spain and had served Charles V and Philip II with distinction before being chosen as viceroy. His administration in Peru marked the end of the tumultuous period after the Spanish Conquest. He made tours of inspection through the territories, reorganized governmental administration and finance, and attempted to reform conditions in the church. Whenever possible, he adopted the ancient Inca laws. He broke the power of the *encomenderos* (the large estate owners), reducing them to obedience to the crown and to the viceroy. He reorganized the Univ. of San Marcos. The one great blot on his administration was the unjust execution (1571) of the Inca leader, Tupac Amaru, after trouble between the Spanish and the Incas. See biography by Arthur F. Zimmerman (1938).

Toledo, city (1970 pop. 44,382), capital of Toledo prov., central Spain, in New Castile, on a granite hill surrounded on three sides by a gorge of the Tagus River. Historically and culturally it is one of the most important cities of Spain. Toledo is of pre-Roman origin; known in ancient times as Toletum, it fell to the Romans in 193 B.C. The city became an early archiepiscopal see; its archbishops, who still wield enormous power, are the primates of Spain. In the 6th cent. Toledo prospered as a capital of the Visigothic kingdom, and it was the scene of several important church councils. Its greatest prosperity began under Moorish rule (712–1085), first as the seat of an emir and after 1031 as the capital of an independent kingdom. Under the Moors and later under the kings of Castile, who made it their chief residence, Toledo was a center of the Moorish, Spanish, and Jewish cultures. Toledo sword blades were famous throughout the world for their strength, elasticity, and craftsmanship; the art was introduced by Moorish craftsmen, and it is still carried on. Other important products were silk and wool textiles. In the 15th cent. Valladolid superseded Toledo as chief royal residence, but Emperor Charles V again resided there during much of his reign (1516–56). Its commercial decline began in the 16th cent., but at the same time Toledo gained increased importance as the spiritual capital of Spanish Catholicism. The somber seat of the Grand Inquisitors, it was also the center of the mysticism symbolized by its adopted citizen, El Greco, whose name has become inseparable from that of Toledo. The city's general aspect has changed little since El Greco painted his famous *View of Toledo.* Its chief landmark, the alcázar (fortified palace), was originally a Moorish structure, restored in the 13th cent. and transformed (1535, 1576) to serve as residence for Charles V and Philip II. It was largely destroyed (1936) in the Spanish civil war, when the Nationalists, with their women and children, shut themselves up inside and withstood a Loyalist siege for two months, until relieved by Franco's forces; after the war the fortress was again restored. Toledo is surrounded by partly Moorish, partly Gothic walls and gates. Of Moorish origin also is the Alcántara bridge across the Tagus. The Gothic cathedral, begun in 1226, is one of the finest in Spain and houses El Greco's *Espolio* and other paintings by him in its lovely baroque chapels. Among the other many famous buildings are the Church of Santo Tomé, with El Greco's *Burial of the Conde de Orgaz;* the Church of Santa María la Blanca (12th–13th cent.; formerly a synagogue); the Convent of San Juan de los Reyes (15th cent.), with five Gothic cloisters; the Hospital of San Juan Bautista (15th–16th cent.), which has some paintings by El Greco; the former Tránsito synagogue, in Mudéjar style; and the Greco Museum.

Toledo (təlē'dō), city (1970 pop. 383,818), seat of Lucas co., NW Ohio, on the Maumee River at its junction with Lake Erie; inc. 1837. With a fine natural harbor and a vast system of railroads and highways, Toledo is a port of entry and one of the chief shipping centers on the Great Lakes. Oil, coal, farm products, and numerous manufactures are exported; iron ore is the principal import. Toledo is also an industrial and commercial center, with large oil refineries, a glassmaking industry, shipyards, and plants that manufacture jeeps, automobile parts, machinery, scales, and chemicals. Other products are paints, metal stampings, tools, die castings, plastics, and cosmetics. Gen. Anthony Wayne built Fort Industry there in 1794 after the battle of Fallen Timbers. The city was settled (1817) as Port Lawrence on that site and in 1833 was consolidated with nearby Vistula as Toledo. In 1835–36 occurred the "Toledo War," an Ohio-Michigan boundary dispute, which was settled by Congress in favor of Ohio when Michigan became a state. Steps in the development of the city included the opening of the canals in the 1840s, the arrival of numerous railroad lines, the development of the Ohio coal fields, the tapping of gas and oil deposits in the late 19th cent., and the establishment of the Libbey glassworks in 1888. When Samuel M. Jones became mayor in 1897, an era of municipal reform was initiated. Jones died in 1904 and was succeeded by Brand Whitlock. The Toledo plan of labor conciliation (1946) has been adopted by other cities. The city is the seat of the Univ. of Toledo, Mary Manse College, the Medical College of Ohio at Toledo, several technical colleges, and a state mental hospital. Points of interest include the Toledo Museum of Art, a large zoological park, and the Anthony Wayne suspension bridge (1931). The site of the battle of Fallen Timbers, a national historic landmark, is in a nearby state park. See H. T. Shenefield and J. 0. Garber, *Toledo, Our Community* (1932); J. L. Stinchcombe, *Reform and Reaction: City Politics in Toledo* (1968).

Toledo, University of, at Toledo, Ohio; coeducational; chartered 1872, opened 1875, and received its first municipal support in 1884. Its present name was adopted in 1940, and in 1967 the university was transferred to the state.

Tolentino (tōlāntē'nō), town (1971 pop. 16,780), in the Marche, central Italy, on the Chienti River. In 1797, Pope Pius VI signed at Tolentino a humiliating treaty with Napoleon Bonaparte, under which the pope gave up considerable territory and numerous works of art. Murat was defeated by the Austrians near the city in 1815 and lost the throne of Naples.

Tollens, Hendrik Franciscus (hĕn'drək fränsĭs'kəs tôl'əns), 1780–1856, Dutch poet. Among the leading Dutch romantics, he was popular for his homely and sincere patriotic verse. His principal work (1819) was an account of the Barentz expedition (1596–97), translated into English as *The Hollanders in Nova Zembla* (1884). He added the patronymic Caroluszoon to his name.

Toller, Ernst (ĕrnst tôl'ər), 1893–1939, German dramatist and poet of the expressionist school. He was imprisoned (1919–24) for participating in the Communist Bavarian revolution. In 1932 he left Germany, and in 1936 he went to New York City, where he committed suicide. His plays of social protest include *Die Wandlung* (1919, tr. *Transfiguration,* 1935); *Masse Mensch* (1920, tr. *Man and the Masses,* 1924); *Die Maschinen-stürmer* (1922, tr. *The Machine-Wreckers,* 1923), based on the Luddite riots in England; *Hinkeman* (1924, tr. *Brokenbow,* 1926); and *Pastor Hall* (tr. 1939), about Martin Niemoeller. *Schwalbenbuch* [swallow book] (1923), a collection of lyric verse, and *Briefe aus dem Gefängnis* [letters from prison] (1935), an account of his imprisonment, appeared together in English translation as *Look Through the Bars* (1937). See his autobiography, *Eine Jugend in Deutschland* (1933, tr. *I Was a German,* 1934); study by J. M. Spalek (1968).

Tolman, Edward Chace, 1886–1959, American psychologist, b. West Newton, Mass., grad. Massachusetts Institute of Technology, 1911; Ph.D. Harvard, 1915. He taught (1915–18) at Northwestern Univ. before joining the faculty of the Univ. of California at Berkeley, where he became (1928) professor of psychology. Rejecting narrow behavioristic theories of stimulus and response, Tolman postulated purpose as the core of behavior in his classic work *Purposive Behavior in Animals and Men* (1932). His other works include *Drives Toward War* (1942).

Tolpuddle Martyrs, name given to six English agricultural laborers who in 1834 were prosecuted for trade union activities and sentenced to transportation. In 1833 these laborers, led by George and James Loveless (or Lovelace), formed a branch of the Friendly Society of Agricultural Laborers at Tolpuddle, in Dorset. With the approval of the Whig government, which feared a renewal of the agricultural agitation of 1831, they were arrested on the trumped-up charge of administering illegal oaths and were sentenced to seven years transportation to Australia. Public reaction throughout the country made the six into popular heroes, and the sentence was finally remitted in 1836 after continuous agitation. One of the six returned to Tolpuddle; the others emigrated to Canada.

Tolstoy, Aleksey Konstantinovich (tŏl'stoi, Rus. əlyĭksyä' kənstəntyē'nəvĭch təlstoi'), 1817–75, Russian poet, dramatist, and novelist. He was a distant cousin of Leo Tolstoy. Together with two cousins he wrote nonsense verse and humorous works under the pseudonym Kozma Prutkov. These works are primarily satire directed against government bureaucracy. Tolstoy also wrote narrative lyrics and epics in both romantic and humorous veins. *Prince Serebryany* (1863, tr. *A Prince of Outlaws,* 1927) is a historical novel set in the time of Ivan the Terrible. He also treated this period in a trilogy of historical dramas in blank verse, *The Death of Ivan the Terrible* (1865, tr. 1926), *Tsar Fyodor Ivanovitch* (1868, tr. 1922), and *Tsar Boris* (1870). Tolstoy's works reflect his vitality and erudition. See study by Margaret Dalton (1972).

Tolstoy, Aleksey Nikolayevich (nyĭkəlī'əvĭch), 1882–1945, Russian writer. He was distantly related to Leo Tolstoy. Of aristocratic origin, he opposed the Bolsheviks in 1917 and emigrated to Western Europe. He returned in 1922 and accepted the Soviet regime, becoming one of its most popular writers. A master storyteller, he is best known for his vivid historical novels, including the trilogy *The Road to Calvary* (1918–23, tr. 1946), in which he traces the effect of the Revolution and the civil war on a group of intellectuals. His *Peter I* (1929–34, tr. *Peter the Great,* 1936) gives a broad picture of Russia during a period of Europeanization. Some of Tolstoy's short stories are translated in *A Week in Turenevo* (1958). *Nikita's Childhood* (1921) is a charming narrative based on his own youth. Tolstoy took an active part in Soviet propaganda activities during World War II.

Tolstoy, Leo, Count, Rus. *Lev Nikolayevich Tolstoi* (lyĕf), 1828–1910, Russian novelist and philosopher, considered one of the world's greatest writers. Of a noble family, he was born at Yasnaya Polyana, his parents' estate near Tula. Orphaned at nine, he was brought up by his aunts and privately tutored. At 16 he was sent to the Univ. of Kazan, at which he studied languages and law. His classes bored him, and he left without a degree. He returned to his estate in 1849 and made several abortive attempts to aid and educate the serfs there. Tolstoy then began a profligate life in Moscow and St. Petersburg. In 1851 he followed his brother into army service in the Caucasus, where he wrote *Childhood* (1852). This became the first part of an autobiographical trilogy, which includes *Boyhood* (1854) and *Youth* (1857). In 1854 he took part in the defense of Sevastopol, descriptions of which were published in Nekrasov's journal the *Contemporary,* attracting considerable attention for their unvarnished picture of war. He left army service in 1855 and for several years divided his time between his estate and the literary circles of St. Petersburg. His diary of the period reveals his intense dissatisfaction with his libertine existence. He set up a school for peasant children on his estate, emphasizing a spontaneous approach to learning. When his school proved impractical, he visited Western Europe and there began to question the bases of modern civilization. In 1862, Tolstoy married Sophia Andreyevna Bers, a young, well-educated girl who bore him 13 children. His candor concerning his infidelities and his harsh conception of her wifely duties contributed to the instability of their marriage. During this time he wrote *The Cossacks* (1863) and his masterpieces *War and Peace* (1862–69) and *Anna Karenina* (1873–76). *War and Peace* is a vast prose epic of the Napoleonic invasion of 1812. It illustrates Tolstoy's view of history as proceeding inexorably to its own ends, a view in which mankind appears as an accidental instrument. This thesis is conveyed by a stream of brilliantly conceived characters and incidents. *Anna Karenina,* his most popular work, concerns the tragedy of a woman's faith in romantic love. About 1876 the doubts that had beset Tolstoy since youth, fed by his puritan temperament in conflict with his sensuality, gathered force. The result of his painful self-examination was his conversion to the doctrine of Christian love and acceptance of the principle of nonresistance to evil. The steps in his conversion are set forth in his *Confession* (1879). For the rest of his life Tolstoy dedicated himself to the practice and propagation of his new faith, which he expounded in a series of works, among them *A Short Exposition of the Gospels* (1881), *What I Believe In* (1882), *What Then Must We Do?* (1886), and *The Law of Love and the Law of Violence* (1908). He preached nonviolence and a Rousseauistic simplicity of life. He was an anarchist to the extent that he considered wrong all organizations based on the premise of force, including both the government and the church. A Tolstoy cult grew up in Russia and abroad, and his estate became a place of pilgrimage; because of his prestige the government did not interfere with his activities, although the Russian Church excommunicated him in 1901. Moral questions are central to his later works, which include the story "The Death of Ivan Ilyich" (1884), the drama *The Power of Darkness* (1886), and the novel *The Kreutzer Sonata* (1889). To his last period belongs the essay *What Is Art?* (1897–98), in which he argued for the moral responsibility of the artist to make his work understandable to most people; he denounced acknowledged masterpieces, including his own earlier works. His last works also include the novels *Hadji Murad* (1896–1904) and *Resurrection* (1899–1900) and the drama *The Living Corpse* (pub. 1911). Tolstoy's insistence on putting his beliefs into practice and abandoning all earthly goods led to a permanent breach between himself and his wife. His children, with the exception of the youngest daughter, Alexandra, sided with their mother. In 1910, at 83, Tolstoy left home with Alexandra without a specific destination. He caught a chill and died at the railroad stationmaster's house at Astapovo. Tolstoy's works are available in many English translations. See the reminiscences of his wife, Sophia (tr. 1928 and 1936); his children Sergei (tr. 1926), Tatiana (tr. 1951), Ilya (tr. 1971), and Alexandra (tr. 1953, repr. 1973); his friends Maxim Gorky (tr. 1920), A. B. Goldenweizer (tr. 1923, repr. 1969), Valentin Bulgakov (tr. 1971), and V. G. Chertkov (tr. 1922, repr. 1973); biographies by Aylmer Maude (1931), E. J. Simmons (1946), and Henri Troyat (tr. 1967); collections of critical essays, ed. by R. E. Matlaw (1967) and by Henry Gifford (1972); Isaiah Berlin, *The Hedgehog and the Fox* (1953).

Toltec (tŏl'tĕk), ancient Indian civilization of Mexico. The name in Nahuatl means "master builders." The Toltec formed a warrior aristocracy that gained ascendancy in the Valley of Mexico A.D. c.900 after the fall of Teotihuacán. Their early history is obscure but they seem to have had ancient links with the MIXTEC and the ZAPOTEC. Their capital was Tollán (see TULA). In architecture and the arts they were masters; they were influenced by Teotihuacán and the OLMEC culture. CHOLULA is considered to be a Toltec site. Toltec civilization was materially far advanced. They smelted metals, and their stonework was highly developed. Their polytheistic religion in later days seems to have centered about QUETZALCOATL. Their ceremonies included human sacrifice, sun worship, and a sacred ball game, *tlatchli.* They are said to have discovered pulque (a fermented drink), and they had considerable astronomical knowledge, as shown in their calendar cycle of 52 years of 260 days each. A period of southward expansion began c.1000 and resulted in Toltec domination of the MAYA of Yucatán from the 11th to the 13th cent. Nomadic peoples (collectively termed the CHICHIMEC) brought about the fall of Tula and of the Toltec empire in the 13th cent., thus opening the way for the rise of the AZTEC. See also PRE-COLUMBIAN ART AND ARCHITECTURE.

tolu or **tolu balsam:** see BALSAM.

Toluca (tōlōō'kä), city (1970 pop. 220,192), capital of Mexico state, central Mexico. Located on the central plateau, Toluca (alt. c.8,760 ft/2,670 m) has a year-round cool climate. It was established as a settlement in 1530 by Hernán Cortés, who had received the Valle de Toluca as a grant from Emperor Charles V. The surrounding plain is fertile, producing grain, fruits, and vegetables. Cattle raising is important. The city has flour, cotton, and woolen mills and a brewery. Toluca is known for its basket weaving, pottery, and embroidery. Two small rivers run through the town, and nearby is an inactive volcano, the Nevado de Toluca, called also Xinantecatl and Cinantécatl.

toluene (tŏl'yōōēn") or **methylbenzene** (mĕth"-əlbĕn'zēn), C_7H_8, colorless liquid aromatic hydrocarbon that melts at −95°C and boils at 110.8°C. It is insoluble in water but highly soluble in most organic solvents. Toluene is obtained from coal tar and petroleum by distillation. It is used as a solvent and as a starting material for the synthesis of many compounds, including dyes and explosives. When toluene is treated with a mixture of nitric and sulfuric acids (a process known as nitration), trinitrotoluene (TNT) is produced.

Tom (tôm), river, c.525 mi (840 km) long, rising in the Ala-Tau range, S Siberian USSR. It flows N through the Kuznetsk Basin past Novokuznetsk, Kemerovo, and Tomsk into the Ob River. It is navigable from Novokuznetsk.

tomahawk [from an Algonquian dialect of Virginia], hatchet generally used by North American Indians as a hand weapon and as a missile. The earliest tomahawks were made of stone, with one edge or two edges sharpened (sometimes the stone was globe shaped). The stone was fastened to a wooden handle in various ways, such as by putting the stone into a hole through the wood, tying the stone to a handle with thongs, or splitting the handle and tying it about the stone with thongs. After the arrival of the European traders the stone implements were rapidly replaced by European-manufactured tomahawks of steel (trade tomahawks). Some tomahawks were also equipped with a pipe bowl and a hollow stem, which were used for smoking. The ceremonial tomahawk usually was richly decorated with feathers and paint. Some Indians had the custom of ceremonially burying a tomahawk after peace had been reached with an enemy. This custom is supposedly the origin of the colloquial phrase, "to bury the hatchet." See H. L. Peterson, *American Indian Tomahawks* (1965).

Tomakomai (tōmä"kō'mī), city (1970 pop. 101,573), Hokkaido prefecture, S Hokkaido, Japan, on the Pacific Ocean. It is a commercial port and the site of Japan's largest paper and newsprint industry.

Tomar (tōōmär'), town (1960 pop. 14,118), central Portugal, in Ribatejo. It has paper and textile mills and other industries but is noted chiefly as the center of the Knights Templars and later of the Military Order of Christ. The knights under Gualdim Pais in 1190 successfully resisted the assault of Yakub and his Almohad forces—an important event in the Christian reconquest of Portugal. The Templars were suppressed early in the 14th cent., but the Order of Christ was founded (1319–20) immediately afterward. The great convent-castle on the hill overlooking Tomar dates from the most glorious days of the order, just after it was under Prince Henry the Navigator, although there are mementos of the earlier years. There are other churches, principally of this period. The order grew rich from Portugal's overseas expansion, and the city flourished. In 1581 it was chosen by Philip II of Spain for the proclamation of his rule. Thereafter it declined.

Tomás, Américo de Deus Rodrigues (əmĕr'ēkōō dĭ dĕ'ōōsh rōōdrē'gəsh tōōmäsh'), 1894–, Portuguese admiral and statesman. After serving in the navy in World War I he joined (1919) the hydrographic board of the marine ministry. He was made (1936) special assistant to the minister of the navy and became minister of the navy himself in 1944. For almost 15 years Tomás was instrumental in developing Portuguese shipping and fishing facilities; he was promoted to rear admiral in 1951. He served as president of Portugal from June, 1958, to April, 1974, when he was deposed by a military coup and exiled to Madeira and later to Brazil. His surname also appears as Thomaz.

Tomaszów Mazowiecki (tômä'shōōf mäzôvyĕts'-kē), city (1970 pop. 54,911), E central Poland. It is a railroad junction and has industries manufacturing woolens, synthetic textiles and fibers, and farm implements. In the city is a 19th-century palace.

tomato, plant *(Lycopersicon esculentum)* of the family Solanaceae (NIGHTSHADE family), related to the potato and eggplant. Although cultivated in Mexico and Peru for centuries before the European conquest, the tomato is one of the newest plants to be used on a large scale for human food. When the Spanish explorers brought back seed from South America, the plant was grown merely for ornament; it was known as the love apple. Though described as a salad plant before 1600, it was commonly regarded as poisonous, and only within the last century has it become recognized as a valuable food. It was reintroduced to the United States as a food plant c.1800 and now ranks third among our vegetable crops. It is very popular as a salad vegetable, yet three quarters of the crop is processed into juice, canned tomatoes, soups, catsup, and tomato pastes. It is the most widely used canned vegetable. Numerous varieties (ranging from the small cherry tomato to the large beefsteak) are cultivated in practically all parts of the United States except the warmest regions. One of the worst tomato pests is the CUTWORM. Tomatoseed oil (from waste seed of canning processes) is sometimes extracted, chiefly in Italy. An antibiotic, tomatine, is also extracted from the seed. Technically the tomato is a fruit, although it is commonly considered a vegetable because of its uses. The tomato is classified in the division MAGNOLIOPHYTA, class Magnoliopsida, order Polemoniales, family Solanaceae.

tomb, vault or chamber constructed either partly or entirely above ground as a place of interment. Although it is often used as a synonym for GRAVE, the word is derived from the Greek *tymbos* [burial ground]. It may also designate a memorial shrine erected above a grave. The concept of the tomb as a chamber or dwelling place for the dead is the most widespread. It may have originated in the practice, known in prehistoric times and common among so-called primitive peoples of today, of burying the dead underneath their place of dwelling. Sometimes the survivors continue to live in the house; sometimes they seal and abandon it after a burial. This may account for the recurrence in different periods and places of the domed or conical funeral mounds and chambers (such as the prehistoric BARROW, the beehive tomb of MYCENAEAN CIVILIZATION, the MAUSOLEUM of Persian and Roman royalty, and the STUPA of Asia) and of the artificial caves commonly called rock-cut tombs (such as those found in Petra, Jordan; Thebes, Egypt; and in various parts of Asia). When corpses were buried outside the house, the purpose of protecting the body and possibly confining the spirit was often served by heaping stones above the grave. This may have been the initial structure that gave rise to the MASTABA and later to the PYRAMID of Egypt. Such heaps of stones also served as markers or shrines where offerings might be left to the spirits of the dead. Christian tombs, relatively simple at first, had by the Middle Ages become quite splendid. It became the custom to build a church over the grave of a martyr. For centuries, kings and other privileged persons were buried within the church buildings, their graves often surmounted by a little shrine or by a SARCOPHAGUS bearing an effigy of the deceased. In Great Britain many important personages have been entombed in WESTMINSTER ABBEY. Famous funerary structures of modern times include the TAJ MAHAL, at Agra, India; the Dôme des INVALIDES, Paris, which contains the tomb of Napoleon; General Grant's tomb, New York City; and the Lenin mausoleum, Moscow. See BURIAL; CEMETERY; CRYPT; FUNERAL CUSTOMS.

Tombalbaye, Ngarta (ən-gär'tä tŏmbəlbä'yä), 1918–, president of Chad (1960–). Born François Tombalbaye, he Africanized his given name in 1973. A businessman and school official, he became involved in territorial politics in the 1950s and served (1959–60) as premier. Elected president in 1960, he established dictatorial control. Opposition to his policies culminated in open rebellion in 1965 by the mainly Arab north. Despite an agreement with the rebels in 1971, fighting continued.

Tombigbee (tŏmbĭg'bē), river, c.400 mi (640 km) long, rising in NE Miss. and flowing SE into W Alabama, then generally south to join the Alabama River and form the Mobile River before entering into Mobile Bay at Mobile. The Tombigbee is an important artery for manufactured goods. Dams and locks improve navigation on the river. In 1972 construction was begun on a canal between the Tombigbee and Tennessee rivers. Scheduled for completion in the 1980s, the 253-mi (407-km) waterway will be a link in a navigable system from the Tennessee Valley to the Gulf Coast.

Tombstone, city (1970 pop. 1,241), Cochise co., SE Ariz.; inc. 1881. With its pleasant climate and legendary past, it is a well-known tourist attraction. The city became a national historic landmark in 1962. Silver was discovered there in 1877 by Ed Schieffelin, a prospector, who two years later laid out and named the city. Tombstone quickly became one of the richest and most lawless mining towns in the Southwest. Its newspaper, *Epitaph*, was first published in 1880. The city was county seat from 1881 to 1929. Large-scale mining ended by 1890. Among Tombstone's many picturesque landmarks are Boot Hill Graveyard, where many desperados are buried; Bird Cage Theater, now a museum; and O.K. Corral, scene of a climactic gun battle between the Clanton gang and Wyatt Earp, his brother Virgil, and Doc Holliday. The city's violent past is reenacted each year at the 3-day Helldorado celebrations. Nearby are the beautiful Dragoon Mts., onetime stronghold of the Indian chief Cochise. See Odie B. Faulk, *Tombstone* (1973).

tomcod: see COD.

Tomlin, Bradley Walker, 1899–1953, American painter, b. Syracuse, N.Y., grad. Syracuse Univ. (1921). He also studied painting in London and Paris. His early work includes cover designs for *Vogue* and *House and Garden* magazines. In the 1930s and 1940s he developed consistently toward abstraction. His late, entirely abstract, works are mosaics of ribbonlike, calligraphic strokes. Among his paintings in museums are *Still Life* (Whitney Mus. of American Art, New York City), *Number 20, 1949* (Mus. of Modern Art, New York City), and *Number 10, 1952–53* (Munson-Williams-Proctor Inst., Utica, N.Y.). See study by John Baur (1957).

Tomlinson, Henry Major, 1873–1958, English novelist. A dock worker, then a journalist and war correspondent, he was (1917–23) literary editor of the *Nation and Athenaeum.* Probably his best-known novel is the sea story *Gallions Reach* (1927). Others include *Pipe All Hands* (1937) and *Morning Light* (1946). *All Our Yesterdays* (1930) is a semifictional history of World War I. Among his travelogues are *The Sea and the Jungle* (1912), *South to Cadiz* (1934), and *Below London Bridge* (1935). See his autobiographical sketches, *A Mingled Yarn* (1953).

Tommaseo, Niccolò (nēk-kōlô' tōm-mäzā'ō), 1802–74, Italian poet and critic, b. Sibenik, Dalmatia. In addition to his poetry, novels, and literary criticism, he wrote well in almost every field, including history, philosophy, lexicography, and philology. He was perhaps most distinguished as a philologist, and his *Dizzionare dei sinonimi* (1830) still remains in use. *Una serva* (1837), stories in verse, is among the best of Italian romantic poetry. Tommaseo also collected the popular poetry of Tuscany, Corsica, Illyria, and Greece. His attacks on the Austrian rule of Italy resulted in a long exile, interrupted by his participation in the unsuccessful Revolution of 1848 in Venice.

Tompion, Thomas, 1639?–1713, English clockmaker. When the Royal Observatory at Greenwich was established in 1676, Tompion was chosen to make two clocks, to be wound only once a year, which proved to be more accurate timepieces than those available to other observatories. Utilizing the new inventions of the cylinder escapement (which enabled the making of flat watches) and the balance spring (discovered by Robert Hooke), he raised clockmaking and watchmaking to a fine art. Several of his clocks survive and still run, including one originally constructed for William III at Hampton Court Palace.

Tompkins, Daniel D., 1774–1825, American political figure, Vice President of the United States (1817–25), b. Scarsdale, N.Y. A leader of the Jeffersonian group in New York state, he was elected to Congress in 1804, but he preferred to accept an appointment to the New York supreme court. He was governor of New York from 1807 to 1817. Slavery was abolished in the state during his administration. In an effort to prevent the chartering of a banking institution in New York, he took (1812) the unique step of proroguing the legislature. He was elected Vice President in 1816 and held office through both Monroe administrations. His college essays were collected in *A Columbia College Student in the Eighteenth Century* (ed. by R. W. Irwin and E. L. Jacobsen, 1940).

Tomsk (tŏmsk, Rus. tômsk), city (1970 pop. 338,000), capital of Tomsk oblast, W central Siberian USSR, on the Tom River. It is a major river port and freight transit point. Machine tools, electric motors, ball bearings, instruments, and chemicals are made.

Founded in 1604 around a fort built by Boris Godunov, Tomsk was a major Siberian trade center until bypassed by the construction of the Trans-Siberian RR in the 1890s. It is a major educational center of Siberia, with a university (founded 1880) and a medical school (founded 1888).

Tom Thumb, 1838-83, American entertainer, whose original name was Charles Sherwood Stratton, b. Bridgeport, Conn. His career as General Tom Thumb began in 1842, when the showman P. T. Barnum gave him the title and arranged with the child's parents for his exhibition as a midget. His height then was less than 2 ft (.61 m), and at no time did it exceed 33 in. (84 cm). Barnum aroused the intense curiosity of people throughout the world by consummately skillful publicity and satisfied this curiosity through profitable display of the general in many countries, bringing Tom Thumb wealth and fame. At the age of 10 the general had already been the guest of President Polk, Queen Victoria, Isabella of Spain, and King Louis Philippe of France. His courtship of Lavinia Warren, a dwarf, led to a fashionable wedding in New York's Grace Church in 1863. In the course of their wedding trip President Lincoln received them at the White House. The general and his wife continued to entertain audiences in the United States and abroad until their retirement in 1882. Of his enormous earnings Tom Thumb spent tens of thousands of dollars for yachts, horses, and precious stones. He died at the age of 45, and Mrs. Tom Thumb died at 77.

tom-tom, name popularly applied to high-pitched hand drums, usually barrel-shaped and having either one or two drumheads of skin. They are tunable

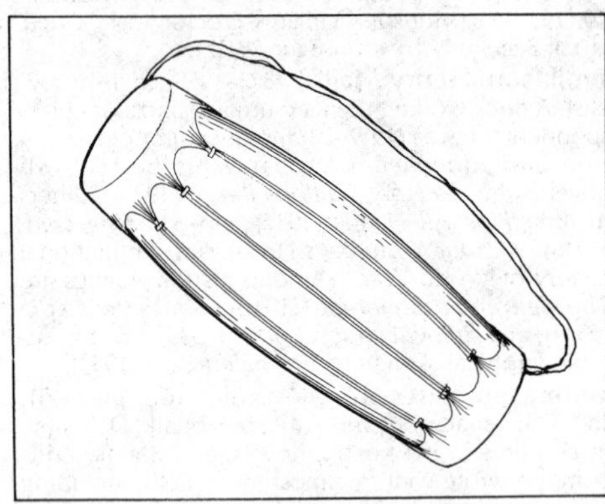

Tom-tom

to specific pitches. Supposedly of American Indian or Oriental origin, they are sometimes used in modern dance orchestras for special effects. The terms *tom-tom* and *tam-tam* are sometimes confused; the latter is another name for the gong.

ton: see ENGLISH UNITS OF MEASUREMENT.

tonality (tōnăl'ĭtē), in music, quality by which all tones of a composition are heard in relation to a central tone called the keynote or tonic. In music that has HARMONY the terms KEY and *tonality* are practically synonymous; those who make a distinction are unable to state it precisely. Some relationship to a tonic is characteristic of all music except that in which it is deliberately avoided (see ATONALITY and SERIAL MUSIC). The term *tonality* is also used in contrast to *modality* (see MODE).

Tonawanda (tŏnəwŏn'də), city (1970 pop. 21,898), Erie co., NW N.Y., on the Niagara River at the terminus of the Barge Canal; inc. as a village 1854, as a city 1903. An industrial suburb of Buffalo and a lake port, Tonawanda is a commercial center and a transshipment point; its manufactures include steel, office equipment, and plastics.

Tonbridge (tŭn'brĭj), urban district (1971 pop. 31,006), Kent, SE England. Tonbridge is mainly residential with light industry including printing and sawmilling. It is a railroad junction. The public school was founded in 1553.

Tønder (tö'nər), Ger. *Tondern,* town (1970 com. pop. 11,631), Sønderjylland co., SW Denmark, near the West German border. It has long been famous for its lace industry and also has breweries and meat-packing plants. The picturesque town was held by Prussia from 1864 to 1920.

Tone, Theobald Wolfe, 1763-98, Irish revolutionary. He was called to the bar in 1789 but soon turned his attention to politics. Inspired by the example of the French Revolution, he helped found (1791) the United Irish Society (see UNITED IRISHMEN), which worked to unite Roman Catholics and Protestants in a common cause against English oppression of Ireland. He played a leading role in the Catholic convention of 1792 that pressed the British government to pass the Catholic Relief Act (1793). In 1794 he was implicated in the intrigues for a French invasion of Ireland, but was allowed to leave the country for the United States. He negotiated (1795) with the French minister concerning French aid in an Irish rebellion and in 1796 went to Paris. He organized several ill-fated expeditions to Ireland, finally joining one intended to aid the 1798 rebellion in Ireland. His force was defeated by an English squadron off Lough Swilly (Donegal), and Tone was captured. He was court-martialed and convicted of treason, but he committed suicide before his execution could be carried out. He was the author of a number of political pamphlets. These, with his autobiography and journals, were edited (1826) by his son. See his letters (ed. by Bulmer Hobson, 1920); biography by Frank MacDermot (1939).

tone. In music, a tone is distinguished from noise by its definite pitch, caused by the regularity of the vibrations which produce it. Any tone possesses the attributes of pitch, intensity, and quality. Pitch is determined by the frequency of the vibration, measured in cycles per second; intensity (or loudness) is determined by the amplitude, measured in decibels. Quality is determined by the overtones (see HARMONIC), the distinctive timbre of any instrument being the result of the number and relative prominence of the overtones it produces. When two fairly loud tones of equal volume but different pitch are sounded together, a fainter resultant tone, representing either the sum of their two rates of vibration (summation tone) or the difference (difference tone) may be heard. The term whole tone or whole step refers to the INTERVAL of a major second or its equivalent; the term half tone, semitone, or half step denotes a minor second (see SCALE).

tone poem: see SYMPHONIC POEM.

Tonga (tŏng'gə), island kingdom (1972 est. pop. 92,360), 270 sq mi (699 sq km), South Pacific, c.2000 mi (3,220 km) NE of Sydney, Australia. Tonga is the only surviving independent kingdom in the South Pacific. The more than 150 islands constitute three main groups: Tongatabu (the seat of NUKUALOFA, the capital) in the south, Vavau in the north, and Haapai in the center. Most of the islands are volcanic, with active craters, but several are coral atolls. The native Polynesians grow subsistence crops and export copra and bananas. Because of compulsory primary education, the literacy rate is relatively high. Every male Tongan over the age of 16 is entitled to an allotment of land; but the shortage of land precludes a holding for many. Dutch navigators discovered the northern islands in 1616 and the rest of the group in 1643. Capt. James COOK visited the islands in 1773 and 1777 and named them the Friendly Islands. English missionaries arrived in 1797 and helped to strengthen British political influence. Internal wars in the early 19th cent. ended with the accession of King George Tupou I (1845-93), who unified the nation and gave it a constitution (1862), a legal code, and an administrative system. His successor, King George Tupou II (1893-1918) concluded a treaty making Tonga a British protectorate in 1900. Tonga remained self-governing, with the British responsible for foreign and defense affairs. A new treaty in 1968 reduced British controls, and complete independence was attained on June 4, 1970. Tonga is a member of the Commonwealth of Nations. The present ruler is King Taufaahau Tupou IV, son of the late queen Salote Tupou III (1918-65). In addition to the king, there is a partially elected legislative assembly, a privy council, and a cabinet headed by a prime minister.

Tongariro (tŏng″gərē'rō), volcanic peak, 6,458 ft (1,968 m) high, on North Island, New Zealand. Hot springs are on its slopes and a lake is on the summit.

Tongeren (tông'ərən), Fr. *Tongres,* town (1970 pop. 17,028), Limburg prov., E Belgium. It is the trade center of the productive Hesbaye farm region. As a center of Gaul, it was a major Roman stronghold, flourishing in the reign of Tiberius (A.D. 14-37). The town was destroyed (4th cent.) by the Salian Franks and again (881) by the Norsemen. Of note are the Church of Notre Dame (9th-15th cent.), with Romanesque cloisters, as well as the town's Roman walls and its many houses dating from the 16th and 17th cent.

Tongres: see TONGEREN, Belgium.

tongue, muscular organ occupying the floor of the mouth in higher animals. In some animals, such as lizards, anteaters, and frogs, it serves a food-gathering function. In humans it functions principally in chewing, swallowing, and speaking. The human tongue is covered by a mucous membrane containing small projections called papillae, which give it a rough surface. Tiny taste organs, or buds, are scattered over the entire surface of the papillae, with large numbers concentrated on the circumvallate papillae, toward the back of the tongue. The appearance of the tongue is often an indication of body health; normal is a pinkish-red color. In impairment of the digestion and in certain feverish diseases, a yellowish coating forms. Local infection of the tongue is called THRUSH.

tonic, in music: see HARMONY; KEY; SCALE; TONALITY.

tonic sol-fa: see MUSICAL NOTATION.

tonka bean (tŏng'kə), black-skinned, aromatic, almondlike single seed from the pod of any tall leguminous tree of the genus *Dipteryx* in the family Leguminosae (PULSE family) of tropical South America. It contains coumarin, a fermented substance that has a vanillalike aroma and is used as a vanilla substitute and in the manufacture of perfumes, sachets, soaps, tobacco, and food. Natural coumarin has been almost completely replaced by a synthetic product. The name of the bean also appears as tonqua bean and tonquin bean. Plants producing tonka beans are classified in the division MAGNOLIOPHYTA, class Magnoliopsida, order Rosales, family Leguminosae.

Tonkin (tŏn'kĭn', tŏng'—), historic region (c.40,000 sq mi/103,600 sq km), SE Asia, now forming the heartland of North Vietnam. The capital was HANOI. Tonkin was bordered on the north by China, on the east by the Gulf of Tonkin, on the south by the historic region of ANNAM (which is now divided between North and South Vietnam), and on the S and W by Laos. The region of Tonkin was conquered in 111 B.C. by the Chinese, who ruled until they were ousted in A.D. 939, at which time the area became independent. The inhabitants began a southward expansion, and by 1471 they had acquired the kingdom of CHAMPA. After the division of the Vietnamese lands between two dynasties in 1558, the northern half was ruled from the city of Tonkin (modern Hanoi); thus the name of Tonkin came to be applied by Europeans to the whole area. The two regions were reunited in 1802 under the rule of the restored line of Hue as part of the empire of Vietnam. To open the Red River to French trade, French expeditions were sent into Tonkin in 1873 and 1882; that of 1882 resulted in a full-scale colonial war, complicated by Chinese intervention (China also claimed the region) against the French. In 1884, Annam accepted a French protectorate, conceding France a separate protectorate over Tonkin with control more direct than over Annam. In 1887, Tonkin became part of the Union of Indochina. In World War II, the region was occupied (1940-45) by the Japanese. After the war Tonkinese and Annamese nationalist leaders joined in demanding independence for the state of Vietnam, and Tonkin was torn by guerrilla warfare between the French and the Viet Minh nationalists led by Ho Chih Minh. The name also appears as Tongking and Tonking.

Tonkin, Gulf of, NW arm of the South China Sea, c.300 mi (480 km) long and 150 mi (240 km) wide, between North Vietnam and China. The shallow gulf (less than 200 ft/60 m deep) receives the Red River. Haiphong, North Vietnam, and Peihai (Pakhoi), China, are the chief ports. An alleged attack (Aug., 1964) by North Vietnamese gunboats against U.S. naval forces stationed in the gulf led to increased U.S. involvement in the Vietnam War.

Tonkin Gulf resolution, in U. S. history, Congressional resolution passed in 1964 that authorized military action in Southeast Asia. On August 4, 1964, North Vietnamese torpedo boats in the Gulf of Tonkin attacked U. S. destroyers that were reporting intelligence information to South Vietnam. President Lyndon B. Johnson and his advisers decided upon immediate air attacks on North Vietnam in retaliation; he also asked Congress for a mandate for future military action. On August 7, Congress passed a resolution drafted by the administration authorizing all necessary measures to repel attacks against U. S. forces and all steps necessary for the defense of U.S. allies in Southeast Asia. Although there was disagreement in Congress over the precise meaning of the Tonkin Gulf resolution, Presidents Johnson and Richard M. Nixon used it to justify later military action in Southeast Asia. The measure was repealed by Congress in 1970.

Tônlé Sap (tŏn'lā säp) [great lake], lake, central Cambodia; largest lake of SE Asia. It occupies the depression of the Cambodian plain and is fed by many streams; the Tônlé Sap River, c.70 mi (110 km) long, drains the lake S into the Mekong River near Phnom Pénh. At low water in the dry season (November–May), the lake covers c.1,100 sq mi (2,850 sq km). During the summer floods, however, the waters of the Mekong back up into Tônlé Sap (which forms a natural reservoir) raising the lake's level c.30 ft (9 m) and more than tripling its area. Approximately 2,500 sq mi (6,475 sq km) of surrounding forest are inundated by the floodwaters and provide a breeding ground for fish. The fisheries of the lake are one of Cambodia's major natural resources. The Tônlé Sap lake and river are also part of an important inland waterway system.

Tönnies, Ferdinand (fĕr'dēnänt tön'yəs), 1855–1936, German sociologist and political scientist. He is noted for his analysis of the distinction between the older form of spontaneous community based on mutual aid and trust and the modern kind of society in which self-interest predominates. See his *Gemeinschaft und Gesellschaft* (1877; tr. *Community and Society,* 1957); selected writings, ed. by W. J. Cahnman and Rudolf Heberle (1971).

tonqua bean: see TONKA BEAN.

Tønsberg (tŏns'bĕr), city (1970 pop. 10,862), capital of Vestfold co., SE Norway, a port on the Skagerrak near the mouth of the Oslofjord. It is a shipping and whaling center and has industries that manufacture forest products and processed food. Tønsberg was founded c.870 and is the oldest city of Norway.

tonsils, name commonly referring to the palatine tonsils, two ovoid masses of lymphoid tissue situated on either side of the throat at the back of the tongue. The pharyngeal tonsils, or ADENOIDS, are masses of similar tissue located in the nasopharynx, and the lingual tonsils are rounded masses of tissue on the back of the tongue. The tonsils act as a filter against disease organisms. However, they often become a site of infection, a condition known as tonsillitis, and sometimes become enlarged. This condition is more prevalent during childhood, since tonsil tissue tends to regress with age. Removal of the tonsils is sometimes advised if frequent inflammation poses a threat to health. See RESPIRATION.

Tonson, Jacob (tŏn'sən), 1656?–1736, English publisher. He and his brother Richard purchased the publication rights to Milton's *Paradise Lost,* a transaction later claimed as the firm's most profitable. With John Dryden he published a series of miscellany volumes (6 vol., 1684–1709), edited by Dryden and often referred to as Dryden's miscellany or Tonson's miscellany. Tonson was secretary of the Kit-Cat Club, a literary club which he founded c.1700, and was publisher of works by Addison, Steele, and Pope, among others. See study by K. M. Lynch (1971).

Tonstall, Cuthbert: see TUNSTALL, CUTHBERT.

tonsure (tŏn'shər) [Lat.,=to shave], formerly, practice in some Christian churches of cutting some of the hair from the scalp of clerics. In the West the tonsure consisted of a circular patch on the crown of the head from which the hair was kept cut; some tonsures kept the entire head shaved above the ears, and some retained a broad band of hair around the head. Different religious orders had different tonsures. In the 6th and 7th cent. one of the outstanding questions between the Celtic use and the Roman use was the tonsure, which the Celts made by cutting the hair off the front part of the head. The Roman Catholic Church abolished the practice of tonsure in 1972. See ORDERS, HOLY.

Tonti or **Tonty, Henri de** (both: äNrē' də tôNtē'), c.1650–1704, French explorer in North America, b. Italy. Serving in the French army, he lost a hand in battle; his skillful use of the appliance with which the hand was replaced was later to lead American Indians to believe him possessed of special powers. In 1678, Tonti accompanied the explorer LA SALLE to Canada as his lieutenant and was dispatched to Niagara where, among hostile Indians, he constructed the *Griffon,* the first sailboat to ply the Great Lakes W of Ontario. Tonti preceded La Salle westward to Detroit and penetrated into the country of the Illinois Indians, whom he won over to the French interest. In 1680, left by La Salle at Starved Rock to construct a fort, he was faced by desertion of his men and the hostility of the Indians and was forced to winter in Wisconsin. Meeting La Salle at Mackinac the following year, he traveled with him down the Mississippi to its mouth; they proclaimed the entire Mississippi watershed the domain of France. Tonti returned alone to the Illinois River, where he was rejoined by La Salle, and together they completed (1682–83) Fort St. Louis at Starved Rock. When La Salle returned to France, Tonti was left in charge of the fort. La Salle did not return, for he failed in his attempt to find the mouth of the Mississippi by sea. Having no word, Tonti in 1686 descended the river in a hopeless search for La Salle. The following year he took part with a band of Illinois Indians in the raid by the marquis de DENONVILLE against the Iroquois. Tonti remained at Fort St. Louis, developing the new empire, until 1700, when he joined Iberville's colony at the mouth of the Mississippi. Pierre Margry included Tonti's account in *Mémoires et documents pour servir à l'histoire des origines francaises des pays d'outre-mer* (6 vol., 1879–1888; tr. *Relation of Henri de Tonty,* 1898). See J. C. Parish, *The Man with the Iron Hand* (1913); C. B. Reed, *Masters of the Wilderness* (1914); E. R. Murphy, *Henry de Tonty, Fur Trader of the Mississippi* (1941).

Tonto Basin, depression S of the Mogollon Rim, central Ariz. The wild country around Tonto Creek, which flows c.45 mi (70 km) south from the basin to enter the lake behind Roosevelt Dam, has been much celebrated in cowboy stories.

Tonto National Monument: see NATIONAL PARKS AND MONUMENTS (table).

Tonton Macoutes (tŏntŏn' mäko͞ot') [Haitian Creole,=bogeymen], personal police force of dictator François DUVALIER of Haiti. They secured Duvalier's position in power by murdering hundreds of his political opponents, sometimes hanging the corpses in the marketplaces to serve as warnings. They were directly responsible only to Duvalier, who gave them virtual license to torture and kill. Wearing steel-rimmed sunglasses and wielding submachine guns, they prowled the streets, terrorizing the populace. After Duvalier's death (1971), they were replaced by a corps of armed men known as the Leopards, who were organized allegedly to fight Communism.

Tonty, Henri de: see TONTI, HENRI DE.

Tooele (to͞oĭl'ə), city (1970 pop. 12,539), seat of Tooele co., N central Utah, in a farm area; inc. 1853. Major source of employment is the U.S. army ordnance depot, a huge installation that includes the Dugway Proving Ground. Tooele also has a lead-ore smelting industry; the Elton Tunnel (4 mi/6 km long; built 1937–42) in the Oquirrh Mts. leads to the source of the ores in Bingham Canyon. The city was settled (1849) by Mormons on a California wagon route. Of interest are the remains of various stagecoach and pony-express stops.

Tooke, John Horne, 1736–1812, English radical politician and philologist. Born John Horne, he adopted the name Tooke in 1782 after being designated heir to the estate of a rich friend, William Tooke. He became (1760) an Anglican priest but soon abandoned his clerical duties for politics. He was a strong supporter of John WILKES until 1771, when he broke with him and founded the Constitutional Society to promote parliamentary reform and support for the American colonists. He was fined and imprisoned (1778) for attempting to raise funds to aid the victims of the government "murder" at Lexington and Concord. In 1794, in a period of repression of radical agitation, Tooke was tried for treason but acquitted. In 1801 he was elected to Parliament, but in the same year the government passed an act (specifically directed against him) that disqualified clergy from sitting in the House of Commons. Tooke's later years were devoted to literary pursuits. His *Epea Pteroenta, or the Diversions of Purley* (1786–1805) was an early attempt at scientific language study.

Tooke, Thomas, 1774–1858, English economist. His *History of Prices . . . 1793–1856* (6 vol., 1838–57) is a classic exposition. He was a free trader, opposing any governmental restriction on foreign trade.

Toombs, Robert, 1810–85, American statesman, Confederate leader, b. Wilkes co., Ga. A successful lawyer in Georgia, he entered politics as a Whig, serving in the state legislature and in Congress (1845–53). He favored the Compromise of 1850 and with Howell COBB and Alexander H. STEPHENS canvassed Georgia to have it ratified. With them also he organized the short-lived Constitutional Union party, which elected him (1852) to the U.S. Senate, in which he served until 1861. A brilliant orator, Toombs was a firm supporter of Southern measures but did not become an avowed secessionist until after the election of Abraham Lincoln. Thereafter he played a leading role in the Georgia secession and in the organization of the Confederacy. Made secretary of state in the new government, he soon resigned to become a brigadier general commanding Georgia troops in Virginia. He fought in the Peninsular campaign, the second battle of Bull Run, and the Antietam campaign in the Civil War, resigning when he was refused promotion. Toombs, who had coveted the Confederate presidency, belonged to the faction that opposed the policies of Confederate President Jefferson Davis. After the war he fled to Europe, returning in 1867. He continued to be important in Georgia politics, especially after Reconstruction. He himself remained "unreconstructed," refusing to the end to take the oath of allegiance to the United States. See biographies by U. B. Phillips (1913, repr. 1968) and W. Y. Thompson (1966).

tooth: see TEETH.

toothache tree: see PRICKLY ASH.

tooth shell: see MOLLUSCA.

toothwort, any species of the genus *Dentaria* [Lat. *dens*=tooth, for the toothed rhizomes of some species], slender perennials of the family Cruciferae (MUSTARD family), native to north temperate regions. North American species are found chiefly in the eastern half of the continent and in the Pacific coastal region. The edible rhizomes have a pungent flavor similar to that of watercress, giving the name pepperwort to some species. *D. diphylla,* also called crinkleroot, is common to the E United States and was eaten raw or boiled by the Iroquois Indians. It is sometimes cultivated for its large white or purple blossoms. Toothworts are classified in the division MAGNOLIOPHYTA, class Magnoliopsida, order Capparales, family Cruciferae.

Toowoomba (təwo͞om'bə), city (1971 pop. 59,476), Queensland, E Australia, in the Eastern Highlands, at the edge of the Darling Downs, c.2000 ft (610 m) above sea level. The city is an agricultural market center with food-processing and farm-machinery industries and railroad workshops. It is also a summer resort.

top, toy with a tapering point on which it can be made to spin. Tops were known in antiquity and appeared in Europe during the Middle Ages; they are used today in many different regions of the world by both primitive and advanced societies. The principle of its motion is utilized in the GYROSCOPE.

topaz (tō'păz), aluminum silicate mineral with either hydroxyl radicals or fluorine, $Al_2SiO_4(F,OH)_2$, used as a gem. It is commonly colorless or some shade of pale yellow to wine-yellow; pale blue and pale green also occur, but natural red stones are uncommon. Some natural yellow stones lose their yellow coloring when heated and become permanently pink ("pinked" topaz). The stone is transparent with a vitreous luster. It has perfect cleavage on the basal pinacoid, but it is nevertheless hard and durable. The brilliant cut is commonly used. Topaz crystals, which are of the orthorhombic system, occur in highly acid igneous rocks, e.g., granites and rhyolites, and in metamorphic rocks, e.g., gneisses and schists. Important sources of topaz are in Russia, Siberia, Brazil, Australia, Mexico, and in New Hampshire, Colorado, and Utah in the United States. The name topaz is commonly but incorrectly used for various other yellow stones, e.g., for citrine QUARTZ.

tope: see STUPA.

Topeka (təpē'kə), city (1970 pop. 125,011), state capital and seat of Shawnee co., NE Kansas, on the Kansas River; inc. 1857. In a rich agricultural region, it is an important shipping point for cattle and wheat and a wholesaling, marketing, and processing center for farm products. There are railroad shops and offices, insurance businesses, printing and publishing firms, grain mills, meat-packing houses, and plants that make tires and rubber products, shoes, and cellophane. The city is an important center for psychiatric research and therapy; the world famous Menninger Clinic, a veterans mental hospital, and a state mental hospital are there. It is also a popular convention city. A ferry was established there in 1842 on the Oregon Trail. The city was laid out in 1854 by Free State settlers from Lawrence and New England and was founded as the center for C. K. Holliday's projected railroad (the Atchison, Topeka, and Santa Fe). A short-lived Free State constitution was framed in the city in 1855. Topeka was selected state capital when Kansas was admitted to the Union in 1861. It is the seat of Washburn Univ. of Topeka. A city of broad, tree-shaded streets, Topeka has the museum and library of the state historical society, the Mulvane Art Museum, the state library, a notable Episcopal cathedral, and a park system that includes a beautiful rose garden. The capitol is designed after the one in Washington, D.C. Forbes Air Force Base is nearby.

Töpffer, Rodolphe (rôdôlf' töp'fər), 1799–1846, Swiss novelist, b. Geneva. His humorous tales and novels of Swiss life were often illustrated with his own apposite drawings. Töpffer's travelogues of fanciful voyages through the Alps, *Voyages en zigzag* (1844), enjoyed a great vogue.

Tophel (tō'fəl), place in Sinai peninsula, near where the Israelites halted. Deut. 1.1.

Tophet (tō'fĭt), place near Jerusalem, in the valley of HINNOM, associated with the worship of MOLECH. Tophet became a name for HELL. 2 Kings 23.10; Isa. 30.33; Jer. 7.31–33.

topi: see DAMALISK.

topiary work (tō'pēēr"ē), pruning and training of shrubs and trees into ornamental shapes, used in landscape gardening. Elaborate topiary work in which trees and shrubs are clipped to resemble statuary (e.g., birds, nymphs, urns) or are planted to form mazes or intricate geometrical patterns was once popular but now can be seen only in old-fashioned or specialized private gardens or in formal parks and botanical displays. Arborvitae, box, privet, and yew are among the plants most used for topiary gardening. See ESPALIER.

topography (təpŏg'rəfē), description or representation of the features and configuration of land surfaces. Topographic maps use symbols and coloring, with particular attention given to the shape and elevations of terrain. Relief is portrayed by means of contour lines, hachures, shading, or coloring to represent elevations, depressions, and depths of water (see CONTOUR); natural and man-made features, such as rivers, sand dunes, forests, urbanized areas, bridges, tunnels, roads, and power lines, are indicated by means of symbols and color overlays. *Topography* is often used incorrectly as a synonym for *relief*.

topology, branch of MATHEMATICS, formerly known as analysis situs, that is concerned with those properties of geometric figures that are invariant under continuous transformations. A continuous transformation, also called a topological transformation or homeomorphism, is a one-to-one correspondence between the points of one figure and the points of another figure such that points that are arbitrarily close on one figure are transformed into points that are also arbitrarily close on the other figure. Figures that are related in this way are said to be topologically equivalent. Topology is sometimes referred to popularly as "rubber-sheet geometry" because a figure can be changed to an equivalent figure by bending, stretching, twisting, and the like, but not by tearing or cutting; the former transformations are a special type of topological transformation called a continuous deformation. Two figures (e.g, certain types of knots) may be topologically equivalent, however, without being changeable into one another by a continuous deformation. Topology may be roughly divided into point-set topology, which considers figures as SETS of points having such properties as being open or closed, compact, connected, and so forth; combinatorial topology, which, in contrast to point-set topology, considers figures as combinations (complexes) of simple figures (simplexes) joined together in a regular manner; and algebraic topology, which makes extensive use of algebraic methods, particularly those of GROUP theory. There is considerable overlap among these branches. It is intuitively evident that all simple closed curves in the plane and all polygons are topologically equivalent to a circle; similarly, all cylinders, cones, polyhedra, and other simple closed surfaces are equivalent to a sphere. On the other hand, a closed surface such as a torus (doughnut) is not equivalent to a sphere, since no amount of bending or stretching will make it into a sphere, nor is a surface with a boundary equivalent to a sphere, e.g., a sphere with a hole in it, which may be stretched into a disk (a circle plus its interior). There are various properties of a figure, in general, and of a surface such as a sphere, torus, or disk, in particular, that may be used to distinguish between such figures topologically. One property is the number of boundaries the surface has, if any. Another property is orientability; a surface is orientable if a circle drawn on it with a given orientation (clockwise or counterclockwise) always retains that orientation as it is moved around the surface. A sphere and a torus are both orientable, but a Möbius strip (a one-sided surface made by twisting a strip of paper and joining the ends so that opposite edges correspond) is a nonorientable surface, since an oriented circle moved around the strip will return to its original position with its orientation reversed. Another topological property of a surface is its Euler-Poincaré characteristic, which describes the way in which the surface can be divided up into regions, like a map. If V is the number of points (vertices) in the map, E is the number of line segments (edges), and F is the number of regions (faces), then the characteristic is given by $\chi = V - E + F$ and is the same for all possible maps that can be drawn on the given surface. For a sphere, $\chi = 2$, and the formula is identical with Euler's formula for the vertices, edges, and faces of a general polyhedron, to which the sphere is topologically equivalent. For a torus, $\chi = 0$. The Euler-Poincaré characteristic for an orientable surface is $\chi = 2 - 2p$, where p is called the genus of the surface. Any orientable closed surface is topologically equivalent to a sphere with p handles attached to it; e.g., the torus, having $\chi = 0$, is of genus 1 and is equivalent to a sphere with one handle, and a double torus (two-hole doughnut), equivalent to a sphere with two handles, is of genus 2 and has $\chi = -2$. For a nonorientable surface, $\chi = 2 - q$, where q is the number of cross-caps that must be added to a sphere to make it equivalent to the surface. (A cross-cap is a cap with a twist like a Möbius strip in it.) Closely related to the Euler-Poincaré characteristic is the connectivity number of a surface, which is equal to the largest number of closed cuts (or cuts connecting points on boundaries or on previous cuts) that can be made on the surface without separating it into two or more parts. The connectivity number is equal to $3 - \chi$ for a closed surface and to $2 - \chi$ for a surface with boundaries (e.g., a disk). A surface with a connectivity number of 1, 2, or 3 is said to be simply connected, doubly connected, or triply connected, respectively, and similarly for more complex surfaces; a sphere is simply connected, while a torus is triply connected. Thus, any surface can be classified by its boundary curves (if any), its orientability, and its Euler-Poincaré characteristic or connectivity number; and any surface is topologically equivalent to a sphere with an appropriate number of handles, cross-caps, or holes. A surface is a simple example of a topological space, the basic entity studied in topology. Different types of topological spaces are defined according to axioms satisfied by the sets of points that constitute the space. Especially important are topological spaces for which a distance function is defined for every pair of points in the space; such spaces are called metric spaces. A full treatment of the properties of topological spaces of arbitrary dimension requires various concepts of an advanced nature, e.g., homology theory, and is beyond the scope of a general article.

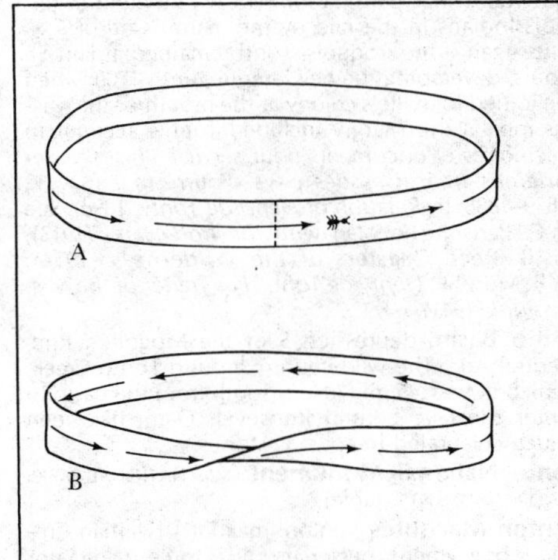

Möbius strip: On the ordinary flat loop (A), an ant walking along the middle of the strip will pass only around the outside of the strip. If the strip is cut along the dotted line, twisted once, and rejoined to form the Möbius strip (B), different topological space results; the ant walking along the middle of the strip will pass around both inside and outside.

Torah (tôr'ə), [Heb.,=teachings or learning], Hebrew name for the five books of Moses—the Law of Moses or the Pentateuch, the first five books of the Bible. The Torah is believed by Orthodox Jews to have been handed down to Moses on Mt. Sinai and transmitted by him to the Jews. It laid down the fundamental laws of moral and physical conduct. The Torah begins with a description of the origin of the universe and ends on the word *Israel,* after the story of the death of Moses, just before the conquest of Canaan by the Israelites. In a wider sense the Torah includes all teachings of Judaism, the entire Old Testament and the Talmud.

Torbay, county borough (1971 pop. 108,888), Devon, SW England. Torbay, created in 1968, comprises the former municipal borough of Torquay and the urban districts of Paignton and Brixham. On Tor Bay, it is a noted resort area, known as the "English Riviera." William of Orange landed at Brixham in 1688. A cave on Windmill Hill contains animal bones and flint implements from the Paleolithic period. An annual yachting regatta is held at Torbay.

Torcello (tōrchĕl'lō), village, on a small island of the same name in the Lagoon of Venice, NE Italy, NE of Venice. A prosperous town until the early Middle Ages, it has a Byzantine cathedral (founded 639; rebuilt 867 and 1008) that is decorated with fine Byzantine mosaics (12th–13th cent.). Also of note is the Romanesque Church of Santa Fosca (late 11th cent.).

Tordesillas, Treaty of (tōr"thāsē'lyäs), 1494, agreement signed at Tordesillas, Spain, by which Spain and Portugal divided the non-Christian world into two zones of influence. In principle the treaty followed the papal bull issued in 1493 by Pope Alexander VI, which fixed the demarcation line along a circle passing 100 leagues W of the Cape Verde Islands and through the two poles. This division gave the entire New World to Spain and Africa and India to Portugal. However, the Treaty of Tordesillas shifted the demarcation line to a circle passing 370 leagues W of the Cape Verde Islands and thus gave Portugal a claim to Brazil. There was little geographic knowledge at the time the treaty was signed, and it remains controversial whether the Portuguese then knew of the existence of Brazil.

Torgau (tôr'gou), city (1970 pop. 21,688), Leipzig district, S central East Germany, a port on the Elbe River. Manufactures include chemicals, glass, pottery, and agricultural machinery. Long a strategic crossing point on the Elbe, Torgau was chartered in the 13th cent. In 1526 the Protestant princes founded the Torgau League there. The articles of the league were written (1530) by Luther, Melanchthon, and others, and they served as a basis for part of the Augsburg Confession. In the Thirty Years War, Gustavus II of Sweden and his allies held (1631) an important council of war in Torgau. In the Seven Years War, Frederick II of Prussia defeated (1760) the Austrians under Daun near the city. Torgau passed in 1815 to Prussia. On April 27, 1945, near the end of World War II, advance elements of the U.S. and Soviet armies made contact for the first time there. Noteworthy buildings of the city include the 16th-century city hall; a late Gothic church in which Luther's wife, Katharina von Bora, is buried; and the Renaissance-style Hartenfels castle (16th cent.), a residence of the electors of Saxony.

Torino: see TURIN, Italy.

tornado, dark, funnel-shaped cloud containing violently rotating air that develops below a heavy cumulonimbus cloud mass and extends toward the earth. The funnel twists about, rises and falls, and where it reaches the earth causes great destruction. The diameter of a tornado varies from a few feet to a mile; the rotating winds attain velocities of 200 to 300 mi (320–480 km) per hr, and the updraft at the center may reach 200 mi per hr. A tornado is usually accompanied by thunder, lightning, heavy rain, and a loud "freight train" noise. In comparison with a CYCLONE, a tornado covers a much smaller area but is much more violent and destructive. The atmospheric conditions required for the formation of a tornado include great thermal instability, high humidity, and the convergence of warm, moist air at low levels with cooler, drier air aloft. In the United States a tornado forms typically over the central and southern plains and the Gulf states, usually several hundred miles southeast of a cyclone. It travels in a generally northeasterly direction with a speed of 20 to 40 mi (32–64 km) per hr. The length of a tornado's path along the ground varies from less than one mile to several hundred. Cyclone cellars are generally constructed near farm dwellings to afford protection in areas where tornadoes are common. Tornadoes occurring over water are called WATERSPOUTS.

Torneälv (tōr'nəĕlv), Finnish *Torniojoki,* river, c.320 mi (510 km) long, rising in N Sweden at the Norwegian border. The river, which drains Torneträsk lake (126 sq mi/326 sq km), flows SW into the Gulf of Bothnia. It receives the Lainioälv at Anttis and forms the Swedish-Finnish frontier below its junction with the Muonioälv (Finnish *Muoniojoki*), its chief tributary. The Muonioälv forms the Swedish-Finnish frontier from its source at the Norwegian border to its confluence with the Torneälv. The Torneälv has several falls and is rich in salmon. Haparanda (Sweden) and Tornio (Finland) are located at its mouth.

Torngat Mountains, N Labrador, Canada, northernmost range of the Laurentian Plateau, between the Atlantic coast and the Quebec border, extending c.120 mi (190 km) north-south and rising to 5,160 ft (1,573 m) in Cirque Mt.

Tornio (tôr'nēō), Swed. *Torneå*, city (1970 pop. 7,481), Lappi prov. (Lapland), NW Finland, at the mouth of the Torneälv on the Gulf of Bothnia. It is a trade center and export point for forest products. It was chartered in 1621 and has the oldest extant wooden church (1684) in Finland.

Toronto (tərŏn'tō), city (1971 pop. 712,786; metropolitan pop. 2,628,043), provincial capital, S Ont., Canada, on Lake Ontario. Toronto is the second largest city in Canada. It is a port of entry and an important commercial, financial, and industrial center as well as the banking and stock-exchange center of the country and its chief wholesale-distributing point. Its importance as a port and transshipment point has increased since the opening (1959) of the St. Lawrence Seaway. Toronto's industries include slaughtering and meat packing, printing and publishing, and the manufacture of aircraft, farm implements, electrical machinery, and metal products. The site was an early fur-trading center. The French built (1749) Fort Rouille there to counteract British influence in the Niagara country, but the post was destroyed (1759) to prevent its occupation by the British. The British purchased the site from Indians in 1787 and it became the home of many American Loyalists. It was chosen by Sir John Simcoe in 1793 to be the capital of Upper Canada (see ONTARIO) and was named York. In the War of 1812 the city was raided twice by the Americans, and many buildings were destroyed. In 1834 it was incorporated as Toronto. The city was the scene of the insurrection led by William Lyon Mackenzie in 1873. Toronto has many buildings of historical interest and numerous parks. Exhibition Park is the site of the annual Canadian National Exhibition. The Toronto city hall is a modernistic structure completed in 1965. The Univ. of Toronto was chartered in 1827 and opened in 1843 as King's College. It was renamed in 1850 and is Canada's largest university and most important graduate research center. York Univ. is also in Toronto. Other notable institutions are the Pontifical Institute of Medieval Studies; the Osgoode Hall law school; and the Royal Ontario Museum, housing an important collection of Chinese art. Toronto has Anglican and Roman Catholic bishoprics and is the headquarters of the United Church of Canada.

Toronto, University of, at Toronto, Ont., Canada; nondenominational; provincially supported; coeducational; founded 1827 as King's College. It achieved university status in 1849. It has faculties of arts and science, architecture, urban and regional planning and landscape architecture, music, dentistry, education, management studies, applied science and engineering, library science, food science, social work, forestry, law, medicine, nursing, and pharmacy, as well as schools of graduate studies, hygiene, and physical and health education.

torpedo, fish: see RAY.

torpedo, in naval warfare, a self-propelled submarine projectile loaded with explosives, used for the destruction of enemy ships. Although there were attempts at subsurface warfare in the 16th and 17th cent., the modern torpedo had its origin in the efforts of David Bushnell who, during the American Revolution, experimented with a SUBMARINE for attaching underwater explosives to British ships. His attempts failed, but later Robert Fulton experimented with similar ideas. In the 19th cent. torpedoes developed at first as stationary mines placed in the water; these were used extensively by the Russians in the Crimean War and by the Confederacy in the U.S. Civil War. The first truly self-propelled torpedo was designed and built at Fiume in 1866 by Robert Whitehead, an Englishman. It was driven by a small reciprocating engine run by compressed air; a hydrostatic valve and pendulum balance, connected to a horizontal rudder, controlled the depth at which it ran. Directional accuracy was achieved in 1885 when John Adams Howell developed the gyroscope to control the vertical rudder. Torpedoes were used by Japan in the Russo-Japanese War and were widely employed in World War I. The torpedoes used in World War II were usually 20 to 24 ft (6.1-7.3 m) long, carrying up to 600 lb (272 kg) of explosives at a speed of 50 knots for more than 10,000 yd (9,144 m). The type of torpedo used in World War II has been largely superseded by the homing torpedo. In contrast to the older type, which traveled in a straight line on a preset course, the homing torpedo automatically changes its course to seek out its target. Most homing torpedoes are activated by sounds coming from the target (e.g., propeller or machinery noises), and they follow the sounds until making contact with the target. A homing torpedo runs through three phases: the enabling run, which takes it to the vicinity of the target; the search pattern, in which it maneuvers to find the target; and the homing, in which it pursues the target. The modern torpedo is generally propelled by an electric motor, but some of the newer, faster, high-diving torpedoes, designed for effectiveness against nuclear submarines, have solid-propellant-driven turbines. Some also may be equipped with nuclear warheads. Torpedoes can be fired from shore stations, surface vessels, and aircraft, as well as from submarines. See Bureau of Naval Personnel, *Principles of Naval Ordnance and Gunnery* (1959); Robert Fulton, *Torpedo War and Submarine Explosions* (1810, repr. 1971).

torpedo boat, small fast warship built specially for using the torpedo as a means of attack. The first modern TORPEDO boat was the *Lightning,* built for the British navy in 1877 by the shipyards of Sir John Isaac Thornycroft. Torpedo boats were adopted by most of the world's major navies, but as they increased in size the DESTROYER was developed as an effective defense against them. They diminished in importance after the Russo-Japanese War (1904-5) and were used sparingly in World War I, but they were widely employed in World War II. At that time torpedo boats were commonly used in attacking enemy coastal shipping and light naval forces under cover of darkness and bad weather. They were usually wooden vessels 75 to 125 ft (22.8-38.1 m) long, powered by gasoline or diesel engines and capable of very high speeds. See *Jane's Fighting Ships* (pub. annually since 1897); Bryan Cooper, *The Battle of the Torpedo Boats* (1970).

Torquay: see TORBAY.

torque, in physics, that which tends to change the rate of rotation of a body; also called the MOMENT OF FORCE. The torque produced by rotating parts of an electric motor or internal-combustion engine is often used as a measure of its ability to do useful work. The magnitude of the torque acting on a body is equal to the product of the force acting on the body and the distance from its point of application to the axis around which the body is free to rotate. Only the component of the force lying in the plane of rotation and perpendicular to the radius from the axis of rotation to the point of application contributes to the torque. This radius is called the moment arm, or lever arm. The net torque acting on a body is always equal to the product of the body's moment of inertia about its axis of rotation and its observed angular ACCELERATION. If a body undergoes no angular acceleration, there is no net torque acting on it. Units of torque are units of force multiplied by units of distance, e.g., newton-meters, dyne-centimeters, and foot-pounds (or pound-feet).

Torquemada, Juan de (hwän dā tôrkāmä'thä), 1388-1468, Spanish churchman, cardinal of the Roman Catholic Church; an uncle of Tomás de Torquemada. He entered (1403) the Dominican order and later participated in the councils of Constance and Basel, where he strenuously defended the supreme papal authority against the conciliar theory. He was made a cardinal by Pope Eugene IV in 1439 and was sent on diplomatic missions. He wrote several theological works.

Torquemada, Tomás de (tōmäs'), 1420-98, Spanish churchman and inquisitor. A Dominican, he became confessor to Ferdinand II and Isabella I and in 1483 was appointed inquisitor general of Castile and Aragón, charged with the centralization of the Spanish INQUISITION. He was largely instrumental in bringing about the expulsion of the Jews in 1492. His great authority was contested by colleagues and was diminished in some measure by the pope, but he remained preeminent until his death. Torquemada owes his reputation for cruelty to the harsh rules of procedure that he devised for the Inquisition and to the rigor with which he had them enforced.

Torrance, industrial city (1970 pop. 134,584), Los Angeles co., S Calif.; inc. 1921. It has large aircraft, electronics, and oil industries. Among the many other manufactures are aluminum products, steel, chemicals, and oil-field equipment. A junior college is there.

Torre Annunziata (tôr'rä än-nōōntsyä'tä), city (1971 pop. 58,906), Campania, S Italy, on the Bay of Naples and at the foot of Mt. Vesuvius. It is a port and seaside resort. Founded in the early 14th cent., the city was destroyed by the eruption of Vesuvius in 1631.

Torre del Greco (tôr'rā dĕl grĕ'kō), city (1971 pop. 92,610), Campania, S Italy, on the Bay of Naples, near Mt. Vesuvius. It is a fishing port and a popular seaside resort. The coral industry has been a specialty of the town since the 16th cent. Torre del Greco has been damaged a number of times by volcanic eruptions.

Torremolinos (tôrāmōlē'nōs), town, Málaga prov., S Spain, in Andalusia, on the Mediterranean Sea. It is a very popular resort.

Torrens, Sir Robert Richard (tŏr'ənz), 1814-84, Australian statesman, b. Ireland. Son of Col. Robert Torrens (1780-1864), one of the founders of South Australia, he went to that colony in 1839. There he served (1851-55) in the colonial legislature. When self-government was introduced (1856) he entered the assembly, and he was briefly prime minister in 1857. He secured the passage (1858) of a landholding reform known as the Torrens Act, which substituted public registration for the old conveyance system, in which land transfer could only be accomplished through a complicated tracing of deeds. The Torrens system has since been widely copied. Torrens resigned from the assembly to administer the act. Pensioned in 1863, he settled in England and served in Parliament from 1868 to 1874.

Torrens, Lake, shallow salt lake, 2,230 sq mi (5,776 sq km), central South Australia state, Australia. In a rift valley, it is 120 mi (193 km) long and is Australia's second largest lake. It becomes partially dry in the summer.

Torreón (tôrāōn'), city (1970 pop. 257,045), Coahuila state, N Mexico, on the Nazas River. It is the metropolis of the LAGUNA DISTRICT, where the land, extensively irrigated, is some of Mexico's finest. Cotton and wheat are the principal crops, and cattle raising is important. Torreón's industries include a rubber factory, foundries, cotton and flour mills, a brewery, and a large smelter. The city is also one of the leading commercial and rail centers of N Mexico. It was founded in 1893.

Torres, Juan José (hwän hōsā' tōr'rās), 1921–, president of Bolivia (1970-71). An army general of Indian background, he assumed the presidency in a counter coup (Oct., 1970) after the ouster of President Ovando Candia. As president, he expropriated U.S. companies, ousted the U.S. Peace Corps, outlawed political parties, and strengthened economic ties with Communist countries. He was deposed by a military-civilian coalition, which installed Col. Hugo Banzer in his place. In exile, Torres organized the National Left Alliance against the rightist government.

Torres Bodet, Jaime (hī'mä tôr'rās bôdĕt'), 1902-74, Mexican poet, diplomat, short-story writer, and essayist. Torres Bodet's first book of poems, *Fervor* (1918), reveals the influence of symbolism and *modernismo*, but his later poetry shows the effect of the European avant-garde and is cosmopolitan in tone. His outstanding early poems were collected in *Poesías* (1926). *Sin tregua* (1957) and *Selected Poems* (bilingual ed. 1964) contain later verse. Narratives collected in *Margarita de niebla* (1927), *Proserpina rescatada* (1931), and *Nacimiento de Venus* (1941) reveal his refined, erudite playfulness. *Contemporáneos* (1938) and *Tres inventores de realidad* (1955) contain some of his major critical essays. Torres Bodet has held many important government posts. See study by Sonja Karsen (1971).

Torres Naharro, Bartolomé de (bärtōlōmā' thā tō'rās nä-ä'rō), fl. 1531, Spanish dramatist and lyric poet, b. Extremadura. As a young man he went to Italy and became a priest. Greatly influenced by the Italian Renaissance, he is considered the originator of the modern Spanish secular theater. He is known for his *Propaladia* (1517), a collection of eight plays and a prologue; the prologue is the first theoretical exposition of dramatic precepts for the Spanish stage. See his *Propaladia and Other Works,* ed. by J. E. Gillet (4 vol., 1943-61); study by J. G. Gillet (1961).

Torres Strait (tŏr'ĭz, -rĭs), channel, c.95 mi (153 km) wide, between New Guinea and Cape York Peninsula of Australia. It connects the Arafura and Coral seas. The strait is shallow, with many reefs and islands, and is hazardous for navigation. Pearl fishing is the main activity in the strait. Discovered in 1606, it is named for Spanish explorer Luis Torres.

Tôrres Vedras (tō'rəsh vā'drəsh), town (1960 pop. 13,196), Lisboa dist., W central Portugal, in Estremadura. Wine and minor manufactures are produced. The town was captured from the Moors by Alfonso I soon after he took Lisbon (1147) but was reconquered by the Almohads briefly in 1189. Tôrres Vedras was an important fortress and royal residence throughout the Middle Ages and was an important strategic point in the Peninsular War (1810).

Torrey, John, 1796–1873, American botanist and chemist, b. New York City, M.D. College of Physicians and Surgeons, 1818. He was professor of chemistry (1827–55) at his alma mater and professor of chemistry and natural history (1830–54) at Princeton. From 1853 he was chief assayer in the U.S. assay office in New York City. His herbarium was presented (1860) to Columbia, and in 1899 it was transferred to the New York Botanical Garden. He was a founder of the New York Academy of Sciences and of the Torrey Botanical Club. A genus of evergreen trees, *Torreya,* is named for him. He wrote *A Flora of the State of New York* (1843) and, with Asa Gray, *A Flora of North America* (2 vol., 1838–43). See study by A. D. Rodgers (1965); catalog of Torrey's manuscripts in the New York Botanical Garden Library, comp. by Sara Lenley et al. (1973).

Torricelli, Evangelista (āvänjālĕ'stä tōr-rēchĕl'lē), 1608–47, Italian physicist and mathematician. He was Galileo's secretary (1641–42) and his successor as professor of philosophy and mathematics at Florence. He invented the barometer (1643), called the Torricelli tube, and a microscope, and he improved the telescope.

torrid zone: see TROPICS.

Torrigiano, Pietro (pyĕ'trō tōr-rējä'nō), 1472–1528, Florentine Renaissance sculptor. Upon leaving Florence in 1492, he worked in Rome and small Italian cities until his departure for the Netherlands, where he worked for the court. By 1511 he was in England, where his gilt bronze masterpiece, the tomb of King Henry VII and his queen, is preserved in Westminster Abbey. In Spain from c.1522, he executed the fine terra-cotta statues of St. Jerome and the *Virgin and Child* (both: Seville Mus.). Two male portrait busts in the Metropolitan Museum exemplify his firmly modeled, refined, and dignified style. Torrigiano is said to have broken Michelangelo's nose in a quarrel when they were fellow students.

Torrijos Herrera, Omar (ōmär' tōrē'hōs ārā'rä), 1929–, Panamanian military and political leader. He joined the national guard in 1952 and as a lieutenant colonel led, together with Col. Boris Martínez, the coup that ousted President Arias in Oct., 1968. In March, 1969, he exiled Martínez, becoming effective ruler of Panama and promoting himself to brigadier general. After Dec., 1969, when he thwarted an attempt by younger officers to depose him, he tightened his grip on the country, curtailing some civil liberties. He instituted wide-ranging economic and social reforms, espousing birth control, expropriating land, and attacking the powerful families that had long controlled Panama's wealth. He vigorously pushed Panama's claim to the Canal Zone, negotiating firmly with the United States. In Sept., 1972, a newly elected assembly granted Torrijos full civil and military powers for a period of six years.

Torrington, George Byng, Viscount (bĭng, tŏr'ĭngtən), 1663–1733, British admiral. Early in his career he helped win the support of the navy for William of Orange in the Glorious Revolution of 1688. After thwarting attempted Jacobite invasions in 1708 and 1715 and defeating a Spanish fleet in the Strait of Messina in 1718, he was raised to the peerage in 1721. He was the father of Admiral John Byng. See *Byng Papers* (ed. by Brian Tunstall, 3 vol., 1930–33).

Torrington, city (1970 pop. 31,952), Litchfield co., NW Conn., on the Naugatuck River; inc. 1740. It is the industrial and commercial hub of NW Connecticut and is known for its metal (especially brass) and machinery manufactures. The first machine-made brass goods in the country were produced in Torrington in 1834. The city was also the site of the world's first condensed-milk plant, and the process of homogenization was invented in Torrington. The abolitionist John Brown was born there; his birthplace burned in 1918 and the spot is now marked by a plaque. Points of interest include the Santa Claus Christmas village, operated annually by the city; a wildlife sanctuary and conservation area, noted for its beautiful mountain laurel; and a museum with early American glass exhibits and a John Brown room. A two-year branch of the Univ. of Connecticut is in Torrington.

Torroja y Miret, Eduardo (ā"dwär'thō tō-rō'hä ē mērĕt'), 1900–1961, Spanish structural architect. With José Maria Aguirre he founded (1934) an experimental institute to develop new uses and theories for reinforced concrete. Examples of his building technique are the Algeciras market (1933), in which the shell construction spans a diameter of 156 ft (48 m), and the Madrid hippodrome (1935), featuring a 73-ft (22-m) cantilevered roof.

Tórshavn or **Thorshavn** (both: tôrs"houn'), city (1966 pop. 9,738), capital of the Faeroe Islands, on SE Streymoy Island, Denmark. It is the commercial and shipping center of the Faeroe Islands and is also a major fishing port. The city has fish-processing plants and a shipyard. Tórshavn was probably founded in the 10th cent. During World War II it was occupied by the British (1942–45).

torsion, stress on a body when external forces tend to twist it about an axis. See STRENGTH OF MATERIALS.

torsion balance, instrument used to measure small forces. It is based on the principle that a wire or thread resists twisting with a force that is proportional to the stress. The torsion balance consists essentially of a wire or thread attached at one end and arranged in such a way that a force applied at the other, or free, end tends to twist it out of shape. The force is measured by the extent to which the wire or thread is so twisted. Torsion balances are used to measure small electric, magnetic, and gravitational forces. One type is used to measure small weights. The invention of the torsion balance is commonly credited to the English geologist John Michell, who made his instrument c.1750, and to the French physicist Charles A. de Coulomb, who independently devised such a balance c.1777.

Torstensson, Lennart (lĕn'närt tōr'stənsōn), 1603–51, Swedish general in the THIRTY YEARS WAR. He was one of the generals trained by GUSTAVUS II in the new techniques of war. As commander of the Swedish artillery at Breitenfeld (1631) and the Lech (1632), he was responsible for the success of the new mobile field artillery. Captured after an unsuccessful attack on Wallenstein, Torstensson was held (1632–33) prisoner. After the death of Baner, Torstensson succeeded to command of the Swedish troops in 1641. He infused new morale into the mutinous army and led the Swedes to numerous victories in Saxony, Moravia, Silesia, and Bohemia, including the second battle of Breitenfeld (1642). In 1643–44 he overran Denmark, which opposed Sweden, but after the indecisive battle of Kolberg Heath (1644) he left Karl Gustav Wrangel in charge of the Danish war and reentered Germany. His brilliant victory at Jankau (1645) cleared the way to Prague and Vienna. Sickness forced him to resign (1646) command to Wrangel. He was made count of Ortala in 1647 and held high civil posts in Sweden. He was the military teacher of Charles X. The name also appears as Torstenson.

tort, in law, the violation of some duty wholly set by law. The duty is imposed equally upon all persons in the jurisdiction, and when it is breached the injured party has the right to institute suit for compensatory DAMAGES. Today civil wrongs are commonly divided into torts and breaches of CONTRACT. A breach of contract differs from a tort in that the parties themselves have determined, at least in part, their obligations. Certain torts, e.g., NUISANCE, may be suppressed by INJUNCTION. Many crimes are also torts, e.g., burglary often constitutes TRESPASS. The history of Anglo-American tort law can be traced back to the action for trespass to property or to the person. Not until the late 18th cent. was the currently observed distinction made between injury willfully inflicted and that which is unintentional, and both types were punished equally. In the early 19th cent. NEGLIGENCE was distinguished as a separate tort, and it has come to supply the bulk of tortious litigation. The general tendency today is to rule that the breach of any duty constitutes a tort, rather than to rule that an alleged tort must fit into some previously recognized variety, such as assault, false imprisonment, or libel. Some courts treat any willful unjustified injury as tortious (e.g., erecting a wall on one's property solely to shut off a neighbor's light), while others hold that the act must be defined as tortious by law, regardless of the perpetrator's motive.

tortoise (tôr'təs), common name for a terrestrial TURTLE, especially one of the family Testudinidae. Tortoises inhabit warm regions of all continents except Australia. They have club-shaped feet with reduced toes, adapted for walking on land, and nearly all have high-domed shells. The limbs are covered with hard scales and when the limbs and head are withdrawn into the shell, the animal is completely closed off. Most tortoises belong to the genus *Testudo.* Most famous are the giant tortoises of islands in the Indian Ocean (*Testudo gigantea*) and of the Galapagos islands (*T. elephantopus*). Galapagos tortoises may reach a length of over 4 ft (120 cm) and weigh over 500 lb (225 kg). There are about a dozen races of the Galapagos tortoise, most of them isolated on separate islands. These tortoises were a major source of meat for sailors in the 17th and 18th cent., and were often slaughtered wantonly. Once so abundant that the islands were named for them (*galapago* is Spanish for tortoise), they are now extinct on some islands and are endangered on most of the others. The tortoises are now protected by law, but their eggs are preyed upon by rats, and by feral dogs and cats. North American tortoises, genus *Gopherus,* are burrowing forms with flattened feet and heavy nails. Three of the four species are very similar. The desert tortoise, *Gopherus agassizii,* inhabits deserts from S Nevada to NW Mexico; the Texas tortoise, *G. berlandieri,* lives in arid brush country and open woods from S Texas to NE Mexico; the gopher tortoise, *G. polyphemus* (known locally as the gopher) is found in high, sandy areas of Florida and the U.S. Gulf and Atlantic coasts. The desert and gopher tortoises reach a length of 13 in. (33 cm), while the Texas tortoise is about 8½ in. (21.6 cm) long. The Mexican tortoise, *G. flavomarginatus,* is a large species of NW Mexico. It has been much used for food and the survival of the species is threatened. Tortoises are extremely long-lived; there are authenticated cases of individuals living over 150 years. They are classified in the phylum CHORDATA, subphylum Vertebrata, class Reptilia, order Chelonia, family Testudinidae.

tortoiseshell, horny, translucent, mottled plates covering the carapace of the tropical hawksbill turtle. The plates, too thin for most purposes in their original form, are usually built up in layers that are molded or compressed after the surfaces have been liquefied by heat; thus, a firm union is effected after resolidification. Inlays can be imbedded in the shell with a hot iron. Tortoiseshell has been used in veneering since ancient times; its chief use today is in the manufacture of toilet articles and decorative objects. It is imitated in products of celluloid and horn, but the laminated structure of most genuine work aids in identifying the real shell.

tortoiseshell cat: see CAT.

Tortola, largest of the British VIRGIN ISLANDS.

Tortosa (tōrtō'sä), city (1970 pop. 46,376), Tarragona prov., NE Spain, in Catalonia, on the Ebro River. It has a fishing industry and light manufacturing. Agricultural products are traded. A Roman colony (then known as Dertosa), the town later fell (8th cent.) to the Moors, who held it against repeated Christian onslaughts until its conquest (1148) by Raymond Berenger IV. There is a seismological observatory nearby.

Tortue, Île de la: see TORTUGA.

Tortuga (tōrtōō'gä) [Span.,=turtle], island, c.70 sq mi (180 sq km), off N Haiti. It was a notorious rendezvous of pirates in the 17th cent. It is called Île de la Tortue by the Haitians.

Toruń (tô'rōōnyə), Ger. *Thorn,* city (1970 pop. 129,152), N central Poland, on the Vistula. It is a river port and a railway junction. The major industries produce machinery, precision instruments, electrical equipment, textiles, and chemicals. It grew around a castle founded in 1231 by the Teutonic Knights. A flourishing trade center, it was a member of the Hanseatic League (14th–16th cent.). Toruń's importance made it an object of dispute between Poland and the TEUTONIC KNIGHTS. The First Peace of Toruń (1411) resulted in a short-lived settlement of the struggle. When Toruń recognized the Polish crown in 1454, it was taken and burned by the Knights. The ensuing war between Poland and the Knights ended with the Second Peace of Toruń (1466), by which Poland gained Toruń, extensive Prussian territories, access to the sea, and suzerainty over the area left to the Knights. A synod (1595) of Polish and Lithuanian Protestants and a synod (1645) of Polish Protestants and Catholics (known as the Colloquium Charitativum) were held in the city. In the early 17th cent. Toruń's population (30,000) was equal to that of Warsaw, but the city suffered heavily in the Swedish invasion. A religious riot there (1724) caused Russia and Prussia to guarantee the rights of religious minorities in Poland. The city passed to Prussia in 1793 and again in 1815, after its occupation by Napoleon I. It reverted to Poland in 1919. Toruń has preserved several fine Gothic buildings, the most notable of which are the churches of St. John (13th–14th cent.), St. James (14th cent.), and the Virgin (14th cent.). It was the birthplace of Copernicus; its university (founded 1945) bears his name.

Tory, Geofroy (zhôfrwä' tōrē'), c.1480–1533, Parisian printer, typographer, and author, b. Bourges. After study in Italy, he won distinction as a professor in Paris and became editor to the printer Henri

ESTIENNE. He took up drawing and engraving and returned to Italy to study (1516–18). He worked as a bookbinder, GROLIER being one of his clients. As designer and engraver he produced beautiful initials, borders, and illustrations, as well as his famous printer's mark (a broken jar) and that of Robert Estienne (an olive tree). His *Book of Hours,* which first appeared in 1525, introduced type design free from dependence on handwriting and established book designing as an art in France. His part in establishing French 16th-century printing of superb quality was recognized by his appointment as printer to the king (Francis I). Tory's writings include *Champfleury* (1529), wherein he explains and illustrates the theory governing his designs of roman capitals. Tory advocated the use of the French language; he introduced accents, the apostrophe, and the cedilla into the printing of French.

Tory (tô'rē), English political party. The term was originally applied to certain Roman Catholic outlaws in Ireland and was adopted as a derogatory name for supporters of the duke of York (later James II) at the time (c.1679–1680) when the 1st earl of SHAFTESBURY was proposing the duke's exclusion from the succession because of his adherence to Roman Catholicism. (The Shaftesbury group came to be known as the WHIG party.) Thus the term *Tory* came to designate the group of men sharing beliefs in ecclesiastical uniformity, strong use of the royal prerogative, and the doctrine of divine, hereditary right to the throne. The GLORIOUS REVOLUTION of 1688, which many Tory leaders supported, forced most Tories to accept some concept of limited royal power, but the party retained its close identification with the Church of England, favoring the restriction of the rights of non-Anglicans. The party at that time represented primarily the country gentry, who, in addition to their staunch Anglicanism, tended to oppose England's involvement in foreign wars. The Tories were favored by Queen Anne and reached the zenith of their early power (1710–14) under the leadership of Robert HARLEY, earl of Oxford, and Henry ST. JOHN. Their hegemony was broken after the accession of George I, and the party was discredited for its connections with the JACOBITES. Supremacy for the next 50 years passed to the Whig factions. After the accession of George III (1760) Tory sympathizers supported the power of the sovereign as the "king's friends." William PITT revitalized the faction after 1783, giving it a more solid parliamentary basis. The Tories again became reactionary under the impact of the French Revolution but entrenched themselves so firmly in control of the government that they were not dislodged until 1830. In the 1820s the Tories made some attempt to adopt a program of reform, but the Reform Bill of 1832 (see REFORM BILLS) demoralized the party and destroyed its strength in the House of Commons. The party that grew up thereafter from the remnants of the Tory group came to be known as the CONSERVATIVE PARTY. Conservatives to the present day are often referred to as Tories. In the American colonies during the American Revolution, the term *Tory* was used to signify those who adhered to the policies of the mother country, the LOYALISTS. See Keith Feiling, *History of the Tory Party, 1640–1714* (1924, repr. 1959) and *The Second Tory Party, 1714–1832* (1938, repr. 1959).

Toscana: see TUSCANY, Italy.

Toscanelli, Paolo dal Pozzo (pä'ōlō däl pôt'tsō tōskänĕl'lē), 1397–1482, Italian cosmographer and mathematician. A physician by training, he was also known as Paul the Physician. He was for a time librarian at Florence. It is said that his map of the world was used by Columbus on the 1492 voyage to America. The Italian architect Brunelleschi may have learned principles of perspective from Toscanelli.

Toscanini, Arturo (ärtōō'rō tōskänē'nē), 1867–1957, Italian conductor, internationally recognized as one of the world's great conductors. He studied cello at the Parma Conservatory, from which he was graduated in 1885. After performing as a cellist with various minor orchestras in Italy, he went to Rio de Janeiro in 1886 to play in the opera orchestra there. Substituting as conductor, he demonstrated his ability to elicit an electrifying performance from the musicians, and he was engaged for the rest of the season. Toscanini returned to Italy the next season (1886–87), and there subsequently conducted the premieres of Leoncavallo's *Pagliacci* (1892) and Puccini's *La Bohème* (1896) and the Italian premiere of Wagner's *Götterdämmerung* (1895). In 1898, Toscanini was appointed chief conductor and artistic director at La Scala, Milan, where he presented many new operas and the Italian premieres of many others, including Wagner's *Die Meistersinger* (1898) and *Siegfried* (1899). From 1908 to 1914 he conducted at the Metropolitan Opera, New York City, where he gave American premieres of Puccini's *Girl of the Golden West* (1910), Wolf-Ferrari's *Le donne curiose* (1912), and other works. Toscanini returned to Italy during World War I. With the reorganized La Scala Orchestra he toured (1920–21) Europe and the United States and was artistic director of La Scala from 1921 to 1929. Upon his return to the United States, he conducted the New York Philharmonic Orchestra from 1926 to 1936 and the NBC Symphony Orchestra, which was formed for him, from 1937. His other important engagements included the Bayreuth Festivals (1930, 1931), of which he was the first non-German conductor, the Salzburg Festivals (1934–36), and the Lucerne Festivals (1937–39). In 1936 he conducted the inaugural concert of the Palestine Symphony Orchestra in Tel Aviv. Consistently antifascist, he refused several times to appear in fascist countries. In 1954 he retired as conductor of the NBC Symphony Orchestra. Toscanini commanded perfection from his orchestras and instilled them with remarkable energy. A tempestuous personality, he was nevertheless greatly respected by performers and was widely emulated by conductors. His artistry is preserved in recordings, notably of the symphonies of Beethoven and works by Brahms, Wagner, Verdi, and many others. See B. H. Haggin, *Conversations with Toscanini* (1959); biographies by H. H. Taubman (1950), S. Chotzinoff (1956), D. Ewen (rev. ed. 1960), and B. H. Haggin (1967); studies by R. C. Marsh (1956) and P. C. Hughes (2d enl. ed. 1970).

Tosefta (tōsĕf'tə), pl. **Toseftoth** (-tōth) [Aramaic,= additional], collection of ancient Jewish teachings supplementing the MISHNA or Oral Law and closely allied to it in organization. Like the Mishna, it was compiled by the TANNAIM. Many of its teachings, called Baraitot, do not appear in the Mishna; others are merely elucidations or alternative versions of mishnaic material. It contains a larger percentage of aggadic material than does the Mishna. The Tosefta is an independent work and has been made the subject of commentaries. See H. L. Strack, *Introduction to Talmud and Midrash* (1931, repr. 1969); Saul Lieberman, *Tosefta Kifshuta* (1955).

Tosti, Sir Francesco Paolo (fränchās'kō pä'ōlō tô'stē), 1846–1916, Italian composer and teacher. Having been court singing teacher in Rome, he went in 1875 to London, where he became singing master (1880) to the royal family and professor (1894) at the Royal Academy of Music. *Serenade* and *Goodbye* are the best known of his many songs. He was knighted in 1908.

Tostig (tŏs'tĭg), d. 1066, earl of Northumbria; son of Earl Godwin of Wessex. He was banished with his father in 1051 and returned with him in their armed invasion of 1052. Made earl of Northumbria in 1055, Tostig jointly invaded (1063) Wales with his brother Harold (later King HAROLD of England). The Northumbrians revolted against Tostig's severe rule in 1065 and chose Morcar, brother of the earl of Mercia, to be their earl. Tostig fled to Flanders. The next year he raided the English coast, then joined the Norwegian king HAROLD III in defeating Morcar. Tostig and his ally were killed by Tostig's brother Harold at Stamford Bridge.

totalitarianism (tōtăl"ĭtâr'ēənĭzəm), modern form of autocratic government in which the state involves itself in all facets of society. A totalitarian government seeks to control the daily life of its citizens by actively controlling not only all economic and political matters but all other features of society, including the attitudes, values, and beliefs of its population. Totalitarian regimes erase the distinction between state and society and deny the existence of a private sphere of living. All social roles become virtually indistinguishable from political life, and the citizen's duty to the state becomes the primary concern of the community. An entity distinct from and superior to its components, the totalitarian state has as its purpose the replacement of existing society with a perfect society. Various totalitarian systems, however, have different ideological goals. For example, of the most notable totalitarian states—the Soviet Union, Nazi Germany, and the People's Republic of China—the Communist regimes of the Soviet Union and China seek the universal fulfillment of mankind through the establishment of a classless society (see COMMUNISM); German NATIONAL SOCIALISM, on the other hand, arose partly in reaction to Communism and attempted to establish the superiority of the so-called Aryan race. Despite the many differences among totalitarian states, they have several characteristics in common, of which the two most important are: the existence of an ideology that covers all aspects of life and explains the means by which to attain the final goal, and a single party through which this ideology is implemented. The party is generally led by a single DICTATOR and, typically, participation in politics, especially voting, is compulsory. The party has full control of the governmental system, and dissent is systematically suppressed. For this reason the use of terror and the employment of secret police in addition to a powerful regular police force are common features of totalitarian systems. Finally, the party, through the government, has a monopoly of control over the economy, communications, and the military establishment. Autocracies through the ages have attempted to exercise control over the lives of their subjects, by whatever means were available to them, including the use of secret police and military force. However, it is only with the advent of modern technology that government control of society has acquired the means to become all encompassing. Because of its reliance on modern technology, totalitarianism is, historically, a recent phenomenon. However, despite the defining characteristics outlined above, the term *totalitarianism* lacks clarity. Constitutional DEMOCRACY and totalitarianism, two forms of government that appear to be antithetical to one another, actually share many of the same characteristics. For example, in modern democracies, as in totalitarian systems, those in authority have a monopoly on the use of the nation's military power and on certain forms of mass communication; and the suppression of dissent, especially during times of crisis, often occurs in democracies. The ideology espoused by a totalitarian state may differ little from that propounded by nations professing democracy to be the perfect system. Moreover, one-party systems are found in some nontotalitarian states, as are government-controlled economies and even dictators. It is clear, therefore, that each type of political system, whether characterized as totalitarian or democratic, shares some of the attributes of the other, and the two should not be regarded as polarities. There is no single cause for the growth of totalitarianism, although some scholars trace its theoretical roots to the collectivist political theories of such thinkers as Plato, Jean Jacques Rousseau, and Karl Marx. It seems likely that a given totalitarian government is more the result of a specific set of historical forces and developments than of any set of philosophical beliefs. For example, the political, social, and economic chaos that followed in the wake of World War I allowed or encouraged the establishment of totalitarian regimes in several European nations, while the sophistication of modern weapons and communications enabled them to extend and consolidate their power. See Erich Fromm, *Escape From Freedom* (1941, repr. 1960); Ernest Barker, *Reflections on Government* (1942, repr. 1958); Hannah Arendt, *The Origins of Totalitarianism* (1958, new ed. 1966); Hans Buchheim, *Totalitarian Rule* (1962, tr. 1968); William Ebenstein, *Totalitarianism: New Perspectives* (1962); C. J. Friedrich and Z. K. Brezinski, *Totalitarian Dictatorship and Autocracy* (2d ed. 1967); J. A. Gregor, *Contemporary Radical Ideologies* (1968); J. L. Talmon, *The Origins of Totalitarian Democracy* (1952, repr. 1970).

totem (tō'təm), an object, usually an animal or plant (or all animals or plants of that species), that is revered by members of a particular social group because of a mystical or ritual relationship that exists with that group. The totem—or rather, the spirit it embodies—represents the bond of unity within a tribe, a clan, or some similar group. Generally, the members of the group believe that they are descended from a totem ancestor, or that they and the totem are "brothers." The totem may be regarded as a group symbol and as a protector of the members of the group. In most cases the totemic animal or plant is the object of taboo: It may be forbidden to kill or eat the sacred animal. The symbol of the totem may be tattooed on the body, engraved on weapons, pictured in masks, or (among Indians of the Pacific Northwest) carved on totem poles. In some cultures males have one totem and females another, but, generally speaking, totemism is associated with clans or blood relatives. Marriage between members of the same totemic group is commonly prohibited. See J. G. Frazer, *Totemism and Exogamy* (4 vol., 1910; repr. 1968); Émile Durkheim, *The Elementary Forms of the Religious Life* (1915, repr. 1965); Sigmund Freud, *Totem and Taboo* (1918, repr. 1960); Alexander Goldenweiser, *History, Psychology, and Culture* (1933); Claude Lévi-Strauss, *Totemism* (tr. 1963).

Totila (tŏt′ĭlə) or **Baduila** (bădyo͞oĭl′ə), d. 552, last king of the Ostrogoths (541–52). By defeating the Byzantines at Faenza and Mugello (542) and by taking Naples (543) and Rome (546), he became master of central and S Italy. BELISARIUS, the Byzantine commander, recovered Rome in 547 but was recalled in the following year. Rome again fell in 550 and left only Ravenna, Ancona, Otranto, and Crotona in Byzantine hands. Totila sent his fleet against Sicily, Corsica, Sardinia, and Illyria and made several peace offers to Emperor Justinian I. Instead of yielding, Justinian sent (552) NARSES to Italy at the head of a well-equipped army. Totila was thoroughly routed by Narses near Taginae, in the Apennines W of Ancona, and perished in the battle. Thus Byzantium regained temporary control over Italy.

Totleben or **Todleben, Eduard Ivanovich** (both: ĕdwärt′ ēvä′nəvĭch tôt′lyĕbyĭn), 1818–84, Russian general and military engineer. He won his chief renown in the Crimean War by his defense of SEVASTOPOL (1854–55). In a very short time Totleben constructed a system of fortifications that enabled the garrison to hold out for nearly a year. Totleben is considered the originator of a new technique of fortification. He planned the siege of PLEVEN in the later Russo-Turkish War (1877–78) and subsequently received the command of the entire Russian army and was created a count.

Totnes, George Carew, earl of: see CAREW, GEORGE, BARON CAREW OF CLOPTON.

Totowa (tŏt′əwə), borough (1970 pop. 11,580), Passaic co., NE N.J., a suburb of Paterson on the Passaic River; inc. 1898. Perfumes, furniture, plastics, detergents, spices, and food products are made. A state training school is there.

Tottel, Richard (tŏt′əl), c.1530–1594?, London publisher. He is chiefly remembered as the compiler of the poetry anthology *The Book of Songs and Sonnets* (1557), known as Tottel's miscellany. It is important because it preserves the extant original verse of Sir Thomas Wyatt and Henry Howard, earl of Surrey, and because it inaugurated the long series of poetry anthologies that were popular in Elizabethan England.

Tottori (tōt-tō′rē), city (1970 pop. 113,029), capital of Tottori prefecture, S Honshu, Japan, a port on the Sea of Japan. Lumber, raw silk, and fruit are exported. The city also produces wood and paper items and is a market for the rice that is grown in Tottori prefecture (1970 pop. 568,651), 1,347 sq mi (3,489 sq km).

Tou (tō′o͞o), same as TOI.

Touareg: see TUAREG.

toucan (to͞okăn′, to͞o′kän), perching bird of the New World tropics, related to the woodpeckers. Toucans vary in size from the jay-sized toucanets to the 24-in. (62-cm) tocos of the Amazon basin. They are notable for their enormous, often brightly colored, canoe-shaped bills, which consist of a lightweight porous substance covered by a horny shell with serrated edges. This bill is well adapted to cutting up the fruits and berries that form their diet. Most brilliantly plumaged are the aracaris and hill toucans of the mountain forests of South America. Toucans are gregarious and, like the woodpeckers, nest in cavities. Toucans are classified in the phylum CHORDATA, subphylum Vertebrata, class Aves, order Piciformes, family Rhamphastidae.

touch, sensation received by the skin, enabling the organism to detect objects or substances in contact with the body. End organs (nerve endings) in the skin convey the impression to the brain. Touch sensitivity varies in different parts of the body, depending on the number of end organs present in any one area. The tip of the tongue, lips, and fingertips are the most sensitive areas, the back and massive parts of the limbs the least so. The sense of touch is very closely related to the other four sensations received by the skin: pain, pressure, heat, and cold. There is a specific kind of sensory receptor for each of the five so-called cutaneous senses. For example, light-touch receptors convey only the sensation that an object is in contact with the body, while pressure receptors convey the force, or degree, of contact. The sense of touch can be developed to a remarkable degree, especially by those who must substitute it for sight or hearing. The blind learn to read by the Braille system by making use of the sensitivity to touch of the fingertips.

touch-me-not, common name for any plant of the genus *Impatiens* of the JEWELWEED family. *I. balsamina* is also called balsam.

Touggourt (to͞ogo͞ort′), town and oasis (1966 pop. 26,486), E Algeria, in the Sahara. It is an important administrative, commercial, and tourist center that was once famous for its abundant date crops but is now a center of the Saharan oil industry. In the 18th cent. it paid tribute to the Turks. French forces captured the town in 1854. An alternate spelling of the name is Tugurt.

Toukhachevski, Mikhail Nikolayevich: see TUKHACHEVSKY, MIKHAIL NIKOLAYEVICH.

Toul (to͞ol), town (1968 pop. 15,199), Meurthe-et-Moselle dept., NE France, on the Moselle River. It is largely an agricultural center but has clothing and glass industries. A Gallo-Roman city, it became a bishopric in the 4th cent. During the Middle Ages, Toul, along with METZ and VERDUN, was one of the bishoprics vital to the defense of France's eastern border. These bishoprics were almost continuously independent until their seizure by Henry II of France in 1552. Confirmed as a French possession by the Peace of WESTPHALIA in 1648, Toul played a significant role during the Franco-German conflicts of succeeding centuries. A suppression of the episcopal see (c.1801) led to a decline in the city's civil importance. Although severely damaged in the FRANCO-PRUSSIAN WAR (1870–71) and in World War II, Toul preserves the Church of St. Gengoult (13th and 16th cent.); the Cathedral of St. Étienne (13th–14th cent.); an interesting 17th-century fortified enclosure; and ramparts from Gallo-Roman times and from the 16th cent.

Toulon (to͞olôN′), city (1968 pop. 178,489), Var dept., SE France, in Provence, on the Mediterranean Sea. An important commercial port and industrial center, Toulon is the principal naval center of France; shipbuilding and ship repairing are major industries. Chemicals, machinery, furniture, and cork are also produced. Toulon first achieved eminence as a hostel for errant Crusaders during the Middle Ages. The city was fortified by Vauban in the 17th cent. and was the scene of many historic naval battles, including the Battle of 1793 in which the royalists surrendered the city to the English. The same year the young Napoleon Bonaparte gained distinction by retaking the city for the French. After 1815, Toulon became the center of French naval power. During World War II much of the French fleet was scuttled (1942) to avoid its capture by the Germans. Although it suffered considerable damage during World War II, the city has preserved the fortifications by Vauban and the Church of St. Marie Majeure (17th–18th cent.).

Toulouse (to͞olo͞oz′), city (1968 pop. 380,340), capital of Haute-Garonne dept., S France, on the Garonne River. One of the great cultural and commercial centers of France, it is also the center of the French aeronautic industry. Originally part of Roman Gaul, Toulouse became an episcopal see in the 4th cent. It was the capital of the Visigoths from 419 until the conquest by Clovis I in 508 and was capital of the Carolingian kingdom of AQUITAINE from 781 until 843. In 843, Toulouse and the surrounding area became a separate county. Toulouse was an artistic and literary center of medieval Europe. In the late 12th cent. the counts of Toulouse were suzerains of practically the entire region of Languedoc; their vassals included the lords of FOIX, QUERCY, and ROUERGUE. Ruling with great wisdom and tolerance (particularly toward the Jews, many of whom settled in Languedoc), the counts held a brilliant court that attracted the best TROUBADOURS and was the center of southern French literature. Although rival dynastic claims to Aquitaine brought recurrent warfare with England, the region itself was barely affected. However, between 1208 and 1229 the area was laid waste when northern lords, under the guise of stamping out the ALBIGENSIAN heresy, plundered Toulouse. The counts fell from power, and in 1271 the county passed to the French crown and from that time on formed much of Languedoc prov. After the annexation the province retained much autonomy in government until the French Revolution. After the suppression of Albigensianism, Toulouse experienced a cultural rebirth. The Univ. of Toulouse was established in 1230 and the Académie des Jeaux Floraux c.1323. Among the many outstanding buildings of Toulouse are the Romanesque Basilica of St. Sernin (11th–12th cent.), the Cathedral of St. Étienne (12th–15th cent.), the Assezat mansion (16th cent.), the *capitole* [town hall] (18th cent.), several excellent museums, and an old quarter left almost intact since the 18th cent.

Toulouse-Lautrec, Henri de (äNrē′ də to͞olo͞oz′-lōtrĕk′), 1864–1901, French painter and lithographer; b. Albi. Son of a wealthy nobleman, Lautrec fell and broke both legs when he was a child and his growth was permanently stunted. Showing an early gift for drawing, he studied with Bonnat and Cormon and set up a studio of his own when he was 21. As a youth he was attracted by sporting subjects and admired and was influenced by the work of Degas. His own work was, above all, graphic in nature, the paint never obscuring the strong, original draftsmanship. He detailed the music halls, circuses, brothels, and the cabaret life of Paris with a remarkable objectivity born, perhaps, of his own isolation. His garish and artificial colors, the orange hair and electric green light of his striking posters, caught the atmosphere of the life they advertised. Lautrec's technical innovations in color lithography created a greater freedom and a new immediacy in poster design. His posters of the dancers and personalities at the Moulin Rouge cabaret are world renowned and have inspired countless imitations. After a life of enormous productivity and debauchery, Lautrec suffered a mental and physical collapse and died at the age of 37. His life has inspired numerous biographies of varying accuracy. Although exhibitions of his work were not well received in his lifetime, he is now represented in the major museums of France and the United States. Many of his sketches and some paintings are in the Musée Lautrec of his native Albi. His painting *At the Moulin de la Galette* (1892) is in the Art Institute, Chicago; the lithograph *Seated Female Clown* (1896) is at the Philadelphia Museum of Art. See his correspondence (ed. by L. Goldschmidt and H. Schimmel, 1969); complete lithographs and drypoints (ed. by J. Adémar, 1965) and posters (intr. by E. Julien, 1966); biographies by H. Perruchot (1960) and P. Huisman (1964, repr. 1968); studies by D. Cooper (1969) and F. Novotny (1969).

Toungoo (toung′go͞o′, toung′o͞o′), town, S Burma, on the Sittang River. It is a railway junction. From the late 14th cent. it was the center of one of the three chief states of Burma; in the late 16th cent., under the Pagan kings, it preceded Pegu as the capital of a unified Burmese kingdom.

Touraine (to͞orĕn′), region and former province (until the French Revolution), W central France, centering around Tours (the historic capital) and drained by the Loire, Cher, and Vienne rivers. Roughly coextensive with Indre-et-Loire dept., Touraine, with its fertile valleys, orchards, and vineyards, is known as the "garden of France." Its numerous châteaus (see CHINON, AZAY-LE-RIDEAU, CHAMBORD, AMBOISE), built mainly in the 15th and 16th cent., are noted tourist attractions. Descartes, Rabelais, and Balzac were born in Touraine, and the latter two celebrated their birthplace in their writings. Originally the county of Tours, Touraine passed (10th cent.) to the counts of Blois, who ceded it (11th cent.) to the counts of Anjou. Touraine then passed (1152) under English domination and was retaken (1204) by Philip II of France and united with the French crown.

Tourane: see DA NANG, South Vietnam.

Tourcoing (to͞orkwăN′), city (1968 pop. 99,369), Nord dept., N France, in French Flanders. With the adjacent city of ROUBAIX, it forms one of the most important textile centers of France. In 1491, Albert Maximilian I granted Tourcoing a city charter in recognition of its important textile industry. Albert Roussel, the composer, was born in Tourcoing.

Touré, Sékou (sä′ko͞o to͞orā′), 1922–, African political leader, president (1958–) of the republic of Guinea. The son of a poor farmer, Touré became active in the labor movement and in 1945 was named general secretary of the postal workers' union. After holding a series of high union posts, he organized (1956) the Union Générale des Travailleurs d'Afrique Noir. Touré's political activity began in 1946 when, with other African nationalist leaders, including Félix Houphouët-Boigny, he was a founder of the Rassemblement Démocratique Africain. In 1956 he was elected Guinea's deputy to the French national assembly and mayor of Conakry. When his country left (1958) the French Community, he became president of Guinea. A Marxist, he sought and received aid from the Soviet bloc of nations. He had stormy relations with other African nations, particularly Senegal and Ivory Coast.

Tourgée, Albion Winegar (to͞orzhā′), 1838–1905, American author and lawyer, b. Williamsfield, Ohio, studied at the Univ. of Rochester. After serving in the Union army he was for a few years a carpetbagger lawyer and political judge in North Carolina. Of his several novels, the best known are *A Fool's Errand* (1879) and *Figs and Thistles* (1879). They are valuable for their picture of the politics of the Reconstruction period. See biography by O. H. Olsen (1965).

tourmaline (to͝or'məlĭn, -lēn), complex borosilicate mineral with varying amounts of aluminum, iron, magnesium, sodium, lithium, potassium and sometimes other elements, used as a gem. It occurs in prismatic crystals, commonly three-sided, six-sided, or nine-sided, and striated vertically. Different crystal forms are usually present at opposite ends of the vertical axis. The luster is vitreous. Colors are red and pink (rubellite), blue (indicolite, or Brazilian sapphire), green (Brazilian emerald), yellow, violet-red, and black (schorl). Colorless varieties are called achroite. Two or more colors may occur in the same stone, the colors being arranged in zones or bands with sharp boundaries between them. Some Brazilian stones have a red core with a green exterior, separated by a colorless band; some stones from California are green within and red outside. The variations in color are, of course, dependent on the variations in chemical composition. Tourmalines are found in pegmatite veins in granites, gneisses, schists, and crystalline limestone. Sources of the gem include Elba, Madagascar, Burma, Sri Lanka (Ceylon), the Urals, Siberia, Brazil, and Maine, Connecticut, and California in the United States.

Tournachon, Gaspard-Félix: see NADAR.

Tournai (to͝ornā'), Flemish *Doornik,* city (1970 pop. 32,794), Hainaut prov., SW Belgium, on the Scheldt River. The manufactures of this commercial and industrial center include textiles, carpets, cement, and processed food. One of Belgium's oldest cities, Tournai was the fortified capital of a Roman province and in the 5th cent. became a seat of the Merovingian kings of Austrasia. The city was destroyed by the Normans in 881. It belonged to France from 1187 to 1521, when Emperor Charles V captured it and attached it to the Spanish (from 1714, Austrian) Netherlands. Tournai joined in the rebellion of the Spanish Netherlands and was a Calvinist stronghold until its capture (1581) by Alessandro Farnese. It was taken several times by the French in the wars of the 17th–18th cent. Tournai has been a cultural center since the 12th cent. Of note are the Cathedral of Notre Dame (11th–12th cent.), with many art treasures; a 15th-century tower named for Henry VIII of England (who took the city in 1513 and made Cardinal Wolsey bishop of Tournai); the clothworkers hall (17th cent.); and a well-known art museum. Alternate spellings are Tournay (French) and Doornijk (Flemish).

tournament or **tourney,** in the Middle Ages, public contest between armed horsemen in simulation of real battle. In this military game, which flourished from the 12th to the 16th cent., combatants were frequently divided into opposing factions, each led by a champion. It differed from the joust, a single combat bout fought with weapons of war. Tournaments perhaps originated in trials by battle (see ORDEAL) or in the earlier gladiatorial combats. The tournament, a typical feature of the Middle Ages, was based on the ideals of chivalry. Thought to have originated in France in the 11th cent., tourneys spread to Germany, England, and S Europe; laws governing them became more or less universal. Such affairs, usually held at the invitation of kings or nobles, were the occasion of much pageantry. Knights with their entourages camped near the field of combat, and their qualifications were examined by judges of the day. The typical tournament field, or lists, was an oval or rectangular area enclosed by barriers and flanked by pavilions for important personages, the ladies who sponsored the combatants, and the judges. Heralds announced the participants, and then, with a fanfare of trumpets, the warriors made their entrance, clad in armor and astride richly caparisoned horses. Their weapons were usually blunted lances or swords. The events of the day normally began with combat between individuals and ended with a collective contest. Prizes were awarded the victors by the queen of beauty, chosen to preside over the tournament. Knights were often killed or gravely injured at tournaments, and to lessen that danger a barrier, or tilt, was sometimes stretched along the length of the lists. The combatants fought across it, and this version of the sport was known as tilting. Although attempts were made to suppress or regulate tournaments, the practice continued until changed social conditions caused a decline in its popularity. See study by F. H. Cripps-Day (1918).

Tourneur, Cyril (tûr'nər), 1575?–1626, English dramatist and poet. Little is known of his life. *The Transformed Metamorphosis* (1600), an allegorical satire, was his first published work. His reputation rests on two gloomy, violent plays, *The Revenger's Tragedy* (1607), of which his authorship has been questioned, and *The Atheist's Tragedy* (1611). See his complete works (ed. by Allardyce Nicoll, 1930).

tourney: see TOURNAMENT.

tourniquet (to͝or'nĭkĕt, -kā, tûr'-), compression device used to cut off the flow of blood to a part of the body, most often an arm or leg. It may be a special surgical instrument, a rubber tube, a strip of cloth, or any flexible material that can be tightened to exert pressure. Compression should not be maintained for more than 20 min at a time because of the danger of congestion and gangrene. In cases of a bleeding emergency, a tourniquet is used to stop the flow of blood if other means, e.g., the application of a pressure bandage to the wound, are not effective. In arterial hemorrhage (bright red blood spurting out in jets) the tourniquet is applied above the wound, i.e., between the wound and the heart. In hemorrhage from a vein (an even flow of dark red blood) the tourniquet is applied below the wound, i.e., away from the heart.

Touro Synagogue National Historic Site: see NATIONAL PARKS AND MONUMENTS (table).

Tours (to͝or), city (1968 pop. 132,861), capital of Indre-et-Loire dept., W central France, in Touraine, on the Loire River. It is a wine market and a tourist center, with metallurgical, chemical, electrical, clothing, and printing industries. An old Gallo-Roman town, it grew rapidly after the death (397) of its bishop, Saint Martin, whose remains are buried in the Basilica of St. Martin (built 1887–1924). The city was a center of medieval Christian learning, notably under Gregory of Tours and Alcuin. It was there that Charles Martel halted (732) the Moorish conquest of Europe. The city became an archdiocese in 853. The history of Tours is essentially that of TOURAINE, of which it was the capital. It was favored by many kings, including Louis XI, who held his States General there and who died in the nearby château of Plessis-lès-Tours. The city has produced great painters, sculptors, goldsmiths, and tapestry weavers. During the Franco-Prussian War (1870–71), Tours was the headquarters of the government of national defense. In World War II it was briefly (June, 1940) the seat of the French government. Points of interest include Gallo-Roman ruins and the splendid Gothic Cathedral of St. Gatien (13th–16th cent.).

Tourville, Anne Hilarion de Cotentin, comte de (än ĕlăryôN' də kôtäNtăN' kôNt də to͝orvēl'), 1642–1701, French naval commander. He served in the wars of King Louis XIV and was made commander of the French fleet in the War of the Grand Alliance. His great victory over the English and the Dutch at Beachy Head (1690) probably marked the height of French sea power, but in 1692 he was defeated by the English and Dutch at La Hogue. He was later victorious (1693) near Cape St. Vincent, Portugal. Tourville was one of the greatest naval technicians of his time.

Toussaint L'Ouverture, François Dominique (fräNswä' dômēnēk' to͞osăN' lo͞ovĕrtür'), c.1744–1803, Haitian Negro patriot and martyr. A self-educated slave freed shortly before the uprising in 1791, he joined the Negro rebellion to liberate the slaves and became its organizational genius. Rapidly rising in power, Toussaint joined forces for a brief period in 1793 with the Spanish of Santo Domingo and in a series of fast-moving campaigns became known as L'Ouverture [the opening], a name he adopted. Although he professed allegiance to France, first to the republic and then to Napoleon, he was singleheartedly devoted to the cause of his own people and advocated it in his talks with French commissioners. Late in 1793 the British occupied all of Haiti's coastal cities and allied themselves with the Spanish in the eastern part of the island. Toussaint was the acknowledged leader against them and, with the Negro generals DESSALINES and CHRISTOPHE, recaptured (1798) several towns from the British and secured their complete withdrawal. In 1799 the mulatto general André RIGAUD enlisted the aid of Alexandre PÉTION and Jean Pierre BOYER, asserted mulatto supremacy, and launched a revolt against Toussaint; the uprising was quelled when Pétion lost the southern port of Jacmel. In 1801, Toussaint conquered Santo Domingo, which had been ceded by Spain to France in 1795, and thus he governed the whole island. By then professing only nominal allegiance to France, he reorganized the government and instituted public improvements. Napoleon sent (1802) a large force under General LECLERC to subdue Toussaint, who had become a major obstacle to French colonial ambitions in the Western Hemisphere; the Haitians, however, offered stubborn resistance, and a peace treaty was drawn. Toussaint himself was treacherously seized and sent to France, where he died in a dungeon at Fort-de-Joux, in the French Jura. His valiant life and tragic death made him a symbol of the fight for liberty, and he is celebrated in one of Wordsworth's finest sonnets and in a dramatic poem by Lamartine. See C. L. R. James, *The Black Jacobins* (1938, 2d ed. 1963); Ralph Korngold, *Citizen Toussaint* (1944, repr. 1965); Stephen Alexis, *Black Liberator* (1949); Charles Moran, *Black Triumvirate: A Study of L'Ouverture, Dessalines, Christophe* (1957).

Tout, Thomas Frederick (tout), 1855–1929, English historian. Educated at Oxford, he taught at the Univ. of Manchester from 1890 to 1925. Considered an outstanding authority on medieval history, Tout emphasized the importance of the administrative aspect of historical development. His writings include *Edward the First* (1893), *The Empire and the Papacy* (1898), *The Place of the Reign of Edward II in English History* (1914), *Chapters in the Administrative History of Medieval England* (6 vol., 1920–33), and numerous textbooks.

Tovey, Sir Donald Francis (tō'vē), 1875–1940, English pianist and musicologist, grad. Oxford, 1898. As a pianist he appeared in England and on the Continent after 1900 and in the United States in 1925 and 1927. He was professor of music (1914–40) at the Univ. of Edinburgh. Although he was an accomplished composer, he is best remembered for his analytical writings on music, which include *Essays in Musical Analysis* (7 vol., 1935–45), a collection of his program annotations; *Musical Form and Matter* (1934); *A Companion to Beethoven's Pianoforte Sonatas* (1931); and *Beethoven* (1944). He was adviser on music for the 14th edition of *The Encyclopaedia Britannica;* many of his articles for this and previous editions were collected and published in 1945. Tovey edited Bach's *Art of the Fugue* and wrote (1932) a companion essay to it. He was knighted in 1935.

tower, structure, the greatest dimension of which is its height. Towers have belonged to two general types. The first embodies practical uses such as defense (characteristic of the Middle Ages), to carry bells or beacons, and to utilize maximum floor space in a given area, as in modern skyscraper towers. The second type is used to symbolize the authority and power of religious and civic bodies, as in the churches and town halls of Europe. The earliest use of tall structures for ritual and symbolism is seen in the Babylonian ZIGGURAT. The temple architecture of India had a variety of pyramidal and cylindrical masonry towers. The many-storied PAGODA in wood was a part of early Chinese and Japanese temple architecture. The MINARET belongs to Islamic religious architecture. Used for defensive purposes in the early Middle Ages in Western Europe, towers with massive masonry walls served as refuges and lookouts. Many 9th- and 10th-century round defense towers remain in Ireland and a few in Scotland, including one at Brechin. Castles had their donjons or keeps, of which the 11th-century TOWER OF LONDON shows a high development. Of the fortified towers that Italian nobles built even for their city dwellings numerous examples remain, notably at San Gimignano. The growth of centralized governments made the tower less essential in the great castles of the late Middle Ages. The earliest existing church towers in Europe were those of the 5th and 6th cent. in Ravenna, Italy. There the bell tower, or CAMPANILE, stood detached from the church building itself; another example is the celebrated bell tower at Pisa (1174). In English and French Romanesque churches a high tower rises over the crossing of nave and transepts, and the west end generally possesses lower twin towers. The relatively simple Romanesque towers generally had square or round shafts with many blind arcades in horizontal tiers and were topped by a simple octagonal or conical spire. They developed into the higher, elaborate type of Gothic, decorated with pinnacles and canopied niches. Towers of extreme lightness and intricacy were developed in the late Gothic period, as in the cathedrals at Rouen, Vienna, and Antwerp. With the Renaissance the classical orders and other elements of Roman architecture were incorporated into tower design. Particular success was attained in the tapering pyramidal compositions of Sir Christopher Wren's numerous London towers, including those of St. Paul's Cathedral. English churches, e.g., St. Martin's-in-the-Fields by James Gibbs, set the pattern for the typical New England church with the wooden tower and steeple rising directly over the entrance vestibule. In the 20th cent. towers have often taken the form of skyscrapers. Notable modern towers of varied design and function include the highly original Einstein Tower at Potsdam by Erich

Mendelsohn; Frank Lloyd Wright's Johnson tower with glass tubing at Racine, Wis.; and the WATTS TOWER, Calif., by Simon Rodilla, constructed of bits of steel, wire, glass, ceramics, and rubbish.

Tower Hamlets, borough (1971 pop. 164,948), of Greater London, SE England. Tower Hamlets was formed in 1965 by the merger of the metropolitan boroughs of Bethnal Green, Poplar, and Stepney. The southern boundary of Tower Hamlets fronts on the Thames and includes some of London's busiest docks. The borough's industries include furniture making, dressmaking, and brewing. Both the Tower of London and the Royal Mint are in the borough.

Tower of London, ancient fortress in London, England, just east of the City and on the north bank of the Thames, covering about 13 acres (5.3 hectares). Now used mainly as an arsenal, it was a royal residence in the Middle Ages. Later it was a jail for illustrious prisoners. The Tower is enclosed by a dry moat, within which are double castellated walls surrounding the central White Tower. Although Roman foundations were discovered as additions and changes were made, and tradition makes Julius Caesar the founder, the White Tower was built c.1078 by Gundulf, bishop of Rochester; the exterior was restored by Sir Christopher Wren. Various towers subsequently built were used as prisons; one of them now houses a collection of medieval arms and armor, and another (the Wakefield Tower) contains the crown jewels. The Traitors' Gate (giving access by water from the Thames) and the Bloody Tower are associated with many historically noted persons, including Queen Elizabeth I (when still princess), Sir Thomas More, Anne Boleyn, Catherine Howard, Lady Jane Grey, the 2d earl of Essex, Sir Walter Raleigh, and the duke of Monmouth. Many persons beheaded within the Tower precincts, or on the neighboring Tower Hill, were buried in the Chapel of St. Peter ad Vincula. The Yeomen of the Guard ("Beefeaters"), dressed in Tudor garb, still guard the Tower. Its north bastion was destroyed in air raids in 1940. See R. J. Minney, *The Tower of London* (1971).

towhee (tō'hē, tōhē', tou'hē), common name for a North American bird of the family Fringillidae (FINCH family). Towhees are also called chewinks, for their call, and ground robins, because like robins they are ground feeders—often detected by the rustling noise they make searching through dry underbrush for insects. In the male red-eyed towhee, found E of the Great Plains and in parts of Canada, the upper parts are glossy black and the underparts white with patches of chestnut-brown on the sides. The white-eyed towhee is found in the South, and the inconspicuous brown and Abert's towhees in the West. The green-tailed towhee is a western mountain bird. The various species of towhees all belong to the genus *Pipilo*. Towhees are classified in the phylum CHORDATA, subphylum Vertebrata, class Aves, order Passeriformes, family Fringillidae.

town, in the United States. In the New England states the town is the basic unit of LOCAL GOVERNMENT. The New England town government's unique feature is the town meeting, much praised as a nearly pure form of democracy. At the annual meeting of voters, town officers are elected and local issues such as town tax rates are decided. Elsewhere in the United States the term *town* has little political use, signifying only a place incorporated as a town or simply a population center. However, *township* has legal meaning—a geographical division of the COUNTY, established in land surveys and usually made up of 36 sections, each with an area of 1 sq mi (2.6 sq km). Except in the Middle Atlantic states, townships are seldom units of local government.

Towneley Plays, a cycle of 32 plays preserved in a manuscript of c.1460 by the Towneleys, a Lancashire family. Intended for production by the guilds of Wakefield, they are sometimes called the Wakefield Plays. The well-known *Second Shepherd's Play* is one of this collection. See MIRACLE PLAY.

Townes, Charles Hard, 1915–, American physicist and educator, b. Greenville, S.C. He was educated at Furman Univ., Duke, and the California Institute of Technology (Ph.D., 1939), was on the technical staff of the Bell Telephone Laboratories (1939–48), and taught at Columbia (1948–59). After serving as vice president and director of research of the Institute for Defense Analyses, Washington, D.C., he was provost of the Massachusetts Institute of Technology (1961–66). Townes is known for his work on the theory and application of the MASER, on which he obtained the fundamental patent, and other work in quantum electronics connected with both maser and LASER devices. He shared the 1964 Nobel Prize in Physics with N. G. Basov and A. M. Prochorov for contributions to this field.

town planning: see CITY PLANNING.

Townsend, Francis Everett (toun'zənd), 1867–1960, American reformer, leader of an old-age pension movement, b. Fairbury, Ill., grad. Univ. of Nebraska medical school, 1903. He practiced medicine in several Western states before he settled (1919) at Long Beach, Calif. In 1933, at the height of the economic depression, he produced the Townsend plan, which called for a pension of $200 per month for citizens of 60 years of age or older, on condition that the $200 be spent in the United States within a month after receipt. The funds were to be raised principally by a 2% Federal sales tax. The simplicity of the proposal, the apostolic zeal of Townsend, and the organization of the Townsendites into a formidable pressure group brought increasing support for the plan despite its condemnation by competent economists. Bills to establish the Townsend plan were continually defeated in Congress after 1935, and the strength of the movement declined after the economy began to recover and the effects of SOCIAL SECURITY were felt in the United States. Townsend modified a few of the provisions of his plan in the 1940s.

Townsend, Mount, 7,260 ft (2,213 m) high, SE New South Wales, in the Australian Alps. Discovered by Polish Count Strzelecki, and thought to be Australia's highest peak, it was at first called Mt. Kosciusko, in honor of a Polish patriot. When a higher peak, the present Mt. Kosciusko, was discovered, the name was changed to Mt. Townsend.

Townsend plan: see under TOWNSEND, FRANCIS EVERETT.

Townshend, Charles Townshend, 2d Viscount (toun'zĕnd), 1674–1738, English statesman. A leading Whig in the reign of Queen Anne, he served as a commissioner to negotiate the union (1707) with Scotland and as ambassador (1708–11) to the Netherlands. He strongly supported the Hanoverian succession, and when George I became king (1714) Townshend was appointed a secretary of state. He was somewhat overshadowed by his colleague James Stanhope (later 1st Earl STANHOPE), and in 1716 Stanhope and the 3d earl of SUNDERLAND undermined his influence with the king and secured his dismissal. With his brother-in-law Robert WALPOLE, who left office with him, Townshend formed an opposition group, led nominally by the prince of Wales (later George II). He returned to office in 1720, and after the fall of Sunderland and the death of Stanhope, he became (1721) secretary of state again, sharing leadership of the ministry with Walpole. He negotiated the Treaty of Hanover (1725) with Prussia and France to counter the alliance between Spain and Austria and, after a brief war in which the Spanish besieged Gibraltar, concluded the Treaty of Seville (1729) with Spain. Foreign policy disagreements with Walpole led to Townshend's resignation in 1730. He retired to the country, where, as an experimental farmer, he became known as Turnip Townshend.

Townshend, Charles, 1725–67, English statesman; grandson of the 2d Viscount Townshend. Distrusted for his marked instability, he held relatively minor offices until the 1st earl of CHATHAM made him chancellor of the exchequer in 1766. Because of Chatham's illness Townshend became the leading figure in the ministry. He effectively sabotaged Chatham's plan to bring India under the sovereignty of the crown and undertook the ill-fated American import levies known as the TOWNSHEND ACTS. He died shortly after the passage of the measures.

Townshend Acts, 1767, originated by Charles TOWNSHEND and passed by the English Parliament shortly after the repeal of the STAMP ACT. They were designed to collect revenue from the colonists in America by putting customs duties on imports of glass, lead, paints, paper, and tea. The colonials, spurred on by the writings of John DICKINSON, Samuel Adams, and others, protested against the taxes. The Boston merchants again boycotted English goods, the Massachusetts Assembly was dissolved (1768) for sending a circular letter to other colonies explaining the common plight, and British troops sent to enforce these laws and keep peace were involved in unpleasant incidents, notably the BOSTON MASSACRE. The boycott decreased British trade, and in 1770 most of the Acts were repealed, but retention of the tea tax caused the BOSTON TEA PARTY.

township: see TOWN.

Townsville, city (1971 pop. 71,109), NE Queensland, Australia, on Cleveland Bay. It is a major port. Wool, hides, meat, copper, and sugar are the chief exports. Copper and sugar refining, meat packing and freezing, and cement making are other industries. Townsville was founded in 1864. James Cook Univ. of North Queensland (1970) is located there.

Towson (tou'sən), uninc. city (1970 pop. 77,809), seat of Baltimore co., N Md., a residential and industrial suburb of Baltimore; settled c.1750. It has varied manufactures and is the seat of Goucher College and Towson State College. Nearby Hampton National Historic Site is a Georgian mansion (c.1790) with formal gardens.

Towton Field (tou'tən), West Riding of Yorkshire, N England, near Tadcaster. It was the scene (1461) of a bloody and decisive battle in which the forces of Edward IV defeated the Lancastrians. See ROSES, WARS OF THE.

toxaphene: see INSECTICIDE.

toxemia (tŏksē'mēə), disease state caused by the presence in the blood of bacterial TOXINS or other harmful substances. The effects of the bacterial toxins known as endotoxins are relatively uniform, regardless of which bacterial species the toxin comes from, and are separate from the effects caused by the infecting bacterium itself. A small amount of endotoxin produces one or more fever episodes, thought to be caused by release of a fever-inducing substance from damaged white blood cells. Large quantities of endotoxin cause shock and death. Exotoxins are bacterial proteins that have specific effects on target tissues, e.g., botulinus toxin affects the nervous system. The term *toxemia* is also used for a disorder occurring during the latter half of pregnancy characterized by high blood pressure, the appearance of protein in the urine, and edema. If not treated it can result in convulsions and coma. The cause of toxemia of pregnancy has not been established with certainty. See ECLAMPSIA.

toxicology, study of poisons, or toxins, from the standpoint of detection, isolation, identification, and determination of their effects on the human body. Toxicology may be considered the branch of PHARMACOLOGY devoted to the study of the poisonous effects of drugs. It is also a division of forensic medicine concerned with the detection of the criminal use of poisons.

toxin, poison produced by living organisms. Toxins are classified as either exotoxins or endotoxins. Exotoxins are a diverse group of soluble proteins released into the surrounding tissue by living bacterial cells. Exotoxins have specific reaction sites in the host; e.g., tetanus and botulinum exotoxins affect nerve tissue, and streptococcal toxins attack vascular tissue. Plants and animals also produce protein toxins. Some, such as cobra venom, are enzymes that destroy substances in host tissue. Endotoxins are polysaccharide and phospholipid substances found in the cell walls of bacteria that are freed when the cells die and break up. The pathologic effects of endotoxins, similar for all bacterial sources, include fever, shock, and intestinal hemorrhage. In sufficiently low doses toxins stimulate the production of ANTIBODIES, or ANTITOXINS, in the host, and toxins of a specific bacterial species have been injected to elicit formation of antibodies against the disease caused by the bacteria. Toxoids are protein toxins that have been heated or chemically treated to deprive them of their toxicity but not of the ability to induce the formation of antibodies. See VENOM.

toxin-antitoxin, mixture of a poisonous substance, or TOXIN, with an ANTITOXIN, or ANTIBODY, in such proportion that a large percentage of the toxin is neutralized by the antitoxin. Although formerly used to immunize an individual against disease, toxin-antitoxin mixtures have been largely supplanted by TOXOIDS. See IMMUNITY.

toxoid, protein TOXIN treated by heat or chemicals so that its poisonous property is destroyed but its capacity to stimulate the formation of toxin ANTIBODIES, or ANTITOXINS, remains. Because toxoids can be given in large quantities with no risk of tissue damage, they have superseded the highly poisonous toxins as immunizing agents against such diseases as diphtheria and tetanus.

Toy, Crawford Howell, 1836–1919, American biblical scholar, b. Norfolk, Va., M.A. Univ. of Virginia, 1856. He also studied (1859–60) at the Southern Baptist Theological Seminary, Greenville, S.C., served as a chaplain in the Confederate army, and continued (1866–68) his studies at Berlin. He resigned the professorship he held (1869–79) at the Southern Baptist Theological Seminary because of theological controversy. From 1880 until his retirement (1909) he was Hancock professor of Hebrew and other Oriental languages at Harvard, and he was (1880–1903) Dexter lecturer on biblical literature. A member (1901–6) of the editorial board of *The Jewish Encyclopedia* and a contributor to learned journals, he wrote *Judaism and Christianity* (1890), *A Critical and Exegetical Commentary on the Book of Proverbs* (1899), and *Introduction to the History of Religions* (1913).

toy, article designed to be played with, chiefly for children. Archaeological research has revealed numerous playthings from prehistoric civilizations. Early Egyptian, Greek, and Roman dolls, tops, balls, rattles, hoops, and miniature representations of furniture, houses, and dishes have been preserved. Mechanical toys, often created for the amusement of adults, have been popular since the Middle Ages. Toys made by individual craftsmen were early distributed in Germany; they were at first sold chiefly by peddlers at fairs. The use of sheet-metal stamping in Nuremberg c.1850 introduced the first large-scale manufacturing methods. The manufacture of toys is an important industry in most countries. Although many new toys are created each year, some, especially dolls, balls, art materials, and blocks, retain their popularity year after year. Educators and psychologists, beginning with Friedrich Wilhelm August Froebel and Maria Montessori, have stressed the role of toys in the mental, emotional, social, and physical development of children. See Antonia Fraser, *A History of Toys* (1966); Gwen White, *Antique Toys and Their Background* (1971).

Toyama (tōyä'mä), city (1970 pop. 269,268), capital of Toyama prefecture, E central Honshu, Japan, on Tokyo Bay. It is the main center of Japan's patent medicine industry and also has industries that produce cotton and rayon yarn and pulp. Toyama prefecture (1970 pop. 1,029,690), 1,644 sq mi (4,258 sq km), is a rice-growing area.

toy dog, classification used by breeders and kennel clubs to designate very small breeds of dogs kept as pets. Some are selectively bred diminutive forms of larger breeds and others are naturally small. The following 17 toy breeds are registered with the American Kennel Club: AFFENPINSCHER, BRUSSELS GRIFFON, CHIHUAHUA, ENGLISH TOY SPANIEL, ITALIAN GREYHOUND, JAPANESE SPANIEL, MALTESE, MINIATURE PINSCHER, PAPILLON, PEKINGESE, POMERANIAN, PUG, SHIH TZU, SILKY TERRIER, toy POODLE, toy MANCHESTER TERRIER, and YORKSHIRE TERRIER. See DOG.

Toynbee, Arnold (toin'bē), 1852–83, English economic historian, philosopher, and reformer. After his graduation in 1878 he was a tutor at Balliol College, Oxford, and was active in reform work outside the university, particularly among the London poor. His influence on his students and contemporaries was great, although he lived to be only 31. Toynbee was interested in applying historical method to the study of economics. He objected to Marxism, believing that the best interests of labor and capital lay in cooperation. His lectures to workingmen were published as *Lectures on the Industrial Revolution of the 18th Century in England* (1884), a pioneer work in economic history. Toynbee Hall in London, the first settlement house, was named for him. See biographies by Alfred Milner (1901) and F. C. Montague (1889, repr. 1973).

Toynbee, Arnold Joseph, 1889–, English historian; nephew of Arnold Toynbee. Educated at Oxford, he served in the British foreign office during World Wars I and II and was a delegate (1919) to the Paris Peace Conference. He was professor of Greek language and history (1919–55) at the Univ. of London and from 1925 to 1955 was director of studies at the Royal Institute of International Affairs. A prolific scholar, Toynbee achieved his greatest fame for his monumental work, *A Study of History* (12 vol., 1934–61), which appeared in an abridgment by D. C. Somervell (2 vol., 1946–57). In the *Study of History,* an investigation into the growth, development, and decay of civilizations, the problems of history are considered in terms of great cultural groups rather than in terms of nationalities. The main thesis of the work is that the well-being of a civilization depends upon its ability to respond successfully to challenges, human and environmental. Of 26 civilizations in man's history, according to Toynbee, only one—Western Latin Christendom—is currently alive, and perhaps even this is in decline. He has been criticized for arbitrary generalization, for inevitable factual error, and for overreliance on religion as a regenerative force. However, he has also been praised for a historical approach that, unlike that of Oswald Spengler, stresses psychic factors rather than materialistic forces. Toynbee also helped to write and edit many volumes of *A Survey of International Affairs,* and he produced works on a multitude of historical topics. For critical evaluations of Toynbee's work see M. F. Ashley-Montagu, ed., *Toynbee and History* (1956); E. T. Gargan, ed., *The Intent of Toynbee's History* (1961); biography by R. N. Stromberg (1972).

Toynbee Hall: see BARNETT, SAMUEL AUGUSTUS.

Toyohashi (tōyō'hä'shē), city (1970 pop. 288,538), Aichi prefecture, central Honshu, Japan. It is a leading silk and cotton production center. Toyohashi was formerly an important castle town of the Matsudaira clan.

Toyokuni (tōyō'kōōnē), 1769–1825, Japanese colorprint artist, whose name in full was Toyokuni Utagawa. He was one of the leading masters of the period of the popular ukiyoe school. After many failures to appeal to the public taste, he attained great success with portrayals of stage favorites in dramatic situations. His work shows vigorous, sweeping lines and striking color contrasts. It attracted numerous imitators and a host of pupils.

toyon: see CHRISTMASBERRY.

Toyota (toi-ō'tə, Jap. tōyō'tä), city (1970 pop. 197,193), Aichi prefecture, central Honshu, Japan. It is a major industrial center dominated by the Toyota Automatic Loom Works.

Tozzi, Federigo (fādärē'gō tôt'tsē), 1883–1920, Italian novelist. He was a follower of Verga and D'Annunzio but, unlike D'Annunzio, became concerned with moral problems. His novels, bitter and dispassionate, are powerfully written; outstanding are *Tre croci* (1920, tr. *Three Crosses,* 1921) and *Il podere* [the farm] (1921). His other works include short stories, plays, and verse.

TPN, in biochemistry, abbreviation for triphosphopyridine nucleotide, a COENZYME now usually called nicotinamide adenine dinucleotide phosphate, or NADP.

Trabzon (träb"zōn') or **Trebizond** (trĕb'ĭzŏnd"), city (1970 pop. 81,528), capital of Trabzon prov., NE Turkey, a port on the Black Sea. A commercial center, it exports food products and tobacco. Known in ancient times as Trapezus, the city was founded in the 8th cent. B.C. by Greek colonists from Sinop. It grew in importance after its conquest (1st cent. B.C.) by Mithradates VI and after its incorporation (1st cent. A.D.) into the Roman Empire. Although it suffered from invasions by barbarians after the 3d cent., it again became a prosperous port under the Byzantine Empire. It reached its greatest splendor after the establishment (1204) by the Comneni of the empire of Trebizond, which endured until 1461, when it was annexed by the Ottoman Empire. Under the rule of Alexius III (1349–90) the city was one of the world's leading trade centers and was renowned for its great wealth and artistic accomplishment. Under the Ottomans it became the starting point of caravans to Persia. Trabzon was included (1920) in the short-lived independent state of Armenia. The city's large Greek population was deported in 1922–23. Trabzon has many historic monuments. The best preserved is the 13th-century Church of Aya Sophia (now a museum), an excellent example of Byzantine architecture.

tracer, an identifiable substance used to follow the course of a physical, chemical, or biological process. In chemistry the ideal tracer has the same chemical properties as the molecule it replaces and undergoes the same reactions, but can at all times be detectible and quantitatively assessed. In biochemistry tracers have been in use since the beginning of the 20th cent. Using synthetic methods, Franz Knoop in 1904 made various derivatives of fatty acids, the degradation of which he studied by feeding the derivatives to dogs and by monitoring the appearance of unusual products in the dogs' urine. From these studies were obtained the first descriptions of the metabolic pathway for fatty acid catabolism. About these sorts of experiments, however, the argument could always be made that the derivatives were "unphysiological," that is, did not occur naturally and might be handled by the enzymes of the body differently than "physiological" compounds. This difficulty was overcome in 1935 when Rudolf Schoenheimer and David Rittenberg described the use of the isotope deuterium (identical to the hydrogen atom except containing one extra neutron) in following biochemical reactions. They argued persuasively that deuterium-labeled compounds (those having a deuterium atom in substitution for a hydrogen) were essentially indistinguishable from non-labeled compounds, as far as metabolic processes were concerned, but that the amount of deuterium in any given sample could be quantitatively determined by the properties of the water produced upon combustion of the sample. Although this was the first declaration of the general usefulness of the approach, George Hevesy in 1923 was the first investigator to use an isotope in metabolic studies; he explored lead transport in the bean plant using radioactive thorium. Radioactive isotopes are more easily detected than nonradioactive ones, such as deuterium; therefore, when the radioactive isotopes of various atoms commonly occurring in organic molecules became widely available after World War II, metabolic studies proliferated. Isotopes in common use today include carbon-14, iodine-131, nitrogen-15, phosphorus-32, sulfur-35, and tritium (hydrogen-3).

tracery, bands or bars of stone, wood, or other material, either subdividing an opening or standing in relief against a wall and forming an ornamental pattern of solid members and open spaces. The term refers especially to the subdivisions in the arched openings of Gothic architecture. In Romanesque design the enclosing of twin openings within a single arch created a wall space above them, where a circular or quatrefoil opening was pierced as an ornament. This plate tracery became more complex in 12th-century rose windows of the Cathedral of Chartres and in early Gothic English churches. Later, windows became larger, areas of solid stone smaller, and masonry members more slender; the patterns in the spaces above the arches were created by bars of stone rather than by a pierced design. Such bar tracery (e.g., in the cathedral at Rheims) prevailed in both France and England by the first half of the 13th cent., creating circles, trefoils, quatrefoils, and other

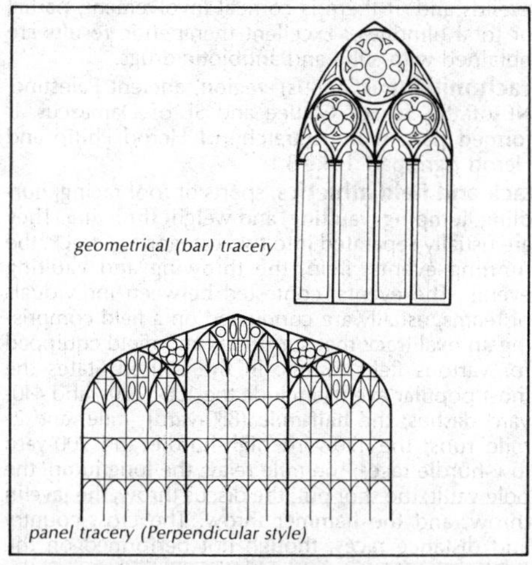

Types of tracery

varied geometrical designs. The terminations of these shapes, termed *cusps,* were finished in square or sharp points or in ornamental blobs. Tracery came gradually to be used also for ornamenting buttresses, gables, spires, interior walls, and choir screens. In France, Rayonnant-style tracery was marked by a multiplication of thin vertical bars within a rational, geometrical order. In England there appeared in the mid-13th cent., mainly in window heads, a new curvilinear tracery of free, flowing curves. The French developed that type into the elaborate, flamboyant tracery of the 15th cent., which produced windows and architectural adornment of amazing lightness and intricacy, as in the cathedral at Rouen and in the wood choir stalls of Amiens. In England, however, the flowing forms were abandoned c.1375, and emphasis passed to perpendicular mullions running the entire height of the windows. By the early part of the 16th cent. the severe tracery of the Perpendicular style, with its closely spaced verticals, was dominant in both windows and wall adornment, providing a contrast to the elaborate fan vaulting, as in the Henry VII Chapel in Westminster and King's College Chapel, Cambridge. Medieval tracery achieved extraordinary effect in the great French rose windows of STAINED GLASS.

trachea (trā'kēə) or **windpipe,** principal tube that carries air to and from the lungs. It is about 4½ in. (11.4 cm) long and about ¾ in. (1.9 cm) in diameter in the adult. It extends from the LARYNX to the bronchial tubes and is situated in front of the esophagus (see RESPIRATION). The trachea consists of a supporting layer of connective and muscular tissue in which are embedded from 16 to 20 U-shaped rings of hard cartilage that encircle the front of the tube. Tiny hairs, or cilia, in the mucous membrane lining keep dust and other foreign particles from entering the lungs. The foreign material becomes trapped in the mucus and is swept by the beating cilia to the nose or mouth, where it is discharged from the body. The air tubes of insects and other arthropods are also called trachea.

tracheotomy (trākēŏt'əmē), surgical incision into the trachea, or windpipe. The operation is performed when the windpipe has become blocked, e.g., by the presence of some foreign object or by swelling of the larynx. A curved or flexible tube is inserted into the trachea to facilitate breathing. In diseases such as pneumonia that cause the lungs to fill with fluids, this same incision may be used to drain the lungs. A tracheostomy is the surgical formation of a rounded opening into the trachea and differs from a tracheotomy in that the former procedure establishes a permanent opening.

trachoma (trəkō'mə), infection of the mucous membrane of the eyelids, caused by a virus. Although rare in the United States, trachoma is the most common disease known to man, with the exception of the common cold. It is highly contagious and is transmitted by direct contact with infected persons or articles (e.g., towels, handkerchiefs). Trachoma occurs under conditions of poor hygiene and is especially prevalent in Asia and Africa. It was formerly widespread among American Indians and in the southern mountainous regions of the United States. Trachoma begins as congestion and swelling of the eyelids with tearing and disturbance of vision. The cornea is often involved. If left untreated, scar tissue forms, which causes deformities of the eyelids and, if there is corneal involvement, partial or total blindness. Excellent therapeutic results are obtained with sulfa and antibiotic drugs.

Trachonitis (trăk"ənī'tĭs), region, ancient Palestine, NE of the Sea of Galilee and SE of Damascus. It formed part of the tetrarchy of Herod Philip and Herod Agrippa I. Luke 3.1.

track and field athletics, sports of foot racing, hurdling, jumping, vaulting, and weight throwing. They are usually separated into two categories—track, the running events; field, the throwing and vaulting events. The events, contested between individuals or teams, usually are conducted on a field comprising an oval track that surrounds an infield equipped for various field events. In the United States the most popular events include the 100-, 220-, and 440-yard dashes; the half-mile (880-yard), mile, and 2-mile runs; the 120-yard high-hurdle and 200-yard low-hurdle races; the mile relay; the long jump, the pole vault, the shot put, the discus throw, the javelin throw, and the hammer throw. The cross-country and distance races, though not performed on the field, are usually classed with these events, as are the marathon and walking races. Winter indoor meets are popular in major cities and include running events (from 60 yd to 2 mi), high hurdles (60 yd), and field events. In the modern OLYMPIC GAMES and many other international meets, track events include the 100-, 200-, 400-, 800-, 1,500-, 5,000-, and 10,000-meter runs; a marathon run (26 mi 385 yd/42.20 km); the 110- and 400-meter hurdle races; the 400- and 1,600-meter relay; the 3,000-meter steeplechase; and the 20,000- and 50,000-meter walks. The Olympic games include, in addition to the field events already named, the triple jump, formerly known as the running hop-step-and-jump. The decathlon is the major composite event contested in Olympic track and field competition, while the pentathlon is contested in the U.S. national championships. All the events described are primarily men's events. There are also equivalent events for women in U.S. and Olympic games competition. In ancient Greece track and field athletics dominated the original Olympic games and other games; there were also less important and separate games for women. Such organized contests were also popular in Rome but lapsed in the early Middle Ages. In England they were revived in the 12th cent. and thereafter steadily increased in popularity. The first college track and field meet occurred in England (1864) between Oxford and Cambridge. Other European countries soon turned to the sport. Track and field athletics in the United States date from the 1860s. The Intercollegiate Association of Amateur Athletes of America, the nation's first national athletic group, held the first collegiate meet in 1876, and in 1888 the Amateur Athletic Union held its first championships. Those two groups, along with the National Collegiate Athletic Association, regulate the sport in the United States. The mid-20th cent. has been marked by a continuous improvement in track and field accomplishments. Performances previously considered unattainable, such as the 4-minute mile, are now common. Other major track and field accomplishments include the 70-foot shot put, the 7-foot high jump, the 29-foot long jump, and the 18-foot pole vault. Professional track and field was begun (1973) by the International Track Association, the world's first professional track and field group. See R. L. Quercetani, *A World History of Track and Field Athletics, 1864–1964* (1964); Cordner Nelson, *Track and Field, the Great Ones* (1970); J. A. Gordon, *Track and Field* (2d ed. 1972).

Tractarian movement: see OXFORD MOVEMENT.

tractor, in agriculture, automotive vehicle used to draw such equipment as plows, cultivators, harvesters, and mowing machines; to power stationary devices such as saws and winches; and to push implements such as snowplows and bulldozers. Formerly tractors were steam-driven; now they are generally powered by gasoline or diesel fuel. The two main types of tractor are the wheeled tractors and the tracklayers, also called crawler, or caterpillar, tractors, which move on treads. Both are adapted in size and horsepower for various demands, from heavy field work to light garden cultivation; the tank used in war is an adaptation of the crawler tractor. The tractor brought profound changes in farm management, displacing not only draft animals but also many farm workers. The small general-purpose tractor was introduced c.1924, and the use of pneumatic tires, affording increased speed, easier operation, lower fuel consumption, and longer wear, was introduced c.1933. Tractors with spiked metal wheels or cleated treads are sometimes used for especially heavy work. See F. R. Jones, *Farm Gas Engines and Tractors* (4th ed. 1963).

Tracy, Benjamin Franklin, 1830–1915, American lawyer, cabinet member, and soldier, b. Owego, N.Y. He was admitted to the bar in 1851 and later served (1853–59) as district attorney of Tioga co., N.Y. He helped organize (1854) the Republican party in his county and served (1862) in the state assembly. In the Civil War he recruited volunteers for the Union army, was wounded in battle, and was mustered out as brigadier general. Tracy served as U.S. district attorney (1866–73) for the eastern district of New York and was defense counsel to Henry Ward Beecher in the adultery suit brought against him by Theodore Tilton. He was (1881–82) judge of the New York court of appeals before becoming Secretary of the Navy (1889–93) under President Benjamin Harrison. Tracy was (1896) chairman of the commission that drafted the charter for Greater New York and served (1899) as counsel for Venezuela in the arbitration of the boundary dispute with Great Britain. See study by B. F. Cooling (1973).

Tracy, Honor, pseud. of Lilbush Wingfield, 1915– , British writer, b. Bury St. Edmonds, Suffolk. She has been European and Far Eastern correspondent for the London *Observer* and Irish correspondent for the British Broadcasting Corp. Tracy's witty, satirical novels celebrate unreasonable human nature, particularly that of the Irish. Her many works include such novels as *The Straight and Narrow Path* (1956) and *The Quiet End of Evening* (1972) and travel books including *Winter in Castille* (1974).

Tracy, Spencer, 1900–1967, American film actor, b. Milwaukee, Wis. He began his career as an actor in summer stock and went into film work in 1930. His fine character portrayals won him Academy Awards for *Captains Courageous* (1937) and *Boys Town* (1938). An actor of rugged strength and sensitivity, he appeared in *Cass Timberlane* (1947), *Father of the Bride* (1950), *The Last Hurrah* (1958), and as the only character in *The Old Man and the Sea* (1958). Tracy and Katharine Hepburn, together in nine films, provided the screen with a delightful, intelligent team. See G. Kanin's *Tracy and Hepburn* (1971).

Tracy, city (1970 pop. 14,724), San Joaquin co., central Calif., in the San Joaquin valley; inc. 1910. Food products and glass are made. A pumping plant in Tracy is part of the Central Valley project.

trade, traffic in goods. Conducted by gift, barter, or sale, trade is one of the most widespread of all social institutions. The discovery of nonlocal objects at many archeological sites suggests that trade existed in prehistoric times. Anthropologists and other explorers have found trade institutions among diverse peoples throughout the world. The ceremonially elaborate kula trade ring of the Trobriand Islands, the gift-giving potlatch of NW Canada's Kwakiutl Indians, and the desert caravan of N Africa and the Arabian Peninsula are among the more famous examples. In the Western world a number of peoples, including the Egyptians, Sumerians, Cretans, Phoenicians, Greeks, Venetians, Spanish, and English have at one time or another dominated world trade. Today the world's major trading powers are the United States, the countries of Western Europe, and Japan. The Crusades did much to widen European trade horizons and prefaced the passing of trade superiority from Constantinople to Venice and other cities of N Italy. In the 15th and 16th cent., with the sudden expansion of Portugal and Spain, the so-called commercial revolution reached a high point. In N and central Europe, the earlier supremacy of the Hanseatic League, the Rhenish cities, and the cities of N France and Flanders was eclipsed by the rise of national states. Antwerp began its long career of glory when the Spanish were losing their hegemony, and the Dutch briefly triumphed in the race for world commerce in the 17th cent. The Dutch in turn lost to British-French rivalry, which by 1815 left Britain paramount. The Industrial Revolution of the 18th and 19th cent. further aided the development of commerce. The expansion of trade was further promoted by the rise, under the auspices of the national state, of the CHARTERED COMPANY and by the modern corporation, which later displaced it. World commerce was also aided materially by the invention of the astrolabe, the mariner's compass, and the sextant; by the development of iron and steel construction; and by the application of steam to both land and water transport. The later development of communication devices such as the telephone, telegraph, cable, and radio, and inventions such as refrigeration, the gasoline engine, the electric motor, and the airplane have also contributed to the growth of trade. The theory of commerce as imposed by the national state has varied from the MERCANTILISM of the 17th and 18th cent. and the protective tariff of the 19th and 20th cent. to the FREE TRADE that Britain long upheld. Since World War II a realization of the need for commercial expansion has led to the creation of regional customs unions, the prime example being the COMMON MARKET. Less geographically restricted trade systems, such as the General Agreement on Tariffs and Trade, have also arisen. In modern times international trade has had an important political role. Nations often use trade either to solidify old political relationships or to create new ones. Thus, the expansion of U.S.-Soviet and U.S.-Chinese trade in the early 1970s was seen by many as a sign of decreased political tension between the United States and the two great Communist powers. Internally, most nations seek to encourage trade among different sections of the country. Internal trade in the United States is regulated by the Interstate Commerce Commission (created 1887). The principles of efficient MARKETING have been applied to domestic trade, which has attained enormous volume. Trade between regions and between countries is natural where each produces some commodity that the other needs. For example, modern industrial countries need certain metals and other raw materials, which they must obtain by trade if they do not have them or do not produce them in sufficient quantity at home. See D. B. Marsh, *World Trade and Investment* (1951); J. H. Harold, *Foreign Commerce* (1953); P. V. Horn, *International Trade* (4th ed. 1959).

trade association, group of businessmen in the same trade or industry organized for the advancement of common interests. The trade association differs from the CHAMBER OF COMMERCE in that membership is by industry rather than by locality. The common interests binding the members of the trade association may include credit, public relations, relations with employees, sales development, output, or prices. Some associations publish official journals, and some maintain bureaus at the national and state capitals.

trademark, distinctive mark placed on or attached to goods by a manufacturer or dealer to identify them as made or sold by him. The use of a trademark indicates that the maker or dealer believes that the quality of the goods will enhance his standing or good will, and a known trademark indicates to a buyer the reputation that is staked on the goods. Registration of a trademark is necessary in some countries to give exclusive right to it. In the United States, Canada, and Great Britain, the sufficient use of a trademark not previously used establishes exclusive right to it, but registration is provided as an aid in defending that right. In the United States trademarks are registered with the Patent Office. Imitations of a trademark wrong both the owner of the trademark and the buyer who is misled as to the source of goods, and such infringements of a trademark are punishable by law. See Milton Wright, *Inventions, Patents, and Trade-marks* (2d ed. 1933).

trade rat: see PACK RAT.

trade union: see UNION, LABOR.

trade winds, movement of air toward the equator, from the NE in the Northern Hemisphere and from the SE in the Southern Hemisphere. The trade winds originate on the equatorial sides of the HORSE LATITUDES, which are two belts of high air pressure, one lying between 25° and 30° north of the equator and the other lying between 25° and 30° south of it. The high air pressure in these belts forces air to move toward a belt of low air pressure along the equator called the DOLDRUMS. The air converging at the doldrums rises high over the earth, recirculates poleward, and sinks back toward the earth's surface in the region of the horse latitudes, thus completing a cycle. The air does not move directly north or south because it is deflected by the rotation of the earth. See WIND.

Trafalgar, battle of (trəfăl'gər), naval engagement fought off Cape Trafalgar on the SW coast of Spain on Oct. 21, 1805, in which the British fleet under Horatio Nelson won a famous victory over the allied French and Spanish fleets under Pierre de Villeneuve. Nelson's strategy was to divide his own fleet into two sections, one led by himself in the *Victory*, the other led by Cuthbert Collingwood in the *Royal Sovereign*, and to penetrate the enemy line in two places. This maneuver resulted in the capture of 20 enemy ships (one was blown up). The British lost no ships. Among the dead was Nelson himself, struck by a bullet from the French ship *Redoutable*. The decisive English victory ended Napoleon I's power on the sea and made a French invasion of England impossible. The words signaled by Nelson at the beginning of the battle—"England expects that every man will do his duty"—became immortal. See studies by D. A. Howarth (1969) and Oliver Warner (1971).

Trafalgar Square, in Westminster, London, England, named for Lord Nelson's victory at the battle of Trafalgar. The statue surmounting the Nelson memorial column (185 ft/56 m high) was executed (1840-43) by E. H. Baily. On the northern side of the square stand the National Gallery and the Church of St. Martin's-in-the-Fields.

traffic regulation, control of the movement of vehicles and pedestrians, chiefly on city streets. Formal regulation of motor vehicle traffic was instituted in New York City in 1903; a set of *Rules for Driving* was issued by the police commissioner, and a traffic squad was formed. Similar systems were soon adopted in cities all over the world. Since that time, as the volume of traffic has increased, a variety of control mechanisms have been developed to regulate the safe flow of traffic. The control of traffic at crossings by the use of traffic lights is common on streets and highways. Traffic lights may be locally operated by a traffic officer; they may be automatic, the lights changing periodically; or they may be operated by remote control. Many cities now control signals by a progressive system: The driver, when starting at the beginning of one traffic block with a green, or clear, signal, sees at the next traffic block a red light; however, by traveling at a constant speed, the driver arrives at the next block when the red light has turned to green. Other devices include traffic signs (the United Nations has encouraged the adoption of a set of signs common to all nations, i.e., pictorial rather than verbal), road markings (which indicate such things as no-passing zones), computerized traffic control systems that aid in determining changes in traffic patterns, and rapid accident reporting. The routing of traffic has also become a focal point of traffic regulation. One-way street systems (which may be reversed at different times of the day) have been found to ease congestion and have been adopted in many parts of the world. Special truck routes through uncongested areas of a city speed the flow of traffic, as do through-street systems that grant the driver the right of way against cross traffic. Traffic regulation also includes the control or elimination of parking on streets and highways, the designation of specific zones for loading and unloading trucks, and special protection for pedestrians. In a number of cities, notably Rome, efforts have been made to reduce traffic congestion by banning the use of private automobiles in the central city. In other areas, various attempts to ease congestion have been made, such as providing free bus service. Traffic regulation requires enforcement; drivers have to be licensed according to specific age, health, and intelligence qualifications. Accidents must be investigated and attempts made to keep erratic or intoxicated drivers off the roads. Finally, as automobile technology and traffic laws have become increasingly complex, driver education has become more important. Courses may be taken privately or within public school systems; some businesses offer them to employees. See T. R. Horton, ed., *Traffic Control Theory and Instrumentation* (1965).

tragacanth (trăg'əkănth) or **gum tragacanth,** gummy exudation from the leguminous shrub *Astragalus gummifer* and related PULSE family plants of SE Europe and W Asia. It is obtained through incisions in the stem of the plant. The gum is produced chiefly in Iran. Tragacanth is almost insoluble in water but swells in it to form a stiff gel. It is used as an emulsifying agent, as a component of pills, hand lotions, and medicinal lubricating jellies, as a demulcent, and as a sizing material. A gum (sometimes called Indian tragacanth) from a plant of the STERCULIA family is sold as a cheaper substitute.

tragedy, form of drama, central to the Western literary tradition, in which a person of superior intelligence and character, a leader of the community, is overcome by the very obstacles he is struggling to remove. Often he is brought low by a flaw in his character. The earliest tragedies were part of the Attic religious festivals held in honor of the god Dionysus (5th cent. B.C.). The ritual entailed the presentation of four successive plays (three tragedies, one comedy). Each was based on situations and characters drawn from myth, and the tragedies ended in catastrophe for the heroes and heroines. The most famous ancient tragedies are probably the *Oresteia* (a trilogy) of Aeschylus, Sophocles' *Oedipus Rex*, and Euripides' *Trojan Women*. In his definitive analysis of tragedy in the *Poetics* (4th cent. B.C.), Aristotle points out its ritual function: The spectators, a congregation as much as an audience, are purged of their own emotions of pity and fear through their vicarious participation in the drama. The plays of the Roman tragedian Seneca—including *Hercules, Medea, Phaedra*, and *Agamemnon*—were based on certain conventions, notably violence, revenge, and the appearance of ghosts. These works are significant not for intrinsic grandeur but for their usefulness as models for such Renaissance dramas as Christopher Marlowe's *Tamburlaine* (1587) and *The Spanish Tragedy* (1594) of Thomas Kyd. These in turn served as models for the towering tragedies of the period, Marlowe's *Dr. Faustus* (1588); Shakespeare's *Othello, Macbeth, Hamlet*, and *King Lear* (1600-1607); and John Webster's *Duchess of Malfi* (1614). As their titles suggest, these plays dramatize the conflicts of kings, conquerors, or, at the very least, geniuses. The tradition of the tragic hero was to continue for the next 300 years, reinforced not only by English dramatists but by such European playwrights as the Spaniards Lope de Vega and Calderón de la Barca; the Frenchmen Pierre Corneille and Jean Racine; and the Germans G. E. Lessing, Goethe, and Schiller. Tragedy can also be a vision of life, one shared by most Western cultures and having its roots in the Judeo-Christian tradition. To reflect this wider sense of the human dilemma, where men feel compelled to confront evil, yet where evil prevails, a second dramatic tradition evolved. Its roots go back once again to religious drama, in this case the mystery and morality plays of medieval England, France, and Germany (see MIRACLE PLAY; MORALITY PLAY). Unlike classical drama, these plays, of which *Everyman* is the best known, emphasize the accountability of ordinary people. Even plays about the divine Christ stress human suffering and sacrifice. The tragic lot of the common man thus found its way into the dramatic repertory of later ages. George Lillo's *London Merchant* (1731) is an early example of domestic tragedy, as Georg Büchner's *Danton's Death* (1835) is of political tragedy. Henrik Ibsen's *Doll's House* (1879) and *An Enemy of the People* (1882) are also superb examples of the domestic and the political tragedy, respectively. In these plays, ordinary people display heroic conduct, thereby acknowledging their faith in the validity of the tragic vision. The cataclysmic events of the 20th cent.—two world wars, the destructive use of atomic power, the disintegration of family and community life—have caused a radical diminution of that vision. Its shrinkage is evident in such plays as Eugene O'Neill's *Mourning Becomes Electra* (1931) and *Long Day's Journey Into Night* (1956), Bertolt Brecht's *Mother Courage* (1941), Arthur Miller's *Death of a Salesman* (1949), and Samuel Beckett's *Waiting for Godot* (1953). In these works life is depicted as so horrible, meaningless, and absurd that heroic behavior is not only impossible, it is irrelevant. Even so, each of these works can be labeled tragedy, if rather loosely. The pattern first seen by Aristotle is still discernible. The protagonist is, as always, defeated by opposing forces—Freudian behavior patterns, wartime attrition, loss of identity, Deus Abscondus, drugs, or alcohol, if not pride, ambition, and jealousy. And still felt is the mysterious cathartic exaltation at the end of a powerful theatrical experience. Despite quibbling about the exact meaning and application of the word *tragedy*, most critics would agree in saying that some of the works of such 20th-century dramatists as Anton Chekhov, August Strindberg, Luigi Pirandello, Gabriele d'Annunzio, Ugo Betti, Michel de Ghelderode, Sean O'Casey, Jean Anouilh, and Tennessee Williams may be classed as tragedy. See also DRAMA, WESTERN; COMEDY; and individual articles on all writers mentioned in this entry. See Barrett H. Clark, ed., *European Theories of the Drama* (rev. ed. 1947); H. J. Muller, *The Spirit of Tragedy* (1956); R. B. Sewall, *The Vision of Tragedy* (1959); R. W. Corrigan, ed., *Tragedy* (1965); Geoffrey Brereton, *Principles of Tragedy* (1968).

Traherne, Thomas (trəhûrn'), 1636?-1674, English poet and prose writer, one of the METAPHYSICAL POETS. He was schooled at Brasenose College, Oxford, and was chaplain to the Lord Keeper from 1667 until his death. His writings express an ardent, childlike love of God and a firm belief in man's relation to the divine. Although *Roman Forgeries* and *Christian Ethicks* were published in 1673 and 1675 respectively, his finest work was lost for many years. In 1896 a manuscript of his poetry and prose was discovered in a London bookstall and subsequently was published as *Poems* (1903) and *Centuries of Meditations* (1908). See his poems ed. by A. Ridler (1966); biography by G. I. Wade (1944, repr. 1969); study by A. L. Clements (1969).

Traikov, Georgi, (gēôr'gē trīkôf'), 1898-, Bulgarian politician and agronomist. Active in agrarian politics from the end of World War I, he rose to become minister of agriculture in the Bulgarian Communist government established in 1946. From 1949 to 1964 he was first deputy prime minister. As head of the Bulgarian national assembly (1964-72), Traikov was nominal chief of state.

Trail, city (1971 pop. 11,149), SE British Columbia, Canada, on the Columbia River just N of the Wash. border. It is a metal-smelting center for a mining area that produces lead, zinc, silver, and gold. Sulfuric acid and fertilizers are manufactured there.

trailing arbutus, Mayflower, or **ground laurel,** one of the best-loved American wild flowers, said by Whittier to have been the first blossom seen on these shores by the Pilgrims (introduction to "The Mayflowers"). The plant blooms in early spring; its creeping stems bear clusters of sweetly fragrant pink or white flowers that are sometimes hidden by the hairy evergreen leaves. The leaves were once used in making a diuretic tea and were also said to be astringent and tonic. Roots of the trailing arbutus live in a partnership arrangement (mycorrhiza) with a fungus (see SYMBIOSIS). The plant is difficult to cultivate, and its existence is endangered by the zeal of flower pickers. In its native habitat, arbutus seems to prefer the acid soil of pinewoods of the eastern part of North America. It is the provincial flower of Nova Scotia and the state flower of Massachusetts, where a law protects the plant. The trailing arbutus (*Epigaea repens*) should not be confused with *Arbutus*, a related botanic genus (including the madroño) also of the HEATH family. The names Mayflower and laurel are also used for other plants. Trailing arbutus is classified in the division MAGNOLIOPHYTA, class Magnoliopsida, order Ericales, family Ericaceae.

Trajan (Marcus Ulpius Trajanus)(trā'jən), A.D. c.53-A.D. 117, Roman emperor (A.D. 98-A.D. 117). Born in Spain, he was the first non-Italian to become head of the empire. Trajan served in the East, in Germany, and in Spain. He was adopted in A.D. 97 by Emperor NERVA, who died shortly afterward. A capable man, Trajan set about strengthening his regime by embarking on a vigorous foreign policy. In two wars against DACIA he brought that region, the parent of modern Rumania, under Roman control. This conquest is commemorated by the sculptured Trajan's Column, which stands in the Forum of Trajan in Rome. Trajan then annexed Arabia Petraea, and in three campaigns he conquered the greater part of the Parthian empire, including Armenia and Upper Mesopotamia. On his way home from this campaign, he died in Cilicia. He was succeeded by Hadrian. Trajan was an able military organizer and civic administrator. He partially drained the Pontine Marshes and restored the Appian Way, and at Rome he built an aqueduct, a theater, and the immense Forum of Trajan, containing basilicas and libraries. See B. W. Henderson, *Five Roman Emperors* (1927); F. A. Lepper, *Trajan's Parthian War* (1948); Tino Rossi, *Trajan's Column and the Dacian Wars* (1972).

Trakl, Georg (gāôrk träk'əl), 1887–1914, Austrian expressionist poet. Trakl's work, influenced by French impressionist poetry, reveals his disgust with imperialistic society. An absorption with sorrow and decay permeates his *Gedichte* [poems] (1913), the only collection published during his lifetime. A pharmacist in the German army, Trakl died from an overdose of drugs. Posthumous publications of his work include *Der Herbst des Einsamen* [the autumn of the lonely] (1920) and *Gesang des Abgeschiedenen* [song of the departed] (1933). See selection of his poems ed. by Christopher Middleton (1968); biography by H. S. Lindenberger (1971); study by T. J. Casey (1964).

Tralee (trəlē', trā–), urban district (1971 pop. 12,227), county town of Co. Kerry, SW Republic of Ireland, on the Lee River. It is a seaport linked with Blennerville on Tralee Bay by a 1-mi-long (1.6-km) canal. Boots, shoes, knitwear, and plastics are produced, and there is a tannery. Tourism is also important in Tralee.

Trälleborg: see TRELLEBORG, Sweden.

Tralles (trăl'ēz), ancient Carian city, W Asia Minor. It is the modern AYDIN, Turkey.

Trani (trä'nē), town (1970 pop. 40,606), in Apulia, S Italy, on the Adriatic Sea. It is a seaport, a beach resort, and an agricultural center, famous for its wine. Trani enjoyed great prosperity at the time of the Crusades (11th–13th cent.) and again in the 15th–16th cent. Its *ordinamenta maris* of 1063 probably constitute the first medieval code of maritime law. Landmarks include the Romanesque Cathedral of San Nicolà Pellegrino, with fine bronze doors (1179) and a lofty campanile; a 13th-century castle; and a large public garden.

tranquilizer, drug whose action calms the central NERVOUS SYSTEM, decreasing emotional agitation without impairing alertness. Tranquilizing drugs differ from hypnotic drugs such as BARBITURATES in that they do not act on the brain's cortical areas but rather on its lower portions, e.g., the HYPOTHALAMUS. They have been found helpful in the treatment of tension and mental illness. RESERPINE, which appeared on the market in 1952, was the first tranquilizer to be used in modern Western medicine. Other drugs used as tranquilizers include the PHENOTHIAZINES, MEPROBAMATE, certain muscle relaxants and anticonvulsants, and lithium carbonate. See also PSYCHOPHARMACOLOGY. See Erwin Lear, *Chemistry and Applied Pharmacology of Tranquilizers* (1966).

transactinide elements (trăns"ăk'tənīd"), in chemistry, elements with atomic numbers greater than that of lawrencium (at. no. 103), the last member of the actinide series. See TRANSURANIUM ELEMENTS.

transactional analysis: see GROUP PSYCHOTHERAPY.

Trans-Alai (trăns-älī', trănz-), mountain range, central Asia, a part of the Pamir-Alai mountain system. The Trans-Alai extends c.125 mi (200 km) W from the China-USSR border into the USSR along the Kirghiz SSR-Tadzhik SSR border. It rises to 23,382 ft (7,127 m) in the Lenin Peak.

Trans-Amazon Highway, road, c.3,000 mi (4,830 km) long, traversing N central Brazil. The highway, stretching from the Atlantic coast to the Peruvian border, is an important factor in the economic development of the Amazon region.

Transandine Railway, 156 mi (251 km) long, between Mendoza, Argentina, and Los Andes, Chile, traversing the Andes at Uspallata Pass. Opened to traffic in 1910, the railway rises to c.10,500 ft (3,200 m) at the long tunnel on the international boundary. A glacial flood in 1934 destroyed 77 mi (124 km) of the Argentine section, but it was later rebuilt. Tunnels and snowsheds protect selected sections of the line.

Transantarctic Mountains, mountain chain stretching across Antarctica from Victoria Land to Coats Land; separating the E Antarctic and W Antarctic subcontinents. Mt. Markham (14,275 ft/4,351 m high), near the Ross Ice Shelf, is the highest peak. Its basement rocks, similar to rocks found in Australia, S Africa, and South America, give credibility to the theory of continental drift.

Transbaykalia or **Transbaikalia** (both: trăns"bīkä'lyə, trănz"-), Rus. *Zabaykalye* (zŭbīkä'lyĭ), region, SE Siberian USSR, extending from Lake Baykal to the Amur River. It consists of plateaus and mountain ranges separated by wide, deep, river valleys. There are gold deposits along the Vitim Plateau. Chita is the chief city of the region.

***trans*-butenedioic acid,** IUPAC name for FUMARIC ACID.

Trans-Canada Highway, c.4,800 mi (7,700 km) long, S Canada; completed 1962. The world's longest national highway, it traverses North America from St. John's, N.F., to Victoria, British Columbia. Ferry routes form vital links at the eastern and western ends of the highway. The Alaska Highway joins the Trans-Canada Highway at Calgary, Alta.

Transcarpathian Oblast: see ZAKARPATSKAYA OBLAST, USSR.

Transcaspian Oblast: see TURKMEN SOVIET SOCIALIST REPUBLIC.

Trans-Caspian Railroad, transportation line linking the republics of Central Asian USSR to one another and with the rest of the USSR. Built in the late 19th cent., the line begins at Krasnovodsk on the Caspian Sea and passes through Ashkhabad, Bukhara, Samarkand, and Tashkent. There are branches to the Fergana Valley. The Trans-Caspian line connects at Arys with the more recent Turkistan-Siberia RR and the Kazalinsk line to Orenburg. It was formerly also known as the Central Asiatic RR.

Transcaucasia (trănz"kôkā'zhə, –shə, trăns"–), region of the USSR, extending from the Greater Caucasus to the Turkish and Iranian borders, between the Black and Caspian seas. It comprises the GEORGIAN SOVIET SOCIALIST REPUBLIC, the ARMENIAN SOVIET SOCIALIST REPUBLIC, and the AZERBAIJAN SOVIET SOCIALIST REPUBLIC. TBILISI, BAKU, BATUMI, YEREVAN, and KUTAISI are the major cities. Between the Greater Caucasus in the north and the Lesser Caucasus in the south is the Colchis lowland. The Kura, Rion, Inguri, and Alazan rivers are important for both hydroelectricity and irrigation. The region's natural resources are oil, manganese, copper, clays, and building stones. Manufactures include oil industry machinery, mining equipment, metal products, automobiles, chemicals, plastics, cotton and silk cloth, and leather footwear. Transcaucasia is second only to Central Asia in the USSR as a region of irrigated agriculture. The area's chief crops are cotton, grain, sugar beets, sunflowers, tobacco, citrus fruits, tea, and plants for essential oils. Transcaucasia's mineral springs have given rise to numerous health resorts; seaside resorts also abound. The population consists of Georgians, Armenians, Azerbaijani, Assyrians (Christians), Ossets, Abkhas, Talyshin, Kurds, and Tats. An independent federal democratic Transcaucasian republic existed in 1917–18. The federation was dissolved in May, 1918, into the republics of Armenia, Azerbaijan, and Georgia. After the three republics were conquered by the Red Army, the Transcaucasian Soviet Federated Socialist Republic was formed; it joined the USSR in Dec., 1922, becoming one of the four original federated republics. In 1936, Armenia, Azerbaijan, and Georgia were reestablished as separate union republics.

transcendentalism (trăn"sĕndĕn'təlĭzəm) [from Lat.,=overpassing], in literature, philosophical and literary movement that flourished in New England from about 1836 to 1860. It originated among a small group of intellectuals who were reacting against the orthodoxy of Calvinism and the rationalism of the Unitarian Church, developing instead their own faith centering on the divinity of man and nature. Transcendentalism derived some of its basic idealistic concepts from romantic German philosophy, notably that of Immanuel KANT, and from such English authors as Carlyle, Coleridge, and Wordsworth. Its mystical aspects were partly influenced by Oriental religious teachings. Although transcendentalism was never a rigorously systematic philosophy, it had some basic tenets that were generally shared by its adherents. The beliefs that God is immanent in man and nature and that individual intuition is the highest source of knowledge led to an optimistic emphasis on individualism, self-reliance, and rejection of traditional authority. The ideas of transcendentalism were most eloquently expressed by Ralph Waldo EMERSON in such essays as "Nature" (1836), "Self-Reliance," and "The Over Soul" (both 1841), and by Henry David THOREAU in his book *Walden* (1854). The movement began with the occasional meetings of a group of friends in Boston and Concord to discuss philosophy, literature, and religion. Originally calling themselves the Hedge Club (after one of the members), they were later dubbed the Transcendental Club by outsiders because of their discussion of Kant's "transcendental" ideas. Besides Emerson and Thoreau, its most famous members, the club included F. H. HEDGE, George RIPLEY, Bronson ALCOTT, Margaret FULLER, Theodore PARKER, and others. For several years much of their writing was published in *The Dial* (1840–44), a journal edited by Fuller and Emerson. The cooperative community Brook Farm (1841–47) grew out of their ideas on social reform, which also found expression in their many individual actions against slavery. Primarily a movement seeking a new spiritual and intellectual vitality, transcendentalism had a great impact on American literature, not only on the writings of the group's members, but on such diverse authors as Hawthorne, Melville, and Whitman. See anthologies ed. by P. G. Miller (1957) and by G. W. Cooke (1903, repr. 1971); Myron Simon and T. H. Parsons, ed., *Transcendentalism and Its Legacy* (1966); Joel Porte, *Emerson and Thoreau* (1966); O. B. Frothingham, *Transcendentalism in New England* (1876, repr. 1972).

transcendentalism, in philosophy, term descriptive of systems that hold that there are modes of being and principles of existence beyond the reach of mundane experience and manipulation. The term is now closely associated with Kantian theory, although some conception of transcendent being has been common to most forms of philosophical idealism. In Immanuel Kant's work he states that transcendent elements of thought cannot be perceived directly through experience; they nevertheless add to empirically derived knowledge. These transcendent elements include conception of space and time and categories of judgment. In Kant's terminology transcendent objects that cannot be known through the evidence of the senses are the noumena (as opposed to phenomena).

transcendental number: see NUMBER.

Transcona (trănskō'nə), city (1971 pop. 22,490), SE Man., Canada. It is a suburb of Winnipeg.

transcontinental railroad, in U.S. history, rail connection with the Pacific coast. In 1845, Asa Whitney presented to Congress a plan for the Federal government to subsidize the building of a railroad from the Mississippi River to the Pacific. The settlement of the Oregon boundary in 1846, the acquisition of western territories from Mexico in 1848, and the discovery of gold in California (1849) increased support for the project; in 1853, Congress appropriated funds to survey various proposed routes. Rivalry over the route was intense, however, and when Senator Stephen Douglas introduced (1854) his KANSAS-NEBRASKA ACT, intended to win approval for a line from Chicago, the ensuing sectional controversy between North and South forced a delay in the plans. During the Civil War, a Republican-controlled Congress enacted legislation (July 1, 1862) providing for construction of a transcontinental line. The law provided that the railroad be built by two companies; each received Federal land grants of 10 alternate sections per mile on both sides of the line (the amount was doubled in 1864) and a 30-year government loan for each mile of track constructed. In 1863 the Union Pacific RR began construction from Omaha, Nebr., while the Central Pacific broke ground at Sacramento, Calif. The two lines met at Promontory Point, Utah, and on May 10, 1869, a golden spike joined the two railways, thus completing the first transcontinental railroad. Others followed. Three additional lines were finished in 1883: the Northern Pacific RR stretched from Lake Superior to Portland, Oregon; the Santa Fe extended from Atchison, Kansas, to Los Angeles; and the Southern Pacific connected Los Angeles with New Orleans. A fifth line, the Great Northern, was completed in 1893. Each of those companies received extensive grants of land, although none obtained government loans. The promise of land often resulted in shoddy construction that only later was repaired, and scandals, such as Crédit Mobilier (see CRÉDIT MOBILIER OF AMERICA), were not infrequent. The transcontinental railroads immeasurably aided the settling of the west and hastened the closing of the frontier. They also brought rapid economic growth as mining, farming, and cattle-raising developed along the main lines and their branches. See Julius Grodinsky, *Transcontinental Railway Strategy, 1869–1893* (1962); R. W. Howard, *The Great Iron Trail* (1962); L. M. Beebe, *The Central Pacific and Southern Pacific Railroads* (1963); Gary Hogg, *Union Pacific: The Building of the First Transcontinental Railroad* (1967, repr. 1970); C. E. Ames, *Pioneering the Union Pacific* (1969); J. J. Stewart, *The Iron Trail to the Golden Spike* (1969).

transducer, device that accepts an input of ENERGY in one form and produces an output of energy in some other form, with a known, fixed relationship between the input and output. One widely used class of transducers consists of devices that produce an electric output signal, e.g., microphones, phonograph cartridges, and photocells. Other widely used transducers accept an electric input, e.g., loudspeakers, light bulbs, and solenoids. Transducers are distinguished as active or passive; active transducers require a source of energy in addition to the input signal to produce the output signal, while passive transducers require only an input signal. Thus, a battery-operated transistor radio is an active transducer, while a "crystal set" radio is a passive transducer. The term *transducer* is sometimes applied to devices producing an output in the same form as their input, e.g., transformers and filters.

transduction, in genetics: see RECOMBINATION.

transept (trăn'sĕpt"), term applied to the transverse portion of a building cutting its main axis at right angles or to each arm of such a portion. Transepts are found chiefly in churches, where, extending north and south from the main body, they create a cruciform plan. They may consist of a central portion as wide as the church nave, with two side aisles or with only one. The rectangular or square space formed by the intersection with the nave is termed the crossing. The cross-hall of vaulted Roman basilicas probably inspired the builders of early Christian churches; examples of the elementary form of transept—an unbroken hall passing directly in front of the apse—are seen in early churches, especially in Rome. This position of the transept remained unchanged. In Romanesque churches the transept became universal, while the development of vaulting unified it organically with the body of the building. Its height equaled that of the nave, while the heavy piers of the crossing frequently supported an exterior dome or tower. Transepts furnished additional space for altars and chapels. In some French Gothic cathedrals transepts projected only slightly from the building. Their ends, however, were richly emphasized externally, with sculptured portals and rose windows, as at Chartres and Amiens, or with a tower, as at Le Mans. In England the transepts, furnishing practically the only opportunity for altars, were long and of deep projection. The need for still more space resulted in the frequent provision of a second and minor transept farther east, behind the choir, as at Salisbury.

transference, term given to the relationship between patient and therapist in PSYCHOANALYSIS. The analyst is believed to become a symbolic representative of a person important in the patient's life, and the patient transfers his feelings about the person to the analyst. See also PSYCHOTHERAPY.

Transfiguration, in the Bible, manifestation wherein Jesus appeared "shining" before Peter, James, and John. Mat. 17; Mark 9; Luke 9.28–36. The traditional explanation is that in it Jesus' divine glory shone in his earthly body. Mt. Tabor is usually said to be the mountain where it took place. The event is commemorated in the feast of the Transfiguration on Aug. 6.

transfinite number, cardinal or ordinal NUMBER designating the magnitude (power) or order of an infinite SET; the theory of transfinite numbers was introduced by Georg Cantor in 1874. The cardinal number of the finite set of integers $\{1, 2, 3, \ldots, n\}$ is n, and the cardinal number of any other set of objects that can be put in a one-to-one correspondence with this set is also n; e.g., the cardinal number 5 may be assigned to each of the sets $\{1, 2, 3, 4, 5\}$, $\{2, 4, 6, 8, 10\}$, $\{3, 4, 5, 1, 2\}$, and $\{a, b, c, d, e\}$, since each of these sets may be put in a one-to-one correspondence with any of the others. Similarly, the transfinite cardinal number $\aleph_0$ (aleph-null) is assigned to the countably infinite set of all positive integers $\{1, 2, 3, \ldots, n, \ldots\}$. This set can be put in a one-to-one correspondence with many other infinite sets, e.g., the set of all negative integers $\{-1, -2, -3, \ldots, -n, \ldots\}$, the set of all even positive integers $\{2, 4, 6, \ldots, 2n, \ldots\}$, and the set of all squares of positive integers $\{1, 4, 9, \ldots, n^2, \ldots\}$; thus, in contrast to finite sets, two infinite sets, one of which is a subset of the other, can have the same transfinite cardinal number, in this case, $\aleph_0$. It can be proved that all countably infinite sets, among which are the set of all rational numbers and the set of all algebraic numbers, have the cardinal number $\aleph_0$. Since the union of two countably infinite sets is a countably infinite set, $\aleph_0 + \aleph_0 = \aleph_0$; moreover, $\aleph_0 \times \aleph_0 = \aleph_0$, so that in general, $n \times \aleph_0 = \aleph_0$ and $\aleph_0{}^n = \aleph_0$, where n is any finite number. It can also be shown, however, that the set of all real numbers, designated by c (for "continuum"), is greater than $\aleph_0$; the set of all points on a line and the set of all points on any segment of a line are also designated by the transfinite cardinal number c. An even larger transfinite number is 2^c, which designates the set of all subsets of the real numbers, i.e., the set of all real-valued functions whose domain is the real numbers. Transfinite ordinal numbers are also defined using a one-to-one correspondence between sets, provided this correspondence preserves the ordering of a set. The transfinite ordinal number of the positive integers is designated by ω, that of the negative integers by ω^*, and that of all integers by π. Since a one-to-one correspondence between the positive and negative integers cannot be made that preserves the order of both sets, $\omega \neq \omega^*$. Thus, although the two sets have the same cardinal number, $\aleph_0$, they do not have the same ordinal number, as would be the case with finite sets. The importance of order is also seen in the fact that $\omega^* + \omega = \pi$, but $\omega + \omega^* \neq \pi$.

transformation, in genetics: see RECOMBINATION.

transformer, electrical device used to transfer an alternating current or voltage from one electric circuit to another by means of electromagnetic INDUCTION. The simplest type of transformer consists of two coils of wire, electrically insulated from one another and arranged so that a change in the current in one coil (the primary) will produce a change in voltage in the other (the secondary). In many transformers the coils are wound on a core made of a material with high magnetic permeability; this intensifies the magnetic field induced by the current in the primary and thus increases the efficiency with which energy is transferred to the secondary. Neglecting power losses (which are made small by careful design), the ratio of primary voltage to secondary voltage is the same as the ratio of the number of turns in the primary coil to the number of turns in the secondary coil. The primary and secondary currents are in inverse proportion to the number of turns in the coils. The primary and secondary IMPEDANCES are in the same ratio as the squares of the numbers of turns in the primary and secondary coils. For example, if a 10-volt, 2-ampere alternating current is applied to a transformer with a 10-turn primary and 20-turn secondary coil, a 20-volt, 1-ampere alternating current is produced; the output impedance is four times as great as the input impedance. Transformers are frequently classified according to their uses; the details of construction depend on the intended application. Power transformers are generally used to transmit power at a constant frequency, usually with an increase (step-up) or decrease (step-down) in voltage. Audio transformers are designed to operate over a wide range of frequencies with a nearly flat response, i.e., a nearly constant ratio of input to output voltage. Radio frequency (rf) transformers are designed to operate efficiently within a narrow range of high frequencies.

Trans-Himalaya: see HIMALAYAS.

Trans-Ili Ala-Tau, mountains, Asia: see ALA-TAU.

transistor, electronic device used as a voltage and current amplifier and for many other functions for which the vacuum tube (see ELECTRON TUBE) has also been used. In contrast to a vacuum tube, which consists of an arrangement of wires (electrodes) separated by a vacuum, the transistor is an arrangement of SEMICONDUCTOR materials that share common physical boundaries. Materials most commonly used are silicon and germanium, into which impurities have been introduced. In *n*-type semiconductors there is an excess of electrons, or negative charges, while in *p*-type semiconductors there is a deficiency of electrons and therefore an excess of positive charges. The invention of the transistor by American physicists John Bardeen, Walter H. Brattain, and William Shockley, later jointly awarded a Nobel Prize, was announced by the Bell Telephone Laboratories in 1948; since then many types have been designed. The *n-p-n* junction transistor consists of two *n*-type semiconductors separated by a thin layer of *p*-type semiconductor; the three segments are called emitter, base, and collector, respectively, and are usually sealed in glass, with a wire extending from each segment to the outside, where it is connected to an electric circuit. The transistor action is such that if the electric potentials on the segments are properly determined, a small current between the emitter and base connections results in a large current between the emitter and collector connections, thus producing current amplification. The *p-n-p* junction transistor, consisting of a thin layer of *n*-type semiconductor lying between two *p*-type semiconductors, works in the same manner except that all polarities are reversed. A very important type of transistor developed later is the field-effect transistor (FET). It draws no power from an input signal, overcoming a major disadvantage of the junction transistor. An *n*-channel FET consists of a bar (channel) of *n*-type semiconductor material that passes between and makes contact with two small regions of *p*-type material near its center. The terminals attached to the ends of the channel are called the source and the drain; those attached to the two *p*-type regions are called gates. A voltage applied to the gates is directed so that no current exists across the junctions between the *p*- and *n*-type materials; for this reason it is called a reverse voltage. Variations of the magnitude of the reverse voltage cause variations in the resistance of the channel, enabling the reverse voltage to control the current in the channel. A *p*-channel device works the same way but with all polarities reversed. The metal-oxide semiconductor field-effect transistor (MOSFET), or insulated-gate field-effect transistor (IGFET), is a variant in which a single gate is separated from the channel by a layer of metal oxide, which acts as an insulator, or dielectric. The electric field of the gate extends through the dielectric and controls the resistance of the channel. In this device the input signal, which is applied to the gate, can increase the current through the channel as well as decrease it. Transistors have rapidly displaced tubes in many applications, including radio receivers, electronic computers, and automatic control instrumentation (e.g., space flight and guided missiles). Because a transistor has no filament, there is no warm-up period, and resultant heat problems do not occur. Transistors also have excellent durability, can be made very small, and have a high resistance to shock. See MICROELECTRONICS.

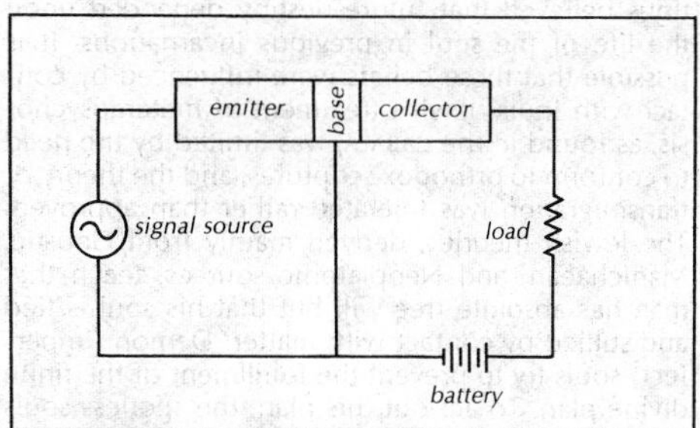

Simple transistor circuit

transit, in astronomy, passage of a body across a meridian or passage of a small body across the visible disk of a larger one. (The passage of a large body across a smaller one is called an ECLIPSE or OCCULTATION.) All of the fixed stars transit the CELESTIAL MERIDIAN once daily; an observer can determine either his LONGITUDE or the SIDEREAL TIME by noting the time at which a given star transits his meridian and by referring to tables. Transits of small bodies across larger ones can be observed only within the bounds of the solar system. The innermost moons of Jupiter are so close to the planet that they transit it at every orbit. Of the planets, only Mercury and Venus, whose orbits lie inside the earth's orbit, can transit the sun. When such a transit occurs, the planet appears in a special solar telescope as a small black dot on the sun's disk. A solar transit can only occur when one of the two planets is in inferior CONJUNCTION and at one of its NODES on the plane of the ecliptic. For Mercury, solar transit can occur only in May or November. The interval between November transits is 7, 13, or 46 years; May transits occur at intervals of 13 or 46 years. Exact timing of Mercury's transits have offered experimental confirmation of the theory of RELATIVITY. For Venus, solar transit occurs in June or December. Currently, two transits take place within about 8 years of each other, with an interval of 52½ or 60½ years between pairs of transits. The next two solar transits of Venus will occur in June, 2004 and June, 2012. Venus's solar transits have been used in determining the ASTRONOMICAL UNIT.

transit compass: see SURVEYING.

transit instrument or **transit,** telescope devised to observe stars as they cross the meridian and used for determining time. Its viewing tube swings on a rigid horizontal axis restricting its movements to the arc of the meridian. In the field of view of the eyepiece are threads of spider web or fine lines ruled on thin glass. The threads or lines are parallel in a north-south direction and odd in number. Precise adjustment places the middle line exactly on the meridian. After the observer has noted the times at which each line is passed by the star, he averages them to learn the instant at which the star was on the meridian. In modern transits, known as meridian circles or meridian telescopes, the observer merely presses a button as the star crosses each line. Electrical impulses are recorded on a revolving drum at one or two second intervals as they pass through a chronograph. The meridian circle is equipped with precisely graduated circles mounted on the horizontal axis. Stationary verniers, or reading microscopes, mounted on the fixed supports of the telescope enable the observer to read the circles. The meridian telescope gives the altitude of a star as well as the transit time. This information yields the right ascension and declination, i.e., the location of the star in the celestial sphere. The meridian circle has largely replaced the transit as the equipment of observatories, although the older transit instrument is still used to some extent for determining SIDEREAL TIME. For a discussion of the transit used by engineers, see SURVEYING.

transition elements or **transition metals,** in chemistry, group of elements characterized by the filling of an inner *d* or *f* electron orbital as atomic number increases. This includes the elements of group VIII and the b groups (I through VII) of the PERIODIC TABLE. Many of the chemical and physical properties of the transition elements are due to their unfilled *d* or *f* orbitals; since these orbitals are filled in the elements of group IIb (zinc, cadmium, and mercury), those elements are not always considered transition elements. In the elements of the lanthanide series and the actinide series the inner *f* orbital is filled as atomic number increases; those elements are often called the inner transition elements. Transition elements generally exhibit high density, high melting point, magnetic properties, variable valence, and the formation of stable coordination complexes. Their variable valence is due to the electrons in the *d* or *f* orbitals. The study of the COMPLEX IONS and compounds formed by transition metals is an important branch of chemistry. Many of these complexes are highly colored and exhibit paramagnetism. See E. M. Larsen, *Transitional Elements* (1965).

Trans-Jordan or **Transjordania:** see JORDAN.

Trans-Juba: see SOMALI DEMOCRATIC REPUBLIC.

Transkei, The (trănskī′), semiautonomous black African homeland, or Bantustan, c.16,500 sq mi (42,730 sq km), E Republic of South Africa. The capital and main city is UMTATA. Almost all the inhabitants are black Africans, most of whom speak a Xhosa language. The Transkei is bounded by the Great Kei River in the south, by the Indian Ocean in the east, by Natal in the north, and by Lesotho in the northwest. Part of the Drakensberg Range is in the west. Much of the territory is hilly or mountainous, and there is little good farmland. Cattle and sheep are raised. Most of the Transkei's income is provided by citizens who work as migrant laborers in the mines and factories of the Orange Free State and the Transvaal. The Transkei's Indian Ocean coastline, known as the Wild Coast, has excellent beaches and good fishing, especially for sardines. In the 1830s and 40s the Transkei was the scene of fighting between European settlers and black Africans over the possession of cattle and grazing land. Much of the territory was annexed in 1848 by Britain as Kaffraria, which in 1865 was joined to Cape Province. In the late 19th cent. the region, called the Transkeian Territories, was given a limited, mainly advisory, form of representative government. In 1955 the government was granted taxing power. The Transkei was separated from Cape Province in 1963 to become the first of a projected nine internally self-governing black African areas within South Africa. The Transkei legislative assembly includes a majority of hereditary chiefs and a minority of elected representatives. The assembly controls many internal matters, but its decisions are subject to veto by the president of South Africa.

translation [Lat.,=carrying across], the rendering of a text into another language. Applied to literature, the term connotes the art of recomposing a work in another language without losing its original flavor, or of finding an analogous substitute, for example, Scott Moncrieff's *Remembrance of Things Past* for Proust's *À la recherche du temps perdu,* which, translated literally, means "Looking for Lost Time." Translations of the most ancient texts extant into modern languages are called decipherment. Two well-known examples are the decoding of the Egyptian hieroglyphs on the ROSETTA STONE by Jean François Champollion and the decoding of the Persian cuneiform inscriptions on the rock of Behistun by Henry Rawlinson. Translating sacred texts has always been the chief means by which a culture transmits its values to posterity. Important translations of the Bible began with the Vulgate (Hebrew and Greek into Latin) of St. JEROME in the 4th cent. A.D. English translations of the Bible include that of John WYCLIF in the 14th cent. (from Latin), William Tyndale's in the 16th cent. (from Hebrew and Greek), and the great Authorized Version of 1611, the King James Version, which has been called the most influential work of translation in any language. The Renaissance was a golden age of translations, especially into English. Renewed interest in the Latin classics created a demand for renderings of Ovid's *Metamorphoses* (tr. by Arthur GOLDING, 1565–67), Vergil's *Aeneid* (tr. by Gawin DOUGLAS, c.1515; Henry Howard, earl of SURREY, c.1540; and Richard Stanyhurst, 1582), and Plutarch's *Lives* (tr. by Sir Thomas North, 1579). The flavor of these renderings is indicated in the opening lines of Stanyhurst's *Aeneid:* "Now manhood and garbroyles [battles] I chaunt, and martial horror." In addition there were translations of important contemporary works into English: Castiglione's *Courtier* (tr. by Sir Thomas Hoby, 1561), Montaigne's *Essais* (tr. by John FLORIO, 1603), and Cervantes's *Don Quixote* (tr. by John Shelton, 1612). Notable translations of the 19th and 20th cent. include Baudelaire's translations of the works of Edgar Allan Poe, Scott Moncrieff's translation of Proust, and Eustache Morel's translation of James Joyce. American authors whose works have been translated into several European languages include Mark Twain, Jack London, Ernest Hemingway, John Dos Passos, Pearl Buck, Margaret Mitchell (*Gone With The Wind*), and Upton Sinclair, who set a record with translations into 47 languages.

Transleithania: see AUSTRO-HUNGARIAN MONARCHY.

transmigration of souls or **metempsychosis** (mətĕm″səkō′sĭs) [Gr.,=change of soul], passage of the soul from one body to another, either human, animal, or inanimate. It is a belief common to many cultures. The Australian aborigines believe that an infant is a reincarnation of deceased ancestors and that the soul is continually reborn. Some Indonesian peoples hold that ancestral souls reside in sacred animals, sometimes in preparation for a new incarnation. Metempsychosis is a fundamental doctrine of several religions originating in India. In HINDUISM the individual soul enters a new existence after the death of the body. The sum total of past moral conduct, or KARMA, determines the condition of the soul and the quality of its rebirth. The cycle of rebirth is eternal, unless the soul is released by knowledge or arduous effort (see YOGA). This release (*moksha* or *mukti*) is the Hindu conception of salvation and is possible only for the most devout. Buddhist doctrine does not accept the soul or transmigration as such, treating both as illusory. Rather, there is an eternal, undifferentiated stream of being (*samsara*). Out of this, existences are produced and prolonged according to karma, or past actions, but rebirth as such is an illusion. The metempsychosis of BUDDHISM stresses the essential solidarity and oneness of the universe. The individual is not a separate entity but rather a grouping of elements. They revert to the original primal stream when desire, the cause of the transmigratory cycle, ceases. Only devout Buddhists or saints (i.e., those who abandon all desire) are able to realize this oneness. The Celtic version of metempsychosis does not have the ethical aspect of its Indian counterpart. The Druids of Gaul supposedly taught that after death the soul left one body to enter another, but the second body was not necessarily earthly; little else is known of their beliefs. Examples of metempsychosis in pre-Christian Irish legends indicate that these transmigrations occurred only in the lifetime of heroes. The belief in transmigration was rare in ancient Egypt, although occasional instances occur of a soul uniting with a god, a soul entering an animal for a lifetime, or a voluntary metamorphosis of a person into another form for his own benefit. The Greek version was not borrowed from Egypt, as many ancient writers thought, but was an indigenous product. Although it appeared in the ORPHIC MYSTERIES, its best-known proponent was PYTHAGORAS. He believed that souls were reincarnated in various bodily shapes. Empedocles, in his poem *Purification,* accepted Orphic and Pythagorean beliefs. Plato's views on metempsychosis are derived from these same sources. Plotinus believed that future destiny depended upon the life of the soul in previous incarnations. It is possible that these beliefs were influenced by contact with India. Jewish treatment of metempsychosis, as found in the CABALA, was limited by the need to conform to orthodox scriptures, and the theory of transmigration was tolerated rather than approved. The Jewish theories, derived mainly from Gnostic, Manichaean, and Neoplatonic sources, teach that man has absolute free will but that his soul is tied and sullied by contact with matter. Demon (imperfect) souls try to prevent the fulfillment of the finite divine plan. To act out this plan, the spotless souls descend from their original abode in heaven and are incarnated. Punishment and atonement for sins is achieved by another incarnation; but before this happens, the now impure soul flits about as a disembodied spirit. If the pious suffer, it is for sins committed in a previous existence. At the end of the cycles, when all the incarnated souls are once again pure, the Messianic period begins. No theories of transmigration are admitted into Christian religion. See Joseph Head, ed., *Reincarnation in World Thought* (1967); A. W. Holzer, *Born Again* (1970).

transmission, in automobiles, system of parts connecting the engine to the wheels. Suitable torque, or turning force, is generated by the engine only within a narrow range of engine speeds, i.e., rates at which the crankshaft is turning. However, the wheels must turn with suitable torque over a wide range of speeds. While its speed is held roughly constant, the engine turns an input shaft on the transmission whose output shaft can be adjusted to turn the wheels at an appropriate speed. The simplest forms of automotive transmission are manual and consist of a system of interlocking gear wheels. These wheels are arranged so that by operating a lever the driver can choose one of several ratios of speed between the input shaft and the output shaft. These ratios are called gears, first gear being the arrangement that gives the lowest output speed, second gear the next lowest, and so forth. To allow smooth shifting from one gear to another, a clutch is provided to disengage the engine from the transmission. The commonly used dry single disk clutch has a steel disk with a friction lining that is sandwiched between a flywheel on the engine shaft and a pressure plate on the transmission input shaft. When the driver takes his foot off the clutch pedal, springs squeeze the friction disk into the space between the flywheel and the pressure plate, enabling the engine shaft to turn the transmission. For many cars and for normal driving conditions a transmission with three forward gears and one reverse gear is sufficient. In cars having small engines transmissions with four or five forward speeds are used; racing cars often have as many as six forward speeds. A synchromesh transmission is a manual transmission in which all forward gear wheels are held in mesh at all times. Used on most American cars with a manual transmission, it allows the driver to shift gears more smoothly and makes the car run more quietly. The automatic transmission, introduced in 1939, switches to the optimum gear without driver intervention except for starting and going into reverse. The type of automatic transmission used on current American cars usually consists of a fluid device called a torque converter and a set of planetary gears.

transmutation of elements, conversion of one chemical element into another. The expression has both historical and contemporary significance. The transmutation of certain metals into gold by means of a substance called the philosopher's stone was one of the two most ambitious quests of the alchemists (see ALCHEMY); the other was for the elixir of life that would cure all diseases, restore youth to the aged, and make youthfulness eternal. The possibility of finding the philosopher's stone harmonized with ideas long generally held, and honest and able men were hopeful of finding it. Now and then a charlatan professed to have found it. In modern times it has been found that a transmutation from one element to another actually does occur in the process of natural RADIOACTIVITY. Transmutation of elements can be achieved artificially by the bombardment of elements with high-speed particles by means of such machines as the cyclotron (see PARTICLE ACCELERATOR). Both artificial and natural transmutations involve changing the number of protons in the atomic NUCLEUS. The TRANSURANIUM ELEMENTS are created in this manner. When a nucleus is bombarded with neutrons from an atomic pile or nuclear reactor, some of the neutrons will be absorbed, resulting in an unstable nucleus. The nucleus then becomes more stable by converting one of its neutrons into a proton by beta decay, becoming a nucleus of the next heavier element in the process.

Transpadane Republic: see CISALPINE REPUBLIC.

transpiration, in botany, the loss of water by evaporation in terrestrial plants. Some evaporation occurs directly through the exposed walls of surface cells, but the greatest amount takes place through the stomates, or intercellular spaces (see LEAF). Transpiration functions to effect the ascent of SAP from the roots to the leaves (thus supplying the food-manufacturing cells with water needed for photosynthesis) and to provide the moisture necessary for the diffusion of carbon dioxide into and oxygen out of these cells. The rate of transpiration is almost always far greater than the above functions would seem to warrant; in most plants 200 to 1,000 lb (90-450 kg) of water are transpired for each pound of solid material added to the plant. Various factors influence the transpiration rate. Photosynthesis, induced by light, has the effect of increasing the water pressure in the guard cells that bound each stomate and that, in expanding, pull apart to widen the stomate aperture and thereby increase water loss. Low humidity promotes the diffusion of water vapor from the air passages inside the leaf into the outside air. A lack of water in the soil cuts down the water supply to the cells, thus limiting expansion of the guard cells. Therefore the rate is highest on a bright, dry day and lowest at night or in drought conditions. Physiological factors such as reduced leaf surfaces, a heavy cuticle layer on the leaves, and stomates recessed below the other epidermal cells also lower the rate; desert plants such as conifers and cacti conserve water in these ways. Plants also lose some water by guttation, a process whereby water is exuded directly through pores called hydathodes. The reaction of a plant to excessive water loss is wilting, and, eventually, death.

transplantation, medical, process by which a tissue or organ is removed and replaced by a corresponding part, either from another part of the body or from another individual. Human tissue grafting was first performed about 100 years ago by a Swiss surgeon, Jacques Reverdin. In 1912 the French surgeon Alexis Carrel developed a method of joining blood vessels that made the transplantation of organs feasible and stimulated the use of transplantation in experimental biology. The first successful transplant of a human kidney was made at Loyola Univ. in Chicago in 1950, and the first human heart transplant was performed by the South African surgeon Christiaan Barnard in 1967. Transplantation to replace such diseased or defective tissue as corneas and heart necessarily requires a dead donor; paired organs such as kidneys, or large or regenerating organs or tissues such as skin, bowel, or blood, can be donated by live donors (see BLOOD TRANSFUSION). Skin autografts, employing skin from the patient's own body, are used to replace skin lost, by burning for example; autograft transplants are also done with bowel, bone, cartilage, and other connective tissue. Organs such as the heart must be transplanted as soon after the death of the donor as possible. Skin, corneas, bone, and some blood fractions can be stored for longer periods of time. In transplanting complex organs, but not small tissue grafts, the larger blood vessels are surgically connected to those of the recipient. Connective tissue cells gradually link together the graft and host tissue. The main obstacle to successful transplantation is the rejection of foreign tissue by the host (see IMMUNITY). Transplanted tissue from another individual (i.e., homograft, or allograft, tissue) contains antigens that stimulate an immune response by the host's lymphocytes. Homograft tissue is destroyed within a few weeks; the rejection mechanism is similar to the mechanism by which the body resists infection. The greater the number of foreign antigens on the donor organ, the more rapid and severe the rejection reactions. Organs donated from one identical twin to another are usually viable because such organs are antigenically identical, but even organs transplanted between individuals who are fairly closely matched antigenically, such as siblings, have a good chance of being rejected. Some kidney and heart transplants, stabilized by available IMMUNOSUPPRESSIVE DRUGS, have been successful for up to five years, and lung transplants for about a month. An antigenic typing system similar to blood typing is being developed to identify histocompatibility, or sufficient similarity, of donor and recipient tissue and to minimize rejection. Noncellular tissues or tissues where the donor cells are not important to the graft (e.g., bone and cartilage) can usually be successfully transplanted. In these transplants the grafts provide nonliving structural support within which the recipient's living cells gradually become established. Corneal transplants have a high success rate largely because there are so few blood vessels in the cornea that corneal antigens may never enter the host's system to stimulate an immune reaction. In animals, transplant recipients can be made immunologically tolerant of donor antigens by injecting the recipient before or shortly after birth with cells from the donor; such methods are not yet adaptable to human transplantation. Implantation of artificial organs, such as artificial bone, is successful because such organs (prostheses) do not produce antigenic substances. Artificial joints made of stainless steel have been developed; recent implants have used nonrusting titanium joints with the midsection of bone substitute composed of lightweight polyethylene. Mammalian fetuses can be considered homografts because their cells contain foreign (i.e., paternal) antigens. Fetuses are not rejected because fetal antigens do not ordinarily cross the placenta into the mother and because the layer of fetal cells in contact with maternal tissue does not act antigenically. The development of heart transplantation has produced an ongoing reexamination of the traditional biological and legal definitions of death, since obtaining a healthy organ for transplantation depends in large part on the earliest possible establishment of the donor's death. However, by the early 1970s heart transplantation was generally superseded by more conservative surgical procedures, e.g., removing obstructions from diseased coronary arteries or bypassing them with arterial transplants from the patient's own body. Transplantation is an important tool in experimental biology: It is used to investigate endocrine gland functions, to study the interactions of cells in developing embryos, and to culture malignant tissue in cancer research. See Donald Longmore, *Spare-part Surgery* (1968); F. T. Rapaport and Jean Dausset, ed., *Human Transplantation* (1968); F. D. Moore, *Transplant* (1972).

transplanting, in horticulture, the process of removing a plant from the place where it has been growing and replanting it in another. The major requirement in transplanting (especially of larger plants) is a sufficient water supply, since the roots are almost inevitably injured in the process. In most cases the roots should be pruned well before replanting, both to stimulate new and compact growth and to eliminate the injured portions. The "balling" of tree roots seems to ensure the survival of the plant when transplanted. Topping (see PRUNING) is usually also required to balance the amount of foliage with the reduced root surface, otherwise more moisture is lost in transpiration than can be absorbed by the roots. Transplanting at a time of minimal evaporation (e.g., an evening or a cloudy day) or of minimal growth (e.g., the dormant season) can help minimize the shock to the plant. Crop and garden plants as well as trees are often started in greenhouses or nurseries under conditions carefully controlled to ensure maximal sprouting and vigorous early growth; they are then transplanted as seedlings or young plants to their permanent environment. See Norman Taylor, ed., *Encyclopedia of Gardening* (4th ed. 1961); bulletins of the U.S. Dept. of Agriculture.

transportation, conveyance of goods and people over land, over water, and through the air. Land transportation first began with the carrying of goods by men. The ancient civilizations of Central America, Mexico, and Peru transported materials in that fashion over long roads and bridges. Primitive man used a sledge made from a forked tree with crosspieces of wood. The North American Indians of the Great Plains made a travois consisting of two poles each fastened at one end to the sides of a dog or a horse, the other end dragging on the ground; the back parts of the two poles were attached by a platform or net, upon which goods were loaded. The first road vehicles were two-wheeled carts, with crude disks fashioned from stone serving as the wheels. Used by the Sumerians (c.3000 B.C.), such simple wagons were precursors of the chariot, which the Egyptians and Greeks, among others, developed from a lumbering cart into a work of beauty. Under the Chou dynasty (c.1000 B.C.), the Chinese constructed the world's first permanent road system. In Asia the camel CARAVAN served to transport goods and people; elsewhere the ox and the ass were the beasts of burden. Four-wheeled carriages were developed toward the end of the 12th cent.; they transported only the privileged until the late 18th cent., when Paris licensed omnibuses, and stagecoaches began to operate in England. In the United States the demands of an ever-extending frontier led to the creation of the CONESTOGA WAGON and the PRAIRIE SCHOONER, so that goods and families could be transported across the eastern mountains, the Great Plains, and westward. The great period of railroad building in the second half of the 19th cent. made earlier methods of transportation largely obsolete within the United States. Where just a self-sufficient settlement might have been established before, a metropolis would come into existence, with isolated farms tributary to it. After World War I, however, automobiles, buses, and trucks came to exceed the railroads in importance. Little is known of the origins of water transportation. As long ago as 3000 B.C. the Egyptians were already employing large cargo boats. The first great system of transportation by sailing vessels, that of the Phoenicians, connected the caravan routes with seaports, chiefly those in the Mediterranean area. Goods of high value and little bulk, such as gems, spices, perfumes, and fine handiwork, made up the cargoes; to King Solomon came "ships of Tarshish bringing gold, and silver, ivory, and apes, and peacocks" (2 Chron. 9.21). As metropolitan centers developed, the transportation of grain became important. In addition to a famous network of paved roads throughout the vast empire, built primarily for military reasons, Rome made much use of ships. In the late Middle Ages, leadership in transportation by sea passed to Spain and Portugal. Maritime transportation between Europe and North America in the Age of Discovery began the English dominance of the seas that lasted until World War I. The forests of New England encouraged the building of wooden sailing vessels, and American schooners and clippers came to carry a large share of the world's SHIPPING, until they were supplanted by steel-hulled steamships in the late 19th cent. Diesel power soon replaced steam, and in the mid-20th cent. the first nuclear powered vessels were launched. Inland water transportation grew with the extensive CANAL construction of the 16th and 17th cent. Transportation by air became a reality in the 20th cent. The modern jet airplane now makes comfortable travel to virtually any point on the globe possible in just one day. Moreover, the controversial supersonic transport promises, if adopted, to reduce long-distance air travel time by one half. Perhaps the most spectacular transportation development of all time was the inauguration of manned space travel. Following the Soviet Union's launching (1957) of Sputnik I, the world's first man-made satellite, space technology developed rapidly. Less than a decade elapsed between the first manned space flight of the USSR's Yuri A. Gagarin (1961) and the epoch-making moon exploration of U.S. astronauts Neil Armstrong and Edwin Aldrin (1969). Already scientists have been able to employ space technology in the development of satellite-based communication, surveying, and meteorological systems. See COMMERCE. See Abraham Berglund, *Ocean Transportation* (1931); R. E. Westmeyer, *Economics of Transportation* (1952); J. R. Rose, *American Wartime Transportation* (1955); M. L. Fair and E. W. Williams, *Economics of Transportation* (rev. ed. 1959); C. I. Savage, *An Economic History of Transportation* (1962, repr. 1966); H. S. Firestone, *Man on the Move* (1967); Wilfred Owen, *Wheels* (1967).

Transportation, United States Department of, executive department of the U.S. government, established by the Department of Transportation Act of 1966. Its chief executive officer, the Secretary, is a member of the President's cabinet. Its principal constituent organizations include the U.S. coast guard, the Federal Aviation Administration, The National Highway Traffic Safety Administration, the Urban Mass Transportation Administration, the Federal Highway Administration, the Federal Railroad Administration, and the Saint Lawrence Development Corporation. The National Transportation Safety Board is an entity within the department but maintains its own statutory responsibilities and executive authority.

transposing instrument, a musical instrument whose part in a score is written at a different pitch than that actually sounded. Such an instrument is usually referred to by the keynote of its natural scale—the clarinet in A, for example—in which case A is sounded when the tone C appears in the musical notation. Since A is a minor third below C, the part for this instrument must be written a minor third higher than it is to sound. Transposing instruments were necessary in the 17th and 18th cent. when the natural brasses and the clarinets could be played easily in only a few keys; they were therefore built in specific keys. The improvements in the 19th cent. have obviated this necessity. Transposing instruments are still useful in families of instruments that have identical fingering systems, permitting identical fingerings on all instruments of the family to be represented by the same note, whatever pitch is actually sounded. This facilitates performance by the same player on, for instance, different clarinets. Transposing instruments are burdensome for the composer or the reader of a score and composers increasingly score all parts at actual pitch, leaving transposition to the copyist or player. All CLARINETS, the ENGLISH HORN, OBOE, FRENCH HORN, TRUMPET, alto FLUTE, CORNET, and most SAXOPHONES are transposing instruments. Parts for the piccolo, double bass, and contrabassoon are written an octave below or above actual pitch to avoid ledger lines, but this is not, strictly speaking, transposition.

Trans-Siberian Railroad, rail line, linking the European USSR with the Pacific coast. Its construction began in 1891, on the initiative of Count S. Y. Witte, and was completed in 1905. The original line began at Chelyabinsk and ran generally E through Omsk, Novosibirsk, Krasnoyarsk, Irkutsk, and Chita; it traversed Manchuria and reentered Russian territory before ending at Vladivostok. The Manchurian section of the line is known as the Chinese Eastern Railroad. The present Trans-Siberian RR branches off from the original line at Chita to follow, roughly, the Amur and Ussuri rivers and reaches Vladivostok by way of Khabarovsk; it lies entirely in Soviet territory. The Trans-Siberian RR now has several branch lines, notably the line connecting Omsk with Sverdlovsk. A branch to Ust-Kut, N of Lake Baykal, was completed in 1954. The railroad is linked with the TURKISTAN-SIBERIA RAILROAD. The completion of the railroad greatly affected the subsequent history of the USSR by opening up Siberia.

transubstantiation: see EUCHARIST.

transuranium elements, in chemistry, radioactive elements with atomic numbers greater than that of URANIUM (at. no. 92). Of these elements only NEPTUNIUM (at. no. 93) and PLUTONIUM (at. no. 94) occur in nature; they are produced in minute amounts in the radioactive decay of uranium. All the transuranium elements of the ACTINIDE SERIES were discovered as synthetic radioactive isotopes at the Univ. of California at Berkeley or at Argonne National Laboratory. Much study of the transuranium elements has taken place at the Lawrence Radiation Laboratory (at Berkeley) and at Dubna in the Soviet Union; workers at both locations have claimed discovery of the very unstable elements 104 and 105, which are TRANSACTINIDE ELEMENTS. Properties of these elements have been predicted from their positions in the periodic table; element 104 is expected to be chemically similar to hafnium, and element 105 to tantalum. On the basis of theories of nuclear structure, physicists have predicted that certain other transactinide elements may have relatively stable isotopes. An isotope of element 110 with mass number 184 is expected to be so stable that it could occur naturally. Chemically, it would resemble platinum; it has been searched for in platinum metal and ores. An isotope of element 114 with mass number 298 should be very stable and resemble lead in its chemical properties, but attempts to synthesize it have been unsuccessful.

Transvaal (trănzväl'), province (1970 pop. 8,600,060), 110,450 sq mi (286,065 sq km), NE Republic of South Africa. PRETORIA is the capital and JOHANNESBURG the largest city. Other leading cities include BRAKPAN, GERMISTON, KRUGERSDORP, SPRINGS, and VEREENIGING. The Transvaal is bounded on the N and W by the Limpopo River, which forms the border with Rhodesia and Botswana, on the E by Mozambique and Swaziland, and on the S by the Vaal River, the border with the Orange Free State. It is mainly situated in the highveld, at an altitude of 3,000 to 6,000 ft (910–1,830 m). Cattle and sheep are raised, and maize, wheat, tobacco, citrus fruits, cotton, groundnuts, and temperate-zone crops are cultivated. The Transvaal's wealth, however, lies mainly in its minerals. Since 1886, when gold was discovered on the WITWATERSRAND, mines in the province have supplied much of the world's gold. In addition, the province produces most of the country's diamonds, coal, asbestos, and uranium and all of its platinum and chromium. Furthermore, roughly half the total industrial production of the republic occurs within the Transvaal; concentrated on and around the Witwatersrand (particularly in Johannesburg, Pretoria, Germiston, and Vereeniging), industries produce iron and steel, explosives, mining equipment, and varied consumer goods. The province is well served by railroads and roads. The nearest ocean port is Lourenço Marques, Mozambique, which handles much of the Transvaal's foreign trade. The Transvaal's numerous educational institutions include, in Pretoria, the Univ. of Pretoria and the Univ. of South Africa and, in Johannesburg, the Univ. of the Witwatersrand. KRUGER NATIONAL PARK, one of the world's largest wildlife sanctuaries, is in the northeast. The Transvaal, inhabited by Bantu-speaking black Africans in the early 19th cent., was settled in the mid-1830s by BOER farmers (see TREK), mainly from the Cape Colony (see CAPE PROVINCE). Having forced out most of the Africans, the Boers scattered over the huge territory but were unable to form a strong government. In the Sand River Convention (1852) Great Britain, which at the time also held Cape Colony and NATAL, recognized the right of the Boers beyond the Vaal River to administer their own affairs. In 1857 the South African Republic was inaugurated in the SW Transvaal but claimed sovereignty over the whole territory. Martin Pretorius, son of the Boer leader Andries PRETORIUS, was its first president. In the 1860s and 70s the South African Republic expanded in size, and there were isolated finds of gold, diamonds, and copper. However, by the late 1870s the republic was bankrupt. In 1877, Britain, seeking to unify S Africa, annexed the South African Republic after only a mild formal protest by its president, T. F. Burgers. In late 1880, however, the Boers began an armed revolt against the British and proclaimed a new republic. After defeats at Laing's Nek, Ingogo, and MAJUBA HILL (all in Feb., 1881), Britain granted the South African Republic internal self-government. In 1883, S. J. P. KRUGER (Oom Paul Kruger) became the new republic's first president. In 1886 large gold deposits were discovered on what later came to be called the Witwatersrand, and many foreigners, especially Britons and Germans, entered the republic. The foreigners, called Uitlanders, brought different customs and beliefs and threatened to overwhelm the tradition-minded Boers, whom they soon outnumbered by more than two to one. The Boers denied political rights to the foreigners and taxed them heavily. In Dec., 1895, Leander Starr JAMESON, believing erroneously that he was following the wishes of Cecil RHODES, then prime minister of Cape Colony, staged a raid into the Transvaal that was intended to trigger an uprising by foreigners against President Kruger. However, only a minor revolt materialized, and Jameson was captured. Tension between Boers and Britons in S Africa increased after the Jameson Raid, and in 1899 the SOUTH AFRICAN WAR broke out. The Transvaal was annexed by Britain in 1900, but guerrilla fighting continued. The Treaty of Vereeniging (1902) ended the war and made the Transvaal (as well as the Orange Free State) a crown colony of the British Empire. The Transvaal, led by Jan Christiaan SMUTS and Louis BOTHA, was granted self-government in 1907 and in 1910 became a founding province of the Union of South Africa.

transvestism: see HOMOSEXUALITY.

Transylvania (trăn"sĭlvā'nyə), Rum. *Transilvania* or *Ardeal*, Hung. *Erdély*, Ger. *Siebenbürgen,* historic region and province (21,292 sq mi/55,146 sq km), central Rumania. CLUJ is the chief city; other major urban centers are BRAŞOV, SIBIV, and TÎRGU-MUREŞ. A high plateau, Transylvania is separated in the S from Walachia by the Transylvanian Alps and in the E from Moldavia and Bukovina by the Carpathian Mts. (of which the Transylvanian Alps are a continuation). In the north and west Transylvania borders on Crişana-Maramureş and in the SW on the Banat. The Transylvanian plateau, 1,000 to 1,600 ft (305–488 m) high, is drained by the Mureşul River and other tributaries of the Danube. Economically and culturally one of the most advanced regions of Rumania, Transylvania is rich in mineral resources, notably lignite, iron, lead, manganese, gold, copper, natural gas, salt, and sulfur. There are large iron and steel, chemical, and textile industries. Stock raising, agriculture, wine production, and fruit growing are important occupations. Timber is another valuable resource. Sizable Hungarian and German minorities, as well as some Jews and Gypsies, live in Transylvania. The area now constituting Transylvania was the nucleus of the Dacian (Getic) kingdom, which in A.D. 107 became part of the Roman province of DACIA. After the withdrawal (A.D. 271) of the Romans from the region it was overrun, between the 3d and 10th cent., by the Visigoths, the Huns, the Gepidae, the Avars, and the Slavs. The Magyar tribes first entered the region in the 10th cent., but they did not fully control it until 1003, when King Stephen I placed it under the Hungarian crown. The valleys in the east and southeast were settled by the Székely, a Turkic people akin to the Magyars. It is not known, however, whether they came into Transylvania with or before the Magyars. In the 12th and 13th cent. the areas in the south and northeast were settled by German colonists called (then and now) Saxons. Siebenbürgen, the German name for Transylvania, derives from the seven principal fortified towns founded there by the Saxons. The German influence became more marked when, early in the 13th cent., King Andrew II of Hungary called on the Teutonic Knights to protect Transylvania from the Cumans, who were followed (1241) by the Mongol invaders. Large numbers of Rumanians, called Vlachs or Walachians, were in the region by 1222, although the exact date that their penetration began is disputed. Originally seminomadic shepherds, the Vlachs soon settled down to agriculture. The administration of Transylvania was in the hands of a royal governor, or voivode, who by the mid-13th cent. controlled the whole region. Society was divided into three privileged "nations," the Magyars, the Székely, and the Saxons. These "nations," however, corresponded to social rather than strictly ethnic divisions. Although the nonprivileged class of serfs consisted mostly of Vlachs, it also included some people of Saxon, Székely, and Magyar origin. A few Vlachs, notably John Hunyadi, hero of the Turkish wars, joined the ranks of the nobility. After the suppression (1437) of a peasant revolt the three "nations" solemnly renewed their union; the rebels were cruelly repressed, and serfdom became more firmly entrenched than ever. When the main Hungarian army and King Louis II were slain (1526) in the battle of Mohács, John Zapolya, voivode of Transylvania, took advantage of his military strength and put himself at the head of the nationalist Hungarian party, which opposed the succession of Ferdinand of Austria (later Emperor Ferdinand I) to the Hungarian throne. As John I he was elected king of Hungary, while another party recognized Ferdinand. In the ensuing struggle Zapolya received the support of Sultan Sulayman I, who after Zapolya's death (1540) overran central Hungary on the pretext of protecting Zapolya's son, John II. Hungary was now divided into three sections: W Hungary, under Austrian rule; central Hungary, under Turkish rule; and semi-independent Transylvania, where Austrian and Turkish influences vied for supremacy for nearly two centuries. The Hungarian magnates of Transylvania resorted to a policy of duplicity in order to preserve independence. The Báthory family, which came to power on the death (1571) of John II, ruled Transylvania as princes under Ottoman, and briefly under Hapsburg, suzerainty until 1602, but their rule was interrupted by the incursion of Michael the Brave of Walachia and by Austrian military intervention. In 1604, Stephen Bocskay led a rebellion against Austrian rule, and in 1606 he was recognized by the emperor as prince of Transylvania. Under Bocskay's successors—especially Gabriel Bethlen and George I Rákóczy—Transylvania had its golden age. The principality was the chief center of Hungarian culture and humanism, the main bulwark of Protestantism in E Europe, and the only European country where Roman Catholics, Calvinists, Lutherans, and Unitarians lived in mutual tolerance. However, Orthodox Rumanians were denied equal rights. After the Turkish defeat near Vienna (1683), Transylvania vainly battled the growing Austrian influence, and its alliance with Turkey under Emeric Thököly and with France under Francis II Rákóczy proved fatal to its independence. In 1711, Austrian control was definitely established over all Hungary and Transylvania, and the princes of Transylvania were replaced by Austrian governors. The proclamation (1765) of Transylvania as a grand principality was a mere formality. The pressure of Austrian bureaucratic rule gradually eroded the traditional independence of Transylvania. In 1791 the Rumanians petitioned Leopold II of Austria for recognition as the fourth "nation" of Transylvania and for religious equality. The Transylvanian diet rejected their demands, restoring the Rumanians to their old status. In 1848 the Magyars proclaimed the union of Transylvania with Hungary, promising the Rumanians abolition of serfdom in return for their support against Austria. The Rumanians rejected the offer and instead rose against the Magyar national state. In the fighting that followed (1849) between the Hungarians and the Austro-Russian forces (supported by the Rumanians and most of the Saxons), the Hungarian republic of Louis Kossuth was suppressed. The ensuing period of Austrian military government (1849–60) was disastrous for the Magyars but greatly benefited the Rumanian peasants, who were given land and otherwise favored by the Austrian authorities. However, in the compromise (*Ausgleich*) of 1867, which established the Austro-Hungarian Monarchy, Transylvania became an integral part of Hungary, and the Rumanians, having tasted equality, were once more subjected to Magyar domination. After World War I the Rumanians of Transylvania proclaimed at a convention at Alba Iulia (1918) their union with Rumania. Transylvania was then seized by Rumania and was formally ceded by Hungary in the Treaty of Trianon (1920). The expropriation of the estates of Magyar magnates, the distribution of the lands to the Rumanian peasants, and the policy of cultural Rumanization that followed were major causes of friction between Hungary and Rumania. It was now the turn of the Magyar and German nationalists to complain of Rumanian oppression. During World War II, Hungary annexed (1940) N Transylvania, which was, however, returned to Rumania after the war. Many of the Saxons of Transylvania fled to Germany before the arrival of the Soviet army. In 1952 the mainly Székely districts of Transylvania were constituted, for the purpose of local self-government, as the Magyar Autonomous Region (4,728 sq mi/12,246 sq km).

Transylvania Company, association formed to exploit and colonize the area now comprising much of Kentucky and Tennessee. Organized first (Aug., 1774) as the Louisa Company, it was reorganized (Jan., 1775) as the Transylvania Company. At Sycamore Shoals on the Watauga River, the Cherokee Indians deeded (March 17, 1775) to Richard HENDERSON and other members of the association all the territory embraced by the Ohio, Kentucky, and Cumberland rivers. Henderson had already dispatched Daniel BOONE to lead the way to the Kentucky River and, with additional settlers, soon followed Boone over his Wilderness Road to Boonesboro, the first settlement. Henderson hoped to make Transylvania, as the region was called, a proprietary colony similar to Pennsylvania and Maryland, but the project did not have British approval and, more importantly, was immediately denounced by both Virginia and North Carolina, within whose chartered limits Transylvania lay. A provisional, democratic government was organized in May, 1775, but the Continental Congress ignored Transylvania's plea to be recognized as the 14th colony. Virginia created (Dec., 1776) Kentucky co. in its portion of Transylvania and voided (Nov., 1778) the company's land titles there. Henderson then turned to the development of the Cumberland River area, employing James ROBERTSON to lead this project. However, North Carolina also voided (1783) this section of the grant. Virginia and North Carolina each awarded Henderson and his associates 200,000 acres (81,000 hectares) for their labor and expenses in promoting western colonization. See Archibald Henderson, *The Conquest of the Old Southwest* (1920); W. S. Lester, *The Transylvania Colony* (1935).

Transylvanian Alps, Rumanian *Carpaţii Meridionali,* southern branch of the Carpathian Mts., extending c.225 mi (360 km) E across central Rumania from the Danube River at the Iron Gate. Moldoveanu (8,343 ft/2,543 m) and Negoiu are the highest peaks. The range, composed of crystalline massifs, is densely forested and is a famous hunting ground. Its subalpine meadows are used for extensive sheep grazing. There are coal, iron, and lignite deposits. Turnu Roşu is the most important of several passes linking Transylvania with Walachia to the south.

Transylvania University, at Lexington, Ky.; Disciples of Christ; coeducational; chartered 1780; opened 1783 as a seminary near Danville, Ky.; moved 1788. In 1798 it became Transylvania Univ., but after a merger (1865) the name Kentucky University was used. In 1878 the agricultural and mechanical college withdrew to become a state college, and in 1908 the university reverted to the name Transylvania University.

Traoré, Moussa (mous'sä trourä'), 1936–, president of Mali (1968–). A lieutenant in the army of Mali, he led the army coup that overthrew Modibo KEITA and assumed the presidency. In 1969 he also became prime minister.

Trapani (trä'pänē), city (1971 pop. 69,771), capital of Trapani prov., W Sicily, Italy, a seaport on a promontory in the Mediterranean Sea. The city's exports include marsala wine, macaroni, olives, and tuna fish. Known in ancient times as Drepanum, the city was an important Carthaginian naval base and fell to Rome after the battle of the Aegates (241 B.C.). Of note in Trapani are the Church of the Annunciation (14th–17th cent.) and the Villa Margherita. The picturesque Egadi Islands (Aegadian Isles) are nearby.

trap-door spider, SPIDER of the same family as the native American TARANTULA. Trap-door spiders dig burrows, which they line with silk and protect by constructing one or two circular, hinged trap doors. The spiders emerge through the snug-fitting camouflaged doors to search for prey. Usually the burrow entrance has a door, the outer surface of which is camouflaged to blend in with the surrounding terrain. If a second door is present, it is usually below the entrance door. Trap-door spiders are classified in the phylum ARTHROPODA, class Arachnida, order Araneae, family Ctenizidae.

trapezoid, closed plane figure bounded by four line segments, or sides, two of which are parallel and two of which are nonparallel. The parallel sides of a trapezoid are called bases and the nonparallel sides legs; in an isosceles trapezoid the legs are of equal length. The median of a trapezoid is the line segment connecting the midpoints of the legs; it is parallel to the bases and equal to half the sum of their lengths. The altitude of a trapezoid is the perpendicular distance between the bases. The area of a trapezoid is equal to half the product of the altitude and the sum of the bases, i.e., to the product of the altitude and the median.

Trapezus: see TRABZON.

trapping, most broadly, the use of mechanical or deceptive devices to capture, kill, or injure animals. It may be applied to the practice of using birdlime to capture birds, lobster pots to trap lobsters, and seines to catch fish. Usually, however, trapping means the capture of land animals larger than rodents by means of deadfall, pitfall, and, especially in modern times, spring-snapped, steel-jawed steel traps. In societies where hunting and fishing are the staple occupations, trapping is necessary to supply food and, in colder climates, furs for clothing. Since antiquity trapping has been the basis of the fur trade (see FUR). It still occupies a great many people over large sections of the globe, especially in the colder regions, such as N Siberia and N Canada. Trapping has also been used to rid an area of animals thought to endanger the lives of human beings or domestic animals. Spurred by bounty laws, the practice of trapping in the United States in the 19th cent. helped lead to the extinction or near-extinction of many mammals, such as various species of bears, mountain lions, wolves, and coyotes. Modern game management frowns upon trapping and recognizes the importance of predators in the ecosystem. Such trapping as is permitted today in the United States is strictly regulated by law. See WILDLIFE REFUGE; ENDANGERED SPECIES.

Trappists, popular name for an order of Roman Catholic monks, officially (since 1892) the Reformed CISTERCIANS or Cistercians of the Stricter Observance. They perpetuate the reform begun at La Trappe, Orne dept., France, by Armand de RANCÉ (c.1660). The reformer's aim was to restore primitive Cistercian (hence also primitive Benedictine) life; actually the Trappists surpassed both St. Benedict and St. Bernard in austerity. The reform was acclaimed in the world, but many Cistercians resisted it. The whole order was affected, but some abbeys never accepted the reform as such. The life of Trappists is one of strict seclusion from the world. Working hours are devoted to common and private worship, labor (often manual), and study; there is no recreation, no meat is eaten by the healthy, and silence is observed except under unusual circumstances, but not by vow. Lay brothers do much of the farming, a peculiarly Cistercian interest. In the 19th and 20th cent. the Trappists shared in the revival of MONASTICISM and expanded greatly. There are 12 abbeys in the United States. The head of the order, the abbot general of Cîteaux, lives in Rome. See Thomas Merton, *The Silent Life* (1957); L. J. Lekai, *The Rise of the Cistercian Strict Observance in Seventeenth Century France* (1968).

traprock: see TRIASSIC PERIOD.

trapshooting: see SHOOTING.

Trasimeno (trāzēmā'nō), Lat. *Trasimenus,* lake, c.50 sq mi (130 sq km), in Umbria, central Italy, W of Perugia. It is also called Lake of Perugia. The shallow circular lake (max. depth 19 ft/6 m) often floods its shores, which are sparsely populated. There is no natural outlet, but a subterranean channel to a tributary of the Tiber was opened in 1898. In 217 B.C., lake Trasimeno was the scene of Hannibal's victory over the Romans under Flaminius.

Trás-os-Montes (trä'zōōzhmōn"tĕsh), former province of NE Portugal, comprising the districts of Bragança and Vila Real. The capital was BRAGANÇA. It is now included with other territory in Trás-os-Montes e Alto Douro prov. (4,162 sq mi/10,780 sq km). The terrain is rough and the winters cold except along the Douro River in the hilly vineyard district, which yields the famed port wine grapes, and in warm tributary valleys, where olives and other crops are grown. Mining is an important industry in the mountains.

Trastevere: see *Renaissance and Modern Rome* under ROME.

Traunsee, lake, Austria: see SALZKAMMERGUT.

Trautenau: see TRUTNOV, Czechoslovakia.

Travancore (trăvənkôr'), former princely state, 7,622 sq mi (19,741 sq km), SW India, on the Arabian Sea. It is now in Kerala state. The region of Travancore has coastal lowlands (protected by lagoons) and a hilly interior, including the Cardamom Hills. Rainfall is heavy, and rice, sugarcane, coconuts, and cotton are important lowland crops. The hill region provides half of India's cardamom and much coffee, tea, rubber, and timber. There is a large Christian minority. The region was brought under the control of a local prince, Martanda Varma, in the 18th cent. The prince accepted British guarantees against HAIDAR ALI and Tippoo Sahib in 1788. Revolts against British overlordship in the early 19th cent. were quickly suppressed. Travancore became noted for its efficient government and its high rate of literacy (about 50%).

traveler's-joy: see CLEMATIS.

Traven, B., 1890?–1969, novelist. For many years no facts about Traven's life were known. It is now thought that his name was Berick Traven Torsvan, that he was born in Chicago to Swedish parents, and that he lived in Germany during World War I and subsequently in Mexico. His novels are often set in exotic locations and usually treat exploiters and those they exploit. Among his works are *The Death Ship* (1926), *The Treasure of the Sierra Madre* (1927), *The Rebellion of the Hanged* (1934), and *The Night Visitors* (1966).

Traverse, Lake (trăv'ərs), c.30 mi (50 km) long, on the Minn.-S.Dak. line, drained to the N by the Bois de Sioux River. The lake is impounded by White Rock Dam (completed 1948).

Traverse City, city (1970 pop. 18,048), seat of Grand Traverse co., N Mich., at the head of the West Arm of Grand Traverse Bay, in a resort and cherry-growing region; inc. 1881. Tourism and food processing are major industries. Wall decorations, gear sets, tools and dies, and cranes are among the manufactures. Protestant missionaries came to the area in 1839. The production of lumber was the major economic activity until c.1915, when the supply was depleted and farming begun. A junior college and a state park are in Traverse City. A huge flock of wild swans live on the bay there. Many ski resorts are in the nearby mountains.

travertine (trăv'ərtĭn, –tēn), form of massive calcium carbonate, $CaCO_3$, resulting from deposition by springs or rivers. It is often beautifully colored and banded as a result of the presence of iron compounds or other (e.g., organic) impurities. This material is variously known as calc-sinter and calcareous tufa and (when used for decorative purposes) as onyx marble, Mexican onyx, and Egyptian or Oriental alabaster. Travertine is generally less coarse-grained and takes a higher polish than stalactite and stalagmite, which are similar in chemical composition and origin.

Traviès de Villers, Charles Joseph (shärl zhôzĕf' trävyĕs' də vēlĕr'), 1804–59, French caricaturist and painter, b. Switzerland. He founded and was a prolific contributor to the popular journal *Charivari* (1831) and drew for *Caricature* (1838). His witty burlesques of Parisian life were very popular. He helped to illustrate Balzac's works (1848–55).

Travis, William Barrett (trăv'ĭs), 1809–36, hero of the Texas Revolution, b. Edgefield co., S.C. He moved to Claiborne, Ala., where he practiced law. Travis later moved (1831) to Texas and soon acquired local prominence. He was ardent in urging the revolt of the American settlers against Mexican rule. In the Texas Revolution he served as a colonel. After the Texans had taken the ALAMO, he was sent to reinforce them and became commander of the fort. The little force was beset by the Mexican army of General SANTA ANNA (March, 1836). The Alamo fell, and all of its defenders, among them Travis, James Bowie, and David Crockett, were massacred. The defense became a symbol of heroism.

travois (trăvoi'), device used by North American Indians of the Great Plains for transporting their tepees and household goods. It consisted of two poles, lashed one on either side of a dog or, later, a horse, with one end of each pole dragging on the ground. It had straps or wooden crosspieces between the poles near the open end that served as a carrier. Like the sledge, the travois was used by Indians before any use of wheels was known to them.

treacle: see MOLASSES.

treason, legal term for various acts of disloyalty. The English law, first clearly stated in the Statute of Treasons (1350), originally distinguished high treason and petit (or petty) treason. Petit treason was the murder of one's lawful superior, e.g., murder of his master by an apprentice. High treason constituted a serious threat to the stability or continuity of the state. It included attempts to kill the king, the queen, or the heir apparent or to restrain their liberty; to counterfeit coinage or the royal seal; and to wage war against the kingdom. Especially cruel methods were used in executing traitors. Court decisions developed the English law of treason into an instrument for suppressing resistance to governmental policy. Any degree of violence in expressing opposition to parliamentary enactments was held to be a levy of war and a threat to the king's life. In the 19th cent. the English law was reformed; petit treason was abolished, cruel methods of executing traitors were forbidden, and many types of treason (e.g., counterfeiting) were made felonies that involved a lesser penalty than death. To avoid the abuses of the English law, treason was specifically defined in the U.S. Constitution (definitions of other crimes were not deemed necessary). Article 3 of the Constitution thus provides that treason shall consist only in levying war against the United States or in giving aid and comfort to its enemies and that conviction may be had only on the testimony of two witnesses to the same overt act or on confession in open court. There have been less than 40 Federal prosecutions for treason and even fewer convictions. Several men were convicted of treason in connection with the Whiskey Rebellion (1794) but were pardoned by George Washington. The most famous treason trial, that of Aaron BURR in 1807, resulted in acquittal. Politically motivated attempts to convict opponents of the Jeffersonian Embargo Acts and the Fugitive Slave Law of 1850 all failed. In the 20th cent., treason has become largely a wartime phenomenon, and the treason cases of World Wars I and II were of minor significance. Most states have provisions in their constitutions or statutes similar to those in the U.S. Constitution. There have been only two successful prosecutions for treason on the state level, that of Thomas Dorr in Rhode Island and that of John Brown in Virginia. See Nathaniel Weyl, *Treason* (1950); Margaret Boveri, *Treason in the Twentieth Century* (tr. 1961); Bradley Chapin, *The American Law of Treason: Revolutionary and Early National Origins* (1964).

treasure-trove, in English law, buried or concealed money or precious metals without any ascertainable owner. Such property belongs to the crown. The present practice in Great Britain is for the crown to pay the finder for the treasure-trove if it is of historic or artistic value. In the United States the government does not assert a claim to apparently ownerless property but allows the finder to keep it.

Treasury, United States Department of the, Federal executive department established in 1789. It is charged with advising the President on fiscal policy, acting as fiscal agent for the Federal government, and performing certain law enforcement tasks through the SECRET SERVICE. Under the Articles of Confederation the limited financial administration of the United States was taken care of by a superintendent of finance, who was replaced in 1784 by a treasury board. One of the first necessities, after the new government was set up in 1789 under the Constitution of the United States, was machinery for the collection of taxes, the custody of Federal funds, and the keeping of accounts. To this end the Dept. of the Treasury was created and its head, the Secretary of the Treasury, became the second-ranking cabinet member (after the Secretary of State). Alexander HAMILTON was the first Secretary. The office of U.S. Treasurer was also created in 1789 to receive and pay out money for the Federal government. Divisions that were added over the years include the Bureau of the Mint (1795), the Internal Revenue Service (1862), the Office of the Comptroller of the Currency (1863), the Bureau of Engraving and Printing (1877), the U.S. Secret Service (1860), the Bureau of Customs (1927), the Fiscal Service (1940), and the U.S. Savings Bonds Division (1945). Until 1829 the department supervised the U.S. postal service and until 1849 the General Land Office; before 1903 the department was also charged with many duties pertaining to commerce. See BANK OF THE UNITED STATES; FEDERAL RESERVE SYSTEM; INDEPENDENT TREASURY SYSTEM; SUBTREASURY.

Treat, Robert, 1622?–1710, American colonial governor of Connecticut, b. England. He was taken to America when a child; his father was an early settler of Wethersfield, Conn., and a patentee of the royal charter granted in 1662. Robert Treat settled (1639) in Milford and became a prominent citizen, serving in the colonial assembly and on the governor's council. When the colonies of New Haven and Connecticut were united, Treat was a leader of the group of settlers who, discontented with the new arrangement, went to New Jersey and founded (1666) the city of Newark. He later returned (1672) to Milford and was commander in chief of the Connecticut forces in King Philip's War (1675–76) and in other clashes with the Indians, especially the Narragansett tribe. Deputy governor after 1676, he became governor of Connecticut in 1683. When the English government planned to unite the New England colonies, Treat led the opposition to the surrender of the Connecticut charter. He is supposed to have had some part in concealing the charter in the CHARTER OAK to prevent its falling into the hands of Gov. Edmund ANDROS, but there is excellent reason to believe that the whole Charter Oak story is a myth. Treat served on Andros's council, and when that unpopular governor was ousted (1689), he resumed the governorship of Connecticut, retaining it until 1698. He again served (1698–1708) as deputy governor.

treaty, in international law, formal agreement between sovereign states or organizations of states. A treaty ordinarily deals with the rights and duties of nations, but treaties may also grant specific rights to private individuals. In some countries treaties are a part of the law of the land and are binding upon all persons. In the United States the Supreme Court has held that a treaty automatically abrogates any state or Federal statute in conflict with it. Treaties are designed to regularize the intercourse of nations, and, as such, they are the source of most international law. The term *treaty* is ordinarily confined to important formal agreements, while less formal international accords are called conventions, acts, declarations, or protocols. Treaties have existed ever since states came into existence. Records survive of Mesopotamian treaties dating before 3000 B.C., and in the Old Testament many treaties are mentioned. The Greeks and the Romans had elaborate ceremonials to emphasize the sanctity of treaties, and many current treaty practices have classical antecedents. Although treaties deal with a great variety of subjects, they are commonly classified under a few heads. Political treaties deal (among other things) with alliances, war, cessions of territory, and rectification of boundaries. Commercial treaties may govern fisheries, navigation, tariffs, and monetary exchange. Legal treaties concern extradition of criminals, patent and copyright protection, and the like. A treaty is negotiated by duly accredited representatives of the executive branch of the government; for the United States negotiations are ordinarily conducted by officials of the Dept. of State under the authority of the President. The preliminaries are not usually open to the public, but the record of all PROTOCOL (i.e., the minutes) is preserved for use in case the treaty provisions require subsequent interpretation. Technical experts draft the text, which the government representatives then sign. The treaty is next ratified by the signatory states in accordance with their regular practice. In the United States the Constitution requires that a treaty must be approved by two thirds of the Senate (executive agreements, however, which are undertaken through the President's powers and do not need the Senate's approval, account for a large number of the international agreements of the United States). A treaty comes into effect when the ratifications are formally exchanged. It has been argued that such wartime agreements as those made by President Franklin Delano Roosevelt at the YALTA CONFERENCE were in effect secret treaties. Members of the United Nations are required to register their treaties with that organization (following the like practice of the League of Nations), and a treaty that has not been registered may not be invoked before a UN agency. If treaties between UN members conflict with their obligations under the Charter of the United Nations, the Charter takes precedence. The interpretation of treaties, like that of all legal documents, may present great difficulties. There is no tribunal with compulsory and final jurisdiction to interpret a treaty; parties may, however, voluntarily submit a dispute to the International Court of Justice (World Court) or the Permanent Court of Arbitration (Hague Tribunal). Treaties may come to an end in various ways. Most provide for a date of expiration or a time at which notice to terminate must be given if the treaty is not to continue in effect for another specified period. Treaties terminate if one of the signatory states becomes politically extinct or (in the case of political treaties) if the parties are at war with one another. The outbreak of war need not necessarily bring a treaty to an end, however, and provisions compatible with a state of hostilities remain in force, as long as they are not expressly terminated. Treaties relating to the laws of war, of course, remain in effect during hostilities. A treaty may be terminated by mutual consent, and breach of a treaty by one party entitles the other to abrogate it. See Hans Blix, *Treaty-making Power* (1960); E. M. Byrd, *Treaties and Executive Agreements in the United States* (1960); A. D. McNair, *The Law of Treaties* (rev. ed. 1961); L. W. Beilenson, *The Treaty Trap* (1969).

treaty port, port opened to foreign trade by a treaty. The term is usually confined to ports in those countries that formerly strongly objected to foreign trade or attempted altogether to exclude it. Thus it is used especially in reference to Japan and China. Those countries had admitted trade with the West in the 16th cent. but soon reversed themselves, with Japan permitting only a trickle of Dutch commerce through Nagasaki, and China shutting off all trade until the opening of Canton in 1834. Great Britain, determined to increase commerce, provoked the OPIUM WAR with China. The Treaty of Nanking (1842), which restored peace, provided for five treaty ports—Amoy, Canton, Fu-chou, Ning-po, and Shanghai. As in all the 69 Chinese treaty ports that were finally opened, zones were established for foreign residence that enjoyed EXTRATERRITORIALITY. Most of the ports were on the seacoast or on large rivers. A similar system came into being in Japan after the country was reopened to Western trade by Matthew Perry in 1854. With the abolition of extraterritoriality, the system of treaty ports also disappeared. This occurred in 1899 in Japan but not until 1946 in China. See J. K. Fairbank, *Trade and Diplomacy on the China Coast: The Opening of the Treaty Ports, 1842–1854* (1953, repr. 1969).

Trebbia (trĕb'byä), river, c.70 mi (110 km) long, rising in the Ligurian Apennines, N Italy, and flowing generally NE past Bobbio to join the Po River near Piacenza. Near that city in 218 B.C. Hannibal won a decisive victory over the Romans. In 1799 the Trebbia was the scene of a Russo-Austrian victory over the French.

Trebizond, Turkey: see TRABZON.

Trebizond, empire of, 1204–1461. When the army of the Fourth Crusade overthrew (1204) the Byzantine Empire and established the Latin Empire of Constantinople, several Greek successor states sprang up. These were the empire of Nicaea, the despotate of Epirus, and the empire of Trebizond. The last of these was founded by two members of the former imperial Comnenus family, David and his brother Alexius I (reigned 1204–22) of Trebizond, who took the titles of Grand Comnenus and emperor, which were assumed by all his successors. The empire comprised the entire southern coastal region of the Black Sea except its westernmost section, which belonged to Nicaea. Trebizond, the capital, and Sinope were the chief cities. The western part of the empire was the conquest of David Comnenus, who soon lost his dominions to Nicaea. The empire of Trebizond was further diminished when Sinope fell (1214) to the Seljuk Turks, and the emperor became a vassal of the sultan of Iconium; for the remainder of its existence Trebizond was restricted to the SE Black Sea coastal region. When the Byzantine Empire was restored (1261) under Nicaean leadership, Trebizond remained separate and independent, although it was often forced to pay tribute to the succeeding dominant powers of Asia Minor. After the Mongol invasion the empire experienced tremendous economic prosperity. It became the commercial route through Asia Minor, leading into the great trade route to the Far East that the Mongols had opened, and its position on the trade routes from Russia and from the Middle East to Europe furthered its importance. Its commercial life was controlled by the Genoese and the Venetians, and the empire profited much from the added opportunity to export the produce of its own rich hinterland. The empire reached its greatest prosperity under Alexius II (1297–1330), but with the decline of Mongol power after 1320, Trebizond suffered increasingly from Turkish attacks, civil wars, and domestic intrigues. In this period the emperors attempted to gain strength by marrying the princesses of the Comnenus dynasty to Turkish princes. Relations between Trebizond and the Muslims were generally friendly, but after the Turkish conquest of Constantinople (1453), David Comnenus, the last emperor of Trebizond, promoted an alliance of the non-Ottoman Asian states against Sultan Muhammad II. In 1461, Muhammad forced David to surrender, and a few years later the sultan had him put to death together with all the Comnenus males but one. Trebizond was annexed to the Ottoman Empire. At the height of its wealth and power the court of the Grand Comneni was a great artistic and cultural center and, though Oriental in character, made Trebizond the last refuge of Hellenistic civilization.

See William Miller, *Trebizond, the Last Greek Empire* (1926).

treble, highest part in choral music, thus synonymous with soprano. The term appeared in 15th-century English polyphony, probably as an Anglicization of the Latin *triplum,* the name given in medieval polyphony to the part that was often the highest (see MOTET). The treble clef, however, is the G clef, one of the two clefs commonly used today for vocal music and for most instrumental music. The soprano clef is a C clef placing middle C on the bottom line of the staff; it was used in vocal music as late as Bach's time but is now nearly obsolete for voice. See MUSICAL NOTATION.

Treblinka: see CONCENTRATION CAMP.

Trebonius, Caius (trēbō'nēəs), d. 43 B.C., Roman politician. When tribune (55 B.C.) of the plebs he proposed the *Lex Trebonia* by which Pompey obtained Spain, Crassus obtained Syria, and Caesar obtained Gaul and Illyricum. As Caesar's protégé he became praetor (48 B.C.), propraetor in Spain (47), and consul (45). Notwithstanding the promise by Caesar of the province of Asia, he was a leading conspirator against his patron. He was slain in Smyrna by Dolabella.

Tredyakovsky, Vasily Kirilovich (vəsē'lyē kĭrē'ləvĭch trĕdyəkôf'skē), 1703–69, Russian poet, translator, and scholar. Tredyakovsky rose from humble origins to membership in the Academy of Sciences and a position as court poet, only to die in poverty and obscurity. He is remembered chiefly for his treatise *A Brief New Method of Composing Russian Verse* (1735), with which he began a reform of Russian prosody. His own verse is uneven.

Tree, Ellen: see KEAN, EDMUND.

Tree, Sir Herbert Beerbohm, 1853–1917, English actor-manager, whose original name was Herbert Draper Beerbohm. He was a half brother of Max Beerbohm. His first success (1884) was as the curate in *The Private Secretary,* and he thereafter became prominent as a romantic actor. In 1883 he married the distinguished actress **Helen Maud Holt** (1863–1937), who became his leading lady. She was a well-educated and very versatile actress, especially adept at comedy. Tree achieved his greatest distinction as a manager with his staging of Shakespeare at the Haymarket theater (1887–97) and at Her Majesty's Theatre, which he built and opened in 1897. In the manner of his day, he stressed visual elements with elaborate, imaginative, and detailed effects. He was knighted in 1909. See his *Thoughts and Afterthoughts* (1913) and *Nothing Matters* (1917); biographies by Max Beerbohm (1920) and Hesketh Pearson (1956, repr. 1971).

tree, perennial woody plant with a single main STEM (the trunk, or bole) from which branches and twigs extend to form a characteristic crown of foliage. In general, a tree differs from a shrub in that it has a single trunk, it reaches a greater height at maturity, it branches at a greater distance from the ground, and it increases in size by producing new branches and expanding in girth while a shrub produces new shoots from ground level. Trees and shrubs are either deciduous, with broad leaves that are shed at the end of the growing season, or evergreen (see CONIFER), with needlelike or scalelike leaves that are shed at intervals of from 2 to 10 years, thus maintaining green foliage at all seasons. There are, however, broad-leaved shrubs that follow the conifer pattern; most of these are tropical, although some (e.g., holly and laurel) are found in relatively cold climates. A few trees with needlelike leaves (e.g., the larch) shed their leaves as do other deciduous varieties; some palms have several trunks growing from the same root system; and various plants called trees (e.g., bamboo and banana) are herbaceous rather than woody. Shedding the leaves has the effect of cutting down water loss through transpiration at a time when the freezing of water in the ground and within the plant would disrupt the normal functions of osmosis, photosynthesis, and sap conduction. Trees are identified both by the characteristic color and shape of the LEAF and by their overall appearance, e.g., the degree and angle of branching, the shape of the crown, and the texture of the bark. Besides their enormous importance in providing oxygen and moisture for the atmosphere, trees are a source of food, of WOOD, and of numerous products (e.g., resins, rubber, quinine, turpentine, and cellulose for the manufacture of paper and various synthetic materials) derived from their wood, bark, leaves, and fruits. See U.S. Dept. of Agriculture, *Trees: the Yearbook of Agriculture* (1949); G. A. Petrides, *A Field Guide to Trees and Shrubs* (2d ed. 1972); Hugh Johnson, *The International Book of Trees* (1973); R. L. Hudson, *The Pruning Handbook* (1973).

Treece, Henry, 1912–66, English poet and novelist. He served as an intelligence officer in the Royal Air Force during World War II, after which he taught school for many years. He is noted chiefly for his poetry, which is characterized by precise observation and intense, vivid imagery. Among his works are *Towards a Personal Armageddon* (1940) and *The Exiles* (1952), volumes of poetry, and the novels *The Dark Island* (1952) and *The Green Man* (1966). See biography by Margery Fisher et al. (1969).

tree fern, any FERN having a treelike trunk. Sometimes other similar primitive plants are also called tree fern, e.g., species of CYCAD.

tree frog, name for any of the small tree- or shrub-inhabiting FROGS of the family Hylidae, characterized by an adhesive disk on the tip of each of the clawlike toes. This family has about 300 species distributed throughout most tropical and temperate regions, with the greatest number found in the New World tropics. Tree frogs, sometimes called tree toads, are usually under 3 in. (7.5 cm) long. They are gray, green, or brown, often blending with the natural background; in most species the color varies with the temperature and other conditions. Most tree frogs lay their eggs in or near water, where the tadpole develops. Many species, such as the spring peeper (*Hyla gratiosa*) and the chorus frogs (*Pseudacris* species), are known for the song they produce when they gather near ponds to breed in the spring. In one group of tree frogs the eggs are carried in a mass on the back of the female, exposed or in a pouch of skin. The tadpoles either are deposited in the water or continue their development in the pouch. A few members of the family, such as the North American cricket frog (*Acris crepitans*), are not arboreal. Tree frogs are classified in the phylum CHORDATA, subphylum Vertebrata, class Amphibia, order Anura, family Hylidae.

treehopper, any member of a cosmopolitan family of winged INSECTS, remarkable for their curious shapes. The shapes are due to the enlargement of the dorsal (upper) covering of the first thoracic section (the region behind the head), which may project upward in a hump or extend forward over the head and backward over the body, and may be ornamented with variously shaped projections. Many treehoppers resemble small thorns and are protectively colored in green or brown. In other species, especially in the tropics, the shapes are quite complex and bizarre. Both larval and adult treehoppers feed on plant juices. The adults, usually under ½ in. (1.2 cm) long, jump from one place to another. Females lay their eggs in slits in bark, which sometimes damages the tree; however, few species are important pests. The buffalo treehopper, *Stictocephala bubulus,* common in the United States, causes stunting of fruit trees. Treehoppers are classified in the phylum ARTHROPODA, class Insecta, order Homoptera, family Membracidae.

tree mouse: see MOUSE; VOLE.

tree of heaven: see AILANTHUS.

tree shrew, small, arboreal PRIMATE of the family Tupaiidae, found in S Asia. Tree shrews superficially resemble squirrels, and are commonly brown, reddish, or olive in color. They have large eyes and good vision and can use their hands effectively for holding food. Their fingers have sharp claws, rather than the flat nails characteristic of other primates. Tree shrews are territorial, omnivorous, and extremely active; they dart about constantly in the trees screaming and fighting with one another. The common tree shrew, *Tupais glis,* looks like a squirrel with an elongated, shrewlike snout. Its body is about 8 in. (20 cm) long, and it has a bushy tail about 7 in. (18 cm) long. It is found from India to Malaysia. The pen-tailed tree shrew, *Ptilocercus lowi,* of Sumatra, Borneo, and the Malay Peninsula is the most distinctive tree shrew; it is a mouse-sized nocturnal animal, dark gray above and yellow below, with a naked, black tail bearing two fringes of white hair at the end. Tree shrews bear some anatomical resemblance to the true SHREW and were formerly classified along with shrews as INSECTIVORES. However, they are anatomically more like the primate LEMUR, and they are now usually classified as primates; they actually constitute a transitional form between the two groups. There are about 20 tree shrew species, classified in 4 genera of the phylum CHORDATA, subphylum Vertebrata, class Mammalia, order Primates, family Tupaiidae.

tree surgery, practice of repairing damaged trees to restore their appearance and to arrest disease. Injured or diseased parts are first removed (even small cavities in the bark may harbor injurious fungi and insects), the surfaces are treated with antiseptics and healing aids, and the cavity may be filled with cement or some special material, e.g., composition filler or elastic cement. Professional tree surgeons commonly perform many tasks in addition to surgery that are difficult for the individual gardener e.g., large-scale pruning and providing proper support when needed.

tree toad: see TREE FROG.

trefoil (trē'foil) [O.Fr.,=three-leaf], in botany, name for several plants, chiefly legumes, having trifoliate leaves. Best known of the trefoils is clover. The bird's-foot trefoil (*Lotus corniculatus*) is an Old World forage plant and weed that has been naturalized in North America; the prairie trefoil (*L. americanus*) is a related native American plant. The shrubby trefoil is the HOP tree. Tick trefoil is a name for the tickseed, or BEGGARWEED.

Treitschke, Heinrich von (hīn'rĭkh fən trĭch'kə), 1834–1896, German historian. A fervid partisan of Prussia, he left Baden at the outbreak of the Austro-Prussian War (1866) and became professor of history at Kiel (1866), Heidelberg (1867), and Berlin (1874). He edited (1866–89) the monthly *Preussische Jahrbücher* and became (1886) Prussian state historiographer. As a young man, he was strongly nationalistic and liberal; as he grew older his political views became more nationalistic and less liberal. Although a member of the Reichstag, he was not especially successful as a practical politician. His writings, however, reflected his political views, his deep hope for the unity and greatness of Germany under Prussian leadership, and his admiration of Bismarck and the Hohenzollerns. They also reflected his strong anti-Semitism. His theories had great impact on the new generation and in academic circles. Treitschke's histories, stirring and graphic and excellent in workmanship, are nevertheless distorted by his fanatic nationalism and his pernicious biases. His masterpiece is his *History of Germany in the Nineteenth Century* (tr., 7 vol., 1915–19). Among his other works are *Politics* (tr. 1916) and *Origins of Prussianism* (tr. 1942). See biography by Andreas Dorpalen (1957); study by H. W. Davis (1915, repr. 1973).

trek (trĕk) [Du.,=draft], Afrikaans term originally meaning merely a journey by ox wagon. In English usage it generally signifies an organized migration, especially of farmers. The best-known trek is the Great Trek (1835–36), in which Boer farmers left the Cape of Good Hope to escape British domination and founded Natal, Transvaal, and the Orange Free State. Those who made the trek were called voortrekkers. A more recent trek (1902) was that of some 700 Boers who, after the British victory in the South African War, left their homes in Transvaal to settle in S central Kenya. See Eric Walker, *The Great Trek* (5th ed. 1965).

Trelawny, Edward John, 1792–1881, English adventurer. A friend of Byron and Shelley, he was at Leghorn when Shelley was drowned, and later served with Byron in the Greek War of Independence. He wrote *Recollections of the Last Days of Shelley and Byron* (1858), and a partly autobiographical novel, *The Adventures of a Younger Son* (1831). See his letters (ed. by Harry Buxton Forman, 1910, repr. 1973); biographies by R. G. Grylls (1951) and M. N. Armstrong (1940, repr. 1973).

Trelleborg (trĕləbôr'yə), city (1970 pop. 23,565), Malmöhus co., extreme S Sweden, a port on the Baltic Sea. Manufactures include machinery, rubber, cement, and refined sugar. There are ferry connections with Rügen Island, East Germany. Trelleborg was founded in the Middle Ages, and its main growth dates from the late 19th cent. The name is sometimes spelled Trälleborg.

trematode: see FLUKE; PLATYHELMINTHES.

tremolite: see AMPHIBOLE.

Trench, Richard Chenevix, 1807–86, Irish clergyman and author, b. Dublin. He was dean of Westminster, 1856–63, and Protestant archbishop of Dublin, 1863–84. His many theological writings were eclipsed by his works in philology and poetry, which include *The Study of Words* (1851), *English, Past and Present* (1855), and *Collected Poems* (1865).

trench: see OCEAN.

Trenchard, Hugh Montague Trenchard, 1st **Viscount,** 1873–1956, British air marshal. He entered the army in 1893 and served in the South African War. During World War I he commanded the Royal Flying Corps. As chief of air staff (1918, 1919–29), Trenchard shaped the offensive air strategy (to the neglect of air defense) that the Royal Air Force adhered to into World War II. He was (1931–35) commissioner of the London police force and was created a peer in 1936. See biography by Andrew Boyle (1962).

trench fever: see RICKETTSIA.

trench mouth, common term for Vincent's infection, an ulcerative membranous infection of the gums and mouth. Although its cause is not known, poor oral hygiene, nutritional deficiencies, and debilitating diseases are predisposing factors. Epidemics of trench mouth often occur in crowded unsanitary environments, and in former years among soldiers in the field, hence the name "trench mouth." In addition to ulcerations on the gums and mouth, which are painful and bleed freely, there are usually foul breath, increased salivation, and difficulty in swallowing and talking. The acute phase of the disease yields to antibiotic treatment and oxygenating mouth rinses, but attention must also be paid to the underlying dental and medical factors to prevent its recurring or becoming chronic.

trench warfare. Although trenches were used in ancient and medieval warfare, in the American Civil War, and in the Russo-Japanese War (1904–5), they did not become important until World War I. The introduction of rapid-firing SMALL ARMS and artillery made the infantry charges of earlier wars virtually impossible, and the war became immobile, with the contenders digging thousands of miles of opposing trenches fronted by barbed wire. To break the stalemate various methods and new weapons were tried; tremendous artillery barrages sought to devastate the enemy and blow a gap in his trenches; trench mortars, hand grenades, poison gas, and tanks were used. It nevertheless remained a war of attrition, with artillery duels and infantry attacks behind creeping artillery barrages. The idea of an uninterrupted line defense held the imagination of the French and German general staffs between the two world wars, and they built lines of field fortifications known as the Maginot Line and the Siegfried Line. The advent of MECHANIZED WARFARE made such defense illusory, and World War II was a war of movement. However, in the last stages of the Korean war both sides established fortified positions across the Korean peninsula, and a stalemated situation similar to that of World War I came into play. See Leon Wolff, *In Flanders Fields: the 1917 Campaign* (1958).

Trenck, Franz, Freiherr von der (fränts frī'hĕr fən dĕr trĕngk), 1711–49, Austrian officer and adventurer, b. Reggio di Calabria, Italy. A daring soldier known for his duels and love affairs, he raised at his own expense (1741) a Croatian regiment for Maria Theresa in the War of the Austrian Succession. Its atrocities led to his court-martial (1747) and to his life imprisonment in the notorious Spielberg fortress at Brno (Brünn), where he died. His memoirs, published several decades later, increased Trenck's notorious reputation.

Trent, Ital. *Trento,* Latin *Tridentum,* city (1971 pop. 91,767), capital of Trentino-Alto Adige and of Trent prov., N Italy, on the Adige River and on the road to the Brenner Pass. It is an industrial and tourist center. Manufactures include leather goods, textiles, printed materials, and food products. Probably founded in the 4th cent. B.C., Trent was later the seat of a Lombard duchy (6th cent.) and of a Frankish march (8th cent.). To safeguard their road into Italy the emperors invested (11th cent.) the bishops of Trent with temporal powers over a sizable territory; a succession of prince-bishops ruled, except for a few short intervals, until 1802, when the bishopric was secularized and became a part of TYROL in Austria. Because Trent had always been Italian in language and culture, there developed a strong movement for union with Italy (see IRREDENTISM). Union was achieved in 1919 by the Treaty of Saint-Germain. Among the city's monuments are the Lombard Romanesque cathedral; the Castello del Buon Consiglio (13th–16th cent.), once the episcopal residence, later a political prison, and now the seat of the National Museum; and a bronze statue of Dante Alighieri (1896). The Council of Trent met there in the 16th cent.

Trent, river, c.170 mi (270 km) long, rising on Biddulph Moor, Staffordshire, W England. It flows generally NE through central England before joining with the Ouse River to form the Humber estuary. The Trent, the third longest river of England, passes through the Potteries district, Burton upon Trent, and Nottingham. Its chief tributary is the Dover River. There is a high tidal bore in the lower course of the Trent. It is navigable for barges to Nottingham; canals connect it with other river systems. Water from the Trent is used as coolant in thermal power plants along its course.

Trent, Council of, 1545–47, 1551–52, 1562–63, 19th ecumenical council of the Roman Catholic Church, convoked to meet the crisis of the Protestant Reformation. Earlier efforts at reforming the church had already produced the Fifth LATERAN COUNCIL (1512–17), but it had proved ineffectual. The rise of Lutheranism brought forth a reforming party within the church that was strongly anti-Lutheran. It hoped for a new council, and when Paul III was elected pope in 1534 such a council seemed assured (see REFORMATION, CATHOLIC). The obstacles, however, took 10 years to overcome, for now that a known reformer was pope, those opposing reform were not eager for a meeting. The Protestants at first stipulated that it be held in Germany, while the pope insisted on an Italian venue. Mantua was chosen, but its duke refused; then Venice prevented a meeting at Vicenza. Finally Trent, an imperial city, almost in Italy, was selected as a compromise between the papal party and that of Holy Roman Emperor Charles V. There was an abortive start in 1542. In 1544 the pope convened the council definitively. There were no Protestant delegates. The work of the council embraced dogmatic definition and correction of abuses, and it was so planned that discussion of doctrine and of reforms of practices could be carried on at the same time. The 10 years of delay bore good fruit, for the reformers arrived at the council intensively prepared in every question likely to be studied. The chief functions of the council were occasional solemn one-day sessions (25 in all, of which 10 dealt with formalities only) for the purpose of making the final decisions and declarations; the hard work of the council was done at informal, sometimes private, meetings. The council met at first in three great committees, later as a whole. As at every ecumenical council, the presence of the papal legates was necessary to conduct it, and at Trent they drew up the agenda. The sessions of the council fell into three periods: 1–10 (1545–47), under Paul III; 11–16 (1551–52), under Julius III; and 17–25 (1562–63), under Pius IV. The two great interruptions were chiefly occasioned, first, by an impasse over the place of meeting after most of the bishops had left Trent for fear of the plague (1547), and, second, by the lack of interest of Paul IV (1555–59). Furthermore, the swiftly changing events of German politics often made delays seem wise. The numbers attending the council varied; in the first group of sessions there were less than 200, in the second group somewhat less, and in the third considerably more. The work of the council was confirmed by Pius IV (in the papal bull *Benedictus Deus,* 1564), and its most important prescription, the issuance of an explicit account of the beliefs of the church, was fulfilled by the publication (1566) of the *Catechism of the Council of Trent,* or *Roman Catechism* (which, in fact, was not catechetical but descriptive in form). The dogmatic definitions and the reform decrees of the first group of sessions treated the Scriptures (canon, text, interpretation, and function), original sin, justification, the sacraments in general, baptism, and confirmation; and also the regulation of education, preaching, and alms collecting and the duties and obligations of bishops and beneficiaries. The canons on justification (6th session), the product of seven months of discussion, are among the chief work of the council. The second period of the council was notable for the work of the Jesuits, especially Diego LAINEZ. The subjects treated were the Eucharist, penance, extreme unction, episcopal jurisdiction and office, clerical discipline, and benefices. The third period was dominated by St. CHARLES BORROMEO; its definitions and regulations covered communion in both kinds, the Mass, the sacraments of orders and matrimony, the veneration and invocation of the saints, the cult of relics and images, the list of forbidden books, the priesthood in all its phases, ecclesiastical foundations, education, marriage, religious orders, feasts and fasts, and the service books of the church. The doctrinal canons of the Council of Trent cover most of the controverted points in Roman Catholic dogma, and the definitions are so clear and lucid that the language of the council is often quoted in definitions. The reform measures of the council were tremendously far-reaching and their enforcement was probably the most thoroughgoing reform in the history of the church. The Catholic Reformation afterwards was to a great extent occupied with carrying out the principles and requirements laid down at Trent. The modern Roman Catholic Church can be understood only in the light of the work of the Council of Trent. The most complete history is found in Ludwig Pastor's history of the popes; there is an English translation of the dogmatic canons and decrees and of the Roman Catechism, which includes much from the conciliar canons. See Hubert Jedin, *History of the Council of Trent* (2 vol., tr. 1957–61); study by J. A. Froude (1896, repr. 1969).

Trent Affair, incident in the diplomatic relations between the United States and Great Britain, which occurred during the American Civil War. On Nov. 8, 1861, the British mail packet *Trent,* carrying James M. MASON and John SLIDELL, Confederate commissioners to London and Paris respectively, was halted in the Bahama Channel by the U.S. warship *San Jacinto,* commanded by Capt. Charles WILKES. The commissioners and their secretaries were forcibly removed from the *Trent* and taken to Boston, where they were interned in Fort Warren. This act was strictly opposed to the laws of the sea as they had been previously upheld by the United States, since Wilkes did not seize the vessel and bring it in for admiralty adjudication but merely exercised search and seizure of the men. Nevertheless, Wilkes's action was greeted with wild acclaim and he was thanked by the U.S. House of Representatives. In Great Britain the act aroused popular indignation. The British drafted a sharp note to the U.S. government, the terms of which were softened by Prince Albert; they demanded the release of the commissioners and an explanation. A seven-day limit was set for reply. It seemed for a time that Great Britain would not only recognize the Confederacy but declare war against the Union. However, Lord Lyons, the British minister to the United States, delayed presentation of the note for several days, meanwhile notifying Secretary of State William H. Seward of its contents. The note was presented Dec. 23, 1861. By that time popular feeling in the United States had died down, and the prospect of war with Britain was anything but welcome. A cabinet meeting on Dec. 26 led to a decision to send to Britain a note by Seward disavowing Wilkes's act and promising to release the prisoners. They were released in Jan., 1862, and trouble with Great Britain was averted.

Trent Canal, waterway system, 240 mi (386 km) long, S Ont., Canada, connecting Lake Ontario, from the Bay of Quinte, with Lake Huron at Georgian Bay; built 1833–48. It utilizes the Trent River to Rice Lake, the Otonabee River through Peterborough, the Kawartha Lakes and artificial channels to Lake Simcoe and Lake Couchiching, and the Severn River to Georgian Bay. The system, with numerous dams and locks, has only 20 mi (32 km) of artificial channels. It was designed primarily to shorten the shipping route between lakes Ontario and Huron but has proved more valuable as a source of water power. Used mainly by pleasure craft, it is open to navigation from May to October.

Trentino-Alto Adige (trāntē'nō-äl'tō ä'dĕjā), region (1971 pop. 839,025), 5,256 sq mi (13,613 sq km), N Italy, bordering on Switzerland in the northwest and on Austria in the north. From 1919 to 1947 it was called Venezia Tridentina. TRENT (Ital. *Trento*) is the capital of the region, which is divided into Trento and Bolzano provs. The provincial capitals alternate biennially as the site of the regional parliament. The provinces have considerable autonomy. Most of the inhabitants of Bolzano province, and roughly 40% of the total population of the region, are German-speaking; the rest speak Italian or, a tiny minority, Rhaeto-Romanic. The terrain is almost entirely mountainous, except for a narrow strip along the upper Adige River, where most of the population is concentrated. The region includes the Tyrolean Alps south of the Brenner Pass and, in the east, part of the Dolomites. Agriculture forms the backbone of the regional economy, with cereals, fruit, and dairy cattle the principal items. The chief manufactures are aluminum, forest products, processed food, and chemicals. There is also a large tourist industry. Most of the region was included from the 11th cent. to 1802–3 in the episcopal principalities of TRENT and BRESSANONE; in 1815 it was put under direct Austrian administration and incorporated into the TYROL. After Trento passed to Italy in 1866, the Austrians pressed for increased Germanization in Bolzano. This led to IRREDENTISM among the Italian minority there. After World War I, the Treaty of Saint-Germain (1919) gave Bolzano to Italy, which resulted in agitation by its German-speaking population. The Italian Fascist government's program of intensive Italianization and the enforcement of Italian as the sole official language met with violent opposition. An agreement in 1938 between Hitler and Mussolini provided for extensive forced migration of the German-speaking population to Germany or to other parts of Italy. However, this program was extremely unpopular and soon collapsed. Following an agreement (1946) between the Italian and Austrian governments, the republican constitution of Italy (1947) granted the region considerable autonomy. Both German and Italian were made official languages, and German schools were permitted in Bolzano prov. However, the German-speaking population in the province (called Südtirol, or South Tyrol, by the Germans) continued to demand greater autonomy. They received the backing of Austria, which charged that the German-speaking population in Bolzano had not been given the autonomy envisaged in the 1946 Austro-Italian agreement. This led to serious tension between the two countries. In 1960 the Bolzano problem was debated, at Austria's request, at the United Nations, on whose recommendation Italy and Austria entered into direct negotiations. Their efforts were partially vitiated by acts of terror committed in the region in 1961. It was only in 1971 that a treaty was signed and ratified; this agreement stipulated that disputes in Bolzano would be submitted for settlement to the International Court of Justice in The Hague, that the province would receive increased legislative and administrative autonomy from Italy, and that Austria would not interfere in Bolzano's internal affairs.

Trento: see TRENT, Italy.

Trenton, town (1971 pop. 14,589), SE Ont., Canada, on the Bay of Quinte at the mouth of the Trent River and at the south end of the Trent Canal. Its manufactures include textiles, electronic components, and paper and steel products. A Royal Canadian Air Force base is to the east.

Trenton. 1 City (1970 pop. 24,127), Wayne co., SE Mich., on the Detroit River opposite Grosse Ile, in a farm area; settled 1816, inc. as a city 1957. An early river port, it has oil refineries and plants making steel and iron molds, chemicals, automobile engines, and building materials. **2** City (1970 pop. 104,638), state capital (since 1790) and seat (since 1719) of Mercer co., W N.J., at the head of navigation on the Delaware River; settled by Friends 1679, inc. as a city 1792. Situated between Philadelphia and New York City, it is an important transportation hub and industrial center. Its pottery industry dates from Colonial times. Other leading manufactures are steel cables, rubber goods, automobile parts, textiles, plastics, and a great variety of metal products. The settlement was first called the Falls, then Stacy's Mills, and finally Trenton. In the American Revolution, Trenton was the scene of a battle when Washington crossed (Dec. 25, 1776) the ice-clogged Delaware and surprised and captured (Dec. 26) 918 Hessians. The Americans, avoiding a British relief force led by Cornwallis, then struck at Princeton. A 155-ft (47-m) granite monument topped by a statue of Washington commemorates the battle, and the place where the Americans crossed the Delaware is marked in a state park. Trenton grew as a commercial center and became the site of many industries; the famous Roebling Works, where wire rope is manufactured, was established in 1848. The city's noteworthy buildings include the golden-domed capitol (1792), much remodeled and enlarged; the capitol annex (1931); the state cultural center; the World War I memorial building (1932); the old barracks, built in 1758 and restored as a museum; and the William Trent House (1719), the city's oldest standing building, now a museum. Joseph Bonaparte's mistress, Annette Savage, lived at "Bow Hill." Zebulon Pike was born in Lamberton, now part of Trenton. In the city are Trenton State College, Rider College, a junior college, and a state prison and other state institutions. The annual state fair is held there in September; the fair grounds include an international speedway. See Trenton Historical Society, *A History of Trenton, 1679–1929* (1929); H. J. Podmore, *Trenton, Old and New* (rev. and ed. by M. J. Messler, 1964).

Trent University, at Peterborough, Ont., Canada; founded 1963. It has faculties of arts and science and graduate studies. Teaching takes the form of tutorial and seminar work in small groups.

trepang (trəpăng'): see SEA CUCUMBER.

Tresco: see SCILLY ISLANDS.

Tres Marías, Las (läs trās märē'äs), archipelago, in the Pacific Ocean, c.60 mi (100 km) W of Nayarit state, Mexico. Of the four islands, two—María Madre, which is the largest (c.56 sq mi/145 sq km) and is also a federal penal colony, and María Magdalena—produce maguey, salt, and lumber (especially cedar and lignum vitae).

trespass, in law, any physical injury to the person or to PROPERTY. In English COMMON LAW the action of trespass first developed (13th cent.) to afford a remedy for injuries to property. The two early forms were trespass *quare clausum fregit,* used in instances of breaking into real property, and trespass *de bonis asportatis,* used when personal property was removed without consent. To sue for trespass the plaintiff must have had possession of the property. Although the offense of trespass required the use of force, the courts quickly decided that the mere act of breaking in or of taking goods was in itself forceful. Trespass in time was applied to injuries to the person involving force, such as ASSAULT, BATTERY, and unlawful imprisonment. Out of the law of trespass developed many of the TORTS that are now commonly recognized. In present-day usage the term *trespass* is usually applied only to unlawful entry into private property. If a trespasser refuses a request to leave the premises, he may be removed by force.

Tres Tabernae (trēs təbûr'nē), ancient town of Latium, Italy, on the Appian Way, 30 mi (48 km) SE of Rome. It is mentioned in Acts 28.15 as the place where St. Paul was met by his friends on his journey to Rome. The Authorized Version translates *Tres Tabernae* as Three Taverns.

Trevelyan, Sir Charles Edward (trĭvĕl'yən), 1807–86, British colonial administrator. After a period of service in India, he returned (1838) to England and was (1840–59) assistant secretary of the treasury. He was knighted (1848) for his administration of Irish famine relief. In 1853 he headed, with Sir Stafford Northcote (later earl of Iddesleigh), the important commission that recommended recruitment to the civil service by competitive examination. He was governor of Madras (1859–60) and finance minister in India (1862–65), promoting public works. Trevelyan was father of the historian George Otto Trevelyan and brother-in-law of Thomas Macaulay.

Trevelyan, George Macaulay, 1876–1962, English historian; son of Sir George Otto Trevelyan. Educated at Cambridge, he became professor of modern history there in 1927 and was master of Trinity College from 1940 to 1951. He was a master of the so-called "literary" school of historical writing, and his reaction against "scientific" history has had tremendous influence. He did not, however, ignore the scientific aspects of historical scholarship; rather he asserted that the historian must elucidate his subject through imaginative speculation, based on all possible evidence, and present it by means of highly developed literary craftsmanship. His most ambitious works are an extended study of Garibaldi (3 vol., 1907–11) and a history of *England under Queen Anne* (3 vol., 1930–34). He is perhaps better known for his one-volume *History of England* (1926), his *British History in the Nineteenth Century* (1922), and *England under the Stuarts* (1907). Other works include biographies of John Bright (1913), Lord Charles Grey (1920), his father, Sir George Otto Trevelyan (1932), and Lord Grey of Fallodon (1937); *The English Revolution, 1688–1689* (1938); *English Social History* (1942; pub. in an illustrated version in 4 vol., 1949–52); and *An Autobiography and Other Essays* (1949). See study by J. H. Plumb (1955, repr. 1969).

Trevelyan, Sir George Otto, 1838–1928, British historian and politician. He served as a Whig member of the House of Commons from 1865 to 1897. He held posts under W. E. Gladstone as civil lord of the admiralty (1868–70), secretary to the admiralty (1880–82), chief secretary for Ireland (1882–84), and chancellor of the duchy of Lancaster (1884–85). In 1876, Trevelyan produced a biography of his uncle, Thomas Macaulay. His *Early History of Charles James Fox* (1880) firmly established his reputation as a historian. His study of the times of Fox was continued in the *American Revolution* (4 vol., 1899–1907) and completed with *George the Third and Charles Fox* (1912). Trevelyan's Whig sympathies led to his condemnation of George III and praise for the American Revolutionary leaders, an attitude that contributed to the great popularity of his work in the United States, but that detracted from its objectivity. See biography by his son, G. M. Trevelyan (1932).

Treves or **Trèves:** see TRIER, West Germany.

Trevisa, John of (trəvē'sə), c.1326–c.1402, English writer. He was the vicar of Berkeley. In 1387 he translated into English Ranulph Higden's *Polychronicon,* a history of the world, and in 1398, Bartholomew de Glanville's *De proprietatibus rerum,* an encyclopedia of natural science. Both translations became standard authorities of the later Middle Ages and were printed by the early presses.

Treviso (trāvē'zō), city (1971 pop. 90,945), capital of Treviso prov., Venetia, NE Italy. Situated in the center of the fertile Venetian plain, it is an agricultural and industrial center. Manufactures include machinery, chemicals, and food products. In the early Middle Ages, Treviso was the seat of a Lombard duchy, then of a Frankish march. It later became a free commune, submitted to various powers, and in 1339 fell to Venice. Severely damaged in the two world wars, Treviso remains picturesque, with canals, old houses, narrow winding streets, and fortifications of the 16th and 17th cent. Of special note are the cathedral (16th cent.) and the municipal museum, whose rich holdings include paintings by Pâris Bordone, born (1500) in Treviso.

Trevithick, Richard (trĕv'ĭthĭk), 1771–1833, English engineer and inventor. He is known as the father of locomotive power because of his invention (1800) of the high-pressure steam engine. He built a steam carriage that on Christmas Eve, 1801, in London, carried the first passengers transported by steam power. In 1804 a steam locomotive he constructed was used in Wales on a railway, the first vehicle to be so operated. Trevithick also developed steam engines for use in mines and invented a steam threshing machine. See L. T. C. Rolt, *The Cornish Giant* (1960).

Trevor-Roper, Hugh Redwald, 1914–, British historian. He was educated at Oxford, where he became Regius professor of modern history in 1957. Trevor-Roper is a prolific writer whose topics range from medieval to contemporary history; his *The Last Days of Hitler* (1947) is considered a classic on the end of the Third Reich. He also wrote *Archbishop Laud* (1940), *The Gentry, 1540–1640* (1953), *The Rise of Christian Europe* (1966), *Religion, The Reformation and Social Change* (1967), *The European Witch-Craze of the 16th and 17th Centuries* (1969).

Triad Society, name given to a number of Chinese antidynastic secret societies by 19th-century Western observers. Most of these groups claimed descent from the Heaven and Earth Society (T'ien-ti hui) or the Triad Society (San-ho hui), two secret societies of the late 17th cent. that had originated in Fukien prov. The avowed purpose of these societies was to overthrow the alien Manchu CH'ING dynasty and to restore the native Chinese MING dynasty. Societies sharing a similar ideology, ritual, and terminology spread all along the SE China coast. In times of peace the secret societies functioned as fraternal organizations, but they often became involved in criminal activities and at times armed conflict with rival groups occurred. Poor peasants, itinerant workers, and others who lacked strong kinship ties found security in the fraternal ties and in the protection offered by the societies. The TAIPING REBELLION (1850–64) brought a revival of secret-society militancy and anti-Manchu sentiment, but local groups continued to function independently and no hierarchic organization was achieved. Branches of the Triads assisted SUN YAT-SEN and other revolutionaries to carry out armed insurrection against the Ch'ing dynasty in the decade before the republican revolution of 1911. The Communist government of China launched (1949–50) a campaign to eliminate secret societies soon after assuming power. For the activities of secret societies in N China during the Ch'ing period, see WHITE LOTUS REBELLION; BOXER UPRISING.

trial: see PROCEDURE.

trial by battle: see ORDEAL.

triangle, in mathematics, plane figure bounded by three straight lines, the sides, which intersect at three points called the vertices. Any one of the sides may be considered the base of the triangle. The perpendicular distance from a base to the opposite vertex is called an altitude. The area of a triangle is equal to one half the product of the base and the corresponding altitude. The line segment joining the midpoint of a side to the opposite vertex is called a median. All three altitudes of a triangle go through a single point, and all three medians go through a single (usually different) point. In Euclidean geometry the sum of the angles of a triangle is equal to two right angles (180°). If all three angles of a triangle are equal, the triangle is called equilateral. An isosceles triangle has two equal angles. A scalene triangle is one in which all three angles are different. A right triangle has one right angle. In geometry it is shown that two triangles are congruent (i.e., are the same shape and size) if, in general, any three independent parts (sides or angles) of one are the same as the corresponding three parts of the other. The rules of congruency make it possible, in trigonometry, to compute the sides and the angles of a triangle when three of these values are known. The triangle is the simplest of the polygons (i.e., it has the least possible number of sides). Since any polygon can be broken up into triangles by drawing various diagonals, a complete theory of the measurement of triangles provides a complete theory of the measurement of all polygons. In non-Euclidean geometries, the angles of a triangle are either less than two right angles (hyperbolic geometry) or more than two right angles (elliptic geometry).

triangle, in music, percussion instrument consisting of a steel rod bent into a triangle, open at one angle, and struck with a steel rod. Only since the end of the 18th cent. has it been an orchestral instrument,

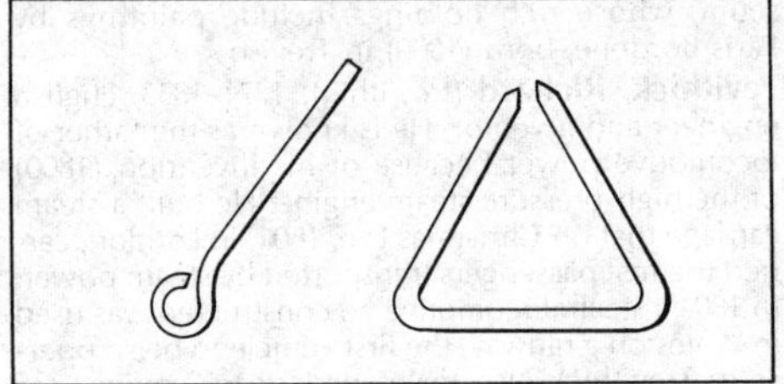

Triangle

although it appeared in Europe much earlier. Its tinkling sound is of indefinite pitch and therefore blends with whatever harmonies the orchestra produces. The triangular SPINET was also termed triangle in the 17th and 18th centuries.

triangulation: see GEODESY.

Trianon (trēänôN'), two small châteaux in the park of VERSAILLES, Seine-et-Oise dept., N France. The Grand Trianon was built by J. H. Mansart in 1687 for Louis XIV; Napoleon I sometimes used it as a retreat. The Petit Trianon was built in 1762 by J. A. Gabriel for Louis XV. It was a favorite residence of Marie Antoinette and of the Empress Eugénie.

Trianon, Treaty of, 1920, agreement following World War I in which the Allies disposed of Hungarian territories. The internal chaos in HUNGARY that followed the dissolution (1918) of the Austro-Hungarian Monarchy delayed the signing of a peace treaty with the Allies of World War I (excluding the United States and Russia) until June 4, 1920. The treaty, signed at the Grand Trianon Palace at Versailles, France, reduced the size and population of Hungary by about one third, divesting it of virtually all areas that were not purely Magyar. Rumania received Transylvania, part of the adjoining plain, and part of the Banat, including Timisoara. Czechoslovakia was confirmed in possession of Slovakia and Ruthenia. Yugoslavia (then the kingdom of the Serbs, Croats, and Slovenes) obtained Croatia, Slavonia, and the western section of the Banat. Austria was awarded the Burgenland, but the city of Sopron and its vicinity were returned to Hungary after a plebiscite (1921). Thus, Hungary was deprived of access to the sea and of some of its most valuable natural resources. The military establishment of the country was reduced to an army of 35,000. The Hungarian delegation signed the treaty under protest. Hungarian agitation for revision began immediately and was supported by the majority of the more than 3 million Magyars transferred to Rumania, Yugoslavia, and Czechoslovakia. Although Hungary recovered part of its lost territories in 1939–40, it was again reduced to its 1920 boundaries by the peace treaty signed in 1947 at Paris.

Triassic period (trīăs'ĭk), first period of the MESOZOIC ERA of geologic time (see GEOLOGIC ERAS, table). Throughout the Triassic, E North America, as a result of the mountain-building episode that formed the Appalachians in the late PALEOZOIC ERA, was elevated above sea level. California and Nevada, however, were submerged. In the Lower Triassic the sea extended E to Idaho, Colorado, and Wyoming; in the Middle Triassic it submerged British Columbia; in the Upper Triassic it extended into Alaska. In Lower and Upper Triassic time the west coast, from Alaska to British Columbia, was disturbed by violent and widespread volcanic activity. The Triassic formations of W North America are chiefly marine shale and limestone, with considerable igneous intrusions. Near the end of the period, the only Triassic formation of E North America was deposited in downfaulted troughs, parallel to the Appalachians, from Nova Scotia to North Carolina. Composed of shale, conglomerate, and sandstone, this Newark series is comprised of sediments from the Appalachians. It is widely interrupted by so-called traprock—diabase dikes and sills—which forms ridges and cliffs, such as the Palisades of the Hudson near New York City. The end of the Triassic in North America was marked by extensive faulting and tilting of the Newark series, called the Palisade disturbance, and by the emergence of W North America. The Triassic deposits of Germany form three series. In the Bunter series, the land was emergent, and red sandstone and sandy shale, with some salt and gypsum, were deposited. The Muschelkalk series saw the transgression of the land by the sea and the deposition of marine shale and limestone; the Keuper series saw the land again emergent and shale, sandstone, and gypsum being formed. In England there was no marine phase corresponding to the Muschelkalk; the Triassic of England is commonly called the New Red Sandstone. The Tethys, a great seaway, extended through the Mediterranean region E through the Middle East to the Himalayas and to E India. Its northern shore lay just N of the Black Sea, extending E across S Russia. Its southern boundary reached the Sinai peninsula as far as the shore of the Dead Sea. The climate of the Triassic was semiarid to arid. In the plant life, marine algae were abundant, ferns and tree ferns less important than in the Paleozoic, conifers dominant among the trees, and a new group, the cycads, just appearing. Many Paleozoic invertebrates appeared for the last time in the Triassic. The ammonites became very important, then were reduced at the end of the Triassic to one species, but were destined to be numerous again in the succeeding Jurassic period. Amphibians were apparently not as numerous as in the Paleozoic, but some types were more highly developed. The dominant animals of the Triassic were the reptiles; although the Triassic reptiles were less specialized than those of the Jurassic, there were already a number of types of dinosaurs, pterosaurs, and marine reptiles. The Triassic rocks contain the fossils of the earliest known mammals.

tribe, social group, usually with a distinguishing area, dialect, cultural homogeneity, and unifying social organization. It may include several subgroups, such as sibs or VILLAGES. A tribe ordinarily has a leader and may have a common ancestor, as well as a patron deity. The families or small communities making up the tribe are linked through economic, social, religious, family, or blood ties. For many anthropologists, however, the term has acquired a far more restricted technical meaning: for them it usually refers to the widest territorially defined, politically independent unit in a tribal society. It no longer refers to the culturally and ethnically distinct tribal society as a whole except where, as in such tribal states as Baganda or Ruanda, tribe and society coincide. While it is always easy to describe the tribe in terms of territoriality, its political aspects are not always easily defined, especially in tribes without chiefs or other formally installed rulers.

Tribonian (Tribonianus) (trĭbō'nēən), d. 545?, Roman jurist. Under the command of JUSTINIAN I, he directed the compilation of the CORPUS JURIS CIVILIS. It is not possible to determine exactly what Tribonian himself contributed; in all likelihood he wrote largely from his encyclopedic knowledge of Roman law.

Triborough Bridge, New York City, connecting the boroughs of Manhattan, the Bronx, and Queens. Completed in 1936, it comprises three separate sections—a suspension bridge crossing the East River, a vertical-lift bridge spanning the Harlem River, and a fixed bridge across the Bronx Hills. Including the viaducts that connect the sections, the bridge's total length is c.3 mi (4.8 km).

tribune, in ancient Rome, one of various officers. The history of the office of tribune is closely associated with the struggle of the PLEBS against the PATRICIAN class to achieve a more equitable position in the state. From c.508 B.C. the military tribunes (*tribuni militum*) were the senior officers of the legions, elected by the people and with the rank of magistrate; a plebeian could hold the position. The office of military tribune with the power of consul (*tribuni militum consulari potestate*) was established in 444 B.C. The office meant that certain of the military tribunes were invested with the political power of the consul. Although military tribunes were abolished (367 B.C.), the office of tribune of the plebs (*tribuni plebis*) designed to protect plebeian rights, especially against abuse by magistrates, had been formed (493 B.C.). The original number of such tribunes is uncertain, but by 449 B.C. there were 10. These tribunes were plebeians elected by an assembly of plebs. The power of the tribune derived from two basic prerogatives, the right of the tribune to inflict punishment upon a magistrate who disregarded either his injunction or the inviolability (*sacrosanctitas*) of the tribune's person. Gradually the tribune gained the *intercessio* or the right to veto a decision of a magistrate—which in effect was a veto over any official act of administration—and the right to prosecute corrupt magistrates before a public body. He further acquired (3d cent. B.C.) the power to attend and convene the senate and to lay before it matters for consideration. As the plebeians came to occupy more and more public offices, the tribune became less the champion of a class and more the representative of the individual over the state. With the reforms of the GRACCHI in the late 2d cent. B.C., the office of tribune acquired wider significance, but later SULLA, combating these reforms, tried to remove the tribuneship as a factor in Roman government. Pompey restored the tribunes to their old power. Under the empire the tribuneship was held by the emperors. This gave to the emperors few powers that they did not otherwise possess, but the tradition of the office as a defender of popular rights and its inviolability was useful to them.

tricarboxylic acid cycle: see CITRIC ACID CYCLE.

Tricca, ancient Greece: see TRÍKKALA.

triceps, any muscle having three heads, or points of attachment, but especially the triceps brachii at the back of the upper arm. One head originates on the shoulder blade and two on the upper-arm bone, or humerus. Uniting part of the way down the arm, the heads swell into the belly, or muscle proper. This tapers to a tendon that rounds the elbow and attaches to the ulna, the larger of the two forearm bones. Since contraction of the triceps straightens the arm, the muscle is called an extensor. It also helps lock the elbow when the forearm pushes forward against resistance. The triceps works in coordination with a flexor muscle, the BICEPS of the upper arm.

Triceratops (trīsĕr'ətŏps), a fossil herbivorous quadruped DINOSAUR of the Cretaceous period of geologic time. Characteristically it had three horns, one on the nose and one over each eye, and a bony shield projecting backward from the skull to serve as a protection to the neck and fore part of the body. The head was large (about 8 ft/2.4 m long), the body (about 20 ft/6 m long) was bulky and barrel shaped, and the limbs were massive and of equal length. Bones of *Protoceratops*, a related hornless form, and eggs probably belonging to it were found in Mongolia. The *Triceratops* is classified in the phylum CHORDATA, subphylum Vertebrata, class Reptilia, order Ornithischia.

trichina (trĭkī'nə), common name for species of roundworm of the class Nematoda. The species *Trichinella spiralis* is an important parasite, occurring in rats, pigs, and man, and is responsible for the disease TRICHINOSIS. The small adult worms mature in the intestine of an intermediate host such as a pig. Each adult female produces batches of up to 1,500 live larvae, which bore through the intestinal wall, enter the blood and lymphatic system, and are carried to striated muscle tissue. Once in the muscle, they encyst, or become enclosed in a capsule. Larvae encysted in the muscles remain viable for some time. When the muscle tissue is eaten by a human, the cysts are digested in the stomach; the released larvae migrate to the intestine to begin a new life cycle. Female trichina worms live about six weeks and in that time may release 15,000 larvae. The migration and encystment of larvae can cause fever, pain, and even death. Encysted larvae in pork are destroyed by thorough cooking or long periods of low-temperature storage. Trichina are classified in the phylum ASCHELMINTHES, class Nematoda.

Trichinopoly, India: see TRICHURAPALLI.

trichinosis (trĭk"ĭnō'sĭs) or **trichiniasis** (trĭk"ĭnī'əsĭs), parasitic disease caused by the roundworm *Trichinella spiralis*. It follows the eating of raw or inadequately cooked meat, especially pork. The larvae are released, reach maturity, and mate in the intestines, the females producing live larvae. The parasites are then carried from the gastrointestinal tract by the bloodstream to various muscles, where they become encysted. It is estimated that 10% to 20% of the adult population of the United States suffers from trichinosis at some time. In many people the disease exhibits no symptoms and is discovered only at autopsy. In others it causes diarrhea and other gastrointestinal symptoms as the worms multiply in the digestive tract. When the larvae circulate through the bloodstream, the patient experiences edema, irregular fever, profuse sweating, muscle soreness and pain, and prostration. There may be involvement of the central nervous system, heart, and lungs; death occurs in about 5% of clinical cases. Once the larvae have imbedded themselves in the muscle tissue, the cysts usually become calcified; however, the infestation usually causes no further symptoms except fatigue and vague muscular pains. There is no specific treatment for trichinosis.

trichloromethane: see CHLOROFORM.

Trichur (trĭchōōr'), city (1971 pop. 76,248), Kerala state, SE India. It is a market for betel and cashew nuts and has a wood-carving industry. Trichur, a district administrative center, is thought to be one of the oldest communities on the Malabar Coast. The city is known for its ancient temples and churches.

trident (trī'dənt), in Greek mythology, three-pronged fork borne by Poseidon. It was variously represented as a fishing spear, a goad, or forked lightning.

Tridentum: see TRENT, Italy.

Trier (trēr), Latin *Augusta Treverorum,* city (1970 pop. 103,724), Rhineland-Palatinate, W West Germany, a port on the Moselle (Ger. *Mosel*) River, near the Luxembourg border. It is also known, in English, as Treves (trēvz) and, in French, as Trèves (trĕv). Trier is an industrial city and the main center of the Moselle wine region. Manufactures include textiles, rolled steel, metal products, and precision instruments. One of the oldest cities in Germany, Trier has played an important role in its history since Roman times and retains many Roman monuments. Founded by Augustus c.15 B.C., the city was made (1st cent.) the capital of the Roman province of Belgica and later became (3d cent.) the capital of the prefecture of Gaul; it was named after the Treveri, a people of E Gaul. Under the Roman Empire Trier attained a population of c.50,000 and became a major commercial center, with a large wine trade. It was a frequent residence of the Western emperors from c.295 until its capture (early 5th cent.) by the Franks. The city was made an episcopal see in the 4th cent. and an archiepiscopal see c.815. Its archbishops became powerful temporal princes, whose territories extended along both sides of the Saar and Moselle rivers and across the Rhine; they ranked second among the spiritual ELECTORS of the Holy Roman Empire and were, ex officio, archchancellors for Gaul and Burgundy (with little real authority). Under the rule of the archbishops, Trier flourished as a commercial and cultural center. It was the seat of a university from 1473 until it was occupied by the French in 1797. The archbishopric of Trier was secularized and was formally ceded to France in 1801 by the Treaty of Lunéville. At the Congress of Vienna the city and most of the archbishopric were awarded (1815) to Prussia; territory E of the Rhine was given to Nassau and, with Nassau, passed to Prussia in 1866. Trier again became an episcopal see in 1821. It was occupied by France after World War I and suffered considerable damage in World War II. Among the city's Roman monuments are the Porta Nigra (early 4th cent.), an imposing and well-preserved fortified gate; an amphitheater (c.100), which can seat about 25,000 persons; ruins of the imperial baths (4th cent.); and the basilica (probably built in the early 4th cent.; now a church). Trier also has a Romanesque cathedral, built (11th–12th cent.) around a 4th-century nucleus and containing the Holy Coat of Treves (supposed to be the seamless coat of Jesus). Other noteworthy buildings include the Gothic Church of Our Lady (13th cent.; Ger. *Liebfrauenkirche*); the baroque electoral palace (17th–18th cent.); and the baroque Church of St. Paulinus (1732–54; designed by B. Neumann). The rare exhibitions (e.g., in 1844, 1891, 1933, and 1959) of the Holy Coat of Treves have been the occasions of large pilgrimages. The remains of St. Matthew are preserved in a shrine in the pilgrimage church of St. Matthew (built in the 12th cent. around an earlier Benedictine monastery). Trier also has a theological seminary, a school of viticulture, and several museums, including one in the house where Karl Marx was born (1818).

Trieste (trēĕ'stā), Serbo-Croatian *Trst,* city (1971 pop. 269,819), capital of Friuli-Venezia Giulia and of Trieste prov., extreme NE Italy, on the Gulf of Trieste (at the head of the Adriatic Sea). A major seaport with large shipyards, it is also a commercial and industrial center. Manufactures include steel, petroleum, and textiles. An ancient settlement, it was made a Roman colony (2d cent. B.C.), called Tergeste. It prospered under the Romans, was later held by the Lombards, and was taken by Charlemagne in the late 8th cent. In the 12th cent. it became a free commune. After two centuries of struggle with its rival Venice, Trieste placed itself (1382) under the control of the duke of Austria, although it retained administrative autonomy until the 18th cent. In 1719 it was made a free port. As the sole Austrian port and as a natural outlet for central Europe, Trieste flourished, and in 1867 the crownland of Trieste was made the capital of Küstenland prov. Despite its Austrian status, Trieste preserved linguistic and cultural ties with Italy. It was a center of IRREDENTISM, and after World War I Trieste and its province were annexed (1919) by Italy. However, its prosperity declined under Italian rule. After World War II the area was claimed by Yugoslavia, mainly because the population outside the city of Trieste is predominantly Slovenian. The Western powers opposed Yugoslavia's claim. As a compromise, a new state, the Free Territory of Trieste, was created (1947) under the protection of the UN Security Council. The Free Territory included the city of Trieste and a coastal zone of Istria, running from Duino along the Gulf of Trieste to Cittanova. When the Security Council was unable to agree on a governor for the territory, Anglo-American forces occupied Zone A, consisting of Italian-speaking Trieste and its environs, while the Yugoslavs occupied Zone B, the remainder of the Free Territory. Tension between Italy and Yugoslavia continued until 1954, when, in a compromise agreement reached under Western auspices, Zone A was placed under Italian administration and Zone B under Yugoslav civil administration. The solution amounted to a partition of the Free Territory, which then ceased to exist. Trieste has some Roman ruins, including those of an amphitheater. On a hill commanding a fine view are the Romanesque Cathedral of San Giusto (part of which dates from the 5th cent.) and an imposing castle (14th–17th cent.). On a small promontory northwest of the city is Miramar castle (1854–56), built for Archduke Maximilian of Austria, who sailed from there on his ill-fated Mexican adventure. Trieste has a university, founded in 1924.

triforium (trīfôr'ēəm), in church architecture, an arcaded gallery above the arches of the nave. In the interiors of medieval churches each bay of the nave wall customarily had three divisions in its height—arcade, triforium, and clerestory. The triforium was thus located beneath the clerestory windows and above the side-aisle vaults and corresponded on the exterior to the lean-to roof over the aisle. In Italian basilical churches this interior surface was generally decorated with paintings or mosaics. In the north the triforium had arched openings with apertures in the wall behind it to ventilate the roof space over the aisle. In most Romanesque churches it appeared as a second-story vaulted gallery over the aisle and was equal to it in depth and sometimes also in height. In Gothic churches, the depth behind the triforium arcades was generally limited to the thickness of the nave wall, into which a narrow passageway was built to furnish a second-story circulation around the church. Developed French Gothic flattened the pitch of the aisle roofs, thus leaving the outside wall of the triforia exposed and free for glazing. The inside face retained its rich open tracery arcades. Late Gothic subordinated the triforium between the higher main arcades and clerestory and sometimes omitted it entirely.

triggerfish, any of several species of tropical reef fishes with laterally compressed bodies, heavy scales, and tough skins. They are named for the mechanism of the three spines of the dorsal fin: when the fish is alarmed the first of these spines is locked upright by the second and drops only when the latter is pressed like a trigger. The function of this reaction is to lock the fish firmly in a mass of coral; when attacked, the fish dives into the coral and erects the spine, releasing it only when the danger has passed. Triggerfishes have powerful, chisel-like teeth adapted for cracking the coral and mollusks on which they feed. They average 1 lb (0.45 kg) in weight and 1 ft (30 cm) in length and are common around the West Indies and Florida. The common triggerfish is variably colored in mottled browns, yellows, or grays, and the queen triggerfish is strikingly colored in blue, green, and yellow. The ocean triggerfish is up to 2 ft (60 cm) long and weighs 3 to 5 lb (1.4–2.3 kg). Triggerfish are classified in the phylum CHORDATA, subphylum Vertebrata, class Osteichthyes, order Tetraodontiformes, family Balistidae.

Triglav (trē'gläv), peak, 9,392 ft (2,863 m) high, NW Yugoslavia, in the Julian Alps, near the Italian and Austrian borders. It is the highest peak in the Julian Alps and in Yugoslavia.

triglyceride, ESTER formed from GLYCEROL and one to three FATTY ACIDS. FATS AND OILS are triglycerides. In a simple triglyceride such as PALMITIN or STEARIN, all three fatty-acid groups are identical. In a mixed triglyceride, two or even three different fatty-acid groups are present; most fats and oils contain mixed triglycerides.

trigonometry [Gr.,=measurement of triangles], study of certain mathematical relations originally defined in terms of the angles and sides of a right triangle, i.e., one containing a right angle (90°). Six basic relations, or trigonometric functions, are defined. If *A, B,* and *C* are the measures of the angles of a right triangle (C=90°) and *a, b,* and *c* are the lengths of the respective sides opposite these angles, then the six functions are expressed for one of the acute angles, say *A*, as various ratios of the opposite side (*a*), the adjacent side (*b*), and the hypotenuse (*c*), as set out in the table. Although the actual lengths of the sides of a right triangle may have any values, the ratios of the lengths will be the same for all similar right triangles, large or small; these ratios depend only on the angles and not on the actual lengths. The functions occur in pairs, e.g., sine and cosine, called cofunctions. Since in ordinary (Euclidean) plane geometry the sum of the angles of a triangle is 180°, angles *A* and *B* must add up to 90° and therefore are complementary angles. From the definitions of the functions, it may be seen that $\sin B = \cos A$, $\cos B = \sin A$, $\tan B = \cot A$, and so forth; in general, the function of an angle is equal to the cofunction of its complement. Since the hypotenuse (*c*), is always the longest side of a right triangle, the values of the sine and cosine are always between zero and one, the values of the secant and cosecant are always equal to or greater than one, and the values of the tangent and cotangent are unbounded, increasing from zero without limit. For certain special right triangles the values of the functions may be calculated easily; e.g., in a right triangle whose acute angles are 30° and 60° the sides are in the ratio $1 : \sqrt{3} : 2$, so that $\sin 30° = \cos 60° = 1/2$, $\cos 30° = \sin 60° = \sqrt{3}/2$, $\tan 30° = \cot 60° = 1/\sqrt{3}$, $\cot 30° = \tan 60° = \sqrt{3}$, $\sec 30° = \csc 60° = 2/\sqrt{3}$, and $\csc 30° = \sec 60° = 2$. For other angles, the values of the trigonometric functions are usually found from a set of tables or a slide rule. For the limiting values of 0° and 90°, the length of one side of the triangle approaches zero while the other approaches that of the hypotenuse, resulting in the values $\sin 0° = \cos 90° = 0$, $\cos 0° = \sin 90° = 1$, $\tan 0° = \cot 90° = 0$, and $\sec 0° = \csc 90° = 1$; since division by zero is undefined, cot 0°, tan 90°, csc 0°, and sec 90° are all

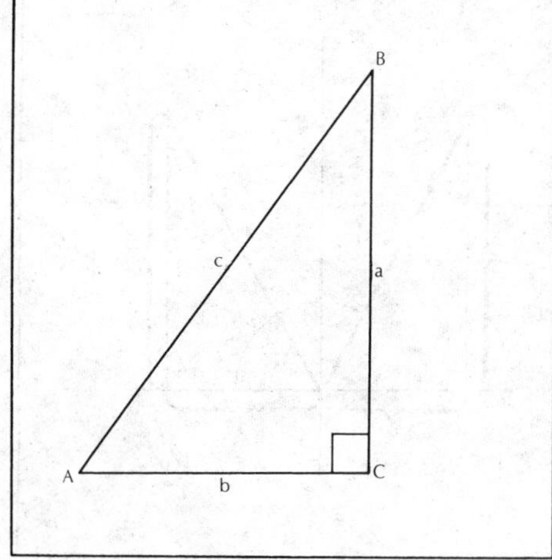

The trigonometric functions are defined in terms of the angles and sides of a right triangle.

TRIGONOMETRIC FUNCTIONS

Function (abbreviation)	Definition
sine (sin)	$\frac{\text{opposite}}{\text{hypotenuse}}$ $\sin A = \frac{a}{c}$
cosine (cos)	$\frac{\text{adjacent}}{\text{hypotenuse}}$ $\cos A = \frac{b}{c}$
tangent (tan)	$\frac{\text{opposite}}{\text{adjacent}}$ $\tan A = \frac{a}{b}$
cotangent (cot or ctn)	$\frac{\text{adjacent}}{\text{opposite}}$ $\cot A = \frac{b}{a}$
secant (sec)	$\frac{\text{hypotenuse}}{\text{adjacent}}$ $\sec A = \frac{c}{b}$
cosecant (csc)	$\frac{\text{hypotenuse}}{\text{opposite}}$ $\csc A = \frac{c}{a}$

undefined, having infinitely large values. The notion of the trigonometric functions can be extended beyond 90° by defining the functions with respect to CARTESIAN COORDINATES. Let *r* be a line of unit length from the origin to the point *P* (x,y), and let θ be the angle *r* makes with the positive *x*-axis. The six functions become $\sin\theta = y/r = y$, $\cos\theta = x/r = x$, $\tan\theta = y/x$, $\cot\theta = x/y$, $\sec\theta = r/x = 1/x$, and $\csc\theta = r/y = 1/y$. As θ increases beyond 90°, the point *P* crosses the *y*-axis and *x* becomes negative; in quadrant II the functions are negative except for $\sin\theta$ and $\csc\theta$. Beyond $\theta = 180°$, *P* is in quadrant III, *y* is also nega-

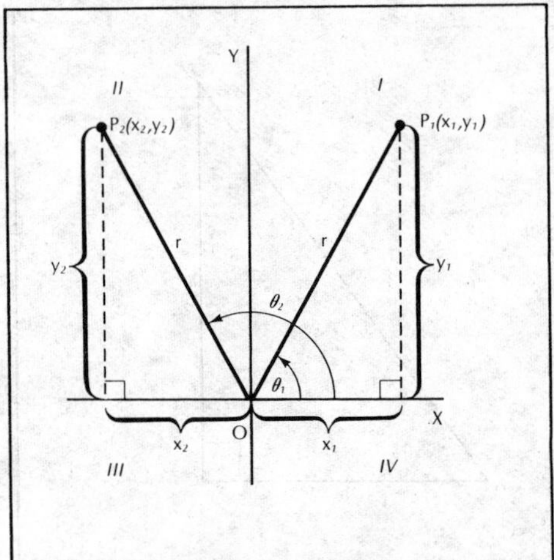

The trigonometric functions of the angle formed by the x*-axis and the line* r *terminating at point* P *may be expressed in terms of* r *and the* x*- and* y*-coordinates of* P. *For* θ_1 *both* x *and* y *are positive; for* θ_2 x *is negative.*

tive, and only $\tan\theta$ and $\cot\theta$ are positive, while beyond $\theta = 270°$ *P* moves into quadrant IV, *x* becomes positive again, and $\cos\theta$ and $\sec\theta$ are positive. Since the positions of *r* for angles of 360° or more coincide with those already taken by *r* as θ increased from 0°, the values of the functions repeat those taken between 0° and 360° for angles greater than 360°, repeating again after 720°, and so on. This

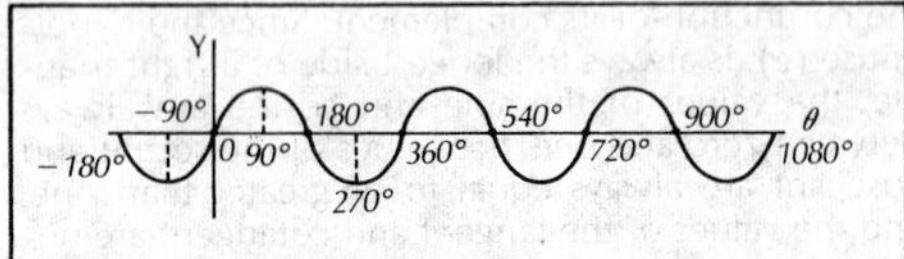

Graph of y = *sin* θ *as a function of the angle* θ. *The values of sin* θ *repeat every 360°.*

repeating, or periodic, nature of the trigonometric functions leads to important applications in the study of such periodic phenomena as light and electricity. A general triangle, not necessarily containing a right angle, can also be analyzed by means of trigonometry, and various relationships are found to exist between the sides and angles of the general triangle (see SINE; COSINE; TANGENT). Spherical trigonometry is concerned with the study of triangles on the surface of a sphere rather than in the plane; it is of considerable importance in surveying, navigation, and astronomy.

Tríkkala (trē'kälä), ancient. *Tricca,* town (1971 pop. 34,794), capital of Tríkkala prefecture, N central Greece, in Thessaly. It is the commercial center of an agricultural and pastoral region. Tricca claimed to be the birthplace of Asclepius, the legendary physician, and was a center of the Asclepian cult. Much of Tríkkala was destroyed by earthquakes in 1954.

Trikora Peak, 15,518 ft (4,730 m) high, in the Djajawidjaja Mts., Irian Barat, the second highest peak in Indonesia. The snow-covered peak was formerly called Mt. Wilhelmina.

trill, in music, ORNAMENT consisting of the more or less rapid alternation of two adjacent notes. Indicated by any of several conventional symbols, it varies in speed and duration and in the manner of its beginning and ending according to context. Originating in the Renaissance, the trill became the most important of ornaments during the baroque period. In British usage the term *shake* is more common.

Trilling, Lionel, 1905–, American critic and author, b. New York City, grad. Columbia (B.A., 1925; M.A., 1926; Ph.D., 1938). He began teaching literature at Columbia in 1932 and became a full professor in 1948. His essays—collected as *The Liberal Imagination* (1950), *The Opposing Self* (1955), and *A Gathering of Fugitives* (1956)—combine social, psychological, and political insights with literary criticism and scholarship. Among his other works are a novel entitled *Middle of the Journey* (1947), *Matthew Arnold* (1939), *E. M. Forster* (1943), and *The Life and Work of Sigmund Freud* (1962). In *Sincerity and Authenticity* (1972), Trilling studies American life in the 1970s.

trillium or **wake-robin** (trĭl'ēəm), any plant of the large genus *Trillium,* attractive spring wild flowers of the family Liliaceae (LILY family), native to North America and E Asia. The leaves, petals, and sepals are characteristically in threes, and the single flower may be white, pink, dark red, yellow, or green. The plants have a perennial rootstock that in *T. erectum* (also called birthroot) was used medicinally by both the Indian and white man. Trillium is classified in the division MAGNOLIOPHYTA, class Liliatae, order Liliales, family Liliaceae.

trilobite (trī'ləbīt″), any of a large group of extinct marine animals that were abundant in the Paleozoic era. The trilobite body was generally oval and flat and was divided into three roughly equal sections: the head, thorax, and tail. The name *trilobite* refers to a pair of furrows along the length of the animal that divided the body into three longitudinal regions. The body was covered by a shell made of

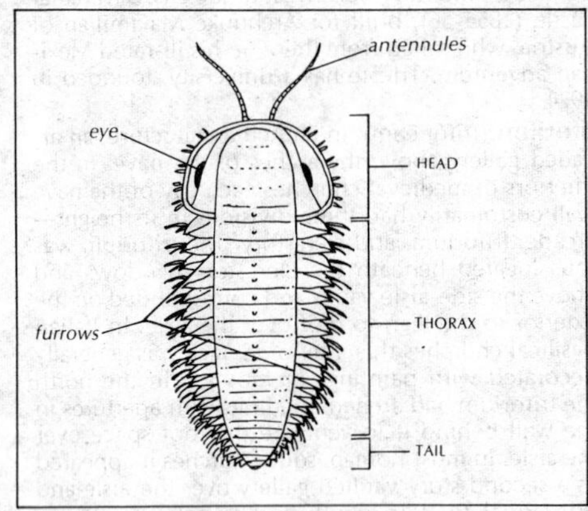

Dorsal view of a trilobite

chitinous plates. Because the dorsal, or upper, shell was thicker than the under shell, it has been the part best preserved in fossil form. Trilobites were the most abundant inhabitants of the Cambrian and Ordovician geological periods. They declined thereafter and became extinct in the Permian period. The relationship of the trilobites to other members of the phylum Arthropoda is still unclear. Some zoologists regard them as ancestral to both the chelicerates, which include the horseshoe crabs and spiders, and the mandibulates, which include insects and crustaceans. Trilobites are classified in the phylum ARTHROPODA, subphylum Trilobitomorpha.

Trincomalee (trĭng″kəməlē'), town (1968 est. pop. 39,000), capital of Eastern prov., NE Sri Lanka (Ceylon), on the Bay of Bengal. Trincomalee has one of the world's finest natural harbors and can accommodate the largest vessels. Since the 1960s congestion and labor problems at the port of Colombo have forced the use of Trincomalee's port, little used commercially in previous years, for modest export trade. Tea is the chief export; hides and dried fish are also shipped. Trincomalee is a railroad terminus and an important road junction and is noted for its rice and coconut plantations. There is some pearl fishing. The Hindu Temple of a Thousand Columns, built by early Tamil settlers from S India, was destroyed (1622) by the Portuguese; on its site is Fort Frederick, built (1676) by the Dutch. Because control of Trincomalee was a key to domination over the Coromandel Coast of India, Britain and France sought (18th cent.) to wrest the city from the Dutch; it was captured (1795) by the British. During World War II, Trincomalee was the British naval headquarters in the Pacific theater and had an airfield from which U.S. planes operated against the Japanese in Burma and Malaya. A British naval base remained at Trincomalee until 1957, when Ceylon abrogated its defense agreement with Britain and took over the base.

Trinidad (trēnēthäth'), town (1970 pop. 31,474), Las Villas prov., central Cuba. Tobacco processing is the chief industry. During the colonial period, Trinidad flourished as a port and was attacked several times by the British. The town is a living relic of the colonial period and has been declared a national monument. Nearby is a large sanatorium.

Trinidad and Tobago (trĭn'ĭdăd, təbā'gō), country (1970 pop. 945,200), 1,980 sq mi (5,129 sq km), West Indies, a member of the Commonwealth of Nations. The capital is PORT OF SPAIN. The country consists of two islands: Trinidad (1,864 sq mi/4,828 sq km) and Tobago (116 sq mi/300 sq km). Lying just north of the Orinoco River delta in Venezuela, Trinidad is largely flat or undulating except for a range of low mountains (the highest point is Mt. Aripo, 3,085 ft/940 m) in the north. Pitch Lake, in the southwest, is the world's largest (114 acres/46 hectares) basin of natural asphalt. Tobago, just NE of Trinidad, is the exposed top of a mountain ridge (maximum height 2,000 ft/610 m) that is densely forested with large reserves of hardwoods. The climate of both islands is warm and humid, and rainfall (from June to Dec.)

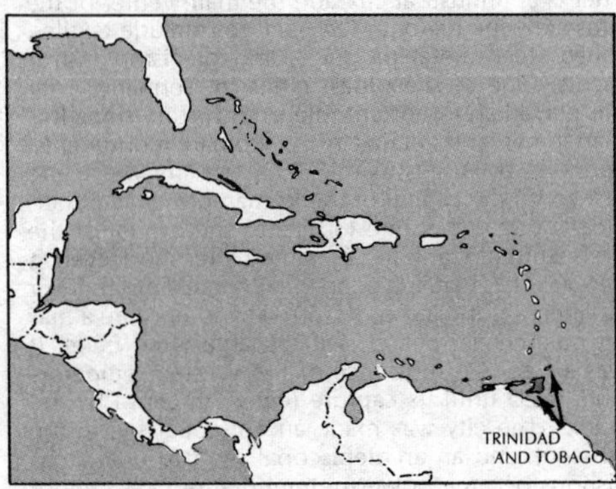

is abundant, particularly where the trade winds sweep in over the eastern coasts. The population of the islands is predominantly of black African descent; about one third of the people are East Indian, and the remainder are of European, Middle Eastern, or Chinese origin. English is the official language, but a French patois is widely spoken. The main exports are sugar, cocoa, petroleum products, asphalt, and chemicals. Crude petroleum must be imported, since domestic supplies have been exhausted. Copra, coffee, bananas, citrus fruits, and angostura bitters are also exported. The islands have a large tourist industry. Trinidad was discovered by Christopher Columbus in 1498 but was not colonized because of the lack of precious metals. It was raided by the Dutch (1640) and the French (1677, 1690) and by British sailors. Britain captured it in 1797 and received formal title in 1802. Tobago had been settled by the English in 1616, but the settlers were driven out by the indigenous Carib Indians. The island was held by the Dutch and the French before being acquired by the British in 1803. The islands were joined politically in 1888. Before becoming an independent nation in 1962, the islands were part of the short-lived West Indies Federation (see WEST INDIES) from 1958 to 1962. The country has a parliamentary form of government. See Gertrude Carmichael, *The History of the West Indian Islands of Trinidad and Tobago, 1498–1900* (1961); J. A. De Suze, *The New Trinidad and Tobago* (14th ed. 1965); F. C. Evans, *A First Geography of Trinidad and Tobago* (1968).

trinitrotoluene or **TNT** (trī″nī″trōtŏl'yo͞oēn), $CH_3C_6H_2(NO_2)_3$, crystalline, aromatic compound that melts at 81°C. It is prepared by the nitration of toluene. Trinitrotoluene is a high EXPLOSIVE, but, unlike nitroglycerin, it is unaffected by ordinary shocks and jarring, and must be set off by a DETONATOR. Because it does not react with metals, it can be used in filling metal shells. It is often mixed with other explosives, e.g., with ammonium nitrate to form amatol.

Trinity [Lat.,=three-foldness], fundamental doctrine in Christianity, by which GOD is considered as existing in three persons. The doctrine was defined very early, but received much amplification at the first ecumenical councils. For systems denying the Trinity, see UNITARIANISM. The usual statement of the doctrine is that God exists in three persons, all coequal, coeternal, and indivisible, of the same substance—God the Father, God the Son (who became incarnate as JESUS), begotten of the Father, and God the HOLY GHOST, proceeding from the Father and the Son (see CREED **1**). The Trinity is considered by most Christian teachers to be a mystery, i.e., its nature cannot be fully understood or known by human intelligence. It is therefore called a truth of revelation.

This mystery is commemorated liturgically in the Western Church on TRINITY SUNDAY.

Trinity, river rising in N Texas in three forks; the Clear Fork runs into the West Fork at Fort Worth, and the Elm Fork joins the West Fork at Dallas. The Trinity then flows c.510 mi (820 km) SE to Trinity Bay, an arm of Galveston Bay. The waters of upper tributaries and the main stream are impounded in numerous reservoirs that provide water for the Dallas-Fort Worth metropolitan area; flood control; and water for irrigation. The largest reservoir, Garza-Little Elm, is impounded by Lewisville Dam (completed 1955) on the Elm Fork. The Trinity valley has a greater population and more industrial development than any other river basin in Texas. On the lower coastal plain, much use is made of the Trinity's waters for irrigating rice fields.

Trinity Bay, inlet of the Atlantic Ocean, 80 mi (129 km) long, SE N.F., Canada, between the Avalon Peninsula and the mainland. There are small fishing settlements and canneries on its shores. Trinity, a small port on the west shore, was the western terminal of the first permanent transatlantic cable laid (1866) by Cyrus West Field.

Trinity College, Ireland: see DUBLIN, UNIV. OF.

Trinity College, at Hartford, Conn.; mainly for men; chartered 1823, opened 1824 as Washington College. Its present name was adopted in 1845.

Trinity Sunday, first Sunday after PENTECOST, observed as a feast of the Trinity. It was an innovation in medieval England and spread through the Western Church in the 14th cent. The Sundays until Advent are counted either from Pentecost or Trinity.

triode (trī'ōd), electronic device having three terminals, or electrodes; the term is reserved for a device receiving power from a source other than its input and is usually used in reference to an ELECTRON TUBE containing a cathode, single grid, and anode.

Triolet, Elsa (Elsa Blick) (ĕlsä' trĕôlĕ'), c.1896–1970, Russian-French author, b. Moscow. In 1928 she married the French writer Louis ARAGON. Her novels often combine a sweeping Russian grandeur with acute observations of French life. They include *Le cheval blanc* (1943; tr. *The White Charger,* 1946), *Personne ne m'aime* [nobody loves me] (1946), *Les Fantômes armées* [the phantom armies] (1946), and *L'Inspecteur des ruines* (1948; tr. *The Inspector of Ruins,* 1953). Among her collections of stories is *Le Premier Accroc du coûte deux cents francs* (1945; tr. *A Fine of 200 Francs,* 1947).

Triple Alliance, in European history, any of several coalitions. The Triple Alliance of **1668** was formed by the Netherlands, England, and Sweden against France after Louis XIV had invaded the Spanish Netherlands in the War of DEVOLUTION. Largely because of the initiative of the Dutch statesman Jan de Witt, the alliance represented a sufficient threat to Louis XIV to induce him to negotiate the Treaty of AIX-LA-CHAPELLE. The Triple Alliance of **1717** was a treaty signed by Great Britain, France, and the Netherlands. Designed to strengthen the terms of the Peace of Utrecht, it was joined in 1718 by the Holy Roman emperor and became the QUADRUPLE ALLIANCE. For the Triple Alliance of **1872,** see THREE EMPERORS' LEAGUE. For that of **1882,** see TRIPLE ALLIANCE AND TRIPLE ENTENTE.

Triple Alliance, War of the, 1865–70, fought between Paraguay on one side and an alliance of Argentina, Brazil, and Uruguay on the other. Brazil's military reprisals for injuries to Brazilian subjects in Uruguay's civil war brought a declaration of war against Brazil from Francisco Solano LÓPEZ, Paraguayan dictator, who favored the Blanco regime in Uruguay. Imprudently, he also declared war on Argentina after Bartolomé Mitre refused to allow Paraguayan troops to cross Argentine territory. A secret alliance, made by Brazil and Argentina with Gen. Venancio Flores of the Colorado faction (traditional enemies of the Blancos), brought Uruguay into the war. The heroic defense of Paraguay against powerful invaders lasted five years until the final stand at Cerro Corá, where even women and children rallied around López. By the end of the war Paraguay was devastated and a considerable part of its male population killed. The war was the brutal consequence of López's provocations as well as of the abusive aggressiveness of the larger powers. It nevertheless opened the way for a development of constitutional government in Paraguay.

Triple Alliance and Triple Entente (äntänt'), two international combinations of states that dominated the diplomatic history of Western Europe from 1882 until they came into armed conflict in World War I. *Formation of the Triple Alliance.* In 1871 two new major states of Europe had been formed—the German Empire and the kingdom of Italy. The new German Empire, under the hand of Otto von BISMARCK, was steered carefully, always with an eye upon France, for the Franco-Prussian War (1870–71) had left France thirsting for revenge and for recovery of the lost provinces of Alsace and Lorraine. Germany had allied itself with Russia and Austria-Hungary in the THREE EMPERORS' LEAGUE, but Austria-Hungary and Russia were not the best of friends, partly because they were at odds over the Balkans and partly because Russia represented the Pan-Slavic movement, whose program threatened the very existence of Austria-Hungary. The Treaty of SAN STEFANO (1878), following the Russo-Turkish War, furthered the cause of Pan-Slavism through the creation of a large Bulgarian state and offended Austria-Hungary as well as Great Britain. A European conference (1878; see BERLIN, CONGRESS OF), called to revise the treaty, caused a sharp decline in the friendship between Russia on the one hand and Austria-Hungary and Germany on the other; Bismarck formed (1879) a secret defensive alliance—the Dual Alliance—with Austria-Hungary. In 1882, Italy, angry at France chiefly because France had forestalled an Italian advance by occupying Tunis, signed another secret treaty, which bound it with Germany and Austria-Hungary. Thus was the Triple Alliance formed. It was periodically renewed until 1913. In 1882, Serbia joined the alliance, in effect, through a treaty with Austria-Hungary. Rumania joined the group in 1883, and a powerful Central European bloc was created. Italy was from the first not so solidly bound to either of its allies as Germany and Austria-Hungary were to each other. Italy was in fact a rival of Austria-Hungary in the Balkans and particularly for control of the Adriatic; moreover, there remained unsettled territorial problems (see IRREDENTISM). The Triple Alliance, however, turned diplomatic history into new channels.
Formation of the Triple Entente. The Three Emperors' League died a slow death, but in 1890 its day was over: Germany refused to renew its reinsurance treaty with Russia, and Russia in consequence sought a rapprochement with France. At the same time France, face to face with an increasingly powerful Germany and a hostile Central European combination, felt great need of an ally, and French diplomats began to make overtures to Russia for an agreement to counterbalance the Triple Alliance. French capital aided Russian projects, especially the Trans-Siberian RR, and friendly diplomatic visits were exchanged. In 1891 there was a definite understanding between the powers; this was strengthened by a military convention in 1893, and by 1894 the Dual Alliance between Russia and France was in existence. It was publicly acknowledged in 1895. Meanwhile, the fall of Bismarck, after the accession of WILLIAM II to the throne of the German Empire, was followed by the appearance of more adventurous foreign policies. Germany committed itself to colonial and commercial expansion. The German plan for a BAGHDAD RAILWAY was viewed with alarm by the powers with interests in the Middle East. The German commercial rivalry with Great Britain not only brought direct trouble but nourished German desire for sea power and a large navy. Great Britain, long in "splendid isolation" from the other European nations, was being propelled by its interests to make some move toward protective international alliance. There had been some efforts to achieve a Franco-German rapprochement, but these ultimately had no effect. In 1898, Théophile DELCASSÉ took control of French foreign policy; he was opposed to Germany and hoped for a rapprochement with Great Britain, his object being the isolation of Germany. Friendship between Britain and France did not seem possible because of their traditional enmity and, more important, their colonial quarrels in Africa. Moreover Great Britain and Germany were traditional friends, and the two countries were bound by dynastic and cultural ties. There had been and continued to be active expressions of Anglo-German amity, but Delcassé's diplomacy, aided by the accession (1901) of Francophile Edward VII to the British throne, ultimately bore fruit. Although Great Britain and France had been on the verge of war over the FASHODA INCIDENT in 1898, the matter was settled and the way opened for further agreements between the two powers. Though there was no alliance, the Entente Cordiale—a friendly understanding—was arrived at in 1904. Colonial rivalries of Russia and Britain had in the late 19th cent. made those powers hostile; the field of contest was Asia—Turkish affairs, Persia, Afghanistan, China, and India. But after the defeat of Russia in the Russo-Japanese War, and particularly after Sir Edward Grey gained influence in the British foreign office, Britain came to favor a friendly settlement. This was finally achieved in the Anglo-Russian entente of 1907. That agreement created the international group opposing the Triple Alliance—France, Great Britain, and Russia had formed the Triple Entente.
The Rising Storm. The two principal problems that caused outright conflict involved MOROCCO and the Balkans. The militarism of the chief countries of Europe was prompted by a growing sense of international hysteria, which was, in turn, increased by military preparations. The crisis in Morocco in 1905 almost precipitated war. More serious still were the Balkan crises brought about by the annexation of BOSNIA AND HERCEGOVINA by Austria-Hungary in 1908, the Italo-Turkish War (1911–12), and the BALKAN WARS (1912–13). The trouble between Austria and Serbia reached a peak after the assassination of Archduke Francis Ferdinand in 1914, and World War I resulted. Italy's interests had long been more or less divorced from those of the Triple Alliance; as early as 1902 a Franco-Italian accord on North Africa had been reached in a secret treaty. With the outbreak of the war, both Italy and Rumania refused to join the Central Powers. The Triple Alliance formally came to an end in 1914 when Italy issued a declaration of neutrality. After much secret negotiation, Italy in 1915 joined the Allies, and the next year Rumania did likewise. Germany and Austria-Hungary gained new support in the Ottoman Empire (Turkey) and Bulgaria; the war ushered in a new diplomatic period, with new diplomatic alignments. See B. E. Schmitt, *The Coming of the War, 1914* (1930, repr. 1966); W. L. Langer, *European Alliances and Alignments, 1871–1890* (2d ed. 1950, repr. 1964) and *The Diplomacy of Imperialism, 1890–1902* (2d ed. 1951, repr. 1965); Luigi Albertini, *The Origins of the War of 1914,* Vol. I (tr. 1952); A. J. P. Taylor, *The Struggle for Mastery in Europe, 1848–1918* (1954, repr. 1971); S. B. Fay, *The Origins of the World War* (2d ed. 1966).

tripletail: see BASS.

Tripoli (trĭp'əlē) or **Tarabulus** (tärăb'o͝olo͝os), ancient *Tripolis,* city (1971 est. pop. 175,000), NW Lebanon, on the Mediterranean Sea. Citrus fruits, cotton, and other goods are exported from Tripoli. It has an oil refinery and is the terminus of an oil pipeline from Iraq. It was probably founded after 700 B.C., as there is no mention of it until Persian times when it was the capital of the Phoenician federation of Tyre, Sidon, and Aradus and was divided into three sections. The city flourished under the Seleucid and Roman empires. In A.D. 638 it was captured by the Arabs. After a long siege it was taken (1109) by the Crusaders; during the siege its great library was destroyed. Tripoli was sacked by the sultan of Egypt in 1289 and was later rebuilt. The British conquered it from the Turks in 1918, and it became part of Lebanon in 1920. The old part of the city, around the harbor, contains the remains of fortified towers and walls.

Tripoli (trĭp'əlē), ancient *Oea,* Arab. *Tarabulus,* city (1971 est. pop. 162,200), capital of Libya and of Tripoli dist., NW Libya, a port on the Mediterranean Sea. It is a commercial, industrial, administrative, and transportation center. Manufactures include processed food, textiles, tobacco products, and woven goods. Located on the edge of a large oasis, the city was founded (probably in the 7th cent. B.C.) as Oea by Phoenicians from Tyre. The main city of the historic region of Tripolitania, it was later captured by the Romans (1st cent. B.C.), the Vandals (5th cent. A.D.), and the Arabs (7th cent.). The city was a terminus of important trans-Saharan caravan routes. Captured in 1510 by the Spanish, Tripoli was granted (1528) to the Knights of St. John who held it until 1551, when it was taken by the Ottoman Turks. From 1711 to 1835, Tripoli was the seat of the Karamanlı dynasty, which ruled most of what later became Libya with little control from Constantinople. The city was a major base of the Barbary pirates, whom the United States fought (1801–5) in the TRIPOLITAN WAR. In 1911, Tripoli passed to Italy, and later it was made the capital of the Italian colony of Libya. During World War II, the city was captured (1943) by the British. Parts of the Roman walls and an arch of Marcus Aurelius remain. Of note also are the Karamanlı mosque (begun 1736) and the large Gurgi mosque (19th cent.).

tripoli, very fine-grained siliceous material used as an abrasive, as a filler, and as a facing for foundry molds. It is found in Arkansas, Illinois, Missouri, Oklahoma, and Pennsylvania. Tripoli is also called infusorial earth or rottenstone.

Trípolis (trē'pôlĭs), town (1971 pop. 20,209), capital of Arcadia prefecture, S Greece, in the Peloponnesus. It is a transportation and agricultural center and a summer resort. Textiles and leather are produced. Founded c.1467 near the sites of the ancient cities of Mantinea, Pallantium, and Tegea, it was the seat of the Ottoman governors of Morea (the Peloponnesus). The town was devastated (1825) in the Greek War of Independence. It was formerly known as Tripolitza.

Tripolis: see TRIPOLI, Lebanon.

Tripolitania (trĭp″əlĭtā′nēə), historic region, W Libya, bordering on the Mediterranean Sea. TRIPOLI is the chief city. The original inhabitants of the region were probably Berbers. In the 7th cent. B.C. the Phoenicians established colonies on the coast at LEPTIS, Oea (later Tripoli), and Sabratha. The coastal zone was later held by Carthage and was taken by NUMIDIA in 146 B.C. Rome captured Tripolitania in 46 B.C., and in the following centuries, as Roman rule was extended far into the south, the region prospered as a trade and agricultural center. In A.D. 435, Tripolitania fell to the Vandals, and it was captured by the Byzantines a century later. In the 7th cent. the Arabs gained control of Tripolitania, and from the 9th to the 11th cent. numerous Arabs settled there. The Normans briefly held the region in the mid-12th cent., and from the mid-13th to the mid-15th cent. Tripolitania was ruled from Tunisia. The Ottoman Turks captured the region in 1553 and it became a stronghold of Barbary pirates. For later history, see LIBYA.

Tripolitan War (trĭpŏl′ĭtən), 1800–1815, conflict between the United States and the Barbary States. Piracy had become a normal source of income in the N African Barbary States long before the United States came into existence. The newly formed republic adopted the practice common to European nations of paying tribute to buy immunity from raids. Difficulties began in 1800 when William BAINBRIDGE, the officer who took tribute to the dey of Algiers, was compelled to go under the Turkish flag to Constantinople. When the pasha of Tripoli demanded (1800) more tribute than previously agreed upon, the United States refused payment. Hostilities broke out in 1801, but Commodore Richard Dale's blockade of Tripoli failed to daunt the pirates. President Thomas Jefferson then decided to settle the affair by negotiation, but Richard Valentine Morris, the officer he sent to Tripoli, could not reach an agreement with the pasha. The war continued. Tunis was more or less drawn into the struggle because of ill feeling between the bey's court and William Eaton, the U.S. consul there. After Eaton and Morris quarreled over the conduct of the campaign, the blockade of Tripoli was lifted, and the U.S. government considered resuming tribute payments. At this juncture Edward Preble succeeded Morris as the U.S. commander in the Mediterranean. Preble dispatched the frigate *Philadelphia* under Bainbridge to resume the blockade of Tripoli. A storm drove the ship aground in the outer harbor. She was captured, and Bainbridge and his crew were imprisoned. Stephen Decatur and a small group of men were sent (Feb., 1804) into the harbor. They set fire to the *Philadelphia* and destroyed her. Despite this exploit Preble was still unable to take Tripoli, and, in Sept., 1804, he was succeeded by Samuel Barron. Meanwhile William Eaton had won the U.S. government to his plan of supporting a rival claimant for the rule of Tripoli by a land expedition. Eaton landed in Egypt and after an arduous march westward took the port of Derna. Before he could advance farther, the war was ended. John Rodgers, sent out with a strong force in May, 1805, negotiated a settlement in June. The U.S. prisoners were ransomed, and Tripoli renounced all rights to halt or to levy tribute on American ships. Though the most favorable agreement yet made with a Barbary power, the treaty was not a brilliant triumph. It did not end the threat of piracy to U.S. shipping. During the later Napoleonic Wars and the War of 1812, the Barbary pirates increased their raids on American commerce. Algiers actually declared war on the United States. In 1815 a squadron under Decatur forced the dey of Algiers to sign a treaty renouncing U.S. tribute, and the so-called Algerine War was ended. After 1815 the United States no longer paid tribute to any Barbary State. See G. W. Allen, *Our Navy and the Barbary Corsairs* (1905, repr. 1965); D. B. Chidsey, *The Wars in Barbary* (1971).

Triptolemus (trĭptŏl′əməs): see DEMETER.

Tripura (trĭ′pŏŏrä), state (1971 pop. 1,556,822), 4,036 sq mi (10,453 sq km), NE India, bordered by Bangladesh on the north, west, and south. The capital is AGARTALA. Tripura lies in a mountainous region but has lush lowlands with cane brakes, swamps, and dense jungles. The population, which is mainly engaged in agriculture, is predominantly Hindu, although aborigines live in the hills. Bengali is the main language. The region was annexed by the Mogul empire in 1733, passed under British rule in the 19th cent., and was joined to India in 1949. Tripura became a union territory in 1956 and a state in 1972. Many pilgrims visit the 16th-century Hindu temple at Radhakishorepur. It is governed by a chief minister and cabinet responsible to an elected unicameral legislature. The states of Assam, Nagaland, Meghalaya, Manipur, and Tripura and the union territories of Mizoram and Arunachal Pradesh have a common governor appointed by the president of India.

trireme: see GALLEY.

trisection of an angle: see GEOMETRIC PROBLEMS OF ANTIQUITY.

Trissino, Gian Giorgio (jän jôr′jō trēs-sē′nō), 1478–1550, Italian poet and philologist. His play *Sofonisba* (written 1515, produced 1557) introduced classical Greek dramatic techniques to Italian drama. Also well known is his epic poem *Italia liberata dai Goti* (1547). His treatise advocating a blending of dialects in literary Italian was attacked by Machiavelli and by Bembo, who supported the Tuscan dialect.

Trist, Nicholas Philip, 1800–1874, American diplomat, b. Charlottesville, Va. He attended West Point, studied law under Thomas Jefferson, whose granddaughter he married, and was private secretary to Andrew Jackson. He served as U.S. consul (1833–41) in Havana, Cuba, and was chief clerk of the Dept. of State when he was sent (1847) to Mexico as a special agent to conduct negotiations to end the MEXICAN WAR. A short armistice was reached after the battles of Contreras and Churubusco (Aug., 1847), but negotiations were unsuccessful and war was resumed. President Polk had Trist recalled. Trist had reopened negotiations before his recall arrived and decided to ignore the order. He succeeded in negotiating the Treaty of GUADALUPE HIDALGO. Polk supported the treaty but declared Trist in disgrace. Trist did not recover his unpaid salary and expenses until 1871.

Tristan: see TRISTRAM AND ISOLDE.

Tristan da Cunha (trĭs′tăn də kōō′nə), group of volcanic islands (1970 est. pop. 280), in the S Atlantic, about midway between S Africa and S America. The only habitable island of the group is Tristan da Cunha, formed by a volcano rising to c.6,760 ft (2,060 m); the other islands are Gough, Nightingale, and Inaccessible, the last being the home of the flightless rail, an almost extinct bird. The first inhabitants came from St. Helena in the 19th cent. Fishing is the chief industry. The island group was discovered by the Portuguese in 1506 and was visited by whalers, seal hunters, and explorers. In 1816 it was annexed by Great Britain, and in 1938 it became a dependency of the colony of St. Helena. An important meteorological and radio base was set up in 1942. The volcano, long dormant, erupted in 1961; the population was evacuated, eventually being transported to England, where their curious 19th-century speech was studied by linguists. In 1962, however, the islanders announced their displeasure with life in England and voted overwhelmingly to return to Tristan da Cunha the next year. See A. Falk-Rønne, *Back to Tristan* (1967).

Tristan L'Hermite, François, pseud. of **François L'Hermite** (fräNswä′ trĕstäN′ lĕrmĕt′), 1601–55, French playwright and poet. Poor and plagued by ill health, he was a page in the court of Henry IV but fled to England, Norway, and Spain after a series of duels. Returning to France in 1620 he recounted his adventures in *Le page disgracié* (1645). In addition to writing poetry, Tristan produced several successful plays, including the tragedies *La Mariane* (1636), *La Mort de Sénèque* (1644), *La Morte de Crispe* (1645), *Osman* (1650), and the burlesque *Le Parasite* (1654).

Tristram and Isolde (trĭs′trəm, ĭsōl′də, ĭzōl′-), medieval romance. The earliest extant version (incomplete) was written (c.1185) by Thomas of Britain in Anglo-Norman French verse. About 1210, Gottfried von Strassburg wrote in German verse a version based on that of Thomas. The story, originally independent of the ARTHURIAN LEGEND, was later incorporated with it. In the 15th cent. Sir Thomas Malory included Tristram and Isolde in his *Morte d' Arthur.* The story is mainly Irish in origin, with details from other sources. Although the many versions of the story naturally differ, the basic plot is much the same in all of them. Sir Tristram is sent to Ireland to bring Isolde the Fair back to Cornwall to be the bride of his uncle, King Mark. A potion that Tristram and Isolde unwittingly swallow binds them in eternal love. According to most versions of the story, after many trysts the lovers become estranged, and Tristram marries another Isolde, Isolde of the White Hands. Later, dying of a battle wound, Tristram sends for Isolde the Fair. Deceived into believing she is not coming, Tristram dies of despair, and Isolde, on finding her lover dead, dies of grief beside him. The names of the two chief characters appear in various forms, such as Tristran, Tristrem, or Tristan and Isolt, Yseult, or Iseult. Modern versions of the story include Matthew Arnold, *Tristram and Iseult;* A. C. Swinburne, *Tristram of Lyonesse;* Joseph Bédier, *Tristan and Iseult;* and E. A. Robinson, *Tristram.* Wagner's opera *Tristan und Isolde* is based on the version of Gottfried von Strassburg. For translation of the version by Thomas of Britain, see R. S. Loomis, *The Romance of Tristram & Ysolt* (rev. ed. 1951); for translation of the version by Gottfried von Strassburg, see A. T. Hatto, *Tristan* (1960). See W. T. H. Jackson, *Anatomy of Love: A Study of the Tristan of Gottfried von Strassburg* (1971).

tritium (trĭt′ēəm), radioactive isotope of HYDROGEN with mass number 3. The tritium nucleus, called a triton, contains one proton and two neutrons.

Triton (trĭt′ən), in astronomy, innermost and largest of the two known moons, or natural satellites, of NEPTUNE.

Triton, in Greek mythology, son of Poseidon. He was a creature of the sea, the upper half of his body being human, the lower fishlike. Later legends speak of many Tritons, sometimes described as riding over the sea on horses. Tritons characteristically blew trumpets of conch shells.

triumphal arch, monumental structure embodying one or more arched passages, frequently built to span a road and designed to honor a king or general or to commemorate a military triumph. This form of monument was probably invented by the Romans, who built them throughout the empire. Examples exist in Italy, France, Spain, Asia Minor, and North Africa, dating from the empire. The typical Roman triumphal arch had a single arched opening in the earliest examples, e.g., the Arch of Titus, Rome (A.D.

Triumphal arch

81); after the 2d cent. a large arch flanked by two smaller ones became common. The piers were faced with columns and enriched with sculptures or bas-reliefs relating to the events commemorated, while above the entablature was an attic story for dedicatory inscriptions supporting a quadriga, a sculptured four-horse chariot group. Among the Roman arches remaining are that of Trajan, at Benevento, Italy (114), relating the story of the emperor's life, and those of Septimius Severus (203) and of Constantine (c.315) at Rome, honoring the military victories of the two emperors. In modern times some arches have been built to celebrate military triumphs. Among them in Paris are the Porte Saint-Denis and the Porte Saint-Martin, both erected under the reign of Louis XIV, and the Arc de Triomphe du Carrousel and the ARC DE TRIOMPHE DE L'ÉTOILE, both built at the decree of Napoleon I. Other well-known arches are the Brandenburg Gate in Berlin; the Victory Gate in Munich; the Marble Arch in London; and the Washington Arch in New York City. Many modern arches have been memorials or civic adornments rather than triumphal monuments in the Roman sense.

Triumvirate (trīŭm′vĭrĭt, -vĭrāt″), in ancient Rome, ruling board or commission of three men. Triumvirates were common in the Roman republic. The **First Triumvirate** was the alliance of Julius CAESAR, POMPEY, and Marcus Licinius CRASSUS formed in 60 B.C. This was not strictly a triumvirate, since the alliance had no official sanction. The three men were able to control Rome, and the alliance aided Caesar's rise to power by giving him the opportunity to pursue the GALLIC WARS. The **Second Triumvirate** was legally established as the *tresviri rei publicae constituendae* [triumvirate for reestablishing the public welfare] in 43 B.C. for five years; it was renewed in 37 B.C. The members were Octavian (AUGUSTUS), Marc ANTONY, and LEPIDUS. This group was granted enormous power by the senate. Lepidus was deposed in 36 B.C., and Antony was defeated at Actium in 31 B.C., leaving Octavian at the head of the Roman Empire.

Trivandrum (trĭvăn'drəm), city (1971 pop. 409,761), capital of Kerala state, SW India, a port on the Arabian Sea. Manufactures include tires, tile, plywood, and titanium products. Trivandrum was the capital of the former state of Travancore and of Travancore-Cochin.

Trivulzio, Gian Giacomo (jän jä'kōmō trēvo͞ol'tsēō), 1441?–1518, Italian CONDOTTIERE. Leaving the service of his native Milan, he fought in the ITALIAN WARS for Naples and in 1495 went over to the French. In 1499 he headed the French forces that took Milan, and he was made marshal of France by Louis XII. As a key figure in the subsequent campaigns, he shared responsibility for the rout at Novara (1513) and the victory of Marignano (1515). The jealousy of his colleague, Lautrec, caused Trivulzio's disgrace with Francis I, and the aged marshal died in resentful retirement.

Trnava (tûr'nävä), Ger. *Tyrnau,* Hung. *Nagyszombat,* city (1970 pop. 38,393), S Czechoslovakia, in Slovakia. The market for a fertile agricultural region, it has steelworks and sugar refineries and manufactures agricultural machinery and railroad cars. The city is also a Roman Catholic episcopal see. Founded in the 6th or 7th cent., Trnava was a center of Slovak Catholicism in the Middle Ages; it is called the Slovak Rome because of its many churches and monasteries, notably the fine Gothic cathedral.

Trnovo or **Tirnovo** (both: tûr'nōvō), city (1968 est. pop. 42,300), N central Bulgaria, on the Yantra River. It is a commercial center and produces foodstuffs, textiles, and leather. Trnovo is the seat of an Eastern Orthodox metropolitan. The site was probably a Roman fortress. The second Bulgarian kingdom came into existence at Trnovo when Ivan I was proclaimed czar in 1186. It was the capital of Bulgaria under Ivan II, who built (1230) the Church of the Forty Martyrs. The city fell to the Turks in 1393. A Bulgarian constitution was drafted in 1879 at Trnovo, where the full independence of Bulgaria was proclaimed in 1908.

Troas (trō'ăs) or **the Troad** (trō'ăd), region about ancient TROY, on the northwest coast of Asia Minor, in present NW Turkey. Traversed by Mt. Ida (Kaz Dağı) and strategically located on the Hellespont (Dardanelles), it was involved in various struggles to control the straits. Troas was the scene of the events of the *Iliad* and was an ancient center of Aegean civilization. The region has yielded to archaeologists a wealth of antiquities. For the Troas of the Bible, see ALEXANDRIA TROAS.

Trobriand Islands (trō'brēănd", trō"brēănd'), small volcanic island group off SE New Guinea, part of Papua New Guinea. Kiriwana is the largest of the group's 22 islands. Yams, pearl shell, and trepang are the major products. The islands were made famous in the writings of anthropologist Bronislaw MALINOWSKI.

Trochu, Louis Jules (lwē zhül trôshü'), 1815–96, French general. He fought in Algeria, in the Crimean War, and in the Italian war of 1859. In *L'Armée française en 1867* (1867), he criticized the French army and urged its reorganization. He was military governor of Paris when the Franco-Prussian War broke out (1870). He did not attempt to prevent the overthrow, at Paris, of the Second Empire after the French rout at Sedan (Sept., 1870), and he accepted the presidency of the government of national defense, hoping to conduct an honorable rather than a victorious defense. Trochu's inactivity in defense of Paris was severely criticized. He resigned after the capitulation of Paris in Jan., 1871. He wrote several volumes of apologia.

Troelstra, Pieter Jelles (pē'tər yĕl'ĕs tro͞ol'strä), 1860–1930, Dutch Socialist. In 1893 he founded what later became the *Sociaaldemocrata,* the official Socialist paper, and in 1900 he assumed editorship of his party's daily, the *Volk.* Opposing the ultraradical wing of the Socialists, Troelstra organized the Dutch Social Democratic Labor party in 1894 and represented it in parliament from 1897 to 1900. He wrote several books on social legislation and his memoirs, *Gedenkschriften* (1927).

Trogir (trō'gēr), Ger. *Trau,* town (1971 pop. 18,424), W Yugoslavia, partly on the Adriatic island of Čiovo and partly on the mainland, separated by a channel. A small port, it is also a seaside resort. Founded by the Greeks in the 3d cent. B.C., Trogir passed to Venice in 1420 and to Austria in 1797. It was included in Yugoslavia in 1920. The town is of great architectural interest, having retained a 9th-century church, a splendid 13th-century cathedral, a 15th-century town hall, and several medieval and Renaissance palaces. Nearby are the ruins of the Roman city of Salonae.

trogon (trō'gŏn), family of tropical jungle birds related to the roadrunners and including the QUETZAL. Trogons are sedentary arboreal birds, 10 to 14 in. (25.4–35.6 cm) long, with short rounded wings, long squared tails, and small weak legs. Their soft, colorful plumage—metallic green or brown above with red, green, blue, or yellow on the head, breast, and belly—blends with the shadowy light of the jungle. Their cooing, ventriloquial call resembles that of the peacock. Trogons feed on insects and fruits and nest in cavities. The coppery-tailed trogon ranges into the S United States. Trogons are classified in the phylum CHORDATA, subphylum Vertebrata, class Aves, order Trogoniformes, family Trogonidae.

Trogus (Cnaeus Pompeius Trogus) (trō'gəs), fl. A.D. 5, Roman historian of Gallic origin. His history of the world, which survives only in excerpts by Justin, dealt with the Orient, Greece, Macedon and the other Hellenistic kingdoms, Rome, Gaul, and Spain. His source was independent of the patriotic tradition of other Roman historians.

Trogyllium (trōjĭl'ēəm), promontory, W Asia Minor, jutting out into the Aegean Sea just S of Samos. St. Paul stopped there (Acts 20.15).

Troilus and Cressida (troi'ləs, krĕs'ĭdə), a medieval romance distantly related to characters in Greek legend. Troilus, a Trojan prince (son of Priam and Hecuba), fell in love with Cressida (Chryseis), daughter of Calchas. When she was exchanged for a Trojan prisoner of war, Cressida swore to be faithful to Troilus, but then deceived him with Diomed. Troilus was killed by Achilles. This story appeared first in Benoît de Sainte-More, from whom Boccaccio drew for his *Filostrato.* Chaucer and Shakespeare also used this legend.

Trois Rivières (trwä rēvyĕr') or **Three Rivers,** city (1971 pop. 55,869), S Que., Canada, at the confluence of the St. Lawrence and St. Maurice rivers. It is a port and an industrial center. The city was founded (1634) by Champlain and took its name from the three channels through which the St. Maurice enters the St. Lawrence. It became a major French trading post and fortified port and was the starting point of many explorers and missionaries. In 1737 the first iron forges in Quebec were built in Trois Rivières. During the 19th cent. lumbering was the major industry, but with the utilization of water power after 1900 the pulp and paper industry became dominant.

Troitse-Sergiyeva Lavra: see ZAGORSK, USSR.

Trojan asteroids, two groups of asteroids that revolve about the sun in the same orbit as Jupiter; one group is about 60° ahead of the planet in the orbit, the other about 60° behind it. The Trojan asteroids represent one possible special solution to the famous three-body problem (see CELESTIAL MECHANICS), with each group forming an equilateral triangle with Jupiter and the sun. The first Trojan asteroid discovered was Achilles, observed in 1904 by the German astronomer Max Wolf; all of these asteroids are named for heroes of the Trojan War.

Trojan War, in Greek mythology, war between the Greeks and the people of Troy. The strife began after the Trojan prince Paris abducted Helen, wife of Menelaus of Sparta. When Menelaus demanded her return, the Trojans refused. Menelaus then persuaded his brother Agamemnon to lead an army against Troy. At Aulis, troopships gathered, led by the greatest Greek heroes—Achilles, Patroclus, Diomed, Odysseus, Nestor, and the two warriors named Ajax. In order to win favorable winds for the journey, Agamemnon sacrificed his daughter Iphigenia to Artemis. The winds came and the fleet set sail for Troy. For nine years the Greeks ravaged Troy's surrounding cities and countryside, but the city itself, well fortified and commanded by Hector and other sons of the royal household, held out. Finally the Greeks built a large hollow wooden horse in which a small group of warriors were concealed. The other Greeks appeared to sail for home, leaving behind only the horse and Sinon, who deceitfully persuaded the Trojans, despite the warnings of Cassandra and Laocoön, to take the horse within the city walls. At night the Greeks returned; their companions crept out of the horse and opened the city gates, and Troy was destroyed. The gods took great interest in the war. Poseidon, Hera, and Athena aided the Greeks, while Aphrodite and Ares favored the Trojans. Zeus and Apollo, although frequently involved in the action of the war, remained impartial. The events of the final year of the war constitute the main part of the *Iliad* of Homer. The Trojan War probably reflected a real war (c.1200 B.C.) between the invading Greeks and the people of Troas, possibly over control of trade through the Dardanelles.

troll (trōl), in Scandinavian folklore, dwarfish or gigantic creature of caves and hills. Variously friendly or malicious, trolls toiled as smiths. The mountain king in Ibsen's *Peer Gynt* is a troll.

trolley: see STREETCAR.

Trollhättan (trôl'hĕ"tän), city (1970 pop. 40,042), Älvsborg co., S Sweden, on the Götaälv River near Lake Vänern. The Götaälv River, which falls 108 ft (33 m) in about 1 mi (1.6 km) at Trollhättan, is used to generate much hydroelectricity; the ready availability of electricity has helped to make the city a major industrial center. Manufactures include locomotives, metal goods, airplane engines, footwear, clothing, and motor vehicles.

Trollope, Anthony (trŏl'əp), 1815–82, one of the great English novelists. After spending seven unhappy years in London as a clerk in the general post office, he transferred (1841) to Ireland and became post-office inspector; he held various other responsible positions in the postal service until his resignation in 1867. He published several unsuccessful novels before he achieved fame with *The Warden* (1855), the first in the series of Barsetshire novels. Others in the series are *Barchester Towers* (1857), *Doctor Thorne* (1858), *Framley Parsonage* (1861), *The Small House at Allington* (1864), and *The Last Chronicle of Barset* (1867). In his later novels Trollope shifted his interest from the rural scene to urban society and politics. These books include *The Claverings* (1867), *Phineas Finn* (1869), *He Knew He Was Right* (1869), *The Eustace Diamonds* (1873), *The Way We Live Now* (1875), *The Prime Minister* (1876), and *The American Senator* (1877). His extensive journeys, many in the service of the post office, resulted in various books of travel, including an account of his visit to the United States. He was an industrious and prolific author, and besides his novels and travel books he wrote several biographical works and a highly praised autobiography (1883). According to Henry James, Trollope's greatness lies in his "complete appreciation of the usual." The Barsetshire novels, upon which his fame rests, depict in detail the lives of a group of ordinary but interesting people who live in the county of Barsetshire. The series as a whole presents a fascinating microcosm of Victorian society. See his autobiography ed. by M. Sadleir (1883, repr. 1968); biographies by M. Sadleir (1927, new ed. 1961) and Hugh Walpole (1928); studies by A. O. J. Cockshut (1955), D. Smalley (1969), A. G. Freedman (1971), and T. Pope-Hennessy (1971). Trollope's mother, **Frances Trollope,** 1780–1863, was also a writer. Her account of her travels in the United States, *The Domestic Manners of the Americans* (1832), was very offensive to Americans but sold well in England and was the beginning of her career as a successful writer. She continued to write travel books and began a steady stream of novels, of which the best are *The Vicar of Wrexhill* (1837) and *The Widow Barnaby* and its sequels (1839–56). See biographies by F. E. Trollope (1895, repr. 1927) and James Pope Hennessy (1972); studies by R. M. Polhemus (1968) and A. O. J. Cockshut (1955, repr. 1968); L. P. and R. P. Stebbins, *The Trollopes* (1945, repr. 1968).

trombone [Ital., = large trumpet], brass wind musical instrument of cylindrical bore, twice bent on itself, having a sliding section that lengthens or shortens it and thus regulates the pitch. The descendant of the SACKBUT, it was developed in the 14th cent. by adding a slide to the trumpet. Early representations of the instrument show it nearly in its present form. Despite its continuous possession of a complete chromatic scale, which was lacking in early trumpets and the FRENCH HORN, the trombone was far behind them in acceptance into the orchestra. In the 16th cent. it became popular for court and church music. In the 18th cent. it entered the opera orchestra, and Beethoven introduced it into symphonic music. In the enlarged orchestra of the 19th cent., the trombone became increasingly important, being valued for its wide range in pitch and dynamics. It is more often used as an ensemble than as a solo instrument in the orchestra, and it has little solo literature. Three trombones are standard in the orchestra, formerly alto, tenor, and bass. The tenor is most often used today, often with extra tubing that can be cut in by a valve to give it the lower notes of

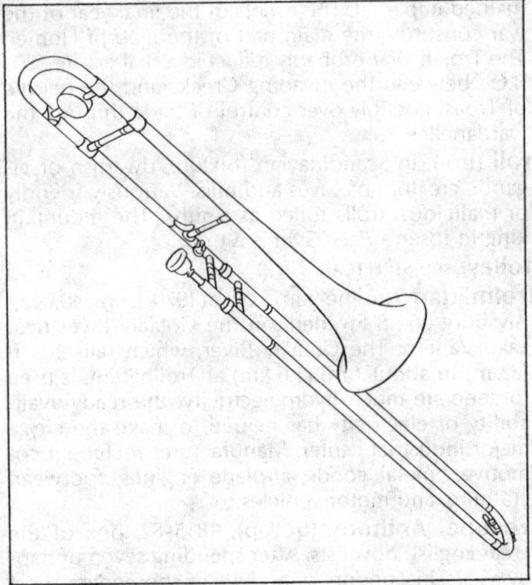

Trombone

the old bass trombone. The trombone is also widely used in jazz and dance bands. A valved trombone is frequently used in Latin countries but is inferior in tone quality to the slide trombone. See Robin Gregory, *The Trombone* (1973).

Tromp, Cornelis (kôrnā'lĭs trômp), 1629–91, Dutch admiral in the second and third of the Dutch Wars; son of Maarten Tromp. In 1665 he was made commander of the Dutch fleet, but he was replaced by M. A. de RUYTER in the same year. In June, 1666, he commanded the rear squadron of the fleet in the Four Days battle or battle of the Downs, but in Aug., 1666, he lost his command because of de Ruyter's complaints. Tromp was reinstated in 1672; in operations against Sweden he was successful at Gotland and Rügen (1676).

Tromp, Maarten Harpertszoon (mär'tən här'pərtsōn), 1597–1653, Dutch admiral. A sailor from childhood, he joined the navy and rose to the rank of lieutenant admiral in 1637. In 1639, by remarkable tactics, he was able to blockade and crush a Spanish fleet in the Downs of the English Channel; this defeat marked the passing of Spanish sea power. In June, 1652, his refusal to lower his flag in deference to the English Admiral Robert Blake started the first of the DUTCH WARS. He won control of the English Channel by his victory (Dec., 1652) over the English off Dungeness, but he was soon forced to withdraw before superior forces. The inferiority of his fleet caused the loss (June, 1653) of 20 ships near Gabbard Shoal. He effected a union with Cornelius de Witt's squadron and joined in the attack (Aug., 1653) on the English off Scheveningen. Though Tromp and de Witt were defeated, this action broke the blockade of the Dutch coast and was the last major conflict of the war. Tromp was killed in the battle. See his *Journal Anno 1639* (tr. by C. R. Boxer, 1930).

trompe l'oeil (trôNp lö'yə): see ILLUSIONISM.

Troms (trôms, trōōms), county (1972 est. pop. 138,000), c.10,070 sq mi (26,080 sq km), N Norway, bordering on the Norwegian Sea (an arm of the Atlantic Ocean) in the west and on Sweden and Finland in the east. Tromsø is the capital. The county has many deep fjords and numerous offshore islands, including some of the Vesterålen group. Fishing, canning, stock raising, and boatbuilding are the main industries, and there is also some mining and farming.

Tromsø (trôms'ö", trōōms'ö"), city (1970 pop. 39,145), capital of Troms co., NW Norway, on the island of Tromsøy; chartered 1794. The chief city of arctic Norway, it has large herring fisheries and is a base for seal hunters. Manufactures include ships and rope. It is also a starting point for cruise ships. In World War II, the German battleship *Tirpitz* was sunk (Nov. 12, 1944) by British planes just off Tromsø.

Trondheim (trôn'hām), city (1970 pop. 127,595), capital of Sør-Trøndelag co., central Norway, a port on the Trondheimsfjord (an arm of the Atlantic Ocean). It is also known by its original name, Nidaros. The second largest city of Norway, it is a commercial, industrial, and shipping center. Manufactures include metal goods, construction materials, processed food, and forest products. Founded in 997 by Olaf I, the first Christian king of Norway, the city was the political and religious capital of medieval Norway. In 1152, Nicholas Breakspear (later Pope Adrian IV) made it an archiepiscopal see. The city was also an important trade center until the Hanseatic period, when its trade was largely diverted (14th cent.) to Bergen. Olaf Engelbrektsson, archbishop of Nidaros, strongly resisted (early 16th cent.) the attempt of King Christian III to force the Reformation on Norway and defended the rights of Norway as a separate kingdom. However, in 1537, Engelbrektsson was obliged to flee, and in the same year the Reformation was introduced and Norwegian bishoprics were abolished. Renamed Trondheim (or Trondhjem), the city declined considerably after this blow to its religious ascendancy. In 1681 it was severely damaged by a fire. Only in the mid-19th cent. did Trondheim reemerge as an important economic center. Its position was enhanced when Haakon VII was crowned (1906) in Nidaros Cathedral as the first king of modern, independent Norway; subsequent rulers of Norway have also been crowned there. In World War II, Trondheim was occupied by the Germans on the first day (April 9, 1940) of their invasion of Norway. It became a major German naval base and as such was frequently bombed by the Allies. Today Trondheim is a well-planned city. Its celebrated cathedral, originally a church erected over the tomb of Olaf II (St. Olaf) in the 11th cent., was built in the 12th and 13th cent., but it was later ravaged by several fires. Reconstruction was begun in 1869, and the completed structure, built of Norwegian blue soapstone and white marble, is considered by many to be the finest Gothic-style cathedral in Scandinavia. Also of note in the city is the *Stiftsgaard,* a large wooden building (18th cent.) that serves as a royal residence.

Trondheimsfjord (trôn'hām"sfyôr), inlet of the Norwegian Sea, c.80 mi (130 km) long, W central Norway. It is considered a natural boundary between N and S Norway. Trondheim is on a peninsula in the fjord. The valleys draining into the fjord comprise one of the most fertile agricultural regions of Norway.

Trophimus (trŏf'ĭməs), Ephesian companion of Paul. Acts 20.4; 21.29; 2 Tim. 4.20.

Trophonius (trəfō'nēəs), in Greek mythology, famous architect. He and his brother Agamedes built the temple of Apollo at Delphi and the treasury of King Hyrieus. According to one legend, Trophonius was swallowed up by the earth at Lebadea in Boeotia, which became the site of a famous subterranean oracle.

tropical medicine, study, diagnosis, treatment, and prevention of certain diseases prevalent in the tropics. The warmth and humidity of the tropics and the primitive and unsanitary conditions under which so many people live in those areas contribute to the development and dissemination of many infectious diseases and parasitic infestations. Much has been achieved in combating such typical tropical diseases as MALARIA, YELLOW FEVER, amebiasis (amebic DYSENTERY), and filariasis (ELEPHANTIASIS). Better public health measures and, in some cases, specific therapeutic agents have assisted in the fight. The realization of local government authorities of the needs of the people, the efforts of the United States and other Western countries with economic and political interests in tropical regions, and the assistance of the World Health Organization and of philanthropic foundations have all combined to bring about medical advances. Specific projects that were hampered by tropical disease also furthered the conquest of those diseases; e.g., during the construction of the Panama Canal there was a concerted effort against—and ultimate conquest of—yellow fever. The deployment of American troops in malaria-infested regions has spurred the search for more efficient synthetic antimalarial drugs. DDT, introduced in World War II to eradicate the malaria-carrying mosquito, is still being used despite the emergence of DDT-resistant mosquitoes and the more recently discovered drawbacks of chemical insecticides. There have also been advances against filariasis, hookworm, leprosy, and other tropical maladies.

tropical year, time between successive vernal EQUINOXES; 365 days, 5 hr, 48 min, 46 sec of MEAN SOLAR TIME. The tropical year is the basis of the YEAR used in the Gregorian CALENDAR.

Tropic of Cancer, parallel of latitude at 23°27′ north of the equator; it is the northern boundary of the TROPICS. This parallel marks the farthest point north at which the sun can be seen directly overhead at noon; above the parallel the sun appears less than 90° from the southern horizon at any day of the year. The sun reaches its vertical position over the Tropic of Cancer at about June 22, the summer SOLSTICE in the Northern Hemisphere. When the Tropic of Cancer was named, the sun was in the constellation CANCER at the time of the summer solstice.

Tropic of Capricorn, parallel of latitude at 23°27′ south of the equator; it is the southern boundary of the TROPICS. This parallel marks the farthest point south at which the sun can be seen directly overhead at noon; below the parallel the sun appears less than 90° from the northern horizon at any day of the year. The sun reaches its vertical position over the Tropic of Capricorn at about Dec. 22, the summer SOLSTICE for the Southern Hemisphere. The term *Capricorn* comes from the Latin words *caper* [goat] and *cornu* [horn] and is the name given to one of the 12 constellations in the ZODIAC.

tropics, also called tropical zone or torrid zone, all the land and water of the earth situated between the TROPIC OF CANCER at lat. 23½°N and the TROPIC OF CAPRICORN at lat. 23½°S. Every point within the tropics receives the perpendicular rays of the sun at noon on at least one day of the year. The sun is directly overhead at lat. 23½°N on June 21 or 22, the summer solstice, and at lat. 23½°S on Dec. 21 or 22, the winter solstice. Since the entire tropical zone receives the rays of the sun more directly than areas in higher latitudes, the average annual temperature of the tropics is higher and the seasonal change of temperature is less than in other zones. The seasons in the tropics are marked by changes in wind or rainfall (as in the monsoon areas) rather than temperature. Several different climatic types can be distinguished within the tropical belt, since latitude is only one of the many factors determining climate in the tropics. Distance from the ocean, prevailing wind conditions, and elevation are all contributing elements. The tropics contain the world's largest regions of tropical rain-forest climate (Amazon and Congo basins). Toward the northern and southern limits are low-latitude savanna, steppe, and desert climates (with decreasing seasonal rainfall). Tropical highland climates (having the characteristics of temperate climates) also occur where high mountain ranges lie in the zone. Rubber, tea, coffee, cocoa, spices, bananas, pineapples, oils and nuts, and lumber are the leading agricultural exports of the countries in the tropical zone. Progress in tropical medicine, advancing technology, and the pressure of increasing populations have led in recent years to the cultivation and settlement of some rain-forest areas. See Marston Bates, *Where Winter Never Comes* (rev. ed. 1963); Pierre Gourou, *The Tropical World* (4th ed. 1966); B. W. Hodder, *Economic Development in the Tropics* (1968); P. W. Richards, *The Life of the Jungle* (1970).

tropism (trō'pĭzəm), involuntary response of an organism, or part of an organism, involving orientation toward (positive tropism) or away from (negative tropism) one or more external stimuli. The term *tropism* is usually applied to growth and turgor movements in plants; an involuntary orientation of an animal or of a motile unicellular plant toward or away from an external stimulus is commonly called a taxic movement, or TAXIS—e.g., the negative phototaxis of certain protozoans that move away from light. Tropistic stimuli include light, heat, moisture, gravity, electricity, and chemical agents. Plant stems are positively phototropic and negatively geotropic, i.e., they grow toward light and against gravity; roots are the reverse, as well as positively hydrotropic (moisture-seeking). Tropistic growth movements in plants are believed to be triggered by the presence of plant hormones (see AUXIN) that promote cell growth. Auxin action is apparently inhibited by light; hence, if a plant is placed in a position of unequal lighting, the cells on the shadier side elongate faster than those on the illuminated side, and the plant bends toward the light. There is also evidence that auxins are affected by gravity, i.e., they accumulate in the lower portions of the plant organs. Since an overconcentration of these hormones inhibits growth, the cells on the underside of a root elongate more slowly than those on the upper side, resulting in the root's downward growth. Generalized plant responses to a stimulus are called nastic movements, or nasties. These include the opening of bud scales and of flower petals, growth movements that occur in response to stimuli such as light and heat without regard for the direction of the stimulus. Some spring flowers exhibit thermonasties, i.e., their flowers open in response to warmth rather than the amount of light. Turgor movements are effected by changes in the water content of cells and are often quite rapid. Examples are the "sleep movements" of clover, the sudden drooping of the leaves of the sensitive plant (mimosa) when touched (thigmotropism), and the reactions of insectivorous plants to the presence of their prey. The exact mechanism controlling the sudden loss of water pressure in certain cells, producing turgor movements, is not clearly understood.

tropopause: see ATMOSPHERE.

troposphere: see ATMOSPHERE.

Troppau: see OPAVA, Czechoslovakia.

Troppau, Congress of (trôp'ou), 1820, international conference convened at the behest of Czar Alexander I of Russia under the provisions of the Quadruple Alliance. The congress met at Troppau, in Austrian Silesia (now Opava, Czechoslovakia). Its purpose was to consider the means of suppressing the liberal uprisings against FERDINAND I of the Two Sicilies and FERDINAND VII of Spain. The Austrian and Russian emperors represented their countries in person but were accompanied by Metternich and Capo d'Istria. Prussia was represented by the crown prince and by K. A. von Hardenberg. Great Britain, shifting away from European commitments, merely sent the British ambassador at Vienna, and the French representatives also were of secondary rank. No decisions were taken on the problems under consideration, which were referred to later meetings (see LAIBACH, CONGRESS OF, and VERONA, CONGRESS OF). However, Austria, Russia, and Prussia signed a protocol (proposed by Alexander I) that threatened armed action against any revolutionary attempts to disturb the status quo. Britain and France refused to adhere to the protocol, marking the first serious weakening of the congress system.

Trotsky, Leon (trŏt'skē, Rus. lā'ən trôt'skē), 1879–1940, Russian Communist revolutionary, one of the principal leaders in the establishment of the USSR. He was born of Jewish parents in the S Ukraine; his original name was Lev Davidovich Bronstein. His father, a prosperous farmer, sent him to Odessa, where he became an outstanding student in a German secondary school. He early became a populist, and he began to be attracted to Marxism in late 1896. In 1898 he was arrested for the first of many times. Exiled to Siberia in 1900, he escaped in 1902, using a forged passport under the name of Trotsky, the head jailer of the Odessa prison in which he had earlier been held. He went to London and collaborated with Vladimir Ilyich Lenin on the revolutionary journal *Iskra* [spark]. After the split (1903) in the Russian Social Democratic party he was for a short time a leading Menshevik spokesman, but he later established an independent course, wavering for years between BOLSHEVISM AND MENSHEVISM. Returning to Russia in 1905, he became chairman of the short-lived St. Petersburg soviet and was arrested during its last meeting. While in prison, he developed his theory of permanent revolution; he declared that in Russia a bourgeois and a socialist revolution would be combined and that a proletarian revolution would then spread throughout the world. Banished again to Siberia, he escaped to Vienna, where he worked (1907–14) as a journalist. At the outbreak of World War I, he went to Switzerland and then to Paris, where he was active in pacifist and radical propaganda. Expelled from France, he moved (Jan., 1917) to New York City, where he edited, with Nikolai Ivanovich BUKHARIN and Aleksandra Mikhailovna KOLLONTAI, the paper *Novy Mir* [new world]. He returned (May, 1917) to Russia after the overthrow of Nicholas II, and, by July, 1917, was a member of the Bolshevik party, taking part with Lenin in the unsuccessful Bolshevik uprising of that month. He was imprisoned by the Aleksandr Kerensky government but was released in September. He was one of the chief organizers of the October Revolution (see RUSSIAN REVOLUTION), which brought the Bolsheviks to power.

In Power. Trotsky became (Nov., 1917) people's commissar for foreign affairs under Lenin. He was a principal figure in negotiations for a separate peace between Russia and the central powers. At first rejecting the arbitrary German *Diktat* in Jan., 1918, and advocating a policy of "neither war nor peace," Trotsky soon yielded to Lenin's appeal for peace in face of the renewed German offensive and the serious split within Bolshevik party ranks. In the Treaty of BREST-LITOVSK (Feb., 1918) Russia submitted to even more humiliating conditions than those offered a few weeks earlier. Trotsky, having resigned as commissar for foreign affairs over the Brest-Litovsk treaty, became commissar of war in 1918. He organized the Red Army in the civil war that followed the revolution, accomplishing the monumental task of welding an efficient fighting force from the tattered remnants of the czarist army and various disparate elements. It was during the civil war that enmity grew between Trotsky and Joseph STALIN. In the trade-union debate (1920–21) within the party, Trotsky clashed with Lenin by demanding strict state control of unions. But the two leaders were again drawn together as a result of the anti-Bolshevik Kronstadt Revolt (1921), the military suppression of which Trotsky directed. As Lenin's health declined, Stalin, more skillful in party infighting, gained prominence. As a result of the tenth party congress (1921), at which the trade-union issues were debated, Stalin was named (1922) general secretary of the party. On Lenin's death (1924) titular power passed to a triumvirate consisting of Stalin, Lev KAMENEV (Trotsky's brother-in-law), and Grigori ZINOVIEV. Advocating world revolution, Trotsky came into increasing conflict with Stalin's plans for "socialism in one country." Trotsky enjoyed great prestige as a revolutionary leader and had followers in the army and state administration, but Stalin effectively controlled the party machine. The triumvirate, although shaky, firmly opposed Trotsky. Stalin refused to expel Trotsky from the party at this time, but he was dismissed as commissar of war in 1925. Zinoviev and Kamenev belatedly joined forces with Trotsky in 1926 in a desperate attempt to check Stalin's power. Trotsky was expelled from the politburo in 1926 and from the party in 1927. In Jan., 1928, he was exiled to Alma Ata (Turkestan), and in 1929 he was ordered to leave the USSR.

In Exile. Refused admission by most countries, Trotsky was granted asylum by Turkey, where he lived on the Princes' Islands near Istanbul. In 1933 he was allowed to move to France, and in 1935 he found refuge in Norway. In the public treason trials held at Moscow in 1936, 1937, and 1938, Trotsky was charged with heading a plot against the Stalinist regime. The accusations, which Trotsky bitterly denied, cloaked Stalin's real purpose of purging the party ranks of all who might prove disloyal to him. In Dec., 1936, the Soviet government obtained the expulsion of Trotsky from Norway, and he settled with his family in a suburb of Mexico City. There he continued to challenge the Stalinist regime in his writings. He also founded the Fourth International, a minor, but highly articulate, group that advocated Trotsky's program of world revolution and the establishment of pure Communism. An unsuccessful attack on Trotsky's life was made in May, 1940. A second attack came in Aug., 1940; Trotsky died of wounds inflicted with an alpenstock. His assassin, Spanish-born Ramón Mercader posing under the assumed name Frank Jackson, had gained access to Trotsky's entourage for several months before the murder. He may have been a Stalinist agent, although this charge was not proved in the trial. The court sentenced him (1943) to imprisonment for 20 years; he was released in 1960. Trotsky's prolific writings are marked by his superlative intelligence—unquestioned even by his enemies—by his indomitable aggressiveness, and by his incisive, always polemical style; they did considerable damage to the Stalinist cause outside the Soviet Union. Among his translated writings are *The Defense of Terrorism* (1921), *Literature and Revolution* (1925), *Lenin* (1925), *My Life* (1930), *History of the Russian Revolution* (3 vol., 1932), *The Revolution Betrayed* (1937), *The Stalin School of Falsification* (1937), *Stalin* (1941), and *Diary in Exile, 1935* (1958). See also study by R. B. Day (1973); B. D. Wolfe, *Three Who Made a Revolution* (1948); Isaac Deutscher, *The Prophet Armed* (1954), *The Prophet Unarmed* (1959), and *The Prophet Outcast* (1963); Isaac Deutscher, ed., *The Age of Permanent Revolution: A Trotsky Anthology* (1964); Nicolas Krasso, ed., *Trotsky* (1972); Francis Wyndham and David King, *Trotsky: A Documentary* (1972).

trotter: see STANDARDBRED HORSE.

trotting races: see HORSE RACING.

troubadours (tro͞o'bədôrz), aristocratic poet-musicians of S France (Provence) who flourished from the end of the 11th cent. through the 13th cent. Many troubadours were noblemen and crusader knights; some were kings, e.g., Richard I, Cœur de Lion; Thibaut IV, king of Navarre; and Alfonso X, king of Castile and León. Of the more than 400 known troubadours living between 1090 and 1292 the most famous are Jaufré Rudel de Blaia, Bernart de Ventadorn, Peire VIDAL, Raimbaut de Vaqueiras, FOLQUET DE MARSEILLE (archbishop of Toulouse), BERTRAND DE BORN, Arnaut Daniel, Gaucelm Faidit, Raimon de Miraval, Arnaut de Mareuil, and Guiraut Riquier. Of lower birth were the JONGLEURS who performed the troubadours' works and perhaps assisted in their composition. Troubadour lyrics were sung and accompanied by instruments that probably duplicated the melody (all the music preserved is monophonic). The poems were written in the southern dialect called *langue d'oc.* The most common forms were *sirventes* (political poems), *plancs* (dirges), *albas* (morning songs), pastorals, and *Jeux partis* (disputes); the favorite subjects were courtly love, war, and nature. After the Albigensian Crusade (see ALBIGENSES), in which many troubadours were caught up because their noble patrons were either sympathetic to the heretics or heretics themselves, Provençal culture declined. The influence of the widely traveling troubadours spread to central and N France, where their counterparts were the TROUVÈRES. In Germany they were imitated by the MINNESINGERS. The tradition was also carried to Spain and Italy. In France annual festivals known as the JEUX FLORAUX were established in the 14th cent. to revive troubadour art. See Maurice Valency, *In Praise of Love* (1958); H. J. Chaytor, *The Troubadours* (1970); R. D. L. Jameson, *Trails of the Troubadours* (1970).

Troubetzkoy, Paul, Prince (tro͞obĕtskoi', tro͞obĕts'koi, Rus. tro͞obyĭtskoi'), 1866–1938, Russian sculptor, b. Italy. The son of a Russian nobleman and an American woman, Troubetzkoy worked in Russia, France, Italy, and the United States. His sculpture was influenced by the impressionism of Rodin. Troubetzkoy's finest portraits and animal sculptures date from the early 1900s. Among his illustrious sitters were Tolstoy, Rodin, Anatole France, and George Bernard Shaw. An equestrian portrait is in the Detroit Institute of Arts, and other works are in many major collections.

Troup, George Michael, 1780–1856, governor of Georgia (1823–27), b. McIntosh Bluff, on the Tombigbee River, Ala. (then a part of Georgia). As governor, he was an extreme supporter of states' rights. The final removal of the Creek Indians from Georgia and the cession of their lands to the state was due in great part to his belligerent and uncompromising attitude toward both the Indians and the Federal government. He was also a U.S. Representative (1807–15) and Senator (1816–18, 1829–33).

trout: see SALMON.

trouvères (tro͞ovĕr'), medieval poet-musicians of central and N France, fl. during the later 12th and the 13th cent. The trouvères imitated the TROUBADOURS of the south. Written in the dialect called *langue d'oïl*, their songs include love lyrics, romances, and the heroic CHANSONS DE GESTE. Chief among the trouvères were Conon de Béthune, Le Châtelain de Coucy, Colin Muset, Renaut de Beaujeu, and ADAM DE LA HALLE. See Hendrik van der Werf, *The Chansons of the Troubadours and Trouvères* (1973).

Trouville-sur-Mer (tro͞ovēl'), town (1968 pop 6,577), Calvados dept., N France, on the English Channel. It is a popular beach resort.

Trowbridge (trō'brĭj, trou'–), urban district (1971 pop. 19,245), Wiltshire, S England. It is a market town and a long-established center for the manufacture of woolen goods. The 13th-century parish church contains the tomb of the poet George Crabbe, rector of Trowbridge from 1814 to 1832. There is a College of Further Education in Trowbridge.

Troy, ancient city made famous by Homer's account of the TROJAN WAR. It is also called Ilion or, in Latin, Ilium. Its site is almost universally accepted as the mound now named Hissarlik, in Asian Turkey, c.4 mi (6.4 km) from the mouth of the Dardanelles. Accepting Greek tradition and details in Homeric poems as reliable, Heinrich Schliemann identified the site and conducted excavations there beginning in 1871. Nine successive cities or villages have occupied the site, the earliest dating from the Neolithic period. Attempting to determine which stratum of the mound was the Troy of the Trojan War, Schliemann first gave this distinction to the third stratum and then to the second. Excavations conducted by Wilhelm Dörpfeld in the 1890s indicated that the sixth stratum, representing the sixth settlement of the city, was the Homeric Troy. However, later discoveries by the Univ. of Cincinnati expedition under C. W. Blegen indicated that the seventh level was the Troy of Homer's period. At any rate, it has been definitely established that the Troy of the Trojan War was a Phrygian city and the center of a region known as TROAS. The culture of the Trojans dates from the Bronze Age. The Romans, believing that they themselves were descendants of Aeneas and other Trojans, favored the city, and the ninth of the settlements on the site was of some importance in Roman times. See Heinrich Schliemann, *Troy and Its Remains* (1875) and *Ilios: The City and the Country of the Trojans* (1881, repr. 1968); J. L. Angel, *Troy* (1951); C. W. Blegen, ed., *Troy* (4 vol., 1950–58; supplementary monographs, 1961–63) and *Troy and the Trojans* (1963).

Troy. 1 City (1970 pop. 11,482), seat of Pike co., SE Ala., on the Conecuh River; inc. 1843. Products include lumber and wood items, textiles, truck bodies, feed, and pecans. As late as 1940 voodoo was still practiced in the area. Troy State Univ. and the county museum are there. 2 City (1970 pop. 39,419), Oakland co., SE Mich., a suburb of Detroit; settled 1821, inc. 1955. Its varied manufactures include automobile and electronic parts. The city contains many historic buildings and is the site of Walsh College of Accountancy and Business Administration. 3 City (1970 pop. 62,918), seat of Rensselaer co., E N.Y., on the east bank of the Hudson River; inc. 1816. It is known especially for its manufacture of collars and shirts. Other important products are abrasives, auto parts, instruments, railroad supplies, and apparel. Henry Hudson explored (1609) the area near present Troy, and the site was included in the patroonship given to Kiliaen Van Rensselaer by the Dutch West India Company. The town was laid out in 1786. From 1812 to 1920 it was industrially prosperous and many inventions were made there. During the last 50 years Troy has suffered from the urban blight of many river towns and has lost a large number of its industries. It is the seat of Rensselaer Polytechnic Institute, Russell Sage College, a junior college, and the Emma Willard School. Samuel Wilson of Troy, who was concerned with army beef supply in the War of 1812, is said to have been the original "Uncle Sam." Many buildings of architectural and historic interest are preserved. 4 City (1970 pop. 17,186), seat of Miami co., W central Ohio, on the Great Miami River, in a farm area; inc. 1814. Food-processing machinery, motor generators, gummed paper, and tools are manufactured. Growth and industrialization came with the arrival of the Miami and Erie Canal in 1837. A disastrous flood in 1913 resulted in the creation of the first flood protection district in the United States.

Troyes (trwä), city (1968 pop. 77,009), capital of Aube dept., NE France, on the Seine River. It is an industrial town. Hosiery is the main product. Troyes became an episcopal see in the 4th cent. and the capital of Champagne in the 11th cent. Its commercial importance was reflected in its annual fairs, which attracted merchants from throughout the known world. The fairs set standards of weights and measures for the whole of Europe, the troy weight having survived to this day. Troyes was the first town taken by Joan of Arc on her march to Rheims. The city has some fine Gothic structures, including the Cathedral of St. Peter and St. Paul (13th–16th cent.) and the Church of St. Urban (begun 1262).

Troyes, Treaty of, 1420, agreement between HENRY V of England, CHARLES VI of France, and PHILIP THE GOOD of Burgundy. Its purpose, ultimately unsuccessful, was to settle the issues of the Hundred Years War. Henry was to marry Charles's daughter Catherine and was recognized as "heir of France." Charles was permitted to retain the royal title until his death. The dauphin (later CHARLES VII) was disinherited by the treaty, which he subsequently repudiated.

Troyon, Constant (kôNstäN' trwäyôN'), 1810–65, French painter of the BARBIZON SCHOOL, famous for his pictures of animals, particularly cows, in landscape. Among his paintings are *Oxen at Work* (Louvre) and *Holland Cattle* and *Road in the Woods* (Metropolitan Mus.).

troy weights: see ENGLISH UNITS OF MEASUREMENT.

truce of God, in the Middle Ages, an attempt by the church to limit private warfare. It is also known as the peace of God. Fighting was usually prohibited from Thursday evening until Monday morning and on certain religious holidays. Violators were threatened with excommunication. The practice began in France in the early 11th cent. and had spread to Flanders, Germany, and Italy by the next century. The increasing power of kings and the subsequent rise of strong national governments rendered the truce of God unnecessary and ineffective for enforcing internal peace.

Trucial Oman: see UNITED ARAB EMIRATES.

truck, automotive vehicle designed primarily for the transportation of goods. A truck is constructed on the general lines of the automobile but uses larger and heavier parts. It may be powered by a gasoline internal-combustion engine or a diesel engine. In some trucks propulsion is supplied through a single front or rear axle, in others through two rear axles, and in still others through both front and rear axles. Many trucks have automatic or semiautomatic transmissions. Most trucks are built as a single unit, but larger trucks are frequently combinations of a truck tractor, which contains an engine, transmission, and cab, and a semitrailer, which is a trailer that the tractor hauls. The semitrailer has no forward axle, so that its front end must be supported by a swivel mount, known as the fifth wheel, which is found on the rear of the truck tractor. A full trailer, which can be attached to the rear of a semitrailer, has a front axle and one or two rear axles. In the United States some states place restrictions on the length of a truck and on the maximum weight that can be carried on a single axle. As common carriers, motor trucks have made serious inroads on the earnings of the railroads and are carrying freight over increasingly long distances. Trucks are used today in most parts of the world, and in Asia and Africa they are replacing the camel caravan and human carriers. Those adapted for special purposes include the fire truck; the refrigerated truck, for transporting frozen foods; the tank truck, unlined for oil, glass-lined for milk; and the concrete truck, whose circular body slowly revolves during transit to keep the concrete mixed.

Truckee (trŭk'ē), river, c.100 mi (160 km) long, rising in Lake Tahoe on the Calif.-Nev. line and flowing NE to Pyramid Lake, W Nev. Lake Tahoe Dam of the Newlands project is on the Truckee; Boca Dam is on one of its tributaries.

truck farming, horticultural practice of growing one or more vegetable crops on a large scale for shipment to distant markets. It is usually less intensive and diversified than MARKET GARDENING. At first this type of farming depended on water transportation to markets, but as the use of railroads and large-capacity trucks expanded and refrigerated carriers were introduced, truck farms grew up on the cheaper lands of the West and South to produce and ship seasonal vegetables and also fruits for market in areas where their cultivation is limited by climate. The major truck-farming areas are in California, Texas, Florida, along the Atlantic Coastal Plain, and in the Great Lakes area. Centers for specific crops vary with the season. The most important truck crops are tomatoes, lettuce, melons, beets, celery, radishes, onions, cabbage, and strawberries. See G. J. Stout, *Successful Truck Farming* (1959); G. W. Ware and J. P. McCollum, *Producing Vegetable Crops* (1968); J. W. Tiller, *The Texas Winter Garden* (1971).

Trudeau, Edward Livingston (trōō'dō), 1848–1915, American physician, b. New York City, M.D. Columbia, 1871. As a result of taking care of his brother, who had tuberculosis, he developed the disease. He went to live in the Adirondacks, spending much time in the open, and regained his health. Seeking to aid others suffering from tuberculosis, he founded (1884) at Saranac Lake the Trudeau Sanatorium, where he employed the open-air treatment of the disease and organized (1894) the first laboratory for the study of tuberculosis. The sanatorium closed in 1954 for lack of patients, modern methods of early diagnosis and of treatment having drastically reduced incidence of the disease. See his autobiography (1916); biography by K. E. Harrod (1960); Lawrason Brown et al., *Edward Livingston Trudeau: A Symposium* (1935).

Trudeau, Pierre Elliott (trōōdō'), 1919–, Canadian political leader. A lawyer and law professor known for championing liberal causes, he was elected (1965) to the House of Commons as a Liberal. He became minister of justice and attorney general in Lester Pearson's government in 1967. He succeeded Pearson as Liberal party leader and prime minister in 1968 and won a landslide victory in elections called shortly after he took office. Pursuing independence from U.S. influence, he recognized (1970) the People's Republic of China and promoted Canadian control of its own economy. In 1970, after terrorist activities by the FRONT DE LIBÉRATION DU QUÉBEC, he temporarily instituted martial law. Although the Liberal party lost its majority in Parliament in the general elections of Oct., 1972, Trudeau remained in office, relying on the support of the small New Democratic party to give him a parliamentary majority. His government was defeated (May, 1974) on a motion of no confidence brought against the budget, but in the ensuing elections (July, 1974) Trudeau and the Liberals regained their parliamentary majority. See his *Conversation with Canadians* (1972); study by Walter Stewart (1971).

True, Alfred Charles, 1853–1929, American agricultural expert and educator, b. Middletown, Conn., grad. Wesleyan Univ. (B.A., 1873). Associated with the U.S. Dept. of Agriculture from 1889, he was director of its Office of Experiment Stations (1893–1915) and of its States Relations Service (1915–23). He was noted for his work in agricultural education and became dean of the graduate school of agriculture of Ohio State Univ. in 1923.

Truffaut, François (fräNswä' trüfō'), 1932–, French film director and critic. Among the first and most original of the "new wave" directors of the late 1950s and 60s, Truffaut made consistently charming and engrossing films of outstanding visual power. His *400 Blows* (1959) and *Jules and Jim* (1961) are classic works exploring difficult human relationships with humor and sensitivity. Truffaut's other major films include *Shoot the Piano Player* (1960), *Stolen Kisses* (1968), *The Wild Child* (1971), *Bed and Board* (1972), and *Day for Night* (1973). See studies by Graham Petrie (1970) and C. G. Crisp (1972).

truffle (trŭf'əl) [Fr.], subterranean edible fungus found chiefly in W Europe. Truffles are small, solid, fleshy saprophytic plants that usually grow close to the roots of trees in woodlands. There are several species, varying in color from gray or brown to nearly black. Their flavor is piquant and aromatic, and they have been esteemed a delicacy from ancient times; recipes for their use are found in Greek and Roman writings. The truffles found in the forests of Périgord, France, have been highly regarded since the 15th cent., and their collection is an important industry. Some are canned for export. Truffles have not been successfully cultivated. They are usually hunted with dogs or hogs, which are able to scent them out underground. In the United States, truffles are occasionally found along the Pacific coast and in scattered areas of the eastern half of the country. Truffles are classified in the division FUNGI, class Basidiomycetes, order Tuberales, family Tuberaceae.

Trujillo: see SANTO DOMINGO, city, Dominican Republic.

Trujillo (trōōhē'yō), city (1969 est. pop. 149,000), capital of La Libertad dept., NW Peru, in a fertile oasis of the coastal desert. A thriving commercial and industrial center, Trujillo processes sugarcane and rice and produces textiles, leather goods, food products, and cocaine. Founded in 1534, the city played a significant role in the struggle against Spanish rule. It declared its independence in 1820, served as provisional capital of Peru in 1825, and was the main headquarters for Simón BOLÍVAR. Points of interest include the remains of a wall built in 1617 to defend against English pirates and the Univ. of La Libertad (founded 1824). The pre-Inca ruins of CHANCHAN are nearby.

Trujillo, town (1970 est. pop. 27,000), capital of Trujillo state, W Venezuela. It is an agricultural market. Trujillo was founded in 1578 and was sacked by French pirates in 1678. It was there in 1813 that Simón Bolívar proclaimed his "war to the death" against the Spanish.

Trujillo Molina, Rafael Leonidas (räfäĕl' lāōnē'thäs trōōhē'yō mōlē'nä), 1891–1961, president of the Dominican Republic (1930–38, 1942–52). Trained by U.S. marines during U.S. occupation of the country, he was army chief in the presidency of Horacio VÁSQUEZ, whom he ousted in 1930. He became dictator and retained power until his death even when not in the presidency. His autocratic, efficient, and ruthless regime accomplished considerable material progress. Terroristic methods were used, however, not only to repress Dominican opposition, but also against neighboring Haiti; in 1937, to stop Haitian infiltration, Dominican troops crossed the border and massacred between 10,000 and 15,000 Haitians. Generalissimo Trujillo was constantly embroiled in difficulties with other Caribbean countries, charging that plots were being hatched against him abroad. In 1956 rumor blamed the Trujillo regime for the disappearance from New York City of Jesús de Galíndez, a Columbia Univ. instructor who had sharply criticized Trujillo. Trujillo was assassinated in 1961. See R. D. Crassweller, *Trujillo: The Life and Times of a Caribbean Dictator* (1966); Jesús de Galíndez, *The Era of Trujillo* (pub. after his disappearance, 1973).

Truk (trŭk, trōōk), island group (1970 pop. 15,153), c.39 sq mi (100 sq km), W Pacific, in the E CAROLINE ISLANDS. Truk consists of c.55 volcanic islands surrounded by an atoll reef and many islets. The chief products are copra and dried fish. During World War II, Truk was the site of an important Japanese naval base. Along with neighboring islands, the Truk group constitutes one of the six administrative districts of the Trust Territory of the PACIFIC ISLANDS.

Trullan synod: see CONSTANTINOPLE, THIRD COUNCIL OF.

Truman, Harry S., 1884–1972, 33d President of the United States, b. Lamar, Mo. He grew up on a farm near Independence, Mo., worked at various jobs, and tended the family farm. He served as a captain of field artillery in France in World War I. On his return from the war he married (1919) Elizabeth (Bess) Virginia Wallace; they had one daughter, Mary Margaret. After a brief partnership in a haberdashery store, Truman turned to politics and, with support from the Democratic machine of Thomas J. PENDERGAST, was elected judge (1922–24) and president judge (1926–34) of Jackson co., Mo. He attended (1923–25) the Kansas City school of law. In 1934 he was elected a U.S. Senator. In the Senate he was a firm supporter of the New Deal policies of President Franklin Delano Roosevelt, but the administration was cool toward Truman because of his connection with Pendergast. By 1940 the Pendergast machine had been broken, and Truman had a hard fight for reelection. In his second term he achieved national prominence as chairman of a Senate committee to investigate government expenditures in World War II. His vigorous investigations revealed startling inefficiency and bungling on war contracts. Because he was acceptable both to the conservative Democrats and the New Dealers as well as to powerful labor leaders, Truman was nominated for Vice President in 1944 and was elected to office along with President Roosevelt. On the death (April 12, 1945) of Roosevelt, Truman succeeded to the presidency. He assumed power at a very critical time. He was immediately confronted with the problems of concluding the war and preparing for the difficulties of international postwar readjustment. The war in Europe ended with Germany's unconditional surrender on May 8, 1945, and in July Truman attended the POTSDAM CONFERENCE to discuss the postwar European settlement. To end the conflict with Japan, he authorized the dropping of the atomic bomb on Hiroshima and Nagasaki. That action did bring the war to an immediate end, but the morality of it continues to be debated. At home, inflation and demobilization were the chief worries of reconversion to a peacetime economy. Although Truman began quietly to eliminate the old New Dealers from the administration, his domestic policies were essentially a continuation of those of the New Deal. His program (later labeled the Fair Deal) called for guaranteed full employment, a permanent Fair Employment Practices Committee (against racial discrimination), an increased minimum wage and extended social security benefits, price and rent controls, public housing projects, and public health insurance. However, Congress, which was controlled by the Republicans after the 1946 elections, blocked most of these projects, while passing other legislation—notably the TAFT-HARTLEY LABOR ACT (1947)—over Truman's veto. In foreign affairs Truman found his chief adversary in the USSR. Relations with that country deteriorated rapidly after Potsdam. The two powers were unable to agree to feasible plans for the unification of Germany, general disarmament, or the establishment of a United Nations armed force. Truman took an increasingly tough stand against what he considered to be the threat of Communist expansion in S and W Europe. In 1947 he proposed a program of economic and military aid to Greece and Turkey, stating that it should be a principle of U.S. policy "to support free peoples who are resisting attempted subjugation by armed minorities or by outside pressures." Enunciation of the so-called Truman Doctrine signaled the beginning of the policy of "containment" of Communism. It was implemented by the adoption of the MARSHALL PLAN (1947), designed to effect the economic reconstruction of Europe, by the POINT FOUR PROGRAM (1949) of technical aid to underdeveloped countries, and, above all, by the creation (1949) of the NORTH ATLANTIC TREATY ORGANIZATION. In 1948, Truman announced a major civil rights program and ordered the desegregation of the armed forces. As a result, a bloc of southern Democrats bolted the party and sponsored J. Strom THURMOND for President in the election of that year. Truman was also challenged on the left by Henry A. WALLACE of the Progressive party. Although he won renomination, the President was thought to have little chance of reelection. But Truman embarked on a vigorous whistlestop campaign across the country, blaming the Republican Congress for most of the nation's ills and highlighting its inactivity by calling a special session of Congress, at which he urged the Republicans to enact into law their own moderately liberal party platform. The campaign was a resounding success. Contrary to all the predictions, Truman defeated his Republican opponent, Thomas E. DEWEY, and Democratic majorities swept into the House and Senate. In his second administration Truman made little progress with his Fair Deal programs, although he did secure passage of a housing act (1949). Domestic affairs were increasingly dominated by the fear of Communist subversion. Truman had instituted (1947) a loyalty program for civil servants, but the government came under increasing attack for loose security, especially after the conviction of Alger HISS. Truman dismissed the charges of internal subversion as a "red herring" and in 1950 vetoed the McCarran Internal Security Act, which provided for the registration of Communist and Communist-front organizations. Congress, however, passed the act over his veto. Overseas developments contributed considerably to the tide of fear within the United States. Truman's administration was blamed by many for the collapse of the regime of Chiang Kai-shek (toward which the administration had been cool) and the victory of the Communists in China. The success of the Chinese Revolution was followed hard by the outbreak (1950) of the KOREAN WAR. Truman immediately sent U.S. troops to Korea under the aegis of the United Nations. However, in 1951 he raised the controversy that had been building up around American foreign policy to a new pitch of intensity when he dismissed Gen. Douglas MACARTHUR from his Far Eastern command for insubordination in publicly advocating an attack on Communist China. At home Truman became involved in further controversy when he seized (1952) the steel industry in order to prevent a strike. He claimed that the action was justified by the President's inherent powers in time of emergency, but the Supreme Court overruled him. Disclosures of corruption among Federal officials were also politically damaging during this period. Truman declined renomination in 1952 and pressed the presidential candidacy of Adlai Stevenson, who was, however, overwhelmingly defeated by the Republican candidate, Dwight D. Eisenhower. Truman remained active in politics for many years after his retirement, campaigning around the country for Democratic candidates and commenting on national issues. He also contributed much time to the Harry S. Truman Library, which opened in 1957 in Independence, Mo. Truman died on Dec. 26, 1972. Since Truman did not have great success with his domestic programs (although many of his reform proposals were later enacted into law) his reputation depends largely on his foreign policy. Thrust into office largely ignorant of foreign affairs, he acted decisively in erecting the machinery of "containment" against the threat of Communist expansion and committing the United States to a new internationalism. Some historians, however, have challenged the assumption of a Communist threat on which Truman's actions were based. They argue that the cold war confrontation between the United States and the Soviet Union could have been averted by a more conciliatory attitude on the part of the Truman administration. Truman's achievements, therefore, remain a subject of great controversy. Truman wrote *Year of Decisions* (1955), *Years of Trial and Hope* (1956), and *Mr. Citizen* (1960). See biographies by Jonathan Daniels (1950, repr. 1971), Alfred Steinberg (1962), and by his daughter, Margaret Truman (1972); C. B. H. Phillips, *The Truman Presidency* (1966); Bert Cochran, *Harry Truman and the Crisis Presidency* (1973); A. L. Hamby, *Beyond the New Deal* (1973); Merle Miller, *Plain Speaking* (1974).

Trumbull, John, 1750–1831, American poet, b. Westbury (now Watertown), Conn. He passed the entrance examinations to Yale when he was seven, but did not enter until he was thirteen. While tutoring at Yale he wrote *The Progress of Dulness* (1772–73), a satire on educational follies. In 1773 he entered the law office of John Adams and was drawn into the political fervor of his times, writing the bombastic *An Elegy of the Times* (1774) and the mock-epic burlesque of Tory politics, *M'Fingal* (1775–82). One of the CONNECTICUT WITS, he contributed to the *Anarchiad* and the *Echo* and was an ardent Federalist.

Trumbull, John, 1756–1843, American painter, b. Lebanon, Conn.; son of Gov. Jonathan Trumbull. He served in the Continental Army early in the Revolution as an aide to Washington. He resigned his commission in 1777 and devoted himself to painting. In 1780 he went to London to study under Benjamin West. There he was imprisoned on suspicion of treason and finally deported. In 1784 he returned to London, where, at the suggestion of West and with the encouragement of Thomas Jefferson, he began his famous national history, which occupied most of his life. His small paintings (for the engraver) at Yale Univ., such as the *Battle of Bunker's Hill* (1786) and *Death of Montgomery at Quebec* (1788), are among his finest works. Trumbull excelled in small-scale painting, especially of oil miniatures (studies for the historical series), the best of which were done in the United States between 1789 and 1793. In the latter year he returned to London as secretary to John Jay and remained for 10 years as one of the commissioners to carry out provisions of the Jay Treaty. He returned to the United States in 1804 with a collection of old masters. He painted portraits, panoramas, and landscapes, and designed the meetinghouse in Lebanon, Conn. In London from 1808 to 1816 he tried unsuccessfully to establish himself as a fashionable portraitist. Returning to New York in 1816, he finally secured a commission from Congress to decorate the Capitol rotunda; his *Signing of the Declaration of Independence, Surrender of Burgoyne at Saratoga, Surrender of Cornwallis at Yorktown,* and *Resignation of Washington* are of interest chiefly for their documentary value. In 1831 he founded the Trumbull Gallery at Yale, one of the earliest art museums in the English-speaking colonies, depositing much of his work in exchange for an annuity. He is well represented in the Museum of Fine Arts, Boston; the Wadsworth Athenaeum, Hartford, Conn.; Yale Univ.; and the Metropolitan Museum, New York City Hall, and the New-York Historical Society. See his autobiography (1841; new ed., by Theodore Sizer, 1953); studies by Theodore Sizer (1950 and 1967).

Trumbull, Jonathan, 1710–85, colonial governor of Connecticut, b. Lebanon, Conn. He was prominent in the colony after 1733, serving in the assembly, of which he became speaker, and in other offices. He was chief justice of the superior court and deputy governor before becoming governor in 1769. He served until 1784 and rendered great services to George Washington in the American Revolution. There is a tradition that the name Brother Jonathan, for an American, arose from a remark of Washington about Trumbull. See biographies by Jonathan Trumbull (1919), a descendant, and Glenn Weaver (1956).

Trumbull, Lyman, 1813–96, U.S. Senator from Illinois (1855–73), b. Colchester, Conn. He taught school in Georgia, was admitted to the bar, and in 1837 moved to Illinois. After serving in the state legislature (1840), as Illinois secretary of state (1841–43), and as a justice of the state supreme court (1848–53), he was elected (1854) to the House of Representatives but was appointed to the Senate before Congress convened. Formerly a Democrat, he became a Republican and a staunch supporter of Abraham Lincoln. Often allied with the radical Republicans on Reconstruction measures, he nevertheless refused to follow them in their attempt to remove Andrew Johnson from office. In the impeachment trial he was one of the handful of Republican Senators who supported the President. In 1872 he was a leader of the LIBERAL REPUBLICAN PARTY, but eventually returned to the Democratic fold. He was one of the counsels for Samuel J. Tilden in the contested Hayes-Tilden election of 1876. See biographies by Horace White (1913) and M. M. Krug (1965).

Trumbull, town (1970 pop. 31,394), Fairfield co., SW Conn.; settled in the 1660s, inc. 1797. It has some light industry.

Trümmelbach, Switzerland: see LAUTERBRUNNEN.

trumpet, brass wind musical instrument of cylindrical bore, in the shape of a flattened loop and having three piston valves to regulate the pitch. Its origin is ancient; records of a type of simple valveless trumpet are found in China from as early as 2000 B.C., and it is mentioned in the Bible and in Greek and Roman history. It attained its present shape early in the 15th cent., at which time it became an important ceremonial instrument. It was used in the opera or-

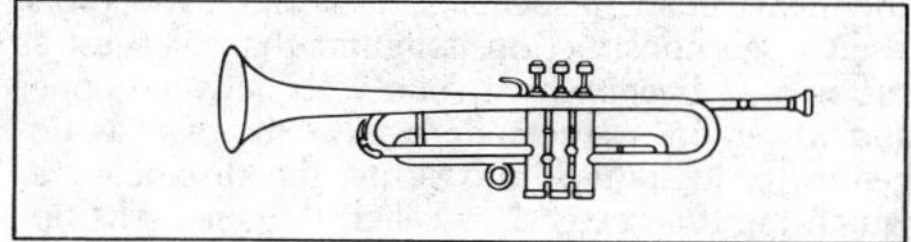

Trumpet

chestra as early as Monteverdi's *Orfeo* (1607) and became a standard orchestral instrument later in the century. At this time the trumpet lacked valves, and a highly developed technique existed for playing in the upper register of the instrument, where a complete diatonic scale was available. The trumpet parts of Bach and Handel were written for such a style. Later in the 18th cent. this bright quality was not desired, and the trumpet was used more in its lower register. The instrument will accept a MUTE, used to repress some of its stridency. Crooks, additional lengths of tubing, were added to the natural trumpet to allow the adjustment of pitch. This was a fairly clumsy method, however, and was superseded in the early 19th cent., when valves were added. A TRANSPOSING INSTRUMENT, it is now most often in B flat. A bass trumpet in C was first called for by Wagner. The trumpet is an important member of most dance and jazz bands.

trumpet creeper and **trumpet vine:** see BIGNONIA.

trunkfish, any member of a family of fishes, also called boxfishes, that have short triangular bodies covered by firmly united hexagonal bony plates. Only the jaw, the bases of the fins, and the tail protrude from this carapace, and the locomotion of these fishes is necessarily peculiar. The dorsal and anal fins propel the fish with a rotary motion, while the tail acts as a rudder. The ventral fins move continually, forcing air through the constricted gill openings. Many trunkfishes are patterned in bright colors. They are sluggish, frequenting shallow water and feeding on minute plant and animal matter. Members of some species have been found to secrete a poison, fatal to other fishes, when disturbed. Trunkfishes are most abundant in tropical waters. The cowfish, one of the larger trunkfish species, is up to 1 ft (30 cm) long and has a short spine over each eye. Trunkfish have palatable flesh and are served baked in their shells by the inhabitants of some South Pacific islands. They are classified in the phylum CHORDATA, subphylum Vertebrata, class Osteichthyes, order Tetraodontiformes, family Ostraciidae.

Truro (trŏŏr'ō), town (1971 pop. 13,047), central N.S., Canada, near the head of Cobequid Bay, an arm of the Bay of Fundy. It is a railroad and industrial center, with lumber mills, printing plants, and other factories. The Nova Scotia Agricultural College there is the headquarters of the provincial agricultural extension service. An early Acadian settlement called Cobequid, the town was destroyed (1755) when the Acadians were expelled. After 1759 it received settlers from New England and Northern Ireland, who named the town for Truro, England.

truss, in architecture and engineering, a supporting structure or framework composed of beams, girders, or rods commonly of steel or wood lying in a single plane. A truss usually takes the form of a triangle or combination of triangles, since this design ensures the greatest rigidity. Trusses are used for large spans and heavy loads, especially in bridges and roofs. Their open construction is lighter than, yet just as strong as, a beam with a solid web between upper and lower lines. The members are known as tiebeams, posts, rafters, and struts; the distance over which the truss extends is called the span. The upper and lower lines or beams are connected by web members.

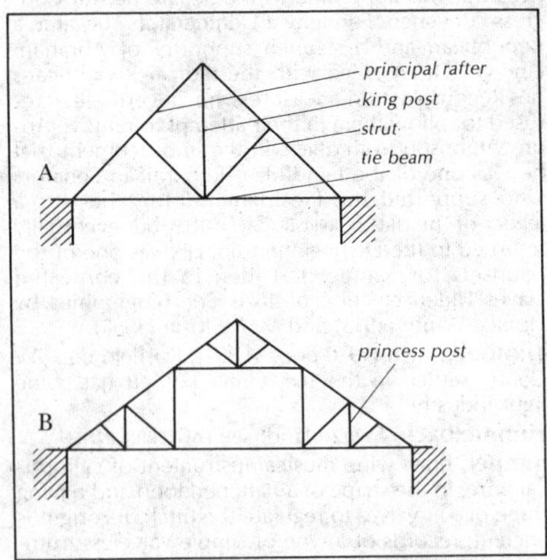

A. *King post truss*

B. *Queen, with princess posts*

trust, in law, arrangement whereby property legally owned by one person is administered for the benefit of another. Three parties are ordinarily needed for the relation to arise: the settlor, who bequeaths or deeds his property for another's benefit; the trustee, in whose hands the control of the property is vested and who receives a fee fixed by law; and the beneficiary, for whose use the proceeds of the property are to be applied. In some cases the settlor may name himself trustee or beneficiary, but it is indispensable that the trustee (legal owner) and the beneficiary (equitable owner) be different persons. The trustee's duty is to make the capital or earnings available to the beneficiary in the manner prescribed by the settlor and to manage the property prudently and honestly. The beneficiary may bring suit if this duty is breached. In modern times banks and trust companies, with their special facilities for handling investments, are often named the trustees of substantial properties. The arrangement at which the SHERMAN ANTITRUST ACT was directed was a business application of the trust form. The Standard Oil Company, for example, induced stockholders in various enterprises to assign their stock to a board of trustees and to receive dividend-bearing trust certificates in return. The board was thus able to manage simultaneously enterprises that many believed should have been in active competition. Soon most business combinations in restraint of trade came to be called trusts, whether in the legal form of a trust or otherwise. A horizontal trust is a combination of corporations engaged in the same line of business. A vertical trust is an organization that controls all or part of a series of operations extending from the procuring of the raw materials to the retailing of the finished products. In Europe the term CARTEL is applied to a monopoly or trust, but the term is broader in that it may have international scope, and there, as in the United States, it may be either vertical or horizontal. Trusts have been opposed as monopolies, and laws have been enacted to prohibit or control them. They have been defended as reducing costs through large-scale operations and avoiding the expenses of competition. In the United States trusts grew rapidly from 1880, and by 1905 most of the important mergers in American industry had been formed. The Sherman Antitrust Act, passed by Congress in 1890, made illegal all "agreements in restraint of trade" and all "attempts to monopolize" industry; but the law was not vigorously enforced. The CLAYTON ANTITRUST ACT (1914) was designed to stop various practices of "unfair" competition, and the Federal Trade Commission was given power to issue "cease and desist" orders when violations were found. To protect small retailers the states in the 1920s began to regulate chain stores by means of heavy taxation. In 1936 the Robinson-Patman Act made it illegal for sellers to discriminate as to price between large and small buyers in the wholesale market. This was followed by the Miller-Tydings Act (1937), which permits manufacturers to fix the price at which retailers may sell their product and prevents large retailers from unfairly underselling smaller ones. The effect of much of this legislation was to limit competition and thus favor monopoly, while it tended to equalize the conditions under which large and small retailers do business. See MONOPOLY. See A. A. Berle, Jr., and G. C. Means, *The Modern Corporation and Private Property* (1932, rev. ed. 1969); Wendell Berge, *Cartels* (1944); R. R. B. Powell, *Cases and Materials on Trusts and Wills* (1960); Milton Handler, *Cases and Materials on Trade Regulations* (4th ed. 1967); Alex Hunter, ed., *Monopoly and Competition* (1969).

trusteeship, territorial, system of UN control for territories that are not self-governing. It replaced the MANDATES of the League of Nations. Provided for under chapters 12 and 13 of the Charter of the United Nations, the trusteeship system is intended to promote the welfare of the native inhabitants and to advance them toward self-government. Trust territories were created out of former mandate territories of the League of Nations (with the exception of SOUTH WEST AFRICA, which remained under mandate) and former possessions of the Axis powers. Other dependent territories (colonies) remain outside the trusteeship system but come under the jurisdiction of chapter 11 of the Charter of the United Nations, which obligates members responsible for dependencies to promote the welfare of their inhabitants. The trusteeship system is supervised by the UN Trusteeship Council, which consists of the members of the United Nations administering trust territories and an equal number of other member nations, including all permanent members of the Security Council that do not administer such territories. Each territory is governed by the provisions of a trusteeship agreement. Agreements that cover nonstrategic areas are approved by the General Assembly and agreements concerning strategic areas are approved by the Security Council. Unlike territories under mandate, trusteeship territories may be fortified. The powers of the administering state usually include full legislative, administrative, and judicial authority and, in certain cases, the right to treat the territory as if it were part of the administering state. Each year the Trusteeship Council submits to the responsible state a detailed questionnaire concerning each territory, with special emphasis on measures taken to increase self-government and educational opportunities. The council considers petitions from inhabitants of the territories and periodically makes inspection tours. It meets at least once a year and by majority vote (not subject to veto) adopts recommendations. In 1949 the General Assembly, by virtue of the League of Nations mandate over Palestine, declared Jerusalem a trust territory under the administration of the whole United Nations. Because of the opposition of Israel and Jordan, the two occupying states, the implementation of this recommendation had to be postponed indefinitely. By 1973, only two territories, New Guinea and the Pacific Islands, remained under the trusteeship system. Italian Somaliland joined British Somaliland to become (1960) Somalia; British Togoland joined (1956) Ghana, and French Togoland became (1960) Togo; French Cameroons became (1960) Cameroon and was joined by the southern part of British Cameroons; the northern part was joined to Nigeria. Tanganyika gained its independence in 1961, Samoa in 1962, and Ruanda-Urundi became two separate states, Rwanda and Burundi, in 1962; Nauru became independent in 1968. See J. N. Murray, Jr., *The United Nations Trusteeship System* (1957); C. E. Toussaint, *The Trusteeship System of the United Nations* (1957); A. G. Mezerik, ed., *Colonialism and the United Nations* (1964).

Truth, Sojourner, c.1797–1883, American abolitionist, a freed slave, originally called Isabella, b. Ulster co., N.Y. Convinced that she heard heavenly voices, she left (1843) domestic employment in New York City, adopted the name Sojourner Truth, and traveled throughout the North preaching emancipation and woman's rights. A remarkable personality, she spoke with much effectiveness even though she remained illiterate. See Olive Gilbert, *Narrative of Sojourner Truth* (1878, repr. 1968); biographies by A. H. Fauset (1938, repr. 1971) and H. E. Pauli (1962).

Trutnov (trōōt'nôf), Ger. *Trautenau,* city (1970 pop. 24,892), N Czechoslovakia, in Bohemia, near the Polish border. It is a center of the Czech linen industry.

Truxtun, Thomas, 1755–1822, American naval officer, b. near Hempstead, L.I., N.Y. In the American Revolution he won a name as a privateer, seizing many British prizes. Later he was a sea captain in merchant trade until the U.S. navy was organized. In the "near war" with France (1798–1800), he commanded the CONSTELLATION and earned an outstanding reputation. He captured the French frigate *L'Insurgente* (1799) and then later defeated *La Vengeance* (1800), although he was prevented by a storm from taking the latter ship as a prize. Shortly afterward he retired from the navy. His name also appears as Truxton. See E. S. Ferguson, *Truxtun of the Constellation* (1956).

Tryon, Dwight William (trī'ən), 1849–1925, American landscape painter, b. Hartford, Conn., studied in Paris under C. F. Daubigny and Jacquesson de la Chevreuse. Upon his return to the United States he became established as an artist and teacher in New York City. He later taught at Smith for 38 years and donated to the college the art gallery that bears his name. He painted rosy, atmospheric landscapes. Large collections of his work are at Smith and in the Freer Gallery of Art, Washington, D.C. See study by H. C. White (1930).

Tryon, William, 1729–88, English colonial governor in North America. After a distinguished army career he was appointed (1764) lieutenant governor of North Carolina and succeeded (1765) Arthur Dobbs as governor. Tryon was an able administrator but became unpopular with the colonists because of his rigorous suppression (1771) of the REGULATOR MOVEMENT. In 1771 he was appointed governor of New York, and at the outbreak of the American Revolution he was forced to remain on a British ship in the harbor. Tryon returned to power when William Howe took the city (1776), and later (1777, 1779) he led Tory raids in Connecticut. See M. D. Haywood,

Governor William Tryon and the Administration of the Province of North Carolina (1903).

trypanosome (trĭp'ənəsōm''), microscopic, one-celled organism of the genus *Trypanosoma,* typically living as an active parasite in the bloodstream of a vertebrate; hundreds of species are known. A trypanosome is long and pointed and possesses a flagellum. The flagellum arises at the front, or anterior, end of the parasite and curves back to form the edge of a long, undulating membrane used in locomotion. Trypanosomes have a complex life cycle; most species undergo part of their development in the digestive tract of insects, which spread the parasite by biting. Many do not appear to harm their hosts, but a number of species cause serious diseases in man or domestic animals. *Trypanosoma gambiense* causes African sleeping sickness and is transmitted by tsetse flies. *Trypanosoma cruzi* is the cause of Chagas' disease, prevalent in South America, which affects the nervous system and heart; it is transmitted by the bite of ASSASSIN BUGS. Other species, restricted in distribution to Africa and Asia, cause diseases of horses and cattle. Control measures include elimination or reduction of the insect carrier populations and measures to reduce the likelihood of bites. Trypanosomes are classified in the phylum PROTOZOA, subphylum Mastigophora.

trypanosomiasis (trəpăn''əsōmī'əsĭs), infectious disease caused by a protozoan organism, the TRYPANOSOME, which exists as a parasite in the blood of a number of vertebrate hosts. The three variations of the disease that predominate in humans are transmitted by an insect vector: Two types of African sleeping sickness are caused, respectively, by *Trypanosoma rhodesiense* and *T. gambiense,* both transmitted by the bite of the tsetse fly. South American trypanosomiasis, or Chagas' disease, is caused by *T. cruzi,* which is transmitted by certain species of bugs; the parasite enters the skin when infected bug feces are rubbed into the site of the bite. The characteristic symptoms of Chagas' disease are edema, hard, red nodular outbreaks of the skin, and damage to the heart muscle; there is no effective treatment. Symptoms of African sleeping sickness may appear at once, after several weeks, or even after years in the Gambian type. Early disturbances include inflammation at the site of the bite, intermittent fever, enlargement of the spleen; in the Gambian variety the lymph nodes are enlarged. Subsequent signs of heart damage, personality changes, and headache develop. The final stages are marked by tremor, disturbed speech and gait, emaciation, and a prolonged comatose state. African trypanosomiasis is treated with suramin sodium and other drugs, which are most effective when injected in early stages of the disease, i.e., before the central nervous system is affected. Such drugs will also provide protection against infection for 2 months or more. Even with treatment, the disease is often fatal and the prognosis becomes grave after the nervous system is invaded. Prevention of sleeping sickness involves the use of insecticides and the clearing of vegetation that harbors the tsetse fly.

Tryphena (trīfē'nə) and **Tryphosa** (trīfō'sə), two Christian women at Rome. Rom. 16.12.

trypsin, ENZYME that acts to degrade PROTEIN; it is often referred to as a proteolytic enzyme, or proteinase. Trypsin is one of the three principal digestive proteinases, the other two being PEPSIN and CHYMOTRYPSIN. In the digestive process, trypsin acts with the other proteinases to break down dietary protein molecules to their component peptides and amino acids. Trypsin continues the process of digestion (begun in the stomach) in the small intestine where a slightly alkaline environment (about *p*H 8) promotes its maximal enzymatic activity. Trypsin, produced in an inactive form by the pancreas, is remarkably similar in chemical composition and in structure to the other chief pancreatic proteinase, chymotrypsin. Both enzymes also appear to have similar mechanisms of action; residues of HISTIDINE and SERINE are found in the active sites of both. The chief difference between the two molecules seems to be in their specificity, that is, each is active only against the peptide bonds in protein molecules that have carboxyl groups donated by certain amino acids. For trypsin these amino acids are arginine and lysine, for chymotrypsin they are tyrosine, phenylalanine, tryptophan, methionine, and leucine. Trypsin is the most discriminating of all the proteolytic enzymes in terms of the restricted number of chemical bonds that it will attack. Good use of this fact has been made by chemists interested in the determination of the amino acid sequence of proteins; trypsin is widely employed as a reagent for the orderly and unambiguous cleavage of such molecules.

tryptophan (trĭp'təfăn), organic compound, one of the 22 α-AMINO ACIDS commonly found in animal proteins. Only the L-stereoisomer appears in mammalian protein. It is one of several essential amino acids needed in the diet; human beings cannot synthesize it from simpler metabolites. Young adults require about 7 mg of this amino acid per day per kg (3 mg per lb) of body weight. Nicotinic acid (niacin), a VITAMIN of the B complex, can be made from tryptophan in the body, but evidently the rate of transformation is insufficient for the demands of normal growth and maintenance, and hence nicotinic acid must be supplied in the diet. Deficiency of tryptophan in the diet enhances the progress of the vitamin-deficiency disease PELLAGRA, which is treated by restoring nicotinic acid to the diet, usually supplemented with tryptophan. Bacteria in the intestine break tryptophan down to compounds such as skatole and indole, which to a great extent are responsible for the unpleasant odor of feces. Tryptophan contributes to the structure of proteins into which it has been incorporated by the tendency of its side chain to participate in hydrophobic interactions (see ISOLEUCINE). The amino acid was isolated from casein (milk protein) in 1901, and its structure was established in 1907.

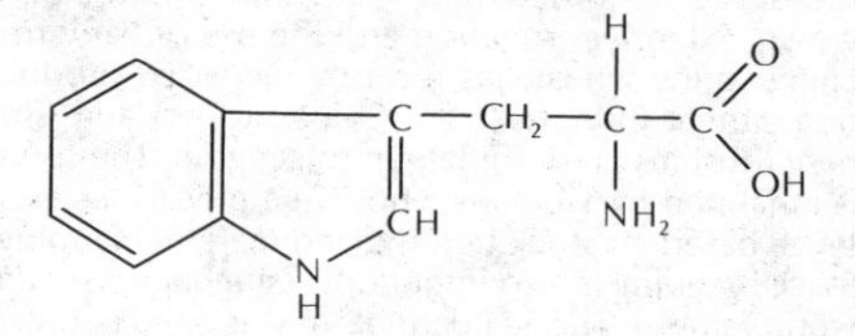

tryptophan

trystie: see GUILLEMOT.

Tsaidam (tsī'däm), Mandarin *Ch'i-ta-mu,* arid basin, c.350 mi (560 km) long and c.100 mi (160 km) wide, between two branches of the Kunlun range, central Tsinghai prov., W China. A salt marsh occupies most of the area. Oil fields and refineries are found in W Tsaidam, and iron ore is mined in the southern part.

Ts'ai Yüan-p'ei (tsī yüän-pā), 1867–1940, Chinese educator and intellectual leader. He achieved distinction as a classical scholar but later joined (1904) the anti-Manchu revolutionary movement at Shanghai. Ts'ai studied philosophy in Germany (1907–11). He returned to China during the republican revolution of 1911 and was appointed education minister in the early cabinets of SUN YAT-SEN and YÜAN SHIH-K'AI. After further study in Germany and France (1912–16), Ts'ai was appointed (1916) chancellor of Peking Univ. He encouraged a critical reevaluation of Chinese culture and promoted freedom of thought, thereby paving the way for the intellectual revolution (1917–21) known as the MAY FOURTH MOVEMENT. After the establishment of the Nanking government (1928), Ts'ai used his prestige as a KUOMINTANG party elder to promote civil liberties and oppose political control of the student movement.

Tsaldaris, Panayoti (pänäyō'tē tsälthä'rēs), 1868–1936, Greek politician. A leader of the Populist (royalist) party, he succeeded Eleutherios VENIZELOS as premier in Nov., 1932, and again, after a brief return to power by Venizelos, in March, 1933. In 1935 the Venizelists rose against the royalist policy of Tsaldaris, but they were crushed by General KONDYLIS. Tsaldaris's government won in the 1935 elections, from which the republicans abstained; however, he was ousted by Kondylis in Oct., 1935. A relative of Tsaldaris, **Constantine Tsaldaris,** 1884–1970, leader of the Populist party, became (1946) the first elected postwar premier of Greece. He faded from prominence after 1951, when new elections dealt a severe blow to his party.

Tsamkong: see CHAN-CHIANG, China.

Tsana: see TANA, lake, Ethiopia.

Tsangpo, river, Tibet: see BRAHMAPUTRA.

Tsankov, Alexander (tsän'kôf), 1879–1959, Bulgarian politician. A professor of political economy at the Univ. of Sofia, he was instrumental in the overthrow (1923) of the dictatorship of Alexander STAMBULISKI. As premier (1923–26), he mercilessly fought members of the Peasants' and Communist parties, and his administration's relations with Greece and Yugoslavia were strained. After his government fell, Tsankov remained active in right-wing politics and favored the Nazis. In 1944 he fled Bulgaria. He died in Buenos Aires. His name is also spelled Tsankoff, Zankoff, or Zankov.

Tsankov, Dragan (drä'gän), 1828–1911, Bulgarian politician. As journalist and later as professor he played an important part in achieving the autonomy of the Bulgarian Church from the patriarchate of Constantinople and in establishing the Bulgarian state. He was vice president of the constituent assembly, founded the Russophile Liberal party, and became (1879) diplomatic agent at Constantinople. Made premier in 1880, he disagreed with Prince Alexander and was imprisoned (1882–83). He formed a government when Alexander abdicated, but it was soon replaced by a regency.

Tsaritsyn: see VOLGOGRAD, USSR.

Tsarskoye Selo: see PUSHKIN, USSR.

Tsavo National Park (tsä'vō), 8,034 sq mi (20,808 sq km), SE Kenya; est. 1948. Located on the semiarid plains, it is a sanctuary for the large animals of E Africa. Lava cones and the Mzimi Springs are found there.

Tschaikovsky, Nikolai Vasilyevich: see CHAYKOVSKY, NIKOLAI VASILYEVICH.

Tschaikowsky, Piotr Ilich: see TCHAIKOVSKY.

Tse Hsi, Chinese empress dowager: see T'ZU HSI.

Tselinny Kray (tsā'lĭnē krī) or **Virgin Lands Territory,** former administrative division, c.231,000 sq mi (598,300 sq km), Central Asian USSR, in Kazakhstan. Created in 1960 by the merger of Kokchetav, Kustanay, North Kazakhstan, Pavlodar, and Akmolinsk oblasts to administer the grain-producing areas of the Kazakh steppe, it was abolished in the late 1960s.

Tselinograd (tsĭlyē''nōgrät'), city (1970 pop. 180,000), capital of Tselinny Kray, Central Asian USSR, in Kazakhstan, on the Ishim River. It is a railroad junction and a center for the production of agricultural machinery and chemicals. The city was founded as a fortress in 1824. It was called Akmolinsk and was the capital of the former Akmolinsk oblast until 1961, when it was renamed.

Tseng Kuo-fan (dzŭng gwô-fän), 1811–72, Chinese general and statesman of the Ch'ing dynasty. He organized (1853) the Hunan army, the first of the great regional armies that were raised to suppress the Taiping Rebellion. Appointed governor-general of Kiangsu, Anhwei, and Kiangsi provs. (1860), Tseng coordinated the military campaign that crushed the Taiping main forces and took the rebel capital at Nanking in 1864. He advocated a policy of conciliation with the Western powers and military self-strengthening. Under his sponsorship the Kiangnan Arsenal was established at Shanghai in 1865. In addition to producing the first modern weapons and ships, the arsenal's translation bureau played a major role in introducing Western technology and thought to China. Tseng was appointed a grand secretary (1867) and was made (1868) governor-general of Chihli (Hopei) prov. With the death of Tseng and the involvement of TSO TSUNG-T'ANG in suppressing the Muslim rebellion in NW China, LI HUNG-CHANG became the leader of the self-strengthening movement. See study by W. J. Hail (1927, repr. 1964).

Tsesis: see CESIS, USSR.

tsetse fly (tsĕt'sē), name for any of several blood-sucking African FLIES of the genus *Glossina,* and in the same family as the HOUSEFLY. The larva of the tsetse fly develops inside the body of the mother until it is ready to pupate in the soil. A number of the 21 species can transmit to humans the trypanosomes that cause the Gambian and Rhodesian forms of African sleeping sickness (see TRYPANOSOMIASIS; ENCEPHALITIS). The tsetse fly also carries the trypanosomes that cause nagana and other diseases of wild and domestic animals. Clearing the brush that the flies inhabit helps to get rid of them; DDT (see separate article) has also been used to exterminate them. Tsetse flies are classified in the phylum ARTHROPODA, class Insecta, order Diptera, family Muscidae. See INSECT.

Tshombe, Moise Kapenda (mô-ēs' kəpĕn'dä chŏm'bā), 1919–69, political leader in the Republic of the Congo (now Zaïre). He was related to the royal family of the Lunda tribe and received his education at mission schools. In 1951 he was elected to the advisory provisional council of Katanga (now Shaba) and later became (1959) president of the Belgian-supported Conakat, the strongest political party in Katanga. In 1960 he attended the Brussels Congo Conference, where he pressed for a loose federation of independent states in the Congo. In the general elections of 1960 Conakat gained control of the Katanga provincial legislature, and, when the Congo became an independent republic,

Tshombe proclaimed Katanga's secession from the country. He worked closely with Belgian business interests, appointed a Belgian officer to command his army, and refused to cooperate with either the United Nations or the central government led by Patrice LUMUMBA. In Aug., 1960, he was elected president of Katanga; he maintained a large mercenary army to fight against UN troops. He was charged by a UN investigation commission with complicity in the murder (Jan., 1961) of Lumumba in Katanga. In April, 1961, Tshombe was arrested by the central government but was released when he pledged to reunite Katanga with the Congo. He quickly repudiated the promise and continued to defy the central government. Finally forced to capitulate, Tshombe went into exile in Europe in 1963. He returned, however, in 1964, and, in July, President Kasavubu named him premier of a government of national reconciliation. He served until Oct., 1965, when Kasavubu dismissed him. Accused (1966) of treason against the government, Tshombe went into exile in Spain and was sentenced (1967) to death in absentia. In June, 1967, a plane in which he was flying was hijacked to Algeria, where he was first jailed and then kept incommunicado until his death in 1969. See his *My Fifteen Months in Government* (tr. 1967); biography by I. G. Colvin (1968).

Tsienfotung: see TUN-HUANG, China.

Tsientang, river, China: see CH'IEN-TANG.

Tsimshian Indians (tsĭm'shēən), North American Indians, speaking a language probably falling within the Penutian linguistic stock (see AMERICAN INDIAN LANGUAGES). They lived around the Skeena and the Nass rivers and southward along the coast of British Columbia and northward into Alaska. Tsimshian culture, like that of the Haida and the Tlingit, was typical of the Northwest Coast area. They depended largely on fishing for subsistence, on the codfish and halibut of the deep sea as well as the salmon and candlefish that come upstream in spring. They hunted seals and sea lions and, in the interior, bears, mountain goats, and deer. The Tsimshian were subdivided into four matrilineal phratries. The Episcopalian missionary William Duncan established (1857) a mission at the Tsimshian village of Metlakahtta, which is 15 mi (24 km) S of Port Simpson, B.C. Duncan moved, however, in 1887 to Port Chester, or New Metlakahtta, on Annette Island, and most of the Tsimshian followed him. Today the Tsimshian, numbering some 6,000, live on reservations in British Columbia and Alaska, where they earn their living mainly by fishing and forestry. Chimmesyan is another spelling for Tsimshian. See Franz Boas, *Tsimshian Mythology* (1916, repr. 1970); Theresa Durlach, *The Relationship Systems of the Tlingit, Haida, and Tsimshian* (1928, repr. 1974).

Tsin (dzĭn) or **Chin** (jĭn), dynasty of China that ruled from 265 to 420, after the period of the THREE KINGDOMS. Tsin was the dynastic name assumed by the Wei general Ssu-ma Yen who usurped the throne, and who by 280 had completed the conquest of China. The reunification of China was of short duration. On Ssu-ma Yen's death in 290, the empire fell apart again in the dynastic struggle known as the Revolt of Eight Kings. Only in 317 was a semblance of unity restored under a pretender to the throne who established himself at Nanking. Meanwhile a revolt had deprived the empire of Szechwan (302), and there were extensive losses to the Hsiung-nu (Huns) in the north. A series of dynasties, mainly of barbaric origin, ruled N China for about 250 years. After the Tsin regained Szechwan (347), they became stronger and occupied many areas in the southeast, where Chinese culture had not previously penetrated. The population of the Tsin state was greatly increased, and its cultural level was raised by the heavy influx of Chinese refugees from the north. The Tsin saw the continued growth of Buddhism and of specialized types of learning, notably regional gazetteers, which were produced in abundance. An important material advance was the extensive use of coal. In the period between the collapse of the Tsin and the founding of the Sui dynasty, China was never united. The most notable of the many local dynasties was the Northern Wei (it had no connection with the Tsin), which conquered most of N China by 439 and ruled until 535. The Northern Wei were originally a Turkic tribe, the T'oba (or T'opa). They left many colossal rock carvings, Buddhist monuments of a mixed Indian and Bactrian Greek character.

Tsinan: see CHI-NAN, China.

Tsinghai (chĭng'hī'), Mandarin *Ch'ing-hai,* province (1967 est. pop. 2,000,000), c.250,000 sq mi (647,500 sq km), W China. HSI-NING is the capital. Tsinghai lies in the Tibetan highlands at an average elevation of 9,800 ft (3,000 m) and is mainly a high, desolate plateau. The central region has the vast, swampy TSAIDAM [Mongolian,=salt marshes] basin, and in the northeast there is the large KOKO NOR or Tsinghai [Mongolian and Chinese,=blue sea] salt lake for which the province is named; it is the largest lake in China. In the precipitous mountain gorges of the south rise some of E Asia's greatest rivers, the Huang Ho (Yellow), the Yangtze, and the Mekong. The chief economic area and the most densely settled part of the province is in the NE around Hsi-ning; there coal is mined and grain and potatoes are grown. Extensive irrigation and the use of early-ripening spring wheat has recently increased production. Ethnic Chinese (from China proper) and Chinese Muslims predominate in this region. The south is inhabited by Tibetans who live a precarious existence based on stock herding and marginal farming. Stock breeding is also important; Tsinghai horses are world famous. The Tsaidam basin was once peopled only by a scattered population of Tibetan, Kazakh, and Mongol herdsmen, but from the 1950s to the 1970s there was an influx of Chinese to work in the mineral extraction industries there (oil, iron ore, salt, borax, and potash). Salt is so abundant that it is used for building blocks and for road pavement. Thousands of miles of highways have been constructed to link Hsi-ning and the Tsaidam basin with adjoining provinces; a railroad links Hsi-ning with Lan-chou, in Kansu prov. Historically a part of Tibet, the Tsinghai region passed to the Mongol overlords of China in the 14th cent., when it became part of Kansu. It came under Chinese (Ch'ing dynasty) control after 1724 and was administered from Hsi-ning as the Koko Nor territory. Over the centuries Chinese settlers have proceeded up the Hsi-ning and Huang Ho rivers from Lan-chou, penetrating deeply into ethnic Tibetan territory in the northeast. In 1928, Tsinghai became a province of China. The Communist government established autonomous districts for the Tibetan, Chinese Muslim, Kazakh, and Mongol minorities. The noted KUMBUM lamasery is SW of Hsi-ning.

Tsingtao: see CH'ING-TAO, China.

Tsingyuan: see PAO-TING, China.

Tsining: see CHI-NING, China.

Tsinkiang: see CH'ÜAN-CHOU, China.

Tsinling or **Ch'in Ling** (both: chĭn lĭng), mountain range, outlier of the Kunlun mts., between the Wei and Han rivers, Shensi prov., central China; T'ai-pai Shan (13,494 ft/4,113 m) is the highest peak. The range is wooded, and coal is mined in the central region. The Tsinling, with the Huai River to the east, marks the geographical boundary between N and central China; rice and citrus fruits are generally not found south of this line. The range is also a natural barrier impeding north-south movement; it checked the Mongol advance in the 13th cent. and divided the Muslim and Taiping rebellion areas in the 19th cent.

Tsiolkovsky, Konstantin Eduardovich (kənstəntyĕn' ĕdwär'dəvĭch' tsēōlkŏv'skē), 1857–1935, Russian inventor and rocket expert. He lost his hearing in childhood, and, as he could not attend the usual schools, he educated himself. His most important work was concerned with the possibility of rocket flight into outer space. Tsiolkovsky's *The Investigation of Outer Space by Means of Reaction Apparatus* was presented in 1903. In this work, he discusses in mathematical terms the problems involved in overcoming the earth's gravitational pull by means of rockets. He also suggests the use of reaction vehicles for interplanetary flight. In 1929, Tsiolkovsky presented a design for a multistage rocket, which he called a rocket train. He also proposed the construction of artificial earth satellites, including manned space platforms to be used as way stations in interplanetary travel.

Tsiranana, Philibert (fēlēbâr' tsēränä'nä), 1910–, president of the Malagasy Republic (1960–72). He served in the legislature of Madagascar and represented the island in the French national assembly before becoming (1958) prime minister. When Madagascar gained its independence as the Malagasy Republic (1960), he became the first president and head of state. In 1972 he was forced out of office by Gen. Gabriel Ramanantsoa.

Tsitsihar: see CH'I-CH'I-HA-ERH, China.

Tskhinvali (tskhĭn'välĭ), city (1970 pop. 30,000), capital of South Ossetian Autonomous Oblast, Georgian Republic, S European USSR. The city has lumber mills and electrical products plants. Its name was changed to Staliniri in 1934 but was changed back to Tskhinvali in 1961.

Tso Tsung-t'ang (dzô dzo͝ong-täng), 1812–85, Chinese general and statesman of the Ch'ing dynasty. He directed (1852–59) resistance to the TAIPING REBELLION in his native Hunan and later organized (1860) a volunteer corps that fought the Taipings in Kiangsi and Anhwei provs. Appointed governor of Chekiang (1862–63) and governor-general of Chekiang and Fukien (1863–66), Tso drove the Taipings from those provinces and planned rehabilitation. He led troops that participated (1868) in the encirclement and annihilation of the Nien forces (see NIEN REBELLION). As governor-general of Shensi and Kansu provs., Tso suppressed (1868–77) the Muslim rebellion on the northwest frontier. In the struggle for military funds between those officials who stressed coastal defense (notably LI HUNG-CHANG) and those who stressed frontier defense, he argued that Western powers fought for commercial privileges and could be contained by skillful diplomacy, whereas strong frontier defense was necessary to forestall Russia's territorial ambitions. In retirement after 1882, he was recalled in 1884 to plan defense of the Fukien coast during the war with France (1884–85) for control of Annam (Vietnam). See biography by W. L. Bales (1937).

Tsu (tso͞o), city (1970 pop. 125,282), capital of Mie prefecture, S Honshu, Japan, on Ise Bay. It is a commercial and manufacturing center, with glass and food-processing factories. In the city are a feudal castle, testimony to its bygone role as a castle town, and several large Buddhist temples. Tsu also has two universities.

Tsuchiura (tso͞ochē'o͞orä), city (1970 pop. 89,958), Ibaraki prefecture, central Honshu, Japan. It is an agricultural and commercial center.

Tsugaru Strait (tso͞ogä'ro͞o), c.100 mi (160 km) long and from 15 to 25 mi (24–40 km) wide, separating Honshu and Hokkaido, N Japan, and connecting the Sea of Japan with the Pacific Ocean.

Tsu Hsi, Chinese empress dowager: see T'ZU HSI.

Tsumeb (tso͞o'mĕb), town (1970 pop. 12,338), N South West Africa. It is the commercial and distribution center for a region where copper, lead, and zinc are mined.

tsunami (tso͞onä'mē) or **seismic sea wave,** series of catastrophic ocean waves generated by submarine movements, which in turn are caused by earthquakes, volcanic eruptions, or landslides beneath the ocean. Their formation is analogous to the formation of concentric ripples when a stone is dropped into a pool of water. In the open ocean, tsunamis may have wavelengths of up to several hundred miles and travel at speeds up to 450 mi per hr (720 km per hr), yet have wave heights of less than 3 ft (1 m). Because the ratio of length to height is so large, tsunami waves pass unnoticed beneath a ship at sea. In spite of their great speed, the period between crests of tsunami waves varies from 10 min to about 1 hour. When tsunamis approach shallow water along a coast, they are slowed, causing their length to shorten and their height to rise sometimes as high as 100 ft (30 m), and when they break, often destroying piers, buildings, and beaches and taking human life. The height of tsunami waves as they crash upon the shore depends almost entirely upon the geometry of the submarine topography offshore. They tend to rise to greater heights along gently sloping shores, along submarine ridges, or in embayments along a coast. There is little warning of approach; when a train of tsunami waves approaches a coastline, the first indication is often a sharp swell, not unlike an ordinary storm swell, followed by a sudden outrush of water that often exposes offshore areas as the first wave trough reaches the coast. After several minutes, the first huge wave crest strikes, inundating the newly exposed beach and rushing inland to flood the coast. Generally, the third to eighth wave crests are the largest. Since tsunamis principally occur following shallow-focus earthquakes of magnitude over 6.5 on the RICHTER SCALE, one of the best means of predicting their possible generation is the detection of such earthquakes on the ocean floor with a seismograph network (see SEISMOLOGY). In addition, wave gauges sensitive primarily to long-period waves of high amplitude can detect tsunamis. Such gauges have been emplaced as part of a Tsunami Warning System operated by the U.S. Coast Guard for the Pacific regions. Probably the most destructive and best-documented tsunamis occurred following the explosive eruption of the volcano Krakatoa in the East Indies on Aug. 27, 1883, when over 36,000 people were killed as a result of associated tsunami activity. Waves 100 ft (30 m) high carried away the town of Merak, located about 30 mi (48 km) from the volcano. Traveling at speeds between 350 and 450 mi per hr (560–720 km per hr), its passage was traced as far away as Panama.

Tsunetaka, Tosa (tsōōnätä'kä), fl. 12th cent., Japanese painter. He held the title of vice lord of Tosa, and later artists of the Tosa clan claimed him as the founder of their school, although there is no proof of any lineal relationship between them. No work of Tsunetaka remains today.

Tsun-i or **Tsunyi** (both: dzōōn-yē), town (1970 est. pop. 275,000), N Kweichow prov., SW China. It is on the main highway to Szechwan and is the commercial and agricultural distribution center of N Kweichow. Iron and manganese ore are mined, food is processed, and textiles (cotton and silk), chemicals, and machine tools are manufactured.

Tsuruga (tsōōrōō'gä), city (1970 pop. 56,444), Fukui prefecture, central Honshu, Japan, a port on the Sea of Japan. It was long a center for commerce with Korea. Among the city's principle products are rayon and cement.

Tsuruoka (tsōōrōō'ōkä), city (1970 pop. 95,136), Yamagata prefecture, NE Honshu, Japan. It is an agricultural center.

Tsushima (tsōō'shēmä), two Japanese islands in Korea Strait. The islands are rocky, and fishing is the main occupation. Nearby, in May, 1905, occurred the major naval battle of the RUSSO-JAPANESE WAR. The Russian Baltic fleet, under command of Admiral Rozhdestvenski, suffered nearly total disaster in its encounter with the Japanese fleet under Count Togo. Only a few of the Russian ships escaped to neutral ports or reached their destination (Vladivostok); the majority were sunk or captured. It was in this battle that naval radio was first used (by Count Togo). The defeat convinced Russia that further struggle was hopeless, and in August a treaty of peace was signed at Portsmouth, N.H.

Tsutsugamushi fever: see TYPHUS.

TTP (thymidine triphosphate): see THYMINE.

Tuamotu Islands (tōōämō'tōō) or **Low Archipelago,** coral group (1970 pop. 6,664), South Pacific, part of FRENCH POLYNESIA. They comprise c.80 atolls in a 1,300-mi (2,092-km) chain, with a total land area of c.330 sq mi (850 sq km). Rangiroa is the largest island; Fakarava is the most important commercially. The islands have coconut, pandanus, and breadfruit trees and produce pearl shell and copra. The Tuamotu Islands were discovered by the Spanish in 1606, came under a French protectorate in 1844, and were annexed by France in 1881. A small part of the group is governed with the GAMBIER ISLANDS; MAKATEA Island is under the administration of the SOCIETY ISLANDS. The Tuamoto group was formerly called Paumotu, or Dangerous Archipelago, because hundreds of ships have been wrecked on its reefs and atolls. Some islands of the group are used for French nuclear experiments.

Tuan Ch'i-jui (dwän'chē-jōōē), 1865–1936, Chinese general and political leader. He studied military science in Germany and held high positions in the army under the Ch'ing dynasty. After the overthrow of the monarchy, Tuan, a consistent supporter of YÜAN SHIH-K'AI, served as minister of war (1912–14) and as premier several times between 1912 and 1918. His power group was called the Anhwei clique. He was provisional president of China (1924–26).

Tuapse (tōōəpsyĕ'), city (1970 pop. 51,000), Krasnodar Kray, SE European USSR, on the Black Sea. It is a major petroleum port and the terminal of the pipeline from the Grozny oil fields. The city refines oil, manufactures equipment for the oil industry, and repairs ships. Tuapse was founded as a fortress in 1838.

Tuareg or **Touareg** (both: twä'rĕg), BERBERS of the Sahara, numbering about 300,000. They have preserved their ancient alphabet, which is related to that used by ancient Libyans. The Tuaregs traditionally maintained a feudal system consisting of a small number of noble families, a large majority of vassals, and a lower class of black non-Tuareg serfs, who performed the agricultural tasks. The upper classes, organized in tribes, convoyed caravans and, until subdued by France, were feared as raiders. The fiercely independent Tuareg resented European hegemony in Africa, and they long resisted conquest. Tuareg men go veiled, while the women are unveiled. Women enjoy respect and freedom, and descent and inheritance are through the female line. Though nominally Muslim, the people still retain many pre-Islamic rites and customs. The traditional way of life for the Tuaregs (e.g., raiding neighboring tribes and exacting taxes from trans-Sahara travelers) is changing; in the 1970s droughts and famines forced many Tuaregs from their desert homes. See F. J. Rennell, *People of the Veil* (1926, repr. 1966); Peter Fuchs, *The Land of Veiled Men* (tr. 1956).

tuatara (tōō"ətär'ə) or **tuatera** (-tā'rə), lizardlike REPTILE, *Sphenodon punctatus,* last survivor of the reptilian order Rhynchocephalia, which flourished in the early Mesozoic era before the rise of the dinosaurs. Also called sphenodon, it is found on a few islands off the New Zealand coast. The olive colored, yellow-speckled tuatara reaches a length of 2 ft (60 cm) or more. It is very lizardlike in external form, with a crest of spines down its neck and back. However, its internal anatomy, its scales, and the attachment of its teeth are quite different from those of lizards. Like certain lizards, it possesses a vestigial third eye (pineal eye) on top of its head, but this organ is probably not sensitive to light. Tuataras usually inhabit the breeding burrows of certain small petrels. They feed on small animals, especially insects, and reproduce by laying eggs. Tuataras lived on the mainland of New Zealand before the arrival of the Maoris but either were exterminated by hunting or died out as a result of the altered environment. Their survival on the offshore islands was threatened by the introduction of sheep, which altered the vegetation by grazing; however, they are now under strict government protection, and their numbers are increasing. Captive tuataras mature in about 20 years, and it appears that their life span may exceed a century. Tuataras are classified in the phylum CHORDATA, subphylum Vertebrata, class Reptilia, order Rhynchocephalia.

Tuatha De Danann (tōō'əthə dā dä'nän), in Irish mythology, invaders of ancient Ireland before the Milesians. They were endowed with great supernatural powers, which enabled them to defeat their predecessors, the Fomors. However, they were themselves defeated by the Milesians.

tuba (tōō'bə) [Lat.,=trumpet], valved brass wind musical instrument. The term *tuba* is applied rather loosely to any low-pitched brass instrument other than the trombone; such instruments vary in size and bore, and are known by various names. The contrabass tuba, which is most common, plays in the same range as the double bass. The helicon and sousaphone are contrabass tubas used in marching bands; they coil around the player and rest on his left shoulder. The baritone and euphonium are small tubas, mainly band instruments, pitched the same as the trombone. Wagner secured the tuba's place in the orchestra in the mid-19th cent. He called for three differently pitched instruments for his *Ring* cycle. The Wagner tuba is a narrow-bore tuba with a French-horn mouthpiece. Tubas appeared first in Berlin in the 1820s, soon after the invention of the valve. They were soon accepted into the band and orchestra, displacing the serpent, ophicleide, and other such instruments of poorer tone quality and intonation.

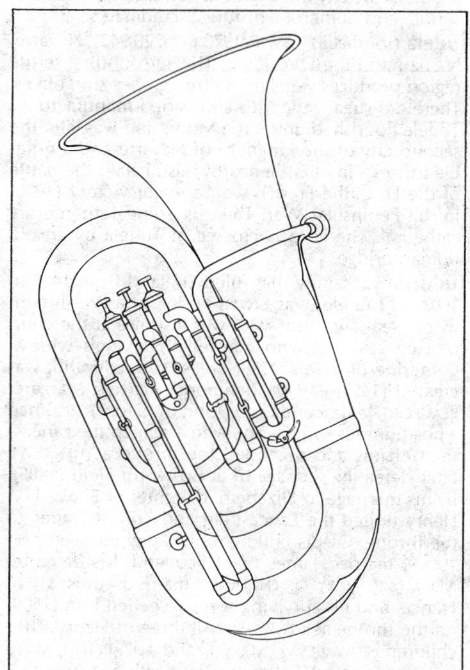

Contrabass tuba

Tubal (tōō'bəl), son of Japheth. Gen. 10.2.

Tubal-cain (tōō'bəl-kān), in the Bible, son of Lamech. He first worked brass and iron. Gen. 4.22.

tube, in electronics: see ELECTRON TUBE.

tuber, enlarged tip of a rhizome (underground stem) that stores food. Although much modified in structure, the tuber contains all the usual stem parts—bark, wood, pith, nodes, and internodes. The eyes of a potato tuber are nodes where sprouts appear, and they are arranged in the same spiral pattern characteristic of buds on an aerial stem.

tubercle (tōō'bərkyōōl") [Lat.,=little swelling], small, usually solid, nodule or prominence. In anatomy the term is applied to natural prominences in certain muscles, to nerve nuclei of the central nervous system, and to eminences on bones, especially in regions where muscles (through tendons) or bones (through ligaments) are attached. In dentistry tubercle refers to the cusp of a tooth. In pathology it describes small morbid growths, particularly the lesions of TUBERCULOSIS. In botany it applies to the nodules on the roots or leaves of plants. In entomology the term is used for a compound or supplementary eye and for the nodules on the bodies of certain insects.

tuberculosis, contagious disease caused by the tubercle bacillus (*Mycobacterium tuberculosis*), first identified in 1882 by Robert Koch. The most common form of the disease is tuberculosis of the lungs (pulmonary consumption, or phthisis), but the intestines, bones and joints, the skin, and the genitourinary, lymphatic, and nervous systems may also be affected. There are three types of tubercle bacilli that affect man—the human type, spread by man himself, the most common one; the bovine type, spread by infected cattle but no longer a threat in areas where pasteurization of milk and the health of cattle is strictly supervised; and the avian type carried by infected birds but occurring very rarely in humans. The tubercle bacillus can live for a considerable period of time in air or dust, and the most common means of acquiring the disease is by inhalation. The bacillus can also be ingested (contaminated food or table utensils), and very rarely it may enter directly through the skin. The nonwhite races are especially vulnerable, as are white persons of fair hair and complexion. Substandard living conditions are a significant factor in any population, as is occupation. Doctors, nurses, and other hospital personnel in contact with tuberculous patients frequently acquire the disease. Among miners, especially those with silicosis, there is a greater than average incidence of tuberculosis. Tuberculosis of the lungs may result in minimal symptoms or in none in its early stages. In many persons the primary lesion becomes calcified and the infection is permanently arrested. In others, the infection progresses until large areas of the lung are destroyed by the tubercle bacilli, when frank symptoms of the disease appear, such as cough, sputum, bleeding from the lungs, fever, drenching sweats, loss of weight, and weakness. X rays of the chest, sputum examinations, and various tuberculin skin tests reveal the presence of the infection. The incidence of tuberculosis of the lungs, the "white plague" that formerly affected millions of persons, has been much reduced by public health and early detection measures and modern therapy. Most effective, however, have been the drugs streptomycin, para-aminosalicylic acid (PAS), and isoniazid. An antituberculosis vaccine (BGG) developed in France and given to more than 50 million children throughout the world under the auspices of the World Health Organization may also have been an important factor in the decline of the disease. Many tuberculosis sanatoriums have been closed because treatment can now be given at home or in general hospitals. In the United States the tuberculosis death rate was reduced 95% in the first half of the 20th cent., and comparable progress has been made in other parts of the world. See René Dubos, *The White Plague* (1955); S. A. Waksman, *The Conquest of Tuberculosis* (1964).

tuberose: see AMARYLLIS.

Tübingen (tü'bĭng-ən), city (1970 pop. 54,892), Baden-Württemberg, SW West Germany, on the Neckar River. It is a cultural and industrial center; manufactures include textiles, machinery, metal goods, precision instruments, and printed materials. Tübingen was chartered c.1200, passed to the counts (later dukes) of Württemberg in the mid-14th cent., and became the second capital of Württemberg in the mid-15th cent. The old part of the city retains its medieval character; noteworthy buildings include the city hall (1435), the late-Gothic Church of St. George (15th cent.), and Hohentübingen, a castle first mentioned in the 11th cent. and later (16th cent.) renovated in Renaissance style. Tübingen is famous for its university (founded 1477), where Melanchthon taught (1512–18); its theological faculty was famous in the 19th cent. as the Tübingen School, founded by F. C. Baur. The poet Uhland was born (1787) in Tübingen, and the poet Hölderlin died (1843) there.

Tübingen School: see BAUR, FERDINAND CHRISTIAN.

Tubman, Harriet, c.1820–1913, American abolitionist, b. Dorchester co., Md. A Negro slave, she escaped in 1849 and became one of the most successful "conductors" on the Underground Railroad. She led more than 300 slaves to freedom, forcing the timid ahead with a loaded revolver. She was a friend of the principal abolitionists, and John Brown almost certainly confided his Harpers Ferry plan to her. In the Civil War, Harriet Tubman attached herself to the Union forces in coastal South Carolina, serving as a nurse, laundress, and spy. At Auburn, N.Y., her home for many years, the Cayuga co. courthouse contains a tablet in her honor. See biographies by Sarah Bradford (1869, new ed. 1961) and Earl Conrad (1942).

Tubman, William Vacanarat Shadrach, 1895–1971, president of Liberia (1944–71). As a young man he was a lawyer, a collector of internal revenue, a teacher, and an officer of the Liberian militia. He was elected to the senate in 1923 but resigned in 1931 after a League of Nations investigation found Liberia (governed by Tubman's party) guilty of selling its people into slavery. He was reelected to the senate in 1934, but he resigned again in 1937 to become an associate justice of the Liberian supreme court. He was elected president in 1943 and took office in 1944. He extended his term several times through constitutional amendments, serving until his death. Tubman greatly modernized the economy of his country and its educational facilities and gave the vote to women and tribesmen. However, he and high officials were often criticized for living in luxury while the vast majority was poor. Other black African leaders accused Tubman of being too much under the influence of the United States. See biographies by A. D. B. Henries (1967) and R. A. Smith (1967); E. R. Townsend, ed., *President Tubman of Liberia Speaks* (1959).

Tubuai Islands: see AUSTRAL ISLANDS.

Tucholsky, Kurt (ko͝ort to͝okhôl'skē), 1890–1935, German political satirist and journalist. Ranging over a wide variety of subjects and styles, Tucholsky's pacifist, antifascist writing marked a high point in German literary journalism. He wrote under four pseudonyms: Ignaz Wrobel (contemporary satire), Peter Panter (theater and literary criticism, travel), Theobald Tiger (poetry), Kaspar Hauser (character of despair, reflecting the drive that led Tucholsky to suicide). Among his works are *Deutschland, Deutschland über alles* (1929), and a collection in English translation, *The World Is a Comedy* (1957), and an anthology of his satirical works, *What If* (tr. 1969).

tuckahoe (tŭk'əhō") [from Algonquian], name applied to two North American Indian foods known also as Indian bread. One of these is the rootstock of certain plants of the ARUM family, especially arrow arum (*Petandrum virginicum*) and golden club (*Orontium aquaticum*). The other form of tuckahoe is a compacted mass of mycelium tissue (called sclerotium) of certain kinds of pore fungus, especially the subterranean *Poria cocos* found on the roots of trees in the S United States.

Tucker, Abraham, 1705–74, English philosopher, b. London. He studied law at Merton College, Oxford, and later devoted himself to independent study. He advanced the ethical view that each man seeks his own interests and that the will of God blends these into a public good. This position is similar to that of the subsequent utilitarianism. Tucker's major work, *The Light of Nature Pursued* (7 vol., 1768–78), was published in part under the pseudonym Edward Search.

Tucker, Richard, 1914–75, American tenor, b. Brooklyn, N.Y. Tucker began his singing career as a cantor and remained one throughout his 30-year operatic career. In 1945 he made his debut at the Metropolitan Opera singing Enzo in Ponchielli's *La Gioconda*. He soon became one of the Metropolitan's leading lyric tenors in the French and Italian repertoire, notably in such roles as Rudolfo in Puccini's *La Bohème* and Radames in Verdi's *Aïda*. Tucker made many concert appearances and world tours. He celebrated his 25th anniversary at the Metropolitan in 1970.

Tucson (to͞o'sŏn"), city (1970 pop. 262,933), seat of Pima co., SE Ariz.; inc. 1877. Situated in a desert valley surrounded by mountains, Tucson is an important transportation and tourist center; its dry, sunny climate attracts vacationers and health seekers throughout the year. The city also has large electronic, optic, and research industries and serves as the processing and distributing center for the cotton and livestock raised in the area and for the many mining (chiefly copper) operations. The first Spanish settlers arrived in the late 17th cent., and in 1700 Father Eusebio Kino founded Mission San Xavier del Bac 9 mi (14.5 km) south of the Indian village of Tucson. The present city was established (1776) as a walled presidio, and Tucson became a military border post of New Spain, of Mexico, and, after its transfer under the Gadsden Purchase, of the United States. Tucson served as territorial capital from 1867 to 1877. In 1873, Fort Lowell was built 2 mi (3.2 km) north of the city for protection against the Indians. The Southern Pacific RR arrived in 1880. Among the city's many points of interest are the "Old Adobe" (1868); Colossal Cave; Fort Lowell (reconstructed, now a museum); the beautiful San Xavier mission nearby (present building erected 1783–97); "Old Tucson," a movie-set replica to the west of the city; and the adjacent Saguaro National Monument. A fiesta and rodeo is held each February. Tucson is the seat of the Univ. of Arizona, state schools for the handicapped, and state botanical and agricultural experiment stations. The city has an international airport. Nearby military installations are Davis-Monthan Air Force Base, a large Strategic Air Command base; and U.S. Fort Huachuca, an army electronic proving ground, with strategic communications headquarters and an intelligence school.

Tucumán, city (1970 pop. 326,208), capital of Tucumán prov., NW Argentina. It is the commercial center of an area that produces sugar, cereals, fruit, and lumber. The city was founded in 1565 and was moved to its present site in 1685. Spanish royalists were defeated in a battle at Tucumán (1812) by forces under Manuel Belgrano. A congress meeting in the city on July 9, 1816, proclaimed the independence of the United Provinces of La Plata from Spain. In the city are a national university, a popular shrine, and numerous historical landmarks.

Tudela (to͞othā'lä), town (1970 pop. 20,942), Navarre, N Spain, on the Ebro River. The surrounding fertile region produces vegetables, fruit, grapes, and olives. There are sugar refineries and varied manufactures. Tudela flourished under the Moors and was later the second city of the kingdom of Navarre and a notable fortress. In a battle nearby, also called the battle of the Ebro, the French won a major victory (1808) in the Peninsular War. There is a fine 12th-century cathedral. The Ebro is crossed at Tudela by an old Roman bridge.

Tudor, royal family that ruled England from 1485 to 1603. Its founder was Owen Tudor, of a Welsh family of great antiquity, who was a squire at the court of Henry V and who married that king's widow, Catherine of Valois. Their eldest son, Edmund, was created (1453) earl of Richmond, married Margaret BEAUFORT (a descendant of John of Gaunt), and had a posthumous son, Henry, who assumed the Lancastrian claims and ascended the throne as HENRY VII after defeating Richard III at Bosworth Field (1485). By his marriage to Elizabeth, daughter of Edward IV, Henry united the Lancastrian and Yorkist claims to the throne. Of his children, his daughter MARGARET TUDOR married James IV of Scotland; his daughter Mary (see MARY OF ENGLAND) married Louis XII of France; and his surviving son succeeded him (1509) on the throne as HENRY VIII. All three of Henry VIII's children, EDWARD VI, MARY I, and ELIZABETH I, were rulers of England. Following the death of Edward VI, there was an unsuccessful attempt to place Mary of England's granddaughter, Lady Jane GREY, upon the throne. The reign of the Tudors was distinguished by considerable governmental reorganization, which strengthened the power of the monarchy; the rise of England as a naval power and a corresponding growth in the sense of national pride; and the Reformation of the English church with attendant religious strife. It was a period of a remarkable flowering of English literature and scholarship. Upon the death of Elizabeth I (1603), the Tudor dynasty was succeeded by the house of Stuart, whose claim to the throne derived from Margaret Tudor. Among the noted historians of the Tudor period are Geoffrey Rudolph ELTON, Sir John Ernest NEALE, and Albert Frederick POLLARD. See also Conyers Read, *The Tudors* (1936); Christopher Morris, *The Tudors* (1955); Michael Foss, *Tudor Portraits* (1974).

Tudor, Antony, 1909–, English choreographer and dancer. Tudor went to the United States at the invitation of the Ballet Theatre, New York City (1931–38); he danced leading roles and created ballets for several English and American companies and was later the artistic director of the Royal Swedish Ballet (1963–64). His ballets, influenced by the expressionism of Fokine and Massine, use the modern idiom. Among Tudor's most popular works are *Lilac Garden* (1938; music by Ernest Chausson), *Gala Performance* (1938), *Pillar of Fire* (1942), *Romeo and Juliet* (1942), *Undertow* (1945), *Offenbach in the Underworld* (1955), and *Echoes of Trumpets* (1963).

Tudor, Owen, d. 1461, founder of the TUDOR dynasty. He belonged to an ancient Welsh family. He was a squire at the court of Henry V, and, probably in 1429, he married Henry's widow, CATHERINE OF VALOIS, by whom he had five children. Twice imprisoned by Humphrey, duke of GLOUCESTER, during Henry VI's minority, he finally escaped to Wales, although Henry later made provision for him in England. Owen, a faithful Lancastrian in the Wars of the Roses, was beheaded by the Yorkists after their victory at Mortimer's Cross.

Tudor style, descriptive of the English architecture and decoration of the first half of the 16th cent., prevailing during the reigns (1485–1558) of Henry VII, Henry VIII, Edward VI, and Mary I. It is the first of the transitional styles between Gothic Perpendicular and Palladian architecture, the other two being Elizabethan and Jacobean. The rise of new trading families to wealth and the enrichment of court favorites by Henry VIII with lands and riches derived from his suppression of monasteries resulted in the building of many manor houses. In these the fortified character of earlier times gave way to increased domesticity and privacy. Although the great hall still remained the focus of the establishment, its importance now decreased with the introduction of other rooms such as parlors, studies, bedrooms in greater number, and quarters for dining. Rooms frequently were fitted with oak paneling, often of linen-fold type; walls and ceilings received rich plaster relief ornament; and articles of furniture came into greater use. Domestic exteriors exhibited Perpendicular features in modified form, notably square-headed, mullioned windows and arched openings of the four-centered or so-called Tudor type. Other characteristics were the use of brickwork combined with half-timber, high pinnacled gables, bay or oriel windows, and numerous chimneys of decorative form. Principal Tudor examples are parts of Hampton Court Palace, begun in 1515, and many colleges of Oxford and Cambridge. Noted country manors include Sutton Place, Surrey; Layer Marney, Essex; and the splendid Compton Wynyates, Warwick. See John Harvey, *Introduction to Tudor Architecture* (1949); James Lees-Milne, *Tudor Renaissance* (1951); R. Edwards and L. G. G. Ramsey, ed., *The Connoisseur Period Guides* (1956).

Tuesday: see WEEK.

tufa: see TRAVERTINE.

Tufts University, mainly at Medford, Mass.; coeducational; chartered 1852 by Universalists as a college. It became a university in 1955. The College of Liberal Arts is for men. Jackson College for women is a coordinate undergraduate college. The Crane Theological School and the Fletcher School of Law and Diplomacy are part of Tufts. The university's medical and dental schools are in Boston.

Tu Fu (do͞o fo͞o, to͞o), 712–70, Chinese poet. Tu Fu is often considered the greatest of Chinese poets. He did not pass the imperial civil service examinations and, although he held a few official positions for brief periods, he spent many poverty-stricken years as a wanderer. His poetry expresses his bitterness concerning his life. It laments the corruption and cruelty that prevailed at court and the sufferings of the poor. Tu Fu's work is pervaded by an ironic awareness of spiritual and social decay. His autobiography was translated (1929–34) by Florence Ayscough. See biographies by William Hung (2 vol., 1952) and A. R. Davis (1971); *Li Po and Tu Fu*, ed. and tr. by Arthur Cooper (1973).

tugboat, small, strongly built vessel, used to warp large oceangoing ships into and out of port and to tow barges, dredging and salvage equipment, and disabled vessels. Tugboats range in overall length from 70 to 210 ft (21–64 m), and their engines generate from 750 to 3,000 horsepower. Steam power dominated tugboat design until diesel and diesel-electric drives were developed. Most tugs are built of wood or metal-sheathed wood; the resiliency of a wooden hull prevents damage to both tugboat and vessel in warping operations.

Tughluq, Muhammad: see DELHI SULTANATE.

Tugurt: see TOUGGOURT, Algeria.

Tugwell, Rexford Guy, 1891–, American economist and political scientist, b. Chautauqua co., N.Y., grad. Wharton School, Univ. of Pennsylvania (B.S., 1915; Ph.D., 1922). He taught economics at the Univ. of Pennsylvania (1915–17), the Univ. of Washington (1917–18), and Columbia (1920–37). Under Franklin Delano Roosevelt, Tugwell was Assistant Secretary (1933) and Under Secretary (1934–37) of Agriculture, and as a member of the BRAIN TRUST he helped draw up the Agricultural Adjustment Act. He was appointed (1938) chairman of the New York City planning commission and later (1941) governor of Puerto Rico. From 1946 to 1957 he taught at the Univ. of Chicago. After 1966, Tugwell was a senior fellow of the Center for the Study of Democratic Institutions. He wrote many books on economics and government, most recently *The Emerging Constitution* (1974). See his autobiography (1962); study by Bernard Sternsher (1964).

tui: see HONEYEATER.

Tuileries (twē'lərēz, Fr. twēlrē'), former palace in Paris. Planned by Catherine de' Medici and begun in 1564 by Philibert DELORME, it occupied part of the present Tuileries gardens. It was rarely used as a royal residence until 1789, when Louis XVI was forced by the revolutionists to move there from Versailles. He and his family were brought back there after their attempted flight (1792) and their arrest at Varennes. A few weeks later (Aug. 10, 1792) a mob attacked the palace (see FRENCH REVOLUTION). Napoleon I made the Tuileries his chief residence, as did Louis XVIII, Charles X, Louis Philippe, and Napoleon III. During the COMMUNE OF PARIS of 1871, the palace was destroyed by fire. The spendid formal gardens, laid out by LENÔTRE, remain and are connected to the LOUVRE museum.

Tuke, William, 1732–1822, English merchant and philanthropist. He succeeded at an early age to the family business at York in wholesale tea and coffee. He is remembered as the chief founder of the York Retreat (opened 1796), an influential early institution for the intelligent and humane care of the insane. His son **Henry Tuke,** 1755–1814, was a cofounder of the retreat. Henry Tuke's son **Samuel Tuke,** 1784–1857, continued in the family business and interested himself in the conditions of the insane. His *Description of the Retreat* (1813) had great influence in reforming the treatment of insanity. Samuel Tuke's son **James Hack Tuke,** 1819–96, also entered the family business and aided in the management of the York Retreat. He long engaged in philanthropic aid to Ireland. His brother **Daniel Hack Tuke,** 1827–95, was an eminent physician whose study of insanity resulted in a valuable treatise, *A Manual of Psychological Medicine* (with J. C. Bucknill, 1858).

Tukhachevsky or **Toukhachevski, Mikhail Nikolayevich** (both: mēkhəyēl' nyĭkəlī'əvĭch to͝okhəchĕf'skē), 1893–1937, Russian marshal. An officer in the czarist army from 1914, he joined (1918) the Bolshevik party after the Russian Revolution and held important commands in the civil war of 1918–20 and the Russo-Polish war of 1920. Tukhachevsky was instrumental in suppressing the Kronstadt rebellion (1921) against Bolshevik rule, and he led the modernization and mechanization of the Red Army (1935–36). In the purges instituted by Stalin in the 1930s he and seven other generals were charged with treason, tried in secret, and executed. His reputation was restored by Premier Khrushchev in 1958.

Tula (to͞o'lä), ancient city in the present state of Hidalgo, central Mexico. It was one of the chief urban centers of the TOLTEC. The city is believed to be Tollán, the legendary Toltec capital mentioned in a number of postconquest sources, including Bernardino de Sahagún's *Historia General de las Cosas de Nueva Espana* (*tr. General History of the Things of New Spain*) as well as in documents in indigenous hieroglyphics known as *códices.* Archaeological investigations in the ceremonial precinct have revealed impressive architectural remains including pyramidal structures and ball courts. One of the former was surmounted by a temple to the Toltec herogod QUETZALCOATL and had unusual sculptured columns in the form of warriors. These columns have been restored. Besides continuing restoration within the ceremonial precinct, archaeologists in recent work have explored outlying residential areas. Architectural and stylistic correspondences between Tula and several Maya centers on the N Yucatán peninsula, primarily at the site of Chichén Itzá, indicate that Toltec influence pervaded the area. This influence is believed to stem from splinter groups of Toltec who migrated into the Maya region and established hegemony in the early Post-Classic period (A.D. 900–1200). See studies in the *Handbook of Middle American Indians,* ed. by Robert Wauchope (13 vol., 1964–73); M. P. Weaver, *The Aztecs, Maya, and Their Predecessors* (1972).

Tula (to͞o'lə), city (1970 pop. 462,000), capital of Tula oblast, N central European USSR, on the Upa River, a tributary of the Oka. It is an important rail and highway hub and a manufacturing city of the Moscow industrial region. Russia's oldest metallurgical center, it also produces mining and transport equipment, deepwater pumps, boilers, ventilators, and armaments. First mentioned in 1146, Tula was included in the Ryazan principality. In the 16th cent., the city became a key fortress of the grand duchy of Moscow. Peter I built Russia's first arms factory at Tula in 1712, based on the discovery nearby of iron and coal deposits. Tula subsequently became a center of the Russian ironworking industry. Serving as the southern anchor of the Moscow defense line during World War II, the city withstood heavy German assaults. The 16th-century kremlin, with turreted walls, has been preserved. Yasnaya Polyana, the home and burial place of Leo Tolstoy, is nearby.

Tulane University of Louisiana (to͝olān', tyo͞o'-), at New Orleans; coeducational; opened 1834, chartered 1835 as a state medical college. It became the Univ. of Louisiana in 1847 but was reorganized in 1884 when it was endowed by Paul Tulane. The college of arts and sciences is for men. The woman's division is Newcomb College (officially H. Sophie Newcomb Memorial College; chartered 1886, opened 1887 through a gift from Josephine L. Newcomb). Tulane's medical school has been noted since its beginning. Special research programs include the Middle American Research Institute, the Urban Studies Center, the Delta Regional Primate Research Center, and the International Center for Medical Research and Training.

Tulare (təlâr', to͞olâr'ē), city (1970 pop. 16,235), Tulare co., S central Calif., in the San Joaquin valley; inc. 1888. It is a processing and shipping center for a farm, cotton, and dairy region. Truck bodies, chalkboard, and aluminum and concrete products are made.

Tulare Lake, intermittent lake, in the Central Valley, central Calif. The Kings, Kaweah, and Kern rivers at one time flowed into the lake, but their waters have been diverted for irrigation. The land in the lake's basin has a high salt content. In dry seasons Tulare Lake is almost without water. Discovered by the Spanish in 1772, the lake then was c.50 mi (80 km) long and c.35 mi (60 km) wide.

tularemia (to͞olərē'mēə) or **rabbit fever,** acute, infectious disease caused by *Pasteurella tularensis.* The greatest incidence of the disease is among those who handle infected wild rabbits. Tularemia may also be transmitted by other infected animals, ticks, or contaminated food or water. Within 10 days of contact the disease begins suddenly with high fever and severe constitutional symptoms. An ulcerating lesion (or several lesions) develops at the site of infection, such as the arm, eye, or mouth. The regional lymph nodes enlarge, suppurate, and drain. The infection may be complicated by pneumonia, meningitis, or peritonitis, and the mortality rate is about 6%. Treatment is with antibiotics, of which streptomycin is the most effective.

Tulchin (to͞ol'chĭn), city, SW European USSR, in the Ukraine, on the Selnitsa River. It is the center of an agricultural district and has food-processing, clothing, and shoe industries. Probably founded by Hungarians, it later became a Polish fortress. After the battles between the Poles and Chmielnicki's Cossacks, it was assigned by the Treaty of Zborov (1649) to the Ukraine. It reverted to Polish rule in 1654 but passed to Russia during the second partition of Poland in 1793. In 1821 the city became the stronghold of the Decembrists. An alternate spelling is Tultchin.

tule elk: see WAPITI.

tulip [Pers.,=turban], any plant of the large genus *Tulipa,* hardy, bulbous-rooted members of the family Liliaceae (LILY family), indigenous to north temperate regions of the Old World from the Mediterranean to Japan and growing most abundantly on the steppes of Central Asia. Cultivated tulips, popular as garden and cut flowers and as potted plants, are chiefly varieties of *T. gesneriana.* They have deep, cup-shaped blossoms of various rich colors. Tulip seeds are said to have been introduced into Europe in 1554 from Turkey, where they were possibly first cultivated. In Holland in the 17th cent. the wild speculation on tulip bulbs became known as tulipomania: single bulbs sometimes brought several thousand dollars until the government was forced to interfere. Dumas has told the story in his *Black Tulip.* Holland is still the most important center of tulip culture. Tulips having a peculiar color flecking or striping known as "breaking" were formerly very popular and were believed to be different varieties but now are thought to be the result of a virus disease carried by aphids. The tulip was so commonly used in the designs of the early Pennsylvania Dutch potters that their ware is often called tulip ware. Holland, Mich., a center of tulip growing in the United States, holds an annual tulip festival. Tulips are classified in the division MAGNOLIOPHYTA, class Liliatae, order Liliales, family Liliaceae. See bulletins of the U.S. Dept. of Agriculture.

tulip tree: see MAGNOLIA.

Tull, Jethro, 1674–1741, English agriculturist and inventor. He studied methods of agriculture in England, France, and Italy and influenced British agriculture through his writings, which include *The Horse-Hoeing Husbandry* (1733). Tull advocated the use of manures, pulverizing the soil, planting with drills, and thorough tilling during the growing period. He invented (c.1701) a mechanical drill for sowing.

Tullahoma (tələhō'mə), city (1970 pop. 15,311), Coffee and Franklin counties, central Tenn.; settled c.1850 as a railroad labor camp, inc. 1903. It is an industrial center in a highland timber and farm area; manufactures include garments, sporting goods, and wood products. In the Civil War, Tullahoma fell (July, 1863) to Federals under Gen. W. S. Rosecrans, who outmaneuvered Gen. Braxton Bragg in the operations preliminary to the CHATTANOOGA CAMPAIGN. The city's cool climate and nearby mineral springs made it a health resort in the late 19th cent. Its growth was spurred during World War II by the establishment nearby of Camp Forrest, an infantry training center. After the war the Camp Forrest reservation became the site of the huge Arnold Engineering and Development Center, a permanent aeronautical research and testing installation serving NASA and the U.S. armed forces. It brought thousands of workers to the area and is the major source of employment in Tullahoma today. The city is the seat of the Univ. of Tennessee Space Institute and a junior college.

Tullamore (tŭl'əmôr), urban district (1971 pop. 6,654), county town of Co. Offaly, central Republic of Ireland. It is a marketing and processing center for a fertile farm area. The Book of Durrow, a copy of the Gospels, was written c.700 at nearby Durrow Abbey (founded 553 by St. Columba; torn down 12th cent.).

Tulle (to͞ol, Fr. tül), town (1968 pop. 21,324), capital of Corrèze dept., S central France. Firearms and other goods are made there. Tulle was built around a 7th-century monastery. It gave its name to tulle cloth, first manufactured in the town. There is an important military school.

Tulloch, John (tŭl'əkh, -ək), 1823–86, Scottish liberal theologian and educator. Ordained (1845) into the Church of Scotland, he was a parish minister until 1854, when he became principal and professor of theology of St. Mary's College, St. Andrews Univ. In 1859 he was appointed a chaplain to Queen Victoria. He was influential in matters of education. In 1878 he was moderator of the General Assembly of the Church of Scotland. Among his many historical works is *Rational Theology and Christian Philosophy in England in the Seventeenth Century* (1872). See memoir by M. O. W. Oliphant (1888).

Tully: see CICERO.

Tulsa (tŭl'sə), city (1970 pop. 330,350), seat of Tulsa co., NE Okla., on the Arkansas River east of its junction with the Cimarron; inc. 1898. It became an inland port with the opening (1971) of the McClellan-Kerr Waterway, a 440-mi (708-km) system linking it with the Gulf of Mexico. It is an important center of the nation's petroleum industry with large refineries and plants that produce petroleum products and related equipment. Some major oil concerns have their business offices and research laboratories there. Mining, metal processing, machinery manufacturing, and the aerospace industry are also important. Tulsa grew as a cattle-shipping village after the coming of the railroad in 1882 and boomed with the discovery of oil nearby in 1901. An extensive park system (which includes Mohawk Park) and well-planned communities characterize the residential aspect of the city. Tulsa is also a cultural and educational center with an opera, a philharmonic orchestra, a civic ballet, a large theater, art and history museums, the Univ. of Tulsa, Oral Roberts Univ., and a junior college.

Tultchin: see TULCHIN, USSR.

T'u-lu-fan (tōō-lōō-fän) or **Turfan** (tōōr'fän'), town and oasis, in the T'u-lu-fan depression (c.5,000 sq mi/12,950 sq km), E Sinkiang Uigur Autonomous Region, China. It is an agricultural center producing cotton and cotton textiles, silk, wheat, grapes, dried fruit, and wine. Oil is in the area. T'u-lu-fan is the chief town of the T'u-lu-fan depression, the lowest point (505 ft/154 m below sea level) in China. The depression was the center (A.D. 200–400) of a flourishing civilization in which Indian and Persian elements were combined. This civilization was later absorbed by the Uigurs, who had their capital there (9th–13th cent.). Archaeological finds made in the early 20th cent. include much Nestorian literature and the bulk of the extant Manichaean literature.

Tumacacori National Monument: see NATIONAL PARKS AND MONUMENTS (table).

Tumaco (tōōmä'kō), city (1968 est. pop. 80,300), SW Colombia, a port on the Pacific Ocean. It is located on a small island just off the coast and has a very hot climate. Tumaco is a commercial center. Coffee, cacao, tobacco, vegetables, and other products of the interior are exported.

tumblebug: see SCARAB BEETLE.

tumbleweed, any of several plants, particularly abundant in prairie and steppe regions, that commonly break from their roots at maturity and, drying into a rounded tangle of light, stiff branches, roll before the wind, covering long distances and scattering seed as they go. The Russian thistle—*Salsola pestifer*, of the family Chenopodiaceae (GOOSEFOOT family) and not a thistle—is one of the most frequent of the tumbleweeds. Naturalized from Asia, it has become a troublesome pest on Western prairies, although in drought years it may serve as forage in the spring before the spines form. Some other common tumbleweeds, such as *Amaranthus graecizans*, are members of the family Amaranthaceae (AMARANTH family), naturalized from tropical America and now common weed pests in Western agricultural fields. Others are the hedge mustards (species of *Sisymbrium*) and several other plants of the goosefoot family, e.g., the winged pigweeds (*Cycloloma*) and the bugseeds (*Corispermum*). Tumbleweeds of the family Chenopodiaceae are classified in the division MAGNOLIOPHYTA, class Magnoliopsida.

Tumkur (tōōmkōōr'), town (1971 pop. 70,475), Karnataka state, S central India. It is a district administrative center and a health center in the Devarayadurga Hills. Tumkur is also a market for vegetable oil, tobacco, chilies, and coconuts. Brick, tile, and iron and steel products are manufactured.

tumor: see NEOPLASM.

Tumulty, Joseph Patrick, 1879–1954, American politician, b. Jersey City, N.J. After his admission to the bar, he practiced law in Jersey City (1902–8) and served in the New Jersey assembly (1907–10). Tumulty supported Woodrow Wilson for the governorship of New Jersey in 1910 and spent the remainder of his public life as secretary to Wilson during the latter's gubernatorial (1911–13) and presidential (1913–21) careers. Initially Wilson relied heavily on him in matters of politics and patronage. Tumulty was the author of *Woodrow Wilson as I Knew Him* (1921). See John M. Blum, *Joe Tumulty and the Wilson Era* (1951, repr. 1969).

tumulus (tōō'myələs), pl. **tumuli** (-lī), in archaeology, a heap of earth or stones placed over a grave. The words MOUND, BARROW, or CAIRN are more common in modern usage.

tuna or **tunny,** game and food fishes, the largest members of the family Scombridae (MACKEREL family) and closely related to the albacore, *Germa alalunga*, and bonito. Of the group called little tunnies, the most important commercially is the little tuna, or false albacore, averaging 10 lb (4.5 kg), found in open Atlantic waters N to Cape Cod. The oceanic bonito, or skipjack, *Katsuwonus pelamis*, is a warm-water fish reaching 20 lb (9 kg) in weight. The Pacific albacore, or long-finned tuna (up to 60 lb/27 kg), is found off the Pacific coast of the United States and in the Mediterranean; its flesh is marketed as "whitemeat tuna." The bluefin tuna, *Thunnus thynnus*, the largest of the great tunnies and the giant of bony fishes, averages 200 to 500 lb (90–225 kg) with adults sometimes reaching 14 ft (427 cm) and ¾ ton (680 kg). The bluefin, also called horse, or jack, mackerel, is cosmopolitan in distribution; in the Atlantic, schools of bluefins travel as far N as Nova Scotia in the spring and summer. The yellowfin tuna, *T. albacares*, is smaller (125 lb/56 kg) and more southerly in range. Tuna fisheries have been important commercially in Europe for centuries and are the backbone of a major canning industry on both coasts of North America. Tunas are classified in the phylum CHORDATA, subphylum Vertebrata, class Osteichthyes, order Perciformes, family Scombridae.

Tunbridge Wells: see ROYAL TUNBRIDGE WELLS, England.

Tun Ch'i-ch'ang (dōōn chē-chäng), 1555–1636, Chinese painter, calligrapher, and a connoisseur of painting of the Ming dynasty. A high official in various public offices, he was also regarded as the greatest art expert of his day. He was the leader of the group who formulated basic principles of the so-called *wên-jên* or *literati* school of painting, which exerted a lasting influence on Chinese and Japanese painting and aesthetics. In his landscape paintings, executed mostly in ink with occasional touches of color, painting and calligraphy were joined harmoniously. Examples of his works may be seen at the Museum of Fine Arts, Boston, and the National Museum, Stockholm.

tundra (tŭn'drə), treeless plains of N North America and N Eurasia, lying principally along the Arctic Circle, on the coasts and islands of the Arctic Ocean, and to the north of the coniferous forest belt. The tundra area is widest in N Siberia on the Kara Sea and reaches as far south as 60° N at the neck of the Kamchatka peninsula. Although sometimes called the Arctic steppe and situated mainly within the Arctic Circle, it reaches southward into the Scandinavian, Timan, and Ural mts. For most of the year the mean monthly temperature is below the freezing point; winters are long and severe. The summers are short and warm, but even in July the mean monthly temperature does not rise above 50°F (10°C). Relatively high temperatures may be reached during a summer day, but the subsoil is perpetually frozen. During this season mosses and lichens appear in abundance, along with some flowering plants. Among the few large animal species found in the tundra are the caribou, the arctic fox, the snowshoe rabbit, and occasionally the polar bear. Precipitation is spread evenly during the year and is slight, varying from 8 to 12 in. (20–30 cm). Evaporation is low, and much of the flat ground in areas of poor drainage becomes swampy during the summer months. Because there are very few species of flora and fauna, the destruction of the tundra is a simple process. The elimination of a single species or the disruption of the permanently frozen subsoil (permafrost) may severely damage this fragile ecosystem. The USSR tundra supports a small human population consisting of the Nensty (Samoyedes) and the Komi. Eskimos inhabit the North American tundra.

Tungchow: see NAN-T'UNG, China.

T'ung-hua or **Tunghwa** (both: tōōng-hwä), city (1970 est. pop. 275,000), SW Kirin prov., China, in a mountainous region, and on a railroad to Korea. Abundant coal and iron reserves are in the area, and the city has iron and steel works. Motor vehicles, machinery, and paper products are also manufactured. The Chinese ski championship was held in T'ung-hua in the winter of 1964–65. The city was formerly the capital of Antung prov. and was part of Liaoning prov. from 1949 to 1954.

Tunghwa: see T'UNG-HUA, China.

tung oil, oil obtained from the seeds of a tropical tree, the tung tree (*Aleurites fordii*) of the SPURGE family, and from seeds of some related species; known also as China wood oil and nut oil. The poisonous seeds found in the heart of the tung fruit (which is the size of a small apple) contain more than 50% tung oil, readily obtained when the seeds are heated, ground, and pressed. The oil is amber-colored and contains a high proportion of eleostearic acid. Because of its wide use as a dryer in varnishes and paints, it has great commercial importance. While the bulk of the product is utilized by the paint and varnish industry, tung oil has additional uses, e.g., as a component of insulating compounds and in the manufacture of linoleum and oilcloth. China was long the chief producer of the oil, but the tree has been introduced in other areas. The U.S. Dept. of Agriculture experimented with tung tree growing early in the 20th cent. and afterward encouraged Southern farmers to cultivate it. In recent years an increasing portion of the commercial supply has been obtained from trees grown in Alabama, Georgia, Florida, Louisiana, Mississippi, and Texas.

Tungshan: see HSÜ-CHOU, China.

tungsten (tŭng'stən) [Swed., =heavy stone], metallic chemical element; symbol W; at. no. 74; at. wt. 183.85; m.p. about 3410°C; b.p. 5927°C; sp. gr. 19.3 at 20°C; valence +2, +3, +4, +5, or +6. Tungsten is a very hard, silver-white to steel-gray metal with a body-centered cubic crystalline structure. In its chemical properties it resembles molybdenum, the element above it in group VIb of the PERIODIC TABLE. It is sometimes called wolfram, and the chemical symbol is taken from this name; in naming compounds of tungsten, use of the name wolfram as a root is preferred. Tungsten is one of the most dense metals and has a higher melting point than any other metal. Pure tungsten is ductile, and wires made of it, even those of very small diameter, have a very high tensile strength. The element is resistant to ordinary acids and aqua regia but dissolves in a mixture of hydrofluoric and nitric acids. It forms compounds with carbon, chlorine, oxygen, sulfur, and some other elements. It is hexavalent in its most important compounds. It forms tungstic acid (H_2WO_4), or wolframic acid, which is the basis of a series of salts called tungstates, or wolframates. Tungsten metal is used extensively for filaments for light bulbs and electronic tubes. CARBOLOY, STELLITE, and tungsten STEELS are of importance in industry because they retain their hardness and strength at high temperatures. Tungsten is usually added to steel in the form of ferrotungsten, obtained by the reduction of ferrous tungstate in an electric furnace. Tungsten carbide is used in place of diamond for dies and as an abrasive. Sodium wolframate is used in the fireproofing of fabrics, in the weighting of silk, and as a mordant in dyeing. Tungsten does not occur uncombined in nature; large deposits of its ores are found in various parts of the world. The trioxide occurs in nature as the mineral wolfram ochre; scheelite and WOLFRAMITE are the chief wolframate minerals. Tungsten is usually prepared from the trioxide by reduction with hydrogen or carbon. Tungsten was first isolated from tungstic acid in 1783 by the de Elhuyar brothers.

Tung-t'ing or **Tungting** (both: dōōng-tĭng), shallow lake, Hunan prov., SE China; one of China's largest lakes. It is fed by the Yüan, Tzu, Hsiang, and many smaller rivers; a canal connects it with the Yangtze River. Depending on the season, the Tung-t'ing varies in size from 1,400 to 4,000 sq mi (3,626–10,360 sq km). It attains its maximum extent during the period of heavy summer rains, when the lake receives the overflow from the Yangtze, which it serves as a natural reservoir. The heavily populated lake basin is one of China's leading rice-producing regions; tea is also an important crop.

tung tree: see SPURGE; TUNG OIL.

Tungus (tōōngōōz'), Siberian ethnic group, numbering about 60,000. They are subdivided into the Evenki, who live in the area from the Yenisi and Ob river basins to the Pacific Ocean and from the Amur River to the Arctic Ocean, and the Lamut, who live on the coast of the Okhotsk Sea. The Tungus are closely related to the Manchus. Certain cultural traits indicate that part of the Japanese population may be descended from this people. Before they were brought under Soviet control, the Tungus practiced a shamanistic religion. The Tungus, or Tunguzic, languages are a family that includes the Manchu literary language; they may be related to the Mongolic and Turkic families. See Ivar Lissner, *Man, God, and Magic* (tr. 1961).

Tunguska (tōōn-gōōs'kə), name of three eastern tributaries of the Yenisei River, E Siberian USSR. The rivers cut across the swampy forests of E Siberia. Furthest north is the **Lower Tunguska** (Rus. *Nizhnyaya Tunguska*) (nyĕzh'nyĭŭ), c.1,590 mi (2,600 km) long. It rises in the Central Siberian Plateau N of Lake Baykal and flows past Tura to join the Yenisei at Turukhansk. Flowing generally west, it is navigable (May–October) for c.1,100 mi (1,770 km). The **Stony Tunguska** (Rus. *Podkamennaya Tunguska*) (pŭtkä'myĭnĭŭ), c.980 mi (1,580 km) long, rises west of the headwaters of the Lower Tunguska. It flows generally NW past Baykit; there are rapids in its lower course. **Upper Tunguska** (Rus. *Verkhnyana Tunguska*) is the name given to the lower course of the Angara River. It flows generally west and joins the Yenisei at Strelka. The area of the three rivers is the home of the TUNGUS.

Tunguska Basin, c.400,000 sq mi (1,036,000 sq km), E Siberian USSR, between the Yenisei and Lena rivers. It has a huge untapped coal reserve. The main settlements there are Norilsk, Igarka, and Yeniseisk.

Tun-huang or **Tunhwang** (both: dōōn-hwäng), town, extreme NW Kansu prov., China. The Caves of the Thousand Buddhas are at nearby Tsienfotung (Ch'ienfotung). The town and its environs were long a gateway between central Asia and China, and the frescoes in the caves, painted from the 5th cent. to the 13th cent., show Indian, Greco-Roman, and Iranian influences. The caves, closed for centuries, were reopened in 1900. There Sir Aurel Stein, an English archaeologist, discovered a library of some 15,000 manuscripts, including the Diamond Sutra, reputed to be the first (A.D. 868) printed book.

tunicate (to͞o'nəkĭt), marine animal of the phylum CHORDATA, which also includes the vertebrates. The adult form of most tunicates (also called urochordates) shows no resemblance to vertebrate animals, but such a resemblance is evident in the larva. The most familiar tunicates are the sea squirts, or ascidians (class Ascidiacea). Adult sea squirts are sedentary, filter-feeding, cylindrical or globular animals, usually found attached to rocks, shells, pilings, or boat bottoms. The soft body is surrounded by a thick test, or tunic, often transparent or translucent and varying in consistency from gelatinous to leathery. The tunic (for which the tunicates are named) is secreted by the body wall of the adult animal. It is composed of cellulose, an almost unique occurrence of that material in the animal kingdom. Two siphons project from the animal's body; water enters the incurrent siphon at the top of the body and leaves the excurrent siphon at the side. Food particles are filtered from the water by the pharynx, which occupies most of the body, and are then passed into the digestive system. Some species reproduce by budding, resulting in the formation of colonies of sea squirts, joined at their bases by slender stalks or embedded in a slab of common tunic material. In addition, nearly all species reproduce sexually and are hermaphroditic. The free-swimming larva, called a tadpole, has a muscular tail and is similar in appearance to a frog tadpole. The larva has the characteristic chordate features also found in the embryos of vertebrates: a dorsal, hollow nerve cord; a stiffening rod, or notochord; and gill slits leading into the pharynx. The tadpole eventually settles and undergoes a drastic metamorphosis into the adult form. A common solitary sea squirt of both coasts of North America is the slender, yellow, transparent *Ciona intestinalis*, about 2 in. (5 cm) tall. The sea peach, *Tethyum pyriforme*, is a round, peach-colored sea squirt found from Maine north. Sea grapes are clusters of the greenish colonial squirt, *Molgula manhattensis*, common from Massachusetts south. Golden stars are colonies of various *Botryllus* species; the bright yellow individual animals are grouped in starlike clusters in a flat, encrusting, greenish tunic. *Amaroucium* species form colonies of minute animals embedded in a grayish, gristly tunic; chunks of such colonies, often washed ashore, are known as sea pork. There are two other groups of tunicates, both found in the plankton of open oceans. The salps (class Thaliacea) are barrel-shaped tunicates, open at both ends; they swim by muscular contractions that force water through the body. The larvaceans (class Larvacea) retain the larval form, with a tail and a notochord, as adults. A commonly held theory maintains that vertebrates evolved from animals like the larvaceans. Larvaceans have no tunics, but secrete gelatinous containers, called houses; these are used to filter food from the water and are continuously discarded and replaced. Tunicates are classified in the phylum Chordata, subphylum Urochordata.

tuning: see TUNING SYSTEMS.

tuning fork, steel instrument in the shape of a U with a short handle. When struck it produces an

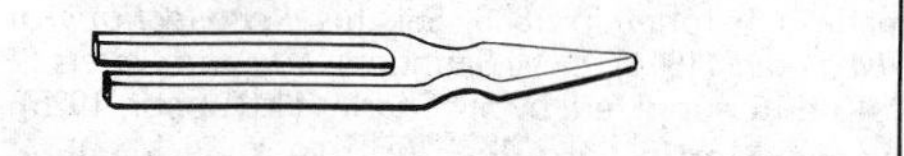

Tuning fork

almost pure tone, retaining its pitch over a long period of time; thus it is a valuable aid in tuning musical instruments. It was invented in 1711 by John Shore, who jokingly called it a pitchfork.

tuning systems, methods for assigning pitches to the twelve pitch names that constitute the octave. The term usually refers to this procedure in the tuning of keyboard instruments. The need for a tuning system hinges on the conflict of pitch relationships in the natural overtone series and the exigencies of musical compositional systems, specifically those utilizing the familiar diatonic scale. Chronologically, the conflict occurred in the early Renaissance when composers had an increasing desire to modulate from one key to another. Implicit in the concept of modulation is the condition of identity of intervals between corresponding scale degrees in different modes or keys. A keyboard instrument tuned to a function of any natural interval except the octave will not satisfy that condition. The Pythagorean system, derived from a scale supposedly invented by PYTHAGORAS (c.550 B.C.), was generated by acoustically perfect fifths. It exhibited an audible difference between the interval of a semitone and the interval resulting from the subtraction of the semitone from the whole tone. The mean-tone system generated the scale with fifths just flat enough to eliminate this difference, producing a scale containing acoustically perfect thirds. Discrepancy between chromatic notes (semitones) rendered this system unsuitable for successive modulations. Equal temperament tuning, which replaced mean-tone tuning in the 18th cent. and is universally accepted today, partitions the octave into twelve equal semitones. All intervals except the octave are acoustically out of tune, but by a tolerable degree, making complex modulations and atonality possible.

Tunis (to͞onĭs), city (1966 pop. 468,997), capital of Tunisia, NE Tunisia, on the Lake of Tunis. Access to the Gulf of Tunis (an arm of the Mediterranean) is by a canal terminating at a subsidiary port, Halq al Wadi (La Goulette). Products include textiles, carpets, and olive oil. There are railroad workshops and a lead smelter. Tunis has notable mosques, the Univ. of Tunis (1960), and a national museum. The ruins of CARTHAGE are nearby, to the northeast. Tunis is probably pre-Carthaginian. Surviving from the Middle Ages are walls, an aqueduct, and a mosque. Tunis became the capital of Tunisia under the powerful Hafsid dynasty (13th–16th cent.) and was a leading center of trade with Europe and the Levant. Turks under Barbarossa took it in 1534 but were temporarily (1535–69, 1573–74) dislodged by the Spanish. After 1591 the Turkish governors (the beys) were practically independent, and the city prospered as a center of piracy and trade. Under the French occupation (1881–1956) a modern European quarter was built and the port was improved. In World War II, Tunis was held by Axis forces from Nov., 1942, to May 7, 1943, and was the base for their final stand in Africa.

Tunisia (to͞onē'zhə, tyo͞o-), Fr. *Tunisie*, republic (1973 est. pop. 5,500,000), 63,378 sq mi (164,150 sq km), NW Africa. The capital is TUNIS. Tunisia, occupying the eastern portion of the great bulge of North Africa, is bounded on the W by Algeria, on the N and E by the Mediterranean Sea, and on the SE by Libya. It has a highly irregular coastline that affords many bays and several fine harbors, notably

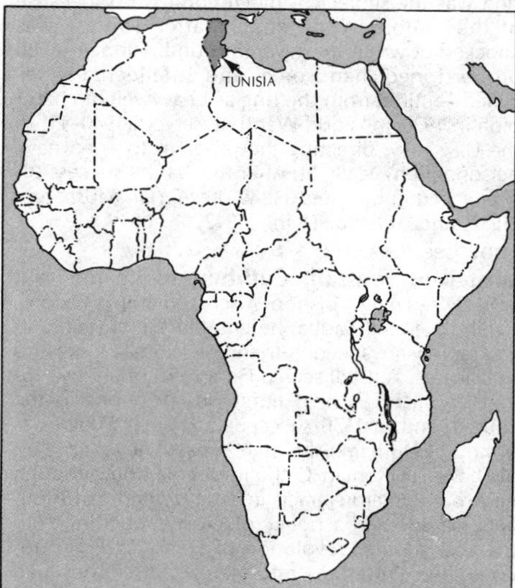

BIZERTE, QABIS, SAFAQIS, and SUSAH. Part of the Atlas Mts. runs through N Tunisia; but, unlike Morocco and Algeria, the mountains in Tunisia rarely exceed 4,000 ft (1,219 m) in elevation. In the south, below the Chott Djerid (a great salt lake), stretches the Sahara Desert. Tunisia's economy is based on agriculture. The leading crops are wheat, barley, grapes, olives, citrus fruits, and dates. Mineral production is the second most important sector of the economy. Phosphates and iron are found in quantity and some zinc and lead are also mined. Petroleum was found (1964) in the Sahara not far from the Algerian border, and production began in 1966. Subsequently other oil fields were discovered, and production has increased substantially. Tunisia's newly established manufacturing industries include steelworks, textile factories, food-processing plants, and sugar refineries. Petroleum, phosphates, and olive oil are the country's leading exports; its imports, which exceed exports, are headed by machinery, metal products, and transportation equipment. France and the United States are the main trade partners. The population is largely Berber and Muslim, Arabic being the official language; there is a Jewish community dating back to ancient times. The coast of Tunisia was settled in the 12th cent. B.C. by Phoenicians. In the 6th cent. B.C., CARTHAGE rose to power, but it was conquered by Rome (2d cent. B.C.), and the region became one of the granaries of Rome. It was held by Vandals (5th cent. A.D.) and Byzantines (6th cent.). In the 7th cent. it was conquered by Arabs, who founded AL QAYRAWAN. The region became known as Ifriqiya and the Berber population was converted to Islam. Successive Muslim dynasties ruled, interrupted by Berber rebellions. The reigns of the Aghlabids (9th cent.) and of the Zirids (from 972), Berber followers of the Fatimids, were especially prosperous. When the Zirids incurred the wrath of the Fatimids in Cairo (1050), the latter sent thousands of Arab tribesmen to ravage Tunisia. The coasts were briefly held by the Normans of Sicily in the 12th cent. In 1159, Tunisia was conquered by the Almohad caliphs of Morocco. The Almohads were succeeded by the Berber Hafsids (c.1230–1574), under whom Tunisia prospered. In the last years of the Hafsids, Spain seized many of the coastal cities, but they were recovered for Islam by the Ottoman Turks. Under its Turkish governors, the beys, Tunisia attained virtual independence. In the late 16th cent. the coast became a pirate stronghold (see BARBARY STATES). The Hussein dynasty of beys, established in 1705, lasted until 1957. In the 19th cent. the heavy debts that the beys had contracted gave European powers cause for intervention. France, Great Britain, and Italy took over Tunisia's finances in 1869. A number of incidents, including attacks on Algeria (a French possession since 1830) by Tunisians, led to a French invasion of Tunisia. The bey was forced to sign the treaties of Bardo (1881) and Mersa (1883), which provided for the organization of a protectorate under a French resident general. The protectorate was opposed by Italy, which had economic interests and a sizable group of nationals in Tunisia. Italy's attitude grew increasingly belligerent, and, in the years immediately preceding World War I, threats of annexation were made. A nationalist movement developed fairly quickly in Tunisia. In 1920 the Destour (Constitutional) party was organized. In 1934 a more radical faction, led by Habib BOURGUIBA, formed the Neo-Destour party. In World War II, Tunisia came under Vichy rule after the fall of France (June, 1940). Major battles of the war in North Africa were fought in Tunisia (see NORTH AFRICA, CAMPAIGNS IN). After the war nationalist agitation intensified. In 1950, France granted Tunisia a large degree of autonomy. The French population in Tunisia, however, opposed further reforms, and negotiations broke down. Bourguiba was arrested (1952), and his imprisonment precipitated a wave of violence. In 1954 the new French premier, Mendès-France, offered to grant Tunisia complete internal self-government, and an agreement to this effect was signed the following year. Full independence was negotiated in 1956, and Bourguiba became prime minister. The country became a republic in 1957 when the bey, Sidi Lamine, was deposed by a vote of the constituent assembly, which then made Bourguiba president. Bourguiba followed a generally pro-Western foreign policy, but relations with France were strained over Algerian independence, which Tunisia supported, and the evacuation of French troops from Tunisia. The French naval installations at Bizerte were the scene of violent confrontation in 1961; France finally agreed to evacuate them in 1963. Relations between Tunisia and Algeria deteriorated after the latter gained (1962) its independence from France, and border disputes between the two countries were not settled until 1970. Bourguiba's support for a negotiated settlement with Israel of the Middle East problem caused strains in its relations with other Arab countries. Bourguiba also accused Egypt (1958) and Algeria (1962) of complicity in attempts by followers of Salah Ben Youssef, the exiled former nationalist leader, to assassinate him. Domestically, Bourguiba's policies emphasized modernization and planned economic growth. An agrarian reform plan, involving the formation of cooperatives, was begun in 1962, but the program was implemented harshly and corruptly, arousing widespread opposition. It was halted in 1969, and the responsible official, Ahmad Ben Salah, was arrested, following his dismissal. In the early 1970s there was increasing conflict within the ruling Destour party between liberals and conservatives. Student demonstrations gave evidence of general unrest, and the succession to Bourguiba, whose health was poor, was a question of increasing importance. Tunisia is governed under the 1959 constitution; the president and national assembly are elected every five years. A cabinet is appointed by the president, and a council, consisting of the cabinet and leaders of the Destour party (the only legal party), advises the president and has power to choose an interim successor. See Ghazi Duwaji, *Economic Development in Tunisia* (1967); D. L. Ling, *Tunisia: From Protectorate to Republic* (1967); Lars Rudebeck, *Party and People: A Study of Political Change in Tunisia* (1969); Winfrid Knapp, *Tunisia* (1970); H. C. Reese et al., *Area Handbook for the Republic of Tunisia* (1970); Rafik Said, *Cultural Policy in Tunisia* (1970); Arthur Marsden, *British Diplomacy and Tunis, 1875–1902* (1972).

Tunja (to͝on'hä), city (1968 est. pop. 72,700), capital of Boyacá dept., central Colombia, on the Pan-American Highway. It is a commercial center and distribution point for the products of the region (coal, emeralds, mineral water, and agricultural products) and for the cattle of the eastern llanos. Tunja was founded in 1539. It declared its independence from Spain in 1811 and shortly thereafter served as Simón BOLÍVAR'S staging point for the victory at BOYACÁ. The city retains many colonial buildings.

Tunkers: see BRETHREN.

Tunki (to͝on'chē'), city, SE Anhwei prov., China. It is a major tea-producing center.

tunnel, underground passage, approximately horizontal, usually made without removing the overlying rock or soil. The origin of tunnel building is disputed. The Egyptians built tunnels as entrances to tombs. The Babylonians built (c.2180 B.C.) a tunnel under the Euphrates. Using what is now called the "cut-and-cover" method, the river was diverted, a wide trench was dug across its bed, and a brick tube was constructed in it and covered up. The ancient Greeks and Romans built tunnels for carrying water and for mining purposes; some of the Roman tunnels are still in use. One of the first notable tunnels in Great Britain was part of the Grand Trunk Canal. It was nearly 2 mi (3.2 km) long and was completed in 1777. Methods of tunneling vary with the nature of the material to be cut through. When soft earth is encountered, the excavation is timbered for support as the work advances; the timbers are sometimes left as a permanent lining for the tunnel. Another method is to cut two parallel excavations in which the side walls are constructed first. Arches connecting them are then built as the material between them is extracted. Portions of the unexcavated center, left temporarily for support, are later removed. A tunnel cut through rock frequently requires no lining. Hard rock is removed by blasting. Tunnels must be built with sufficient gradient for proper drainage. The Mont Cenis Tunnel, nearly 8 mi (12.9 km) long, opened in 1871, and passing through the Alps, was probably the first tunnel built with the use of compressed-air drills. The SIMPLON TUNNEL, the longest railway tunnel in the world, also through the Alps, consists of two parallel single-line tunnels with connecting tunnels at short intervals. Great difficulty was experienced during its building because of the presence of hot spring water. In constructing tunnels under rivers, the ordinary methods can be used as long as a stratum of impermeable material lies between the tunnel and the river bed. In all cases, however, pumping equipment must be installed. Where mud, quicksand, or permeable earth is present in underwater tunneling, it becomes necessary to provide some means of holding back the water while the enclosing sections of the tunnel are placed in position. For this purpose the shield was devised and first used in 1825 by the French-born engineer Sir Marc I. Brunel when boring between Wapping and Rotherhithe, in England. Considered unsuccessful, the device was not employed again until 1869, when the British engineer James H. Greathead and the American inventor Alfred E. Beach developed improvements at about the same time. Their shields were metal cylinders fitting around the outside of the tunnel, the forward end closed by a diaphragm plate. The shield was shoved forward into the earth, headings being cut through openings in the forward end, and the tunnel walls were extended within the cylinder. Greathead introduced the use of compressed air in conjunction with the shield to keep out water and substituted cast-iron ring sections for brick and mortar as a tunnel lining. Beach introduced the use of hydraulic rams to push the shield forward. The use of the pneumatic shield is now universal in tunneling under rivers, the air pressure employed varying with depth and permeability of the earth being bored. River-crossing tunnels are also constructed by dredging a trench in the river bed and then lowering prefabricated tunnel sections through the water into the trench, where they are connected to each other. The trench and tunnel are then covered over. Often, to speed construction, work is started at both ends. This poses no problem with the cut-and-cover method, but when the tunnel is bored from within, it must be assured that the tubes will actually meet in the center. Modern methods accomplish this with high precision. Tunnels may be ventilated by shafts leading to the surface or by exhaust fans at the ends. The first tunnel of importance in the United States was the tunnel through the HOOSAC RANGE in Massachusetts. There are hundreds of miles of tunnels in New York City and its vicinity, e.g., for subways, roads, water systems, and railroads. The DELAWARE AQUEDUCT, which provides part of New York City's water supply, is the longest continuous tunnel in the world. Road tunnels include the Holland Tunnel and the Lincoln Tunnel, which connect New York City with New Jersey, and the Brooklyn-Battery Tunnel, which connects Manhattan with Brooklyn. The Chesapeake Bay Bridge-Tunnel has a length of 18 mi (29 km). Part bridge and part tunnel, it was opened in 1963 and now connects the lower tip of Virginia's eastern shore with the Hampton Roads-Norfolk area. The longest road tunnel in the world is the Mont Blanc Tunnel between Italy and France. It is 7.2 mi (11.6 km) long. See F. E. Dean, *Tunnels and Tunnelling* (1963); G. E. Sandstrom, *Tunnels* (1963); Patrick Beaver, *A History of Tunnels* (1973).

tunnel diode: see DIODE.

Tunney, James Joseph (Gene Tunney), 1898–, American boxer, b. New York City. He began boxing in neighborhood clubs. In World War I, he served in the U.S. marines and in Paris won (1919) the light-heavyweight championship of the American Expeditionary Forces. In 1922 he defeated Battling Levinsky for the American light-heavyweight title, but lost it the same year to Harry Greb—the only fighter to defeat Tunney in the professional ring. Tunney regained this title in 1923. In 1926, Tunney defeated Jack Dempsey in a 10-round decision in Philadelphia and became the world heavyweight champion. In Chicago a year later, Tunney repeated this performance in a return bout with Dempsey; the decision was the subject of much controversy because of the famous "long count" after Tunney was knocked down in the seventh round. Tunney—well proportioned, handsome, and intellectually inclined—retired from the ring as heavyweight champion in 1928. In World War II he served (1940–45) in the U.S. navy, directing the program to keep navy personnel physically fit. After the war he successfully engaged in business. He wrote *A Man Must Fight* (1932) and *Arms for Living* (1942).

tunny: see TUNA.

Tunstall or **Tonstall, Cuthbert** (both: tŭn'stəl), 1474–1559, English bishop. After studying at Oxford, Cambridge, and Padua, he entered the church and was rapidly advanced. A friend of Thomas More and of Erasmus, Tunstall served Henry VIII on many diplomatic missions, held numerous positions in the church, and in 1530 succeeded Thomas Wolsey as bishop of Durham. Although Tunstall never gave up his belief in Roman Catholic dogma and although he wrote numerous tracts in Latin defending his beliefs, he adopted a policy of passive obedience to the ecclesiastical revolution of Henry VIII. He opposed the Protestant reforms, but after they had been passed he helped carry them out. He supported Henry's oath of supremacy, and in 1537 he was made president of the Council of the North. In Edward VI's reign he supported the protectorate of Edward Seymour, duke of SOMERSET, and was imprisoned and deprived after Somerset's fall (1551). Restored to his bishopric at the accession of Mary (1553), he refrained from the persecution of Protestants, and there were no executions in his diocese. Tunstall refused to take the oath of supremacy when Elizabeth I came to the throne, and he was placed in the custody of the archbishop of Canterbury.

Tupac Amaru (to͞opäk' ämä'ro͞o), 1742?–1781, Indian leader in Peru, baptized José Gabriel Condorcanqui. A man of some education and of high moral character, he sympathized with the plight of the Indians of Peru and sought to alleviate their condition. Unable to persuade the government to better conditions in the textile mills, the mines, and the villages, Condorcanqui, under the name of his ancestor, the Inca Tupac Amaru, led a rebellion in 1780. The Indians, regarding him with reverence, flocked to support him, and at first Tupac Amaru was successful. He was later captured and executed with incredible brutality. The revolt continued, notably with the siege of La Paz in 1781, but was finally crushed. All of Tupac Amaru's family were executed or imprisoned, but many of the reforms for which he died were granted.

Tupamaros (to͞opämä'rōs), urban guerrilla organization in Uruguay; it derives its name from the Inca revolutionist, Tupac Amaru. An extreme leftist group, it became active in the early 1960s, operating primarily in Montevideo. At first it aided the poor, stealing food and money and distributing it among them, but by the late 1960s it was engaged in bombings, bank robberies, political kidnappings, and murder. The government under President Pacheco Areco waged a vigorous campaign against the Tupamaros, making numerous arrests, which at first seemed only to provoke more outrageous crimes. By 1973, however, most of the leadership appeared to have been captured, and the group's activities dramatically declined. It is also called the National Liberation Movement.

Tupelo (to͞o'pĭlō, tyo͞o–), city (1970 pop. 20,471), seat of Lee co., NE Miss.; founded 1859, inc. 1870. It is the trade, processing, and shipping center for a cotton and livestock area. A U.S. fish hatchery is there. On the Civil War battlefield of Tupelo, now a national battlefield (see NATIONAL PARKS AND MONUMENTS, table), Union troops repulsed an attack by Gen. N. B. Forrest (July 14, 1864) but nevertheless retreated. Nearby is the scene of a victory of Chickasaw and British forces over the Choctaw and French (May 26, 1736). Tombigbee State Park and the Natchez Trace Parkway visitor center are also in the vicinity.

tupelo: see BLACK GUM.

Tupelo National Battlefield: see TUPELO, Miss.; NATIONAL PARKS AND MONUMENTS (table).

Tupí Indians: see GUARANÍ INDIANS.

Tupolev, Andrei Nikolayevich (əndrā' nyĭkəlī'əvĭch to͞opō'lĕf), 1888–1972, Soviet aeronautical engineer, educated at the Moscow Technical Institute. In 1918 he helped organize the Central Aerodynamics Institute, the first aerodynamics research institution in the USSR. Tupolev was the first in the USSR to design all-metal aircraft. Several of his military designs were widely used during World War II, and he later designed several jet-propelled military and commercial aircraft. Tupolev is widely considered the foremost aircraft designer of the USSR.

Tupper, Sir Charles, 1821–1915, Canadian statesman, b. Nova Scotia. A doctor, he sat (1855–67) in the provincial legislature, became (1864) premier of Nova Scotia, and was a leader in the movement for Canadian confederation. Despite the opposition of Joseph Howe, Tupper eventually brought Nova Scotia into the dominion. A loyal supporter of Prime Minister John Macdonald, he held several important cabinet posts. As minister of railways and canals (1879–84), he helped achieve the completion of the Canadian Pacific Railway. In 1896 he became prime minister of Canada and urged the adoption of a preferential tariff with Great Britain and the colonies, but his Conservative party was defeated that year. Tupper became leader of the opposition, serving until his defeat in the election of 1900. He was made a baronet in 1888. See his *Recollections of Sixty Years* (1914); E. M. Saunders, *Life and Letters* (2 vol., 1916; suppl. ed. by Sir Charles H. Tupper, 1926).

Tupper, Martin Farquhar, 1810–89, English author. He is remembered for his *Proverbial Philosophy* (1838–76), a popular collection of moralizations in blank verse. See his autobiography (1886).

tur: see IBEX.

Tura, Cosmé or **Cosimo** (kōzmā' to͞o'rä, kô'zēmō), c.1430–1495, Italian artist. He was a leading master of the Ferrarese school and court painter to Borso d'Este and Ercole d'Este. His paintings are filled with erudite symbols. At the same time they are peppered with delightful natural details—squirrels, monkeys, diversified landscapes, and fruits. Examples of his art are two organ panels, *Annunciation* and *St. George Slaying the Dragon* (cathedral, Ferrara); *Pietà* (Venice); *Christ on the Cross* (Milan); *St. Jerome* (National Gall., London); *Portrait of a Man* and *Saints* (National Gall. of Art, Washington, D.C.). Attributed to him is a portrait of a member of the Este family, *The Fight into Egypt,* and *St. Louis of Toulouse* (all: Metropolitan Mus.). His works are executed in a harsh, linear, rather angular style, with strident coloring. The total effect is powerful. See biography by Eberhard Ruhmer (1958).

Turan (to͝orän'), desert lowland, in W TURKISTAN, Central Asian USSR, S and E of the Aral Sea. The Amu Darya and Syr Darya rivers divide it into the KARA-KUM desert in the south, the KYZYL-KUM desert in the center, and the Aral Kara-Kum desert in the north. The region has very little precipitation and is sparsely populated, except in the fertile irrigated oases along the Amu Darya and Syr Darya, where cotton, fruit, and rice are grown. Part of the region is used for sheep grazing.

turbellarian: see PLATYHELMINTHES; PLANARIAN.

turbidity current: see OCEAN.

turbine, rotary engine that uses a continuous stream of fluid (gas or liquid) to turn a shaft that can drive machinery. A water, or hydraulic, turbine is used to drive electric generators in hydroelectric power stations. The first such station was built in Wisconsin in 1882. In a hydraulic turbine falling water strikes a series of blades or buckets attached around a shaft, causing the shaft to rotate, this motion in turn being used to drive the rotor of an electric generator. The three most common types of hydraulic turbine are the Pelton wheel, the Francis turbine, and the Kaplan turbine. Toward the end of the 19th cent. two engineers, Sir Charles A. Parsons of Great Britain and Carl G. P. de Laval of Sweden, were pioneers in the building of steam turbines. Continual improvements of their basic machines have caused steam

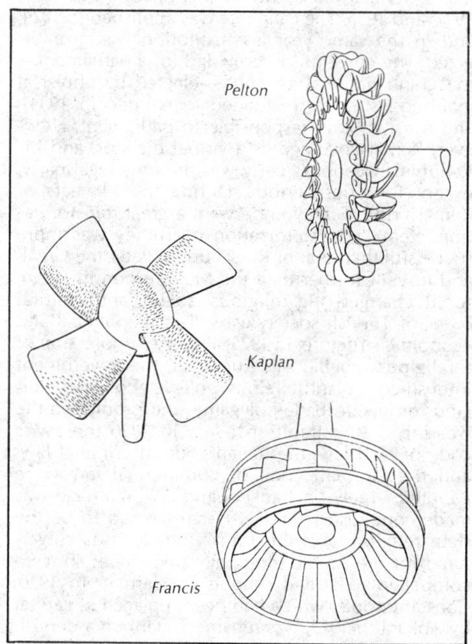

Types of turbines

turbines to become the principal power sources used to drive most large electric generators and the propellers of most large ships. A steam turbine typically consists of a roughly conical, steel shell enclosing a central shaft along which a series of bladed disks are spaced like washers. The blades are curved and extend radially outward from the rim of each disk. In some steam turbines the shaft is surrounded by a drum to which the rows of blades are attached. Between each pair of disks is a row of stationary vanes attached to the steel shell and extending radially inward. Each set of stationary vanes and the bladed disk immediately next to it constitutes a stage of the turbine; most steam turbines are multistage engines. At the inlet end of the turbine high-pressure steam enters from a boiler and moves through the turbine parallel to the shaft, first striking a row of stationary vanes that directs the steam against the first bladed disk at an optimum speed and angle. The steam then passes through the remaining stages, forcing the disks and the shaft to rotate. At one end of the turbine the shaft sticks out and can be attached to machinery. A large steam turbine unit may actually be composed of several turbines that are all using the same shaft and steam. Such a unit might consist of a small, high-pressure turbine, connected to a larger, intermediate-pressure turbine, connected to a still larger, low-pressure turbine. After the steam leaves the turbine, it is sent to a condenser where it is converted back into water before being returned to the boiler. Gas turbines are used mainly as aircraft engines. Some are used to drive electric generators and high-speed tools. The term *gas turbine* is usually applied to a unit whose essential components are a compressor, a combustion chamber, and a turbine that resembles a steam turbine. The turbine drives the compressor, which feeds high-pressure air into the combustion chamber; there it is mixed with a fuel and burned, providing high-pressure gases to drive the turbine, the gases expanding until their pressure drops to atmospheric pressure. In a turboprop engine the turbine is used to turn a propeller as well as the compressor. In a turbojet engine only a small pressure drop is used to drive the turbine, the majority of the pressure drop occurring as the gases are expelled directly out of the engine. A variation of the turbojet is known as the turbofan engine.

turbojet: see TURBINE.

turboprop: see TURBINE.

turbot: see FLATFISH.

Turcoman: see TURKMEN SOVIET SOCIALIST REPUBLIC.

Turenne, Henri de La Tour d'Auvergne, vicomte de (äNrē' də lä to͝or dōvĕr'nyə vĕkôNt' də tərĕn'), 1611–75, marshal of France, one of the greatest of French commanders. The son of the duc de BOUILLON, he was brought up as a Protestant. He began his military career in the Dutch army but soon entered French service. Turenne showed his great capabilities in the THIRTY YEARS WAR, distinguishing himself under Bernhard of Saxe-Weimar in the victory (1638) over the imperial forces at Breisach. In the successful battles of Freiburg im Breisgau (1644) and Nördlingen (1645) he served with the brilliant commander Louis II de Bourbon, prince de Condé; the lives of the two were thereafter intertwined. Turenne, who had been made a marshal in 1643, was—with the Swede Lennart Torstensson—the dominant figure in the last years of the war. His series of victories expedited the long negotiations leading to the Peace of Westphalia (1648). In the war of the Fronde of the Princes (see under FRONDE) he was persuaded by Mme de Longueville, Condé's sister, to take the part of the rebels led by Condé and was defeated (1650) by government forces at Rethel. When the princes of the Fronde had been reconciled with Mazarin, Turenne again became a government commander. He defeated (1652) Condé roundly at the battle of the Faubourg Saint-Antoine near Paris and was again (1658) victorious over Condé in the Battle of the Dunes, when the latter was serving with Spain. In the War of Devolution (see DEVOLUTION, WAR OF) he commanded (1667) in Flanders but had no part in the campaign (1669) of Condé (now reconciled to the government) in Franche-Comté. In the third of the DUTCH WARS he marched with King Louis XIV and Condé into Holland, but the French were checked before Amsterdam by the opening (1672) of the dikes. On the Rhine, Turenne defeated (1674) enemy troops at Sinzheim and ravaged the Palatinate. He was killed in battle against the troops of Raimondo Montecucculi. His emphasis on mobility and surprise and his patient calculation, matched by his personal courage and his popularity with his men, won him much admiration. Late in his life he was converted (1668) to Roman Catholicism. See biography by Maxime Weygand (tr. 1930).

turf: see LAWN.

Turfan: see T'U-LU-FAN, China.

Turgenev, Ivan Sergeyevich (ēvän' syĭrgā'əvĭch to͝orgā'nyĭf), 1818–83, Russian novelist, dramatist, and short-story writer, considered one of the foremost Russian writers. He came from a landowning family in Orel province, and his cruel, domineering mother was a great influence on his life. Turgenev studied in Moscow, St. Petersburg, and Berlin, and he became an enthusiastic advocate of the Westernization of Russia. His early writings were published in Nekrasov's journal *The Contemporary.* He won his first success in 1847 with "Khor and Kalinich," a sympathetic story of peasant life, which was published later, with similar stories, in *A Sportsman's Sketches* (1852). In this book he attacked serfdom, and it is thought that this work helped induce Alexander II to emancipate the serfs. Turgenev's most fruitful period was the decade 1850–60, the latter half of which he spent in Western Europe. In his novels of this period, which include *Rudin* (1855), *A Nest of Gentlefolk* (1859), and *On the Eve* (1860), Turgenev is concerned with Russian social and political issues. His masterpiece, *Fathers and Sons* (1861), deals with nihilist philosophy and personal and social rebellion. The novel was severely criticized, and Turgenev resolved to remain outside Russia, where he could continue his passionate, lifelong love affair with the French singer Pauline Viardot-Garcia. His last long works were *Smoke* (1867) and *Virgin Soil* (1877), both of which treated social themes. Turgenev also wrote several plays, including *A Month in the Country* (1850), in which he made several dramatic innovations that Chekhov later developed, and the comedy *A Provincial Lady* (1851). His superbly crafted short stories are considered his greatest works, including "First Love" (1870), "A Lear of the Steppe" (1870), and "Torrents of Spring" (1871). His works remain enormously popular in the USSR. Almost all of them are available in English. See his *Literary Reminiscences* (1958); his letters (tr. 1960); biographies by David Magarshack (1954), Avrahm Yarmolinsky (rev. ed. 1959), and J. A. T. Lloyd (1942, repr. 1971); study by Richard Freeborn (1960).

Turgot, Anne Robert Jacques (än rōbĕr' zhäk türgō'), 1727–81, French economist, comptroller general of finances (1774–76). The son of a rich merchant, he showed precocious ability at school and at the Sorbonne. He early abandoned plans to enter the priesthood, and in 1752 he entered the royal administration. From 1761 to 1774 he was intendant of LIMOGES. After writing his *Lettres sur la tolérance* (1753–54), Turgot wrote on economic subjects, notably *Réflexions sur la formation et la distribution des richesses.* He advocated the free-trade and free-competition principles of Vincent de GOURNAY and was a disciple of the PHYSIOCRATS. In Limoges, then one of the poorest provinces of France, he applied some of his theories. He encouraged new agricultural methods, introduced new crops, developed industry, promoted local free trade, abolished compulsory labor for public work, built roads, instituted a modicum of public assistance, and removed some tax abuses. Although his reforms were on a modest scale and encountered much local prejudice, he was acclaimed for them, particularly by the philosophes, whom Turgot joined in writing the ENCYCLOPÉDIE. In 1774 the comte de MAUREPAS made him comptroller general of finances in his cabinet. Turgot's program—"No bankruptcy, no increase in taxes, no borrowing, but economy"—necessitated stringent reforms. He abolished some sinecures and monopolies, tried to improve the system of FARMING the taxes, drastically cut government expenses, and redeemed part of the public debt. His edict (1774) restoring free circulation of grain inside France antagonized the grain speculators and was unfortunately followed by a crop failure. Bread riots resulted and were suppressed. This, together with the threat to vested interests posed by his reforms, caused Turgot to lose much of his popularity. He aroused the clergy by favoring toleration of the Protestants and provoked a storm of protest by his six edicts of Jan., 1776. The first four edicts were not of major importance. The fifth abolished guilds, thus ending restrictions on work and occupation. The sixth, the most important, struck at the nobles by eliminating the CORVÉE and proposing taxation of all landholders. Opposition to him now included all privileged groups as well as the queen, Marie Antoinette, whose enmity he had incurred when he refused favors to her protégés. Maurepas persuaded Louis XVI to ask Turgot's resignation (May, 1776). Refusing the offer of a pension, Turgot retired to a life of scientific, historical, and literary study. He was succeeded by Jacques NECKER, and his edicts were repealed. Subsequent events vindicated Turgot's conviction—expressed as early as 1750—that the only alternative to radical reform was still more radical revolution. There is a five-volume edition of his works by Gustave Schelle (1913–23, in French). See Léon Say, *Turgot* (1888, tr. 1888); Douglas Dakin, *Turgot and the Ancien Régime in France* (1939, repr. 1965).

Turin (to͝or'ĭn, tyo͝or'–, tyo͝orĭn'), Ital. *Torino*, city (1971 pop. 1,177,939), capital of Piedmont and of Turin prov., NW Italy, at the confluence of the Po and Dora Riparia rivers. It is a major industrial center and a transportation hub. Manufactures include motor vehicles (especially Fiat and Lancia), tires, textiles, clothing, machinery, electronic equipment, leather goods, furniture, chemicals, and vermouth. It is an international center of clothing fashions. The most important Roman town of the W Po valley, Turin was later a Lombard duchy and then a Frankish county. In spite of the claims of the house of Savoy, it remained a free commune in the 12th and 13th cent. It passed c.1280 to the house of Savoy (see SAVOY, HOUSE OF). Occupied (1536–62) by the French, it was restored to the dukes of Savoy and became the capital of their duchy. From 1720 to 1861 it was the capital of the kingdom of Sardinia. During the War of the Spanish Succession it suffered a long siege, which ended with the victory of Eugene of Savoy over the French. In 1798, Charles

Emmanuel IV of Savoy was obliged by the French to abdicate and to abandon Turin, but Victor Emmanuel I returned in 1814, and the city soon became the center of Italian national aspirations. From 1861 to 1864 it was the capital of the new Italian kingdom. Because of its industrial importance, Turin suffered heavy damage in World War II; most of the important remaining buildings date from the 17th–19th cent. Of note are the Palace of the Marquesses of Caraglio e Senantes (17th cent.); the Palazzo Madama (begun late 13th cent.); the royal palace (17th cent.), which houses a fine collection of arms and armor; the Academy of Science, which contains the rich Egyptian Museum; the Cathedral of San Giovanni (late 15th cent.), which has an urn containing a shroud in which, it is said, Jesus was wrapped after the descent from the Cross; and the Car Museum. On a hill overlooking the city is the basilica of Superga (1717–31), containing the tombs of many of the dukes of Savoy and kings of Sardinia. Turin has a university.

Turkestan: see TURKISTAN.

Turkey, Turk. *Türkiye* (tür"kēyĕ'), republic (1970 pop. 35,666,549), 301,380 sq mi (780,574 sq km), SW Asia and SE Europe, bordering on Iraq in the southeast, on Syria and the Mediterranean Sea in the south, on the Aegean Sea in the west, on Greece and Bulgaria in the northwest, on the Black Sea in the north, and on the USSR and Iran in the east. Asian Turkey (made up largely of Asia Minor), which includes 97% of the country, is separated from European Turkey (made up of E THRACE) by the Bosporus, the Sea of Marmara, and the Dardanelles (which together form a water link between the Black Sea and the Mediterranean). Northeast Asian Turkey includes part of ARMENIA, and SE Asian Turkey includes part of KURDISTAN. ANKARA is the capital of the country, which is divided into 67 provinces (*ils*). European Turkey, which includes EDİRNE and most of İSTANBUL, is largely rolling agricultural land and is drained by the Ergene River. Asian Turkey is mostly made up of highland and mountains, with some narrow strips of lowland in the west on the coasts of the Aegean Sea and the Sea of Marmara and along the Simav, Gediz, and Menderes rivers; in the north on the Black Sea coast and along the Sakarya and Kızıl Irmak rivers; and in the south on the Mediterranean coast and along the Aksu, Göksu, Seyhan, and Ceyhan rivers. The center of W Asian Turkey is made up of the vast semiarid Plateau of Anatolia (average height c.3,000 ft/914 m), which includes lakes Tuz and Beyşehir and which is fringed in the N by the Köroğlu mts. and in the S by the Taurus Mts. In NE Turkey are the Pontic Mts. and in E Turkey are the Eastern Taurus Mts. Great Ararat mountain (16,945 ft/5,165 m), the highest point in Turkey, and Lake Van are in the extreme eastern part of the country. SE Turkey is drained by the upper courses of the Tigris and Euphrates rivers. Although the Turks regard the Osmanlis, or Ottomans, as their ancestors, they are a highly composite ethnic mixture. Ninety percent of the population speaks Turkish, the official language, as its first language, and 6% speaks Kurdish; there are also small Arabic, Circassian, Greek, Armenian, Georgian, and Laze-speaking minorities. Almost 99% of the people are Muslim, mostly of the Sunni branch; there are also small groups of Orthodox Christians (İstanbul is the seat of the Ecumenical Patriarch), Gregorians, Roman Catholics, Protestants, and Spanish-speaking Jews.

The Turkish economy is basically agricultural, with most workers engaged in subsistence or commercial farming. However, since the late 1940s, with the help of considerable aid from the United States, the pace of industrialization in Turkey has accelerated. In the late 1960s agriculture contributed about 34% of the annual national product and industry (including construction) about 26%. The most productive farmland is in W Turkey, and there is extensive pastureland in most parts of the country. The chief crops are wheat, barley, maize, rye, oats, rice, cotton, fruit, and tobacco. Large numbers of sheep, goats (including many mohair-producing Angora goats), and cattle are raised. The principal minerals extracted are coal, lignite, copper and iron ores, chromite, antimony, and mercury. Some petroleum is produced. The leading industrial centers are İstanbul, Ankara, KARABÜK, BURSA, İZMİR, ADANA, SAMSUN, and DİYARBAKIR. The country's chief manufactures include iron and steel, construction materials (especially cement), forest products, cotton and woolen textiles, processed food (especially refined sugar and raisins), wine, refined petroleum, and chemical fertilizer. Turkey is also noted for the manufacture of carpets; Meerschaum pipes and artifacts; and pottery. Much hydroelectric power is generated. There is a substantial, and growing, tourist trade. Turkey's main ports are İstanbul, İzmir, Samsun, İSKENDERUN, MERSİN, and TRABZON. The country has a very limited rail network, which originated with the BAGHDAD RAILWAY. The annual value of imports into Turkey is usually considerably higher than the value of exports. The chief imports are machinery, chemicals, motor vehicles, metals, and textiles; the principal exports are fruit and nuts, cotton, tobacco, and mineral ores. The leading trade partners are West Germany, the United States, Great Britain, and Italy. Since 1964, Turkey has been an associate member of the European Economic Community (Common Market). Large numbers of Turks are employed in Western Europe, especially in West Germany. Universities in Turkey are located at İstanbul, Ankara, İzmir, Erzurum, and Trabzon. The Univ. of the Bosporus (formerly Robert College) is in İstanbul. Although Anatolia (the western portion of Asian Turkey) is one of the oldest inhabited regions of the world, the history of Turkey as a national state began only with the collapse of the Ottoman Empire in 1918. For the earlier history of the region now constituting Turkey, see (for the ancient period) ASIA MINOR; IONIA; PONTUS; THRACE; BYZANTIUM; (for the medieval period) BYZANTINE EMPIRE; ARMENIA; TURKS; KONYA; KARAMAN; NICAEA, EMPIRE OF; TREBIZOND, EMPIRE OF; (for the modern period before 1918) OTTOMAN EMPIRE; EASTERN QUESTION. The Ottoman Empire, which had been tottering since the Treaty of KUCHUK KAINARJI in 1774, was dealt its death blow in World War I. By the Treaty of Sèvres (1920; see SÈVRES, TREATY OF) the victorious Allies reduced the once mighty empire to a small state comprising the northern half of the Anatolian peninsula and the narrow neutralized and Allied-occupied Zone of the Straits. Sultan MUHAMMAD VI accepted the treaty, but Turkish nationalists rallied under the leadership of Mustafa Kemal (from 1934 known as Kemal ATATÜRK) and organized their forces for resistance. In April, 1920, even before the Treaty of Sèvres was signed, a Turkish national government and national assembly began to function at Ankara. The nationalists defied the authority of the sultan, took the offensive against the Allies in Anatolia, and concluded (1921) a treaty of friendship with the USSR, which restored the KARS and Ardahan regions to Turkey in exchange for Batumi. In the meantime the Greeks, encouraged by the Allies, launched an offensive against the nationalists from their base at İzmir. The Turkish counteroffensive, beginning in Aug., 1922, ended with the complete rout of the Greeks and with the Turkish capture of İzmir (Sept., 1922). On Nov. 1, 1922, the Ankara government declared the sultan deposed, but it allowed his brother, Abd al-Majid, to succeed to the spiritual office of caliph. Shortly afterward, a conference opened at Lausanne (see LAUSANNE, TREATY OF) to revise the Treaty of Sèvres. The Treaty of Lausanne (1923) established the present boundaries of Turkey, except for the disputed region of Alexandretta (İskenderun; see ALEXANDRETTA, SANJAK OF), which was acquired by Turkey in 1939. Turkey was to exercise full sovereign rights over its entire territory, except the Zone of the Straits (see DARDANELLES), which was to remain demilitarized; this last restriction was lifted in 1936. Under a separate agreement negotiated at Lausanne in 1923, approximately 1.5 million Greeks living in Turkey were repatriated to Greece and approximately 800,000 Turks living in Greece and Bulgaria were resettled in Turkey. As a result, large numbers of persons, mostly unskilled peasants, had to be absorbed by the shaky Turkish economy, which was simultaneously further weakened by the departure of experienced Greek merchants. Turkey was formally proclaimed a republic in Oct., 1923, with Kemal as its first president; he was reelected in 1927, 1931, and 1935. The caliphate was abolished in 1924, and in the same year a constitution was promulgated. The constitution provided for a parliament—the grand national assembly—elected by universal manhood suffrage (extended to women in 1934), and for a cabinet responsible to parliament. However, Kemal governed as a virtual dictator, and his Republican People's party was the only legal party, except for brief periods. During the 14 years of Kemal's rule, Turkey underwent a great transformation. Kemal's westernization of Turkey was more successful than that of Russia under Peter the Great, and it went further than the Meiji reform in Japan, for it changed the religious, social, and cultural bases of Turkish society as well as its political and economic structure. In 1925, after the suppression of a religious rebellion in Kurdistan, the government intensified its antireligious policy, abolished religious orders, forbade polygamy, and prohibited the wearing of the traditional fez. In 1926 the Swiss code of civil law, the Italian code of criminal law, and the German code of commercial law were adopted largely unchanged, and civil marriage was made compulsory. In 1928, Islam ceased to be the state religion, and the Latin alphabet was substituted for the Arabic script; all Turks under 40 were compelled to attend schools to learn it. In 1930, Constantinople, which had been replaced as capital by Ankara in 1923, was renamed İstanbul; a dervish rebellion was put down and further antireligious measures were taken. In 1934, women who under the Ottoman regime had had few rights, were given suffrage and were fully emancipated. In 1935 every Turkish citizen had to adopt a family name. At the death (1938) of Kemal, Turkey was well on its way to becoming a state on the Western model. In the economic field, Kemal aimed at obtaining self-sufficiency for Turkey without the aid of foreign capital. Foreign investors had virtually taken over the finances of the Ottoman Empire, and one of the major problems of the Turkish republic was to pay off the old Ottoman debt; the refusal of foreign loans thus was a basic point in Kemal's nationalist program. The difficulties of establishing basic heavy industries without foreign investment and in the absence of much domestic capital required the government to assume a large role, and state ownership became the rule in the new industries. In 1934 a Five-Year Plan to develop industry was adopted. In foreign policy, Turkey sought friendly relations with all its neighbors. It entered the League of Nations in 1932, guaranteed its European borders by joining (1934) with Greece, Rumania, and Yugoslavia in the BALKAN ENTENTE, and signed (1937) a treaty (the Saadabad Pact) with Afghanistan, Iran, and Iraq. Although Communism was severely suppressed at home, relations with the USSR were cordial until World War II. Having gained new international prestige, Turkey was able to obtain a revision of the Straits Convention by the MONTREUX CONVENTION of 1936 and gained a satisfactory solution of the Alexandretta dispute through an agreement with France in 1939. Ismet INÖNÜ, who succeeded Kemal as president in 1938, warily steered a neutral course through the first five years of World War II, although Turkey received lend-lease aid from the United States after 1941. The inflation caused by the Turkish mobilization program and by the severe reduction of imports was checked by the imposition of a capital levy, which hit the Christian and Jewish minorities particularly hard. Despite considerable Allied pressure, Turkey declared war on Germany and Japan only in Feb., 1945; as a result of its declaration of war, Turkey took part in the conference (April–June, 1945) at San Francisco that founded the United Nations. Relations with the Soviet Union became acrimonious after the USSR denounced (March, 1945) its friendship pact with Turkey and demanded a thorough revision of the Montreux Convention and joint control of the Straits. Turkey rejected all Soviet demands, and in 1947 it became, with Greece, the recipient of U.S. assistance under the Truman Doctrine (see TRUMAN, HARRY S.). By 1971, the United States had given Turkey about $5.7 billion in aid under various programs. U.S. influence was partly responsible for the relaxation of the Turkish system of state capitalism in favor of free enterprise as well as for the lifting of the ban on opposition parties. The sincerity of the government's move toward political democracy was demonstrated in the elections of 1950, when the government party was defeated and Celal BAYAR, leader of the Democratic party (established in 1946), succeeded İnönü as president. With Adnan MENDERES as premier, the new government followed a policy of firm alignment with the West. Turkish troops fought with distinction in the Korean War, and in 1952 Turkey became a full member of the North Atlantic Treaty Organization; U.S. air and missile bases were subsequently established at İzmir and Adana. Turkey concluded a military defense pact with Yugoslavia and Greece (the Balkan Pact) in 1954 and played a leading part in the creation (1954–55) of the CENTRAL TREATY ORGANIZATION (CENTO; until 1959 known as the Baghdad Pact). Tension with Greece over the island of CYPRUS, whose population is mostly Greek but includes a vocal Turkish minority, began in the mid-1950s and continued after Cyprus became independent in 1960. Partly as a result of aid under the Marshall Plan (European Recovery Program), the Turkish economy expanded considerably after 1950, and foreign capital was attracted by favorable investment laws. The Menderes government gained a decisive victory in the 1954 parliamentary elections. Shortly thereafter, however, poor harvests and overhasty industrialization resulted in a serious economic crisis; growing discontent led to the enactment of restrictive laws by the government. The Democratic party under Menderes was returned to power in 1957, but with a smaller majority. Political controls were further tightened, and, in an effort to gain the support of the rural population, a return to some pre-Kemal religious and cultural practices was encouraged. Many leading journalists were jailed, and tension erupted into the open in April, 1960, when university students in İstanbul and Ankara demonstrated against the government. The attempts to suppress these outbreaks led directly to a coup in May by an army junta headed by Gen. Cemal GÜRSEL. The junta, which favored a return to Kemalist principles, placed Menderes, Bayar, and several hundred other Democratic party leaders on trial for having violated the constitution. Most of the defendants received long prison sentences, but Menderes and several others were executed. In July, 1961, a new constitution, providing for a bicameral legislature and a strong executive was approved in a referendum, thus establishing the second Turkish republic. As a result of elections held in October, General Gürsel was elected president and İnönü became prime minister at the head of a coalition government. In Feb., 1962, a group of young, moderately leftist army officers staged an unsuccessful coup. After a bitter and prolonged debate, an amnesty bill was passed (Oct., 1962) covering the former supporters of Menderes, except Bayar and a few others who remained in prison. During the Cuban missile crisis, which broke out in Oct., 1962, the Turkish government strongly supported U.S. President Kennedy's refusal to close down the U.S. bases in Turkey in exchange for the dismantling of Soviet bases in Cuba; thus, close U.S.-Turkish ties were reaffirmed. Following a reversal in parliament, İnönü resigned in Feb., 1965, and was succeeded as prime minister by Suat Hayri Ürgüplü. After the conservative Justice party won a majority in the lower house of parliament in the general election of Oct., 1965, Süleyman Demirel replaced Ürgüplü as prime minister. Gürsel died in 1966 and was succeeded as president by Cevdet Sunay. In 1969 the United States and Turkey signed a military agreement under which Turkey gained some influence over the number of troops and types of weapons the United States deployed in Turkey. Demirel won the 1969 general elections handily, but his government was soon undermined by civil unrest caused by conflicts between leftists and rightists, by student demonstrations, and by a separatist movement among the Kurds. Western Turkey suffered severe earthquakes in 1970–71. Partly because of the intervention of the military, Nihat Erim replaced Demirel as prime minister in early 1971. Although he declared limited martial law, Erim had little success in curtailing the civil strife and was succeeded by Defense Minister Ferit Melen in early 1972. Melen, too, was unable to steer Turkey on a more stable course and was replaced by Naim Talu in early 1973. Also in 1973, Fahri Korutürk succeeded Sunay as president of the country. National elections were held in Oct., 1973, and after much difficulty in forming a new government, Bülent Ecevit became (1974) prime minister. Turkey maintained its close ties with the United States in the early 1970s and at the same time cultivated better relations with the USSR. Largely as a result of U.S. pressure, the growing of opium poppies in Turkey was banned in 1971 (effective 1972), although in 1974 the government announced it would allow cultivation of opium poppies under state control for medical purposes only. In mid-1974, Turkish troops invaded Cyprus following a Greek-oriented coup d'etat there, and they gained control of important parts of the island. The events on Cyprus led to a marked deterioration in relations between Turkey and Greece, but, largely because of the diplomatic intervention of the United States, Great Britain, and the United Nations, war between the two countries was averted.

Government. Under the 1961 constitution as amended, legislative power is vested in the bicameral grand national assembly, made up of the national assembly and the senate. The national assembly is composed of 450 members elected to four-year terms; the senate includes 150 members elected to six-year terms, 15 members appointed by the president of Turkey, and a small number of life members. The president, who is head of state, is elected by the grand national assembly to one nonrenewable seven-year term. The country's executive is the prime minister, who presides over the council of ministers and who must have the confidence of the national assembly. See E. J. Cohn, *Turkish Economic, Social, and Political Change* (1970); T. D. Roberts et al., *Area Handbook for the Republic of Turkey* (1970); G. E. Bean, *Turkey Beyond the Meander: An Archaeological Guide* (1971); J. C. Dewdney, *Turkey: An Introductory Geography* (1971); F. A. Váli, *Bridge Across the Bosporus: The Foreign Policy of Turkey* (1971).

turkey, common name for a large game and POULTRY bird related to the grouse and the pheasant in the order Galliformes, fowllike birds. Its name derives from its "turk-turk" call. Turkeys are indigenous to the New World; American fossils date back 40 million years to the Oligocene geologic era. The Mexican turkey, taken to Europe in the 16th cent. by the conquistadors, is the original of the domestic race. The wild eastern turkey, *Meleagris gallapavo,* was common in New England at the time of the Pilgrims, but has since been exterminated there and now breeds as far north as Pennsylvania and as far south as Missouri. Turkeys are woodland birds, gregarious except at breeding time. They are nonmigratory, although they are good fliers. Like pheasants, they are polygamous, and the male, who eats little during courtship, depends at this time on a fatty breast appendage for nourishment. The female alone builds the nest on the ground; she lays 8 to 15 eggs per clutch and also broods the young. The colorful ocellated turkey, *Agriocharis ocellata,* measuring 36 in. (91.5 cm) in length, is found in Central America. Turkeys are classified in the phylum CHORDATA, subphylum Vertebrata, class Aves, order Galliformes, family Meleagrididae.

turkey buzzard: see VULTURE.

Turkic (tûr'kĭk), group of languages forming a subdivision of the ALTAIC subfamily of the Ural-Altaic family of languages (see URALIC AND ALTAIC LANGUAGES). The Turkic group of languages has a total of 73 million speakers. TURKISH, the official language of Turkey, is the most important of these tongues and has the largest number of speakers, about 35 million, chiefly in Turkey. Other major Turkic languages include Azerbaijani (also called Azeri), spoken by more than 7 million people, of whom more than 3 million live in the Soviet Union and 4 million in Iran; Uzbek, with 7 million speakers, mainly in the Soviet Union but also in Afghanistan; Tatar, the mother tongue of 5 million in the USSR; Kazakh, with over 4 million speakers in the Soviet Union and 600,000 others in the Sinkiang province of China; Uigur, native to more than 4 million in the Sinkiang Uigur Autonomous Region of China and to some 80,000 in the USSR; Turkoman, the language of more than 1 million in the USSR, with some speakers in Afghanistan; Chuvash, native to 1 million in the Soviet Union; and Kirghiz, spoken by 1 million, also in the USSR. The Turkic languages have been assigned to various groupings, an acceptable arrangement being the division into Southern (Turkish, Azerbaijani, Turkoman, and Chuvash), Eastern (Uzbek and Uigur), and Western (Kirghiz, Kazakh, Tatar, and others). Such a classification is tentative, and more definite grouping awaits the results of further research. Like the other Uralic and Altaic languages, the Turkic tongues are characterized by agglutination and exhibit vowel harmony. They are also noted for an abundance of participles and gerunds. Several different scripts were used in the distant past by the Turkic-speaking peoples, but following their association with Islam in the 9th cent. A.D., they largely turned to the Arabic alphabet. Since 1939, however, the Turkic-speaking peoples in the USSR have adopted modified versions of the Cyrillic alphabet, and those in Chinese territory now use the Roman alphabet as a basis for their scripts. In Turkey proper the change to a modified Roman alphabet was made in 1928. See N. A. Baskakov, *The Turkic Languages of Central Asia* (1954); Geoffrey L. Lewis, *Turkish Grammar* (1967); Karl H. Menges, *The Turkic Languages and Peoples: An Introduction to Turkic Studies* (1968).

Turkish language, member of the Turkic subdivision of the ALTAIC subfamily of the Ural-Altaic family of languages (see URALIC AND ALTAIC LANGUAGES). Turkish is the official language of Turkey and one of the official languages of Cyprus. It is spoken by about 35 million people, most of whom reside in Turkey. There are also some 250,000 speakers of Turkish in Yugoslavia, 200,000 in Bulgaria, 200,000 in Greece, and 110,000 in Cyprus. The speech of educated people in İstanbul is the standard form of the language. Like the other Uralic and Altaic languages, Turkish is characterized by vowel harmony and agglutination. Thus suffixes added to the stem of the verb may indicate passive, reflexive, causative, and other meanings. Postpositions are used instead of prepositions. Both the definite article and grammatical gender are lacking. Turkish was written in the Arabic script following the conversion of the Turks to Islam, but in 1928 the Turkish president, Kemal Atatürk, ordered a change to a modified version of the Roman alphabet. The reform was designed to introduce an alphabet better suited to Turkish than the Arabic script and also to lessen the hold of Islam on Turkey. In the 1930s the Turks attempted to purify their language by eliminating words of foreign, especially Persian and Arabic, origin and to simplify the literary style of the language, making it more similar to colloquial Turkish. See Uriel Heyd, *Language Reform in Modern Turkey* (1954); G. L. Lewis, *Turkish Grammar* (1967); Hikmet I. Sebüktekin, *Turkish-English Contrastive Analysis* (1971).

Turkistan or **Turkestan** (both: tûr"ĭstăn', -stän'), historic region of central Asia. Western or Russian Turkistan extended from the Caspian Sea in the west to the Chinese frontier in the east and from the Aral-Irtysh watershed in the north to the borders of Iran and Afghanistan in the south. Eastern, or Chinese, Turkistan comprised the western provinces of China, now constituting the Sinkiang-Uigur Autonomous Region. Southern, or Afghan, Turkistan referred to a small area of N Afghanistan. Politically, Russian Turkistan (now known officially as Soviet Central Asia) includes the Turkmen, Uzbek, Tadzhik, and Kirghiz republics and the southern portion of the Kazakh Republic. Much of the western part of the Soviet territory is composed of two deserts, the Kara-Kum and the Kyzyl-Kum. The eastern part, rough and hilly, rises to include the mountains of part of the Pamir highland and of the Tien Shan system. Athwart the eastern section extends the Fergana Valley, one of Asia's most fertile regions. Turkistan is Persian for "land of the Turks," but although most of the population speak Turkic languages, the region is not the oldest known home of the Turks, nor do the majority of the Turkish peoples dwell there. Turkistan may be regarded as a single region, however, because a combination of geographical and historical factors made it the bridge linking the Eastern and Western worlds and the route taken by many of the great conquerors and migrating peoples. The Caspian Sea hinders invasions of Turkistan from the Caucasus region; but forces from Asia Minor, Arabia, the Balkan Peninsula, and Africa could skirt the Caspian's southern shores. Invaders from the East (especially Mongolia) had to cross Turkistan in order to pass between the marshes of central Siberia in the north and the great mountain barriers of the Tien Shan, the Pamirs, and the Hindu Kush in the south. Except in the case of the White Huns, such invaders avoided the only other route into Europe, that going N of the Caspian Sea, perhaps because pasturage for their large cavalry was lacking there. Moreover, Turkistan, as the focus of trade between Europe and Asia, had great wealth and large cities (notably BUKHARA, SAMARKAND, and MERV) that could be plundered. Perhaps the earliest empire to bring Turkistan under its sway was that of the Persians, who by 500 B.C. had cleared the Lydian empire from the region around the Caspian Sea. Persia was destroyed by the march of Alexander the Great through S Turkistan, the ancient Bactria, which was colonized by Greeks after his victories. After Alexander's death, Turkistan fell to Seleucus; but by the middle of the 2d cent. B.C. it was divided between Parthia in the west and Bactria in the east. Parthia expanded eastward at Bactria's expense. Bactria around 130 B.C. was bordered on the E by China, which controlled (from the 2d cent. B.C. to the 2d cent. A.D.) much of the area extending from Lake Balkhash S to the Hindu Kush. In the late 1st cent. A.D., the Kushans took Bactria's holdings, and the Huns were disputing the region near Lake Balkhash with China. China's conquest of E Turkistan, meanwhile, opened the way for Chinese travel through Turkistan to India and permitted the introduction of Buddhism in oases along the trade routes in an attempt to convert the warlike nomads to a pacifist philosophy. With the fall (220) of the Han dynasty, however, China lost control of E Turkistan to Persia, which ruled the region between the 3d and 4th cent. and introduced Zoroastrianism. When China reestablished control there in the middle of the 7th cent., it came into contact with Persia, which, under the Sassanids, occupied nearly all the rest of Turkistan except the central zone. The Persian holdings were swept away by the Arab invasion of the 8th cent.; first the Umayyad and then the Abbasid caliphate held all of Turkistan. Zoroastrianism was suppressed, and Islam, which today remains the chief religion of Turkistan, was imposed. The Abbasid caliphate weakened in the middle of the 9th cent.; at the same time, China lost its holdings in the east, and many states, notably KHOREZM, occupied parts of Turkistan. Meanwhile, from the 8th cent., the Seljuk Turks began moving into the region. Their language was adopted by most of the peoples there (with the notable exception of the Tadzhiks), but the Turks themselves tended to adopt the Iranian culture, which in fact was the dominant culture of Turkistan until the 20th cent. All of Turkistan fell to the Mongols in the late 13th cent., and the territory was mostly bestowed upon the khan Jagatai. TAMERLANE conquered Turkistan in the late 14th cent., pushing the Mongols into the steppes of Kazakhstan. After Tamerlane's death (1405), his successors, the Timurids, controlled much of the territory for about a century. The later internal history of Turkistan is mainly one of prolonged struggle involving the khanates of Khiva, Bukhara, and Kokand and the nomadic peoples of the region, most notably Kirghiz, Kazakhs, Turkomans, and Uzbek. In the late 17th and early 18th cent., the vigorous young Ch'ing dynasty of China controlled E Turkistan, but it gradually lost more and more territory to Russia, whose troops invaded the khanate of Kokand in 1865 and took Tashkent. A military administration under a Russian governor general was established in 1867 in the conquered territories. In 1868 the emir of Bukhara and the khan of Khiva were forced to accept a Russian protectorate. An Anglo-Russian treaty of 1881 designated the southern limits of Russian rule in the area. Harsh Russian administration sparked frequent native revolts, but they were suppressed. Following the Russian Revolution of 1917, the Turkistan autonomous soviet republic (1918) and the Bukhara and Khorezm soviet republics (1920) were set up in the region. However, in 1924 the southern part of Russian Turkistan was divided along geographical and ethnic lines into new divisions—the Uzbek SSR, the Turkmen SSR, the Tadzhik SSR (a union republic as of 1929), the Kirghiz autonomous oblast (made an autonomous republic in 1926 and a union republic in 1936), and the Kara-Kalpak autonomous oblast (which became an autonomous republic in 1932); the northern part of Turkistan was included in the Kazakh SSR. During this period, the term *Russian Turkistan* was officially replaced with *Soviet Central Asia*.

Turkistan-Siberia Railroad, abbreviated as **Turk-Sib,** important railroad in Central Asian USSR, providing the shortest link between Siberia and central Asia. Completed in 1931, it runs from the Trans-Siberian RR at Novosibirsk SW to the Trans-Caspian RR, which it joins N of Tashkent. Its principal stations are Semipalatinsk, Barnaul, Alma-Ata, Dzhambul, and Chimkent. The railroad is of vital economic importance.

Turkmanchai, Treaty of (to͝orkmänchī'), 1828, agreement signed by Russia and Persia at the village of Turkmanchai (Torkaman), East Azerbaijan prov., NW Iran. It concluded the Russo-Persian war that had begun in 1825 and forced Persia to cede part of Persian Armenia to Russia and to grant extraterritorial rights.

Turkmen Soviet Socialist Republic or **Turkmenistan** (tûrk"mĕnĭstăn', -stän', Rus. to͝orkmyĕ"-nyĭstän'), constituent republic (1970 pop. 2,158,000), 188,455 sq mi (488,100 sq km), Central Asian USSR. It borders on Afghanistan and Iran in the south, the Uzbek SSR and the Kazakh SSR in the east and northeast, and the Caspian Sea in the west. ASHKHABAD (the capital), KRASNOVODSK, CHARDZHOU, Nebit-Dag, and MARY are the major cities and industrial centers. The Trans-Caspian RR is the main transportation route. The desert lands of Kara-Kum occupy 90% of the total area; the population is concentrated in oases at the foot of the Kopet Dagh mts. in the south and along the Amu Darya, Murgab, and Tedzhen rivers. The republic's numerous mineral resources include oil, natural gas, salt, phosphate, mirabilite, sulfur, ozokerite, iodine, bromine, witherite, bentonite, lignite, barites, clays, and such building stones as limestone and gypsum. More than 90% of the cultivated land is irrigated. Part of the Kara-Kum Canal crosses the desert, furnishing water for irrigation and hydroelectric power. Cotton, grown along the canal and in the Murgab and Tedzhen oases, is the chief crop; wheat, barley, maize, millet, sesame, vegetables, melons, wine grapes, kenaf, jute, and alfalfa are also cultivated. Karakul sheep (which provide wool for the region's famous carpets), horned cattle, horses, and camels are raised, and silkworms are bred. Turkmenistan's industries include cotton ginning, silk spinning, metalworking, ship and railroad car repairing, fish canning (along the Caspian), meat processing, oil refining, and the production of chemicals, textiles, and building materials. The republic has numerous hydroelectric stations. The Turkomans (or Turcomans) make up about 60% of the population; the remainder are Russians, Uzbek, Kazakhs, Tatars, Ukrainians, and Armenians. The Turkomans are a Turkic-speaking people of the Sunnite Muslim religion. Unlike other Central Asian groups, they still retain tribal and clan divisions. They are descendants of the medieval Oguz tribes (to which the Seljuk and Osmanli Turks also belonged). Originally a part of the kingdom of ancient Persia (see MERV), Turkmenistan passed under Arab domination in the 8th cent. In the 11th cent., it was ruled by the Seljuk Turks (see KHOREZM). JENGHIZ KHAN conquered the region in the 13th cent. and TAMERLANE in the 14th cent. After the breakup (late 15th cent.) of the empire of Tamerlane's successors, the Timurids, Turkmenistan came under Uzbek control. In the early 19th cent., the Turkomans became subject to the khan of Khiva. In 1869, Russian military forces founded Krasnovodsk and began to conquer the Turkomans, whose fierce resistance to Russian encroachment was broken in 1881 with the conquest of their stronghold, Geok Tepe. The Russians then established the Transcaspian Oblast, which in 1899 became part of the governate general of Russian Turkistan. Harsh Russian administration provoked revolts by the Turkomans. During the Russian civil war sporadic fighting flared between the Transcaspian provincial government and Bolshevik troops. The Red Army took Ashkhabad in July, 1919, and Krasnovodsk in Feb., 1920. The Transcaspian Oblast was renamed Turkmen Oblast in 1921; the following year, it became part of the Turkistan Autonomous Soviet Socialist Republic, which in 1924 incorporated the Turkmenian districts of the former Bukhara and Khorezm republics. Turkmenistan formally became a constituent Soviet republic in 1925. Large numbers of Turkomans still live in Iran and Afghanistan.

Turkoman: see TURKMEN SOVIET SOCIALIST REPUBLIC.

Turks, term applied in its wider meaning to the Turkic-speaking peoples of Turkey, the Soviet Union, the Sinkiang Region of the People's Republic of China (Chinese Turkistan), Iran, and Afghanistan. They total about 73 million, and they are distributed from E Siberia to the Balkans. The wide differences in physical appearance and culture among the Uigurs of China, the Uzbeks of central Asia and the Osmanlis of Turkey (to cite random instances) make it impossible to speak of Turks as an ethnic or racial group. Although Islam is the religion of the majority of Turks, its importance came relatively late. The most significant unifying link among the Turks is the very close relation of their languages, which are marked by great regularity of pattern and clarity of structure. In the Soviet Union all the nationalities classified as Tatars are Turkic-speaking. It is probable that many peoples who were unrelated to the original Turks adopted either wholly or in part their speech and their social organization. The AVARS were probably Turkic; they and the MAGYARS certainly had adopted the Turkic tribal organization when they appeared in Europe, and many Magyar words are of Turkic origin. The name Turk was first used by the Chinese in the 6th cent. to designate a nomadic people who had established a large empire stretching from Mongolia to the Black Sea. This empire, which was divided into two independent parts, was forced to accept Chinese sovereignty in the 7th cent. The northern empire regained its independence in 682, and the oldest known Turkic inscriptions (see under ORKHON) are related to it. In succeeding centuries control of the area passed from the Oghuz Turks to the Uigurs and to the Kirghiz, who were the last Turkic peoples to reside in Mongolia. They, like their predecessors, migrated to the south and west after they were expelled (924) by the Kitai. Other Turkic peoples, notably the KHAZARS, CUMANS, and PECHENEGS, played important roles in the medieval history of S Russia and SE Europe. The Turkish groups of the greatest import in the history of Europe and W Asia were, however, the Seljuks and the Osmanli or Ottoman Turks, both members of the Oghuz confederations. The Arab annexation of the area of ancient Sogdiana in the 7th cent. brought the Oghuz Turks into direct contact with the Abbasid caliphate and later with the Persian Empire. The Turks embraced the Sunni Muslim faith and began to migrate to the Middle East. At first they were used as mercenaries by the Abbasids, but soon the Turks became the actual rulers of the empire. At the beginning of the 11th cent., a great wave of Seljuk Turks, led by Togrul, conquered Khorezm and Iran. They entered Baghdad in 1055; Togrul was proclaimed sultan. Under his successor, ALP ARSLAN, the Seljuks conquered Georgia, Armenia, and much of Asia Minor, overran Syria, and defeated (1071) the Byzantine emperor Romanus IV at MANZIKERT, opening Byzantium (except for a small area around Constantinople) to Seljuk and Turkmen occupation. This irruption was a major factor in bringing about the CRUSADES, during which a three-part struggle among Christians, Seljuks, and Egyptian Mamelukes developed. Alp Arslan's son, Malik Shah (reigned 1072–92), ably administered and developed his huge empire; he was a protector of OMAR KHAYYAM, who reformed the calendar at his behest. At the start of the 12th cent., the Seljuk empire began to fragment, and various parts achieved virtual independence. The attacks of the Khorezm shah led to the final downfall of the empire in 1157. Among the successor states were the Zangid sultanate of Syria, whose ruler NUR AD-DIN was known for his victories over the Crusaders; the empire of KHOREZM, which at one time nearly attained the limits of the earlier Seljuk empire; and the sultanate of Rum or Iconium (see KONYA), which comprised a large part of Asia Minor. All the Seljuk states were overrun in the 13th cent. by Genghiz Khan and his successors, whose hordes comprised both Mongols and Turks and became generally known as TATARS. The Turco-Tatars now living in the Soviet Union are largely descended from the GOLDEN HORDE of Batu Khan, as are the Uzbeks (see UZBEK SOVIET SOCIALIST REPUBLIC), who ruled a vast empire in the 16th cent. In Asia Minor the sultanate of Konya was taken over, after the Mongol wave had receded, by the emirate of Karamania (see KARAMAN), but the Osmanli Turks completed the overthrow of the Byzantine Empire. A minor tribe and the last of the Turkish invading peoples, the Osmanli had been assigned (13th cent.) to the border area of the Byzantine Empire by their Seljuk overlords. It was largely this position as guards of a constantly contested frontier that allowed them to develop their highly disciplined organization, which in turn enabled them in the 14th cent. to make themselves masters of the ruins of the

Seljuk empire in Anatolia. Their first historic ruler OSMAN I, gave his name both to the nation and to the dynasty that ruled an empire extending, at one period, from Vienna to the Indian Ocean and from Tunis to the Caucasus (see OTTOMAN EMPIRE). The people of modern Turkey, which was founded after the collapse of the Ottoman Empire in 1918, are called Osmanli Turks. The original Osmanlis had merged at an early stage with the Seljuks, and their descendants mixed extensively with Muslim converts from the many dozens of nationalities that made up their empire. See J. R. Krueger, ed., *The Turkic Peoples* (1963); K. H. Menges, *The Turkic Languages and Peoples* (1968); David Hotham, *The Turks* (1972).

Turks and Caicos Islands (kī'kōs), dependency of Great Britain (1970 est. pop. 5,675), 166 sq mi (430 sq km), British West Indies. There are more than 30 cays and islands, of which only 6 are inhabited. The capital is on Grand Turk. The islands are geographically a southeastern continuation of the Bahama Islands. Salt is the main export. The population is largely of black African descent. The islands were discovered (1512) by Ponce de León.

Turk-Sib: see TURKISTAN-SIBERIA RAILROAD.

Turku (to͞or'ko͞o), Swed. *Åbo*, city (1971 pop. 155,069), capital of Turku-and-Pori prov., SW Finland, at the mouth of the Aurajoki River on the Baltic Sea. The center of the fertile agricultural region of SW Finland, it is also the country's largest port and an important industrial city. There are shipyards, steel mills, machine shops, textile mills, and clothing factories. Known as the "cradle of Finnish culture," Turku is among Finland's oldest cities. Swedish Crusaders landed on the site in 1157. It was the seat (1220) of the first bishop of Finland, and the capital of Finland until 1812. The national university was in Turku from 1640 to 1827, when a fire destroyed almost the entire city and the university was moved (1828) to Helsinki. The Treaty of Åbo, by which Sweden ceded part of SE Finland to Russia, was signed in the city in 1743. The great cathedral was begun in the early 13th cent. The 13th-century castle, burned in 1614 and restored in 1961, is now a historic museum. Turku has a Finnish university (founded 1917) and a Swedish university (founded 1918).

Turlock (tûr'lŏk), city (1970 pop. 13,992), Stanislaus co., central Calif.; inc. 1908. It is the center of the Turlock irrigation district, which uses the waters of the Tuolumne River for a rich farm area. The city has canneries and poultry-processing plants. A branch of California State College is there.

turmeric: see GINGER.

turn and bank indicator, aircraft instrument containing one indicator to show turning, or rotation about the vertical axis, and another to show banking, or rotation about the longitudinal axis. The two indicators are essentially separate instruments, but they are customarily placed together. The bank indicator is the simpler of the two and consists of a curved glass tube filled with a damping liquid in which a small steel ball rolls. When the craft is horizontal, the ball is located in the lowest part of the tube; as the craft banks, gravity holds the ball at the lowest point as the tube rotates from side to side. The tube can be calibrated to show the angle of banking. The turn indicator contains a gyroscope that develops a torque when the craft rotates. This torque controls a pointer that indicates to the pilot in degrees per unit of time the rate at which the craft is turning.

Turner, Frederick Jackson, 1861-1932, American historian, b. Portage, Wis. He taught at the Univ. of Wisconsin from 1885 to 1910 except for a year spent in graduate study at Johns Hopkins Univ. From 1910 to 1924 he taught at Harvard, and later he was research associate at the Henry E. Huntington Library. At first he taught rhetoric and oratory but turned to U.S. history, soon focusing on Western history. His doctoral dissertation, *The Character and Influence of the Indian Trade in Wisconsin* (1891; an enlargement of his master's essay), showed the trend of his interest. In 1893, at the meeting of the American Historical Association in Chicago, he delivered an address, "The Significance of the Frontier in American History," which outlined brilliantly the history of the receding frontier and its effect in creating American democracy. Little noticed at the time, it was to prove epoch-making in American history writing. It supplied a large part of a generation of historians with a theme to investigate. Turner's ideas are now generally incorporated in some form in most American history texts; although a historical controversy has raged for decades over the validity of his frontier thesis, few critics reject it entirely. The address and various short papers were reprinted in *The Frontier in American History* (1920). He collaborated with Edward Channing and Albert Bushnell Hart in the revision of *Guide to the Study and Reading of American History* (1912). Though he produced few books—*The Rise of the New West* ("American Nation" series, 1906) and two studies in sectionalism, *The Significance of Sections in American History* (1932) and the posthumously published *The United States, 1830-1850* (1935)—his influence as a teacher and proponent of a new and important theory made him one of the most renowned of all American historians. See *The Early Writings of Frederick Jackson Turner* (with a bibliography by E. E. Edwards and an introduction by Fulmer Mood, 1938, repr. 1969); Lee Benson, *Turner and Beard* (1960); Richard Hofstadter, *Progressive Historians* (1968); Richard Hofstadter and S. M. Lipset, ed., *Turner and the Sociology of the Frontier* (1968); R. A. Billington, *The Genesis of the Frontier Thesis* (1971) and *Frederick Jackson Turner* (1973).

Turner, Joseph Mallord William, 1775-1851, English landscape painter, b. London. Turner was the foremost English romantic painter and the most original of English landscape artists. He received almost no general education but at 14 was already a student at the Royal Academy of Arts and three years later was making topographical drawings for magazines. In 1791 for the first time he exhibited two watercolors at the Royal Academy. In the following 10 years he exhibited regularly, was elected a member (1802), and was made professor of perspective (1807). By 1799 the sale of his work had freed him from drudgery and he devoted himself to the visionary interpretations of landscape for which he became famous. In 1802 he made a trip to the Continent, where he painted his famous *Calais Pier* (National Gall., London). From then on he traveled constantly in England or abroad, making innumerable direct sketches from which he drew material for his studio paintings in oil and watercolor. Turner showed a remarkable ability to distill the best from the tradition of landscape painting. Influence of the Dutch masters is apparent in his *Sun Rising through Vapor* (National Gall., London). In the vein of the French classical landscape painter, Claude Lorrain, he produced the *Liber Studiorum* (1807-19), 70 drawings that were later reproduced by engraving under Turner's supervision. Among the paintings evocative of Claude's style are his *Dido Building Carthage* (National Gall., London) and *Crossing the Brook* (Tate Gall., London). Despite his early and continued success Turner lived the life of a recluse. As his fame grew he maintained a large gallery in London for exhibition of his work, but continued to live an obscure existence with his old father. His painting became increasingly abstract as he strove to portray light, space, and the elemental forces of nature. Characteristic of his later period are his paintings *The Fighting Téméraire* and *Rain, Steam, and Speed* (both: National Gall., London). His late Venetian works, which describe atmospheric effects with brighter colors, include *The Grand Canal* (Metropolitan Mus.) and *Approach to Venice* (National Gall., Washington, D.C.). Turner encountered violent criticism as his style became increasingly free, but he was passionately defended by Sir Thomas Lawrence and the youthful Ruskin. His will, which was under litigation for many years, left more than 19,000 watercolors, drawings, and oils to the nation. Most of these works are in the National Gallery and the Tate Gallery, London. Many of Turner's oils have deteriorated badly. In watercolor he is unsurpassed. See his watercolors (ed. by M. Butlin, 1962); catalog by A. J. Finberg (1968); biographies by A. J. Finberg (2d ed. 1961) and J. Lindsay (1966); studies by J. Rothenstein and M. Butlin (1964), L. Gowing (1966), J. Gage (1969), and W. Gaunt (1971).

Turner, Nat, 1800-1831, American Negro slave, leader of the Southampton Insurrection (1831), b. Southampton co., Va. Deeply religious from childhood, Turner was a natural preacher and possessed some influence among local Negro slaves. Believing himself divinely appointed to lead fellow slaves to freedom, he plotted a revolt with a small band (approximately 60) of followers. After murdering the family of Turner's owner, the band ravaged the neighborhood, killing a total of 55 white people. The revolt was soon crushed, however, and 13 slaves and 3 free Negroes were hanged immediately. Turner himself escaped to the woods, but he was captured six weeks later and hanged. The abortive uprising, by far the most serious in the history of slavery in the United States, led to more stringent slave laws in the South and an end there to the organized abolition movement. See studies by Herbert Aptheker (1943 and 1968), Eric Foner (1971), and John Duff and Peter Mitchell, ed. (1971).

Turner Valley, village (1971 pop. 766), SW Alta., Canada, at the foot of the Rocky mts., on the Sheep River, SW of Calgary. It is in the center of the Turner Valley oil and natural gas fields, opened in 1914. The village has sulfur and propane and pentane gas plants.

Turnhout (türn'hout), city (1970 pop. 38,007), Antwerp prov., N Belgium, near the Dutch border. Manufactures of this industrial city include paper products, textiles, lace, and electrical equipment. Of note is a 13th-century castle, the former seat of the dukes of Brabant and now a judicial center.

turnip, garden vegetable of the same genus of the family Cruciferae (MUSTARD family) as the cabbage; native to Europe, where it has been long cultivated. The two principal kinds are the white (*Brassica rapa*) and the yellow (*B. napobrassica*), which is known as the rutabaga, the Swedish turnip, or the swede. The rutabaga is grown extensively only in Europe, where it is believed to have originated during the Middle Ages as a cross between the white turnip and the cabbage. The turnip is one of the ROOT CROPS used as a stock feed as well as for human food. The green leaves (greens) are often cooked like spinach. The turnip is a biennial cool-weather crop, grown mostly in cool climates. The worst turnip pests are the root maggot and the flea beetle; it is also attacked by clubroot fungus. Turnips are classified in the division MAGNOLIOPHYTA, class Magnoliopsida, order Capparales, family Cruciferae.

turnpike, road paid for partly or wholly by fees collected from travelers at tollgates. It derives its name from the hinged bar that prevented passage through such a gate until the toll was paid. In England tollgates were first authorized by law in 1346. Although American colonists from Scotland and Ireland, as well as from England, knew the turnpike system, it was not introduced in the United States until after the Revolution. It was then that the business interests of growing cities first required through roads, most of which could not be built and maintained by local funds in unsettled or sparsely settled regions. The tollgate, like the later gasoline tax, was a device to make the traffic pay for the road. The first American turnpike road was a state enterprise, authorized by a Virginia act of 1785. The first American turnpike to be constructed and operated by a private corporation was the Lancaster Turnpike built (1792) in Pennsylvania. Thereafter turnpikes were regularly private enterprises, and turnpike corporations held the leadership in the development of the American corporation system. The construction of turnpikes proceeded rapidly, and by 1825 a map of the Eastern states showing the turnpikes would have looked much like a present-day map showing the railroads. Famous turnpikes included the post road from New York to Boston (now part of U.S. 1), the two roads from New York to Albany (on the two sides of the Hudson River), and the roads from Albany to Buffalo, main lines of communication with the developing West. Construction of one of the early roads usually began with felling trees and uprooting stumps. Swamps were crossed by corduroy, i.e., logs laid side by side. The surface of the turnpike was sometimes of earth, but often of broken stone or of planks. The total costs were often from $5,000 to $7,000 a mile and sometimes as much as $10,000 a mile. American turnpikes thrived from c.1800 to c.1840, as did the passenger stagecoach and the Conestoga wagon. The coach had places for 8 to 14 passengers and was drawn by four or six horses; the wagon, for freight, was drawn by six or eight horses. The traffic over the turnpikes also included droves of horses, cattle, and sheep. Settlers going West often used turnpikes on the first part of their route. Tollgates were 6 to 10 mi (9.7-16.1 km) apart, and tolls were commonly from 10¢ to 25¢ for a vehicle, depending on its type. Turnpikes that were not profitable were turned over to the states. After the coming of canals and railroads, abandonment became general. In more recent times the multilane expressways have often followed the abandoned rights-of-way of the old turnpikes. The opening (1940) of the first multilane superhighway, the Pennsylvania Turnpike, began a new era in tollroad construction. Since then every state has constructed at least one superhighway on either a toll or nontoll basis. Those that do charge tolls are generally located E of the Mississippi River. Virtually every major American superhighway is part of the National System of Interstate and Defense Highways, a network of controlled-access express roads throughout the country. Authorized (1944) by an act of Congress, the interstate system is designed to provide an efficient national transportation system for ordinary use as well as in case of war or other emergency. Construction of the system began in 1956; the network is eventually expected to encompass some 44,000 mi (70,800 km) of roads. The system is financed largely by the Federal Highway Trust Fund (established 1956), into which are paid the revenues from most highway-related Federal taxes. The states now also derive considerable income from various forms of road and motor-vehicle taxation, reducing the need for toll collection. See ROAD. See J. A. Durenberger, *Turnpikes* (1931, repr. 1968).

Turnus (tûr'nəs), in Roman legend, king of the Rutulians. In the *Aeneid* he is a spirited warrior. When his betrothed, Lavinia, daughter of King Latinus, was given to the Trojan Aeneas by her father, Turnus led a combined force of Latins and Rutulians against the Trojans. After several bloody battles, Turnus was killed by Aeneas.

Turnu-Severin (to͝or'no͞o-sĕvĕrĕn'), city (1970 est. pop. 55,000), SW Rumania, in Walachia, on the Danube River opposite Yugoslavia. It is a river port and has large shipyards, a plywood factory, and several food-processing plants. The surrounding area is known for its extensive rose gardens and its white wine. Turnu-Severin was founded on the site of Drobeta, an ancient town believed to be the oldest Roman settlement in Rumania. Nearby are the ruins of a bridge across the Danube, erected (A.D. 103) by Emperor Trajan.

Turnverein (to͝orn'fərīn), society of a type originated in Prussia by Friedrich Ludwig JAHN. The first hall of such a society was built in 1811 on the Hasenheide athletic grounds, near Berlin. The organization emphasized gymnastic exercises, but it also had important social and patriotic functions. In the beginning it was an effective instrument in organizing opposition to French domination of Germany, and it had official approval and support. Similar societies were at once organized throughout Germany. After the fall of Napoleon, the Turnverein movement began to dissolve because German governments disapproved of the Turnvereins as centers from which liberal ideas might be disseminated. The Turnvereins were supported loyally by their members, and new groups were organized in other countries, including the United States, by members who migrated to those countries. Today the word *Turnverein* is used in German-speaking countries to refer to any gymnasium or similar site of physical recreation. The example of the Turnvereins has encouraged organizations under other names to combine gymnastic exercises with discussion and social pleasures.

turpentine, yellow to brown semifluid oleoresin exuded from the sapwood of pines, firs, and other conifers. It is made up of two principal components, an ESSENTIAL OIL and a type of RESIN that is called ROSIN. The essential oil (oil of turpentine) can be separated from the rosin by steam distillation. Commercial turpentine, or turps, is this oil of turpentine. When pure, it is a colorless, transparent, oily liquid with a penetrating odor and a characteristic taste. It contains a large proportion of pinene, a compound from which camphor is manufactured. Turpentine is obtained in large amounts from several species of pines of the SE United States; its physical properties, e.g., boiling point, depend on its source. It is used chiefly as a solvent and drying agent in paints and varnishes.

turpentine tree: see TEREBINTH.

Turpin, Dick, 1706–39, English robber. After a short and brutal career of horse stealing and general crime he was hanged at York. The fame—or notoriety—that he later achieved derives mainly from W. H. Ainsworth's romance, *Rookwood* (1834), which is based upon his life. Turpin's famous ride from London to York on his mare, Black Bess, is fiction, and his actual exploits were not of a romantic character.

Turquino (to͝orkē'nō), peak, 6,560 ft (1,999 m) high, SE Cuba, in the Sierra Maestra range. It is the highest point on the island. The mountain, called Pico Turquino in Spanish, was the scene of intense guerrilla activity during the revolution led by Fidel Castro.

turquoise, hydrous phosphate of aluminum and copper, $Al_2(OH)_3PO_4 \cdot H_2O + Cu$, used as a gem. It occurs rarely in crystal form, but is usually cryptocrystalline. Turquoise is opaque and has a waxy luster; the color varies from greenish gray to sky-blue. The sky-blue varieties are the most valued as gems, but because of their porosity they easily absorb dirt and grease and change in color to an unattractive green. Exposure to heat or sunlight is also injurious to the color of the turquoise. The finest specimens come from Iran; other sources are the Sinai peninsula and the SW United States, especially New Mexico, Nevada, Arizona, and Colorado. Turquoise matrix is a rock including fragments of turquoise, cut as a gem stone. Variscite, the hydrated phosphate of aluminum, is sometimes used as a substitute for turquoise. It occurs in crystals of the orthorhombic system and in massive form; minable deposits are found in Utah.

Turrialba (to͞orēäl'bä), inactive volcano, 10,974 ft (3,345 m) high, E central Costa Rica. It is difficult to ascend. On its lower slopes is the city of Turrialba, seat of the Inter-American Institute of Agricultural Sciences for experiments in tropical agriculture.

turtle, a REPTILE of the order Chelonia, with an armorlike shell and strong, beaked, toothless jaws. The shell usually consists of bony plates overlaid with horny shields. The upper portion, or carapace, covers the turtle's back and sides, and the lower portion, or plastron, covers the belly; the two parts are joined at the sides. Nearly all turtles can pull their heads into their shells for protection. Most pull the head straight back, the neck folding into an S-shaped curve; however, in the SIDE-NECKED TURTLES of the Southern Hemisphere, the head is swung sideways and tucked next to the shoulder. Turtles are found throughout most of the temperate and tropical world; however, there are none native to the British Isles, and only side-necked turtles are found in Australia. Different types of turtle are variously adapted to living on land, in fresh water, or in the ocean, but all turtles breathe air by means of lungs, and all lay eggs on land. The land-living species, especially those of the family Testudinidae, are commonly called TORTOISES. The name terrapin is generally applied to large freshwater or brackish water species, especially those used for food. Nearly all turtles are omnivorous, although the preferred proportions of animal and vegetable matter vary in different species. Turtles range in length from a few inches to over 7 ft (11 m), most being between 5 and 15 in. (13–38 cm) long. Many specimens have lived over 50 years in captivity and some over 100 years. The 200 to 300 species of turtle are classified in 12 families. The largest family of the Northern Hemisphere is the family of common freshwater turtles (Emydidae), which includes about a third of all turtle species and is most abundant in S and E Asia, E North America, and Central America. Members of this group have webbed feet. Many are found in freshwater ponds or marshes and spend most of the time in the water. Some live in brackish marshes and estuaries. They include such well-known North American turtles as the pond turtles (including the spotted, wood, and Muhlenberg's turtles), the painted turtle, the sliders, the diamondback terrapin, the map turtle, and the Blanding's turtle. The BOX TURTLE, which is primarily terrestrial, is also a member of this family. The second largest family is the tortoise family (Testudinidae). The tortoises have high-domed shells and club-shaped feet adapted for walking on land. They are found in warm regions throughout the world. The musk turtles and mud turtles (family Kinosternidae) are common small turtles of the E United States; the family is found only in the New World. The soft-shelled turtles (family Trionychidae) are flat-bodied freshwater turtles of the Northern Hemisphere, with a leathery covering instead of horny shields on their shells. The SNAPPING TURTLE family (Chelydridae) is a North American group that includes the common snapper and the alligator snapper. Marine turtles are classified in two families. The family Chelonidae includes four SEA TURTLE species of tropical and subtropical distribution: the green turtle, the loggerhead, the hawksbill (or tortoiseshell turtle), and the ridley. The family Dermochelidae includes a single species, the LEATHERBACK, or leatherneck, largest of all turtles. Marine turtles lack toes, and their legs are oarlike in shape. They tend to have reduced shells. Many turtles are valued as food; among the important edible species are the green turtle (traditional ingredient of turtle soup), the diamondback terrapin, and the soft-shelled turtles. The eggs are also eaten in many parts of the world, a practice that has contributed to a serious decline in numbers of many species, especially of marine turtles. The hawksbill is the source of TORTOISESHELL. The turtles commonly sold as pets are usually young slider or map turtles. Proper nutrition and heat and light conditions are essential for the survival of pet turtles. Painting the shell is harmful. Turtles are the oldest living group of reptiles; they existed in the Triassic period, at the time of the earliest dinosaurs. These early turtles could not retract their necks. Many of the living families of turtles existed in the Cretaceous period and have undergone very little change since then. Turtles are classified in the phylum CHORDATA, subphylum Vertebrata, class Reptilia, order Chelonia. See Archie Carr, *So Excellent a Fishe: A Natural History of Sea Turtles* (1967); Maxwell Knight, *Tortoises and How to Keep Them* (rev. ed. 1970); C. H. Ernst and R. W. Barbour, *Turtles of the United States* (1972).

turtledove: see PIGEON.

turtle stone: see CONCRETION.

Tuscaloosa (təskəlo͞o'sə), city (1970 pop. 65,773), seat of Tuscaloosa co., W central Ala., on the Black Warrior River; inc. 1819. It is a transportation, manufacturing, and medical center, with industries centered on the region's coal, iron, cotton, and timber. Food is processed, and rubber tires, chemicals, paper, adhesives, petroleum products, plastics, and textiles are manufactured. The city is primarily known as the seat of the Univ. of Alabama. Stillman College is also there. Tuscaloosa was settled (1816) on the site of an Indian village after the Creek revolt of 1813. It was state capital from 1826 to 1846. Points of interest include many beautiful antebellum homes, as well as the Old Tavern (1827).

Tuscan order: see DORIC ORDER.

Tuscany (tŭs'kənē), Ital. *Toscana*, region (1971 pop. 3,470,915), 8,876 sq mi (22,989 sq km), N central Italy, bordering on the Tyrrhenian Sea in the west and including the Tuscan Archipelago. FLORENCE is the capital of the region, which is divided into the provinces of Arezzo, Florence, Grosseto, Leghorn, Lucca, Massa-Carrara, Pisa, Pistoia, and Siena (named for their principal cities). The region is mostly hilly and mountainous. There is much fertile soil, especially in the Arno River valley and in the MAREMMA, a coastal strip. The Apennines are in northern and eastern Tuscany; in the northwest are the Alpi Apuane, where the famous Carrara marble is quarried; and there are also mountains in the south, where iron, magnesium, and quicksilver are produced. In addition, borax is produced in the Maremma, and iron is mined on Elba island. Along the northern coast, which is low and sandy, are fine pine woods. Farm products of the region include cereals, olives, tobacco, and grapes; sheep, goats, and hogs are widely raised. Tuscany has considerable industry, although farming is still the chief occupation. Manufactures include cotton and woolen textiles, chemicals, machinery, motor vehicles, precision instruments, glass, refined petroleum, and fertilizer. The wine produced in the Chianti district near Siena is world famous. Modern Tuscany corresponds to the larger part of ancient ETRURIA, and most of our knowledge of ETRUSCAN CIVILIZATION is derived from findings there. The Romans conquered the region in the mid-4th cent. B.C. After the fall of Rome, it was a Lombard duchy (6th-8th cent. A.D.), with Lucca as its capital, and later a powerful march under the Franks (8th–12th cent.). MATILDA (d.1115), the last Frankish ruler, bequeathed her lands to the papacy, an act which long caused strife between popes and emperors. In spite of the dual claims, most cities became (11th–12th cent.) free communes; some of them (Pisa, Lucca, Siena, and Florence) developed into strong republics. Commerce, industry, and the arts flourished. Guelph (pro-papal) and Ghibelline (pro-imperial) strife, however, was particularly violent in Tuscany, and there were strong rivalries both within and among cities. After a period of Pisan hegemony (12th–13th cent.), Florence gained control over most Tuscan cities in the 14th–15th cent.; Siena (1559) was the last city to fall under Florence's influence. Under the MEDICI, the ruling family of Florence, Tuscany became (1569) a grand duchy, and thus again a political entity; only the republic of Lucca and the duchy of Massa and Carrara remained independent. After the extinction of the Medici line, Tuscany passed (1737) to ex-duke Francis of Lorraine (later Holy Roman Emperor FRANCIS I), who was succeeded by Grand Duke Leopold I (1765–90; later Emperor LEOPOLD II) and then by Ferdinand III (1790–1801; 1814–24). The French Revolutionary armies invaded Tuscany in 1799, and it was briefly included in the kingdom of Etruria (1801–7) and was ruled under the duchy of Parma, before it was annexed to France by Napoleon I. In 1814, Tuscany again became a grand duchy, under the returning Ferdinand III and then under Leopold II (1824–59) and briefly under Ferdinand IV (1859–60). In 1848, Leopold was forced to grant a constitution, and in 1849 he had to leave Tuscany briefly when it was for a short time a republic. However, in 1852 he was able, with the help of Austria, to rescind the constitution. In 1860, Tuscany voted to unite with the kingdom of Sardinia. In the late Middle Ages and throughout the Renaissance, Tuscany was a center of the arts and of learning. The Tuscan spoken language became the literary language of Italy after Dante Alighieri, Petrarch, and Boccaccio used it. Notable schools of architecture, sculpture, and painting developed from the 11th cent. in many cities, particularly Florence, Pisa, Siena, and Arezzo. From the 16th cent., however, intellectual and artistic life was almost wholly concentrated in Florence. There are universities at Florence, Pisa, and Siena.

Tuscarora Indians (təskərôr'ə): see IROQUOIS CONFEDERACY.

Tusculum (tŭs'kyŏŏləm), city of ancient Latium. The ruins of this city are near modern Frascati, 15 mi (24 km) SE of Rome, Italy. According to legend, Tusculum was founded by Telegonus, son of Ulysses, and it early became an important city. It was a favorite summer residence of Roman nobles; Pliny the Younger, Cicero, and the emperors Nero and Titus were among those who built villas there. It continued to be important until 1191, when it was razed by the Romans. Ruins include those of villas, an amphitheater, and a theater.

Tuskegee (təskē'gē), city (1970 pop. 11,028), seat of Macon co., SE Ala., in a cotton, corn, and dairy region; settled before 1763, inc. 1843. It has gristmills and plants making cottonseed oil and fertilizer. In 1960 a Supreme Court decision voided a 1957 Alabama law that had excluded black residents from the city's population by altering Tuskegee's city limits. A U.S. veterans hospital is there, and antebellum houses remain. Nearby is a national forest. Tuskegee is best known as the seat of the Tuskegee Institute, chartered and opened in 1881 by Booker T. Washington as Tuskegee Normal and Industrial Institute.

Tuskegee Institute, at Tuskegee, Ala.; coeducational; chartered and opened 1881 by Booker T. WASHINGTON as Tuskegee Normal and Industrial Institute. Its present name was adopted in 1937. One of the first important schools to provide adequate education for the Negro, it has since its beginning stressed the practical application of learning. George Washington CARVER conducted his famous experiments and taught there. The Carver Foundation and Tuskegee's Agricultural Research and Experiment Station continue to do research in the natural sciences. There are schools of arts and sciences, engineering, nursing, home economics, education, mechanical industries, and veterinary medicine. The institution's other facilities include the Tuskegee Archives, containing information on black history since 1896.

Tussaud, Marie Gresholtz (tŏŏsō', tüsō'), 1760–1850, Swiss modeler in wax. She learned her art from her uncle, J. C. Curtius, proprietor of wax museums in Paris from 1762. Tussaud was imprisoned during the Reign of Terror, and many heads of famous persons were brought to her for modeling. In 1802 she inherited her uncle's museums and immigrated to London, where she established Madame Tussaud's Exhibition, a museum that remains a principal tourist attraction. See J. T. Tussaud, *The Romance of Madame Tussaud's* (1920); S. P. Martin, *I, Madame Tussaud* (1957), a fictionalized account.

Tustin (tŭs'tĭn), residential city (1970 pop. 21,178), Orange co., S Calif.; founded 1868, inc. 1927. Lumber, plumbing and piping, plastics, office equipment, and food products are made there. This rapidly growing city (its population increased almost tenfold between 1960 and 1970) is part of the greater Los Angeles area. Two U.S. marine corps air stations are in the vicinity.

Tutankhamen or **Tutenkhamon** (tōōt''ängkä'mən, -ĕngk-), fl. c.1350 B.C., king of ancient Egypt, of the XVIII dynasty. He was the son-in-law of IKHNATON and succeeded to the throne after a brief reign by Ikhnaton's successor. Under Ikhnaton the god Amon had been replaced by Aton, and the reaction in favor of Aton ended under Tutankhamen; thus, the king who had been known as Tutankhaton, changed his name. He also abandoned Ikhnaton's new capital, Akhetaton (Tel-el-Amarna), to return to Thebes, sacred to Amon; he restored the name of Amon, deleted from the monuments by Ikhnaton. The chief officer of state, HOREMHEB, controlled affairs, successfully stemming the tide of dissolution that had threatened to engulf the kingdom under Ikhnaton. The tomb of Tutankhamen was found (1922) almost intact by Howard Carter and the earl of Carnarvon in the Valley of the Tombs near Luxor. Its great wealth of objects afforded a new store of knowledge on Egyptian sculpture and life of the XVIII dynasty. The contents of the tomb, including the mummy and the gold sarcophagus, are now in Cairo. See studies by Howard Carter and A. C. Mace (3 vol., 1923–33; abr. ed. 1972); Christiane Desroches-Noblecourt (tr., abr. ed. 1965); Michael Carter (1972); Barry Wynne (1973).

Tuticorin (tōō''tĭkôrĭn'), city (1971 pop. 154,804), Tamil Nadu state, SE India. An important fishing center, it has a Fishing Technological Institute and is also famous for its pearl oysters. Other products include cotton cloth, embroidery, boats, and salt. Tuticorin was founded c.1540 by the Portuguese, captured by the Dutch in 1658, and ceded to the British in 1825.

Tutsi (tōōt'sē, tōō'-) or **Watutsi** (wä-), cattle-raising people of central Africa, particularly in BURUNDI and RWANDA. The original Tutsi homeland was probably in Ethiopia, and c.400 years ago they migrated south to around Lake Kivu. Here they established the native kingdoms of Rwanda and Burundi, ruled by a mwami (king). An aristocratic people, the Tutsi long held the peasant Bahutu, or Hutu, in feudal subjugation. The Tutsi are spectacularly tall, often 7 ft (2.1 m) in height.

Tuttle, Daniel Sylvester, 1837–1923, American Episcopal bishop, b. Windham, N.Y. In 1867 he was consecrated bishop of Montana. He became (1886) bishop of Missouri and from 1903 was presiding bishop of his denomination in the United States.

Tutuila (tōōtōōē'lä), island (1970 pop. 24,548), 52 sq mi (135 sq km), largest island of AMERICAN SAMOA. The principal town and harbor is PAGO PAGO. The island has a rugged eastern area, with a fertile plain in the southwest. Near the center is Matafao Peak (2,141 ft/653 m), the highest point on Tutuila. Copra, canned fish, and handicrafts are the island's chief products.

Tuva Autonomous Soviet Socialist Republic (tōō'və, Rus. tōōvä') or **Tuvinian Autonomous Soviet Socialist Republic**, administrative division (1970 pop. 231,000), 65,830 sq mi (170,500 sq km), extreme S Siberian USSR, on the Mongolian border. Kyzyl is the capital. The area is a mountain basin, c.2,000 ft (610 m) high, encircled by the Sayan and Tannu-Ola ranges. The eastern part is forested and elevated, and the west is a drier lowland. The area includes the upper course of the Yenisei River. There are many glacial lakes. Cattle, horses, sheep, goats, reindeer, and camels are raised in the elevated steppe areas, and grain is cultivated in the irrigated lowlands. Lumbering is carried on extensively. The fur trade remains important in the northeast. Among the republic's industries are food processing; leather making; woodworking; auto repairing; and the manufacture of building materials. Tuvinians make up about 50% of the population and Russians (who live primarily in urban areas) around 35%. Traditionally nomadic herdsmen who engaged in supplemental hunting and agriculture, the Tuvinians have been encouraged under the Soviet government to adopt a sedentary mode of life and have turned increasingly to collectivized agriculture. They are a Turkic-speaking people with Mongol strains; their religion is Tibetan Buddhism. The Tuvinians have a rich folklore and are skilled artisans in silver, bronze, wood, and stone. Controlled by the Mongols from the 13th to 18th cent., they belonged to the Chinese Empire from 1757 to 1911. During the 1911 revolution in China, czarist Russia fomented a separatist movement among the Tuvinians, whose territory became nominally independent before being made a Russian protectorate in 1914. The chaos accompanying the Russian Revolution of 1917 allowed the Tuvinians to again proclaim their independence; but in 1921 the Bolsheviks established a Tuvinian People's Republic, popularly called Tannu-Tuva. It was annexed by the USSR in 1944 as an autonomous oblast and became an autonomous republic in 1961.

Tuwim, Julian (yōōl'yän tōō'vĕm), 1894–1953, Polish poet. A leader of the Skamander group of experimental poets, he was also a major figure in his nation's literature. In his principal collection of poetry, *Slowa we krwi* [words bathed in blood] (1926), he wrote with fervor and violence of the emptiness of urban existence. Tuwim's other works include the collection of poems for children *Locomotive* (1938, tr. 1940) and brilliant translations of Pushkin and other Russian poets. See his selected poems, ed. by Adam Gillon (tr. 1968).

Tuxtla (tōōs'tlä) or **Tuxtla Gutiérrez** (gōōtyär'räs), city (1970 pop. 69,326), capital of Chiapas state, SE Mexico, in the fertile Grijalva valley and at the foot of the Chiapas highlands. Agriculture and cattle raising are the chief occupations, and there is trade in timber. Tuxtla's excellent communications facilities have made it the focal distribution point for the products of the region. The city is the seat of an episcopal see. Near Tuxtla are the remarkable Maya ruins of BONAMPAK.

Túy (tōō'ē), town (1970 pop. 12,600), Pontevedra prov., NW Spain, in Galicia, on the Miño River, opposite the Portuguese town of Valença do Minho. The capital of the Visigothic King Witiza (early 8th cent.), Túy played later an important role in the wars between Castile and Portugal. There is an imposing fortresslike Romanesque cathedral (12th cent.; later restored).

Tuz, Lake (tōōz), shallow salt lake, c.625 sq mi (1,620 sq km), central Turkey. Salt is mined there.

Tuzigoot National Monument: see NATIONAL PARKS AND MONUMENTS (table).

Tuzla (tōōz'lä), city (1971 pop. 107,124), central Yugoslavia, in Bosnia and Hercegovina. It has chemical, coking, and textile industries. Plums are grown in the vicinity, lignite and salt are mined, and some oil is extracted. The city's salt springs were known in Roman times. Tuzla was under Turkish rule from 1463 until its incorporation into Yugoslavia after World War I.

TVA: see TENNESSEE VALLEY AUTHORITY.

Tver: see KALININ, USSR.

Twachtman, John Henry (twäkt'mən), 1853–1902, American landscape painter and etcher, b. Cincinnati. He studied in Cincinnati under Duveneck and in Munich and Paris, but was influenced principally by the impressionists. Many of his exquisite and atmospheric landscapes in oil and pastel were inspired by the countryside near his home in Greenwich, Conn. He also painted a series of landscapes at Yellowstone Park and at Niagara Falls. He did not live to enjoy the high reputation his work now holds. Twachtman is represented in many American galleries. Characteristic works are *Waterfall* (Metropolitan Mus.), *The Hemlock Pool* (Addison Gall. of American Art, Andover, Mass.), and *Summer* (Phillips Memorial Gall., Washington, D.C.).

Twain, Mark, pseud. of **Samuel Langhorne Clemens,** 1835–1910, American author, b. Florida, Mo. As humorist, narrator, and social observer, Twain is unsurpassed in American literature. His novel *The Adventures of Huckleberry Finn*, a masterpiece of humor, characterization, and realism, has been called the first modern American novel. After the death of his father in 1847, young Clemens was apprenticed to a printer in Hannibal, Mo., the Mississippi River town where he spent most of his boyhood. He first began writing for his brother's newspaper there, and later he worked as a printer in several major Eastern cities. In 1857, Clemens went to New Orleans on his way to make his fortune in South America, but instead he became a Mississippi River pilot—hence his pseudonym, "Mark Twain," which was the river call for a depth of water of two fathoms. The Civil War put an end to river traffic, and in 1862 Clemens went W to Carson City, Nev., where he failed in several get-rich-quick schemes. He eventually began writing for the Virginia City *Examiner* and later was a newspaperman in San Francisco. Soon the humorist "Mark Twain" emerged, a writer of tall tales and absurd anecdotes. He first won fame with the comic masterpiece "The Celebrated Jumping Frog of Calaveras County," first published in 1865 in the New York *Saturday Press* and later (1867) used as the title piece for a volume of stories and sketches. When he returned from a trip to Hawaii financed by the Sacramento *Union* in 1866, Twain became a successful humorous lecturer. The articles he wrote on a journey to the Holy Land were published in 1869 as *The Innocents Abroad*. In 1870 he married Olivia Langdon of Elmira, N.Y., and settled down in Hartford, Conn., to be "respectable," although *Roughing It* (1872) presented anecdotes of his less genteel past on the Western frontier. In Hartford, Twain wrote some of his best work: *The Gilded Age* (1873), a satirical novel written with Charles Dudley Warner about materialism and corruption in the 1870s; two evocations of his boyhood in Hannibal, *The Adventures of Tom Sawyer* (1876) and *The Adventures of Huckleberry Finn* (1884); *The Prince and the Pauper* (1882), a novel for children, blending the simplicity of a fairy tale with realistic social criticism; and the nonfictional *Life on the Mississippi* (1883). He also produced a travel book, *A Tramp Abroad* (1880), and *A Connecticut Yankee in King Arthur's Court* (1889), in which satirical overtones reflect a profound seriousness. Some of Twain's later works are forced attempts at humor—

The American Claimant (1892) and two sequels to *Tom Sawyer.* His distinctly bitter *Tragedy of Pudd'nhead Wilson* (1894) underscores his increasingly melancholy attitude. Over the years Twain had invested a great deal of money in unsuccessful printing and publishing ventures, and in 1893 he found himself deeply in debt. To recoup his losses he wearily lectured his way around the world, being funny at whatever cost, and recording his experiences in *Following the Equator* (1897). His later life was shadowed by the deaths of two of his daughters and by the long illness and death in 1904 of his wife. Some critics think that the fierce pessimism of his later works derives from these tragedies. Whatever the reason, he abandoned the optimistic tone of *The Personal Recollections of Joan of Arc* (1896), and wrote such somber works as *The Man Who Corrupted Hadleyburg* (1899), *What Is Man?* (1905), *The Mysterious Stranger* (1916), and *Letters from the Earth* (1962). The strange contradiction in personality between the genial humorist and the declared misanthrope has long intrigued commentators and makes Twain a fascinating biographical subject. Twain's literary reputation rests most particularly on *The Adventures of Huckleberry Finn.* In its hero, a resourceful, unconventional boy with an innate sense of human values, Twain created one of the most memorable characters in fiction. The narrative device of a raft carrying Huck and a runaway slave down the Mississippi enabled Twain to achieve a realistic portrait of American life in the 19th cent. Through his use of authentic vernacular speech he revolutionized the language of American fiction and exerted a great influence on many subsequent American writers. See his love letters, ed. by Dixon Wecter (1949); letters to his publisher, ed. by Hamlin Hill (1966), and to William Dean Howells, ed. by Frederick Anderson et al. (1967); notebooks, ed. by A. B. Paine (1935); autobiography, ed. by Charles Neider (1959); biographies by A. B. Paine (1912, new ed. 1935), Dixon Wecter (1952), DeLancey Ferguson (1942, repr. 1966), and Justin Kaplan (1966); studies by W. D. Howells (1910), Bernard De Voto (1932), J. M. Cox (1966), Van Wyck Brooks (rev. ed. 1933, repr. 1970), and Maxwell Geismar (1970); Frederick Anderson and K. M. Sanderson, ed., *Mark Twain: The Critical Heritage* (1972).

twayblade: see ORCHID.

Tweed, William Marcy, 1823-78, American politician and Tammany leader, b. New York City. A bookkeeper, he became (1848) a volunteer fireman and as a result acquired influence in his ward. He was an alderman (1852-53) and sat (1853-55) in Congress. By 1857 he was a power in TAMMANY. As chairman of the Tammany general committee and later as grand sachem, "Boss" Tweed gained absolute power in the city Democratic party, controlling party nominations and party patronage. He also became a state senator in 1868 and extended his influence into state politics. He engaged in various business deals, and through political services to Jay Gould and James Fisk he became a director of the Erie RR. But it was chiefly from the rich plums plucked through the control of New York City expenditures that Tweed made his great fortune. For a time the **Tweed Ring**, consisting of Tweed and his henchmen—Peter Sweeny, city chamberlain; Richard B. Connolly, city comptroller; and A. Oakey Hall, mayor—controlled the city without interference. They defrauded the city to the extent of at least $30 million through padded and fictitious charges and also profited extravagantly from tax favors. Votes were openly bought and other nefarious vote-getting methods were employed. City judges became notoriously corrupt. Attempts within Tammany to oust the Tweed Ring failed, and in 1870 Tweed forced through the state legislature a charter that greatly increased the powers of the ring. Tweed maintained personal popularity because of his openhandedness and charity to the poor. The immediate cause of Tweed's downfall was the publication in the New York *Times* of evidence of wholesale graft revealed by M. J. O'Rourke, a new county bookkeeper. The effective cartoons of Thomas NAST aroused public indignation. A committee of 70, organized to fight Tammany, elected most of its candidates in 1871, although Tweed himself was returned to the state senate. Largely through the efforts of Samuel J. TILDEN, Tweed was tried for felony, but the jury could not reach a verdict. In a second trial he was convicted and given a 12-year prison sentence; this, however, was reduced by a higher court, and he served one year. Arrested once more on other charges, he escaped and went to Cuba and then to Spain, but was extradited (1876) to the United States. He died in prison two years later. See D. T. Lynch, *"Boss" Tweed* (1927, repr. 1974); W. A. Bales, *Tiger in the Streets* (1962); S. J. Mandelbaum, *Boss Tweed's New York* (1965); A. B. Callow, *The Tweed Ring* (1966).

Tweed, river, 97 mi (156 km) long, rising in the Southern Uplands of Scotland. It flows E through S Scotland then NE, forming part of the Scotland-England border before entering the North Sea at Berwick, NE England. The Tweed system drains most of SE Scotland; the Gala, Ettrick, and Teviot are its chief tributaries. In Scotland the Tweed waters a sheep-farming region and passes Peebles, Melrose, and Kelso. The Tweed has rich salmon fisheries.

tweed, rough, unfinished woolen fabric, of a soft, open, flexible texture resembling cheviot or homespun, but more closely woven. It is made in either plain or twill weave and may have a check, twill, or herringbone pattern. Subdued, interesting color effects (heather mixtures) are obtained by twisting together different-colored woolen strands into a two- or three-ply yarn. Tweeds are desirable for outer wear, being moisture resistant and very durable.

Tweeddale, John Hay, 2d **earl** and 1st **marquess of,** 1626-97, Scottish statesman. In the English civil war he left the party of Charles I and fought for Parliament at Marston Moor (1644), but when Charles promised to support Presbyterianism, he fought for the king at Preston (1648). At the Restoration (1660) he was made a privy councilor for Scotland and advanced to president of the council in 1663. He was dismissed (1674) from office because he favored leniency toward the COVENANTERS, but he later served Charles II and James II as commissioner of the treasury and privy councilor. Supporting the accession (1688) of William III, he was again made privy councilor and a lord of the treasury (1689), high chancellor of Scotland (1692), and marquess (1694). In 1695 he conducted the inquiry into the massacre at GLENCOE. The next year he was dismissed from the chancellorship for approving in the king's name the DARIEN SCHEME.

Tweeddale, Scotland: see PEEBLESSHIRE.

Tweed Ring: see TWEED, WILLIAM MARCY.

Tweedsmuir, John Buchan, 1st **Baron:** see BUCHAN, JOHN.

Twelfth Night, Jan. 5, the vigil or eve of EPIPHANY, so called because it is the 12th night from Christmas, counting Christmas as the first. In England, Twelfth Night has been a great festival marking the end of the Christmas season, and popular masquerading parties are typical entertainment.

Twelve Apostles or **Twelve Disciples:** see APOSTLE.

Twelve Tables, early code of Roman law. Most modern authorities accept the traditional date of 450 B.C., but several place the work later. The tables were supposedly written in response to the protest of the plebeians' protest that the patrician judges were able to discriminate against them with impunity because the principles governing legal disputes were known only orally. Two decemvirs [10-man commissions] were appointed to state the law in writing, and they first produced 10 tablets, probably wooden, with laws inscribed thereon; in the next year they produced two more. Exact quotations of the Twelve Tables are exceedingly rare, but from references in later Latin writings their content has been approximately reconstructed. They appear to have been an exceedingly formalistic statement of the customary law. In later times the Twelve Tables were regarded with reverence as a prime legal source.

twelve-tone music: see SERIAL MUSIC.

twenty-one: see BLACKJACK.

Twenty-one Demands (1915), instrument by which Japan secured temporary hegemony over China. Japan used its declaration of war against Germany (Aug., 1914) as grounds for invading Kiaochow, the German leasehold in Shantung prov., China. Disregarding the Chinese request to withdraw, Japan secretly presented (1915) President Yüan Shih-K'ai with an ultimatum comprising 21 demands divided into five sections. These provided that Japan assume Germany's position in Kiaochow; that Manchuria and Mongolia be reserved to Japan for exploitation and colonization; that Japan control the main coal deposits of China; that the other powers be excluded from further territorial concessions; and that Japan guide China's military, commercial, and financial affairs. The demands for control of Chinese policy were dropped, partly at the insistence of the United States. The remainder of the demands were accepted by President Yüan after the Japanese threatened to extend their invasion. Treaties were signed (May 25) extending Japan's lease of the Liaotung peninsula (see LIAONING) and of the Manchurian railroads and granting Kiaochow to Japan. The demands, setting a pattern for Japanese domination, were forced on China, but the treaties were not ratified by the Chinese legislature. The Japanese reinforced their claims in 1917 and forced a second agreement from the Chinese in 1918. At the Versailles Conference, Japan, by reason of secret treaties signed in 1917, was awarded the German possessions in Shantung over strong Chinese protest. China refused to sign the Versailles treaty, and this event led directly to the MAY FOURTH MOVEMENT of 1919. At the Washington Conference (1921-22), Japan agreed to withdraw its troops from Shantung and restore full sovereignty to China.

Twickenham: see RICHMOND UPON THAMES.

twilight, period between sunset and total darkness or between total darkness and sunrise. Total darkness does not occur immediately when the sun sinks below the horizon because light from the sun that strikes the atmosphere is scattered (both by the air itself and by suspended matter, e.g., dust and smoke). Civil twilight ends when the center of the sun is 6° below the horizon. Although it is still not very dark, it is necessary to use artificial light to carry out most activities. Nautical twilight ends when the sun's center is 12° below the horizon; at about this time the light is too dim for the user of a sextant to see a sharp horizon. Astronomical twilight ends when the sun's center is 18° below the horizon; by this time even the faintest stars overhead can be seen. (Similar definitions apply to morning twilight.) During twilight, Venus or Mercury is often seen as the evening star or morning star. The length of twilight depends on latitude and the time of year. Twilight is generally shorter at the equator, where the sun's path toward the horizon is more nearly vertical than at higher latitudes; typically, astronomical twilight may last for 1 hr at the equator and 1½ hr in New York City.

twine: see CORDAGE.

Twin Falls, city (1970 pop. 21,914), seat of Twin Falls co., S Idaho, in the Snake River valley; inc. 1905. The city was begun as a center of a private irrigation project, which is now supplemented by the Minidoka project of the U.S. Bureau of Reclamation. One of the falls of Twin Falls in the nearby gorge is harnessed for hydroelectric power. Sugar beets, potatoes, corn, beans, and grains are processed, as well as livestock and dairy products. Several trout farms are in the area. Scenic attractions include the deep Snake River canyon and Shoshone Falls (212 ft/65 m high). A junior college is in Twin Falls, and Craters of the Moon National Monument is nearby.

twinkling, in astronomy: see SEEING.

twins: see MULTIPLE BIRTH.

Twins, The, English name for GEMINI, a CONSTELLATION.

2, 4-D: see HERBICIDE.

Two Rivers, city (1970 pop. 13,553), Manitowoc co., E Wis., on Lake Michigan at the mouth of the Twin River; inc. 1878. Two Rivers is closely associated with its twin city, Manitowoc, both of which are highly industrialized. A U.S. Coast Guard station (est. 1872) is in Two Rivers, and to the north are a nuclear power plant and a petrified forest.

Two Sicilies, kingdom of the. The name Two Sicilies was used in the Middle Ages to mean the kingdoms of Sicily and of Naples (see SICILY and NAPLES, KINGDOM OF). ALFONSO V of Aragón, who in 1442 reunited the two kingdoms under his rule, styled himself king of the Two Sicilies. Under his successors the kingdoms were again separate, but the title was revived during Spanish domination (1504-1713) of both kingdoms and after the accession (1759) of a cadet branch of the Spanish line of BOURBON to Naples and Sicily. Ferdinand IV of Naples (Ferdinand III of Sicily) officially merged the two kingdoms in 1816 and called himself FERDINAND I of the Two Sicilies. Both the Sicilians, who thus lost their autonomy, and the pope, who saw his theoretical suzerainty over the two kingdoms ignored, protested the change. A popular uprising (1820) instigated by the CARBONARI forced Ferdinand to concede a constitution, but Austrian intervention (1821) after the Congress of LAIBACH restored his absolute power. The reactionary regimes of his successors FRANCIS I, FERDINAND II, and FRANCIS II finally ended when Sicily and Naples fell to the forces of GARIBALDI in 1860. In 1861, Gaeta, Francis's last fortress, surrendered to Victor Emmanuel II of Sardinia, and the Two Sicilies became part of the kingdom of Italy. See studies by H. M. M. Acton (1956 and 1962); G. T. Romani, *The Neapolitan Revolution of 1820–*

1821 (1950); Benedetto Croce, *History of the Kingdom of Naples* (tr. 1970).

Tyana (tī'ənə), town of ancient Cappadocia, at the northern foot of the Taurus range, in present S central Turkey. A powerful military fortress and a prosperous commercial center as early as the 5th cent. B.C., it was incorporated into the Roman Empire in A.D. 272. The city was the birthplace of Apollonius of Tyana. There are extensive ruins on the site.

Tyard, Pontus de (pôNtüs' də tēär'), 1521?-1605, French poet of the PLÉIADE. The sonnets in his *Erreurs amoureuses* (3 vol., 1549-55) are imitative of Petrarch and are among the earliest written in France. He was bishop of Châlons from 1578 to 1592.

Tyche (tī'kē): see FORTUNA.

Tychicus (tĭk'ĭkəs), companion of Paul. Acts 20.4; Eph. 6.21; Col. 4.7; 2 Tim. 4.12; Titus 3.12.

Tycho Brahe: see BRAHE, TYCHO.

Tydeus (tī'dēəs), in Greek legend, son of Oeneus. He was killed in the expedition of the SEVEN AGAINST THEBES. His son, Diomed, avenged his father's death in the expedition of the EPIGONI.

Tydings, Millard Evelyn (tī'dĭngz), 1890-1961, American politician, b. Havre de Grace, Md. He was admitted (1913) to the bar, soon built a successful law practice, and became (1916) a member of the Maryland legislature. In World War I he saw action in France. He again served (1920-23) in the Maryland legislature before becoming a Democratic member (1923-27) of the U.S. House of Representatives. In the U.S. Senate after 1927, Tydings opposed much New Deal legislation and on several occasions opposed President Franklin Delano Roosevelt's foreign policy. In 1950 he headed the Senate subcommittee appointed to investigate Sen. Joseph R. McCarthy's allegations of Communist infiltration of the Dept. of State. The committee's report cleared the department and denounced McCarthy as a liar. Tydings was defeated for reelection the same year.

Tygart (tī'gərt), river, c.160 mi (260 km) long, rising in E West Virginia and flowing north to join the West Fork and form the Monongahela at Fairmont. Tygart River Dam (completed 1938), near Grafton, forms a large reservoir in Tygart Lake State Park.

Tylenol (tī'lənôl), trade name for acetaminophen, an ANALGESIC used as a substitute for ASPIRIN.

Tyler, John, 1790-1862, 10th President of the United States, b. Charles City co., Va. Educated at the College of William and Mary, he studied law under his father, John Tyler (1747-1813), governor of Virginia from 1808 to 1811, and was admitted (1809) to the bar. A state legislator (1811-16, 1823-25) and U.S. Representative (1817-21), Tyler was an unswerving states' rights Democrat. He joined the condemnation of Andrew Jackson's actions in Florida and voted against the Missouri Compromise. Governor of Virginia (1825-27) and a U.S. Senator (1827-36), Tyler reluctantly supported Jackson as the least objectionable of the presidential candidates in 1828 and 1832. Although he did not approve South Carolina's nullification act, he violently opposed Jackson's measures against it (see FORCE BILL). The President's fiscal policies further alienated him, so that he was eventually drawn to the new WHIG PARTY, joining its states' rights Southern wing, which differed with many of the nationalistic policies associated with the Clay leadership. He resigned from the Senate rather than abide by the instructions of the Virginia legislature to vote for the motion to expunge Henry Clay's censure of Jackson from the records. In 1840, Tyler was chosen running mate to the Whig presidential candidate, William Henry HARRISON, and they waged their victorious "Tippecanoe and Tyler too" campaign. One month after his inauguration Harrison died, and on April 4, 1841, Tyler became the first Vice President to succeed to the presidency. His antipathy toward many Whig policies soon became apparent (he had never concealed it), and a rift developed between him and Henry CLAY, the party leader. After his second veto of a measure creating a national bank with branches in the states (on the grounds that it violated the constitutional rights of the states), his cabinet, except for Daniel WEBSTER, resigned (Sept., 1841). Webster stayed on as Secretary of State until the negotiations for the Webster-Ashburton Treaty with the British were completed (May, 1843). Bitterly denounced by the Whigs and with few friends among the Democrats, Tyler became a President without a party. Nevertheless he accomplished much toward the annexation of Texas. Abel P. UPSHUR, Webster's successor, was killed when a gun on the U.S.S. *Princeton* blew up, and John C. CALHOUN continued Upshur's negotiations for a treaty with Texas. The treaty was rejected by the Senate. Tyler then supported a plan for a joint resolution to annex Texas and had the satisfaction of seeing it accepted by Texas just before he left office in 1845. The completion of annexation was brought about under James K. POLK, Tyler's Democratic successor. Tyler, nominated by a small Democratic faction, had withdrawn from the 1844 election. In Feb., 1861, he presided over the unsuccessful conference at Washington that attempted to find some last-minute solution to avert the Civil War. Later, he served in the provisional Confederate Congress and was elected to the permanent Confederate Congress, but he died before he could take his seat. See Lyon Gardiner Tyler (his son), *Letters and Times of the Tylers* (3 vol., 1884-96, repr. 1970); biography by O. P. Chitwood (1939, repr. 1964); study by R. J. Morgan (1954).

Tyler, Moses Coit, 1835-1900, American writer on intellectual history, b. Griswold, Conn. He moved to Michigan as a boy. Graduated from Yale (1857) and from Andover Theological Seminary, he entered the Congregational ministry, but remained in it only two years. He was professor of English (1867-81) at the Univ. of Michigan and of American history (1881-1900) at Cornell Univ. and was an organizer of the American Historical Association. The two books upon which his fame chiefly rests are *A History of American Literature, 1607-1765* (1878) and *The Literary History of the American Revolution* (1897). His life of Patrick Henry for the "American Statesmen" series and his *Three Men of Letters* (1895) also added to his reputation as a sympathetic and accurate biographer. His wide knowledge of both history and literature enabled him to write authoritatively on both. See biography by Howard Mumford Jones (1933).

Tyler, Royall, 1757-1826, American jurist, author, and playwright, b. Boston, grad. Harvard, 1776. He served in the colonial army during the American Revolution and later in the suppression of Shays's Rebellion. Tyler was admitted to the bar in 1780; he practiced law in Maine, later in Massachusetts, and after 1790 in Vermont, where he was (1807-13) chief justice of the supreme court and professor of jurisprudence (1811-14) at the Univ. of Vermont. He is remembered for his play *The Contrast* (1787), which was the first American comedy produced by a professional company. He also wrote other plays and a novel, the *Algerine Captive* (1797). With Joseph Dennie he wrote witty Federalist verse and essays for the *New Hampshire Journal.* See his *Four Plays* (ed. by A. W. Peach and G. F. Newbrough, 1941). See study by G. T. Tanselle (1967).

Tyler, Wat, d. 1381, English rebel. His given name appears in full as Walter; his surname signifies the trade of a roof tiler. He came into prominence as the leader of the rebellion of 1381, known as the Peasants' Revolt. The revolt had its ultimate origins in the plague of 1348-49, which had swept away nearly a third of the population of England. The result was a scarcity of labor and a rise in wages. In 1351, Parliament passed the Statute of Labourers to hold down wages. This proved almost impossible to enforce but aroused much resentment among the peasantry. Another source of discontent was the fact that landlords were attempting to stem the new mobility of labor by asserting their ancient manorial rights. This unrest flared into rebellion when the poll tax was increased in 1380. The first outbreak came in Essex, but the trouble soon spread to Kent, where Tyler was chosen as leader. The rebels seized Canterbury and then proceeded to London, their number increasing on the way. After an unsuccessful attempt to interview RICHARD II, Tyler led the mob into the city, where it plundered and burned many houses (including the Savoy Palace, residence of John of Gaunt) and the Fleet and Newgate prisons. On June 14 the king met some of the rebels at Mile End and agreed to their demands to abolish serfdom, feudal service, market monopolies, and restrictions on buying and selling. At the same time, however, or immediately thereafter, Tyler and another group of rebels captured the Tower of London and killed the archbishop of Canterbury and several other officials. The following day Tyler met the king at Smithfield, where he presented new demands, including one for the confiscation of all church property. In an exchange of blows with the mayor of London, Tyler was mortally wounded and died soon afterward. The king, with remarkable courage, cowed the mob and held them at bay until the mayor brought up armed support. The rebels dispersed, and the revolt, which had raged over all England, was put down with severity. King Richard immediately revoked the Mile End grants. See Charles Oman, *The Great Revolt of 1381* (1906, repr. 1969); R. B. Dobson, ed., *The Peasants' Revolt of 1381* (1970).

Tyler, city (1970 pop. 57,770), seat of Smith co., E Texas; inc. 1850. In the heart of the rich East Texas oil field, Tyler has refineries and other oil-based industries. It also has a foundry, and plants manufacturing pipes, tires, and electrical equipment. The city's rose-growing industry is one of the nation's largest. There is a huge municipal rose garden, and in season every street and yard is colored with blooms. Tyler is the seat of a junior college, two private business colleges, a museum of art, and a planetarium. It has a symphony orchestra and a civic theater. The East Texas fairgrounds are there. Nearby is a state park.

Tylor, Sir Edward Burnett, 1832-1917, English anthropologist. His extensive researches helped to develop interest in anthropological science in England. Tylor became (1883) keeper of the University Museum at Oxford and was professor of anthropology there from 1896 to 1909. His work on the mentality of primitive peoples, and especially on animism, made an important contribution to the study of primitive religion. Tylor's pioneering book, *Anthropology* (1881, abr. ed. 1960), is still essentially modern in its cultural theories and concepts. His other works include *Researches into the Early History of Mankind* (1865) and *Primitive Culture* (1871, repr. 1958). See study by R. R. Marett (1936).

tympanum (tĭm'pənəm). In architecture, the triangular space of a PEDIMENT, or low-pitched gable, above a portico, door, or window. Its boundaries are generally cornice moldings. The term also designates the solid wall space above an arched window or door. Sculptured tympanums of this type, within

Tympanum (west pediment, temple of Aphaia at Aegina)

round or pointed arches, occurred above the doors of the recessed portals in the medieval churches. They were universal in both Romanesque and Gothic periods, and were especially fine in France. The usual subjects are biblical and symbolic, often arranged in horizontal tiers with numerous figures to illustrate a complete legend. Over the central doorway of Notre-Dame de Paris is a depiction of the Last Judgment. In Italy tympanums were sometimes decorated with mosaic or fresco.

Tynan, Kenneth Peacock (tī'nən), 1927-, English drama critic, author, and theatrical executive, b. Birmingham, England. During the 1950s, while writing for *The Observer,* Tynan became widely regarded as Britain's most influential drama critic. He espoused a new theatrical realism best exemplified in the works of the ANGRY YOUNG MEN. In 1963 he became literary manager of the British National Theatre. Tynan has published several books including *Curtains* (1961) and *Tynan Right and Left* (1967). In 1969 he helped devise the controversial review *Oh, Calcutta!,* which featured a nude cast.

Tyndale, Tindal, or **Tindale, William** (all: tĭn'dəl), c.1494-1536, English biblical translator (see BIBLE) and Protestant martyr. He was probably ordained shortly before entering (c.1521) the household of Sir John Walsh of Gloucestershire as chaplain and tutor. His sympathy with the new learning led to disputes with the clergy, and he moved to London, determined to translate the New Testament into English. Finding that publication could not be accomplished in England, Tyndale went to Hamburg in 1524, visited Martin Luther in Wittenberg, and at Cologne began (1525) the printing of the New Testament. Interrupted by an injunction, he had the edition completed at Worms. When copies entered England, they were denounced by the bishops and suppressed (1526); Cardinal Wolsey ordered Tyndale seized at Worms. Living in concealment, Tyndale pursued his translation, issuing the Pentateuch (1530) and the Book of Jonah (1536). His work was later the basis of the King James Version of the Bible. His tracts in defense of the principles of the English Reformation, *The Obedience of a Christian Man* (1528) and *The Parable of the Wicked Mammon* (1528), were denounced by Sir Thomas More. *The Practice of Prelates* (1530), condemning the divorce of Henry VIII, drew the wrath of the king. Occupied with revising his translations, Tyndale was seized (1535) in Antwerp and confined in Vilvoorde Castle, near Brussels. His trial ended in condemnation for heresy, and he was strangled at the stake before his body was burned. See biographies by J. F. Mozley (1937) and C. H. Williams (1969); study by E. W. Cleaveland (1911, repr. 1972).

Tyndall, John (tĭn'dəl), 1820–93, British physicist, b. Ireland. He became (1853) professor of natural philosophy at the Royal Institution and in 1867 succeeded Michael Faraday, his friend and colleague, as superintendent there. His chief researches were in the fields of light, sound, and radiant heat. He made significant studies of Alpine glaciers. He was known as a lecturer and writer, and his gifted expositions of science for the layman were widely translated. The Tyndall effect (see COLLOID) is named for him.

Tyndall effect: see COLLOID.

Tyndareus (tĭndâr'ēəs): see LEDA.

Tyne (tīn), river, c.30 mi (50 km) long, NE England, formed near Hexham, Northumberland, by the confluence of the North Tyne (33 mi/53 km long; rising in SW Cheviot Hills) and the South Tyne (32 mi/52 km long; rising in the N Pennines). The Tyne flows eastward through the Tyneside conurbation to the North Sea at Tynemouth. The lower Tyne is lined with docks, shipbuilding yards, a variety of industrial plants, and coal-mining and ironworking towns. The Tyne was made navigable to Newcastle upon Tyne, its chief port, at the turn of the 20th century; South Shields, Gateshead, Jarrow, and Wallsend are important ports on the river. Three bridges cross the Tyne at Newcastle upon Tyne; the Tyne Tunnel (opened 1967) connects Jarrow and Willington.

Tyne and Wear, metropolitan county (1972 est. pop. 1,209,000), NE England, created under the Local Government Act of 1972 (effective 1974). It is subdivided into five metropolitan districts. Tyne and Wear comprises the county boroughs of GATESHEAD, NEWCASTLE UPON TYNE, SOUTH SHIELDS, SUNDERLAND, TYNEMOUTH, and parts of the former counties of DURHAM and NORTHUMBERLAND.

Tynemouth (tĭn'məth, tīn'-), county borough (1971 pop. 68,861), Northumberland, NE England, on the Tyne River. Tynemouth is highly industrialized; it is a shipbuilding center and a coal and fishing port. Its manufactures include furniture, textiles, glassware, machine tools, and die castings. It is also a resort. There are remains of a priory founded by King Edwin of Northumbria early in the 7th cent. In 1974, Tynemouth became part of the new metropolitan county of Tyne and Wear.

type, for PRINTING, was invented in China. Related devices, such as seals and stamps for making impressions in clay, had been used in ancient times in Babylon and elsewhere. Movable types made from metal molds were used in Korea a half-century before they were used in Europe. However, there is no evidence that the European invention of movable type attributed to Johann GUTENBERG was not independent of Eastern developments. The first dated printing from movable types in Europe is a papal indulgence, printed at Mainz in 1454. The first dated book printed from movable type was a Psalter printed by FUST and Schoeffer on the Gutenberg press at Mainz in 1457. Gutenberg's MAZARIN BIBLE, completed at Mainz not later than 1455, is believed to be the first book printed in Europe from movable type. The type used in these beginnings of European printing was of the kind known as black letter or Gothic, represented now by such types as Old English and German. The forms of the letters were derived from popular handwriting styles. Other styles suggested the letter forms of roman and italic type. Roman type was used by several printers before Nicolas JENSON so improved it as to ensure its triumph as the standard type. Italic type was first used by ALDUS MANUTIUS, who also introduced small capitals. Roman type is of two basic sorts, old style and modern. The modern type emphasizes the contrast between light and heavy lines and has conspicuous level serifs; the old style type keeps its lines of nearly the same weight and has inconspicuous serifs, some of them sloping. Qualities of old style and modern types are often combined. Type characters are usually made by pouring type metal into previously cut matrices, by photomechanic techniques (see COLD TYPE), and, less frequently, by processes using plastics and other synthetic materials. Type may be set by hand, one line at a time, or cast by machine. Famous designers of types include, in addition to those named above, Geofroy TORY, Claude GARAMOND, Robert GRANJON, Christopher van DYCK, William CASLON, John BASKERVILLE, Giambattista BODONI, François Ambroise DIDOT, William MORRIS, Bruce ROGERS, and F. W. GOUDY. See TYPOGRAPHY. See Hellmut Lehmann-Haupt, *One Hundred Books about Bookmaking* (1949); W. T. Berry and A. F. Johnson, *Encyclopaedia of Type Faces* (1953); D. B. Updike, *Printing Types* (3d ed. 1962); J. R. Biggs, *An Approach to Type* (2d. ed. 1962); A. L. Lawson, *Printing Types* (1971).

type metal, alloy of lead with antimony, tin, and sometimes copper, so named because of its extensive use for making printing type. Expanding upon solidification, the alloy takes a fine and clear impression of the mold in which it hardens. It has a low melting point. In addition to its use for type, it is also employed in making the metal parts of various musical instruments and for ornaments of intricate design and pattern. The percentages of the metals in the alloy vary, according to the use to which it is to be put.

typesetting: see PRINTING.

typewriter, instrument for producing by manual operation characters similar to those of printing. Corresponding to each key on the instrument's keyboard is a steel type. Activated through a series of levers when its key is pressed, the type strikes the paper in the machine through an inked ribbon; the carriage holding the paper then automatically moves, providing space for the next character. The first recorded patent for a typewriter was taken out in England by Henry Mill in 1714. In the United States the typographer of William Austin Burt, patented in 1829, was the first practical writing machine. An improved French machine appeared in 1833. The early models were chiefly for the blind and produced embossed writing. A practical commercial machine invented in the United States in 1867 by Christopher Latham Sholes and his associates, Carlos Glidden and Samuel Soulé, was manufactured by Philo Remington and placed on the market in 1874. This early model had only capital letters. A shift-key model, permitting change of case, appeared in 1878. An electric typewriter, requiring less effort than the ordinary manual machine, came into use c.1935. The modern electric typewriter offers a number of advantages, including speed and uniformity of type impression. In the Selectric, introduced by International Business Machines (IBM) in 1961, the usual type bars are replaced by type raised on the surface of a metal globe that moves across the surface of a stationary paper holder, which replaces the moving carriage of the ordinary typewriter; interchangeable globes provide a variety of typefaces and special symbols, allowing a single typewriter to be utilized for scientific writing, foreign languages, or other uses. The stock ticker, suggested as early as 1867, is a form of typewriter that records on a narrow strip a telegraphed message. The teletypewriter, invented in 1904, transmits typing over an electric circuit such as the telephone or telegraph; an electric impulse actuates the proper key in the receiving typewriter.

Typhoeus: see TYPHON.

typhoid fever, acute, generalized infection caused by *Salmonella typhosa*. The main sources of infection are contaminated water or milk and, especially in urban communities, food handlers who are carriers. The symptoms of typhoid appear 10 to 14 days after infection; they include high fever, rose-colored spots on the abdomen and chest, diarrhea or constipation, and enlargement of the spleen. Complications, especially in untreated patients, may be numerous, affecting practically every body system, and they account for the mortality rate of 7% to 14%. Perforation of the intestine with hemorrhage is not uncommon. Chloramphenicol is the most effective drug in combating typhoid, and in very toxic patients a cortisone derivative may be helpful. Skilled nursing care is still of the utmost importance, as is a high caloric diet to prevent wasting of the body. Vaccination against typhoid is a valuable preventive measure, especially for persons in military service and for those who travel to poorly sanitized regions.

Typhon (tī'fŏn) or **Typhoeus** (tīfē'əs), in Greek mythology, fierce and monstrous son of Gaea. He was the father of Echidna—a monster half woman and half dragon—and of Cerberus, Hydra, the Sphinx, and the Chimera. Typhon was so frightful that Zeus set him afire and buried him alive under Mt. Aetna.

typhoon: see HURRICANE.

typhus, any of a group of infectious diseases caused by microorganisms classified between bacteria and viruses, known as rickettsias. Typhus diseases are characterized by high fever and an early onset of rash and headache. They respond to antibiotic treatment with tetracycline and chloramphenicol and can be prevented by vaccination. Epidemic typhus, the most serious in the group, is caused by *Rickettsia prowazeki*, which is transmitted in the feces of body lice. It occurs in crowded, unsanitary conditions and has historically been a major killer in wartime. It occurs more commonly in cooler climates and seasons. Brill's disease, also called recrudescent typhus, is believed to be a milder recurrence of epidemic typhus. Endemic murine typhus is primarily a disease of rodents and is spread to humans by rat fleas. The symptoms are milder than those of epidemic typhus. Scrub typhus (Tsutsugamushi fever) is carried to humans by infected mites. It occurs primarily in East Asia and the Southeast Pacific islands.

typography (tīpŏg'rəfē), the art of PRINTING from movable type. The term typographer is today virtually synonymous with a master printer skilled in the techniques of type and paper stock selection, ornamentation, and composition. Before the development of typography, related arts flourished for centuries. Scribes in ancient Egypt and the Middle East perfected the craft of writing on papyrus scrolls and clay tablets. Hellenistic and Roman makers of books developed the art, which reached a peak of aesthetic perfection in the exquisite illuminated MANUSCRIPTS of the Middle Ages (see ILLUMINATION, in art). The first European typographers imitated these manuscripts, but the introduction of metal types in the 15th cent. brought about a radical transformation. Crisp and uncompromising, metal types imposed new standards of composition. A highly conservative art, modern typography adheres closely to tradition. Since legibility is of the utmost importance, the forms that print most legibly are retained. New typographic styles continue to develop, however, to suit myriad uses in the design of advertisements, posters, newspapers, greeting cards, almanacs, and fine books. For bibliography and a list of notable type designers, see TYPE. See J. R. Biggs, *Basic Typography* (1969); Warren Chappell, *A Short History of the Printed Word* (1970).

Tyr: see TIW.

Tyrannosaurus (tĭrăn"ōsôr'əs, tĭr-) [Gr.,=tyrant lizard], genus of a biped carnivorous DINOSAUR, about 50 ft (15 m) in length and about 20 ft (6 m) tall, weighing 10 tons, having an elongated skull and large, sharp, daggerlike teeth in jaws that could open to a 4-ft (122-cm) gape. The short forelimbs had three fingers armed, like the three digits of the powerful hind limbs, with sharp, recurved claws; on the foot was a spurred toe not reaching to the ground. The largest and probably the most ferocious terrestrial carnivore that ever lived, the *Tyrannosaurus* is believed to have existed only for a short time in the late Cretaceous period and to have dominated the North American continent at that time; parts of a few skeletons have been found in Montana and South Dakota. Only one species (*Tyrannosaurus rex*) is known. The *Tyrannosaurus* is classified in the phylum CHORDATA, subphylum Vertebrata, class Reptilia, order Saurischia.

Tyrannus (tĭrăn'əs), teacher of Ephesus at whose school Paul preached. Acts 19.9.

tyrant, in ancient history, ruler who gained power by usurping the legal authority. The word is perhaps of Lydian origin and carried with it no connotation of moral censure. With the growth of the constitutional, democratic form of government, especially at Athens, in the 5th cent. B.C. the word took on its negative sense. Many tyrants ruled well and with benefit to their subjects. Greek tyranny was in the main an outgrowth of the struggle of the rising popular classes against the aristocracy or plutocracy. The usual procedure was for a leader to win popular support, overthrow the existing government, and seize power for himself. The 7th cent. B.C. saw the rise of the tyrant Cypselus and his son, PERIANDER, of Corinth, and the 6th cent. B.C. was the time of the tyrants CLEISTHENES of Sicyon in the Peloponnesus, POLYCRATES of Samos, and PISISTRATUS of Athens, followed by his sons HIPPARCHUS and HIPPIAS. The tyrants of Sicily were the products of more or less the same causes as those in Greece, but tyranny was prolonged by the threat of Carthaginian attack, which facilitated the rise of military leaders with the people united behind them. Such Sicilian tyrants as GELON, HIERO I, HIERO II, DIONYSIUS THE ELDER, and DIONYSIUS THE YOUNGER maintained lavish courts and were patrons of culture. The THIRTY TYRANTS were not tyrants in the usual sense. See P. N. Ure, *The Origin of Tyranny* (1922); Anthony Andrewes, *The Greek Tyrants* (1956, repr. 1968).

tyrant flycatcher: see FLYCATCHER.

Tyrconnel, Richard Talbot, duke and **earl of** (tôl'-bət, tərkŏn'əl), 1630–91, Irish Jacobite. He escaped from Ireland after Oliver Cromwell's punitive campaign there (1649) and was party to various intrigues to restore the monarchy. After the Restoration (1660) he joined the household of the duke of York (later James II) and used his influence at court to promote his own interests. He was arrested and exiled for supposed complicity in the Popish Plot (see OATES, TITUS), but after the accession (1685) of James II, he was created earl (1685) and sent as commander in chief of the forces in Ireland. In this capacity and as lord deputy (1687-88) he placed Catholics in many key positions. After the Glorious Revolution of 1688, James crossed to Ireland and created Tyrconnel a duke—a title recognized only by the Jacobites. After defeat in the battle of the Boyne (1690) Tyrconnel went to France for aid. He returned in 1691, but died suddenly just before the fall of Limerick.

Tyrconnel, Rory O'Donnell, earl of, 1575-1608, Irish chieftain; brother of Hugh Roe O'Donnell, lord of Tyrconnel, whom he succeeded as chief of the clan in 1602. After the rebellion in which his brother had been a leading figure, Rory went to London (1603) to submit to James I. He was knighted, created earl, and made sheriff of Donegal. However, he soon engaged in a conspiracy with Spain to seize Dublin Castle and the government and to start a general uprising. His flight (1607) with Hugh O'Neill, 2d earl of TYRONE, after the discovery of the plot, signified the end of political power of the Irish tribal chieftains. He died at Rome and was posthumously attainted (1613) by the Irish Parliament.

Tyrconnell, ancient kingdom in NW Ireland in what is the modern Co. Donegal. The kingdom was founded by Conall Gulban in the 5th cent.; kings of Tyrconnell reigned until 1071.

Tyre (tīr), ancient city of PHOENICIA, S of Sidon. It is the present-day Sur in Lebanon, a small town on a peninsula jutting into the Mediterranean from the mainland of Syria S of Beirut. It was built on an island just off the mainland, but the accumulation of sand around a mole built by Alexander the Great to facilitate his siege of the city (333-332 B.C.) has formed a causeway more than .5 mi (.8 km) wide. The date of the founding of the city is extremely uncertain, but by 1400 B.C. it was a flourishing city. The maritime supremacy of Tyre was established by 1100 B.C., and by that date its seamen seem to have sailed around the Mediterranean and to have founded colonies in Spain, S Italy, and N Africa. Tyrians founded the city of Carthage in the 9th cent. B.C. Tyre was famous for its industries, such as textile manufactures, and particularly for the purple Tyrian dye. Throughout its long history Tyre frequently came under foreign rule. It was besieged by the Assyrians and the Chaldaeans and fell to the Persians. The city was sacked by Alexander the Great but recovered quickly. In 64 B.C. it became a part of the Roman Empire. In spite of competition offered by newer cities such as Alexandria, it prospered and was able to retain varying degrees of autonomy. Christianity was introduced early into Tyre, and a splendid cathedral, of which there are remains, was built in the 4th cent. After the rise of Islam, Tyre came under Muslim rule and later under that of the Crusaders. It was destroyed by the Muslims in 1291 and never recovered its former greatness. The principal ruins of the city today are those of buildings erected by the Crusaders. There are some Greco-Roman remains, but any left by the Phoenicians lie underneath the present town. Tyre is mentioned frequently in the Bible. See W. B. Fleming, *History of Tyre* (1915).

Tyrnau: see TRNAVA, Czechoslovakia.

Tyrol (tĭr'ŏl, tĭrōl'), Ger. *Tirol*, province (1971 pop. 539,000), 4,882 sq mi (12,644 sq km), W Austria. Innsbruck is the capital. Bordering on West Germany in the north and on Italy and Switzerland in the south, it is an almost wholly Alpine region, traversed by the Inn River. The main part of the province is separated from the fertile East Tyrol (Ger. *Osttirol*) by a corridor belonging partly to Italy and partly to Salzburg prov., Austria. The Tyrolean Alps, which culminate in the ÖTZTAL ALPS, are famed for their idyllic beauty and attract many tourists, thus supplementing income from the exploitation of the province's limited natural resources. Tourist centers include Kitzbühel, Kufstein, Sankt Anton, and Zell am See. Subsistence farming, cattle raising, forestry, and viticulture are the main occupations. Some industry is located at Innsbruck, Landeck, and Kufstein. The saltworks near Solbad Hall are an important source of revenue. The now little-worked silver and copper mines of Tyrol, known since antiquity, and its strategic position commanding the Brenner Pass across the Alps gave the region a fairly important role in European history. The Tyrol was inhabited by Rhaetic tribes when it was conquered (15 B.C.) by the Romans. It was invaded (6th cent. A.D.) by Teutonic tribes, the Baiovarii and the Lombards, and later by the Franks, who held all Tyrol by the 8th cent. Large parts of S Tyrol (now in Italy) were ruled from the 11th cent. to 1802-3 by the bishops of TRENT and by the bishops of Brixen (see BRESSANONE). The two bishoprics were secularized and fell to Austria in consequence of the Peace of Lunéville (1801) between France and Austria. The northern section (constituting the present Tyrol), first divided into petty counties, was united under the counts of Tyrol and passed, with the abdication (1363) of MARGARET MAULTASCH, to Austria. In 1805 the Treaty of Pressburg awarded all Tyrol to Napoleon's ally, Bavaria, but when war broke out (1809) between France and Austria the Tyrolean peasants, led heroically by Andreas HOFER, rose in revolt and stubbornly defied the French and Bavarian troops. In 1810, Napoleon, at variance with Maximilian I of Bavaria, attached most of S Tyrol to Italy. Both parts were restored (1815) to Austria by the Congress of Vienna. The Treaty of Saint-Germain (1919) awarded S Tyrol (the predominantly German-speaking province of Bolzano and the predominantly Italian-speaking province of Trento) to Italy. The ruthless Italianization policy of the Fascist government created much unrest and friction in the period between the two World Wars (see TRENTINO-ALTO ADIGE). The Italian constitution of 1947, however, gave S Tyrol the status of an autonomous region, with full protection of minority rights.

Tyrone, Hugh O'Neill, 2d **earl of,** 1540?-1616, Irish chieftain. He was the son of Matthew O'Neill, the illegitimate son of the 1st earl. Hugh succeeded his murdered older brother, Brian, as Baron Dungannon in 1562 and was sent to England for safety. He returned (1568) to Ulster following the death of his cousin Shane O'NEILL. He served with the English against the rebel Gerald Fitzgerald, earl of DESMOND, in 1580 and in 1585 was made earl of Tyrone. In 1593 he displaced his kinsman Turlough Luineach O'Neill as the O'Neill chieftain and quickly became the most powerful nobleman in Ulster. Dissatisfied with the English government's persistent policy of playing the chiefs against one another, Tyrone was also angered by the English refusal to restore the lands granted to his grandfather. At last he formed an alliance with the other Irish chiefs and sought aid against Protestant England from Catholic Spain. He achieved something like unity among his allies and, after 1595, defeated some of Queen Elizabeth's best commanders in Ireland. In 1599 he made a short-lived truce with the 2d earl of ESSEX. In 1601 Tyrone's Spanish allies landed in the S of Ireland, where they were besieged at Kinsale by the English lord lieutenant, Lord Mountjoy. Tyrone marched south to relieve the siege but was defeated, as were the Spanish later. His Irish allies dispersed, and Tyrone retreated to Ulster. In 1603 he made peace with the English, surrendering his tribal authority. His friend King James I pardoned him, but he never recovered his power in Ireland. In 1607, Tyrone suspected that a summons to London to settle a quarrel was a pretext to obtain his imprisonment, and he fled to Flanders with Rory O'Donnell, earl of TYRCONNEL, and a boatload of other Irish noblemen. The "flight of the earls" marked the end of tribalism in Ireland. Eventually Tyrone lived in Rome, pensioned by Spain and the pope. See Seán O'Faoláin, *The Great O'Neill* (1942).

Tyrone (tĭrōn'), county (1971 pop. 138,975), 1,261 sq mi (3,266 sq km), Northern Ireland, the largest county in Northern Ireland. The county town is OMAGH. There are uplands in the north and center, rising to Mt. Sawel (2,240 ft/683 m) in the Sperrin Mts. In the east and west are lowlands. The main rivers are the Derg, Strule, Ballinderry, and tributaries of the Mourne and the Blackwater. Dairy and beef cattle are raised and barley, potatoes, and oats are grown. Manufactured products include linens, woolens, and other textiles, whiskey, and processed foods. Tourism is significant. The ancestors of the O'Neill family dominated the region after the 5th cent. Tyrone was organized as a shire in the beginning of the 17th cent., after the English defeated the O'Neills in 1603.

tyrosine (tĭ'rəsēn), organic compound, one of the 22 α-AMINO ACIDS commonly found in animal proteins. Only the L-stereoisomer appears in mammalian protein. It is not essential to the human diet, since it can be synthesized in the body from PHENYLALANINE. When the enzyme that catalyzes the transformation of phenylalanine to tyrosine is not active because of a hereditary defect, the serious disease known as PHENYLKETONURIA (PKU) results. Other defects in tyrosine metabolism include the rare hereditary disorder known as alkaptonuria, characterized by discharge of a urine which darkens on standing exposed to air. Tyrosine is a precursor of the adrenal

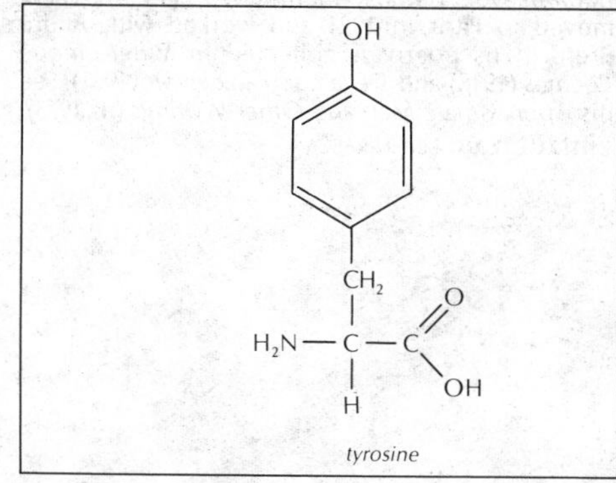

tyrosine

hormones EPINEPHRINE and NOREPINEPHRINE as well as of the thyroid hormones, including THYROXINE. MELANIN, the skin and hair pigment, is also derived from this amino acid. Tyrosine residues in enzymes have frequently been shown to be associated with active sites. Modification of these residues with various chemicals often results in a change in the specificity of the enzyme toward its substrates or even in total destruction of its activity. In 1846 tyrosine was obtained as a product of the degradation of the protein casein (from cheese). It was synthesized in the laboratory in 1883, and its structure was thus determined.

Tyrrell, Joseph Burr (tĭr'əl), 1858-1957, Canadian explorer and geologist, b. Ontario. In 1881 he joined the Canadian Geological Survey as an explorer and in 1883 accompanied G. M. Dawson on his expedition to the Canadian Rockies. He made other explorations in W and N Canada, but his best-known feat was his crossing (1893) of the barren grounds from Lake Athabaska to Chesterfield Inlet; his total journey, largely by canoe, covered some 3,200 mi (5,150 km). See his *Documents Relating to the Early History of Hudson Bay* (1931, repr. 1968). Tyrrell's brother, **James Williams Tyrrell,** 1863-1945, accompanied him on the expedition across the barren grounds and wrote an account of it in *Across the Sub-Arctics of Canada* (1897).

Tyrrhenian Sea (tĭrē'nēən), Ital. *Tirreno*, part of the Mediterranean Sea, c.475 mi (760 km) long and from 60 to 300 mi (97-483 km) wide, between the Ligurian Sea, the Italian peninsula, Sicily, Sardinia, and Corsica. The Strait of Messina connects it with the Ionian Sea. The sea is named for the Tyrrhenoi (an ancient name for the Etruscans). Naples and Palermo are the chief ports.

Tyrtaeus (tərtē'əs), fl. 7th cent. B.C. at Sparta, Greek elegiac poet. Fragments of his martial elegies in Dorian Greek, which were written to spur Spartan soldiers to victory, are extant. An Athenian legend relates that Athens sent Tyrtaeus, a lame schoolmaster, to Sparta when Sparta needed help in war.

Tyrwhitt, Thomas (tĭr'ĭt), 1730-86, English scholar. He was noted for his studies of Shakespeare (1766) and for his edition of Chaucer's *Canterbury Tales* (5 vol., 1775-78). Tyrwhitt revealed in 1777 that the "Rowley Poems" were not actually Middle English poems, but a fabrication by young Thomas Chatterton.

Tyumen (tyōōmĕn'yə), city (1971 pop. 269,000), SW Siberian USSR, on the Tura River. On the Trans-Siberian RR, Tyumen is a major transfer point for river and rail freight. It has shipyards and machine plants. The surrounding area is rich in petroleum and natural gas. Tyumen was founded in 1585 by YERMAK and is the oldest city in Siberia. It was formerly an important center of trade with China. The name is sometimes spelled Tiumen.

Tyutchev, Feodor Ivanovich (fyô'dər ēvä'nəvĭch tyōō'chĭf), 1803-73, Russian lyric poet and essayist. Most of Tyutchev's adult life was spent abroad in the diplomatic service. Although he was encouraged by Nekrasov and Turgenev, his poetry, little of which was published, was not fully appreciated until the rise of symbolism. His philosophical poems express his complex view of nature. He also wrote poignant love lyrics. See translations of his poetry by Charles Tomlinson (1960) and Vladimir Nabokov

(1944, repr. 1969); his letters, ed. by Jesse Zeldin (tr. 1973); biography by R. A. Gregg (1965).

Tzara, Tristan (trĕstäN' tsä'rä), 1896–1963, French writer, b. Rumania. He studied at the Univ. of Zürich, where he and his friends formulated the dadaist movement initially as a pacifist statement (see DADA). His theories are expressed in *Sept manifestes dada* [seven dadaist manifestos] (1924). Tzara moved to Paris in 1921 and worked with André Breton. His poetry is collected in *Vingt-cinque Poèmes* (1918) and *De la coup aux lèvres* (1961). See his *Approximate Man and Other Writings* (tr. 1973).

Tzintzuntzan: see TARASCAN.

Tz'u Hsi, Tsu Hsi, or **Tse Hsi** (all: tso͞o shē), 1834–1908, dowager empress of China (1861–1908) and regent (1861–73, 1874–89, 1898–1908). Her failure to realize the gravity of the foreign threat to China kept her from wholeheartedly supporting modernization, thus driving reformers into opposition to the CH'ING dynasty. She was a consort of Emperor Hsien Feng (d. 1861) and bore his successor, T'ung Chih. On her child's death (1875) she named her infant nephew KUANG HSÜ to the throne, although he was not in the direct line of succession. In 1898 she resumed the regency after he had attempted to institute political reforms against her wishes, and thereafter she ruled directly. She resisted foreign encroachment by encouraging the unsuccessful BOXER UPRISING (1898–1900). In her last years Tz'u Hsi abandoned her conservatism to some extent and consented to several modernizing measures; schools were established, the traditional civil service examinations were discontinued, the army was reorganized by YÜAN SHIH K'AI, railroad building was encouraged, and opium cultivation was suppressed. Her last official act was the appointment of Pu Yi, a remote claimant, as emperor. See biographies by Princess Der Ling (1929), Charlotte Haldane (1965), and Marina Warner (1972).

U

U, 21st letter of the ALPHABET, corresponding to the Greek upsilon [Gr., = u without the aspirate]. Until the late Middle Ages the capital was *V*, the minuscule *u*, no distinction being made between the consonantal and vocalic uses of the letter. The fixing of modern orthography, however, has restricted *u* to the vowel, *v* to the consonant. In phonetics *u* usually represents a high back rounded vowel, rather like *o͝o* in *foot;* English *ū* is a triphthong of *y, o͝o,* and *w* as in *utensil; o͞o* is a diphthong of *o͝o* and *w* as in *glue.* In chemistry U is the symbol of the element URANIUM.

U, honorific meaning "minister," used in Burma. See second part of name (e.g., THANT, U).

Uaxactún: see MAYA.

Ubangi (o͞obăng'gē, yo͞obăng'-), Fr. *Oubangui*, river, c.700 mi (1,130 km) long, formed on the Zaïre-Central African Republic border, central Africa, by the confluence of the Uele and Bomu rivers. It flows west and south, forming part of the boundary between Zaïre and the Central African Republic and Zaïre and the Congo Republic, before emptying into the Congo River, of which it is the chief northern tributary. The river is navigable to Bangui.

Ubangi-Shari: see CENTRAL AFRICAN REPUBLIC.

Ube (o͞o'bā), city (1970 pop. 152,933), Yamaguchi prefecture, SW Honshu, Japan, on the Inland Sea. It has a modern harbor and an important chemical industry. Coal is mined under the sea near Ube.

Ubico, Jorge (hôr'hā o͞obē'kō), 1878-1946, president of Guatemala (1931-44). An army general, Ubico as president established financial stability and political order. He built an extensive network of roads and modernized local administrations to include increased health and school facilities. His methods, however, were arbitrary. He sternly suppressed opposition and twice engineered constitutional changes to extend his term of office. His efficient and honest but tyrannical rule ended when he was driven into exile by a democratic revolution following the revolt in Salvador that deposed Maximiliano HERNÁNDEZ MARTÍNEZ.

Ubundi (o͞obo͞on'dē), formerly **Ponthierville** (pôNtyävēl'), town, Haut-Zaïre region, N central Zaïre. It is connected to Kisangani by a railroad that rounds the Stanley Falls of the Congo River. Palm products are shipped.

Ucal (yo͞o'kăl), name appearing with Ithiel in translations of Prov. 30.1. Modern critics agree with the Vulgate in regarding them as mistranslations of common nouns; see the translations in the margin of RV and in Douay.

Ucayali (o͞okäyä'lē), river, c.1,000 mi (1,610 km) long, formed by the confluence of the APURÍMAC and URUBAMBA rivers, E Peru, and flowing generally north through a mountain and jungle wilderness to the MARAÑÓN River, SW of Iquitos. It is a main headstream of the Amazon River. The Ucayali is navigable for its entire course by small craft. It is an important communications link for Iquitos.

Uccello, Paolo (pä'ōlō o͞ot-chĕl'lō), c.1396-1475, Florentine painter. One of the earliest masters of perspective, Uccello was little appreciated in his own time. Much of his work has been destroyed or is in poor condition. Although first apprenticed to Ghiberti, he shows the later influence of Masaccio. In 1425 he went to Venice and worked on mosaics for St. Mark's. After about five years he returned to Florence and painted *Creation* scenes in the cloister of Santa Maria Novella. In 1436 he was commissioned to paint an equestrian figure of Sir John Hawkwood in monochrome for the cathedral. He also depicted four prophets for the clockface of the cathedral. Uccello's most significant contribution is his cycle of *Noah* for Santa Maria Novella. According to Vasari, he represented the dead, the tempest, the fury of the winds, and the terror of men. Indeed, in the *Deluge* he combined a rigorous system of perspective with details of unsparing realism. Uccello's most famous scenes are from the *Battle of San Romano* (Uffizi; Louvre; and National Gall., London), notable for their rich, decorative panoply, for their solid, wooden toylike figures and for the experiments he made in foreshortening. See his complete work ed. by John Pope-Hennessy (2d ed. 1969).

Uccialli, Treaty of: see MENELIK II.

Udaipur (o͞odī'po͝or', o͞odī'po͝or) or **Mewar** (māwär'), city and former princely state, now part of Rajasthan state, NW India. The Udaipur region, thickly wooded in the south and west, is mostly an alluvial plain watered by many intermittent streams. Grains and cotton are grown. Udaipur was probably founded in the early 8th cent. It was a center of resistance to the Muslim invaders of India, who never completely subjected it. Udaipur accepted British overlordship in 1818. In 1948 it joined Rajasthan.

Udaipur, city (1971 pop. 162,394), capital of the former state, was founded c.1560. It is an agricultural market and a weaving and embroidery center. The city, surrounded by a battlemented wall, is especially noted for its maharaja's palace, which overlooks scenic Pichola Lake.

Udall, Udal (both: yo͞o'dəl), or **Uvedale, John** (yo͞o'dəl, yo͞ov'dăl), 1560?-1592, English clergyman, educated at Cambridge. He adopted Puritan sympathies and aided John PENRY in issuing the anticlerical pamphlets published under the pseudonym Martin Marprelate. Udall was responsible for two tracts (1588) denouncing the episcopacy, *The State of the Church of England* and *A Demonstration of the Truth.* In 1590 he was arrested, charged with the authorship of the pamphlets, and sentenced to death. He was pardoned but died in prison shortly thereafter. His well-known *Key to the Holy Tongue*, a Hebrew grammar and dictionary, was published posthumously in 1593.

Udall, Nicholas, 1505-56, English dramatist, educated at Oxford. He was headmaster of Eton (1534-41) and of Westminster School (from 1554). His one extant play, *Ralph Roister Doister* (c.1545), is regarded as the first complete English comedy. The influence of Plautus and Terence is evident, but the play is distinguished by its elements of native English humor.

Udall, Stewart Lee (yo͞o'dôl), 1920-, U.S. cabinet member, b. St. Johns, Ariz. After serving in World War II, Udall practiced law in Tucson until elected to the U.S. House of Representatives in 1954. As a member of the Committee on Interior and Insular Affairs he gained a reputation as a conservationist and as an advocate of public works. An early supporter of John F. Kennedy for the presidency, he became in Jan., 1961, the first Arizonan to hold a cabinet post. As Secretary of the Interior under both Kennedy and Lyndon B. Johnson, he stressed government dam building to generate increased public power and advocated enlargement of the national park system. See his *National Parks of America* (1966), *The Quiet Crisis* (1963, repr. 1967), and *1976: Agenda for Tomorrow* (1968).

udder: see MAMMARY GLAND.

Uddevalla (ŭ'dəvä"lä), city (1970 pop. 35,459), Göteborg och Bohus co., SW Sweden, a port on the Byfjorden, an arm of the Skagerrak. Manufactures of this industrial center include textiles, clothing, furniture, and machinery. There are shipyards in the city.

Udine (o͞o'dēnā), city (1971 pop. 100,768), capital of Udine prov., Friuli-Venezia Giulia, NE Italy. Manufactures include machinery, textiles, clothing, and chemicals. In the 10th cent. Emperor Otto II gave the city to the patriarchs of Aquileia, who made it their capital (13th cent.). Udine has been the chief city of FRIULI since the 15th cent. It passed to Venice in 1420 and to Austria in 1797 and 1814, and it was annexed by Italy in 1866. In World War I the city was the headquarters of the Italian army (1915-17) and was occupied by Austria (1917-18). In the Piazza della Liberta, the main square, are the Loggia di San Giovanni (16th cent.), with a clock tower; the Gothic town hall (1457); and a fine fountain (16th cent.). Overlooking Udine is a castle (early 16th cent.), which was the seat of the Venetian governors and now houses a museum of painting and numismatics. Nearby is Campo Formio, where a treaty between France and Austria was signed (1797).

Udmurt Autonomous Soviet Socialist Republic (o͞od'mo͞ort, Rus. o͞odmo͞ort'), autonomous republic (1970 pop. 1,417,000), 16,255 sq mi (42,100 sq km), E European USSR, in the forested foothills of the Urals, between the Kama and Vyatka rivers. IZHEVSK (the capital), SARAPUL, and VOTKINSK are the chief cities. The terrain is mostly low and hilly, with wide river valleys. Railroads are the main form of transportation; but the Kama is navigable, and the Cheptsa and Kilmez rivers are used for lumber flotage. Although soil fertility is low, grain (especially rye), flax, hemp, sugar beets, peas, and potatoes are cultivated. The republic's extensive timber, peat, and oil shale resources are only partially exploited because of transportation difficulties. There are also deposits of quartz sand, clays, limestone, coal, and other minerals. The Udmurt ASSR is an important part of the Urals industrial area; its growth was particularly spurred by the evacuation during World War II of many industries from W Russia to the less vulnerable Urals region. Engineering, steel milling, metallurgy, lumbering, machine building, and food and flax processing are important industries. The republic is one of the most heavily populated areas of the Urals. Udmurts (formerly known as Votyaks or Votiaks) make up around 40% of the population; Russians constitute some 55%, and there are Mari and Tatar minorities. The Udmurts, representing the eastern branch of the Finno-Ugrian nationalities, are related to the Mari and the Komi. They are known for their embroidery, weaving, and wood carving. Some Udmurts are Orthodox Christians; others belong to an ancestor-worshiping cult. The predecessors of the Udmurts inhabited the region between the Kama and the Vyatka in Neolithic times. They were controlled by the Bulgar state from the 8th to 13th cent. The S Udmurts were subject to the Kazan khanate from the 13th to the late 15th cent., while the northern territory constituted the Vyatka republic. The Russians gradually brought the Udmurts under their rule in the 16th cent., particularly after Czar Ivan IV's conquest of Kazan in 1552. The area became the Votyak Autonomous Oblast in 1920, the Udmurt Autonomous Oblast in 1932, and an autonomous republic in 1934.

UDP (uridine diphosphate): see URACIL.

Uel (yo͞o'əl), Jew who had a foreign wife. Ezra 10.34.

Uele or **Welle** (both: wĕ'lā), river, c.700 mi (1,130 km) long, rising in NE Zaïre, central Africa, and flowing west to merge with the Bomu River and thus form the Ubangi River at the Zaïre-Central African Republic border. Its course has many rapids.

Ufa (o͞ofä'), city (1970 pop. 771,000), capital of Bashkir Autonomous Republic, E European USSR, at the confluence of the Belaya and Ufa rivers. An industrial center in the Urals, Ufa produces electrical and mining equipment and has oil refineries and a major chemical industry. The Russians took Ufa in 1574 and built a fortress and settlement.

Uffizi (o͞of-fē'tsē), palace in Florence, Italy, built in the 16th cent. by Giorgio Vasari for Cosimo I de' Medici as public offices. It houses the state archives of Tuscany and the **Uffizi Gallery,** one of the richest art collections in the world. Besides the Florentine, all the Italian as well as the Dutch and Flemish schools are well represented, with works by Botticelli, Raphael, Leonardo, Michelangelo, Titian, and Rubens, to name only a few. It houses the world-famous statue of the Venus of the Medici (Greek, 3d cent. B.C.), with other Greek, Roman, and Renaissance sculpture. The Uffizi contains a fine collection of artists' self-portraits.

UFO: see UNIDENTIFIED FLYING OBJECTS.

Uganda (yo͞ogăn'də, o͞ogăn'dä), republic (1972 est. pop. 10,461,500), 91,133 sq mi (236,036 sq km), E central Africa, bordering on Tanzania and Rwanda in the south, on Zaïre in the west, on Sudan in the north, and on Kenya in the east. KAMPALA is Uganda's capital and its largest city; other cities include ENTEBBE, Gulu, JINJA, and Mbale. The country is divided into four administrative regions, which are subdivided into a total of 18 districts. Most of Uganda, which lies astride the equator, is made up of a fertile plateau (average elevation, 4,000 ft/1,220 m), in the center of which is Lake Kyoga. The plateau is bounded on the W by the western branch of the Great Rift Valley, which includes lakes Albert and Edward (in each case about half of the lake is in Uganda) and the Albert Nile River; on the SW by the Ruwenzori Range, which includes Margherita Peak (16,794 ft/5,119 m), Uganda's loftiest point, and by the Virunga mts.; on the S by Victoria Nyanza (Lake Victoria), about half of which is in Uganda; and on the E and N by several mountain ranges. The eastern mountains include Mt. Elgon (14,178 ft/4,321 m), part of which is in Kenya, and Mt. Moroto (10,114 ft/3,083 m). Altogether, about 18% of Uganda is made up of water surface and about 7% comprises highland situated at more than 5,000 ft (1,520 m).

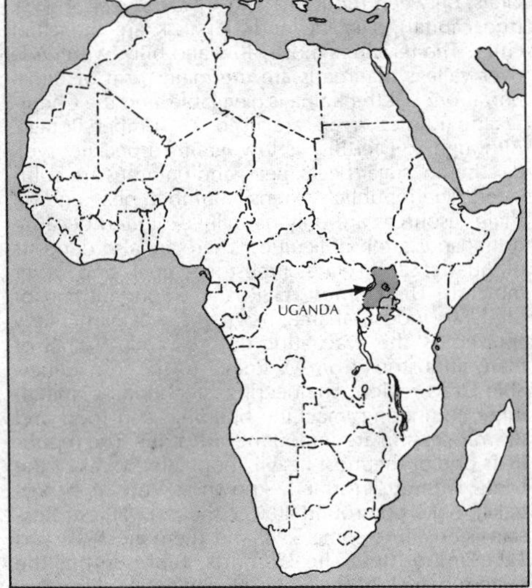

Virtually all of Uganda's inhabitants are black Africans, and about 90% of the people live in rural areas. Approximately 66% of the people speak one of the Bantu languages; the main Bantu ethnic groups, all of which live in the southern half of the country, are the Ganda (who make up about 15% of the country's total population), the Soga, the Ankole, the Nyoro, and the Toro. Other language groups in Uganda are the Nilotic (principally the Acholi, the Lango, and the Alur), whose speakers live in the north and make up about 15% of the population; the Nilo-Hamitic (mainly the Kramojong, the Pokot, the Teso, and the Turkana), whose members live in the northeast and make up about 13% of the population; and the Sudanic (the Lugbara), whose speakers live in the northwest and make up about 5% of the population. English is the country's official language; Swahili is widely spoken in commercial centers. Most of the people follow traditional religious beliefs; in addition, about 30% are Christian and about 5% are Muslim. The economy of Uganda is overwhelmingly agricultural, and farming employs about 90% of the work force. Most of the farms are small in size. The chief food crops are cassava, sweet potatoes, plantains, millet, sorghum, maize, and pulses. The principal cash crops are cotton, coffee, tea, tobacco, sugarcane, and groundnuts. Large numbers of poultry, cattle, goats, and sheep are raised. There is a sizable fishing industry, and much hardwood (especially mahogany) is cut. Copper ore (found in the Ruwenzori Range) is by far the leading mineral produced; other minerals extracted include tin and iron ores, manganese, beryl, chromite, and wolfram. Uganda's few manufactures are limited mainly to processed agricultural goods (especially cured coffee and ginned cotton) and basic consumer items, but they also include textiles, cement, chemical fertilizer and insecticides, and metal goods. There is a large hydroelectric plant at Owen Falls, located on the Victoria Nile River where it leaves Victoria Nyanza. Uganda has two main rail lines; one traverses the southern part of the country, the other connects Tororo on the Kenya border with Gulu in the north. The country is linked by rail with Mombasa, Kenya, on the Indian Ocean. The annual value of Uganda's exports is usually considerably higher than the value of its imports. The principal exports are coffee (which accounts for about 50% of the total value of exports), cotton, copper, and tea. The leading imports are transportation equipment, machinery, manufactured consumer goods, chemicals, and foodstuffs. The main trade partners are Great Britain, the United States, Japan, and West Germany. Uganda is a member of the East African Community.

History. The earliest history of Uganda is not clear, but archaeological remains indicate that the country was the site of Paleolithic and Neolithic civilizations. Around A.D. 1100, Bantu-speaking people migrated into SW Uganda from the west. By the 14th cent. they were organized in several kingdoms (known as the Cwezi states), which had been established by Hima (also called Tutsi) migrants from present-day SW Ethiopia. Around 1500, Nilotic-speaking Lwo people from present-day SE Sudan conquered the Cwezi states and established the Bito dynasties of Buganda (in some Bantu languages, the prefix "Bu" means state; thus, "Buganda" means "state of the Ganda people"), Bunyoro, and Ankole. Later in the 16th cent., other Lwo-speakers conquered N Uganda, forming the Alur and Acholi ethnic groups. The peoples of the north adopted Nilotic languages, but in the south Bantu languages continued to predominate. In the 17th cent. the Lango and Teso migrated into Uganda. During the 16th and 17th cent. Bunyoro was the leading state of S Uganda, controlling an area that stretched into present-day Rwanda and Tanzania. From about 1700, Buganda began to expand (largely at the expense of Bunyoro), and by 1800 it controlled a large territory bordering Victoria Nyanza from the Victoria Nile to the Kagera River. Buganda was centrally organized under the autocratic kabaka (king), who appointed regional administrators and maintained a large bureaucracy and a powerful army. The Ganda raided widely for cattle, ivory, and slaves. In the 1840s Muslim traders from the Indian Ocean coast reached Buganda, and they exchanged firearms, cloth, and beads for the ivory and slaves of Buganda. Beginning in 1869, Bunyoro, ruled by Kabarega and using guns obtained from traders from Khartoum, challenged Buganda's ascendency. By the mid-1880s, however, Buganda again dominated S Uganda. In 1862, John Hanning SPEKE, a British explorer interested in establishing the source of the Nile, became the first European to visit Buganda. He met with Mutesa I, as did Henry M. STANLEY, who reached Buganda in 1875. Mutesa, fearful of attacks from Egypt, agreed to Stanley's proposal to allow Christian missionaries (who Mutesa mistakenly thought would provide military assistance) to enter his realm. Members of the British Protestant Church Missionary Society arrived in 1877, and they were followed in 1879 by representatives of the French Roman Catholic White Fathers; each of the missions gathered a group of converts, which in the 1880s became fiercely mutually antagonistic. At the same time, the number of Ganda converts to Islam was growing. In 1884, Mutesa died and was succeeded as kabaka by Mwanga, who soon began to persecute the Christians out of fear for his own position. In 1885, Bishop James Hannington, an Anglican, was killed as he tried to enter Buganda from the east, and numerous Ganda Christians were murdered in 1886. In 1888, Mwanga was deposed by the Christians and Muslims and replaced by his brother Kiwewa. A month later the Muslims ousted Kiwewa and replaced him with another brother, Kalema. In 1889, Mwanga, assisted by Ganda Christians and by Charles Stokes, a British trader, regained his throne, only to lose it to the Muslims again after a few weeks. In early 1890, Mwanga permanently regained his throne, but at the expense of losing much of his power to Christian chiefs. During the period in 1889 when Mwanga was kabaka, he was visited by Carl Peters, the German colonialist, and signed a treaty of friendship with Germany. Great Britain grew alarmed at the growth of German influence and the potential threat to its own position on the Nile. In 1890, Great Britain and Germany signed a treaty which, in part, gave the British rights to what was to become Uganda. Later that year Frederick LUGARD, acting as an agent of the Imperial British East Africa Company (IBEA), arrived in Buganda at the head of a detachment of troops, and by 1892 he had established the IBEA's authority in S Uganda and had also helped the Protestant faction defeat the Roman Catholic party in Buganda. The British Parliament sent Sir Gerald Portal to investigate the situation, and in 1893 he signed a treaty of protection with Mwanga. In 1894, Great Britain officially made Uganda a protectorate. The British at first ruled Uganda through Buganda, but when Mwanga opposed their growing power, they deposed him, replaced him with his infant son Daudi Chwa, and began to rule more directly. From the late 1890s to 1918, the British established their authority in the rest of Uganda by negotiating treaties and by using force where necessary. In 1900 an agreement was signed with Buganda that gave the kingdom considerable autonomy and also transformed it into a constitutional monarchy controlled largely by Protestant chiefs. In 1901 a railroad from Mombasa on the Indian Ocean reached Kisumu, on Victoria Nyanza, which in turn was connected by boat with Uganda; in 1923 the railroad was extended to Jinja, and in 1931 to Kampala. In 1902 the Eastern prov. of Uganda was transferred to the British East Africa Protectorate (Kenya) for administrative reasons. In 1904 the commercial cultivation of cotton was begun, and cotton soon became the major export crop; coffee and sugar production accelerated in the 1920s. The country attracted few permanent settlers, and the cash crops were mostly produced by African smallholders and not on plantations as in other colonies. Many Asians (Indians, Pakistanis, and Goans) settled in Uganda, where they played a leading role in the country's commerce. During the 1920s and 30s the British considerably reduced Buganda's independence, partly by ignoring the authority of the kabaka, partly by controlling the parliament (lukiko), and partly by curtailing the power of the influential prime minister, Sir Apolo Kagwa. In 1921 a legislative council for the protectorate was established; its first black African member was admitted only in 1945, and it was not until the mid-50s that a substantial number of seats was allocated to the Africans. In 1953, Mutesa II was deported for not cooperating with the British; he was allowed to return in 1955, but the rift between Buganda and the rest of Uganda remained. In subsequent years, as Great Britain prepared Uganda for independence, Buganda intermittently demanded to be set up as a separate state. In 1961 there were three main political parties in Uganda—the Uganda People's Congress (UPC), whose members were mostly non-Ganda; the Democratic party, made up chiefly of Roman Catholic Ganda; and the Kabaka Yekka [Kabaka only] party, comprising only Ganda. On Oct. 9, 1962, Uganda became independent, with A. Milton Obote, a Lango leader of the UPC, as prime minister. Buganda was given considerable autonomy. In 1963, Uganda became a republic, and Mutesa was elected president. The first years of independence were dominated by a struggle between the central government and Buganda. In 1966, Obote introduced a new constitution that ended Buganda's autonomy. The Ganda protested vigorously and seemed on the verge of taking up arms when Obote captured the kabaka's palace at Mengo, forced the kabaka to flee the country, and ended effective Ganda resistance. In 1967 a new constitution was introduced giving the central government—especially the president—much power and dividing Buganda into four districts. In 1969, Obote decided to follow a leftist course in the hope of bridging the country's ethnic and regional differences through a common social policy. However, in Jan., 1971, Obote, at the time outside the country, was deposed in a coup d'etat by Maj. Gen. Idi Amin. Amin was faced with opposition within the army by officers and troops loyal to Obote, but by the end of 1971 he was in firm control of the army and the country. Amin cultivated good relations with the Ganda. In 1972-73 he initiated severe diplomatic wrangles with the United States and Israel, both of which had provided Uganda with military and economic aid and were now accused of trying to undermine the government. In Aug., 1972, Amin ordered Asians who were not citizens of Uganda to leave the country, and within three months all 60,000 had left, most of them for Great Britain. From 1971 to 1973, there were border clashes with Tanzania, partly instigated by exiled Ugandans loyal to Obote, but, in early 1973, Amin and Julius Nyerere, president of Tanzania, reached an agreement that appeared to head off future incidents. See D. A. Low and R. C. Pratt, *Buganda and British Overrule* (1960); Roland Oliver and Gervase Mathew, ed., *History of East Africa,* Vol. I (1963); L. A. Fallers, *The King's Men* (1964); V. T. Harlow and E. M. Chilver, ed., *History of East Africa,* Vol. II (1965); F. B. Welbourn, *Religion and Politics in Uganda, 1952-1962* (1965); D. E. Apter, *The Political Kingdom in Uganda* (2d ed. 1967); P. M. Gukiina, *Uganda: A Case Study in African Political Development* (1972); G. S. Ibingira, *The Forging of an African Nation* (1973).

Ugarit (o͞ogərēt'), ancient city, capital of the Ugarit kingdom, W Syria. Although the name of this city was known from Egyptian and Hittite sources, its location and history were a mystery until the accidental discovery (1928) of an ancient tomb at the small Arab village of Ras Shamrah, near modern Latakia. This led to excavations (begun in 1929 and still continuing) that have established the identity of the mound as the site of ancient Ugarit. The site has been particularly rich in finds, which have yielded much valuable historical information and from which a partial account of the city may be constructed. Ugarit was probably occupied from the first appearance of man in Syria. The lowest level of the mound dates from the Neolithic period, the 5th millennium B.C. It developed as a great center of commerce, having important connections with Mesopotamia. By the 4th millennium Ugarit had reached a high stage of development and was part of the general civilization of ancient Syria. Between 3000 and 2000 B.C., important ethnic changes took place at Ugarit, brought about by the northward migrations of Amorites and Semitic Canaanites. Early in the 2d millennium, because of invasions from the north and east, Ugarit turned to an alliance with Egypt, and from this period Egyptian influence was strong in the city. The city was also the most important center of Minoan trade in Syria. The 15th and 14th cent. B.C. were the period of highest prosperity for Ugarit. Trade developed tremendously, and the city expanded in size. The rich and abundant art of this period shows that an important Mycenaean colony existed in the city. Foreign invasions and economic change in the 12th cent. B.C. caused Ugarit to decline. By the end of the century, although it was not completely abandoned, it had ceased to exist as an important town. Among the more important discoveries at Ugarit are tablets from the 14th cent. B.C. Written in a cuneiform script, in a hitherto unknown language, Ugaritic, they record the poetic works and myths of the ancient Canaanites. They are written in an alphabet that is one of the earliest known. Ugaritic has been identified as a Semitic language, related to classical Hebrew, the language of the Old Testament, and these tablets, the first authentic specimens of pagan Canaanite literature, have been of great importance to students of language and of the Bible. They offer evidence that the stories of the Old Testament were based on written Canaanite documents as well as being passed down orally. See C. F. A. Schaeffer, *The Cuneiform Texts of Ras Shamra-Ugarit* (1939); Julian Obermann, *Ugaritic Mythology* (1948); C. H. Gordon, *Ugaritic Literature* (1949); D. A. Rolles, *Canaanite Myths and Legends* (1956); C. H. Gordon, *Ugaritic Textbook* (1965) and *Ugarit and Minoan Crete* (1966).

Uglich (o͞o'glyĭch), city, N central European USSR, on the Volga River. It is a river port and rail terminus and has textile and paper mills, food-processing plants, sawmills, and a large hydroelectric station. Founded in 1148, Uglich became the center of an independent principality in 1218. It joined the grand duchy of Moscow in the first half of the 14th cent. Czarevich Dmitri was allegedly murdered (1591) in the city's 15th-century fortress, which has been preserved.

Ugolino della Gherardesca (o͞ogōlē'nō dĕl'lä gärärdä'skä), d. 1289, Italian nobleman. A leader of the Guelph, or pro-papal, faction in predominantly Ghibelline (pro-imperial) Pisa, he was made podesta [chief magistrate] of Pisa in 1284 to negotiate a peace with Pisa's Guelph enemies. His attempts to consolidate his power in Pisa, which was anti-Guelph, failed, and he fell victim to a conspiracy. Ugolino was arrested for treason and shut in a tower to starve to death with his sons and grandsons. Dante relates the episode in the *Inferno.*

Ugrian (yo͞o'grēən, o͞o'-) or **Ugric** (yo͞o'grĭk, o͞o'-), subgroup of the Finno-Ugric group of languages, which is, in turn, a subdivision of the Uralic subfamily of the Ural-Altaic family of languages. See FINNO-UGRIC LANGUAGES; URALIC AND ALTAIC LANGUAGES.

Uhland, Ludwig (lo͝ot'vĭkh o͞o'länt), 1787–1862, German poet, leader of the Swabian group. He studied and practiced law at Tübingen, held various official posts, and taught German literature. His lyrics and ballads, almost all written in his youth, made him one of the most popular German poets of the romantic period. Noted for their lucid, polished style, they include "The Minstrel's Curse," "The Good Comrade," and "Taillefer." His other works include *Gedichte* [poems] (1815), *Vaterländische Gedichte* [songs of the fatherland] (1816), and the unsuccessful drama *Ludwig der Bayer* (1819), which, however, contains some of his best verse.

Uigurs or **Uighurs** (both: wē'go͝orz), Turkic-speaking people of Asia who live mainly in W China. They were the Yue-che of ancient Chinese records and first rose to prominence in the 7th cent. when they supported the T'ang Chinese in central Asia. In 744 the Uigurs seized control of Mongolia and established their capital on the ORKHON River, near the site of later KARAKORUM. Ousted (840) from Mongolia by the Kirghiz, they moved to TU-LU-FAN, in Sinkiang prov., China, where they founded an empire that lasted until the Mongol onslaught of the 13th cent. Unlike other peoples of central Asia, the Uigurs were not exclusively nomadic but practiced some agriculture and trade. They were converted to Manichaeism, but later became Sunni Muslims. The Uigurs transmitted their script to the Mongols. Today most of the population of Sinkiang prov. (reorganized as the Uigur Autonomous Region in 1955) is of Uigur descent; there they number about 4 million. See Colin Mackerras, ed., *The Uighur Empire* (1968, repr. 1973).

Uijongbu (o͞o'ē'jŭng'bo͞o'), city (1966 pop. 74,800), NW South Korea. It is an agricultural center.

Uinta Mountains (yo͞oĭn'tə), range of the Rocky Mts. extending c.120 mi (190 km) E from NE Utah to SW Wyoming. It rises to Kings Peak (13,528 ft/4,123 m), the highest point in Utah. The Uinta Mts., the largest east-west range in the United States, are almost totally part of national forests. Phosphates are mined there.

Uist, North (yo͞o'ĭst, o͞o'-), and **South Uist,** islands, two of the Outer Hebrides, Inverness-shire, NW Scotland. North Uist (1971 pop. 1,732), is 18 mi (29 km) long and 13 mi (21 km) wide, with a much indented coast (Lochs Maddy, Eport, and others). The east is hilly and boggy, but the west has some fertile land. Lochmaddy is the chief town. Most of the inhabitants are crofters. South Uist (1971 pop. 3,781) is c.22 mi (35 km) long and 7 mi (11 km) wide, with Lochs Boisdale, Eynort, and Skiport indenting the east coast. A testing range for rockets was erected there in 1954. Lochboisdale is the leading town, and the village of Milton was the birthplace of the Jacobite heroine Flora Macdonald.

Uitenhage (yo͞o'tənhāg", oi'tənhä"gə), town (1970 pop. 69,048), Cape Prov., S South Africa, on the Zwartkops River. It is an industrial center, with large railroad workshops, wool washeries, textile mills, and motor vehicle assembly plants. The town also serves as the commercial center for the surrounding agricultural region. Uitenhage was founded in 1804 and named after Jacob A. Uitenhage de Mist, commissioner-general of the Dutch-held Cape Colony. There is a technical college in the town.

Uitlander: see SOUTH AFRICAN WAR.

Uji (o͞o'jē), town (1970 pop. 103,497), Kyoto prefecture, S Honshu, Japan. It is a resort and is noted for its tea and for cormorant fishing. Uji is best known for its 11th-century monastery, Byodo-in, with its beautiful pavilion, Phoenix Hall.

Ujiji: see KIGOMA-UJIJI, Tanzania.

Uji-yamada: see ISE, Japan.

Ujjain (o͞ojīn', o͞o'jīn), city (1971 pop. 209,118), Madhya Pradesh state, central India, on the Sipra River. Many pilgrims visit Ujjain, which Hindus consider one of the holiest places in India. The town is comparatively new, but nearby is a ruined ancient city, which may have been inhabited in the late 2d millennium B.C. This city has been identified as the capital of the semilegendary kingdom of Avanti, which was described in Buddhist chronicles as one of the greatest Indian states. Later it was the central city of the Malwa kingdoms, and in the 8th cent. A.D. it became the center of Sanskrit learning. Muslims captured the city in 1235 and destroyed most of the Hindu temples. Akbar conquered it in 1562, and not until it became (c.1750) part of Gwalior was Ujjain restored to Hindu control. Today Ujjain is a district administrative headquarters and the seat of Vikram Univ.

Újpest: see BUDAPEST, Hungary.

Ukerewe: see VICTORIA NYANZA, lake, Africa.

Ukiah (yo͞okī'ə), city (1970 pop. 10,095), seat of Mendocino co., W Calif., in a lumber and fruit-growing region; inc. 1876. Masonite is manufactured. An international latitude observatory and a state hospital are there.

Ukraine (ū'krān, ūkrān') or **Ukrainian Soviet Socialist Republic,** Ukr. *Ukraina,* constituent republic (1970 pop. 47,136,000), 232,046 sq mi (601,000 sq km), SW European USSR. KIEV is the capital. The Ukraine borders on Poland in the northwest; on Czechoslovakia, Hungary, Rumania, and the Moldavian SSR in the southwest; on the Black Sea and the Sea of Azov in the south; on the Russian Soviet Federated Socialist Republic (RSFSR) in the east and northeast; and on the Belorussian SSR in the north. In terms of population, economic value, and historic importance, the Ukraine ranks second after the RSFSR among the Soviet Union's 15 constituent republics. Drained by the Dnepr, the Dnestr, the Southern Bug, and the Donets rivers, the Ukraine consists largely of fertile steppes, extending from the Carpathians and the Volhynian-Podolian uplands in the west to the Donets Ridge in the southeast. The Dnepr divides the republic into right-bank and left-bank Ukraine. In the north and northwest parts of Ukraine is the wooded area of the Pripyat Marshes, with gray podsol soil and numerous swamps; wooded steppes extend across the central Ukraine, and a fertile, treeless, black-earth *(chernozem)* steppe covers the south. The continental climate of the republic is greatly modified by proximity to the Black Sea. The Ukraine supplies approximately 25% of the USSR'S foodstuffs. The steppe is one of the chief wheat-producing regions of Europe. Other major crops include corn, rye, barley, potatoes, sugar beets, melons, sunflowers, and flax. The Ukraine possesses numerous raw materials and power resources, and its central and eastern regions form one of the world's densest industrial concentrations. About 30% of the Soviet Union's heavy industrial output comes from the Ukraine. The heavy metallurgical, machine-building, and chemical industries are based on the iron mines of KRIVOY ROG, the manganese ores of NIKOPOL, and the coking coal and anthracite of the DONETS BASIN. The DNEPROGES dam powers one of the world's greatest hydroelectric stations and has made the Dnepr navigable for nearly its entire length. The region also produces aluminum, zinc, mercury titanium, nickel, oil, natural gas, and bauxite. The iron and steel industries of the Communist countries of Eastern Europe depend on Ukrainian coal, ore, and other raw materials. The Ukraine's main industrial centers are KHARKOV, DNEPROPETROVSK, DONETSK, ZAPOROZHYE, MAKEYEVKA, ZHDANOV, and VOROSHILOVGRAD. ODESSA is the principal Ukrainian port on the Black Sea. The Western Ukraine, although mainly agricultural, has large petroleum centers at DROGOBYCH and Borislav, natural gas at Dashava, coal industries at Novovolynsk, and rich salt deposits. LVOV is a major industrial city. ZHITOMIR and VINNITSA are the main agricultural centers. The republic's leading industrial products include machinery, cast iron, steel, rolled metals, tractors, cement and other building materials, mineral fertilizers, glass, paper, plywood, pottery, china, furniture, textiles, clothing, and leather footwear. Food processing, notably the refining of sugar, is also a major industry. About 20% of the USSR's people live in the Ukraine. Ukrainians make up more than three fourths of the population; Russians constitute around 17%, Jews around 2%, and there are Polish, Belorussian, Moldavian, and Hungarian minorities. More than half the population is urban. The majority of those belonging to a religious faith are Russian Orthodox. The West Ukrainian Catholic Church, which in 1596 established unity with the Roman Church, was forced by the Soviet government to sever its ties with Rome in 1946 and to join with the Russian Orthodox Church. The republic's many educational and cultural institutions include seven universities. In ancient times a major part of the present-day Ukraine was inhabited by the Scythians (see SCYTHIA), who were later displaced by the Sarmatians (see SARMATIA). Early in the Christian era, a series of invaders (Goths, Huns, Avars) overran the Ukrainian steppes, and in the 7th cent. the KHAZARS included much of the Ukraine in their empire. The Ukrainians themselves can be traced to Neolithic agricultural tribes in the Dnepr and Dnestr valleys. The Antes tribal federation (4th–7th cent.) represented the first definitely Slavic community in the area. In the 9th cent., a Varangian dynasty from Scandinavia established itself at Kiev. Having freed the Slavs from Khazar domination, the Varangians united them in powerful Kievan Russia. Thus, the Ukrainians, Russians, and Belorussians originated from a single nationality that formed the backbone of Kievan Russia. Following YAROSLAV'S reign (1019–54), which marked the zenith of Kiev's power, Kievan Russia split into principalities, including the western duchies of Galich (see GALICIA) and Vladimir (see VLADIMIR-VOLYNSKI and VOLHYNIA). These and the rest of the western region, which included PODOLIA, had separate histories after the conquest of Kievan Russia (13th cent.) by the Mongols of the GOLDEN HORDE. In the mid-14th cent. Lithuania began to expand eastward and southward, liberating the Ukraine from the Tatars. The dynastic union between Poland and Lithuania in 1386 also opened the Ukraine to Polish expansion. The Ukraine had flourished under Lithuanian rule, and its language became that of the state; but after the organic union of Poland and Lithuania in 1569, the

Ukraine came under Polish rule, enserfment of the Ukrainian peasants proceeded apace, and the Ukrainian Orthodox Church suffered persecution. In 1596 the Ukrainian Orthodox bishops, confronted with the power of Polish Catholicism, established the Uniate, or Greek Catholic, faith, which recognized papal authority but retained the Orthodox rite. Meanwhile, the Black Sea shore, ruled by the khans of CRIMEA, was absorbed into the Ottoman Empire in 1478. The term *Ukraine*, which may be translated as "at the border" or "borderland," came into general usage in the 16th cent. At that time, Poland-Lithuania and the rising principality of Moscow, or Muscovy, were vying for control of this vast area south of their borders. The harsh conditions of Polish rule led many Ukrainians to flee serfdom and religious persecution by escaping beyond the area of the lower Dnepr rapids. There they established a military order called the Zaporozhye Sich ("clearing beyond the rapids."). These fugitives became known as Cossacks or Kozaks, an adaptation of the Turkic work *kazakh*, meaning "outlaw" or "adventurer." In 1648 the Cossacks, led by Hetman Bohdan CHMIELNICKI, successfully waged a revolution against Polish domination. The Ukraine, however, was too weak to stand alone, and in 1654 Chmielnicki recognized the suzerainty of Moscow in the Treaty of Pereyaslavl. By the terms of the treaty, the Ukraine was to be largely independent; but Russia soon began to encroach upon its rights (the czars contemptuously referred to the Ukrainians as "Little Russians," as contrasted with the "Great Russians" of the Muscovite realm). Through a treaty with Poland in 1658, the Ukraine attempted to throw off Russian protection. The ensuing Russo-Polish war ended in 1667 with the Treaty of Andrusov, which partitioned Ukraine. Russia obtained left-bank Ukraine, east of the Dnepr River and including Kiev; Poland retained right-bank Ukraine. Hetman Ivan MAZEPA, presiding over a diminished Cossack state, sought once again to free the Ukraine from Russian domination; he thus joined Sweden against Russia in the Northern War, but their defeat at Poltava by Czar Peter I in 1709 sealed the fate of the Ukraine. Mazepa's fall crushed the last hopes for Ukrainian independence and further curtailed Ukrainian autonomy. Finally, the last of Ukraine's hetmans was forced by Empress Catherine II to resign in 1764; the Zaporozhye Sich was razed by Russian troops in 1775, and the Ukraine, its political autonomy terminated, was divided into three provinces. In 1783, Russia annexed the khanate of Crimea. The Polish partition treaties of 1772, 1793, and 1795 (see POLAND, PARTITIONS OF) awarded Podolia and Volhynia to Russia, thus reuniting left-bank and right-bank Ukraine; E Galicia went to Austria. Colonization of the steppes proceeded apace in the 19th cent., and in the 1870s the great Ukrainian coal and metallurgical industrial region was established. Despite a Russian ban on use of the Ukrainian language in the schools and in publications, a movement for Ukrainian national and cultural revival blossomed in the late 19th cent. There was also renewed agitation for Ukrainian independence and for the union of all Ukrainian lands, including those of Austria-Hungary-Galicia, Bukovina, and Ruthenia (see ZAKARPATSKAYA OBLAST) under a single state. The Galician Ukrainians, who emerged as a political nationality during the 1848 Austrian revolution, made Galicia a haven abroad for the nationalist movement in Russian Ukraine. This movement was spearheaded by secret educational groups called *hromadas*, that were repeatedly suppressed by the czar. Following the overthrow of the czarist regime in 1917, a Ukrainian central council was set up with Mikhails HRUSHEVSKY as president; in June, 1917, it formed a government with Vladimir VINNICHENKO as premier and Simon Petlura as war minister. Originally declaring itself a republic within the framework of a federated Russia, Ukraine proclaimed complete independence in Jan., 1918, after the Bolshevik Revolution. Soviet troops were sent into the Ukraine; but the Central Powers, having acknowledged Ukrainian independence, then overran the territory with their own soldiers and forced the Red Army, through the Treaty of Brest-Litovsk (March, 1918) to withdraw. The World War I armistice of Nov., 1918, in turn forced the withdrawal from the Ukraine of the Central Powers. Meanwhile, with the disintegration of Austria-Hungary, an independent republic in W Ukraine had been proclaimed in Lvov. In Jan., 1919, the union of the two Ukraines was proclaimed; however, Soviet troops immediately occupied Kiev. A four-cornered struggle ensued among Ukrainian forces, the counterrevolutionary army of DENIKIN, the Red Army, and the Poles. Soviet troops eventually regained control of the Ukraine, which in 1922 became one of the original constituent republics of the USSR. Lenin's attempts to assuage Ukrainian nationalism through a measure of cultural autonomy were abandoned by Stalin, who also imposed agricultural collectivization on Ukraine and requisitioned all grain for export. Millions of Ukrainians died in the resulting famine. Mykola Shrypnyk and other Ukrainian Communist leaders who opposed Stalinist measures were purged and executed. During World War II, many Ukrainians at first viewed the Germans as liberators and collaborated with them against the USSR. However, the Nazis' scorn for all Slavs and their harsh occupation (1941–44) of the Ukraine turned many Ukrainians into anti-German guerrilla fighters. The republic suffered severe wartime devastation. Several major territorial changes occurred in the Ukraine during this period. South Bessarabia, recovered from Rumania in 1940, was incorporated into the Ukraine, while the former Moldavian ASSR was detached from the republic and merged with central Bessarabia as the Moldavian SSR. The northern parts of Bukovina and Bessarabia were added to the Ukraine, as was E Galicia, including Lvov, formally ceded by Poland in 1945. Zakarpatskaya Oblast, which had been part of Czechoslovakia since 1919, was also ceded in 1945, thus completing the process by which all Ukrainian lands were united into a single republic. Crimea was annexed to the Ukraine in 1954. Although russification has intensified in the Ukraine (as in other Soviet republics) since the war, Ukrainian nationalism has remained strong, and a small dissident movement has actively pressed for greater cultural and political freedom. During the 1960s, Ukrainians emerged as tacit junior partners of the Russians in governing the Soviet Union. Leonid Brezhnev, General Secretary of the Soviet Communist Party, was born in the Ukraine and held important party posts there before being called to Moscow. Former Soviet ruler Nikita Khrushchev, although a Russian by birth, served as First Secretary of the Ukrainian Communist party during the 1930s and carried out the Stalinist purges in Ukraine. The Ukraine, along with the USSR and Belorussia, is a member of the United Nations.

Ukrainian language, also called Little Russian: see RUSSIAN LANGUAGE; SLAVIC LANGUAGES.

Ukrainian literature. Kievan CHURCH SLAVONIC texts of the 11th cent. and W Ukrainian texts of the 13th cent. show Ukrainian characteristics in their language. Ukrainian linguistic features predominate in the Galician-Volhynian chronicle of the 13th cent. and in much of the writing of the 14th–16th cent. The great body of Ukrainian oral literature attained its zenith in the 16th cent. with the Cossack epic songs, the *dumy*. The first books printed in Ukrainian were translations of the Gospels (16th cent.). Early books were usually religious, but a grammar appeared in 1596 and a dictionary in 1627. Ukrainian cultural life of the 17th cent. centered around the Kievan academy, established in 1633. The outstanding poet and philosopher of the 18th cent. was Gregory Skovoroda (1722–94). A leading figure in the Ukrainian literary revival of the early 19th cent. was Ivan Kotliarevsky (1769–1838), whose travesty of the *Aeneid* and operetta *Natalka Poltavka* are major works of Ukrainian classical literature. Classicism predominates also in the writings of the novelist Gregory Kvitka (1778–1843) and in the plays of Vasil Gogol (d. 1825). Interest in folklore and ethnography is represented in the works of Levko Borovykovsky (1806–89) and Ambros Metlynsky (1814–70), poets of the Kharkov romantic school. With the founding in the 1830s of a university in Kiev, the capital became once again the cultural center of the Ukraine. The leading scholar of the period was the historian Mikola Kostomarov (1817–85). The poet Taras SHEVCHENKO was the great figure of Ukrainian romanticism, which predominates also in the dramatic works of Michael Staritsky (1840–1904), Marko Kropivnitsky (1840–1910), and Ivan Tobilevich (1845–1907). Realism in Ukrainian prose found expression in the works of Boris Hrinchenko (1863–1910) and Ivan Nechuy-Levitsky (1838–1918) and in the naturalistic tales of Marko Vovchok (pseud. of Maria Markovich, 1834–1907). Modern Ukrainian literature is represented by the outstanding writer Ivan FRANKO and the poet Lesia UKRAINKA. Masters of impressionist prose were Michael Kotsiubynsky (1864–1913) and Vasil Stefanyk (1871–1936). The novelist Olha Kobylanska (1868–1942) and the novelist and political writer Vladimir VINNICHENKO were among the major literary figures of the early 20th cent. Many Ukrainian writers were killed or deported by the Soviet regime during the 1930s, among them the dramatist Mikola Kulish (1892–1934), the humorist Ostap Vyshnia, and the theorist of neoclassicism Mikola Zerov. One of the leading writers of the proletarian age, Mikola Khvylovy (1893–1933), proposed the reorientation of Ukrainian literature toward the West. Important writers who survived the purges of the 1930s include the master of subjective verse Maxim Rylsky, the neo-romantic poet Mikola Bazhan, the lyric poet Pavlo Tychyna, the dramatist Aleksandr Korneichuk, and the novelists Oles Honchar and Michael Stelmakh. See C. A. Manning, *Ukrainian Literature* (1944); George Luckyj, *Literary Politics in the Soviet Ukraine, 1917–1934* (1956) and *Between Gogol and Sevcenko* (1971).

Ukrainka, Lesia (lās'yə o͝okrĭn'kə), 1871–1913, Ukrainian poet and dramatist, whose original name was Larisa Kvitka-Kosach. Ukrainka spent most of her life abroad fighting to recuperate from tuberculosis. Her early collections of lyric poetry, *On the Wings of Song* (1892), *Thoughts and Dreams* (1899), and *Responses* (1902), reflect the liberal and revolutionary ideals of Heinrich Heine and Taras Shevchenko. Her principal plays, using themes from Western and classicial literature, include *Cassandra* (1908) and *In the Desert* (1909). *The Forest Song* (1912) is her dramatic poem based on Slavic mythology.

ukulele (yo͞okəlā'lē), Hawaiian musical instrument developed from the Portuguese guitar. It has a fretted fingerboard and four strings that are plucked or strummed. Patented in 1917, the ukulele became popular in the United States in the 1920s. It is also spelled ukelele. See FRETTED INSTRUMENT.

Ukulele

Uladislaus I, king of Hungary: see LADISLAUS III, king of Poland.

Uladislaus II (o͞o"lä'dĭslous), Hung. *Ulászló II,* c.1456–1516, king of Hungary (1490–1516) and, as Ladislaus II, king of Bohemia (1471–1516); son of CASIMIR IV of Poland. Designated by George of Podebrad as his successor, he was elected to the Bohemian throne. Matthias Corvinus, king of Hungary, invaded his territories and in 1478 acquired Moravia, Silesia, and Lusatia from him. In Bohemia, Uladislaus openly favored the Roman Church against the HUSSITES. His weak rule enabled the nobles to pass laws in the diets of 1487 and 1497 that made the peasants virtual serfs. On the death of Matthias Corvinus (1490), the Hungarian magnates elected Uladislaus king in preference to Maximilian of Hapsburg (later Holy Roman Emperor MAXIMILIAN I). In Hungary, the nobles also exploited the king's weakness, abolishing the reforms of Matthias Corvinus and worsening the lot of the peasants. When Cardinal BAKOCZ issued the call for a crusade against the Turks, the peasants revolted and were cruelly repressed by John Zapolya (later JOHN I). In 1515, Uladislaus concluded with Maximilian I a treaty that eventually brought Hungary and Bohemia under Hapsburg rule—his daughter Anna was promised to Archduke Ferdinand (later Holy Roman Emperor FERDINAND I); his son and successor, LOUIS II, was to marry Ferdinand's sister, Mary; if Louis died childless (as he did), Hungary and Bohemia were to pass to the Hapsburgs.

Ulai (yo͞o'lā), biblical river, probably the Karun River in Iran. Dan. 8.2,16.

Ulala: see GORNO-ALTAI AUTONOMOUS OBLAST, USSR.

Ulam (yo͞o'lăm). **1** Manassite. 1 Chron. 7.16,17. **2** Family of archers. 1 Chron. 8.39,40.

Ulan Bator (o͞olän' bä'tôr) [Mongolian,=red hero], Chinese *Kulun,* city (1971 est. pop. 282,000), capital of the Mongolian People's Republic, E central Outer Mongolia, on the Tola River. It is situated at the foot of the Bogdo Ula (Po-ko-to), which rises 3,000 ft (914 m) above the city. It is the political, cultural, economic, and transportation center of the country. Manufactures include woolen textiles and related goods, leather and footwear, soap, paper, iron castings, matches, glassware, beer and spirits, and processed foods. Coal mined nearby provides power. Ulan Bator is the junction point of the country's major roads and caravan routes and lies on the Trans-Siberian RR, which links (since 1955) the USSR with Peking. The city has the only university (founded 1942) in the country and a library with ancient Mongolian, Chinese, and Tibetan manuscripts. In the center of the city is the Sukhe Bator Square (with an equestrian statue of the Mongolian revolutionary leader for whom the city is named). Founded in 1649 as a monastery town, Ulan Bator still preserves the monastery section, the former center of the city, and the residence of the Living Buddha, once Mongolia's spiritual leader. In the 1860s the town prospered as a commercial center on the tea route between Russia and China. There in 1911 autonomous Mongolia was first proclaimed. During the Russian civil war the city was (1921) the headquarters of the White army of Baron von Ungern-Sternberg. It was made capital of the Mongolian republic in 1924, when its name was changed from Urga [palace] to Ulan Bator. The city was developed with aid from the Soviet government, and the first industrial combine was established there in 1934.

Ulanova, Galina (gälyē'nə o͞olä'nōvə), 1910–, Russian ballerina. Of a family of ballet dancers, Ulanova made her formal debut in 1928. After 1944 she was prima ballerina of the Bolshoi Theatre, Moscow, with which she first appeared in 1935, and she received numerous awards from the Soviet government. Noted for her lyric grace and beauty and her superb acting, she excelled especially in *Swan Lake* and *Giselle* and in Lavrovski's version of Prokofiev's *Romeo and Juliet* (1940), in which she created the role of Juliet. First appearing abroad in 1951, she has been lauded as one of the greatest ballerinas since Pavlova. After her official retirement in 1962 she continued to teach at the Bolshoi. See A. E. Kahn, *Days with Ulanova* (1962).

Ulan-Ude (o͞olän"-o͞odĕ'), city (1970 pop. 254,000), capital of the Buryat Autonomous Soviet Socialist Republic, SE Siberian USSR, on the Selenga River near its confluence with the Uda. A major transportation hub, it is a river port, a junction on the Trans-Siberian RR, and the starting point of a railway to Peking. Industries include railroad maintenance, boatbuilding, ship repairing, sawmilling, food and wool processing, meat canning, and the manufacture of machinery and locomotives. Founded in 1649 as a Cossack winter encampment, Ulan-Ude became a fortress in 1689 and a city in 1775. It developed as an important trade center of Transbaykalia, along the tea route to China. The city became the capital of the Far Eastern republic in 1920 and of the Buryat-Mongol Autonomous SSR in 1923. Formerly called Udinsk and Verkhneudinsk, it was named Ulan-Ude in 1934.

Ulbricht, Walter (väl'tər o͞ol'brĭkht), 1893–1973, Communist leader in the German Democratic Republic. A founder of the German Communist party, he fled Germany in 1933 and went to Moscow, where he was a member of the politburo of the exiled German Communist party. Ulbricht entered Germany with the Russian troops in 1945. In 1949 he became deputy premier of the German Democratic Republic and in 1950 was named secretary general of the Socialist Unity party, successor to the Communist party. Leader of East Germany from that time, he became chairman of the council of state in 1960. A hard-line Communist who was opposed to normalizing relations with West Germany, Ulbricht was responsible for the building (1961) of the Berlin Wall. He strongly supported close ties with the USSR and sent troops to join the Soviet invasion of Czechoslovakia in 1968. In 1971 he was replaced as secretary general by Erich Honecker. See biography by Carola Stern (tr. 1965).

ulcer, open sore or circumscribed erosion, usually slow to heal, on the skin or mucous membranes. It may develop as a result of injury; because of a circulatory disturbance, e.g., in varicose veins or after prolonged bed rest; or in association with such diseases as tuberculosis, syphilis, or leprosy. Corneal ulcers, which result from infection, allergy, or foreign objects in the eye, can cause visual impairment if not treated promptly. Some ulcers may develop into cancer. The underlying cause must be treated as well as the ulcerous lesion. Peptic ulcer occurs in the mucous membrane of the intestinal tract in areas accessible to the hydrochloric acid secreted by the stomach. Most commonly, it occurs in the stomach (gastric ulcer) or at the beginning of the small intestine (duodenal ulcer) and causes abdominal pain, especially between meals. Peptic ulcer is found more frequently in men, and the duodenum is its most common site. It is estimated that about 10% of the U.S. population suffer from duodenal ulcer. The exact cause of peptic ulcer is not known, but increased acid secretion, tissue vulnerability to acid secretion, and emotional disturbance are all believed to play a part. Usual treatment of peptic ulcer includes some alteration in diet, although the value of the smooth, bland foods commonly prescribed in the past is now in question. In addition, antacids, gels, and anticholinergic drugs are recommended to relieve symptoms; physicians usually resort to surgery in severe cases. Hemorrhage or perforation of peptic ulcers requires emergency medical treatment.

Uleåborg, Finland: see OULU.

Ulfilas (ŭl'fĭləs) or **Wulfila** (wo͝ol'fĭlə) [Gothic,=little wolf], c.311–383, Gothic bishop, translator of the Bible into Gothic. He was converted to Christianity at Constantinople and was consecrated bishop (341) by the Arian bishop Eusebius of Nicomedia. Ulfilas then returned to the Visigoths as a missionary; it was partly as a result of Ulfilas's work that the Goths became and remained Arians for so long in the face of triumphant Catholicism. Of Ulfilas's Bible only fragments remain—parts of Genesis, Nehemiah, most of the Gospels, and the whole of 2 Corinthians, with several more fragments. Ulfilas is said to have invented the alphabet that he used.

Ulhasnagar (o͞ol'həsnəgər), city (1971 pop. 168,128), Maharashtra state, W central India. It is a residential and industrial suburb of Bombay.

Ulithi (o͞olē'thē), atoll comprising 40 islets, 1.75 sq mi (4.53 sq km), W Pacific, in the W CAROLINE ISLANDS (see PACIFIC ISLANDS, TRUST TERRITORY OF THE). Mokomok is the chief village. The atoll became (1920) part of the Japanese mandate in the Pacific and was strongly fortified. The main atoll has an excellent lagoon for anchoring large ships, and after the American capture (1944) of Ulithi in World War II, it was used as a rendezvous station for naval units.

Ulla (ŭl'ə), Asherite. 1 Chron. 7.39.

Ulloa, Antonio de (äntô'nyō thā o͞olyō'ä), 1716–95, Spanish scientist and naval officer. As a young man he went to Peru with a scientific expedition, remaining in the country from 1736 to 1744; the result was an account of the people and the country published in 1748. The book was translated into English as *A Voyage to South America* (1758, 5th ed. 1807). Sent to New Orleans (1766) as governor of Louisiana after that province had been ceded by France to Spain, he was harassed in his administration by the rebellious attitude of the French colonists and by inadequate military and financial support. After an uprising in 1768 he was forced to leave.

Ulloa, Francisco de (fränthēs'kō), d. c.1540, Spanish explorer in Mexico. Against the orders of Viceroy Antonio de Mendoza, Hernán Cortés sent Ulloa to explore the Gulf of California. In 1538–39 he sailed to the head of the gulf, thus proving that lower California was a peninsula.

Ullswater, lake, 7½ mi (12.1 km) long, on the Cumberland-Westmorland boundary, NW England; second largest in the country. It is divided into three reaches. The waterfall of Aira Force (65 ft/20 m high) and Helvellyn mt. are nearby. Gowbarrow, west of the lake, is said to have been the source of inspiration of William Wordsworth's poem "Daffodils."

Ulm (o͞olm), city (1970 pop. 92,943), Baden-Württemberg, S West Germany, on the Danube (Donau) River. It is an active river port, rail junction, and industrial center. Manufactures include textiles, clothing, processed food, beer, and foundry products. A canal links Ulm with the Neckar River. Known in 854, Ulm became (14th cent.) a free imperial city in Swabia and ruled a considerable territory N of the Danube. It was one of the greatest commercial centers and one of the most powerful cities of the medieval empire, reaching its zenith in the 15th cent. Changes in international trade routes during the 15th and 16th cent. and the religious wars in Germany (e.g., the Thirty Years War, 1618–48) caused its decline. Ulm accepted the Reformation c.1530 and was a member of the Schmalkaldic League. The city and its territory were awarded to Bavaria in 1803 at the Diet of Regensburg, but were transferred to Württemberg in 1810. Bavaria built Neu-Ulm on the opposite shore of the Danube, which forms the state boundary there. The industrial development of Ulm dates from the 19th cent. In World War II more than half of the city, including many old and historic buildings, was destroyed. The famous Gothic minster, begun in 1377, is the largest Gothic church in Germany after the Cologne Cathedral and has one of the world's highest church towers (528 ft/161 m). The city has a university and several museums. Albert Einstein was born (1879) in Ulm.

ulna: see ARM.

Ulpian (ŭl'pēən) (Dometius Ulpianus) (ŭl'pēən), d. 228, Roman jurist. He was a member of the council of the jurist Papinian. As Praetorian prefect from 222, he enjoyed the favor of the emperor Alexander Severus, and he was murdered by the jealous Praetorian Guard. Ulpian's *Libri ad edictum* [edicts], a statement of the policy he would follow while in office, survives only in excerpts. Much of the CORPUS JURIS CIVILIS is extracted from Ulpian's writings.

Ulrich von Lichtenstein (o͞ol'rĭkh fən lĭkh'-tənshtīn), c.1200–1275, German MINNESINGER. His chief work, *Frauendienst* [service of his lady] (1255), is a record in verse of a long and convention-bound courtship. His dialogue *Frauenbuch* (1257) laments the decay of chivalric courtship.

Ulsan (o͞ol'sän'), city (1970 pop. 159,340), SE South Korea, a port on the Korea Strait. It is an industrial center, with oil refineries, chemical plants, and a large sugar refinery.

Ulster, northernmost of the historic provinces of Ireland. Modern Ulster consists of nine counties. Six (Antrim, Armagh, Down, Fermanagh, Londonderry, and Tyrone) now make up Northern Ireland (see IRELAND, NORTHERN), which is often referred to as Ulster; the remaining three (Cavan, Donegal, and Monaghan) are in the Republic of Ireland.

Ulster cycle: see GAELIC LITERATURE.

ultimatum (ŭl"tĭmā'təm), in international law, final, definitive terms submitted by one disputant nation to the other for immediate acceptance or rejection. Since refusal to accept the terms may lead to war or hostile measures, an ultimatum usually constitutes a conditional declaration of war. An ultimatum is written and indicates how its nonacceptance will be regarded. When a brief time limit is imposed, the crisis becomes more intense, because there is less opportunity for mediation or arbitration. The contracting powers at the second Hague Conference (1907) agreed to begin hostilities only after giving warning. These provisions were superseded by the Covenant of the League of Nations and later by the Charter of the United Nations, which limited the right of states to use war as an instrument of national policy. An ultimatum presented by Austria to Serbia on July 23, 1914, was the immediate cause of World War I. Hitler also presented several ultimatums (to Czechoslovakia and Poland) in the year before the outbreak of World War II. Japan, however, began its war with the United States with an attack rather than an ultimatum.

ultraísmo: see BORGES, JORGE LUIS.

ultramarine, blue PIGMENT used chiefly as a coloring material and as a bluing agent. A double silicate of sodium and aluminum with some sulfur, it is prepared commercially from kaolin, sulfur, soda ash, and other inexpensive ingredients. It was formerly produced by grinding the rare mineral lapis lazuli and was very costly.

ultramicroscope: see MICROSCOPE.

ultramontanism (ŭl"trəmŏn'tənĭzəm) [Lat.,=beyond the mountains, i.e., the Alps], formerly, point of view of Roman Catholics who supported the pope as supreme head of the church, as distinct from those who professed GALLICANISM or other tendencies opposing the papal jurisdiction. The term was used principally in France by Gallicans, especially before the French Revolution, but it was revived in 19th-century Germany by the group that left the church as OLD CATHOLICS after the First VATICAN COUNCIL. The term is now obsolete, since all those in communion with the pope accept his supremacy. See PAPACY.

ultrasonics, study and application of the energy of SOUND waves vibrating at frequencies greater than 20,000 cycles per second, i.e., beyond the range of human hearing. The application of sound energy in the audible range is limited almost entirely to communications, since increasing the pressure, or intensity, of sound waves increases loudness and therefore causes discomfort to human beings. Ultrasonic waves, however, being inaudible, have little or no effect on the ear even at high intensities. They are produced, commonly, by a TRANSDUCER containing a piezoelectric substance, e.g., a quartz-crystal oscillator that converts high-frequency electric current into vibrating ultrasonic waves. Ultrasonics has found wide industrial use. For nondestructive testing an object is irradiated with ultrasonic waves; variation in velocity or echo of the transmitted waves indicates a flaw. Fine machine parts, ball bearings, surgical instruments, and many other objects can be cleaned ultrasonically. They are placed in a liquid, e.g., a detergent solution or a solvent, into which ultrasonic waves are introduced. By a phenomenon called cavitation, the vibrations cause large numbers of invisible bubbles to explode with great force on the surfaces of the objects. Film or dirt is thus removed even from normally inaccessible holes, cracks, and corners. Radioactive scale is similarly removed from nuclear reactor fuel and control rods. In medicine ultrasonic devices are used to examine internal organs without surgery and are safer to genetic material than X rays. The waves with which the body is irradiated are reflected and refracted; these are recorded by a sonograph for use in diagnosis. Metals can be welded together by placing their surfaces in contact with each other and irradiating the contact with ultrasound. The molecules are stimulated into rearranged crystalline form, making a permanent bond. Ultrasonic whistles, which cannot be heard by human beings, are audible to dogs and are used to summon them.

ultraviolet radiation, invisible ELECTROMAGNETIC RADIATION between visible violet light and X rays; it ranges in wavelength from about 4,000 to 40 angstrom units and in frequency from about 10^{15} to 10^{18} hertz. It is a component (less than 5%) of the sun's radiation and is also produced artificially in arc lamps, e.g., in the mercury arc lamp. Much of the ultraviolet radiation in sunlight is absorbed in the ozone layer of the atmosphere before it reaches the earth's surface; the OZONE is formed when ordinary oxygen absorbs the energy of the ultraviolet radiation. That radiation which passes through is largely absorbed by ordinary window glass or impurities in the air (e.g., water, dust, and smoke) or is screened by clothing. This is beneficial, since overexposure to ultraviolet rays may be harmful; the rays induce sunburn and tanning of the skin and are believed to have a role in causing skin cancer. Vitamin D is produced by the action of ultraviolet radiation on ergosterol, a substance present in the human skin and in some lower plants (e.g., yeast), and treatment or prevention of rickets often includes exposure of the body to natural or artificial ultraviolet light. The radiation also kills germs; it is widely used to sterilize rooms, exposed body tissues, blood plasma, and vaccines. Ultraviolet radiation can be detected by the FLUORESCENCE it induces in certain substances. It may also be detected by its photographic and ionizing effects. The long-wavelength, "soft" ultraviolet radiation, lying just outside the visible spectrum, is often referred to as black light; low intensity sources of this radiation are often used in mineral prospecting and in producing unusual lighting effects in conjunction with bright-colored fluorescent pigments. See L. R. Koller, *Ultraviolet Radiation* (2d ed. 1965).

Ulúa (o͝olo͞o'ä), river, c.200 mi (320 km) long, rising in the Sierra de Gujiquiro, W Honduras, and flowing north to the Caribbean Sea. The Ulúa, with its tributaries, drains almost the entire western half of the country. The valley, once a center of the CHOROTEGA civilization, is one of the most productive in Honduras.

Ulugh-Beg or **Ulug-Beg** (both: o͞o'lo͞og bĕg), 1394–1449, Timurid ruler and astronomer. The grandson of Tamerlane, he succeeded to the Timurid domain in 1447. A patron of the arts and sciences, he established an astronomical observatory at Samarkand and is said to have been the first since Ptolemy to compile a star catalog. His work, written in Arabic, was translated into Persian, and a Latin version appeared in England in the 17th cent.

Ulugh Muz Tagh, peak, China: see KUNLUN.

Ulyanov, Vladimir Ilyich: see LENIN.

Ulyanovsk (o͞olyä'nəfsk), city (1970 pop. 351,000), capital of Ulyanovsk oblast, W central European USSR, a port on the Volga and Svigaya rivers. It is a major rail and water transport center and trades in grain, wool, and potash. Industries include food processing, flour milling, brewing, vodka distilling, and the manufacture of motor vehicles, machine tools, and metal and milling equipment. Ulyanovsk was founded in 1648 on the site of a Tatar village as a strongpoint to defend Russia's southern frontier. It also developed as a trade center. It was taken by the Cossack leader Stenka Razin in 1670, was the scene of fighting during the Pugachev insurrection of 1773–74, and was virtually destroyed by fire in 1864. The city was the birthplace of V. I. Lenin, the founder of Soviet Russia, as well as of such famous figures as A. F. Kerensky, the head of the 1917 provisional Russian government; the novelist I. A. Goncharov; and the historian and writer N. M. Karamzin. The house where Lenin was born and the school that he attended are now national shrines. The city, formerly called Simbirsk, was renamed in 1924 in honor of Lenin (whose original name was Vladimir I. Ulyanov).

Ulysses: see ODYSSEUS.

Uman (o͞omän'), city (1969 est. pop. 64,000), SW European USSR, in the Ukraine, at the confluence of the Kamenka and Umanka rivers. It is a rail junction and has industries that include poultry processing, fruit preserving, and the production of machinery, bricks, clothing, and vitamins. Mentioned in 1659 as a strongpoint, Uman was the seat of the wealthy Potocki nobility until 1834. In the late 17th cent. it was an important fortress for protection against Crimean Tatar attacks on right-bank Ukraine. In 1768 the city was the scene of a Ukrainian peasant and Cossack uprising that resulted in a general massacre and that Taras Shevchenko later depicted in his poem "Haydamaki." Uman passed to Russia in 1793 during the second partition of Poland.

Umanak (o͞o'mənäk), town (1969 pop. 1,006), in Umanak dist. (1969 pop. 2,369), W Greenland, on an inlet of Baffin Bay. A hunting and fishing base, it has a canning factory and is a center for sealing operations. Marble is quarried there.

Umar (o͞omär') or **Omar** (ō'mär), c.581–644, 2d caliph (see CALIPHATE). At first hostile to Islam, he was converted by 618 and was adviser to Muhammad. He was responsible for the choice of ABU BAKR as 1st caliph in 632, and he himself succeeded Abu Bakr without opposition in 634. In his reign Islam became an imperial power. The Muslim generals pushed conquests far and wide—into Syria, Egypt, and the Persian Empire. Umar also laid the administrative base of the empire, creating the office of kadi and establishing fixed taxes. He reopened the canals of Mesopotamia and the waterway from the Nile to the Red Sea. Umar was assassinated by a foreign slave. He had appointed a group to select his successor, and the choice fell on UTHMAN.

Umatilla (ŭm"ətĭl'ə), river, c.85 mi (140 km) long, rising in NE Oregon in the Blue Mts. It flows W past Pendleton, then NW to the Columbia River at the city of Umatilla (1970 pop. 679). The Umatilla project taps two of the river's tributaries to irrigate c.30,000 acres (12,140 hectares).

Umayyad (o͞omä'yäd), Arabian dynasty of caliphs. The powerful Umayyad clan was at first hostile to Islam, but a member of the family, UTHMAN, became a son-in-law of the Prophet and was the 3d caliph. After his murder ALI became caliph, and he was succeeded by his son HASAN. The Umayyad leader MUAWIYA was, however, disaffected. As governor of Syria, he opposed Ali, and in 658 he spread his power to Egypt. Hasan was forced to resign, and Muawiya was recognized in the older Muslim provinces. He made the caliphate hereditary (though the principle was not firmly maintained) and created the Umayyad dynasty. The accession of the Umayyads brought about the great schism between the SUNNI and the SHIITES. There were 14 Umayyad caliphs before 750. **1** Muawiya, caliph 661–80; **2** Yazid, caliph 680–83; **3** Muawiya II, caliph 683; **4** Marwan I, caliph 683–85; **5** Abd al-Malik, caliph 685–705; **6** Walid I, caliph 705–15; **7** Sulayman, caliph 715–17; **8** Umar II, caliph 717–20; **9** Yazid II, caliph 720–24; **10** Hisham, caliph 724–43; **11** Walid II, caliph 743; **12** Yazid III, caliph 743–44; **13** Ibrahim, caliph 744; **14** Marwan II, caliph 744–50. The Umayyad capital was usually Damascus, and they gave that city its splendor until 750, when Marwan II was defeated and killed by ABBASIDS, who then perpetrated a general massacre of the Umayyad family. One member escaped to Spain, where he established himself over the MOORS as ABD AR-RAHMAN I, emir of Córdoba, in 756. This emirate, changed to a caliphate by Abd ar-Rahman III in the 10th cent., survived until 1031. It came to include most of Muslim Spain. The rulers were Hisham I (reigned 788–96), Hakim I (reigned 796–822), Abd ar-Rahman II (reigned 822–59), Muhammad (reigned 859–86), Mundhir (reigned 886–88), Abdullah (ruled 888–912), Abd ar-Rahman III (reigned 912–61; caliph 929–61), Hakim II (caliph 961–76). The early emirs pushed into S France, then sought to oppose the invasion of Charlemagne. They were troubled by raids of the Norsemen along the coast and by numerous revolts and finally by the reconquests of the Christian kings, but they built a brilliant civilization that reached its apex under Abd ar-Rahman III, when art, literature, and science flourished. The great Arabic library was collected largely by his successor, Hakim II. Local dissensions were by that time tearing the state apart, but the able general al-MANSUR in the late 10th cent. carried Umayyad power across almost all of Spain, sacking Santiágo and Barcelona. The last Umayyad rulers (Hisham II and Hisham III) were, however, inconsiderable, and the Almoravids had little difficulty in taking over Spain. For bibliography, see CALIPHATE; MOORS; SPAIN.

umber: see OCHER.

umbilical cord (ŭmbĭl'ĭkəl), cordlike structure about 22 in. (56 cm) long in the pregnant human female, extending from the abdominal wall of the fetus to the PLACENTA. Its chief function is to carry nourishment and oxygen from the placenta to the fetus and return waste products to the placenta from the fetus. It consists of a continuation of the membrane covering the fetus and encloses a mucoid jelly in which lie one vein, carrying oxygenated blood, and two arteries, carrying unoxygenated blood. After birth the cord is clamped off and cut. It is sometimes abnormal in length, and sometimes it breaks or forms loops or knots, which may asphyxiate the fetus. The stump of the cord that is left attached to the infant withers and drops off, leaving the scar known as the navel.

umbra: see ECLIPSE.

umbrella, a small canopy used as a protection against the sun in China, Egypt, and elsewhere in remote antiquity. It was often an emblem of rank. During the Middle Ages the umbrella became almost extinct in Europe; its usefulness was not rediscovered until the late 16th cent., when it was introduced as the *parapluie* (Fr.,=against the rain). Its use did not become general, however, until the late 18th cent., when it is said to have been introduced in England by Jonas Hanway; umbrellas were first manufactured on the Continent after 1787. Their construction has not varied greatly through the ages though modern materials, such as steel for the ribs and synthetic fabrics for the covering, have replaced the oiled paper, bamboo, and wood of the ancient versions. In the mid-19th cent. the *parasol* (Fr.,= against the sun) emerged, distinguished from the umbrella in being solely a sunshade, and became, until the coming of the automobile, a necessary accessory of dress. Within the obvious limitations of its form, the modern umbrella has taken on a variety of shapes, from nearly flat to the long, curved birdcage design. In the 1960s a taste for transparent plastic, clear and colored, was developed.

umbrella bird: see COTINGA.

umbrella tree: see MAGNOLIA.

Umbria (o͞om'brēä), region (1971 pop. 772,601), 3,265 sq mi (8,456 sq km), central Italy. PERUGIA is the capital of the landlocked region, which is divided into the provinces of Perugia and Terni (named for their capitals). Crossed by the Apennines in the east, Umbria is almost entirely mountainous or hilly. The Tiber and the Nera are the main rivers; Lake Trasimeno is in the west. Farming, mostly on a small scale, is the chief occupation. Cereals, grapes, and olives are grown, and cattle and hogs are raised. In the 20th cent., industrialization has been facilitated by the construction of several hydroelectric plants, particularly on the Nera at Terni. Manufactures of the region include chemicals, iron and steel, processed food, and cotton and woolen textiles. There are a number of popular tourist spots, including Assisi, Spoleto, Perugia, Orvieto, and Castiglione. The Umbri were among the first inhabitants of the region, settling there by 600 B.C. Knowledge of them is derived mainly from inscriptions found in Umbria, especially the IGUVINE TABLES discovered (1444) at Gubbio. There are also many Etruscan remains from a later period. Umbria was conquered by the Romans in the 3d cent. B.C., and after the fall of Rome it passed to the Goths and then to the Byzantines. From the 6th to the 11th cent. it was usually included in the powerful Lombard duchy of Spoleto. In the 12th cent. free communes developed in most cities. Local autonomy and petty tyrannies prevailed until the 16th cent., when the popes conquered Umbria (except Gubbio); Perugia, the region's leading city, was the last to fall (1540) under the papacy. Umbria was held by France from 1798 to 1800 and from 1808 to 1814, when it was restored to the papacy. There were several revolts (1831, 1848, 1859) against papal rule, and in 1860 the region voted to join the kingdom of Sardinia. Art has long flourished in the region, and a school of painting (15th–16th cent.) founded by Niccolò da Foligno, included the masters Pinturicchio and Perugino There is a university at Perugia.

Umbrian (ŭm'brēən), extinct language belonging to the Italic subfamily of the Indo-European family of languages. See ITALIC LANGUAGES.

Umbriel (ŭm'brēĕl"), in astronomy, one of the five known moons, or natural satellites, of URANUS.

Umeå (ü'məō"), city (1970 pop. 48,805), capital of Västerbotten co., NE Sweden, on an inlet of the Gulf of Bothnia and at the mouth of the Umeälv River; founded 1622. Manufactures of this industrial center include forest products, furniture, and machinery. Nearby Holmsund serves as its port. Umeå is the cultural center of Upper Norrland and has a university.

Umeälv (ü'mə ĕlv), river, c.285 mi (460 km) long, rising in N Sweden in a lake on the Norwegian border. It flows SE through Storuman and Overuman lakes to the Gulf of Bothnia at Umeå. The Vindelälven (c.280 mi/450 km long) is its chief tributary. There is a large hydroelectric power station at Stornorrfors.

umkokola, small, thorny S African tree (*Dovyalis caffra*, also called kei-apple), widely cultivated in its native area for the round or oval bright yellow fruits. Their juicy pulp, acid in flavor, is used for preserves and jams. A related and similarly grown tree of Ceylon and India, the kitembilla, or Ceylon gooseberry (*D. hebecarpa*), bears somewhat smaller and sweeter dark purple fruits. Both species have been introduced into the American tropics and are sometimes cultivated in other warm regions as hedge plants. Umkokolas are classified in the division MAGNOLIOPHYTA, class Magnoliopsida, order Violales, family Flacourtiaceae.

umlaut (ōōm'lout) [Ger.,=transformed sound], in INFLECTION, variation of vowels of the type of English *man* to *men*. In this instance it is the end product of the effect of a *y* (long since disappeared) that was present in the plural; the *y* caused the vowel before the *n* to be pronounced higher and more forward in the mouth in the plural than in the singular; eventually there was replacement of the vowel in the plural. Other examples are *mouse, mice; tooth, teeth; to fall, to fell; doom, deem.* Umlaut is also called mutation and inflection. For the variation of *sing, sang,* see ABLAUT. Umlaut is also the name for the diacritical symbol placed above a vowel to indicate a sound change in Germanic languages, as in the German *Fräulein* and the Swedish *fröken* (see ACCENT).

Ummah (ŭm'ə), city, NW Palestine. It is a mistranslation for Acco (see AKKO). Joshua 19.30.

Umm al-Qaiwain (ōōm äl-kīwīn'), sheikhdom (1968 pop. 3,740), c.300 sq mi (780 sq km), part of the federation of UNITED ARAB EMIRATES, E Arabia, on the Persian Gulf. Fishing and agriculture are the main economic activities, although oil production began in 1964. The sheikhdom, formerly a British protectorate, became part of the United Arab Emirates in 1971.

Umnak (ōōm'năk), island, c.83 mi (134 km) long, off SW Alaska, one of the largest of the Aleutian Islands. A volcanic peak, Mt. Vsevidof, 7,236 ft (2,206 m) high, is there.

UMP (uridine monophosphate): see URACIL.

Umpqua Indians (ŭmp'kwə), North American Indians of the ATHABASCAN branch of the Nadene linguistic stock (see AMERICAN INDIAN LANGUAGES). In the mid-19th cent. the Umpqua were settled on the upper Umpqua River in SW Oregon. They then numbered some 400, but have since then become almost extinct. They subsisted by fishing in the Umpqua River. Some of the Umpqua, the Nahankhuotana, lived along Cow Creek. The Lower Umpqua were distinct from the others; they were part of the Siuslaw subdivision of the Penutian linguistic stock.

Umtali (ōōmtä'lē), city (1973 est. pop., with suburbs, 54,000), E Rhodesia, near the Mozambique border. Umtali is the commercial center for a rich agricultural and gold-mining region. Its industries include automobile assembly, petroleum refining, and the manufacture of textiles. The city is connected by rail with the port of Beira in Mozambique. Founded in 1890, Umtali grew after the coming (1899) of the railroad.

Umtata (ōōmtä'tə), town (1970 pop. 24,805), capital of The TRANSKEI, an African homeland, or bantustan, SE South Africa, on the Umtata River. The town is chiefly an administrative center. Umtata, founded in 1860 as a military post, became capital of the newly created Transkei African homeland in 1963. An Anglican cathedral and St. John's College are in the town.

Unalaska (ŭn"əlăs'kə, ōō"nə-), rugged island, 30 mi (48 km) long, off SW Alaska, one of the largest Aleutian Islands. Discovered (c.1759) by Russian explorers, the island was a center of Russian fur trade until it was superseded by Kodiak. Spruces planted on Unalaska by the Russians remain among the few trees in the Aleutians. The main towns on the island are Unalaska and Dutch Harbor.

Unamuno, Miguel de (mēgĕl' dā ōōnämōō'nō), 1864–1936, Spanish philosophical writer, of Basque descent, b. Bilbao. The chief Spanish philosopher of his time, he was professor of Greek at the Univ. of Salamanca and later rector there. His criticism of the monarchy and especially of the dictator Miguel Primo de Rivera, caused his removal from the university in 1920 and his exile from Spain (1924–30), but with the establishment of the republic (1931), he was reinstated as rector. At first a supporter of the republic, he became critical of it and sided briefly (1936) with the rebels, only to rebuke them sharply just before his death. In his chief work, *Del sentimiento trágico de la vida en los hombres y los pueblos* (1913; Bollingen Series tr., *The Tragic Sense of Life in Men and Nations,* 1968), he expresses his highly individualistic philosophy—one of faith in faith itself, not in any affirmation or denial of faith. Other important volumes are *La vida de don Quijote y Sancho* (1905; Bollingen Series tr., *Our Lord Don Quixote,* 1958–59) and *La Agonía del cristianismo* (1925; Bollingen Series tr., *The Agony of Christianity,* 1973). His poetry, as serious as his essays, includes *Poesías* (1907), *Rosario de sonetos líricos* (1911), and *El Cristo de Velázquez* (1920). His novels also express his impassioned concern with life and death; they are *Niebla* (1914; tr. *Mist,* 1928), *Tres novelas ejemplares y un prólogo* (1920; tr. *Three Exemplary Novels and a Prologue,* 1930), and *La tía Tula* (1921). His complete works were published in Spanish in 1951–52. See studies by Demetrios Basdekis (1969), Martin Nozick (1971), M. J. Valdes (1973), and Victor Oumiette (1974).

Uncas (ŭng'kəs), c.1588–c.1683, chief of the MOHEGAN INDIANS. Uncas was a subchief of the PEQUOT INDIANS, but because of trouble with the chief, Sassacus, he withdrew with his followers and formed a separate tribe, the Mohegan. These people flourished under Uncas's leadership. Uncas was ambitious and sought British support. He was constantly at war with MIANTONOMO, the Narragansett chief. Both sided with the British in the Pequot War, but despite a treaty of peace (1638) signed between them through the instrumentality of the British, trouble continued. Uncas finally captured Miantonomo in 1643 and killed him, with British acquiescence. For the remainder of his life Uncas was involved in various troubles with the British and other Indians. See A. J. Peale, *Uncas and the Mohegan-Pequot* (1939).

uncertainty principle, physical principle, enunciated by Werner Heisenberg in 1927, that places an absolute, theoretical limit on the combined accuracy of certain pairs of simultaneous, related measurements. The accuracy of a measurement is given by the uncertainty in the result; if the measurement is exact, the uncertainty is zero. According to the uncertainty principle, the mathematical product of the combined uncertainties of simultaneous measurements of position and momentum in a given direction cannot be less than PLANCK'S CONSTANT h divided by 2π. The principle also limits the accuracies of simultaneous measurements of energy and of the time required to make the energy measurement. The value of Planck's constant is extremely small, so that the effect of the limitations imposed by the uncertainty principle are not noticeable on the large scale of ordinary measurements; however, on the scale of atoms and elementary particles the effect of the uncertainty principle is very important. Because of the uncertainties existing at this level, a picture of the submicroscopic world emerges as one of chaos, of statistical probabilities rather than measurable certainties. On the large scale it is still possible to speak of causality in a framework described in terms of space and time; on the atomic scale this is not possible. Such a description would require exact measurements of such quantities as position, speed, energy, and time, and these quantities cannot be measured exactly because of the uncertainty principle. The principle can be conceived as resulting from the fact that any measurement requires an interaction between the measurer (and his instruments) and the thing being measured; such an interaction necessarily disturbs the thing being measured, even if only very slightly. The uncertainty principle, as a physical principle, makes very specific statements about limita[illegible] does not limit the accuracy of [illegible] of nonsimultaneous measureme[illegible] neous measurements of pairs of [illegible] than those specifically restricted by [illegible] Even so, its restrictions are sufficient to p[illegible] entists from being able to make absolute [illegible] tions about future states of the system being [illegible] ied. The uncertainty principle has been elevated [illegible] some thinkers to the status of a philosophical principle, called the principle of indeterminacy, which has been taken by some to limit causality in general. See QUANTUM THEORY. See Werner Heisenberg, *The Physical Principles of the Quantum Theory* (tr. 1949).

uncial: see PALEOGRAPHY; CALLIGRAPHY.

Uncle Sam, name used to designate the U.S. government. The term arose in the War of 1812 and seems at first to have been used derisively by those opposed to the war. Possibly it was an expansion of the letters "U.S." on uniforms and government property, but some sources attribute the origin of the term to Samuel Wilson (1766–1854) of Troy, N.Y. Wilson, whose nickname was Uncle Sam, was an inspector of army supplies. The "U.S." stamped on supplies was referred to as "Uncle Sam" by the workmen. Regardless of origin, the term found wide application and became permanent.

Uncompahgre (ŭn"kəmpä'grē), river, c.75 mi (120 km) long, rising in the San Juan Mts., SW Colo., and flowing NW past Montrose to the Gunnison River at Delta. Its waters are used for irrigation. Gunnison Tunnel diverts water from the Gunnison River to the Uncompahgre valley.

Uncompahgre Peak, 14,309 ft (4,361 m) high, SW Colo., in the San Juan Mts. of the Rockies and NE of Ouray.

unconscious, in psychology, that aspect of mental life that is apart from immediate consciousness and is not subject to recall at will. It is also called the subconscious. Freud regarded the unconscious as a submerged but vast portion of the mind. In his view, one part of the unconscious, known as the *id,* is composed of instinctual drives, acts as the motivating force in human behavior, and contains the residue of unacceptable experiences and desires that the individual hides, or represses, from conscious recognition. The system that acts to restrain and control id impulses, which Freud termed the *superego,* also acts partly on an unconscious level. Conscious cognitive processes, such as thinking, are performed by the ego and part of the superego (see PSYCHOANALYSIS). Conflict between conscious and unconscious impulses are said to give rise to ANXIETY and DEFENSE MECHANISMS. The strongest empirical evidence for the existence of the unconscious was found by Freud to be the fact that under hypnosis the individual is able to remember experiences that he cannot recall when in a normal state(see HYPNOTISM). To the Freudian concept C. G. Jung added the idea of an inherited unconscious, i.e., the capacity of humans to generate concepts. The idea of the unconscious is rejected by some psychological schools; however, the majority of psychoanalysts attempt to bring repressed unconscious material to CONSCIOUSNESS. The term *unconscious* is also sometimes used for latent, or unretrieved, memories, or to describe stimuli too weak to enter an individual's conscious awareness.

underground: see GUERRILLA WARFARE.

underground coal mining: see COAL MINING.

Underground Railroad, in U.S. history, loosely organized system for helping fugitive slaves escape to Canada or to areas of safety in free states. It was run by local groups of Northern ABOLITIONISTS, both white and free Negro. The metaphor first appeared in print in the early 1840s, and other railroad terminology was soon added. The escaping slaves were called passengers; the homes where they were sheltered, stations; and those who guided them, conductors. This nomenclature, along with the numerous, somewhat glorified, personal reminiscences written by conductors in the postwar period, created the impression that the Underground Railroad was a highly systematized, national, secret organization that accomplished prodigious feats in stealing slaves away from the South. In fact, most of the help given to fugitive slaves on their varied routes north was spontaneously offered and came not only from abolitionists or self-styled members of the Underground Railroad, but from anyone moved to sympathy by the plight of the runaway slave before his eyes. The major part played by free Negroes, of both North and South, and by slaves on plantations along the way in helping fugitives escape to freedom was

…stimated in nearly all early accounts of the …ailroad. Moreover, the resourcefulness and daring of the fleeing slaves themselves, who were usually helped only after the most dangerous part of their journey (i.e., the Southern part) was over, were probably more important factors in the success of their escape than many conductors readily admitted. In some localities, like Philadelphia, Cincinnati, Wilmington, Del., and Newport, Ind. (site of the activities of Levi COFFIN), energetic organizers did manage to loosely systematize the work; Quakers were particularly prominent as conductors, and among the free Negroes the exploits of Harriet TUBMAN stand out. In all cases, however, it is extremely difficult to separate fact from legend, especially since relatively few enslaved Negroes, probably no more than a few thousand a year between 1840 and 1860, escaped successfully. Far from being kept secret, details of escapes on the Underground Railroad were highly publicized and exaggerated in both the North and the South, although for different reasons. The abolitionists used the Underground Railroad as a propaganda device to dramatize the evils of slavery; Southern slaveholders publicized it to illustrate Northern infidelity to the FUGITIVE SLAVE LAWS. The effect of this publicity, with its repeated tellings and exaggerations of slave escapes, was to create an Underground Railroad legend that correctly represented a humanitarian ideal of the pre-Civil War period, but that strayed far from reality. The pioneer study is W. H. Siebert, *The Underground Railroad from Slavery to Freedom* (1898, repr. 1968); for an extensively revised account, see Larry Gara, *The Liberty Line* (1961).

Underhill, John, c.1597–1672, military commander in the American colonies, b. England. In 1630 he accompanied John Winthrop (1588–1649) to Massachusetts Bay, and in 1637 he distinguished himself as a commander with John MASON (c.1600–1672) in the Pequot War, of which he wrote an account in *Newes from America* (1638). Because of his ardent support of Anne HUTCHINSON in the antinomian controversy, he fled (1638) to Dover, N.H., where he was briefly governor, opposing Massachusetts's claims to authority over the area. He returned to Massachusetts, was reinstated (1640) in the church, then moved to Stamford, Conn. Later in New Netherland he commanded (1644) for the Dutch against the Algonquin Indians; he opposed Peter Stuyvesant and had to leave (1653) the colony but returned after the British conquest of 1664. See biography by H. C. Shelley (1932).

Underwood, Oscar Wilder, 1862–1929, American political leader, U.S. Senator from Alabama (1915–27), b. Louisville, Ky. A lawyer in Birmingham, Ala., he became important in Democratic party politics. In the U.S. House of Representatives (1895–96, 1897–1915) he introduced the Underwood Tariff Act of 1913. The act drastically reduced tariff schedules and transferred many articles to the free list but was only in force briefly because of the outbreak (1914) of World War I. In the Senate (1915–27) he was a leading exponent of President Wilson's foreign policy. Underwood was a prominent contender for the Democratic presidential nomination in 1912 and 1924. He wrote *Drifting Sands of Party Politics* (1928).

undine (əndēn′, ŭn′dēn), in folklore, female water sprite who could acquire a soul by marrying a human being. If, however, her lover proved unfaithful, she had to return to the sea. The legend is the subject of Baron de La Motte-Fouqué's *Undine* and Jean Giraudoux's *Ondine.*

Undset, Sigrid (sĭ′grĭd o͝on′sĕt), 1882–1949, Norwegian novelist. Poverty forced Undset to do secretarial work for a time (1898–1908). Her early novels of seamy contemporary life, among them *Jenny* (1911, tr. 1921), were frank and realistic works in which she upheld traditional institutions. Her writing, always strongly ethical, deepened in religious intensity after her conversion (1924) to Roman Catholicism. Undset is most famous for her historical novels dealing with human problems of continuing significance. *Kristin Lavransdatter* (3 vol., 1920–22; tr. 1923–27), considered her masterpiece, tells of love and religion in medieval Norway. It was followed by the excessively detailed and more explicitly religious *Olav Audunsson* (4 vol., 1925–27; tr. *The Master of Hestviken,* 4 vol., 1928–30). Her later works include tales of contemporary family life, among them *Ida Elisabeth* (1932, tr. 1933), *The Faithful Wife* (1936, tr. 1937), and *Madame Dorthea* (1939, tr. 1940), and the autobiographical *The Longest Years* (1934, tr. 1935) and *Return to the Future* (1942). Undset came to the United States after the Nazi invasion of Norway (1940), returning home in 1945. She was awarded the 1928 Nobel Prize in Literature. See biography by A. H. Winsnes (tr. 1953, repr. 1970).

undulant fever: see BRUCELLOSIS.

unearned increment, gain in the value of property not due to any act of the owner. There may be unearned increment in the value of SECURITIES, rarities, and objects of art, and the value of land may be enhanced by the progress of a community.

unemployment, condition of one who is able to work but unable to find work. Formerly assumed to be voluntary, idleness was punishable by law; however it is now recognized that unemployment arises from factors beyond the control of the individual worker. Unemployment may be due to seasonal layoffs (e.g., in agricultural jobs), technological changes in industry (particularly by increased automation), racial discrimination, lack of adequate skills by the worker, or fluctuations in the economy. In developing countries, unemployment is often caused by the urban migration that generally precedes the industrial development needed to employ those migrants. In industrial nations, most unemployment is the result of economic recessions and depressions. In the Great Depression of the 1930s unemployment rose to 25% of the work force in Germany, Great Britain, and the United States. During the 1950s and 60s most of Western Europe and Japan generally kept their unemployment levels below 3%, and by the late 60s the rate in the United States, where there had been far more fluctuation, was down to less than 4%. In the 1970s, however, worldwide economic difficulties began to push unemployment up again. As Keynesian economics (see KEYNES, JOHN MAYNARD) gained influence among policymakers, more countries committed themselves to finding ways to approach full employment through government intervention. Governments, in addition to trying to increase employment opportunities by stimulating business, have also taken other measures to deal with the problem. In the United States, the Social Security Act of 1935 and the Employment Act of 1946 represented moves in this direction; in Great Britain, labor exchanges were set up and a contributory unemployment insurance system established. In the Soviet Union and in the People's Republic of China, unemployment has been eliminated by socializing the means of production and distribution and by directing labor into more productive channels. See DEPRESSION. See A. C. Pigou, *The Theory of Unemployment* (1933); R. C. Wilcock and Walter H. Franke, *Unwanted Workers* (1963); Arthur Okun, ed., *The Battle Against Unemployment* (1972).

unemployment insurance, insurance against loss of wages during the time that an able-bodied worker is involuntarily unemployed. The goal of such insurance is to maintain unemployed workers until they are reabsorbed into industry. Compulsory unemployment insurance makes such protection legally obligatory for certain classes of workers under prescribed conditions. Voluntary unemployment insurance is maintained by private organizations sanctioned, encouraged, or subsidized by the state. The first attempts to establish unemployment insurance plans began toward the end of the 19th cent. in Germany, Italy, and Switzerland (see SOCIAL SECURITY). Most Western European states adopted such plans in the early part of the 20th cent.: France, 1905; Great Britain, 1911; the Netherlands, 1916; Italy, 1919; and Germany, 1927. In the United States an unemployment insurance program, along with other welfare programs, was introduced by the Social Security Act of 1935. That act, amended many times, provides for a sliding scale of payroll taxes on industry. For example, employers whose records show that their business experiences little unemployment receive lower rates. The Unemployment Service of the Dept. of Labor is responsible for administering the law. Over the years Congress has extended the program to many workers initially not covered. In response to an economic recession, Congress in 1958 enacted the Temporary Unemployment Compensation Act to extend benefits for longer periods of time than the Social Security Act of 1935 had allowed. The Area Redevelopment Act (1961) was designed to create new jobs in areas of chronic unemployment. The act authorizes the appropriation of funds in loans and grants for such purposes as construction and modernization of plants, improvement of public facilities, and retraining of workers. Each state has its own unemployment insurance law and operates its own program. By the early 1970s over three quarters of the work force was covered by unemployment insurance. See William Haber, *Unemployment Insurance in the American Economy* (1966); Daniel Nelson, *Unemployment Insurance; the American Experience, 1915–1935* (1969); M. G. Murry, *Income for the Unemployed* (1971); L. P. Adams, *Public Attitudes toward Unemployment Insurance* (1971).

UNESCO: see UNITED NATIONS EDUCATIONAL, SCIENTIFIC, AND CULTURAL ORGANIZATION.

Unfederated Malay States: see MALAYSIA, FEDERATION OF.

Ungaretti, Giuseppe (jo͞ozĕp′pā o͞ongärĕt′tē), 1888–1970, Italian poet and translator, b. Alexandria, Egypt. The remarkable purity of Ungaretti's poetic style was achieved by his condensing it to essentials. His elaborate, difficult works are in the tradition of the French SYMBOLISTS. Ungaretti was educated in France and lived and taught for six years in Brazil before settling in Italy. His works are collected in 12 volumes under the title *Vita d'un Uomo* (tr. *Life of a Man,* 1958). See his *Selected Poems* (tr. 1972).

Ungava: see LABRADOR-UNGAVA, peninsula, Canada.

Ungava Bay (ŭng″gä′və, –gā′-), inlet of the Atlantic Ocean, N Que., Canada, extending c.200 mi (320 km) S from Hudson Strait between the N Quebec mainland and the north tip of the Labrador peninsula. It is 160 mi (257 km) wide at its mouth.

Uni (o͞o′nē), fl. c.2325 B.C., Egyptian official of the VI dynasty. His career is known through his private inscription. After rising from an obscure court position to a position of command, he defeated the Bedouins five times and pursued them as far as Palestine. As governor of the south under Pepi I, he established water connections with the quarries just above the First Cataract of the NILE by a series of canals cut through the granite and shipped granite blocks down the river to be used for the royal pyramid.

Uniates or **Uniats:** see ROMAN CATHOLIC CHURCH.

unicorn (yo͞o′nĭkôrn), fabulous equine beast with a long horn jutting from the middle of its forehead. Once thought to be native to India, the unicorn was reportedly seen throughout the world. It was often considered as a composite creature, having the features of various animals. The unicorn is depicted as a beautiful animal, usually pure white in color. It has been used to represent virginity, but also has religious significance in connection with the Virgin Mary and Christ. The hunting of the unicorn was a subject in tapestries of the late Middle Ages and the Renaissance.

unidentified flying object or **UFO,** an object or light reportedly seen in the sky whose appearance, trajectory, and general dynamic and luminescent behavior do not suggest a logical, conventional explanation. Some of these phenomena have been photographed and others correlated with radar echoes. Throughout history there have been reports of strange objects in the sky. In the 20th cent. a number of observers claim to have seen vehicles, or "flying saucers," which some believe are space ships visiting the earth from other planets. Because the objects are often shining and in that part of the sky opposite the sun, most investigators, official and unofficial alike, tend to interpret them as reflections of the sun's rays from airplanes. Some UFOs, when pursued by planes, have proved to be weather balloons or other objects of unquestionably terrestrial origin. Fireballs, meteors, and other meteorological phenomena account for most of the relatively few UFOs that observers report seeing at night. However, there are some sightings that investigators are unable to explain in terms of known phenomena. See U.S. Air Force Project, *Blue Book Special Report No. 14* (1955); Edward J. Ruppelt, *The Report on Unidentified Objects* (1956, repr. 1965); D. H. Menzel and L. G. Boyd, *The World of Flying Saucers* (1963); P. J. Klass, *UFO's Identified* (1968); G. I. R. Lore and H. H. Deneault, *Mysteries of the Skies* (1968); E. U. Condon, *Final Report of the Scientific Study of Unidentified Flying Objects* (1969); J. Allen Hynek, *The UFO Experience: A Scientific Inquiry* (1972); D. E. Keyhoe, *Aliens from Space* (1973); Carl Sagan and Thornton Page, eds., *UFO's: A Scientific Debate* (1973).

uniformitarianism, in geology, doctrine holding that changes in the earth's surface that occurred in past geologic time are referable to the same causes as changes now being produced upon the earth's surface. This doctrine, the basic concept of which was first advanced by the Scottish geologist James Hutton in his *Theory of the Earth* (1785, 1795), was further expounded by another Scotsman, John Playfair, in his *Illustrations of the Huttonian Theory*

(1802). It made little progress, however, against the teachings of the school of Abraham Gottlob Werner, a German geologist, and as a theory of dynamic geology it was overshadowed by the doctrine of CATASTROPHISM, of which the major supporter was the French naturalist G. L. Cuvier. This was in large measure because uniformitarianism seemed in several ways to be contrary to religious beliefs. It required an immensely long period of time for the consummation of geological processes (thus disturbing the accepted biblical chronology) and set aside all remarkable catastrophies (thus, it would seem, denying the Flood). Uniformitarianism had its day in the 19th cent., when it was widely accepted as a result of the efforts of the English geologist Sir Charles Lyell. The more recent tendency has been to effect somewhat of a synthesis of the two theories, based mainly upon Lyell's conception of the slow operation, over extremely long periods of time, of forces at work in historic time, but admitting the existence in earth history of periods when such activity was accelerated and intensified.

Unimak (o͞o'nĭmăk, yo͞o'-), volcanic island, 70 mi (113 km) long, off W Alaska, one of the Aleutian Islands, nearest of the chain to the Alaska Peninsula.

Union. **1** Township (1970 pop. 52,878), Union co., NE N.J.; settled 1749 by colonists from Connecticut, set off from Elizabethtown 1808. Steel and metal products and paints are manufactured. Union was the site of a Revolutionary battle (1780). It is the seat of Newark State College at Union. **2** City (1970 pop. 10,775), seat of Union co., N S.C.; settled 1791, inc. 1837. Textiles, fertilizer, and metal products are made. Neal Shoals hydroelectric plant is there. Many antebellum houses remain.

Unión, La (lä o͞onyōn'), city (1968 est. pop. 15,000), SE El Salvador, on the Gulf of Fonseca, an arm of the Pacific Ocean. With Cutuco, its subsidiary port, La Unión is the southern terminus of an important railroad system and a major port of the country, handling the bulk of its foreign trade. It is on the Inter-American Highway and at the foot of the Conchagua volcano. The city was severely damaged in 1947 when the volcano erupted simultaneously with an earthquake.

Unión, La, town (1970 pop. 13,145), Murcia prov., SE Spain. It is a center for the rich lead, silver, iron, and zinc mines of the vicinity, which have been worked since Carthaginian times. The ores are exported from Portman on the Mediterranean.

Union, Act of. For the union of England and Scotland (1707), see GREAT BRITAIN; for the union of Ireland (1800) with Great Britain, see IRELAND. For both, see UNITED KINGDOM OF GREAT BRITAIN AND NORTHERN IRELAND.

Union, Fort: see FORT UNION.

union, labor, association of workers for the purpose of improving their economic status and working conditions through collective bargaining with employers. Historically there have been two chief types of unions: the horizontal, or craft, union, in which all the members are skilled in a certain craft (e.g., the International Brotherhood of Carpenters and Joiners); and the vertical, or industrial, union, composed of workers in the same industry regardless of their particular skill (e.g., the United Automobile Workers of America). A company union is an employer-controlled union having no affiliation with other labor organizations. Although there were associations of journeymen under the medieval system of GUILDS, labor unions were essentially the product of the Industrial Revolution. In Great Britain after the French Revolution, fear of uprisings by the working classes led to passage of the Combination Acts, declaring unions illegal. Although those acts were repealed (1824), little progress was made in union growth until the organization of miners and textile workers in the 1860s, after which the struggle for legal recognition was waged with vigor. After the Trade Union Act of 1871, British labor unions were guaranteed legal recognition, although it required the laws of 1913 and 1915 to assure their status. In the latter part of the 19th cent. the socialist movement made headway among trade unionists, and James Keir HARDIE induced (1893) the trade unions to join forces with the socialists in the Independent Labour party (see LABOUR PARTY). The central organization of the British trade unions, the Trades Union Congress was formed in 1868 to coordinate and formulate policy on behalf of the whole labor movement. Labor unions developed differently on the Continent than they did in Great Britain (and in the United States), mainly because the European unions organized along industrial rather than along craft lines and because they engaged in more partisan political activity. In Germany the printers' and cigarmakers' unions were started after the uprisings of 1848; German unions until World War I were responsible for much social legislation. In France labor unions were organized in the early part of the 19th cent. but received no legal recognition until 1884. In most European countries labor organizations either are political parties or are affiliated with political parties, usually left-wing ones. In some European countries, notably Italy, Belgium, and the Netherlands, there are rival Christian and Socialist trade-union movements; the former are linked to the World Confederation of Labour, which exists in Latin America as well as in Europe and claimed a membership of over 12 million by the early 1970s. In Russia, trade unions first appeared on a considerable scale in the revolution of 1905 but were later stamped out. They reappeared in the 1917 revolution and became highly organized in a national movement under Communist control. Thereafter the trade-union movement in the Soviet Union was mainly an instrument of the state in the drive for higher industrial production. Organized labor in nonindustrial nations, although small numerically, has played a disproportionately large role in political developments in those countries. Many union movements in the underdeveloped countries, particularly in Asia and Africa, rising on the wave of nationalism, have led anticolonial movements toward political independence; the leaders of many newly independent nations have owed their rise largely to the support of workers they have organized. In Latin America, too, labor unions are a powerful force, constituting as they do the most important mass political organizations in the nations of that region. Internationally, world trade unionism was split after 1949 between two rival organizations: the, largely Communist, World Federation of Trade Unions (WTFU), originally set up in 1945, and the International Confederation of Free Trade Unions (ICFTU), founded in 1949 by member unions that had withdrawn from the WTFU in protest against its Communist domination. By the early 1970s the WTFU claimed a membership of 150 million; the ICFTU had a membership of around 50 million in 1970. There has been keen rivalry between the ICFTU and the WTFU in stimulating the growth of unions in the underdeveloped countries, with the ICFTU particularly active in India and in Africa. The international federations are recognized by the United Nations Educational, Scientific, and Cultural Organizations (UNESCO), and there is close cooperation between the ICFTU and UNESCO in the field of education. The INTERNATIONAL LABOR ORGANIZATION is a specialized agency of the United Nations; some of its aims include raising living standards, improving working conditions, gaining recognition of the right to collective bargaining, and the protection of workers' health. In the United States unionism in some form is almost as old as the nation itself. Crafts that formed local unions in the late 18th and early 19th cent. included printers, carpenters, tailors, and weavers. Their chief purpose was to keep up craft standards and to prevent employers from hiring untrained workers and importing foreign labor. From 1806 there were numerous prosecutions by employers of unions as combinations in restraint of trade. The early 1830s, a period of industrial prosperity and inflation, was a time of union development; however, the financial Panic of 1837 halted this growth. After the Civil War, in 1866, the National Labor Union was formed; it had such objectives as the abolition of convict labor, the establishment of the eight-hour workday, and the restriction of immigration, but it collapsed with its entry into politics in 1872. Among the most important of the early national organizations was the KNIGHTS OF LABOR (1869–1917), organizing among both skilled and unskilled workers. That policy brought them into conflict with the established craft unions, who joined together to form the American Federation of Labor (AFL; see AMERICAN FEDERATION OF LABOR AND CONGRESS OF INDUSTRIAL ORGANIZATIONS) in the 1890s under Samuel Gompers. The Knights, thereafter, declined in numbers and effectiveness. The leaders of the AFL opposed the entry of the federation into politics. In 1905 a huge, unwieldy but militant industrial body arose—the INDUSTRIAL WORKERS OF THE WORLD (IWW). It concentrated on unskilled workers—lumbermen, migrant workers, and miners. With the conviction of most of its leaders under the Espionage Act during and after World War I, IWW membership shrank, and the organization became ineffective in the 1920s. During the depression of the 1930s, unions experienced a rapid growth in membership. At this time the Congress of Industrial Organizations (CIO) was formed; it was made up at first of dissident unions of the AFL and was led by John L. LEWIS. During the administration of President Franklin Delano Roosevelt, steps were taken to restore seriously deteriorated standards of employment and to facilitate the development of trade-union organization. The accomplishment of those goals were sought through the passage of such acts as the National Labor Relations (Wagner) Act of 1935, an enactment that enlarged the rights of unions and created the NATIONAL LABOR RELATIONS BOARD, and by protective labor legislation such as the Fair Labor Standards Act (1938) and the Social Security Act (1935). There were often severe conflicts between the AFL and the CIO during the 1930s and 40s. It was therefore considered a momentous step when in 1955 the two labor groups merged to form the AFL-CIO. The AFL, the larger of the two organizations, was given a proportionate share of the offices of the new federation, and its president, George Meany, was unanimously elected president of the combined body. Industrial unions of the CIO were given a department of their own within the merged organization. The AFL-CIO issued a series of ethical-practice codes to govern the behavior of union officers; it also created machinery for the enforcement of the codes, providing expulsion as the ultimate penalty for unions failing to conform (the TEAMSTERS UNION was expelled in 1957). Nevertheless the entire labor movement found itself on the defensive in the late 1950s, following the disclosures made by the Senate Committee on Improper Activities in the Labor or Management Field (popularly known as the McClellan Committee); the committee exposed such abuses as collusion between dishonest employers and union officials, extortions and the use of violence by certain segments of labor leadership, and the misuse of funds by high-ranking union officials. As a result of the findings of the McClellan Committee, the LANDRUM-GRIFFIN ACT of 1959 was enacted to correct abuses in labor-management relations. By the late 1960s trade-union membership in the United States was estimated at around 17 million; it has remained substantially unchanged since the 1955 merger despite drives by the AFL-CIO to increase membership. Unlike European union movements, American organized labor has avoided the formation of a political party and has remained within the framework of the two-party system. For British unions, see Sidney and Beatrice Webb, *The History of Trade Unionism* (new ed. 1920, repr. 1965); V. L. Allen, *Power in Trade Unions: A Study of Their Organization in Great Britain* (1954); G. D. H. Cole, *An Introduction to Trade Unionism* (1955); B. C. Roberts, *The Trades Union Congress, 1868–1921* (1958); for American unions, see R. A. Lester, *As Unions Mature: An Analysis of the Evolution of American Unionism* (1958); Joseph G. Rayback, *A History of American Labor* (1959, repr. 1966); Solomon Barkin, *The Decline of the American Labor Movement* (1961); Albert Rees, *The Economics of Trade Unions* (1962); J. R. Commons, *History of Labor in the United States* (4 vol., 1918–35, repr. 1966); W. R. van Tine, *The Making of the Labor Bureaucrat* (1973). See also V. R. Lorwin, *The French Labor Movement* (1955); J. B. Carey, *Trade Unions and Democracy* (1957); Walter Galenson, ed., *Comparative Labor Movements* (1952, repr. 1968) and *Trade Union Democracy in Western Europe* (1961); Eric Jacobs, *European Trade Unionism* (1973).

Union City. **1** Residential city (1970 pop. 14,724), Alameda co., W Calif., in a farm region; inc. 1959 with the merger of Decoto and Alvarado districts. Steel and iron products, aluminum, and sugar are manufactured there. **2** City (1970 pop. 58,537), Hudson co., NE N.J., on the Palisades overlooking the Hudson River, directly opposite New York City; inc. 1925. This densely populated city has many small firms, most of them in the embroidery field. **3** City (1970 pop. 11,925), seat of Obion co., W Tenn., near the Ky. line; inc. 1867. It is a trade, processing, and shipping center in a rich livestock, grain, and cotton region. Automobile parts, shoes, aluminum and sheet-metal products, and textiles are made. Three Civil War battles were fought in the vicinity in 1862–63. The city has a Civil War cemetery, a monument to unknown Confederate dead, and an eternal-flame memorial. A state vocational training school is there.

Uniondale, uninc. residential city (1970 pop. 22,077), Nassau co., SE N.Y., on Long Island.

Union League Clubs, in U.S. history, organizations formed throughout the North in the Civil War after the military defeats and Republican election losses of 1862. A convention at Cleveland (May, 1863) provided for national headquarters of the Union League at Washington. The clubs distributed war literature, raised money for soldier relief, and recruited both white and black volunteers for the army. In the South after the war, the league, led by officials of the Freedmen's Bureau, carpetbaggers, and scalawags, developed into a strong Republican political organization that controlled the black vote. Its influence was curtailed by the rise of the Ku Klux Klan and vanished with the end of Reconstruction. The Union League Clubs of New York City, Philadelphia, and Chicago survived as conservative social organizations. See studies of the New York club by Will Irwin and others (1952) and of the Chicago club by Bruce Grant (1955).

Union of Burma: see BURMA, UNION OF.

Union of South Africa: see SOUTH AFRICA, REPUBLIC OF.

Union of Soviet Socialist Republics (USSR), Rus. *Soyuz Sovetskikh Sotsialisticheskikh Respublik*, republic (1973 est. pop. 248,500,000), 8,649,489 sq mi (22,402,200 sq km), E Europe and N Asia. It is also known as the Soviet Union. The USSR borders on Rumania, Hungary, Czechoslovakia, and Poland in the west; on the Baltic Sea, Finland, and Norway in the northwest; on the Barents, Kara, Laptev, East Siberian and Chukchi seas (arms of the Arctic Ocean) in the north; on the Bering Sea, Sea of Okhotsk, and Sea of Japan (arms of the Pacific Ocean) in the east; on China, Mongolia, and Afghanistan in the south; and on Iran, the Caspian Sea, Turkey, and the Black Sea in the southwest. MOSCOW is the country's capital and largest city. Other cities with more than one million inhabitants are BAKU, GORKY, KHARKOV, KIEV, KUYBYSHEV, LENINGRAD, NOVOSIBIRSK, SVERDLOVSK, and TASHKENT. The Soviet Union is the successor of the Russian Empire, which ended with the Russian Revolution of 1917. Covering about one seventh of the earth's land area, the USSR is the world's largest nation and ranks third (after China and India) in population. Its maximum extent from east to west is about 6,800 mi (10,940 km) and from north to south about 2,800 mi (4,510 km). The USSR is made up of 15 constituent or union republics and can be divided into four regions. European USSR stretches from the country's western boundary to the Urals and Caspian Sea. It includes the Estonian Soviet Socialist Republic, or ESTONIA (capital: TALLINN), the Latvian Soviet Socialist Republic, or LATVIA (RIGA), the Lithuanian Soviet Socialist Republic, or LITHUANIA (VILNIUS), the Belorussian Soviet Socialist Republic, or BELORUSSIA (MINSK), the Ukrainian Soviet Socialist Republic, or UKRAINE (Kiev), the MOLDAVIAN SOVIET SOCIALIST REPUBLIC (KISHINEV), the GEORGIAN SOVIET SOCIALIST REPUBLIC (TBILISI), the ARMENIAN SOVIET SOCIALIST REPUBLIC (YEREVAN), the AZERBAIJAN SOVIET SOCIALIST REPUBLIC (Baku), and part of the RUSSIAN SOVIET FEDERATED SOCIALIST REPUBLIC, or RSFSR (Moscow). Central Asian USSR includes that part of the S Soviet Union from the Caspian Sea to just beyond the Irtysh River. It is made up of the TURKMEN SOVIET SOCIALIST REPUBLIC (ASHKHABAD), the KAZAKH SOVIET SOCIALIST REPUBLIC (ALMA-ATA), the UZBEK SOVIET SOCIALIST REPUBLIC (Tashkent), the TADZHIK SOVIET SOCIALIST REPUBLIC (DUSHANBE), and the KIRGHIZ SOVIET SOCIALIST REPUBLIC (FRUNZE). Siberian USSR (see SIBERIA) comprises the vast region of the RSFSR between the Urals and the western boundaries of Chukchi National Okrug, Magadan Oblast, Khabarovsk Kray and Amur Oblast. The SOVIET FAR EAST, or Far Eastern USSR, the fourth region, is made up of the extreme eastern part of the RSFSR. European USSR lies generally below 1,000 ft (300 m), except for the Urals, the Caucasus, and scattered highlands (for instance, in W Ukrainian SSR). In the north is a narrow belt of tundra extending along the entire length of the country and characterized by permafrost and a light cover of vegetation. The tundra zone in the European USSR includes the KOLA PENINSULA, the islands of KOLGUYEV and NOVAYA ZEMLYA, FRANZ JOSEF LAND, and the mouths of the Onega, Northern Dvina, and Pechora rivers. South of the tundra is a somewhat wider belt of taiga, or evergreen forest, that fans out E of the Urals to include most of Siberian USSR and the Soviet Far East. The taiga zone in European USSR includes lakes Ladoga and Onega (both near the border with Finland), the largest lakes in Europe. South of the taiga is a vast region known as the Russian Plain or Fertile Triangle, which stretches from the country's western boundary to the Yenisei River (in Central Siberian USSR) and takes in the rest of European USSR, except for the arid region between the Black and Caspian seas, which is made up largely of the Caucasus and has a climate and soil cover similar to Central Asian USSR. The Russian Plain includes the country's most fertile and productive farmland. It is drained by several large rivers, including the Dnepr, Don, Volga, Oka, Western Dvina, Neman, Dnestr, Southern Bug, and Kama in European USSR and the Irtysh and Ob in Siberian USSR. The chief rivers of European USSR are connected with one another by a system of artificial waterways; among them are the Baltic-White Sea canal, the Moscow-Volga canal, the VOLGA-BALTIC WATERWAY, and the Volga-Don canal. The vast Pripyat Marshes are in W European USSR. There is a narrow subtropical strip along the Black Sea littoral of the S Crimea and of the Caucasus. Central Asian USSR is an arid region of poor soils. Most of the western part is low lying, but there are highlands in the east and lofty mountains in the south and southeast. Mt. Communism (24,590 ft/7,495 m), the highest point in the USSR, is located in the Pamir range in the extreme south. Central Asian USSR also includes the Aral Sea; lakes Tengiz, Balkhash, and Issyk Kul; the Syr Darya River and parts of the Amu Darya, Ural, Irtysh, and Ili rivers; and the Kyzyl-Kum and Kara-Kum deserts. The tundra zone of Siberian USSR includes the SEVERNAYA ZEMLYA archipelago, the NEW SIBERIAN ISLANDS, and Bolshoy Lyakhov Island in the Arctic Ocean, and the mouths of the Ob, Yenisei, Khatanga, Lena, Yana, and Indigirka rivers. The rest of the region can be divided into three areas—the West Siberian Plain, which lies between the Urals and the Yenisei River and is part of the Russian Plain; the Central Siberian Plateau, which is situated between the Yenisei and Lena rivers; and a mountainous area, which lies E of the Lena and continues into the Soviet Far East. Much of the West Siberian Plain is marshland; the area is drained chiefly by the Ob and Irtysh rivers. Bordering the plain in the southeast is a mountainous area that

includes the Sayan Mts. The Central Siberian Plateau averages about 2,000 ft (610 m) in height and is covered with taiga. Notable rivers there include the Lower Tunguska, the Stony Tunguska, the Angara, the Olenek, and the Vilyuy. The mountainous area in E Siberian USSR, also covered with taiga, includes the Verkhoyansk and Cherskogo (Cherski) ranges in the center and the Patom Plateau, the Yablonovy Range, and Lake Baykal in the southwest. Most of the Soviet Far East, including SAKHALIN Island in the Pacific Ocean, is covered with taiga; however, the north and northeast (extending to the center of KAMCHATKA Peninsula) is covered with tundra. The tundra zone also includes WRANGEL ISLAND in the Arctic Ocean and Cape Dezhnev on the Bering Strait opposite Alaska. The Soviet Far East is largely mountainous, although there are fertile lowlands in the northeast and southeast. In the northeast are the Chukotsk Mts. (situated on the CHUKCHI PENINSULA), the Kolyma Range (see under KOLYMA, river), and Koryaksky Range; in the east is the Dzhugdzhur Range; and in the southeast are the Sikhote-Alin and Bureya ranges. The Amur and Ussuri rivers (which form parts of the boundary with China) are located in the southeast, and the Anadyr and Penzhina rivers are in the northeast. The USSR includes more than 100 ethnic groups. The major ones, according to the 1970 census, were the Russians (129 million), Ukrainians (41 million), and Belorussians (9 million), who all speak Slavic languages and together make up 74% of the country's population; the Uzbek (9 million), Tatars (6 million), Kazakhs (5 million), and Azerbaijan (4.4 million), who all speak a Turkic language; the Armenians (3.6 million); the Georgians (3.2 million); the Lithuanians (2.7 million); and the Moldavians (2.7 million). Between the censuses of 1959 and 1970 the population of the USSR grew by 33 million or 16% (from 209 million to 242 million). In 1970, 56% of the country's inhabitants were classified as urban. About 75% of the population live in European USSR. Russian is the country's official language. Under the ideology on which the Soviet Union is grounded, religion plays a relatively small role in the nation's affairs. The majority of those professing religious faith in the USSR adhere to the Russian Orthodox Church, whose head is the patriarch of Moscow and All Russia (see ORTHODOX EASTERN CHURCH); in the late 1960s it was estimated that the Russian Orthodox Church had 30 million regular worshippers. Also important are the Armenian Orthodox Church and the Georgian Orthodox Church, each of which is an independent body headed by a patriarch. Roman Catholics are numerous in Lithuania, with substantial minorities in Latvia, Belorussia, and W Ukraine; in 1946 about 3.5 million Uniates in Ukraine transferred their allegiance from the Pope in Rome to the Russian Orthodox patriarch in Moscow. Protestantism is represented chiefly by Lutherans, who are concentrated in the Baltic republics (especially Latvia and Estonia), and by Evangelical Christian Baptists. After Christianity, the largest religious following is that of Islam, whose members (about 30 million in the late 1960s) are mostly Turkic-speaking persons living in the southwestern part of the country. The majority of the Muslims belong to the Sunni branch. There are about 2.2 million Jews (virtually all of whom live in European USSR and approximately 500,000 Buddhists. Church and state and church and education are constitutionally separated in the USSR. Education is free, and 8 years of schooling is compulsory; in 1974 a proposal to extend compulsory education to 10 years was being considered. There are more than 800 institutions of higher learning, and education is unusually vocational and scientific in character. The country has 50 universities, the most noteworthy of which are located at Moscow, Leningrad, Kharkov, ODESSA, TARTU, KAZAN, SARATOV, TOMSK, Kiev, Minsk, Baku, Riga, Tashkent, and Alma-Ata. There are also 60 technical universities. A large proportion of higher study is carried on through correspondence schools and in night schools. The Academy of Sciences (the highest academic institution in the USSR) supervises scientific research, directing the work of about 2,650 institutes, departments, and branches.

Economy. When the Bolsheviks came to power in 1917 the Soviet Union was an overwhelmingly agricultural country (more than 80% of its population being classified as rural), although there had been considerable industrial development since the late 19th cent. The economy was devastated by the destruction incurred during World War I and the civil war that followed the Communist takeover. Between 1918 and 1921, a period called "war communism," the state took control of the whole economy. This led to inefficiency and confusion, and in 1921 there was a partial return to the market economy with the adoption of the NEW ECONOMIC POLICY (NEP). In 1928, the NEP was abandoned, and the first FIVE-YEAR PLAN (1928–32) was drawn up by Gosplan (the state planning commission), setting goals and priorities for virtually the entire economy. Under the first plan and subsequent plans to 1970 the production of capital goods was emphasized, and consumer goods were largely neglected. The plan for the period from 1971 to 1975 was the first to set a higher growth rate for the manufacture of consumer goods, but the larger capital-goods sector of the economy was still allocated a greater share of funds. Under that plan capital investment was to be divided chiefly among heavy industry (40%), agriculture (22%), housing (15%), transport and communications (10%), light consumer goods (5%), and consumer services (1%). In the 1970s the state owned and operated the industrial and service sectors of the economy. State farms (sovkhozy), whose land is directly owned and operated by the state, and COLLECTIVE FARMS (kolkhozy), whose land is rented by a group of farmers at no cost and in perpetuity from the state and which are run by elected officials, embraced more than 95% of the country's cultivated land in the early 1970s. However, about 30% of the country's total agricultural output was produced on the small amount of privately held cultivated land; this land, composed of very small household plots (the legal maximum size being 3.7 acres/1.5 hectares), was owned principally by collective farmers. Because the Soviet Union and other Communist countries use a system of national economic accounting that differs from the one employed in the West, and because complete statistics are not available, it is difficult to compare the output of the USSR with that of Western nations. However, Western economists estimated that Soviet output in the early 1970s was equal roughly to half the U.S. gross national product (GNP). This level of production indicates the high level of growth achieved by the USSR in its short history despite the costly changeover from a market economy to a socialist economy and the great destruction and loss of manpower suffered in World War II. Using the Soviet economic measurement of gross social product (which leaves out aspects of the economy such as education, public administration, and defense, which are included in the GNP), in 1971 industry and transport accounted for 78% of output (compared to 42% in 1913), and agriculture contributed 16% (compared to 58% in 1913). In the late 1960s the civilian work force numbered about 110 million, of whom approximately 50% were women. About 34% of the workers were employed in manufacturing and construction, 30% in agriculture and forestry, 11% in education and health, 8% in transport and communications, and 6% in commerce. Soviet farmers cultivate a vast area and produce large quantities of many agricultural commodities. The amount of cultivated land increased from 321 million acres (130 million hectares) in 1933 to 511 million acres (207 million hectares) in 1971, mostly as a result of the campaign (begun in 1954) to open Central Asian USSR and W Siberian USSR to the cultivation of grain. Although 30% more land is farmed in the USSR than in the United States, Soviet farm output is only about 80% of that of the United States. The main reasons for the lower yield per acre are a shorter growing season, more frequent natural impediments (e.g., drought and early frost), and lesser amounts of modern farm machinery and fertilizer. Some analysts also maintain that the lack of enough monetary incentive for farmers on state and collective farms also inhibits output. The following are some of the main agricultural commodities produced in the Soviet Union (with the USSR's world rank in 1972 in terms of quantity produced): wheat (1st); maize (4th); barley (1st); rye (1st); oats (1st); rice (11th); butter (1st); cheese (3d); beef and veal (2d); pork (2d); mutton, lamb, and goat meat (2d); lard (1st); raw sugar (1st); honey (1st); tea (5th); tobacco (3d); cotton (2d); and wool (2d). The main wheat-growing regions are in the Ukraine, in the KUBAN steppe, on the steppes east of the middle Volga River, in N Kazakh SSR, and in SW Siberian USSR. Large numbers of poultry, cattle, hogs, sheep, goats, horses, camels, and reindeer are raised. In 1971 the Soviet Union was the world's third leading fishing nation in terms of the total weight of fish caught. The catch is principally made up of marine fish such as cod, haddock, and herring. In addition, specialties such as sturgeon and black caviar (processed sturgeon roe) are produced in the Caspian Sea and elsewhere. The leading fishing port is ARKHANGELSK, on the White Sea; Okhotsk, on the Sea of Okhotsk, also has important fisheries. In 1971 the USSR ranked 4th in the world in the number of whales caught. Approximately one third of the land area in the Soviet Union is covered with forest, about three quarters of which is made up of softwood coniferous trees. Virtually all the forest land is owned and exploited by the state. The USSR is the world's leading producer of timber. The Soviet Union is extremely rich in mineral resources. The following are the main minerals produced (with the country's rank in 1972 in quantity extracted): antimony (4th); asbestos (2d); bauxite (4th); chromite (1st); coal and lignite (1st); cobalt (3d); copper ore (5th); fluorite (3d); gold (2d); iron ore (1st); lead (2d); manganese ore (1st); mercury (2d); molybdenum (3d); nickel (2d); crude petroleum (2d); phosphate rock (2d); platinum (1st); potash (1st); pyrite (1st); salt (3d); silver (3d); sulfur (4th); tin (3d); tungsten (1st); and zinc ore (2d). Coal and lignite are found mainly in the DONETS BASIN (Ukraine), around VORKUTA (NE European USSR), in the MOSCOW BASIN, in the KUZNETSK BASIN (east of Novosibirsk), in the Karaganda Basin (Kazakh SSR), on the Taymyr Peninsula, and in the TUNGUSKA BASIN and Lena Basin (both in E Siberian USSR). Petroleum is produced principally in W Siberian USSR (notably at Agansk and around TYUMEN) and also at Baku, GROZNY, and MAIKOP in the Caucasus and in the Ural-Volga region at Kuybyshev, in the BASHKIR AUTONOMOUS SOVIET SOCIALIST REPUBLIC, and around PERM. Iron ore is mined in the Urals, at KRIVOY ROG, around Kursk, in Kazakh SSR, and in many other areas; manganese ore is found at NIKOPOL (Ukraine) and CHIATURA (Georgian SSR); chromite is mined in Kazakh SSR; gold is produced in E Siberian USSR, notably in the Kolyma Gold Fields and at ALDAN; diamonds are found in the Vilyui River Basin in the YAKUT AUTONOMOUS SOVIET SOCIALIST REPUBLIC; and bauxite is mined in W Siberian USSR, near Leningrad, and in Kazakh SSR. The Soviet Union is a great industrial nation whose factories produce a wide range of manufactures. There has been a heavy emphasis on the production of capital goods, but in the late 1960s and early 70s growing attention was given to consumer goods such as passenger vehicles, household appliances, and clothing. The country's leading industrial centers are also its largest cities, and most of them are situated in European USSR—Moscow, Leningrad, Gorky, Kuybyshev, ROSTOV-NA-DONU, and VOLGOGRAD in the RSFSR; Kiev, Kharkov, Odessa, DNEPROPETROVSK, and DONETSK in the Ukraine; Baku and Tbilisi in the Transcaucasus; and SVERDLOVSK in the Urals. Increasingly, however, cities in other parts of the country are becoming major industrial centers; they include Ashkhabad, Tashkent, Alma-Ata, Novosibirsk, Chita, and Vladivostok. In 1971 and 1972 the Soviet Union was the world's leading producer of crude steel, a position formerly held by the United States (and regained by a slim margin in 1973). The Soviet Union has great amounts of energy resources, notably coal, petroleum, natural gas, and water power. Between 1940 and 1971 the production of electricity increased 16-fold, reaching 800 billion kilowatt hours in 1971 (about half the U.S. output and second in the world). Large hydroelectric facilities are located on the Dnepr, Volga, Kama, Angara, and Yenisei rivers. Nuclear power is also being developed. European USSR has a dense rail network, as does Siberian USSR between the Urals and Novosibirsk. The TRANS-SIBERIAN RAILROAD runs along S Siberia to Vladivostok on the Pacific Ocean; it is linked with the TURKISTAN-SIBERIA RAILROAD, which in turn is connected with the TRANS-CASPIAN RAILROAD. All major rail lines use broad-gauge tracks, unlike those of other European countries. The country's all-weather road system is relatively poor, and most freight transportation is by train rather than by truck. Most of the USSR is linked by airplane, and there is service to numerous foreign cities. The Soviet Union has access to several seas, but most of its ports are icebound in winter. Its only ice-free ports are those on the Black Sea (notably Odessa, NIKOLAYEV, and ZHDANOV); KALININGRAD, on the Baltic; and MURMANSK, on the Arctic Ocean. Other large ports include Arkhangelsk, Leningrad, Riga, and Vladivostok. The country's great rivers, many of which are joined by artificial waterways, provide important inland traffic lanes. The Soviet Union carries on a substantial foreign trade, although not as large as might be expected given the output of its economy. In 1972 the total value of Soviet international trade was equivalent to $38 billion, whereas that of the United States was $108 billion and that of West Germany $103 billion. In the period from 1964 to 1972 the USSR had a small annual trade deficit five times and an annual trade surplus four times. The principal exports are machinery, crude petroleum, iron and steel, and timber; the chief imports are machinery, manufactured consumer goods, and foodstuffs. About two thirds of Soviet trade is with the Communist nations of Eastern Europe, notably East Germany, Poland, Czechoslovakia, and Bulgaria. International trade is a monopoly of the state, and it is conducted in accordance with the government's overall goals for the economy. A noteworthy feature of Soviet trade relations in the late 1960s and early 70s were the agreements with private Western firms to build major installations in the USSR. Thus, Fiat of Italy helped build (1967–70) a motor-vehicle factory at Togliatti, a U.S. firm agreed (1973) to build a large international trade center in Moscow , and a West German consortium contracted (1974) to construct a huge iron and steel plant at KURSK. The USSR is a member of the COUNCIL FOR MUTUAL ECONOMIC ASSISTANCE (COMECON)

Government. Soviet Russia was the first state to be based on Marxist SOCIALISM (see also MARXISM; COMMUNISM). As officially created by the treaty of union of 1922, which joined the RSFSR, the Ukraine, Belorussia, and TRANSCAUCASIA (divided in 1936 into the Georgian, Armenian, and Azerbaijan republics), the USSR comprised Russia and the remainder of the Russian Empire (for its earlier history see RUSSIA) as it had emerged from the Russian Revolution of 1917 and the ensuing civil war. The civil war had been complicated by Allied intervention and by war (1920) with Poland. The peace treaty (1921) with Poland (see RIGA, TREATY OF), the declarations of independence of Finland, Estonia, Latvia, and Lithuania, and the seizure by Rumania of Bessarabia had greatly reduced the size of the former Russian Empire, establishing what the governments of Western Europe called a cordon sanitaire (quarantine belt) separating Communist Russia from the rest of Europe. Temporarily accepting this quarantine, Vladimir I. LENIN and the other leaders of the Soviet Union set about repairing the damage caused by the revolution and the civil war. The constitution of 1924 was based theoretically on the dictatorship of the proletariat and founded economically on the public ownership of the land and the means of production according to the revolutionary proclamation of 1917. In 1936 a new constitution (called the Stalin constitution) was promulgated, and it was still in effect in 1975. The 1936 constitution had a veneer of radical innovation (for instance, direct elections and the secret ballot were introduced), but in practice the state operated much as it had before, with the Communist party of the Soviet Union (CPSU; see COMMUNIST PARTY, in the USSR) continuing to be by far the most important political organization in the country. The party indirectly controls all levels of government, and the general secretary of the Communist party is usually the most powerful person in the USSR. The CPSU had about 14.5 million members in the early 1970s. The chief administrative divisions of the USSR were set up so that each included one preponderant ethnic group that was given formal autonomy but little actual power. The USSR is made up of 15 constituent republics (listed above), each of which has its own government (modeled after the national system) and is entitled, under the constitution, to maintain a separate army and to have its own foreign representation. However, no separate military forces are in fact maintained, and the only republics to have diplomats abroad are the Ukrainian SSR and the Belorussian SSR, which in 1945 were admitted into the United Nations. In practice, the governments of the constituent republics (and of the other administrative divisions) have authority only in the field of cultural affairs and are mostly concerned with implementing national policy. The constituent republics have the constitutional right to secede from the USSR, but it is highly unlikely that they will ever exercise this right. The next most important administrative divisions, after the constitutent republics, are the autonomous republics, of which there are 20 (16 in the RSFSR, two in the Georgian SSR, and one each in the Azerbaijan SSR and the Uzbek SSR); each has a unicameral supreme soviet and a council of ministers. Each of the other administrative divisions has only a unicameral soviet. These divisions include autonomous oblasts (five in the RSFSR and one each in the Georgian SSR, the Azerbaijan SSR, and the Tadzhik SSR); oblasts; national okrugs (all 10 in the RSFSR); krays; and urban and rural districts (Rus. *rayons*). Under the 1936 constitution national legislative power is vested in the Supreme Soviet (Rus. *Verkhovny Soviet*). It is divided into the Soviet of the Union, elected by universal suffrage on the basis of one deputy for every 300,000 citizens, and the Soviet of the Nationalities, also elected by universal suffrage and containing 32 representatives from each of the constituent republics, 11 representatives from each of the autonomous oblasts, and 1 representative from each of the national okrugs. Members of the Supreme Soviet must be either members of the Communist party or so-called nonparty persons (the only legal political party being the Communist party); they serve four-year terms. Laws are passed by a simple majority in both houses; constitutional amendments require a two-thirds majority. The Supreme Soviet usually meets for a short session twice a year. In a joint session, it elects a presidium, or permanent committee, headed by a chairman, or president (who is the official head of state of the USSR), and also including one deputy chairman from each constituent republic, a secretary, and 20 members. Among the presidium's various functions are convening (or dissolving) the Supreme Soviet, carrying out the functions of the Supreme Soviet when it is not in session, interpreting existing laws, issuing edicts, and conducting national referenda. The Supreme Soviet appoints the council of ministers (called the council of people's commissars until 1946), headed by a chairman (known as the country's premier), which is the chief executive and administrative body of the state and whose members direct the country's ministries and some of its committees and departments. The chairmen of the councils of ministers of the constituent republics are ex officio members of the national council of ministers. Communications media (especially newspapers, films, radio, and television) are important arms of the government. The leading daily newspapers are *Pravda* (circulation 7.5 million) published by the central committee of the CPSU, and *Izvestia* (circulation 8 million), put out by the presidium of the Supreme Soviet. *Pravda* generally contains the most important articles on public policy and is read closely by CPSU members and officials, as well as by foreign journalists and scholars.

Armed Forces. The military in the USSR is headed by the minister of defense and is divided into an army, navy, air force, air defense command, and strategic rocket force. In the early 1970s it was estimated that the Soviet Union had 3.3 million soldiers in uniform, compared with approximately 590,000 in 1927, 1.4 million in 1937, 11.4 million in 1945, 5.8 million in 1955, and 2.4 million in 1960. In 1955 the USSR organized and became a charter member of the WARSAW TREATY ORGANIZATION.

History. The Russian Revolution of 1917, Soviet Russia's withdrawal from World War I, and the civil war (1918–20) are covered in the articles RUSSIAN REVOLUTION and BREST-LITOVSK, TREATY OF. The fundamental policy of the Communist party of the Soviet Union (CPSU) from its beginning has been complete socialization. In 1922, Germany recognized the Soviet Union (see RAPALLO, TREATY OF), and most other Western nations except the United States followed suit in 1924. A struggle for leadership followed Lenin's death in early 1924; Joseph V. STALIN and Leon TROTSKY were the two main protagonists, with Stalin emerging victorious by the late 1920s. Stalin's program called for a more gradual transformation of Soviet society than did Trotsky's and had as its primary objective the consolidation of Communism in the USSR rather than Trotsky's ideal of immediate world revolution. Nevertheless, the Soviet Union continued to guide the Communist parties abroad through the Third International, or COMINTERN, and at home the New Economic Policy instituted in 1921 was replaced by full government planning with the adoption of the first Five-Year Plan (1928–32). A system of collective and state farms was imposed over widespread peasant opposition, which was expressed notably in the slaughter of livestock. Those comparatively prosperous peasants (called kulaks) who refused to join the new agricultural institutions were "liquidated" by drastic means. More than 5 million peasant households were eliminated, their property was confiscated, and most of the peasants were sent as forced laborers to Siberia. By the end of the 1930s, 99% of the cultivated land was in collective farms (the system of state farms was established successfully only after World War II). Industrialization was accelerated, and the production of desperately needed industrial raw materials and capital equipment was stressed at the expense of consumer goods. One of the major results of the successive Five-Year Plans was the spectacular industrial and agricultural development of the Urals, Siberian USSR, and Central Asian USSR. The level of literacy, very low in 1917, was steadily raised in all parts of the country, and free medical and social services were extended to the population. At the same time, the state (and behind it, the CPSU) increased its hold over all political, social, and cultural aspects of life. Education and media of public information passed under state control. Freedom of movement was severely restricted. All criticism of public policy, if not authorized by the state, was banned. The SECRET POLICE became a major instrument of state control, and much power was given to the civil service. The system of controls gave rise to a large and powerful bureaucracy, called the "new class" by some analysts. Religious bodies were severely persecuted in the early years of the Soviet Union, but in the mid-1930s there was a measure of relaxation in official policy, probably because antireligious propaganda in the schools had already taken effect among the younger generation. However, relations with the Roman Catholic Church and with the Jewish community remained hostile. The mid-1930s also saw a conservative trend in official attitudes toward culture: Family life was emphasized again, and divorces and abortions were made difficult to obtain; great men and events in pre-1917 Russian history were extolled in literature (e.g., in works by Aleksey N. TOLSTOY) and in films (especially those of Sergei EISENSTEIN); and experimentation in education gave way to a return to structure and discipline. In 1936 the Stalin constitution was issued, and it included many features of Western democracies, which, however, were more window-dressing than true indications of the distribution of power in the Soviet system. The CPSU continued to control the government and run the country, and Stalin, as the Wisest of the Wise, was firmly in control of the party. Following the murder (1934) of Sergei M. KIROV, one of Stalin's closest associates, and the announcement of the discovery of an alleged plot against Stalin's regime headed by the exiled Trotsky, there began a series of purges that culminated in the great purge from 1936 to 1938. The armed forces and the CPSU were purged of all allegedly dissident persons; the victims were generally sentenced to death or to long terms of hard labor. Much of the purge was carried out in secret, and only a few cases were tried in public "show trials." Among the many thousand victims of the purges were such prominent CPSU leaders as Grigori E. ZINOVIEV, Lev B. KAMENEV, Karl RADEK, Nikolai BUKHARIN, and Aleksey I. RYKOV and military figures like Marshal Mikhail N. TUKHACHEVSKY. Independent influence in society was thus ended, and monolithic unity under Stalin was achieved by 1939. Soviet foreign policy, long hampered by the hostility of the nations of Europe and America and by pervasive mutual distrust, was carried out first by Georgi CHICHERIN and from 1930 by Maxim M. LITVINOV. In 1933 the United States recognized the USSR, and in 1934 the Soviet Union was admitted into the League of Nations. In the mid-1930s the USSR sought friendly relations with its neighbors, declared its renunciation of imperialistic expansion, and advocated total disarmament. Soviet-controlled Communist parties in other countries became friendlier to more moderate socialists and to liberals and in 1936 joined leftist Popular Front coalitions in France and Spain. The Western nations did not invite the USSR to take part in the negotiations with Germany leading to the MUNICH PACT (1938), and a radical shift in Soviet foreign policy ensued. V. M. MOLOTOV replaced Litvinov as foreign minister. On Aug. 23, 1939, the USSR concluded a nonaggression pact with Nazi Germany, which shortly afterward invaded Poland, precipitating WORLD WAR II. Soviet troops also entered (Sept., 1939) Poland, which was divided between Germany and the USSR. Lithuania, Latvia, and Estonia were occupied (Sept.-Oct., 1939) by the Soviet Union, and in mid-1940 were transformed into constituent republics of the USSR. Finland opposed Soviet demands, and the FINNISH-RUSSIAN WAR of 1939–40 resulted; it ended in a hard-earned Soviet victory. Finland ceded territory, which was organized into the Karelo-Finnish SSR (which in 1956 became part of the RSFSR as the Karelian Autonomous Soviet Socialist Republic). Rumania was forced (1940) to cede Bessarabia and N Bukovina, and the Moldavian SSR was created. In April, 1941, a nonaggression treaty with Japan was signed. Although defense preparations were accelerated (probably in anticipation of eventual war with Germany), when Germany attacked on June 22, 1941, the Soviet Union was caught by surprise. Rumania, Finland, Hungary, Slovakia, and Italy joined in the invasion of the USSR. By the end of 1941 the Germans had overrun Belorussia and most of the Ukraine, had surrounded Leningrad, and were converging on Moscow. A Soviet counter-offensive saved Moscow, but in June,

1942, the Germans launched a new drive directed against Stalingrad (now called Volgograd) and the Caucasus petroleum fields. Stalingrad held out, and the surrender (Feb. 2, 1943) of 330,000 Axis troops there marked a turning point in the war. The Soviets drove the invaders back in an almost uninterrupted offensive and in 1944 entered Poland and the Balkan Peninsula. Early in 1945, German resistance in Hungary was overcome, and Soviet troops marched into East Prussia. The converging Soviet armies then closed in on BERLIN in a climactic drive. On May 2, 1945, Berlin fell; on May 7 the USSR together with the Western Allies accepted the surrender of Germany. The Soviet victory was obtained at the great price of at least 20 million lives (including civilian casualties) and staggering material losses. The United States contributed much aid to the USSR through LEND-LEASE. Understandings concerning the conduct of war and postwar policies had been reached by the USSR, the United States, and Great Britain at the MOSCOW CONFERENCES (1941–47), the TEHERAN CONFERENCE (1943), the YALTA CONFERENCE (1945), and the POTSDAM CONFERENCE (1945). In accordance with a previous agreement, the Soviet Union declared war on Japan on Aug. 8, 1945. A swift campaign brought Soviet forces deep into Manchuria and Korea by the date (Sept. 2, 1945) Japan surrendered. As a direct result of the war, the USSR received the southern half of Sakhalin Island and the KURIL ISLANDS from Japan; the northern part of East Prussia from Germany; and some additional territory from Finland. By agreements in 1945 with Poland and Czechoslovakia the USSR also vastly increased the area of the Belorussian and Ukrainian republics. Cooperation between the USSR and the Western powers—already shaky during the war—ceased soon after the armistice, and relations between the Soviet Union and the United States (which emerged from the war as the two chief powers in the world) became increasingly strained, leading to the international tension of the COLD WAR. Friction became particularly acute in the jointly occupied countries of Germany, Austria, and Korea and in the UNITED NATIONS (of which the USSR was a charter member), preventing the conclusion of joint peace treaties with Germany, Austria, and Korea and agreements over REPARATIONS and the control of nuclear weapons. Increasing Soviet influence in Poland, Czechoslovakia, Hungary, Rumania, Bulgaria and Albania and the continued tight control of East Germany created fears in the Western world of unlimited Soviet expansion, as did the creation (1947) of the COMINFORM (which in a limited sense was the successor of the Comintern). The USSR, on the other hand, justified its policies by its fears of encirclement by hostile capitalist nations. In 1948, Yugoslavia declared its independence from the "Soviet bloc," as the Communist nations of East Europe came to be known. In 1948 and 1949 the USSR unsuccessfully tried to prevent supplies from reaching the sectors of Berlin occupied by the Western Allies. In 1949, the USSR recognized the newly established Communist government of China, and a 30-year alliance was signed in early 1950. Relations with the Western powers worsened considerably after the outbreak of the KOREAN WAR (1950–53), which the West ascribed to Soviet instigation, and Stalin's dictatorship took on an increasingly tyrannical character.

The Khrushchev Era (1953–64). The death of Stalin on March 5, 1953, ushered in a new era in Soviet history. "Collective leadership" at first replaced one-man rule, and after the arrest (June, 1953) of Lavrenti P. BERIA the power of the secret police was curtailed. Soviet citizens began to gain a greater degree of personal freedom and civil security. Georgi MALENKOV succeeded Stalin as premier, while Nikita S. KHRUSHCHEV, as first secretary of the central committee of the CPSU, played an increasingly important role in policy planning. In 1955, Malenkov was replaced as premier by Nikolai BULGANIN. At the 20th All Union Congress (Feb. 1956), Khrushchev bitterly denounced the dictatorial rule and personality of Stalin in a secret speech that was later obtained by foreigners. Khrushchev replaced Bulganin as premier in 1958, thus becoming leader of both the government and the CPSU; he modified some of the more dictatorial aspects of Stalin's rule, but the CPSU continued to dominate all facets of Soviet life. Khrushchev retained many of Stalin's basic economic policies, but there were important changes. Management of the economy (especially industry) was decentralized (1957) in an attempt to reduce the inefficiency and delays resulting from central bureaucratic control. Numerous national ministries were disbanded. In agriculture, vast tracts of virgin land (especially in Central Asian USSR and W Siberian USSR) were opened to the cultivation of grain, notably maize; taxation of collective farmers' private plots was reduced; and the Machine Tractor Stations, established in the late 1920s and 30s as a means of supervising the collective farms by controlling their use of farm machinery, were abolished in 1958 and their equipment sold to the collectives. Somewhat larger amounts of consumer goods were manufactured. In 1957–58 the noted author Boris L. PASTERNAK was heavily censured for his novel *Doctor Zhivago*, which contained a general criticism of life in the Soviet Union immediately after the Revolution. Foreign policy became more flexible; the Soviet Union negotiated a peace treaty with Austria (1955), established diplomatic relations with West Germany (1955), restored the Porkkala naval base to Finland (1955), dissolved the Cominform (1956), allowed foreigners to travel in the USSR, and set up cultural exchanges with Western nations. In addition, it was considered proper beginning in 1955 to form alliances with, and give aid to, the non-Communist nations of the Middle East, especially Egypt and Syria, and other non-Communist underdeveloped countries. Relations with the Communist countries of Eastern Europe were formalized and strengthened by the establishment of the Council for Mutual Economic Assistance and the Warsaw Treaty Organization. In June, 1956, a revolt against Soviet influence in Poland was defeated by the Polish army, but the Poles managed to gain some concessions from Moscow; an uprising in Hungary in Oct., 1956, was crushed ruthlessly by Soviet troops. In the technological race between the Soviet Union and the West (principally the United States), the USSR exploded (1953) a hydrogen bomb; announced (1957) the development of intercontinental ballistic missiles; orbited (1957) the first artificial earth satellite (called Sputnik); and in 1961 sent Yuri GAGARIN in the first manned orbital flight. In Sept., 1959, Khrushchev undertook a 10-day tour of the United States. In May, 1960, a four-power (USSR, United States, France, and Great Britain) summit conference scheduled for Paris was aborted when a U. S. reconnaissance airplane ("U-2") crashed in the Soviet Union and U.S. President Dwight D. Eisenhower refused to apologize for the aerial spying. The USSR participated in the international negotiations on nuclear DISARMAMENT and agreed (1958) to a voluntary moratorium on nuclear tests, but resumed testing in 1961. In 1963, the USSR signed a milestone treaty with the United States and Great Britain banning atmospheric nuclear tests. The question of divided Berlin (a focal point of the cold war) remained unresolved through several rounds of negotiations and a number of "Berlin crises." In June 1964, the Soviet Union signed a separate peace treaty with East Germany. At the 22d CPSU congress in 1961 the attack on Stalin was continued, and the reputations of many purge victims of the 1930s were rehabilitated. Stalin's body was removed from its place of honor in the Kremlin next to Lenin's; his name was erased from the geography of the USSR (e.g., Stalingrad was renamed Volgograd), and pictures and statues of him were removed. Also at the 22d congress the Sino-Soviet conflict (which had begun in the late 1950s) emerged, stated at first in terms of a dispute with Albania (a close ally of China). Among other things, China had accused the USSR of betraying Marxism-Leninism by attempting to negotiate with the West, while Khrushchev and his administration insisted that Communist expansion could be accomplished in conjunction with a policy of "peaceful coexistence" with states having different social and economic systems. In Oct., 1962, despite seemingly improved relations with the West, the USSR came into sharp conflict with the United States over the presence of Soviet missiles in CUBA. The United States demanded the removal of the missiles and blockaded the island to keep out Soviet ships. Backing down, Khrushchev agreed to withdraw the missiles, and the crisis passed. Some analysts maintain that the "Cuban missile crisis" marked a turning point in U.S.-Soviet relations because the USSR realized the extent to which the United States would protect what it considered its vital interests. In 1963 a "hot line" (direct and instantaneous teletype communications) was set up between the heads of government of the USSR and the United States.

The USSR since 1965. In a well-prepared and bloodless move by CPSU leaders, Khrushchev was ousted from his positions of power Oct. 14–15, 1964. He was replaced as first secretary of the CPSU by Leonid I. BREZHNEV (who in 1960 had become chairman of the presidium of the Supreme Soviet) and as premier by Alexei N. KOSYGIN. The official reasons given for Khrushchev's ouster were his advanced age (70) and his declining health. The real reason was dissatisfaction with the policies and style of his government. Specifically, Khrushchev was criticized for the inadequate performance of the economy, especially the agricultural sector (there had been a bad harvest in 1963); for the humiliation of the USSR in the Cuban missile crisis; for the widening rift with China; and for his flamboyant personal style, which it was said created a "cult of personality." Several persons closely associated with Khrushchev also lost their posts; they included his son-in-law Alexei I. Adzhubei, the editor of the government newspaper *Izvestia*. In July, 1964, Anastas I. MIKOYAN succeeded Brezhnev as chairman of the presidium; Mikoyan was replaced in Dec., 1965, by Nikolai V. PODGORNY. The new leaders stressed collective leadership (as opposed to Khrushchev's one-man rule), but because of his position at the head of the CPSU Brezhnev held an advantage and by 1970 was clearly the most powerful person in the country, followed at a considerable distance by Kosygin. In 1966 the position of first secretary of the CPSU again was called general secretary (as it had been until 1952), and the presidium of the supreme soviet reverted to the name politburo (short for political bureau). Becoming a member of the CPSU was made much more difficult than under Khrushchev. In 1973, Defense Minister Andrei A. GRECHKO, security police chief Yuri V. ANDROPOV, and Foreign Minister Andrei A. GROMYKO—all close associates of Brezhnev—were made full members of the politburo in the first major shake-up of that important body since 1964. In the later 1960s the official attitude toward Stalin became somewhat less hostile. In internal affairs the new leaders stressed economic development, and in foreign affairs they generally pursued peaceful coexistence with the West (although there were several major indirect confrontations). Claiming that Khrushchev's policy of decentralizing administration had been ill advised, his successors reestablished 28 national ministries in 1965. However, at the same time a major program to decentralize decision-making in industry was begun. In doing this the Soviet leaders generally followed the ideas of Yevsei G. Liberman, a professor of economics, who held that capitalist price and profit mechanisms should be used to guide industrial firms; it was argued that they more accurately reflected supply and demand conditions than did national directives, which tended to be abstract. Under the Liberman system individual firms made their own decisions on levels of production based on prevailing prices, and their efficiency was judged individually on the amount of profit they made. By the early 1970s the vast majority of industrial firms were operating on this basis. The new system allowed much more latitude to the individual firms, but they still had to operate within the constraints of the overall Five-Year Plans, which established the basic course of the Soviet economy, and of the annual national government budget. Industrial production (and the productivity of individual workers) increased steadily after 1964, but not as rapidly as the leadership desired, largely because available technology was not sufficiently advanced. To make up for this deficiency, a number of major contracts were signed (beginning in the late 1960s) with Western firms to build factories and other installations incorporating the latest technology. Agricultural production increased dramatically. However, in 1972 there was a very bad grain harvest because of unfavorable weather conditions, and the Soviet Union was forced to purchase 28 million metric tons of grain from the West (mainly from the United States). In 1973 the grain harvest reached the record level of 222 million metric tons; from 1961 to 1965 the average annual harvest had been 130 million metric tons. Beginning in the mid-1960s leading writers, scientists, and intellectuals protested certain aspects of Soviet life, especially curbs on the free flow of ideas, corruption in government, and inefficiency. Although the dissidents were small in number and had little popular support, they were treated harshly by the government, many being sentenced to terms in prison or being forced into exile. The leading dissidents included the writers Andrei Sinyavsky (whose pen name was Abram Tertz), Yuri Daniel (whose pen name was Nikolai Arzhak), Anatoly V. Kuznetsov (who defected to Great Britain in 1969), Aleksandr I. SOLZHENITSYN (who was forced to leave the country in early 1974), Aleksandr Ginzburg, Yuri Galanskov, and Andrei Amalrik; the editor Aleksandr Tvardovski; the nuclear physicist Andrei D. Sakharov; the geneticist Zhores A. Medvedev (who left the country in 1973 and was not allowed to return); the economist Viktor Krasin; and the historian Pyotr Yakir. Stalin's daughter, Svetlana ALLILUYEVA, defected to the West in 1967 and took up residence in the United States. From the later 1960s many Jews asked to leave the country, mainly in order to settle in Israel. For a time the government made emigration for them exceptionally difficult (for instance, by charging a high "emigration tax" allegedly to cover the cost of the person's education in the USSR), but in the early 1970s considerable numbers of Jews were able to emigrate (partly because the emigration tax was suspended). Between 1971 and 1973 about 75,000 Jews left the USSR, compared to approximately 2,000 annually in preceding years. In 1974 the USSR agreed to ease its emigration policy in return for favored-nation trade status with the United States. Also contributing to disquiet in the country were the spokesmen of several ethnic groups (notably the Lithuanians, Latvians, and Tatars) who vociferously demanded increased autonomy for their people. Formal Soviet-U.S. relations continued to be good after 1964, but there were serious indirect conflicts in Vietnam (where the USSR gave North Vietnam much material aid, but did not send troops, to oppose U.S. forces active in South Vietnam), during the Indo-Pakistani War of 1971 (when the USSR aided India and the United States backed Pakistan), and during the 1973 Arab-Israeli War (when U.S. President Richard M. Nixon, believing that the Soviet Union was about to send troops to back the Arab side, instituted a worldwide precautionary alert of U.S. forces). In a meeting at Glassboro, N.J., in 1967, Premier Kosygin and U.S. President Lyndon B. Johnson discussed Middle Eastern affairs and other matters. In 1969, the USSR, the United States, and about 100 other nations signed a treaty banning the spread of nuclear weapons to countries not possessing them. Strategic arms limitation talks (SALT) between the Soviet Union and the United States began in 1969, and they were continuing in 1974. When President Nixon visited Moscow in 1972, an agreement partially limiting strategic arms was signed, (an agreement that was renewed during Nixon's 1974 visit to the USSR), along with accords on cooperation in space exploration, environmental matters, and trade. By this time Soviet-U.S. relations were described as having entered an era of détente, and the cold war was said to have ended. In 1973, Brezhnev toured the United States and met with Nixon. In 1968, Soviet relations with the Communist nations of Eastern Europe reached a critical stage when Soviet troops (and forces of some of the other Warsaw Treaty Organization members) invaded (Aug. 21) Czechoslovakia in a successful effort to curb the trend toward liberalization there (and indirectly to reduce Czechoslovakia's increasing contact with Western European nations). Brezhnev declared (in what became known as the "Brezhnev doctrine") that Communist countries had the right to intervene in other Communist nations whose actions threatened the international Communist movement. Rumania and Yugoslavia explicitly denounced the Brezhnev doctrine, but relations between the USSR and Eastern Europe soon improved, and by the early 1970s there was much less friction. A major objective of Soviet foreign policy in the early 1970s was to gain official recognition of the post-World War II settlement in Europe. In 1970 a landmark treaty with West Germany was signed (ratified in 1972) confirming existing boundaries in Europe (notably the eastern border of East Germany) and also renouncing the use of force to settle disputes. In 1972 the USSR, the United States, Great Britain, and France signed an accord regularizing the position of Berlin, thus making future "Berlin crises" unlikely. In the same year meetings were held to set up a European security conference, which the USSR hoped would also help make permanent the status quo in Europe, and the conference formally opened in 1973. Also in 1973 the North Atlantic Treaty Organization and the Warsaw Treaty Organization began negotiations on the mutual and balanced reduction of military forces in Europe. The Sino-Soviet conflict worsened after 1964. In 1969 there were numerous border clashes, including a major one over control of Damansky Island in the Ussuri River. Both countries enlarged their border forces and maintained them in the early 1970s despite somewhat less tense relations. In the 1967 Arab-Israeli War, the Soviet Union backed the Arabs rhetorically but gave them little material assistance. In 1970-71 the USSR equipped Egypt's army with modern weapons and also sent about 16,000 military advisers and soldiers. However, in mid-1972 Egypt forced virtually all Soviet military personnel to leave the country, apparently feeling that the USSR was delivering insufficient quantities of sophisticated arms. Soviet-Egyptian relations improved soon thereafter, however, and during the 1973 Arab-Israeli War the Soviet Union played a major role in equipping both the Egyptian and Syrian armies. The USSR continued to give considerable assistance to underdeveloped countries after 1964. At Tashkent in 1966, Kosygin mediated a dispute between India and Pakistan over Kashmir. In the early 1970s there was a notable increase in both the size and quality of the Soviet military, especially the navy. In the "space race" with the United States, the USSR did not place a man on the moon (as the United States did in 1969) but made other important, but less spectacular, exploratory probes of space. In 1973, Soviet and American teams began training for a joint manned space flight scheduled for 1975. Geographical works on the USSR include S. S. Balzak et al., ed., *Economic Geography of the USSR* (tr. 1949); Theodore Shabad, *Geography of the USSR: A Regional Survey* (1951, repr. 1958); D. J. Hooson, *The Soviet Union* (1966); P. E. Lydolph, *Geography of the USSR* (1970); C. H. Harris, *Cities of the Soviet Union* (1970); J. C. Dewdney, *A Geography of the Soviet Union* (2d ed. 1971). Two histories of Russia that deal with the USSR extensively are George Vernadsky, *A History of Russia* (5th ed. 1961) and S. S. Harcave, *Russia: A History* (6th ed. 1968). See also G. F. Kennan, *Russia and the West under Lenin and Stalin* (1961); Leonard Schapiro, *The Government and Politics of the Soviet Union* (rev. ed. 1965); R. W. Campbell, *Soviet Economic Power* (2d ed. 1966); J. P. Nettl, *The Soviet Achievement* (1967); Robert Conquest, ed., *Justice and the Legal System in the USSR* (1968), *Religion in the USSR* (1968), and *The Soviet Political System* (1968); Alec Nove, *An Economic History of the USSR* (1969); R. F. Rosser, *An Introduction to Soviet Foreign Policy* (1969); Theodore Shabad, *Basic Industrial Resources of the USSR* (1969); Michael Ellman, *Soviet Planning Today* (1971); Raymond Hutchings, *Soviet Economic Development* (1971); D. W. Treadgold, *Twentieth Century Russia* (3d ed. 1971); Max Beloff, *The Foreign Policy of Soviet Russia, 1929-1941* (2 vol., 1947-49; repr. 1955) and *Soviet Policy in the Far East, 1944-51* (1953, repr. 1972); Georg von Rauch, *A History of Soviet Russia* (6th ed. 1972); Merwyn Matthews, *Class and Society in Soviet Russia* (1973); A. B. Ulam, *Expansion and Coexistence: The History of Soviet Foreign Policy, 1917-1967* (1968), *The Rivals: America and Russia since World War II* (1971), and *Stalin: The Man and His Era* (1974); J. A. Armstrong, *Ideology, Politics, and Government in the Soviet Union* (3d ed. 1974).

Union Pacific Railroad, transportation company chartered (1862) by Congress to build part of the nation's first transcontinental railroad line. Under terms of the Pacific Railroads Act, the Union Pacific was authorized to build a line westward from Omaha, Nebr., to the California-Nevada line, where it was to connect with the Central Pacific RR—which was to be built simultaneously from Sacramento, Calif. Each railroad company, after completion of an initial 40 mi (64 km) of track, was to be granted 6,400 acres (2,589 hectares) of public lands and a loan of from $16,000 to $48,000 for each mile of track laid. In 1864, Congress doubled the land grant, considerably eased the terms of government loans, and allowed the two railroad companies to borrow private capital. Also in 1864 and again in 1866, the Central Pacific was authorized to build eastward beyond the Nevada line. In 1865 construction of the Union Pacific was begun from Omaha westward, and a long succession of harrowing construction problems, Indian troubles, and delays were encountered. Nevertheless, on May 10, 1869, the Union Pacific joined the Central Pacific, NW of Ogden, Utah, thus connecting the Missouri River and the Pacific Ocean by rail and completing the nation's first transcontinental railroad. The joining of the roads was marked in ceremony by the driving of a golden spike. Construction of both roads involved tremendous profiteering, and in 1872 the scandal involving the CRÉDIT MOBILIER OF AMERICA, an ephemeral holding company to which most of the Union Pacific's liquid assets had been transferred (1867), was unearthed. The fraud, combined with later mismanagement and overextensions, left the Union Pacific with heavy financial burdens, and in 1893 the company went into receivership. It was reincorporated (1897) as the Union Pacific Railroad Company in Utah, and under the management of Edward H. HARRIMAN the railroad was expanded, vastly improved, and stabilized. In 1901, Harriman added the Southern Pacific (see SOUTHERN PACIFIC COMPANY) and the Central Pacific to his expanding railroad empire, and his spectacular attempt to control the Northern Pacific led to the formation of the Northern Securities Company, a huge rail monopoly that controlled transportation throughout the Northwest. Under pressure from President Theodore Roosevelt, the giant holding company was dissolved by the Supreme Court in 1904. Four years later the court ordered the Union Pacific Railroad Company to relinquish its control of the Southern Pacific, and in 1913 the separation was completed. Soon the Union Pacific acquired large holdings in railroads in the East and later gained control over Western motor-coach lines. In 1936 the railroad initiated its development of Sun Valley, Idaho, into a popular winter resort. Today the Union Pacific Company is a highly diversified organization, with some 10,000 mi (16,093 km) of track in the W United States and interests in a number of ventures only remotely connected with transportation. See J. P. Davis, *The Union Pacific Railway* (1894, repr. 1973); G. M. Dodge, *How We Built the Union Pacific Railway* (1910, repr. 1966); Nelson Trottman, *The History of the Union Pacific* (1923).

Union party, in American history. **1** Coalition of Republicans and War Democrats in the election of 1864. Abraham Lincoln was renominated for President with Andrew Johnson, the Democratic war governor of Tennessee, as his running mate. The Union party was hardly more than a name; very few Democrats were attracted, and the party reverted to its Republican designation in 1868. **2** In 1936 various radical groups discontented with the New Deal formed the Union party at a convention in Cleveland, Ohio. Father Charles E. COUGHLIN, Dr. Francis E. TOWNSEND, and Gerald L. K. Smith, who had succeeded the recently assassinated Huey Long as the leader of the Share-the-Wealth movement, were the prime movers in the new party. William Lemke, a Republican congressman from North Dakota, was put forward as presidential nominee, and Thomas C. O'Brien of Boston, a labor lawyer, was nominated for Vice President. Although some believed that the Union ticket might deprive Franklin Delano Roosevelt of many normally Democratic votes, Lemke failed to get on the ballot in many states and polled only 882,000 votes. The strange coalition that had created the Union party fell apart immediately, and the party disappeared. See D. H. Bennett, *Demagogues in the Depression* (1969).

union shop: see CLOSED SHOP AND OPEN SHOP.

Union Theological Seminary, in New York City; interdenominational; coeducational; opened 1836, chartered 1839. Auburn Theological Seminary (Presbyterian; chartered 1820, opened 1821 at Auburn, N.Y.) became associated with it as an autonomous unit in 1939; the Auburn Seminary, however, no longer matriculates and graduates students, and is now known as the Auburn Program at Union Seminary. There is a noted school of sacred music and a seminary library that houses outstanding theological collections, particularly in materials relating to the biblical and historical fields. Since 1928, Union has had a reciprocal educational relationship with Columbia.

Uniontown, city (1970 pop. 16,282), seat of Fayette co., SW Pa., near the W.Va. line; settled c.1767, inc. as a city 1916. It is a farm-trade center and an industrial city. Formerly noted for its production of coal and coke, the city now has industries with diversified manufacturing. Products include meters, trailers, aircraft parts, steel scaffolding, stone crushers, and tires. The city is the seat of the Fayette campus of Pennsylvania State Univ. Each autumn a foliage festival is held in Uniontown. Gen. George C. Marshall was born there. Nearby, on the old National Road, is Fort Necessity, built by George Washington. Gen. Edward Braddock is buried near the fort.

Union University, an association of independent undergraduate and graduate schools chartered in 1873. It includes Union College (at Schenectady; coeducational; chartered and opened 1795), noted for its pioneer work in the teaching of engineering, Albany Medical College (1839), Albany Law School (1851), Dudley Observatory (1852), and Albany College of Pharmacy (1881)—all in Albany, N.Y.

unison, in music, tones identical in pitch produced by two or more parts or voices. In popular usage a vocal composition is said to be sung in unison even though some of the voices are separated from others by the interval of an octave.

Unitarianism, in general, the form of Christianity that denies the doctrine of the TRINITY, believing that God exists only in one person. While there were previous antitrinitarian movements in the early Christian Church, like Arianism and Monarchianism, modern Unitarianism originated in the period of the Protestant Reformation. In Geneva, Michael SERVETUS was burned at the stake (1553) for his antitrinitarian views. Under Faustus SOCINUS a strong center of Unitarian belief developed in Poland. In Transylvania, Francis Dávid laid the foundation (c.1560) for the Unitarian Church there. In the 17th and 18th cent. Socinian ideas took root in England, especially under the influence of John BIDDLE, called the father of English Unitarianism. The development of a separate Unitarian body came about gradually through the efforts of such men as Joseph Priestley and Thomas Belsham. Originally a scripturally oriented movement, in the mid-19th cent. Unitarianism became a religion of reason under the leadership of James Martineau in England and Ralph Waldo Emerson and Theodore Parker in the United States. Reason and conscience were considered the only guides to religious truth; complete religious toleration, the innate goodness of man, and universal salvation were preached. Unitarianism took hold in the liberal wing of the Congregational churches of New England. At King's Chapel, Boston, in 1785, trinitarian doctrines were removed from the liturgy. In 1796, Priestley, who had fled to America to escape persecution, established a Unitarian church in Philadelphia. Liberal Congregationalists in New England gradually formed themselves into a new denomination, to which the name Unitarian was given (c.1815) by their conservative opponents. The final separation from Congregationalism was hastened by the choice of Henry WARE (1764–1845), a liberal, as Hollis Professor of Divinity at Harvard Univ. in 1805 and by the ordination sermon defending the liberals preached (1819) by William Ellery CHANNING in Baltimore. Channing's statement of Unitarian beliefs became the platform of the denomination. The American Unitarian Association was formed in 1825, and in 1865 a national conference was organized. A congregational form of government prevails in the Unitarian churches, each congregation having control of its own affairs. Neither ministers nor members are required to make profession of any particular doctrine, and no creed has been adopted by the church. The covenant in general use is simply, "In the love of truth, and in the spirit of Jesus, we unite for worship of God and the service of man." In 1961 the Universalist Church of America merged with the American Unitarian Association to form the UNITARIAN UNIVERSALIST ASSOCIATION. See J. F. Clarke, *Manual of Unitarian Belief* (20th ed., rev., 1924); E. M. Wilbur, *A History of Unitarianism: in Transylvania, England, and America* (1952); Conrad Wright, *The Beginnings of Unitarianism in America* (1955); D. B. Parke, *The Epic of Unitarianism: Original Writings from the History of Liberal Religion* (1957); D. W. Howe, *The Unitarian Conscience* (1970).

Unitarian Universalist Association, Protestant church in the United States formed in 1961 by the merger of the American Unitarian Association (see UNITARIANISM) and the UNIVERSALIST CHURCH OF AMERICA. Having largely shared common concerns and positions throughout the 19th and 20th cent., the two churches formed a Council of Liberal Churches in 1953 as a preliminary step to merger. The convention in May, 1961, at which the merger was approved by delegates from both churches, adopted a constitution for the merged church and elected Dana McLean Greeley, formerly Unitarian president, the first president of the new association. The principal purpose of the merger was to link the churches' headquarters organizations and to enable them to speak as one on social and political questions. See H. H. Cheetham, *Unitarianism and Universalism* (1962); G. N. Marshall, *Challenge of a Liberal Faith* (1970).

Unitas, John, 1933–, American football player, b. Pittsburgh. Unlike the majority of athletic stars, Unitas had difficulty obtaining both a college scholarship and a professional offer. After being released by the Pittsburgh Steelers in 1955, he played semiprofessional football until he was signed by the Baltimore Colts of the National Football League. He rapidly developed into one of the game's finest quarterbacks and powered the Colts to three championship seasons (1958, 1959, 1968). Traded to the San Diego Chargers before the 1973 season, Unitas announced his retirement in July, 1974. He holds the lifetime record for most passes completed (2,830) and most yards gained passing (40,239).

Unitas Fratrum: see MORAVIAN CHURCH.

United Arab Emirates, federation (1968 pop. 179,138), c.30,000 sq mi (77,700 sq km), E Arabia, on the Persian Gulf and the Gulf of Oman. The federation consists of seven emirates: ABU DHABI, AJMAN, DUBAI, FUJAIRAH, RAS AL-KHAIMAH, SHARJAH, and UMM AL-QAIWAIN. The states were formerly known as the Trucial States, Trucial Coast, or Trucial Oman. The term *trucial* refers to the fact that the sheikhs ruling the seven constituent states were bound by truces concluded with Great Britain in 1820 and by an

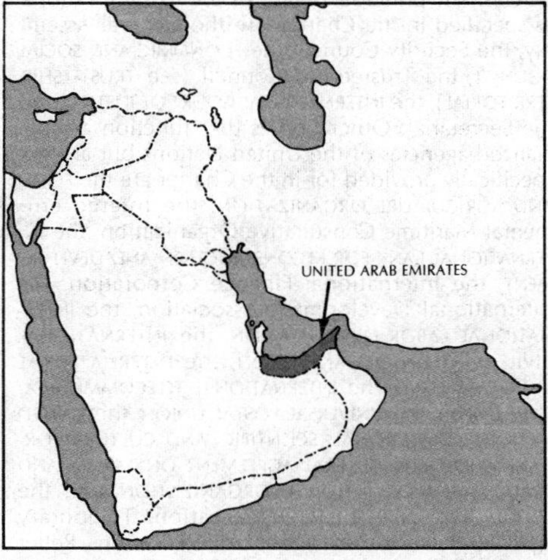

agreement made in 1892 accepting British protection. Before British intervention, the area was notorious for its pirates and was called the Pirate Coast. After World War II the British granted internal autonomy to the sheikhdoms. Discussion of federation began in 1968 when Britain announced its intended withdrawal from the Persian Gulf area by 1971. Originally BAHRAIN and QATAR were to be part of the federation, but after three years of negotiations they chose to be independent. Ras al-Khaimah at first opted for independence but reversed its decision in Feb., 1972. The highest legislative body in the federation is the supreme council, and a representative federal council holds executive power. Local matters are dealt with by the sheikhs. Sheikh Zaid ibn Sultan an-Nahatan, the ruler of Abu Dhabi, is the first president of the federation. Abu Dhabi is the temporary capital, pending the building of a new one on the border between Abu Dhabi and Dubai. The United Arab Emirates is a member of the United Nations and the Arab League. Most of the inhabitants are Arabs, but there are also Persians, Baluchis, and Indians. The majority are Sunni Muslims, although some Shi'a Muslims live in Dubai. The area is rich in oil deposits, which have been exploited since the early 1960s. Fishing and pearling are also important occupations. See Donald Hawley, *The Trucial States* (1971); Stanford Research Institute, *Area Handbook for Peripheral States of the Arabian Peninsula* (1971); M. T. Sadik and W. P. Snavely, *Bahrain, Qatar, and the United Arab Emirates* (1972).

United Arab Republic, political union (1958–61) of EGYPT and SYRIA. The capital was Cairo. The two countries were merged (1958) into a single unit comprising the Southern (Egypt) and the Northern (Syria) Regions, with Gamal Abdal NASSER as president. As an initial step toward creating a pan-Arab union, the republic abolished Syrian and Egyptian citizenship, termed its inhabitants Arabs, and called the country "Arab territory." It considered the Arab homeland to be the entire area between the Persian Gulf and the Atlantic coast. With Yemen, it formed (1958) a loose federation called the United Arab States. In 1961, Syria withdrew from the union after a military coup, and Yemen soon followed, thus ending the union.

United Brethren in Christ: see EVANGELICAL UNITED BRETHREN CHURCH.

United Church of Canada, Protestant denomination formed (1925) by the union of the Methodist, Congregational, and Presbyterian churches in Canada. A large number of Presbyterian congregations, however, remained outside the union. In 1968 the Canada Conference of the Evangelical United Brethren Church also joined the union. The United Church of Canada is ecumenical in orientation and attempts to allow diversity among the different denominations. In the early 1970s the union claimed more than one million members.

United Church of Christ, American Protestant denomination formed in 1957 by a merger of the General Council of Congregational Christian Churches (see CONGREGATIONALISM) and the EVANGELICAL AND REFORMED CHURCH. The constitution for the new body was adopted in July, 1961, thus completing the union. The statement of faith promulgated in 1959 maintains the noncreedal position common to both religious bodies, holding only to baptism and communion as sacraments, ordination as an act of laying on of hands, and local autonomy in all matters of worship, doctrine, and congregational life. The church has about 2,000,000 members. A general synod of the whole church meets biennially, and establishes the various agencies through which its social action, ecumenical, and missionary work is carried out. See Douglas Horton, *The United Church of Christ* (1962).

United Colonies of New England: see NEW ENGLAND CONFEDERATION.

United Empire Loyalists, in Canadian history, name applied to those settlers who, loyal to the British cause in the American Revolution, migrated from the Thirteen Colonies to Canada. Some emigrated during the Revolution, but the greatest number left the colonies in 1783–84, after the Treaty of Paris had failed to make adequate provision for the LOYALISTS. Numbers estimated at up to 50,000 went to British North America—principally to Nova Scotia and Quebec. In Nova Scotia so many settled north of the Bay of Fundy that this region was separated from Nova Scotia and organized as the province of New Brunswick in 1784. Others, flocking to the region north of the Great Lakes and the St. Lawrence River, were numerous enough to cause the creation (1791) of Upper Canada (Ontario). See studies by W. S. Wallace (1914, repr. 1972) and A. G. Bradley (1932, repr. 1972).

United Irishmen or **United Irish Society,** Irish political organization. It was founded at Belfast in 1791 by Theobald Wolfe TONE. Disgruntled by the use of English patronage to control Irish politics, the organization aimed at legislative reform "founded on the principles of civil, political, and religious liberty." Yet there was, from the outset, an undercurrent of revolutionary striving toward independence that was encouraged by the progress of the French Revolution. Tone, with James Napper TANDY, started a branch at Dublin; this became the center of the movement, which spread rapidly throughout Ireland. The society was suppressed in 1794 and became a secret revolutionary organization. Tone was exiled and went to France to request aid. A French force did attempt an invasion in 1796, but it was wrecked off the southwest coast of Ireland. The British government waged a campaign of brutal repression in Ulster in an attempt, largely successful, to break up the cohesive center of the movement. In March, 1798, several southern leaders were arrested, and when rebellion did break out in May, it was in isolated, sporadic bursts. The only appreciable success was in Co. Wexford, but the rebels there were defeated in the battle of Vinegar Hill, June 21. Two months later a small French force landed, but it received almost no support and surrendered. A larger invasion force, led by Tone, was intercepted by the British navy, and Tone was captured. The force of the movement was spent, and it was not revived. See studies by R. R. Madden (1858–60), Rosamond Jacob (1937), and Thomas Pakenham (1969).

United Kingdom of Great Britain and Northern Ireland: see GREAT BRITAIN.

United Methodist Church, in the United States, religious body formed by the union in 1968 of the EVANGELICAL UNITED BRETHREN CHURCH and the Methodist Church (see METHODISM), involving some 11 million members. Emphasizing ecumenism, the newly united church, the second largest Protestant church in the United States, proposed further amalgamation with other Protestant groups. The church also attempted to broaden its social involvement, concentrating its efforts not only on spiritual, but on material aspects of the individual's well-being. Assailing racism and sexism, the church moved to stamp out both in its own hierarchy. Politically active, shortly after its formation the church denounced U.S. involvement in the Vietnam War.

United Methodist Church or **United Methodists,** nonconformist community in England formed by the incorporation in one body, in 1907, of three branches of METHODISM, the Methodist New Connection, the United Methodist Free Churches, and the Bible Christians. The United Methodists, in the still broader reunion of 1932, were merged with the Wesleyan Methodist Church and the Primitive Methodist Church to form the Methodist Church in Great Britain.

United Mine Workers of America (UMW), international labor union formed (1890) by the amalgamation of the National Progressive Union (organized 1888) and the mine locals under the Knights of Labor. Earlier unions of miners in the United

States had been the American Miners' Association (founded 1860); the Miners' National Association of the United States of America (founded 1873); the Ohio Miners' Amalgamated Association (founded 1882), later to become (1883) the Amalgamated Association of Miners of the United States; and the National Federation of Miners and Mine Workers (founded 1885). The newly formed UMW affiliated with the American Federation of Labor (AFL). It is an industrial union, including all workers in the coal industry. The lack of continuity of employment, the prevalence of company-owned towns, and the extreme occupational hazards have led to numerous strikes and constant efforts to improve conditions by collective bargaining. The UMW strengthened its position in 1894 and 1897 by successful strikes, and in 1898, under the leadership of John Mitchell, the fight for an 8-hour workday was won. A no-strike pledge was kept during World War I, but strikes in 1919-20 led to the establishment by the U.S. government of the Bituminous Coal Commission, which awarded the miners a substantial wage increase. In 1920 the anthracite operators recognized the UMW as a bargaining body. John L. LEWIS became president of the union in 1920, and under his militant leadership most of the union's aims were accomplished, including a health and welfare fund assuring a pension of $100 per month to all miners over 62. The UMW was a leader in the formation (1935) of the Committee for Industrial Organization (later the Congress of Industrial Organizations, or CIO) and was expelled from the AFL in 1937. However, in 1942 the UMW withdrew from the CIO; it was readmitted to the AFL in Jan., 1946, but was again disaffiliated in 1947, when Lewis refused to sign the non-Communist affidavit required by the Taft-Hartley Act. A strike (1943) during World War II brought about governmental seizure of the mines. Strikes in 1945-47, although successful, cost both Lewis and the union heavy fines for violation of the injunction barring the union from striking. Lewis resigned as president in 1959, and his place was taken in 1960 by Thomas Kennedy, long a vice president of the UMW. Upon the death of Kennedy, W. A. (Tony) Boyle was elected (1963) president. Throughout the 1960s, Boyle was increasingly criticized by a portion of the rank and file membership. Dissidents rallied to the campaign of Joseph A. Yablonski in 1969, but Yablonski lost to Boyle. A few weeks later Yablonski was murdered. In 1972, Boyle and other top union officials were convicted of making illegal political contributions with union funds. In the same year, a Federal judge invalidated the 1969 election, and Arnold Miller, a Yablonski supporter, defeated Boyle for the presidency. Miller immediately set about reforming the union by replacing Boyle appointees, stopping Boyle's pension, and reducing the salaries of union officials. In 1974 Boyle, charged with having ordered Yablonski's killing, was convicted of murder. See M. S. Baratz, *The Union and the Coal Industry* (1955).

United Nations (UN), international organization established immediately after World War II. It replaced the LEAGUE OF NATIONS. The name United Nations was coined by President Franklin Delano Roosevelt in 1941 to describe the countries fighting against the Axis. It was first used officially on Jan. 1, 1942, when 26 states joined in the Declaration by the United Nations, pledging themselves to continue their joint war effort and not to make peace separately. The need for an international organization to replace the League was first stated officially on Oct. 30, 1943, in the Moscow Declaration issued by China, Great Britain, the United States, and the USSR. At the Dumbarton Oaks Conference (Aug.-Oct., 1944), those four countries drafted specific proposals for a charter for the new organization, and at the YALTA CONFERENCE (Feb., 1945) further agreement was reached. All the states that had ultimately adhered to the 1942 declaration and that had declared war on Germany or Japan by March 1, 1945, were called to the founding conference held in San Francisco (April 25-June 26, 1945). The San Francisco Conference drafted the governing treaty, the United Nations Charter. It was signed on June 26 and ratified by the required number of states on Oct. 24 (officially United Nations Day). The General Assembly first met in London on Jan. 10, 1946; seven days later the Security Council held its first meeting. It was decided to locate the UN headquarters in the E United States. In Dec., 1946, the General Assembly accepted the $8.5 million gift of John D. Rockefeller, Jr., to buy a tract of land along the East River, New York City, for its headquarters. The principal buildings there, the Secretariat, the General Assembly, and the Conference Building, were completed in 1952. The Dag Hammarskjöld Memorial Library was dedicated in 1961.

Organization and Principles. The UN Charter comprises a preamble and 19 chapters divided into 111 articles. The principal organs of the United Nations, as specified in the Charter, are the General Assembly, the Security Council, the ECONOMIC AND SOCIAL COUNCIL, the Trusteeship Council (see TRUSTEESHIP, TERRITORIAL), the INTERNATIONAL COURT OF JUSTICE, and the Secretariat. Other bodies that function as specialized agencies of the United Nations but are not specifically provided for in the Charter are the FOOD AND AGRICULTURE ORGANIZATION, the Intergovernmental Maritime Consultative Organization, the INTERNATIONAL BANK FOR RECONSTRUCTION AND DEVELOPMENT, the International Finance Corporation, the International Development Association, the INTERNATIONAL LABOR ORGANIZATION, the INTERNATIONAL CIVIL AVIATION ORGANIZATION, the INTERNATIONAL MONETARY FUND, the INTERNATIONAL TELECOMMUNICATION UNION, the UNIVERSAL POSTAL UNION, the UNITED NATIONS EDUCATIONAL, SCIENTIFIC, AND CULTURAL ORGANIZATION, the GENERAL AGREEMENT ON TARIFFS AND TRADE, the WORLD HEALTH ORGANIZATION, and the World Meteorological Organization. Temporary agencies have included the United Nations Relief and Rehabilitation Administration, the International Refugee Organization (whose responsibilities were later assumed by the Office of the UNITED NATIONS HIGH COMMISSIONER FOR REFUGEES), and the United Nations Relief and Works Agency for Palestine Refugees, which is still in existence. The Charter sets forth the purposes of the United Nations as: the maintenance of international peace and security, the development of friendly relations between states, and the achievement of cooperation in solving international economic, social, cultural, and humanitarian problems. It expresses a strong hope for the equality of all men and the expansion of basic freedoms. All UN administrative functions are handled by the Secretariat, with the secretary general at its head. The Charter does not prescribe a term for the secretary general, but a five-year term has become standard. Trygve LIE, the first secretary general, was succeeded in 1953 by Dag HAMMARSKJÖLD, who was reelected in 1957 and served until his death in 1961. U THANT became acting secretary general and in 1962 was elected secretary general. He was reelected in 1966 and served until the end of 1971, when he was succeeded by Kurt WALDHEIM. The secretary general transcends a merely administrative role by his authority to bring situations to the attention of various UN organs, by his position as an impartial party in effecting conciliation, and especially by his power to "perform such . . . functions as are entrusted to him" by other UN organs. Also strengthening the office of secretary general is the large Secretariat staff, which is recruited on a wide geographic basis and is required to work exclusively in the interests of the organization. The only UN body provided by the Charter on which all member states are represented is the General Assembly. Here, as throughout the United Nations, the official

UNITED NATIONS MEMBERS *(including year of entry)*

Afghanistan, 1946	Germany, West, 1973	Nigeria, 1960
Albania, 1955	Ghana, 1957	Norway, 1945
Algeria, 1962	Grenada, 1974	Oman, 1971
Argentina, 1945	Greece, 1945	Pakistan, 1947
Australia, 1945	Guatemala, 1945	Panama, 1945
Austria, 1955	Guinea, 1958	Paraguay, 1945
Bahamas, 1973	Guinea-Bissau, 1974	Peru, 1945
Bahrain, 1971	Guyana, 1966	Philippines, 1945
Bangladesh, 1974	Haiti, 1945	Poland, 1945
Barbados, 1966	Honduras, 1945	Portugal, 1955
Belgium, 1945	Hungary, 1955	Qatar, 1971
Belorussian Soviet Socialist Republic, 1945	Iceland, 1946	Rumania, 1955
	India, 1945	Rwanda, 1962
Bhutan, 1971	Indonesia, 1950	Saudi Arabia, 1945
Bolivia, 1945	Iran, 1945	Senegal, 1960
Botswana, 1966	Iraq, 1945	Sierra Leone, 1961
Brazil, 1945	Ireland, 1955	Singapore, 1965
Bulgaria, 1955	Israel, 1949	Somalia, 1960
Burma, 1948	Italy, 1955	South Africa, 1945
Burundi, 1962	Ivory Coast, 1960	Spain, 1955
Cambodia (Khmer Republic), 1955	Jamaica, 1962	Sri Lanka (Ceylon), 1955
Cameroon, 1960	Japan, 1956	Sudan, 1956
Canada, 1945	Jordan, 1955	Swaziland, 1968
Central African Republic, 1960	Kenya, 1963	Sweden, 1946
Chad, 1960	Kuwait, 1963	Syria, 1945
Chile, 1945	Laos, 1955	Tanzania, 1961
China, Republic of, 1945-71	Lebanon, 1945	Thailand, 1946
China, People's Republic of, 1971	Lesotho, 1966	Togo, 1960
Colombia, 1945	Liberia, 1945	Trinidad and Tobago, 1962
Congo, 1960	Libya, 1955	Tunisia, 1956
Costa Rica, 1945	Luxembourg, 1945	Turkey, 1945
Cuba, 1945	Malagasy Republic, 1960	Uganda, 1962
Cyprus, 1960	Malawi, 1964	Ukrainian Soviet Socialist Republic, 1945
Czechoslovakia, 1945	Malaysia, 1957	
Dahomey, 1960	Maldives, 1965	Union of Soviet Socialist Republics, 1945
Denmark, 1945	Mali, 1960	
Dominican Republic, 1945	Malta, 1964	United Arab Emirates, 1971
Ecuador, 1945	Mauritania, 1961	United Kingdom, 1945
Egypt, 1945	Mauritius, 1968	United States, 1945
El Salvador, 1945	Mexico, 1945	Upper Volta, 1960
Equatorial Guinea, 1968	Mongolia, 1961	Uruguay, 1945
Ethiopia, 1945	Morocco, 1956	Venezuela, 1945
Fiji, 1970	Nepal, 1955	Yemen Arab Republic, 1947
Finland, 1955	Netherlands, 1945	Yemen, People's Democratic Republic of, 1967
France, 1945	New Zealand, 1945	
Gabon, 1960	Nicaragua, 1945	Yugoslavia, 1945
Gambia, 1965	Niger, 1960	Zaïre, 1960
Germany, East, 1973		Zambia, 1964

languages are Chinese, English, French, Russian, and Spanish. The working languages of the General Assembly are English, French, and Spanish (in the Security Council only English and French are working languages). The General Assembly meets in a regular

United Nations Secretaries General (*including nationality and dates in office*)
Trygve Halvdan Lie [Norwegian], 1946–53 Dag Hammarskjöld [Swedish], 1953–61 U Thant [Burmese], 1962–71 Kurt Waldheim [Austrian], 1972–

annual session beginning the third Tuesday in September; special sessions are sometimes held. It has seven main committees set up to deal with specific matters designated as (1) political and security, (2) economic and financial, (3) social, humanitarian, and cultural, (4) trusteeship, (5) administrative and budgetary, (6) legal, (7) special political. It also has procedural, standing, and many ad hoc committees. The assembly passes on the budget and sets the assessments of the member countries. It may conduct studies and make recommendations, but may not make advisements on any matter under the consideration of the Security Council, unless by request of the Security Council. In the assembly, decisions on routine matters are taken by a simple majority of members voting; a two-thirds majority of those voting is required for matters of importance. Among the matters decided by a two-thirds majority are the admission of new members, the revision of the Charter, and budgetary and trusteeship questions. While the General Assembly was envisaged in the Charter as primarily a deliberative body to deal chiefly with general questions of a political, social, or economic character, the Security Council was constructed as an organ with primary responsibility for preserving peace. Unlike the assembly, it was given power to enforce measures and was organized as a compact executive organ. Also unlike the General Assembly, the Security Council in theory functions continuously at the seat of the United Nations. The council has 15 members. Five—China (until 1971 the Republic of China; since then the People's Republic of China), France, Great Britain, the United States, and the USSR—are permanent. The 10 nonpermanent members are elected for two-year terms by the General Assembly, which by the Charter is required in choosing them to consider the contribution to peace made by the candidates as well as equitable geographic distribution. Customarily there are five nonpermanent members from African and Asian states, one from Eastern Europe, two from Latin America, and two from Western Europe and elsewhere. In the council the presidency is occupied for one-month terms in the alphabetical order of the members' names in English. There are two systems of voting in the Security Council. On procedural matters the affirmative vote of any nine members is necessary, but on substantive matters the nine affirmative votes required must include those of the five permanent members. This requirement of Big Five unanimity embodies the so-called veto. In practice the council has, on most substantive matters, not treated an abstention by a permanent member as a veto. In two situations, however, those of recommending applicants for UN membership and of approving proposed amendments to the Charter, the actual concurrence of all permanent members has been required. Although the veto provision was strongly opposed at the San Francisco Conference, especially by many smaller nations, because of the danger of paralyzing UN action and violating the principle of sovereign equality of states, it was passed largely because of the belief that the resolution of major crises would in any case require the agreement of the major world powers. Under the Charter the council appears able to take measures on any occurrences dangerous to world peace. It may act upon complaint of a member or of a nonmember, on notification by the secretary general or by the General Assembly, or of its own volition. In general the council considers matters of two sorts. "Disputes" (or situations that may give rise to them) that might endanger peace constitute one category. In this category the council is limited to making recommendations to the parties after it has exhausted other methods of reaching a solution. In the case of more serious matters, such as "threats to the peace," "breaches of the peace," and "acts of aggression," the council may take enforcement measures. These may range from full or partial rupture of economic or diplomatic relations to military operations of any scope deemed necessary. By the terms of the Charter, the United Nations was forbidden to intervene in matters "which are essentially . . . domestic," but this limitation was explicitly not intended to hinder Security Council measures to prevent threats to peace. The UN Charter was thus somewhat ambiguous regarding domestic issues that could also be construed as threats to peace, and left a potential opening for intervention in domestic issues that threatened dangerous international repercussions.

Evolution and Accomplishments. In practice the United Nations has not evolved as was first envisaged. Originally it was composed largely of the Allies of World War II, mainly European countries, British Commonwealth countries, and nations of the Americas. It was conceived as an organization of "peace-loving" nations, who were combining to prevent future aggression and for other humanitarian purposes. Close cooperation among members was expected; the Security Council especially was expected to work in relative unanimity. Hopes for essential accord were soon dashed by the frictions of the COLD WAR, which affected the functioning of the Security Council and other UN organs. The Charter had envisaged some sort of regular military force available to the Security Council and directed the creation of the Military Staff Committee to make appropriate plans. The committee—consisting of the chiefs of staff (or their deputies) of the Big Five—was unable to reach agreement on the structure and command over such forces, with the USSR and the other four states on opposing sides. Thus no regular forces were made available to the Security Council. The same split that existed in the Military Staff Committee frustrated the activities of two special Security Council bodies, the Atomic Energy Commission and the Commission on Conventional Armaments. Hence no arrangements were concluded for regulating the production of atomic bombs or reducing other types of armaments. In 1952 a new Disarmament Commission (see DISARMAMENT, NUCLEAR) was given jurisdiction over negotiations for both atomic and conventional weapons, but was unable to reconcile the conflict between East and West. The Charter anticipated that regional security agreements would supplement the overall UN system, but in fact such comprehensive alliances as the NORTH ATLANTIC TREATY ORGANIZATION (NATO), the ORGANIZATION OF AMERICAN STATES, the SOUTHEAST ASIA TREATY ORGANIZATION, and the WARSAW TREATY ORGANIZATION have to an extent bypassed the UN system. There were some early instances of Soviet cooperation with the United States and other powers that allowed for UN successes in restoring or preserving peace. These included the settlement (1946) of the complaint of Syria and Lebanon that France and Great Britain were illegally occupying their territory; the partitioning of Palestine (see ISRAEL); the fighting over Kashmir between India and Pakistan (see INDIA-PAKISTAN WARS); and the withdrawal of the Dutch from Indonesia. However, in many other issues of more direct importance to the security of the great powers, conflict between the USSR and the remaining members of the Big Five loomed as a major factor. The Security Council was crippled by casting of the veto, which by the end of 1955 had been used 78 times, 75 of them by the Soviet Union. In reaction, the other great powers and other nations tried to develop the General Assembly beyond its original scope. In the assembly the United States and Great Britain had strong support from among the Commonwealth and Latin American countries and generally commanded a majority. The Soviet Union could muster only a smaller bloc, sufficient to create debate between East and West but less effective in voting. An early assembly innovation to bypass the veto was the establishment (1947) of the Interim Assembly to meet in permanent session; it was staunchly opposed by the USSR, which charged that it usurped Security Council functions, and it has never fulfilled its purpose. Of great importance were procedures evolved in the Korean crisis in 1950. At that time the Soviet Union was boycotting the Security Council because of the UN refusal to admit Communist China as a member. Since the USSR was not present to cast a veto, the Security Council was enabled to establish armed forces to repel the North Korean attack on South Korea (see KOREAN WAR). Thus, at a time when the young organization had begun to seem politically sterile, it gave birth to the first UN army and to the widest "collective security" action in history, although the United States provided the bulk of both fighting personnel and matériel. In addition, firmer UN action in future crises was prepared for when, in Nov., 1950, the assembly adopted the "Uniting for Peace" resolution, which permitted it to take its own measures when use of the veto paralyzed the council. Although the assembly has been convened a few times under this resolution, its authority to require action by members has remained vague, and it has never developed workable enforcement machinery. Some areas were opened for UN intervention, however, where world opinion and great power responsiveness favored it. In the struggle for independence in Morocco, Algeria, and elsewhere, the ruling colonial powers claimed these conflicts to be domestic; with their seats on the Security Council they were in a position to veto assembly resolutions, and with the official governments of rebellious territories under their control they were enabled to forestall UN intervention. In the Hungarian revolt (1956), requests that the USSR withdraw its troops from Hungary and that UN observers be admitted to the country were rejected by the Soviet Union. In the Suez crisis (1956), however, the General Assembly resolution for an immediate cease-fire and for withdrawal of invading forces was heeded by Great Britain, France, and Israel (see ARAB-ISRAELI WARS). Parallel to the growing activity of the assembly was the expanding role of the secretary general. Trygve Lie, as secretary general, had made vigorous efforts to muster world opinion in such difficulties as the Korean crisis, but his precipitate labeling of North Korea as the aggressor, among other statements, had earned him Soviet enmity and thus limited the effectiveness of his office. Under the "quiet diplomacy" of Dag Hammarskjöld the secretary generalship gained greater scope. The secretary general, not the deadlocked Security Council, had been entrusted with organizing and establishing UN forces in the Suez crisis. He worked closely with the General Assembly on other issues. In 1958, when an assembly resolution asking for a strong force of UN observers in Lebanon had been vetoed by the council, the secretary general nevertheless followed the assembly's recommendation. In 1959 he acted in direct contravention of Soviet wishes when he visited Laos and assigned a special UN ambassador there. Beyond such missions Hammarskjöld interpreted his office as responsible for preserving peace even when the assembly itself was deadlocked and could issue no definite instructions. In practice he operated largely under a General Assembly mandate but frequently took executive steps that could not be completely detailed by instructions, such as in the many diplomatic tasks entrusted to him by the assembly. Thus the office of secretary general showed signs of becoming the United Nations' de facto executive authority in matters of international conflict, and the Security Council began to meet much less frequently. By the late 1950s the UN was being revolutionized by a change in membership. Since the inception of the United Nations there had been a steady growth of feeling that the organization should comprise all the nations of the world. But new membership was long blocked by East-West rivalry; each side was antagonistic to admission of new members unfavorable to its views, and as non-Communist countries outnumbered Communist ones the USSR was especially intransigent. From 1947 to 1955 only Yemen (1947), Pakistan (1947), Burma (1948), Israel (1949), and Indonesia (1950) gained admission. The way to a compromise was led by Canada in 1955; 16 new members were admitted in that year, and thereafter expansion was rapid. Accompanying expansion came voting realignment. The clear majority of the United States and its allies disappeared as the Afro-Asian group of nations (see AFRO-ASIAN BLOC) obtained over half of the assembly seats. New voting blocs formed, including the NATO nations, the Arab nations, the Commonwealth nations and, increasingly, a general Afro-Asian bloc. Latin America shifted some of its earlier support of U.S. proposals. Other themes began to equal that of the cold war in assembly debates, and more militant stands were taken against remnants of colonialism. The changed nature of the United Nations was revealed in UN policy regarding Africa in the early 1960s. The United Nations acted strongly in the crisis in the Republic of the Congo (see ZAIRE), and during its involvement there the secretary general developed his office to an unprecedented extent. When the United Nations was invited (1960) by the Congo government to send troops there, a UN force was quickly organized by Hammarskjöld from among neutral European and African states. The UN troops, confronted by social and political chaos, engaged in direct military action to force Katanga province (see SHABA) to reintegrate with the Congo, which it finally did in 1963. UN action in the

Congo and later in sending peacekeeping forces to Cyprus (1964) demonstrated a willingness to intervene in basically internal situations, both to restore order and to prevent the spread of disorder to neighboring states. This willingness was especially evident in the attention paid to the remaining colonial areas, mainly in Africa. The United Nations repeatedly condemned the colonial policies of Portugal (until that country began to free its colonies after the 1974 coup) and the racial policies of South Africa and Rhodesia, against which severe economic sanctions were applied. These resolutions and sanctions appeared to have little effect and stand as examples of lessening UN influence in world political affairs, due largely to a diminishing support of the United Nations by major world powers. Having lost its automatic majority in the assembly, the United States has, in effect, joined the Soviet Union in limiting UN power and authority, mainly by keeping major issues within the purview of the Security Council and the veto, with inaction the usual result. There has been a corresponding decline in the freedom of movement allowed the secretary general. In the wake of Hammarskjöld's Congo operation and accidental death, the Soviet Union's "troika" plan for a three-man secretary general—an Eastern, a Western, and a neutralist member, each with a veto—was a sign that the USSR would not tolerate another activist secretary general. Although its plan was defeated, the USSR's goal has been largely achieved, since both U Thant and Kurt Waldheim have consistently avoided actions that might be controversial. Severe financial pressures have also served to restrict UN action. A number of countries, including the USSR, have refused to pay for UN actions, such as the Congo operation, not directly approved by the Security Council. The United States, for its part, has made it official policy to reduce its assessment to a maximum of 25% of the UN budget, instead of underwriting an average of one third of the United Nations' operating expenses. Finally, the major powers have tended to deal with each other outside the framework of the United Nations. While certain agreements in peripheral areas of disarmament and international cooperation have been worked out within the United Nations—e.g., the peaceful use of atomic energy (see ATOMIC ENERGY AGENCY, INTERNATIONAL), cooperation in outer space, and arms limitation on the international seabed—the major negotiations and agreements have been on a bilateral basis. As a result, the United Nations has played a relatively secondary role in most recent world crises, including the Arab-Israeli Wars of 1967 and 1973; the India-Pakistan War of 1971; and the Vietnam War. As the United Nations' peacekeeping role has declined, it has been expanding its activities in the economic and technological development of the less developed countries, who are now a majority of the membership. The United Nations and its related agencies have had a significant impact in areas such as disease control, aid to refugees, and technological cooperation. Over the years, however, its focus has changed from rebuilding the countries ravaged by World War II to raising the living standards of the world's poor. It has provided a mechanism through which developed countries can jointly contribute with a minimum of national antagonism and from which less developed countries can receive aid with a minimum of suspicion and resentment. Following the World Food Conference of 1974, a new UN agency, the World Food Council, was set up to coordinate efforts to deal with the critical problem of food shortages in many parts of the world. The United Nations has also been active in setting standards of human dignity and freedom, such as in the Universal Declaration of Human Rights and the establishment of international labor standards. As it begins its second quarter-century, the United Nations can look back upon a history marked with less success than many had hoped for but with enough achievement to maintain expectations of a useful future. It enters this period, moreover, with a membership that for the first time approaches encompassment of all the nations of the world. The seating of the Communist Chinese (1971) and the entry of East Germany and West Germany (1973) make the United Nations more truly a meeting place for all the nations of the world

Bibliography. The United Nations publishes a series of comprehensive yearbooks (1947-) and the useful *Everyman's United Nations* (8th ed. 1965, supplement 1970). See Carnegie Endowment for International Peace, *United Nations Studies* (Vol. I-XI, 1947-62); L. M. Goodrich and A. P. Simons, *The United Nations and the Maintenance of International Peace and Security* (1955); Gabriella Rosner, *The United Nations Emergency Force* (1963); L. M. Goodrich and N. J. Padelford, *The United Nations in the Balance* (1965); D. A. Kay, *The United Nations Political System* (1967); R. A. Divine, *Second Chance* (1967); Maurice Waters, *The United Nations* (1967); L. M. Goodrich, E. I. Hambro, and A. P. Simons, *Charter of the United Nations: Commentary and Documents* (3d ed. 1969); C. M. Eichelberger, *UN: The First Twenty-Five Years* (4th ed. 1970); Andrew Boyd, *Fifteen Men on a Powder Keg* (1971); H. G. Nicholas, *The United Nations as a Political Institution* (1971); Mahdi Elmandjra, *The United Nations System: An Analysis* (1973); D. W. Wainhouse, *International Peacekeeping at the Crossroads* (1973); L. M. Goodrich, *The United Nations in a Changing World* (1974).

United Nations Atomic Energy Commission: see DISARMAMENT, NUCLEAR.

United Nations Children's Fund (UNICEF), an affiliated agency of the United Nations. It was established in 1946 as the United Nations International Children's Emergency Fund. UNICEF is concerned with assisting children and adolescents throughout the world, particularly in devastated areas and developing countries. Unlike most United Nations agencies, UNICEF is financed through voluntary contributions from governments and individuals, rather than by regular assessments. National UNICEF committees collaborate with UNICEF in various projects. UNICEF was awarded the Nobel Peace Prize in 1965.

United Nations Commission for the Investigation of War Crimes: see WAR CRIMES.

United Nations Commission on Conventional Armaments: see UNITED NATIONS .

United Nations Development Program (UNDP), agency of the United Nations, established in 1965 to unify the operations of the Expanded Program of Technical Assistance and the United Nations Special Fund, which continued as separate components of UNDP until full unification in 1971. The UNDP provides developing countries with technical and preinvestment assistance in such areas as resource planning and utilization, educational and training institutes, the application of modern technology to development, and the building of the economic and social infrastructure needed for development and for the attraction of larger development funds. As the largest multinational source of technical and preinvestment aid, the UNDP works both with the developing countries and with various UN-associated agencies involved in development activities. It is funded by voluntary contributions from UN members.

United Nations Economic and Social Council: see ECONOMIC AND SOCIAL COUNCIL.

United Nations Educational, Scientific, and Cultural Organization (UNESCO), specialized agency of the United Nations, with headquarters in Paris. Its counterpart in the League of Nations was the International Committee for Intellectual Cooperation. UNESCO was founded in 1945, and in 1946 it became an agency of the United Nations. In 1972 it had 131 members and associate members, several of whom did not belong to the United Nations (Monaco, Switzerland, South Vietnam, and South Korea). The organization's policies are decided by the general conference, which meets every two years; it consists of one representative for each member. The executive board, with 34 members elected for three-year terms, and a secretariat, headed by a director general, carry out the program. National commissions or cooperating bodies of member states act as liaison between UNESCO and national educational, scientific, and cultural organizations. UNESCO seeks to further world peace by removing social, religious, and racial tensions, encouraging free interchange of ideas and of cultural and scientific achievements, and improving and expanding education. After World War II, UNESCO worked for the physical reconstruction of the educational facilities of war-devastated countries by building up library and museum collections. Since 1950 it has organized projects for primary education in Latin America, Asia, and Africa; it has also encouraged cultural exchanges between East and West, undertaking translations of important writings and organizing personal exchanges. A most important long-range UNESCO program concerns the problem of "fundamental education"—teaching people to read and write and to meet the problems of their environment. Centers to train educators have been established in Cambodia, India, South Korea, Liberia, Thailand, and Turkey, and fundamental education centers have been set up in Latin America and in the Middle East. In 1959, UNESCO set up an international committee to preserve and restore cultural property, which played a leading role in preserving Egyptian monuments threatened by the construction of the Aswan High Dam (see under ASWAN). Funds were collected and experts assembled from all over the world in a successful effort to save the monuments, including the famous Abu Simbel temples of Rameses II. UNESCO has placed increasing emphasis on the advancement of scientific research and on cooperation and aid to developing countries. See W. H. C. Laves and C. A. Thomas, *UNESCO* (1957, repr. 1968); G. H. Evans, *The United States and UNESCO* (1971).

United Nations General Assembly: see UNITED NATIONS.

United Nations High Commissioner for Refugees (UNHCR), **Office of the,** established Jan., 1951, by the General Assembly. It superseded the International Refugee Organization. Its purpose is to seek a permanent solution to the refugee problem, to offer international protection to refugees under its mandate, to coordinate the activities of voluntary agencies, and to assist the most needy refugee groups. It was awarded the 1954 Nobel Peace Prize. In the late 1950s the office of UNHCR was active in providing for refugees from Hungary, Algeria, Morocco, and Tunisia, and for Chinese refugees in Hong Kong. In the 1960s and early 70s most of its economic assistance went to aid the refugees generated by various tribal and political conflicts and civil wars on the African continent and in Chile. See Louise Holborn, *Refugees, a Problem for Our Time: The Work of the United Nations High Commissioner for Refugees, 1950–1970* (1974).

United Nations Relief and Rehabilitation Administration (UNRRA), organization founded (1943) during World War II to give aid to areas liberated from the Axis powers. There were finally 52 participating countries, each of which contributed funds amounting to 2% of its national income in 1943. A sum of nearly $4 billion was expended on various types of emergency aid, including distribution of food and medicine and restoration of public services and of agriculture and industry. China, Czechoslovakia, Greece, Italy, Poland, the Ukrainian SSR, and Yugoslavia were the chief beneficiaries. UNRRA returned some 7 million displaced persons to their countries of origin and provided camps for about 1 million refugees unwilling to be repatriated. More than half the funds were provided by the United States, and the three directors general—Herbert H. Lehman, Fiorello La Guardia, and Gen. Lowell Rooks—were American. UNRRA discontinued its operations in Europe on June 30, 1947. Its remaining work, chiefly in China, ended on March 31, 1949. The functions of UNRRA were transferred to other UN agencies, chiefly the INTERNATIONAL REFUGEE ORGANIZATION, the Food and Agriculture Organization, and the International Children's Fund. See George Woodbridge, ed., *UNRRA: the History of the United Nations Relief and Rehabilitation Administration* (3 vol., 1950).

United Nations Relief and Works Agency for Palestine Refugees (UNRWA), agency of the United Nations, with headquarters in Beirut. Established in 1949, it replaced the United Nations Relief for Palestine Refugees in 1950 as the major UN agency dealing with Palestine refugees. The refugees, defined as those who have been displaced by the various Arab-Israeli Wars, were estimated by the agency to number nearly 1.5 million before the 1973 war; however, this estimate is challenged by Israel and others as being greatly inflated. Originally the agency was charged with the care of these refugees until they could be repatriated, compensated, or resettled; UNRWA has, in fact, found itself faced with the job of housing, feeding, and educating hundreds of thousands of people, many of them in special camps throughout the Middle East. During this period, it has had the difficult task of dealing with the competing interests of Israel, the Arab states, and the Palestine guerrilla movement. In 1972 the agency had a budget of over $50 million, of which more than half was paid by the United States. See E. H. Buehrig, *The UN and the Palestinian Refugees* (1971).

United Nations Security Council: see UNITED NATIONS.

United Nations Trusteeship Council: see TRUSTEESHIP, TERRITORIAL.

United Presbyterian Church, denomination of PRESBYTERIANISM. It was formed in Scotland by the union (1847) of the United Secession Church with the majority of the congregations of the Relief Church. In 1900 the United Presbyterian Church and the Free Church of Scotland joined as the United Free Church of Scotland. This United Free Church in 1929 merged with the Church of Scotland. The United Presbyterian Church of North America was constituted (1858) by the union of the Associate Presbyterian Church with the Associate Reformed Presbyterian Church. **The United Presbyterian Church in the U.S.A.** was formed in 1958 by the merger of the United Presbyterian Church of North America and the Presbyterian Church in the U.S.A. In 1958 and again in 1967 the church adopted a new confessional position that emphasizes God's work of reconciliation and man's role in the fulfillment of this work. It thus committed its members to find solutions to contemporary social and political problems. Its membership is over 3 million.

United Press: see NEWS AGENCY.

United Provinces: see NETHERLANDS.

United Provinces, former state, N India, now almost coextensive with the modern state of Uttar Pradesh. The United Provinces embraced the plain of the Ganges, the heartland of India. This region was the scene of the ancient Hindu epics, the *Ramayana* and the *Mahabharata*. Invasions, battles, and the rise of great kingdoms occurred there. Many Hindu pilgrims flock to the holy cities along the Ganges, notably ALLAHABAD and VARANASI. The east, as the scene of Buddha's life, remains sacred to Buddhism. Though the region was overwhelmingly Hindu in population, it was under Muslim rule from the 12th to the 18th cent. Great Britain first acquired territory there in 1764. The United Provinces of Agra and Oudh was formed in 1877 by merging the presidency of Agra and the kingdom of OUDH. The provincial area was occupied by rebels in the INDIAN MUTINY. After the partition of India in 1947, many Muslims migrated from the United Provinces to Pakistan. In 1950 the new state of Uttar Pradesh was formed.

United Service Organizations (USO), organization that supplies social, recreational, welfare, and spiritual facilities to members of the armed services. The associated agencies include the YMCA, the YWCA, the National Catholic Community Service, the Salvation Army, the Jewish Welfare Board, and the National Travelers Aid Association. USO was organized in 1941; its services, discontinued at the end of 1947, were resumed early in 1949 at the request of President Truman. It is supported by voluntary contributions, and many thousands of volunteers assist in its programs, which include live entertainment. The USO maintains over 200 off-post clubs and hospitality centers.

United States, republic (1970 pop. 203,235,298; 1973 est. pop. 210,000,000), 3,615,191 sq mi (9,363,353 sq km), North America, consisting of 50 states and a federal district; WASHINGTON, D.C., is the capital. The full name is the United States of America. The outlying territories and areas of the United States include: in the West Indies, PUERTO RICO (since 1952 a commonwealth associated with the United States) and the VIRGIN ISLANDS of the United States (purchased from Denmark in 1917); in the Pacific Ocean, GUAM (ceded by Spain after the Spanish-American War), AMERICAN SAMOA, WAKE ISLAND, CANTON ISLAND, Enderbury Island, and several other islands. The United States also has trusteeship under the United Nations of the Caroline, Marshall, and part of the Marianas island chains. The PANAMA CANAL ZONE is held under lease from the government of Panama. Excluding Alaska and Hawaii, the conterminous United States stretches across central North America from the Atlantic Ocean on the east to the Pacific Ocean on the west, and from Canada on the north to Mexico and the Gulf of Mexico on the south. The state of Alaska is located in extreme NW North America between the Arctic and Pacific oceans and is bordered by Canada on the east. The state of HAWAII, an island chain, is situated in the central Pacific Ocean c.2,100 mi (3,400 km) SW of San Francisco. The conterminous United States may be divided into several regions: the New England states (MAINE, NEW HAMPSHIRE, VERMONT, MASSACHUSETTS, RHODE ISLAND, and CONNECTICUT), the Middle Atlantic states (NEW YORK, NEW JERSEY, PENNSYLVANIA, DELAWARE, MARYLAND, VIRGINIA, and WEST VIRGINIA), the Southeastern states (NORTH CAROLINA, SOUTH CAROLINA, GEORGIA, FLORIDA, ALABAMA, MISSISSIPPI, LOUISIANA, ARKANSAS, TENNESSEE, and KENTUCKY), the states of the Midwest (OHIO, INDIANA, ILLINOIS, MICHIGAN, WISCONSIN, MINNESOTA, IOWA, and MISSOURI), the Great Plains states (NORTH DAKOTA, SOUTH DAKOTA, NEBRASKA, KANSAS, OKLAHOMA, and TEXAS), the Mountain states (MONTANA, IDAHO, WYOMING, COLORADO, and NEW MEXICO), and the states of the Far West (WASHINGTON, OREGON, CALIFORNIA, NEVADA, UTAH, and ARIZONA). ALASKA is the largest state in area (586,412 sq mi/1,518,807 sq km) but has the smallest population (1970 pop. 300,382); Rhode Island is the smallest state in area (1,214 sq mi/3,144 sq km), while California has the largest population (1970 pop. 19,953,134). The largest U.S. cities are NEW YORK, CHICAGO, LOS ANGELES, and PHILADELPHIA; among the major cities are BOSTON, BALTIMORE, Washington, D.C., ATLANTA, MIAMI, BUFFALO, PITTSBURGH, CLEVELAND, CINCINNATI, DETROIT, MILWAUKEE, MINNEAPOLIS, SAINT LOUIS, KANSAS CITY, MEMPHIS, NEW ORLEANS, HOUSTON, DALLAS, DENVER, SAN FRANCISCO, SEATTLE, SAN DIEGO, and HONOLULU.

Physical Geography, Economy, and People. The conterminous United States may be divided into seven broad physiographic divisions: from east to west, the Atlantic-Gulf Coastal Plain; the Appalachian Highlands; the Interior Plains; the Interior Highlands; the Rocky Mountain System; the Intermontane Region; and the Pacific Mountain System. An eighth division, the Laurentian Uplands, a part of the CANADIAN SHIELD, dips into the United States from Canada in the Great Lakes region. It is an area of little local relief, with an irregular drainage system and many lakes, as well as some of the oldest exposed rocks in the United States. The Atlantic-Gulf Coastal Plain extends along the east and southeast coasts of the United States from E Long Island to the Rio Grande; Cape Cod and the islands off SE Massachusetts are also part of this region. Although narrow in the north, the Atlantic Coastal Plain widens in the south, merging with the Gulf Coastal Plain in Georgia. The Atlantic and Gulf coasts are essentially coastlines of submergence, with numerous estuaries, embayments, islands, sandspits, and barrier beaches backed by lagoons. The northeast coast has many fine natural harbors, such as those of NEW YORK BAY and CHESAPEAKE BAY, but south of the great capes of the North Carolina coast (Fear, Lookout, and Hatteras) there are few large bays. A principal feature of the lagoon-lined Gulf Coast is the great delta of the MISSISSIPPI River. The Atlantic Coastal Plain rises in the west to the rolling Piedmont (the falls along which were an early source of waterpower) at the foot of the APPALACHIAN MOUNTAINS. These ancient mountains, a once-towering system now worn low by erosion, extend SW from SE Canada to the Gulf Coastal Plain in Alabama. In E New England, the Appalachians extend to the Atlantic Ocean, forming a rocky, irregular coastline. The Appalachians and the ADIRONDACK MOUNTAINS of New York (which are geologically related to the Canadian Shield) include all the chief highlands of E United States; Mt. MITCHELL (6,684 ft/2,037 m high), in the Black Mts. of North Carolina, is the highest point of E North America. Extending more than 1,000 mi (1,610 km) from the Appalachians to the Rocky Mts. and lying between the Great Lakes in the north and the Gulf Coastal Plain in the south are the undulating Interior Plains. Once covered by a great inland sea, the Interior Plains are underlain by sedimentary rock. Almost all of the region is drained by one of the world's greatest river systems—the Mississippi-Missouri-Ohio. The Interior Plains may be divided into two sections: the fertile central lowlands, the agricultural heartland of the United States; and the GREAT PLAINS, a treeless plateau that gently rises from the central lowlands to the foothills of the Rocky Mts. The BLACK HILLS of South Dakota form the region's only upland area. The Interior Highlands are located just W of the Mississippi River between the Interior Plains and the Gulf Coastal Plain. This region consists of the rolling Ozark Plateau (see OZARKS) to the north and the OUACHITA MOUNTAINS, which are similar in structure to the ridge and valley section of the Appalachians, to the south. West of the Great Plains are the lofty ROCKY MOUNTAINS. This geologically young and complex system extends into NW United States from Canada and runs S into New Mexico. There are numerous high peaks in the Rockies; the highest is Mt. ELBERT (14,433 ft/4,399 m). The Rocky Mts. are divided into four sections—the Northern Rockies, the Middle Rockies, the Wyoming Basin, and the Southern Rockies. Along the crest of the Rockies is the CONTINENTAL DIVIDE, separating Atlantic-bound drainage from that heading for the Pacific Ocean. Between the Rocky Mts. and the ranges to the west is the Intermontane Region, an arid expanse of plateaus, basins, and ranges. The COLUMBIA PLATEAU, in the north of the region, was formed by volcanic lava and is drained by the COLUMBIA River and its tributary the SNAKE River, both of which have cut deep canyons into the plateau. The enormous COLORADO PLATEAU, an area of sedimentary rock, is drained by the COLORADO River and its tributaries; there the Colorado River has entrenched itself to form the GRAND CANYON, one of the world's most impressive scenic wonders. West of the plateaus is the basin and range province, an area of extensive desert and semidesert. The lowest point in North America, in DEATH VALLEY NATIONAL MONUMENT (282 ft/86 m below sea level), is there. The largest basin in the region is the GREAT BASIN, an area of interior drainage (the HUMBOLDT River is the largest stream) and of numerous salt lakes, including the GREAT SALT LAKE. Between the Intermontane Region and the Pacific Ocean is the Pacific Mountain System, a series of ranges generally paralleling the coast, formed by faulting and volcanism. The CASCADE RANGE, with its numerous volcanic cones, extends S from SW Canada into N California, and from there is continued S by the SIERRA NEVADA, a great fault block. Mt. WHITNEY (14,495 ft/4,418 m), in the Sierra Nevada, is the highest peak in the conterminous United States. West of the Cascades and the Sierra Nevada and separated from them by a structural trough are the COAST RANGES, which extend along the length of the U.S. Pacific coast. The Central Valley in California, the Willamette Valley in Oregon, and the Puget Sound lowlands in Washington are part of the trough. The San Andreas Fault, a crack in the earth's crust, parallels the trend of the Coast Ranges from San Francisco Bay to NW Mexico; earthquakes are common along its entire length. The Pacific Coastal Plain is narrow, and in many cases the mountains plunge directly into the sea. A coastline of emergence, it has few islands, except for the Channel Islands (see SANTA BARBARA ISLANDS) and those in Puget Sound; there are few good harbors besides PUGET SOUND and SAN FRANCISCO BAY. Alaska may be divided into four physiographic regions; they are, from north to south, the Arctic Lowlands, the coastal plain of the Arctic Ocean; the Rocky Mountain System, of which the BROOKS RANGE is the northernmost section; the Central Basins and Highlands Region, which is dominated by the YUKON River basin; and the Pacific Mountain System, which parallels Alaska's southern coast and which rises to Mt. MCKINLEY (20,320 ft/6,194 m), the highest peak of North America. The islands of SE Alaska and those of the ALEUTIAN ISLANDS chain are partially submerged portions of the Pacific Mountain System and are frequently subjected to volcanic activity and earthquakes. The Hawaiian Islands may also be considered part of the Pacific Mountain System. These islands are the tops of volcanoes that rise from the floor of the Pacific Ocean; MAUNA KEA and MAUNA LOA are active volcanoes. The terrain of N United States was formed by the great continental ice sheets that covered N North America during the Pleistocene epoch. The southern edge of the ice sheet is roughly traced by a line of moraines extending W from E Long Island and then along the course of the Ohio and Missouri rivers to the Rocky Mts.; land north of this line is covered by glacial material. Alaska and the mountains of NW United States had extensive mountain glaciers and were heavily eroded. Large glacial lakes (see BONNEVILLE, LAKE; LAHONTAN, LAKE) occupied sections of the Great Basin; the Great Salt Lake and the other lakes of this region are remnants of the glacial lakes. The United States has an extensive inland waterways system, much of which has been improved for navigation and flood control and developed to produce hydroelectricity and irrigation water by such agencies as the U.S. Bureau of Reclamation, the U.S. Corps of Engineers, and the TENNESSEE VALLEY AUTHORITY. Some of the world's largest dams, man-made lakes, and hydroelectric power plants are on U.S. rivers. The Mississippi-Missouri–Red Rock river system (c.3,890 mi/6,300 km long), is the longest in the United States and the second longest in the world. With its hundreds of tributaries, chief among which are the RED RIVER, the OHIO, and the ARKANSAS, the Mississippi basin drains more than half of the nation. The Yukon, Columbia, Colorado, and RIO GRANDE also have huge drainage basins. Other notable river systems include the CONNECTICUT, HUDSON, DELAWARE, SUSQUEHANNA, POTOMAC, JAMES, ALABAMA, BRAZOS, SAN JOAQUIN, and SACRAMENTO. The Great Salt Lake and ILIAMNA are the largest U.S. lakes outside of the GREAT LAKES and LAKE OF THE WOODS, which are shared with Canada. Since the opening of the SAINT LAWRENCE SEAWAY (1959) the Great Lakes have become a fourth U.S. seacoast, enabling oceangoing vessels to reach Duluth, Minn. The ILLINOIS WATERWAY connects the Great Lakes with the Mississippi River, and the NEW YORK STATE BARGE CANAL links them with the Hudson. The INTRACOASTAL

PACIFIC OCEAN
C A N
CAPE FLATTERY
Puget Sound
Seattle
Olympia
WASH.
Spokane
Portland
Columbia R.
Salem
COAST RANGES
CASCADE RANGES
ROCKY MOUNTAINS
Helena
MONT.
Missouri R.
N. DAK.
Bismarck
Yellowstone R.
OREGON
IDAHO
Boise
Snake R.
S. DAK.
Pierre
WYO.
GREAT PLAINS
Humboldt R.
GREAT SALT LAKE DESERT
Great Salt Lake
Salt Lake City
Cheyenne
NEBR.
Platte R.
GREAT BASIN
NEV.
Carson City
Sacramento
San Francisco Bay
San Francisco
San Jose
SIERRA NEVADA
UTAH
Colorado R.
Denver
COLO.
KANSAS
Arkansas R.
CALIF.
DEATH VALLEY
Las Vegas
GRAND CANYON
POINT CONCEPTION
Santa Barbara
MOJAVE DESERT
Rio Grande
Santa Fe
OKLA.
Los Angeles
SANTA BARBARA ISLANDS
ARIZ.
Albuquerque
Colorado R.
San Diego
Phoenix
N. MEX.
Tucson
Gulf of California
TEXAS
Pecos R.
San Antonio
MEXICO
Rio Grande
ARCTIC OCEAN
U.S.S.R.
Bering Strait
BROOKS RANGE
ALASKA
ARCTIC CIRCLE
SEWARD PENINSULA
Fairbanks
CANADA
ST. LAWRENCE ISLAND
Yukon R.
ALASKA RANGE
Bering Sea
Anchorage
Lake Iliamna
KENAI PENINSULA
Gulf of Alaska
Juneau
ALASKA PENINSULA
KODIAK ISLAND
ALEXANDER ARCHIPELAGO
ALEUTIAN IS.
PACIFIC OCEAN
KAUAI
Kauai Channel
OAHU
Honolulu
Kaiwi Channel
MOLOKAI
MAUI
HAWAII
Alenuihaha Channel
Hilo
HAWAII
PACIFIC OCEAN

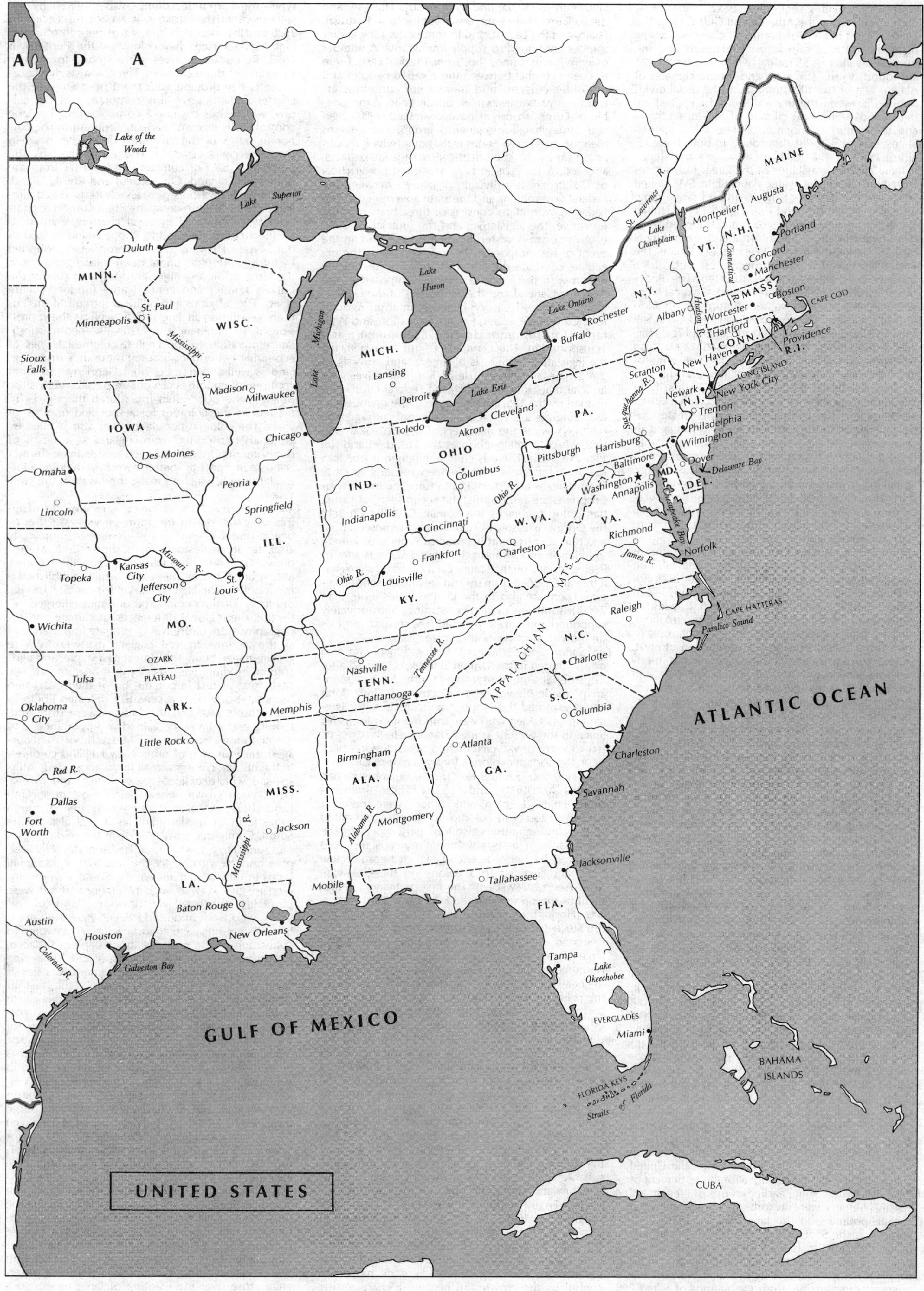
ADA
Lake of the Woods
Lake Superior
Duluth
MINN.
St. Paul
Minneapolis
WISC.
Mississippi R.
Sioux Falls
Lake Michigan
Lake Huron
MICH.
Lansing
Madison
Milwaukee
Detroit
Lake Erie
IOWA
Chicago
Toledo
Cleveland
Akron
Des Moines
OHIO
Omaha
Columbus
Peoria
IND.
Lincoln
Springfield
Indianapolis
ILL.
Cincinnati
Kansas City
Missouri R.
Frankfort
Topeka
Jefferson City
St. Louis
Ohio R.
Louisville
KY.
Wichita
MO.
OZARK PLATEAU
Nashville
TENN.
Tennessee R.
Tulsa
Chattanooga
Oklahoma City
ARK.
Memphis
Little Rock
Birmingham
Atlanta
Red R.
ALA.
GA.
MISS.
Dallas
Fort Worth
Jackson
Alabama R.
Montgomery
Mississippi R.
LA.
Mobile
Tallahassee
Baton Rouge
Austin
Houston
New Orleans
Colorado R.
Galveston Bay
GULF OF MEXICO
UNITED STATES
Lake Ontario
Rochester
Buffalo
N.Y.
St. Lawrence R.
Lake Champlain
Montpelier
VT.
N.H.
Connecticut R.
MAINE
Augusta
Portland
Concord
Manchester
MASS.
Boston
CAPE COD
Albany
Worcester
Hudson R.
Hartford
CONN.
Providence
R.I.
New Haven
LONG ISLAND
Scranton
Susquehanna R.
Newark
N.J.
New York City
Trenton
PA.
Philadelphia
Wilmington
Pittsburgh
Harrisburg
Baltimore
Dover
Delaware Bay
MD.
DEL.
Washington
Annapolis
Chesapeake Bay
Ohio R.
W. VA.
VA.
Richmond
Charleston
James R.
Norfolk
APPALACHIAN MTS.
Raleigh
N.C.
CAPE HATTERAS
Pamlico Sound
Charlotte
S.C.
Columbia
ATLANTIC OCEAN
Charleston
Savannah
Jacksonville
FLA.
Tampa
Lake Okeechobee
EVERGLADES
Miami
FLORIDA KEYS
Straits of Florida
BAHAMA ISLANDS
CUBA

WATERWAY provides sheltered passage for shallow draft vessels along the Atlantic and Gulf Coasts. The United States has a broad range of climates, varying from the tropical rain-forest of Hawaii and the tropical savanna of S Florida (where the EVERGLADES are found) to the subarctic and tundra climates of Alaska. East of the 100th meridian (the usual dividing line between the dry and humid climates) are the humid subtropical climate of SE United States and the humid continental climate of NE United States. Extensive forests are found in both these regions. West of the 100th meridian are the steppe climate and the grasslands of the Great Plains; trees are found along the water courses. In SW United States are the deserts of the basin and range province, with the hottest and driest spots in the United States. Along the Pacific coast are the Mediterranean-type climate of S California and, extending N into SE Alaska, the marine West Coast climate. The Pacific Northwest is one of the wettest parts of the United States and is densely forested. The Rocky Mts., Cascades, and Sierra Nevada have typical highland climates and are also heavily forested. In addition to the Grand Canyon in Arizona and Great Salt Lake in Utah, widely publicized geographical marvels of the United States include NIAGARA FALLS, on the New York-Canada border; the pink cliffs of BRYCE CANYON NATIONAL PARK, in Utah; and the geysers of YELLOWSTONE NATIONAL PARK, primarily in Wyoming (for others, see NATIONAL PARKS AND MONUMENTS, table). The United States is the greatest industrial nation in the world. Its mineral and agricultural resources are tremendous. Although it has been virtually self-sufficient in the past, an enormous increase in consumption, especially of energy, is making it increasingly dependent on certain imports. It is, nevertheless, the world's largest producer of both electrical and nuclear energy. It leads all nations in the production of natural gas, lead, copper, aluminum, sulfur, and salt. With the Soviet Union it is the leading producer of coal and steel. It ranks second in the production of crude oil, iron ore, silver, and zinc. The United States produces 69% of the world's mica, 68% of its molybdenum, 54% of its uranium, and 46% of its magnesium. It leads the world in the production of pig iron and ferroalloys, motor vehicles, and synthetic rubber. Agriculturally, the United States is first in the production of meat, cheese, corn, soybeans, and tobacco; second in cattle, hogs, cow's milk, butter, cotton lint, oats, and wheat; third in barley; and fourth in sugar. (For more detailed accounts of agricultural and industrial products, see separate articles on the states, cities, towns, and villages.) Major U.S. exports in the early 1970s were motor vehicles and parts, aircraft and parts, food, iron and steel-mill products, chemicals, and electronic computers and parts. The leading imports included ores and metal scraps, petroleum and petroleum products, machinery, transportation equipment (especially automobiles), paper and paper products, and metal manufactures. Major trading partners were Canada, Japan, West Germany, and the United Kingdom. The volume of trade has been steadily increasing. By 1972 the nation's gross national product, also steadily rising, had passed the $1-trillion mark. The development of the economy has been spurred by the growth of a complex network of communications not only by railroad, highways, inland waterways, and air but also by telephone, telegraph, radio, and television. More than half of the population is urban, and the great majority of the inhabitants are of European descent. About 11% of the total population is black; there are smaller groups of Orientals, with Japanese and Chinese in Hawaii and on the Pacific coast and large groups of Chinese in some of the Eastern cities. Living for the most part on reservations are remnants of the aboriginal inhabitants, the heterogeneous Indian tribes (see INDIANS, NORTH AMERICAN). Until the immigration law of 1924, the United States was the "melting pot" of nations. In addition to the original group of British settlers in the colonies of the Atlantic coast, numerous other national groups were introduced by immigration. Large numbers of Negro slaves were imported chiefly to work on the plantations of the South. When the United States was developing rapidly with the settlement of the West (where some earlier groups of French and Spanish settlers were absorbed), immigrants from Europe poured into the land. An important early group was the Scotch-Irish. Just before the middle of the 19th cent., Irish and German immigrants were predominant. A little later the Scandinavian nations supplied many settlers. After the Civil War, the immigrants came mainly from the nations of S and E Europe: from Italy, Greece, Russia, the part of Poland then in Russia, and from Austria-Hungary and the Balkans. There were lesser strains from Portugal, Spain, and the Levant, and to some extent the earlier sources continued to supply immigrants. A number of immigrants came, too, from the Far East. There has been conflict between these varied peoples and the older citizens, and there were conscious attempts at AMERICANIZATION, but in general the people of European origin have coalesced into a new and somewhat homogeneous group. The government of the United States is that of a federal republic set up by the CONSTITUTION OF THE UNITED STATES, adopted by the FEDERAL CONSTITUTIONAL CONVENTION of 1787. There is a division of powers between the Federal government and the state governments. The Federal government consists of three branches: the executive, the legislative, and the judicial. The executive power is vested in the President and, in the event of his incapacity, the Vice President. The executive conducts the administrative business of the nation with the aid of a cabinet composed of the Attorney General and the Secretaries of the Departments of State; Treasury; Defense; Interior; Agriculture; Commerce; Labor; Health, Education, and Welfare; Housing and Urban Development; and Transportation. The CONGRESS OF THE UNITED STATES, the legislative branch, is bicameral and consists of the Senate and the House of Representatives. The judicial branch is formed by the Federal courts and headed by the U.S. SUPREME COURT. The members of the Congress are elected by universal suffrage (see ELECTION) as are the members of the ELECTORAL COLLEGE, which formally chooses the President and the Vice President. There is complete religious freedom in the United States, and the overwhelming majority of Americans are Christians. In turn, the majority of Christians are Protestants; the second largest Christian group embraces the Roman Catholic Church; the Orthodox Eastern Church is also represented. In addition, a considerable group of Americans adhere to Judaism. Education in the United States is administered chiefly by the states. Each of the 50 states has a free and public primary and secondary school system. There are also in the United States more than 2,000 institutions of higher learning, both privately supported and state supported (see separate articles on individual colleges and universities).

Exploration and Settlement. Exploration of the area now included in the United States was spurred after Christopher Columbus, sailing for the Spanish monarchy, made his voyage of discovery in 1492. John CABOT explored the North American coast for England in 1498. Men who were important explorers for Spain in the present United States include PONCE DE LEÓN, CABEZA DE VACA, Hernando DE SOTO, and CORONADO; important explorers for France were Giovanni da VERRAZANO, Samuel de CHAMPLAIN, Louis JOLLIET, Jacques MARQUETTE, and LA SALLE. These three nations—England, Spain, and France—were the chief nations to establish colonies in the present United States, although others also took part, especially the Netherlands in the establishment of NEW NETHERLAND (explored by Henry HUDSON), which became New York, and Sweden in a colony on the Delaware River (see NEW SWEDEN). The first permanent settlement in the present United States was SAINT AUGUSTINE (Florida), founded in 1565 by the Spaniard Pedro MENÉNDEZ DE AVILÉS. Spanish control came to be exercised over Florida, West Florida, Texas, and a large part of the West, including California. For the purposes of finding precious metals and of converting heathens to Catholicism, the Spanish colonies in the present United States were relatively unfruitful and thus were never fully developed. The French established strongholds on the St. Lawrence River (Quebec and Montreal) and spread their influence over the Great Lakes country and along the Mississippi; the colony of Louisiana was a flourishing French settlement. The French government, like the Spanish, tolerated only the Catholic faith, and it implanted the rigid and feudalistic seignorial system of France in its North American possessions. Partly for these reasons, the French settlements attracted few colonists. The English settlements, which were on the Atlantic seaboard, developed in patterns more suitable to the New World, with greater religious freedom and economic opportunity. The first permanent English settlement was made at JAMESTOWN (Virginia) in 1607. The first English settlements in Virginia were managed by a chartered commercial company, the Virginia Company; economic motives were paramount to the company in founding the settlements. The Virginia colony early passed to control by the crown and became a characteristic type of English colony—the royal colony. Another type—the corporate colony—was initiated by the settlement of the PILGRIMS at PLYMOUTH COLONY in 1620 and by the establishment of the more important Massachusetts Bay colony by the Puritans in 1630. Religious motives were important in the founding of these colonies. The colonists of Massachusetts Bay brought with them from England the charter and the governing corporation of the colony, which thus became a corporate one, i.e., one controlled by its own resident corporation. The corporate status of the Plymouth Colony, evinced in the MAYFLOWER COMPACT, was established by the purchase (1626) of company and charter from the holders in England. Connecticut and Rhode Island, which were offshoots of Massachusetts, owed allegiance to no English company; their corporate character was confirmed by royal charters, granted to Connecticut in 1662 and to Rhode Island in 1663. A third type of colony was the proprietary, founded by lords proprietors under quasi-feudal grants from the king; prime examples are Maryland (under the Calvert family) and Pennsylvania (under William PENN). The religious and political turmoil of the Puritan Revolution in England, as well as the repression of the Huguenots in France, helped to stimulate emigration to the English colonies. Hopes of economic betterment brought thousands from England as well as a number from Germany and other continental countries. To obtain passage across the Atlantic, the poor often indentured themselves to masters in the colonies for a specified number of years. The colonial population was also swelled by criminals transported from England as a means of punishment. Once established as freedmen, former bondsmen and transportees were frequently allotted land with which to make their way in the New World.

Colonial America. The colonies were subject to English MERCANTILISM in the form of NAVIGATION ACTS, begun under Cromwell and developed more fully after the Stuart Restoration. As shown by C. M. Andrews, G. L. Beer, and later historians, the colonies at first benefited by these acts, which established a monopoly of the English market for certain colonial products. Distinct colonial economies emerged, reflecting the regional differences of climate and topography. Agriculture was of primary importance in all the sections. In New England many crops were grown, maize being the closest to a staple, and agricultural holdings were usually of moderate size. FUR TRADE was at first important, but it died out when the NEW ENGLAND CONFEDERATION defeated Philip in KING PHILIP'S WAR and the Indians were dispersed. Fishing and commerce gained in importance, and the economic expansion of Massachusetts encouraged the founding of other New England colonies. In the middle colonies small farms abounded, interspersed with occasional great estates, and diverse crops were grown, wheat being most important. Land there was almost universally held through some form of feudal grant, as it was also in the South. Commerce grew quickly in the middle colonies, and large towns flourished, notably Philadelphia and New York. By the late 17th cent. small farms in the coastal areas of the South were beginning to give way to large plantations; these were profitably developed with the slave labor of Negroes, who were imported in ever-increasing numbers. Plantations were almost exclusively devoted to cultivation of the great Southern staples—tobacco, rice, and, later, indigo. Fur trade and lumbering were long important. Although some towns developed, the Southern economy remained the least diversified and the most rural in colonial America. In religion, too, the colonies developed in varied patterns. In Massachusetts the religious theocracy of the Puritan oligarchy flourished. By contrast, Rhode Island allowed full religious freedom; there Baptists were in the majority, but other sects were soon in evidence. New Jersey and South Carolina also allowed complete religious liberty, and such colonies as Maryland and Pennsylvania established large measures of toleration. Maryland was at first a haven for Catholics, and Pennsylvania similarly a haven for Quakers, but within a few decades numerous Anglicans had settled in those colonies. Anglicans were also much in evidence further south, as were Presbyterians, most of them Scotch-Irish. Politically, the colonies developed representative institutions, the most important being the vigorous colonial assemblies. Popular participation was somewhat limited by property qualifications. In the proprietary colonies, particularly, the settlers came into conflict with the executive authority. Important points of difference arose over the granting of large estates to a few, over the great power of the proprietors, over the failure of the proprietors (who generally lived in England) to cope with problems of defense, and over religious grievances, frequently stemming from a struggle for dominance between Anglicans and other groups. In corporate Massachusetts religious grievances were created by the zealous Puritan demand for conformity. These conflicts, together with England's desire to coordinate empire defenses against France and to gain closer control of the colonies' thriving economic life, stimulated England to convert corporate and proprietary colonies into royal ones. By 1702, New Hampshire, Massachusetts, and New Jersey had been made royal colonies, and later the Carolinas and Georgia were transferred to royal control. Pennsylvania and Maryland remained nominally proprietary, but modifications of their charters in effect brought them under royal sway. Only Connecticut and Rhode Island remained substantially free of royal interference and, as corporate colonies, continued to select their own governors. In general, royal control brought more orderly government and greater religious toleration, but it also focused the colonists' grievances on the mother country. The policies of the governors, who were the chief instruments of English will in the colonies, frequently met serious opposition. The colonial assemblies clashed with the governors—notably with Edmund ANDROS and Francis NICHOLSON—especially over matters of taxation. The assemblies successfully resisted royal demands for permanent income to support royal policies and used their powers over finance to expand their own jurisdiction. As the 18th cent. progressed, colonial grievances were exacerbated. The British mercantile regulations, beneficial to agriculture, impeded the colonies' commercial and industrial development, and the pattern of trade enforced by the Navigation Acts kept the colonies denuded of specie. However, economic and social growth continued, and by the mid-18th cent. there had been created a greater sense of a separate, thriving, and distinctly American, albeit varied, civilization. In New England, Puritan values were modified by the impact of commerce and by the influence of the Enlightenment, while in the South the planter aristocracy developed a lavish and gentlemanly mode of life. Enlightenment ideals also gained influential adherents in the South. Higher education flourished in such institutions as Harvard, William and Mary, and King's College (now Columbia Univ.). The varied accomplishments of Benjamin FRANKLIN epitomized colonial common sense at its most enlightened and productive level. A religious movement of importance emerged in the revivals of the GREAT AWAKENING, stimulated by Jonathan EDWARDS; the movement ultimately led to a strengthening of METHODISM. Also inherent in this movement was egalitarian sentiment, which progressed but was not to triumph in the colonial era. One manifestation of egalitarianism was the long-continued conflict between the men of the frontiers and the wealthy Eastern oligarchs who dominated the assemblies, a conflict exemplified in the REGULATOR MOVEMENT. Colonial particularism, still stronger than national feeling, caused the failure of the ALBANY CONGRESS to achieve permanent union. However, internal strife and disunity remained a less urgent issue than the controversy with Great Britain. After the British and colonial forces had combined to drive the French from Canada and the Great Lakes region in the French and Indian War (1754–60; see under FRENCH AND INDIAN WARS), the colonists felt less need of British protection; but at this very time the British began colonial reorganization in an effort to impose on the colonists the costs of their own defense. Thus was set off the complex chain of events that united colonial sentiment against Great Britain and culminated in the AMERICAN REVOLUTION (1775–83; the events are described under that heading).

The States in Union. The Revolution resulted in the independence of the Thirteen Colonies: Massachusetts, New Hampshire, Connecticut, Rhode Island, New York, New Jersey, Pennsylvania, Delaware, Maryland, Virginia, North Carolina, South Carolina, and Georgia; their territories were recognized as extending N to Canada and W to the Mississippi River. The Revolution also broadened representation in government, advanced the movement for separation of church and state in America, increased opportunities for westward expansion, and brought the abolition of the remnants of feudal land tenure. The view that the Revolution had been fought for local liberty against strong central control reinforced the particularism of the states and was reflected in the weak union established under the Articles of Confederation (see CONFEDERATION, ARTICLES OF). Before ratification of the Articles (1781), conflicting claims of states to Western territories had been settled by the cession of Western land rights to the Federal government; the ORDINANCE OF 1787 established a form of government for territories and a method of admitting them as states to the Union. But the national government floundered. It could not obtain commercial treaties or enforce its will in international relations, and, largely because it could not raise adequate revenue and had no executive authority, it was weak domestically. Local economic depressions bred discontent that erupted in SHAYS'S REBELLION, further revealing the weakness of the Federal government. Advocates of strong central government bitterly attacked the Articles of Confederation; supported particularly by professional and propertied groups, they had a profound influence on the Constitution drawn up by the FEDERAL CONSTITUTIONAL CONVENTION of 1787. The Constitution created a national government with ample powers for effective rule, which were limited by "checks and balances" to forestall tyranny or radicalism. Its concept of a strong, orderly Union was popularized by the *Federalist* papers (see FEDERALIST, THE) of Alexander HAMILTON, James MADISON, and John JAY, which played an important part in winning ratification of the Constitution by the separate states. The first man to be elected President was the hero of the Revolution, George WASHINGTON. Washington introduced many government practices and institutions, including the cabinet. JAY'S TREATY (1794) allayed friction with Great Britain. Hamilton, as Washington's Secretary of the Treasury, promulgated a strong state and attempted to advance the economic development of the young country by a neomercantilist program; this included the establishment of a protective tariff, a mint, and the first BANK OF THE UNITED STATES as well as assumption of state and private Revolutionary debts. The controversy raised by these policies bred divisions along factional and, ultimately, party lines. Hamilton and his followers, who eventually formed the FEDERALIST PARTY, favored wide activity by the Federal government under a broad interpretation of the Constitution. Their opponents, who adhered to principles laid down by Thomas JEFFERSON and who became the Democratic Republican or DEMOCRATIC PARTY, favored narrow construction—limited Federal jurisdiction and activities. To an extent these divisions were supported by economic differences, as the Democrats largely spoke for the agrarian point of view and the Federalists represented propertied and mercantile interests. A significant divergence between the factions concerned the French Revolution, which seemed heroically egalitarian to the Democrats and dangerously radical to the Federalists; the latter favored friendship with England, while the Democrats sought bonhomie with France. Political differences reflected divergent visions of American civilization. Although Americans generally were proud of the absence of a privileged aristocracy and feudal encumbrances on their land, they differed on more subtle questions of egalitarianism and progress. Extreme democrats like Thomas PAINE had ebullient faith in popular government and popular mores; Joel BARLOW, too, envisioned a great popular culture evolving in America. From such optimists came schemes for broad popular education and participation in government. Men like John ADAMS had mixed views on the good sense of the masses, and many more conservative thinkers associated the "people" with vulgarity and ineptitude. The Federalists generally represented a pessimistic and the Democrats an optimistic view of man's inherent ca-

PRESIDENTS OF THE UNITED STATES (*with Vice Presidents, political parties, and dates in office*)

George Washington, 1789-97
John Adams

John Adams [Federalist] 1797-1801
Thomas Jefferson

Thomas Jefferson [Democratic-Republican] 1801-9
Aaron Burr, 1801-5
George Clinton, 1805-9

James Madison [Democratic-Republican] 1809-17
George Clinton, 1809-12
(no Vice President, April, 1812-March, 1813)
Elbridge Gerry, 1813-14
(no Vice President, Nov., 1814-March, 1817)

James Monroe [Democratic-Republican] 1817-25
Daniel D. Tompkins

John Quincy Adams [Democratic-Republican] 1825-29
John C. Calhoun

Andrew Jackson [Democratic] 1829-37
John C. Calhoun, 1829-32
(no Vice President, Dec., 1832-March, 1833)
Martin Van Buren, 1833-37

Martin Van Buren [Democratic] 1837-41
Richard M. Johnson

William Henry Harrison [Whig] 1841
John Tyler

John Tyler [Whig] 1841-45
(no Vice President)

James Knox Polk [Democratic] 1845-49
George M. Dallas

Zachary Taylor [Whig] 1849-50
Millard Fillmore

Millard Fillmore [Whig] 1850-53
(no Vice President)

Franklin Pierce [Democratic] 1853-57
William R. King, 1853
(no Vice President, April, 1853-March, 1857)

James Buchanan [Democratic] 1857-61
John C. Breckinridge

Abraham Lincoln [Republican] 1861-65
Hannibal Hamlin, 1861-65
Andrew Johnson, 1865

Andrew Johnson [Democratic/National Union] 1865-69
(no Vice President)

Ulysses Simpson Grant [Republican] 1869-77
Schuyler Colfax, 1869-73
Henry Wilson, 1873-75
(no Vice President, Nov., 1875-March, 1877)

Rutherford Birchard Hayes [Republican] 1877-81
William A. Wheeler

James Abram Garfield [Republican] 1881
Chester A. Arthur

Chester Alan Arthur [Republican] 1881-85
(no Vice President)

Grover Cleveland [Democratic] 1885-89
Thomas A. Hendricks, 1885
(no Vice President, Nov., 1885-March, 1889)

Benjamin Harrison [Republican] 1889-93
Levi P. Morton

Grover Cleveland [Democratic] 1893-97
Adlai E. Stevenson

William McKinley [Republican] 1897-1901
Garret A. Hobart, 1897-99
(no Vice President, Nov., 1899-March, 1901)
Theodore Roosevelt, 1901

Theodore Roosevelt [Republican] 1901-9
(no Vice President, Sept., 1901-March, 1905)
Charles W. Fairbanks, 1905-9

William Howard Taft [Republican] 1909-13
James S. Sherman, 1909-12
(no Vice President, Oct., 1912-March, 1913)

Woodrow Wilson [Democratic] 1913-21
Thomas R. Marshall

Warren Gamaliel Harding [Republican] 1921-23
Calvin Coolidge

Calvin Coolidge [Republican] 1923-29
(no Vice President, 1923-25)
Charles G. Dawes, 1925-29

Herbert Clark Hoover [Republican] 1929-33
Charles Curtis

Franklin Delano Roosevelt [Democratic] 1933-45
John N. Garner, 1933-41
Henry A. Wallace, 1941-45
Harry S. Truman, 1945

Harry S. Truman [Democratic] 1945-53
(no Vice President, 1945-49)
Alben W. Barkley, 1949-53

Dwight David Eisenhower [Republican] 1953-61
Richard M. Nixon

John Fitzgerald Kennedy [Democratic] 1961-63
Lyndon B. Johnson

Lyndon Baines Johnson [Democratic] 1963-69
(no Vice President, 1963-65)
Hubert H. Humphrey, 1965-69

Richard Milhous Nixon [Republican] 1969-74
Spiro T. Agnew, 1969-73
(no Vice President, Oct. 10, 1973-Dec. 6, 1973)
Gerald R. Ford, 1973-74

Gerald Rudolph Ford [Republican] 1974-
(no Vice President, Aug. 9, 1974-Dec. 19, 1974)
Nelson A. Rockefeller, 1974-

pacity to govern and develop himself; in practice, however, the values held by these two groups were often mixed. That a long road to democracy was still to be traveled is seen in the fact that in the late 18th cent. few but the economically privileged took part in political affairs. The Federalists were victorious in electing John Adams to the presidency in 1796. Federalist conservatism and anti-French sentiment were given vent in the ALIEN AND SEDITION ACTS of 1798 and in other acts. Deteriorating relations with France were seen in the XYZ AFFAIR and the "half war" (1798–1800), in which U.S. warships engaged French vessels in the Caribbean. The so-called Revolution of 1800 swept the Federalists from power and brought Jefferson to the presidency. Jefferson did bring a plainer and more republican style to government, and under him the Alien and Sedition Acts and other Federalist laws were allowed to lapse or were repealed. He moved toward stronger use of Federal powers, however, in negotiating the LOUISIANA PURCHASE (1803). In foreign policy Jefferson steered an officially neutral course between Great Britain and France, resisting the war sentiment roused by British IMPRESSMENT of American seamen and by both British and French violations of American shipping. He fostered the drastic EMBARGO ACT OF 1807 in an attempt to gain recognition of American rights through economic pressure, but the embargo struck hardest against the American economy, especially in New England. Under Jefferson's successor, James MADISON, the continued depredations of American shipping, combined with the clamor of American "war hawks" who coveted Canada and Florida, led to the WAR OF 1812, which was, however, opposed in New England (see HARTFORD CONVENTION). The Treaty of Ghent (see GHENT, TREATY OF) settled no specific issues of the war, but did confirm the independent standing of the young republic. Politically, the period that followed was the so-called era of good feeling. The Federalists had disintegrated under the impact of the country's westward expansion and its new interests and ideals. Democrats of all sections had by now adopted a Federalist approach to national development and were temporarily in agreement on a nationalist, expansionist economic policy. This policy was implemented in 1816 by the introduction of internal improvements, a protective tariff, and the second Bank of the United States. The same policies were continued under James MONROE. The MONROE DOCTRINE (1823), which proclaimed U.S. opposition to European intervention or colonization in the American hemisphere, introduced the long-continuing U.S. concern for the integrity of the Western Hemisphere. Domestically, the strength of the Federal government was increased by the judicial decisions of John MARSHALL, who had already helped establish the power of the U.S. Supreme Court. By 1820, however, sectional differences were arousing political discord. The sections of the country had long been developing along independent lines. In the North, merchants, manufacturers, inventors, farmers, and factory hands were busy with commerce, agricultural improvements, and the beginnings of the Industrial Revolution. In the South, Eli Whitney's cotton gin had brought in its wake a new staple; cotton was king, and the new states of Alabama, Louisiana, and Mississippi were the pride of the cotton kingdom. The accession of Florida (1819) further swelled the domain of the South. The American West was expanding as the frontier rapidly advanced. Around the turn of the century settlement of territory W of the Appalachians had given rise to the new states of Kentucky, Tennessee, and Ohio. Settlers continued to move farther west, and the frontier remained a molding force in American life (the importance of frontier influence was later described by Frederick Jackson TURNER and other historians). The MISSOURI COMPROMISE (1820) temporarily resolved the issue of slavery in new states, but under the presidency of John Quincy ADAMS sectional differences were aggravated. Particular friction, leading to the NULLIFICATION movement, was created by the tariff of 1828, which was highly favorable to Northern manufacturing but a "Tariff of Abominations" to the agrarian South. In the 1820s and 30s the advance of democracy brought manhood suffrage to many states and virtual direct election of the President, and party nominating conventions replaced the caucus. Separation of church and state became virtually complete. An era of political vigor was begun with the election (1828) of Andrew JACKSON to the presidency. If Jackson was not, as sometimes represented, the incarnation of frontier democracy, he nonetheless symbolized the advent of the common man to political power. He provided powerful executive leadership, attuned to popular support, committing himself to a strong foreign policy and to internal improvements for the West. His stand for economic individualism and his attacks on such bastions of the moneyed interests as the Bank of the United States won the approval of the growing middle class. Jackson acted firmly for the Union in the nullification controversy. But the South became increasingly dissident, and John C. CALHOUN emerged as its chief spokesman with his STATES' RIGHTS doctrine. Opponents of Jackson's policies, including both Northern and Southern conservative propertied interests, amalgamated to form the WHIG PARTY, in which Henry CLAY and Daniel WEBSTER were long the dominant figures. Jackson's successor, Martin VAN BUREN, attempted to perpetuate Jacksonian policies, but his popularity was undermined by the panic of 1837. In 1840, in their "Log Cabin and Hard Cider" campaign, the conservative Whigs adopted and perfected the Democratic party's techniques of mass appeal and succeeded in electing William Henry HARRISON as President. The West was winning greater attention in American life, and in the 1840s expansion to the Pacific was fervently proclaimed as the "manifest destiny" of the United States. Annexation of the republic of Texas (which had won its own independence from Mexico), long delayed primarily by controversy over its slave-holding status, was accomplished by Harrison's successor, John TYLER, three days before the expiration of his term. Tyler's action was prompted by the surprising victory of his Democratic successor, James K. POLK, who had campaigned on the planks of "reoccupation of Oregon" and "reannexation of Texas." The annexation of Texas precipitated the MEXICAN WAR; by the Treaty of GUADALUPE HIDALGO the United States acquired two fifths of the territory then belonging to Mexico, including California and the present American Southwest. In 1853 these territories were rounded out by the GADSDEN PURCHASE. Although in the dispute with Great Britain over the Columbia River country (see OREGON), Americans demanded "Fifty-four forty or fight," under President Polk a peaceful if more modest settlement was reached. Thus the United States gained its Pacific Northwest, and "manifest destiny" was virtually fulfilled. In California the discovery of gold in 1848 brought the rush of forty-niners, swelling population and making statehood for California a pressing question. The westward movement was also stimulated by many other factors. The great profits from open-range cattle ranching brought a stream of ranchers to the area (this influx was to reach fever pitch after the Civil War). The American farmer, with his abundant land, was often profligate in its cultivation, and as the soil depleted he continued to move farther west, settling the virgin territory. Soil exhaustion was particularly rapid in the South, where a one-crop economy prevailed, but because cotton profits were frequently high the plantation system quickly spread as far west as Texas. Occupation of the West was also sped by European immigrants hungry for land. MORMONS seeking a permanent home settled Utah.

Disunion and Reunion. By the mid-19th cent. the territorial gains and westward movement of the United States were focusing legislative argument on the extension of slavery to the new territories and breaking down the Missouri Compromise of 1820. The WILMOT PROVISO illustrated Northern antislavery demands, while Southerners, too, became increasingly intransigent. Only with great effort was the COMPROMISE OF 1850 achieved, and it was to be the last great compromise between the sections. The new Western states, linked in outlook to the North, had long since caused the South to lose hold of the House of Representatives, and Southern parity in the Senate was threatened by the prospective addition of more free states than slaveholding ones. The South demanded stronger enforcement of FUGITIVE SLAVE LAWS and, dependent on sympathetic Presidents, obtained it from Millard FILLMORE and especially from Franklin PIERCE and James BUCHANAN. The passage of the KANSAS-NEBRASKA BILL (1854), which repealed the Missouri Compromise, led to violence between factions in "bleeding Kansas" and spurred the founding of the new REPUBLICAN PARTY. Although there was sentiment for moderation and compromise in both North and South, it became increasingly difficult to take a middle stand on the slavery issue, and extremists came to the fore on both sides. Southerners, unable to accept the end of slavery, upon which their entire system of life was based, and fearful of slave insurrection (especially after the revolt led by Nat TURNER in 1831), felt threatened by the ABOLITIONISTS, who regarded themselves as leaders in a moral crusade. Southerners attempted to uphold slavery as universally beneficial and biblically sanctioned, while Northerners were increasingly unable to countenance the institution. Vigorous antislavery groups like the FREE-SOIL PARTY had already arisen, and as the conflict became more embittered it rent the older parties. The Whig party was shattered, and its Northern wing was largely absorbed in the new antislavery Republican party. The Democrats were also torn, and the compromise policies of Stephen A. DOUGLAS were of dwindling satisfaction to a divided nation. Moderation could not withstand the impact of the decision in the DRED SCOTT CASE, which denied the right of Congress to prohibit slavery in the territories, or the provocation of John Brown's raid on HARPERS FERRY (1859). The climax came in 1860 when the Republican Abraham LINCOLN defeated three opponents to win the presidency. Southern leaders, feeling there was no possibility of fair treatment under a Republican administration, resorted to secession from the Union and formed the CONFEDERACY. The attempts of the seceding states to take over Federal property within their borders (notably Fort Sumter in Charleston, S.C.) precipitated the CIVIL WAR (1861–65), which resulted in a complete victory for the North and the end of all slavery. The ensuing problems of RECONSTRUCTION in the South were complicated by bitter struggles, including the impeachment of President Andrew JOHNSON in 1868. Military rule in parts of the South continued through the administrations of Ulysses S. GRANT, which were also notable for their outrageous corruption. A result of the disputed election of 1876, in which the decision was given to Rutherford B. HAYES over Samuel J. TILDEN, was the end of Reconstruction and the reentry of the South into national politics.

Expansion, Reform, and World Involvement. The remainder of the 19th cent. was marked by railroad building (assisted by generous Federal land grants) and the disappearance of the American frontier. Great mineral wealth was discovered and exploited, and important technological innovations sped industrialization, which had already gained great impetus during the Civil War. Thus developed an economy based on steel, oil, railroads, and machines, an economy that a few decades after the Civil War ranked first in the world. Mammoth corporations such as the Standard Oil trust were formed, and "captains of industry" like John D. ROCKEFELLER and financiers like J. P. Morgan (see under MORGAN, family) controlled huge resources. Into the "land of promise" poured new waves of immigrants; some acquired dazzling riches, but many others suffered in a competitive and unregulated economic age. Behind the facade of the "Gilded Age," with its aura of peace and general prosperity, a whole range of new problems was created, forcing varied groups to promulgate new solutions. In the 1870s the expanding GRANGER MOVEMENT attempted to combat railroad and marketing abuses and to achieve an element of agrarian cooperation; this movement stimulated some regulation of utilities on the state level. Labor, too, began to combine against grueling factory conditions, but the opposition of business to unions was frequently overpowering, and the bulk of labor remained unorganized. Some strike successes were won by the KNIGHTS OF LABOR, but this union, discredited by the HAYMARKET SQUARE RIOT, was succeeded in prominence by the less divisive American Federation of Labor (see AMERICAN FEDERATION OF LABOR AND CONGRESS OF INDUSTRIAL ORGANIZATIONS). Massachusetts led the way (1874) with the first effective state legislation for an 8-hr day, but similar state and national legislation was sparse (see LABOR, HOURS OF), and the Federal government descended harshly on labor in the bloody strike at Pullman, Ill., and in other disputes. Belief in laissez faire and the influence of big business in both national parties, especially in the Republican party, delayed any widespread reform. The Presidents of the late 19th cent. were generally titular leaders of modest political distinction; however, they did institute a few reforms. Both Hayes and his successor, James A. GARFIELD, favored CIVIL SERVICE reforms, and after Garfield's death Chester A. ARTHUR approved passage of a civil service act; thus the vast, troublesome presidential patronage system gave way to more regular, efficient administration. In 1884 a reform group, led by Carl SCHURZ, bolted from the Republicans and helped elect Grover CLEVELAND, the first Democratic President since before the Civil War. Under President Benjamin HARRISON the SHERMAN ANTITRUST ACT was passed (1890). The attempt of the GREENBACK PARTY to combine sponsorship of free coinage of silver (see FREE SILVER) and other aids to the debtor class with planks favorable to labor had failed, but reform forces were gathering strength, as witnessed by the rise of the POPULIST PARTY. The reform movement was spurred by the economic panic of 1893, and in 1896 the Democrats nominated for President William Jennings BRYAN, who had adopted the Populist platform. He orated eloquently for free silver, but was defeated by William MCKINLEY, who gained ardent support from big business. By the 1890s a new wave of expansionist sentiment was affecting U.S. foreign policy. With the purchase of Alaska (1867) and the rapid settlement of the last Western territory, Oklahoma, American capital and attention were directed toward the Pacific and the Caribbean. The United States established commercial and then political hegemony in the Hawaiian Islands and annexed them in 1898. In that year expansionist energy found release in the SPANISH-AMERICAN WAR, which resulted in U.S. acquisition of Puerto Rico, the Philippine Islands, and Guam and in a U.S. quasi-protectorate over Cuba. American ownership of the Philippines involved military subjugation of the people, who rose in revolt when they realized that they would not be granted their independence; the Philippine Insurrection (1899-1901) cost more American lives and dollars than the Spanish-American War. U.S. rule, once firmly established, was generally beneficent; many internal improvements were introduced, and the standard of living in the various dependencies was raised. The American reforming zeal was most dramatically seen in the work of Walter REED and W. C. GORGAS, who eradicated yellow fever in Cuba. Widening its horizons, the United States formulated the OPEN DOOR policy (1900), which expressed its interest in China. Established as a world power with interests in two oceans, the United States intervened in the Panama revolution to facilitate construction of the PANAMA CANAL; this was but one of its many involvements in Latin American affairs under Theodore ROOSEVELT and later Presidents. By the time of Roosevelt's administration (1901-9), the progressive reform movement had taken definite shape in the country. Progressivism was partly a mode of thought, as witnessed by the PROGRESSIVE EDUCATION program of John DEWEY; as such it was a pragmatic attempt to mold modern institutions for the benefit of all. Progressives, too, were the MUCKRAKERS, who attacked abuse and waste in industry and in society. In its politics as shaped by R. M. LA FOLLETTE and others, progressivism adopted many Populist planks but promoted them from a more urban and forward-looking viewpoint. Progressivism was dramatized by the magnetic Roosevelt, who denounced "malefactors of great wealth" and demanded a "square deal" for labor; however, in practice he was a rather cautious reformer. He did make some attacks on trusts, and he promoted regulation of interstate commerce as well as passage of the Pure Food and Drug Act (1906) and legislation for the CONSERVATION OF NATURAL RESOURCES. Roosevelt's hand-picked successor, William H. TAFT, continued some reforms but in his foreign policy and in the PAYNE-ALDRICH TARIFF ACT, passed in his administration, favored big business. Taft's conservatism antagonized Roosevelt, who split with the Republican party in 1912 and ran for the presidency on the ticket of the PROGRESSIVE PARTY (see also INSURGENTS). But the presidency was won by the Democratic reform candidate, Woodrow WILSON. Wilson's "New Freedom" brought many progressive ideas to legislative fruition. The FEDERAL RESERVE SYSTEM and the FEDERAL TRADE COMMISSION were established, and the Adamson Act and the CLAYTON ANTITRUST ACT were passed. Perhaps more than on the national level, progressivism triumphed in the states in legislation beneficial to labor, in the furthering of education, and in the democratization of electoral procedures. Wilson did not radically alter the aggressive Caribbean policy of his predecessors; U.S. marines were sent to Nicaragua, and difficulties with Mexico were capped by the landing of U.S. forces in the city of Veracruz and by the campaign against Francisco (Pancho) VILLA. The nation's interest in world peace had already been expressed through participation in the HAGUE CONFERENCES, and when World War I burst upon Europe, Wilson made efforts to keep the United States neutral; in 1916 he was reelected on a peace platform. However, American sympathies and interests were actively with the Allies (especially with Great Britain and France), and although Britain and Germany both violated American neutral rights on the seas, German submarine attacks constituted the more dramatic provocation. On April 6, 1917, the United States entered the war on the side of the Allies and provided crucial manpower and supplies for the Allied victory. Wilson's FOURTEEN POINTS to insure peace and democracy captured the popular imagination of Europe and were a factor in Germany's decision to seek an armistice; however, at the Paris Peace Conference after the war, Wilson was thwarted from fully implementing his program. In the United States, isolationist sentiment against participation in the LEAGUE OF NATIONS, an integral part of the Treaty of Versailles (see VERSAILLES, TREATY OF), was led by Senator William E. BORAH and other "irreconcilables." The majority of Republican Senators, led by Henry Cabot LODGE, insisted upon amendments that would preserve U.S. sovereignty, but Wilson fought for his original proposals, and they were rejected. Isolationist sentiment prevailed during the 1920s, and while the United States played a major role in the NAVAL CONFERENCES for disarmament and in the engineering of the KELLOGG-BRIAND PACT, which outlawed war, its general lack of interest in international concerns was seen in its highly nationalistic economic policies, notably its insistence (later modified) on collecting the WAR DEBTS of foreign countries and the passage of the HAWLEY-SMOOT TARIFF ACT.

From Prosperity to Depression. The country voted for a return to "normalcy" when it elected Warren G. HARDING President in 1920; but the ensuing period was a time of rapid change, and the old normalcy was not to be regained. The Republican governments of the decade, although basically committed to laissez faire, actively encouraged corporate mergers and subsidized aviation and the merchant marine. Harding's administration, marred by the TEAPOT DOME scandal, gave way on his death to the presidency of Calvin COOLIDGE, and the nation embarked on a spectacular industrial and financial boom. In the 1920s the nation became increasingly urban, and everyday life was transformed as the "consumer revolution" brought the spreading use of automobiles, telephones, radios, and other appliances. The pace of living quickened, and mores became less restrained, while fortunes were rapidly accumulated on the skyrocketing stock market, in real estate speculation, and elsewhere. To some it seemed a golden age. But agriculture was not prosperous, and industry and finance became dangerously overextended. In 1929 there began the GREAT DEPRESSION, which reached worldwide proportions. In 1931, President Herbert HOOVER proposed a moratorium on foreign debts, but this and other measures failed to prevent economic collapse. In the 1932 election Hoover was overwhelmingly defeated by the Democrat Franklin D. ROOSEVELT. The new President immediately instituted his NEW DEAL with vigorous measures. To meet the critical financial emergency he instituted a "bank holiday." Congress, called into special session, enacted a succession of laws, some of them to meet the economic crisis with relief measures, others to put into operation long-range social and economic reforms. Some of the most important agencies created were the NATIONAL RECOVERY ADMINISTRATION, the AGRICULTURAL ADJUSTMENT ADMINISTRATION, the PUBLIC WORKS ADMINISTRATION, the CIVILIAN CONSERVATION CORPS, and the TENNESSEE VALLEY AUTHORITY. This program was further broadened in later sessions with other agencies, notably the SECURITIES AND EXCHANGE COMMISSION and the Works Progress Administration (later the WORK PROJECTS ADMINISTRATION). Laws also created a SOCIAL SECURITY program. The program was dynamic and, in many areas, unprecedented. It created a vast machinery by which the state could promote economic recovery and social welfare. Opponents of these measures argued that they violated individual rights, besides being extravagant and wasteful. Adverse decisions on several of the measures by the U.S. SUPREME COURT tended to slow the pace of reform and caused Roosevelt to attempt unsuccessfully to revise the court. Although interest centered chiefly on domestic affairs during the 1930s, Roosevelt continued and expanded the policy of friendship toward the Latin American nations which Herbert Hoover had initiated; this full-blown "good-neighbor" policy proved generally fruitful for the United States (see PAN-AMERICANISM). Roosevelt was reelected by an overwhelming majority in 1936 and won easily in 1940 even though he was breaking the no-third-term tradition.

World War II. The ominous situation abroad was chiefly responsible for Roosevelt's continuance at the national helm. By the late 1930s the Axis nations (Germany and Italy) in Europe as well as Japan in the Far East had already disrupted world peace. As wars began in China, Ethiopia, and Spain, the United States sought at first to bulwark its insular security by the NEUTRALITY ACT. As Axis aggression led to the outbreak of the European war in Sept., 1939, the United States still strove to stay out of it, despite increasing sympathy for the Allies. But after the fall of France in June, 1940, the support of the United States for beleaguered Britain became more overt. In March, 1941, LEND-LEASE aid was extended to the British and, in November, to the Russians. The threat of war had already caused the adoption of SELECTIVE SERVICE to build the armed strength of the nation. Hemisphere defense was enlarged, and the United States drew closer to Great Britain with the issuance of the ATLANTIC CHARTER. In Asian affairs the Roosevelt government had vigorously protested Japan's career of conquest and its establishment of the "Greater East Asia Co-Prosperity Sphere." After the Japanese takeover of French Indochina (July, 1941), with its inherent threat to the Philippines, the U.S. government froze all Japanese assets in the United States. Diplomatic relations grew taut, but U.S.-Japanese discussions were still being carried on when, on Dec. 7, 1941, Japanese bombs fell on PEARL HARBOR. The United States promptly declared war, and four days later Germany and Italy declared war on the United States. (For an account of military and naval events, see WORLD WAR II.) The country efficiently mobilized its vast resources, transforming factories to war plants and building a mighty military force which included most able-bodied young men and many young women. The creation of a great number of government war agencies to control and coordinate materials, transportation, and manpower brought unprecedented government intervention into national life. Rationing, price controls, and other devices were instituted in an attempt to prevent serious inflation or dislocation in the civilian economy. The war underscored the importance of U.S. resources and the prestige and power of the United States in world affairs. A series of important conferences outlined the policies for the war and the programs for the peace after victory; among these were the MOSCOW CONFERENCES, the CASABLANCA CONFERENCE, the CAIRO CONFERENCE, the TEHERAN CONFERENCE, and the YALTA CONFERENCE, at which Roosevelt, Winston Churchill, and Joseph Stalin planned for postwar settlement. Roosevelt was also a key figure in the plans for the UNITED NATIONS. After his sudden death in April, 1945, Harry S. TRUMAN became President. A month later the European war ended when Germany surrendered on May 7, 1945. Truman went to the POTSDAM CONFERENCE (July-August), where various questions of the peacetime administration of Europe were settled, many on an ad interim basis, pending the conclusion of peace treaties. Before the war ended with the defeat of Japan, the United States developed and used a fateful and revolutionary weapon of war, the ATOMIC BOMB. The Japanese surrender, announced Aug. 14, 1945, and signed Sept. 2, brought the war to a close. Peacetime readjustment was successfully effected. The government's "G.I. Bill" enabled many former servicemen to obtain free schooling, and millions of other veterans were absorbed by the economy, which boomed in fulfilling the demands for long-unobtainable consumer goods. The shortening of the postwar factory work week and the proportionate reduction of wages precipitated a rash of strikes, causing the government to pass the TAFT-HARTLEY LABOR ACT (1947). Some inflation occurred by 1947 as wartime economic controls were abandoned. Congress passed a host of Truman's measures relating to minimum wages, public housing, farm surpluses, and credit regulation; thus was instituted acceptance of comprehensive government intervention in times of prosperity. The nation's support of Truman's policies was signified when it returned him to the presidency in 1948 in an upset victory over Thomas E. Dewey.

The United States in a Divided World. The most striking postwar development was America's new peacetime involvement in international affairs. U.S. support for the United Nations symbolized its desire for peace and order in international relations. However, relations between the United States and the Soviet Union worsened during the late 1940s. In addition, a serious human problem was presented by Europe, prostrated and near starvation after years of war. The Truman Doctrine attempted to thwart Soviet expansion in Europe; massive loans, culminating in the MARSHALL PLAN, were vital in reviving European economies and thus in diminishing the appeal of Communism. As the COLD WAR intensified, the United States took steps (1948) to nullify the Soviet blockade of BERLIN and played the leading role in forming a new alliance of Western nations, the NORTH ATLANTIC TREATY ORGANIZATION (NATO). In the KOREAN WAR, U.S. forces played the chief part in combating the North Korean and Chinese attack on

South Korea. Thus the United States cast off its traditional peacetime isolationism and accepted its position as a prime mover in world affairs. International policy had significant repercussions at home. The fear of domestic Communism and subversion almost became a national obsession, culminating in such sensational events as the Alger HISS case and the trial and execution of Julius and Ethel Rosenberg (see ROSENBERG CASE). Security measures and loyalty checks in the government and elsewhere were tightened, alleged Communists were prosecuted under the Smith Act of 1940, and employees in varied fields were dismissed for questionable political affiliations, past or present. The most notorious prosecutor of alleged Communists was Senator Joseph MCCARTHY, whose extreme methods were later recognized as threats to freedom of speech and democratic principles. Two decades of Democratic control of the White House came to an end with the presidential election of 1952, when Dwight D. EISENHOWER was swept into office over the Democratic candidate, Adlai E. STEVENSON. Although it did not try to roll back the social legislation passed by its Democratic predecessors, the Eisenhower administration was committed to a laissez-faire domestic policy. By the mid-1950s, America was in the midst of a great industrial boom, and stock prices were skyrocketing. In foreign affairs the Eisenhower administration was internationalist in outlook, although it sternly opposed Communist power and threatened "massive retaliation" for Communist aggression. Some antagonism came from the neutral nations of Asia and Africa, partly because of the U.S. association with former colonial powers and partly because U.S. foreign aid more often than not had the effect of strengthening ruling oligarchies abroad. In the race for technological superiority the United States exploded (1952) the first hydrogen bomb, but was second to the USSR in launching (Jan. 31, 1958) an artificial satellite and in testing an intercontinental guided missile. However, spurred by Soviet advances, the United States made rapid progress in SPACE EXPLORATION and missile research. In the crucial domestic issue of racial INTEGRATION, the U.S. Supreme Court in a series of decisions supported the efforts of black citizens to achieve full civil rights. In contrast to the increased liberalism of the Supreme Court was the appearance of such ultraconservative political groups as the JOHN BIRCH SOCIETY. In 1959, Alaska and Hawaii became the 49th and 50th states of the Union. Despite hopes for "peaceful coexistence," negotiations with the USSR for nuclear disarmament failed to achieve accord, and Berlin remained a serious source of conflict. In 1961, Eisenhower, the oldest President ever to hold office, gave way to the youngest President ever elected, John F. KENNEDY, who defeated the Republican candidate, Richard M. Nixon. President Kennedy called for "new frontiers" of American endeavor, but had difficulty securing Congressional support for his domestic programs (integration, tax reform, medical benefits for the aged). Kennedy's foreign policy combined such humanitarian innovations as the PEACE CORPS and the ALLIANCE FOR PROGRESS with the traditional opposition to Communist aggrandizement. After breaking relations with Cuba, which, under Fidel Castro, had clearly moved within the Communist orbit, the United States supported (1961) an ill-fated invasion of Cuba by anti-Castro forces. In 1962, in reaction to the presence of Soviet missiles in Cuba, the United States blockaded Soviet military shipments to Cuba and demanded the dismantling of Soviet bases there. The two great powers seemed on the brink of war, but within a week the USSR acceded to U.S. demands. In the meantime the United States achieved an important gain in space exploration with the orbital flight around the earth in a manned satellite by Col. John H. GLENN. The tensions of the cold war eased when, in 1963, the United States and the Soviet Union reached an accord on a limited ban of nuclear testing. On Nov. 22, 1963, President Kennedy was assassinated while riding in a motorcade in Dallas, Texas. His successor, Lyndon B. JOHNSON, proclaimed a continuation of Kennedy's policies and was able to bring many Kennedy measures to legislative fruition. Significant progress toward racial equality was achieved with a momentous Civil Rights Act (1964), a Voting Rights Act (1965), and the 24th Amendment to the Constitution, which abolished the poll tax. Other legislation, reflecting Johnson's declaration of a "war on poverty" and his stated aim of creating a "Great Society," included a comprehensive Economic Opportunity Act (1964) and bills providing for tax reduction, medical care for the aged, an increased minimum wage, urban rehabilitation, and aid to education. Public approval was given in the landslide victory won by Johnson over his Republican opponent, Senator Barry Goldwater, in the 1964 presidential election. The victory also represented voter reaction against Senator Goldwater's aggressive views on foreign policy. Ironically, international problems dominated Johnson's second term, and Johnson himself pursued an aggressive course, dispatching (April, 1965) troops to the Dominican Republic during disorders there and escalating American participation in the VIETNAM WAR. Authorization for the latter was claimed by Johnson to have been given (Aug., 1964) by Congress in the Gulf of Tonkin Resolution, which was passed after two U.S. destroyers were reportedly attacked by North Vietnamese PT boats in the Gulf of Tonkin. The resolution recognized the maintenance of peace in Southeast Asia as vital to American interests and authorized the President to "take all necessary measures to repel any armed attack" and to "prevent further aggression." President Johnson subsequently instituted (1965) extensive air attacks against North Vietnam, increased the number of U.S. troops in Vietnam from 16,000 to more than 500,000, and committed them to an extensive air, sea, and ground war in defense of South Vietnam. The Federal military budget soared, and inflation became a pressing problem. The Vietnam War provoked increasing opposition at home, manifested in marches and demonstrations in which casualties were sometimes incurred and thousands of people were arrested. An impression of general lawlessness and domestic disintegration was heightened by serious race riots that erupted in cities across the nation, most devastatingly in the Watts district of Los Angeles (1965) and in Detroit and Newark (1967), and by various racial and political assassinations, notably those of Martin Luther KING, Jr., and Senator Robert F. KENNEDY (1968). Other manifestations of social upheaval were the increase of drug use, especially among youths, and the rising rate of crime, most noticeable in the cities. Opposition to American involvement in the Vietnam War so eroded Johnson's popularity that he chose not to run again for President in 1968; his position as leader of the Democratic party had been seriously challenged by Senator Eugene McCarthy, who ran as a peace candidate in the primary elections. Antiwar forces in the Democratic party received a setback with the assassination of Senator Kennedy, also a peace candidate, and the way was opened for the nomination of Vice President Hubert H. HUMPHREY, a supporter of Johnson's policies, as the Democratic candidate for President. Violence broke out during the Democratic national convention in Chicago when police and national guardsmen battled some 3,000 demonstrators in what a national investigating committee later characterized as "a police riot." The Republican candidate, Richard M. NIXON, ran on a platform promising an end to the Vietnam War and stressing the need for domestic "law and order"; he won a narrow victory, receiving 43.4% of the popular vote to Humphrey's 42.7%. A third-party candidate, Gov. George C. WALLACE of Alabama, carried five Southern states. The Congress remained Democratic. Pronouncing the "Nixon doctrine"—that thenceforth other countries would have to carry more of the burden of fighting Communist domination, albeit with substantial American economic aid—Nixon began a slow withdrawal of American troops from Vietnam. Criticism that he was not moving fast enough in ending the war increased after the revelation (1969) of a long hushed-up massacre of Vietnamese civilians by American soldiers in the hamlet of My Lai and the publication (1971) of excerpts from the PENTAGON PAPERS, a top-secret study of U.S. involvement in Vietnam that suggested serious policy errors as well as deception on the part of the government. Massive antiwar demonstrations continued, and when Nixon in the spring of 1970 ordered U.S. troops into neutral Cambodia to destroy Communist bases and supply routes there, a wave of demonstrations, some of them violent, swept American campuses. Four students were killed by national guardsmen at Kent State Univ. in Ohio, and 448 colleges and universities temporarily closed down. Antiwar activity declined, however, when American troops were removed from Cambodia after 60 days. The institution of draft reform, the continued withdrawal of U.S. soldiers from Vietnam, and a sharp decrease in U.S. casualties all contributed toward dampening antiwar sentiment and removing the war as an issue from public debate. Racial flare-ups abated after the tumult of the 1960s (although the issue of the busing of children to achieve integration continued to arouse controversy); a measure of domestic unrest was still seen in sporadic terrorist bombings (a wing of the Capitol was one target), serious prison riots, and increased revolutionary activity by militant blacks. The growing movement of women demanding social, economic, and political equality with men also reflected the changing times. A dramatic milestone in the country's space program was reached in July, 1969, with the landing of two men on the moon, the first of several such manned flights. Significant unmanned probes of several of the planets followed, and in 1973 the first space station was orbited. In domestic policy Nixon appeared to favor an end to the many reforms of the '60s. He was accused by civil rights proponents of wooing Southern support by seeking delays in the implementation of school integration. Such actions by his administration were overruled by the Supreme Court. Nixon twice attempted to appoint conservative Southern judges to the U.S. Supreme Court and was twice frustrated by the Senate, which rejected both nominations. In an attempt to control the spiraling inflation inherited from the previous administration, Nixon concentrated on reducing federal spending. He vetoed numerous appropriations bills passed by Congress, especially those in the social service and public works areas, although he continued to stress defense measures, such as the establishment of an antiballistic missiles (ABM) system, and foreign aid. Important legislative accomplishments included the Postal Reorganization Act (1970), which converted the Post Office into an independent government agency, and a "revenue-sharing" bill (1972), which provided direct Federal payments to the states for local needs, a significant step toward the decentralization of government. Federal budget cuts contributed to a general economic slowdown but failed to halt inflation, so that the country experienced the unprecedented misfortune of both rising prices and rising unemployment; the steady drain of gold reserves after almost three decades of enormous foreign aid programs, a new balance-of-trade deficit, and the instability of the dollar in the international market also affected the economy. In Aug., 1971, Nixon resorted to the freezing of prices, wages, and rents; these controls were continued under an ensuing, more flexible but comprehensive program known as Phase II. Another significant move was the devaluation of the dollar in Dec., 1971; it was further devalued in 1973 and again in 1974. In keeping with his announced intention of moving the United States from an era of confrontation to one of negotiation, Nixon made a dramatic visit to the People's Republic of China in Feb., 1972, ending more than 20 years of hostility between the two countries and opening the way for a normalization of relations. A trip to Moscow followed in the spring, culminating in the signing of numerous agreements between the United States and the Soviet Union, the most important being two strategic arms limitations accords, reached after lengthy talks begun in 1969. The attainment of a degree of friendly relations with China and the USSR was especially surprising in view of the provocative actions that the United States was taking at that time against North Vietnam. Although U.S. ground troops were being steadily withdrawn from Vietnam, U.S. bombing activity was increasing, and after the North Vietnamese staged a massive drive directly across the demilitarized zone in the spring of 1972, the United States mined Haiphong and other North Vietnamese harbors and resumed the full-scale bombing raids north of the 20th parallel that had been halted by President Johnson in 1968. Meanwhile, peace talks with North Vietnamese representatives, initiated under President Johnson in 1968, continued in Paris. A cease-fire in Vietnam was not achieved until Jan., 1973. When the peace talks snagged in the middle of Dec., 1972, Nixon ordered the heaviest bombing attacks in history against North Vietnam. Widely condemned by both U.S. and world opinion, they were halted after two weeks. However, U.S. bombing attacks on Communist positions in both Laos and Cambodia continued even after the cease-fire in Vietnam, and although a cease-fire soon followed in Laos, heavy U.S. bombing of Cambodia persisted. In May-June, 1973, Congress voted to cut off all funds for the continued bombing, and Nixon, after vetoing the bill, struck a compromise whereby he promised to end the bombing on Aug. 15. Congress subsequently passed a bill, overriding Nixon's veto, limiting the President's power to commit U.S. troops to combat abroad without Congressional approval. In the presidential election of 1972, the Democratic party reforms that increased the power of women and minority groups in the convention resulted in the nomination of Senator George S. MCGOVERN for President. Senator McGovern called for an immediate end to the Vietnam War and for a drastic cut in defense spending and a guaranteed minimum income for all citizens. His candidacy was damaged by the necessity to replace his original choice for Vice President and by the continuing perception of McGovern as a dangerous radical. Nixon was reelected (Nov., 1972) in a landslide, losing only Massachusetts and the District of Columbia. But Nixon's second term was marred, and finally destroyed, by the WATERGATE AFFAIR, which began when five men (two of whom were later discovered to be direct employees of Nixon's reelection committee) were arrested after breaking into the Democratic party's national headquarters at the Watergate apartment complex in Washington, D.C. In March, 1973, one of the convicted burglars charged that there had been a massive coverup of the burglary involving many present and former officials of the Nixon administration. Hearings were held by a special Senate committee investigating corrupt campaign practices, and one of the witnesses, John Dean, former White House counsel, accused Nixon of approving the coverup. During the course of the hearings it was discovered that presidential conversations had been tape-recorded in the White House since 1971. The special Watergate prosecutor, Archibald Cox, sued Nixon to obtain the tapes, and Nixon responded by firing him (Oct., 1973). The dismissal of Cox caused a tremendous public outcry and led the House of Representatives to empower its Judiciary Committee to initiate an impeachment investigation. In early 1974 several high-ranking former officials of the Nixon administration were indicted in the coverup, and Nixon was named an unindicted co-conspirator. The President's efforts to bolster his position—which included the appointment of a new special prosecutor, Leon Jaworski, the release (April, 1974) of edited transcripts of his taped conversations, and several abortive public relations attempts at "candor"—all failed to stem the erosion in confidence. In July, 1974, the Judiciary Committee adopted three articles of impeachment against Nixon, charging him with obstruction of justice, abuse of the office of President (an article that encompassed numerous other scandals not directly related to Watergate), and failure to respond to a House subpoena. On Aug. 5, in response to a Supreme Court ruling, Nixon released the transcripts of three recorded conversations that were among those to be given to Jaworski. At that time he admitted that he had attempted to halt a Federal Bureau of Investigation inquiry into the break-in. Nixon resigned on Aug. 9, the first president in the history of the republic to be driven from office under the threat of impeachment. He was succeeded by Vice President Gerald R. FORD. (Nixon's first Vice President, Spiro T. AGNEW, had resigned in Oct., 1973, after being charged with income tax evasion.) Ford promised to continue Nixon's foreign policy, particularly the improvement of relations with China and the USSR (in his last days in office, Nixon had made trips to the Middle East and the Soviet Union to promote peace). In domestic affairs, Ford attempted to formulate new policies to stem the ever-increasing inflation rate, which by late 1974 had reached the most severe levels since the period following World War II. He was also confronted with mounting unemployment, with the continuing economic impact caused by the high price of petroleum, and with the threat of a devastating world food crisis. Ford's popularity suffered a sharp setback when he granted Nixon (Sept. 8) a complete and unconditional pardon for any crimes that Nixon may have committed during his term as President. The public disapproval of this decision, along with the deteriorating economy, contributed to a sharp reversal in Republican fortunes in the elections of 1974. In Dec., 1974, Nelson A. Rockefeller, a former governor of New York, was sworn in as Vice President following extensive hearings before Congressional committees. Thus, neither the President nor the Vice President had been popularly elected, both having been chosen under the terms of the Twenty-fifth Amendment.

Bibliography and Related Articles. There are articles on all Americans of major importance, on the principal government agencies and departments, and on numerous topics of American history, e.g., WHISKEY REBELLION, OHIO COMPANY, INDEPENDENT TREASURY SYSTEM, and STAR ROUTE. There are also articles on more than 2,000 cities, towns, and villages in the United States. The state articles supply bibliographies for state history. Aspects of American culture are discussed under AMERICAN ARCHITECTURE, AMERICAN ART, AMERICAN LITERATURE, and JAZZ. Many general articles (e.g., SLAVERY; DIPLOMATIC SERVICE) have useful material and bibliographies relating to the United States. The writings on American history are voluminous. Useful bibliographies are Oscar Handlin et al., ed., *The Harvard Guide to American History* (1954, repr. 1967); Library of Congress, *A Guide to the Study of the United States of America* (1960); and Harvard Univ. Library, *American History* (5 vol., 1967). P. M. Hamer, ed., *Guide to Archives and Manuscripts in the United States* (1961) is the most complete work of its kind. Other reference works are Richard B. Morris and Henry S. Commager, ed., *Encyclopedia of American History* (rev. ed. 1970); T. C. Cochran and Wayne Andrews, *Concise Dictionary of American History* (1962); H. S. Commager, ed., *Documents of American History* (8th ed. 1968); and J. F. Jameson, *Dictionary of American History* (rev. ed. by A. E. McKinley, 1971). The still usable cooperative "American Nation" series (ed. by A. B. Hart, 28 vol., 1904–18) has been largely superseded by the "New American Nation Series" (ed. by H. S. Commager and R. B. Morris, 1954–). Another cooperative work is the "History of the South" series (ed. by W. H. Stephenson and E. M. Coulter, 10 vol., 1947–67). The "History of American Life" series (ed. by Arthur M. Schlesinger and Dixon R. Fox, 13 vol., 1927–55) remains the most comprehensive survey of American social history. The "Yale Chronicles of America" series (ed. by Allen Johnson, 50 vol., 1918–21; 6-vol. supplement ed. by Allan Nevins, 1950–51) remains important. Some of the classic works on American history are those of Henry ADAMS, C. M. ANDREWS, George BANCROFT, Charles A. BEARD, Carl L. BECKER, G. L. BEER, Edward CHANNING, John FISKE, J. B. MCMASTER, E. P. OBERHOLTZER, H. L. OSGOOD, Francis PARKMAN, Vernon Louis PARRINGTON, Ulrich B. PHILLIPS, James Ford RHODES, and Frederick Jackson TURNER. Other works of significance are by Bernard BAILYN, S. F. BEMIS, Ray Allan Billington, Daniel Boorstin, Bruce CATTON, H. S. COMMAGER, David DONALD, D. S. FREEMAN, L. H. GIPSON, Richard HOFSTADTER, John F. JAMESON, Perry MILLER, S. E. MORISON, R. B. MORRIS, Allan NEVINS, A. M. SCHLESINGER, A. M. SCHLESINGER, JR., T. J. WERTENBAKER, and C. Vann WOODWARD. Brief general histories include S. E. Morison, *The Oxford History of the American People* (1965); Allan Nevins and H. S. Commager, *A Short History of the United States* (5th rev. ed. 1966); H. J. Carman, H. C. Syrett, and Bernard Wishy, *A History of the American People* (3d ed., 2 vol., 1967); Dexter Perkins and G. G. Van Deusen, *The United States of America: A History* (2d ed., 2 vol., 1968); and S. E. Morison and H. S. Commager, *The Growth of the American Republic* (6th ed. 1969). Special topics are treated in F. A. Shannon, *America's Economic Growth* (3d ed. 1951); O. W. Larkin, *Art and Life in America* (rev. ed. 1960); Merle Curti, *The Growth of American Thought* (3d ed. 1964); E. S. Gausted, *A Religious History of America* (1966); R. A. Billington and J. B. Hedges, *Westward Expansion* (3d ed. 1967); T. A. Bailey, *A Diplomatic History of the American People* (8th ed. 1969); L. M. Hacker, *The Course of American Economic Growth and Development* (1970); A. H. Kelly and W. A. Harbison, *The American Constitution* (4th ed. 1970); M. J. Frisch, ed., *American Political Thought* (1971); S. E. Ahlstrom, *A Religious History of the United States* (1972); R. E. Spiller et al., ed., *Literary History of the United States* (3d ed., 3 vol., 1963–72); M. E. Armbruster, *The Presidents of the United States and Their Administrations from Washington to Nixon* (5th ed., rev. 1974). Geographical works include N. M. Fenneman, *Physiography of Western United States* (1931) and *Physiography of Eastern United States* (1938); R. H. Brown, *Historical Geography of the United States* (1948); U.S. Geological Survey, *National Atlas of the United States* (1948); P. E. James and C. F. Jones, ed., *American Geography: Inventory and Prospect* (1954); D. J. Bogue and C. L. Beale, *Economic Areas of the United States* (1961); C. L. White and E. J. Foscus, *Regional Geography of Anglo-America* (3d ed. 1963). Guides to individual states are found in the Federal Writers' Project's "American Guide" series. See also U.S. Bureau of the Census, *Statistical Abstract of the United States* (latest ed.).

United States, Great Seal of the, official impression that validates a United States government document. It was adopted by the Continental Congress in 1782 and, with only minor changes in the design, remains in use today. In the center of the seal is an American eagle. It holds in its beak a scroll inscribed "E pluribus unum"; in one talon is an olive branch; in the other, a bundle of thirteen arrows. A shield with thirteen alternate red and white stripes covers the eagle's breast, and over its head a cloud surrounds a blue field containing thirteen stars. The Secretary of State is the official custodian of the seal, and it is only affixed to certain classes of documents (e.g., foreign treaties, presidential proclamations, and commissions installing cabinet officers and other high executive officials). See Gaillard Hunt, *History of the Seal of the United States* (1909); U.S. Dept. of State, *The Seal of the United States* (1957).

United States Air Force Academy, at Colorado Springs, Colo.; for training young men to be officers in the U.S. air force; authorized in 1954 by Congress. Temporary quarters were opened at Lowry Air Force Base at Denver in 1955. The permanent campus opened in 1958. Candidates must be between 17 and 22 years of age and meet special physical and educational qualifications. An applicant must obtain a nomination to be considered for an appointment to the academy. The sources of nomination are the President of the United States (who may appoint 100 cadets each year); the Vice President (5 attending the academy at any one time); U.S. Senators and Representatives (5 each at any one time); the mayor of the District of Columbia (5 at any one time); the governor of the Panama Canal Zone (1 at any one time); the resident commissioner and governor of Puerto Rico (6 at any one time); the governors of American Samoa, Guam, and the Virgin Islands (1 at any one time); sons of deceased and disabled veterans or of military or civilian personnel in a missing status (40 at any one time); regular air force (85 each year); air force reserve and national guard (85 each year); honor graduates of military and naval schools and air force ROTC and Junior ROTC (20 at any one time); sons of Medal of Honor recipients (unlimited); the Republic of the Philippines (4 at any one time); and the American republics (20 at any one time). Cadets undergo a four-year course of instruction; they receive free tuition and room and board and receive a monthly allotment to pay for supplies, clothing, and personal expenses.

United States Coast Guard Academy, at New London, Conn.; for training young men to be officers of the U.S. Coast Guard; established 1876, opened 1877 as United States Revenue Cutter Service School of Instruction, took its present name in 1915. The academy, differing from other U.S. military academies, gains its candidates through a nationwide competition. There are no congressional appointments or geographical quotas. Each applicant must be between the ages of 17 and 22. A cadet's education consists of military and academic instruction, including professional training at sea. Cadets receive full scholarships to the academy as well as pay and allowances. See Irving Crump, *Our United States Coast Guard Academy* (1961).

United States Government Printing Office: see GOVERNMENT PRINTING OFFICE, U.S.

United States–Japan Security Treaty, military defense agreement between the United States and Japan. Originally concluded in 1952, the treaty was revised in 1960 in response to Japanese dissatisfaction with many of its provisions. According to the original agreement, the United States assumed responsibility for Japan's defense in case of external attack. In return, U.S. forces had unrestricted use of their Japanese bases and could, if requested by the Japanese government, be used to suppress internal disorders. Those provisions, combined with the treaty's open-ended termination date, led the Japanese to seek a renegotiation of the agreement, finally achieved in 1960. Under terms of the revised treaty, the United States must consult with Japan's government before using its Japanese bases for combat in Asia. The new treaty also had a 10-year limitation. Despite such changes, ratification of the new agreement sparked massive anti-American demonstrations during the spring of 1960, culminating in the resignation of prime minister Nobusuke Kishi's government in July. The Japanese government's decision to extend the treaty automatically in 1970 sparked another round of leftist demonstrations. The treaty remains a major target of Japan's left wing.

United States Merchant Marine Academy, at Kings Point, N.Y.; for the training of merchant marine officers; established 1936, opened 1942. Candidates must be between the ages of 17 and 22, be nominated for candidacy by their Representative or Senator, and pass a competitive examination. In 1974 the academy became coeducational.

United States Military Academy, at WEST POINT, N.Y.; for training young men to be officers in the U.S. army; founded and opened in 1802. The original act provided that the Corps of Engineers stationed at West Point should constitute a military academy, but the growing threat of war with England in 1812 resulted in congressional action to increase the corps and to expand the academy's facilities. Changes in curriculum and organization made by Sylvanus THAYER, superintendent from 1817 to 1833, earned him the title Father of the Military Academy. In the 19th cent. the military academy was one of the nation's major sources of civil engineers and its graduates made excellent records in the Mexican War and especially in the Civil War. After 1866 the academy was no longer formally related to the Corps of Engineers. The academy is now under the general direction and supervision of the Dept. of the Army. Its enrollment has greatly expanded since its founding and at present is about 4,400 cadets. The curriculum, too, has been greatly modernized, notably under Douglas MacArthur, its superintendent from 1919 to 1922. An applicant must obtain a nomination to be considered for an appointment to the academy. The sources of nomination are the President of the United States (100 cadets), the Vice President (5), U.S. Senators and Representatives (5 each), the mayor of the District of Columbia (5), the governor of the Canal Zone (1), the resident commissioner and governor of Puerto Rico (6), the governors of Guam, the Virgin Islands, and America Samoa (1 each), regular army (85), army reserve and national guard (85), sons of deceased and disabled veterans (about 10), honor graduates of military and naval schools and the Reserve Officers' Training Corps (20), sons of persons awarded the Medal of Honor (unlimited), Republic of the Philippines (1), and the American republics (20). Candidates must be between the ages of 17 and 22 and must meet certain physical and educational qualifications. Cadets undergo a four-year course of instruction on full scholarship, with summers devoted to practical military training, and are paid $283.05 a month plus a ration allowance. The West Point Museum contains ordnance and military trophies of historical interest. It is one of the most important college museums in the United States. George W. CULLUM compiled a valuable biographical register of West Point cadets. See T. J. Fleming, *West Point* (1969); Joseph Ellis and Robert Moore, *School for Soldiers* (1974).

United States National Museum: see SMITHSONIAN INSTITUTION.

United States National Science Foundation: see NATIONAL SCIENCE FOUNDATION.

United States Naval Academy, at Annapolis, Md.; for training young men to be officers of the U.S. navy or marine corps. George BANCROFT, Secretary of the Navy, founded and opened (1845) it as the Naval School at Annapolis. In 1850–51 the school was reorganized under the present title. During the Civil War it was moved to Newport, R.I., but was returned to Annapolis in 1865. Candidates for admission must be between 17 and 22 years of age and meet certain physical and educational qualifications. An applicant must obtain a nomination to be considered for an appointment. The following are sources of nomination: the President of the United States (who may appoint 100 midshipmen each year); the Vice President (5 attending the academy at any one time); U.S. Senators, Representatives, the delegate to the Congress from the District of Columbia, and the resident commissioner of Puerto Rico (each of whom may have 5 attending at any one time); regular and naval marine corps (85 each year); naval and marine corps reserve (85 each year); naval ROTC (10 each year); honor graduates of naval and military schools (10 each year); and sons of deceased or disabled veterans, prisoners of war, or servicemen missing in action (65 at any one time). Residents of Puerto Rico, the Canal Zone, the Virgin Islands, Guam, and American Samoa may apply to their governors for nomination and sons of Medal of Honor winners to the superintendent of the academy. Midshipmen receive a monthly allotment to pay for supplies, clothing, and personal expenses. The four-year course includes scientific and general studies as well as technical courses on naval subjects and practical work on cruises. John Paul Jones is buried at the naval academy. In 1963 the academy was designated a national historic site. See John Crane and J. F. Kiely, *United States Naval Academy: the First Hundred Years* (1945); Kendall Banning, *Annapolis Today* (6th ed. 1963).

United States Naval Observatory, the federal astronomical OBSERVATORY, located in Washington, D. C. It evolved from the Navy's oldest scientific institution, the Depot of Charts and Instruments, founded in 1830; the observatory was completed in 1844 and moved to its present site in 1893. It was formerly administered through the Bureau of Navigation and is now under the jurisdiction of the chief of naval operations. The principal instrument at the Washington headquarters is a 26-in. refracting telescope, which has been in continuous operation since its installation in 1873, when it was the largest of its kind in the world. Other equipment includes a number of ordinary refracting and reflecting telescopes and special telescopes (photographic zenith tubes) used in the precise determination of time. The observatory's Flagstaff Station in Arizona has 61-in. and 40-in. reflecting telescopes. The main programs of the Naval Observatory involve continual observations of the positions and motions of celestial bodies for astronomical and navigational purposes and for the derivation and broadcasting of accurate time signals. Atomic clocks are used for the observatory's time system, which is accurate to within 100 millionths of a second per day. Since 1894 the U. S. Naval Observatory has included the Nautical Almanac Office, which publishes the *American Ephemeris and Nautical Almanac.* The observatory also has an extensive library.

United States Supreme Court: see SUPREME COURT, U.S.

United Transportation Union (UTU), U.S. railroad union, member of the American Federation of Labor and Congress of Industrial Organizations (AFL-CIO); headquarters at Lakewood, Ohio. It was founded in 1969 by a merger of the Brotherhood of Locomotive Firemen and Enginemen (founded 1873), the Brotherhood of Railroad Trainmen (founded 1883), the Order of Railway Conductors and Brakemen (founded 1868), and the Switchmen's Union of North America (founded 1894). It has about 260,000 members in some 1,750 locals.

United Way of America: see COMMUNITY CHEST.

United Zion Church: see RIVER BRETHREN.

Unity, religious movement incorporated as the Unity School of Christianity, with headquarters at Lee's Summit, Mo. Although the movement used the name *Unity* from 1891, it was founded earlier by Charles and Myrtle Fillmore as a faith-healing cult, with affinities to both Christian Science and New Thought. Unity professes to follow closely the "Jesus Christ preaching" and has an ordained ministry. The Bible is interpreted allegorically, not literally; but its revelation is not final, for revelation is a continuing process. Men attain salvation through development of their Christ consciousness, and ultimately all men will be saved. Emphasis is placed on man's ability to heal ills of mind and body by prayer and right thinking. See Marcus Bach, *They Have Found a Faith* (1946, repr. 1971); Eric Butterworth, *Unity of All Life* (1969).

universal gas constant: see GAS LAWS.

Universalist Church of America, Protestant denomination originating in the 18th cent. and represented almost entirely in the United States. Universalism is the belief that it is God's purpose to save every individual from sin through divine grace revealed in Jesus Christ. The doctrine is old, but no organized body of believers took it as a distinctive feature of their church until modern times. The Universalist denomination in the United States originated with John MURRAY, a convert to Universalism as taught by James Relly in England. Murray arrived in New Jersey in 1770. After preaching there and in New York and New England, he settled in Gloucester, Mass., where in 1779 he became pastor of the first Universalist church in the United States. The movement spread; in 1790 a convention in Philadelphia decided upon a congregational polity and drew up a profession of faith. Until the middle of the 19th cent. little thought was given to organization, as attention was chiefly devoted to settling points of doctrine and disseminating the belief. Murray's Universalism was of the Calvinistic type; under Hosea BALLOU, the most influential force in the denomination from c.1796 to 1852, the movement was separated from its Calvinistic associations. Ballou's doctrine of "Christ's subordination to the Father" gave Universalism a position very similar to that of UNITARIANISM. The doctrinal position of the church, called the Winchester Profession, was adopted in 1803 by the General Convention. In 1899 a briefer statement of essential principles was accepted. Later, in 1935, the Washington Avowal of Faith was taken as the official statement of principles of American Universalism. These principles are the universal fatherhood of God; the spiritual authority and leadership of Jesus Christ, His son; the trustworthiness of the Bible as containing a revelation from God; the certainty of just retribution for sin; and the final harmony of all souls with God. Organizationally, the individual church or parish is considered an independent unit. The church established Tufts Univ. (1852) and Tufts Divinity School (1861). The name Universalist General Convention (adopted 1866) was changed (1942) to the Universalist Church of America. In 1961 it merged with the American Unitarian Association to form the UNITARIAN UNIVERSALIST ASSOCIATION. See Richard Eddy, *Universalism in America* (2 vol., 1884–86); J. H. Allen and Richard Eddy, *A History of the Unitarians and the Universalists in the United States* ("American Church History" series, Vol. X, 1894); H. H. Cheetham, *Unitarianism and Universalism* (1962); E. A. Robinson, *Story of American Universalism* (1970); Ernest Cassara, *Universalism in America* (1971).

universal language, a language intended to further communication and goodwill among peoples speaking different languages without necessarily replacing their native tongues. See INTERNATIONAL LANGUAGE.

Universal Postal Union (UPU), specialized agency of the United Nations, with headquarters at Bern, Switzerland. Established in 1875 following adoption of the Universal Postal Convention, it is one of the oldest extant international governmental organizations. The union was brought into association with the United Nations in 1947. The Universal Postal Congress, the governing body, usually meets every five years to consider the activities of the executive council of 31 members elected on a geographical basis. Countries that belong to the union form a unified postal territory with easy international exchange of mail. The union also provides technical assistance and advice in attempts to improve postal service, especially in developing countries. By 1972 the UPU had 146 members.

universals, in philosophy, term applied to general or abstract objects such as concepts, qualities, relations, and numbers, as opposed to particular objects. The exact nature of a universal deeply concerned thinkers in the Middle Ages. The extreme realists, following Plato, maintained that universals exist independently of both the human mind and particular things. In NOMINALISM universals are considered arbitrary constructions of the human mind. In CONCEPTUALISM universals exist as the pattern to which particular things are related. Conceptualism led to the moderate REALISM of St. Thomas Aquinas and John of Salisbury. See R. I. Aaron, *Theory of Universals* (2d ed. 1967); C. A. Landesman, ed., *The Problems of Universals* (1971).

universal time: see GREENWICH MEAN TIME.

universe, totality of MATTER and ENERGY in existence. The study of the origin of the universe, or cosmos, is known as cosmogony, and that of its structure and evolution, COSMOLOGY. The matter in the universe is subject to various forces, but the greatest force on the cosmological scale is GRAVITATION. This force pulls matter together to form STARS, which either exist alone or are part of BINARY STAR or MULTIPLE STAR systems. Gravitation also acts to group billions of stars into GALAXIES and to group galaxies into clusters and superclusters. The main source of energy in the universe is the conversion of the matter of the stars into energy through thermonuclear reactions (see NUCLEAR ENERGY). These reactions continue throughout the different stages of STELLAR EVOLUTION (see also STELLAR POPULATIONS) until the star has consumed all its available nuclear fuel. The first systematic theory of the size and shape of the universe that attempted to explain observed data was constructed by Ptolemy in the 2d cent. In this theory the SOLAR SYSTEM was thought to be the entire universe, with the earth at its center and the distant stars located just beyond the farthest planet. This belief was held until the 16th cent., when Copernicus advanced the idea that the sun, rather than the earth, is at the center of the system and that the stars are at very great distances compared to the planets. During the first part of the 20th cent., astronomers discovered that the sun is only one of billions of stars in the MILKY WAY galaxy and is located far from the galactic center. Estimates of the size of the universe have been refined as methods of measuring galactic and extragalactic distances have improved. Close stellar distances were at first found by measuring a star's trigonometric PARALLAX. A more powerful contemporary method is to analyze the light reaching the earth from an object by means of a spectroscope; the distance of a very faint object can be estimated by comparing its apparent brightness to those of similar objects at known distances. Another method depends on the fact that the universe as a whole appears to be expanding, as indicated by red shifts (see DOPPLER EFFECT) in the spectral lines of distant galaxies. HUBBLE'S LAW makes it possible to estimate their distances from the speed with which they are rushing away from the earth. At present the universe is believed to be at least 10 billion LIGHT-YEARS in diameter. One problem with estimating the size of the universe is that space itself (or more properly, space-time) may be curved, as held by the general theory of RELATIVITY. This curvature would affect measurements of distance based on the passage of light through space from objects as far away as 5 billion light-years or more. The age of the universe depends on which theory of cosmology one accepts. According to the big bang theory, favored by many scientists, the universe is between 8 and 13 billion years old. The steady-state theory holds that the universe has been in existence for all time. See A. S. Eddington, *The Expanding Universe* (1933); J. H. Jeans, *The Universe Around Us* (4th ed. 1953); George Gamow, *The Creation of the Universe* (1961); Fred Hoyle, *Man in the Universe* (1966); L. B. Young, ed., *Exploring the Universe* (2d ed. 1971).

University City, city (1970 pop. 46,309), St. Louis co., E Mo., a residential suburb of St. Louis; inc. 1906.

University Heights, city (1970 pop. 17,055), Cuyahoga co., NE Ohio, a residential suburb of Cleveland; inc. 1925. It is the seat of John Carroll Univ.

University Park, city (1970 pop. 23,498), Dallas co., N Texas, surrounded by Dallas on three sides; inc. 1924. A residential suburb, the city is the seat of Southern Methodist Univ.

university press, publishing house associated with a university and nearly always bearing the university's name in its imprint. There is no unanimity of opinion among the American university presses concerning the aims and purposes of the institution. It is generally agreed that the university press is normally a specialized publishing house emphasizing serious books, monographs, and periodicals that aid in the dissemination of knowledge to scholars and to well-informed laymen. The first English-language university presses were those of Oxford and Cambridge, both of which were officially established by the end of the 16th cent. Both presses have enjoyed since the 17th cent. a monopoly in Great Britain on the publication of the Bible and the Book of Common Prayer granted them by royal charter, giving them a financial resource such as no university press in North America enjoys. Several university presses in the United States were started in order to centralize the printing and publishing needs of the university. They issued the official bulletins of the university and student and alumni publications, as many still do. Others began by publishing the scholarly works of the university's faculty, in cooperation with commercial publishing houses. The first use of the term "university press" in the United States was at Cornell Univ. in 1869. This venture, like the one begun at the Univ. of Pennsylvania the following year, failed in its early efforts (the presses operating at these universities today were started in 1930 and 1920, respectively); the oldest American university press in continuous existence is the Johns Hopkins Press (1878). It was followed in 1891 by the Univ. of Chicago Press and in 1893 by Columbia Univ. Press and the Univ. of California Press. By 1920 there were recognized presses at the following American universities: Fordham (1907), Yale (1908), Univ. of Washington (1909), Princeton (established in its present form, 1910), Loyola (1912), Harvard (1913), New York Univ. (1916), and Univ. of Illinois (1918). In 1935 there were 17 university presses which published five or more books, and they published 6% of all the books produced by publishers of that size. By 1949 the number of university presses had risen to 30, publishing 7.2% of the books put out; in that year, in addition to the presses listed above, university presses included those of Duke, the Univ. of Georgia, Iowa State College, Louisiana State Univ., the Univ. of Michigan, the Univ. of Minnesota, the Univ. of Nebraska, the Univ. of New Mexico, the Univ. of North Carolina, the Univ. of Oklahoma, Rutgers, Stanford, and the Univ. of Wisconsin and the University Press in Dallas. This growth was accompanied, especially in the larger presses, by a broadening of scope. University presses undertook more and more to present the results of scholarly research to laymen, to encourage regional literature, and to supply texts for new educational programs of the universities. University presses expanded to keep pace with the extraordinary growth of the institutions with which they were affiliated. In the early 1920s the Association of American University Presses was founded, and in 1937 it was given formal organization. The association conducted a survey of its 35 member presses in 1948-49, upon which was based Chester Kerr's *Report on American University Presses* (1949). Since that time the number of university presses has continued to grow; Helen Sears's comprehensive survey of the field, *American University Presses Come of Age* (1959), listed 42 university presses and 7 outside institutions that are affiliated with the Association. By 1974 there were about 90 university presses operating in the United States. They published some 4,000 titles per annum or nearly 12% of all book titles published in the United States. Expansion tapered off in the field in the late 1960s, reflecting diminishing growth of education systems generally. Individual presses have sought to diversify their production by making films, tapes, and other audio-visual materials; others have attempted collaborative efforts to solve increasing problems of economic pressure. The journal *Scholarly Publishing,* founded in 1969, has become recognized as the unofficial professional journal of university press publishing. See R. G. Underwood, *Production and Manufacturing Problems of American University Presses* (1960); Gene R. Hawes, *To Advance Knowledge* (1967); Herbert S. Bailey, Jr., *The Art and Science of Book Publishing* (1970).

Unknown Soldier, Tomb of the, form of memorial to a nation's war dead, adopted by many countries after World War I. A memorial to the American dead of World Wars I and II and the Korean War is in ARLINGTON NATIONAL CEMETERY, just outside Washington, D.C. On Nov. 11, 1921, an unidentified soldier who had been killed in France was buried there in a temporary crypt over which a marble slab was placed: the completed tomb, a sarcophagus of Colorado marble placed on the original base, was dedicated as the Tomb of the Unknown Soldier on Nov. 11, 1932. On Memorial Day, May 30, 1958, the bodies of two other unknown soldiers—one of whom had lost his life in World War II, the other during the Korean War—were buried in the tomb, which was then renamed the Tomb of the Unknowns. In 1973, Congress approved a bill authorizing the burial of an unknown soldier of the Vietnam War in the tomb. The best known of other such memorials are those in Westminster Abbey in London and under the Arc de Triomphe in Paris, where a perpetual flame is kept burning. There are innumerable memorials to the war dead that more or less honor unknown soldiers. Especially notable is the cenotaph in Whitehall, London.

unlawful assembly: see RIOT, ROUT, AND UNLAWFUL ASSEMBLY.

Unni (ŭn'ī). **1** Temple musician. 1 Chron. 15.18,20. **2** Family in the return of Zerubbabel. Neh. 12.9.

UNRRA: see UNITED NATIONS RELIEF AND REHABILITATION ADMINISTRATION.

Unruh, Fritz von (frĭts fən o͝on'ro͞o), 1885-1970, German dramatic poet. Son of a Prussian general, Unruh was himself an officer, but he became a pacifist after World War I. His early expressionist plays include *Offiziere* (1912), *Louis Ferdinand Prinz von Preussen* (1913), and the antiwar *Ein Geschlecht* [a family] (1917) and its sequel, *Platz* (1920). The prose epic written during the siege of Verdun, entitled *Opfergang* (1918; tr. *The Way of Sacrifice,* 1928), is powerful antiwar propaganda. After the publication of *Bonaparte* (1927, tr. 1928), his warning against the coming dictatorship, Unruh left Germany, returning in 1948. His other works include *The End Is Not Yet* (tr. 1947), an anti-Nazi novel, and a play, *Odysseus auf Ogygia* (1968). See biography by Alwin Kronacher (1946).

unsaturated fats: see SATURATED FATS.

Untermeyer, Louis (ŭn'tərmīər), 1885-, American poet and anthologist, b. New York City. Although a first-rate poet, he is known best for his anthologies, notably *Modern American Poetry* (1919), *Modern British Poetry* (1920), *This Singing World* (1923), *Fifty Modern American and British Poets: 1920-1970* (1973), and many others, all of which have been revised numerous times. The high quality of his own poetry and his talent as a parodist are best represented in his *Selected Poems and Parodies* (1935). His prose works include *Lives of the Poets* (1960) and several volumes of criticism. See his autobiography, *From Another World* (1939), and *The Letters of Robert Frost to Louis Untermeyer* (1963). His first wife was **Jean Starr Untermeyer**, 1886-1970, poet, b. Zanesville, Ohio. Her volumes of poetry include *Steep Ascent* (1927) and *Love and Need* (1940). See her autobiography, *Private Collection* (1965).

Untermyer, Samuel, 1858-1940, American lawyer and civic leader, b. Lynchburg, Va., grad. Columbia law school, 1878. He gained fame as a lawyer and took part in some of the country's most important litigation. He served as counsel to the congressional committee headed by Arsène PUJO that investigated (1912) money trusts, and to the Lockwood committee of the New York legislature, which probed (1921-22) statewide housing conditions. As special counsel until 1933 in the famous New York City transit suits, he helped maintain the five-cent subway fare. Untermyer was a staunch advocate of stock-market regulations, government ownership of railroads, and various legal reforms. A leading crusader against anti-Semitism, Untermyer was active in the movement to boycott Germany after Hitler rose to power.

Unterwalden (o͝on'tərväldən), canton, central Switzerland, one of the FOUR FOREST CANTONS. A mountainous, forested, and chiefly pastoral region, Unterwalden is divided into the half cantons of Obwalden (1970 pop. 24,509), 190 sq mi (492 sq km), in the west, with its capital at Sarnen (1970 pop. 6,952), and Nidwalden (1970 pop. 25,634), 106 sq mi (275 sq km), in the east, with its capital at Stans (1970 pop. 5,180). Dairying and woodworking are the main occupations of Obwalden, while Nidwalden has orchards, cement works, and glassworks. The population of Unterwalden is German-speaking and Roman Catholic. In 1291, Unterwalden formed with the cantons of Uri and Schwyz a league that became the nucleus of the Swiss Confederation (see SWITZERLAND).

untouchables: see PARIAH.

Unwin, Sir Raymond (ŭn'wĭn), 1863-1940, English architect and town planner. He designed the first English garden city near Letchworth, the New Earwick development in Yorkshire, and Hampstead Garden suburb near London. He lectured on housing and city planning at the Univ. of Birmingham (1911-14) and at Columbia Univ. (1936-40). After World War I he served in the ministry of health as housing chief. His *Town Planning in Practice* (1909) is a standard work in its field. Unwin was knighted in 1932.

Upanishads (o͞opăn'ĭshădz), speculative and mystical scriptures of HINDUISM, regarded as the wellspring of Hindu religious and speculative thought. The Upanishads, which form the last section of the literature of the VEDA, were composed beginning c.900 B.C. Of the 112 Upanishads extant, about 13 date from the Vedic period and the rest are later, sectarian works. The principal early Upanishads develop fully answers to questions posed in the *Rig-Veda* and the *Brahmanas* as to the source and controlling power of the world and the individual and the real significance of the Vedic sacrifice. They are best known for their doctrine of brahman, the ultimate and universal reality of pure being and consciousness, and the identity of brahman with the inner self, or atman, of man. This equation is expressed in the famous utterances "That art thou" and "All this is brahman." The Upanishads are not a systematic exposition of concepts but a heterogeneous compilation of material from different sources. In addition to brahman-atman teachings, they contain information about allegorical interpretation of the sacrifice, death and rebirth processes, and yogic practice and experience. They are the basis for the later philosophical schools of VEDANTA. For bibliography see VEDA.

upas tree (yo͞o'pəs): see MULBERRY.

Updike, Daniel Berkeley (ŭp'dīk"), 1860-1941, American printer and historian of typography, b. Providence, R.I. At the Merrymount Press, which he founded in 1893 in Boston, his stated purpose was "to do common work well." Here, the excellence of his printing, influenced by William MORRIS, inspired and instructed other printers. At Harvard Univ. he taught the first college course in the United States on the history of type and the practice of printing. In his books he added the care and scope of the scholar to the knowledge of a master printer. *Printing Types: Their History, Forms, and Use* (1922, 2d ed. 1937) is the standard work on the subject and a basic book for all interested in the graphic arts. Updike's other works include *In the Day's Work* (1924) and *Some Aspects of Printing* (1941). See G. P. Winship, *Daniel Berkeley Updike and the Merrymount Press* (1947); *Updike: American Printer and the Merrymount Press* (1948), a symposium.

Updike, John, 1932-, American author, b. Shillington, Pa., grad. Harvard, 1954. His novels and stories, written in a well-modulated style, usually treat the tensions, frustrations, lesions, and tragedies of contemporary life. The novel *Rabbit,Run* (1961), set in Pennsylvania in the 1950s, concerns a young man who yearns for his days as a high school athlete and deserts his wife and child; in *Rabbit Redux* (1971), the same hero personally confronts the explosive American issues of the 1960s—racial tension, job obsolescence, sexual freedom, drugs, violence, and the alienation of the young. Updike's other works include the novels *The Poorhouse Fair* (1959), *The Centaur* (1962), *Of the Farm* (1965), *Couples* (1968), and *A Month of Sundays* (1975); volumes of poetry such as *The Carpentered Hen* (1958) and *Midpoint and Other Poems* (1969); the short-story collections *Pigeon Feathers* (1962), *The Music School* (1967), *Bech: a Book* (1970), and *Museums and Women and Other Stories* (1972); and the play *Buchanan Dying* (1974), a closet drama about President James Buchanan.

Upernavik (o͝opĕr'nävĭk), town (1969 pop. 730) in Upernavik dist. (1969 pop. 1,907), W Greenland, on a small island in Baffin Bay. It is an important sealing and whaling base.

Uphaz (yo͞o'făz), country known for its gold. It is perhaps a variant of OPHIR. Jer. 10.9; Dan. 10.5.

upholstery, general term for household fittings, hangings, curtains, cushions, and covers. It refers to stuffed, padded, and spring-cushioned furniture, such as chairs and sofas, or to the usually decorative materials and fabrics that cover them. The first furniture upholstery was probably leather, stretched on without padding. Italian Renaissance chairs were cushioned with leather, velvet, or embroidery; the French made ornate chairs covered with tapestries and embroideries; England developed upholstery in Elizabethan and Jacobean reigns. The use of springs is comparatively modern. Hair, fiber, flock, foam rubber, down, and kapok are used for padding in modern upholstery, and woven fabrics, plastics, leather, and synthetic leather serve as coverings.

Upjohn, Richard, 1802–78, American architect, b. England. He came to the United States in 1829. A skilled cabinetmaker and draftsman, he lived first in Manlius, N.Y., and then in New Bedford, Mass., where he set himself up as an architect. His first commission (1833) was a private house (now Symphony House) in Bangor, Maine. He had executed St. John's Church, Bangor (1836–39), and several smaller commissions when in 1839 he was engaged to rebuild Trinity Church, New York City. He moved to New York City at that time and established an office there. The new Trinity Church, completed in 1846, was carefully modeled on English examples and inaugurated a new phase in the Gothic revival. Upjohn designed the old St. Thomas's Church in New York City (later burned), several churches in Brooklyn, the chapel of Bowdoin College, other smaller Gothic churches, and many residences. He was a founder of the American Institute of Architects and its first president (1857–76). His son, Richard Michell Upjohn (1828–1903), was associated with his father. See E. M. Upjohn, *Richard Upjohn, Architect and Churchman* (1939).

Upland, city (1970 pop. 32,551), San Bernardino co., S Calif., in a citrus-fruit region at the foot of the San Gabriel Mts.; inc. 1906. Citrus fruits and grapes are packed and processed, and paint, orchard heaters, auto parts, and feed products are made.

upland cress: see WINTER CRESS.

Upolu (o͞opō'lo͞o), volcanic island, WESTERN SAMOA, S Pacific, the most populous of the Samoan islands. Upolu's land area is c.430 sq mi (1,110 sq km); the highest peak is Vaaifetu (c.3,600 ft/1,100 m). The island is well watered, and its fertile soil yields cacao, rubber, bananas, and coconuts. APIA, the capital of Western Samoa, is the chief port and major city of the island. At Saluafata, the second port, is a U.S. naval station. Robert Louis STEVENSON spent his last years on Upolu, residing at his home, Vailima.

Upper Arlington, city (1970 pop. 38,630), Franklin co., central Ohio, a residential suburb of Columbus; inc. 1918.

Upper Austria, Ger. *Oberösterreich,* province (1971 pop. 1,244,000), 4,625 sq mi (11,979 sq km), NW Austria. Linz is the capital. Bordering on West Germany in the west and Czechoslovakia in the north, the province is predominantly hilly and forested. It is drained by the Danube River and two of its tributaries, the Enns and the Traun, and includes a large part of the SALZKAMMERGUT resort area. Agriculture is the chief occupation. Industry is centered at Linz, Steyr, and Ranshofen. The area of Upper Austria was included in the Roman province of Noricum. In 1156 it was made a duchy by Frederick I and given to the Babenberg dukes of Austria. The province was invaded by the Turks in the 16th cent. It was a site of battles during the Thirty Years War (1618–48) and during the campaigns of Napoleon I.

Upper Avon, river: see AVON **3,** river, England.

Upper Canada: see ONTARIO.

Upper Hutt, city (1971 pop. 20,001), S North Island, New Zealand, on the Hutt River. It is largely residential but has some light industries.

Upper Palatinate, Germany: see PALATINATE.

Upper Volta (vōl'tə), Fr. *Haute-Volta,* republic (1973 est. pop. 5,655,000), 105,869 sq mi (274,200 sq km), W Africa, bordering on Mali in the west and north, on Niger in the northeast, on Dahomey in the southeast, and on Togo, Ghana, and Ivory Coast in the south. OUAGADOUGOU is the capital and largest city; other cities include Bobo-Dioulasso, Koudougou, Kaya, and Ouahigouya. The country is made up mainly of vast monotonous plains and of low hills that rise to c.2,300 ft (700 m) in the southwest. Precipitation is low (nowhere exceeding 45 in./114 cm annually), and the soil is of poor quality. Rainfall is heaviest in the southwest, which is covered largely with savanna; the rest of the country is semidesert. Upper Volta has several rivers, none of which are navigable. In the southwest is the Komoé (Comoé) River, which flows through Ivory Coast to the Gulf of Guinea; in the center are the Black, Red, and White Volta rivers, which join in Ghana to form the Volta River; and in the northeast are several small tributaries of the Niger. The population of Upper Volta is made up of black Africans. The main ethnic

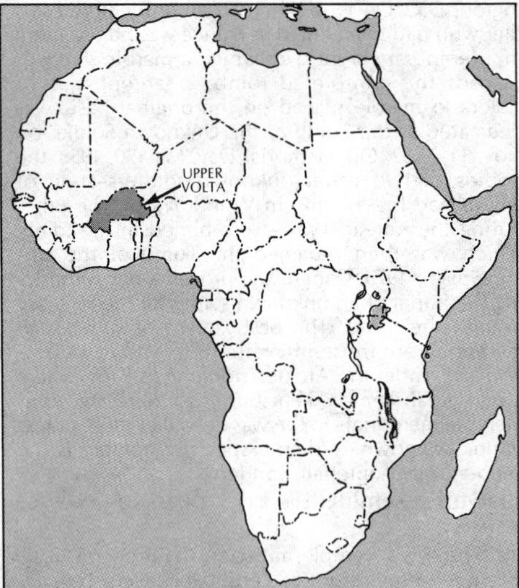

groups are the Mossi (about 48% of the total population), Lobi (about 7%), Bobi (about 7%), and Gurunsi (about 6%), all of whose members speak a Voltaic language; Fulani (about 11%); Mande (about 7%); and Senufo (about 6%). French is the country's official language. Most of the inhabitants follow traditional religious beliefs; there are also about 1 million Muslims and approximately 220,000 Roman Catholics. Upper Volta is a poor agricultural country, with the great majority of its workers engaged in subsistence farming. Less than 10% of the country's land area is cultivable, and most of this land has a poor crop yield. The principal agricultural commodities are sorghum, millet, maize, groundnuts, karite nuts (gathered from shea trees), rice, cotton, yams, and sesame. Large numbers of cattle, sheep, and goats are raised. The country's manufactures, which are limited largely to basic consumer goods, include processed foods, beverages, ginned cotton, textiles, bicycles, construction materials, leather, cigarettes, and matches. Upper Volta has a small mining industry that produces manganese and limestone; there are also small, and as yet untapped, deposits of copper ore, bauxite, and uranium. The country has a good road network; a railroad runs from Ouagadougou to the seaport of Abidjan, Ivory Coast, via Bobo-Dioulasso. The annual cost of Upper Volta's imports is usually much higher than its earnings from exports. The principal imports are foodstuffs, machinery, motor vehicles, textiles and clothing, and metals; the leading exports are live animals, cotton, groundnuts and groundnut oil, and hides and skins. The chief trade partners are France, Ivory Coast, and Ghana. Each year some 500,000 Upper Voltaians migrate to Ivory Coast and (to a lesser extent) to Ghana to work in factories and on farms; about one quarter of the migrants take up permanent residence in those countries. The money the workers bring (or send) back to Upper Volta constitutes a major contribution to the country's economy. In 1974, Upper Volta became a charter member of the West African Economic Community, linking six former French territories.

History. Neolithic remains have been found in N Upper Volta. By about 1100 A. D. the principal inhabitants of the western part of the country were the Bobo, Lobi, and Gurunsi. Around 1,400 invaders on horseback from present-day Ghana conquered central and E Upper Volta, establishing the Mossi states of Ouagadougou, Yatenga, and Tengkodogo in the center and the state of Gourma in the east. The conquerors were far outnumbered by their subjects, but by using religion (based on ancestor worship) and a complex administrative system (which allowed for some local autonomy) they created powerful states that endured for more than 500 years. Ouagadougou, which still existed in nominal form in the early 1970s, was headed by the Morho Naba and at its peak was divided into several provinces, which were subdivided into a total of about 300 districts. The Mossi states had strong armies, which included cavalry units, and were able to repel most attacks by the Mali and Songhai empires during the period from the 14th to 16th cent. Near the end of the 19th-century scramble for African territory among the European powers, France gained control over the region of Upper Volta. In 1895 the French peacefully negotiated a protectorate over Yatenga, in 1896 they forcefully occupied Ouagadougou, and in 1897 they annexed Gourma and the lands of the Bobo, Lobi, and Gurunsi peoples. An Anglo-French agreement in 1898 established the boundary with the Gold Coast (now Ghana). The region of Upper Volta was administered as part of Soudan (then called Upper Senegal-Niger and now mostly part of Mali) until 1919, when it was made a separate protectorate. In 1932, Upper Volta was divided among Ivory Coast, Soudan, and Niger for administrative convenience. In 1947, Upper Volta was reestablished as a separate territory within the FRENCH UNION and received its own territorial assembly. By the mid-1950s the Voltaic Democratic Union (UDV) was the leading political party; it was headed by Ouezzin Coulibably and Maurice Yaméogo. In 1958, Upper Volta became an autonomous republic within the FRENCH COMMUNITY, and on Aug. 5, 1960, it achieved full independence. The constitution of 1960 established a strong presidential government, and Yaméogo became the first president. He managed to reduce the traditional power of the Mossi states, but his authority was weakened by ethnic conflicts and by the poor performance of the economy. In late 1965 Yaméogo was overwhelmingly reelected president, but in Jan., 1966, at the height of trade union demonstrations against the government's austerity program, he was ousted in a bloodless coup d'etat by a group of army officers headed by Lt. Col. Sangoulé Lamizana, who became head of state. Lamizana dissolved the national assembly and temporarily prohibited political activity. In 1970 a new constitution was approved in a national referendum under which the chief executive officer was the president (popularly elected to a five-year term) and legislative power was vested in a 57-member unicameral national assembly (whose members were also popularly elected to five-year terms). As an interim measure, Lamizana was to remain in power until 1975, when he would be replaced by an elected president. In elections in Dec., 1970, the UDV won 37 seats in the national assembly, and Gérard Kango Ouedraogo became prime minister after being nominated for the post by Lamizana. However, in Feb., 1974, the army, headed by Lamizana, again intervened in the political process, dissolving the national assembly, ousting Ouedraogo, and suspending the 1970 constitution. Lamizana maintained that the army acted because political factionalism (caused in part by jockeying for position in the scheduled presidential elections) was undermining the welfare of the nation; it was also reported that Lamizana feared that Yaméogo might again be elected president. During the 1960s and early 1970s Upper Volta received much financial aid from France. The country (especially the north) was severely affected by the long-term drought that began in the late 1960s and was continuing unabated in 1974. See E. P. Skinner, *The Mossi of the Upper Volta: The Political Development of the Sudanese People* (1964); P. B. Hammond, *Yatenga: Technology in the Culture of a West African Kingdom* (1966).

Uppsala (ŭp'sələ, -sä"lä), city (1970 pop. 111,294), capital of Uppsala co., E Sweden, on the Fyrisån River. It is an industrial and cultural center and a railroad junction. Manufactures include metal goods, clothing, footwear, processed food, and printed materials. The city developed near Gamla

Uppsala, now a small village, which became the pagan capital of Sweden in the 6th cent. An archiepiscopal see was established at present-day Uppsala in 1270, and the cathedral of Uppsala (13th cent.), the finest Gothic church in Sweden, became the usual coronation place of Swedish kings and is the burial place of Gustavus I, the botanist Linnaeus, and the scientist and religious teacher Swedenborg. The Univ. of Uppsala, founded in 1477 by Sten Sture, the Elder, and Archbishop Jakob Ulvsson, is the oldest university of N Europe and has ranked among the world's great universities since its reorganization in 1595. The university's library contains more than 1 million volumes and about 20,000 manuscripts, notably the Codex argenteus of Bishop ULFILAS. Other institutions in Uppsala include the Royal Society of Sciences, the Gustav Werners institute of high-energy physics and radiation biology, the Victoria Museum, and the Linnaean Museum.

Uppsala, University of, at Uppsala, Sweden; founded 1477. Its activities were suspended in 1510 as a result of religious disputes. It was reorganized in 1595. The university has faculties of theology, law, medicine, arts, social science, science, and pharmacy, and an institute of African studies.

Upshur, Abel Parker (ŭp'shər), 1790–1844, American cabinet officer, b. Northampton co., Va. Admitted (1810) to the bar, he practiced law in Richmond, Va., and held state offices. When most of the Whig cabinet resigned in disagreement with President Tyler, Upshur was appointed (1841) U.S. Secretary of the Navy. Upon Daniel Webster's resignation, he became Secretary of State (1843–44). An ardent advocate of slavery, Upshur reopened negotiations with Texas for its admission to the Union as a slave state and thus played an important role in the movement for the annexation of Texas. He was killed by the explosion of a cannon on the battleship *Princeton*. See biography by C. H. Hall (1964).

Ur (ûr), ancient city of Sumer, S Mesopotamia. The city is also known as Ur of the Chaldees. It was an important center of Sumerian culture (see SUMER) and is identified in the Bible as the home of Abraham. The site was discovered in the 19th cent., but it was not until the excavations of C. Leonard Woolley in the 1920s and 30s that a partial account of its history could be constructed. Remains found at the site seem to indicate that Ur existed as far back as the late Al' Ubaid period (see MESOPOTAMIA) and that the city was an important commercial center even before the first dynasty was established (c.2500 B.C.). Among the most important remains of the first dynasty, which has revealed a luxurious material culture, are the royal cemetery, where the standard of Ur was found, and the Temple of Ninhursag at Ubaid, bearing the inscriptions of the kings of the first dynasty. Ur was captured c.2340 by Sargon, and this era, called the Akkadian period, marks an important step in the blending of Sumerian and Semitic cultures. After this dynasty came a long period of which practically nothing is known except that a second dynasty rose and fell. The third dynasty was established c.2060 B.C. under King UR-NAMMU, who built the great ziggurat that has stood, although crumbled and covered with sand, throughout the centuries. An inscription in the Museum of the Ancient Orient in Istanbul was identified (1952) as a fragment of the code of Ur-Nammu. It predates the code of Hammurabi by 300 years and is the oldest known law code yet discovered. The third dynasty of Ur fell (c.1950 B.C.) to the Elamites and later to Babylon. The city was destroyed and rebuilt throughout the years by various kings and conquerors, including Nebuchadnezzar and Nabonidus in the 6th cent. About the middle of the 6th cent., Ur went into a decline from which it never recovered. A record dated 324 B.C. mentions it as being inhabited by Arabs, but by that time its existence as a great city was forgotten. The change in the course of the Euphrates, which had been the source of the city's wealth, probably contributed to the final decline of Ur. Ur is mentioned often in the Bible (Gen. 11.28,31; 15.7; Neh. 9.7) and was at one period known to the Arabs as Tall al-Muqayyar [mound of pitch]. See C. J. Gadd, *History and Monuments of Ur* (1929); C. L. Woolley, *Ur of the Chaldees* (1930, repr. 1965) and *Excavations at Ur* (1954, repr. 1965).

uracil (yŏŏr'əsĭl), organic base of the PYRIMIDINE family. It was isolated from herring sperm and also produced in a laboratory in 1900–1901. When combined with the sugar ribose in a glycosidic linkage, uracil forms a derivative called uridine (a nucleoside), which in turn can be phosphorylated with from one to three phosphoric acid groups, yielding respectively the three NUCLEOTIDES UMP (uridine monophosphate), UDP (uridine diphosphate), and UTP (uridine triphosphate). The analogous nucleosides and nucleotides formed from uridine and deoxyribose occur only very rarely in living systems; such is not the case with the other pyrimidines. The nucleotide derivatives or uracil perform important functions in cellular metabolism, particularly in carbohydrate metabolism; UTP acts as a COENZYME in the biosynthesis of sucrose in plants, lactose and glycogen in mammals, and chitin in insects. It can also readily donate one of its phosphate groups to adenosine diphosphate (ADP) to form ADENOSINE TRIPHOSPHATE (ATP), an extremely important intermediate in the transfer of chemical energy in living cells. Since the uracil nucleotides contain only ribose and not deoxyribose, UTP is the source of uridine only in ribonucleic acid (RNA); there is no uridine in deoxyribonucleic acid (DNA). Its involvement in the biosynthesis of RNA demonstrates that uracil is important in the translation of genetic information (see NUCLEIC ACID). A few laboratory derivatives of uracil have been designed as experimental antimetabolites (see METABOLITE) for use in cancer chemotherapy.

Ural (yŏŏr'əl, Rus. ōōräl'), river, c.1,580 mi (2,540 km) long, rising in the S Urals, SE Russian Republic, USSR. It flows S past Magnitogorsk and Orenburg, then through NW Kazakhstan, past Uralsk, and into the Caspian Sea at Guryev. At Magnitogorsk there is a water reservoir which supplies the area's metallurgical industry. The Ural River is a transport route to the north for oil, fish, and lumber; grain and cattle are generally shipped south on the river. It is a source of water supply for the towns and agricultural areas in the steppe area in W Kazakhstan.

Uralic and Altaic languages (yŏŏrăl'ĭk, ăltā'ĭk), two groups of related languages thought by many scholars to form a single Ural-Altaic linguistic family. However, other authorities hold that the Uralic and Altaic groups constitute two unconnected and separate language families. The Ural-Altaic tongues are spoken by about 90 million people, who inhabit discontinuously a vast area that reaches from E Europe across Russia and Asia to the Pacific Ocean. The Ural-Altaic family takes its name from the Ural Mts., which separate Europe and Asia, and the Altai, a central Asian mountain range, where the languages of this family are believed to have originated. The speakers of the Ural-Altaic languages apparently began to migrate from this original homeland to their present dwelling areas many centuries ago. If the Ural-Altaic tongues are regarded as forming one family, this family consists of two subfamilies, the Uralic and the ALTAIC. The Uralic subfamily has 20 million speakers and can be divided into two principal subdivisions, Finno-Ugric (see FINNO-UGRIC LANGUAGES) and Samoyedic. The languages of the Samoyedic subdivision have only about 25,000 speakers, who reside in NW Siberia and NE Europe. Samoyed is the chief language of this subdivision and the tongue of 22,000 people. Two important features that characterize the Ural-Altaic languages with few exceptions are agglutination and vowel harmony. It is these two points of similarity that have led a number of authorities to accept Ural-Altaic unity. In an agglutinative language, different linguistic elements, each of which exists separately and has a fixed meaning, are often joined to form one word. In these languages multiple suffixes are added to a root while prefixes are almost totally lacking. Vowel harmony refers to the agreement between the vowels in the root of a word and the vowels in the word's suffix or suffixes. Such agreement is illustrated in the Turkish words *ev* [house] and *evde* [at the house]; *masa* [table] and *masada* [at the table]. Thus, most suffixes have a double form, one with a front vowel (e.g., *e, i, ö, ü*) to correspond to a root with a front vowel, and one with a back vowel (e.g., *a, ı, o, u*) to match a root with a back vowel. Grammatical gender (with its distinctions of masculine, feminine, and neuter) is generally lacking in the Ural-Altaic languages. Stress varies in the different tongues. The Ural-Altaic languages also have a small common vocabulary consisting of basic words, among them some personal pronouns, some words indicating kinship (e.g., mother, father), and some words that denote plants and animals, name occupations, and the like. This rudimentary vocabulary is common to all the tongues and is considered by some to be additional evidence for Ural-Altaic unity. At the same time, speakers of the Ural-Altaic languages also borrowed words from the various tongues of other peoples with whom they came in contact. See Nicholas Poppe, *Introduction to Altaic Linguistics* (1965); Björn Collinder, *Survey of the Uralic Languages* (2d ed. 1969).

Urals or **Ural Mountains,** E European USSR, forming, together with the Ural River, the traditional boundary between Europe and Asia and separating the Russian plain from the W Siberian lowlands. The Urals extend c.1,500 mi (2,400 km) north and south from the Arctic tundra to the deserts N of the Caspian Sea. The polar section (north of lat. 64°N) is covered by tundra. The northern section (between lat. 64°N and lat. 61°N), a rocky treeless range, has the highest peaks, Naroda and Telpos-Iz. The central Urals (between lat. 61°N and lat. 55°N) are also known as the Ore Urals and have many low passes. The southern section (between lat. 55°N and lat. 51°N), known as the MUGODZHAR HILLS, consists of several high, parallel ridges that rise to 5,377 ft (1,639 m) in the Yaman-Tau. The S Urals are drained by the Ural River into the Caspian Sea. The waterways in the west are the Kama and Belaya rivers, tributaries of the Volga, and, in the east, the Ob-Irtysh drainage system. The Trans-Siberian RR crosses the central Urals, and the Kuybyshev-Tashkent RR crosses the S Urals. To the west, the Ural foothills slope gradually to the Volga. The eastern slope drops abruptly to the W Siberian lowlands. Except in the polar and northern sections, the mountains are densely forested, and lumbering is an important industry. The great mineral resources of the USSR are in the Urals. Iron ore is mined in the south, and there are rich deposits of coal, copper, manganese, gold, aluminum, and potash. Oil fields and refineries along the Kama and Belaya rivers in the W Urals produce much of the USSR's oil. Emeralds, chrysoberyl, topaz, and amethyst are mined, as are deposits of bauxite, asbestos, zinc, lead, silver, platinum, nickel, chrome, and tungsten. The Urals industrial area (c.290,000 sq mi/751,100 sq km), a major Soviet metallurgical region, is in the central and S Urals and the adjacent lowlands. Huge industrial centers are found at SVERDLOVSK, MAGNITOGORSK, CHELYABINSK, PERM, BEREZNIKI, NIZHNI TAGIL, ORSK, ORENBURG, UFA, and ZLATOUST. The population consists primarily of Russians, with some Bashkirs, Tatars, Udmurts, and Komi-Permyaks. Known to medieval Russia as the Stone Belt, the Urals were reached in the early 12th cent. by colonists and fur traders from Novgorod. Colonization developed rapidly in the late 16th cent. The first ironworks were established in the 1630s, and metallurgy was encouraged by Peter the Great. In the late 18th and early 19th cent., the Urals area was a major iron producer, but its relative importance declined in the late 19th cent. Under the first two Five-Year plans (1929–39), the tremendous industrial development of the Urals was based on Ural iron ore and coking coal shipped by rail from the KUZNETSK BASIN. During World War II, industries were transplanted from European USSR to the Urals, strategically situated in the heart of the USSR. Since the war, coking coal from the Karaganda Basin, Ural coal mixed with better imported grades, and hydroelectric power support the metallurgical industry, which has been enormously expanded. To increase the power resources of the Urals area, plans were made for construction of atomic power stations.

Uralsk (yŏŏrälsk', Rus. ōōrälsk'), city (1970 pop. 134,000), capital of Uralsk oblast, Kazakhstan, W Central Asian USSR, on the Ural River. Among its industries are the repair of agricultural equipment, food processing, tanning, and the manufacture of engine and motor parts. Uralsk was founded in 1622 by the Ural Cossacks, who fought with Stenka Razin in the uprising of 1667 and against the Bolsheviks in 1918–19. It was an important trade center on the border of European Russia and Kazakhstan.

Urania (yŏŏrā'nēə): see APHRODITE; MUSES.

uraninite: see PITCHBLENDE.

uranium (yŏŏrā'nēəm), radioactive metallic chemical element; symbol U; at. no. 92; at. wt. 238.03; mass no. of most stable isotope 238; m.p. 1132°C; b.p. 3818°C; sp. gr. 19.1 at 25°C; valence +3, +4, +5, or +6. Uranium is a hard, dense, malleable, ductile, silver-white, radioactive metal of the ACTINIDE SERIES in group IIIb of the PERIODIC TABLE. At ordinary temperatures it has an orthorhombic crystalline structure. It is a highly reactive metal and reacts with almost all the nonmetallic elements and their compounds, especially at elevated temperatures. It dissolves readily in nitric acid but resists attack by alkalies. It forms solid solutions and intermetallic compounds with many of the metals. Naturally occurring uranium is a mixture of three ISOTOPES. The most abundant and most stable is uranium-238 (half-life 4.5×10^9 years); also present are uranium-235 (half-life 7×10^8 years) and uranium-234 (half-life 2.5×10⁵ years). There are 12 other known isotopes. Uranium-238 is the parent substance of the 18-member radioactive decay series known as the uranium series (see RADIOACTIVITY). Some relatively long-lived members of this series include uranium-234, thorium-230, and radium-226; the final stable member of the series is lead-206. Uranium-235, also called actinouranium, is the parent substance of the so-called actinium series, a 15-member radioactive decay series ending in stable lead-207; protactinium-231 and actinium-227 are the relatively stable members of this series. Because the rate of decay in these series is constant, it is possible to estimate the age of uranium samples (e.g., minerals) from the relative amounts of parent substance and final product (see radioactive DATING). Uranium is widely distributed in its ores but is not found uncombined in nature. It is a fairly abundant element in the earth's crust, being about 40 times as abundant as silver. The most important mineral is PITCHBLENDE, mined in the Congo River basin and NW Canada. Coffinite (a uranium silicate) and carnotite (a potassium uranate-vanadate) are important minerals found in Colorado and Utah. Ores with as little as 0.1% uranium are mined and processed. Most ores are processed by chemical methods including leaching and solvent extraction. The uranium is obtained as pure uranyl nitrate, $UO_2(NO_3)_2 \cdot 6H_2O$, which is typically decomposed to the trioxide, UO_3, by heating and reduced to the dioxide, UO_2, with hydrogen. The dioxide is chemically and physically stable at high temperatures, and is the form most often used as nuclear reactor fuel. The dioxide may be converted to the tetrafluoride, UF_4, by treatment with hydrogen fluoride gas, HF. The pure metal is obtained by electrolysis or by chemical reduction of the tetrafluoride or by chemical reduction of the dioxide. Before the discovery of nuclear fission by O. Hahn and F. Strassmann in 1939, the principal use of uranium (chiefly as the oxides) was in pigments, ceramic glazes, and a yellow-green fluorescent glass. It has also been added to steels to increase their strength and toughness. However, because of the high toxicity (both chemical and radiological) of uranium and its compounds, and because of their importance as nuclear fuel, these earlier uses have been largely curtailed. Uranium gained importance with the development of practical uses of NUCLEAR ENERGY. Uranium-235 is the only naturally occurring nuclear fission fuel, but this isotope is only about 1 part in 140 of natural uranium; the balance is mostly uranium-238. Because the supply of uranium-235 is limited, the use of fast breeder reactors that convert nonfissionable uranium-238 to fissionable plutonium-239 is becoming increasingly important (see NUCLEAR REACTOR). Uranium-235 can be separated from uranium-238 by a diffusion process using the gaseous hexafluoride, UF_6; the compound of the lighter isotope diffuses faster. Discovery of uranium is commonly credited to M. H. Klaproth, who, in 1789, while experimenting with pitchblende, concluded that it contained a new element, which he named after the planet Uranus, discovered only eight years earlier. However, the substance that Klaproth identified was not pure uranium, but an oxide. E. M. Péligot isolated the element in 1841. A. H. Becquerel discovered its radioactivity in 1896.

Uranium City, town, NW Sask., Canada, on Lake Athabasca near the Northwest Territories line. It is the center of a large uranium-mining area developed in the 1950s.

Uranus (yo͝or'ənəs, yo͝orā'-), in astronomy, 7th planet from the sun, at a mean distance of 1.78 billion mi (2.85 billion km), with an orbit lying between those of Saturn and Neptune; its period of revolution is slightly more than 84 years. The first planet discovered in modern times with the aid of a telescope, Uranus was detected in 1781 by Sir William Herschel, who originally thought it to be a comet. It has a diameter of c.29,200 mi (46,700 km), roughly 4 times that of the earth, and a mass about 15 times the earth's mass. Like the giant planets Jupiter and Saturn, Uranus has a thick atmosphere of hydrogen, helium, methane, and ammonia; a relatively low density; and a rapid period of rotation of about 10 hr, 48 min, which causes a polar flattening of over 6%. Viewed through a telescope, Uranus appears as a greenish disk, slightly elliptical because of its rapid rotation. Its surface temperature is estimated to be about −330°F (−200°C), and at this temperature the ammonia, the main constituent of the visible cloud cover, would exist in the form of ice crystals. Uranus has five known natural satellites with diameters ranging in size from 600 mi (970 km) down to 200 mi (320 km); the largest, Titania, is about a quarter the size of the moon. Their orbits lie in a single plane that coincides with the equatorial plane of the planet. Uranus is unique in that its equatorial plane is inclined about 98° with respect to its orbital plane. This extreme inclination gives the planet a retrograde rotation, i.e., rotation opposite to the direction of revolution. All the satellites revolve in this retrograde direction. Because the calculated orbit of Uranus did not compare accurately with the observed orbit, astronomers concluded that a disturbing influence was present. A study of its irregularity led to the discovery of Neptune in 1846.

Uranus, in Greek mythology, the heaven, first ruler of the universe, son of Gaea (the earth). He was the father of Gaea's children, the Titans, the Cyclopes, and the Hundred-handed Ones (the Hecatoncheires). Fearing that his children would rebel against him, he imprisoned them, but Cronus, a Titan, with the help of Gaea, castrated him, thereby taking away his power. From the blood of Uranus that fell on Earth sprang the three Furies (the Erinyes), the goddesses of revenge. According to Hesiod, Aphrodite was born of Uranus' discarded flesh and the foaming sea.

Urartu (o͞orär'to͞o), ancient kingdom of ARMENIA, centered about Lake Van in present-day E Turkey. It was the biblical Ararat. Urartu flourished from the 13th cent. to the 7th cent. B.C., but it was most powerful in the 8th cent. B.C., when it ruled over most of N Syria. The Urartians were constantly at war with Assyria; Shalmaneser I, Shalmaneser III, and Sargon all attacked Urartu but never completely subdued it. In the 7th cent. B.C. repeated invasions by the Cimmerians, the Scyths, and the Medes finally brought about the downfall of the Urartian kingdom. Recent excavations, particularly at such sites as Toprak Kale and Karmir Blur, have shown that Urartu had an advanced agricultural and commercial civilization, which was largely influenced by Assyria. The use of cuneiform was also borrowed from the Assyrians. Urartian technique of metalworking and of stone masonry (especially in the construction of fortresses) was highly advanced. See Boris Piatrovski, *Ancient Civilization of Urartu* (1969).

Urawa (o͞orä'wä), city (1970 pop. 269,397), capital of Saitama prefecture, central Honshu, Japan. It is a commercial center and has a university.

Urban II, c.1042–1099, pope (1088–99), a Frenchman named Odo (or Eudes) of Lagery; successor of Victor III. He studied at Rheims and became a monk at Cluny. He went to Rome, as prior of Cluny, early in the reign of St. Gregory VII. The pope kept him there, finding in Odo one of his ablest assistants in the great reform; he made him cardinal and bishop of Ostia. Odo worked especially as legate in Germany. When he was elected pope, Urban pursued the cause of reform, undaunted by the opposition of Holy Roman Emperor Henry IV and his antipope, Clement III (Guibert of Ravenna). He began work in the lands that recognized him, those of the Normans (S Italy), of the Countess Matilda (Tuscany), and the Lombard cities. He could not stay in Rome until 1093, when the antipope was expelled. Urban's method was to travel about, summoning great councils of the whole population, to advertise and gain popularity for the reforms. The principal councils were at Piacenza (March, 1095), Clermont (Nov., 1095), Rome (1097), Bari (1098), and Rome again (1099). At Clermont, Urban preached a sermon that brought forth the First Crusade (see CRUSADES). At Bari the reunion of East and West was the theme; St. Anselm was the apologist for the West. Urban's resolute condemnation of Philip I of France in the matter of Philip's repudiation of his wife exemplifies his fearlessness. Without Urban's work, most of Gregory's reform movement would probably have been ephemeral. He was succeeded by Paschal II. Urban was beatified in 1881. See study by F. J. Gossman (1960).

Urban IV, d. 1264, pope (1261–64), a Frenchman (b. Troyes) named Jacques Pantaléon; successor of Alexander IV. In the pontifical service he was sent on missions into N Germany; then he was made bishop of Verdun (1253) and Latin patriarch of Jerusalem (1255). On his election he inherited the struggle between the HOHENSTAUFEN and the church, which he continued with vigor and success. It was Urban who dealt the Hohenstaufen the fatal stroke by a definite renewal of the offer of the Sicilian throne to Charles of Anjou. Urban restored the papal finances to solvency, and he established the feast of Corpus Christi. He was succeeded by Clement IV.

Urban V, 1310–70, pope (1362–70), a Provençal named Guillaume de Grimoard; successor of Innocent VI. He was a Benedictine renowned for his knowledge of canon law. The great event of Urban's pontificate was the abortive attempt to return the papacy from Avignon to Rome. The success of Cardinal ALBORNOZ in reconquering the Papal States and the continued agitation by the devout, among them St. Bridget of Sweden, for the restoration of the Holy See, persuaded Urban to depart for Rome in 1367. The return made a great impression, and in 1368, Holy Roman Emperor Charles IV came to visit and reaffirmed his allegiance. The Byzantine emperor, John V, also came and submitted to the pope. In 1370, Urban, disturbed by the resumption of war between France and England, returned to Avignon hoping to end the conflict. He had been further encouraged to leave Rome by the worsening political situation following the death of Albornoz. Urban's quarrel with Edward III of England over the payment of the annual tribute (dating back to King John) occasioned the antipapal polemics of John Wyclif. Urban was a patron of the arts and founded universities at Orange, Kraków, and Vienna. He was succeeded by Gregory XI. Urban was beatified in 1870.

Urban VI, 1318?–1389, pope (1378–89), whose election was the immediate cause of the Great SCHISM; a Neapolitan named Bartolomeo Prignano; successor of Gregory XI. He was made archbishop of Acerenza (1364) and of Bari (1377). On the death of Gregory, the conclave, with French cardinals in the majority, fell into factions and was threatened by a Roman mob demanding the election of an Italian to prevent the return of the papacy to Avignon. At the suggestion of Cardinal de LUNA, Prignano was elected. Urban, before his election peaceable and modest, now became upbraiding and harsh and alienated all the cardinals. They went to Anagni, then to Fondi, and declared Urban's election invalid on the ground that they had been intimidated by the mob. With the consequent election of a new "pope," ROBERT OF GENEVA (antipope Clement VII), began the Great Schism. Urban was recognized from the first by most of Italy and Germany, by Flanders, and by England and English territories. Until 1380, St. Catherine of Siena lived at Rome, working for Urban's recognition. Urban alienated his political allies by his behavior; he probably murdered five cardinals (he had created a new sacred college) who had plotted against him, and thus horrified all Europe. Many believe Urban was insane. His election is now generally considered canonical. He was succeeded by Boniface IX.

Urban VIII, 1568–1644, pope (1623–44), a Florentine named Maffeo Barberini; successor of Gregory XV. Throughout his pontificate the THIRTY YEARS WAR raged in Germany. For various political reasons, Urban gave little help to the Catholics. The old story that Urban rejoiced at Protestant victories because he hated the Hapsburgs is, however, false. His policy in Italy was unsuccessful, and he was humiliated by defeat at the hands of the Farnese of Parma. Urban was very active in church affairs: he published the revised breviary, normalized liturgical practice, canonized many saints, instituted new orders, and continued the reformation of the church. He built and decorated extensively in Rome. Urban sanctioned the condemnation of Galileo and later freed him. He condemned the posthumous work of Cornelis Jansen, *Augustinus.* Urban's strict legislation against easy acceptance of miracles is still in effect. He was succeeded by Innocent X.

Urban, Joseph Maria (ûr'bən), 1872–1933, American architect and scene designer, b. Vienna. He won distinction with his architectural work, including the bridge across the Neva at Leningrad, and with his decorative work at the Paris exposition, 1900. At the St. Louis exposition, 1904, he decorated the Austrian building. He emigrated to the United States in 1911 and was naturalized in 1917. He was active as scene designer for the Metropolitan Opera and for the Ziegfeld Follies. Urban was art consultant for the Chicago Century of Progress Exposition, held in 1933–34.

Urbana (ûrbăn'ə). **1** City (1970 pop. 32,800), seat of Champaign co., E central Ill., adjoining CHAMPAIGN; inc. 1833. With Champaign, its twin city, Urbana is a trade, medical, and educational center in a rich farm area. Electronic systems are manufactured. Urbana is best known as a seat of the Univ. of Illinois at Urbana-Champaign. A tablet in the county courthouse commemorates a speech made by Lincoln in 1854. Chanute Air Force Base, a technical-training center concerned chiefly with land-to-air missiles, is near the city, as is a state park. **2** City (1970 pop. 11,237), seat of Champaign co., W central Ohio, in a rich farm and livestock area; inc. 1814. It has hatcheries and plants that make airplane lights, plastics, paper, fans, and welded products. During the War of 1812, Urbana was an outfitting point for the Great Lakes area; c.14,000 soldiers were quartered there. The soldiers' monument in the city was done by John Quincy Adams Ward. The grave of Simon Kenton, a famous Indian fighter, is in Oak Dale cemetery. The Ohio Caverns are nearby, and several lakes are in the area. The city is the seat of a junior college.

Urbandale, city (1970 pop. 14,434), Polk co., central Iowa, a residential suburb of Des Moines; inc. 1917. It has light industry and warehousing.

Urbane, Roman Christian. Rom. 16.9.

Urban League, National, voluntary nonpartisan community service agency, founded in 1910, whose goal is to help end racial segregation and discrimination in the United States and to help economically and socially disadvantaged groups to share equally in every aspect of American life. It provides direct service in the areas of employment, housing, education, social welfare, health, family planning, mental retardation, law and consumer affairs, youth and student affairs, labor affairs, veterans affairs, and community and minority business development. The Urban League has about 50,000 members.

Urbino (o͞orbē'nō), town (1971 pop. 16,234), in the Marche, central Italy. It is an agricultural and tourist center, located on the site of a former Roman community. The town flourished under the Montefeltro family (12th–16th cent.) and then under the Della Rovere family (1508–1631), before coming under the papacy. The court of Federigo da Montefeltro, 2d duke of Urbino (1444–82), was a great artistic center during the Renaissance. Urbino was particularly noted for its school of painting (15th–17th cent.) and for the manufacture of majolica ware. The Palazzo Ducale (1444–82) today houses a major museum, with paintings by Raphael (born in the town), Titian, Piero della Francesca, and others. Also of interest are St. John's Oratory and Raphael's house (now a museum).

Urchard, Sir Thomas: see URQUHART, SIR THOMAS.

Urdu (o͞or'do͞o), language belonging to the Indic group of the Indo-Iranian subfamily of the Indo-European family of languages (see INDO-IRANIAN LANGUAGES). The official tongue of Pakistan, Urdu is also one of the 15 languages recognized in the 1950 Indian constitution. Urdu has been described as the written or literary variant of HINDUSTANI that is used by Muslims. It is written in a modified form of the Arabic alphabet, and its basically Indic vocabulary has been enriched by borrowings from Arabic and Persian. However, grammatically and phonetically, Urdu is an Indic language. About 20 million persons in Pakistan and India understand Urdu. See M. C. Saihgal, *Hindustani Grammar* (Urdu edition, 1945); Ernest Bender, *Urdu Grammar and Reader* (1967); Franklin Southworth, *Student's Hindi-Urdu Reference Manual* (1971).

urea (yo͞orē'ə), organic compound that is the principal end product of nitrogen metabolism in most mammals. Urea was the first animal metabolite to be isolated in crystalline form; its crystallization was described in the early 18th cent., and in 1773 it was noted that urea gave off ammonia when heated. This discovery provided a clue to its structure. In 1828 urea also became the first organic compound to be synthesized from inorganic materials (lead or

$$\mathrm{C}{=}\mathrm{O}\ (\mathrm{NH_2})_2$$

NH$_2$ / C=O \ NH$_2$

urea

silver cyanate and ammonia); this work was done by German chemist Friedrich Wöhler in 1828. Years of investigation of the biosynthesis of urea culminated in the proposal of the ornithine cycle (sometimes known as the Krebs urea cycle, named for German-born chemist Hans Krebs) in 1932. The proposed cycle, which has since been amended only in detail, involved the addition of one molecule of ammonia and one molecule of carbonic acid to ornithine, with the elimination of one molecule of water and the formation of citrulline. The second reaction was the combination of a second molecule of ammonia with citrulline, with the loss of a second molecule of water and the formation of ARGININE. The third was the addition of water to arginine to split it into one molecule of urea and one molecule of ornithine, which could then repeat the cycle. The first ammonia molecule to enter the cycle has been shown to come from the α-amino group of GLUTAMIC ACID and the second is provided by the α-amino group of ASPARTIC ACID. The other amino acids that make up protein can, during degradation, donate their α-amino groups to aspartic and glutamic acids; thus most of the nitrogen in protein is eventually converted to nitrogen in urea. These reactions have been shown to occur in the liver. Urea is transported in the blood to the kidneys, where it is filtered out; its concentration in urine is about 60 to 70 times as great as that in blood.

uremia (yo͞orē'mēə), condition resulting from advanced stages of kidney failure in which urea and other nitrogen-containing wastes are found in the blood. Some of the early signs of uremia are lethargy, mental depression, loss of appetite and edema; later symptoms include diarrhea, anemia, convulsions, coma, and a gray-brown coloration resulting from the accumulation of urinary pigments in the skin. Treatment of uremia is directed at the underlying kidney disease. See NEPHRITIS; NEPHROSIS.

ureter (yo͞orē'tər), thick-walled tube that conveys urine from the KIDNEY to the urinary bladder. It is approximately 10 in. (25.4 cm) long, with the upper half located in the abdomen and the lower half in the pelvic region. Urine is transported down this tube under the impetus of gravity assisted by contractions of the smooth muscles that line the ureteral walls. A blocked ureter can result from congenital abnormality, a tumor, or the formation of kidney stones. Blockage may require surgery to prevent loss of urinary function and eventual urea poisoning. See URINARY SYSTEM.

urethra (yo͞orē'thrə), canal in most mammals that carries urine from the BLADDER to the outside of the body; in the male it also serves as a genital duct. In humans the urethra is about 1½ in. long (3.8 cm) in women, terminating above the vaginal opening. In men the urethra is about 8 in. (20 cm) long and terminates in an opening at the end of the penis. In the male the urethra is connected to the PROSTATE GLAND and to the seminal vesicles and testes. It transports semen received from those organs as well as urine. See also URINARY SYSTEM.

Urey, Harold Clayton (yo͞or'ē), 1893–, American chemist, b. Walkerton, Ind., grad. Univ. of Montana (B.S., 1917), Ph.D. Univ. of California, 1923. He taught at Johns Hopkins (1924–29), at Columbia (1929–45; as head of the department of chemistry from 1939 to 1942), and at the Univ. of Chicago (1945–58). He became professor-at-large at the Univ. of California in 1958. For his isolation of deuterium (heavy hydrogen) he received the 1934 Nobel Prize in Chemistry; he later isolated heavy isotopes of oxygen, nitrogen, carbon, and sulfur. During World War II, Urey took part in the research leading to the production of the atomic bomb; his special work was on methods of separating uranium isotopes and the production of heavy water. With A. E. Ruark he wrote *Atoms, Molecules, and Quanta* (1930).

Urfa (o͞or'fä), city (1970 pop. 100,231), capital of Urfa prov., SE Turkey. It is the trade center for a productive agricultural region. The city was called EDESSA until its incorporation in the Ottoman Empire in 1637. Its once large Christian population—mostly Armenian—suffered severe massacres in the late 19th cent. A former spelling is Orfa.

Urfé, Honoré d' (ōnōrā' dürfā'), 1567–1625, French novelist. He was the author of *L'Astrée* (5 vol., 1607–10), the principal French PASTORAL novel. It portrays shepherds and shepherdesses living in Urfé's native Auvergne in the 5th cent. An embodiment of courtly manners and conversation in artificially learned style, the novel had wide popularity during the author's lifetime and it influenced Rousseau.

Urga: see ULAN BATOR.

Urgench (o͞orgĕnch'), city (1970 pop. 76,000), capital of Khorezm oblast, Central Asian USSR, in Uzbekistan, on the Amu Darya River, in the Khiva oasis. It is a large port and has cotton and food-processing industries.

Urgench (o͞orgyĕnch'), ancient city of central Asia, on the site of present-day Kunya-Urgench, in the Turkmen Soviet Socialist Republic. It lies c.85 mi (140 km) NW of present Urgench. A major trade and craft center from the 10th to 13th cent., Urgench became the capital of the khanate of Khorezm in the 12th cent. The city was destroyed by the Mongols in the early 13th cent., partially rebuilt, and finally abandoned in the 16th cent. Ruins of an 11th-century minaret and mosque, mausoleums, shops, and the portal of the Caravanserai Gates (14th cent.) have been uncovered.

Uri (yo͞o'rī). **1** Father of BEZALEEL **1.** **2** Father of GEBER **2.** **3** Porter. Ezra 10.24.

Uri (o͞o'rē), canton (1970 pop. 34,091), 415 sq mi (1,075 sq km), central Switzerland, one of the FOUR FOREST CANTONS. ALTDORF is the capital. The most sparsely populated of the Swiss cantons, Uri is an Alpine region of glaciers and pastures, with forests and meadows in the Reuss River valley. Its inhabitants are German-speaking and Roman Catholic. The region became (853) a fief of the Fraumünster convent at Zürich. It was incorporated into the Holy Roman imperial bailiwick of Zürich after 1098. Under Emperor Frederick II it was granted (1231) the status of a dependency of the emperor. The scene of the events of the William TELL legend, Uri in 1291 formed with Schwyz and Unterwalden the league that became the nucleus of Switzerland. It rejected the Reformation and in 1845 joined the Catholic SONDERBUND.

Uriah (yo͞orī'ə), husband of BATH-SHEBA. 2 Sam. 11. Urias: Mat. 1.6. For others called Uriah in the Bible, see URIJAH.

Urias (yo͞orī'əs), Greek form of URIAH.

uric acid (yo͞or'ĭk), white, odorless, tasteless crystalline substance formed as a result of PURINE degradation in man, other primates, dalmatians, birds, snakes, and lizards. The last three groups of animals also channel all AMINO ACID degradation into the formation of GLYCINE, ASPARTIC ACID, and GLUTAMINE, which combine to form purines and finally uric acid; these so-called uricotelic organisms thus excrete uric acid as the major end-product of the metabolism of all nitrogen-containing compounds. Uric acid is a very weak organic acid that is barely soluble in water and insoluble in alcohol and ether. The urates are its salts. Uric acid is present in human urine only in extremely small amounts, but constitutes a large part of the body waste matter of birds (see GUANO) and of reptiles. It collects sometimes in the human kidneys or bladder in calculi, or stones, and is responsible, when present in tissues or deposited upon bones in the form of urates, for gouty conditions. It occurs also in normal human blood. The pure acid is obtained from guano and other similar substances. Upon decomposition urea is obtained. A common test for the presence of the acid in urine depends upon the formation of murexide (an ammonium salt), which is an intense reddish purple. Nitric acid is added to the urine, which is then evaporated. If uric acid is present, murexide is formed when ammonia is added to the residue.

Uriel (yo͞o'rēəl). **1, 2** Two descendants of Kohath. 1 Chron. 6.24; 15.5,11. **3** Man whose daughter became mother of King Abijah of Judah. 2 Chron. 13.2. The name appears in the pseudepigrapha for an archangel. 2 Esdras 4.1–11. He is introduced in Milton's *Paradise Lost* as the angel of the sun.

Urijah (yo͞orī'jə). **1** High priest under King Ahaz. 2 Kings 16.10–16. Uriah: Isa. 8.2. **2** Prophet killed by King Jehoiakim. Jer. 26.20–23. **3** Ancestor of a priestly family. Neh. 3.4,21. Uriah: Ezra 8.33. **4** Companion of Ezra. Neh. 8.4.

Urim and Thummim (yo͞o'rĭm, thŭm'ĭm), name of two sacred LOTS mentioned in the Bible. Ex. 28.30; Lev. 8.8; Num. 27.21; Deut. 33.8. The meaning of the two names is uncertain, as is the nature of the lots; they were connected in some way, however, with the EPHOD.

urinalysis (yo͞or"ənăl'ĭsĭs), clinical examination of URINE for the purpose of medical diagnosis. Urine is initially examined for such characteristics as color, odor, and specific gravity. It is routinely tested for acidity, as indicated by its *p*H reading, and screened for sugar, ketone bodies, proteins, and bile content. Benedict's solution, for example, may be used to test for simple sugars, a high level of which is a possible indicator of diabetes mellitus. Ketone bodies, e.g., acetone and acetoacetic acid, in the urine indicate the substitution of fats for sugar in the energy cycle and are another indication of diabetes mellitus. Abnormal levels of protein may be signs of kidney disease. A high concentration of bile in the urine is a sign of liver malfunction or blockage of the bile duct. Urine is examined microscopically to determine blood count. High levels of erythrocytes, or red blood cells, and leukocytes, or white blood cells, may be a result of bleeding and infection, respectively, in the urinary tract. Casts, crystals, and other substances, whose origins may be ascertained by determining their chemical structures, can be observed microscopically. Additional studies are performed when specific malfunctions are suspected. Clearance tests, for instance, will determine the ability of the kidneys to remove waste substances from the blood plasma per unit of time. The urine of patients with melanotic cancer will often contain melanin, a skin pigment. A diagnosis of drug addiction may be confirmed by the presence of specific chemical substances in the urine. Urinalysis is also employed to test for pregnancy. Pregnant women secrete high levels of gonadotrophic, or ovary-regulating, hormones from the placenta. A reagent containing gonadotrophic hormones is mixed with a sample of urine from the patient, and gonadotrophic antigens are added to it. Failure of the antigens to clump, or agglutinate, is positive evidence of pregnancy.

urinary system, group of organs of the body concerned with excretion of urine, that is, water and the waste products of metabolism. The kidneys are two small organs situated near the vertebral column at the small of the back, the left lying somewhat higher than the right. They are bean-shaped, about 4 in. (10 cm) long and about 2½ in. (6.4 cm) wide. Their purpose is to separate urea, mineral salts, toxins, and other waste products from the blood, and at least one kidney must function properly for life to be maintained. Each kidney contains several million filtering units called nephrons. One end of the nephron is expanded into a structure called the renal corpuscle, or glomerulus, which surrounds a cluster of blood capillaries. The remainder of the nephron consists of a very long narrow tubule, in alternately convoluted and looping sections. Blood containing waste products enters the glomerulus through an afferent arteriole from the renal artery. The cells of the tubule extract the water and waste products as the blood leaves through the outgoing blood vessel (the

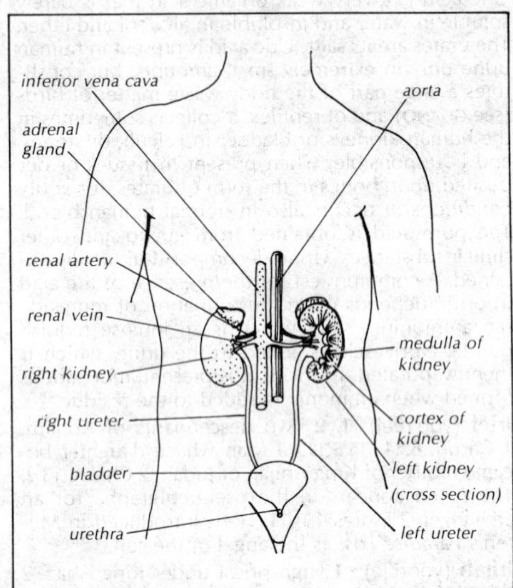

Urinary system

efferent arteriole) of the glomerulus. Blood leaving the glomerulus flows through the network of capillaries that surrounds each tubule; there the substances that the body still needs, such as water and certain salts, are restored to the blood. The purified blood returns to the general circulation through blood vessels leading to the renal vein. The ends of the tubules unite to form collecting tubules, which empty the urine into the kidney pelvis, a collecting chamber in the middle of the kidney. Urine from the kidney pelvis then passes into the ureters, a pair of tubes 16 to 18 in. (40–45 cm) long. Muscles in the walls of the ureters send the urine in small spurts into the bladder, a collapsible sac found on the forward part of the cavity of the bony pelvis that allows temporary storage of urine. The outlet of the bladder is controlled by a sphincter muscle. A full bladder stimulates sensory nerves in the bladder wall that relax the sphincter and allow release of the urine. However, relaxation of the sphincter is also in part a learned response under voluntary control. The released urine enters the urethra, a tube lined with mucus membrane that conveys the urine to the outside. The male urethra, about 8 in. (20 cm) long, terminates at the tip of the penis and is also the passage through which semen is released (see REPRODUCTIVE SYSTEM). The female urethra is less than 2 in. (5 cm) long and opens just in front of the entrance to the vagina; it has no function other than excretion of urine. There are many types of urinary system disorders, including congenital malformation, injury, infection, presence of kidney stones, or calculi, other types of obstruction, and tumors. See NEPHRITIS; NEPHROSIS. Abnormal urine output may indicate other diseases, such as diabetes.

urine, clear, amber-colored fluid formed by the kidneys that carries metabolic wastes out of the body (see URINARY SYSTEM). As the blood circulates it collects excretory products from the tissues and these substances are separated from the blood by the kidneys and eliminated chiefly in the urine. The urine is then stored in the BLADDER and passes out of the body via the URETHRA. The amount passed depends on fluid intake and other factors. Urine is 95% water, in which are dissolved urea, uric acid, creatinine, and other waste products. Normal urine also contains small amounts of substances ordinarily utilized by the body, such as sodium, potassium, and calcium; these substances are excreted by the kidneys when excessive amounts are present in the bloodstream. Analysis of the urine is important in detecting diseases of the urogenital organs, as well as disorders of other body systems.

Uris, Leon (yo͞orĭs'), 1924–, American novelist, b. Baltimore, Md. A popular author who has written many best-selling novels, Uris is probably best known for *Exodus* (1958), a fictional account of the early history of Israel. His other novels include *Battle Cry* (1953), *The Angry Hills* (1955), *Mila 18* (1961), *Topaz* (1967), and *QB VII* (1970).

Urmia, city and lake, Iran: see REZAIYEH.

Ur-Nammu (ŭr-näm'o͞o), fl. 2060 B.C., king of the ancient city of Ur, sometimes called Zur-Nammu or Ur-Engur. He founded a new Sumerian dynasty, the third dynasty of Ur, that lasted a century. Ur-Nammu was the promulgator of the oldest code of law yet known, older by about three centuries than the code of Hammurabi. It consists of a prologue and seven laws; the prologue describes Ur-Nammu as a divinely appointed king who established justice throughout the land. This code is of great importance to the study of biblical law, which it predates by about five centuries. The two most famous monuments of Ur-Nammu's reign are the great ziggurat (temple) at Ur and his stele, of which fragments remain.

Urquhart, David (ûr'kərt), 1805–77, British diplomat and writer. He served (1831–37) in various diplomatic capacities in Constantinople but was recalled because of his hostility to Russia. Subsequently in Parliament (1847–52) and through the press he attacked the British government's Middle Eastern policies, deprecating the interference in Turkey's domestic affairs before the Crimean War. As vehicles for his views, Urquhart founded the *Portfolio* (1835) and the *Free Press* (1855; called the *Diplomatic Review* after 1866). His numerous writings include *England, France, and Turkey* (1834) and *The Crisis* (1840). See biography by Gertrude Robinson (1920, repr. 1970).

Urquhart or **Urchard, Sir Thomas** (both: ûr'kərt), 1611–60, Scottish translator and author. A royalist, he was knighted (1641) by Charles I and fought in the civil wars. He wrote treatises on mathematics and linguistics, but he is noted especially for his superb translation of three books (first two, 1653; third, 1693) of the *Gargantua* of Rabelais.

Urquiza, Justo José de (ho͞o'stō hōsā' thā o͞orkē'sä), 1801–70, Argentine general and politician, president of the confederation (1854–60). As the caudillo of Entre Ríos prov., he helped sustain the power of Juan Manuel de ROSAS. In 1851, resentful of the economic and political dominance of Buenos Aires, he revolted against his chief. Supported by Brazil and the Uruguayan liberals, he forced Manuel ORIBE to capitulate, ending the long siege of Montevideo (Oct., 1851), and defeated Rosas at Monte Caseros (Feb. 3, 1852). Urquiza immediately began the task of national organization. He became provisional director of the Argentine confederation in May, 1852. A constituent assembly adopted (1853) a constitution based primarily on the ideas of J. B. ALBERDI, and Urquiza was inaugurated president in March, 1854. In his administration foreign relations were improved, public education was encouraged, colonization was promoted, and plans for railroad construction were initiated. His work of national organization was, however, hindered by the opposition of Buenos Aires prov, which seceded from the confederation. Open war broke out in 1859. Urquiza defeated at Cepeda the provincial army led by Bartolomé MITRE (Oct., 1859), and Buenos Aires agreed to reenter the confederation. Constitutional amendments proposed by Buenos Aires were adopted in 1860. The settlement was short-lived, and further difficulties culminated in civil war. Urquiza met the army of Buenos Aires, again led by Mitre, at Pavón (Sept., 1861). The battle was indecisive, but Urquiza withdrew from the field, leaving the victory with Mitre. He retired to Entre Ríos, where he ruled with patriarchal autocracy until his assassination.

Urraca (o͞orä'kä), d. 1126, Spanish queen of Castile and León (1109–26), daughter and successor of Alfonso VI. Her first husband, Raymond of Burgundy, died in 1107, and in 1109 she was married to ALFONSO I of Aragón. Her reign was disturbed by strife among the powerful nobles and especially by recurrent warfare with her husband, who had seized her lands. The marriage was annulled in 1114, and Urraca recovered most of her lands with the help of her son by her first husband. He succeeded her as Alfonso VII.

Ursa Major (ûr'sə) and **Ursa Minor** [Lat.,=the great bear; the little bear], two conspicuous northern CONSTELLATIONS. Known to many peoples from ancient times, these constellations have had various names; the configuration of the seven brightest stars has been called the Bear, Septentriones (the seven plowing oxen), the Plow, Charles's Wain, and the Wagon. Ursa Minor was once known as Cynosura (from the Greek for "dog's tail"). In the United States part of Ursa Major is called the Big Dipper (or the Drinking Gourd) and part of Ursa Minor, the Little Dipper. Four of the seven bright stars in the Big Dipper form the bowl and three the handle; five of these stars are of second magnitude. The middle star in the handle of the Big Dipper is Mizar (Zeta Ursae Majoris). A fainter star, Alcor, which appears to be near Mizar, was observed from ancient times. These two stars are sometimes called a double star, but since they do not revolve around a common center of gravity they are not true doubles. Mizar itself is, however, a visual BINARY STAR and was the first to be recognized as such—by G. B. Riccioli in 1650. It was also the first spectroscopic binary to be discovered; this observation resulted from studies of the spectrum of the brighter component of Mizar, which revealed it as a binary consisting of a pair of stars of almost equal brightness. The two end stars in the bowl of the Big Dipper are known as the Pointers. A line extended through them to about five times the distance between them leads to the polestar (POLARIS, or the North Star). Polaris is at the extreme end of the Little Dipper. Including Polaris there are three stars in the handle of the Little Dipper and four forming the bowl. The handles of the two Dippers extend in opposite directions, and when one bowl is upright the other is inverted. Ursa Major reaches its highest point in the evening sky in April and Ursa Minor its highest point in June. However, for observers in the middle and northern latitudes of the Northern Hemisphere both constellations are circumpolar and thus are visible throughout the year.

Ursins, Marie Anne de la Trémoille, princesse des (mārē' än də lä trāmwä'yə präNsĕs' däzürsăN'), 1642–1722, French noblewoman and unofficial diplomat. After the death of her first husband, she married (1675) Duke Flavio Orsini, whose name was gallicized into Ursins. She soon separated from her husband. In 1698 she solicited papal approval for the choice of a French prince, Philip of Anjou (later King Philip V), to succeed King Charles II on the throne of Spain. She arranged the marriage of Philip V with María Luisa of Savoy, whose lady-in-waiting she became in 1701. Until the queen's death (1714) Mme des Ursins exerted virtually dictatorial power at the court of Madrid. She defied Philip's grandfather, King Louis XIV of France, insisting on a Spanish policy of independence from France. It was largely because of her energy that Philip V kept the throne in the War of the Spanish Succession (see SPANISH SUCCESSION, WAR OF THE) despite both his enemies and allies. When María Luisa died, Mme des Ursins advised Philip to marry Elizabeth Farnese, who, when queen, had her expelled (1714) from Spain. Ill-received in France, she went to the Netherlands and later to Rome. Her correspondence has been published.

Ursúa, Pedro de (pā'thrō thā o͞orso͞o'ä), c.1526–1561, Spanish conquistador and explorer in South America. Arriving in New Granada in 1545, he served as temporary governor at Bogotá. Ursúa subjugated the neighboring Indians and searched for El Dorado and the legendary kingdom of Omagua, founding a number of towns. A restless adventurer, he joined the Peruvian viceroy, the marqués de Cañete, in Panama, where he subdued the *cimarrones* (escaped Negro slaves) before going with Cañete to Peru in 1558. The viceroy sent him (1560) to explore the MARAÑÓN and search for El Dorado. On the voyage Lope de AGUIRRE and a band of rebels mutinied and murdered Ursúa.

Uruapan (o͞orwä'pän), city (1970 pop. 104,475), Michoacán state, W Mexico. An attractive city with fine gardens and parks, it is in a semitropical, mountainous agricultural region. The city, founded in 1540, is the center of the manufacture of gourd lacquerware by the Tarascan Indians. Local craftsmen also produce glassware, woodwork, and embroideries. Not far from Uruapan is the volcano Paricutín.

Urubamba (o͞oro͞obäm'bä), river, c.450 mi (720 km) long, rising in the Andes mts., S Peru, and flowing generally north to join the Apurímac River to form the Ucayali. The Urubamba is extensively used for irrigation, and its valley is heavily populated; Cuzco, Peru, is located there. High above the Urubamba's gorge are the ruins of the terraced Inca city of Machu Picchu.

Uruguay (yo͞o'rəgwā, -gwī, Span. o͞oro͞ogwi', o͞o-ro͞owī'), republic (1971 est. pop. 2,900,000), 68,536 sq mi (177,508 sq km), SE South America. The capital is MONTEVIDEO. The smallest country in South America, Uruguay extends from a short Atlantic coastline along the north bank of the Rió de la Plata to the Uruguay River, which separates it on the west from Argentina. To the north is Brazil. The land is an area of topographical transition from the humid Argentine Pampa to the uplands of S Brazil. North of the alluvial plain, known as the Banda Oriental [Span.,=east bank, i.e., of the Uruguay and the Rió de la Plata], Uruguay generally has long, sweeping slopes and grasslands, wooded valleys with slow-moving rivers, and long ranges of low hills, with some huge granite blocks that stand out against the

horizon. The land has a faint purplish hue. Although Uruguay is within the temperate zone, climatic variations are moderate; generally the climate is warm, with rainfall evenly distributed through the seasons, but in some years there are severe droughts. Uruguay's greatest natural resource is its rich agricultural land, more than 70% of which is devoted to livestock raising. Sheep and cattle are so important that public rights of way have been built for driving the herds. Grains for cattle fattening and human consumption make up the bulk of the harvested crops. Wheat is the major food crop, followed by rice, an important export crop. Corn is the principal feed concentrate. Oats, barley, and grain sorghums are also grown, and oil crops (flaxseed and sunflower seed) and sugar beets and sugarcane are important. In the vicinity of SALTO there are many orchards and vineyards. The country has abundant fisheries. Despite Uruguay's basically agricultural-pastoral economy, its dependence upon imports for most raw materials, and its lack of fuel resources, there is considerable industrialization. Hydroelectric power has been developed. The processing of agricultural and animal products accounts for about half of the manufacturing activity; FRAY BENTOS and PAYSANDÚ are noted for their meat-freezing and canning plants. Meat, wool, and hides and skins constitute about 80% of Uruguay's exports. Other manufactures include beverages, textiles, construction and building materials, chemicals, metallurgical goods, and petroleum and coal derivatives. A large refinery near Montevideo processes imported crude oil. Marble, stone, and granite were long thought to be the only important mineral resources, but in the late 1960s iron ore and some uranium were found (these deposits have not yet been mined). Uruguay's magnificent beaches, such as those at PUNTA DEL ESTE, are great economic assets; tourists, chiefly vacationing Argentines, contribute much to the national income. The country's transportation facilities are extensively developed. The state owns the railroad, as well as the power, telephone, oil refining, and other industries; about one third of the workers are on the government payroll. Most of the population is concentrated in the south; almost half live in Montevideo. Most are of European descent, Spanish and Italian predominating; there are few Negroes and pure Indians. The original inhabitants, the Charrúa Indians, were absorbed into the Spanish and Portuguese populations after long resistance; today the mestizo element (about 10% of the total population) is found principally in N Uruguay. Although the Rió de la Plata was explored as early as 1515, it was not until 1624 that the Spanish established the first permanent settlement, at Soriano in SW Uruguay. The Portuguese founded (1680) a short-lived settlement at Colonia, and in 1717 they fortified a hill on the site of Montevideo. Fearing encroachment and competition, the Spanish drove them out (1724) and from then until the wars of independence controlled the Banda Oriental. Uruguay's position between Spanish and Portuguese settlements, and later between Argentina and Brazil, helped determine the emergence of Uruguay as an independent state. On the pampas stock raising spread; gradually the unbounded range gave way to huge estancias and small settlements concentrated about the ranch buildings. It was the rough and hardy GAUCHO who fought for independence, and the traditions, personal loyalties, and rivalries of the gauchos helped to keep the nation in almost continual strife for three quarters of a century after independence was won. When the revolutionary banner was raised in the Argentine in 1810, the leaders of the Banda Oriental, notably ARTIGAS, accepted the cause, but in 1814 Artigas broke with the military junta of Buenos Aires and began a struggle for Uruguayan independence that lasted until the Brazilian occupation of Montevideo in 1820. Five years later a small group, known as the Thirty-three Immortals, under the guidance of LAVALLEJA, declared Uruguay independent; in 1827 at Ituzaingó Brazil was defeated. Great Britain, opposing Brazilian expansion S to the Río de la Plata, helped ultimately to create an independent Uruguay as a buffer state between Argentina and Brazil. The peace (1828) stipulated that the new Uruguayan constitution should be acceptable to both the larger nations. When it was adopted in 1830, Fructuoso RIVERA was chosen as president. He was promptly faced with revolts led by his old rival, Lavalleja, and when he was succeeded in office by Manuel ORIBE, he himself revolted against Oribe, who was in sympathy with Juan Manuel de ROSAS of Argentina. In the long fratricidal struggle that ensued, the two dominant political parties of Uruguay emerged, Rivera's Colorados [reds] and Oribe's Blancos [whites]. Oribe was driven out in 1838, but later with the aid of Rosas returned to begin the long siege of Montevideo. The Italian patriot Garibaldi fought in the Uruguayan wars from 1842 to 1846. In 1851 the Argentine general URQUIZA drove out Rosas and brought an end to the Uruguayan civil war. When in 1864 Brazil presented a claim for damages to property and nationals during the civil wars, Uruguay refused to accept it. Brazil invaded and, aided by the Uruguayan general Vanancio Flores (a Colorado), overthrew the Blanco president. Paraguay, under Francisco Solano LÓPEZ, came to the assistance of the Blancos, whereupon Argentina, Brazil, and Uruguay formed a tripartite alliance against Paraguay (see TRIPLE ALLIANCE, WAR OF THE). During the 19th and 20th cent. waves of immigration, chiefly from Europe, augmented the Uruguayan population. Until the rise of BATLLE Y ORDÓÑEZ early in the 20th cent., Uruguay experienced many revolutions and counterrevolutions. In Batlle's second term as president (1911–15), however, began the social and material progress that made Uruguay one of the more stable and prosperous nations of Latin America. By a coup d'etat in 1933, Gabriel TERRA suspended the constitution of 1919, and his rule was strongly personalistic. Yet, under Terra's rule, which ended in 1938, the socialistic measures for public welfare were not reversed but forwarded; the labor code was broadened, social benefits increased, and industry further nationalized. Batlle's influence on Uruguayan political practice did not end with his death; concerned lest the country again fall prey to dictatorial caudillos, he had advocated the creation of an executive governing council. This reform, inspired by the Swiss multiple-executive system of government, was adopted in 1951; the office of president was abolished and replaced by a nine-man council with a president, chosen from the majority party, to act as titular head of state. The plural executive, however, proved ineffectual; factionalism and apathy within the council hindered action on social and economic problems, which became pressing in the mid-1950s and acute during the 60s. The increasing use of synthetic fibers and the steadily declining price of wool cut deeply into Uruguay's exports of wool and leather, and the country suffered an increasingly unfavorable balance of trade. A runaway inflation ensued; unemployment rose as high as 12%. The vast, intricate, and inefficient bureaucracy became a burden to the economy, which could not support the great numbers on the government payroll, including the thousands on pensions. In 1958 the Colorados, who had been in power for over 93 years, were overwhelmingly defeated by the conservative Blancos, who won again in 1962 by a narrower margin. Throughout the 1960s and early 70s the economic decline continued relentlessly, intensified by droughts and floods and accompanied by massive social unrest—riots, paralyzing strikes, and the emergence of a terrorist Marxist guerrilla group, the well-organized Tupamaro National Liberation Front. In 1967 a new constitution abolished the plural executive and reinstated a powerful president. That same year the Colorado party returned to power, with Oscar Gestido as president. Gestido died after several months in office and was succeeded by his vice president, Jorge Pacheco. Pacheco and his hand-picked successor, José María Bordaberry (who was elected in 1972), ruled with increasingly dictatorial powers, imposing strict economic controls and suppressing many civil liberties. As the Tupamaros increased their terrorist activities, kidnapping foreign diplomats and assassinating high officials, the army assumed tremendous power, moving against the Tupamaros with arrests and torture, and even pressuring President Bordaberry (June, 1973) to dissolve the congress. Uruguay has long been remarkable for its contributions to literature and the arts (see SPANISH AMERICAN LITERATURE). The Univ. of the Republic is in Montevideo. See G. G. Lindahl, *Uruguay's New Path: A Study in Politics during the First Colegiado, 1919–33* (1962); George Pendle, *Uruguay* (3d ed. 1965); R. H. Fitzgibbon, *Uruguay, Portrait of a Democracy* (1954, repr. 1966); R. H. Brannon, *The Agricultural Development of Uruguay* (1968); J. H. Ferguson, *The River Plata Republics* (1968); Marvin Alisky, *Uruguay: A Contemporary Survey* (1969); T. E. Weil et al., *Area Handbook for Uruguay* (1971); M. E. Gilio, *The Tupamaro Guerrillas* (tr. 1973).

Uruguay, river, c.1,000 mi (1,610 km) long, rising in S Brazil and flowing in an arc W, SW, and S to the Río de la Plata, an estuary; it forms part of the Brazil-Argentina border and the entire Argentina-Uruguay line. The Río Negro is an important tributary. The lower river is navigable for oceangoing vessels for 130 mi (209 km) upstream. Its upper course is broken by waterfalls. Salto Grande Falls is the site of a joint hydroelectric project of Argentina and Uruguay. Concordia, Argentina, and Salto and Paysandú, Uruguay, are on the river.

Uruk: see ERECH.

Urumchi: see WU-LU-MU-CH'I, China.

urus: see AUROCHS.

Usambara (o͞osämbä'rä), mountains, c.70 mi (110 km) long and from 20 to 40 mi (30–60 km) wide, NE Tanzania. On its slopes, which rise to c.8,000 ft (2,440 m), coffee, sisal, tea, and cinchona are produced; rice is grown in the swampy foothills. The region was among the first in E Africa to be settled (1902) by European farmers.

U.S. Customary System of weights and measures: see ENGLISH UNITS OF MEASUREMENT.

Usedom (o͞o'zədôm) or **Uznam** (o͞oz'näm), island, 164 sq mi (425 sq km), in the Baltic Sea. Formerly in Pomerania prov., Germany, it was divided in 1945 between East Germany (which received most of the island) and Poland. Usedom is separated from the mainland by Stettin Lagoon and from the neighboring island of Wolin by the Świna Channel. The chief towns are Świnioujście (Swinemünde) in the Polish section and Usedom in the East German section. It is generally lowland, with forests and several lakes.

Grain and potatoes are the principal agricultural products; the main sources of income are tourism and fishing.

Ushant (ŭsh′ənt), Fr. *Ouessant*, island, 10 sq mi (25.9 sq km), Finistère dept., off Brittany, in the Atlantic, c.10 mi (16 km) from the mainland. The chief occupations are sheep raising and fishing; many men are in the merchant marine. In 1778 and 1794 naval battles occurred near there between the French and English. Ushant has a very powerful lighthouse.

Usher, James: see USSHER, JAMES.

Ushuaia (o͞oswī′ä), city (1970 pop. 5,677), Tierra del Fuego Territory, S Argentina, a port on the Beagle Canal, on Ushuaia Bay. Settled in the 1870s by English missionaries, it was taken over by Argentine naval forces in 1884.

Usk, Thomas (ŭsk), d. 1388, English politician and author. He was under-sheriff of London. While in Newgate Prison he wrote *Testament of Love*, an allegory in prose describing and justifying the political actions that resulted in his imprisonment. The work is useful in dating Chaucer's *Troilus and Criseyde*, from which it borrows. Usk was executed in 1388.

Usk, river, c.60 mi (100 km) long, rising in the Black Mts., S Wales and flowing generally SE to Bristol Channel near Newport. The upper Usk is noted for its beauty and its excellent fishing. It is the river associated with the legend of King Arthur.

Üsküdar (üskü′där) or **Scutari** (sko͞o′tərē), urban district (1970 pop. 143,938), part of İstanbul, Turkey, on the Asian side of the Bosporus. It is a commercial and industrial center. Known as Chrysopolis in ancient times, it enjoyed its greatest prosperity after the Ottoman conquest (15th cent.). As the gateway to Constantinople (İstanbul), it was embellished with many mosques, caravansaries, and other public buildings. During the Crimean War, Üsküdar was a base (1854–56) of the British army and the site of the military hospital made famous by the work of Florence Nightingale.

Uslar Pietri, Arturo (ärto͞o′rō o͞os′lär pyā′trē), 1906–, Venezuelan novelist and essayist. Uslar Pietri is considered one of the most powerful regional writers in modern Spanish American letters. His masterpiece is the historical novel *Las Lanzas coloradas* (1931), a vivid depiction of the Venezuelan campaign of Simón Bolívar. Other works include *Red* (1936) and *Treinta hombres y sus sombras* (1949), short stories; *El Camino de El Dorado* (1948), a biography of Lope de Aguirre; and three collections of essays—*Las visiones del camino* (1945), *Letras y hombres de Venezuela* (1948), and *Las Nubes* (1956).

USO: see UNITED SERVICE ORGANIZATIONS.

Uspallata Pass (o͞ospäyä′tä), c.12,500 ft (3,810 m) high, over the Andes between Mendoza, Argentina, and Santiago, Chile. A trail—and later a rough road—for men and pack animals was used before the Transandine Railway was built. The Pan-American Highway now runs through the pass. In 1817 José de San Martín sent part of his patriot army through the pass to fight the Spanish royalists in Chile. The Christ of the Andes stands in the pass. Mt. Aconcagua towers to the north.

Ussachevsky, Vladimir (vlədyē′mĭr o͞osəchĕf′skē), 1911–, Russian-American composer, b. Manchuria. Ussachevsky emigrated to the United States in 1930 and studied at the Eastman School. He joined the faculty of Columbia Univ. in 1947. After composing many works for traditional instruments, Ussachevsky began working in electronic music in 1951, in collaboration with his former teacher Otto LUENING. The two, together with Milton BABBITT and Roger SESSIONS, became (1959) directors of the Columbia-Princeton Electronic Music Center in New York City. Ussachevsky has written *A Piece for Tape Recorder* (1956) and the choral work *Creation*, which can be performed electronically or with live performers and electronic sounds.

Ussher or **Usher, James** (both: ŭsh′ər), 1581–1656, Irish prelate and scholar. While a fellow (1599–1605) of Trinity College, Dublin, he was ordained (1601). By 1605 he was chancellor of St. Patrick's Cathedral, Dublin. In 1615 a convocation of clergy called upon him to draft the articles of doctrine and discipline of the Irish Protestant church. These showed a Calvinistic tendency. In 1620 or 1621 he became bishop of Meath and later (1625) archbishop of Armagh. He often went to England, where he enjoyed association with noted scholars and statesmen. He was there when the Irish rebellion of 1641 broke out, and he never returned to Ireland. Although he refused to sit (1643) in the Westminster Assembly and upheld the doctrine of the divine right of kings, he was in 1647 elected preacher of Lincoln's Inn; by Cromwell's order he was given a state funeral in Westminster Abbey. His learning, attested by his numerous works in Latin and English, awakened great admiration. In his chronological study, the *Annales Veteris et Novi Testamenti* (2 vol., 1650–54), Ussher worked out a system of dates (setting the creation at 4004 B.C.) afterward long used in some editions of the King James Version of the Bible. His works were edited by C. R. Elrington and J. H. Todd (17 vol., 1847–64). See W. B. Wright, *The Ussher Memoirs* (1889) and the biography by R. B. Knox (1967).

USSR: see UNION OF SOVIET SOCIALIST REPUBLICS.

Ussuri (o͞oso͞o′rē), Mandarin *Wu-shu-li*, river, c.365 mi (590 km) long, formed by the confluence of the Ulukhe and Daubikhe rivers, S Primorsky Kray, Far Eastern USSR. It flows N to the Amur River at Khabarovsk, forming part of the USSR-China border. The Ussuri abounds in fish, and it is used to transport timber. The Ussuri-Khanka lowland is a fertile agricultural region. Armed border clashes between Soviet and Chinese forces occurred (1972) along the river.

Ussuriysk (o͞o″so͞orēsk′), city (1970 pop. 128,000), Primorsky Kray, Far Eastern USSR, on the Suyfun River. It is a coal-mining center. Whaling, sugar refining, and the manufacture of motors and agricultural machinery are also important. The city was called Nikolsk-Ussuriski until 1935 and Voroshilov until 1957.

Uster (o͞os′tər), town (1970 pop. 21,819), Zürich canton, NE Switzerland, between Pfäffiker and Greifen lakes. Textiles and machinery are made in the town.

Ústí nad Labem (o͞os′tyē näd lä′bĕm), Ger. *Aussig*, city (1970 pop. 72,299), NW Czechoslovakia, in Bohemia, on the Elbe and Bilina rivers and near the East German border. It is a river port, railroad hub, and industrial center in a lignite-mining area. The city has ironworks and chemical, machine-building, and food-processing industries. Founded in the 13th cent., Ústí nad Labem was ceded to Germany in 1938 by the Munich Pact but reverted to Czechoslovakia in 1945. In the city are several Gothic and Renaissance churches.

Ustinov, Peter (yo͞os′tənôf), 1921–, English writer, director and actor, b. London. A witty, charming man, he has an international reputation for his talent and versatility. Among the plays he has written are *Romanoff and Juliet* (1956), *The Unknown Soldier and His Wife* (1967), and *Who's Who in Hell* (1974). His works of fiction include a volume of short stories, *Add a Dash of Pity* (1959), and *Krumnagel* (1971), a novel. Also noted as an actor—his most famous role being that of Nero in the movie *Quo Vadis* (1951)—he has appeared in his own plays and in such films as *Billy Budd* (1962) and *Hot Millions* (1971). See study by Tony Thomas (1971).

Ust-Kamenogorsk (o͞ost″kəmyĭnəgôrsk′), city (1970 pop. 230,000), capital of East Kazakhstan oblast, Central Asian USSR, in Kazakhstan, on the Irtysh River and in the foothills of the W Altai mts. It is a river port and an industrial center with zinc, lead, and titanium-magnesium smelters. There is a large hydroelectric station nearby. The city was founded in 1720 as the Russian military outpost of Ust-Kamennaya.

Ust-Sysolsk: see SYKTYVKAR, USSR.

Ust Urt: see USTYURT, USSR.

Ustyurt (o͞ost″yo͞ort′), desert plateau, c.62,000 sq mi (160,600 sq km), Central Asian USSR, between the Caspian and Aral seas. It rises to between c.490 and 980 ft (150–300 m). It occupies the southern part of the Kazakh Republic, the northern part of the Kara-Kalpak Autonomous Republic, and the Turkmen Republic. Its seminomadic population raises sheep, goats, and camels. The name is sometimes spelled Ust Urt.

Usulután (o͞oso͞olo͞otän′), city (1968 est. pop. 17,000), S El Salvador. Near the volcano of the same name, the city is the commercial center of an agricultural region.

Usumacinta (o͞o″so͞omäsĕn′tä), river, c.600 mi (970 km) long, formed at the Guatemala-Mexico border by the Chixoy and Pasion rivers and flowing NE through Tabasco state, Mexico, to the Bay of Campeche. It is navigable for c.300 mi (480 km) upstream by small boats and is used to move logs and chicle downstream. Near its mouth some of the channels of the Usumacinta merge with the Grijalva River. To increase agricultural production there, Mexico is constructing irrigation and hydroelectric facilities.

Usumbura: see BUJUMBURA, Burundi.

usury: see INTEREST.

Utah (yo͞o′tô″, –tä″), state (1970 pop. 1,059,273), 84,916 sq mi (219,932 sq km), including 2,577 sq mi (6,674 sq km) of inland water surface, W United States, one of the Rocky Mt. states; admitted 1896 as the 45th state of the Union. SALT LAKE CITY is the capital and largest city; it is also the headquarters of the Church of Jesus Christ of LATTER-DAY SAINTS (see also MORMONS), which founded the state and to a large extent still dominates it. Other important cities are OGDEN and PROVO. Utah is bounded on the N by Idaho, on the NE by Wyoming, on the E by Colorado, on the S by Arizona, and on the W by Nevada. The state has two dissimilar regions abruptly separated by the Wasatch Range (part of the Rocky Mts.), which runs generally south from the Idaho border. To the east of the Wasatch rise massive mountains and irregular plateaus; along its western foothills lie the major cities of Utah, while further west is the Great Basin. In the northeast the snow-capped Uinta Mts. reach the state's highest elevation in Kings Peak (13,528 ft/4,123 m). The dissected Colorado Plateau stretches southward, rugged and largely uninhabitable except in isolated river valleys. Deep, tortuous canyons cut by the Colorado River and its tributaries impede travel but create vistas of remarkable grandeur. Western Utah, part of the Great Basin, was once submerged beneath an extensive Pleistocene lake, Lake Bonneville. During many thousands of years the amount of water in the lake fluctuated, then subsided, leaving behind a salt-strewn desert, wide expanses of arid but nonalkaline soil, and a series of lakes. GREAT SALT LAKE, the largest

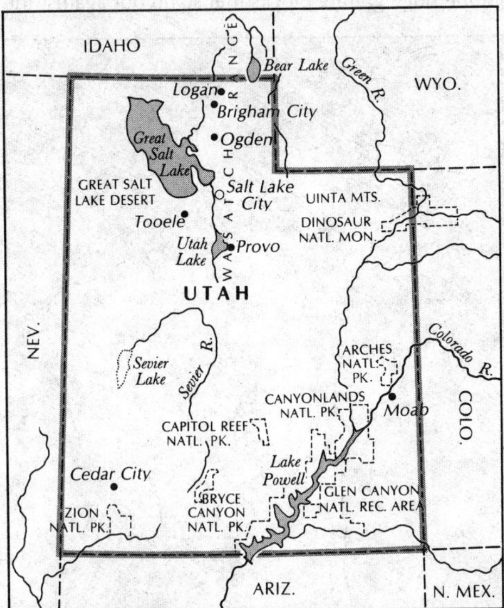

of these, has through evaporation reached a concentration of mineral salts several times that of the ocean. Gulls, pelicans, and blue herons are found around the lake and have rookeries on its islands. Much of the lake shore is bordered by mud and salt flats. The haze-covered Oquirrh Mts., rising south of the lake, dip to form pleasant beaches at the water's edge, then emerge as islands within the lake and rise again in the Promontory Mts. on the northern lake shore. Utah Lake, to the south, is the largest natural body of fresh water in the state and drains into Great Salt Lake through the Jordan River. Between Great Salt Lake and the Wasatch Range and curving southwest toward the Arizona line is a river-crossed strip, an agricultural oasis and the center of the life of Utah. On terraces left by the ancient Lake Bonneville are situated the major cities. Irrigation of the rich but arid land has long been a vital problem in Utah's agricultural development. Major reclamation projects, such as the Weber River, Weber River Basin, Moon Lake, and Strawberry Valley projects, assist numerous private enterprises in storing water for distribution and in aiding flood control. Construction on the $325 million CENTRAL UTAH PROJECT began in 1967; when completed, a vast complex of dams, canals, and aqueducts will carry water across the Wasatch Range to the Salt Lake valley. Lake Powell, reservoir of Glen Canyon Dam just beyond the Arizona line, and Flaming Gorge Dam are important parts of the COLORADO RIVER STORAGE PROJECT in Utah. Yet the arduous task of converting deserts to productive soil has confined the tilled land, including isolated farms in river valleys and a considerable amount of dry-farming land, to a small percentage of the state's total area. A typical rural scene consists of a group of small, intensively cultivated farms situated close to a general store and a Mormon religious edifice. Major crops are hay, wheat, barley, and sugar beets, but the bulk of income from agriculture is based on livestock and livestock products, including sheep and an expanding poultry industry. Abundant sunshine provides some compensation for inadequate rainfall, and the climate is moderate, except in the high altitudes. Agrarian life was well suited to the principles of the Mormons when they came to found their Zion there; the difficulties of agriculture in the dry land were an advantage since the Mormons offered little inducement to outsiders. The development of resources other than agricultural ones was more or less frowned upon by the Mormon Church and, in general, was initiated by non-Mormons (called Gentiles by the Mormons). However, a wealth of minerals made mineral exploitation almost inevitable and, in turn, stimulated the construction of railroads. Today much of the population is directly or indirectly engaged in mining. Copper is the chief metal; in 1970 Utah was second in the nation in its production (Bingham Canyon has one of the largest open-pit copper mines in the country). Copper is followed in economic importance by petroleum (first discovered in the late 1950s), coal, and molybdenum (Utah ranked third in its production in 1970). It also ranked first in the production of beryllium (the first major discovery was in 1960); second in the production of asphalt; third in silver, lead, tin, gold, and fluorspar; and fourth in mercury, vanadium, potassium salts, manganiferous ore, and uranium. For many years high freight rates and the long distances from markets, together with a Mormon distrust of industrialization, tended to discourage extensive manufacturing. However, the establishment of defense plants and U.S. armed forces installations in the state during World War II spurred a phenomenal industrial growth. The proximity of high-grade iron, coal, and limestone have made Provo the most important steel mill center in the west. Industrial plants now extend from Provo to Brigham City, with the largest concentration in the Salt Lake City area. Utah is a center for aerospace research and the production of all kinds of missiles, spacecraft, electronic systems, and related items. Other major manufactures are processed foods, machinery, fabricated metalware, and petroleum products. Tourism is becoming increasingly important to the state's economy. Thousands of visitors come annually to view the many natural wonders, most notably Great Salt Lake and the spectacular Bryce Canyon and Zion national parks. Other attractions are Canyonlands and Arches national parks; Natural Bridges, Cedar Breaks, Dinosaur, Hovenweep, Rainbow Bridge, and Timpanogos Cave national monuments; Glen Canyon National Recreation Area; and Golden Spike National Historic Site (see NATIONAL PARKS AND MONUMENTS, table). The Bonneville Salt Flats are famous as an automotive speedway. There are many national forests and a number of Indian reservations. Capitol Reef National Park contains ancient cliff dwellings (see CLIFF DWELLERS), caves with interesting glyphs, and numerous artifacts of prehistoric man. Recent anthropological studies have produced evidence that the Utah area was inhabited as early as c.9,000 B.C. Although some of Coronado's men under García López de Cárdenas may have entered S Utah in 1540, the first definite penetration by Europeans did not occur until 1776, when the Spanish missionaries Silvestre Vélez de Escalante and Francisco Atanasio Domínguez opened the route for the Old Spanish Trail between Santa Fe and Utah Lake. By the Treaty of 1819 between the United States and Spain, the large area of which Utah was a part was officially recognized as a Spanish possession (it passed to the United States in 1848 with the Treaty of Guadalupe Hidalgo after the Mexican War). In the 1820s the MOUNTAIN MEN, in search of rich beaver streams, made their way over the difficult terrain, thoroughly exploring the region. The discovery of Great Salt Lake is generally credited to James Bridger, but Étienne Provot, Jedediah S. Smith, and others also have claims. The Canadian fur trader Peter Skene Ogden led four Snake River expeditions into the area and is commemorated in the name of one of Utah's leading cities. Between 1824 and 1830 the riches in furs were exhausted, and a decade was to pass before the arrival of the next transients—westward-bound emigrants. In 1841 the first California-bound emigrant train, usually called the Bidwell party, left the Oregon Trail and made its way across the Great Salt Lake Desert. Several years later Miles Goodyear became Utah's first settler when he set up a trading post at the site of present-day Ogden, naming it Fort Buenaventura. The ill-fated DONNER PARTY broke trail over the difficult mountains E of Great Salt Lake in 1846 and proceeded in their tragic journey westward across the desert. Permanent settlement began in 1847 with the arrival of the first of the hosts of persecuted Mormons, seeking a "gathering place for Israel" in some undesired and isolated spot. It is said that when Brigham Young, their leader, surmounted the Wasatch Range and looked out over the green valley of Great Salt Lake, he knew that the place had been found. On July 24, 1847, now celebrated as Pioneer Day, he entered the valley. Young was to prove himself one of the greatest administrators and leaders in 19th-century America. Under his direction and in communal fashion the ground was plowed and planted, the Temple foundation was laid, and Salt Lake City was platted directly on compass lines. Gradually the Latter-Day Saints assembled, their ranks swelled by streams of emigrants from the United States and abroad (particularly Great Britain and the Scandinavian countries). More and more of the arid land yielded to their pioneering irrigation. In the next 50 years they not only had to learn the techniques of wresting a living from the desert, of combating frequent invasions of grasshoppers, and of warding off Indian attacks, but they also had to face opposition from the Federal government. In 1850 a large area, of which the present state was a part, was constituted Utah Territory and Young was appointed governor. The name Deseret [honeybee], chosen by the Mormons, was discarded, but the beehive remains a ubiquitous symbol of Mormon activity throughout Utah. The Indians, dispossessed of their lands and foreseeing further encroachment, became embittered, and the Mormons were threatened by the powerful Ute Indians, eventually leading to the Walker War (1853-54) and the Black Hawk War (1865-68). There were also conflicts between the Mormons and the California-bound immigrants, but the real trouble came with the gradual disintegration of relations between the Mormons and the Federal government. Numerous petitions for statehood were denied because of the practice of polygamy, publicly avowed by the Mormons in 1852. Friction was increased by the assigning to Utah of non-Mormon, and often incompetent, Federal judges, and clashes between church and Federal interpretation of the law were frequent. Stories of Mormon violence toward non-Mormon settlers circulated in the East, and antagonism, much of it based on misunderstanding, grew out of proportion. In 1857 a "state of substantial rebellion" was declared by the Federal government; Young was removed from his post, and President James Buchanan directed U.S. army troops to proceed against the Mormons. The Mormons prepared for warfare, calling in outlying settlers, and guerrilla bands harrassed the westward-bound troop supply trains of Albert S. Johnston. The affair, known as the "Utah War" or the "Mormon campaign," was finally settled peacefully, but great ill feeling had developed, particularly after the massacre at MOUNTAIN MEADOWS. Some settlers who during the disturbances had made an exodus to land S of the Utah Valley remained to spread colonization there. This turbulent episode was succeeded by several difficult decades. Congressional acts forbidding polygamy were passed in 1862, 1882, and 1887. In the attempt to enforce them, civil liberties were infringed upon and some Mormon church properties were expropriated. In 1890 a church edict advising members to abstain from the practice of polygamy was ratified, and civil rights and church properties were restored. Long before Utah became a state in 1896, its area had been reduced to its present size by the creation of the territories of Nevada and Colorado in 1861 and Wyoming Territory in 1868. The influx of settlers included many non-Mormon groups, and cultural and economic isolation had been broken by the development of mining as well as by the completion of the Union Pacific RR, which in 1869 joined the Central Pacific RR (NW of Ogden), completing the nation's first transcontinental railroad. Agriculture was hampered by a court interpretation of water rights in 1880 that favored a concept of water as private property. Not until the Reclamation Act of 1902 was the principle designating water as public property restored, buttressed by the state act of 1903 that vested the ownership of water in the state. In political life the violent conflict between Mormons and non-Mormons has disappeared, as citizens have largely learned to ignore religious differences and to fine common causes and understanding in their mutual problems. Urbanization has proceeded rapidly. World War II spurred industrial growth, and the development of hydroelectric power during the 1950s attracted new industries. Utah still operates under its first constitution, adopted in 1895 and effective with statehood in 1896. The state's executive branch is headed by a governor elected for a four-year term; so far no governor has served more than two terms. Utah's bicameral legislature has a senate with 30 members elected for four-year terms and a house of representatives with 69 members elected for two years. The state sends 2 Senators and 2 Representatives to the U.S. Congress and has 4 electoral votes. From 1932 to 1950 Utah was predominantly Democratic and for the next 20 years it was largely Republican, but Calvin L. Rampton, a Democrat, was elected governor in 1968 and reelected in 1972. The state's leading institutions of higher learning include Brigham Young Univ., at Provo; the Univ. of Utah, at Salt Lake City; and Utah State Univ., at Logan. See H. M. Beardsley, *Joseph Smith and His Mormon Empire* (1931); R. J. Dwyer, *The Gentile Comes to Utah* (1941); Maurine Whipple, *This Is the Place: Utah* (1945); D. L. Morgan, *The Great Salt Lake* (1947); W. D. Stout, *History of Utah* (3 vol., 1967–71); F. J. Buttle, *Utah Grows* (1970); R. W. Taylor, *Uranium Fever* (1970); G. O. Larson, *The Americanization of Utah for Statehood* (1971); Jules Remy and Julius Brenchley, *A Journey to Great-Salt-Lake-City* (2 vol., 1861, repr. 1972); Federal Writers' Project, *Utah: A Guide to the State* (1941, repr. 1972).

Utah, University of, at Salt Lake City; coeducational; state supported; opened 1850, chartered 1851 as Univ. of Deseret, closed 1851–67. It was empowered to give degrees in 1884 and renamed in 1892. The university's diverse research programs include studies of the American West, biomedical engineering, industrial relations, and isotope geology. The state engineering experiment station is there.

Utah Indians: see UTE INDIANS.

Utah Lake, c.145 sq mi (380 sq km), N central Utah; largest freshwater lake in the state. It drains through the Jordan River to the Great Salt Lake. The waters of Utah Lake were formerly much used for irrigation and in the 1930s showed signs of exhaustion. The PROVO River project and the STRAWBERRY VALLEY PROJECT now irrigate the region.

Utah State University, mainly at Logan; coeducational; land-grant and state supported; chartered 1888, opened 1890. The university has branches at Ephraim and Cedar City.

Utah War, in U.S. history, conflict between Mormons and the U.S. government. In the spring of 1857, President James Buchanan appointed a non-Mormon, Alfred Cumming, as governor of the Utah Territory, replacing Brigham YOUNG, and dispatched troops to enforce the order. The Mormons prepared to defend themselves and their property; Young declared martial law and issued an order on Sept. 15, 1857, forbidding the entry of U.S. troops into Utah. The order was disregarded, and throughout the winter sporadic raids were conducted by the Mormon militia against the encamped U.S. army. Buchanan dispatched (April, 1858) representatives to work out a settlement, and on June 26, the army entered Salt Lake City, Cumming was installed as governor, and peace was restored. See L. R. and A. W. Hafen, ed., *The Utah Expedition, 1857-58* (1958); N. F. Furniss, *The Mormon Conflict, 1850-1859* (1960).

Utamaro, Kitagawa (kētä'gäwä o͞otä'märo), 1753–1806, Japanese color-print artist, best known for his portrayals of women. Although he enjoyed enormous success during his lifetime, not much is known about his life except that he was imprisoned for a short time when his prints were supposed to have offended the Tokugawa government. His were among the first Japanese prints to become familiar in the West, as they were especially popular with the Dutch exporters of Nagasaki. Following Kiyonaga, Utamaro depicted women in an idealized manner, accenting sensuous beauty. His book of *Insects* (1788) reveals a keen observation of nature. His draftsmanship and use of color (especially reds and black) show a striking originality that made him the first of the greater masters of the ukiyo-e school. The New York Public Library has a collection of 133 of his prints.

Ute Indians (yo͞ot, yo͞o'tē), North American Indians whose language belongs to the Shoshonean group of the Uto-Aztecan branch of the Aztec-Tanoan linguistic stock (see AMERICAN INDIAN LANGUAGES). In the early 19th cent. the Ute occupied W Colorado and E Utah. They were fierce, nomadic warriors, who, after the introduction of the horse, ranged into New Mexico and Arizona, menacing and sometimes destroying the villages of the Pueblo Indians. Once the Ute discovered that the Spanish were conducting slave raids against Indians, they entered the market, taking captured Indians to slave markets in New Mexico. Early in 1855 the Ute began to attack Mexican settlements in the San Luis valley of Colorado; they were put down by U.S. troops, and a treaty was extracted. Retaining their hatred for the Navaho and other traditional enemies, some of the Ute fought with Kit Carson during the American Civil War in campaigns against the Navaho. In 1868 they were placed on a large reservation in Colorado. A group of Ute killed (1879) the Indian agent Nathan Meeker and several employees of the agency, but serious repercussions were avoided, mainly through the peaceful efforts of Chief Ouray. By a treaty signed in 1880 the Ute were moved from rich mineral and agricultural lands to areas less desirable to white settlers. Today, although some Ute own land individually, most of them live on reservations in Colorado and Utah, where they number some 3,000; their income is derived largely from oil and gas leases, farming, and raising livestock. Ute culture was typical of the western part of the Plains culture area; they lived in tepees, which were frequently decorated with brilliantly colored paintings, or in brush or sod shelters. The bear dance and the sun dance were important features of their culture; the Ute also became adherents of PEYOTISM. See Wilson Rockwell, *The Utes: A Forgotten People* (1956); Lyman Tyler, *The Ute People* (1964); George Fay, *Land Cessions in Utah and Colorado, by the Ute Indians, 1861-1899* (1970).

uterus, in most female mammals, hollow muscular organ in which the fetus develops and from which it is delivered at the end of PREGNANCY. The human uterus is pear-shaped, about 3 in. (7.6 cm) long (it expands greatly during pregnancy); it normally lies in the pelvis, where it is supported by a ligament on either side extending to the pelvic wall. The body of the uterus tapers down to a necklike structure (cervix) that leads into the vagina. On either side of the uterus is an oviduct (called fallopian tube in humans) from 3 to 5 in. (7.6-12.7 cm) long, one end opening into the uterus and the other, wide-mouthed, ends in close proximity to an OVARY. These oviducts serve as passageways for the ova to reach the uterus. Fertilization is believed to occur in the oviduct; the fertilized ovum then continues into the uterus, where it becomes implanted in the lining of that organ. If fertilization does not occur, the ovum and the lining of the uterine wall pass out of the body through the vagina (see MENSTRUATION). Venous tissues then build up again in the uterus in anticipation of the next release of an ovum. See also REPRODUCTIVE SYSTEM.

Uthai (yo͞o'thāī, yo͞othā'ī). **1** See ATHAIAH. **2** Returned exile. Ezra 8.14.

Uther Pendragon: see ARTHURIAN LEGEND.

Uthman (o͞oth'män) or **Othman** (ōth'-), c.574-656, 3d caliph (644-56); son-in-law of Muhammad. He belonged to the great Umayyad family and was selected as caliph after the murder of Umar. Muslim conquests were continued and extended to Bactria and Cyprus. To strengthen his control over the distant provinces, he replaced the generals and governors appointed by Abu Bakr and Umar with members of his own family. He recognized only one revised version of the Koran, destroying all other versions. These highhanded methods aroused deep resentment, and subsequent revolts in Egypt and Mesopotamia were very serious. In 656 a mob of malcontents in Medina stormed Uthman's house and murdered him. Ali succeeded to the caliphate. Osman is the Turkish form of Othman.

Utica (yo͞o'tĭkə), ancient N African city, c.25 mi (40 km) NW of Carthage. According to tradition, it was founded by Phoenicians from Tyre c.1100 B.C. Second in importance to Carthage, Utica usually allied itself with that city, but in the Third Punic War it sided with Rome against Carthage. Upon the destruction of Carthage (146 B.C.), Utica was made the capital of the Roman province of Africa. In the 3d cent. A.D. the town became an episcopal see. It fell (A.D. 439) to the Vandals, was recaptured (534) by the Byzantines, and was finally destroyed (c.700) by the Arabs. Excavations at the site have yielded two Punic cemeteries and Roman ruins, including baths and a villa with mosaics.

Utica, city (1970 pop. 91,611), seat of Oneida co., central N.Y., on the Mohawk River and the Barge Canal, in a large dairy region; inc. 1862. It is a port of entry, and its manufactures include textiles, electronic and aviation equipment, tools, and firearms. Settled in 1773 on the site of old Fort Schuyler (1758), it was destroyed (1776) in an Indian and Tory attack and resettled after the Revolution. Its location on the Erie and other canals and on the railroads stimulated its industrial development. Utica has an extensive park system, with winter and summer sports facilities. It is the seat of Utica College (a branch of Syracuse Univ.), a junior college, and the oldest New York state mental hospital.

utilitarianism (yo͞o"tĭlĭtâr'ēənĭzəm, yo͞otĭ"-), in ethics, the theory that the rightness or wrongness of an action is determined by the goodness or badness of its consequences. Jeremy BENTHAM measured happiness by the intensity, duration, certainty, propinquity, fecundity, purity, and extent of pleasures. John Stuart MILL argued that pleasures differ also in virtue and that the highest good involves qualitative as well as quantitative pleasure. Herbert SPENCER developed an evolutionary utilitarian ethics in which the principles of ethical living are based on the evolutionary changes of organic development. He held that the doctrine identifying pleasure with happiness as the base of morality could be related to physiological and psychological health and to natural sociological development. G. E. Moore, in his *Principia Ethica* (1903), presented a version of utilitarianism in which he rejected the traditional equating of good with pleasure. See T. K. Hearn, ed., *Studies in Utilitarianism* (1971); J. J. C. Smart, *Utilitarianism: For and Against* (1973).

utility, in economics: see VALUE.

utility, public, industry required by law to render adequate service in its field at reasonable prices to all who apply for it. Such an industry is said to be "affected with a public interest" (a phrase coined by Chief Justice Waite in 1876) and therefore subject to a degree of government regulation from which other businesses are exempt. Opinions differ as to the characteristics that an industry must possess to merit classification as a public utility, since all industries in a sense serve the public. By its nature a public utility is often a monopoly and so not prevented by competition from charging exorbitant prices. It usually operates under a license or franchise by which it enjoys special privileges, such as the right of eminent domain. Finally, it may supply an essential service, such as water or light, the unavailability of which would injuriously affect public health and welfare. From an early period there was public regulation of canals, turnpikes, toll roads and ferries, inns, gristmills, and pawnshops. Docks, sleeping cars, commodity exchanges, warehouses, insurance companies, banks, housing, milk, coal mines, and (in the 20th cent.) broadcasting, are other types of goods and services held to be affected with public interest. Important utilities that satisfy the vital needs of large populations include: water, gas, and electric companies; transportation facilities, such as subways, bus lines, and railroads; and communication facilities, such as telephones and telegraphs. In nearly all European nations such industries are owned by the state. In the United States, however, most public utilities are privately owned. In the United States public-utility rates and standards of service are established by direct legislation and are administered by state regulatory commissions and by such Federal agencies as the Interstate Commerce Commission, the Federal Power Commission, the Securities and Exchange Commission, and the Federal Communications Commission. The Federal agencies supervise utilities conducting interstate business. Rates are subject to review by the courts, which have held that they must provide a "fair" return on a "fair" valuation of investment. How valuation is to be determined, whether on the basis of prudent investment, present earning power, or present cost of production, has been the subject of much controversy. That a utility may not earn excessive profits is an established principle of regulation. The means of regulation include supervision of accounting and control of security issues. Municipalities dissatisfied with the results of public regulation of privately owned local utilities have often acquired ownership of such enterprises, especially in the case of urban public transportation systems (see PUBLIC OWNERSHIP). To keep rates down and make utilities available to more people, the United States has formed public corporations or agencies, such as the Tennessee Valley Authority, which has served as a yardstick for measuring the efficiency of privately owned utilities, and the National Railroad Passenger Corporation (Amtrak), which operates virtually all intercity passenger rail lines in the United States. See Edward Hungerford, *The Story of Public Utilities* (1928); J. C. Bonbright, *Principles of Public Utility Rates* (1961); W. G. Shepherd, ed., *Utility Regulation* (1966).

Uto-Aztecan (yo͞o'tō-ăztĕk'ən), branch of the Aztec-Tanoan linguistic stock. The languages belonging to this stock are spoken in North and Central America. See AMERICAN INDIAN LANGUAGES.

Utopia (yo͞otō'pēə) [Gr.,=no place], title of a book by Sir Thomas MORE, published in Latin in 1516. The work pictures an ideal state where all is ordered for the best for mankind as a whole and where the evils of society, such as poverty and misery, have been eliminated. The popularity of the book has given the generic name *Utopia* to all concepts of ideal states. The description of a utopia enables an author not only to set down criticisms of evils in the contemporary social scene but also to outline vast and revolutionary reforms without the necessity of describing how they will be effected. Thus, the influence of utopian writings has generally been inspirational rather than practical. The name utopia is applied retroactively to various ideal states described before More's work, most notably to that of the *Republic* of Plato. St. Augustine's *City of God* in the 5th cent. enunciated the theocratic ideal that dominated visionary thinking in the Middle Ages. With the Renaissance the ideal of a utopia became more worldly, but the religious element in utopian thinking is often present thereafter, such as in the politico-religious ideals of 17th-century English social philosophers and political experimenters. Among the famous pre-19th-century utopian writings are François Rabelais's description of the Abbey of Thélème in *Gargantua* (1532), *The City of the Sun* (1623) by Tommaso CAMPANELLA, *The New Atlantis* (1627) of Francis BACON, and the *Oceana* (1656) of James HARRINGTON. In the 18th-century Enlightenment, Jean Jacques Rousseau and others gave impetus to the belief that an ideal society—a Golden Age—had existed in the primitive days of European society before the development of civilization corrupted it. This faith in natural order and the innate goodness of man had a strong influence on the growth of visionary or utopian socialism. The end in view of these thinkers was usually an idealistic communism based on economic self-sufficiency or on the interaction of ideal communities. SAINT-SIMON, Étienne CABET, Charles FOURIER, and Pierre Joseph PROUDHON in France and Robert OWEN in England are typical examples of this sort of thinker. Actual experiments in utopian social living were tried in Europe and the United States, but for the most part the efforts were neither long-lived nor more than partially successful. The humanitarian socialists were largely displaced after the middle of the 19th cent. by political and economic theorists, such as Karl Marx and Friedrich Engels, who preached the achievement of the ideal state through political and revolutionary action. The utopian romance, however, became an extremely popular literary form. These novels depicted the glowing, and sometimes frightening, prospects of the new industrialism and social change. One of the most important of these works was *Looking Backward* (1888), by Edward BELLAMY, who had a profound influence on economic idealism in America. In England, *Erewhon* (1872), by Samuel BUTLER, *News from Nowhere* (1891), by William MORRIS, and *A Modern Utopia* (1905), by H. G. WELLS, were notable examples of the genre; in Austria an example was Theodor Hertzka's *Freiland* (1890). The 20th cent. saw a veritable flood of these literary utopias, most of them "scientific utopias" in which mankind enjoys a blissful leisure while all or most of the work is done for him by docile machines. The adjective *utopian* has come into some disrepute and is frequently used contemptuously to mean impractical or impossibly visionary. The device of describing a utopia in satire or for the exercise of wit is almost as old as the serious utopia. The satiric device goes back to such comic utopias as that of Aristophanes in *The Birds.* Bernard MANDEVILLE in *The Fable of the Bees* (1714) and Jonathan SWIFT in parts of *Gulliver's Travels* (1726) are in the same tradition. Pseudo-utopian satire has been extensive in modern times in such novels as Aldous Huxley's *Brave New World* (1932). The rise of the modern totalitarian state has brought forth several works, notably *Nineteen Eighty-four* (1949), by George Orwell, which describe the unhappy fate of the individual under the control of a supposedly benevolent despotism. Connected with the literary fable of a utopia has been the belief in an actual ideal state in some remote and undiscovered corner of the world. The mythical ATLANTIS, described by Plato, was long sought by Greek and later mariners. Similar to this search were the vain expeditions in search of the Isles of the Blest, or FORTUNATE ISLES, and EL DORADO. See V. L. Parrington, *American Dreams* (2d ed. 1964); Lewis Mumford, *The Story of the Utopias* (rev. ed. 1966); Mark Holloway, *Heavens on Earth* (2d ed. 1966); Glenn Negley and J. M. Patrick, *The Quest for Utopia* (1952, repr. 1971).

UTP (uridine triphosphate): see URACIL.

Utraquists: see HUSSITES.

Utrecht (yōō'trĕkt, Du. ü'trĕkht), province (1971 pop. 816,400), c.500 sq mi (1,290 sq km), central Netherlands, bounded by the IJsselmeer in the north. Utrecht, which is the capital, and Amersfoort are the chief cities. It is made up largely of low-lying land and is drained by the Lower Rhine (Neder Rijn) River. Its economy is mixed, with prosperous farms and diverse industries.

Utrecht, city (1971 pop. 278,417), capital of Utrecht prov., central Netherlands, on a branch of the Lower Rhine (Neder Rijn) River. It is a transportation, financial, and industrial center. Manufactures include machinery, cement, processed minerals, food products, and chemicals. It is the site of a major trade fair. Utrecht was founded by the Romans as *Trajectum ad Rhenum* [Lat.,=ford of the Rhine]. In the late 7th cent. it was made an episcopal see for St. Willibrord, the Apostle to the Frisians. The bishops of Utrecht, as princes of the Holy Roman Empire, later ruled the area around the city and the lordship (now province) of Overijssel. There was a recurring power struggle between the bishops and the city's merchants. Utrecht received a liberal charter in 1122, but its difficulties with the bishops continued sporadically until 1527, when the bishop was forced to transfer his territorial rights to Emperor Charles V. One of the most important commercial centers of the Netherlands in the Middle Ages, Utrecht was incorporated with the rest of the Hapsburg-held Netherlands by Charles V. Utrecht joined (1577) in the rebellion against Philip II of Spain, and on Jan. 23, 1579, the seven provinces of the N NETHERLANDS, from then on known as the United Provinces, the nucleus of the Dutch republic, drew together for their common defense in the Union of Utrecht. In the 17th cent. Utrecht became a center of Jansenism (see under JANSEN, CORNELIS). In 1713 several treaties forming part of the Peace of Utrecht were signed there. Today Utrecht is a picturesque city, crossed by numerous sunken canals. It is the site of a 14th-century cathedral and a famous university (founded 1636). It is the see of the Roman Catholic primate of the Netherlands.

Utrecht, Peace of, series of treaties that concluded the War of the SPANISH SUCCESSION. It put an end to French expansion and signaled the rise of the British Empire. By the treaty between England and France (April 11, 1713), Louis XIV recognized the English succession as established in the house of Hanover and confirmed the renunciation of the claims to the French throne of Louis's grandson, Philip V of Spain. The French fortifications of Dunkirk were to be razed and the harbor filled up, and the Hudson Bay territory, Acadia, St. Kitts, and Newfoundland were ceded to England. By a commercial treaty England and France granted each other most-favored-nation treatment. By a treaty with the Netherlands (April 11, 1713) France agreed to surrender to Austria the Spanish Netherlands still in French hands; these were to be held in trust by the Netherlands until the conclusion of a treaty between the Netherlands and the Holy Roman emperor. A commercial treaty between France and the Netherlands was also signed. France furthermore restored Savoy and Nice to VICTOR AMADEUS II, recognizing him as king of Savoy. France also signed a treaty with Portugal and one with Prussia confirming the kingship of the Prussian rulers. The Anglo-Spanish treaty (July 13, 1713) confirmed the clauses of the Anglo-French treaties relating to the English and French successions. Spain ceded Gibraltar and Minorca to Great Britain and ceded Sicily (exchanged in 1720 for SARDINIA) to Savoy. Britain and Spain signed the Asiento, an agreement giving Britain the sole right to the slave trade with Spanish America. The Treaty of Rastatt (March 7, 1714) between Louis XIV and Holy Roman Emperor Charles VI and the Treaty of Baden (Sept. 7, 1714), which completed the settlement, restored the right bank of the Rhine to the empire and confirmed Austria in possession of the formerly Spanish Netherlands, of Naples, and of Milan. The Third Barrier Treaty (Nov. 15, 1715) regulated trade relations between the Dutch and Austrian Netherlands. See J. W. Gerard, *The Peace of Utrecht* (1885).

Utrera (ōōträ'rä), city (1970 pop. 35,775), Seville prov., S Spain, in Andalusia, on a branch of the Guadalquivir River. It is a rail junction and processing center of a fertile agricultural region. Horses are bred, and bulls are raised for the ring. There are a Gothic church and ruins of a medieval castle and walls.

Utrillo, Maurice (ōōtrē'lō, Fr. mōrēs' ütrēlō'), 1883–1955, French painter. He was the son of the painter Suzanne VALADON and was adopted by the writer Miguel Utrillo. His mother taught him to paint in order to divert him from the alcoholism that ravaged him from a very early age. Utrillo's favorite themes were the street scenes of Paris, particularly of Montmartre, and Montmagny. Within an almost hallucinatory vision, he developed a personal style based on a modified CUBISM and a fine sense of atmosphere and composition. In his later years he lost much of his original power. An extremely prolific painter, Utrillo is well represented in American and European collections. See biographies by W. George (1960) and P. de Polnay (rev. ed. 1969).

Utsunomiya (ōōtsōōnō'mēä), city (1970 pop. 301,239), capital of Tochigi prefecture, central Honshu, Japan. It is a tobacco-processing center and a tourist resort. Landmarks include the Peace Cannon statue and the 9th-century Oyaji temple.

Uttar Pradesh (ōō'tär prä'dĭsh), state (1971 pop. 88,364,779), 113,454 sq mi (293,846 sq km), N central India, bordered on the N by Nepal and Tibet. The capital is LUCKNOW. Other important cities are ALLAHABAD, BAREILLY, KANPUR, and VARANASI. The most populous state of India, it was formed in 1950 by merging the United Provinces and the former princely states of Benares, Rampur, and Tehri. Hindi is the main language. The northern area falls within the Himalaya zone, with many peaks higher than 20,000 ft (6,096 m), and there is a hilly region along the southern border; most of the state, however, is a low-lying fertile plain formed by the Jumna, Ganges, and Gogra rivers. The moderate rainfall is supplemented by an extensive system of river irrigation. The mild climate generally permits two harvests a year; wheat, rice, millet, sugarcane, tobacco, cotton, and jute are grown. The economy is predominantly agricultural, and industry is centered on processing sugar and cotton; the once-important manufacture of brooches and artwares, such as ornamental brasses, has declined. Building stone and high-grade sand for the glass industry are abundant. Adequate railroads and roads ensure efficient distribution. Five universities are supported by this prosperous state. The state is governed by a chief minister and cabinet responsible to a bicameral legislature with one elected house and by a governor appointed by the president of India.

Uusikaupunki (ōō'sēkou"pōōngkē), Swed. *Nystad,* city (1970 pop. 7,452), Turku ja Pori prov., SW Finland, on the Gulf of Bothnia. A local trade center and port, it has sawmills, machine shops, granite quarries, and a shipyard. It was chartered in 1616 and was the scene (1721) of the signing of the Treaty of Nystad (see NORTHERN WAR).

Uvalde (yōōvăl'dē), city (1970 pop. 10,764), seat of Uvalde co., SW Texas; founded c.1854, inc. as a city 1921. A large plaza and many pecan and oak trees lend grace to the town, which draws wealth from surrounding ranches and an irrigated farm area. It has cattle-feed lots, meat-packing houses, grain-storage facilities, and great asphalt mines. Tourism is increasing in importance; there is excellent hunting and fishing in the area, which has brushy hills and deep canyons, with underground caverns and springs. Uvalde was the seat of John Nance Garner's political power. A junior college and a research and extension center of Texas A & M Univ. are there. Garner state park is nearby.

Uvedale, John: see UDALL, JOHN.

uvula: see PALATE.

Uxbridge, England: see HILLINGDON.

Uxmal (ōōshmal', ōōz-), ancient city, northern Yucatán peninsula, Mexico. A Late Classic period MAYA center situated in the Puuc hills, Uxmal flourished between 600 and 900. It is one of the finest expressions of Maya architecture known as the Puuc style. The site has such impressive structures as the unique Pyramid of the Magician; the Nunnery, with elaborately decorated facades of stone mosaic friezes; and the Governor's Palace (320 ft/98 m long, 40 ft/12.2 m wide, and 26 ft/8.9 m high), with some 20,000 carved stone elements in its facade. The site was abandoned shortly after 950 but was reoccupied briefly in the 15th cent. by the Xiu, a Mexican group who soon abandoned the site after wresting power from the Cocom Itzá at Mayapán. See studies in the *Handbook of Middle American Indians,* ed. by Robert Wauchope (13 vol., 1964–73); M. P. Weaver, *The Aztecs, Maya, and Their Predecessors* (1972).

Uz (ŭz). **1** Grandson of Shem. Gen. 10.23; 1 Chron. 1.17. **2** Grandson of Seir. Gen. 36.28; 1 Chron. 1.42. **3** Land of Job, variously placed in Aram, Edom, or N Arabia. Job 1.1; Jer. 25.20; Lam. 4.21.

Uzai (yōō'zāī), father of PALAL.

Uzal (yōō'zăl), descendant of Shem whose clan settled in S Arabia. Gen. 10.27; 1 Chron. 1.21. Also called Javan. Ezek. 27.19.

Uzbek Soviet Socialist Republic (ōōz' bĕk, ōōzbĕk', Rus. ōōzbyĕk') or **Uzbekistan** (ōōz"bĕkĭstăn', -stän', Rus. ōōzbyĕkĭstän'), constituent republic (1970 pop. 11,963,000), 173,552 sq mi (449,500 sq km), Central Asian USSR. TASHKENT (the capital) and SAMARKAND are the chief cities. The republic borders on Afghanistan in the south, on the Turkmen SSR in the southwest, on the Kazakh SSR in the west and north, and on the Kirghiz SSR and the Tadzhik SSR in the east. The Kara-Kalpak Autonomous SSR is included in Uzbekistan. The terrain of the republic encompasses two unequal sections: the larger northwest area, which is part of the Kyzyl-Kum desert; and the smaller southeast area, which has fertile loess soil and touches on the Tien Shan mountain system. The Aral Sea lies on the northwest frontier. Central Asia's two major rivers—the Amu Darya and Syr Darya—pass through Uzbek territory. The Khiva oasis is irrigated by the Amu Darya, the fertile Fergana Valley by the Syr Darya and its tributaries, the Tashkent oasis by the Chirchik and Angren rivers, and the Samarkand and Bukhara oases by the Zeravshan. Uzbekistan has a dry continental climate. The rivers and many irrigation canals furnish water for the cotton crop, which supplies the USSR with about 65% of its cotton. Half of the country's rice also comes from Uzbekistan (notably from the Zeravshan valley). Other crops include cereals, alfalfa, fruits, wine grapes, kenaf, sesame, tobacco, and sugarcane. The republic ranks first in the USSR as a region of irrigated agriculture. Livestock are raised in the more arid western areas; Uzbekistan is a leading Soviet producer of Karakul sheep pelts. Cotton, silk, and wool provide the basis for Uzbekistan's extensive textile industry. Industrialization has proceeded apace, particularly since the transfer during World War II of many industries from European Russia to the less vulnerable Uzbek region. Machine building, metallurgy, food processing, hydroelectric power production, and the manufacture of iron and steel, machine tools, chemicals, fertilizer, building materials, and clothing are leading industries. Uzbekistan is rich in mineral resources. The Fergana Valley, an important cotton, silk, and wine region, is also the site of oil fields. Western Uzbekistan has large natural gas deposits. Coal, zinc, copper, tungsten, molybdenum, lead, fluorspar, wolfram, ozokerite, sulfur, limestone, marl, and clays are also found. Uzbekistan has more than 20 hydroelectric power plants. The Trans-Caspian RR and its two branch lines are the republic's main transportation routes. More than 60% of the people of Soviet Central Asia live in Uzbekistan. The Uzbek, a Turkic-speaking group of Persian culture and Sunnite Muslim religion, make up nearly two thirds of the population. Russians (who live mostly in the cities) constitute around 14%, and there are Tatar, Kazakh, and Tadzhik minorities. About 35% of the population is urban. Uzbekistan was the site of one of the world's oldest civilized regions. The ancient Persian province of SOGDIANA, it was conquered in the 4th cent. B.C. by Alexander the Great. Turkic nomads entered the area in the 6th cent. A.D. It passed in the 8th cent. to the Arabs, who introduced Islam, and in the 12th cent. to the Seljuk Turks of KHOREZM. JENGHIZ KHAN captured the region in the 13th cent., and in the 14th cent. TAMERLANE made his native Samarkand the center of his huge empire. The realm was much reduced under his successors, the TIMURIDS, and began to disintegrate by the end of the 15th cent. Throughout these turbulent times, the cities of Samarkand, Bukhara, and Tashkent, situated on major trade routes to China, India, Persia, and Europe, were centers of prosperity, culture, and fabulous luxury. In the early 16th cent., the Uzbek, formerly called Sarts, invaded the region from the northwest. A remnant of the empire of the GOLDEN HORDE, they took their name from Uzbeg Khan (d. 1340), from whom their dynasty claimed descent. Later in the 16th cent., the Uzbek leader Abdullah extended his domain over parts of Persia, Afghanistan, and Chinese Turkistan; but the empire soon broke up into separate principalities, notably Khiva, Kokand, and Bukhara. Weakened by internecine warfare, these states were conquered by Russian forces, who took Tashkent in 1865, Samarkand and Bukhara in 1868, and Khiva in 1873. Kokand was annexed outright to the Russian empire, but Khiva and Bukhara remained under their native rulers as vassal states of Russia. Efforts by Uzbek leaders to establish a European-style democratic republic in the aftermath of the Russian Revolution of 1917 were unsuccessful. In 1918 the Turkistan Autonomous SSR was organized on Uzbek territory, in 1920 the Khorezm and Bukharan People's Republics were established, and finally, in 1924, the Uzbek-populated areas were united in the Uzbek SSR. Tadzhikistan was part of the Uzbek SSR until 1929, when it became a separate republic. In 1936 the Kara-Kalpak Autonomous SSR was joined with Uzbekistan.

Uzhgorod (o͞ozh'gərət), Czech *Užhorod*, Ukr. *Uzhhorod*, Hung. *Ungvár*, city (1970 pop. 65,000), capital of ZAKARPATSKAYA OBLAST, SW European USSR, in the Ukraine, in the SW Carpathian foothills and on the Uzh River. It is a rail and highway junction and the economic and cultural heart of Transcarpathian Ukraine. There is trade in lumber and cattle. Industries include metalworking, automobile repairing, meat packing, winemaking, brandy distilling, and the manufacture of plywood, furniture, bricks, tiles, clothing, and footwear. Tourism is also economically significant. The city has long been important militarily because of its position guarding the southern approach to the Uzhok Pass over the Carpathians. One of the earliest Slavic settlements, Uzhgorod was founded in the 8th or 9th cent. and belonged to Kievan Russia in the 10th and 11th cent. Conquered by the Magyars at the end of the 11th cent., the city remained under Hungarian rule until it passed to Austria-Hungary in 1867. Uzhgorod became a bishopric of the Ukrainian Catholic Uniate Church in 1775 and was the center of the Ukrainian national and Russophile movements in the 19th and early 20th cent. The city passed to Czechoslovakia in 1919, was under Hungarian occupation from 1938 to 1944, and was included in the Ukraine after World War II. Uzhgorod has a university, a 15th-century castle, and an 18th-century cathedral.

Uznam, island, East Germany and Poland: see USEDOM.

Uzza or **Uzzah** (ŭz'ə). **1** Israelite who met sudden death after touching the Ark of the Covenant. 2 Sam. 6.3–8; 1 Chron. 13.7–11. **2** Benjamite. 1 Chron. 8.7. **3** Descendant of Merari. 1 Chron. 6.29. **4** One who returned with Zerubbabel. Ezra 2.49.

Uzzen-sherah (ŭz'ən-shē'rə), unidentified village built by SHERAH. 1 Chron. 7.24.

Uzzi (ŭz'ī). **1** High priest. 1 Chron. 6.5,6,51; Ezra 7.4. **2** Son of Tola. 1 Chron. 7.2,3. **3** Levitical overseer in Jerusalem. Neh. 11.22. **4,5** Benjamites. 1 Chron. 7.7; 9.8. **6** Priest. Neh. 12.19,42.

Uzzia (ŭzī'ə), hero of David. 1 Chron. 11.44.

Uzziah (ŭzī'ə). **1** King of Judah, son and successor of Amaziah. He rebuilt Elath, port on the Gulf of Aqaba. He was stricken with leprosy after usurping the duties of high priest. He was succeeded by Jotham. 2 Chron. 26. He is called Azariah in 2 Kings 15. Ozias: Mat. 1.8,9. **2** Levite: see AZARIAH **5.** **3** Father of one of David's officers. 1 Chron. 27.25. **4** Man with a foreign wife. Ezra 10.21. **5** Judahite. Neh. 11.4.

Uzziel (ŭz'ēĕl, ŭzī'əl). **1** Kohathite Levite mentioned often. Ex. 6.18. **2** Captain of David. 1 Chron. 4.42. **3** See AZAREEL **2.** **4** Head of a Benjamite family. 1 Chron. 7.7. **5** Levite. 2 Chron. 29.14. **6** Goldsmith. Neh. 3.8.

V

V, 22d letter of the ALPHABET (see U). It is a usual symbol for a voiced labiodental spirant, as in the English *vat.* In Roman numerals it corresponds to Arabic 5. In chemistry V is the symbol of the element VANADIUM.

Vaal (fäl), river, c.750 mi (1,210 km) long, rising in SE Transvaal, NE Republic of South Africa, S Africa, and flowing SW to the Orange River. It forms most of the Transvaal-Orange Free State border. The river's flow is almost totally regulated and provides water power for industries on the Witwatersrand. Vaal Dam, one of the country's largest, is located SE of Vereeniging; it stores water for use by the mines. The Vaalhartz Dam, near the junction of the Vaal and the Hartz rivers, is an important part of the Vaal River Development Project.

Vaasa (vä'sä), Swed. *Vasa,* city (1970 pop. 49,084), capital of Vaasa prov., W Finland, on the Gulf of Bothnia. It is a port and agricultural market. Many products are made, including iron and steel. Chartered in 1606, Vaasa was rebuilt closer to the sea after a devastating fire in 1852. From 1855 to 1917 it was called Nikolainkaupunki or Nikolaistad (after Czar Nicholas I). It was the capital of White Finland during the civil war of 1918. Both Swedish and Finnish are spoken in the city.

Vác (väts), Ger. *Waitzen* (vī'tsůn), town (1970 pop. 27,946), N central Hungary, on the Danube River. A commercial center producing textiles, cement, and photographic articles, it is also a favorite summer resort of Budapest residents. Dating from Roman times, Vác was made (1008) a bishopric by St. Stephen. It has an 18th-century cathedral, an episcopal palace, and an 18th-century triumphal arch. The name was formerly spelled Vacz or Vacs.

Vaca, Cabeza de: see CABEZA DE VACA, ÁLVAR NÚÑEZ.

Vaca de Castro, Cristóbal (krēstō'bäl vä'kä thā kä'strō), fl. 1540–45, Spanish colonial administrator in Peru. A judge of the royal audiencia at Valladolid, he was chosen by Charles V to restore order between the Pizarro and the Almagro factions. He was a man of integrity, sagacity, and courage. Arriving in 1541 and learning of the assassination of Francisco PIZARRO, he assumed the governorship. Supported by Francisco de CARVAJAL, he put down the uprising headed by Almagro the younger (son of Diego de ALMAGRO), who was defeated in 1542. Vaca de Castro was succeeded by the first viceroy of Peru, NÚÑEZ VELA, in 1544. The viceroy, suspecting Vaca de Castro of sympathizing with the rebellion of Gonzalo Pizarro, had him arrested. Returned to Spain in disgrace, Vaca de Castro was imprisoned for 12 years before he was cleared of all charges and restored to his honors. He probably died at some time after 1571.

Vacaville (văk'əvĭl, vä'-), city (1970 pop. 21,690), Solano co., central Calif., in a farm area; inc. 1892. Food products are made. A state prison medical facility is there, and Travis Air Force Base and Hospital are to the south.

vaccination, means of producing active IMMUNITY against disease by the introduction of live, attenuated (weakened), or killed microorganisms. Vaccination was first introduced to the Western world in 1796 by the English physician Edward Jenner, although it was practiced in other parts of the world previously. Jenner demonstrated that rubbing or scraping the cowpox virus into the skin produced only a local lesion, but was sufficient to stimulate the production of antibodies that would defend the body against the more virulent smallpox. Immunization against smallpox lasts for five to seven years or more. Vaccines are also used for immunization against other infections including diphtheria, typhoid, hydrophobia, and poliomyelitis.

Vaclav, Saint: see WENCESLAUS, SAINT.

vacuum, theoretically, space without matter in it. A perfect vacuum has never been obtained; the best man-made vacuums contain less than 100,000 gas MOLECULES per cc, compared to about 30 billion billion (30×10^{18}) molecules for air at sea level. The most nearly perfect vacuum exists in intergalactic space, where it is estimated that on the average there is less than one molecule per cc. In ancient times the belief that "nature abhors a vacuum" was held widely and persisted without serious question until the late 16th and early 17th cent., when the experimental observations of Galileo and the Italian physicist Evangelista Torricelli demonstrated its essential fallacy. Torricelli obtained a nearly perfect vacuum (Torricellian vacuum) in his mercury BAROMETER. A common but incorrect belief is that a vacuum causes "suction." Actually the apparent suction caused by a vacuum is the pressure of the atmosphere tending to rush in and fill the unoccupied space. There are various methods for producing a vacuum, and several different kinds of **vacuum pumps** have been devised for removing the molecules of gas or vapor from a confined space. In the rotary oil-sealed pump a rotor turning in a cylinder allows gas to enter through an inlet valve from a space to be evacuated and then pushes it through an outlet valve into the atmosphere. In the oil or mercury diffusion pump, gas enters the pump through an inlet and is then swept toward an outlet by heavy, fast-moving oil or mercury vapor molecules. The outlet is connected to a rotary pump that expels the gas into the atmosphere. A cryogenic pump removes gas from a container by condensing the gas molecules on an extremely cold surface in the container. An ion pump consists of a chamber containing a source of electrons that are used to bombard gas molecules from a container to be evacuated. Collisions between the electrons and gas molecules ionize the molecules, causing them to be drawn to, and held by, a collector in the pump. The first vacuum pump was invented by the German physicist Otto von Guerricke in 1650. There are many practical applications of vacuums in industry and scientific research, e.g., in vacuum distillation, vacuum processing of food, in devices such as the vacuum tube, vacuum bottle, and barometer, and in research machines.

vacuum cleaner, mechanical device using a draft of air to remove dust, loose dirt, or other particulate matter from dry surfaces. It is especially useful on highly textured surfaces, such as carpets and upholstery, that are difficult to clean by wiping or brushing. Usually, an electrically powered fan is used to produce a zone in which the air pressure is below atmospheric pressure, causing a draft of air to flow through the material to be cleaned, carrying the small particles with it. The draft passes through a filter bag which traps the particles, and the flow of air is then discharged back into the atmosphere. In some machines the electric motor and wiring are sealed so that wet surfaces can be cleaned safely.

vacuum tube: see ELECTRON TUBE.

Vacz: see VÁC, Hungary.

Vadsø (väd'sö), town (1970 pop. 5,570), capital of Finnmark co., NE Norway, an ice-free arctic port on the Varangerfjord. It is a whaling and fishing base and a trade center for reindeer meat and skins, dried fish, herring oil, and guano. In World War II the town was severely damaged (1944) by the Germans.

Vadstena (väd'stā"nä), town (1970 pop. 4,926), Östergötland co., S Sweden, on Lake Vättern. The town is a tourist center and a port on the Göta Canal; it has a noted lace-making industry. First mentioned in the early 14th cent., Vadstena is the site of the most important medieval cloisters in Sweden, the Convent of St. Birgitta (Bridget), founded c.1370. The town has many historic buildings, including the original convent and Vadstena castle, built by Gustavus I in 1545.

Vaduz (vädo͞ots'), town (1970 pop. 3,921), capital of Liechtenstein, W Liechtenstein, on the Rhine River. It is a tourist center. A beautiful medieval castle (now an art museum) dominates the town. Vaduz was destroyed (1499) in the war between the Swiss and the Holy Roman Empire and was rebuilt in the early 16th cent.

Vaga, Perino del: see PERINO DEL VAGA.

Vagarshapat: see ECHMIADZIN, USSR.

vagrancy, in law, term applied to the offense of persons who are without visible means of support or DOMICILE while able to work. State laws and municipal ordinances punishing vagrancy often also cover loitering, associating with reputed criminals, prostitution, and drunkenness. The punishment is usually a fine or several months in jail. Instead of arresting vagrants, local officials often attempt to induce them to move on. Beginning in the 1960s vagrancy laws came under constitutional attack. The vague statutory language was often held to be too broad, in violation of the due process requirements of the Fourteenth Amendment to the U.S. Constitution: individuals were not adequately warned of what conduct was forbidden and police had too much discretion in deciding whether to make an arrest. It was ruled that enforcement of the laws often violated the protections of the First Amendment, especially when police used them against political demonstrators and unpopular groups. U.S. vagrancy laws generally punish the status of being a vagrant and not some overt act. This approach derives from English laws of the 16th cent. that generally failed to distinguish between the indigent and the criminal and that set harsh punishments, including whipping and transportation to the colonies. England gradually modified its POOR LAWS and today punishes only overt acts dangerous to the community. Vagrants are often tolerated as scavengers, and in certain Oriental countries they are ascribed semireligious qualities, revered, but also feared, for their spiritual powers. Vagrants are basically a product of unemployment and their numbers swell during depressions. See C. J. Ribton-Turner, *The History of Vagrants and Vagrancy* (1887, repr. 1972).

Váh (väkh), Hung. *Vág,* river, c.245 mi (390 km) long, E Czechoslovakia. It is formed by the union of the Biély Váh, rising in the High Tatra, and the Cierny Váh, rising in the Low Tatra, and flows SW into the Danube at Komárno. The Orava and Nitra rivers are its chief tributaries.

Vaida-Voevod, Alexander (vä'ēdä voivōd'), 1871–1950, Rumanian statesman, b. Transylvania. He was (1906–18) a member of the Hungarian parliament, in which he advocated the cause of the Rumanians in Transylvania. In 1918, on the collapse of the Austro-Hungarian Monarchy, he led in proclaiming the union of Transylvania with Rumania, and in 1919 he was made premier and foreign minister of Rumania. He secured recognition of the incorporation of Transylvania and Bessarabia into Rumania, although Russia refused to concede the loss of Bessarabia, and he had Rumanian troops intervene in Hungary to oust the Communist regime of Bela Kun. He resigned in 1920, but was later premier in 1932 and 1933 at the head of the National Peasants' party. Withdrawing from that party, he associated with the reactionary, pro-German, and anti-Semitic elements in Rumanian politics and set up in 1935 the right-wing Rumanian Front.

Vaigach: see VAYGACH, island, USSR.

Vaihinger, Hans (häns fī'hĭng-ər), 1852–1933, German philosopher. Educated at Tübingen, Leipzig, and Berlin, he served at Strasbourg first as tutor and then as professor of philosophy. One of the great Kant scholars, in 1884 he went to Halle, where he became full professor in 1892. His studies of Kant culminated in *Kant—ein Metaphysiker?* (1899). His own system was set forth in 1911 and was translated into English as *The Philosophy of "As If"* (1924). He argued that since reality cannot be truly known, human beings construct systems of thought to satisfy their needs and then assume that actuality agrees with their constructions; i.e., people act "as if" the real were what they assume it to be. See H. F. Wolf, *Philosophy for the Common Man* (1951).

Vaillant, George Clapp (văl'yănt), 1901–45, American archaeologist, b. Boston; grad. Harvard (B.A., 1922; Ph.D., 1927). At the American Museum of Natural History he became associate curator (1930) and honorary curator (1941) of Mexican archaeology, and later he served (1941–45) as director of the Univ. of Pennsylvania museum. He carried out archaeological expeditions in the Southwest (1921–22, 1922–25), in Egypt (1923–24), and in Central

America (1926, 1928–36). During World War II he organized archaeological programs throughout Latin America. Vaillant was known for his reconstruction of the early stages of Mexican culture and for his synthesis of Aztec history, presented in popular form in *The Aztecs in Mexico* (1944). His other writings include numerous monographs on Middle American excavations and *Indian Arts in North America* (1939).

Vaiont Dam, 858 ft (262 m) high, on the Vaiont River, a tributary of the Piave River, in Venetia, NE Italy, near Belluno. Vaiont Dam, one of the highest in the world, was completed in 1961 and is used to generate electricity. After heavy rains in 1963, landslides into the Vaiont reservoir caused the stored water to spill over the dam, sweeping away the village of Longarone and flooding nearby hamlets; some 2,000 people drowned.

Vaisheshika (vī"shəshē'kə): see INDIAN PHILOSOPHY.

Vajezatha (vəjĕz'əthə), one of Haman's sons. Esther 9.9.

Vajrayana Buddhism: see TIBETAN BUDDHISM.

Vakhtangov, Yevgeni (yĭvgā'nyē väkhtän'gôf), 1883–1922, Russian actor, producer, and founder of the Moscow theater that bears his name. A pupil and friend of Stanislavsky, Vakhtangov joined the Moscow Art Theatre, and in 1914, in charge of an affiliated studio, he produced an enormously successful *Macbeth.* In 1920 his studio became independent, and he began to mount his own productions. Vakhtangov is celebrated for using grotesque realism and fantasy to great effect, as in *Turandot,* which was presented after his death. See biography by Ruben Simonov (tr. 1969).

Valaam, island, USSR: see LADOGA, LAKE.

Valadon, Suzanne (süzän' välädôN'), 1867–1938, French painter. After abandoning successful careers as an acrobat and as artist's model to many of the major impressionists, Valadon, encouraged by Toulouse-Lautrec and Degas, became a painter. Her fresh, intensely personal works, including landscapes, nudes, and portraits, are executed in vibrant colors with heavy black outlines. Valadon was the mother of the painter Maurice UTRILLO.

Valais (välā'), Ger. *Wallis,* canton (1970 pop. 206,563), 2,021 sq mi (5,234 sq km), S Switzerland. SION is the capital. Bordering on France and Italy, the Valais extends from the Bernese Alps in the north to the Pennine Alps in the south, with the fertile upper Rhône valley between them. It has some of the highest peaks (Matterhorn, Dufourspitze, Dom, and Weisshorn) in Switzerland. Mainly a livestock-raising and agricultural canton, it is also known for its fine wines. The Valais has a well-developed hydroelectric system, and its industries produce metal products and chemicals. Zermatt is the largest of its numerous resorts and winter sports centers. Most of the population is French-speaking and Roman Catholic. Taken by the Romans in 57 B.C., the region later passed to the Burgundians and to the Franks. In 999, Rudolf III of Burgundy made the bishop of Sion lord of Valais, but the country later split, with the Lower Valais passing to Savoy. In 1475, the bishop of Sion and the communes of the Upper Valais, which had gained considerable autonomy, defeated the duke of Savoy, and from then until 1798 the Lower Valais was held in subjection by the Upper Valais. Made a canton of the HELVETIC REPUBLIC in 1798, an independent republic in 1802, and a French department in 1810, the Valais became a canton of the Swiss Confederation in 1815.

Valama or **Valamo**, island, USSR: see LADOGA, LAKE.

Valday Hills or **Valdai Hills** (both: väldī', Rus. vəldī'), upland region, NW European USSR, composed of a series of glacial moraines that rise to c.1,100 ft (340 m). The region forms the watershed of the upper Volga, the Western Dvina, and the Dnepr rivers and also of the rivers that flow into Lake Ilmen. Numerous glacial lakes are found there; Lake Seliger is the largest.

Valdemar. For Danish rulers thus named, see WALDEMAR.

Val-de-Marne (väl-də-märn), department (1968 pop. 1,100,000), N central France, adjoining Paris on the southeast. CRÉTEIL is the capital.

Valdés, Armando Palacio: see PALACIO VALDÉS.

Valdés, Juan de (hwän thā väldās'), c.1500–1540, Spanish reformer, b. Cuenca. Suspected by the Inquisition, he went soon after 1530 to Naples, where he became the center of a circle of men interested in religious reform. Valdés had already published an attack on many ecclesiastical abuses. He never openly abjured Catholicism, but he was a principal influence on many reformers, e.g., Bernardino OCHINO and Pietro Martire VERMIGLI. He seems to have held the doctrine of justification by faith alone. Many consider him a Socinian or Unitarian.

Valdés Leal, Juan de (lāäl'), 1622–90, Spanish baroque painter and etcher, active mainly in Seville and Córdoba. He is especially famous for grimly moralizing subjects, as in *Allegory of Vanity* (Wadsworth Athenaeum, Hartford, Conn.) and *Hieroglyphs of Death* (Seville). He also executed moving religious paintings, using an inventive palette, e.g., *Way to Calvary* (Hispanic Society, New York City), and fine portraits. See study by Elizabeth du Gué Trapier (1960).

Valdez (väldēz'), city (1970 pop. 1,005), Valdez-Chitina-Whittier census div., S Alaska, at the head of Valdez Arm inside Prince William Sound; inc. 1901. It has tourist and fishing industries. Salmon spawning grounds are there. The city's excellent landlocked, ice-free harbor was explored and named by the Spaniards in 1790. Valdez was established (1898) as a debarkation point for men seeking a route to the Yukon gold fields that would obviate the necessity of paying duty to Canada. The city was devastated by the 1964 earthquake; it was rebuilt at a location 5 mi (8 km) west of the old site. Carefully planned, many of its new buildings are of Swiss design. Valdez is the southern terminus of the oil pipeline that originates in Prudhoe Bay. Its port facilities were greatly enlarged in the mid-1970s.

Valdivia, Pedro de (pā'dhrō dā väldē'vyä), c.1500–1554, Spanish conquistador, conqueror of Chile. One of Francisco Pizarro's best officers in the conquest of Peru, educated, energetic, somewhat less cruel and avaricious than his fellow conquerors, Valdivia obtained permission from Pizarro to subdue Chile. In Jan., 1540, he began his march south through the Desert of Atacama, following the route used by his unfortunate predecessor, Diego de ALMAGRO. Although Santiago was founded in 1541 and other settlements in the next few years, the colony was not prosperous; gold was scarce and the Araucanian Indians warlike. To secure additional aid and confirm his claims to the conquered territory, Valdivia returned in 1547 to Peru, where he supported the viceroy, Pedro de la GASCA, against the rebellion of Gonzalo Pizarro. He received the title of governor of Chile and returned to his domain in 1549, continuing his march S to the Bío-Bío River, where he founded Concepción, and farther S to Valdivia (1552). Ostensibly the conquest was complete. Toward the end of 1553, however, the Indians under LAUTARO revolted. Valdivia, sallying forth with 40 men to stamp out the rebellion, was ambushed. As each successive wave of Indian attackers was wiped out or beaten off, Lautaro sent another, until the entire company, including Valdivia, was massacred. See biographies by R. B. C. Graham (1926, repr. 1973) and I. W. Vernon (1969); study by H. R. Pocock (1968).

Valdivia, city (1970 pop. 90,942), capital of Valdivia prov., S central Chile, on the Valdivia River. It is a leading commercial and industrial center. Founded in 1552, it was a fortress in the defense against the Araucanian Indians and was a royalist center during the war of liberation. The city did not grow until the arrival in the mid-19th cent. of German immigrants who founded the first industries (beer and shoes). Valdivia was devastated by an earthquake in 1960 but has been largely rebuilt.

Val-d'Oise (väl-dwäz), department (1968 pop. 693,269), N central France, N of Paris. PONTOISE is the capital.

Val d'Or (väl dôr), town (1971 pop. 17,421), SW Que., Canada, SE of Rouyn. It is a mining center. Gold was discovered in the region in 1909; copper, zinc, lead, and molybdenum are also mined.

Valdosta (väldŏs' tə), city (1970 pop. 32,303), seat of Lowndes co., S Ga., near the Fla. line, in a lake region; inc. 1860. Valdosta is a large naval stores market and a processing, distributing, and commercial center for a tobacco, cotton, watermelon, and livestock area. Manufactures include turpentine, pine lumber, wood products, paper, textiles, fertilizer, and metal goods. Valdosta State College is there, and Moody Air Force Base is to the north.

Valence (väläNs'), city (1968 pop. 64,134), capital of Drôme dept., SE France, in Dauphiné, on the Rhône River. Its many manufactures include metallurgical products, textiles, leather goods, jewelry, and munitions. It is also a processing and trade center for a fertile farm area. An old Roman town, it was taken by the Visigoths (413) and the Arabs (c.730), then changed hands many times. Although nominally under the control of various European powers, it was actually ruled by its own bishops from 1150 until the 15th cent., when its citizens put themselves under the protection of the dauphin. Its Romanesque cathedral (11th cent.; partially restored) is a tourist attraction. Its university was founded in 1452.

valence, combining capacity of an ATOM expressed as the number of single bonds the atom can form or the number of electrons an element gives up or accepts when reacting to form a compound (see CHEMICAL BOND). Atoms are called monovalent, divalent, trivalent, or tetravalent according to whether they form one, two, three, or four bonds. For purposes of describing chemical behavior, an atom can be considered as a positively charged nucleus surrounded by negatively charged electrons orbiting in concentric spherical shells. The number of positive charges in the nucleus determines how many electrons normally surround the nucleus; as ATOMIC NUMBER increases, the electron shells are filled starting with those nearest the nucleus. The valence of an atom is determined by the number of electrons in the outermost, or valence, shell. The atom exists in its most stable configuration when its outermost shell is completely filled; in combining with other atoms, it thus tends to gain or lose valence electrons in order to attain a stable configuration. If the valence shell of the atom is nearly complete, as in chlorine and other nonmetals, the atom will tend to accept electrons to complete it; if the valence shell has few electrons, as in potassium and other metals, the atom will tend to lose these electrons so that the next shell below the valence shell becomes a completed outermost shell. The valence of many elements is determined from their ability to combine with hydrogen or to replace it in compounds. For example, one oxygen atom combines with two hydrogen atoms to form water and the valence of oxygen is thus determined to be 2. Similarly, chlorine accepts one electron in combining with a single atom of hydrogen to form hydrogen chloride, HCl, and chlorine's valence is 1. Zinc does not combine with hydrogen but does replace it in compounds; in a typical replacement reaction, one zinc atom replaces two hydrogen atoms, as in the equation $Zn + H_2SO_4 \rightarrow ZnSO_4 + H_2$, so that zinc has a valence of 2. Atoms are assigned numbers, called valence numbers, oxidation numbers, or oxidation states, which range in value from -4 through 0 to $+7$ and describe the combining behavior of the atoms in chemical reactions, particularly oxidation-reduction reactions (see OXIDATION AND REDUCTION). Metals, which commonly donate electrons and form compounds in which they exist in the positive, or cationic, state, are assigned positive oxidation numbers (see CATION). For a metal such as zinc, which donates two electrons to achieve a stable electron configuration, the oxidation number is $+2$. Nonmetals, which commonly accept electrons and in compounds exist in the negative, or anionic, state, are assigned negative oxidation numbers (see ANION). The oxidation number is -1 for chlorine and the other halogens, which accept one electron to complete their valence shell. Some elements, like the transition metals, have electron configurations in which electrons from their inner shells can also be used as valence electrons; these elements can have several different oxidation states. For example, iron can have a valence of $+2$ or $+3$ and chromium can have a valence of $+2$, $+3$, or $+6$. Iron in the $+3$ oxidation state, Fe^{+3}, acts as an oxidizing agent, accepting one electron to attain the Fe^{+2} state, while ferrous iron, Fe^{+2}, by donating an electron in going to the $+3$ state, acts as a reducing agent.

Valencia, Guillermo (gēyär'mō välän'syä), 1873–1943, Colombian poet, one of the leaders of MODERNISMO. He came from an aristocratic family, received solid classical training, and became active politically as an orator. Valencia was a disciple of José Asunción SILVA. His austere and subtle verses display his considerable culture and extreme sensibility. The only collections of his work published in his lifetime are *Ritos* [rites] (1898) and *Catay* (1928). Valencia was constantly preoccupied with the fate of the poet in an indifferent world.

Valencia (välăn'thēä), region (1970 pop. 3,073,255) and former kingdom, E Spain, on the Mediterranean. It now comprises the provinces of Alicante, Castellón de la Plana, and Valencia. The country is chiefly mountainous, with a fertile coastal plain, on which most of the population is concentrated. The Mediterranean climate has helped to make Valencia the "garden of Spain." Irrigation and an intensive system of cultivation were started by the Moors. Citrus and other fruits, rice, vegetables, cereals, olive oil, and wine are now produced. Many of these products (especially Valencia oranges) are exported. The mulberry tree has been cultivated for silk since ancient times, but the silk industry has declined. Processed foods, ceramics, metal products, and textiles are the chief manufactures. Many prehistoric remains have been found in Valencia. Inhabited by the Iberians in early times, it was later colonized by Greek and Carthaginian traders. It was a battlefield between the Carthaginians and the Romans (see SAGUNTO). It passed to the Moors in the 8th cent. At the fall of the caliphate of Córdoba it became (1022) an independent emirate. The CID ruled briefly the city and district of Valencia (1094-99). The rule of the Almoravids and Almohads was followed by a brief period of independence. Valencia was ruled (1238-52) by James I of Aragón. It preserved its political identity within the Aragonese confederation and later in the Spanish state, but its privileges were completely abolished (18th cent.) by Philip V. The 14th and 15th cent. were a period of economic prosperity and artistic flowering; decline came after the expulsion of the Moors (1609). The region has had an economic revival in the 20th cent.; increased tourism has been an important factor.

Valencia, city (1970 pop. 653,690), capital of Valencia prov., E Spain, on the Turia River. The third largest city of Spain, it lies in a fertile garden region a short distance from its busy Mediterranean port, El Grao, on the Gulf of Valencia. It is an active industrial and commercial center producing textiles, metal products, chemicals, furniture, and *azulejos* [colored tiles]. There also are important shipyards. First mentioned in the 2d cent. B.C., Valencia was a Roman colony. Under the Moors, from the 8th to the 13th cent., it was twice the seat of an independent state (see VALENCIA region). From 1094 to 1099 it was ruled by the CID. After its conquest (1238) by James I of Aragón, Valencia rose to great commercial and cultural importance and rivaled Barcelona. Its university was founded in 1501. In the 15th and 16th cent., through the work of Auzias March and others, Valencia achieved literary and intellectual eminence. It experienced an economic revival in the 19th and 20th cent. During the civil war Valencia served (1936-37) as the seat of the Loyalist government. A popular winter resort, the city is very picturesque, with blue-tiled church domes and narrow streets in the old quarter and fine tree-lined avenues and promenades in the modern section. Among its chief landmarks are the cathedral (13th-15th cent.), called La Seo, with a Gothic belltower (the Miguelete); the Torres de Serranos, 14th-century fortified towers built on Roman foundations; the Gothic silk exchange, called La Lonja; and the Renaissance palace of justice. The city also has a fine art gallery. The *Tribunal de las Aguas,* which settles disputes over the irrigation of the outlying garden region, has met regularly in the city since the 10th cent.

Valencia (vălĕn′syä), city (1970 est. pop. 232,000), capital of Carabobo state, N Venezuela. It is Venezuela's fourth largest city and one of its major industrial centers. Products include motor vehicles, chemicals, textiles, cattle feed, and consumer goods. Lying in a leading agricultural region, the city is a market for sugarcane and cotton and for cattle driven from the Orinoco llanos. Valencia was founded in 1555. It was briefly the national capital in 1812 and again in 1830, when a convention held there proclaimed Venezuela's secession from Greater Colombia. Valencia's industrialization dates from the 1950s.

Valencia or **Valentia** (both: vəlĕn′shēə), island (1966 pop. 847), c.7 mi (11.3 km) long and 2 mi (3.2 km) wide, off the coast of Co. Kerry, SW Republic of Ireland. Valencia was named by Spanish traders. Its slate, once famous, is no longer quarried, and the island is now best known as the eastern terminus of the first permanent transatlantic cable, laid (1866) by the *Great Eastern* and connecting Valencia with Trinity Bay, Newfoundland. The cable station is at Knightstown. Glanleam, the old estate of the knight of Kerry, has subtropical gardens.

Valenciennes (väläNsyĕn′), city (1968 pop. 47,464), Nord dept., N France, on the Escaut (Scheldt) River. It is located in a rich coal basin, which fuels its textile, machinery, and metallurgical industries. An important place in medieval HAINAUT, it became famous (15th cent.) for its lace industry.

Valens (vā′lənz), c.328-378, Roman emperor of the East (364-78). Brother and coregent of VALENTINIAN I, Valens followed in most respects his brother's policies but, unlike him, embraced Arian Christianity (see ARIANISM). An intolerant man, he sporadically persecuted orthodox Christians. At the beginning of his reign he put down the revolt of Procopius. He initiated warfare against the VISIGOTHS under Athanaric and defeated them in 369. His attitude toward the Persian threat to Armenia was indecisive, but in 376 peace was made. He admitted the Visigoths under Fritigern into the empire. Dissatisfied with the Romans, they rebelled, and in 378, Valens was killed in the battle of Adrianople, in which two thirds of the Roman army was destroyed, leaving the Eastern Empire virtually defenseless. He was succeeded by Theodosius I.

Valentia: see VALENCIA, island, Ireland.

Valentine, Saint, d. c.270, Roman martyr priest. The customs connected with him in English-speaking countries are probably a survival from a period when a pagan festival associated with love occurred about Feb. 14, his feast day. He is now popularly considered the patron of lovers and the helper of those unhappily in love. The lovers' greeting cards sent on this day (and the parodies of them) are called valentines for him.

Valentine's Day: see SAINT VALENTINE'S DAY.

Valentinian I (văl″əntĭn′ēən), 321-75, Roman emperor of the West (364-75). He held high military rank under Julian and Jovian. After the death of Jovian, Valentinian was proclaimed emperor; he appointed his brother VALENS coregent in the East. Valentinian defeated the Alemanni several times, and his general THEODOSIUS successfully defended the empire in Britain and in Africa. To protect the frontiers of his empire, Valentinian ordered the construction of fortresses on the Rhine and the Danube rivers. He reduced taxation and promoted education. Although he was an orthodox Christian, he allowed religious freedom to Arians and to pagans. He was succeeded by his sons Valentinian II and GRATIAN.

Valentinian II, 371?-392, Roman emperor of the West (375-92), son of Valentinian I. Upon the death of his father, he was proclaimed emperor with his brother GRATIAN as coregent. After the death (378) of VALENS, Gratian made THEODOSIUS I ruler in the East. Valentinian's reign during minority was troubled by the religious struggle between the Arians, supported by his mother, Justina, and the Nicene Christians led by Gratian and St. AMBROSE. In 383, Gratian was killed by order of MAXIMUS, and the personal rule of Valentinian began. He was expelled (387) from Italy by Maximus, but was restored by Theodosius in 388. Valentinian was murdered four years later, probably by the Frankish general Arbogast, who then named the puppet Eugenius as emperor.

Valentinian III, 419-55, Roman emperor of the West (425-55). Two years after the death of his uncle, HONORIUS, he was placed on the throne by his cousin Theodosius II, who deposed the usurper John. Valentinian's mother, GALLA PLACIDIN, was regent during his minority, but from 433 to 454 the general AETIUS was the actual ruler in the West. In Africa, BONIFACE was defeated (430) by the Vandals under GAISERIC; by 442, Aetius was obliged to acknowledge Vandal independence. The empire was also disturbed by the war between Aetius and Boniface, by general barbarian unrest, and by peasant revolts. Valentinian proved an indolent and ineffectual ruler, although he supported the efforts of Pope Leo I (see LEO I, SAINT) to enforce ecclesiastical order in the West. The terrible invasions of the Huns under ATTILA began in 441; although defeated (451) in Gaul by Aetius, Attila briefly invaded N Italy in 452. In 454, Valentinian murdered Aetius, and shortly afterward Valentinian was himself assassinated. He was succeeded by Maximus.

Valentino, Rudolph (văləntē′nō), 1895-1926, American film actor, b. Italy. He emigrated to the United States in 1913 and, after a brief career as a dancer and bit player, was an instant success in the film *The Four Horsemen of the Apocalypse* (1921). Such films as *The Sheik* (1921), *Blood and Sand* (1922), and *Monsieur Beaucaire* (1924) made him the idol of millions. He was the first "Latin lover" in motion pictures. Valentino's screen personality and his early death, both surrounded by mystery, made him a cult figure. See biographies by Alan Arnold (1954) and Robert Oberfirst (1962).

Valentinus (vălənti′nəs), fl. c.135-c.160, founder of the Valentinians, the most celebrated of the Gnostic sects (see GNOSTICISM) of the 2d cent. The little that is known of his life is found in the works of early Christian theologians who refuted him, such as St. Irenaeus and Clement of Alexandria. Probably born in Egypt, Valentinus received his education in Alexandria and after c.135 taught in Rome, where he attracted brilliant converts. Valentinus viewed ultimate reality as a procession of aeons, 33 in all, issuing in pairs from the primal aeons, abyss and silence. From these came mind and truth, in turn engendering word (logos) and life. The thirtieth aeon, Sophia, by her inordinate desire to penetrate the abyss, caused great disorder within the pleroma (divine realm). Her passion was banished to a formless existence outside the pleroma. It is for the restoration of order and the salvation of the progeny issuing from the expelled passion that the last three aeons are produced—Christ, the Holy Spirit, and Jesus the Savior, who is the "common fruit" of the pleroma. Ruler of the outcast world is the proud Demiurge, identified with the deity of the Old Testament, who created the forms of life by which man is ensnared. Jesus appears in the world to reveal the knowledge (gnosis) that will restore man to the divine order. Valentinus wrote letters, homilies, and psalms, of which fragments survive. The recently discovered Coptic manuscript Gospel of Truth may be by Valentinus. See Hans Jonas, *The Gnostic Religion* (1958); Jean Doresse, *The Secret Books of the Egyptian Gnostics* (tr. 1960); Kendrick Grobel, *The Gospel of Truth* (1960).

Vale Press, celebrated British establishment for fine printing. It was one of the presses founded in London in 1896 during the revival of the art and craft of making books. The Vale type and the other types (Avon and King's Fount) used by the Vale Press were designed and the printing of Vale Press books were supervised by the artist Charles RICKETTS; the presswork was by the Ballantyne Press. The masterpiece of the Vale Press is *The Works of Shakespeare,* in 39 volumes (1900-1903). The work of the press, encompassing 45 titles, ended in 1904, and Ricketts then destroyed the types. See also KELMSCOTT PRESS; ASHENDENE PRESS; DOVES PRESS.

Valera, Diego de (dyā′gō dā välä′rä), 1412?-1488?, Spanish adventurer and writer. Reared at the Castilian court, he was page to John II and later became one of his diplomatic agents. He took part in the campaigns against the Hussites. After the death of John II he retired to scholarly pursuits, but he returned to public life in 1474 to become majordomo of Isabella I and chronicler of Ferdinand II, whom he incited to the conquest of Granada. His works range from poetry to philosophy and genealogy, but his chief importance is as a historian. His *Crónica abreviada,* a universal history from the creation to John II, is continued by chronicles of the reigns of Henry IV of Castile and of Ferdinand and Isabella.

Valera, Eamon de: see DE VALERA, EAMON.

Valera y Alcalá Galiano, Juan (hwän välā′rä ē älkälä′ gälyä′nō), 1824-1905, Spanish writer and diplomat. Of a leading liberal family, Valera was a diplomat until 1858, and he later became a senator and an ambassador. Among his major works are *Cartas americanas* (4 vol., 1889), on Spanish-American writers, and *Florilegio de poesías castellanas del siglo XIX* (5 vol., 1902-3), an anthology of Spanish poetry. His first novel, *Pepita Jiménez* (1874, tr. 1886), won international fame. Other novels include *El comendador Mendoza* (1877, tr. *Commander Mendoza,* 1893) and *Juanita la Larga* (1895).

Valerian (Publius Licinius Valerianus) (vəlēr′ēən), d. after 260, Roman emperor (253-60). He held important posts, both civil and military, under the emperors Decius and GALLUS. After the short reign of the former general Aemilianus, Valerian was proclaimed emperor. In 257 he organized a general persecution of the Christians. Although not an incapable man, he was nevertheless unsuited to rule in such a critical time, for N Italy, Greece, and Asia Minor were falling to the barbarians and to the Persians. Appointing his son, GALLIENUS, as coregent, Valerian undertook a campaign in the East against SHAPUR I of Persia, who destroyed the Roman army and took (260) the emperor prisoner. Valerian died in captivity and was succeeded by Gallienus.

valerian, common name for some members of the Valerianaceae, a family chiefly of herbs and shrubs of temperate and colder regions of the Northern Hemisphere; a few species, however, are native to the Andes. The name valerian is popularly used for plants of the genus *Valeriana* and also for other related plants that are cultivated in flower gardens or borders for the numerous small and fragrant blossoms. The common valerian (*V. officinalis*) is sometimes grown under the name garden heliotrope, although it is unrelated to the true heliotropes. A perennial herb, it was used as a condiment during the Middle Ages and later as the source of a perfume oil (from the scented roots and rhizomes). It is still cultivated in parts of N Europe and in some Oriental countries for the essential oil, sometimes substituted for that of the related SPIKENARD, and for the dried roots and rhizomes, also called valerian and used medicinally as a sedative and carminative. In the N United States the common valerian is found naturalized in the North, and several species grow indigenously elsewhere, e.g., *V. ciliata* on the

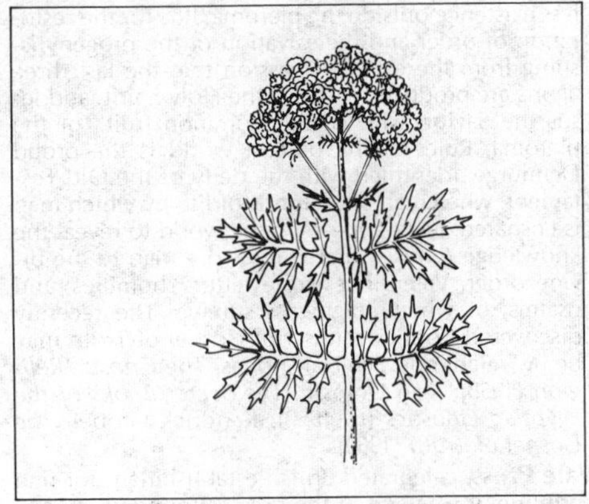

Valerian, Valeriana officinalis

prairies and *V. uliginosa* in eastern swamps and moist woodlands. The red valerian, or Jupiter's-beard (*Centranthus ruber*), and the African valerian (*Fedia cornucopiae*) are among other ornamental species native to the Old World. Some unrelated plants are also called valerian, e.g., the Greek valerian or Jacob's-ladder (see PHLOX). The valerian family is classified in the division MAGNOLIOPHYTA, class Magnoliopsida, order Dipsacales.

Valerian Way: see ROMAN ROADS.

Valerius Maximus (vəlĕr'ēəs măk'sĭməs), c.49 B.C.–c.A.D. 30, Roman author. Little is known of his life. His *Factorum ac dictorum memorabilium libri IX* [nine books of memorable deeds and sayings] was written A.D. c.30 and is a miscellany of anecdotes about a variety of subjects. The work was widely popular, especially as a source for writers and orators.

Valéry, Paul (pōl vălārē'), 1871–1945, French poet and critic. A follower of the SYMBOLISTS, Valéry was one of the greatest French poets of the 20th cent. He was encouraged by Pierry Loüys and by Mallarmé to publish a few poems in several small reviews, but he soon turned from poetry to prose with *La Soirée avec M. Teste* (1896; tr. *An Evening with Mr. Teste,* 1925). In 1912, Gide and other admirers urged him to publish a collection of his early poems. A brief valedictory to poetry, which he had planned to add to the collection, grew into his masterpiece, *La Jeune Parque* (1917). It is a long and somewhat obscure poem, which, together with *Le Cimetière marin* (1920; tr. *The Graveyard by the Sea,* 1932), offers the best example of Valéry's poetics. In 1920 appeared *Odes* and *Album de vers anciens,* followed in 1922 by *Charmes.* His prose works include five collections of essays, all called *Variété* (1924–44; partial tr. *Variety,* 1927, 1938), and four dialogues on subjects ranging from the arts to mathematics and the sciences. He succeeded Anatole France in the French Academy in 1925. Between the world wars Valéry was a member of the Committee of Letters and Arts of the League of Nations, serving as its president in the 1930s. Valéry held the chair of poetry at the Collège de France. A recipient of many honors, he was accorded a state funeral at his death. Publication (in English) of a projected 15-volume edition of *The Collected Works of Paul Valéry,* edited by Jackson Mathews, was begun in 1956. See studies by H. A. Grubbs (1968), W. N. Ince (2d ed. 1970), and C. M. Crow (1972); bibliography by A. J. Arnold (1970).

Valhalla or **Walhalla** (both: vălhăl'ə, -hăl'ə), in Norse mythology, Odin's hall for slain heroes. This martial paradise was one of the most beautiful halls of ASGARD. The dead warriors, brought to Valhalla by the Valkyries, fought during the day and feasted at night.

valine (văl'ēn), organic compound, one of the 22 α-AMINO ACIDS commonly found in animal proteins.

$$H_2N-\underset{\displaystyle H}{\overset{\displaystyle \overset{\displaystyle CH_3\quad CH_3}{CH}}{C}}-C\overset{\displaystyle O}{\underset{\displaystyle OH}{}}$$

valine

Only the L-stereoisomer appears in mammalian protein. It is one of several essential amino acids needed in the diet, as the human body cannot synthesize it from simpler metabolites. Young adults need about 23 mg of this amino acid per day per kilogram (10 mg per lb) of body weight. Valine can be degraded into simpler compounds by the enzymes of the body; an inherited defect in one of the enzymes involved in this process results in a rare disorder called maple syrup urine disease. Valine contributes to the structure of proteins into which it has been incorporated by the tendency of its side chain to participate in hydrophobic interactions. The structure of valine was established in 1906, after it had been first isolated from albumin in 1879. See ISOLEUCINE.

Valkyries (vălkĕr'ēz), in Germanic mythology, warrior maidens of Odin. They presided over battles, chose those who were to die, and brought the souls of the dead heroes back to VALHALLA. Chief among them was BRUNHILD. They were usually represented as riding through the air on horseback, helmeted and carrying a spear. The Valkyries play a prominent role in *Die Walküre* of Richard Wagner.

Valla, Lorenzo (lōrān'tsō väl'lä), c.1407–1457, Italian humanist. He knew Greek well and was chosen by Pope Nicholas V to translate Herodotus and Thucydides into Latin. His earliest known work, now lost, demonstrated his polemical style and his attempt to reform the analysis of the classics. In a pioneer work of criticism, he proved that the long suspect Donation of Constantine (see CONSTANTINE, DONATION OF) was a forgery. At 26 he wrote *De Voluptate,* a triad of dialogues that constitute an analysis of pleasure and a humanist condemnation of scholasticism and monastic asceticism. Aggressive in tone, it was received with hostility. His masterwork, *De elegantia linguae latinae* (composed, 1435–44), was a brilliant philological defense of classical Latin, in which he contrasted the elegance of the ancient Romans' works with the clumsiness of medieval and Church Latin. This enormously influential work ran to 60 editions before 1536. Valla's investigations into the textual errors in the Vulgate spurred Erasmus to undertake the study of the Greek New Testament.

Valladolid (välyäthōlēth'), city (1970 pop. 236,341), capital of Valladolid prov., N central Spain, in León, at the confluence of the Pisuerga and Esgueva rivers and on the Canal de Castilla. A communications and industrial center, Valladolid is also an important grain market. The city has played an important role in Spanish history. Of obscure origin (its name is derived from the Arabic), it was conquered by the Christians from the Moors in the 10th cent., rose to prominence in the 12th and 13th cent., and largely replaced Toledo as the chief residence of the kings of Castile in the 15th cent. Valladolid was famous for its lavish festivals and tournaments under John II, and in 1469 it was the scene of the marriage of Ferdinand and Isabella. Christopher Columbus died (1506) in the city, Emperor Charles V often resided there, and Philip II was born there in 1527. It declined greatly after 1561, when Philip II made Madrid the Spanish capital (the capital was returned to Valladolid 1600–1606). Today Valladolid remains an important cultural center and archiepiscopal see. Its university, founded in 1346, has a rich library with valuable manuscripts. The house of Columbus and the house where Cervantes wrote part of *Don Quixote* have been preserved. Other landmarks include the late Renaissance cathedral; the Colegio de Santa Cruz, built in the plateresque style, now housing a museum; the Colegio de San Gregorio (15th cent.), with a lavishly adorned facade; the former royal palace; and the churches of San Pablo and Santa María Antigua (12th–13th cent.).

Vallandigham, Clement Laird (vəlăn'dĭghăm", —găm"), 1820–71, American political leader, leader of the COPPERHEADS in the Civil War, b. New Lisbon (now Lisbon), Ohio. He became (1842) a lawyer, was elected to the Ohio legislature (1845, 1846), and was editor (1847–49) of the Dayton *Empire,* a Democratic weekly. A strong upholder of states' rights, Vallandigham was a U.S. Representative from 1858 to 1863, being defeated for reelection in 1862. On May 1, 1863, in a political speech at Mt. Vernon, Ohio, he declared, among other things, that the Civil War was being fought not to save the Union but to free the Negroes and enslave the whites. Gen. Ambrose E. Burnside, then commanding the Dept. of the Ohio, accused him of violating "General Order No. 38," which threatened punishment for those declaring sympathy for the enemy, and Vallandigham was arrested, court-martialed, and sentenced to imprisonment for the rest of the war. President Lincoln commuted the sentence to banishment behind Confederate lines. The Peace Democrats of Ohio nevertheless nominated (July, 1863) Vallandigham for governor, but he was defeated by John BROUGH. He made his way from the Confederacy to Canada, and from there he returned to the United States and was allowed to go unmolested. In the presidential campaign of 1864, the Democratic platform, representing his views, demanded immediate cessation of hostilities. Made commander of the Sons of Liberty (see KNIGHTS OF THE GOLDEN CIRCLE), he was the most prominent of the Copperheads. After the war he was an unsuccessful aspirant to Congress. See biography by his brother, J. L. Vallandigham (1872, repr. 1972); study by F. L. Klement (1970).

Valle, Pietro della (pyĕ'trō dĕl'lä väl'lä), 1586–1652, Italian traveler in Asia. He sailed (1614) from Venice; spent a year in Constantinople, where he studied Turkish and Arabic; then traveled in Egypt, the Holy Land, Arabia, Persia, and India, returning to Italy in 1626. An account of his travels based on his letters appeared in two volumes (1650–58); a part appeared in English with a life of Della Valle as *The Travels of Pietro della Valle in India* (ed. by Edward Gray, Hakluyt Society, Vol. LXXXIV and LXXXV, 1892).

Valle Inclán, Ramón del (rämōn' dĕl vä'lyā ēnklän'), 1866?–1936, Spanish writer, a member of the GENERATION OF '98. Valle Inclán was deeply influenced by foreign literary trends, especially by MODERNISMO. An eccentric who cultivated bizarre legends about himself, he published a collection of sensational, erotic tales, *Femeninas* (1895). He used himself as the model for the old libertine hero of his *Sonatas* (1902–5, tr. *The Pleasant Memoirs of the Marquis de Bradomín,* 1924). His symbolist aesthetic is expressed in his poetic works such as *Aromas de leyenda* (1907). Among his plays are *Aquila de blasón* [eagle of honor] (1907) in prose, and *La Marquesa Rosalinda* (1913) in verse. In his later works he satirized Spanish life in grotesque caricatures that he called *esperpentos.* Reminiscent of the nightmare etchings of Goya, these include *Luces de Bohemia* (1920). See study by Robert Lima (1972).

Vallejo, César (sā'sär väyä'hō), 1895–1938, Peruvian poet. Vallejo was one of the most influential yet least imitated figures of modern Spanish American letters. He identified himself with the sufferings of the underprivileged and dedicated himself to the cause of social progress. Himself a cholo—a mestizo of Indian and white origin—he was deeply distressed by the exploitation of the Indian. His poems in *Heraldos negros* (1918) blend symbolism and caustic observation in terse classical form. He was imprisoned on false charges in 1920; in jail he wrote a part of *Trilce* (1922). The book is somber and tragic in tone and dramatically experimental in form. In 1923 he went to Europe in self-imposed exile, espoused the Marxist cause, and aligned himself with the Republicans in the Spanish civil war. He also wrote *Tungsteno* (1931), a moving novel about the Indians. Vallejo made a meager living from journalism and died in poverty. Two volumes of his work were published posthumously, *Poemas humanos* (1939) and *España, aparta de mi este cáliz* [Spain, let this cup pass from me] (1940). See anthology of his poetry ed. by James Higgins (1970).

Vallejo (vălā'hō, -lā'ō, və-), city (1970 pop. 71,710), Solano co., W Calif., on San Pablo Bay at the mouth of the Napa River; inc. 1866. It is a port and a trade and processing center for farm products. Its main source of employment is the U.S. naval shipyard on Mare Island, just west of the city. Founded by Admiral David Farragut in 1854, it covers 1,500 acres (607 hectares) and has four drydocks and eight shipbuilding ways. Submarines and destroyers are built and repaired there. Vallejo was created on the property of Gen. Mariano G. Vallejo to be the state capital; it was the nominal capital from 1852 to 1853. A junior college and the California Maritime Academy are in Vallejo. A state park is nearby.

Valletta (vəlĕt'ə), city (1970 est. pop. 15,547), capital of Malta, NE Malta. It is strategically located on a rocky promontory between two deep harbors. Dockyards line the harbors and employ more workers than any other industry. A 16th-century town, with many relics of the Knights of St. John of Jerusalem (the Knights Hospitalers, or Knights of Malta), Valletta contains a 16th-century cathedral, the old governor's palace, the Royal Univ. (1769), and a library with a museum of antiquities. The city was severely damaged by air raids in World War II.

Valleyfield, city (1971 pop. 30,173), S Que., Canada, on the Beauharnois canal, at the northeast end of Lake St. Francis, SW of Montreal. A port of entry and industrial center, it has cotton and synthetic textile mills, a zinc refinery, and plants making chemicals, clothing, asbestos, and felt.

Valley Forge, on the Schuylkill River, NE Pa., NW of Philadelphia. There, during the American Revolution, the main camp of the Continental Army was established (Dec., 1777–June, 1778) under the command of Gen. George Washington. The winter was severe, food and clothing was inadequate, and there was much illness and suffering. The number of ragged and half-starved troops dwindled through desertion, and the remaining men, about 11,000, talked of mutiny but were held together by their loyalty to Washington and the patriotic cause. Two distinguished foreigners, French General Lafayette and Prussian General Steuben, shared the misery of the troops; Steuben drilled and organized the men, transforming the loose-jointed army into an integrated force. The site is now in a state park.

Valley of Ten Thousand Smokes: see KATMAI NATIONAL MONUMENT.

Valley Station, uninc. town (1970 pop. 24,471), Jefferson co., N central Ky.

Valley Stream, village (1970 pop. 40,413), Nassau co., SE N.Y., on Long Island, a residential suburb of New York City; inc. 1925. It is the original site and home office of a chain of Long Island luxury restaurants and food services. Valley Stream State Park is there, and Kennedy International Airport is to the west.

Vallombrosa (väl-lōmbrô'zä), village, Tuscany, central Italy, near Florence, beautifully situated in the Apennine forest at an altitude of 4,000 ft (1,219 m). It is a well-known summer resort and has a Benedictine abbey dating from the 11th cent.

Vallotton, Félix (fālĕks' välətôN'), 1865–1925, Swiss woodcut artist and painter. Associated with the NABIS, he worked in Paris. Vallotton rejuvenated the woodcut medium as a creative technique. His boldly cut designs, conceived as arrangements in black and white, depict Parisian society with wit and intelligence. A painting, *Swiss Landscape*, is in the Lyman Allyn Museum, New London, Conn.

Valmy (välmē'), village (1968 pop. 291), Marne dept., NE France, in the Argonne region. The "cannonade of Valmy," a Franco-Prussian artillery skirmish, was fought near there on Sept. 20, 1792. This was the first important engagement in the FRENCH REVOLUTIONARY WARS. Although heavy rain brought an inconclusive halt, the encounter revealed the superiority of French artillery.

Valois, Dame Ninette de (väl'wä), 1898–, English ballet director, b. Ireland. She was originally named Edris Stannus. After attaining distinction as a dancer, she became choreographic director of both the Abbey Theatre and the Old Vic Theatre in 1926. In 1931 she established the Sadler's Wells Ballet School. As the director of the Vic-Wells Ballet (later the Royal Ballet), she did much to increase the prestige of ballet in England. Also a choreographer of note, she was made a Dame of the British Empire in 1951. De Valois retired in 1964 and was named Life Governor of the Royal Ballet. She wrote *Invitation to the Ballet* (1937) and *Come Dance With Me* (1957).

Valois (välwä'), royal house of FRANCE that ruled from 1328 to 1589. At the death of Charles IV, the last of the direct CAPETIANS, the Valois dynasty came to the throne in the person of PHILIP VI, son of CHARLES OF VALOIS and grandson of Philip III. The direct Valois line ended (1498) with Charles VIII; the dynasty was continued by LOUIS XII (Valois-Orléans) and, after his death (1515), by the Valois-Angoulême line, of which FRANCIS I was the first to rule. At the death of HENRY III (1589), the house of Bourbon, descending from a younger son of Louis IX, succeeded to the throne in the person of Henry IV.

Valois, historic region, now comprised in Aisne and Oise depts., N France. Crépy-en-Valois was its historic capital. It is a rich agricultural area. A county and later a duchy, Valois was the appanage of the royal house of Valois, which succeeded the elder Capetian line (see CAPETIANS) on the French throne. It was incorporated into the royal domain in 1515.

Valona: see VLORË, Albania.

Valparaiso (vălpərī'zō), Span. *Valparaíso* (bälpäräē'sō) [Span., = vale of paradise], city (1970 pop. 251,459), capital of Valparaiso dept., central Chile. It is the chief port and second-largest city of Chile and the terminus of a trans-Andean railroad. An important industrial center, it manufactures textiles, sugar, paint, enamelware, cottonseed oil, shoes and leather goods, chemicals, and metal products. From a narrow waterfront terrace, steep hills rise to make Valparaiso an amphitheater, with wharves and business quarters at the base and residential sections above. So steep is the ascent that funicular railways are used. The city faces a wide bay, which, although partly protected by breakwaters, often carries severe northern gales in winter. However, Valparaiso's climate is generally mild, and thousands of tourists visit the region, particularly nearby Viña del Mar. Valparaiso was founded in 1536 by the Spanish conquistador Juan de Saavedra but was not permanently established until 1544 by Pedro de Valdivia. It was frequently raided by English and Dutch pirates throughout the 16th and 17th cent. Relatively unimportant in colonial times, the city grew in the late 19th cent. It has a technical school, a Catholic university, and a Chilean naval academy.

Valparaiso (vălpərā'zō), city (1970 pop. 20,020), seat of Porter co., NW Ind.; inc. 1850. Ball and roller bearings, magnets, electric switches, food-processing equipment, and automobile parts are among its many manufactures. The city is the seat of Valparaiso Univ. (noted for its huge chapel) and a technical institute (est. 1874).

Valtellina (vältāl-lē'nä), Alpine valley of the upper Adda River, c.75 mi (120 km) long, in Lombardy, N Italy, extending from Lake Como to the Stelvio Pass. The main towns are Sondrio and Tirano. The valley is a fertile agricultural region, known for its wine. With the adjoining counties of Bormio and CHIAVENNA, the Valtellina was seized (1512) from Milan by the GRISONS, which subsequently ruled the district—its richest and most populous possession—as a subject territory. By the start of the Thirty Years War (1618–48), the stoutly Roman Catholic inhabitants of the Valtellina were ready for revolt against the Grisons, the majority of whose population was Protestant; in 1620 they rose and massacred their Protestant masters. These internal troubles quickly assumed European proportions, because the valley commanded the passages between Austria and the Grisons and Venice and Spanish-held Milan. The Valtellina became the pawn of the participants in the Thirty Years War and the victim of their complicated intrigues. The massacre of 1620 led to a series of military interventions by Spain, Austria, the pope, the Catholic party of the Grisons, France, and the Protestant majority of the Grisons (largely financed by Venice). The valley was sacked in turn by these armies and in 1627 passed under Spanish control; transportation of Spanish reinforcements through the Valtellina into Germany contributed to several victories by the imperial party, notably at Nördlingen (1634). When France fully entered the war on the Protestant side, a French army was again dispatched (1635) to the Valtellina. Henri de ROHAN conquered the valley but failed to restore it to the full control of his Grisons allies. Incensed, the Grisons Protestants, led by the preacher-soldier George Jenatsch, secretly negotiated with the Catholic powers, who promised to restore the Valtellina to the Grisons if the French were expelled. However, Rohan, ill and weakly supported by the French government, had to evacuate the Grisons in 1637. By the Peace of Milan (1639) the Grisons fully recovered the Valtellina; it remained in the Grisons until 1797, when it was incorporated into the Cisalpine Republic. The Valtellina passed (1815) to the Lombardo-Venetian kingdom (held by Austria) and later (1859) to Italy.

value, in colorimetry: see COLOR.

value, in economics, worth of a commodity or service in terms of other commodities or services, or in terms of money. When expressed in terms of money it is called PRICE. Value depends on both desirability and scarcity. Water, although desirable, is usually not scarce and hence costs little. Diamonds, on the other hand, have much value because they are both scarce and desirable. The marginal theory of value takes account of both scarcity and desirability by holding that the total value of a good depends on the utility rendered by the last unit consumed. It developed in opposition to the labor theory of value, which holds that the value of a good is determined by the amount of labor necessary to produce it. The position of the marginal theory is that in addition to value in exchange, there is also value in use, or the utility of a commodity for satisfying a human want, which is subjective. The subjective value of a loaf of bread to a starving man, for instance, is much greater than it is to a man who has just eaten a full meal; but it can be bought at the same market price by both men. See Edward Chamberlin, *Towards a More General Theory of Value* (1957); Gail M. Inlow, *Values in Transition* (1972); M. H. Dobb, *Theories of Value and Distribution Since Adam Smith* (1973).

value-added tax, levy imposed on business at all levels of the manufacture and production of a good or service, and based on the increase in price, or value, provided by each level. Because it is the consumer who ultimately pays a higher price for the taxed commodity, a value-added tax is essentially a hidden sales tax. Originally introduced in France (1954), it is now a major part of the tax structure of most Western European nations.

valve, device for controlling the flow of fluids (liquids and gases). Valves vary in construction and size depending upon their function. Some are classified according to their method of operation or design, e.g., butterfly, gate, globe, lift, needle, piston, and slide valves. Valves are also named for the functions they perform, e.g., check valve (which permits flow in one direction only) and cutoff, bypass, exhaust, intake, safety (see SAFETY VALVE), and throttle valves. Valves are operated automatically, by hand, or by special mechanism. Valves are employed in the carburetor, diesel engine, internal-combustion engine, pump, and steam engine. In Great Britain an ELECTRON TUBE may be referred to as a valve. In anatomy and physiology the term *valve* includes the flaps of tissue that help to control the direction of the flow of blood in the heart.

Vambery, Arminius or **Hermann** (văm'bārī), Hung. *Ármin Vámbéry* (är'mĭn), 1832–1913, Hungarian Orientalist and traveler. In Constantinople (1857–63) he learned several Oriental languages and dialects and then traveled through Armenia and Persia dressed as an Asiatic. He was professor of Oriental languages at the Univ. of Budapest from 1865 to 1905 and wrote many books on his travels and on Asiatic languages and ethnology. See his autobiography (1884) and his memoirs, *The Story of My Struggles* (1904), both in English.

vampire, in folklore, animated corpse that sucks the blood of humans. Belief in vampires has existed from the earliest times and has given rise to an amalgam of legends and superstitions. They were most commonly thought of as spirits or demons that left their graves at night to seek and enslave their victims; it was thought that the victims themselves became vampires. The vampire could be warded off with a variety of charms, amulets, and herbs and could finally be killed by driving a stake through its heart or by cremation. Sometimes the vampire assumed a nonhuman shape, such as that of a bat or wolf (see LYCANTHROPY). Probably the most famous vampire in literature is Count Dracula in the novel *Dracula* by Bram STOKER. See Anthony Masters, *The Natural History of the Vampire* (1972).

vampire bat, name for the blood-drinking BATS of the family Desmodontidae, found in the New World tropics. Vampire bats feed exclusively on the blood of living animals and are thus the only true parasites among mammals. There are three species ranging from Argentina to N Mexico. They are small (about 3 in./7.5 cm long), round-bodied bats with large, pointed ears and naked snouts. Unlike most bats, vampire bats can walk on all fours with the body lifted off the ground; it is in this manner that they approach their sleeping prey. The bat uses its razor-sharp incisors to make a neat incision, usually without waking the victim, then laps the blood with its tongue. Its saliva contains an anticoagulant that causes the wound to seep for several hours. Vampire bats parasitize a variety of animals, chiefly mammals. Although the quantity of blood they take is insufficent to harm a large animal, they are dangerous to livestock and humans because they transmit serious diseases such as rabies and Chagas' disease. Vampire bats live in caves, tree hollows, and houses. They are mutual groomers, and an effective method of reducing their numbers is to coat a captured bat with a sticky poison and release it; when the bat returns to its roost the poison will be licked by other bats. Members of another bat family, the Megadermatidae, of the Old World tropics, are known as false vampire bats. They are exclusively carnivorous, but do not feed on blood. The generic name *Vampyrus* belongs to a large, fruit-eating bat of Central and South America that was once mistakenly believed to suck blood. True vampire bats are classified in the phylum CHORDATA, subphylum Vertebrata, class Mammalia, order Chiroptera, family Desmodontidae.

Van (vän), city (1970 pop. 47,057), capital of Van prov., E Turkey, near the eastern shore of Lake Van, at an altitude of 5,659 ft (1,725 m). It is the trade center for a fruit- and grain-growing region. Van was the cradle of an ancient Armenian civilization. It was the capital of the old Vannic kingdom of URARTU or Ararat. The city fell to the Seljuk Turks (1071) after the defeat of the Byzantines at Manzikert and to the Ottoman Turks in 1543. Near the city is the mound of Toprakkale where excavations in the 19th cent. uncovered the remains of the town of Urartu. Many tablets with so-called Vannic inscriptions relating to early Armenian history were found. In 1939 archaeologists discovered fortifications and various materials dating from the 8th cent. B.C. Many of the Armenians living in the region were massacred by the Turks in 1895. **Lake Van**, c.1,450 sq mi (3,760 sq km), is the largest lake in Turkey. It is alkaline and has no apparent outlet.

vanadium (vənā'dēəm), metallic chemical element; symbol V; at. no. 23; at. wt. 50.942; m.p. about 1890°C; b.p. above 3000°C; sp. gr. about 6 at 20°C; valence +2, +3, +4, or +5. Vanadium is a soft, ductile, silver-grey metal. It is the element above niobium in group Vb of the PERIODIC TABLE. In its properties it resembles chromium. It is corrosion resistant at normal temperatures, but oxidizes above 660°C. It resists attack by hydrochloric and sulfuric acids, salt water, or alkalies. Vanadium forms numerous compounds, including vanadates and complex organic compounds. Vanadium pentoxide, V_2O_5, is commercially important. Vanadium is not found uncombined in nature but occurs widely distributed in minerals. Important ores include carnotite, patronite, roscoelite, and vanadinite. In the United States vanadium ores are mined in Arizona, Colorado, and Utah; other sources are Peru and Africa. Vanadium is recovered from these ores largely as the pentoxide; the pentoxide is also recovered during phosphorus production in Idaho and from certain crude oils and petroleum ashes. The principal use of vanadium is in alloys, especially with STEEL. In tool and spring steels it is a powerful alloying agent; a small amount (less than 1%) adds strength, toughness, and heat resistance. It is usually added in the form of ferrovanadium, a vanadium-iron alloy. Vanadium compounds, especially the pentoxide, are used in the ceramics, glass, and dye industries, and are important as catalysts in the chemical industry. Although high-purity vanadium metal can be produced by chemical reduction of the trichloride, most commercial production of the metal is by calcium reduction of the pentoxide. Vanadium was discovered in 1801 by A. M. del Rio, who called it erythronium; however, it was mistaken for impure chromium. The element was rediscovered and named in 1830 by N. G. Sefström, a Swedish chemist. The element was first isolated in 1867 by H. E. Roscoe.

Van Allen radiation belts, two belts (sometimes considered as a single belt of varying intensity) of radiation outside the earth's atmosphere, extending from c.400 to c.40,000 mi (c.650–c.65,000 km) above the earth. Their existence was confirmed from information secured by launching the first U.S. earth satellite, Explorer I, sent up during the International Geophysical Year of 1957–58. The belts were named for James A. Van Allen, the American astrophysicist who was first to interpret the findings of the Explorer satellite. The region of belts has been given the name of magnetosphere to distinguish it from the ATMOSPHERE. The charged particles, or high-energy protons and electrons, of which the belts are composed circulate along the earth's magnetic lines of force. These particles are believed to originate in gigantic solar flares that occur periodically. After crossing through space they become trapped by the earth's magnetic field and are possibly responsible for the aurora seen about both polar regions where the belts dip into the upper regions of the atmosphere. Recent studies of the earth's magnetic field indicate that it periodically reverses its direction and even disappears for a time. When this happens the magnetosphere likewise vanishes. Van Allen belts have been created artificially by nuclear explosions in outer space.

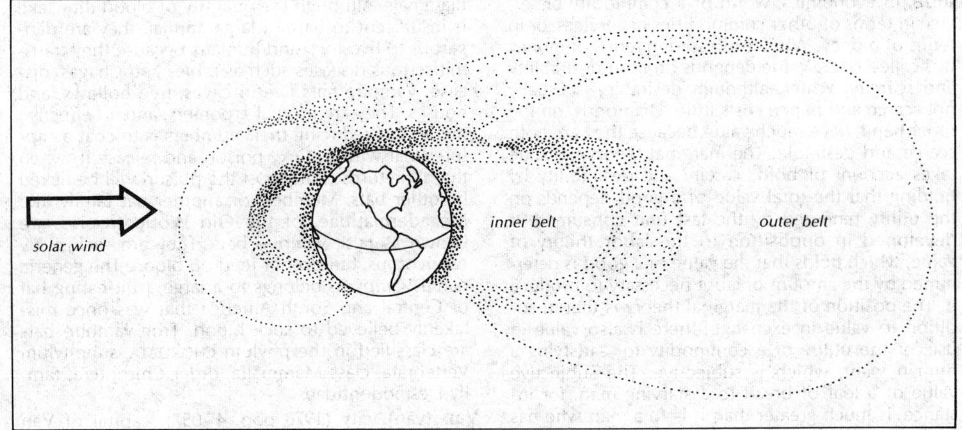

Van Allen radiation belts: The solar wind, a stream of protons, electrons, and ions coming from the sun, gives the belts their asymmetrical shape.

Vanbrugh, Sir John (vănbrōō', văn'brə), 1664–1726, English dramatist, architect, soldier, and adventurer, b. London, of Flemish descent. In 1686 he obtained a commission in the army. He was arrested for espionage in 1690 and spent two years in a French prison. After his return from France he turned to writing for the stage. His first play, *The Relapse* (1696), was a counterblast to Colley Cibber's *Love's Last Shift.* Vanbrugh's masterpiece, *The Provoked Wife* (1697), was attacked (1698) by Jeremy Collier in his famous diatribe on the immorality of the English stage. Vanbrugh was an inventive playwright, imbued with the wit and cynicism that was common to the Restoration dramatists. As his reputation as an architect grew, Vanbrugh turned away from the stage. He became Wren's principal colleague and his style, expansive, ostentatious, and theatrical, is derived from Wren and from Hawksmoor. His best-known buildings are Blenheim Palace (the perfect example of his genius for the heroic and the culmination of English baroque), Castle Howard, the Queen's Theatre in the Haymarket, and Greenwich Hospital. Vanbrugh's later plays include *The Confederacy* (1705) and *A Journey to London* (completed by Cibber as *The Provoked Husband,* 1728). He was knighted in 1714. See his complete works, including letters (ed. by Bonamy Dobrée and Geoffrey Webb, 4 vol., 1927–28); biography by Laurence Whistler (1938, repr. 1971).

Van Buren, Martin, 1782–1862, 8th President of the United States (1837–41), b. Kinderhook, Columbia co., N.Y. He was reared on his father's farm, was educated at local schools, and after reading law was admitted (1803) to the bar. He practiced law successfully and soon became active in politics. After he was (1808–13) surrogate of Columbia co., he served (1813–20) in the state senate and became prominent in the state Democratic party. While still a senator Van Buren was made state attorney general in 1815, but because of his mounting rivalry with De Witt Clinton, the governor of New York, he was removed from this post in 1819. Meanwhile he had helped to secure the election (1816) of Daniel D. Tompkins as Vice President. He served (1821–28) in the U.S. Senate, where he firmly backed the tariffs of 1824 and 1828. His record there was inconsistent as to states' rights, slavery, and internal improvements; this wavering was later brought up against him by his political enemies. Van Buren was far more important as a political leader than as a legislator. He organized the closely knit political group known as the ALBANY REGENCY and was a leading supporter of William H. Crawford, who ran for President in 1824. After the election of John Quincy Adams, Van Buren gradually swung his power to the support of Andrew JACKSON. Elected (1828) governor of New York state, Van Buren resigned in 1829, after Jackson had become President, to become his Secretary of State. Probably the most influential of Jackson's advisers, Van Buren, although essentially opposed to the doctrine of NULLIFICATION, did not at first take a conspicuous part in the rising hostilities between Vice President John C. CALHOUN and the President. Van Buren further strengthened his position with Jackson by being courteous to Peggy Eaton (see O'NEILL, MARGARET). His resignation (1831) as Secretary of State brought about that of the other cabinet officers and enabled Jackson to eliminate the supporters of Calhoun from the cabinet. Jackson immediately appointed Van Buren minister to Great Britain, but the deciding vote of Calhoun in the Senate prevented him from being confirmed in the post. Thoroughly in accord with Jackson's policies, Van Buren was nominated for Vice President by the Democratic party in 1832 and was elected to office along with President Jackson. It was largely through Jackson's influence that Van Buren was chosen as Democratic candidate for President in 1836. The Whig party was still in the formative stage, and there was no well-organized opposition; Van Buren, therefore, was easily swept into office. The new President announced his intention of following Jackson's policies, but the Panic of 1837 and the hard times that followed brought Van Buren a great deal of unpopularity. To meet the economic crisis, Van Buren, wary of the existing banking system, backed after 1837 the INDEPENDENT TREASURY SYSTEM. Not until 1840, however, did Congress pass measures establishing it. In foreign affairs, Van Buren attempted to conciliate differences with Great Britain arising out of the CAROLINE AFFAIR and the AROOSTOOK WAR. He was again the presidential candidate of the Democratic party in 1840, but he was defeated in the "log cabin and hard cider" campaign by William Henry Harrison. The Whigs unfairly painted Van Buren as a man of great wealth who was ignorant of, and disdainful toward, the common man. In 1844, Van Buren was the leading possibility as Democratic candidate for the presidency, but he flatly opposed the annexation of Texas because he felt it would provoke war with Mexico and because he opposed the extension of slavery. Although he held a majority in the nominating convention, he was unable (largely as a result of the efforts of Robert J. WALKER) to obtain the two-thirds majority necessary to win the nomination. Van Buren, bitterly disappointed, saw James K. POLK elected President. He remained prominent in Democratic party politics, and helped lead the BARNBURNERS in their violent struggle with the HUNKERS. In 1848 he was the presidential candidate of the newly organized FREE-SOIL PARTY and managed to take enough New York votes away from the Democratic candidate, Lewis CASS, to aid Zachary TAYLOR, the Whig party candidate, in winning the election. He voted for the Democratic candidate in the elections of 1852, 1856, and 1860, but supported Abraham Lincoln during the secession crisis. *An Inquiry into the Origin and Course of Political Parties of the United States* (1867) was written by Van Buren, edited by one of his sons, and published posthumously. See his autobiography (1920, repr. 1973); R. V. Remini, *Martin Van Buren and the Making of the Democratic Party* (1959, repr. 1970); J. C. Curtis, *The Fox at Bay* (1970).

Vance, Zebulon Baird, 1830–94, American political leader, Confederate governor of North Carolina (1862–65) in the Civil War, b. Buncombe co., N.C. A lawyer and a Whig, he served in the state legislature (1854) and in Congress (1858–61). Opposed to secession until President Lincoln's call for troops, he promptly urged support of the Confederacy. He distinguished himself in the Seven Days battles (June–July, 1862) before assuming the governorship. Vance was loyal to the Southern cause, but for him the interests of North Carolina superseded those of the Confederate government of Richmond. After the war he was arrested but soon released. Elected to the U.S. Senate in 1870, he was denied his seat. In 1876 he was again elected governor, but resigned in 1878 to enter the Senate, where he was an important figure and a popular orator until his death. See biographies by F. R. Shirley (1963) and Glenn Tucker (1966).

vancomycin (văn"kōmī'sĭn), ANTIBIOTIC resembling PENICILLIN in the way it acts. It is derived from the bacterium *Streptomyces orientalis,* which was isolated from soil of India and Indonesia. Vancomycin destroys Gram positive bacteria, especially staphylococci and enterococci (see GRAM'S STAIN). It seems to function by inhibiting the formation of the bacterial cell wall, as does penicillin; it may also cause damage to the cell membrane. The drug is intensely irritating to tissues and is usually used only for infections where microorganisms are resistant to penicillin (see DRUG RESISTANCE). Vancomycin must be administered intravenously because it is not absorbed through the gastrointestinal tract. Mutant microorganisms resistant to vancomycin are rare.

Van Corlaer, Arent: see VAN CURLER, ARENT.

Van Cortlandt, Jacobus (jəkō'bəs văn kôrt'lənd), 1658–1739, colonial American merchant, b. New Amsterdam (later New York City); brother of Stephen Van Cortlandt. He served (1710 and 1719) as mayor of New York. He purchased land in Yonkers and was thus founder of the estate that was bought (1899) by New York City and converted into Van Cortlandt Park, a tract of 1,132 acres (459 hectares). The manor house in the park was built by Jacobus's son Frederick in 1748.

Van Cortlandt, Stephen or **Stephanus** (stĭfā'nəs), 1643–1700, colonial American merchant and politician, b. New Amsterdam (later New York City); brother of Jacobus Van Cortlandt. A successful merchant, he held a number of high political offices. In 1677 he became the first native-born mayor of New York City, a position he held again in 1686–87. He was also a councilor for many years, associate justice of the provincial supreme court (of which he was appointed chief justice shortly before his death), and commissioner of customs. The owner of large tracts of land in and near New York City, Van Cortlandt was granted a royal patent in 1697 making his estates a manor. The greater part of his property was an 87,000-acre (35,208-hectare) tract on the east bank of the Hudson River, extending from Croton River to Anthony's Nose. The Van Cortlandt house at Croton-on-Hudson has been restored and is now a museum.

Vancouver, George, 1757–98, English navigator and explorer. He sailed on Capt. James Cook's second and third voyages. After 1780 he served under Admiral George Rodney in the West Indies, taking part in the great victory (1782) over Admiral de Grasse. In 1791, a commander, he set out for the northwest coast of America, charged with a double mission—to take over the territory at Nootka Sound that had been assigned to England by the Nootka Convention and to explore and survey the N Pacific coast. Vancouver rounded the Cape of Good Hope, made new explorations on the coasts of Australia and New Zealand, and visited Tahiti and the Hawaiian Islands. He arrived at the northwest coast of America in 1792 and for three years (1792–94) thoroughly explored and surveyed it. In the course of his journeyings he circumnavigated the island now called Vancouver Island in his honor. After arriving (1795) in England again he began to prepare an account of his voyage for publication, a task not quite completed at his death. His brother, with the aid of Peter Puget, Vancouver's lieutenant, finished the book, which was published as *A Voyage of Discovery to the North Pacific Ocean and round the World* (3 vol. and an atlas, 1798, repr. 1968). Another first-hand account was that of Archibald Menzies; part of his journal was edited in 1923 by C. F. Newcombe. See biographies by G. H. Anderson (1923), George Godwin (1931), and Bern Anderson (1959, repr., 1966).

Vancouver, city (1971 pop. 426,256, metropolitan pop. 1,082,352), SW British Columbia, Canada, on Burrard Inlet of the Strait of Georgia, opposite Vancouver Island and just N of the Wash. border. It is the largest city in W Canada and the chief Canadian Pacific port, with an excellent year-round harbor. It is also the major western terminus of trans-Canadian railroads, highways, and airways. Its location on hills with views of the harbor and the mountains of the Coast Range as well as its mild winter climate make it a year-round tourist center. The city's industries include shipbuilding, fish processing, and sugar and oil refining. It has textile and knitting mills and plants making metal, wood, paper, and mineral products. Vancouver is the western terminus of the tramontane pipeline bringing oil to the west coast from Edmonton. At Point Grey in metropolitan Vancouver is the Univ. of British Columbia. Stanley Park (900 acres/364 hectares), one of the city's many parks, has a zoo and famous gardens and specimens of native trees. The city was settled before 1875 and called Granville; it was incorporated in 1886, after a rail link was built, and named in honor of Capt. George Vancouver.

Vancouver, city (1970 pop. 42,493), seat of Clark co., SW Wash., on the Columbia River opposite Portland, Oregon, with which it is connected by a bridge; inc. 1857. An important deepwater port, it has shipyards, lumber mills, and an enormous grain elevator. Power from the nearby Bonneville Dam supplies its industries; manufactures include aluminum ingots and aluminum parts, paper products, telephone equipment, and sportswear. Founded by the Hudson's Bay Company as Fort Vancouver in 1825–26 (see MCLOUGHLIN, JOHN), it was an important fur center and an early focus for settlement in the state. After the area was ceded to the United States in 1846, the U.S. army established (1849) a fort there; it is still in operation and contributed to Vancouver's importance during World War II, when the city's shipping and manufacturing boomed. Vancouver has a junior college, a veterans hospital, and state schools for the blind and deaf. It is the headquarters for Gifford Pinchot National Forest. Historic attractions include Fort Vancouver National Historic Site (see NATIONAL PARKS AND MONUMENTS, table); Covington House (1845), one of the oldest houses in the state; and the Ulysses S. Grant house and museum, where Grant lived when he was stationed there in 1852–53. A state trout hatchery is nearby.

Vancouver Island (1971 est. pop. 360,000), 12,408 sq mi (32,137 sq km), SW British Columbia, Canada, in the Pacific Ocean; largest island off W North America. It is c.285 mi (460 km) long and c.30 to 80 mi (50–130 km) wide and is separated from the mainland by Queen Charlotte, Georgia, and Juan de Fuca straits. The rugged island, a partially submerged portion of the Coast Mts., rises to 7,219 ft (2,200 m) at Golden Hinde Mt. Level plains extend inland from the eastern coastline. The Pacific coastline is deeply indented by numerous fjords and inlets. The island has a mild humid climate; W Vancouver Island receives the greatest amount of precipitation in North America. There are many lakes and streams but no navigable rivers. The island is heavily forested, and lumbering and wood processing are major industries. Vancouver Island is underlaid by a mineral-rich batholith, from which iron, copper, and gold are mined. Coal is extracted from a depression at the edge of the batholith; the mines at Nanaimo provide most of the coal for British Columbia. Fishing, agriculture, and tourism are other important economic activities. Pacific Rim National Park, Fort Rodd Hill National Historic Park, and Strathcona Provincial Park are there. Population is concentrated along the east coast; Victoria (the provincial capital), Nanaimo, Port Alberni, and Esquimalt (site of a large naval base) are the largest cities. There are many small ports and fishing settlements. Both Spain and Britain claimed the island; it was sighted (1774) by Juan Pérez, the Spanish explorer, and Capt. James Cook was the first (1778) to land there. In 1788, John Meares, an English trader, built a fort on NOOTKA SOUND, which was later occupied by Spanish forces. In 1792 the island was circumnavigated and chartered by Capt. George Vancouver. British sovereignty over Vancouver was confirmed (1846) when the U.S.–Canada line was drawn through Juan de Fuca Strait. Vancouver Island was made a crown colony in 1849 and in 1866 became part of British Columbia.

Van Curler or **Van Corlaer, Arent** (är'ənt văn kûr'lər, văn kôr'lär), 1619–67, Dutch colonist in New Netherland. He came (1637) to the colony to assist in the management of Rensselaerswyck, the estate of his cousin Kiliaen VAN RENSSELAER, and from 1642 to 1644 was administrator. He made friends of the Indians and on several occasions successfully mediated between them and the colonists. Purchasing a tract of land on the Mohawk River, Van Curler founded (1662) Schenectady there. He was drowned in Lake Champlain on his way to Canada.

Vandalia (văndā'lyə), city (1970 pop. 10,796), Montgomery co., W central Ohio, a suburb of Dayton; inc. 1848.

Vandals, ancient Germanic tribe. They originated in N Jutland and, along with other Germanic peoples, settled in the valley of the Oder about the 5th cent. B.C. They appeared in Pannonia and Dacia in the 3d cent. A.D., apparently under imperial aegis. In the early 5th cent., the Vandals began a migration that was to take them farther than any other Germanic people. They invaded (406) Gaul, where the Franks, as allies of Rome, refused them permission to settle. In 409 they crossed the Pyrenees to Spain. After meeting opposition there, they concluded a peace with Roman Emperor Honorius, who recognized their right to the land, subject to imperial authority. While in Spain, however, they continued to fight the Romans and Visigoths and were able to develop their maritime power. In 428, Gunderic, the Vandal king, died and was succeeded by his brother, GAISERIC, whose leadership carried the tribe to its greatest heights. Pressed by the Goths, and taking advantage of unsettled conditions in Africa, the Vandals crossed (429) to that continent and defeated the Roman general Boniface. The tradition that they came at Boniface's invitation is probably false. By 435 the Vandals controlled most of the Roman province of Africa, and in 439 they took Carthage. Their vessels made pirate attacks on ships in the Mediterranean, and they went on plundering expeditions to Sicily and S Italy. In 442, Valentinian III recognized Gaiseric as an independent ruler, and Vandal migration ceased. The next years were spent in building a powerful kingdom. Their fleet controlled the Mediterranean, and even the Eastern Empire felt their power. In 455, Rome was sacked by Gaiseric's troops, and Empress Eudoxia and her two daughters were taken as hostages. The Vandals were Arian Christians, and, especially under Gaiseric and his son, Hunneric, they harshly persecuted Orthodox Christianity. The Roman emperors Marjorian and Leo I made attempts to destroy Vandal power, but Zeno was forced to make peace (476) with Gaiseric. After the death (477) of Gaiseric, however, the Vandals declined quickly as a dominant power. In 533, JUSTINIAN I sent against them an army under BELISARIUS, which after meeting weak resistance captured Carthage. With this overwhelming defeat the Vandals ceased to exist as a nation. The Vandals were not an artistic people, and they left no monuments of their reign. The modern use of their name is probably derived from the fear and hatred felt toward them by African Catholics and a reminiscence of the sack of Rome. See J. B. Bury, *The Invasion of Europe by the Barbarians* (1928, repr. 1967); J. M. Wallace-Hadrill, *The Barbarian West, 400–1000* (3d ed. 1967).

Van de Graaff, Robert Jemison (văn dĭ grăf), 1901–67, American physicist, b. Tuscaloosa, Ala., grad. Univ. of Alabama (B.S., 1922), Ph.D. Oxford, 1928. He was research associate at Massachusetts Institute of Technology (1931–34) and associate professor from 1934. He developed an electrostatic particle accelerator used in nuclear research.

Vandenberg, Arthur Hendrick, 1884–1951, American politician, b. Grand Rapids, Mich. He was editor and publisher of the Grand Rapids *Herald* from 1906 to 1928, when he was appointed to fill a U.S. Senate vacancy. He won election to the seat in the same year. In the upper house he became an influential Republican leader. Before World War II he was generally considered an isolationist, but by 1945 his views on foreign affairs had changed, and he became one of the chief proponents of a bipartisan foreign policy. He served as U.S. delegate to the San Francisco United Nations Conference in 1945 and as a delegate to the General Assembly of the United Nations (1946). As chairman of the Senate Committee on Foreign Affairs (1946–51), Vandenberg was the leading proponent of bipartisan support for President Truman's foreign policy. He was instrumental in securing Senate approval of the Marshall Plan and the North Atlantic Treaty Organization. He wrote several studies about Alexander Hamilton. See *The Private Papers of Senator Vandenberg* (ed. by A. H. Vandenberg, Jr., and J. A. Morris, 1952); biography by C. D. Tompkins, (1970).

Vandenberg Air Force Base, U.S. military installation, 3,456 acres (1,399 hectares), SW Calif., near Lompoc; chief Pacific coast launch site for military satellites. It has an ICBM range on constant standby alert.

Vanderbilt, Cornelius, 1794–1877, American railroad magnate, b. Staten Island, N.Y. As a boy he ferried freight and passengers from Staten Island to Manhattan, and he soon gained control of most of the ferry lines and other short lines in the vicinity of New York City. He further expanded his shipping lines and came to be known as Commodore Vanderbilt. In 1851, when the gold rush to California was at its height, Vanderbilt opened a shipping line from the East Coast to California, including land transit across Nicaragua along the route of the proposed Nicaragua Canal. In Central America he came to be a violent opponent of the military adventurer William WALKER. After the outbreak of the Civil War, he entered the railroad field, and by 1867 he had gained control of the New York Central RR. Although his efforts to gain control of the Erie RR proved unsuccessful, Vanderbilt vastly expanded his railroad empire and by 1873 connected Chicago with New York City by rail. He amassed a great fortune and gave $1 million to found VANDERBILT UNIVERSITY. See biography by W. J. Lane (1942); Wayne Andrews, *The Vanderbilt Legend* (1941). A son, **William Henry Vanderbilt,** 1821–85, b. New Brunswick, N.J., succeeded Cornelius Vanderbilt as president of the New York Central RR and augmented the family fortune. He gave liberally to Vanderbilt Univ., to the College of Physicians and Surgeons (now part of

Columbia Univ.), and to various other institutions. **Cornelius Vanderbilt,** 1843–99, b. Staten Island, N.Y., was a son of William H. Vanderbilt. He took over the family holdings and helped to establish in New York City the Vanderbilt Clinic (affiliated with Columbia-Presbyterian Hospital) and the Cathedral of St. John the Divine. Another son of William H. Vanderbilt was **William Kissam Vanderbilt,** 1849–1920, b. Staten Island, N.Y., who also helped establish the Vanderbilt Clinic. He was a yachtsman, and his wife was a well-known society leader. A fourth son of William H. Vanderbilt was **George Washington Vanderbilt,** 1862–1914, b. Staten Island, N.Y. He engaged in numerous philanthropies, giving to agricultural research and donating land for the establishment of Teachers College, Columbia Univ. He also built the estate "Biltmore" near Asheville, N.C. One of the sons of Cornelius Vanderbilt the younger was **Alfred Gwynne Vanderbilt,** 1877–1915, b. New York City. A noted horse breeder, he went down on the Lusitania. One of the sons of William K. Vanderbilt, **Harold Sterling Vanderbilt,** 1884–1970, born Suffolk co., Long Island, N.Y., gained note as a sportsman. He won the America's Cup yachting races three times. The modern game of contract bridge was largely invented by him. A grandson of the younger Cornelius Vanderbilt, **Cornelius Vanderbilt, Jr.,** 1898–1974, became a well-known writer, newspaper publisher, and movie producer. See his *Man of the World; My Life on Five Continents* (1959). See also E. P. Hoyt, *The Vanderbilts and Their Fortunes* (1962).

Vanderbilt Mansion National Historic Site: see NATIONAL PARKS AND MONUMENTS (table).

Vanderbilt University, at Nashville, Tenn.; coeducational; chartered 1872 as Central University of Methodist Episcopal Church, founded and renamed 1873, opened 1875 through a gift from Cornelius Vanderbilt. Until 1914 it operated under the auspices of the Methodist Church. Major facilities at Vanderbilt include the Dyer Observatory for astronomical research, the Vanderbilt Medical Center, and the Graduate Science Laboratory. Cooperative instruction is carried on with George Peabody College for Teachers and Scarritt College.

Van der Goes, Hugo: see GOES, HUGO VAN DER.

Vanderlyn, John (văn'dərlĭn), 1776–1852, American portrait and historical painter, b. Kingston, N.Y. Under the patronage of Aaron Burr he studied with Gilbert Stuart and in Paris. From 1796 to 1815 much of his life was spent in Paris and in Rome. He achieved a high reputation with such compositions as *Marius amid the Ruins at Carthage* (M. H. de Young Memorial Mus., San Francisco), which was awarded a gold medal by Napoleon, and *Ariadne* (Pa. Acad. of the Fine Arts). He was able to assist his former patron when Burr fled to Paris in disgrace. Vanderlyn returned to America in 1815. His ambitious historical compositions found no market, and his admirable portraits were so slowly executed that few had the patience to pose for him. Late in life he was commissioned to paint the *Landing of Columbus* (Capitol, Washington, D.C.), but was obliged to employ assistants to execute it. He died impoverished and embittered. A self-portrait is in the Metropolitan Museum. The Senate House Museum, Kingston, N.Y., has numerous paintings attributed to Vanderlyn.

Vanderlyn, Pieter (pē'tər), c.1687–1778, American colonial painter, b. Holland. He reached New York c.1718 and became a portrait painter and land speculator and practiced other trades, settling in Kingston, N.Y. The portrait most certainly ascribed to him is that of Mrs. Petrus Vas, his mother-in-law. John Vanderlyn was his grandson.

Van der Meer, Jan or **Johannes,** Dutch painter of Delft: see VERMEER, JAN OR JOHANNES.

Vander Meer, John Samuel, 1914–, American baseball player, b. Prospect Park, N.J. Playing for the Cincinnati Reds of the National League, he established an outstanding major league record in 1938 by pitching two consecutive no-hit, no-run games, the first against the Boston Braves and the second against the Brooklyn Dodgers.

Vandervelde, Émile (āmēl' vändĕrvĕl'də), 1866–1938, Belgian statesman and Socialist leader. He entered parliament in 1894, and served in many cabinets, notably as minister of justice (1918–21), foreign minister (1925–27), and vice premier and minister of public health (1936–37). He resigned in protest when the cabinet, headed by Paul van Zeeland, recognized the Franco government in the Spanish civil war. Influential in Belgian politics and in the European labor movement, Vandervelde played a leading role in the Second, or Socialist, International (1889–1914), serving as the first president of the International Socialist Bureau. He also taught political economy at the Univ. of Brussels from 1924 until his death and wrote several works on political science.

van der Waals, Johannes Diderik (yōhä'nəs dē'dərĭk vän dər väls), 1837–1923, Dutch physicist. It had been known for some time that the behavior of real gases differs from that of an ideal gas as predicted by THERMODYNAMICS and the KINETIC-MOLECULAR THEORY OF GASES. Van der Waals was led to the hypothesis of the continuity of the gaseous and liquid states of matter by combining the kinetic theory of gases with Laplace's theory of capillarity. In his theory of corresponding states (1880) he presented an equation of state (now named for him) for homogeneous substances in terms of pressure, volume, and temperature (see GAS LAWS); unlike the ideal gas law, his equation contains constant factors (different for each real substance) to account for the fact that molecules are of finite size and experience weak forces of mutual attraction (now called van der Waals forces). For that work and for discovering the law of binary mixtures he received the 1910 Nobel Prize in Physics. He was professor (1877–1907) at the Univ. of Amsterdam.

van der Waals equation: see GAS LAWS.

van der Waals forces: see INTERMOLECULAR FORCES.

Van der Weyden, Roger: see WEYDEN, ROGER VAN DER.

Van DerZee, James, 1886–, American photographer, b. Lenox, Mass. The son of Ulysses S. Grant's maid and butler, Van DerZee opened his first studio in Harlem, New York City, in 1909. For 60 years, working in obscurity, he made a visual record of Harlem life unsurpassed in scope and detail. In 1967 the Metropolitan Museum of Art discovered Van DerZee's remaining 40,000 prints and negatives and exhibited many of them. See monograph by Liliane de Cock and Reginald McGhee (1973).

Van Devanter, Willis (văn dēvăn'tər), 1859–1941, American jurist, Associate Justice of the U.S. Supreme Court (1910–37), b. Marion, Ind. He practiced law (1881–84) in Indiana and, after he removed to Wyoming, became (1889) chief justice of the Wyoming supreme court. He had a prominent role in Republican party politics and served as Assistant U.S. Attorney General (1897–1903) and U.S. circuit court judge (1905–10). Appointed to the Supreme Court by President Taft, Van Devanter sternly adhered to the letter of the U.S. Constitution and was one of the quartet of conservative justices who opposed most of the New Deal legislation. After retiring from the Supreme Court, he returned (1938) to judicial service as a U.S. district court judge.

van de Velde: see VELDE, VAN DE.

Van Diemen's Land: see TASMANIA, Australia.

Van Dine, S. S.: see WRIGHT, WILLARD HINTINGTON.

Van Doren, Carl (Clinton), 1885–1950, American editor and author, b. Hope, Vermilion co., Ill., grad. Univ. of Illinois, 1907, Ph.D. Columbia, 1911; brother of Mark Van Doren. He lectured at Columbia from 1911 and was an associate in English until 1930. He was literary editor of the *Nation* (1919–22) and *Century Magazine* (1922–25), managing editor of *The Cambridge History of American Literature* (1917–21) and editor of the Literary Guild (1926–34). His writings include critical works, such as *Many Minds* (1924), *American Literature: an Introduction* (1933), a study of Sinclair Lewis (1933), and *The American Novel, 1789–1939* (1940); fiction, such as *The Ninth Wave* (1926); historical works, such as his *Secret History of the American Revolution* (1941) and *The Great Rehearsal* (1948); and biographies, such as those of Thomas Love Peacock (1911), Jonathan Swift (1930), and Benjamin Franklin (1938; Pulitzer Prize). See his autobiography, *Three Worlds* (1936).

Van Doren, Mark 1894–1973, American poet and critic, b. Hope, Vermilion co., Ill., grad. Univ. of Illinois, 1914, Ph.D. Columbia, 1920; brother of Carl Van Doren. He became assistant professor of English at Columbia in 1920 and was professor from 1942 to 1959. He was a renowned and dedicated teacher; among his pupils were John Berryman, Thomas Merton, Allen Ginsberg, and Lionel Trilling. Van Doren was also on the staff of the *Nation* (1924–28, 1935–38). In 1922 he married Dorothy Graffe, also a writer, who was associate editor of the *Nation* (1926–36). With Carl Van Doren he wrote *American and British Literature since 1890* (1939). He wrote critical studies of various authors, including John Dryden (1920) and Nathaniel Hawthorne (1949), and compiled several anthologies, including *Anthology of World Poetry* (rev. ed. 1936). With Theodore Spencer, Van Doren wrote *Studies of Metaphysical Poetry* (1939), and he collected his own lectures on poetry in *The Noble Voice* (1946); his lectures on Cervantes are published in *Don Quixote's Profession* (1958). As a poet Van Doren was deeply influenced by Wordsworth. Among his volumes of poems are *Collected Poems, 1922–1938* (1939; Pulitzer Prize), *The Seven Sleepers and Other Poems* (1944), *The Country Year* (1946), and *Morning Worship and Other Poems* (1959). Other writings include several novels and a play, *The Last Days of Lincoln* (1959). He also wrote the influential *Liberal Education* (1943). See his collected stories (3 vol., 1962–68) and collected poems (1963 and 1969); his autobiography (1958); the memoirs of his wife, Dorothy Graffe Van Doren, *The Professor and I* (1959).

Van Druten, John William (văn drōō'tən), 1901–1957, English dramatist. His best-known plays, primarily light comedies, include *Old Acquaintance* (1940), *The Voice of the Turtle* (1943), *I Remember Mama* (1944), *Bell, Book and Candle* (1950), and *I Am a Camera* (1951). In 1944 he became a U.S. citizen. See his autobiographies, *The Way to the Present* (1938) and *The Widening Circle* (1957).

Van Dyck or **Vandyke, Sir Anthony** (both: văn dīk), 1599–1641, Flemish portrait and religious painter and etcher, b. Antwerp. In 1618 he was received as a master in the artists' guild, but even before this he produced independent paintings in his studio. For a few years he was the skilled assistant and close collaborator of Rubens. In 1620 he was summoned to England by James I, whose portrait (now lost) he painted. The next year he went to Italy, where he studied the works of the great Venetians and painted a series of portraits of the Genoese nobility. These pictures, many of them still in the palaces of the Doria, Balbi, Durazzo, and Grimaldi families, show Van Dyck's extraordinary gift for aristocratic portraiture. An outstanding example is the portrait of Marchesa Elena Grimaldi (National Gall., Washington, D.C.). Van Dyck returned to Antwerp in 1627 where he rivaled Rubens in popularity and painted a famous series of religious pictures. In his portraits Van Dyck conferred upon his sitters elegance, dignity, and refinement, qualities pleasing to royalty and aristocracy. In 1632 he was invited to England by Charles I. His most successful portraits of the monarch are in the Louvre and in Buckingham Palace. He was made court painter, was knighted, and was overwhelmed with commissions. Assistants were employed to enlarge his small black and white sketches and to paint the drapery from clothes lent by the sitter. With this preparation he was able to complete pictures very rapidly. From 1634 to 1635 he spent some time in Antwerp, where he painted his masterly *Lamentation,* as well as some of his best portraits. The work of Van Dyck differs radically from that of his great master, Rubens, although it is similar in technique. The color is much more restrained, the form more refined, although his best work has an essential vigor which the English painters strove in vain to surpass. In his delineations of English aristocrats, he created a patrician image that greatly influenced the development of English portrait painting. Van Dyck is well represented in the major European galleries. In the United States splendid examples are in the Art Institute of Chicago, the Fine Arts and the Gardner museums, Boston, the Frick Collection, New York City, the National Gallery, Washington, D.C., and many others. The Metropolitan Museum has several portraits including those of James Stuart, the Marchesa Durazzo, and Lucas van Uffel. Van Dyck produced a fine series of etched portraits known as the *Iconography.* The British Museum has an excellent collection of these prints. See H. Gerson and E. H. Ter Kuile, *Art and Architecture in Belgium* (1960); study by L. Puyvelde (1964).

Van Dyck, Cornelius Van Alen, 1818–95, American missionary, b. Kinderhook, N.Y. In 1840 he went to Syria as a medical missionary. In 1846 he was ordained in the Congregational ministry. Besides being the author of textbooks in Arabic and the translator of scientific and religious writings, he translated the Bible into Arabic, completing the work begun by Eli Smith.

Vandyke, Sir Anthony: see VAN DYCK, SIR ANTHONY.

van Dyke, Henry, 1852–1933, American clergyman, educator, and author, b. Germantown, Pa., grad. Princeton, 1873, and Princeton Theological Seminary, 1874. He was pastor of the Brick Presbyterian Church, New York City (1883–99), professor of English literature at Princeton (1899–1923), and U.S. minister to the Netherlands (1913–16). Among his popular inspirational writings is the Christmas story *The Other Wise Man* (1896). The themes of his sermons are also expressed in his poetry and the essays collected in *Little Rivers* (1895) and *Fisherman's Luck* (1899). He translated (1902) *The Blue Flower* of Novalis. See biography by his son, Tertius van Dyke (1935).

Vane, Sir Henry, 1589-1655, English courtier; father of the Puritan leader Sir Henry Vane, the younger. He gained the favor of James I, was knighted in 1611, and acquired wealth by the purchase of profitable offices. He served in every Parliament from 1614 to 1640 and was successively made comptroller (1629) and treasurer (1639) of the household and secretary of state (1640). He also served Charles I on diplomatic missions to Holland (1629-30) and to Gustavus Adolphus (1631). Vane's appointment as secretary of state was opposed by the earl of STRAFFORD. In the latter's trial, Vane, with genuine or pretended reluctance, testified that Strafford had advocated the use of the Irish army against Parliament. As a result he lost favor with the king and was dismissed from office. Joining the parliamentary opposition, he served as lord lieutenant of Durham (1642) and as a member of the committee for both kingdoms. He never became important in the new government.

Vane, Sir Henry, 1613-62, English statesman; son of Sir Henry Vane (1589-1655). Early converted to Puritanism, he went to New England in 1635 and became governor of Massachusetts in 1636. His religious tenets and his support of Anne HUTCHINSON embroiled him in political quarrels, especially with John WINTHROP (1588-1649), and he returned to England in 1637. His governorship was notable chiefly for the founding of Harvard College and the start of the Pequot War. He was made (1639) joint treasurer of the navy, sat in the Short Parliament (1640), and was knighted (1640). Vane allowed a paper of his father's to be copied by John PYM, who later used it in the prosecution of the earl of STRAFFORD, and in the Long Parliament he was a leading advocate of the abolition of episcopacy. As a result Charles I dismissed him (1641) from his treasurership of the navy, but Parliament reappointed him as sole treasurer in 1642. During the English civil war, Vane was a consistent moderate and proved himself a very able administrator. Although he was largely responsible for securing (1643) the Solemn League and Covenant with Scotland, he opposed an established Presbyterian church. An advocate of religious toleration and a constitutional monarchy, he was one of the committee that negotiated vainly (1648) with Charles I, and he refused to take part in the king's execution (1649). Nonetheless, he became (1649) a member of the council of state of the Commonwealth and remained very influential until he clashed with Oliver Cromwell over the latter's dissolution (1653) of the Rump Parliament. In 1656 he was imprisoned briefly for writing the pamphlet *A Healing Question*, in which he attacked arbitrary government. Vane sat in Parliament under Richard Cromwell but, at the fall of Richard's government, argued for the restoration of the Long Parliament. Suspected, probably without reason, of conspiring with Gen. John Lambert to establish a dictatorship, he became generally unpopular. In 1662 he was convicted of treason by the Restoration government and executed. His numerous writings on religion and government include *The Retired Man's Meditations* (1655) and the pamphlets on *The Trial of Sir Henry Vane, Kt.* (1662). See biography by J. H. Adamson and H. F. Folland (1973).

Vänern (vĕ'nərn), lake, c.2,145 sq mi (5,560 sq km), SW Sweden, fed by the Klarälven and drained by the Götaälv SW into the Kattegat. It is the largest lake in Sweden and the third largest in Europe. The deep lake, traversed by the Göta Canal, accommodates small oceangoing vessels. There are vast stands of forest north of the lake; pulp and paper mills line the shore. Karlstad is the principal city on the lake.

Vänersborg (vĕnərsbôr'yə), city (1970 pop. 19,465), capital of Älvsborg co., SW Sweden, at the southwest tip of Lake Vänern; founded in the mid-17th cent. It is an industrial center and a port on the Göta Canal. Manufactures include footwear, machines, forest products, and bricks.

Van Fleet, James Alward, 1892-, American general, b. Coytesville, N.J., grad. West Point, 1915. He commanded a machine gun battalion in World War I, advanced through the grades, and was a colonel at the beginning of World War II. In 1944 he distinguished himself leading his regiment in the landing on Utah Beach in Normandy and was soon made a major general. After heading (1948-50) the successful American military mission to Greece, he was (1951-53) field commander of UN forces in Korea. He retired from active service in 1953 but served (1961-62) as a consultant to the Secretary of the Army on guerrilla warfare.

Van Gogh, Vincent (văn gō, Dutch vĭnsĕnt' văn khôkh), 1853-90, postimpressionist painter, b. the Netherlands. Van Gogh's works are perhaps better known generally than those of any other painter. His brief, turbulent, and tragic life is thought to epitomize the mad genius legend. His work was represented, during his lifetime, in two very small exhibitions and two larger ones. Only one of Van Gogh's paintings was sold while he lived. The great majority of the works by which he is remembered were produced in 29 months of frenzied activity and intermittent bouts with epileptoid seizures and profound despair that finally ended in suicide. In his grim struggle Vincent had one constant ally and support, his younger brother Théo, to whom he wrote revealing and extraordinarily beautiful letters detailing his conflicts and aspirations. As a youth Vincent worked for a picture dealer, antagonizing customers until he was dismissed. Compulsively humanitarian, he tried to preach to oppressed mining families and was jeered at. His difficult, contradictory personality was rejected by the women he chose to fall in love with, and his few friendships usually finished in bitter arguments. Ten years before his death he decided to be a painter, fully conscious of the sacrifices this decision would require of him. His early work, the Dutch period of 1880-85, consists of dark greenish-brown, heavily painted studies of peasants and miners, e.g., *The Potato Eaters* (1885; Municipal Mus., Amsterdam). He copied the work of Millet, whose idealization of the rural poor he admired. In 1886 he joined Théo in Paris, where he met the foremost French painters of the postimpressionist period. The kindly Pissarro convinced him to adopt a colorful palette and thereby made a tremendously significant contribution to Vincent's art. His painting *Père Tanguy* (1887; Niarchos Coll., Paris) was the first complete and successful work in his new colors. Impressed by the theories of Seurat and Signac, Vincent briefly adopted a pointillist style. Two years later, in ill health and longing for release from Paris and what he felt was his imposition upon Théo's life, he took a house at Arles. There he painted with the heavy impasto and rhythmic linear style that is so completely identified with him. At Arles he was joined by Gauguin for a brief period fraught with tension, during which he mutilated his left ear in the course of his first attack of the dementia that was to torment him the rest of his days. The paintings of these months were the most ecstatic and tortured that he produced. They include the incomparable series of sunflowers (1888; one version: National Gall., London); *The Night Café* (Yale Univ.); and *The Public Gardens in Arles* (Phillips Coll., Washington, D.C.). During his illness he was confined first to the Arles Hospital, then to the asylum at Saint-Rémy where, in 1889, he painted the swirling, climactic *Starry Night* (Mus. of Modern Art, New York City). During the remaining two years of his life Vincent was lucid for long intervals. His last three months were spent in Auvers near Pissarro, painting the postman Roulin and the sympathetic, eccentric Dr. Gachet, a physician and collector who watched over him. Vincent's consciousness of his burden upon Théo, by then married and a father, increased. His work tempo was pushed to the limit; one of his last paintings, *Wheat Field With Crows* (Van Gogh Foundation, Amsterdam), projected ominous overtones of distress. He despaired and shot himself, dying two days later in the arms of his brother, whose own life was thereafter destroyed by his grief. In his letters to Théo, Vincent wrote: "I paint as a means to make life bearable. . . . Really we can speak only through our paintings." See his works ed. by J. B. de la Faille (rev. ed. 1970); his *Complete Letters* (tr. 1958); studies by M. Schapiro (1950), A. M. Hammacher (1968), J. Leymarie (1968), and M. E. Tralbaut (1969).

Van Heemskerck, Maarten: see HEEMSKERCK.

Van Horne, Sir William Cornelius, 1843-1915, president (1888-99) and chairman of the board (1899-1915) of the Canadian Pacific Railway, b. Illinois. He worked on U.S. railways before becoming (1881), on the recommendation of James J. Hill, general manager of the Canadian Pacific railway. He supervised its construction (1881-85) and was active in the development of Canadian transportation in general. A naturalized citizen, he was knighted in 1894. See biography by Walter Vaughan (1926).

Vaniah (vənī'ə), Jew who had a foreign wife. Ezra 10.36.

Vanier, formerly **Eastview,** town (1971 pop. 22,477), SE Ont., Canada, at the confluence of the Rideau and Ottawa rivers. It is an industrial suburb of Ottawa.

vanilla, a plant of the genus *Vanilla* of the family Orchidaceae (ORCHID family). Vines of hot, damp climates, they are indigenous to Central America, especially Mexico, but are now cultivated in other tropical regions. The fruits yield vanilla, a flavoring popular since pre-Columbian times, when the Aztecs used it in making chocolate. The commercial vanilla plant is usually *V. fragrans.* Since its natural pollinating agents (certain bees and hummingbirds) are uniquely adapted for this function, commercial plants must be pollinated by hand. The source of the flavor is an aromatic essence, vanillin, which crystallizes on the outside of the seed pod after a series of curing and drying processes. Vanilla flavoring is also obtained from the TONKA BEAN, although now it is most commonly manufactured by the cheaper process of artificially synthesizing vanillin, as from coal tar, clove oil, or lignin, a byproduct of paper manufacture. Vanilla is usually marketed as an alcoholic extract for use as food and tobacco flavoring and in perfumery. Vanilla is classified in the division MAGNOLIOPHYTA, class Liliatae, order Orchidales, family Orchidaceae.

Vanini, Lucilio (lo͝ochē'lyō vänē'nē), c.1585-1619, Italian philosopher, who gave himself the name Julius Caesar. A freethinker, he was persecuted for his ideas and driven from one European country to another. His works, published in 1615 and 1616, caused suspicion, and he was finally condemned and burned at the stake at Toulouse, France, for atheism and witchcraft. A part of the movement to break with the dogmas of scholasticism and the authority of Aristotle, Vanini made a courageous contribution to the foundations of a new philosophy. His writings are available in Italian.

Vanloo (väNlō', vänlō'), family of French painters of Dutch origin. **Jacob** or **Jacques Vanloo,** 1614-70, b. Holland, went to Paris in 1662, where he had great success as a portrait painter. His portrait of Michel Corneille is in the Louvre. His grandson, **Jean Baptiste Vanloo,** 1684-1745, became a popular portrait painter and a member of the Académie royale. He painted the portraits of Louis XV and Marie Leszczynska. In London, where he was highly acclaimed, he did portraits of Colley Cibber, Sir Robert Walpole, and others. He was also known for his historical paintings and frescoes. His brother, **Carle** or **Charles André Vanloo,** 1705-65, enjoyed an international reputation as a decorative painter. He worked on a cycle of the life of St. Gregory for the dome of the Invalides. His *Marriage of the Virgin* and *Halt during a Hunt* (both: Louvre) are good examples of his work. The son of Jean Baptiste, **Louis-Michel Vanloo,** 1707-71, was a well-known portrait painter. He was (1735-46) painter to Philip V, king of Spain, and executed portraits of Louis XV and others in the French royal family.

van Loon, Hendrik Willem (văn lōn), 1882-1944, American author and journalist, b. Rotterdam, Netherlands. He emigrated to the United States in 1903 and studied at Harvard and Cornell (B.A., 1905). He was an Associated Press correspondent in Russia during the revolutionary outbreak of 1905 and in Belgium at the beginning of World War I. His numerous popular histories include *The Story of Mankind* (1921), *The Story of the Bible* (1923), *Tolerance* (1925), *America* (1927), and *R. v. R.* (1930), a fictional biography of Rembrandt.

Vannes (vän), town (1968 pop. 40,724), capital of Morbihan dept., NW France, in Brittany, on the Gulf of Morbihan. It is an important agricultural and tourist center with food-processing and textile factories and flour mills. The surrounding region is noted for its pre-Christian megalithic monuments; Vannes has an archaeological museum (the former House of Parlement of Brittany) containing many prehistoric antiquities. Vannes was the capital of the kingdom (later duchy) of Brittany (9th-16th cent.). Points of interest include the Cathedral of St. Peter (13th-19th cent.), which contains the tomb of St. Vincent Ferrer, and ramparts built during the 13th cent. Francis I (reigned 1515-47) was born in Vannes.

Vannucci, Pietro: see PERUGINO.

Van Ostade, Adriaen: see OSTADE, ADRIAEN VAN.

Van Rensselaer, Kiliaen (kē'lēän văn rĕn'sələr, rĕn'səlĕr''), c.1580-1644, Dutch merchant and patroon, b. Amsterdam. He was a wealthy diamond and pearl merchant and helped found (1621) the Dutch West India Company, later becoming one of its directors. He was one of the first to develop a patroonship in New Netherland, having purchased a vast tract of land near what is now Albany. It was called Rensselaerswyck and comprised a large part of the present-day counties of Albany, Rensselaer, and Columbia. Van Rensselaer himself never visited his estate, which was the largest of its kind, but he sent his cousin Arent VAN CURLER to manage it. His first name is also spelled Killian. See Maunsell Van Rensselaer, *Annals of the Van Rensselaers in the United States* (1888).

Van Rensselaer, Martha, 1864–1932, American home economist and pioneer in the development of extension courses for women in rural areas, b. Randolph, N. Y. In 1900 she joined the faculty of Cornell Univ. to give extension courses in home economics. These courses, with others, developed into New York State College of Home Economics, of which she was a director.

Van Rensselaer, Stephen, 1764–1839, American political leader and soldier, called the Patroon, b. New York City. He spent some years managing his property, which included most of the present-day Albany and Rensselaer counties of New York state, before entering politics. An ardent Federalist, he served in the state assembly (1789–90, 1808–10), in the state senate (1790–95), as lieutenant governor (1795–1801), and as a Congressman (1822–29). His unexpected vote (1825) in the House of Representatives for John Quincy Adams for President, instead of William H. Crawford, to whom his vote was committed, secured Adams's election as President. He was a delegate to the constitutional convention of 1801, a member of the New York state commission that recommended (1811) building the ERIE CANAL, and president (1825–39) of the canal commission. As major general in the state militia during the War of 1812, he commanded troops along the northern frontier and was badly defeated in an attack on QUEENSTON in Canada; he thereupon resigned his command. Van Rensselaer founded (1824) a technical school at Troy, N.Y., which later (1826) was incorporated as RENSSELAER POLYTECHNIC INSTITUTE. See biography by W. B. Fink (1950).

Van Schaick, Goose (gō'sə văn skīk), 1736–89, American Revolutionary soldier, b. Albany, N.Y. He fought in the French and Indian War, becoming (1760) lieutenant colonel of a New York regiment. As a colonel in the Revolution, he led (1779) a successful expedition against the Onondaga Indians. Gen. James Clinton placed him in command of forces completing the Sullivan-Clinton campaign against the Indians in the Mohawk valley. He was brevetted brigadier general in 1783.

Vansittart, Nicholas, 1st **Baron Bexley** (văn'sĭtärt), 1766–1851, British politician. He entered Parliament in 1796, was joint secretary of the treasury (1801–4, 1806–7) and briefly secretary for Ireland (1805), and in 1812 he became chancellor of the exchequer under the 2d earl of Liverpool. He held office for the unusual period of 12 years, during which he had to deal with the problems of economic adjustment following the end of the Napoleonic Wars. A loyal follower of Viscount Sidmouth, he resigned (1823) not long after Sidmouth. He was raised to the peerage in 1823 and remained in the cabinet as chancellor of the duchy of Lancaster until 1828.

Vansittart, Robert Gilbert Vansittart, 1st **Baron,** 1881–1957, British diplomat. After serving in a number of diplomatic positions, he was (1920–24) private secretary to Lord Curzon, who was then foreign secretary. In 1930 he became permanent undersecretary of state for foreign affairs. In this influential position, he consistently advocated an anti-German, though noninterventionist, policy. Vansittart served as chief diplomatic adviser to the foreign secretary from 1938 to 1941, when he was raised to the peerage. He continued throughout the war to advocate a "hard peace" for Germany. See his memoirs, *Lessons of My Life* (1945) and *The Mist Procession* (1958); study by I. G. Colvin (1965).

van't Hoff, Jacobus Hendricus (yäkō'bəs hĕndrē'kəs vänt hôf), 1852–1911, Dutch physical chemist. He taught at the universities of Amsterdam (1878–96) and Berlin (from 1896). For his work in chemical dynamics and osmotic electrical conductivity (which led to Arrhenius's theory of electrolytic dissociation or ionization) he received the first Nobel Prize in Chemistry (1901). His studies in molecular structure laid the foundation of stereochemistry.

Van Twiller, Wouter, fl. 1632–1640, Dutch director general of New Netherland. A nephew of Kiliaen VAN RENSSELAER, he was appointed to succeed Peter MINUIT and arrived in New Amsterdam in 1633. Kind to the Indians but blundering with his opponents, he left (1637) to his successor, Willem KIEFT, a colony fraught with confusion. Van Twiller managed his uncle's estate.

Van Tyne, Claude Halstead, 1869–1930, American historian, b. Tecumseh, Mich. An assistant professor at the Univ. of Michigan (1903–6) and a professor there from 1906 to his death, he became head of the department of history in 1911. Among his books are *The Loyalists in the American Revolution* (1902); *The American Revolution, 1776–1783* ("American Nation" series, 1905); *The Causes of the War of Independence* (1922); *India in Ferment* (1923); *England and America, Rivals in the American Revolution* (1927); and *The War of Independence: American Phase* (1929), for which he was posthumously awarded the 1930 Pulitzer Prize in history.

Vanua Levu (vänōō'ä lā'vōō) or **Sandalwood Island,** volcanic island, 2,137 sq mi (5,535 sq km), S Pacific, second largest of the FIJI Islands. Mt. Thruston (3,139 ft/960 m) is the highest peak. The Ndreketi is the principal river. The large east peninsula is connected with the rest of the island by a narrow isthmus. There are gold mines and sugarcane plantations on Vanua Levu.

Van Vechten, Carl (văn vĕk'tən), 1880–1964, American music critic, novelist, and photographer, b. Cedar Rapids, Iowa, grad. Univ. of Chicago, 1903. While he was a leading music critic in New York City, he wrote *The Music of Spain* (1918) and other critical works. At 40 he began writing novels, the best known of which, written in the sophisticated style of the '20s, are *Peter Whiffle* (1922), *The Tattooed Countess* (1924), *Nigger Heaven* (1926), and *Spider Boy* (1928). After completing his autobiographical *Sacred and Profane Memories* (1932), he turned to photography and distinguished himself in that field. Van Vechten is well known for his efforts to promote better interracial relations. See studies by E. G. Lueders (1965) and Bruce Kellner (1968).

Van Wert (văn wûrt), city (1970 pop. 11,320), seat of Van Wert co., NW Ohio, near the Ind. line, in a rich grain-farming area; inc. 1848. Fabricated metal products, electronic equipment, cheeses, cigars, and woodworking machinery are made. The city is known for its peonies, which blossom all over town during the first two weeks in June. An annual peony festival is held.

Van Zeeland, Paul (pōl văn zā'länt), 1893–1973, Belgian political leader. He was a professor of law and later director of the institute of economic science at the Univ. of Louvain and vice governor of the national bank of Belgium. In 1935 he was made premier of a government of national unity. Given decree powers, he weathered the Belgian economic crisis by stringent measures that included devaluation of the currency. In 1936, he instituted reform and social legislation and suppressed the turbulent Rexists (the Belgian fascists) after proclaiming martial law. In his administration Belgium denounced (1936) its military alliance with France, reverting to its policy of neutrality, and received (1937) a German guarantee of its inviolability. In 1937, accused by the Rexists of political corruption, Van Zeeland was completely exonerated. Nevertheless, he resigned his post. He remained an unofficial adviser and in 1938 vainly urged a conference of the great powers to restore international economic cooperation. In 1939 he became president of the committee on refugees, established at London, and throughout World War II he continued to work for international economic cooperation. Van Zeeland was made (1944) high commissioner for the repatriation of displaced Belgians. A leader of the Catholic party, he later served as foreign minister in several cabinets and also as a financial adviser to the Belgian government and to the North Atlantic Treaty Organization's council of ministers.

Vaphio cups (vä'fēō), pair of gold cups of Minoan workmanship, probably dating from c.1500–1400 B.C. Shaped like teacups and about 3½ in. (8.9 cm) high, they were formed by fastening together two plates of gold, the inner one smooth, the outer in low-relief *repoussé*. The designs represent a bull hunt; on one the bulls are grazing, on the other they are captured in nets. Found in a grave at Vaphio in Laconia, the cups are preserved in Athens.

vaporization, change of a liquid or solid substance to a gas, or vapor. There is fundamentally no difference between the terms *gas* and *vapor,* but gas is used commonly to describe a substance that appears in the gaseous state under standard conditions of pressure and temperature, and vapor to describe the gaseous state of a substance that appears ordinarily as a liquid or solid. Although most substances undergo changes of state in the order of solid to liquid to gas as the temperature is raised, a few change directly from solid to gas in a process known as SUBLIMATION. When heat is added to a liquid at its BOILING POINT, with the pressure kept constant, the molecules of the liquid acquire enough energy to overcome the INTERMOLECULAR FORCES that bind them together in the liquid state, and they escape as individual molecules of vapor until the vaporization is complete. Vaporization at the boiling point is known simply as boiling. The temperature of a boiling liquid remains constant until all of the liquid has been converted to a gas. For each substance a certain specific amount of heat must be supplied to vaporize a given quantity of the substance. This amount of heat is known as the LATENT HEAT of vaporization of the substance. The quantity of heat applied for each gram (or each molecule) undergoing the change in state depends on the substance itself. For example, the amount of heat necessary to change one gram of water to steam at its boiling point at one atmosphere of pressure, i.e., the heat of vaporization of water, is approximately 540 calories. Other substances require other amounts. Liquids can also change to gases at temperatures below their boiling points. Vaporization of a liquid below its boiling point is called EVAPORATION, which occurs at any temperature when the surface of a liquid is exposed in an unconfined space. When, however, the surface is exposed in a confined space and the liquid is in excess of that needed to saturate the space with vapor, an equilibrium is quickly reached between the number of molecules of the substance going off from the surface and those returning to it. A change in temperature upsets this equilibrium; a rise in temperature, for example, increases the activity of the molecules at the surface and consequently increases the rate at which they fly off. When the temperature is maintained at the new point for a short time, a new equilibrium is soon established. The pressure exerted by the vapor of a liquid in a confined space is called its vapor pressure. It differs for different substances at any given temperature, but each substance has a specific vapor pressure for each given temperature. At its boiling point the vapor pressure of a liquid is equal to atmospheric pressure. For example, the vapor pressure of water, measured in terms of the height of mercury in a barometer, is 4.58 mm at 0°C and 760 mm at 100°C (its boiling point).

vapor pressure, PRESSURE exerted by a vapor that is in equilibrium with its liquid. A liquid standing in a beaker is actually a dynamic system: some molecules of the liquid are evaporating to form vapor and some molecules of vapor are condensing to form liquid. At equilibrium the rates of the two processes are equal and the system appears to be stationary (see CHEMICAL EQUILIBRIUM). The vapor, like any gas, exerts a pressure, and this pressure at equilibrium is called the vapor pressure. Vapor pressure depends on various factors, the most important of which is the nature of the liquid. If the molecules of liquid bind to each other very strongly, there will be less tendency for the molecules to escape as gas and a consequent lower vapor pressure; for example, polar molecules that can form hydrogen bonds between themselves, e.g., water molecules and the alcohols, have relatively low vapor pressures. If there is only weak interaction between the liquid molecules, there will be a greater tendency for the molecules to evaporate and a higher vapor pressure. Temperature also affects the vapor pressure. If the system in equilibrium is perturbed by raising the temperature, then according to LE CHÂTELIER'S PRINCIPLE the system should react to relieve this stress; as the temperature is increased, the evaporation process, which absorbs heat, is speeded up to a greater degree than the condensation process, which gives off heat, so that the vapor pressure is higher when equilibrium is restored at the new temperature. If the temperature is increased enough to raise the vapor pressure until it equals atmospheric pressure, the liquid will boil. If the external pressure is reduced, as in a vacuum system, then the liquid will boil much more readily than under atmospheric pressure. This fact is used in the vacuum distillation process to obtain relatively pure samples of liquids with high boiling points. Some solids, e.g., iodine and carbon dioxide, are capable of subliming (going directly from a solid to a gas) at atmospheric pressure and room temperature; thus, such solids also have significant vapor pressures under these conditions. Another factor affecting vapor pressure is the presence of dissolved substances in the liquid or solid; according to RAOULT'S LAW, the vapor pressure of a pure liquid or solid is lowered by the addition of a solute.

Var, department (1968 pop. 555,926), SE France, in Provence. DRAGUIGNAN is the capital.

varactor: see DIODE.

Varanasi (vəränʹəsē), formerly **Benares** (bənäʹrĭz), city (1971 pop. 560,296), Uttar Pradesh state, N central India, on the Ganges River. Although a rail hub and trade center, Varanasi is chiefly important as a holy city. Thought to be one of the world's oldest cities, it is the holiest city of the Hindus, who call it Kasi. There are about 1,500 temples, palaces, and shrines. Few of these, however, date back further than the 17th cent., since Muslim invasions destroyed many Hindu religious sites. The most famous Hindu temples are the Golden temple, dedicated to Siva, and the Durga temple with its swarms of sacred monkeys. The banks of the Ganges in the city are bordered by ghats, or flights of steps, that Hindus descend in order to bathe in the sacred river. Hindus believe that to die in Varanasi releases them from the cycle of rebirths and enables them to enter heaven. About one million religious pilgrims visit the city annually. Varanasi is of importance to other religions also. Buddha is said to have begun preaching at Sarnath, 4 mi (6.4 km) outside the city. The mosque of the emperor Aurangzeb stands on the city's highest ground and is the most notable building of the Muslim period in India. Varanasi is also famous for its silk brocades and brassware. The city is an educational center, especially for Sanskrit studies; Benares Hindu Univ. (1916) is there.

Varangians (vərănʹjēənz), name given by Slavs and Byzantine Greeks to Scandinavians who began to raid the eastern shores of the Baltic and penetrate Eastern Europe by the 9th cent. Their leader, RURIK, established himself at Novgorod in 862, thus laying the traditional foundation for KIEVAN RUSSIA. The Varangians, some of whom were known also as Rus or Rhos, made their way down the Dnepr and established the great trade route from Kiev to Byzantium. In the 9th and 10th cent. they repeatedly threatened Constantinople. During the 10th and 11th cent. they served as soldiers of East Slavic princes, but they gradually merged with the Slavs, adopting Slavic culture. Other Varangians served as mercenary troops to the emperors at Constantinople. Varangian migrations paralleled to those of the Norsemen and Vikings in the West.

Varchi, Benedetto (bānādĕtʹtō värʹkē), 1502?–1565, Italian poet and historian. A protégé of Filippo Strozzi and Cosimo de' Medici, he was commissioned to write the history of Florence. His *Storia fiorentina* (16 vol.) covers the period from 1527 to 1538 and is generally an excellent history, far superior to the usual recollections and commentaries of his day.

Vardaman, James Kimble, 1861–1930, U.S. political leader, b. near Edna, Jackson co., Texas. Admitted to the Mississippi bar in 1881, he practiced law and was a newspaper editor before entering politics. He served (1890–96) in the Mississippi state assembly and was (1894) its speaker. After two unsuccessful campaigns (1895, 1899) for governor, Vardaman was elected (1903) after a campaign in which he exploited the racial prejudices of poor white farmers toward blacks. As governor (1904–8), he increased taxes on railroads and large corporations and initiated prison reforms. Elected to the U.S. Senate in 1912, he vigorously opposed America's entry into World War I. Vardaman's vote against a declaration of war was responsible for his failure to be renominated in 1918. See biography by W. F. Holmes (1970).

Vardar (värʹdär), river, c.240 mi (390 km) long, rising in the Šar Planina, S Yugoslavia, and flowing northeast then southeast in a fertile valley, past Skopje, through NE Greece to the Aegean Sea near Thessaloníki. The Vardar valley forms part of the principal corridor of the Balkan Peninsula.

Vardø (värʹdö), town (1970 pop. 4,095), Finnmark co., extreme NE Norway, on the island of Vardøya in the Arctic Ocean, near the entrance to the Varangerfjord. It is an ice-free port and has fish-processing plants. The northernmost fortress in the world was built at Vardø in 1307 and was rebuilt in the early 18th cent. Chartered in 1789, the town was long the center of a lively trade with Russia and Finland. Fridtjof Nansen used Vardø as the base for his important arctic expedition of 1893–96.

Vardon, Harry, 1870–1939, British golfer, b. Jersey. A former caddie, he became at 20 a professional golfer. He won six British Open championships (1896, 1898, 1899, 1903, 1911, and 1914). Vardon, rated by many as second only to Bobby Jones, was known for his accurate drives and for his introduction of the overlapping grip on the golf club. He toured the United States several times and in 1900 won the U.S. Open. He won over 60 important golf tournaments before retiring in 1934. He wrote *The Complete Golfer* (1913) and *The Gist of Golf* (1923). See his autobiography (1933).

Vare, William Scott, 1867–1934, American political leader, b. Philadelphia. He engaged in machine politics and became (1898) a member of the select council of Philadelphia. He was recorder of deeds (1902–12) and—with his brothers Edward and George—came to control the Republican machine in Philadelphia. He later succeeded Boies PENROSE as political boss of Pennsylvania. Vare served (1912–27) in Congress but, elected (1926) to the U.S. Senate, was barred from his seat on the grounds of excessive campaign expenditures. He wrote *My Forty Years in Politics* (1933).

Varenius, Bernhardus (bŭrnhärʹdəs vərēʹnēəs) or **Bernhard Varen** (bĕrnʹhärt fäʹrən), 1622–50, Dutch geographer. He studied to be a physician, but turned his attention to geography. His first work was a geography and history of Japan, *Descriptio regni Japoniae* (1649); he is best known for his *Geographia generalis* (1650), standard for a century and translated into many languages. Newton took part of it in the production of the English Cambridge edition (1682) and used the work in his teaching. Varenius attempted to define the field of geography as a science and to classify, organize, and coordinate its branches.

Varèse, Edgard (värĕzʹ), 1885–1965, French-American composer. In Paris he first studied mathematics and science but became more interested in music. He then studied composition with Roussel and D'Indy at the Schola Cantorum and with Widor at the Conservatory. After founding and conducting orchestras and choruses in Paris and Berlin, he went (1916) to the United States, where he founded (1921) the International Composers' Guild for the advancement of experimental music. A bold innovator whose early works aroused angry protests, Varèse explored entirely new rhythms and sounds in such compositions as *Hyperprism* (1923), for wind instruments and percussion; *Intégrales* (1931), for chamber orchestra; *Ionisation* (1931), a sonata for percussion instruments and sirens; and *Poème Electronique* (1958), which was performed at the Brussels Exposition. Varèse achieved highly dissonant effects by using the extreme registers of orchestral instruments in combination with electronically produced sounds. In his later years he completely rejected traditional rhythms, sonorities, and instruments, and became a leading proponent of modern ELECTRONIC MUSIC. See biographies by F. Ouellette (tr. 1968) and his wife, Louise (Vol. I, 1972).

Varese (väräʹzä), city (1971 pop. 83,150), capital of Varese prov., Lombardy, N Italy, near the Swiss border. Situated in the Alpine foothills, near several Italian lakes, it is a popular tourist center. Manufactures include silk, machinery, and leather goods. The Este palace in Varese (1768–80) has lovely gardens. On a nearby hill is a church originally founded (late 4th cent.) by St. Ambrose.

Vargas, Getúlio Dornelles (zhətōōʹlyō dôrnĕʹlĭs värʹgəs), 1883–1954, Brazilian statesman, twice president (1930–45, 1951–54). The popular governor of Rio Grande do Sul (1928–30), he ran for the presidency in 1930, was defeated, charged fraud, and led a successful revolt. He established and maintained dictatorial control. A new constitution guaranteeing states' rights and forbidding reelection of the president was altered in 1937; a corporative state, the *Estado Novo,* was established on the model of Portugal. Industrial development and agricultural diversification were encouraged by a strong central government. In 1945, Vargas promised elections, but he was suspected of planning to remain in power and was ousted by a group of army officers. Still popular with the masses, he was elected senator two months later. He was again elected president in 1950, and was inaugurated in 1951. Three years later, under pressure from the army and threat of impeachment, he resigned and committed suicide. See biography by J. W. Dulles (1967); study by R. M. Levine (1970).

Vargas Llosa, Mario (märʹyō värʹgäs yōʹsä), 1936–, Peruvian novelist and short-story writer. Although his works contain much external realism emphasizing the ugly and grotesque, he often delves into the minds of his characters, rejecting both time and space. His works of fiction include *Los jefes* [the bosses] (1958), *La ciudad y los perros* (1962; tr. *The Time of the Hero,* 1966), *La casa verde* (1966; tr. *The Green House,* 1968), and *Conversation in the Cathedral* (tr. 1975).

Vargas Zapata y Luján Ponce de León, Diego de (dyāʹgō dā värʹgäs thäpäʹtä ē lōōhänʹ pōnʹ thā dā lāōnʹ), c.1643–1704, Spanish governor and captain general of NEW MEXICO, b. Spain. As governor (1691–97) he reconquered (1692) and resettled New Mexico for the Spanish after the Pueblo revolt in 1680 had driven the Spanish settlers from the region. In 1696 he suppressed another Pueblo revolt. He was reappointed governor in 1703 and conducted a campaign against the Apache in 1704. See J. B. Bailey, *Diego de Vargas and the Reconquest of New Mexico* (1940); J. M. Espinosa, tr. and ed., *First Expedition of Vargas into New Mexico, 1692* (1940) and *Crusaders of Rio Grande* (1942).

variable star, star that varies, either periodically or irregularly, in the intensity of its light. Other physical changes are usually correlated with the fluctuations in brightness, such as pulsations in size, ejection of matter, and changes in spectral type, color, or temperature. The 20,000 known variable stars are grouped into three broad classes: the pulsating variables, the eruptive variables, and the eclipsing variables. The class to which a variable star belongs is determined by a plot of its light curve, which is a graph of the star's apparent brightness versus time. The light curve reveals its maximum and minimum brightness and gives evidence for periodicity, if any exists. Pulsating variables account for more than half of the known variable stars. They are characterized by slight instabilities that cause the star alternately to expand and contract. This pulsation is accompanied by changes in absolute luminosity and temperature. The pulsating variables can be further divided into the following subclasses: short-term, long-term, semi-regular, and irregular. Short-term variables have well-defined periods ranging from less than one day to more than 50 days. Relatively rare among this subclass are the historically important CEPHEID VARIABLES. These yellow supergiant stars, having periods roughly proportional to their absolute brightness, provide a means of measuring galactic and extragalactic distances. Cepheid variables are classed as either population I cepheids, which are found in the spiral arms of galaxies, or population II cepheids, also known as W Virginis stars, which are found in STAR CLUSTERS (see also STELLAR POPULATIONS). About 600 cepheids of both types have been found in our galaxy. A commoner short-term variable is of the R R Lyrae group; about 2,500 of this type are known in our galaxy and are concentrated in globular clusters. They have periods of less than one day, and all have roughly the same intrinsic brightness. The latter feature, along with their wide distribution throughout the galaxy, makes them another useful distance indicator. The long-term variables are the most numerous of all pulsating stars. They are red giant and supergiant stars with periods ranging from 80 to 300 days. The best known of these stars is Omicron Ceti, also known as Mira Ceti. About every 11 months, it brightens by about 7 magnitudes and then suddenly dims. Semiregular variables are stars whose periodic variations are occasionally interrupted by sudden bursts of light. The best-known example is the red supergiant Betelgeuse, in Orion. Irregular variables show no periodicity in their variations in brightness. The amplitude of their fluctuations in brightness is in general smaller than the fluctuations of the long-term regular variables. The eruptive variables are highly unstable stars that suddenly and unpredictably increase in brightness. T Tauri stars are the least violent of these explosive stars. Novas and supernovas are much more dramatic. Novas are small, very hot stars that suddenly increase thousands of times in luminosity. Their decline in luminosity is much slower, taking months or even years. Some stars are known to undergo repeated nova explosions. SUPERNOVAS, upon exploding, increase millions of times in brightness and are totally destroyed. Fifty supernovas have been observed, but only three within our own galaxy. Eclipsing variables are not true (intrinsic) variables but rather are BINARY STAR systems, i.e., pairs of stars revolving around their common centers of mass. The apparent brightness of an eclipsing variable fluctuates because the orbit of the pair is seen edgewise, so that first one star and then the other regularly blocks the light of its companion. Best known of this type is Algol (Beta Persei).

variation, in biology: see DARWINISM.

variation, in music, a compositional device in which certain features of a musical unit, e.g., phase, are altered while others are retained in a subsequent statement of the unit. Modifications include melodic, harmonic, and rhythmic. Variation is fundamental in Western music, serving to identify the unique features of a composition by partitioning those features. Gregorian chant exhibits much melodic variation, and all music from the Middle Ages through the 20th cent. employs the technique in some form. Specifically the term refers to a musical form, also called "theme and variations," in which the varied item is an entire brief movement. The form originated in baroque dance suites, in which all movements have the same theme, and was popular during the 18th and 19th cent. Bach's Goldberg Variations and Beethoven's Diabelli Variations are famous examples of the genre.

varicella: see CHICKENPOX.

varicose vein, superficial vessel that is abnormally lengthened, twisted, or dilated, seen most often on the legs and thighs. Varicose veins develop spontaneously, and are usually attributed to a hereditary weakness of the vein; the valves in the vein that keep the blood circulating upward toward the heart are usually incompetent. Increased pressure from long standing or exertion, or internal factors such as pregnancy, or lessened support by the tissues surrounding the veins that occurs with aging and obesity causes the weakened veins to dilate. Mild varicosities often cause no discomfort. Persons with more severe cases may develop swelling of the legs, ankles, and feet, and local eczema or ulcers. Mild varicosities may be treated with rest, elevation of the legs, and the use of elastic bandages or stockings. In severe cases surgical treatment (tying off and removing a vein segment) may be necessary. Varicose veins that occur around the rectum are called hemorrhoids, and those that form in the scrotum are called varicoceles.

variscite: see TURQUOISE.

Varkaus (vär'kous), town (1970 pop. 24,307), Kuopio prov., S central Finland, on Lake Saimaa. In an abundant forest region, it is a major timber, pulp, and paper-manufacturing center.

Varley, John, 1778–1842, English painter in watercolor; one of the founders of the Old Water Colour Society. He is best known for his paintings of Welsh mountain country. He was also an influential teacher, an astrologer, and a writer; among his writings are *Landscape Design* (1816) and *A Treatise on Zodiacal Physiognomy* (1828), which was inspired by works of William Blake, a good friend. His work is well represented at the Victoria and Albert Museum and the British Museum.

Varna (vär'nä), city (1968 est. pop. 206,300), E Bulgaria, on the Black Sea. It is a major port and an industrial center, with shipyards and one of Bulgaria's largest cotton textile industries. Other products include foodstuffs, machinery, metal goods, soap, chemicals, ceramics, and household appliances. Varna is also an international summer resort. Founded in 580 B. C. as the Greek colony of Odessus, it passed to the Roman Empire in the 1st cent. A.D. The Bulgarians defeated Byzantine emperor Constantine IV at Varna in 679. The city passed to the second Bulgarian kingdom in 1201, was captured by the Turks in 1391, and became an active seaport under their rule. In 1444 the Turks under Murad II won a decisive victory over Crusader forces led by Ladislaus III of Poland and Hungary, who was killed. The battle of Varna was the last major attempt by Christian Europe to stem the Ottoman tide. Varna was (1854) the chief naval base of the British and French forces in the Crimean War. The city was liberated from Turkish rule in 1878 and ceded to newly independent Bulgaria. It now has a university (founded 1920), a polytechnic institute, a naval academy, an archaeological museum, and ruins of a 5th-century basilica and a 6th-century Byzantine fortress. From 1949 to 1956 the city was named Stalin.

Varnhagen von Ense, Karl August (kärl ou'gŏŏst färn'hägən fən ĕn'zə), 1785–1858, German poet, historian, and journalist. He collaborated with Chamisso and other writers and wrote *Biographische Denkmaler* [biographical monuments] (5 vol., 1824–30). The Berlin salon of his wife, Rahel Antoine Friederike Levin Varnhagen von Ense (1771–1833), was frequented by leading romantics, among them Heine, Gutzkow, and Laube.

varnish, homogeneous solution of gum or of natural or synthetic resins in oil (oil varnish) or in a volatile solvent (spirit varnish), which dries on exposure to air, forming a thin, hard, usually glossy film. It is used for the protection or decoration of surfaces and may be transparent, translucent, or tinted. For oil varnishes a hard gum or resin, often a fossilized plant exudation such as kauri or copal, is dissolved in oil (commonly linseed oil or tung oil) and is diluted with a volatile solvent such as turpentine. Spirit varnishes are commonly made of soft resins or gums, such as SHELLAC, dammer, mastic, or sandarac, dissolved in a volatile solvent, e.g., alcohol, benzene, acetone, or turpentine. Enamel is varnish with added pigments. Lacquer may be a cellulose derivative dissolved in a volatile solvent, or it may be a natural varnish made in the Orient from the sap of trees. Among the varnishes named either for their constituents or for the proposed use are japanner's gold size, cabinet, carriage, bookbinder's, patent-leather, insulating, photographic, shellac, and copal picture varnish. Varnish has been known from antiquity; the Egyptians coated mummy cases with a pastelike form made of soft resins dissolved in oil and applied when warm. Another early use was for coating oil paintings. Stradivarius and other violinmakers used a slow-drying linseed oil varnish on their instruments. See Oil & Colour Chemists' Assoc., *Paint Technology Manual* (2 vol., 1961, 1962); C. R. Martens, *Technology of Paints, Varnishes, and Lacquers* (1968).

Varnsdorf (värns'dôrf), Ger. *Warnsdorf*, city (1970 pop. 13,927), NW Czechoslovakia, in Bohemia, on the East German border. It is a railway junction and has industries that produce hosiery, cotton, velvet, linen textiles, dyes, and wooden articles. The village was known in the 14th cent.; the city was founded in 1849 through the union of six settlements.

Varona y Pera, Enrique José (ānrē'kā hōsā' värō'nä ē pā'rä), 1849–1933, Cuban philosopher and vice president of Cuba (1913–17). Varona was a professor at the Univ. of Havana and was a dominant intellectual influence in Cuba for 50 years. Varona's interests lay in the philosophy of logic, psychology, and ethics. His orientation was towards empiricism and positivism. In logic, he analyzed the ways man thinks and learns, using John Stuart Mill's work on induction as a base. His psychological approach was physiological and deterministic, although he felt that man could avoid automaton status, since through intelligence man can learn to understand and direct laws of causal determination, which is "tantamount to overcoming them." In ethics, Varona wrote that the proper approach is genetic, i.e., man is moral by virtue of being social, and society is a consequence of evolutionary development.

Varro, Caius Terentius (kā'yəs tĭrĕn'shəs vâr'ō), fl. 216 B.C., Roman statesman and general. Consul in 216 B.C., he opposed HANNIBAL at the battle of CANNAE, where the Roman army was destroyed. Probably more blame for this disaster may be ascribed to the Roman system of alternate command than to Varro's incompetence. One of the few survivors, Varro rallied the remnants of his army at nearby Canusium (now Canosa di Puglia). He received official commendation from the senate.

Varro, Marcus Terentius, 116 B.C.–27? B.C., Roman man of letters. Known as the most erudite man and the most prolific writer of his times, Varro is estimated to have written about 620 volumes. He served as Pompey's legate in Spain and fought at Pharsala, but was reconciled with Caesar, who made him director of the proposed public library. At the time of the Second Triumvirate his villa was plundered, and he himself was proscribed. He fled, but was pardoned by Augustus. In his writing scarcely a field of contemporary learning was left untouched. Of his many works only one remains intact, *De re rustica libri III* [three books on farming]. This is one of the most important books of its kind extant from antiquity. Six books (V–X) out of the original 25 remain of *De lingua latina* [on the Latin language], and about 600 fragments from his *Satirae Menippeae* survive.

Varuna (vûr'ŏŏnə): see VEDA.

Varus (Publius Quintilius Varus) (vâr'əs), d. A. D. 9, Roman general. In 13 B. C. he was consul with Tiberius Claudius Nero (later emperor as TIBERIUS) and later was governor of Syria. Although unsuited for the position, he was appointed governor of Germany by AUGUSTUS. In A. D. 9, to suppress an uprising, he led three legions across the Rhine into the Teutoburg Forest where they were massacred by the troops of ARMINIUS. Varus himself committed suicide. This defeat was a major catastrophe for the Romans. It is said that afterward Augustus would start up from sleep, crying, "Varus, Varus, bring me back my legions!"

varve, in geology, pair of thin sedimentary layers formed annually by seasonal climatic changes. Usually found in glacial lake deposits, varves consist of a coarse-grained, light-colored summer deposit and a finer-grained, dark-colored winter deposit formed when fine sediment settles out from the water under the ice cover. Varves, and the pollen they contain, are useful for interpreting recent climatic history.

varying hare, any of several medium-sized hares, sometimes known as snowshoe rabbits, having white fur in winter and turning brownish in summer. They are 18 to 19 in. (45–48 cm) long and have very large back feet and relatively small ears for hares. Varying hares range over the northern half of North America. Most species feed on foliage, twigs, and other succulent vegetation in summer and on bark in winter. The varying hare is classified in the phylum CHORDATA, subphylum Vertebrata, class Mammalia, order Lagomorpha, family Leporidae.

Vasa (vä'zə), Pol. *Waza*, royal dynasty of Sweden (1523–1654) and Poland (1587–1668). GUSTAVUS I, founder of the dynasty in Sweden, was succeeded by his sons ERIC XIV (reigned 1560–68) and John III (reigned 1568–92). John III married the sister of Sigismund II of Poland, and their son was elected (1587) king of Poland as SIGISMUND III. On John's death Sigismund succeeded to the Swedish throne, but his Catholicism led to his deposition (1599) in Sweden, where his uncle CHARLES IX (reigned 1604–11) succeeded him. The house was thus split into a senior Catholic line (in Poland) and a cadet Protestant line (in Sweden), and the two lines engaged in chronic warfare. Charles IX of Sweden was succeeded by GUSTAVUS II; on Gustavus's death (1632) his daughter CHRISTINA ascended the throne. With Christina's abdication (1654) in favor of her first cousin, Charles X, the Swedish throne passed to the ZWEIBRÜCKEN line of the house of Wittelsbach. In Poland, Sigismund III was succeeded (1632) by his son LADISLAUS IV, who was succeeded (1648) by his brother JOHN II. John abdicated in 1668.

Vasari, Giorgio (jôr'jō väzä'rē), 1511–74, Italian architect, writer, and painter. He is best known for his entertaining biographies of artists, *Vite de' più eccellenti architetti, pittori e scultori italiani* (1550, rev. ed. 1568). The standard modern edition is that annotated by Gaetano Milanesi (1878), translated into English by Gaston de Vere as *Lives of the Artists* (10 vol., 1912–14). Vasari is most enlightening in the discussion of his contemporaries and less trustworthy for 14th- and 15th-century artists. His work is the basic source of our knowledge of Renaissance and mannerist artists. A mannerist himself, he executed paintings in the Palazzo Vecchio at Florence and the Sala Regia in the Vatican and made portraits of the Medici. His major architectural works include the Uffizi in Florence and churches and palaces in Arezzo and in Pisa. See study by E. Rud (1963).

Vasco da Gama: see GAMA, VASCO DA.

Vasconcelos, José (hōsā' väskōnsā'lōs), 1882–1959, Mexican educator and writer. He headed (1920–24) the National Univ. of Mexico and, as minister of education under Álvaro OBREGÓN, worked vigorously and with considerable success to establish schools, to persuade the Mexican people of the importance of education, and to raise the literacy rate. For this task he enlisted the aid of prominent figures, notably the poet Gabriela MISTRAL. In 1929 he was defeated in the presidential race and was forced into exile by Plutarco Elías Calles. As teacher, propagandist, and writer, he attracted a large youthful following, and his fierce localism and belief in Latin American culture as the response of a unique mixture of peoples to a unique physical environment had an effect abroad as well as in Mexico. In later years he became an ardent Roman Catholic and a zealous apologist for the Spanish tradition. He denounced democracy and tended to glorify force and racism. Among his well-known works are *La raza cósmica* (1925) and *Indología* (1927). The first volume of his four-volume autobiography (1935–39) is *Ulises criollo*—also the general title for the whole work, which includes *La tormenta, El desastre*, and *El proconsulado*. See biographies by Gabriella de Beer (1966) and J. H. Haddox (1967).

vascular bundle, in botany, the strand of conducting tissue extending lengthwise through the stems and roots of higher plants, including the ferns, fern allies, gymnosperms, and angiosperms. The vascular bundle consists of xylem, or WOOD, which conducts water and dissolved mineral substances from the soil to the leaves, and phloem, which conducts dissolved foods, especially sugars, from the leaves to the storage tissues of the stem and root. The structure of vascular bundles varies among the different plant groups.

vas deferens: see REPRODUCTIVE SYSTEM; VASECTOMY.

vase, vessel of pottery, glass, metal, stone, wood, or synthetic material. The pottery vase was anciently employed as a container for water (a hydria), wine (an amphora), or oil (a lekythus), or for mixing and serving wine and water (a crater). It had one or two handles, sometimes a lip or spout, and frequently a base or foot; sometimes it was pointed to thrust into the ground or was set into a frame holder for support. Large covered vases were used for general storage purposes. The cinerary (cremation) vase, or urn, has been common throughout historical times, a famous one being the PORTLAND VASE. Modern vases are widely used for flowers. Beautiful in form and embellished with incised patterns, modeled or painted figures or scenes, and sometimes inscriptions, the vase became a work of art in early times. Greek painted vases are in form and color among the most exquisite examples of ancient art. Vases or their fragments discovered in burial chambers and through excavations in various countries serve as records of the manners, customs, and history of their peoples. Buddhist and Christian altar objects include the vase, usually of silver or gold with chased or modeled designs of exquisite workmanship. Bronze and brass are much employed for vases in the Far East, as well as porcelain, carved jade, and crystal in China and enamelware in the Satsuma and Kutani vases of Japan. The vase of CLOISONNÉ is also much in evidence in the Orient. The Persian pottery type is famous for its blue-green color, French Sèvres for miniature medallions, English Wedgwood for cameo reliefs, and American Rookwood for rich tones and underglaze painting.

vasectomy, male sterilization by surgical excision of the vas deferens, the thin duct that carries sperm cells away from the testicles. Vasectomy is becoming an increasingly popular method of BIRTH CONTROL: the number of men undergoing the operation in the United States increased from about 50,000 per year in the mid-1960s to about 540,000 in 1973. Excision of the vas deferens is a minor surgical procedure that can be performed in a physician's office in less than half an hour. A small incision is made on one side of the scrotum (the external sac housing the testes) and the vas deferens is located, cut, and the ends tied off. The excision is closed and the procedure is repeated on the other side. After surgery it is necessary to wait until a negative sperm count is obtained before discarding other means of contraception, because viable sperm cells are retained in the seminal vesicles (the pair of storage pouches where sperm is mixed with other components of semen) and along the various sperm ducts. In addition it is usually advised that the patient be reexamined after a year, because the severed ends of the vas deferens occasionally reknit. Sterility resulting from vasectomy is considered to be permanent, since attempts at surgically reversing vasectomy, called vasovasotomy, have resulted in successful impregnations in only 25% of the cases tried. Efforts to overcome the irreversibility of vasectomy have also led to experimentation with the implantation of faucet-like devices that can be made to open or close the sperm duct in a simple operation. Such devices have functioned successfully in animals, but are still considered experimental in humans because of their unproved reversibility, high cost, and the degree of surgical skill needed to implant them. Another option suggested to those undergoing vasectomy is to preserve their fertility by depositing semen in sperm banks. Such semen samples are frozen in liquid nitrogen below −300°F (−185°C) and are considered to be viable for an indefinite period. However, there is considerable debate over the scientific and ethical aspects of sperm freezing, and the practice is still considered experimental. Researchers are also examining the possible negative physiological effects of vasectomy. Some doctors believe that the retention of sperm may upset the body's immunological system. Reabsorbed by the body, sperm products may trigger the production of antibodies that attack newly produced sperm cells, and could conceivably increase susceptibility to certain disorders, like rheumatoid arthritis, that are related to autoimmune reactions.

Vašek, Vladimir: see BEZRUČ, PETR.

Vashni (văsh'nī), same as JOEL **14.**

Vashti (văsh'tī), queen whom Ahasuerus deposed for disobedience. Esther 1.

Vasily III (Vasily Ivanovich) (vəsē'lyē ēvä'nəvĭch), 1479–1533, grand duke of Moscow (1505–33). Carrying on the policies of his father, IVAN III, he rounded out the territorial consolidation of the Russian state, formally annexing Pskov (1510), Ryazan (1517), and Novgorod-Seversk (1523) and gaining Smolensk (1514) in a war with Sigismund I of Poland and Lithuania. In 1525, he forced his childless first wife to become a nun and soon remarried. His older son from this marriage succeeded him as Ivan IV.

vasopressin (văz"ōprĕs'ĭn): see ANTIDIURETIC HORMONE.

Vásquez, Horacio (ōrä'syō vä'skās), 1860–1936, president of the Dominican Republic (1899–1903, 1903–7, 1924–30). A dominating figure in the nation, even when out of office, Vásquez in his third term attempted to continue the material reforms begun during U.S. occupation (1916–24). In 1928 he requested Charles G. Dawes to head a commission to recommend badly needed fiscal changes. He adopted the commission's report, ousted many political henchmen, and extended his term, but was shortly overthrown and exiled by insurgents led by Rafael TRUJILLO MOLINA.

Vásquez de Ayllón, Lucas: see AYLLÓN.

Vásquez de Coronado, Francisco: see CORONADO.

vassal: see FEUDALISM.

Vassar, Matthew (văs'ər), 1792–1868, American philanthropist, founder of Vassar College, b. England. He emigrated to the United States with his father in 1796. In 1811, after his father's successful brewery in Poughkeepsie, N. Y., had burned, the son opened another, which in time became immensely prosperous. In 1861 he founded Vassar Female College, to which he gave more than $800,000; he also contributed to local charities and churches. See his autobiography and letters (ed. by E. H. Haight, 1916).

Vassar College (văs'ər), at Poughkeepsie, N.Y.; coeducational; chartered 1861 by Matthew Vassar, opened 1865 as Vassar Female College, renamed 1867. A leading institution of higher education for women, it pioneered in music and physical education and had the first department of euthenics, devoted to applying scientific principles to living conditions. The school became coeducational in 1969. There are several museums and a fine library with collections relating to printing and literature.

Västerås (vĕs"tərōs'), city (1970 pop. 110,457), capital of Västmanland co., E Sweden, a port on Lake Mälaren at the mouth of the Svartån River. It is the main center of the Swedish electrical goods industry; other manufactures include metal goods, textiles, and glass. Founded by 1100, Västerås was one of Sweden's great medieval cities, with a cathedral (13th cent.) and a fortified castle (14th cent.). Eleven important diets convened there, notably the Västerås Recess (1527), which created the Lutheran state church, and the diet of 1544, which made the Swedish throne hereditary.

Västervik (vĕ'stərvēk"), city (1970 pop. 20,473), Kalmar co., SE Sweden, on an inlet of the Baltic Sea. Manufactures of this industrial center include paper, furniture, matches, and prefabricated houses. There are also shipyards, iron foundries, and fisheries. Gustavus I built a major shipyard at Västervik in the 16th cent., and the city was Sweden's second largest Baltic port into the 19th cent.

Vatel, François (fräNswä' vätĕl'), fl. 17th cent., French chef, famous in the time of Louis XIV. Mme Marie de Sévigné, in her letters, speaks of him as the chef of the prince of Condé and says that on a Friday, when the king was coming to dinner and the fish failed to arrive in time, Vatel committed suicide. The authenticity of this story is doubtful.

Vatican (văt'ĭkən), residence of the pope at Rome (see PAPACY; ROMAN CATHOLIC CHURCH). Since the so-called Roman Question was ended by the LATERAN TREATY of 1929 between Pope Pius XI and King Victor Emmanuel III (negotiated by Cardinal GASPARRI and Mussolini), the **Vatican City** has been an independent state (108.7 acres/44 hectares), with the pope as its absolute ruler. It may be said to correspond politically to the former PAPAL STATES, but its origin is not connected with them. The Vatican City is a roughly triangular tract of land within Rome, on the west bank of the Tiber River and west of the Castel Sant' Angelo. In its southeast corner is the piazza of SAINT PETER'S CHURCH surrounded by the splendid colonnade. North of the piazza is a quadrangular area containing administrative buildings and the Belvedere Park. West of Belvedere Park are the pontifical palaces, and beyond the palaces lie the Vatican Gardens, which make up half the area of the little state. The Leonine Wall forms the western and southern boundaries. In the city of Rome are certain important basilicas, churches, and other buildings to which the Italian government extends the rights of extraterritoriality and tax exemption but not papal sovereignty. The basilicas include San Giovanni in Laterno (St. John LATERAN), Santa Maria Maggiore (St. Mary Major), and San Paolo fuori le Mura (St. Paul outside the Walls). The palace of San Callisto at the foot of the Janiculum also shares the immunity of the Vatican, as does the papal summer residence at CASTEL GONDOLFO, in the Alban Hills outside Rome. The political freedom of the Vatican is guaranteed and protected by Italy. The state has its own citizenship, issues its own currency and postage stamps, and has its own flag and a large diplomatic corps. The civil government of the Vatican City is run by a lay governor and a council, all appointed by and responsible to the pope. The law is the CANON LAW and the courts are part of the judicial system of the church. The only court special to Vatican City is a court of first instance for civil and criminal cases arising in the city. The Vatican is above all the seat of the central government of the Roman Catholic Church. Because of the papacy's vast interest in temporal as well as spiritual affairs, an elaborate bureaucracy has been developed over the course of centuries. The pope's privy council and cabinet is the college of CARDINALS. He may act as he chooses without their consent, but in practice he relies on the cardinals for advice as well as for administration of the church government. The whole administrative body surrounding the pope and responsible to him is called the Curia Romana. The papal court has all the characteristics of a royal court, such as elaborate rituals and uniforms, and complex rules of precedence; however, since the reign of Pope John XXIII (1958–63) and the Second Vatican Council, many of the Vatican ceremonies have been greatly simplified. The bodyguard of the pope is the corps of SWISS GUARDS, founded in the 16th cent. and made up of a small group of Roman Catholic Swiss. Its members wear the splendid Renaissance uniforms designed by Michelangelo. The palaces themselves form an irregular mass of three-story and four-story buildings, built on long plain lines and broken by additions and alterations. The papal residence and offices occupy the portion near the colonnade, and the rest is given over to museums and the Vatican Library. The Vatican museums are among the most important in the world; they are the Museo Pio-Clementino, founded in the 18th cent. and containing one of the world's great collections of antiquities; the Chiaramonti Museum, founded in the early 19th cent. and holding a collection of Greek sculptures and Renaissance imitations; the Braccio Nuovo, considered by many to be the most beautiful of all the museums; the Egyptian Museum and the Etruscan Museum, opposite the Braccio Nuovo; and the Pinacoteca Vaticana (opened in 1932), which contains paintings by Giotto, Guercino, Caravaggio, Poussin, and others. The museums, however, house only part of the Vatican's treasure, for many of the Renaissance and modern paintings are found in the galleries surrounding the various courtyards, such as the Cortile del Belvedere and the Cortile San Damasco. Adjoining the Cortile San Damasco is the building containing the Borgia apartments on the first floor and the Raphael rooms on the second. The works of Raphael and his followers in the building make it one of the most famous artistic monuments in the world. The Vatican Library lies all along the western side of the Giardino della Pigna and Cortile del Belvedere. The principal chapel in the Vatican is the SISTINE CHAPEL, the ceiling of which was painted (1508–12) by Michelangelo. The history of the Vatican as a papal residence dates from the 5th cent., when, after Emperor Constantine I had built the basilica of St. Peter's, Pope Symmachus built a palace nearby. The pope usually resided in the Lateran Palace until the "Babylonian captivity" (14th cent.) in Avignon, France. After the return

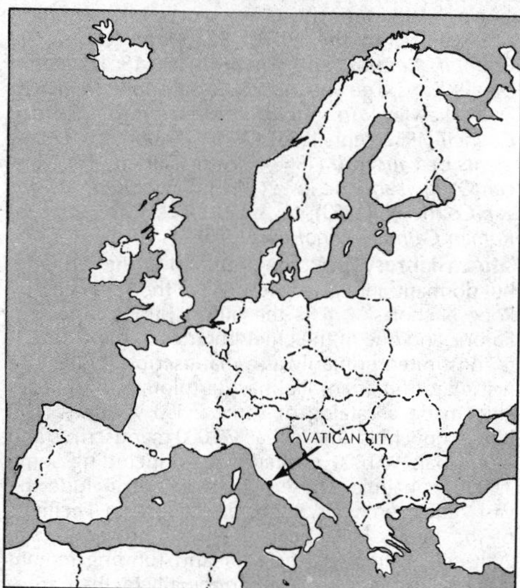

of the papacy to Rome (1377) the Vatican became the usual residence. The Renaissance popes, principally Sixtus IV, Innocent VIII, Alexander VI, Julius II, Leo X, and Clement VII, were great patrons of the arts, and it was they who began to assemble the great collections and to construct the wonderful galleries. Gregory XIII and Sixtus V spent huge sums on the Vatican and also began the Quirinal, a palace that served as the papal residence from the 17th to the 19th cent., was the Italian royal palace from 1870 to 1946, and is now the home of the president of Italy. The Vatican is open to visitors all year, and the pope receives callers in public and private audiences. The Vatican City has its own newspaper (*Osservatore Romano*), railroad station, and broadcasting facility (first established by Marconi under Pius XI). The seven Vatican universities, including the Pontifical Gregorian Univ., are located in Rome. See M. T. Bonney, *The Vatican* (photographs with explanations, 1940); Karl Isper, *Vatican Art* (1953); Bernard Wall, *The Vatican Story* (1956); Robert Neville, *The World of the Vatican* (1962); P. M. Letarouilly, *Vatican* (2 vol., 1954–64); Angelo Lipinsky, *The Vatican* (tr. 1968); Nino Lo Bello, *The Vatican Wealth* (1971).

Vatican Council, First, 1869–70, the 20th ecumenical council of the Roman Catholic Church (see COUNCIL, ECUMENICAL), renowned chiefly for its enunciation of the doctrine of papal INFALLIBILITY. The council was convened by Pope PIUS IX, who announced his intention in 1864. Because of the Italian political situation (the Papal States were the only bar to a united Italy) the advisability of having a council at all was questioned by the Catholic powers, who traditionally opposed strong action on the part of the church. In 1868 it was widely rumored in Europe that the enunciation of papal infallibility as a dogma was the purpose of the council and that it would confirm the papal denunciations of modernistic rationalism and liberalism. As a result there was a widespread attack on the prospective council in non-Catholic circles of France, Great Britain, and Germany. Within the church several prominent persons denounced the enunciation of infallibility as a dogma. Chief of these were Johann Joseph Ignaz von DÖLLINGER in Germany, Lord ACTON in England, and the comte de MONTALEMBERT in France. The council was convened Dec. 8, 1869, in St. Peter's, and it was attended by some 600 of the higher clergy (patriarchs, archbishops, bishops, abbots, generals of orders, and theologians) from all over the world. The Eastern Churches in schism were invited, and the Protestants were officially informed. Late in 1870 the council was brought to a halt by the entrance of Italian soliders into Rome, and a month later the pope prorogued the council indefinitely; it was never reconvened. Two constitutions were promulgated by the Vatican Council and confirmed by the pope. The first was on the faith, consisting of four chapters holding chiefly that God is personal, that man knows God by reason and revelation, that faith is a supernatural virtue, and that faith and reason are complementary, never contradictory. The second constitution concerned the papacy; after defining the primacy of papal jurisdiction it goes on to enounce definitively the dogma of infallibility. This, the one official statement of the doctrine, reads in its significant part as follows: "the Roman pontiff when he speaks ex cathedra, that is, when he, in the exercise of his office of his supreme apostolic authority, decides that a doctrine concerning faith or morals is to be held by the entire Church, he possesses, in consequence of the divine aid promised him in St. Peter, that infallibility which the Divine Savior wished to have His Church furnished for the definition of doctrines concerning faith or morals; and that definitions of the Roman pontiff are of themselves, and not in consequence of the Church's consent, irreformable." Past definitions are included in the statement. In the council there was a long dispute over the enunciation. In the first vote it stood 451 in favor, 88 opposed, and 62 conditionally in favor; at the last vote 433 were in favor of the promulgation, two opposing, 55 abstaining. All the fathers of the council accepted the dogma as true. After the council a great deal of discussion of infallibility took place among non-Catholics; violent attacks were made on the pope, the church, and the council. Within the church the papal infallibility had been generally believed for many centuries. A few groups departed from the church. The most important was the OLD CATHOLICS in Germany, under Döllinger; in France a small group headed by Père Hyacinthe (Charles LOYSON) also seceded. The political results were numerous: Otto von Bismarck gave the definition as the reason for the KULTURKAMPF, and Austria used it as an excuse to abrogate its concordat with the Holy See. The French government denounced it in a memorandum, which was acceded to by Britain, Spain, and Portugal. The anger of the states reflected the chief political effect of the enunciation of papal infallibility: since the doctrine made GALLICANISM and similar claims obsolete, governments could no longer use them to interfere in church affairs. See E. C. Butler, *The Vatican Council, 1869–1870* (1930, repr. 1962); Alvan Ryan, ed., *Newman and Gladstone: The Vatican Decrees* (1962).

Vatican Council, Second, popularly called **Vatican II,** 1962–65, the 21st ecumenical council (see COUNCIL, ECUMENICAL) of the Roman Catholic Church, convened by Pope JOHN XXIII and continued under PAUL VI. Its announced purpose was spiritual renewal of the church and reconsideration of the position of the church in the modern world. The most spectacular innovation of the council, which convened Oct. 11, 1962, was the invitation extended to Protestant and Orthodox Eastern churches to send observers; the meetings were attended by representatives from many of those churches. Another obvious feature was the diversity of national and cultural origins shown among those who attended from all over the world. One of the announced aims of the conference was to consider reform of the liturgy, primarily to bring the layman into closer participation in the church services and therefore to encourage some diversity in language and practice. Great emphasis was also laid from the beginning upon the pastoral duties of the bishops, as distinguished from administrative duties. The procedure at the conference accorded with democratic practice, and there was lively debate between the so-called "progressive" and "conservative" groups. By the time of its adjournment the council had issued four constitutions, nine decrees, and three declarations. The nature of these statements was conciliatory, avoiding rigid definitions and condemning anathemas. Session II (Sept.–Dec., 1963) produced the Constitution on the Sacred Liturgy (permitting vernacularization of the liturgy and stressing greater lay participation in the ritual) and the decree on the media of social communication. Out of Session III (Sept.–Nov., 1964) came the Dogmatic Constitution on the Church (which espoused the principle of episcopal collegiality with the pope), the decrees on ecumenism and on the Eastern Catholic churches, and the proclamation of the Blessed Virgin Mary as the "Mother of the Church." Pope Paul VI opened Session IV (Sept.–Dec., 1965) with the announcement that he was establishing an episcopal synod to assist the pope in governing the church. That final session issued the Dogmatic Constitution on Divine Revelation and the Pastoral Constitution on the Church in the Modern World; the decrees on the bishops' pastoral office, on the appropriate renewal of the religious life (i.e., the life of the religious orders), on education for the priesthood, on the ministry and life of priests, on the apostolate of the laity, and on the church's missionary activity; and declarations on Christian education, on religious freedom, and on the relationship of the church to non-Christian religions (which included an important passage condemning anti-Semitism and recognizing "the bond that spiritually ties the people of the New Covenant to Abraham's stock"). Before the close of the council Pope Paul began to establish a series of commissions to implement the council's wide-ranging decisions. The process of implementation continued into the 1970s. See Hans Kung, *The Council, Reform, and Reunion* (tr. 1961); Henry Daniel-Rops, *The Second Vatican Council* (tr. 1962); D. C. Pawley, *An Anglican View of the Vatican Council* (1962, repr. 1973); W. M. Abbot, ed., *Documents of Vatican II* (1966); Arthur Gilbert, *The Vatican Council and the Jews* (1968); Xavier Rynne, *Vatican Council II* (1968); G. A. Lindbeck, *The Future of Roman Catholic Theology* (1970).

Vatican Library, in Rome, founded in the 4th cent. but dormant until given new life in the 15th cent. by Pope Nicholas V. It is the oldest public library in Europe and one of the chief libraries of the world. It is constituted primarily as a manuscript library. The first major librarian, Platina (Bartolommeo de' Sacchi), made a catalog of some 2,500 volumes. The library now holds more than 75,000 manuscripts and more than 900,000 printed books, including some 7,000 incunabula. These figures do not include the vast Vatican archives, a separate collection. Facilities of the library have been greatly improved in the 20th cent., although the staff and funding remain small. With funds supplied principally by the Carnegie Endowment for International Peace, librarians from the United States did much work (1927–30) in cataloging and classifying the contents of the library. Microfilms of most of the library's great manuscript collection were deposited at St. Louis Univ. in 1957.

Vatnajökull (vät'näyö'ko͞ol), glacier, c.3,150 sq mi (8,160 sq km), SE Iceland; largest glacier in Europe. At an elevation of from 4,200 to 6,100 ft (1,280–1,860 m), it covers a huge volcanic plateau. It descends in some 40 branches into adjoining valleys. Some peaks rise above the ice, notably Öraefajökull.

Vattel, Emerich de (ä'mərĭkh də vätĕl'), 1714–67, Swiss philosopher and jurist. He served (1746–58) as Saxon minister at Bern and later in the cabinet of Augustus III at Dresden. He is famous for one book, *Droit des gens; ou, Principes de la loi naturelle appliqués à la conduite et aux affaires des nations et des souverains* (1758; tr. *Law of Nations,* 1760). This book, founded on the writings of Christian von Wolff, was important chiefly because it supplied a justification for liberal revolution. It also illustrated the growing attention to international law based on natural laws that were superior to positive legislation. See P. P. Remec, *The Position of the Individual in International Law* (1960).

Vättern (vĕ'tərn), lake, 733 sq mi (1,898 sq km), c.80 mi (130 km) long and up to 20 mi (32 km) wide, S central Sweden, drained by the Motala Ström E into the Baltic Sea. It is the second largest lake in Sweden. The Göta Canal crosses the northern part of the deep lake. Visingsö (c.10 sq mi/25 sq km) is the largest island in the Vättern; a prehistoric burial mound is there. Motala and Jönköping are the principal cities on the lake.

Vaucluse (vōklüz'), department (1968 pop. 353,966), SE France, in Provence. AVIGNON is the capital.

Vaud (vō), Ger. *Waadt,* canton (1970 pop. 511,851), 1,239 sq mi (3,209 sq km), W Switzerland. LAUSANNE is the capital. Bordering on France in the west, it lies roughly between the Lake of Geneva, the Lake of Neuchâtel, the Jura mts., and the Bernese Alps. Cereals, tobacco, and other crops are grown, livestock is raised, and wine is produced in its large, fertile central region. There are watchmaking towns in the west. Montreux and Vevey are among its numerous resorts. The population is French-speaking and mainly Protestant. Originally occupied by Celts, the region was conquered by the Romans in 58 B.C. Under Roman rule many towns achieved great prosperity, particularly Avenches. Vaud passed (6th cent.) to the Franks and was under the rule of Transjurane BURGUNDY from 888 to 1032. It subsequently was subjected partly to the prince-bishops of Lausanne and partly to the counts of Savoy. In 1536 it was conquered by Bern and forced to accept the Reformation. In 1798, having revolted under the leadership of Frédéric César de La Harpe against its Bernese rulers, it became the canton of Leman in the HELVETIC REPUBLIC. In 1803 it joined the Swiss Confederation under its present name.

vaudeville (vôd'vĭl), originally a light song, derived from the drinking and love songs formerly attributed to Olivier Basselin and called *Vau,* or *Vaux, de Vire.* Similar to the English MUSIC-HALL, American vaudeville was a stage entertainment consisting of unrelated songs, dances, acrobatic and magic acts, and humorous skits and sketches. From humble origin in barrooms and "museums," vaudeville came to be the attraction in hundreds of theaters throughout the United States from 1881, when Tony Pastor gave the first "big time" vaudeville show in New York City, until 1932, when its greatest center, the Palace Theatre, was closed. Such headliners as George M. Cohan, Harry Houdini, Eva Tanguay, W. C. Fields, Fay Templeton, Will Rogers, Ed Wynn, Eddie Cantor, Jimmy Durante, Irene Franklin, Fred Allen, Jack Benny, and Edgar Bergen began their careers by playing the circuits. There was an invigorating influx of performers from England and France who were a major influence on the growing sophistication and high quality of vaudeville. The popularity of radio and motion pictures caused vaudeville's decline, but television brought about a revival of vaudeville revues. See historical studies by Joe Laurie (1953, repr. 1971); Marion Spitzer, *The Palace* (1969); J. E. DiMeglio, *Vaudeville U.S.A.* (1974).

Vaudois: see WALDENSES.

Vaudreuil-Cavagnal, Pierre de Rigaud, marquis de (pyĕr də rēgō' märkē' də vōdrö'yə-kävänyäl'), 1698–1765, last French governor of New France, b. Quebec. He was the son of Philippe de Rigaud, marquis de Vaudreuil (1643–1725), also governor (1705–25). After entering the army he became governor of

Trois Rivières (1733) and of Louisiana (1742). In 1755 he became governor of New France. Devoted to those who, like himself, were Canadian-born, he nevertheless failed to check his thieving intendant, François BIGOT. During the last of the French and Indian Wars, Vaudreuil sought to discredit General MONTCALM with the home government and to hamper his conduct of military affairs. After Vaudreuil's surrender of all Canada to the British in 1760, he was charged with maladministration, tried in France, and acquitted.

Vaugelas, Claude Favre de (klōd fä'vrə də vōzhəlä'), 1585–1650, French grammarian. He set up, in his *Remarques sur la langue française* (1647), the usage of cultured people as the standard for French.

Vaughan, Henry (vôn), 1622–95, one of the English METAPHYSICAL POETS. Born in Brecknockshire, Wales, he signed himself Silurist, after the ancient inhabitants of that region. After leaving Oxford, where he did not take a degree, he turned to the study of law. Later he switched to medicine and spent his life as a highly respected physician. His greatest poetry is contained in *Silex Scintillans* (1650; second part, 1655), which includes "The Ascension Hymn," "The World," "Quickness," "The Retreat," and "They are all gone into the world of light." Though he openly admitted his indebtedness to George HERBERT, where Herbert celebrates the institution of the Church, Vaughan is more interested in natural objects and in a mystical communion with nature. Vaughan's other works include *Poems* (1646), *Olor Iscanus* (1651), *Thalia Rediviva* (1678), *The Mount of Olives* (1652), and *Flores Solitudinis* (1654). See edition of his works edited by L. C. Martin (2d ed. 1957); biography by F. E. Hutchinson (1947); studies by Elizabeth Holmes (1932, repr. 1967), Ross Garner (1959), and R. A. Durr (1962).

Vaughan, Herbert, 1832–1903, English churchman, cardinal of the Roman Catholic Church. Educated at Stonyhurst College and on the Continent, Vaughan was ordained in 1854 and joined the Oblate Fathers. He was vice president of the seminary at Ware and left there (1861) to go on a trip to America to raise money for foreign missions. The fruit of that labor is a college for foreign missionaries at Mill Hill near London. In 1871 he traveled to the United States to examine the spiritual state of the Negroes, which had always concerned him. On his return Vaughan was made bishop of Salford, E Lancashire. When Cardinal Manning died, Vaughan succeeded him as archbishop of Westminster, the Catholic primate of England; in 1893 he was created cardinal. He improved the position of Catholic schools in the archdiocese and the seminaries of England, and he cooperated widely with non-Catholics.

Vaughan Williams, Ralph, 1872–1958, English composer, considered the outstanding composer of his generation in England. He graduated from Trinity College, Cambridge, in 1894 and took composition with Parry and Stanford at the Royal College of Music, London, as well as organ and piano with several teachers. Although he also studied abroad with Max Bruch (1897–98) and Ravel (1909), his style remained individual and English. Receiving a Doctorate in Music from Cambridge in 1901, he was appointed organist at Lambeth and his interest in English folk music dates from his stay there. He used the folk idiom first in the orchestral piece *The Fen Country* (1904), continuing the same style in the three *Norfolk Rhapsodies* (1905–7). Elements of English music of the Tudor period interested him and are apparent in his *Fantasia for Double Stringed Orchestra on a Theme by Thomas Tallis* (1910) and in his Mass in G Minor (1923). His full orchestral works include *A London Symphony* (1914; revised 1920), *A Pastoral Symphony* (1921), and the important Sixth Symphony (1947). Among his many vocal compositions are the song cycles *On Wenlock Edge* (1909, texts by A. E. Housman) and *Five Mystical Songs* (1911, texts by George Herbert). In his opera *Sir John in Love* (1929; based on Shakespeare's *Merry Wives of Windsor*), he incorporated the traditional song "Greensleeves," which he also transformed into various instrumental arrangements. Other operas include *Hugh the Drover* (1924), *Riders to the Sea* (1937; from the play by J. M. Synge), and *The Pilgrim's Progress* (1951; libretto after John Bunyan). See his *National Music* (1934) and *The Making of Music* (1955); biographies by James Day (1961), Ursula Vaughan Williams (1964), and pictorial biography by J. E. Lunn and Ursula Vaughan Williams (1971); studies by E. S. Schwartz (1964) and Michael Kennedy (1964, repr. 1971).

vault, ceiling over a room, formed in any one of a variety of curved shapes. A vault is generally composed of separate units of material, such as bricks, tiles, or blocks of stone, so shaped or cut that when assembled they form a tightly wedged and stable construction whose weight can be concentrated upon the proper supports. Vaults are also formed in a homogeneous material, as when built in concrete. In modern work, ceilings in the form of masonry vaults are often merely of plaster applied against a curved framework of wood or metal. Vaults constructed of numerous blocks of material pressing against one another exert not only the accumulated downward weight of the material and of any superimposed load but also a side thrust or tendency to spread. To avoid collapse, adequate resistance against this thrust must thus be concentrated at the haunches (lower portions) of the vault. The resistance may take the form of thickened walls at the haunches; of BUTTRESSES placed at points of concentrated thrust as in Romanesque and Gothic architecture; or of vaults so placed that their thrusts oppose and counteract. This necessity has controlled the evolution of masonry vaulting and its use in buildings. In ancient Egypt brick vaulting was used, chiefly for drains. The Chaldeans and Assyrians used vaults for the same purpose but seem also to have made architectural use of high DOMES and barrel vaults. The Greeks made no use of vaults. The vaulting technique of the Etruscans was absorbed by the Romans, who started in the 1st cent. A.D. the development of a mature vaulting system. Casting concrete in one solid mass, the Romans created vaults of perfect rigidity, devoid of external thrust, and requiring no buttresses. Thus vaults and domes could be easily erected over vast spaces, producing the impressive and complex thermae, amphitheaters, and basilicas. The Roman vaults were the basis on which more complex and varied forms were developed in the Middle Ages. The tunnel, or barrel, vault spans between two walls, like a continuous arch. The cross, or groined, vault is formed by the intersection at right angles of two barrel vaults, producing a surface that has arched openings for its four sides and concentration of load at the four corner points of the square or rectangle. The semicircular arch was universally employed in Romanesque vaulting throughout Europe, and the Roman cross vault was the type used for covering square or rectangular compartments. Ribs to strengthen the groins and sides of a cross vault were first employed in the Church of Sant'Ambrogio, Milan (11th cent.). When the system of using ribs to form a complete organic supporting skeleton was developed, it became one of the basic principles of perfected Gothic architecture. The use of ribs led to increasing complexity beginning in the 12th cent., in vault forms. The pointed arch, which was dominant in medieval architecture from the 13th cent. onward, helped to overcome the difficulties of vaulting oblong compartments exclusively with semicircular sections and to bring the various ribs of unequal spans to a crown at the same height. Some vaulting compartments or bays were divided by ribs into six segments and were known as sexpartite vaults, but the four-part vault generally prevailed. In England the multiplication of ribs for structural and decorative purposes culminated in the 15th cent. in the elaborate fan vault of the Perpendicular style. The architects of the Renaissance and baroque abandoned Gothic methods and returned to the basic Roman vault forms, to which new devices were added, including barrel vaults of semi-elliptical section, domes mounted on drums, and cross vaults with groins of elliptical section. In modern times reinforced concrete produces lightweight vaults devoid of thrust. Since antiquity, vault surfaces have been enriched at various times in diverse ways, with coffers, carvings, plaster decorations, mosaics, or frescoes. See John Fitchen, *The Construction of Gothic Cathedrals* (1961).

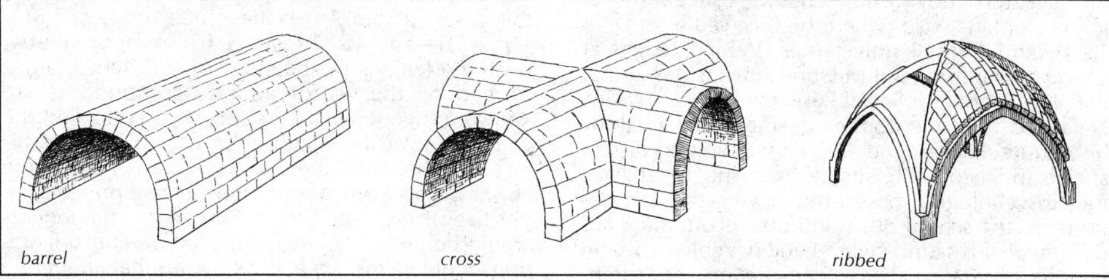

Vaults

Vaux, Calvert (vôks), 1824–95, American landscape architect, b. London. He emigrated (1857) to the United States with A. J. Downing, with whom he was first associated. Later he worked with Frederick Law Olmsted and with him developed Central Park in New York City, the state reservation at Niagara Falls, N.Y., Prospect Park in Brooklyn, N.Y., and other parks. He made the plans for the Metropolitan Museum and the American Museum of Natural History. Vaux was a member of many important commissions. His published work includes *Villas and Cottages: a Series of Designs Prepared for Execution in the United States* (1857).

Vavilov, Nikolai Ivanovich (nyĭkəlī' ēvä'nəvĭch vəvē'ləf), 1887–1943?, Russian botanist and geneticist. He is reported to have died in a Soviet concentration camp after losing political favor to Trofim Lysenko, whose theories he opposed. He served earlier as professor at the Leningrad Agricultural Institute and as director of the All-Union Institute of Plant Industry. In 1918 he discovered in Transcaucasia a variety of wheat that grows at an altitude of nearly 3,000 ft (914 m) and is resistant to rust and mildew. His genetic study of wheat variations led to an attempt to trace the locales of origin of various crops by determining the areas in which the greatest number and diversity of their species are to be found. In 1936 he reported that his studies indicated Ethiopia and Afghanistan as the birthplaces of agriculture and hence of civilization. Vavilov divided cultivated plants into those that were domesticated from wild forms, e.g., oats and rye, and those known only in the cultivated form, e.g., corn. Since the ouster of Lysenko, Vavilov's work has regained prestige in the Soviet Union. His *Immunity of Plants to Infectious Diseases* (1918) includes a summary in English.

Vavilov, Sergei Ivanovich (syĭrgā' ēvä'nəvĭch), 1891–1951, Russian physicist. In 1932 he became director of the P. N. Lebedev Physical Institute, which he organized around the laboratory of the Soviet Academy of Sciences. In 1945 he became president of the academy. He is known for his work in radiation, luminescence, the creation of cold light through the conversion of ultraviolet rays, and optics.

Växjö (vĕk'shö"), city (1970 pop. 36,467), capital of Kronoberg co., S Sweden. Manufactures include textiles, machines, sporting goods, and furniture. An old city, Växjö became the seat of a bishop c.1170 and was chartered in 1342. It has an impressive cathedral (12th cent.) and the Småland Museum, which contains a notable collection of glassware.

Vaygach or **Vaigach** (both: vīgäch'), island, 1,312 sq mi (3,398 sq km), Nenets National Okrug, off NE European USSR, in the Arctic Ocean, between the mainland and Novaya Zemlya. A continuation of the Pay-Khoy range, the island is covered with tundra and has zinc, copper, and lead deposits. Two settlements, Vaygach and Varnet, are on the island. It is named after the Russian mariner who discovered it in the 16th cent.

Vazov, Ivan (ĭvän' vä'zôf), 1850–1921, Bulgarian poet, novelist, and playwright, the first professional man of letters in Bulgaria. His work was inspired by the political upheavals of the period from 1890 to 1920 and by indignation over the sufferings of his countrymen before their liberation from Turkish rule. *Under Our Heaven* (1900), *Songs of Macedonia* (1914), and *It Will Not Perish* (1920) contain some of his best poetry. His novel *Under the Yoke* (1893, tr. 1893) is internationally famous. *Vagabonds* (1894) is his best-known play. Among his other works are the novels *New Country* (1894) and *The Empress of Kazalar* (1902) and the plays *Borislav* (1909) and *Ivaylo* (1911). Vazov's patriotic views forced him to flee Bulgaria many times.

veal, flesh of a calf from two to three months old weighing usually less than 300 lb (135 kg). Veal is obtained from specially bred calves who are fed a diet lacking herbaceous food but high in protein; this produces the desired white color of good veal. It contains gelatin in large proportion and is therefore excellent for making soup stock. Flesh from week-old calves disposed of by the dairy industry is used in certain meat products but is not, properly speaking, veal. Veal is sold almost entirely as fresh meat. The main cuts are the leg, loin, ribs (or rack), shoulder, and breast. The brains, liver, kidneys, sweetbreads, and tongue are considered delicacies.

Veblen, Thorstein (thôr'stĭn vĕb'lən), 1857–1929, American economist and social critic, b. Cato Township, Wis. Of Norwegian parentage, he spent his first 17 years in Norwegian-American farm communities. After studying at Carleton College and at Johns Hopkins, Yale (where he received a Ph.D. in 1884), and Cornell universities, Veblen taught at Chicago, Stanford, and Missouri universities and at the New School for Social Research, New York City. Detached from the dominant American society by his cultural background, Veblen was able to dissect social and economic institutions and to analyze their psychological bases, thus laying the foundations for the school of institutional economics. His dry, involved, satiric style enabled Veblen to coin famous phrases such as "conspicuous consumption." In his criticism of the price system, his analysis of the business cycle, and his interpretation of the role of technical men in modern society, there are implications for social engineering. Veblen did not achieve popular acclaim in his time but has since exerted an increasingly pervasive and profound influence. His works include *The Theory of the Leisure Class* (1899), *The Theory of Business Enterprise* (1904), *The Engineers and the Price System* (1921), and *Absentee Ownership and Business Enterprise in Recent Times* (1923). He also translated *The Laxdoela Saga* (1925) from the Icelandic. *Essays in Our Changing Order* was published in 1934. Anthologies of his writings have been edited with introductions by W. C. Mitchell (1936) and Max Lerner (1948). See selected writings ed. by W. C. Mitchell (1936, repr. 1964) and Max Lerner (1950). See also biographies by Joseph Dorfman (1934, repr. 1966), J. A. Hobson (1936, repr. 1971), and D. F. Dowd (1964); studies by R. V. Teggert (1932, repr. 1966), D. F. Dowd, ed. (1958), and C. C. Qualey, ed. (1968); J. S. Gambs, *Beyond Supply and Demand* (1946).

Vecchietta, Il: see LORENZO DI PIETRO.

Vecchio, Il: see AMATO, GIOVANNI ANTONIO D'.

Vecellio: see TITIAN.

vector, quantity having both magnitude and direction; it may be represented by a directed line segment. Many physical quantities are vectors, e.g., force, velocity, and momentum. Thus, in specifying a force, one must state not only how large it is but also in what direction it acts. The simplest representation of a vector is as an arrow connecting two

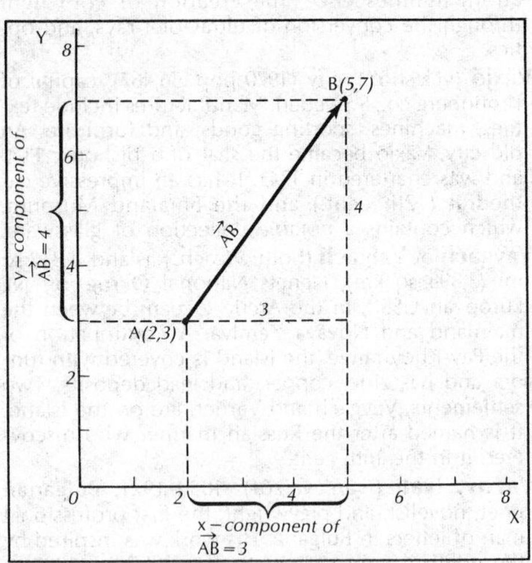

The components of the vector $\vec{AB}$ are given by its projections on each of the coordinate axes.

points. Thus, $\vec{AB}$ designates the vector represented by an arrow from point A to point B, while $\vec{BA}$ designates a vector of equal magnitude in the opposite direction, from B to A. In order to compare vectors and to operate on them mathematically, however, it is necessary to have some reference system that determines scale and direction. CARTESIAN COORDINATES are often used for this purpose. In the plane, two axes and unit lengths along each axis serve to determine magnitude and direction throughout the plane. For example, if the point A mentioned above has coordinates (2,3) and the point B coordinates (5,7), the size and position of the vector are thus determined. The size of the vector in the x-direction is found by projecting the vector onto the x-axis, i.e., by dropping perpendicular line segments to the x-axis. The length of this projection is simply the difference between the x-coordinates of the two points A and B, or $5-2=3$. This is called the x-component of the vector. Similarly, the y-component of the vector is found to be $7-3=4$. A vector is frequently expressed by giving its components with respect to the coordinate axes; thus, our vector becomes [3,4]. Knowledge of the components of a vector enables one to compute its magnitude—in this case, 5, from the Pythagorean theorem $[(3^2+4^2)^{1/2}=5)]$—and its direction from trigonometry, once the lengths of the sides of the right triangle formed by the vector and its components are known. (Trigonometry can also be used to find the component of the vector as projected in some direction other than the x-axis or y-axis.) Since the vector points from A to B, both its components are positive; if it pointed from B to A, its components would be $[-3,-4]$ but its magnitude and orientation would be the same. It is obvious that an infinite number of vectors can have the same components [3,4], since there are an infinite number of pairs of points in the plane with x- and y-coordinates whose

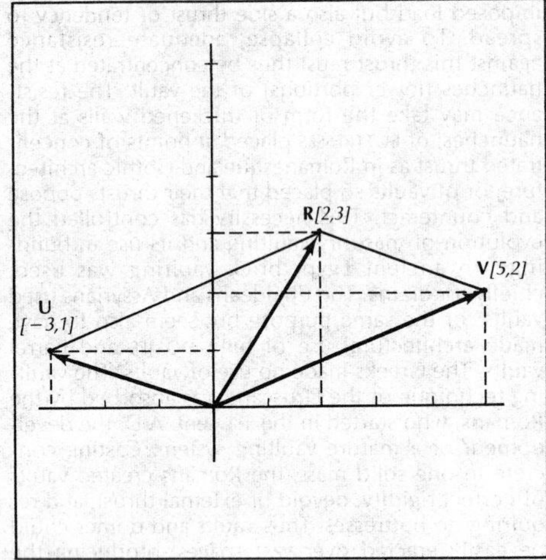

Addition, or composition, of the vectors **U**$[-3,1]$ *and* **V**$[5,2]$ *to form the resultant vector* **R**$[2,3]$.

respective differences are 3 and 4. All these vectors have the same magnitude and direction, being parallel to one another, and are considered equal. Thus, any vector with components a and b can be considered as equal to the vector [a,b] directed from the origin (0,0) to the point (a,b). The addition, or composition, of two vectors can be accomplished either algebraically or graphically. For example, to add the two vectors **U** $[-3,1]$ and **V** [5,2], one can add their corresponding components to find the resultant vector **R** [2,3], or one can graph **U** and **V** on a set of coordinate axes and complete the parallelogram formed with **U** and **V** as adjacent sides to obtain **R** as the diagonal from the common vertex of **U** and **V**. The concept of a vector can be extended to three or more dimensions. Two different kinds of multiplication are defined for vectors in three dimensions. The scalar, or dot, product of two vectors, **A** and **B**, is a scalar, or quantity that has a magnitude but no direction, rather than a vector, and is equal to the product of the magnitudes of **A** and **B** and the cosine of the angle θ between them, or $\mathbf{A}\cdot\mathbf{B}=|\mathbf{A}||\mathbf{B}|\cos\theta$. The vector, or cross, product of **A** and **B** is a vector, $\mathbf{A}\times\mathbf{B}$, whose magnitude is equal to $|\mathbf{A}||\mathbf{B}|\sin\theta$ and whose orientation is perpendicular to both **A** and **B** and pointing in the direction in which a right-hand screw would advance if turned from **A** to **B** through the angle θ. The vector product is an example of a kind of multiplication that does not follow the COMMUTATIVE LAW, since $\mathbf{A}\times\mathbf{B}=-\mathbf{B}\times\mathbf{A}$. The components of a vector need not be constants but can also be variables and FUNCTIONS of variables. For example, the position of a body moving through space can be described by a vector whose x, y, and z components are each functions of time. The methods of the CALCULUS may be applied to such vector functions, leading to the branch of mathematics known as vector analysis. The more general extension of vectors leads to the concept of a vector space. A vector space is a set of elements, **A**, **B**, **C**, . . ., called vectors, for which the operations of addition of vectors and multiplication of a vector by a scalar are defined and which satisfies ten axioms relating to such properties as closure under both operations, associativity, commutativity, and existence of a zero vector, an additive inverse (negative of a vector), and a unit scalar. See J. H. Taylor, *Vector Analysis* (1939); R. M. Thrall and Leonard Tornheim, *Vector Spaces and Matrices* (1957, repr. 1970).

Veda (vā'də, vē'də) [Sanskrit,=knowledge, cognate with English *wit* from a root *know*], oldest scriptures of HINDUISM and the most ancient religious texts in an Indo-European language. The authority of the Veda as stating the essential truths of Hinduism is still accepted to some extent by all Hindus. The Veda is the literature of the ARYANS who invaded NW India c.1500 B.C. and pertains to the fire sacrifice that constituted their religion. The Vedic hymns were probably first compiled after a period of about 500 years during which the invaders assimilated various native religious ideas. The end of the Vedic period is about 500 B.C. Tradition ascribes the authorship of the hymns to inspired seer-poets (*rishis*). Composed according to an advanced poetic technique and complex metrical system, the Veda consists of four types of literature: *Samhita, Brahmana, Aranyaka,* and UPANISHAD. Most important are the four *Samhitas,* which are the basic Vedas. The earliest is the *Rig-Veda* (*rig*=stanza of praise), a collection of 1,028 hymns. The *Sama-Veda* (*saman*=chant) consists of stanzas taken from the *Rig-Veda* meant to be sung to fixed melodies. The *Yajur-Veda* (*yajus*=sacrificial prayer), compiled a century or two later than the *Rig-Veda,* contains prose and verse formulas that were to be pronounced by the priest performing the manual part of the sacrifice. These three Vedas were recognized as canonical and called *Trayi Vidya* [the threefold knowledge]. The *Atharva-Veda* (*atharvan*=charm), written at a later period, was included in the canon only after a long struggle. Influenced by popular religion, it included spells and incantations for the practice of magic. Each of these Vedas was taught in different schools, and each school produced commentarial literature. The *Brahmanas* are prose explanations of the sacrifice, while the *Aranyakas,* or forest treatises, give instruction for the mental performance of the sacrifice through meditation, thus forming a transition to the *Upanishads,* works of mysticism and speculation. In the Vedic sacrifice a god or gods are invoked by the hymns or MANTRAS. Offerings of food, butter, or SOMA are prepared and offered to the fire, which as an intermediary god, conveys these to the other gods. The total number of Vedic gods is said to be 33, although more than this number are actually mentioned in the Veda. The three main kinds of gods are celestial, atmospheric, and terrestrial. Their attributes shift, and one god can be identified with another or take on his powers. The most important gods are Agni, the fire god, who plays a central role in the sacrifice, and Indra, the warrior god and thunder god, celebrated for his slaying of the drought demon Vritra. Several solar deities are found, including Surya, Savitri, Pushan, and VISHNU. Varuna is the all-seeing god of justice, guardian of the cosmic order or *rita.* Soma personifies the plant whose intoxicating juice was offered as an oblation. With the passage of time the sacrifice became increasingly elaborate, and priests became highly skilled specialists. The conception of the sacrifice's meaning also developed. Correlations were made between parts of the sacrifice and of the cosmos. The sacrifice came to be regarded as the fundamental agency of creation, embodied in brahman, the mystical power of speech in the mantras. Theories of cosmogony and the idea of a single underlying reality found clear expression in philosophical hymns and the later interpretive works. See Maurice Bloomfield, *The Religion of the Veda* (1908, repr. 1973); A. B. Keith, *The Religion and Philosophy of the Vedas and Upanishads* (1923, repr. 1971); Moriz Winternitz, *History of Indian Literature* (3 vol., tr. 1927–33); R. C. Majumdar, *The Vedic Age* (1951, repr. 1957); E. V. Arnold, *The Rigveda* (1960, repr. 1972).

Vedanta (vĭdän'tə, -dăn'-), one of the six classical systems of INDIAN PHILOSOPHY. The term "Vedanta" has the literal meaning "the end of the Veda" and refers both to the teaching of the UPANISHADS, which constitute the last section of the VEDA, and to the knowledge of its ultimate meaning. By extension it is the name given to those philosophical schools that base themselves on the *Brahma Sutras* (also called the *Vedanta Sutras*) of Badarayana (early centuries A.D.), which summarize the Upanishadic doctrine. The best-known and most influential of the schools of Vedanta is that of Shankara (A.D. 788–820), known as the non-dualist or *advaita* Vedanta. Shankara attempted to show that the teaching of the Upanishads was a self-consistent whole. According to Shankara, the ultimate reality is Brahman or the Self, which is pure reality, pure consciousness, and pure bliss. The world has come into being from Brahman and is wholly dependent on it. The criteria of reality are immutability and permanence. Since the world is constantly changing, and since its existence is not absolute but dependent on Brahman, the world is called illusion or MAYA. Brahman exists as the Absolute, without qualities (*nirguna*), and also exists with qualities (*saguna*) as a personal god, *Ishvara*, who presides over the world of appearance. Shankara divided the Veda into two sections, that dealing with duties and ritual actions (*karmakanda*) and that dealing with knowledge of reality (*jnanakanda*) contained in the Upanishads. Spiritual liberation is achieved not by ritual action, which is for those of inferior spiritual capacity, but by eradication of the ignorance (*avidya*) that sees the illusory multiplicity of the world as real, and by attainment of knowledge of the Self. The qualified non-dualism or *vishishtadvaita* of Ramanuja (1017–1137) argued against Shankara, holding that Brahman is not devoid of qualities, but rather is the possessor of divine qualities. The world and individual souls are not illusion, but have intrinsic reality, although they are dependent on God. Ramanuja, a worshipper of VISHNU, advocated devotion or BHAKTI as a means of salvation. The dualist or *dvaita* Vedanta of Madhva (1197–1276) attacked the monistic followers of Shankara and defended a pluralist standpoint. He asserted the permanently separate reality of the world, souls, and God, who is identified with Vishnu. Vedanta in one or the other of its forms has had a pervasive influence on the intellectual and religious life of India, and it is still a living tradition. Well-known modern Vedantists include Sarvepalli RADHAKRISHNAN, Swami VIVEKANANDA, and Aurobindo GHOSE (Sri Aurobindo). See bibliography under INDIAN PHILOSOPHY.

Vedder, Elihu, 1836–1923, American painter, illustrator, and author, b. New York City, studied in Paris. From 1867 his permanent residence was Rome. He often used romantic landscape as a setting for allegorical images. Among his works are *The African Sentinel* and *The Pleiades* (Metropolitan Mus.) and *The Keeper of the Threshold* (Carnegie Inst., Pittsburgh). He is known for his illustrations for Fitzgerald's translation of *The Rubaiyat.* His symbolic and decorative murals include five lunettes representing good and bad government (Library of Congress). He wrote *Digressions of V.* (1910), *Miscellaneous Moods in Verse* (1914), and *Doubt and Other Things* (1923). See biography by Regina Soria (1971).

Veen, Maarten van: see HEEMSKERCK.

veery: see THRUSH.

Vega, Garcilaso de la, called **the Inca:** see GARCILASO DE LA VEGA.

Vega (vā'gə), brightest star in the constellation LYRA; Bayer designation Alpha Lyrae; 1970 position R.A. $18^h35.9^m$, Dec. +38°45′. A white main-sequence star of SPECTRAL CLASS A0 V, its apparent MAGNITUDE is 0.1, making it the fifth brightest star in the sky. Vega is about three times the size of the sun and 50 times as luminous. Its distance from the earth is 26 light-years. Its name is from the Arabic for "falling eagle," referring to the figure that the Arabs associated with the constellation Lyra.

Vega Carpio, Lope de: see LOPE DE VEGA CARPIO.

vegetable, term originally used for any plant, now the popular name for many food plants, most of them annuals, and for their edible parts. There is no clear distinction between the vegetables and fruits. Most of our common vegetables were first brought into cultivation in the Eastern Hemisphere; the Indians of the New World developed cultivation of the potato, tomato, and corn and some varieties of squashes and peppers. Most vegetables consist largely of water, plus starches, sugars, proteins, and the mineral salts that are one of their chief contributions to the diet. Dried legume seeds contain a large proportion of proteins and can be used to some extent as meat substitutes. Many vegetables, especially those with green and yellow coloring, are valuable sources of vitamins. In the United States the demand for fresh vegetables at all seasons has been met by improved methods of handling and shipment and the development of large commercial truck farms and market gardens, especially in California, Florida, and Texas. Even vaster acreages supply vegetables for canning and quick freezing.

vegetable ivory: see TAGUA.

vegetable marrow: see GOURD; PUMPKIN.

vegetarianism, theory and practice of eating only fruits and vegetables, thus excluding animal flesh, fish, or fowl and often butter, eggs, and milk. The basis of the practice may be religious or ethical, economic, or nutritional, and its followers differ as to strictness of observance. Certain Hindu and Buddhist sects are vegetarian, as are Seventh-Day Adventists. As a general movement vegetarianism arose about the middle of the 19th cent.; it made considerable progress in Great Britain and in the United States. Vegetarianism is now assisted by the increasing production of meatless high-protein foods, often distributed through what are known as health food stores.

vegetative propagation, the ability of plants to reproduce without sexual reproduction, by producing new plants from existing vegetative structures, as in the regeneration or spontaneous sprouting of roots. Some plants, such as the Canada thistle and certain bamboos, send out long underground stems that produce new plants, often at considerable distances from the original plant. Such plants form enormous colonies of new plants within a relatively few years. Many trees, such as the beech and aspen, send up root sprouts, and large colonies of new trees thus arise. In other trees, the lower branches may produce roots where they rest upon the ground, and new trees are produced. The leaves of many plants take root and develop into new plants when they fall naturally onto moist soil; others produce buds at their edges, which develop in turn into miniature plants that fall off and take root. Specialists in the fields of agriculture and horticulture take advantage of the regenerative ability of plants through such techniques as the rooting of cuttings; grafting and budding of fruit trees; layering, or inducing the tips of branches to produce new plants; the cutting apart of clusters of certain plants, such as rhubarb, into individual plants; the cutting of plants (such as the common potato) into pieces that are then planted separately, each with a bud ("eye"); and numerous other techniques. The vegetative propagation of economically important and useful plants is now so widespread that most horticultural varieties are now only reproduced clonally, and many of them will no longer breed true from seed.

Vegetius (Flavius Vegetius Renatus) (vĭjē'shəs), fl. 385, Roman writer. He is the author of *Epitoma rei militaris* [a summary of military matters], which is an important source of information about the Roman military system.

Vehmgericht (fām'gərĭkht), **Vehme** (fā'mə), or **vehmic court** (fā'mĭk), in medieval Germany, a type of criminal tribunal. The inability of the Holy Roman emperors to exercise effective central control over their lands and the extensive feudal warfare of the period brought increasing disorder. To control this lawlessness, there emerged in WESTPHALIA near the end of the 12th cent. extralegal but efficient criminal tribunals, the Vehmgerichte. Probably the outgrowths of the Frankish courts, they had presumably received their original jurisdiction from the royal court in Carolingian times. In the legal fragmentation of medieval Germany they represented the remnants of royal, as opposed to territorial, jurisdiction; they were supported by the Holy Roman emperor until the 16th cent. They combined old traditions with new legal forms and filled an important gap in German medieval criminal law. Operating where ordinary seignorial or territorial justice failed, they were strongest in Westphalia; in 1382, Holy Roman Emperor Wenceslaus granted them jurisdiction elsewhere in Germany, and they subsequently appeared in Frankfurt (1386), Cologne (1387), and Lübeck (1399). Originally public, they became increasingly secret after the 14th cent. and were operated by "holy bands" sworn to secrecy on pain of death. Any freeman could become a member. Accusations were made mysteriously, often by nailing a notice to a tree, and failure to appear for trial was punished by death. The possible trial verdicts were hanging or acquittal. Despite apparently terroristic methods, the Vehmgerichte were less severe than tradition has made them. They were most powerful in the 15th cent. Thereafter increasing corruption and abuse, and the consolidated power of the petty princes, brought a general move against them, and in the 16th cent. the Vehmgerichte largely disappeared; they were entirely eliminated only in the 19th cent. Their secret and solemn proceedings and fear-inspiring methods made them fit material for romantic historical novels such as Sir Walter Scott's *Anne of Geierstein.* The name is also spelled Fehmgericht or Femgericht.

Veii (vē'ī), ancient city of Etruria, 11 mi (18 km) NW of Rome, Italy. One of the most powerful member cities of the Etruscan League, it was constantly at war with Rome. It fell (c.396 B.C.) to the Roman army under Camillus after a 10-year siege. The city was an important center of ETRUSCAN CIVILIZATION and was especially noted for its statuary. Near the modern Isola Farnese there are ruins of the ancient city and tombs, which have yielded Etruscan antiquities.

veil, a feature of female costume from antiquity, especially in the East, where it was worn primarily to conceal the features. In modern times it is worn to enhance the face. The Egyptian woman of rank, after Muslim influence, wore a transparent white gauze veil; the Greek woman wore a linen veil over the back of her head; the Roman woman favored the beautiful *palliolum,* a veil that was arranged over the hair and fell to the shoulders. The Middle Ages saw an abundance of veils decorating the extravagant headdresses (see HAT) of the times. In England, during the reign of Elizabeth I, veils of a shawl-like nature were fashionable, and it was at that time that the white bridal veil probably became popular in England. The black crepe veil has been worn for mourning since early times. The Spanish mantilla, usually a black or white triangular veil of blonde lace, is worn on the head and falling over the shoulders. The veils of nuns and nurses are patterned after the early forms of the veil. The 20th cent. brought forth a great variety of veils—from large veils worn during the early years of the automobile to delicate, decorative nose veils. The modern veil, of chiffon or net, is often embroidered or embossed. Veils have often had symbolic meanings—of modesty, of religious humility, of bondage; only since c.1925 have Muslim women been allowed to remove their veils, long symbolic of their servile position.

vein, blood vessel that returns blood to the HEART. Except for the pulmonary vein, which carries oxygenated blood from the lungs to the heart, veins carry deoxygenated blood. The oxygen-depleted blood passes from the CAPILLARIES to the venules (small veins). The venules feed into larger veins, which eventually merge into the superior and inferior vena cavae, large vessels that consolidate the

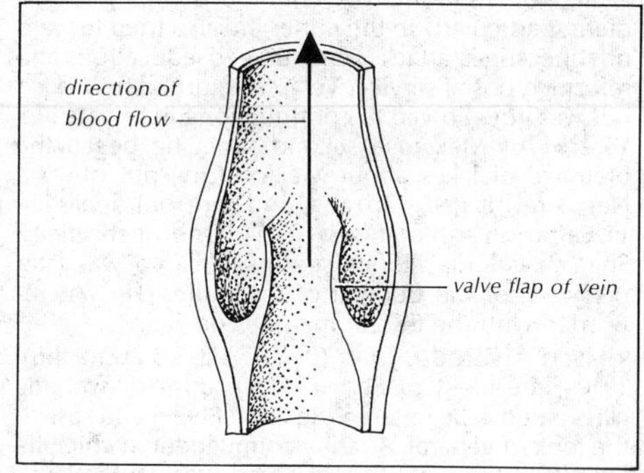

Cross section of vein showing valves

blood flow from the head, neck, and arms and from the trunk and legs, respectively (see also CIRCULATORY SYSTEM). The vena cavae direct the blood back into the heart. The walls of a vein are formed of three layers like the walls of an artery. However, they are thinner and less muscular and collapse when empty. Most veins contain valves, formed by pouches in their inner coats, that keep the blood from flowing backward. Valves are most numerous in the veins of the extremities and are absent in the smallest veins. Veins are subject to inflammation, dilatation or enlargement (as in a VARICOSE VEIN), rupture, and blockage by blood clots (THROMBOSIS).

Veit, Philipp (fē'lĭp fīt), 1793–1877, German historical painter; grandson of Moses Mendelssohn. In Rome he joined the NAZARENES and was one of the most interesting members of the group. With them he assisted in the fresco decorations of the Casa Bartholdy and Villa Massimi. From 1830 to 1843 he was director of the Städel Institute, Frankfurt-am-Main, for which he painted *The Triumph of Christianity.* The last part of his life was spent in Mainz, where he designed the decorations for the cathedral.

Vejle (vī'lə), city (1970 com. pop. 49,847), capital of Vejle co., central Denmark, a seaport at the head of the Vejle Fjord. It is a commercial and industrial center and a rail junction. Manufactures include textiles, soap, and leather goods. Of note in Vejle is St. Nicholas Church (13th cent.; restored).

Vela, Blasco Núñez: see NÚÑEZ VELA, BLASCO.

Velasco, José María (hōsā' märē'ä väläs'kō), 1840–1912, Mexican landscape painter; teacher of Diego Rivera. A gifted craftsman descended from a family of shawl weavers, he entered the art academy of San Carlos in 1858. His early work is reminiscent of Corot. Feeling that scientific knowledge would enable him to depict most expressively the natural beauty of the Valley of Mexico, he studied anatomy, botany, geology, and other sciences. He became extremely fluent in oil technique and developed an immense variety of shades of coloring. He portrayed nature with minute attention to detail, as in his painting *The Bridge of Metlac* (1881); his paintings of rocks manage to convey the effects of time and weather. He deviated from academic standards and in 1907 was removed from a professorship at the Mexican National Academy which he had held since 1868. His paintings, rejected in Mexico, won first place at the Paris exposition (1889). Altogether he painted more than 400 oils and worked also in pencil and watercolor. Almost forgotten after his death, he commanded new praise at a large retrospective exhibition (1942) in Mexico City.

Velasco, Luis de (lwēs' thā), d. 1564, Spanish administrator, second viceroy (1550–64) of New Spain (now Mexico), successor to Antonio de MENDOZA. His rule was remarkably energetic, humanitarian, and free of corruption. He did much to improve the condition of the Indians and thus aroused the opposition of many of the powerful Spaniards in Mexico. In 1553 the Univ. of Mexico was founded. Exploring expeditions were sent out—Francisco de IBARRA conquered Nueva Vizcaya and LÓPEZ DE LEGASPI conquered the Philippines. Velasco was beloved by the people of Mexico, especially the Indians. His son, **Luis de Velasco,** 1534–1617, was viceroy of New Spain (1590–95, 1607–11) and of Peru (1595–1604). In Mexico he helped to quell the rather obscure conspiracy in which Martín Cortés, the son of the conqueror, was involved. Appointed viceroy after distinguished service in Spain, Velasco continued the work of his father in aiding the Indians, encouraged weaving and other native industries, beautified Mexico City, strengthened fortifications at Veracruz, and extended the conquest to the north, pacifying the Indians. As viceroy of Peru he again worked to improve conditions among the Indians, particularly in the mines; he also tried to ward off buccaneer attacks, encouraged education, and reformed postal service. Velasco returned to Mexico but was not allowed to continue long in private life. Viceroy of Mexico a second time, he began the drainage of lakes about Mexico City, put down a Negro revolt near Orizaba, and sent out Sebastián Vizcaíno on explorations (1611). One of the finest Spanish colonial administrators, Velasco was later president of the Council of the Indies. He was rewarded with the title of marqués de Salinas.

Velasco Alvarado, Juan (hwän väläs'kō älvärä'thō), 1910–, president of Peru (1968–). Born of working class parents, he entered the army (1929) and rose to the rank of general. As army commander in chief, he led (1968) the junta that deposed President Belaúnde Terry after his failure to expropriate U.S.-owned oil operations. Velasco appointed an all-military cabinet, and immediately seized the disputed oil fields. He restricted the press, launched a sweeping agrarian reform aimed at breaking up the country's large estates, and worked toward the nationalization of selected industries.

Velasco Ibarra, José María (hōsā' märē'ä väläs'kō ēbä'rä), 1893–, president of Ecuador (1934–35, 1944–47, 1952–56, 1960–61, 1968–72). A brilliant orator, noted for his mercurial temperament, he was twice elected president and deposed before succeeding Galo PLAZA LASSO as president in 1952. Although he high-handedly censored the press, he spurred the construction of new schools and roads; the country prospered, and he managed to complete his term. Elected again in 1960, he announced a program of economic reform but soon became unpopular as a result of austerity measures. He quarreled with congress and was forced (Nov., 1961) by an army junta to resign. Reelected again in 1968, he faced a hostile congress, overwhelming economic problems, and increasing political chaos. After rioting by thousands of university students, he disbanded congress and, with the backing of the army, established a dictatorship (June, 1970). In Feb., 1972, after Velasco Ibarra insisted upon holding elections in which populist leader Assad Bucaram seemed certain to win, military leaders overthrew Velasco Ibarra and replaced him with a junta headed by Gen. Guillermo Rodriguez Lara.

Velay (vəlā'), region, E central France, in the MASSIF CENTRAL and partly in Haute-Loire dept. Partly volcanic in origin, the region has many high arid plateaus, some of startling beauty. Le Puy, the chief city and ancient capital (see PUY, LE), is set in a fertile basin. Velay is noted for its lace. The region was held in turn by the counts of Toulouse and the English rulers of Aquitaine and was united with the French crown by Louis VIII in the 13th cent.

Velázquez, Diego de (vəlăs'kwĭz, Span. dyā'gō dā vāläth'kāth), c.1460–1524?, Spanish conquistador, first governor of Cuba, b. Cuéllar, Spain. He sailed with Christopher Columbus on his second voyage (1493) to Hispaniola and in 1511 commanded an expedition sent by Diego Columbus to conquer Cuba. Landing at BARACOA, where he established the seat of government, by 1514 he had completed occupation of the island with the aid of his friend and chief lieutenant, Pánfilo de NARVÁEZ. Velázquez continued the colonization of Cuba and founded many of its principal towns. Before he sailed for Cuba, there had been ill feeling between him and Diego Columbus; soon after conquering Cuba, Velázquez established himself as governor of the island and declared himself independent of Columbus's authority. He was connected with the expedition of Fernández de Córdoba to Yucatán (1517) and in 1518 sent out an expedition under Juan de Grijalva, who explored the Mexican coast. Late in 1518 the Spanish king made Velázquez adelantado (civil and military governor) of Cuba and any territories that might be discovered under his orders. Hernán Cortés was placed in command of a third expedition that sailed in 1519 for the conquest of Mexico. Distrusting Cortés, Velázquez in 1520 sent Pánfilo de Narváez to compel his return to Cuba, but Narváez was defeated and the remainder of his forces joined Cortés. In 1521, Velázquez was replaced as governor of Cuba, but in 1523 he was restored to his post.

Velázquez, Diego Rodríguez de Silva y (rôthrē'gāth thā sēl'vä ē vāläth'kāth), 1599–1660, b. Seville. He was the most celebrated painter of the Spanish school. At 11 he was apprenticed to Francisco de Herrera the elder, whom he soon left for the studio of Pacheco, where he remained for five years. There he came into contact with the most intellectual society of Seville and with the work of the Spanish naturalist painters and the great Italian masters. His earliest paintings, such as *Christ and the Pilgrims of Emmaus* (Metropolitan Mus.), show great vigor and a strong naturalistic point of view. In 1618 Velázquez married Pacheco's daughter Juana, and five years later moved to Madrid. Under the protection of the condé de Olivares, he was introduced to the court and painted an equestrian portrait of Philip IV (destroyed) which won him immediate recognition. At 25 he was made court painter and given a studio in the royal palace. During his first years at court, Velázquez painted the portrait of Olivares (Hispanic Society, New York City) and full-length portraits of Philip IV and Don Carlos, a bust portrait of Philip IV, and the celebrated *Borrachos* [the drunkards] (all: Prado). In 1629, shortly after a visit by Rubens to the Spanish court, Velázquez made his first visit to Italy, returning in 1631. During his stay he copied some works of Tintoretto and painted two large figure compositions, *The Forge of Vulcan* (Prado) and *Joseph's Coat* (Escorial). To his second period (1631–49) belong the great equestrian portraits of Olivares and the king, *Christ on the Cross,* the magnificent *Surrender of Breda,* the series of dwarfs and buffoons of the court, the *Aesop,* the *Menippus* (all: Prado), and the three-quarter-length portrait of Philip IV (Frick Coll., New York City). In 1649, Velázquez paid a second visit to Italy to buy statues and paintings for the king and returned two years later having enriched the Spanish royal collection by many Italian masterpieces. While in Italy he painted the superb portrait of Pope Innocent X (Doria Palace), and two small, exquisite landscapes of the Villa Medici gardens (Prado). His only nude, *Venus and Cupid*—also called the *Rokeby Venus*—(c.1650; National Gall., London) exemplifies his moral view of mythology, emphasizing the vanity of the goddess. To the last years (1651–60) belong the *Coronation of the Virgin, St. Anthony the Abbot and St. Paul the Hermit,* the famous full-length portraits of Mariana of Austria (Philip's second wife), and the Infanta Margarita, the *Fable of Arachne,* and *Las Meninas* (all: Prado). Also of this period are the head of the Infanta (Louvre) and the portrait of Philip IV as an old man. Throughout his career Velázquez enjoyed the close friendship of the king; he was made marshal of the palace and administrator of the royal galleries. His duties often interfered with his freedom to paint. He died shortly after organizing the marriage ceremonies of Marie Thérèse of Austria to Louis XIV. His development as an artist was uncommonly steady. His first forms were monumental and powerful, enveloped in a strong chiaroscuro. Velázquez slowly evolved an extraordinarily subtle and intellectual art based on exquisite color values, of which he remains the unrivaled master. His cool palette and consummate use of silver tones in conjunction with brilliant color sometimes recall El Greco, whose work he knew and admired. In spirit, however, he is far removed from the art of El Greco in his worldliness and compassion for all levels of mankind. He imbued all human beings from dwarfs to kings with a sense of dignity and individual worth. Velázquez had many followers. His son-in-law Mazo imitated his portrait style so successfully that many minor works now thought to be his were formerly attributed to Velázquez. Murillo learned much from Velázquez. But in his great works Velázquez has never been successfully imitated. His mature works are very few—some say not more than 100. He was obliged to produce replicas of many of his court portraits. Some of these were executed by Mazo, and all are inferior to the originals. Velázquez can be fully appreciated only in Madrid, although more or less authentic examples of his work are to be seen in many galleries in Europe and the United States. See studies by E. Lafuente Ferrari (tr. 1960), J. López-Rey (1968), and J. E. White (1969).

veld or **veldt** (both: vĕlt, Du. fĕlt) [Du.,=field], term applied to the grassy undulating plateaus of the Republic of South Africa and of Rhodesia. The veld comprises territory of varying elevation—the highveld (4,000–6,000 ft/1,220–1,830 m), the middle veld (2,000–4,000 ft/610–1,220 m), and the lowveld (500–2,000 ft/150–610 m). The highveld, the largest of the plateaus, is in the Republic of South Africa. Abundant crops of potatoes and maize are grown, large cattle herds are grazed, and industrial and mining centers are found there.

Velde, van de (vän də vĕl'də), 17th-century Dutch family of artists. **Jan van de Velde,** 1593–1641, was a draftsman and engraver as well as a painter. His cousin **Esaias van de Velde,** c.1591–1630, a painter of genre and battle scenes, is best known for his clearly delineated landscapes. His *Ferry Boat* (Rijks Mus.) is indicative of the trend Dutch landscape was soon to follow. Esaias's pupil Jan van Goyen was greatly influenced by his work. His brother **Willem van de Velde,** the elder, 1611–93, a marine painter, accompanied the Dutch fleet and depicted its victories over the English. He settled in England in 1672 and executed many works preserved at Hampton Court; he is also well represented in Amsterdam. He is thought to have worked often in collaboration with his son **Willem van de Velde,** the younger, 1633–1707, who was the most renowned marine painter of his day and is considered the father of English marine painting. Willem, the younger, was with his father in the fleet and in England and was commissioned by Charles II to portray naval engagements, being court painter from 1677. The National Maritime Museum in London has an important collection of his paintings. His brother, **Adriaen van de Velde,** 1636–72, was a landscape painter who showed a keen perception of the changes in light due to the season and the hour of the day. Most of his landscapes contain figures, and he often painted the figures in the landscapes of other painters, including his brother Willem, the younger, Hobbema, Ruisdael, his master Wynants, and Jan van der Heyden. **Jan Jansz van de Velde,** 1620–63, the son of Jan van de Velde, painted still lifes with fine, coloristic subtlety. His *Still-life Study* is in the National Gallery, London.

Velde, Henri van de (äNrē' väN də vĕld), 1863–1957, Belgian designer and architect. Beginning as a painter, critic, and crafts designer in Belgium and in France, he received his first great acclaim for the interiors that he exhibited at Dresden in 1897. Van de Velde played a leading role in the development of Jugendstil, the German equivalent of art nouveau. His designs for furniture and tableware are of especially high quality. With ideas deriving in part from Ruskin and William Morris, he taught at his own school, the Weimar School of Arts and Crafts. Van de Velde's architectural activity was considerable. His best work is found in his own house near Brussels (1895) and in the studio building for his school at Weimar (1906), but his architecture never had the quality, importance, or influence of his crafts and his numerous writings. His first book was *Die Renaissance in modernen Kunstgewerbe* (1901).

Vélez de Escalante, Silvestre: see ESCALANTE, SILVESTRE VÉLEZ DE.

Vélez de Guevara, Luis (lo͞oĕs' vä'lāth thā gävä'rä), 1579?-1644, Spanish playwright and novelist. He was a follower of Lope de Vega and wrote many popular plays noted for their poetic quality. Among these the most important are *La luna de la sierra* [the mountain moon] and *Reinar después de morir* [to reign after death]. His well-received romance of roguery, *El diablo cojuelo* [the limping devil] (1641), was widely imitated and was adapted by Le Sage as *Le Diable boiteux*. Despite lifelong poverty, he was a joyous, vigorous man.

Vélez-Málaga (vä'lāth-mä'lägä), town (1970 pop. 42,454), Málaga prov., S Spain, in Andalusia, on the Vélez River. It is an agricultural center. Recovered from the Moors by Ferdinand V in 1487, it has a Moorish castle and a fine church, which tradition claims was founded by St. Peter.

Veliki Bečkerek: see ZRENJANIN, Yugoslavia.

Veliki Ustyug (vyĭlyĕ'kē o͝ostyo͝ok'), city (1967 est. pop. 35,000), N central European USSR, a port on the Northern Dvina River. Industries include shipbuilding and the production of textiles, bristles and brushes, and silver handicrafts. First mentioned as Ustyug in the 12th cent., the city later became (16th-17th cent.) a wealthy and important trade and transport center on the road from Moscow to Arkhangelsk and from European Russia to Siberia. Veliki Ustyug also became a noted center of painting and artistic handicrafts (particularly in silver) during the 17th and 18th cent. Its commercial role declined after the founding of St. Petersburg in 1703. City landmarks include the Voznesensky Church and several monasteries.

Velikiye Luki (vyĭlyē'kēə lo͞o'kē), city (1969 est. pop. 84,000), W central European USSR, on the Lovat River. A railroad junction, it has industries producing foodstuffs, bricks, radios, and furniture. Dating from the 12th cent., the city was controlled first by Novgorod, then by Lithuania, and, from 1448, by Moscow. During the Livonian war it was captured by Stephen Bathory of Poland (1580), who controlled it until 1582.

Vellore (vĕlôr'), town (1971 pop. 138,220), Tamil Nadu state, SE India, on the Palar River. It is a district administrative center and an agricultural market town. In the 18th cent. Vellore was the stronghold of the Indian leaders Haidar Ali and his son Tippoo Sahib. An ancient fort, a 14th-century temple of the Hindu god Siva, and a medical college are in the town.

vellum: see PARCHMENT.

velocity, change in displacement with respect to time. Displacement is the VECTOR counterpart of distance, having both magnitude and direction. Velocity is therefore also a vector quantity. The magnitude of velocity is known as the speed of a body. The average velocity or average speed of a moving body during a time period t may be computed by dividing the total displacement or total distance by t. Computation of the instantaneous velocity at a particular moment, however, usually requires the methods of the calculus.

Velsen (vĕl'sən), municipality (1971 pop. 67,501), North Holland prov., W Netherlands, near the mouth of the North Sea Canal. It is a center of the Dutch steel industry, and it includes the port of IJMUIDEN.

velvet, fabric having a soft, thick, short pile, usually of silk, and a plain twill or satin weave ground. The pile surface is formed by weaving an extra set of warp threads that are looped over wires as in Wilton carpet, the rods being withdrawn after the weft thread is placed, leaving a row of loops or tufts across the breadth. The loops may remain uncut, forming terry velvet, or be cut, automatically in machine weaving or by a special tool in handlooming. The fabric may also be woven double, face to face, then cut apart. Velvet is supposedly one of the silk weaves developed on the ancient shuttle looms of China. The most beautiful weaves, such as brocades, are still done by hand. India has produced velvet from remote times, often richly embroidered, for the furniture and trappings of royalty. Many fine velvets were made in Turkey, and Persia was famous for its beautiful designs and colors. Magnificent velvets were used in Europe in 12th- and 13th-century religious and court ceremonials. Lucca and Genoa apparently were the first cities to make fine velvets and excelled through the 16th and 17th cent. Genoese velvet was notable for designs formed by contrasts of cut and uncut pile. Venetian and Florentine fabrics were sumptuous brocades, floral designs on contrasting grounds or on cloth of gold. Utrecht made a rich, heavy velvet used for wall and furniture coverings. Modern velvets are of many types and grades. Lyons velvet has a stiff ground and erect pile. Transparent velvet has a sheer foundation. Panne velvet is a long-napped weave, pressed. Plush and velveteen resemble velvet and are sometimes used as substitutes; the weft loops, rather than the warp loops, form the pile on these substitutes.

velvetweed or **velvetleaf:** see MALLOW.

Ven: see LANDSKRONA, Sweden.

Venaissin: see COMTAT VENAISSIN, France.

Venantius Fortunatus, Saint (Venantius Honorius Clementianus Fortunatus) (vĕnăn'shəs fôr"tyo͞onā'təs), d. c.600, Latin poet, b. near Treviso, Italy. A priest in Gaul and later bishop of Poitiers, he wrote a long poem on St. Martin of Tours and also the hymn *Vexilla Regis prodeunt*, sung on Good Friday in the Roman Catholic Church. Another of his hymns supplied the first line and the meter for the later *Pange lingua*. He was the last of the Gallic Latin poets. Feast: Dec. 14.

Vendée (väNdā'), department (1968 pop. 421,250), W France, on the Bay of Biscay, in POITOU. The offshore islands of Noirmoutier and Yeu are included in the department. Largely an agricultural (wheat, cattle raising) and forested region, the Vendée has many beach resorts and fishing ports. Canned fish, leather, textiles, fishing boats, and uranium are the chief products, and the construction industry is important. La Roche-sur-Yon (the capital) and Les Sables d'Olonne are the main towns. The department gave its name to the insurrection of 1793 to 1796, which began there. The peasants of the Vendée, who had lived amiably with the local nobility, began violently to oppose the French Revolution when it turned against the Roman Catholic Church. Under Henri La Rochejaquelein and others, an army of more than 50,000 men was raised to clear the region of Revolutionary authorities. The army occupied Saumur and planned to continue through Brittany, Maine, and Normandy to join the CHOUANS, the anti-Revolutionary peasants of those regions. However, the important city of NANTES held out against the Vendeans, who marched as far north as Granville but were then forced by lack of discipline to return south late in 1793. Overtaken at Le Mans and Savenay by the republican army, they were totally defeated and suffered terrible reprisals (see NOYADES). Robespierre's overthrow led to the peace of La Jaunaie (1795), by which the government granted an amnesty and freedom of worship to the Vendeans. Renewed conflict began in 1796, when royalist émigrés, backed by Great Britain, tried to land at Quiberon in Brittany; they were routed by government forces under Gen. Lazare Hoche. The comte d'Artois (later Charles X), who had landed on the isle of Yeu, took fright and abandoned the Vendean leaders to capture and execution. Smaller royalist uprisings occurred in 1815 (against Napoleon I) and in 1832, when the duchess de Berry tried to stir up the Vendée for the Bourbon cause against Louis Philippe.

Vendémiaire (väNdāmyĕr'), first month of the FRENCH REVOLUTIONARY CALENDAR. 13 Vendémiaire of the year IV (Oct. 5, 1795) was the day when Napoleon Bonaparte, until then an obscure general, won fame by putting down a serious insurrection. The Parisian electorate had revolted against certain decrees designed to perpetuate the power of the leaders of the Convention in the Directory, which was about to be established. Napoleon, with the blessings of BARRAS, crushed the rebels with artillery fire—which he later described as "a whiff of grapeshot."

vendetta (vĕndĕt'ə) [Ital.,=vengeance], feud between members of two kinship groups to avenge a wrong done to a relative. Although the term originated in Corsica, the custom has also been practiced in other parts of Italy, in other European countries, and among the Arabs. It generally reflects a society where the family is the only social unit with authority or where there is no centralized government to compel order. After a society attains cohesion and will no longer tolerate private vengeance, COMPOSITION for offenses may be compelled. In time the state itself punishes antisocial acts, and a system of CRIMINAL LAW takes form. The vendetta may prevail also where the government is feared or distrusted to such an extent that private justice is considered more equitable. The obligation to carry on the vendetta usually rests primarily on the male who is next of kin to the wronged person. Among some peoples, vengeance may be taken on any member of the group of the person who has done the wrong. The most striking form of the vendetta is the blood FEUD, or the taking of a life for a life. While the vendetta is almost universally proscribed by law, it persists in areas that are remote or lack trusted police protection.

vending machine, coin-operated, automatic device for selling goods. Many vending machines are capable of making change, and some of the more sophisticated ones accept paper money. The first vending machine was invented by Richard Carlisle, English publisher and bookshop owner, for selling books. Until 1926 vending machines were restricted chiefly to selling penny gum and candy. In that year the invention of a cigarette-vending machine by William Rowe, an American, started a trend toward selling higher-priced merchandise. Soft drink and nickel-candy machines followed in the 1920s and 30s. Today vending machines sell a wide variety of items, e.g., milk, sandwiches, soap, and newspapers. Operators maintain and service machines and pay rent, usually a commission on sales, to the owners of the location sites. Some luncheonettes consist entirely of unattended vending machines. See study by R. D. Burkett (1967).

Vendôme, César, duc de (sāzär' dŭk də väNdōm'), 1594-1665, French general and politician; son of King Henry IV and his mistress Gabrielle d'Estrées. Legitimized in 1595, he was made duke of Vendôme in 1598, and also acquired Brittany through marriage. He rebelled against Marie de' Medici (1614-16) and against the duc de Luynes (1620) and was imprisoned (1626-30) for conspiring against Cardinal Richelieu. In 1641 he was forced to flee after being accused of plotting against Richelieu. Returning after Richelieu's death, he was exiled (1643) for conspiring against Cardinal Mazarin. However, he was reconciled, married his son to a niece of Mazarin's, and fought on the government side in the Fronde; he captured (1653) Bordeaux, and in 1655 he defeated a Spanish fleet at Barcelona.

Vendôme, François de: see BEAUFORT, FRANÇOIS DE VENDÔME, DUC DE.

Vendôme, Louis Joseph, duc de (lwē zhōzĕf'), 1654-1712, marshal of France; grandson of César de Vendôme and son of Laure Mancini. He fought in the War of the Grand Alliance. In the War of the Spanish Succession he was appointed (1702) commander in Italy and decisively defeated his cousin, the Austrian commander Prince Eugene of Savoy, at Cassano (1705). Sent to Flanders to repair the French defeat at Ramillies (1706), he was at first successful against the duke of Marlborough and Eugene but was defeated at Oudenarde (1708). In 1710 he went to the aid of King Philip V of Spain, Louis XIV's grandson, and by his victories at Brihuega and Villaviciosa helped ensure Philip's retention of the Spanish crown.

Vendôme, town (1968 pop. 16,728), Loir-et-Cher dept., N central France, in Orléanais. It is a manufacturing town with food processing and metal and electrical industries. The town developed around the Abbey of the Trinity (11th cent.) and during the Middle Ages was the prosperous center of the county (duchy after 1515) of Vendôme. Henry IV inherited the duchy as part of the Bourbon lands, united it with the royal domain in 1589, and gave the title of the duke of Vendôme to his illegitimate son César in 1598. Among the numerous monuments are the ruins of a château built during the 12th, 14th, and 15th cent.

veneer (vənēr'), thin leaf of wood applied with glue to a panel or frame of solid wood. The art of veneer developed with early civilization. It produces richly grained effects cheaply and is used also on structural parts that must be cut with the grain for strength. The grain pattern varies with the direction of the cut, woods cut across the grain in general displaying more effective patterns, e.g., burr and oyster walnut, bird's-eye maple. Rosewood, satinwood, maple, walnut, and mahogany are frequently employed for veneers. Hand-cut veneers were 1/10 to 1/8 in. thick; the modern machine-cut sheets are rarely thicker than 1/32 in. Veneering executed in inlaid sheets is known as MARQUETRY. PLYWOOD and beams or planks of compounded woods are developed by a veneering process.

venereal disease (vənēr'ēəl), term for infections acquired mainly through sexual contact. These infections include notably GONORRHEA and SYPHILIS and, less commonly, granuloma inguinale, lymphogranuloma venereum, and chancroid. In some instances two or more infections may be present concurrently. Granuloma inguinale is caused by *Donovania granulomatis*, an organism whose classification is uncertain (i.e., it may be a protozoan or a bacterium). Early lesions appear as buttonlike elevations on the skin of the genital and pelvic regions, succeeded by a spreading ulceration of the tissues. If not treated, the condition becomes chronic and may lead to death through anemia and general debility. Treatment is with chloramphenicol and the tetracycline drugs. Lymphogranuloma venereum is caused by a psittacosis-type microorganism (i.e., classified as a bacterium but having some viral characteristics). The primary genital lesion is often overlooked. The lymphatic structures about the pelvic and rectal region then become involved; blockage of such structures may cause disfigurement and scarring of external genitals. Fever and chills are other constitutional symptoms. Severe involvement of the rectal mucosa may cause intestinal obstruction or stricture. Treatment is also with the tetracycline drugs and chloramphenicol. Chancroid is an acute localized infection caused by a bacterium called *Hemophilus ducreyi.* It results in vascular changes and necrosis of the affected area. Involvement of the lymph nodes occurs in more than half the cases. Usually the disease is self-limited, but it may cause destruction of tissue. Sulfa drugs and tetracycline are the most effective compounds used in treatment. In order to lessen dangers of venereal infection caused by ignorance, the U.S. government just before and after World War II encouraged publicity on the matter, for the taboo long associated with public discussion of these contagious diseases had given rise to serious public health problems. A nationwide campaign was initiated in 1937 by Thomas Parran, then serving as U.S. surgeon general, in the course of which both press and radio discussed the incidence, cause, and cure of venereal diseases. As a result, the number of new cases in the United States steadily declined each year; infant deaths from venereal diseases also diminished. However, in the 1950s a rise in the incidence of venereal diseases in general was noted especially among teenagers and young adults. Public authorities undertook energetic measures to cope with the problem, coordinating their efforts with those of private agencies especially to identify and isolate promptly all sources of infection. The incidence of venereal disease nevertheless continued to rise, especially among young people age 15-24. From 1962 to 1972 the reported cases of gonorrhea almost tripled. However, there was a slight decline in reported cases of syphilis from 1961 to 1970, probably accounted for by increased efforts to control the disease. The rate began to rise again in 1971 and 1972. See Theodor Rosebury, *Microbes and Morals* (1971); K. L. Jones et al., *VD* (1974).

Veneti (vĕn'ətī), Celtic people of ancient Gaul, who inhabited an area of NW France, now in Morbihan dept. Forming the most important of the Gallic maritime states, they rebelled in 57 B.C. against Roman rule. They were decisively defeated by Julius Caesar and Decimus Junius Brutus in a naval battle, in which, according to Caesar's account, they lost 220 vessels.

Veneti, people of ancient Italy. They occupied the shore of the Adriatic from Trieste to the mouth of the Po River and spoke an Illyrian language. Friendly toward Rome, they came under Roman rule in the 2d cent. B.C.

Venetia (vənē'shə), Ital. *Veneto* or *Venezia Euganea,* region (1971 pop. 4,109,787), 7,095 sq mi (18,376 sq km), NE Italy, bordering on the Gulf of Venice (an arm of the Adriatic Sea) in the east and on Austria in the north. VENICE is the capital of the region, which is divided into the provinces of Belluno, Padua, Rovigo, Treviso, Venice, Verona, and Vicenza (named for their capitals). Venetia falls into two geographic zones, a mountainous and hilly area in the north, which includes parts of the Dolomites and Carnic Alps (Alpi Carniche), and the fertile Venetian Plain in the south, which is partly marshy near the Adriatic. Venetia's main rivers are the Po (which forms the boundary with Emilia-Romagna in the south), the Mincio (which forms part of the boundary with Lombardy in the west), the Adige, and the Piave. The region borders on Lake GARDA in the west. Most of Venetia's workers are engaged in agriculture; the leading crops are cereals, fruit, sugar beets, and hemp. Mulberry trees are grown for use in sericulture. Manufactures include textiles, chemicals, paper, processed food, wine, and ships. Chioggia is a major fishing port. Tourism is important, especially at Venice, and Cortina d'Ampezzo is a well-known winter-sports center. Venetia derives its name from the VENETI, a people who settled the region c.1000 B.C. and who came under Roman rule in the 2d cent. B.C. Emperor Augustus joined Venetia and Istria to form a separate province, whose capital was AQUILEIA. Venetia was devastated by Attila, king of the Huns, in the mid-5th cent. A.D. About the 10th cent., the towns of the region began to reacquire importance. They were ruled at first by their bishops, and later developed into free communes. Some towns (including Verona and Padua) grew powerful under the rule of noble families, but the republic of Venice gradually became dominant, and by the early 15th cent. its territories included virtually all of present-day Venetia. By the Treaty of CAMPO FORMIO (1797), Venetia passed to Austria, and by the Treaty of PRESSBURG (1805) it was made part of the Napoleonic kingdom of Italy. In 1814, Venetia was restored to Austria, which held it to the end of the Austro-Prussian War (1866), when it was ceded to Italy. After World War II, Udine prov. in the east was detached from Venetia and was combined with that part of VENEZIA GIULIA not ceded by Italy to Yugoslavia to form the region of Friuli-Venezia Giulia. Venetia suffered severe flooding in 1966. There are universities at Padua and Venice.

Venezia: see VENICE, Italy.

Venezia Giulia (vānā'tsyä jo͞o'lyä), former region, 3,356 sq mi (8,692 sq km), NE Italy, on the Adriatic Sea. It was formed after World War I from part of the territories ceded by Austria to Italy in 1919, and included E Friuli, Trieste, Istria, and part of Carniola. Fiume was added in 1921. Except along the coast, the population is Slovenian, and after World War II most (c.2,890 sq mi/7,485 sq km) of Venezia Giulia was ceded by Italy to Yugoslavia. Most of Istria was joined with Croatia; part of Friuli and Carniola was combined with Slovenia and another portion (c.285 sq mi/740 sq km) formed the Free Territory of Trieste (divided in 1954 between Italy and Yugoslavia). The rest of Venezia Giulia (c.180 sq mi/470 sq km), part of Gorizia prov., remained Italian and was merged with Udine prov. to form the new region of FRIULI-VENEZIA GIULIA.

Veneziano, Domenico: see DOMENICO VENEZIANO.

Venezia Tridentina: see TRENTINO-ALTO ADIGE, Italy.

Venezuela (vĕnəzwā'lə, Span. vānāswā'lä), republic (1973 est. pop. 11,300,000), 352,143 sq mi (912,050 sq km), N South America. The capital is CARACAS. Venezuela has a coastline 1,750 mi (2,816 km) long on the Caribbean Sea in the north. It is bordered on the S by Brazil, on the W and SW by Colombia, and on the E by Guyana. Dependencies include MARGARITA Island, Tortuga Island, and many smaller island groups in the Caribbean. The republic consists of 20 states, 2 federal territories, and the federal district, of which Caracas is a part. Geographically Venezuela is a land of vivid contrasts, with four major divisions: the Venezuelan highlands, the coastal lowlands, the basin of the Orinoco River, and the Guiana Highlands. An almost inaccessible and largely unexplored wilderness S of the Orinoco, the Guiana Highlands occupy more than half of the national territory and are noted for scenic wonders such as Angel Falls. Iron ore, gold, diamonds, and other minerals are found near CIUDAD BOLIVAR. The dense forests of the region yield rubber, tropical hardwoods, and other forest products. The boundary with Brazil is mostly mountainous. The Orinoco, one of the great rivers of South America, has its source in this region. The Orinoco basin is a great pastoral area. North of the Orinoco and about the Apure River and its tributaries are the llanos, the vast, hot Orinoco plains, where there is a great cattle industry. Oil is found N of the Orinoco in Anzoátegui and Monagas states. The most vital region economically, however, is an area in the coastal plains, the lowlands around Lake Maracaibo. There, since 1918, Dutch, British, and American interests have developed the astonishingly rich oil fields. The coastal lowlands are exceedingly hot, but coastal ranges rise abruptly from the Caribbean to cool altitudes of 6,000 to 7,000 ft (1,830-2,130 m). These ranges soon become a region of hills, intermontane basins, and plateaus known as the Venezuelan highlands and are a spur of the Andes. Further to the southwest, close to BARQUISIMETO, the mountains rise to their greatest height at Pico Bolívar (16,427 ft/5,007 m) in the Sierra Nevada de Mérida. Densely populated, the highland region is the political and commercial hub of the nation. Coffee, the keystone of the economy before the oil boom, comes from the slopes and cocoa from the lower foothills. VALENCIA and MARACAY are, next to Caracas, the chief cities of the mountain basins. Economically dominant in the 19th cent., they are still major urban centers, despite some loss of power because of the oil boom along the coast. Cattle from the llanos are fattened on the rich valley grasses near Lake Valencia. Field crops are intensively cultivated in the vicinity. The mountains long impeded Venezuela's economic development because of the communications problems they presented; today, however, the country has a fine highway system. Because of its oil riches Venezuela has the highest per capita national income in Latin America. Oil accounts for about 90% of the export income, 70% of government revenues, and 20% of the gross national product. Other exports are iron ore (Venezuela is a major supplier of the United States), coffee, cocoa, rice, and cotton. The main imports are manufactured goods—especially machinery, vehicles, and chemicals—and food. The United States and Canada buy most of the exports, and the United States, West Germany, and Japan supply most of the imports. A large amount of oil is exported to the Netherlands Antilles for refining. MARACAIBO, PUERTO CABELLO, La Guaira (see GUAIRA, LA), and CUMANÁ are the important ports. The government has used oil revenues to stimulate manufacturing industries. Food processing and the manufacture of textiles, shoes, chemicals, and automobiles have become well established. Heavy metal works are being established on the Orinoco near Santo Tomé de Guayana (Ciudad Guayana). Despite recent government reform programs, Venezuela's great wealth remains in the hands of a small minority. A disproportionately high percentage of the population lives in conspicuous poverty. Many cities have squalid slums, and in the countryside the majority are still propertyless tenant farmers. The landowning class is mainly of Spanish descent. Over all, about 65% of the population is mestizo, 20% white, 8% Negro, and 7% Indian. The rate of population growth is one of the highest in the world. There is no established church, but nearly all Venezuelans are Roman Catholic. There are eight universities in the country. Venezuela is governed under a 1961 constitution. The president and members of congress are elected for five-year terms. The president may not succeed himself. Senators are apportioned among the states and the federal district; members of the chamber of deputies are apportioned by population with at least two from each state. Each state has a unicameral legislature and a governor appointed by the president. The major parties are the Social Christian party; the Democratic Action party; the People's Electoral Movement, a left-wing offshoot of the Democratic Action party; and the National Civic Crusade, organized by the exiled dictator, Pérez Jiménez. There are a number of smaller parties, including the Communist party, which was banned in 1962 but made legal again in 1969. Columbus discovered the mouths of the Orinoco in 1498. In 1499 the Venezuelan coast was explored by Alonso de OJEDA and Amerigo VESPUCCI. The latter, coming upon an island off the Paraguaná peninsula (probably Aruba), nicknamed it Venezuela (little Venice) because of Indian villages built above the water on stilts; the name held and was soon applied to the mainland. Spanish settlements were established on the coast at Cumaná (1520) and CORO

(1527), but the major task of the conquest was accomplished by German adventurers—Ambrosio de Alfinger, George of Speyer and especially Nikolaus FEDERMANN—in the service of the Welsers, German bankers who had obtained rights in Venezuela from Emperor Charles V. During part of the colonial period the area was an adjunct of NEW GRANADA. Cocoa cultivation was the mainstay of the colonial economy. From the 16th to the 18th cent. the coastline was attacked by British buccaneers, and in the 18th cent. there was a brisk smuggling trade with the British islands of the West Indies. In 1795 there was an uprising against Spanish control, but it was only after Napoleon had taken control of Spain that a real revolution began (1810) in Venezuela, under Francisco de MIRANDA. In 1811 complete independence was declared. The revolution encountered difficulties. An earthquake in 1812 destroyed cities held by the patriots and helped to forward the cause of the royalists. Later, however, Simón BOLÍVAR (born in Venezuela) and his lieutenants, working from Colombia, were able to liberate Venezuela despite setbacks administered by the royalist commander, Pablo MORILLO. The victory of Carabobo (1821) secured independence from Spain. Venezuela and other territories became part of the federal republic of Greater Colombia. Almost from the beginning, however, Venezuela was restive. José Antonio PÁEZ, who had conquered the last Spanish garrison at Puerto Cabello in 1823, favored independence. He was a caudillo with a strong following among the hardy cattlemen, the llaneros. In 1830 the separatists gained the upper hand, and Venezuela became an independent state. Páez was the leading figure. Although conservative and liberal parties appeared, the actual control of Venezuela was held mainly by caudillos from the landholding class. After Páez, José Tadeo MONAGAS and his brother entrenched (1846) themselves in power, but not before a bitter struggle was waged to prevent the refractory Páez from keeping a large measure of political control. The Monagas brothers were overthrown in 1858, and civil war among caudillos became chronic. A brief liberal regime under Juan Falcon created the decentralized United States of Venezuela in 1864. From 1870 to 1888, GUZMÁN BLANCO dominated Venezuela. He improved education, communications, and finances, crushed the church, and enriched himself. He was overthrown in 1888, but dictatorship was resumed four years later under Joaquín CRESPO. During Crespo's regime began the VENEZUELA BOUNDARY DISPUTE with Great Britain over the border with British Guiana. Cipriano CASTRO, a new dictator, came to power in 1899. The financial corruption and incompetence of his administration helped to bring on a new international incident, that of the VENEZUELA CLAIMS. In 1908 began the rule of one of the longest-lasting of all Latin American dictators, Juan Vicente GÓMEZ, who stayed in power until his death in 1935. His rule was that of total and absolute tyranny, although he did force the state (with the help of foreign oil concessions) into national solvency and material prosperity. His death was followed by popular celebration. Eleazar López Contreras became president (1935–41) and increased Venezuela's share of the oil companies' profits; under his legally elected successor, Isaías Medina Angarita, Venezuela sympathized with the Allies and finally entered World War II on the Allied side in 1945. Later in 1945 a military junta committed to democracy and social reform and headed by Rómulo BETANCOURT of the Democratic Action party gained control of the government. A new constitution promulgated in 1947 provided, for the first time in Venezuelan history, for the election of a president by direct popular vote. The first president elected under the new constitution was the eminent novelist GALLEGOS RÓMULO. His administration, however, was short-lived. A military coup in Nov., 1948, overthrew the Gallegos government, and a repressive military dictatorship was established. By 1952, Col. Marcos Pérez Jiménez had become dictator, and he made wide use of police state techniques. A popular revolt, supported by liberal units of the armed forces, broke out early in 1958; Pérez Jiménez fled. Elections held that year restored democratic rule to Venezuela. Rómulo Betancourt, now president, adopted a moderate program of gradual economic reform and maintained friendly relations with the United States despite the association of U.S. interests with Pérez Jiménez. A new constitution (1961) was adopted. The country, long out of debt because of the oil revenues, reached a peak of prosperity, but the new administration was nevertheless gravely challenged. Left-wing groups, particularly the Communists, bitterly opposed the administration, and their activities, combined with the restiveness of the poorer classes and the dissidence of leftist elements in the military, led to numerous uprisings. In May and June of 1962 two Communist-inspired revolts by marine corps garrisons were suppressed only after bloody fighting. Extreme right-wing elements also plotted against the Betancourt regime. Betancourt was succeeded in 1964 by Raúl Leoni. Following an outbreak of leftist terrorism in Caracas in 1966, the army occupied the Central Univ. and seized weapons found there. In 1968 the Social Christian party came to power when Rafael Caldera won the close presidential election. Relations with Colombia and Guyana have been strained by border disputes. At issue with Colombia have been control over offshore oil reserves and also the illegal movement of many Colombians into Venezuela to work. In 1973, Venezuela joined the Andean Group, an economic association of Latin American nations. The 1973 presidential election was won by Carlos Andrés Pérez of the Democratic Action party. In early 1974 he announced Venezuela's intention to nationalize major industries, including oil production, iron ore mining, and iron and steel manufacturing. See Irving Rouse and J. M. Cruxent, *Venezuelan Archaeology* (1963); Guillermo Morón, *A History of Venezuela* (tr. 1964); Edwin Lieuwen, *Venezuela* (2d ed. 1965); J. D. Powell, *Political Mobilization of the Venezuelan Peasant* (1971); D. K. Rudolph and G. A. Rudolph, *Historical Dictionary of Venezuela* (1971); T. E. Weil et al., *Area Handbook for Venezuela* (1971); W. J. Burggraaff, *The Venezuelan Armed Forces in Politics, 1935–1959* (1972); D. H. Levine, *Conflict and Political Change in Venezuela* (1973).

Venezuela Boundary Dispute, diplomatic controversy, notable for the tension caused between Great Britain and the United States during much of the 19th cent. Of long standing, the dispute concerned the boundary between Venezuela and British Guiana; the Venezuelan claim, extending E to the Essequibo River (and thus taking in most of the settled areas of British Guiana) had been inherited from Spain, and that of Great Britain, stretching W to the Orinoco, was acquired from the Dutch in 1810. The controversy did not gain importance until Great Britain in 1841 had a provisional line (the Schomburgk Line) run. Discovery of gold in the region intensified the dispute. Great Britain refused to arbitrate concerning the settled area; Venezuela, however, maintained that the British were delaying in order to push settlements farther into the disputed area. Venezuela sought aid from the United States and in 1887 broke off diplomatic relations with Great Britain. President Grover Cleveland's Secretary of State, Thomas Francis BAYARD, began negotiations, but the matter lapsed. In 1895, Secretary of State OLNEY, invoking a new and broader interpretation of the MONROE DOCTRINE, virtually demanded arbitration, basing the right of the United States to intercede on the ground that any state whose interests or prestige is involved in a quarrel may intervene. Lord Salisbury, the British prime minister, offered to submit some of the area to arbitration but refused to allow British settlements to be submitted to adjudication. That reply, a rebuff to Olney, brought Cleveland's momentous message to Congress on Dec. 17, 1895, which denounced British refusal to arbitrate and maintained that it was the duty of the United States to take steps to determine the boundary and to resist any British aggression beyond that line once it had been determined. The message caused a commotion; Congress supported the President but, although there was some war talk, neither nation desired to fight. Salisbury, involved in European troubles and disturbed by difficulties in South Africa, sent a conciliatory note recognizing the broad interpretation of the Monroe Doctrine. An American commission was appointed, and the line that was finally drawn in 1899 made an award generally favorable to Great Britain.

Venezuela Claims. In 1902, due to civil strife and to gross mismanagement during the administration of Cipriano CASTRO, Venezuelan finances were chaotic. Great Britain, Germany, and Italy were determined to seek redress for unpaid loans and sent a joint naval expedition to the Venezuelan coast; seaports were blockaded and shelled by German and British vessels, and Venezuelan gunboats were captured. The matter was embarrassing to the United States because of the MONROE DOCTRINE. The powers, taking a conciliatory step, disclaimed territorial ambitions. Germany in particular had already brought its claims to U.S. attention. Theodore Roosevelt refused a request to act as arbitrator, but the United States worked toward an amicable settlement. The claims were adjusted at Caracas in 1903, but further complications arose as to whether Venezuela should pay off the debts owed to the blockading powers before settling the claims of neutral nations; in 1904 the Hague Tribunal decided in favor of the blockading powers. The dispute became significant in international law because the scope of the Monroe Doctrine was not extended to include such cases as this; further, the heated resentment of other Spanish American nations over violation of the sovereignty of one of them resulted in the DRAGO DOCTRINE.

Venice (vĕn'ĭs), Ital. *Venezia*, city (1971 pop. 364,063), capital of Venetia and of Venice prov., NE Italy, built on 118 alluvial islets within a lagoon in the Gulf of Venice (an arm of the Adriatic Sea). The city is connected with the mainland, 2.5 mi (4 km) away, by a rail and highway bridge. Between the islands run about 150 canals, mostly very narrow, crossed by some 400 bridges. The Grand Canal, shaped like a reversed letter *S*, is the main traffic artery; its chief bridge is the RIALTO, named after the island that was the historical nucleus of Venice. Gondolas and other boats are the only means of conveyance, but there are numerous lanes (*calles*), public squares, and a few streets. Houses are built on piles. Venice is a tourist, commercial, and industrial center. The tourist trade is stimulated by many annual festivals, including ones devoted to painting, motion pictures, drama, and contemporary music. Manufactures include lace, jewelry, flour, and MURANO glass, and the city is a center for shipbuilding. Porto Marghera, the modern port of Venice (founded in the 1920s), located on the mainland, is a major shipping facility and also has considerable industry. With Istria, Venice formed a province of the Roman Empire. In the late 5th cent. refugees fleeing the Lombard invaders of N Italy sought safety on the largely uninhabited islands. The communities organized themselves (697) under a doge [from Lat. *dux*=leader]. Favorably situated for handling seaborne trade between East and West, the communities grew, and by the 9th cent. they had formed the city of Venice. The city secured (10th cent.) most of the coast of DALMATIA, thus gaining control of the Adriatic, and began to build up its eastern empire, obtaining trade and other privileges in the ports of the eastern Mediterranean. The influence of the Middle East, particularly Byzantium, which characterizes much Venetian art and architecture, is most clearly expressed in SAINT MARK'S CHURCH (rebuilt 1063–73), located on the city's principal square. In 1204 the doge, Enrico Dandolo (see under DANDOLO, family), led the host of the Fourth Crusade (see CRUSADES) in storming Constantinople. Strategic points in the Ionian, the Aegean, and the E Mediterranean were taken, notably Crete (1216). The great traveller Marco POLO represented the enterprising spirit of Venice in the 13th and 14th cent. After defeating (1380) its rival Genoa in the War of CHIOGGIA, Venice was indisputably the leading European seapower; its sea consciousness was expressed in the symbolic marriage ceremony of the doges with the Adriatic, celebrated with great pomp on the huge gilded gondola, the *Bucentaur*. All citizens shared in the prosperity, but the patrician merchants obtained political privileges. Membership in the great council, which by then had replaced the general citizenry as an electorate in the election of the doges, became restricted to an oligarchy. In reaction to an unsuccessful conspiracy in 1310, the Council of Ten (see TEN, COUNCIL OF) was instituted to punish crimes against the state. The Ten, by means of a formidable secret police, acquired increasing power, and the doge became a figurehead. In the 15th cent. Venice, known as the "queen of the seas," reached the height of its power. The city engaged in a rich trade, especially as the main link between Europe and Asia; all VENETIA on the mainland was conquered; and Venetian ambassadors, creators of the modern DIPLOMATIC SERVICE, made the power of the city felt at every court of the known world. The arsenal (founded 1104; rebuilt in the 15th and 16th cent.), where ships were built, was one of the world's wonders. The decline of Venice can be dated from the fall (1453) of Constantinople to the Turks, which greatly reduced trade with the Levant, or from the discovery of America and of the Cape of Good Hope route to Asia, which transferred commercial power to Spain and other nations to the west of Italy. The effects were not felt immediately, however, and Venice continued its proud and lavish ways. In the ITALIAN WARS, it challenged both the emperor and the pope; the League of Cambrai, formed (1508) by Pope Julius II to humble Venice, merely resulted in a few minor losses of the city's territory; the naval victory of LEPANTO (1571) gave Venice renewed standing by undoing Turkish seapower. The Renaissance marked the height of Venice's artistic glory. Architects like the LOMBARDO family, Jacopo SANSOVINO, and PALLADIO, and the Venetian school of painting, which besides its giants—TITIAN and TINTORETTO—also included Giovanni BELLINI, GIORGIONE, Jacopo PALMA (Palma Vecchio), and VERONESE, gave Venice its present aspect of a city of churches and palaces, floating on water, blazing with color and light, and filled with art treasures. Freedom of expression was complete except to those who actively engaged in politics; the satirist Aretino, the "scourge of princes," chose Venice as his place of residence, and JOHN OF SPEYER, Nicolas JENSON, and ALDUS MANUTIUS made the city a center of printing. Although the dramatist GOLDONI and painters such as TIEPOLO and CANALETTO still made Venice the most original artistic city of 18th-century Italy, they represented to some extent the decadence that accompanied the city's commercial and military decline. The fall of CYPRUS (1571), Crete (1669), and the Peloponnesus (1715; see GREECE) to the Turks ended Venetian dominance in the E Mediterranean. Politics in 18th-century Venice was aristocratic and stagnant. When, in 1797, Napoleon I delivered Venice to Austria in the Treaty of CAMPO FORMIO, the republic fell without fighting. During the Risorgimento, however, Venice played a vigorous role under the leadership of Daniele MANIN; having expelled the Austrians in 1848, it heroically resisted siege until 1849. In 1866, Venice and Venetia were united with the kingdom of Italy. The center of animation in Venice is St. Mark's Square and the Piazzetta, which leads from the square to the sea. On the square are St. Mark's Church; the Gothic Doges' Palace (14th-15th cent.), from which the BRIDGE OF SIGHS (c.1600) leads to the former prisons; the Old and New Law Courts (16th-17th cent.); the campanile (325 ft/99 m high; built in the 10th cent.; rebuilt after it collapsed in 1902); the Moors' Clocktower (late 15th cent.); the elegant Old Library (1553); St. Moses' Church; and the twin columns supporting the statues of St. Theodore stepping on a crocodile and of a winged lion of St. Mark (the emblem of Venice). On an island facing the Piazzetta is the Church of San Giorgio Maggiore (1566-1610) and on a nearby tip of land is the Church of Santa Maria della Salute (17th cent.). Among the city's numerous other points of interest are the churches of Santa Maria Gloriosa del Frari (with paintings by Titian), San Zanipolo (1234-1430), and San Zaccaria (with a *Madonna* by Bellini); the Academy of Fine Arts, with fine paintings by Bellini, Carpaccio, Mantegna, Giorgione, Veronese, and others; the Scuola di San Rocco, with a series of paintings by Tintoretto; the Scuola degli Schiavoni, with paintings by Carpaccio; and the palaces Ca' d'Oro (1440; late Gothic), Rezzonico (1680), and Pesaro (1710; baroque). The fashionable beach resort of Lido di Venezia is on a nearby island. See P. G. Molmenti, *Venice* (tr., 6 vol. 1906-8); Alberto Tenenti, *Piracy and the Decline of Venice, 1560-1615* (tr. 1967); Maurice Andrieux, *Daily Life in Venice in the Time of Casanova* (tr. 1972); Oliver Logan, *Culture and Society in Venice, 1470-1790* (1972); J. R. Hale, *Renaissance Venice* (1973); James Morris, *The World of Venice* (1974); W. H. McNeill, *Venice: The Hinge of Europe, 1081-1797* (1974).

Veni Creator Spiritus (vā'nē krāā'tôr spē'rētōōs) [Lat.,=come, Creator Spirit] and **Veni Sancte Spiritus** (sängk'tā) [Lat.,=come, Holy Ghost], Pentecostal hymns of the Roman Catholic Church. The first, much the older, has seven four-line stanzas, unrhymed, of iambic eight-syllable lines. It is used in the office of Pentecost and at solemnities such as papal elections and ordinations. In translation it is used at Anglican ordinations. *Veni Sancte Spiritus*, the sequence of Pentecost, was written before 1200. Its 10 stanzas are of three seven-syllable lines, with the first two lines of each stanza rhyming with each other; the third lines rhyme throughout the hymn.

venison (vĕn'ĭzən) [O.Fr.,=hunting], term formerly applied to the flesh of any wild beast or game hunted and used for food but now restricted to the flesh of members of the deer family. The meat is best if the animal is plump, forest fed, and at least five years old; it is improved by hanging in a cool, airy place. In Alaska, N Canada, and Siberia the domestication and breeding of reindeer developed a new meat supply (somewhat resembling beef).

Venite (vēnī'tē) [Lat.,=come], Ps. 95, so called from its opening, "O come, let us sing unto the Lord." It is the opening psalm of the Roman Catholic matins and of the Anglican morning prayer.

Venizelos, Eleutherios (ĕlĕfthâr'yôs vĕnēzĕ'lôs), 1864-1936, Greek statesman, b. Crete. After studying at the Univ. of Athens, he returned to CRETE and played a prominent part in the Cretan insurrection of 1896-97. In 1905 he led the Cretan assembly to declare the union of Crete with Greece; this union actually was not completed until 1913. In 1909 he was called to Athens by the members of the so-called Military League, who wanted political reform. The League brought him to power. During his first term as Greek premier (1910-15), Venizelos completed the revision of the constitution (1911), undertook military and financial reform, and led Greece through the BALKAN WARS (1912-13), in which its territory was greatly increased. After the outbreak of World War I he strongly favored the Allied cause, and pro-German King CONSTANTINE I forced him to resign (March, 1915). An electoral victory made Venizelos premier again in August, but when the Allies landed forces at Thessaloníki (see SALONICA CAMPAIGNS), Constantine again compelled his resignation (Oct., 1915). In 1916 Venizelos established a provisional government at Thessaloníki, which declared war on Germany and Bulgaria, and in 1917, on Constantine's abdication, he became premier for the third time. Greece fully entered the war on the Allied side, and Venizelos took part in the Paris Peace Conference. In 1920 his cabinet fell, and King Constantine was restored. The Greek defeat in the war with Turkey restored the Venizelists; Constantine abdicated in 1922, and Venizelos became (1924) premier after an overwhelming electoral victory. Soon afterward a plebiscite declared Greece a republic. Having fallen out with the military leaders, Venizelos retired from office even before the plebiscite took place. After several years of political chaos, he was recalled (1928) to the premiership. Venizelos, now elderly, overlooked the political corruption that weakened the republic. He secured rapprochements with Italy (1928), Yugoslavia (1929), and Turkey (1930). Growing royalist opposition forced his resignation in 1932; he returned to power briefly in 1933. Fearing the restoration of the monarchy, Venizelos joined a last desperate attempt at stemming the royalist tide by armed uprisings (1935) in Athens, Macedonia, and Crete. Crete held out longest against the government forces, but the rebellion was soon put down by General KONDYLIS. Venizelos fled to France, where he died.

Venlo (vĕn'lō), municipality (1971 pop. 63,077), Limburg prov., SE Netherlands, on the Maas (Meuse) River, near the West German border. It is a trade center for fruit and vegetables. Manufactures include lumber and chemicals. Venlo was formerly a fortress city; it frequently changed hands during the wars of the 16th, 17th, and 18th cent. Noteworthy buildings include a 15th-century Gothic church and the 16th-century town hall.

Vennberg, Karl, 1910-, Swedish poet. Vennberg's work reflects a skeptical attitude toward life, exemplified in *Reckoning of Time* (1945), *Crossing the Street* (1952), and *Points of View* (1954). He has been an influential critic of modern Swedish literature.

venom or **zootoxin,** any of a variety of poisonous substances produced by animals. In poisonous snakes, venom is secreted in two poison glands, one on each side of the upper jaw, and enters the fang by a duct. Snake venom is a complex substance, containing various enzymes and TOXINS. Venoms differ in their effect according to the preponderance in them of hemotoxic, hemolytic, or neurotoxic agents. Hemotoxins perforate the blood vessels, causing hemorrhage, and hemolysins dissolve the red blood cells. The venom of the fer-de-lance is chiefly hemotoxic; that of the rattlesnake, the copperhead, and the moccasin is both hemotoxic and hemolytic. Neurotoxins produce paralysis, often of the nerve centers that control breathing, thus causing a quicker death from suffocation. Cobras, coral snakes, scorpions, and spiders produce neurotoxic venoms. The venom of the gaboon viper is both hemotoxic and neurotoxic. Venoms may also contain agglutinins, which promote coagulation of blood, or anticoagulants, which have the opposite effect. The venoms of various snakes have been used medicinally, according to their specific properties, as painkillers (in arthritis, cancer, and leprosy), antispasmodics (in epilepsy and asthma), and blood coagulants (in hemophilia). The venom of the Russell's viper has been used as a coagulant in tonsillectomies and for bleeding gums. The effect of any SNAKEBITE necessarily depends on the quantity and kind of toxin it contains, as well as on the resistance of the victim. Immune serum against snake venom, or antivenin, can be prepared by repeatedly injecting sublethal doses of venom into an animal such as the horse. The immune serum thereby produced in the animal can be extracted and used to treat snakebite victims. Poisons are produced by animal species of every phylum; examples include the poison in the rounded warts of the skin of toads, the venoms of spiders, scorpions, bees, and other arthropods, and the poison of jellyfish and other coelenterates. Certain protozoans, such as dinoflagellates and blue-green algae, produce toxins as a by-product of metabolism. When conditions permit growth of large populations of such organisms, human illness and fish kills may result.

ventilation, process of supplying fresh air to an enclosed space and removing from it air contaminated by odors, gases, or smoke. Proper ventilation requires also that there be a movement or circulation of the air within the space and that the temperature and humidity be maintained within a range that allows adequate evaporation of perspiration from the skin. It was formerly believed that the discomfort, headache, and lethargy commonly associated with poor ventilation were caused entirely by the increase in the amount of carbon dioxide and the decrease in the oxygen content of the air. There is evidence to show, however, that the deleterious effects result largely from interference with the heat-regulating mechanism of the body. Lack of air currents and the increase in relative humidity and temperature (especially noticeable in crowded, poorly ventilated places) prevent normal evaporation of perspiration and loss of heat from the surface of the skin. Natural ventilation depends on winds outside and convection currents inside a building. Winds raise air pressure slightly on the windward side of a building and lower it slightly on the lee side. The pressure difference promotes circulation into the building on the windward side and out of it on the lee side. Convection currents are caused by the sinking of colder and therefore heavier air, which displaces the warmer air. A building may have a roof ventilator to allow the rising warm air to escape. If there is an opening to the outside at the bottom of the building, fresh, cool air will be drawn in. A simple roof ventilator is essentially an opening in the roof with a cover to keep out rain and to prevent winds from interfering with its functioning. Natural convection is an appreciable aid to ventilation in a large building only if it contains sources of large amounts of heat. A further useful adjunct is a FAN in the roof ventilator. The addition of distribution ducts to the fan and a system for forcing air into the building provides greater efficiency. Outlets are designed to attain maximum mixing of air and to move large amounts of air at low velocity so that temperature layers are eliminated. Factories have special suction hoods and enclosures to draw away localized dust, fumes, and heat. Incoming air may be cleaned of dust by filters or electrostatic precipitators. Deep mines, underwater tunnels, and other subterranean and submarine environments require elaborate mechanically operated systems for maintaining the air supply in a healthful condition. The lives of those working in, or traveling through, such areas depend upon a constant supply of fresh air; not only must the systems used be highly efficient, but there should be provision for emergencies in case of failure of the apparatus in operation. An outgrowth of studies of problems of ventilation is the development of methods of AIR CONDITIONING. Such systems, unlike ordinary methods of ventilation, are independent of outdoor atmospheric conditions and can, therefore, maintain the indoor atmosphere at the most healthful temperature and humidity and can free the air of dust and other undesirable materials. They accomplish this, however, at a considerable cost in energy. See Institution of Heating and Ventilating Engineers, *A Guide to Current Practice* (rev. ed. 1960).

Ventimiglia (väntēmē'lyä), Fr. *Vintimille*, town (1971 pop. 25,554), Liguria, NW Italy, on the Ligurian Sea and the Italian Riviera, near the French border. It is a seaport, a popular beach resort, and a major flower market. Landmarks include the 11th-century Church of San Michele and the cathedral (11th-12th cent.), with a 5th-century piscina. In nearby Grimaldi are grottoes in which prehistoric remains have been found.

Ventnor City, city (1970 pop. 10,385), Atlantic co., SE N.J.; inc. 1903. A seaside resort adjacent to Atlantic City, it is located on a 10-mi (16-km) sand bar known as Absecon Beach.

ventriloquism: see PUPPET.

Ventris, Michael George Francis, 1922–56, English linguist. Ventris was a student of architecture, but he became interested in the untranslated Mycenaean scripts, particularly Linear B, which was found at Cnossus, Pylos, and other sites. In 1952 he collaborated with John Chadwick in the decipherment and subsequent publication of *Documents in Mycenaean Greek* (1956). His theory, now generally accepted by scholars, indicates that Linear B was an archaic form of the Greek language. Ventris died at 34 as the result of an automobile accident.

Ventspils (vĕnts'pēls), Ger. *Windau,* city (1970 pop. 40,000), W European USSR, in Latvia, on the Baltic Sea, at the mouth of the Venta River. An ice-free seaport, it also has shipyards, fisheries, and varied manufactures. The city grew around a 13th-century castle of the Livonian Knights and was chartered in 1314.

Ventura (vĕntōō'rə), city (1970 pop. 55,964), seat of Ventura co., SW Calif., on the Pacific coast in a farm and oil region; inc. 1866. Fruit and vegetable packing, petroleum production, and research (especially in electronics and missiles) are the major industries. A mission called San Buenaventura (still the official name of the city), founded by Junípero Serra in 1782, has been restored. The Ventura city hall is on the national register of historic places. There is a junior college.

Venturi, Adolfo (ädôl'fō väntōō'rē), 1856–1941, Italian art historian. Director of Galleries and Museums in Italy, Venturi completed his exhaustive history of Italian art as far as the 16th cent. He was skilled in interpreting the authenticity of art works and made several significant judgments concerning important Renaissance pieces. His son, **Lionello Venturi,** 1885–1961, taught the history of art at the Univ. of Rome. Central to his thought was the notion that a work of art must be judged as to how well it expresses the intention of its creator. Venturi was primarily interested in modern art, believing that it informs and illuminates the art of the past. His major work is his *History of Art Criticism* (tr. 1936).

Venturi, Robert, 1925–, American architect, b. Philadelphia. Embracing the billboard and neon-sign atmosphere of the contemporary American landscape, Venturi uses it in his building designs to emphasize the ugly, bleak, and ordinary. Among his large works are the Humanities and Social Sciences building at the State Univ. of New York, Purchase, N.Y. (1968–70). His residential designs include the Trubeck and Wislocki houses, Nantucket, Mass. (1970). A characteristic design is Venturi's entry for the Football National Hall of Fame competition (1967, not built), the facade of which is a gigantic, illuminated ballpark scoreboard. He is the author of *Complexity and Contradiction in Architecture* (1966) and *Learning from Las Vegas* (1972).

Venus, in astronomy, 2d planet from the sun; it is often called the EVENING STAR or morning star and is brighter than any object in the sky except the sun and the moon. Because its orbit lies between the sun and the orbit of the earth, Venus passes through phases like those of the moon, varying from a large bright crescent when the planet is near inferior CONJUNCTION (nearest the earth) to a smaller silvery disk when it is at superior conjunction (farthest from the earth). Since its greatest ELONGATION (the angle made between the sun, the earth, and Venus) is 47°, it can never be seen much longer than 3 hr after sunset or 3 hr before sunrise. Venus revolves around the sun at a mean distance of c.67 million mi (107 million km) in a nearly circular orbit, and its period of revolution is about 225 days. It comes closer to the earth than any other planet, being c.26 million mi (42 million km) away at inferior conjunction. Venus is often referred to as the sister planet of the earth, because it is only slightly smaller in both size and mass. Several important differences, however, exist between the two planets. Although Venus is covered with a thick blanket of clouds that hides its surface from view, much has been learned of the conditions on Venus from recent U.S. and Soviet space probes. These probes indicate a surface temperature of about 800°F (427°C) and an atmospheric pressure as great as 100 times that at the earth's surface. The thick atmosphere is composed mainly of carbon dioxide, with a slight amount of water vapor and a trace of nitrogen and other elements. The high surface temperature is assumed to result partly from the so-called greenhouse effect; radiation passing through the atmosphere heats the surface, but the heat is blocked by the enveloping carbon dioxide from escaping back out through the atmosphere. Studies also indicate that Venus rotates on its axis in a retrograde direction (opposite to the direction of revolution about the sun) with a period of about 243 days. Despite this slow rotation there is little observed temperature difference between the lighted and unlighted sides of the planet. The surface of Venus is thought to be relatively smooth, although radio-wave data indicate the possible existence of two long mountain ranges. No strong magnetic field comparable to that of the earth has been detected.

Venus, in Roman religion, goddess of vegetation. Later, she became identified (3d cent. B.C.) with the Greek APHRODITE. In imperial times she was worshiped as Venus Genetrix, mother of Aeneas; Venus Felix, the bringer of good fortune; Venus Victrix, bringer of victory; and Venus Verticordia, protector of feminine chastity. The most famous representations of Aphrodite or Venus in sculpture are the *Venus of Milo* or *Melos* (Louvre); the *Venus of Medici* or *Medicean Aphrodite* (Uffizi); the *Venus of Capua* (national museum, Naples); and the *Capitoline Venus* (Capitoline Mus., Rome). The *Venus of Milo* is a Greek statue in marble, generally dated to the 2d or 1st cent. B.C. Found (1820) on the island of Melos, it was taken by the French ambassador to Turkey and was eventually presented by Louis XVIII to the Louvre. The *Venus of Medici* belongs to the 3d cent. B.C. It is probably derived from Praxiteles' *Aphrodite of Cnidus,* which was destroyed.

Venus's flower-basket: see PORIFERA.

Venus's-flytrap, insectivorous or carnivorous bog plant *(Dionaea muscipula)* native to the Carolina savannas and now widely cultivated as a novelty. The leaves, borne in a low rosette, resemble bear traps. They are hinged at the midrib, each half bearing sensitive bristles; when a bristle is touched—as by an insect—the halves snap shut and the marginal teeth interlock to imprison the insect until it has been digested. Related genera of insectivorous bog plants, notably the widespread sundews (genus *Drosera*), are found in many other parts of the world. Venus's-flytrap is classified in the division MAGNOLIOPHYTA, class Magnoliopsida, order Sarraceniales, family Droseraceae.

Venus's girdle: see CTENOPHORA.

Venus's looking-glass: see BELLFLOWER.

Veracruz (väräkrōōs') [Span.,=true cross], state (1970 pop. 3,813,613), 27,759 sq mi (71,896 sq km), E central Mexico. The capital is JALAPA DE ENRIQUEZ. Stretching c.430 mi (690 km) along the Gulf of Mexico and reaching from 30 to 100 mi (48–161 km) inland, Veracruz rises from a tropical coastal plain into the temperate valleys and highlands of the Sierra Madre Oriental. The state shares with neighboring Puebla the highest peak in Mexico, Orizaba. Most of central Veracruz is mountainous. The few navigable rivers are the Coatzacoalcos, Papáloapan, Pánuco, and Tamesí. Abundant rainfall and extremely fertile soil permit the cultivation of numerous crops. The state is a leading national producer of coffee, sugarcane, beans, maize, and rice; cacao, vanilla, tobacco, cotton, fruits, and vegetables are also grown. Cattle raising is practiced in the semitropical and temperate zones. From the tropical forests come dyewoods and hardwoods, chicle, and rubber, and in the colder regions maguey, various cacti, and coniferous forests are found. The state's principal natural resource is oil. The mountains contain relatively unexploited deposits of gold, silver, iron, and coal. Veracruz ranks high in the production of foods and beverages. In ancient times the area was a hub of pre-Columbian civilizations, including the OLMEC, the HUASTEC, and the Totonac-speaking tribes of the REMOJADAS culture. Some Indian groups were tributary to the Aztecs by the time Juan de GRIJALVA discovered the coast in 1518. Veracruz became a state in 1824. The major cities are Veracruz, Orizaba, and Cordoba.

Veracruz, city (1970 pop. 242,351), Veracruz state, E central Mexico, on the Gulf of Mexico. Rivaling Tampico as the country's main port, it is also the commercial and industrial center of an important oil region, as well as a major tourist resort with beautiful scenery, fine beaches, and excellent accommodations. The city stands on a low, sandy plain surrounded by dunes and swamps, some of which have been reclaimed and are very fertile. In 1519 the Spanish explorer Hernán Cortés landed near the site later chosen (1599) for the present city. Veracruz was easy prey for the buccaneers of the 17th and 18th cent. The harbor is guarded by the fortress of San Juan de Ulúa, which was begun in the 17th cent. and was the last stronghold of the Spanish before their expulsion in 1821. Veracruz was blockaded in 1838 by the French, who sought compensation for damages suffered by French nationals. In 1847, U.S. troops under Gen. Winfield Scott landed at Veracruz to begin the major campaign of the Mexican War. The War of the Reform involved foreign intervention in Veracruz; in Dec., 1861, Spanish troops landed there as the first contingent of a joint European force. French and British forces arrived the following month. When it became apparent that France was bent on actual conquest, the Spanish and British withdrew from the joint force. The adventure of the empire of MAXIMILIAN ensued. In 1914 an incident involving U.S. sailors in Tampico led President Woodrow Wilson to land troops in Veracruz, where they briefly invested the customhouse. Mexico responded by severing diplomatic relations. Veracruz is the seat of an episcopal see.

verb, PART OF SPEECH typically used to indicate an action. English verbs are inflected for person, NUMBER, TENSE and partially for MOOD; compound verbs formed with auxiliaries (e.g., *be, can, have, do, will*) provide a distinction of VOICE. Some English verblike forms have properties of two parts of speech (e.g., participles may be used as adjectives and gerunds as nouns). Verbs are also classified as transitive (requiring a subject) or intransitive. In Latin verb INFLECTION, voice and mood are indicated in every form. Most languages have a form class resembling that of English verbs. In many of them, unlike English, these words may form complete sentences; e.g., in Spanish, "I am singing" is expressed by the single word *canto.* Some languages (e.g., Turkish) can convey a great deal of information through modifications of form in the verb stem and ending, without the aid of auxiliary forms. A single word, for example, can indicate reciprocity, reflexivity, necessity, time, infinitive, number, person, and voice, as well as negative, causative, imperative, and intensive meanings.

Verbano: see MAGGIORE, LAGO.

Verbeck, Guido Herman Fridolin (gē'dō hûr'mən frē'dōlĭn vərbĕk'), 1830–98, American missionary in Japan, b. Netherlands. He came to the United States in 1852. After study at Auburn Theological Seminary he was ordained (1859) and sent to Japan as a missionary of the Reformed Church in America. In 1869, at the invitation of the Japanese government, Verbeck assumed direction of the school in Tokyo that later became the Imperial Univ. His *History of Protestant Missions in Japan* was published in 1883.

verbena: see VERVAIN.

Vercelli (värchĕl'lē), city (1971 pop. 56,494), capital of Vercelli prov., Piedmont, N Italy, on the Sesia River. It is an important rice market and has food-processing and textile industries. A Roman town and later a prosperous free commune, it passed to the Visconti of Milan in 1335 and was ceded by them to the house of Savoy in 1427. Of note is the Gothic basilica of Sant' Andrea (13th cent.), which has a Renaissance cloister and a convent. The only school of painting in Piedmont flourished at Vercelli in the 15th–16th cent. In the library of the cathedral (16th–18th cent.) is the Vercelli Book or *Codex Vercellensis,* a late 10th-century Anglo-Saxon manuscript that contains a collection of religious poems, including *Elene* by CYNEWULF.

Vercingetorix (vûr"sĭnjĕt'ərĭks), d. 46 B.C., leader of the Gauls, a chieftain of the Arverni. He was the leader of the great revolt against the Romans in 52 B.C. Julius Caesar, upon hearing of the trouble, rushed to put it down. Vercingetorix was, however, an able leader and adopted the policy of retreating to heavy natural fortifications and burning the Gallic towns to keep the Roman soldiers from living off the land. Caesar and his chief lieutenant Labienus lost in minor engagements, but when Vercingetorix shut himself up in ALESIA and summoned all his Gallic allies to attack the besieging Romans, the true brilliance of Caesar appeared. He defeated the Gallic relieving force and took the fortress. Vercingetorix was captured to enhance Caesar's triumph in Rome and then was put to death.

Vercors (vĕrkôr'), 1902–, French writer and illustrator, whose original name was Jean Bruller. Vercors served in the French resistance movement and helped to found Les Éditions de Minuit, an underground publishing firm. For them he wrote *Le Silence de la mer* (1942, tr. *The Silence of the Sea,* 1944). This story and the later *La marche à l'étoile* (1943) deal with the moral impossibility of collaboration with the Germans. Among his many later works are *Les Yeux et la lumière* (1948), *Sylva* (1961, tr. 1962), *Quota* (1966, tr. 1966), and *Sillages* (1972).

Verdaguer, Jacinto (hāthĕn'tō vārthägär'), 1845–1902, Catalan poet, considered the national poet of Catalonia and the most beloved poet of the Catalan Renaissance of the 19th cent. Religious troubles and poor health frequently darkened his life. Known as a saintly priest, he wrote works of religious fervor including *Idilis y Cants mistichs* (1879). He depicted the Catalan countryside in his long *Canigó* (1886). In his masterpiece, the great epic *La Atlántida* (1877), he dealt with prehistoric myths of the Iberian peninsula; it was the basis for an opera-oratorio by Manuel de Falla.

verd antique: see SERPENTINE.

Verde (vûrd'ē, vĕrd'ē), river, c.190 mi (310 km) long, rising in central Ariz. and flowing S to the Salt River. The valley supported early Indian civilizations and is dotted with ruins, such as those at Tuzigoot National Monument (see NATIONAL PARKS AND MONUMENTS, table). Bartlett and Horseshoe dams are on the river.

Verde, Cape (vûrd) [Port.,=green], Fr. *Cap Vert,* peninsula, extending into the Atlantic Ocean, W Senegal; the westernmost point of Africa. Dakar is located there. The cape was discovered by the Portuguese in 1445. The Cape Verde Islands are c.350 mi (560 km) to the west.

Verdi, Giuseppe (vâr'dē, Ital. jōōzĕp'pā vĕr'dē), 1813–1901, foremost Italian composer of opera, b. Le Roncole. Verdi, the son of an innkeeper, showed a precocious talent for the organ but was refused entrance to the Milan Conservatory as having been inadequately trained. He studied with Lavigna of La Scala, and in 1841 his first opera, *Oberto, conte di San Bonifacio,* was produced. His third opera, *Nabucodonosor* (1842, also known as *Nabucco*; the story of Nebuchadnezzar), was enormously successful. The next work *I Lombardi alla prima Crociata,* concerning the First Crusade, assured Verdi's position at La Scala. Among his major successes of the next years were *Ernani* (1844), *Rigoletto* (1851), considered his first masterpiece, *Il Trovatore* (1853), and *La Traviata* (1853). These works showed him to be a master of dramatic composition and established him securely. Verdi's style was further developed in *Un ballo in maschera* [a masked ball] (1859) and *La forza del destino* [the power of destiny] (1862). In *Aïda* (1871) all the elements of his earlier style reach maturity, the music assuming a new dramatic importance to the story. Verdi next composed his great *Requiem* (1874) in memory of the writer Manzoni. Verdi greatly admired Shakespeare, on whose plays three of his operas are based—*Macbeth* (1847; rev. version 1865) and the masterpieces of his old age, *Otello* (1887) and *Falstaff* (1893; based on *The Merry Wives of Windsor*), for both of which Boito was librettist. In these two late works, finished at ages 73 and 80, Verdi astonished the musical world with a power, subtlety, and brilliance that marked the culmination of Italian grand opera. Verdi was greatly honored during his lifetime. He was nominated a senator and offered a marquisate, which he declined. His superbly melodic works are performed throughout the world. See his letters, ed. by Charles Osborne (1971); biographies by Frank Walker (1962), G. W. Martin (1963), and Joseph Wechsberg (1974).

verdict, in law, official decision of a JURY respecting questions of fact that the judge has laid before it. In the United States, verdicts must be unanimous in Federal courts, but majority verdicts are constitutionally permissible in state courts. The jury may be instructed to render a general verdict, a special verdict, or both. A general verdict requires the jury to decide whether the defendant is guilty (or liable, in civil cases). The jury's decision is theoretically based on whether it was convinced of the occurrence of all the facts necessary to substantiate a given violation of the criminal or civil law. A special verdict answers a specific question; e.g., did a deceased person die naturally or by violence? If the jury is required only to return a special verdict, the judge must himself decide whether the law was violated. In civil suits the judge may often modify or set aside verdicts. In criminal cases, however, a verdict of not guilty generally cannot be modified, and the accused must be discharged; the judge may in certain circumstances disregard a verdict of guilty. See JEOPARDY; SENTENCE.

verdigris (vûr'dəgrēs''), one of three copper acetates: blue verdigris, $Cu(CH_3COO)_2 \cdot CuO \cdot 6H_2O$; green verdigris, $2Cu(CH_3COO)_2 \cdot CuO \cdot 6H_2O$; or neutral verdigris, $Cu(CH_3COO)_2 \cdot H_2O$; or a mixture of them. It is a poisonous gray-green to green-blue substance that is formed by the action of acetic acid on copper or copper oxide; e.g., verdigris can form on copper pots used to cook acidic foods such as tomatoes. Verdigris is used as a mordant in dyeing, as a pigment, and in making PARIS GREEN. *Verdigris* may also be used to mean PATINA.

Verdun (vərdŭn'), city (1971 pop. 74,718), S Que., Canada, on the south shore of Montreal island, on the St. Lawrence River. It is a residential suburb of Montreal.

Verdun (vĕrdŭn', Fr. vĕrdöN'), town (1968 pop. 24,716), Meuse dept., NE France, in Lorraine, on the Meuse River. A strategic transportation center, Verdun has varied industries, including textiles, candy making, and printing. The town was a prosperous commercial center in Roman times and also during the Carolingian period in the 800s. An episcopal see since the 4th cent., Verdun, with its surrounding area, was one of the three bishoprics (with Metz and Toul) seized (1552) by Henry II of France from the Holy Roman Empire. The town itself was a free imperial city before it passed to France. The Peace of WESTPHALIA (1648), ending the Thirty Years War, confirmed Verdun in French possession. Fortified by Sébastien Vauban during the reign of Louis XIV, Verdun thereafter became important strategically. After 1871 the town became the principal French fortress facing Germany and was surrounded by a ring of defenses. The longest battle of World War I was fought at Verdun in 1916 (see VERDUN, BATTLE OF). In 1918 the Americans and French were victorious in the Verdun sector and at SAINT-MIHIEL. Almost totally destroyed, Verdun was rebuilt after the war. The town and the battlefield of Verdun, with their huge military cemeteries and numerous impressive monuments, form a national sanctuary. Other points of interest are the cathedral (11th–12th cent.) and the town hall (17th cent.), which is now a war museum.

Verdun, battle of, the longest and one of the bloodiest engagements of WORLD WAR I. Two million men were engaged. It began on Feb. 21, 1916, when the Germans, commanded by Crown Prince Frederick William, launched a massive offensive against Verdun, an awkward salient in the French line. The outlying forts of Douaumont and Hardaumont soon fell, but the French rallied under General Pétain (with the cry "They shall not pass") and resistance stiffened. A British offensive on the Somme relieved the pressure on Verdun in July, 1916, and by December the French had recovered most of the ground lost. The intention of the Germans had been a battle of attrition in which they hoped to bleed the French army white. In the end, they sustained almost as many losses as the French: 328,500 to the French 348,000. See Alistair Horne, *The Price of Glory: Verdun, 1916* (1962); William Hermanns, *The Holocaust* (1972).

Verdun, Treaty of, the partition of Charlemagne's empire among three sons of LOUIS I, emperor of the West. It was concluded in 843 at Verdun on the Meuse or, possibly, Verdun-sur-le-Doubs, Soâne-et-Loire dept., E France. LOUIS THE GERMAN received the eastern portion (later Germany); CHARLES II (Charles the Bald) became king of the western portion (later France); LOTHAIR I received the central portion (Low Countries, Lorraine, Alsace, Burgundy, Provence, and most of Italy) and also kept the imperial title. Though superseded in 870 by the Treaty of MERSEN, the Treaty of Verdun was significant as marking the end of political unity in Western Europe. It also marked the beginning of the long struggle by France to reach the Rhine boundary.

Vere, Edward de: see OXFORD, EDWARD DE VERE, 17TH EARL OF.

Vereeniging (fərē'nĭkhĭng) [Afrikaans,=union], city (1970 pop. 169,553), Transvaal, NE South Africa on the Vaal River. An industrial center, its chief products are iron, steel, pipes, bricks and tiles, and processed lime and coal. Thermal power plants there supply electricity to nearby goldfields. The city, founded in 1892, owed its early growth to nearby coal mines. The Treaty of Vereeniging (1902), which ended the SOUTH AFRICAN WAR, was negotiated there and signed in Pretoria.

Veregin, Peter: see DUKHOBORS.

Vérendrye, Pierre Gaultier de Varennes, sieur de la (pyĕr gōtyā' də vărĕn' syör də lä vārăNdrē'), 1685–1749, explorer in W Canada and the United States, b. Trois Rivières (Three Rivers), Que. His father was the sieur de Varennes, for a time governor of Trois Rivières. Pierre entered the French colonial army and served in Queen Anne's War and for a time (1707–11) in its European counterpart, the War of the Spanish Succession. In 1727–28 he was a prominent figure in the extension of New France on its far frontiers and in the search for an overland Northwest Passage to the Western Sea, serving as commander of the trading posts on Lake Nipigon. In 1729 he returned to Quebec and sought to secure official permission and aid in an expedition to search for the Western Sea. Obtaining a monopoly of the fur trade in the West, but no financial support, he entered into partnership with some Montreal merchants and set out in 1731 with three of his sons, Jean Baptiste, Pierre, and François, and a nephew, La Jeremaye. The party founded a number of posts—one on Rainy Lake; Fort St. Charles on the Lake of the Woods; and Fort Maurepas, which was at first on Red River and later on Lake Winnipeg. He returned to Quebec in 1734 but went back to the West with still another son, Louis Joseph. In the years that followed the Vérendryes continued to explore in the hope of reaching the Western Sea. The eldest of the sons, Jean Baptiste, was killed (1736) by the Sioux. In 1738, Vérendrye made his memorable journey from the Assiniboine River to the Missouri River, where he visited the Mandan Indians. He returned to Fort La Reine on the Assiniboine, and it is said that he discovered Lake Manitoba in 1739. The most-discussed voyage undertaken by the Vérendryes was that of 1742–43, which was accomplished by two of the sons, probably Louis Joseph (who is generally agreed to have been the son known as the Chevalier) and François. They made a fairly long journey westward, but because of the difficulty of identifying places and Indian tribes, there is no certainty at all as to their route. The earlier hypotheses were shaken when in 1913 some school children discovered near Pierre, S.Dak., the lead plate that had been buried by the explorers when they reached the Missouri on their return. Chiefly because of this discovery, it is now generally thought that the journey did not extend farther west than the Black Hills. The elder Vérendrye sent out next an expedition that went to the Saskatchewan River and also founded two forts, Dauphin and Bourbon, on Lake Winnipegosis, probably in 1741. How far the explorers in this region went it is impossible to say; they may have entered present-day Wyoming. In 1744, Vérendrye was retired and replaced as commander in the West. In 1749 he was again appointed to that post and was given the Cross of St. Louis. He died before he could accomplish anything further in exploration. His sons wished to continue the work but received no government aid. *The Journals and Letters of Pierre Gaultier de Varennes de la Vérendrye and His Sons* were edited by Lawrence J. Burpee for the Champlain Society (1927). See also Burpee, *Pathfinders of the Great Plains* (1914); biography by N. M. Crouse (1972).

Vereshchagin, Vasily Vasilyevich (vəsē'lyē vəsēl'yəvĭch vyĕrĭshchä'gĭn), 1842–1904, Russian painter, soldier, and traveler. He is best known for his military pictures, which portrayed war in all its horror and brutality. He is known also for his studies of Turkistan and Oriental life and the canvases dealing with Anglo-Indian history. Among his most famous pictures are *Before the Attack, After the Attack, The Apotheosis of War, Left Behind, The Presentation of the Trophies, All Quiet at the Shipka Pass, The Graves at Shipka,* and *Blessing the Dead.* Most of his works are collected in the Tretyakov Gallery, Moscow. He was killed in the explosion of the flagship *Petropavlovsk* in the Russo-Japanese War. See his autobiography (tr. 1887).

Verga, Giovanni (jōvän'nē vĕr'gä), 1840–1922, Italian novelist, b. Sicily. He abandoned the study of law for literature and wrote several novels of passion in the style of the French realists. His later works, written in a different style, are marked by simplicity and strict accuracy. They deal with the Sicilian middle class and sympathetically treat the poverty and struggles of the peasantry. Verga's technique gave rise to the term *verismo,* denoting the realistic school. He is considered one of the outstanding writers of modern Europe and has been compared with Flaubert and Zola. His works include *Cavalleria rusticana* (1880, tr. with other stories in the same volume, by D. H. Lawrence, 1928), *I Malavoglia* (1881, tr. *The House by the Medlar Tree,* 1890), *Novelle rusticane* (1883, tr. by D. H. Lawrence, *Little Novels of Sicily,* 1925), and *Mastro-Don Gesualdo* (1889, tr. by D. H. Lawrence, 1923). The dramatization of *Cavalleria rusticana* was produced in 1884, and Mascagni's opera, based on it, in 1890. A stage version of *La lupa,* one of his best stories, was produced in 1896 (tr. *The Wolf Hunt,* 1921). See biography by Alfred Alexander (1972).

Vergennes, Charles Gravier, comte de (shärl grävyä' kôNt də vĕrzhĕn'), 1717–87, French statesman. After serving as ambassador at Trier, Constantinople, and Stockholm (where in 1772 he participated in the coup d'etat of Gustavus III), he was made (1774) foreign minister by Louis XVI. He supported the American Revolution, at first secretly through Pierre de BEAUMARCHAIS, then officially after signing, with Benjamin Franklin, the alliance of Feb. 6, 1778. Vergennes was the chief French representative at the peace negotiations between Great Britain and the United States, France, and Spain at the close of the American Revolution (see PARIS, TREATY OF, 1783). He also assisted in negotiating the Treaty of Teschen (1779) between Austria and Prussia at the close of the War of the Bavarian Succession. See J. J. Meng, *The Comte de Vergennes* (1932).

Vergil or **Virgil** (Publius Vergilius Maro) (both: vûr'-jil), 70 B.C.–19 B.C., Roman poet, b. Andes dist., near Mantua, in Cisalpine Gaul. Vergil's father, a farmer of the yeoman class, took his son to Cremona for his education. Thereafter Vergil continued his studies in Milan, Naples, and Rome. The poet's boyhood experience of life on the farm was an essential part of his education. After his studies in Rome, Vergil is believed to have lived with his father on the farm for about 10 years, engaged in farm work, study, and writing poetry. In 41 B.C. the farm was confiscated to provide land for soldiers. Vergil went to Rome, where he became a part of the literary circle patronized by Maecenas and Augustus and where his *Eclogues*, or *Bucolics*, were completed in 37 B.C. In these poems he idealizes rural life in the manner of his Greek predecessor Theocritus. From the *Eclogues*, Vergil turned to rural poetry of a contrasting kind, realistic and didactic. In his *Georgics*, completed in 30 B.C., he seeks, as had the Greek Hesiod before him, to interpret the charm of real life and work on the farm. His perfect poetic expression gives him the first place among pastoral poets. For the rest of his life Vergil worked on the *Aeneid*, a national epic narrating the adventures of AENEAS, which is unquestionably one of the greatest long poems in world literature. Vergil made Aeneas the paragon of the most revered Roman virtues—devotion to family, loyalty to the state, and piety. In 12 books, Vergil tells how Aeneas escaped from Troy to Carthage, where he became intimate with Dido and related his adventures to her. He then left Dido, went to Sicily, visited Hades, and landed in Italy. There he established the beginnings of the Roman state and waged successful war against the natives. The work ends with the death of TURNUS at the hands of Aeneas. The verse, in dactylic hexameters, is strikingly regular, though Vergil's death left the epic incomplete and some of the lines unfinished. Other writers were forbidden by Augustus to complete or "improve" the work. The sonority of the words and the nobility of purpose make the *Aeneid* a masterpiece. Vergil is the dominant figure in all Latin literature. Despite his paganism, his influence continued through the Middle Ages, and many poets since Dante have acknowledged their great debt to him. Minor poems ascribed to Vergil are of doubtful authorship. The spelling *Virgil* is not found earlier than the 5th cent. A.D. For a prose translation of the *Aeneid* see W. F. Jackson Knight (1956, rev. ed. 1958); for a verse translation see Rolfe Humphries (1951). See biographical studies by F. J. H. Letters (1946), Tenney Frank (1922, repr. 1965), and Brooks Otis (1966); A. G. McKay, *Vergil's Italy* (1970); W. F. Jackson Knight, *Vergil, Epic and Anthropology* (1967) and *Roman Vergil* (3d ed. 1971).

Vergil or **Virgil, Polydore,** 1470?–1555?, historian and humanist, b. Urbino, Italy. He studied at Bologna and Padua, served as secretary to the duke of Urbino, was chamberlain to Pope Alexander VI, and was sent to England as subcollector of PETER'S PENCE in 1501 or 1502. He secured the patronage of Henry VII, held many ecclesiastical preferments, and became an English subject in 1510. In 1515 he was briefly imprisoned for his criticism of Thomas Wolsey. Vergil remained largely aloof from the religious controversies of the time. He returned to Italy a few years before his death. His chief work was his *Anglicae historicae libri XXVI* [26 books of English history] (1534). This work is the first critical history of England and the first interpretive study of Henry VII. He made use of documentary as well as chronicle sources, and though his critical techniques do not meet modern standards, he marks the beginning of modern English historical criticism. See biography by Denis Hay (1952).

Vergniaud, Pierre Victurnien (pyĕr vĕktürnyăN' vĕrnyō'), 1753–93, French revolutionary. A brilliant lawyer, he gained attention (1790) when defending peasants who had burned a castle. Elected a deputy to the legislative assembly from the Gironde, he was a leader of the GIRONDISTS and was one of the greatest orators of the French Revolution. His most noted speeches include his address (1792) in favor of beginning the war against Austria. He led the fight against the bloc known as the MOUNTAIN and against Maximilien Robespierre. He fell with the Girondists, and was guillotined.

Verhaeren, Émile (āmēl' värärĕn', vərhä'rən), 1855–1916, Belgian poet and critic, a Fleming who wrote in French. His dominant passion for social reform found expression successively in a disgust with mankind, as in the naturalistic verse of *Les Flamandes* (1883); in pessimism over the growth of urban industrialization, as in *Les Villages illusoires* and *Les Villes tentaculaires* (both 1895); and finally in optimistic glorification of the energy of man, as in the lyrical *Les Forces tumultueuses* (1902) and *La Multiple Splendeur* (1906). A period of gloom and melancholic unrest in which he traveled over Western Europe and spent much time in London is reflected in a trilogy of poetic works—*Les Soirs* and *Les Débâcles* (both 1888) and *Les Flambeaux noirs* (1891). He also wrote for his wife, Marthe Massin, a trilogy of love poems—*Les Heures claires* (1896, tr. *The Sunlit Hours,* 1916), *Les Heures de l'après-midi* (1905, tr. *Afternoon,* 1917), and *Les Heures du soir* (1911, tr. *The Evening Hours,* 1918). Outstanding among his dramas, which combine verse and prose, is *Hélène de Sparte* (1912, tr. 1916). The poems in *Les Ailes rouges de la guerre* [the red wings of war] (1917) are his bitter protest against war. See study by Stefan Zweig (1914); Amy Lowell, *Six French Poets* (1915, repr. 1967).

Veria, Greece: see VÉROIA.

verism (vĕr'ĭzəm), artistic style in which photographic realism is combined with hallucinatory or ironic images. Its practitioners, including Salvador DALI and Yves TANGUY, often make use of Renaissance concepts of perspective and various academic conventions. The style is also termed veristic SURREALISM.

Veríssimo, Érico Lopes (ĕ'rēkō͞o lō͞opəs vərēs'-sēmō͞o), 1905–, Brazilian writer. Veríssimo has lectured and taught in the United States. He wrote (in English) *Brazilian Literature* (1945). His best-known novel is *Caminhos cruzados* (1935, tr. *Crossroads,* 1943). His other works include two studies of North American culture and *Mexico* (1957, tr. 1960). He was director (1953–56) of the Dept. of Cultural Affairs of the Pan American Union. Veríssimo's fiction has been published as *Ficção completa* (1966–67).

Verkhneudinsk: see ULAN-UDE, USSR.

Verkhoyansk (vyĕrkhəyänsk'), town, Yakut Autonomous Republic, NE Siberian USSR, on the Yana River, near the Arctic Circle. A river port, a fur-collecting depot, and the center of a livestock-raising area, it lies in the coldest area of the earth. The lowest temperature recorded there was −90°F (−68°C). Founded in 1638, it was a place of political exile until 1917.

Verkhoyansk Range, mountain chain, c.600 mi (970 km) long, E Siberian USSR, in the Yakut Autonomous Republic. It forms a vast arc along the Lena and Aldan rivers and rises to c.8,150 ft (2,480 m) in the south. There are coal, silver, lead, and zinc deposits. The world's lowest temperatures for inhabited places have been recorded in this region.

Verlaine, Paul (pōl vĕrlĕn'), 1844–96, French poet. He gained some notice with the Parnassian poetry of *Poèmes saturniens* (1866) and *Fêtes galantes* (1869) and became a figure in the bohemian literary world of Paris. Verlaine's turbulent marriage broke up as a result of his liaison with his young protégé, Arthur RIMBAUD. The two poets traveled in Belgium and England; their relationship ended in tragedy when Verlaine shot and wounded Rimbaud and was imprisoned in Belgium for two years. In prison he was brought back to the Catholic faith of his childhood and wrote some noble religious poetry that appeared in *Sagesse* (1881). From that time also dates his *Romances sans paroles* (1874), which shows Verlaine as one of the first of the SYMBOLISTS. The sensitive appreciation of the common incidents and sights of life and the haunting and simple music of his verse, combined with the melancholy and unreal disillusion of the decadents, distinguish his poetry. More striking, however, is the candor of Verlaine himself. Through the degrading incidents of his later life, which was marked by drunkenness, poverty, and debauchery, he preserved his honesty and inverted naïveté. *Jadis et Naguère* (1884) and *Parallèlement* (1889) were perhaps the best of his later volumes of poetry. Of his prose works the only one of importance is *Les Poètes maudits* (1884), sketches of his fellow symbolists, particularly Mallarmé and Rimbaud. The original and unorthodox phraseology and onomatopoeic music of Verlaine's verse are exemplified in the well-known "Il pleure dans mon coeur" from *Romances sans paroles.* Fine translations of some lyrics were made by Arthur Symons and Ernest Dowson, and many poems were translated by Gertrude Hall (1912), C. F. MacIntyre (1948), and Brian Hill (1957). See biographies by L. and E. Hanson (1957) and Joanna Richardson (1971); study by A. E. Carter (1969).

Vermandois (vĕrmäNdwä'), region, N France, now in Somme and Aisne depts. The region is largely agricultural (wheat, beets) but has some industry (metallurgy, textiles, rubber) located principally at SAINT-QUENTIN, the former capital. Vermandois became an earldom under Charlemagne (9th cent.), and its lords were among the most powerful in N France. The region was annexed to the French crown (c.1200), ceded to Burgundy (1435), recovered by Louis XI (1477), and incorporated into the province of PICARDY.

Vermeer, Jan or **Johannes** (vərmēr', Dutch yän vərmār', yōhän'əs), 1632–75, Dutch genre and landscape painter. He was born in Delft, where he spent his entire life. He was also known as Vermeer of Delft and as Jan or Johannes van der Meer. Carel Fabritius is presumed to have influenced him greatly. In 1653 he was admitted to the painters' guild, of which he was twice made dean. He enjoyed only slight recognition during his short life, and his work was forgotten or confused with that of others during the following century. Today he is ranked among the greatest Dutch masters and considered one of the foremost of all colorists. His most frequent subjects were intimate interiors, often with the solitary figure of a woman. Although his paintings are modest in theme, they exhibit a profound serenity and a splendor of execution that are unsurpassed. No painter has depicted more exquisitely luminous blues and yellows, pearly highlights, and the subtle gradations of reflected light, all perfectly integrated within a strictly ordered composition. Vermeer apparently produced only one or two pictures a year during his period of greatest activity. His career is a mystery to art historians because, although his work was of the finest quality, his output was too small to have been the sole support of his family of 11 children. Only about 35 paintings can be attributed to him with any certainty. Among them are *The Milkmaid* and *The Letter* (Rijks Mus.); *The Procuress* (Dresden); *Artist and Model* (Vienna); *View of Delft* (The Hague); *Soldier and Laughing Girl* (Frick Coll., New York City); *Girl Asleep* and *Young Woman with a Water Jug* (Metropolitan Mus.); *Woman Weighing Gold* and *Young Girl with a Flute* (National Gall., Washington, D.C.); and *The Concert* (Gardner Mus., Boston). Forgeries of Vermeer's work have been frequent, Hans van Meegeren's being the most successful (see FORGERY, in art). See biographies by A. Vries (1948) and F. W. Thienen (1949); studies by P. L. Hale (repr. 1937), P. Descargues (tr. 1966), L. Goldschieder (rev. ed. 1967), and L. Gowing (new ed. 1970). See also P. B. Coreman's study of Van Meegeren's forgeries (tr. 1949).

Vermeylen, August (ou'gō͞ost vĕrmī'lən), 1872–1945, Flemish writer and critic. Active in the Flemish literary revival, he was the chief founder (1893) of the journal *Van Nu en Straks* [today and tomorrow]. He was professor of literature and of art history at the Univ. of Brussels (1901–23), and in 1930 he was named rector of the Flemish Univ. of Ghent. In addition to many works of literary and art criticism, he wrote poetry and a novel, *De wandelende Jood* [the wandering Jew] (1906).

vermicelli: see MACARONI.

Vermigli, Pietro Martire (pyĕ'trō märtē'rā värmē'-lyē), 1500–1562, Italian Protestant reformer, also known as Peter Martyr. He joined the Augustinian canons and in that order received high honors as a scholar and preacher. At Naples he was influenced by Juan de VALDÉS and, accused of heresy, was forbidden to preach for some time. In 1541 he was appointed prior at Lucca, where he became the center of a group known as the Lucchese Reformers. Vermigli began to publicize Protestant views in such doctrinal matters as the interpretation of the Eucharist solely as a spiritual remembrance. Threatened with arrest, he fled to Pisa, to Switzerland, and then to Strasbourg. At the invitation of Archbishop Cranmer, he went to England, where he was professor at Oxford from 1547 until the restoration of Roman Catholicism by Mary I in 1553. While there he had some influence on episcopal changes and was consulted about the revision of the Book of Common Prayer. Vermigli returned to Strasbourg as professor; he then went to Zurich, where he was professor of theology from 1556 until his death. He was a Protestant representative at the unsuccessful attempt at Catholic-Protestant reconciliation at the Colloquy of POISSY (1561). Vermigli's works were widely read and were influential in developing a Protestant theology.

vermilion, vivid red PIGMENT of durable quality. It is a chemical compound of mercury and sulfur and is known as red sulfide of mercury; it was formerly obtained by grinding pure cinnabar but is now commonly prepared synthetically. Vermilion is a good pigment for protecting iron and steel and is therefore used in paints. It is commonly adulterated because of its high cost. Certain other materials are sometimes called vermilion; among them is imitation vermilion, prepared from a combination of red lead or basic lead chromate and certain other chemicals.

Vermont (vərmŏnt') [Fr.,=green mountain], state (1970 pop. 444,732), 9,609 sq mi (24,887 sq km), NE United States, in NEW ENGLAND, admitted to the Union in 1791 as the 14th state. MONTPELIER is the capital, BURLINGTON the largest city. Vermont is bounded on the N by the Canadian province of Quebec, on the E by New Hampshire (the Connecticut River forms the line), on the S by Massachusetts, and on the W by New York (Lake Champlain constitutes more than half this boundary). The forested Green Mts. constitute the dominant physiographical feature of the state. They consist of at least four distinct groups, all traversing the state generally in a north-south direction. Largest and most important are the Green Mts. proper, which extend down the center of the state from the Canadian border to the

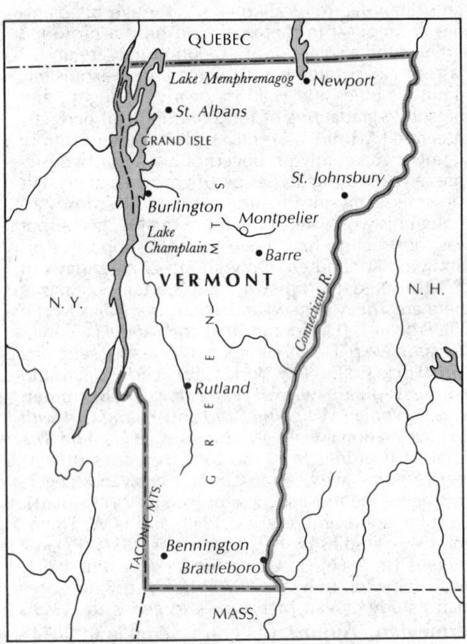

Massachusetts line, rising to Vermont's highest peak in Mt. Mansfield (4,393 ft/1,339 m). The Taconic Mts., occupying the southwestern portion of the state, contain Vermont's important marble deposits. East of the Green Mts. and extending from the Canadian border to somewhat below the middle of the state are the Granite Hills, so called because of their valuable stone. The fourth group, sometimes called the Red Sandrock Hills, extends along the Vermont shore of Lake Champlain. In E Vermont there are also isolated peaks or monadnocks not connected with the principal ranges. The rivers of Vermont (the only completely inland state of New England) flow either into the Connecticut River or into Lake Champlain. The Winooski rises E of the Green Mts. and cuts directly through them to Lake Champlain. Grand Isle co., comprising several islands and a peninsula jutting down into Lake Champlain from Canada, is connected to Vermont proper by causeways. Vermont has the variable climate of the northeast temperate zone, with abundant rainfall and a growing season that varies from 120 days in the Connecticut valley to 150 in the Lake Champlain region. Winter brings heavy snows, which usually cover the ground for at least three full months, but because the state's good roads are almost always kept clear, this season no longer forces complete isolation on rural communities. With its rugged terrain, much of it still heavily wooded, Vermont has limited areas of arable land, but the state is well suited to grazing (the Justin Morgan breed of horses was developed there). Dairy farming has long been dominant in agriculture, and the state ships milk in huge quantities to the great metropolitan markets of Boston and New York. Hay is the state's chief crop, and Vermont is famous for its maple syrup; apples and potatoes are other important products. The state's most valuable mineral resources are stone, asbestos, sand and gravel, and talc. In RUTLAND and Proctor industry is based on the quarrying and finishing of marble, and at BARRE the famous Vermont granite is quarried and processed. The manufacture of nonelectric machinery is a major industry. The textile industry, once important in Burlington, has generally declined, but the manufacture of computer components, food products, pulp and paper, and plastics has helped to compensate for this loss. Tourism is also vitally important to the state economy. Every summer thousands of vacationers are drawn by the scenic mountains and the picturesque New England villages, while climbers attack the many accessible peaks and hikers take on the Long Trail that runs the length of the state along the Green Mt. ridge. In the winter thousands of skiers flock to the slopes at Mad River Glen, Bromley, Stowe, and elsewhere. The first white man known to have entered the area that is now Vermont was Samuel de CHAMPLAIN, who, after beginning the colonization of Quebec, journeyed south with a Huron war party in 1609 to the beautiful lake to which he gave his name. The French did not attempt any permanent settlement until 1666, when they built a fort and a shrine to Ste Anne on the ISLE LA MOTTE in Lake Champlain. However, this and later French settlements were abandoned, and until well into the 18th cent. the region was something of a no man's land. Fort Dummer, built (1724) by the English near the site of BRATTLEBORO to protect settlers from Indians, is considered the first permanent settlement in what is now Vermont. However, Vermont's history may be said to have really begun in 1741, when Benning WENTWORTH became royal governor of New Hampshire. According to his commission New Hampshire extended W across the Merrimack River until it met "with our [i.e., the king's] other Governments." Since the English crown had never publicly proclaimed the eastern limits of the colony of New York, this vague description bred considerable confusion. Wentworth, assuming that New York's modified boundary with Connecticut and Massachusetts (20 mi/32 km E of the Hudson River) would be extended even farther north, made (1749) the first of the NEW HAMPSHIRE GRANTS—the township called Bennington—to a group that included his relatives and friends. However, New York claimed that its boundary extended as far east as the Connecticut River, and Gov. George Clinton of New York (father of Sir Henry Clinton) promptly informed Governor Wentworth that he had no authority to make such a grant. Wentworth thereupon suggested that the dispute between New York and New Hampshire over control of Vermont be referred to the crown. The outbreak of the last of the FRENCH AND INDIAN WARS in 1754 briefly suspended interest in the area, but after the British captured Ticonderoga and Crown Point in 1759, Wentworth resumed granting land in the area of present Vermont. In 1764 the British authorities upheld New York's territorial claim to Vermont. New York immediately tried to assert its jurisdiction—Wentworth's grants were declared void, and new grants (for the same lands) were issued by the New York authorities. Those who held their lands from New Hampshire resisted, and a hot controversy, long in the making, now exploded. New York and New Hampshire land speculators had most at stake, with the New Hampshire grantees, first on the scene, having the advantage. Regional pride among the New England settlers played a large part in creating resistance to New York authority. Chief among the leaders of this resistance was Ethan ALLEN, who organized the GREEN MOUNTAIN BOYS. New York courts were forcibly broken up, and armed violence was directed against New Yorkers until the outbreak of the American Revolution in 1775, when the British became the major threat. At the beginning of the Revolution, Ethan Allen and the Green Mountain Boys captured TICONDEROGA, and Seth WARNER took CROWN POINT. In Jan., 1777, Vermont (as its citizens were soon calling the region) proclaimed itself an independent state at WESTMINSTER. Chiefly because of the opposition of New York, the Continental Congress refused to recognize Vermont as the 14th colony or state. The convention that met at WINDSOR in July reaffirmed Vermont's independent status and adopted a constitution, notable chiefly because it was the first in the United States to provide for universal manhood suffrage. Thomas CHITTENDEN was elected the first governor. The Green Mountain Boys under Seth Warner and John STARK made an important contribution to the American cause with their victory at Bennington in Aug., 1777 (see SARATOGA CAMPAIGN). Later, Ethan Allen and his brother Ira ALLEN, acting on their own, entered into devious negotiations with British agents, possibly with the intent of annexing Vermont to Canada. The talks were inconclusive and ended when the Americans finally triumphed at Yorktown in 1781. For ten years Vermont remained an independent state, performing all the offices of a sovereign government (such as coining money, setting up post offices, naturalizing new citizens, and appointing ambassadors) and gradually becoming more and more independent. Not until 1791, after many delays and misunderstandings and, most important, after the dispute with New York was finally adjusted (1790) by payment of $30,000, did Vermont enter the Union. It was the first state to be admitted after the adoption of the Constitution by the 13 original states. In the next two decades Vermont had the greatest population increase in its history, from 85,425 in 1790 to 217,895 in 1810. As in the earliest days, most of the settlers migrated from S New England, and, since the more desirable lands in the river valleys were soon taken up, many of them settled in the less hospitable hills. Although the EMBARGO ACT OF 1807 aided the development of many small manufacturing establishments, it was bitterly opposed in Vermont for its disruption of the profitable trade with Canada. The WAR OF 1812 was unpopular in Vermont as in the rest of New England, and during the war extensive smuggling across the Canadian border was carried on. Vermont was threatened by British invasion from Canada until the Americans, under Thomas MACDONOUGH, won (1814) the battle on Lake Champlain. At this early period in its history, Vermont, lacking an aristocracy of wealth, was the most democratic state in New England. Jeffersonian Democrats held control for most of the first quarter of the 19th cent. Beginning in the 1820s political and social life in Vermont was considerably affected by the activities of those opposed to Freemasonry, and in the presidential election of 1832 Vermont was the only state carried by William Wirt, candidate of the ANTI-MASONIC PARTY. Anti-Masonry agitation was soon succeeded by even more vigorous efforts in behalf of another cause—the one against slavery. In the Mexican War, which it viewed as an undertaking solely to increase slave territory, Vermont was very apathetic, but no Northern state was more energetic in support of the Union cause in the Civil War, and Vermonters strongly favored Lincoln over Vermont-born Stephen Douglas. One of the most bizarre incidents of the war was the Confederate raid (1864) on SAINT ALBANS, a town which, after the war, also figured in the equally bizarre attempt of the Fenians to invade Canada in the cause of Irish independence. The economy of the state, meanwhile, was in the midst of a series of sharp dislocations. The rise of manufacturing in towns and villages during the early 19th cent. had created a demand for foodstuffs for the nonfarming population. Consequently, commercial farming began to crowd out the subsistence farming that had predominated since the mid-18th cent. Grain and beef cattle became the chief market produce, but when the rapidly expanding West began to supply these commodities more cheaply and when wool textile mills began to spring up in S New England, Vermont turned to sheep raising. After the Civil War, however, the sheep industry, unable to withstand the competition of Western, Australian, and South American wool, began to diminish. The rural population declined as many farmers migrated westward or turned to the easier life of the cities, and abandoned farms became a common sight. The transition to dairy farming in the 20 years following the war staved off a permanent decline in Vermont's agriculture. In politics the Republican party continued to dominate the state for nearly a century behind such leaders as Justin S. Morrill. Two Republican Presidents, Chester A. Arthur and Calvin Coolidge, were born in Vermont. The extent of the state's great devotion to the party was indicated by the presidential elections of 1912 and 1936, when in each case Vermont was one of the two states in the Union that voted Republican. In 1958, however, Vermonters sent a Democrat to Congress for the first time since the emergence of the Republican party, in 1962 they elected a Democratic governor, and in 1964 they preferred a Democratic presidential candidate for the first time in 108 years. Vermont nevertheless remains a fundamentally conservative state, perhaps most notably in its vigorous opposition to any form of Federal aid or intervention in its affairs. Vermont is governed under a constitution adopted in 1793. The state legislature, called the general assembly, consists of a senate with 30 members and a house of representatives with 150 members, all elected to serve two-year terms. The governor is elected for a two-year term; Thomas Salmon, a Democrat, was elected in 1972 and reelected in 1974. Vermont sends two Senators and one Representative to the U.S. Congress, and has three electoral votes. Among Vermont's institutions of higher education are Bennington College, Middlebury College, and the Univ. of Vermont, at Burlington. See Walter H. Crockett, *Vermont, the Green Mountain State* (5 vol., 1921–23); Harold F. Wilson, *The Hill Country of Northern New England: Its Social and Economic History, 1790–1930* (1936); Federal Writers' Project, *Vermont: A Guide to the Green Mountain State* (3d ed. 1968); M. B. Jones, *Vermont in the Making, 1750–1777* (1939, repr. 1968); R. N. Hill et al., comp., *Vermont* (1969); A. M. Hemenway, *Abby Hemenway's Vermont*, ed. by B. C. Morrissey from the 5-volume Vermont Historical Gazetteer of 1881 (1972).

Vermont, University of, officially named the Univ. of Vermont and State Agricultural College, at Burlington; land-grant and state supported; chartered 1791, opened 1800. The university has a state agricultural experiment station, a forestry research center, and a museum of art.

vermouth (vərmo͞oth'), blend of white wines fortified with additional alcohol and flavored with aromatic herbs, spices, and roots. It contains up to 19% alcohol. The sweeter, darker type of vermouth is sometimes called Italian vermouth, and the lighter, drier type, French vermouth. Vermouth is used as an appetizer and as a mixer in cocktails.

Vernadsky, George (vĕrnät'skē), 1887–1973, American historian, b. Russia. He emigrated to the United States in 1927 and was research associate in history (1927–46) and professor of Russian history (1946–56) at Yale. His many books on Russian and Ukrainian history include *Political and Diplomatic History of Russia* (1936), *Bohdan, Hetman of Ukraine* (1941), and his one-volume *History of Russia* (5th rev. ed. 1961). He also wrote a five-volume work, *A History of Russia* (1943–69). The first two volumes, written with Michael Karpovich, are *Ancient Russia* and *Kievan Russia*. The other volumes are *The Mongols and Russia, Russia at the Dawn of the Modern Age,* and *The Tsardom of Moscow.*

vernal equinox: see EQUINOX.

Verne, Jules (vûrn; zhül vĕrn), 1828–1905, French novelist, originator of modern science fiction. After completing his studies at the Nantes lycée, he went to Paris to study law. He early became interested in the theater and wrote (1848–50) librettos for operettas. For some years his concerns alternated between business and the theater, but after 1863 he drew upon his interest in science and geography to write a series of romances of extraordinary journeys, in which he anticipated, with remarkable foresight, many scientific and technological achievements of the 20th cent. He is especially known to English readers in translations of his *Five Weeks in a Balloon* (1863), *A Journey to the Center of the Earth* (1864), *From the Earth to the Moon* (1865), *Twenty Thousand Leagues under the Sea* (1870), *The Tour of the World in Eighty Days* (1873), *The Mysterious Island* (1875), and *Michael Strogoff* (1876). Verne became extremely popular, and by his death he had written more than 50 books. Plays and motion pictures have been made from many of his works, which are still widely read, particularly by the young. See study by I. O. Evans (1966).

Verner, Karl Adolf (vûr'nər, Dan. kärl ä'dôlf vĕr'nər), 1846–96, Danish philologist. Verner was a librarian at the Univ. of Halle (now in E Germany) and a professor of Slavonic languages at the Univ. of Copenhagen. His fame rests on **Verner's law,** a linguistic formulation showing that certain consonantal alternations in Germanic languages are the result of patterns of alternation in the position of word accent in the parent language. This formulation contained modifications of GRIMM'S LAW.

Vernet (vĕrnā'), French family of painters. **Claude Joseph Vernet,** 1714–89, marine painter, b. Avignon, studied with his father, Antoine Vernet, a decorative painter, and in Rome, where he acquired a reputation for fine work. He was summoned to Paris in 1753 and commissioned by the king to paint the famous series of seaports of France. He finished 14 of them (Louvre). His son **Antoine Charles Horace Vernet,** 1758–1835, called Carle Vernet, rose to fame under the empire with his drawings of the Italian campaign and his paintings *The Battle of Marengo* (Versailles) and *Morning of Austerlitz.* Under the Restoration he was popular as a lithographer and painter of dogs, horses, and scenes of the hunt. His son **Émile Jean Horace Vernet,** 1789–1863, was one of the most popular military painters of the 19th cent. He is best known for his decorations of the Constantine Room at Versailles and his *Defense of the Barrier at Clichy* (Louvre).

vernier (vûr'nēr), auxiliary scale, either straight or an arc of a circle, designed to slide along a fixed scale. Its unit divisions, usually smaller than those on the fixed scale, permit a far more precise reading. The vernier is attached to the scales of instruments employed for very accurate linear or angular measurements; these include the transit, sextant, barometer, compass, and caliper. It was devised by a French mathematician, Pierre Vernier, who described it in his *Construction, usage et propriétés du quadrant nouveau de mathématiques* (1631). Certain auxiliary control mechanisms used for fine measurements or adjustments are often called verniers.

Vernon, Edward, 1684–1757, British admiral. He entered the navy in 1700 and rose steadily in rank. A member of Parliament from 1722, he opposed the government of Sir Robert Walpole and urged war with Spain. When war was finally declared (see JENKINS'S EAR, WAR OF), Vernon won great popularity by his capture (1739) of Portobelo. However, the failure of his joint expedition (1741) with the incompetent General Wentworth against Cartagena and Santiago de Cuba led to his recall. Vernon's nickname, "Grog," was given to the drink—rum diluted with water—that he ordered served to his sailors to curb their drunkenness. George Washington's half brother Lawrence named the Washington estate, Mt. Vernon, for the admiral, under whom he had served. See study by Cyril Hartmann (1953).

Vernon, city (1971 pop. 13,283), S British Columbia, Canada, near the north end of Okanagan Lake. The center of a fruit-growing area, it has packing and dehydrating plants. There are lumber mills and sawmills in the district.

Vernon. 1 Town (1970 pop. 27,237), Tolland co., N Conn.; settled c.1726, inc. 1808. Manufactures include electronic components, silk screens, and textiles. Vernon merged with Rockville in 1965 and is closely associated with the nearby towns of Ellington and Tolland in the greater Hartford area. **2** City (1970 pop. 11,454), seat of Wilbarger co., N Texas, near the Okla. line; inc. 1890. Vernon is headquarters for the 500,000-acre (202,300-hectare) W. T. Waggoner Ranch. Founded in 1880 on the cattle trail to Dodge City not far from Doan's Crossing on the Red River, it was a roistering trail town until Swiss and Wendish farmers came. A highway center, it is known to tourists.

Vero Beach (vēr'o), city (1970 pop. 11,908), seat of Indian River co., E Fla., on Indian River (a lagoon and part of the Intracoastal Waterway), in a citrus-fruit region; founded c.1888, inc. 1919. Nearby are the noted McKee Jungle Gardens (opened 1931).

Véroia or **Veria** (both: vĕ'rēä), town (1971 pop. 29,528), capital of Imathía prefecture, N Greece, in Macedonia. It is a lignite-mining and textile-milling center. In ancient times the town was known as Berea or Beroea. Paul and Silas preached there (Acts 17.10).

Verona (vərô'nä), city (1971 pop. 263,589), capital of Verona prov., Venetia, NE Italy, on the Adige River. It is an industrial and agricultural center, with noted annual agricultural fairs. Manufactures include food products, textiles, and chemicals. Verona's position on the Brenner road to central Europe has given it commercial and strategic importance since Roman times. The date of its founding is obscure, but it was an important settlement before its conquest by Rome in 89 B.C. During the barbarian invasions of Rome (5th–6th cent. A.D.) Odoacer made it his fortress, and Theodoric later made it his favorite residence. Verona later became the seat of a Lombard duchy and then of Frankish counts. In the 12th cent. it was made a free commune. Along with other communes of Venetia, Verona formed (1164) the Veronese League, which joined (1167) the Lombard League in opposing Emperor Frederick I. Ezzelino da Romano ruled the city from 1226 to 1259. The story of *Romeo and Juliet* embodies the strife between Guelphs (of whom Romeo's family were members) and Ghibellines (Juliet's family) that tore Verona in the 13th and 14th cent. The Ghibelline Della Scala (or Scaligeri) family became lords of Verona in the 1260s; under Can Francesco (Can Grande) della SCALA (1291–1329) the city reached its greatest power. His successors gradually lost all the city's possessions, and in 1387 Verona fell to Milan. Venice conquered Verona in 1405, and the city fared well under Venetian rule (to 1797). During the Renaissance, Verona produced major artists, e.g., the architects Giocondo and Sanmichele and the painters Pisanello and Paolo Veronese, who embellished both Verona and Venice. In the 19th cent. Austria, which then ruled Venetia, made Verona one of its chief fortresses in N Italy. The Congress of Verona (see VERONA, CONGRESS OF) was held there in 1822. After Austrian rule of Venetia was ended as a result of the Austro-Prussian War (1866), Verona joined the kingdom of Italy. Because of its strategic position Verona was the target of heavy Allied bombings in World War II and suffered considerable damage. It was further damaged by retreating Germans in April, 1945. Among the numerous points of interest in Verona (some reconstructed after 1945) are the Romanesque Church of San Zeno Maggiore (9th–15th cent.), which has a fine triptych (1459) by Mantegna; the large Roman amphitheater (1st cent. A.D.); a Roman theater; the castle and bridge of the Scaligeri (both 1354); the Gothic tombs of the Scaligeri; the Romanesque cathedral (12th–15th cent.); the Gothic Church of Sant' Anastasia (13th–15th cent.); the Giusti Gardens (c.1580); and the Renaissance-style Loggia del Consiglio (15th cent.).

Verona (vərō'nə), borough (1970 pop. 15,067), Essex co., NE N.J.; inc. 1907.

Verona, Congress of, 1822, at Verona, Italy, the last European conference held under the provisions of the Quadruple Alliance of 1814. The main problem discussed was the revolution in Spain against FERDINAND VII, and the congress decided that a French army, under mandate of the Holy Alliance, should suppress the rebellion. This decision was protested by the British foreign minister, George CANNING, and led to a growing rift between Great Britain and the other powers.

Veronese, Paolo (pä'ōlō vārōnā'zā), 1528–88, Italian painter of the Venetian school. Named Paolo Caliari, he was called Il Veronese from his birthplace, Verona. Trained under a variety of minor local artists, he was more influenced by the works of Giulio Romano, Parmigianino, and particularly Titian. In 1553 he was in Venice, where he began to develop his characteristic opulent use of color. His talent was quickly recognized. Commissioned to work on the ceilings in the ducal palace, he painted *Age and Youth* and *Hera Presenting Gifts to Venice.* His pictures are crammed with figures arranged in a sinuous spatial pattern. Complex mannerist devices are evident in the Giustiniani altarpiece (San Francesco della Vigna, Venice) and in the many works he executed for the Church of San Sebastian. About 1566 he decorated the villa at Maser (near Vicenza). Depicting landscapes, mythological scenes, and portraits, he achieved one of the most ingenious examples of illusionism. Veronese is known chiefly for his religious feast scenes, which he interpreted in a notably secular manner. Such canvases were the *Supper at Emmaus* (Louvre), the *Marriage at Cana* (1562; Louvre), and the *Feast in the House of the Pharisee* (c.1570; Milan). In these scenes he emphasized splendor of color and lavish accessories, banquet delicacies, highly fashionable courtiers, and soldiers, musicians, horses, dogs, apes, and magnificent buildings. In 1573 the artist was called before the Inquisition because certain details in the *Feast in the House of Levi* (now in the Academy, Venice) were considered irreverent. He defended himself valiantly but was required to change the offending details. In 1576 he painted one of his most famous works, *The Rape of Europa,* now in the ducal palace. After the fire of 1577 he was employed in the reconstruction of the ducal palace, where he executed the splendid *Triumph of Venice* and *Venice Ruling with Justice and Peace.* Veronese ranks among the greatest of Venetian decorative painters. His harmonious tonalities and rich textures place him among the best colorists. Many of his works are in American museums, including *Venus and Mars* (Metropolitan Mus.), two allegorical paintings (Frick Coll., New York City), *Lady with her Daughter* (Walters Art Gall., Baltimore), *Creation of Eve* (Art Inst., Chicago), a family portrait (California Palace of the Legion of Honor, San Francisco), and a family portrait and *Rest on the Flight to Egypt* (Ringling Mus. of Art, Sarasota, Fla). See biography by Antoine Orliac (1940).

veronica, in botany: see FIGWORT.

veronica (vərŏn'ĭkə) [Lat., probably connected with Greek *Berenice*], relic preserved in St. Peter's Church, Rome. It is said to be a veil that a woman used to wipe the face of Jesus as he was on the way to Calvary. The cloth retained the print of his face. The woman, often called Veronica, is not listed in official calendars of saints. The relic is commonly called Veronica's veil.

Verrazano, Giovanni da (jōvän'nē dä vĕr"rätsä'nō; vĕr"əzä'nō), c.1480–1527?, Italian navigator and explorer, in the service of France, possibly the first European to enter New York Bay. Sailing west to reach Asia, Verrazano explored (1524) the North American coast probably from North Carolina to Maine. In 1526, or later, sailing from France, he explored the West Indies, where he was killed by the natives. Based on his discoveries, his brother Gerolamo's maps (1529) showed a new concept of North America. The name is sometimes spelled Verrazzano. See L. C. Wroth, *The Voyages of Giovanni da Verrazzano* (1970).

Verrazano-Narrows Bridge, vehicular suspension bridge, New York City, across the Narrows at the entrance to New York harbor, linking the boroughs of Brooklyn and Richmond (Staten Island). Designed by O. H. Ammann, the bridge was completed in 1964. It is the longest suspension bridge in the United States, with a main span of 4,260 ft (1,298 m). There are two levels, each holding six traffic lanes.

Verres, Caius (kā'əs vĕr'ēz), c.120 B.C.–43 B.C., Roman administrator. He held various posts before serving as governor of Sicily (73–71 B.C.). His corruption and extortion were notable even in an era when corruption among Roman governors was taken for granted. He was brought to trial, and Cicero began to issue his thundering Verrine Orations against him. Undeniably the trial was a political maneuver to bolster the senatorial party and the denunciations by Cicero were highly colored, but Verres' lawyer, Hortensius Quintus, was unable to offer an adequate defense. Verres fled to Massilia (modern Marseilles). In 46 B.C., Marc Antony proscribed Verres, who lived in Massilia until his death.

Verrius Flaccus (vĕr'ēəs flăk'əs), fl. 20 B.C., Roman grammarian. A freedman, he was appointed by Augustus to educate his grandsons and died at an advanced age during the reign of Tiberius. Of his numerous works, only one, his treatise *De verborum significatu* [on the meaning of words], survives, in an abridgment by Sextus Pompeius FESTUS. This work is a source of information about Latin grammar and Roman literature, customs, and myths.

Verrocchio, Andrea del (ändrē'ä dĕl vār-rôk'kyō), 1435–88, Florentine sculptor and painter, whose real name was Andrea di Michele di Francesco di Cioni. He was a leading figure in the early Renaissance, and his workshop was a center for the training of young artists in Florence. A virtuoso metalworker, Verrocchio was primarily concerned with the spirited rendering of movement and the elaboration of detail. Many of his paintings are lost. Of the remaining panels, his hand is evident in the *Baptism of Christ* (Uffizi), assisted by Leonardo da Vinci. In the Pistoia altarpiece he was aided by Lorenzo di Credi. Other attributions are *Tobias and the Angel* (National Gall., London), two paintings of the *Madonna and Child* (National Gall., London; Berlin), and a *Crucifixion with Saints* (Argiano). Most of Verrocchio's achievements in sculpture have survived. He may have received his first training under Donatello. His earlier work includes the bold group *Incredulity of St. Thomas* (Orsanmichele). In 1472 he designed the tombs of Piero and Giovanni de' Medici (San Lorenzo). In the same period he created the graceful *Boy with a Dolphin* and a lithe portrayal of *David* (Bargello). He went to Venice (c.1480) to work on the equestrian monument of the condottiere Bartolomeo Colleoni. Verrocchio designed an awesome figure of the commander, which was not cast until after the sculptor's death. Examples of his bronze work are in the Metropolitan Museum, and there are two portrait busts of Giuliano and Lorenzo de' Medici in the National Gallery of Art, Washington, D.C. See his complete sculptures, paintings, and drawings, ed. by Gunther Passavant (1969).

Versailles (vərsī', Fr. vĕrsī'), city (1968 pop. 94,915), capital of Yvelines dept., N central France. It was an insignificant village made famous by Louis XIV, who built (mid-17th cent.) the palace and grounds that have become almost synonymous with the name Versailles. The growth of the town began in 1682, when Louis moved his court there. The huge structure, representing French classical style at its height, was the work of Louis Le Vau, J. H. Mansart, and Charles Le Brun. André Le Nôtre laid out the park and gardens, which are decorated with fountains, reservoirs, and sculptures by such artists as Antoine Coysevox. A huge machine was built at MARLY-LE-ROI to supply water for the fountains. The park contains two smaller palaces, the Grand TRIANON and the Petit Trianon, as well as numerous temples, grottoes, and other decorative structures. The scene of the beginnings of the French Revolution, Versailles never again became a royal residence (the Tuileries in Paris replaced it in this function); under Louis Philippe it became a national monument and museum. The palace was the scene of the proclamation of the German Empire (1871) and of the Third French Republic. Several important treaties were signed at Versailles, most notably the 1919 treaty ending World War I and establishing the League of Nations. Versailles is today one of the greatest tourist centers in France. The city has some industry, such as the manufacture of trailers, insulators, chemical products, and watches.

Versailles, Treaty of, any of several treaties signed in the palace of Versailles, France. For the Treaty of Versailles of **1783,** see PARIS, TREATY OF, 1783. The Preliminary Treaty of Versailles of **1871** was signed at the end of the Franco-Prussian War by Otto von Bismarck for Germany and by Adolphe Thiers for France. It was ratified (1871) in the Treaty of Frankfurt. France ceded Alsace (except the Territory of Belfort) and part of Lorraine, including Metz, to Germany and agreed to pay an indemnity of 5 billion francs ($1 billion). German occupation troops were to remain until payment had been completed (only until 1873, it turned out, because of prompt French payment). The most important treaty signed at Versailles (in the Hall of Mirrors) was that of **1919.** It was the chief among the five peace treaties that terminated World War I. The other four (for which see separate articles) were Saint-Germain, for Austria; Trianon, for Hungary; Neuilly, for Bulgaria; and Sèvres, for Turkey. Signed on June 28, 1919, by Germany on the one hand and by the Allies (save Russia) on the other, the Treaty of Versailles embodied the results of the long and often bitter negotiations of the Paris Peace Conference of 1919. The outstanding figures in the negotiations leading to the treaty were Woodrow WILSON for the United States, Georges CLEMENCEAU for France, David LLOYD GEORGE for England, and Vittorio Emanuele ORLANDO for Italy—the so-called Big Four. Germany, as the defeated power, was not included in the consultation. Among the chief causes of Allied dissension was Wilson's refusal to recognize the secret agreements reached by the Allies in the course of the war; Italy's refusal to forego the territorial gains promised (1915) by the secret Treaty of London; and French insistence on the harsh treatment of Germany. Wilson's FOURTEEN POINTS were, to a large extent, sacrificed, but his main objectives, the creation of states based on the principle of national self-determination and the formation of the LEAGUE OF NATIONS, were embodied in the treaty. However, the U.S. Senate refused to ratify the treaty, and the United States merely declared the war with Germany at an end in 1921. The treaty formally placed the responsibility for the war on Germany and its allies and imposed on Germany the burden of the REPARATIONS payments. The chief territorial clauses were those restoring Alsace and Lorraine to France; placing the former German colonies under League of Nations MANDATES; awarding most of West Prussia, including Poznan and the POLISH CORRIDOR, to Poland; establishing Danzig (see GDAŃSK) as a free city; and providing for plebiscites, which resulted in the transfer of Eupen and Malmédy to Belgium, of N Schleswig to Denmark, and of parts of Upper Silesia to Poland. The Saar Territory (see SAARLAND) was placed under French administration for 15 years; the RHINELAND was to be occupied by the Allies for an equal period; and the right bank of the Rhine was to be permanently demilitarized. The German army was reduced to a maximum of 100,000 men, the German navy was similarly reduced, and Germany was forbidden to build major weapons of aggression. Germany, after futile protests, accepted the treaty, which became effective in Jan., 1920. Subsequently, German dissatisfaction with the terms of the treaty played an important part in the rise of NATIONAL SOCIALISM, or the Nazi movement. While Gustav STRESEMANN was German foreign minister, Germany by a policy of fulfillment succeeded in having some of the treaty terms eased. Reparations payments, the most ruinous part of the treaty, were suspended in 1931 and were never resumed. In 1935 Chancellor Adolf HITLER unilaterally canceled the military clauses of the treaty, which in practice became a dead letter; in 1936 he began the remilitarization of the Rhineland. A vast literature has been written on the Paris Peace Conference and on the Treaty of Versailles, and controversy continues as to whether the treaty was just, too harsh, or not harsh enough. See J. M. Keynes, *Economic Consequences of the Peace* (1919, repr. 1971); H. W. V. Temperley, ed., *A History of the Peace Conference of Paris* (6 vol., 1920–24); Carnegie Endowment for International Peace, *The Treaties of Peace, 1919–1923* (1924); Harold Nicolson, *Peacemaking, 1919* (1933, repr. 1965); Lord Riddell et al., *The Treaty of Versailles and After* (1935); W. E. Stephens, *Revisions of the Treaty of Versailles* (1939); Paul Birdsall, *Versailles Twenty Years After* (1941, repr. 1962); F. S. Marston, *The Peace Conference of 1919* (1944); Étienne Mantoux, *The Carthaginian Peace* (1946, repr. 1965).

Verschaffelt, Pieter Anton (pē'tər än'tôn vĕrskhäf'-əlt), 1710–93, Flemish rococo sculptor. He spent about 10 years in Rome, where he executed a monument to Pope Benedict XIV. In 1752 he settled at Mannheim, Germany, where he became director of the academy. His most important works are there—decorations for the Jesuit church and for the library of the ducal palace, and a statue of Elector Charles Theodore. In the cathedral at Ghent is his tomb of Bishop Maximilian Antoine van der Noot.

versification, principles of metrical practice in poetry. In different literatures poetic form is achieved in various ways; usually, however, a definite and predictable pattern is evident in the language. In ancient Greek poetry the pattern was in the quantity of the syllables, i.e., the duration of the time required to express a syllable. Intricate metrical patterns were devised by the Greek poets and adapted by the Romans. Greek terminology is still used in the analysis of metrics, although in modern languages stress has been substituted for quantity. The line or verse of poetry is a fundamental unit of meter and is divided somewhat arbitrarily into feet according to the major and minor stresses. In the stanza beginning, "Thirty days hath September," there are four stresses in the first line; there is no unstressed syllable between the second and third stressed ones. The types of feet retain the ancient Greek names: iambus u-; trochee -u; spondee - -; pyrrhic uu; anapest uu-; and dactyl -uu. Accordingly the number and type of feet determine the name of the meter, e.g., iambic PENTAMETER, five iambic feet; iambic hexameter (see ALEXANDRINE), six iambic feet; dactylic hexameter, six dactylic feet. A patterned arrangement of lines into a group is called a stanza. RHYME, which developed after the classical period, perhaps to reinforce rhythm when the old quantitative verse was no longer used, is an important element in stanzaic structure. Rhyme was developed to a high degree in Romance languages, especially in Provençal and French. Germanic poetry, entirely unrelated to Greek origins, developed characteristics of its own, many of which are reflected in modern poetry. Anglo-Saxon and Icelandic poetry have strong accents or stresses, usually four to a line; a caesura or definite break in the middle of the line; and a pattern of alliteration (repetition of consonant sounds), usually of three of the stressed syllables of the line, or sometimes of only two. Much of Middle English poetry is alliterative verse, while the rest follows the French forms of rhyme and rhythm. Chaucer is credited with inventing the first characteristically English stanza form, the rhyme royal. Later popular English forms were the BALLAD, the SONNET, and the stanza developed by Edmund SPENSER, called Spenserian. Blank verse became the great dramatic line in the 16th cent., while the heroic couplet was the dominant form in 18th-century English verse. Modern poets, such as Gerard Manley Hopkins, have recognized both the time and stress measures of verse and have experimented with assonance, alliteration, and sprung rhythm (see FREE VERSE). See George Saintsbury, *A History of English Prosody* (3 vol., 1906–10); Karl Shapiro, *A Bibliography of Modern Prosody* (1948) and with Robert Beum, *A Prosody Handbook* (1965); J. B. Mayor, *Chapters on English Metre* (2d ed. 1968); W. K. Wimsatt, *Versification* (1972).

vers libre: see FREE VERSE.

vertebral column: see SPINAL COLUMN.

vertebrate, any animal having a backbone or SPINAL COLUMN. In the adults of nearly all forms the backbone consists of a series of vertebrae. All vertebrates belong to the subphylum Vertebrata of the phylum CHORDATA. There are five classes of vertebrates: fish, amphibians, reptiles, birds, and mammals. General characteristics of vertebrate animals include their comparatively large size, the high degree of specialization of parts they exhibit, their bilaterally symmetrical structure, and their wide distribution over the earth. In addition to an internal skeleton of bone and cartilage or of cartilage alone, vertebrates have a spinal cord, a brain enclosed in a cranium, a closed circulatory system, and a heart divided into two, three, or four chambers. Most have two pairs of appendages that are variously modified as fins, limbs, or wings in the different classes. All animals without backbones are called INVERTEBRATES; these do not form a homogeneous group as do vertebrates. See J. Z. Young, *The Life of Vertebrates* (2d ed., 1962).

vertical circle, in astronomy, the great circle on the celestial sphere that passes from the observer's zenith through a given celestial body. In the HORIZON COORDINATE system the ALTITUDE of a body is measured along its vertical circle.

vertical takeoff and landing aircraft (VTOL), craft capable of rising and descending vertically from and to the ground, thus requiring no runway. While a BALLOON or an AIRSHIP has obvious VTOL capability, both are very inefficient at moving parallel to the earth's surface. The AUTOGIRO and the HELICOPTER offer some improvement in this respect, but still have very limited performance. A large number of VTOL designs have been produced and tried. The pogostick, or tail-sitting, type was similar in appearance to a conventional airplane except for a special tail on which it took off and landed. This type was abandoned, partly because of the difficulty in maintaining fine control when its fuselage was positioned vertically, e.g., during a landing. Convertiplanes are VTOL craft that can fly horizontally with the same effectiveness as a conventional airplane. In one helicopter-type convertiplane, a rigid rotor that spins about a vertical axis provides lift during takeoff and landing. During forward flight, some of the lift is provided by short fixed wings, and forward thrust is supplied by a pusher propeller. In other convertiplanes conventional-looking aircraft tilt their propellers so that their axes are vertical during takeoff and landing and are horizontal during forward flight. By 1968 a jet fighter convertiplane, using vanes that could direct the thrust of its engine upward or forward, and capable of flight at approximately the speed of sound, was developed. The military consider such a craft to be highly desirable because it cannot be neutralized by destroying runways.

vertigo (vûr'tĭgō), sensations of moving in space or of objects moving about a person and the resultant difficulty in maintaining equilibrium. True vertigo, as distinguished from faintness, lightheadedness, and other forms of dizziness, occurs as a result of a disturbance of some part of the body's balancing mechanism, located in the inner ear (e.g., vestibule, semicircular canals, auditory nerves). Labyrinthitis, or infection and irritation of the middle and inner ear, is a common cause of vertigo. Elimination of infectious, toxic, or environmental factors underlying the disturbance is essential for permanent relief.

Verulamium, England: see SAINT ALBANS.

vervain, common name for some members of the Verbenaceae, a family of herbs, shrubs, and trees (often climbing forms) of warmer regions of the world. Well-known wild and cultivated members of the family include species of the shrubby *Lantana* and of *Verbena;* many species of both are native to the United States. Many cultivated verbenas (herbs or shrubs) have fragrant blossoms and leaves that are sometimes used for distillation of oils or for tea, as are those of the similar lemon verbena (*Lippia citriodora*) of tropical America and Africa. Wild American species are more frequently called vervains. The European vervain (*V. officialis*), now naturalized in the United States, was sacred to the Greeks, Romans, and Druids and is associated in Christian tradition with the Crucifixion. Plants of the genus *Avicennia* are a characteristic constituent of tropical MANGROVE vegetation. Economically, the most important member of the family is TEAK. The family is classified in the division MAGNOLIOPHYTA, class Magnoliopsida, order Lamiales.

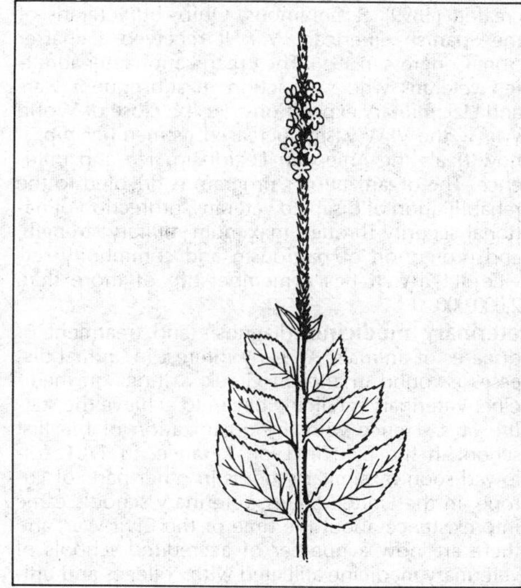

Hoary vervain, Verbena stricta

vervet: see MONKEY.

Verviers (vĕrvyā'), city (1970 pop. 33,587), Liège prov., E Belgium, on the Vesdre River and at the foot of the Ardennes. Manufactures of this industrial center include textiles and machinery. Nearby is a large reservoir, the Barrage de la Gileppe (built 1867–78).

Vervins, Treaty of (vĕrvăN'), 1598, peace treaty signed at the small town of Vervins, Aisne dept., N France, by the representatives of Henry IV of France and Philip II of Spain. It ended the French Wars of Religion by obliging Philip to withdraw his troops from France, thus depriving the Catholic League of Spanish support. The Edict of Nantes (see NANTES, EDICT OF), which defined the rights of French Protestants, was signed in the same year.

Verwey, Albert (äl'bĕrt vĕrvī'), 1865–1937, Dutch poet. His early verse was melodious, spontaneous, and evocative and showed the influence of Wordsworth; later works became increasingly dissonant and complex. Verwey came to believe that the primary role of poetry was to function as a social force, and he promoted his views in his periodical, the *Bewiging* [movement] (1905–19), and as professor of Dutch literature at Leiden (1924–35).

Verwoerd, Hendrik Frensch (hĕn'drək frĕnsh fərvōōrt'), 1901–66, South African political leader, b. Holland. He was taken as an infant to South Africa when his parents emigrated as missionaries. He graduated from Stellenbosch Univ. and studied further in Germany, where he came into contact with the nascent National Socialist (Nazi) party. He became (1927) professor of psychology and sociology at Stellenbosch. In 1928 he was named editor of the *Transvaaler,* an Afrikaans nationalist newspaper. His editorial policy reflected enmity toward the British, the Africans, and the Jews. Following a series of important posts in the Nationalist party, he became a senator (1948) and minister of native affairs (1950). In 1958 he was elected to parliament and, upon the death of J. G. Strijdom, became prime minister. A harsh proponent of white supremacy, Verwoerd, in response to foreign criticism, reformulated the apartheid policy as "separate development," meaning physical segregation of the races. When South Africa became (1961) a republic, he severed its connections with the British Commonwealth. An attempt was made (1960) on his life; its failure was interpreted by Verwoerd as God's approval of his work. A second assassination attempt succeeded in Sept., 1966.

Very, Jones, 1813–80, American poet, b. Salem, Mass., studied at Harvard Divinity School. His mystical poems express his belief in total surrender to the will of God and his reverence for nature as a symbol of the Divine. Emerson edited Very's *Essays and Poems* (1839). Posthumous volumes of Very's works were *Poems* (1883) and *Poems and Essays* (ed. by J. F. Clarke, 1886).

Vesalius, Andreas (vĭsā'lēəs), 1514–64, Flemish anatomist. He made many discoveries in anatomy and became noted as professor of anatomy (1537?–1546?) at the Univ. of Padua. There he produced his chief work, *De humani corporis fabrica* (1543), based on studies made by dissection of human cadavers; the notable illustrations are attributed to Jan von Calcar. Vesalius's condensation (1543) appeared in English as *The Epitome of Andreas Vesalius* (1949). His work overthrew many of the hitherto-uncontested doctrines of the second-century anatomist Galen and caused a storm of criticism to be directed against himself. He left Padua, becoming physician to Emperor Charles V and to his son Philip II. In 1563 he made a pilgrimage to Jerusalem and on the return voyage died in Greece. See biography by C. D. O'Malley (1964); H. W. Cushing, *Bio-bibliography of Andreas Vesalius* (2d ed. 1964); J. B. de C. M. Saunders and C. D. O'Malley, *Illustrations from the Works of Andreas Vesalius* (1950, repr. 1973).

Vesey, Denmark, 1767?–1822, American Negro leader. After many years as a slave he won (1800) $1,500 in a lottery and purchased his freedom. An intelligent and energetic person, he acquired considerable wealth and influence in South Carolina. Using church meetings as a cover, he planned (1822) a slave insurrection with the intention of taking over Charleston and, if necessary, fleeing to the Caribbean. Betrayed by informers, Vesey was hanged along with 34 others. See Herbert Aptheker, *American Slave Revolts* (1943); John Lofton, *Insurrection in South Carolina* (1964); Robert S. Starobin, ed., *Denmark Vesey* (1970).

Vesoul (vəzōōl'), town (1968 pop. 18,240), capital of Haute-Saône dept., E France, in Franche-Comté. Agricultural and mechanical equipment and metal and wood products are the chief manufactures. Formerly an earldom, Vesoul was decimated by the plague in 1586. It became part of France in 1678. There are several old buildings, including St. George Church (18th cent.).

Vespasian (Titus Flavius Vespasianus) (vĕspā'zhən), A.D. 9–A.D. 79, Roman emperor (A.D. 69–A.D. 79), founder of the Flavian dynasty. The son of a poor family, he made his way in the army by sheer ability. He served in Germany and in Britain (where he conquered the Isle of Wight) and was made consul (A.D. 51). Later he was proconsul in Africa under Nero. In A.D. 66, Nero put him in charge of the war against the Jews, and he was in Judaea when the emperor died. He recognized OTHO and then VITELLIUS, but when he himself was proclaimed emperor by the soldiers in Judaea and Alexandria, he set out to make good his claim. He arrived in Italy late in A.D. 69. He set about restoring the state and its finances and gave an example of frugal living that contrasted greatly with the life of Nero. His son Titus, whom he had left to prosecute the Jewish war, destroyed Jerusalem and returned to Rome to enjoy the triumph with his father. To commemorate the beginning of an era of peace (which lasted a century), Vespasian closed the gates of the temple of Janus and built the temple of Pax. He also erected the Colosseum. The principal external events of Vespasian's reign were the revolt of the Batavii (see CIVILIS) and the campaigns and administration of AGRICOLA in Britain. He was succeeded by his son TITUS; his other son, DOMITIAN, later succeeded Titus. The reign of Vespasian was noted for its order and prosperity. See B. W. Henderson, *Five Roman Emperors* (1927, repr. 1969); M. W. McCrum and A. G. Woodhead, *Select Documents of the Principates of the Flavian Emperors* (1961).

vespers (vĕs'pərz) [Lat.,=evening], in the Christian Church, principal evening office. In the Roman rite, vespers have consisted since the 6th cent. of a few prayers, five psalms, a lesson, the *Magnificat,* and an antiphon. The Anglican evening prayer, often called vespers, is made up largely of the Roman vespers and compline (the final evening office).

Vespers, Sicilian: see SICILIAN VESPERS.

Vespucci, Amerigo (ämārē'gō väspōōt'chē), 1454–1512, Italian navigator in whose honor America was named, b. Florence. He entered the commercial service of the Medici and in 1492 moved to Seville. He accompanied Alonso de OJEDA in 1499, but by agreement the two separated shortly before land was sighted in the West Indies, and Vespucci alone discovered and explored the mouths of the Amazon. Subsequently he sailed along the northern shore of South America and among the islands. He returned to Spain in 1500, and in 1501 he entered Portuguese service to explore the southern coast of South America. Vespucci found the mouth of the Río de la Plata and probably went as far as lat. 50°S. He explored c.6,000 mi (9,700 km) of coastline, but it is in the scientific application of his discoveries that his achievements are remarkable. He evolved a system for computing nearly exact longitude (previously determined by dead reckoning); he arrived at a figure for the earth's equatorial circumference only 50 mi (80 km) short of the correct measurement. Vespucci accepted South America as a new continent, not part of Asia. Consequently cosmography was radically altered, and in 1507, with the publication of Martin Waldseemüller's *Cosmographiae introductio,* the name *America* first appeared as applied to the continent. His voyage completed in 1502, Vespucci returned to Spain, where in 1508 he was made pilot major, a high and prestigious position. He died of malaria contracted on his voyages. Vespucci's achievements were long belittled by scholars, but the conclusions of Alberto Magnaghi in the 1920s and 30s are now widely accepted, and the pilot major is given his due. An edition of Vespucci's letters and other documents appeared in English in 1894. See biographies by Germán Arciniegas (tr. 1955) and F. J. Pohl (1966); J. B. Thacher, *The Continent of America* (1971).

Vesta (vĕs'tə), in astronomy, 4th ASTEROID to be discovered. It was found in 1807 by H. Olbers. It is the third-largest asteroid, with a diameter of c.240 mi (385 km). Its average distance from the sun is 2.36 ASTRONOMICAL UNITS, and the period of its orbit is 1,325 days. Vesta is the only asteroid that can be seen with the naked eye; it can be seen only when it is in the right position in the sky relative to the earth and sun, namely, when it is at opposition and perihelion simultaneously.

Vesta, in Roman religion, hearth goddess. She was highly honored in every household from early times to the beginning of Christianity. Her public cult maintained a sacred building in which her priestesses, the vestal virgins, tended the communal hearth and fire, which was never allowed to die out. Vesta was identified with the Greek Hestia.

Vest-Agder (vĕst'-äg"dər), county (1972 est. pop. 126,000), 2,810 sq mi (7,278 sq km), S Norway, bordering on the Skagerrak in the south. Kristiansand is the capital. Farming, shipping, fishing, and the manufacture of forest products are the chief occupations. LINDESNES, Norway's southernmost point, is in Vest-Agder.

vestal (vĕs'təl), in Roman religion, priestess of Vesta. The vestals were first two, then four, then six in number. While still little girls, they were chosen from prominent Roman families to serve for 30 (originally 5) years, during which time they could not marry. Their duties included the preparation of sacrifices and the tending of the sacred fire. If any vestal broke her vow of chastity, she was entombed alive. The vestals had great influence in the Roman state.

Vester-. For Swedish place names beginning thus, see VASTER-.

Vesterålen Islands, Norway: see LOFOTEN.

Vestfjarða (vĕst'fyär"thä), peninsula, c.80 mi (130 km) long, NW Iceland, between Breiðafjörður and Húnaflói and extending into the Denmark Strait. The peninsula, c.90 mi (140 km) wide at its head, is connected with the rest of Iceland by an isthmus c.6 mi (10 km) wide. It is mountainous and is indented by many fjords, the largest of which is Ísafjörður. The town of Ísafjörður is the chief commercial center of the peninsula.

Vestfold (vĕst'fôl"), county (1972 est. pop. 178,000), c.900 sq mi (2,330 sq km), SE Norway, bordering on the Skagerrak in the south and on the Oslofjord in the east. Tønsberg is the capital. Farming and shipping are the chief occupations, according to, with much of the Norwegian merchant marine registered at Vestfold ports, notably Tønsberg, Sandefjord, and Larvik.

Vestmannaeyjar (vĕst'mänäā"yär), group of 15 small islands, c.10 mi (16 km) S of Iceland. In English they are known as the Westman Islands. The largest and most populous is Heimaey [home island]. The people live by fishing and fowling; great colonies of gannets and other waterfowl breed in these islands. The chief town is Vestmannaeyjar (1970 pop. 5,183) on Heimaey. In 1627, Algerian pirates ravaged the islands and carried nearly 300 people into slavery. In 1963 a volcanic eruption created the island of Surtsey. The eruption of a volcano on Heimaey in 1973 damaged Vestmannaeyjar and curtailed the fishing industry.

vestments, garments worn by ecclesiastics in ceremonial functions. The cassock, a close-fitting gown buttoning down the front and reaching to the feet, is not a vestment so much as the daily uniform of the Western priest. Among most Protestants the vestments are generally limited to full gowns, much like academic gowns, sometimes with white bands worn around the neck and tied in front. Some Anglicans and Lutherans approximate the Roman Catholic use. In the Roman Catholic Church the priest's vestments at Mass are the most important. They are often elaborately worked and are usually made of linen or silk. They have remained largely the same since the early Middle Ages; in origin they are the upper-class "Sunday dress" of the late Roman Empire. Certain of them match in color; this "liturgical color" varies according to the Mass being said for that day, e.g., white for Easter and black for requiem Masses. The vestments for Mass are put on over the cassock as follows: the amice, a rectangular white strip covering the shoulders and having strings put around the neck; over this the alb, a long white gown with tight sleeves; the girdle, a rope of hemp or linen with tassels, usually white, confining the alb; the maniple (of the liturgical color), a broad band hanging over the left forearm; the stole (of the liturgical color), a long band hanging around the neck and crossed in front; over all the chasuble (of the liturgical color), a cloak with a hole for the head, cut in at the sides to give the arms freedom of action, often covering only the shoulders and reaching only part way down in front and back. Of these the stole is worn uncrossed when the alb is not worn (as when the priest distributes communion), or diagonally from the left shoulder to the right side (by a deacon). The deacon's vestment par excellence is the dalmatic (of the liturgical color), a coat reaching to the knees, with wide, short sleeves. The cope is a great cape worn by the priest in processions, in giving absolution to the dead, at benediction, and on some other occasions. The vestments proper to a bishop celebrating Mass, in addition to the priest's vestments, are miter, gloves, buskins (stockings), and sandals (slippers). Not properly a vestment but frequently seen in churches is the surplice or cotta, a loose-fitting white linen garment reaching to the waist or knees. The only vestment peculiar to the Anglican communion is the chimer worn by some bishops, a black gown with white balloon sleeves of lawn. Related to the chimer, but shorter and sleeveless, is the manteletta of Roman Catholic bishops. See PALLIUM. For bibliography, see LITURGY; MASS.

Vestris, Gaetan (gäätäN' vĕs'trēs), 1729-1808, Italian-French classical dancer, b. Florence. Vestris is esteemed one of the greatest dancers of the 18th cent. Born of an Italian theatrical family, he studied dance with Louis Dupré at the Royal Academy in Paris, then joined the Paris Opéra and served as dancing master to Louis XVI. Vestris was the first dancer to discard the mask and to use his face in mime. He taught his son, **Auguste Vestris** (1760-1842), b. Paris, who, in turn, was considered the greatest male dancer of his time. Auguste made his debut at 12 with the Paris Opéra and was the company's leading dancer for 36 years. After his retirement he trained many great dancers of the 19th cent., including Fanny ELSSLER and Jules PERROT.

Vestris, Lucia Elizabeth (Bartolozzi) (bärtōlôt'sē vĕs'trĭs), 1797-1856, English actress and manager, the first woman to be a lessee of a theater. The daughter of a music and fencing teacher, she made an unsuccessful marriage at 16 to Armand Vestris, her ballet master. Following her debut (1815) in Italian opera, she acted at the Comédie Française with Talma, who suggested to her the ideas on realism in costuming that she was later to develop. After her success as Don Giovanni in a burlesque of Mozart's opera in 1820, Vestris became known for her natural style as a ballad-singing comedienne in light opera and in breeches parts (male roles). Not satisfied with contemporary methods of production, she leased the Olympic Theatre, London, in 1831, and was an instant success as manager and director. At great expense, she redecorated the theater and used realistic stage settings and real props; she was perhaps the first to use the box set complete with ceiling. Vestris produced Shakespearean comedies, with attention to text and historical accuracy, as well as burlesques and farces. She married Charles James Mathews in 1838 on the eve of what was to be an unsuccessful American tour and from 1839 to 1842 managed Covent Garden with him. In 1841 they produced Boucicault's *London Assurance.* In 1847 they took over the Lyceum, where they introduced French plays to England. See Rosamond Gilder, *Enter the Actress* (1931); W. W. Appleton, *Madame Vestris and the London Stage* (1974).

Vestspitsbergen, island: see SPITSBERGEN, Norway.

Vesuvius (vəso͞o'vēəs), Ital. *Vesuvio,* only active volcano on the European mainland, S Italy, on the eastern shore of the Bay of Naples, SE of Naples. The height of the main cone changes with each eruption, varying within a few hundred feet of the 4,000-ft (1,219-m) level; in 1969 the height was 4,190 ft (1,277 m). The second summit, Monte Somma (3,770 ft/1,149 m) is a ridge that half encircles the cone and is separated from it by a valley (c.3 mi/5 km long). The sides of Vesuvius are deeply scarred by lava flow, but its lower slopes are extremely fertile, dotted with villages, and covered with vineyards which produce the famous Lachryma Christi wine. The base of the mountain (circumference c.45 mi/70 km) is encircled by a railroad, and a chairlift reaches almost to the rim of the crater (diameter c.2,300 ft/700 m). On the western slope, at 1,995 ft (608 m), there is a seismological observatory (built 1840-45). The outline of Vesuvius forms part of the backdrop of Naples; it is often surmounted by a faint plume of smoke. The earliest recorded eruption (A.D. 79) was described by Pliny the Younger in two letters to Tacitus; the eruption buried Pompeii, Herculaneum, and Stabiae under cinders, ashes, and mud. Pliny the Elder was killed by the eruption, which he had come to investigate. Frequent eruptions have been recorded since then, notably in 512, in 1631, six times in the 18th cent., eight times in the 19th cent. (notably in 1872), and in 1906, 1929, and 1944. The eruptions vary greatly in severity.

Veszprém (vĕ'sprām), town (1970 pop. 35,158), W Hungary, near the Lake of Balaton. It is a commercial center producing chemicals, knitted goods, and foodstuffs. Made a bishopric by St. Stephen in 1001, Veszprém has an 18th-century episcopal palace, a cathedral (rebuilt many times), a former citadel, and a museum containing Roman remains. The tall Turkish minaret is now a fire tower.

Vetch, Samuel, 1668-1732, British soldier and colonial administrator, b. Scotland. He settled in Albany, N.Y., in 1699 and became an Indian trader. Author of a plan to capture French Canada, he was empowered (1709) by the British government to raise troops for the attack. He was adjutant general of the expedition that captured (1710) Port Royal (now Annapolis Royal, N. S.) and became military governor (1710-13) and civil governor (1715-17) of the conquered territory. See biographies by J. C. Webster (1929) and G. M. Waller (1960).

vetch, common name for many weak-stemmed leguminous herbs of the genus *Vicia* of the family Leguminosae (PULSE family). The vetches are chiefly annuals, distributed over temperate regions of the Northern Hemisphere and of South America. Most of the species cultivated for food and forage are Old World in origin. The common vetch (*V. sativa*), also called spring vetch, is a purple- or pink-flowered climber native to Europe, where it is grown for fodder. It is extensively grown on the Pacific coast and in other sections of the United States for green fodder and hay and as a cover and green-manure crop. The hairy vetch (*V. villosa*), used almost as widely, is a hardy biennial with narrower, silvery leaves and blue flowers. Valued as an enricher of the nitrogen content of soil, it grows almost anywhere in the United States and is considered the best legume to plant where red clover does not thrive. It is also known as sand, Siberian, Russian, and winter vetch. Vetch seed is often inoculated with nitrogen-fixing bacteria when grown in soil of low fertility. In areas of grain cultivation vetches sometimes escape into grainfields and become weedy pests. In Europe the principal cultivated species of *Vicia* is the broad bean (*V. faba*), the only edible bean native to the Old World. Tare is a common name sometimes used as a synonym for any vetch, most frequently for the common vetch. Vetches are classified in the division MAGNOLIOPHYTA, class Magnoliopsida, order Rosales, family Leguminosae. See bulletins of the U.S. Dept. of Agriculture.

Veterans' Day, holiday formerly observed in the United States as Armistice Day in commemoration of the signing of the Armistice ending World War I. November 11th officially became Veterans' Day on May 24, 1954, by act of Congress. The day is set aside in honor of all those who have fought in defense of the United States.

Veterans of Foreign Wars (VFW), organization created (1899) at Columbus, Ohio, by veterans of the Spanish-American War. It received a charter from Congress in 1936. The organization later admitted veterans who saw action in subsequent wars and U.S. military expeditions . At the close of World War II, the VFW vastly increased its membership; it now rivals the American Legion in size and influence. The organization's program is devoted to the rehabilitation of disabled veterans, protection of national security through maximum military strength, and promotion of patriotism and community service activity. It has a membership of more than 2,000,000.

veterinary medicine, diagnosis and treatment of diseases of animals. An early interest in animal diseases is found in ancient Greek writings on medicine. Veterinary medicine began to achieve the stature of a science with the organization of the first school in the field in Lyons, France, in 1761, followed soon by similar schools in other parts of Europe. In the United States, veterinary schools came into existence about the time of the Civil War, and there are now a number of accredited schools of veterinary medicine affiliated with colleges and universities. In 1884 the Bureau of Animal Industry was established in the U.S. Dept. of Agriculture to deal with animal disease problems in the fast-growing livestock industry. Veterinary research has made important contributions to medical science in general. Forms of vaccination for animals devised by Louis Pasteur and Robert Koch were found effective for man also. Veterinarians inaugurated the inspection of meat and milk to prevent the spread of tuberculosis. The development since World War II of live-virus and modified live-virus vaccines and of antibiotics, sulfonamides, and other biological products has brought about a marked change in veterinary medicine. An important innovation was the mass immunization of poultry through sprays, dusts, and agents added to drinking water. Many animal diseases hitherto considered incurable can now be prevented or controlled by these new therapeutic agents, and this in turn has greatly increased the output of livestock and poultry products. See B. W. Bierer, *A Short History of Veterinary Medicine in America* (1955); U.S. Dept. of Agriculture, *Animal Diseases* (1956); *The Merck Veterinary Manual* (4th ed. 1973).

veto [Lat.,=I forbid], in government, power of the chief executive to refuse assent to laws passed by the legislature. In the United States, Article I, Section 7, of the Constitution gives the President the power to veto any bill passed by Congress. The President's veto power is limited, however, in that it may not be used on constitutional amendments and it may be overridden by a two-thirds vote of the Congress. In practice the veto is used only occasionally by the President, and once vetoed, a bill is rarely reapproved by Congress. American states, in general, have given a similar power of veto to their governors. In Great Britain the crown technically has veto power over acts of Parliament, but the power has not been exercised since 1707. Because all five permanent members of the UNITED NATIONS Security Council must approve proposed measures, a negative vote by only one amounts to a veto. In this case the veto power has been used to the point where it hinders the proper functioning of the United Nations.

Veuster, Damien de: see DAMIEN, FATHER.

Vevey (vəvā'), town (1970 pop. 17,957), Vaud canton, W Switzerland, on the Lake of Geneva. It is a resort. Various goods are manufactured, including chocolate, pharmaceuticals, and metal products. About every 25 years a great wine festival is held.

Vexin (vĕksăN'), region of N France. It is mainly agricultural, with some industry in the valleys. By the Treaty of Saint-Clair-sur-Epte (911), the northernmost part (Vexin Normand) was assigned to Rollo of Normandy; the rest (Vexin Français) remained with the French crown. PONTOISE, Gisors, and Les Andelys (see ANDELYS, LES) are the chief towns.

Via Appia: see APPIAN WAY; ROMAN ROADS.

viaduct (vī'ədŭkt") [Lat.,=road conveyor], type of bridge for carrying a highway or railroad over a valley, over low ground, or over a road. It is commonly constructed in the form of several towers or piers that support arches on which the roadway rests. Viaducts are usually constructed of steel or concrete; in the past they were built of wood or stone. The Pulaski Skyway, connecting Jersey City and Newark, N.J., is an example of a concrete and steel viaduct. It spans the New Jersey marshes for a distance of c.3 mi (5 km).

Via Mala (vē'ä mä'lä), narrow gorge of the Hinterrhein River, a headstream of the Rhine, c.3½ mi (6 km) long, Grisons canton, E Switzerland. One of the most wild and picturesque gorges in Switzerland, it is walled by vertical limestone cliffs c.1,600 ft (490 m) high. The Splügen Road (see SPLÜGEN) passes above the gorge.

Vian, Boris (bôrēs' vyăN), 1920–59, French novelist. He patterned his literary style on that of terse American crime fiction. His best-known work is *J'irai cracher sur vos tombes* [I will spit on your graves] (1946), a novel about a fugitive black man hunted by whites. Other novels include *L'arrache-cœur* (1953; tr. *Heartsnatcher,* 1968) and *Les bâtisseurs d'empire* (1959; tr. *The Empire Builders,* 1967). See biography by Alfred Cismaru (1974).

Viana, Charles of: see CHARLES OF VIANA.

Vianney, Saint Jean-Baptiste (zhäN-bätēst' vyänā'), 1786–1859, French parish priest, popularly known as the Curé d'Ars, b. Dardilly, near Lyons. He came of poor peasant stock and received scant education until, as a youth, he struggled through the seminary. As a young curé he was sent to the little village of Ars. Vianney found that the people there had lost their faith, and he vowed to make the community "the property of God." He beautified the church, lived like the poorest of the poor, and fasted and prayed for the people. His skill as a confessor drew people from outside his parish, and neighboring priests complained and sought to have him removed. Vianney himself signed their petitions. He began an orphanage for girls that served as a model throughout France. Many miracles were attributed to him during his lifetime, and in his last years thousands from all over France came annually to his confessional. He was canonized in 1925. In 1929 he was made universal patron of parish priests. Feast: Aug. 8. See biographies by Henri Ghéon (tr. 1929) and Jean de la Varende (1959).

Viardot-Garcia, Pauline (pōlēn' vyärdō'-gärsēä'), 1821–1910, French mezzo-soprano; sister of Maria Malibran; pupil of her father, Manuel GARCÍA. Following her concert debut in Brussels in 1837 and her opera debut in London in 1839, she became celebrated for her wide range, fine technique, and histrionic ability. She created the role of Fidès in Meyerbeer's *Prophète* (1849), developed a teaching method, and composed songs and an opera, *Le dernier Sorcier* (1869). She retired from the stage in 1863 and taught (1871–75) at the Paris Conservatory.

Viareggio (vēärĕd'jō), city (1971 pop. 55,382), Tuscany, N central Italy, on the Tyrrhenian Sea. It is a fishing center and a fashionable beach resort. The body of the poet Shelley was cremated there after his death by drowning near La Spezia in 1822.

viaticum (vīăt'ĭkəm) [Lat.,=provision for a journey], in the Roman Catholic Church, Communion given to the dying by a priest. Catholics are obliged to receive the viaticum if they are able and to procure it for others. The dying person is usually confessed before receiving the viaticum but need not be fasting. The confession, viaticum, and ANOINTING OF THE SICK are called the last rites of the church.

Viaud, Julien: see LOTI, PIERRE.

Viborg (vē'bôr), city (1970 com. pop. 36,227), capital of Viborg co., N central Denmark. It is a commercial and industrial center and a rail junction. Manufactures include tobacco and textiles. It is one of the oldest Danish cities and became an episcopal see in 1065. The city's cathedral (c.1130), the largest granite church in Denmark, was restored (1862–76) in its original Romanesque style. There is also a 13th-century Dominican abbey church with a remarkable 16th-century Flemish altarpiece.

Viborg: see VYBORG, USSR.

Vibo Valentia (vē'bō välän'tyä), town (1971 pop. 31,206), Calabria, S Italy, near the Tyrrhenian Sea. It is an agricultural and commercial center. A flourishing Roman town, Vibo was destroyed by the Arabs in the 9th cent. and was rebuilt by Emperor Frederick II in the 13th cent. The town has suffered from numerous earthquakes (especially in 1783 and 1905), but Frederick II's castle still stands. There are also Greek ruins. Vibo was known until 1928 as Monteleone di Calabria.

vibration, in physics, commonly an oscillatory motion—a movement first in one direction and then back again in the opposite direction. It is exhibited, for example, by a swinging pendulum, by the prongs of a tuning fork that has been struck, or by the string of a musical instrument that has been plucked. Random vibrations are exhibited by the molecules in matter (see BROWNIAN MOVEMENT). Any simple vibration is described by three factors: its amplitude, or size; its frequency, or rate of oscillation; and the phase, or timing of the oscillations relative to some fixed time (see HARMONIC MOTION). Sound is produced by the vibrations of a body and is transmitted through material media in pressure waves (see WAVE) made up of alternate condensations (forcing of the molecules of the medium together) and rarefactions (pulling of the molecules of the medium away from one another). In sound the vibration is longitudinal, for the movement is to and fro along the direction in which the sound is traveling. When a sound wave of one frequency strikes a body that will vibrate naturally at the same frequency, the vibration of the body is called sympathetic vibration. A reinforcement of sound resulting from sympathetic vibration is called resonance. When the vibrations of a sound-producing body cause another body to vibrate in the same frequency, not normally its own, the vibration is known as forced vibration. Light is propagated in electromagnetic waves; the vibratory movement is, however, transverse, since the motion is at right angles to the direction that the light waves are taking. Heat is commonly defined as the energy of molecules, part of which consists of the energy of their vibrational motion.

viburnum: see HONEYSUCKLE.

Vicente, Gil (Port. zhēl vēsĕnt'ə, Span. hēl vēthĕn'tā), 1470?–1536?, Portuguese dramatist and poet, considered second only to Camões. Vicente was attached to the courts of the Portuguese kings Manuel I and John II, and he may have been identical with, or related to, an accomplished goldsmith of the same name at the court. He was a humanist, and his writings reveal the influence of Renaissance Italy, the thought of Erasmus, and, in his early plays, the works of Encina. Vicente's lyric plays and entertainments were created (c.1500–c.1536) for production at court, and they varied from slight farcical interludes to full comedies and tragicomedies. They vividly portray the breadth of Portuguese society. Some are profoundly religious, some especially satirical; Vicente was antagonistic to the corrupt clergy and pretentious parvenus at the court, and he decried the superficial glory of empire that hid the increasing poverty in Portugal. His writing, in Portuguese, in Spanish, and in an arbitrary combination of the two, was important in shaping modern Spanish and Portuguese drama. An accomplished musician, he interspersed his plays with exquisite songs. Although his works were suppressed by the Inquisition and his fame waned, he is now recognized as one of the principal figures of the Iberian Renaissance. See study by J. H. Parker (1967).

Vicenza (vēchān'tsä), city (1971 pop. 115,747), capital of Vicenza prov., Venetia, NE Italy. It is an agricultural, commercial, and industrial center. Manufactures include machinery, chemicals, and processed food. Originally a Roman town, later the seat of a Lombard duchy, Vicenza became a free commune and joined (12th cent.) the Lombard League. It was stormed by Emperor Frederick II in 1236 and later fell to various powers (including Verona and Milan) before being annexed (1404) by Venice. Andrea Palladio (1508–80) made Vicenza famous for his interpretation of classical architecture. The basilica, the Loggia del Capitano, the Teatro Olimpico, the Villa Capra (called La Rotonda), and the Palazzo Chiericato (now housing a museum), all designed by Palladio, inspired the Georgian style in England and the Colonial style in the United States. Vicenza also has a noted Gothic cathedral, with a polyptych (1356) by Lorenzo Veneziano. Bartolomeo Montagna was the founder, in the late 15th cent., of the Vicenza school of painting.

Vichy (vĭsh'ē, Fr. vēshē'), city (1968 pop. 33,898), Allier dept., central France, on the Allier River. Vichy's hot mineral springs have made it one of the foremost spas in Europe. In addition to bottled Vichy water, pharmaceuticals, clothing, and cosmetics are manufactured. The **Vichy government** was the regime set up there by Marshal Henri Pétain in July, 1940, subsequent to the Franco-German armistice of June 22. Its effective control extended only to unoccupied France and its colonies. The Third Republic was voted out of existence by a truncated parliament, and a new constitution established a corporate state (see FASCISM). The Vichy government, which was never recognized by the Allies, became a German tool in the hands of such men as Pierre Laval, Jean François Darlan, and Jacques Doriot, although German expectations were never completely satisfied. When the Allies invaded North Africa in Nov., 1942, Hitler annulled the armistice of 1940 and occupied all France. The Vichy government continued a shadowy existence, eventually fleeing before the Allied advance to Sigmaringen, Germany, where it collapsed when Germany surrendered in 1945. See Paul Farmer, *Vichy* (1955); Robert Aron and Georgette Elgey, *The Vichy Regime: 1940–1944* (tr. 1958); R. O. Paxton, *Vichy France* (1972).

Vicksburg, city (1970 pop. 25,478), seat of Warren co., W Miss., on bluffs above the Mississippi River at the mouth of the Yazoo; inc. 1825. An important port, it is the commercial, processing, and shipping center for a cotton, timber, and livestock area. Its many manufactures include lumber and related products, lighting fixtures, machinery, mobile homes, chemicals, feed, fertilizers, and food products. There was a French fort near there in the early 18th cent., and the Spanish established Fort Nogales in 1791. The area, known to the English as Walnut Hills, came into U.S. possession in 1798. Rev. Newitt Vick founded a mission nearby c.1812 and in 1819 began laying out lots for a town. Vicksburg became a busy river port, and in the Civil War it was a major objective in Grant's VICKSBURG CAMPAIGN. The city fell July 4, 1863, after 14 months of naval shelling, 7 months of land assault, and 47 days of total siege. River traffic, which fell off greatly in the late 19th and early 20th cent., has been aided by the U.S. Mississippi River Commission, whose headquarters are at Vicksburg. Nearby is the U.S. Waterways Experiment Station. Antebellum homes are in the city and the surrounding area. In April, 1973, sections of the city were inundated as the level of the Mississippi and Yazoo rivers rose in flood. In Vicksburg National Military Park (see NATIONAL PARKS AND MONUMENTS, table) are preserved trenches and fortifications of the Civil War siege. North of the city is a national cemetery containing 18,113 Civil War dead, including c.13,000 unknown Union soldiers brought from temporary burial places all over the South. Most of the Confederate soldiers killed in the campaign were buried in the Vicksburg city cemetery.

Vicksburg campaign, in the American Civil War, the fighting (Nov., 1862–July, 1863) for control of the Mississippi River. The Union wanted such control in order to split the Confederacy and to restore free commerce to the politically important Northwest. New Orleans and Memphis fell to Union forces in the spring of 1862, but an attempt to take Vicksburg, Miss., by water failed (May–June). As a result the South still held 200 mi (320 km) of the river between Port Hudson, La., and Vicksburg. Early in Nov., 1862, Gen. Ulysses S. GRANT, commanding the Dept. of the Tennessee, planned a converging assault on Vicksburg; Gen. William T. SHERMAN led an expedition down the river from Memphis to attack the city from the north, while Grant himself advanced overland from the east. However, Confederate cavalry under Earl Van Dorn and Nathan B. FORREST cut Grant's line of communications, forcing him to retreat, and Sherman was repulsed in the battle of Chickasaw Bluffs (Dec. 29, 1862). In Jan., 1863, Grant concentrated his army across the river from Vicksburg. He took over the command of John A. MCCLERNAND, who had succeeded Sherman. After several unsuccessful experiments to gain an approach to the seemingly impregnable city (Feb.–March, 1863), Grant in April began a brilliant movement to take it from the south. To divert the attention of the Confederate commander, John C. PEMBERTON, Grant left Sherman before the city and ordered a cavalry raid through central Mississippi. On the night of April 16–17, David Dixon PORTER ran gunboats and transports down the river past Vicksburg, and in the following days Grant marched his army south to meet the fleet and be transported across the river at Bruinsburg (c.30 mi/48 km S of Vicksburg). On May 1, McClernand and James B. MCPHERSON defeated the Confederates at Port Gibson, forcing them to abandon their batteries at Grand Gulf, which Grant seized as a base. When Sherman joined him on May 7, 1863, Grant left Grand Gulf, marched northeast, and on May 12 defeated the Confederates at Raymond. At Jackson (May 14), he met Gen. Joseph E. JOHNSTON, Confederate commander in the West, who retreated. Turning west toward Vicksburg, Grant defeated Pemberton in successive battles (May 16, 17) at Champion's Hill and at the bridge over the Big Black River, forcing him back into Vicksburg. After two unsuccessful attempts at storming the city's fortifications, Grant opened siege. With the Union forces between them, Pemberton and Johnston were unable to unite, and after about six weeks of gallant resistance Vicksburg's defenders surrendered on July 4, 1863. The fall of Port Hudson a few days later placed the Mississippi River entirely in Union hands. See J. D. Milligan, *Gunboats Down the Mississippi* (1965); A. A. Hoehling, *Vicksburg* (1969).

Vico, Giovanni Battista (jōvän'nē bät-tē'stä vē'kō), 1668–1744, Italian philosopher and historian, also known as Giambattista Vico, b. Naples. In 1699, Vico became professor of rhetoric at the Univ. of Naples, and in 1734 he was appointed historiographer to the king of Naples. Vico is regarded by many as the first modern historian; he was the first to formulate a systematic method of historical research, and he developed a theory of history that was far in advance of his times. For Vico, history is the account of the birth and development of human societies and their institutions. He thus departed from previous systems of writing history—either as the biographies of great men, or as the development of God's will. Opposing the antihistorical elements of the prevailing Cartesianism (see DESCARTES, RENÉ), he asserted that history is a valid object of human knowledge because man himself created history. Vico urged the study of language, mythology, and tradition as techniques for the investigation of history. As a philosopher, Vico believed that every period in history had a distinct character, and that similar periods recur throughout history in the same order. He departed from the old cyclical theories of history, however, in asserting that these periods do not recur in exactly the same form, but are subject to the modifications that new circumstances and developments impose. Thus the historian can never be a prophet. Vico also wrote on law, affirming an innate human sense of justice and natural law. Vico's major theories were developed in his *New Science* (1725), which he revised completely (1730; 1744). Vico's work was little known in his own time, and his importance was not recognized until the 19th cent. See his autobiography (tr. by M. H. Finch and T. G. Bergin, 1944); Giorgio Tagliacozzo and H. V. White, ed., *Giambattista Vico* (1969); H. P. Adams, *The Life and Writings of Giambattista Vico* (1935, repr. 1970); Benedetto Croce, *The Philosophy of Giovanni Battista Vico* (1913, repr. 1970); Frederick Vaughan, *The Political Philosophy of Giambattista Vico* (1972).

Victor Amadeus II (ămədē'əs), 1666–1732, duke of Savoy (1675–1713), king of Sicily (1713–20), king of Sardinia (1720–30). Succeeding his father, Charles Emmanuel II, as duke of Savoy, he overthrew the regency of his mother in 1683. Finding himself caught between France and the house of Hapsburg, he steered an opportunistic course in foreign policy, guided in part by his desire to rid Savoy of French influence, in part by his appetite for territorial aggrandizement. Under French pressure he took (1686) severe measures against the WALDENSES, but in 1690 he joined the League of Augsburg (see AUGSBURG, LEAGUE OF) against the French king Louis XIV and returned to a more tolerant policy at home. Although defeated by the French in the War of the GRAND ALLIANCE, he concluded a favorable separate peace in the Treaty of Turin (1696), which restored Pinerolo to Savoy and caused the collapse of the alliance. In the War of the Spanish Succession (1701–13) he at first sided with France, but changed sides once more in 1703. The French occupied Savoy, but were obliged to lift the siege of Turin after Victor Amadeus and his cousin, Eugene of Savoy, had thoroughly defeated them in 1706. The peace (see UTRECHT, PEACE OF) awarded him Sicily with the royal title and gave him additional territory in N Italy, including Alessandria. When the Spanish seized (1718) Sicily, the QUADRUPLE ALLIANCE was formed and humbled Spain. Victor Amadeus in 1720 ceded his claim to Sicily to Holy Roman Emperor Charles VI in exchange for the island of Sardinia and became king of Sardinia. He abdicated in 1730 in favor of his son, Charles Emmanuel III.

Victor Amadeus III, 1726–96, king of Sardinia (1773–96), son and successor of Charles Emmanuel III. He declared war on France in 1792 after French Revolutionary troops had occupied Savoy and Nice. With Austrian help he defended Piedmont until 1796, when Bonaparte (see NAPOLEON I) forced him to conclude the armistice of Cherasco. His son, Charles Emmanuel IV, succeeded him (see SAVOY HOUSE OF).

Victor Emmanuel I, 1759–1824, Italian king of Sardinia (1802–21). His brother and predecessor, Charles Emmanuel IV, lost (1798) all his territories except the island of Sardinia to France in the French Revolutionary Wars. Victor Emmanuel accompanied his brother to Sardinia and succeeded him on his abdication. After Napoleon's fall he returned (1814) to Turin, recovered Piedmont, Savoy, and Nice, and received Liguria with Genoa. He abolished many Napoleonic reforms and refused to grant a constitution. An uprising (1821) in Piedmont, largely the work of the CARBONARI, forced him to abdicate in favor of his brother Charles Felix (see SAVOY, HOUSE OF).

Victor Emmanuel II, 1820–78, Italian king of Sardinia (1849–61) and first king of united Italy (1861–78). He fought in the war of 1848–49 against Austrian rule in Lombardy-Venetia and ascended the throne when his father, CHARLES ALBERT, abdicated after the defeat at Novara. With the skillful collaboration of CAVOUR, whom he appointed premier in 1852, he became the symbol and the central figure of the RISORGIMENTO, the movement for Italian unification. Popular in Sardinia because of his liberal reforms and his respect for the constitution, he increased Sardinian prestige abroad by engaging in the Crimean War as an ally of France, Britain, and Turkey. In conjunction with Napoleon III of France, with whom Cavour had formed an alliance, he fought against Austria in the Italian War of 1859. After the battle of Solferino, France signed a separate armistice with Austria at VILLAFRANCA DI VERONA; Victor Emmanuel was not consulted, but the terms were ratified in the Treaty of Zürich. When, in 1860, Tuscany, Romagna, Parma, and Modena voted for union with Sardinia (contrary to the treaty terms), Victor Emmanuel secured French consent to their incorporation in exchange for the cession of Savoy and Nice. He favored the expedition (1860) of GARIBALDI into the kingdom of the TWO SICILIES and joined forces with Garibaldi after crossing the Papal States and defeating the papal army at Castelfidardo. Plebiscites in Naples and Sicily and in the Marches and Umbria (two provinces of the Papal States) favored union with Sardinia, and in 1861 the kingdom of Italy was proclaimed with Victor Emmanuel as king. The capital was transferred from Turin to Florence in 1865. Siding (1866) with Prussia in the AUSTRO-PRUSSIAN WAR, Victor Emmanuel was awarded Venetia in the peace settlement. The remaining Papal States were protected by the troops of Napoleon III, but when he fell in 1870, Italian troops seized the Papal States, and Rome was made (1871) the capital of Italy. Pope Pius IX and his successors protested, and the so-called Roman Question remained a serious problem until the Lateran Treaty of 1929. The remainder of Victor Emmanuel's reign was spent in the consolidation of the new kingdom. His son Humbert I succeeded him. See biography by C. S. Forester (1927).

Victor Emmanuel III, 1869–1947, king of Italy (1900–1946), emperor of Ethiopia (1936–43), king of Albania (1939–43), son and successor of Humbert I. In 1896 he married Princess Helena of Montenegro. Though involved with Germany and Austria-Hungary in the Triple Alliance, he sought cordial relations with France and Great Britain. He favored the war of 1911–12 against Turkey, thus acquiring Libya. Though first advocating neutrality, he finally joined (1915) the Allies in World War I. He was unable to handle the confused internal situation of ITALY after the war, refused to oppose the Fascist march on Rome, and asked (1922) MUSSOLINI to form a government. Under the Fascist regime he was king in name only, but Mussolini's conquests added to his list of titles. During World War II, when the Fascist grand council voted (1943) against continued support of Mussolini, the king dismissed the dictator, placed him under arrest, and named Pietro BADOGLIO premier. German troops occupied Rome after Italy surrendered to the Allies, and Victor Emmanuel fled to S Italy. Unpopular because of his long association with Mussolini, he was obliged to transmit (1944) his royal prerogatives to his son, Humbert II, in whose favor he abdicated in 1946. He died in exile in Egypt.

Victoria (Alexandrina Victoria), 1819–1901, queen of Great Britain and Ireland (1837–1901) and empress of India (1876–1901). She was the daughter of Edward, duke of Kent (fourth son of George III), and Princess Mary Louise Victoria of Saxe-Coburg-Saalfeld. Her father died before she was a year old. Upon the death (1830) of George IV, she was recognized as heir to the British throne, and in 1837, at the age of 18, she succeeded her uncle, William IV, to the throne. With the accession of a woman, the connection between the English and Hanoverian thrones ceased in accordance with the Salic law of Hanover. One of the young queen's advisers was Baron STOCKMAR, sent by her uncle, King LEOPOLD I of the Belgians. Her first prime minister, Viscount MELBOURNE, became her close friend and adviser. In 1839, when Melbourne's Whig cabinet resigned, Victoria refused to dismiss her Whig ladies of the bedchamber, the accepted gesture of confidence in the incoming party. The Tory leader, Sir Robert PEEL, declined to form a cabinet, and Melbourne remained in office. In 1840, Victoria married her first cousin, Prince ALBERT of Saxe-Coburg-Gotha. Albert, with whom she was very much in love, became the dominant influence in her life. Her first child, Victoria, later empress of Germany, was born in 1840, and the prince of Wales, later EDWARD VII, in 1841. Victoria had nine children. Their marriages and those of her grandchildren allied the British royal house with those of Russia, Germany, Greece, Denmark, Rumania, and several of the German states. Through Albert's efforts, Victoria was reconciled with the Tories, and she became very fond of Peel during his second ministry (1841–46). She was less happy with the Whig ministry that followed, taking particular exception to the adventurous foreign policy of Viscount PALMERSTON. The resulting friction was a factor in Palmerston's dismissal from office in 1851. The queen and Albert also influenced the formation of Lord Aberdeen's coalition government in 1852. Royal popularity was increased by the success of the Crystal Palace exposition (1851), planned and carried through by Albert. However, it began to wane again when it was rumored on the eve of the Crimean War that the royal couple was pro-Russian. After the outbreak (1854) of the war, Victoria took part in the organization of relief for the wounded and instituted the Victoria Cross for bravery. She also reconciled herself to Palmerston, who became prime minister in 1855 and proved a vigorous war leader. In 1861, Albert (who had been named prince consort in 1857) died. Victoria's grief was so great that she did not appear in public for three years and did not open Parliament until 1866; her prolonged seclusion damaged her popularity. Her reappearance was largely the work of Benjamin DISRAELI, who, together with William GLADSTONE, dominated the politics of the latter part of Victoria's reign. Disraeli, adroit in his personal relations with Victoria, became the queen's great favorite. In 1876 he secured for her the title empress of India, which pleased her greatly; she was ardently imperialistic and intensely interested in the welfare of her colonial subjects, particularly the Indians. Victoria's relations with Gladstone, on the other hand, were very stiff; she disliked him personally and disapproved of many of his policies, especially Irish Home Rule. After Gladstone's retirement (1894) she aroused criticism by choosing the earl of ROSEBERY as prime minister instead of Sir William HARCOURT. Nevertheless, in her old age, Victoria was enormously popular. Jubilees were held in 1887 and 1897 to celebrate the 50th and 60th years of the longest English reign. The queen was not highly intelligent, but her conscientiousness and strict morals helped to restore the prestige of the crown and to establish it as a symbol of public service and imperial unity. See her letters (9 vol., 1907-30); *The Girlhood of Queen Victoria* (extracts from her journal, ed. by Lord Esher, 1912); biographies by Lytton Strachey (1921, repr. 1960), Edith Sitwell (1936), Roger Fulford (1951), Elizabeth Longford (1964), and Cecil Woodham-Smith (1972); study by J. A. R. Marriott (1934).

Victoria (Victoria Adelaide Mary Louisa), 1840-1901, empress of Germany, daughter of Victoria of England. In 1858 she married the German crown prince (later Emperor Frederick III). After her husband's death in 1888, she was generally known as Empress Frederick. A dogmatic English liberal, she was bitterly hostile to the imperial chancellor Otto von BISMARCK but was unable to make her dislike effective. Her letters were published in English in 1928. See biography by Richard Barkeley (1956).

Victoria, Guadalupe: see GUADALUPE VICTORIA.

Victoria, Tomás Luis de (tōmäs' lo͞oēs' dā vēktō'ryä), c.1548-1611, Spanish composer. He went to Rome in 1565 to study for the priesthood at the Collegium Germanicum. In 1571 he became music master of the Collegium Romanum, succeeding Palestrina, who may have been his teacher. Mutual influence is evident in their works. In 1578, Victoria gave up the position he had held since 1573 as music master at the Collegium Germanicum to become a resident priest at the Church of San Girolamo. All of Victoria's known compositions are religious. His first book of motets (1572) contains the well-known *O quam gloriosum* and *O vos omnes.* He also composed masses, canticles, settings of all the hymns for the church year (1581), and settings of the biblical accounts of the Passion. His polyphonic technique, equal to any in the Renaissance, expresses a passionate mysticism that is essentially Spanish. In 1594 or 1595 he returned to Spain to be chaplain and choirmaster to Empress Mary (wife of Emperor Maximilian II), in whose memory he composed his last and greatest work, *Officium defunctorum* (pub. 1605).

Victoria (vĭktô'rēə), state (1970 est. pop. 3,443,000), 87,884 sq mi (227,620 sq km), SE Australia. It is bounded on the S and E by the Indian Ocean, Bass Strait, and the Tasman Sea. MELBOURNE is the capital. Other important cities are GEELONG, BALLARAT, and BENDIGO. The second smallest state of the commonwealth, Victoria is also the most densely populated state. The Australian Alps and other mountains of the Eastern Highlands traverse the state; the highest point is Mt. Bogong (6,508/1,984 m). The climate is generally temperate and pleasant. The large, but frequently dry, rivers such as the Campaspe and the Mitta Mitta are important for irrigation purposes; about one half of the irrigated land in Australia is in Victoria. Hume Reservoir, on the New South Wales border, irrigates an extensive agricultural and pastoral area in the north. Despite its small size, Victoria is one of Australia's leading agricultural states. Wheat, grown largely in the northeast, is the most important crop, followed by oats, barley, fruits, and vegetables. Livestock and dairying are also important. Sheep are raised in the southwest and dairy cattle in the south. Victoria was the first state in Australia to develop industry. The manufacture of automobiles is the state's largest industry, followed by textiles, clothing, and food processing. Gold mining has declined sharply; however, the mining of rich brown coal, mainly in the Latrobe Valley E of Melbourne, has increased dramatically. Unsuccessful attempts at settlement were made in 1803 and 1826 on the site of the present Melbourne. Settlement began in the 1830s when sheep ranchers from Tasmania came looking for pasture. Known as the Port Phillips District, the area that is now Victoria became part of the colony of New South Wales in 1836. In 1851, Victoria was made a separate British colony, which was granted full constitutional self-government in 1855. The discovery of gold in 1851 led to a rapid population increase. Victoria was federated as a state of the Commonwealth of Australia in 1901. Executive power rests nominally in the governor, who is appointed by the crown on advice of the cabinet. The premier and the cabinet are responsible to the bicameral state parliament.

Victoria, city (1971 pop. 61,761; metropolitan pop. 195,800), capital of British Columbia, SW Canada, on Vancouver Island and Juan de Fuca Strait. It is the largest city on the island and its major port and business center. In addition to its importance as the seat of provincial government, Victoria is noted as a residential city because of its mild climate, beautiful scenery, many parks (including Beacon Hill Park) and drives. It is also a popular center for American and Canadian tourists. It has sawmills and woodworking plants, fish-processing factories, grain elevators, and cold-storage plants. The city is the base of a deep-sea fishing fleet; a large naval installation is nearby. Founded (1843) as Fort Camosun, a Hudson's Bay Company post, the city was later called Fort Victoria. When Vancouver Island became a crown colony, a town was laid out on the site (1851-52), named Victoria, and made the capital of the colony. With the discovery (1858) of gold on the British Columbia mainland, Victoria became the port, supply base, and outfitting center for miners on their way to the Cariboo gold fields. In 1866, when the island was administratively united with the mainland, Victoria remained the capital of the colony and became the provincial capital in 1871. It is the seat of the Dominion Astrophysical Observatory and the Univ. of Victoria.

Victoria: see HONG KONG.

Victoria or **Ciudad Victoria** (syo͞othäth' vēktō'ryä), city (1970 pop. 94,304), capital of Tamaulipas state, NE Mexico, on the San Marcos River and at the foot of the Sierra Madre Oriental. It lies on the Inter-American Highway and on a major rail line. Henequen and citrus fruits are the principal products, and pine forests are exploited. Victoria, founded in 1750, is the seat of an episcopal see.

Victoria, city (1970 pop. 41,349), seat of Victoria co., S Texas, on the Guadalupe River, in a prosperous farm, cattle, and oil area. The Victoria Barge Canal (completed in 1962) connects the city with the Intracoastal Waterway. Victoria has food-processing plants, aircraft shops, and factories manufacturing petrochemicals, concrete, metal, machinery, clothing, and boats. The Mexican settlement of Nuestra Señora de Guadalupe de Victoria attracted early American colonists, and after Texas independence the prosperous American city attracted many German immigrants. In architecture and spirit it has a leisurely Southern air. There is a junior college, a zoo, and museums of history and fine arts. To the south are the Padre Island National Seashore and a national wildlife refuge.

Victoria, Lake, Africa: see VICTORIA NYANZA.

Victoria and Albert Museum, South Kensington, London, opened in 1852 as the Museum of Manufacturers at Marlborough House. It originally contained a nucleus of contemporary objects of applied art bought from the Great Exhibition of 1851 at the instigation of the Prince Consort, and collections from the Government School of Design. The collection was soon expanded to include objects of all styles and periods, and the name was changed to Museum of Ornamental Art. In 1857 it was moved to its present site in South Kensington, to become part of the collective museum known as the South Kensington Museum. The present building, designed by Sir Aston Webb, was begun in 1899, at which time the museum was given its present name by Queen Victoria. When this building was opened in 1909, it became purely an art museum; the scientific collections were renamed the Science Museum. The museum embraces the Royal College of Art, an extensive art library, and the collections of the India Museum, which it absorbed. Its collections of paintings and sculpture (especially of early Italian works) are celebrated; other collections of note include ceramics, glass, jewelry, textiles, medieval enamels, ivories, miniatures, metalwork, engravings, and furniture. Raphael's cartoons for the Sistine Chapel tapestries are among its most famous treasures.

Victoria de las Tunas (vēktō'ryä thä läs to͞o'näs), city (1970 pop. 53,739), Oriente prov., E Cuba. It is the marketing center for an important livestock-raising area and is located on major road and rail lines.

Victoria Falls, waterfall, c.1 mi (1.6 km) wide with a maximum drop of 420 ft (128 m), in the Zambezi River, S central Africa, on the Zambia-Rhodesia border. The falls are formed as the Zambezi plummets into a narrow chasm (c.400 ft/120 m wide) carved by its waters along a fracture zone in the earth's crust. Numerous islets at the crest of the falls divide the water to form a series of falls. The thick mist and loud roar produced there are perceptible from a distance of about 25 mi (40 km). The Boiling Pot, the beginning of a winding gorge (c.50 mi/80 km long) through which the river flows below the falls, is spanned by a 650 ft (198 m) long bridge that is 310 ft (94 m) above the river. The discovery (1855) of the falls is generally credited to David Livingstone, the British explorer, who named them for Queen Victoria.

Victoria Island, c.81,930 sq mi (212,200 sq km), part of the Arctic Archipelago, Franklin dist., Northwest Territories, N Canada; third largest island of Canada. On the southeast coast is Cambridge Bay, a U.S.-Canadian weather station and trading post. The island was discovered by the British explorers Thomas Simpson and Peter W. Dease in the late 1830s; John Rae explored it in 1851.

Victoria Land, part of E ANTARCTICA, S of New Zealand; Cape Adare is to the northeast. Bounded on the E by the Ross Sea and on the W by Wilkes Land, it consists of ranges of the Transantarctic Mts., with a high plateau in the interior. The region was discovered during the expedition (1839-43) of Sir James Clark Ross and was first carefully studied by the Douglas Mawson expedition (1911-14).

Victoria Nile, river, section of the White Nile, c.260 mi (420 km) long, central Uganda, E central Africa. It drains from the northern end of Lake Victoria at Jinja and flows generally north and west, over Ripon Falls and Owen Falls (both now submerged), through shallow Lake Kyoga, and thence over Murchison Falls to Lake Albert. Hydroelectric plants are located at Owen and Murchison falls. The river is navigable from Lake Albert to Murchison Falls.

Victorian style, in architecture, an eclectic fashion based on revivals of older styles. Although the trend occurred during the reign (1837-1901) of Victoria, it was Prince Albert who was the actual promoter of taste. Although he sponsored the forward-looking construction of iron and glass known as the Crystal Palace (1851), he also promulgated a dry Tuscan Renaissance revival, e.g., in the rebuilding for Queen Victoria of Osborne House on the Isle of Wight. During the Victorian era there was also a romantic harking back to Gothic architecture (see GOTHIC REVIVAL). Government buildings, such as the Houses of Parliament by Sir Charles Barry and A. W. N. Pugin, and churches by William Butterfield were designed in the Gothic style. Nevertheless, modern means of mass production were employed extensively for building materials and furniture. See H. R. Hitchcock, *Early Victorian Architecture in Britain* (1954); John Gloag, *Victorian Comfort* (1961); R. Dutton, *The Victorian Home* (1964); P. Ferriday, ed., *Victorian Architecture* (1964).

Victoria Nyanza (nēăn'zə, nī-), largest lake of Africa and the world's second largest freshwater lake, c.26,830 sq mi (69,490 sq km), E central Africa, on the Uganda-Tanzania-Kenya border. Victoria Nyanza (c.255 mi/410 km long and c.155 mi/250 km wide) occupies a shallow depression (c.250 ft/75 m deep) on the Equatorial Plateau (alt. 3,725 ft/1,135 m) between two arms of the Great Rift Valley. It has an irregular shoreline and many small islands. Numerous streams, including the Kagera River, feed Victoria Nyanza, which is one of the chief headwater reservoirs of the Nile; the Victoria Nile drains the lake to the north. At Owen Falls Dam on the Victoria Nile the lake's waters are used to generate hydroelectricity. The lake basin is densely populated and intensely cultivated, and the lake is an important fishery. Ships regularly call at lakeside towns, including Entebbe, Mwanza, Bukoba, and Kisumu. The first European to see Victoria Nyanza (originally called Ukerewe) was John Speke, the British explorer, in 1858; Henry Stanley explored the region in 1875. It is also called Lake Victoria.

Victoriaville, town (1971 pop. 22,047), S Que., Canada, at the confluence of the Nicolet and Bulstrode rivers, SE of Trois-Rivières. An industrial center, it has factories that make furniture, clothing, and farm equipment.

Victorinus (Caius Marius Victorinus Afer) (vĭktərī'nəs), fl. 361, Roman grammarian, b. Africa. He became renowned as a teacher of rhetoric in Rome and as an advocate of Neoplatonism. Becoming a Christian in his later life, he was forbidden to teach by Emperor Julian. His works include a book on definitions, a treatise on Cicero's *De inventione,* an unoriginal grammar, several tracts against Arianism, and some Pauline commentaries. Some hymns and several other treatises have been attributed to him.

Victorio, d. 1880, chief of the Ojo Caliente [warm spring] Apache Indians, at one time a lieutenant of Mangas Coloradas. When his people were removed from their ancestral home to the desolate reservation at San Carlos, Victorio bolted (1880) for Mexico with a group of followers. He and his people terrorized the border country with repeated raids and massacres, always managing to elude their pursuers. It took the combined efforts of the Mexican army, the Texas Rangers, and c.2,000 U.S. soldiers to defeat Victorio, a master strategist, and his warriors, who numbered less than 200. Victorio died in the battle. See D. L. Thrapp, *Victorio and the Mimbres Apaches* (1974).

Victory of Samothrace: see NIKE.

vicuña (vĭkōō'nyə, vĭkyōō'nə), wild South American hoofed mammal, *Vicugna vicugna,* the smallest member of the camel family. It is 30 in. (75 cm) high at the shoulder, with a long, slender neck and pale fawn coloring. Vicuñas live in herds on high plateaus of the Andes, at altitudes of 14,000 to 18,000 ft (4,300–5,500 m); they feed on grasses and other vegetation. Their fleece is exceptionally soft and silky, and in the time of the Incas was reserved for royal robes. The vicuña has never been successfully domesticated; however, the Indians periodically round up the wild herds for shearing. Hunted nearly to extinction for its wool and flesh, it is now protected in Peru. It is classified in the phylum CHORDATA, subphylum Vertebrata, class Mammalia, order Artiodactyla, family Camelidae.

Vicuña Mackenna, Benjamin (bānhämĕn' vēkōō'nyä mäkä'nä), 1831–86, Chilean historian and journalist. A vigorous opponent of the conservative government of Manuel Montt, he was sentenced to death for his part in the revolution of 1851–52, but escaped and spent some years in exile. He returned to Chile in 1856 and remained active in politics, running unsuccessfully for the presidency in 1875. He visited Mexico, the United States, and Europe and became a collector of manuscripts on early Chilean history. His historical works, based on immense knowledge and scholarship, number more than 100 volumes and include biographies of Antonio José de Sucre, Bernardo O'Higgins, and Diego Portales and a detailed chronicle of the War of the Pacific.

Vida, Marco Girolamo (mär'kō jĕrô'lämō vē'dä), c.1490–1566, Italian poet, b. Cremona. After joining the humanist court of Pope Leo X, he was given a priory at Frascati and was commissioned by Leo to compose a Christian epic, which took form as the *Christiad* or *Christias* (1535). He became bishop of Alba in 1532. In the *Christiad,* the first epic to deal with the redemption and with episodes from the Gospels, he attempted to blend medieval Christian thought with classical formalism. Vida's didactic poems on the silkworm and on chess made him famous, but his most celebrated poem is the long *Ars poetica,* advocating emulation of the classics. Vida wrote in an elegant and readable Latin. See study by M. A. Di Cesare (1963).

Vidal, Peire (pĕr vēdäl'), fl. 1180–1206, Provençal troubadour, b. Toulouse. He spent much of his career in S France and traveled widely in Italy, Cyprus, Hungary, Spain, and Malta. Richard I (Richard Cœur de Lion) was one of his patrons. A high-spirited gallant, Vidal involved himself in numerous escapades. His poems, excellent examples of troubadour love poetry, are notable for their strong personal feeling and simple style.

Vidal de la Blache, Paul (pôl vēdäl' də lä bläsh), French geographer, 1845–1918, the father of French human geography. He was educated at the École Normale Supérieure, Paris, and had an avid interest in history and geography. He taught geography in Nancy and Paris and was a member (1898–1905) of the Faculté des Lettres, Paris, holding the geography chair. Vidal believed that there was an interrelationship between the natural environment and man's activities. He was the founder (1891) and editor of *Annales de géographie.* Among his works are *États et nations de l'Europe* (1889), *Tableau de la géographie de la France* (1903), and the posthumous *Principes de géographie humaine* (1923; tr. *Principles of Human Geography,* 1926) and *Géographie universelle* (15 vol., 1927–48, completed by Lucien Gallois).

Vidin (vē'dĭn), city (1968 est. pop. 176,500), extreme NW Bulgaria, a port on the Danube River. Metal goods, ceramics, and gold and silver filigree work are produced. Vidin is the seat of the Bulgarian metropolitan. Founded in the 1st cent. A.D. as the Roman fortress of Bononia, Vidin became (14th cent.) the capital of the independent West Bulgarian kingdom under Ivan Sratsimir. It was captured by the Turks in 1396. Under Turkish rule it served (1794–1807) as the residence of the pasha Osman Pazvantoğlu. Vidin has several mosques, old churches, synagogues, a bazaar, and ruins of a medieval fortress.

Vidocq, Eugène François (ûzhĕn' fräNswä' vēdôk'), 1775–1857, French detective. After a career of crime for which he had been imprisoned, he joined the Paris Sûreté (security police) as a police spy in 1809. He became head of the detective branch, but incurred the enmity of his colleagues. In 1832 he was removed from office on the charge of instigating a crime for the purpose of uncovering it. He is the prototype of M. Lecoq in the stories of Émile Gaboriau. Vidocq's memoirs (4 vol., 1828–29; partial tr. by E. G. Rich, 1935) were written with the assistance of L. F. L'Héritier de l'ain, who is said to have taken great liberties with the facts. Vidocq only authorized volumes I and II. See biography by J. P. Stead (1954).

Vidzeme: see LIVONIA, USSR.

Viebig, Clara (klä'rä fē'bĭkh), 1860–1952, German novelist of the naturalist school. A skillful and sympathetic portrayer of working-class women, she wrote many novels, among them *Das Weiberdorf* [the women's village] (1900), *Das tägliche Brot* (1900, tr. *Our Daily Bread,* 1909), *Die Wacht am Rhein* [the watch on the Rhine] (1902), *Das schlafende Heer* (1904, tr. *The Sleeping Army,* 1929), *Das Kreuz im Venn* [the cross in Venn] (1908), *Töchter der Hekuba* (1917, tr. *The Daughters of Hecuba,* 1922), and a historical novel *Der Vielgeliebte und die Vielgehasste* [the much-loved man and the much-hated woman] (1935).

Vieira, Antonio (əntô'nyōō vyā'ērə), 1608–97, Portuguese Jesuit orator and missionary. Born in Lisbon, he grew up in Brazil. He was sent by the Jesuits to Portugal to salute the new king, John IV, and there he became court preacher and an ambassador. Returning (1652) to Brazil as a missionary, he championed the exploited natives until he was expelled by the colonists. Back in Portugal he experienced varying fortunes and was imprisoned (1665–67) by the Inquisition. Vieira spent the years 1669–75 in Rome, where he was papal preacher and pled for the persecuted Jews of Portugal. In 1681 he returned to Portugal. His voluminous letters and sermons are couched in a classical although occasionally florid style, and his gracefully flowing phrases are quite vivid. He is now generally considered the foremost prose writer of 17th-century Portugal as well as one of the great preachers of his day.

vielle (vyĕl), bowed string instrument used throughout Europe from the 13th cent. through the 15th cent. The vielle resembles the VIOLIN, of which it is a direct precursor, but it has a longer body and five strings, one of which was used as a drone. In the 15th cent. the word vielle referred to the hurdy-gurdy *(vielle à roue).*

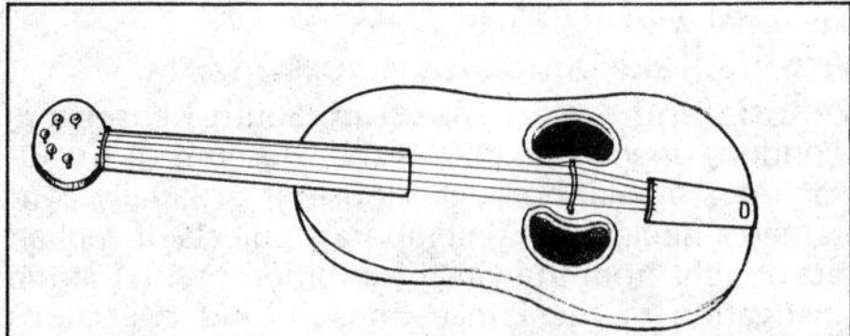

Vielle

Vien, Joseph-Marie (zhôzĕf'-märē' vyăN'), 1716–1809, French neoclassical painter. A protégé of the comte de Caylus, he won the Prix de Rome and studied in Italy. He was appointed director of the French Academy in Rome in 1775. He is best known as Jacques-Louis David's teacher. His own works, primarily allegories and anecdotes, reflect the ideas of Winckelmann. *Marchande d'amours* (Fontainebleau) is one of Vien's better paintings. He enjoyed tremendous prestige in his day.

Vienna (vēĕn'ə), Ger. *Wien,* city and province (1971 pop. 1,614,800), 160 sq mi (414 sq km), administrative seat of Lower Austria and capital of Austria, NE Austria, on the Danube River. The former residence of the Holy Roman emperors and, after 1806, of the emperors of Austria, Vienna is one of the great historic cities of the world and a melting pot of the Germanic, Slav, Italian, and Hungarian peoples and cultures. Located on a plain surrounded by the Wienerwald (Vienna Woods) and the Carpathian foothills, it is a cultural, industrial, commercial, and transportation center, although, since World War II, no longer an important port. The city is divided into 23 districts grouped roughly in two semicircles around the Innere Stadt, or Inner City. Vienna's industries, mainly concentrated on the left bank of the Danube and in the southern districts, produce machinery, textiles, chemicals, and furniture. There are also large oil refineries, breweries, and distilleries. The production of handicrafts (fashion articles, ceramics, and leather) occupies a large portion of the population. The annual Wiener Messe, an industrial fair (est. 1921), attracts buyers from all over the world. Vienna's musical and theatrical life, its parks, coffeehouses, and museums, make it a great tourist attraction. Originally a Celtic settlement, Vienna, then called Vindobona, became an important Roman military and commercial center; Emperor Marcus Aurelius resided there and died there (A.D. 180). After the Romans withdrew (late 4th cent.), it rapidly changed hands among the invaders who overran the region. The Magyars, who gained possession of Vienna early in the 10th cent., were driven out by Leopold I of BABENBERG, the first margrave of the Ostmark (see AUSTRIA). Construction on Vienna's noted Cathedral of St. Stephen began c.1135. Several decades later Henry Jasomirgott, first duke of Austria, transferred his residence to the town, made it capital of the duchy, and erected a castle, Am Hof. The town was fortified by Ottocar II of Bohemia, who conquered Austria in 1251. In 1282, Vienna became the official residence of the house of HAPSBURG. The city was occupied (1485–90) by Matthias Corvinus of Hungary and was besieged by the Turks for the first time in 1529. In the critical second siege (1683) by the Turks under Kara MUSTAFA and their Hungarian allies under Thokoly, the city, heroically defended by Ernst von STARHEMBERG, was on the verge of starvation when it was saved by JOHN III (John Sobieski) of Poland. Early in the 18th cent. a new circle of fortifications was built around the city and many magnificent buildings were erected. Bernhard FISCHER VON ERLACH drew up new plans for the Hofburg (the imperial residence) and built the beautiful Karlskirche; Johann von Hildebrandt designed St. Peter's Church, the Belvedere (summer residence of Prince Eugene of Savoy), and the Kinsky Palace; together they planned the Schwarzenburg Palace and the winter residence of Prince Eugene. Empress Maria Theresa (reigned 1740–80) enlarged the old university, founded in 1365, and completed the royal summer palace of SCHÖNBRUNN, started by her father, Charles VI (1711–40). Joseph II (1765–90) opened the Prater, a large imperial garden, which now contains an amusement park, to the public. Haydn, Mozart, Beethoven, and Schubert lived in Vienna and gave it lasting glory. In 1805 and 1809, Vienna was occupied by Napoleon. The era of political reaction under Prince Metternich, which followed the Congress of Vienna (1814–15), was also famous for the waltzes of Joseph Lanner and the Strauss family, and for the farces of Nestroy, the comedies of Raimund, and the tragic dramas of Grillparzer. During the Revolution of 1848, revolutionists in Vienna forced Metternich to resign, but they were eventually suppressed by WINDISCHGRÄTZ. The modern city dates from Francis Joseph's reign (1848–1916). By 1860 the old ramparts about the inner city had been replaced by the famous boulevard, the Ringstrasse. The principal edifices on or near the Ringstrasse are the neo-Gothic Rathaus, with many statues and a tower 320 ft (98 m) high; the domed museums of natural history and of art, in Italian Renaissance style; the Votivkirche, one of the finest of modern Gothic churches; the parliament buildings, in Greek style; the palace of justice; the famous opera house and the Burgtheater, both in Renaissance style; the Künstlerhaus, with painting exhibitions; the Musikverein, containing the conservatory of music; and the Academy of Art. In the late 19th and early 20th cent., Vienna flourished again as a cultural and scientific center. Rokitansky, Wagner-Jauregg, and Billroth (to whom Brahms dedicated the string quartets Op. 51) worked at the General Hospital; at the same time Freud was developing his theory of psychoanalysis. Vienna attracted Brahms, Mahler, Richard Strauss, and Arnold Schönberg and his disciples, who gave it a further period of musical greatness. Krauss, Werfel, Hofmannsthal, Schnitzler, and Wassermann dominated the literary scene. Vienna suffered hardships during World War I. Amidst food shortages and revolution it became, at the end of the war, the capital of the small republic of Austria. In 1922, Vienna became an autonomous province *(Bundesland)* of Austria. The highly successful Social Democratic city government headed by Mayor Karl Seitz (1923–34) initiated a program of municipal improvements. In public housing Vienna set an example for the world. Model apartment houses for workers, notably the huge Karl Marx Hof, began to replace the city's slums. The projects were badly damaged in the civil war of Feb., 1934, between Viennese Socialists and the Austrian government of Chancellor DOLLFUSS. On March 15, 1938, Adolf Hitler triumphantly entered Vienna, and Austria was annexed to Germany. During World War II the city suffered considerable damage. The Jewish population (115,000 in 1938), residing mainly in the Leopoldstadt district (designated the official ghetto in the 17th cent.), was reduced to 6,000 by the end of the war. The Russian army entered Vienna in April, 1945. Vienna and Austria were divided into four occupation zones by the victorious Allies. The occupation lasted until 1955, when, by treaty, the four powers reunited Austria as a neutral state. Vienna became the headquarters of the International Atomic Energy Agency in 1957. President Kennedy and Premier Khrushchev met in the city in 1961, and the United States and the USSR held disarmament talks there in 1970 and 1971. See A. J. May, *Vienna in the Age of Franz Josef* (1966); Erik von Wickenburg, *A Pocket History of Vienna* (tr. 1972).

Vienna. **1** Town (1970 pop. 17,152), Fairfax co., N Va., a residential suburb of Washington, D.C.; inc. 1890. It has some research industry. Originally called Springfield, it became the site of Fairfax county's first courthouse in 1742. It grew mainly after World War II. Filene Center for the Performing Arts is on the city's outskirts. Dulles International Airport is nearby. **2** Industrial city (1970 pop. 11,549), Wood co., NW W. Va., on the Ohio River; laid out 1794, inc. 1935. Glass is manufactured there.

Vienna, Congress of, Sept., 1814–June, 1815, one of the most important international conferences in European history, called to remake Europe after the downfall of Napoleon I. The Austrian emperor Francis I (formerly Holy Roman Emperor FRANCIS II) was the host. Among the many monarchs to attend the congress the most important were Czar Alexander I of Russia and King Frederick William III of Prussia. Fürst von METTERNICH was the chief Austrian negotiator and presided over the congress; Viscount Castlereagh and, for a time, the duke of Wellington represented Great Britain; the Russian delegation included Count Nesselrode, Count Capo d'Istria, and Carlo Andreo Pozzo di Borgo; among the Prussian diplomats were Karl August von Hardenberg, Wilhelm von Humboldt, and Karl vom und zum Stein. A peace settlement with defeated France had been reached before the congress convened (see PARIS, TREATY OF, 1814), but France was represented by Charles Maurice de TALLEYRAND, who, by skillfully exploiting differences among the allies, soon obtained an equal voice with the four great victorious powers. All other European states, large and petty, that had legally existed before the Napoleonic upheaval were represented by an army of delegates and agents, but the important work was carried out in committees under the tutelage of the major powers. The problems confronting the congress were extremely thorny and complex, for the French Revolution and the Napoleonic Wars had swept away the entire structure of Europe. Although the principle of legitimacy—restoration of the pre-Revolutionary dynastic and territorial states—was often ceremoniously invoked, it was the determination to achieve a balance of power for the preservation of peace that guided congress decisions. In place of the defunct Holy Roman Empire or its several hundred princes, the GERMAN CONFEDERATION was created. Major territorial changes were unavoidable, partly because of previous secret agreements reached among individual allies and partly because of the pressure of power politics. The principle of national self-determination, although invoked in certain cases, was neglected in practice. The congress opened with a round of magnificent balls and entertainments, while its serious business was stalled by intrigues and rivalries. Major points of friction were the settlement of the Polish question, the conflicting claims of Sweden, Denmark, and Russia, and the adjustment of the borders of the German states. Russia and Prussia were generally opposed by Austria, France, and Britain, which at one point (Jan., 1815) went so far as to conclude a defensive triple alliance. The shock of this crisis and of the return of Napoleon I from Elba so upset the delegates that the congress began to find solutions for its many difficulties. The constitution of the German Confederation was accepted on June 8, 1815, and was incorporated into the Final Act of the congress, signed on June 9, nine days before Napoleon's defeat at Waterloo. The restoration of Louis XVIII in France and of Ferdinand VII in Spain was confirmed. Italy was dealt with as a geographic rather than a political entity, and its hopes for unity were dashed. Naples and Sicily were reunited under Bourbon rule; the Papal States were restored; the duchies of Parma, Piacenza, and Guastalla were awarded to French Empress MARIE LOUISE for her lifetime; Tuscany and Modena were restored to the house of Hapsburg-Lorraine; the Lombardo-Venetian kingdom was set up under Austrian rule to compensate Austria for its loss of the Austrian Netherlands; and the formerly Venetian part of Dalmatia also went to Austria. The kingdom of Sardinia was restored and recovered Savoy, Nice, and Piedmont, and it received Liguria with Genoa. Poland was redivided among Russia, Prussia, and Austria, with Russia benefiting primarily; part of Poland, with Warsaw, was set up as a kingdom in personal union with Russia; Kraków and its surrounding territory was made a republic under the protection of Russia, Austria, and Prussia. Since Austria received Italian territories to compensate for Russian gains, Prussia was awarded much of Saxony as well as important parts of Westphalia and Rhine Province. Great Britain, more interested in acquiring strategic colonial territories, retained the former Dutch colonies of Ceylon and Cape Colony, received parts of the West Indies at the expense of the Netherlands and Spain, kept Malta and Helgoland, and obtained a protectorate over the Ionian islands. The former Austrian Netherlands was united with the former United Provinces as the kingdom of the Netherlands, under the house of Orange. Russia retained the formerly Swedish Finland. The congress confirmed the transfer of Norway from the Danish to the Swedish crown; W Pomerania, the claim to which Sweden had ceded to Denmark in the Treaty of Kiel (1814), was given to Prussia, which compensated Denmark with the duchy of Lauenburg. Bavaria received its approximate present-day boundaries, as did Württemberg and Baden. SWITZERLAND was enlarged, and Swiss neutrality was guaranteed. As regards France, a new peace settlement was reached on Nov. 20, 1815 (see PARIS, TREATY OF, 1815). The Final Act of Vienna was subsequently ratified by the powers concerned, but several separate treaties were required to complete the settlement. Although the territorial changes did not endure long in entirety, they represented a practical if not always equitable solution and an attempt at dealing with Europe as an organic whole. The QUADRUPLE ALLIANCE and the HOLY ALLIANCE, designed to uphold the decisions of Vienna and to settle disputes and problems by means of conferences, were an important step toward European cooperation. The CONCERT OF EUROPE, which functioned—even though imperfectly—through the 19th cent., may be credited to the Congress of Vienna. An auxiliary accomplishment of the congress was the adoption of standard rules of diplomacy. Serious defects were the disregard of the growing national aspirations and the social changes that brought about the revolutions of 1848, and the failure to include the Ottoman Empire (Turkey) in the settlement and to deal satisfactorily with the Eastern Question. See Harold Nicolson, *The Congress of Vienna* (1946, repr. 1970); Henry Kissinger, *A World Restored* (1957, repr. 1964); Hilde Spiel, ed., *The Congress of Vienna: An Eyewitness Account* (1968).

Vienna University, at Vienna, Austria; founded 1365. It was reorganized in 1377, 1384, and 1850. It has faculties of Roman Catholic theology, Protestant theology, law and political science, medicine, and philosophy and natural sciences.

Vienne (vyĕn), department (1968 pop. 340,256), W central France, in POITOU. POITIERS is the capital.

Vienne, town (1968 pop. 30,276), Isère dept., SE France, on the Rhône River. It is a farm trade center with textile, metallurgical, and pharmaceutical industries. The capital of the Allobroges, Vienne (then Vienna) became one of the chief cities of Roman Gaul, one of the first archiepiscopal sees (suppressed in 1790), and the seat of several kings of Burgundy (5th–9th cent.; see under BURGUNDY). A council held there abolished (1312) the KNIGHTS TEMPLARS. Rich in Roman remains, Vienne has the temple of Augustus and Livia (c.25 B.C.), which rivals the Maison Carrée of Nîmes. The Church of St. Pierre (partly 6th cent.), the Church of St. André-le-Bas (12th cent.), and the Church of St. Maurice (12th–16th cent.) are also of interest. Recent excavations have unearthed a Roman cultural center.

Vienne, river, 230 mi (370 km) long, rising in the Massif Central, central France, and flowing W past Limoges, then N into the Loire near Saumur.

Vienne, Council of, 1311–12, 15th ecumenical council of the Roman Catholic Church, held at Vienne, France. It was convened by Pope CLEMENT V at the behest of PHILIP IV of France as a further move in the plan of the French king to destroy the KNIGHTS TEMPLARS. The council voted to hear the knights in their own defense but, under pressure from Philip, reversed itself and recommended that the order be suppressed. The pope dissolved the order by papal bull a few days later. The council also passed minor doctrinal decrees and condemned the errors of the BEGHARDS.

Vientiane (vē″əntyĕn′, vyăNtyän′), city (1970 est. pop. 150,000), administrative capital and largest city of Laos, N central Laos, on the Mekong River, c.130 mi (210 km) southeast of the royal capital of Luang Prabang. A railroad links the two capitals. Vientiane is a trading center for forest products, lac, textiles, and hides. Many commodities are ferried across the Mekong to Thailand, where they are transported by rail to Bangkok. Chinese and Vietnamese minorities dominate retailing and commerce in Vientiane. The city is noted for its canals, its houses built on stilts, and its numerous pagodas, one of which now houses an architectural museum. There is an international airport. Vientiane was the capital of a Lao kingdom from 1707. It was sacked by the Siamese in 1827. It passed under French rule in 1893 and became the capital of the French protectorate of Laos in 1899. The ruins of the old capital are near the modern city.

Vieques (vyā′kās), island (1970 pop. 7,767), 51 sq mi (132 sq km), off E Puerto Rico. It is hilly, with a dry, warm climate. Products are pineapples, cattle, and hogs. The only town, **Vieques** (1970 pop. 2,378), commonly called Isabel Segunda, was founded in 1843. The island has gained popularity as a holiday resort.

Vierge, Daniel Urrabieta (dänyĕl′ o͞oräbyā′tä vyăr′-hā), 1851–1904, Spanish illustrator. He went to Paris before 1870 and won recognition for his drawings of scenes of the Commune of Paris. He worked for the *Monde illustré* and the *Vie moderne,* and he illustrated works of Hugo, Zola, Poe, and Quevedo. Most famous, however, are his illustrations for *Don Quixote* (4 vol., 1906–7). Paralyzed on his right side at the age of 30, Vierge learned to draw with his left hand. His pen-and-ink drawings had a marked influence on the art of modern illustration.

Viersen (fēr′zən), city (1970 pop. 85,326), North Rhine-Westphalia, W West Germany. It is a textile-manufacturing center; other products include machinery, leather goods, and processed food. Viersen passed to Prussia in 1713 and was chartered in 1856.

Vierwaldstättersee: see LUCERNE, LAKE OF.

Viet Cong (vēĕt′ kông), officially *Viet Nam Cong San* [Vietnamese Communists], Communist insurgents in South Vietnam. The term originally referred to the Communist troops (about 10,000) left in hideouts in South Vietnam after the Communists withdrew to North Vietnam in accordance with agreements reached at the Geneva Conference of 1954, which followed the French Indochina War (1946–54). Supported and later directed by North Vietnam, the Viet Cong first tried subversive tactics to overthrow the South Vietnamese regime, then resorted to open warfare (see VIETNAM WAR). They were subsequently reinforced by huge numbers of North Vietnamese troops infiltrating south.

Viète or **Vieta, François** (fräNswä′ vyĕt, vyātä′, vīē′-tə), 1540–1603, French mathematician. As a founder of modern algebra, he introduced the use of letters as algebraic symbols and correlated algebra with geometry and trigonometry. A prominent lawyer, he was attached for a time to the parliament of Brittany and served as privy councillor to Henry IV, for whom he decoded messages sent by Philip II of Spain to his soldiers in the Netherlands.

Viet Minh (vē-ĕt′ mĭn), officially *Viet Nam Doc Lap Dong Minh* [League for the Independence of Vietnam], a coalition of Communist and nationalist groups that opposed the French and the Japanese during World War II. The Viet Minh spearheaded

Vietnamese resistance to French rule in the French Indochina War (1946–54). The organization was soon dominated by Communists, and in 1951 its Communist elements were absorbed by the Communist party of North Vietnam.

Vietnam (vēĕt'näm), former state, Southeast Asia, now divided into the Democratic Republic of Vietnam (North Vietnam) and the Republic of Vietnam (South Vietnam). It was formed (1949–50) by the union of the historic areas of TONKIN (N Vietnam), ANNAM (central Vietnam), and COCHIN CHINA (S Vietnam). The region of Vietnam is covered largely by forested mountains and plateaus. In the north is the delta of the Red River and in the south that of the Mekong River. The central section of Vietnam lies between the Annamese Cordillera and the South China Sea. The region has a tropical monsoon climate, modified by local conditions. Agriculture is the principal occupation of the population, and rice is by far the leading crop. The Vietnamese (more than 80% of the population) are a basically Mongoloid people. Most consider themselves Buddhists,

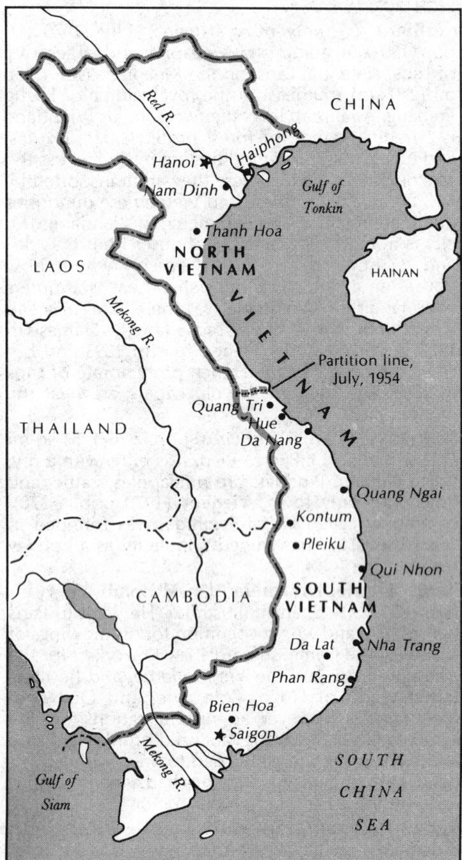

but religious practice typically combines elements of Taoism, Confucianism, ancestor worship, and animism as well. Religious activity has been somewhat curtailed in North Vietnam, although a sizable number of Roman Catholics still worship there. South Vietnam has an even larger Roman Catholic minority. Principal highland tribes are the Thai, Muong, Nung, Meo, and Man in the north and the Montagnards in the south. Cambodians (Khmers) are found near the Cambodian border and at the mouth of the Mekong River. There are large numbers of Chinese in the urban centers, notably in the Cholon area of Saigon. The early history of Vietnam is that of Tonkin, Annam, and Cochin China. The first Europeans to arrive were the Portuguese in 1535. Dutch, French, and English traders came in the 17th cent., at which time missionaries entered the area, winning many converts to Roman Catholicism. The persecution of missionaries and of their Vietnamese converts by the ruler of Vietnam was a factor prompting French conquest in the 19th cent. The French captured Saigon in 1859, and after a period of warfare, organized (1867) the colony of Cochin China. In 1884, France declared protectorates over Tonkin and Annam; in 1887 it merged Tonkin, Annam, and Cochin China with Cambodia to form a union of INDOCHINA, to which Laos was added in 1893. A nationalist movement arose in Vietnam in the early 20th cent. and gained momentum during the Japanese occupation in World War II. The Japanese allowed the French Vichy administration to continue as a figurehead power until March, 1945, when they ousted it and established the autonomous state of Vietnam (comprising Tonkin, Annam, and Cochin China) under the rule of BAO DAI, the emperor of Annam. The Bao Dai government quickly collapsed, and at the end of World War II, the VIET MINH party (the League for the Independence of Vietnam, a coalition of nationalist and Communist groups), headed by HO CHI MINH, established a republic with its capital at Hanoi. The Chinese Nationalists, who occupied North Vietnam for seven months after the war (in accordance with a decision made at the POTSDAM CONFERENCE), did not challenge Ho's power. The French attempted to reassert their authority in Vietnam following the war, and the British, who occupied South Vietnam, permitted French troops to land and assisted them in suppressing native resistance. In March, 1946, France signed an agreement with Ho Chi Minh, recognizing Vietnam as a free state within the Indochina federation and the French Union. French troops were then permitted to replace the Chinese in the north. However, differences immediately arose over whether Cochin China was included in the independent state of Vietnam; in June, 1946, France supported the establishment of a separate republic of Cochin China. Fighting broke out (Nov., 1946) between Vietnamese and French troops in Haiphong, and French ships shelled the city, killing some 6,000 civilians. The next month the Viet Minh attacked the French at Hanoi, ushering in the prolonged and bloody guerrilla conflict that became known as the French Indochina War (1946–54). In an attempt to win popular support, the French in 1949 reinstalled Bao Dai as the ruler of Vietnam, of which Cochin China was then recognized to be a part. Spurred by the Communist takeover of mainland China, which brought Chinese Communist forces to the northern border of Indochina by Dec., 1949, France concluded a treaty (ratified Feb., 1950) granting Vietnam independence within the French Union. The new state was promptly recognized by the United States, Great Britain, and other states; meanwhile the Ho regime was recognized by the USSR, Communist China, and other Soviet allies. Except for Thailand (which recognized Bao Dai), the states of Southeast Asia held aloof from both regimes. Bao Dai failed to win the general support of the Vietnamese, many of whom saw him as a French puppet. Thousands of non-Communists joined the Viet Minh, and the war reached an eventual stalemate, with the French controlling the cities and a few isolated outposts and the Viet Minh occupying most of the countryside. France formally asked U.S. aid for the Bao Dai regime in Feb., 1950. By 1954, the United States was paying about 80% of the French war costs in Vietnam. The French military situation deteriorated rapidly in early 1954 as Viet Minh forces closed in on DIENBIENPHU, upon which the French had staked the defense of the Red River delta. Dienbienphu fell in May, and at the Geneva Conference of 1954, France had to accept disadvantageous terms for an armistice. The truce agreement was signed by representatives of the French Union and of the Viet Minh forces. As a temporary expedient, Vietnam was divided into two parts along a line approximating the 17th parallel (latitude 17°N). North Vietnam, where the Viet Minh were the strongest, went to the Communist government of Ho Chi Minh, while South Vietnam was placed under the control of the French-backed government of Bao Dai. Freedom of movement between the two areas was to be permitted for a period of 300 days, thereby facilitating the regroupment of Communist forces in the north and non-Communist forces in the south. The unification of the country under one government was to be effected through general elections, later scheduled for July, 1956. These elections, which were considered likely to favor the Communists, were never held; the South Vietnamese government refused to participate on the grounds that it had not signed the Geneva agreements and was therefore not bound by them. **North Vietnam** or the Democratic Republic of Vietnam (1973 est. pop. 22,300,000), 61,293 sq mi (158,750 sq km), includes all of Tonkin and a portion of Annam. The capital is HANOI. It is bordered by China on the north, the Gulf of Tonkin on the east, South Vietnam on the south, and Laos on the west. The northern and western sections have high mountain masses which are continuations of the mountains of the Chinese provinces of Yünnan and Kwangsi to the north. The mountains give way in the east to an alluvial plain—the delta of the Red River and other streams that empty into the Gulf of Tonkin. To the south is a narrow coastal strip backed by mountains that extend almost to the gulf. Population is concentrated in the fertile Red River delta, where an elaborate network (c.2,700 mi/4,350 km) of dikes, dams, canals, and locks provide irrigation and flood control. In the delta are the great rice fields and the major cities of Hanoi (the capital) and HAIPHONG (the chief harbor). Although only 15% of the total land is arable, the economy is basically agricultural. Farming is largely unmechanized; water buffalo and oxen are used, and irrigation pumps are manually controlled. Rice fields comprise almost all of the cultivated land, but corn, sweet potatoes, cassava, taro, and beans are also grown, as are some industrial crops (cotton, jute, hemp, sugarcane, oilseeds). Before the division of Vietnam in 1954, the north depended upon the south for supplemental rice supplies; now considerable wheat and other grains are imported from China and the USSR. The mountainous areas contain dense rain forests, and timber is the country's most valuable economic crop. Fishing is also important. North Vietnam has virtually all of Vietnam's mineral deposits; coal is by far the most abundant resource, and tin, iron, zinc, lead, gold, chromite, manganese, uranium, and phosphate are also mined. Industrial progress has been hampered by the many years of war; the massive U.S. bombings (1965–68, 1972) virtually destroyed the country's limited industrial plant, but much has been reconstructed (see recent history, below). After the partition of Vietnam (1954), some 900,000 people fled south during the period permitting free movement between the two zones. Many of the emigrants were Catholics, but many were also fleeing the land-reform program initiated even before the defeat of the French. The program, featuring a "free hand to the masses," provoked (1956) an open revolt in the province of Nghe An, which was suppressed by the army. The revolt is believed to have resulted in the deaths of more than 50,000 people; at least 2,000 landlords were executed. Ho Chi Minh, who dominated North Vietnamese politics until his death in 1969, maintained good relations with both China and the USSR, receiving enormous aid from both countries while skillfully protecting independence. A three-year economic rehabilitation program (1958–60) and a five-year plan (1961–66), financed with Soviet and Chinese aid, were aimed at improving both industry and agriculture. Electric power production was increased fifteenfold, new mineral deposits were located, mining operations were expanded, and many new industries were established, especially in Hanoi and Haiphong. Also constructed were a large iron-and-steel complex at Thai Nguyen, a chemical combine at Viet Tri, and a textile complex at Nam Dinh. Much national effort was also devoted to the support of Communist insurgents in South Vietnam (the VIET CONG), who operated under the leadership of the National Liberation Front, an organization alleged to be indigenous to South Vietnam. (The North Vietnamese also supported Communist insurgency movements in Laos and, later, in Cambodia.) North Vietnamese troops and supplies were soon infiltrating South Vietnam by way of what came to be known as the Ho Chi Minh Trail in Laos. Open warfare inevitably resulted, and the United States, deeply committed to the support of the non-Communist government of South Vietnam, became increasingly involved (see VIETNAM WAR). The U.S. bombing of North Vietnam began after two U.S. destroyers were reportedly attacked (Aug., 1964) by North Vietnamese torpedo boats in the Gulf of Tonkin. The bombing, directed at military and industrial targets, extended to Hanoi and Haiphong and continued systematically until March, 1968, when raids north of latitude 19°N were halted to promote peace negotiations. In Nov., 1968, all bombing ceased. U.S. "protective reaction" air strikes against military installations south of latitude 19°N were resumed by 1970, however. In April, 1972, in response to a major Communist drive from North Vietnam, the United States reinstituted mass bombings throughout the country; Haiphong harbor and six other North Vietnamese ports, as well as rivers and canals, were mined and effectively closed to shipping. Heavy, concentrated air strikes (as many as 340 a day) continued, with one temporary halt (Oct. 24–Dec. 18) until Dec. 30, 1972, inflicting enormous damage. The country's industrial plant was destroyed, transportation lines were cut, and many non-military targets—including the extensive system of dikes in the Red River delta and numerous residential areas—were hit. Morale nevertheless remained high; damaged transportation facilities were constantly repaired, and "ant tactics" kept supplies laboriously moving from Communist China. After the cease-fire (Jan.,

1973), reconstruction began with foreign aid, and in less than a year the shipyards at Haiphong, the iron and steel works at Thai Nguyen, and many small factories were again in operation. The constitution of North Vietnam (adopted Dec., 1959) provides for a national assembly, which meets, however, only twice a year and serves largely as a rubber stamp for the executive. The president is elected by the national assembly, but since the death of Ho Chi Minh, that office has been largely honorific. True authority resides in the Communist party, which is now under the collective leadership of the politburo, headed by first secretary Le Duan. North Vietnam's numerous colleges and universities include the Univ. of Hanoi, the Hanoi Polytechnic College, and specialized institutions. **South Vietnam** or the Republic of Vietnam (1973 est. pop. 19,700,000), 67,108 sq mi (173,809 sq km), includes Cochin China and the major part of Annam. The capital is SAIGON. It is bounded by North Vietnam on the north, the South China Sea on the east and south, and Cambodia and Laos on the west. Population is concentrated in the fertile Mekong delta, which occupies the southern two fifths of the country. With heavy rainfall and rich alluvial soil, it is one of the world's greatest rice-growing regions. To the north, the Annamese Cordillera—the southern spur of a mountain range that originates in China—rise to more than 8,000 ft (2,440 m). They contain a notable plateau known as the Central Highlands (alt. 600–1,600 ft/180–490 m), which, although sparsely populated, contains rubber, coffee, and tea plantations. East of the Annamese Cordillera are the Central Lowlands (central to all of Vietnam), a narrow coastal strip where short, often torrential rivers, flowing west to east, form fertile deltas given over to the growing of rice. South Vietnam is predominantly agricultural, and rice is the chief crop; fiber plants, peanuts, tea, coffee, and sugarcane are secondary crops. Normally the Mekong delta and adjacent areas produce enough food for export, but agricultural output declined some 30% during the Vietnam War and after 1964 rice had to be imported. The production of rubber, once an important export item, declined by more than 50%. Massive U.S. aid has rebuilt war-torn areas and financed public works and irrigation projects. Fishing is widespread, especially along the coast, and forestry is important. Unlike North Vietnam, the south is poor in mineral resources. There is one exploitable coal field, and small amounts of gold, lead, copper, iron, and molybdenum have been found. Silica, limestone, and clay support small glass, cement, and ceramic enterprises. Before the division of Vietnam, almost all industry was concentrated in the north. Investments spurred southern industrial growth, but almost exclusively in the Saigon area, where textile mills, assorted manufacturing plants, and establishments processing the food and forest products of the country (e.g., rice, timber, fish) are found. A few months after the partition of Vietnam in 1954, South Vietnam withdrew from the French Union and thus attained complete sovereignty. In a referendum held in Oct., 1955, the electorate deposed Bao Dai as chief of state and approved the establishment of a republic with Ngo Dinh DIEM as president. The republic, proclaimed on Oct. 26, 1955, was recognized as the legal government of Vietnam by the United States, France, Great Britain, and other Western powers. Diem was faced with a war-torn economy and serious political chaos as numerous factions and individuals vied for power. He suppressed the Cao Dai, a religious sect with its own private army (the Binh Xuyen), and the Hoa Hao, an occultist religious group, both of which opposed him. But his authoritarian policies—rigid press censorship, interference with elections, restriction of opposition parties, and mass arrests—drew increasing criticism. His land reform programs were ineffective, and by late 1961, the Viet Cong, supported by North Vietnam, had won control of virtually half the country with little local opposition. The United States increased its military and economic aid to combat the Communist threat and at the same time put pressure on President Diem for democratic reforms. In April, 1961, Diem was reelected president, but many voters boycotted the election. Resentment against the government was dramatized by the Buddhist crisis, which erupted in May, 1963, as a result of government persecution. A number of self-immolations by Buddhist monks followed. Large antigovernment demonstrations provoked police shootings, mass arrests, and more repressive government measures. These actions, along with the increasing loss of territory to the Viet Cong, prompted Diem's own military commanders to resort to a coup (Nov. 1, 1963), in which Diem and his brother, Ngo Dinh Nhu (who headed the secret police), were murdered. A period of great political instability followed, with frequent changes in government, mounting disorders, and continued religious unrest (both Buddhist and Catholic). In 1964 regular units of the North Vietnamese army began infiltrating into South Vietnam to assist the Viet Cong, and the guerrilla conflict expanded into the Vietnam War. In June, 1965, a military junta came to power with Gen. Nguyen Van THIEU as chief of state and Air Vice Marshal Nguyen Cao KY as prime minister. Their regime was strengthened by the capture (1966) of Buddhist rebel strongholds in Da Nang and Hue. A new constitution (approved March, 1967) provided for a strong executive and a bicameral legislature. In Sept., 1967, Thieu and Ky were elected president and vice president respectively. The problems they faced were aggravated by the rapidly accelerating war. Heavy fighting in the rural areas forced thousands of people to seek refuge in the cities, where serious overcrowding ensued. Heavy damage was sustained in the Tet offensive of 1968, especially in Hue and in the Saigon area. The country became increasingly dependent upon U.S. aid, which reached massive proportions, and the presence of U.S. troops, whose numbers peaked at almost 550,000 in 1969, dislocated the traditional agricultural economy. In Oct., 1971, President Thieu was reelected for another four-year term; he ran unopposed as other candidates, fearing a rigged election, refused to run. In his second term President Thieu faced serious problems. The gradual withdrawal of U.S. troops, which had begun in 1969, adversely affected the economy, bringing a severe recession. At the same time, the endless war fed a raging inflation. The cease-fire, concluded in Paris in Jan., 1973, did not bring peace; North Vietnamese and Viet Cong attacks persisted, and half the national budget continued to be consumed by defense activities. In 1974, South Vietnam came into direct conflict with Communist China, which seized the disputed Paracel Islands in the South China Sea. President Thieu gradually assumed dictatorial powers; he abolished local self-government, restricted the press, arrested thousands of suspected Viet Cong sympathizers, and increased the number of executions. Mass protest demonstrations (Oct., 1974) in Saigon caused Thieu to reorganize his cabinet in an attempt to quiet the opposition. In early 1974 the constitution was amended to permit him to seek a third term in 1975, at the same time increasing that term from four to five years. South Vietnam has five universities and several colleges; these include the Univ. of Saigon (the largest and most important), Van Hanh Univ. (also in Saigon), and universities in Hue, Da Lat, and Can Tho. See Tran Van Tung, *Vietnam* (1959); Robert Scigliano, *South Vietnam: Nation under Stress* (1963); W. G. Burchett, *Vietnam* (2d ed. 1965); Chester Bain, *Vietnam: The Roots of Conflict* (1967); Bernard Fall, *The Two Vietnams* (2d rev. ed. 1967); P. J. Honey, ed., *North Vietnam Today* (1962), *Communism in North Vietnam* (1963, repr. 1973), and *Genesis of a Tragedy* (1968); J. F. Cairns, *The Eagle and the Lotus: Western Intervention in Vietnam, 1847–1968* (1969); J. T. McAlister, *Vietnam: The Origins of Revolution* (1969) and *The Vietnamese and Their Revolution* (1970); Piero Gheddo, *The Cross and the Bo-tree: Catholics and Buddhists in Vietnam* (1970); D. G. Marr, *Vietnamese Anticolonialism, 1855–1925* (1971); Joseph Buttinger, *Vietnam: A Political History* (1968) and *A Dragon Defiant: A Short History of Vietnam* (1972); J. H. M. Chen, *Vietnam: A Comprehensive Bibliography* (1973); W. F. Vella, ed., *Aspects of Vietnamese History* (1973).

Vietnam War, conflict in Southeast Asia, primarily fought in South Vietnam between government forces aided by the United States and guerrilla insurgents aided by North Vietnam. The war began soon after the GENEVA CONFERENCE provisionally divided (1954) Vietnam at 17° N lat. into the Democratic Republic of Vietnam (North Vietnam) and the Republic of Vietnam (South Vietnam); escalated from a Vietnamese civil war into a limited international conflict in which the United States was deeply involved; and was substantially halted by peace agreements in 1973. In part the war was a legacy of France's colonial administration of Indochina, which effectively ended in 1954 with the French army's catastrophic defeat at DIENBIENPHU and the acceptance of the Geneva Conference agreements (see VIETNAM). The end of hostilities was followed by refugee movements between zones and by reprisals by each regime against suspected enemies. Elections scheduled for 1956 in South Vietnam for the reunification of Vietnam were cancelled by President Ngo Dinh DIEM. The cancellation was denounced by HO CHI MINH and the Communist government of North Vietnam. The Communists expected to benefit from any elections held in South Vietnam because of the popular support they had there. After 1956, Diem's government faced increasingly serious opposition from insurgents known as the VIET CONG, who were aided by North Vietnam. The Viet Cong, following the tactics of North Vietnam's Vo Nguyen GIAP, became masters of guerrilla warfare. Diem's army received U.S. advice and aid but was unable to suppress the guerrillas, who established a political organization, the National Liberation Front (NLF) in 1960. In 1961, South Vietnam signed a military and economic aid treaty with the United States that led to the arrival (1961) of the first U.S. support troops and the formation (1962) of the U.S. Military Assistance Command. Mounting dissatisfaction with the ineffectiveness and corruption of Diem's government culminated (Nov., 1963) in a military coup engineered by Duong Van MINH and in Diem's execution. No one person or group was able to establish control in South Vietnam until June, 1965, when Nguyen Cao KY became premier. During this interim, U.S. military aid to South Vietnam increased, especially after the U.S. Senate passed the TONKIN GULF RESOLUTION (Aug. 7, 1964) at the request of President Lyndon B. Johnson. In early 1965 the United States began air raids on North Vietnam and on Communist-controlled areas in the South, attempting to stop the flow of men and supplies to the South; by 1966 there were 190,000 U.S. troops in South Vietnam. North Vietnam, meanwhile, was receiving armaments and technical assistance from the Soviet Union and other Communist countries. Despite massive U.S. military aid, heavy bombing, the growing U.S. troop commitment (which reached nearly 550,000 in 1969), and the achievement of some political stability in South Vietnam after the election (1967) of Nguyen Van THIEU as president, the United States and South Vietnam were unable to inflict permanent setbacks on the Viet Cong and North Vietnamese. Optimistic U.S. military reports were discredited in Feb., 1968, by the devastating Tet offensive of the North Vietnamese army and the Viet Cong, which involved attacks on more than 100 towns and cities and a month-long battle for HUE in South Vietnam.

The End of the War. Although initial efforts for a negotiated settlement were rejected by both sides, progress was made after President Johnson's decision not to seek reelection in 1968. Contacts between North Vietnam and the United States in Paris in 1968 were expanded in 1969 to include South Vietnam and the NLF. The United States, under the leadership of President Richard M. Nixon, altered its tactics to combine U.S. troop withdrawals with intensified bombing and the invasion of Communist sanctuaries in Cambodia (1970). The length of the war, the high U.S. casualties, and the exposure of U.S. involvement in war crimes such as the massacre at My Lai (see MY LAI INCIDENT) helped to turn many in the United States against the war. Politically, the movement was led by Senators James William FULBRIGHT, Robert F. KENNEDY, Eugene J. McCARTHY, and George S. McGOVERN; there were also huge public demonstrations in Washington, D.C., as well as in many other cities in the United States and on college campuses. Even as the war continued, peace talks in Paris progressed, with Henry KISSINGER as U.S. negotiator. Hopes for peace were temporarily dashed in Dec., 1972, when a break in negotiations was followed by U.S. saturation bombing of North Vietnam. However, a peace agreement was reached in Jan., 1973, and the formal document was signed by the United States, North Vietnam, South Vietnam, and the NLF's provisional revolutionary government on Jan. 27, 1973. The accord provided for the end of hostilities, the withdrawal of U.S. and allied troops (several Southeast Asia Treaty Organization countries had sent token forces), the return of prisoners of war, and the formation of a four-nation international control commission to ensure peace. Although many problems were settled by the peace, fighting between South Vietnamese and the Communists for additional territory continued and hostility between North and South Vietnam remained undiluted. U.S. casualties in Vietnam during the era of direct U.S. involvement (1961–72) were more than 50,000 dead; South Vietnamese dead were estimated at more than 400,000 and Viet Cong and North Vietnamese at over 900,000. See also CAMBODIA; LAOS. See Bernard Fall, *The Two Vietnams* (2d rev. ed. 1967); D. J. Duncanson, *Government and Revolution in Vietnam* (1968); W. R. Fishel, ed., *Viet-*

nam: Anatomy of a Conflict (1968); Robert Shaplen, *The Lost Revolution* (rev. ed. 1966) and *The Road from War* (1970); C. L. Cooper, *The Lost Crusade* (1970); Anthony Austin, *The President's War* (1971); Marvin Kalb and Elie Abel, *Roots of Involvement* (1971); Frances Fitzgerald, *Fire in the Lake* (1972); David Halberstam, *The Best and the Brightest* (1972); Raphael Littauer and Norman Uphoff, ed., *The Air War in Indochina* (1972).

Vieuxtemps, Henri (äNrē' vyötäN'), 1820–81, Belgian violinist and composer. He toured Europe and the United States as a concert violinist and taught in St. Petersburg (1846–52), where he was also court violinist, and at the Brussels Conservatory (1871–73). His six violin concertos are still in the standard repertory.

Vigée-Lebrun, Élisabeth (ālēzäbĕt' vēzhā'-ləbröN'), 1755–1842, French portrait painter; pupil of her father, Louis Vigée. She was influenced by Greuze. Summoned to Versailles in 1779 to paint Marie Antoinette, she embarked upon a long and successful career. She became painter and friend to the queen; two of her best-known portraits are of Marie Antoinette—one holding a rose and the other with her two children (both: Versailles). At the outbreak of the Revolution, Vigée-Lebrun escaped to Italy and in the following years visited Vienna, Berlin, St. Petersburg, Dresden, and London, finding acclaim and prominent sitters everywhere. Her representations show great elegance and facility of execution. Well known are her portraits of Mme de Staël, C. J. Vernet, and two of herself and her daughter (Louvre). She is also highly esteemed for her work in pastel.

Vigeland, Gustav (gōōs'täv vĕ'gəlän), 1869–1943, Norwegian sculptor. Vigeland's sculpture owed much to Rodin in stylistic realism, but it was imbued with an unrestrained romanticism and emotionalism that far surpassed that of Rodin. His great undertaking in Frogner Park, Oslo, occupied Vigeland for 40 years. He planned the park and designed numerous granite and bronze sculptural groups, illustrating the development of man.

vigil (vĭj'əl) [Lat.,=watch], in Christian calendars, eve of a feast, a day of penitential preparation. In ancient times worshipers gathered for vespers before a great feast and then waited outside the church until dawn for the liturgy (Mass). Traces of this practice survive in the East, but the Western Church abolished it early because of disorders in the night watch. The Roman liturgy assigns a proper Mass for the vigil of each important older feast; two of them, Holy Saturday (Easter Eve) and the vigil of Pentecost, have special ceremonies.

vigilantes (vĭjĭlăn'tēz), members of a vigilance committee. Such committees were formed in U.S. frontier communities to enforce law and order before a regularly constituted government could be established or have real authority. They were most common in mining communities, but were also known in cow towns and in farming settlements. The extreme penalty inflicted by the vigilantes was LYNCHING. Among the most famous of the vigilante groups were those formed in San Francisco in 1851 and reorganized in 1856 to bring order to the notorious BARBARY COAST. Measures taken by vigilance committees were at best extralegal. When such committees were formed in a community with a well-constituted government and a police force, they were strictly illegal and usually were merely the expression of mob violence. See Wayne Gard, *Frontier Justice* (1949, repr. 1968); S. A. Coblentz, *Villains and Vigilantes* (rev. ed. 1957); A. C. Valentine, *Vigilante Justice* (1956); J. H. Jones, *The Minutemen* (1968); Arnold Madison, *Vigilantism in America* (1973).

Vigilantius (vĭj"ĭlăn'shəs), fl. 400, Christian priest of Gaul who was violently opposed by St. JEROME. Jerome's letters and a tract, *Liber contra Vigilantium,* declare that Vigilantius denied the efficacy of relics, prayers to the saints, almsgiving, celibacy of the clergy, and monasticism. His works are not extant.

Vigilius (vĭjĭl'ēəs), pope (537–55), a Roman; successor of St. SILVERIUS. Empress THEODORA exiled Silverius and made Vigilius pope in the expectation that he would compromise with the Monophysites. After Silverius' death Vigilius' pontificate was legalized. Vigilius at first resisted coercion, refusing to condemn the Three Chapters in the quarrel over MONOPHYSITISM. Emperor Justinian forced him to come to Constantinople, where he eventually consented to their condemnation by the Second Council of Constantinople, provided that the canons of the Council of Chalcedon would not be thereby discredited. His action was intensely disliked in the West. He remained a virtual prisoner at Constantinople for eight years. He died on his way back to Rome. He was succeeded by Pelagius I.

Vignemale (vēnyəmäl'), mountain, 10,820 ft (3,298 m) high, S France, on the Franco-Spanish border. It is the highest peak in the French Pyrenees.

Vignola, Giacomo da (jä'kōmō dä vēnyō'lä), 1507–73, one of the foremost late Renaissance architects in Italy. His real name was Giacomo Barozzi or Barocchio. Appointed (1550) papal architect to Pope Julius III, he spent his later life in Rome, where most of his important works are found. After Michelangelo's death, Vignola succeeded him as architect in charge of the work on St. Peter's. His finest productions are the Villa Caprarola, near Viterbo, for Cardinal Alessandro Farnese, and the beautiful Villa Giulia for Pope Julius III in Rome. As designer of the interior (1568) of the Church of the Gesù, in Rome, mother church of the Jesuit order, he developed a plan that greatly influenced ecclesiastical architecture. In the Gesù he combined the longitudinal axis of medieval churches with the central domical scheme of the Renaissance. He greatly expanded the nave, reducing the side aisles to a series of chapels. His designs for the facade of the Gesù were rejected in favor of those by Giacomo della Porta. Vignola is universally known for his treatise (1562) on the five orders of architecture. Based upon the work of Vitruvius, it undertook to formulate definite and minute rules for proportioning the classical orders appearing in the buildings of the Romans. This work, which has been in continuous use, has been scrupulously adhered to by many as an almost inviolable authority. Such was not Vignola's real intention, however, and his own designs, even when utilizing the classical orders, showed notable originality and freedom.

Vigny, Alfred Victor, comte de (älfrĕd' vĕktôr' kôNt də vēnyē'), 1797–1863, French poet, novelist, and dramatist. One of the foremost romantics, Vigny expressed a philosophy of stoical pessimism, stressing the lonely struggle of the individual in a hostile universe. Though physically weak, he was sent to military school and became an officer in 1814, resigning in 1827. His best-known poems are found in *Poèmes antiques et modernes* (1826), containing "Éloa" and his famous "Moïse," and in *Destinées* (1864). His prose works include the novels *Cinq-Mars* (1826, tr. *The Spider and the Fly,* 1925), *Stello* (1832), *Servitude et grandeur militaires* (1835, tr. *The Military Necessity,* 1953), and *Chatterton* (1835, tr. 1908), a play. A selection of his own notes comprises *Journal d'un poète* (1867). Unlike other romantics of his period, he did not emphasize personal emotion; instead he presented his ideas through general symbols with dramatic force. His reputation, temporarily dimmed by that of Hugo and Lamartine, was revived by the time of Baudelaire. See studies by J. Doolittle (1967) and A. Whitridge (1933, repr. 1971).

Vigo, Francis (vē'gō, vĭ'gō), 1747–1836, American frontier trader and merchant, supporter of the American Revolution. He was born at Mondovi, Italy, and originally named Giuseppe Maria Francesco Vigo. Having enlisted in the Spanish army, he was sent to Cuba and to New Orleans, where he became interested in the fur trade. After his military service, he went to St. Louis and was secretly an agent of the Spanish governor while he built up a successful business among the Indians. After George Rogers CLARK captured Kaskaskia (1778), Vigo took up the American cause, and his assistance with money, supplies, and information helped make possible Clark's recapture of Vincennes. In 1783, Vigo settled in Vincennes, where he became an American citizen. His claims for his advances to Clark were not honored until long after his death. See biography by Bruno Roselli (1933).

Vigo, Jean (zhäN vēgō'), 1905–34, French movie director, whose original name was Jean Almereyda. His reputation is based on two superb short films: *Zéro de Conduite* (1932) and *L'Atalante* (1934). *Zéro de Conduite* is a surrealistic depiction of Vigo's years in boarding school and shows a poetic expressiveness and a marked feeling for the strange and unexpected. *L'Atalante* is a haunting evocation of life on a Paris river barge and in the city's river-front districts. See biography by P. E. S. Gomes (1971).

Vigo (vē'gō), city (1970 pop. 197,144), Pontevedra prov., NW Spain, in Galicia, on an inlet of the Atlantic Ocean. It is a naval base and one of the most active ports of Spain and a center of tuna and sardine fishing. It also has shipyards, canneries, petroleum and sugar refineries, and various light industries. In 1702 a Franco-Spanish fleet, escorting galleons loaded with American gold and precious stones, was destroyed in the Bay of Vigo by the British and the Dutch; several galleons were sunk, and it is believed that much of the treasure is still at the bottom of the bay. The port was captured by the British in 1719.

Viipuri: see VYBORG, USSR.

Vijayanagar (vē'jəyənŭ'gər) [Sanskrit,=city of victory], ruined city, SE India. It was the capital (14th–16th cent.) of the Hindu Vijayanagar empire, which embraced all India S of the Kistna River and shielded S India from the Muslim kingdoms of the north. At its height during the reign (c.1510–c.1530) of Krishnadeva Raya, the empire had dealings with many Asian and European countries. The city of Vijayanagar, then some 60 mi (95 km) in circumference, flourished as a prosperous trade center and was noted for its artists, writers, and temples. After a crushing defeat of the Hindus at Talikota (1565) Muslim forces utterly demolished the city, and, except for a brief revival, the empire was destroyed.

Vijayawada (vĭjä"yəväd'ə), formerly **Bezwada,** city (1971 pop. 316,448), Andhra Pradesh state, SE India, near the Krishna River delta. It is a transportation and administrative hub and the trade center for the Eastern Ghats. Chromite is mined in the vicinity. Vijayawada is a religious center, with Brahmanic cave temples (7th-century Dravidian) nearby.

Vikings, Scandinavian warriors who raided the coasts of Europe and the British Isles from the 9th cent. to the 11th cent., thereby giving the period the name of the Viking Age. During the Neolithic period the Scandinavians had lived in small autonomous communities as farmers, fishermen, and hunters. At the beginning of the Viking Age they were the best shipbuilders and sailors in the world; they later ventured as far as Greenland and North America (see VINLAND). At the height of the Viking Age, the typical Viking warship, the "long ship," had a high prow, adorned with the figure of an animal, and a high stern (see SHIP). It seated up to 30 oarsmen and had an average crew of 90. Its square sails were perpendicularly striped in many colors, and the entire ship was vividly painted and elaborately carved. On both sides of the ship hung a row of painted round shields. This is the most familiar Viking ship; the many other types varied according to purpose and period. Among the causes that drove the Vikings from their lands were overpopulation, internal dissension, quest for trade, and thirst for adventure. The Vikings were exceedingly cruel and rapacious on their raids, and the dread they inspired facilitated their conquests. Many local kingdoms came into existence in Scandinavia, and from them stemmed the kingdoms of Norway, Denmark, and Sweden. The Vikings' religion was paganism of the Germanic type; their mythological and heroic legends form the content of OLD NORSE LITERATURE. The Viking Age ended with the introduction of Christianity into Scandinavia, with the emergence of the three great Scandinavian kingdoms, and with the rise of European states capable of defending themselves against further invasions. Many Vikings settled where they had raided. The Scandinavian raiders in Russia were known as VARANGIANS; their leader Rurik founded the first Russian state. Elsewhere the Vikings came to be known as Danes, Northmen, NORSEMEN, or NORMANS. See T. D. Kendrick, *A History of the Vikings* (1930, repr. 1968); J. B. Brondsted, *The Vikings* (new tr. 1965); Gwyn Jones, *A History of the Vikings* (1968, repr. 1973); Peter Foote and D. M. Wilson, *The Viking Achievement* (1970); Ole Klindt-Jensen, *The World of the Vikings* (tr. 1971); P. H. Sawyer, *The Age of the Vikings* (2d ed. 1972).

Viljandi (vĭl'yändē), Ger. *Fellin,* town (1967 est. pop. 19,000), NW European USSR, in Estonia. It is a rail terminus and has flax-spinning, fur-processing, canning, textile, and match factories. Founded in 1283, Viljandi was an important medieval trade center and a member of the Hanseatic League. It passed to Poland-Lithuania in 1561 and to Sweden in 1629 and was captured by Russia in 1710. Ruins of the castle of the grand master of the Livonian Knights remain standing.

Villa, Francisco (fränsēs'kō vē'yä), c.1877–1923, Mexican revolutionary, nicknamed **Pancho Villa**. His real name was Doroteo Arango. When he came of age, he declared his freedom from the peonage of his parents and became notorious as a bandit in Chihuahua and Durango. His vigorous fighting in the revolution of 1910–11 was largely responsible for the triumph of Francisco I. MADERO over Porfirio Díaz. When Victoriano HUERTA overthrew Madero (Feb., 1913), Villa joined Venustiano CARRANZA and the Constitutionalists in the fight against Huerta.

The Constitutionalists met with continual success. Villa, at the head of his brilliant cavalry, *Los Dorados*, gained control of N Mexico by the audacity of his attacks; Huerta resigned in July, 1914. Antipathy and suspicion had always existed between Villa and Carranza; now, with their common enemy eliminated, an open break occurred after the Convention of AGUASCALIENTES. A bloody contest ensued, with Álvaro OBREGÓN taking the side of Carranza. In the midst of chaos, Villa, with Emiliano ZAPATA, occupied Mexico City (Dec., 1914) but later evacuated the capital (Jan., 1915). Obregón pursued Villa, and their armies engaged at Celaya (April, 1915). Decisively defeated, Villa was driven north and out of military significance. In the winter of 1915 he campaigned disastrously against Plutarco E. CALLES in Sonora. Villa's waning power was further diminished by President Wilson's recognition of Carranza (Oct., 1915), which angered Villa. In Jan., 1916, a group of Americans were shot by bandits in Chihuahua, and on March 9, 1916, some of Villa's men raided the U.S. town of Columbus, N.Mex., killing some American citizens. It is not certain that Villa participated in these assaults, but he was universally held responsible. Wilson ordered a punitive expedition under General Pershing to capture Villa dead or alive. The expedition pursued Villa through Chihuahua for 11 months (March, 1916–Feb., 1917) but failed in its objective. Carranza violently resented this invasion and it embittered relations between Mexico and the United States. Villa continued his activities in northern Mexico throughout Carranza's regime, but in 1920 he came to an amicable agreement with the government of Adolfo de la HUERTA. Three years later Villa was assassinated at Parral. In a sense he was a rebel against social abuses; at times he worked a rough justice but he was a violent and undirected destructive force. His daring, his impetuosity, and his horsemanship made him the idol of the masses, especially in N Mexico, where he was regarded as a sort of Robin Hood. The Villa myth is perpetuated in numerous ballads and tales. See biography by W. D. Lansford (1965); M. L. Guzmán, *The Eagle and the Serpent* (tr. 1930); Edgcumb Pinchón, *Viva Villa!* (1933, repr. 1970); H. Braddy, *Cock of the Walk* (1955, repr. 1970); C. C. Clendenen, *The United States and Pancho Villa* (1961, repr. 1972).

villa. Although used to designate any country residence, especially in Italy and S France, the term *villa* particularly refers to a type of pleasure residence with extensive grounds favored by the Romans and richly developed in Italy in the Renaissance. The Roman villa of the empire is described in several contemporary literary accounts and particularly by Pliny. Favored locations were at Tivoli near Rome and along the shores of the Bay of Naples. The dwelling quarters, consisting of several low buildings, included recreation facilities and lodgings for the servants. The farmhouse type (*villa rustica*) had barns, orchards, and vineyards, and the type used as a pleasure retreat (*villa urbana*) had formal gardens adorned with fountains and sculptures. The luxurious villa of Emperor Hadrian near Tivoli, of which extensive ruins remain, is said to have covered more than 7 sq mi (18 sq km); many works of art were exhumed there during the Renaissance. In the late 15th cent. the classic villas, rediscovered along with the rest of the Roman past, furnished the Renaissance nobles with patterns for pleasure estates of their own, e.g., the Villa Madama, Rome, designed by Raphael and the many villas built by Palladio in N Italy. In the early quattrocento (15th cent.), villas developed from the medieval type of semifortified residence even before the antique villas were excavated. Fine examples of these early Renaissance types are the old Tuscan villas at Careggi and Cafaggiolo converted by Michelozzo into graceful living quarters for the Medici. Many of these villas had hillside locations, which called forth the fullest ingenuity of the garden designers. Their pictorial compositions blended with the variable elements of nature the formal qualities of the house, the incidental garden architecture, and the fountains. Baroque villas displayed the most fanciful variety of garden frivolities—grotesque sculptures, grottoes lined with rock and shell decorations, fantastic water displays, and ingenious transitions between different levels. Isola Bella on Lake Maggiore is a striking example. Among the finest villas are the FARNESINA; the VILLA D'ESTE at Tivoli; the Villa Farnese at Caprarola by Vignola; the BORGHESE VILLA; and the VILLA DORIA PAMPHILI.

Villach (fĭl'äkh), city (1971 pop. 34,600), Carinthia province, S Austria, on the Drava River. It is an industrial and rail center. Manufactures include forest products, machinery, and chemicals. Nearby is a mineral spa. Originally a Roman settlement, Villach belonged to the bishopric of Bamberg from the early 11th cent. to 1759, when it passed to Austria. The city has Gothic and baroque churches and a museum with prehistoric artifacts.

Villa d'Este (vē'lä dĕ'stā), name of two famous villas in Italy. One lies near Tivoli, c.20 mi (30 km) E of Rome. Built in 1550 by Pirro Ligorio for Cardinal Ippolito II d'Este, it is decorated with paintings and statues and is surrounded by one of the most beautiful Renaissance gardens in Italy. The garden is adorned with many picturesque fountains. The other Villa d'Este, built (16th cent.) on the west shore of Lake Como, 3 mi (4.8 km) N of Como, with an elaborate park, is now one of the celebrated hotels of Europe. See study by D. R. Coffin (1960).

Villa Doria Pamphili (vĕl'lä dô'ryä päm'fēlē), Roman villa, built in the 17th cent. for Camillo Pamphili, nephew of Pope Innocent X, from plans designed by Alessandro Algardi. It was situated against the western walls of Rome near the San Pancrazio gate. The Romans called it Belrespiro.

Villafranca di Verona (vēl''läfräng'kä dē värō'nä), town (1971 pop. 22,366), Venetia, NE Italy. In 1859, Napoleon III and Emperor Francis Joseph of Austria met there after the Austrian defeats at Magenta and SOLFERINO and signed a preliminary peace treaty, which was formalized the same year by the Treaty of Zürich. Sardinia, Napoleon's ally, was not represented. Austria ceded Lombardy, which was added to Sardinia; Venetia remained Austrian. The rulers of Tuscany were to be reinstated, and the Italian states were to form a confederation under the presidency of the pope. Sardinia ignored the last two clauses; to obtain Napoleon's consent for this course, Victor Emmanuel II of Sardinia ceded Nice and Menton to France (1860). The exclusion of Sardinia from the Treaty of Villafranca, an act that nearly deprived Victor Emmanuel of his leading role in the RISORGIMENTO, was deeply resented throughout Italy and greatly harmed Franco-Italian relations.

village, small rural population unit, held together by common economic and political ties. Based on agricultural production, a village is smaller than a town and has been the normal unit of community living in most areas of the world throughout history. The **village community,** comprising the people living in a village, consists of a group, possibly linked by blood, using land, sometimes held communally, for purposes of cultivation and pasturage. The village community, noted in the history of many cultures, is thought to have originated in the area of present-day Iraq and Iran, and its establishment seems to have paralleled the transformation of tribal life from nomadic hunting to stable agriculture. Although innumerable variations in patterns of village life have existed, the typical village was small, consisting of perhaps 5 to 30 families. Homes were situated together for sociability and defense, and land surrounding the living quarters was farmed. This farmland might extend for as much as a mile (1.6 km) and was generally parceled out in varying proportions to each family. There were also woods and meadows used for pasturage, firewood, and hunting, which were often held in common. The village was in ancient times largely self-sufficient, but with the development of the town and city the village became more integrated economically and politically with the larger society. At one time there was a great debate amongst anthropologists as to whether villages arose out of the independent settlement of a kindred group that held property communally or whether they were established by a hierarchial authority such as the Roman Empire, in which land was controlled privately or by the state. Today it is generally agreed that there may have been separate and different origins of the village, each area developing independently according to its specific history. For this reason village life once found in Wales, Mexico (see EJIDO), the Balkans, Russia (see MIR), China, Africa, Sweden, India, and Java may all differ considerably from each other. In England property was at one time held largely in common and each village member was comparatively equal to all others. Sometime between the 5th and 10th cent., however, something resembling a feudal pattern emerged, with a lord ruling each village. After the Norman conquest (1066) this feudal hold was solidified, and village life changed considerably, especially in its property relations (see FEUDALISM; MANORIAL SYSTEM). In the United States the village life found today bears little resemblance to the small villages of past eras. Moreover, most farming in the United States takes place on land privately owned and may thus differ from the aforementioned village agricultural pattern. However, the village is still the predominant form of community organization in many parts of the world, including much of Asia, Africa, and Latin America. See Henry Maine, *Village-Communities in the East and West* (1871); Erwin Nasse, *On the Agricultural Community of the Middle Ages* (tr. 1871); P. H. Ditchfield, *Old Village Life* (1920); G. G. Coulton, *The Medieval Village* (1925, repr. 1960); J. M. Halpern, *The Changing Village Community* (1967); Donald Fraser, *Village Planning in the Primitive World* (1968); George Dalton, ed., *Economic Development and Social Change: The Modernization of Village Communities* (1971).

Villahermosa (vē''yäärmō'sä), city (1970 pop. 71,000), capital of Tabasco state, SE Mexico, on the Grijalva River. The city, which has good communications facilities, is the commercial and distribution center for the surrounding region. Oil is the chief product. Villahermosa was founded in the 16th cent. On the city's outskirts is a large collection of Olmec stone sculptures.

Villa-Lobos, Heitor (ā'tôr vē'lä-lô'bôs), 1887–1959, Brazilian composer, educated in Brazil but self-taught in composition. He developed an interest in Brazilian folk music, which became the strongest influence on his works. A series of compositions which he called *Chôros*, ranging from an instrumental solo to an orchestral work, employ a synthesis of the different modes of Brazilian folk and popular music. Outstanding are *Chorôs* No. 7 (1924), for strings and woodwinds, No. 10 (1925), for orchestra and chorus, and No. 11 (1928; premiere, 1942), for piano and orchestra. He visited Paris (c.1923–26), conducted various orchestras in Europe, and became well known there; but it was not until his music was played at the New York World's Fair (1939–40) that he became known in the United States. In 1932 he was appointed director of musical education in Brazil. He came to the United States (1944–45) to conduct various orchestras in performances of his works. His compositions, including five symphonies, several operas, concertos, chamber music, and songs, number about 2,000. Although these are of uneven quality, his best works, such as *Bachiana's brasileira's* No. 1 (1930), written in homage to Bach, display great originality and vitality.

Villani, Giovanni (jōvän'nē vĕl-lä'nē), c.1275–1348, Italian historian of Florence. As a functionary in the Florentine government, he took part in some of the events he narrates. His history of Florence (in 12 books), written as a universal history from ancient times to 1348, is quite reliable for Florentine events during Villani's own time. It is an early monument of Italian prose and helped fix the Tuscan language as the standard of Italy. Villani died in the plague.

Villanovan culture, the culture of a people of N Italy in the early Iron Age (c.1100–700 B.C.). The term is derived from the town of Villanova, near Bologna, where the first excavations of a Villanovan cemetery were conducted (1853–55). The Villanovans are believed to have come into Italy from Central Europe, the third of a wave of Central European-Danubian invasions. The Villanovans brought with them a reasonably advanced Iron Age culture, closely related to the Hallstatt culture of the E Alps. They lived over a large part of central Italy, including Etruria, Latium, and the region around Bologna. The Villanovans cremated their dead and buried the ashes in urns. The Villanovans were followed by the Etruscans (see ETRUSCAN CIVILIZATION). See David Randall-MacIver, *Villanovans and Early Etruscans* (1924); H. J. Rose, *Primitive Culture in Italy* (1926, repr. 1971); Lawrence Barfield, *Northern Italy before Rome* (1971).

Villanova University (vĭlənō' və), at Villanova, Pa., near Philadelphia; Roman Catholic; primarily for men; est. 1842.

Villanueva, Carlos Raul (kär'lōs räōōl' vē''yänwā'-vä), 1900–, Venezuelan architect, b. England. Villanueva studied at the École des Beaux-Arts in Paris and thereafter sought to introduce modern design into Venezuelan building. Known for his daring compositional effects, Villanueva made striking use of polychromy and exposed concrete. He has collaborated with numerous painters and sculptors. His major works for University City in Caracas include University Hospital and Medical School (1945), the Technical-Industrial School (1945), and the School of Architecture and Urbanism (1937). Among his other buildings is the Institute for Petroleum Engineering at the Univ. of Zulia, Maracaibo (1956). See study by Dorothea Moholy-Nagy (1964).

Villa Park, village (1970 pop. 25,891), Du Page co., NE Ill., a residential suburb of Chicago; inc. 1914.

Villard, Henry (vĭlärd'), 1835–1900, American journalist and financier, b. Germany. His first name was originally Hilgard. He attended universities in Germany, and after he reached (1853) the United States he did newspaper reporting. He won distinction in 1858 by reporting the Lincoln-Douglas debates, and in the Civil War he was a correspondent for New York newspapers. In 1873 he acted as agent for holders of Western railroad securities and soon became active in railroad financing. He organized (1879) the Oregon Railway and Navigation Company and gained a solid foothold in the transportation of the Pacific Northwest area. He then obtained a controlling interest in the Northern Pacific RR and became (1881) its president, but completion of the building of that railroad through the mountains bankrupted him (1883). With new capital Villard once more gained control of the Northern Pacific and in 1889 became chairman of the board of directors. He merged (1890) smaller companies to form the Edison General Electric Company (later the General Electric Company) and was its president until 1893. Villard obtained (1881) control of the New York *Evening Post,* which later (1897) came under the management of his son, Oswald Garrison Villard. He generously contributed to the Univ. of Oregon. See his autobiography (1904, repr. 1969); study by J. B. Hedges (1930; repr. 1967).

Villard, Oswald Garrison, 1872–1949, American editor and author, b. Wiesbaden, Germany, grad. Harvard (B.A., 1893; M.A., 1896). The son of Henry Villard and the grandson, on his mother's side, of William Lloyd Garrison, he was a lifelong liberal and a pacifist. In 1897 he became an editorial writer on the New York *Evening Post* and after inheriting the paper from his father was its editor until he sold it in 1918. He retained its weekly edition, the *Nation,* and as its editor made it a leading liberal journal; he sold it in 1932, remaining as publisher and contributor until 1935, but finally severed all connections when the *Nation* became nonpacifist in 1940. His writings include *John Brown: A Biography Fifty Years After* (1910), *Newspapers and Newspaper Men* (1923), and an autobiography, *The Fighting Years* (1939).

Villari, Pasquale (päskwä'lä vĕl'lärē), 1826–1917, Italian historian and statesman. He took part in the Revolution of 1848, served in the legislative chamber (1867–82), and was minister of education (1889–92). His first work on Savonarola (1859, tr. *The History of Girolamo Savonarola and His Times,* 1863) gained him an appointment (1859) as teacher of modern history at Pisa. He also taught at Florence. His vivid and keenly observant writings include *The Life and Times of Niccolò Machiavelli* (3 vol., 1877–82; tr. of 4th ed.1929); biographies of Dante, Cavour, and Garibaldi; and studies of Galileo and the experimental method and of Sicilian socialism. See his studies, ed. by Linda Villari (1907, repr. 1968).

Villarrica (vē"yärē'kä), city (1972 pop. 17,448), capital of Guairá dept., SE Paraguay. It is a commercial center and shipping point in a region that produces cattle, tobacco, mate, cotton, sugarcane, lumber, wine, and citrus fruits. A large portion of the population is of German descent. Villarrica's cathedral is a pilgrimage center.

Villars, Claude Louis Hector, duc de (klōd lwē ĕktôr' dük də vēlär'), 1653–1734, marshal of France, the last of the great generals of Louis XIV. He fought in the Dutch War (1672–78) and in 1687 went to Bavaria, where he helped strengthen the new French alliance with the elector of Bavaria; he fought with the elector against the Turks at Mohács. After serving (1698–1701) as ambassador at Vienna he was given a command in the War of the Spanish Succession and made his reputation by his victories at Friedlingen (1702) in Baden and Höchstädt (1703) in Bavaria. In 1704 he quelled the revolt of the CAMISARDS. Defeated (1709) by the duke of Marlborough and Eugene of Savoy at Malplaquet, he successfully defended the French frontier during the succeeding years; in 1712 he defeated Eugene at Denain and in 1713–14 negotiated the Treaty of Rastatt. He was a member of the regency council (1715–23) and of the succeeding administrations and was in supreme command in the War of the Polish Succession at the time of his death. Villars left important memoirs. See C. C. Sturgill, *Marshall Villars and the War of the Spanish Succession* (1965).

Villa Umberto I: see BORGHESE VILLA.

Villaurrutia, Xavier (hävē'är vē"yōōrōō'tyä), 1903–50, Mexican poet and playwright. Villaurrutia was deeply influenced by Ramón LÓPEZ VELARDE. He worked on the Mexican literary review *Contemporáneos* (1928–31) and in 1928 founded the first experimental theater in Mexico. His poetic writing includes *Reflejos* (1926) and *Nocturnos* (1933). Villaurrutia's intense preoccupation with death permeates the poems in *Nostalgia de la muerte* (1938) and *Decima muerte* [tenth death] (1941); it is also the subject of his play *Invitacíon a la muerte* (1941). His most notable theatrical works are the short dramatic pieces, *Autos profanos,* included in *Poesiá y teatro completos* (1953). Villaurrutia greatly influenced the work of younger Mexican poets, notably Alí Chumacero.

Villavicencio (vēlyävēsān'syō), city (1968 est. pop. 80,700), capital of Meta dept., central Colombia, on the Meta River. Located in the eastern foothills of the Andes, it is the chief urban center of the llanos and forests of E Colombia. Cattle, coffee, bananas, rice, and rubber are the main products of the region. The surrounding area was the scene of large-scale banditry in the civil strife that rocked the country from 1948 to 1958.

Villaviciosa (vē"lyävēthēō'sä), town (1970 pop. 17,213), Oviedo prov., NW Spain, in Asturias, on the Bay of Biscay. It is a major fishing port with cider distilleries. Emperor Charles V disembarked in the town (1517) when he first came to Spain. Nearby is the 9th-century Church of San Salvador de Valdedíos.

Villeda Morales, Ramón (rämōn' vēyā'thä mōrä'lās), 1909–71, president of Honduras (1957–63). A physician, he was prominent in the Liberal party and served as Honduran ambassador to the United States and to the Organization of American States. Selected president of Honduras by a constituent assembly, he launched a Liberal, pro-labor regime that aroused considerable opposition; he introduced numerous welfare benefits, a social security law, and a new labor code. In 1963, 10 days before scheduled presidential elections in which the Liberal candidate appeared likely to win, Villeda was overthrown in an army coup led by Col. Osvaldo López. Villeda later served as head of the Honduran delegation to the United Nations. He died in New York City.

Villefranche-sur-Saône (vēlfräNsh'-sür-sōn), town (1968 pop. 26,846), Rhône dept., E central France, on the Morgon River. Its industries include weaving, the dyeing of cotton fabric, and the manufacture of clothing and agricultural tools. The town is also a river port and the trade center for Beaujolais wine, which is made in the region. Villefranche-sur-Saône was founded in 1212 and became capital of Beaujolais in the 14th cent. Points of interest include the Church of Notre-Dame-de-Marais (12th–16th cent.), and several Renaissance houses.

Villehardouin (vēlärdwăN'), French noble family that ruled the PELOPONNESUS from 1210 to 1278. **Geoffroi I de Villehardouin,** d. 1218, nephew of the historian and marshal of Champagne and Rumania, set out on the conquest of Morea (as the Peloponnesus was then called) in 1205, with his friend Guillaume de Champlitte. With some 100 knights the two men rapidly subdued the Greeks, who were beset by internal quarrels, and, in 1205, Champlitte proclaimed himself prince of all Achaia. On the return of Champlitte to France, Villehardouin succeeded him (1210) as prince. Achaia, organized on the feudal model of the Latin Kingdom of Jerusalem, comprised virtually the whole Peloponnesus save several ports held by the Venetians, and it was a fief held under the Latin Empire. Its capital was Mistra, near Sparta. The principality prospered under the strong rule of Geoffroi I and of his son **Geoffroi II de Villehardouin,** d. 1246, who like his father was an excellent administrator. Geoffroi II's brother and successor, **Guillaume de Villehardouin,** d. 1278, was a warlike prince. Captured (1259) at the battle of Pelagonia by Emperor Michael VIII of Nicaea, who in 1261 was to recover Constantinople and to restore the Byzantine Empire, he refused to accept freedom in exchange for the cession of Achaia. In 1262 the so-called Ladies' Parliament, held by the wives and widows of the captive or slain nobles of Morea, met some of Michael's demands and ceded the Greeks a foothold in SE Morea, including Mistra but not Sparta, which became the new Latin capital. Released, Guillaume gained the alliance of King Charles I of Naples and Sicily, to whom he gave the hand of his elder daughter, Isabelle, and who received (1267) the nominal suzerainty over Achaia from the exiled Latin emperor, Baldwin II. Guillaume's death in 1278 ended the male line of Villehardouin.

Villehardouin, Geoffroi de, c.1160–c.1212, French historian and Crusader. As marshal of Champagne, he was a leader of the Fourth Crusade (see CRUSADES), which resulted in the conquest (1204) of Constantinople and the creation of the Latin Empire of Constantinople. Villehardouin, in his *De la conquête de Constantinople* (first pub. 1585; available in several English editions), described the Crusade and the subsequent struggles of the Latin nobles against their Greek and Bulgarian neighbors, from 1198 to 1207, with vivid detail and disarming frankness. Reliable as a historical source, Villehardouin's account stands as an early masterpiece of French prose. For his services in the Crusade he received the title of marshal of Rumania (the name then given to Thrace) and a rich fief in Thrace. His nephew, Geoffroi I de Villehardouin, founded the Villehardouin dynasty in the Peloponnesus.

villein (vĭl'ən) [O.Fr.,=village dweller], peasant under the MANORIAL SYSTEM of medieval Western Europe. The term applies especially to SERFS in England, where by the 13th cent. the entire unfree peasant population came to be called villein. The localism of medieval economy has made a general definition of villein status exceedingly difficult. The villein was a person who was attached to the manor and who performed the servile work of the lord and in some respects was considered the property of the lord. Various distinctions of **villeinage,** or serfdom, were sometimes made. In privileged villeinage the services to be rendered to the lord were certain and determined; in pure villeinage the services were unspecified, and the villein was, in effect, subject to the whim of the lord. The villein was theoretically distinguished from the freeholder by the services and duties he owed to the lord; these included week-work (a specified number of days' work on the lord's demesne each week throughout the year) and boon days (work required at busy periods during the seasonal year, as at plowing or harvesting time), payment on the marriage of the villein's daughter, payment of tallage on demand, and the like. In practice, however, distinctions blurred, and all land tenure on the manor tended to approach a common level. The villein in England was protected by law against all except his lord, and some guarantee against the lord's power was gradually extended by the royal courts. In the 14th cent. English villeinage began to disappear. A contributing factor in its decline was the increasing substitution of money payments for manual services; rents replaced labor dues. The Black Death of 1349 (see PLAGUE), by greatly reducing the population and thus making labor scarce, made the demands of villeins more difficult to refuse and thus hastened the decline. The growth of towns also influenced the breakdown of the older class distinctions and the building up of new. For bibliography, see MANORIAL SYSTEM; FEUDALISM.

Ville Lasalle: see LASALLE, Que., Canada.

Villèle, Jean Baptiste Séraphin Joseph, comte de (zhäN bätēst' säräfăN' zhôzĕf' kôNt də vēlĕl'), 1773–1854, French statesman and premier (1822–28). Elected (1815) a deputy after the Bourbon restoration, he became leader of the extreme royalists in the chamber of deputies. He entered the ministry of the duc de Richelieu in 1820, and in 1822 King Louis XVIII named him president of the council, or premier. He stabilized France's finances to such a degree that they remained sound until the 20th cent. His reactionary government suppressed press freedom; intervened (1823) in Spain against Spanish revolutionaries; prolonged (1824) the term of the chamber of deputies from four to seven years; gave the Roman Catholic Church increasing control of education; and indemnified (1825) the émigrés for lands confiscated during the French Revolution. Assailed in 1827 by both the liberals and the extreme ultraroyalists, who found his methods too slow, he dissolved the chamber. He was defeated in the new elections and resigned.

Villella, Edward, 1936–, American ballet dancer, b. Long Island, N.Y. Villella studied at George Balanchine's School of American Ballet, joining the New York City Ballet in 1957. He soon became a principal dancer with a large repertoire of roles, most notably *The Prodigal Son.* Villella's dancing is remarkable for its tremendous vigor and dynamic style.

Villemain, Abel François (äbĕl' fräNswä' vēlmăN'), 1790–1870, French scholar and critic. He was a professor at the Sorbonne from 1816, held several government posts after 1830, and was permanent secretary of the French Academy from 1832. As minister of public instruction (1839–44) he was largely responsible for a reorganization of libraries in France and for promoting the passage of a law assuring academic freedom. His reputation as a literary critic was established by his *Cours de littérature française* (1830), several times reedited and enlarged, which included his notable *Tableau de la littérature au* *moyen âge* and *Tableau de la littérature française au XVIIIe siècle.*

Villeneuve, Pierre de (pyĕr də vĕlnöv'), 1763–1806, French admiral. He commanded the rear guard of the fleet in the disastrous battle of ABU QIR (1798). His defeat at the battle of TRAFALGAR (1805) was partly due to the unpreparedness of his fleet and to his initial refusal to leave Cádiz when ordered to by Napoleon I. Taken prisoner by the English, he was released and committed suicide after returning to France.

Villeroi, François de Neufville, duc de (fräNswä' də növēl' dük də vĕlrwä'), 1644–1730, marshal of France and favorite of King Louis XIV. In the War of the Grand Alliance, he succeeded (1695) Marshal Luxembourg as commander in Flanders, where he was unsuccessful against King William III of England. In the War of the Spanish Succession, he replaced Nicolas Catinat in Italy, was defeated by the Austrian commander Prince Eugene of Savoy at Chiari (1701), and was taken prisoner at Cremona (1702). In 1706 he was defeated by the duke of Marlborough at Ramillies. Villeroi held several high posts between 1717 and 1722, when he fell into disgrace for intriguing against the regent. He died, in virtual exile, as governor of Lyons.

Ville-sous-La-Ferté (vēl-so͞o-lä-fĕrtā'), village (1968 pop. 1,854), NE France. It is famous for its nearby abbey (now a prison) of Clairvaux, founded (1115) by St. Bernard of Clairvaux. The abbey was suppressed in the French Revolution.

Villeurbanne (vēlürbän'), city (1968 pop. 122,898), Rhône dept., E central France, a suburb E of LYONS. It is a major industrial center; metals, machines, electrical equipment, jewelry, and printed material are produced there.

villi: see DIGESTIVE SYSTEM.

Villiers, Barbara: see CLEVELAND, BARBARA VILLIERS, DUCHESS OF.

Villiers, George: see BUCKINGHAM, GEORGE VILLIERS, 1ST DUKE OF; BUCKINGHAM, GEORGE VILLIERS, 2D DUKE OF.

Villiers, George William Frederick: see CLARENDON, GEORGE WILLIAM FREDERICK VILLIERS, 4TH EARL OF.

Villiers de l'Isle-Adam, Philippe Auguste Mathias, comte de (fēlēp' ōgüst' mätyäs' kôNt də vēyä' də lē'l-ädäN'), 1838–89, French novelist. His works, in the romantic style, are often fantastic in plot and filled with mystery and horror. Important among them are the drama *Axel* (revision, 1890), the novel *L'Ève future* (1886), and the short-story collection, *Contes cruels* (1883, tr. *Sardonic Tales,* 1927).

Villmanstrand: see LAPPEENRANTA, Finland.

Villon, François (fräNswä' vēyôN'), 1431–1463?, French poet, b. Paris, whose original name was François de Montcorbier or François Des Loges. One of the earliest great poets of France, Villon was largely rediscovered in the 19th cent. He was brought up by the chaplain of Saint-Benoît-le-Bétourné, Guillaume de Villon, whose name he adopted. Knowledge of the facts of Villon's life is drawn from his poems and from the police records concerning him; it is believed that he died shortly after receiving a sentence of 10 years' exile from Paris, commuted from the death sentence. Confessedly a vagabond and rogue from his student days at the Sorbonne, Villon killed a man in 1455. During his subsequent banishment from Paris he fell in with the *coquillards,* a band of thieves that ravaged France at the close of the Hundred Years War, and for them he composed his ballads in thieves' jargon. The preservation of Villon's works was principally due to Clément Marot, who collected and edited them (1533). Villon used the medieval forms of versification, but his intensely personal message puts him in the rank of the moderns. Besides his ballads in jargon, Villon's work consists of his *Lais* (also known as the *Little Testament*), written in 1456; the *Testament* or *Grand Testament* (1461); and a number of poems including the "Débat du cœur et du corps de Villon" [debate between Villon's heart and body] and the "Épitaphe Villon," better known as the "Ballade des pendus" [ballad of the hanged], written during Villon's expectation of the same fate. The *Lais* (a pun on the words *lais,* or lays, and *legs,* or legacy) is a series of burlesque bequests to his friends and enemies. The *Testament* follows the same scheme (not uncommon in medieval literature), but is far superior in depth of emotion and in poetic value. The work is filled with irony, repentance, constant preoccupation with death, ribald humor, rebellion, and pity. The *Testament* is interspersed with ballads and rondeaux, including the "Ballade de la grosse Margot," his bequest to a prostitute, and "Ballade des dames du temps jadis" with the famous refrain "But where are the snows of yester-year?" There have been many English translations of the poems, including those by Rossetti and Swinburne, and more recently (1973) by Peter Dale. The standard French edition of the works was made by Auguste Longnon (1892, several revisions). See biography by D. B. Wyndham Lewis (1928); study by J. H. Fox (1963).

Villon, Jacques, 1875–1963, French painter, brother of Marcel DUCHAMP and Raymond DUCHAMP-VILLON. Villon became an exponent of CUBISM in 1911 and is best known for his refinement of the cubist style. His works are noted for their free use of color and carefully structured composition (e.g., *Portrait of the Artist's Father,* 1924; Guggenheim Mus.).

Vilna: see VILNIUS, USSR.

Vilnius (vĭl'nēo͞os), Rus. *Vilna,* Pol. *Wilno,* city (1970 pop. 372,000), capital of the Lithuanian Soviet Socialist Republic, W European USSR, on the Neris River. It is a rail and highway junction, a commercial and industrial city, and a center of education and the arts. Industries include machine building, metallurgy, food and tobacco processing, and the manufacture of electrical equipment, machine tools, and construction materials. Vilnius was officially founded in 1323 when the Lithuanian prince Gediminas made it his capital and built his castle there. The city also became (1415) the metropolis of the Lithuanian Orthodox Eastern Church. Vilnius gained importance both as a strategic point and as a trade and transportation center. The city declined after the merger of Lithuania and Poland, and its Lithuanian-Belorussian culture was replaced by Polish institutions. In the third partition of Poland (1795), Vilnius passed to Russia, where it became a provincial capital (1801–1815). After World War I the city was disputed between Poland and the newly independent Lithuania, which claimed it as its capital. The Paris Peace Conference assigned the city to the Lithuanians, to whom the Russians gave it (1920) after capturing it from the Poles. In the same year, however, Poland retook Vilnius, which became part of Poland (1922) after a plebiscite of doubtful validity. A theoretical state of war between Poland and Lithuania continued until 1927, and diplomatic relations were resumed only in 1938, when Lithuania abandoned its claim to Vilnius. In 1939, Soviet troops occupied the city, and it was transferred to Lithuania, which in 1940 was incorporated into the USSR. Vilnius was occupied by the Germans in World War II and was heavily damaged. The city's university, founded by Stephen Báthory as a Jesuit academy in 1579, is one of Europe's oldest. Vilnius is also the seat of the Lithuanian Academy of Sciences (founded 1941). The city was a leading East European center of Jewish culture from the 16th cent. until the virtual extermination of its large Jewish population by the Germans in World War II. The city's historic nucleus contains numerous old churches and synagogues. The old town hall is now a museum. Also of interest is the Ausros Vartai (Pol. *Ostra Brama*), or Pointed Gate, the sole remnant of the city walls built (1552) by Sigismund I Jagiello. Above the gate is a shrine containing an image of the Virgin, long an object of pilgrimage. Ruins of the 14th-century castle built by Gediminas still remain.

Vilyui (vĭlyo͞o'ē), river, c.1,520 mi (2,450 km) long, rising in the central Siberian uplands, E Siberian USSR, in the Yakut Autonomous Republic, and flowing east through an agricultural area into the Lena River. It is navigable for c.750 mi (1,210 km) upstream and abounds in fish. In the Vilyui basin there are deposits of diamonds, iron ore, coal, and gold. The Vilyui Range, which rises to 3,300 ft (1,006 m) separates the Lena and Olenek river basins.

Vimeiro (vēmā'rō), village (1970 pop. 945), Lisboa dist., W central Portugal, in Estremadura. It was the scene of a battle (1808) of the Peninsular War, in which Wellington defeated Junot, thus ending the first French invasion of Portugal.

Viminal, hill: see *Rome before Augustus* under ROME.

Viña del Mar (vē'nyä dĕl mär) [Span., = vineyard by the sea], city (1970 pop. 184,332), central Chile. Practically a suburb of VALPARAISO, Viña del Mar is one of the most famous and popular resort cities in South America. There are luxurious hotels, villas, clubs, and gardens and fine beaches. The city has several industries—textile mills, an oil refinery, and a large sugar refinery. It is also a market for the agricultural products of the region. A naval base is there. The city was founded in 1874.

Vincennes, Jean Baptiste Bissot, sieur de (vĭnsĕnz'; zhäN bätēst' bēsō' syör də văNsĕn'), 1668–1719, Canadian explorer and leader of the Miami Indians, b. Quebec. He was sent to the Miami country by Frontenac (c.1696); he established a fort and trading post there and quickly won the esteem and confidence of the Indians. In 1712 he helped to defeat the hostile Fox Indians. He died in a Miami village near the site of Fort Wayne. His son, **François Marie Bissot, sieur de Vincennes** (fräNswä' märē'), 1700–1736, b. Montreal, was called François Margane after his godfather and uncle. He served as a cadet under his father from 1718 until his father's death, and, like him, won the high respect of the Miami. After 1730 he established a fort on the Wabash (where the French and later the Spanish had previously had a post), and the settlement that developed there was named after him.

Vincennes, town (1968 pop. 49,297), Val-de-Marne dept., N central France, an industrial and residential suburb E of Paris. Radio, electrical, and photographic equipment; typewriters; bicycle accessories; machinery; and machine tools are produced. A royal residence since the 12th cent., Vincennes was a favorite of Louis IX, who liked to administer justice sitting under an oak tree in the forest. The huge castle dates in part from the 14th cent. Its interior fortress, the keep, in which many famous prisoners were held, has been converted into a museum. Among the many kings of France who lived at Vincennes were Charles V, Charles IX, and Francis I; Henry V of England and Cardinal Mazarin died in the castle. Vincennes also has one of the most famous zoos in Europe.

Vincennes (vĭnsĕnz'), city (1970 pop. 19,867), seat of Knox co., SW Ind., on the Wabash River; inc. 1814. The city is the center of an extensive farm area. Its many manufactures include storage batteries; spring assemblies; fabricated steel, glass, wood, paper, and plastic products; fertilizer; seed; farm implements; and food products. The oldest town in Indiana, Vincennes is proud of its long past. Although 1702 is a traditional date for its founding, French fur traders had almost certainly come long before that time. By 1732 it had been fortified by the younger sieur de Vincennes and was an important French settlement. Occupied by the British in 1763, the town, in the American Revolution, was a main object of the expedition of George Rogers Clark. Aided by Francis Vigo, François Bosseron, and Father Gibault, Clark triumphantly took the British Fort Sackville from its commander, Henry Hamilton, in Feb., 1779. Vincennes was capital (1800–13) of Indiana Territory until succeeded by Corydon. A treaty with the Indians was signed there in 1805. The old French settlement changed its character, as German immigrants, Yankees, and others made it into an American river port. Many historic marks and old buildings recall the past. A magnificent memorial (dedicated 1936) to George Rogers Clark was included (1966) in George Rogers Clark Historical Park. "Grouseland," the home of William H. Harrison (built 1803–4), is a national historic landmark. Vincennes Univ., actually a junior college, dates from 1801. See A. W. Derleth, *Vincennes* (1968).

Vincent, George Edgar, 1864–1941, American educator, organizer, and sociologist, b. Rockford, Ill., grad. Yale, 1885, Ph.D. Univ. of Chicago, 1896; son of Bishop John Heyl Vincent. He was associated with his father in the Chautauqua movement and was president (1907–15) of the Chautauqua Institution. Always a popular lecturer, he became noted for his wit and clear thinking. Vincent taught sociology at the Univ. of Chicago from 1894 to 1911 and was dean of the faculty of arts, literature, and science from 1907. In 1911 he became president of the Univ. of Minnesota. From 1917 until his retirement in 1929 he headed the Rockefeller Foundation, which under him expanded its activities, especially in medical aid and research. He wrote *An Introduction to the Study of Society* (with A. W. Small, 1894) and *Social Mind and Education* (1897).

Vincent, John Heyl, 1832–1920, American Methodist bishop, b. Tuscaloosa, Ala. In 1857 he was assigned to an Illinois conference, where he held various pastorates. His work in improving teaching methods in Sunday schools had widespread results. Vincent founded (1866) the periodical the *Sunday School Teacher;* from 1868 to 1888 he was editor of Methodist Sunday school publications and corresponding secretary of the Sunday School Union. With Lewis Miller he organized (1874) at Chautauqua, N.Y., a Sunday school teachers' institute, which included secular as well as religious instruction, out of which grew the CHAUTAUQUA MOVEMENT. He was active in planning and directing (1878–88) Chautauqua programs. In 1888 Vincent was made bishop. From 1900 until his retirement in 1904 he was head of the work of his denomination in Europe, making his residence in Zurich. His books include *The Chautauqua Movement* (1886) and *The Modern Sunday School* (1900). George E. Vincent was his son.

Vincent de Paul, Saint, 1580?–1660, French priest renowned for charitable work, b. Gascony. He was ordained in 1600. There are conflicting stories about his capture by pirates and enslavement in Tunis and his subsequent escape. In Rome he came to the attention of Pope Paul V, who sent him on a mission to the French court of Henry IV, where Vincent remained as chaplain to the queen. His activism, and the holiness of his life brought about the revival of French Catholicism. He inspired many of the court to an interest in the poor of Paris and was the founder of organized charity in France. In 1625 he founded an order of secular priests to work in rural areas; it became the Congregation of the Mission, called Lazarists or Vincentians. With these priests, St. Vincent conducted retreats, founded seminaries, and achieved widespread reform among the French clergy. For city work he founded the Sisters of Charity. St. Vincent's influence, through his spirit and through his institutions, is incalculable. He was canonized in 1737. Feast: July 19. See Joseph Leonard, ed., *Letters of St. Vincent de Paul* (1938); biographies by Henri Daniel-Rops (1961) and Mary Purcell (1963); Pierre Coste, *The Life and Works of Saint Vincent de Paul* (3 vol., tr. 1952).

Vincent Ferrer, Saint (fĕr'ər), 1350?–1419, Spanish Dominican preacher, b. Valencia. He studied at Barcelona, taught at Lérida, and later studied at Toulouse. After 1379 he became a friend and protégé of Pedro de Luna, later antipope Benedict XIII. St. Vincent became widely known as a preacher even in his youth. He considered himself called to summon sinners to repent and prepare for the Judgment. He was tremendously successful, and many thousands were converted by him. He was especially interested in converting the Spanish Jews and Muslims. St. Vincent traveled over Europe, visiting France, N Italy, and Flanders. He preached his last two years in Brittany and died in Vannes. St. Vincent's life was severely ascetic, and his followers were inspired to imitate his austerities. Vincent's surname is also spelled Ferrier. Feast: April 5. See Henri Ghéon, *Saint Vincent Ferrer* (tr. 1939).

Vincent of Beauvais (bōvā'), c.1190–c.1264, French Dominican friar. He was the author of three of the four parts of the *Speculum majus,* of great value as a summary of the knowledge of his time. The part entitled "Morals" is of unknown authorship, but is not by him. The three parts written by him are entitled "Nature," "Instruction," and "History." In "Nature," the order followed is that of the six days of creation described in Genesis. "Instruction" ranges from the liberal arts to the mechanical arts. The "History" epitomizes the story of man since Adam as it was understood by 13th-century scholars. See Asztrik Gabriel, *The Educational Ideas of Vincent of Beauvais* (2d ed. 1962).

Vincent's infection: see TRENCH MOUTH.

Vinci, Leonardo da: see LEONARDO DA VINCI.

Vindhya Range (vĭn'dyə), chain of hills, c.600 mi (970 km) long, rising to c.3,000 ft (910 m), Madhya Pradesh state, central India. The Vindhya Range has been the historic dividing line between N and S India, separating the Sanskrit-speaking ARYAN invaders from the DRAVIDIAN peoples of the Deccan. The massive sandstone of the range, long an important building material, was used for the famous group of Buddhist stupas at Sanchi (built 3d cent. B.C.–11th cent. A.D.), the 11th-century Jain and Brahman temples at Khajraho, and the 15th-century palaces of GWALIOR.

vine, CLIMBING PLANT or trailing plant. The GRAPE is often called "the vine."

vinegar, sour liquid consisting mainly of acetic acid and water, produced by the action of bacteria on dilute solutions of ethyl alcohol derived from previous yeast FERMENTATION. The coloring and flavoring are characteristic of the alcoholic liquor (as cider, beer, wine, fermented fruit juices, solutions of barley malt, hydrolyzed cereals, starches, or sugars) from which the vinegar is made. Vinegar is used as a salad dressing, a preservative, a household remedy to allay irritations, a mild disinfectant, and, in cooking, as a fiber softener. Vinegar has been known from antiquity as a natural by-product of wine; the name is derived from the French *vin aigre* [sour wine]. The manufacture as a separate industry began in France in the 17th cent. The wasteful slow, or natural, process, a spontaneous fermentation in casks half full of beechwood shavings exposed to the atmosphere by bung holes, was superseded in the early 19th cent. by the quick, or generator, method. The generator used in present-day commercial manufacture is usually a tall, truncated cone or vertical wood tank with a false bottom perforated to admit air that is generally forced through by a blower. The alcoholic solution is allowed to drip through a filling of hard-wood shavings or other material presenting a large surface area. Vinegar made by this method must be aged to remove a natural harshness. It is generally clarified, then pasteurized. Some vinegars are subjected to distillation which removes most of the flavorings other than acetic acid. In another process, the solution is aerated directly by a spinning rotor. The wood shavings are not needed in this case, and the process runs continuously. Acetic fermentation may be impeded by an excessive growth of mother of vinegar, a slimy mass of bacteria, or of the parasitic vinegar eel, a minute, threadlike worm.

vinegar eel, small (2 mm) nematode often found living in unpasteurized vinegar. The vinegar eel is a single species, *Turbatrix aceti;* it subsists on the "mother," a fungus mat that develops in natural vinegars. Enormous numbers of nematodes may develop in vinegar, and classroom population studies are sometimes carried out with *Turbatrix.* Eggs are stored in the female uterus before being deposited. The larvae undergo several molts before reaching maturity. Vinegar eels are classified in the phylum ASCHELMINTHES, class Nematoda.

Vineland, city (1970 pop. 47,399), Cumberland co., S N.J., in a poultry and fruit area; settled 1861, inc. 1952 when combined with Landis township. It has cooperative markets, large glassworks (with offices designed by William Lescaze), and food-processing and clothing industries. A junior college is there.

Vinet, Alexandre Rodolphe (älĕksäN'drə rôdôlf' vēnā'), 1797–1847, Swiss Protestant theologian and historian of literature. In 1817 he became professor of French language and literature at Basel, and in 1819 he was ordained into the Reformed ministry. His reputation as an intellectual leader among French Protestants was soon established, and at the same time he won distinction by the fine quality of his critical literary studies. He was made (1837) professor of theology at the Academy of Lausanne. Liberty of conscience and separation of church and state were advocated in his *Mémoire en faveur de la liberté des cultes* (1826) and other works. In 1845, Protestant liberties were curbed in the canton of Vaud; Vinet soon resigned his professorship and joined the secession in the Free Church of Vaud. His works include *Chrestomathie française* (3 vol., 1829–30) and a number of writings published posthumously from notes of his courses—*Études sur Blaise Pascal* (1848), *Études sur la littérature française au XIXème siècle* (3 vol., 1849–51), *Histoire de la littérature française au dix-huitième siècle* (1853, tr. 1854, repr. 1970), *Moralistes de XVIème et XVIIème siècles* (1859), and *Poètes du siècle de Louis XIV* (1861). See study by P.T. Fuhrmann (1964).

vineyard, area of ground upon which the cultivation of the GRAPE—known as viticulture—takes place. Biblical references to vineyards and allusions made to them by Vergil and Homer indicate their existence in remote antiquity. As many as 40 varieties of *Vitis vinifera* are known. All but the few that grow wild and are generally not used require great care to make them produce good fruit. The primary purpose of the vineyard in the past has been the production of WINE, and on the whole it still is. Yet in thousands of vineyards—largely those of the New World—the grapevines are cultivated to provide fresh grapes for eating, grape juice for drinking, and dried grapes, or raisins. Vine culture is an exacting endeavor, with success dependent upon such factors as sunny exposure, congenial soil, suitable vines, moisture, wind, and disease-control methods. The best wines are made in warm and dry vintage years. A vineyard is begun by transplanting vines from an active vineyard into new soil; these are in turn propagated by cuttings of the past season's growth of wood with two or three buds. Traditionally introduced to Europe by the Phocaeans c.600 B.C., the cultivation of the vine was widespread in the Mediterranean region in ancient times. Emperor Domitian decreed (A.D. 81) restrictions in use of Italy's land for vineyards, for fear of grain scarcity. Later the Romans carried the vine to England, where its cultivation was attempted sporadically in the south and southwest until the 19th cent., with scant success. On the Continent the results were the opposite. Large areas of France, Italy, the Rhineland, Spain, and Portugal proved to be more hospitable and the elements most accommodating. Greece, North Africa, the Canary Islands, and the Azores were some of the other regions in which *V. vinifera* was well received. Attempts to transplant it to the New World began early in the 17th cent. They continued, but even Tuscan vinegrowers in Virginia (working for Thomas Jefferson) and German immigrants from the Rhineland to Pennsylvania failed. The reason for the failure was not known until the late 19th cent., when it was discovered that the cause was the insect PHYLLOXERA. Grape growing was first successful in the United States when John Adlum introduced the Catawba grape in 1830 and E. W. Bull introduced the Concord grape in 1849. These varieties of native species were resistant to phylloxera. Calamitously, however, the pest was taken to Europe on an American vine. Havoc there was prompt and widespread. Many of the vineyards were completely ruined, and others were seriously damaged. France, seeing the possible extinction of the huge wine industry, evolved a technique of using American vines as stock upon which to graft *V. vinifera;* the vineyards were thus saved. The European vine now grows in the majority of U.S. vineyards, but that majority is entirely on the Pacific coast. Two thirds of the grape vines grown in the United States are in California. New York is second among the states. The vineyards of the San Francisco Bay area provide the bulk of grapes needed for the growing American wine industry. The scourge of grapevines, the phylloxera, is not native on the Pacific coast, nor is its equal as a vine destroyer, MILDEW, at home there, and stringent state regulations have prevented their introduction. A few of the other pests and afflictions that beset vineyards in the E United States are the grape-berry moth, which destroys fruit by causing it to color prematurely; the grapevine beetle, which eats the new buds in spring; climbing cutworms, which hide in the ground during the day and feed on the buds at night; and black rot, which shrivels the fruit. The *V. vinifera* of the Pacific slope is harassed by an even greater variety of pests and diseases, including black measles, little-leaf, nematodes, red spiders, rabbits, and gophers. Prophylaxis of the healthy vines and treatment of the afflicted ones are but one aspect of the intensive and continuous efforts that go into viticulture. From the early stages of tending a vineyard, when appropriate vines must be selected and congenial soil chosen for them, through the operations of cutting, layering, and grafting, planting, and fertilizing, up to the gathering of the crop, the skill and the knowledge of the vineyardist must match his industry. The grapes comprising the blue, black, white, or red cluster, if pale, bitter, or shriveled, will quickly disclose his failings, or if rotund, sweet, and juicy, will testify to his ability.

vingt-et-un (văN-tā-ōN'): see BLACKJACK.

Vinh (vĭn), city, SE North Vietnam, near the Song Ca River and the Gulf of Tonkin coast. It is on the highway and railroad from Hanoi south to the demarcation line and has a lumber industry.

Vinje, Aasmund Olafsson (ôs'mo͝on ō'läfs-sôn vĭn'yə), 1818–70, Norwegian essayist and poet. After establishing a reputation as a successful journalist, Vinje earned a law degree. In 1858 he founded *Dølen,* a periodical intended to promote the use of *Nynorsk,* the New Norwegian language. *Ferdaminni* [travel memories] (1861) is his best-known work. Vinje's writing is noted for its subtle irony.

Vinland or **Wineland,** section of North America discovered by LEIF ERICSSON in the 11th cent. The sources for the knowledge of Leif Ericsson's exploration differ as to whether it was planned or accidental, but it is definitely known that he found a land containing grapes and self-sown wheat, which he called Vinland. Later expeditions, particularly that of THORFINN KARLSEFNI, attempted to rediscover that land. There has been much speculation as to the identification of Vinland. Places from Newfoundland to Virginia have been suggested, but from the examination of the evidence that is available or may be deduced, pertaining to directions, distances, topography, climate, and flora and fauna, the southern coast of New England has been generally accepted. Efforts such as those by Eben N. Horsford, who in the late 19th cent. definitely located Vinland on the banks of the Charles River at Gerry's Landing, Cambridge, Mass., have usually met with little agreement. Inscriptions and relics have been sought to throw light on the subject. The discovery of the KENSINGTON RUNE STONE has been connected by Hjalmar R. Holand with the expedition of Paul Knutson to America. Holand has further claimed that the Newport Tower (or Old Stone Mill), in Touro Park, Newport, R.I., was the headquarters of Knutson's expedition, but some scholars maintain that the tower was built in colonial times. See William Hovgaard, *The Voyages of the Norsemen to America* (1914, repr. 1971); Halldor Hermannsson, *The Problem of Wineland* (1936, repr. 1966); H. R. Holand, *Explorations in America Before Columbus* (2d ed. 1958); F. J. Pohl, *The Lost Discovery* (1952); R. A. Skelton, *The Vinland Map and the Tartar Relations* (1965); W. E. Washburn, ed., *Vinland Map Conference: Proceedings* (1971).

Vinnichenko, Vladimir (vlədyē'mĭr vyĕnĭchăn'kō), 1880–1951, Ukrainian writer and statesman. Vinnichenko's early tales are naturalistic; his later novels concern the individual's conflict with society. Vinnichenko's witty and satirical dramas, including *The Black Panther and the White Bear* (1911), were internationally popular. He was repeatedly persecuted by the czarist government for revolutionary activities. In 1918 he was named president of the Ukrainian directorate, for a while heading the People's Republic. His *Rebirth of a Nation* (3 vol., 1920) deals with the history of the revolution (1917–1920) in the Ukraine. After the revolution failed, Vinnichenko lived in France.

Vinnitsa (vĭn'ĭtsä, Rus. vē'nyĭtsə), city (1970 pop. 212,000), capital of Vinnitsa oblast, in Podolia, the Ukraine, SW European USSR, on the Southern Bug River. A railroad junction in a sugar beet district, the city has food-processing and other industries. It was taken by Russia from Poland in 1793.

Vinogradoff, Sir Paul (vĭnəgrä'dəf), 1854–1925, English historian, b. Russia. Resigning (1901) his professorship at the Univ. of Moscow in protest against the repressive measures of the czarist government, he was professor of jurisprudence at Oxford from 1903 to his death. He became a British subject in 1918. Vinogradoff's study of medieval institutions and the history of law was marked by his special interest in the historic importance of the village community. His principal works include *Villainage in England* (1892), *The Growth of the Manor* (1904), and *Outlines of Historical Jurisprudence* (2 vol., 1920–23).

Vinson, Frederick Moore, 1890–1953, 13th Chief Justice of the United States (1946–53), b. Louisa, Ky. He received his law degree from Centre College in 1911. He served (1923–29, 1931–38) in the U.S. House of Representatives, where he was notable mainly as a fiscal expert. He resigned from Congress to become associate justice of the U.S. Court of Appeals for the District of Columbia and later chief justice of the U.S. Emergency Court of Appeals. He was director of the Office of Economic Stabilization (1943–45) and served briefly as Federal loan administrator (March, 1945) and as director of the Office of War Mobilization (April–July, 1945) before becoming Secretary of the Treasury (1945–46). Chief Justice Harlan F. Stone's death led to his appointment as Chief Justice by President Truman; he served until his death.

Vinson Massif, peak, 16,860 ft (5,139 m) high, W Antarctica, in the Ellsworth Mts.; highest peak in Antarctica.

Vintimille: see VENTIMIGLIA, Italy.

vinyl plastics, group of thermoplastics used in molded products, flexible tubing, material for raincoats, and laminated safety glass. Vinyl PLASTICS are POLYMERS and copolymers of vinyl derivatives (i.e., derivatives of ethylene, $H_2C{=}CH_2$), e.g., vinyl chloride ($H_2C{=}CHCl$), vinyl alcohol ($H_2C{=}CHOH$), and vinyl acetate ($H_2C{=}CH{-}OOC{-}CH_3$). POLYETHYLENE may be considered the simplest of the vinyl polymers, and POLYVINYL CHLORIDE is an important member of this group. Polytetrafluoroethylene, or TEFLON, is also sometimes classed as a vinyl polymer.

Vinyon, trademark for a noncellulose man-made fiber, made from vinyl resin, which is derived from natural gas or coal, salt, water, and air. Vinyon is made as a continuous filament and as a short staple. The staple form is mixed with cotton or wool for use in felt and for fabrics in which creases or folds must be retained. Vinyon yarn is not affected by moths, mildew, or age. It does not support combustion, and its water absorbency is low. It is ideal for acid- and alkali-resisting clothing, shower curtains, fireproof awnings, industrial filter fabrics, fishing tackle, electric insulation, waterproof covering, and protective pipe covering.

viol, family of bowed stringed instruments, the most important ensemble instruments from the 15th to the 17th cent. The viol's early history is indefinite, but it is recognizable in depictions from as early as the 11th cent. During the second half of the 17th cent. it lost its dominant position to the VIOLIN family and became practically extinct until the general revival of interest in early music and instruments in the 20th cent. The viol differs from the violin in the manner of playing, in its shape, and in having frets and typically six strings, tuned in fourths rather than in fifths. Most viols are properly played upright, resting on or between the knees, with the bow held with the palm upward. The viol usually has sloping shoulders, a flat back, and deeper ribs than the violin. It is a chamber instrument with a soft, sweet tone, incapable of the dynamic extremes and brilliance of the violin; this helps to account for its decline. The viol was built in four principal sizes—treble, alto, tenor, and bass—which were used in ensemble, or "consort." The double-bass viol, or *violone,* survived all the others, becoming, with some modification, the present DOUBLE BASS. The bass viol was the principal solo instrument of the family, possessing a large literature from the 16th to the 18th cent. It later became known as *viola da gamba* [Ital.,=knee viol]—originally the name of the whole family, to distinguish them from those of the *viola da bracchio* (arm viol) family, the forerunners of the violin. The *viola d'amore,* a member of the viol family, originated in the 17th cent. and was especially popular in the 18th cent. It has from five to seven strings, tuned in thirds and fourths, and an

Viol

equal number of sympathetic strings running through the bridge and under the fingerboard. Unlike most viols, it is held, like the violin, under the chin. It was and is principally a solo instrument, possessing a modest literature from all periods, including the 20th cent.

viola: see VIOLIN.

viola da gamba: see VIOL.

viola d'amore: see VIOL.

violet, common name for some members of the Violaceae, a family of chiefly perennial herbs (and sometimes shrubs) found on all continents. Violets, including the genus *Viola* and similar related species, are popular as florists', garden, and wild flowers. Of this large group, with its fragrant blossoms ranging from deep purple to yellow or white, over 60 species are native to the United States and well over 100 varieties are offered in trade as ornamentals. Florists' violets are usually the sweet, or English, violet (*V. odorata*). Garden violets (often called violas) are generally hybrids and may be purple, blue, rose, yellow, white, or combinations of these, sometimes with double flowers. The violet has long been regarded as a symbol of modesty. It became the flower of Athens; followers of Napoleon, who promised to return from Elba with violets in the spring, used the blossom as a badge; and in the United States a violet is the floral emblem of three states (New Jersey, Rhode Island, and Wisconsin). Various species, particularly the sweet violet, have been used for perfume, dye, and medicine and have been candied. The common pansy was originally derived, long ago, from the Old World *V. tricolor,* one of several species called heartsease and Johnny-jump-up; the Eastern field pansy, a wild flower of North America, is a separate species. A resemblance to the human face is often seen in pansy blossoms, and the plant has come to signify remembrance, a tradition reflected in the name heartsease. Some unrelated plants are also called violets, e.g., the African violet of the family Gesneriaceae (gesneria family) and the dog-toothed violet of the family Liliaceae (lily family). Violets are classified in the division MAGNOLIOPHYTA, class Magnoliopsida, order Violales, family Violaceae.

violin, family of stringed musical instruments having wooden bodies whose backs and fronts are slightly convex, the fronts pierced by two f-shaped resonance holes. The smallest instrument of this group is also called violin, and its four strings, tuned in fifths,

Violin

run from the tailpiece at the base of the body over a bridge in the lower center, along the fingerboard, and into the pegbox. It is played by drawing a horsehair BOW, held in the right hand, across the strings; the body is supported by the shoulder and held firm by the chin. The fingers of the left hand are used to stop the strings against the fingerboard, thus changing the pitch by shortening the vibrating length of the strings. Within certain limitations more than one note can be played at once and the instrument is capable of producing harmonic effects and, with a mute clamped to the bridge, hushed, ethereal tones. The instrument first appeared about 1510 as the *viola da bracchio* (arm viol) and soon spread through Europe. During the 16th cent. three sizes were known, a soprano (corresponding to the modern viola), a tenor (a fifth lower), and a bass (a tone lower than the present violoncello). The present-day violin appeared only near the end of the 16th cent. The earliest-known makers of the new instrument worked in Lombardy in the mid-16th cent. They were followed by Andrea AMATI, founder of the Cremona school of violinmaking made famous by the GUARNERI family and by Antonio STRADIVARI. In Stradivari's work the peak of violinmaking seems to have been reached barely a century after the emergence of the instrument itself. The instruments of the violin family have been the dominant bowed instruments because of their versatility, brilliance, and balance of tone, and their wide dynamic range. A variety of sounds may be produced, e.g., by different types of bowing or by plucking the string (see PIZZICATO). The violin has always been the most important member of the family, from the beginning being the principal orchestral instrument and holding an equivalent position in chamber music

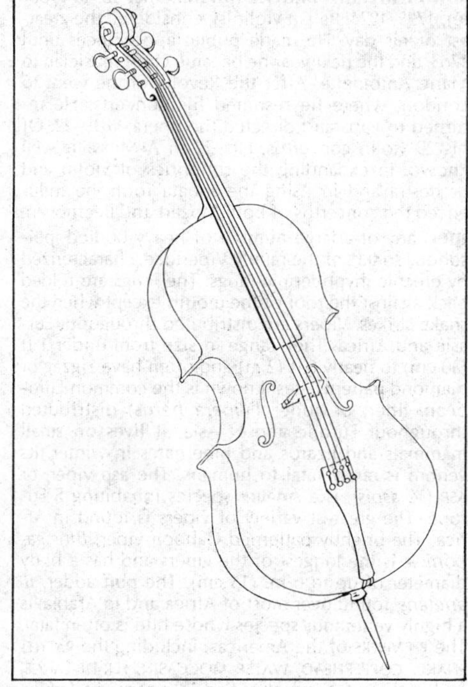
Violoncello

and as a solo instrument. The technique of the violin was developed much earlier than that of the viola or violoncello. Being the smallest, it is the most agile of the family, and it has the greatest variety of tone color. The viola is about one seventh larger than the violin and tuned a fifth lower. It is the only original member of the violin family to exist continuously in the same size. Its tone is deeper and less brilliant than that of the violin. In the 17th and early 18th cent. it was used mainly as an accompanying instrument in the orchestra, but the classical period made it much more independent. It is used mainly in the orchestra and chamber music, but recently has become increasingly popular as a solo instrument. The violoncello, often called cello, is about twice as large as the violin and has four strings tuned an octave lower than those of the viola. As the bass *viola da bracchio* it was originally tuned a tone lower than it now is, but the present tuning had become standard by 1700. Because of its size, it is played between the knees like members of the VIOL family. The bass viol was favored for solo playing in the 17th and early 18th cent., and the violoncello became an important solo instrument only after the disappearance of the viols and the subsequent refinement of cello technique by Jean Louis Duport (1749–1819). The cello was, from its beginning, an important member of the orchestra and is also indispensable in chamber music. It now has an extensive solo literature of its own.

Viollet-le-Duc, Eugène Emmanuel (özhĕn' ĕmänüĕl' vyôlā'-lə-dük), 1814–79, French architect and writer. He was the most prominent exponent of the Gothic revival in France, and was internationally celebrated for his restoration work upon historic French buildings. He studied architecture in Paris, traveled in Italy, and painstakingly studied medieval monuments throughout France. After restoring various churches and town halls in small towns of S France, he was employed, with J.-B. A. Lassus, to restore the Sainte-Chapelle in Paris. With Lassus he later did important work (1845–55) upon Notre-Dame de Paris, including the design of the pulpit and a replacement for the original central spire. His other important restorations include the cathedrals of Amiens, Chartres, and Rheims; the château of Pierrefonds; and the city of Carcassonne. Viollet-le-Duc wrote a number of books of permanent archaeological value, in which he emphasized the structurally organic quality of Gothic edifices. They include *Dictionnaire raisonné de l'architecture française du XI au XVI siècle* (10 vol., 1854–69) and *Dictionnaire du mobilier français de l'époque carlovingienne à la Renaissance* (1855), both of these great standard works containing illustrations by Viollet-le-Duc; *Monographie de Notre-Dame de Paris* (1856), with the baron de Guillermy; and *Entretiens sur l'architecture* (2 vol., 1858–72, tr. *Discourses on Architecture,* 1959 ed.).

violoncello: see VIOLIN.

Vionnet, Madeleine: see under FASHION.

Viotti, Giovanni Battista (jōvän'nē bät-tēs'tä vyôt'-tē), 1755–1824, Italian violinist, considered the greatest of his day. He made public appearances until 1783, and the next year he became court musician to Marie Antoinette. After the Revolution he went to London, where he resumed his concerts. He returned to Paris and directed the opera, 1819–22. Of his 29 violin concertos, No. 22 in A Minor is well known. In expanding the sonorities of violin and orchestra and in using the sonata form, he influenced the concertos of both Mozart and Beethoven.

viper, any of a large number of heavy-bodied, poisonous SNAKES of the family Viperidae, characterized by erectile, hypodermic fangs. The fangs are folded back against the roof of the mouth except when the snake strikes. Vipers are distributed throughout Eurasia and Africa. They range in size from under 1 ft (30 cm) to nearly 6 ft (2 m) and often have zigzag or diamond patterns. Best known is the common European viper, or adder (*Vipera berus*) distributed throughout Europe and N Asia. It lives on small mammals and lizards and hibernates in winter. Its venom is rarely fatal to humans. The asp viper, or ASP (*V. aspis*), is a smaller species inhabiting S Europe. The greatest variety of vipers is found in Africa. The brightly patterned Gaboon viper, *Bitis gabonica,* is the longest of the vipers and has a body diameter of up to 6 in. (15 cm). The puff adder, *B. arietans,* found over most of Africa and in Arabia, is a highly venomous species whose bite is often fatal. The PIT VIPERS of the Americas, including the RATTLESNAKE, COPPERHEAD, WATER MOCCASIN, FER-DE-LANCE, and BUSHMASTER, are classified in a separate family. Vipers are classified in the phylum CHORDATA, subphylum Vertebrata, class Reptilia, order Squamata, family Viperidae.

Virchow, Rudolf (ro͞o'dôlf fĭr'khō), 1821–1902, German pathologist, a founder of cellular pathology. He became professor at the Univ. of Würzburg (1849) and professor and director of the Pathological Institute, Berlin (1856). He contributed to nearly every branch of medical science as well as to anthropology, and he introduced sanitary reforms in Berlin. Virchow was a member of the Prussian lower house and later of the Reichstag (1880–93) and he was a leader of the liberal Progressive party opposed to Bismarck. He founded (1847) the *Archiv für pathologische Anatomie und Physiologie und für klinische Medizin* and wrote numerous works, including *Die Cellularpathologie* (1858, tr. 1860). See Erwin H. Ackerknecht, *Rudolf Virchow* (1954).

vireo, small, migratory songbird of the New World. Some species nest in the United States, but the majority are tropical. Vireos (also called greenlets) range from 4 to 6 1/2 in. (10.2–16.5 cm) in length; they are greenish above and white or yellowish below and have either stripes above or rings around the eyes. They search methodically through vegetation for insects. Vireos are known for their loud, persistent call and for their cup-shaped nest that is suspended in the fork of a tree limb. American vireos include the red-eyed, white-eyed, warbling, Philadelphia, yellow-throated, and blue-headed, or solitary, vireos. Vireos are classified in the phylum CHORDATA, subphylum Vertebrata, class Aves, order Passeriformes, family Vireonidae, genus *Vireo.*

Virgil: see VERGIL.

Virgil, Polydore: see VERGIL, POLYDORE.

Virgin, The, English name for VIRGO, a CONSTELLATION.

virginal, musical instrument: see SPINET.

Virgin Gorda, one of the British VIRGIN ISLANDS.

Virginia, state (1970 pop. 4,648,494), 40,815 sq mi (105,711 sq km), E United States, most northerly of the Southern states, the first of the Thirteen Colonies. It is officially styled a commonwealth. RICHMOND is the capital, and NORFOLK the largest city; other large cities are NEWPORT NEWS; PORTSMOUTH; and ALEXANDRIA and ARLINGTON, both suburbs of Washington, D.C. Virginia is roughly triangular in shape. Its base rests on North Carolina and Tennessee to the south, and in the north it touches on West Virginia and Maryland; its eastern side is bounded by Maryland and the Atlantic Ocean and its western side by Kentucky and West Virginia. The small section of Virginia that with Maryland and Delaware occupies the Delmarva peninsula between Chesapeake Bay and the Atlantic Ocean is separated from the main part of Virginia and is called the Eastern Shore. The coastal plain or TIDEWATER region of E Virginia, generally flat and partly swampy, is cut by four great tidal rivers—the Potomac (forming most of the line with Maryland), the Rappahannock, the York, and the James—all of which empty into Chesapeake Bay. In the tidewater region stretch vast forests of pine and hardwood, highlighted in early spring by flowering redbud and dogwood. At its western extension, the tidewater rises to c.300 ft. (90 m) at the fall line (passing through Richmond) and gives way to the Piedmont—rolling, generally fertile country that broadens gradually as it extends south to the North Carolina line. Rising rather abruptly in the western Piedmont is the Blue Ridge range, carpeted with bluegrass and ablaze in spring with rhododendron and mountain laurel; the Blue Ridge rises to the state's highest peak in Mt. Rogers (5,720 ft/1,743 m). Between the Blue Ridge and the westward-lying Allegheny Mts., both part of the Appalachian range, lies the valley and ridge province, commonly called the Valley of Virginia. Chief of the valleys, which are joined by narrow gaps, is the rich, beautiful, and historic valley of the Shenandoah. Crowning the hilltops and river bluffs from the Chesapeake region west to the Blue Ridge and adding to the grace and elegance of the Virginia landscape are the classic, Greek revival homes and public buildings with their characteristic stately porticos. The overall climate of Virginia is mild, and rainfall is well distributed. Virginia's economy is among the most diversified in the South, but agriculture is still the basic element. Tobacco, Virginia's traditional staple, leads among crops, but hay, corn, peanuts, sweet potatoes, and apples (especially in the Shenandoah valley) are also important. Livestock and livestock products are a major source of agricultural income; the Valley of Virginia is well known as a cattle area, and dairy and poultry farms are also important there. The coastal fisheries are large, and Virginia shellfish—especially oysters and crabs—yield a large annual catch. Coal is Virginia's chief mineral; stone and cement and sand and gravel are also important. The manufacture of chemical products is Virginia's leading industry. The nation's tobacco manufacture has long been focused in Richmond. ROANOKE is a center for the rail transport equipment industry, and a high proportion of the nation's shipyards are concentrated on the shores of HAMPTON ROADS. Norfolk serves as a major U.S. naval base, and Portsmouth as a U.S. naval shipyard; HAMPTON is an important center for aeronautical research. Other leading industries include the manufacture of food and textile and paper products. Virginia (named for Elizabeth I, the Virgin Queen) at first designated the whole vast area of North America not held by the Spanish or French. The colony on ROANOKE ISLAND, organized by Sir Walter RALEIGH, failed, but the English soon made another attempt slightly farther north. In 1606, James I granted a charter to the LONDON COMPANY (later better known as the Virginia Company), a group of merchants lured by the thought of easy profits in mining and in the Indian trade. The company sent three ships and 144 men under captains Christopher NEWPORT, Bartholomew GOSNOLD, and John Ratcliffe to establish a base, and the tiny force entered Chesapeake Bay in April, 1607. On a peninsula in the James River they founded (May 13, 1607) the first permanent English settlement in America, which they called JAMESTOWN. It soon became clear that the company's original plans were unrealistic, and the Jamestown settlers began a long and unexpected struggle to live off the land. By 1608, despite the firm and resourceful leadership of John SMITH, hunger and disease had reduced their numbers to 38. The company responded by sending supplies and men and new leadership in Sir Thomas GATES, who was to take charge as deputy governor under the authority of a new charter (1609). Gates arrived in 1610 to find that only a handful of settlers had survived the terrible winter (the "starving time") of 1609–10. He decided to take them back to England, but he had just

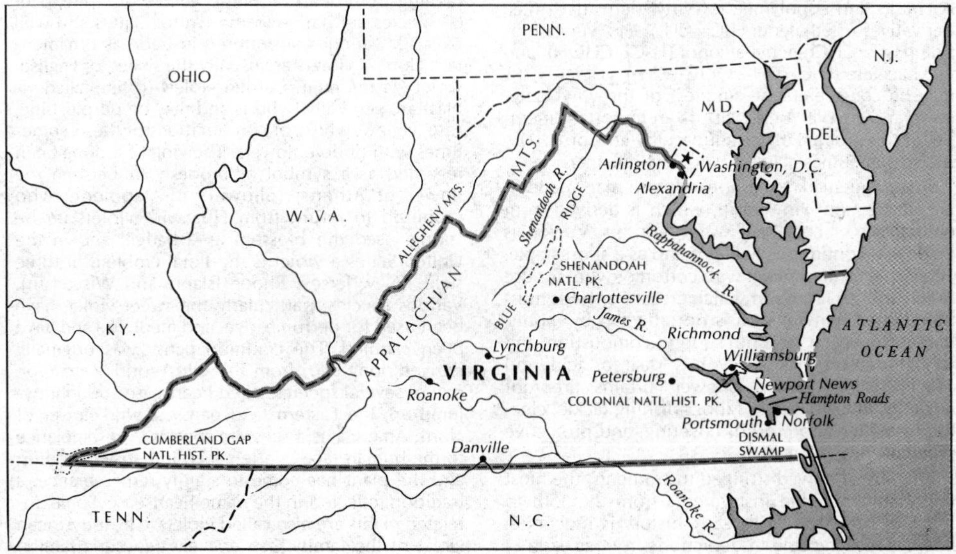

set sail in June, 1610, when his superior, Governor Thomas West, Baron DE LA WARR, ordered them to reoccupy Jamestown. Although sickness and starvation continued to take a heavy toll, the settlement at last began to make headway under the harsh regimes of Sir Thomas DALE, De la Warr's successor in 1611, and later under that of Sir Samuel ARGALL. Tobacco, first cultivated by John ROLFE in 1612, gave the company new hope of a profitable return on its investment. To encourage settlement and improve agricultural productivity it granted colonists (still technically employees and shareholders) the right to own private gardens, then, at the urging of Sir Edwin SANDYS, promised to give 100 acres (40 hectares) of its land to purchasers of stock and 50 acres (20 hectares) to settlers who brought over other settlers at his own expense (the "head-right" system). The company also set up smaller joint-stock companies to settle vast tracts known as "colonies" or "hundreds." As additional incentives to immigration the company instructed Governor George YEARDLEY in 1619 to form a house of burgesses—the first representative assembly in the New World—and in 1620 began to import women. But although these various expedients did succeed in attracting new settlers and strengthening the colony, the company itself failed to prosper. Rolfe's marriage (1614) to POCAHONTAS, daughter of chief POWHATAN, had secured good relations with the Indians for a time, but in 1622 Powhatan's son Opechancanough led the POWHATAN CONFEDERACY in a surprise attack on the colony and massacred 350 settlers (about one third of the total community). English retaliation effectively ended serious Indian troubles, except for a final uprising of the Confederacy in 1644. However, the 1622 attack had delivered a fatal blow to the company, and in 1624, beset by internal dissension, it surrendered its charter to the crown. After almost two decades as a private enterprise, Virginia became a royal colony, the first in English history. Partly because the English kings were occupied with affairs at home, the Virginia house of burgesses was able to continue its functions, and it won formal recognition in the late 1630s; thus representative government under royal domain was assured. By 1641, when Sir William BERKELEY became governor, the colony was well established and extended on both sides of the James up to its falls. Three fourths of the settlers (about 7,500 in 1641) had come as indentured servants or apprentices, but many of them became freemen and small farmers. In 1641 there were also about 250 Negroes (the first had arrived in 1619 on a Dutch ship), most of whom were indentured servants rather than slaves. The freeholders, together with the merchant class (from which were descended most of the first families of Virginia), controlled the government. Only whites were enfranchised, and property qualifications for voting continued during and after the colonial period. Most of the settlers were Anglicans, and during the civil war in England, many well-to-do Englishmen (mainly Anglicans and supporters of Charles I, if not actually Cavaliers) came to Virginia. The colony was understandably loyal to the crown until 1652, when an expedition sent by Oliver Cromwell forced it to adhere to the Puritan Commonwealth. With the Commonwealth busy at home, Virginia was practically independent until 1660, engaging in free trade with foreigners, especially the Dutch, and enjoying the profits of the expanding tobacco and fur trade. This prosperous era came to an end with the Restoration in 1660. The NAVIGATION ACTS forced the tobacco trade to use only English ships and English ports, which were at first insufficient to handle it; tobacco piled up in Virginia and in England, and prices plummeted. The wealthy planters weathered this depression, but the small farmers faced ruin. Serious discontent spread and was aggravated by Governor Berkeley's high-handed policies, by his favoritism for the wealthy tidewater planters, and by his refusal to sanction a campaign against the Indians who had been attacking the frontier; these grievances brought the eruption of BACON'S REBELLION in 1676. The unfortunate death of Nathaniel BACON left the yeomen leaderless, and they were put down so ruthlessly that Berkeley was recalled to England. The next governors—the 2d Baron CULPEPER and his successor, Lord Howard of Effingham (1683-89)—succeeded in slightly weakening the house of burgesses, but its basic powers remained, and after the Glorious Revolution in England (1688-89), it gained more full respect. The 1690s also brought renewed prosperity, as the Navigation Acts began to be applied more beneficially and Virginia tobacco was profitably marketed in Europe. Expansion of the plantation system was made possible only with the use of Negro slave labor (first recognized in law in 1662), and tens of thousands of Negroes were being imported every year by the end of the century. Small independent cultivators, unable to compete with the plantation-slave system, formed the nucleus of a poor white class that drifted southward or pioneered to the west. Also contributing to westward settlement were the French Huguenots, who came to Virginia by the end of the 17th cent. and began to settle the Piedmont. Westward movement was stimulated under Gov. Alexander SPOTSWOOD, who himself discovered (1716) the Swift Run Gap in the Blue Ridge mts., leading into the Shenandoah valley. Spotswood also imported (1714-17) Germans to work his iron furnaces in the Piedmont area, and numerous Germans followed their countrymen. They helped settle the Shenandoah valley (beginning c.1730) as did many newcomers from Pennsylvania—German Lutherans, English Quakers, Scotch-Irish Presbyterians, and a lesser number of Welsh Baptists. Soil exhaustion from continuous tobacco cultivation speeded the westward march, as did the settlement activities of land speculators like Spotswood and William BYRD (d. 1744). Many land speculators were indebted eastern planters who hoped to salvage their fortunes. The OHIO COMPANY grant (1749) furthered exploration beyond the Allegheny Mts. and brought conflict with the French. The activities and interests of the new frontier settlements contrasted sharply with the plantation life of the tidewater region, where the lavish material life of the planter aristocracy was complemented by high cultural accomplishments and by the spread of the ideas of the Enlightenment. The last of the FRENCH AND INDIAN WARS, in which Virginians—notably Col. George WASHINGTON—were prominent, ended the French obstacle to westward migration. After the war many indebted planters were disturbed by British limitations on westward settlement. With Massachusetts, Virginia was a leader in the movement that culminated in the AMERICAN REVOLUTION, although Virginia was never as politically discontented or as radical as Massachusetts, despite the burning oratory of Patrick HENRY and the enlightened political writings of Thomas JEFFERSON and other brilliant spokesmen. In 1773 the burgesses at WILLIAMSBURG (the capital since 1699), led by Richard Henry LEE, formed an intercolonial committee of correspondence. The Virginia leaders proposed (May, 1774) a congress of all the colonies; delegates were chosen at the First Virginia Convention (Aug.) and in September, Virginia's Peyton RANDOLPH was elected president of the First Continental Congress. The next year, in June, George Washington was made commander in chief of the Continental Army. After the patriots forced the royal governor, John Murray, earl of DUNMORE, to flee, the Fifth Virginia Convention (May 6-June 29, 1776) declared the colony's independence, instructed the Virginia delegates to the Continental Congress to propose general colonial independence (resulting in the Declaration of Independence written by Thomas Jefferson), and adopted a declaration of rights and the first constitution of a free American state, both drawn up by George MASON. Patrick Henry was elected the first governor. Although the British had burned Norfolk in Jan., 1776, they did not invade the state in full force until 1779, when they took Portsmouth and Suffolk. Continentals under Lafayette came to Virginia in 1780, and the British cause was lost as American land forces and a French fleet combined to bring about Cornwallis's surrender (Oct. 19, 1781) in the YORKTOWN CAMPAIGN. Meanwhile, George Rogers CLARK and his Virginians had wrested (1779) from the British the Northwest Territory, and in 1784 Virginia yielded its claim to this area to the Federal government. During the Revolution a degree of religious freedom had been instituted in Virginia under the lead of Jefferson. Other reforms had removed entail and primogeniture from land tenure, liberalized the legal code, and abolished further importation of slaves. A liberal law for formal emancipation of slaves was passed in 1782 and remained in force for more than 20 years. In 1786 a statute for religious freedom, championed by James MADISON, completed the disestablishment of the Anglican Church and established complete religious equality for all Virginians. In replacing the unsatisfactory Articles of Confederation with the Constitution of the United States, Virginians, especially James Madison, again played leading roles. Other able leaders such as Patrick Henry, Edmund PENDLETON, and Edmund RANDOLPH at various times opposed the document, but the state ratified it (June 26, 1788) with tidewater and western support, and another Virginian, Chief Justice John MARSHALL, later gave it much of its strength. The Old Dominion ceded (1789) a portion of its Potomac lands to the United States for the creation of the District of Columbia. In 1792, Kentucky, a Virginia county since 1776, was admitted to the Union as a separate state. After Madison and Jefferson raised an opposition to the financial program of Treasury Secretary Alexander HAMILTON, Virginia supported the emerging Democratic-Republican party's struggle against the Federalists and became a hotbed of states' rights sentiment (see KENTUCKY AND VIRGINIA RESOLUTIONS). Of the first 12 Presidents of the United States, seven were Virginians—Washington, Jefferson, Madison, James MONROE (these four comprising the "Virginia Dynasty"), William Henry HARRISON, John TYLER, and Zachary TAYLOR. These Presidents sometimes expanded national power and national development to an extent which many states' rights Virginians deemed unconstitutional. However, Virginia itself, stimulated by western complaints, embarked on a vigorous policy of internal improvements in the second and third decades of the 19th cent. The tidewater majority made few concessions to western demands for manhood suffrage and other reforms in the constitution of 1830. Economically, however, the whole state benefited from transportation improvements, from the growth of scientific agriculture and the spread of wheat cultivation, and from the growth of such industries as tobacco processing and iron manufacture. In the east cotton replaced tobacco as the staple, and as the newer Southern states eclipsed Virginia in cotton production the tidewater became a breeding ground for the slaves they needed. Elsewhere in the state, especially in the west, antislavery sentiment was strong in the early 19th cent., and following the slave insurrection (1831) of Nat TURNER the house of delegates voted down a bill to abolish slavery by the narrow margin of seven votes. The insurrection did result in harsher laws and more conservative policies regarding Negroes. A liberal political spirit triumphed in the constitution of 1851, which granted suffrage to "every white male citizen," and effected reapportionment of representation. For the most part Virginians labored to avert conflict between North and South. But "fire-eaters" such as Edmund RUFFIN and abolitionists such as John BROWN of HARPERS FERRY fame, shaped the course that led to the Civil War. Secession came (April 17, 1861) only after all attempts to keep peace had failed. Virginia joined the Confederacy, and Richmond became the Confederate capital. Robert E. LEE entered the military service of the new Southern government, but not a few Virginians such as Winfield SCOTT, George H. THOMAS, and David G. FARRAGUT remained loyal to the Union. Most Virginians W of the Appalachians also opposed secession, and on June 20, 1863, this section was admitted to the Union as the new state of West Virginia. Virginia was the chief battleground of the Civil War. In the beginning the Union armies were repeatedly set back—at the first battle of BULL RUN (July 21, 1861), in the SEVEN DAYS BATTLES of the PENINSULAR CAMPAIGN (April-July, 1862) after the MONITOR and MERRIMACK had clashed in Hampton Roads, and in lesser but related campaigns such as the triumph of Thomas J. (Stonewall) JACKSON in the Shenandoah valley. The second battle of Bull Run (Aug., 1862) was a smashing victory for Lee, but in the ANTIETAM CAMPAIGN (Sept., 1862) he fared no better than Union Gen. George B. MCCLELLAN in invading enemy country. However, in the battles of FREDERICKSBURG (Dec. 13, 1862) and CHANCELLORSVILLE (May 2-4, 1863), the Federals under Gen. Ambrose E. BURNSIDE and then under Gen. Joseph HOOKER were again handsomely repulsed. Thus encouraged, Lee and his lieutenants—James LONGSTREET, R. S. EWELL, A. P. HILL, and J. E. B. STUART—undertook another invasion of the North but failed against George G. MEADE in the GETTYSBURG CAMPAIGN (June-July, 1863). That marked the beginning of the end for the Confederacy, although it took considerable bloody pounding by Gen. U. S. GRANT in the WILDERNESS CAMPAIGN (May-June, 1864) and the siege of PETERSBURG (1864-65) before Lee surrendered the remnants of his Army of Northern Virginia at APPOMATTOX COURTHOUSE on April 9, 1865. President Jefferson Davis had already fled Richmond, and the Confederacy soon collapsed. The war left its marks on the land and the people. The Shenandoah valley was particularly desolate after the campaigns of Confederate Gen. Jubal A. EARLY and Union Gen. Philip H. SHERIDAN in 1864. But poverty-stricken as it was from the war, the state, under Gov. Francis H. PIERPONT, had the consolation of escaping the worst aspects of RECONSTRUCTION. Radical Republicans were but briefly in power. On the recommendation (1869) of President

Ulysses Grant, Congress allowed Virginia to vote without coercion, and the state passed the essential clauses of a constitution which the Radicals had drafted (1868), providing for free public schools and heavy taxes on land. More important, Virginia was enabled to elect to office its own moderate party, the "white Republicans," led by Gen. William MAHONE. Radical sway was ended. In 1870, after the Virginia assembly had ratified the 14th and 15th amendments to the Constitution, the state was readmitted to the Union. The end of slavery and the hard agricultural times of postwar decades also ended the plantation system in Virginia and brought some increase in farm tenancy, but the economy benefited from diversification as fruit farming and the cigarette industry became important. To offset declines in demand for dark Virginia tobacco, bright-leaf tobacco was increasingly grown. Politically the state was troubled for more than a decade by the debt question. The "Funders"—mainly Conservatives (old Whigs and Democrats)—wanted to pay the debt in full and to sell the state's railway to private enterprise; the "Readjusters," led by Mahone, wanted to reduce debt payments and to use remaining funds for a free public school system. The Readjusters carried their program in 1879, and a more traditional political pattern returned when the Democratic party, reunited under its old name, came to power in 1883. In many districts Republicans continued strong. Agrarian discontent was reflected in politics by the brief strength of the POPULIST PARTY in Virginia. In 1902 a new state constitution invoked rigorous literacy tests for voting, completing the long process of reducing the Negro electorate. During the years preceding World War I, Virginia's prosperity grew as dairy farming in particular gained importance, and during the war agriculture boomed, as did industry, especially the important shipbuilding works at Hampton Roads. The name of Woodrow WILSON lengthened the list of Virginian Presidents. In the mid-1920s, Harry Flood BYRD assumed direction of the state's powerful Democratic organization, formerly headed by U.S. Senator Thomas S. Martin and Methodist Episcopal Bishop James Cannon, Jr. Byrd, governor from 1926 to 1930 and U.S. Senator from 1933 until 1965, became the most influential figure in the state. As chief executive he put through a sound reorganization of the state government, brought about the passage of the first antilynching law of any state, and improved the highway system. However, the organization's chief boast was that the state was entirely free of debt due to a rigid "pay-as-you-go" policy. Liberals criticized this financial policy for scrimping on public education and welfare. In the Great Depression of the 1930s the state fared better than many states. Its industries had not been overexpanded, and, more important, the state's economy was built around consumer goods—foods, textiles, and tobacco—which remained in relatively high demand. Farmers benefited from the Agricultural Adjustment Administration, but conservative Virginians resisted some of the economic policies of the New Deal. In World War II, Virginia was the scene of much military training, and the shipyards at Hampton Roads and other industries again aided the war effort. In the prosperous postwar period the conservative Byrd organization maintained its power. After the 1954 Supreme Court decision on integration, attempts at desegregating Virginia's schools proceeded slowly. After Virginia courts and Federal courts ruled illegal the order by Gov. J. Lindsay Almond, Jr., to close public schools in nine counties, a lame compromise of "local option" was adopted. With the exception of Prince Edward co., where schools remained closed from 1959 until 1964, all parts of Virginia had accepted token integration by the mid-1960s. The Virginia constitution was revised extensively in the late 1960s. The legislature (called the general assembly) consists of a house of delegates of 100 members, elected to two-year terms, and a senate with 30 members, elected to four-year terms. The governor serves a four-year term and is ineligible for reelection. Linwood Holton, the first Republican to be elected since Reconstruction, became governor in 1970. He was succeeded by another Republican, Mills E. Godwin, Jr., in 1974. Despite the state's long tradition as a stronghold of the Democratic party, the Republicans grew in strength throughout the 1950s and 1960s. Richard Nixon carried Virginia in the presidential elections of 1960, 1968, and 1972. Virginia sends 10 Representatives and 2 Senators to the U.S. Congress and has 12 electoral votes. Virginia's shores, mountains, mineral springs, natural wonders, and numerous historic sites draw thousands of visitors annually. Major tourist attractions are Shenandoah National Park, Colonial National Historical Park, and Arlington House National Memorial. Other historic points of interest include Appomattox Court House National Historical Park; Manassas and Richmond national battlefield parks; Booker T. Washington and George Washington Birthplace national monuments; Jamestown National Historic Site; National Capital Parks (shared with Washington, D.C., and Maryland); and several national cemeteries and military parks (see NATIONAL PARKS AND MONUMENTS, table). Among Virginia's institutes of higher learning are the Univ. of Virginia, mainly at Charlottesville, with Mary Washington College at Fredericksburg; the College of William and Mary in Virginia, mainly at Williamsburg; Hampton Institute, at Hampton; Randolph-Macon College, at Ashland; Randolph-Macon Woman's College, at Lynchburg; Sweet Briar College, at Sweet Briar; Virginia Military Institute and Washington and Lee Univ., at Lexington; Virginia Polytechnic Institute and State Univ., at Blacksburg; and Virginia State College, at Petersburg. See E. G. Swem, *A Bibliography of Virginia* (4 vol., 1916–32); M. P. Andrews, *The Soul of a Nation* (1943) and *Virginia, the Old Dominion* (1937, repr. 1963); M. W. Fishwick, *The Virginia Tradition* (1956); F. B. Simkins et al., *Virginia: History, Government, Geography* (1957); C. H. Ambler, *Sectionalism in Virginia from 1776 to 1861* (1910, repr. 1964); P. A. Bruce, *Social Life of Virginia in the Seventeenth Century* (1907, repr. 1964); *Institutional History of Virginia in the Seventeenth Century* (2 vol., 1910; repr. 1964), *Economic History of Virginia in the Seventeenth Century* (2 vol., 1896; repr. 1966) and *The Virginia Plutarch* (2 vol., 1929; repr. 1971); H. J. Eckenrode, *The Revolution in Virginia* (1916, repr. 1964) and *The Political History of Virginia during the Reconstruction* (1904, repr. 1971); Jean Gottman, *Virginia in Our Century* (1969); C. C. Pearson, *The Readjuster Movement in Virginia, 1847–1861* (1917, repr. 1969); Virginius Dabney, *Virginia, the New Dominion* (1971); Federal Writer's Project, *Virginia, a Guide to the Old Dominion* (1940, repr. 1972).

Virginia, city (1970 pop. 12,450), St. Louis co., NE Minn., on the Mesabi range; inc. 1892. In addition to its iron mines—both open-pit (these are tourist attractions) and underground—the city has foundries and plants that manufacture garments and chipboard. It is also the trade center of a resort area. A junior college and the Minnesota Museum of Mining are there. The Laurentian Divide is to the north, and a state park, with an abandoned mine, is nearby.

Virginia, Confederate name for the ironclad *Merrimack.* See MONITOR AND MERRIMACK.

Virginia, in Roman legend, daughter of the centurion Virginius. Her father stabbed her to save her from the lust of Appius CLAUDIUS Crassus, decemvir. This precipitated the fall of the decemvirs. The story occurs often in literature.

Virginia, University of, mainly at Charlottesville; state supported; coeducational; chartered 1819, opened 1825 with Thomas Jefferson as its rector. Jefferson also planned the organization and curriculum and designed its first buildings. A leading Southern university, it was the first U.S. university to use the elective system. Mary Washington College (for women; chartered 1908) at Fredericksburg was consolidated with the Univ. of Virginia in 1944. The university operates a 4-year liberal arts college at Wise. It is known for its law school and for its library, which contains collections in American literature and international law. Its colonnaded buildings and rectangular "Lawn" are part of the spacious campus.

Virginia Beach, resort city (1970 pop. 172,106), independent and in no county, SE Va., on the Atlantic coast; inc. 1906. In 1963, Princess Anne co. and the former small town of Virginia Beach (1960 pop. 8,091) were merged, giving the present city an area of 302 sq mi (782 sq km). It begins at the North Carolina state line, extends N for 28 mi (45 km) along the Atlantic to the mouth of the Chesapeake Bay and to Norfolk, varying in width from c.7 to 15 mi (11–24 km). Its economy centers on tourism, agriculture (truck crops and livestock), and four large military bases now within the city limits: Oceana Naval Air Station, a huge base with hundreds of carrier planes; Dam Neck, the U.S. fleet anti-air warfare training center; a naval amphibious training center at Little Creek; and Fort Story, a U.S. army transportation command. Virginia Beach was long a popular resort, with beautiful beaches and excellent sportfishing. The huge area now added to the city offers additional fishing as well as game hunting. One section is famous for its thoroughbred horses and another for its Guernsey cows—it sends breeding stock abroad and is the nation's largest producer-distributor of Guernsey milk. Among the many points of interest in the city are the Cape Henry memorial cross, site of the landing of the first colonists in 1607; the Cape Henry lighthouse (1791; restored); the nation's oldest brick residence (1636; restored); and the Alan B. Shepard civic center, a geodesic aluminum-domed structure. Seashore State Park is within the city limits, and Virginia Wesleyan College is on the Norfolk–Virginia Beach border. The spectacular Chesapeake Bay Bridge-Tunnel (opened 1964) links Virginia Beach with the Eastern Shore of Virginia and Maryland.

Virginia bluebell: see BORAGE.

Virginia Company, name of two English colonizing companies, chartered by King James I in 1606. By the terms of the charter, the Virginia Company of London (see LONDON COMPANY) was given permission to plant a colony 100 mi (160 km) square between lat. 34°N and lat. 41°N; the Virginia Company of Plymouth (see PLYMOUTH COLONY), to found a colony between lat. 38°N and lat. 45°N. The overlapping area was open to settlement by either company, though neither might establish a colony within 100 mi of the other. A local council was to be set up in each colony, but the king, through a council in England, had the final authority. By 1609 the Plymouth Company had become inactive, and the London Company was granted its own individual charter in that year. The Plymouth Company later received (1620) a new charter as the Council for New England.

Virginia cowslip: see BORAGE.

Virginia creeper, native woody vine (*Parthenocissus quinquefolia*) of the family Vitaceae (GRAPE family), tall growing and popular as a wall covering. It has blue-black berries and clings by disk-tipped tendrils, some branches hanging free in graceful festoons. The five-fingered leaves—brilliant in the fall—are sometimes confused with the three-fingered poison ivy. The Virginia creeper belongs to the same genus as the Boston, or Japanese, ivy. Other names are American ivy, woodbine, and AMPELOPSIS. Virginia creeper is classified in the division MAGNOLIOPHYTA, class Magnoliopsida, order Rhamnales, family Vitaceae.

Virginia Military Institute, at Lexington; for men; state supported; chartered and opened 1839 as the first state military college in the United States. Although one of the leading U.S. military institutions, it grants degrees in engineering, science, and the liberal arts. During the Civil War, the institute's corps of cadets served as a unit in the Confederate army under Gen. T. J. (Stonewall) Jackson.

Virginia Polytechnic Institute and State University, at Blacksburg; land-grant and state supported; coeducational; chartered and opened 1872 as an agricultural and mechanical college. In 1896 it became Virginia Agricultural and Mechanical College and Polytechnic Institute. In 1944 its name was shortened to Virginia Polytechnic Institute, and in 1970 its present name was adopted. A women's division at Radford (Radford College, opened 1913 as a state normal school, later a state teachers college) was consolidated with the institute in 1944. The university maintains a Water Resources Research Center as well as numerous agricultural research stations throughout the state.

Virginia Resolutions: see KENTUCKY AND VIRGINIA RESOLUTIONS.

Virginia State College, at Petersburg; coeducational; land-grant and state supported; chartered 1882 as a normal and collegiate institute, opened 1883. It became a normal and industrial institute in 1902, was renamed Virginia State College for Negroes in 1930, and took its present name in 1946. The college's research facilities include a farm service center and a computer center.

Virgin Islands, group of about 100 small islands, West Indies, E of Puerto Rico. The islands are divided politically between the United States and Great Britain. Although constituting the westernmost part of the Lesser Antilles, the Virgin Islands form a geological unit with Puerto Rico and the Greater Antilles; they are of volcanic origin overlaid with limestone. The islands are subject to occasional hurricanes between August and October and suffer from light earthquakes. The water supply is almost completely dependent on rainfall and is preserved in cisterns. The tropical climate, with its cooling northeast trade winds, and the picturesque quality of the islands, enhanced by their Old World architecture, have encouraged a large tourist trade. But the population, predominantly black, remains poor.

The islands were discovered and named by Columbus in 1493. The **Virgin Islands of the United States** (1970 pop. 62,468), 133 sq mi (344 sq km), were purchased from Denmark in 1917 for $25 million because of their strategic position alongside the approach to the Panama Canal. Under a law passed in 1954, the islands are administered by the U.S. Dept.

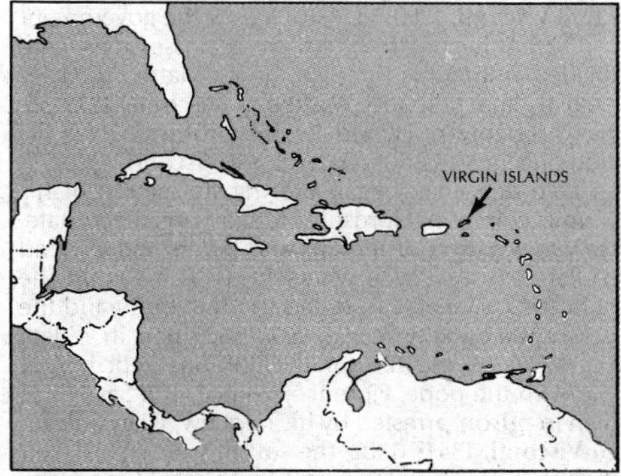

of the Interior; a governor and senate are locally elected. The capital is Charlotte Amalie on St. Thomas; other cities are Christiansted and Frederiksted, both on St. Croix. Although 68 islands comprise the group, only the three largest are of importance—St. Croix (80 sq mi/207 sq km), St. Thomas (32 sq mi/83 sq km), and St. John (20 sq mi/52 sq km). St. Thomas is mountainous, almost completely cultivated, and encloses many snug harbors and bays. Charlotte Amalie is noted for one of the finest harbors in the Caribbean. St. Croix, with a flatter terrain, is predominantly agricultural. Food crops are raised; sugarcane is no longer grown but rum is still distilled. The people on all three islands raise cattle, and meatpacking is a growing industry. The VIRGIN ISLANDS NATIONAL PARK covers most of St. John. Settlement of St. Thomas was begun by the Danish West India Company in 1672; St. John was claimed by Denmark in 1683, and St. Croix was purchased from France in 1733. The islands became a Danish royal colony in 1754. In 1801 and again from 1807 to 1815 the islands were in British hands. See Waldemar Westergaard, *The Danish West Indies, 1671–1754* (1917); H. W. Hannau, *The Virgin Islands: St. Thomas, St. Croix, St. John* (1965); D. C. Canegata, *St. Croix at the 20th Century* (1968); J. A. Jarvis, *The Virgin Islands and Their People* (1944, repr. 1971); E. A. O'Neill, *Rape of the American Virgins* (1972). Immediately to the northeast are the **British Virgin Islands**, a colony (1970 pop. 10,484), 59 sq mi (153 sq km). They are ruled by a governor (appointed by the crown) and an executive and a legislative council. There are more than 30 islands; 16 are inhabited. The principal ones are Tortula, Anegada, and Virgin Gorda. Road Town, the capital, is on Tortula. Livestock raising, farming, and fishing are the principal economic activities, in addition to tourism. Britain acquired the islands from the Dutch in 1666.

Virgin Islands National Park, 14,419 acres (5,835 hectares), St. John, Virgin Islands; est. 1956. The park, with beaches, coves, and headlands, is rich in tropical-plant, animal, and marine life. Bordeaux Mt., 1,277 ft (389 m) high, is the highest point on the island. Prehistoric Carib Indian relics and the remains of Danish colonial sugar plantations are in the park.

virginium: see FRANCIUM.

Virginius affair, 1873, incident that came near to causing war between the United States and Spain. The *Virginius,* a filibustering ship, was fraudulently flying the American flag and carrying arms to the Cubans in the TEN YEARS WAR. It was captured by the Spanish off Cuba, Oct. 31, 1873. The captain, Joseph Fry, and 52 of the crew and passengers—among them several Americans—were executed. More would have been killed but for the intervention of the British ship, *Niobe.* After the incident, negotiations were undertaken by Daniel Edgar Sickles, U.S. minister to Spain, whose intemperate attitude worsened the situation. However, Secretary of State Hamilton FISH (1808–93) took negotiations out of Sickles's hands and a settlement was reached. Spain paid the United States an indemnity of $80,000.

Virgin Lands Territory: see TSELINNY KRAY, USSR.

Virgin Mary: see MARY.

virgin's-bower: see CLEMATIS.

Virgo (vûr'gō) [Lat.,=the virgin], CONSTELLATION lying on the ECLIPTIC (the sun's apparent path through the heavens) between Libra and Leo, and SW of Boötes; it is one of the constellations of the ZODIAC. Virgo is traditionally depicted as a maiden holding an ear of grain to symbolize the harvest; various civilizations identified her with such figures as Ceres, Isis, Ishtar, and Rhea. The most prominent star is SPICA (Alpha Virginis), a white star of first magnitude. In 1936 a supernova was discovered in Virgo. A famous cluster of 2,500 galaxies, the Virgo cluster, lies in the constellation; the radio galaxy Virgo A is also found there. Virgo reaches its highest point in the evening sky in late May.

Viriatus (vērēā'təs), d. 139 B.C., leader of the Lusitani (see LUSITANIA). One of the survivors of the massacre of the Lusitani by the Roman praetor Servius Sulpicius Galba, Viriatus rose as a popular leader and persuaded his countrymen to resist Roman rule. He gathered an army and in 147 B.C. defeated the Romans. During the next two years he established control over a considerable area. In 145, Rome sent the consul Fabius Maximus, who was successful in restricting Viriatus' activities. The next year, however, Viriatus defeated the successor of Maximus and reestablished his power. One Roman defeat followed another. The victories of Viriatus encouraged the Celtiberians to renew their resistance to Rome. The senate then sent an army under Fabius Maximus Servilianus, which Viritus succeeded in trapping. He might have ended the war by destroying this army, but instead he concluded a peace and allowed the army to leave. For this act of clemency he was declared a friend of Rome by the senate. In 139, however, the successor of Servilianus, Servilius Caepio, with the tacit consent of the senate, renewed the war. Viriatus, probably swayed by his countrymen, who were weary of the war, opened negotiations with Caepio, who brought the war to an end by bribing the emissaries of Viriatus to kill him. His rule collapsed after his assassination.

virology, study of viruses and their role in disease. Many viruses, such as animal RNA viruses and viruses that infect bacteria, or BACTERIOPHAGES, have become useful laboratory tools in genetic studies and in work on the cellular metabolic control of gene expression (see NUCLEIC ACIDS). Because viruses can sometimes carry extra genetic material into host cells, they have been used to experimentally transfer genetic material, specifying a particular enzyme, into nuclei of mammalian host cells that lacked the ability to synthesize that enzyme. The ability of viruses to transfer genetic material has also been extensively studied in bacteria (see RECOMBINATION). Virus-mediated gene transfers are medically interesting because of the possibility that in the future enzyme-specifying genes might be transferred into humans with hereditary enzyme-deficiency diseases. Virus interference is a phenomenon in which host cells, while infected by one virus, are protected against infection by other viruses; the technique has been used experimentally as a form of temporary immunization. Interferon, a protein produced by virus-infected cells that inhibits viral growth within the cells, has been studied with a view toward preventing or controlling virus-caused diseases. Viruses continue to be investigated because they are held to be possible causative agents of some human cancers, and because under certain conditions the body's immune response to virus infection may cause tissue damage.

virtue [Lat.,=manliness], in philosophy, quality of good in human conduct. The cardinal virtues, as presented by Plato, were wisdom (or prudence), courage, temperance, and justice. They are to be interpreted as descriptive of conduct rather than the initiating force. These virtues are achieved through proper training and discipline. They have been called natural virtues, as contrasted with the Christian theological virtues of faith, hope, and charity. The theological virtues are regarded as dispositions for good residing in humans. As early as the 14th cent. the Christian virtues were combined with the Platonic virtues and called the seven cardinal virtues, figuring largely, with the opposing seven deadly sins, in such medieval literature as Dante's *Divine Comedy.*

Virunga (vērōōng'gä), volcanic range of mountains, E Zaïre, N Rwanda, and SW Uganda, central Africa, NE of Lake Kivu. It extends along the eastern rim of the Great Rift Valley and separates the basins of the Nile and Congo (Zaïre) rivers. Karisimbi (14,786 ft/4,507 m) is the highest peak, and the range includes active volcanoes. It is also called the Mfumbiro range.

virus, organism composed mainly of NUCLEIC ACID within a protein coat that is usually too small to be seen with the light microscope. In one stage of their life cycle, in which they are free and infectious, virus particles do not carry out the functions of other living cells, such as respiration and growth; however, in the other stage of the life cycle, viruses enter living plant, animal, or bacterial cells and make use of the host cell's chemical energy and its protein- and nucleic acid-synthesizing ability to replicate themselves. The existence of submicroscopic infectious agents was suspected by the end of the 19th cent.; in 1892 the Russian botanist Dmitri Iwanowski showed that the sap from tobacco plants infected with mosaic disease, even after being passed through a porcelain filter known to retain all bacteria, contained an agent that could infect other tobacco plants. In 1900 a similarly filterable agent was reported for foot-and-mouth disease of cattle. In

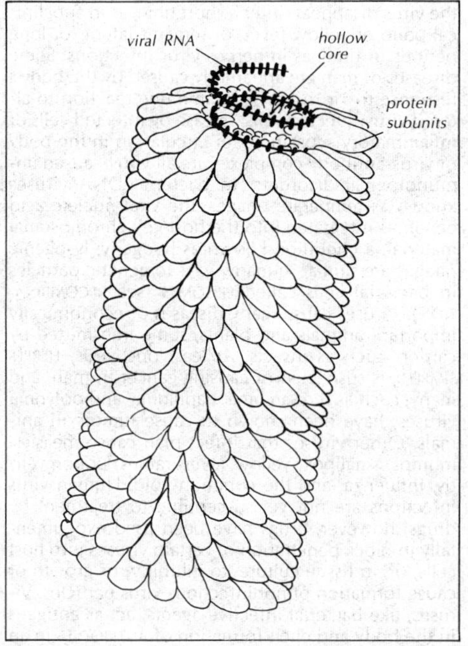

Structure of a tobacco mosaic virus, an RNA-containing virus

1935 the American virologist W. M. Stanley crystallized tobacco mosaic virus; for that work Stanley shared the 1946 Nobel Prize. Later studies of virus crystals established that the crystals were composed of individual virus particles, or virions. Typically, the protein coat, or capsid, of a virion is composed of several protein subunits, or capsomeres. Viruses have three main types of symmetry: cubic, as in the icosahedral herpes virus; helical, as seen in the tobacco mosaic virus; and complex, typical of large viruses such as the pox viruses and the larger bacterial viruses, or BACTERIOPHAGES. Viruses range in size from 100 to 2000 ANGSTROMS; they can therefore only be seen with an electron microscope, which uses an electron beam whose wavelength is smaller than the dimensions of the virus. Certain viruses, such as bacteriophages, also have complex protein tails; some viruses contain enzymes or other substances, and some also have an outer nonprotein envelope. The inner viral genetic material—the nucleic acid—may be double-stranded, with two complementary strands, or single-stranded; it may be deoxyribonucleic acid (DNA) or ribonucleic acid (RNA). The nucleic acid specifies information for the synthesis of from one to 50 different proteins, depending on the type of virus. A free virus particle may be thought of as a packaging device, by which viral genetic material can be introduced into the host cell. A bacterial virus infects the cell by attaching with fibers of its protein tail to a specific receptor site on the bacterial cell wall and then injecting the nucleic acid into the host, leaving the empty capsid outside. In other viruses the entire capsid enters the cell cytoplasm, either by PINOCYTOSIS or by a process in which the outer viral envelope merges with the host cell membrane and the capsid passes into the cell cytoplasm; in the case of such viruses the nucleic acid core dissociates from the protein coat inside the cell. Within the cell the virus nucleic acid uses the protein-synthesizing components of the host, i.e., the ribosomes and small molecules, and transcribes the information in the viral nucleic acid into virus enzymes, the head and tail proteins of the virus, and more viral nucleic acid. The site of protein synthesis varies with the virus; for example, polio virus components are synthesized in the cell cytoplasm, and herpes virus components in the cell nucleus. The details of the process by which the information in viral nucleic acid is expressed vary according to the type of nucleic acid the virus contains. As viral components are formed within a host cell, virions are created by a self-assembly process; that is, capsomere subunits spontaneously assemble into a protein coat around the nucleic acid core. Release of virus particles from the host may occur by means of reverse pinocytosis, as with some animal viruses, or, as in bacteria, by the action of enzymes that dissolve the cell wall, resulting in the host cell's lysis. Some viruses do not kill host cells but transform them into a cancerous state (see CANCER). In many virus infections of animals, including man, the host does not develop obvious illness and the virus disappears after a short time, as in subclinical polio or yellow fever, or remains latent for long periods of time, as in herpes virus infections. Some diseases of man are apparently caused by the body's response to virus infection: immune reaction to altered virus-infected cells, release by infected cells of inflammatory substances, or circulation in the body of virus-antibody complexes are all virus-caused immunological disorders. In bacterial DNA viruses known as temperate phages, the viral nucleic acid becomes integrated into the host cell chromosomal material, a condition known as lysogeny; lysogenic phages are similar in many ways to genetic particles in bacterial cells called EPISOMES (see RECOMBINATION). Viruses cause many diseases of economically important animals and plants, some transmitted by carriers such as insects. At least one virus, HERPES SIMPLEX, is suspected of causing cancer in man, and many, such as the sarcoma, papilloma, and polyoma viruses, have been shown to cause tumors in animals. Other viruses that infect man cause measles, mumps, smallpox, yellow fever, rabies, poliomyelitis, influenza, and the common cold. Human virus infections are not yet susceptible to treatment by drugs; however, drugs have been used experimentally to block penetration of certain viruses into host cells, or, in tissue culture, to inhibit virus growth or cause formation of noninfectious virus particles. Viruses, like bacterial infective agents, act as antigens in the body and elicit formation of ANTIBODIES in an infected individual (see IMMUNITY). Indeed, vaccines against diseases such as smallpox were developed before the causative agents were known. Some viruses stimulate cellular production of a protein, called interferon, that inhibits viral growth within the infected cell. Viruses are not usefully classified into conventional taxonomic groups but are usually grouped according to such properties as size, the type of nucleic acid they contain, the structure of the capsid and the number of protein subunits in it, host species, and immunological characteristics.

Vis (vēs), Gr. *Issa,* Ital. *Lissa,* island (1971 pop. 5,054), 35 sq mi (91 sq km), W Yugoslavia, off the Dalmatian coast in the Adriatic. A popular resort, it is the center of the Yugoslav fish-canning industry and is noted for its wine. Its chief town, also named Vis, is a picturesque village on the north coast. Ancient Issa was a Greek colony from the 4th cent. B.C. and later prospered under the Romans. From 996 to 1797 it was a Venetian possession, and in the Napoleonic Wars (1803–15) it changed hands among the Austrians, the French, and the British. From the Congress of Vienna (1815) until 1918 the island belonged to Hungary. Two important naval battles occurred off Vis: in 1811, the British won a victory over the French, and in the Austro-Prussian War of 1866 the Austrians under Admiral Wilhelm von Tegetthoff thoroughly defeated the Italian fleet. There are many ancient remains on the island, notably Roman baths, mosaic pavements, and several old Roman Catholic and Orthodox Eastern churches.

Visakhapatnam (vĭsäk″əpŭt′nəm), city (1971 pop. 351,249), Andhra Pradesh state, SE India, a port on the Bay of Bengal. Established by the British in the 17th cent., Visakhapatnam was famous for cloth and for local handicrafts, especially ornamental objects of ivory, horn, and silver. Today it is a district administrative center and a health resort and has a naval base, a shipyard, and an oil refinery. Andhra Univ. is on the outskirts of the city.

Visalia (vəsāl′yə), city (1970 pop. 27,268), seat of Tulare co., S central Calif., in the San Joaquin Valley; founded 1852, inc. 1874. Its economy is centered chiefly around agriculture. Electronic products are also manufactured. A junior college is there. Sequoia and Kings Canyon national parks (see NATIONAL PARKS AND MONUMENTS, table) are to the east.

Visayan Islands (vĭsī′ən), large island group (1970 est. pop. 10,000,000), c.24,000 sq mi (62,160 sq km), in and around the Visayan Sea, central Philippines. The group includes Bohol, Cebu, Leyte, Masbate, Negros, Panay, Samar, and hundreds of smaller islands. Samar and Leyte, on the east, act as buffers, protecting the other islands from storms and giving them a mild, Mediterranean-type climate that permits intensive cultivation. The coastal plains of Samar and Leyte are densely populated. Cebu, Negros, and Panay are the commercial heart of the Visayan Islands, and Cebu city—second in size and importance only to Manila—is the region's trade, transportation, industrial, and cultural center.

Visby (vēs′bə) or **Wisby** (wĭz′bē), city (1970 pop. 19,245), capital of Gotland co., SE Sweden, on Gotland Island and on the Baltic Sea. It is an industrial center and a popular resort and has a modern ice-free port. Manufactures include cement and refined sugar. The city is a Lutheran episcopal see. Visby was a pagan religious center. In the 11th cent. it became a prominent international trade center of the HANSEATIC LEAGUE. An independent republic, the city was the commercial center of N Europe, minting its own coins and developing an influential international maritime code. The ruins of 10 fine churches and the restored Cathedral of St. Mary, all from the 12th and 13th cent., testify to its former greatness. Visby's decline began in 1280, when Sweden conquered Gotland while the city was suffering civil strife. It was sacked (1361) and captured (1362) by the Danes, who returned (1370) it to the Hanseatic League. Pirates made it their stronghold for the next two centuries, and its trade was taken over by Lübeck. Visby passed to Denmark in 1570, and again came under Sweden in 1645. The city only began to recover its trade in the 19th cent.

Vischer, Friedrich Theodor (frē′drĭkh tā′ōdôr fĭsh′ər), 1807–87, German aesthetic philosopher. He taught at Tübingen, and later at Zürich and Stuttgart. Vischer was not only one of the most individual and independent critics of his century, but also a gifted author. His chief work is his *Ästhetik; oder Wissenschaft des Schönen* (6 vol., 1846–57). He also wrote the humorous and satirical *Auch Einer* [one more] (1879) and a parody of part of Goethe's *Faust,* as well as poems and numerous critical and philosophical works.

Vischer, Peter (pā′tər), the elder, c.1455–1529, German sculptor, foremost of the bronze founders in Germany. Beginning as the assistant of his father, Hermann Vischer, Peter set up his own establishment at Nuremberg and in time had his five sons working with him. Italian influence is noticeable in certain works, particularly the reliquary of St. Sebald at Nuremberg, Vischer's masterpiece; its rich ornamentation combines medieval and Renaissance characteristics. Of the other tombs from his workshop, the most important are those of Archbishop Ernst (cathedral, Magdeburg) and Graf Otto IV von Henneberg (Stadtkirche, Römhild). In 1513 Vischer, at the summons of Emperor Maximilian, went to Innsbruck, where he made two statues of Theodoric and Arthur for the great tomb of the Hapsburg. Of the sons who carried on their father's work, **Hermann Vischer,** the younger, c.1486–1517, and **Peter Vischer,** the younger, 1487–1528, were the most celebrated. Both sons are said to have gone to Italy and were influenced by the art of antiquity. Hermann's monumental achievement was the tomb of Elisabeth and Hermann VIII of Henneberg (Stadtkirche, Römhild). Peter the Younger made several reliefs of *Orpheus and Eurydice* and other mythological figures. He also executed the tomb of Frederick the Wise (Schlosskirche, Wittenberg).

Visconti (vēskôn′tē), Italian family that ruled Milan from the 13th cent. until 1447. In the 12th cent. members of the family received the title of viscount, from which the name is derived. **Ottone Visconti,** 1207–95, archbishop of Milan, was recognized (1277) as lord of the city after he had defeated the opposition of the Della Torre family, established leaders of the popular party. To keep the lordship in the family, he had **Matteo I Visconti,** 1255–1322, elected captain of the people in 1287. Exiled (1302–10) by the Della Torre faction, Matteo returned with the help of Holy Roman Emperor Henry VII and became imperial vicar. He established his overlordship in all Lombard cities, but Guelph opposition (see GUELPHS AND GHIBELLINES) obliged him to retire (1322) in favor of his son, **Galeazzo I Visconti,** 1277?–1328, who continued the struggle against popes and Guelphs. Galeazzo's son **Azzone Visconti,** 1302–39, consolidated the state, made peace with the pope, and increased the Milanese territories. At his death his two uncles, Lucchino and Giovanni, were proclaimed dukes. **Lucchino Visconti,** 1292–1349, who in fact ruled alone, continued his predecessor's conquests, acquiring territory in Piedmont, Tuscany, and the present Ticino canton of Switzerland. The expansion of Milan aroused the other Italian states, and coalitions were repeatedly formed against Lucchino and his successors. Lucchino's brother, **Giovanni Visconti,** 1290–1354, took over the government in 1349. At his death the Milanese possessions were divided among his three nephews, Matteo II, Galeazzo II, and Bernabò. **Matteo II Visconti,** 1319–55, was probably poisoned by his brothers, who divided his possessions. **Galeazzo II Visconti,** 1320–78, an able diplomat, began the transformation of his various communal lordships into an organized state. He was a patron of the arts and letters and a friend of Petrarch. At Pavia, where he held his court, he built the castle and founded the university and the library. **Bernabò Visconti,** 1323–85, ruled in Milan. His intrigues and territorial ambitions kept him at war with the pope, Florence, Venice, and Savoy. He died in prison, arrested by his nephew, **Gian Galeazzo Visconti,** 1351?–1402, the son of Galeazzo II. Left the sole ruler of all Visconti possessions, Gian Galeazzo embarked on a systematic program of conquest, first in Venetia, then in central Italy. He withstood hostile coalitions partly by skillful diplomacy, partly by employing the best condottieri of his time. He bought (1395) his investiture as hereditary duke of Milan from Holy Roman Emperor Wenceslaus and defeated (1401) Holy Roman Emperor Rupert when Rupert sought to restore imperial rule over Italy. Gian Galeazzo's ambition was to establish an Italian kingdom, but he died of the plague while preparing a final attack on Florence, his chief enemy. He reformed and centralized the government and promoted the arts and industries. During his reign the cathedral of Milan and the CERTOSA DI PAVIA were begun. He allied his family with the ruling house of France by marrying Isabella, daughter of John II. His daughter by a second marriage, Valentina, married Louis d'ORLÉANS; it was through her that Louis XII and Francis I of France derived their claim to Milan in the Italian Wars. See D. M. Bueno de Mesquita, *Giangaleazzo Visconti* (1941). During the regency of Gian Galeazzo's widow for her son, **Giovanni Maria Visconti,** 1389–1412, many cities were lost and political chaos prevailed. On reaching his majority Giovanni Maria revealed himself a dissolute and cruel ruler. He was assassinated, and the duchy passed to his brother, **Filippo Maria Visconti,** 1392–1447, who employed both diplomacy and force to restore the duchy. In his wars with Venice and Florence he was at first aided, then opposed, by CARMAGNOLA. His daughter and sole heir, Bianca Maria, married Francesco I SFORZA, who became duke of Milan after the fall of the short-lived Ambrosian Republic (1447–50), set up after Filippo Maria's death.

Visconti, Ennio Quirino (ĕn′nyō kwērē′nō), 1751–1818, Italian archaeologist. He was conservator of the Capitoline Museum, Rome, and one of the consuls of the brief Roman republic (1798). A political refugee in Paris from 1799, he became curator of antiquities at the Louvre (1799) and professor and member of the Institut de France (1803). He wrote *Iconographie grecque* (1808) and the first volume of *Iconographie romaine* (4 vol., 1817–26), which was completed by Antoine Mongez. His father, **Giovanni Battista Antonio Visconti,** 1722–84, was prefect of antiquities at Rome from 1768. He reorganized the Museo Pio-Clementino at the Vatican and edited the first volume of its noted catalog with the assistance of his son, who continued the work alone.

Visconti, Luchino (lo͝okē′nō), 1906–, Italian film director and writer, b. Milan; his original name was Luchino Visconti de Modrone. One of Italy's most acclaimed directors, Visconti has been called the father of neorealism for his early film *Obssessione* (1942). His later films have been studies of decadence. He is particularly adept at conveying a sense of place and past time. Among his films are *La Terra Trema* (1948), *Rocco and His Brothers* (1960), *The Leopard* (1964), *The Damned* (1969), *Death in Venice* (1971), and *Ludwig* (1973). He has also directed many plays and operas.

Visconti-Venosta, Emilio, marchese di (āmē′lyō märkā′zā dē vēskôn′tē-vānō′stä), 1829–1914, Italian patriot and statesman. At first a follower of Giuseppe Mazzini, he broke with him after the unsuccessful revolution of 1853 in Milan and became a supporter of Camillo Benso di Cavour. He held the foreign ministry several times in rightist cabinets between 1863 and 1901 and promoted friendly relations with France. In 1886 he became a senator.

viscose process (vĭs'kōs), method widely used for the commercial preparation of RAYON. Cellulose, prepared from either wood pulp or, less commonly, cotton linters, is treated with sodium hydroxide (an alkali) and then with carbon disulfide, the resulting product being a substance called cellulose xanthate. Dissolved in sodium hydroxide, this alkaline cellulose xanthate forms a thick solution called viscose. Rayon yarn is made by forcing the viscose through tiny openings in a spinneret into an acid solution, which coagulates it in the form of fine strands. Most of the rayon manufactured today is produced by this method, although other processes are also in use. The viscose process was discovered in 1892 by the English chemist Charles Frederick CROSS and his collaborator, Edward John Bevan.

viscosity, resistance of a fluid to flow. This resistance acts against the motion of any solid object through the fluid and also against motion of the fluid itself past stationary obstacles. Viscosity also acts internally on the fluid between slower and faster moving adjacent layers. All fluids, i.e., all liquids and gases, exhibit viscosity to some degree. Viscosity may be thought of as fluid FRICTION, just as the friction between two solids resists the motion of one over the other but also makes possible the acceleration of one relative to the other (e.g., the friction between the wheels of an automobile and a highway), so viscosity resists the motion of a solid through a fluid but also makes it possible for a propeller or other device to accelerate the solid through the fluid. When a fluid is moving through a pipe or a solid object is moving through a fluid, the layer of fluid in contact with the sides of the pipe or the surface of the object tends to be in the same state of motion as the object with which it is in contact; that is, the layer of fluid along the side of the pipe is at rest, while that in contact with the moving object is carried along at the same velocity as the object. If the difference in velocity between the fluid at the sides of the pipe and that at the center, or between the moving object and the fluid through which it is moving, is not too great, then the fluid flows in continuous, smooth layers; that is, the flow is laminar. The difference in velocity between adjacent layers of the fluid is known as a velocity gradient and is given by v/x, where v is the velocity difference and x is the distance between the layers. To keep one layer of fluid moving at a greater velocity than the adjacent layer, a force F is necessary, resulting in a shearing stress F/A, where A is the area of the surface in contact with the layer being moved. The ratio of the shearing stress to the velocity gradient is a measure of the viscosity of the fluid and is called the coefficient of viscosity η, or $\eta = Fx/Av$. The cgs unit for measuring the coefficient of viscosity is the poise. Experiments have shown that the coefficient of viscosity of liquids decreases with increasing temperature, while the coefficient of viscosity of gases increases with increasing temperature. In liquids, an increase in temperature is associated with the weakening of bonds between molecules; since these bonds contribute to viscosity, the coefficient is decreased. On the other hand, intermolecular forces in gases are not as important a factor in viscosity as collisions between the molecules, and an increase in temperature increases the number of collisions, thus increasing the coefficient of viscosity. A striking result of the kinetic theory of gases is that the viscosity of a gas is independent of the density of a gas. Viscosity is the principal factor resisting motion in laminar flow. However, when the velocity has increased to the point at which the flow becomes turbulent, pressure differences resulting from eddy currents rather than viscosity provide the major resistance to motion.

Viscount Melville Sound, 250 mi (402 km) long and 100 mi (161 km) wide, arm of the Arctic Ocean, N Northwest Territories, Canada, between Victoria and Prince of Wales islands on the south and Melville and Bathurst islands on the north. It is a section of the Northwest Passage. Through McClure Strait on the west it is linked with the Beaufort Sea; Barrow Strait and McClintock Channel lead east and southeast. A crossroads of arctic waterways, it is navigable only under favorable weather conditions. The western part was discovered (1850-53) by Sir Robert McClure.

Visé (vēzā'), town (1970 pop. 6,880), Liège prov., E Belgium, on the Meuse River and on the Albert Canal, near the Dutch border. It is a center of cement manufacture. The first battle of World War I was fought there on Aug. 4, 1914. It is also known as Wezet.

Viseu (vēzā'ōō), town (1960 pop. 17,365), capital of Viseu dist. and Beira Alta, N central Portugal. The town has agricultural-processing and textile industries. It was founded by the Romans, captured by the Moors (893), and retaken (1058) from the Moors by Ferdinand I of Castile. Noteworthy are a cathedral of mixed style, remains of ancient fortifications, and a museum.

Vishinsky or **Vyshinsky, Andrei Yanuarievich** (both: əndrā' yənōōär'yĭvĭch vĭshĕn'skē), 1883-1954, Russian diplomat and jurist. He studied law at the Univ. of Kiev, early entered the Social Democratic party, and fought in the Bolshevik ranks during the civil war (1918-20). Professor of law and later rector at the Univ. of Moscow, he became deputy state prosecutor (1933) and chief prosecutor (1935) of the USSR. Vishinsky served as Stalin's legal aide in the Communist party purges, and he was chief prosecutor at the Moscow treason trials (1936-38). In 1938 he was appointed vice premier. With the outbreak of World War II, Vishinsky became deputy commissar for foreign affairs (1940-49) and represented the Soviet Union on Allied commissions for the Mediterranean and Italy. He later (1944-45) represented Russian interests in the Balkans, forcing King Michael of Rumania to appoint a pro-Communist as premier by threatening military reprisals. As a major Russian figure in the United Nations, he acquired a reputation for biting wit as well as for the violence of his attacks on the United States. He was foreign minister of the USSR from 1949 until 1953, when he was succeeded by Molotov and became permanent Soviet delegate to the United Nations. He died in New York City. Among his writings is *The Law of the Soviet State* (tr. 1948).

Vishniac, Roman (vĭsh'nēăk), 1897-, Russian-American biologist, photographer, linguist, art historian, and philosopher, b. Pavlosk, near St. Petersburg. Vishniac took degrees in medicine, philosophy, art history, and biology. He fled in 1920 to Berlin, where he conducted research in endocrinology and worked as a photojournalist. From 1933 to 1939 he produced a photographic record of Jewish communities in Central and Western Europe. A part of this unique humanitarian document was published in 1947 under the title *Polish Jews.* In the mid-1930s he was imprisoned 11 times and forced to do hard labor in two concentration camps. He escaped and emigrated to the United States in 1940. At Yeshiva Univ. he was appointed research associate (1957) at the Albert Einstein College of Medicine and became professor of biological education there in 1961. A pioneer in time-lapse cinematography and light-interruption photography as well as the color photomicroscopy of living organisms, Vishniac became, in 1960, project director and filmmaker for the Living Biology film series sponsored by the National Science Foundation. His chief biological researches have been in the field of marine microbiology, the physiology of ciliates, and circulation systems in unicellular plants. He has proposed the hypothesis that the first living organisms were multicellular structures that emerged many times in many places by different biochemical pathways (polyphyletic origin). A volume of his color microphotographs of proteins, vitamins, and hormones, *Building Blocks of Life,* was published in 1971. Widely read and fluent in most modern and ancient European and Asian languages, Vishniac is a specialist in Far Eastern art and philosophy. He has taught in several fields at many universities, including the City Univ. of New York, Pratt Institute, and Case Western Reserve Univ.

Vishnu (vĭsh'nōō), one of the greatest gods of HINDUISM, also called Narayana. First mentioned in the Veda as a minor deity, his theistic cults, known as Vaishnavism, or Vishnuism, grew steadily from the first millennium B.C., absorbing numerous different traditions and minor deities. By his worshipers Vishnu is regarded as the supreme God, of whom other gods are secondary manifestations. The early epics the MAHABHARATA and the RAMAYANA show considerable Vaishnavite influence. The later *Puranas* fully elaborate the myths of Vishnu and his AVATARA (incarnations): Matsya (the fish), Kurma (the tortoise), Varaha (the boar), Narasimha (the man-lion), Vamana (the dwarf), Parashurama (Rama with the ax), Rama, KRISHNA, BUDDHA, and Kalkin (who is yet to appear). Vishnu is generally depicted as dark blue in color, crowned, and bearing in his four hands his emblems, the conch, discus, mace, and lotus. His mount is the eagle Garuda, and his consort is Lakshmi, or Shri, the goddess of wealth.

Visigoths (West Goths), division of the Goths, one of the most important groups of GERMANS. Having settled in the region W of the Black Sea in the 3d cent. A.D., the Goths soon split into two divisions, the OSTROGOTHS and the Visigoths. By the 4th cent. the Visigoths were at the borders of the East Roman Empire, raiding across the Danube River, and peacefully infiltrating the trans-Danubian provinces. Constantine I was troubled by the Visigoths, but they became a real menace only after the middle of the 4th cent. At that time groups of Visigoths had settled in Dacia as agriculturalists, and many had accepted Arian Christianity (see ARIANISM), partly as a result of the work of ULFILAS. About 364 a group of Visigoths devastated Thrace, and punitive measures were undertaken against them. They were also involved in the revolt (366) of Procopius, and until 369 Emperor VALENS waged war successfully against the Visigoths, who were led by ATHANARIC. Athanaric asserted his supremacy over FRITIGERN, a rival Visigothic leader who then retired into the Roman Empire and obtained Roman aid against Athanaric. However, the internal affairs of the Goths became of secondary importance to the invasion (c.375) of their lands by the HUNS. Athanaric retired to Transylvania, and the majority of the Visigoths joined Fritigern and fled (376) into the empire. Subjected to oppressive measures by Roman officials, these Visigothic settlers soon rose in revolt. Opposed by Emperor Valens at Adrianople in 378, the Goths won a decisive victory. They then swept across the upper Balkan Peninsula and ravaged Thrace. THEODOSIUS I immediately took up arms against them. In 382 peace was finally concluded, and the Goths under Athanaric were settled in Thrace. However, friction continued. In 395, after the death of Theodosius I, the Visigothic troops in Roman service proclaimed ALARIC I their leader; under his strong guidance they first developed the concept of kingship. Alaric led a revolt in the Balkan Peninsula but was checked by STILICHO. In 401 Alaric began his attacks on Italy; he was halted by Stilicho, but after Stilicho's death he succeeded in his invasion, and the Visigoths became masters of Italy. Negotiations between Alaric and Emperor HONORIUS failed, and in 410 the Visigoths sacked Rome. Alaric died soon afterward, and under ATAULF the Visigoths left (412) Italy and went into S Gaul and N Spain. They increased their territories in Spain (which was evacuated by the VANDALS), acquired AQUITAINE, and extended their influence to the Loire valley, making Toulouse their capital. The height of Visigothic power was reached under EURIC (466-84), who completed the conquest of Spain. In 507, ALARIC II was defeated at Vouillé by the Franks under Clovis, to whom he lost nearly all his possessions N of the Pyrenees. Toledo became the new Visigothic capital, and the history of the Visigoths became essentially that of SPAIN. Weakened by warfare with the Franks and the Basques and by Byzantine penetration in S Spain, the kingdom recovered its vigor in the late 6th cent. under LEOVIGILD and under RECARED, whose conversion to Catholicism facilitated the fusion of the Visigothic and the Hispano-Roman populations of Spain. King RECCESWINTH imposed (c.654) a Visigothic common law on both his Gothic and his Roman subjects, who previously had lived under different codes (see GERMANIC LAWS). The church councils of Toledo became the main force in the government, and the royal power was weakened accordingly. King Wamba, who succeeded Recceswinth, was deposed after a civil war, and thereafter the kingdom was torn by civil strife. When the last king, RODERICK, seized the throne, his rivals appealed to the Muslim leader TARIK IBN ZIYAD, whose victory (711) in a battle near Medina Sidonia ended the Visigothic kingdom and inaugurated the Moorish period in the history of Spain. See Thomas Hodgkin, *Italy and Her Invaders,* Vols. I-III (2d ed. 1892-96, repr. 1967); E. A. Thompson, *The Goths in Spain* (1969).

vision, sense of sight by which the form, color, size, movements, and distance of objects are perceived. The human EYE functions somewhat like a camera; that is, it receives and focuses light upon a photosensitive receiver, the retina. The light rays are bent and brought to focus as they pass through the cornea and the lens. The shape of the lens can be changed by the action of the ciliary muscles so that clear images of objects at different distances and of moving objects are formed on the retina. This ability to focus objects at varying distances is known as accommodation. The retina—the embryonic outgrowth of the brain—is a very complex tissue. Its most important elements are its many light-sensitive nerve cells—the rods and cones. The cones secrete the pigment iodopsin and are most effective in bright light; they alone provide color vision. The rods, which secrete a substance called visual purple, or rhodopsin, provide vision in dim light or semi-darkness; since rods do not provide color vision, objects in such light appear in shades of gray. Light rays brought to focus on the rods and cones produce a chemical reaction in those cells, in which the two pigments are broken down to form a protein and a vitamin A compound. This chemical process, by some unknown mechanism, stimulates an electrical impulse which is sent to the brain. The decomposition of pigment is normally balanced by the formation of new pigment through the recombination of the protein and vitamin A compound; thus vision is uninterrupted. The division of function between rods and cones is a result of the different sensitivity of their pigments to light. The iodopsin of cone cells is less sensitive than rhodopsin and therefore is not activated by weak light, while in bright light the highly sensitive rhodopsin of rod cells breaks down so rapidly that it soon becomes inactive. There is a depression near the center of the retina called the fovea that contains only cone cells. It provides the keenest possible vision when an object is viewed directly in bright light. In dim light, objects must be viewed somewhat to one side so that the light rays fall on the area of the retina that contains rod cells. The nerve impulses from the rods and cones are transmitted by nerve fibers across the retina to an area where the fibers converge and form the optic nerve. The area where the optic nerve passes through the retina is devoid of rods and cones and is known as the blind spot. The optic nerve from the left eye and that from the right eye meet at a point called the optic chiasma. There each nerve separates into two branches. The inner branch from each eye crosses over and joins the outer branch from the other eye. Two optic tracts exit thereby from the chiasma, transferring the impulses from the left side of each eye to the left visual center in the cerebral cortex (see BRAIN) and the impulses from the right half of each eye to the right cerebral cortex. The brain then fuses the two separate images to form a single image. The image formed on the retina is an inverted one because the light rays entering the eye are refracted and cross each other. However, the mental image as interpreted by the brain is right side up. How the brain corrects the inverted image to produce normal vision is unknown, but the ability is thought to be acquired early in life, with the aid of the other senses. No fully satisfactory hypothesis to explain color vision has been developed. The most widely accepted one was devised more than a century ago by Thomas Young and H. L. F. Helmholtz. The Young-Helmholtz theory is based on the assumption that there are three fundamental color sensations—red, green, and blue—and that there are three different groups of cones in the retina, each group particularly sensitive to one of these three colors. Light from a red object, for example, stimulates the cones that are more sensitive to red than the other cones. Other colors (besides red, green, and blue) are seen when the cone cells are stimulated in different combinations. The sensation of white is produced by the combination of the three primary colors, and black results from the absence of stimulation. Man normally has binocular vision, i.e., separate images of the visual field are formed by each eye; by some unknown means, the two images fuse to form a single impression. Because each eye forms its own image from a slightly different angle, a stereoscopic effect is obtained, and depth and distance and solidity of an object are appreciated. Defects of vision include ASTIGMATISM, COLOR BLINDNESS, FARSIGHTEDNESS, and NEARSIGHTEDNESS. See Matthew Luckiesh, *Light, Vision, and Seeing* (1944); M. H. Pirenne, *Vision and the Eye* (2d ed. 1967); G. H. Begbie, *Seeing and the Eye* (1969); R. L. Gregory, *Eye and Brain: The Psychology of Seeing* (2d ed. 1973).

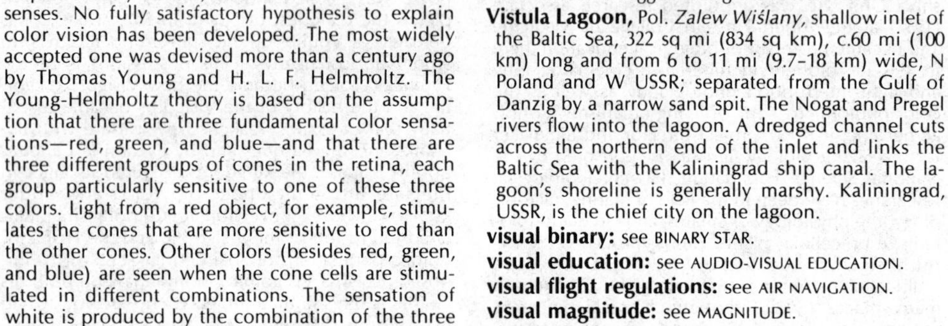

Optic nerve

visit and search: see SEARCH, RIGHT OF.

Visitation of Our Lady: see MARY.

Viso, Monte (môn'tā vē'zō) or **Monviso** (mōnvēz'-ō), peak, 12,602 ft (3,841 m) high, on the French-Italian border; highest of the Cottian Alps. The Po River rises there.

Visser't Hooft, Willem Adolph (vĭl'əm ä'dôlf vĭs'-ĕrt hōft), 1900–, Dutch clergyman, a leader of the Protestant ecumenical movement, b. Haarlem, educated at the Univ. of Leiden. In 1924 he was named secretary of the world committee of the YMCA, and in 1936 he was ordained a minister of the Reformed Church in Geneva. In 1938 he became the first general secretary of the World Council of Churches. He has written many books, in French and English, on the ecumenical movement and on the Christian calling. Among them are *Anglo-Catholicism and Orthodoxy* (1933), *The Kingship of Christ* (1947), *The Ecumenical Movement and the Racial Problem* (1954), and *A Responsible University in a Responsible Society* (1971).

Vista (vĭs'tə), uninc. town (1970 pop. 24,688), San Diego co., S Calif., near the Pacific coast, in an agricultural and resort area; inc. 1963. A junior college is in nearby San Marcos.

Vistrítsa, river: see ALIAKMON, river, Greece.

Vistula (vĭs'cho͝olə), Pol. *Wisła,* longest river and principal waterway of Poland, c.665 mi (1,070 km) long. It rises in the West Beskid range of the Carpathians, S Poland, and flows NE past Kraków, NW past Warsaw and Toruń, and N past Grudziądz and Tczew to the Gulf of Danzig on the Baltic Sea. The two main branches of its estuary are the Nogat, which flows past Malbork to the Vistula Lagoon, and the Martwa Wisła [dead Vistula], which flows past Gdańsk. Navigable for small craft for almost its entire length, the Vistula is connected by canals with the Oder, Dnepr, Neman, and Pregel rivers. Among its tributaries are the Dunajec, San, and Narew (with the Bug) rivers. Coal is transported from SW Poland, and lumber is logged along the lower Vistula.

Vistula Lagoon, Pol. *Zalew Wiślany,* shallow inlet of the Baltic Sea, 322 sq mi (834 sq km), c.60 mi (100 km) long and from 6 to 11 mi (9.7–18 km) wide, N Poland and W USSR; separated from the Gulf of Danzig by a narrow sand spit. The Nogat and Pregel rivers flow into the lagoon. A dredged channel cuts across the northern end of the inlet and links the Baltic Sea with the Kaliningrad ship canal. The lagoon's shoreline is generally marshy. Kaliningrad, USSR, is the chief city on the lagoon.

visual binary: see BINARY STAR.

visual education: see AUDIO-VISUAL EDUCATION.

visual flight regulations: see AIR NAVIGATION.

visual magnitude: see MAGNITUDE.

visual purple: see VISION.

vital statistics, primarily records of the number of births and deaths in a POPULATION. Other factors, such as number of marriages and causes of death, by age groups, are regularly included. From these records can be computed birthrates and death (or mortality) rates from which trends are determined. The earliest known system of vital statistics was in China. In England the clergy was required as early as the 16th cent. to keep records of christenings, marriages, and burials; during the 17th cent. the clergy in France, Italy, and Spain began to keep similar records. The oldest continuous national records system is that of Sweden (since 1741). The clergy and government officials in the colonies of North America began to record vital statistics in the 17th cent.; on a national level, the U.S. government started publishing annual records of deaths in 1900 and of births in 1915. The most striking trend shown by recent vital statistics is the rapid increase of the populations of nonindustrial countries due to a sharp decline in the mortality rate and an acceleration of the birthrate. See United Nations Statistical Office, *Handbook of Vital Statistics Methods* (1955); Roland Pressat, *Demographic Analysis* (tr. 1972).

vitamin, group of organic substances that are required in the diet of man and animals for normal growth, maintenance of life, and normal reproduction; very often either the vitamins themselves are COENZYMES, or they form integral parts of coenzymes. A substance that functions as a vitamin for one species does not necessarily function as a vitamin for another species. The vitamins differ in structure, and there is no chemical grouping common to them all. They were first called accessory factors because in 1906 it was found by English biochemist Sir F. G. Hopkins that most foods contain—besides carbohydrates, proteins, fats, minerals, and water—other substances necessary for health. The word *vitamin* was derived from the term *vitamine* used by Polish-American biochemist Casimir Funk to describe an amine (organic base) that was essential to life (it was later found to be thiamine). Hopkins and Funk in 1912 formulated the vitamin hypothesis of deficiency disease, that is, that certain diseases are caused by a dietary lack of specific vitamins. A well-balanced diet having sufficient amounts of milk, fruits, vegetables, eggs, and meat, fish, or fowl (in other words, any good protein source) usually satisfies the minimum vitamin requirements of human beings. The chemical structures of the vitamins are all known, and all of them have been synthesized; the vitamins in foods are identical to the synthetic ones. Vitamins were originally classified according to their solubility in water or fats, and as more and more were discovered they were also classified alphabetically. The fat-soluble vitamins are A, D, E, and K; the B complex and C vitamins are water soluble. **Vitamin A** is derived in the body from various carotenoids, chiefly CAROTENE, a pigment that occurs in leafy green vegetables and in yellow fruits and vegetables such as peaches, squash, sweet potatoes, carrots, and corn; other carotenoids can be found in fish liver, milk, cheese, butter, and egg yolk. Vitamin A is essential to skeletal growth and to the health of the skin and mucous membranes; the aldehyde form is important in the visual process, especially vision in dim light. In the deficiency state there is cessation of skeletal growth, night blindness, and various abnormalities of the skin and linings of the genitourinary system and gastrointestinal tract. The eye disorders that result from a deficiency of vitamin A may eventually lead to permanent blindness. As with the other fat-soluble vitamins, conditions that lead to inability to absorb fats, such as obstruction of bile flow or excessive use of mineral oil, can produce a deficiency state. Prolonged overdosage of vitamin A can cause irritability, painful joints, thickening of bones, itching, and loss of hair. Polar bear liver is quite poisonous to human beings because of its extremely high content of vitamin A. The recommended daily dietary allowance of vitamin A, as published by the U.S. Food and Nutrition Board, National Academy of Sciences–National Research Council, varies from 1500 to 8000 international units, depending upon age and other physical parameters. Commonly grouped as the **vitamin B complex** are about a dozen water-soluble factors. Thiamine (vitamin B_1, or antiberiberi factor) is a necessary ingredient for the biosynthesis of the coenzyme thiamine pyrophosphate; in this latter form it plays an important role in carbohydrate metabolism. Good sources are lean pork, liver, green beans, peas, yeast, whole grains, and thiamine-enriched flour and bread. This vitamin is a factor in the maintenance of appetite, normal intestinal function, and in the health of the cardiovascular and nervous systems. A deficiency of the vitamin may lead to BERIBERI; the disease was first shown to result from a dietary deficiency by Dutch physician Christian Eijkman. The recommended daily allowance of thiamine varies from 0.2 to 1.5 mg per day. Riboflavin (vitamin B_2, or lactoflavin) is used to synthesize two coenzymes that are associated with several of the respiratory enzymes of plants and animals (including humans) and is therefore important in biochemical oxidations and reductions. Deficiency leads to fissures in the corners of the mouth, inflammation of the tongue showing a reddish-purple coloration, skin disease, and often severe irritation of the eyes. The need for this vitamin (as for the other vitamins) is increased in women during the latter half of pregnancy and while lactating; during such periods the recommended allowance is as much as 1.8 to 2.0 mg per day. Otherwise the recommendation varies between 0.4 and 1.7 mg per day, depending on sex and age. Riboflavin is widely distributed in plant and animal tissues; liver, kidney, milk, yeast, wheat germ, and leafy green vegetables are good sources. Niacin (nicotinic acid) and niacinamide (nicotinamide) are commonly known as preventatives of PELLAGRA, which in 1912 was shown by American medical researcher Joseph Goldberger to result from a dietary deficiency. Niacin, a derivative of pyridine, was first synthesized in 1867. Niacin and niacinamide function in the biochemistry of man and other organisms as components of the two coenzymes nicotinamide adenine dinucleotide (NAD) and nicotinamide adenine dinucleotide phosphate (NADP); these operate in many enzyme-catalyzed oxidation and reduction reactions. The deficiency state in humans causes skin disease, diarrhea, dementia, and ultimately death. The deficiency state in dogs analogous to pellagra in humans is called blacktongue disease. Liver, lean meats, fish, wheat germ, yeast, peanuts, and soybeans are among the best sources of niacin; niacin-enriched bread and flour also provide significant quantities. Adequate uptake of the amino acid TRYPTOPHAN also appears necessary to prevent niacin deficiency in humans. The recommended daily allowance of niacin ranges from 5 to 20 "milligram equivalents" (60 mg of dietary tryptophan can substitute for 1 mg of niacin) per day. Pyridoxine, pyridoxal, pyridoxamine, and their phosphorylated forms make up the vitamin B_6 group. Pyridoxal phosphate functions as a coenzyme with certain enzymes engaged in the metabolism of amino acids. The best sources of B_6 vitamins are wheat germ, milk, yeast, meat (especially liver and kidney), and egg yolk. In infants pyridoxine deficiency can lead to convulsions; more generally the effects of deficiency include inadequate growth or weight loss, a decrease in the body's ability to manufacture hemoglobin (with resulting anemia), gastrointestinal disturbances, and skin diseases. The recommended daily allowance of vitamin B_6 varies from 0.2 to 2.5 mg, depending on sex, age, and physical condition. Pantothenic acid, another B vitamin, is present in perhaps all animal and plant tissues, as well as in many microorganisms. Large quantities of it are found in egg yolk, kidney, liver, and yeast; most vegetables are only fair sources. It is a component of the important substance coenzyme A, which is involved in the metabolism of many biochemical substances including fatty acids, steroids, phospholipids, heme, amino acids, and carbohydrates. The adrenal gland is an important site of pantothenic acid activity. This vitamin's nutritional role in man has not been firmly established, but much evidence from experimental animals points to deficiency symptoms that include lesions of the skin, of the neuromuscular system, and of the gastrointestinal system. In cases in which death occurs it appears to result from dehydration caused by inability to synthesize steroids such as aldosterone. On the basis of data obtained from experimental animals, it has been concluded that a daily intake of 10 mg of pantothenic acid should satisfy human needs. Biotin is a B vitamin that functions as a coenzyme in the metabolism of carbohydrates, fats, and amino acids. Although it is vitally necessary to the body, only exceedingly small quantities are needed, and since biotin is synthesized by intestinal bacteria, naturally occurring biotin deficiency disease is virtually unknown. The disease state can be produced artificially by including large quantities of raw egg white in the diet; the whites contain avidin, a biotin antagonist. Especially good sources of this widely distributed vitamin include egg yolk, kidney, liver, tomatoes, and yeast. Folic acid (pteroylglutamic acid, or folacin) occurs abundantly in green leafy vegetables, liver, kidney, and yeast. Derivatives of this vitamin are directly involved in the synthesis of nucleic acids; for this reason cells in the body that are subject to rapid synthesis and destruction are especially sensitive to folic acid deprivation. For example, the retarded synthesis of blood cells in folic acid deficiency results in several forms of anemia, while failure to replace rapidly-destroyed cells in the intestinal wall results in a disease called sprue. Several chemical antagonists to the action of folic acid have been developed in the hope that they might inhibit the growth of rapidly dividing cancer cells; one such compound, methotrexate (amethopterin) is used to treat leukemia in children. The recommended daily dietary allowance of folic acid ranges from 0.05 mg for infants to 0.8 mg for pregnant women. Para-aminobenzoic acid, which is incorporated into the folic acid molecule, is often listed separately as a B vitamin, although there is no evidence that it is essential to the diet of man. The molecular structure of vitamin B_{12} (cyanocobalamin), the most complex of all known vitamins, was announced in 1955 by several scientists, including British biochemists A. R. Todd and Dorothy Hodgkin. In 1973 the vitamin was reported to have been synthesized by organic chemists. Although its physiological role remains somewhat obscure, vitamin B_{12} and closely related cobalamins appear to be involved in the metabolism of amino and fatty acids. American physicians G. R. Minot and W. P. Murphy in 1926 fed large amounts of liver to patients with pernicious anemia and cured them; the curative substance in this case was probably vitamin B_{12}. However, pernicious anemia in man is caused not by vitamin B_{12} deficiency in the diet, but rather by the absence of a substance called the intrinsic factor, ordinarily secreted by the stomach and responsible for facilitating the absorption of B_{12} from the intestine. When a person's body cannot produce intrinsic factor, the standard treatment today is to inject vitamin B_{12} directly into the bloodstream. Minot and Murphy's therapy worked because the liver they fed their patients contained such large quantities of B_{12} that sufficient amounts of the vitamin were absorbed without the assistance of intrinsic factor. Inadequate absorption of B_{12} causes anemia, numbness and tingling, especially in the hands and feet, poor muscular coordination, psychological disturbances, and eventually death. The only site of cobalamin synthesis in nature appears to be in microorganisms; neither animals nor higher plants are capable of making these vitamin B_{12} derivatives. Nevertheless, such animal tissues as the liver, kidney, and heart of ruminants contain relatively large quantities of vitamin B_{12}; the vitamin stored in these organs was originally produced by the bacteria in the ruminant gut. Bivalves (clams or oysters), which siphon microorganisms from the sea, are also good sources. Plants, on the other hand, are poor sources of B_{12}. The recommended daily dietary allowance of this vitamin is said to vary between 1 and 8 micrograms. Two other substances which are sometimes classified as B vitamins are choline and inositol. Choline is an essential constituent of some fats (such as the lecithins) and of acetylcholine, the neurotransmitter. Since choline can be synthesized in the body from the amino acid serine, its classification as a vitamin is somewhat dubious. The richest sources are heart, brain, and egg yolk. The need for inositol in human nutrition is not yet established; the chick, pig, guinea pig, mouse, and rat, however, require this vitamin for normal growth. Good sources include muscle (especially shark muscle), heart, whole grains, beans, and nuts. **Vitamin C,** or ascorbic acid, a water-soluble vitamin, was first isolated (from adrenal cortex, oranges, cabbage, and lemon juice) in the laboratories of American biochemists Albert Szent-Gyorgyi and Charles King in the years 1928–33. Szent-Gyorgyi found the Hungarian red pepper to be an exceptionally rich source; other excellent sources include citrus fruits, tomatoes, berries, fresh green vegetables, and potatoes. The vitamin is readily oxidized and therefore is easily destroyed in cooking and during storage. All animals except man, other primates, and guinea pigs are able to synthesize ascorbic acid. The biochemical functions of ascorbic acid have not yet been fully elucidated, but it is known to be necessary for proper COLLAGEN synthesis; it apparently serves as a coenzyme during the formation of hydroxyproline residues from proline residues in the unfinished collagen molecule. Deficiency of vitamin C results in SCURVY, the symptoms of which are largely related to inadequate collagen synthesis and defective formation of intercellular materials. Ascorbic acid is metabolized slowly in man, and symptoms of scurvy are usually not seen for three or four months in the absence of any dietary vitamin C. The usefulness of ascorbic acid in prophylaxis and therapy of the common cold is quite controversial. The recommended daily allowance for this vitamin varies from 35 mg for infants to 60 mg for pregnant women. **Vitamin D** is a name given to two fat-soluble compounds: calciferol (vitamin D_2) and activated 7-dehydrocholesterol (vitamin D_3). The latter plays an essential role in the utilization of calcium and phosphorus by the body and prevents RICKETS in children. It has been argued that the term "vitamin" is inappropriate when used to describe these compounds because a plentiful supply of 7-dehydrocholesterol exists in the human skin and needs only to be activated by ultraviolet light (such as that of sunlight) to become fully potent. Rickets is really caused by a lack of exposure to sunlight, rather than a dietary deficiency. Nevertheless the disease can be prevented and its course halted by the intake of vitamin D_2 (found in irradiated yeast and used in some commercial preparations of the vitamin) or vitamin D_3 (found in fish liver oils and in irradiated milk). Symptoms of vitamin D deficiency in children include bowlegs, knock-knees, and more severe (often crippling) deformations of the bones. In adults deficiency results in osteomalacia, characterized by a softening of the bones. Vitamin D is essential to general well-being, but excessive doses may cause nausea, loss of appetite, kidney damage, and deposits of insoluble calcium salts in certain tissues. The daily dietary allowance has been set at 400 international units and is thought to be independent of age, sex, and physical condition. **Vitamin E** (tocopherol) occurs in at least seven molecular forms designated alpha-, beta-, gamma-, delta-, epsilon-, zeta-, and eta-tocopherol; all exist as light-yellow, viscous oils. The best sources include green leaves, peanut and corn oil, wheat germ, and eggs. Rancid fats in food destroy this vitamin. Tocopherol is essential to normal reproduction in some animals, but there is no evidence that it plays a role in human reproduction. The significance of vitamin E in human nutrition is not clear, but it is assumed that man requires the vitamin. The recommended daily dietary allowance for vitamin E ranges from 5 to 30 international units. **Vitamin K** consists of substances that are essential for the clotting of blood. It was identified in 1934 by Danish biochemist Henrik Dam. Two groups of K vitamins have been isolated: K_1, an oil purified from alfalfa concentrates, and K_2, a series of oils obtained from fish meal. Both are derived from the synthetic compound menadione (sometimes called vitamin K_3), a yellow crystalline solid that is as potent in its ability to promote BLOOD CLOTTING as the natural vitamins. The best sources are liver, leafy green vegetables, and bacteria (including the intestinal bacteria). Vitamin K is required for the synthesis in the liver of several blood-clotting factors, including prothrombin. The coumarin derivatives, used in medicine to prevent blood coagulation in certain cases, act by antagonizing the action of vitamin K. In the deficiency state an abnormal length of time is needed for blood to clot, and there may be multiple hemorrhaging in various tissues. The deficiency occurs in hemorrhagic disease of the newborn infant, in liver damage, and in cases where the vitamin is not absorbed properly by the intestine. This deficiency is rarely of dietary origin and the daily requirement is not known. Vitamin K is not effective in the treatment of hemophilia. A group of substances which decrease blood capillary fragility, called the **vitamin P** group, are no longer considered to be vitamins. See R. J. Kutsky, *Handbook of Vitamins and Hormones* (1973).

Vitebsk (vē'tĕpsk, vĕ'tyĭpsk), city (1970 pop. 231,000), capital of Vitebsk oblast, Belorussia, W European USSR, on the Western Dvina River. It is a river port and large railroad junction in an agricultural district. Manufactures include processed food, textiles, and building materials. Vitebsk dates from the 11th cent. and was the capital of a Russian principality that came under (14th cent.) Lithuanian rule. It passed to Russia again in 1772.

Vitellius, Aulus (ō'ləs vĭtĕl'ēəs), A.D. 15–A.D. 69, Roman emperor (A.D. 69). He was made commander of the legions on the lower Rhine by Galba in A.D. 68. On Galba's death he was proclaimed emperor at Colonia Agrippina (now Cologne). The generals who favored him defeated his rival, OTHO, in Italy, and Vitellius was briefly the emperor. He distinguished himself by extravagance, debauchery, and general incompetence. When his rival in the East, VESPASIAN, moved into Italy, Vitellius quickly lost his supporters. His troops were defeated at Cremona, and Vitellius fought with Vespasian's brother, Flavius Sabinus, in Rome. When Vespasian's troops entered Rome, Vitellius was captured while in hiding and murdered.

Viterbo (vētär'bō), city (1971 pop. 54,626), capital of Viterbo prov., Latium, central Italy, near Lake Bolsena. It is an agricultural center with food-processing industries. A Roman colony called Vicus Elbii, the city later (11th cent.) passed to the papacy. It became a favorite residence of the popes, and several conclaves were held there. The city has a picturesque medieval quarter, with palaces and houses built in the 13th-14th cent. and with numerous fountains. Landmarks include the pinnacled palace of the popes and the Gothic loggia (both 13th cent.); the Romanesque Cathedral of San Lorenzo (12th cent.), with a fine campanile; and the former Convent of St. Mary (11th and 14th-15th cent.), which now houses the municipal museum.

Viti: see FIJI.

Viti Levu (vē'tē lā'vōō) or **Naviti Levu** (nä-), volcanic island, 4,010 sq mi (10,386 sq km), S Pacific, largest and most important of the FIJI Islands. On Viti Levu are SUVA, the capital and chief port of the Fijis, and Lautoka, an important town. Mt. Victoria (c.4,340 ft/1,320 m), the highest peak in the Fijis, is on the island. Sugarcane, pineapples, rice, coconuts, and cotton are the major products; dairying and gold mining are also important industries. Sugar and copra are the chief exports.

Vitim (vētyēm'), river, c.1,140 mi (1,830 km) long, rising in the Transbaykalian Mts., E Siberian USSR, in the Buryat Autonomous Republic, and flowing S, NE, then N into the Lena River at Vitim. It is navigable for five months of the year from its mouth to Bodaybo, its chief port. Its lower course crosses the Vitim gold-mining plateau. The Vitim is a freight route for coal and grain.

Vitória (vētô'rēə), city (1970 pop. 123,809), capital of Espírito Santo state, E Brazil, on an island in Espírito Santo Bay of the Atlantic Ocean. It is one of Brazil's chief ore ports and is linked by rail with rich iron deposits at Itabira, in Minas Gerais state. Besides processing ore, the city produces sugar, leather goods, coffee, furniture, and paper bags. Vitória was founded in 1535 as a defensive position against the Indians. The city repelled several French attacks and the English pirate Thomas Cavendish (late 16th cent.), as well as an attempted Dutch invasion in 1625.

Vitoria (vētō'rēä), city (1970 pop. 136,873), capital of Álava prov., N Spain, in the Basque Provinces. The city is c.1,750 ft (530 m) above sea level. It is a manufacturing and administrative center. It was probably founded in the 6th cent. by the Visigoths; in 1181 Sancho the Wise of Navarre named it Vitoria to commemorate a victory over the Moors. At Vitoria in 1813 Wellington won the decisive battle of the Peninsular War against the French under Joseph Bonaparte and Jourdan. The 12th-century church of San Miguel is noted for its woodwork.

Vitoria da Conquista (vētô'rēə dä kōōng-kē'stə), city (1970 pop. 125,901), Bahia state, E Brazil, in the Batalha Mts. It is a major cattle-breeding and marketing center.

vitriol: see SULFURIC ACID.

Vitruvius (Marcus Vitruvius Pollio) (vĭtrōō'vēəs), fl. late 1st cent. B.C. and early 1st cent. A.D., Roman writer on architecture, engineer and architect for Augustus. In his one work, *De architectura* (tr. 1914), he discusses in 10 volumes city planning, building materials, temples and the Greek orders of architecture, public and private buildings, interior decorations, waterworks, chronometric instruments, machines to be used in construction, military machines, and human proportions as well. Its value lies in its uniqueness and its encyclopedic nature. The theories of Vitruvius were much used by Renaissance artists and architects in the CLASSIC REVIVAL.

Vitry-le-François (vētrē'-lə-fräNswä'), town (1968 pop. 17,562), Marne dept., NE France, on the Marne River. Woolens, earthenware, metal products, containers, and lumber are the chief manufactures. The town was founded by Francis I in 1545. During World War I it was the headquarters of General Joseph Joffre; in World War II the town was almost completely destroyed. Monuments include the Notre Dame Church (17th-18th cent.).

Vitry-sur-Seine (vētrē'-sür-sĕn), city (1968 pop. 79,242), Val-de-Marne dept., N central France, on the Seine River; an industrial suburb SE of Paris. The chief products are lighting and heating equipment, paper and cardboard, and chemicals. The city also has a thermo-electric station. In the St. Germain Church (13th-14th cent.) are the tombs of the former lords of Vitry.

Vittoria, Alessandro (äläs-sän'drō vēt-tô'rēä), 1525-1608, Italian sculptor. A leader of the Venetian Renaissance and a student of SANSOVINO, Vittoria was influenced by the MANNERISM of Ammanati and Michelangelo. He was celebrated for his portrait busts and decorative work, much of which was created for the restoration of the Palazzo Ducale. Vittoria worked in collaboration with Palladio and Veronese on the Villa Barbaro at Maser.

Vittoria, city (1971 pop. 45,717), SE Sicily, Italy; founded 1607. It is an important center of wine and olive oil production and export.

Vittorini, Elio (ĕ'lyō vēt-tōrē'nē), 1908-66, Italian novelist, b. Syracuse, Sicily. Between 1934 and 1941 Vittorini translated the works of D. H. Lawrence, Poe, Faulkner, Hemingway, T. S. Eliot, W. H. Auden, and others. His first novel, *In Sicily* (1938, tr. 1949), caused his imprisonment by the Fascist government. Vittorini's works, among them *The Twilight of the Elephant* (1947, tr. 1951) and *The Red Carnation* (1948, tr. 1952), make a serious attempt to assess the Fascist experience. His later works include *The Dark and the Light* (1956, tr. 1961); *Diario in pubblico* (1957), essays; and *Le città nel mondo* (1969). See Donald Heiney, *Three Italian Novelists* (1968).

Vittorino da Feltre (vēt-tōrē'nō dä fĕl'trā), 1378-1446, Italian humanist and teacher, b. Feltre. His real name was Vittorino Ramboldini. He studied at Padua and later taught there, but after a few years he was invited by the marquis of Mantua to educate his children. At Mantua, Vittorino set up a school at which he taught the marquis's children and the children of other prominent families, together with many poor children, treating them all on an equal footing. He not only taught the humanistic subjects, but placed special emphasis on religious and physical education. Many of his methods were novel, particularly in the close contacts between teacher and pupil and in the adaptation of the teaching to the ability and needs of the child. He was one of the first modern educators to develop during the Renaissance. Many of 15th-century Italy's greatest scholars, including Guarino da Verona, Bracciolini Poggio, and Francesco Filelfo sent their sons to study under Vittorino da Feltre. See W. H. Woodward, *Vittorino da Feltre and Other Humanist Educators* (1897, repr. 1964).

Vittorio Veneto (vēt-tô'ryō vānĕ'tō), town (1971 pop. 30,881), Venetia, NE Italy, in the Alpine foothills. It is an industrial and commercial center and a spa. There, in Oct.-Nov., 1918, the Italians won a decisive victory over the Austrians, which led to the Austro-Hungarian surrender to Armando Diaz on Nov. 3.

Vitu Islands (vē'tōō), volcanic group, 37 sq mi (96 sq km), in the BISMARCK ARCHIPELAGO, part of Papua New Guinea. Garove and Unea are the largest islands. The group is the chief copra center of Papua New Guinea. Formerly called the French Islands, the group is sometimes known as the Witu Islands.

Vitus, Saint (vī'təs), 4th cent.?, Sicilian martyr. As one of the saints called the Fourteen Holy Helpers he is invoked against many diseases, including St. Vitus's dance. He is traditionally the patron of dancers and actors. Guy is the English form of his name. His nurse and her husband, St. Crescentia and St. Modestus, martyred with St. Vitus, share his feast, June 15.

Vivaldi, Antonio (äntô'nyō vēväl'dē), c. 1675-1741, Italian composer. He was the greatest master of Italian baroque, particularly of violin music and the concerto grosso. Vivaldi received his early training from his father, a violinist at St. Mark's, Venice, and later studied with Giovanni Legrenzi. Ordained a priest in 1703, Vivaldi spent most of his life after 1709 in Venice, teaching and playing the violin and writing music for the Pietà, one of Venice's four music conservatories for orphaned girls. Although he produced quantities of vocal music (including 46 operas), he is remembered chiefly for his instrumental music—sonatas; concerti grossi, including four famous ones known as *The Four Seasons;* and 447 concertos for violin and other instruments. Vivaldi's style is characterized by driving rhythm, clarity, and lyrical melody. He helped standardize the three-movement concerto form later used by J. S. Bach and others. Vivaldi's brilliant allegros and impassioned slow movements were greatly admired by Bach, who arranged 10 of the solo concertos for other instruments. After Vivaldi's death his music was forgotten, but in the early 20th cent. his works were rediscovered. See biographies by M. Pincherle (tr. 1957) and W. Kolneder (tr. 1971).

Vivarais (vēvärā'), region, roughly coextensive with Ardèche dept., SE France. Its mountainous terrain rises to 5,753 ft (1,754 m) in the Mézenc. Cattle raising and silk manufacturing are the chief occupations. Privas is the principal town. The medieval county of Viviers or Vivarais, a part of the kingdom of Arles, was held in fief by the counts of Toulouse, who lost it to the French crown in 1229.

Vivarini (vēvärē'nē), Italian family of painters originating in Murano. They executed innumerable altarpieces that reflect the trends of the 15th cent. in northern Italian painting, from Gentile da Fabriano to Giovanni Bellini. **Antonio Vivarini,** b. c.1415, d. between 1476 and 1484, established a thriving workshop with his brother-in-law, Giovanni d'Alemagna. A joint work is *Madonna Enthroned* (Academy, Venice). Work signed only by Antonio includes an altarpiece in the cathedral of Parenzo and one in the Vatican. His brother was **Bartolomeo Vivarini,** c.1432-c.1499, who copied the style of Mantegna. Several of his altarpieces are in the Academy, Venice. **Alvise Vivarini,** c.1446-c.1503, son of Antonio, painted altarpieces (Academy, Venice; Naples) and some portraits.

Vivekananda (vē"vəkənŭn'də), 1863-1902, Hindu mystic, major exponent of Vedanta philosophy. He was born of a well-to-do family in Calcutta, and his given name was Narendra Nath Datta. As a young man he met RAMAKRISHNA and thereafter devoted himself completely to his teachings. After Ramakrishna's death in 1886, he traveled throughout India as a wandering monk. In 1893 he went to the United States where he represented Hinduism at the World Parliament of Religions in Chicago. After four years of teaching in the West he returned to India, where he organized the Ramakrishna Mission and engaged in a strenuous campaign to encourage a national renaissance. See his *Complete Works* (7 vol., 1922-31); biography by Romain Rolland (5th ed. 1960); study by S. L. Mukherji (1971).

Vives, Juan Luis (hwän lōōēs' vē'vās), 1492-1540, Spanish humanist and philosopher; friend of Erasmus. At the invitation of King Henry VIII he went to England, where he lectured at Oxford and served as tutor to Princess Mary (later Queen Mary I). Opposed to the divorce of Henry and Katharine of Aragón, he left England and until his death lived in Bruges. Vives, a vigorous and adventurous thinker, opposed the authority of Aristotle and the conventions of scholasticism. He was the forerunner of Francis Bacon by his application of induction to philosophical and psychological inquiry and by his pragmatic testing of hypotheses. In *De anima et vita* (1538) Vives produced one of the first works on modern psychology. Another one of his books, *De disciplinis* (1531), is an important analysis of educational theory. See study by G. E. McCully (1967); R. P. Adams, *The Better Part of Valor* (1962).

Viviani, René (rənā' vēvyänē'), 1863-1925, French statesman. He entered politics as a Socialist and joined Jean Jaurès in founding the journal *Humanité* and in forming (1905) the united French Socialist party. He headed (1906-9) the newly created labor ministry in the cabinet of Georges Clemenceau and also in the Aristide Briand cabinet (1909-10). Viviani became premier in June, 1914. At the start of World War I his appeal for a "sacred union" of all parties resulted in the formation of a coalition defense cabinet. He resigned as premier in 1915, but served as minister of justice until 1917. In 1921-22 he represented France at the naval conference in Washington.

Vivien, in Arthurian legend: see MERLIN.

vivisection (vĭv"ĭsĕk'shən), dissection of living animals for experimental purposes. More recently the use of the term has been expanded to include all experimentation on living animals rather than just dissection alone. The practice of vivisection dates at least from the beginning of the scientific study of living organisms in ancient Greece. It contributed to the outstanding progress that was made in the 17th cent. by William Harvey in understanding the circulation of the blood. However, the use of research animals in the laboratory did not become widespread in Europe until the 19th cent. Animals most frequently used in the laboratory include rats, mice, guinea pigs, and rabbits. When animals more closely resembling humans in size and structure are needed, dogs and chimpanzees are frequently utilized. Animal experimentation is especially advantageous if offspring of several generations are to be observed. About 5 generations of mice can be observed in a year; in humans the same experiment would require over 100 years. Some individuals and groups have voiced concern over the use of animals in this way, amounting to outright opposition in some cases. There have been attempts to legislate an end to animal experimentation and, although they have not been successful, antivivisectionists have attempted to influence lawmakers to that end in countries where such practices are widespread, especially in the United States and Great Britain. The National Society for Medical Research was established in 1945 to explain the nature of and necessity for experimental procedures on animals. A number of organizations are concerned with determining and disseminating strict codes for the treatment of experimental subjects, and their interest has kept scientists on the alert for any laxity in maintaining humane experimental procedures. The United Nations Educational, Scientific, and Cultural Organization (UNESCO), the United States Government Institute of Laboratory Animal Resources of the National Research Council, and the Laboratory Animal Bureau in Great Britain are examples of governmental agencies that assume advisory or regulatory roles in the practice of vivisection. Private organizations in the United States include the Animal Care Panel, the American Society for the Prevention of Cruelty to Animals (ASPCA), and numerous local humane societies. Efforts of the latter have been successful in preventing the use of stray dogs and cats in research.

Vizcaíno, Sebastián (sävästyän' vĕthkäē'nō), c.1550–c.1628, Spanish explorer and merchant. After an unsuccessful attempt to plant a colony in Lower California (1596), he sailed (1602) to explore the California coast, where he discovered and named Monterey Bay. In 1611 he was sent out on an unsuccessful venture to search for the fabled Pacific islands of Rica de Oro and Rica de Plata and to promote relations with Japan.

Vizcaya: see BASQUE PROVINCES.

Vizianagram (vĭzyŭ'nəgrəm), city (1971 pop. 86,548), Andhra Pradesh state, E India, near the Bay of Bengal. It is a market for grain, peanuts, and sugar. There are leather-tanning and jute-processing industries. On the city's outskirts is the largest ferromanganese plant in India.

Vizsla (vĭzh'lə), breed of large SPORTING DOG introduced into Europe by the Magyar invasion of the 10th cent. and perfected in Hungary over hundreds of years; also called Hungarian pointer. It stands between 21 and 24 in. (53.3–60.9 cm) high at the shoulder and weighs between 40 and 60 lb (18.1–27.2 kg). Its short, smooth coat may be various shades of solid rusty gold or sandy yellow. Its tail is docked. Developed to exhibit the caution and alertness necessary for hunting on the plains of Hungary, the Vizsla is particularly suited for hunting in flat, open country. It is used on a variety of upland game and waterfowl and can be trained to point and retrieve on both land and water. See DOG.

Vlaardingen (vlär'dĭng-ən), city (1971 pop. 81,097), South Holland prov., SW Netherlands, on the Nieuwe Maas (New Meuse) River, near Rotterdam. It is an industrial city, a major port, and a fishing center, especially for herring and cod.

Vlachs: see WALACHIA.

Vlad IV, 1431?–1476, prince of Walachia (1448, 1456–62, 1476), known as Vlad the Impaler. He was the son of Prince Vlad Dracul (Vlad the Devil) and is therefore also called Dracula or son of the Devil. Vlad IV seized the Walachian throne briefly in 1448 and definitively in 1456 with the support of John Hunyadi, whom he had helped against the Ottoman Turks. Ruling with firmness and with cruelty toward his opponents, he created an orderly administration, developed commerce, and strengthened the army. In 1462, however, a campaign against him by the Ottoman Sultan Muhammad II resulted in his deposition. Vlad sought aid from the Hungarian king Mathias Corvinus but was instead imprisoned in Hungary for 12 years. In late 1476, Vlad, with Transylvanian aid, regained the Walachian throne only to be defeated and killed by the Turkish-supported prince, Laiota Basarab. The novel *Dracula* by Bram Stoker, although not based on Vlad's historical exploits, made the name *Dracula* well-known in literature. See R. T. McNally and Radu Florescu, *Dracula* (1973).

Vladikavkaz: see ORDZHONIKIDZE, USSR.

Vladimir I or **Saint Vladimir** (vlăd'əmēr, Rus. vlədyē'mĭr), d. 1015, first Christian grand duke of Kiev (c.980–1015); son of SVIATOSLAV. In 970, Vladimir was sent by his father to govern Novgorod. After Sviatoslav's death Vladimir vied with his two brothers, Yaropolk and Oleg, for the succession. About 980, he defeated his brothers and became grand duke of Kiev. During his reign he conquered and united under KIEVAN RUSSIA distant Slavic tribes and waged successful wars on the Lithuanians, the Bulgars, and the Byzantines in Crimea. At first a fervent pagan, he converted to Christianity, probably influenced by the political and economic advantages of an alliance with Byzantium. His baptism, in 988 or 989, was followed by his marriage to Anna, sister of the Byzantine Emperor Basil II. After the wedding he returned Kherson (in Crimea) to Byzantium. Vladimir renounced his profligate ways and made Greek Orthodox Christianity the religion of his people. He devoted the remainder of his life to the building of churches, including the splendid Cathedral of the Tithes (989), and to the establishment of schools and libraries. He also enacted several statutes concerning the legal status and courts of the church. Feast: July 15.

Vladimir II (Vladimir Monomakh), 1053–1125, grand duke of Kiev (1113–25); son of Vsevolod I, prince of Pereyaslavl and grand duke of Kiev (ruled 1078–93). On his father's death he became prince of Pereyaslavl, but supported his cousin Sviatopolk for grand duke of Kiev in order to avoid warfare among the princes of Russia. Vladimir gained popularity as a result of his successful campaigns (1103 and 1111) against the Cumans, nomadic invaders who were a constant threat to Russian lands. When Sviatopolk died Vladimir succeeded him. Under his reign the state flourished and grew in power. He enacted social legislation, extended colonization in the northeastern forests, and built new towns.

Vladimir (vlədyē'mĭr), city (1970 pop. 234,000), capital of Vladimir oblast, W central European USSR, on the Klyazma River. A rail junction, it has industries producing machinery, tractors, chemicals, cotton textiles, and plastics. Founded in the early 12th cent. by Vladimir II of Kiev, it was (c.1157–1238) the capital of the grand duchy of Vladimir-Suzdal, which became the chief principality after the breakup of Kievan Russia. Vladimir was destroyed (1238) by the Mongols under Batu Khan, who killed the grand duke in battle. The dukes of Moscow emerged as the most powerful Russian princes, and in 1364 they acquired Vladimir; they assumed the title of grand dukes and for a time afterward had themselves crowned there. The city's landmarks include the Uspensky (Assumption) Cathedral (1158–61) with a museum of religious art and tombs of the early princes of Vladimir; the Demetrius Cathedral (1193–97); the Golden Gate, a city gate erected in 1164; and several monasteries built (12th–13th cent.) of white stone in the Vladimir-Suzdal style (see RUSSIAN ART AND ARCHITECTURE).

Vladimir-Volynski (vlədyē'mĭr-vəlĭn'skē), Pol. *Włodzimierz,* city (1967 est. pop. 23,000), W European USSR, in the Ukraine. One of the oldest Ukrainian settlements, it was founded in the 9th cent. and supposedly refounded in 988 by the Grand Duke Vladimir I of Kiev. It became an Eastern Orthodox bishopric and the capital of the grand duchy of Vladimir or Lodomeria. The settlement was fortified and became a large trading center between the 10th and 13th cent. Originally dependent on Kiev, the duchy became independent in 1154 and for some time included all of VOLHYNIA. It was united with the duchy of Galich in 1188 to form the Galich-Volhynian duchy, of which it was the capital from 1300. The city passed to Lithuania in the late 14th cent. It changed hands often, but finally went to Russia in 1795. The Treaty of Riga (1921) awarded the city to Poland, but it was included in the Ukraine in 1939. Notable architectural monuments are the Mstyslavsky or Uspensky Cathedral (1157–60), remains of old fortress walls (12th–13th cent.), a rotunda church (13th–14th cent.), and a 16th-century bishop's palace (restored in the 19th cent.).

Vladislav (vlä'dyĭsläf), Czech version of the name Ladislaus. Two kings of Bohemia who were thus named were Vladislav I (who was LADISLAUS V, king of Hungary) and Vladislav II (who was ULADISLAUS II, king of Hungary).

Vladivostok (vlă"dĭvŏ'stŏk, –vəstŏk', Rus. vlä"-dyēvəstôk'), city (1970 pop. 442,000), capital of Primorsky Kray (Maritime Territory), Far Eastern USSR, on a peninsula that extends between two bays of the Sea of Japan. It is the chief Soviet port on the Pacific (kept open in winter by icebreakers), the terminus of the Trans-Siberian RR and the Northern Sea Route, the chief base of the Soviet navy in the Pacific, and a base for fishing and whaling fleets. The city has large shipyards, chemical and engineering factories, fish canneries, and food plants. The Russians founded a military post on the site in 1860, and it became an important outpost for Russian expansion in the Far East. Vladivostok became capital of Primorsky Kray in 1888 and grew rapidly after the completion (1903) of the Trans-Siberian RR. It developed as a naval base after the loss (1905) of Port Arthur to Japan. In World War I the Allies used the city as a major supply depot, and after the Russian Revolution of 1917 they occupied it. Most of the occupying forces were Japanese, but there were also about 7,500 Americans and contingents of British, Italian, and French troops. By 1920, when Vladivostok was included in the newly proclaimed Far Eastern Republic, the Japanese continued to occupy the region and installed a counterrevolutionary Russian puppet government. By 1922 all the interventionist forces had withdrawn and the city came under Soviet control. In World War II, Vladivostok was a major port for lend-lease supplies. The city is the chief Soviet cultural center in the Far East. Among its many educational institutions are the Far Eastern branch of the Soviet Academy of Sciences and the Far Eastern University (reopened 1956). Russians and Ukrainians comprise most of the city's population.

Vlaminck, Maurice de (mōrēs' də vlămăNk'), 1876–1958, French painter, writer, and printmaker. At first an avid racing cyclist, he supported himself (c.1900) as a musician and taught himself to paint. Vlaminck early adopted the strident palette and twisted lines of Van Gogh. He rejected the intellectual approach of CUBISM, but became associated with FAUVISM, applying exuberant colors to the canvas directly from the paint tube. Vlaminck was one of the first artists to be influenced by African sculpture. He advanced from the fauvist style to paint strong, often grim landscapes (e.g., *Village in the Snow,* Philadelphia Mus. of Art). He repeated these so often that they lost much of their original power. Vlaminck also wrote several novels and books of reminiscences. See his autobiography tr. by M. Ross (1967); illustrated biographies by P. MacOrlan (1958) and J. Selz (1963).

Vlissingen (vlĭs'ĭng-ən) or **Flushing** (flŭsh'ĭng), city (1971 pop. 41,085), Zeeland prov., SW Netherlands, on the southern coast of the former island of WALCHEREN. It has oil refineries, shipyards, machinery factories, and iron and steel plants and is an important port for traffic with England. Chartered in 1247, Vlissingen was one of the first Dutch towns to rebel (1572) against Spain. Because it dominates the approach (via the Western Scheldt) to Antwerp, Vlissingen has been the scene of several battles. During World War II the Allies captured (1944) the city from the Germans after bitter fighting.

Vlona or **Vlonë:** see VLORË, Albania.

Vlorë (vlô'rə) or **Valona** (vəlō'nə), city (1970 pop. 50,000), capital of Vlorë prov., SW Albania, on Vlorë Bay of the Adriatic Sea. Vlorë is a major seaport and a commercial center. Its industries produce foodstuffs, leather products, cement, and tobacco products. A commercial fishing fleet is based at Vlorë. Petroleum, natural gas, bitumen, and salt deposits are found nearby. The Stalin (Kuçovë) oil field near Berat is linked to Vlorë by pipeline. Vlorë Bay, strategically located at the mouth of the Adriatic Sea, has long been the site of military installations. In the 5th cent. Vlorë became an episcopal see. The city was prominent in the struggle (11th–12th cent.) between the Normans of Sicily and the Byzantines. It passed to Serbia in 1345 and to the Ottoman Empire in 1464; it was held by the Turks until 1912 when Albanian independence was proclaimed there. Vlorë was occupied by the Italians from 1914 to 1920 and from 1939 to 1944; it was bombed during World War II. It is also known as Vlonë, Vlona, and Vlora.

Vlotslavsk: see WŁOCŁAWEK, Poland.

Vltava (vəl'tävä), Ger. *Moldau,* longest river of Czechoslovakia, c.270 mi (430 km) long, rising in the Bohemian Forest, SW Czechoslovakia, and flowing SE, then N, past České Budějovice and Prague, to the Elbe River at Mělník. There are several large hydroelectric stations on the river; Orlická Dam (300 ft/91 m high; opened 1964) has a 330,000-kw generating capacity.

vocal cords: see LARYNX.

vocational education, training designed to advance an individual's general proficiency, especially in relation to his present or future occupation. The term does not normally include training for the professions. Prior to the Industrial Revolution, the APPRENTICESHIP system and the home were the principal sources of vocational education. Since then society has been forced by the decline of handwork and the specialization of occupational functions to develop institutions of vocational education. Manual training, involving general instruction in the use of hand tools, developed initially in Scandinavia (c.1866) in response to the doctrines of Friedrich Froebel and Johann Pestalozzi. It became popular in the elementary schools of the United States after 1880. While the immediate object of this training was not vocational, it developed gradually into extended courses in industrial training. Courses in bookkeeping, stenography, and allied commercial work in both public and private institutions were other early forms of vocational education. Among the early private trade schools were Cooper Union (1859) and Pratt Institute (1887). Hampton Institute (1868) and Tuskegee Institute (1881) were pioneers in industrial, agricultural, and home economics training for Negroes. The agricultural high school (1888) of the Univ. of Minnesota was the first regularly established public vocational secondary school and introduced extensive public instruction in agriculture. Since 1900 the number of public and private vocational schools has greatly increased. Under the Smith-Hughes Act (1917) the Federal government agreed to assist states in financing industrial, home economics, and agricultural courses. This aid was extended in the George-Deen Act (1936) to include teacher education and training for certain other occupations. The Manpower Development Training Act (1962), the Vocational Education Act (1963), and the Vocational Education Amendments (1968) were a series of Federal bills designed to upgrade the nation's work force and extend vocational training to disadvantaged youth. Large communities frequently have separate public schools devoted to specific occupational fields, and some counties and states sponsor regional vocational training establishments. These public schools work closely with interested industries and trades in establishing curricula and in GUIDANCE programs. The cooperative training technique, in which the student works part time in the job for which he is preparing, is a common feature of these schools. COMMUNITY COLLEGES often provide vocational training courses. Many industries have instituted extensive vocational education programs for their employees, and virtually all trades require apprenticeship and on-the-job training. Vocational correspondence courses in great numbers were formed to meet the growing demand for training. Many of these were poorly designed and without value, but were improved under the informal supervision of the National Home Study Council (1926) working with the Federal Trade Commission. Advances in the techniques of vocational education were made by the armed services during World War II. The need for technicians was so great that civilian life could not supply them, and special training methods stressing graphic presentation and practical work were used to meet the demand. Further impetus to vocational training resulted from the Servicemen's Readjustment Act of 1944 (popularly, the G. I. Bill of Rights), which allowed World War II veterans to receive tuition and subsistence during extended vocational training. Subsequent bills have provided funds for the vocational education of veterans of the Korean and Vietnam wars. Theorists in vocational training have emphasized that its aim is to improve the worker's general culture as well as to further his technical training. That policy is evident in the academic requirements of public vocational schools and in the work of public continuation and evening schools. Various academic courses are provided so that workers who have not completed the public school requirements may do so while engaged on regular jobs. In some localities attendance at continuation schools is compulsory for those who are of school age. While continuation and evening schools are often primarily vocational, they frequently include general courses that attract older workers. Labor organizations also have established vocational and cultural centers for their members. See SCHOOL and PROGRAMMED INSTRUCTION. See publications of the U.S. Office of Education; Alfred Kähler and Ernest Hamburger, *Education for an Industrial Age* (1948); F. J. Keller, *The Double-Purpose High School* (1953, repr. 1970); R. W. Roberts, *Vocational and Practical Arts Education* (3d ed. 1971); Rupert N. Evans, *Foundations of Vocational Education* (1971); *Vocational Education: Today and Tomorrow* (ed. by Gerald G. Somers and J. Kenneth Little, 1971).

vocational guidance: see GUIDANCE.

vocative (vŏk'ətĭv) [Lat.,=calling], in the grammar of certain languages (e.g., Latin), the CASE referring to a person addressed. In English a special intonation expresses the vocative, as in *Look, Jack.*

Vodena, Greece: see EDHESSA.

vodka (vŏd'kə), traditional spirituous drink of Russia, the Baltic states, and Poland; it is now consumed internationally. The best vodka is distilled from rye and barley malt, but the cheaper maize and potatoes are commonly employed. The high alcoholic strength of over 90% is generally diluted before marketing. A characteristic of vodka is that it has little or no distinctive odor or taste.

Vogau, Boris Andreyevich: see PILNYAK, BORIS.

Vogler, Georg Joseph (gā'ôrkh yō'zĕf fō'glər), 1749–1814, German composer and organist, known as Abbé Vogler. He traveled widely, giving organ concerts and demonstrating his innovations in organ construction. In 1775 he went to Mannheim as court chaplain and was court music director at Stockholm (1786–89) and at Darmstadt (1807–14). Vogler composed operas, organ music, masses and other church music, and some instrumental music. He was the teacher of Meyerbeer and Weber. Robert Browning idealized him in his poem "Abt Vogler."

Vogüé, Eugène Marie Melchior, vicomte de (ōzhĕn' mārē' mĕlkyôr' vēkôNt' də vôgüā'), 1848–1910, French critic. He fought in the Franco-Prussian War and was imprisoned for six months at Magdeburg. He served (1876–82) in the embassy at St. Petersburg and became interested in Russian literature. Preferring romanticism to naturalism, Vogüé wrote a series of essays, *Le Roman russe* (1886, tr. *The Russian Novel,* 1913), which introduced Russian novelists to France and had a wide influence on French literary thought.

voice, sound produced by living beings. The source of the sound in human speaking and singing is the vibration of the vocal cords, which are inside the LARYNX, and the production of the sounds is called phonation. The vocal cords are set into vibration by air from the lungs that moves through the windpipe passing over them, and they in turn produce resonance in the column of air enclosed by the pharynx. The mouth and throat are variable in size and shape, thus permitting alteration of vowel sound and PITCH. At puberty the vocal cords of the male become approximately double their original length, with the result that the average adult male voice is about an octave lower in pitch than the female. Not only is the voice man's principal means of communication, but it was undoubtedly his first musical instrument. The principal difference between singing and speaking is that in singing the vowel sounds are sustained and given definite pitch. Despite the innate and natural quality of singing, the training of the singing voice for artistic purposes is among the most subtle and difficult branches of music pedagogy. The instrument is within the performer, and the condition of the vocal apparatus, and thus the quality of the voice, is strictly dependent on the physical and mental condition of the singer. Since the vocal impulse cannot actually be described, the teacher's task is to provide the pupil with concepts, usually systematized into a vocal "method," that will free the vocal apparatus from restrictive tensions and lead ultimately to the complete coordination of all the faculties involved. Because of the great changes that have taken place in the art of singing within Western musical culture, modern singers can only approximate the vocal timbre of previous eras. Gregorian chant may have been sung with a nasal timbre resembling Oriental technique. The Neapolitan operatic school developed the virtuoso art of *bel canto,* in which brilliance of vocal technique was stressed rather than romantic expression or dramatic interpretation. The sound of the *castrato* (see EUNUCH), for which many 17th- and 18th-century soprano and alto roles were intended, is approached by several contemporary COUNTERTENORS using FALSETTO techniques. The foundation of the scientific study of the voice was laid in the middle of the 19th cent. by Manuel Patricio Rodríguez García, a successful voice teacher and writer, who invented the laryngoscope (used to examine the interior of the larynx). Singing voices are classified according to range as SOPRANO and contralto, the high and low female voices, with mezzo-soprano as an intermediate classification; and as TENOR and BASS, the high and low male voices, with BARITONE as an intermediate classification. Within these ranges there are specific designations of the quality of a voice, e.g., coloratura soprano. Choral music generally requires a range of about an octave and a half for each voice; a solo singer must have at least two octaves, and some have been known to possess ranges of three, even three and a half, octaves. See SONG. See Denis Stevens, ed., *A History of Song* (1960); Richard Luchsinger and G. E. Arnold, *Voice, Speech, Language* (1965); Robert Rushmore, *The Singing Voice* (1971).

voice, grammatical category according to which an action is referred to as done by the subject (active, e.g., *men shoot bears*) or to the subject (passive, e.g., *bears are shot by men*). In Latin, voice is a category of INFLECTION like mood or tense. In ancient Greek, verbs were conjugated in three voices: active, passive, and middle (reflexive).

Voice of America, broadcasting service of the United States Information Agency, est. 1942. It produces and broadcasts radio programs in English and foreign languages in order to promote a favorable impression of life in the United States in other, primarily Communist, countries. Programming includes news, reports from correspondents on the scene, and analysis of events from Washington, D.C., presentation of conflicting views on topical issues, feature programs, and music.

Voisin, La: see POISON AFFAIR.

Voiture, Vincent (văNsăN' vwätür'), 1597–1648, French man of letters and poet. He wrote in the precious manner of the salon of the Hôtel de Rambouillet, in which he was a leading figure.

Vojvodina or **Voivodina** (both: voi"vōdē'nä), autonomous province (1971 pop. 1,950,268), 8,301 sq mi (21,500 sq km), NE Yugoslavia, in Serbia. NOVI SAD is the chief city. A part of the great Danubian plain, it is watered by the Danube, the Tisza, and the Sava rivers and is one of the most densely populated and most prosperous parts of Yugoslavia. About 60% of the land is under cultivation. It is the breadbasket of Yugoslavia; fruit (notably plums, used for brandy), grapes, and vegetables are extensively cultivated. Cattle raising is also important, and food processing is the most significant industry. Besides Novi Sad, the chief cities are Subotica, Zrenjanin, Sombor, and Pančevo. The region was part of Hungary and Croatia before its conquest by the Turks in the 16th cent., and it was restored to the Hungarian crown by the Treaty of Passarowitz (1699). Parts of the region were included in the military frontier of S Hungary in the 18th cent., and the whole region was settled with Serbian and Croatian fugitives from the Ottoman Empire, as well as by German colonists. The present population is still mixed and includes Serbs, Croats, Magyars, Rumanians, and Slovaks. The region was ceded (1920) to Yugoslavia by the Treaty of Trianon, and it received autonomy in 1946. As constituted in 1946, the Vojvodina consists of three sections—the Srem, in the southwest, which was part of Croatia-Slavonia until 1918; the Backa, in the northwest, which was an integral part of Hungary; and the western part of the Banat of Temesvar.

volcano, aperture in the earth's crust through which gases, molten rock, or LAVA, and solid fragments are discharged. The term *volcano* is commonly applied both to the vent and to the conical mountain (cone) built up around the vent by the ejected rock materials. Usually the mountain has as its apex a cavity, or crater, in which is the mouth of the vent. Volcanoes are described as active, dormant, or extinct. About 500 are known to be active. Belts of volcanoes are found in the ocean along the crest of the mid-ocean ridge system (see SEA-FLOOR SPREADING). Belts of volcanoes also occur where a crustal plate is being subducted into the earth's interior along converging crustal plate boundaries (see PLATE TECTONICS). One such belt is associated with volcanic island arcs and ocean trenches surrounding the Pacific Ocean; another occurs along the north shore of the Mediterranean Sea and extends eastward through Asia Minor and the Himalayan mts. Isolated volcanoes in the mid-ocean area of the Pacific are apparently unrelated to crustal plate boundaries and have given rise to the abundant sea mounts and volcanic island chains, such as the Hawaiian chain. Volcanic eruptions may take one or more of four chief forms, or phases, known as Hawaiian, Strombolian, Vulcanian, and Peleean. In the Hawaiian phase there is a relatively quiet effusion of basaltic lava unaccompanied by explosions or the ejection of fragments; the eruptions of Mauna Loa on the island of Hawaii are typical. The Strombolian phase derives its name from the volcano Stromboli in the Lipari, or Aeolian, Islands, N of Sicily. It applies to continuous but comparatively mild discharges in which viscous lava is emitted in recurring explosions; the ejection of incandescent material produces luminous clouds. A more explosive volcanic eruption is the Vulcanian. In this phase the magma (lava before emission) accumulates in the upper level of the vent but is blocked by a plug of hardened lava that forms at the orifice between consecutive explosions. When the explosive gases have reached a critical pressure within the volcano, masses of solid and liquid rock erupt into the air and clouds of vapor form over the crater; unlike in the Strombolian phase the clouds are not incandescent. The Peleean is the most violent phase of volcanic action, manifesting emission of fine ash, hot, gas-charged fragments of lava, and superheated steam in an incandescent "cloud" that travels downhill at great speed. This phase derived its name from Mont Pelée, on Martinique, which erupted in this fashion in 1902; a series of violent explosions formed a cloud that annihilated all life in its path; finally the mountain itself was blown apart. Eruptions are often accompanied by torrential rains caused by the condensation of steam. The erupted fragments vary in size; they include minute particles of volcanic dust and ash, lapilli (cinders or pellets), bombs (rounded or ellipsoidal masses of hardened magma), and huge masses called blocks. Explosive eruptions build up steep-sided cones, while the nonexplosive ones usually form broad, low lava cones. Eruptions also occur under the sea. The soil resulting from decomposition of volcanic materials is extremely fertile, and the ash itself is a good polishing and cleansing agent. Notable eruptions within historic times have been those of Vesuvius, in Italy (A.D. 79); Jorullo, in Mexico (1759); Tamboro, in the East Indies, where between 30 and 50 cu mi (125–210 cu km) of molten and shattered rock were blown into the air (1815); Consequina, in Nicaragua, where 2½ cu mi (10.4 cu km) of ash hurled into the air darkened all Central America for two or three days; Krakatoa, near Java, material from which was sent 17 mi (27 km) into the atmosphere to be carried around the entire globe, causing unusually beautiful sunsets for several years afterward (1883); Bandai, in Japan (1888); Soufrière, on St. Vincent (1902); Santa Maria, in Guatemala (1902); Parícutin, in Mexico, the volcano that began in a cornfield (1943); Hibok Hibok, on Camiguin island in the Philippines, which killed 84 people (1948); Besymianny, in Kamchatka, USSR, where 2 cu mi (8 cu km) of material were hurled into the air (1956); the peak of Tristan da Cunha, whose eruption caused the entire settlement to be evacuated (1961); and Agung, in Bali, which killed 1,100 people (1963). Other notable volcanoes are Cotopaxi and Chimborazo (Ecuador), Izalco (El Salvador), Ixtacihuatl and Popocatepetl (Mexico), Lassen Peak and Katmai (United States), and Etna (Sicily). In 1963 the birth of a volcanic island near Iceland was observed. In November of that year events began with a submarine eruption along the Mid-Atlantic Ridge. In six months the originally submerged volcano had grown into a volcanic island, 1 mi (1.6 km) wide and c.600 ft (180 m) high, now named Surtsey. See F. M. Bullard, *Volcanoes in History, in Theory, in Eruption* (1962); Alfred Rittmann, *Volcanoes and Their Activity* (1962); G. A. MacDonald, *Volcanoes* (1972).

Volcano Islands, Jap. *Kazan-retto,* island group, c.11 sq mi (30 sq km), W Pacific. The group consists of three islands, of which IWO JIMA is the most important. The highest peak (3,181 ft/970 m) is on Minami-iwo-jima. There are sugarcane plantations and sulfur mines on the Volcano Islands. The inhabitants are Japanese, Koreans, and Formosans. Japanese fishermen and sulfur miners arrived in 1887, and Japan annexed the islands in 1891. Captured by U. S. forces in World War II, the islands were placed under U.S. administration from 1945 until 1968, when they were restored to Japan.

vole, name for a large number of mouselike RODENTS, related to the LEMMINGS. Most range in length from 3½ to 7 in. (9–18 cm) and have rounded bodies with gray or brown coats, blunt muzzles, small ears concealed in the long fur, and short tails. They are found in a wide variety of habitats. Of the approximately 70 vole species, over 40, distributed throughout North America, Eurasia, and North Africa, are classified in the genus *Microtus.* These voles typically make runways under dense vegetation or shallow burrows in the ground. They feed chiefly on grasses but also eat bark, leaves, seeds, and insects. They are known in North America as field mice or meadow mice (the Old World field mice are not voles). Like lemmings and various other small rodents, these voles periodically undergo population explosions which cause them to swarm over the countryside. Of similar distribution are the five species of red-backed voles, genus *Clethrionomys,* which spend much of their time in shrubs and bushes. Species of the North American genus *Phenacomys* nest in trees and are known as tree mice or lemming mice. The sagebrush vole, *Lagarus curtatus,* is found in the W United States. Other *Lagarus* species, found in S Russia and Mongolia, are misleadingly called steppe lemmings. The water vole, *Arvicola,* of Europe and W Asia, is a large, semiaquatic vole, somewhat resembling the closely related MUSKRAT. Voles are classified in the phylum CHORDATA, subphylum Vertebrata, class Mammalia, order Rodentia, family Crecetidae. See also MOUSE.

Volendam (vô"ləndäm'), town (1970 pop. c.12,000), North Holland prov., N central Netherlands, on the IJsselmeer, near Amsterdam. A picturesque town largely unchanged since the 17th cent., it is a famous tourist spot and is much frequented by artists.

Volga (vŏl'gə, Rus. vôl'gə), river, c.2,300 mi (3,700 km) long, central and E European USSR. It is the longest river of Europe and the principal waterway of the USSR, being navigable (with locks bypassing the dams) almost throughout its course. Its basin forms about one third of European USSR. Rising at an altitude of only 742 ft (226 m) in the Valday Hills, it winds E past Rzhev and Kalinin, through the RYBINSK RESERVOIR, and past Shcherbakov, Yaroslavl, Kostroma, and Gorky to Kazan, where it turns south and continues its broad, majestic course past Ulyanovsk, Kuybyshev, Saratov, and Volgograd. From Volgograd (c.300 mi/480 km upstream) the Volga River flows in a course below sea level through the Caspian lowland. There a distributary parallels the mainstream and is connected with the Volga by numerous channels. The Volga enters the Caspian Sea through a wide delta below Astrakhan. The Volga's chief tributaries are the Oka, Sura, Vetluga, Kama, and Samara rivers. The VOLGA-BALTIC WATERWAY links the Volga with the Baltic Sea and with the Baltic-White Sea Canal; the Volga-Don Canal links the Volga with the Azov and Black Seas; the Moscow Canal connects it directly with Moscow. In its upper course the Volga traverses numerous lakes. Below Gorky it broadens considerably and is lined on its right (western) bank by the bluffs of the Volga Hills, which contrast sharply with the steppe that extends from the left bank. The Zhiguli Mts. cause the river to make a sharp bend (the Samara Bend), which reaches its easternmost point at Kuybyshev. The Volga is navigable from late April to late November at Shcherbakov and from early March to mid-December at Astrakhan. A tranquil, regular stream, it has a flood stage in May and June and a low-water stage in the late summer, when shoals and sandbars impede navigation. Numerous dams and reservoirs have been constructed in the Volga basin for flood control, improved navigation, irrigation, and hydroelectric power. There are many important hydroelectric stations, notably at Uglich, at Shcherbakov, and at Ivankovo, all along the upper Volga. At Ivankovo, NW of Moscow, a dam creates the vast Volga Reservoir or Moscow Sea, covering an area of c.125 sq mi (320 sq km); this is connected with the Moskva River by the Moscow Canal. Large hydroelectric stations have been built at Gorky, Kuybyshev, Kama, Volgograd, and Votkinsk. The chief ports are Kalinin, Gorky, Kazan, Kuybyshev, Volgograd, Astrakhan, Saratov, Yaroslavl, and Rybinsk. The Volga has played an incalculably important part in the life of the Russian people, and it is characteristically named in Russian folklore, "Mother Volga." For centuries it has served as the chief thoroughfare of Russia and as the lifeline of Russian colonization to the east. It carries one half of the total river freight of the USSR and irrigates the vast steppes of the lower Volga region. Grain, oil (chiefly from Baku, shipped across the Caspian Sea), salt, fish, and caviar (from the Volga delta and the Caspian Sea) are shipped upstream; lumber is the main commodity shipped downstream. The Volga was known to the ancient Greeks as the Rha, but little was known about the river until the early Middle Ages, when Slavic tribes settled along its upper course, the Bulgars (see BULGARS, EASTERN) along its middle course, and the KHAZARS in the south. Its importance as a trade route dates from that time. The Russians soon extended their control as far as Nizhny Novgorod (Gorky), founded in 1221. The Mongol invasion of the 13th cent. resulted in the direct control by the Golden Horde of the Volga below Nizhny Novgorod and in the creation (15th cent.) of the Tatar khanates of KAZAN and ASTRAKHAN, which fell to Moscow only in the 16th cent. Sarai, on the Volga River near modern Volgograd, was the capital of the empire of the Golden Horde. The conquest of these territories was largely the work of the Cossacks, who used the Volga and its tributaries for their epic forays into Siberia (under Yermak in the 16th cent.) and into the Caspian Sea (under Stenka Razin, in the 17th cent.). Many of the Finnic and Turco-Tatar nationalities still live in the middle and lower Volga regions, notably in the Chuvash ASSR, the Mari ASSR, the Mordvinian ASSR, the Tatar ASSR, and the Udmurt ASSR. The Kalmyrs settled in the lower Volga region in the early 17th cent. The lower Volga was the center of the great peasant rebellions under Stenka Razin and Pugachev. After their suppression Catherine II settled many German colonists in the region around Saratov.

Volga-Baltic Waterway, canal and river system, c.685 mi (1,100 km) long, N European USSR. It links the Volga River and the Leningrad industrial area. It consists of the Moscow-Volga Canal, the VOLGA River, the RYBINSK RESERVOIR, the Mariinsk system (composed of the Sheksna River, the White Lake Canal, the Kovzha River, the Mariinsk Canal, and the Vytegra River), the Onega Canal, the Svir River, the Ladoga Canals, and the Neva River to Leningrad. The waterway was begun in 1709 to connect St. Petersburg with the interior. The major canals were built in the 1930s. The waterway has been reconstructed and modernized (reopened May, 1964), the principal addition being a dam across the Sheksna River near Cherepovets, which deepened the waterway as far as the Kovzha River, facilitating the use of larger vessels. Although more extensive, this waterway follows the historic Baltic-Volga trade route, in use since the 9th cent.

Volgograd (vôlgəgrät'), formerly **Stalingrad,** city (1970 pop. 818,000), capital of Volgograd oblast, SE European USSR, a port on the Volga River and the eastern terminus of the Volga-Don Canal. As a transshipment point, the port handles oil, coal, ore, lumber, and fish. Volgograd is also a major rail center, with connections to Moscow, the Donets Basin, the Caucasus, and SW Siberia. One of the world's largest hydroelectric power dams stands on the Volga just above the city. A center of heavy industry, Volgograd has shipyards, oil refineries, iron, steel, and aluminum mills, and tank, tractor, cable, machinery, and chemical factories. Other industries include food processing, flour milling, distilling, sawmilling, tanning, and the manufacture of farm and oilfield equipment. Founded in 1589 as a stronghold to defend Russia's newly acquired land along the Volga, the city was originally called Tsaritsyn. It fell to the Cossack rebels under Stenka Razin in 1670 and Yemelyan Pugachev in 1774. In the 19th cent. it became an important commercial center. During the Russian civil war the city was defended (1918) by Soviet forces under Stalin, Voroshilov, and Budenny, but White troops under Denikin took it in 1919–20. The city was named Stalingrad in 1925. It was virtually destroyed during World War II in a battle that marked a major turning point in the war and a landmark in military history. In Sept., 1942, a German army exceeding 500,000 men (including Italians, Hungarians, and Rumanians) and commanded by Gen. Friedrich von Paulus began an all-out attack on Stalingrad, which was defended by 16 Soviet divisions under Gen. Vasily I. Chuikov. Stalin ordered that the city be held at all costs. After two months of house-to-house fighting, the Germans had taken most of the city; but the Soviet garrison, receiving supplies from the east bank of the Volga, continued to hold out, thus giving Gen. Grigori Zhukov time to prepare a counter-offensive. Hitler reaffirmed his intention to take Stalingrad, despite great losses and lack of reserves. He refused, against the advice of his general staff, to allow Paulus to withdraw. In Nov., 1942, two Soviet forces, advancing from the north and south in a pincers movement, encircled the Germans. In December a German relief force was routed. Paulus surrendered the remnants of his army on Feb. 2, 1943. The combined German and Soviet losses during the battle were staggering—the Germans alone suffered approximately 300,000 casualties. The Soviets followed up their victory with a mighty westward drive and generally remained on the offensive for the remainder of the war. Rebuilding of Stalingrad began immediately after the city's liberation. It was renamed Volgograd in 1961, following Nikita Khrushchev's renewed denunciations of Stalin's dictatorship.

Volhynia (vŏlĭ'nyə), Rus. *Volyn,* Pol. *Wołyń,* historic region, SW European USSR, in the Ukraine, around the headstreams of the Pripyat and Western Bug rivers in an area of forests, lakes, and marshlands. One of the oldest Slavic settlements in Europe, it derived its name from the extinct city of Volyn or Velyn, said to have stood on the Western Bug. Volhynia's early history from c.981 coincides with that of the duchies of Vladimir (see VLADIMIR-VOLYNSKY) and Galich. After the disintegration (c.1340) of the grand duchy of Galich-Vladimir, Volhynia was divided (c.1388) between Poland (western part) and Lithuania (eastern part). With the Polish-Lithuanian union of 1569,

Volhynia became a quasi-autonomous province of Poland. During the second and third partitions of Poland (1793, 1795), Volhynia passed to Russia and was made (1797) a province. In 1921 the Treaty of Riga returned W Volhynia to Poland, but the rest passed to the Ukraine. Poland ceded its section of Volhynia to the USSR in 1939, and the Soviet-Polish border agreement of 1945 confirmed it as a Soviet possession. This section now constitutes the Volyn oblast, a rich agricultural lowland and coal-mining area.

Volk, Leonard Wells, 1828–95, American sculptor, b. Wellstown (now Wells), N.Y. In 1848 he went to St. Louis, where he studied drawing and worked at funerary sculpture. With the aid of Stephen A. Douglas he studied in Rome, and in 1857 he opened a studio in Chicago. He closely studied both Lincoln and Douglas during their famous debates and also made a life mask of Lincoln and casts of his hands. A leading figure in the Chicago art world, Volk was active in founding the Chicago Academy of Design. His colossal Douglas monument is in Chicago, and statues of Lincoln and Douglas are in the capitol at Springfield, Ill. He executed many portrait busts and military monuments.

Vollard, Ambroise (äNbrwäz' vôlär'), 1867–1939, French art dealer, collector, and publisher. He was noted for his early recognition and sponsorship of leading artists of the SCHOOL OF PARIS, especially Van Gogh, Cézanne, Matisse, Picasso (for whom he held the first one-man exhibitions), and Rouault. He made numerous comparatively small but very fortunate investments when there was no market for the works of these and other artists destined for tremendous fame. He accumulated their works for years and slowly sold them to eager collectors and dealers, thus acquiring great wealth. Vollard's interest in publishing dated from the beginning of his career. His *Albums des peintres-graveurs* (1896–99) and *Parallèlement* (1900) included prints by most of the major French masters working at that time. Thereafter he concentrated on the production of fine editions illustrated with original prints by Picasso, Dufy, Redon, Rouault, and others, works that are now highly prized by collectors and museums. Vollard wrote anecdotal biographies of his friends Cézanne, Renoir, and Degas, as well as the autobiographical *Recollections of a Picture Dealer* (tr. 1936).

volleyball, outdoor or indoor ball and net game played on a level court. An upright net, the top of which stands 8 ft (2.44 m) from the ground, divides the court—60 ft (18.29 m) long and 30 ft (9.14 m) wide—in half. Smaller courts are generally used when women or children play the game. Three forwards and three backs, covering equal areas of the court, compose a volleyball team. The inflated rubber or leather volleyball, about 27 in. (69 cm) in circumference, is served from behind the back lines of the court. The ball is batted with the open hand or fist and must clear the top of the net; it may go into any part of the opponents' court. Only one try is allowed on the serve. The ball must be returned without allowing it to touch the ground and must be volleyed within the boundaries of the court. Any part of the body may be used to bat the ball, and a maximum of three hits (in passing the ball from player to player on one team) is permitted before the ball is returned. Only the team that is serving scores, and if the receiving team wins the volley, it gains the next serve after the players rotate their positions clockwise. The team scoring 15 points first wins the game, but if the score is tied at 14, the first team to lead by two points wins. Volleyball was originated (1895) by William G. Morgan at Holyoke, Mass. The game was fostered by the Young Men's Christian Association in its early years, but since 1928 the governing body in the United States has been the U.S. Volleyball Association. The association is a charter member of the International Volleyball Federation (founded 1947). In 1955 volleyball was included in the Pan American games, and since 1964 it has been included in the Olympic games. See W. H. Peck, *Volleyball* (1970).

Volney, Constantin François de Chasseboeuf, comte de (kôNstäNtäN' fräNswä' də shäsbôf' kôNt də vôlnā'), 1757–1820, French scholar. He traveled in Egypt and Syria in the 1780s and wrote an account of his journey, *Voyage en Syrie et en Égypte* (1787); notable for its exact descriptions, it was useful to Napoleon during his Egyptian campaign. Volney served as deputy (1789) to the States-General, as secretary (1790) of the National Assembly, and later, after spending some time in the United States, as senator under Napoleon, who made him a count in 1808; he was also a member of the chamber of peers under Louis XVIII. His principal work, *Les Ruines; ou, Méditation sur les révolutions des empires* (1791), which popularized religious skepticism, was influential not only in France but also in England and the United States; it went through many translations and editions and stimulated much controversy. His writings also include works on the United States, on ancient history, and on Arabic.

Vologda (vô'ləgdə), city (1970 pop. 178,000), N central European USSR, on the Vologda River. It is a major river and rail junction in a dairying region. There are shipyards, machine factories, lumber mills, and flax-processing plants. Vologda is famed for its lace. Founded in 1147 by merchants from Novgorod, it passed to Moscow in the 15th cent. and was from the 15th to 17th cent. a major trade center and transit point to NE Russia, Siberia, and W Europe. It declined in the 18th cent. but revived in the late 19th cent. with the development of the lumber industry and the coming of the railroad. In Vologda's old kremlin are the 18th-century bishop's palace and the Cathedral of St. Sophia, built (1568–70) by Ivan IV. The Spasso-Priluki monastery (founded 1371) is nearby.

Vólos (vô'lôs), city (1971 pop. 51,290), capital of Magnisia prefecture, E Greece, in Thessaly, on the Gulf of Vólos, an inlet of the Aegean Sea. The principal port of Thessaly, Vólos is a transportation, commercial, and industrial center. Its leading exports are tobacco, wheat, wine, and olives. Vólos is located near the sites of the ancient towns of Pagasae and Demetrias. It was known as Gholos under Ottoman rule and was modernized after it passed to Greece in 1881. An earthquake in 1955 damaged much of the city.

Volscians (vŏl'shənz) or **Volsci** (vŏl'sī), people of ancient Italy. They occupied the country SE of the Alban Hills. They were early opponents of the Romans and Latins, and the story of CORIOLANUS reflects the fierceness of the Volscian attacks on Rome. Warfare apparently continued from the 6th cent. B.C. until the 4th cent. B.C., when the Volscians were conquered and Romanized.

Volsinii (vŏlsĭn'ēī), ancient city of Etruria, Italy, probably on the site of modern Orvieto. It was a powerful member of the Etruscan League, and the spirit of the league was broken when Romans conquered and thoroughly sacked Volsinii in 280 B.C. A new Volsinii was founded near Lacus Volsiniensis (Lake Bolsena).

Volsk (vôlsk), city (1970 pop. 69,000), S central European USSR, a port on the Volga River. It has food and metal processing and cement industries.

Volstead, Andrew Joseph (vŏl'stĕd), 1860–1947, American legislator, b. Goodhue co., Minn. A lawyer, he held several local offices in Minnesota before serving (1903–23) in the U.S. House of Representatives. He sponsored many measures in Congress and became a national figure as the author of the **Volstead Act.** That federal prohibition act, passed in 1919 over the veto of President Wilson, made provisions for the enforcement of the Eighteenth Amendment. The act defined an intoxicating beverage as one containing more than .5% alcohol by volume. It also gave Federal agents the power to investigate and prosecute violations of the amendment. The act was modified (1933) in order to permit the sale of 3.2% beer and wine, and became void after the repeal of the Eighteenth Amendment late in 1933. See J. A. Krout, *Origins of Prohibition* (1925, repr. 1967); Andrew Sinclair, *Prohibition* (1962, repr. 1964).

Volsungasaga (vŏl'sŏŏng-gəsä'gə) [Icelandic, = saga of the Volsungs], Icelandic prose SAGA founded on earlier poetic materials, which are represented in Germany by the Nibelungenlied (see under NIBELUNGEN), and probably assembled late in the 13th cent. Its heroine is GUDRUN, who accomplishes the ruin of the Volsungs, the principal of whom is Sigurd (see SIEGFRIED). William Morris translated the saga and also based on it his story of *Sigurd the Volsung and the Fall of the Niblungs* (1876). See Stefan Einarsson, *History of Icelandic Literature* (1957).

volt [for Alessandro Volta], abbr. V, unit of voltage or more technically of electric potential and electromotive force. It is defined as the difference of electric potential existing across the ends of a conductor having a resistance of 1 ohm when the conductor is carrying a current of 1 ampere. The kilovolt (1,000 V), the millivolt (0.001 V), and the microvolt (0.000001 V) are units derived from the volt. See VOLTMETER.

Volta, Alessandro, Conte (älĕs-sän'drō kôn'tā vôl'tä), 1745–1827, Italian physicist. He was professor of physics at the Univ. of Pavia from 1779 and became famous for his work in electricity. Napoleon I made him a count and a senator of the kingdom of Lombardy. Volta invented the so-called Volta's pile (or voltaic pile); the ELECTROPHORUS; an electric CONDENSER; and the VOLTAIC CELL. The VOLT, a unit of electrical measurement, is named for Volta.

Volta (vól'tə), river, c.290 mi (470 km) long, formed in central Ghana, W Africa, by the confluence of the Black Volta (c.840 mi/1,350 km long) and the White Volta (c.450 mi/720 km long), both of which rise in Upper Volta. The river flows generally south, through a large delta, to the Gulf of Guinea at Ada. The Volta River system drains c.150,000 sq mi (388,500 sq km). Lake Volta (c.3,275 sq mi/8,480 sq km), one of the world's largest man-made lakes, extends c.280 mi (450 km) upstream behind Akosombo Dam, SE Ghana, in the Ajena Gorge. The dam (370 ft/113 m high; completed 1965), the principal unit of the Volta Development Project, regulates the flow of the Volta River, stores water for irrigation, and generates hydroelectricity (750,000-km capacity) that supports a large aluminum industry.

Volta, Lake, Ghana: see VOLTA, river.

voltage, term commonly used in place of ELECTROMOTIVE FORCE and POTENTIAL, ELECTRIC.

voltage divider: see POTENTIOMETER.

voltaic cell, a simple device with which chemical energy is converted into electrical energy. Two dissimilar metals (e.g., copper and zinc) are immersed in an electrolyte (e.g., a dissolved sulfate). If the metals are connected by an external circuit, one metal is reduced (i.e., gains electrons) while the other metal is oxidized (i.e., loses electrons). In the example above, copper is reduced and zinc is oxidized. The difference in the oxidation potentials of the two metals provides the electric power of the cell. The voltaic cell is sometimes also called the galvanic cell. The names refer to the 18th-century Italian scientists Alessandro Volta and Luigi Galvani.

Voltaire, François Marie Arouet de (fräNswä' märē' ärwā' də vôltĕr'), 1694–1778, French philosopher and author, whose original name was Arouet. One of the towering geniuses in literary and intellectual history, Voltaire personifies the ENLIGHTENMENT. The son of a notary, he was born at Paris and was educated at the Jesuit Collège Louis-le-Grand. Because of insults to the regent, Philippe II d'Orléans, wrongly ascribed to him, Voltaire was sent to the Bastille (1717) for 11 months. There he rewrote his first tragedy, *Œdipe (1718),* and began an epic poem on Henry IV, the *Henriade.* It was at this time that he began to call himself Voltaire. *Œdipe* won him fame and a pension from the regent. Voltaire acquired an independent fortune through speculation; he was often noted for his generosity, but displayed a shrewd business acumen throughout his life and became a millionaire. In 1726 a young nobleman, the chevalier de Rohan, resenting a witticism of Voltaire at his expense, had Voltaire beaten. Far from obtaining justice, Voltaire was imprisoned in the Bastille through the influence of the powerful Rohan family, and he was released only upon his promise to go to England. The episode left an indelible impression on Voltaire, who for the rest of his life exerted himself to his utmost in struggling against judicial arbitrariness. During his more than two years in England, Voltaire met, through his friend Lord Bolingbroke, the literary men of the period. He was impressed by the greater freedom of thought in England and was deeply influenced by Newton and Locke. Voltaire's *Letters concerning the English Nation* (1733, in English), which appeared (1734) in French as *Lettres philosophiques,* may be said to have initiated the vogue of English philosophy and science that characterized the literature of the Enlightenment. The book was formally banned in France. While in England, Voltaire wrote the first of his historical works, a history of Charles XII of Sweden, which remains a classic in biography. Returning to France in 1729, he produced several tragedies, among them *Brutus* (1730) and *Zaïre* (1732). In 1733 he met Mme Du Châtelet, the mathematician and physicist, whose interests, particularly in science, accorded with his own. They took up residence together at Cirey, in Lorraine, under the Marquis Du Châtelet's tolerant eye. The connection with Émilie Du Châtelet lasted until her death in 1749. At Cirey, Voltaire worked on physical and chemical experiments, began his long correspondence with Crown Prince Frederick of Prussia (later FREDERICK II), and wrote *Éléments de la philosophie* *de Newton* (1736); a burlesque treatment of the Joan of Arc legends, *La Pucelle* (1755); and the dramas *Mahomet* (1742), *Mérope* (1743) and *Sémiramis* (1748). Through the influence of Mme de Pompadour, Voltaire was made royal historiographer, gentleman of the king's bedchamber, and a member of the French Academy. He first visited Berlin in 1743 and after Mme Du Châtelet's death he accepted Frederick II's invitation to live at his court. His relations with Frederick, a man whose unbending nature matched his own, were generally stormy. Voltaire's interference in the quarrel between MAUPERTUIS and König led to renewed coldness on the part of Frederick, and in 1753 Voltaire hastily left Prussia. At a distance, the two men later became reconciled, and their correspondence was resumed. Unwelcome in France, Voltaire settled in Geneva, where he acquired the property "Les Délices"; he also acquired another house near Lausanne. The Genevese authorities soon objected to Voltaire's holding private theatrical performances at his home and still more to the article "Genève" written for Diderot's *Encyclopédie,* on Voltaire's instigation, by Alembert. The article, which declared that the Calvinist pastors of Geneva had seen the light and ceased to believe in organized religion, stirred up a violent controversy. Voltaire purchased (1758) an estate, Ferney (see FERNEY-VOLTAIRE), just over the French border, where he lived until shortly before his death. He conducted an extensive correspondence with most of the outstanding men and women of his time; received hosts of visitors who came to do homage to the "patriarch of Ferney"; employed himself in seeking justice for victims of religious or political persecution; contributed to the *Encyclopédie;* managed his estate; took an active interest in improving the condition of his tenants; edited the works of Corneille and wrote commentaries on Racine; and turned out a stream of anonymous novels and pamphlets in which he attacked the established institutions of his time with unremitting virulence. Ironically, it is one of these disavowed works, *Candide* (1759), that is most widely read today. It is the masterpiece among his "philosophical romances," which also include the inimitable short tale *Jeannot et Colin* (1764), perhaps the quintessence of Voltaire's style. In *Candide* Voltaire attacked the philosophical optimism made fashionable by Leibniz. Its conclusion, "Let us cultivate our garden" (instead of speculating on unanswerable problems), expresses succinctly Voltaire's practical philosophy of common sense. Voltaire attained the most subtly comical effects through an imperceptible turn of a phrase; his sentences flow with facility; his expressions are always felicitous and unlabored; his irony is as devastating as its touch is light. Brevity and lucidity characterize all his writings. The *Dictionnaire philosophique* (1764) is a compendium of Voltaire's thought on the most varied subjects. In his serious poetic works, the perfection of his style is usually combined with a coldness that has robbed them of lasting appeal, although they tower above those of other 18th-century imitators of Racine. Voltaire was significant in helping to introduce to the theater authentic costumes, and he labored successfully for the improvement of the social status of actors. In his philosophy, based on skepticism and rationalism, he was indebted to Locke as well as to Montaigne and Bayle. Despite Voltaire's passion for clarity and reason, he frequently contradicted himself. Thus he would maintain in one place that man's nature was as unchangeable as that of animals and would express elsewhere his belief in progress and the gradual humanization of society through the action of the arts, sciences, and commerce. In politics he advocated reform but had a horror of the ignorance and potential fanaticism of people and the violence of revolution. In religion Voltaire felt that Christianity was a good thing for chambermaids and tailors to believe in, but for the use of the elite he advocated a simple deism. He opposed the atheism and materialism of Helvétius and Holbach. His line, "If God did not exist, he would have to be invented," has become proverbial. His celebrated slogan, *Écrasez l'infâme!* [crush the infamous thing!], has been interpreted as addressed either against the church or against the *ancien régime* in general. Voltaire's influence in the popularization of the science and philosophy of his age was incalculably great. Perhaps his most lasting and original intellectual contribution was made in the field of history. His *Siècle de Louis XIV* (1751) embodies in part the ideas of his historical masterpiece, *Essai sur l'histoire générale et sur les mœurs et l'esprit des nations* (7 vol., 1756; tr. 1759), the first attempt at writing a history of the world as a whole; Voltaire laid as much emphasis on culture and commerce as on politics and war, and he avoided national parochialism. In 1778, his 84th year, Voltaire attended the first performance of his tragedy *Irène,* in Paris. His journey and his reception were a triumph and apotheosis, but the emotion was too much for him and he died in Paris soon afterward. In order to obtain Christian burial he signed a partial retraction of his writings. This was considered insufficient by the church, but he refused to sign a more general retraction. To a friend he gave the following written declaration: "I die adoring God, loving my friends, not hating my enemies, and detesting persecution." An abbot secretly conveyed Voltaire's corpse to an abbey in Champagne, where he was buried. His remains were brought back to Paris in 1791 and buried in the Panthéon. The first "complete" edition of Voltaire's work was the so-called Kehl edition, by Beaumarchais (70 vol. in octavo or 92 vol. in duodecimo, 1784–89); a later edition is that of M. Beuchot (72 vol., 1828–40; rev. and enl., 52 vol., 1883). Publication of a complete collection of Voltaire's huge correspondence was started in 1953 under the editorship of Theodore Besterman and is continuing. There are English translations of Voltaire's most widely read works. Biographies and studies of Voltaire reflect continued controversy as to Voltaire's real thought and beliefs. See biographies by Gustave Lanson (1906, in French; tr. by Robert A. Wagoner, 1966) and H. N. Brailsford (1935, repr 1963); studies by Peter Gay (1959) and V. W. Topazio (1966); René Pomeau, *La Religion de Voltaire* (1956, in French, new ed. 1969); Ira O. Wade, *Voltaire and Madame du Châtelet* (1941, repr. 1967) and *The Intellectual Development of Voltaire* (1969).

Volta Redonda (vôl'tä rĕdôN'dä), city (1970 pop. 120,645), Rio de Janeiro state, E Brazil, on the Paraíba River. Its proximity to sources of hydroelectricity and basic raw materials and to the industrial centers of Rio de Janeiro and São Paulo favored its selection as the site of a huge government-run steel mill. The city was founded in 1941, and construction of the steel mill began the following year, with production starting in 1946. Within a decade Volta Redonda, one of the most ambitious industrial projects in South America, was producing more than half of Brazil's ingots and rolled steel. Near the mills is a model residential community for the steel workers.

Volterra, Daniele da (dänyā'lā dä vōltĕr'rä), 1509–66, Italian mannerist painter and sculptor. His family name was Ricciarelli, but he was known by the name of his birthplace. He was active primarily in Rome, and his works reveal the influence of his friend Michelangelo, of whom he executed portraits in sculpture. His best-known painting is *Descent from the Cross* (c.1545; Trinità dei Monti, Rome). Other paintings include *Massacre of the Innocents* (1557; Uffizi) and *David Killing Goliath* (c.1555; Louvre). He was nicknamed Il Braghettone [breeches maker] because of his commission to paint clothes over the nudes in Michelangelo's *Last Judgment.*

Volterra, town (1971 pop. 15,824), Tuscany, central Italy. A powerful Etruscan town, it later (12th–13th cent.) was a free commune and passed to Florence in the 14th cent. Of note are well-preserved Etruscan gates and tombs, medieval walls, a Romanesque cathedral, and the Palazzo dei Priori (13th cent.). The powerful fortress (built 14th–15th cent.) is now a prison. There is an Etruscan museum in the town.

voltmeter, instrument used to measure differences of electric POTENTIAL, commonly called voltage, in volts or units that are multiples or fractions of volts. A voltmeter is usually combined with an ammeter and an ohmmeter in a multipurpose instrument. Most voltmeters are based on the d'Arsonval GALVANOMETER and are of the analog type, i.e., they give voltage readings that can vary over a continuous range as indicated by a scale and pointer. However, digital voltmeters, which provide voltage readings that are composed of a group of digits, are becoming increasingly common. Since an oscilloscope is capable of giving a calibrated visual indication of voltage, it can be called a voltmeter. See also POTENTIOMETER.

Volturno (vōltōōr'nō), chief river of S Italy, 109 mi (175 km) long, rising in the Apennines of Molise and flowing SE, then SW through Campania, past Capua, to the Tyrrhenian Sea. On its banks Guiseppe Garibaldi defeated (1860) the troops of Francis II of the Two Sicilies.

volume, measure of solid content or capacity, usually expressed in units that are the cubes of linear units, such as cubic inches and cubic centimeters, or in units of dry and liquid measure, such as bushels, gallons, and liters.

FORMULAS FOR THE VOLUMES OF SOME COMMON SOLIDS

Solid	*Volume**	*Solid*	*Volume**
cube	l^3	right rectangular parallelepiped	lwh
prism	Bh	right circular cylinder	$\pi r^2 h$
pyramid	$\frac{1}{3}Bh$	right circular cone	$\frac{1}{3}\pi r^2 h$
sphere	$\frac{4}{3}\pi r^3$		

* Abbreviations: B=area of base; h=height; r=radius; l=length; w=width.

Volunteers of America, nonsectarian, nondenominational, religious and philanthropic organization, founded (1896) by General and Mrs. Ballington Booth (see BOOTH, family) after their withdrawal from the Salvation Army. The Volunteers' aim is to act as auxiliary to the churches; converts won by evangelistic efforts are urged to join the denomination of their preference. They also conduct worship services, missions, and Sunday schools where needed. Ministration to social and physical needs has developed into an extensive system of welfare activities, including day-care centers, employment centers, fresh-air camps, maternity homes, hostels for women, clubs and homes for the aged, and services to prisoners. The Volunteers have a democratic form of government, although the society is military in its titles, uniforms, and movements of officers. The organization has its headquarters in New York City and is supported by voluntary contributions.

Volyn: see VOLHYNIA, USSR.

vomiting, ejection of food and other matter from the stomach through the mouth, often preceded by NAUSEA. The process is initiated by stimulation of the vomiting center of the brain by nerve impulses from the gastrointestinal tract or other part of the body. The vomiting center then sends out nerve impulses that precipitate spasmodic muscular contractions of the stomach wall and downward spasms of the diaphragm. The pressure generated then forces up the contents of the stomach. The vomiting mechanism may be in response to local irritation (diseases or disorders of the gastrointestinal tract, overburdening of the capacity and digestive capabilities of the stomach, ingestion of harmful foods or substances). It may also result from a metabolic disturbance (as in pregnancy) or from disorders or stimulation of the nervous system (e.g., migraine, motion sickness, infectious disease, brain tumor or injury, disagreeable odors). Vomiting may also be a reflex action to other spasmodic conditions (whooping cough, gagging).

Von. For some German names beginning thus, see under the proper name; e.g., for Von Bismarck, see BISMARCK, OTTO VON.

von Braun, Wernher (vôn broun), 1912–, American rocket expert, b. Germany, grad. Berlin Technological Institute (B.S., 1932), Ph.D. Univ. of Berlin, 1934. After 1930, von Braun assisted Hermann Oberth in early experiments in building and firing small liquid fuel rockets. From 1937 to 1945, von Braun was technical director of the German rocket research center at Peenemünde and was research professor there from 1943. At Peenemünde he was responsible for the successful development of the German V-2 liquid fuel rocket and also for other rocket weapons. At the close of World War II, von Braun was brought to the United States, and from 1945 to 1950 he was technical adviser at the White Sands Proving Grounds and also project director at Fort Bliss, Texas. He went to Huntsville, Ala., in 1950, first as chief of the guided missile development division, Redstone Arsenal (1950–56), and then as director of the development operations division of the Army Ballistic Missile Agency (now the George C. Marshall Space Flight Center), where he developed rockets for the manned lunar program. In 1970 he became deputy associate administrator of the National Aeronautics and Space Administration. Von Braun has been an ardent advocate of rocket development and space flight since the days of his youth. He became a U.S. citizen in 1955. His writings include *Across the Space Frontier* (1952), *The Exploration of Mars,* with Willy Ley (1956), and *First Men to the Moon* (1960). See biography by H. M. David (1967).

Vondel, Joost van den (yōst vän dĕn vôn'dəl), 1587–1679, Dutch poet and dramatist, b. Cologne. He is generally considered the greatest Dutch writer. During the emergence of the Dutch nation Vondel was the national poet; his occasional verse celebrated the triumphs of the United Provinces in a vigorous oratorical style. In 1621 he fell victim to a sort of manic-depressive melancholia which may have hindered his work for a while. His drama *Palamedes* (1625), concerning a contemporary religious-political martyrdom, made him suspect to the Calvinist officials. At this time he joined the Remonstrants, whose Arminian opposition to dogmatic Calvinism appealed to him, and later, when national independence was virtually assured, he converted (c.1641) to Roman Catholicism as a more universal faith. Many poems were inspired by his conversion and also by his grief at the death of his wife (1635) and of three of his five children. Vondel's verse is melodious, sonorous, and seemingly effortless and spontaneous; it is marked by vowel elision, which he brought into full use in Dutch poetry, and by rhythmic patterns reminiscent of the French. His dramatic style has been called high baroque. Built on the medieval mystery play and on classical models, his plays are Christian and semitragic and illuminate a recurring theme—the conflict between man's will to rebel and his desire to give himself to God. Probably the most famous are *Gysbrecht van Aemstil* (1637), on a medieval Dutch theme, and the magnificent *Lucifer* (1654, tr. 1898), which may have influenced Milton. Vondel's immense production includes numerous translations from French, Latin, Italian, and Greek, including works of Sophocles, Euripides, Vergil, Ovid, Horace, Seneca, and Tasso. See A. J. Barnouw, *Vondel* (1925).

Vo Nguyen Giap: see GIAP, VO NGUYEN.

Vonnegut, Kurt, Jr. (vŏn'əgət) 1922–, American novelist, b. Indianapolis, Ind. After serving in World War II, he worked as a police reporter. During the late 1960s, Vonnegut was considered the most popular writer on college campuses. In his works he protests the horrors of the 20th cent.—mass death, dehumanization, pollution of the environment—and recommends a turn toward peace and love. Often labeled science fiction, his novels have fantastic plots, involving trips in outer space, time faults, and apocalyptic destruction. Vonnegut treats his grim themes with wry charm and dark humor. His works of fiction include *Player Piano* (1951), *Mother Night* (1962), *Cat's Cradle* (1963), *Welcome to the Monkey House* (1969), *Slaughterhouse Five* (1969), and *Breakfast of Champions* (1973). *Wampeters, Foma and Granfalloons* (1974) is a collection of essays.

Von Neumann, John (noi'män), 1903–57, American mathematician, b. Hungary, Ph.D. Univ. of Budapest, 1926. He came to the United States in 1930 and was naturalized in 1937. He taught (1930–33) at Princeton and after 1933 was associated with the Institute for Advanced Study. In 1954 he was appointed a member of the Atomic Energy Commission. A founder of the mathematical theory of games (see GAMES, THEORY OF), he also made fundamental contributions to quantum theory and to the development of the atomic bomb. He was a leader in the design and development of high-speed electronic computers; his development of *maniac*—an acronym for *m*athematical *a*nalyzer, *n*umerical *i*ntegrator, *a*nd *c*omputer—enabled the United States to produce and test (1952) the world's first hydrogen bomb. With Oskar Morgernstern he wrote *Theory of Games and Economic Behavior* (1944, rev. ed. 1953). Von Neumann's other writings include *Mathematical Foundations of Quantum Mechanics* (1926, tr. 1955), *Computer and the Brain* (1958), and *Theory of Self-reproducing Automata* (ed. by A. W. Burks, pub. posthumously, 1966). See his collected works (Vol. I–III, 1961–62; Vol. IV–VI, 1963).

Vonnoh, Bessie Potter (vŏn'ō), 1872–1955, American sculptor, b. St. Louis, studied under Lorado Taft at the Art Institute of Chicago. She was Taft's assistant in his work for the World's Columbian Exposition at Chicago in 1893. Her small bronzes—*Young Mother, Dancing Girl, Reading Girl,* and others—are in the museums of New York City, Chicago, Detroit, Pittsburgh, and other cities. Her fountain figures also are notable for their delicate charm and sentiment. She was married in 1899 to **Robert Vonnoh,** 1858–1933, American portrait painter, b. Hartford, Conn., studied at the Massachusetts Normal Art School and in Paris. He was a portraitist of distinction in the linear academic style; he also painted landscapes. He taught at the school of the Boston Museum of Fine Arts, the Pennsylvania Academy of the Fine Arts, and elsewhere. Among his works are his portrait of Silas Weir Mitchell (Pa. Acad. of the Fine Arts) and *La Mère Adèle* (Metropolitan Mus.).

Von Sternberg, Joseph (Joseph Stern), 1894–1969, Austrian-American film director and screenwriter. Von Sternberg, who worked in the United States from 1925, made films that were noted for their dazzling visual impact and attention to physical detail. His early works include *The Salvation Hunters* (1925), *Underworld* (1927), and *Docks of New York* (1928). His masterpiece was *The Blue Angel* (1930) with Emil Jannings and Marlene Dietrich, made in Germany. The film depicts, with a dreadful intimacy and a striking control of contrasting atmospheres, a stuffy professor's desire for a nightclub singer and his subsequent shattering humiliation. Von Sternberg directed Dietrich in several other films (including *Morocco,* 1930; *Shanghai Express,* 1932; and *The Devil Is a Woman,* 1935) and thereby fashioned her enduring screen image. Von Sternberg wrote most of his films' screenplays, relying in later years on romantic formulas. Among his later films are *Jet Pilot* (1950) and *Macao* (1951). See his autobiography (1965); study by H. G. Weinberg (1967).

Von Stroheim, Erich (Hans Erich Marie Stroheim von Nordenaall) (ā'rĭkh fən shtrō'hīm), 1885–1957, Austrian-American film director, writer, and actor. He came to the United States in 1909, and his first appearance as an actor was in Griffith's *Birth of a Nation.* In 1918 he wrote, directed, and acted in his first film, *Blind Husband,* and in 1923 his *Greed,* a landmark in film realism, brought him acclaim. As a director, his attention to minute detail soon earned him a reputation as a spendthrift. Especially noted for his portrayals of Prussian officers, he is perhaps best remembered for *Grand Illusion* (1937). His last film role in the United States was in *Sunset Boulevard* (1950). One of the most important directors in film history, Von Stroheim was an inspiring force as the champion of artistic integrity. See Thomas Curtiss, *Von Stroheim* (1971, repr. 1973).

voodoo (vo͞o'do͞o), religious beliefs and practices, African in origin, held by certain Caribbean peoples, particularly in Haiti. Similar observances have been found sporadically in parts of the United States and in the Guianas. A highly developed voodooistic religion known as candomblé is found in Brazil. The basic features of voodoo were brought by slaves from W Africa (particularly those from what is now Dahomey), where the name originated. Ecstatic trances and magical practices play an important role in voodooistic ritual. In the New World, Christian elements were soon introduced; the African deities became identified with various saints. The magical aspects of voodoo are related to superstitious beliefs and practices found throughout the world. Although attempts have been made to suppress it, voodoo continues to flourish. See MAGIC; ZOMBI. See Alfred Métraux, *Voodoo in Haiti* (tr. 1959); Francis Huxley, *The Invisibles* (1966).

Vophsi (vŏf'sī), father of Nahbi. Num. 13.14.

Voragine, Jacobus de: see JACOBUS DA VARAGINE.

Vorarlberg (fōr"ärl'bĕrkh), province (1971 pop. 274,000), 1,004 sq mi (2,600 sq km), extreme W Austria, bordering on Switzerland, Liechtenstein, and West Germany. Bregenz, on the eastern shore of the Lake of Constance (Bodensee), is the capital. The province is a cattle-raising and dairy-farming region noted for its Alpine scenery. It has considerable industry. Hydroelectric works dot the Bregenzer Ache and Ill rivers, and textile mills are found in almost every town. Beautiful embroidery and lace are produced by artisans. Vorarlberg has numerous popular winter sports resorts. The province is bounded on the west by the Rhine River. Vorarlberg was part of the Roman province of Rhaetia and was acquired by the powerful counts of Montfort in the Middle Ages. The Hapsburgs gained possession of it piecemeal in the 14th, 15th, and 16th cent., and in 1523 it became a crownland, administered by the Tyrol. Culturally related to the Swiss, the inhabitants of Vorarlberg voted for unification with Switzerland after World War I. The attempt failed because of Allied and Swiss opposition.

Vorkuta (vərko͞otä'), city (1970 pop. 90,000), Komi Autonomous Republic, NE European USSR, above the Arctic Circle. It is the industrial center of the Pechora coal basin. Founded in 1932 as the site of large Soviet forced-labor camps, Vorkuta became a city in 1942. Some of the camps may still exist, though they were reportedly dissolved after Stalin's death in 1953.

Voronezh (Rus. vərô'nyĭsh), city (1970 pop. 666,000), capital of Voronezh oblast, E central European USSR, on the Voronezh River. A river port and a major industrial center in a black-earth agricultural region, it has industries producing machinery, locomotives, synthetic rubber, oil, and food products. A nuclear power station operates at Voronezh. Founded in 1586 as a frontier fortress against Crimean and Nogai Tatar attacks from the southern steppe, it became a shipbuilding center in the Azov campaign (1695–96) of Peter I. It has been important as a commercial and cultural center since the 1830s. During World War II it was largely destroyed (1942–43) when a German advance was stopped there; it was rebuilt completely after the war. The architectural monuments, the Nikolsk church (early 18th cent.), and the Potemkin palace (18th cent.) were restored. The Univ. of Voronezh, originally the Univ. of Tartu, was transferred there in 1918. The poet Koltsov was born at Voronezh. There are Scythian burial mounds outside the city.

Voroshilov, Kliment Yefremovich (vôrəshē'lôf, Rus. klyĭmyĕnt' yəfrĕm'əvĭch vərəshē'ləf), 1881–1969, Russian military leader and public official. A Bolshevik from 1903, he was an active revolutionary prior to the Russian Revolution of 1917 and an outstanding Red Army commander in the civil war (1918–20) that followed it. As commissar for military and naval affairs, later defense (1925–40), Voroshilov helped reorganize the Red Army. In World War II he served as commander of the northwestern front. Voroshilov was a member of the politburo of the central committee of the Communist party from 1926 and a member of the Supreme Soviet from 1937. A close associate of Stalin, he became chairman of the presidium of the supreme council of the USSR (i.e., president of the USSR) on Stalin's death (1953). Implicated by KHRUSHCHEV in the 1957 "antiparty faction" against Khrushchev, he was forced to resign in 1960 and was dropped from the central committee in 1961. After Khrushchev's ouster he was reelected to the central committee (1966).

Voroshilov: see USSURIYSK, USSR.

Voroshilovgrad (vərəshē'ləfgrät), city (1970 pop. 384,000), capital of Voroshilovgrad oblast, S central European USSR, in the Ukraine, at the confluence of the Lugan and Olkhov rivers, in the Donets Basin. Its products include locomotives, steel pipes, mining equipment, machine tools, textiles, and processed food. It was founded in 1796 around a cannon foundry, and is the oldest center of the Donets Basin. Named Lugansk in 1889, it was called Voroshilovgrad from 1935 to 1958, Lugansk from 1959 to 1969, and renamed Voroshilovgrad in 1970.

Vörösmarty, Mihály (mĭ'hälyə vö'röshmōr"tē), 1800–1855, Hungarian poet. Considered one of the greatest Hungarian poets, he created a new poetic language and combined the characteristics of the national and classical schools in his work. He is best known abroad for his patriotic lyrics, especially *The Call* (1837). His national epics, notable for their splendor of language, include *Zalan's Flight* (1825), *Erlan* (1825), and *Two Neighboring Castles* (1831). Vörösmarty also wrote dramas and critical works and translated the *Thousand and One Nights* and works of Shakespeare.

Vorster, Balthazar Johannes (yōhän'əs bältäzär' fôr'stər), 1915–, South African political leader. A lawyer, John Vorster became involved in the Afrikaner nationalist movement and helped found a militant anti-British organization. His opposition to the Allied war effort in World War II led to his internment from 1942 to 1944. Entering politics after the war, he was elected (1953) to the South African Parliament as a member of the Nationalist party and became a leader of the party's right wing. In 1958, Vorster was named a deputy minister in Hendrik Verwoerd's cabinet. Responsible for education, he rigidly enforced the Bantu Education Act, an apartheid measure. Later, as minister of justice (1961–66), Vorster repressed opponents of apartheid. After the assassination of Verwoerd (Sept., 1966), he became prime minister of the Republic of South Africa. While maintaining strict internal security, Vorster attempted a somewhat more conciliatory foreign policy, seeking a solution to the problem of South West Africa (Namibia) in response to international pressure for the territory's independence and allowing (1973) interracial competition in national and international sports.

vortex (vôr'tĕks), mass of fluid in whirling or rotary motion. To simplify the analysis, vortex motion usually describes motions in a frictionless fluid. In such cases the absence of friction would make it impossible to create or to destroy vortex motion. Motion in such a fluid would be a permanent flow pattern; the velocity of the fluid element instantaneously passing through a given point in space would be constant in time. Lines drawn so that their direction is that of the axis of rotation of the fluid are called vortex lines, and if these lines close on themselves they are called vortex rings. Hermann von Helmholtz was probably the first to investigate the properties of vortex motion; Lord Kelvin developed a theory of the material atom as a vortex ring; and J. C. Maxwell worked out a theory of electromagnetism, assuming that every magnetic tube of force was a vortex with an axis of rotation coinciding with the direction of the force. Many properties have been mathematically proved for the perfect frictionless fluid. In practice, however, their full realization is impossible because no frictionless fluid exists. To maintain a vortex motion a continuous energy supply to overcome friction is needed. A smoke ring is a familiar example of a typical vortex motion in which the medium is air. In this case the rings are stable for a short time because of the comparatively slight friction in air. An illustration of vortex motion in a liquid medium is the small whirlpool formed by water as it drains from a wash basin. In nature, illustrations of vortical motion on a larger scale are seen in waterspouts, whirlpools, and tornadoes. Investigations of sunspots reveal enormous vortices in the gases surrounding them. The principles of vortex motion are applied in aerodynamics, e.g., to explain the movement of air behind the trailing edge of a wing.

vorticism (vôr'tĭsĭzəm), short-lived 20th-century art movement related to FUTURISM. Its members sought to simplify forms into machinelike angularity. Its principal exponent was a French sculptor, GAUDIER-BRZESKA. The movement, however, had its largest following in England, where Wyndham Lewis, Ezra Pound, James Joyce, and T. S. Eliot wrote about it. See W. C. Wees, *Vorticism and the English Avant-Garde, 1910–1915* (1972).

Vortigern (vôr'tĭgərn), 5th cent., tribal king of Britons in Wales and S England. Tradition transmitted by Bede says that Vortigern invited the Germanic leaders HENGIST AND HORSA to Kent to help withstand the Picts and Scots. Later he quarreled and fought with Hengist and Horsa.

Vos, Cornelis de (kôrnā'lĭs də vōs), 1584–1651, Flemish portrait and figure painter. He was a contemporary of Rubens, who sent many sitters to him. Although of the school of Rubens, Vos developed an individual style of portraiture in which cool grays predominate. His representations of children were particularly successful. An example of his many portraits is that of Abraham Grapheus (Antwerp). His brother, **Paulus de Vos,** c.1596–1678, was an excellent painter of animals and hunting scenes. His paintings show the influence of his brother-in-law, Frans Snyders. His work is best seen in the museums of Madrid and Leningrad.

Vos, Marten de (mär'tən), c.1536–1603, Flemish painter. He studied with Floris in Antwerp and is said to have assisted Tintoretto in Venice. In 1558 he returned to Antwerp after seven years in Italy. Vos was a mannerist and painted chiefly ambitious figure compositions in imitation of the Venetians. Characteristic are his *Temptation of St. Anthony* and *Triumph of Christ* (Antwerp). Much of his work in the churches of Antwerp was destroyed by the iconoclasts.

Vos, Paulus de: see under VOS, CORNELIS DE.

Vosges (vōzh), department (1968 pop. 388,201), E France, largely in Lorraine. Épinal is the capital.

Vosges, mountain range, E France, between the Alsatian plain in the east and the plateau of S Lorraine in the west. It extends generally north and parallel to the Rhine River for c.120 mi (190 km) from the Belfort Gap. The Vosges, old crystalline mountains flanked by sandstone, have gently rounded or nearly flat summits. The highest point is the Ballon de Guebwiller (4,672 ft/1,424 m). The slopes (steep in Alsace, gentle in Lorraine) are forested (chiefly by pines) up to c.3500 ft (1,070 m). Vineyards, producing Riesling and other wines, grow on the Alsatian slopes. Lumbering, dairying, and paper and textile manufacturing are the chief occupations. There are resorts, notably Plombières-les-Bains. The Moselle, Meurthe, Sarre, and Ill rivers rise in the Vosges.

Votiak: see UDMURT AUTONOMOUS SOVIET SOCIALIST REPUBLIC.

voting, method of registering collective approval or disapproval of a person or a proposal. The term generally refers to the process by which citizens choose candidates for public office or decide controversial questions submitted to them. However, it may also describe the formal recording of opinion of a group on any subject. In either sense it is a means of transforming numerous individual desires into a coherent and collective basis for decision. In the early history of mankind voting was simply the communication of approval or disapproval by tribal members of certain proposals offered by the chieftain, who himself held elected office. Eventually in political voting, the BALLOT came into use, a sophisticated form of which is the VOTING MACHINE. In modern democracies voting is generally considered the right of all adult citizens. In the past, however, voting was often a privilege limited by stringent property qualifications and restricted to the upper classes, and it is only in recent times that universal suffrage has become a fact. In the United States this was accomplished in 1920 when women were given the right to vote by the Nineteenth Amendment. While in democracies voting is a voluntary right, in totalitarian systems it is virtually a compulsory duty, and nonvoting may be considered an act of disapproval of government policies. In recent years a great deal of study has been devoted to the analysis of voting behavior in nonauthoritarian nations. Through the use of complex sampling surveys attempts have been made to determine on what basis the voter makes his decisions. Findings reveal that voting is influenced not only by political differences but also by religious, racial, and economic dissimilarities. For this reason nearly all politicians rely on a sampling survey, or POLL, to gauge the attitudes of their constituencies. Also a subject for considerable study in the United States is that large segment of the population that refrains from voting. Research has shown that nonvoting is caused by factors that include social cross pressures, new residency in the community, and relative political ignorance or disinterest. See ELECTION. See Gabriel Almond and Sidney Verba, *The Civic Culture* (1963); Angus Campbell et al., *The American Voter* (1960); Robert Lane, *Political Life* (1959); Lester Milbraith, *Political Participation* (1965); Robin Farquharson, *The Theory of Voting* (1969); Fred Greenstein, *The American Party System and the American People* (2d ed. 1970).

voting machine, instrument for recording and counting votes. The voting machine itself is generally positioned in a booth, closed off by a curtain to assure secrecy for the voter. As the voter enters the booth and closes the curtain behind him, the machine unlocks for voting. The titles of all elective offices are listed on the face of the machine along with the party candidates running for each office. Above each name is a lever which, when depressed, indicates a vote for that candidate. The machine is designed so that only one candidate for each office may be selected, thereby eliminating the errors and spoiled votes common to the paper ballot. Votes may be cast for persons not nominated by writing in their names in a space provided on a paper roll. If a proposition is to be voted upon, it is placed at the top of the ballot, and levers marked "yes" and "no" are used to record the vote. At any time while inside the booth the voter may change his vote by returning the lever to its original position and selecting another. Only when the voter opens the curtain to leave does the machine automatically register the vote and clear itself for use by the next person. The voting machine was first used in New York state in 1892, and its use is now widespread in local and national elections throughout the United States. Because it automatically records each vote as it is cast, it is much more rapid and accurate in tabulating the total vote than the paper ballot. Other advantages include the virtual elimination of voting errors and the reduced need for election officials. Perhaps its greatest asset is the protection it affords against voting fraud. However, critics of the voting machine claim that it intimidates some citizens into nonvoting, that machines often break down, and that fraud is not completely eliminated. The United States is the only country that uses voting machines extensively. Their high cost and the less frequent elections of many nations combine to make them an impractical device for worldwide use.

Votkinsk (vôt'kĭnsk), city (1970 pop. 74,000), Udmurt Autonomous Republic, E European USSR, on a tributary of the Kama River. It has machine plants, sawmills, and brickyards. Founded in 1759 as Votkinski Zavod, a metal industry settlement, it was pillaged by PUGACHEV in 1774. The home of Tchaikovsky, who was born in Votkinsk, is now a museum. The city is named for the Votyaks, now called Udmurts.

Votyak: see UDMURT AUTONOMOUS SOVIET SOCIALIST REPUBLIC.

Vouet, Simon (sēmôN' vwā), 1590–1649, French portrait and decorative painter. He first established himself as a successful painter in Rome. Recalled to France in 1627 as court painter to Louis XIII, he decorated several of the royal palaces. Vouet was the first to introduce the Italian baroque style into France. After his return to Paris, he began to work in a more classical and decorative vein. He created new devices in illusionism and developed a splendid manner that formed the foundation of French 17th-century painting. Le Brun, Mignard, and Le Sueur were among the pupils who perpetuated his style. Several of his paintings are in the Louvre.

Voyageurs National Park: see NATIONAL PARKS AND MONUMENTS (table).

Voysey, Charles Francis Annesley, 1857–1941, English decorator and architect. He was the first modern English architect to design houses almost free of stylistic reminiscences. He also incorporated truly original features in fenestration and semiopen planning. In 1898, Voysey designed what is considered to be his finest work, "Broadleys," on Lake Windermere. Horizontality is emphasized by the low-pitched roof; a vertical counterpoint is established by three groups of rounded bay windows; and the main hall rises through two stories. Voysey's designs were imitated by architects in Europe and America.

Voznesensky, Andrei Andreyevich (əndrā' əndrā'əvĭch vəznyəsyān'skē), 1933–, Soviet poet, b. Moscow. Voznesensky studied at the Moscow Architectural Institute and later became a close friend and protégé of Boris Pasternak. After publishing his first poems in 1958, Voznesensky became immensely popular and presented numerous public readings of his works. In 1963 the government antimodernist campaign curtailed his writing. Gradually his poetry appeared again, but his dramatic work, though not political in content, had to be withdrawn (1970) and he was placed under close surveillance in 1971. Voznesensky's poetry is marked by brilliant use of language, fine craftsmanship, a wide range of subject matter, and a profound knowledge of the Russian poetic tradition. See his *Selected Poems,* ed. Herbert Marshall (1966); *Antiworlds,* ed. by Patricia Blake and Max Hayward (1967); *Dogalypse: San Francisco Poetry Reading* (1972).

Vrangel, Baron Ferdinand Petrovich von: see WRANGEL, BARON FERDINAND PETROVICH VON.

Vrangelya, island, USSR: see WRANGEL ISLAND.

Vratsa (vrä'tsä), city (1968 est. pop. 45,000), NW Bulgaria, in the foothills of the Balkan Mts. It is a commercial and crafts center and a railway junction. Vratsa has textile, metal processing, and ceramics industries. It was an administrative and garrison town under Ottoman Turkish rule (15th–19th cent.).

Vrchlický, Jaroslav (yä'rôsläf vŭrkh'lĭtskē), pseud. of **Emil Bohuslav Frída,** 1853–1912, Czech writer. Vrchlický, a poetic virtuoso, produced nearly 85 volumes of lyric verse, much of which is sensual and affirmative. In his narrative poetry he introduced numerous foreign trends, being greatly influenced by Victor Hugo and several French and Italian poets. A scholar of great erudition, Vrchlický translated poetry from many languages. His literary influence was great, and a school of young poets formed around him.

Vries: see also DE VRIES.

Vries, Adriaen de (ä'drēän də vrēs), c.1560–c.1626, Dutch sculptor. Having studied in Florence under Giovanni Bologna, he carried into Bohemia and Germany the influence of the Italian Renaissance. In Prague he worked under the patronage of Emperor Rudolf II, of whom he made busts and reliefs, which are now in Vienna. His finest works, done in Augsburg, are the *Mercury* and *Hercules and the Hydra* fountains. Among his bronzes are *Mercury and Psyche* (Louvre) and *Triton* (Metropolitan Mus.).

Vries, David Pietersen de (dä'vĕt pē'tərsən), b. c.1593, Dutch merchant captain and colonizer. An experienced mariner, Vries, in partnership with directors of the Dutch West India Company, founded (1631) a settlement (Swanendael) on Delaware Bay, later destroyed by the Indians. After trading trips to America (1634–36), he established patroonships on Staten Island (1639) and at Tappan (1640). When both colonies were ravaged by the Indians, he returned to Holland and wrote his *Korte Historiael* (1655), a valuable source for the history of New Netherland. Portions of his book are translated in *Narratives of New Netherland* (ed. by J. F. Jameson, 1909). See C. M. Parr, *The Voyages of David de Vries* (1969).

Vrindaban (vrĭn''dəbŭn'), formerly **Brindaban,** town (1971 pop. 29,475), Uttar Pradesh state, central India, on the Jumna River. Legends about the youth of the Hindu god Krishna center about the town, which is a popular pilgrim site. There are c.1,000 shrines, chiefly from the 16th cent., including the elegant Red Temple of Krishna.

VTOL aircraft: see VERTICAL TAKEOFF AND LANDING AIRCRAFT.

Vuelta Abajo (vwĕl″tä äbä′hō) or **Vueltabajo** (vwĕl″täbä′hō), district, c.90 mi (140 km) long and c.10 mi (16 km) wide, Pinar del Rio prov., W Cuba, along the southern piedmont of the Órganos Mts. Famous for the fine quality of its tobacco, which is some of the world's best, Vuelta Abajo supplies about one half of the total Cuban crop.

Vuillard, Édouard (ādwär′ vüēyär′), 1868–1940, French painter and lithographer; a member of the NABIS. He is known for his scenes of Montmartre and especially for his canvases that evoke the quiet intimacy of home life. Such paintings as *Mother and Sister of the Artist* (Mus. of Modern Art, New York City) have a brooding tension that was supplanted by works in a lighter, more decorative vein after 1900. See study by A. C. Ritchie (1954).

Vulcan, in astronomy, hypothetical planet whose existence was proposed by Leverrier to explain part of the advance of the perihelion of MERCURY, not all of which could be accounted for by gravitational effects of the other planets under the Newtonian theory of GRAVITATION. The general theory of RELATIVITY explains the observed advance of the perihelion of Mercury as being caused by the curvature of space in the vicinity of the sun as a result of the sun's large mass.

Vulcan, in Roman religion, fire god. Chiefly a god of destructive fire, Vulcan seems to have originated as a god of volcanoes. His festival, the Volcanalia, was held on August 23. He was later identified with the Greek Hephaestus.

vulcanization (vŭl″kənəzā′shən), treatment of RUBBER to give it certain qualities, e.g., strength, elasticity, and resistance to solvents, and to render it impervious to moderate heat and cold. Chemically, the process involves the formation of cross-linkages between the polymer chains of the rubber's molecules. Vulcanization is accomplished usually by a process invented by Charles Goodyear in 1839, involving combination with sulfur and heating. A method of cold vulcanization (treating rubber with a bath or vapors of a sulfur compound) was developed by Alexander Parkes in 1846. Rubber for almost all ordinary purposes is vulcanized; exceptions are rubber cement, crepe-rubber soles, and adhesive tape. Hard rubber is vulcanized rubber in which 30% to 50% of sulfur has been mixed before heating; soft rubber contains usually less than 5% of sulfur. After the sulfur and rubber (and usually an organic accelerator, e.g., an aniline compound, to shorten the time or lower the heat necessary for vulcanization) are mixed, the compound is usually placed in molds and subjected to heat and pressure. The heat may be applied directly by steam, by steam-heated molds, by hot air, or by hot water. Vulcanization can also be accomplished with certain peroxides, gamma radiation, and several other organic compounds. The finished product is not sticky like raw rubber, does not harden with cold or soften much except with great heat, is elastic, springing back into shape when deformed instead of remaining deformed as unvulcanized rubber does, is highly resistant to abrasion and to gasoline and most chemicals, and is a good insulator against electricity and heat. Many synthetic rubbers undergo processes of vulcanization, some of which are similar to that applied to natural rubber. The invention of vulcanization made possible the wide use of rubber and aided the development of such industries as the automobile industry.

Vulcano, island, Italy: see LIPARI ISLANDS.

Vulgar Latin, vernacular form of the LATIN LANGUAGE spoken in ancient Rome and the Roman Empire, as distinguished from classical or literary Latin. Vulgar Latin, rather than classical Latin, is the true parent of the individual ROMANCE LANGUAGES.

Vulgate (vŭl′gāt) [Lat. *Vulgata editio*=common edition], most ancient extant version of the whole BIBLE. It is the official, Latin version of the Roman Catholic Church. It was made c.383–405 by St. JEROME at the instance of Pope St. DAMASUS I, his protector, and was intended to replace the Old Latin version (the Itala), which had been translated from the Greek. The Old Testament is a careful translation of the Hebrew Masoretic text; for this purpose Jerome sought the aid of several rabbis. The Psalms had a special history; Jerome made three versions: the Roman Psalter, a mild revision of the Old Latin translation of the Septuagint; the Gallican Psalter, a revision of the Old Latin to make it more parallel to the Hebrew Masoretic text; and the Hebrew Psalter, a new translation of the Hebrew Masoretic text. Texts of the Vulgate now contain the Gallican Psalter. As to the deuterocanonical books of the Old Testament, Jerome made hasty translations of Tobias, Judith, and the additions to Daniel; the rest he did not touch, hence the Vulgate includes Old Latin versions of them. The New Testament was undertaken by Jerome first; he revised the Old Latin Gospels carefully, leaving the text as it stood unless it was actually incorrect; the Gospels were translated in 382–83. The rest of the New Testament shows many fewer changes from the Old Latin, and it has not been definitely established whether Jerome also revised these books. From the 5th cent. the Vulgate was popular in the West; by the early Middle Ages it was used everywhere by the Roman Catholic Church, and all the early vernacular translations were from the Vulgate. The texts naturally varied considerably. In 1546 the Council of Trent made the Vulgate the official version of the Catholic Church, and in 1592 the official text with no variants was promulgated by Clement VIII. All subsequent editions of the Vulgate published with the church's imprimatur represent this Clementine edition. In the 20th cent. the Benedictines, deputed (1933) by the Holy See, began a thorough revision of the Vulgate from all good ancient manuscripts. The work of revision continues under a commission appointed by Pope Paul VI in 1965.

Vulpius, Christian August (krĭs′tyän ou′go͝ost vo͝ol′pēo͞os), 1762–1827, German writer. He wrote several picaresque novels. His sister **Christiane Vulpius,** 1765–1816, lived with GOETHE for many years and was married to him in 1806.

vulture, common name for large birds of prey of temperate and tropical regions. The Old World vultures (family Accipitridae) are allied to hawks and eagles; the more ancient American vultures and condors are of a different family (Cathartidae) with distant links to storks and cormorants. American vultures have no syrinx and are thus voiceless, emitting weak hisses. They feed voraciously and indiscriminately, chiefly on carrion; because they have weak beaks and lack the strength of other birds of prey, they rarely attack other than helpless animals. Most vultures have dark plumage and small, naked heads. In the adult turkey vulture, or turkey buzzard, *Cathartes aura* (wingspread 6 ft/1.9 m), the head is red; in the smaller black vulture it is black; and in the tropical king vulture (with cream and black plumage) it is orange, crimson, and purple, with a neck ruff of gray down. Vultures have keen sight and are effortless soarers, skillful at riding the thermal updrafts of their mountain habitats. They are normally solitary but will gather in crowds to feed. As valuable scavengers they are protected by law. A vulture of the Pleistocene epoch was the largest bird that ever existed, with a wingspread of 16 to 17 ft (4.9–5.1 m). Vultures are frequently called buzzards, although the name is more correctly applied to hawks of the genus *Buteo.* Vultures are classified in the phylum CHORDATA, subphylum Vertebrata, class Aves, order Falconiformes, families Cathartidae and Accipitridae.

VX (vee-ĕks), NERVE GAS several times more toxic than sarin but less volatile. It kills within minutes if inhaled or deposited on the skin; protection from VX would require both protective suits and masks. The compound was first prepared in the 1950s during research for new insecticides; its chemical formula is classified by the U.S. government as secret. VX contaminates for several days ground on which it is released. Accidental release of VX in Utah in 1968 caused the death of thousands of sheep, some of them as far as 40 mi (64 km) from where the gas escaped.

Vyatka: see KIROV, USSR.

Vyatka (vyät′kə), river, c.850 mi (1,370 km) long, rising in the foothills of the central Urals, E European USSR, and flowing first N, then NW past Kirov, and finally SE into the Kama River near Mamadysh. It is navigable below Kirov and is important for logging and fishing.

Vyazma (vyäz′mə), city (1967 est. pop. 39,000), N central European USSR, on the Vyazma River, a tributary of the Dnepr. It is a rail junction and has machine building, auto repair, food- and flax-processing, and tanning industries. Founded in the 9th cent., Vyazma became an important trade and military center that was an object of contention among Russia, Lithuania, and Poland. During World War II it was held by the Germans, who destroyed it prior to withdrawal.

Vyborg (vĭ′bərk), Finnish *Viipuri*, Swed. *Viborg*, city (1969 est. pop. 69,000), NW European USSR, NW of Leningrad and near the Finnish border, on Vyborg Bay and the Gulf of Finland. A Baltic port and railroad junction, it is an export center for lumber. It also has shipyards and industries producing machinery, electrical equipment, food products, furniture, and paper. Vyborg was a trading point for Novgorod in the 12th cent. but actually grew around a Swedish castle built there in 1293. Vyborg became a port for the Hanseatic League and was chartered in the 15th cent. In 1710 Peter the Great seized Vyborg, and it was incorporated with Finland (then under Russian sovereignty) in 1812. Before 1917, it was a key transit point for revolutionary literature, arms, and agitators going into Russia. Vyborg remained Finnish until 1940, when it was occupied by the Soviet Union. It was recaptured by Finnish forces in 1941 and was finally seized by the Soviets in 1944 and awarded to them by the Finnish-Soviet peace treaty (1947). In the city are a tower (1550), several towers of the town hall (15th–17th cent.), and a fort (18th cent.).

Vychegda (vĭ′chĕgdä), river, c.700 mi (1,130 km) long, rising in several headstreams in the Urals, NE European USSR, and flowing generally W into the Northern Dvina River at Kotlas. It is navigable (April–November) c.595 mi (960 km) to Voldino and is used for timber flotation. Solvychegodsk and Syktyvkar are two of its chief ports. In the 16th cent. the Vychegda was an important water route to Siberia.

Vyg (vĭg), Finn. *Uikujärvi*, Rus. *Vygozero*, lake, c.300 sq mi (780 sq km), NW European USSR, in Karelia, between Lake Onega and the White Sea. It is fed by the Vyg River, which also drains it into the White Sea. The lake is a part of the Baltic–White Sea Canal.

Vyshinsky, Andrei Yanuarievich: see VISHINSKY.

Vysokaya (vĭsō′käyä), mountain, c.1,235 ft (380 m) high, E European USSR, in the central Urals, NW of Nizhni Tagil. It has rich magnetite deposits, which have been mined since 1721.

Vytautas: see WITOWT.

Vytegra (vĭ′tyĭgrə), river, c.45 mi (70 km) long, rising near Lake Kovzhas, NW European USSR and flowing generally NW into Lake Onega. It is one of the most important parts of the Volga-Baltic Waterway. At its mouth is the city of Vytegra, a center for the lumber industry and for ship and farm-implement repairs.

W

W, 23d letter of the ALPHABET, in form a doubled *u* or *v.* It is the usual symbol of a voiced bilabial semivowel, as in the English *wing.* The same semivowel occurs as second member of the dipthongs *au* (as in *house*), *ō,* and *o͞o.* In *twice* the *w* represents a voiceless semivowel, which is heard also in some dialects that distinguish between *where* and *wear.* In chemistry W is the symbol for the element TUNGSTEN.

Waag: see VÁH, river, Czechoslovakia.

Waal (väl), main arm of the Rhine River, 52 mi (84 km) long, branching off the Rhine near the West German border and flowing W through central Netherlands, past Nijmegen to join the Maas (Meuse) near Gorinchem. The joined rivers form the upper Merwede.

Waals, Johannes Diderik van der: see VAN DER WAALS, Johannes Diderik.

Wabash (wô'băsh"), city (1970 pop. 13,379), seat of Wabash co., N central Ind., on the Wabash River; inc. 1849. Wabash is in a fertile area that yields grain, vegetables, and fruit. Rubber products, paperboard, temperature controls, insulation, and electrical parts are manufactured. The U.S. government built (1820) a mill there for the Miami Indians. A treaty concluded (1826) with the Indians opened the way for the first permanent white settlers, who arrived in 1827. Wabash was the world's first electrically lighted city; one of the original street lamps is on exhibition in the county courthouse. Nearby Salamonie and Mississinewa dams (completed 1966 and 1967) provide flood protection and water recreation.

Wabash, river, c.475 mi (765 km) long, rising in Grand Lake, W Ohio, and flowing NW into Ind., then generally SW through Ind., becoming the Ind.-Ill. border before emptying into the Ohio River; largest northern tributary of the Ohio. The Wabash's major tributaries are the Tippecanoe and White rivers. Dams on the Wabash control floods, produce hydroelectricity, and regulate navigation; sand and gravel barges constitute the chief traffic on the river. In the fertile Wabash basin corn and livestock are raised. Vincennes, Terre Haute, and Lafayette, Ind., and Danville, Ill., are on the Wabash.

Wabash Case, popular name for *Wabash, St. Louis & Pacific Railroad Company* vs. *Illinois,* decided by the U.S. Supreme Court in 1886. The decision narrowed earlier ones (see MUNN VS. ILLINOIS) favorable to state regulation of those phases of interstate commerce upon which Congress itself had not acted. The court declared invalid an Illinois law prohibiting long- and short-haul clauses in transportation contracts as an infringement on the exclusive powers of Congress granted by the commerce clause of the Constitution. The result of the case was denial of state power to regulate interstate rates for railroads, and the decision led to creation of the Interstate Commerce Commission.

Wabash College, Crawfordsville, Ind.; for men; opened 1833, chartered 1834 as Wabash Manual Labor College and Teachers Seminary; renamed 1851.

WAC (Women's Army Corps), U.S. army organization created (1942) during World War II to enlist women as auxiliaries for noncombatant duty in the U.S. army. Before 1943 it was known as the Women's Auxiliary Army Corps (WAAC). Its first director was Oveta Culp HOBBY. During World War II, WACs served as medical technicians, cartography clerks, secretaries, and the like in the United States and in all the theaters of war. Almost 100,000 had joined the WAC by 1945. Enlistment ended with the war's end, and rapid demobilization followed. But by 1946 the War Dept. asked for reenlistments to meet shortages in army hospitals and personnel centers. In 1948 a bill was passed by Congress formally establishing the WAC within the regular army. There is a permanent training center for WAC recruits at Fort McClellan, Ala. See M. E. Treadwell, *The Women's Army Corps* (1954).

W. A. C. Bennett Dam: see PEACE, river, Canada.

Wace (wās), c.1100–1174, Norman-French poet of Jersey. King Henry II made him canon of Bayeux. His *Roman de Brut* (1155) is a long rhymed chronicle of British history based on the *Historia* of Geoffrey of Monmouth. Wace's account is much more personal, vigorous, and dramatic than Geoffrey's. The *Brut* of Layamon is an English adaptation of Wace's chronicle; both were important in the development of the ARTHURIAN LEGEND. Wace's *Roman de Rou* is a chronicle of the dukes of Normandy and contains a famous description of the battle of Hastings.

Wace, Alan John Bayard, 1879–1957, English archaeologist. From 1914 to 1923 he was director of the British School at Athens. He served as professor of classical archaeology at Cambridge (1934–44) and at Farouk I Univ., Alexandria (1943–52). Wace excavated at Sparta, Mycenae, Troy, Thessaly, Corinth, and Alexandria. His writings include *Prehistoric Thessaly* (1912); *Mycenae, an Archaeological History and Guide* (1949); and *A Companion to Homer* (1962).

Wachsmann, Konrad, 1901–, American architect, b. Frankfurt an der Oder, Germany. Intrigued by mass production, Wachsmann advocates an architecture based on MODULES designed to fit into complex structures. In the 1940s, Wachsmann designed a system of aircraft-hangar construction for the U.S. air force in which the principal structure could be enlarged by the addition of steel struts.

Wachusett Reservoir (wôcho͞o'sĭt), on the South Branch of the Nashua River, central Mass., NE of Worcester; built 1897–1905. Impounded by Wachusett Dam (completed 1906), it receives some of its water from Quabbin Reservoir and supplies the Boston area.

Waco (wā'kō), city (1970 pop. 95,326), seat of McLennan co., E central Texas, on the Brazos River, just below the mouth of the Bosque; inc. 1856. It is a trading, shipping, and industrial center. Tires, glass, and paper are among the manufactures. The Hueco (Waco) Indians once had villages there, and the site had attracted white men years before the city was laid out in 1849. Rich blacklands supported cotton plantations and cattle ranches before the Civil War, but the city suffered a severe decline after the war. Prosperity returned when its suspension bridge (still a tourist attraction) was built across the Brazos (1870) and the railroad arrived (1881). Broad, shady streets and parkways, huge Cameron Park in a residential area, and artificial Lake Waco (created 1923) on the nearby Bosque give an air of ease and opulence. Waco is the seat of Baylor Univ., Paul Quinn College, a technical institute, and a junior college. Of interest are several historic homes and a reconstructed Texas Ranger fort (built 1837). A fair and rodeo are held there annually.

Wadai (wädī'), former sultanate, N Chad, E of Lake Chad. Founded in the 16th cent., it was from time to time loosely subject to Darfur. Toward the end of the 19th cent., Wadai came under the influence of the Sanusi. The sultanate was gradually taken over (1903–13) by the French.

Waddell, James Iredell (wŏdĕl'), 1824–86, Confederate naval officer in the American Civil War, b. Pittsboro, N.C. He was appointed a midshipman in the U.S. navy in 1841. On return from duty in the Orient in 1862, he resigned his commission as lieutenant and in March took the same rank in the Confederate navy. In 1864 he took command of the *Shenandoah,* one of the outstanding CONFEDERATE CRUISERS, which remained in action after the fall of the Confederacy; Waddell was not apprised of the Confederacy's fall until Aug., 1865. Later he was master of a passenger ship between San Francisco and Yokohama. See his memoirs, *C.S.S. Shenandoah* (ed. by J. D. Horan, 1960).

Waddington, William Henry, 1826–94, French statesman and archaeologist, of English descent. Waddington was minister of education (1876–77) and was appointed foreign minister in 1877. He represented France at the Congress of Berlin (1878). In 1879 he headed a cabinet but was soon replaced by Charles de Freycinet. Waddington served as ambassador to Great Britain from 1883 to 1893. He wrote several works on archaeology.

Wade, Benjamin Franklin, 1800–1878, U.S. Senator from Ohio (1851–69), b. near Springfield, Mass. He moved (1821) to Ohio and studied law. He was successively prosecuting attorney of Ashtabula co., state senator, and presiding judge of the third judicial district in Ohio before becoming a Whig Senator. He was reelected as a Republican. An uncompromising abolitionist, he denounced the fugitive slave laws, the Kansas-Nebraska Act, and other proslavery measures. During the Civil War, Wade and his radical Republican colleagues set up the meddlesome committee on the conduct of the war, of which he was chairman. The Wade-Davis Bill, drawn up with Representative Henry W. DAVIS, was approved (July, 1864) by Congress as the committee's plan of RECONSTRUCTION. Lincoln, who had already begun a more lenient program, killed it with a pocket veto, for which he was vindictively attacked in the Wade-Davis Manifesto (Aug. 5, 1864). Later the congressional plan prevailed over the opposition of President Andrew Johnson. As president pro tempore of the Senate, Wade was next in line for the presidency, and he eagerly awaited Johnson's conviction on impeachment charges. Not long after Johnson's acquittal Wade was denied reelection to the Senate and returned to law practice.

Wadi Halfa (wä'dē häl'fə), town, N Sudan, on the Nile. It is the terminus of a railroad from Khartoum and is the point at which cotton, wheat, livestock, and other goods are transferred to steamers going down the Nile into Egypt. Archaeological expeditions have worked to excavate and preserve the area's numerous Egyptian antiquities, which faced inundation from the reservoir of the Aswan High Dam. Founded in the 19th cent., Wadi Halfa became (1885–98) the headquarters of the Anglo-Egyptian army as it prepared to reconquer Sudanese territory from the Mahdi. The railroad up the Nile to Wadi Halfa was built to support Lord Kitchener's forces during the reconquest. During World War II the town served as a staging post on the Allied communication line with Egypt via central Africa.

Wad Madani (wäd mädä'nē), city (1969 est. pop. 71,000), capital of Blue Nile prov., E Sudan, on the Blue Nile River. It is linked by rail with Khartoum and is the chief center of the Al Jazirah cotton-growing region. Wheat, barley, and livestock are other products of the city. Wad Madani has an agricultural research station. A small Turco-Egyptian administrative post in the 19th cent., the city grew rapidly after the implementation (1925) of a program to develop the Al Jazirah region.

Wadsworth, city (1970 pop. 13,142), Medina co., NE Ohio, an industrial suburb of Akron; settled c.1816, inc. 1866. Matches, iron and steel valves, and rubber products are manufactured there.

Wafd (wŏft), in modern Egyptian history, a political party. It arose out of the delegation [Arabic *wafd*= delegation] headed by ZAGHLUL PASHA that was to have visited Great Britain in 1918 to urge Egypt's independence. Zaghlul formed the party in 1919. In addition to espousing independence, the Wafdists called for extensive social and economic reforms. In the first parliament elected (1924) under the constitution of 1923, the Wafd won a large majority. King Fuad I, who bitterly opposed the party, dissolved parliament and would not call a new election until 1926. Again the Wafd won, and in 1928 its new leader, NAHAS PASHA, became prime minister. That year the government introduced a measure forbidding the king to rule without parliament. Fuad, asserting that this would give the Wafd absolute control of the country, refused his assent and suspended the constitution. Nevertheless, in 1930 the Wafd was again victorious. Fuad soon dismissed the new cabinet and appointed a conservative prime minister, who made the party illegal. When the constitution of 1923 was restored in 1935, the Wafd returned to power. They formed the cabinet in 1936–37. Relations with the new king, Farouk, were scarcely more cordial than those with his father. In World War II the party, which was anti-Axis, was installed in office from 1942 to 1944 at the insistence of Great Britain, which feared pro-Axis elements. In the elections of 1950 the Wafd triumphed again, and Nahas Pasha returned as prime minister. The party lost much of its popularity because of charges of corruption and the support it had given the British during the war. On Jan. 26, 1952, King Farouk took advantage of riots in Cairo to dismiss the Wafd from power. When the Egyptian revolution took place in July, 1952, Wafd politicians were discredited, and the party was forced to disband. See Z. M. Quraishi, *Liberal Nationalism in Egypt* (1967).

Wagadugu: see OUAGADOUGOU, Upper Volta.

wages, payment received by an employee in exchange for his labor. It may be in goods or services, but is customarily in money. The term in a broad sense refers to what is received in any way for labor. Thus the farmer receives wages as part of the price of his product or in the product if he uses it himself. The term *salary* is usually distinguished from wages as implying a more fixed and permanent form of income (e.g., payment by the month rather than by the hour). In economic theory, wages reckoned in money are called nominal wages, as distinguished from real wages, i.e., the amount of goods and services that the money will buy. Real wages depend on the price level, as well as on the nominal or money wages. To explain the nature of wages many theories have been advanced. The first of them was the subsistence theory of wages, also called the "iron law of wages," of which David Ricardo was one of the main exponents. The theory maintains that wages cluster around the bare subsistence level of workers. A wage rate much above the subsistence level causes an increase in the number of workers; competition will then lead to a depression of wages back toward the cost of subsistence. Wages that are below subsistence reduce the size of the working population; in that case competition will raise wages, but only up to the subsistence level again. In the surplus-value theory as propounded by Karl Marx, the value produced by the worker in excess of what is paid to him in wages is called surplus value. The surplus value, exacted from the worker, constitutes the capitalist's profit. The wage-fund theory is that wages are advanced out of a fixed fund of capital, from which an excess withdrawal, either through legislation or through union pressure, will ultimately reduce the amount available for other workers. Any increase in wages would also have to be taken out of profits, and their reduction would cause a decline in savings, which provide the capital from which the wage fund is derived. The marginal-productivity theory maintains that employers will only pay a wage that is, at most, equal to the amount of extra value added to the total product by one additional worker. Thus, the prevailing wage is determined by the marginal productivity of a single worker. The bargaining theory modifies the marginal-productivity theory by taking into consideration other factors (e.g., laws and social and political changes) that might affect the determination of wage levels and by acknowledging that certain basic assumptions (equal bargaining power of employer and employee, free competition between the two, and mobility of labor) that characterize the marginal-productivity theory do not hold in our present economic system. See MINIMUM WAGE. See R. S. Stockton, *Wage Policies and Wage Surveys* (1960); Albert Rees and D. P. Jacobs, *Real Wages in Manufacturing, 1890–1914* (1961); E. H. P. Brown, *A Century of Pay* (1968).

Wages and Hours Act (also called Fair Labor Standards Act), passed by U.S. Congress in 1938 to establish minimum living standards for workers engaged directly or indirectly in interstate commerce. The act provided an initial minimum wage of 25¢ per hr and a maximum workweek of 44 hr, set up a seven-year schedule under which minimum wages were gradually lifted to 40¢ per hr and the workweek was reduced to 40 hr. A Wage and Hour Division was created in the Dept. of Labor, headed by an administrator. He was empowered to hasten the legal schedule for raising minimum standards in an industry if a committee representing the public as well as employers and labor recommended the change. Classes of workers exempt from the act included agricultural and seasonal laborers, handlers of perishable foods, and workers in certain industries covered by collective bargaining. A Supreme Court decision (1941) upheld the law. Amendments set up provisions for Puerto Rico and the Virgin Islands. After 1942 the Wages and Hours Act was administered jointly with the Walsh-Healy Public Contracts Act (1936), which requires that employers holding government contracts in excess of $10,000 must pay the prevailing minimum wage as determined by the Secretary of Labor. In Jan., 1950, an amendment to the Wages and Hours Act went into effect to meet the rising costs of living. The minimum wage was increased to 75¢ per hr, regular-time work was redefined, and provisions were amended for time-and-a-half payments for overtime hours worked in excess of the 40-hr week by employees earning less than $75 per week. New categories of employees (e.g., switchboard operators and those engaged in the fish-canning industry) were included, while other groups of workers (e.g., workers connected with forestry and irrigation) were exempted. By 1956 the minimum wage had been raised to $1.00 per hr; in May, 1961, Congress approved amendments that extended the act to cover retail, service, and transit employees engaged in producing goods for interstate commerce. Minimum pay was increased to $1.15 per hr, and a raise to $1.25 went into effect in Sept., 1963. A bill passed in Sept., 1966, set a new minimum wage of $1.40 effective Feb., 1967, and $1.60 in Feb., 1968. The Equal Pay Act of 1963 required that women working in jobs covered by the Federal minimum wage must be paid the same salary as men performing the same work. In 1966 coverage was extended to employees in laundries, transit systems, and logging firms; included also were some hospital workers and farm workers employed on a farm that hired at least seven full-time workers. To ease the impact of the extended coverage, a $1 per hr minimum wage was set for these new categories; it was to be raised over several years until it reached the prevailing minimum wage. To meet the rising cost of living, amendments periodically raise the minimum wage. In 1974 Congress passed a bill providing for a gradual increase from the prevailing $1.60 per hr to $2.30 per hr by 1976. In addition, the bill extended coverage to some 8 million previously exempted laborers, including all state and local government employees and most domestic workers.

Wagga Wagga (wŏg'ə wŏg'ə), city (1971 pop. 28,814), New South Wales, SE Australia, on the Murrumbidgee River. It is the center of an agricultural district with food-processing and rubber-goods plants and foundries. There is a Roman Catholic cathedral in the city. Wagga Wagga also has teacher-training, technical, and agricultural colleges.

Wagley, Charles Walter (wăg'lē), 1913–, American anthropologist, b. Clarksville, Tex., grad. Columbia (Ph.D., 1941). He began teaching at Columbia in 1940, serving as professor from 1953 to 1971. He was appointed director of the Latin American Institute in 1961. Wagley carried out field research in Brazil and Guatemala and served on various inter-American economic and cultural missions. His books include *Social and Religious Life of a Guatemalan Village* (1949) and *The Latin American Tradition* (1968).

Wagner, Adolf Heinrich Gotthilf (ä'dôlf hīn'rĭkh gôt'hĭlf väg'nər), 1835–1917, German economist and socialist, studied at Göttingen and Heidelberg. He taught economics at several universities before becoming professor of economics at the Univ. of Berlin, a post he held for many years. He was an authority on banking and public finance and was a member of the Christian Socialist party. He promulgated a theory, known as Wagner's law, that governments increasingly assume responsibility for the economic welfare of their peoples.

Wägner, Elin (ä'lĭn vĕg'nĕr), 1882–1949, Swedish novelist. Wägner was a leading feminist. In early works such as *Pennskaftet* [the penholder] (1910), she deals with the social, economic, and political questions confronting self-supporting urban women. Her later works, including her best-known novel, *Åsa-Hanna* (1918), and the family saga *Silverforsen* [the silver rapids] (1924), concentrate more heavily on religious and moral questions.

Wagner, Honus (hō'nŭs wăg'nər), 1874–1955, American baseball player, b. Mansfield (now Carnegie), Pa. His real name was John Peter Wagner. He played semiprofessional ball in Ohio and was given a contract (1896) by the Paterson, N.J., club before entering (1897) major-league play with the Louisville (Ky.) club of the National League. He played infield and outfield positions, and when Pittsburgh replaced (1900) Louisville in the National League, Hans (a nickname also much used) soon anchored himself at shortstop with the Pirates. Wagner, called the Flying Dutchman by his fans, came to be regarded as one of the outstanding players of baseball. He led the National League in batting eight times (1900, 1903–4, 1906–9, 1911), had a lifetime batting average of .329 (batting over .300 in 17 consecutive years), made 3,430 base hits, scored close to 1,800 runs, and played in 2,785 games. Wagner, agile though massively built, excelled at fielding; he also led the National League five times in stolen bases. In 1917 he retired from baseball, but returned to the Pirates as coach (1933–52). In 1936 he was elected to the National Baseball Hall of Fame.

Wagner, Otto (ôt'ō väg'nər), 1841–1918, Austrian architect. A structural rationalism was exhibited in his stations for the Vienna city railroad, built in the 1890s. His later works, showing an individual and monumental style, include the Vienna Postal Savings Building and the Steinhof Church (1906). He became a professor at the Imperial Academy of Art in 1894. His many executed designs, his projects, his teaching, and his *Moderne Architektur*, of which there were four editions (1896–1914), were all widely influential both in Austria and abroad.

Wagner, Richard, 1813–83, German composer, b. Leipzig. Wagner's operas represent the fullest musical and theatrical expression of German romanticism. His ideas exerted a profound influence on the work of later composers. For the principle of sharply differentiated RECITATIVE and aria, Wagner substituted his "endless melody" and his *Sprechgesang* [sung speech], calling his operas music-dramas to signify the complete union of music and drama that he sought to achieve. He thought that music could not develop further with the resources it had employed since Beethoven's time, and he maintained that the music of the future must be part of a synthesis of the arts. Adapting German mythology to his dramatic requirements, Wagner applied to it an increased emotional intensity, derived from the harmonic complexity and power of Beethoven's music, to produce what he termed a "complete art work." He achieved a remarkable dramatic unity due in part to his development of the leitmotif, a brief passage or fragment of music used to characterize an episode or person and brought in at will to recall it to the audience. At the same time, Wagner greatly increased the flexibility and variety of his orchestral accompaniments. He was responsible for the productions of his works from libretti to details of sets and costumes. Wagner was reared in a theatrical family, given a classical education, and began composing at 17. He studied harmony and the works of Beethoven and in 1833 became chorus master of the theater at Würzburg, the first of a series of theatrical positions. *Die Feen* (composed 1833), his first opera, was in the German romantic tradition begun by Weber; *Das Liebesverbot* (1835–36) demonstrated his assimilation of the Italian style. In Paris he completed *Rienzi* (1838–40) but was unable to have it performed there. Its production in Dresden in 1842 was highly successful, and in 1843 Wagner was made musical director of the Dresden theater. *Der Fliegende Holländer* (1841) was less successful. It was based on Heine's version of the legend of the FLYING DUTCHMAN, and it foreshadows the idea, developed in *Tannhäuser* (1843–44) and prevalent in later works, of redemption by love. *Tannhäuser,* based in part on the actual life of TANNHÄUSER, and *Lohengrin* (1846–48) brought the German romantic opera to culmination. In *Lohengrin,* Wagner for the first time is more interested in his characters as symbols than as actual personages in a drama. Wagner participated in the Revolution of 1848, fled Dresden, and with the help of Liszt escaped to Switzerland, where he stayed eight years. There he wrote essays, including *Oper und Drama* (1851), which defines the aesthetic ideas governing all his subsequent works. *Der Ring des Nibelungen* (1853–74), his tetralogy based on the Nibelungenlied (see under NIBELUNGEN), embodies the most complete adherence to his stated principles. In 1857, having completed the composition of the first two works of the cycle, *Das Rheingold* (1853–54) and *Die Walküre* (1854–56), and two acts of *Siegfried* (1856–69), Wagner laid the *Ring* aside without hope of ever seeing it performed and composed *Tristan und Isolde* (1857–59) and *Die Meistersinger von Nürnberg* (1862–67), his only comic opera. *Tristan,* based on the legend of TRISTRAM AND ISOLDE, was so utterly in opposition to the operatic conventions of the day that it required the intercession and support of Louis II of Bavaria to have it produced (1865) in Munich. In 1872, Wagner moved to BAYREUTH, where in 1874 he finished *Die Götterdämmerung,* the last work of the *Ring* cycle. There, too, he was able to build a theater, Das Festspielhaus, adequate for the proper performance of his works, in which the complete *Ring* was presented in 1876. At Bayreuth, Wagner entertained the great musicians of his day. *Parsifal* (1877–82), his last work, is a religious festival play. Wagner experienced both great financial hardship and considerable critical success. Although during his lifetime opposition to him and to his ideas went to fantastic lengths, Wagner's operas held a position of complete dominance in the next generation, retaining their enormous popularity in the 20th cent. See his prose works (8 vol., tr. 1892-99); his letters (ed. by John N. Burk, 1950); his autobiography, *My Life* (tr. 1911, repr. 1974); biography by Ernest Newman (4 vol., 1933-46); studies by Geoffrey Skelton (1965) and R. W. Gutman (1968). Wagner's second wife, **Cosima Wagner,** 1837-1930, was the daughter of Liszt and the comtesse d'Agoult. From 1857 to 1870 she was the wife of Hans von BÜLOW. In 1870 she married Wagner and involved herself closely with his work. After his death she was largely responsible for the continuing fame of the Bayreuth festivals. See biographies by R. M. F. du Moulin-Eckart (2 vol., tr. 1930) and A. H. Sokoloff (1969). Their son, **Siegfried Wagner,** 1869-1930, composed 11 operas, orchestral and chamber music, and some vocal pieces, but was known chiefly as a conductor. With his wife, Winifred Williams, he directed the Bayreuth festivals, a tradition carried on by their two sons, Wieland and Wolfgang, after World War II.

Wagner, Robert Ferdinand (wăg'nər), 1877-1953, American legislator, b. Germany. He arrived with his family in the United States in 1885 and grew up in poor surroundings in New York City. After he received his law degree, he became attached to Tammany Hall and was elected (1904) to the New York state assembly. In the state senate (1910-18), Wagner was noted for his investigations of factory conditions; as justice (1919-26) of the state supreme court, he did much to protect the rights of labor. He served (1927-49) in the U.S. Senate, where he was one of the chief leaders in directing New Deal legislation, particularly the acts establishing the National Recovery Administration (1933), the NATIONAL LABOR RELATIONS BOARD (1935), social security, and the U.S. Housing Authority (1937). In the 1940s he sponsored bills calling for the extension of Federal housing. He resigned from the Senate in 1949 because of ill health. His son, **Robert Ferdinand Wagner, Jr.,** 1910–, b. New York City, entered politics with his father's encouragement. He was a member of the New York state assembly (1938-41), and after service in the air force in World War II, he became successively New York City tax commissioner (1946), commissioner of housing and buildings (1947), chairman of the City Planning Commission (1948), and president of the borough of Manhattan (1949). Elected mayor of New York in 1953, he was overwhelmingly reelected in 1957. Wagner broke (1961) with the Tammany organization after long association and, after defeating the organization candidate in the primary election, won a third term as mayor. In 1965 he chose not to run for reelection. He was appointed (1968) U.S. Ambassador to Spain, but he resigned in Feb., 1969, and ran unsuccessfully in the New York Democratic mayoral primary in June of that year.

Wagner-Jauregg, Julius (yo͞o'lyo͝os väg'nər-you'-rĕk), 1857-1940, Austrian neurologist and pioneer in fever therapy. He was professor at the Univ. of Vienna from 1893 to 1928. He introduced the treatment of paresis by inoculation with the organisms causing malaria, attributing the success of the procedure to the induced malarial fever. For this work he received the 1927 Nobel Prize in Physiology and Medicine.

wagon: see CARRIAGE.

wagon train, in U.S. history, a group of covered wagons used to convey people and supplies to the West before the coming of the railroad. The wagon replaced the pack, or horse, train in land commerce as soon as proper roads had been built. The first frontier region in which wagoning became highly developed was across the Allegheny barrier in the late 18th cent. There were few routes through the mountains, and in the days of the westward movement they were well-traveled by the migrants' wagons and by the wagon trains of professional wagoners carrying goods between the Ohio settlements and the cities on the coast. Used in this trade was the CONESTOGA WAGON, the most efficient freight carrier of the age. On the prairies of the Middle West and on the Great Plains, wagons could be used without the necessity of making roads, and there the covered wagon, or PRAIRIE SCHOONER, of the migrant predominated. It was in crossing the Great Plains that the typical wagon train was developed. The vast distances through unsettled country and the danger from Indians made it necessary to travel in large parties. Such a train was organized with an almost military discipline for defense. A contract, or constitutional paper, was drawn up, setting forth the objects of the migration, the terms of joining, the rules to be followed, and the officers to be elected. All joining signed this paper and then participated in the election of officers. Sometimes both a military captain and a president with civil powers were chosen. More often the offices were combined in one individual. Aides or lieutenants were elected, and a guide was usually hired for the more difficult parts of the route. The order of wagons both on the trail and in camp was strictly regulated. At night the wagons were drawn into a circular corral, and a strict guard was kept to prevent a surprise attack by hostile Indians. Freighters who supplied the early army posts and mining camps also usually traveled in parties for the same reason as the migrants. The wagon trains disappeared in the East in the 1840s and 50s, and the Western trails lost importance in the later 19th cent. See H. P. Walker, *The Wagonmasters* (1966).

Wagram (vä'gräm) or **Deutsch-Wagram** (doich-), town, Lower Austria prov., NE Austria, in the Marchfeld, near Vienna. On July 5-6, 1809, Napoleon I gained one of his most brilliant victories there. Despite their heroic conduct and the able leadership of Archduke Charles, the Austrians were forced to fall back by French field artillery fire. Napoleon's "grand battery" of 100 guns was the largest concentration of artillery that had until then been used for massed fire. Six days later, Austria was forced to conclude an armistice.

wagtail: see PIPIT.

Wahabi (wähä'bē), Arabian reform movement in ISLAM, the religion of the ruling family of Saudi Arabia. It was founded by Muhammad ibn Abd al-Wahab (c.1703-1791), who taught that all accretions to Islam after the 3d cent. of the Muslim era—i.e., after c.950—were spurious and must be expunged. This view, involving essentially a purification of the Sunni sect, regarded the veneration of saints, ostentation in worship, and luxurious living as the chief evils. Accordingly, Wahabi mosques are simple and without minarets, and the adherents of the cult dress plainly and do not smoke tobacco or hashish. Driven from Medina for his preaching, the founder of the Wahabi sect went into the NE Nejd and converted the Saud tribe. The sheik, convinced that it was his religious mission to wage holy war (jihad) against all other forms of Islam, began the conquest of his neighbors in c.1763. By 1811 the Wahabis ruled all Arabia, except Yemen, from their capital at Riyadh. The Ottoman sultan, nominally suzerain over Arabia, had vainly sent out expeditions to crush them. Only when the sultan called on Muhammad Ali of Egypt for aid did he meet success; by 1818 the Wahabis were driven into the desert. In the Nejd they collected their power again and from 1821 to 1833 gained control over the Persian Gulf coast of Arabia. The domain thereafter steadily weakened; Riyadh was lost in 1884, and in 1889 the Saud family fled for refuge into the neighboring state of Kuwait. The Wahabi movement was to enjoy its third triumph when IBN SAUD advanced from his capture of Riyadh in 1902 to the reconstitution in 1932 of nearly all his ancestral domain under the name SAUDI ARABIA. The Wahabi movement, although mainly in Arabia, at an early date was also carried eastward to India and Sumatra and westward to North Africa and the Sudan. Wahabis were urged to fight against nonbelievers. In India, native Muslims under Sayid Ahmad warred against the Sikhs in 1830, even capturing Peshawar for a short time. As late as 1870 bands of Wahabis continued sporadic disorders in India. Today, however, the once austere Wahabi code is more liberal.

Wahiawa (wä"hēəwä'), residential city (1970 pop. 17,598), Honolulu co., Hawaii, on central Oahu, in a pineapple region. The U.S. army's Schofield Barracks adjoins the city.

Wahlstatt: see LEGNICA, Poland.

wahoo: see STAFF TREE.

Waialeale, peak, Hawaii: see KAUAI, island.

Waianae Mountains (wīänä'ä), volcanic range, W Oahu island, Hawaii. It rises to Mt. Kaala (4,025 ft/1,227 m), the highest point on the island.

Waikato (wī'kä"tō), river, 270 mi (435 km) long, rising in Lake Taupo, central North Island, New Zealand, and flowing NW into the Tasman Sea. It is New Zealand's longest river. The Waikato's hydroelectric stations are the main source of power for North Island. Coal is mined in the reclaimed swamplands of the Waikato basin. Dairy farming is an important activity in the basin. The river is navigable for 80 mi (129 km) up to Cambridge.

Waikiki (wīkēkē'), famous beach and resort center SE of Honolulu on SE Oahu island, Hawaii. Surfboard riding is the major sport at Waikiki, which is noted for its huge waves. The Honolulu Zoo is in nearby Kapiolani Park.

Waimea (wīmā'ə), town (1970 pop. 1,569), Hawaii, on the southern coast of Kauai island, NW of Hanapepe and near the Waimea River, in a sugarcane region. James Cook landed on the site in 1778, and the first missionaries to come to Hawaii settled there. Nearby are the remains of a fort built by the Russians in 1815, when they tried to gain influence in Hawaii.

Wain, John, 1925–, English novelist and critic, b. Stoke on Trent, Staffordshire, grad. Oxford (B.A., 1946; M.A., 1950). He was ranked with England's ANGRY YOUNG MEN after the publication of *Hurry on Down* (1953), a novel satirizing the British class system. His later novels, often comedies about people in uncomfortable situations, all stress the importance of human dignity. His works include the novel *A Winter in the Hills* (1970); *Arnold Bennett* (1967) and *A House for the Truth* (1972), critical works; and *Samuel Johnson* (1975), a biography. See his autobiography (1962).

Wainewright, Thomas Griffiths (wān'rīt), 1794-1852, English art critic and criminal. He contributed essays on the arts to the *London Magazine* under the pseudonyms Egomet Bonmot and Janus Weathercock, exhibited several paintings at the Royal Academy, and wrote *Some Passages in the Life of Egomet Bonmot* (1827). He is thought to have poisoned his uncle (whose property he inherited), his mother-in-law, and his sister-in-law (whose life he had heavily insured). He went to France (1831), but on returning to England (1837) was arrested, convicted on an old forgery charge, and transported to Tasmania for life. See Charles Norman, *The Genteel Murderer* (1956).

Wainwright, Jonathan Mayhew, 1883-1953, American general, b. Walla Walla, Wash. Commissioned in the army in 1906, he reached the rank of brigadier general in 1938. In World War II he was stationed in the Philippines when the Japanese attacked in Dec., 1941. Wainwright took command after Gen. Douglas MacArthur was ordered to leave and led (March-May, 1942) the gallant but vain fight that ended in the surrender of Bataan and Corregidor. He described his hard experiences as a prisoner of war in *General Wainwright's Story* (1946). Released (1945) from a prison camp in Manchuria, he witnessed (1945) the Japanese surrender in Tokyo Bay and then returned to the United States and was given the Medal of Honor. He was made a full general in 1945 and in 1947 retired from the army.

Wainwright, town (1971 pop. 3,872), E Alta., Canada, SE of Edmonton and near the Sask. border. It is a trade center and railroad division point for an oil and natural gas area. It has oil refineries, grain elevators, and flour mills. Nearby is a military base.

Waite, Morrison Remick (wāt), 1816-88, American jurist, seventh Chief Justice of the U.S. Supreme Court (1874-88), b. Lymé, Conn. Admitted to the bar in 1839, he became prominent when he represented the United States in prosecuting the ALABAMA CLAIMS. It was Waite's task as Chief Justice to help interpret the amendments to the Constitution that were adopted after the Civil War. His interpretation of the due process clause of the FOURTEENTH AMENDMENT was long influential. Waite maintained that only businesses "clothed with a public interest" might be subject to economic regulation by the states; e.g., a state might set the rates charged by a grain elevator but not the prices of a haberdasher. The Supreme Court essentially adhered to this position until the 1930s. See biographies by B. R. Trimble (1938, repr. 1970) and C. P. Magrath (1963).

Waitz, Georg (gä'ôrk vīts), 1813-86, German historian. In the Frankfurt Parliament in 1848 he defended the idea of a unified Germany, including Austria and Prussia. He was professor at Göttingen after 1849. His great knowledge of the literature and sources of history enabled him to direct the *Monumenta Germaniae historica* after 1875 and to prepare with Dahlmann an indispensable *Quellenkunde zur deutschen Geschichte* [sources on German history] (ed. 1869, 1874, 1883; 9th ed. 1931). Waitz also wrote an eight-volume work (1844-78) on German constitutional history to the middle of the 12th cent.

Waitzen: see VÁC, Hungary.

Wakamatsu: see AIZU-WAKAMATSU; KITAKYUSHU.

Wakashan (wäkăsh'ən, wô'kəshän", -shôn"), branch of the Algonquian-Wakashan linguistic family, or stock, of North America and spoken by American Indians of W Canada and the state of Washington. See AMERICAN INDIAN LANGUAGES.

Wakatsuki, Reijiro (rä'jērō wäkätsōō'kē), 1866–1949, Japanese statesman. He served (1906, 1908–11) as vice minister of finance, was elected to parliament in 1911, and was minister of finance from 1912 to 1915. He helped draft (1925) the Universal Manhood Suffrage Law and the Peace Preservation Law. He was leader of the Kenseikai party in 1925 and headed the Minseito party from 1927 to 1934. He was briefly (1926–27, 1931) prime minister. In 1930 he was chief delegate to the London Naval Conference. From 1933 to 1936 he spoke out strongly against Japanese militarism.

Wakayama (wäkä'yämä), city (1970 pop. 365,180), capital of Wakayama prefecture, SW Honshu, Japan, on the Inland Sea. It is a railroad hub and a manufacturing center where cotton and flannel textiles are produced. The city has a castle built in 1585 by Hideyoshi. Wakayama prefecture (1970 pop. 1,042,635), 1,824 sq mi (4,724 sq km), yields lumber and agricultural products.

wake, watch kept over a dead body, usually during the night preceding burial. Ancient peoples in various parts of the world observed the custom. As an ancient ritual, it was rooted in a concern that no person should be buried alive. After it was adopted by Christians and as it is practiced today, the wake serves the primary purpose of allowing friends and relatives of the deceased an opportunity to adjust collectively to the changed conditions. Typically there are traditional songs and laments. Prayers for the deceased and eating and drinking by the assembled mourners are features of the wake. Wakes may vary from part of one night to three nights in length. See FUNERAL CUSTOMS.

Wakefield, Edward Gibbon, 1796–1862, British colonial statesman. He was attached to the British embassies in Turin (1814–16) and Paris (1820–26), but in 1826 was convicted of an attempt to marry an heiress by trickery. While in prison (1827–30) Wakefield prepared material for a book on capital punishment (pub. 1831) and studied colonial affairs. He evolved his important theory of systematic colonization, embodied in such works as *A Letter from Sydney* (1829) and *A View of the Art of Colonization* (1849). Concerned by the problems of increasing population, with resultant poverty and crime, he advocated the settlement of the colonies by ordinary citizens rather than by transported convicts. He argued that land should be sold in small lots at a moderate fixed price instead of given away (the funds thus gathered to be used to support further colonization), and some self-government should be allowed. These influential ideas led to the founding (1834) of the South Australian Association and the establishment of the South Australian colony. Wakefield accompanied (1838) Lord DURHAM to Canada as an adviser and influenced Durham's report on Canadian government. In 1839 he founded the New Zealand Land Company, which colonized part of that territory. He went to New Zealand in 1852 and entered into politics there, but suffered a complete breakdown in 1854. See his collected works, ed. by M. F. Lloyd Prichard (1968); biographies by Irma O'Connor (1929) and Paul Bloomfield (1961); R. C. Mills, *The Colonization of Australia* (1915, repr. 1968).

Wakefield, county borough (1971 pop. 59,650), administrative center of the West Riding of Yorkshire, N central England, on the Calder River. It has been a center of the cloth industry from the 14th cent. Modern manufactures include woolen goods, chemicals, machine tools, and power presses. It is also a railroad junction and farm center, with an important cattle market. There are coal mines in the borough. The site was occupied by the Danes and Saxons; Richard, duke of York, was defeated and slain in the battle of Wakefield in 1460. The Towneley Plays (see MIRACLE PLAY) originated in Wakefield. Notable buildings are All Saints' Church (mainly 15th cent.), the chantry chapel on the bridge over the Calder (c.1350; restored 1847), and the grammar school (1591). There is a technical college in Wakefield. In 1974, Wakefield became part of the new metropolitan county of West Yorkshire.

Wakefield, town (1970 pop. 25,402), Middlesex co., NE Mass., a suburb of Boston; settled 1639, inc. 1812. It is chiefly residential, but there is some industry.

Wakefield, family estate of George Washington, on the Potomac River, E. Va.; part of the George Washington Birthplace National Monument (see NATIONAL PARKS AND MONUMENTS, table). John Washington, the great-grandfather of George, settled there in 1664. The house in which George was born was built by his father, Augustine Washington. It was destroyed by fire in 1779, but on its original foundations a new house, similar to the original, was completed in 1931.

Wakefield Master: see SECOND SHEPHERD'S PLAY.

Wakefield Plays: see TOWNELEY PLAYS; MIRACLE PLAYS.

Wake Forest University, at Winston-Salem, N.C.; Southern Baptist; coeducational; chartered 1833, opened 1834 at Wake Forest, moved 1956. The school achieved university status in 1967.

Wake Island, atoll with three islets (Wake, Wilkes, and Peale) (1970 pop. 1,647), 3 sq mi (7.8 sq km), central Pacific, between Hawaii and Guam. It is a U.S. commercial and military base under the jurisdiction of the Federal Aviation Agency. There is no indigenous population. Wake Island was discovered by the Spanish in 1568, visited by the British in 1796 and named after Capt. William Wake, and annexed by the United States in 1898. The island became (1935) a commercial air base on the route to the Orient and later served as a U.S. military base. In Dec., 1941, Wake Island was seized by the Japanese. U.S. forces bombed the island from 1942 until Japan's surrender in 1945.

wake-robin, name for several plants, particularly TRILLIUM.

Waksman, Selman Abraham (wäks'mən), 1888–1973, American microbiologist, b. Priluka, Russia, grad. Rutgers (B.S. 1915), Ph.D. Univ. of California, 1918. He went to the United States in 1910 and was naturalized in 1916. He taught at Rutgers from 1918 and was a professor there from 1930. At the New Jersey State Agricultural Experiment station, where he became microbiologist in 1921, Waksman and his associates made studies of the decomposition of organic matter by microorganisms, of the origin and nature of humus, and of the production of substances detrimental to certain bacteria. For his discovery of the antibiotic streptomycin and of its value in treating tuberculosis, he was awarded the 1952 Nobel Prize in Physiology and Medicine. In addition to many scientific papers Waksman wrote *Enzymes* (with W. C Davison, 1926); *Principles of Soil Microbiology* (1927); *The Soil and the Microbe* (with R. L. Starkey, 1931); *Humus* (1936); *Microbial Antagonisms and Antibiotic Substances* (1945); *The Conquest of Tuberculosis* (1964); and *The Actinomycetes* (1967).

Walachia or **Wallachia** (both: wälā'kēə, wə–) historic region (29,568 sq mi/76,581 sq km), S Rumania. The Transylvanian Alps separate it in the NW from Transylvania and the Banat; the Danube separates it from Yugoslavia in the west, Bulgaria in the south, and N Dobruja in the east; in the northeast it adjoins Moldavia. BUCHAREST, the Rumanian capital, is its chief city. The Oltul River, a tributary of the Danube, divides Walachia into Muntenia or Greater Walachia (20,265 sq mi/52,486 sq km) in the east and Oltenia or Lesser Walachia (9,303 sq mi/24,095 sq km) in the west. With the rich PLOIEŞTI oil fields and the industrialized area near Bucharest, Walachia is economically the most developed region of Rumania. Its industries (notably chemicals, heavy machinery, and shipbuilding) provide employment for about half of the country's labor force. Walachia is also a rich agricultural area and the "bread basket" of Rumania. The overwhelming majority of the population is Rumanian, but there are also Bulgarians, Jews, and Serbs. The region was part of the Roman province of Dacia and has retained its Romanic speech despite centuries of invasion and foreign rule. Although theoretically part of the Byzantine Empire, Walachia was successively occupied (6th–11th cent.) by the Lombards, the Avars, and the Bulgarians. By the 12th cent. it had passed under the Cumans, who in turn succumbed (1240) to the Mongols. When the Mongol wave receded, the native inhabitants descended from their mountain refuges, and the principality of Walachia was founded (c.1290) by their leader Radu Negru or Rudolf the Black. The name *Vlachs* (or *Walachs* or *Wallachs*) was given them by their Slavic neighbors. Although some claim that the Vlachs are direct descendants of the Dacians (mainly on the ground that they preserved their Latin speech), it is more than likely that they represent a composite ethnic mixture. The sister principality, MOLDAVIA, came into existence about the same time as Walachia. Cîmpulung, the earliest capital of Walachia, was later replaced by Curtea-de-Arges. Mircea the Great of Walachia (reigned 1386–1418) shared in the defeats of Kossovo (1389) and Nikopol (1396) at the hands of the Turks and was obliged to pay tribute to the sultan. Walachia continued to be governed by its own princes under Turkish suzerainty. Like Moldavia, it was torn by strife among the great landowners (or boyars) and among rival claimants to the throne; lawlessness prevailed. Prince Vlad the Impaler (reigned 1456–62) restored some order by putting 20,000 persons to death within six years. He refused tribute to the sultan, defeated the Turks, and impaled the Turkish prisoners. His rivalry with Stephen the Great of Moldavia cost him his throne. A last attempt to free all Rumanians from foreign domination was made (1593–1601) by Michael the Brave, who massacred the Turks in Walachia and conquered Transylvania and Moldavia. His death delivered Walachia back into the hands of the Turks. The alliance (1711) of Prince Constantine Brancovan with Peter I of Russia and his subsequent downfall resulted in a tightening of Turkish control. Instead of native princes, governors (hospodars), mostly Greek Phanariots (see under PHANAR), were appointed. In the Russo-Turkish Wars of the 18th cent. Walachia was repeatedly occupied by Russian and Austrian troops. The oppressive rule of the Phanariots lasted until 1822, when the Rumanians rebelled against the Greeks, who at the same time began their war of independence against Turkey. Native governors were again appointed, and the Treaty of Adrianople (see ADRIANOPLE, TREATY OF) in 1829 made Walachia an almost autonomous state, tributary to Turkey but under Russian protection. A Rumanian national uprising (1848–49) in Walachia was suppressed by Russian intervention. Russian troops occupied (1853) Walachia and Moldavia early in the Crimean War; however, to purchase Austrian neutrality, they evacuated the lands in 1854, and the two Danubian Principalities (as Walachia and Moldavia were called) passed under Austrian occupation. The Congress of Paris (1856), which ended the Crimean War, guaranteed the principalities virtual independence under the nominal suzerainty of Turkey. With the accession (1859) of Alexander John Cuza as prince of both Moldavia and Walachia, the history of modern Rumania began.

Walafrid Strabo (Walafrid the Squinter), c.809–849, German scholar, b. Swabia. Educated at the abbey of Reichenau, he wrote, at 18, a Latin verse account of a journey to the hereafter, *Visio Wettini*. In 842 he returned to Reichenau as abbot. There he encouraged the production and exchange of manuscripts which made the library and scriptorium famous. Among Walafrid's writings, renowned throughout the Middle Ages for their distinguished Latin, are *Hortulus*, a poem describing the monastery garden; a scriptural commentary; and notes on contemporary liturgy, still valuable as a source. See H. J. Waddell, *The Wandering Scholars* (1927, repr. 1968).

Wałbrzych (väl'bzhĭkh), Ger. *Waldenburg*, city (1970 pop. 125,048), SW Poland. Coal mining is the chief economic activity. The city's importance dates from the 19th-century industrialization of the Lower Silesian coal basin. Wałbrzych sustained great damage during World War II, after which it passed from Germany to Poland.

Walburga, Saint (wôlbûr'gə), d. c.779, English missionary in Germany; sister of St. Willibald. She went there to assist St. Boniface, settling at Heidenheim, near Eichstätt (NW of Ingolstadt), where another brother, Winnebald (or Wynbald), had an abbey. St. Walburga's convent became a principal center of civilization in Germany and an important shrine. Feast: Feb. 25. *Walpurgisnacht*, the traditional German witches' sabbath held in the HARZ mountains, is named after her for unknown reasons. It is held on the eve of one of her feasts, May 1. There is a famous Walpurgisnacht scene in Goethe's *Faust*. Other forms of her name are Walpurgis and Vaubourg.

Walcheren (väl'khərən), region, Zeeland prov., SW Netherlands, on the North Sea at the entrance to the Scheldt estuary. Middelburg is the chief city and is also the capital of Zeeland prov. Dunes line the North Sea coast, and diked lowlands predominate elsewhere. Agriculture and cattle raising constitute the mainstays of Walcheren's economy; the main crops are wheat, vegetables, fruit, and sugar beets. Walcheren also has a considerable tourist trade, attracted largely by the medieval buildings in Middelburg. Walcheren was occupied by the Germans and suffered heavy bombardment during World War II. The dikes were bombed and the region largely flooded in order to force German evacuation. In the autumn of 1944, British troops landed on Walcheren, drove out the remaining Germans, and went on to capture the Belgian port of Antwerp, which became a major Allied base.

Wald, Lillian D. (wôld), 1867–1940, American social worker and pioneer in public health nursing. In 1893 she organized a visiting nurse service, which became the nucleus of the noted Henry Street Settlement in New York City. The U.S. Children's Bureau (founded 1912) was suggested by her, as were other public health services and social reforms. See her autobiographical books *The House on Henry Street* (1915) and *Windows on Henry Street* (1934, 4th ed. 1937); biographies by R. L. Duffus (1938) and B. W. Epstein (1960).

Waldeck (väl'dĕk), former principality, E West Germany, now an administrative district (c.420 sq mi/ 1,090 sq km) of Hesse. Arolsen was the capital. An agricultural region, hilly and forested, it is drained by the Eder and Diemel rivers. An immediate county of the Holy Roman Empire from c.1200, Waldeck was united with the county of Pyrmont in the late 17th cent., and its rulers were later raised (1712) to princely rank. In 1867 the prince of Waldeck-Pyrmont renounced most of his sovereign prerogatives in favor of Prussia; the title, however, continued in the family. Waldeck-Pyrmont became a republic in 1918. By a plebiscite in 1922, Pyrmont passed to Prussia and was incorporated into Hanover prov.; by another plebiscite (1929) Waldeck proper became part of the Hesse-Nassau prov. of Prussia. After World War II it was made part of Hesse.

Waldeck-Rousseau, René (rənā' väldĕk'-ro͞osō'), 1846–1904, French statesman. Belonging to the republican left, he was twice minister of the interior (1881, 1883–85), and in 1884 he was responsible for the passage of the Waldeck-Rousseau law, legalizing the creation of trade unions. In 1893 he was defense counsel for A. Gustave EIFFEL in the Panama Canal scandal trial. President Émile Loubet appointed him to head a cabinet in 1899, at the height of the DREYFUS AFFAIR, and he succeeded in securing a presidential pardon for Dreyfus. Although Waldeck-Rousseau himself advocated moderate measures, the repressive anticlerical legislation that grew out of the affair began during his ministry. His Associations Law (1901) virtually abolished the right of free association of religious orders, and thousands of monks and nuns went into exile. Waldeck-Rousseau resigned (1902) because of failing health and was succeeded by Émile Combes.

Waldemar. For Russian rulers thus named, see VLADIMIR.

Waldemar I (Waldemar the Great) (wăl'dəmär), 1131–82, king of Denmark (1157–82). In 1147, Waldemar, Sweyn III, and Canute each claimed the Danish throne. After a war Waldemar received Jutland as his share of Danish territory. When Canute was assassinated (probably on Sweyn's orders), Waldemar conducted a campaign against King Sweyn, whom he defeated (1157) in a great battle near Viborg. Although now supreme in Denmark, Waldemar found his country overrun by the WENDS. With Henry the Lion of Saxony and Albert the Bear of Brandenburg he subjugated the Wends and forced them to accept Christianity. He became the vassal of Holy Roman Emperor Frederick I in order to gain German support, but was later powerful enough to free himself from that control. Waldemar codified the laws and gained Norwegian territory. The marriages of his daughters to the sons of Frederick I, Eric X of Sweden, and Philip II of France increased his prestige. Archbishop ABSALON was his adviser in ecclesiastical, political, and military affairs. Waldemar was succeeded by his son, Canute VI (reigned 1182–1202).

Waldemar II, 1170–1241, king of Denmark (1202–41), second son of Waldemar I. In the reign of his brother, Canute VI, he defended Denmark from German aggression and then extended Danish control over Schwerin. After his accession, the king of Norway paid him homage (1204). When his German conquests had been confirmed (1214) by Frederick II, the German king, he undertook a crusade against the Estonians and became master of much of the Baltic region. In 1223 he was treacherously seized by his vassal the count of Schwerin and held prisoner for three years. He was released only after he had been forced to relinquish much of his territory. He then attempted a reconquest, but was defeated (1227) at Bornhöved and spent the remainder of his life in codifying Danish law and in forwarding internal reform. He was succeeded by his son, Eric IV.

Waldemar IV (Valdemar Atterdag), c.1320–1375, king of Denmark (1340–75). He became king of a land completely dismembered by foreign rulers, but his ambition, unscrupulousness, and military ability enabled him to unite his kingdom by 1361. Waldemar IV married his daughter MARGARET I to Haakon VI, king of Norway, in an effort to unite Denmark and Norway. He interfered in Germany on behalf of his kinsman, the margrave of Brandenburg. His conquest of Skane, in violation of a treaty with the Swedish king, gave him control of the lucrative fishing industry, and his defeat (1362) of the HANSEATIC LEAGUE secured him temporary possession of GOTLAND. In 1368, however, the Hanseatic towns, Mecklenburg, Sweden, and Holstein formed a coalition against him. Defeated, Waldemar was forced to consent (1370) to the humiliating Treaty of Stralsund, which granted freedom of trade in Denmark to the Hanseatic League. He was succeeded by Margaret's son, Olaf, under his parents' regency. See Fletcher Pratt, *The Third King* (1950).

Waldenburg: see WAŁBRZYCH, Poland.

Walden Pond, Mass.: see CONCORD 2.

Waldenses (wôldĕn'sēz) or **Waldensians,** Protestant religious sect of medieval origin, called in French *Vaudois.* They originated in the late 12th cent. as the Poor Men of Lyons, a band organized by Peter Waldo, a wealthy merchant of Lyons, who gave away his property (c.1176) and went about preaching apostolic poverty as the way to perfection. Being laymen, they were forbidden to preach. They went to Rome, where Pope Alexander III blessed their life but forbade preaching (1179) without authorization from the local clergy. They disobeyed and began to teach unorthodox doctrines; they were formally declared heretics by Pope Lucius III in 1184 and by the Fourth Lateran Council in 1215. In 1211 more than 80 were burned as heretics at Strasbourg, beginning several centuries of persecution. The Waldenses proclaimed the Bible as the sole rule of life and faith. They rejected the papacy, purgatory, indulgences, and the mass, and laid great stress on gospel simplicity. Worship services consisted of readings from the Bible, the Lord's Prayer, and sermons, which they believed could be preached by all Christians as depositaries of the Holy Spirit. Their distinctive pre-Reformation doctrines are set forth in the Waldensian Catechism (c.1489). They had contact with other similar groups, especially the Humiliati. The Waldenses were most successful in Dauphiné and Piedmont, and had permanent communities in the Cottian Alps SW of Turin. In 1487 at the instance of Pope Innocent VIII a persecution overwhelmed the Dauphiné Waldenses, but those in Piedmont defended themselves successfully. In 1532 they met with German and Swiss Protestants and ultimately adapted their beliefs to those of the Reformed Church. In 1655 the French and Charles Emmanuel II of Savoy began a campaign against them. Oliver Cromwell sent a mission of protest; that occasion also prompted John Milton's famous poem on the Waldenses. At the time of the revocation of the Edict of Nantes (1685), the Waldensian leader, Henri ARNAUD, led a band into Switzerland, then later led them back to their valleys. After the French Revolution the Waldenses of Piedmont were assured liberty of conscience, and in 1848, King Charles Albert of Savoy granted them full religious and civil rights. A group of Waldensians settled in the United States at Valdese, N.C. The Waldensian Church is included in the Alliance of Reformed Churches of the Presbyterian Order. The principal Waldensian writer was Arnaud. See J. A. Wye, *History of the Waldenses* (1880).

Waldheim, Kurt (ko͝ort vält'hīm), 1918–, Austrian diplomat, secretary general of the United Nations (1971–). Son of an Austrian government official, he entered diplomatic service at the end of World War II. He served in France and Canada, where he became the Austrian ambassador. When Austria entered the United Nations in 1958, Waldheim became a member of its delegation and was (1965–68) Austria's permanent representative. After serving (1968–70) as Austria's foreign minister and losing (1971) an election for the presidency of Austria, he returned to the United Nations as permanent representative. He was elected to a five-year term as secretary general in Dec., 1971, replacing the retiring U Thant.

Waldo, Peter: see WALDENSES.

Waldseemüller, Martin (mär'tĭn vält"zāmül'ər), Gr. *Ilacomilus,* 1470?–1522?, German cosmographer. One of a group of humanists known as the Gymnasium Vosagense, he lived at Saint-Dié, Lorraine, during the latter part of his life. He was the first cartographer to call the New World *America.* He sketched the New World in two maps (the first to show North and South America separate from Asia) that he published in 1507 together with an explanatory treatise, *Cosmographiae introductio,* and Amerigo Vespucci's account of his voyages to the New World. A first edition of this rare work is in the New York Public Library. Waldseemüller also prepared with his colleagues a new edition of Ptolemy, published in 1513. See *The Cosmographiae Introductio of Martin Waldseemüller in Facsimile* (U.S. Catholic Historical Society, 1907, repr. 1969).

Waldstein, Albrecht Wenzel Eusebius von: see WALLENSTEIN, ALBRECHT WENZEL EUSEBIUS VON.

Waldwick, borough (1970 pop. 12,313), Bergen co., NE N.J.; inc. 1919. It is a residential community NW of New York City.

Walensee, lake, Switzerland: see WALLENSTADT, LAKE OF.

Wales, Welsh *Cymru,* western peninsula (1971 pop. 2,723,596) of Great Britain, 8,016 sq mi (20,761 sq km), W of England; politically united with England since 1536. Wales is bounded on the N by the Irish Sea, on the S by the Bristol Channel, on the E by the English counties of CHESHIRE, HEREFORD and WORCESTER, and GLOUCESTER (prior to 1974 the English border counties were Cheshire, SHROPSHIRE, and HEREFORDSHIRE), and on the W by Cardigan Bay and St. George's Channel. Across the Menai Strait is the former Welsh island county of ANGLESEY. The other 12 old counties of Wales were CAERNARVONSHIRE, DENBIGHSHIRE, FLINTSHIRE, MERIONETHSHIRE, and MONTGOMERYSHIRE in the north and CARDIGANSHIRE, RADNORSHIRE, BRECKNOCKSHIRE, PEMBROKESHIRE, CARMARTHENSHIRE, GLAMORGANSHIRE, and MONMOUTHSHIRE in the south. As a result of the British Local Government Act of 1972, Wales was reorganized, effective 1974, into eight counties: CLWYD, DYFED, GWENT, GWYNEDD, MID GLAMORGAN, POWYS, SOUTH GLAMORGAN, and WEST GLAMORGAN. The Cambrian Mts. cover most of Wales, with high points at SNOWDON (3,560 ft/1,085 m), PLYNLIMON (2,468 ft/752 m), and Cader Idris (2,970 ft/905 m). The eastern rivers—the Dee, the Severn, and the Wye—drain into England. The Usk flows through Monmouthshire into the Bristol Channel. The Towy, Teifi, Taff, Dovey, and Conway rivers lie completely in Wales. The eastern boundary, drawn in 1536, united England and Wales politically but disregarded cultural and linguistic distribution. Welsh-speaking areas were added to Herefordshire, Shropshire, and Gloucestershire (in England); the language survived in Herefordshire until the 18th cent. and survives to a small extent in Shropshire today. Wales has maintained a distinctive culture despite its long union with England. In 1971 more than 41,000 inhabitants of Wales spoke Celtic Welsh only, and more than 673,000 spoke Welsh in addition to English. The northern counties of Wales are characterized by farms and pastoral highlands, although there has been some recent industrial development around the coal fields of Denbighshire and Flintshire. The coastal towns of the Lleyn Peninsula (Caernarvonshire) are tourist and vacation centers for N England's industrial cities. The industrial wealth of Wales is concentrated in the southern counties bordering on the Bristol Channel. This area has large steelworks (Port TALBOT), oil refineries (MILFORD HAVEN), tinplate and copper foundries, and the S Wales coal fields, which have been revitalized since World War II. Other important industrial cities and ports are NEWPORT, CARDIFF, SWANSEA, and Tenby. The labor force has tended to drift into the southern industrial areas, leaving the north sparsely populated. The Univ. of Wales was created in 1893 by royal charter; it is the collective name of four constituent colleges—three of them created before the incorporation—at Aberystwyth (1872), Cardiff (1883), Bangor (1884), and Swansea (1920); the national school of medicine is also in the system.

Independence, Invasion, and Union. Welsh tradition stretches back into prehistory (see CELT; GREAT BRITAIN). In the first centuries A.D., Celtic-speaking clans of shepherds, farmers, and forest dwellers defended their homes against Roman invaders, who penetrated the N to found Segontium (near Caernarvon) and the S to found Maridunum (now Carmarthen). But the Roman impress upon Wales was light, and Welsh clans continued to dominate large areas of Great Britain, N to the Clyde and the Firth of Forth and S past the Bristol Channel into present Somerset, Devonshire, and Cornwall. They were converted to Christianity by Celtic monks, notably St. DAVID. Although the Anglo-Saxon conquest of E Britain (late 5th cent.) did not seriously affect the Welsh, the invaders did thrust between the main body of Welsh and those S of the Bristol Channel (who nevertheless maintained their national identity for centuries). Border wars were chronic between the Welsh and the seven English kingdoms known as the heptarchy. The sturdy Welsh fighters, who took the name *Cymry* [compatriots], withstood the forces of the kings of MERCIA and WESSEX and later the harrying of the Norsemen. The disparate clans of pastoral people gradually coalesced. Hywel Dda, king of Wales in the mid-10th cent., collected Welsh law and custom into a unified code. At the same time the position of the BARD was formalized, to yield later a wealth of poetry, music, and learning. Defense of the besieged hills went on, and GRUFFYDD AP LLEWELYN, the ruler of Wales, maintained Welsh independence until his death in 1063. William I of England tried to deal with the Welsh by setting up border earldoms to protect his newly won kingdom from their incursions. The power of the border earls (see WELSH MARCHES) grew steadily, and Wales was increasingly threatened with English conquest, although Welsh foot soldiers, moving swiftly and secretly over the mountain paths, resisted through 200 years of guerrilla warfare. When the English made inroads in the north, Rhys ap Tewdr held sway in the south, and only after his death (1093) did the Anglo-Norman barons take full possession of the Vale of Glamorgan. Dissension within England in the early 12th cent. relaxed pressure on the Welsh princes, and medieval Welsh culture approached its full blossom (see EISTEDDFOD; MABINOGION). Nevertheless, although invasions from England were repeatedly thwarted and although LLEWELYN AP IORWERTH (d. 1240) united the Welsh and gained power by skillfully intervening in the troubled English affairs of King John, the end was certain. During the reign of Llewelyn's grandson, LLEWELYN AP GRUFFYDD, English conquest of Wales was finally accomplished by Edward I in 1282. The Statute of Rhuddlan (1284) established English rule. To placate Welsh sentiment, Edward had his son (later Edward II), who had been born at Caernarvon Castle, made prince of Wales in 1301; thus originated the English custom of entitling the king's eldest son prince of Wales. Changes in Welsh life, although few, included a gradual cultural decline and the growth of market towns through trade with England. Wool became a staple source of revenue. The Norman barons were left undisturbed in their marcher lordships. Early in the 15th cent. OWEN GLENDOWER led a revolt that had a brief but amazing success, and Welsh leaders continued to seek advantage from disturbances in the domestic affairs of their conquerors. HENRY VII, the first Tudor king, who ascended the English throne in 1485, was the grandson of Owen TUDOR, a Welshman. Tudor policy toward Wales was one of assimilation on a basis of equality. Welsh lands, including the marches, were converted into shires, and PRIMOGENITURE replaced the old Welsh system of tenure (see GAVELKIND). Leading Welsh families held their lands from the king; the others became leaseholders and tenants after the English pattern. The feudal aristocracy became versed in English manners and were received at the English court. Thus a deep breach, fostered by economic inequality, opened between landlord and tenant and remained unhealed for centuries. A judicial council of Wales, dating from the 15th cent., enhanced royal authority. The Act of Union (1536) and supplementary legislation completed the process of administrative assimilation by abolishing all Welsh customary law at variance with the English and by establishing English as the language of all legal proceedings. Welsh representatives entered the English Parliament; from 1536 onward, the separate history of Wales was mainly religious and cultural.

Modern Wales. The Reformation came belatedly to Wales. Catholic tradition died slowly under Elizabeth I and James I; Puritanism was stoutly resisted, and the Welsh supported Charles I in the ENGLISH CIVIL WAR. Oliver Cromwell had to use oppressive measures to get the Welsh to adopt Puritan practices. In the 18th cent. Wales turned rapidly from the Established Church to dissent with strong Calvinist leanings. This was accompanied by great advances in the field of popular education, which attained unusually high standards. Welsh evangelicism had links with the English movement but was actually a native development. The CALVINISTIC METHODIST CHURCH gathered in great numbers of Welsh from the Church of England and bolstered Welsh nationalism, one of the most successful nonpolitical nationalist movements of the world. The strong hold of evangelical Protestantism on Wales was to make the establishment of the Church of England there the dominant question in Welsh politics in the later 19th cent.; one of the last acts of Parliament that applied to Wales alone was the disestablishment of the church in 1914. Long before that time the tenor and tempo of Welsh life had been changed by the Industrial Revolution. The mineral wealth of Wales was opened to exploitation, at first in the north, then in the rich coal fields of the south. The accent shifted from the sheep walks and farms to the coal pits and factories. By the early 19th cent. the effects of industrialization threatened both cottage industry and agriculture. The distress of rural Wales was dramatically evidenced in the Rebecca Riots of 1843, when poor farmers destroyed toll booths, and in the emigration of large numbers of Welshmen, many to the United States. Numerous company towns sprang up in S Wales, which by the late 19th cent. was the world's chief coal-exporting region. With the benefits of industrialization, however, came poverty and unemployment, which intensified in the years of economic decline following World War I, particularly in the late 1920s and the 1930s. Although Welsh interests had spokesmen in the British government in the early 20th cent.—the flamboyant David LLOYD GEORGE and the Welsh supporters of the Liberal party—chronic poverty and increasing unemployment continued almost unchecked until World War II. After the wartime industrial boom the Labour government, which drew substantial support from the socialist stronghold of S Wales, undertook a full-scale program of industrial redevelopment. This included reorganization of the coal mines and tinplate manufacture under government control, introduction of diversified industry, and improvement of communications, housing, and technical education. As in earlier days, a revived Welsh nationalism turned to education and the arts. The modern National Eisteddfod perpetuates interest in Welsh language, poetry, and choral music. Since 1944 primary and secondary schools have been established with Welsh as the sole language of instruction. Yet political nationalism survives and has been manifested in the Plaid Cymru party, which elected a member to Parliament in 1966. See also WELSH LITERATURE. See A. H. Williams, *An Introduction to the History of Wales* (2 vol., 1962); David Williams, *A Short History of Modern Wales, 1485 to the Present Day* (3d ed. 1962); K. O. Morgan, *Wales in British Politics 1868–1922* (1963); John Rhys and D. B. Jones, *The Welsh People* (1906, repr. 1969); Graham Humphrys, *South Wales* (1972).

Wales, University of, at Cardiff; founded 1893 through the organization of three university colleges already existing in Wales into a unified system for the purpose of degree examinations. The university presently comprises the Univ. College of Wales (1872) at Aberystwyth, Univ. College of North Wales (1884) at Bangor, Univ. College (1883) at Cardiff, Univ. College of Swansea, Univ. of Wales Institute of Science and Technology at Cardiff, the Welsh National School of Medicine at Cardiff, and St. David's Univ. College at Lampeter.

Walewska, Countess Maria (märē′ä välĕf′skä), 1789–1817, Polish noblewoman. She became (1807) the mistress of Emperor Napoleon I and bore (1810) him a son, Alexandre Walewski.

Walewski, Alexandre Florian Joseph Colonna, Comte (älĕksäN′drə flôryäN′ zhôzĕf′ kôlônä′ kôNt välĕfskē′), 1810–68, French diplomat, b. Poland; illegitimate son of Maria Walewska and Emperor Napoleon I. He went to France after the Restoration, returned to Poland in 1830 and joined the Polish uprising, and subsequently went to England to plead the Polish cause. When the insurrection was suppressed, Walewski returned to France, was naturalized, and entered the army, resigning in 1837 to take up journalism. When his cousin, Louis Napoleon (later Napoleon III), came to power in 1848, Walewski was sent on diplomatic missions to Italy, England, and Spain. Foreign minister (1855–60) and minister of state (1860–63), Walewski helped to prepare the Congress of Paris (1856) and presided over it. He also served as a senator and was president of the legislative assembly.

Waley, Arthur, 1889–1966, English orientalist, b. London as Arthur David Schloss, educated at Cambridge. He is considered one of the world's great Oriental scholars. His most important works include his translations of Chinese poetry and of the Japanese poem *The Tale of Genji* (1925–33) by MURASAKI SHIKIBU. Among his other works are *The No Plays of Japan* (1921), *The Poetry and Career of Li Po* (1959) and *The Secret History of the Mongols and Other Pieces* (1964). He never traveled to the Orient. See his bibliography by F. A. Johns (1968).

Walfisch Bay: see WALVIS BAY, South West Africa.

Walhalla, in Germanic mythology: see VALHALLA.

Walke, Henry (wôk), 1808–96, American naval officer, b. Princess Anne co., Va. Walke was appointed a midshipman in 1827, served in the Mexican War, and was later made a commander. In wisely removing the garrison at Pensacola, Fla., to New York early in 1861, he technically violated orders, but a court-martial sentence of admonishment was lightly carried out. Walke's subsequent service on the Mississippi River was outstanding. His gunboats supported Ulysses S. Grant in that general's first Civil War battle, at Belmont, Mo. (Nov., 1861), and as commander of the *Carondelet* he had an important part in the victories at Forts Henry and Donelson, ISLAND NO. 10, Fort Pillow, and Memphis. Promoted to captain (July, 1862), he commanded the *Lafayette,* an ironclad ram, in the Vicksburg campaign. From Sept., 1863, to the end of the war, Walke commanded the *Sacramento* in a search for Confederate cruisers in the Atlantic. He retired (1871) as a rear admiral. See his *Naval Scenes and Reminiscences of the Civil War* (1877), illustrated with his own drawings.

Walker, Amasa, 1799–1875, American economist, b. Woodstock, Conn. He became a merchant in Boston but retired from business in 1840. He lectured (1842–48) on political economy at Oberlin College, which he was influential in founding. He was a delegate to the peace congresses at London (1843) and Paris (1849). An abolitionist, he was elected secretary of state (1851–53) for Massachusetts by the Free-Soil party; he filled out a term (1862–63) as U.S. Congressman. Walker was examiner (1853–60) in economics at Harvard and lecturer (1859–69) at Amherst. His *Science of Wealth* (1866) was long a popular textbook on economics.

Walker, Sir Emery, 1851–1933, English master printer, typographic designer, and engraver. He was, along with William MORRIS and others, one of the moving spirits behind the revival of fine printing at the end of the 19th cent. in England. He helped to found the KELMSCOTT PRESS and later was the partner of Cobden-Sanderson in the DOVES PRESS. Walker was responsible for much of the successful work of the Doves Press, though he and Cobden-Sanderson quarreled, and most of the public credit went to Cobden-Sanderson. Walker exerted great force as a teacher. He was also interested in the improvement of ordinary books and had tremendous influence in changing book design. He was knighted in 1930.

Walker, Francis Amasa, 1840–97, American economist, statistician, and educator, b. Boston, grad. Amherst; son of Amasa Walker. In the Civil War he was brevetted brigadier general. Walker's activities in the U.S. government included service as director of the 10th Census (1880) and as U.S. commissioner of Indian Affairs (1871–72). From 1872 to 1880 he was professor of political economy at Yale, and from 1881 to his death he was president of the Massachusetts Institute of Technology. As an economist, Walker is especially known for his theories on wages and profits (promulgated in *The Wages Question,* 1876) and for his advocacy of international bimetallism. Other works by him include *Money* (1878), *Political Economy* (1883), *Land and Its Rent* (1883), and *International Bimetallism* (1896). See biography by J. P. Munroe (1923); study by Bernard Newton (1968).

Walker, George, 1618–90, Irish Anglican clergyman and commander. As joint governor of Londonderry during the siege (1689) of that city by the army of the deposed James II, Walker roused the people by his courage and inspiring sermons and was able to hold the city for 105 days until it was relieved. He received the thanks of Parliament, was given £5,000 by William III for the citizens of Londonderry, and was designated bishop of Derry. He published *A True Account of the Siege of Londonderry* (1689) and, in answer to charges of self-seeking, a *Vindication* (1690). Walker was killed in the battle of the Boyne.

Walker, Horatio, 1858–1938, Canadian painter, b. Ontario, largely self-taught. Though he lived in Rochester and New York City, he painted chiefly scenes from the simple life of the inhabitants of the Île d'Orléans in the St. Lawrence. His work has been compared to that of the painter J. F. Millet. Examples of his art are *The Woodcutter* and *Milking* (City Art Mus. of St. Louis).

Walker, James John, 1881–1946, American politician, b. New York City. Dapper and debonair, Jimmy Walker, having tried his hand at song writing, engaged in Democratic politics and in 1909 became a member of the state assembly. After studying law at St. Francis Xavier College and at New York Univ. law school, he was admitted (1912) to the bar. He attracted the notice of several Tammany leaders and, under the tutelage of Alfred E. Smith, was elected (1914) to the state senate. In 1921 he became minority leader of the senate and effectively pushed through liberal legislation. With Tammany backing, he defeated John F. Hylan, the incumbent, and F. D. Waterman to become mayor of New York City in 1925. In office Walker backed the adoption of an extensive transit system, unified the public hospitals, and created the department of sanitation. Immensely popular with the electorate, he was returned to office in 1928, defeating Fiorello H. LaGuardia. As a result of several frauds exposed in the municipal government in Walker's second administration, the state legislature ordered an investigation headed by Samuel SEABURY. Extensive corruption was revealed, and 15 charges were leveled at the mayor. Walker hastily resigned (Sept., 1932) before the hearings were closed and went to Europe, where he lived for a number of years. Later he returned to the United States and in 1940 was appointed by Mayor LaGuardia as a municipal arbiter for the garment industry. See Gene Fowler, *Beau James* (1949, repr. 1970).

Walker, Mary Edwards, 1832–1919, American surgeon and feminist, b. Oswego, N.Y., grad. Syracuse Medical College, 1855. At the beginning of the Civil War she offered her services to the Union army. For the first three years she served as a nurse, but in 1864 she was commissioned assistant surgeon, the first woman to have such a commission, and was awarded a medal for her service. She adopted male attire, which she wore to the end of her life, and was active in the struggle for woman suffrage and other reforms. Her book of essays, *Hit* (1871), presents the essence of her ideas on woman's rights. See biography by C. M. Snyder (1962).

Walker, Mickey, 1901–, American boxer, originally named Edward Walker, b. Elizabeth, N.J. He had a turbulent youth and was expelled from school for fighting. Walker's willingness to fight anyone, regardless of weight class, earned him the title of "Toy Bulldog." In 1922 he won the welterweight title, which he held until 1926 when he defeated Tiger Flowers for the middleweight championship. In 1931 he relinquished the middleweight title, and one month later Walker (at 162 lb) fought Jack Sharkey (at 198 lb) to a draw. Later he fought such light heavyweights as Tommy Loughran and Maxie Rosenbloom and the heavyweight Max Schmeling. In 140 matches Walker won 91 fights, including 51 by knockout. In the 1940s he became interested in art and his paintings met with some success. He also worked as a sportswriter. See his *Will to Conquer* (1953) and *Mickey Walker* (1961).

Walker, Robert, d. 1658?, English painter, a follower of Van Dyck and favorite portraitist of Oliver Cromwell. His portraits of Cromwell and his family and followers are convincing studies of Puritan temperament. Examples are in the National Portrait Gallery, London, and the Metropolitan Museum.

Walker, Robert John, 1801–69, American public official, b. Northumberland, Pa. His middle name is sometimes given as James but he was generally known as Robert J. Walker. A lawyer, he practiced for a time in Pittsburgh. In 1826 he moved to Natchez, Miss. As a Democratic Senator (1836–45) from Mississippi, Walker was an ardent advocate of U.S. expansion and became a leader in the drive to annex Texas. James K. Polk made him Secretary of the Treasury (1845–49), and he had an influential voice in government policies. He reestablished the independent treasury system and helped to improve Anglo-American relations (strained by the Oregon dispute) by the Walker Tariff of 1846, a moderate protective tariff that lowered the rates on many items. His financial administration (he was a firm hard-money advocate) is generally considered one of the most able in the history of the Treasury. In March, 1857, he reluctantly accepted appointment as governor of KANSAS. Walker was committed to Stephen A. Douglas's popular sovereignty theory, and believed that the majority of Kansans favored admission to the Union as a free state. When President Buchanan refused to support Walker's contention that the proslavery Lecompton Constitution (see under LECOMPTON) was fraudulently adopted and should be put to popular vote, he resigned (Dec., 1857). He subsequently supported the Union in the Civil War and served as a financial agent in Europe. An expansionist to the end, he had a part in the purchase of Alaska. See biographies by W. E. Dodd (1914, repr. 1967) and J. P. Shenton (1961).

Walker, William, 1824–60, American filibuster in Nicaragua, b. Nashville, Tenn. Walker was a qualified doctor, a lawyer, and a journalist by the time he was 24, but sought a more adventurous career. After a short stay in San Francisco, his filibustering expeditions began with an invasion of Lower California (1853–54) intended to wrest the region together with Sonora from Mexico. The invasion failed miserably. He was tried for violating neutrality laws but was acquitted by a sympathetic jury. In June, 1855, Walker set out on another filibustering expedition, this time to Nicaragua, at the invitation of one of the country's revolutionary factions. His capture of Granada brought an end to the fighting, and, after obtaining recognition (May, 1856) from the United States for the new government, Walker declared himself president of Nicaragua in July, 1856. An alliance of hostile Central American states and the enmity of his former friend, Cornelius Vanderbilt, whose Accessory Transit Company controlled Walker's supply lines, led to his defeat and surrender to the U.S. navy in May, 1857. Considered a hero by many Americans, Walker was again acquitted of violating neutrality, but then alienated U.S. public opinion by blaming his defeat on the U.S. navy. From the Bay Islands of Honduras, Walker made a final abortive attempt (1860) to conquer Central America, but was forced to surrender to the British navy. He was turned over to Honduras and was shot by a firing squad Sept. 12, 1860. See his own book, *War in Nicaragua* (1860, repr. 1971); W. O. Scroggs, *Filibusters and Financiers* (1916, repr. 1969); Laurence Greene, *The Filibuster* (1937, repr. 1974); biography by A. H. Carr (1963).

Walker Lake, salt lake, c.105 sq mi (270 sq km), W Nev., SE of Carson City. Fed by the Walker River, it is a remnant of prehistoric Lake Lahontan and has no outlet.

walking fish: see CLIMBING PERCH.

walking stick or **stick insect,** names applied to extremely longbodied, slow-moving, herbivorous INSECTS, forming a single family in the order Orthoptera. Walking sticks have green, gray, or brown bodies that closely resemble twigs or grass stems. Most are wingless and have long antennae. They range from less than 1 in. to over 1 ft (2–33 cm) in length, thus including the longest insects in the world. The winged forms have two pairs of wings; the hind wings are often colored. Their excellent camouflage protects them from predators; in addition, walking sticks can emit a foul-smelling substance as a means of defense. Some tropical species bear sharp spines resembling thorns. Walking sticks, unlike most insects, have the ability to regenerate lost limbs. Their eggs, which look like seeds, are deposited randomly on the ground; these often pass two winters before hatching in the spring. The young resemble the adults but are smaller. Although principally tropical and Oriental in distribution, walking sticks are also found in temperate regions of Europe and North America. One species, *Megaphasma dentricus,* is the longest insect in the United States, attaining a length of 7 in. (17.5 cm). Walking sticks are classified in the phylum ARTHROPODA, class Insecta, order Orthoptera, suborder Phasmotodea, family Phasmatidae. See also LEAF INSECT.

Walküre: see VALKYRIES.

Wall, Richard, 1694–1778, Spanish statesman. Born in France of Irish parents, Wall entered the Spanish military service as a young man and later held important diplomatic posts. He helped negotiate the Treaty of Aix-la-Chapelle (1748) ending the War of the Austrian Succession, and he cemented friendly Anglo-Spanish relations as ambassador in London (1748–52). In Madrid, he served (1752–64) as minister of state under Ferdinand VI and Charles III.

wall, in architecture, protective, enclosing, or dividing vertical structure. Its thickness is determined by the material, height, and stress. It may be of studding and lath, either boarded or plastered; adobe; RAMMED EARTH; brickwork or stonework; concrete; tile; or of steel in combination with one or more of the preceding materials. The wall serves two functions. A bearing wall is used as a support, e.g., for the floors and roof. Usually raised on foundations, it is thicker at the bottom than at the top and is often buttressed. A nonbearing wall, such as a partition SCREEN or curtain wall, is used to separate and define spaces and is generally much thinner. A party wall is one common to two adjoining buildings, and a gable wall is one at right angles to the roof ridge. A fire wall, or bulkhead, separates hazardous equipment from the rest of a structure to prevent the spreading of fire; in ships the bulkhead is also watertight. The front wall or face of a building is termed the FACADE. Exterior walls may be finished with STUCCO or GRAFFITO and enhanced by bas-relief, tile, mosaic, or painted decoration. Arcade, rustication, and vermiculated work are means of ornamenting brick and stone masonry. In engineering a retaining wall either of CYCLOPEAN or of wet masonry protects an embankment from washing; a sea wall, or BREAKWATER, is for harbor protection; and a DAM is an earth, masonry, or concrete wall to stop the natural flow of a stream to conserve a water supply or create power. The defensive walls of a city or other political division (see CHINA, GREAT WALL OF) are frequently two or three concentric ramparts, often including FORTIFICATION and watchtowers. Great portals form the gateways. Notable walls of antiquity were those of Thebes, Troy, Jericho, and Babylon; an example of a medieval wall is that at Carcassonne in France.

wallaby: see KANGAROO.

Wallace, Alfred Russel, 1823–1913, English naturalist. From his study of comparative biology in Brazil and in the East Indies, he evolved a concept of evolution similar to that of Charles DARWIN. Like Darwin, he was greatly influenced by the writings of Malthus and Lyell and based his theories on careful observation. His special contribution to the evidence for evolution was in biogeography; he systematized the science and wrote *The Geographical Distribution of Animals* (2 vol., 1876) and a supplement, *Island Life* (1881). His research in this field is commemorated in the name WALLACE'S LINE. He assisted H. W. BATES in evolving an early concept of mimicry. His other works include *Contributions to the Theory of Natural Selection* (1870), *Darwinism* (1889), *Social Environment and Moral Progress* (1913), and an autobiography (2 vol., 1905). See study by H. L. McKinney (1972).

Wallace, Edgar, 1875–1932, English novelist and playwright, b. Greenwich. He was the author of more than 150 detective and adventure novels, of which as many as 5 million were sold in a year. *The Terror* (1930), which is typical of his work, still ranks high as a thriller. He wrote several plays and the scenarios for such films as *King Kong* (1933). See biographies by his wife, E. V. Wallace (1932), and by Margaret Lane (1939, repr. 1964).

Wallace, George Corley, 1919–, governor of Alabama (1963–67, 1971–), b. Clio, Ala. Admitted to the bar in 1942, he was active in the Democratic party in Alabama, serving in the state assembly (1947–53) and as a district court judge (1953–59). In 1962 he ran successfully for governor as an avowed segregationist and promised to defy Federal orders to integrate Alabama schools. In June, 1963, Wallace blocked the path of two black students attempting to enter the Univ. of Alabama, but capitulated when President John F. Kennedy federalized the Alabama national guard. Prevented by state law from succeeding himself as governor in 1966, he had his wife, Lurleen Burns Wallace (1926–1968), run successfully in his place. As the leading spokesman against the civil rights movement, Wallace ran for president in 1968 on a third-party ticket and capitalized on anti-Negro feeling in both the North and the South. In 1970, he was reelected governor of Alabama. In 1972, he entered the Democratic presidential primaries; Wallace's campaign ended abruptly on May 15, 1972, when an assassination attempt by Arthur H. Bremer critically wounded him and left him paralyzed below the waist. He was overwhelmingly reelected governor in 1974. See biographies by W. G. Jones (1966) and Marshall Frady (1968).

Wallace, Henry, 1836–1916, American agricultural leader, b. West Newton, Pa., grad. Jefferson (later Washington and Jefferson) College, 1859. He studied (1861–63) theology and went (1863) to Iowa as a home missionary of the United Presbyterian Church. He later turned to farming, pioneering in several aspects of agriculture, and began writing agricultural articles for the *Iowa Homestead.* He was made its managing editor, but his efforts in the early 1890s to curb railroad powers led to his removal from the editorship. In 1895 he joined with his son Henry Cantwell Wallace in founding the newspaper that later was called *Wallaces' Farmer.* This journal soon won recognition as a leading agricultural newspaper of the country. "Uncle Henry," as he was affectionately known, was a popular speaker and a counselor of Republican statesmen. He served (1908) as a member of President Theodore Roosevelt's Country Life Commission. Wallace's works include *Clover Farming* (1898) and *Letters to the Farm Folk* (1915). His autobiography, *Uncle Henry's Own Story of His Life* (1917), dealt chiefly with his boyhood.

Wallace, Henry Agard, 1888–1965, Vice President of the United States (1941–45), b. Adair co., Iowa. He was (1910–24) associate editor of *Wallaces' Farmer,* an influential agricultural periodical run by his family, and when his father, Henry Cantwell Wallace, died in 1924, he became editor. Henry A. Wallace had developed several strains of hybrid corn that were to be used extensively by farmers of the American Corn Belt, and his writings on farm economics and plant genetics quickly won him recognition as an agrarian authority. A Republican until 1928, Wallace helped swing Iowa to the Democratic party in the 1932 election. In 1933 he was appointed Secretary of Agriculture by President Franklin Delano Roosevelt and soon led in the reorganization of the Dept. of Agriculture and in the supervision of the Agricultural Adjustment Agency. He became a highly regarded leader in the New Deal, and in 1940 he was elected Vice President of the United States. He went on several missions to Latin America and the Far East and served (1942-43) as head of the Board of Economic Warfare. In 1944, Wallace failed to receive the vice presidential nomination again. In 1945, shortly before Roosevelt's death, he became Secretary of Commerce. He held that position until Sept., 1946, when he was forced to resign because of his open opposition to President Truman's foreign policy. He then edited (1946-48) the *New Republic.* In 1948, Wallace helped launch a new Progressive party, which charged the Truman administration with primary responsibility for the cold war. As its presidential candidate that year he polled slightly over 1,150,000 votes (mostly in New York state), but won no electoral votes. Wallace left the party in 1950 after it had repudiated his endorsement of the U.S.-UN intervention in Korea. Wallace's numerous books on agricultural problems and politics include *Agricultural Prices* (1920), *New Frontiers* (1934), *The Century of the Common Man* (1943), *Toward World Peace* (1948), and *The Long Look Ahead* (1960). With E. N. Bressman he wrote *Corn and Corn Growing* (1923), and with W. L. Brown he wrote *Corn and Its Early Fathers* (1956). See biographies by Dwight Macdonald (1948) and E. L. Schapsmeier (2 vol., 1968-70); Russell Lord, *The Wallaces of Iowa* (1947); K. M. Schmidt, *Henry Wallace: Quixotic Crusade, 1948* (1960).

Wallace, Henry Cantwell, 1866-1924, American agricultural leader and cabinet officer, b. Rock Island, Ill., grad. Iowa State College of Agriculture, 1892; son of Henry WALLACE (1836-1916). Harry Wallace, as he often was called, was associated with his father in founding *Wallaces' Farmer* and served as assistant editor until 1916, then becoming editor. He held government posts in World War I, and later (1921) President Warren G. Harding appointed him Secretary of Agriculture. In spite of opposition from the packing interests, Wallace continued to serve under President Calvin Coolidge. He reorganized the department and died in office. His views were set forth in his book, *Our Debt and Duty to the Farmer* (1925). See study by D. L. Winters (1970).

Wallace, Irving, 1916-, American writer, b. Chicago. An extraordinarily prolific writer, Wallace has written over 500 articles for magazines, biographies for encyclopedias, film scripts, and such best-selling novels as *The Chapman Report* (1960), *The Prize* (1962), *The Man* (1964), *The Plot* (1967), *The Seven Minutes* (1969) and *The Fan Club* (1974). See biography by John Leverence (1974).

Wallace, Lew (Lewis Wallace), 1827-1905, American novelist and diplomat, b. Brookville, Ind. He served in both the Mexican and Civil wars. After returning to his law practice in Indiana, he became governor of the Territory of New Mexico (1878-81) and minister to Turkey (1881-85). His famous book, *Ben Hur* (1880), has been one of the best-selling novels in American publishing history and was made into several motion pictures. Among his other novels are *The Fair God* (1873), a story of the conquest of Mexico, and *The Prince of India* (1893). See his autobiography (1906).

Wallace, Sir Richard, 1818-90, English art collector. The illegitimate son of the marquess of Hertford, he inherited in 1871 his father's superb collection of continental art, which he had helped to build. Wallace, created baronet in 1871, was a member of Parliament (1873-85). Lady Wallace bequeathed the **Wallace Collection** to the government in 1897. Especially fine in the 18th-century French schools, it has been open to the public since 1900 in Hertford House, London. See H. C. Shelley, *The Art of the Wallace Collection* (1913).

Wallace, Sir William, 1272?-1305, Scottish soldier and national hero. The first historical record of Wallace's activities concerns the burning of Lanark by Wallace and 30 men in May, 1297, and the slaying of the English sheriff, one of those whom EDWARD I of England had installed in his attempt to make good his claim to overlordship of Scotland. After the burning of Lanark many joined Wallace's forces, and under his leadership a disciplined army was evolved. Wallace marched on Scone and met an English force of more than 50,000 before Stirling Castle in Sept., 1297. The English, trying to cross a narrow bridge over the Forth River, were killed as they crossed, and their army was routed. Wallace crossed the border and laid waste several counties in the North of England. In December he returned to Scotland and for a short time acted as guardian of the realm for the imprisoned king, John de BALIOL. In July, 1298, Edward defeated Wallace and his army at Falkirk, and forced him to retreat northward. His prestige lost, Wallace went to France in 1299 to seek the aid of King Philip IV, and he possibly went on to Rome. He is heard of again fighting in Scotland in 1304, but there was a price on his head, and in 1305 he was captured by Sir John de Menteith. He was taken to London in Aug., 1305, declared guilty of treason, and executed. The best-known source for the life of Wallace is a long romantic poem attributed to BLIND HARRY, written in the 15th cent. See biography by J. Fergusson (1938, rev. ed. 1948).

Wallaceburg, town (1971 pop. 10,550), SE Ont., Canada, on the Sydenham River near Lake St. Clair. It is a port of entry with some light industry.

Wallace Collection: see under WALLACE, SIR RICHARD.

Wallace's line, imaginary line postulated by A. R. Wallace as the dividing line between Asian and Australian fauna in the Malay Archipelago. It passes between Bali and Lombok islands and between Borneo and Celebes, then continues S of the Philippines and N of the Hawaiian Islands.

Wallachia: see WALACHIA.

Wallack, James William (wŏl'ək), c.1795-1864, Anglo-American actor and manager. Of a theatrical family, he was a leading actor (1812-32) in both comedy and melodrama at Drury Lane. After 1852 he lived in the United States. In New York City he managed Wallack's National (1837-39), Wallack's Lyceum (1852), and Wallack's (1861), where he maintained one of the best theatrical companies in New York. His son, **Lester Wallack** (John Johnstone Wallack), 1820-88, also an actor-manager, gained experience in Dublin and London and made his New York debut in 1847. He was best in comic and romantic roles. Lester succeeded to the management of Wallack's in 1861; in 1882 he simultaneously operated another Wallack's at Broadway and 30th St. He wrote, produced, and played in a variety of dramas, but his best production was his own play *Rosedale* (1863). See his *Memoirs of Fifty Years* (1889).

wallaroo: see KANGAROO.

Wallas, Graham (wŏl'əs), 1858-1932, English political scientist and psychologist. He joined (1886) the FABIAN SOCIETY and was the author of one of the *Fabian Essays.* In 1914, Wallas became professor of political science at the Univ. of London. In his lectures and writings he studied the psychological factors in politics and advocated government by specially trained persons. Wallas wrote a biography of Francis Place (1898), *Human Nature in Politics* (1908), *The Great Society* (1914), *Our Social Heritage* (1921), and *The Art of Thought* (1926). See study by M. J. Wiener (1971).

Wallasey (wŏl'əsē), county borough (1971 pop. 97,061), Cheshire, W central England, on the tip of Wirral peninsula at the mouth of the Mersey River. There is some industry, including flour milling and ship repairing, but Wallasey is largely residential. The borough includes New Brighton, a seaside resort. In 1974, Wallasey became part of the new metropolitan county of Merseyside.

Walla Walla (wŏl'ə wŏl'ə), city (1970 pop. 23,619), seat of Walla Walla co., SE Wash., at the junction of the Walla Walla River and Mill Creek, near the Oregon line; inc. 1862. It is a trade, processing, and distributing center for a rich farm area. Fruits and vegetables (especially green peas) are canned and frozen in numerous plants there, grain is processed for animal feeds, and cans are manufactured. The city also has a pulp and paper mill. The old fur-trading Fort Walla Walla was established near that site in 1818, and in 1836 the mission of Marcus Whitman was also built nearby. Wagon trains began bringing settlers in the 1840s, and Steptoeville (later Walla Walla) grew around the U.S. military Fort Walla Walla (est. 1856; now a veterans hospital). The name was changed when the settlement became county seat in 1859. Walla Walla is the seat of Whitman College, the state's first institution of higher learning. Walla Walla College, a junior college, and the state penitentiary are also in the city. The Whitman mission nearby has been restored as a national historic site.

Wallensee: see WALLENSTADT, LAKE OF, Switzerland.

Wallenstadt, Lake of (väl'ənshtät"), Ger. *Walensee* or *Wallensee,* narrow mountain lake, c.9 sq mi (23 sq km), between St. Gall and Glarus cantons, E Switzerland. It is connected with Zürich by the Linth Canal. Wallenstadt, on the east shore, is a summer resort and the chief town on the lake.

Wallenstein or **Waldstein, Albrecht Wenzel Eusebius von** (wäl'ənstīn, Ger. äl'brĕkht vĕn'tsəl oizā'bēo͞os fən-väl'ənshtīn, vält'shtīn), 1583-1634, imperial general in the THIRTY YEARS WAR, b. Bohemia. He attended the Lutheran academy at Altdorf but at the age of 20 converted to Roman Catholicism. He advanced his fortune by marriage to a wealthy widow, and for his support of Archduke Ferdinand of Styria (Holy Roman Emperor FERDINAND II) before, during, and after the Bohemian revolt that started the Thirty Years War, he was well rewarded, becoming prince and then (1625) duke of Friedland. He built up a magnificent estate in Bohemia, expanding his fortune at the expense of the Bohemian Protestants, whose lands he confiscated with Ferdinand's authorization. In 1625, Wallenstein raised a large army for Ferdinand II and became chief imperial general, cooperating with the general of the Catholic League, Count TILLY, in the Danish phase of the war. Wallenstein in 1626 defeated Ernst von MANSFELD at the Dessau bridgehead, and some of his men helped Tilly to defeat the Danish king CHRISTIAN IV at Lutter. The next year Wallenstein destroyed the remnants of Mansfeld's army and later defeated Christian IV's forces. Now at the height of his wealth and power, Wallenstein, having driven the dukes of Mecklenburg from their lands, was granted that duchy as a hereditary fief from the Holy Roman emperor. He was also given the title of admiral, but his hopes of founding a maritime empire were set back by the failure of the siege of Stralsund (1628) on the Baltic. Wallenstein had powerful enemies, particularly among the German princes, from whom he had extorted money for the support of the army. Finally, in 1630, they prevailed on Ferdinand to dismiss him. The failure of his successor, Tilly, against King GUSTAVUS II of Sweden brought Wallenstein back to power (1632). With a huge army he cleared Bohemia and began a contest with the Swedish king that ended at Lützen (1632), where Wallenstein was defeated and the Swedish king was killed. Embittered by his earlier dismissal, Wallenstein was then determined to become more powerful than ever, controlling not only military decision, but imperial policy also. His secret negotiations with the enemy brought down on his head accusations of treason. A number of his generals, including Matthias GALLAS and Ottavio PICCOLOMINI, were drawn into a conspiracy against him. Ferdinand secretly removed Wallenstein from command on Jan. 24, 1634. Wallenstein renewed his attempts to negotiate with the Swedes and with a few hundred troops fled to Eger (CHEB), where he was treacherously murdered (Feb., 1634). His assassin later had the emperor's favor. Wallenstein is the central figure in a dramatic trilogy by Schiller. See Francis Watson, *Wallenstein, Soldier under Saturn* (1938).

Waller, Edmund, 1606-87, English poet. He studied at Eton and Cambridge and became a prominent speaker in Parliament at a young age. He married twice (1631 and 1644), but his early poems are addressed to "Sacharissa," Lady Dorothy Sidney, who refused to marry him. Although at first an antiroyalist, he later supported Charles I against Parliament and conceived "Waller's plot" (1643) to secure the city of London for the king. The plot was discovered, and Waller was fined and banished. He was pardoned in 1651 and after the Restoration was again in Parliament, where he served until his death. His verse is noted for its smoothness and polish, but aside from a few amatory poems his importance rests on his contributions in style, most notably the development of the heroic couplet. The first collection of his works appeared in 1645 and immediately went through several editions. His best-known lyrics are "Go, Lovely Rose" and "On a Girdle." See his poems ed. by George Thorn Drury (1893, repr. 1968); A. W. Allison, *Toward an Augustan Poetic* (1962).

Waller, Fats, 1904-43, American jazz musician, singer, and composer, whose original name was Thomas Wright Waller, b. New York City. Waller began playing the piano as a child, and later studied with Carl Bohm and Leopold Godowsky. He became a protégé of James P. Johnson, who gave him piano lessons and furthered his career. From about 1920, Waller appeared in night-clubs and theaters, and in the 1930s he began recording. Waller's style influenced many jazz pianists. His compositions include

Ain't Misbehavin', Black and Blue, Honeysuckle Rose, and *London Suite.* See biography by Charles Fox (1961).

Waller, Sir William, 1597-1668, English parliamentary general. He fought (1620-22) in the Thirty Years War and was knighted in 1622. A zealous Puritan, he sat in the Long Parliament (see ENGLISH CIVIL WAR), became a colonel in the parliamentary army, and achieved a series of victories that gained him the popular title of William the Conqueror. In 1643, however, he was defeated by the royalists at Roundway Down. He received fresh troops and continued campaigning with mixed results until the creation of the New Model Army (which he had originally proposed). The Self-Denying Ordinance (1645) prohibited his serving in that army because he was a member of Parliament. A leader of the Presbyterian party in Parliament, he was imprisoned (1648-51) by the army and again under the Protectorate. He promoted the return of Charles II and was returned (1660) to Parliament by General Monck's influence, but after the Restoration he retired.

walleye: see STRABISMUS.

walleye or **walleyed pike:** see PERCH.

wallflower, Mediterranean perennial (*Cheiranthus cheiri*) of the family Cruciferae (MUSTARD family), particularly popular in Europe, where it flourishes on old walls. An old-fashioned garden flower, it is similar in appearance to the related stock and is also sometimes called gillyflower. The early spring blossoms are often much doubled; yellow, red, and brown are the prevailing colors. Related species are also called wallflower, e.g., the orange-flowered Siberian, or western, wallflower (*Erysimum asperum*), which occurs both wild and in cultivation in North America. Wallflowers are classified in the division MAGNOLIOPHYTA, class Magnoliopsida, order Capparales, family Cruciferae.

Wallingford, town (1970 pop. 35,714), New Haven co., S Conn.; inc. 1670. Its silverware industry dates from c.1835. Fruit growing and the manufacture of plastics, steel, precision instruments, and hardware are among the town's other industries. Several old buildings remain. In Wallingford is the Choate preparatory school for boys, now coordinated with Rosemary Hall, a girls' preparatory school formerly located at Greenwich, Conn. A branch of the Oneida Community was founded in the town in 1851. Lyman Hall was born there.

Wallington, borough (1970 pop. 10,284), Bergen co., NE N.J., on the Passaic River opposite Passaic; inc. 1895. Manufactures include paints, chemicals, and textile products.

Wallis, John (wŏl'ĭs), 1616-1703, English mathematician. He was Savilian professor of geometry at Oxford Univ. from 1649. He systematized the use of formulas, introduced the symbol ∞ for infinity, and made a study of the quadrature of curves, which he recorded in *Arithmetica infinitorum* (1655). His collected mathematical works appeared in three volumes (1693-99). He wrote also on grammar, logic, theology, and cryptography.

Wallis and Futuna Islands (wŏl'ĭs, fo͞oto͞o'nä), French overseas territory (1969 pop. 8,546), South Pacific, W of Samoa and NE of Fiji. Comprising two small groups, the Wallis Islands and the Hoorn Islands, which are c.120 mi (190 km) apart, it is sometimes called Wallis Archipelago. The main volcanic islands are Uvea, Futuna, and Alofi; the chief town is Matautu. Copra was an important export until the mid-1960s, when an attack of rhinoceros beetles ravaged the islands' palm trees. Timber is still exported. The islands came under French control in 1842 and became an overseas territory in 1961. They are governed by an administrator and a territorial assembly.

Wallon, Henri Alexandre (äNrē' älĕksäN'drə välôN'), 1812-1904, French historian and politician. He was elected (1871) to the national assembly, and it was his proposal (1875) that led to the adoption of the organic laws that formed the constitution of the Third Republic. As minister of public instruction (1875-76), he was accused of supporting Roman Catholic interests and was forced to resign. Wallon's major field of historical scholarship was the French Revolution. His *Histoire du tribunal révolutionnaire* (6 vol., 1880-82) contained much new material and connected the work of the tribunal with the general revolutionary movement.

Walloons (wŏlo͞onz'), general term applied to the French-speaking people of BELGIUM (mostly in the provinces of Hainaut, Liège, Namur, Luxembourg, and the southern part of Brabant), in contrast to the Dutch-speaking Flemings of the northern provinces. Walloon in its proper meaning is a French dialect spoken in the Liège region; the movement for reviving Walloon literature centered in Liège in the 19th cent. The periodical *Wallonie* had considerable influence. Since medieval times the economic and social background of the Walloons has differed radically from that of the Flemings, and the cleavage became even more pronounced with the Industrial Revolution. The Walloon part of Belgium contains major mining areas and heavy industries, while the Flemings engage mainly in agriculture, manufacturing (particularly textiles), and shipping. Tension between Walloons and Flemings has long been a critical political issue. In 1970 a plan was approved that recognized the cultural autonomy of Belgium's three national communities: the Dutch-speaking Flemings of the north, the French-speaking Walloons of the south, and bilingual Brussels. The name *Walloons* was also applied to Huguenot refugees in America by the Dutch, who made no distinction between French and Walloon Protestants. See H. H. Turney-High, *Château-Gerard; the Life and Times of a Walloon Village* (1953).

Wallowa Lake (wəlou'ə), c.3 mi (4.8 km) long, NE Oregon, at the foot of the Wallowa Mts. An irrigation reservoir, it is drained by the Wallowa River NW to the Grande Ronde River. The lake is the center of a resort region; a state park is there.

wallpaper was used in Europe in the 16th and 17th cent. as an inexpensive substitute for costly hangings. The French developed marbled papers, introduced from the East via Italy and used at first for box coverings, into larger sheets for wall coverings and also made other papers in small designs. Outlines were block-printed, and the color was filled in with brush or stencil. The flock technique of printing designs with an adhesive and sprinkling with fine bits of wool or silk was probably first adapted to wallpaper c.1620 in France, but by the 18th cent. England had become the principal manufacturer. Sets of painted Chinese paper were imported in the 17th cent. and by the 18th had become highly popular and were widely imitated. In France, Jean Papillon established in 1688 the first large wallpaper factory, where he made matching designs that would be continuous when pasted. In the 18th cent. paper was glued into continuous rolls before printing. Wallpaper was manufactured in the American colonies from the mid-18th cent. Colonial homes displayed various scenic and pictorial papers, often with tropical themes. The mid-19th cent. brought modern printing on roll paper, mass production, and decadence in design. The English Pre-Raphaelite artists, particularly William MORRIS, promoted a renaissance in wallpaper designs, and the 20th cent. has seen its fulfillment in England, France, and the United States. American designers have revived interest in landscape papers and have greatly developed frieze and panel papers through the medium of hand block printing. See Phyllis Ackerman, *Wallpaper* (1923); E. A. Entwistle, *The Book of Wallpaper* (1954).

Wallsend (wôlz'ĕnd''), municipal borough (1971 pop. 45,793), Northumberland, NE England, on the Tyne River. In a coal-mining region, Wallsend has ship building and engineering industries. Wallsend is the eastern terminus of Hadrian's Wall. In 1974, Wallsend became part of the new metropolitan county of Tyne and Wear.

Wall Street, narrow street in the lower part of Manhattan island, New York City, extending E from Broadway to the East River. It is the center of one of the greatest financial districts in the world, and by extension the term "Wall St." has come to designate U.S. financial interests. In the district, which extends several blocks N and S of Wall St., are the major U.S. stock exchanges (the New York and the American) as well as exchanges for cotton, coffee, produce, metals, maritime goods, and other commodities. There are also brokerage houses and the main offices of numerous banking firms, insurance, railroad, and steamship companies, and large industrial corporations. Facing Wall St., on the west side of Broadway, is Trinity Church. The Subtreasury Building, now Federal Hall National Memorial (see NATIONAL PARKS AND MONUMENTS, table), one block east, was erected on the site of the former Federal Hall, where George Washington was inaugurated in 1789 and where the first Congress met. Wall St. received its name from a stockade, or wall, built in 1653 by Dutch colonists to protect the settled area south of it from assault by the English and by Indians.

walnut, common name for some members of the Juglandaceae, a family of chiefly deciduous, resinous trees characterized by large and aromatic compound leaves. Species of the walnut family are indigenous mostly to the north temperate zone, but also range from Central America along the Andes to Argentina and through tropical Asia to Java and New Guinea. Several trees of the Juglandaceae are of commercial importance for the edible nuts and for lumber. The nuts, usually enclosed in a leathery or woody hull, include many of the most valuable food nuts of the United States—the walnut and the butternut of the walnut genus *Juglans* and the pecan, hickory nut, pignut, and mockernut of the HICKORY genus *Carya.* The single-seeded nuts contain no endosperm; the edible portion is the corrugated, meaty seed leaves of the embryo itself. Lumber is obtained chiefly from *Juglans, Carya,* and *Englehardtia.* The latter genus is now restricted to the Orient except for one Central American species, but fossil

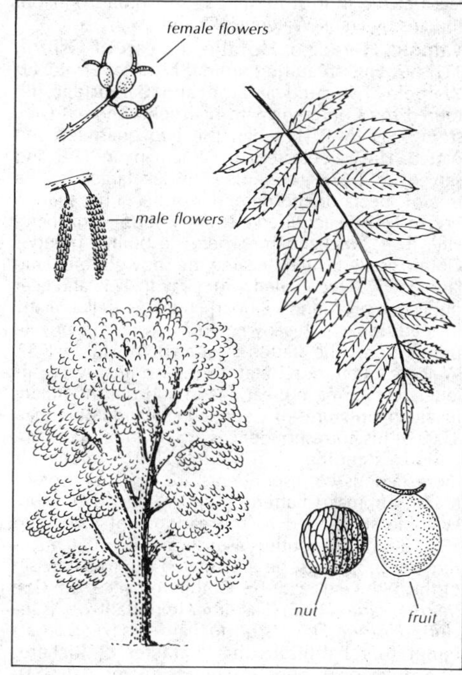

Black walnut, Juglans nigra

trees have been found in the United States. Species of these and other genera (e.g., *Pterocarya,* the Asiatic wingnuts) are often planted as ornamental shade trees. Walnut as a common name is used for species of *Juglans* (from Lat. *Jovis glans*=nut of Jove), the largest and most widely distributed genus of the family. The dark-colored timber of the black walnut (*J. nigra*), found in hardwood forests in the eastern half of North America, and of the Persian, or English, walnut (*J. regia*), native to W Asia, is unusually hard and durable and is valued for furniture, interior paneling, gunstocks, musical instruments, and other uses. Black walnut has been the foremost cabinet wood of North America since colonial times. The closer-grained English walnut, usually sold as lumber under the name Circassian walnut, is widely cultivated in S Europe and the Orient and has been introduced with great success into California, now the major producing area of the world. The nut of this tree is more easily extracted from the shell than that of the black walnut and is the one usually sold commercially for use as a table nut and for confectionery, flavorings, and sometimes pickling. A decoction of the leaves, bark, and hulls is used for a brown wool dye and the crushed leaves for an insect repellent. The butternut, or white walnut (*J. cinerea*), of approximately the same range as the black walnut, has a sweet and oily nut that is gathered locally but is not of commercial importance. The butternut is also timbered; the wood is softer than that of the black and English walnuts. Sugar is sometimes obtained from its sap, and the hulls yield a yellow to gray dye that gave color to the homespun of pioneers and to the "butternut" uniforms of some of the Confederate soldiers. The inner root bark, called butternut bark, has been used in domestic remedies, as have the hulls of the English walnut. Other American and Old World walnuts are also used and esteemed locally for timber, dyes, and food. The walnut family is classified in the division MAGNOLIOPHYTA, class Magnoliopsida, order Juglandales.

Walnut Canyon National Monument: see NATIONAL PARKS AND MONUMENTS (table).

Walnut Creek, residential city (1970 pop. 39,844), Contra Costa co., W Calif., in the San Francisco Bay area; inc. 1914. Numerous industrial research firms, corporate headquarters, and a naval weapons station are there.

Walpi (wäl'pē) [Hopi,=place of the gap], pueblo, NE Ariz., on a mesa NE of Flagstaff; founded c.1700. Its inhabitants are Pueblo Indians who speak the Hopi language (Uto-Aztecan linguistic stock). One of the most picturesque pueblos of the Southwest, it is a major tourist attraction. The pueblo was founded as a refuge in anticipation of Spanish retaliation for the revolt of the Pueblo Indians (1680). The antelope ceremony is held there in August on even years, and the famous Hopi snake dance in August on odd years. The pueblo, however, is gradually being deserted for the new village of Polacca at the foot of the mesa. See studies on Hopi Indians by Frank Waters (1963 and 1969).

Walpole, Horace or **Horatio,** 4th **earl of Orford,** 1717–97, English author; youngest son of Sir Robert Walpole. Educated at Eton and Cambridge, he toured the Continent with his friend Thomas Gray from 1739 to 1741, when the two quarreled and parted. He was elected to Parliament in 1741 and served until 1767, confining himself largely to the role of spectator and defender of his father's memory. In 1747 he acquired a country house, Strawberry Hill, near Twickenham, where he built a pseudo-Gothic castle, which became the showplace of England. He was reconciled with Gray in 1745 and later published his friend's Pindaric odes, as well as many first editions of his own works from the private printing press he started at Strawberry Hill in 1757. Walpole's literary reputation rests primarily on his letters, which have great charm and polish and are invaluable pictures of Georgian England. More than 3,000 of his correspondences are extant and cover a period extending from 1732 to 1797. Among his more famous correspondents are Gray, Sir Horace Mann, Thomas Chatterton, and Mme DU DEFFAND. Walpole succeeded to the earldom of Orford in 1791. Besides his enthusiasm for medieval architecture and trappings, he anticipated the romanticism of the 19th cent. with his Gothic romance *The Castle of Otranto* (1765). His other important works include *Historic Doubts on Richard III* (1768), an attempt to rehabilitate the character of Richard; *Anecdotes of Painting in England* (4 vol., 1762–71); and posthumous works, *Reminiscences* (1798) and memoirs of the reigns of George II (1822) and George III (1845, 1859). See Yale edition of the letters by W. S. Lewis (vol. 1–36; 1937–73); biographies by W. S. Lewis (1961) and R. W. Ketton-Cremer (rev. ed. 1964); study ed. by W. H. Smith (1967).

Walpole, Sir Hugh Seymour, 1884–1941, English novelist, b. New Zealand, educated at Cambridge. His first two novels were failures, but with *Fortitude* (1913) he achieved financial and literary success. He was an uneven writer who turned out colorful, descriptive prose at a rapid pace; his best-known works include the historical Herries novels—*Rogue Herries* (1930), *Judith Paris* (1931), *The Fortress* (1932), and *Vanessa* (1933). *Portrait of a Man with Red Hair* (1925) is probably his best horror story. There are autobiographical elements in *Jeremy* (1919), *Jeremy and Hamlet* (1923), *Jeremy at Crale* (1927), and *The Cathedral* (1922). He also wrote short stories, several plays, biographies of Joseph Conrad (1916) and Anthony Trollope (1928), and the screenplay for the film *David Copperfield* (1934). Walpole was knighted in 1937. See his autobiography (3 vol., 1924, 1932, 1940); biographies by Rupert Hart-Davis (1952) and Elizabeth Steele (1972).

Walpole, Robert, 1st **earl of Orford,** 1676–1745, English statesman. He was the younger son of a prominent Whig family of Norfolk. After the death of his father and elder brothers he was returned (1701) to Parliament from the family borough of Castle Rising, and in 1702 he took the seat for King's Lynn, from which he was regularly returned thereafter. Walpole soon made his mark as a hard-working administrator. In 1708 he was appointed secretary of war and later (1710–11) was treasurer of the navy. As a Whig, he led the opposition in Parliament to the Tory administration of 1710–14 and as a consequence was falsely convicted (1712) of corruption and spent some months in the Tower of London. The accession of George I (1714) returned the Whigs to power, and Walpole served variously as paymaster of the forces, first lord of the treasury, and chancellor of the exchequer (1715) under his brother-in-law, Viscount TOWNSHEND, and James Stanhope (later 1st Earl Stanhope). The dismissal of Townshend led to Walpole's resignation (1717), and together they formed an opposition nominally headed by the prince of Wales (later George II). The two returned to office in 1720. The same year Walpole was called upon to salvage the financial wreckage resulting from the SOUTH SEA BUBBLE, in which he himself lost a substantial amount of money. This marked the turning point of his career. His successful handling of this matter led to his appointment (1721) as first lord of the treasury and chancellor of the exchequer. He shared power with John Carteret (later 1st Earl GRANVILLE) until 1724 and with Townshend, whom he left in charge of foreign affairs, until 1730, but thereafter his ascendancy was complete until 1742. He enjoyed the confidence of both George I and George II, influencing the latter through his friendship with the queen, CAROLINE OF ANSBACH, and handled Parliament with unprecedented skill. His control of Parliament was due partly to the dispensation of royal patronage, partly to the electoral management of Thomas Pelham-Holles, duke of NEWCASTLE, but also to Walpole's own debating skills and the popularity of many of his policies. In financial policy, his strongest point, he created the sinking fund to reduce the national debt. He mollified the largely Tory gentry by reduction of the land tax and promoted trade by awarding bonuses for exports and encouraging the production of raw materials by the colonies. Walpole's plan to reduce smuggling and make London a free port by replacing tariffs on wine and tobacco with an excise tax was defeated in 1733, largely because of widespread popular prejudice against excise. After this debacle Walpole dismissed all the officeholders who had voted against him, an action that created a much stronger opposition group than he had previously faced. It was on foreign policy that the opposition against him finally coalesced. Walpole had pursued a policy of friendship with France and avoidance of war, and he had managed (against fierce opposition) to keep Great Britain neutral during the War of the Polish Succession (1733–35). In 1739, however, the war party forced him into the War of Jenkins's Ear (1739–41; see JENKINS'S EAR, WAR OF), which in turn involved Britain in a general European war (see AUSTRIAN SUCCESSION, WAR OF THE). Military reverses increased the opposition, and Walpole was forced to resign in 1742. He was created earl of Orford and remained politically powerful until his death. Walpole is usually described as the first prime minister of Great Britain, but he was not a prime minister in the modern sense. Although management of Parliament, and particularly the House of Commons, was an essential part of his power, so too was royal favor, on which he ultimately depended. The purge of his ministry in 1733, sometimes hailed as a major step in the development of cabinet solidarity, could not have been accomplished without royal support. Moreover, the contention that there was any idea of cabinet solidarity is refuted by the fact that when Walpole left office his most important colleagues remained in the ministry. Walpole's primacy was achieved and maintained through his own political talents and the circumstances of the time; he made little impact on constitutional development. See biographies by C. R. Stirling Taylor (1931) and J. H. Plumb (2 vol., 1956–61, repr. 1973); study by H. T. Dickinson (1973).

Walpole, Sir Spencer, 1839–1907, English historian. He held a number of minor public offices and served as private secretary in the home office to his father, Sir Spencer Horatio Walpole, whose biography he wrote (1874). He contributed to the newly founded *Pall Mall Gazette* but is chiefly remembered for his *History of England from 1815* (5 vol., 1878–86) and its continuation, *History of Twenty-five Years* (4 vol., 1904–8), which covers the period from 1856 to 1880. His biography of the 1st Earl Russell appeared in 1889. He was knighted in 1898.

Walpole, town (1970 pop. 18,149), Norfolk co., E Mass., SW of Boston; settled 1659, inc. 1724. Textiles and paper products are the chief manufactures.

Walpurga or **Walpurgis, Saint:** see WALBURGA, SAINT.

Walpurgis Night: see WALBURGA, SAINT.

Walras, Léon, 1834–1910, French economist. He abandoned his studies in mining engineering and became a free-lance journalist, espousing the causes of economic and social reform. He was a professor of political economy at the Univ. of Lausanne from 1870 to 1892. His economic theory was unique at the time in that he applied mathematical analysis to the study of the general economy. Walras was also an early exponent of a managed currency. See his correspondence, ed. by William Jaffé (3 vol., 1965).

walrus, marine mammal, *Odobenus rosmarus,* found in Arctic seas. Largest of the fin-footed mammals, or pinnipeds (see SEAL), the walrus is also distinguished by its long tusks and by cheek pads bearing quill-like bristles. Adult males are 10 ft (3 m) long or more, and weigh up to 3,000 lb (1,400 kg); females weigh about two thirds as much as males. The tusks, which are elongated upper canine teeth, may reach a length of 3 ft (90 cm) in large males and weigh over 10 lb (4.5 kg). The hide of a walrus is very thick and wrinkled, and is light brown and nearly hairless. Beneath the hide is a layer of fat several inches thick. Like sea lions, walruses can turn their hind flippers forward for walking on land; their foreflippers are weaker than those of sea lions and they are not as strong swimmers. They live in shallow water and spend much of the time on ice floes and beaches, where they congregate in herds of about 100 animals of both sexes. They dive for food to a depth of 240 ft (70 m); their diet consists chiefly of shellfish, especially mollusks. The cheek teeth are rounded and are used for crushing shells. Walruses use their tusks for prying shellfish from the ocean floor, as well as for pulling themselves up onto ice floes. The herds tend to follow the ice line, moving south in winter and north in summer. Walruses have been very important in the economy of the Eskimo, who hunt them for food and clothing; the introduction of firearms greatly increased the size of the kill. Commercial hunting of walruses for blubber, hides, and ivory has been extensive since the 16th cent. and has greatly reduced the walrus population. Several nations now have protective laws; Canada and the USSR prohibit walrus hunting except by peoples for whom it is a traditional part of the economy. There are two walrus races, the Atlantic and the Pacific. The Atlantic race, which formerly was found as far S as Nova Scotia and occasionally Massachusetts, is now considered endangered. Walruses are classified in the phylum CHORDATA, subphylum Vertebrata, class Mammalia, order Carnivora, suborder Pinnipedia, family Odobenidae. See Richard Perry, *The World of the Walrus* (1968).

Walsall (wôl'sôl), county borough (1971 pop. 184,606), Staffordshire, W central England, in the Black Country. Coal mining, iron and brass founding, limestone quarrying, and the manufacturing of leather goods and aircraft parts are among the industries of Walsall. In 1974, Walsall became part of the new metropolitan county of West Midlands.

Walsh, Thomas James (wôlsh), 1859–1933, American political leader, b. Two Rivers, Wis. A lawyer, he was Democratic Senator from Montana from 1913 until his death. Walsh helped write the Eighteenth and Nineteenth amendments and worked for the abolition of child labor. Noted for his debating ability, he fought for the League of Nations and the World Court and advocated arms limitations. He became a popular figure when the Senate Investigating Committee, which he headed (1922–23), exposed the fraudulent practices of the Harding administration in the leasing of naval oil reserves at TEAPOT DOME. In 1924 he refused the vice presidential nomination of the Democratic party. Walsh supported Franklin Delano Roosevelt in 1932 and was appointed U.S. Attorney General, but he died suddenly before he was able to take office. See biography by Josephine O'Keane (1955); J. L. Bates, ed., *Tom Walsh in Dakota Territory* (1966).

Walsingham, Sir Francis (wôl'sĭng-əm), 1532?–1590, English statesman. A zealous Protestant, he went abroad during the reign of Queen Mary I but returned on the accession (1558) of Elizabeth I. He entered Parliament (1559) and soon was employed by William Cecil, Baron BURGHLEY, in obtaining intelligence from abroad. Joint secretary of state after 1573, he built up an elaborate and effective spy system, which later implicated the imprisoned Mary Queen of Scots in a conspiracy against Elizabeth (1586) and led to her execution. His system in 1587 also provided England with minute details of the impending attack of the Spanish Armada. Walsingham, as a Protestant, favored an alliance of England, France, and the Netherlands against Spain. But, although he was employed on numerous missions and knighted in 1577, he was never able to persuade Elizabeth to adopt his policies of militant Protestantism. The responsibility for the debts he assumed (1586) at the death of his son-in-law, Sir Philip Sidney, put him in financial difficulties, and he died in debt. See Conyers Read, *Mr. Secretary Walsingham and the Policy of Queen Elizabeth* (3 vol., 1925, repr. 1967).

Walsingham, rural district (1971 pop. 17,416), Norfolk, E central England. It is the site of Walsingham

Abbey, one of the great shrines of medieval England.

Walter, Bruno, 1876–1962, German-American conductor, b. Berlin as Bruno Walter Schlesinger. Walter studied at the Stern Conservatory in Berlin. After he had conducted in several German cities, Gustav Mahler appointed him (1901) assistant conductor of the Vienna State Opera, where he remained until 1912. Walter was musical director of the Munich Opera (1912–22) and of the Municipal Opera, Berlin (1925–29), and appeared at Covent Garden and the Salzburg Festival. He made his American debut in 1923. While conductor of the Gewandhaus Concerts in Leipzig (1929–33), he was forced by the Nazis to leave Germany. He returned to the Vienna Opera in 1935 but left in 1938, when the Nazis dominated Austria. Walter became a permanent resident of the United States in 1939. He conducted the Metropolitan Opera, the NBC Symphony, the New York Philharmonic, and other American ensembles, being permanent conductor of the New York Philharmonic from 1947 to 1949. Walter was renowned as an interpreter of the German and Austrian classics and was a friend and champion of Mahler. He wrote *Gustav Mahler* (tr. 1941), an autobiography, *Theme and Variations* (1946), and *Of Music and Music-Making* (1961).

Walter, Hubert, d. 1205, English archbishop and statesman. He was clerk to his uncle, Ranulf de Glanvill, and in 1186 he was made dean of York. In 1189 he was appointed bishop of Salisbury, and he accompanied RICHARD I on crusade in 1190. He returned to England in 1193 to be made archbishop of Canterbury and justiciar of the realm at the instigation of the now captive Richard. He was responsible for raising Richard's ransom and forestalling a rebellion planned by John (later King JOHN). After Richard again departed (1194), Hubert was virtual ruler of England. Despite his manifest avarice, he was responsible for tax reforms and important administrative reforms in town and county government. In 1196, Walter caused the Church of St. Mary-le-Bow to be set afire in order to drive out the leader of the revolting London craftsmen, William FitzOsbert, who had taken sanctuary there. This and other unclerical actions led the pope to demand Walter's resignation from secular office in 1198. However, upon the accession (1199) of John he became chancellor and continued to wield enormous influence. He died shortly after frustrating the king's plan for another French campaign. See biography by C. R. Young (1968).

Walter, Lucy, 1630?–1658, mistress (1648–50) of Charles II of England during his exile in Holland and France. She was the mother by him of James Scott, duke of MONMOUTH, whom the Whigs supported as heir to the throne in their attempt to exclude James, duke of York (later James II), from the succession. It was rumored at that time that Charles had actually married Lucy and that proof of the marriage was contained in a mysterious black box. Charles always denied the report. Lucy herself was a courtesan before and after her connection with Charles. She was arrested (1656) in London as a spy but was released and sent abroad. She died in Paris.

Walter, Thomas Ustick, 1804–87, American architect, b. Philadelphia. In 1819 he entered the office of William Strickland in Philadelphia as a student. In 1830 he began practice, the county prison (1831) at Moyamensing, Philadelphia co., being his first important work. The main building of Girard College in Philadelphia, which he designed in 1833 and completed in 1847, was one of the most ambitious works of the classic revival. In 1851, Walter was appointed to design extensions for the Capitol at Washington, D.C., which had remained unchanged since the completion of Bulfinch's plans in 1830. Holding the post of government architect until 1865, Walter added the wings for the Senate and House of Representatives, as well as the central dome of cast iron, replacing Bulfinch's low dome, and rebuilt the west front. At Washington, D.C., Walter also designed the interior of the Library of Congress and built extensions for the Post Office, the Patent Office, and the Treasury. His works in Philadelphia included the Biddle and Cowperthwaite country residences. For the Venezuelan government he designed a breakwater at La Guaira. One of the original organizers of the American Institute of Architects in 1857, he held its presidency from 1867 until his death. Walter's designs possessed fine classic and monumental character, and he stood highest among American architects of his time.

Walter of Henley or **Walter de Henley,** fl. 13th cent., English writer on agriculture. His treatise *Husbandry,* written in Norman French in the mid-13th cent., was the great medieval authority in England, covering all aspects of rural economy from the sowing and manuring of land to the management of labor. It was not superseded until 1523. See translation by Elizabeth Lamond, *Walter of Henley's Husbandry* (1890).

Walter Reed Army Medical Center, major hospital complex in Washington, D.C., and Forest Glen, Md.; est. 1923 and named for U.S. army surgeon Walter Reed. It is composed of seven units including a general hospital and a research institute. There are 1,500 beds.

Walter the Penniless, Fr. *Gautier Sans-Avoir,* d. 1096, French Crusader, a disciple of PETER THE HERMIT. He and his followers left for the Holy Land well in advance of the main army of the First Crusade (see CRUSADES). They passed peacefully through Germany and Hungary, but plundered the Belgrade area and were set upon by the Bulgarians, who killed many of them. Walter and the remnants of his army were joined at Constantinople by the forces of Peter the Hermit. The Byzantine emperor Alexius I provided transport for the combined forces to Asia Minor. There they were utterly defeated (1096) by the Seljuk Turks, and Walter was killed.

Waltham (wôl'thăm, –thəm), city (1970 pop. 61,582), Middlesex co., E Mass., a suburb of Boston, on the Charles River; settled c.1634, set off from Watertown 1738, inc. as a city 1884. Electronic equipment and parts, precision instruments, and small tools are among its varied manufactures. It was known as the seat of the Waltham Watch Company, which produced clocks and watches there from 1854 until 1950. Brandeis Univ. and Bentley College are in the city.

Waltham Forest (wôl'təm, –thəm), borough (1971 pop. 233,528) of Greater London, SE England. The borough was formed in 1965 by the merger of the municipal boroughs of Chingford, Leyton, and Walthamstow. Waltham Forest is primarily residential. William Morris lived in Water House. The hunting lodge of Queen Elizabeth I is now a museum.

Waltham Holy Cross, urban district (1971 pop. 14,585), Essex, SE England. The great abbey, the Norman nave of which is now used as a parish church, was built in 1030 to contain a cross found in Somerset and believed to have miraculous powers. The abbey was enlarged in 1060 by King Harold, who is thought to have been buried there.

Walthamstow: see WALTHAM FOREST.

Walther von der Vogelweide (väl'tər fən dĕr fō'gəlvī"də), c.1170–c.1230, German minnesinger of noble birth, probably the finest lyric poet of medieval Germany. He wandered from court to court singing songs for which he wrote both words and music. In addition he was noted for his *Sprüche,* or maxims, which were frequently political.

Walton, Ernest Thompson Sinton, 1903–, Irish physicist, educated at Methodist College (Belfast), Trinity College (Dublin), and Cambridge. He became a fellow of Trinity College in 1934 and professor of natural and experimental philosophy there in 1946. The 1951 Nobel Prize in Physics was awarded jointly to Walton and Sir John Cockcroft for their pioneer work in transmuting atomic nuclei by bombarding elements with artificially accelerated atomic particles.

Walton, George, 1741?–1804, American Revolutionary patriot, signer of the Declaration of Independence, b. near Farmville, Va. He moved to Savannah, Ga., where he established a law practice. Walton was a delegate to the Continental Congress (1776–78, 1780–81). He was captured by the British at the fall of Savannah (1778) but was exchanged in 1779 and later was governor of Georgia (1779–80, 1789) and served briefly as U.S. Senator (1795–96).

Walton, Izaak, 1593–1683, English writer. He wrote one of the most famous books in the English language, *The Compleat Angler; or, the Contemplative Man's Recreation.* The first edition appeared in 1653, and it was reissued frequently with additional material; the last edition in Walton's lifetime appeared in 1676. The book not only describes the technique of angling, but draws a picture of peace and simple virtue that was Walton's protest against the civil wars taking place at the time. He also wrote several biographies, including ones of John Donne (1640), Sir Henry Wotton (1651), and George Herbert (1670), all of whom were his friends. See study by David Novarr (1958); John R. Cooper, *The Art of The Compleat Angler* (1968).

Walton, Sir William Turner, 1902–, English composer, b. Oldham. Walton studied at Oxford. One of his earliest works was a piano quartet (1918–19). In 1923, *Facade,* satirical poems by Edith Sitwell read to Walton's music, had enormous success in London. His orchestral works, noted for eloquent melodic structure, include the overtures *Portsmouth Point* (1925) and *Scapino* (1940) and two symphonies (1935, 1961). He wrote an oratorio, *Belshazzar's Feast* (1931), and coronation marches for George VI (1937) and Elizabeth II (1953). Walton's concerto for viola and orchestra (1929), a violin concerto (1939), and a sonata for violin and piano (1950) are also well known. Among the films for which he composed musical scores are *Henry V* (1944), *Hamlet* (1947), and *Richard III* (1954). Walton wrote the opera *Troilus and Cressida* in 1954 and the one-act extravaganza *The Bear* in 1967. He was knighted in 1951. See study by F. S. Howes (rev. ed. 1974).

Walton and Weybridge (wā'brĭj), urban district (1971 pop. 51,004), Surrey, SE England. It is largely a residential suburb of London. There are market gardening, an aircraft works, and other industries.

Walton-le-Dale, urban district (1971 pop. 26,841), Lancashire, N England. There are engineering works and textile and paper industries. An 11th-century church was rebuilt in 1748. Oliver Cromwell's headquarters before the battle of Preston (1648) were in Walton-le-Dale.

waltz, romantic dance in moderate triple time. It evolved from the German *Ländler* and became popular in the 18th cent. The dance is smooth, graceful, and vital in performance. The waltz in Vicente Martin's opera *Una cosa rara,* produced in Vienna (1776), is regarded as the first Viennese waltz. This type was later made famous by the two Johann Strausses, father and son. The younger Strauss composed the *Blue Danube Waltz,* the most popular of the Viennese style. The waltz was introduced in the United States via England in the early 19th cent. Mozart, Chopin, Berlioz, Brahms, Richard Strauss, and Ravel have also composed waltzes.

Walvis Bay (wôl'vĭs), city (1970 pop. 21,725), W central South West Africa, on Walvis Bay, an arm of the Atlantic Ocean. With the surrounding area, c.430 sq mi (1,110 sq km), it is an exclave of South Africa, although it is administered by South West Africa. Walvis Bay is the principal port of South West Africa and is the terminus of a railroad from the hinterland. Whaling and fishing fleets are stationed there, and the city has fish canneries. The town of Walvis Bay and its surrounding region were annexed by Great Britain in 1878 and incorporated into the Cape Colony. When South West Africa was annexed (1884) by Germany, Walvis Bay became a British exclave administered by the Cape Colony. It is also known as Walfisch Bay and Walvisbaai.

Wampanoag Indians (wäm"pənō'ăg), North American Indians whose language belongs to the Algonquian branch of the Algonquian-Wakashan linguistic stock (see AMERICAN INDIAN LANGUAGES). In the early 17th cent. they occupied the region extending E from Narragansett Bay to the Atlantic Ocean, including Nantucket and Martha's Vineyard. The Wampanoag were sometimes referred to as the Pokanoket Indians, from the name of their principal village. When the Pilgrims settled (1620) at Plymouth, the Wampanoag, although reduced by the pestilence of 1617, were powerful, living in some 30 villages. Their chief, MASSASOIT, was very friendly to the settlers. His son, Philip, however, was the central figure of the deadliest war with the colonists, KING PHILIP'S WAR (1675). The victory of the English brought ruin to the tribe. The Wampanoag were harried almost out of existence, the remnant consolidating with the Saconnet. There are still a few Indians of Wampanoag descent, living mainly in Massachusetts. The Wampanoag were of the Eastern Woodlands culture area. See M. A. Travers, *The Wampanoag Indian Federation of the Algonquian Nation* (rev. ed. 1961).

wampum (wäm'pəm) [New England Algonquian,= white string of beads], beads or disks made by American Indians from the shells of mollusks found on the eastern coast or along the larger rivers of North America, used as a medium of exchange. In general, wampum beads were cylindrical. They were highly prized by the Indians, particularly by those of the Eastern Woodlands and Plains cultural areas. On the Pacific coast, shell ornaments (especially gorgets) were also used, but wampum was principally important in trade in what is now the NE United States. Wampum was passed by trade to inland tribes. Used as a currency or SHELL MONEY, there were two varieties—the white, which is the only sort properly called wampum, and the more valuable purple (usually made from the purple portion of a clam shell), to which different names were applied by the various tribes. Wampum was used for the ornamentation of such things as necklaces and collars. Wampum belts were of particular ceremonial importance because they were typically exchanged when a treaty of peace was signed. Frequently the belts had pictograph designs on them. Wampum was also used by white fur traders in their trade with the Indians in the early part of the 17th cent. because of a lack of European currency.

Wanamaker, John (wŏn'əmā"kər), 1838–1922, American merchant, b. Philadelphia. He went into the men's clothing business in Philadelphia with Nathan Brown, his brother-in-law, in 1861. The firm was Wanamaker and Brown until the death of Brown in 1868, and from 1869 it was John Wanamaker and Company. In 1875, Wanamaker bought the site of the old Pennsylvania RR freight station and opened a new dry goods and clothing store, which later became one of the first and best-known department stores. He was Postmaster General (1889–93) in Benjamin Harrison's cabinet and greatly improved the efficiency of the service. He extended his business into New York City in 1896, when he took over the store which had formerly been A. T. Stewart and Company. He was identified with religious work in Philadelphia, as a paid secretary (1857–61) and later president (1870–83) of the Young Men's Christian Association and as superintendent of the Bethany Presbyterian Sunday School for many years. See biographies by H. A. Gibbons (1926) and J. H. Appel (1970).

Wandering Jew, in literary and popular legend, a Jew who mocked or mistreated Jesus while he was on his way to the cross and who was condemned therefore to a life of wandering on earth until Judgment Day. The story of this wanderer was first recorded in the chronicles of Roger of Wendover and Matthew of Paris (13th cent.), but not until the early 17th cent. was he identified as a Jew. The story is common in Western Europe, but it presents marked national variations. Among the innumerable treatments of the subject is Shelley's *Queen Mab.* See G. K. Anderson, *The Legend of the Wandering Jew* (1965).

wandering jew, common name for several creeping plants of the genera *Tradescantia* and *Zebrina* in the SPIDERWORT family. *Zebrina pendula* is most commonly cultivated in window boxes and hanging pots. Wandering jew is classified in the division MAGNOLIOPHYTA, class Liliatae, order Commelinales, family Commelinaceae.

Wandsworth, borough (1971 pop. 298,931) of Greater London, SE London, on the Thames River. The borough was created in 1965 by the merger of the metropolitan borough of Battersea with most of the metropolitan borough of Wandsworth. An area along the Thames is industrialized, with gasworks and breweries. In the 18th cent. there were cloth industries worked by Huguenots who had come to England after the revocation of the Edict of Nantes in 1685. Battersea Park, along the Thames between the Albert and Chelsea bridges, contains a lake, amphitheater, and theater. Wandsworth Technical College and Battersea Technical College are in the borough.

Wang An-shih (wäng än-shûr), 1021–86, Chinese Sung dynasty statesman. As a chief councilor (1069–74, 1075–76) he directed sweeping administrative and fiscal reforms that drew strong conservative opposition. His aim was to strengthen the central government, but the poor also benefited from reforms such as the graduated land tax, cheap government credit, and reduction of the forced labor levy. Wang revived government price and commodity controls, local police administration, and the militia system. Followers of Wang competed with conservative bureaucratic opponents for high office after his resignation. See biography by H. R. Williamson (2 vol., 1935–37, repr. 1973); J. T. C. Liu, *Reform in Sung China* (1959).

Wanganui (wŏng"ənōō'ē, wŏng"gə-), city (1971 pop. 35,782), SW North Island, New Zealand, near the mouth of the Wanganui River. Wanganui is a distribution center and port for coastal trade. It was founded in 1840.

Wang Ching-wei (wäng jĭng-wā), 1883–1944, Chinese revolutionary and political leader. A supporter of Sun Yat-sen, Wang was sentenced (1910) to life imprisonment for attempting to assassinate the regent of China. After being freed (1912) by the republican revolution, he studied in France until 1917. He and Hu Han-min were Sun's leading disciples, and after Sun's death (1925) Wang led the left-wing of the Kuomintang. He revolted several times against Chiang Kai-shek's leadership of the party, but he was premier (1932–35) and deputy leader of the Kuomintang (1938). Wary of the Communists, and dubious of China's ability to sustain a protracted war, Wang advocated peace with Japan in 1938 and broke with Chiang. From 1940 to his death he was premier of the Japanese puppet government at Nanking. See study by G. E. Bunker (1972).

Wang Ch'ung-hui (wäng chōōng-hwē), 1881–1958, Chinese jurist. He was educated in China, Japan, Europe, and the United States. He was greatly influenced by Sun Yat-sen. Wang became (1912) the first minister of justice of the Chinese republic. An important figure in the Kuomintang, he held numerous positions in the field of Chinese and international law. He was chief justice of the Chinese supreme court (1920), minister of justice (1922, 1927–31), deputy judge (1923–25), and judge of the World Court (1931–36). Wang was also minister of education (1926), president of the Judicial Yuan (1928–31, 1948–58), and foreign minister (1937–41).

Wang Mang (wäng mäng), 45 B.C.–A.D. 23, Chinese HAN dynasty regent who usurped the throne and ruled as emperor of the Hsin [new] court, carrying out many reforms. Although he portrayed his government as a revival of the idealized state of early CHOU times, his reforms were aimed essentially at strengthening the bureaucracy and solving the current financial crisis. To refill the imperial coffers, Wang Mang instituted government monopolies, debased the currency, and introduced agricultural reforms. In his most famous reform he decreed (A.D. 9) that the large tax-free estates be dissolved and that the land be redistributed to the peasants, who were to pay taxes. Pressure from the aristocracy, however, forced him (A.D. 12) to rescind the measure. Wang Mang's control ultimately collapsed in the face of the social disorder and rebellion that spread following a disastrous change in the lower course of the Huang Ho. He died at the hands of rebels when his capital, Changan (Hsi-an), was sacked; his centralized bureaucracy was destroyed at the same time. A battle for the throne continued until A.D. 25, when LIU HSIU restored the Han and began the long process of rebuilding the central administration.

Wang Wei (wäng wā), 699–759, Chinese poet. He was an extremely versatile man, being a physician and painter as well as a poet. He wrote quatrains almost exclusively; these verses portray quiet scenes like those depicted in his few surviving paintings. Wang Wei's delicate landscapes, famed for their depiction of water and mist, were drawn in black ink. He is considered the first master of atmosphere and the founder of Southern Chinese landscape art. Forced to serve at court until aged, Wang Wei entered a Buddhist monastery after the death of his wife. His poems were translated (1959) by Chang Yin-nan and L. C. Walmsley.

Wang Yang-ming (wäng yäng-mĭng), 1472–1529, Chinese philosopher. He developed an idealist interpretation of CONFUCIANISM that denied the rationalist dualism of the orthodox philosophy of CHU HSI. Wang believed that universal moral law is innate in man and discoverable through self-cultivation. In contrast to the orthodox Confucian reliance on classical studies (see CHINESE LITERATURE) as a means to self-cultivation, Wang stressed self-awareness and the unity of knowledge and action. One school of his followers emphasized achievement of mystical enlightenment in a manner strikingly similar to ZEN BUDDHISM.

Wan-hsien (wän-shēĕn), city (1970 est. pop. 175,000), E Szechwan prov., China, an important port on the Yangtze River at the beginning of the Yangtze gorges. It is a major tung-oil exporting point.

Wankel engine: see INTERNAL-COMBUSTION ENGINE.

Wankie (wŏng'kē), city (1973 est. pop., with suburbs, 24,000), W Rhodesia. It is a coal-mining center. The city was founded in 1903 and named for a local black African chief. A game preserve is nearby.

Wanne-Eickel (vä'nə-ī'kəl), city (1970 pop. 99,156), North Rhine-Westphalia, W West Germany, a port on the Rhine-Herne Canal. It is a coal-mining and industrial center of the RUHR district. Its manufactures include chemicals, processed food, and electrical goods. The city was formed in 1926 by the merger of the twin cities of Wanne and Eickel.

Wanstead and Woodford: see REDBRIDGE.

Wantagh (wŏn'tô), uninc. residential city (1970 pop. 21,873), Nassau co., SE N.Y., on the S shore of Long Island. A causeway leads to Jones Beach State Park.

Wapentake: see HUNDRED.

wapiti (wŏp'ĭtē), large North American deer, *Cervus canadensis,* closely related to the Old World red deer. It is commonly called ELK in America although the name *elk* is used in Europe to refer to the MOOSE. The wapiti is grayish brown, with a chestnut mane and yellowish rump patch and short tail. It is the largest of the deer family besides the moose; the male stands up to 5 ft (150 cm) at the shoulder and weighs up to 1,000 lb (450 kg). The male has antlers with 5 or more points on each branch and up to a 5-ft (150-cm) spread. Once abundant throughout temperate North America, the wapiti was slaughtered for food, leather, and sport and for its canine teeth (used as charms). It has been completely exterminated in the E United States and reduced in numbers elsewhere. Several varieties now exist, mostly under protection in national parks and wildlife refuges. Two of these are the Rocky Mountain elk, found from N Mexico to central Alberta, and the Roosevelt, or Olympic, elk, found in forests of the Pacific coastal belt from British Columbia to N California. Related to the wapiti is the dwarf, or tule elk, *C. nannodes,* a small, light-colored deer of E California. The Old World red deer, *C. elaphus,* is smaller than the wapiti; males stand about 4 ft (120 cm) at the shoulder and have antlers up to 4 ft (120 cm) long. Its coat is reddish brown. It is found in wooded areas throughout the cold and temperate portions of Eurasia and in N Africa. Several other species of the genus *Cervus* are found in Asia. The sambar, *C. unicolor,* is a large brown deer of SE Asia. These and other deer are classified in the phylum CHORDATA, subphylum Vertebrata, class Mammalia, order Artiodactyla, family Cervidae.

Wappers, Gustave, Baron (güstäv' bärôN' väpĕrs', väp'ərs), 1803–74, Belgian historical and genre painter. For many years director of the Antwerp Academy, he introduced the romantic school into Belgium. The last 15 years of his life were spent in Paris. His most famous work is *Episode of the Belgian Revolution of 1830* (Brussels).

Wappinger Indians (wŏp'ĭnjər), confederation of North American Indians of the Algonquian branch of the Algonquian-Wakashan linguistic stock (see AMERICAN INDIAN LANGUAGES). In the early 17th cent. they occupied the east bank of the Hudson River from Poughkeepsie to Manhattan Island and ranged E into Connecticut. They were closely related to the Mahican to the north and the Delaware to the southwest, and there is much argument about assigning various groups to any one of the three peoples. The Wappinger, however, included many groups, the most important of which were the Wappinger proper, the Kitchawong, the Sint Sink, the Tankiteke, the Weckquaesgeek, the Manhattan, the Siwanoy, the Nochpeem, and the Mattabesec. The power of the Wappinger confederacy, which numbered about 5,000 at its peak, was broken in a war with the Dutch (1640–45), and gradually they lost their lands and retired to the protection of the neighboring Indians. Some joined the Nanticoke, some the Delaware, and some the Mahican. The Wappinger were of the Eastern Woodlands cultural area.

war, armed conflict between sovereign states (international war) or between factions within a state (civil war), prosecuted by force and having the purpose of compelling the defeated side to do the will of the victor. Among the causes of war are ideological, political, racial, economic, and religious conflicts. Imperialism, nationalism, and militarism have been called the dynamics of modern war. According to Karl von CLAUSEWITZ, war is a "continuation of political intercourse by other means." As such it often takes place when arbitration (see ARBITRATION, INTERNATIONAL), MEDIATION, and negotiation have failed to remove its cause. War has been a constant feature of history since primitive times. In ancient states warfare was usually a community enterprise, but as society divided on a functional basis a warrior class developed, and the ARMY and NAVY became component parts of the state. In many instances, both recent and historic, the military has ruled the state. The use of fighting forces as instruments of war became a scientific art with the development of STRATEGY AND TACTICS. Modern war has been even more greatly influenced, however, by industrial development, scientific progress, and the spread of popular education; a new era of machine warfare, prosecuted by masses of troops obtained through CONSCRIPTION, rather than by rulers and the military class alone, developed after the wars of Napoleon I. Modern total war calls for the regimentation and coordination of peoples and resources; the state is compelled to demand a surrender of private rights in order that unity of purpose may enable it to prosecute the war to a victorious conclusion. Total wars are waged not only against a nation's government and armed forces but also against a nation's economic means of existence and its civilian population in order to destroy the means and will to continue the struggle. The U.S. Civil War was the first modern total war. Major wars thereafter became increasingly total and destructive with the development of new weapons, including the atomic bombs that devastated Japan at the end of World War II. Organized efforts to put an end to war began with the PEACE CONGRESSES of the 19th cent. and culminated in the formation of the LEAGUE OF NATIONS after World War I and the UNITED NATIONS after World War II. Since the days of the COLD WAR the threat of nuclear retaliation has served to restrain the use of large-scale nuclear weapons; instead there has been an arms race, a succession of limited wars, and a proliferation of GUERRILLA WARFARE. For efforts to retard the arms race, see DISARMAMENT, NUCLEAR. See studies by Quincy Wright (2d ed. 1965), Geoffrey Blainey (1973), and John Stoessinger (1974).

war, laws of, in INTERNATIONAL LAW, rules and principles regulating an armed conflict between nations. These laws are designed to minimize the destruction of life and property, to proscribe cruel treatment of noncombatants and PRISONERS OF WAR, and to establish conditions under which the belligerents may consult with one another. To mitigate the effects of insurrections and civil wars, established governments often recognize the BELLIGERENCY of domestic opponents and conduct conflicts with them according to the laws of war. In the Middle Ages the ideals of knighthood restrained some cruelties in warfare, but systematic legal codes did not appear until the 17th cent. The great work of GROTIUS, *De jure belli ac pacis* [on the laws of war and peace] (1625) and the works of Vattel had much influence in introducing humane practices. Detailed international treaties governing war are mostly a product of the 19th and 20th cent. The Declaration of Paris (1856; see PARIS, DECLARATION OF), the accords concluded at the HAGUE CONFERENCES (1899, 1907), and the Geneva Conventions (1864, 1906, 1929, 1949) are the main bodies of formulated law. There is no convention to which all the major powers of the world have acceded, and many conventions provide that their terms shall be inoperative if any of the belligerents is not a signatory or if an enemy commits a violation. Despite such provisions, many nations have adopted the laws of war, and the conditions of warfare have undoubtedly been ameliorated, particularly in the treatment of prisoners and the consideration shown to the sick and wounded. The care of the sick and the wounded is facilitated by making medical personnel noncombatants and by clearly marking hospitals and similar installations, thus sparing them from attack. Conventions restricting the use of certain weapons probably have not materially mitigated the horrors of war. For the most part, only those weapons that are of limited military use, e.g., poison gas, have been effectively banned, while efforts to prohibit militarily effective weapons, e.g., atomic weapons and submarine mines, have not succeeded. The laws of war have had as their objective the protection of civilian populations by limiting all action to the military. A distinction was made between combatants and noncombatants, the former being defined in terms of traditional military units. Thus combatants must have a commander responsible for subordinates, wear a fixed and recognizable emblem, carry arms openly, and follow the laws of war. But the development of aerial bombing in World War I and of guerrilla forces dependent on civilians has tended to make all enemy territory part of the theater of operations. New practices and categories have yet to be worked out to protect civilian centers adequately. Civilians in territory occupied by the enemy are, however, supposed to be entitled to certain protections. There may not be imprisonment without cause, and fines may not be levied upon a whole civilian population for individual offenses. Private property also receives limited protection, and it may not be confiscated for military use unless fair compensation is paid. Special rules govern such actions against property as the taking of a PRIZE at sea or in port, the confiscation of CONTRABAND, and the use of the BLOCKADE. Property destroyed in the course of action against the enemy is, of course, not compensable. Places of religious, artistic, or historical importance should not be attacked unless there is military need. No direct diplomatic relations exist between belligerents, but neutral diplomats are often given custody of property in enemy territory and are entrusted with negotiations. In the field of combat, passports, safe-conducts, and flags of truce permit consultations between opposing commanders. Hostilities may even be totally suspended by an armistice, which is often the prelude to surrender. Violations of the laws of war have probably occurred in all major conflicts; a nation confident of victory will frequently not be deterred even by fear of reprisals. After World War II the military and civilian leaders of the Axis Powers who were responsible for violations were tried for WAR CRIMES, and some Americans were tried for war crimes in the Vietnam War (see MY LAI INCIDENT). See also NEUTRALITY; SEAS, FREEDOM OF THE. See Morris Greenspan, *The Modern Law of Land Warfare* (1959) and *The Soldier's Guide to the Laws of War* (1969); S. D. Bailey, *Prohibitions and Restraints in War* (1972).

Warangal (vərŭng'gəl), city (1971 pop. 207,130), Andhra Pradesh state, SE India. It is a district administrative center and a market town for grain and oilseed. Carpets and ironware are produced.

Warbeck, Perkin, 1474?-1499, pretender to the English throne, b. Tournai. He lived in Flanders and later in Portugal and arrived in Ireland in the employ of a silk merchant in 1491. There adherents of the Yorkist party persuaded him to impersonate Richard, duke of York, the younger brother of EDWARD V of England. His claim was supported by Holy Roman Emperor Maximilian I, by James IV of Scotland, and by Margaret of Burgundy, sister of Edward IV (and thus Richard's aunt) and the chief supporter of the Yorkist exiles. Warbeck's attempt to invade England in 1495 failed, and he went to Scotland where he married Catherine Gordon, a cousin of James IV. In 1497 Warbeck landed in Cornwall, proclaimed himself Richard IV, and raised a rebel army. His forces were met by those of Henry VII at Exeter, and the pretender fled. He was captured, admitted the whole story of his adventure, and was imprisoned. In 1499 he and the earl of Warwick (son of the duke of Clarence) were hanged for plotting against the king. See biography by James Gairdner in his *History of the Life and Reign of Richard the Third* (1898, repr. 1969).

warble fly: see BOTFLY.

warbler, name applied in the New World to members of the wood warbler family (Parulidae) and in the Old World to a large family (Sylviidae) of small, drab, active songsters, including the hedge sparrow, the KINGLET, and the tailorbird of SE Asia, *Orthotomus sutorius,* named for its habit of sewing leaves together to make its nest. The American warblers number 119 species of small, generally insectivorous birds of mediocre singing ability. Those found in North America are migratory, spending only the summer north of tropical regions. They are brightly plumed in the spring, usually yellow marked with black, gray, olive green, or white, but after the autumn molt they become uniformly drab. Most are arboreal insect catchers; some, e.g., the black-and-white, the yellow-throated, and the pine warblers, crawl on trees like nuthatches and are sometimes called creepers, e.g., the honey creeper of tropical America. Best known are the yellow warbler, or summer yellowbird (also called wild canary), which often nests in gardens; the myrtle warbler, with a yellow rump patch, found along the Massachusetts coast; the redstart and Blackburnian warblers, both with vivid black and orange plumage; the Maryland yellowthroat, with a distinctive black mask; the black-throated blue and green warblers; and the pileolated, or Wilson's, warbler. There are a few exceptions to the generally low level of vocal ability in the New World warblers. The yellow-breasted chat, the largest (7½ in./18.8 cm) of the warblers, is an excellent singer and mimic. The North American ovenbird, which looks like a miniature thrush, has a melodious flight song and is not to be confused with the true ovenbirds, which belong to the family Furnariidae. The water thrush is also a superior singer. Most warblers build open, cup-shaped nests at moderate heights; they are favored victims of the parasitic cowbird. Warblers are unusual in that they hybridize. They are of inestimable value as destroyers of insect enemies of forest trees. Warblers are classified in the phylum CHORDATA, subphylum Vertebrata, class Aves, order Passeriformes, families Parulidae and Sylviidae.

Warburg, Otto Heinrich (ŏt'ō hīn'rĭkh vär'-bo͝orkh), 1883-1970, German physiologist. He was director (1931-53) of the Kaiser Wilhelm Institute (now Max Planck Institute) for cell physiology at Berlin. He investigated the metabolism of tumors and the respiration of cells, particularly cancer cells. For his discovery of the nature and the mode of action of (Warburg's) yellow enzyme, he won the 1931 Nobel Prize in Physiology and Medicine. He edited *The Metabolism of Tumours* (tr. 1931) and wrote *New Methods of Cell Physiology* (1962).

Warburton, Bartholomew Elliott George (Eliot Warburton), 1810-52, Irish author. He is best known for *The Crescent and the Cross* (1844), an account of his travels in the Near East.

Warburton, William, 1698-1779, English bishop and author. Ordained in 1727 and serving successively in several rectories, he became chaplain to Frederick Louis, prince of Wales, in 1738, preacher to Lincoln's Inn in 1746, and chaplain to George II in 1754. He was made prebendary of Durham in 1755, dean of Bristol in 1757, and bishop of Gloucester in 1760. His writing, most of which was ecclesiastical, is noted for its arrogance and its often prejudiced scholarship. *The Alliance between Church and State* (1736) was followed by *The Divine Legation of Moses,* a learned antideist polemic, the first six books of which appeared in 1737-38 and 1741 and the ninth in 1788. Warburton and Alexander Pope became warm friends with the appearance of *A Vindication of the Essay on Man* (1739-40). Warburton edited Shakespeare with Pope, and, as Pope's literary executor, edited his works (1751). *The Doctrine of Grace* (1763) was an assault upon Methodism that invoked replies from its leaders, John and Charles Wesley and George Whitefield. Bishop Hurd prefaced his edition of Warburton's works (1788) with a life, which was separately published in 1860. See A. W. Evans, *Warburton and the Warburtonians* (1932); Isaac D'Israeli, *Quarrels of Authors* (3 vol., 1814; repr. 1970).

war crimes, in international law, violations of the laws of war (see WAR, LAWS OF). Those accused have been tried by their own military and civilian courts, by those of their enemy, and by expressly established international tribunals. The records of the war crimes trials after World War II provide one of the most comprehensive formulations of the concept of war crimes. During that war the Allies agreed to try Axis war criminals. In Aug., 1945, Great Britain, France, the USSR, and the United States established a tribunal at Nuremberg to try military and civilian Axis leaders whose alleged crimes were directed at more than one national group. The trial opened in Nov., 1945. Voluminous evidence was presented to prove the plotting of aggressive warfare, the extermination of civilian populations (especially the Jews), the widespread use of slave labor, the looting of occupied countries, and the maltreatment and murder of prisoners of war. Among those sentenced to death (1946) were Hermann GOERING, Joachim von RIBBENTROP, and Julius STREICHER. Hjalmar SCHACHT and Franz von PAPEN were acquitted. The court did not convict Nazi organizations or the German general staff. A trial of 28 alleged Japanese war criminals was conducted (1946-47) by an 11-nation tribunal in Tokyo. Evidence similar to that presented against the Nazis brought death sentences to Hideki TOJO and others. The U.S. Supreme Court refused an appeal that was based on the ground that the international court was unlawful. There were many trials in national civil and military courts, including those of the Japanese generals Tomoyuki YAMASHITA and Masaharu Homma. In 1961, Israel captured, tried, and later executed Adolf EICHMANN. Critics have questioned the legal basis of some of the charges at the post-World War II trials. Individuals were found guilty of acts considered legal, or even required, by their nation at the time; such findings represent a violation of the concept of SOVEREIGNTY. The plotting or carrying out of aggressive war had not been previously and explicitly called criminal, and the judges tended to define it very narrowly. A defendant was generally found guilty only if he had been involved in developing the policy, but not if he had just carried it out. Critics have also termed the trials an act of vengeance by the victors and questioned their practical use as a precedent. Personal liability for national action is very difficult to prove conclusively, and a nation will be reluctant to try its own leaders. Therefore, effective prosecution may be possible only if a nation is defeated (and then perhaps only if the documents are captured, as they were after World War II). Both critics and supporters of the U.S. role in the Vietnam War have justified their positions on the basis of the post-World War II trials. Several Americans were tried for war crimes in this war, and William Calley was found guilty (see MY LAI INCIDENT). See Sheldon Glueck, *War Criminals* (1944); Robert H. Jackson, *The Case against the Nazi War Criminals* (1946); J. J. Heydecker and Johannes

Leeb, *The Nuremberg Trial* (tr. 1962); Telford Taylor, *Nuremberg and Vietnam* (1970).

Ward, Artemas (är'tĭməs), 1727–1800, American general in the American Revolution, b. Shrewsbury, Mass. He was active in colonial politics and served in the last French and Indian War. As head of the Massachusetts troops, he was chief commander at the siege of Boston (1775) until the arrival of George Washington. After the withdrawal of the main army to New York he was commander at Boston until March, 1777. Later he served in the Continental Congress (1780–81) and the U.S. Congress (1791–95). See biography by Charles Martyn (1921).

Ward, Artemus, pseud. of **Charles Farrar Browne,** 1834–67, American humorist, b. Waterford, Maine. As a reporter on the Cleveland *Plain Dealer,* he began in 1858 a series of "Artemus Ward's Letters" that made him famous on both sides of the Atlantic. The letters were supposedly written by a carnival manager who commented on current events in a New England dialect that was augmented by bad grammar and misspelled words. In 1859, Browne joined the staff of the New York humorous weekly *Vanity Fair* and later turned successfully to lecturing. See his *Selected Works* (ed. by A. J. Nock, 1924); biography by James C. Austin (1964).

Ward, Barbara, 1914–, British writer. Educated at the Sorbonne and at Oxford, she joined the staff of the *Economist* in 1939 and became foreign editor in 1940. From 1946 to 1950 she served as a governor of the British Broadcasting Corporation. In 1968 she was appointed Schweitzer professor of international economic development at Columbia Univ. Among her several popular and penetrating works on international relations are *The West at Bay* (1948), *Policy for the West* (1951), *The Interplay of East and West* (1957; new ed. with new epilogue,1962), *The Rich Nations and the Poor Nations* (1962), and *Nationalism and Ideology* (1966); she edited, with others, *The Widening Gap* (1971). Ward has stressed the need for unity and farsighted ideals in the West and for understanding and liberal economic and political policies toward developing nations.

Ward, Bernard Nicholas: see WARD, WILLIAM GEORGE.

Ward, Edgar Melville: see WARD, JOHN QUINCY ADAMS.

Ward, Frederick Townsend, 1831–62, American adventurer, b. Salem, Mass. A soldier of fortune, he served with William WALKER in Nicaragua and with the French forces in the Crimean War. Ward arrived in Shanghai in 1859, when the TAIPING REBELLION was at its height. Hired by the Chinese authorities to help quell it, he raised troops, cleared the Shanghai area of rebels, and won many successes near Shanghai and Ningpo. Killed in an attack, he was buried in a tomb at Sungkiang, which had been his headquarters. His armed force became the nucleus of the victorious army of Charles George GORDON (Chinese Gordon). See biographies by Holger Cahill (1930) and Hallet Abend (1947).

Ward, Mrs. Humphry, 1851–1920, English novelist, whose maiden name was Mary Augusta Arnold; granddaughter of Thomas Arnold. She was born in Tasmania but was brought to England and grew up in Oxford; there, in 1872, she married Thomas Humphry Ward, an editor of the Oxford *Spectator.* Her first publications were translations of Spanish literature and a children's book, *Millie and Olly* (1881). *Robert Elsmere* (1888), a story defending an ethical rather than mystical interpretation of the Bible, made her reputation. Her novels dramatized her view concerning the social application of religious belief and included *Fenwick's Career* (1906) and *The Case of Richard Meynell* (1911). Mrs. Ward was also a dedicated social worker; her achievements include the founding of the Invalid Children's School in 1891. See her autobiography, *A Writer's Recollections* (1918); biographies by her daughter, J. P. Trevelyan (1923), and E. H. Jones (1973).

Ward, James, 1843–1925, English philosopher. He was professor of mental philosophy at Cambridge from 1897 until 1925. Among his most important writings are *Heredity and Memory* (1913), *Psychological Principles* (1918), and *Essays in Philosophy* (with a memoir by Olwen Ward-Campbell, 1927). See study by A. H. Murray (1937).

Ward, John Quincy Adams, 1830–1910, American sculptor, b. Urbana, Ohio. He was trained under H. K. Brown, whom he assisted in the execution of the equestrian statue of George Washington in New York City. His *Indian Hunter* (1864) was the first of many works for Central Park, New York City. His later commissions were for portrait statues and monuments. These include the equestrian statue of General Thomas, the Garfield monument, and General Sherman, Washington, D.C.; Lafayette, Burlington, Vt.; George Washington, in front of the Subtreasury, and Horace Greeley, New York. In 1903, with the collaboration of P. W. Bartlett, he made the pediment sculptures for the New York Stock Exchange. His work is marked by liveliness and strength. He was a founder and president of the National Sculpture Society (1893–1904) and president of the National Academy of Design (1874). See Adeline Adams, *John Quincy Adams Ward* (1912). His brother **Edgar Melville Ward,** 1839–1915, was a genre painter; his *Coppersmith* is housed in the Metropolitan Museum.

Ward, Lester Frank, 1841–1913, American sociologist and paleontologist, b. Joliet, Ill. Largely self-educated, he eventually took degrees in medicine and law. He worked as a government geologist and paleontologist from 1881 to 1906, when he became professor of sociology at Brown. One of the first and most important of American sociologists, Ward developed a theory of planned progress called telesis, whereby man, through education and development of intellect, could direct social evolution. His theories and those of his contemporary, William Graham Sumner, represent two main trends in 19th-century American sociology. Among his important works are *Dynamic Sociology* (1883), *Psychic Factors of Civilization* (1893), *Pure Sociology* (1903), and *Glimpses of the Cosmos* (6 vol., 1913–18). See Samuel Chugerman, *Lester F. Ward, the American Aristotle* (1939, repr. 1965).

Ward, Nathaniel, 1578–1652, English clergyman and author. Educated at Cambridge, he turned from law to Puritan ministry and sailed to Massachusetts in 1634. He was chief compiler of the Body of Liberties (1641), the earliest code of law in New England. In 1646 he returned to England. There he published *The Simple Cobbler of Aggawam* (1647), a satire on religious toleration and the fashions of the day.

Ward, William George, 1812–82, English Roman Catholic apologist, educated at Oxford. He became (1834) a fellow at Balliol College, Oxford, and was ordained in the Church of England. At first a Broad Churchman, he joined the OXFORD MOVEMENT in 1838. Thereafter he became the most extreme of his group, and as a result of his vigorous support of *Tract 90* he lost his teaching positions in the university. His long work, *The Ideal of a Christian Church* (1844), which compared all churches in England unfavorably with the Roman Catholic Church, brought his official degradation from his university degrees (1854); he was soon afterward received into the Roman Catholic Church, where he remained a layman. Ward was lecturer in moral theology in St. Edmund's College, Ware, from 1851 to 1858. From 1863 to 1878 he edited the *Dublin Review.* He was uncompromising in his religious views, especially with respect to Ultramontanism. He was an eager and hasty controversialist, and his metaphysical subtlety made him a formidable opponent. Ward's friends included men of very divergent opinions. His son, **Wilfrid Philip Ward,** 1856–1916, was his father's biographer (1893). He also wrote a biography of Cardinal Newman and accounts of Cardinal Wiseman and Aubrey de Vere. Wilfrid Philip Ward, like his father, opposed liberalism in the church but, unlike him, took a more conciliatory position, notably in the modernist controversy. He edited the *Dublin Review* from 1906. See Maisie Ward, *The Wilfrid Wards and the Transition* (2 vol., 1934–37). William George Ward's third son, **Bernard Nicholas Ward,** 1857–1920, was a distinguished churchman; he was president of St. Edmund's College, Ware, and first bishop of Brentwood. He wrote on the history of the Roman Catholic Church in England.

ward: see GUARDIAN AND WARD.

war debts. This article discusses the obligations incurred by foreign governments for loans made to them by the United States during and shortly after World War I. For international obligations arising out of World War II, see LEND-LEASE. As early as 1914 the United States began to extend credits for the purchase of American goods to the European Allies, and in 1915 the first of many long-term war loans was made to the Allied powers. In addition to loans made during the war itself, loans and credits were extended for several years after the armistice, both to allied and former enemy nations. All the debtor nations except Russia (where the USSR had replaced the Russian Empire) recognized their obligations. In 1922 the World War Foreign Debt Commission of the United States negotiated with 15 European countries and set the funded indebtedness, based on capacity to pay, at slightly more than $11.5 billion. A 62-year period of repayment was arranged for, and thus principal and interest charges would have amounted to more than $22 billion. The United States refused to reduce the debt further, but the serious European financial situation caused U.S. agreement on some reductions in 1925–26. Payments were made until 1931, largely out of the REPARATIONS that the Allies received from Germany. In 1931, in the face of the worldwide economic depression, President Hoover's proposal for a one-year moratorium on all intergovernmental obligations was adopted. In the Lausanne Pact of 1932 the debtors greatly reduced German reparations in the hope that the United States would release all claims. The United States refused. Six countries made token payments in 1933, but in 1934 all the debtors formally defaulted except Hungary, which paid interest until 1939, and Finland, which continued to pay in full.

War Department, United States, Federal executive department organized (1789) to administer the military establishment. It was reconstituted (1947) as the Dept. of the Army when the military administration was reorganized (see DEFENSE, UNITED STATES DEPARTMENT OF). During the American Revolution, military affairs were largely supervised by the Continental Congress, and under the Articles of Confederation a secretary of war was put in charge of defense matters. In Aug., 1789, the U.S. War Dept., headed by the Secretary of War with cabinet rank, was created to organize and maintain the U.S. army—under the command of the President in time of peace and war. Subsequent legislation expanded the department's organization, and until 1903 the commanding general of the army and various staff departments aided the Secretary in guiding the military establishment. Its supervision of naval affairs was soon transferred (April, 1798) to the U.S. Dept. of the Navy. At times the War Dept. supervised quasi-military matters—e.g., the distribution of bounty lands, pensions (see INTERIOR, UNITED STATES DEPARTMENT OF THE), Indian affairs (see INDIAN AFFAIRS, BUREAU OF), and the Reconstruction of the South after the Civil War, but by the 20th cent. the only such responsibilities that remained were the construction of public works in connection with rivers and harbors and the maintenance and operation of the Panama Canal. Meanwhile, the purely military functions of the department were vastly expanded in war periods, and after the Spanish-American War the War Dept. was thoroughly reorganized (1903). The office of the commanding general of the army was abolished, and the general staff corps was established to coordinate the army under the direction of the chief of staff, who was charged with supervising the planning of national defense and with the mobilization of the military forces. Thereafter the War Dept. absorbed several new functions; it was given supervision over the newly created NATIONAL GUARD, and under the National Defense Act of 1916 the officers' reserve corps was created within the department's organization. This act also established the office of Assistant Secretary of War to coordinate the procurement of munitions. After World War I the War Dept. was again revamped (1922). Its scope of military activities, however, remained wide, stretching from the supervision of the U.S. Military Academy (West Point) to the guidance of insular affairs and occupied territories and to the intricate organization of defense. In World War II plans were laid to coordinate the activities of the armed services, and with the creation (1947) of the National Military Establishment—which later became (1949) the U.S. Dept. of Defense—the War Dept. was reconstituted as the Dept. of the Army, which became a division of the Dept. of Defense. The Secretary of War, holding a post with high cabinet rank, became the Secretary of the Army, an office without cabinet rank, and several of the department's functions, notably those connected with the air arm, were transferred.

Wardha (wär'də, vŭr'də), town (1971 pop. 68,990), Maharashtra state, central India, on the Bombay-Nagpur RR. It is a district administrative center and a market for cotton. Wardha, founded in 1866, is the headquarters of the All-India Village Industries Association.

Ware, Henry, 1764–1845, American clergyman, instrumental in the founding of UNITARIANISM in the United States, b. Sherborn, Mass., grad. Harvard, 1785. As pastor (1787–1805) of the First Church, Hingham, Mass., he became known for his liberal inclinations. His appointment in 1805 as Hollis professor of divinity at Harvard aroused opposition in the orthodox division of the Congregational churches. The questions brought into prominence by his appointment helped to hasten the separation of the Unitarians from the Congregationalists and change their organization into an independent denomination. Later, in an interchange of views with Dr. Leonard Woods, Ware wrote his *Letters to Trinitarians and Calvinists* (1820) and other controversial works. In 1816 he took up his work as professor of theology in the newly founded Harvard divinity school. In 1842 he published some of his lectures under the title *An Inquiry into the Foundation, Evidences, and Truths of Religion.* His son **Henry Ware,** 1794–1843, b. Hingham, Mass., grad. Harvard, 1812, was pastor (1817–30) of the Second Unitarian Church, Boston, and was professor in the Harvard divinity school until 1842. He was an editor (1819–22) of the first organ of Unitarianism, the *Christian Disciple,* and one of the leaders in the development of the denomination.

Ware, Isaac, d. 1766, English architect of the Georgian period. After travels in Italy he was employed in 1729 as clerk of the works at Windsor Castle. For Philip, earl of Chesterfield, he built (1749) Chesterfield House, Mayfair, of which his work *The Complete Body of Architecture* (1756) contains illustrations. In 1737, Ware produced a translation of Palladio. Ware and William Kent designed mantelpieces, ceilings, and other details for Robert Walpole's house, Houghton, built by Thomas Ripley, and did drawings for Ripley's book on this house.

Wareham, town (1970 pop. 11,492), Plymouth co., SE Mass., on an inlet of Buzzards Bay; settled 1678, inc. 1739. It is a resort as well as a shipping point for cranberries and shellfish. Other industries include the manufacture of boats and nails.

warfare, violent conflict between armed enemies. In modern times warfare has usually been conducted by the armed forces (e.g., army, navy, and air force) of a nation or other politically organized group. The way in which WAR is carried out is governed by the principles of STRATEGY AND TACTICS, by the type of weapons employed (see articles on individual weapons), and by the type of communication and transportation facilities available. Thus, throughout history the methods of warfare have changed. See AIR POWER; AMPHIBIOUS WARFARE; CHEMICAL WARFARE; BIOLOGICAL WARFARE; FORTIFICATION; MECHANIZED WARFARE; TRENCH WARFARE; GUERRILLA WARFARE; SIEGE.

warfarin (wôr'fərĭn), ANTICOAGULANT used to treat blood clots. In large doses it causes bleeding. Warfarin, mixed with bait, is used in rodent control.

Wargla: see OUARGLA, Algeria.

Warham, William (wôr'əm), 1450?–1532, English churchman, archbishop of Canterbury. He studied at Oxford and became widely known in England for his legal ability, went often on diplomatic missions, and was made (1502) bishop of London. He was a generous supporter of humanist learning and a patron of Erasmus. In 1504, Warham was made lord chancellor by Henry VII and archbishop of Canterbury by the pope. In the early years of Henry VIII's reign his influence was paramount, but before many years Thomas WOLSEY, archbishop of York, began to displace him. In 1515, Wolsey was created cardinal and Warham willingly resigned the chancellorship to him. Thereafter, Warham was second in the church in England. In the matter of Henry VIII's divorce, in which Warham was involved from 1527, his actions were subservient to the king's will, and in 1530 he was a signer of the petition to the pope for the divorce. Eventually, in 1532, after Warham had allowed a gradual encroachment by the king on ecclesiastical rights, he reversed himself and formally protested just before his death all acts derogatory to the papal authority.

Warhol, Andy, 1930?–, American artist and filmmaker, b. Philadelphia? The leading exponent of the POP ART movement, Warhol chooses his imagery from the world of commonplace objects such as dollar bills and soup cans. He is variously credited with attempting to ridicule and to celebrate American middle-class values by erasing the distinction between popular and high culture. Monotony and repetition became the hallmark of his multi-image, mass-produced silk-screen paintings; for many of these, such as the portraits of Marilyn Monroe and Jacqueline Kennedy, he employed newspaper photographs. In the early 1960s Warhol began making films, suppressing the personal element in marathon essays on boredom. In *The Chelsea Girls* (1966), a seven-hour voyeuristic look into hotel rooms, he used projection techniques that constituted a startling divergence from established methods. Among his later film productions are *Trash* (1971), *L'Amour* (1973), and his gory satires on sex-and-horror films, *Frankenstein* (1974) and *Dracula* (1974). The last two were directed by Paul Morrissey, who worked as Warhol's assistant and sound engineer on earlier films. In 1973, Warhol originated the magazine *Interview.* See his autobiographies (1969 and 1971); biographies by Rainer Crone (1970) and Peter Gidal (1971); Stephen Koch, *Stargazer* (1973).

Warka: see ERECH.

Warley, county borough (1971 pop. 163,388), Worcestershire, central England. Constituted in 1966, Warley comprises substantially the former county borough of Smethwick and the municipal boroughs of Oldbury and Rowley Regis. The borough is highly industrialized. Its manufactures include scales and weighing machines, steel tubes, chemicals, tar, nails and screws, and electrical appliances. There are also glass, iron, brass, and engineering works. In 1974, Warley became part of the new metropolitan county of West Midlands.

warlord, in modern Chinese history, autonomous regional military commander. In the political chaos following the death (1916) of republican China's first president and commander in chief, YÜAN SHIH-K'AI, central authority fell to the provincial military governors and regional military groups emerged based on personal loyalties. During the next decade there was a series of wars between shifting coalitions of military cliques in N China for the collection of provincial and national revenues and for control of the republican government at Peking. Between 1926 and 1928 the NORTHERN EXPEDITION of the Kuomintang party and the army under CHIANG K'AI-SHEK in alliance with prorevolutionary militarists wrested control of N China from the regional armies of CHANG TSO-LIN, WU P'EI-FU, and Sun Ch'uan-fang. However, the new KUOMINTANG government at Nanking was able to establish central administrative and fiscal hegemony over only a few provinces in SE China. Most provinces continued to be controlled by local militarists until the unification of China following the Communist victory in 1949.

Warmia: see ERMELAND, Poland.

Warming, Johannes Eugenius Bülow (yōhän'əs ēōōgä'nēōōs bü'lou värm'ĭng), 1841–1924, Danish botanist, a founder of the science of plant ecology. He was a professor at the Univ. of Copenhagen (1885–1911) and wrote a pioneer work in his field, *Plantesamfund* (1895), which, rewritten and enlarged, appeared in English as *Oecology of Plants* (1909). He also wrote *A Handbook of Systematic Botany* (1878; tr., 2d ed. 1904).

Warm Springs, watering place, Meriwether co., W Ga., famous in treating and studying the aftereffects of poliomyelitis. The salutary properties of the water springing from Pine Mt. were known to the Indians, and white men learned of them in the late 18th cent. By the 1830s a resort was established. It was destroyed by fire in 1865 but was rebuilt and was fashionable at the end of the 19th cent. Franklin D. Roosevelt, who found the water beneficial after his attack of poliomyelitis, established (1927) the Georgia Warm Springs Foundation to help other victims of the disease, and he gave the foundation his 2,600-acre (1,052-hectare) farm there. He retained the cottage known as the Little White House (now a national shrine), in which he died in 1945. The foundation grew, especially after Roosevelt became President. Nearby is the city, incorporated in 1924 as Warm Springs (1970 pop. 523), formerly named Bullochville. A national fish hatchery is there. See Turnley Walker, *Roosevelt and the Warm Springs Story* (1953).

Warner, Charles Dudley, 1829–1900, American editor and author, b. Plainfield, Mass., grad. Hamilton College, 1851, LL.B. Univ. of Pennsylvania, 1858. After practicing law in Chicago, he was associate editor and publisher of the Hartford, Conn., *Courant.* The many travel articles he contributed to the *Courant* and to *Harper's Magazine* were later published in book form. Warner edited the "American Men of Letters" series, for which he wrote a life of Washington Irving, and the "Library of the World's Best Literature" (30 vol., 1896–97). He wrote several novels and collaborated with Mark Twain on *The Gilded Age* (1873). *My Summer in a Garden* (1871) is one of several collections of his polished, charming essays.

Warner, Glenn Scobey, 1871–1954, American football coach, commonly known as "Pop" Warner, b. Springville, N.Y., grad. Cornell (LL.B., 1894). He excelled as guard (1892–94) on the Cornell football team. As coach (1895–96) of the Univ. of Georgia eleven, he had an undefeated, untied team in 1896. He later coached at Cornell (1897–98, 1904–6) and at the Carlisle Indian School (1899–1903, 1907–14), where he developed several outstanding football stars, notably Jim THORPE and Chief Bender, and gained a nationwide reputation. At the Univ. of Pittsburgh (1915–23) Warner again developed several powerful teams, three of which held (1915–17) undefeated records, and at Stanford (1924–32) he produced three Rose Bowl teams. Warner coached (1933–38) at Temple Univ. and was advisory coach at San Jose (Calif.) State College (1939). Warner is credited with introducing the double-wing formation, the practice of numbered plays, and dummy scrimmaging.

Warner, Rex, 1905–, English author, b. Birmingham, grad. Oxford, 1928. A classical scholar noted for his translations from Greek and Latin, Warner has taught in England, Egypt, and the United States. He was profoundly influenced by Kafka, and his early novels are expressionist allegories concerning problems of power; they include *The Wild Goose Chase* (1937) and *The Aerodome* (1941). Among Warner's other works are several historical novels, including *The Young Caesar* (1958) and *Pericles the Athenian* (1963); and *Men of Athens* (1973), a collection of essays about great Athenians of the 5th century B.C.

Warner, Seth, 1743–84, hero of the American Revolution, b. Roxbury, Conn. One of the group who, under Ethan ALLEN, resisted the New York claim to the New Hampshire Grants (now Vermont), he was outlawed by New York authorities. He became a leader of the GREEN MOUNTAIN BOYS, and in May, 1775, he gained his claim to fame by the capture of Crown Point from the British. He later took part in the expedition against Canada that failed at Quebec. He also participated in the fighting that took place after the abandonment of Ticonderoga and was defeated (1777) at Hubbardtown. He was with John STARK at Bennington (1777) and in other operations against General Burgoyne.

Warner, Sylvia Townsend, 1893–, English novelist and poet. Her first published work was poetry, *The Espalier* (1925), but she became more generally known with two novels of gentle fantasy—*Lolly Willowes* (1926) and *Mr. Fortune's Maggot* (1927). In *The Corner That Held Them* (1948), generally regarded as her masterpiece, she tells the story of a 13th-century convent with a scholar's knowledge of the period, in a style that combines poetry, wit, and irony. She has written several volumes of short stories, including *Swans on an Autumn River* (1966) and *The Innocent and the Guilty* (1971), and a highly regarded biography of T. H. WHITE (1967).

Warner, William, 1558?–1609, English poet. He is remembered for *Albion's England,* a history in prose and verse first published in 1586.

Warner Robins, city (1970 pop. 33,491), Houston co., central Ga., in an agricultural region; inc. 1943. The surrounding area yields peanuts, grain, fruit, and livestock. The city grew with the construction of the adjacent Robins Air Force Base, and its economy is centered around that vast military complex, now one of the largest air force installations in the South and headquarters of the Continental Air Command. Before World War II a small country hamlet called Wellston (pop. c.50) existed on that site. After the air force base and a major air force supply depot were established, a boom city grew around them. The city and base were named for Gen. Warner Robins (1882–1940), considered the originator of the air force's present systems of supply and maintenance.

War of 1812, armed conflict between the United States and Great Britain, 1812–15. It followed a period of great stress between the two nations as a result of the treatment of neutral countries by both France and England during the French Revolutionary and Napoleonic Wars, in which the latter two were antagonists (1793–1801, 1803–14). American shippers took advantage of the hostilities in Europe to absorb the carrying trade between Europe and the French and Spanish islands in the West Indies. By breaking the passage with a stop in a U.S. port, they evaded seizure under the British rule of 1756, which forbade to neutrals in wartime trade that was not allowed in peacetime. In 1805, however, in the *Essex* Case, a British court ruled that U.S. ships breaking passage at an American port did not circumvent the prohibitions set out in the rule of 1756. As a result the seizure of American ships by Great Britain increased. The following year Great Britain instituted a partial blockade of the European coast. The French emperor, Napoleon I, retaliated with a blockade of the British Isles. Napoleon's Continental System, which was intended to exclude British goods or goods cleared through Britain from countries under French control, and the British orders in council (1807), which forbade trade with France except after touching at English ports, threatened the American merchant fleet with confiscation by one side or the other. Although the French subjected American ships to considerable arbitrary treatment, the difficulties with England were more apparent. The IMPRESSMENT of sailors alleged to be British from U.S. vessels was a particularly great source of anti-British feeling, a famous incident of impressment being the CHESAPEAKE affair of 1807. Despite the infringement of U.S. rights, President Jefferson hoped to achieve a peaceful settlement with the British. Toward this end he supported a total embargo on trade in the hope that economic pressure would force the belligerents to negotiate with the United States. The Nonimportation Act of 1806 was followed by the EMBARGO ACT OF 1807. Difficulty of enforcement and economic conditions that rendered England and the Continent more or less independent of America made the embargo ineffective, and in 1809 it gave way to a Nonintercourse Act. This in turn was superseded by Macon's Bill No. 2, which repealed the trade restrictions against Britain and France with the proviso that if one country withdrew its offensive decrees or orders, nonintercourse would be reimposed with the other. In 1809, after the passage of the Nonintercourse Act, a satisfactory agreement was reached with the British minister in Washington, David Erskine, who promised repeal of the orders in council. The pact was disavowed by Foreign Secretary George Canning, however, and Erskine was replaced by F. J. Jackson, who soon proved himself persona non grata to the U.S. government. Subsequently, by a dubious commitment, Napoleon tricked James Madison, who had succeeded Jefferson as President, into reimposing (1811) nonintercourse on England. Negotiations with Britain for repeal of the orders in council continued without result; just before the declaration of war, yet too late to prevent it, the orders in council were repealed. However, it was not so much the infringement of neutral rights that occasioned the actual outbreak of hostilities as the desire of the frontiersmen for free land, which could only be obtained at the expense of the Indians and the British. Moreover, the West suspected the British, with some justification, of attempting to prevent American expansion and of encouraging and arming the Indians. Matters came to a head after the battle of Tippecanoe (1811); the radical Western group believed that the British had supported the Indian confederacy and dreamed of expelling the British from Canada. Their militancy was supported by Southerners who wished to obtain West Florida from the Spanish (allies of Great Britain). Among the prominent "war hawks" in the 12th Congress were Henry CLAY, John C. CALHOUN, Langdon CHEVES, Felix GRUNDY, Peter Porter, and others, who managed to override the opposition of John RANDOLPH and of the moderates. War was declared June 18, 1812. It was not until hostilities had begun that Madison discovered how woefully inadequate American preparations for war were. The rash hopes of the "war hawks," who expected to take Canada at a blow, were soon dashed. The American force under Gen. William HULL, far from gaining glory, disgracefully surrendered (Aug., 1812) at Detroit to a smaller Canadian force under Isaac Brock. On the Niagara River, an American expedition was repulsed after a successful attack on Queenston Heights, because the militia under Stephen Van Rensselaer would not cross the New York state boundary. On the sea, however, the tiny American navy initially gave a good account of itself. The victory of the *Constitution*, under Isaac Hull, over the *Guerrière* and the capture of the *Macedonian* by the *United States* (Stephen DECATUR commanding) were two outstanding achievements of 1812. The smaller vessels also did well, and American privateers carried the war to the very shores of England. In 1813 the British reasserted their supremacy on the sea; the *Chesapeake,* under Capt. James LAWRENCE ("Don't give up the ship!"), accepted a challenge from the *Shannon* and met with speedy defeat. Most of the American ships were either captured or bottled up in harbor for the duration of the war. However, it was on inland waters that the American navy achieved its most notable triumphs—victories that had an important bearing on the course of the war. In Jan., 1813, at the Raisin River, S of Detroit, American troops suffered another defeat. But with the victory of Capt. Oliver PERRY on Lake Erie in Sept., 1813, American forces, under Gen. William Henry HARRISON, were able to advance against the British, who burned Detroit and retreated into Canada. Harrison pursued and defeated them in a battle at the Thames River (see THAMES, BATTLE OF THE), in which Tecumseh, the Indian chief, was killed. Yet the feeble efforts of James Wilkinson along the St. Lawrence River did nothing to improve the situation on the New York border. The first months of 1814 held gloomy prospects for the Americans. The finances of the government had been somewhat restored in 1813, but there was no guarantee of future supplies. New England, never sympathetic with the war, now became openly hostile, and the question of secession was taken up by the HARTFORD CONVENTION. Moreover, with Napoleon checked in Europe, Britain could devote more time and effort to the war in America. In July, 1814, the American forces along the Niagara River, now under Gen. Jacob BROWN, maintained their own in engagements at Chippawa and LUNDY'S LANE. Shortly afterward, Sir George PREVOST led a large army into New York down the west side of Lake Champlain and seriously threatened the Hudson valley. But when his accompanying fleet was defeated near Plattsburgh (Sept., 1814) by Capt. Thomas MACDONOUGH, he was forced to retreat to Canada. In August, a British expedition to Chesapeake Bay won an easy victory at BLADENSBURG and took Washington, burning the Capitol and the White House. The victorious British, however, were halted at FORT MCHENRY before Baltimore. This setback and the American victory at Plattsburgh helped to persuade British statesmen to agree to end the war, in which no decisive gains had been made by either side. For some time negotiations for peace had been taking place. Although Great Britain had refused an early Russian offer to mediate between it and the United States, the British entered into direct peace negotiations at Ghent in mid-1814. The American delegation to the meeting at Ghent was headed by John Quincy Adams, Henry Clay, and Albert Gallatin. After long and tortuous discussions, a treaty (see GHENT, TREATY OF) was signed (Dec. 24, 1814), providing for the cessation of hostilities, the restoration of conquered territories, and the setting up of boundary commissions. The final action of the war took place after the signing of the treaty, when Andrew JACKSON decisively defeated the British at New Orleans on Jan. 8, 1815. This victory, although it came after the technical end of the war, was important in restoring American confidence. Although the peace treaty failed to deal with the matters of neutral rights and impressment that were the ostensible cause of the conflict, the war did quicken the growth of American nationalism. In addition, the defeats suffered by the Indians in the Northwest and in the South forced them to sign treaties with the U.S. government and opened their lands for American expansion. See G. W. Cullum, *Campaigns of 1812-15* (1879); Theodore Roosevelt, *The Naval War of 1812* (1882, repr. 1968); A. T. Mahan, *Sea Power in Its Relation to the War of 1812* (2 vol., 1905, repr. 1968); J. W. Pratt, *Expansionists of 1812* (1925, repr. 1957); Henry Adams, *The War of 1812* (ed. by H. A. DeWeerd, 1944); Francis Beirne, *War of 1812* (1949, repr. 1965); Glenn Tucker, *Poltroons and Patriots* (2 vol., 1954); C. S. Forester, *The Age of Fighting Sail: The Story of the Naval War of 1812* (1956); A. H. Z. Carr, *The Coming of War* (1960); Reginald Horsman, *The Causes of the War of 1812* (1962, repr. 1972) and *The War of 1812* (1969).

warp: see WEAVING.

War Production Board (WPB), former U.S. government agency, established (Jan., 1942) by executive order to direct war production and the procurement of materials in World War II. The chairman (Donald M. Nelson, 1942–44; Julius A. Krug, 1944–45) was granted sweeping powers over the nation's economic life. The WPB converted and expanded the peacetime economy to maximum war production; controls included assignment of priorities to deliveries of scarce materials and prohibition of nonessential industrial activities. During its three-year existence the WPB supervised the production of $185 billion worth of weapons and supplies. Businessmen serving with the WPB were sharply criticized by a Senate committee headed by Harry S. TRUMAN. WPB organization changed frequently, and disputes with the armed services occurred. After the defeat of Japan, most restrictions were quickly lifted, and the WPB was abolished in Nov., 1945. The Civilian Production Administration was set up to take over the remaining WPB reconversion functions.

warrant, in law, written order by an official of a court directed to an officer. The SEARCH WARRANT and the warrant of ARREST are the most frequently used types. Warrants of attachment order the seizure of a defendant's goods pending trial or judicial determination of ownership and in certain other cases. Warrants are usually issued by a judge or court clerk. They are directed to sheriffs, marshals, constables, and other officers of the peace. The strictest compliance with legal forms and rules for serving a warrant is ordinarily necessary if it is to be effective.

Warren, Charles, 1868–1954, American jurist, b. Boston. He was admitted to the Massachusetts bar in 1892. An assistant U.S. Attorney General (1914–18), he served as a special master in important cases decided by the U.S. Supreme Court. Warren is noted for his scholarly studies of constitutional history, especially *The Supreme Court in United States History* (3 vol., 1922; rev. ed., 2 vol., 1926, repr. 1960), which won the Pulitzer Prize. He also wrote *Congress, the Constitution, and the Supreme Court* (1925, enl. ed. 1935, repr. 1969), *The Making of the Constitution* (1928, repr. 1967), and *Odd Byways in American History* (1942).

Warren, Earl, 1891–1974, American public official and 14th Chief Justice of the United States (1953–69), b. Los Angeles. He graduated from the Univ. of California Law School in 1912. Admitted (1914) to the bar, he practiced in Oakland, Calif., and held several local offices. He served (1939–43) as state attorney general and was governor of California from 1943 to 1953. In 1948 he was unsuccessful Republican candidate for Vice President on the ticket headed by Thomas E. Dewey. In Oct., 1953, President Eisenhower appointed him Chief Justice to succeed Fred M. Vinson. One of the most dynamic of Chief Justices, Warren, a liberal, led the court toward a number of landmark decisions in the fields of civil rights and individual liberties. Among these were the 1954 unanimous decision of the court, written by Warren, ending segregation in the nation's schools (see BROWN VS. BOARD OF EDUCATION OF TOPEKA, KANSAS); the one man, one vote rulings, which opened the way for legislative and Congressional reapportionment; and the decisions in criminal cases guaranteeing the right to counsel and protecting the accused from police abuses. While Chief Justice, Warren headed the commission that investigated the assassination of President Kennedy (see WARREN COMMISSION). He retired from the bench in 1969. His public papers were edited by Henry M. Christman (1959). See biography by J. D. Weaver (1967); study ed. by R. H. Sayler et al. (1969).

Warren, Gouverneur Kemble (gəvərnēr'), 1830–82, Union general in the American Civil War, b. Cold Spring, N.Y. An army engineer, he assisted in the survey of the Mississippi delta and also engaged in surveying in the West. In the Civil War he commanded a brigade of the Army of the Potomac in the campaigns of 1862, distinguishing himself particularly at Gaines's Mill in the Seven Days battles. In the GETTYSBURG CAMPAIGN Warren, who was then chief engineer, saved the Round Tops by promptly diverting troops to their defense, July 2, 1863. He took part in the indecisive operations following Gettysburg and saw action in the Wilderness campaign and in the fighting around Petersburg (1864–65). At Five Forks (April 1, 1865) Gen. Philip H. Sheridan, alleging dilatoriness on Warren's part, removed him from command. Warren made repeated requests for an official examination of Sheridan's charges; soon after his death in 1882, a court of inquiry exonerated him. After the war he continued in the engineers corps. His *Account of the 5th Army Corps* (1866) is a vindication of his conduct. See biography by E. G. Taylor (1932).

Warren, Joseph, 1741–75, political leader in the American Revolution, b. Roxbury, Mass. A Boston physician, he participated in the agitation against the Stamp Act (1765). He became a member of the Boston Committee of Safety and in 1774 drafted the Suffolk Resolves, advocating forcible resistance to the British; they were endorsed by the Continental Congress. On the night of April 18, 1775, he dispatched William DAWES and Paul REVERE to warn Sam Adams and John Hancock that the British were marching on Concord. Warren was killed in the battle of Bunker Hill (1775). See biographies by Richard Frothingham (1865, repr. 1971) and John Cary (1961).

Warren, Josiah, 1798–1874, American reformer and anarchist, b. Boston. An early follower of Robert Owen, he soon rejected Owen's political socialism, advocating instead anarchy based on "the sovereignty of the individual." He founded several "equity" stores, based on the idea of exchanging goods for an equivalent amount of labor and on the principle that cost should be the limit of price. He also established three utopian colonies; the most successful (1851–c.1860) was Modern Times (now

Brentwood), Long Island, N.Y. The most important of his publications was *True Civilization* (1863; 5th ed. 1875). See study by William Bailie (1906, repr. 1971).

Warren, Mercy Otis, 1728-1814, American writer, b. Barnstable, Mass.; sister of James Otis and wife of James Warren. An ardent patriot, she conducted a political salon during the pre-Revolutionary days and wrote two satirical plays, *The Adulateur* (1773) and *The Group* (1775), against the Tories. Her history of the American Revolution (3 vol., 1805) is still important for factual information as well as for its sketches of contemporary figures. See studies by K. S. Anthony (1958, repr. 1972) and Jean Fritz (1972).

Warren, Robert Penn, 1905–, American novelist, poet, and critic, b. Guthrie, Ky., educated at Vanderbilt Univ. (B.A., 1925), Univ. of California (M.A., 1927), and as a Rhodes scholar at Oxford (B.Litt., 1930). At Vanderbilt he became associated with John Crowe Ransom and the group of Southern agrarian poets who made the *Fugitive* (1922–25) an important literary magazine. Warren has taught at several universities. He was managing editor with Cleanth Brooks of the *Southern Review*. With Brooks, he also wrote and compiled several textbooks, including *Understanding Poetry* (1938) and *Modern Rhetoric* (1949). Warren first gained recognition as a poet. His early verse was much influenced by the METAPHYSICAL POETS, but his later poetry is simpler and more regional. Among his volumes of poetry are *Thirty-six Poems* (1935); *Brother to Dragons* (1953; Pulitzer Prize), a long, dramatic poem; *Promises* (1957; Pulitzer Prize); *Selected Poems: New and Old* (1966); *Incarnations* (1968); *Audubon: A Vision* (1969); and *Or Else* (1974). He is also an important novelist, his most famous novel being *All the King's Men* (1946; Pulitzer Prize), which concerns the rise to power of a political demagogue resembling Huey LONG. Among his other novels are *World Enough and Time* (1950), *Band of Angels* (1955), *The Cave* (1959), *Wilderness* (1961), *Flood* (1964), and *Meet Me in the Green Glen* (1971). An acute sense of the moral dilemma of the modern world pervades all of his work. His other publications include a collection of short stories, *The Circus in the Attic* (1948), and his *Selected Essays* (1958). See studies by Leonard Casper (1960) and L. H. Moore (1970).

Warren, Samuel, 1807–77, English lawyer and author. He wrote many legal texts, *Passages from the Diary of a Late Physician* (1832), and the extremely popular novel *Ten Thousand a Year* (1841).

Warren, Whitney, 1864-1943, American architect, b. New York City, studied at the École des Beaux-Arts. He began practice in New York City in 1894. Later he joined with Charles D. Wetmore in a firm that had one of the most extensive practices of its time and was known for the designing of large hotels. Warren and Wetmore's New York works include the Grand Central Terminal (1903–13, built in collaboration with the firm Reed and Stem), the New York Central office building, the Chelsea docks, and the Ritz-Carlton, Biltmore, Commodore, and Ambassador hotels. After World War I they were entrusted with the reconstruction of the historic library of the Univ. of Louvain, Belgium, which had been destroyed by the Germans who again demolished it in 1940.

Warren. 1 City (1970 pop. 179,260), Macomb co., SE Mich., a suburb of Detroit; est. 1837, inc. as a city 1957. It is an important metalworking center. Steel is processed, and tools and dies, and automobile engines, bodies, and parts are made. Military vehicles are manufactured at the Detroit Arsenal there. The city's growth and industrialization were spurred by World War II. A large General Motors technical center and a junior college are in Warren. **2** City (1970 pop. 63,494), seat of Trumbull co., NE Ohio, in the fertile Mahoning valley; settled 1799, inc. as a city 1905. Steel, metal-forming machinery, electrical equipment, and automobile and truck parts are the principal manufactures. The Trumbull Branch of Kent State Univ. is in the city. **3** Borough (1970 pop. 12,998), seat of Warren co., NE Pa., on the Allegheny River; inc. 1832. Warren is located in beautiful wooded country near oil and natural gas reserves. Oil is refined, and electrical equipment and metal products are made. A Seneca Indian village there was burned by Colonel Brodhead in 1781. Laid out c.1795, Warren was an early lumbering center. It had an oil boom in 1860. The headquarters of Allegheny National Forest are there, and nearby are Edinboro State College and the Cornplanter Indian Reservation. **4** Town (1970 pop. 10,523), Bristol co., E R.I., a suburb of Providence on the Kickemuit River and Narragansett Bay; inc. 1747. An early whaling and shipbuilding center, it still has an active boatbuilding industry. Other manufactures are luggage, electrical items, and jewelry. Warren was transferred from Massachusetts to Rhode Island in 1746. Brown Univ. was first chartered there (1764) as Rhode Island College. During the American Revolution Lafayette made his headquarters in Warren after taking command (1778) of the American forces in the area.

Warren Commission, popular name given to the U.S. Commission to Report upon the Assassination of President John F. Kennedy, established (Nov. 29, 1963) by executive order of President Lyndon B. Johnson. The commission, which was given unrestricted investigating powers, was directed to evaluate all the evidence and present a complete report of the event to the American people. The members of the commission were Earl Warren, Chief Justice of the United States; U.S. Senators Richard B. Russell (Democrat from Georgia) and John Sherman Cooper (Republican from Kentucky); U.S. Representatives Hale Boggs (Democrat from Louisiana) and Gerald R. Ford (Republican from Michigan); Allen W. Dulles, former Director of the Central Intelligence Agency; and John J. McCloy, former president of the World Bank. The commission named former U.S. Solicitor General James Lee Rankin as its general counsel and also appointed 14 assistant counsels and an additional staff of 12. The proceedings began Dec. 3, 1963, and the final report was delivered to the President on Sept. 24, 1964. During its investigation the commission weighed the testimony of 552 witnesses and the reports of 10 Federal agencies, most important of which were the Secret Service, the Federal Bureau of Investigation, the Dept. of State, the Central Intelligence Agency, and military intelligence. The hearings were closed to the public unless the person giving testimony requested otherwise; only two witnesses made that request. The commission, in its findings, attempted to reconstruct the exact sequence of events of the assassination. Foremost among its conclusions was refutation of speculation that the assassination was part of a conspiracy, either domestic or foreign, or that any elements of the government had a hand in the event. The report maintained that Lee Harvey OSWALD, acting alone and without accomplices, shot and killed the President and wounded Texas Governor John Connally from the sixth floor window of the Texas School Book Depository Building in Dallas on Nov. 23, 1963. Oswald was also declared the murderer of Police Patrolman J. D. Tippit, who tried to apprehend Oswald some 45 min after the shooting. In addition, Jack Ruby, a Dallas restaurant owner who killed Oswald the day after the assassination (Nov. 24), was found innocent of conspiracy; no connection was found between Oswald and Ruby. The commission concluded its report by recommending reform in presidential security measures, and it offered specific proposals to improve the Secret Service. The commission's findings came under attack from a number of persons who felt it served as a "whitewash." In 1966, New Orleans district attorney, Jim Garrison, began an independent inquiry based on the assumption that the assassination had resulted from a conspiracy. He brought charges against a New Orleans businessman, who, however, was acquitted in 1969. For a summary of the commission's findings, see *Report of the President's Commission on the Assassination of President John F. Kennedy* (1964). The commission's proceedings and conclusions are criticized in E. J. Epstein, *Inquest* (1966) and Mark Lane, *Rush to Judgment* (1966).

Warrensburg, city (1970 pop. 13,125), seat of Johnson co., W Mo.; inc. as a city 1855. It is situated in a dairy and farm region. Local manufactures include clothing, lawnmowers, and electronic components. Central Missouri State Univ. is in the city; Whiteman Air Force Base is nearby.

Warrensville Heights, city (1970 pop. 18,925), Cuyahoga co., NE Ohio, a suburb of Cleveland; inc. 1927. Although chiefly residential, it has plants that manufacture machinery, automobile equipment, and cardboard containers. It is the home of a summer stock musical theater-in-the-round. A local attraction is a black oak tree estimated to be more than 300 years old.

Warri (wôr'rē), city (1969 est. pop. 64,000), S Nigeria, a port on the Warri River. It is a transshipment point where oceangoing vessels meet Niger River boats. The main items shipped from Warri are rubber, palm products, cacao, groundnuts, and hides and skins. The city's industries include bicycle assembly, rubber processing, and ship repair. Traditional artisans make canoes, rope, and mats. According to legend, Warri was founded in the 15th cent. by a BENIN prince. By the 17th cent. it was independent of Benin, and in the 19th cent. it became wealthy in the palm oil trade. Warri came under British protection in 1884.

Warrington, county borough (1971 pop. 50,342), Lancashire, NW England, on the Mersey River and on the Manchester Ship Canal. Manufactures include wire and other metal products, chemicals, soap, leather goods, and beer. The site was occupied very early; the Church of St. Elphin has a Saxon crypt. The grammar school dates from 1526, and there are several half-timbered houses. Warrington academy for religious dissenters (1757–83) included Joseph Priestley among its faculty. In 1974, Warrington became part of the new nonmetropolitan county of Cheshire.

Warrington, uninc. residential town (1970 pop. 15,848), Escambia co., extreme NW Fla., a suburb of Pensacola, on Pensacola Bay. Although chiefly residential, it has shipyards and waterfront industries.

Warrior, river, Ala.: see BLACK WARRIOR.

Warsaw (wôr'sô), Pol. *Warszawa*, city (1970 pop. 1,308,112), capital of Poland and of Warsaw prov., central Poland, on both banks of the Vistula River. It is a political, cultural, and industrial center, a major transportation hub, and one of Europe's great historic cities. The city has industries producing steel machinery, motor vehicles, chemicals, electrical equipment, and textiles. Although settlements existed on the site of Warsaw in the 11th cent., the city probably grew around a castle built in the 13th cent. by a duke of Masovia. In 1413, Warsaw became the capital of the duchy of Masovia, which was incorporated with Great Poland in 1526. After Kraków burned, Warsaw replaced it (1596) as Poland's capital. Warsaw grew rapidly as a commercial and cultural center, despite frequent invasions and pillages. It fell temporarily to the Swedes under Charles X (1655–56) and Charles XII (1702), was occupied by the Russians in 1792 and 1794, and passed to Prussia in 1795. Liberated by Napoleon I in 1806, it became (1807) the capital of the grand duchy of Warsaw (see POLAND) and was the scene in 1812 of a diet that proclaimed the reestablishment of Poland. In 1813, however, the city fell to the Russians, and in 1815 it became the capital of the nominally independent kingdom of central Poland, awarded by the Congress of Vienna to the Russian crown. Warsaw was the principal center of unsuccessful Polish uprisings against Russian domination in 1830 and 1863. German forces took the city in 1915, during World War I. In Nov., 1918, it was liberated by Polish troops and proclaimed capital of the restored Polish state. In 1920 the Polish defense of Warsaw, led by the French general Maxime Weygand, turned the tide of the Russo-Polish War. The city was the scene in 1926 of a military coup that established Marshal Joseph Pilsudski's dictatorship. During World War II the city was occupied (1939–45) by German troops and subjected to systematic destruction. In 1940 the Germans isolated the Jewish ghetto, which in 1942 contained about 500,000 persons. In reprisal for a Jewish uprising (Feb., 1943) in the ghetto, the Germans killed an estimated 40,000 of the Jews who had survived the battle. When Warsaw was liberated (Jan., 1945) by Soviet troops, only about 200 Jews remained. From Aug. to Oct., 1944, the Polish nationalist underground and German troops battled for Warsaw; while the battle was raging, the Soviet army, across the Vistula, remained inactive. The Germans, following their victory, expelled Warsaw's inhabitants and deliberately demolished the city. The postwar decision to retain Warsaw as the national capital resulted in a large-scale reconstruction. The medieval Stare Miasto [old town], with its market place and 14th-century cathedral, was rebuilt according to the prewar pattern. Among Warsaw's most notable buildings are the Holy Cross Church, the 15th-century St. Carmelite Church, several fine palaces, and the monuments to Copernicus and Adam Mickiewicz. Warsaw has many educational and cultural institutions, including the Univ. of Warsaw (founded in 1818) and the Polish Academy of Sciences.

Warsaw Treaty Organization, alliance set up under a mutual defense treaty signed in Warsaw, Poland, in 1955 by Albania, Bulgaria, Czechoslovakia, East Germany, Hungary, Poland, Rumania, and the Soviet Union. The organization is the Soviet bloc's equivalent of the North Atlantic Treaty Organization. Initiated as an alliance made necessary by the remilitarization of West Germany under the Paris Pacts of 1954, the treaty was binding for 20 years but would lapse in the event of a general European collective security treaty. A unified military command, with headquarters in Moscow, directs the united forces, which include Soviet divisions stationed in some of the member nations prior to the signing of the treaty. In 1962, Albania was no longer invited to Warsaw Treaty meetings and formally withdrew in 1968. In the same year, the organization sent forces to occupy Czechoslovakia after that country began to take steps toward democratization.

warship, any ship built or armed for naval combat. The forerunners of the modern warship were the men-of-war of the 18th and early 19th cent., such as the SHIP OF THE LINE, FRIGATE, CORVETTE, sloop of war (see SLOOP), BRIG, and CUTTER. With the advent of steel construction and steam propulsion in the latter half of the 19th cent., warships evolved into their modern form. The key naval vessels used in modern warfare are the AIRCRAFT CARRIER and the SUBMARINE; other modern warships include the BATTLESHIP, CRUISER, DESTROYER, GUNBOAT, and TORPEDO BOAT. See *Jane's Fighting Ships* (pub. annually since 1897); J. M. Thornton, *Warships 1860–1970* (1973).

Warszawa: see WARSAW, Poland.

wart, circumscribed outgrowth of the skin caused by a filterable virus that is readily transmitted. Warts may appear anywhere on the skin but are most common on the hands. They may disappear spontaneously or persist for many years. However, there is also a tendency to develop new lesions. Warts are treated by surgical excision (sometimes by electrocautery), bloodless removal by freezing with liquid nitrogen, or repeated applications of ointments or creams. Those on the soles of the feet (plantar warts) are the most painful and most difficult to treat, since on pressure-bearing areas they may become depressed beneath the surface of the skin.

Warta (vär'tä), river, c.475 mi (760 km) long, rising in the Jura Krakowska, S Poland, and flowing N and W past Częstochowa and Poznań to the Oder River at Kostrzyn. It is connected with the Vistula River by the Noteć River, its tributary, and by the Bydgoszcz Canal. The Warta is navigable for large craft to Poznań and for small craft for about half its course. The lower course of the river, formerly in Germany, became (1945) part of Poland as a result of the Potsdam Conference.

Wartburg (värt'bŏŏrk), castle near Eisenach, in the former state of Thuringia, central Germany (now in East Germany). Built c.1070, later enlarged, and renovated in the 18th cent., it was the seat of the medieval landgraves of Thuringia. It was the scene in 1207 of the *Sängerkrieg*, a contest of minnesingers in which Heinrich von Ofterdingen, Wolfram von Eschenbach, and Walther von der Vogelweide, among others, took part and which Richard Wagner used (with some poetic license) as the setting for a famous scene in the opera *Tannhäuser*. St. Elizabeth of Hungary lived in Wartburg until 1227. In 1521, Martin LUTHER was brought to the castle for his protection by the elector of Saxony, and there he completed his translation of the New Testament. The spot on the wall of Luther's study where Luther allegedly threw an inkpot at a vision of the devil is still shown to visitors. In 1817 the first general assembly of the Burschenschaften, the nationalist German student organizations, met at Wartburg.

Warton, Joseph, 1722–1800, English critic and poet, brother of Thomas Warton. Educated at Winchester and Oxford, he took holy orders in 1744 and served several cures. He spent an unsuccessful tenure as headmaster at Winchester, resigning in 1793. In London he met Samuel Johnson and became part of Johnson's literary group. His poems show a preference for the primitive over the civilized life. *The Enthusiast* (1744) and his subsequent volume of odes (1746) are early examples of romantic nature poetry. His chief work was his *Essay on the Genius and Writings of Pope* (2 vol., 1756 and 1782). Though an admirer of Pope, he criticized the classical tendencies of 18th-century poetry and longed for a revival of imagination and passion. He edited a nine-volume edition of Pope in 1797. See Joan Pittock, *The Ascendancy of Taste: The Achievement of Joseph and Thomas Warton* (1973).

Warton, Thomas, the elder, c.1688–1745, English poet, father of Joseph and Thomas Warton. He was professor of poetry at Oxford from 1718 to 1728. His collected poems, edited by Joseph Warton, and published posthumously in 1748, are primitive and biblical in tone; some are runic odes and may have influenced Thomas GRAY.

Warton, Thomas, 1728–90, English poet and literary historian, grad. Trinity College, Oxford (1747), brother of Joseph Warton. He was ordained and eventually served as professor of poetry at Oxford from 1757 to 1767. In 1785, the year he was named poet laureate, he became Camden professor of history. More important as a literary scholar than as a poet, he did much to awaken the public interest in medieval and Elizabethan literature. Although his first important scholarly work was his *Observations on the Faerie Queene of Spenser* (1754), his major work was the *History of English Poetry* (1774–81), which covered the 11th through the 16th cent. Though it was condemned for its inaccuracies, it is still regarded as an extremely valuable scholarly work. As a poet, Warton was more inclined toward light and humorous verse. He also edited *The Oxford Sausage* (1764), an anthology of Oxford wit. See biographies by W. P. Ker (1911) and Clarissa Rinaker (1916); study by Edmund Gosse (1915); Joan Pittock, *The Ascendancy of Taste: The Achievement of Joseph and Thomas Warton* (1973).

Warwick, Guy de Beauchamp, earl of (bē'chəm, wŏr'ĭk), d. 1315, English nobleman. He was active in Edward I's campaigns in Scotland. A leading opponent of Piers GAVESTON, he became (1310) one of the lords ordainers and procured Gaveston's banishment. He was largely responsible for Gaveston's death in 1312, although he did not participate in the actual execution.

Warwick, John Dudley, earl of: see NORTHUMBERLAND, JOHN DUDLEY, DUKE OF.

Warwick, Richard de Beauchamp, earl of, 1382–1439, English nobleman; son of Thomas de Beauchamp, earl of Warwick. He fought for Henry IV against Owen Glendower in Wales and the Percys at Shrewsbury (1403). In 1408 he set out for the Holy Land, visiting monarchs and fighting in a tournament en route; he made a similarly active return trip through Russia, Poland, and Germany. After his return (1410), Beauchamp performed several royal missions, including that as chief English lay envoy to the Council of Constance (1414). He fought with notable success in Henry V's French campaigns and on Henry's death (1422) became a member of the council for the infant Henry VI. He served as tutor to the young king from 1428 to 1437, when he was appointed lieutenant of France and Normandy. Richard de Beauchamp was a man of piety and courtesy and was famed throughout Europe as a chivalrous knight. His daughter Anne married and brought the earldom to Richard Neville, earl of Warwick.

Warwick, Richard Neville, earl of (nĕv'əl), 1428–71, English nobleman, called the Kingmaker. Through his grandfather, Ralph Neville, 1st earl of WESTMORLAND, he had connections with the house of Lancaster; he was also the nephew of Cecily Neville, wife of Richard, duke of YORK. Through his wife, Anne de Beauchamp, he inherited the earldom of Warwick and the vast Beauchamp estates. Thus by virtue of his family and lands, Warwick was the most powerful noble in England and the principal baronial figure in the Wars of the Roses (see ROSES, WARS OF THE). With his father, the earl of Salisbury, Warwick supported Richard of York in his bid for the protectorship of HENRY VI (1454) and took up arms when York lost his office. Warwick was largely responsible for the Yorkist victory at the first battle of St. Albans (1455) and was appointed to the strategic post of governor of Calais. In 1459 when fighting broke out again, York, Salisbury, and Warwick were forced to flee the country, but in 1460 they returned and captured the king at the battle of Northampton. The queen, MARGARET OF ANJOU, raised an army in the north, defeated and killed York and Salisbury at Wakefield (1460), and defeated Warwick and recaptured Henry at the second battle of St. Albans (1461). But York's son, Edward, won the battle of Mortimer's Cross (1461), entered London, and was proclaimed king as EDWARD IV. Henry and Margaret were decisively defeated at Towton (1461), and Edward was crowned. Warwick was now the most powerful man in England, and the Nevilles received extensive royal favors; but Edward resented the earl's domination. In the midst of negotiations by Warwick to marry Edward to Bona of Savoy, the sister-in-law of Louis XI of France, the king announced (1464) that he had secretly married Elizabeth WOODVILLE. Edward now favored a Burgundian alliance against France, the Woodvilles received favor, and Warwick was gradually pushed into the background. He formed an alliance with the king's brother George, duke of CLARENCE, to whom he married his daughter, against Edward's orders. Together they rose against Edward in 1469, defeated the king's forces, and placed Edward in captivity. By the end of the year, however, Edward had regained control, and in 1470, after another abortive rising, Warwick and Clarence fled to France. There Louis XI persuaded them to make up their differences with Margaret of Anjou, and in Sept., 1470, Warwick invaded England as a Lancastrian, defeated Edward (who fled abroad), and restored Henry VI. Within six months Edward secured Burgundian aid, landed in England, and was joined by Clarence. Edward and Warwick met in battle at Barnet; the earl was defeated and was slain in flight. Although an able diplomat and a man of great energy, Warwick owed much of his greatness to his birth and marriage. By the marriage of his daughter to Clarence and the marriage after his death of another daughter to the duke of Gloucester, later Richard III, all of Warwick's property went to the royal house. See P. M. Kendall, *Warwick the Kingmaker* (1957).

Warwick, Thomas de Beauchamp, earl of, d. 1401, English nobleman, of an ancient and powerful family. He was one of the governors of the young RICHARD II. After Richard assumed power, Warwick joined the barons who opposed the acts of Richard's favorite courtiers and was one of the lords appellant (1388) who accused them of treason and curbed Richard's power. When Richard resumed control (1389), Warwick retired to his estates until his sudden arrest on a fabricated charge of treason in 1397. He was imprisoned in the Tower of London (in the Beauchamp Tower, named for him) and then banished to the Isle of Man until the accession of Henry IV, when he was restored to his estates.

Warwick, municipal borough (1971 pop. 18,289), county town of Warwickshire, central England, on the Avon River. Although there is some commerce and manufacturing, Warwick is best known for Warwick Castle, located on the site of a fortress built by Æthelflæd, the daughter of King Alfred, in 915. The castle was begun in the 14th cent. and was converted into a mansion in the 17th. St. Mary's Church dates partly from the 12th cent.; partially burned in 1694, it was rebuilt by William Wilson, a pupil of Wren. The Beauchamp Chapel (1443–64) is noteworthy. In the church are a Norman crypt and monuments to Richard de Beauchamp, earl of Warwick, to his countess, and to Robert Dudley, earl of Leicester.

Warwick (wôr'wĭk, wŏ'rĭk), city (1970 pop. 83,694), Kent co., central R.I., at the head of Narragansett Bay; settled by Samuel Gorton 1642, inc. as a city 1931. Its textile industry dates from 1794. Other manufactures include machinery, pipes and tubing, and fluorescent-lighting fixtures. The town includes the villages of Apponaug, on Greenwich Bay; Hillsgrove, site of the state airport; Warwick; and several resorts. Warwick village was nearly destroyed (1676) in King Philip's War. Gaspee Point, S of Pawtuxet, was the scene of the burning of the British revenue cutter GASPEE in 1772; annual "Gaspee Days" commemorate the event. Warwick is the seat of the Seminary of Our Lady of Providence. Nathanael Greene was born in the city.

Warwickshire (wŏ'rĭkshĭr), county (1971 pop. 2,079,799), 975 sq mi (2,525 sq km), central England. The county town is WARWICK. The terrain is gently rolling, with outcroppings of the Cotswold Hills in the south. The Avon, flowing southwesterly, is the chief river. There are vestiges of the ancient Forest of Arden. The region is a varied one, largely given to agriculture (wheat and other grains, dairying, sheep and cattle grazing). It also contains the great industrial centers of BIRMINGHAM and COVENTRY, which have more than 50% of the population. There are many industries including the manufacture of motor vehicles, aircraft, and textiles. There are deposits of limestone, fireclay, and, in the northeast, coal. One of England's most famous public schools is at RUGBY. There are numerous traces of Roman occupation; ecclesiastical remains, such as the abbeys of Merevale and Stoneleigh; and the ruins of the castle at KENILWORTH. Warwick Castle is largely intact. The mansion at Compton Wynyates is one of the finest surviving pieces of early Tudor architecture. The county is rich in literary associations as well. Shakespeare's birthplace at STRATFORD-UPON-AVON, with the great memorial theater, is one of England's most popular literary shrines. In 1974, Warwickshire was reorganized as a nonmetropolitan county. See study by Vivian Bird (1973).

Wasatch Range (wô'săch), part of the Rocky Mts., extending c.250 mi (400 km) south from SE Idaho to central Utah. Mt. Timpanogos, the highest peak (12,008 ft/3,660 m), is the site of Timpanogos Cave National Monument. Many streams on the western flank of the Wasatch carry water into the fertile Salt Lake oasis, which stretches along the foothills; all of Utah's principal cities and most of the state's population are found there. Emigrant Canyon, a site of early Mormon activities, is now a major winter resort area.

Wash, The, inlet of the North Sea, 20 mi (32 km) long and 15 mi (24 km) wide, between Lincolnshire and Norfolk, E England. It receives the Witham, Wellend, Nene, and Ouse rivers. It is mostly shallow with sandbars and low, marshy shores. Dredged ship channels lead to King's Lynn and Boston.

Washburne, Elihu Benjamin, 1816-87, American politician and diplomat, b. Livermore, Maine. On leaving home in 1830 he added an *e* to his family name. Admitted to the bar in Massachusetts, he opened (1840) his law practice in Galena, Ill. As a U.S. Representative from Illinois (1853-69) he became a radical Republican noted for his efforts to limit expenses. Washburne helped to promote the fortunes of Ulysses S. Grant early in the Civil War, and when Grant became President he made (1869) his benefactor Secretary of State, although Washburne was completely unqualified for that post. However, he resigned within two weeks to become minister to France (1869-77). In the Franco-Prussian War, Washburne was the only foreign diplomat to remain in Paris throughout the siege of the city and the period of the Commune. He later lived in Chicago. See his *Recollections of a Minister to France, 1869-1877* (1877); Gaillard Hunt, *Israel, Elihu, and Cadwallader Washburn* (1925, repr. 1971).

washing soda: see SODIUM CARBONATE.

Washington, Booker Taliaferro, 1856-1915, black American educator, b. Franklin co., Va. His mother was a mulatto slave on a plantation, his father a white man. After the Civil War, he worked in salt furnaces and coal mines in Malden, W. Va., and attended school part time, until he was able to enter the Hampton Institute (Va.). A friend of the principal paid his tuition, and he worked as a janitor to earn his room and board. After three years (1872-75) at Hampton he taught at a school for black children in Malden, then studied at Wayland Seminary, Washington, D.C. Appointed (1879) an instructor at Hampton Institute, he was given charge of the training of 75 Indians, under the guidance of Gen. S. C. Armstrong. He later developed the night school. In 1881 he was chosen to organize a normal and industrial school for blacks at Tuskegee, Ala. Under his direction, Tuskegee Institute became one of the leading black educational institutions in America. Its programs emphasized industrial training as a means to self-respect and economic independence for black people. Washington gave many lectures in the interests of his work, both in the United States and in Europe, and he was counted among the ablest public speakers of his time. In 1895 at Atlanta, Ga., Washington made a highly controversial speech on the place of the black man in American life. In it he maintained that it was foolish for blacks to agitate for social equality before they had attained economic equality. His speech pleased many whites and gained financial support for his school, but his position was denounced by many black leaders, among them W. E. B. DuBois. Washington was the organizer (1900) of the National Negro Business League, a group committed to black economic independence. He received honorary degrees from Dartmouth and Harvard. Among his many published works are his autobiography, *Up From Slavery* (1901, repr. 1963), *The Future of the American Negro* (1899), *Tuskegee and Its People* (1905, repr. 1969), *Life of Frederick Douglass* (1907, repr. 1968), *The Story of the Negro* (1909, repr. 1969), and *My Larger Education* (1911). See biographies by E. J. Scott and L. B. Stowe (1916, repr. 1972), Basil Mathews (1948, repr. 1969), S. R. Spencer, Jr. (1955), Arna Bontemps (1972), and L. R. Harlan (1972); studies by Hugh Hawkins, ed. (1962) and E. L. Thornborough, ed. (1969).

Washington, Bushrod, 1762-1829, American jurist, b. Westmoreland co., Va.; nephew of George Washington. He was an original member of Phi Beta Kappa at the College of William and Mary, where he was graduated in 1778. Having served (1780-82) in the American Revolution, he was a member of the Virginia house of delegates and of the Virginia convention that adopted (1788) the Constitution. In 1798 he was appointed Associate Justice of the Supreme Court. He was executor of George Washington's estate and aided John Marshall in writing his biography of Washington. He helped organize the American Colonization Society in 1816.

Washington, George, 1732-99, 1st President of the United States (1789-97), commander in chief of the Continental army in the American Revolution, called the Father of His Country. He was born on Feb. 22, 1732 (Feb. 11, 1731, O.S.), the first son of Augustine Washington and his second wife, Mary Ball Washington, on the family estate (later known as WAKEFIELD) in Westmoreland co., Va. Of a wealthy family, George embarked upon a career as a surveyor and in 1748 was invited to go with the party that was to survey Baron Fairfax's lands W of the Blue Ridge. In 1749 he was appointed to his first public office, surveyor of newly created Culpeper co., and through his half-brother Lawrence Washington he became interested in the OHIO COMPANY, which had as its object the exploitation of Western lands. After Lawrence's death (1752), George inherited part of his estate and took over some of Lawrence's duties as adjutant of the colony. As district adjutant, which made (Dec., 1752) him Major Washington at the age of 20, he was charged with training the militia in the quarter assigned him. Washington first gained public notice late in 1753 when he volunteered to carry a message from Gov. Robert DINWIDDIE of Virginia to the French moving into the Ohio country, warning them to quit the territory which was claimed by the British. In delivering the message Washington learned that the French were planning a further advance. He hastened back to Virginia, where he was commissioned lieutenant colonel by Dinwiddie and sent with about 400 men to reinforce the post at the junction of the Allegheny and Monongahela rivers that Dinwiddie had ordered built. The French, however, captured the post before he could reach it, and on hearing that they were approaching in force Washington retired to the Great Meadows to build (July) an entrenched camp (FORT NECESSITY). Late in May he had won his first military victory (and his colonelcy) when he surprised (through the intelligence of his Indian allies) a small body of French troops. The French soon avenged this defeat, overwhelming him with a superior force at Fort Necessity on July 3, 1754. He surrendered on easy terms on July 4 and returned to Virginia with the survivors of his command. These battles marked the beginning of the last of the French and Indian Wars in America, in which Washington continued to figure. As an aide to Edward BRADDOCK he acquitted himself with honor in that general's disastrous expedition against Fort Duquesne in 1755. After the debacle he was appointed commander in chief of the Virginia militia to defend the frontier, and in 1758 he commanded one of the three brigades in the expedition headed by Gen. John Forbes that took an abandoned Fort Duquesne. With this episode his pre-Revolutionary military career ended. In 1759, he married Martha Dandridge Custis, a rich young widow, and settled on his estate at Mt. Vernon. He was a member (1759-74) of the house of burgesses, became a leader in Virginian opposition to the British colonial policy, and served (1774-75) as a delegate to the Continental Congress. After the American Revolution broke out at Concord and Lexington, the Congress organized for defense, and, largely through the efforts of John ADAMS, Washington was named (June 15, 1775) commander in chief of the Continental forces. He took command (July 3, 1775) at Cambridge, Mass., and found not an army but a force of unorganized, poorly disciplined, short-term enlisted militia, officered by men who were often insubordinate. He was faced with the problem of holding the British at Boston with a force that had to be trained in the field, and he was constantly hampered by congressional interference. Washington momentarily overcame these handicaps with the brilliant strategic move of occupying Dorchester Heights, forcing the British to evacuate Boston on March 17, 1776. Against his wishes the Continental Congress compelled him to attempt to defend New York City with a poorly equipped and untrained army against a large British land and sea force commanded by Sir William HOWE. He was not yet experienced enough to conduct a large-scale action, and he committed a military blunder by sending part of his force to Brooklyn, where it was defeated (see LONG ISLAND, BATTLE OF) and surrounded. With the British fleet ready to close the only escape route, Washington saved his army with a masterly amphibious retreat across the East River back to Manhattan. Seeing that his position was completely untenable, he began a retreat northward into Westchester co., which was marked by delaying actions at Harlem Heights and White Plains and by the treacherous insubordination of Charles LEE. The retreat continued across the Hudson River through New Jersey into Pennsylvania, as Washington developed military skill through trial and error. With colonial morale at its lowest ebb, he invaded New Jersey. On Christmas night, 1776, he crossed the Delaware, surrounded and defeated the British at Trenton, and pushed on to Princeton (Jan. 3, 1777), where he defeated a second British force. In 1777 he attempted to defend Philadelphia but was defeated at the battle of Brandywine (Sept. 11). His carefully planned counterattack at Germantown (Oct. 4, 1777) went awry, and with this second successive defeat certain discontented army officers and members of Congress tried to have Washington removed from command. Horatio GATES was advanced as a likely candidate to succeed him, but Washington's prompt action frustrated the so-called CONWAY CABAL. After Germantown, Washington went into winter quarters at VALLEY FORGE. Seldom in military history has any general faced such want and misery as Washington did in the winter of 1777-78. He proved equal to every problem, and in the spring he emerged with increased powers from Congress and a well-trained striking force, personally devoted to him. The attack (June 28, 1778) on the British retreating from Philadelphia to New York was vitiated by the actions of Charles Lee, but Washington's arrival on the field prevented a general American rout (see MONMOUTH, BATTLE OF). The fortunes of war soon shifted in favor of the colonial cause with the arrival (1780) of French military and naval forces, and victory finally came when General CORNWALLIS surrendered to Washington on Oct. 19, 1781. Washington made the American Revolution successful not only by his personal military triumphs but also by his skill in directing other operations. At the war's end he was the most important man in the country. He retired from the army (at Annapolis, Md., Dec. 23, 1783), returned to Mt. Vernon, and in 1784 journeyed to the West to inspect his lands there. Dissatisfied with the weakness of the government (see CONFEDERATION, ARTICLES OF), he soon joined the movement intent on reorganizing it. In 1785 commissioners from Virginia and Maryland met at Mt. Vernon to settle a dispute concerning navigation on the Potomac. This meeting led to the Annapolis Convention (1786) and ultimately to the FEDERAL CONSTITUTIONAL CONVENTION (1787). Washington presided over this last convention, and his influence in securing the adoption of the CONSTITUTION OF THE UNITED STATES is incalculable. After a new government was organized, Washington was unanimously chosen the first President and took office (April 30, 1789) in New York City. He was anxious to establish the new national executive above partisanship, and he chose men from all factions for the administrative departments. Thomas JEFFERSON became Secretary of State, and Alexander HAMILTON Secretary of the Treasury. His efforts to remain aloof from partisan struggles were not successful. He approved of Hamilton's nationalistic financial measures, and although he was by no means a tool in the hands of the Secretary of the Treasury, he consistently supported Hamilton's policies. In the Anglo-French war (1793) he decided against Jefferson, who favored fulfilling the 1778 military alliance with France, and he took measures against Edmond Charles Édouard GENÊT. Jefferson left the cabinet, and despite Washington's efforts to preserve a political truce the Republican party (later the DEMOCRATIC PARTY) and the FEDERALIST PARTY emerged. Washington was unanimously reelected (1793), but his second administration was Federalist and was bitterly criticized by Jeffersonians, especially for JAY'S TREATY with England. Washington was denounced by some as an aristocrat and an enemy of true democratic ideals. The WHISKEY REBELLION and trouble with the Indians, British, and Spanish in the West offered serious problems. The crushing of the rebellion, the defeat of the Indians by Anthony Wayne at FALLEN TIMBERS, and the treaty Thomas PINCKNEY negotiated with Spain settled some of these troubles. Foreign affairs remained gloomy, however, and Washington, weary with political life, refused to run for a third term. Washington's *Farewell Address* (Sept. 17, 1796), a monument of American oratory, contained the famous (and much misquoted) passage warning the United States against "permanent alliances" with foreign powers. Washington returned to Mt. Vernon, but when war with France seemed imminent (1798) he was offered command of the army. War, however, was averted. He died on Dec. 14, 1799, and was buried on his estate. There are many portraits and statues of Washington, among them the familiar, idealized portraits by Gilbert Stuart; the statue by Jean Antoine Houdon, who also executed the famous portrait bust from a life mask; and paintings by Charles Willson Peale, John Trumbull, and John Singleton Copley. The national capital is named for him; one state, several colleges and universities, and scores of counties, towns, and villages of the United States bear his name. Wakefield and Mt. Vernon are national shrines. The definitive edition of Washington's writings (39 vol., 1931–44) was edited by John C. Fitzpatrick. His journals—that of his Barbados journey in 1751–52 (1892), that of his journey to the West (1905), and his diaries (ed. by John C. Fitzpatrick, 4 vol., 1925)—were also edited separately. An old standard edition of his writings is that by Worthington C. Ford (14 vol., 1889–93), and Saxe Commins edited a one-volume selection, *Basic Writings* (1948). Other standard sources of his works are *The Washington Papers* (1955, repr. 1967), edited by Saul K. Padover, and *The George Washington Papers* (1964), edited by Frank Donovan. There have been innumerable editions of his *Farewell Address* and many separate editions of others of his works. His figure has bulked large in drama, poetry, fiction, and essays in American literature. There have been a great many studies of phases and incidents of his career and a continual stream of biographies; the definitive biography is by Douglas Southall Freeman (7 vol., 1948–1957; abr. ed. 1968); Volume VII was written after Freeman's death by John Alexander Carroll and Mary Wells Ashworth of his staff. The biography (1940) begun by Nathaniel W. Stephenson and completed by Waldo H. Dunn is full and eminently useful; so is the four-volume biography by James T. Flexner (1965–72). The early biography by "Parson" M. L. Weems is important chiefly because it contained many of the now famous Washington legends, such as that of the cherry tree. Biographies of Washington by eminent men of another day include those by John Marshall, Jared Sparks, Washington Irving, and Woodrow Wilson. Among the shorter biographies are those by P. L. Ford (1896, repr. 1971), Woodrow Wilson (1896, repr. 1969), John Corbin (1930, repr. 1972), L. M. Sears (1932), J. C. Fitzpatrick (1933, repr. 1970), and North Callahan (1972). See also W. C. Ford, *Washington as Employer and Importer of Labour* (1889, repr. 1971); T. G. Frothingham, *Washington, Commander in Chief* (1930); G. A. Eisen, *Portraits of Washington* (3 vol., 1932); C. H. Ambler, *George Washington and the West* (1936, repr. 1971); E. S. Whitely, *Washington and His Aides-De-Camp* (1936, repr. 1968); F. R. Bellamy, *The Private Life of George Washington* (1951); C. P. Nettels, *George Washington and American Independence* (1951); Marcus Cunliffe, *George Washington: Man and Monument* (1958); L. M. Sears, *George Washington and the French Revolution* (1960); Bernhard Knollenberg, *Washington and the Revolution* (1940, repr. 1968) and *George Washington, the Virginia Period, 1732–1775* (1964); T. N. Dupuy, *The Military Life of George Washington* (1969); Forest MacDonald, *The Presidency of George Washington* (1974).

Washington, Martha, 1731–1802, wife of George Washington, b. New Kent co., Va. The daughter of John Dandridge and Frances Jones Dandridge, she first married (1749) Daniel Parke Custis. She bore him four children, but the first two died in childhood. Custis himself died in July, 1757, leaving Martha one of the wealthiest women in Virginia. Washington first met her in March, 1758, lost no time in proposing, and was just as quickly accepted. They were married in Jan., 1759, and Washington took Martha and her family, John Parke Custis (d. 1781) and Martha Parke Custis (d. 1773), to his MOUNT VERNON estate. They had no children of their own, but John Parke Custis had four, and after John's death Washington adopted the youngest two, Eleanor Parke Custis and George Washington Parke Custis, whose daughter married Robert E. Lee. See biographies by A. H. Wharton (1897, repr. 1967), A. C. Desmond (1942), and E. Thane (1960).

Washington, state (1970 pop. 3,409,169), 68,192 sq mi (176,617 sq km), including 1,483 sq mi (3,841 sq km) of inland water surface, extreme NW United

States, in the Pacific Northwest, admitted 1889 as the 42d state. OLYMPIA is the capital; SEATTLE, SPOKANE, and TACOMA are the largest cities. Washington is bounded on the N by the Canadian province of British Columbia, on the E by Idaho, on the S by Oregon (with the Columbia River marking much of the boundary), and on the W by the Pacific, with Puget Sound in the northwest and two inlets, Grays Harbor and Willapa Bay, farther south. The deep cut of Puget Sound creates the Olympic Peninsula—a wet region with dense rain forests of spruce, fir, cedar, and hemlock—much of it included in Olympic National Park, where the Olympic Mts. rise 7,965 ft (2,428 m) in Mt. Olympus. Puget Sound, the focal point of Washington's economic development, is entered from the Pacific by the Juan de Fuca Strait or the Strait of Georgia. It is navigable and has many beautiful bays, on which are situated such important commercial and industrial cities as Seattle, Tacoma, and Everett. More than 300 islands dot Puget Sound; they include the picturesque and historic San Juan Archipelago (see SAN JUAN BOUNDARY DISPUTE) and Whidbey Island. Another of Washington's bold topographical features is the lofty Cascade Range, which runs north and south, rising to 14,410 ft (4,392 m) in Mt. Rainier, and divides the state into western and eastern sections of quite contrasting physical (and corresponding economic) characteristics. The Cascades block the eastward movement of warm ocean air from the Japanese Current, creating abundant rainfall to the west and almost semiarid conditions to the east. Thus, the coastal region is one of the wettest areas in the country, averaging in some places as much as 150 in. (381 cm) of rainfall per year and containing some of the heaviest stands of timber in the world. In contrast, the dry eastern section is comparatively treeless (except in the Rocky Mts. to the north and the Blue Mts. in the extreme southeast), with just sufficient rainfall for the dry farming of wheat and hay and for cattle and sheep raising. Spokane is the commercial and transportation hub of the entire region between the Cascades and the Rockies, an area extending into British Columbia, Idaho, Montana, and Oregon. However, irrigation has converted many of the river valleys E of the Cascades (especially the Yakima and Wenatchee) into garden areas. Washington leads the country in the production of apples and is also a major wheat-producing state. Miles of apple and cherry orchards in the irrigated area just E of the Cascades create the landscape of spring beauty for which the state is famous. Washington is the nation's second largest producer of sweet cherries, as well as of asparagus and green peas. Other major crops are hay and potatoes. Cattle, dairy goods, and poultry are also economically important. Washington's great water resources provide not only irrigation but enormous hydroelectric power. The impact of the Columbia River on the life and economy of the state can scarcely be overestimated. In early days the river was a means of transport and a salmon-fishing field for the many Indian tribes. Because of the rapid drop from its origin to its mouth, the Columbia is one of the greatest sources of hydroelectric power in the world. It flows from British Columbia in the northeast, makes a great bend westward just after receiving the Spokane, and later turns in another large bend generally southward. After being joined by its greatest tributary, the Snake, it continues west again as the Washington-Oregon line, cutting its way through the Cascades and the Pacific Coast Range in magnificent gorges to reach the Pacific. Grand Coulee Dam, one of the world's largest concrete dams and greatest potential power-producing structures, and Bonneville Dam have been supplemented, on the river's upper course, by Chief Joseph and Rocky Reach dams (completed 1961), Priest Rapids Dam (1962), and Wanapum Dam (1963), and, on its lower course, by The Dalles Dam (1957), John Day Dam (1968), and McNary Dam (1953), all shared with Oregon. The dams on the lower course were designed as power, flood-control, and navigation projects, whereas the dams on the upper course are integral to the COLUMBIA BASIN PROJECT (with the Grand Coulee as the key unit), providing not only power and flood control but extensive irrigation to the Columbia Plateau. The Snake River in the east and the Yakima River in S central Washington also have important irrigation projects, and dams on the Skagit River (including Ross and Diablo, two of the world's highest) supply power to Seattle and the surrounding area. Seattle, a great shipping point for the Orient and a natural gateway to Alaska (because of the protected Inland Passage) is one of the large cities in the United States and a center for the state's leading industry, the manufacture of jet airplanes, missiles, and spacecraft. Washington's second largest industry is food processing; this is based on the state's diversified irrigated farming and dairying as well as on its abundant fishing resources. Salmon is the biggest catch, but halibut, bottomfish, oysters, and crabs are also caught in significant numbers. Despite the vast acres of semiarid land E of the Cascades, more than one half of the state's area is forested, and the old lumber and wood-products industry, so important in the early development of the state, is today its third largest industry. Many of Washington's cities (Tacoma, Bellingham, Everett, Anacortes) began as sawmill centers, and lumber, pulp, paper, and related items are still their major products. Other important manufactures in the state are chemicals and primary metals, especially aluminum. The abundant water power and the rich aluminum and magnesium ores found in the Okanogan Highlands in the northeast part of the state have made Washington the nation's leading aluminum producer. Washington's chief minerals are sand and gravel, cement, stone, uranium, and diatomite. Gold, silver, lead, and zinc are also found in the Okanogan Highlands. Tourism is an increasingly important industry. Thousands of visitors are annually attracted to Mount Rainier National Park, Olympic National Park, North Cascades National Park (created 1968), Fort Vancouver and Whitman Mission national historic sites, and Coulee Dam National Recreation Area (see NATIONAL PARKS AND MONUMENTS, table). Rugged mountain slopes and the simple grandeur of the scenery draw many climbers during the summer months, and in winter excellent snowfields near Seattle and Tacoma attract crowds of skiers. Washington's early history is shared with that of the whole Oregon Territory. The perennial search for the NORTHWEST PASSAGE aroused initial interest in the area. Of the early explorers along the Pacific coast, Spanish expeditions under Juan Pérez (1774) and Bruno Heceta (1775) are the first known to have definitely skirted the coast of what is now Washington. Capt. James Cook's English expedition (1778) first opened up the area to the maritime fur trade with China, and British fur companies were soon exploring the West and encountering Russians pushing southward from posts in Alaska. In 1787, Charles William Barkley found the inland channel, which the following year John Meares named the Juan de Fuca Strait (after the sailor who is alleged to have discovered it). In 1792, the British explorer George Vancouver and the American fur trader Robert Gray crossed paths along the Washington coast. Vancouver sailed into Puget Sound and mapped the area, and Gray, convinced of the existence of a great river that the other explorers rejected, found the entrance, crossed the dangerous bar, and sailed up the Columbia, establishing U.S. claim to the areas that it drained. The Lewis and Clark expedition, which reached the area in 1805, and the establishment of John Jacob Astor's settlement, ASTORIA, both helped to further the American claim; but in 1807 the Canadian trader David Thompson traveled the length of the Columbia, mapping the region and establishing British counter claims. After Astoria was sold to the NORTH WEST COMPANY in the War of 1812, British interests appeared paramount, although in 1818 a treaty provided for 10 years (later extended) of joint rights for the United States and Great Britain in the Columbia River country. The HUDSON'S BAY COMPANY absorbed the North West Company in 1821 and, under the patriarchal guidance of Dr. John McLoughlin, dominated the region until challenged by the Americans in the 1840s. Fort Vancouver, on the site of present-day Vancouver, sheltered American overland traders—particularly Jedediah Smith, Benjamin Bonneville, and Nathaniel Wyeth—and later the American missionaries, who were the first real settlers in the area N of the Columbia. Marcus Whitman established (1836) a mission at Waiilatpu (near present Walla Walla), which for a decade not only served the Indians as a medical and religious center but also provided an indispensable rest stop for immigrants on the OREGON TRAIL. Meanwhile the British, although despairing of control over the area S of the Columbia, were still determined to retain the region to the north; the Americans, on the other hand, demanded the ouster of the British from the whole of the Columbia River country up to a lat. of 54°40'N. "Fifty-four forty or fight" became a slogan in the 1844 election campaign, and for a time war with Britain threatened. However, diplomacy prevailed, and in 1846 the boundary was set at lat. 49°N. Peace with the British did not, however, preclude Indian conflict, and in 1847 the whole area was thrown into turmoil with the massacre of the Whitmans and other settlers at the hands of the Indians. Partly as a protective measure, the Oregon Territory, embracing the Washington area, was created the following year; but in 1853 the region was divided, and Washington Territory (containing a part of what is now Idaho) was set up, with Isaac Stevens as the first governor. (The Idaho section was cut away when Idaho Territory was formed in 1863.) Meanwhile, some of the pioneers on the Oregon Trail began to turn northward, and a small settlement sprang up at New Market, or Tumwater (near present Olympia). After word of the needs of California gold seekers for lumber and food spread northward, settlers recognized the potential of the Puget Sound country and poured into the area in ever-increasing numbers. Lumber and fishing industries arose to supply the demand to the south, and other towns, including Seattle, were founded. Meanwhile Stevens, who also served as superintendent of Indian affairs, set about persuading the Indians to sell much of their lands and settle on reservations. Treaties with the coast tribes were quickly concluded, but the more warlike inland tribes revolted, and hostilities with the Cayuse, the Yakima, and the Nez Percé tribes continued for many years. (Today about half of Washington's Indians, who number about 33,000, live in or near reservations.) Gold was first discovered in Washington in 1852 by a Hudson's Bay Company agent at Fort Colville, but the Yakima War was then in progress and hindered extensive mining activity. In 1860 the Orofino Creek and Clearwater River deposits were uncovered, bringing a rush of prospectors to the Walla Walla area. The great influx of settlers was delayed, however, until the 1880s, when transport by rail became possible (the first of three transcontinental railroads linked to Washington was completed in 1883). The population almost quadrupled between 1880 and 1890; although the majority of the new settlers were from the East and Midwest, the territory also absorbed large numbers of foreign immigrants. Chinese laborers had been brought in during the 1860s to aid in placer mining; after 1870 they were followed by substantial groups of Germans, Scandinavians, Russians, Dutch, and Japanese immigrants. By the time Washington became a state in 1889, the wide sagebrush plains of E Washington had been given over to cattle and sheep, agriculture was flourishing in the fertile valleys, and the lumber industry had been founded. Although some agrarian and labor dissatisfaction with the railroads and other big corporations existed, giving rise to the GRANGER MOVEMENT and the POPULIST PARTY, the discovery of gold in Alaska in 1897 brought renewed prosperity. Seattle, the primary departure point for the Klondike, became a boom town. Labor and election reform laws were enacted, and the primary, the initiative, the referendum, and the recall were adopted. At the same time came labor clashes that gave Washington a reputation as a radical state. The extreme policies of the INDUSTRIAL WORKERS OF THE WORLD (IWW) proved appealing to the shipyard and dock workers and to the loggers, and in 1917 the War Dept. was forced to intervene in a lumber dispute. A general strike after the war had a crippling effect on the state's economy; antilabor feeling increased, and the famous incident at Centralia resulted in bloody strife between the IWW and the American Legion. The alarmed reaction of management to radical labor policies produced a confrontation situation that hindered the institution of remedial measures until the onset of the lean days of the 1930s and the emergence of the New Deal. Washington was an important center of the defense industry during World War II, particularly with the immense aircraft industry in Seattle and the Atomic Energy Commission's Hanford Works at Richland (today a center for nuclear research). The large Japanese-American population in the state (more than 15,000 persons) was moved eastward, suffering great physical and emotional hardship. In the postwar period the climate of public affairs began to change, owing in part to the political power of Dave Beck and organized labor, and also to the continuing widespread prosperity brought by booming aircraft production, expanding uranium and aluminum-processing industries, and a growing transarctic air trade with the Far East. Washington still operates under its first constitution, adopted in 1889. Its executive branch is headed by a governor elected for a four-year term. The bicameral legislature has a senate with 49 members elected for four-year terms and a house of representatives with 98 members elected for two-year terms. The state sends 2 Senators and 7 Representatives to the U.S. Congress and has 9 electoral votes. Washington has generally divided its allegiance fairly equally between the two major political parties; Daniel J. Evans, a Republican, won an unprecedented third term as governor in 1972. Among the state's institutions of higher learning are the Univ. of Washington and Seattle Univ., at Seattle; Washington State Univ., at Pullman; Gonzaga Univ., at Spokane; Pacific Lutheran Univ., at Tacoma; and Whitman College, at Walla Walla. See Lancaster Pollard and Lloyd Spencer, *A History of the State of Washington* (4 vol., 1937); E. I. Stewart, *Washington: Northwest Frontier* (4 vol., 1957); M. W. Avery, *Washington: A History of the Evergreen State* (1965); P. L. Beckett, *From Wilderness to Enabling Act* (1968); W. S. Lee, ed., *Washington State: A Literary Chronicle* (1969); Joan Olson and Gene Olson, *Washington Times and Trails* (1970); Federal Writers' Project, *Washington: A Guide to the Evergreen State* (1941, repr. 1972).

Washington, new town (1971 pop. 25,269), Durham, NE England. Washington was designated one of the NEW TOWNS in 1964 to alleviate overpopulation in the Tyneside-Wearside area. Its population goal is 80,000. The new town takes in most of the urban district of Washington, whose industries include the production of chemicals and iron and steel, coal mining, and stone quarrying. In 1974, Washington became part of the new metropolitan county of Tyne and Wear.

Washington. **1** City (1970 pop. 11,358), seat of Daviess co., SW Ind.; settled 1805, inc. as a city 1871. It has railroad shops and a rubber industry. **2** City, SW Ohio: see WASHINGTON COURT HOUSE, Ohio. **3** City (1970 pop. 19,827), seat of Washington co., SW Pa., in a bituminous coal region; settled 1769, laid out 1781, inc. as a city 1924. Chief among its many manufactures are glass, steel, and electronic products. David Bradford House, erected in 1788, was a meeting place in the Whiskey Rebellion (1794). Le Moyne House (1812) was the home of Dr. Francis Le Moyne, an abolitionist leader. Washington and Jefferson College (1781; oldest college W of the Alleghenies) is there. Also in the city are a race track and a trolley museum.

Washington, D.C., capital of the United States (1970 pop. 756,510), coextensive (since 1878, when GEORGETOWN became a part of Washington) with the DISTRICT OF COLUMBIA, on the Potomac River; inc. 1802. It is the center of a metropolitan area (1970 pop. 2,861,123) extending into Maryland and Virginia. It is the legislative, administrative, and judicial center of the United States and, in a sense, the political capital of the Western world. It has little industry; its business is government, and the city's Federal civilian employees total c.300,000. Washington is also a major tourist attraction, drawing millions of visitors every year. In 1790 the rivalry of Northern and Southern states for the capital's location ended when Jefferson's followers supported Hamilton's program for Federal assumption of state debts in return for an agreement to situate the national capital on the banks of the Potomac River. George Washington selected the exact spot. The "Federal City" was designed by Pierre L'Enfant and laid out by Andrew Ellicott. Construction began on the WHITE HOUSE in 1792 and on the CAPITOL the following year. John Adams was the first President to occupy the White House. Congress held its first session in Washington in 1800, moving there from Philadelphia, and Thomas Jefferson was the first President to be inaugurated in the new capital. In the War of 1812 the British captured and sacked (1814) Washington, burning most of the public buildings, including the Capitol and the White House. The city grew slowly. Even after 1850 it was still "a sea of mud," and not until the 20th cent. did it cease to be an unkempt, rural city and assume its present gracious and urban aspect. Though strongly manned during the Civil War, it was several times threatened by the Confederates, notably by Gen. Jubal A. Early in 1864. After 1901, Washington was developed on the basis of the resurrected L'Enfant plan—a gridiron arrangement of streets cut by diagonal avenues radiating from the Capitol and White House, with an elaborate system of parks. The stately city spreads out over 69 sq mi (179 sq km), including 8 sq mi (20.7 sq km) of water surface, with broad tree-shaded thoroughfares and open vistas at frequent intervals. The numerous impressive government buildings are built of white or gray stone in the classical style, and there are also many fine homes. Among other attractive buildings are the embassies and legations of many foreign countries, many of them lining "embassy row" on Massachusetts Ave. The larger of the city's fine parks are West Potomac Park, which extends S from the Lincoln Memorial and includes the Tidal Basin, flanked by the famous Japanese cherry trees; East Potomac Park, an area of reclaimed land jutting S from the Jefferson Memorial; Rock Creek Park, with almost 1,800 acres (728 hectares) of natural woodlands and extensive recreation facilities, and the adjoining National Zoological Park; and Anacostia Park, adjacent to the National Arboretum. Besides the Capitol and the White House, some other important government buildings and places of historic interest are the Senate office buildings and the House of Representatives office buildings, the Supreme Court Building, the PENTAGON (in Virginia), the new Federal Bureau of Investigation building, the LIBRARY OF CONGRESS, the National Archives Building, and Constitution Hall. Ford's Theatre, where Lincoln was shot, has been restored. Best known of the city's many statues and monuments are the WASHINGTON MONUMENT, at the western end of the long grass Mall; the LINCOLN MEMORIAL, with its pool reflecting the marble shaft of the Washington Monument; and the THOMAS JEFFERSON MEMORIAL, overlooking the Tidal Basin. The Arlington Memorial Bridge across the Potomac connects the capital with ARLINGTON NATIONAL CEMETERY. In the Potomac itself lies Theodore Roosevelt Island, a thickly wooded islet with many foot trails. Among Washington's famous churches are the Washington National Cathedral (Protestant Episcopal) on Mt. St. Alban, which contains the tomb of Woodrow Wilson; and the National Shrine of the Immaculate Conception, the largest Roman Catholic church in the United States. The city's many institutions of higher education include American Univ., the Army War College, the Catholic Univ. of America, Georgetown Univ., George Washington Univ., and Howard Univ. Among the many cultural attractions of the capital are the NATIONAL GALLERY OF ART, the Freer Gallery of Art, and the other centers under the auspices of the SMITHSONIAN INSTITUTION; the John F. Kennedy Center for the Performing Arts; the Corcoran Gallery of Art; the Phillips Collection and the Phillips Gallery of Art; and the Folger Shakespeare Library. The U.S. Naval Observatory, the U.S. Naval Research Laboratory, the Smithsonian Institution, the BROOKINGS INSTITUTION, the National Institutes of Health, and the Carnegie Institution of Washington are among the institutions dedicated to scientific research and education. Also in Washington are Walter Reed Army Medical Center, including the Army Medical School and Walter Reed Army Hospital, and the U.S. Soldiers Home (1851), the oldest in the country. Military installations in the area include Fort McNair, Fort Myer, Andrews Air Force Base, and Bolling Air Force Base. Of historic interest is Fort Washington (built 1809, destroyed 1814, rebuilt by 1824). In 1970 work was begun on the construction of a 98-mi (158-km) subway system. The capital's main transit points are Union Station, National and Dulles International airports (both in Virginia). In 1974 the Admiral's House on the grounds of the U.S. Naval Observatory was designated the temporary official residence of the Vice President. Through the years the city has been a focus for national political activity; during the 1960s and early 1970s an unusual number of demonstrations were staged there, both for civil rights and against the war in Vietnam. Washington has long been a gateway for blacks emigrating from the South, and today its population is predominantly black. Many of these citizens live in poverty conditions, and there are serious problems of housing and crime. In April, 1968, the assassination of Martin Luther King, Jr., touched off six days of violence, looting, and burning in Washington. Army troops were called in to quell the disorders and to protect important government buildings. In 1871, Washington lost its charter as a city and a territorial government was inaugurated to govern the entire District of Columbia. Congress took direct control of the District's government in 1874, providing for a mayor appointed by the President and a commission chosen by Congress; the residents were disfranchised. The Twenty-third Amendment (1961) to the Constitution gave inhabitants the right to vote in presidential elections; the District of Columbia was accorded three electoral votes, the minimum number. In 1970 legislation was enacted authorizing election of a nonvoting delegate to the House of Representatives. The present system of government, approved in a referendum in May, 1974, provides for an elected mayor and a 13-member city council but reserves for Congress the right to review the budget and legislation passed by the council and to retain direct control over an enclave containing most of the Federal buildings and monuments. The first elections were held in Nov., 1974. See Federal Writers' Project, *Washington: City* *and Capital* (1942, repr. 1968); C. M. Green, *Washington, 1800–1878* (1962) and *Washington: Capital City, 1879–1950* (1963); *The New York Times Guide to the Nation's Capital* (1967); J. W. Reps, *Monumental Washington* (1967).

Washington, Fort, N.Y.: see FORT WASHINGTON.

Washington, Mount, N.H.: see PRESIDENTIAL RANGE.

Washington, Treaty of, May, 1871, agreement concluded between the United States and Great Britain in Washington, D.C. Its principal articles provided for determination of the ALABAMA CLAIMS by an international commission. The treaty also provided for arbitration of the SAN JUAN BOUNDARY DISPUTE and of the Canadian-American fisheries controversy. Hamilton FISH , who was chiefly responsible for bringing about the treaty, headed the five American commissioners in the negotiations. The British delegation was led by the 2d earl (later 1st marquess) of Ripon.

Washington, University of, at Seattle; state supported; coeducational; chartered and opened 1861 as the Territorial Univ. of Washington, renamed 1889. There are noted schools of medicine and engineering, and the university operates laboratories for the marine sciences. Also of note is the Washington State Museum, which is located on campus and houses collections in natural history and anthropology. See C. M. Gates, *The First Century at the University of Washington, 1861–1961* (1961).

Washington and Jefferson College, at Washington, Pa.; founded for men; formed 1865 with the merger of Washington College (chartered 1787, opened 1789 as an academy; became a college 1806) and Jefferson College (opened c.1791, chartered 1794 as an academy; rechartered as a college 1802). In 1970 female undergraduates were admitted. See history by H. T. W. Coleman (1956).

Washington and Lee University, at Lexington, Va.; for men; founded and opened 1749 as Augusta Academy. It was called Liberty Hall in 1776, Liberty Hall Academy (a college) in 1782, Washington Academy (following a gift from George Washington) in 1798, Washington College in 1813, and Washington and Lee Univ. in 1871. Robert E. Lee was president from 1865 to 1870, and his tomb is in the university chapel. The university's front campus was designated a national historic landmark in 1972.

Washington Conference: see NAVAL CONFERENCES.

Washington Court House, city (1970 pop. 12,495), seat of Fayette co., SW Ohio, on Paint Creek, in a productive farm, dairy, and poultry area; laid out and founded c.1810, inc. 1831. Its many manufactures include shoes, gloves, and automobile and aircraft parts.

Washington Island, atoll (1968 pop. 437), 3 sq mi (7.8 sq km), central Pacific, one of the LINE ISLANDS and part of the British colony of the GILBERT AND ELLICE ISLANDS. Discovered by the American explorer Edmund FANNING in 1798, it was annexed by Great Britain in 1889 and became part of the colony in 1916. Copra is the only export. Its former name was Prospect Island.

Washington Island, c.20 sq mi (50 sq km), NE Wis., in NW Lake Michigan, just off the northern tip of the Door Peninsula. It includes the town of Washington (1970 pop. 446). The island was visited by the French explorers Radisson (1657) and La Salle (1679). It has a large Icelandic settlement and is a popular resort area.

Washington Monument, hollow shaft, 555 ft 5⅛ in. (169.3 m) high, located on a 106-acre (43-hectare) site at the west end of the Mall, Washington, D.C.; dedicated 1885. In 1783, Congress passed a resolution approving an equestrian statue of George Washington, and in 1791 architect Pierre L'Enfant included a site for the statue near the present location of the monument in his plans for the Federal city. However, Washington objected to the idea. After Washington's death in 1799, plans for a memorial were discussed but none were adopted until 1832, when the Washington National Monument Society, a private group, was formed. Its activity brought gifts of money, as well as blocks of stone from each state, some foreign governments, and private individuals. These "tribute blocks" carry inscriptions on the inside walls of the monument. Architect Robert Mills's elaborate Greek temple design was accepted for the monument, and on July 4, 1848, the cornerstone was laid. Work on the project was interrupted by political quarreling in the 1850s and, then, by the Civil War, funds became scarce. It was not until 1876 that Congress took over the project and appropriated money for the monument. The base, entirely different from Mills's design, was completed in 1880; the aluminum top was positioned in 1884; and the monument was opened to the public in 1888. The top may be reached by stairs or elevator.

Washington-on-the-Brazos, former town, S central Texas, on the Brazos River; settled 1821. It was the scene of the Texas declaration of independence from Mexico on March 2, 1836, and in 1842 it was the seat of the Republic of Texas's government. A state park on the site commemorates the town's historical importance.

Washington Square Players: see THEATRE GUILD.

Washington State University, at Pullman; land-grant and state supported; chartered 1890, opened 1892 as an agriculture college. From 1905 to 1959 it was the State College of Washington. The university's College of Agriculture carries on important agricultural research and instruction throughout the state. The school's other facilities include a nuclear radiation center and an environmental research center.

Washington University, at St. Louis, Mo.; coeducational; est. as Eliot Seminary 1853, opened 1854, renamed 1857. It has a well-known medical school and school of social work; also of note is its institute of radiology.

Washita (wŏsh'ĭtô), river, c.450 mi (720 km) long, rising in the Texas Panhandle near the Okla. line and flowing generally SE across Oklahoma to Lake Texoma or the Red River. The name is Indian—another spelling of Ouachita. The battle of the Washita (1868), in which General Custer defeated the Cheyenne Indians, took place on the river, near Cheyenne. Fort Cobb Dam on Pond Creek and Foss Dam on the Washita both serve the Washita basin project.

Washo Indians (wä'shō), North American Indians occupying in the mid-19th cent. the region around Washo and Tahoe lakes in W Nevada and E California. The Paiute were the inveterate enemies of the Washo; before the coming of white settlers the Paiute defeated and drove back the Washo, and again in the period 1860 to 1862 they conquered the Washo. Today the Washo live on reservations in California and Nevada, where they number less than 900. Their original material culture is of undetermined status, and their language belongs to the Hokan-Siouan linguistic stock (see AMERICAN INDIAN LANGUAGES). See J. F. Downs, *The Two Worlds of the Washo* (1966); E. M. Dangberg, comp., *Washo Tales* (tr. 1968).

wasp, name applied to many winged INSECTS of the order Hymenoptera, which also includes the ant and the bee. Most wasps are carnivorous, feeding on insects, grubs, or spiders. They have biting mouthparts, and the females have stings with which they paralyze their prey. The sting can be used repeatedly. The thorax of a wasp is attached to the abdomen by a narrow stalk (hence the term "wasp-waisted"). Some wasps are solid black or dark blue, but most have red, orange, or yellow wings or markings. Stripes are common. The great majority of the 20,000 species are solitary, but one family (the Vespidae) includes both social forms (the paper wasps, hornets, and yellow jackets) and solitary forms (e.g., the potter wasps). In the social wasps there are usually three castes: the egg-laying queens (one or more per colony), the workers, or sexually undeveloped females, and the drones, or males. Social wasps build nests of a coarse, papery material, prepared by masticating wood fiber. The eggs are deposited in the compartments, or cells, of the nest, where they develop into larvae and then pupae, emerging as adults. Adult social wasps feed chiefly on nectar and plant sap but feed the larvae with masticated animal food. In temperate regions a colony lasts a single season, the drones and workers dying in the fall. The mated queens take shelter during the winter and in spring lay eggs and start new colonies. In the tropics colonies continue indefinitely, dividing when they grow very large. The paper wasps (*Polestes*), of nearly worldwide distribution, usually hang their nests, consisting of a single comb (layer of cells), from eaves, branches, or other shelters. The hornets and yellow jackets (*Vespa*), found throughout the Northern Hemisphere, build a large, round nest of many combs, covered with a paper sheath; in some species this nest is built underground. Among the solitary wasps, each species usually favors a particular type of prey. The female seals a single egg in a nest provided with paralyzed prey on which the developing larva feeds. In many species the nest is in a burrow or small hole dug by the female. The jug-shaped nests of the potter, or mason, wasps (*Eumenes*) of Europe and North America are made of mud and fastened to plants. Often seen under bridges and eaves are the "organ-pipe" nests of the mud-dauber wasps (*Sceliphron*), consisting of long, narrow, adjacent cells of mud. Other solitary wasps are the tarantula hawks (*Pepsis*) and cicada killers (*Sphecius*) of the SW United States, which hunt prey much larger than themselves. Some wasps are parasitic. The cuckoo wasps (family Chrysididae), of worldwide distribution, are brilliantly colored wasps that lay their eggs in other wasps' nests. The ICHNEUMON FLIES are wasps that lay their eggs in the larvae of other insects. The gall wasps (see GALL) lay eggs in plant tissues. Wasps that prey on harmful insects have been introduced in various regions to control these pests. The name wasp is sometimes restricted to the so-called true wasps, members of the superfamilies Vespoidae and Sphecoidae. Wasps are classified in the phylum ARTHROPODA, class Insecta, order Hymenoptera. See H. E. Evans and M. J. W. Eberhard, *The Wasps* (1970).

wassail (wŏs'əl, wŏs'āl), ancient salutation used in England in presenting a cup of wine to a guest or in drinking a health. It signifies "be whole" or "have health," the answer being "drink hail." The words by association came to mean any liquor in which healths are drunk, especially the spiced drinks served as a feature of medieval Christmas celebrations. By a natural transition, *wassail* also came to refer to revelries, carousals, and drinking songs.

Wassermann, August von (wŏs'ərmən, Ger. ou'gōōst fən väs'ərmän), 1866–1925, German physician and bacteriologist. In Berlin he was director of the department of experimental therapy and serum research (1906–13) at Koch Institute and director of experimental therapy (from 1913) at the Kaiser Wilhelm Institute. In addition to developing inoculations against cholera, typhoid, and tetanus, he devised the **Wassermann test** (1906), used in the diagnosis of syphilis. A positive reaction when the blood or spinal fluid of the patient is tested indicates the presence of antibodies formed as a result of infection with syphilis (even though symptoms of the disease may not be observable at the time). A few other diseases, however (such as leprosy), also sometimes produce a positive Wassermann reaction.

Wassermann, Jakob (yä'kôp), 1873–1934, Austrian novelist, b. Bavaria. He won international fame with *Christian Wahnschaffe* (1919, tr. *The World's Illusion,* 1920), a novel whose moral intensity and characterization have suggested comparison to Dostoyevsky. Other works popular in his lifetime include the novels *Casper Hauser* (1908, tr. 1928), *Das Gänsemännchen* (1915, tr. *The Goose Man,* 1922), *Ulrike Woytich* (1923, tr. *Gold,* 1924), and *Der Fall Maurizius* (1928, tr. *The Maurizius Case,* 1929). He also wrote an autobiography, *Mein Weg als Deutscher und Jude* (1921, tr. *My Life as German and Jew,* 1933), plays, biographies, and essays. See study by J. C. Blankenagel (1942).

waste: see SOLID WASTE.

Wast Water (wŏst), lake, 3 mi (4.8 km) long and ½ mi (.8 km) wide, in the Lake District, NW England, SW of Keswick. It is the deepest lake in England (maximum depth 258 ft/79 m). The ravine of Wastdale Head is nearby.

Watauga (wŏtô'gə), river, 60 mi (97 km) long, rising in the Blue Ridge Mts., NW N.C., and flowing NW to the south fork of the Holston River near Kingsport, Tenn. Watauga Dam (completed 1949), a unit of the Tennessee Valley Authority, provides flood control and power (50,000-kw capacity). Settlement on the river began in 1768; Sycamore Shoals Monument, a national historic landmark, marks the site of early historic events on the river (see ELIZABETHTON, Tenn.).

Watauga Association, government (1772–75) formed by settlers along the Watauga River in present E Tennessee. Virginians made the first settlements in 1769, and after the collapse of the REGULATOR MOVEMENT in North Carolina, citizens from that colony under James ROBERTSON established homes farther west on the river. For their mutual protection these settlements united in 1772 and drew up a written agreement, called the Watauga Association. A five-man court constituted the government. Other settlements along the Holston and Nolichucky rivers also adhered to the Watauga Association. In 1772 the Wataugans secured a 10-year lease from the Cherokee Indians for the land along the river; in 1775 they organized as Washington district, but in 1776, at their own request, they came under the protection of North Carolina, which created (1777) Washington co. for the area. After the American Revolution the Wataugans belonged to another new, short-lived government (see FRANKLIN, STATE OF) before Tennessee became a state in 1796.

watch, small, portable timepiece usually designed to be worn on the person. Other kinds of timepieces are generally referred to as CLOCKS. At one time it was generally believed that the first watches were made in Nuremburg, Germany, c.1500. However, there is now evidence that watches may have appeared at an earlier date in Italy. Early watches were ornate, very heavy, and made in a variety of shapes, e.g., pears, skulls, and crosses; the faces were protected by metal latticework. Watch parts were made by hand until c.1850, when machine methods were introduced by watch manufacturers in the United States. The introduction of machine-made parts not only cut manufacturing costs but increased precision and facilitated repairs. To insure the accuracy of a watch over a long period, bearings made of jewels (usually synthetic sapphires or rubies) are utilized at points subject to heavy wear. The mechanical watch contains a mainspring to drive the watch's mechanism. Part of the mechanism includes a hairspring and an oscillating balance wheel to control the rate at which the mechanism moves. The mainspring is wound by the wearer when he turns a knob outside the watch's casing. The automatic, or self-winding, watch has a mainspring that is wound by an oscillating weight, contained in the watch, that is set into motion by the movements of the wearer. The stopwatch can be stopped or started at will by pressing a tiny button on its edge and is used for timing such events as races. The electric watch, which was introduced by the Hamilton Watch Company in 1957, also uses a hairspring and a balance wheel to regulate the rate at which its mechanism moves, but it has no mainspring. One of the various devices used to drive the mechanism consists mainly of a permanent magnet and an electromagnet whose mutual attraction is used to push the balance wheel to keep it and the rest of the mechanism moving. In recent years sophisticated electronic watches have been developed. One type uses the vibrations of an electrically driven tuning fork to determine the rate at which a small motor drives the hands. In another type a crystal oscillator provides a signal that regulates this motion. In yet a third type a crystal oscillator is joined to digital counting and digital display circuits, thus eliminating all moving parts. Watches using a crystal oscillator are accurate to within several seconds per month. Electric and electronic watches are powered by tiny long-lasting batteries. See CHRONOMETER. See Eric Bruton, *Clocks and Watches 1400–1900* (1967); George Daniels, *English and American Watches* (1967); Kenneth Welch, *The History of Clocks and Watches* (1972).

Watchung Mountains, two long low ridges of volcanic origin, from 400 to 500 ft (122–152 m) high, N central N.J. They curve c.40 mi (60 km) between Paterson and Somerville. Basalt is quarried there. The Watchungs have been the scene of extensive suburban development.

Watenstedt-Salzgitter: see SALZGITTER, West Germany.

water, odorless, tasteless, transparent liquid that is colorless in small amounts but exhibits a bluish tinge in large quantities. It is the most familiar and abundant liquid on earth. In solid form (ice) and liquid form it covers about 70% of the earth's surface. It is present in varying amounts in the atmosphere. Most of the living tissue of man is made up of water; it constitutes about 92% of blood plasma, about 80% of muscle tissue, about 60% of red blood cells, and over half of most other tissues. It is an important component as well of the tissues of most other living things. Chemically, water is a compound of hydrogen and oxygen, having the formula H_2O. It is chemically active, reacting with certain metals and metal oxides to form bases, and with certain oxides of nonmetals to form acids. It reacts with certain organic compounds to form a variety of products, e.g., alcohols from alkenes. Because water is a polar compound, it is a good solvent. Although completely pure water is a poor conductor of electricity, it is a much better conductor than most other pure liquids because of its self-ionization, i.e., the ability of two water molecules to react to form a hydroxide ION, OH^-, and a hydronium ion, H_3O^+. Its polarity and ionization are both due to the high dielectric constant of water. Water has interesting thermal properties. When heated from 0°C, its melting point, to 4°C, it contracts and becomes more dense; most other substances expand and become less dense when heated. Conversely, when water is cooled in this temperature range, it expands; it expands greatly as it freezes. Ice is less dense than water, and floats on it. Because of hydrogen bonding between water molecules, the LATENT HEATS of fusion and of evaporation and the HEAT CAPACITY of water are all unusually high. For these reasons, water serves both as a heat-transfer medium (e.g., ice for cooling and steam for heating) and as a temperature regulator (the water in lakes and oceans helps regulate the climate). Many of the physical and chemical properties of water are due to its structure. The atoms in the water molecule are arranged with the two H—O bonds at an angle of about 105° rather than on directly opposite sides of the oxygen atom. The asymmetrical shape of the molecule arises from a tendency of the four electron pairs in the valence shell of oxygen to arrange themselves symmetrically at the vertices of a tetrahedron around the oxygen nucleus. The two pairs associated with covalent bonds (see CHEMICAL BOND) holding the hydrogen atoms are drawn together slightly, resulting in the angle of 105° between these bonds. This arrangement results in a polar molecule, since there is a net negative charge toward the oxygen end (the apex) of the V-shaped molecule and a net positive charge at the hydrogen end. The electric dipole gives rise to

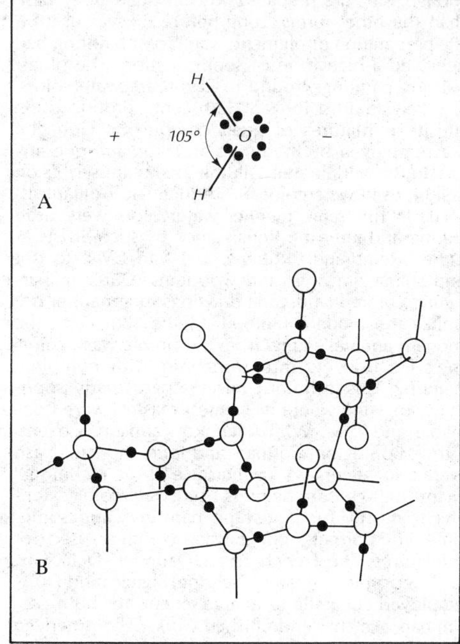

A. *Water molecule*

B. *Structure of ice: Each oxygen atom (white circles) is bonded to four other oxygen atoms by hydrogen bonds, the hydrogen atom (black circles) in each bond being closer to one of the oxygens than to the other.*

attractions between neighboring opposite ends of water molecules, with each oxygen being able to attract two nearby hydrogen atoms of two other water molecules. Such hydrogen bonding, as it is called, has also been observed in other hydrogen compounds. Although considerably weaker than the covalent bonds holding the water molecule together, hydrogen bonding is strong enough to keep water liquid at ordinary temperatures; its low molecular weight would normally tend to make it a gas at such temperatures. Various other properties of water, such as its high specific heat, are due to these hydrogen bonds. As the temperature of water is lowered, clusters of molecules form through hydrogen bonding, with each molecule being linked to others by up to four hydrogen bonds, each oxygen atom tending to surround itself with four hydrogen atoms in a tetrahedral arrangement. Hexagonal rings of oxygen atoms are formed in this way, with alternate atoms in either a higher or lower plane than their neighbors to create a kinked three-dimensional structure. In ice, each molecule forms the maximum number of hydrogen bonds, resulting in crystals composed of open, hexagonal columns. Because these crystals have a number of open regions and pockets, normal ice is less dense than water. However, other forms of ice also exist at conditions of higher pressure, each of these different forms (designated ice II, ice III, etc.) having greater density and other distinct physical properties that differ from those of normal ice, or ice I. As many as eight different forms of ice have been distinguished in this manner. The higher pressures creating such forms cause rearrangements of the hexagonal columns in ice, although the basic kinked hexagonal ring is common to all forms. When ice melts, it is thought that the fragments of these structures fill many of the gaps that existed in the crystal lattice, making water denser than ice. This tendency is the dominant one between 0°C and 4°C, at which temperature water reaches its maximum density. Above this temperature, expansion due to the increased thermal energy of the molecules is the dominant factor, with a consequent decrease in density. According to present theories, water in the liquid form contains three different molecule populations. At the highest temperatures single molecules are the rule, with little hydrogen bonding because of the high thermal energy of the molecules. In the middle range of temperatures there is more hydrogen bonding, and clusters of molecules are formed. At lower temperatures aggregates of clusters also form, these aggregates being the most common arrangement below about 15°C. On the basis of these three population types and the transitions between them, many aspects of the anomalous behavior of water can be explained. For example, the tendency of water to freeze faster if it has been cooled rapidly from a relatively warm temperature than if it has been cooled at the same rate from a lower temperature is explained in terms of the greater number of irregularly shaped cluster aggregates in the cooler water that must find a suitable means of fitting together with a neighboring aggregate. The discovery in the late 1960s of "superwater," or "polywater," helped to shed light on some aspects of the structure of water. This substance was thought by some to be a giant polymer of water molecules, 40 times denser and 15 times more viscous than ordinary water. Studies showed, however, that these new and unexplained properties were connected with the presence of contaminants in the water. Even so, the interaction of the water molecules with these other substances may be helpful in understanding the way in which water molecules interact with each other. See David Eisenberg and Walter Kauzmann, *The Structure and Properties of Water* (1969); A. K. Biwas, *History of Hydrology* (1970); Cynthia Hunt and R. M. Garrels, *Water: The Web of Life* (1972).

water, desalination of, process of removing soluble salts from water to render it suitable for drinking, irrigation, or industrial uses. The principal methods used include DISTILLATION (or evaporation), electrodialysis, freezing, ion exchange, and reverse osmosis. In distillation salt water is heated in one container to make the water evaporate, leaving the salt behind. The desalinated vapor is then condensed to form water in a separate container. Although long known, distillation has found limited application in water supply because of the fuel costs involved in converting salt water to vapor. Representative of man's early attempts in this direction were the solar distillation methods employed (c.49 B.C.) by the legions of Julius Caesar for using water from the Mediterranean. Modern technological advances led to the development of more efficient distillation units using solar energy; however, since these units have small capacities, their utility is restricted. Distillation plants having high capacities and using combustible fuels employ various devices to conserve heat. In some systems a vacuum is applied to reduce the boiling point of the water; in others a spray or thin film of water is exposed to high heat causing flash evaporation. Another method of desalination is by electrodialysis. When salt dissolves in water, it splits up into charged particles called ions. An electrodialysis unit consists basically of a container with a positively charged electrode at one end and a negatively charged electrode at the other. The electrodes are separated by a series of selectively permeable membranes. After the container is filled with salt water, the salt ionizes and the ions are filtered by the membranes as they are attracted toward the electrodes. The ions become concentrated in the space between some membranes and depleted in the space between others, leaving there a supply of desalinated water that can be tapped. The first large installation using this process began operating in South Africa in 1958. Another way to desalinate water is the freezing method, based on the principle that water excludes salt when it crystallizes to ice. In the ion-exchange method, water passes through a bed of specially treated synthetic resins that are capable of extracting ions of the salt from the solution and replacing them with ions that form water. In the reverse osmosis process pressure is applied to salt water to force it through a special membrane. Only pure water passes, however, leaving the salt behind. For emergency use, i.e., in lifeboats, various systems are available in addition to solar or fuel-heated distillation devices. One device made of flexible plastic is worn around the waist of the user to employ body heat for evaporation. Another type is an empty hollow sphere of semipermeable material that is lowered into the sea. The water flowing into the sphere is fresh, since the salt is excluded by the membrane that covers the entire sphere and is its guard. The Office of Saline Water established (1952) by the U.S. government has engaged in much research to reduce the cost of desalination of water. A number of large desalination plants, some with capacities of 1,000,000 or more gallons (3,800,000 or more liters) per day have been constructed in the United States. However, the use of such plants has been much more widespread outside the United States, especially in underdeveloped countries.

Water Bearer, The, English name for AQUARIUS, a CONSTELLATION.

water beetle, name for aquatic BEETLES of several families. They should not be confused with WATER BUGS, which are true bugs (order Hemiptera). The predaceous diving beetles (family Dytiscidae) are a large group, widespread in quiet streams and ponds. They are black, brown, or greenish, .08 to 1.57 in. (3–40 mm) long, with smooth oval bodies and hairy, oarlike hind legs. There is a cavity beneath the wings for holding an air supply, so the diving bettle can remain submerged for long periods; however, the insect often hangs head down from the surface, exposing the openings (spiracles) of the last two of its breathing tubes, located at the tip of the abdomen. Both the adults and the long, conspicuously segmented larvae prey on a variety of animals, including snails and fish much larger than themselves. Adults of most species are strong fliers, and many are attracted to lights at night. The water scavenger beetles (family Hydrophilidae), of similar appearance, are abundant in marshy places in warm parts of the world and feed on water plants and decaying matter. Their larvae are predaceous. The whirligig beetles (family Gyrinidae) are oval, shiny, blue-black to dark brown beetles, about 3/4 in. (19 mm) long. They are found in groups in sheltered places, spinning around on the surface of the water. They feed on small insects on the surface and seldom dive. There are several other groups of water beetles, all classified in the phylum ARTHROPODA, class Insecta, order Coleoptera.

water boatman: see WATER BUG.

waterbuck: see MARSH ANTELOPE.

water buffalo: see BUFFALO.

water bug, name for a large number of water-living BUGS, comprising several families of the order Hemiptera (true bugs). All have jointed, sharp, sucking beaks, breathe air, and undergo gradual metamorphosis (see INSECT). They are found on or below the surface of almost all quiet streams and ponds; a few forms live in rapidly flowing water. The water boatmen (family Corixidae) are abundant in lakes and ponds throughout most of the world. They are oval-bodied, with flattened, oarlike hind legs used for propulsion; the short front legs are used for gathering food and for anchoring the bug to aquatic vegetation. Water boatmen store air in a concavity beneath the wings and are thus able to remain submerged for long periods. They feed on algae and other small aquatic organisms and, unlike the predaceous water bugs, do not bite humans. The other wager bugs are carnivorous and prey, according to their size, on young fishes, snails, crustaceans, and the adults and larvae of other insects. The BACKSWIMMERS (family Notonectidae) resemble the water boatmen in appearance, but swim upside down. The water striders, or water skaters (family Gerridae), have two pairs of long, slender legs that enable them to move over the surface film of quiet waters, where they often congregate in large numbers. They also have a pair of short, grasping forelegs, used for catching insects on the surface. All live in fresh water except those of the genus *Halobates,* which are found in oceans. The giant water bugs (family Belostomatidae), with wide, flat bodies and grasping forelegs, are the world's largest bugs and among the largest of the insects. Members of some North American species grow 2 in. (5 cm) long, while one South American form attains a length of more than 4 in. (10 cm). They fly well and are attracted to lights at night, hence their other common name, electric-light bug. In some species the female glues her eggs to the back of the male, where they remain until they hatch. The water scorpions (family Nepidae) are named for the breathing tube that protrudes from the rear of the abdomen. There are several other water bug families. The term *water bug* is also sometimes applied to the various WATER BEETLES. True water bugs are classified in the phylum ARTHROPODA, class Insecta, order Hemiptera.

Waterbury, city (1970 pop. 108,033), New Haven co., W Conn., on the Naugatuck River; settled 1651, inc. as a city 1853. Its brass industry dates from the mid-18th cent. Clocks and watches, tools, instruments, plastics, and electronic parts are among the many other manufactures of Waterbury. The city's historical society has notable collections. Waterbury is the site of a branch of the Univ. of Connecticut, two junior colleges, and a state technical college.

water chestnut: see SEDGE.

water clock: see CLEPSYDRA.

water clover, common name for various species of aquatic FERNS.

watercolor painting, in its wider sense, refers to all pigments mixed with water rather than with oil and also to the paintings produced by this process; it includes FRESCO and TEMPERA as well as aquarelle, the process now commonly meant by the generic term. Gouache and distemper are also watercolors, although they are prepared with a more gluey base than the other forms. Long before oil was used in the preparation of pigment, watercolor painting had achieved a high form of sophistication. The oldest existing paintings, found in Egypt, are watercolors. The Persian artist Bihzad (15th cent.) produced exquisite miniatures of great complexity. Gouache was employed by Byzantine and Romanesque artists. In the Middle Ages, illuminated manuscripts on vellum used watercolor to produce flat, brilliant effects. In this same manner watercolors were used during and after the Renaissance by such artists as Dürer, Rembrandt, Rubens, and Van Dyck to tint and shade drawings and woodcuts. Dürer in particular colored landscape drawings in a manner not unlike the modern method. In the 18th cent. the modern aquarelle grew from the simple wash coloring of a drawing into a technique of complete painting. This technique became particularly popular in England, where its greatest masters were Constable and J. M. W. Turner. Rowlandson, Cozens, Girtin, Bonington, Cotman, and John and Paul Nash were also celebrated for their use of the technique. Many 19th-century painters used watercolor extensively, mostly for landscape paintings and sometimes for portraits, but it was no longer used for miniatures. The French artists Daumier, Delacroix, and Géricault, and later, Cézanne, Signac, and Dufy, employed aquarelle to a large extent, for both preliminary sketches and finished works. The American John Singer Sargent became well known for his aquarelles. Other painters in the United States, including Homer, Whistler, Prendergast, Marin, and Sheeler, painted noteworthy watercolors. The advantages of watercolor lie in the ease and quickness of its application, in the transparent effects achievable, in the brilliance of its colors, and in its relative cheapness. Aquarelles have a delicacy difficult to achieve in oil and are equally flexible and lend themselves to immediate expression of a visual experience. Their handling demands considerable skill as overpainting of flaws is usually impossible. Watercolor is a comparatively perishable medium; it is vulnerable to sunlight, dust, and contact with glass surfaces. See G. Reynolds, *A Concise History of Water Colors* (1971).

watercress, hardy perennial European herb (*Nasturtium officinale*) of the family Cruciferae (MUSTARD family), widely naturalized in North America, found in or around water. Often cultivated commercially for the small, pungent leaflets, it is used as a peppery salad green or garnish. Other plants of the genus are sometimes called watercress and are used similarly. Watercress was formerly used as a domestic remedy and against scurvy. The ornamental plant whose common name is NASTURTIUM is unrelated. Watercress is classified in the division MAGNOLIOPHYTA, class Magnoliopsida, order Capparales, family Cruciferae.

Wateree (wôtərē'), river, c.395 mi (635 km) long, rising in the Blue Ridge, W N.C., as the Catawba River and flowing SE to the Congaree, which it joins to form the Santee SE of Columbia. Catawba Dam (completed 1925) and Wateree Dam (1919) are on the river in South Carolina.

waterfall, sudden drop in a stream formed where the stream passes over a layer of harder rock—often igneous—to an area of softer, and therefore more easily eroded, rock. Normally, as a stream grows older, the waterfall, by undercutting and by the erosion of the brink and of the stream bed above the fall, moves upstream and loses height until it eventually becomes a series of rapids and finally disappears. Because of the waterpower that waterfalls and rapids can provide, their existence is a determinant of the location of cities. For example, there is a string of cities in the United States that grew up along the line where streams from the Appalachians descend suddenly to the coastal plain. The early textile cities of New England used power from waterfalls, and Minneapolis flour mills used the Falls of St. Anthony of the Mississippi. Immense hydroelectric plants have been established at many falls, e.g., at Niagara. Waterfalls noted for their height, volume of flow, or beauty include ANGEL FALL, the world's highest, in Venezuela; NIAGARA FALLS and those at Yosemite and Yellowstone national parks in the United States; VICTORIA FALLS between Rhodesia and Zambia; the Falls of GERSOPPA in India; SUTHERLAND FALLS in New Zealand; IGUAÇU FALLS between Argentina and Brazil; Tugela Falls in South Africa; Guaira Falls between Brazil and Paraguay; and Stanley Falls in Zaïre.

water fern, common name for various species of aquatic FERNS.

water flea: see CRUSTACEAN.

Waterford (wô'tərfərd), county (1971 pop. 45,237), 710 sq mi (1,839 sq km), S Republic of Ireland. The county town is the port city of Waterford. Although the terrain is largely hilly, there are lowlands in the east. Principal rivers are the Blackwater, the Bride, and the Suir, which forms most of the northern boundary. The coastline, on the south, is indented by Dungarvan Harbour and Waterford Harbour and by Youghal Bay and Tramore Bay. The county has much farming and grazing land; dairy and beef cattle and sheep are important. Fishing, food processing, tanning, and glassmaking are other industries. Waterford was rebellious under English domination, notably in the latter part of the 16th cent., when it suffered severely during the revolt of the Desmonds.

Waterford, county borough (1971 pop. 31,695), county town of Co. Waterford, S Republic of Ireland, on the Suir River near the head of Waterford Harbour. The city is a port for the produce, especially dairy products and meat, of S Ireland. Other industries are fishing, food processing, and the manufacture of footwear and fertilizers. The making of Waterford glass, famous in the 18th cent., died out in the mid-19th cent. but has been revived. Established very early as a walled Danish settlement, Waterford was taken in 1170 by Richard, earl of Pembroke, who used Reginald's Tower (built 1003; still standing) as a fort. King John granted the first charter in the 13th cent. In 1618 the charter was withdrawn because the people refused to accept the religious supremacy of the king of England. Waterford was besieged by Oliver Cromwell in 1649 and taken by Henry Ireton in 1650. The borough contains remains of 13th-century Franciscan and Dominican foundations that were suppressed in the 16th cent.; there are also Protestant and Roman Catholic cathedrals. Waterford is the seat of the united Protestant dioceses of Cashel, Emly, Waterford, and Lismore and of the Roman Catholic dioceses of Waterford and Lismore. St. John's College is a Protestant theological seminary.

Waterford, town (1970 pop. 17,227), New London co., SE Conn., on Long Island Sound; settled c.1653, inc. as a separate town from New London, 1801. It is mainly residential, with some publishing and other light industry. Both commercial and sport fishing are carried on. The Millstone atomic power plant produces the town's electricity. Harkness Memorial State Park is in Waterford.

waterfowl, common term for members of the order Anseriformes, wild, aquatic, typically freshwater birds including ducks, geese, and screamers. In Great Britain the term is also used to designate species kept for ornamental purposes on private lakes or ponds, while in North America it is used for quarry species and is sometimes extended to refer to wading birds of the order Charadriiformes, such as plovers and sandpipers, as well as to other edible water birds. The hunting of any of these birds is known most generally as duck hunting. In Britain quarry species are referred to as wildfowl and their hunting as wildfowling. British wildfowling, formerly done with nets, is now done with shotguns, as is duck hunting in North America, but the practices differ in some respects. In North America the birds are typically shot as they approach to investigate rubber, wooden, plastic, or other decoys. The British, however, manipulate the birds by deliberately feeding them at certain places, a practice generally outlawed in North America, where hunting tends to be more strictly legislated. Waterfowl are classified in the phylum CHORDATA, subphylum Vertebrata, class Aves, orders Anseriformes and Charadriiformes.

water gardening: see HYDROPONICS.

water gas, colorless poisonous gas that burns with an intensely hot, bluish (nearly colorless) flame. The gas is a mixture of carbon monoxide and hydrogen with very small amounts of other gases, e.g., carbon dioxide, and is almost entirely combustible as a result. Water gas is so named because of the use of water (steam) in its preparation. This process involves treating white-hot hard coal or coke with a blast of steam; carbon monoxide and hydrogen are formed. The gas is manufactured in vast quantities for commercial use. It is of much importance in the preparation of hydrogen and as a fuel in the making of steel and in other industrial processes, e.g., the FISCHER-TROPSCH PROCESS.

Watergate affair, in U.S. history, series of scandals involving the administration of President Richard M. Nixon; more specifically, the burglarizing of the Democratic party national headquarters in the Watergate apartment complex in Washington, D.C. On June 17, 1972, police apprehended five men attempting to break into and wiretap Democratic party offices. With two other accomplices they were tried and convicted in Jan., 1973. Two of the seven were employees of President Nixon's reelection committee, and many persons, including the trial judge, John J. Sirica, suspected a conspiracy involving higher-echelon government officials. In March, James McCord, one of the convicted burglars, wrote a letter to Sirica charging a massive coverup of the burglary. His letter transformed the affair into a political scandal of unprecedented magnitude. When a special Senate committee investigating corrupt campaign practices, headed by Senator Sam Ervin, began nationally televised hearings into the Watergate affair, former White House counsel John Dean testified that the burglary was approved by former Attorney General John Mitchell and that chief White House advisers John Ehrlichman and H. R. (Bob) Haldeman were involved in the coverup; he further accused President Nixon of approving the coverup. Attorney General Elliot Richardson appointed (May, 1973) a special prosecutor, Archibald Cox, to investigate the entire affair; Cox and his staff began to uncover widespread evidence of political espionage by the Nixon reelection committee, illegal wiretapping of citizens by the administration, and corporate contributions to the Republican party in return for political favors. In July, 1973, it was revealed that presidential conversations in the White House had been tape recorded since 1971; Cox sued Nixon to obtain the tapes, and Nixon responded by firing him (Oct., 1973). Nixon's action led to calls from the press, from government officials, and from private citizens for his impeachment, and the House of Representatives empowered its Judiciary Committee to initiate an impeachment investigation. Meanwhile, in response to a public outcry against the dismissal of Cox, President Nixon appointed a new special prosecutor, Leon Jaworski, and released to Judge Sirica the tapes of the Watergate conversations subpoenaed by Cox. Jaworski subsequently obtained indictments and convictions against several high-ranking administration officials; one of the grand juries investigating the Watergate affair named Nixon as an unindicted coconspirator and turned its evidence over to the Judiciary Committee. Responding to public pressure, in April, 1974, Nixon gave the Judiciary Committee edited transcripts of his taped conversations relating to Watergate; however, Nixon's actions failed to halt a steady erosion of confidence in his administration, and by the middle of 1974 polls indicated that a majority of the American people believed that the President was implicated in the Watergate coverup. On July 24, 1974, the Supreme Court affirmed a lower court ruling that ordered Nixon to turn over to special prosecutor Jaworski additional subpoenaed tapes relating to the coverup. Meanwhile, the House Judiciary Committee completed its investigation and adopted (July 27–30) three articles of impeachment against President Nixon; the first article, which cited the Watergate break-in, charged President Nixon with obstruction of justice. On Aug. 5, Nixon made public the transcripts of three recorded conversations that were among those to be given to Jaworski; at that time he admitted that he had been aware of the Watergate coverup shortly after the break-in occurred and that he had tried to halt the Federal Bureau of Investigation's inquiry into the break-in. Several days later (Aug. 9) Nixon resigned and was succeeded by Gerald R. Ford. President Ford issued a pardon to Nixon for any and all crimes that he might have committed while President. However, Nixon's chief associates, Haldeman, Ehrlichman, and Mitchell, were among those convicted (Jan. 1, 1975) for their role in the affair. In addition to the governmental upheaval that resulted from the Watergate affair, the scandal provoked widespread loss of confidence in public officials and tended to foster a general suspicion of government agencies. See Lewis Chester et al., *Watergate: The Full Inside Study* (1973); W. B. Dickinson, Jr., ed., *Watergate: Chronology of a Crisis* (1973); Michael Myerson, *Watergate: Crime in the Suites* (1973); Carl Bernstein and Bob Woodward, *All the President's Men* (1974).

water glass or **soluble glass,** colorless, transparent, glasslike substance available commercially as a powder or as a transparent, viscous solution in water. Chemically it is SODIUM SILICATE, potassium silicate, or a mixture of these. It is prepared by fusing sodium or potassium carbonate with sand or by heating sodium or potassium hydroxide with sand under pressure. Water glass is very soluble in water, but the glassy solid dissolves slowly, even in boiling water. Water glass has adhesive properties and is fire resistant. It is used as a detergent; as a cement for glass, pottery, and stoneware; for fireproofing paper, wood, cement, and other substances; for fixing pigments in paintings and cloth printing; and for preserving eggs (it fills the pores in the eggshell, preventing entrance of air).

water hemlock: see POISON HEMLOCK.

water hog: see CAPYBARA.

Waterhouse, Alfred, 1830–1905, English architect. He won competitions for the Manchester assize court (1859) and the Manchester city hall (1868). This work placed him in the forefront of the Victorian Gothic revival. His most important work, the Natural History Museum, South Kensington, in a modified Romanesque style, was notable for its revival of the use of terra-cotta; although a well-studied design, it illustrates the inherent incongruity between medieval forms and the needs of modern secular buildings. Waterhouse also executed important buildings for Balliol College, Oxford; Pembroke College, Cambridge; Prudential Assurance Company, Holborn, London; and the City and Guilds College, South Kensington (1881).

Waterhouse, Benjamin, 1754–1846, American physician, b. Newport, R.I. He studied at the universities of Edinburgh and Leiden. In 1783 he became professor on the first faculty of the Harvard medical school. In 1800 he inoculated members of his household with vaccine obtained from England, thus introducing the method of Edward Jenner into America. Inoculation had been used by Zahdiel Boylston and others, but Waterhouse was the first American physician to establish it as a general practice.

water hyacinth: see PICKERELWEED.

waterleaf, common name for the Hydrophyllaceae, a family of herbs and some shrubs, widely distributed but especially abundant in W and SW North America. Best known in the United States are the waterleafs (genus *Hydrophyllum*), forest herbs; the yerba santa (*Eriodictyion californicum*), a common chaparral shrub; and species of *Nemophila*, including the cultivated baby blue-eyes (*N. menziesii*) of California. Waterleaf is classified in the division MAGNOLIOPHYTA, class Magnoliopsida, order Polemoniales.

water lily, common name for some members of the Nymphaeaceae, a family of freshwater perennial herbs found in most parts of the world and often characterized by large shield-shaped leaves and

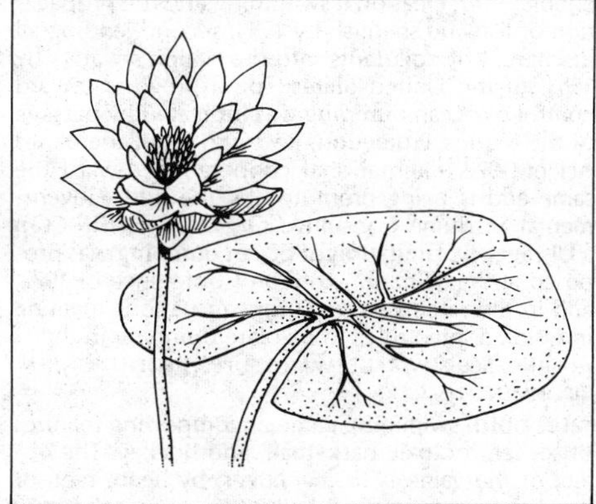

Fragrant water lily, Nymphaea odorata

showy, fragrant blossoms of various colors. Among the plants of the family are the water lilies, lotuses, and pond lilies (called also cow lilies and spatterdocks) of the genera *Nymphaea, Nelumbo,* and *Nuphar*, respectively; however, the common names often overlap; e.g., "water lily" is used for most species of the family and even for other unrelated aquatic plants with similar flowers. Most species of *Nymphaea* in cultivation are tropical, but some of the hardy kinds are native to the United States and to the corresponding temperate areas of the Southern Hemisphere. Both day- and night-blooming species open at fairly definite hours. Included in the genus is the blue or white Egyptian lotus (*Nymphaea caerulea* or *N. lotus,* respectively), sacred from remote times and the national emblem of Egypt. The lotus flower is traditional in Egyptian art and architecture, as in the lotus CAPITAL. The genus *Nelumbo* contains two species: the American, or yellow, lotus, also called water chinquapin, is found in E North America; the Indian lotus, or sacred bean, is sacred to Hinduism and to several other Oriental religions, e.g., Buddhism. Its large pink blossom is used symbolically in religion and art. Most species of *Nuphar* are native to North America. Many members of the water lily family have seeds or tubers that have been used for food; however, the fruit of the LOTUS-EATERS of classical literature has been most often identified as that of the jujube of the buckthorn family or the nettle-tree of the elm family. *Lotus* is also the botanical name for a genus of the pea family. Water lilies are classified in the division MAGNOLIOPHYTA, class Magnoliopsida, order Nymphales, family Nymphaeaceae.

Waterloo (vä'tərlō), town (1970 pop. 17,764), Brabant prov., central Belgium, near Brussels. The battle of Waterloo (see WATERLOO CAMPAIGN) was fought just south of there on June 18, 1815. The battle is commemorated by a large monument (built 1823–27).

Waterloo (wôtərlōō'). **1** City (1971 pop. 36,677), SE Ont., Canada. It is a suburb of Kitchener. Several large insurance companies have their main offices there. Its industries include distilleries and plants making furniture, farm machinery, and metal products. The district was settled (1800–1805) by Mennonites from Pennsylvania. The Univ. of Waterloo and Waterloo Lutheran College are there. **2** Town (1971 pop. 4,936), S Que., Canada, SE of Montreal. It is the center of a farming region known for its mushrooms. Manufactures include plastics, wire goods, and baby carriages.

Waterloo, city (1970 pop. 75,533), seat of Black Hawk co., NE Iowa, on the Cedar River; inc. 1868. Originally a center for sawmills and flour mills, Waterloo is now a trade and industrial center in a farm and livestock area. The city's chief industries are meat-packing and the manufacture of farm machinery, plastics, and heating and air-conditioning equipment. The National Dairy Cattle Congress is held there annually. A 10-acre (4-hectare) replica of the island where the protagonist of Defoe's *Robinson Crusoe* was shipwrecked has been built in the Cedar River at Waterloo.

Waterloo, University of, at Waterloo, Ont., Canada; nondenominational; founded 1959. It has faculties of arts, science, engineering, and mathematics as well as schools of architecture, optometry, physical education and recreation, and urban and regional planning.

Waterloo campaign, last action of the Napoleonic Wars, ending with the battle of Waterloo. Napoleon I, who escaped from Elba in Feb., 1815, and entered Paris on March 20, soon faced a European coalition. His only hope lay in attacking before the enemy could attack him, although he could count on only about 125,000 men in the immediate future. His plan was to destroy the British and Prussian forces under Wellington and Blücher on the northern frontier, before dealing with the Austrians and Russians under Prince Schwarzenberg then gathering on the eastern frontier. To effect this, he decided to concentrate his forces near Charleroi, between Blücher's force of about 120,000 and Wellington's of about 93,000, and thus prevent their junction. Setting out for the front on June 12, he seized Charleroi while the allies still believed he was in Paris, and he defeated Blücher at Ligny (June 16). Assuming that the Prussians were retreating toward their base in Namur, he detached GROUCHY with 33,000 men to pursue them. Meanwhile, Marshal Ney was battling Wellington at QUATRE BRAS; Napoleon now turned to his assistance, and Wellington, though victorious, was compelled to retreat toward Brussels. Wellington took up a strong position S of Waterloo, between Mont-Saint-Jean and Belle-Alliance, and awaited attack. On June 18, about noon, Napoleon began a massed attack against the British center, but the British stemmed the tide until the overdue arrival, late in the day, of the Prussian forces, who had eluded Grouchy by marching on Wavre instead of Namur. This event proved the turning point of the battle. Routed, the French retreated with the Prussians in pursuit. Napoleon left the field and signed (June 22) his second abdication. French casualties were about 32,000, the coalition's about 23,000. The campaign was marked by confusion and miscalculation on all sides. The battle figures prominently in European literature. See John Naylor, *Waterloo* (1960); D. A. Howarth, *Waterloo: Day of Battle* (1968); Ugo Pericoli, *1815: The Armies at Waterloo* (1974).

watermark: see PAPER.

watermelon, plant of the family Curcurbitaceae (GOURD family) native to Africa and introduced to America by the Negroes. Watermelons are now extensively cultivated in the United States and are popular also in S Russia. The fleshy, juicy fruit is eaten fresh, the rind is pickled, and in the Orient the seeds are eaten. One white-fleshed variety, the citron melon, is used like citron in preserving. Watermelons are classified in the division MAGNOLIOPHYTA, class Magnoliopsida, order Violales, family Curcurbitaceae.

water moccasin or **cottonmouth,** highly venomous SNAKE, *Ancistrodon piscivorus,* of the swamps and bayous of the S United States. Like the closely related copperhead, it is a PIT VIPER and has a heat sensitive organ for detecting warm-blooded prey. The young are born live. The young snake is a pale reddish brown with transverse dark brown bands edged with white; as it ages the colors dull to a blotched olive or brown and then to an unmarked olive or blackish in old specimens. The maximum length is 6 ft (2 m), the average from 3 to 4 ft (90–120 cm). A good climber, the water moccasin often relaxes on branches overhanging the water. If startled it erects its head and shows the white interior of its mouth—hence the name cottonmouth. It eats both warm-blooded and cold-blooded animals. It is aggressive in the wild state but may become quite tame in captivity. It is classified in the phylum CHORDATA, subphylum Vertebrata, class Reptilia, order Squamata, family Crotalidae.

water mold, common name for members of the order Saprolegniales, a group of FUNGI. Water molds grow most commonly in fresh water, especially ponds, but some also grow in moist soil. They live as SAPROPHYTES, obtaining their metabolic energy from decaying plant and animal material, or as PARASITES, attacking fish, insects, and other small aquatic animals. The cottonlike patches they form on their source of nourishment is characteristic. Occasionally water molds invade the roots of flowering plants, causing abnormal growth. One such disease caused by these fungi is the clubroot disease of cabbages and related plants. Water molds are classified in the division Fungi, class Phycomycetes, order Saprolegniales.

water oats: see WILD RICE.

water on the brain: see HYDROCEPHALUS.

water pollution, contamination of water resources by harmful wastes. In the United States industry is the greatest pollution source, accounting for more than half the volume of all water pollution and for the most deadly pollutants. Some 240,000 industrial plants use huge quantities of fresh water to carry away wastes of many kinds. The waste-bearing water, or effluent, is discharged into streams, lakes, or ocean, which in turn disperse the polluting substances. These pollutants include grit, asbestos, phosphates and nitrates, mercury, lead, caustic soda and other sodium compounds, sulfur and sulfuric acid, oils, and petrochemicals. In addition, numerous plants pour off undiluted corrosives, poisons, and other noxious by-products. The construction industry discharges slurries of gypsum, cement, abrasives, metals, and poisonous solvents. Hot water discharged by factories and power plants causes so-called thermal pollution by increasing water temperatures. Such increases change the level of oxygen dissolved in a body of water, thereby disrupting the water's ecological balance, killing off some plant and animal species while encouraging the overgrowth of others. Towns and municipalities are the second largest source of water pollution. Many U.S. communities discharge untreated or only partially treated sewage into the waterways, threatening the health of their own and neighboring populations. Along with domestic wastes, sewage carries industrial contaminants and a growing tonnage of paper and plastic refuse (see SOLID WASTE). Although thorough sewage treatment would destroy most disease-causing bacteria, the problem of the spread of viruses and viral illness remains. Moreover, most sewage treatment does not remove phosphorus compounds, contributed principally by detergents, which cause EUTROPHICATION of lakes and ponds. Rain drainage is another major polluting agent because it carries such substances as highway debris (including oil and lead from automobile exhausts), sediments from highway and building construction, and acids and radioactive wastes from mining operations into freshwater systems as well as into the ocean. Also transported by rain runoff and by irrigation return-flow are pesticide and fertilizer residues as well as animal waste from feedlots and farms. Large and small craft significantly pollute both inland and coastal waters by dumping their untreated sewage. Oil spilled accidently from tankers and offshore rigs (250,000 metric tons annually) or flushed from ship holds and bilges (1.5 million metric tons annually) sullies beaches and smothers bird, fish, and plant life. In addition oil takes up fat-soluble poisons like DDT, allowing them to be concentrated in organisms that ingest the oil-contaminated water; thus such poisons enter the food chains leading to sea mammals and man (see ECOLOGY). Another pervasive group of contaminants entering food chains is the POLYCHLORINATED BIPHENYL (PCB) compounds, components of lubricants, plastic wrappers, and adhesives. Manufactured and used in many parts of the world, both DDT and PCBs are now widespread in the Atlantic and Pacific oceans. Tarry oil residues are encountered throughout the Atlantic, as are styrofoam and other plastic rubbish. Plastic bits litter sections of the Pacific as far N as Amchitka Island near Alaska. Garbage, solid industrial wastes, and sludge formed in sewage treatment, all commonly dumped into oceans, are other marine pollutants found worldwide, especially along coastal areas. Virtually all water pollutants are hazardous to man as well as lesser species; sodium is implicated in cardiovascular disease, nitrates in blood disorders. Mercury and lead can cause nervous disorders. Some contaminants are carcinogens. DDT is toxic to humans and can alter chromosomes. PCBs cause liver and nerve damage, skin eruptions, vomiting, fever, diarrhea, and fetal abnormalities. Along many shores, shellfish can no longer be taken because of contamination by DDT, sewage, or industrial wastes. Dysentery, salmonella, and hepatitis are among the maladies transmitted by sewage in drinking and bathing water. Federal agencies estimate that 50% of U.S. drinking water comes from sources that receive industrial effluents, raw sewage, effluent from treated sewage, and urban runoff. In approximately 25% of public water systems, pollution exceeds safe levels, one reason being that much groundwater has been contaminated by wastes pumped underground for disposal or by seepage from surface water. When contamination reaches underground water tables, it is difficult to correct and spreads over wide areas. Millions of Americans drink water that, while not technically unsafe, has an unpleasant odor or taste imparted by pollution. In the United States beaches along both coasts, river banks, and lake shores have been ruined for bathers by industrial wastes and municipal sewage. The U.S. Environmental Protection Agency is developing improved standards of water quality mandatory in some localities and recommended in others. The Federal Water Pollution Control Act, as amended in 1972, established machinery and financing to achieve two goals: first, rendering all shores clean enough for recreational swimming and the propagation of fish and shellfish by 1983; second, ending all discharges of pollutants into the nation's waters by 1985. In the United States, some progress toward control of ocean dumping was indicated by passage of the Marine Protection, Research and Sanctuaries Act of 1972. International cooperation toward the same end is being promoted by the Inter-Governmental Maritime Consultive Organization (IMCO), a UN agency. Limitation of ocean dumping was proposed at the 80-nation London Conference of 1972, and in the same year 12 European nations meeting in Oslo adopted rules to regulate dumping in the N Atlantic. See SEWERAGE; WATER SUPPLY; POLLUTION; ENVIRONMENTALISM.

water polo, swimming game encompassing features of soccer, football, basketball, and hockey. The object of the game is to maneuver, by head, feet, or hand, a leather-covered ball 27 to 28 in. (about 70 cm) in circumference into net-enclosed goals at opposite ends of a pool 19 to 30 yd (17.37 to 27.43 m) long and at most 20 yd (18.29 m) wide. The two competing teams consist of seven players each, one of whom is the goalie. Only one hand may be used to advance the ball, which must be carried on the surface. Rough defensive techniques permitted include ducking, i.e., holding a player under water. Water polo was devised in England in the 1870s and became popular in the United States in the early 20th cent. It is mainly played by club teams, although it is also popular in collegiate competition. Water polo has been an Olympic event since 1900. A far rougher version of the game, played with a soft rubber ball in a larger pool and known as American or softball water polo, was formerly popular in the United States. However, its extreme violence brought it into disfavor, and today only the international or hardball game is played throughout the world. See A. F. Lambert and Robert Gaughran, *The Technique of Water Polo* (1969).

water power, mechanical energy derived from falling or flowing water, e.g., rivers, streams, and the overflow of dams. The wooden WATER WHEEL, long utilized for driving machinery in flour mills and factories, was largely supplanted by the steam engine in the early 19th cent. In modern practice, water flowing from a higher level to a lower level (as from a dam or waterfall) is used to activate a TURBINE that drives an electric generator. The amount of power furnished is proportional to the rate of flow of the water and the vertical distance through which it falls. In a pumped-storage plant, water is pumped upward to a high-level reservoir during periods of low electricity demand by using the excess electricity available. During periods of high demand the facility produces electricity by using the water that flows down from the reservoir. The availability of water power along a fall line, which is a boundary between an upland region and a coastal plain, was a reason for the location of many cities in the E United States. In the early 1970s the countries that led the world in installed capacity of hydroelectric power were the United States, USSR, Canada, Japan, and France. For information on some important hydroelectric power projects, see CHURCHILL FALLS; NIAGARA FALLS; COLUMBIA BASIN PROJECT; COLORADO RIVER STORAGE PROJECT; SAINT LAWRENCE SEAWAY; TENNESSEE VALLEY AUTHORITY; DNEPROGES.

waterproof and water-repellent fabrics, materials treated with various substances so as to make them impervious to water. Permanent waterproofing is achieved by first coating fabrics with rubber or plasticized synthetic resins, then vulcanizing or baking them. Fabrics so treated lose porosity and lightness and when rubberized are subject to cracking. Water-repellent fabrics, sprayed with or immersed in synthetic resins, metallic compounds, oils, or waxes, tend to remain porous and to retain their natural characteristics. Earlier treatments, such as tarring the surface (as for tarpaulin) or oiling (as for oilskin), have been supplemented by highly technical and varied processes and by the method of coating the fibers prior to cloth construction. Some woolen fabrics, especially Navaho blankets and tweeds and other napped textiles, are naturally water repellent.

water rights, in law, the qualified privilege of a landowner to use the water adjacent to or flowing through his property. The privilege, also known as riparian rights, may be modified or even denied because of the competing needs of other private property holders or of the community at large. There is no private ownership of such water in most cases, and hence ordinarily it cannot be impounded and sold. The owner, however, may use the water for his ordinary private purposes, such as stock watering or irrigation, and then return the unused residue. Most uses of water affect its purity to some degree, but so long as pollution is not excessive other users may not make legal objection. In certain parts of the United States, especially in the arid and semiarid regions of the Southwest, the prior appropriation rule applies, and the first user of water, whether or not he owns land abutting the water, has the unrestrained right to it without regard to his neighbor's needs. Throughout the United States the rights of private owners in water can be set aside to construct public works, such as dams and irrigation projects. The ownership of a stream bed may depend upon whether the stream is or is not a NAVIGABLE WATER. If it is navigable, some states claim title to the bed, whereas in other states the rule is the same as in the case of nonnavigable streams, namely that an abutting owner's property extends to the middle of the bed and that those with property along both banks of a stretch own the enclosed portion of the bed. If the stream is navigable, the owner must permit public use for passage and transportation; if it is nonnavigable, the owner may exclude all but other riparian owners from using the stream. If the stream shifts course, ownership of the former bed is not affected. Underground and percolating waters have no easily determined course, and the usual American practice is not to restrict a landowner who taps and exploits these waters; however, in some states the rights of those who may be adversely affected must be considered. See J. H. Beuscher, *Water Rights* (1967).

waters, territorial, all waters within the jurisdiction of a country. Certain waters by their situation can be controlled only by one nation. These waters include inland seas, wholly enclosed lakes, and enclosed rivers. The control of bounding rivers and lakes extends to the middle of the navigable channel, but agreements to share the use of such waters and of waters that flow through more than one country (e.g., the Rhine, the Danube) are common. When a body of water that is almost completely bordered by one country lies along an international route of navigation (e.g., the Panama Canal, the Bosporus), treaties often make it available to all ships. By international law a country enjoys complete civil and criminal jurisdiction over the unenclosed coastal waters for a certain distance. Although the generally accepted distance has been approximately three mi (4.8 km; a marine league), only a relatively small number of countries advocate retention of this distance. Many advocate a limit of 12 mi (19.3 km); still others favor wider limits, ranging up to 200 mi (322 km). Ecuador claims a 200-mi limit. These waters may be used by all ships in time of peace (called the right of innocent passage), but during war the naval vessels of belligerents are excluded. Most countries claim control over a wider sea margin for certain purposes, such as protection of fisheries and the effective maintenance of police, sanitation and customs services. In the prohibition period the United States asserted jurisdiction over ships smuggling liquor that were found within an hour's run from the shore.

water scavenger: see WATER BEETLE.

watershed, elevation or divide separating the CATCHMENT AREA, or drainage basin, of one river system or group of river systems from another system or group of systems. The term is also often used as synonymous with drainage basin. The Rocky Mts. and the Andes form the watershed between westward-flowing and eastward-flowing streams; the Mississippi watershed extends from the Rockies to the Appalachians. Often the watershed is a distinct range of mountains, the two sides of which have widely different climatic characteristics, as in the Americas and Australia. The low Valdai Hills are an important watershed of the USSR.

water skater: see WATER BUG.

water skiing, sport of riding on skis along the water's surface while being towed by a motor-propelled boat. It probably originated on the French Riviera in the early 1920s and was already known in the United States by 1927. The American Water Ski Association was founded in 1939 and held the first national championships the same year. In recreational water skiing, the type of ski, length of tow rope, and speed of the boat may vary with individual taste. In championship competitions, skis of hickory, ash, fiber glass, or aluminum are used. They must be at least 39⅜ in. (1 m) long and not more than about 9¾ in. (25 cm) wide. There are usually three events in water ski tournaments: slalom, jumping, and trick riding. In the slalom the skiers are towed through a staggered series of buoys and must ski outside each of them. In jumping, the contestants are towed over an inclined wooden ramp about 21 ft (6 m) long and 6 ft (1.8 m) high; jumps of 150 ft (46 m) from the point of takeoff to the point where the skier's foot enters the water have been recorded. In trick riding, contestants choose their own routines, many of them remarkably intricate. The World Water Ski Union (founded 1949) sponsors biennial international tournaments. See Al Tyll, *Water Skiing* (1966).

Waters of Merom: see HULA, LAKE.

waterspout, TORNADO occurring at sea or over inland waters. The characteristic funnel-shaped cloud is formed at the base of a cumulus-type cloud and extends downward to the water surface, where it picks up spray. Waterspouts are most frequent in tropical regions, but are not uncommon in higher latitudes.

water strider: see WATER BUG.

water supply, process or activity by which water is provided for some use, e.g., to a home, factory, or business. The term may also refer to the supply of water provided in this way. The stringency of the requirements that a supply of water must meet depends on the use to be made of it. For example, water used to wash semiconductor material from which transistors are made must be extraordinarily pure. The more usual requirement, however, is that water be free enough of harmful bacteria, chemicals, and other contamination to be drinkable. It is also desirable that water be free of substances that make its taste or appearance unpleasant. Water that is to be used for washing must be fairly free of salts of calcium and magnesium. Water containing much of these, also called hard water, interferes with the action of soap. The basic source of water is rainfall, which collects in rivers and lakes, under the ground, and in artificial reservoirs. Water from under the ground is called groundwater and is tapped by means of WELLS. Most often water must be raised from a well by pumping. In some cases a well will draw water from a permeable rock layer called an aquifer in which the water is under pressure; such a well needs little or no pumping (see ARTESIAN WELL). Water that collects in rivers, lakes, or reservoirs is called surface water. Most large water supply systems draw surface water through special intake pipes or tunnels and transport it to the area of use through canals, tunnels, or pipelines, which are known as mains or aqueducts. These feed a system of smaller conduits or pipes that take the water to its place of use. A complete water supply system is often known as a waterworks. Sometimes the term is specifically applied to pumping stations, treatment stations, or storage facilities. Storage facilities are provided to reserve extra water for use when demand is high and, when necessary, to help maintain water pressure. Treatment stations are places in which water may be filtered to remove suspended impurities, aerated to remove dissolved gases, or disinfected with chlorine, ozone, ultraviolet light, or some other agent that kills harmful bacteria and microorganisms. Sometimes hard water is softened by a process that exchanges dissolved calcium and magnesium salts for sodium salts, which do not interfere with soap. Salts of iodine and fluorine, which are considered helpful in preventing goiter and tooth decay, are sometimes added to water in which they are lacking. Not all water supply systems are used to deliver drinking water. Systems used for purposes such as irrigation and fire fighting operate in much the same way as systems for drinking water, but the water need not meet such high standards of purity. In most municipal systems hydrants are connected to the drinking water system except during periods of extreme water shortage. Because many cities draw water from the same body into which they discharge sewage, proper sewage treatment has become increasingly essential to the preservation of supplies of useful water (see SEWERAGE; WATER POLLUTION).

Waterton Lakes National Park, 203 sq mi (526 sq km), SW Alta., Canada, SW of Lethbridge and at the U.S. border, adjoining Glacier National Park; est. 1895. It is the Canadian section of Waterton-Glacier International Peace Park, created (1932) by acts of the Canadian Parliament and the U.S. Congress. The area is mountainous, rising to c.9,600 ft (2,930 m) at Mt. Blakiston, and contains the Waterton Lakes, the largest of which extends across the border into Montana.

Watertown. 1 Town (1970 pop. 18,610), Litchfield co., W Conn.; set off from Waterbury and inc. 1780. Synthetic textiles, thread, plastics, chemicals, mattresses, and metal goods are among its manufactures. A method for processing silk thread developed there (1849) and led to the foundation of a major silk industry in the 19th cent. Taft preparatory school and portions of a state park and a state forest are in the town. **2** Town (1970 pop. 39,307), Middlesex co., E Mass., on the Charles River; settled 1630, inc. 1785. It is an industrial suburb of Boston, and its manufactures include machinery, automotive parts, rubber-coated fabrics, clothing, and food products. A Federal arsenal, built in 1816, was greatly enlarged during the two world wars; most of it is now owned by the town, but the U.S. government has retained a section for research. The Perkins School for the Blind (est. in Boston 1829, moved to Watertown 1912) and a junior college are in the town. **3** City (1970 pop. 30,787), seat of Jefferson co., N N.Y., on the Black River, in a dairy region; settled c.1800, inc. as a city 1869. The falls on the river (more than 100 ft/30 m high) provide power for its many small industries. Talc, lead, zinc, and iron are mined in the area. Watertown also has a tourist business as a result of its proximity to Canada, the Adirondacks, and the Thousand Islands resort area. A junior college is in the city, and the huge Camp Drum military reservation (national guard) and an air force station are nearby. **4** City (1970 pop. 13,388), seat of Codington co., NE S.Dak., on the Big Sioux River; inc. 1885. It is the distributing, shipping, and trading center for a large agricultural area, and it has food-processing industries. It is also a recreational site; two large lakes adjoin the city. **5** Industrial city (1970 pop. 15,683), Dodge and Jefferson counties, SE Wis., at the falls of the Rock River, in a farm and dairy area; inc. 1853. Carl Schurz lived there from 1855 to 1857. His wife, Margarethe, established (1856) the first kindergarten in the United States there; it has been restored and moved to the grounds of the Octagon House (c.1849), the city's historical museum.

water turkey: see DARTER.

Waterville, city (1970 pop. 18,192), Kennebec co., S. Maine, at the falls of the Kennebec River; settled 1754, inc. as a city 1888. It is the trade and medical center of a lake resort area, with railroad shops as well as textile and paper and pulp mills. During the early 1900s the town had five shipyards that built many ocean and river vessels. Present-day Waterville is the seat of Colby College and of Thomas College.

Watervliet (wô"tərvlēt', wô'-, wŏ'-), industrial city (1970 pop. 12,404), Albany co., E N.Y., on the Hudson River, opposite Troy, near the terminus of the New York State Barge Canal; founded by the Dutch 1735, inc. as a city 1896. The U.S. arsenal there, which specializes in the production of heavy ordnance, was established in 1813. In 1776, Ann Lee founded in Watervliet the first American community of Shakers.

waterway, natural or artificial navigable inland body of water, or system of interconnected bodies of water, used for transportation, e.g., a lake, river, canal, or any combination of these. The existence of natural waterways has been an important factor in the development of regions, for the waterways have served first as paths of exploration and new settlement and later as avenues of commerce and trade. The world's great river systems have opened up the interior of continents and have aided their growth; large lakes have also facilitated the movement of people and goods. In many instances lesser waterways, because of their excellent location, have played major roles in local development. Natural waterways are supplemented and connected by CANALS. Great quantities of goods are moved on waterways. Although slower than rail, road, and air transport, water shipping is less expensive and attracts such bulk cargoes as coal, ores, grain, and lumber. Navigation on waterways may be improved by the construction of dams, locks, levees, and dikes; cuts are made to straighten and shorten water courses. Dredging is carried on to maintain minimum depths. Waterways vary in size from very shallow streams and channels on which rafts move, to barge-carrying rivers and canals and the deep seaways that accommodate oceangoing vessels. Waterways of international importance, either because they border or run through more than one country or because other nations wish to use them for trade, have long caused friction among nations; a number of these waterways have been internationalized.

water wheel, device for utilizing the power of flowing or falling water. The Norse wheel is the oldest type known. Despite its name it probably originated in the Middle East, where the swift stream required by this type of wheel is common. The Norse wheel has a vertical shaft directly connected at the top to a millstone; the lower end of the shaft, with vanes or paddles attached, dips into the flowing stream. In the 1st cent. B.C. a horizontal shaft came into use; the wheel attached to it had radial vanes around its edge. Among the early forms of this wheel are the overshot wheel, used where water falls from a height, striking the vanes from above; the breast wheel, employed where the height of the water is less than the height of the wheel so that the water strikes the wheel about midway; and the undershot wheel, usable where the water flows more or less on a level but with a swift current and strikes the vanes on the under part of the wheel. One of the first uses of the steam engine was to drive a pump that raised water into a millpond whose spillway drove a water wheel. Today the water wheel has been largely replaced by the TURBINE. See HYDRAULIC MACHINE.

waterworks: see WATER SUPPLY.

Watford, municipal borough (1971 pop. 78,117), Hertfordshire, SE England. Watford's great publishing industry produces many of the nation's periodicals. Other industries are engineering, the manufacture of woolen and silk goods, paper, and chemicals, and brewing. There is a technical college and a teacher-training school.

Watkins, Vernon, 1906–67, British poet, b. Maesteg, Wales, educated at Cambridge. Like his close friend Dylan THOMAS, Watkins was profoundly influenced by his Welsh background. His poetry combines serious meditation with an ecstatic acceptance of the world. Among his volumes of poetry are *The Ballad of Mari Lwyd and Other Poems* (1941), *Selected Poems* (1948), *The Death Bell and Other Poems* (1954), *Affinities* (1962), and *Uncollected Poems* (1969). See his edition of his correspondence with Dylan Thomas (1957).

Watkins Glen (wŏt'kĭnz), resort village (1970 pop. 2,716), seat of Schuyler co., W central N.Y., in the Finger Lakes region, at the southern end of Seneca Lake; inc. 1842. It is in a grape and wine area and has extensive saltworks. Its setting of cliffs, waterfalls, and unusual rock formations made by an interwinding stream attracts many visitors. The resort hotel there is famed for its mineral spring water. An international Grand Prix sports-car race is held there annually. Watkins Glen State Park adjoins the village.

Watling Island or **Watlings Island:** see SAN SALVADOR.

Watling Street (wŏt'lĭng), important ancient road in England, built by the Romans in the course of their military occupation. It ran from London generally north to the intersection with the Fosse Way, c.13 mi (21 km) SW of Leicester, and thence in a westerly direction to Wroxeter in Salop, SE of Shrewsbury, a distance of more than 100 mi (161 km). The principal town through which it passed was St. Albans (ancient Verulamium). Its later importance arose from its use as a thoroughfare throughout the Middle Ages and into modern times. In places the ancient Roman road is still in daily use, and in others it has been used as a base for modern thoroughfares. Some other Roman roads in England are also called Watling Street, notably the extension which led from London to Dover.

Watson, James Dewey, 1928–, American biologist and educator, b. Chicago, Ill., grad. Univ. of Chicago, 1947, Ph.D. Univ. of Indiana, 1950. With F. H. C. Crick he began (1951) research on the molecular structure of deoxyribonucleic acid at the Cavendish Laboratory of Cambridge Univ. Their findings, published in 1953, resulted in the joint award to them and to M. H. F. Wilkins (on whose work in X-ray diffraction their studies were partly based) of the 1962 Nobel Prize in Medicine and Physiology. Since 1955, Watson has been on the faculty at Harvard. His chief researches have been in the fields of bacteriophage reproduction and bacterial genetics. See his *The Double Helix* (1968).

Watson, John Broadus, 1878–1958, American psychologist, b. Greenville, S.C. He taught (1903–8) at the Univ. of Chicago and was professor and director (1908–20) of the psychological laboratory at Johns Hopkins. Watson originated the school of psychology called BEHAVIORISM, in which behavior is described in terms of physiological response to stimuli; the concept of conscious or unconscious mental activity is rejected. From his work with infants he concluded that there are three unconditioned (unlearned) responses in newborns—fear, love, and rage. He wrote *Psychology from the Standpoint of a Behaviorist* (1919), *Behaviorism* (1925), and *Psychological Care of Infant and Child* (1928).

Watson, Thomas, 1557?–1592, English poet and scholar. He translated into Latin the *Antigone* of Sophocles and the *Aminta* of Tasso and wrote *The Hecatompathia; or, Passionate Century of Love* (1582), one of the earliest collections of sonnets in English.

Watson, Thomas Edward, 1856–1922, American political leader, b. Columbia co., Ga. A successful lawyer, he practiced in Thomson, Ga., before serving (1882–83) in the state legislature and as a Farmers' Alliance Democrat in Congress (1891–93), where he worked for rural free delivery of mail. He was a spokesman for Populism, and in 1896 the Populists nominated him for Vice President; in 1904 he was their presidential nominee. He was elected to the Senate as a Democrat in 1920 and served until his death. In the course of his career he published *Tom Watson's Magazine, Watson's Jeffersonian Magazine,* the *Weekly Jeffersonian,* the *Sentinel,* and numerous books, including biographies of Thomas Jefferson (1903) and Andrew Jackson (1912). Watson launched virulent attacks on Roman Catholics, Negroes, Jews, and Socialists, and was prosecuted for *The Roman Catholic Hierarchy* (1910), a diatribe against Catholics. Although indicted three times, he was never convicted. See biography by C. V. Woodward (1938, repr. 1963).

Watson, Sir William, 1715–87, English apothecary, physician, and electrician. As a Fellow of the Royal Society who was well-versed in many fields, he regularly reported on the work of foreign scientists such as Carolus Linnaeus of Sweden. Watson carried out numerous electrical experiments, especially involving the discharge of Leyden jars, and gave the first description of Benjamin Franklin's electrical studies to the Royal Society. His own theory of electricity, which was superseded by Franklin's, traced attraction and repulsion to currents of a subtle "aether."

Watson, Sir William, 1858–1935, English poet. His first great success was *Wordsworth's Grave* (1890), followed by a meditative elegy on Tennyson, *Lachrymae Musarum* (1892). He is also remembered for sonnets and lyrics. He was knighted in 1917.

Watson Lake, village (1971 pop. 553), SE Yukon Territory, Canada, near the Liard River and the British Columbia border. It is a Royal Canadian Mounted Police Post, with an airfield and a radio station, located near the Alaska Highway.

Watsonville, city (1970 pop. 14,569), Santa Cruz co., W Calif., on the Pajaro River near Monterey Bay; inc. 1868. It is a trade and processing center for vegetables, fruits (especially apples), and flowers. Granite is quarried, and bricks, aluminum parts, and pajamas are made. The site was discovered by the Portola expedition in 1769. A yearly rally of operable antique aircraft is held there. Nearby are beach and mountain resorts and several state parks.

Watt, James, 1736–1819, Scottish inventor. While working at the Univ. of Glasgow as an instrument maker, Watt was asked to repair a model of Thomas Newcomen's steam engine. He devised improvements that resulted in a new type of engine (patented 1769) with a separate condensing chamber, an air pump to bring steam into the chamber, and parts of the engine insulated. He also perfected a rotary engine. Matthew Boulton financed Watt's work and was his partner (1775–80) in manufacturing the engines at Soho near Birmingham. Watt coined the term *horsepower.* The watt, a unit of electrical power, was named for him. See his correspondence, *Partners in Science,* ed. by E. H. Robinson and Douglas McKie (1970); study by E. H. Robinson and A. E. Musson (1969).

watt [for James Watt], abbr. W, unit of power, or work done per unit time, equal to 1 joule per second. It is used as a measure of electrical and mechanical power. One watt is the amount of power that is delivered to a component of an electric circuit when a current of 1 ampere flows through the component and a voltage of 1 volt exists across it. The derivative units are kilowatt (1,000 W) and megawatt (1,000,000 W), used in electric power systems, and milliwatt (0.001 W) and microwatt (0.000001 W), used in electronics.

Watteau, Jean-Antoine (wätō', Fr. zhäN'-äNtwäN' vätō'), 1684–1721, French painter of Flemish descent, b. Valenciennes. Until 1704 poverty forced him to work in the shops of mediocre artists, where he produced genre and devotional subjects. In 1704–8 he studied in the studio of Claude Gillot, an adept painter of scenes of theatrical life, which later became the subject of some of Watteau's finest paintings, such as *Love in the Italian Theatre* and *Love in the French Theatre* (both: Berlin). In 1708–9 Watteau worked with the decorator Claude Audran. Watteau attracted the attention of eminent patrons in his last years, including the comte de Caylus, his biographer, and in 1717 he was made a full member of the Académie royale. *The Embarkation for Cythera* (1717; Louvre) is characteristic of his art; it is a delicate, courtly fantasy, represented in warm and shimmering pastel tones that place him among the great colorists of all time. A lyric, Giorgionesque quality pervades his airy, gay, and sensuous scenes, which have a poignancy that none of his followers attained. Out of the most fleeting aspects of life he created an enduring and individual art. His exquisite paintings influenced fashion and garden design in the 18th cent. Other outstanding works include *Gilles* (Louvre), *Perspective* (Mus. of Fine Arts, Boston), *Mezzetin* (Metropolitan Mus.), and *Gersaint's Shop Sign* (1719; Berlin). Watteau was also a superb draftsman. Many of his exquisite drawings are known only from engravings. See his complete paintings (introd. by John Sunderland and notes by Ehore Camesasca, 1971); studies by Anita Brookner (1967), René Huygne (1970), K. T. Parker (1931, repr. 1970), and Malcolm Cormack (1971).

Wattenscheid (vät'ənshĭt''), city (1970 pop. 80,756), North Rhine-Westphalia, W West Germany, an industrial center of the RUHR district. Its manufactures include metal goods, electrical equipment, and textiles.

Watterson, Henry, 1840–1921, American journalist, b. Washington, D.C. Throughout most of his life he was known as "Marse Henry." Early in life he became a Washington newspaper reporter. He served with the Confederate army in the Civil War and for a time edited the Chattanooga (Tenn.) *Rebel.* After working on newspapers in Alabama, Ohio, and Tennessee, Watterson became an editor of the Louisville (Ky.) *Journal.* In 1868 he merged that paper with the competing Louisville *Courier* to form the *Courier-Journal,* which soon became locally influential and nationally famous. In his editorials Watterson argued compellingly for the rights of Negroes and the restoration of home rule to the South. In 1876–77 he served in Congress and vigorously supported S. J. Tilden for President in 1876. He was sharply critical of President Grover Cleveland and opposed William J. Bryan and free silver. His editorials urging the United States to declare war on Germany earned him a Pulitzer Prize. He supported Woodrow Wilson only intermittently, bitterly attacking American participation in the League of Nations. In 1923 a volume of his editorials, edited by Arthur Krock, was published. See his autobiography, *"Marse Henry"* (1919, repr. 1973); biography by J. F. Wall (1956).

wattle, in botany: see ACACIA.

wattlebird: see HONEYEATER.

Watts, George Frederic, 1817–1904, English painter and sculptor. He studied at the Royal Academy and in Italy, where he developed an enthusiasm for Renaissance painting and Greek sculpture that greatly influenced his work. He executed several decorative commissions, including his large fresco *Justice* (Lincoln's Inn, London), modeled after Raphael's *School of Athens.* Many of his allegorical pictures are in the Tate Gallery, London. The National Portrait Gallery, London, contains a large collection of his portraits of eminent contemporaries. The Metropolitan Museum has his *Ariadne in Naxos.* He was married to Ellen TERRY and later to Mary Fraser-Tytler, who wrote a biography of him (3 vol., 1912). His home at Compton is now the Watts Gallery. See also studies by C. T. Bateman (1901) and G. K. Chesterton (1904).

Watts, Isaac, 1674–1748, English clergyman and hymn writer, b. Southampton. He was one of the most eminent Dissenting divines of his day. As a pastor in London he was known for his sermons, but beginning in 1712 poor health caused him to live in semiretirement. His several hundred hymns embodied the stern doctrines of Calvinism but were assuaged with a gentleness and sympathy. The few hymns that are included in present-day hymnals are among the finest examples of English metrical hymnody. Those beginning "Jesus shall reign where'er the sun," "When I survey the wondrous cross," "Joy to the world," and "O God, our help in ages past," appeared in his *Psalms of David Imitated* (1719). See biography by A. P. Davis (1943); study by H. Escott (1962).

Watts-Dunton, Theodore (Walter Theodore Watts-Dunton), 1832–1914, English poet, novelist, and critic. A member of the staff of the *Examiner* (1874–76), he became editor of the *Athenaeum* (1876–98). He was the benefactor of Swinburne, whose life he organized and who lived with him from 1879 to 1909. Watts-Dunton edited many literary classics and contributed important articles to *The Encyclopaedia Britannica.* Among his works are *The Coming of Love* (1897); *Aylwin* (1898), a romantic novel about gypsies; *The Christmas Dream* (1901); and *Old Familiar Faces* (1916), a volume of recollections. See biography by James Douglas (1904, repr. 1973); Max Beerbohm, "No. 2 The Pines," in *And Even Now* (1920); Mollie Panter-Downes, *At the Pines* (1971).

Watt's Dyke: see OFFA'S DYKE.

Watts Towers, group of towers built by Simon Rodilla (also spelled Rodia, 1879–1965) between 1921 and 1954 in Watts, Los Angeles. They are unique and extraordinarily fanciful structures that are sculptural in appearance and reminiscent of Antoni Gaudí's imaginative architecture. A monument to Rodilla's inventiveness, they are constructed of stone, steel, cement, and discarded elements such as bottle caps, china shards, bits of glass, and seashells.

Watutsi: see TUTSI.

Waubeshiek (wô'bəshēk), c.1794–c.1841, North American Indian prophet, also known as White Cloud. He was a friend and adviser of Black Hawk and by prophesying victory was chiefly responsible for the continuance of the Black Hawk War. He was captured with Black Hawk, imprisoned, and taken to Washington, D.C. He spent his last days peacefully in Iowa.

Waugh, Evelyn Arthur St. John (ēv'lĭn wô), 1903–66, English writer, considered the greatest satirist of his generation. Educated at Oxford, he was briefly an art student and a teacher but spent much of his time traveling. He served with distinction in World War II. Waugh burst upon the literary scene with a group of hilarious novels satirizing 20th-century life with savage and sophisticated wit; they include *Decline and Fall* (1928), *Vile Bodies* (1930), and *A Handful of Dust* (1934). He was even more mordantly satiric in *Black Mischief* (1932) and *Scoop* (1938), both treating Africa, and *Put Out More Flags* (1942), a fictional comment on the English war effort. His most popular novel is *Brideshead Revisited* (1945), which recounts the spiritual regeneration of a wealthy Catholic family. In a novella, *The Loved One* (1948), he examined the mortuary customs of Hollywood, Calif. His series of novels on World War II includes *Men at Arms* (1952), *Officers and Gentlemen* (1955), and *The End of the Battle* (1961). In addition to these and other works of fiction, he wrote amusing travel books, biographies of Rossetti (1928) and Edmund Campion (1935), and *A Little Learning* (1964), the only completed volume of a projected three-volume autobiography. All these works reflect his superb command of the English language. Though labeled an archconservative by some critics, Waugh was essentially a moralist who devoted himself to attacking social institutions and customs with impersonal scorn. See the biography by his brother Alec (1968); studies by Christopher Hollis (1954), J. F. Carens (1966), P. A. Doyle (1969), W. J. Cook (1971), David Lodge (1971), and David Price-Jones (1973). Waugh's older brother **Alec Waugh** (1898–)is the author of numerous novels and travel books. Among his best-known works are *The Loom of Youth* (1918), *Island in the Sun* (1956), and *The Fatal Gift* (1973).

Waukegan (wôkē'gən), residential and industrial city (1970 pop. 65,269), seat of Lake co., NE Ill., on Lake Michigan; inc. 1859. It has a good harbor and is the first port of call in Illinois on the St. Lawrence Seaway route. Its industries are closely allied with those of neighboring North Chicago. Pharmaceuticals, chemicals, and iron, steel, and wood products are among the area's many manufactures. Waukegan was settled (1835) as Little Fort near an old French stockade established on the site of an Indian village.

Waukesha (wô'kĭshô), city (1970 pop. 40,258), seat of Waukesha co., SE Wis., on the Fox River; inc. 1896. An industrial center in a dairy area, it became a health resort after the Civil War. Its bottled waters are shipped widely. Manufactures include engines, bearings, castings, aluminum products, and electrical and electronic equipment. Carroll College, a county technical institute, and an extension center of the Univ. of Wisconsin are there. Old Indian mounds are preserved in the city's Cutler Park.

Wausau (wô'sô), city (1970 pop. 32,806), seat of Marathon co., central Wis., on the Wisconsin River; settled 1839, inc. 1872. It is an industrial and commercial city in the heart of Wisconsin's dairy region. Its industries include paper, paper products, machinery, and insurance. A branch of the Univ. of Wisconsin is in Wausau. Rib Mountain State Park is nearby.

Wauwatosa (wôwətō'sə), city (1970 pop. 58,676), Milwaukee co., SE Wis., an industrial suburb adjacent to Milwaukee, on the Menominee River; settled 1835, inc. as a city 1897. Metal products are among its manufactures.

wave, in oceanography, disturbance in the surface of a body of water. Wind, gravitational attraction between the earth and moon (see TIDE), and submarine earthquakes, volcanic eruptions, and landslides all create waves. Generally, waves seen on the surface of the ocean are wind waves. They are generated by the stresses in the water from the wind blowing across it. Waves consist of a series of crests and troughs that move through the water body. Wavelength is the distance between two successive crests (or successive troughs). The wave height is the vertical distance between the crest and the adjacent trough. As the wind-generated waves pass, the water particles are set in motion, following vertical circular orbits. In deep water, the diameter of the circular path at the water surface is equal to the height of the wave. Water particles momentarily move forward as the wave crest passes and backward as the trough passes. Thus, except for a slight forward drag, the water particles remain in essentially the same place as successive waves pass. The orbital motion of the water particles decreases in size at depths below the surface, so that at a depth equal to about one half of the wave's length, the water particles are barely oscillating back and forth. Thus, for even the largest wind waves, their effect is virtually zero beyond a depth of 300 m (980 ft). The height and period of waves are determined by wind velocity, the duration of the wind, and the fetch (the distance the wind has blown across the water). In stormy areas, the waves are not uniform but form a confusing pattern of many waves of different periods and heights. That pattern is called "sea." As these waves leave the storm area, the longer-period waves, because of their higher velocity, will move ahead of the shorter waves, which tend to die out. The waves sort themselves out by size to produce a swell, or regular pattern of long-period waves. When the swell approaches a shore, the orbital motion of the water particles becomes influenced by the bottom of the body of water. The wavelength decreases as the wave is slowed, but the period remains relatively constant. The wave steepens when the water depth is about one half the wavelength. As the water becomes shallower the wave steepens further until it "breaks" in a breaker, or surf, carrying the water forward and up onto the beach in a turbulent fashion. Because waves usually approach the shore at an angle, a longshore (littoral) current is generated parallel to the shoreline. These currents can be effective in eroding and transporting sediment along the shore (see COAST PROTECTION; BEACH). In many enclosed or partly enclosed bodies of water such as lakes or bays, a particular wave form called a standing wave, or seiche, commonly develops as a result of sudden storms or rapid changes in air pressure. These waves do not move forward, but the water surface moves up and down at antinodal points, while it remains stationary at nodal points. Such waves, which can be dangerous to ships in harbors, can be simulated in a cup of water by tilting the cup and then allowing the high side of the cup to drop; a standing wave will develop that causes the water to spill first out of one side of the cup and then the other. Internal waves can form within waters that are density stratified. In many respects they are similar to wind-driven waves. They usually cannot be seen on the surface, although oil slicks, plankton, and sediment tend to collect on the surface above troughs of internal waves. Any condition that causes waters of different density to come into contact with one another can lead to internal waves. They tend to have lower velocities but greater heights than surface waves. Very little is known about internal waves. It is possible that they can move sediment on deeper parts of continental shelves. Just as a rock dropped into water produces waves, unusual and severe conditions can generate trains of large and catastrophic waves of short duration. Landslides and earthquakes can produce very high energy waves of short duration that can devastate coastal regions (see TSUNAMI). Hurricanes traveling over shallow coastal waters can generate storm surges that in turn can cause devastating coastal flooding (see TIDAL WAVE).

wave, in physics, the transfer of ENERGY by the regular VIBRATION, or oscillatory motion, either of some material medium or by the variation in intensity of the FIELD vectors of an electromagnetic field (see ELECTROMAGNETIC RADIATION). Waves may be classified according to the direction of vibration relative to that of the energy transfer. In longitudinal, or compressional, waves the vibration is in the same direction as the transfer of energy; in transverse waves the vibration is at right angles to the transfer of energy; in torsional waves the vibration consists of a twisting motion as the medium rotates back and forth around the direction of energy transfer. The three types of waves are illustrated by an example in which a coil spring is held stretched out by two persons. If the person holding one end pulls a few coils toward himself and releases them, a longitudinal wave will travel along the spring, with coils alternately being pressed closer together, then stretched apart, as the wave passes. If the first person then shakes his end up and down or from side to side, a transverse wave will travel along the spring. Finally, if he grabs several coils and twists them around the axis of the spring, a torsional wave will travel along the spring. A wave may be a combination of types. Water waves in deep water are mainly transverse. However, as they approach a shore they interact with the bottom and acquire a longitudinal component. When the longitudinal component becomes very large compared to the transverse component, the wave breaks. The maximum displacement of the medium in either direction is the amplitude of the wave. The distance between successive crests or successive troughs (corresponding to maximum displacements in the same direction) is the wavelength of the wave. The frequency of the wave is equal to the number of crests (or troughs) that pass a given fixed point per unit of time. Closely related to the frequency is the period of the wave, which is the time lapse between the passage of successive crests (or troughs). The frequency of a wave is the inverse of the period. One full wavelength of a wave represents one complete cycle, that is, one complete vibration in each direction. The various parts of a cycle are described by the phase of the wave; all waves are referenced to an imaginary synchronous motion in a circle; thus the phase is measured in angular degrees, one complete cycle being 360°. Two waves whose corresponding parts occur at the same time are said to be in phase. If the two waves are at different parts of their cycles, they are out of phase. Waves out of phase by 180° are in phase opposition. The various phase relationships between combining waves determines the type of INTERFERENCE that takes place.

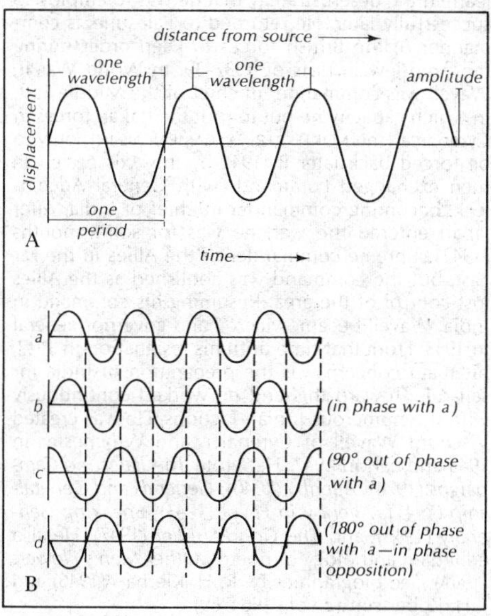

A. *Diagram of wave: Wave travels one wavelength during one period*

B. *Diagram of wave: Phase relationships*

The speed of a wave is determined by its wavelength λ and its frequency ν, according to the equation $v=\lambda\nu$, where v is the speed, or velocity. Since frequency is inversely related to the period T, this equation also takes the form $v=\lambda/T$. The speed of a wave tells how quickly the energy it carries is being transferred. It is important to note that the speed is that of the wave itself and not of the medium through which it is traveling. The medium itself does not move except to oscillate as the wave passes. In the graphic representation and analysis of wave behavior, two concepts are widely used—wave fronts and rays. A wave front is a line representing all parts of a wave that are in phase and an equal number of wavelengths from the source of the wave. The shape of the wave front depends upon the nature of the source; a point source will emit waves having circular or spherical wave fronts, while a large, extended source will emit waves whose wave fronts are effectively flat, or plane. A ray is a line extending outward from the source and representing the direction of propagation of the wave at any point along it. Rays are perpendicular to wave fronts. Many familiar phenomena are associated with energy transfer in the form of waves. SOUND is a longitudinal wave that travels through material media by alternatively forcing the molecules of the medium closer together, then spreading them apart. LIGHT and other forms of electromagnetic radiation travel through space as transverse waves; the displacements at right angles to the direction of the waves are the field intensity vectors rather than motions of the material particles of some medium. With the development of the QUANTUM THEORY, it was found that particles in motion also have certain wave properties, including an associated wavelength and frequency related to their momentum and energy. Thus, the study of waves and wave motion has applications throughout the entire range of physical phenomena.

wave guide, device that controls the propagation of an electromagnetic wave so that the wave is forced to follow a path defined by the physical structure of the guide. Wave guides, which are useful chiefly at MICROWAVE frequencies, typically take the form of hollow metal tubes. A wave guide of a given dimension will not propagate electromagnetic waves lower than a certain frequency (the cutoff frequency). Generally speaking, the electric and magnetic fields of an electromagnetic wave have a number of possible arrangements when the wave is traveling through a wave guide. Each of these arrangements is known as a mode of propagation. Specification of all of these modes can be extremely complex, but the mode of propagation for a wave at the cutoff frequency is called the dominant mode.

Wavell, Archibald Percival Wavell, 1st Earl (wā'vəl), 1883–1950, British field marshal and viceroy of India. Wavell first saw service in the South African War and in India. During World War I he fought in France (and lost an eye) and in Palestine, where, under the command of General Allenby, he first learned the desert strategy that he was to employ so successfully later. He returned to Palestine as commander of the British forces to keep order during the Arab-Jewish riots of 1937–39. In World War II, Wavell was commander in chief of the Middle East, in which capacity he put to rout the Italian forces in Cyrenaica (see NORTH AFRICA, CAMPAIGNS IN), only to be forced back later in 1941 by the Axis drive. He then exchanged commands with General Auchinleck, becoming commander in chief of India. After Japan entered the war, he was for some months (1942) supreme commander of the Allies in the Far East, but the command was abolished as the Allies lost control of the area. Resuming his command in India, Wavell became viceroy and governor general in 1943. From that time until his resignation in 1947, his main concern was the preparation of India for self-rule; toward this end he worked continuously with the numerous Indian factions. He was created Viscount Wavell of Cyrenaica and Winchester in 1943 and earl in 1947. He wrote *The Palestine Campaigns* (1928), *Allenby* (1940), *Generals and Generalship* (1941), *Allenby in Egypt* (1943), *Speaking Generally* (1946), and *The Good Soldier* (1947). He also edited an anthology of poetry, *Other Men's Flowers* (1944). See biographies by R. H. Kiernan (1946) and J. H. Robertson (2 vol., 1964–69).

wave mechanics: see QUANTUM THEORY.

Waves (Women Appointed for Voluntary Emergency Service), U.S. navy organization, created (1942) in World War II to release male naval personnel for sea duty. The organization was commanded until 1946 by Mildred Helen McAfee. Waves served in communications, air traffic control, naval air navigation, and clerical positions in the United States, Hawaii, Alaska, and the Caribbean. Recruiting ended in 1945, with a peak enrollment of 86,000. Waves forces were reduced when the war ended, and after the passage (1948) of the Women's Armed Service Integration Act women were enlisted into the regular navy; they continued to be known as Waves.

wax, substance secreted by glands on the abdomen of the bee and known commonly as beeswax; also various substances resembling beeswax. Waxes are mixtures comprising chiefly esters of monohydroxy alcohols, besides other esters and free fatty acids, free alcohols, and higher hydrocarbons. They differ from fats in that fats contain chiefly esters of glycerol. Waxes are generally harder and less greasy than fats, but like fats they are less dense than water and are soluble in alcohol and ether but not in water. Among the waxes derived from plants are carnauba wax, obtained from the leaves of a PALM grown in Brazil, and candelilla wax, produced by a Mexican plant (*Euphorbia antisyphilitica*). Those of animal origin include wool wax, or lanolin, obtained from the surface of wool fibers and used in making certain creams, ointments, and soaps, in the processes of finishing and softening leather, and as an ingredient of some paints and varnishes; SPERMACETI, obtained from the sperm whale, and Chinese wax, which is deposited on certain trees in parts of Asia (especially China and India) by a species of scale insect. Mineral waxes include OZOCERITE and PARAFFIN, both composed of hydrocarbons. Japan wax and bayberry (or myrtle) wax are composed chiefly of fats. See Lillian Roth and Jack Weiner, *Waxes, Waxing and Wax Modifiers* (1961); Harry Bennett, *Industrial Waxes* (2 vol., 1963).

Waxahachie (wŏk"sĭhăch'ē), city (1970 pop. 13,452), seat of Ellis co., N Texas; inc. 1861. A market center (especially for cattle) in the rich blackland prairie, it also has small manufacturing industries. Southwestern Junior College of the Assemblies of God is there.

waxbill, common name for small, brightly colored weaver finches of the Estrildini tribe of the family Estrildidae. Most are African with the exception of two S Asian species of avadavats, and one Australian species (*Estrilda temporalis*), which may not properly belong in this group. Considerable adaptive radiation may be seen in the African species, which include a number of small seedeaters such as the lavender finch (*E. subflava*); larger seedeaters such as the bluebills (genus *Spermophaga*); large-headed and large-billed species (genus *Pirenestes*); the arboreal, insect-catching Negro finches (genus *Nigrita*); and the tiny, short-billed, omnivorous flowerpecker finch (*Parmoptila woodhousei*). Timid, social birds, waxbills are typically found in small flocks but may sometimes descend upon a field en masse. They tend to form stable, long-lasting pairs, and both mates share in nesting, incubation, and the care of the offspring. Their pure white eggs number from 4 to 10 per clutch. Their young are curiously marked on palate and tongue; a five-dot, domino pattern on the palate is common and is displayed by the nestlings when begging for food. Waxbills are classified in the phylum CHORDATA, subphylum Vertebrata, class Aves, order Passeriformes, family Estrildidae.

wax figures, sculptures usually made of beeswax or tallow, which is susceptible to modeling, casting, and coloring. The Egyptians, Greeks, and Romans used wax to make sacred images or death masks. Wax has been employed in the CIRE PERDUE casting process for sculpture; it is also used in the preparatory stages by sculptors as a sketch or model for the finished work. Polychrome wax portraits were popular in Europe throughout the 18th cent. In the 19th cent., wax dolls came into fashion, and exhibits of wax figures, often portraits of notorious people, were popular. Among such collections Mme Tussaud's, London, and the Musée Grévin, Paris, are famous. See F. Eliscu, *Direct Wax Sculpture* (1969); R. McDermott Miller, *Figure Sculpture in Wax and Plaster* (1971).

wax moth, greater: see BEE MOTH.

wax myrtle: see BAYBERRY.

wax painting: see ENCAUSTIC.

wax plant: see MILKWEED.

waxwing, any of three species of perching songbirds of the Northern Hemisphere. Waxwings have crests (raised only in alarm) and sleek brownish-gray plumage with flecks of red pigment resembling sealing wax on the wings and a yellow band on the tail tip. The cedar waxwing, called cherry bird and cedar bird, breeds throughout most of Canada and the United States. The Bohemian, or greater, waxwing is more northern in distribution, ranging into the U.S. only rarely in winter. It is found in N Europe and Asia as well as in N North America. The third species, the Japanese waxwing, is found only in NE Asia. Waxwings are classified in the phylum CHORDATA, subphylum Vertebrata, class Aves, order Passeriformes, family Bombycillidae, genus *Bombycilla*.

Waycross, city (1970 pop. 18,996), seat of Ware co., SE Ga.; settled 1818, inc. 1874. Waycross is a rail and highway center in a productive pine lumber, livestock, tobacco, and pecan area. It has railroad shops, a tobacco auction market, and a great variety of manufactures. Waycross is the gateway to Okefenokee Swamp Park (a national wildlife refuge). A state park is also nearby.

wayfaring tree: see HONEYSUCKLE.

Wayland, Francis, 1796–1865, American clergyman and educator, b. New York City, grad. Union College, 1813, and studied at Andover Theological Seminary. As pastor (1821–26) of the First Baptist Church, Boston, he became known for his able preaching. After a brief professorship at Union College, he was president (1827–55) of Brown. He enlarged the scope of the institution through a vigorous program of reforms and was a pioneer in progressive ideas in higher education, such as flexible entrance requirements and elective systems. His founding of a free library at Wayland, Mass., inspired legislation that empowered towns to support public libraries by taxation. After retirement he gave his attention to benevolent works, notably prison reform. His many books include *Elements of Moral Science* (1835), *Elements of Political Economy* (1837), and *Elements of Intellectual Philosophy* (1854). See biography by his son Francis Wayland (2 vol., 1867); study by T. R. Crane (1962). His son **Francis Wayland,** 1826–1904, b. Boston, grad. Brown, 1846, studied at Harvard law school and was (1873–1903) dean of the Yale law school. A graduate course in law, the first of its kind in America, was established under his auspices.

Wayland, town (1970 pop. 13,461), Middlesex co., E Mass., W of Boston; settled c.1638, inc. 1835. Electronic and chemical research is carried on.

Wayland Smith, in English folklore, a skillful blacksmith and great armor maker, whose forge was near the White Horse (Berkshire). He appears in the Old English *Beowulf* and *Deor* and in Sir Walter Scott's *Kenilworth*. The story of his Norse cognate, Völund, appears at length in the *Elder Edda*. To the German peoples he is known as Wieland.

Wayne, Anthony, 1745–96, American Revolutionary general, b. Chester co., Pa. Not inclined toward academic studies, Wayne became a surveyor in 1763. In 1765 he was engaged to survey the land for, and promote the settlement of, a proposed colony in Nova Scotia, a venture from which he withdrew in 1766. He returned to the business of farming and tanning at Waynesborough, on the farm that his grandfather had established and that he inherited. He represented Chester co. in the Pennsylvania assembly (1774–75), was an agitator against British policies, and was active in preparations to defend the cause of the colonists. When the Continental army was formed, he organized and commanded a regiment from Chester co., and in Jan., 1776, he was commissioned a colonel and given command of the 4th Pennsylvania Battalion. As agent for the Pennsylvania committee of safety, he built defenses for the Delaware River. In the spring of 1776 he covered the retreat of the Americans after their failure in the Quebec campaign. The next winter he spent in command at Fort Ticonderoga. In 1777 he was commissioned brigadier general and joined George Washington's army at Morristown, N.J. In the battle of Brandywine, Wayne commanded a division at Chadds Ford. Later he was defeated by General Howe's forces at Paoli, Pa.; to silence rumors that the defeat had been caused by his negligence, Wayne requested a court-martial and was acquitted with honor. He fought at Germantown, made successful raids on British supplies for the troops encamped at Valley Forge, and served in the battle of Monmouth. His most famous achievement, however, was his capture of the British outpost at Stony Point, N.Y., by a night attack in July, 1779. He aided General Lafayette in Virginia and participated in the YORKTOWN CAMPAIGN. Later he fought successfully against the Indians in Georgia, and, after Nathanael Greene's army had forced the British evacuation of Charleston, S.C., Wayne occupied the city. In 1783 he returned to Pennsylvania, and in 1784 he was again elected to represent Chester co. in the general assembly. The following year he returned to Georgia and tried unsuccessfully to work the land which the Georgia assembly had given him in gratitude for his services. In 1791 he was elected to Congress as a representative from Georgia but was unseated because of irregularities in the election and in his residence qualification. In 1792 he succeeded Arthur St. Clair as commander of the American army in the Northwest Territory. After the failure of peace negotiations with the Indians there—which Wayne opposed, feeling that war was inevitable—he decisively defeated (Aug., 1794) the Indians at Fallen Timbers near present Toledo, Ohio. He secured (1795) the Treaty of Greenville with the chiefs of the defeated tribes, who ceded lands in the Northwest Territory. This was the first treaty in which Indian title to lands within the boundaries of the new United States was overtly recognized. Impetuous and hot-headed, Wayne was sometimes known as "mad Anthony," but he was an able general. Wayne's activities in the Old Northwest are recorded in *The Wayne-Knox-Pickering-McHenry Correspondence* (ed. by R. C. Knopf, 1960). See H. B. Dawson, *The Assault on Stony Point* (1863); J. W. De Peyster, *Major General Anthony Wayne* (1886); C. J. Stillé, *Major General Anthony Wayne and the Pennsylvania Line in the Continental Army* (1893, repr.

1968); biographies by Thomas Boyd (1929), J. H. Preston (1930), H. E. Wildes (1941), and Glenn Tucker (1973).

Wayne, John, 1906–, American movie actor, b. Winterset, Iowa; his original name was Marion Michael Morrison. An extraordinarily popular movie star for more than 40 years, Wayne plays tough yet affable heroes, usually in Westerns or war films. John FORD directed many of his most successful movies—*Stagecoach* (1939), *Fort Apache* (1948), *Rio Grande* (1950), *The Quiet Man* (1952), *The Searchers* (1956), and *Donovan's Reef* (1963). Wayne's other films include *The High and the Mighty* (1954), *The Alamo* (1960; also produced and directed), and *True Grit* (1969). See studies by Mike Tomkies (1971) and George Carpozi (1972).

Wayne, city (1970 pop. 21,054), Wayne co., SE Mich., a suburb of Detroit, on the Lower Rouge River; inc. as a village 1869, and with surrounding areas as a city 1960. It has automobile and aircraft industries and other varied manufactures.

Waynesboro. **1** Borough (1970 pop. 10,011), Franklin co., S Pa., near the Md. line; laid out 1797, inc. 1818. A trade, processing, and shipping center in an agricultural area (dairy farms and fruit orchards), it is also a manufacturing city. Pottery, prefabricated homes, and machine tools are produced. Two state parks are nearby. **2** City (1970 pop. 16,707), surrounded by but politically independent of August co., central Va., in the Shenandoah valley; settled c.1736, inc. as a city 1948. A manufacturing center in a farm area, it has plants making a wide variety of products. In the battle of Waynesboro (March, 1865), Gen. Jubal Early's heavily outnumbered Confederate troops were severely defeated by a detachment of Sheridan's army under Custer. A boys' military school and a girls' preparatory school are in the city. Nearby are Sherando Lake Recreation Area (in George Washington National Forest) and a game refuge.

Wayne State University, at Detroit, Mich.; state supported; coeducational; established 1956 as a successor to Wayne University (formed 1934 by a merger of five city colleges). The university includes schools of medicine and nursing and colleges of education, liberal arts, and engineering; it also maintains an extensive adult education division.

Waynflete, William (wān'flēt), 1395?–1486, English prelate and lord chancellor. He was master of Winchester College before 1429, and in 1443 he became provost of the newly founded Eton College. In 1447 he became bishop of Winchester. Soon afterward he received patents to found a hall at Oxford for the study of theology and philosophy. The buildings, which incorporated the earlier Magdalen Hall, were completed in 1480, largely through Waynflete's own generosity, and Magdalen College still bears his arms. The bishop's political career was largely devoted to matters of personal aid to Henry VI. Waynflete negotiated for peace with Jack CADE and with Richard, duke of YORK. He was a privy councilor, in which capacity he tried to obtain (1454) Henry's consent to a regency by York; in 1456 he was made lord chancellor. Waynflete presided at the Parliament (1459) at Coventry that attainted the Yorkists, but after the Yorkist victory in 1460, he was well treated, although deprived of the chancellorship.

Waziristan (wəzē'rĭstän''), region (1961 pop. 395,000), 4,473 sq mi (11,585 sq km), North-West Frontier Province, Pakistan, on the Afghanistan border. An extremely arid and mountainous region, it is divided into N Waziristan, inhabited by farming Wazir tribes, and S Waziristan, populated by seminomad Mahsuds. The two tribes, both of Pathan descent, have constant blood feuds and supplement their meager incomes by brigandage. They live in fortresslike mountain villages or tent camps and export some timber and firewood, hides, ghee (clarified butter), and iron to other parts of Pakistan for cash income. Fertile valleys in parts of N Waziristan support wheat, maize, barley, and millet; livestock are also raised. In S Waziristan the hills are used for grazing, and forests on the higher slopes provide timber. Protected by the mountain fastness, the Wazirs and Mahsuds historically resisted British authority. When the Durand Line was established as the border between Afghanistan and British India in 1893, Waziristan became an independent territory outside the bounds of effective British rule. Since Waziristan became part of Pakistan in 1947, the government has continued the British practice of pacification through payment of subsidies to tribal chieftains; it has also tried to persuade the tribesmen to move to more settled areas. The tribes, led by the Faqir of Ipi, have reportedly received arms from Afghanistan, which has agitated for an independent Pushtunistan composed of all border Pathan tribal lands.

Wazzan (wäzän'), Fr. *Ouezzane,* town (1960 pop. 26,203), N Morocco. It is a sacred city, the seat of an important Muslim brotherhood.

weakfish: see CROAKER.

Weald, the (wēld), area between the North Downs and the South Downs, SE England, forming part of the counties of East Sussex, West Sussex, Surrey, Hampshire, and Kent. Formerly forested and once noted for its iron industry, the Weald is now largely agricultural.

wealth, goods possessing economic VALUE. Wealth may be measured by price. It does not include such necessaries of life as air, sunlight, and water when these are free, and it does not include unmarketable human qualities. Many economists believe that the economic value, or price, of wealth is necessarily less than the total satisfaction supplied by it. The gap between the two is thought to give rise to the consumers' surplus. National wealth may include the value of all the material economic goods within a nation's boundaries or the value of all material economic goods within and outside the country that are owned by its citizens. See J. A. Hobson, *Work and Wealth* (1914, repr. 1933); W. A. Robson, *The Relation of Wealth to Welfare* (1925); C. F. Carter, *Wealth* (1969, repr. 1971).

Wear (wēr), river, c.65 mi (100 km) long, rising in the Pennines, W Durham, NE England, and flowing to the North Sea at Sunderland. Navigable for barges to Durham, the river waters a rich agricultural area. The lower Wear passes through an industrial region.

weasel, name for certain small, lithe, carnivorous mammals of the family Mustelidae (weasel family). Members of this family are generally characterized by long bodies and necks, short legs, small rounded ears, and medium to long tails. All have scent glands, generally used for territorial markings but in some animals for defense. True weasels belong to the genus *Mustela,* with species found in Eurasia, N Africa, and the Americas. Weasels are very active and chiefly terrestrial but able to climb trees. They prey on small animals by night, often killing more than they eat, and spend the day in dens made in holes in the ground, rock piles, or hollow stumps. Although they are notorious for destruction of poultry, the damage they do is far outweighed by their value as destroyers of rodents. Weasels are usually brown, with white underparts. Species living in snowy regions acquire white coats in winter and are then known as ERMINE. The most widely distributed weasel, *Mustela erminea,* is known in Europe as the stoat and in North America as the short-tailed weasel. It is about 16 in. (40 cm) long including the 5-in. (13-cm) tail; it has a white winter coat through much of its range and a characteristic black tail tip the year around. It ranges from the Arctic Ocean to central Asia, S Europe and the central United States. The much smaller *M. nivalis,* known in Europe simply as weasel, is found in Europe, N and central Asia, and N Africa. It turns white only in the extreme northern parts of its range. Among the New World weasels is the tiny least weasel, measuring only 7 or 8 in. (18–20 cm) in total length; it ranges from the N central United States to N Canada and Alaska. There are many other true weasel species, mostly in the Old World. Besides these, the genus *Mustela* includes the POLECAT, FERRET, and MINK. African animals of several genera in the weasel family are called striped weasels; they are characterized by conspicuous black and white markings and, in some cases, by the use of scent for defense. Among these is a skunklike animal with a powerful odor known as the ZORILLA. The weasel family also includes the MARTEN, FISHER, and WOLVERINE, as well as the more distantly related SKUNK, BADGER, HONEY BADGER (or ratel), and OTTER. Weasels are classified in the phylum CHORDATA, subphylum Vertebrata, class Mammalia, order Carnivora, family Mustelidae. See Bil Gilbert, *The Weasel* (1970).

weather, state of the atmosphere at a given time and place with regard to temperature, air pressure (see BAROMETER), wind, humidity, cloudiness, and precipitation. The term *weather* is restricted to conditions over short periods of time; conditions over long periods are referred to as CLIMATE. The earliest evidence of scientific activity in the field of METEOROLOGY is from the 4th cent. B.C.; Aristotle wrote what is probably the first treatise on the subject. The first attempt to chart weather from reports over a considerable area was made (1820) in Europe by H. W. Brandes, but it was not until after the invention of the telegraph that the rapid collection of weather data from remote stations became possible. In the United States, a government weather service was established (1870) under the army Signal Corps. In 1891 the weather service was transferred to the U.S. Weather Bureau under the Dept. of Agriculture, and it later came (1940) under the jurisidiction of the Dept. of Commerce. The U.S Weather Bureau has since been renamed the U.S. National Weather Service and transferred to the National Oceanic and Atmospheric Administration. The central forecast office is the National Meteorological Center (NMC), in Suitland, Md.; first-order stations are located chiefly in the larger cities, and numerous substations for special purposes (e.g., observing river stages, measuring depth of snow, and maintaining records of climate) are distributed throughout the country. Devices used for meteorological observations include rockets, weather satellites, RADIOSONDES, barometers, anemometers, WEATHER VANES, PSYCHROMETERS, THERMOMETERS, and radar. By means of high-speed telecommunications, information from all over the world is sent to the NMC. Here the data is decoded and plotted both automatically and by hand. These data are used to create weather maps based on simultaneous weather observations at different atmospheric levels over any desired geographic region. All such charts are prepared at least twice each day. On a typical map the various weather elements are shown by figures and symbols; ISOBARS are drawn to show areas of low pressure (CYCLONES) and high pressure (anticyclones); FRONTS (boundaries between AIR MASSES) and areas of precipitation are indicated. By using computer models based on mathematical formulations of the evolution of the atmosphere, weather charts are also produced as prognostics of future weather patterns. The many simplifying assumptions required in these formulations, as well as the incompleteness of weather data, limit the accuracy of the computer predictions. Meteorologists interpret and modify such prognostics according to their knowledge of the prognostics' reliability and their familiarity with local influences, such as topography and proximity to large bodies of water, in order to derive the best possible weather forecasts. Forecasts are disseminated by television, radio, telegraph, telephone, mail, and newspapers. A signal flag system is used on the coasts to announce storm warnings. Specific forecasts can usually be made only for a short future period (generally 48 hr or less). Forecasts for up to five days can usually predict departures from normal temperature and precipitation fairly well; longer-range predictions are more general and less accurate, being based on the known normal weather of the area. See D. S. Halacy, Jr., *The Weather Changers* (1968); Herbert Riehl, *Introduction to the Atmosphere* (2d ed. 1972); P. D. Thompson, *Weather* (1973).

weather balloon, BALLOON used in the measurement and evaluation of atmospheric conditions. Information may be gathered during the vertical ascent of the balloon through the atmosphere or during its motions once it has reached a predetermined maximum altitude. Helium, which is less dense than air (see BUOYANCY), is usually used to inflate weather balloons. A pilot balloon is a small balloon (diameter c.1 m/39 in.) whose ascent is followed visually to obtain data for the computation of the speed and direction of winds at different altitudes. A ceiling balloon is a slightly smaller version of the pilot balloon and is used to determine the altitude of cloud bases. A much larger, teardrop-shaped balloon is used to carry a RADIOSONDE aloft. The balloon expands as it rises, usually reaching an altitude of at least 90,000 ft (27,400 m) before it bursts. Teardrop-shaped balloons are also used for horizontal sounding of the atmosphere. A predetermined level of inflation allows the balloon to rise only to some desired altitude, where it becomes neutrally buoyant, and winds then carry it along. Atmospheric pressure information may be sent by radio from the balloon; monitoring of its movement provides information about winds at its flight level. A technique has been developed whereby many horizontal sounding balloons can be monitored by earth-orbiting SATELLITES, which relay information on the balloons' positions to earth-based stations. The tetroon is a tetrahedral balloon used for horizontal sounding. It was developed to withstand the extremely low pressures of high-altitude flight; the straight seals joining its four triangular faces are stronger than the curved seals of the more traditionally shaped balloons. Tetroons have been used extensively in tracing low-level atmospheric currents by following their movement with radar; they have thus increased the meteorologist's understanding of atmospheric turbulence, low-level vertical motions, and air pollution dispersion.

Weatherford, William, c.1780–1824, North American Indian chief, b. present-day Alabama. He is also called Red Eagle. In the War of 1812 he led the Creek war party, stirred by Tecumseh, against the Americans. On Aug. 30, 1813, he attacked Fort Mims, a temporary stockade near the confluence of the Tombigbee and Alabama rivers, where his warriors, refusing to heed his plea for restraint, massacred some 500 whites. In the battle of HORSESHOE BEND on the Tallapoosa River (March 27, 1814), Gen. Andrew Jackson completely broke the power of Weatherford and his nation. Weatherford was pardoned by Jackson, who admired his courage, and he lived peaceably in Alabama until his death. See G. C. Eggleston, *Red Eagle & the Wars with the Creek Indians of Alabama* (1878).

Weatherford, city (1970 pop. 11,750), seat of Parker co., N central Texas; inc. 1856. It is in a fertile region that yields peanuts, watermelons, and peaches. Oilfield equipment is manufactured. A junior college and a railroad museum are there. Fort Wolters, a major helicopter center, is nearby.

weathering, collective term for the processes by which rock at or near the earth's surface is disintegrated and decomposed by the action of atmospheric agents, water, and living things. Some of these processes are mechanical, e.g., the expansion and contraction caused by sudden, large changes in temperature, the expansive force of water freezing in cracks, the splitting caused by plant roots, and the impact of running water; others are chemical, e.g., oxidation, hydration, carbonization, and loss of chemical elements by solution in water. Weathering is important because it aids in the formation of soil, prepares materials for EROSION, and causes discoloration and weakening of building stone.

weather map: see WEATHER.

weather satellite, artificial SATELLITE used to gather data on a global basis for improvement of weather forecasting. Information is provided about cloud cover, storm location, temperature, and heat balance in the earth's atmosphere. The first weather satellites were those of the Tiros series, which began in 1960. Tiros was succeeded by the Nimbus series, which moved in a polar orbit. The Earth Resources Technology Satellite (ERTS), launched in 1972, provided photographs to help forecasting. The Environmental Science Services Administration (ESSA) has also launched weather satellites. Meteorological data has also been obtained by the Soviet Meteor and Cosmos series.

weather vane or **wind vane,** instrument used to indicate wind direction. It consists of an asymmetrically shaped object, e.g., an arrow or a rooster, mounted at its center of gravity so it can move freely about a vertical axis. Regardless of the design, the portion of the object with greater surface area (usually the tail) offers greater resistance to the wind and thus positions the vane so that the forward part points in the direction from which the wind is blowing. The compass direction of the wind may then be determined by reference to an attached compass rose; alternatively, the orientation of the vane may be relayed to a remote calibrated dial. The wind vane must be mounted at a distance from the nearest obstacle equal to at least twice the height of the obstacle above the vane if the observed wind direction is to be representative of meteorologically significant wind patterns; for this reason, the vane is often mounted on a pole or tower that is in turn mounted on the roof of a tall building.

Weaver, James Baird, 1833–1912, American political leader, b. Dayton, Ohio. Reared in frontier areas of Michigan and Iowa, he practiced law in Iowa. He served in the Union army in the Civil War and rose from the rank of private to that of brevet brigadier general. He held several offices in Iowa before he adopted the cause of reform and was elected (1878) to the U.S. House of Representatives on the Greenback party ticket. In 1880 he was the unsuccessful presidential candidate of the Greenback party. Again (1885–89) in Congress with the backing of the Democratic and the Greenback-Labor parties, Weaver continued to advocate "soft-money" views. He helped form the Farmers' Alliance—an agrarian reform movement—and when that organization became the POPULIST PARTY, Weaver ran (1892) as its presidential candidate. He recorded his political views in *A Call to Action* (1892). Although defeated, he polled more than one million popular and 22 electoral votes. Weaver became one of the important leaders of the free-silver movement, backed William Jennings Bryan in the 1896 presidential campaign, and after the decline of Populism retired from national politics. See biography by F. E. Haynes (1919).

Weaver, Robert Clifton, 1907–, U.S. Secretary of Housing and Urban Development (1966–68), b. Washington, D.C. He was successively adviser to the Secretary of the Interior (1933–37) special assistant with the Housing Authority (1937–40), and an administrative assistant with the National Defense Advisory Commission (1940). During World War II he held several offices concerned with mobilizing black labor. After holding various teaching assignments and working with the John Hay Whitney Foundation, Weaver was (1955–59) New York state rent commissioner. In 1961, President John F. Kennedy appointed him to the post of administrator of the Housing and Home Finance Agency. In 1966, President Lyndon B. Johnson appointed him head of the newly created Department of Housing and Urban Development (HUD); he was the first black to hold a cabinet post. After leaving HUD he was (1969–70) president of Bernard M. Baruch College. His works include *Negro Labor: A National Problem* (1946), *The Negro Ghetto* (1948), *The Urban Complex: Human Values in Urban Life* (1964), and *Dilemmas of Urban America* (1965).

Weaver, Warren, 1894–, American scientist, b. Reedsburg, Wis., grad. Univ. of Wisconsin. He taught mathematics at Wisconsin (1920–32), was director of the division of natural sciences at the Rockefeller Institute (1932–55), and was science consultant (1947–51), trustee (1954), and vice president (from 1958) at the Sloan-Kettering Institute for Cancer Research. Weaver's chief researches are in the problems of communication in science and in the mathematical theory of probability. He is one of the founders of INFORMATION THEORY, or communication theory. His writings include *The Mathematical Theory of Communication* (with C. E. Shannon, 1949).

weaver bird, name for the Ploceidae, a family of Old World seed-eating birds closely resembling finches (hence the alternate name weaver finch). It includes a number of so-called goldfinches and waxbill finches that are actually weaver birds, rather than true finches of the family Fringillidae. The weavers are named for the highly complex woven nests built by many species, though others build only crude nests, and the parasitic widow weavers build no nests at all. Most weavers are sedentary, noisy, gregarious, and polygynous, with elaborate courtship rituals. The weaver group is divided into the buffalo, sparrow, typical, and widow weavers. The African buffalo weavers are black-and-brown birds 8 to 10 in. (20.3–25.4 cm) long, that travel in small flocks and build bulky compartmented nests with separate chambers for two or more pairs. Of the 35 sparrow weavers the best known, and in fact one of the most widely distributed and familiar small birds in the world, is the ENGLISH SPARROW native to Europe, W Asia, and N Africa. It is the most successful town and city dweller among birds, and has followed European civilization wherever it has gone; it was introduced to North America in 1852. As common in the Orient is the Eurasian tree sparrow (also introduced in the United States), a nuisance in rice fields and sold in great quantities for food. These birds build untidy domed nests with side entrances. Most specialized of the sparrow weavers is the social weaver of Africa, famous for its apartment-house nest, in which 100 to 300 pairs have separate flask-shaped chambers entered by tubes at the bottom. They build these structures, which may be 10 ft (3 m) high and 15 ft (4.5 m) across, high in a sturdy tree, beginning with a roof of straw thatch. Of the 100 or more African and Asian typical weavers, the small quelea, only 5 in. (12.7 cm) long, sometimes causes huge crop losses in Africa by feeding on grain in flocks numbering as many as one million birds. The African widow weavers (named for the long, drooping black tail plumes of the breeding male), or whydahs, are notable for their selective parasitic nesting habits; they lay their eggs in the nests of waxbills, and their eggs are white, as are those of the waxbill, rather than spotted, as are those of all other weavers. Many of the weaver family are kept as cage birds, especially the colorful waxbills (e.g., the Java sparrow, mannikin, munia, grenadier, cutthroat, and cordon-bleu and the locust, parrot, Gouldian, and fire finches). Weaver birds are classified in the phylum CHORDATA, subphylum Vertebrata, class Aves, order Passeriformes.

weaver finch: see WEAVER BIRD.

weaving, the art of forming a fabric by interlacing at right angles two or more sets of yarn or other material. It is one of the most ancient fundamental arts as indicated by archaeological evidence. The earliest literatures often mention the products of the loom. In primitive cultures the craft was practiced mainly by women. Although weaving sprang up independently in different parts of the world and was early known in Europe, its high development there in the Middle Ages was brought about by Eastern influences operating through Muslim and Byzantine channels of culture. Byzantium became a center of silk weaving in the 6th cent. In the 9th cent., Greece, Italy, and Spain became proficient. In Flanders a high degree of skill was attained by the 10th cent., especially in the weaving of wool. Flemish weavers brought to England by William the Conqueror and later by Queen Elizabeth I gave a great impetus to the craft there, and Lancashire became an important center. TAPESTRY weaving was brought to a high art in France. In colonial America weaving was a household industry allied with agriculture. The 18th-century weaving and spinning inventions marked the transition from the old era of domestic craftsmanship to the tremendous, organized industry of today. The factory system of machine weaving produces quantities of standardized material for mass consumption; the result is a loss of the distinctive elements of quality and design. Some of the finest silks, velvets, table linens, and carpets are still woven on handlooms. The first step in weaving is to stretch the warp, or longitudinal, yarns, which must be very strong. The weft, woof, or filling crosses the warp, binding the warp threads at either side to form the selvage. The three essential steps after the warp is stretched are: shedding, or raising every alternate warp yarn or set of yarns to receive the weft; picking, or inserting the weft; and battening, or pressing home the weft to make the fabric compact. In most primitive weaving these operations were performed by the hands alone, as in making rush mats and baskets. Gradually frames for holding the warp evenly stretched and devices for throwing the weft came into use (see LOOM). Woven fabrics are classified as to weave or structure according to the manner in which warp and weft cross each other. The three fundamental weaves, of which others are variations, are the plain, twill, and satin. In plain weave, also known as calico, tabby, taffeta, or homespun weaves, the weft passes over alternate warp threads, requiring two harnesses only. The relatively simple construction suits it to cheap fabrics, heavy yarns, and printed designs. Variations are produced by the use of groups of yarns, as in basket weave and monk's cloth, or by alternating fine and coarse yarns to make ribbed and corded fabrics, as the warp-ribbed Bedford cord, piqué, and dimity and the weft-ribbed poplin, rep, and grosgrain. The second primary weave, twill, shows a diagonal design made by causing weft threads to interlace two to four warp threads, moving a step to right or left on each pick and capable of variations, such as herringbone and corkscrew designs. Noted for their firm, close weave, twill fabrics include gabardine, serge, drill, and denim. Satin weave has floating or overshot warp threads on the surface which reflect light, giving a characteristic luster. When the uncrossed threads are in the weft, the weave is called sateen. Pile fabrics have an additional set of yarns drawn over wires to form loops, and may be cut or uncut. Warp-pile fabrics include terry and plush; weft-pile, velveteen and corduroy. In double-cloth weave two cloths are woven at once, each with its warp and filling threads, and combined by interlacing some yarns or by adding a fifth set. The cloth may be made for extra warmth or strength, to permit use of a cheaper back, or to produce a different pattern or weave on each surface, e.g., steamer rugs, heavy overcoating, and machine belting. Velvet is commonly woven as a double cloth. In swivel weaving, extra shuttles with a circular motion insert filling yarns to form simple decorations, such as the dots on swiss muslin. Figure weaves are made by causing warp and weft to intersect in varied groups. Simple geometric designs may be woven on machine looms by using a cam or a dobby attachment to operate the harnesses. For curves and large figures each heddle must be separately governed. The Jacquard loom attachment permits machine weaving of the most complicated designs. See M. E. Pritchard, *A Short Dictionary of Weaving* (1956); Anni Albers, *On Weaving* (1965); Herman Blum, *The Loom Has a Brain* (rev. ed. 1966); T. M. Nye, *Swedish Weaving* (1972); S. E. Held, *Weaving* (1973).

Webb, Beatrice Potter, 1858–1943, English socialist economist; daughter of a wealthy industrialist. She took an early interest in social problems and worked with Charles BOOTH on his survey of working life in London. Her *Cooperative Movement in Great Britain* was published in 1891. In 1892 she married **Sidney James Webb,** 1859–1947, a civil servant and a contributor to *Fabian Essays* (1890). Thereafter they worked together, complementing each other's qualities in an unusual partnership. They were of first importance in the FABIAN SOCIETY, in the building up of the British Labour party, and in the creation (1895) of the London School of Economics. In 1913 they founded the *New Statesman.* Most of the political and social reforms of their period owe much to their indefatigable research and political acumen. Together they produced *The History of Trade Unionism* (1894; rev. ed. extended to 1920, 1920), *Industrial Democracy* (1897), *English Local Government* (9 vol., 1906–29), *Consumers' Cooperative Movement* (1921), and *Soviet Communism: A New Civilization?* (2 vol., 1935). In 1922 Sidney Webb was elected to Parliament. He was president of the board of trade in the 1924 Labour government and secretary for the colonies from 1929 to 1931. In 1929 he was created Baron Passfield, a title his wife refused to share. See Beatrice Webb's autobiographical *My Apprenticeship* (1926) and *Our Partnership* (1948); her diaries (ed. by M. I. Cole, 2 vol., 1952–56); biographies by M. I. Cole (1945) and Kitty Muggeridge and Ruth Adam (1968); M. I. Cole, ed. *The Webbs and Their Work* (1949).

Webb, Mary (Meredith), 1881–1927, English novelist. Her native Shropshire is the scene of all her novels, which are somber, passionate, and infused with an intense feeling for the countryside. Although her work was little known in her lifetime, her literary reputation grew after her death. The emotional intensity of such novels as *Gone to Earth* (1917) and *Precious Bane* (1924) compensates for their lack of originality in plot and characterization. An anthology of her writings was published in 1940. See biographies by Hilda Addison (1931) and Thomas Moult (1932); study by D. P. H. Wrenn (1964).

Webb, Philip Speakman, 1831–1915, English architect. His influence, together with that of R. N. Shaw and W. E. Nesfield, established after the mid-19th cent. a revival of residential architecture based upon the Queen Anne and Georgian styles and upon the use of materials for their own artistic values. He became the assistant of G. E. Street, and he was an intimate friend of William Morris and a supporter of his aesthetic creeds. Webb's first commission was the historic Red House, Bexley Heath, built (1859) for Morris, in which the theories of both owner and architect received their practical crystallization. Its planning and specially designed furnishings led to the establishment (1861) of Morris's celebrated decorating business, the firm of Morris, Marshall, Faulkner, and Company, important in the development of the arts and crafts movement. Webb was one of the six members of this firm, and for it he designed furniture, tiles, and stained glass. Additional designs by Webb were Lord Carlisle's house, Kensington; and offices at Lincoln's Inn Fields. See study by W. R. Lethaby (1935).

Webb, Sidney James: see under WEBB, BEATRICE POTTER.

Webb, Walter Prescott, 1888–1963, U.S. historian, b. Panloa co., Texas. He joined the faculty of the history department at the Univ. of Texas in 1918, received his Ph.D. in 1932, and became full professor the following year. A distinguished scholar and teacher, Webb was Harkness lecturer in American history at the Univ. of London in 1938 and Harmsworth professor of American history at Oxford Univ. (1942–43). He became president of the Mississippi Valley Historical Association (1953) and the American Historical Association (1958). His works, which deal mainly with the history of the American West, include *The Great Plains* (1931), *The Texas Rangers* (1935, 2d ed. 1965), *Divided We Stand* (1937), *The Great Frontier* (1952), and *An Honest Preface and Other Essays* (1959). See biography by W. A. Owens (1969).

Weber, Carl Maria Friedrich Ernst von (frē'drĭkh ĕrnst fən vā'bər), 1786–1826, German composer and pianist; pupil of Michael Haydn and Abbé Vogler. He made his debut as a pianist at 13 and began to compose at about the same time. Weber enjoyed favor at court and became musical director and conductor of opera at Breslau (1804–6), Prague (1813–16), and Dresden (1816–26). He is considered the founder of German romantic opera, combining in his works strong nationalistic emotion with supernatural elements from German folklore. Of his 10 operas, *Der Freischütz* [the marksman] (1821) and *Oberon* (1826) were influential and continue to be performed. *Euryanthe* (1823) is without spoken dialogue and is thus a landmark in opera history. Weber's instrumental works, including *Invitation to the Dance* (1819), for piano, and the *Concertstück* (1821), for piano and orchestra, emphasize virtuoso technique. Nearly all of his nonoperatic works, including three Masses, incidental dramatic music, and many songs, have disappeared from the concert repertoire. See biographies by his son Max Maria von Weber (2 vol., 1965, repr. 1969), John Warrack (1968), and William Saunders (2d ed. 1969).

Weber, Ernst Heinrich (ĕrnst hīn'rĭkh), 1795–1878, German physiologist. He was a professor at the Univ. of Leipzig (1821–71) and is known for his work on touch and for the formulation of Weber's law—that the increase in stimulus necessary to produce an increase in sensation is not fixed but depends on the strength of the preceding stimulus. With his brother Eduard Friedrich Weber (1806–71) he discovered the inhibitory power of the vagus nerve (1845). With another brother, W. E. Weber, he made studies of acoustics and wave motion.

Weber, Joe: see WEBER AND FIELDS.

Weber, Max (māks), 1864–1920, German sociologist and political economist. At various times he taught at Berlin, Freiburg, Munich, and Heidelberg. One of Weber's chief interests was in developing a methodology for social science, and his works had a considerable influence on 20th-century social scientists. As a technique of sociological analysis, he devised the concept of "ideal types," generalized models of historical situations that could be used as a basis for comparing societies. He opposed the Marxian view that economics is the preeminent determining factor in social causation and instead stressed the plurality and interdependence of causes. Weber emphasized the role of religious values, ideologies, and charismatic leaders in shaping societies. In his *Protestant Ethic and the Spirit of Capitalism* (1920, tr. 1930) he developed a thesis concerning the intimate connection between the ascetic ideal fostered by Calvinism and the rise of capitalist institutions. A keen observer of politics in his own time, he first admired, then repudiated Otto von Bismarck, and he later advocated for Germany a democratic form of government somewhat on the American model. Among his other books are *Wirtschaft und Gesellschaft* [economy and society] (4th ed. 1956) and *General Economic History* (1924, tr. 1927). See *From Max Weber: Essays in Sociology* (with a biography and appraisal by H. H. Gerth and C. Wright Mills, 1946); studies by Julian Freund (1968), Arthur Mitzman (1969), W. G. Runciman (1972), David Beetham (1974), and W. J. Mommsen (1974).

Weber, Max (wĕb'ər), 1881–1961, American painter, b. Russia. At 10 he accompanied his family to Brooklyn, N.Y. He studied art at Pratt Institute and in 1905 went abroad. In Paris he studied under J. P. Laurens, later visiting Spain and Italy and returning to New York in 1909. Weber's work in the following decade was fauvist and then cubist inspired. Characteristic of the latter trend is his well-known *Chinese Restaurant* (Whitney Mus., New York City). He began to introduce Jewish subjects into his work c.1917. During the 1920s, Weber alternated painting with teaching. Contemporary and social themes were his subjects in the 1930s, when his work became increasingly abstract and revealed a new energetic use of line. Weber is represented in leading galleries throughout the United States. He is the author of several essays on art theory. See study by Lloyd Goodrich (1949).

Weber, Wilhelm Eduard (vĭl'hĕlm ā'dōōärt vā'bər), 1804–91, German physicist. He was professor (1831–37, 1849–91) at the Univ. of Göttingen, where he worked with C. F. GAUSS on terrestrial magnetism and devised an electromagnetic telegraph. He introduced the absolute system of electrical units. The coulomb was once known as the weber; now the weber is a magnetic unit. With a brother, E. H. WEBER, he wrote (1825) a book on wave motion; with another brother, E. F. Weber, he made a study of walking.

Weber (wē'bər), river, c.125 mi (200 km) long, rising in the Uinta Mts., N central Utah, and flowing north and northwest to join the Ogden River at Ogden. The combined stream flows to the Great Salt Lake. The Weber has long been used for irrigation and is now part of the U.S. Bureau of Reclamation's Weber basin project, which irrigates more than 80,000 acres (32,380 hectares) and provides water for industrial and municipal use. Among the dams on the Weber are Wanship Dam (completed 1957) and Echo Dam (completed 1931). Water is also diverted to the Provo River project.

weber (vā'bər, wē–, wĕb'ər), abbr. Wb, unit of magnetic FLUX in the MKS SYSTEM of weights and measures; 1 Wb is equal to 1 volt-second. The weber per square meter, recently named the tesla (abbr. T), is the unit of magnetic flux density, which is a measure of the strength of a magnetic field in a given region. See ELECTRIC AND MAGNETIC UNITS.

Weber and Fields (wĕb'ər), American comedy team. The partners were Joe Weber (Joseph Maurice Weber), 1867–1942, and Lew Fields (Lewis Maurice Schanfield), 1867–1941, both born in New York City. At the age of eight they were performing together on the Bowery, and shortly afterward they began their professional career. Appearing in beards, loud checked clothes, and low-crown derbies, they were beloved by millions and became the prototypes of future comedy teams. Fields was tall and aggressive, while Weber was short and the brunt of the jokes. They were noted for their slapstick antics, their dialect jokes, and their burlesques of popular plays. They opened and managed Weber and Fields Music Hall on Broadway (1896–1904), where they presented many of the leading stars of the time. A quarrel separated them in 1904, but they resumed their partnership in 1912. Both went into semiretirement after 1930.

Webern, Anton von (än'tōn fən vā'bərn), 1883–1945, Austrian composer and conductor; pupil of Arnold Schoenberg. He conducted theater orchestras in Prague and in various German cities until 1918, devoting himself thereafter to composition and teaching. His first composition, a passacaglia for orchestra (1908), which showed the postromantic influence of Mahler, gave no hint of the exclusive use of the 12-tone technique (see ATONALITY) of Schoenberg that was to characterize the rest of his output. In his relatively few works, mostly for small chamber combinations or for voice, he reduced music to its barest essentials, depriving it of traditional harmonic concepts. He concentrated many fragmented musical events, ordered by intricate contrapuntal, rhythmic, and dynamic patterns, into extremely contracted time spans. For example, 6 *Bagatelles* (1913) for string quartet are to be played in 3 minutes, 37 seconds, and the whole of *Five Pieces for Orchestra* (1911–13) contains only 76 measures. In later works, such as *Variations* (1940) for orchestra, he strove for total variation, the opposite of traditional developmental technique. His individual style was both poetic and intensely expressive, and his music is increasingly influential, although it remains outside the popular taste. Webern was accidentally killed by a sentry during the American occupation of Germany. See his letters, ed. by Josef Polnauer (tr. 1967); his *The Path to the New Music,* ed. by Willi Reich (tr. 1963); biography by Friederich Wildgans (tr. 1966); study by René Leibowitz (tr. 1949, repr. 1970).

Webster, Daniel, 1782–1852, American statesman, lawyer, and orator, b. Salisbury (now in Franklin), N.H. He graduated (1801) from Dartmouth College, studied law, and, after an interval as a schoolmaster, was admitted (1805) to the bar. Webster practiced law at Boscawen and Portsmouth, N.H., and rapidly gravitated toward politics. As a Federalist and a defender of the New England shipping interests, he sat (1813–17) in the U.S. House of Representatives, where he opposed James Madison's administration, although he did not join forces with members of the HARTFORD CONVENTION. In 1816 he transferred his residence to Boston. Before he was returned (1822) to the House, Webster won fame as a lawyer, defending (1819) his alma mater in the DARTMOUTH COLLEGE CASE and the Bank of the United States in MCCULLOCH VS. MARYLAND. Again in Congress (1823–27), Webster began to gain repute as one of the greatest orators of his time; his brilliant speeches in the House were matched by his eloquent public addresses—notably the Plymouth address (1820), the Bunker Hill oration (1825), and the speech (1826) on the deaths of Thomas Jefferson and John Adams. As a U.S. Senator from Massachusetts (1827–41), he became a leading political figure of the United States. The dominant interest of his constituency had changed from shipping to industry, so Webster now abandoned his earlier free-trade views and supported the tariff of 1828. In the states' rights controversy that followed he took a strong pro-Union stand, defending the supremacy of the Union in the famous debate with Robert Y. HAYNE in 1830. Although Webster supported President Jackson in the nullification crisis, he vehemently opposed him on most issues, especially those concerning financial policy. He became a leader of the WHIG PARTY and in 1836 was put forward as a presidential candidate by the Whig groups in New England. However, he won only the electoral votes of Massachusetts. His prominence brought him into consideration in later presidential elections, but he never attained his ambition. After William Henry HARRISON was elected (1840) President on the Whig ticket, Webster was appointed (1841) U.S. Secretary of State. Although every other cabinet officer resigned (1841) after John TYLER had succeeded to the presidency and had broken with the Whig leaders, Webster remained at his post until he had completed the settlement of the WEBSTER-ASHBURTON TREATY (1843). Again (1845-50) in the Senate, Webster opposed the annexation of Texas and war with Mexico and faced the rising tide of sectionalism with his customary stand: Slavery was an evil, but disunion was a greater one. He steadily lost his following and was sorely disappointed when the Whig party nominated Zachary Taylor for President in 1848. Cherishing the preservation of the Union above his own popularity, Webster, in one of his most eloquent and reasoned speeches, backed the COMPROMISE OF 1850 and was reviled by antislavery groups in the North and by members of his own party. He served again (1850-52) as Secretary of State under President Millard Fillmore. His writings were edited by J. W. McIntyre (18 vol., 1903). See biographies by G. T. Curtis (1869), C. M. Fuess (1930, repr. 1968), J. B. McMaster (1939), and R. N. Current (1955); N. D. Brown, *Daniel Webster and the Politics of Availability* (1969); R. F. Dalzell, *Daniel Webster and the Trial of American Nationalism, 1843-1852* (1972); Sydney Nathans, *Daniel Webster and Jacksonian Democracy* (1973). The diary kept by his second wife, Caroline Le Roy Webster, was published as *Mr. W. & I* (1942).

Webster, John, 1580?-1634, English dramatist, b. London. Although little is known of his life, there is evidence that he worked for Philip HENSLOWE, collaborating with such playwrights as Dekker and Ford. Webster's literary reputation rests almost entirely on his two great tragedies, *The White Devil* (c.1608) and *The Duchess of Malfi* (c.1614). Both plays treat the theme of revenge and generate a brooding, somber mood. Despite the fact that the plays often degenerate into sensationalism, Webster's highly graphic language and profound understanding of human suffering create a true tragic pathos and force. See his works (ed. by F. L. Lucas, 4 vol., 1927); studies by Clifford Leech (1951, repr. 1970), Ralph Berry (1972), and R. F. Whitman (1973).

Webster, Margaret, 1905-72, American actress, producer, and director, b. New York City; daughter of Ben Webster and Dame May WHITTY. Webster made her formal acting debut in 1924. After working with several English companies, including the Old Vic (1929-30), she returned to the United States and began (1935) an outstanding career as director and producer. In 1946, together with Eva LE GALLIENNE, she founded and managed the American Repertory Theatre, and from 1948 to 1951 she directed the Margaret Webster Shakespeare Company. Webster directed several operas and notable presentations of Shakespeare in England. She wrote *Shakespeare Without Tears* (1942), *Shakespeare Today* (1957), and the autobiographical *The Same Only Different* (1969) and *Don't Put Your Daughter on the Stage* (1972).

Webster, Noah, 1758-1843, American lexicographer and philologist, b. West Hartford, Conn., grad. Yale, 1778. After serving in the American Revolution, Webster was admitted to the bar in 1781 and practiced law in Hartford. His *Grammatical Institute of the English Language,* in three parts, speller, grammar, and reader (1783-85), was the first of a list of publications which made him for many years the chief American authority on English. The first part, often revised, was his famous *Elementary Spelling Book,* or "Blue-backed Speller," with which he helped to standardize American spelling. Pioneer families on the frontiers taught their children to read from it; in the schools it was a basic textbook, and in settlements and villages its lists were read out for lively spelling matches. By 1850, when the total population of the United States was less than 23,200,000, the annual sales of Webster's spelling book were about 1,000,000 copies, and the figures increased yearly. The difficulty of copyrighting his works in 13 states led Webster to agitate for many years for a national copyright law; it was passed in 1790. An active Federalist, he became a pamphleteer for centralized government and wrote his *Sketches of American Policy* (1785), proposing the adoption of a constitution. In 1793 he left Hartford to support Washington's administration by editing the newspaper *American Minerva* (later the *Commercial Advertiser*) in New York; he was also editor, at various times, of several magazines. Webster wrote scholarly studies on a great diversity of subjects, including epidemic diseases, mythology, meteors, and the relationship of European and Asian languages. During most of his later life he lived in New Haven, Conn., and Amherst, Mass., and was a member of the first board of trustees of Amherst College. Deriving his income from his schoolbooks, he devoted most of the rest of his life to compiling dictionaries. After his *Compendious Dictionary* was published in 1806, he worked on another, *The American Dictionary of the English Language* (1828), which included definitions of 70,000 words, of which 12,000 had not appeared in such a work before. Its definitions were excellent, and the dictionary's sales reached 300,000 annually. This work, Webster's foremost achievement, helped to standardize American pronunciation. Webster completed the revision of 1840, and the dictionary, revised many times, has retained its popularity. See also DICTIONARY. See his letters, ed. by H. R. Warfel (1953); biographies by H. R. Warfel (1936) and H. E. Scudder (6th ed. 1971); Emily Skeel, *A Bibliography of the Writings of Noah Webster* (ed. by E. H. Carpenter, Jr., 1958).

Webster, Pelatiah, 1726-95, American writer, b. Lebanon, Conn., grad. Yale, 1746. A Philadelphia businessman, he is remembered for his advocacy in his *Dissertation of the Political Union and Constitution of the Thirteen United States of North America* (1783) of a revision of the Articles of Confederation by creating a new constitution. He was a Federalist in the fight for ratification of the Constitution, and his able arguments, based on historical and economic principles, were of great weight. He also wrote many books on economics.

Webster, Richard Everard: see ALVERSTONE, RICHARD EVERARD WEBSTER, 1ST VISCOUNT.

Webster, town (1970 pop. 14,917), Worcester co., S Mass., near the Conn. line; settled c.1713, set off from Dudley and Oxford and inc. 1832. The chief manufactures are footwear, fabrics, and textiles. Webster was named for Daniel Webster and became a textile center in the early 19th cent. through the efforts of Samuel Slater, a pioneer in the U.S. textile industry.

Webster-Ashburton Treaty, Aug., 1842, agreement concluded by the United States, represented by Secretary of State Daniel Webster, and Great Britain, represented by Alexander Baring, 1st Baron Ashburton. The treaty settled the NORTHEAST BOUNDARY DISPUTE, which had caused serious conflicts, such as the AROOSTOOK WAR. Over 7,000 sq mi (18,100 sq km) of the disputed area, including the Aroostook valley, were given to the United States, and several waterways, including the St. Johns River, were opened to free navigation by both countries. The Webster-Ashburton Treaty also settled the disputed position of the U.S.-Canada border in the Great Lakes region. Other clauses provided for cooperation in the suppression of the slave trade and for mutual extradition of criminals. Some disputes between the United States and Britain, notably the one concerning the Oregon boundary, were ignored. The treaty, however, served as a precedent in peaceful settlements of disputes between the two countries. See H. S. Burrage, *Maine in the Northeastern Boundary Dispute* (1919).

Webster Groves, city (1970 pop. 27,455), St. Louis co., E Mo., a residential suburb of St. Louis; inc. 1896. It is the seat of Webster College and Eden Theological Seminary.

Wechsler Adult Intelligence Scale (WAIS): see PSYCHOLOGICAL TESTS.

Weddell Sea (wĕd'əl), arm of the Atlantic Ocean, W Antarctica, SE of South America, bordered by the Antarctic Peninsula and Coats Land. The vast Ronne and Filchner ice shelves are at the head of the sea. Named for James Weddell, a British navigator who claimed to have discovered the sea in 1823, it was investigated by the British explorer William Bruce from 1902 to 1904 and was studied most fully during the International Geophysical Year (1957-58).

Wedekind, Frank (frängk vā'dəkĭnt), 1864-1918, German dramatist. He was also a journalist and publicist, and he worked on the staff of *Simplicissimus.* A forerunner of the expressionists, he employed grotesque fantasy and unconventional characters in order to attack the bourgeois ideals and hypocrisy of his society. Wedekind was particularly concerned with sexual themes, stressing the primacy of man's instincts. His plays include *Frühlings Erwachen* (1891, tr. *The Awakening of Spring,* 1909), *Der Erdgeist* (1895, tr. *Earth Spirit,* 1914), and *Die Büchse der Pandora* (1903, tr. *Pandora's Box,* 1918). Alban Berg compiled the libretto for his opera *Lulu* (1934) from the latter two. See study by Sol Gittleman (1969).

Wedemeyer, Albert Coady (wĕd'ĕmī"ər), 1897-, American general, b. Omaha, Nebr., grad. West Point, 1918. After service in China, the Philippines, and Europe, he was graduated (1936) from the general staff school at Fort Leavenworth, Kansas, and was sent to the German general staff school. In World War II he was (1941-43) a member of the war plans division of the general staff and in 1944 was named to succeed Joseph Stilwell as commander of the U.S. forces in China. Promoted (1945) to lieutenant general, Wedemeyer made (1947) a survey of China and Korea for President Harry S. Truman and was named (1949) commander of the U.S. 6th Army. He retired from active service in 1951. Wedemeyer became a business executive and was an active anti-Communist. See his *Wedemeyer Reports!* (1958).

wedge, piece of wood or metal thick at one end and sloping to a thin edge at the other; an application of the INCLINED PLANE. It is employed in separating two objects from each other or in separating one part of a solid object from an adjoining part, as in splitting wood. The thin edge is applied to the surface of the solid or to the crack between two solids, and force is applied to the opposite thick edge. The ax, chisel, knife, nail, and carpenter's plane are wedges, and the CAM is a rotating wedge.

Wedgwood, Cicely Veronica, 1910-, English historian. She was educated privately and at Oxford (B.A., 1931). She has written prolifically on the period of the English civil war, her works including *Strafford* (1935; rev. ed. as *Thomas Wentworth,* 1961), *Oliver Cromwell* (1939, rev. ed. 1973), *Montrose* (1952), *The King's Peace* (1955) and *The King's War* (1958), and *A Coffin for King Charles* (1964). She is also the author of *William the Silent* (1944) and *Milton and His World* (1969). A member of the Institute of Advanced Studies at Princeton (1953-68) and an honorary fellow of Lady Margaret Hall, Oxford, from 1962, she was created a dame of the British Empire in 1968.

Wedgwood, Josiah, 1730-95, English potter, descendant of a family of Staffordshire potters and perhaps the greatest of all potters. At the age of nine he went to work in the plant of his brother Thomas in Burslem, and in 1751, with a partner, he started in business. In 1753 he joined Thomas Whieldon of Fenton, then one of the foremost potters of Staffordshire. In 1759, Wedgwood started his own business at the Ivy House Works, Burslem. He obtained a site near Stoke-on-Trent, where he built a village, Etruria, for his workmen and opened a new works in 1769. In that year he took into partnership Thomas Bentley, who remained a valuable ally until his death in 1780. At Etruria, Wedgwood specialized in ornamental products to supplement the utilitarian wares of Burslem. Wedgwood entered the field of pottery at a time when it was still a backward and minor industry and by his skill, taste, and organizing abilities transformed it into one of great importance. He combined with experiments in his art an interest in improved roads, canals, schools, and living conditions for the workmen. He soon acquired a reputation for his cream-colored earthenware, known as queen's ware, and at the same time produced decorative objects, candlesticks, and vases of a black composition known as basalt or Egyptian stoneware. He also produced a mottled and veined ware in imitation of granite and a translucent, smooth, unglazed semiporcelain, which gave way to his most notable product, jasper ware (best known in a delicate blue with Greek figures in white embossed upon it; see PORTLAND VASE). He invented and perfected this ware and in it gave expression to the interest of his day in the revival of classical art. He employed the best talent available for his finer pieces, many of which were designed by John Flaxman. His terra-cottas of various hues were made with one color in relief upon another. Wedgwood made a dinner service for Catherine the Great. His work is found in many museums and private collections; the Fogg Museum of Art, Cambridge, Mass., has a collection. He published several pamphlets, and his *Address to the Young Inhabitants of the Pottery* appeared in 1783. For his invention of a pyrometer for measuring temperatures Wedgwood was made a fellow of the Royal Society (1783). The extensive potteries he established have been perpetuated by his descendants. See Wolf Mankowitz, *Wedgwood* (1953); Alison Kelly, *The Story of Wedg-*

wood (1962); Eliza Meteyard, *The Life of Josiah Wedgwood* (1865, repr. 1970).

Wednesday: see WEEK.

Weed, Thurlow (thûr'lō), 1797–1882, American journalist and political leader, b. Cairo, N.Y. After working on various newspapers in W New York, Weed joined the Rochester *Telegraph* and was influential as a supporter of John Quincy Adams. For a short time he published the *Anti-Masonic Enquirer* and as a leader of the ANTI-MASONIC PARTY opposed Martin Van Buren. He wielded much political influence as editor of the Albany *Evening Journal* after 1830 and was a staunch opponent of the ALBANY REGENCY. Becoming a Whig, Weed in 1840 helped secure the election of William H. Harrison as President. In 1844 he helped bring about the presidential nomination of Henry Clay, and in 1848 he backed Zachary Taylor. Though paying lip service to various reforms, notably the abolition of slavery, Weed was more at home with the problems of patronage and lobbying and came to be regarded as the silent boss of the Whig party. After the Whig party disintegrated over the slavery issue, Weed joined (1855) the new Republican party and worked in close cooperation with William H. SEWARD. Seward was his close personal friend as well as political ally, and Weed carefully shepherded Seward's career as state legislator, governor of New York, and U.S. Senator. He failed, however, to secure for Seward the Republican presidential nomination in 1860. Both Weed and Seward nevertheless came to be President Lincoln's staunch supporters. During the Civil War, Weed went on a special diplomatic mission to France and England. His political power in the Republican party was destroyed by his support of the Reconstruction policies of Andrew Johnson in 1866, and he was never again able to exert great political influence. His travels were turned to account in his *Letters From Europe and the West Indies* (1866). See *The Life of Thurlow Weed* (2 vol., 1883–84, including his autobiography and a memoir by his grandson); biography by G. G. Van Deusen (1947, repr. 1969).

weed, common term for any wild plant, particularly an undesired plant, growing in cultivated ground, where it competes with crop plants for soil nutrients and water. In their natural habitat, wild flowers and herbs not only provide beauty but function in many useful ways, e.g., as a source of food for insects and animals and to enrich the earth, loosen hard-packed soils, and help prevent erosion. However, when they invade cultivated areas they often interfere with the desired crop by appropriating space, sunlight, moisture, and soil chemicals. Weeds may also harbor and spread insect and fungus pests. Dried weeds along roadsides are often the starting point for brush and forest fires. Their habits of growth and of propagation must be considered in attempting to eradicate them. Control methods include continual soil cultivation, blanketing the soil with some material (e.g., mulch) to thwart weed growth, and the use of various herbicides (see SPRAYING). A growth-regulating chemical called 2,4-D (dichloro-phenoxyacetic acid) has the effect of telescoping the life cycle of most broad-leaved plants (which include many weeds) but has no effect on narrow-leaved plants and is therefore applied to lawns and grainfields. Plants which are cultivated in one region may become weeds when introduced in another, e.g., the oxeye daisy, imported to the United States from Europe; the Russian thistle, called tumbleweed in America; and burdock, which in Japan is grown as a vegetable. Crabgrass and ragweed are weeds well known to gardeners and to hay-fever sufferers. See T. J. Muzik, *Weed Biology and Control* (1970); R. E. Wilkinson and H. E. Jaques, *How to Know the Weeds* (2d ed. 1973).

weed killer: see HERBICIDE.

Weehawken (wē'hôkən, wēhô'kən), township (1970 pop. 12,958), Hudson co., NE N.J., on the Hudson River opposite New York City, with which it is connected by the Lincoln Tunnel; inc. 1859. It has railroad shops and varied industries. "Highwood," the James Gore King estate, was the scene in 1804 of the duel between Aaron Burr and Alexander Hamilton. A bronze bust commemorates Hamilton, who was fatally wounded.

week, period of time shorter than the month, commonly seven days. The ancient Egyptians used a 10-day period, as did the French under the short-lived FRENCH REVOLUTIONARY CALENDAR. In many regions a four-day to eight-day market week is based on the recurrence of market days; the early Romans observed an eight-day market week. This period also corresponds roughly with the moon's quarter phases, which come every 7 or 8 days. The seven-day week is said to have originated in ancient times in W Asia, probably in Mesopotamia. This is thought to have been a planetary week predicated on the astrological concept of the influence of the planets, which were long erroneously believed to be seven celestial bodies revolving around the earth; these were the sun and moon and five of the bodies recognized today as planets—Mars, Mercury, Jupiter, Venus, and Saturn. The Hebrew week is based chiefly on the religious observance of the SABBATH, which comes every seventh day and is usually associated with the seventh day of creation, when the Lord rested from his labors. The Christian week and the Muslim week were probably derived chiefly from the Hebrew week, although the weekly holy days are different (Hebrew, Sabbath, seventh day; Christian, Sunday, first day; Muslim, Friday, sixth day). The influence of the weeks of Chaldaeans, Christians, and Jews slowly made itself felt in the Roman Empire, and elements of the systems were probably merged. The planetary week was at first preeminent, and the use of planetary names, based on names of pagan deities, continued even after Constantine (c.321) made the Christian week, beginning on Sunday, official in the civil calendar. The Roman names for the days of the week pervaded Western Europe; in most languages the forms are translations from Latin or attempts to assign corresponding names of divinities. The Latin names, their translations, the English equivalents, and their derivations follow: *dies solis* [sun's day], Sunday; *dies lunae* [moon's day], Monday [moonday]; *dies Martis* [Mars' day], Tuesday [Tiw's day]; *dies Mercurii* [Mercury's day], Wednesday [Woden's day]; *dies Jovis* [Jove's or Jupiter's day], Thursday [Thor's day]; *dies Veneris* [Venus' day], Friday [Frigg's day]; and *dies Saturni* [Saturn's day], Saturday.

Weeks, Feast of: see SHAVUOT.

Weelkes, Thomas, c.1575–1623, English composer. His four books of madrigals (1597–1600) mark Weelkes as one of the great English madrigalists. His music is remarkable for melodic characterization and innovative use of chromatic harmonic progressions. *The Triumphs of Oriana* contains his popular "As Vesta was from Latmos hill descending." In 1602, Weelkes became organist of Chichester Cathedral. Of his 10 church services that survive in fragments, all are of interest for their original treatment of the liturgy. He also wrote anthems and a few instrumental works. See study by David Brown (1969).

Weems, Mason Locke, 1759–1825, American author and preacher, b. Anne Arundel co., Md., studied theology in London. He was ordained in 1784 and served various Episcopal parishes. For 30 years after 1794 he was a traveling agent for Mathew Carey, bookseller and publisher. Parson Weems is chiefly known for *The Life and Memorable Actions of George Washington* (c.1800), in the fifth edition of which appears the famous cherry-tree story. He fictionalized this and other biographies he wrote to increase their interest. Weems also wrote moralistic tracts, such as *The Drunkard's Looking Glass* (1812). See biography by Harold Kellock (1928, repr. 1971).

Weenix, Jan Baptist (yän bäptĭst' vā'nĭks), 1621–63, Dutch painter and engraver. About 1649 he settled in Utrecht, becoming in the same year the master of the painters' guild there. Weenix excelled in painting pastoral scenes, with ruins and shepherds or shepherdesses and their flocks. He also painted seaports, portraits, and genre scenes. Examples of his work are in many European galleries. The Metropolitan Museum has his *Italian Seaport.* His son and pupil, **Jan Weenix,** c.1640–1719, began as a painter of seaports in the manner of his father, but later became known for his fine animal paintings, hunting scenes, and studies of dead game; many are now in European museums. The Metropolitan Museum has a study of fruit.

weevil, common name for certain BEETLES of the snout beetle family (Curculionidae), small, usually dull-colored, hard-bodied insects. The mouthparts of snout beetles are modified into down-curved snouts, or beaks, adapted for boring into plants; the jaws are at the end of the snout. The bent antennae usually project from the middle of the snout. The largest weevils are about 3 in. (7.6 cm) long, with the average length being about 1/4 in. (0.6 mm). The snout varies greatly in length among the different species; in the CURCULIOS, or nut weevils, it may be longer than the body. Different weevil species attack different parts of plants—fruits, seeds, leaves, stems, or roots. In most species the female lays her eggs inside the plant tissue, on which the growing larvae feed. The granary weevil and rice weevil are serious pests of stored cereal grains. The thousands of other destructive weevil species include the sweet-potato, vegetable, alfalfa, clover leaf, strawberry, and pine weevils, as well as the cotton BOLL WEEVIL, the most serious weevil pest in the United States. The seed weevils, including the BEAN WEEVIL, are not true weevils, but boring beetles of another family; they feed on leguminous crops, such as peas and beans. Weevils cause millions of dollars' worth of damage annually. The bark beetles, or engraver beetles, are related to the weevils. True weevils are classified in the phylum ARTHROPODA, class Insecta, order Coleoptera, family Curculionidae.

weft: see WEAVING.

Wegener, Alfred Lothar (äl'frĕt lōtär' vĕg'ənər), 1880–1930, German geologist, meteorologist, and arctic explorer. He was professor of meteorology at the Univ. of Graz from 1924. He is known for his theory of CONTINENTAL DRIFT, set forth in his *Die Entstehung der Kontinente und Ozeane* (1915; tr. *The Origin of Continents and Oceans,* 1924). He is also known for his expeditions to Greenland (on the last of which he lost his life) to establish meteorological stations and to ascertain the thickness of the icecap and the rate of drift of Greenland. See the account of his last expedition, *Greenland Journey* (ed. by Else Wegener and F. P. Loewe, tr. 1939); Johannes Georgi, *Mid-Ice* (tr. 1934).

Wei, dynasty of China: see THREE KINGDOMS.

Wei (wā), river, c.450 mi (720 km) long, rising in W Kansu prov. and flowing E through Kansu and Shensi provs. to the Huang Ho. Its wide, alluvial valley was the site of some of the earliest centers of Chinese civilization (such as the Chou dynasty, 1122–255 B.C.) and is now the agricultural and population center of Shensi prov. Cotton, wheat, millet, and fruits are extensively grown. The Wei is navigable below Hsi-an, the capital of Shansi; Pao-chi is also on the river.

Weidenreich, Franz (vī'dĕnrīkh), 1873–1948, German anatomist and physical anthropologist. He was educated at the universities of Munich, Kiel, Berlin, and Strasbourg. In 1921 he became professor of anatomy at the Univ. of Heidelberg; his work there stimulated his interest in anthropology and laid the groundwork for his later achievements in that field. Weidenreich was (1928–35) professor of anthropology at the Univ. of Frankfurt and worked (1935) on the excavation and study of Sinanthropus fossils from caves near Peking, China. Later he was associated with the American Museum of Natural History, New York City. He is known for his descriptions of Peking Man (*Sinanthropus pekinensis*) in 1943 and of Solo Man (*Homo soloensis*) in 1948. His most famous work, *The Skull of Sinanthropus Pekinensis,* was published by the Geological Survey of China in 1943.

Weidman, Charles, 1901–, American modern dancer and choreographer, b. Lincoln, Neb. Weidman performed with the troupe formed by Ruth ST. DENIS and Ted Shawn from 1920 to 1927, when he and Doris HUMPHREY left to form their own company and school. He created many dances that combined abstract movement with gestures based on his own brilliant mime technique. After starting his own company and school in 1945, Weidman continued to teach and perform. In 1960 he established the Expression of the Two Arts Theater in New York City with the graphic artist Mikhail Santaro. Weidman's most renowned pupils include José Limón.

Weierstrass, Karl Wilhelm Theodor (kärl vĭl'hĕlm tā'ōdōr vī'ərshträs), 1815–97, German mathematician. From 1864 he was professor of mathematics at the Univ. of Berlin. His development of the modern theory of functions is described in his *Abhandlungen aus der Funktionenlehre* (1886), which was compiled largely from the lecture notes of his students. He was one of those chiefly responsible for the modern, rigorous approach to ANALYSIS and NUMBER THEORY, and he did much to clarify the foundations of these subjects. He demonstrated (1871) a function that is continuous throughout an interval but that possesses no derivative anywhere in the interval. See E. T. Bell, *Men of Mathematics* (1937).

weigela or **weigelia:** see HONEYSUCKLE.

weighing machine: see BALANCE; SCALE.

weight, measure of the force of gravity on a body (see GRAVITATION). Since the weights of different bodies at the same location are proportional to their masses, weight is often used as a measure of MASS. However, the two are not the same; mass is a measure of the amount of matter present in a body and thus has the same value at different locations, and weight varies depending upon the location of the body in the earth's gravitational field (or the gravitational field of some other astronomical body). A given body will have the same mass on the earth and on the moon, but its weight on the moon will be only about 16% of the weight as measured on the earth. The distinction between weight and mass is further confused by the use of the same units to measure both—the pound, the gram, or the kilogram. One pound of weight, or force, is the force necessary at a given location to accelerate a one-pound mass at a rate equal to the acceleration of gravity at that location (about 32 ft per sec per sec). Similar relationships hold between the gram of force and the gram of mass and between the kilogram of force and the kilogram of mass.

weight-average molecular weight: see MOLECULAR WEIGHT.

weightlessness, the absence of any observable effects of GRAVITATION. This condition is experienced by an observer when he and his immediate surroundings are allowed to move freely in the local gravitational FIELD. All bodies in the weightless environment experience the same acceleration. The more massive bodies (see MASS) in the surroundings experience a stronger gravitational force, but they also have more INERTIA, or resistance to acceleration. As seen by a stationary outside observer, they appear to move together without any constraint. To the observer being accelerated, objects appear to float freely in space and to move with uniform speed in a straight line when given a push. Within a weightless environment, the force of gravitation acting on each object is exactly cancelled by an equal and opposite inertial force arising from the common acceleration. Such forces are called fictitious because they have no external physical origin but are simply consequences of an accelerated state of motion. Three examples of situations where weightlessness is encountered are: (1) an elevator falling freely in a vacuum; (2) a space capsule orbiting the earth; (3) a spacecraft drifting in outer space with its engines off. In the second example, the fictitious inertial force is directed radially outward from the earth and is called the centrifugal force (see CENTRIPETAL FORCE AND CENTRIFUGAL FORCE).

weight lifting, international sport and training technique for athletes in other sports. From the earliest times men have lifted weights as a test of strength. Long popular as a competitive sport in Europe, Egypt, Turkey, and Japan, weight lifting became increasingly popular in the United States after 1900. Meets are conducted according to weight classes: flyweight, bantamweight, featherweight, lightweight, middleweight, light heavyweight, middle heavyweight, heavyweight, and super heavyweight. The man who lifts the greatest total of weights using three standard lifts—two-hand or military press, clean-and-jerk, and snatch—wins. The two-hand press involves lifting the weight from the floor, resting it on the chest, and then lifting it above the body while holding a straight military stance. The clean-and-jerk is similar except that the weight is lifted from the chest at a signal from the referee and there is no need for a military position. In the snatch, contestants use one continuous movement to lift the weight from the floor to a position as high above the head as possible. Although a limited Olympic sport previously, weight lifting has been a regular part of the Olympic program since 1920. The Soviet Union and other E European nations excel in international weight lifting. See Alexander Murray, *Modern Weight-Training* (2d ed. 1971).

weights and measures, units and standards for expressing the amount of some quantity, such as length, capacity, or weight; the science of MEASUREMENT standards and methods is known as metrology. Crude systems of weights and measures probably date from prehistoric times. Early units were commonly based on body measurements and on plant seeds or other objects from agriculture. As civilization progressed, technological and commercial requirements led to increased standardization. For example, because the length of the human foot or the width of the palm varies from individual to individual, it probably became necessary first to specify a particular individual (e.g., the king) and later to reproduce standards based on this commonly accepted unit of length. Units were usually fixed by edict of local or national rulers and were subdivided and multiplied or otherwise arranged into systems of measurement. Standards varied greatly in different localities, although conquest and trade stimulated some correspondence between systems, e.g., between the systems of Egypt, Babylon, and Phoenicia. A high degree of standardization was achieved in the Roman Empire, but after its fall considerable diversity returned. The foot, which was one of the earliest units, is believed to have had as many as 280 variants in Europe as late as the 18th cent. Today the chief systems are the ENGLISH UNITS OF MEASUREMENT and the METRIC SYSTEM. The United States is one of the few countries still using the former system; all other major nations have either converted to the latter or committed themselves to conversion. The English system is much older and less practical than the metric system, and in the United States there has been considerable discussion in favor of adopting the metric system as the principal system. However, attempts to legislate such a change in the U.S. Congress have failed. The basic units of the English system, the YARD of length and the pound of mass, are now defined in terms of the metric standards, the METER of length and the KILOGRAM of mass. Before 1960 the meter was defined as the distance between two scratches on a prototype bar kept at the International Bureau of Weights and Measures (est. 1875) at Sèvres, France, near Paris. In 1960 it was redefined in terms of an atomic standard. This new standard is more stable than the old meter bar, is indestructible, and is easily reproduced, eliminating the need for periodic comparison with a single standard. The kilogram is defined in terms of a prototype cylinder kept at the bureau. In the United States, Congress has the constitutional right to fix standards, but except for purposes of customs and internal revenue, weights and measures legislation has been, for the most part, permissive. Sets of official weights and measures were sent to the states in 1856, but legisla-

COMMON WEIGHTS AND MEASURES

LENGTH	AREA
Metric system	*Metric system*
1 millimeter=1/1,000 meter	1 square centimeter=1/10,000 square meter
1 centimeter=1/100 meter	1 square decimeter=1/100 square meter
1 decimeter=1/10 meter	1 square meter (basic unit of area)
1 meter (basic unit of length)	1 are=100 square meters
1 dekameter=10 meters	1 hectare=10,000 square meters=100 ares
1 kilometer=1,000 meters	1 square kilometer=1,000,000 square meters
American and British units	*American and British units*
1 inch=1/36 yard=1/12 foot	1 square inch=1/1,296 square yard=1/144 square foot
1 foot=1/3 yard	1 square foot=1/9 square yard
1 yard (basic unit of length)	1 square yard (basic unit of area)
1 rod=5½ yards	1 square rod=30¼ square yards
1 furlong=220 yards=40 rods	1 acre=4,840 square yards=160 square rods
1 mile=1,760 yards=5,280 feet	1 square mile=3,097,600 square yards=640 acres
Conversion factors	*Conversion factors*
1 centimeter=0.39 inch	1 square centimeter=0.155 square inch
1 inch=2.54 centimeters	1 square inch=6.45 square centimeters
1 meter=39.37 inches	1 acre=0.405 hectare
1 foot=0.305 meter	1 hectare= 2.47 acres
1 meter=3.28 feet	1 square kilometer=0.386 square mile
1 yard=0.914 meter	1 square mile=2.59 square kilometers
1 meter=1.094 yards	
1 kilometer=0.62 mile	
1 mile=1.609 kilometers	

VOLUME AND CAPACITY (LIQUID AND DRY)	WEIGHT (MASS)
Metric system	*Metric system*
I cubic centimeter=1/1,000,000 cubic meter	1 milligram=1/1,000,000 kilogram=1/1,000 gram
1 cubic decimeter=1/1,000 cubic meter	1 centigram=1/100,000 kilogram=1/100 gram
1 cubic meter=1 stere (basic unit of volume)	1 decigram=1/10,000 kilogram=1/10 gram
1 milliliter=1/1,000 liter=1 cubic centimeter	1 gram=1/1,000 kilogram
1 centiliter=1/100 liter	1 dekagram=1/100 kilogram=10 grams
1 deciliter=1/10 liter	1 hectogram=1/10 kilogram=100 grams
1 liter=1 cubic decimeter (basic unit of capacity)	1 kilogram (basic unit of weight or mass)
1 dekaliter=10 liters	1 metric ton=1,000 kilograms
1 hectoliter=100 liters=1/10 cubic meter	
American and British units	*American and British units: avoirdupois*
1 cubic inch=1/46,656 cubic yard=1/1,728 cubic foot	1 grain=1/7,000 pound=1/437.5 ounce
1 cubic foot=1/27 cubic yard	1 dram=1/256 pound=1/16 ounce
1 cubic yard (basic unit of volume)	1 ounce=1/16 pound
1 U.S. fluid ounce=1/128 U.S. gallon=1/16 U.S. pint	1 pound (basic unit of weight or mass)
1 British imperial fluid ounce=1/160 imperial gallon=1/20 imperial pint	1 short hundredweight=100 pounds
1 pint=1/8 gallon=1/2 quart	1 long hundredweight=112 pounds
1 quart=1/4 gallon	1 short ton=2,000 pounds
1 U.S. gallon (basic unit of liquid capacity in the United States)=231 cubic inches	1 long ton=2,240 pounds
1 imperial gallon (basic unit of liquid capacity in some Commonwealth nations)=277.4 cubic inches	*American and British units: troy and apothecaries'*
1 dry pint=1/64 bushel=1/2 dry quart	1 grain=1/7,000 avoirdupois pound=1/5,760 troy or apothecaries' pound
1 dry quart=1/32 bushel=1/8 peck	1 apothecaries' scruple=20 grains=1/3 dram
1 peck=1/4 bushel	1 pennyweight=24 grains=1/20 troy ounce
1 U.S. bushel (basic unit of dry capacity in the United States) =2,150.4 cubic inches	1 apothecaries' dram=60 grains=1/8 apothecaries' ounce
1 imperial bushel (basic unit of dry capacity in some Commonwealth nations)=2,219.4 cubic inches	1 troy or apothecaries' ounce=480 grains=1/12 troy or apothecaries' pound
	1 troy or apothecaries' pound=5,760 grains=5,760/7,000 avoirdupois pound
Conversion factors	*Conversion factors*
1 cubic centimeter=0.06 cubic inch	1 milligram=0.015 grain
1 cubic inch=16.4 cubic centimeters	1 grain=64.8 milligrams
1 cubic yard=0.765 cubic meter	1 gram=0.035 avoirdupois ounce
1 cubic meter=1.3 cubic yards	1 avoirdupois ounce=28.35 grams
1 milliliter=0.034 fluid ounce	1 troy or apothecaries' pound=0.82 avoirdupois pound=0.37 kilogram
1 fluid ounce=29.6 milliliters	1 avoirdupois pound=1.2 troy or apothecaries' pounds=0.45 kilogram
1 U.S. quart=0.946 liter	1 kilogram=2.205 avoirdupois pounds
1 liter=1.06 U.S. quarts	1 short ton=0.9 metric ton
1 U.S. gallon=3.8 liters	1 metric ton=1.1 short tons
1 imperial gallon=1.2 U.S. gallons= 4.5 liters	
1 liter=0.9 dry quart	
1 dry quart=1.1 liters	
1 dekaliter=0.28 U.S. bushel	
1 U.S. bushel=0.97 imperial bushel=3.5 dekaliters	

tion and enforcement are largely state prerogatives. The Federal government permitted the use of the metric system in 1866 and established a conversion table based on the yard and the pound; in 1893 the yard and the pound were redefined in terms of the metric prototypes of the meter and the kilogram. The major arguments against total conversion to the metric system in the United States are that it would involve great expense in industry and would cause widespread confusion among the general public. See Stacy Jones, *Weights and Measures* (1963); L. J. Chisholm, *Units of Weights and Measure: International and U.S. Customary* (U.S. National Bureau of Standards, 1967).

Wei-hai-wei or **Weihaiwei** (wä-hī-wā), city, NE Shantung prov., China, a seaport on the Po Hai. The harbor is protected by Liu-kung Island. The city was part of a territory (c.285 sq mi/740 sq km), also called Wei-hai-wei, which was leased by Great Britain from 1898 to 1930. The British leasehold comprised the city, a strip of land along the coast, and nearby islands. Under the British, the city was developed from a small village into a major port and coaling station, and a naval base (Port Edward) was established on Liu-kung Island.

Weil, Simone (sēmôn' vīl), 1909–43, French philosopher and mystic. After receiving her *baccalauréat* with honors at 15, she studied philosophy for four years, then entered (1928) the prestigious École Normale Supérieure, from which she graduated in 1931. She then taught in secondary schools and contributed many articles to socialist and Communist journals. She was active in the Spanish civil war until her health failed. Originally Jewish, she became strongly attracted in 1940 to Christianity, believing that Christ on the Cross was a bridge between God and man, and became a practicing Roman Catholic. Most of her works, published posthumously, consist of some notebooks and a collection of religious essays. They include, in English, *Waiting for God* (1951), *Gravity and Grace* (1952), *The Need for Roots* (1952), *Notebooks* (2 vol., 1956), *Oppression and Liberty* (1958), and *Selected Essays, 1934–1943* (1962). See Jacques Cabaud, *Simone Weil* (tr. 1965); Richard Rees, *Simone Weil* (1966); bibliography by J. P. Little (1973).

Weill, Kurt (ko͝ort' vīl), 1900–1950, German-American composer, b. Dessau, studied with Humperdinck and Busoni in Berlin. He first became known with the production of two short, satirical, surrealist operas, *Der Protagonist* (1926) and *Der Zar lässt sich photographieren* [the czar has himself photographed] (1928). More popular than these, however, was his melodious *Dreigroschenoper* (1928), a modern version of John Gay's *Beggar's Opera,* with book by Bertolt BRECHT. Translated and adapted by Marc Blitzstein as *The Threepenny Opera,* it was first produced in New York City in 1933; revived in 1954, it ran for more than six years and has become one of the classics of the musical stage. Brecht was also the librettist of Weill's satiric opera *Aufstieg und Fall der Stadt Mahagonny* [rise and fall of the city Mahagonny] (1927; revised 1930). All these works were condemned as decadent by the rising followers of Hitler, and, in 1933, Weill left Germany for France. In 1935 he emigrated to the United States, where he began writing sophisticated musicals, the most notable being *Johnny Johnson* (1936), *Knickerbocker Holiday* (1938; written with Maxwell Anderson), *Lady in the Dark* (1941), and *One Touch of Venus* (1943; written with Ogden Nash). In these works Weill employed with great facility advanced techniques, including multiple rhythms and polytonality, combined with the idiom of American popular music and jazz. His last works, in a more serious vein, included *Street Scene* (1947), *Down in the Valley* (1948), and *Lost in the Stars* (1949; written with Maxwell Anderson). His wife, the singer Lotte LENYA, played many of the leading roles in his works. Weill also wrote some instrumental works and a cantata, *Lindbergh's Flight* (1929). He became a U.S. citizen in 1943.

Weimar (vī'mär), city (1970 pop. 63,689), Erfurt district, S East Germany, on the Ilm River. It is an industrial, transportation, and cultural center. Manufactures include textiles, agricultural machinery, electrical equipment, chemicals, pharmaceuticals, printed materials, and processed food. Known in the 10th cent., Weimar became important only in the 16th cent. when it was made the capital of the duchy (after 1815 the grand duchy) of SAXE-WEIMAR. It developed as a cultural center of international importance. Under Elector John Frederick I, the painter Lucas Cranach, the elder, worked there (16th cent.), and from 1708 to 1717 Johann Sebastian Bach was court organist and concertmaster at Weimar. Under Dowager Duchess Amalia (1739–1807) and her son, Charles Augustus (1775–1828), Weimar reached the peak of its fame as a cultural center. C. M. Wieland at first dominated the scene in the late 18th cent., but after the arrival (1775) of Goethe at the court, Weimar and Goethe became virtually synonymous. Goethe not only made Weimar the literary capital of Europe during his lifetime, but he also attracted such men as Herder and Schiller, established and directed the Weimar theater, and as chief minister of Charles Augustus was active in the physical improvement of the city. The Weimar state theater was the site of the first performances of most of Goethe's and many of Schiller's plays. After Goethe's death (1832) Weimar lived mainly on its past reputation, but its active cultural life continued. Franz Liszt was musical director there in the mid-19th cent., and Richard Wagner's opera *Lohengrin* was first performed (1850) in Weimar. The fact that Friedrich Nietzsche (1844–1900) lived and died at Weimar resulted in the foundation there of the important Nietzsche Archives by his sister. In 1919, Weimar was the scene of the German national assembly that established the republican government known as the "Weimar Republic." The Bauhaus art school was first established (1919) in Weimar. Among the landmarks of the city are the parish church, with the graves of Lucas Cranach and Herder and with an altarpiece by Cranach; the former grand ducal palace (built 1789–1803) and the ducal crypt with the graves of Goethe and Schiller; Belvedere castle (1724–32); the residences of Goethe, Schiller, and Liszt; Goethe's garden cottage; the state theater; the Goethe National Museum; and the nearby ducal castle of Tiefurt. The city has a state college of music and an academy of art and architecture, and it is the seat of the Goethe and Schiller archives. BUCHENWALD, the Nazi concentration camp (1937–45), was located nearby.

Weimaraner (vī'mərä"nər, wī'mərä"-), breed of large, muscular SPORTING DOG developed in Germany in the early 19th cent. It stands between 23 and 27 in. (58.4–68.6 cm) high at the shoulder and weighs between 55 and 85 lb (25–38.6 kg). Its short, smooth coat ranges in color from mouse-gray to silver-gray. The tail is docked to approximately 6 in. (15.2 cm). Although originally they hunted game such as wildcats, wolves, deer, mountain lions, and bears, the dwindling population of these animals in Germany led the Weimaraner to be bred increasingly for upland bird hunting. Today it is used as both bird dog and water retriever. See DOG.

Weimar Republic: see GERMANY.

Weinberger, Jaromir (wīn'bûrgər, Czech. yä'rômēr wīn'bĕrgĕr), 1896–1967, Czech composer. Weinberger studied at the conservatories of Prague and Leipzig. In 1939, after extensive travels, he settled in New York City. His most popular works are the polka and fugue from the opera *Schwanda the Bagpiper* (1927) and his orchestral variations *Under the Spreading Chestnut Tree* (1939). Other works are the operas *Outcasts of Poker Flat* (1932; based on the story by Bret Harte) and *Wallenstein* (1937), and the ballet *Saratoga* (1941).

Weingartner, Felix (fā'lĭks vīn'gärtnər), 1863–1942, Austrian conductor and composer, b. Dalmatia, studied at the Leipzig Conservatory and with Liszt. After holding several appointments in Germany, including those of conductor (1891–98) of the Royal Opera in Berlin and conductor (1898–1903) of the Kaim Orchestra in Munich, he conducted (1908–10) at the Vienna State Opera, where he was successor to Mahler. He was music director (1912–14) at Hamburg and conductor from 1919 to 1924 of the Vienna Volksoper and from 1919 to 1927 of the Vienna Philharmonic. Afterward he directed the Basel Conservatory until 1934, when he returned to the Vienna State Opera for two seasons. He composed, among other works, six symphonies, three symphonic poems, and several operas. His writings on music include an important essay on conducting, and he edited (1899) the complete works of Berlioz. See his *Lebenserinnerungen* (1928, tr. *Buffets and Rewards, a Musician's Reminiscences,* 1937).

Weir, Julian Alden (wēr), 1852–1919, b. West Point, N.Y., American painter, studied with his father Robert Walter Weir, a landscape painter of the HUDSON RIVER SCHOOL; at the National Academy; and with Gérôme in Paris. He was one of the earliest American impressionist painters. Subtle gradations of light and tone characterize his work. He was a founder of the Society of American Artists (1877), a member of the National Academy (1886), and its president (1915–17). When the Ten American Artists formed a separate group (1898), he joined them. His works include *Idle Hours, The Green Bodice,* and *The Red Bridge* (all: Metropolitan Mus.); a portrait and *Autumn* (Corcoran Gall.); and *Midday Rest in New England* (Pa. Acad. of the Fine Arts). See his letters with a biography by his daughter, Dorothy Weir Young (ed. by L. Chisolm, 1960). Weir's brother, **John Ferguson Weir** (1841–1926), was a painter, sculptor and author, noted for small genre scenes and for his biography of John Trumbull.

weir, barrier or dam built in a stream to raise its level and to direct its course for such purposes as making a fish pond, flooding irrigation furrows, turning a waterwheel, or canalizing the stream. The weir may be constructed so that all or part of it can be opened or closed, raised or lowered, to allow the water to flow freely, or else it may be designed simply to obstruct the stream so that it is forced to flow over the crest of the weir. The overflow sections, e.g., spillways, of other types of dams are also called weirs. In early England simple mesh weirs for fishing purposes were made of twigs and branches. Weirs are also used to measure the flow of water, e.g., in streams and sewers.

Weirton, city (1970 pop. 27,131), Brooke and Hancock counties, NW W.Va., in the industrial Northern Panhandle, on the Ohio River; settled 1790s, inc. 1947. It is a steel-manufacturing center in an area of coal mines.

Weise, Christian (krĭs'tyän vī'zə), 1642–1708, German didactic poet and dramatist. He wrote more than 60 plays, many of them written for production in schools. Perhaps the best-known are the comedy *Bäurischer Macchiavellus* [the village Machiavelli] (1679) and the tragedy *Masaniello* (1688). His plays are marked by realism and the use of natural dialects. He also wrote novels, mostly political satires, e.g., *Die drei argsten Erznarren* [the three archest fools] (1672).

Weiser, Conrad (wī'zər), 1696–1760, American pioneer, b. Württemberg, Germany. Arriving in America in 1710, his family settled in Livingston Manor, N.Y., and later at Schoharie. While still a youth, Weiser lived for some time among the Mohawks and learned their language and customs. Going (1729) to Tulpehocken, Pa., he became (1731) the official Pennsylvania Indian interpreter and soon gained fame as a wise and honorable mediator between the whites and the Indians. Coming under the influence of Johann Conrad BEISSEL, he moved (1739) to Ephrata and, leaving his family, entered the Baptist cloister there. Within two years, however, he withdrew, returned to Tulpehocken, and entered local politics. He later aided in establishing Berks co. and in developing Reading, became a Lutheran adherent, and continued as an Indian mediator until his death. See biography by P. A. W. Wallace (1945, repr. 1971).

Weismann, August (ou'go͝ost vīs'män), 1834–1914, German biologist. He taught zoology at the Univ. of Freiburg from 1866 to 1912. He is known as the originator of the germ-plasm theory of HEREDITY. His doctrine, formerly called Weismannism, stresses the unbroken continuity of the germ plasm and the nonheritability of acquired characteristics. His works include *The Germ-Plasm* (1892, tr. 1893) and a series of essays translated into English as *Essays upon Heredity and Kindred Biological Problems* (2d ed., 2 vol., 1891–92). See G. J. Romanes, *An Examination of Weismannism* (1903).

Weiss, Paul, 1901–, American philosopher, b. New York City, grad. City College of New York, 1927, Ph.D Harvard, 1929. He taught at Bryn Mawr (1931–46) and then at Yale (1946–69) until his retirement, when he became associated with Catholic Univ. In his philosophy he has combined the thought of the American philosophers C. S. Peirce and William James with that of contemporary European thinkers. He has also written in the field of aesthetics. He founded (1947) the *Review of Metaphysics* and was one of the editors of *The Collected Papers of Charles S. Peirce* (8 vol., 1931–58). Among his works are *Reality* (1938), *Nature and Man* (1947), *Man's Freedom* (1950), *Modes of Being* (1958), *The World of Art* (1961), *Nine Basic Arts* (1961), *Religion and Art* (1963), and *Sport: A Philosophic Inquiry* (1969). See I. C. Lieb, ed., *Experience, Existence and the Good: Essays in Honor of Paul Weiss* (1961).

Weiss, Peter (pā'tər), 1916–, German-Swedish dramatist, novelist, film director, and painter. Weiss's early novels *Abschied von den Eltern* (1961; tr. *Leavetaking,* 1962) and *Fluchtpunkt* (1962; tr. *Vanishing Point,* 1967) draw upon his emigration experience. His philosophic drama on the nature of revolution, *The Persecution and Assassination of Jean Paul Marat as Performed by the Inmates of the Asy-*

lum of Charenton under the Direction of the Marquis de Sade (1964; tr. 1965), effectively conveys the atmosphere of an insane asylum as a social microcosm. Both this and his play *Die Ermittlung* (1965; tr. *The Investigation,* 1966) were international successes. Later works include the documentary drama *Trotzki im Exil* (1970; tr. *Trotsky in Exile,* 1971) and *The Song of the Lusitanian Bogey* (tr. 1970). See study by Ian Hilton (1970).

Weissenburg in Bayern (vīˈsənbo͝ork ĭn bīˈyərn) or **Weissenburg,** town (1970 pop. 13,964), Bavaria, S West Germany. It is a manufacturing center of Middle Franconia; products include gold and silver lace, processed wood, and metal goods. Weissenburg was founded in the 9th cent. on a Roman site. It became a free imperial city in the mid-14th cent. and passed to Bavaria in 1806. Points of interest in the picturesque town include remains of Roman fortifications and of the town's medieval walls; the late Gothic town hall (1476); and the Carmelite church (15th cent.).

Weissenfels (vīsˈənfĕls), city (1970 pop. 46,120), Halle district, S East Germany, on the Saale River. It is an industrial city and lignite-mining center. Manufactures include shoes, paper, and machinery. Chartered in the 12th cent., Weissenfels passed to Prussia in 1815. The baroque palace (17th cent.) served as the residence of the dukes of Saxe-Weissenfels from 1680 to 1746.

Weisshorn (vīsˈhôrn″), peak, 14,782 ft (4,506 m) high, Valais canton, S Switzerland, one of the highest in the Pennine Alps.

Weizmann, Chaim (khīmˈ vītsˈmän), 1874–1952, scientist and Zionist leader, first president (1948–52) of Israel, b. Russia, grad. Univ. of Freiburg, 1899. He lectured in chemistry at the Univ. of Geneva (1901–3) and later taught at the Univ. of Manchester. Active in ZIONISM from his youth, Weizmann first visited Palestine in 1907. He became a British subject in 1910, and in World War I he was (1916–19) director of the British admiralty laboratories. He became famous when he developed a synthetic acetone to be used in the manufacture of explosives. In 1917 he helped procure the pro-Zionist declaration of Arthur James BALFOUR. A founder of so-called synthetic Zionism, Weizmann supported grass-roots colonization efforts as well as higher-level diplomatic activity. After 1920 he assumed leadership in the world Zionist movement, serving twice (1920–31, 1935–46) as president of the World Zionist Organization. In World War II he was (1939–45) honorary adviser to the British ministry of supply and did research on synthetic rubber and high-octane gasoline. When the republic of Israel was founded (1948), Weizmann became the first president. At Rehoboth, where he lived, Weizmann founded a research institute (now the Weizmann Institute of Science). He wrote many papers for scientific journals. See his autobiography (1949); his letters and papers (3 vol., 1968–72); biography ed. by M. W. Weisgal and Joel Carmichael (1962); studies by Isaiah Berlin (1958) and Israel Kolatt (1970); Paul Goodman, ed., *Chaim Weizmann: A Tribute* (1959).

Wekerle, Alexander (vĕˈkĕrlĕ), 1848–1921, Hungarian premier. He became minister of finance in 1889 and retained that post during his first two terms as premier (1892–95, 1906–10). In his first term civil marriage was made obligatory, and the power of the church was lessened as a result. His second cabinet was a coalition of parties; it carried out financial reforms and supported the annexation of BOSNIA AND HERCEGOVINA. Werkerle headed four successive cabinets in 1917–18. On Oct. 16, 1918, he declared the dissolution of all bonds between Hungary and Austria except the personal union of the two countries under the same monarch. He resigned shortly afterward.

wel: see CATFISH.

Welch, William Henry, 1850–1934, American pathologist, b. Norfolk, Conn., grad. Yale (B.A., 1870), M.D. College of Physicians and Surgeons (now part of Columbia Univ., 1875). After studying abroad he taught (1879–84) at Bellevue Hospital Medical College, introducing laboratory methods of instruction. He was associated with Johns Hopkins Univ., as professor of pathology (1884–1916), dean of the medical faculty (1893–98), director of the school of hygiene (1916–26), and professor of the history of medicine (1926–30). He was chairman of the board of the Rockefeller Institute for Medical Research (now Rockefeller Univ.) from 1901. His research includes studies of the Welch bacillus of gas gangrene and of embolism, thrombosis, and diphtheria. See biographies by Simon Flexner and J. T. Flexner (1941, repr. 1966) and Donald Fleming (1954, repr. 1972).

Weld, Theodore Dwight, 1803–95, American abolitionist, b. Hampton, Conn. In 1825 his family moved to upstate New York, and he entered Hamilton College. While in college he became a disciple of the evangelist Charles G. FINNEY and was influenced by Charles Stuart, a retired British army officer who urged Weld to enlist in the cause of Negro emancipation. While studying for the ministry at Oneida Institute he traveled about lecturing on the virtues of manual labor, temperance, and moral reform. After 1830 he became one of the leaders of the antislavery movement working with Arthur TAPPAN and Lewis TAPPAN, New York philanthropists, James G. BIRNEY, Gamaliel BAILEY, and Angelina GRIMKÉ and Sarah GRIMKÉ. He married Angelina Grimké in 1838. Weld chose Lane Seminary at Cincinnati, Ohio, for the ministerial training of other Finney converts and studied there until the famous antislavery debates he organized (1834) among the students led to his dismissal. Almost the entire student body then requested dismissal, and it was from these theological students that Weld and Henry B. Stanton selected agents for the American Anti-Slavery Society. The "Seventy," as the agents were called, gave character and direction to the antislavery movement and successfully spread the abolitionist gospel throughout the North. From 1836 to 1840, Weld worked at the New York office of the antislavery society, serving as an editor of the society's paper, the *Emancipator,* and contributing antislavery articles to newspapers and periodicals. He also directed the national campaign for sending antislavery petitions to Congress and assisted John Quincy ADAMS when Congress tried Adams for reading petitions in violation of the gag rule. While in Washington he advised the Northern antislavery Whigs, many of whom (e.g., Ben Wade, Thaddeus Stevens) were converted to the cause by Weld or one of his agents. After 1844 he retired from public participation in the movement to found a school, Eaglewood, near Raritan, N.J. During the Civil War, at the urging of William Lloyd GARRISON, he came out of retirement to speak for the Union cause and campaign for Republican candidates. Most famous of his writings (none was published under his own name) was *American Slavery As It Is* (1839), on which Harriet Beecher Stowe partly based *Uncle Tom's Cabin* and which is regarded as second only to that work in its influence on the antislavery movement. Many historians regard Weld as the most important figure in the abolitionist movement, surpassing even Garrison, but his passion for anonymity long made him an unknown figure in American history. See *Letters of Theodore Dwight Weld, Angelina Grimké Weld and Sarah Grimké 1822–1844,* ed. by G. H. Barnes and D. L. Dumond (2 vol., 1934); biography by B. P. Thomas (1950); G. H. Barnes, *The Antislavery Impulse, 1830–1844* (1933).

welding, process for joining separate pieces of metal in a continuous metallic bond. Cold-pressure welding is accomplished by the application of high pressure at room temperature; forge welding (forging) is done by means of hammering, with the addition of heat. In most processes in common use, the metal at the points to be joined is melted; additional molten metal is added as a filler, and the bond is allowed to cool. In the Thomson process, resistance to an electric current, passed through the sections to be joined, causes them to melt. Other notable methods include the THERMITE process, oxyacetylene, electric arc, oxyhydrogen, and the atomic hydrogen flame. In this last-named method, molecules of hydrogen gas passing through an electric arc are broken up into atoms of hydrogen by absorbing energy; when outside the arc, the atoms reunite into molecules, yielding in the process enough heat to weld the material. Another process, the argon-arc method, is widely used with metals such as stainless steel, aluminum, magnesium, and titanium, which require an inert atmosphere for successful welding. The use of argon prevents slag from forming in the weld and greatly increases the speed of the welding. See A. C. Davies, *The Science and Practice of Welding* (6th ed. 1972).

Welfs: see GUELPHS.

Welhaven, Johan Sebastian (yōhänˈ säbäsˈtyän vĕlˈhävən), 1807–73, Norwegian poet and critic. His charming and reflective poetry, tending toward the classical in style, drew much inspiration from Norwegian landscape, legend, and history. As a critic Welhaven led the intellectual opposition to the zealous democrat WERGELAND. However, Welhaven shared Wergeland's liberal ideals in modified form, and after Wergeland's death he became the most important arbiter of taste in Norway.

Welkom (vĕlˈkəm), city (1970 pop. 66,217), Orange Free State, central South Africa. It is a commercial center, and there are mines in the vicinity. Founded in 1947, Welkom is a planned city.

well, aperture in the earth's surface through which substances in a natural underground reservoir, such as water, gas, oil, salt, and sulfur, can flow or be pumped to the surface. In the United States until some years after the Civil War, the majority of wells were "open," i.e., holes dug in the ground and lined, or cased, with brick, stone, or wood. Although they are sometimes dug with picks and shovels, most wells today are made by rotary or percussion drills. An ARTESIAN WELL, the most desirable type of water well, is always drilled because rock layers must be cut through to reach the water. Oil wells are usually drilled using a rotary-drill method, in which a drilling bit set in the bottom of a drilling pipe is rotated by machinery on the ground level. As the cut deepens, more sections of pipe are fastened to the sections already in use. A special mixture called drilling mud is sent down through the pipe to wash away the drillings and also to cool the cutting bit. Some oil wells are drilled by a percussion method known as cable-tool drilling. In this procedure a heavy metal bit attached to a cable is alternately raised and dropped, pulverizing the rock beneath it. Water is pumped into the well and mixed with the rock cuttings, the mixture being bailed out when it becomes thick enough to interfere with the action of the bit. Regardless of the drilling method, well walls are usually cased with iron or steel to prevent cave-ins. Casing is inserted when the desired depth has been reached or, in some cases, as the well is being drilled. Minerals, such as salt and sulfur, can be pumped to the surface through a well if they are first liquefied by some process; for example, salt may be brought up if water is first pumped to the bottom of the well to dissolve the salt.

Welland (wĕlˈənd), city (1971 pop. 44,397), SE Ont., Canada, on the Welland Ship Canal. It is a canal port and an industrial center. Cotton, iron, steel, and many other goods are made in Welland. The city is also a distributing center for a fruit-growing area

Welland Ship Canal, 27.6 mi (44.4 km) long, SE Ont., Canada, connecting Lake Ontario with Lake Erie and bypassing Niagara Falls. Built between 1914 and 1932 by Canada to replace a canal opened in 1829, it can accommodate (minimum depth 27 ft/8 m) the largest lake ships. Its eight locks overcome a 326-ft (99-m) difference in level between the lakes. The Lake Ontario entrance is near Port Dalhousie; the Lake Erie entrance is at Port Colborne. It is part of the St. Lawrence Seaway system.

Welle, river, Zaïre: see UELE.

Weller, Thomas Huckle, 1915–, American microbiologist and physician, b. Ann Arbor, Mich., B.A. Univ. of Michigan, 1936, M.D. Harvard, 1940. In 1936 he began teaching at Harvard, and as a specialist in tropical medicine he became professor in the school of public health in 1954. Together with J. F. Enders and F. C. Robbins he was awarded the 1954 Nobel Prize in Physiology and Medicine for work in growing polio viruses in cultures of different tissues.

Welles, Gideon (wĕlz), 1802–78, American statesman, b. Glastonbury, Conn. He was (1826–36) editor and part owner of the Hartford *Times,* one of the first New England papers to support Andrew Jackson. An organizer of the Jacksonian forces in Connecticut, Welles served in the state legislature (1827–35). He was three times elected state comptroller of public accounts and was postmaster of Hartford. He was also chief of the Bureau of Provisions and Clothing for the U.S. navy (1846–49). Leaving the Democratic party on the slavery issue, he helped found (1856) the Hartford *Evening Press,* a Republican paper, and in 1861 became Secretary of the Navy in Abraham Lincoln's cabinet. Incorruptible, efficient, and something of a curmudgeon, Welles built the powerful Union navy of the Civil War. The construction of the *Monitor* and the other ironclads resulted largely from his support, and the victorious admirals David C. Farragut and David D. Porter were men of his choice. One of the first to recognize Lincoln's essential greatness, he thoroughly disliked some of his cabinet colleagues, notably William H. Seward and Edwin M. Stanton. Welles was a moderate who favored Lincoln's Reconstruction plan and, retaining his post under Andrew Johnson, stood by the President in his struggle with the radical Republicans in Congress. He returned to the Democratic party in 1868. Welles wrote *Lincoln and Seward* (1874), and his salty diary (ed. by H. K. Beale, 3 vol.,

1960) is of immense value to the historian. See biographies by R. S. West, Jr. (1943) and John Niven (1973).

Welles, Orson, 1915–, American actor, director, and producer, b. Kenosha, Wis. Welles made his New York stage and radio debuts in 1934. In 1937 he directed several Federal Theatre productions and organized the Mercury Theatre company in New York. He achieved national recognition when in 1938 he shocked a radio audience with his realistic adaptation of H. G. Wells's *War of the Worlds.* In his first Hollywood venture he wrote, produced, directed, and starred in *Citizen Kane* (1939), a film noted for its technical brilliance, structural complexity, and literate treatment of a controversial biographical subject. He directed, with greatly reduced artistic freedom, several Hollywood productions, including *The Magnificent Ambersons* (1942) and *Touch of Evil* (1958). His later, European-produced films (e.g., *The Trial,* 1963, and *Chimes at Midnight,* 1966) allowed him greater personal control within small budgets. Welles also acted in many films made by other directors, including *Jane Eyre* (1943), *Compulsion* (1958), *Crack in the Mirror* (1960), and *Catch 22* (1970). See H. J. Mankiewicz and Pauline Kael, *The Citizen Kane Book* (1971); studies of his films by Charles Higham (1970) and Peter Cowie (1972).

Welles, Sumner, 1892–1961, American diplomat, b. New York City. Welles began his diplomatic career as secretary of the U.S. embassy at Tokyo (1915–17). Attached to the embassy at Buenos Aires (1917–19), he then served as assistant chief (1920–21) and chief (1921–22) of the division of Latin American affairs of the Dept. of State. As commissioner to the Dominican Republic in 1922, he helped prepare for the evacuation of American troops from that country; later he was sent to offer mediation in the Honduras revolution of 1924. He wrote a book on the Dominican Republic, *Naboth's Vineyard* (1928), and was an influential member of the Dawes financial mission to the Dominican Republic (1929). President Franklin Delano Roosevelt appointed him Assistant Secretary of State in 1933 and in the same year sent him as ambassador to Cuba. There he was unable to bring about successful mediation between the opposing groups in the revolution against Gerardo MACHADO in 1933, and in the midst of political turmoil he was recalled and resumed his duties as Assistant Secretary of State. He later (1937–42) was Undersecretary of State and served as U.S. delegate to several Pan-American conferences. In 1940 he went on a confidential fact-finding mission to Europe, and he took part in the meeting at sea between Roosevelt and Winston Churchill that produced the Atlantic Charter (1941). Some of his speeches were collected in *The World of the Four Freedoms* (1943); his other writings include *The Time for Decision* (1944), *The Intelligent American's Guide to Peace* (1945), *Where Are We Heading?* (1946), and *Seven Decisions That Shaped History* (1950).

Wellesley, Richard Colley Wellesley, Marquess, 1760–1842, British colonial administrator; brother of Arthur Wellesley, 1st duke of WELLINGTON. He became earl of Mornington on his father's death (1781) and took his seat in the Irish House of Lords. He entered the English House of Commons in 1784 and gave his support to William Pitt, who in 1793 appointed him to the board of control for India. In 1797 he was created Baron Wellesley and sent as governor-general to India. He was created marquess in 1799. Under Wellesley's rule British influence in India was greatly extended. He was an excellent administrator, wiped out the French hold in India, and crushed the power of TIPPOO SAHIB of Mysore. Aided by the military talents of his brother Arthur (later duke of Wellington), he checked the power of native rulers in a great struggle with the MAHRATTAS. However, the policy of subsidiary alliances that he introduced as a means of bringing the weaker Indian states under British control, and the expenses of his military exploits caused discontent at home, and he was recalled to England in 1805. Chagrined at charges unsuccessfully brought in Parliament against his administration in India, he refused a cabinet post but went to Spain as ambassador in 1809. He served as foreign secretary (1810–12) under Spencer Perceval. A supporter of CATHOLIC EMANCIPATION, Wellesley became lord lieutenant of Ireland in 1821. He resigned (1828) when his brother, then an opponent of Catholic Emancipation, became prime minister, but he served again as lord lieutenant for a brief period (1833–34) after the issue of Catholic Emancipation had been settled. See biographies by G. B. Malleson (1889) and W. H. Hutton (1893, repr. 1961); study by P. E. Roberts (1929, repr. 1961).

Wellesley, town (1970 pop. 28,051), Norfolk co., E Mass., a residential suburb SW of Boston; settled 1660, inc. 1881. Its many educational institutions include several private preparatory schools, Babson College, and Wellesley College.

Wellesley College, at Wellesley, Mass.; for women; chartered 1870, opened 1875. Long a leader in women's education, it was the first woman's college to have scientific laboratories. With Lake Waban and 500 acres (202 hectares) of wooded hills, the campus is noted for its beauty. The Jewett Arts Center has a collection of classical, medieval, and contemporary art, and the library has a large Browning collection. See Florence Converse, *Wellesley College* (1939); Wellesley Alumnae Magazine, special centennial issue, *A Women's Place* (1974).

Wellesz, Egon (ā'gŏn vĕl'ĕs), 1885–1974, Austrian composer and musicologist. Wellesz studied with Schoenberg at the same time as Berg and Webern. His early compositions show the influence of Mahler, but the clarity and articulation that characterize his later works are already evident. He is the author of studies of Byzantine and Arabic music, including *Eastern Elements in Western Chant* (1947) and *A History of Byzantine Music and Hymnology* (1948). From 1939 he lived in England; there he taught at Oxford and composed operas, ballets, chamber music, liturgical works, and symphonies.

Wellhausen, Julius (yo͞ol'yo͝os vĕl'hou''zən), 1844–1918, German Orientalist and one of the leading biblical scholars of the 19th cent. A pioneer in the science of textual comparison, Wellhausen helped to clarify the development of the Old Testament. *Prolegomena to the History of Israel* (1882; tr. 1885) is the best known of his many works of scholarship.

Wellingborough, urban district (1971 pop. 18,433), Northamptonshire, central England. It is a very old market town. Formerly known for its chalybeate spring, Wellingborough is now a rail center with leather factories, iron foundries, breweries, flour mills, and chemical works. It has a public school that was founded in 1595.

Wellington, Arthur Wellesley, 1st duke of, 1769–1852, British soldier and statesman. He entered the army in 1787 and, aided by his brother Richard (later Marquess WELLESLEY), rose rapidly in rank. He held a command in Flanders (1794–95) and in 1796 went with his regiment to India. After his brother's appointment (1797) as governor-general of India, he received command of a division in the invasion of Mysore and became (1799) governor of Seringapatam. In 1800 he defeated the robber chieftain, Dhundia Wagh, and in 1802 he was made major general. In 1803 he moved against the MAHRATTAS, breaking their force of about 40,000 with an army of about 10,000 in a surprise attack. A valuable civil and military adviser to his brother, he returned with him to England in 1805 and was knighted. His election (1806) to Parliament and appointment (1807) as Irish secretary did not prevent him from leading (1807) an expedition against the Danes. In 1808 he led an expedition to assist Portugal in its revolt against the French. He defeated the French at Roliça and Vimeiro, but was superseded in command. In 1809 he returned to the Iberian Peninsula, where he ultimately assumed command of the British, Portuguese, and Spanish forces in the PENINSULAR WAR. Taking advantage of the irregular terrain, Portuguese and Spanish nationalism, and Napoleon's preoccupation with other campaigns and projects, he drove the French beyond the Pyrenees by 1813, though his campaigns were rendered difficult by poor support from the British government. Late in 1813 he invaded S France, and he was at Toulouse when news of Napoleon's abdication (April, 1814) arrived. Returning to England, he received many honors and was created duke of Wellington. He served for a short time as ambassador to Paris, then succeeded Viscount Castlereagh at the peace conference in Vienna; but when Napoleon returned from Elba, he took command of the allied armies. There followed his most famous victory, that in the WATERLOO CAMPAIGN, won in conjunction with the Prussian general, Gebhard Leberecht von Blücher. Wellington, again lavishly honored, took charge of the army of occupation in France, exerting his influence to restrain harsh treatment of the defeated French. Wellington, "the iron duke," with the soldier's taste for discipline and order and the aristocrat's distrust of democratic institutions, lent his great prestige to the Tory policy of repression at home and took a cabinet post as master general of the ordnance (1819). He represented England at the Congress of Verona (1822), where he opposed intervention in the Spanish revolt, and at the conference at St. Petersburg (1826) that concerned itself with the revolt in Greece; but he was not in sympathy with the liberal foreign policy of George CANNING and resigned (1827) when Canning became prime minister. In 1828, however, Wellington himself reluctantly became prime minister. He bowed to public clamor and allowed the repeal of the Test Act and Corporation Act and the passage of the CATHOLIC EMANCIPATION bill (reforms he had previously opposed); but he lost the support of much of the Tory party as a consequence. When he declared against parliamentary reform, the ministry fell (1830), and his unpopularity subjected him to an assault by a mob. He refused to form a government in 1834, but served under Sir Robert PEEL as foreign secretary (1834–35) and again (1841–46) as minister without portfolio. On the repeal of the corn laws he supported Peel, while not wholly approving his policy. In 1842 he was made commander in chief for life. He is buried in St. Paul's Cathedral. See his dispatches and other papers (pub. in 3 series, 1834–39, 1858–72, 1867–80); biographies by J. W. Fortescue (1925, 3d ed. 1960), Philip Guedalla (1931), Sir Charles Petrie (1956), Elizabeth Longford (2 vol., 1969–72), and Sir Arthur Bryant (1971); study by Godfrey Davies (1954).

Wellington, city (1971 pop. 135,677), capital of New Zealand, extreme S North Island, on Port Nicholson, an inlet of Cook Strait. It is a great communications and transportation center and is an important port for coastal trade. Wellington has garment, transportation-equipment, food-processing, and textile industries. It was founded in 1840 and supplanted Auckland as the capital in 1865. Notable are the governor-general's residence, the Parliament building, the National Art Gallery, and the Dominion Museum. Victoria Univ. of Wellington was founded in 1962. Wellington has a symphony orchestra and ballet as well as opera companies. It is the seat of a Roman Catholic archbishopric.

Wells, David Ames, 1828–98, American economist, b. Springfield, Mass., grad. Williams, 1847, and Lawrence Scientific School, Cambridge, Mass., 1851. Early in life he wrote several popular books on science. In 1864 his pamphlet *Our Burden and Our Strength,* dealing with the financial problems of the Civil War, attracted considerable attention. While serving as special commissioner of the U.S. Revenue Commission he wrote a series of reports (1866–69) concerned particularly with indirect taxes. He favored free trade and opposed the Federal income tax. He wrote many books and pamphlets, including *Robinson Crusoe's Money* (1876), *Our Merchant Marine* (1882), and *The Theory and Practice of Taxation* (1900). See study be F. B. Joyner (1939).

Wells, Henry, 1805–78, American pioneer expressman, b. Thetford, Vt. As a child he moved with his family to central New York state. In 1843 he established express service between New York City and Buffalo and successfully competed with the U.S. Post Office by carrying mail at less than the government rate. His association with William G. FARGO began in 1844, when Wells & Company was organized. In 1846, Wells temporarily abandoned most of his other commercial interests to concentrate on the trans-Atlantic trade. Together with William Fargo, he organized (1852) Wells, Fargo & Company to handle express service to California and the West. Wells made his home in Aurora, N.Y., where he founded Wells Seminary (now Wells College). A stammerer, he established several schools for those similarly afflicted. See N. M. Loomis, *Wells Fargo* (1968).

Wells, Herbert George (H. G. Wells), 1866–1946, English author. Although he is probably best remembered for his works of science fiction, he was also an imaginative social thinker, working assiduously to remove all vestiges of Victorian social, moral, and religious attitudes from 20th-century life. He was apprenticed to a draper at 14 and was later able through grants and scholarships to attend the Univ. of London (grad. 1888). Inspired by the teaching of T. H. Huxley, Wells taught biology until 1893, when he began his career as a novelist. His early books, full of fantasy and fascinating pseudoscientific speculations, exemplify the political and social beliefs of his time. They include *The Time Machine* (1895), *The Wonderful Visit* (1895), *The Invisible Man* (1897), and *The War of the Worlds* (1898). In the novels of his middle period he turned from the fantastic to the realistic, delineating with great energy and color the world he lived in. These books, considered his finest achievement, include *Kipps* (1905), *Tono-Bungay* (1909), and *The History of Mr. Polly* (1910). His later books are primarily novels of ideas in which he sets forth his view of the plans and concessions man must make in order to survive. Included among these final works, which became increasingly pessimistic as Wells aged, are *The World of William Clissold* (1926), *The Shape of Things to Come* (1933), *World Brain* (1938), and *Mind at the End of Its Tether* (1945). His other works include the immensely popular *Outline of History* (1920) and *The Science of Life* (1929), which was written in collaboration with his son G. P. Wells and Julian Huxley. See his *Experiment in Autobiography* (1934); biographies by Lovat Dickson (1969) and Norman and Jeanne MacKenzie (1973); studies by M. R. Hillegas (1967) and G. N. Ray (1974).

Wells, municipal borough (1971 pop. 11,170), Somerset, SW England. Primarily a cathedral town, it has changed little since medieval times. The first church was erected by King Ine of Wessex in the early 8th cent. The earliest part of the present cathedral dates from 1176. The towers were built in the 14th cent., and much of the woodwork dates from the 15th cent. There are more than 300 13th-century sculptured figures. The grounds of the present bishop's palace include ruins of the original 13th-century structure and the complete 14th-century moat and wall. There is a theological college in Wells.

Wells College, at Aurora, N.Y.; for women; chartered and opened 1868 by Henry Wells as a seminary; became a college in 1870.

well-tempered, in music: see TUNING SYSTEMS.

Wels (vĕls), city (1971 pop. 47,300), Upper Austria province, W Austria, on the Traun River. It is an industrial and rail center and an agricultural market. Manufactures include machinery, paper, and textiles. Nearby are natural gas wells. A town in Roman times, Wels later became a stronghold against the Avars and the Magyars. Noteworthy buildings include the parish church and the castle where Emperor Maximilian I died in 1519.

Welsbach, Carl Auer, Baron von (kärl ou'ər bärōn' fən vĕls'bäkh), 1858–1929, Austrian chemist. He discovered the rare earth elements neodymium and praseodymium (1885) and lutetium (c.1908, independently of the French chemist Georges Urbain). He is known also for the invention of the Welsbach mantle.

Welsbach mantle or **Welsbach burner** [for the Austrian chemist C. A. von Welsbach], cylindrical framework of gauze impregnated with oxides of thorium and cerium. When heated in a gas flame, it produces a very bright light because of the incandescence of the oxides. It is now used in outdoor and camp lamps.

Welser (vĕl'zər), German family of wealthy merchants and bankers at Augsburg. It reached the height of its prosperity under **Bartholomäus Welser,** 1488–1561, who had advanced large sums to Holy Roman Emperor Charles V. Unable to repay his debts, Charles granted (1528) virtual sovereignty over present Venezuela to his creditor, who sent out agents and had the territory explored. Charges (probably false) of oppressive administration brought a prolonged trial (1541–56); the Welser concession was revoked in 1556. A niece of Bartholomäus Welser, **Philippine Welser,** 1527–80, was famed for her beauty and erudition. She secretly married (1557) Archduke Ferdinand, second son of Holy Roman Emperor Ferdinand I.

Welsh corgi: see CARDIGAN WELSH CORGI; PEMBROKE WELSH CORGI.

Welsh language, member of the Brythonic group of the Celtic subfamily of the Indo-European family of languages. See CELTIC LANGUAGES.

Welsh literature. The earliest Welsh literature is preserved in about half a dozen manuscripts written with one exception after the 12th cent. However, the literature was highly developed well before the Norman Conquest. Of early extant works the most important, the so-called "Four Ancient Books of Wales," are *The Book of Aneurin, The Book of Taliesin, The Black Book of Caemarthen,* and *The Red Book of Hergest.* Much of the poetry in these manuscripts is credited to four late 6th-century bards—Aneurin, Taliesin, Myrddin (the Merlin of Arthurian romance), and Llywarch Hen—and most of the anonymous poetry is marked by style and subject as belonging to their various schools. Early Welsh poetry is epic, romantic, and historical; songs in praise of heroes (many pre-Christian and mythological) and elegiac poems of desolation and longing frequently appear. They are marked by a rich, musical style, displaying the verbal felicity of a highly developed art. Among early prose survivals, the classic is the *Mabinogion* (set down c.1060). In this work the cycle of stories concerning the old Celtic gods and heroes—similar to those in Irish and Arthurian literature—is expanded by the addition of later stories and partly transformed by numerous Welsh revisions. Early medieval prose includes *The History of the Kings of Britain* and romances and stories of the Holy Grail, partly adopted from French and other sources, but showing native Welsh style and story innovations. In poetry, the *Gogynfeirdd* (early medieval period) eulogized the heroes of the North, but it is lyrical rather than epic. From c.1150 the bardic system, with its archaisms, its prescribed themes and meters, and its aim of "exquisiteness" flowered; of the several levels of bardic verse, eulogy was considered the highest and was preserved. In the 14th cent., a golden age in South Wales, DAFYDD AP GWILYM, the greatest Welsh poet, broke the classical eulogistic traditions of the bards and established new horizons. Dafydd was influenced by Provençal poetry, but his verse was more informal and spontaneous. With a simpler, more personal diction and a fuller cognizance of nature than had been present in Welsh verse, he elevated love poetry over the eulogistic variety. Dafydd influenced Welsh poetry for 200 years, inaugurating the *Cywyddwyr* period named after the *cywydd* meter (a 7-syllable rhymed couplet with alternating endings in masculine and feminine genders), which he introduced. This poetry achieved perfection in the 15th cent. but declined from the mid-16th. The bards overlaid the *cywydd* with an excessively formal, alliterative style, as they did with the more natural, spontaneous English poetry that began to be popular in the 16th cent. After the 16th cent., social and political changes in Wales had marked effects, especially the anglicization of the Welsh gentry and the gradual decline of patronage for the native language. Influence from religious sources grew. Early modern Welsh prose standards were partly set by Bishop William Morgan's translation of the Bible (1583). Welsh humanist prose of the 16th and 17th cent., although not much published in the original tongue, was polished and musical. In the 18th cent. theological and pedagogical writings dominated, but such authors as Morgan Llwyd, Theophilus Evans, and Ellis Wynn created clear, elegant prose classics. Religious feeling and the interest of the clergy were significant in keeping alive Welsh poetry in the 18th cent.; while the priest Goronwy Owen and other members of the "Morris School" attempted to assimilate the early, free *cywydd* poetry to modern situations, the great Methodist hymnodists, William Williams (Pantycelyn) and Ann Griffiths, deriving elements from the abundant folk verse (*penillion*), created a more personal poetry in "free" meters. They were a potent influence on the 19th-century lyric poets, Ceiriog and Islwyn. In addition several factors, including scholarship, the Welsh-language publications of the Society for the Dissemination of Christian Knowledge, improved popular education, and increased Welsh political consciousness—as exemplified in the 19th cent. by the writings of Daniel Owens, "the Welsh Dickens"—gave rise to a literary revival that reached a high point in the 20th cent. The poetic revival, which produced both nationalist and cosmopolitan works, was tied to the founding in 1872 of the new Univ. of Wales. Attempts at language purification, interest in Welsh mythology, and a turning away from earlier Welsh puritanism have accompanied influences ranging from the Greek classics to modern French symbolists. Dominating other trends are the love of nature, the boldness of imagery, and the lilt of language, best represented in the free-metered works of W. J. Gruffydd and the more classical poetry of T. Gwynn-Jones. The short story has been developed to a high level by Dewi Williams, Islwyn Williams, and Kate Roberts. The principal novelists of the 20th cent. include Kate Roberts, Tegla Davies, T. Rowland Hughes, and Islwyn Ffowc Ellis. Realistic drama was developed by R. G. Berry, D. T. Davies, Saunders Lewis, and W. J. Gruffydd. A more symbolic and psychological dramatic literature followed with the works of Huw Lloyd Edwards, T. Parry, and Gwilym R. Jones. The poet and dramatist Saunders Lewis has enriched Welsh critical writing. The EISTEDDFOD remains a vigorous cultural force. See anthologies of Welsh poetry, ed. by Gwyn Williams (1950 and 1953) and Thomas Parry (1962); Gwyn Williams, *An Introduction to Welsh Poetry* (1953); Thomas Parry, *A History of Welsh Literature* (1955); Ifor Williams, *The Beginnings of Welsh Poetry* (1972).

Welsh Marches, lands in Wales along the English border. After the Norman conquest of England in the 11th cent., William I established the border earldoms of Chester, Shrewsbury, and Hereford to protect his English kingdom. Norman barons were encouraged by William's successors to conquer and hold other earldoms in the east of Wales. These nobles ruled as petty feudal princes, owing allegiance only to the king. Attempts to control the resulting lawlessness were made by Edward I and by Edward IV, who set up the Council of Wales and the Marches in 1471. Finally the act of Union (1536) abolished the more than 100 marcher lordships, providing for their division into Welsh shires or their incorporation into English counties.

Welsh pony, breed of small HORSE of European origin. First bred primarily in Saxony, it later became localized in Wales. Although the breed is of ancient type, it presently bears traces of the ARABIAN HORSE and shows influences of the THOROUGHBRED HORSE. It is a popular children's pony and has been used extensively for light labor, especially in the harness, having trotting tendencies similar to those of the STANDARDBRED HORSE. The Welsh pony is taller than the SHETLAND PONY, averaging just over 12 hands (48 in./120 cm). It is usually of solid color, grays, whites, and chestnuts predominating.

Welsh springer spaniel, breed of medium-sized SPORTING DOG developed several centuries ago in Wales. It stands about 17 in. (43.2 cm) high at the shoulder and weighs between 30 and 40 lb (13.6–18.1 kg). Its straight, dense, silky coat is rich dark red and white in color and forms fringes, or feathers, on the ears, chest, underside, back of legs, and stern. The tail is docked. A hardy, all-purpose gundog, the Welsh springer can be trained to retrieve waterfowl as well as upland game birds. See DOG.

Welsh terrier, breed of medium-sized TERRIER developed in Wales more than a century ago. It stands about 15 in. (38 cm) high at the shoulder and weighs about 20 lb (9 kg). Its close-lying, harsh, wiry coat may be black and tan or black, grizzle, and tan in color. The direct descendant of the old English wire-haired black-and-tan sporting dogs from which have come many of the present-day terriers, the Welsh terrier was renowned for its gameness on badger, fox, and otter. In recent times it has been raised chiefly as a pet. See DOG.

Welty, Eudora, 1909–, American author, b. Jackson, Miss., grad. Univ. of Wisconsin, 1929. One of the important American regional writers of the 20th cent., Welty usually writes about the inhabitants of rural Mississippi. Her characters are alive—comic, eccentric, often grotesque, but nonetheless charming—and their reality is augmented by Welty's skill at capturing the dialect and speech patterns of the Mississippi area. Among her collections of short stories are *A Curtain of Green* (1941), *The Wide Net* (1943), *The Golden Apples* (1949), and *The Bride of Innisfallen* (1955). Her novels include *Delta Wedding* (1946), about a 20th-century plantation family; *The Ponder Heart* (1954; dramatized 1956), a comic fantasy concerning a soft-hearted, foolish man; *Losing Battles* (1970), which uses the framework of a large family reunion in the 1930s to describe various characters' lost battles against time and change; and *The Optimist's Daughter* (1972; Pulitzer Prize), about the contemporary loosening of home and family ties and its effect on grief, love, and the acknowledgment of loss. She has also published a novelette, *The Robber Bridegroom* (1942), and a collection of her own photographs of Mississippi in the 1930s, *One Time: One Place* (1972).

Welwyn Garden City (wĕl'ĭn), urban district (1971 pop. 40,369), Hertfordshire, E central England. It is a GARDEN CITY, founded by Sir Ebenezer Howard in 1920. Its industries, which employ most of the local population, produce a variety of products including radio and television sets. After World War II the district's growth was planned to relieve London of overpopulation.

Wembley: see BRENT.

wen, benign, slow-growing, painless cyst of the skin resulting from obstruction of the sebaceous gland ducts. It is frequently found on the scalp, ears, face, back, or scrotum. Usually no treatment is required. Large wens may be surgically removed.

Wenatchee (wĭnăch'ē), city (1970 pop. 16,912), seat of Chelan co., central Wash., on the Columbia River in the foothills of the Cascade Range; inc. 1892. It is a resort and a commercial center in a fertile fruit-growing valley famous for its apples. An apple-blossom festival is held annually in the spring. Wenatchee's major industries are food processing and the production of aluminum. In the city are Wenatchee Valley College, an agriculture experiment and research station, and a museum containing prehistoric Indian artifacts. Nearby Rock Island Dam, the first hydroelectric dam on the Columbia River, supplies Wenatchee with power.

Wenceslaus, Saint (wĕn'səsləs), d. 929, duke of Bohemia. He was reared in the Christian faith by his grandmother, St. Ludmilla. He became duke at an early age, and during his minority his mother, Drahomira, acted as regent. She, like many other Czech nobles, opposed Christianity and persecuted the Christians. She incurred the enmity of the German king, Henry I (Henry the Fowler), by aiding the Wends, a Slavic people, against Henry; Henry invaded Bohemia. Wenceslaus, who had then begun to rule, recognized the futility of resistance and negotiated a peace. During his reign Wenceslaus was noted for his piety; he worked vigorously to strengthen Christianity in Bohemia. His religion and his friendly relations with Henry I caused much discontent among the nobles, and he was assassinated by his brother Boleslav I, who succeeded him. By the beginning of the 11th cent., he was already recognized as the patron saint of Bohemia. Vaclav is the Czech form of his name. Feast: Sept. 28.

Wenceslaus, 1361–1419, Holy Roman emperor (uncrowned) and German king (1378–1400), king of Bohemia (1378–1419) as Wenceslaus IV, elector of Brandenburg (1373–76), son and successor of Emperor Charles IV. He was, even more than his father, a Bohemian rather than German king. Although gifted, he was given to drunkenness and violent fits of temper. It was largely through his support that his half-brother SIGISMUND was able to take possession (1387) of Hungary. Residing in Bohemia, Wenceslaus could do little to end the conflict in Germany between the nobles and the imperial towns. In the general war from 1386 to 1389, Wenceslaus finally sided with the nobles, who were favored by the Peace of Eger (or Peace of Cheb). In the Great SCHISM, Wenceslaus, like his father, at first supported the Roman pope, Urban VI, but in 1398 he agreed with Charles VI of France that both rival popes should resign and a new pope be elected. The two weak monarchs were unable to execute this plan. As early as 1380, Wenceslaus's neglect of German affairs caused the princes to demand that he name a vicar for Germany. Dissatisfied with his appointment (1396) of Sigismund, they were further provoked by his entente with France and his sale (1395) of Milan as a hereditary fief to Gian Galeazzo VISCONTI. They deposed him from the German kingship and elected (1400) RUPERT of the Palatinate. Wenceslaus refused to recognize the deposition, but he retired to Bohemia; in 1411, after Rupert's death, he surrendered his claim to Germany to Sigismund. In Bohemia, Wenceslaus was early embroiled with the nobles and higher clergy, especially with the archbishop of Prague. Constant civil war with the nobles twice led to Wenceslaus's imprisonment (1394, 1402–3); Sigismund was both times involved in the plot. As an enemy of the higher clergy, Wenceslaus supported John HUSS, the Czech religious reformer. The Decree of Kutna Hora (1409), which gave the Czechs preponderance in voting for the rector of the Univ. of Prague led to the election of Huss as rector. The king attempted to prevent the burning of the writings of John WYCLIF and the termination of Huss's preaching and sought to persuade John XXIII (see COSSA, BALDASSARE) to suspend proceedings against Huss. When the interdict was laid on Prague (1412), he persuaded the reformer to leave the city, but continued to support him covertly. Wenceslaus avoided suppressing the national and religious outburst that followed the burning of Huss, but pressure from Sigismund, then German king, and the rise of the radical Hussite leader John ZIZKA cooled his feelings toward the Hussites. The reform took on a rebellious character, and after serious riots several town councilors appointed by the king were thrown from the windows of the town hall (the first Defenestration of Prague, July 30, 1419) and were killed. Wenceslaus died shortly afterward and was succeeded by Sigismund as king of Bohemia. The HUSSITE WARS prevented Sigismund from being accepted as king until 1436.

Wenceslaus I, d. 1253, king of Bohemia (1230–53), son and successor of Ottocar I. He invited large numbers of Germans to settle in the villages and towns of Bohemia and Moravia. In some villages peasants of Czech origin became a minority or were forced to submit to German-style feudal obligations. Many towns were granted self-rule, with charters modeled on that of MAGDEBURG. After resisting the invasion of BATU KHAN (1241), Wenceslaus and his nobles built or rebuilt many castles, giving them German names. Wenceslaus received Holy Roman Emperor Frederick II's support in his attempt to acquire Austria but later backed Pope Gregory IX against the emperor. He was succeeded by his son, Ottocar II.

Wenceslaus II, 1271–1305, king of Bohemia (1278–1305) and of Poland (1300–1305), son and successor of OTTOCAR II. From the death (1278) of his father until 1283 the regency was exercised by Otto, margrave of Brandenburg, appointed by the German king Rudolf I of Hapsburg. Otto abused his power, and the Bohemians suffered greatly until Rudolf's intervention reestablished order. After Wenceslaus's entry (1283) into Prague, his mother's secret husband, Zavis of Falckenstein, rose to power. Zavis's intrigues and his hostility to Rudolf I, whose daughter Judith was the wife of Wenceslaus, led to Zavis's downfall. In 1290, Wenceslaus had Zavis beheaded and began his personal rule. Although poorly educated, Wenceslaus planned to codify Bohemian law, and he reformed the currency. Wenceslaus soon adopted Zavis's anti-Hapsburg policy and greatly extended his power. At the invitation of some Polish lords he accepted (1291) the duchy of Kraków and in 1300 was crowned king of all Poland. In 1301 he accepted for his son (later Wenceslaus III) the crown of Hungary. The new German king, Albert I of Hapsburg, and Pope Boniface VIII demanded that Wenceslaus give up Poland and Hungary and the rights to the rich silver mines of Kutna Hora, key to Bohemian strength. Wenceslaus repulsed Albert's invasion (1304) and was preparing to invade Austria when he died.

Wenceslaus III, c.1289–1306, king of Bohemia (1305–6) and of Hungary (1301–5), son and successor of Wenceslaus II. On the death of Andrew III of Hungary, last of the Arpad dynasty, he was elected (1301) king of Hungary. Unable to assert his authority in Hungary, he relinquished (1305) his claim to Duke Otto of Bavaria. Wenceslaus tried, however, to assert his hereditary claim to the Polish crown, but he was assassinated at Olomouc while marching to Poland. He was the last of the dynasty of the Premyslids. After an interregnum, John of Luxemburg, who married Wenceslaus's sister, was elected (1310) king of Bohemia.

Wenceslaus IV, king of Bohemia: see WENCESLAUS, Holy Roman emperor.

Wen-chou: see WENCHOW, China.

Wenchow or **Wen-chou** (wŭn-jō), city (1970 est. pop. 250,000), SE Chekiang prov., SE China. It is a small deep-sea port on the Ou River 12 mi (19 km) from the East China Sea and a major trade center for an area producing tea, cotton, and oranges. Manufactures include condensed milk, paper and bamboo products, fertilizer, and handicrafts. Founded in the 4th cent. A.D., Wenchow retains many ancient buildings.

Wendell, Barrett (wĕn'dəl), 1855–1921, American teacher and scholar, b. Boston, grad. Harvard, 1877. He taught at Harvard (1880–1917) and lectured at Cambridge and the Sorbonne. Among his works are a study of Cotton Mather (1891) and *A Literary History of America* (1900), the outgrowth of the first course in the subject at Harvard. See M. A. De W. Howe, *Barrett Wendell and His Letters* (1924).

Wenden: see CESIS, USSR.

Wends or **Sorbs,** Slavic people (numbering over 300,000) of E Germany, in Lusatia. They speak Lusatian (also known as Sorbic or Wendish), a West Slavic language with two main dialects: Upper Lusatian, nearer to Czech, and Lower Lusatian, nearer to Polish. The towns of Bautzen (Upper Lusatia) and Cottbus (Lower Lusatia) are their chief cultural centers. In the Middle Ages the term *Wends* was applied by the Germans to all the SLAVS inhabiting the area between the Oder River in the east and the Elbe River and the Saale River in the west. German conquest of their land began in the 6th cent. and was completed under Charlemagne (8th cent.). A coalition of Wendish tribes in the 10th cent. and again in the early 12th cent. temporarily halted German expansion. A crusade against the pagan Wends was launched in 1147 under the leadership of HENRY THE LION of Saxony and ALBERT THE BEAR of Brandenburg. The crusade itself was, on the whole, a failure, but in subsequent years Henry the Lion, aided by Waldemar I of Denmark, Albert the Bear, and other princes, carried out a systematic campaign of conquest. By the end of the 12th cent. nearly all Germany except East Prussia had been subjected to German rule and was Christianized. However, a group of Slavic-speaking Wends has maintained itself to the present day in Lusatia. They call themselves *Srbi* and hence are known also in English as Lusatian Sorbs or Serbs. See Gerald Stone, *The Smallest Slavonic Nation: The Sorbs of Lusatia* (1972).

Wengen (vĕng'ən), mountain resort, Bern canton, S central Switzerland, in the Bernese Alps. It is a summer and winter recreation area. The nearby **Wengern Alp** (vĕng'ərn ălp), at 6,160 ft (1,878 m), has a beautiful view of the Jungfrau peak.

Wentworth, Benning, 1696–1770, American colonial governor, b. Portsmouth, N.H. A leading merchant of Portsmouth, he served in the colonial assembly and council, and, when New Hampshire was established as a separate province, he was appointed (1741) governor; he served until 1767. With no legal justification he made vast grants of land W of the Connecticut River in the region claimed by New York, including among the beneficiaries his friends, his relatives, and himself. The New Hampshire Grants (later the state of Vermont) thus became a much-disputed area. Bennington, Vt., took its name from his first name.

Wentworth, Sir John, 1737–1820, colonial governor of New Hampshire, b. Portsmouth, N.H. On the forced resignation of his uncle, Benning Wentworth, he was commissioned (Aug., 1766) to succeed him both as governor of New Hampshire and as surveyor of the king's woods in North America. Assuming the governorship in June, 1767, Wentworth was at first popular. However, he was thoroughly loyal to the king and prorogued the assembly when it attempted to form (1774) a committee of correspondence. On the outbreak of the American Revolution, he was forced to flee. In 1783 he was reappointed surveyor of what remained of the king's woods in North America, and from 1792 to 1808 he was governor (although he only had the title of lieutenant governor) of Nova Scotia. He was knighted in 1795. While governor of New Hampshire, Wentworth granted (1769) Dartmouth College its charter and was a member of its original board of trustees. See L. S. Mayo, *John Wentworth, Governor of New Hampshire, 1767–1775* (1921); W. C. Abbott, *Conflicts with Oblivion* (1924, repr. 1969).

Wentworth, Thomas: see STRAFFORD, THOMAS WENTWORTH, 1ST EARL OF.

Wentworth, William Charles, 1793?–1872, Australian statesman. His exploration (1813) of the Blue Mts. in Australia revealed vast pasturelands in the western part of the continent. In 1816 he went to Great Britain to study law; while there he published (1819) a description of Australia. He returned (1824) to Australia, where he set up a lucrative law practice, championed the cause of the "emancipists" (liberated convicts), and founded (1824) a newspaper, the *Australian*, to promulgate his views on Australian self-government. Wentworth took a prominent part in the legislative council of New South Wales, formed in 1842, and was the leading figure in the fight for the constitution of 1855. In 1849 he put through the bill for the founding of the Univ. of Sydney. After 1857 he resided mainly in England. He wrote *Australasia* (1823), a poem about his native country.

werewolf: see LYCANTHROPY.

Werfel, Franz (fränts vĕr'fəl), 1890–1945, Austrian writer, b. Prague. He expressed his belief in the brotherhood of man in lyric verse, in expressionist and conventional plays, and in large-scale novels that have become internationally famous. He fled from Nazi-occupied Austria to France and, after the fall of France, to the United States. Besides several volumes of poems, his work includes the dramas *Bockgesang* (1921, tr. *Goat Song*, 1926), *Juarez und Maximilian* (1924, tr. 1926), *Paulus unter den Juden* (1926, tr. *Paul Among the Jews,* 1928), and *Das Reich Gottes in Böhmen* [the Kingdom of God in Bohemia] (1930); and the comedy *Jacobowsky und der Oberst* (1945; adaptation by S. N. Behrman, *Jacobowsky and the Colonel,* 1944). He is best known in the United States for the novels *Vierzig Tage des Musa Dagh* (1933, tr. *The Forty Days of Musa Dagh,* 1934), recounting the struggle of the Armenians against the Turks in World War I, and *Das Lied von Bernadette* (1941, tr. *The Song of Bernadette,* 1942), about the saint from Lourdes.

Wergeland, Henrik (hĕn'rĭk vĕr'gəlän), 1808–45, Norwegian writer and patriot. A champion of liberty, democracy, and international cooperation, he worked zealously for popular education and reform. His strong personality and his extreme nationalism involved him in violent controversies. He was considered the Norwegian literary genius of his era, and his influence was felt long after his death. Wergeland's poems include *Creation, Man, and Messiah* (1830), a long verse drama, and *The Jew* (1842) and *The Jewess* (1844), in support of Jewish immigrants. *The English Pilot* (1844) voiced his final aim, the liberation of the human mind. See Halvdan Koht and Sigmund Skard, *The Voice of Norway* (1944).

wergild: see COMPOSITION.

Werner, Abraham Gottlob (ä'brähäm gôt'lōp vĕr'nər), 1750–1817, German geologist. In 1775 he became inspector and teacher in the mining academy at Freiberg, which through his efforts became one of the leading schools in Germany. In the last part of the 18th cent. he was the most notable figure in the investigation of rocks and minerals; he called the new science geognosy and defined it as the study of the layers of mineral matter. He was the first to classify minerals systematically. According to his theory of neptunism, the earth was originally an ocean of water from which were precipitated the solid rocks now forming most of the dry land. Although much of his theory has been rejected, geology is indebted to him for the application of chronology to rock formations as well as for his precise definitions.

Werner, Anton Alexander von (än'tôn älĕksän'dər fən vĕr'nər), 1843–1915, German historical painter, portraitist, and illustrator. He was director (1875–1915) of the Berlin Academy. In the Franco-Prussian War he accompanied the 3d Army Corps in an unofficial capacity as painter. Of this period are his portrait of von Moltke, *In Quarters before Paris* and *Episode of War*. His best-known illustrations are those for Scheffel's poems.

Werner, Pierre (pyĕr vĕr'nər), 1913–, political leader in Luxembourg. A lawyer, he held various posts in the ministry of finance after World War II. Secretary to the council of government (1949–53), he was (1953–58) minister of finance and of the armed forces. He became prime minister in 1959, holding other ministerial posts concurrently. Named chairman of the Common Market Committee on Monetary Union in 1970, he was instrumental in coordinating the member countries' economic and monetary policies. He resigned in 1974 after his party lost the election.

Werner, Zacharias (Friedrich Ludwig Zacharias Werner) (tsäkhärē'äs), 1768–1823, German dramatist. After a life of dissipation, he was converted to Roman Catholicism and became a priest of intense piety. His plays, which established the "fate-tragedy" school, include *Die Söhne des Thales* (1803–4, tr. *The Sons of the Valley*, 1903); the very popular *Martin Luther; oder, Die Weihe der Kraft* [Martin Luther; or, the consecration of strength] (1807), which, after his conversion, he repudiated in the allegorical poem *Die Weihe der Unkraft* [the consecration of weakness] (1813); *Attila* (1808); and *Der Vierundzwanzigste Februar* (1815, tr. *The 24th of February*, 1844).

Wernher der Gartenaere (Wernher the Gardener) (vĕr'nər dĕr gär'tənĕrə), 13th-century German poet. His *Meier Helmbrecht* (written between 1270 and 1282) is the satirical tale of a young farmer who, to elevate his social status, becomes a robber-knight. He is hanged by the peasants he tried to rise above. A lively and well-written verse narrative, it is also a contribution to social history.

Wernigerode (vĕrnēgərō'də), city (1970 pop. 32,662), Magdeburg district, W East Germany, at the northern foot of the Harz mts. It is an industrial city and a tourist center. Manufactures include machinery, paper, processed food, and pharmaceuticals. Noteworthy buildings in the picturesque city include a medieval castle (rebuilt in the 19th cent.), formerly the seat of the princes of Stolberg-Wernigerode; two Romanesque-early Gothic churches; and a 15th-century city hall.

Wertenbaker, Thomas Jefferson (wûr'tənbākər), 1879–1966, American historian, b. Charlottesville, Va. He taught history at the Agricultural and Mechanical College of Texas (1907–9) and at the Univ. of Virginia (1909–10). After 1910 he taught at Princeton. A specialist in the colonial history of Virginia, he wrote *Virginia under the Stuarts* (1914), *Patrician and Plebeian in Virginia* (1916), and *Planters of Colonial Virginia* (1922)—all republished in one volume, *The Shaping of Colonial Virginia* (1958). His other books on the South include *Norfolk—Historic Southern Port* (1931) and *The Old South—the Founding of American Civilization* (1942). His general histories of the United States are *The American People* (1926) and *The United States of America* (1931; with Donald E. Smith). He also wrote *The Puritan Oligarchy* (1947), *Father Knickerbocker Rebels: New York City during the Revolution* (1948), and *Give Me Liberty* (1958). In 1939–40 he occupied the chair in U.S. history established at Oxford for visiting American scholars.

Wertheimer, Max (mäks vĕrt'hīmər), 1880–1943, German psychologist, b. Prague. He studied at the universities of Prague, Berlin, and Würzburg (Ph.D., 1904). His original researches, while he was a professor at Frankfurt and Berlin, placed him in the forefront of contemporary psychology. With the advent of Hitler he came to the United States, where he immediately joined the graduate faculty of the New School for Social Research; he was also visiting lecturer (1934) at Columbia Univ. Wertheimer's discovery (1910–12) of the phi phenomenon (concerning the illusion of motion) gave rise to the influential school of GESTALT psychology. His early experiments, in collaboration with Wolfgang Köhler and Kurt Koffka, introduced a new approach (macroscopic as opposed to microscopic) to the study of psychological problems. In the latter part of his life he directed much of his attention to the problem of learning; this research resulted in a book, posthumously published, called *Productive Thinking* (1945).

Werve, Claus van de (klous vän də vĕr'və), d. 1439, Flemish sculptor. The nephew and student of Claus SLUTER, Werve succeeded his uncle as chief sculptor to Philip the Bold, whose tomb he designed. His squat chunky figures were close in style to Sluter's.

Wescott, Glenway, 1901–, American author, b. Kewaskum, Wis. He grew up in Wisconsin, which serves as the background for several of his novels and short stories. During the 1920s he lived in Europe, mainly in Germany and in France. His early publications include poetry (*Natives of the Rocks*, 1926) and short stories (*Good-bye Wisconsin*, 1928), but it is as a novelist that he made his reputation. His first novel, *The Apple of the Eye*, appeared in 1924. It was followed by *The Grandmothers* (1927), a carefully wrought story concerning the sorrows and frustrations of a pioneer Midwestern family. His later novels include *The Pilgrim Hawk* (1940), a love story set in Paris, and *Apartment in Athens* (1945), which describes the effects of the Nazi occupation on a Greek family. *Images of Truth* (1962) is a collection of his remembrances and critical writings.

Wesel (vā'zəl), city (1970 pop. 44,633), North Rhine-Westphalia, W West Germany, on the Rhine River near the mouth of the Lippe River. It is a river port, a transshipment point, and an industrial center in the RUHR district. Manufactures include precision instruments, processed food, glass, and iron goods. First mentioned in the 8th cent., Wesel passed to the counts of Cleves in the early 13th cent. and in 1407 joined the Hanseatic League. The city came under the control of Brandenburg in 1666. Wesel was almost totally destroyed in World War II. In March, 1945, the Allies crossed the Rhine there in a major amphibious and airborne operation. The city contains a Gothic church, the Willibrordikirche (1424–1506).

Weser (vā'zər), river, c.300 mi (480 km) long, formed at Münden, E central West Germany, by the junction of the Fulda and Werra rivers. It flows generally N past Minden, where it passes through the Porta Westphalia into the North German plain. It enters the North Sea through a long estuary N of Bremen. The Hunte and Aller rivers are among its chief tributaries. Navigable to Kassel on the Fulda River, the Weser is connected by the Midland canal system with the Rhine, the Ems, and the Elbe rivers.

Wesker, Arnold, 1932–, English playwright, b. London. At various times he has been a carpenter's mate, a seed sorter, and a pastrycook. His plays *Chicken Soup with Barley* (1958), *Roots* (1958), and *I'm Talking about Jerusalem* (1960) form a trilogy about a family of Jewish Communist intellectuals. His socialist point of view is reflected in his other plays, notably *The Kitchen* (1961), *Chips with Everything* (1962), and *The Four Seasons* (1969). See studies by Glenda Leeming and Simon Trussler (1971) and Ronald Hayman (1973).

Weslaco (wĕs'lĭkō), city (1970 pop. 15,313), Hidalgo co., extreme S Texas, in the irrigated region of the lower Rio Grande valley; inc. 1921. It has a giant citrus-canning plant, fruit- and vegetable-processing companies, a garment factory, and other agriculture-related industries. Agricultural research is also conducted. The city's name was derived from the initials of the W. E. Stewart Land Company, which promoted the townsite in 1917. Its Spanish-style architecture and palm-lined streets abloom with flowers give it a leisurely air. It is linked to Mexico by an international bridge. A wildlife preserve is nearby.

Wesley, Charles, 1707–88, English Methodist preacher and hymn writer. As a student at Oxford he devoted himself to systematic study and to the regular practice of religious duties; he and companions whom he persuaded to adopt the same orderly course were taunted as "methodists." They formed a society, sometimes referred to as the Holy Club, of which his older brother John Wesley became the leader in 1729. Charles Wesley was ordained in the Church of England in 1735, and the same year both brothers sailed for Georgia, Charles to act as secretary to James Oglethorpe. The following year, however, he returned to England in ill health. After experiencing evangelical conversion in May, 1738, he began writing hymns and preaching at the great revival meetings led by the two Wesleys and George Whitefield. For 17 years Charles made continual evangelistic journeys, but after 1756 he worked mainly in Bristol and London. He was firmly opposed to all suggestion of separation from the Church of England. He is said to have produced about 6,500 hymns, many of which are still used in Protestant churches; among the best known are "Hark! the Herald Angels Sing" and "Jesus, Lover of My Soul." See his journal, ed. by Thomas Jackson (1849); biography by F. C. Gill (1964).

Wesley, John, 1703–91, English evangelical preacher, founder of METHODISM, b. Epworth, Lincolnshire. He was ordained a deacon in the Church of England in 1725, elected a fellow of Lincoln College, Oxford, in 1726, and ordained a priest in 1728. At Oxford he took the lead (1729) in a group of students that included his younger brother, Charles WESLEY, and George WHITEFIELD. They were derisively called "methodists" for their methodical devotion to study and religious duties. In 1735 the Wesleys accompanied James Oglethorpe to Georgia, John to serve there as a missionary and Charles to act as secretary to Oglethorpe. During John Wesley's two-year stay in the colony he was deeply influenced by Moravian missionaries; upon his return to England he made many Moravian friends. On May 24, 1738, at a meeting of a small religious society in Aldersgate St., London, Wesley experienced a religious conversion while listening to a reading of Martin Luther's preface to the Epistle to the Romans. This experience of salvation through faith in Christ alone was the burden of his message for the rest of his life. He soon became involved in evangelistic work, in the course of which he is said to have preached 40,000 sermons and to have traveled 250,000 mi (400,000 km). On the advice of Whitefield, Wesley undertook open-air, or field, preaching, first in Bristol, then elsewhere. In 1739 a group in London requested him to aid them in forming a society and to act as their leader. An old foundry at Moorfields was purchased; it remained until 1778 the center of Methodist work in London. Because of his Arminianism and belief in Christian perfection, Wesley repudiated (c.1740) the Calvinist doctrine of election. This led to a break with Whitefield, although the personal friendship of the two Methodist leaders remained firm. In 1784, Wesley executed the deed of declaration by which the Methodist societies became legally constituted; it was in essence the charter of the Wesleyan Methodists. In the same year he became convinced that he must ordain a superintendent to administer sacraments and to serve the Methodist societies in America, although he had long hesitated to assume the authority of ordination. Wesley ordained Dr. Thomas COKE to this office; Francis Asbury was to serve as associate superintendent. It was not Wesley's intention to found a separate church, but toward the end of his life the Methodist Episcopal Church had already come into existence in America, and it became apparent that in England the Methodists could not work within the Anglican Church. He therefore made plans for his societies to go on independently after his death, although both Wesleys remained clergymen of the Church of England to the end of their lives. During John Wesley's later years admiration for his abilities largely replaced the rejection he had endured in earlier days. See John Wesley's letters (ed. by John Telford, 8 vol., 1831); the standard edition of his journal (ed. by Nehemiah Curnock, 4 vol., 1909–16); biographies by Dobree Bonamy (1933, repr. 1974), Oscar Sherwin (1961), V. H. Green (1964, repr. 1971), and Dorothy Marshall (1965); studies by Frank Baker (1970) and W. J. Warner (1930, repr. 1967).

Wesleyan College, at Macon, Ga.; United Methodist; for women; chartered 1836 as Georgia Female College. The present form of the name was adopted in 1919. Wesleyan College was the first college chartered to award degrees to women.

Wesleyan University, at Middletown, Conn.; coeducational; chartered and opened 1831. There are special cooperative study programs with the California Institute of Technology and the engineering department of Columbia Univ. Wesleyan is noted for its undergraduate programs of tutorial instruction and independent study. The university's research facilities include the African-American Institute, a computer laboratory, and a science center.

Wessel, Johann (yō'hän vĕs'əl), c.1420–1489, Dutch theologian and precursor of the Protestant Reformation, also known as Wessel Harmenss Gansfort or Goesevoyrd. He was one of the Brethren of the Common Life, among whom he had his early instruction at Zwolle, although he rejected their narrowness of view. From c.1470 he lived in Paris, where he was known for his teachings. His later years (from 1479) were spent in Holland, partly in Groningen, partly near Zwolle, in the midst of friends and pupils. His writings belong to that period and are made up chiefly of short treatises. After his death his manuscripts were gathered together and sent to Martin Luther and Huldreich Zwingli. Luther edited his writings (c.1521). While he looked backward to Augustine and Bernard, Wessel also had views that prefigured the great Protestant Reformation in Germany. He regarded the Scriptures as the sole repository of truth and rejected the decrees of church councils, although he accepted papal authority.

Wessex (wĕs'ĭks), one of the Anglo-Saxon kingdoms in England. It may have been settled as early as 495 by Saxons under CERDIC, who is reputed to have landed in Hampshire. Cerdic's grandson, Ceawlin (560–93), annexed scattered Saxon settlements in the Chiltern Hills and drove the Celts from the region between the upper Thames valley and the lower Severn. But Ceawlin himself was finally expelled from Wessex, and until the end of the 8th cent. the country was overshadowed successively by Kent, Northumbria, and Mercia. King Cædwalla (reigned 685–88) conducted several successful campaigns; and his successor INE consolidated the western expansion through Somerset and exacted tribute from Kent. After Ine's death, however, the kingdom relapsed into anarchy. EGBERT (802–39) became overlord of all England, but his successors were forced to relinquish many of his gains and to concentrate on defending their lands against the invading Danes. With the reign of ALFRED (871–99) and the halting of the Danes, the history of Wessex becomes that of England. In the 10th cent., Edward the Elder, Athelstan, Edmund, and Edred gradually acquired firm control over all England, including the Danelaw. This unity ended, however, after the quiet reign of Edgar (959–75), for ÆTHELRED (978–1016) could offer no effective resistance to the invading Vikings. Canute established Danish rule in 1016. The end of his line caused the recall of Edward the Confessor (1042–66), last of the Wessex line of Alfred. In the novels of Thomas Hardy, Wessex is used to mean the SW counties of England, mainly Dorsetshire.

West, Benjamin, 1738–1820, American historical painter who worked in England. He was born in Springfield, Pa., in a house that is now a memorial museum at Swarthmore College. After some instruction from a local artist named William Williams, he set up as a portrait painter in Philadelphia at 18, subsequently moving to New York City. In 1760 he went to Europe, where he remained for the rest of his life. For three years he studied in Italy. Working under the tutelage of Anton Mengs, he was also inspired by the classical research of Johann Winckelmann. He then settled in London, becoming a leader of the neoclassical movement. Under the patronage of George III, commissions came to him in great numbers, and in 1772 he was appointed historical painter to the king. A founder of the Royal Academy, he succeeded Sir Joshua Reynolds as its president in 1792. West executed more than 400 canvases, chiefly historical, mythological, and religious subjects painted on a heroic scale. He had many pupils and was a generous friend and adviser to younger artists, particularly American painters studying in England, among whom were Washington Allston, Samuel Morse, Charles Willson Peale, Gilbert Stuart, and John Singleton Copley. His influence on American painting of the period was predominant. Among West's best-known works are *Death of General Wolfe* (Grosvenor Gall., London) and *Penn's Treaty with the Indians* (Pa. Acad. of the Fine Arts). In these paintings he created a new departure in historical painting by clothing his figures in the costume of their period instead of the traditional classical garb. At the same time, he maintained the balanced compositional elements of the neoclassical painters. Sometimes his paintings were more turbulent and colorful and indeed prefigured romanticism, such as *Death on a Pale Horse* (Pa. Acad. of the Fine Arts). See studies by John Galt (1816), Henry Jackson (1900), and Grose Evans (1959).

West, Jessamyn, 1907–, American novelist, b. Indiana. A Quaker, she is best known for her novel *The Friendly Persuasion* (1945), about the conflicts felt by a Quaker farm family during the Civil War. Her other works include the novels *Cress Delahanty* (1954) and *Except For Me and Thee* (1969), sequel to *The Friendly Persuasion; Love, Death, and the Ladies Drill Team* (1955), a collection of stories; and *Hide and Seek* (1973), an autobiography.

West, Mae, 1892–, American stage and movie comedienne, b. Brooklyn, N.Y. The unparalleled mistress of double entendre, West began her career in burlesque and continued on stage and in films to treat sex in a broad and humorous form. She wrote and starred in a number of plays, including *Sex* (1926) and *Diamond Lil* (1928). Among her typical films are *She Done Him Wrong* (1933) and *My Little Chickadee* (1939), written with her co-star W. C. Fields. In 1969 West appeared in *Myra Breckenridge.* See her autobiography, *Goodness Had Nothing to Do with It* (1959), and *The Wit and Wisdom of Mae West* (1967).

West, Morris, 1916–, Australian novelist, b. Melbourne. He has been an intelligence officer in the Australian Signal Corps, a member of the Christian Brothers Order, and secretary to William Morris Hughes. This background is reflected in his best-selling novels; e.g., *The Shoes of the Fisherman* (1963) concerns a Soviet cardinal who is named pope during an international crisis. His other novels include *The Devil's Advocate* (1959), *Daughter of Silence* (1961), and *Harlequin* (1974).

West, Nathanael, 1903–40, American novelist, whose real name was Nathan Weinstein, b. New York City, grad. Brown Univ., 1924. An innovative, highly original author, West revealed the sterility and grotesqueness underlying the American dream; his vision has profoundly influenced subsequent writers. After spending two years in Paris, he worked as a hotel manager in New York. His first novel, *The Dream Life of Balso Snell* (1931), is a garish satire that foreshadowed the work to follow. *Miss Lonelyhearts* (1933), his most successful novel, relates the painful life of a columnist for the lovelorn whose misguided priestliness leads him to a tragic and ironic involvement with his suffering correspondents. He also edited and wrote for several magazines and in 1935 moved to Hollywood, where he became a scriptwriter. *A Cool Million* (1934) was West's bitter indictment of a materialistic world. His last novel, *The Day of the Locust* (1939), presents a gallery of horrifying misfits living in a vacuous, surreal Hollywood atmosphere. West was never a commercial success in his own time, but his popularity rose after his premature death at 37 in an automobile accident. The *Complete Works of Nathanael West* was published in 1957. See biography by Jay Martin (1970); studies by Randall Reid (1967) and J. F. Light (2d ed. 1971).

West, Dame Rebecca, 1892–, English novelist and critic, whose real name is Cicily Fairfield, b. Ireland. At various times she has served as a literary critic and political writer for American and British journals. Her novels are detailed studies of the psychology of the individual and include *The Return of the Soldier* (1918), *The Judge* (1922), *The Thinking Reed* (1939), *The Fountain Overflows* (1956), and *Birds Fall Down* (1966). Her critical work includes essays in *The Strange Necessity* (1928), studies of Henry James (1916) and St. Augustine (1933), and *The Court and the Castle* (1957). *Black Lamb and Grey Falcon* (1942) is an extraordinary travel book, political study, and commentary on Yugoslavia. *The Meaning of Treason* (1947) is based on her reports of treason trials growing out of World War II. In 1959 she was made a Dame Commander, Order of the British Empire. See Peter Wolfe, *Rebecca West, Artist and Thinker* (1971); G. N. Ray, *H. G. Wells and Rebecca West* (1974).

West, Thomas: see DE LA WARR, THOMAS WEST, 12TH BARON.

West Allis, city (1970 pop. 71,649), Milwaukee co., SE Wis., a suburb of Milwaukee; inc. 1902. Mobile equipment, electronic products, generators, and heavy machinery are among its manufactures. The Wisconsin state fair and annual international skating and auto races are held there. A veterans' hospital is nearby.

West Bend, industrial city (1970 pop. 16,555), seat of Washington co., E Wis., on the Milwaukee River; inc. 1885, consolidated with Barton in 1961. Tools and dies, machine tools, washers, dairy items, and leather products are made there. A two-year branch of the Univ. of Wisconsin is located in West Bend, and a state park is nearby.

West Bengal: see BENGAL.

West Berlin: see under BERLIN.

Westborough, town (1970 pop. 12,594), Worcester co., E central Mass., on the Assabet River; inc. 1717. The town, which is largely residential, produces abrasives, electronic components, tools, dyes, and other products. The birthplace of Eli Whitney, the inventor of the cotton gin, is preserved.

West Bromwich (brŭm'ĭj, -ĭch, brŏm'wĭch), county borough (1971 pop. 166,626), Staffordshire, W central England. The borough's area was enlarged in 1966 by the addition of most of the borough of Wednesbury and other areas. On the site of a 12th-century Benedictine priory, the town has coal mines, foundries, and electrical engineering and chemical works. There is a technical college. In 1974, West Bromwich became part of the new metropolitan county of West Midlands.

Westbrook, city (1970 pop. 14,444), Cumberland co., SW Maine, an industrial suburb W of Portland; founded 1657, inc. as a city 1891. Its manufactures include shoes and paper and wood products. An industrial park opened in the city in 1969.

Westbury, residential village (1970 pop. 15,362), Nassau co., SE N.Y., on Long Island; settled 1650, inc. 1932. Harness races are held at Roosevelt Raceway there.

West Caldwell, borough (1970 pop. 11,887), Essex co., NE N.J., a residential suburb of Newark and New York City; inc. 1904. It has some light manufacturing.

West Carrollton, city (1970 pop. 10,748), Montgomery co., SW Ohio, a suburb of Dayton on the Miami River.

West Chester, borough (1970 pop. 19,301), seat of Chester co., SE Pa., W of Philadelphia; inc. 1799. Primarily residential, West Chester is also the trade and processing center of a fertile agricultural region. The borough's chief manufactures are pharmaceuticals, canned mushrooms, and fire-fighting equipment. West Chester State College is there, and Brandywine State Historical Park, on the site of the battle of BRANDYWINE (1777), is nearby. The Turk's Head Inn (1747), an early stage coach stop, still stands.

Westchester, village (1970 pop. 20,033), Cook co., NE Ill., a suburb W of Chicago; inc. 1925.

West Chicago, city (1970 pop. 10,111), Du Page co., NE Ill.; inc. 1906.

Westcott, Brooke Foss, 1825–1901, English prelate and scholar. From 1870 to 1890 he was regius professor of divinity at Cambridge. With F. J. A. Hort, he published *The New Testament in the Original Greek* (2 vol., 1881). From 1890 until his death he was bishop of Durham. He was known for his many scriptural commentaries.

Westcott, Edward Noyes, 1846–98, American novelist and banker, b. Syracuse, N.Y. He is known for his popular novel, *David Harum* (pub. posthumously, 1898), which concerns a shrewd, humorous country banker.

West Covina, city (1970 pop. 68,034), Los Angeles co., S Calif., in the San Gabriel valley; inc. 1923. Before World War II it was a small rural community where walnuts, wheat, and livestock were raised.

West Des Moines (də moin'), city (1970 pop. 16,441), Polk co., S central Iowa, a suburb W of Des Moines; inc. 1893 as Valley Junction, renamed 1938. Products manufactured there include cement, metal nozzles, and pumps.

Westerly, town (1970 pop. 17,248), Washington co., extreme SW R.I., between the Pawcatuck River and Block Island Sound; inc. 1669. Its large textile industry dates from 1814, and granite has been quarried there since c.1850. Westerly has other varied manufactures and a substantial trade market. It is also famous as a summer resort. The town actually embraces 11 villages, among them Westerly, on the Pawcatuck River; Watch Hill, a resort severely damaged in the hurricanes of 1938 and 1954; and Avondale. Points of interest include many old buildings. A bridge built in 1932 connects the village of Westerly with Connecticut. A lighthouse and a U.S. coast guard station are maintained at Watch Hill.

Westermann, William Linn, 1873–1954, American classical scholar, b. Belleville, Ill. He taught (1902–6) Latin and Greek at the Univ. of Missouri before teaching history at the Univ. of Minnesota (1906–8), the Univ. of Wisconsin (1908–20), and Cornell (1920–23). After 1923 he taught at Columbia, becoming professor emeritus in 1948. He served on international peace commissions concerned with Middle Eastern affairs, contributed to various historical and philological journals, and edited *Westermann's Classical and Historical Map Series* (1918). He collaborated in writing a series of four volumes about Greek papyri (1926–40); his other writings include *Upon Slavery in Ptolemaic Egypt* (1929) and *Slave Systems of Greek and Roman Antiquity* (1955).

Westermarck, Edward Alexander (vĕs'tərmärk, wĕs'-), 1862–1939, Finnish social philospher and anthropologist. He was professor of sociology at the Univ. of London (1907–30) and professor of philosophy at the Univ. of Turku (until 1935). Westermarck was an authority on the history of morals and of marriage customs, his best-known work being *The History of Human Marriage,* written in English (1891; 5th ed., 3 vol., 1921). On it he based *A Short History of Marriage* (1926). He wrote several books on Moroccan customs. Other books (all in English) include *The Origin and Development of the Moral Ideas* (2 vol., 1906–8; 2d ed. 1912–17), *Ethical Relativity* (1932), *The Future of Marriage in Western Civilization* (1936), and *Christianity and Morals* (1939). See his letters (1940); autobiography (tr. 1929).

Western Australia, state (1971 pop. 1,030,469), 975,920 sq mi (2,527,633 sq km), Australia, comprising the entire western part of the continent. It is bounded on the N, W, and S by the Indian Ocean. PERTH is the capital. Other important cities are KALGOORLIE, a gold-mining center; FREMANTLE, the chief port; and Bunbury, a port S of Perth. Western Australia is the largest state of the commonwealth, but only its southwest corner is fertile and substantially settled; the rest is arid and scarcely habitable. Half the population lives in the Perth metropolitan area; there are also 10,000 aborigines living on reservations throughout the state. State-owned goldfields cover much of Western Australia, and there is a vast central desert. The King Leopold, Hamersley, and Stirling ranges are actually high plateaus. The large lakes in the interior are usually dry, and the northern rivers (the Fortescue, Fitzroy, and Ashburton) are intermittent; the only important river is the Swan in the southwest. The climate is tropical in the north and temperate in the southwest. Agriculture is confined primarily to the southwest and around Perth. About one half of the cultivated land is in wheat. Sheep graze in the north and southwest, and wool is a major product. Meat, dairy products, and timber are also important. The mining of gold, coal, iron, and other minerals is steadily increasing. Industry expanded significantly during the 1960s; industrial metals, machinery, and transportation equipment are the main manufactures. Dirck Hartog, a Dutchman who arrived in 1616, was the first white man known to have visited the coast. A penal colony was founded at Albany in 1826, and the first free settlement was established in the Perth-Fremantle area in 1829. During the 1850s, Britain sent some 10,000 convicts to aid the settlers, most of whom had migrated from E Australia. In the 1860s the first livestock farmers arrived in the northwest. Gold was discovered in the 1880s. Governed at first by New South Wales, Western Australia received its own governor in 1831 and a full constitution as a separate colony in 1890. In 1901 it became a state of the Commonwealth of Australia. The state government consists of a premier, a cabinet, and a bicameral parliament. The nominal chief executive is the governor, appointed by the British crown on advice of the cabinet.

Western Desert, Egypt: see LIBYAN DESERT.

Western Dvina: see DVINA (Western Dvina).

Western Empire: see *Roman Empire* under ROME and see CHARLEMAGNE.

Western European Union (WEU): see INTERNATIONAL GOVERNMENTAL ORGANIZATIONS.

Western Federation of Miners (WFM), a radical labor union that organized the miners and smelter workers of the Rocky Mountain states. Created in 1893 by the merger of several local miners' unions, the WFM had a reputation for violent strikes and militant action from its beginning. On several occasions pitched battles occurred between union members and company guards, and state militia and Federal troops were sometimes dispatched to keep order in strike areas, such as Leadville, Colo., and Coeur d'Alene, Idaho. When Frank Steunenberg, a former governor of Idaho, was murdered in 1905, attempts were made to fix the responsibility on the WFM. Charles Moyer, president of the union, William D. HAYWOOD, secretary, and George Pettibone, a former member, were arrested and stood trial for Steunenberg's murder; defended by Clarence S. Darrow, they were acquitted. The WFM had joined the American Federation of Labor in 1896, but the conservative policies of that organization caused the WFM to withdraw the following year, and, in 1898, to attempt to organize a rival federation, the Western Labor Union. In 1901 the WFM adopted a socialist program, and after the failure of the Western Labor Union it joined in the formation of the Industrial Workers of the World (IWW) in 1905. Factionalism within the IWW led to the defection of the WFM, which then rejoined (1911) the American Federation of Labor. The failure of several strikes and the depression of 1914 injured the union, and it suffered from antiradical feeling. Declining in membership and power, the union changed its name in 1916 to International Union of Mine, Mill, and Smelter Workers. See Vernon H. Jensen, *Heritage of Conflict* (1950, repr. 1968); S. H. Holbrook, *The Rocky Mountain Revolution* (1956).

Western Ghats, mts., India: see GHATS.

Western Islands, Scotland: see HEBRIDES, THE.

Westernizers, in Russian history: see SLAVOPHILES AND WESTERNIZERS.

Western Michigan University, at Kalamazoo, Mich.; coeducational; founded in 1903 as Western State Normal School, became accredited in 1927 as a college, gained university status in 1957. In 1960 the university began participation in the development of a technical college at Ibadan, Nigeria. The university's research facilities include the Institute of International and Area Studies, the Educational Resources Center, and the Kleinstuck Nature Preserve.

Western Ontario, University of, at London, Ont., Canada; non-denominational; coeducational; chartered 1878. It has faculties of arts, science, music, social science, engineering, dentistry, medicine, law, and graduate studies as well as schools of education, library and information science, nursing, and business administration.

Western Province, formerly **Barotseland** (bərŏt'-səlănd), province (1969 pop. 410,087), c.63,000 sq mi (163,170 sq km), W Zambia. The capital is Mongu. The area, covered mostly by savanna, is drained by the Zambezi River. Livestock and grain are raised, and teak is produced. In the early 19th cent. the province was the site of the kingdom of the Lozi (or Barotse) people; they were conquered in 1838 by Kalolo invaders from what is now Lesotho, but regained power in 1864. In 1890 and 1900, Lewanika, the Lozi paramount chief, signed treaties with the British South Africa Company, which gave the company extensive trading and mining rights. Later, Barotseland became (1911) a province of the British protectorate of Northern Rhodesia, although it retained considerable autonomy. There was some separatist sentiment among the Lozi after Northern Rhodesia became independent as Zambia in 1964. The province was renamed after independence.

Western red cedar: see JUNIPER, ARBORVITAE.

Western Reserve, tract of land in NE Ohio, on the southern shore of Lake Erie, retained by Connecticut in 1786 when it ceded its claims to its western lands (see NORTHWEST TERRITORY). In 1792, Connecticut gave 500,000 acres (202,350 hectares), called "firelands," to its citizens whose property was burned during the American Revolution. The Connecticut Land Company bought the remaining land in 1795; the next year, one of its directors, Moses Cleaveland, established the first permanent settlement in the reserve, Cleveland. The reserve did not have a permanent government until 1800, when it was included in the Northwest Territory as Trumbull co. Later this region was divided into 10 counties and parts of 4 others. The chief cities are Akron, Ashtabula, Cleveland, Lorain, Sandusky, and Youngstown. See study by H. H. Hatcher (rev. ed. 1966).

Western Reserve University: see CASE WESTERN RESERVE UNIV.

Western Samoa, independent state (1971 pop. 146,635), South Pacific, comprising the western half of the SAMOA island chain. There are nine major islands: UPOLU, SAVAI'I, Apolima, Manono, Fanuatapu, Namua, Nuutele, Nuula, and Nuusafee, with a total land area of 1,097 sq mi (2,842 sq km). APIA, the capital, is on Upolu. All the islands are mountainous, fertile, and surrounded by coral reefs; extensive volcanic activity occurred on Savai'i early in the 20th cent. The population, which is Polynesian, is engaged largely in subsistence agriculture; the chief exports are copra, cocoa, and bananas. Tourism is important. All of the Samoan islands west of long. 171°W were awarded to Germany under the terms of an 1899 treaty between Germany, the United States, and Great Britain. New Zealand seized the islands from Germany in 1914 and obtained a mandate over them from the League of Nations in 1921. The United Nations made Western Samoa a trusteeship of New Zealand in 1946. New Zealand rule was unpopular, and in the 1930s a resistance movement (known as *mau*) emerged among Europeans and native Polynesians. In 1961 a UN-supervised plebiscite was held, and on Jan. 1, 1962, independence was proclaimed. Western Samoa, a constitutional monarchy, has a 45-member legislative assembly, two members of which are elected by universal suffrage and the remainder by the titled heads of families (*matai*). Executive power rests in the head of state, who is selected by the assembly from among the royal families; the head of state in turn chooses a prime minister and cabinet from among members of the assembly. Samoan and English are the official languages. Western Samoa is a member of the Commonwealth of Nations.

Western Springs, village (1970 pop. 12,147), Cook co., NE Ill., a suburb of Chicago; inc. 1886.

Western Union Telegraph Company, enterprise created (1851) to provide telegraphic communications services in the United States. In 1970 it was reorganized as one division of the Western Union Corporation. Originally known as the New York and Mississippi Valley Printing Telegraph Company, Western Union built the nation's first transcontinental telegraph line in 1861. The company briefly entered the telephone field but, after losing a court battle with Bell Telephone in 1879, turned completely to telegraph communications. Western Union's telegraph business grew rapidly, and by 1943, after acquiring Postal Telegraph and some 500 other competitors, it was easily the largest company in its field. During the 1960s, faced with steeply declining telegraph revenues and rising costs, the company moved into a number of other nontelegram fields, such as time-sharing computer systems, teleprinters, and satellite communications. Today telegrams sent by individuals account for only a small portion of Western Union's total revenue. See R. L. Thompson, *Wiring a Continent: The History of the Telegraph Industry in the United States* (1947, repr. 1972).

Westerville, city (1970 pop. 12,530), Delaware and Franklin counties, central Ohio; inc. 1858. Seed and grain cleaners, fabricated steel, and dairy products are made. Otterbein College is there, and Hoover reservoir is to the east.

Westfalen, Germany: see WESTPHALIA.

Westfield. 1 City (1970 pop. 31,433), Hampden co., SW Mass., a residential and industrial suburb of Springfield, on the Westfield River; settled c.1660, inc. as a city 1920. Bicycles, machinery, and paper and metal products are made. Westfield State College is there. **2** Town (1970 pop. 33,720), Union co., NE N.J.; settled late 17th cent. as part of Elizabethtown, inc. 1903. It is completely residential. A Revolutionary War cemetery is there.

West Flanders, Flemish *West-Vlaanderen* (vĕst-vlän'dərən), Fr. *Flandre Occidentale,* province (1970 pop. 1,054,429), W Belgium, bordering on the North Sea in the west, on the Netherlands in the northeast, and on France in the south. The chief cities are Bruges (the capital), Kortrijk, Oostende, Ypres, and Roeselare. West Flanders is drained by the Leie and Yser rivers and has many small canals. It has considerable fertile soil; grain, flax, and dairy cattle are raised. Fishing is pursued in the North Sea. The province's varied manufactures include textiles and linen, both long-standing industries. West Flanders is mainly Flemish-speaking. For its history, see FLANDERS.

West Florida Controversy, conflict between Spain and the United States concerning possession of Florida. By the Treaty of Paris of 1763, Britain received Florida from Spain, and from France that portion of Louisiana lying between the Mississippi and Perdido rivers (exclusive of New Orleans). The British organized this territory into the provinces of East Florida (most of the present state of Florida) and West Florida (the strip on the Gulf Coast formed by parts of the present states of Florida, Alabama, Mississippi, and Louisiana). The Apalachicola River was the boundary. In 1764 they arbitrarily moved the northern boundary of West Florida from 31°N to a line running from the mouth of the Yazoo River east to the Chattahoochee River (32°28'N). After the American Revolution the British ceded Florida back to Spain, but without clear definition of its boundaries. A controversy immediately developed over the northern boundary of West Florida. The Spanish demanded the 1764 line; the United States insisted on the old line of 31°N. The issue was settled by Pinckney's Treaty (1795), in which Spain recognized the American claim. With the transfer of

Louisiana from Spain to France and its subsequent purchase (1803) by the United States, another dispute over West Florida's boundaries developed. Based on the treaty of cession with France, which did not specify the boundaries of the Louisiana Purchase, the United States claimed that part of West Florida (between the Perdido and the Mississippi rivers) that had been part of Louisiana before 1763. The Spanish insisted that Louisiana, as held and administered by them, had not included this area. Lengthy and inconclusive negotiations ensued. At the same time American settlers moved into the area and resisted Spanish control. In 1810, after a revolt against Spanish rule in West Florida, President Madison ordered United States occupation of the disputed area, which was incorporated into the Territory of Orleans (which became the state of Louisiana in 1812) and the Mississippi Territory. Spain refused to recognize the American occupation, and American expansionists contemplated taking East Florida. The issue was finally settled in 1819, when, by the Adams-Onís Treaty between U.S. Secretary of State John Quincy Adams and the Spanish minister Luis de Onís, Spain renounced its claims to West Florida and also ceded East Florida to the United States. See I. J. Cox, *The West Florida Controversy, 1798–1813* (1918, repr. 1967).

Westford, town (1970 pop. 10,368), Middlesex co., NE Mass., a suburb of the greater Boston area; settled 1653, set off from Chelmsford and inc. 1729. There are apple orchards, granite quarries (which have long been in operation), and a book lithography firm. The major manufacture is textile machinery. Although chiefly a residential community today, it was once a busy industrial town, attracting many French and Irish immigrants. Its many colonial structures include two 17th-cent. saltbox houses and the Old Fletcher Tavern (1713).

West Glamorgan (glәmôr'gәn), nonmetropolitan county, S Wales, created under the Local Government Act of 1972 (effective 1974). It comprises the county borough of SWANSEA and portions of the former county of GLAMORGANSHIRE.

West Ham: see NEWHAM.

West Hartford, town (1970 pop. 68,031), Hartford co., central Conn., a suburb of Hartford; settled c.1679, inc. 1854. Tobacco is sorted and packed, and machine tools and parts, aircraft accessories, air conditioners, electrical equipment, vacuum cleaners, and typewriter ribbons are among the many manufactures. The town has numerous commercial and professional offices. It is the seat of St. Joseph College, the Univ. of Hartford, and the American School for the Deaf (1817). Of interest is Noah Webster's birthplace.

West Haven, town (1970 pop. 52,851), New Haven co., S Conn., a suburb across the West River from New Haven; settled 1638, inc. as a separate borough 1873. Although chiefly residential, there is some manufacturing industry. The Univ. of New Haven is there.

West Helena (hĕl'әnә), city (1970 pop. 11,007), Phillips co., E Ark.; inc. 1917. Originally a suburb of Helena, its expanding industry has caused it to grow larger than Helena. Wood products are its chief manufactures. St. Francis National Forest is nearby.

West Hempstead, uninc. city (1970 pop. 20,375, including Lakeview), Nassau co., SE N.Y., on Long Island. It is residential.

West Highland white terrier, breed of sturdy, compact TERRIER developed in Scotland in the early 19th cent. It stands about 11 in. (27.9 cm) high at the shoulder and weighs from 13 to 20 lb (5.9–9.1 kg). Its white, water-resistant double coat consists of a short, dense, soft underlayer and a hard, curl-free topcoat about 2 in. (5 cm) long. The West Highland white, descending from the same ancestral stock as the cairn, Dandie Dinmont, and Scottish terrier, was used to hunt small game both on land and in the water. In recent times it has been popular chiefly as a house pet. See DOG.

West Indies, archipelago, between North and South America, curving c.2,500 mi (4,020 km) from Florida to the coast of Venezuela and separating the Caribbean Sea and the Gulf of Mexico from the Atlantic Ocean. The archipelago, sometimes called the Antilles, is divided into three groups, the BAHAMA ISLANDS, the Greater Antilles (CUBA, JAMAICA, HAITI, the DOMINICAN REPUBLIC, and PUERTO RICO), and the Lesser Antilles (LEEWARD ISLANDS, WINDWARD ISLANDS, TRINIDAD AND TOBAGO, BARBADOS), and the Dutch and Venezuelan islands off the northern coast of Venezuela. The British West Indies comprise the CAYMAN ISLANDS, the TURKS AND CAICOS ISLANDS, the British Leeward Islands (ANTIGUA, SAINT KITTS-NEVIS, Anguilla, MONTSERRAT, and the British VIRGIN ISLANDS), the British Windward Islands (DOMINICA, SAINT LUCIA, SAINT VINCENT, and GRENADA), and Barbados. The Dutch West Indies (called the Netherlands Antilles) include CURAÇAO, ARUBA, BONAIRE, SAINT EUSTATIUS, SABA, and part of SAINT MARTIN. The French West Indies are made up of GUADELOUPE and dependencies and MARTINIQUE. The U.S. possessions are the Virgin Islands of the United States. Puerto Rico is a self-governing commonwealth associated with the United States. MARGARITA belongs to Venezuela. Many of the islands are mountainous, and some have partly active volcanoes. Hurricanes occur frequently, but the warm climate (tempered by northeast trade winds) and the clear tropical seas have made the West Indies a very popular resort area. Some 25 million people live on the islands, and the majority of inhabitants are of black African descent. Several of the islands were discovered (1492) by Christopher COLUMBUS. In 1496 the first permanent European settlement was made by the Spanish on HISPANIOLA. By the middle 1600s the English, French, and Dutch had established settlements in the area, and in the following century there was constant warfare among the European colonial powers for control of the islands. Some islands flourished as trade centers and became targets for pirates. Large numbers of Africans were imported to provide slave labor for the sugarcane plantations that developed there in the 1600s. The political status of the islands varies: Barbados, Cuba, Haiti, the Dominican Republic, Jamaica, the Bahama Islands, and Trinidad and Tobago are independent. The Netherlands Antilles officially have equal status with Holland in the Kingdom of the Netherlands. Guadeloupe and Martinique are overseas departments of France, Puerto Rico is a commonwealth in association with the United States, and the U.S. Virgin Islands have territorial status. In 1958, 10 British territories joined to form the **West Indies Federation.** Trinidad and Tobago, Jamaica, and Barbados were the principal members, but the federation included most of the British Leeward and Windward islands. The seat of government was Port-of-Spain, Trinidad. Slated for independence in 1962, the federation did not survive its troubled infancy. Jamaica, the most populous and prosperous member, voted (1961) to leave the federation, fearing that it would have to shoulder the burdens of the economically underdeveloped members; Trinidad and Tobago followed suit, and the federation was dissolved in May, 1962. Jamaica became an independent member of the COMMONWEALTH OF NATIONS in 1962, as did Barbados in

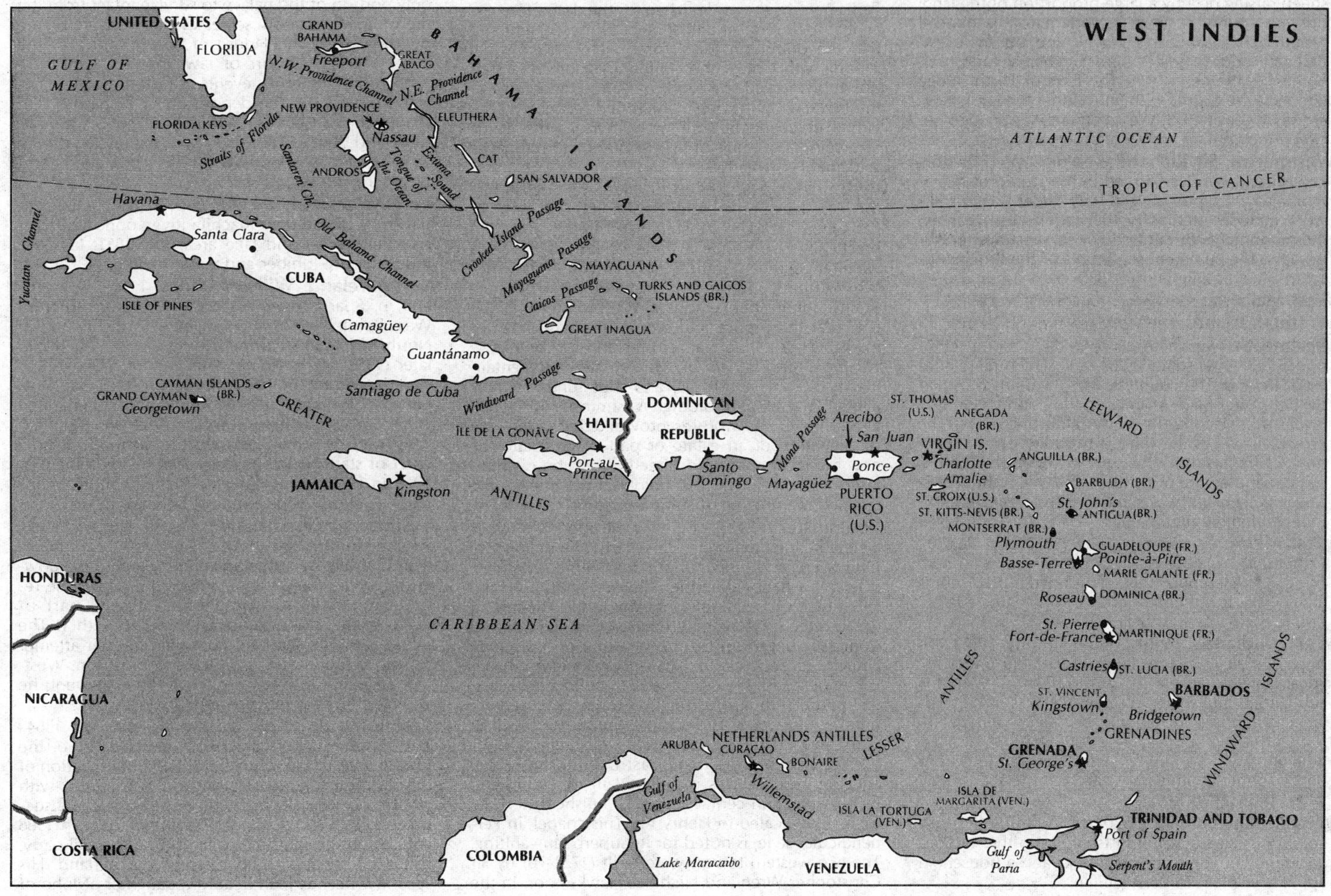

1966 and the Bahama Islands in 1973. In 1967 the West Indies Associated States were created, made up of Antigua, St. Kitts-Nevis, Dominica, Grenada, St. Lucia, and St. Vincent. Each of the states is voluntarily associated with Great Britain and is fully self-governing in its internal affairs. See R. C. West and J. P. Augelli, *Middle America* (1966); G. K. Lewis, *The Growth of the Modern West Indies* (1968); Sir John Mordecai, *The West Indies: The Federal Negotiations* (1968); E. E. Williams, *From Columbus to Castro: The History of the Caribbean, 1492–1969* (1970); M. M. Horowitz, comp., *Peoples and Cultures of the Caribbean: An Anthropological Reader* (1971); J. H. Parry and P. M. Sherlock, *A Short History of the West Indies* (3d ed. 1971); Tad Szulc, ed., *The United States and the Caribbean* (1971); David Lowenthal and Lambros Comitas, comp., *Consequences of Class and Color: West Indian Perspectives* (1973).

Westinghouse, George, 1846–1914, American inventor and manufacturer, b. Central Bridge, N.Y. In the Civil War he served in the Union army and navy. Among his inventions in the railroad field were a reversible frog, the air brake (1868), and automatic signal devices. The Westinghouse Air Brake Company was organized in 1869 and the Union Switch and Signal Company in 1882. Westinghouse was a pioneer in introducing into the United States the high-tension alternating current system for transmission of electricity. In 1866 the Westinghouse Electric Company was incorporated. The inventor also patented devices for the transmission of natural gas. Over 400 patents were credited to him in his lifetime. See biographies by F. E. Leupp (1919), H. G. Garbedian (1943), and H. G. Prout (1921, repr. 1972).

West Irian: see IRIAN BARAT, Indonesia.

West Lafayette, city (1970 pop. 19,157), Tippecanoe co., W Ind., on the Wabash River; inc. 1924. Purdue Univ. is there. Nearby is the Tippecanoe battlesite, where William Henry Harrison fought (1811) the Indian chief Tecumseh.

Westlake, city (1970 pop. 15,689), Cuyahoga co., NE Ohio, a suburb of Cleveland; inc. as a city 1956. Among its manufactures are ink and plastics.

West Lothian (lō'thēən), formerly **Linlithgowshire** (lĭnlĭth'gōshĭr), county (1971 pop. 108,474), 123 sq mi (319 sq km), S central Scotland, on the Firth of Forth. The county town is LINLITHGOW. The land slopes from the Forth to the hills (c.1,000 ft/305 m high) along the southern border. Principal streams are the Avon and the Almond. Dairy farming and sheep raising occupy a large proportion of the land, but the county is more important for its mineral wealth (coal, sand and gravel, and oil shale). At Bathgate and Armdale there are heavy industries. Bo'ness is the chief port. The famous Forth Bridge connects the county with Fife. Under the Local Government Act of 1973, West Lothian was divided between the Lothian and Central regions.

Westmacott, Sir Richard (wĕst'məkŏt), 1775–1856, English sculptor. He worked in the studio of his father, also a sculptor, and in Italy under Canova. His work includes statues in the neoclassical manner, the monuments of Pitt and Fox in Westminster Abbey, and the pediment sculptures of the British Museum. He was knighted in 1837.

West Malaysia: see MALAYSIA, FEDERATION OF.

Westman Islands: see VESTMANNAEYJAR, Iceland.

Westmeath (wĕstmēth', wĕst'mēth), county (1971 pop. 53,557), 681 sq mi (1,764 sq km), central Republic of Ireland. The county town is Mullingar. A part of the central plain of Ireland, the county is mostly level and fertile, with many lakes and bogs. The principal river is the Inny, a tributary of the Shannon. Cattle raising is the chief occupation. There is some manufacture of textiles. ATHLONE is the largest town. Westmeath was separated from Meath as an independent county in 1543.

West Memphis (mĕm'fĭs), city (1970 pop. 26,070), Crittenden co., NE Ark., near the Mississippi (there bridged to Memphis, Tenn.); founded c.1910, inc. as a city 1935. It is a timber and cotton center. A greyhound-racing park is there.

West Midlands, metropolitan county (1972 est. pop. 2,790,000), central England, created under the Local Government Act of 1972 (effective 1974). It is subdivided into 7 metropolitan districts. West Midlands comprises the county boroughs of BIRMINGHAM, COVENTRY, DUDLEY, SOLIHULL, WALSALL, WARLEY, WEST BROMWICH, and WOLVERHAMPTON, and portions of the former counties of STAFFORDSHIRE, WORCESTERSHIRE, and WARWICKSHIRE.

West Mifflin, borough (1970 pop. 28,070), Allegheny co., SW Pa., a suburb of Pittsburgh, on the Monongahela River. There are steelworks and a household appliances plant in West Mifflin.

Westminster. 1 Residential city (1970 pop. 59,874), Orange co., S Calif.; founded 1870 as a temperance colony for Presbyterians, inc. 1957. It has several industrial parks. A U.S. naval weapons station and Los Alamitos Naval Air Base are nearby. **2** City (1970 pop. 19,432), Adams and Jefferson counties, N central Colo., a residential suburb of Denver; inc. 1911. Telephone-switching equipment and electro-mechanical products are manufactured in the city. Standley Lake there provides the city with both water and recreation. Stapleton International Airport is nearby.

Westminster, City of, borough (1971 pop. 225,632) of Greater London, SE England, on the Thames River. The borough was created in 1965 by the merger of the metropolitan boroughs of the City of Westminster, Paddington, and St. Marylebone. Westminster is the location of the principal offices and residences of Great Britain's national government. Important offices and departments are in WHITEHALL and DOWNING streets. The monarch lives in BUCKINGHAM PALACE. Parliament meets in WESTMINSTER PALACE. Paddington has an important railroad terminal. In St. Marylebone are the administrative offices of the British Broadcasting Corp., London's chief shopping district, and Harley St., a center of medical practice. There is also a clothing industry in St. Marylebone. Westminster School is a leading public school, founded in the 14th cent. and reestablished by Queen Elizabeth I in 1560. Other notable features of the borough are Westminster Cathedral, WESTMINSTER ABBEY, SAINT JAMES'S PALACE, the NATIONAL GALLERY, the TATE GALLERY, the Imperial College of Science and Technology, St. James's Park, HYDE PARK, parts of Regent's Park and Kensington Gardens, Mme Tussaud's waxworks, and Kensal Green Cemetery, resting place of several literary figures. Westminster Bridge is the second-oldest bridge in London.

Westminster, Provisions of: see PROVISIONS OF OXFORD.

Westminster, Statute of, 1931, in British imperial history, an act of the British Parliament that gave formal recognition to the autonomy of the dominions of the British Empire and was in effect the founding charter of the British COMMONWEALTH OF NATIONS. It declared that the Commonwealth was a free association of autonomous dominions and the United Kingdom, bound only by common allegiance to the throne, and specified that the British Parliament might not legislate for the dominions except at their request and subject to their assent and that the dominion legislatures were on an equal footing with that of the United Kingdom. The statute implemented the work of various meetings of the IMPERIAL CONFERENCE, which had recognized the virtual independence of the dominions that came into being as a result of World War I and the peace settlements thereafter.

Westminster, Statutes of, in medieval English history, legislative promulgations made by EDWARD I in Parliament at Westminster. Westminster I (1275) practically constitutes a code of law; it covers a wide range, incorporating much unwritten law into the written code, and is a sweeping ordinance against administrative abuses. Westminster II (1285) is similar in purpose and scope; it is especially remarkable for its judicial reforms and for the clause *De donis conditionalibus,* which fostered the entailing of estates (see ENTAIL) and thus fundamentally altered English landholding. Westminster III (1290), also called *Quia emptores,* provided that in the case of alienation of an estate or part of an estate the new holder should hold directly from the overlord rather than from the old holder. Thus, the statute stopped the process of subinfeudation.

Westminster Abbey, originally the abbey church of a Benedictine monastery (closed in 1539) in London. One of England's most important Gothic structures, it is also a national shrine. The first church on the site is believed to date from early in the 7th cent. It was erected by Æthelbert, king of Kent. Edward the Confessor began c.1050 the building of a Norman church, consecrated in 1065. In 1245, Henry III began to demolish the edifice and to build a new eastern portion, thus initiating centuries of construction. The fine octagonal chapter house was built in 1250, and in the 14th cent. the cloisters, abbot's house, and principal monastic buildings were added. The nave was completed in the 16th cent. Early in the 16th cent. Henry VIII finished the Lady Chapel, dedicated to Henry VII. This chapel, in Perpendicular style, is noted for its superb fan vaulting. The two western towers were built (1722–40) by Sir Christopher Wren and Nicholas Hawksmoor. In the late 19th cent. Sir George Gilbert Scott supervised extensive restoration. From that time memorial statues by many academic Victorian sculptors have been added to the decor. The present church is cruciform in plan; both nave and transept have side aisles. The choir is apsidal in plan, and its ring of chapels exhibits the only complete chevet in England. French influence is also seen in the height of the nave, the loftiest in England, and in the strongly emphasized flying buttresses. Nearly every English king and queen since William I has been crowned in Westminster, and it is the burial place of 18 monarchs. England's most notable statesmen and distinguished subjects have been given burial in the Abbey since the 14th cent. In the Poets' Corner in the south transept rest the tombs of Chaucer, Browning, Tennyson, and other great English poets. See descriptive and historical works by W. R. Lethaby (1906 and 1925), H. F. Westlake (1923), A. E. Henderson (1937), L. E. Tanner (1953), and Edward Carpenter (1966); Council of Christians and Jews, *The Corners of the Earth . . . Westminster Abbey in the 900th Anniversary Year* (1966).

Westminster Conference, 1866–67, held in London to settle the plan for confederation of the Canadian provinces. The resolutions on confederation that had been framed at the Quebec Conference (1864) were the basis for those promulgated at the Westminster Conference and incorporated in the British North America Act (1867), under which the dominion of Canada was created.

Westminster Confession: see CREED **6**.

Westminster Palace or **Houses of Parliament,** in Westminster, London. The present enormous structure, of Perpendicular Gothic design, was built (1840–60) by Sir Charles Barry to replace an aggregation of ancient buildings almost completely destroyed by fire in 1834. Edward the Confessor constructed the original palace buildings on a site where a still earlier royal residence is thought to have stood. The complex served as a royal abode until the 16th cent., when it was adopted as the assembly place for the House of Commons and the House of Lords. The Great Hall was built by William II at the end of the 11th cent. The superbly constructed hammer-beam roof spanning its width of 68 ft. (20.7 m), part of a subsequent rebuilding of the hall by Richard II, was the finest extant example of medieval open-timber work; it was burned by incendiary bombs in 1941. Westminster Hall was the only portion of the palace to survive intact from the fire of 1834 and now serves as the entrance of the building. In it the House of Lords, sitting as the highest English court of law, met for centuries. Among the numerous events of historic renown enacted there were the deposition of Richard II, the sentencing of Charles I, and the trials of Sir Thomas More and Warren Hastings. Damage inflicted during air raids during World War II has since been completely repaired.

West Monroe, city (1970 pop. 14,868), Ouachita parish, N La., on the Ouachita River, opposite Monroe, in a forest and lake area; inc. 1851. Its chief industries are lumber and paper milling.

Westmoreland, William Childs, 1914–, U.S. general, b. Spartanburg co., S.C. He graduated from West Point in 1936 and fought with distinction in North Africa and Europe during World War II and later (1952–53) in Korea. After serving (1960–64) as superintendent of West Point, Westmoreland attained (1964) the rank of general and commanded (1964–68) U.S. military forces in Vietnam (see VIETNAM WAR). He then assumed the position of army chief of staff, which he held until his retirement in 1972. In 1974 he was defeated in the Republican primary election for governor of South Carolina.

Westmorland, Charles Neville, 6th **earl of** (nĕv'ĭl, wĕst'mərlənd), 1543–1601, English nobleman. A Roman Catholic by birth and connected with the powerful Howard family by marriage, he joined the rebellion (1569) led by Thomas Percy, earl of NORTHUMBERLAND against Queen Elizabeth I. The rebels captured Durham but failed in their attempt to rescue Mary Queen of Scots from prison. Westmorland fled, to live in exile on the Continent; he was attainted by Parliament in 1571.

Westmorland, Ralph Neville, 1st **earl of,** 1364–1425, English nobleman. His family was one of the most powerful in England and shared domination of the northern counties with the Percy family, with whom the Nevilles were closely allied. Neville succeeded his father as Baron Neville of Raby in 1388 and supported Richard II against the baronial party. In 1397 he was created earl of Westmorland. His second wife was Joan Beaufort, daughter of John of

Gaunt and half sister of Henry of Lancaster (later HENRY IV). When, in 1399, Henry revolted against Richard, Westmorland supported Lancaster. He continued to support Henry as king and helped to put down the Percy revolt in 1403. When a new anti-Lancastrian revolt broke out in 1405, Westmorland captured two of the leaders, Archbishop Richard Le SCROPE and the earl marshal of England, by trickery, but he had nothing to do with their quick execution. He was the father of a large family, many of whom made advantageous marriages. His daughter Cecily Neville married Richard, duke of York, and became the mother of Edward IV and Richard III; another of his grandsons was Richard Neville, earl of WARWICK, called the Kingmaker.

Westmorland, county (1971 pop. 72,724), 789 sq mi (2,044 sq km), N England. The county town is Appleby; Kendal is the administrative center. Much of the county lies in the picturesque region known as the LAKE DISTRICT. The county is largely mountainous. Mt. Helvellyn, on the Cumberland border, rises to a height of 3,118 ft (950 m). Chief among the numerous streams are the Eden, the Lune, and the Kent. The lakes of Grasmere, Rydal Water, and Ullswater are shared with Cumberland, and Lake Windermere, the largest lake in England, lies between Westmorland and Lancashire. The county is primarily a pastoral land (dairy farming and sheep and cattle grazing). There is some quarrying (limestone, granite, and slate), and minor manufacturing is carried on. The beauty of the scenery attracted Wordsworth, who lived most of his life in the county and is buried at Grasmere. In 1974, Westmorland became part of the new nonmetropolitan county of Cumbria.

Westmount (wĕst'mount), city (1971 pop. 23,606), S Que., Canada, on Montreal island. A western residential suburb of Montreal, it became a city in 1908.

West New Guinea: see IRIAN BARAT, Indonesia.

West New York, town (1970 pop. 40,627), Hudson co., NE N.J., atop the Palisades across the Hudson River from New York City; settled 1790, inc. 1898. It is a residential town with some light industry. West New York is the leading embroidery center in the United States. The waterfront on the Hudson is 1 mi (1.6 km) long and can accommodate oceangoing vessels.

Weston, Edward, 1886–1958, American photographer, b. Highland Park, Ill. Weston began to make photographs in Chicago parks in 1902. Four years later he moved to California; the Western landscape soon became his principal subject matter. In the 1930s, Weston and several other photographers, including Ansel Adams, Immogen Cunningham, and Willard van Dyke, formed the *f*64 group, which greatly influenced the aesthetics of American photography (see PHOTOGRAPHY, STILL). In 1937, Weston received the first Guggenheim Fellowship awarded to a photographer. His sharp, stark, brilliantly printed images of sand dunes, nudes, vegetables, rock formations, trees, cacti, shells, water, and human faces are considered to be among the finest of 20th-century photographic works; their influence on the art remains inestimable. Weston made his last photographs at his beloved Point Lobos, Calif., in 1948; that year he was stricken with Parkinson's disease. See *The Daybooks of Edward Weston*, ed. by Nancy Newhall (2 vol., 1961 and 1966), *The Flame of Recognition*, ed. by Nancy Newhall (1965), and *My Camera on Point Lobos* (1968); Nancy Newhall, *The Photographs of Edward Weston* (1946); Cole Weston, *Edward Weston: Fifty Years* (1973). His second son **Brett Weston**, 1911–, and his fourth son **Cole Weston**, 1919–, are both photographers in their father's tradition.

Weston, town (1970 pop. 10,870), Middlesex co., E Mass., W of Boston; settled c.1642, set off from Watertown and inc. 1713. The town is mainly residential. Regis College and the Weston College Geophysical Observatory are there. Weston has many 18th-century buildings.

Weston-super-Mare (wĕst'ən-so͞o'pər-mâr), municipal borough (1971 pop. 50,794), Somerset, SW England, on the Bristol Channel. It is a seaside resort with attractions that include Worlebury Hill, with its Iron Age hill fort and a fine view of the opposite coast of Wales; a long esplanade; and Brean Down, a bird sanctuary. There are light industries with products that include shoes, aluminum window frames, and scientific instruments. In 1974, Weston-super-Mare became part of the new nonmetropolitan county of Avon.

West Orange, town (1970 pop. 43,715), Essex co., NE N.J., a residential suburb of Newark; set off from Orange 1862, inc. 1900. "Glenmont," Thomas Edison's home in Llewellyn Park, and his laboratory (now a museum) are included in the Edison National Historic Site (see NATIONAL PARKS AND MONUMENTS, table). The Edison plant manufactures electrical equipment.

West Palm Beach, city (1970 pop. 57,375), seat of Palm Beach co., SE Fla., on Lake Worth (a lagoon) opposite Palm Beach, with which it is connected by bridges; inc. 1894. It is a winter resort and a center for the research and production of aeronautical and electronic equipment. The city was developed by Henry M. Flagler in 1893 as a commercial center for Palm Beach. A canal extends from West Palm Beach to Lake Okeechobee. The city is a gateway to the Everglades. In the city are the Norton Gallery and School of Art, a science museum and planetarium, and the county fairgrounds, which include an automobile speedway. Nearby is Palm Beach International Airport.

West Paterson (păt'ərsən), borough (1970 pop. 11,692), Passaic co., NE N.J., a suburb of Paterson; inc. 1914. Electric, electronic, and photographic products are made. A junior college is there.

Westphalia (wĕstfāl'yə), Ger. *Westfalen,* region and former province of Prussia, W West Germany. Münster was the capital of the province. After 1945 the province was incorporated into the West German state of North Rhine–Westphalia. The region of Westphalia occupies, roughly, a triangle formed by a line drawn eastward from the Rhine River at the Dutch border to the Weser River at Minden, a line drawn from Minden southwestward to Siegen (near the border with Hesse), and a line drawn to the northwest from Siegen and parallel to the Rhine. The region is drained by the Ems, Weser, Ruhr, and Lippe rivers; it is hilly in the east and south and forms a low plain in the northwest. The land consists partly of fertile soil and partly of sandy tracts, moors, and heaths. The Ruhr valley, in the west, is part of the great Westphalian coal basin and of the RUHR district, one of the world's most important industrial regions. The Ruhr district is connected with the Ems River by the Dortmund-Ems Canal and with the Elbe River by the Midland Canal. Westphalia first appears as the name of the western third of the duchy of SAXONY in the 10th cent. Unlike Eastphalia, the eastern third of the duchy of Saxony, Westphalia survived the breakup (1180) of the Saxon duchy as a regional concept, although it lost political unity. The larger part of Westphalia came under the rule of ecclesiastical princes—the bishops of MÜNSTER, OSNABRÜCK, MINDEN, and PADERBORN and the archbishops of Cologne, who obtained the region around Arnsberg, known as the duchy of Westphalia. Among the temporal fiefs that emerged from the breakup of Saxony were the counties of LIPPE, RAVENSBERG, and Mark. All these territories were later included in the Westphalian Circle of the Holy Roman Empire (formed c.1500), which also encompassed considerable non-Westphalian land. The anarchy caused by numerous local feudal lords and robber barons led, in the 12th cent., to the creation of the secret VEHMGERICHT, a criminal tribunal, which had its center at Arnsberg. In the later Middle Ages most of the important Westphalian towns—e.g., Münster, Osnabrück, Paderborn, Bielefeld, and SOEST—prospered as members of the Hanseatic League. As a result of the demise of the house of Cleves, which held the counties of Ravensberg and Mark, and as a result of the Thirty Years War (terminated in 1648 by the Peace of Westphalia, signed at Münster and Osnabrück), the elector of Brandenburg obtained Ravensberg, Mark, and the bishopric of Minden; thus Prussia obtained a foothold in western Germany. The Protestant Reformation made considerable gains among the people of Westphalia in the 16th cent., but much of the population was reconverted to Catholicism after the Catholic Reformation (late 16th cent.). The bishoprics of Münster, Paderborn, and Osnabrück and the duchy of Westphalia were secularized only in 1803 by the Diet of Regensburg as a result of the French Revolutionary Wars; they were at first partitioned among Prussia, Hanover, Hesse-Darmstadt, Hesse-Kassel, and the grand duchy of Berg. However, in 1807, after the signing of the Treaty of Tilset, Napoleon seized all Prussian possessions W of the Elbe, as well as the electorates of Hesse-Kassel and Hanover and the duchy of Brunswick; the northern section of these territories, including Münster, was directly annexed by France, and the southern section was constituted as the kingdom of Westphalia, with Napoleon's brother Jérôme Bonaparte (see BONAPARTE, family) as king and with Kassel as the capital. The choice of the name was misleading, for only a small part of Westphalia was included in that kingdom, which collapsed in 1813. At the Congress of Vienna the major part of Westphalia proper was awarded (1815) to Prussia; and Hanover, Hesse-Kassel, and Brunswick were restored. Westphalia continued as a Prussian province until 1945.

Westphalia, Peace of, 1648, general settlement ending the THIRTY YEARS WAR. It marked the end of the Holy Roman Empire as an effective institution and inaugurated the modern European state system. The chief participants in the negotiations were the allies Sweden and France; their opponents, Spain and the Holy Roman Empire; and the various parts of the empire (which had been riven by the war) together with the newly independent Netherlands. Earlier endeavors to bring about a general peace had been unsuccessful. The compact known as the Peace of Prague (May, 1635) marked a step in the direction of peace and signaled the belief of the Protestant powers that the Swedish forces on which they depended would not be able to maintain a preponderant role in Germany. The conditions of the compact were not in accord with Richelieu's design to break up the imperial power, however, and the war continued despite offers of mediation from the pope and the king of Denmark. Congresses were proposed and discarded. It was not until Dec. 25, 1641, that a preliminary treaty provided for two concurrent conferences—at Münster and Osnabrück. The conferences, fixed for 1643, met in 1644 and began serious work in 1645. The treaties were signed Oct. 24, 1648. Through the French and Swedish "satisfactions" the power and influence of the HOLY ROMAN EMPIRE and of the house of Hapsburg were lessened. The sovereignty of the German states was recognized, and the empire continued only in name. France, emerging as the dominant European power, had its sovereignty over three bishoprics (Metz, Toul, and Verdun) and over Pinerolo confirmed. Breisach was made over to France. ALSACE was ceded despite ambiguity of title, and France was allowed to fortify a garrison at Philippsburg. Sweden obtained W Pomerania, including Stettin and the island of Rügen; the archbishopric (but not the city) of Bremen and the adjoining bishopric of Verden; and Wismar and the island of Pöl. It was agreed that the Upper Palatinate and the old electoral vote should remain with Bavaria, while the Rhenish Palatinate, with a new electoral vote, was assigned to Charles Louis, the son of Frederick the Winter King. The Swiss Confederation and the independent Netherlands were explicitly recognized. The elector of Brandenburg received compensation for Pomerania; the duke of Mecklenburg, for Pöl and part of Wismar. The outcome of the religious deliberations was significant. Territorial rulers continued to determine the religion of their subjects, but it was stipulated that a subject could worship as he had in 1624. Terms of forced emigration were eased; Calvinism was recognized; and rulers could allow full toleration, at their discretion. Finally, religious questions could no longer be decided by a majority of the imperial estates. Future disputes were to be resolved by a compromise between the confessions. The era of religious warfare was over, and a general attempt had been made toward religious toleration. See C. V. Wedgwood, *The Thirty Years War* (1938).

West Point, U.S. military post, since 1802 seat of the UNITED STATES MILITARY ACADEMY. On the high west bank of the Hudson River N of New York City, West Point was the site of Revolutionary forts guarding the Hudson. Constitution Island, in the river, is also in the reservation. The plan of Benedict ARNOLD to surrender (1780) West Point to the British was discovered with the capture of Major John André.

Westport, residential town (1970 pop. 27,414), Fairfield co., SW Conn., on Long Island Sound at the mouth of the Saugatuck River; settled 1645–50, inc. 1835. It is a summer resort and a residence for New York City commuters, especially artists and writers. The town has a summer theater. William Tryon landed at Compo Beach before his raid on Danbury in 1777. A number of 18th-century houses remain. Nearby are a state park and a fish hatchery.

West Prussia, Ger. *Westpreussen,* former province of Prussia, 9,867 sq mi (25,556 sq km), NE Germany, extending S from the Baltic Sea, between Pomerania on the west and East Prussia on the east. Danzig was the capital. The larger part of the region belonged to Poland until the Polish partitions of 1772 and 1793 and included Pomerelia (Ger. *Pommerellen;* see POMERANIA). The province also included, prior to World War I, the western portion of originally East Prussian territory, including the cities of Elbing,

Marienburg, and Marienwerder. The Treaty of Versailles (1919) gave most of West Prussia to Poland (see POLISH CORRIDOR) and made Danzig and its environs a free city. The remainder of West Prussia was divided between the Prussian province of Grenzmark Posen-West Prussia and the district of West Prussia, incorporated with the province of East Prussia. The whole territory was again annexed to Germany at the outbreak (1939) of World War II, but in 1945 the Potsdam Conference placed it under Polish administration.

West Quoddy Head, promontory extending into the Atlantic Ocean, SE Maine, SE of Lubec; the easternmost point in the continental United States. A lighthouse is there.

West Riding: see YORKSHIRE.

West River, China: see SI.

West Roman Empire: see *Roman Empire* under ROME.

West Saint Paul, city (1970 pop. 18,799), Dakota co., SE Minn., a suburb of St. Paul; inc. 1889. Meat is processed, and plastics, textiles, and clothing are manufactured.

West Spitsbergen, island: see SPITSBERGEN, Norway.

West Springfield, industrial town (1970 pop. 28,461), Hampden co., SW Mass., on the Connecticut River opposite Springfield; settled 1654, set off from Springfield and inc. 1774. Paper, ignition systems, and hair care preparations are manufactured. Storrowton, a reconstructed colonial village, is on the grounds of the annually held Eastern States Exposition.

West Suffolk, England: see under SUFFOLK.

West Sussex, nonmetropolitan county (1972 est. pop. 610,000), SE England, created under the Local Government Act of 1972 (effective 1974). It is composed of the former county of West Sussex, as well as parts of the former counties of East Sussex and Surrey.

West University Place, residential city (1970 pop. 13,317), Harris co., S Texas, completely surrounded by the city of Houston; inc. 1925.

West Virginia, state (1970 pop. 1,744,237), 24,181 sq mi (62,629 sq km), E central United States, admitted (1863) as the 35th state of the Union. CHARLESTON is the capital and second largest city; HUNTINGTON is the largest city. WHEELING and PARKERSBURG are also important centers. Extremely irregular in both outline and terrain, West Virginia has two narrow projections—the Northern Panhandle, which cuts north between Ohio and Pennsylvania, and the Eastern Panhandle, which cuts east between Maryland (with the Potomac River forming the state line) and Virginia. The jagged Virginia-West Virginia line continues SW from the Eastern Panhandle, roughly following the eastern escarpment of the Allegheny Plateau (known as the Allegheny Front) to shape West Virginia's eastern border. In the south the state is bounded by Virginia. In the southwest it is bounded by Kentucky (the Tug Fork forms the state line) and in the west by Ohio (from which it is separated by the Ohio River). Nicknamed the "Mountain State," West Virginia is very hilly and rugged, with the highest mean altitude (1,500 ft/457 m) of any state E of the Mississippi. Nearly all of West Virginia is in the Allegheny Plateau. The Eastern Panhandle, a part of the Appalachian ridge and valley country, contains the state's lowest point (240 ft/73 m) near Harpers Ferry where the Shenandoah River joins the Potomac, as well as its highest point, Spruce Knob (4,860 ft/1,481 m). West Virginia is well drained; its important rivers include the Tug Fork, the Big Sandy River, the New River, the Kanawha, the Little Kanawha, the Cheat, and the Monongahela, all of which find their way to the Ohio. The New River and the Kanawha combine to form the most important waterway entirely within the state. West Virginia's rainfall and temperature vary considerably, though the climate is generally of the humid continental type, with hot summers (except in the highest areas) and cool to cold winters. Except for the river-bottom lands, a few small plateaus, and the northern end of the rolling, fertile Valley of Virginia in the Eastern Panhandle, farming is not extensive. (The population nevertheless is about 60% rural.) Hay, apples, corn, and tobacco are the principal crops, while cattle, dairy products, apples, and eggs lead in market receipts. West Virginia has extensive natural resources; it ranks fourth among the states in the value of its mineral production, it is the nation's leading producer of bituminous coal (its reserves total more than 60 million tons), and its production of natural gas is the highest of any state E of the Mississippi. Stone, cement, salt, and oil are also important. Utilizing these mineral resources the state has major glass and chemical (including synthetic textile) industries; they are concentrated in the highly industrialized Ohio and Kanawha river valleys, with Charleston a leading center; Huntington and Parkersburg are also important. Other manufactures include primary and fabricated metals and machinery. Steel mills extend S from Pittsburgh into the Northern Panhandle; Wheeling is a major manufacturing hub in that area. Lumber has long been an important resource in the state; about 65% of the land is still forested, most of it in valuable hardwoods. West Virginia's natural beauty is spectacular, and the excellent hunting, fishing, hiking, camping, and skiing offered there attract a growing tourist industry. The state has 20 state parks, 11 public hunting areas, 9 state forests, Monongahela National Forest, and a portion of George Washington National Forest (most of which is in Virginia). Numerous mineral springs are scattered throughout the state, notably at the resorts of Berkeley Springs and of White Sulphur Springs. Other tourist attractions include Harpers Ferry National Historical Park (see NATIONAL PARKS AND MONUMENTS, table) and various prehistoric Indian mounds, most notably Grave Creek Mound in Moundsville, one of the nation's largest. The Mound Builders were the earliest known inhabitants. When the first white men arrived, however, the region was for the most part unpopulated, serving as a common hunting ground (and therefore a battleground) for the settlers and the Indians. This part of Virginia, which later became West Virginia, was penetrated by explorers and fur traders as early as the 1670s. It was cut off from the eastern regions by rugged mountains and remained uninhabited for more than a century after Virginia had thriving colonies. What is now the Eastern Panhandle attracted the first settlers. They were Germans and Scotch-Irish, and they came not over the Blue Ridge mts. from Virginia but rather down the valleys from Pennsylvania. German families established (c.1730) a settlement on the Potomac and named it Mecklenburg; now called Shepherdstown, it is the oldest town in the state. Homes sprang up along the rivers, but the formidable Allegheny Mt. barrier was not crossed until after the British government, concerned about French claims to the Ohio valley, granted (1749) the Ohio Company large tracts of land in the trans-Allegheny region. Settlers began laboriously making their way over the mountains, and they eventually came into conflict with the French; this conflict was the direct cause of the last French and Indian War (1754–63). During the war, massacres at the hands of Indians were so numerous that most settlers fled the area. They returned after the English captured Fort Duquesne in 1758 and broke the French hold on the Ohio valley. Great numbers poured back over the mountains, ignoring the British proclamation of 1763, which, in the hopes of avoiding Indian troubles, forbade settlement W of the Alleghenies. The Indians resented this encroachment on their hunting grounds, and their hostility was fed by often unjust treatment at the hands of white settlers. The brutal murder of the family of Indian chief James Logan provoked a series of Indian massacres that resulted in Lord Dunmore's War (see DUNMORE, JOHN MURRAY, 4TH EARL OF), in which the Indians were decisively defeated (Oct. 10, 1774). During the American Revolution the area was disturbed by three major Indian invasions, led by the British. After the American conquest of the Northwest by an army (consisting mostly of western Virginians) under George Rogers Clark, the British threat to the area was virtually removed and Indian hostility abated. Western Virginians overwhelmingly supported ratification of the U.S. Constitution; they wanted a strong Federal government that would quell further Indian disturbances and that would enrich commerce along the Ohio, a river of central importance to their economic life. Population growth and prosperity were spurred by the opening of the Mississippi River with the Louisiana Purchase in 1803, by the resulting expansion and improvement of river-borne commerce, and by the completion (1818) of the National Road at Wheeling. The area became an increasingly important part of Virginia, but the predominance of small farms and the almost total absence of slavery were already contributing to a sense of estrangement from the eastern part of the state. Virginia was politically dominated by the wealthy tidewater planters, who were overrepresented in the state legislature because slaves were counted in apportioning representation. As a result the western Virginians suffered from inequitable taxation, and their demands for internal improvements and public education were not met. A new Virginia constitution, ratified in 1830, brought no reform, but another charter (1851) effected a compromise by which representation in the lower house was based on white population and under which universal white manhood suffrage was granted. It was not enough; tidewater domination of the state legislature continued, and the two sections were being pulled further apart by economic differences—western Virginia was becoming an industrialized coal and steel center—and by the increasing prominence of the slavery issue. At the outset of the Civil War the northwestern counties of Virginia overwhelmingly opposed the state's ordinance of secession (April 17, 1861). Unable to halt Virginia's secession from the Union, westerners in the state were quick to take advantage of a long-awaited opportunity for their own separation from Virginia. Protected by Federal troops, delegates representing most of Virginia's western counties met at Wheeling on June 11, 1861, and nullified the Virginia ordinance of secession, declared the offices of the state government at Richmond to be vacated, and formed the "restored government" of Virginia, with Francis H. Pierpont as governor. Creation of a new state was overwhelmingly approved in the referendum of Oct. 24, and in November another convention at Wheeling began to draft the state constitution that was approved in April, 1862. President Lincoln proclaimed (April 20, 1863) admission of a new state, West Virginia, to be effective 60 days thence, and on June 20, 1863, Arthur I. Boreman was inaugurated as its first governor. Pierpont and his "restored government" of Virginia had, of course, consented to the formation of the new state, thereby technically fulfilling the requirement in the U.S. Constitution that a state consent to its own division. Pierpont continued to act as governor of occupied Virginia throughout the war. Meanwhile, the Confederates had failed to hold on to the region militarily; Union forces, under the command of Gen. George B. McClellan and then under Gen. William S. Rosecrans, were victorious in battles at Philippi (June 3, 1861), Rich Mt. (July 11), Corrick's Ford (July 13), and Carnifax Ferry (Sept. 10). Gen. Robert E. Lee's attempt to rally the Confederate forces ended in defeat at Cheat Mt. (Sept. 12–13), and a year later Rosecrans's victory at Gauley Bridge extended Union control to the lower Kanawha valley. The Confederates made no serious endeavor to recover the territory W of the Alleghenies, although guerrilla attacks persisted throughout the war. The strategically important Eastern Panhandle, on the other hand, was the scene of continual fighting; not originally a part of West Virginia, it had been quickly annexed (1863) because it contained the Baltimore and Ohio RR. (West Virginia's possession of this area was confirmed by the U.S. Supreme Court in 1871.) Of the many West Virginians who remained loyal to the old state, Virginia, the most notable was Gen. Thomas J. (Stonewall) Jackson; his only sister, however, was a staunch Union supporter. Such a division in allegiance was common in many families, and these divisions affected West Virginia's politics for several decades after the war. Slavery was abolished in 1865, but it was not until 1872 that the state established the Negro's right to vote and to hold public office. In 1866, Radical Republicans disenfranchised all persons who had aided the Confederacy, but after the Democrats came to power (which they held for 25 years), this act was annulled (1871) by the Flick Amendment. In 1885 the capital, which had been shuttled back and forth between Wheeling and Charleston, became fixed at Charleston. Three years earlier, along the

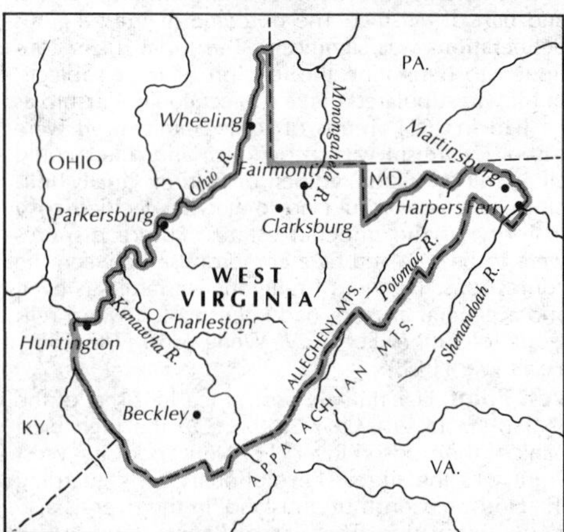

border region between West Virginia and Kentucky, there had begun the now famous Hatfield-McCoy feud, which was to encompass many killings and embroil the governors of the two states in lengthy and heated controversy. The blood of West Virginia Hatfields and Kentucky McCoys was shed until 1896. Of great significance to West Virginia was the state's industrial expansion in the late 19th cent. Based on rich resources and supported by the immigration of Southern Negroes and northern laborers, industrialization marked a change from the largely self-sufficient economy of local communities to one of dependence on industry's profits and labor's wages. West Virginia's great chemical industry was founded during World War I when German chemicals could no longer be imported, and it was greatly expanded during World War II. Both wars also brought unprecedented boom periods to the mines and the steel mills. The state's rapid industrialization, however, was long accompanied by serious labor problems. This was especially true in the coal mines, where wages were low and working conditions dangerous. Unionization was bitterly resisted by mine owners, and strikes throughout the latter part of the 19th cent. and the first third of the 20th cent. were often marked by serious and extended violence, particularly in 1912–13 and in 1920–21. The Great Depression in 1930 intensified difficulties, but reform measures under the New Deal finally assured the miners their right to organize; membership in the United Mine Workers of America soared, and by 1937 labor leaders enjoyed tremendous political power in the state. During the 1950s economic weakness in the coal industry, combined with the mechanization and automation that enabled mines to operate at top efficiency with far fewer employees, helped bring about the highest unemployment rate in the country and a major exodus of population—down 7.2% from 1950 to 1960 and another 6.2% from 1960 to 1970. Economic conditions improved during the 1960s, as Federal aid poured into the state and massive efforts were made to attract new industry. More recently, the ravages of surface, or "strip," mining have become a major political issue; in March 1971, the state legislature took initial steps toward control. West Virginia's first constitution was ratified in 1862; it was amended in 1863 to provide for the gradual abolition of slavery, as required by Congress before the granting of statehood. The present constitution dates from 1872. West Virginia's executive branch is headed by a governor elected for a four-year term. The state's bicameral legislature has a senate with 34 members elected for four-year terms and a house of delegates with 100 members elected for two-year terms. The state sends two Senators and four Representatives to the U.S. Congress and has six electoral votes. Democrats have played the dominant role in West Virginia politics since the Great Depression, but growing Republican strength was seen in the election of Arch A. Moore, Jr., a Republican, as governor in 1968; he was reelected in 1972, defeating his secretary of state, John D. Rockefeller IV, a Democrat. The state's leading institution of higher learning is West Virginia Univ., which has two main campuses at Morgantown. See C. H. Ambler, *Sectionalism in Virginia from 1776 to 1861* (1910) and, with F. P. Summers, *West Virginia, the Mountain State* (2d ed. 1958); J. M. Callahan, *Semicentennial History of West Virginia* (1913) and *History of West Virginia* (1923); P. M. Conley, ed., *The West Virginia Encyclopedia* (1929); P. M. Conley, *Beacon Lights of West Virginia History* (2 vol., 1939); R. F. Munn, *Index to West Virginia* (1960); F. A. Zeller and W. J. Smith, *Economic Development in West Virginia* (1969); J. P. Hale, *Trans-Allegheny Pioneers* (3d ed. 1971); O. K. Rice, *The Allegheny Frontier: West Virginia Beginnings, 1780–1830* (1969) and *West Virginia: The State and Its People* (1972); Federal Writers' Project, *West Virginia: A Guide to the Mountain State* (1941, repr. 1972).

West Virginia University, mainly at Morgantown; coeducational; land-grant and state supported; est. and opened 1867 as an agricultural college, renamed 1868. It operates Potomac State College (coeducational; two years) at Keyser as well as its graduate and professional programs at Morgantown. The university maintains the state agricultural experiment station, an extensive university farm system, forestry and engineering camps, experimental forests, and a biological station. The university also manages the Center for Appalachian Studies and Development (organized 1963) and is involved in agricultural research in E Africa.

West Warwick (wôr'wĭk, -ĭk), town (1970 pop. 24,323), Kent co., central R.I., on the Pawtuxet River; set off from Warwick and inc. 1913. Textile manufacturing is a leading industry. West Warwick includes the village of River Point.

Westwego (wĕstwē'gō), city (1970 pop. 11,402), Jefferson parish, SE La., a suburb of New Orleans.

Westwood. 1 Residential town (1970 pop. 12,750), Norfolk co., E Mass., in the greater Boston area; settled 1640, inc. 1897. It has several early 18th-century buildings. **2** Residential borough (1970 pop. 11,105), Bergen co., NE N.J., a suburb in the New York-northern New Jersey metropolitan area; inc. 1894. Some light manufacturing is carried on.

Westwood Lakes, uninc. village (1970 pop. 12,811), Dade co., SE Fla., a residential suburb of Miami.

West Yorkshire, metropolitan county (1972 est. pop. 2,053,000), N central England, created under the Local Government Act of 1972 (effective 1974). It is subdivided into 5 metropolitan districts. West Yorkshire comprises the county boroughs of BRADFORD, LEEDS, HALIFAX, DEWSBURY, HUDDERSFIELD, and WAKEFIELD, and portions of the former county of YORKSHIRE (West Riding).

Wethersfield (wĕth'ərzfēld), town (1970 pop. 26,662), Hartford co., central Conn., on the Connecticut River, adjoining Hartford on the north; settled 1634 by colonists from Watertown, Mass.; inc. 1637. Wethersfield, which is largely residential, manufactures tools, machinery, aircraft parts, and other products. The oldest permanent English settlement in Connecticut, Wethersfield has preserved many Colonial buildings. They include the Joseph Webb House, where Gen. George Washington and the Comte de Rochambeau met secretly in 1781 to coordinate the efforts of French forces with the American army in the Revolutionary War.

Wettekind, Saxon historian: see WITTEKIND.

Wetterhorn (vĕt'ərhôrn"), peak, c.12,150 ft (3,700 m) high, Bern canton, S central Switzerland, in the Bernese Alps N of the Finsteraarhorn.

Wettin (vĕt'ĭn), German dynasty, which ruled in Saxony, Thuringia, Poland, Great Britain, Belgium, and Bulgaria. It takes its name from a castle on the Saale near Halle. The family gained prominence in the 10th cent. as leaders in the German drive to the east, which made Saxony and Lusatia German. It acquired (c.1100) the margravate of Meissen and soon expanded its domains to include most of SAXONY and THURINGIA. In 1423, Frederick the Warlike of Meissen was granted Saxony and became (1425) elector of Saxony as FREDERICK I. The Wettin holdings were repeatedly subdivided. The most important division (1485) established the Ernestine line and the Albertine line, named for Frederick II's sons Ernest and Albert. The electoral title and most of Saxony passed in 1547 from the Ernestine to the Albertine line. The Ernestine line retained its possessions in Thuringia but split into several collateral branches. In 1918, when the house of Wettin was deposed in Thuringia and Saxony, its Thuringian holdings consisted of Saxe-Weimar-Eisenach, a grand duchy (see under SAXE-WEIMAR), and of Saxe-Coburg-Gotha (see under SAXE-COBURG), SAXE-MEININGEN, and SAXE-ALTENBURG, which were duchies. From the branch of Saxe-Coburg-Gotha the Belgian, the English, and the Bulgarian dynasties were descended through, respectively, LEOPOLD I of the Belgians, Prince ALBERT (consort of Queen Victoria), and Czar FERDINAND of Bulgaria. The English house changed its name to WINDSOR; the Bulgarian branch was deposed in 1946. A cousin of Prince Albert married Queen Maria II of Portugal and became king consort as FERDINAND II of Portugal. The Albertine line ruled in Saxony, obtaining hereditary royal rank in 1806; it also ruled Poland from 1697 to 1763 (see AUGUSTUS II; AUGUSTUS III).

Wettingen (vĕt'ĭng-ən), town (1970 pop. 19,900), Aargau canton, N Switzerland. It is the site of the Zürich power station and of industries that produce textiles and metal goods. In the town is a former Cistercian monastery, founded in 1227 and now a school, which contains outstanding stained glass and the tomb of the Holy Roman Emperor Albert I.

Wetzlar (vĕts'lär), city (1970 pop. 36,618), Hesse, central West Germany, on the Lahn River. Situated in a region where iron ore is mined, the city has a metallurgical industry. Other manufactures include optical equipment (cameras, microscopes, and binoculars), machinery, and textiles. Wetzlar was a free imperial city from 1180 to 1803. The supreme court of the Holy Roman Empire (Ger. *Reichskammergericht*) was located in the city from 1693 to 1806. Goethe was a young lawyer in Wetzlar when he met (1772) Charlotte Buff, the Lotte in his novel *Die Leiden des jungen Werthers* (1774). The city passed to Prussia in 1815 and formed an enclave between Nassau and Upper Hesse. It suffered considerable damage in World War II. Noteworthy structures include the cathedral (9th cent.) and the ruins of Kalsmunt castle (13th cent.).

WEU: see INTERNATIONAL GOVERNMENTAL ORGANIZATIONS.

Wexford (wĕks'fərd), county (1971 pop. 85,892), 910 sq mi (2,357 sq km), SE Republic of Ireland. The county town is the port city of WEXFORD. Most of the land is low and fertile, but on the western border Mt. Leinster in the Blackstairs Mts. rises to 2,610 ft (796 m). The Slaney is the principal river. Wexford is chiefly an agricultural region; wheat is the chief crop, and cattle and pigs are raised. There is fishing in the Slaney and the Barrow. The chief port is Rosslare. The name of the county is Danish in origin, and much evidence of the early Danish occupation of Wexford survives today.

Wexford, urban district (1971 pop. 11,744), county town of Co. Wexford, SE Republic of Ireland, on Wexford Harbour, which is formed by the Slaney River estuary. Wexford is a business center. Products include woolens, agricultural machinery, furniture, mineral water, and cured bacon. Malting and tourism are other industries. English invaders landed there and signed a treaty with the Irish in 1169; Oliver Cromwell sacked the town in 1649; and the United Irishmen made it their headquarters in 1798. Selskar, or St. Sepulchre, Abbey dates from the 12th cent. Of interest are the Church of St. Patrick and the old Bull Ring (scene of bullfights). Wexford was once noted for its fairs and tourneys.

Weyburn (wā'bərn), city (1971 pop. 8,815), SE Sask., Canada, SE of Regina. A trade center for a wheat-growing and oil-producing region, it has grain elevators and a feed mill. Power-line and transmission cables, and plastic pipes and fittings are manufactured.

Weyden, Roger van der (vän dər vī'dən), c.1400–1464, major early Flemish master, known also as Roger de la Pasture. He is believed to have studied with Robert Campin. His early works also show the influence of Jan van Eyck. Van Eyck, however, had been a master of objective observation, whereas Roger in his work portrayed intangible emotions with an assurance that has not been surpassed. His piety is reflected in the early masterpiece *Descent from the Cross* (c.1435; Prado); he depicted with incredible restraint the profound grief of the mourners grouped around the tragic figure of Christ. His composition strongly affected later representations of the theme. Roger became City Painter in Brussels in 1436. He then produced a series of undated altarpieces including the *Last Judgment* (hospital, Beaune), the *Braque Triptych* (Louvre), *Crucifixion with Donors* (Vienna), and *Adoration of the Magi* (Berlin), which vary in execution from the typically Flemish presentation of sumptuous details to an almost Italianate sculptural rendering of the figures. An early source indicates that Roger made a pilgrimage to Italy in the holy year 1450. Whether this supposed excursion had any effect on his style is much debated. It has been shown that his *Entombment* (Uffizi) bears an affinity to the Tuscan treatment of the subject, particularly by Fra Angelico, and that Roger's *Virgin and Child with Saints* (Frankfurt) has a strong resemblance to the Italian religious art of the day. His style is, however, highly individual. His religious paintings and his portraits have simplicity blended with the monumental. The portraits, such as that of a young lady (National Gall. of Art, Washington, D.C.) and of Francesco d'Este (Metropolitan Mus.) exhibit a simple clarity of contour and psychological penetration. Other notable works are his *St. Luke Painting the Virgin,* of which a version or replica is in the Museum of Fine Arts, Boston, the *Crucifixion* (Philadelphia Mus.), and paintings in the museums of Chicago, Houston, and San Marino, Calif. Roger's influence was great, and his tradition was carried on by such painters as Dierick Bouts and Hans Memling. See Erwin Panofsky, *Early Netherlandish Painting* (1953); Martin Davies, *Roger van der Weyden* (1972).

Weygand, Maxime (mäksēm' vāgäN'), 1867–1965, French general, b. Belgium. A career army officer, he was (1914–23) chief of staff to Marshal Foch, and in 1920 he directed the defense of Warsaw against the Soviet army and turned the tide of the Russo-Polish War in favor of Poland. Weygand subsequently served France as high commissioner in Syria (1923–24), chief of the general staff, and commander in the Middle East (1939–40). In World War II he replaced (May, 1940) General Gamelin as supreme Allied commander, but he could not avert the fall of

France. After the Franco-German armistice (June), Weygand served in the Vichy government as minister of defense, delegate general to French Africa, and governor general of Algeria. Dismissed (1941) as delegate general and arrested (1942) as a hostage for Gen. Henri Giraud (who had gone over to the Allies), Weygand was held by the Germans until 1945. After his return to France he was accused of collaboration with Germany, but was exonerated in 1948. See his memoirs, *Recalled to Service* (tr. 1952); study by P. C. F. Bankwitz (1967).

Weyler y Nicolau, Valeriano (välāryä'nō wä'lĕr ē nēkōlä'o͞o), 1838–1930, Spanish general. After graduation from the Toledo military academy he was sent to Santo Domingo and later to Cuba, where he served during the TEN YEARS WAR. He returned to Spain in 1873 and fought against the Carlists (1875–76). While captain general of the Canary Islands (1878–83) he was created marqués de Tenerife. Later he held a series of high posts, becoming captain general of the Philippines in 1888. In 1896 he replaced Arsenio Martínez de Campos in Cuba to suppress the rebellion there, but his cruel methods were protested by the United States, and he was recalled (1897). Weyler was war minister three times between 1901 and 1907. While captain general of Catalonia he suppressed the anarchist rebellion in Barcelona, which culminated in the execution of Francisco FERRER GUARDIA (1909). In the mid-20s he was accused of plotting against Primo de Rivera, but he was acquitted.

Weymouth (wā'məth), town (1970 pop. 54,610), Norfolk co., E Mass., a suburb of Boston on Hingham Bay; settled 1622, inc. 1635. It is chiefly residential. A generating plant there supplies electric power to the Boston area. Abigail Adams was born in Weymouth.

Weymouth and Melcombe Regis (wā'məth, mĕl'kəm rē'jĭs), municipal borough (1971 pop. 42,332), Dorset, SW England, on Weymouth Bay. It is a port and a resort town with wide beaches. The port was active in the wool trade in the Middle Ages. Today grain, fertilizers, and Portland stone are exported, and potatoes, flowers, and tomatoes are imported. The resort facilities are mostly in Melcombe Regis; Elizabeth I amalgamated the two towns in 1571. Weymouth was an embarkation base for the invasion of Normandy in 1944.

Weyprecht, Karl (kärl vī'prĕkht), 1838–81, German arctic explorer. With Julius von Payer he made a voyage to Novaya Zemlya in 1871. Weyprecht and Payer were leaders of an Austrian expedition (1872–74) to the arctic in the course of which Franz Josef Land was discovered. Weyprecht became an advocate of internationally coordinated exploration of the polar regions; his views were influential in the formation of the first International Polar Year of 1882–83. See Julius von Payer, *New Lands within the Arctic Circle* (1876).

whale, aquatic mammal of the order Cetacea, found in all oceans of the world. Members of this order vary greatly in size and include the largest animals that have ever lived. They never leave the water, even to give birth. Like other mammals, whales breathe air, are warm-blooded (i.e., possess an efficient system for maintaining a constant body temperature), and produce milk for feeding their young. Their adaptations for aquatic life include a fishlike form, nearly hairless skin, and an insulating layer of blubber (up to 12 in./30 cm thick in some species). The forelimbs of whales are modified into flippers, and the hind legs are reduced to internal vestiges. In some species there is a dorsal fin. The tail is flattened horizontally and is used for propulsion. The head is very large, and there is no external neck. Whales have lungs, with one or two nostril openings, called blowholes, located far back on the top of the head; the nostrils are equipped with valves that close when the whale dives. Most whales must surface every 15 to 20 min to breathe, but some of the toothed whales can remain submerged for 60 min. Spouting, sometimes visible for miles, occurs when the whale surfaces and is caused by condensation of hot, moist air as it is exhaled from the blowhole. The shape of the spout is characteristic of each type of whale. Although whales have small eyes, designed to withstand great pressures, their vision is good. They have excellent hearing, and many species use echolocation (sonar) for underwater navigation. Whales cruise and rest on the surface of the ocean. Most large whales travel in small schools, or pods, but some of the smaller ones form schools of up to several thousand individuals. Large whales are found in open ocean, where they migrate thousands of miles. Smaller whales are sometimes found in offshore waters. A few dolphin species are found in tropical rivers. Females of most species give birth to a single calf every other year, after a gestation period of 10 or 12 months. The newborn calf is pushed to the surface by the mother or by another adult; it is able to swim almost immediately but is nursed for about six months. There are two major groups, or suborders, of whales—the toothed whales (suborder Odontoceti) and the toothless, or baleen, whales (suborder Mysticeti). Toothed whales are predators, most species living on fish or squid. They have a single blowhole and wide throats designed to accommodate large prey. Most use their teeth to catch and hold the prey, which is swallowed whole. The larger ones can dive to great depths; sperm whales may go as far down as 1 mi (1.6 km). The toothed whales range in length from 8 to 50 ft (2.4–15 m). They include the beaked whales and bottlenose whales (family Ziphiidae), as well as the SPERM WHALE, or cachalot (family Physeteridae), both families of worldwide distribution; the BELUGA, or white whale, and the NARWHAL (family Monodontidae), small polar whales with only a few teeth; and several families of small whales better known as DOLPHINS and PORPOISES. The KILLER WHALE and pilot whale are types of dolphin. The white whale Moby Dick, of Melville's novel, was not a beluga, but an albino sperm whale. Baleen whales are large species, usually over 30 ft (9 m) long. They are filter feeders, living on plankton and small fish. They lack teeth but have fringed sheets of a horny material (similar to that of fingernails) called baleen, or whalebone, suspended from the roof of the mouth. They swim with their mouths open, alternately taking in and expelling water; as water is expelled from the mouth, enormous quantities of plankton are trapped behind the baleen strainers. Baleen whales have narrow throats and paired blowholes. There are three families of baleen whales: the RIGHT WHALE family (Balaenidae); the gray whale family (Eschrichtidae), with a single species found in the N Pacific Ocean; and the rorqual family (Balaenopteridae). Rorquals, the most familiar of the large whales, are characterized by large, pouchlike throats with many furrows running from mouth to belly. The rorqual family includes the humpback whale, the finback whale, or common rorqual, the sei whale, and the BLUE WHALE, or blue rorqual, which may attain a length of 100 ft (30 m) and a weight of 150 tons. All species of large whales have been drastically reduced in numbers by centuries of intensive whaling. Most of the right whales and rorquals are considered endangered species, and the blue whale and humpback whale are particularly close to extinction. Whale products include WHALE OIL, SPERM OIL, SPERMACETI, AMBERGRIS, and whalebone, as well as meat, bone meal, and liver oil. Whales are classified in the phylum CHORDATA, subphylum Vertebrata, class Mammalia, order Cetacea. See L. H. Matthews, ed., *The Whale* (1968); F. D. Ommanney, *Lost Leviathan* (1971); G. L. Small, *The Blue Whale* (1971).

whalebone: see WHALE.

whale oil, oil extracted from the blubber and other parts of certain species of whales. It varies in composition, color, and the degree of fishy odor according to the method and extent of refining. Formerly widely used as an illuminant, it was superseded by petroleum products. It is used today in soapmaking, as a leather dressing, and as a lubricant. Some is hydrogenated to form edible fats. The term is also sometimes used to include SPERM OIL.

Whales, Bay of: see ROSS SEA; ANTARCTICA.

whale shark, large, plankton-eating shark, *Rhincodon typus,* found in all tropical seas of the world. The largest known specimens are 50 ft (15 m) long, making them the largest fish in the world. The whale shark feeds largely on plankton, as well as on small fish and crustaceans. It is the only large shark with its mouth at the front of its head rather than on the underside. The mouth is equipped with many rows of tiny teeth, and the throat has numerous long slender structures called gill rakers, which form a fine mesh for straining food from the water. The whale shark's body is stout but streamlined, like that of a whale. It is dark brown above, with many white or yellow spots, and white or yellow below. The whale shark is a docile, torpid fish; it does not attack, even on provocation, but has been known to collide with boats. It is classified in the phylum CHORDATA, subphylum Vertebrata, class Chondrichthyes, order Selachii, family Rhincodontidae.

whalesucker: see REMORA.

whaling. The hunting of whales is thought to have been first pursued by the Basques—from land as early as the 10th cent. and in Newfoundland waters by the 14th cent. It is not until the middle of the 16th cent., however, that the appearance of Basques in those waters is established by record. Whaling on a large scale was first organized at SPITSBERGEN at the beginning of the 17th cent., largely by the Dutch who, with the Basques, apparently developed methods of flensing and boiling still largely used. The Dutch were at first in competition with the English Muscovy Company of London, but before its collapse in 1625 they had gained ascendancy; in 1623 they established the port of Smeerenberg. Large profits continued only until c.1640, when the scarcity of whales forced the Dutch farther out into the northern waters in search of them. By the middle of the 17th cent. whaling from the land was established in America. Its centers, at first on Long Island and Cape Cod, shifted to Nantucket and then New Bedford, the greatest whaling port in the world until the decline (c.1850) of the industry. With the capture (1712) of a sperm whale by a Nantucket fisherman, the superior qualities of SPERM OIL were immediately discovered, and American whalers began fishing farther south in search of the sperm whale, which superseded the right whale in value. The American fisheries were set back by the American Revolution, but in 1791 the first Americans rounded Cape Horn to hunt in the S Pacific. Another, but temporary, setback occurred in the War of 1812, but the outcome spelled the complete defeat of British whaling, and from 1820 until shortly before the Civil War, Americans sailed the Pacific from south to north, often gone as long as three or four years, in search of the whale. Melville's *Moby Dick* gives an account of a voyage in this period. The advent of the Civil War, together with a decrease in the demand for sperm oil and in the number of whales, brought the decline of the industry. The invention (c.1856), by the Norwegian Sven Foyn, of a harpoon containing an explosive head may be said to have inaugurated modern whaling. Besides insuring the whale's immediate death this type of harpoon can now also shoot compressed air into the whale, so that it will not sink before it can be hauled on board. The development of the factory ship, equipped to take on board and completely process whales caught by the smaller chasers, has brought increased safety and the ability to catch the larger blue whale. It also allows for the use of all parts of the whale; formerly only the blubber and head could be procured, and the job of flensing from the side of the ship was a hazardous one. In 1904 operations commenced from a whaling station on South Georgia, an island in the S Atlantic, and the modern industry found in antarctic waters the last rich whaling fields on the globe. The number of expeditions from the antarctic islands was restricted by Great Britain, which had secured sovereignty over these areas. In 1925 the first floating factory was sent to the antarctic regions; that innovation led to the greatest expansion in the history of whaling. In 1930 the modern whaling industry reached its zenith, with 6 shore stations, 41 floating factories, and 232 whale catchers in the antarctic regions, of which 3 stations, 27 factory ships, and 147 catchers were Norwegian and 2 stations, 27 floating factories, and 68 catchers were British. During World War II most of the world's whaling fleet was lost, but afterwards Norway, Britain, and Japan (which had started antarctic expeditions in 1935) soon reestablished their prewar positions, and in addition the Soviet Union, the Netherlands, and South Africa appeared in the antarctic regions for the first time. The main whalers are now the Japanese and the Russians, the traditional Norwegian dominance having been curtailed by the high cost of labor and supplies, as well as by the diminishing use of whale oil and by-products in Western Europe. In 1932–33 the first attempts were made to regulate and restrict the catch by international agreement. After World War II the International Whaling Convention was signed in Washington, D.C., by 17 nations, including all those operating in the antarctic regions. The convention, which regulates most of the world's whaling activity, limits the season to a few months of the year and prohibits the taking of right whales, gray whales, and all females with calves. However, those regulations have no compulsion, and the whale continues to be over-hunted. The blue whale, once the mainstay of the American whaling industry, now numbers only about 2,000, and other species have also been seriously depleted. See J. T. Travis, *A History of the Whale Fisheries* (1921); Clifford Ashley, *The Yankee Whaler* (1926, 2d ed. 1942); Albert Church, *Whale Ships and Whaling* (1938); F. R. Dulles, *Lowered Boats: A Chronicle of American Whaling* (1933); Edouard Stackpole, *The Sea-Hunters: The*

New England Whaleman . . . 1635–1835 (1953); Frank Crisp, *The Adventure of Whaling* (1954); Addison Whipple, *Yankee Whalers in the South Seas* (1954); Eric Ash, *Whaler's Eye* (1962); L. H. Matthews, et al., *The Whale* (1968); G. L. Small, *The Blue Whale* (1971).

Whalley, Edward (hwā'lē, hwô'-), d. 1675?, English regicide. During the English civil war he served under his cousin Oliver Cromwell in the parliamentary army. He was given custody of Charles I for a time in 1647, served on the high court of justice that tried him, and signed the death warrant. After 1655, Whalley was one of the major generals who ruled the country until the restored Long Parliament withdrew his commission and those of other prominent Cromwellians. At the Restoration (1660), Whalley, with his son-in-law, William GOFFE, fled to New England. He lived successively in Boston, New Haven, Milford (Conn.), and Hadley (Mass.), hunted by English agents but never betrayed.

Whampoa: see HUANG-PU, China.

Whangarei (hwäng"gərā'), city (1971 pop. 30,746), N North Island, New Zealand, on the Pacific Ocean. It is the leading city on the Northland Peninsula and an important port for coastal trade. There is an oil refinery in the city.

Whangpoo, Hwangpoo, or **Huang-p'u** (all: hwäng'po͞o'), river, 60 mi (97 km) long, rising in the lake district of Shanghai Municipality, E China, and flowing NE past Shanghai into the Yangtze estuary at Wu-sung. It is a major navigational route. Its dredged channel, lined with wharves, warehouses, and industrial plants, provides access to Shanghai for oceangoing vessels.

Wharton, Edith (Newbold Jones), 1862–1937, American novelist, b. New York City, noted for her subtle, ironic, and superbly crafted fictional studies of New York society at the turn of the century. The daughter of a socially elect family, she was educated privately in New York and in Europe. In 1885 she married Edward Wharton, a Boston banker; after the first few years of marriage Edward Wharton became mentally ill, and the burden of caring for him fell upon his wife. Finally, in 1913, after she had settled permanently in France, Edith Wharton terminated the marriage by divorce. Her early stories and tales were collected in *The Greater Inclination* (1899), *Crucial Instances* (1901), and *The Descent of Man* (1904); somewhat narrow in scope, they nevertheless show the unity of mood and the lucid, polished prose style of her more mature works. Much of her writing bears a resemblance to the fiction of Henry James, who was her close friend; but the similarities are superficial, and in her best and most characteristic novels—*The House of Mirth* (1905) and *The Age of Innocence* (1920; Pulitzer Prize)—she asserts herself as a distinctive artist. Re-creating the atmosphere of the unadventurous, ceremonious society of New York, she depicts in these and other works the cruelty of social convention and the conflicts that arise between money values and moral values. In the novella *Ethan Frome* (1911)—one of her best-known, most successful, and least characteristic works—she evokes the tragic fate of three people against the stark background of rural New England. Among her many other novels are *The Valley of Decision* (1902), a historical novel of 18th-century Italy; *The Custom of the Country* (1913); *Hudson River Bracketed* (1929) and its sequel, *The Gods Arrive* (1932); and an unfinished novel, *The Buccaneers* (1938). Later collections of short stories include *Xingu and Other Stories* (1916), *Certain People* (1930), and *Ghosts* (1937). She is also the author of travel books *(Italian Backgrounds,* 1905), literary criticism, and poetry. In 1915 she was awarded the Cross of the Legion of Honor by the French government for her services during World War I. See her autobiography, *A Backward Glance* (1964); biography by Louis Auchincloss (1971); studies by Millicent Bell (1965), Percy Lubbock (1947, repr. 1969), and Geoffrey Walton (1971).

Wharton, Francis, 1820–89, American clergyman and jurist, b. Philadelphia, grad. Yale, 1839. Admitted to the Pennsylvania bar in 1843, he became an authority on criminal law and wrote *A Treatise on the Criminal Law of the United States* (1846). He was (1856–63) professor of history and literature at Kenyon College. He was ordained (1862) an Episcopalian minister, and he was (1871–81) professor of canon law at the Episcopal Theological School in Cambridge, Mass. During this period he wrote *A Treatise on the Conflict of Laws* (1872). As head of the legal division of the U.S. Dept. of State (1885–88), he edited *A Digest of the International Law of the United States* (3 vol., 2d ed. 1887) and *The Revolutionary Diplomatic Correspondence of the United States* (6 vol., 1889, 2d ed. 1969). See biography by H. E. Wharton (1891).

Wharton, Thomas Wharton, 1st marquess of, 1648–1715, English politician. Before his entry into Parliament (1673) he had acquired the reputation as a rake and gambler that he retained for life. After 1679 he became active in Whig politics, supporting the attempt to exclude the duke of York (later James II) from the succession. He composed the words of the popular satirical ballad "Lilliburlero" (set to music by Henry Purcell), with which, he boasted, he sang James II out of his kingdom in 1688. William III made Wharton a privy councilor and comptroller of the household (1689). Queen Anne removed him because of her personal dislike and distrust of him on religious grounds, but he remained one of the powerful Whig politicians. He was a commissioner for the union with Scotland, was created (1706) earl, and served as lord lieutenant of Ireland (1708–10). George I made him lord privy seal (1714) and a marquess (1715).

Whately, Richard (hwāt'lē), 1787–1863, English prelate and writer. Fellow and tutor of Oriel College, Oxford, he published a witty work aimed at extreme skeptics, *Historic Doubts Relative to Napoleon Bonaparte* (1819). In 1822 he gave the Bampton Lectures at Oxford entitled *The Use and Abuse of Party Feeling in Matters of Religion.* As archbishop of Dublin (from 1831) he worked to free religious instruction from sectarianism and urged state endowment of the Roman Catholic clergy. He was an influential supporter of the Broad Church party. Among his many works are *Elements of Logic* (1826) and *Elements of Rhetoric* (1828). See his *Life and Correspondence,* ed. by his daughter, E. J. Whately, (1866); memoirs by W. J. Fitzpatrick (2 vol., 1864).

wheat, cereal plant of the genus *Triticum* of the family Gramineae (GRASS family), a major food and an important commodity on the world grain market. It was one of the first of the grains domesticated by man (see GRAIN). Its cultivation began in the NEOLITHIC PERIOD. Bread wheat is known to have been grown in the Nile valley by 5000 B.C., and its apparently later cultivation in other regions (e.g., the Indus and Euphrates valleys by 4000 B.C., China by 2500 B.C., and England by 2000 B.C.) indicate that it spread from Mediterranean centers of domestication. The civilizations of W Asia and of the European peoples have been largely based on wheat, while rice has been more important in E Asia. Since agriculture began, wheat has been the chief source of bread for Europe and the Middle East. It was introduced into Mexico by the Spaniards c.1520 and into Virginia by English colonists early in the 17th cent. For its early growth, wheat thrives best in cool weather. The wheat plant is an annual, probably derived from a perennial; the ancestry of and precise distinctions between species are no longer always clear. Among the more ancient, and now less frequently cultivated, species are einkorn (*T. monococcum*), emmer (*T. dicoccum*), and spelt (*T. spelta*). Modern wheat varieties are usually classified as winter wheats (fall-planted and unusually winter hardy for grain crops) and spring wheats. Approximately three fourths of the wheat grown in the United States is winter wheat. Flour from hard wheats (varieties evolved for the most part from *T. aestivum*) contains a high percentage of GLUTEN and is used to make bread and fine cakes. The hardest-kerneled wheat is durum (*T. durum*); its flour is used in the manufacture of macaroni, spaghetti, and similar pasta products. White- and soft-wheat varieties are paler in color and have starchy kernels; their flour is preferred for piecrust, biscuits, and breakfast foods. Wheat is used in the manufacture of whiskey and beer, and the grain, the bran (the residue from milling), and the vegetative plant parts make valuable livestock feed. Before the introduction of maize into Europe, wheat was the principal source of starch for sizing paper and cloth. Although in many regions wheat is still harvested and threshed by hand and stone-milled, in the United States, and increasingly elsewhere, it is combine-harvested and mechanically milled. It is susceptible to many pests and diseases, the more destructive including RUST, bunt (see SMUT), and the HESSIAN FLY and CHINCH BUG. All wheat-producing countries carry on breeding experiments to improve existing varieties or to obtain new ones with such dominant characteristics as disease resistance, increased hardiness under specific environments, and greater yield. High-yield wheat, one of the grains resulting from the GREEN REVOLUTION, requires optimal growth conditions, e.g., adequate irrigation and high concentrations of fertilizer. Large-scale mechanized farming and continued planting of wheat without regard to crop rotation has exhausted the soil of large areas. The great wheat-producing countries of the world are the United States, China, and the USSR; extensive wheat growing is carried on also in India, W Europe, Canada, Argentina, and Australia. In the United States the wheat belt covers the Ohio Valley, the Prairie States, and E Oregon and Washington; Kansas leads the states in production. Wheat is classified in the division MAGNOLIOPHYTA, class Liliatae, order Cyperales, family Gramineae. See publications issued by the U.S. Dept. of Agriculture; R. F. Peterson, *Wheat* (1965); P. T. Dondlinger, *The Book of Wheat* (1908, repr. 1973).

wheatear: see THRUSH.

wheat fly, name for several insects harmful to wheat, e.g., the HESSIAN FLY, the wheat gallfly, the wheat MIDGE, and others.

wheat grass, any plant of the genus *Agropyron,* cool-season perennials of the family Gramineae (GRASS family). Species of wheat grass, both native and introduced, are important range forage grasses in the prairie states. Wheat grasses are also valuable for revegetation because of their drought resistance and winter hardiness. Important species are the crested wheat grass (*A. cristatum*), introduced from the N USSR, and the native Western wheat grass (*A. smithii*). The weed QUACK GRASS also belongs to this genus. Wheat grass is classified in the division MAGNOLIOPHYTA, class Liliatae, order Cyperales, family Gramineae.

Wheatley, Henry Benjamin, 1838–1917, English bibliographer and antiquarian, a founder of the Early English Text Society and of the Index Society. Wheatley's work on the indexing of books, *How to Make an Index* (1902), is a classic. He edited Pepys's diary (10 vol., 1893–99) and wrote *Samuel Pepys and the World He Lived In* (1880).

Wheatley, Phillis, 1753?–1784, American poet, considered the first important black writer in the United States. Brought from Africa in 1761, she became a slave of the Boston merchant John Wheatley, who, recognizing her intelligence and wit, educated her and encouraged her talent. Her work, which was derivative, includes *Poems on Various Subjects* (1773). Although she obtained her freedom and traveled to England, where she was much admired, she eventually died in poverty. See her *Life and Works* (1916, repr. 1969).

Wheaton, Henry, 1785–1848, American jurist and diplomat, b. Providence, R.I., grad. Rhode Island College (now Brown), 1802. After translating the Code Napoléon into English, he practiced law, held various judicial offices, and was (1816–27) reporter of the decisions of the U.S. Supreme Court. While reporter he prepared *A Digest of the Decisions of the Supreme Court of the United States, 1789–1820* (1821). Wheaton's diplomatic career began with his service (1827–35) as chargé d'affaires in Denmark. While in Denmark he wrote his *History of the Northmen* (1831), which maintained that America had been discovered by Scandinavians before the voyage of Columbus. Wheaton represented (1835–46) the United States at the Prussian court. The U.S. Senate ratified treaties he negotiated with Prussia respecting the rights of immigrants, but it rejected the reciprocal trade agreements he considered his greatest achievement. Wheaton's crowning work as a jurist was his *Elements of International Law* (1836) and the companion work, *A History of the Law of Nations* (1845). See biographies by W. V. Kellen (1902) and E. F. Baker (1937, repr. 1971).

Wheaton. 1 City (1970 pop. 31,138), seat of Du Page co., NE Ill., a residential suburb of Chicago; inc. 1859. Wheaton College is there. Elbert H. Gary was born nearby. **2** Uninc. city (1970 pop. 66,247), Montgomery co., central Md., a residential suburb of Washington, D.C. It grew (1860s) around a tavern established there in the early 1700s and was named for Union Gen. Frank Wheaton, who defended nearby Fort Stevens in the Civil War.

Wheaton College, at Norton, Mass.; for women; opened 1835, chartered 1837. Organized by Mary LYON, it was one of the earliest women's schools. It became a college in 1912.

Wheat Ridge, city (1970 pop. 29,795), Jefferson co., N central Colo., a residential suburb of Denver; inc. 1969. An annual carnation festival is held there.

Wheatstone, Sir Charles (hwēt'stōn, -stən), 1802–75, English physicist and inventor. He was professor at King's College, London, from 1834. A pioneer in telegraphy, he was coinventor with Sir W. F. Cooke of an electric telegraph (patented 1837) and inventor of many other devices, including an automatic transmitter, an electric recording apparatus, and an automatic telegraph. He is credited with the invention of the concertina and with improving the stereoscope and the dynamo. He is known also for his research on light (color vision and spectra), sound, and electricity; he popularized a method for the measurement of electrical resistance using a network now known as the Wheatstone bridge. He was knighted in 1868. See his collected *Scientific Papers* (1879).

wheel. Through the many millennia of the Paleolithic period and the Neolithic period no use of the wheel was known to man. Its use was not known to the American Indians until the white man introduced it. In the Old World it came into use in the Bronze Age, when oxen and horses were first used as draft animals and wheeled vehicles were devised. Wheels for vehicles were at first solid wooden disks; spoked wheels were introduced c.2700 B.C. The potter's wheel was invented in the Bronze Age, earlier pottery being made, like that of the American Indians, without the use of the wheel. See GEAR; WHEEL AND AXLE. See R. J. Forbes, *Studies in Ancient Technology* (1955); Edwin Tunis, *Wheels* (1955); Wilfred Owen et al., ed. *Wheels* (1972).

wheel and axle, simple MACHINE consisting of a wheel mounted rigidly upon an axle or drum of smaller diameter, the wheel and the axle having the same axis. It is fundamentally a form of LEVER, the center common to both the wheel and the axle corresponding to the fulcrum, the radii of the two parts to the arms. The effort (applied to the wheel) needed to overcome the resistance (acting upon the axle) is relatively small. The mechanical advantage gained by the use of the wheel is equal to the ratio of the radius of the wheel to the radius of the axle.

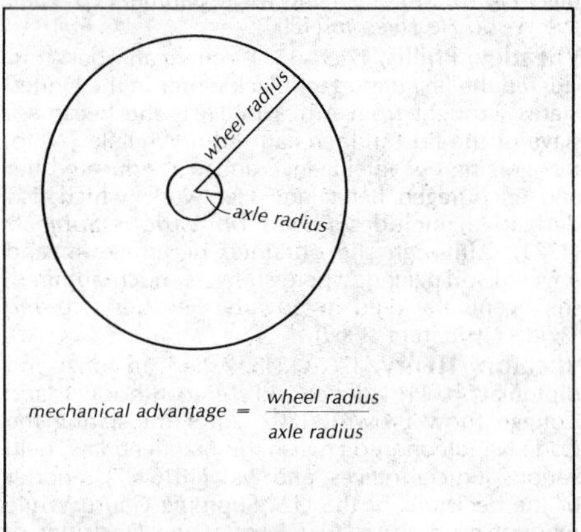

Wheel and axle

The wheel and axle is not as efficient as the lever, since a part of the effort must be used to overcome the resistance of FRICTION. In common use, a crank or handle often takes the place of the wheel. Applications of the wheel and axle are numerous in everyday life; examples are the steering wheel of an automobile, the doorknob, and the windlass. The effort is applied through a greater distance than is the resistance, but this effort is applied conveniently in a circle. In the treadmill, the windmill, and the waterwheel, the wheel and axle led the way to the utilization of power in modern machinery. Clockmakers were pioneers in devising ways of transmitting and controlling power by the use of the wheel and axle.

wheel bug: see ASSASSIN BUG.

Wheeler, Benjamin Ide, 1854–1927, American educator and classical scholar, b. Randolph, Mass. Wheeler was a professor of Greek and comparative philology at Cornell Univ. before serving as president of the Univ. of California in the years of its greatest development (1899–1919). He wrote works in classics and in linguistics, among them *Dionysos and Immortality* (1899), *Alexander the Great* (1900), and *The Whence and Whither of the Modern Science of Language* (1905).

Wheeler, Burton Kendall, 1882–1975, U.S. Senator (1923–47), b. Hudson, Mass. He practiced law in Butte, Mont. Wheeler was (1911–13) a member of the state legislature and was appointed (1913) Federal attorney by President Woodrow Wilson. He was elected (1922) to the Senate from Montana on the Democratic ticket, but in 1924 was the vice presidential candidate of the Progressive party on the ticket with Robert La Follette. He soon returned to the Democratic party and backed much of the New Deal legislation. With the outbreak of World War II he became a leading exponent of isolationism and by 1940 had broken with President Franklin Delano Roosevelt. In 1946, Wheeler was defeated in the Democratic primaries. See his autobiography, *Yankee from the West* (with Paul F. Healy, 1962).

Wheeler, Joseph, 1836–1906, Confederate general in the American Civil War, b. Augusta, Ga. He resigned from the U.S. army in April, 1861, to fight for the Confederacy. He commanded a regiment at Shiloh (April, 1862) and became chief of cavalry in the Army of Tennessee (Oct.). Wheeler took part in Braxton Bragg's Kentucky campaign and in the Chattanooga campaign, in which he destroyed William Rosecrans's supplies in a brilliant raid through middle Tennessee (Oct.). Wheeler operated against William T. Sherman in the Atlanta campaign, the march to the sea, and the advance through the Carolinas. He surrendered with Joseph E. Johnston's army in April, 1865. After the war Wheeler, a lawyer and planter in Alabama, served in the House of Representatives (1881–82, 1883, 1885–1900). A major general of volunteers in the Spanish-American War, he commanded cavalry in the invasion of Cuba. He also led a brigade in the Philippine insurrection (1899–1900). He was made a brigadier general in the regular army shortly before he retired in Sept., 1900. Wheeler wrote *The Santiago Campaign* (1899). See biography by J. P. Dyer (rev. ed. 1961).

Wheeler, Wayne Bidwell, 1869–1927, American prohibitionist and lawyer, b. Brookfield, Ohio. After his graduation (1898) from Western Reserve law school, he became increasingly important in the Ohio Anti-Saloon League. Under his direction the league opposed and helped to defeat the incumbent and antiprohibition governor of Ohio, Myron T. Herrick, in 1906. As attorney for the National Anti-Saloon League, Wheeler was prominent in the fight for prohibition legislation, notably the Eighteenth Amendment to the Constitution and the Volstead Act. See biography by Justin Steuart (1928, repr. 1970).

Wheeler, William Almon, 1819–87, American legislator, Vice President of the United States (1877–81), b. Malone, N.Y. He was admitted to the New York bar in 1845. In New York he was district attorney of Franklin co. (1846–49), Whig member of the state assembly (1850–51), and a Republican member and president pro tempore of the state senate (1858–59). After 1851 he turned from law to banking and railroad finance. He presided over the New York constitutional convention of 1867–68, and he sat (1861–63, 1869–77) in the U.S. House of Representatives. His most notable service in Congress was devising the Wheeler compromise, which settled (1875) a disputed election in Louisiana. Wheeler was little known when the Republicans nominated him for Vice President in 1876. He was elected with Rutherford Hayes in the disputed election of that year.

Wheeling. 1 Village (1970 pop. 14,746), Cook co., NE Ill., a suburb of Chicago; founded c.1830, inc. 1894. **2** City (1970 pop. 48,188), seat of Ohio co., W. Va., in the Northern Panhandle, on the Ohio River; settled 1769, inc. as a city 1836. It is an important manufacturing and commercial center in an area rich in coal and natural gas. Its many industrial products include steel, iron, chemicals, ceramics, glass, tobacco, plastics, and textiles. Fort Fincastle, renamed Fort Henry, was built (1774) to protect the settlement from Indian raids; in 1782 it was the scene of one of the last skirmishes of the American Revolution, in which a party of British and Indian attackers was driven off. Wheeling became the western terminus of the National Road in 1818, a port of entry in 1831, and a railhead in 1852. A center of pro-Unionist activity during the Civil War, the town was the site of the Wheeling Conventions (1861–62), which provided a means of forming a new state out of the northern and western counties of Virginia. Wheeling became the first capital of West Virginia in 1863 (see CHARLESTON). The city has a symphony orchestra, an opera workshop, and a racetrack. It is the seat of Wheeling College. Points of interest include the site of Fort Henry, St. Joseph's Cathedral, and Oglebay Park, with museums, a nature center, and an outdoor theater.

Wheelock, Eleazar (ĕlēā'zər hwē'lŏk), 1711–79, American clergyman, founder of DARTMOUTH COLLEGE, b. Windham, Conn., grad. Yale, 1733. He became (1735) the pastor of a Congregational church in the part of Lebanon, Conn., that is now Columbia. Here he became interested in Indian education, and he founded and conducted (1754–67) an Indian charity school. One of his first students, Samson Occom, went to England and helped to raise funds for the project, and when an endowment of some $50,000 had been collected, Wheelock moved to what is now Hanover, N.H., and established (1770) Dartmouth. He became its first president and guided the college through the early days of the American Revolution. See biography by J. D. McCallum (1939, repr. 1969).

wheel window: see ROSE WINDOW.

Wheelwright, John, c.1592–1679, American Puritan clergyman, founder of Exeter, N.H., b. Lincolnshire, England. He studied at Cambridge and was vicar (1623–33) of Bilsby. Suspended by Archbishop Laud on a charge of nonconformity, he emigrated to New England in 1636. While pastor of a Puritan church at Mt. Wollaston (now Quincy), Mass., he alienated himself from the parent church in Boston by publicly defending the views of Anne HUTCHINSON, his sister-in-law. The General Court in Boston banished him from the colony in 1638, whereupon he formed a settlement at Exeter, N.H. When the new town was claimed as within the limits of Massachusetts, the minister, with part of the church he had established, moved in 1643 to Wells, Maine. The next year, upon his acknowledging some error on his own part, the sentence of banishment was withdrawn. He held a pastorate in Hampton, N.H. After visiting England, he returned to America; his last pastorate, from 1662, was at Salisbury, N.H. See memoir by C. H. Bell in the 1876 ed. of Wheelwright's works; biography by John Heard, Jr. (1930).

whelk, large marine GASTROPOD snail found in temperate waters. The whelk is sometimes eaten, but when food is plentiful, fishermen frequently use it for bait. Whelks are scavengers and carnivores, equipped with an extensible proboscis, tipped with a filelike radula, with which they bore holes through the shells of crabs and lobsters, and a large, muscular foot with which they hold their victims. The thick-lipped, spiral shell has an uneven surface with many protuberances. The knobbed whelk, the largest species, ranging up to 16 in. (40.6 cm), and the channeled whelk, slightly smaller, are both found south of Cape Cod, Mass. In summer the strings of pale, disk-shaped egg cases are common along the shore. The whelk is sometimes mistakenly called CONCH. Whelks are classified in the phylum MOLLUSCA, class Gastropoda, order Neogastropoda.

Whetstone, George, 1551?–1587, English dramatist and poet. His chief work, the play *Promos and Cassandra* (1578), is important in the development of English domestic drama and was a source for Shakespeare's *Measure for Measure.* Whetstone was also the author of *Rock of Regard* (1576), a miscellany of verse and prose; *A Remembrance* (1577), a poem in honor of his friend George Gascoigne; *An Heptameron of Civil Discourses* (1582); and *A Mirror for Magistrates of Cities* (1584). His works, full of grave moral utterances, are of value to literary and social historians.

whetstone, natural or manufactured stone used as an abrasive solid to sharpen tools. It is used dry, with water, or with oil. Such a stone of the finer grade used with oil is usually called an oilstone.

Whig, English political party. The name, originally a term of abuse first used for Scottish Presbyterians in the 17th cent., seems to have been a shortened form of *whiggamor* [cattle driver]. It was applied (c.1679) to the English opponents of the succession of the Roman Catholic duke of York (later James II), a group led by the 1st earl of SHAFTESBURY. The GLORIOUS REVOLUTION of 1688, in which the Whigs were joined by many Tories (see TORY), assured a Protestant succession and the constitutional supremacy of Parliament over the king. Political parties during the 18th cent. were essentially groups of factions allied on specific issues. After the accession of William III advocacy of a constitutional monarchy no longer distinguished the Whigs, and during the reign of Queen Anne they became identified increasingly with aristocratic large landholders and the wealthy merchant interests. Under George I and George II most governments were composed of those with aristocratic connections, loosely Whig. The disgrace of Anne's Tory ministers who negotiated for the return of James II on her death, and the Jacobite risings of 1715 and 1745 stigmatized the Tories as supporters of absolute monarchy, and the Whig ministries of Robert WALPOLE and Henry Pelham dominated the period. After the accession (1760) of George III there were at first no real issues around which parties could polarize, but a Whig party gradually emerged, united largely in opposition to William Pitt, under the leadership of Charles James FOX. This party became identified with dissent, industrial interests, and social and parliamentary reform, and also with the Prince Regent, later George IV. Whig ministries under the 2d Earl GREY and Lord MELBOURNE were in power from 1830 to 1841, passing the first parliamentary reform bill. After this the Whigs became a part of the rising Liberal party, in which they constituted the conservative element. See Basil Williams, *The Whig Supremacy* (2d ed. 1962).

Whig party, one of the two major political parties of the United States in the second quarter of the 19th cent. As a party it did not exist before 1834, but its nucleus was formed in 1824 when the adherents of John Quincy Adams and Henry CLAY joined forces against Andrew Jackson. This coalition, which later called itself the NATIONAL REPUBLICAN PARTY, increased in strength after the election of Jackson in 1828 and was joined in opposition to the President by other smaller parties, the most notable being the ANTI-MASONIC PARTY. By 1832, Jackson had also earned the enmity of such diverse groups as states' rights advocates in the South, proponents of internal improvements in the West, and businessmen and friends of the Bank of the United States in the East. This opposition was built up and correlated by Henry Clay in the election of 1832. Two years later all of the various groups were combined in a loose alliance. However, they were not unified or strong enough to join behind a single presidential candidate in the 1836 presidential election; instead several Whig candidates ran for office. The most prominent were Daniel WEBSTER in New England, William Henry HARRISON in the Northwest, and Hugh Lawson WHITE in the Southwest. The election went to the Democrat, Martin Van Buren, but in opposition the Whigs grew steadily stronger. The two great leaders of the party were Clay and Webster, but neither was ever to head a victorious national ticket. This failure was partly a result of the sectional variations in the party, which had only one common aim, opposition to the Democrats, and partly a result of the power held by intraparty forces opposed to them, including the political bosses of New York, Thurlow WEED and William SEWARD. The party went on to victory in 1840 with the rousing "Log Cabin and Hard Cider" campaign, which put William H. Harrison in the White House. Harrison died after only one month in office and was succeeded by his Vice President, John TYLER of Virginia. A definite break now ensued between Tyler and the Whig leaders in Congress—a break that illustrated the Whig philosophy of government. The Whigs had originated in objection to what they considered the excessive power of the executive branch under Andrew Jackson. To them the legislative branch of the government represented the wishes of the people, and the task of the executive was to serve as the enforcing agent of the legislative branch. When Tyler ignored the counsel of his cabinet and vetoed bills that sought to reestablish the Bank of the United States, about 50 Whig members of Congress met in caucus and read Tyler out of the party. At the behest of Clay the entire cabinet resigned; even Webster retired after completing the Webster-Ashburton Treaty (1843). Clay became the standard-bearer in 1844 but was defeated by James K. Polk. In 1848, Weed and his associates swung the nomination from Webster and Clay to Zachary TAYLOR, who had gained wide popularity as a commander in the Mexican War. This move temporarily prevented a division of the party, and although Taylor died while Clay was formulating the Compromise of 1850 in Congress, Millard FILLMORE, his Vice President and presidential successor, kept the faith of the Whig party. However, the disintegration of the party was already manifest; in 1848 several important Whigs joined the new FREE-SOIL PARTY along with the abolitionists. In New England a bitter struggle developed between antislavery "Conscience Whigs" and proslavery "Cotton Whigs," in other places between "lower law" Whigs and "higher law" Whigs (the term "higher law" had originated from a famous speech by William H. Seward who declared that there was a higher law than the Constitution). In the election of 1852, the party was torn wide open by sectional interests. Both Clay and Webster died during the campaign, and Winfield SCOTT, the Whig presidential candidate, won only 42 electoral votes. This brought about a quick end to the party, and its remnants gravitated toward other parties. The newly formed (1854) REPUBLICAN PARTY and the sharply divided Democratic party absorbed the largest segments. Other Whigs, led by Fillmore, drifted into the KNOW-NOTHING MOVEMENT. See A. C. Cole, *The Whig Party in the South* (1913, repr. 1962); E. M. Carroll, *Origins of the Whig Party* (1925, repr. 1970); G. R. Poage, *Henry Clay and the Whig Party* (1936, repr. 1965); R. J. Morgan, *A Whig Embattled: The Presidency under John Tyler* (1954).

whippet, breed of small, slender HOUND developed in England in the mid-18th cent. It stands between 18 and 22 in. (45.7–55.8 cm) high at the shoulder and weighs about 20 lb (9 kg). Its close-lying, smooth coat may be any color but is usually white, tan, or gray. Developed from crosses of greyhound, terrier, and, later, Italian greyhound, the whippet was used for coursing hares in an enclosed area, a sport that became popular when bullbaiting and bearbaiting were outlawed. Today it is raised primarily as a race dog and pet. See DOG.

Whipple, Abraham, 1733–1819, American Revolutionary naval officer, b. Providence, R.I. In 1759–60, as captain of the privateer *Game Cock* in the French and Indian Wars, he captured numerous prizes. Whipple commanded the party of Rhode Islanders that captured and burned the British revenue cutter GASPEE in Narragansett Bay in 1772, one of the most provocative instances of resistance to the British in the pre-Revolutionary period. At the beginning of the American Revolution he was made commodore of Rhode Island's small fleet and then became fourth-ranking captain in the Continental navy. With the *Columbus* in 1776 he fought the first sea fight of the war. In 1778, Whipple, commanding the *Providence,* evaded the British blockade of Narragansett Bay and carried important government dispatches to France. His most daring exploit occurred in 1779 when, as commander of several vessels, he encountered the large, well-protected British Jamaica fleet. Whipple, concealing the guns of his flagship, the *Providence,* hoisted the British flag and fell in with the fleet for several days. Each night he cut out one of the merchant ships, manned it from his own crew, and sent it to an American port. Eight of the 11 captured ships reached port, making this one of the richest hauls of the war. In 1780 he was charged with the naval defense of Charleston, S.C.; the city fell and Whipple was captured and held prisoner for the rest of the war.

Whipple, Amiel Weeks, 1818–63, American soldier and topographical engineer, b. Greenwich, Mass. He became (1841) a topographical engineer in the U.S. army and engaged in surveying the U.S. borders with Canada (1844–49) and Mexico (1849–53). Whipple then made (1853–56) a survey of the region from Fort Smith, Ark., to Los Angeles to determine the route for a projected transcontinental railroad. His diary of this expedition became a valuable anthropological record of the little-known Indians of the Southwest. Later he took part in broadening the channels of the St. Clair Flats and St. Marys River, as a result of which the Great Lakes were opened to navigation by larger boats. He fought in the Civil War, reaching the rank of major general, but he was killed at the battle of Chancellorsville. See his *Whipple Report,* ed. by E. I. Edwards (1961); biography by Grant Foreman (1941).

Whipple, George Hoyt, 1878–, American pathologist, b. Ashland, N.H., M.D. Johns Hopkins, 1905. He taught at Johns Hopkins (1909–14) and at the Univ. of California (1914–21) and was professor of pathology and dean of the school of medicine and dentistry at the Univ. of Rochester (1921–54). His work included studies of metabolism, blood regeneration, and anemia. For his independent researches on the treatment of pernicious anemia by the use of liver he shared the 1934 Nobel Prize in Physiology and Medicine with G. R. Minot and W. P. Murphy.

Whipple, Henry Benjamin, 1822–1901, American Episcopal bishop, b. Adams, N.Y. He was ordained a priest in 1850, and in 1859 he was consecrated the first bishop of Minnesota. With James Lloyd Breck he founded (1860) in Faribault, Minn., the Bishop Seabury Mission, which developed into the Seabury Divinity School. Bishop Whipple's influence was great with the Indians, among whom he worked and by whom he was called "Straight Tongue"; he was successful in obtaining some government reforms in the administration of Indian affairs.

Whipple, William, 1730–85, political leader in the American Revolution, signer of the Declaration of Independence, b. Kittery, Maine. Whipple, who had been a sea captain, was a merchant of Portsmouth, N.H., before he served as a delegate to the Continental Congress from New Hampshire (1776–79) and as commander in the Saratoga campaign (1777).

whippoorwill: see GOATSUCKER.

whipray: see RAY.

whirligig beetle: see WATER BEETLE.

whirlpool, revolving current in an ocean, river, or lake. It may be caused by the configuration of the shore, irregularities in the bottom of the body of water, the meeting of opposing currents or tides, or the action of the wind upon the water. There are no true whirlpools really dangerous to shipping; the Maelstrom, near Norway, and CHARYBDIS, near Sicily, are subjects of legend and myth, and CORRIEVREKIN, near Scotland, was feared by the sailors of small boats. The Whirlpool Rapids below Niagara Falls are remarkable for their volume and violence, caused by an irregularity in the Niagara River channel. There is also a whirlpool below Victoria Falls, in South Africa.

whirlwind, revolving mass of air resulting from local atmospheric instability, such as that caused by intense heating of the ground by the sun on a hot summer day. Examples of whirlwinds are WATERSPOUTS, TORNADOES, small whirls of dust or leaves, and the sand whirls of the desert, called dust devils or dust whirls.

whiskey [Gaelic,=water of life], spirituous liquor distilled from a fermented mash of grains, usually rye, barley, oats, wheat, or corn. Inferior whiskeys are made from potatoes, beets, and other roots. The standard whiskeys of the world are Scotch (commonly spelled *whisky*), Irish, American, and Canadian. The Scotch Highland whiskey (made in pot stills) and that of the Lowlands (patent stills) differ in the percentage of barley used, quality of the water, quantity of peat employed in curing the malt, manner of distilling, and kind of casks in which they are matured. Practically all Scotch whiskeys are blends. Irish whiskey resembles Scotch, but no peat is used in the curing, and instead of the dry, somewhat smoky flavor of Scotch, it has a full, sweet taste. American whiskeys are divided into two main varieties, rye and bourbon, a corn whiskey that derives its name from Bourbon co., Ky. They have a higher flavor and a much deeper color than Scotch or Irish and require from two to three years longer to mature. Newly made whiskey is colorless, the rich brown of the matured liquor being acquired from the cask in which it is stored. Canadian whiskey has a characteristic lightness of body and must, according to law, be produced from cereal grain only. Whiskey was made in England in the 11th cent., chiefly in monasteries, but in the 16th cent. distilling was carried on commercially. No whiskey can be released from bond in Great Britain until it has matured in wood at least three years, and in practice most whiskey is stored seven or eight years before marketing. In the United States bonded whiskey must stay a minimum of four years in bond before it can be labeled as bonded rye or bourbon. The illicit manufacture of whiskey to avoid payment of excise taxes has been common. In the United States this is known as moonshining.

Whiskey Rebellion, 1794, uprising in the Pennsylvania counties W of the Alleghenies, caused by Alexander Hamilton's excise tax of 1791. The settlers, mainly Scotch-Irish, for whom whiskey was an important economic commodity, resented the tax as discriminatory and detrimental to their liberty and economic welfare. There were many public protests, and rioting broke out in 1794 against the central government's efforts to enforce the law. Troops called out by President Washington quelled the rioting, and resistance evaporated. Nevertheless Hamilton sought to make an example of the settlers and illustrate the newly created government's power to enforce its law; many were arrested. President Washington pardoned the two rebels who were convicted of treason. The government's power to enforce its laws had been proved. See L. D. Baldwin, *Whiskey Rebels: The Story of a Frontier Uprising* (rev. ed. 1967).

Whiskey Ring, in U.S. history, a group of distillers and public officials who defrauded the Federal government of liquor taxes. Soon after the Civil War these taxes were raised very high, in some cases to eight times the price of the liquor. Large distillers, chiefly in St. Louis, Milwaukee, and Chicago, bribed government officials in order to retain the tax proceeds. The Whiskey Ring was a public scandal, but it was considered impregnable because of its strong political connections. U.S. Secretary of the Treasury Benjamin H. BRISTOW resolved to break the conspiracy. To avoid warning the suspects, he assigned secret investigators from outside the Treasury Dept. to collect evidence. Striking suddenly in May, 1875, he arrested the persons and seized the distilleries involved. Over $3 million in taxes was recovered, and of 238 persons indicted 110 were convicted. Although President Grant's secretary, Orville E. Babcock, was acquitted through the personal intervention of the President, many persons believed that the Whiskey Ring was part of a plot to finance the Republican party by fraud. See John MacDonald, *Secrets of the Great Whiskey Ring* (1880, repr. 1969).

Whiskeytown-Shasta-Trinity National Recreation Area: see NATIONAL PARKS AND MONUMENTS (table).

whist, card game for four players, those on opposite sides of the table being partners. The full pack of 52 cards is dealt. The dealer's last card is turned up to indicate trump, and after he draws this card in hand, the player on the left of the dealer leads. Cards rank from ace down through two, and the highest card of the suit or the highest trump wins the trick. Partners collect their tricks in one pile. Six tricks make a book, and each trick over the book in one game counts one point. The partners who first score seven points win. Famous variations include duplicate whist, bid whist, solo whist, and Norwegian whist. Whist originated in England, where it was a development of earlier games (e.g., triumph) that were known in the 16th cent. In 1742, Edmond Hoyle published *A Short Treatise on the Game of Whist,* but it was Henry Jones (see CAVENDISH, pseud.) who first compiled (1862) a complete system of scientific whist play. The game spread to other European countries in the 19th cent., and tournaments were organized. Whist gave rise in the late 19th cent. to the game of BRIDGE, which quickly surpassed the parent game in popularity.

Whistler, James Abbott McNeill, 1834–1903, American painter, etcher, wit, and eccentric, b. Lowell, Mass. Whistler was dismissed from West Point for insufficient knowledge of chemistry and from the U.S. Coast and Geodetic Survey, where he had learned etching and map engraving, for erratic attendance. In 1855 he went to Paris, where he acquired a lifelong appreciation for the works of Velázquez and for Oriental art, particularly the Japanese print. From these sources he developed a delicate sense of color and design evident in most of his mature works. His early work was largely inspired by the realism of Courbet. Settling in London in 1859, he became known as an etcher, a wit, and a dandy. *The Little White Girl* (National Gall., Washington, D.C.) brought him his first major success in the Salon des Refusés (1863). To advertise and defend his credo of art for art's sake, Whistler resorted to elaborate exhibits, lectures, polemics, and more than one lawsuit. In connection with his *Falling Rocket: Nocturne in Black and Gold* (Detroit Inst. of Arts) he sued Ruskin in 1878 for writing that Whistler asked "two hundred guineas for flinging a pot of paint in the public's face." Whistler explained that the harmonious arrangement of light, form, and color was the most significant element of his paintings. To de-emphasize their subjective content, he called them by fanciful, abstract titles such as *Nocturne in Black and Gold,* and *Arrangement in Gray and Black* (the famed portrait of the artist's mother, 1872; Louvre). Whistler won the argument in court but payment of the court costs left him bankrupt. Toward the end of his life Whistler won wide recognition for his admirable draftsmanship, exquisite color, and extreme technical proficiency both as painter and etcher. As an etcher he achieved a high reputation. More than 400 superb plates remain. He also excelled in lithography, watercolor, and pastel. Fine examples of his painting are in the galleries of London, Paris, Pittsburgh, Washington, D.C., Chicago, and New York City. The most representative collection is that in the Freer Gallery of Art, Washington, D.C., which also contains an entire room that he decorated in a style that anticipated ART NOUVEAU, for the Leyland home in London—the so-called Peacock Room. *Nocturne in Green and Gold, Cremorne Gardens at Night,* portraits of Sir Henry Irving, Connie Gilchrist, Theodore Duret, and several others are all in the Metropolitan Museum. Other important works are his portrait of Thomas Carlyle (Glasgow) and *Old Battersea Bridge* (Tate Gall., London). He was the author of brilliant critical essays and aphorisms. The lecture published under the title *Ten o'clock* (1888) was of enormous influence in art theory. *The Gentle Art of Making Enemies* (1890) was a clever selection of snippets from the critics, accompanied by acerbic rejoinders from Whistler. See catalog by Denys Sutton (1966); biographies by E. R. Pennell and Joseph Pennell (1908, repr. 1973), Hesketh Pearson (1952), Horace Gregory (1959), Roy McMullen (1973), and Stanley Weintraub (1974); studies by Denys Sutton (1965), Tom Pocock (1970), and Tom Prideaux and others (1970).

whistler: see MARMOT.

Whiston, William, 1667–1752, English clergyman and mathematician. He won favor through his *New Theory of the Earth* (1696) and in 1701 was made deputy to Sir Isaac Newton, whom he succeeded (1703) as Lucasian professor of mathematics at Cambridge. Well-known as a preacher, Whiston aroused opposition by proclaiming his opinion that the faith of the early Christian centuries was Arian. In 1710 he was dismissed from the university for heresy. He propounded his Arian views in *Primitive Christianity Revived* (5 vol., 1711–12), lectured on scientific and religious subjects in London and elsewhere, and continued his scientific experiments. His translation (1737) of the writings of Josephus has been many times reprinted. See his memoirs (3 vol., 1749–50).

Whitaker, Charles Harris (hwĭt'əkər), 1872–1938, American architect and author, b. Rhode Island, studied art abroad. Editor (1913–27) of the journal of the American Institute of Architects, he became widely known through his fight against "pork barrel" appropriations for public buildings. He was a forceful advocate of government housing and community planning. He wrote *Rameses to Rockefeller* (1934), a history of architecture.

Whitby, town (1971 pop. 25,324), SE Ont., Canada, NE of Toronto, on Lake Ontario. It has a good harbor. The town's manufactures include tires and electronic equipment.

Whitby, Synod of, called by King Oswy of Northumbria in 663 at Whitby, England. Its purpose was to choose between the usages of the Celtic and Roman churches, primarily in the matter of reckoning Easter (see CALENDAR; CELTIC CHURCH). Among those involved in the synod were Cædmon, the poet, and St. HILDA, the abbess of Whitby, who favored the Celtic usages. Oswy decided for the Roman usages and in so doing determined that the English church would be associated with the Roman in the main stream of Western European Christianity. Only a few of the Celtic clergy returned to the monastery of Iona and to their old ways. The traditional date (from Bede) of 664 has recently been interpreted as Sept. or Oct., 663.

White, Andrew Dickson, 1832–1918, American educator and diplomat, b. Homer, N.Y., briefly attended Geneva (now Hobart) College, grad. Yale, 1853. He studied in France and Germany, served (1854–55) as attaché in St. Petersburg (now Leningrad), and toured Europe. While teaching history (1857–63) at the Univ. of Michigan, he developed the idea of a university detached from all sects and parties and free to pursue truth without deference to dogma. After his father died (1860) he returned (1863) to New York a comparatively rich man. He sat (1864–67) in the New York state senate and was chairman of the education committee, which dealt with the founding of a land-grant college. With the financial aid of a fellow senator, Ezra CORNELL, the land grant was made available for the institution that became Cornell Univ. White, as first president (1867–85), expanded the institution to teach not only agriculture and mechanical arts but also other fields of knowledge. He was one of the first educators to use the system of free elective studies. As Cornell was nonsectarian, the charge of "godlessness" was made against it. White, a practicing Episcopalian, maintained that freedom was beneficial to religion and wrote his *History of the Warfare of Science with Theology in Christendom* (1896) and *Seven Great Statesmen in the Warfare of Humanity with Unreason* (1910) to develop his concept of free inquiry. Later White was minister to Germany (1879–81) and to Russia (1892–94). He was also ambassador to Germany (1897–1902) and was chairman of the American delegation to the First Hague Conference (1899). He persuaded Andrew Carnegie to build the Palace of Justice to house the Hague Tribunal. See his autobiography (1905); study by W. P. Rogers (1942).

White, Bouck (bouk), 1874–1951, American clergyman and author, b. Middleburg, N.Y. He was ordained as a Congregational minister in 1904 but was dismissed from his post at Trinity House, Brooklyn, N.Y., in 1913 because of his *Call of the Carpenter* (1911), which portrayed Jesus as a social agitator. He then founded the Church of the Social Revolution in New York City and soon acquired a reputation as an eccentric radical. He was imprisoned several times for actions connected with his socialistic views. In the 1930s he retired to a mountain retreat in Voorheesville, N.Y.

White, Byron Raymond, 1917–, Associate Justice of the U.S. Supreme Court (1962–), b. Fort Collins, Colo. He was an All-America football player as well as a member of Phi Beta Kappa at the Univ. of Colorado. After graduation (1938), he played a season of professional football as "Whizzer" White, then went to Oxford as a Rhodes scholar (1939–40). He later played (1940–41) with the Detroit Lions while attending Yale law school. He received his law degree in 1946 after serving in the navy in World War II. White was (1946–47) law clerk for Chief Justice Fred Vinson before going to Denver, Colo., to practice corporation law. He supported John F. Kennedy for the presidency in 1960 and was appointed Deputy Attorney General by President Kennedy in 1961. In March, 1962, Kennedy appointed him to succeed Charles E. Whittaker on the Supreme Court. After President Nixon's conservative appointments to the court, White became known as a "swing" justice, sometimes siding with the liberals but more often joining the strict constructionists in their opinions.

White, Clarence Cameron, 1880–1960, American composer and violinist, b. Clarksville, Tenn., studied at the Oberlin Conservatory and in Europe. In addition to activities as violinist and teacher in Boston (1912–23) and New York City, he was director of music at West Virginia State College (1924–30) and at Hampton Institute (1932–35). His compositions for the violin include *Bandanna Sketches* and arrangements of Negro spirituals, and he also wrote an opera *Ouanga* (1932), based on Haitian history.

White, E. B. (Elwyn Brooks White), 1899–, American writer, b. Mt. Vernon, N.Y., grad. Cornell, 1921. He is noted as a witty, satiric observer of contemporary society. A member of the staff of the early *New Yorker* magazine, White wrote "The Talk of the Town"; some of these columns were collected in *The Wild Flag* (1946). In addition to much light, graceful, and humorous verse, he has written *Is Sex Necessary?* (with James Thurber, 1929), *Quo Vadimus?* (1939), *One Man's Meat* (1942), *Here is New York* (1949), and *The Points of My Compass* (1962). He edited *A Subtreasury of American Humor* (1941) with his wife, Katherine. A superb literary stylist himself, White revised *The Elements of Style* (1959) by William Strunk, Jr. He has written three delightful stories for children, *Stuart Little* (1945), *Charlotte's Web* (1952), and *The Trumpet of the Swan* (1970). See study by E. C. Sampson (1974).

White, Edward Douglass, 1845–1921, Associate Justice of the U.S. Supreme Court (1894–1910), ninth Chief Justice of the United States (1910–21), b. Lafourche parish, La. He attended the Jesuit College in New Orleans and Georgetown College (now Georgetown Univ.), Washington, D.C. After service in the Confederate army he practiced law. White became (1879) judge of the Louisiana supreme court and served (1891–94) in the U.S. Senate until he was appointed (1894) Associate Justice of the U.S. Supreme Court by President Cleveland. Made Chief Justice by President Taft, White—the first Southerner since Roger Taney to head the Supreme Court—was generally a conservative on the bench. He wrote the "rule of reason" decisions, which differentiated between legal and illegal business combinations, in the antitrust cases against the American Tobacco Company and the Standard Oil Company in 1911. In 1916 he wrote the decision upholding the constitutionality of the Adamson Act, which established an eight-hour day for railroad workers. See biographies by M. C. C. Klinkhamer (1943) and Gerard Hagemann (1962).

White, Elijah, 1806–79, American missionary in the Oregon country. A physician, he left Boston in 1836 to join the Methodist mission established by Jason Lee. After friction with his associates, he left in 1840. His fame rests on the fact that, returning overland to Oregon with an appointment as an Indian agent in 1842, he led the first large party of settlers (more than 100) to Oregon.

White, Ellen Gould (Harmon), 1827–1915, leader of the Seventh-Day Adventists, b. Gorham, Maine. Converted at the age of 15 to the beliefs of the ADVENTISTS, she began to receive visions accepted as prophetic by many members of that sect. In 1846 she married James White, a minister of Adventist convictions. After her husband's death in 1881, she traveled widely as a missionary. Her numerous writings include *The Ministry of Healing* (1942) and *The Desire of Ages* (1944). See biographies by T. H. Jemison (1955) and René Noorbergen (1972); study by F. D. Nichol (1952).

White, Sir George Stuart, 1835–1912, British field marshal. He first achieved distinction in the Afghan War of 1878–80. In Burma (1885–87), where he was knighted in 1886, in Baluchistan (1889–93), and later as commander in chief in India (1893–98), he was an instrument of Great Britain's "forward" policy of combating any Russian advance toward India by aggressive campaigns, military and diplomatic, in the borderlands. His greatest fame came in the South African War when he defended Ladysmith against a 118-day siege by the Boers (1899-1900). He became governor of Gibraltar (1900-1904) and was made field marshal in 1903.

White, Gilbert, 1720-93, English naturalist. He served as curate at Selborne and nearby parishes from 1751. He recorded his detailed observations of nature in letters to other naturalists, and on these he based *The Natural History and Antiquities of Selborne* (1789), a classic in scientific writing noted for its highly literary style.

White, Henry, 1850-1927, American diplomat, b. Baltimore. He studied abroad and traveled widely. White—often called the first career diplomat in the United States—entered the foreign service as secretary (1883-84) of the U.S. legation in Vienna. He served (1884-93) with the U.S. embassy at London, and in 1896 President McKinley appointed him secretary of the embassy. He later was ambassador at Rome (1905-7) and at Paris (1907-9); as head of the U.S. delegation to the Algeciras Conference (1906), White helped in the settlement of the Moroccan Crisis between Germany and France. He was sent (1910) as a special emissary to Chile and in 1918 was appointed a commissioner to the Paris Peace Conference by President Wilson. See biography by Allan Nevins (1930).

White, Hugh Lawson, 1773-1840, American political leader, b. Iredell co., N.C. He moved (1787) to what is now E Tennessee and served in the wars against the Creek and Cherokee Indians. He was (1793) secretary to Gov. William BLOUNT, studied law in Lancaster, Ohio, and began (1796) practice in Knoxville, Tenn. He held various judicial offices in Tennessee and was a state senator (1807-9, 1817-25) before becoming a U.S. Senator in 1825. A supporter of Andrew Jackson and his policies, he split with the President when Jackson backed Martin Van Buren for President. White, in protest, ran (1836) for the presidency as a Whig party candidate and secured the electoral votes of Tennessee and Georgia. He resigned (1840) from the U.S. Senate after he fought, in opposition to the instructions of the Tennessee legislature, Van Buren's plan for the Independent Treasury System.

White, John, 1575-1648, English colonizer. An Anglican priest of moderate Puritan belief, White wished to establish a colony for Puritans. He helped form (1628) the New England Company, which later became (1629) the Massachusetts Bay Company, but he himself never went to America.

White, John, fl. 1585-93, artist, cartographer, and Virginia pioneer, b. probably in England. In 1585 he was commissioned to go with the expedition to ROANOKE ISLAND to depict life in the New World. His paintings provide some of the earliest and most valuable source materials on the natural history of the North American continent. It is believed, though by no means proved, that he is the same John White whom Sir Walter Raleigh appointed governor of the second Roanoke colony in 1587.

White, Leslie Alvin, 1900-, American anthropologist, b. Salida, Colo., grad. Columbia, 1923, Ph.D. Univ. of Chicago 1927. He taught at the Univ. of Buffalo and was curator of anthropology at the Buffalo Museum of Science from 1927 to 1930. In 1930 he joined the faculty of the Univ. of Michigan, where he became professor of anthropology in 1943. While retaining his post at Michigan, White served as visiting professor at many other universities. His earlier years were devoted largely to research among the Pueblo Indians, which resulted in a number of monographs, such as *The Acoma Indians* (1932), *The Pueblo of San Felipe (1932),* and *The Pueblo of Santa Ana, New Mexico* (1942). In later years he turned increasingly to ethnological theory. His views are set forth in two major works, *The Science of Culture* (1949) and *The Evolution of Culture: The Development of Civilization to the Fall of Rome* (1959).

White, Patrick, 1912-, Australian novelist, b. London. Educated at Cheltenham College and Cambridge, he returned to Australia after World War II, earning his living by farming and writing. His novels are often set in the Australian outback, and they usually portray the suffering of extraordinary people. He writes in a hypnotic style distinguished by description rather than plot. His novels include *The Happy Valley* (1939), *The Aunt's Story* (1948), *The Tree of Man* (1955), *Riders in the Chariot* (1961), *Vivisector* (1970), and *The Eye of the Storm* (1974). *The Cockatoos* (1975) is a collection of short stories. In 1973, White was awarded the Nobel Prize in Literature.

White, Peregrine, 1620-1704, first child born to English parents in New England. He was born on the *Mayflower* as she lay at anchor in Cape Cod Bay on Nov. 20. He became a citizen of Marshfield, Mass., and held minor offices.

White, Richard Grant, 1821-85, American journalist, writer, and Shakespearean scholar, b. New York City. He had a varied career and was at different times music critic and coeditor (1851-59) of the New York *Courier and Enquirer,* a founder and editor (1860-61) of the *World,* and chief clerk in the New York Customs House (1861-78). In 1853 he published a series of articles in *Putnam's Magazine* that exposed as fraudulent the marginalia that John Payne COLLIER had discovered on certain Shakespearean manuscripts. White's own annotated 12-volume edition of Shakespeare appeared from 1857 to 1866 and was republished, in three volumes, as *The Riverside Shakespeare* in 1883. His other works include a *Handbook of Christian Art* (1853) and two dogmatic manuals of English usage—*Words and Their Uses* (1872) and *Every-Day English* (1880).

White, Stanford, 1853-1906, American architect, b. New York City; son of Richard Grant White. In 1872 he entered the office of Gambrill and Richardson in Boston, at the time when H. H. Richardson was at the peak of his fame. There White worked upon the design for Trinity Church, Boston. After studying in Europe, he entered (1879) into partnership with C. F. McKim and W. R. Mead, a firm that was to affect the course of American architecture over a long period. White had a passionate love of beauty; his special talents were for the decorative elements of a building and for its interior design and furnishing. He also possessed a wide knowledge of antiques. Among the buildings executed by the firm, those that are commonly ascribed as his individual accomplishments include the first Madison Square Garden, Madison Square Presbyterian Church, the New York Herald Building, Washington Arch, and the Century Club, all in New York City; only the last two still stand. These buildings illustrated his characteristic concentration upon rich and graceful effects and especially upon beautifully sculptured Renaissance ornament. White was shot and killed in Madison Square Roof Garden by Harry K. Thaw because of his love affair with Thaw's wife, Evelyn Nesbit Thaw. After his death the firm continued to design buildings in his style that later were erroneously attributed to White himself, e.g., the Harvard Club, New York City. See biography by C. C. Baldwin (1931, repr. 1971); Gerald Langford, *The Murder of Stanford White* (1962).

White, Stewart Edward, 1873-1946, American author, b. Grand Rapids, Mich., grad. Univ. of Michigan, 1895. The stories collected in *The Claim Jumpers* (1901) and *The Blazed Trail* (1902) reflect his own adventures in the Black Hills gold rush and in a Michigan lumber camp, respectively. His ambitious trilogy, *The Story of California* (1927), consists of three historical novels, *Gold* (1913), *The Gray Dawn* (1915), and *The Rose Dawn* (1920). In addition to books for children he recounted his own life in *Dog Days* (1930) and *Speaking for Myself* (1943).

White, Terence Hanbury, 1906-64, British author, b. Bombay, India. His best-known work, the tetralogy *The Once and Future King* (1939-58), is a dramatic and delightfully idiosyncratic retelling of the story of King Arthur and his knights. An authority on medieval life and legend, T. H. White was also the author of *The Goshawk* (1951), a book on falconry, and *A Book of Beasts* (1954), an annotated translation of a 12th-century Latin bestiary. See biography by Sylvia Townsend Warner (1968); study by John Crane (1974).

White, Walter Francis, 1893-1955, American Negro leader, b. Atlanta, Ga., grad. Atlanta Univ., 1916. From 1931 until his death he was secretary of the National Association for the Advancement of Colored People and tirelessly fought against racial discrimination and violence in the United States. He served on several government commissions. White's defense of Negro rights is vividly recorded in his autobiography, *A Man Called White* (1948). His works include *Fire in the Flint* (1924), *Flight* (1926), *Rope and Faggot* (1929), *Rising Wind* (1945), and *How Far the Promised Land* (published posthumously in 1955). See biography by Poppy Cannon (Mrs. Walter White), *Gentle Knight* (1956).

White, William, 1748-1836, American Episcopal bishop, b. Philadelphia, grad. College of Philadelphia (now the Univ. of Pennsylvania), 1765. He was ordained in England in 1772, returning to become assistant rector, then rector, of Christ Church, Philadelphia. Instrumental in organizing the Protestant Episcopal Church in the United States, White drafted its first constitution and also aided in the American revision of the Book of Common Prayer. He was elected bishop of Pennsylvania in 1786. His works include *Memoirs of the Protestant Episcopal Church in the United States of America* (2d ed. 1836). See his *Life and Letters* (ed. by W. H. Stowe, 1937).

White, William Allen, 1868-1944, American author, b. Emporia, Kansas, studied (1886-90) at Kansas State Univ. He bought the Emporia *Gazette* in 1895, editing it the rest of his life and making it and himself famous throughout the nation as representatives of grass roots political opinion. In 1896 his famous editorial, "What's the Matter with Kansas?" attacked the Populists and aided the Republicans in electing McKinley. Another of his well-known essays is "Mary White," a eulogy for his daughter, who died at the age of 17. A spokesman for small town life and a liberal Republican, White feared the results of excessive industrialization. His fiction reflects his social and political views and includes the short stories *In Our Town* (1906) and the novel *A Certain Rich Man* (1909). Among his other works are a biography of Woodrow Wilson (1924), two of Calvin Coolidge (1925, 1938), and two collections of his newspaper writings, *The Editor and His People* (1924) and *Forty Years on Main Street* (1937). See his autobiography (1946; Pulitzer Prize) and selected letters (ed. by Walter Johnson, 1947).

White, William Hale, pseud. **Mark Rutherford,** 1831-1913, English novelist. He studied to become a clergyman, but instead became (1854) a clerk in the admiralty, rising in 1879 to assistant director of naval contracts. The son of a dissenter, White gives in his novels a poignant account of his spiritual disillusionment and growing loneliness. His best-known works are *The Autobiography of Mark Rutherford* (1881), *Mark Rutherford's Deliverance* (1885), and *The Revolution in Tanner's Lane* (1887). See biographies by C. M. Maclean (1955) and W. H. Stone (1955); study by Irvin Stock (1956).

white alder, deciduous shrub or small tree (*Clethra alnifolia*) native to the Appalachians, named for the resemblance of its leaves to those of the unrelated true alders. It is cultivated as an ornamental for the fragrant white or pinkish blossoms. Similar in appearance and also cultivated are the sweet pepper bush, or summer sweet (*C. acuminata*), of a somewhat wider range, and a Japanese species (*C. barbinersis*), whose young leaves are eaten with rice by peasants in its native localities. Most other *Clethra* species are of tropical America. They are good honey plants. White alder is classified in the division MAGNOLIOPHYTA, class Magnoliopsida, order Ericales, family Clethraceae.

white ant: see TERMITE.

White Bear Lake, city (1970 pop. 23,313), Ramsey and Washington counties, SE Minn., on White Bear Lake; inc. 1922. It is a residential and resort suburb of Minneapolis-St. Paul. A junior college is there, and Bald Eagle Lake is nearby.

white blood cell: see BLOOD.

Whiteboys, members of small illegal, largely Roman Catholic, peasant bands in 18th-century Ireland. First organized (c.1759) in protest against the large-scale enclosure of common lands and other causes of agrarian distress, they were so called because on their nocturnal raids they often wore white disguises. They were heavily suppressed (1765), but outbreaks of similar activity recurred during periods of extreme agricultural hardship. Hostility (1775-85) was largely aimed at tithe collectors. There were similar, although shortlived, Protestant groups in Ulster, the Oakboys (1763) and the Steelboys (1770). Terrorist activity hastened the establishment of the Irish Parliament (1782), in which Henry GRATTAN attempted to reform the system of tithes. Although the Whiteboys were suppressed, they set a pattern for agrarian unrest that continued under various names and later became politicized.

White Cloud: see WAUBESHIEK.

white-collar workers, broad occupational grouping of workers engaged in nonmanual labor; frequently contrasted with blue-collar (manual) employees. American in origin, the term has close analogues in other industrial countries. Managers, salaried professionals, office workers, sales personnel, and proprietors are generally included in the category. Professionals and managers, however, are occasionally excluded. Since World War II the number of white-collar workers in the U.S. labor force has increased dramatically. Today they account for almost 50% of the labor force, outnumbering blue-collar workers by approximately 11 million persons. There is considerable difference of opinion concerning the political and social attitudes of white-collar workers. Some authorities, such as C. Wright Mills, author of *White Collar* (1951), contend that members of the group identify with the institutions for which they work and hence tend toward political conservatism. Others, pointing to white-collar unions such as the American Federation of Teachers and the Distributive Workers of America, claim that white-collar workers tend to identify with manual laborers and others who do not own the means of production.

white dwarf, in astronomy, an unusual type of star that is abnormally faint for its white-hot temperature (see MASS-LUMINOSITY RELATION). Typically, a white dwarf star has the mass of the sun and the radius of the earth. The physical conditions inside the star are quite unusual; the central density is about 1 million times that of water. The existence of white dwarfs is intimately connected with STELLAR EVOLUTION. The first white dwarf discovered (1844) was the faint companion in the binary star Sirius. Although invisible to the telescopes of the day, the white dwarf's mass was large enough to produce a noticeable wavy motion of its very bright partner as the two stars revolved around each other.

white-eye, common name for warblerlike, arboreal birds, including 85 species in the family Zosteropidae, and for certain species of ducks. The members of Zosteropidae, with the exception of a few species, are marked by a ring of tiny, white feathers surrounding the eye and are also known as silver-eyes and spectacle birds. They are predominantly olive to yellow-green above, with whitish or grayish abdomens. With the exception of a few species of the genus *Zosterops,* such as *Z. erythropleura* of NE China, white-eyes are tropical, dwelling in wooded habitats from sea level to timberline and ranging from sub-Saharan Africa to Asia and Australia. They are typically small, except for several giant species such as two in the South Pacific genus *Woodfordia,* which also lack the white eye ring. Aided by their short, pointed, slightly decurved bills and brushlike tongues, white-eyes feed on a varied diet consisting of insects, fruits, berries, and nectar. They are much disliked by farmers because of their habit of piercing fruit with their bills. White-eyes are highly gregarious birds, given to constantly calling in a soft, warbling song. They build their deep, cup-shaped nests in tree forks, in which the female deposits two or three white or pale blue eggs. Incubation periods may be as short as 10½ days, among the shortest known of any bird. The common name *white-eye* is also given to certain of the unrelated pochards (ducklike birds) of the family Anatidae and especially to the white-eyed pochard (*Nyroca ferina*). These are probably called white-eyes for their tiny irises set in a large white sclera. Although these white-eyes are worldwide in distribution, they are found primarily in the Northern Hemisphere. *N. ferina* is found throughout Great Britain and Europe. In its breeding plumage, it has a chestnut-red head with a light gray body bordered in black on the breast and tail. With their webbed feet set far back on their bodies, pochards are poor walkers, but they are among the best of the diving birds. They feed on a variety of aquatic animals, using their muscular tongues as pistons to pump water through their bills. The water is strained through bony plates lining the inner edges of the bill. Their young are especially well developed at birth and rapidly take to water. White-eyes are classified in the phylum CHORDATA, subphylum Vertebrata, class Aves, order Passeriformes, family Zosteropidae; or order Anseriformes, family Anatidae.

Whitefield, George, 1714–70, English evangelistic preacher, leader of the CALVINISTIC METHODIST CHURCH. At Oxford, which he entered in 1732, he joined the Methodist group led by John WESLEY and Charles WESLEY. Ordained (1736) a deacon in the Church of England, Whitefield soon demonstrated his power as a preacher. The first of his seven trips to America was made in 1738, when he spent a short time in Georgia in the mission post vacated by John Wesley. He returned to England to seek funds for an orphanage in Georgia and to take orders as an Anglican priest, but his connection with the Wesleys and the evangelical character of his preaching led to his exclusion from most of the pulpits of the Church of England. He then began a series of open-air meetings in Bristol and elsewhere, to which huge audiences were attracted. He persuaded John Wesley to carry on the work while he again visited (1739–41) America; there he was an influential figure in the GREAT AWAKENING, preaching to congregations in the large settlements from Georgia to New England. About 1741 he adopted Calvinistic views, especially in regard to predestination. Breaking away from the Wesleys, he became the leader of the Calvinistic Methodists, whose greatest numbers were in Wales. However, Whitefield's personal friendship with John Wesley continued. In London his work was centered in the Moorfields Tabernacle, near Wesley's church. Returning to England after another evangelistic tour (1744–48) in America, he was appointed a chaplain in the Connexion, the Methodist association sponsored by the countess of HUNTINGDON. Whitefield's evangelistic tours in Great Britain and America continued to draw throngs; in 1756 the noted Tottenham Court Chapel, London, was opened for him. His last sermon was delivered in the open air at Exeter, Mass., the day before he died in Newburyport, where he is buried. See his works (6 vol., 1771–72); biographies by Luke Tyerman (2 vol., 1876) and S. C. Henry (1957); studies by A. A. Dallimore (1970) and J. C. Pollock (1972).

whitefish: see SALMON.

Whitefish Bay, village (1970 pop. 17,402), Milwaukee co., SE Wis., a residential suburb of Milwaukee on Lake Michigan; inc. 1892.

Whitehall. 1 City (1970 pop. 25,263), Franklin co., central Ohio, a suburb of Columbus; inc. 1948. Manufactures include water coolers and packaged meats. A large Federal defense construction supply center is there. **2** Borough (1970 pop. 16,551), Allegheny co., SW Pa., a residential suburb of Pittsburgh; inc. 1948.

Whitehall, street in Westminster borough, London, England. Because of the many British government offices on the street, *Whitehall* has become a synonym for the government. The name derives from Whitehall Palace, first built for Hubert de Burgh in the 13th cent. and rebuilt for Cardinal Wolsey in the 16th cent. A new palace was built on the site by Inigo Jones in 1622. The Banqueting House survives today and is used for official receptions. There is a World War I memorial cenotaph on the street.

Whitehaven (hwĭt'hāvən), municipal borough (1971 pop. 26,720), Cumberland, NW England, at the mouth of Solway Firth. Whitehaven is a seaport and industrial town. There are coal mines (some of which extend under the sea), iron foundries, and other industries. Whitehaven was attacked by John Paul Jones in 1778 and by a German submarine in 1918. In 1974, Whitehead became part of the new nonmetropolitan county of Cumbria.

Whitehead, Alfred North, 1861–1947, English mathematician and philosopher, grad. Trinity College, Cambridge, 1884. There he was a lecturer in mathematics until 1911. At the Univ. of London he was a lecturer in applied mathematics and mechanics (1911–14) and professor of mathematics (1914–24). From 1924 he was professor of philosophy at Harvard. Whitehead's distinction rests upon his contributions to mathematics and logic, the philosophy of science, and the study of metaphysics. In the field of mathematics Whitehead extended the range of algebraic procedures and, in collaboration with Bertrand Russell, wrote *Principia Mathematica* (3 vol., 1910–13), a landmark in the study of logic. His inquiries into the structure of science provided the background for his metaphysical writings. He criticized traditional categories of philosophy for their failure to convey the essential interrelation of matter, space, and time. For this reason he invented a special vocabulary to communicate his concept of reality, which he called the philosophy of organism. He formulated a system of ultimate and universal ideas and justified them by their fruitful interpretation of observable experience. His philosophic construction as applied to religion offered a concept of God as interdependent with the world and developing with it; he rejected the notion of a perfect and omnipotent God. In 1945 he received the Order of Merit. His works include *The Organisation of Thought* (1916), *Principles of Natural Knowledge* (1919), *The Concept of Nature* (1920), *The Principle of Relativity* (1922), *Science and the Modern World* (1925), *Religion in the Making* (1926), *Symbolism* (1927), *The Aims of Education and Other Essays* (1929), *Process and Reality* (1929), *Adventures of Ideas* (1933), and *Essays in Science and Philosophy* (1947). See J. W. Blyth, *Whitehead's Theory of Knowledge* (1941, repr. 1973); P. A. Schilpp, ed., *The Philosophy of Alfred North Whitehead* (2d ed. 1951, repr. 1971); A. H. Johnson, *Whitehead's Philosophy of Civilization* (1958, repr. 1962); V. A. Lowe, *Understanding Whitehead* (1962); D. M. Emmett, *Whitehead's Philosophy of Organism* (1966); Charles Hartshorne, *Whitehead's Philosophy: Selected Essays, 1935–1970* (1972); D. L. Hall, *The Civilization of Experience* (1973).

Whitehead, William, 1715–85, English poet and playwright. He wrote several plays based on ancient Greek models, including *Creusa, Queen of Athens* (1754). Whitehead was appointed poet laureate in 1757. Although his light verse had been admired, the more grandiose works that he was required to write as laureate were ridiculed.

White Hill, battle of the: see WHITE MOUNTAIN.

Whitehorse, city (1971 pop. 11,217), S Yukon, Canada, on the Yukon River. Since 1952 it has been the territorial capital. Whitehorse is on the Alaska Highway and is the terminal of the White Pass and Yukon Railway from Skagway, Alaska. The city is the center of a copper-mining, hunting, and fur-trapping region that attracts tourists. It is headquarters of the Royal Canadian Mounted Police for S Yukon and has an airport, a radio station, and a weather station. It was an important supply and stage center during the Klondike gold rush (1897–98). During World War II it was the center of the Canol oil project (closed in 1945).

White Horse, Vale of the, Oxfordshire, S central England. The vale is the valley of the Ock River. The region is rich in associations with Alfred the Great, who was born in Wantage, the central town of the vale. According to tradition, his victory at Ashdown in 871 was commemorated by the White Horse on White Horse Hill, although it is probably of a much earlier date. The figure of the horse, over 350 ft (107 m) long, is at Uffington, near Wantage, and its outline is visible for miles. It was formed by cutting away the turf to expose the white chalk of the hillside beneath. An Iron Age fort, Uffington Castle, is on the hill top. There are other "white horses" of various ages in Wiltshire, Berkshire, Yorkshire, and elsewhere, but that at Uffington is the most famous.

White House, official name of the executive mansion of the President of the United States. It is on the south side of Pennsylvania Ave., Washington, D.C., facing Lafayette Square. The building, constructed of Virginia freestone, is of simple and stately design. The porte-cochere on the north front, which forms the main entrance, is a portico of high Ionic columns reaching from the ground to the roof pediment; it is balanced by a semicircular colonnaded balcony on the south with a second-floor porch, completed in 1948. The main building (four stories high) is about 170 ft (52 m) long by 85 ft (26 m) wide. The east and west terraces, the executive office (1902), the east wing (1942), and a penthouse and a bomb shelter (1952) have been added. The colonnade at the east end is the public entrance. The executive office is approached by an esplanade. Large receptions are usually held in the East Room, which is 40 ft (12 m) by 82 ft (25 m). The elliptical Blue Room is the scene of many social, diplomatic, and official receptions. The Red Room and the Green Room are used for private and quasi-official gatherings. The White House, designated "the Palace" in the original plans, was designed by James Hoban on a site chosen by George Washington. It is the oldest public building in Washington, its cornerstone having been laid in 1792. John Adams was the first President to live there (1800). The building was restored after being burned (1814) by British troops, and the smoke-stained gray stone walls were painted white. Despite popular myth the cognomen "White House" was applied to the building some time before it was painted. The name became official when President Theodore Roosevelt had it engraved upon his stationery. Part of the house was rebuilt (1949–52) on a steel-supporting frame. The grounds, which cover about 18 acres (7 hectares) are attractive with broad lawns, fountains, trees, and gardens. They were planned by Andrew Jackson DOWNING. See Perry Wolff, *A Tour of the White House with Mrs. John F. Kennedy* (1962); Charles Hurd, *The White House Story* (1966).

White Huns or **Hephthalites** (hĕf'thəlīts"), people of obscure origins, possibly of Tibetan or Turkish stock. They were called Ephthalites by the Greeks, and Hunas by the Indians. There is no definite evidence that they are related to the HUNS. The White Huns were an agricultural people with a developed set of laws. They were first mentioned by the Chinese, who described them (A.D. 125) as living in Dzungaria. They displaced the Scythians and conquered Transoxiana and Khurasan before 425. They crossed (425) the Syr Darya (Jaxartes) River and invaded Persia. Held off at first by Bahram Gur, they later (483-85) succeeded in making Persia tributary. After a series of wars (503-13) they were driven out of Persia, permanently lost the offensive, and were finally (557) defeated by Khosru I. The White Huns also invaded India and succeeded in extending their domain to include the Ganges valley. They temporarily overthrew the Gupta empire but were eventually driven out of India in 528 by a Hindu coalition. Although in Persia they had little effect, in India the White Huns influenced society by altering the caste system and disrupting the hierarchy of the ruling families. Some of the White Huns remained in India as a distinct group.

white iron pyrites: see MARCASITE.

Whitelaw, William (William Stephen Ian Whitelaw), 1918-, British politician. A Scottish landowner and cattle farmer, he was elected to Parliament as a Conservative in 1955 and served as parliamentary private secretary in various ministries (1956-64). As lord president of the council and leader of the House of Commons (1970-72) he was one of Prime Minister Edward Heath's closest advisers. In March, 1972, with the institution of direct British rule in Northern Ireland, Whitelaw became secretary of state for the province. He attempted to bring the Roman Catholic and Protestant political groups into negotiations with each other, lifted the ban on protest marches, and relaxed the policy of internment of suspected members of the Irish Republican Army. He was instrumental in bringing about creation of a new legislative assembly (June, 1973), elected on a basis of proportional representation, and of a new Northern Ireland executive in which Protestants and Catholics shared power (Dec., 1973)—both, however, shortlived. As secretary of state for employment from Dec., 1973, he supervised the government's unsuccessful attempt to reach a wage settlement with the miners' union, whose ban on overtime, followed by a strike, threw Britain into a severe economic crisis. After the Conservative defeat in the general election of Feb., 1974, he became chairman of the Conservative party.

white lead, heavy, white substance, poisonous, insoluble in water, extensively used as a white PIGMENT and base in paints. It is one of the oldest paint pigments used by man. Chemically, it is basic LEAD carbonate, a mixture of lead carbonate and lead hydroxide. It is prepared in various ways. When used in paints, it is first ground into a fine powder and mixed with linseed oil. Its covering power is greater than that of most other white pigments, but its use has certain disadvantages. It reacts with hydrogen sulfide and some other sulfur compounds in the atmosphere, the lead combining with the sulfur to form lead sulfide, a dark substance. In paints made with white lead a chalky film is formed after some time. White lead is extremely poisonous, and painters who apply it are often afflicted with painter's colic (see LEAD POISONING) because of the absorption of too great a quantity into the body. White lead is used also in making putty and in the manufacture of certain pottery. Sublimed white lead is the basic sulfate of lead mixed with lead oxide and zinc oxide; it is also used as a white pigment. White lead is often adulterated with barite.

Whitelocke, Bulstrode (bŏŏl'strōd hwĭt'lŏk), 1605-75, English statesman. A lawyer and member of the Long Parliament, he was head of the committee that managed the prosecution of Thomas Wentworth, earl of Strafford. Always an advocate of moderation, he took part in attempts to make terms with King Charles I in 1643, 1644, and 1645, and refused to participate in the trial of the king. He was commissioner of the great seal (1648, 1649, 1654-55, 1659) and ambassador to Sweden (1653-54). He was elected (1659) president of the council of state after the collapse of the Protectorate. At the Restoration (1660) he was pardoned, and thereafter he lived quietly. The most important of his voluminous writings are his *Memorials of the English Affairs* (1682), a source work for the period 1625-60, and *Journal of the Swedish Embassy* (1772).

Whitelocke, John, 1757-1833, British general. He served against the French in the West Indies and in 1807 was given command of the expedition to recover Buenos Aires. The British attack on Buenos Aires failed (July 5, 1807); two days later Whitelocke surrendered to Jacques de LINIERS. Returning to England, Whitelocke was cashiered from the army by court-martial (1808).

White Lotus Rebellion, Chinese anti-Manchu uprising that occurred during the Ch'ing dynasty. It broke out (1796) among impoverished settlers in the mountainous region that separates Szechwan prov. from Hupei and Shensi provs. It apparently began as a tax protest led by the White Lotus Society, a secret religious society that forecast the advent of the Buddha, advocated restoration of the native Chinese Ming dynasty, and promised personal salvation to its followers. At first the corrupt Ch'ing administration of HO-SHEN sent inadequate and inefficient imperial forces to suppress the ill-organized rebels. On assuming effective power in 1799, however, Emperor Chia Ch'ing (reigned 1796-1820) overthrew the Ho-shen clique and gave support to the efforts of the more vigorous Manchu commanders as a way of restoring discipline and morale. A systematic program of pacification followed in which the populace was resettled in hundreds of stockaded villages and organized into militia. In its last stage, the Ch'ing suppression policy combined pursuit and extermination of rebel guerrilla bands with a program of amnesty for deserters. Although the Manchu finally crushed (1804) the rebellion, the myth of the military invincibility of the Manchu was shattered, perhaps contributing to the greater frequency of rebellions in the 19th cent.

Whiteman, Paul, 1891-1967, American conductor, b. Denver. Whiteman played viola in the Denver Symphony Orchestra and in 1915 joined the San Francisco Symphony. During World War I he was an army band leader. In 1924 he inaugurated the period of "symphonic jazz" when he introduced Gershwin's *Rhapsody in Blue* in New York City. Whiteman encouraged the composition of concert jazz works by establishing the annual Whiteman Award. He was influential in the formation of large jazz ensembles. His books include *Jazz* (1926) and *Records for the Millions* (1948).

white metal: see BABBITT METAL; ANTIFRICTION METAL.

White Mountain or **White Hill,** Czech *Bílá Hora,* hill near Prague, Czechoslovakia. There, in Nov., 1620, the Czech Protestants under CHRISTIAN OF ANHALT were routed by the combined armies of the empire and of the Catholic League, under Tilly. The battle ended the independence of Bohemia for 300 years and was the first engagement of the THIRTY YEARS WAR.

White Mountains, part of the Appalachian system, N N.H. and SW Maine, rising to 6,288 ft (1,917 m) at Mt. Washington in the Presidential Range and to 5,249 ft (1,600 m) at Mt. Lafayette in the Franconia Mountains. Crawford Notch separates these two main groups. Formed in the latter part of the Paleozoic era, the White Mts. are remnants of a much higher mountain mass. They are composed chiefly of granite and have been extensively glaciated. Much of the mountain area, c.1,200 sq mi (3,110 sq km), is included in White Mountain National Forest. Nationally noted for their varied and beautiful scenery, the White Mts. have long been one of the most popular year-round resort areas in the country.

White Nile, river, one of the chief tributaries of the Nile, E Africa. The name is sometimes used for the 600 mi (970 km) long section of the river known as the Bahr el Abiad which extends upstream from Khartoum to the junction of the Bahr el Jebel and the Bahr el Ghazal at Lake No, c.100 mi (160 km) above Malakal. In a wider sense it is applied to the entire c.2,300 mi (3,700 km) long stem of the Nile draining from the headwaters of Victoria Nyanza (Lake Victoria). In this wider sense, its remotest headstream is the Luvironza River in Burundi, which flows into the Ruvuvu River and which, in turn, is a tributary of the Kagera River, one of the principal headstreams feeding into Victoria Nyanza. Known as the Victoria Nile for approximately the next 260 mi (430 km), it flows N and W through Uganda into Lake Albert. It leaves Lake Albert as the Albert Nile and flows north c.100 mi (160 km) to Nimule, where it enters the Sudan and becomes the Bahr el Jebel. From Nimule to Rejaf is a zone of rapids. At Juba it leaves the highlands of central Africa and enters the broad Sudan plain; downstream at Bor, it flows through the Sudd, a vast swampy area named after the floating vegetation (sudd) that sometimes hinders navigation. At Lake No it receives the Bahr el Ghazal and continues E to Khartoum, where it joins with the Blue Nile to form the Nile.

White Oak, uninc. community (1970 pop. 19,769), Montgomery and Prince Georges counties, central Md., in the suburbs of Washington, D.C. It is the site of a naval ordnance laboratory.

White Pass, 2,888 ft (880 m) high, in the Coast Mts., on the Alaska-British Columbia border, NE of Skagway. A hazardous trail through the pass was made (1897) by prospectors going to the Klondike, as an alternate route to the Chilkoot Pass. Between 1898 and 1900 the White Pass and Yukon Railway was built from Skagway to White Horse, Yukon, to provide transportation from the Pacific tidewater to the Yukon valley.

White Plains, city (1970 pop. 50,346), seat of Westchester co., SE N.Y., N of New York City; settled by Puritans from Connecticut in 1683; inc. as a village 1866, as a city 1916. Mainly residential, the city has some light industries and serves as the headquarters for several corporations and laboratories. The state convention that ratified the Declaration of Independence met (1776) in White Plains. The battle of White Plains (1776), a principal engagement of the Revolutionary War, followed Gen. George Washington's retreat from New York City. Washington briefly made his headquarters (1738) in White Plains at the Elijah Miller House, which still stands. Other buildings from the Revolutionary period are also preserved. White Plains is the site of the Westchester County Center, where concerts and sports events are held, and of the College of White Plains.

White River. 1 River, c.690 mi (1,110 km) long, rising in the Boston Mts., NW Ark., and flowing first N into SW Missouri, then generally SE through NE Arkansas to the Mississippi River. Its chief tributaries are the Black and Little Red rivers. Near its mouth, the White is joined to the Arkansas River by a cutoff channel. The White is navigable for shallow-draft vessels c.300 mi (480 km) upstream. Bull Shoals Dam (340,000-kw capacity; completed 1957), Table Rock Dam (200,000 kw; 1959), and Beaver Dam (112,000 kw; 1965) are major projects on the river. Bull Shoals Lake (111 sq mi/288 sq km), on the Ark.-Mo. line, is the largest reservoir. **2** River, 307 mi (494 km) long, rising near Muncie, E Ind., and flowing SW through Indianapolis to the Wabash River. With the White East Fork (282 mi/454 km long), its chief tributary, the White drains much of S Indiana. **3** River, 507 mi (816 km) long, rising in NW Nebraska and flowing N then E through S South Dakota to the Missouri River near Chamberlain. It drains much of the Badlands.

White Rock, city (1971 pop. 10,349), SE British Columbia, Canada, on Georgia Strait and on the U.S. border. The city is a customs port and resort center with a residential area.

White Russia: see BELORUSSIA, USSR.

White Sands, uninhabited desert area, S central N.Mex. It is a center for U.S. military-weapons research and testing. On July 16, 1945, the first atomic bomb was exploded at Holloman Air Force Base (formerly Alamogordo Air Base). Each military branch maintains facilities at White Sands Missile Range, the busiest U.S. missile range. The area encloses White Sands National Monument (see NATIONAL PARKS AND MONUMENTS, table) and San Andres National Wildlife Refuge.

White Sea, Rus. *Beloye More,* c.36,680 sq mi (95,000 sq km), NW European USSR, an inlet of the Barents Sea. Its northern section, opening into the Barents Sea between the Kola and Kanin peninsulas, is connected with the southern body of the sea by a narrow strait c.100 mi (160 km) long and 30 to 35 mi (48-56 km) wide. Kandalashka Bay, in the southern section, is the deepest part of the sea (1,115 ft/340 m). The Mezen, the Northern Dvina, and the Onega rivers empty into large bays of the White Sea. The Solovetski Islands lie at the entrance to Onega Bay. Near the mouth of the Northern Dvina is Arkhangelsk (Archangel), the chief port. A canal system (140 mi/225 km long) connects the White Sea, at Belomorsk, with the Baltic Sea, at Leningrad. Icebreakers keep the major sections of the sea open in winter. There are lumber exports, fisheries (herring and cod), and seal herds. The White Sea was known by the people of Novgorod in the 11th cent. and was significant in the 16th cent. as the only sea outlet for Muscovite trade.

White Settlement, city (1970 pop. 13,449), Tarrant co., NE Texas, a suburb of Fort Worth.

white shark, large, ferocious shark, *Carcharodon carcharias.* Also known as the maneater, this aggressive shark attacks swimmers and boats without provocation. Although not abundant anywhere, it is widely distributed in tropical and temperate oceans and is found in both inshore and deep waters; it is most common on the Atlantic coast of the United States. Like the other members of its family, the MAKO and the porbeagle, it is a fast swimmer, with large pectoral fins and a nearly symmetrical tail fin. Despite its name, the white shark is usually whitish only on the underside, the back being some shade of gray. It has dark-tipped fins and a conspicuous black spot behind the pectorals. It reaches a length of over 20 ft (6 m) and a weight of over 7,000 lb (3,180 kg). It feeds on large fish and other animals; a

100-lb (45-kg) sea lion was recovered from the stomach of one specimen. The white shark's serrated, triangular teeth were used as arrowheads by Indians of the Florida coast. The white shark is classified in the phylum CHORDATA, subphylum Vertebrata, class Chondrichthyes, order Selachii, family Isuridae.

white-slave traffic: see PROSTITUTION.

white snakeroot, North American woods perennial (*Eupatorium urticaefolium*) of the family Compositae (COMPOSITE family), having a flat-topped cluster of small white flowers. It is of the same genus as the BONESET and JOE-PYE WEED. The herbage contains tremetol, a toxic principle causing "milk sickness," or milk fever. White snakeroot is classified in the division MAGNOLIOPHYTA, class Magnoliopsida, order Asterales, family Compositae.

white-tailed rat: see HAMSTER.

white vitriol: see ZINC SULFATE.

whitewash, white fluid commonly used as an inexpensive, impermanent coating for walls, fences, stables, and other exterior structures. It varies in composition, being generally a mixture of lime (quicklime), water, flour, salt, glue, and WHITING, with other ingredients such as molasses, water glass, or soap sometimes added. Mixed with size and colored, whitewash is occasionally used on interiors as calcimine.

Whitewater, city (1970 pop. 12,038), Jefferson and Walworth counties, SE Wis., in a dairy and farm area; inc. 1885. It has a foundry and plants that make eyeglasses, rakes, television parts, and dairy products. It is the seat of the Univ. of Wisconsin at Whitewater.

white whale: see BELUGA.

whitewood, common name for numerous unrelated trees having light-colored wood, e.g., the tulip tree (see MAGNOLIA), the LINDEN, and the cottonwood (see WILLOW).

Whitgift, John (hwĭt'gĭft), 1530?-1604, archbishop of Canterbury. He was a fellow of Peterhouse, Cambridge. As vice chancellor (1573) he had a leading part in revising the university statutes. He was made dean of Lincoln in 1571 and bishop of Worcester in 1577. He became archbishop of Canterbury in 1583. In his efforts to establish uniformity of discipline in ecclesiastical matters, Whitgift had the full support and favor of Queen Elizabeth. His policy was severe toward the Puritans, and he was attacked in some of the tracts published in the MARPRELATE CONTROVERSY. See his works, ed. by John Ayre (3 vol., 1851-53); biography by H. J. Clayton (1911); studies by P. M. Dawley (1954) and V. J. K. Brook (1957).

Whiting, William Henry Chase, 1825-65, Confederate general in the American Civil War, b. Biloxi, Miss. He served in the U.S. army until Feb., 1861, when he resigned and entered the Confederate service; there he rose to the rank of major general. As chief engineer to Gen. Joseph E. Johnston, Whiting distinguished himself at the first battle of Bull Run (1861). He fought in Stonewall Jackson's command in the Seven Days battles (1862). Appointed (Nov., 1862) commander of the district around Wilmington, N.C., he made FORT FISHER one of the strongest Confederate fortifications. He was wounded and captured when Union forces finally seized the fort in Jan., 1865, and died a prisoner in New York.

whiting, fish: see CROAKER.

whiting, white, powdery substance, prepared by grinding chalk or some other source of calcium carbonate. When mixed with linseed oil it forms PUTTY, and with water and several other substances it constitutes WHITEWASH. It is used as a pigment, called Spanish white, as a filler in paints, for polishing metalware, and for various other purposes.

Whitlam, Gough (gŏf), 1916–, Australian political leader. Edward Gough Whitlam studied law and entered practice near Sydney after serving in World War II. A member of the Labour party, he was elected to Parliament in 1952 and rose in Labour party circles. In 1960 he became deputy leader of the party, and in 1967 he succeeded Arthur Calwell as leader. He attempted to broaden the party's appeal to the middle class in order to reverse the poor electoral showing by Labour in the 1950s and 1960s. In the Dec., 1972, elections he led the party to victory against the Liberal-Country coalition that had dominated Australian politics for years. Emphasizing reform and better treatment for aborigines, as prime minister and foreign minister he also attempted to limit British and U.S. influence in Australia; immediately after taking office he ordered all Australian troops to return from South Vietnam. In Nov., 1973, Whitlam relinquished the office of foreign minister. In the May, 1974, elections his government was returned to power with a small majority.

Whitley Bay, municipal borough (1971 pop. 37,775), Northumberland, NE England, on the North Sea. Formerly the urban district of Whitley and Monkseaton, Whitley Bay was chartered as a municipal borough in 1954 and is the main resort on the Northumberland coast. It is also a residential area for the industrial concentration on the northern bank of the Tyne River. In 1974, Whitley Bay became part of the new metropolitan county of Tyne and Wear.

Whitlock, Brand, 1869-1934, American author and diplomat, b. Urbana, Ohio. After working as a reporter and practicing law, he became reform mayor of Toledo (1905-13). Meanwhile he wrote realistic novels chiefly concerned with politics, among them *The Thirteenth District* (1902) and *The Turn of the Balance* (1907). His service as U.S. minister and ambassador to Belgium from 1913 to 1922 was distinguished for his efforts to defend the British nurse Edith CAVELL and for his care of refugees. His later novels are surpassed by his nonfiction—*Belgium: a Personal Record* (1919) and a fine biography of Lafayette (1929). See his autobiography, *Forty Years of It* (1914), and his letters and journals (ed. with biographical introduction by Allan Nevins, 2 vol., 1936). See also biography by D. D. Anderson (1968); studies by Jack Tager (1968) and R. M. Crunden (1969).

Whitman, Charles Otis, 1842-1910, American zoologist, b. Woodstock, Maine, grad. Bowdoin, 1868, Ph.D. Univ. of Leipzig, 1878. From 1892 he was professor of zoology at the Univ. of Chicago. He founded (1887) and edited the *Journal of Morphology* and was a founder and director (1888-1908) of the Marine Biological Laboratory at Woods Hole, Mass. He wrote on animal behavior, embryology, evolution, microscopical anatomy, and other subjects. *Posthumous Works* (3 vol.) appeared in 1919.

Whitman, Marcus, 1802-47, American pioneer and missionary in the Oregon country, b. Federal Hollow (later Rushville), N.Y. In 1836 he left a country medical practice to go West as a missionary for the joint Presbyterian-Congregationalist board. With his wife, Narcissa Prentiss Whitman, and others, he crossed from Missouri to the Columbia River country and founded a mission at Waiilatpu (now in Whitman National Monument, near Walla Walla, Wash.). Disagreement among the missionaries and a board order (1842) to curtail their work led Whitman to ride back across the continent on horseback during the winter of 1842-43 to settle the various disputes. He was successful and returned with the "great emigration" of 1843 over the Oregon Trail. The Cayuse Indians around Waiilatpu, never friendly, grew more hostile, and on Nov. 29, 1847, they attacked the mission and killed Whitman, his wife, and others. Later, there was argument as to whether Whitman made his ride of 1842-43 in order to "save" Oregon from the British, the boundary still being in dispute. However, this "Whitman legend" has been discredited. See biographies by Nard Jones (1959, repr. 1968) and C. M. Drury (1937, and 2 vol., 1973).

Whitman, Sarah Helen (Power), 1803-78, American poet, b. Providence, R.I. In 1828 she married a Boston lawyer, John W. Whitman; after his death (1833) she returned to Providence and devoted herself to writing. In 1848 she was engaged for a time to Edgar Allan Poe, who wrote the second of his two poems entitled "To Helen" about her. She wrote several poems about Poe and defended him in *Edgar Poe and His Critics* (1860). Her collected poems, *Hours of Life,* appeared in 1853 (enl. ed. 1879).

Whitman, Walt (Walter Whitman), 1819-92, American poet, b. West Hills, Huntington, Long Island, N.Y. Considered by many to be the greatest of all American poets, Walt Whitman celebrated the freedom and dignity of the individual and sang the praises of democracy and the brotherhood of man. His *Leaves of Grass,* unconventional in both content and technique, is probably the most influential volume of poems in the history of American literature. Whitman left school in 1830, worked as a printer's devil and later as a compositor. In 1838-39 he taught school on Long Island and edited the *Long Islander,* a newspaper. By 1841 he had become a full-time journalist, editing successively several papers and writing prose and verse for New York and Brooklyn journals. His active interest in politics during this period led to the editorship of the Brooklyn *Daily Eagle,* a Democratic party paper; he lost this job, however, because of his vehement advocacy of abolition and the "free-soil" movement. After a brief trip to New Orleans in 1848, Whitman returned to Brooklyn, continued as a journalist, and later worked as a carpenter. In 1855 he published at his own expense a volume of 12 poems, *Leaves of Grass,* which he had begun working on probably as early as 1847. Prefaced by a statement of his theories of poetry, the volume included the poem later known as "Song of Myself," in which the author proclaims himself the symbolic representative of the common man. Although the book was a commercial failure, critical reviewers recognized the appearance of a bold new voice in poetry. Two larger editions appeared in 1856 and 1860, and they had equally little public success. The book was criticized because of Whitman's exaltation of the body and sexual love and also because of its innovation in verse form—that it, the use of free verse in long rhythmical lines with a natural, "organic" structure. Emerson was one of the few intellectuals to praise Whitman's work, writing him a famous congratulatory letter. Whitman continued to enlarge and revise further editions of *Leaves of Grass;* the last edition prepared under his supervision appeared in 1892. From 1862 to 1865 he worked as a volunteer hospital nurse in Washington. His poetry of the Civil War, *Drum-Taps* (1865), reissued with *Sequel to Drum Taps* (1865-66), included his two poems about Abraham Lincoln, "When Lilacs Last in the Dooryard Bloom'd," considered one of the finest elegies in the English language, and the much-recited "O Captain! My Captain!" For a while Whitman served as a clerk in the Dept. of the Interior, but he was discharged because *Leaves of Grass* was considered an immoral book. In 1873 he suffered a paralytic stroke and afterward lived in a semi-invalid state. His prose collection *Democratic Vistas* had appeared in 1871, and his last long poem, "Passage to India," was published in the 1871 edition of *Leaves of Grass.* From 1884 until his death he lived in Camden, N.J., where he continued to write and to revise his earlier work. His last book, *November Boughs,* appeared in 1888. Whitman was a complex person. He saw himself as the full-blooded, rough-and-ready spokesman for a young democracy, and he cultivated a bearded, shaggy appearance. Indeed, Whitman's early biographers John Burroughs and R. M. Bucke were so affected by the robust "I" of Whitman's poems and by the poet himself that they depicted him as a rowdy, sensual man, a great lover of women, and the father of several illegitimate children. Most of this was false. In reality Whitman was a quiet, gentle, circumspect man, robust in youth but sickly in middle age, who sired no children and is thought by some critics to have been homosexual. Whitman had an incalculable effect on later poets, inspiring them to experiment in prosody as well as in subject matter. See his correspondence, ed. by E. H. Miller (4 vol., 1961-69); prose works, ed. by Floyd Stovall (2 vol., 1963-64); T. L. Brasher, ed., *Early Poems and Fiction,* (1963); H. W. Blodgett and Sculley Bradley, ed., *Leaves of Grass* (1965); biographies by Newton Arvin (1938, repr. 1969) and G. W. Allen (rev. ed. 1969); studies by R. V. Chase (1961; 1955, repr. 1966), G. W. Allen (1970), J. J. Rubin (1973), and Floyd Stovall (1974).

Whitman, town (1970 pop. 13,059), Plymouth co., SE Mass., S of Boston; settled c.1670, set off from Abington and inc. 1875. It is an industrial town that manufactures shoe polish, plastics, foundry products, burial vaults, and textile machinery. The old Toll House (1709) is restored.

Whitman College, at Walla Walla, Wash.; coeducational; chartered 1859, opened 1866 as a seminary; became a college 1883. It was named for Marcus Whitman.

Whitman Mission National Historic Site: see NATIONAL PARKS AND MONUMENTS (table); WHITMAN, MARCUS.

Whitney, Asa, 1797-1872, American merchant and transcontinental railroad projector, b. North Groton, Conn. He entered the mercantile business in New York City, acted as a foreign buyer for several years, and then was (1842-44) a merchant in China. Upon his return, he toured (1844-51) the United States, carrying on an extensive publicity campaign urging the construction of a railroad from Chicago to the Pacific; he also petitioned (1845) Congress to support his plan. Whitney's proposed route from Lake Michigan through South Pass to the Pacific was not accepted mainly because of the growing sectionalism before the Civil War. He also presented to the British in 1851 an unsuccessful plan for a Canadian transcontinental railroad. He retired in 1852, a decade before the U.S. Congress passed an act for the construction of a transcontinental railroad. He wrote *National Railroad Connecting the Pacific* (1845) and *A Project for a Railroad to the Pacific* (1849). See study by M. L. Brown (1933).

Whitney, Eli, 1765–1825, American inventor of the COTTON GIN, b. Westboro, Mass., grad. Yale, 1792. When he was staying as tutor at Mulberry Grove, the plantation of Mrs. Nathanael Greene, Whitney was encouraged by Mrs. Greene and visiting cotton planters to try to find some device by which the fiber of short-staple cotton could be rapidly separated from the seed. Whitney, whose creative mechanical bent had been evident from boyhood, completed his model gin early in 1793, after about 10 days of work, and by April had built an improved one. With Phineas Miller, Mrs. Greene's plantation manager (and later her husband), he formed a partnership to manufacture gins at New Haven. He was unable to make enough gins to meet the demand, and although the partners received a patent in 1794, others copied his model and soon many gins were in use. After much litigation the partners received (1807) a favorable decision to protect their patent, but Congress in 1812 denied Whitney's petition for its renewal. His invention, which had immense economic and social effects, brought great wealth to many others, but little to Whitney himself. In 1798 he built a firearms factory near New Haven. The muskets his workmen made by methods comparable to those of modern mass industrial production were the first to have standardized, interchangeable parts. See biographies by Jeannette Mirsky and Allan Nevins (1962) and Denison Olmsted (1846, repr. 1972); C. M. Green, *Eli Whitney and the Birth of American Technology* (1956).

Whitney, John Hay, 1904–, American public official and newspaper publisher, b. Ellsworth, Maine. After an active career in business and in various government posts, Whitney served (1957–61) as ambassador to Great Britain. In 1958 his company acquired control of the New York *Herald Tribune,* and in 1961 he became publisher of the newspaper, which ceased publication in 1966. The company continued to publish the International *Herald Tribune.*

Whitney, William Collins, 1841–1904, American financier and political leader, b. Conway, Mass. After attending (1863–64) Harvard law school, he moved to New York City, became successful as a corporation lawyer, and was associated with various public utility companies and transportation interests. He helped lead the fight that brought about the downfall of William Marcy TWEED and the election (1874) of Samuel J. TILDEN as governor. As city corporation counsel (1875–82) he helped save New York City much money. Whitney, important in Democratic politics, served (1885–89) as Secretary of the Navy under President Cleveland and secured legislation for the making of armor-plated war vessels. In 1892 he supported Cleveland for the presidency, but in 1896 he refused to support the candidacy of William Jennings Bryan. He was a society leader and an outstanding sportsman. See biography by M. D. Hirsch (1948, repr. 1969).

Whitney, William Dwight, 1827–94, American Sanskrit scholar and lexicographer, b. Northampton, Mass. After studying in Germany, Whitney became professor of Sanskrit and of comparative philology at Yale. He was outstanding among American Orientalists and philologists and wrote *A Sanskrit Grammar* (1879) and *Language and the Study of Language* (1867). He was also brilliantly successful as editor of *The Century Dictionary.*

Whitney, Mount, peak, 14,494 ft (4,418 m) high, E Calif., in the Sierra Nevada at the eastern border of Sequoia National Park; the second highest peak in the United States (after Mt. McKinley, Alaska). It is connected by a scenic highway with Death Valley. The peak is named for U.S. geologist Josiah D. Whitney, who surveyed it in 1864.

Whitney Museum of American Art, in New York City, founded in 1930 by Gertrude Vanderbilt Whitney. It was an outgrowth of the Whitney Studio (1914–18), the Whitney Studio Club (1918–28), and the Whitney Studio Galleries (1928–30). Opened to the public in 1931, the museum actively supports American art through the purchase and exhibition of the work of living artists. Its extensive permanent collection contains sculpture, paintings, drawings, and prints, which are exhibited regularly. Annual shows in the various media provide comprehensive reviews of each year's American art. The spacious Madison Avenue building designed by Marcel Breuer to house the collection was opened to the public in 1966.

Whitstable (hwĭt'stəbəl), urban district (1971 pop. 25,404), Kent, SE England. It was formerly the port for Canterbury pilgrims. Today it is largely a resort and residential area. Whitstable oysters have long been famous.

Whitsunday: see PENTECOST.

Whittaker, Charles Evans, 1901–73, Associate Justice of the U.S. Supreme Court (1957–62), b. Troy, Kansas. He received his law degree from the Univ. of Kansas City in 1924 and practiced law for many years. He served as judge of the U.S. District Court for Western Missouri (1954–56) and on the U.S. Court of Appeals, 8th circuit (1956–57), before appointment by President Eisenhower to the Supreme Court. Upon his retirement in 1962, he was succeeded by Byron R. White.

Whittier, John Greenleaf (hwĭt'ēər), 1807–92, American Quaker poet and reformer, b. near Haverhill, Mass. Whittier was a pioneer in regional literature as well as a crusader for many humanitarian causes. He received a scanty education but read widely. An introduction at the age of 14 to Robert Burns's poetry inspired him to write verse; his first poems were published (1826) in the Newburyport *Free Press,* edited by William Lloyd Garrison, the abolitionist, who became his lifelong friend. In the years from 1828 to 1832, Whittier edited and contributed stories, sketches, and poems to various newspapers. His first two published books, *Legends of New England* (1831) and the poem *Moll Pitcher* (1832), warmly portrayed everyday life in his rural region. Whittier is depicted so often as the gentle hoary-headed Quaker that the fiery politician within him is often forgotten. He declared himself an abolitionist in the pamphlet *Justice and Expediency* (1833) and went to the unpopular national antislavery convention. In 1834–35 he sat in the Massachusetts legislature; he ran for Congress on the Liberty ticket in 1842 and was a founder of the Republican party. He also worked staunchly behind the political scene to further the abolitionist cause and was an active antislavery editor until 1840, when frail health forced him to retire to his Amesbury home. From there he sent out more of the poems and essays that made him a spokesman for the cause, and he was corresponding editor (1847–59) of the Washington abolitionist weekly, the *National Era.* In addition, Whittier compiled and edited a number of books; the most entertaining was the semifictional *Leaves from Margaret Smith's Journal* (1849). Meanwhile his volumes of verse came out almost biennially; the first authorized collection appeared in 1838. After the Civil War he turned from politics and dedicated himself completely to poetry. Although he liked to think of himself as the bard of the common man, as in *Songs of Labor* (1850), his best work is his careful and accurate delineation of New England life, history, and legend. His most famous poem is *Snow-bound* (1866), an idyllic picture of his boyhood home; other memorable volumes are *The Tent on the Beach* (1867) and *Maud Muller* (1867). Such ballads as "Barbara Frietchie," "Marguerite," and "Skipper Ireson's Ride"; perennial favorites like "The Barefoot Boy" and the war poem "Laus Deo"; and his nearly 100 hymns, of which the best known is "Dear Lord and Father of Mankind," gave him popularity in his time surpassed perhaps only by Longfellow. In current critical estimation, Whittier's ability as a balladist surpassed his ability as a poet. His meters and rhythms were conventional, and his poems tended to be too profuse, but as the voice of the New England villager and farmer prior to industrialization, his work portrays an important period in American history. See biographies by S. T. Pickard (1907, repr. 1969), J. A. Pollard (1949, repr. 1969), Whitman Bennett (1941, repr. 1971), W. J. Linton (1893, repr. 1973), and T. W. Higginson (1902, repr. 1973); studies by L. G. Leary (1961) and Edward Wagenknecht (1967).

Whittier, city (1970 pop. 72,863), Los Angeles co., S Calif.; in a fruit and oil area; inc. 1898. It is chiefly residential but has plants that manufacture potato chips; automobile, aircraft, and missile parts; oil pumps; and clay and steel products. Several companies have their administrative headquarters there. Founded by Quakers in 1887, it was the hometown of President Richard M. Nixon and the seat of Whittier College and a junior college.

Whittingham, Charles (hwĭt'ĭnjəm, -ĭng-əm), 1767–1840, English printer. He established a printery in London in 1789, removing to Chiswick and founding the Chiswick Press in 1810. He was assisted in his work by his nephew, also named **Charles Whittingham,** 1795–1876, who succeeded him. The younger Whittingham revived the use of Caslon's old-style type in 1844. The printery returned to London in 1852. The Chiswick Press printed admirable editions of numerous books for the London publisher William Pickering. Pickering used as his device the anchor and dolphin of Aldus Manutius. William MORRIS began his active association with printing by commissioning the Chiswick Press to print *The Roots of the Mountains* in 1889.

Whittington, Richard, 1358–1423, English merchant and lord mayor of London. He made his fortune as a mercer and then entered London politics to become successively councilman, alderman, sheriff, and finally (1397) lord mayor, an office to which he was elected three times. Like most of the London merchants, Whittington supported the usurpation of the throne by Henry IV in 1399, and in 1400 he was made a merchant of the London and Calais staples. He made several loans to Henry IV and Henry V in return for lucrative trading concessions. Whittington had no children and left his fortune in a trust administered by the Mercers' Company, largely for building purposes in the City of London. The famous story of Dick Whittington and his cat is far removed from the actual life of the lord mayor, who was born the son of a Gloucestershire knight. According to the story, Dick was an orphaned kitchen boy who put his one possession, a cat, on his master's ship in the hope that it might be traded. He then ran away but turned back when he heard the prophetic ringing of Bow Bells ("Turn again, Whittington, lord mayor of London") and found that his cat had been purchased, for a large fortune, by the ruler of Morocco, whose kingdom was plagued with rats and mice. Dick was thus able to marry his master's daughter and become a successful merchant. The story was first recorded in a play, now lost, that was licensed in 1605. See Walter Besant and James Rice, *Sir Richard Whittington* (1894).

Whittle, Sir Frank, 1907–, English aeronautical engineer. Whittle was one of the first men to associate the gas turbine with jet propulsion. Previously the gas turbine had been regarded as a machine for supplying shaft power, but Whittle saw it as an ideal means for providing jet propulsion in aircraft. As a Royal Air Force engineering officer, he patented in 1930 the basic designs for the turbojet engine. During the 1930s and early 1940s he and his associates constructed a number of turbojet engines and jet planes. These experiments led to the modern jet aircraft engine. The Germans and the Italians who constructed and flew the first jet aircraft used the basic engine designs that Whittle patented in the 1930s; the early American jet engines were also based on Whittle's work.

Whittredge, Worthington (hwĭt'rĭj), 1820–1910, American painter, b. Springfield, Ohio. Numbered among the exponents of LUMINISM, Whittredge studied in Europe with G. E. Lessing. His paintings contain a minutely executed tonal quality that expresses a mysterious, atmospheric silence broken by intense illumination. His *Camp Meeting* (1874) is in the Metropolitan Museum of Art.

Whitty, Dame May, 1865–1948, English actress. She made her London debut in 1881. In 1892 she married Ben Webster, an actor, and in 1895 she first appeared in the United States, becoming a favorite on the stage and in films. Her notable films include *Night Must Fall* (1938), *The Lady Vanishes* (1938), and *Mrs. Miniver* (1942). Her forte was the portrayal of kind but strong-minded old ladies. She was made a Dame of the British Empire in 1918. Her daughter was Margaret WEBSTER. See Margaret Webster, *The Same only Different* (1969).

WHO: see WORLD HEALTH ORGANIZATION.

whooping cough or **pertussis,** highly communicable infectious disease caused by the bacterium *Hemophilus pertussis,* predominantly a disease of children. The early or catarrhal stage of whooping cough is manifested by the usual symptoms of an upper respiratory infection with bronchial involvement. After about two weeks the cough becomes paroxysmal; 10 to 15 coughs may follow in rapid succession before a breath is taken, which is the characteristic high-pitched crowing "whoop." An attack of coughing is accompanied by a copious discharge of mucus and, often, vomiting. Antibiotics and hyperimmune human serum are valuable in treatment. Rest and proper nutrition (especially if there is frequent vomiting) are important. Whooping cough is a serious disease, especially in children under four years of age, since it may give rise to such complications as pneumonia, asphyxia, convulsions, and brain damage. For these reasons and since whooping cough occurs most commonly before two years of age, it is recommended that all infants be actively immunized at as early an age as possible (one to two months).

whortleberry: see BLUEBERRY; HUCKLEBERRY.

Whyalla, city (1971 pop. 31,568), South Australia state, S Australia, on Spencer Gulf. The city has shipbuilding and iron and steel industries. Iron ore and iron and steel products are exported.

Whydah, Dahomey: see OUIDAH.

Whymper, Edward (hwĭm'pər), 1840–1911, English illustrator and mountain climber, b. London. Sent to Switzerland to make sketches of mountain scenery, he became interested in mountaineering and in 1865, after six failures, climbed the hitherto unscaled Matterhorn. The descent ended in a fall that killed four of the party of seven, a memorable disaster in the history of mountaineering. He made expeditions to Greenland and later to South America, where he participated (1880) in the first ascent of Chimborazo (20,577 ft/6,272 m). He climbed other major Andean peaks, including Aconcagua and Tupungato. His best-known book is *Scrambles amongst the Alps* (1871, 6th ed. 1936). See biography by Francis S. Smythe (1940).

Wibert: see GUIBERT OF RAVENNA.

Wichita (wĭch'ĭtô), city (1970 pop. 276,554), seat of Sedgwick co., S central Kansas, at the confluence of the Arkansas and the Little Arkansas rivers; inc. 1870. It is the chief commercial and industrial center of S Kansas and the largest city in the state. It has railroad shops, flour mills, meat-packing plants, grain elevators, oil refineries, and a huge aircraft industry. Other manufactures are heaters, air conditioners, and trenching equipment. Wichita is located on the site of a village (1863–65) inhabited by Wichita Indians who had been driven out of Oklahoma and Texas for their Union sympathies during the Civil War. A trading post was established there in 1864 and the city was founded in 1868 by settlers serving the Chisholm Trail. In 1872 the railroad was extended to Wichita and the city boomed as a cow town. After 1880 it became the trade center of an agricultural and livestock region. Oil was discovered just E of Wichita in 1915. Today the city has many civic and cultural facilities, including art museums, a symphony orchestra, a new modernistic convention and cultural complex (Century II), and a large speech-and-hearing rehabilitation center. It has fine parks, a zoo, a "cow-town" restoration, and two large stadiums. It is the seat of Wichita State Univ., Friends Univ., and Kansas Newman College. McConnell Air Force Base is nearby.

Wichita Falls, city (1970 pop. 96,265), seat of Wichita co., N Texas, on the Wichita River; inc. 1889. The city's name comes from the Wichita Indians and from the falls that have since been reduced to an area of rapidly flowing water in the Wichita River. The area was probably settled in the 1870s, but the town did not grow until the coming of the railroad in 1882. Formerly a shipping point for wheat and cattle from nearby ranches, the city achieved tremendous prosperity with the oil booms of 1919 and 1937 in the vicinity. Today the headquarters of numerous oil companies are in Wichita Falls, and oil-field machinery is a leading manufacture. Electrical supplies, medical products, and electronic products are also manufactured there. Agriculture and ranching as well are important to the city's economy. Wichita Falls is the seat of Midwestern Univ. Nearby is Sheppard Air Force Base.

Wichita Indians, North American Indians whose language belongs to the Caddoan branch of the Hokan-Siouan linguistic stock (see AMERICAN INDIAN LANGUAGES). They formerly occupied central Kansas and ranged into Oklahoma and Texas. The Wichita were the people of Quivira, which Francisco Coronado visited in 1541. Juan de Padilla, left by the expedition to undertake the Christianization of the Indians, was the earliest missionary among the Plains Indians. Padilla, however, was killed by the Indians three years later. In 1662 the Wichita were defeated by Diego Dionisio de Peñalosa. By 1765, forced southward by hostile northern and eastern Indians, they had a village on the north fork of the Red River in Oklahoma. Following a severe smallpox epidemic (it reduced them to some 2,500), they abandoned the village, moving to the present site of Fort Sill; later they moved farther, and in the Civil War they fled for a time to Kansas; the site became Wichita, Kansas. In 1872 they ceded all their lands to the United States. Later they were settled on a reservation in W Oklahoma, where they now number some 200. In culture the Wichita were of the Plains area, like their relatives the Pawnee. The French called the Wichita *Panis piqués*, or Pawnee Picts, because the Wichita practiced tattooing. Distinctive to the Wichita was the conical grass house, which resembled a haystack. They practiced a horn dance for agricultural fertility, and in later years they adopted the ghost dance.

Wick, burgh (1971 pop. 7,613), county town of Caithness, N Scotland, on Wick Bay at the mouth of the Wick River. The burgh consists of the villages of Louisburgh, Old Wick, and Pulteneytown. It is an important herring port. Manufactures include knitwear, whiskey, herring oil, and hosiery. Tourism is also economically important.

Wickersham, George Woodward, 1858–1936, American lawyer and government official, b. Pittsburgh. He began law practice in Philadelphia, and after moving (1882) to New York City, he became a prominent corporation lawyer. As U.S. Attorney General (1909–13) under President Taft, he successfully prosecuted many corporations under the Sherman Antitrust Act. His book *The Changing Order* (1914) deals with monopolies. In 1929 he was appointed by President Hoover to head the National Commission on Law Observance and Law Enforcement, which came to be called the Wickersham Commission. It concluded in its final report of 1931 that the Federal machinery for enforcing criminal law in the United States was inadequate. It found in particular that prohibition enforcement had broken down, and the majority (which did not include Wickersham) recommended revision (but not repeal) of the 18th Amendment.

Wickham, William of: see WILLIAM OF WYKEHAM.

wickiup (wĭk'ēŭp"), temporary dwelling of nomadic North American Indians. It is a framework of arched poles covered by brush, bark, rushes, or mats. The wickiup is found among Indians in Arizona, New Mexico, Utah, Idaho, and California. Sometimes other dwellings of tribes in this region are called wickiups even when made of more permanent materials. The name is also spelled wikiup.

Wickliffe, John: see WYCLIF, JOHN.

Wickliffe (wĭk'lĭf), city (1970 pop. 21,354), Lake co., NE Ohio; inc. 1916. Chemicals, machinery, and meters are manufactured. Borromeo College of Ohio is there.

Wicklow (wĭk'lō), county (1971 pop. 66,270), 782 sq mi (2,025 sq km), E Republic of Ireland. The county town is WICKLOW. The Wicklow Mts. and their foothills occupy almost the entire area of the county; Lugnaquilla (3,039 ft/926 m) is the highest peak. The Liffey and the Slaney rivers rise in Wicklow, and there are also lakes and picturesque glens. Sheep and cattle are raised in the region, and grains are cultivated. Wicklow also has copper mines and granite and slate quarries. Its proximity to Dublin makes the region a popular one with tourists. GLENDALOUGH has notable ecclesiastical remains. The people of the mountainous district were long able to maintain their independence of English control, and Wicklow was not organized as a shire until 1606.

Wicklow, urban district (1971 pop. 3,908), county town of Co. Wicklow, E Republic of Ireland, on the Irish Sea. It is a seaport and market for an area of potato growing and cattle and sheep raising. Chemicals, fertilizers, and farm implements are the chief manufactures. There are flour mills in the town.

Wickram, Jörg (yörk vĭk'räm), c.1505–62, German writer. Wickram wrote Meisterlieder, farces such as *Der treue Eckart* [faithful Eckart] (1538), biblical drama such as *Tobias* (1550), and the first original German novel, *Historie von Reinhart und Gabriotto* (1551). His last book, *Von guten und bösen Nachbarn* [of good and bad neighbors] (1556) marked the transition from medieval epic to social novel. *Das Rollwagenbüchlein* [the little wagon book] (1555), a collection of anecdotes and witty tales, is considered his most successful work.

Wiclif, John: see WYCLIF, JOHN.

Widener, Harry Elkins (wĭd'nər), 1885–1912, American bibliophile, b. Philadelphia. He had the greatest Robert Louis Stevenson collection in existence. Widener died at the age of 27 on the *Titanic*. His library went by will to Harvard Univ., where it is installed with other collections in the Harry Elkins Widener Memorial Library, donated by his mother.

Widmanstätten figures: see METEORITE.

Widnes (wĭd'nĭs), municipal borough (1971 pop. 56,709), Lancashire, NW England, on the Mersey River. It is an important alkali-processing center and timber market. Other products are paints, soap, and steel goods. In 1974, Widnes became part of the new nonmetropolitan county of Cheshire.

Widor, Charles Marie (shärl märē' vēdōr'), 1845–1937, French organist and composer. He was organist at St. Sulpice from 1869 until his retirement in 1934. In 1891 he succeeded César Franck as professor of organ at the Paris Conservatory and later also became professor of composition there. Chief among his compositions are 10 symphonies for organ. He composed operas, chamber music, orchestral suites, and piano concertos as well. In 1904 he wrote a supplement to Berlioz's treatise on orchestration. He also made, with Albert Schweitzer, an edition of the organ works of Bach.

Widsith (wĭd'sĭth), 7th-century Anglo-Saxon poem found in the EXETER BOOK. It is an account of the wanderings of a Germanic minstrel and of the legends he relates. The poem gives an excellent description of minstrel life in the Germanic heroic age.

Widukind, Saxon historian: see WITTEKIND.

Widukind (wĭd'ŏŏkĭnd) or **Wittekind** (wĭt'ə-), d. 807?, leader of the Saxons against the Frankish king Charlemagne (later emperor of the West). In 782, when Charlemagne organized Saxony as a Frankish province and ordered forced conversion of the pagan Saxons, the Saxons under Widukind resumed warfare against the Franks. In the course of the war Charlemagne is said to have ordered the massacre (783) of 4,500 Saxon prisoners. Widukind fled to Denmark, but the Saxons fought on all the more fiercely. In 785, Charlemagne offered Widukind a safe-conduct in order to negotiate peace. Widukind met the emperor and accepted baptism; Charlemagne was his godfather. Sporadic Saxon uprisings continued until 804.

Wiechert, Ernst (ĕrnst vē'khĕrt), 1887–1950, German novelist. His works, distinguished by a poetic prose style, generally deal with his native East Prussia and the upheavals of the world wars. They include *Die Magd des Jürgen Doskocil* (1932, tr. *The Girl and the Ferryman,* 1947), *Der Totenwald* (1945, tr. *The Forest of the Dead,* 1947), and *Missa sine nomine* (1950, tr. 1953). Also of interest is the autobiographical novel *Wälder und Menschen* (1936).

Wied, Gustav (gōōs'täf vēth), 1858–1914, Danish novelist, playwright, and short-story writer. Wied was celebrated as a humorist. His vision of humanity was cynical and bitter, reflected in his writing by an amused, scornful tone, somewhat tempered with compassion. Among his best-known works are the novels *Livsens Ondskab* [life's malice] (1899) and *Knagsted* (1902); *Dansemus* [dancing mice] (1905), a play; and *Circus Mundi* (1909), a collection of short stories.

Wieland, Christoph Martin (krĭs'tôf mär'tĭn vē'länt), 1733–1813, German poet and novelist. His style, typical of the German rococo, is elegant, satiric, and often playful. He borrowed subjects from classical antiquity as well as from fairy tales. A political novel, *Der goldene Spiegel* [the golden mirror] (1772), won him employment as a tutor to the princes of Saxe-Weimar. His *Geschichte des Agathon* (1766, tr. *The History of Agathon,* 1773) is an early psychological novel; *Die Abderiten* (1774, tr. *The Republic of Fools,* 1861) is his best-known political satire. Wieland's verse narratives include *Musarion* (1768) and a noted fairy-tale epic, *Oberon* (1780, tr. 1798; by John Quincy Adams, 1799). He edited the influential literary journal *Teutsche Merkur* (1773–1810) and, with his translations of Shakespeare, helped to pave the way for future literary developments in Germany.

Wien, Wilhelm (vĭl'hĕlm vēn), 1864–1928, German physicist. He was professor at the universities of Giessen (1899), Würzburg (1900–20), and Munich (from 1920). He received the 1911 Nobel Prize in Physics for his studies on the radiation of heat from black objects. He is noted also for his work on hydrodynamics, X rays, and the radiation of light.

Wien: see VIENNA, Austria.

Wiener, Norbert, 1894–1964, American mathematician and educator, b. Columbia, Mo., grad. Tufts College, 1909, Ph.D. Harvard, 1913. In 1920 he joined the faculty of the Massachusetts Institute of Technology, where he became (1932) professor of mathematics. He is best known for his theory of cybernetics and for his contributions to the development of electronic computers and calculators. His principal fields of research included the theory of probability, the postulate theory, and the foundations of mathematics. Precocious as a child, Wiener recounted his youth and training in the autobiographical *Ex-Prodigy* (1953). He described his mature years and scientific career in *I Am a Mathematician* (1956). His other writings include *The Human Use of Human Beings* (1950), *Nonlinear Problems in*

Random Theory (1958), and *Cybernetics* (rev. ed. 1961).

Wiener Neustadt (vē'nər noi'shtät), city (1971 pop. 34,800), Lower Austria province, E Austria. It is an industrial and rail center. Manufactures include locomotives, heavy machinery, and textiles. Founded in 1192, Wiener Neustadt was the birthplace of Emperor Maximilian I (1459–1519). The city was severely damaged in World War II. The 12th-century castle of the Babenbergs, dukes of Austria, became a military academy in 1752.

Wienerwald (vē'nərvält) [Ger.,=Vienna forest], forested range, NE Austria, just W of Vienna. An outlier of the Eastern Alps, it rises to 2,930 ft (893 m) in the Schöpfl. The best-known summit, however, is the Kahlenberg (1,585 ft/483 m) near Vienna. The beautiful forests, streams, and hills of the Wienerwald have made it a favorite excursion and resort area for the Viennese.

Wiertz, Antoine Joseph (äNtwän' zhôzĕf' vĕrts), 1806–65, Belgian historical painter. He enjoyed such prestige that the government built him a studio in Brussels, now the Wiertz Museum. He delighted in painting complicated, philosophical subjects and scenes from ancient history. Wiertz invented a type of mat painting and wrote a memoir on Flemish painting.

Wierzyński, Kazimierz (käzē'myĕsh vyĕzhĭ'nyə̆skē), 1894–1969, Polish poet and journalist. Wierzyński was a cofounder with Julian Tuwim of the Skamander group of experimental poets. His *Olympic Laurel* (1927) idealizes the grace and fitness of athletes, and his other early poems also celebrate the joy of living. Later works are more serious and socially conscious. *The Bitter Crop* (1933) includes poems about the United States. His *Forgotten Battlefield* (tr. 1944) contains narratives of World War II. See his *Selected Poems* (tr. 1959). His biography of Chopin appeared in English in 1971.

Wiesbaden (vēs'bä"dən, vĭs'-), city (1970 pop. 250,122), capital of Hesse, central West Germany, on the Rhine River, at the southern foot of the Taunus mts. The city, an industrial center and a market for Rhine wines, is one of the most famous spas of Europe. Manufactures include metal goods, chemicals, plastics, pharmaceuticals, machinery, and textiles. There are also motion picture and television studios. Wiesbaden was founded as a Celtic settlement in the 3d cent. B.C. In the 1st and 2d cent. A.D. it was a popular Roman spa known as Aquae Mattiacorum; there are remains of the Roman water conduits and walls. It later became a free imperial city and passed to the county (later duchy) of Nassau in 1281. In 1806 the city was made the capital of Nassau and with it passed to Prussia in 1866. After World War I, Wiesbaden was the seat (1918–29) of the Allied Rhineland Commission. Noteworthy buildings in the city include the castle (1837–41), the Kurhaus (1905–7), and the State Theater of Hesse (1892–94).

Wieser, Friedrich von (frē'drĭkh fən vē'zər), 1851–1926, Austrian economist and sociologist. He is noted for his formulas applying the principle of marginal utility to cost phenomena. He taught at Prague (1884–1903) and Vienna (1903–17, 1919–22) and served (1917–18) as Austrian secretary of commerce. His works include *Der natürliche Wert* (1889, tr. *Natural Value*, 1893) and *Theorie der gesellschaftlichen Wirtschaft* (1914, tr. *Social Economics*, 1927).

wife: see HUSBAND AND WIFE.

wig, arrangement of artificial or human hair worn to conceal baldness, as a disguise, or as part of a costume, either theatrical, ceremonial, or fashionable. In ancient Egypt the wig was worn to protect the head from the sun; short-haired and in many tiers or long and thickly plaited, the wig was an ingenious structure and rather formalized in appearance. Roman women, who favored light hair, often wore blond wigs. The wig came into popular fashion in Europe in the 17th cent. First worn in France during the reign of Louis XIII, who himself wore a wig of long curls that was meant to simulate real hair, the fashion became widespread during the reign of Charles II of England. As human hair was both difficult to obtain and expensive, the hair of horses and goats was often used. The natural wig eventually gave way to the formal peruke or periwig. Later (c.1690) scented pomade and white powder of starch and plaster of Paris were used on the wigs; pink, gray, and blue powder were fashionable as the fad grew. At its height during the reign of Louis XV, the powdered wig was out of fashion by 1794. The periwig gradually gave way to a smaller wig with horizontal curls above the ears and with the back drawn into a loose queue and tied with a bow. By 1788 men began to wear their own hair tied at the back (and sometimes powdered) in imitation of a wig; wigs however continued their hold on the professional classes and can be seen today in the official dress of English courts. After 1800 as long hair for men lost favor, the wig became a part of women's fashions. Today the use of the wig is dictated by fashion. The late 1960s saw an enormous revival of the ornamental wig for women and men.

Wigan (wĭg'ən), county borough (1971 pop. 14,851), Lancashire, N England, on the Douglas River. There are coal mines in the vicinity. The borough has a wide variety of industries. In the Middle Ages, Wigan was an important market town. It was long noted for the manufacture of pottery and pewter and for bell founding. There were iron works in the 19th cent. Wigan is thought to have been the site of the Roman station Coccium. The fine Church of All Saints has a Norman tower. In 1974, Wigan became part of the new metropolitan county of Greater Manchester.

Wiggin, Kate Douglas (Smith), 1856–1923, American author and educator, b. Philadelphia. In San Francisco she organized the first free kindergartens on the Pacific coast (1878) and with her sister established a training school for kindergarten teachers. As part of her teaching career she wrote her first book, *The Story of Patsy* (1883). The most popular among her many later works for children were *The Birds' Christmas Carol* (1887), *Timothy's Quest* (1890), *Rebecca of Sunnybrook Farm* (1903), and *Mother Carey's Chickens* (1911). See her autobiography, *My Garden of Memory* (1923); biography by her sister, Nora A. Smith (1925).

Wigglesworth, Michael, 1631–1705, American clergyman and poet, b. England, grad. Harvard, 1651. His family emigrated to New England in 1638. A devoted minister at Malden, Mass., he also practiced medicine and wrote didactic poetry. His *Day of Doom* (1662), a ballad of Puritan theology, was extremely popular and was followed by *God's Controversy with New England* (written c.1662; printed 1873), *Meat Out of the Eater* (1670), and lesser writings. Replete with vivid biblical imagery, Wigglesworth's verse reflects his dedication to his austere faith. See his *Diary, 1653–57*, ed. by E. S. Morgan (1951, repr. 1970); *The Day of Doom* (ed. by K. B. Murdock, 1929); memoir by J. W. Dean (2d ed. 1871); biography by Richard Crowder (1962).

Wight, Isle of (wīt), island county (1971 pop. 109,284), 147 sq mi (381 sq km), S England, across the Solent and Spithead channels from Hampshire. The administrative center is Newport. The island is 23 mi (37 km) long from the eastern Foreland to the Needles (detached chalk formations at the western extremity) and 13 mi (21 km) wide. The Medina, which almost bisects the island, and the East Yar and the West Yar are the chief rivers. Numerous small streams on the southern coast have cut a series of picturesque gullies in the soft rock. The climate is mild, and the scenery, as a result of the contrasting geological strata, is varied. Pleasant villages, such as Ventnor, and a beautiful coast line make the island popular as a winter resort. There are shipbuilding, aircraft, and other industries in COWES. Quarrying is also done. The island was conquered by the Romans in A.D. 43 and probably settled later by the Jutes. It was annexed to the kingdom of Wessex in 661 and Christianized c.700. The Isle of Wight was the headquarters of the Danes at the end of the 10th cent. William I bestowed the lordship of the island upon William Fitz-Osbern. In 1293 it returned permanently to the crown. At Carisbrooke Castle, now in ruins, King Charles I was imprisoned (1647–48). In 1890 the island was established as a separate administrative county. Queen Victoria's seaside home, Osborne House, is near the famous yachting center at Cowes.

Wightman Cup: see TENNIS.

Wigmore, John Henry, 1863–1943, American jurist and legal educator, b. San Francisco, grad. Harvard (B.A., 1883; M.A. and LL.B., 1887). He taught (1889–92) Anglo-American law at Keio-Gijuku Univ., Tokyo. After 1893 he was a professor of law at Northwestern Univ.; from 1901 to 1929 he was dean of the law faculty. Wigmore is especially noted for his monumental work usually known as *Treatise on Evidence* (4 vol., 1904; 3d ed., 10 vol., 1940; suppl. 1964). This work is at the same time a lawyer's manual of practice and an incisive and highly critical survey of the law of evidence. His shorter works on evidence include books usually cited as *The Code of Evidence* (3d ed. 1942) and *Students' Textbook of Evidence* (1935). Out of Wigmore's interest in comparative law came his *Panorama of the World's Legal Systems* (3 vol., 1928; repr., 3 vol. in 1, 1936).

Wigner, Eugene Paul (wĭg'nər), 1902–, American physicist, b. Hungary, grad. Technische Hochschule, Berlin, 1925. He was a professor at Princeton Univ. from 1930 to 1936 and again from 1938 to 1971. In 1937 he became a U.S. citizen. During World War II he worked on the Manhattan Project, which resulted in the first atomic bomb. After beginning his association with the Atomic Energy Commission in 1947, he served as a member of its general advisory committee from 1952 to 1957 and from 1959 to 1964. He shared the 1963 Nobel Prize in Physics with U.S. physicist Maria Goeppert-Mayer and German physicist J. H. D. Jensen for work on the structure of the atomic nucleus. Wigner has received other major awards, including the 1960 Atoms for Peace Award.

Wigtownshire (wĭg'tənshĭr), county (1971 pop. 27,335), 487 sq mi (1,261 sq km), SW Scotland. The administrative center is STRANRAER. The coastline is irregular, and there are numerous lakes. The peninsula set off by Loch Ryan and Luce Bay is called the Rhinns. Much of the county is hilly moorland, but the arable land (about half the area) is well cultivated. Agriculture is almost the sole industry. Dairying is most important. Sheep, cattle, and pigs are raised. Vestiges of early occupation include hill forts, standing stones, and Pictish crannogs. Stranraer handles much traffic with Northern Ireland. Under the Local Government Act of 1973, Wigtownshire became part of the Strathclyde region.

wigwam (wĭg'wŏm), dwelling found among the Algonquian Indians of the Eastern woodlands area of the United States. The wigwam was usually conical, arborlike, or domed. Some were small, accommodating a single family; others were large communal dwellings. They were covered with squares of bark, with reed mats, or with thatch. Sometimes the word is incorrectly extended to almost all North American Indian dwellings including the earth lodge and sometimes even the tepee and the wickiup.

Wijk, Netherlands: see MAASTRICHT.

Wijnants, Jan: see WYNANTS, JAN.

wikiup: see WICKIUP.

Wilberforce, Samuel (wĭl'bərfôrs), 1805–73, English prelate; son of William Wilberforce. In 1845 he became bishop of Oxford. He did not support the OXFORD MOVEMENT; instead, he attempted to hold a middle course between the High Church and Low Church factions. As a signer of the remonstrance against the appointment of R. D. Hampden to the bishopric of Hereford and as a participant in other controversies, he was at times an unpopular figure, sometimes referred to by his detractors as "Soapy Sam." A man of oratorical powers and of marked administrative ability, Bishop Wilberforce greatly improved the organization of his diocese and was instrumental in restoring to the English church convocations some of their earlier ecclesiastical authority. In 1869 he was made bishop of Winchester. With his brother Robert he wrote a biography (1838) of his father; his work includes *History of the Protestant Episcopal Church in America* (1844). See biographies by A. R. Ashwell and R. G. Wilberforce (3 vol., 1879) and Standish Meacham (1970).

Wilberforce, William, 1759–1833, British politician and humanitarian. He was elected to Parliament in 1780 and during the campaign formed a lifelong friendship with William Pitt, whose measures he generally supported in the House of Commons. In 1785, during a tour of the Continent, he became converted to evangelicism—a decision that affected his entire outlook and caused him to withdraw from fashionable society. He pressed unsuccessfully for more humane criminal laws and, joining with Thomas CLARKSON and others in the campaign for the abolition of the slave trade, was for 20 years parliamentary leader of this movement. He also organized (1802) the Society for the Suppression of Vice and took part in other evangelical activities for social improvement. Abolition of the slave trade was achieved in 1807. When it became apparent that the measure would not cause the natural demise of slavery, Wilberforce directed his efforts to the suppression of the institution throughout the British Empire. A bill to this effect was passed a month after his death. Wilberforce wrote *A Practical View of the Prevailing Religious System of Professed Christians* (1797), a work that enjoyed wide popularity both in Britain and on the Continent. See his correspondence (1840); biographies by R. I. and Samuel Wilberforce (1835), Reginald Coupland (1923, repr. 1968), and O. M. Warner (1962).

Wilberforce University, at Wilberforce, Ohio, near Xenia; African Methodist Episcopal; coeducational; chartered and opened 1856. In 1863 it absorbed

Union Seminary (est. 1847). The university adopted a work-study program in 1964.

Wilbraham, town (1970 pop. 11,984), Hampden co., S central Mass.; settled 1730, inc. 1763. It is mainly residential. Wilbraham Academy, a preparatory school, is there.

Wilbur, John, 1774–1856, American Quaker leader, b. Hopkinton, R.I. He became the leader of the opposition to the evangelical principles of J. J. Gurney and Elias Hicks, and his expulsion (1843) by the Quakers resulted in the formation of the new New England Yearly Meeting. His followers were called Wilburites. See FRIENDS, RELIGIOUS SOCIETY OF. See Rufus Jones, *The Later Periods of Quakerism* (2 vol., 1921).

Wilbur, Ray Lyman, 1875–1949, American public official and educator, b. Boonesboro, Iowa, grad. Stanford (B.A., 1896; M.A., 1897) and Cooper Medical College, San Francisco, 1899. After studying medicine abroad, Wilbur became a professor (1909–16) and dean (1911–16) of the medical school at Stanford. In 1916 he became president of Stanford. In World War I he served with the U.S. Food Administration and was (1929–33) Secretary of the Interior under President Hoover. He retired as college president in 1943. *The March of Medicine* (1938) and *Human Hopes* (1940) are collections of his speeches and writings. See his memoirs (ed. by E. E. Robinson and P. C. Edwards, 1960).

Wilbur, Richard, 1921–, American poet, b. New York City, grad. Amherst (B.A., 1942) and Harvard (M.A., 1947). A skillful craftsman who writes in traditional verse forms, Wilbur is always original and can be profound and witty, playful and intellectual. His volumes of verse include *The Beautiful Changes* (1947), *Things of This World* (1956; Pulitzer Prize), *Advice to a Prophet* (1961), *The Poems of Richard Wilbur* (1963), and *Walking to Sleep: New Poems and Translations* (1969); *Opposites* (1973) is a collection of his poems for children. He has translated Moliere's *The Misanthrope* (1955) and *Tartuffe* (1963), and, with Lillian Hellman, wrote the libretto for a musical version of Voltaire's *Candide* (1957). See study by D. L. Hill (1967).

Wilbye, John (wĭl'bē), 1574–1638, English madrigal composer. Although only two sets of his madrigals (1598, 1609) are extant, their excellence distinguishes him as perhaps the greatest English madrigalist of the 16th cent.

Wild, Jonathan, 1683–1725, English criminal. He maintained a highly organized gang of thieves in London and long escaped punishment by posing as an instrument of justice and helping the authorities catch other criminals independent of, or rebellious to, his control. He planned robberies and then secured rewards for helping owners recover "lost" property. His thriving business required warehouses, branch offices, artisans to make alterations, and a vessel for trade with the Continent. He was finally convicted (1725) of receiving a reward for returning some stolen lace and was hanged at Tyburn. Literary accounts of Wild's career, such as those of Fielding and Defoe, are partly fictional. See W. R. Irwin, *The Making of Jonathan Wild* (1941); Gerald Howson, *Thief-Taker General* (1970).

wild allspice: see LAUREL.

wild canary: see FINCH; WARBLER.

wild carrot: see QUEEN ANNE'S LACE.

wildcat, common name of two Old World CATS, the European wildcat, *Felis sylvestris,* of Europe and W Asia, and the African wildcat, or kaffir cat, *F. lybica,* of Africa and Asia. The European wildcat resembles a large domestic tabby cat with a heavy tail; its fur is brownish to gray, with a pattern of light stripes. It can and does interbreed with domestic cats. The African wildcat was domesticated by the ancient Egyptians and is probably ancestral to the modern domestic cat. The name *wildcat* is also applied regionally to a variety of small cats. In North America it is a common name for the bobcat (see LYNX).

Wilde, Oscar (Oscar Fingall O'Flahertie Wills Wilde), 1854–1900, Irish author and wit, b. Dublin. He is most famous for his sophisticated, brilliantly witty plays, which were the first since the comedies of Sheridan and Goldsmith to have both dramatic and literary merit. He studied at Trinity College, Dublin, and at Magdalen College, Oxford, where he distinguished himself for his scholarship and wit, and also for his eccentricity in dress, tastes, and manners. Influenced by the aesthetic teachings of Walter PATER and John RUSKIN, Wilde became the center of a group glorifying beauty for itself alone, and he was satirized with other exponents of "art for art's sake" in *Punch* and in Gilbert and Sullivan's operetta *Patience.* His first published work, *Poems* (1881), was well received. The next year he lectured in the United States, where his drama *Vera* (1883) was produced. In 1884 he married Constance Lloyd, and they had two sons, Cyril and Vyvyan. Later he began writing for and editing periodicals; but his active literary career began with the publication of *Lord Arthur Savile's Crime and Other Stories* (1891) and two collections of fairy tales, *The Happy Prince* (1888) and *The House of Pomegranates* (1892). In 1891 his novel *The Picture of Dorian Gray* appeared: A tale of horror, it depicts the corruption of a beautiful young man pursuing an ideal of sensual indulgence and moral indifference; although he himself remains young and handsome, his portrait becomes ugly, reflecting his degeneration. Wilde's stories and essays were well received, but his creative genius found its highest expression in his plays—*Lady Windermere's Fan* (1892), *A Woman of No Importance* (1893), *An Ideal Husband* (1895), and his masterpiece, *The Importance of Being Earnest* (1895), which were all extremely clever and filled with pithy epigrams and paradoxes. Wilde explained away their lack of depth by saying that he put his genius into his life and only his talent into his books. He also wrote two historical tragedies, *The Duchess of Padua* (1892) and *Salomé* (1893). In 1891, Wilde had become intimate with Lord Alfred Douglas, and the marquess of Queensberry, Douglas's father, accused Wilde of homosexual practices. Foolishly, Wilde brought action for libel against the marquess and was himself charged with homosexual offenses under the Criminal Law Amendment, found guilty, and sentenced to prison for two years. His experiences in jail inspired his most famous poem, *The Ballad of Reading Gaol* (1898), and the apology published by his literary executor as *De Profundis* (1905). Released in 1897, he lived in France until his death, plagued by ill health and bankruptcy. See his collected works (ed. by Robert Ross, 1969); letters (ed. by Rupert Hart-Davis, 1962); biography by Philippe Jullian (1969); studies by H. M. Hyde (1963), K. E. Beckson, ed. (1970), and Martin Fido (1974).

wildebeest: see GNU.

Wildenvey, Herman (hĕr'män vĭl'dənvā), 1886–1959, Norwegian poet, whose family name was Portaas (pôr'tōs). He developed a verse line particularly suitable to light, gay subjects, and most of his poetry is concerned with youth and beauty. *Owls to Athens* (1935) is a selection of his verse in English translation.

Wilder, Billy, 1906–, American film director, producer, and writer, b. Austria. Wilder achieved prominence with *The Lost Weekend* (1945), which won him Academy Awards for best direction, best picture, and best screenplay. His screenplay for *Sunset Boulevard* (1950), which he also directed, won another. His later films, often notable for their tough, cynical approach, include *Stalag 17* (1953), *Love in the Afternoon* (1957), *Some Like It Hot* (1959), *The Fortune Cookie* (1966), *The Front Page* (1974), and *The Apartment* (1960), which again won him three Academy Awards. See studies by Axel Madsen (1969) and Tom Wood (1970).

Wilder, Thornton Niven, 1897–, American playwright and novelist, b. Madison, Wis., grad. Yale (B.A., 1920) and Princeton (M.A., 1925). He received most of his early education in China, where his father was in the American consular service. Wilder has taught in colleges and universities in the United States and Europe; he was the Charles E. Norton professor of poetry at Harvard in 1950–51. A serious and highly original dramatist, Wilder often employs nonrealistic theatrical techniques, i.e., scrambled time sequences, minimal stage sets, characters speaking directly to the audience, and the use of a narrator. His plays, like his novels, usually maintain that true meaning and beauty are found in ordinary experience. Wilder's first important literary work was the novel *The Bridge of San Luis Rey* (1927; Pulitzer Prize), which probes the lives of victims of a bridge disaster in Peru. Among his other novels are *The Cabala* (1926); *The Woman of Andros* (1930); *Heaven's My Destination* (1934); *The Ides of March* (1948); *The Eighth Day* (1967), an old-fashioned saga about two families that is also a mystery story and an exploration of chance and human destiny; and *Theophilus North* (1973), a comic account of the experiences of an unusual young man living in Newport, R.I., during the summer of 1929. Although he had written one-act plays, published in *The Angel That Troubled the Waters* (1928) and *The Long Christmas Dinner* (1931), Wilder did not achieve critical recognition as a playwright until the production of *Our Town* (1938; Pulitzer Prize). Now considered a classic of the American theater, *Our Town* is the simple yet panoramic story of life as it is lived in Grover's Corners, N.H. *The Skin of Our Teeth* (1942; Pulitzer Prize), supposedly based on James Joyce's *Finnegan's Wake,* treats man's unending struggle to survive. Wilder's other plays include *The Merchant of Yonkers* (1938), which was revised as *The Matchmaker* (1954) and adapted, by others, into the successful musical *Hello Dolly!* (1963); and *Plays for Bleeker Street* (1962), one-act plays from his projected "Seven Ages of Man" and "Seven Deadly Sins" cycles. In 1965, Wilder was awarded the first National Medal for Literature. See studies by Rex Burbank (1961), Malcolm Goldstein (1965), Donald Haberman (1967), Helmut Papajewski (tr. 1968), and M. C. Kuner (1972).

wilderness, land retaining its primeval character with the imprint of man minimal or unnoticeable. In the United States, the U.S. Wilderness Act of 1964 established the National Wilderness Preservation System with a nucleus of 9 million acres (3,636,000 hectares) of land in 54 different areas, mostly in Western states, and provided for the designation of new wilderness areas. Since then another 2 million acres (808,000 hectares) have been added to the system, also mainly in the West. Pending legislation would authorize wilderness areas in Eastern locations where signs of civilization have been substantially erased. Wilderness lands are to be preserved in their natural condition, wild and undeveloped, both for their own sake and for man's enjoyment of their beauty and solitude. The idea of wilderness has deep roots in American thought (see ENVIRONMENTALISM). In the 17th cent. William Penn decreed that one acre of forest be left wild for every five that were cleared. Henry David Thoreau believed that the existence of wilderness was justified by the inspiration men could draw from it.

Wilderness campaign, in the American Civil War, a series of engagements (May–June, 1864) fought in the Wilderness region of Virginia. Early in May, 1864, the Northern commander in chief, GRANT, led the Army of the Potomac (118,000 strong) across the Rapidan River into the Wilderness, a wild and tangled woodland c.10 mi (16 km) W of Fredericksburg. Grant planned to clear the Wilderness before trying to destroy the smaller Confederate Army of Northern Virginia (60,000 troops) under Robert E. LEE. But Lee advanced on the Union troops while they were still in that area, causing Grant to face about and order an attack. The nature of the terrain made the battle of the Wilderness (May 5–6) a disjointed but bloody fight. After the repulse of a Union attack on May 6 through the opportune arrival of the 1st Corps under James Longstreet, Lee counterattacked, and the battle became stabilized. Grant then pushed ahead by Lee's right, heading toward Spotsylvania Courthouse, c.12 mi (19 km) to the southeast. Lee, anticipating the move, was soon entrenched there. In the battle of Spotsylvania Courthouse (May 8–19), Grant unsuccessfully hammered away at the Confederate lines. The bloodiest fighting of this battle occurred on May 12 when the Union assault on the salient forming the Confederate center (the Bloody Angle) was repulsed after initial success. Lee confronted Grant's next move from a position S of the North Anna River, so impregnable that even Grant did not attack. By the beginning of June both armies were near Richmond. Fearing that Lee might withdraw within the defenses of the capital, Grant made another unsuccessful frontal assault on his strongly entrenched enemy in the battle of Cold Harbor, June 3, 1864. The Union lost 7,000 men in a few hours—the most horrible slaughter of the war. After several days of desultory trench fighting Grant then withdrew, crossed the James River, and moved against PETERSBURG. He had lost about 60,000 men in the campaign, and although Lee's army sustained the proportionately larger loss of 20,000, it was by no means destroyed. See Clifford Dowdy, *Lee's Last Campaign* (1960); Edward Steere, *The Wilderness Campaign* (1960).

Wilderness Road, principal avenue of westward migration for U.S. pioneers from c.1790 to 1840, blazed in 1775 by the American frontiersman Daniel Boone and an advance party of the Transylvania Company. Feeders from the east (Richmond, Va.) and the north (Harpers Ferry, W.Va.) converged at Fort Chiswell in the Shenandoah valley. Boone's road ran southwest from there through the valley, then W across the Appalachian Mts. and through Cumberland Gap into the Kentucky bluegrass region and to the Ohio River. The road followed old buffalo traces and Indian paths, but much of it had to be cut through the wilderness. In the early years, many travelers fell victim to hostile Indians. After

Kentucky became a state in 1792, the road was widened to accommodate wagons. Private contractors, authorized to keep up sections of the road, charged tolls for its use. With the building of the National Road, the Wilderness Road was neglected and finally abandoned in the 1840s. Since 1926 the Wilderness Road has been a section of U.S. Route 25, the Dixie Highway.

wildfowl: see WATERFOWL.

wild hyacinth: see BRODIEA; CAMASS; SQUILL.

wildlife, conservation of: see ENDANGERED SPECIES; WILDLIFE REFUGE; CONSERVATION OF NATURAL RESOURCES.

wildlife refuge, haven or sanctuary for animals, an area of land or of land and water set aside and maintained for the preservation and protection of one or more species of wildlife. In the United States limited game laws were passed in various states in the late 17th cent., but it was not until after the mid-19th cent. that legislation became concerned with the depletion of wildlife. By that time, the populations of many birds and mammals had been alarmingly reduced, and some species had become extinct chiefly because of the rapacious and indiscriminate slaughter of animals for feathers and hides, for food, and for sport and also because of the destruction of breeding places by the draining of swamps and leveling of forests for farming and human settlement. Modern wildlife conservation policy began with a conference of state governors and other officials called by President Theodore Roosevelt in 1908 to inventory the nation's natural resources; its immediate outcome was the appointment of a national conservation commission, followed shortly by the establishment of similar commissions in most of the states (see CONSERVATION OF NATURAL RESOURCES). Milestones in early legislation designed to preserve wildlife in the United States were the Lacey Act (1900), regulating imports of and interstate commerce in birds and mammals and a similar supplementary act for black bass (1926); the establishment (1916) of the National Park Service, which forbids hunting within its parks; international treaties for the protection of migratory birds made by the United States with Canada (1918) and with Mexico (1937); the Norbeck-Andresen Migratory-Bird Conservation Act (1929), which provided for the development of a system of refuges; and an act (1934) requiring hunters of migratory fowl to purchase a stamp, and a similar act (1937) establishing a tax on arms and ammunition, the funds in both cases to be used for wildlife preservation programs. Recent legislation to protect wildlife includes the National Environmental Policy Act of 1970 and other antipollution legislation and the Endangered Species Acts of 1966, 1969, and 1973 (see ENDANGERED SPECIES). The Wildlife Refuge System presently consists of some 330 different areas, comprising 30 million acres (12,120,000 hectares). The system is administered by the Fish and Wildlife Service (Bureau of Sport Fisheries and Wildlife) of the Dept. of the Interior. The service was established in 1940 by consolidation of the Bureau of Biological Survey (est. 1885 in the Dept. of Agriculture) and the Bureau of Fisheries (est. 1871 as an independent office). The work of the service includes biological research, the administration and enforcement of relevant Federal legislation, and numerous related projects. Refuges have been established for big game (e.g., bison, bighorn sheep, and elk), small resident game, waterfowl, and colonial nongame birds (e.g., pelicans, terns, and gulls). By far the most numerous are the waterfowl refuges, which variously supply breeding areas, wintering areas, and resting and feeding areas along major flyways during migration. Although the main purpose of the refuge system is to ensure survival of wildlife by providing suitable cover, food, and protection from man, many refuges permit hunting and fishing in season and other recreational activities such as hiking, boating, and swimming. Some refuges have been designated WILDERNESS areas. Refuges have been established by private individuals and societies (the Isaak Walton League, the Nature Conservancy, and the National Audubon Society are notable for their pioneering conservation work) and by all levels of government. The first state refuge was established by California in 1870; the first Federal refuge was Pelican Island in Florida (1903). Other countries throughout the world also maintain parks, refuges, and game preserves. One of the oldest is the vast Kruger National Park (est. 1898) for the preservation of big game in South Africa. In 1948 an international conference established the International Union for the Conservation of Nature and Natural Resources (IUCN). The first international organization devoted solely to wildlife conservation and environmental protection, the IUCN is now composed of 30 national governments and several hundred governmental and private organizations from more than 80 nations. The IUCN was instrumental in convening the 1973 meeting in Washington, D.C., that drafted the Convention on International Trade in Endangered Species of Wild Fauna and Flora. See George Laycock, *The Sign of the Flying Goose: A Guide to the National Wildlife Refuges* (1965); Robert Murphy, *Wild Sanctuaries* (1968); D. W. Ehrenfeld, *Conserving Life on Earth* (1972).

wild rice, tall aquatic plant *(Zizania aquatica)* of the family Gramineae (GRASS family), of a genus separate from common rice *(Oryza)*. Wild rice (called also Canada rice, Indian rice, and water oats) is a hardy annual with broad blades, reedy stems, and large terminal panicles. It grows best in shallow water along the margins of ponds or lakes in the N United States and S Canada; certain varieties grow also in the Southern states. Its seeds were one of the chief foods of certain Indian tribes, especially in the Great Lakes region. Indians of the Algonquian linguistic family, especially the Ojibwa and Menominee tribes, and certain Sioux tribes warred for centuries for control of the wild-rice fields. The Ojibwa called the grain *manomin* [good berry], and the Menominee are believed to have been named for a variant of this word; it is said to have some 60 synonyms, from which a great number of geographical names have been taken. The Indians gathered the seeds by pulling the grain heads over their canoes and flailing them with paddles; the seeds were sun-dried or parched over a slow fire to crack the hulls, then the grain was threshed by tramping, and winnowed. The harvest was traditionally followed by a thanksgiving festival. The seed is harvested today, especially in Minnesota, for the epicurean market and commands a high price. It is still gathered by primitive methods and has never been cultivated with success. Wild rice is an important source of food and shelter for fish and waterfowl and is sown for this purpose. It is also planted as an ornamental grass in home garden ponds and bogs. The seed is usually sown in the spring; it should first be soaked in water overnight. Manchurian wild rice *(Z. caducifolia)* is a smaller plant native to NE Asia. Wild rice is classified in the division MAGNOLIOPHYTA, class Liliatae, order Cyperiales, family Gramineae.

Wildwood, city (1970 pop. 4,110), Cape May co., SE N.J., on an island off Cape May; settled 1882, inc. as a city 1911. It has large commercial fisheries and is a popular seaside resort.

Wiley, Harvey Washington, 1844–1930, American chemist, b. Kent, Ind., grad. Hanover College, (B.A., 1867), M.D. Indiana Medical College, 1871. After serving (1874–83) as state chemist of Indiana, he was chief chemist of the U.S. Dept. of Agriculture (1883–1912) and professor of agricultural chemistry at George Washington Univ. (1899–1914). A prominent figure in the fight against food adulteration, he was largely responsible for the passage and administration of the Food and Drug Act of 1906. His writings include works on agricultural chemistry and food adulteration.

Wilfrid, Saint, 634–709?, English churchman, b. Northumbria, of noble parentage. He was educated at Lindisfarne and Canterbury. With Benedict Biscop he traveled to Lyons and Rome in 654; St. Wilfrid remained to study in each city. In 661 he returned to England and became abbot of Ripon. Moved by St. Wilfrid's eloquence, King Oswy at the Synod of Whitby (663; see WHITBY, SYNOD OF) rejected Celtic usages, including the reckoning of Easter, and established instead the Roman custom. That year Wilfrid was consecrated bishop of Ripon; in 669 his diocese was extended to include all of Northumbria with its see of York. There ensued a long controversy with the archbishop of Canterbury over division of dioceses in England. It was compromised with the aid of the pope, and Wilfrid ended as bishop of Ripon and Hexham. He made many converts and was responsible for the vigorous growth of Roman ecclesiastical practices in England. Feast: Oct. 12.

Wilhelm. For German rulers thus named, see WILLIAM.

Wilhelmina (vĭl″hĕlmē′nä), 1880–1962, queen of the Netherlands (1890–1948), daughter and successor of William III. Her mother, Emma of Waldeck-Pyrmont, was regent until 1898. Wilhelmina married (1901) Prince Henry of Mecklenburg-Schwerin (d. 1934), who played no active part in the government. The Salic law then having application in Luxembourg, the personal union of that grand duchy with the Netherlands was abrogated at her accession. The queen probably had a large share in the maintenance of Dutch neutrality in World War I and in the granting of asylum to William II of Germany after the war. When the Netherlands was invaded (May, 1940) by the Germans in World War II, Wilhelmina fled to England with her government; she made her formal return to the Netherlands in May, 1945. In 1948, after celebrating the 50th anniversary of her reign amid rejoicings that reflected her great popularity, Wilhelmina abdicated in favor of her daughter, Queen Juliana. See her autobiography (tr. 1960).

Wilhelmina, Mount, Indonesia: see TRIKORA PEAK.

Wilhelmshaven (vĭl″hĕlms-hä′fən), city (1970 pop. 102,732), Lower Saxony, NW West Germany, on Jade Bay, an inlet of the North Sea. It is a major oil port and an industrial center. Manufactures include heavy machinery, automobile chassis, electrical equipment, typewriters, and clothing. The city is also a summer resort. It is connected by a canal with Emden and by an oil pipeline with the RUHR district. Wilhelmshaven was founded in 1869 on territory purchased from Oldenburg in 1853. It was the chief German naval base on the North Sea until the end of World War II, after which its naval installations were dismantled. In 1956 it again was made a naval base. The city has marine biological and geological institutes and an ornithological station.

Wilkes, Charles, 1798–1877, American naval officer and explorer, b. New York City, educated by his father. In 1815 he entered the merchant service and received (1818) an appointment as a midshipman. For his survey (1832–33) of Narragansett Bay he was designated (1833) head of the department of charts and instruments of the navy. In command of a government exploring expedition Wilkes, then a lieutenant, set sail (1838) from Norfolk, Va., with a squadron of six ships; he was accompanied by trained scientists. They sailed around South America, did important research in the S Pacific, and explored the Antarctic. The portion of Antarctica that he is believed to have explored was subsequently named Wilkes Land. Wilkes explored Fiji in 1840, visited the Hawaiian group, and in May, 1841, entered the Strait of Juan de Fuca on the Pacific coast of the United States, and explored the Pacific Northwest. After having completely encircled the globe, he returned to New York in June, 1842. His *Narrative of the United States Exploring Expedition* (5 vol. and an atlas) appeared in 1844. He edited the scientific reports of the expedition (20 vol. and 11 atlases, 1844–74) and was the author of Vol. XI (*Meteorology*) and Vol. XIII (*Hydrography*). The impetuosity of his nature, for which he was twice court-martialed, was demonstrated when early in the Civil War, as commander of the *San Jacinto,* he stopped the British mail ship *Trent* and, contrary to all regulations, forcibly removed Confederate commissioners John Slidell and James M. Mason. The incident almost involved the Union in a war with England (see TRENT AFFAIR). Promoted to the rank of commodore in 1862, he commanded a squadron in the West Indies. See biography by Daniel Henderson (1953, repr. 1971); William Bixby, *The Forgotten Voyage of Charles Wilkes* (1966).

Wilkes, John, 1727–97, English politician and journalist. He studied at the Univ. of Leiden, returned to England in 1746, and purchased (1757) a seat in Parliament. Backed by Earl TEMPLE, Wilkes founded (1762) a periodical, the *North Briton,* in which he made outspoken attacks on GEORGE III and his ministers. In the famous issue No. 45 (1763), Wilkes went so far as to criticize the speech from the throne. He was immediately arrested on the basis of a general warrant (one that did not specify who was to be arrested), but his arrest was adjudged a breach of parliamentary privilege by Chief Justice Charles PRATT, who later ruled also that general warrants were illegal. The government then secured Wilkes's expulsion from Parliament on the grounds of seditious libel and obscenity (Wilkes was notoriously dissolute and the author of an obscene parody of Alexander Pope's *Essay on Man,* which was used against him). He fled (1764) to Paris and was convicted of seditious libel in his absence. He returned in 1768 and was repeatedly elected to Parliament from Middlesex, but each time he was denied his seat by the king's party. The issue, in the eyes of the angry populace, became a case of royal manipulation of parliamentary privilege against Wilkes to restrain the people's right to elect their own representatives. Wilkes was supported by Edmund Burke and the unknown writer JUNIUS, but he was not seated. After 22 months in prison for his libel conviction he was elected sheriff of London (1771) and lord mayor (1774). In 1774 he was again elected and this time allowed to take his seat in Parliament, where he championed the liberties of the American colonies and fought for parliamentary reform. He lost popular favor for his vigorous action as chamberlain of London in suppressing the Gordon riots (1780). Although a demagogue, Wilkes is remembered as a champion of freedom of the press and the rights of the electorate. See biographies by R. W. Postgate (1929), O. A. Sherrard (1930, repr. 1972), C. P. Chenevix Trench (1962), and Louis Kronenberger (1974); I. R. Christie, *Wilkes, Wyvill and Reform* (1962); G. F. E. Rudé, *Wilkes and Liberty* (1962).

Wilkes-Barre (wĭlks-bâr'ē), city (1970 pop. 58,856), seat of Luzerne co., E Pa., on the east bank of the Susquehanna River; settled 1769, inc. as a city 1871. Once a major anthracite coal center, Wilkes-Barre now has factories manufacturing pencils, radios, tires, and oil-refining equipment. The city was named for John Wilkes and Isaac Barre, defenders of the colonies before Parliament. The settlement was burned in 1778 by the British and Indians, just after the Wyoming Valley massacre, and was again burned in the second Pennamite Wars (see WYOMING VALLEY). Wilkes-Barre is the seat of Wilkes College, King's College, and a branch of Pennsylvania State Univ. The city has a symphony orchestra and a racetrack; the Swetland Homestead (early 1800s) is of historical interest. Much of Wilkes-Barre was severely damaged by the flooding of the Susquehanna in June, 1972.

Wilkes Land: see ANTARCTICA.

Wilkie, Sir David, 1785–1841, Scottish genre painter. He studied in Edinburgh and at the Royal Academy and won early popularity with his admirable little scenes of everyday life. Anecdotal painting was established in England with Wilkie's success. After traveling on the Continent, he turned to portraiture and historical painting. He became painter-in-ordinary to George IV and was knighted in 1836. Well-known examples of his work, including *The Blind Fiddler, The Village Festival,* and *Blind Man's Bluff,* are in the National Gallery and in the Tate Gallery, London.

Wilkins, Sir George Hubert, 1888–1958, British explorer, b. Australia. He made a number of trips to Antarctica and to the arctic regions. Valuable experience gained when he accompanied Vilhjalmur Stefansson's expedition (1913–18) to the arctic regions and Sir Ernest Shackleton's expedition (1921–22) to Antarctica prepared Wilkins to assume the leadership in the following years of a number of polar expeditions. A pioneer in the method of air exploration, he was the first to fly (1928) from North America to the European polar regions, traveling from Point Barrow, Alaska, to Spitsbergen; his *Flying the Arctic* (1928) described his observations during the flights. He was knighted that year. He commanded an antarctic exploration (1928–29) when flights were made in the region of Palmer Peninsula, and in 1931 he headed a submarine expedition to the arctic regions, an exploit depicted in his *Under the North Pole* (1931). Though mechanical difficulties made it impossible for his submarine, the *Nautilus,* to reach the North Pole, Wilkins's work was to be very valuable for future arctic exploration by submarine. From 1933 to 1939 he was manager for Lincoln Ellsworth's transantarctic expeditions. His *Thoughts Through Space* (with H. M. Sherman, 1942) recounts the attempts made by Wilkins and Sherman to communicate by mental telepathy during the period when Wilkins was searching (1938) for a group of Russian aviators lost in the arctic. During World War II and afterwards, Wilkins served as a geographer for the British army.

Wilkins, John, 1614–72, English mathematician. Informal gatherings held at his home at Oxford in which scientific experiments were discussed and performed led to the founding of the Royal Society, London. Wilkins disputed Copernicus' claim that the earth was a planet, and he wrote a fanciful account of the moon's inhabitants. His book *Mathematical Magic* (1648) is an account of the fundamental principles of mechanics and contains an argument on the possibility of perpetual motion.

Wilkins, Maurice Hugh Frederick, 1916–, Irish biophysicist, b. New Zealand, Ph.D. Univ. of Birmingham, 1940. He conducted research at the Univ. of St. Andrews, Scotland, and at the Univ. of London. In Berkeley, Calif., he worked (1944) for the Manhattan Project on the separation of uranium isotopes for use in atomic bombs. Shortly thereafter, he discontinued his research in nuclear physics to concentrate on problems in molecular biology, particularly the structure of DNA (see NUCLEIC ACID). In the early 1950s Wilkins successfully extracted some fibers from a gel of DNA. When analyzed by X-ray diffraction, the fibers appeared to have a helical molecular structure. On the basis of this helical structure and other scientific information, F. H. C. Crick and J. D. Watson built a model of the DNA molecule and explained its function. For their work the three men shared the 1962 Nobel Prize in Physiology and Medicine.

Wilkins, Roy, 1901–, American social reformer and civil rights leader; b. St. Louis, Mo.; grad. Univ. of Minnesota (B.A., 1923). While a student, Wilkins served as secretary of the local chapter of the National Association for the Advancement of Colored People (NAACP). Upon graduation, he joined the Kansas City (Mo.) *Call,* a black weekly newspaper, and was its managing editor until 1931, when he became assistant executive secretary of the NAACP and editor of its official magazine, *The Crisis.* In 1955 he became executive secretary of the NAACP and in 1965, when the title of the position was changed, executive director. In 1963 he helped organize the historic civil rights march on Washington, D.C. Devoted to the principle of nonviolence, Wilkins came under increasing attack in the 1960s and early 70s from more militant blacks.

Wilkinsburg, residential borough (1970 pop. 26,780), Allegheny co., SW Pa., a suburb of Pittsburgh; settled c.1800, inc. 1887.

Wilkinson, Charles Burnham (Bud Wilkinson), 1916–, American football coach, b. Minneapolis, Minn. He was an all-around athlete at the Univ. of Minnesota and later was assistant football coach at Syracuse Univ. and the Univ. of Minnesota before entering the U.S. navy in 1943. He became assistant coach at the Univ. of Oklahoma in 1945 and head coach in 1947. His teams won 31 consecutive games in 1948–51, and in 1953–57 they won 47 consecutive games, the longest winning record in modern football history. Oklahoma was national football champion in 1950, 1955, and 1956, and Wilkinson was named coach of the year in 1949 and again in 1950. He used the split-T attack on offense, and his teams were noted for their speed and determination. From 1961 to 1964 he was head of President Kennedy's youth fitness program, and he later served as a consultant to President Nixon.

Wilkinson, Ellen, 1891?–1947, English politician. Of a working-class family, she graduated from the Univ. of Manchester and became a union organizer. A Labour member of Parliament (1924–31, 1935–47), she was an impassioned fighter for socialist causes and became known as Red Ellen. In 1936 she led her constituents from the severely depressed town of Jarrow on a hunger march to London. She was parliamentary secretary to the ministry of home security during World War II and became minister of education in 1945.

Wilkinson, James, 1757–1825, American general, b. Calvert co., Md. Abandoning his medical studies in 1776 to join the army commanded by George Washington, he served as a captain in Benedict Arnold's unsuccessful Quebec campaign. Later he was Gen. Horatio Gate's deputy adjutant general in the Saratoga campaign and was given the honor of bringing to Congress the news of General Burgoyne's defeat. Congress censured Wilkinson for delay in carrying the dispatch but rewarded him by promoting him to brigadier general (1777) and making him secretary to the board of war (1778), a position he was forced to leave because of his implication in the Conway Cabal. He was (1779–81) clothier general of the army but resigned when charged with irregularities in his accounts. Wilkinson moved to Kentucky in 1784. Shortly thereafter, he became a key figure in the plan to induce what was then the SW United States to form a separate nation allied to Spain. Wilkinson apparently took an oath of allegiance to Spain and received a Spanish pension of $2,000 (and later $4,000) a year. To the Spanish authorities in New Orleans he represented his agitation for the separation of Kentucky from Virginia as part of this scheme; there is no indication, however, that he revealed any such motivation to the Kentucky conventions, in which others had expressed sentiments in favor of a separate republic of Kentucky. In 1791, Wilkinson reentered the army as a lieutenant colonel, and in 1792 he again attained the rank of brigadier general, serving under Anthony Wayne. On Wayne's death (1796) Wilkinson became ranking army officer. While governor (1805–1806) of the Louisiana Territory, he became involved in the schemes of Aaron BURR. Alarmed when he realized that his association with Burr was common knowledge, Wilkinson informed President Jefferson that Burr was plotting to disrupt the Union. Although he was chief prosecution witness at Burr's trial, he narrowly escaped indictment. Subsequently (1811) he was cleared, but just barely, by an army board of inquiry. In the War of 1812 he failed signally in the campaign to take Montreal and was relieved of his command. Once again an official inquiry left him untouched. He wrote *Memoirs of My Own Times* (3 vol., 1816) in an attempt to answer his many critics. He died in Mexico, where he spent his last years. See biographies by J. R. Jacobs (1938) and T. R. Hay and M. R. Werner (1941); J. E. Weems, *Men Without Countries* (1969).

Wilkinson, Jemima, 1752–1819, American religious leader, b. Cumberland, R.I. As a girl she was powerfully impressed by the sermons of George WHITEFIELD and also aspired to emulate the example of Ann LEE ("Mother Ann"). She became very ill when she was about 20 and fell into a prolonged coma. On reviving, she maintained that she had died and her original soul had gone to heaven while her body was occupied by the "Spirit of Life," sent by God to warn the world of His impending wrath. Calling herself the "Public Universal Friend," she preached widely through Connecticut and Rhode Island. She established churches at New Milford, Conn., and at Greenwich, R.I. She aroused much hostility by advocating celibacy, and she did not restrain enthusiastic followers from representing her as the Messiah. To escape persecution she founded (c.1790) the colony of "Jerusalem" in Yates co., NW N.Y. (near the present Penn Yan). Dissension later developed in Jerusalem because the "Friend" demanded gifts of her followers and instituted punishments for breaking her rules. She spent her last years in a house far from the other dwellings. After her death the community dispersed. See David Hudson, *Memoir of Jemima Wilkinson* (1824, repr. 1972); H. A. Wisbey, *Pioneer Prophetess* (1964).

will, in law, document expressing the wishes of a person (known as a testator) concerning the disposition of his PROPERTY after his death. If a person dies intestate, i.e., without a valid will, statutes determine how his property is divided up among his relatives; if no relatives can be found, the property escheats (i.e., goes to the government). Wills are made to vary the statutory scheme (e.g., to give a crippled child more money than a healthy child). The will may provide for outright grants or for the establishment of TRUSTS. No particular form of words is necessary in a will, only a clear expression of intent. Statutes usually protect the surviving spouse and children, prescribing for them a set proportion of the estate whatever the provisions of the will. Wills ordinarily must be in writing, but in certain strictly defined circumstances (e.g., in the case of soldiers or sailors in combat) the law may recognize an oral will as reported by a witness. Written wills must be subscribed (i.e., signed below the complete text) by the testator and must bear the signatures of two (or, in some jurisdictions, three) people who witnessed the testator's signature. A person has capacity to make a will only when he is of sound mind and is not unduly influenced by an interested party. Persons below a certain age (usually ranging from 18 to 21) are deemed not to have the capacity. All objections to a will must be made at the PROBATE, which precedes the distribution (administration) of the property. Real and personal property were once passed on by two different systems, but today only remnants of the division remain (e.g., in separate sets of terms). In England the Statute of Wills (1540) lifted many restrictions on the use of wills and permitted the testator to dispose of real property by will. See HEIR.

will, in philosophy and psychology, term used to describe that which is alleged to stimulate the motivation of purposeful activity. It is characteristic of the will that it can be observed only in oneself and can be attributed to others only by inference from their behavior. There is no generally accepted explanation in psychology for the apparent freedom men enjoy to do what they will, i.e., to originate the stimuli necessary to initiate a course of action. Until recently the psychological discussions of the will have been closely related to the philosophical. Disagreements have been extreme. One approach has been the doctrine of determinism, which denies the reality of the will. Another type simply accepts the will—the motive power of the personality—as the faculty or function of the person. This idea is generally based on intuitive grounds and is associated with Plato, Aristotle, Lucretius, St. Thomas Aquinas,

René Descartes, and Immanuel Kant. Others have considered it the externalized result of the interaction of conflicting elements. These include Baruch Spinoza, G. W. von Leibniz, David Hume, J. G. Herbart, Wilhelm Wundt, Herbert Spencer, and Hugo Münsterberg. Still others have considered the will to be the manifestation of the personality striving to accomplish its purposes. Among these are St. Augustine, Duns Scotus, Thomas Hobbes, Arthur Schopenhauer, Friedrich Nietzsche, William McDougall, and John Dewey. Modern psychology has tended to consider the concept of the will as an unscientific principle. The problems involved in dealing with it are largely absorbed in other areas of investigation, such as the psychology of adjustment, the study of unconscious motivation, the concept of attention, and the influence of endocrine balance. See V. J. Bourke, *Will in Western Thought* (1964).

Willaert, Adrian (äd'rēän vĭl'ärt), c.1490–1562, Flemish composer. After brief engagements at Ferrara and Milan, he was choirmaster at St. Mark's, Venice, from 1527 until his death. Willaert was the founder of the Venetian school of composition. His polychoral settings of psalms and the Magnificat helped popularize this technique, and he and his followers were important in the development of the madrigal. Among his works are masses, motets, instrumental *ricercari,* and French and Italian secular songs.

Willamette (wĭlăm'ĭt), river, 294 mi (473 km) long, rising in several headstreams in the Cascade Range, W Oregon. It flows N past Eugene, Salem, and Portland to the Columbia River just NW of Portland. The river is navigable for most of its course. Its wide, fertile valley is a major fruit-growing and dairying region. There is also diversified agriculture, manufacturing, and an important lumber industry. A Federal project begun in 1938 harnesses the river and its tributaries for flood control, navigation, and power production with numerous dams and reservoirs in the Willamette basin. First settled in the 1830s, the valley was the goal of many pioneers traveling west to the Oregon Country on the Oregon Trail. The region quickly became the chief source of food products on the West coast, especially with the California gold rush in the mid-1800s. Rapidly settled after 1846, the valley has long been the most densely populated part of Oregon.

Willamette University, at Salem, Oregon; coeducational; United Methodist; opened 1844 as Oregon Institute; the oldest institution of higher learning in the Far West. It was chartered and renamed in 1853.

Willard, Daniel, 1861–1942, American railroad executive, b. Windsor co., Vt. A self-made man, he started as a track laborer (1879) and rose to be president of the Baltimore and Ohio RR from 1910 to 1941. See biography by Edward Hungerford (1938).

Willard, Emma, 1787–1870, American educator, pioneer in woman's education, b. Emma Hart in Berlin, Conn. She attended and later taught in the local academy and in 1807 took charge of the Female Academy at Middlebury, Vt. Two years later she married Dr. John Willard. In 1814 she opened a school in her home, where she taught subjects not then available to women. In 1818 she addressed to the New York legislature an appeal for support of her plan for improving female education, and Governor Clinton invited her to move to New York state. Her school was opened (1819) at Waterford, but promised financial support was not forthcoming, and in 1821 the Troy Female Seminary was founded under her leadership. Troy became famous, offering collegiate education to women and new opportunity to women teachers. She wrote a number of textbooks, a journal of her trip abroad in 1830, and a volume of poems, including "Rocked in the Cradle of the Deep." In 1838 Willard retired from active management of the school, which was later renamed in her honor. She devoted the remainder of her life to the improvement of common schools and to the cause of woman's education. See Alma Lutz, *Emma Willard, Daughter of Democracy* (1929) and *Emma Willard, Pioneer Educator of American Women* (1964).

Willard, Frances Elizabeth, 1839–98, American temperance leader and reformer, b. Churchville, N.Y., grad. Northwestern Female College, 1859. She was president of Evanston College for Ladies and dean of women at Northwestern Univ. After leaving the university, she helped organize (1874) the WOMAN'S CHRISTIAN TEMPERANCE UNION and in 1879 became its president. She devoted most of her life to the organization of women for the prohibition of alcoholic beverages but was active in other causes, especially that of woman suffrage. See her autobiography, *Glimpses of Fifty Years* (1889); biographies by Mary Earhart (1944) and M. L. Gates (1964).

Willard, Solomon, 1783–1861, American architect and sculptor, b. Petersham, Mass. Arriving in Boston in 1804, he eventually became a leading architect; he both designed and supervised the erection of the Bunker Hill monument. He carved the architectural detail of many Boston buildings, as well as ships' figureheads, including the figure for the frigate *Washington* (U.S. Naval Academy, Annapolis, Md.). He taught drawing and sculpture in Boston, where Horatio Greenough was one of his pupils.

Willemstad (vĭl'əmstät), city (1960 pop. 43,547), CURAÇAO, capital of the Netherlands Antilles. The city is the commercial and industrial center of the Netherlands Antilles as well as a free port and tourist center. It is especially important as a transshipment point and refining center for petroleum sent across the Gulf of Venezuela from MARACAIBO. Neat and attractive, its streets lined by narrow, gabled houses, Willemstad has a distinctive Dutch character.

Willesden: see BRENT.

Willet, Marinus (mərē'nəs wĭl'ĭt), 1740–1830, American Revolutionary soldier, b. Jamaica, N.Y. In the French and Indian War he was (1758) a member of the expeditions against Fort Ticonderoga and Fort Frontenac. He was a leader of the Sons of Liberty in New York and, after the outbreak of the American Revolution, served under Richard Montgomery in the invasion of Canada. He won (1777) a victory over the British under Barry St. Leger while second in command at Fort Stanwix (Fort Schuyler), joined George Washington's army in New Jersey in 1778, and participated (1779) in the Clinton-Sullivan expedition against the Iroquois. From 1780 until the end of the war he commanded New York troops in the Mohawk valley, and there his scouts managed to kill (Oct., 1781) Walter BUTLER after a skirmish with Loyalists. After the war he negotiated (1790) a treaty with the Creek Indians of Georgia. Later Willett, a partisan of Aaron Burr and a Republican, held several local offices in New York City, where he served (1807–8) as mayor. See his *Narrative of the Military Actions of Colonel Marinus Willett* (1831, repr. 1969), biography by Howard Thomas (1954).

William I, 1797–1888, emperor of Germany (1871–88) and king of Prussia (1861–88), second son of the future King Frederick William III of Prussia and Louise of Mecklenburg. Essentially conservative, William fled to England during the revolutionary uprisings of 1848 in Prussia, and upon his return (1849) he commanded the troops that crushed the republican insurrection in Baden. When his brother King Frederick William IV was declared insane, William became (1858) regent, and on Frederick William's death William became king of Prussia. William immediately set about reorganizing and strengthening the army, and when he met the opposition of the legislature, he appointed Otto von BISMARCK his prime minister in 1862. From then until the emperor's death, Bismarck guided the destiny of Prussia and Germany. Opposition to the king's and Bismarck's military program was suppressed, and in 1864 Prussia began its career of military conquest in the war with Denmark over SCHLESWIG-HOLSTEIN. This led to the AUSTRO-PRUSSIAN WAR of 1866, from which Prussia emerged the leading German power. William I commanded in person in the FRANCO-PRUSSIAN WAR of 1870–71, received the surrender of Napoleon III at Sedan, and was proclaimed (Jan. 18, 1871) emperor of Germany in the Hall of Mirrors at Versailles (see GERMANY). Although William often disagreed with Bismarck's policies, he ultimately was always persuaded by his chancellor. William did not favor the KULTURKAMPF (Bismarck's struggle against the Roman Catholic Church) but gave it his tacit consent. As a symbol of reborn German unity he was popular, but his militarism and belief in his divine right to rule drew upon him the hatred of the radical elements. Two attempts on William's life (1878) enabled Bismarck to pass severe legislation against the socialists. William's reign was crucial in European history, for it saw Germany's rise to power on the continent. His son Frederick III succeeded him. See Paul Wiegler, *William the First* (1927, tr. 1929); Theo Aronson, *The Kaisers* (1971).

William II, 1859–1941, emperor of Germany and king of Prussia (1888–1918), son and successor of Frederick III and grandson of William I of Germany and of Queen Victoria of England. He was early alienated from his liberal-minded parents by his belief in the divine nature of kingship, his love of military display, and his impulsiveness. Much has been made of the fact that he had a withered left arm, in order to explain these traits as a compensation for his physical weakness. After studying at the Univ. of Bonn, he entered the army and in 1881 married Princess Augusta Victoria of Schleswig-Holstein. As emperor, William endeavored to maintain and, if possible, to extend the royal prerogative to make Germany a major naval, colonial, and commercial power. Friction soon developed between him and Otto von BISMARCK, the chancellor who had controlled German affairs for nearly 30 years, and Bismarck was forced to resign in 1890. Succeeding chancellors (Leo von CAPRIVI, Prince HOHENLOHE-SCHILLINGSFÜRST, Prince von BÜLOW, and Theobold von BETHMANN-HOLLWEG) were much less influential, and William was in general the dominating force in his own government. In domestic affairs he extended social reform, although he detested the socialists. The conduct of foreign affairs was his major interest, but he had no basic policy and was greatly influenced by his ministers. The reinsurance treaty with Russia, which had been a chief feature of Bismarck's system of alliance, was not renewed in 1890. Although sincerely desirous of maintaining friendly relations with Great Britain, William by his naval program and his colonial and commercial aspirations precluded an alliance between the two countries and drove England into the Entente Cordiale with France (see TRIPLE ALLIANCE AND TRIPLE ENTENTE). The German support of Russia in East Asia and the friendly relations between William and Czar Nicholas II of Russia (as revealed in the "Willy-Nicky" correspondence) were counteracted by the encouragement William gave to Austria in its Balkan policy. The already strained relations with France were further embittered by German interference in French colonial affairs in Africa, especially in MOROCCO. Alarmed at the growing isolation of Germany, William strengthened the Triple Alliance with Austria and Italy and secured Turkish adherence. The emperor was fond of travel, but his state visits frequently engendered ill feeling, as in the Moroccan crisis of 1905. His combined eloquence and impetuousness led him to speak or act unadvisedly on many occasions. Among the more famous incidents was his dispatch of a telegram of encouragement to President Paul KRUGER of the Transvaal after the Boers had repulsed a British raid on the Transvaal (Dec., 1895; see JAMESON, SIR LEANDER STARR). The message aroused British public opinion against Germany and the emperor. Again, in 1908, in the *Daily Telegraph* affair, William's indiscretion caused a public furor in Great Britain and in Germany. In an interview with the London *Daily Telegraph,* William revealed that German naval expansion was not directed at Great Britain, but at Japan. He also stated that German public opinion was anti-British, but that he did not share this sentiment. The affair produced a widespread demand for a check on the emperor's personal rule. After the outbreak of WORLD WAR I William's power declined. From 1917 the military leaders Erich LUDENDORFF and Paul von HINDENBURG were the virtual dictators of Germany. The failure of the great German drive of 1918 was a prelude to the collapse of the Hohenzollern dynasty. The last chancellor of the German Empire, MAXIMILIAN, PRINCE OF BADEN, negotiated for an armistice, but clamor for the emperor's abdication began to be heard in Germany, especially after U.S. President Woodrow Wilson made it a prerequisite of peace negotiations. Naval mutiny and civilian revolt were followed by republican proclamations in leading German cities. On Nov. 9, 1918, Prince Max, without William's consent, announced the emperor's abdication. William fled to Holland and two weeks later formally abdicated in his own name and that of his family. Although the Treaty of Versailles provided that William be tried for promoting the war, the Dutch government refused to extradite him, and he remained in retirement at Doorn. There, after the death of Augusta Victoria, he married the widowed Princess Hermine of Schönaich-Carolath (1922). See his memoirs (tr. 1922); *My Early Life* (tr. 1926); Joachim von Kürenberg, *The Kaiser* (tr. 1954); Theo Aronson, *The Kaisers* (1971); Michael Balfour, *The Kaiser and His Times* (1972).

William, ruler of Albania: see WILLIAM, PRINCE OF WIED.

William I or **William the Conqueror,** 1027?–1087, king of England (1066–87). The illegitimate son of Robert I, duke of Normandy, and Arletta, daughter of a tanner, he is sometimes called William the Bastard. He succeeded to the dukedom on his father's death in 1035. William and his guardians were hard pressed to keep down recurrent rebellions during his minority, and at least once the young duke barely escaped death. In 1047, with the aid of HENRY I of

France, he solidly established his power. William is said to have visited England in 1051 or 1052, when his cousin EDWARD THE CONFESSOR probably promised that William should succeed him as king of England. Despite a papal prohibition, William married Matilda, daughter of Baldwin, count of Flanders, in 1053. The union, which greatly increased the duke's prestige, did not receive papal dispensation until 1059. William's growing power brought him into conflict with King Henry of France, whose invading armies he defeated in 1054 and 1058. The accession (1060) of the child Philip I of France, whose guardian was William's father-in-law, improved his position, and in 1063 William conquered the county of Maine. Soon afterward HAROLD, then earl of Wessex, was shipwrecked on the French coast and was turned over to William, who apparently extracted Harold's oath to support the duke's interests in England. Upon hearing that Harold had been crowned (1066) king of England, William secured the sanction of the pope, raised an army and transport fleet, sailed for England, and defeated and slew Harold at the battle of HASTINGS (1066). Overcoming what little resistance remained in SE England, he led his army to London, received the city's submission, and was crowned king on Christmas Day. Although William immediately began to build and garrison castles around the country, he apparently hoped to maintain continuity of rule; many of the English nobility had fallen at Hastings, but most of those who survived were permitted to keep their lands for the time being. The English, however, did not so readily accept him as their king. A series of rebellions broke out, and William suppressed them harshly, ravaging great sections of the country. Titles to the lands of the now decimated native nobility were called in and redistributed, on a strictly feudal basis (see FEUDALISM), to the king's Norman followers. By 1072 the adherents of EDGAR ATHELING and their Scottish and Danish allies had been defeated and the military part of the NORMAN CONQUEST virtually completed. In the only major rebellion that came thereafter (1075), the chief rebels were Normans. William undertook church reform, appointed LANFRANC archbishop of Canterbury, substituted foreign prelates for many of the English bishops, took command over the administration of church affairs, and established (1076) separate ecclesiastical courts. In 1085-86 at his orders a survey of England was taken, the results of which were embodied in the DOMESDAY BOOK. By the Oath of Salisbury in 1086, William established the important precedent that loyalty to the king is superior to loyalty to any subordinate feudal lord of the kingdom. William fought with his factious son ROBERT II, duke of Normandy, in 1079 and quarreled intermittently with France from 1080 until his death. He invaded the French Vexin in 1087, was fatally injured in a riding accident, and died at Rouen, directing that his son Robert should succeed him in Normandy and his son William (William II) in England. Earnest and resourceful, William was not only one of the greatest of English monarchs but a pivotal figure in European history as well. See biographies by F. M. Stenton (1908, repr. 1967), D. C. Douglas (1964), and David Walker (1968); F. M. Maitland, *Domesday Book and Beyond* (1897, repr. 1966); Frank Barlow, *William I and the Norman Conquest* (1965); F. M. Stenton, *Anglo-Saxon England* (3d ed. 1971).

William II or **William Rufus** (ro͞o'fus), d. 1100, king of England (1087-1100), son and successor of William I. He was called William Rufus or William the Red because of his ruddy complexion. His first act as king was to put down the effort of his uncle, Odo of Bayeux, to seat William I's eldest son, ROBERT II, duke of Normandy, on the English throne. Having quelled the rebellion in England, William invaded (1090) Normandy, secured a portion of Robert's lands, and then agreed to help his brother regain lands, most notably Maine, that Robert had previously lost. After his return to England, William forced MALCOLM III of Scotland to do him homage (1091) and seized (1092) the city of Carlisle from the Scots. Having quarreled with Robert over their agreement of 1091, William again invaded Normandy in 1094 and bribed Philip I of France to withdraw his support from Robert. In 1095 he suppressed an English rebellion led by the earl of Northumberland and made an unsuccessful expedition against the Welsh. A second Welsh campaign in 1097 was also ineffective, but in that year William gained control of the Scottish throne by sanctioning the successful expedition of EDGAR ATHELING to dethrone Malcolm III's son Donald Bane. In the meantime Robert, who needed money to go on the First Crusade, had pledged (1096) his duchy to William in return for the sum of 10,000 marks. From 1097 to 1099 William was engaged primarily in campaigns in France, securing and holding northern Maine but failing in his attempt to seize the French Vexin. At the time of his death he was planning to occupy Aquitaine. William ruled England with a strong hand and aroused the hatred particularly of the church, for which he had utter contempt. He extorted large sums of money from the church by the sale of church appointments and by leaving sees and abbeys vacant so that their revenues would come to him. Although responsible for the appointment (1093) of Saint ANSELM as archbishop of Canterbury, he quarreled with the archbishop over the question of INVESTITURE and finally drove him into exile in 1097. William was killed by an arrow while on a hunting party, and there is some evidence to suggest that his death was not an accident. The English throne was immediately seized by his younger brother, HENRY I. See E. A. Freeman, *The Reign of William Rufus* (1882, repr. 1970); A. L. Poole, *From Domesday Book to Magna Carta* (2d ed., 1955); D. W. Grinnell-Milne, *The Killing of William Rufus* (1968).

William III, 1650-1702, king of England, Scotland, and Ireland (1689-1702); son of William II, prince of Orange, stadtholder of the United Provinces of the Netherlands, and of Mary, oldest daughter of King Charles I of England. He was born at The Hague after his father's death, when the office of stadtholder was suspended and power fell into the hands of Jan de WITT. In 1672, however, a revolution was precipitated by Louis XIV's invasion of the Netherlands; De Witt was overthrown, and William was made stadtholder, captain general, and admiral for life. In the ensuing warfare with France (see DUTCH WARS 3), William was able to drive the French out of the Netherlands. He made peace with England in 1674, and finally with France in 1678. Thereafter he endeavored to build up a European coalition to prevent further French aggression. In 1677, William had married the English Princess Mary (see MARY II), Protestant daughter of the Roman Catholic James, duke of York (later JAMES II). After James's succession (1685) to the English throne, the Protestant William kept in close contact with the opposition to the king. Finally, after the birth of a son to James in 1688, William was invited to England by seven important nobles. He landed in Devon with an army of 15,000 and advanced to London, meeting virtually no opposition. James was allowed to escape to France. Early in 1689, William summoned a Convention Parliament and accepted its offer of the crown jointly with his wife. The GLORIOUS REVOLUTION was thus accomplished in England without bloodshed, and it proved a decisive victory for Parliament in its long struggle with the crown; William was forced to accept the BILL OF RIGHTS (1689), which greatly limited the royal power and prescribed the line of succession, and to give Parliament control of finances and of the army. In Scotland, the JACOBITES resisted violently but after their defeat at Killiecrankie (1689), William was able to make Scottish Presbyterianism secure. He blackened his reputation, however, by apparently condoning the bloody massacre of GLENCOE (1692). In Ireland, after William's victory over the exiled James at the battle of the Boyne (1690) and the conclusion of the Treaty of Limerick (1691), the PENAL LAWS against Roman Catholics were increased in severity. The Jacobite effort in Ireland had been supported by Louis XIV, who hoped thus to divert William from the larger war then being fought on the Continent (see GRAND ALLIANCE, WAR OF THE). William, however, took an English army to the Spanish Netherlands in 1691 and was constantly involved in campaigning until the conclusion of peace by the Treaty of Ryswick (1697). William attempted to ignore the party divisions in England, but he was forced to rely increasingly on Whig ministers because only the Whigs supported his foreign policy fully. His Whig ministers, most notably Charles Montagu, earl of HALIFAX, were responsible for establishment (1694) of the BANK OF ENGLAND and the policy of the national debt. William and the Whigs were also responsible for the Toleration Act (1689), which lifted some of the disabilities imposed on Protestant nonconformists, and for allowing the Licensing Act to lapse (1695), a great step toward freedom of the press. William sought to maintain royal prerogatives but was unable to prevent passage of the Triennial Act (1694), which required a new Parliament every three years, and the Act of SETTLEMENT (1701), which imposed the first statutory limitation on royal control of foreign policy. A center of disaffection from c.1690 was the household of the queen's sister Anne (later Queen ANNE), who, with her favorites, the Marlboroughs, had been alienated by the hostile attitude of William and Mary. William's popularity diminished greatly after the death (1694) of the childless Queen Mary, and his concern near the end of his life with the Partition Treaties and with the War of the Spanish Succession (see SPANISH SUCCESSION, WAR OF THE), in which England was involved in another long duel with France, did nothing to improve it. William's personality was cold and his public policy calculating, but he was an able soldier and an astute politician, and his reign was of momentous constitutional importance. A standard source for William's time is the history of Gilbert BURNET. See biographies by N. A. Robb (2 vol., 1962-66), Stephen Baxter (1966), and H. and B. C. Van der Zee (1973); studies by Lucile Pinkham (1954, repr. 1969) and David Ogg (1956, repr. 1969); G. N. Clarke, *The Later Stuarts* (2d ed. 1956).

William IV, 1765-1837, king of Great Britain and Ireland (1830-37), third son of George III. He went to sea in 1779, served under Admiral George Rodney in action off Cape St. Vincent (1780), and by 1786 was a captain. William became duke of Clarence in 1789 and was advanced by 1799 to the rank of admiral, but he saw little active service after 1790. Meanwhile in the House of Lords he opposed the antislavery movement and supported the extravagances of his oldest brother (later George IV). About 1791 he formed a liaison with Mrs. Jordan, an actress, with whom he lived for over 20 years. He married (1818) Adelaide, daughter of the duke of Saxe-Meiningen, and on the death (1827) of the duke of York, second son of George III, he became heir presumptive to the throne. Made lord high admiral in 1827, he tried to run naval affairs without his council, contrary to law, and was forced to resign (1828). In 1830 he succeeded George IV as king. His most important public act was his promise, given most reluctantly, to the 2d Earl GREY that he would, if necessary, create enough Whig peers to pass the REFORM BILL of 1832. This bill and such reforms as the education act, the new poor law, the municipal corporations act, and the abolition of slavery in the empire marked his reign, but he maintained the generally passive attitude toward politics formed during his many years as younger brother of the king. Political leadership was left to the duke of WELLINGTON, Earl Grey, Viscount MELBOURNE, and Sir Robert PEEL. Good-natured but eccentric and given to ill-considered public utterances, William was only moderately popular. He was succeeded by his niece, Victoria. See biographies by W. G. Allen (1960) and Philip Ziegler (1971).

William I, 1772-1843, first king of the Netherlands and grand duke of Luxembourg (1815-40), son of Prince William V of Orange, last stadtholder of the Netherlands. He commanded (1793-95) the Dutch army in the French Revolutionary Wars, and after the French occupation of the Netherlands he entered the Prussian and later the Austrian service. He returned to the Netherlands in 1813, and the Congress of Vienna gave him (1815) the title king of the Netherlands. His kingdom comprised present BELGIUM as well as the Netherlands, and he was awarded the grand duchy of LUXEMBOURG in compensation for his family holdings in Germany, which he ceded to Prussia. William soon alienated his Belgian subjects by attempting to make Dutch the official language, by granting disproportionate influence to the northern provinces, and by encroaching on the freedom of the Roman Catholic Church. Political unrest in Belgium led to the revolution of 1830, which he stubbornly sought to suppress despite the intervention of England and France (see LONDON CONFERENCE). Belgium won its independence, but final recognition by William came only in 1839. When his Dutch subjects forced him to liberalize the constitution in 1840, he abdicated in favor of his son William II. Though his rule was reactionary, William fostered the development of Dutch agriculture, commerce, and industry.

William II, 1792-1849, king of the Netherlands and grand duke of Luxembourg (1840-49), son and successor of William I. He served with Wellington in the Peninsular War, was wounded at Waterloo, and led the Dutch army in the Belgian revolution (1830), after his father had failed to approve his efforts at conciliation. Called to the throne upon the abdication of his father (1840), William II was immediately confronted with a grave financial problem, which was solved by raising a "voluntary loan" among the people. Demand mounted for constitutional revision, but the king resisted the liberal movement, led by Jan THORBECKE, until the revolutionary spirit of 1848 induced him to grant the desired reforms. He was succeeded by his son, William III.

William III, 1817-90, king of the Netherlands and grand duke of Luxembourg (1849-90), son and successor of William II. William III ruled as a constitutional monarch, and his long reign was unmarred by friction with the States-General. He granted a parliamentary constitution to his Luxembourg subjects and maintained Luxembourg's neutrality in the Franco-Prussian War (1870-71). The leading Dutch statesman during his reign was Jan THORBECKE, who obtained full emancipation of the Dutch Catholics and also promoted economic growth and political reform. With William's death the male Dutch line of the house of Orange-Nassau became extinct. The Netherlands crown passed to his daughter, WILHELMINA, but Luxembourg went to Duke Adolph of Nassau, from a collateral line of the family.

William, king of Scotland: see WILLIAM THE LION.

William II (William the Good), c.1153-1189, king of Sicily (1166-89), son and successor of William I. He married (1177) Joan, daughter of Henry II of England. As an ally of Pope Alexander III and the Lombard League, he was at war with Holy Roman Emperor Frederick I, but in 1184 he made peace in order to resume the attempts of his grandfather, Roger II, to conquer the Byzantine Empire. He took Durazzo and Salonica, but was defeated (1185) by Isaac II. When he died childless, his kingdom was claimed by his aunt CONSTANCE, whom he had designated as his successor, but the crown went instead to his cousin TANCRED of Lecce.

William I, 1781-1864, king of Württemberg (1816-64), son and successor of Frederick I. Before his accession he fought (1812) with the French emperor Napoleon I in Russia and later, when Frederick I had broken his alliance with France, William served with the anti-French forces (1814-15). As king, William granted a constitution in 1819, strove to protect the rights of the smaller German states against both Austria and Prussia, and promoted the ZOLLVEREIN, the German customs union.

William or **Frederick William,** 1882-1951, crown prince of Germany, son of William II. In World War I he commanded (1914) an army on the Western Front and was nominal commander in the German attack (1916) on Verdun. He fled to Holland in Nov., 1918, and renounced his rights to the throne, but returned (1923) to Germany with the permission of the Weimar government. He supported Adolf Hitler for a time.

William I, prince of Orange: see WILLIAM THE SILENT.

William II, 1626-50, prince of Orange, stadholder of the United Provinces of the Netherlands (1647-50), son and successor of Frederick Henry. He married (1641) Mary, eldest daughter of Charles I of England. His ambitious projects brought him into conflict with the great merchants of Amsterdam. He opposed acceptance of the Treaty of Münster (1648), despite its recognition of the independence of the Netherlands, and he immediately began secret negotiations with France, having as his purpose the extension of his territory, the centralization of his government, and the restoration of his brother-in-law, Charles II, to the English throne. The prompt resistance he encountered from the states of Holland was broken by William's imprisonment of its leaders (1650). He next turned his attention to external affairs and was negotiating a treaty with France when he died of smallpox. He was succeeded by his posthumous son, the future William III of England.

William III, prince of Orange: see WILLIAM III, king of England.

William, prince of Wied, 1876-1945, mpret [ruler] of Albania (1914), third son of William, prince of Wied, nephew of Elizabeth of Rumania. A German army officer, he was selected by the great powers of Europe, with consent of the Albanians, to be ruler of the independent Albania that was created after the BALKAN WARS. Civil war soon made his position untenable, and he had no support among the large powers. The coming of World War I broke down all foreign aid. A rebellion under Essad Pasha was successful, and in Sept., 1914, William was forced to retire, although he refused to abdicate.

William, count of Holland, 1227?-1256, German king (1254-56), previously rival king (1247-54) to CONRAD IV. William was chosen by Pope INNOCENT IV to succeed Henry Raspe (d. 1247) as antiking to Conrad IV during the conflict between Innocent and Conrad's father, Holy Roman Emperor FREDERICK II. Although William was recognized as king by most of the German princes after Conrad's death (1254), his rule was only nominal and was never unchallenged. His major support came from the Rhenish towns. He was killed fighting the Frisians.

William and Mary in Virginia, College of, mainly at Williamsburg; state supported; coeducational; chartered 1693, opened 1694 by Episcopalians under James BLAIR. It became a university in 1779. The second oldest institution of higher learning in the United States, it traces its descent from plans for a university of Henrico in 1618, which were put aside after the Indian massacre of 1622. The college was closed when it was occupied (1781) by Revolutionary troops, in the Civil War, and again from 1881 to 1888 for lack of funds (see EWELL, BENJAMIN STODDERT). Phi Beta Kappa was founded there in 1776, and in 1779 the elective system and the honor system were first introduced. William and Mary established the first school of law in the United States and pioneered also in the teaching of political economy, natural philosophy, and modern history and languages. The college also operates Richmond Professional Institute, a four-year college at Norfolk. The Institute of Early American History and Culture, which publishes the historical periodical *The William and Mary Quarterly,* is there. The college library houses noted collections relating to Virginian and U.S. history.

William Henry, Fort: see FORT WILLIAM HENRY.

William Howard Taft National Historic Site: see NATIONAL PARKS AND MONUMENTS (table).

William of Champeaux (shămpō', shäNpō'), c.1070-1121, French scholastic philosopher. William studied and taught in Paris. In 1109 he founded the monastic school of St. Victor, which later became famous. From 1113 until his death he was bishop of Châlons-sur-Marne. Although very little of his writings has survived, William is known for his role in the dispute over the nature of universals in the Middle Ages (see REALISM). An extreme realist, he was forced to change his views after being overcome in a disputation with his pupil Peter ABELARD.

William of Longchamp: see LONGCHAMP, WILLIAM OF.

William of Malmesbury (mämz'bərē), c.1096-1143, English writer, monk of Malmesbury. His most important work is the *Gesta regum Anglorum,* a history of the kings of England from 449 to 1127, with its continuation, *Historia novella* (ed. by William Stubbs, 1887-89). Book V is contemporary history, especially valuable for the reigns of Henry I and Stephen. The work appeared in English as *The Chronicle of the Kings of England* (see ed. by J. A. Giles, 1847, repr. 1968). He also wrote *Gesta pontificum Anglorum,* a source for early ecclesiastical history and for several saints' lives.

William of Newburgh, 1136?-1198?, English chronicler, monk of Newburgh, Yorkshire. He wrote the *Historia rerum Anglicarum,* a history of England from 1066 to 1198. Its chief value lies in the commentary on contemporary events, particularly its analysis of the causes and effects of the anarchy under King Stephen. See the translation of the history by Joseph Stevenson in his *Church Historians of England,* Vol. IV (1856).

William of Occam or **Ockham** (both: ŏk'əm), c.1285-c.1349, English scholastic philosopher. A Franciscan, Occam studied and taught at Oxford from c.1310 until 1324, when he was summoned to the papal court at Avignon to answer charges of heresy in his writings. He waited there until 1328 for a judgment. When it appeared that Pope John XXII was about to condemn his position Occam fled to the protection of Holy Roman Emperor Louis IV, whom he supported in his struggle with Pope John. He is thought to have died in the black plague that swept Europe in the middle of the 14th cent. Occam's teachings mark an important break with previous medieval philosophy, especially with the Aristotelian realism of St. Thomas Aquinas. A nominalist, he denied that the forms of knowledge corresponded to those of being. Men's concepts he saw to be naturally occasioned by the world, but thought could not be taken as a measure of being. Specifically, Occam denied the existence of universals except in men's minds and in language. An empiricist, Occam disputed the self-evidence of principles of Aristotelian logic (like the final cause) and of Christian theology (like the existence of God). For this reason Occam severely restricted the province of philosophy in order to safeguard theology, denying the competence of reason in matters of faith. Just as he had maintained a distinction between men's concepts and being, he saw creation not as a necessary consequence of the divine intellect, as Aquinas had, but as an expression of God's limitless will. In the area of logic, where he had great influence, he is remembered for his use of the principle of parsimony, formulated as "Occam's razor," which enjoined economy in explanation with the axiom, "What can be done with fewer [assumptions] is done in vain with more." Like Marsilius of Padua, Occam strongly opposed the temporal power of the pope and wrote numerous works on the subject. His *Dialogus* is a thorough discussion of political theories. See his philosophical writings (tr. and ed. by Philotheus Boehner, 1957); see also Ernest Addison Moody, *The Logic of William of Ockham* (1935, repr. 1965); A. S. McCrade, *The Political Thought of William of Ockham* (1974).

William of Orange: see WILLIAM THE SILENT; WILLIAM II, prince of Orange; WILLIAM III, king of England.

William of Tyre (tī'ər), b. c.1130, d. before 1185, historian and churchman. Born in the Latin Kingdom of Jerusalem and possibly of French extraction, he received his education at Antioch and in Europe. In 1167 he was appointed archdeacon of Tyre, an important Christian city in the Middle East. He was employed on various embassies by the king, AMALRIC I, and became (c.1170) tutor of Amalric's son and heir (later Baldwin IV). After Amalric's death he became (1174) chancellor of the kingdom, and in 1175 he was made archbishop of Tyre. His chief importance lies in his historical work, which is especially accurate in dealing with his own time. His only extant work, the *History of Deeds Done beyond the Sea,* is a detailed account of the Crusades and the Latin Kingdom from 1095 to 1184.

William of Wykeham or **William of Wickham** (both: wĭ'kəm), 1324-1404, English prelate and lord chancellor. He is thought to have been the son of a serf. Entering the service of the royal court in 1347, he supervised the building of additions to Windsor Castle and rapidly gained influence at the court of Edward III, becoming royal secretary and lord privy seal (1364). He received benefices in all parts of England but was not ordained a priest until 1362. In 1366 he was appointed bishop of Winchester, and he was made lord chancellor the following year. The debility of the aging Edward III and the strife of factions made his political position extremely difficult. In 1371, William was dismissed, largely as a result of the rising tide of anticlericalism. Opposing JOHN OF GAUNT, he supported the attack made on Gaunt's court party in the Good Parliament (1376). As a result he was charged (1376) with previous misuse of government funds, deprived of his temporalities, and harried for almost a year. On Richard II's accession (1377) he was exonerated and devoted most of his remaining life to his episcopal duties, although from 1389 to 1391 he again served as chancellor. His most lasting importance lies in his two great foundations, New College at Oxford (1379) and Winchester College (opened 1394), one of the most famous English public schools. He rebuilt the Norman nave of Winchester Cathedral and repaired many churches of his diocese. A conservative but conscientious churchman, William was a vigorous clerical reformer. See biography by G. C. Heseltine (1932); William Hayter, *William of Wykeham: Patron of the Arts* (1970).

William Rufus: see WILLIAM II, king of England.

Williams, Bill: see WILLIAMS, WILLIAM SHERLEY.

Williams, Daniel Hale, 1858-1931, American surgeon, b. Hollidaysburg, Pa., M.D. Northwestern Univ., 1883. As surgeon of the South Side Dispensary in Chicago (1884-91), he became keenly aware of the lack of facilities for training Negroes like himself as doctors and nurses. As a result he organized the Provident Hospital, the first Negro hospital in the United States. In 1893, Williams performed the first successful closure of a wound of the heart and pericardium. In the same year President Cleveland appointed him surgeon in chief of Freedmen's Hospital, Washington, D.C., and during his five-year tenure there he reorganized the hospital and provided a training school for Negro nurses. From 1899 until his death he was professor of clinical surgery at Meharry Medical College, Nashville, Tenn.

Williams, Eleazer (ĕlēā'zər), c.1787-1858, missionary among North American Indians. He was the son of Thomas Williams, a St. Regis Indian chief, and a white woman; he was educated in private schools in Massachusetts. He became a Protestant Episcopal missionary among the New York Indians. When the Oneida went (1822) to a reservation near Green Bay, Wis., he went with them and remained until 1850, when he returned to New York. He is credited with simplifying the written Mohawk language. Among other things he translated (1853) the Book of Common Prayer into Iroquois and wrote (1859) a *Life of Te-ho-ra-gwa-ne-gen* (the Iroquois name of Thomas Williams, his father). He is remembered for claiming, without substantiation, to have been Louis XVII of France (the Lost Dauphin), the supposed kidnapped son of Louis XVI and Marie Antoinette. *Eleazer* was the form used by Williams himself, although the name occurs also as Eleazar, Lazar, and Lazau. See William Wight, *Eleazer Williams: His Forerunners, Himself* (1896).

Williams, Emlyn, 1905–, Welsh actor and dramatist. His best-known plays are *Night Must Fall* (1935) and *The Corn Is Green* (1941). His *Collected Plays* were published in 1961. As an actor he is noted for his interpretations of Charles Dickens and Dylan Thomas in one-man shows and of Pope Pius XII in Rolf Hochhuth's play *The Deputy* (1964). See his autobiographies, *George* (1961) and *Emlyn* (1973).

Williams, Ephraim, 1715–55, American soldier, founder of WILLIAMS COLLEGE, b. Newton, Mass. After several years as a sailor, he lived in Massachusetts and took part in defending the frontier against the Indians. He was a captain in King George's War. In recognition of his service he was given command of the Massachusetts posts W of the Connecticut River and 200 acres (80.9 hectares) of land in Massachusetts, where Adams and Williamstown now stand. Made a colonel in 1755, Williams was killed leading troops of Sir William Johnson's command in the first action of the battle of Lake George in the final French and Indian War. His will directed that his property be used for establishing a free school. Out of the academy thus founded at Williamstown, Williams College developed.

Williams, Eric, 1911–, prime minister of Trinidad and Tobago (1961–). He attended Oxford Univ. and taught at Howard Univ. in Washington, D.C. (1939–53). Returning to Trinidad, he founded (1955) the country's first formal political party. He became chief minister in 1956 and prime minister in 1961. Elections in 1966 and 1971 reaffirmed his position. He led his country to independence within the British Commonwealth (1962). Williams launched several ambitious five-year development plans, attracting foreign capital through tax incentives and acquiring foreign aid. He concentrated his efforts on the improvement of education and the development and diversification of industry and agriculture. Although of African descent, he faced increasing black militant opposition to his government. His numerous writings include *The Negro in the Caribbean* (1942); *History of the People of Trinidad and Tobago* (1964); *British Historians and the West Indies* (1964); and *From Columbus to Castro* (1970). See his autobiography, *Inward Hunger* (1969).

Williams, Sir George, 1821–1905, English merchant. A vigorous advocate of temperance and an opponent of gambling and tobacco, Williams founded the YOUNG MEN'S CHRISTIAN ASSOCIATION in 1844. In 1894 he was knighted for his lifelong work for boys.

Williams, John, 1664–1729, American clergyman, b. Roxbury, Mass., grad. Harvard, 1683. In 1686 he became the first minister at Deerfield, Mass. During the great Indian massacre at that frontier town in Feb., 1704, he and his family were taken captive. Two of his children were murdered, and his wife was killed on the long journey to Canada. In 1706 he and his surviving children (except one, who remained with the Indians) were released. Williams returned to Deerfield. His story of his adventures, *The Redeemed Captive Returning to Zion* (1707), is one of the best known of the many accounts of Indian captivity.

Williams, John, 1796–1839, English missionary, called the Apostle of Polynesia. Under the London Missionary Society he went (1817) to the Society Islands. He discovered Rarotonga in 1823 and founded missions there. He later translated parts of the Bible and other books into Rarotongan. After a visit to England (1834–38), he returned to the South Seas in a newly outfitted missionary ship. In a region of the New Hebrides where he was not known and where he was planning to start a mission, he was killed by cannibals. His *Narrative of Missionary Enterprise in the South Sea Islands* (1837) threw valuable light on Polynesia. See biographies by E. Prater (1947) and Cecil Northcott (1965).

Williams, Ralph Vaughan: see VAUGHAN WILLIAMS, RALPH.

Williams, Roger, c.1603–1683, clergyman, advocate of religious freedom, founder of RHODE ISLAND, b. London. A protégé of Sir Edward Coke, he graduated from Pembroke College, Cambridge, in 1627 and took Anglican orders. He early espoused Puritanism and emigrated to the Massachusetts Bay colony in 1631. Williams became teacher (1632) and, after a stay at Plymouth, minister (1634) of the Salem church. However, his radical religious beliefs and political theories—he denied the validity of the Massachusetts charter, challenged the Puritans to acknowledge they had separated from the Church of England, and declared that civil magistrates had no power over matters of conscience—alarmed the Puritan oligarchy, and the General Court banished him in 1635. In the spring of 1636 he founded PROVIDENCE on land purchased from the Narragansett Indians. To Providence, a democratic refuge from religious persecution, came settlers from England as well as Massachusetts. There were four settlements in the Narragansett Bay area by 1643, when Williams went to England. Through the influence of powerful friends such as Sir Henry VANE (1613–62), he obtained from the Long Parliament a patent (1644) uniting the Rhode Island towns of Portsmouth, Newport, and Warwick with Providence. In 1651, William CODDINGTON secured a commission annulling the patent, but Williams, with John CLARKE, hastened again to England and had the patent of 1644 restored. (The patent's grant of absolute liberty of conscience was later confirmed by the royal charter of 1663.) On his return in 1654, Williams was elected president of the colony and served three terms. Always a trusted friend of the Indians (he wrote *Key into the Language of America,* 1643), he often used his good offices in maintaining peaceful relations with them. But he was unable to prevent the outbreak of King Philip's War (1675–76), in which he served as a captain of militia. Williams, though he remained a Christian, disassociated himself from existing churches. His writings, reprinted in the *Narragansett Club Publications* (1866–74), reveal the vigor with which he propounded his democratic and humanitarian ideals. *The Bloudy Tenent of Persecution for Cause of Conscience* (1644) was condemned by John COTTON, who was answered with *The Bloudy Tenent Yet More Bloudy* (1652). Other works include *Queries of Highest Consideration* (1644), an argument for complete separation of church and state; *The Hireling Ministry None of Christ's* (1652); and *George Fox Digg'd Out of His Burrowes* (1676), a polemic against Quaker teachings. Of great personal charm and unquestioned integrity, Williams was admired even by those who, like both the elder and the younger John Winthrop, abhorred his liberal ideas. See biographies by S. H. Brockunier (1940), Perry Miller (1953, repr. 1962), Ola Winslow (1957, repr. 1973), E. S. Morgan (1967), and John Garrett (1970).

Williams, Roger John, 1893–, American chemist, b. India, grad. Univ. of Redlands, Redlands, Calif. (B.S., 1914), Ph.D. Univ. of Chicago, 1919; brother of the chemist Robert R. Williams. He taught chemistry at the Univ. of Oregon (1920–32) and at Oregon State College (1932–39) and became professor at the Univ. of Texas in 1939 and also director of the Biochemical Institute of Texas in 1941. He is noted for his work on the vitamin B complex and especially for his discovery of pantothenic acid. He is the author of several textbooks on organic chemistry and biochemistry and is a pioneer in biochemical investigations of alcoholism. In 1970 he announced that ordinary commercial white bread was so nutritionally deficient that in an experiment he conducted a number of laboratory rats given a steady diet of it died of malnutrition after three months.

Williams, Ted (Theodore Samuel Williams), 1918–, American baseball player, b. San Diego, Calif. At the age of 17 he began playing professional ball with the San Diego Padres of the Pacific Coast League. In 1938 he tried out with the Boston Red Sox in spring training, and a year later he joined that club as a regular outfielder. Except for service (1943–45) in World War II and again (1952–53) in the Korean War, Williams played continuously for the Boston Red Sox from 1939 until his retirement in 1960. One of the greatest natural hitters the game has ever known, he batted well over .300 in 1939 and in 1940; in 1941, besides batting .406 to win the batting championship, he led the American League in home runs (37). In 1942 the tall, rangy left-hander was again top batter in the major leagues with a .356 average, while leading the American League in home runs (36) and runs batted in (137). Williams, a controversial personality to some baseball fans, helped lead the Red Sox to a pennant in 1946. Although opposing teams frequently employed the "Williams shift"—moving fielders toward right field, where Williams customarily drove his base hits—he continued to lead the league in batting in 1947 with .343, in 1948 with .369, in 1957 with .388, and in 1958 with .328. Williams had a lifetime batting average of .344 and hit a total of 521 home runs. He managed the Washington Senators from 1969 to 1971 and remained as manager when the franchise became (1972) the Texas Rangers but retired shortly afterward. See his autobiography, *My Turn at Bat* (1970), and *The Science of Hitting* (1972), both coauthored by John Underwood.

Williams, Tennessee (Thomas Lanier Williams), 1914–, American dramatist, b. Columbus, Miss., grad. State Univ. of Iowa, 1938. One of America's foremost playwrights, he achieved his first successes with the productions of *The Glass Menagerie* (1945) and *A Streetcar Named Desire* (1947; Pulitzer Prize). In these plays as in many of his later works Williams explores the intense passions and frustrations of a disturbed and frequently brutal society. An eloquently symbolic poet of the theater, he is noted for his scenes of high dramatic tension and for brilliant dialogue. He is perhaps most successful in his portraits of the hypersensitive and lonely Southern woman, clutching at life, particularly at her memories of a grand past that no longer exists. His later plays, which never quite achieve the poignancy of his first two successes, include *Summer and Smoke* (1948), *The Rose Tattoo* (1950), *Camino Real* (1953), *Cat on a Hot Tin Roof* (1955; Pulitzer Prize), *Sweet Bird of Youth* (1959), *Period of Adjustment* (1959), *Night of the Iguana* (1961), *The Milk Train Doesn't Stop Here Any More* (1963), *The Seven Descents of Myrtle* (1968), *In the Bar of the Tokyo Hotel* (1969), and *Small Craft Warnings* (1972). His one-act plays were collected in *27 Wagons Full of Cotton* (1946) and *The American Blues* (1948). He has also written four collections of short fiction: *One Arm and Other Stories* (1948), *Hard Candy* (1954), *The Knightly Quest* (1969), and *Eight Mortal Ladies Possessed* (1974); a novel, *The Roman Spring of Mrs. Stone* (1950); a volume of verse, *In the Winter of Cities* (1956); and a film script based on two of his short plays, *Baby Doll* (1956). See critical studies by S. L. Falk (1962), Francis Donahue (1964), and E. M. Jackson (1965).

Williams, William, c.1710–c.1790, American painter, b. England. He probably led a seafaring life before settling (c.1747) in Philadelphia, where he was Benjamin West's first instructor in painting. He designed the building and in 1759 painted scenery for the first Philadelphia theater. After painting in New York City in 1775, Williams probably returned (c.1780) to England. He died in a Bristol almshouse, leaving a partly autobiographical manuscript, *The Journal of Llewellin Penrose;* this was published in 1815. His richly colored paintings have a lively naïveté and romantic charm; among those known to be his are portraits of Deborah Hall (Brooklyn Mus., N.Y.) and Benjamin Lay (Historical Society of Pennsylvania). See study by D. H. Dickason (1970).

Williams, William, 1731–1811, political leader in the American Revolution, signer of the Declaration of Independence, b. Lebanon, Conn. He served in the French and Indian War and held many public offices before becoming a Connecticut delegate (1776–78, 1783–84) to the Continental Congress.

Williams, William Carlos, 1883–1963, American poet and physician, b. Rutherford, N.J., educated in Geneva, Switzerland, Univ. of Pennsylvania (M.D., 1906), and Univ. of Leipzig, where he studied pediatrics. He is regarded as one of the most important and original American poets of the 20th cent. Williams began his medical practice in 1910 in Rutherford and was a physician for more than 40 years. His early poetry shows the influences of the various poetic trends of the time—from metaphorical imagism in *Poems* (1909) and *The Tempers* (1913) to free-verse expressionism in *Al Que Quiere!* (1917), *Kora in Hell* (1920), and *Sour Grapes* (1921). Williams observed American life closely, expressed anger at injustice, and recorded his impressions in a lucid, vital style. He developed a verse that is close to the idiom of speech, revealing a fidelity to ordinary things seen and heard. Later volumes of his poetry include *Collected Poems* (1934), *Collected Later Poems* (1950), *Collected Earlier Poems* (1951), *Journey to Love* (1955), *Pictures from Brueghel, and Other Poems* (1963; Pulitzer Prize), and a five-volume, impressionistic, philosophical poem, *Paterson* (1946–58), in which he uses the experience of life in an American city to voice his feelings on the duty of the poet. His essays include those in *In the American Grain* (1925), *Selected Essays* (1954), and *Embodiment of Knowledge* (1974). Among his other works are a collection of short stories, *Make Light of It* (1950); plays, including *A Dream of Love* (1948) and *Many Loves* (1950); and the novels, *A Voyage to Pagany* (1928) and a three-volume chronicle of an immigrant family in America—*White Mule* (1937), *In the Money* (1940), and *The Build-Up* (1952). His autobiography appeared in 1951, and his *Selected Letters* was published in 1957. See biography by J. E. Breslin (1970); studies by James Guimond (1968) and L. W. Wagner (1964 and 1970); Charles Tomlinson, ed., *A Critical Anthology* (1972).

Williams, William Sherley, 1787-1849, American trader and trapper, known as Old Bill Williams, b. Rutherford co., N.C. Much of his early life was spent in Missouri, where he was a traveling preacher. Becoming (c.1822) an independent trapper, he accompanied (1825-26) a surveying party on the Santa Fe Trail. He also trapped in the Yellowstone country and in Texas and went to California on an expedition in 1833-34. After that he spent much time in the mountain country and along the Santa Fe Trail. In 1848, Williams, who was one of the most colorful of the mountain men, joined John C. Frémont's fourth expedition at Bent's Fort as a guide. Frémont, disregarding Williams's advice, led the group toward the headwaters of the Rio Grande, where most of the party perished of cold and starvation. Frémont retreated, blaming the episode on the guide. Williams was killed by Ute Indians while retracing the path of the expedition. See biography by A. H. Favour (new ed., 1962).

Williamsburg, historic city (1970 pop. 9,069), seat of James City co., SE Va., on a peninsula between the James and York rivers; settled 1632 as Middle Plantation, laid out and renamed 1699, inc. 1722. It is a great tourist attraction and is also important as the seat (since 1693) of the College of William and Mary in Virginia. Williamsburg became the temporary capital after the burning of Jamestown (1676) during Bacon's Rebellion, then served as capital of Virginia from 1699 to 1779. It was the scene of important conventions during the movement for American independence, but it declined after the capital was moved (1779) to Richmond. In the PENINSULAR CAMPAIGN of the Civil War a rearguard action was fought there (May 5, 1862) between retreating Confederates and McClellan's forces. In 1926, with the financial support of John D. Rockefeller, Jr., a large-scale restoration of the city was begun; 700 buildings were removed, 83 were renovated, and 413 were rebuilt on their original sites. Today Williamsburg has its colonial appearance, with green formal gardens and many craft shops where revived trades are practiced. Among the historic structures are the colonial capitol (reconstructed); Raleigh Tavern (reconstructed), rendezvous of Revolutionary patriots; the courthouse of 1770; the Bruton Parish Church (1710-15); the governor's palace (reconstructed); the public gaol; the magazine; and many old homes. The Abby Aldrich Rockefeller museum there houses one of the finest folk art collections in the country. The Colonial Parkway passes through Williamsburg, connecting it with the Jamestown and Yorktown sections of Colonial National Historical Park (see NATIONAL PARKS AND MONUMENTS, table). See Marcus Whiffen, *The Public Buildings of Williamsburg* (1958) and *The Eighteenth-Century Houses of Williamsburg* (1960); A. L. Kocher and Howard Dearstyne, *Colonial Williamsburg* (rev. ed. 1971); J. A. Osborne, *Williamsburg in Colonial Times* (1936, repr. 1972).

Williams College, at Williamstown, Mass.; coeducational; chartered 1785, opened as a free school 1791, became a college 1793, named for Ephraim WILLIAMS. The Williams campus, noted for its fine old buildings, includes West College (1790), the Van Rensselaer Manor House (moved from Albany, N.Y.), and the oldest U.S. observatory (Hopkins; 1838). Williams College, the first to establish an institute of politics (maintained until 1934), now has several research institutes. The Chapin Library of Rare Books houses important books, manuscripts, and prints relating to Americana, English literature, and early painting. There is a fine art museum.

William Smith College: see HOBART COLLEGE.

Williamson, Hugh, 1735-1819, American political leader, physician, and scientist, b. West Nottingham, Pa. He studied theology, preached for a short time, and then was (1760-63) professor of mathematics at the College of Philadelphia (now Univ. of Pennsylvania) before studying medicine abroad. He practiced at Philadelphia and became interested in general science. While in England (1774-76), he obtained and delivered to Benjamin Franklin private letters written by Gov. Thomas HUTCHINSON urging harsh measures against the patriots. He later became surgeon general of North Carolina's militia in the American Revolution. Elected (1782) to the state legislature, he was also a member (1782-85, 1788) of the Continental Congress, a delegate (1787) to the Federal Constitutional Convention, and a member (1789-93) of the U.S. House of Representatives. After 1793 he engaged in scientific studies and wrote numerous scientific tracts. See David Hosack, *A Biographical Memoir of Hugh Williamson* (1820).

Williamsport, city (1970 pop. 37,918), seat of Lycoming co., central Pa., on the Susquehanna River; settled 1772, inc. as a borough 1806, as a city 1866. The scene of several Indian massacres in colonial times, Williamsport grew with the development of the lumber industry in the 19th cent. Today it is a tourist center, a manufacturing city, and the trade and distribution point for an agricultural area. The chief manufactures are aircraft engines and parts, wire and rope products, valves, machinery, piping, electronic and photographic equipment, and pajamas. Williamsport is the home of Little League baseball; the Little League world series is held there each year. Also in the city are Lycoming College and Williamsport Area Community College.

Williamstown, city (1971 pop. 29,983), Victoria, SE Australia, part of the Melbourne urban agglomeration, on Hobson's Bay. The city has oil refineries and other industries.

Williams University, at Montreal, Que.: see SIR GEORGE WILLIAMS UNIV.

William the Conqueror: see WILLIAM I, king of England.

William the Lion, 1143-1214, king of Scotland (1165-1214), brother and successor of Malcolm IV. Determined to recover Northumbria (lost to England in 1157), he supported the rebellion (1173-74) of the sons of Henry II of England. The result was that he was captured by Henry, who forced him to sign the Treaty of Falaise (1174), making Scotland a feudal possession of England. Released in 1175, he immediately asked the pope to declare the Scottish church free of English domination. A quarrel with the pope delayed the decision, but, in 1188, Pope Clement III declared the church in Scotland subject only to Rome. In 1189, William was able to buy annulment of the Treaty of Falaise from Richard I of England for 10,000 marks. After the succession (1199) of King John in England, William once more demanded the restoration of Northumbria but was finally forced (1209) by show of arms to abandon the claim. William put down several revolts within Scotland and furthered somewhat the process of feudalization in the kingdom. His alliance (1168) with Louis VII of France began a long friendship between France and Scotland, later to be known as the Auld Alliance. He was succeeded by his son, Alexander II.

William the Silent or **William of Orange** (William I, prince of Orange), 1533-84, Dutch statesman, principal founder of Dutch independence. A descendant of the Ottonian line of NASSAU, he was born at Dillenburg, near Wiesbaden, Germany, of Protestant parents. After inheriting (1544) the principality of ORANGE, in S France, William was reared a Roman Catholic at the insistence of Holy Roman Emperor Charles V, whose favorite page he became. In 1555 he was made stadtholder of Holland, Zeeland, and Utrecht. He ably served Philip II of Spain as a diplomat, particularly in the making of the Treaty of Cateau-Cambrésis (1559). Philip's encroachments on the liberties of the NETHERLANDS and the introduction of the Spanish Inquisition by Cardinal GRANVELLE led William to turn against the king. In 1563, with the help of counts EGMONT and HOORN, he succeeded in obtaining the removal of Granvelle, but under the regency of MARGARET OF PARMA disorders grew in the Netherlands. In 1566 the party of the GUEUX was organized with William's connivance, and when ALBA was sent to the Netherlands to quell the rebels, William withdrew to Germany. He refused Alba's summons to appear before a tribunal, and his property was confiscated. William and his brother Louis of Nassau raised an army to drive the Spanish out of the Netherlands. They at first met defeat, but in 1576 the provinces of the Netherlands, taking advantage of the mutiny of the Spanish army under JOHN OF AUSTRIA, united under William's leadership in the Pacification of Ghent for the purpose of expelling the Spanish. In 1573, chiefly for the sake of policy, William had become a Calvinist. The struggle with Spain continued. The Union of Utrecht (1579) proclaimed the virtual independence of the northern provinces, of which William was the uncrowned ruler, but the victories of the Spaniards under Alessandro FARNESE forced William to seek French support by offering (1580) the rule over the Netherlands to FRANCIS, duke of Alençon and Anjou. Philip II denounced William as a traitor, and a high price was set on his head in 1581. William replied with his famous *Apologia*, in which he not only sought to vindicate his own conduct, but hurled violent accusations at the Spanish king. In the same year the representatives of Brabant, Flanders, Utrecht, Gelderland, Holland, and Zeeland solemnly declared Philip deposed from sovereignty over those provinces. William was chosen count of Holland and Zeeland, which had refused to accept Francis as sovereign. William's support of the unpopular Francis resulted in the wane of William's own popularity during his last years. He was assassinated at Delft by a French Catholic fanatic, while the struggle against Spain was still in a critical stage. William married four times. His first wife was Anne of Egmont and Büren (d. 1558); in 1561 he married Anne, daughter of Elector Maurice of Saxony, in spite of the opposition of Philip II and of Anne's parents; in 1575, two years before Anne's death, he married Charlotte de Bourbon, a French princess and a runaway nun, after securing the approval of several Protestant divines; in 1583 he married Louise de Coligny, daughter of Admiral Coligny. From the first marriage Prince Philip William of Orange (d. 1616) was born; from the second and fourth marriages issued William's successors as stadtholders—Maurice of Nassau and Frederick Henry. See biography by C. V. Wedgwood (1944, repr. 1967).

Willing, Thomas, 1731-1821, American merchant and financier, b. Philadelphia. He studied law in London. Returning to Philadelphia in 1749, he entered his father's business and later established with Robert MORRIS (1734-1806) a prominent importing and exporting firm in Philadelphia. He was elected mayor of Philadelphia in 1763 and was (1767-77) a justice of the Pennsylvania court. As a member (1775-76) of the Continental Congress, he voted against the Declaration of Independence. In 1780, Willing was active in raising money for the Continental army. He was one of the founders of the Bank of North America and its first president (1781-1792). He was also (1791-1811) first president of the Bank of the United States. See B. A. Konkle, *Thomas Willing and the First American Financial System* (1937).

Willingdon, Freeman Freeman-Thomas, 1st **marquess of,** 1866-1941, British colonial administrator. He was a Liberal member of Parliament from 1900 to 1910. He served as governor of Bombay presidency (1913-19) and of Madras presidency (1919-24) and as governor general of Canada (1926-31). As viceroy and governor general of India (1931-36) he repressed passive-resistance campaigns of the Indian National Congress. He was created baron in 1910 and marquess in 1936.

Willis, Nathaniel Parker, 1806-67, American author, b. Portland, Maine, grad. Yale, 1827. He was editor of the periodical the *Legendary* and later of the *Token* before founding (1829) the *American Monthly Magazine* in Boston. In 1831 he merged his magazine with George Pope Morris's *New-York Mirror* and went abroad to write for the *Mirror* and for English magazines. As editor of the *Mirror* after 1840 and of the *National Press* (later the *Home Journal*), which he and Morris founded in 1846, Willis attracted many prominent contributors. His books, popular but ephemeral, were collections of his journalistic work; among them are *Pencillings by the Way* (1835), *Inklings of Adventure* (1836), and short stories in *Dashes at Life with a Free Pencil* (1845). See biography by H. A. Beers (1885, repr. 1969); study by C. P. Auser (1969).

Willis, Thomas, 1621-75, English physician and anatomist. He became professor at Oxford Univ. in 1660 and in 1666 established a practice in London. An authority on the brain and the nervous system, he discovered the 11th cranial nerve and a circle of arteries at the base of the brain (the circle of Willis). He was the first to note the presence of sugar in the urine of diabetics. His works, written in Latin, include *Of the Anatomy of the Brain*, illustrated by Sir Christopher Wren, published in 1664, and translated in *The Remaining Medical Works . . . of Doctor Thomas Willis* (1681).

Williston, city (1970 pop. 11,280), seat of Williams co., NW N.Dak., on the Missouri River; inc. 1904. An early riverboating town, its importance increased with the discovery (1951) of rich oil reserves in the Williston Basin. It is the trade, processing, and shipping center of a spring-wheat and livestock region, with an oil refinery, stockyards, grain elevators, dairy-processing plants, and railroad shops. Huge reserves of lignite, as well as natural gas, salt, and leonardite are in the area. Of interest are a frontier museum and nearby Fort Union Trading Post National Historic Site and Fort Buford State Historic Site. A junior college branch of the Univ. of North Dakota and a state agricultural experiment station are there.

Willkie, Wendell Lewis, 1892–1944, American industrialist and political leader, b. Elwood, Ind. He practiced law in Ohio (1914–23) and in New York (1923–33) before he became president (1933) of the Commonwealth and Southern Corp., a giant utility holding company. Although a Democrat, Willkie became a leading spokesman of business interests opposed to the New Deal. He finally enrolled as a Republican in 1940 and in that year was nominated by the Republican party for the presidency. In his campaign he endorsed President Franklin Delano Roosevelt's foreign policy but attacked the New Deal at home. Although defeated in the election, he polled more than 22 million votes (the largest popular vote received by a defeated candidate up to that time). He later (1941–42) visited England, the Middle East, the Soviet Union, and China as the President's personal representative. He led the fight (1942–44) to liberalize the Republican party, mainly attacking isolationism. He wrote *One World* (1943) and *An American Program* (1944). See biography by William Severn (1967); study by Warren Moscow (1968).

Willmar (wĭl'mär), city (1970 pop. 12,869), seat of Kandiyohi co., central Minn., in a dairy and farm region; settled 1856, inc. as a city 1901. It is a medical center and a railroad division point. It has a turkey hatchery and turkey-processing plant. Food products, plastics, machinery, and clothing are also made. A state junior college, a vocational institute, and a state mental hospital are there.

will-o'-the-wisp, phenomenon known also as *ignis fatuus* and jack-o'-lantern. It is seen at night as a pale, flickering light over marshland. There is no generally accepted explanation for it; it may result from the spontaneous ignition of gases (e.g., methane) produced by the disintegration of dead plant or animal matter, or it may be a form of phosphorescence. The eerie lights have given rise to many superstitions.

Willoughby (wĭl'əbē), city (1970 pop. 18,634), Lake co., NE Ohio, on the Chagrin River, near Lake Erie; settled c.1800, inc. as a city 1951. Manufactures include rubber products, electronic components, clothing, and fused quartz. Nearby is Kirtland Temple (1833–36), a Mormon church.

willow, common name for some members of the Salicaceae, a family of deciduous trees and shrubs of worldwide distribution, especially abundant from north temperate to arctic areas. The family consists of two genera, *Salix* and *Populus,* both of which are propagated easily by cuttings, grow rapidly, and characteristically bear male and female flowers in catkins on separate plants. Many plants of the narrower-leaved willow genus (*Salix*) flourish in cold, wet ground; willows grow farther north than any other woody angiosperm (flowering plant). The poplars (genus *Populus*) usually have heart-shaped or ovate leaves; they include the cottonwoods, aspens, and many species specifically named poplar. The cottonwoods (sometimes also called poplars) characteristically have seeds that are covered with fibrous coats so that when they are released at maturity they clump together in cottony balls. Cottonwoods were a welcome sight to the pioneers pushing westward, for they marked the streams in the otherwise treeless Great Plains. Some of the poplars, especially the aspens, have flattened leaf stalks that permit the pendulous leaves to quiver in the slightest breeze (hence the name quaking aspen). The quaking, or golden, aspen is a common deciduous tree of the mountains of the W United States; it is often the first tree to reforest burned-over woodlands. Because the lumber of this family is so soft it finds little use except for paper pulp (mostly the poplars), for charcoal, and especially in basketry and wickerwork (mostly the willows). The bushes and their twigs used in basketry are often called osiers. Willow buds and bark have also been used medicinally; the chemical predecessor of aspirin was originally isolated from the bark of a willow. The trees are valuable in erosion control along riverbanks because of their rapid growth. Economically the family is most noted for its many species planted as ornamentals, e.g., the Lombardy and the silver, or white, poplars, now naturalized in North America from Eurasia; the weeping willow, indigenous to China; and the pussy willow of North America. *Populus gileadensis,* an ancient horticultural species whose original form is unknown, is one of the plants called BALM OF GILEAD. Yellow poplar is a name sometimes used for the unrelated tulip tree of the magnolia family. Willows are classified in the division MAGNOLIOPHYTA, class Magnoliopsida, order Salicales, family Salicaceae.

willow herb, name for several plants, among them the fireweed (see EVENING PRIMROSE).

Willowick, city (1970 pop. 21,337), Lake co., NE Ohio, a residential suburb of Cleveland on Lake Erie; inc. 1924.

willow-pattern ware, sometimes porcelain but frequently opaque pottery, originated in Staffordshire, England, c.1780. Thomas Minton, then an apprentice potter, developed and engraved the design, presumably after an old Chinese legend. It portrays the garden of a rich mandarin whose young daughter elopes with his secretary. The lovers, overtaken on the bridge by her father, are transformed by the gods into birds and flutter beyond his reach. The scene with its willow tree covers the central part of plate, dish, or bowl, with a border of butterflies, daggers, a fret, or other motif. The blue-and-white chinaware on which it appeared became immensely popular, and the design was reproduced with variations by many European potters and even in the Orient, where it is still constantly employed, most of the ware being exported to Western countries.

Wills, Helen Newington, 1906–, American tennis player, b. Alameda co., Calif. She studied art at the Univ. of California and later gave exhibitions of her paintings and etchings. She gained international attention, however, by tennis playing. She repeatedly won (1923–25, 1927–29, 1931) the U.S. women's singles crown while also taking (1927–30, 1932–33, 1935,1938) the British women's singles title and other championships in France and Holland. Although she defaulted to Helen Hull JACOBS because of a leg injury in the 1933 finals of the U.S. singles, she came back in 1935 and dramatically defeated Jacobs in the Wimbledon finals match. She is generally considered to have been the greatest woman tennis player of her time. She wrote *Tennis* (1928) and *Fifteen-Thirty* (1937).

Wills, Maury (Maurice Morning Wills), 1932–, American baseball player, b. Washington, D.C. He was an outstanding shortstop and base stealer with the Los Angeles Dodgers (1959–66; 1969–72), the Pittsburgh Pirates (1967–68) and the Montreal Expos (1969). From 1960 through 1965, Wills led the National League in stolen bases, amassing a lifetime record of 586 steals. In 1962, Wills, by stealing 104 bases in 165 games, surpassed Ty Cobb's major-league record of 96 steals, which had stood since 1915; although Cobb's record was set in 156 games, Wills stole 97 bases in the same number of games. Wills won the National League's most valuable player award in 1962. See his autobiography (1963).

Willstätter, Richard (rĭkh'ärt vĭl'shtĕtər), 1872–1942, German chemist. He was professor at the Kaiser Wilhelm Institute of Chemistry, Berlin (1912–16), and at the Univ. of Munich (1916–25). He received the 1915 Nobel Prize in Chemistry for his work on chlorophyll and on anthocyanins (red, blue, and violet plant pigments). His later work was on the assimilation of carbonic acids in plants and on the chemical composition of enzymes.

Willughby, Francis (wĭl'əbē), 1635–72, English naturalist. He is known especially for his early systematic work on birds and fishes, in which he made some of the most important contributions before those of Linnaeus. He toured the Continent with John Ray, collecting material for his Ornithologia (1676, in Latin), translated into English by Ray as *The Ornithology of Francis Willughby* (1678). Ray also published Willughby's *De Historia piscium* (1686).

Wilmette (wĭlmĕt'), village (1970 pop. 32,134), Cook co., NE Ill., a residential suburb of Chicago, on Lake Michigan; inc. 1872. A Bahai temple (see BAHAISM), a junior college, and a U.S. coast guard station are there.

Wilmington, Spencer Compton, earl of, 1673?–1743, British politician. He was a member of Parliament (1695–1710, 1713–30) and served as speaker of the House of Commons (1715–27). He was paymaster general (1722–30) and in 1730 was created an earl and lord privy seal by Robert Walpole. He turned against Walpole in 1739 and after the latter's fall served briefly (1742–43) as chief minister. He was merely a figurehead, however, and took no active role in the government.

Wilmington. 1 City (1970 pop. 80,386), seat of New Castle co., NE Del., on the Delaware River and tributary streams, the Christina and the Brandywine; settled 1638, inc. as a city 1832. The largest city in the state, it is a port of entry handling considerable domestic and foreign shipping. It has large shipyards and railroad shops and is a great chemical center, with manufacturing plants and company headquarters. Other industries include copper smelting, automobile assembling, and the manufacture of explosives and munitions, and rubber, leather, and petroleum products. Fort Christina, built there by the Swedes in 1638 (the site is now a state park), was taken by the Dutch (1655) and then by the British (1664). In 1682, William Penn came into possession of the region. Shipping and manufacturing grew early, and industry was well developed when E. I. du Pont established a powder mill on the Brandywine there in 1802. Three junior colleges are in the city. Wilmington's numerous historic buildings include Old Swedes Church, built in 1698. Other points of interest are Rodney Square (civic center), the Delaware Academy of Medicine, the Delaware Art Center, and several museums. **2** Town (1970 pop. 17,102), Middlesex co., NE Mass., a suburb of Boston, on the Ipswich River; settled 1639, inc. 1730. Economic enterprises include space research and plastic and electronics manufacturing. **3** City (1970 pop. 46,169), seat of New Hanover co., SE N.C., a port of entry on the Cape Fear River, c.30 mi (50 km) from its mouth; settled 1732, inc. as a city 1866. It has a fine harbor and is the state's largest port, receiving domestic petroleum products and shipping tobacco, wood products, and scrap metal. Wilmington is also a rail hub, a resort, and a sports fishing center. Among its manufactures are metal and wood products, textiles and clothing, boilers, and fertilizers. Cornwallis held the town in 1781. During the Civil War it was the last Confederate port to close; Confederate blockade runners used it until the fall of FORT FISHER on Jan. 15, 1865. Many large cargo ships were built in the shipyards during World War II. The Univ. of North Carolina at Wilmington and a junior college are in the city. Many old buildings remain, and a national cemetery is there. The U.S.S. *North Carolina* is moored in the river. **4** City (1970 pop. 10,051), seat of Clinton co., SW Ohio, in a farm (chiefly corn and hogs) area; settled 1810, inc. 1828. Wood-boring tools, air compressors, castings, and auto parts are made. Wilmington College is there, and a state park is nearby. See study by A. T. Lincoln (1972).

Wilmot, David, 1814–68, American legislator, b. Bethany, Pa. As a Democratic Congressman (1845–51) he became widely known as the author of the famous WILMOT PROVISO, which helped build up sectional animosity before the Civil War. Ardently opposed to slavery, Wilmot became a leader of the Free-Soil party. He helped to found the Republican party and was (1861–63) a Republican Senator, filling out the unexpired term of Simon Cameron. He then became (1863) judge of the U.S. Court of Claims. See biography by C. B. Going (1924, repr. 1966).

Wilmot, John: see ROCHESTER, JOHN WILMOT, 2D EARL OF.

Wilmot Proviso, 1846, amendment to a bill put before the U.S. House of Representatives during the Mexican War; the bill provided an appropriation of $2 million to enable President Polk to negotiate a territorial settlement with Mexico. David Wilmot, a Democrat from Pennsylvania, introduced an amendment to the bill stipulating that none of the territory acquired in the Mexican War should be open to slavery. In the House, the amended bill was passed, but the Senate adjourned without voting on it. In the next session of Congress (1847), a new bill providing for a $3-million appropriation was introduced, and Wilmot again proposed an antislavery amendment to it. The amended bill passed the House, but the Senate drew up its own bill, which excluded the proviso. The Wilmot Proviso created great bitterness between North and South and helped crystallize the conflict over the extension of slavery. In the election of 1848 the terms of the Wilmot Proviso, a definite challenge to proslavery groups, were ignored by the Whig and Democratic parties but were adopted by the Free-Soil party. Later the Republican party also favored excluding slavery from new territories. See C. W. Morrison, *Democratic Politics and Sectionalism* (1967).

Wilno: see VILNIUS, USSR.

Wilson, Angus, 1913–, English novelist, whose original name was Frank Johnstone. Wilson's novels are solidly rooted in English life. They attempt to delineate a society in which traditional values have lost all force and human relationships, public as well as private, are corrupted by pretension and sham. After the publication of two volumes of short stories his first novel, *Hemlock and After* (1952), appeared. It was followed by *Anglo-Saxon Attitudes* (1956), considered by many to be his major achievement, *The Middle Age of Mrs. Eliot* (1958), *The Old Men at the Zoo* (1961), *Late Call* (1965), and *No Laughing Matter* (1967). Wilson's other writings include *Death Dance: 125 Stories* (1969) and *The World of Charles Dickens* (1970). See biography by K. W. Gransden (1969).

Wilson, Benjamin, 1721-88, English portrait painter and electrician who opposed Benjamin Franklin's theory of positive and negative electricity. Instead, Wilson supported Newton's gravitational-optical ether, which he supposed to differ in density around bodies in accordance with their degrees of electrification. Wilson also opposed Franklin's theory of lightning rods, holding that blunt conductors performed better than pointed ones. His best experimental work was on the electrical properties of the tourmaline. He was elected fellow of the Royal Society in 1751 and received its gold medal in 1760 for his electrical experiments.

Wilson, Charles Erwin, 1890-1961, American industrialist and cabinet officer, b. Minerva, Ohio. He was an electrical engineer with Westinghouse Electric and Manufacturing Company from 1909 to 1919 and designed the first automobile starters made by Westinghouse. In 1919 he joined General Motors Corp., becoming (1926) president of Delco Remy Corp., a subsidiary. Vice president of General Motors from 1929 to 1939, he became executive vice president in 1939 and president in 1941. In World War II he supervised the huge war production activity in which General Motors was engaged. He is credited with formulating the cost-of-living wage formula that General Motors first inserted in its union contract in 1948. From 1953 to 1957 he was President Eisenhower's Secretary of Defense.

Wilson, Charles Thomson Rees, 1869-1959, Scottish physicist, educated at Manchester and Cambridge universities. He was Jacksonian professor of natural philosophy at Cambridge from 1925 to 1934. Noted for his studies of atmospheric electricity, he devised a method for the protection of barrage balloons from lightning during World War II. He invented the Wilson cloud chamber for studying the activity of ionized particles. For this invention he shared with A. C. Compton, a U.S. physicist, the 1927 Nobel Prize in Physics.

Wilson, Colin, 1931-, English writer, b. Leicester. From a proletarian background and self-educated, he has worked as a laborer in England and on the Continent. He first gained critical attention with *The Outsider* (1956). To Wilson the "outsider" is the individual who sees that life is futile and that society is formed in such a manner as to conceal this terrible truth. Among Wilson's many other works are *Beyond the Outsider* (1965), *The Glass Cage* (1966), *Bernard Shaw: A Reassessment* (1969), *Order of Assassins* (1972), and *Hesse, Reich, Borges* (1974). See the biographical study by S. R. Campion (1962).

Wilson, Edmund, 1895-1972, American critic and author, b. Red Bank, N.J. grad. Princeton, 1916. He is considered one of the most important American literary and social critics of the 20th cent. From 1920 to 1921 he was managing editor of *Vanity Fair,* and he was later on the staffs of the *New Republic* (1926-31) and the *New Yorker* (1944-48). In the 1930s he was much interested in the theories of Freud and Marx, which are treated in many of his works. Among his major writings are *Axel's Castle* (1931), a study of symbolism and other imaginative literatures (see SYMBOLISTS); *The Triple Thinkers* (1938); *The Wound and the Bow* (1941); *The Shores of Light* (1952); and *Patriotic Gore* (1962). As a critic Wilson was concerned with the social, psychological, and political conditions that shape literary ideas. His social studies include *To the Finland Station* (1940), a history of the European revolutionary tradition, and *The American Earthquake* (1958), a record of the Great Depression. His versatility is further revealed in *I Thought of Daisy* (1929), a novel; *Memoirs of Hecate County* (1949), short stories; and *Five Plays* (1954). Wilson edited F. Scott Fitzgerald's *The Crack-up* (1945). His later works include *Scrolls from the Dead Sea* (1955), *The Bit Between My Teeth* (1966), *Upstate: Records and Recollections of Northern New York* (1971), *A Window on Russia* (1973), *The Devils and Canon Barham: 10 Essays on Poets, Novelists, and Monsters* (1973). Wilson's third wife was the author Mary McCarthy. See his *Piece of My Mind: Reflections at Sixty* (1956); biography by C. P. Frank (1970); study by Sherman Paul (1965); bibliography by R. D. Ramsey (1971).

Wilson, Edmund Beecher, 1856-1939, American zoologist, b. Geneva, Ill., grad. Yale (Ph.B., 1878), Johns Hopkins Univ. (Ph.D., 1881). He taught at Bryn Mawr (1885-91) and at Columbia (1891-1928), where he initiated research in genetics and attracted many followers. His principal work was on the function of the cell in heredity and on the role of the chromosomes (including the significance of the sex chromosome). He also studied embryology and experimental morphology. His works include *The Cell in Development and Heredity* (1896, 3d ed. 1925) and *The Physical Basis of Life* (1923).

Wilson, Harold (James Harold Wilson), 1916-, British statesman. A graduate of Oxford, he became an economics lecturer there (1937) and a fellow of University College, Oxford (1938). During World War II he held various civil service appointments. Wilson entered Parliament (1945) as a Labour member, and as president of the board of trade (1947-51) he ended many of the wartime controls on industry. In 1951 he resigned with Aneurin Bevan, opposing the introduction of changes within the National Health Service. He thus became a spokesman for the left wing of the Labour party, later opposing party leader Hugh Gaitskell's stand against unilateral nuclear disarmament. After Gaitskell's death (1963), Wilson won the leadership of the party and became prime minister as a result of Labour's electoral victory in 1964. At first his government had only a four-seat majority in Parliament, but it was reelected with a large majority in 1966. The Labour government under Wilson sought to offset Britain's diminishing role outside Europe (in 1968 it announced the withdrawal of all military bases E of the Suez Canal by 1971) by increasing its role in Europe (in 1967 it reapplied for membership in the European Common Market). Wilson also tried unsuccessfully to reach a settlement with the white supremacist regime in Rhodesia, which unilaterally declared itself independent of Britain in 1965. Domestically Wilson imposed strict controls on wages and prices, raised taxes, and devalued (1967) the pound to end the growing economic crisis. By the spring of 1970 the economy seemed to be recovering, and Wilson scheduled a June election, which resulted in an unexpected defeat for the Labour party. In opposition, Wilson led his party to reverse its stand on entry into the Common Market, but a significant minority voted with the Conservative government in favor of entry and thus presented Wilson with the serious problem of maintaining party unity. Another divisive issue arose with the party's espousal (1973) of wide-scale nationalization. Nonetheless, in the general election of Feb., 1974, held at a time of severe economic crisis, Labour was returned to power, and Wilson again became prime minister. Despite the fact that he headed a minority government (and was therefore very vulnerable to defeat in Parliament), Wilson announced his intention of implementing the controversial policies of renegotiation of the terms of Britain's membership in the Common Market and nationalization. His government had to face continuing economic difficulties as well as a deterioration of the political situation and increasing violence in Northern Ireland (which required the reimposition of direct British rule). It was also obliged to mediate between Greece and Turkey in the tense crisis created by the overthrow of Archbishop Makarios in Cyprus and the subsequent Turkish invasion of that island in July, 1974. Wilson called another election in Oct., 1974, and secured a narrow majority in Parliament. See Wilson's own memoirs (*A Personal Record,* 1971) and biographies by Anthony Howard (1965) and Ernest Kay (1967).

Wilson, Henry, 1812-75, American politician, Vice President of the United States (1873-75); b. Farmington, N.H. At 21 he legally changed his name from Jeremiah Jones Colbath, and as Henry Wilson he apprenticed himself to a cobbler at Natick, Mass. Wilson became successful as a shoe manufacturer and as a Whig politician, serving as a state legislator for most of the years from 1841 to 1852. His strong abolitionist convictions led him to leave the Whigs in 1848, when he helped organize the Free Soil party. Elected (1855) to the U.S. Senate by the Know-Nothing legislature, Wilson finally joined (1856) the Republican party because of its clear opposition to slavery. He was a leading radical Republican for the rest of his career. During the Civil War he was chairman of the Senate committee on military affairs. The "Natick cobbler," as he was called, was elected Vice President on the ticket headed by Ulysses S. Grant in 1872, but he died before completing his term. Wilson wrote the *History of the Rise and Fall of the Slave Power in America* (3 vol., 1872-77), the first major history of the coming of the Civil War. See biographies by Ernest McKay (1971) and R. H. Abbott (1972).

Wilson, Sir Henry Hughes, 1864-1922, British field marshal. He saw active service in Burma and in the South African War before becoming commandant of the army staff college at Camberley (1907-10) and director of military operations at the war office (1910-14). A friend of the French general Ferdinand Foch, he formulated the plans by which the British Expeditionary Force went to France on the outbreak of World War I. Wilson was assistant chief of staff of that force. He was later principal liaison officer (1915) between the British and French armies and commander of the 4th army corps (1915-16). In 1917 he went on a military mission to Russia and returned to sit in the Allied Supreme War Council and become (1918) chief of the British imperial general staff. He was made chief marshal in 1919. He retired from the army in 1922 and was elected to Parliament from Northern Ireland. Shortly afterward he was killed by Sinn Fein terrorists. See biographies by C. E. Callwell (2 vol., 1927), Basil Collier (1961), and Bernard Ash (1968).

Wilson, Henry Maitland Wilson, 1st **Baron,** 1881-1964, British field marshal. He served in the South African War and World War I and in 1939 became commander of the British forces in Egypt. He led the ill-fated British expedition in Greece in 1941 and served as commander in chief in the Middle East (1943-44) and as supreme Allied commander in the Mediterranean (1944-45). "Jumbo" Wilson was head of the British joint staff mission in Washington from 1945 to 1947. In 1946 he was created baron.

Wilson, Jack: see WOVOKA.

Wilson, James, 1742-98, American jurist, signer of the Declaration of Independence, b. near St. Andrews, Scotland. He studied at the universities of Glasgow and Edinburgh and, after emigrating to Pennsylvania in 1766, taught Latin at the College of Philadelphia (now Univ. of Pennsylvania). He studied law there under John Dickinson, was later admitted to the bar in 1767, and became a successful lawyer within a few years. He was a member of the Pennsylvania convention (1774) and in the following year was elected a delegate to the Continental Congress. Although he strongly disputed Parliament's authority over the colonies, he opposed independence until July, 1776. Because he vigorously opposed the extremely democratic principles of the Pennsylvania constitution of 1776, he lost (1777) his seat in Congress. He became allied with the conservative faction and argued for it in the Congress of the Confederation (1782-83, 1785-87). Wilson is especially known for his part in the Federal Convention of 1787, where he incorporated into the Constitution the principle that sovereignty resides in the people. His influence in drawing up the Constitution was second only to that of James Madison. He was active in drafting the Pennsylvania constitution of 1790 and served as Associate Justice of the U.S. Supreme Court (1789-98). He was the first professor of law (1789) at the College of Philadelphia. Wilson wrote a number of pamphlets, addresses, treatises, and lectures on law. See biography by C. P. Smith (1956, repr. 1973); the collection of his works, 2 vol., ed by R. G. McCloskey (1804, repr. 1967).

Wilson, James, 1836-1920, American agriculturist and cabinet officer, b. Ayrshire, Scotland. He emigrated to the United States and settled (1851) in Connecticut, later moving (1855) to Tama co., Iowa, where he became a successful farmer. A member of the Republican party, he served in the state legislature (1867-73) and in the U.S. Congress (1873-77, 1883-85). Wilson was (1891-97) director of the agricultural experiment station and professor of agriculture at Iowa State (now Iowa State Univ. of Science and Technology). As Secretary of Agriculture (1897-1913) under Presidents William McKinley, Theodore Roosevelt, and William Howard Taft, he greatly expanded the services of the department; a number of experimental stations were set up over the country, and the aid of experts and scientists was enlisted.

Wilson, James Grant, 1832-1914, American biographer and man of letters, b. Scotland. He was brought to the United States in 1833. After journalistic work in Chicago and service in the Union army in the Civil War, he settled in New York, as a writer and editor principally concerned with biography. With John Fiske he edited *Appleton's Cyclopedia of American Biography* (6 vol., 1886-89; revised with supplementary volume, 1898-99). His other works included a biography of U.S. Grant and its revisions, compilations of military biographies, and editions of the poetry of Bryant and of Fitz-Greene Halleck.

Wilson, John: see NORTH, CHRISTOPHER.

Wilson, Richard, 1713?–1782, British landscape painter, b. Wales. He studied in London and achieved success as a portrait painter, but after a visit to Italy (c.1750–1756) he devoted himself to landscape in the classical tradition of Claude Lorrain. The exhibition of Wilson's *Niobe* in 1760 won him acclaim, and he was made a member and later librarian of the Royal Academy. His work did not become generally popular until after his death. Although his Italian landscapes did not depart from the classical tradition of picturesque Roman ruins and recumbent nymphs, his work shows considerable originality and breadth of treatment, especially in his many fine paintings of English country houses. He exerted a strong influence on subsequent landscape painting in England. *On Hounslow Heath* (National Gall., London) and *Afternoon and Lake Nemi* (both: Metropolitan Mus.) are well-known examples of his work. See monograph by W. G. Constable (1953).

Wilson, William Bauchop, 1862–1934, American labor leader, U.S. Secretary of Labor (1913–21), b. Blantyre, Scotland. Coming as a child to the United States in 1870, he worked in Pennsylvania coal mines after 1871 and helped organize (1890) the United Mine Workers of America. He was (1900–1908) secretary-treasurer of the labor union and, as a Democrat, served (1907–13) in the House of Representatives. As chairman (1912–13) of the House Labor Committee, he helped draft the bill creating the Dept. of Labor. The first Secretary of Labor in U.S. history, William B. Wilson organized the department and introduced machinery for mediation in labor disputes. See R. W. Babson, *W. B. Wilson and the Department of Labor* (1919).

Wilson, William Lyne, 1843–1900, American legislator, cabinet member, and university president, b. Jefferson co., Va. (now in W.Va.). He was a private in the Confederate army in the Civil War, and after teaching (1865–71) Latin at Columbian College (now George Washington Univ.) and practicing law (1871–82) in Charles Town, W.Va., Wilson was (1882–83) president of the Univ. of West Virginia. He entered politics and served (1883–95) as a Democrat in the U.S. House of Representatives. As chairman (1893–95) of the Committee on Ways and Means, he fought for moderate tariff reform. He was active in the repeal of the Sherman Silver Purchase Act and gained wide notice through the Wilson-Gorman Tariff Act of 1894. Wilson had introduced a tariff bill—backed by President CLEVELAND—which substantially reduced rates on many raw materials and manufactured products and levied an income tax. The bill passed the House unchanged, but largely through the efforts of Arthur P. GORMAN and others, it was considerably altered in the Senate, and Wilson's low-tariff principle was lost. Cleveland refused to sign the bill, which became law without his signature. In 1895 the Supreme Court declared the income tax provisions unconstitutional. As Postmaster General (1895–97), Wilson inaugurated the rural free delivery system. He served as president of Washington and Lee Univ. from 1897 to 1900. See Festus P. Summers, ed., *William L. Wilson and Tariff Reform* (1953) and *The Cabinet Diary of William L. Wilson, 1896–1897* (1957).

Wilson, Woodrow (Thomas Woodrow Wilson), 1856–1924, 28th President of the United States (1913–21), b. Staunton, Va. He graduated from Princeton in 1879 and studied law at the Univ. of Virginia. Admitted (1882) to the bar, he practiced in Atlanta, Ga., for a year before going to Johns Hopkins to study political science and jurisprudence. In 1885, he published *Congressional Government,* a significant work. After receiving (1886) his Ph.D. degree, he taught history and political economy at Bryn Mawr (1885–88) and Wesleyan Univ. (1888–90). In 1890 he became professor of jurisprudence and political economy at Princeton and gained a reputation for his eloquent orations. Popular with the student body, Wilson, a descendant of Presbyterian ministers on both sides of his family, was elected (1902) president of Princeton, becoming its first nonclerical head. He strove to raise academic standards, reorganized the curriculum, and introduced the preceptorial system of instruction, which provided for more individualized education. His attempt to change the social and living facilities by eliminating the elite eating clubs for upperclassmen and introducing the quadrangle system, where students from all of the classes would live and eat together, was less successful. It aroused great hostility, which reached a climax in his bitter struggle with the group headed by Dean Andrew F. West. Wilson lost, but with prompting from George B. M. Harvey, a New York publisher with strong connections in the Democratic party, he ran for governor of New Jersey in 1910 soon after resigning his post at Princeton. With the aid of the New Jersey Democratic machine, he secured the nomination and, breaking with the machine to espouse progressive policies, went on to win the election. Despite much resistance from the regular Democrats, Wilson forced through the New Jersey legislature such reforms as an employer's liability act, the direct primary, a corrupt practices act, and revitalization of the state public utilities commission. His gubernatorial record brought him to the forefront of national politics. Although Champ CLARK was the leading contender for the presidential nomination at the Democratic convention in 1912, he could not muster the necessary two-thirds vote, and after he had exhausted his strength, Wilson won on the 46th ballot. He was helped by the switch to him of William Jennings BRYAN (prompted by Edward M. HOUSE). The split in the Republican party, which divided into the regular Republicans supporting William Howard Taft and the PROGRESSIVE PARTY backing Theodore ROOSEVELT, gained the election for Wilson, who captured 435 electoral votes. Wilson revived the custom, abandoned in 1801, of addressing Congress in person and immediately called for a series of reforms, which he had called the "New Freedom" in his presidential campaign. During his administration the tariff was drastically decreased (1913; see UNDERWOOD, OSCAR WILDER); the FEDERAL RESERVE SYSTEM was instituted (1913); the La Follette Seamen's Act, regulating labor conditions aboard ship, became law (1915); the Adamson Act, establishing an eight-hour day for railroad employees, was enacted (1916); and the Federal Farm Loan Act, providing for loans to cooperative farm associations, was passed (1916). Wilson continued the policy of curbing monopoly by creating (1914) the FEDERAL TRADE COMMISSION to investigate and expose unfair practices of corporations, pushed the passage (1914) of the CLAYTON ANTITRUST ACT, and instituted antitrust proceedings in 92 cases. Further, the Seventeenth Amendment, providing for the direct popular election of U.S. Senators, the Eighteenth Amendment, which instituted PROHIBITION, and the Nineteenth Amendment, by which women received the vote, were all launched while Wilson was President. In foreign affairs the Wilson administration was faced with mounting difficulties. In Mexico, a revolution brought (Feb., 1913) Victoriano HUERTA to the presidency. Wilson refused to recognize Huerta on the grounds that he had gained power by assassinating his predecessor, and instead resorted to a policy of "watchful waiting." In 1914, this policy ended when U.S. marines landed in Veracruz in retaliation for the arrest of U.S. sailors in Tampico. Mediation by Argentina, Brazil, and Chile prevented war but failed to settle the aggravated situation. After Huerta was driven from power, new troubles arose from the internal situation in Mexico. The raid of Francisco ("Pancho") VILLA across the U.S. border resulted in the punitive expedition (1916) into Mexico led by John J. PERSHING. Border incidents continued, and relations between the two countries remained unfriendly. During this period, Wilson also sent U.S. troops to Haiti (1915), the Dominican Republic (1916), and Cuba (1917), and established protectorates over the first two. In his Far Eastern policy, notably his refusal (1913) to support loans to China by American bankers, Wilson openly rejected "dollar diplomacy." Despite these concerns, the outbreak of World War I in Europe overshadowed all other problems. Secretary of State William Jennings Bryan, who scrupulously favored neutrality, resigned (1915) and was succeeded by Robert LANSING, who tended to favor intervention on the side of the Allies. Wilson during his first term nevertheless sought by all diplomatic means to maintain an impartial neutrality. American public opinion, however, increasingly mounted against Germany, and the sinking (May 7, 1915) of the LUSITANIA by a German submarine aroused a storm of protest. After the sinking (March 24, 1916) of the American vessel *Sussex,* Wilson issued an ultimatum to which Germany responded with a pledge to cease its unrestricted submarine attacks. Trouble over shipping also occurred with Great Britain in its effort to enforce the blockade of Germany. In the 1916 election, the Democratic campaign slogan, "He kept us out of war," helped return Wilson to the White House; Charles Evans HUGHES was defeated by a very close margin. Wilson immediately attempted to mediate between the warring nations, but without success. Relations with Germany became more and more tense, especially after the announcement (Jan. 31, 1917) by Germany of a renewal of unrestricted submarine warfare. On Feb. 3, Wilson broke diplomatic relations with Germany. Several more U.S. vessels were sunk, and on April 2, 1917, Wilson asked Congress to declare war on Germany. In his war message Wilson stated that "the world must be made safe for democracy" and that the United States would wage war for liberty and peace. War was declared April 6. Wilson's speeches, elaborating his war aims, did much to consolidate U.S. opinion behind his policies as the country mobilized. In addition to the establishment of a fighting force, war industries were placed under government control and the President was given wide powers over the production and distribution of food and fuel. Late in Dec., 1917, Wilson put the railroads under government operation. The Committee on Public Information was established to propagandize for the war. In Jan., 1918, prompted by the publication by the Bolshevik revolutionary government in Russia of secret treaties that revealed the imperialistic war aims of the Allies, Wilson presented the FOURTEEN POINTS to Congress; these outlined the basic provisions that he believed the peace settlement must cover. As the war drew to a close and preparations were begun for a peace conference, Wilson was generally looked upon in Europe as the savior of the future. In the United States, however, he suffered an electoral setback in Nov., 1918, after appealing for the return of a Democratic Congress as an endorsement of his foreign policy; the Republicans captured both houses of Congress. Shortly afterward (December) Wilson set sail for Europe as head of the U.S. delegation to the Paris Peace Conference; his attendance broke all American precedents. Angry at Republican criticism, Wilson did not include any active Republican, or any Senator, on the peace commission. Wilson was received in Europe with warm ovations and set about trying to create a new world society, which would be governed by the "self-determination of peoples," which would be free from secret diplomacy and wars, and, most important, which would have an association of nations to maintain international justice. At the peace conference he became involved in long and bitter wrangles with Georges CLEMENCEAU, David LLOYD GEORGE, Vittorio ORLANDO, and the other representatives of European powers. The resulting treaty (see VERSAILLES, TREATY OF) was far from being the fulfillment of his dream, although he did secure the adoption of the covenant establishing the LEAGUE OF NATIONS. Yet he accepted the treaty as being the best obtainable. At home, opposition to the League had been growing, and when Wilson returned (July, 1919) with the signed treaty, his accomplishments at Paris were received with mixed feelings. In the Senate, quarrels over the ratification of the treaty and the proposed amendments broke out immediately. In the group that emerged as opponents of the League, Henry Cabot LODGE was outstanding. Nevertheless, despite the agitation of a handful of "irreconcilables," the Senate would probably have ratified the treaty if certain reservations protecting U.S. sovereignty had been added. Wilson, however, refused to compromise and sought popular support by making a speaking tour of the United States. He was on his way east from the Pacific coast when fatigue and strain brought on a sudden physical breakdown in Sept., 1919, and forced him to cancel his trip. On Oct. 2, 1919, the President suffered a stroke, which incapacitated him for several months. He never entirely recovered, and for the remainder of his second term, Wilson, bitterly disillusioned, was virtually detached from the political scene. He continued to be uncompromising in his refusal to accept reservations on the League. Three years after the expiration of his term he died. His character and policies have been the subject of acrimonious debate, but even those who have doubted his wisdom have recognized him as one of the pivotal figures of American and world history. His writings on history and jurisprudence include *Division and Reunion, 1829–1889* (1893), *George Washington* (1896), *A History of the American People* (5 vol., 1902), and *Constitutional Government in the United States* (1908). These books are distinguished by a wide knowledge of constitutional law and by the severe and polished literary style that also characterizes *An Old Master and Other Political Essays* (1893) and *Mere Literature and Other Essays* (1893). Wilson's addresses, messages, and speeches, considered among the finest by an American, have been published and republished in various collections; see L. S. Turnbull, *Woodrow Wilson: A Selected Bibliography of His Published Writings, Addresses, and Public Papers* (1948, repr.

1971). Publication of the definitive edition of the Wilson papers was begun in 1966. *The Woodrow Wilsons* (1937), by Eleanor Wilson McAdoo (his daughter) and M. Y. Gaffrey, is an intimate account of his family life. See biographies by W. A. White (1925), H. H. Bellot (1955), J. M. Blum (1956), S. B. McKinley (1957), Herbert Hoover (1958), and Arthur Link (5 vol., 1947–65); R. S. Baker, *Woodrow Wilson and the World Settlement* (3 vol., 1922; repr. 1960) and *Woodrow Wilson: Life and Letters* (8 vol., 1927–39, repr. 1968); William Diamond, *The Economic Thought of Woodrow Wilson* (1943); T. A. Bailey, *Woodrow Wilson and the Lost Peace* (1944, repr. 1963) and *Woodrow Wilson and the Great Betrayal* (1945); Josephus Daniels, *The Wilson Era* (1946); E. H. Buehrig, *Woodrow Wilson and the Balance of Power* (1955, repr. 1968) and *Wilson's Foreign Policy in Perspective* (1957, repr. 1970); Hardin Craig, *Woodrow Wilson at Princeton* (1960); H. W. Bragdon, *Woodrow Wilson: The Academic Years* (1967); Arthur Link, ed., *Woodrow Wilson: A Profile* (1968).

Wilson, city (1970 pop. 29,347), seat of Wilson co., E N.C., in a rich agricultural region; inc. 1849. It is a commercial and industrial center producing textile goods (especially clothing), metal products, and processed foods. Atlantic Christian College is in the city.

Wilson, Mount, peak, 5,710 ft (1,740 m) high, S Calif., in the San Gabriel Mts., NE of Pasadena. It is the site of Mt. Wilson Observatory (est. 1904), which is operated jointly by the Carnegie Institution and the California Institute of Technology and houses a 100-in. (254-cm) telescope.

Wilson cloud chamber: see CLOUD CHAMBER.

Wilson Dam: see TENNESSEE VALLEY AUTHORITY.

Wilson-Gorman Tariff Act: see WILSON, WILLIAM LYNE; GORMAN, ARTHUR PUE.

Wilson's Creek National Battlefield: see NATIONAL PARKS AND MONUMENTS (table).

Wilson's thrush: see THRUSH.

Wilton, municipal borough (1971 pop. 3,815), Wiltshire, S central England. Carpets have been made in Wilton for centuries. Felt and farm machinery are other important products. Three sheep fairs are held annually. Wilton was an ancient capital of WESSEX and the residence of Saxon kings. In the 9th cent. Wilton was the site of a battle between King Alfred and the Danes. It was the seat of a bishopric until 1050. Wilton House, in which Sir Philip Sidney wrote *Arcadia,* was partly designed by Inigo Jones. It is the seat of the earl of Pembroke.

Wilton, town (1970 pop. 13,572), Fairfield co., SW Conn.; settled c.1701, inc. 1802.

Wilton Manors, city (1970 pop. 10,948), Broward co., SE Fla.; inc. 1947. It is a residential community in the greater Fort Lauderdale area. An electronic research firm is there.

Wiltshire (wĭlt'shĭr, -shər) or **Wilts,** county (1971 pop. 486,048), 1,345 sq mi (3,484 sq km), S central England. The county town is Salisbury. More than half of Wiltshire is occupied by the great chalk Salisbury Plain and by the Marlborough Downs. Primarily an agricultural county, Wiltshire affords large areas for sheep grazing in the uplands, and the fertile valleys of the Lower Avon, the East Avon, and the Kennet rivers have extensive dairy farming. Pigs are also raised and grains cultivated. Textiles, metal products, processed foods, farm machinery, and electrical goods are manufactured. SWINDON, the leading industrial center, is known for its locomotive works. The county is rich in historical associations. At STONEHENGE, Avebury, and Silbury Hill are the largest and oldest monuments of the early British, dating back 4,000 years. OLD SARUM was the seat of a bishopric until the 13th cent., when the office was transferred to SALISBURY, famous since then for its cathedral. WILTON, known for its carpets, was once the capital of the powerful Saxon kingdom of Wessex, where in the 9th cent. many of King Alfred's battles against the Danes were fought. His grandson, Athelstan, is buried at MALMESBURY Abbey, and according to legend, Queen Guinevere spent her last days in the nunnery at AMESBURY. Among Wiltshire's famous sons or residents are Joseph Addison, John Dryden, John Gay, George Herbert, and Christopher Wren.

Wimbledon, England: see MERTON.

Winant, John Gilbert (wī'nənt), 1889–1947, American public official, b. New York City. He served in the New Hampshire legislature (1917, 1921–25) and was governor of the state (1925–26, 1931–34). A liberal Republican, he was appointed (1935) chairman of the Social Security Board by President Franklin Delano Roosevelt. He served as assistant director (1935, 1937–39) and then director (1939–41) of the International Labor Organization. From 1941 to 1946 he was ambassador to Great Britain, maintaining close relations with the British government during the difficult years of World War II. His *Letters from Grosvenor Square* (1947) described his experiences. In 1947, while U.S. representative to the United Nations Economic and Social Council, he committed suicide. See biography by Bernard Bellush (1968).

winch, mechanical device for hauling or lifting consisting essentially of a movable drum around which a cable is wound so that rotation of the drum produces a drawing force at the end of the cable. A windlass is essentially the same device as a winch, except that a winch may be power-driven whereas a windlass is usually hand-powered and somewhat less sophisticated. Winches are normally equipped with a ratchet wheel and a pawl to prevent slippage of the load, and brakes that allow a load to be lowered or released at a controlled rate. A hoist is another closely related device, mounted so as to be movable (as in a traveling crane). Winches and hoists are widely used in cargo handling, e.g., in ships, factories, and warehouses, and also function as the power unit in derricks, power cranes, and power shovels. A car puller is a winch with a vertical drum axis, used to position railroad cars in freight yards. Certain military and construction vehicles designed for off-road use are equipped with engine-powered winches that can be used for lifting and hauling or to extricate the vehicle should it become stuck in areas where traction is poor.

Winchelsea (wĭn'chəlsē), village, East Sussex, SE England. Winchelsea was an important member of the CINQUE PORTS.

Winchester (wĭn'chĭstər), municipal borough (1971 pop. 31,041), county town of Hampshire, S central England. It was called Caer Gwent by the Britons, Venta Belgarum by the Romans, and Wintanceastre by the Saxons. Winchester was the capital of the Anglo-Saxon kingdom of Wessex. Even after the Norman Conquest, when London gradually gained political ascendancy, Winchester remained England's center of learning and attracted many religious scholars. At this time it was also a wool center. The city has held a position of great ecclesiastical influence, reflected in its magnificent cathedral. This Norman structure, which replaced a Saxon church, was consecrated in 1093. In the 14th cent. it was enlarged and transformed into the present Gothic cathedral. It is the burial place of Saxon kings and queens and of William of Wykeham, Samuel Wilberforce, Izaak Walton, and Jane Austen. In Winchester are remains of Wolvesey Castle, where Queen Mary I lived in 1554. St. Cross Hospital, founded in the 12th cent., is the setting for Anthony Trollope's *The Warden.* The Norman castle, where several parliaments met, was damaged by Oliver Cromwell's soldiers; a round table, supposedly of King Arthur, hangs in the Great Hall. Winchester is still a historic cathedral town, virtually untouched by modern industry and construction. **Winchester College,** one of the great English public schools, was founded (1382; opened 1394) by William of Wykeham, bishop of Winchester, and is still partly housed in 14th-century buildings.

Winchester (wĭn'chĕ"stər, wĭn'chĭstər). **1** Town (1970 pop. 11,106), Litchfield co., NW Conn., in the Litchfield Hills; settled 1732, inc. 1771. It includes Winsted (1970 pop. 8,954), an industrial center where electrical appliances, machine products, pipe organs, and fishing tackle are manufactured. A junior college is in Winsted, as are many early 18th-century mansions. Of interest are the little red schoolhouse (1815) and the Winchester Historical Society, located in the Rockwell House (1813). Winchester lies at the gateway to the Berkshire Hills, in a region of lakes and mountain laurel. **2** City (1970 pop. 13,402), seat of Clark co., N central Ky.; inc. 1793. The center of a tobacco and livestock area on the edge of the bluegrass country, it has plants making steel tubing, bed springs, synthetic rubber, truck axles, and lamps. Henry Clay made his last speech in Kentucky in the old courthouse there. The city is the headquarters of Cumberland National Forest and the seat of a junior college. Two state parks are in the vicinity. **3** Town (1970 pop. 22,269), Middlesex co., E Mass., a residential suburb of Boston; settled 1640, inc. 1850. **4** City (1970 pop. 14,643), seat of Frederick co., N Va., in the Shenandoah valley; settled 1732 near an Indian village in Lord Fairfax's domain, inc. as a city 1874. It is the trade, processing, and shipping center for an orchard district noted for its apples. Its manufactures include brake linings, cans, furniture, clothing, plastics, and travel trailers. George Washington began his career as a surveyor there in 1748. During the French and Indian War Winchester was a center for defense against Indian raids, and Washington, who commanded the Virginia troops, had his headquarters there. Gen. Daniel Morgan lived in Winchester and is buried in Mt. Hebron Cemetery. During the Civil War the city suffered severely, changing hands many times. Stonewall Jackson headquartered there during the winter of 1861–62, and Gen. Philip Sheridan during the winter of 1864–65. Both headquarters are preserved. Also of interest are Washington's office, the old Presbyterian Church (1790; now an armory), and an annual apple festival. Willa Cather and Richard E. Byrd were born in Winchester.

Winchilsea, Anne Finch, countess of (wĭn'-chəlsē), 1661–1720, English poet. In 1684 she married Heneage Finch, who became (1712) 4th earl of Winchilsea. Though her friendships extended to the foremost literary figures of the day, including Pope and Swift, she never became part of the London literary coterie. Her most celebrated poem, the Pindaric ode "The Spleen," appeared in Charles Gildon's miscellany in 1701. The only early collection of her poems was *Miscellany Poems Written by a Lady* (1713). Her nature poetry was greatly admired by Wordsworth.

Winckelmann, Johann Joachim (yō'hän yōä'khĭm vĭng'kəlmän), 1717–68, German classical archaeologist and historian of ancient art, in which field he was a noted authority. A convert to Roman Catholicism in 1754, he went to Italy the following year. There he spent the rest of his life in study in the Vatican Library and in research in Rome, Florence, and Naples. His chief book was *Geschichte der Kunst des Altertums* [history of the art of antiquity] (1764), which laid the foundation for modern scientific archaeology. See his *Writings on Art* (ed. by David Irwin, 1972); biography by Wolfgang Leppmann (1970).

Winckler, Hugo (hōō'gō vĭngk'lər), 1863–1913, German Orientalist. A professor at the Univ. of Berlin, Winckler was noted for his archaeological work. He helped to excavate the Phoenician city of Sidon. During excavations at Boğazköy in 1906–7 he discovered CUNEIFORM tablets in Hittite (or Kanesian), a principal source for knowledge of the Hittite civilization.

wind, flow of air parallel to the earth's surface. The direction of wind may be indicated by a wind vane, or WEATHER VANE; in meteorological stations the vane is usually connected to an electrical recording device. A wind is named according to the point of the compass from which it blows, e.g., a wind blowing from the north is a north wind. Wind velocity is commonly measured by means of a cup anemometer, an instrument with three or four small hollow metal hemispheres set so that they catch the wind and revolve about a vertical rod. An electrical device records the revolutions of the cups and thus the velocity of the wind. A scale of wind velocity was devised (c.1805) by Admiral Sir Francis Beaufort of the British navy. An adaptation of Beaufort's scale is used by the U.S. National Weather Service; it employs numbers from 0 to 12, representing calm, light air, light breeze, gentle breeze, moderate breeze, fresh breeze, strong breeze, moderate gale, fresh gale, strong gale, whole gale, storm, hurricane. Zero (calm) is a wind velocity of less than 1 mi (1.6 km) per hr, and 12 (hurricane) represents a velocity of over 75 mi (120 km) per hr. The U.S. National Weather Service has estimated that TORNADO winds have reached a velocity of 500 mi (800 km) per hr. Over some areas of the earth, winds blow predominantly from one direction throughout the year; over

BEAUFORT NUMBER	WIND	SYMBOL	WIND SPEED (MPH)
0	calm		less than 1
1	light air		1–3
2	light breeze		4–7
3	gentle breeze		8–12
4	moderate breeze		13–18
5	fresh breeze		19–24
6	strong breeze		25–31
7	moderate gale		32–38
8	fresh gale		39–46
9	strong gale		47–54
10	whole gale		55–63
11	storm		64–75
12	hurricane		more than 75

Beaufort scale of wind speeds

other areas, the prevailing direction changes with the seasons; over still others, winds are so variable from day to day that no prevailing direction is evident. These wind directions are indicative of the mass distribution of the atmosphere and hence of atmospheric pressure over the earth's surface. Around the equator there is a belt of relatively low pressure known as the DOLDRUMS, where the heated air is expanding and rising; at about lat. 30°N and S there are belts of high pressure known as the HORSE LATITUDES, regions of descending air; farther poleward, near lat. 60°N and S, are belts of low pressure, where the POLAR FRONT is located and cyclonic activity is at a maximum; finally there are the polar caps of high pressure. The prevailing wind systems of the earth blow from the several belts of high pressure toward adjacent low-pressure belts. Because of the earth's rotation (see CORIOLIS EFFECT), the winds do not blow directly northward or southward to the area of lower pressure, but are deflected to the right in the Northern Hemisphere and to the left in the Southern Hemisphere. The wind systems

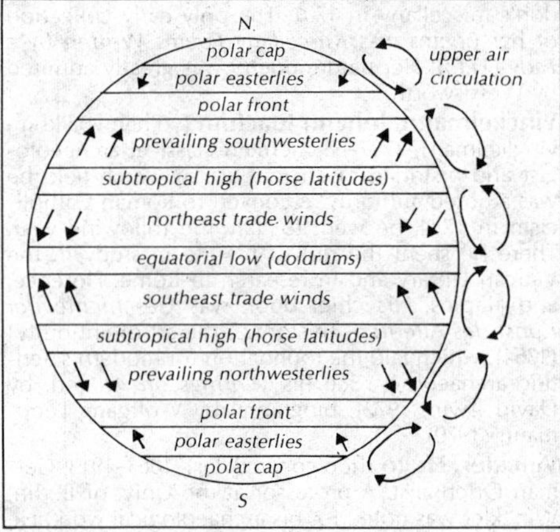

Global wind patterns

comprise the TRADE WINDS; the prevailing westerlies, moving outward from the poleward sides of the horse-latitude belts toward the 60° latitude belts of low pressure (from the southwest in the Northern Hemisphere and from the northwest in the Southern Hemisphere); and the polar easterlies, blowing outward from the polar caps of high pressure and toward the 60° latitude belts of low pressure. This zonal pattern of winds is displaced northward and southward seasonally because of the inclination of the earth on its axis and the consequent migration of the belts of temperature and pressure. In addition, the pattern is considerably modified by the distribution of land and water, especially in the temperate regions, where temperature differences between land and water are greatest. In winter, areas of high pressure tend to build up over cold continental land masses, while vigorous low-pressure development takes place over the adjacent, relatively warm oceans. Exactly the opposite conditions occur during summer, although to a lesser degree. These contrasting pressures over land and water areas are the cause of MONSOON winds, which reverse their direction with the seasons. Superimposed upon the general circulation of winds are many lesser disturbances, such as the extratropical CYCLONE (the common storm of the temperate latitudes), the tropical cyclone, or HURRICANE, and the tornado; each of these storms moves generally along a path that follows the direction of the prevailing winds but within itself maintains a circulatory wind pattern. The diurnal, or daily, heating and cooling of land near a lake or ocean of fairly constant temperature causes air to blow toward the relatively warmer land during the day (sea breeze) and toward the relatively warmer water at night (land breeze). These breezes are shallow and seldom penetrate far inland or attain high velocity. Similar diurnal changes occur on mountain slopes, the air in the valley becoming heated and expanding so that it moves up the slope in the daytime, the cold air settling into the valley at night. Although winds tend to blow along the length of a valley, they may be deflected at an angle from their normal course. Friction with the earth's surface, eddies caused by surface irregularities, and inequalities of heating and radiation with consequent convection currents tend to reduce wind velocity near the surface of the earth and cause winds to blow in gusts. In animistic religions the winds are connected with supernatural powers. In classical mythology Aeolus is the controller of the winds. The various winds, Boreas, Zephyr, Notus, and Argestes, were the children of Eos, goddess of the dawn, and her husband, Astraeus. See also CHINOOK; CLIMATE; ROARING FORTIES; SANDSTORM; SIROCCO; WEATHER. See S. H. Walker, *Wind and Strategy* (1973).

Windau: see VENTSPILS, USSR.

Windaus, Adolf (ä'dôlf vĭn'dous), 1876–1959, German chemist. He was professor of chemistry and director of the chemistry laboratories at the Univ. of Göttingen (1915–44). For his research on sterols, especially in relation to vitamins, he received the 1928 Nobel Prize in Chemistry. He later discovered and prepared synthetically vitamin D_3, the component of vitamin D that is most important in preventing the bone disease rickets.

Wind Cave National Park, 28,059 acres (11,355 hectares), in the Black Hills, SW S.Dak.; est. 1903. Wind Cave, discovered in 1881, was named for the strong air currents that blow alternately in and out of it depending on whether the atmospheric pressure is higher or lower than the air pressure inside the cave. There are 10.5 mi (16.9 km) of explored passageways. The cave's temperature remains constant at 47°F (8°C). Unusual calcite-crystal and boxwork formations make Wind Cave unique. The park's surface is characterized by rolling grasslands with herds of bison, elk, deer, and pronghorn antelope; several prairie dog towns are in the park.

Windermere (wĭn'dərmēr), lake, 10.5 mi (17 km) long and 1 mi (1.6 km) wide, in the Lake District, between Lancashire and Westmorland, NW England. It is c.210 ft (60 m) deep and lies among wooded hills near Scafell and other mountains. The largest lake in England, it is fed by many streams and is drained by the Leven River to Morecambe Bay. The lake's shores are indented to form little bays, and it has several islands. It attracts many tourists.

windflower: see ANEMONE; PASQUEFLOWER.

Windham, William (wĭn'dəm), 1750–1810, British politician. Elected to Parliament in 1784, he was a friend of Edmund Burke, whom he assisted in the impeachment of Warren Hastings. He served (1794–1801) as secretary for war under William Pitt, resigning with Pitt when the king prevented Catholic Emancipation. He was secretary of state for war and colonies (1806–7) in the ministry of Lord Grenville. His political career was not outstanding, but his influence on leading politicians was great, and his written record is an important source for the period. See his diary for the years 1784–1810 (ed. by C. A. Baring, 1866); *The Windham Papers* (1913).

Windham, town (1970 pop. 19,626), Windham co., E Conn.; inc. 1692. It includes the industrial city of Willimantic. At Windham Center (settled c.1688) are several old buildings.

Windhoek (vĭnt'ho͝ok), city (1970 pop. 61,260), capital of South West Africa. It is South West Africa's largest city and its administrative, communications, and economic center. Windhoek is one of the world's major trade centers for Karakul sheep skins. Clothing is manufactured, and meat and bone meal are processed in the city. A transportation hub, Windhoek is linked with the Republic of South Africa's railroad network. Windhoek was originally the headquarters of a Nama chief, who defeated the HERERO inhabitants of the region in the 19th cent. After the occupation of the territory by German forces in 1885, it became the seat of administration and was later (1892) made the capital of the German colony of South West Africa. During World War I, Windhoek was captured by South African troops. Today the city retains a German flavor, and many of its residents are of German background. Windhoek stands 5,428 ft (1,654 m) above sea level and is surrounded by hills, three of which have castles built in German medieval style.

wind instrument, in music, any instrument whose tone is produced by a vibrating column of air. In the pipe ORGAN the column of air is set into vibration by mechanical means. Other wind instruments are blown by the player and are divided into two groups, the woodwinds and the brass winds, or brasses. The woodwinds include the FLUTE family, played without a reed, the CLARINET family, having single-reed mouthpieces, and the OBOE family, having double-reed mouthpieces (see REED INSTRUMENT). The brass winds include the BUGLE, CORNET, OPHICLEIDE, TROMBONE, TRUMPET, and TUBA, all having cup-shaped mouthpieces, and the FRENCH HORN, having a funnel-shaped mouthpiece. In the brasses the lips of the player perform the function of reeds. The wind passage of a wind instrument is called the bore and may be conical or cylindrical; its flared edge is called the bell. Woodwind and brass instruments are now best distinguished according to their mouthpieces, since metal flutes and saxophones remain woodwinds regardless of the material used to make them. See Anthony Baines, *Woodwind Instruments and Their History* (rev. ed. 1963); Adam Carse, *Musical Wind Instruments* (2d ed. 1965); Robert Donington, *Instruments of Music* (3d ed. 1970).

Windisch (vĭn'dĭsh), town (1970 pop. 7,444), Aargau canton, N Switzerland, on the Reuss River near its confluence with the Aare. Textiles and cables are made there. Originally a Helvetian settlement, it later became a Roman camp called Vindonissa. A Roman amphitheater, which accommodated over 10,000 spectators, has been excavated. Nearby are the remains of the once powerful monastery of Königsfelden, erected in 1310 on the site where Holy Roman Emperor Albert I had been murdered. The monastery church is a splendid example of Swiss Gothic architecture, with fine stained glass.

Windischgrätz or **Windisch-Grätz, Alfred, Fürst zu** (äl'frāt fürst tso͞o vĭn'dĭshgrĕts'), 1787–1862, Austrian field marshal. He was military governor of Bohemia when the REVOLUTIONS OF 1848 broke out in the Hapsburg empire. Given command in Vienna, he crushed the insurrection there, but because of the pressure of public opinion he was sent back to Bohemia. Meanwhile Prague had fallen to the revolutionists, and Windischgrätz's wife and eldest son had been killed in the insurrection. Windischgrätz recaptured (June, 1848) Prague after bombarding it and set up a military dictatorship over Bohemia. Vienna, where the revolutionists had again taken over, was also bombarded into submission (Oct., 1848) by Windischgrätz. With Felix zu SCHWARZENBERG, he engineered the abdication (Dec. 2, 1848) of Austrian Emperor Ferdinand in favor of Francis Joseph. Windischgrätz was removed from command in 1849 when his campaign against the Hungarian revolutionists was checked at Godollo. He later held various government posts.

windlass: see WINCH.

windmill, apparatus that harnesses wind power for a variety of uses, e.g., pumping water, grinding corn, driving small sawmills, and driving electricity generators. Windmills were probably not known in Europe before the 12th cent., but thereafter they became familiar landmarks in Holland, England, France, and Germany. The typical Dutch windmill, also called the tower type, has a huge tower of stone, brick, or wood, in contrast to the German, or post, mill, the distinctive feature of which is that the whole building revolves on a central post. At the top of either type there is a revolving apparatus to which four to six arms are attached. The arms, usually 20 to 40 ft (6–12 m) long, bear sails constructed of light wood, or of canvas attached to a frame. A small fan serves as a rudder to keep the wheel facing the wind. Most American windmills have high towers of light steel girders; at the top is a wheel with many sheet-metal concave and "warped" vanes (sails) about 4 ft (1.2 m) long. The wheel is kept automatically facing the wind by a broad tail geared to a shaft. They were once widely used for pumping water in rural parts of the United States. Windmills have been used since 1890 to drive electricity generators, but they are a very minor source of electric energy.

window, in architecture, the casement or sash, fitted with glass, which closes an opening in the wall of a structure without excluding light and air. It may have a square, round, or pointed head; may be single, double, or grouped; and in relation to the wall, may be flush, recessed, or projected. A projected window is called a bay window if polygonal, a bow window if semicircular, an ORIEL if it has corbeled brick or stone supports. A mullioned window is divided by slender bars into panes; when the bars radiate from the center of a circular bar it is called a wheel. It takes the name of ROSE WINDOW when adorned with STAINED GLASS or figure design. The long, narrow window of the English Perpendicular Gothic church is called a lancet; a lunette fills a somewhat crescent-shaped space under a vaulted intersection high upon a wall. A fanlight, characteristic of the American Colonial style, is either a semicircular transom, usually over an entrance, or a small attic window (or often a pair flanking the chimney). A French window reaches the floor and has double casements opening as doors; originating in France in the late Renaissance, it was adopted throughout the Continent and in the Southern states in America. The double-hung sashes (sliding up and down within the frame), first used in Renaissance England, attained wide popularity. In Spain windows are frequently ornate, with stone framework, an elaborate head, and a decorative iron GRILLE. In Indian and Byzantine windows a pierced slab of marble or alabaster often substitutes for glass. Muslims also used cement frames in which colored glass was set in brilliant ARABESQUE forms. Carved and turned wood grilles are found in Syria and Egypt. In China and Japan, rice paper, protected by a sliding wooden shutter, often takes the place of glass. Shell, also used in China, was employed by the Romans, as were thin panes of marble, mica, and horn. In modern architecture the use of windows has greatly increased in dwellings and in the exterior walls of factories and commercial buildings.

windpipe: see TRACHEA.

Wind River Range, part of the Rocky Mts., W Wyo., running southeastward c.120 mi (190 km) and constituting part of the Continental Divide. Gannett Peak (13,785 ft/4,202 m) is the highest point in Wyoming. A number of historic passes cross these mountains; South Pass (alt. 7,550 ft/2,301 m), at the southern end of the range, was the most important Rocky Mts. pass on the Oregon Trail.

Windsor (wĭn'zər), family name of the royal house of Great Britain. The name Wettin, family name of Albert of Saxe-Coburg-Gotha, consort of Queen Victoria, was changed to Windsor by George V in 1917. The new name was adopted by all members of the family. In 1952, Queen Elizabeth II, who married Philip Mountbatten, duke of Edinburgh, decreed that she and her descendants (other than females who marry) should retain the name Windsor. A declaration of 1960, however, restricted the name to those descendants bearing the title prince or princess (i.e., the sovereign's children, the children of the sovereign's sons, and the eldest son of the eldest son of the prince of Wales); all other descendants are to be known as Mountbatten-Windsor.

Windsor, Edward, duke of: see EDWARD VIII.

Windsor, Wallis Warfield, duchess of, 1896–, American-born wife of Edward, duke of Windsor, who, as EDWARD VIII, abdicated the British throne in order to marry her. In 1916 she married a naval lieutenant, from whom she was divorced in 1927. The next year she married Ernest Aldrich Simpson, an American businessman residing in London, where she met Edward, who was then prince of Wales. The friendship between Mrs. Simpson and the prince continued after he succeeded to the throne in Jan., 1936. In Oct., 1936, Mrs. Simpson obtained a divorce decree nisi. Rumors of a projected marriage of Edward and Mrs. Simpson preceded the crisis of Dec., 1936, which resulted in Edward's abdication. On April 27, 1937, the Simpson divorce became final, and Mrs. Simpson legally changed her name to Wallis Warfield. On June 3 she married Edward in France, where they made their home. By special letters patent it was provided that the duchess of Windsor should not share her husband's royal rank. See her memoir, *The Heart Has Its Reasons* (1956).

Windsor. **1** Town (1971 pop. 3,775), central N.S., Canada, at the mouth of the Avon River on an arm of Minas Basin. It is the center of a gypsum and limestone-quarrying area. Manufactures include fertilizers, building materials, and lumber products. Windsor was settled by Acadians (1703) and called Pisiquid. After their expulsion it was settled by New Englanders and renamed in 1764. It is the site of Fort Edward, built (1750) by the British. King's College, the first English university in Canada, was founded in Windsor in 1789 but moved in 1923 to Halifax as part of Dalhousie Univ. **2** City (1971 pop. 203,300), S Ont., Canada, on the Detroit River opposite Detroit, Mich. It is a port of entry and an important industrial center producing automobiles, salt, and chemicals. The city was settled by the French in 1749. After the American Revolution many Loyalists settled in the area. The city is the seat of Windsor Univ.

Windsor, officially **New Windsor,** municipal borough (1971 pop. 30,065), Berkshire, S central England, on the Thames River. There are a few light industries. In Elizabethan times about 70 inns enlivened the town. Sir Christopher Wren built the town hall, and Grinling Gibbons did much of the wood carving in the Church of St. John the Baptist. The real importance of the town has always been derived from **Windsor Castle,** the chief residence of English rulers since William I. The castle was improved and rebuilt by successive sovereigns. Henry II erected the Round Tower, and Edward IV began the construction of St. George's Chapel, one of the most splendid churches in England, where the Knights of the Garter are installed with medieval ceremony. In the chapel are buried several of England's kings. Some of the vaults are now used to store art treasures, national archives, and museum collections. The castle proper lies in the Home Park, and beyond it, separated by the tree-lined Long Walk, is the Great Park. In Frogmore, the royal mausoleum, are buried Queen Victoria and Prince Albert. On the castle grounds is a large lake, Virginia Water. See studies by Olwen Hedley (1967) and A. L. Rowse (1974).

Windsor, town (1970 pop. 22,502), Hartford co., N Conn., at the confluence of the Farmington and Connecticut rivers, just N of Hartford. Settled by Plymouth Colony in 1633, Windsor was the first English settlement in Connecticut and is the state's oldest town. Although primarily residential, the town produces nuclear installations for submarines and generators, tool and machine parts, computer equipment, metal products, paper, and soft drinks. The surrounding area has truck farming and tobacco raising, but Windsor's once renowned tobacco industry has gradually declined. The American statesman Oliver Ellsworth was born in Windsor; his home is now a museum. Also in the city are Fyler House (1640) and the Loomis/Chaffee Institute, a coeducational preparatory school.

Windsor, University of, at Windsor, Ont., Canada; nondenominational; coeducational; founded 1857 as Assumption College. It achieved university status in 1953. It has faculties of arts and science, engineering, graduate studies, education, business administration, law, and physical and health education as well as schools of computer science, nursing, and social work.

Windsor Castle: see under WINDSOR, England.

Windsor Locks, town (1970 pop. 15,080), Hartford co., N Conn., on the Connecticut River; settled 1663, set off from Windsor and inc. 1854. A tobacco-farming center since the 17th cent., it also has a large aircraft plant and paper industries. The town developed industrially after a canal, with locks, was built (1829) around the rapids there. Bradley International Airport, serving both Hartford and Springfield, Mass., is in Windsor Locks.

Windthorst, Ludwig (lo͝ot'vĭkh vĭnt'hôrst), 1812–91, German political leader. As a founder and head of the Catholic Center party, he became the Reichstag's foremost opponent of Chancellor Otto von Bismarck in the dispute between the chancellor and the German Roman Catholics known as the KULTURKAMPF. Remarkable for parliamentary skill, he later helped Bismarck seek a reconciliation with the Roman Catholic Church.

wind tunnel, apparatus for studying the interaction between a solid body and an airstream. A wind tunnel simulates the conditions of an aircraft in flight by causing a high-speed stream of air to flow past a model of the aircraft (or part of an aircraft) being tested. The model is mounted on wires so that lift and drag forces on it can be measured by measuring the tensions in the wire. The paths of the airstream around the model can also be studied by attaching tufts of wool (which align themselves with the wind direction) to various parts of the model, by injecting thin streams of smoke into the tunnel to render the airflow visible, or by using certain optical devices. Pressures on the model surface are measured through small flush openings in its surface. Forces exerted on the model may be determined from measurement of the airflow upstream and downstream of the model. In wind tunnels operating well below the speed of sound, the airstream is created by large motor-driven vanes. At velocities near or above the speed of sound, the airstream is created either by releasing highly compressed air from a tank at the upwind end of the tunnel or by allowing air to rush through the tunnel into a previously evacuated vacuum tank at its downwind end. Sometimes these methods are combined, especially for the production of hypersonic velocities, i.e., velocities at least five times as great as the speed of sound. The effect of wind on other vehicles, e.g., automobiles, and on stationary objects such as buildings and bridges may also be studied in wind tunnels.

wind vane: see WEATHER VANE.

Windward Channel, strait, c.50 mi (80 km) wide, between Cuba and Haiti, connecting the Atlantic Ocean and Caribbean Sea. It provides a direct route from the E United States to the Panama Canal.

Windward Islands, southern group of the Lesser Antilles in the West Indies, curving generally southward for c.300 mi (480 km) from the Leeward Islands toward NE Venezuela. Excluding Barbados, Trinidad, and Tobago, which are in the region but are not part of the group, the Windward Islands consist of French Martinique, GRENADA, and the **British Windward Islands** (c.700 sq mi/1,810 sq km). The British islands consist of Dominica, Saint Lucia, and Saint Vincent. Since 1967 the islands have been associated states of the United Kingdom. They each have complete internal autonomy while Great Britain remains responsible for foreign affairs and defense. The Grenadines, an archipelago of tiny islands strung out between St. Vincent and Grenada, are divided administratively between them. Of volcanic origin, the islands are generally rugged, mountainous, and well forested, and they have many streams and lakes. With an equable climate, ample rainfall, and rich soil, they produce a variety of tropical agricultural crops for export including bananas, spices, limes, and cacao. The islands are subject to hurricanes in the autumn. In recent years small-scale manufacturing has gained importance, but perhaps the most encouraging development has been the growth of the tourist trade. The deep and sheltered harbors encourage considerable interisland commerce. Roseau, on Dominica, and Kingstown, on St. Vincent, are the islands' chief cities. Largely inhabited by persons of black African descent, with some admixture of Carib Indian, Portuguese, and East Indian, the islands are dominated by a class of native-born civil servants and by a small percentage of white families, chiefly British. The culture varies from island to island, but the French influence is strong and many inhabitants speak a French patois. For some time after Columbus's discovery of the islands, they were largely ignored and left to the aboriginal Caribs. In the early 17th cent., colonization was undertaken by the British and the French; settlements and sovereignty overlapped. The long struggle for dominance in the islands was a good part of the worldwide Anglo-French conflict. Several naval battles were fought there; in 1782, off St. Lucia, the French Admiral de Grasse was defeated by Admiral Rodney. In the Napoleonic Wars the islands traded hands, and it was only after the close of the conflict that the Congress of Vienna established the present ownership.

wine, alcoholic beverage made by the FERMENTATION of the juice of the grape. Wines are distinguished by color, flavor, bouquet or aroma, and alcoholic content. Wine is also divided into three main types: still or natural, fortified, and sparkling. Wines are red, white, or rosé (depending on the grape used and the amount of time the skins have been left to ferment in the juice). For red wines the entire crushed grape is utilized; for white wines, the juice only. In rosé wines, the skins are removed after fermentation has begun thus producing a light pink color. Wines are also classified as dry or sweet, according to whether the grape sugar is allowed to ferment completely into alcohol (dry), or whether some residual sugar has been left (sweet). In a natural wine all the alcohol present has been produced by fermentation. Fortified wines, such as sherry, port, Madeira, and Malaga, are wines to which brandy or other spirits have been added. These wines contain a higher alcohol content (from 16% to 35%) than the still wines (from 7% to 15%). Sparkling wines, of which CHAMPAGNE is the finest example, are produced by the process of secondary fermentation in the bottle. In natural-wine making the grapes are gathered when fully ripe (sometimes, as for sauterne, when overripe). Mechanical extraction of the juice, called must, has almost entirely replaced treading. For red wines the must is fermented with the skins and pips, from which the newly formed alcohol extracts coloring matter and tannin. Fermentation starts when wine yeasts (*Saccharomyces ellipsoideus*), existing on the skins of ripe grapes, come in contact with the must. It may take from a few days to several weeks, according to the temperature and the amount of yeast present or introduced. When the new wine has become still and fairly clear, it is run off into large casks, where it undergoes a complicated series of chemical processes including oxidation, precipitation of proteids, and formation of esters that create a characteristic bouquet. The wine is periodically fined (clarified), then racked into smaller casks. After some months, or for certain wines several years, the wine is ripe for bottling. The very rare, superfine natural wines made in good vintage years from perfect grapes of the better varieties and possessing the unaccountable quality that vintners call breed are produced in commmercial quantities in limited areas of the Bordeaux and Burgundy regions in France, of the Rhine valley in Germany, and around Tokaj, Hungary (see TOKAY). The fine SHERRY of Spain and PORT of Portugal are superior fortified wines. Champagne is the only superfine sparkling wine. So ancient that its origin is unknown, wine is mentioned in early Egyptian inscriptions and in the literature of many lands. The term *wine* is also applied to alcoholic beverages made from plants other than the grape, e.g., elderberry wine, dandelion wine.

French wine. France is the greatest wine-producing area in the world, both in quantity and quality, and has developed superfine natural still wines and the finest sparkling wine—champagne. The department of Bordeaux furnishes red wine known as claret and white wine, both dry except for sauterne. The best-known Bordeaux wines are Médoc (red), classified and known by the vineyard names, as Château Lafite, Château Margaux, Château Latour; graves (red or white); sauterne (white), sweet, made from overripe grapes and including the noted Château d'Yquem; and St. Emilion-Pomerol. Burgundy wines, red and white, have more body than the Bordeaux. Connoisseurs prize the Burgundies of the Côte d'Or, especially the white Montrachet, and red Clos Vougeot and Romanée. The Chablis area produces fine, white Burgundy. Good wines are made in the Loire valley (Vouvray), the Rhône valley (Hermitage), Alsace, and the Jura mts. A great quantity of ordinary wine is produced in S France, much of it made into vermouth, distilled into brandy, or used for blending. See Alexis Lichine and W. E. Massee, *Wines of France* (4th ed. 1963).

German wine. Fine German wines are generally light, dry, white wines made from the Riesling grape and characterized by a fresh, flowery bouquet. Hock, derived from the town of Hochheim, is an English term sometimes applied to all Rhine wines. The best white Rhines are from the Rheingau. They include Johannisberger, Rüdesheimer, and Steinberger. Rheinhessen wines are milder and lighter in taste; Liebfraumilch is the best known. The third Rhine district, the Palatinate, produces sweeter, less distinguished wines. Rhine wines were formerly matured for many years in huge casks like the classic Heidelberg Tun, but are now aged in small casks for not more than three years. The most northern viticultural area in the world, situated along the Moselle River and its tributaries the Saar and the Ruwer, furnishes extremely light, delicate wines. Moselle wines are drawn off into green bottles, Rhine wines into brown. Other good wines are made in Baden and in Bavaria, noted for Stein wine.

Italian wine. Italy is the second largest wine-producing country in the world, but few of its wines are of export quality. Italian wines are frequently named for the grape rather than for the region of origin; hence a wine excellent in one locality may be inferior in another. The best known is Chianti, red or white, and properly a Tuscan wine. From Campania come the esteemed Lacrima Cristi, Capri wines, and Falerno, descendant of Horace's Falernian; from Veneto comes Valpolicella, dark red with a rich texture. Sicily makes Marsala, a sweet, amber colored wine, usually fortified.

American wine. Excellent wines are made in the United States, although American vintners, in the past, were satisfied with quantity production and with imitations of foreign wines. Most American wines are blends. Although many states produce wine, California produces approximately nine tenths of the nation's wine. There, grapes of the Old World species, *Vitis vinifera*, are grown. The best wines come from the Napa Valley area N of San Francisco. Distinguished wines from that region include Cabernet Sauvignon, Gamay, and Zinfandel. Eastern wines, most of them from New York state—especially the Finger Lakes region—are made from native grapes such as Concords, Catawbas, and the southern scuppernong. See R. S. Blumberg, *The Fine Wines of California* (1971).

Other Countries. Spain is the third largest wine-producing country in the world. Rioja, a leading table wine, is Spain's most widely exported wine. Portugal, best known for port and Madeira, also produces some excellent table wines. Greek wines, mainly whites and rosés, are often treated with retsina (pine resin). French planting has made Algeria one of the largest wine-producing countries. The Soviet Union, which now ranks as one of the half-dozen largest wine-producing countries, has greatly increased its output since World War II. The best wines from South America come from Chile, which produces both fortified and table wines. Other large wine-producing countries include Argentina, Hungary, South Africa, and Yugoslavia. See A. W. Allen, *A History of Wine* (1962); André Simon, ed., *Wines of the World* (1967) and *A Wine Primer* (rev. ed. 1970); Frank Schoonmaker, *Encyclopedia of Wine* (4th ed. 1969); Hugh Johnson, *The World Atlas of Wine* (1971).

Winebrenner, John: see CHURCHES OF GOD IN NORTH AMERICA.

Wineland: see VINLAND.

Wines, Enoch Cobb, 1806–79, American clergyman and prison reformer, b. Hanover, N.J. After a varied career as a schoolmaster and preacher he became (1861) secretary of the Prison Association of New York and began his most important work. His noted *Report on the Prisons and Reformatories of the United States and Canada* (1867) was partly responsible for the wave of prison reform in the 19th cent.

Winfield, city (1970 pop. 11,405), seat of Cowley co., S central Kansas, on the Walnut River; inc. 1873. The surrounding area is basically agricultural, with some petroleum production. Among the city's manufactures are crayons, gas burners, steel drums, industrial boilers, and aircraft. Southwestern College and St. John's College are in Winfield.

Winfrid: see BONIFACE, SAINT, c.675–754?

wing: see AIRFOIL; FLIGHT; AIRPLANE.

Wingate, Orde Charles (ôrd), 1903–44, British general. He served with the Sudan defense force (1928–33) and on special duty in Palestine (1936–39). It was in Palestine that he first used guerrilla tactics against Arabs attempting to cut the Haifa pipeline. An ardent Zionist, Wingate trained large squads of Jewish youths in military tactics and worked closely with Jewish leaders. The possibility of his acting against the British to secure Jewish independence caused his removal from Palestine. In World War II, although only a major, he commanded (1941) the British and native troops who ousted the numerically superior Italians from Ethiopia and restored Emperor Haile Selassie to his throne. Sent to India and raised to the rank of brigadier in 1942, Wingate trained and led a force of raiders into Japanese-held Burma for a period of seven months (1943). His guerrillas became known as the "Chindits" or "Wingate's raiders." He was made a major general and placed in command of a larger army, which was flown into Burma, but he was killed in an airplane accident two weeks after this operation began. A colorful personality and an unorthodox campaigner, Wingate demonstrated the effectiveness and practicality of jungle guerrilla warfare by Western troops. See Charles Rolo, *Wingate's Raiders* (1944); W. G. Burchett, *Wingate's Phantom Army* (1946); L. O. Mosley, *Gideon Goes to War* (1955); Christopher Sykes, *Orde Wingate* (1959).

Winged Victory: see NIKE.

wingnut: see WALNUT.

wings, FLIGHT organs of the BIRD, the BAT, and the INSECT. Birds' wings are pectoral appendages that are basically the same in skeletal structure as the forelimbs of all higher vertebrates, including the arm of man. Bird bones are specialized for strength and lightness, and the wing bones are further modified to act as a sturdy anchor for the wing feathers and for the powerful muscles and tendons necessary for flight. The main inner part of the bird's wing is like an airplane wing, concave below and convex above, and supplies lift. The secondary flight feathers also function in lifting; they are attached to a "forearm" bone, the ulna. The ulna locks with a parallel bone, the radius, in flight. The wingtip, or primary, feathers attach to the fused "hand" bones; their circular movement in flight provides the thrust to pull the bird forward. The primaries can be spread and maneuvered to control speed and direction. A mobile "thumb," bearing one or more feathers called alulae that lie along the front edge of the wing, can also be lifted to direct airstreams over the wing when its angle is too great (as in climbing) for the air to flow smoothly around it. There is much variation in the size, shape, and strength of wings and in the number and arrangement of their feathers. Soaring birds, such as the eagle and the pelican, have long, broad wings; in gliding and diving birds, like the gull and the albatross, wings are long and narrow; and in hoverers and darters, like the hummingbird and the swallow, wings are narrow and the primaries especially long to facilitate a rapid, erratic flight. The ostrich's vestigial wings are used for balance in running, and the wings of aquatic birds such as the penguin and the puffin are flipperlike for underwater swimming. The wings of bats are really membranes extending from the "arm," "hand," and "finger" bones to the ankles; the elongated finger bones form a frame to support the folds of skin. Insects' wings are not modified limbs but special lateral outgrowths of the cuticle of the thorax comprising a light membrane strengthened by thick-walled veins. The number, kind, and venation of the wings are bases for classification.

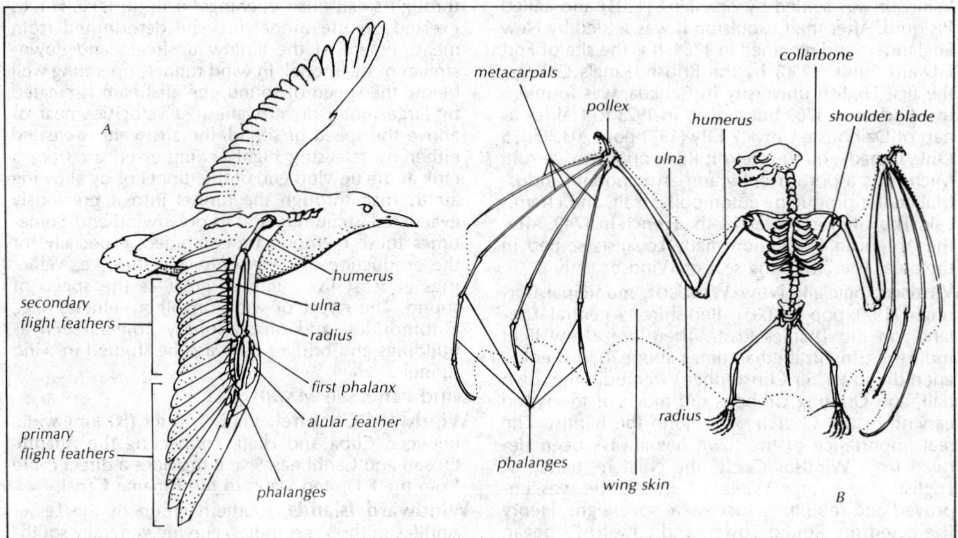

A. *Structure of a bird wing*
B. *Structure of a bat wing*

Winkelried, Arnold von (är'nôlt fən vĭng'kəlrēt), d. 1386, Swiss hero. His action at the battle of Sempach (July 9, 1386) is credited in legend with the Swiss defeat of the Austrians under Duke Leopold. According to the legend, Winkelried saved the battle by throwing himself against the Austrians and gathering against his breast all the spears within reach. He fell dead but he had breached the enemy ranks, and his compatriots rushed to victory. There has been much argument as to the truth of this legend. In 1886 a monument to Winkelried was erected on the battlefield.

Winneba (wĭnā'bə), town (1970 pop. 25,376), S Ghana, a fishing port on the Gulf of Guinea. Coconuts, cassava, and corn are raised. In 1663 the British built a fort at Winneba that served as a gold-trading center. From the 19th cent. the town exported palm oil and cacao, but after the opening of the harbor at TEMA in 1961 its commercial traffic declined considerably.

Winnebago, Lake, 215 sq mi (557 sq km), E Wis.; largest lake in Wisconsin. Fed and drained by the Fox River, the lake is part of an all-water route between the Great Lakes and the Mississippi River. Oshkosh and Fond du Lac are on the lake, which is a major recreation area.

Winnebago Indians, North American Indians whose language belongs to the Siouan branch of the Hokan-Siouan linguistic stock (see AMERICAN INDIAN LANGUAGES). When Father Jean Nicolet encountered them (1634) the Winnebago lived in E Wisconsin, from Green Bay to Lake Winnebago. Except for a war with the Illinois (1671) and one with the Ojibwa (1827), the Winnebago generally were peaceful toward their neighbors such as the Menominee, the Sac and Fox, and the Ottawa. The Winnebago traded with, and were staunch supporters of, the French. After the fall of French power, however, they allied themselves with the British; they fought against the colonists in the American Revolution and in the War of 1812. The Winnebago clandestinely participated in the Black Hawk War (1832). After numerous hardships and much loss of population the Winnebago were finally settled on reservations in Nebraska and Wisconsin. In 1843 they numbered some 4,500, but today they number some 2,000. Winnebago culture was of the Eastern Woodlands area with some Plains area traits. Their many ceremonies were elaborate, e.g., the buffalo dance held in the spring and the winter feast. See Paul Radin, *The Winnebago Tribe* (1923, repr. 1970) and *The Culture of the Winnebago* (1949).

Winnetka (wĭnĕt′kə), village (1970 pop. 14,131), Cook co., NE Ill., a residential suburb of Chicago, on Lake Michigan; inc. 1869. A correspondence school for the blind is there.

Winnetka plan: see PROGRESSIVE EDUCATION.

Winnibigoshish, Lake (wĭn″ĭbĭgō′shĭsh), 179 sq mi (464 sq km), N central Minn., in Chippewa National Forest, E of Bemidji. The outlet of the lake, one of the largest reservoirs of the Mississippi headwaters, is dammed.

Winnipeg (wĭn′ĭpĕg), city (1971 pop. 246,246; metropolitan area pop. 540,262), provincial capital, SE Man., Canada, at the confluence of the Red and Assiniboine rivers. It is the largest city of the Prairie Provinces and one of the world's largest wheat markets. A railroad, commercial, industrial, and distribution center, it has an international airport, railroad shops, grain elevators, stockyards, meatpacking plants, flour mills, and varied manufacturing industries. The city's history reflects the history of early French and British explorers and fur traders. In 1738, the sieur de la Vérendrye built the first post on the site, Fort Rouge, but it was later abandoned. Other posts were built in the Red River region, which was fiercely contested by the North West Company and the Hudson's Bay Company. The conflict reached its height in the struggle over the RED RIVER SETTLEMENT. The two companies were merged in 1821. Fort Gibraltar, a post of the North West Company on the site of present-day Winnipeg, was renamed Fort Garry and became the leading post in the region. In 1835 its name was changed to Winnipeg. Settlement was spurred by the construction of a rail line in 1881. In the city are the Royal Winnipeg Ballet, the Manitoba Theater Group, and a symphony orchestra. The Univ. of Manitoba and the Univ. of Winnipeg are also there.

Winnipeg, river, c.200 mi (320 km) long, issuing from the north end of Lake of the Woods, SW Ont., Canada, and flowing in a winding course generally northwest to the southeast end of Lake Winnipeg, SE Man. There are six hydroelectric stations on its course, supplying most of S Manitoba with electricity; the largest station is at Seven Sisters Falls. The river was first traveled by the sons of Vérendrye, the Canadian explorer, and was much used by explorers and fur traders.

Winnipeg, Lake, third largest lake of Canada, 9,465 sq mi (24,514 sq km), 264 mi (425 km) long and from 25 to 68 mi (40-109 km) wide, S central Man., Canada, N of Winnipeg. It is a remnant of glacial Lake Agassiz. It receives the Red, Winnipeg, and Saskatchewan rivers and many lesser streams and is drained NE by the Nelson River to Hudson Bay. It is surrounded by valuable timber land; there are several summer resorts on its shores. The lake has extensive fishing resources. It was discovered (1733) by the Vérendrye expedition and was an important route of early explorers and fur traders.

Winnipeg, University of, at Winnipeg, Man., Canada; founded 1877. It achieved university status in 1967. It is controlled jointly by the provincial government of Manitoba and the United Church of Canada. It has faculties of arts and science and theology and an Institute of Urban Studies.

Winnipegosis, Lake (wĭn″ĭpəgō′sĭs), 2,086 sq mi (5,403 sq km), 125 mi (201 km) long and 25 mi (40 km) wide, W Man., Canada. It is a remnant of glacial Lake Agassiz. It drains SE into Lake Manitoba and thence into Lake Winnipeg. Lake Winnipegosis has important pike fisheries.

Winnipesaukee, Lake, (wĭn″ĭpəsô′kē), 71 sq mi (184 sq km), E central N.H.; largest in the state. The lake is irregular in shape, with many indentations. It has 283 mi (455 km) of shore line and many small islands. Lake Winnipesaukee drains into the Merrimack River through the 20-mi-long (32-km) Winnipesaukee River. The region around the lake is a popular summer resort.

winnowing: see THRESHING.

Winogradsky, Sergei Nikolayevich (syĭrgā′ nyĭkəlī′əvĭch vyĕnəgräd′skē), 1856-1953, Russian microbiologist, grad. Univ. of St. Petersburg, 1881. He conducted research on microorganisms and their activities at the universities of St. Petersburg (1881-84; 1891-1905), Strasbourg (1885-88), and Zürich (1888-91). Because of the political changes that were made after World War I, Winogradsky left his homeland. He worked (1922-40) at the Pasteur Institute, in France, where he made important contributions to the study of soil microbiology. Winogradsky's studies on the autotrophic bacteria, the nonsymbiotic nitrogen-fixing bacteria, and the bacteriology of cellulose decomposition added greatly to the knowledge of microbiology.

Winona (wĭnō′nə, wī-), city (1970 pop. 26,438), seat of Winona co., SE Minn., on the Mississippi River; inc. 1857. Automotive products, flour, metal, and heavy road equipment are made there. An early trading and lumber center, Winona grew as river traffic increased, and the city developed as a manufacturing and commercial center. St. Mary's College, College of St. Teresa, and Winona State College are there. The sculptor James Earle Fraser was born in Winona.

Winooski, river, 90 mi (145 km) long, rising in NE Vermont and flowing southwest, then northwest, across the state, passing Montpelier and Waterbury and entering Lake Champlain near Burlington and Winooski. There are flood control and hydroelectric power projects on the river.

Winslow, Cameron McRae (wĭnz′lō), 1854-1932, American naval officer, b. Washington, D.C. He served on the *Nashville* in the Spanish-American War, and for his heroism off Cienfuegos, Cuba—where he commanded an expedition that cut the cables between Cuba and Europe—he was advanced five numbers in rank. Winslow was (1905) naval aide to President Theodore Roosevelt and in 1911 was promoted to rear admiral. He served (1911-13) as commander in the Atlantic Fleet and later (1915-16) was commander in chief of the Pacific Fleet.

Winslow, Edward, 1595-1655, one of the founders of PLYMOUTH COLONY in New England, b. England. One of the leaders of the PILGRIMS who traveled to America on the *Mayflower* in 1620, Winslow negotiated (1621) the treaty of peace and friendship with the Indian chief MASSASOIT. Sent back to England (1623-24) as agent of the colony, he wrote *Good Newes from New England,* which Samuel Purchas published in 1625. On his return to Plymouth he was elected an assistant of the colony and was continuously reelected until 1647, except for the years he served as governor (1633-34, 1636-37, and 1644-45), years in which William BRADFORD had declined to hold the governorship. Winslow was an active explorer and was apparently the first Englishman to visit (1632) Connecticut. He was also one of the Pilgrim leaders who successfully undertook to discharge the colony's debts to its English backers. In England again (1635) he was imprisoned for a short time for his religious beliefs and for performing the marriage ceremony in the colony. On still another journey to England, to answer charges made against Plymouth Colony, he issued a vigorous defense in *Hypocrisie Unmasked* (1646). With the Puritan cause triumphant in England, he decided to remain there. He was sent on several missions by Oliver Cromwell, dying on one to the West Indies. He was the father of Josiah Winslow. See G. F. Willison, *Saints and Strangers* (rev. ed. 1965).

Winslow, John Ancrum, 1811-73, American naval officer, b. Wilmington, N.C. Appointed a midshipman in 1827, he served in the Mexican War and was commissioned commander in 1855. In the Civil War, Winslow first served with the Union flotilla operating on the upper Mississippi River. Promoted to captain in 1862, he commanded the *Kearsarge* (1863-64) in pursuit of CONFEDERATE CRUISERS in European waters. On June 19, 1864, in one of the outstanding naval engagements of the war, the *Kearsarge* sank the celebrated raider *Alabama* off Cherbourg. For his victory Winslow was promoted to the rank of commodore and received the thanks of Congress. He commanded the Gulf squadron (1866-67), was made a rear admiral (1870), and was commander of the Pacific squadron (1870-72). See biography by J. M. Ellicott (1902).

Winslow, Josiah, c.1629-1680, American governor of Plymouth Colony, b. Plymouth, Mass.; son of Edward Winslow. Educated at Harvard, he was an assistant of the Plymouth Colony (1657-73) and then governor (1673-80), the first native-born governor of any American colony. Winslow also served (1658-72) as the Plymouth commissioner to the New England Confederation and as commander in chief of the colonial forces in KING PHILIP'S WAR in 1675.

Winsor, Justin, 1831-97, American librarian and historian. He was superintendent (1868-77) of the Boston Public Library and afterwards librarian (1877-97) of Harvard. In addition to important bibliographical work on Shakespeare, Columbus, and the American Revolution, he edited the *Narrative and Critical History of America* (8 vol., 1884-89) and wrote *The Westward Movement* (1897). A founder of the American Library Association (1876), he was its president for a number of years (1876-85; 1897).

Winstanley, Gerrard: see DIGGERS.

Winston-Salem, city (1970 pop. 132,913), seat of Forsyth co., central N.C., in the Piedmont; inc. 1913. North Carolina's third most populous city and its foremost industrial center, Winston-Salem is the nation's chief tobacco manufacturer. Large amounts of tobacco are stored and auctioned in numerous warehouses there. The city also has a brewery, a large bakery, and plants that manufacture clothing, textiles, and electrical equipment and appliances. The village of Bethabara, the first Moravian settlement in North Carolina, was established nearby in 1753. In 1766 the Moravians built their central town, Salem, a few miles away, and most of the industries and residents of Bethabara moved there. Winston was established in 1849 as the county seat. The two communities were united in 1913. Moravian culture has been sustained in the city through long-range efforts to restore the 18th-century village of Old Salem (some 40 buildings erected between 1767 and 1811 are extant). Also of interest is historic Bethabara park. Winston-Salem is the seat of Wake Forest Univ., Winston-Salem State Univ., Salem College, North Carolina School of the Arts, a technical institute, a school of medicine, a Bible college, and Salem Academy (est. 1772).

Wint, Peter de: see DE WINT, PETER.

Winter, William, 1836-1917, American drama critic, biographer, and poet, b. Gloucester, Mass., grad. Harvard Law School, 1857. A member of the literary bohemians who met in Pfaff's Cellar in New York City in the 1850s, he summed up his memories of them—Bayard Taylor, Walt Whitman, and others—in *Old Friends* (1909). As drama critic for the New York *Tribune* (1865-1909), Winter vigorously opposed the advent of dramatic realism. His many studies of theatrical personalities and his *Other Days* (1908) and *The Wallet of Time* (1913), theatrical reminiscences, are useful histories of the period. Winter's poetry was collected in 1909.

winterberry, name for two species of shrubs or small trees of the genus *Ilex* of the family Aquifoliaceae (HOLLY family), native to the eastern half of North America. Both are deciduous but have winter-persistent bright red or yellow berries. The Virginia winterberry, or black alder (*I. verticillata*), has toothed but spineless narrow leaves, hairy beneath. The similar smooth winterberry (*I. laevigata*) has smooth leaves. Winterberry is classified in the division MAGNOLIOPHYTA, class Magnoliopsida, order Celastrales, family Aquifoliaceae.

winter cress or **upland cress,** species of *Barbarea,* herbs of the family Cruciferae (MUSTARD family). The pungent leaves of several species have been used for salads or garnishes, and the plants are sometimes cultivated as ornamentals, e.g., the common winter cress, or yellow rocket (*B. vulgaris*), in garden varieties with variegated leaves and double flowers. Widely naturalized in North America, it is a common weed (called spring mustard) of croplands. A medicinal substance, *Herba Barbaraea,* was formerly made from it and used in Europe for healing wounds. Another species, *B. uverna,* is often sold as cress in Europe. Winter cress is classified in the division MAGNOLIOPHYTA, class Magnoliopsida, order Capparales, family Cruciferae.

wintergreen or **checkerberry,** low evergreen plant (*Gaultheria procumbens*) of the family Ericaceae (HEATH family), native to sandy and acid woods (usually of evergreens) of E North America and frequently cultivated. It has a creeping stem, erect branches, glossy, oval leaves, and small, waxy, white flowers followed by crimson fruits. The aromatic leaves and fruits are edible; the leaves are a source of wintergreen oil (now mostly obtained from the sweet, or black, birch, *Betula lenta,* or synthetically). The oil (see RADICAL) is used in medicine and as a flavoring. A tea has often been made from the leaves, whence two of the many names of the plant, mountain tea and teaberry. There are other species of *Gaultheria* found in W America and elsewhere; one of these, *G. shallon,* is called salal or shallon. Some PIPSISSEWA species, of the family Clethraceae, are sometimes called wintergreen. True wintergreen is classified in the division MAGNOLIOPHYTA, class Magnoliopsida, order Ericales, family Ericaceae.

Winterhalter, Franz Xaver (fränts ksävâr' vĭn'tərhäl"tər), 1806–73, German portrait painter. Most of European royalty sat for him, and his decorative pictures of court figures are in leading European galleries. Empress Eugénie is thought to have posed for his *Florinda* (Metropolitan Mus.). His *Susannah and the Elders* is in the Seattle Art Museum.

Winter Haven, resort city (1970 pop. 16,136), Polk co., central Fla; settled 1883. It is a marketing, processing, and shipping center for one of the state's chief citrus-fruit regions. There are 97 lakes within a radius of 5 mi (8 km) and a boat course of some 17 connected lakes. Tourist attractions include an annual citrus festival and the nearby Cypress Gardens, a famed water-skiing center. A junior college is there.

Winter Park, residential and resort city (1970 pop. 21,895), Orange co., central Fla., just N of Orlando in a citrus area; settled in the 1850s, inc. 1887. It is the seat of Rollins College. Within the city are 12 lakes, some of which are connected by navigable canals. The city is known for its large oak trees and parks. The Temple orange was developed there.

Winters, Yvor, 1900–1968, American poet and critic, b. Chicago, educated at the Univ. of Chicago, Univ. of Colorado (M.A., 1925), and Stanford (Ph.D., 1934). From 1928 until his death he was a member of the English department of Stanford. His controversial criticism was based on the thesis that a work of art should be "an act of moral judgment." *In Defense of Reason* (1947), his major critical work, is a collection of three earlier studies—*Primitivism and Decadence* (1937), *Maule's Curse* (1938), and *The Anatomy of Nonsense* (1943). His poetry, ranging in mood from the austere to the lyrical, appears in *Collected Poems* (1952) and *The Early Poems of Yvor Winters* (1966). See his *Forms of Discovery: Critical and Historical Essays on the Forms of the Short Poem in English* (1967) and *The Uncollected Essays and Reviews of Yvor Winters* (1973).

winter sports: see BOBSLEDDING; CURLING; HOCKEY, ICE; SKATING; SKIING; SNOWSHOES; TOBOGGANING.

Winterthur (vĭn'tərtŏŏr"), city (1970 pop. 92,722), Zürich canton, N Switzerland. An industrial center, it is an important rail junction and has manufactures of railroad equipment (including locomotives and diesel engines), cotton textiles, clothes, and other goods. It is also a cultural center with an old music festival and two excellent art collections. Winterthur was ruled by the counts of Kyburg (whose castle stands south of the city) until 1264, when it passed to the Hapsburgs. It became a free city of the Holy Roman Empire in 1415 and in 1467 was bought by Zürich.

Winthrop, John, 1588–1649, governor of the Massachusetts Bay colony, b. Edwardstone, near Groton, Suffolk, England. Of a landowning family, he studied at Trinity College, Cambridge, and became a prosperous lawyer with strong Puritan leanings. A member of the MASSACHUSETTS BAY COMPANY, he led the group that arranged for the removal of the company's government to New England and was chosen (1629) governor of the proposed colony. He arrived (1630) in the ship *Arbella* at Salem and shortly founded on Shawmut peninsula the settlement that became Boston. He was—with the possible exception of John COTTON—the most distinguished citizen of Massachusetts Bay colony, serving as governor some 12 times. He helped to shape the theocratic policy of the colony and opposed broad democracy. It was while he was deputy governor and Sir Henry VANE (1613–62) was governor that Winthrop bitterly and successfully opposed the antinomian beliefs of Anne HUTCHINSON and her followers, who were supported by Vane. The force of his influence on the history of Massachusetts was enormous. Winthrop's journal, which was edited by J. K. Hosmer and published in 1908 as *The History of New England from 1630 to 1649,* is one of the most valuable of American historical sources. See R. C. Winthrop, *Life and Letters of John Winthrop* (2 vol., 1864–67; repr. 1971); *Winthrop Papers* (5 vol., 1929–47); biographies by J. H. Twichell (1892), E. S. Morgan (1958), and G. R. Raymer (1963); R. S. Dunn, *Puritans and Yankees* (1962, repr. 1971).

Winthrop, John, 1606–76, colonial governor in America, b. Groton, Suffolk, England; oldest son of John Winthrop (1588–1649). He was educated at Trinity College, Dublin, became a lawyer, and emigrated to Massachusetts Bay in 1631. He returned to England in 1634 and in 1635 was commissioned governor of the new colony at Saybrook (now Deep River), Conn., just when other towns were being settled in the Connecticut valley; by agreement he was recognized for a year as titular governor of all. In 1646, Winthrop founded New London, and in 1657 and annually from 1659 to 1676 he was elected governor of Connecticut. After the Stuart restoration (1660), he obtained a charter (1662) that led to the union (1664) of Connecticut and New Haven colonies, and he governed the colony with an administration practically independent of England. He gathered a considerable library and by his interest in chemistry and other sciences helped to promote scientific study in the colonies. Elected a fellow of the Royal Society in 1663, he became the first member resident in America. See biographies by T. F. Waters (1899) and R. C. Black (1966); R. S. Dunn, *Puritans and Yankees* (1962, repr. 1971).

Winthrop, John (Fitz-John Winthrop), 1638–1707, American colonial governor of Connecticut, b. Ipswich, Mass.; son of John Winthrop (1606–76). He is commonly called Fitz-John Winthrop to distinguish him from his father and his grandfather. He left Harvard to serve in the English parliamentary army, returned to America in 1663, and served in King Philip's War (1675–76). He was a member of the council of Gov. Edmund ANDROS, but after the latter's overthrow he helped restore Connecticut's separate government. After serving as commander of the unsuccessful invasion (1690) of Canada in King William's War, he represented Connecticut in England from 1693 to 1697 and was elected governor in 1698. He served ably until his death. See R. S. Dunn, *Puritans and Yankees* (1962, repr. 1971).

Winthrop, John, 1714–79, American scientist, b. Boston, Mass., grad. Harvard, 1732. Because of his study of earthquakes, he is sometimes called the founder of seismology. He made scientific observations of sunspots and other astronomical phenomena, lectured on electricity, and was the first important scientist to teach at Harvard. He was elected a fellow of the Royal Society in 1766.

Winthrop, Robert Charles, 1809–94, American statesman, b. Boston. He studied law under Daniel Webster, was admitted (1831) to the bar, and was (1835–41) a Whig member of the Massachusetts legislature. He served (1842–50) in the U.S. House of Representatives, becoming speaker in 1847. Appointed (1850) to the Senate to complete Daniel Webster's unexpired term, he was defeated (1851) for reelection by Charles Sumner. He was generally considered a moderate in the sectional disputes leading up to the Civil War. He gained a reputation as an orator and was the chief speaker at the laying of the cornerstone of the Washington Monument (1848) and again (1885) at its dedication. After 1851 he chiefly devoted himself to literary and philanthropic work. Winthrop College in South Carolina was named in his honor. His writings include *The Life and Letters of John Winthrop* (1864–67), *Washington, Bowdoin, and Franklin* (1876), and *Memoir of Henry Clay* (1880).

Winthrop, residential and resort town (1970 pop. 20,335), Suffolk co., E Mass., on a peninsula extending into Boston Bay; settled 1635, set off from North Chelsea and inc. 1852. Several houses of historical interest (17th–18th cent.) still stand, including Governor Winthrop's house.

Winwood, Sir Ralph, 1563?–1617, English diplomat and statesman. He served as ambassador to France (1601–3) and agent to the States-General of the Netherlands (1603–14). At The Hague he assisted the Dutch as much as possible in their revolt against Spain. On his return to England he was made (1614) secretary of state, secured the friendship of James I's favorite, the earl of Somerset, and upheld James's subsidy demands and the impositions in the Addled Parliament of 1614. Winwood helped secure the release of Sir Walter RALEIGH from the Tower of London (1616) and urged him on his fatal expedition against the Spanish fleet and possessions. By his death Winwood escaped the consequences of this act.

Winzer, Otto (ô'tō vĭnts'ər), 1902–, East German political leader. A member of the German Communist party from 1925, he left Germany in 1935 during the Hitler era and returned after World War II. He became (1945) a member of the East German Socialist Unity (Communist) party and joined its central committee in 1946. Winzer served as secretary of state (1949–56) and first deputy minister of foreign affairs (1956–65) before becoming foreign minister. In the last position he participated in the negotiations that resulted in the 1970 nonaggression treaty between East and West Germany.

wire, metal filament, strand, or solid rod usually having a round cross section. Metals and alloys used for wiremaking are chosen for high tensile strength and ductility or for their electrical conductivity, weight, melting point, or other properties, depending upon the use to which the wire is to be put. The size of a wire is the measure of its diameter. For convenience, the different wires are numbered in order of decreasing size, the number being known as the gauge, or gage; the higher the gauge the smaller the diameter. The number of gauges used and their sizes differ according to the kind of wire and the country's standards of measurement. In the United States the American wire gauge, known also as the Brown & Sharpe wire gauge (abbr. B. & S.), is used; in Great Britain and Canada the British, or imperial, standard wire gauge (S.W.G.) is employed. For steel wire the steel wire gauge (also known as the Washburn & Moen, the Roebling, or the American Steel & Wire Co.'s wire gauge) is employed. Wire is widely used in conducting electricity and in making fencing, screens, netting, springs, and mesh or cloth. Very thin wire is used in various scientific instruments. A wire mesh is often used in glass (wire glass) to prevent shattering and to increase strength and safety. Wire rope (cable) is made by forming wires into strands that are then wound on a core. Wire has been used since the 3d millennium B.C. In early times the metal was hammered into sheets, then cut in strips and shaped with hammer and file. The modern method of drawing wire is believed to have originated in Europe late in the 13th cent. In this process the metal is pulled, or drawn, through a number of holes, each smaller than the one preceding, until finally it is passed through the hole having the desired diameter. Metal plates with such holes are known as drawplates or dies. Success in drawing wire through the drawplate formerly depended upon the physical strength of the wiredrawer (or wiresmith), since machinery was not used until the introduction of power-driven cylinder blocks to pull and coil the wire. The manufacture of steel wire in the United States dates from 1831, when Ichabod Crane, a blacksmith, began to draw wire using a water wheel for power. He devised many innovations in the process, some of which form the basis for modern wire-drawing machinery. The demand for piano wire and bicycle-wheel spokes and the introduction of barbed-wire fencing advanced production rapidly. With the establishment of telegraph lines in the late 1800s, the production of wire expanded into one of the greatest industries of the 19th cent.

wirehaired pointing griffon, breed of medium-sized SPORTING DOG developed in Holland and France in the late 19th cent. It stands about 22 in. (56 cm) high at the shoulder and weighs between 45 and 60 lb (20.4–27.2 kg). Its harsh, bristly coat may be steel gray, chestnut, or grayish white with chestnut splashes. The tail is docked. Although a slow hunter, the griffon is a strong swimmer and a good pointing retriever with an excellent sense of smell. See DOG.

wireless: see RADIO.

wire saw: see QUARRYING.

wireworm, elongate, cylindrical larva of the CLICK BEETLE. Most wireworms are hard and brown, but members of some species are soft and whitish. Wireworms live in rotten wood or in the ground and feed on roots and seeds, injuring potatoes, grasses, and a wide variety of leguminous field crops. They live for 2 to 10 years before pupating in the ground or in wood. Methods of control include letting the land lie fallow, rotating crops, and special methods of cultivation. Wireworms are classified in the phylum ARTHROPODA, class Insecta, order Coleoptera, family Elateridae. See bulletins of the U.S. Dept. of Agriculture.

Wirral, urban district (1971 pop. 26,834), Cheshire, NW England, on the peninsula between the Mersey and Dee estuaries. Sometimes referred to as "the dormitory of Liverpool," it contains many high-income residential developments and some agricultural land. Formerly the area was a royal forest and game preserve that outlaws used as a hiding place. Arrowe Park was the site of the First Worldwide Boy Scouts Jamboree in 1929. Heswall parish was the birthplace of Lady Hamilton. In 1974, Wirral became part of the new metropolitan county of Merseyside.

Wirt, William (wûrt), 1772–1834, U.S. Attorney General and author, b. Bladensburg, Md. He had little formal schooling but was admitted to the Virginia bar in 1792. His first book was an anonymous collection of sketches called *The Letters of a British Spy* (1803), which purported to be the work of a "meek and harmless" noble visitor to America. *The Rainbow* (1804) and *The Old Bachelor* (1810) are similar collections, attempting the style of Joseph Addison. Wirt's *Life and Character of Patrick Henry* (1817) was his first book to appear under his own name; it presumed to give the text of Henry's speeches. His role as prosecutor in the trial (1807) of Aaron Burr brought him renown as a lawyer. As U.S. Attorney General (1817–29), Wirt initiated the practice of preserving his official opinions so that they could be used as precedents. In 1832 he accepted the nomination for President of the ANTI-MASONIC PARTY.

Wirt, William Albert, 1874–1938, American educator, b. Markle, Ind., grad. DePauw Univ. (Ph.B., 1898; Ph.D., 1916). In 1907 he became superintendent of schools in Gary, Ind., where he developed a plan of school operation (see PROGRESSIVE EDUCATION) known variously as the Gary plan, the platoon system, and Wirt's "Work-Study-Play" plan. This system increased the utilization of the school plant by alternating classes between regular and special teachers.

Wirth, Karl Joseph (kärl yō'zĕf vĭrt), 1879–1956, German statesman. A leader of the Catholic Center party, he succeeded (1920) Matthias Erzberger as minister of finance. In 1921, Wirth became chancellor, pledging the fulfillment of World War I treaty obligations. With Walter RATHENAU he represented Germany at the Genoa reparations conference of 1922 and while there signed the Treaty of Rapallo with the Soviet Union. Currency inflation caused the fall of the Wirth ministry in Nov., 1922, but Wirth later held cabinet posts. He fled Germany in 1933, returned to West Germany after World War II, and favored a neutral, reunified Germany. Increasingly pro-Soviet, he received the Stalin Peace Prize in 1955.

Wirtz, William Willard, 1912–, U.S. Secretary of Labor (1962–69), b. De Kalb, Ill. A professor of law at Northwestern Univ. (1939–42), he served (1943–45) with the War Labor Board and was (1946) chairman of the National Wage Stabilization Board. Wirtz returned to Northwestern, where he again taught law until 1954. Appointed Undersecretary of Labor in 1961, he succeeded Arthur Goldberg as Secretary of Labor and held this post throughout the Kennedy and Johnson administrations. He dealt effectively with the various strikes of the 1960s.

Wisby: see VISBY, Sweden.

Wisconsin (wĭskŏn'sən, -sĭn), state (1970 pop. 4,417,933), 56,154 sq mi (145,439 sq km), including 1,449 sq mi (3,753 sq km) of inland water surface, N central United States, admitted as the 30th state of the Union in 1848. MADISON is the capital and the second largest city; MILWAUKEE is the largest city. Water marks most of Wisconsin's boundaries; to the east lies Lake Michigan and to the north, Lake Superior; between the two, in the northeast corner, Wisconsin is divided from the Upper Peninsula of Michigan partly by the Menominee River. To the west the St. Croix and the Mississippi mark most of the boundary with Minnesota and Iowa, and to the south the line of lat. 42°30′ N separates Wisconsin from Illinois. Despite the tempering effects of the water, winters in the north are cold and summers in the south are warm (from the hot winds of the Mississippi valley); however, most of Wisconsin is known for its pleasantly cool summer temperatures. The most notable physiographical feature of the state is its profusion of lakes, over 8,500, ranging in size from Lake Winnebago (215 sq mi/557 sq km) to relatively tiny glacial lakes of surprising beauty. The Wisconsin River, with its extensive dam system, runs generally southward through the middle of the state until it turns west (just NW of Madison) to flow into the Mississippi, dividing the state into eastern and western sectors. Running a parallel course just to the east, Wisconsin's major watershed extends in a broad arch from north to south; to the east the Menominee, the Peshtigo, the Wolf, and the Fox rivers flow E and NE into Lake Michigan, while to the west the Chippewa, the Flambeau, and the Black rivers make their way to the Mississippi. The rough isolation of the north country is cut by part of the Gogebic range, from which considerable iron ore was extracted before 1965. Iron mining was resumed in Dec., 1969, when the state's first taconite plant began putting out low-grade pellets. Sand and gravel, stone, and zinc are other valuable mineral resources; zinc mines (as well as lead) are found in the DRIFTLESS AREA in the southwest. Important copper deposits were discovered in the north in the early 1970s. The state's greatest natural resource since its earliest days has been lumber. Giant forests (white pines in the north, hardwoods elsewhere) once covered all except the southern prairie. While reckless exploitation in the late 19th cent. drastically reduced the magnificent stands, extensive conservation and reforestation measures have saved the valuable lumber industry, and today c.45% of Wisconsin's land area is forested. The state's accent, however is chiefly pastoral. The nation's largest dairy herds graze there, and Wisconsin is the leading state in the production of milk and cheese. After dairy products and cattle, its most valuable farm commodities are hogs and corn. Wisconsin also ranks first in the production of hay and alfalfa; other important crops are oats, potatoes, cranberries, and a great variety of fruits and vegetables. Food processing, predictably, is one of the state's foremost industries, surpassed only by the manufacture of machinery, which is centered in Milwaukee, Madison, and Racine. The pulp, paper, and paper-products industrial complex in Green Bay and Appleton is the largest (1970) in the nation. Other important manufactures are transportation equipment, metal products, farm implements, and lumber. Almost all Wisconsin's major industries are to be found within the metropolis of Milwaukee, where the traditional industries of beer brewing and meat-packing are rivaled by the manufacture of heavy machinery and diesel and gasoline engines. Wisconsin has 14 ports on the Great Lakes, all capable of accommodating ocean vessels. The superb harbor at Superior (shared with Duluth, Minn.) has sizeable shipyards and among the nation's largest coal and ore docks. Wisconsin's frontage on both lakes Superior and Michigan, as well as its many beautiful lakes, streams, and its northern woodlands, has made it a haven for hunters, fishermen, and water and winter sports enthusiasts. Tourism is a burgeoning industry; there are 49 state parks, 9 state forests, and 2 national forests. Apostle Islands National Lakeshore (see NATIONAL PARKS AND MONUMENTS, table) is also there. The Great Lakes offered an easy access from Canada to the region that is now Wisconsin, and the Frenchman Jean Nicolet arrived at the site of Green Bay in 1634 in search of fur pelts and the Northwest Passage. He was followed by other traders and missionaries, among them Radisson and Groseilliers; Marquette and Joliet, who discovered the upper Mississippi; Aco and Hennepin, from the party of La Salle; and the redoubtable Duluth. Meanwhile the growth of white civilization in the East was bringing the Ottawa, the Huron, and other Indian tribes into Wisconsin, where they in turn unsettled the older Indian inhabitants, the Winnebago, the Kickapoo, and others. Similarly, the Ojibwa drove their kinsmen the Sioux westward from Wisconsin. Only the Menominee remained relatively settled. Nicolas Perrot helped (1667) establish Green Bay as the center of the Wisconsin fur trade, and in 1686 he formally claimed all the region for France. The fur trade flourished despite the 50-year war between the Fox Indians and the French, and the historic Fox-Wisconsin portage was used by generations of traders from Green Bay and Prairie du Chien in their search for beaver and other furs. Like all of New France, Wisconsin fell to the British with the end of the French and Indian Wars (1763). British traders mingled with the French and eventually gained the bulk of the fur trade. The British hold continued even after the end of the American Revolution, when the Old Northwest formally passed (1783) to the United States and was made (1787) a part of the Northwest Territory. After JAY'S TREATY (1794), northwestern strongholds were turned over to the Americans, but the British continued to dominate the fur trade from the Canadian border. In the War of 1812, Wisconsin again fell into British hands. It was only with the Treaty of Ghent (see GHENT, TREATY OF) that effective U.S. territorial control began and that the American Fur Company gained control of much of the fur trade. Present-day Wisconsin was transferred from Illinois Territory to Michigan Territory in 1818. By then the fur trade was diminishing, but the lead mines in SW Wisconsin had long been known, and booming lead prices in the 1820s brought the first large rush of white settlers. The region's great agricultural potential was also apparent, and after 1825 a considerable number of easterners began arriving via the new Erie Canal and the Great Lakes. They settled in the Milwaukee area and along the waterways. The U.S. army preserved order from key forts established at Green Bay (1816), Prairie du Chien (1816), and Portage (1828) and built bridges, trails, and roads throughout the region. The incursions of aggressive white settlers brought trouble with the Indians, culminating in the BLACK HAWK WAR (1832); this revolt, brutally crushed, was the last Indian uprising of serious consequence in the area. In 1836, Wisconsin was made a territory, and the legislators chose a compromise site for the capital, midway between the Milwaukee and western centers of population; thus the city of Madison was founded. By 1840 population in the territory had risen above 130,000, but the people, fearing higher taxes and stronger government, rejected propositions for statehood four times. In addition politicians were at first unwilling to yield Wisconsin claims to a strip of land around Chicago and to what is now the Upper Peninsula of Michigan. However, hopes that statehood would bring improved communications and prosperity became dominant; the claims were yielded, and Wisconsin achieved statehood in 1848. The state constitution provided protection for indebted farmers, limited the establishment of banks, and granted liberal suffrage. These measures and the state's rich soil attracted immigrants from Europe. The influx of Germans was especially heavy, and some parts of Wisconsin assumed the tidy semi-German look that has persisted along with an astonishing survival of the German language. Liberal leaders, like Carl Schurz, came after the failure of the Revolution of 1848 in Germany and added to the intellectual development of the state. Contributions were also made, then and later, by Irish, Scandinavians, Russian Germans from the Volga, and Poles. The state's development was not always smooth. Although the state constitution provided for a system of free public schools, the principle was implemented only slowly. Similarly, the Univ. of Wisconsin (chartered 1848) was slow to assume importance. After a referendum (1852) ended the state constitutional ban on banking, farmers and many others mortgaged their property to buy railroad stocks, only to suffer distress when the state's railways went bankrupt in the Panic of 1857. Wisconsin was steadily antislavery; the FREE-SOIL PARTY gained a large following in the state (although the party's homestead plank and economic program were the major attractions). Wisconsin abolitionists played an important part in the formation of the Republican party. In the Civil War, Wisconsin quickly rallied to the Union. Copperheads were few, but many War Democrats opposed the abridgment of civil liberties and other aspects of the war effort, and some of the German immigrants, who had left Germany because they opposed compulsory military service, opposed even voluntary war service. However, the boom times brought by the war mitigated discontent, and economic and social growth was rapid during the 1860s and after. Railroads and other means of communication linked Wisconsin closely to the East. The meat-packing and brewing industries of Milwaukee began to assume importance in the 1860s. Wheat briefly was dominant especially in S Wisconsin, but was superseded in the 1870s as states further west became wheat producers and Wisconsin shifted to more diversified farming. Its great dairy industry developed, spurred by an influx of skilled dairy farmers from New York and Scandinavia and by the efforts of the Wisconsin Dairymen's Association (est. 1872). In these years the

great pine forests of N Wisconsin began to be greatly exploited, and in the 1870s lumbering became the state's most important industry. Oshkosh and La Crosse flourished. With lumbering came large paper and wood products industries, and the opening of iron mines in Minnesota and Michigan promoted the N Great Lake ports and increased industrial opportunities. Although hard hit in the panics of 1873 and 1898, Wisconsin was generally prosperous in the late 19th cent., and the reform-minded Granger movement and Populist party received less support than in other Midwestern states. A trend toward liberal political views was stimulated in Wisconsin by socialist thought, which was introduced early. Socialism, in a pragmatic and reformist rather than a doctrinaire form, dominated Milwaukee politics for many years and gave the city honest and efficient government, particularly under the leadership of Victor Berger and Daniel Hoan. Stemming from a different source was the reform spirit of specialized and advanced Wisconsin farmers, who recognized the need for a more viable political and economic framework. In the early 20th cent., reform sentiment blossomed in the Progressive movement, under the tutelage of the Republican leader, Robert M. La Follette. This pragmatic attempt to achieve good effective government for all and to limit the excessive power of the few resulted in a direct primary law (1903), in legislation to regulate railroads and industry, in pure food acts, in high civil service standards, and in efforts toward cooperative nonpartisan action to solve labor problems. An important adjunct of progressivism was the "Wisconsin idea"—that of linking the facilities and brainpower of the Univ. of Wisconsin to progressive experiments and legislation. The plan owed much to Charles McCarthy and to the support of university president Charles Van Hise, and it brought such diverse benefits as the spread of scientific agricultural methods and the many labor and other bills drafted by Professor John R. Commons. The progressive movement was temporarily halted by World War I. La Follette, some Socialists, and many German-Americans were critical of U.S. involvement in that war, but they were a distinct minority. Wisconsin was generally prosperous in the 1920s; industrialization made rapid strides, reforestation of the once great but now exhausted timberland was stimulated by state legislation, and the dairying industry continued to grow. Wisconsin was alone in voting for its native son, La Follette, when he ran for President on the Progressive party ticket in 1924, and in the state his policies continued to be carried forward by his sons Robert M. La Follette, Jr., and Philip La Follette. Wisconsin's pioneer old-age pension act (1925) and its unemployment compensation act (1931) served as models for national social security a few years later. The Great Depression of the 1930s struck particularly hard in industrialized Milwaukee, but some relief was provided by the New Deal, and in addition Gov. Philip La Follette attempted, in his "little new deal," to improve agricultural marketing, promote electrification, and enforce fair labor practices. During World War II, Wisconsin's shipbuilding industry flourished. In the prosperous postwar era, urbanization and industrial growth continued. A controversial Wisconsin politician on the national scene was Sen. Joseph McCarthy, but his methods and approach were balanced by other political strains in the state; Milwaukee, in the same period, again elected a Socialist mayor. The Democratic party, long no match for Republican or progressive forces in state elections, gained strength in the late 1950s and 1960s. Wisconsin still operates under its first constitution, adopted in 1848. Its executive branch is headed by a governor elected for a four-year term (before 1970, it was for a two-year term). Patrick J. Lucey, a Democrat, was elected governor in 1970 and reelected in 1974. Wisconsin's bicameral legislature has a senate with 33 members elected for four-year terms and an assembly with 99 members elected for two years. The state elects 2 Senators and 9 Representatives to the U.S. Congress, and has 11 electoral votes. The extensive Univ. of Wisconsin has campuses at Madison, Eau Claire, Green Bay, La Crosse, Milwaukee, Oshkosh, Kenosha, Platteville, River Falls, Stevens Point, Menomonie, Superior, and Whitewater. Other notable institutions of higher learning are Beloit College, at Beloit; Lawrence Univ., at Appleton; and Marquette Univ., at Milwaukee. See F. L. Holmes, *Wisconsin* (1946); B. K. Whyte, *Wisconsin Heritage* (1954); L. D. Epstein, *Politics in Wisconsin* (1958); Larry Gara, *A Short History of Wisconsin* (1962); S. A. Barrett, *Ancient Aztalan* (1933, repr. 1970); C. W. Rowe, *The Effigy Mound Culture of Wisconsin* (1956, repr. 1970); Federal Writers' Project, *Wisconsin: A Guide to the Badger State* (1941, repr. 1973); R. C. Nesbit, *Wisconsin: A History (1973).*

Wisconsin, river, c.430 mi (690 km) long, rising in the lake district, NE Wis., and flowing generally SW across central Wis. to the Mississippi River near Prairie du Chien. At Portage it is connected by a short canal with the Fox River, and thus with Lake Michigan. There are many hydroelectric power facilities on the river. The scenic Dells of the Wisconsin are a famous gorge.

Wisconsin, University of, mainly at Madison; land-grant and state supported; coeducational; chartered 1848, opened 1849. Its history was disturbed by storms over the policies of Glenn FRANK and of Alexander MEIKLEJOHN. It has 13 two-year colleges located throughout the state, as well as 11 liberal arts and teachers colleges. In 1955 the extension division merged with Wisconsin State College at Milwaukee to form the Univ. of Wisconsin—Milwaukee (coeducational; authorized by the legislature 1955, opened 1956). It is an integral part of the Univ. of Wisconsin. Well-known divisions of the university are the colleges of agriculture and engineering, the medical school, and the Institute for Research in the Humanities. Notable among the extensive facilities at Madison are the space astronomy laboratory, the geophysical and polar research laboratory, the numerical analysis laboratory, and the state engineering experiment station, which includes a solar research laboratory. The university library contains excellent collections relating to literature, science, and Russian history. See history by Merle Curti and Vernon Carstenson (1949); study by W. A. Strang (1971).

Wisconsin Rapids, city (1970 pop. 18,587), seat of Wood co., central Wis., on the Wisconsin River; inc. 1869. Paper and pulp, heating equipment, plastics, chemicals, and iron and steel are produced. Dairy farms, agriculture, and a large cranberry industry also contribute to the city's economy. Two towns on the river there, Grand Rapids (east bank) and Centralia (west bank), were consolidated in 1900, and the name was changed in 1920 to Wisconsin Rapids. A state-owned nursery is nearby.

Wisconsin State University System, coordinating unit (est. 1964) consisting of nine coeducational state universities in Wisconsin. Most of the universities began in the 19th cent. as normal schools, became four-year teachers colleges (from 1925 to 1927), became liberal arts colleges (by 1951), and gained university status (by 1964). The various branches are located at Eau Claire (founded 1909), La Crosse (1909), Oshkosh (1871), River Falls (1874), Stevens Point (1894), Superior (1893), Whitewater (1868), Platteville (formed in 1959 by a merger of Wisconsin State College at Platteville, founded 1866, and Wisconsin Institute of Technology, founded 1907), and Menomonie.

Wisdom, Arthur John Terrence Dibben, 1904–, British philosopher, grad. Cambridge (B.A. 1924, M.A. 1934). He taught at St. Andrews Univ., Scotland, and at Cambridge, where he was made (1952) professor of philosophy. In 1968 he became professor at the Univ. of Oregon. Wisdom was strongly influenced by Ludwig Wittgenstein. In his earlier work he was interested specifically in the problems surrounding the idea of logical constructions, a central issue in British philosophy in the 1920s and 30s, and more generally in the nature of philosophical inquiry, which he took to be an inquiry into the ultimate structure of facts: "Philosophic progress does not consist in acquiring knowledge of new facts but in acquiring new knowledge of facts." Later he saw the purpose of philosophy more broadly as a guide to what we can know, as well as showing what we cannot; for example, in his series of essays "Other Minds" (first published in the journal *Mind* 1940–43), he explored the sense in which we can be said to know such things as another person's mind. Wisdom's writings include *Interpretation and Analysis* (1931), *Problems of Mind and Matter* (1934), *Other Minds* (1952), *Philosophy and Psychoanalysis* (1953), and *Paradox and Discovery* (1965).

Wisdom, biblical book included in the Western canon and the Septuagint, but not included in the Hebrew Bible and placed in the Apocrypha in the Authorized Version. It is traditionally named the Wisdom of Solomon. The book opens with an exhortation to seek wisdom, followed by a statement (2.1–20) of the attitude of worldly men. Chapter 3 is an eloquent passage on the immortality of the just and the rewards of the wicked, amplified in the next chapters. Then there is another exhortation (6) and a transition to a section (7–8) praising wisdom, ending with a prayer for it (9). The rest of the book (10–19) is a history of God's care of the Jews from the beginning, with a long parenthesis (13–15) on the natural origin of idolatry and its folly. The style and content of the book lend themselves to quotation; thus there are allusions in St. Paul's epistles to passages from Wisdom. The book is probably of Alexandrian Jewish authorship, and most scholars place the date in the two centuries before Christ. Some see in it a composite work of three parts: 1–6, 7–9, and 10–19, of which the third is said to resemble a Passover haggada. It is a supreme example of what is called wisdom literature, a term for the Jewish philosophical writings of the pre-Christian era. The following other books of the Old Testament represent this type also: Job, Proverbs, Ecclesiastes, and Ecclesiasticus. See John Geyer, *The Wisdom of Solomon* (1963).

Wisdom of Jesus the Son of Sirach (sī'rək): see ECCLESIASTICUS.

Wise, Henry Alexander, 1806–76, American political leader and Confederate general in the Civil War, b. Accomac, Va. A lawyer, he was successively a Jackson Democrat, a Whig, and a Tyler Democrat in Congress (1833–44). He was minister to Brazil from 1844 to 1847. An outspoken defender of slavery, Wise defeated (1855) the Know-Nothing candidate for governor of Virginia by accusing that party of abolitionism, thereby breaking the Know-Nothing movement in the South. One of his last official acts as governor (1856–60) was to sign the death warrant of John Brown. Although he opposed secession, when war broke out he became a Confederate brigadier general, distinguishing himself in the defense of Petersburg against General Grant's first assault (1864) and in the retreat to Appomattox.

Wise, Isaac Mayer, 1819–1900, American rabbi, founder of organized Reform Judaism in the United States, b. Bohemia, studied at the Univ. of Vienna. He settled in the United States in 1846. Wise was liberal in his religious and political views. He was rabbi of Orthodox congregations in Albany, N.Y., and (from 1854) Cincinnati, both of which he turned into Reform synagogues. He energetically pursued his goal by founding (1875) the Hebrew Union College in Cincinnati and by organizing (1873) the Union of American Hebrew Congregations and the Central Conference of American Rabbis (1889). He presided over these organizations until his death. He founded and edited two periodicals, the *American Israelite*, in English, and *Deborah*, in German. He wrote several novels, two plays, his reminiscences (1901), and many historical and religious works, including *History of the Israelitish Nation* (1854). See study by A. F. Key (1962); J. G. Heller, *Isaac Wise: His Life, Work, and Thought* (1965).

Wise, John, 1652–1725, American clergyman, exponent of the democratic principles of modern Congregationalism, b. Roxbury, Mass., grad. Harvard, 1673. He was pastor at Ipswich, Mass., from 1680 until his death, but his influence extended beyond his parish. For a short time, in 1687, he was deprived of his ministerial office by Governor Andros for having led his fellow townsmen in their refusal to pay taxes violating their charter rights. In 1689 he represented Ipswich in the Boston convention for reorganization of the colonial government. In opposition to Increase Mather and Cotton Mather, he resisted the plan to place individual churches under the jurisdiction of associations of ministers, stating his reasons in two pamphlets that carried great influence, *The Churches Quarrel Espoused* (1710) and *A Vindication of the Government of New England Churches* (1717). These expositions of church democracy were reissued and widely read before the American Revolution and again before the Civil War. See biography by G. A. Cook (1952, repr. 1967)

Wise, Stephen Samuel, 1874–1949, American Reform rabbi and Zionist leader, b. Budapest, grad. College of the City of New York, 1891, Ph.D. Columbia, 1901. He served as a rabbi in New York City (1893–1900) and in Portland, Oregon (1900–1906). Returning to New York, he founded (1907) the Free Synagogue, of which he was rabbi until his death. Wise worked for labor reforms, world peace, alleviation of the problems of the Jewish minorities in Europe, and relief for refugees. He was one of the foremost leaders of Zionism and Reform Judaism. Among the many organizations in which he was active were the American Jewish Congress, the World Jewish Congress, and the Zionist Organization of America. He founded (1922) the Jewish Institute of Religion for the training of a modern rabbinate and of Jewish educators and community workers. His writings include *The Great Betrayal* (with Jacob De Haas, 1930), *As I See It* (1944), and his autobiography, *Challenging Years* (1949). See his personal letters (ed. by his children, J. W. Wise and Justine Wise Polier, 1956).

Wise, Thomas James, 1859-1937, English bibliographer and book collector. His famous Ashley Library of rare editions and manuscripts was acquired by the British Museum in 1937. His many bibliographies and catalogs of the works of English literary figures included those on Shelley, Tennyson, Wordsworth, Conrad, Coleridge, and Robert Browning. Wise also privately printed nearly 300 works of English authors, some of which were exposed by John Carter and Graham Pollard as forgeries in *An Enquiry into the Nature of Certain Nineteenth Century Pamphlets* (1934). See *Letters of Thomas J. Wise to John Henry Wrenn* (ed. by F. E. Ratchford, 1944); W. G. Partington, *Forging Ahead* (1939, repr. 1973); and *Thomas J. Wise: Centenary Studies* (1959).

Wiseman, Nicholas Patrick Stephen, 1802-65, English prelate, cardinal of the Roman Catholic Church, b. Seville, Spain, of Irish-English parentage. In 1836 he founded (with Daniel O'Connell) the *Dublin Review.* In 1840 he was taken from his rectorship of the English College at Rome (which he had held since 1828) and made coadjutor to the vicar apostolic of the central district of England. Later he was appointed vicar apostolic of the London district. He was very influential among Catholics and was sympathetic to the OXFORD MOVEMENT. In 1850 the pope restored the hierarchy in England; Wiseman was appointed a cardinal (the first English cardinal in modern times) and was selected as the first archbishop of Westminster, the Catholic primate of England. He succeeded in allaying much of the suspicion that existed between the older Catholic families of England and the newer converts and worked to lessen the anti-Catholic feeling in England. He wrote many books, notably *Fabiola* (1854), a historical novel of early Christianity. Henry Edward MANNING was his assistant and successor. See E. E. Reynolds, *Three Cardinals* (1958); biography by B. Fothergill (1963).

Wise Men of the East, Magi, or **Three Kings,** men who came from the East to adore the newborn Jesus. Mat. 2. They were the first to tell Herod of the birth. A star (the Star of Bethlehem) had been a sign for them. Christian tradition has elaborated the biblical account; it has set their number as three, perhaps from their gifts of gold, frankincense, and myrrh; it has called them kings, perhaps from Ps. 72.10,11 and Isa. 49.7,23 considered as prophecies; and it has given them names, Caspar or Gaspar, Melchior, and Balthazar. They are called sometimes the Three Kings of Cologne because there is a great shrine to them in the cathedral at Cologne. The feast of the EPIPHANY commemorates their visit. In art the visit is called the Adoration of the Magi.

wisent (vē'sənt), name for the European BISON, *Bison bonasus.* It is a close relative of the American bison, *B. bison.* Longer legged and less heavily built than its American cousin, the wisent may reach a height of 54 to 60 in. (137-152 cm) at the shoulder, and a weight of more than 1 ton (908 kg). It has brown hair and short upcurved horns. Its hump is less prominent than that of the American bison and its coat less shaggy. In the wild the wisent is a forest animal; it browses on leaves, ferns, and bark. Females give birth after a gestation period of 9 to 10 months, usually to a single calf. Abundant in Europe in prehistoric times, wisents remained numerous until the early Christian era. Hunted for their meat and displaced from their habitats by farmers, by the 11th cent. they had been reduced to two herds numbering but a few hundred animals. By 1927 fewer than 50 remained. Since the foundation of an international protective society in 1932, their numbers have been growing, but they are no longer found outside of zoos or forest reserves. Wisents are classified in the phylum CHORDATA, subphylum Vertebrata, class Mammalia, order Artiodactyla, family Bovidae.

Wishart, George (wĭsh'ərt), 1513?-1546, Scottish religious reformer, Protestant martyr. He was master of a grammar school in Montrose. In 1538 he fled Scotland to escape charges of heresy; he was in England for a short time, then on the Continent. In 1544 he is thought to have returned to Scotland, where he traveled about at his peril, preaching Christianity as he conceived it. The most eventful result of his preaching was the conversion of John KNOX. Cardinal BEATON instigated Wishart's arrest. He was tried for heresy (1546), convicted, and burned at St. Andrews. His followers murdered Beaton in retaliation. Wishart's translation of the Helvetic Confession was published posthumously (c.1548). See biography by John Knox in his *History of the Reformation in Scotland,* ed. by W. C. Dickinson (2 vol., 1950).

Wishaw, Scotland: see MOTHERWELL AND WISHAW.

Wisła, river, Poland: see VISTULA.

Wismar (vĭs'mär), city (1970 pop. 56,057), Rostock district, NW East Germany, on the Baltic Sea. It is an industrial center and an oil and fishing port. Manufactures include machinery and processed food, and there are shipyards in the city. Wismar was (1256-1306) the residence of the princes of Mecklenburg and later became one of the most flourishing members of the Hanseatic League. Under the Peace of Westphalia (1648) the city passed to Sweden, but in 1803 Sweden pledged it to Mecklenburg-Schwerin with the privilege of recall within 100 years. In 1903, Sweden renounced all rights to the city. Wismar was badly damaged in World War II. There are several Gothic churches and many medieval houses.

Wissler, Clark, 1870-1947, American anthropologist, b. Wayne, Ind., grad. Indiana Univ., 1897, Ph.D. Columbia, 1901. At first a teacher of psychology, he became interested in anthropology under Franz Boas at Columbia. In 1902 he began an affiliation with the American Museum of Natural History that lasted until his retirement in 1942. Wissler increased ethnographic studies by sending out numerous field expeditions and by launching an ambitious publication program of which he was editor. His interest in the geographical foundations and regional distribution of culture led him to the concept of "culture area" that has played an important role in the ordering and interpretation of ethnographic data. Wissler was associated with Yale from 1924 to 1940, first with the new Institute of Psychology and later with its successor, the Institute of Human Relations. He became the first professor in the department of anthropology established at Yale in 1931. In addition to numerous monographs, his works include *North American Indians of the Plains* (1912, 4th ed. 1948), *The American Indian* (1917, 3d ed. 1957), *The Relation of Nature to Man in Aboriginal America* (1926), and *Indians of the United States* (1949).

Wissmann, Hermann von (hĕr'män fən vĭs'män), 1853-1905, German explorer in Africa. He crossed (1880-82) Africa from Luanda to Zanzibar and, on behalf of Leopold II of Belgium, explored (1883-85) the Kasai River system in the Congo basin (now Zaïre). As German commissioner (1889-92) he suppressed an Arab revolt in German East Africa (now part of Tanzania). In the coastal area given up by the sultan of Zanzibar, he founded Moshi on the slopes of Mt. Kilimanjaro. He was (1895-96) governor of German East Africa. His writings include *My Second Journey through Equatorial Africa* (1891, tr. 1891).

Wistar, Caspar (wĭs'tər), 1761-1818, American physician, b. Philadelphia, M.D. Univ. of Edinburgh, 1786; grandson of Caspar Wistar (1696-1752), early Pennsylvania glassmaker. He taught (1789-91) at the College and Academy of Philadelphia, then at the Univ. of Pennsylvania organized (1791) by a merger of the college and academy with another institution. He wrote the first American textbook on anatomy, *A System of Anatomy* (2 vol., 1811-14), and left an anatomical collection that eventually passed to the Wistar Institute of Anatomy and Biology, founded by his great-nephew, Isaac J. Wistar. He was president (from 1815) of the American Philosophical Society, and his home was the weekly meeting place of students and scientists. The plant genus *Wistaria* was named in his honor.

Wistar, Isaac Jones, 1827-1905, American financier, b. Philadelphia; great-nephew of Caspar Wistar. His early manhood was spent adventurously in the West as a muleteer, trapper, and gold miner. In the Civil War he was a brigadier general in the Union army and was wounded four times. After the war he made his fortune by financing railroad building. He established the Wistar Institute of Anatomy and Biology in Philadelphia with gifts of $1 million. See his autobiography (1914).

wistaria: see WISTERIA.

Wister, Owen (wĭs'tər), 1860-1938, American author, b. Philadelphia, grad. Harvard (B.A., 1882; LL.B., 1888). Trips to the West for his health gave him material for his short stories and for his greatest success, *The Virginian* (1902), a novel about Wyoming cowhands. He wrote several biographies, including one in 1930 on his friend Theodore Roosevelt. His other books include the novel *Lady Baltimore* (1906) and the short stories "Lin McLean" (1898) and "Jimmyjohn Boss" (1900). His collected works, in 11 volumes, appeared in 1928. The journals of his Western travels from 1885 to 1895 were published in 1958 as *Owen Wister Out West.*

wisteria (wĭstēr'ēə) or **wistaria** (-târ'-), any plant of the genus *Wistaria,* woody twining vines of the family Leguminosae (PULSE family), cultivated and highly esteemed for the beautiful pendent clusters of pealike flowers, lilac, white, or pink. There are two species (*W. frutescens* and *W. macrostachya*) native to the United States, found mostly in the Southeast, but the showier Asian species are the most commonly cultivated. One variety of the Japanese wisteria (*W. floribunda macrobotrys*) has flower clusters up to 3 ft (1 m) long. Wisteria is classified in the division MAGNOLIOPHYTA, class Magnoliopsida, order Rosales, family Leguminosae.

Witbank (wĭt'băngk), town (1970 pop. 36,923), Transvaal, NE South Africa. It is the industrial center of South Africa's most important coalfield. Aside from coal-processing plants, the town has plants producing carbide, cyanide of potassium, steel, and vanadium. A miners' training college is in Witbank.

witchcraft, exercise of supernatural powers mainly for evil purposes through the use of black magic, sorcery, enchantment, satanism, and other occult arts. The origins of witchcraft in Europe are found in the pre-Christian, pagan cults such as the Teutonic nature cults, in Roman religion, and in the speculations of the Gnostics (see GNOSTICISM), the Zoroastrians, and the Manicheans. These pagan religions and philosophies believed in a power of evil and a power of good within the universe. Later, among certain sects, the worship of good was repudiated as false and misleading. The Cainites, a Gnostic sect, maintained that all that was commended by the Bible was in fact evil, and conversely, all that was condemned was actually good; thus Cain and the rebels were to be admired, and Judas Iscariot was considered to be the only true apostle. As the influence of the Christian church spread in the Western world, it banned pagan beliefs and practices, although many of the common people and clergy retained faith in the old beliefs. The church, seeking to convert all the peoples of Europe to Christianity, was particularly hostile to witchcraft. This attitude, however, resulted in a spread of witch lore and in an explosion of fear and mass hysteria. Religious persecution of supposed witches commenced early in the 14th cent. Trials, convictions, and executions became common throughout Europe and reached a peak during the 16th and 17th cent. Under the authority of the Spanish Inquisition, as many as 100 persons were burned as witches in a single day. The auto-da-fé, as this mass burning was called, took on the qualities of a carnival, where one could buy souvenirs, rosaries, holy images, and food. Suspicion also fell on many who were interested in scientific experimentation. An accusation of witchcraft became at times a means of destroying an enemy or of confiscating an estate. The crusade lasted from the 14th to the 18th cent. The colonies of North America shared in this fanaticism, particularly in Salem, Mass., where in 1692, 20 persons were executed as witches. Witchcraft survives in technologically developed societies as well as in contemporary primitive ones. In primitive cultures witchcraft or sorcery is often blamed as a cause of misfortune, disease, and death. See MAGIC and SHAMAN. See Montague Summers, *The History of Witchcraft and Demonology* (1926, repr. 1965); C. H. L. Ewen, *Witchcraft and Demonianism* (1933, repr. 1970); H. C. Lea and A. C. Howland, *Materials Toward a History of Witchcraft* (1939, repr. 1957); R. H. Robbins, *The Encyclopedia of Witchcraft and Demonology* (1959); J. C. Baroja, *The World of the Witches* (tr. 1964); Gillian Tindall, *A Handbook on Witches* (1966); L. L. Martello, *Witchcraft* (1973).

witch doctor: see MEDICINE MAN; SHAMAN.

witch hazel, common name for some members of the Hamamelidaceae, a family of trees and shrubs found mostly in Asia. The family includes the large genus (*Corylopsis*) of winter hazels, and the witch hazels (genus *Hamamelis*), sweet gums (*Liquidambar*), and witch elders (*Fothergilla*), the latter three genera represented by species in E North America as well as in Asia. The American witch hazel (*H. virginiana*) is a fall-blooming shrub or small tree found E of the Rockies. Its ripening fruits discharge their seeds by a characteristic explosive action, often shooting them several feet. The plant seems to have been named for the resemblance of its leaves to those of the hazel, and the witch hazel branch, like that of the hazel, has been used as a DIVINING ROD. The name "witch hazel" is applied also to an astringent liniment obtained from the leaves and bark of the plant. The sweet gums are characterized by their star-shaped leaves, their unusually brilliant and varied autumn coloring, and their round fruits with hornlike projections. The hard wood is used for cabinetmaking and for various building purposes. The bark, especially that of Asiatic species, is a source of storax or styrax, a fragrant BALSAM used in expectorants and perfumes and sometimes in chewing gum. Witch hazel is classified in the division MAGNOLIOPHYTA, class Magnoliopsida, order Hamamelidales, family Hamamelidaceae.

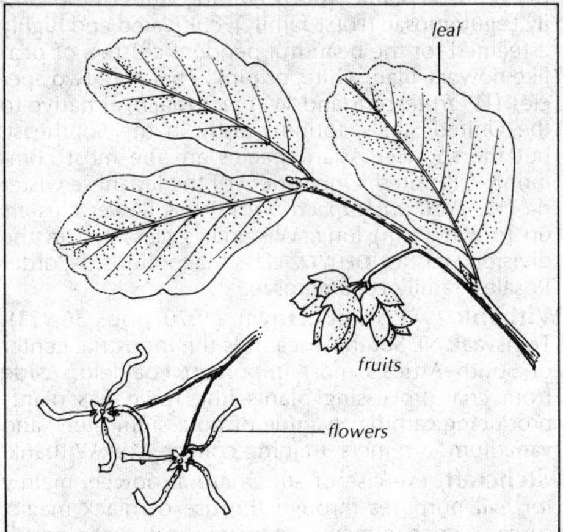

Witch hazel, Hamamelis virginiana

witenagemot (wĭt″ənəgĭmōt′) [Old Eng.,=meeting of counselors], a session of the counselors (the witan) of a king in Anglo-Saxon England. Such a body existed in each of the Anglo-Saxon kingdoms. Composed of the higher churchmen, the earls, and other members of the nobility, it was aristocratic, and its membershp at any one time was dependent upon the appointments of the ruling king or his immediate predecessors. These facts discredit the old argument that the witenagemot was similar to the later representative PARLIAMENT and make it clear that the witan were more analogous to the later Curia Regis. On the other hand, the witenagemot had considerable powers. Although the number of members and the functions varied with each realm and each king, the counsel and assent of the group were usually sought by the king in matters of laws, taxes, foreign negotiations, national defense, and the bestowal of privileged estates. Probably only rarely would the witan directly oppose the king, but their potential independence must have served as a check on the monarch. Furthermore, although records are rather scarce, it appears probable that the witan, especially in Wessex, had the power to elect the king. Since the kingship was largely hereditary, such a ceremony was usually perfunctory, but upon occasion the witan actually selected the king. See Felix Liebermann, *The National Assembly in the Anglo-Saxon Period* (1913, repr. 1961); Sir Frank Stenton, *Anglo-Saxon England* (3d ed. 1971).

Wither, George, 1588–1667, English poet, b. Hampshire, studied at Oxford. While in prison for having written the satires *Abuses Stript and Whipt* (1613), he wrote five pastorals under the title *The Shepherd's Hunting* (1615). Subsequent works include *Fidelia* (1617) and *Fair Virtue* (1622). About 1620 he became a Puritan, and his writings took on a religious tone. He served the Commonwealth during the civil war as a soldier and a politician.

witherite: see CARBONATE.

Witherspoon, Herbert (wĭth′ərspōōn), 1873–1935, American basso, b. Buffalo, N.Y.; grad. Yale, 1895, studied music with Edward MacDowell. He studied both painting and singing in New York City, London, Paris, and Berlin. In 1898 he made his operatic debut, and from 1908 to 1916 he was leading basso of the Metropolitan Opera Company, afterward devoting his time to concerts and to teaching. He was president (1925–29) of the Chicago Musical College, director for a brief time of the Chicago Civic Opera Company, and director (1932–33) of the Cincinnati Conservatory. In 1935 he succeeded Giulio Gatti-Casazza as director of the Metropolitan Opera Company, but he died shortly thereafter.

Witherspoon, John, 1723–94, Scottish-American Presbyterian clergyman, political leader in the American Revolution, and signer of the Declaration of Independence, b. Haddingtonshire (now East Lothian), Scotland. He was educated at the Univ. of Edinburgh. From 1745 to 1768 he occupied pastorates in Scotland. A conservative in religion, he wrote *Ecclesiastical Characteristics* (1753) as an attack on those ministers who preached humanism instead of dogmatic truth, and in his *Serious Enquiry into the Nature and Effects of the Stage* (1757) he maintained that drama was not an innocent recreation but an arouser of immoral passion. In 1768, Witherspoon was appointed president of the College of New Jersey (now Princeton Univ.), where he broadened the curriculum and considerably improved the quality of education. He promoted the growth of the Presbyterian Church in America (often heading the General Assembly) and healed schisms. Despite his original feeling that the clergy should avoid politics, he accepted a position as delegate from New Jersey to the Continental Congress and served almost continuously from 1776 to 1782. His last years were spent in restoring the college at Princeton and in participating in New Jersey politics. His collected works appeared in nine volumes in 1815. See biographies by D. W. Woods (1906) and V. L. Collins (1925, repr. 1969).

witness: see EVIDENCE.

Witold: see WITOWT.

Witos, Wincenty (vĕntsĕn′tĭ vĕ′tôs), 1874–1945, Polish politician. The leader of the Polish Peasant party, he was premier three times (1920–21, 1923, 1926). Witos's government was overthrown by PILSUDSKI in the coup d'état of 1926. Imprisoned (1930) with other opposition leaders, Witos later fled to Czechoslovakia but returned to Poland in 1939. He was again imprisoned during the German occupation.

Witowt or **Witold** (vĭt′ôft,-ôlt), Lithuanian *Vytautas*, 1350–1430, grand duke of Lithuania (1401–30). In 1382, Witowt, as well as his father, was imprisoned by Ladislaus Jagiello (see LADISLAUS II, king of Poland), his cousin, in a dispute over territorial claims and the title of grand duke. Although his father died in prison, Witowt escaped to take refuge with the order of Teutonic Knights. The cousins were reconciled in 1384, and Witowt received from Jagiello, whom he recognized as grand duke of Lithuania, Russian territory as an appanage. After Jagiello became (1386) king of Poland, Witowt plotted to separate Lithuania from its union with Poland and to assume the title of grand duke. With the help of the Teutonic Knights and Vasily I, prince of Moscow, he secured recognition as master of Lithuania (1392); in 1401 Ladislaus granted Witowt the grand ducal title while remaining his suzerain as king of Poland. Witowt sought to reduce the Tatars of the Golden Horde to vassalage but was defeated by them in 1399. In 1410, at the battle of Tannenberg, Witowt and Ladislaus defeated the Teutonic Knights, who had been threatening Polish-Lithuanian independence.

Witt, Cornelius de (kôrnā′lēəs də vĭt), 1623–72, Dutch naval officer; brother of Jan de Witt. Imprisoned on the charge of plotting against William of Orange (later WILLIAM III of England), he and his brother were killed by a mob.

Witt, Jan de (yän), 1625–72, Dutch statesman. Like his father, Jacob de Witt, burgomaster of Dort, he became a leading opponent of the house of Orange and played a vital role in the three successive DUTCH WARS. As leader of the republican party, he was elected (1653) grand pensionary, thus acquiring control of state affairs. He represented the mercantile interests and accordingly encouraged industry and commerce. He ended the disastrous war with England (first of the Dutch Wars) in 1654, but the Restoration in England was considered a danger to Dutch maritime and political freedom and led to the renewal of the war in 1665. The favorable (to the Dutch) terms of the Treaty of Breda (1667) were largely due to Jan de Witt. In order to end the power of the house of Orange he secured passage of the Eternal Edict, which abolished the office of stadtholder. He helped form the TRIPLE ALLIANCE of 1668 against Louis XIV, thus ending the War of Devolution; the Treaty of AIX-LA-CHAPELLE (1668) was the climax of his career. In 1672, Louis XIV invaded Holland and began the third of the Dutch Wars. Jan de Witt sought to negotiate peace, but his offer was spurned by the French. Popular feeling suddenly turned violently against him and in favor of William of Orange (later WILLIAM III of England), who by popular acclaim was made stadtholder. De Witt resigned, but was exonerated of treason charges. However, when he visited his brother, Cornelius de Witt, in prison, a mob gathered outside, fought its way into the prison, and hacked the two brothers to pieces, hanging their scattered limbs on lamp posts. De Witt was one of the greatest of Dutch statesmen and patriots, a patron of the sciences, and a close friend of Spinoza.

Witte, Count Sergei Yulyevich (syĭrgā′ yōō′lyĭvĭch vĭt′ə), 1849–1915, Russian premier. A railway administrator, he became minister of communications (1892) and minister of finance (1892–1903). He introduced the gold standard, reformed finances, encouraged the development of Russian industries with the help of foreign capital, and opened up Siberia to large-scale colonization with the construction of the TRANS-SIBERIAN RR. These measures reduced the gap between the industrial development of Russia and that of Europe and also expanded the Russian industrial proletariat, which was concentrated in a few large cities. Witte was dismissed in 1903, probably because he opposed the aggressive policy of Czar Nicholas II in the Far East, but he was recalled in 1905 at the close of the Russo-Japanese War (1904–5) to negotiate peace with Japan. He secured unexpectedly favorable terms for Russia in the Treaty of Portsmouth and was rewarded with the title of count. Returning to Russia during the Revolution of 1905 (see RUSSIAN REVOLUTION), he was called on by the czar to draw up the manifesto of Oct., 1905, by which Nicholas II promised more liberal government under a duma, or legislative assembly. Appointed premier (Oct., 1905), Witte failed to gain liberal support against the Social Democrats and the reactionaries. He secured a loan from France and suppressed a workers' uprising in Moscow (Dec., 1905–Jan., 1906). His resignation was accepted (April, 1906) by Nicholas II, who restored a more conservative regime. See studies by T. H. von Laue (1963) and H. D. Mehlinger and J. M. Thompson (1971).

Witte, Emanuel de (āmä′nōōĕl də vĭt′ə), 1617–92, Dutch painter. Witte's paintings of architecture, GENRE scenes, seascapes, and portraits were influenced by the work of ELSHEIMER. Witte excelled at moody, majestic paintings of church interiors (e.g., *Interior of a Gothic Church;* Rijks Mus.). He possessed a melancholy nature that ultimately drove him to suicide.

Wittekind, Saxon leader: see WIDUKIND.

Wittekind, Widukind, or **Wettekind** (wĭ′təkənd, wĭ′dōōkĭnd, wĕ′tə-), c.925–c.1004, Saxon historian, a monk, frequently called Wittekind of Corvey. He wrote the *Res gestae Saxonicae*, a history of the Saxons from earliest times to 997.

Wittelsbach (vĭ′təlsbäkh), German dynasty that ruled Bavaria from 1180 until 1918. It takes its name from the ancestral castle of Wittelsbach in Upper Bavaria. In 1180 Holy Roman Emperor Frederick I invested Count Otto of Wittelsbach with the much-reduced duchy of BAVARIA, of which he had deprived the Guelphic duke, Henry the Lion. In 1214 Otto's son, Otto II, also received the Rhenish Palatinate. After Otto's death (1253) the Wittelsbach possessions were divided between an elder branch, which received the Rhenish Palatinate and W Bavaria, and a younger branch, which received the rest. The Wittelsbachs reached their zenith under Duke Louis III, of the elder branch, who became Holy Roman Emperor LOUIS IV (reigned 1314–47). Louis IV temporarily (1324–73) attached BRANDENBURG to his dynasty and through his second marriage added Hainaut, Holland, Zeeland, and Friesland. In 1329, Louis IV subdivided the Wittelsbach lands; the elder branch, descended from Louis's brother Rudolf, received the Rhenish and the Upper Palatinate, while the younger branch, descended from Louis's first marriage, received Bavaria proper. The electoral dignity at first was to alternate between the two branches but was settled permanently on the Palatinate branch by the Golden Bull of 1356. Both branches underwent several subdivisions, but in the early 16th cent. Bavaria was reunited by Duke Albert IV, who introduced succession by primogeniture. (For the subdivisions of the Palatinate branch, which is not treated here in detail, see PALATINATE.) In 1443, Philip the Good of Burgundy seized Hainaut, Holland, Zeeland, and Friesland from Countess Jacqueline, his first cousin. In the 16th and 17th cent. the Bavarian Wittelsbachs championed the Roman Catholic cause while the Palatinate branch were the leading Protestant princes. After the defeat of the elector palatine, known as FREDERICK THE WINTER KING of Bohemia, his electoral voice was transferred (1623) to Duke MAXIMILIAN I of Bavaria, who also received the Upper Palatinate. A new electorate was created in 1648 for Frederick's son, to whom the Rhenish Palatinate was restored. Elector Charles Albert of Bavaria was chosen (1742) Holy Roman emperor as CHARLES VII; with the death (1777) of his son, Maximilian III, the Bavarian branch of the Wittelsbachs died out, and the Palatinate-Sulzbach line acceded in Bavaria in the person of Elector Charles Theodore, who died in 1799 without issue. He was succeeded by the duke palatine of Zweibrücken, senior member of the Palatinate branch, who thus united all Wittelsbach lands under his sole rule and who in 1806 became king of Bavaria as MAXIMILIAN I. His successors as kings of Bavaria were LOUIS I, MAXIMILIAN II, LOUIS II, OTTO I, and LOUIS III, who abdicated in 1918. Empress Elizabeth of Austria, wife of FRANCIS JOSEPH, and Queen Elizabeth of the Belgians, consort of ALBERT I, issued from a collateral line of the dynasty, and the Wittelsbachs have intermarried for centuries with all the royal families of Europe. A line of the Palatinate branch (see ZWEIBRÜCKEN) ruled Sweden from 1654 to 1741. Prince Rupert (d. 1955), son of King Louis III and claimant to the Bavarian throne, also inherited, through a complicated succession, the claim of the STUART dynasty to the British throne.

Witten (vĭt'ən), city (1970 pop. 97,379), North Rhine-Westphalia, W West Germany, on the Ruhr River. It is a modern industrial city, whose manufactures include iron and steel, glass, and chemicals. Witten was first mentioned in the 13th cent. and was chartered in 1825.

Wittenberg (vĭt'ənbĕrkh"), city (1970 pop. 47,151), Halle district, central East Germany, on the Elbe River. A city with a noted history, it is today an industrial and mining center and a rail junction. Manufactures include machinery, chemicals, processed food, and rubber products. First mentioned in the late 12th cent., Wittenberg was (1273–1422) the seat of the Ascanian dukes of Saxe-Wittenberg (see SAXONY), who in 1356 became electors of Saxony. In 1423, Saxe-Wittenberg passed to the margraves of Meissen (members of the house of WETTIN), who in 1425 were given electoral rank. Elector Frederick III founded (1502) the Univ. of Wittenberg, which became the center of the Protestant Reformation when Martin Luther and Philip Melanchthon taught there. In 1517, Luther nailed his 95 theses on the door of the Schlosskirche [castle church], and in 1520 he burned the papal bull against him outside the Elster gate. The first complete Lutheran Bible was printed (1534) at Wittenberg. In 1547 Emperor Charles V captured Wittenberg after the battle of Mühlberg, where Elector John Frederick I of Saxony was captured. By the Capitulation of Wittenberg, in the same year, John Frederick, representing the Ernestine line of the house of Wettin, ceded the electoral dignity and the duchy of Saxony to Maurice, of the collateral Albertine line. Primarily the focus of the Lutheran Reformation, 16th-century Wittenberg was also a center of German art. Lucas Cranach, the elder, founded a school of painting there. The city declined after 1547, when Dresden, residence of the Albertine dukes, replaced it as Saxon capital. In 1815 Wittenberg passed to Prussia, and in 1817 the Univ. of Wittenberg was absorbed by the Univ. of Halle. Among Wittenberg's most notable structures are the Schlosskirche (15th cent.), where Luther and Melanchthon are buried; the town church (14th-15th cent.), where Luther preached; the houses where Luther, Melanchthon, and Lucas Cranach, the elder, lived; and the city hall (16th cent.).

Wittgenstein, Ludwig Josef Johann (lo͝ot'vĭkh yō'zĕf yō'hän vĭt'gənshtīn), 1889–1951, Austrian philosopher, b. Vienna. Originally trained as an engineer, Wittgenstein turned to philosophy, went to Cambridge, where he studied (1912–13) with Bertrand Russell, and further developed his philosophy through solitary study in Norway (1913–14). After serving in the Austrian army in World War I, he taught elementary school (1920–26) in Lower Austria and was an architect in Vienna (1926–28). The *Tractatus Logico-philosophicus,* one of his major works, appeared in 1921 but initially attracted little attention. During the 1920s Wittgenstein came in contact with the so-called Vienna Circle of logical positivists, who were profoundly influenced by the *Tractatus* (see LOGICAL POSITIVISM). Wittgenstein returned to Cambridge in 1929, received his doctorate, and began lecturing in 1930; in 1937 he succeeded G. E. Moore in the chair of philosophy. Retiring in 1947, he worked in seclusion until his death. Wittgenstein's philosophical thought is unified by a constant concern with the relationship between language, mind, and reality; but it divides into two importantly different phases. The first phase, expressed in the *Tractatus,* posits a close, formal relationship between language, thought, and the world; there is a direct logical correspondence between the configurations of simple objects in the world, thoughts in the mind, and words in language. Thus the shape of ideas in the mind and the relationship of words in a sentence are identical in form with the structure of reality or "state of affairs" they represent. Language and thought worked literally like a picture of the real, and to conceive or speak of any state of affairs is to be able to form a "picture" of it. To understand any sentence one must grasp the reference of its constituents, both to each other and to the real: Meaning in thought and language requires a direct reference to the real. The *Tractatus,* however, made a distinction between what language could mean and what it might indicate. The structures of language and thought could indicate, but not represent, an area beyond themselves; unsayable things did exist, and sentences whose structures of meaning amounted to nonsense could result in philosophical insight. Thus the *Tractatus* did not, like the logical positivists, reject the metaphysical; rather, it denied the possibility of stating the metaphysical: "Whereof one cannot speak, thereof one must be silent." The second phase of Wittgenstein's philosophy commenced with his return to Cambridge in 1929 and continued until his death in 1951; his major work of that period is the *Philosophical Investigations* (1953). In this period he revised his own thought in the *Tractatus,* stressing the conventional nature of language. He saw language as a response to, as well as a reproduction of, the real. Its meaning was influenced not only by the formal resemblance of its constituents to reality but by the situation, the "language game," in which it was used. Wittgenstein's work greatly influenced, and indeed in a sense occasioned, what has come to be called ordinary language philosophy, that is, the position that maintains that all philosophical problems arise from the illusions created by the ambiguities of language. Philosophy, therefore, must be chiefly concerned with the analysis and proper use of language. This outlook still forms a dominant trend in Great Britain and the United States. Other of Wittgenstein's posthumous works are *Remarks on the Foundations of Mathematics* (1956), *The Blue and Brown Books: Preliminary Studies for the Philosophical Investigations* (1958), and *Notebooks 1914–1916* (1961). See George Pitcher, *The Philosophy of Wittgenstein* (1964); Justus Hartnack, *Wittgenstein and Modern Philosophy* (1965); K. T. Fann, *Wittgenstein's Conception of Philosophy* (1970); David Pears, *Wittgenstein* (1970); Rush Rhees, *Discussions of Wittgenstein* (1970); E. D. Klemke, *Essays on Wittgenstein* (1971); C. W. K. Mundle, *A Critique of Linguistic Philosophy* (1971); W. W. Bartley, *Wittgenstein* (1973); A. J. P. Kenny, *Wittgenstein* (1973).

Wittkower, Rudolf (wĭt'kou-ər, Ger. vĭt'kōv-ər), 1901–71, German-American art historian. After gaining his doctorate in Berlin, Wittkower became a research assistant and later research fellow at the Biblioteca Hertziana, Rome (1923–33). He was (1934–56) on the staff of the Warburg Institute, London, and became professor at the Univ. of London from 1949 until 1956. Wittkower then headed the department of fine arts and archaeology at Columbia Univ. A man of indomitable energy, he transformed the department into one of the vital centers of scholarship in art history. His highly original works in English include *Architectural Principles in the Age of Humanism* (1949), which was a major influence on modern English architects; *The Drawings of the Carracci* (1952); *Gian Lorenzo Bernini* (1955), a basic reevaluation; *Art and Architecture in Italy, 1600–1750* (1958); *Born under Saturn, the Character and Conduct of Artists* (with Margot Wittkower, 1963); *Essays in the History of Architecture* (1967); *Essays in the History of Art* (1967); and *Baroque Art: The Jesuit Contribution* (with Irma Jaffe, 1972).

Wittlin, Józef (yo͞o'zĕf vĕt'lēn), 1896–, Polish poet, translator, and novelist. Wittlin first became known for his antiwar *Hymns* (1920), and his translation of the *Odyssey* (1924). His lyrical epic novel *Salt of the Earth* (1935, tr. 1939) concerns the experience of a peasant soldier during World War I.

Wittstock (vĭt'shtôk), town (1970 pop. 10,606), Potsdam district, N central East Germany. Manufactures include woolen textiles, machinery, and forest products. At Wittstock in 1636 the Swedes under Baner defeated the Saxon and imperial forces under Melchior Hatzfeldt in an important battle of the Thirty Years War.

Witu Islands: see VITU ISLANDS.

Witwatersrand (wĭtwô'tərzrănd") [Afrik., = white water ridge] or **the Rand,** region, Transvaal, Republic of South Africa. The area, which forms the watershed between the Vaal and Olifants rivers, is c.25 mi (40 km) wide and extends more than 60 mi (100 km) from west to east in a series of parallel ranges 5,000 to 6,000 ft (1,520–1,830 m) above sea level. The Rand is one of the world's richest gold-mining regions. The gold occurs in reefs, or thin bands, that are mined at depths of up to 10,000 ft (3,050 m). Development of the Rand dates from the 1880s. Although many of the older mines are now nearly exhausted, the Rand still produces more than two thirds of South Africa's gold and almost one third of total world output. Silver and iridium are recovered as gold-refining by-products, and the region also has coal mines. The Rand also has such industries as engineering, steel milling, metallurgy, machine building, diamond cutting, food processing, and the manufacture of chemicals, cement, furniture, and clothing. Major cities of the Rand are JOHANNESBURG, BENONI, BOKSBURG, SPRINGS, and GERMISTON.

Witz, Conrad (kôn'rät vĭts), fl. c.1434–c.1447, German painter, active at Basel and Geneva. Many of his works can be seen in Basel. His large altarpieces reveal stubby figures that recall painted sculpture and settings of steeply recessed perspective or topographically accurate landscapes. Witz showed a remarkable understanding of the effects of reflected light on water and landscape. In his realism he is an early follower of van Eyck and Campin, although his forms are more abstract and geometric.

Wladimir. For rulers thus named, see VLADIMIR.

Wladislaw, Wladyslaw, and **Wladislas,** Pol. *Władysław.* For Polish kings thus named, see LADISLAUS.

Włocławek (vlôtslä'vĕk), Rus. *Vlotslavsk,* city (1970 pop. 77,169), central Poland, a port on the Vistula (Wisła) River. It is an agricultural market center and has industries producing farm machinery, chemicals, metalware, paper, cellulose, and pottery. Nearby are salt domes, lignite deposits, and sulfur springs. The city was founded in the 12th cent., passed to Russia in 1815, and reverted to Poland after World War I. Landmarks include a 14th-century Gothic cathedral and a 17th-century episcopal palace.

Włodzimierz: see VLADIMIR-VOLYNSKI, USSR.

woad, name for a perennial plant (*Isatis tinctoria*) of the family Cruciferae (MUSTARD family) and for a blue dye obtained from its leaves. The plant is believed to be native to S Russia, but was in cultivation (and escaped) throughout Europe in early times. The pigment is obtained by fermentation and oxidation of a colorless glucoside, indican. Indican is also present in the leaves of the unrelated INDIGO, the other major blue vegetable dye plant. Although the dye obtained from indigo is superior in vividness of color, fastness, and ease of processing, woad growers and distributors of the Renaissance prohibited the sale of indigo in Europe for more than a century. In 1392 the Saxon town of Erfurt, Germany, had gained enough wealth through the woad trade to establish its own university. By the mid-17th cent., however, woad had been largely replaced by its successor—partly because of the low prices of indigo imports from the New World. Both woad and indigo have been eclipsed by the synthetic aniline dyes perfected in the late 19th cent. Woad was also extensively used for brilliant blue paint pigments. The ancients used it medicinally for ulcers and other ailments, and the early Britons painted their bodies with it. Woad is classified in the division MAGNOLIOPHYTA, class Magnoliopsida, order Capparales, family Cruciferae. See J. B. Hurry, *The Woad Plant and Its Dye* (1930, repr. 1974).

Wobblies: see INDUSTRIAL WORKERS OF THE WORLD.

Woburn (wo͞o'bərn), village, Bedfordshire, S central England. It is famous for Woburn Abbey (seat of the dukes of Bedford), an 18th-century mansion constructed on the site of a Cistercian Abbey founded in 1145. It contains a noteworthy art collection with many classical works brought from Rome in the 18th cent.

Woburn, city (1970 pop. 37,406), Middlesex co., NE Mass.; settled 1640, inc. as a city 1888. It has electrical, chemical, and leather industries, as well as greenhouses. Count Rumford was born there.

Wodehouse, P. G. (Sir Pelham Grenville Wodehouse), 1881–, English novelist and humorist. For over 70 years Wodehouse entertained readers with his comic novels and stories, set in an England that is forever Edwardian and featuring idiotic youths, feckless debutantes, redoubtable aunts, and stuffy businessmen. He is most famous for his many novels about Bertie Wooster and his unflappable valet Jeeves. The "Jeeves" novels include *The Inimitable Jeeves* (1924), *Bertie Wooster Sees It Through* (1955), and *Much Obliged, Jeeves* (1971). In addition to his works of fiction, Wodehouse collaborated with Guy Bolton on several Broadway musicals, including *Anything Goes* (1934) and *Bring On the Girls* (1953). Wodehouse emigrated to the United States in 1910 and became a citizen in 1955. In 1941, while he was a prisoner of the Germans, he made five broadcasts for his captors. He was knighted by Queen Elizabeth II of England in 1975. See his autobiographical *Author! Author!* (1962; originally pub. as *Performing Flea,* 1953); biography by D. A. Jasen (1974); studies by R. A. Usborne (1961), H. W. Warren (1972), and R. A. Hall, Jr. (1974).

Woden (wō'dən; German vō'dĭn), Norse **Odin** (ō'dĭn), in Germanic religion, the supreme god. His cult, although widespread among the Germanic tribes, was sometimes subordinated to that of his son Thor. With his brothers, Woden fashioned the earth and the sky from the dead body of the giant Ymir, and from an ash tree and an alder he created the first man and woman. As chief of the gods of ASGARD he established the laws that governed the universe and controlled the destiny of man. At his court at VALHALLA he was attended by the Valkyries. Woden was widely known as a god of war, but he was important also as a god of learning, of poetry, and of magic. His wife was Frigg, and his children included Thor, Balder, and Tiw. He was identified with the Roman god Mercury, and among Germanic peoples Mercury's day became Woden's day (Wednesday). In Richard Wagner's opera cycle, *Der Ring des Nibelungen,* Woden is called Wotan.

Wodrow, Robert (wŏŏd'rō), 1679–1734, Scottish ecclesiastical historian. His principal work is *The History of the Sufferings of the Church of Scotland from the Restoration to the Revolution* (1721–22).

Woestijne, Karel van de (kä'rəl vän də vōō'stīnə), 1878–1929, Flemish symbolist poet and novelist. He also had some reputation as a painter. He worked for a time as journalist and from 1919 was professor of Dutch literature at the Univ. of Ghent. His early verse was semiautobiographical and explored themes of spiritual and sensual love. Such later works as *De Modderen Man* [the man of mud] (1920), also semiautobiographical, dealt with conflicting emotions and desires and with unrealized dreams. His prose tales were often based on legendary and biblical themes.

Woffington, Peg (Margaret Woffington), 1714?–1760, English actress, b. Dublin. Her charm and beauty as a child attracted attention, and at the age of 10 she acted in the role of Polly Peachum in a Lilliputian production of *The Beggar's Opera.* She made her first important appearance in Dublin in 1737 as Ophelia and followed it with her greatest role, the breeches part (male role) of Sir Harry Windair in Farquhar's *Constant Couple,* which in 1740 led to her engagement by John Rich for Covent Garden. She was Garrick's leading lady in London and Dublin from 1742–48. Her attachment to Garrick was the most publicized of her numerous affairs. Ill health compelled her to retire in 1757. She was best suited for comedy, although her grace and vivacity helped to overcome the harshness of her voice in tragic roles. Charles Reade's play *Masks and Faces* and his novel *Peg Woffington* are based on her life. See biography by Janet Dunbar (1968); Barbara Marinacci, *Leading Ladies* (1961).

Wöhler, Friedrich (frē'drĭkh vö'lər), 1800–1882, German chemist. He studied under the German chemist Leopold Gmelin and J. J. Berzelius, a Swedish chemist, and in 1836 was appointed professor at the Univ. of Göttingen. He devised (1827) a new method for isolating aluminum and in 1828 used the method to isolate beryllium and yttrium. His synthesis (1828) of urea, the first synthesis of an organic compound from inorganic material, opened a new era in organic chemistry and contributed greatly to the theory of isomerism. His work on benzoic acid was important to the chemistry of metabolism. His works on chemistry, widely used as texts, include *Outlines of Organic Chemistry* (1840, tr. 1873).

Wohlgemuth, Michael: see WOLGEMUT, MICHAEL.

Woking (wō'kĭng), urban district (1971 pop. 75,771), Surrey, SE England. Woking is primarily a residential suburb of London. There are printing, rubber, and packing industries. Of interest is a mosque built in 1889, headquarters of the Muslim Society of Great Britain.

Wolcot, John (wŏŏl'kət), pseud. **Peter Pindar,** 1738–1819, English poet. He wrote several satires, notably *Lyric Odes to the Royal Academicians* (1782–83), *Bozzy and Piozzi* (1786), and *The Lousiad* (1785–95). See study by R. L. Vales (1973).

Wolcott, Oliver, 1726–97, political leader in the American Revolution, signer of the Declaration of Independence, b. South Windsor (then in Windsor), Conn.; son of Roger Wolcott. He fought in King George's War, and upon his return to Connecticut he entered a legal and public career. Wolcott held several judicial posts and in 1775 was named an Indian commissioner to obtain the neutrality of the Iroquois in the conflict with Great Britain. He was a general in the Saratoga campaign and a prominent figure in Connecticut politics as a delegate to the Continental Congress (1775–78, 1780–84), lieutenant governor (1786–96), and governor (1796–97).

Wolcott, Oliver, 1760–1833, U.S. Secretary of the Treasury (1795–1800), b. Litchfield, Conn; son of Oliver Wolcott. Admitted to the bar in 1781, he served as Connecticut comptroller (1788–89), auditor of the U.S. treasury (1789–91), and U.S. comptroller (1791–95). A Federalist and loyal follower of Alexander Hamilton, he succeeded Hamilton as Secretary of the Treasury and was bitterly, but unfairly, attacked by Republicans for misappropriating funds. Wolcott left the Federalist party during the War of 1812, and was elected (1817) governor of Connecticut as a Republican, serving until 1827. As president of the 1818 state constitutional convention, he led the successful fight for a wider suffrage, an independent judiciary, and the disestablishment of the Congregationalist Church.

Wolcott, Roger, 1679–1767, American colonial governor of Connecticut, b. Windsor, Conn. A member of an influential Connecticut family, he became a judge and was prominent in the colonial assembly and the executive council before becoming governor (1750–54). He was second-in-command of the expedition that captured (1745) Louisburg in King George's War. Wolcott wrote *Poetical Meditations* (1725), the first book of verse published in Connecticut. He was the father of Oliver Wolcott.

Wolcott, town (1970 pop. 12,495), New Haven co., central Conn.; inc. 1796. Tools and novelties are made. Bronson Alcott was born nearby.

Wolf, Christian von: see WOLFF, CHRISTIAN VON.

Wolf, Hugo (hōō'gō vôlf), 1860–1903, Austrian composer; studied at the Vienna Conservatory. From 1883 to 1887 he wrote musical criticism for the Vienna *Salonblatt.* As a composer he first gained attention when his songs began to be published in 1889. Wolf's more than 300 *lieder* place him with Schubert and Schumann as a supreme master of that form. He wrote many songs with texts by Goethe, Mörike, Eichendorff, and other German poets, but he also used foreign lyrics in translation, as in his *Spanisches Liederbuch* (1889) and *Italienisches Liederbuch* (Part I, 1891; Part II, 1896). Wolf borrowed Wagner's chromatic harmony and symphonic conception of accompaniment, but in his songs he transformed them into his own miniaturistic idiom. He also wrote an opera, *Der Corregidor* (1896; based on Alarcón's *El Sombrero de tres picos*), as well as choral works and some chamber music. In 1897 he had a mental breakdown and later at his own request was committed to a state asylum, where he died. See biographies by E. Newman (1966) and F. Walker (2d. ed. 1968).

wolf, carnivorous mammal of the genus *Canis* in the DOG family. Once distributed over most of the Northern Hemisphere, wolves are now confined to the wilder parts of a reduced range. Three wolf species are generally recognized, although there is much local variation within them. The most widespread is the gray wolf, *C. lupus,* of circumpolar distribution; it is also known as the timber wolf in North America. Extinct in W Europe except in a few isolated pockets, it is still found in SE Europe, Russia, and much of Asia. In the New World it is found in wilderness forests and tundra from Greenland and the shores and islands of the Arctic Ocean to the extreme N United States, and in a few isolated regions in the mountains of the W United States. It is similar in appearance to a German shepherd dog, with a thick, shaggy coat, erect ears, and a bushy tail. Its fur is usually gray mixed with black and brown, but may be nearly black or, in the Arctic, nearly white. An average-sized adult male is about 3 ft (90 cm) high at the shoulder and 4 ft (120 cm) long, excluding the tail, and weighs about 100 lb (45 kg); some individuals weigh twice as much. Active mostly at night, gray wolves prey on birds and small mammals and on weak members of larger species, such as deer; they also eat vegetable matter and some carrion. They can run at speeds of up to 35 mi (56 km) per hour and can clear 16 ft (4.9 m) in a single bound. While hunting they can maintain a speed of about 20 mi (32 km) per hr for many hours, eventually wearing down even the swiftest prey. They roam over large areas and may migrate in response to migrations or numerical fluctuations of their prey species. Gray wolves hunt singly and in family groups, called packs, which typically include about five individuals. Under severe conditions, especially in winter, several families may join together, forming a pack of up to 30 individuals, rarely more. During the mating season a wolf pair establishes a den, usually in a cave or underground burrow, in which they raise the young; both parents bring home food. A pair is believed to remain mated for life. Because of their raids on livestock, gray wolves have been hunted ruthlessly, resulting in their extermination in all but the most sparsely populated areas. North American gray wolves have not been known to attack humans without provocation, although Siberian gray wolves have on occasion attacked riders of horses or horse-drawn vehicles. There are many stories of human children being raised by gray wolves, particularly in India, but none has been authenticated. The red wolf, *C. niger,* is a smaller species found in forest and brush country of the S central United States; it varies in color from reddish gray to nearly black. It is probably similar in behavior to the prairie wolf, *C. latrans,* better known as the COYOTE. Smallest of the wolves, coyotes are still widespread in W North America. Other living members of the genus *Canis* are the JACKAL and the dog. All *Canis* species can interbreed, producing fertile offspring; the Eskimos have interbred wolves and dogs to produce hardy animals for pulling sleds. The maned wolf, *Chrysocyon brachyurus,* found in wooded areas of central South America, is not a true wolf, although it is a canine (member of the dog family). It has extremely long, stiltlike legs and an erectile mane on the neck. Strand wolf is a name for the brown HYENA (not a canine) of Africa. The AARDWOLF is also a member of the hyena family. Wolves are classified in the phylum CHORDATA, subphylum Vertebrata, class Mammalia, order Carnivora, family Canidae. See R. J. Rutter and D. H. Pimlott, *The World of the Wolf* (1967); L. D. Mech, *The Wolf: The Ecology and Behavior of an Endangered Species* (1970); M. W. Fox, *Behaviour of Wolves, Dogs and Related Canids* (1972).

Wolfe, James, 1727–59, British soldier. After a distinguished record in European campaigns, he was made (1758) second in command to Jeffrey Amherst in the last of the French and Indian Wars. Through his skillful siege operations, he became a hero of the capture of Louisburg (1758) from the French, and he was rewarded with the command of an expedition against the French at Quebec, which he himself had urged. After frontal attacks on the positions of General MONTCALM at Quebec had failed, Wolfe took 5,000 men in boats down the St. Lawrence by night and forced an open battle with the French on the Plains of ABRAHAM (Sept. 13, 1759). The British were victorious, but both Wolfe and Montcalm were killed. The battle was decisive in the fall of New France to the British. Wolfe is vividly portrayed in Thackeray's *Virginians.* See biographies by Christopher Hibbert (1959) and D. R. Robin (1960); Francis Parkman, *Montcalm and Wolfe* (1884); Richard Howard, *Wolfe at Quebec* (1965).

Wolfe, Thomas Clayton, 1900–1938, American novelist, b. Asheville, N.C., grad. Univ. of North Carolina, 1920, M.A. Harvard, 1922. An important 20th-century American novelist, Wolfe wrote four mammoth novels, which, although highly autobiographical, present a sweeping picture of American life. He was the son of William Oliver Wolfe, a stonecutter, and Julia Westall Wolfe, a boarding-house keeper and speculator in real estate. Wolfe's early, insistent efforts to become a playwright met with frustration and failure. In 1924 he became an instructor at New York Univ., teaching there until 1930; thereafter he wrote mostly in New York City or abroad. During the late 1920s he was closely associated with Aline Bernstein (the "Esther Jack" of his novels), a noted theatrical designer, who was a major influence in his adult life. In 1929, under the editorial guidance of Maxwell Perkins, he published his first novel, *Look Homeward, Angel.* After the appearance of its sequel, *Of Time and the River* (1935), he broke with Perkins and signed a contract with Harper & Brothers, with Edward Aswell as his editor. Wolfe died at 38 from complications following pneumonia. Aswell arranged from the material left at Wolfe's death two novels—*The Web and the Rock* (1939) and *You Can't Go Home Again* (1940)—and a volume of stories and fragments, *The Hills Beyond* (1941). Wolfe's other publications include *From Death to Morning* (1935), a collection of short stories; and *The Story of a Novel* (1936), a record of how he wrote his second book. Wolfe's works compose a picture, left somewhat incomplete by his premature death. They describe the life of a youth from the rural South through his education to his career in New York City as a teacher and writer. Wolf's major theme was almost always himself—his own inner and outer existence—his gropings, his pain, his self-discovery, and his endless search for an enduring faith. He was obsessed by memory, time, and location, and his novels convey a brilliant sense of place. His writing is characterized by a lyrical and dramatic intensity, by the weaving and reweaving of a web of sensous images, and by rhapsodic incantations. See his letters, ed. by Elizabeth Nowell (1956); biographies by Elizabeth Nowell (1960), Andrew Turnbull (1967), and N. F. Austin (1968); studies by P. H. Johnson (1947), R. S. Kennedy (1962), and R. G. Walser, ed. (1967).

Wolfe, Tom, pseud. of **Thomas Kennerly, Jr.,** 1931–, American journalist, b. Richmond, Va. Wolfe writes studies of contemporary American culture, especially the drug, rock, and car culture of California. The titles of his works indicate his style, a mixture of comic strip, jet set, and academic jargon. His works include *The Kandy-Kolored Tangerine-Flake Streamline Baby* (1965), *The Electric Kool-Aid Acid Test* (1968), *Radical Chic and Mau-mauing the Flak Catchers* (1970), and *The Right Stuff* (1975).

Wolfenbüttel (vôl'fənbüt'əl), city (1970 pop. 40,279), Lower Saxony, E West Germany, on the Oker River, near the East German border. It is an agricultural market and an industrial center. Manufactures include machinery, chemicals, and liquor. Wolfenbüttel developed around an 11th-century castle that became (c.1280) a favorite Guelphic residence. It was the residence of the dukes of Brunswick-Wolfenbüttel (see BRUNSWICK, state) from 1432 to 1753. The famous ducal library, founded in the 17th cent., contains about 350,000 volumes, some 3,000 incunabula, and more than 8,000 manuscripts. Its librarians included Leibniz (1690–1716) and G. E. Lessing (1770–81). Lessing's house, in which he wrote *Nathan the Wise,* still stands. The city's noteworthy buildings include the former ducal palace (15th–18th cent.; now a museum), a 17th-century church, and numerous 17th-century half-timber houses.

Wolff, Caspar Friedrich (käs'pär frē'drĭkh vôlf), 1733–94, German biologist, a founder of observational embryology. In his *Theoria generationis* (1759) he reintroduced the theory of epigenesis to replace the then current theory of preformation, directing attention to the evidence of comparative development in plants and animals. He spent many years of research at the Academy of Sciences in St. Petersburg.

Wolff or **Wolf, Christian von** (krĭs'tyän fən vôlf), 1679–1754, German philosopher. One of the first to use the German language instead of Latin, he systematized and popularized the doctrines of Leibniz. Wolff studied at Jena and taught at Leipzig before going to a professorship at Halle (1706–23). His doctrines of apparent fatalism aroused the Pietists to secure his banishment, which he spent as professor at Marburg (1723–40). Recalled to Halle by Frederick the Great in 1740, he became chancellor of the university in 1743. Wolff's major work was *Vernünftige Gedanken von Gott, der Welt, und der Seele der Menschen* [rational thoughts on God, the world, and the souls of men] (1719). The Leibnizian doctrine of preestablished harmony was more prominent than the monad theory in Wolff's presentation, though both were considerably moderated. He is chiefly remembered for his broad concept of philosophy, his insistence on clarity and precision, and his devotion to the power of reason and mathematics. See study by J. V. Burns (1966).

Wolff, Elisabeth (**Bekker**) (ālē'zäbĕt bĕk'ər vôlf), 1738–1804, Dutch novelist. She wrote satirical articles and poems, but she is most famous for the novels she wrote in collaboration with Agatha Deken (1741–1804). These sentimental novels of the early romantic school are important in Dutch literature, and they show the influence of Richardson and Fielding. Among them are *Historie van Mejuffrouw Sara Burgerhart* (1788) and *Historie van Willem Leevend* (8 vol., 1784–85). Elisabeth Wolff is known also as Elisabeth Wolff-Bekker and Betje Wolff; Agatha Deken as Aagje Deken.

Wolf-Ferrari, Ermanno (ārmän'nō vôlf-fār-rä'rē), 1876–1948, German-Italian composer, b. Venice, studied in Germany. Most of his 12 operas, which adapted the *opera buffa* style of the 18th cent., were first produced in Germany. Best known is *The Secret of Suzanne* (1909). He also wrote a tragic opera, *The Jewels of the Madonna* (1911).

wolf fish: see BLENNY.

Wölfflin, Heinrich (hīn'rĭkh völf'lĭn), 1864–1945, Swiss art historian. Wölfflin's formal stylistic analysis of motifs and composition in art combined cultural history and psychological insight into the creative process to form a complete aesthetic system. His theory of form greatly influenced the development of art criticism. Wölfflin's ideas were spread through his teaching (1893–1934) at the universities of Basel, Berlin, Munich, and Zürich, and through his books, *Renaissance und Barock* (1888), *Classic Art* (1899, tr. 1953), and his most celebrated work, *Principles of Art History* (1915, tr. 1932).

wolfhound: see IRISH WOLFHOUND.

Wolf National Scenic Riverway: see NATIONAL PARKS AND MONUMENTS (table).

wolfram: see TUNGSTEN.

wolframite (wo͝ol'frəmīt"), reddish-brown to grayish-black lustrous mineral, a tungstate of iron and manganese, (Fe,Mn)Wo_4, occurring in crystals of the monoclinic system. It is the chief ore of the metal tungsten. Widely distributed in nature, it is mined in England, Portugal, Bolivia, Burma and the Malay Peninsula, S China, Australia, and W United States.

Wolfram von Eschenbach (vôl'främ fən ĕsh'-ənbäkh), c.1170–c.1220, German poet. He was a knight who led a restless, roving life. In 1203 he was at the court of Landgrave Hermann von Thüringen. His only complete work is his famous *Parzival,* a poem of chivalry notable for its lyricism, humor, and depth of conception (see PARSIFAL). Wolfram's other works include two unfinished epic poems, *Willehalm* and *Titurel,* and lyrics. He appears as a character in Wagner's *Tannhäuser.* Wolfram is not only one of the greatest of the German minnesingers, but he ranks high among the poets of medieval Europe. See the interpretation of *Parzival* by M. F. Richey (1933) and the translation by Jessie Weston (1894); study by J. F. Poag (1972).

Wolf-Rayet star: see SPECTRAL CLASS.

wolfsbane: see ACONITE.

Wolfsburg (vôlfs'bo͝orkh), city (1970 pop. 88,655), Lower Saxony, NE West Germany, on the Midland Canal. A small village in 1937, Wolfsburg grew and prospered as the headquarters of the Volkswagen automobile company.

Wolf Trap Farm Park: see NATIONAL PARKS AND MONUMENTS (table).

Wolfville, town (1971 pop. 2,861), W central N.S., Canada, on the southwest shore of Minas Basin. It is a market center for a dairy and fruit-growing area. Acadia Univ. (1839) is there. Just east is Grand Pré.

Wolgemut or **Wohlgemuth, Michael** (both: mĭkh'äēl vôl'gəmo͞ot), 1434–1519, German painter, wood carver, and engraver who worked mainly in Nuremberg. First instructed by his father and in Munich, he traveled and then returned to Hans Pleydenwurff's shop in Nuremberg where he worked on the *Hofer Altarpiece.* The *Descent from the Cross* panel in this work is treated in a highly patterned, almost abstract style. Wolgemut was the master of Albrecht Dürer. Besides large painted and sculptured altarpieces at Zwickau and Schwabach, executed in his shop, Wolgemut produced hundreds of designs for illustrated books such as the *World Chronicle* of 1493. The vigor of his outlines is in accord with his taste for drama, complex movement, and forceful characterization.

Wolin: see WOLLIN, Poland.

Wollaston, John (wo͝ol'əstən), English portrait painter. Active in America from 1751 to 1769, he worked in New York, Pennsylvania, and the South and painted portraits of Martha Custis (Mrs. Washington) and the Custis children. His work is in museums of New York City and Philadelphia.

Wollaston, William Hyde, 1766–1828, English scientist, M.D. Cambridge, 1793. His wide-ranging scientific achievements include the discovery (1802) of the dark lines (Fraunhofer lines) in the solar spectrum; the invention of the reflecting goniometer (an instrument by which the angles of crystals are measured) and of the camera lucida; a method of making platinum malleable; the discovery of the elements palladium (1803) and rhodium (1804); and establishment of (1801) the equivalence of galvanic and frictional electricity. He created an endowment with the Wollaston medal to be awarded annually by the Geological Society, London, for outstanding research. Wollastonite, a mineral compound of calcium, silicon, and oxygen, was named in his honor.

Wollaston Lake, 796 sq mi (2,062 sq km), NE Sask., Canada, NW of Reindeer Lake. It drains into both the Churchill and the Mackenzie river systems.

Wollin or **Wolin** (both: vô'lēn), island, 95 sq mi (246 sq km), off the coast of Pomerania, in the Baltic Sea, and belonging to Poland. Wollin is separated from the mainland by the Zalew Szczeciński (Stettiner Haff). It is generally a lowland, with forests and several lakes. Fishing and livestock raising are the chief industries. There are numerous bathing resorts. The principal town, Wollin, is a fishing port. A fortress and Slavic settlement once occupied the site of the town, whose history dates from the 9th cent. The island passed to Sweden in 1648, to Prussia in 1721, and to Poland after World War II. It is administratively part of Szczecin prov.

Wollongong (wo͝ol'ən-gŏng), city (1971 pop. 160,902; urban agglomeration pop. 185,890), New South Wales, SE Australia. It is an important iron and steel center. There are other industries, including copper refining and textile and chemical manufacturing. Port Kembla, which was absorbed by Wollongong in 1947, is a major port. A branch of the Univ. of New South Wales is in Wollongong.

Wollstonecraft, Mary (wo͝ol'stənkrăft, -krăft), 1759–97, English author and feminist. She was an early proponent of educational equality between men and women, and her *Vindication of the Rights of Women* (1792) was the first great feminist document. In Paris, where she lived with an American, Gilbert Imlay, during much of the French Revolution, she was close to many of the Revolution's leading political figures. After the birth (1794) of a daughter, Fanny, Imlay deserted her, and in 1797 she married William GODWIN. She died in giving birth to another daughter, Mary, who later became the wife of Percy Bysshe Shelley. See William Godwin, *Memoirs of Mary Wollstonecraft Godwin* (1798); biographies by H. R. James (1932, repr. 1972) and Eleanor Flexner (1972); studies by Emma Clough (1884), R. M. Wardle (1951), George R. S. Taylor (1969), and Margaret George (1970).

Wolof (wōl'əf), black African ethnic group, along the Atlantic coast of W Africa; most live in Senegal, but there is a significant minority in Gambia. Traditional Wolof society was distinguished for its rigid social classes. There were nobles and farmers among the free born; below them were lower classes of artisans and minstrels; slaves were the lowest class. Chiefs were elected by the nobles. By the 14th cent. the Wolof had established a separate state. They were converted to Islam in the 18th cent.

Wolpe, Stefan (shtĕf'än vôl'pə), 1902–72, German composer. Of Jewish ancestry, he went to live in Palestine in 1933, but settled in the United States in 1938. Wolpe wrote several operas and cantatas and a good deal of chamber music. His style embraces many elements, from folk music to modern jazz to a form of twelve-tone technique. His works include the opera *Zeus and Elida* (1927), the cantata *On the Education of Man* (1930), and the ballet *The Man from Midian* (1942).

Wolseley, Garnet Joseph Wolseley, 1st **Viscount** (wo͝olz'lē), 1833–1913, British field marshal. He fought in Burma (1852–53), the Crimea (1854–56), India (1857–58), and China (1860), and was an observer in the American Civil War. Later he went to Canada, where as commander of the Red River expedition (1870), he suppressed the rebellion led by Louis RIEL at Fort Garry. After conducting the Ashanti campaign (1873–74), he served as high commissioner of Cyprus (1878) and as an administrator in South Africa (1879–80). His most famous achievements were his brilliant defeat of Arabi Pasha, leader of an Egyptian army revolt, at Tall al Kabir in 1882 and his attempt to relieve General Gordon at Khartoum (1884–85), for which he was made a viscount. A tireless advocate of army reform, he became (1871) assistant adjutant general at the war office and worked with Viscount CARDWELL to achieve shorter periods of enlistment, the abolition of the purchase of commissions, and the creation of an army reserve. As quartermaster general (1880–82), adjutant general (1882–90), commander in chief for Ireland (1890–95), and commander in chief of the army (1895–1901), he continued to press for reform and was responsible for the modernization of training and equipment. He wrote *The Story of a Soldier's Life* (1903). See his *The American Civil War: An English View,* ed. by J. A. Rawley, (1964); his Khartoum journal, *In Relief of Gordon* (1967), his South African diaries (1971) and journals (1973), all three ed. by Adrian Preston; biography by J. H. Lehmann (1964).

Wolsey, Thomas (wo͝ol'zē), 1473?–1530, English statesman and prelate, cardinal of the Roman Catholic Church. Educated at Magdalen College, Oxford, he served for a while as master of the Magdalen College school. He was ordained a priest in 1498. In 1507 he entered the service of Henry VII as royal chaplain. Upon the accession of HENRY VIII in 1509, Wolsey was appointed royal almoner and privy councilor. He successfully organized an army for the invasion of France in 1513, accompanied Henry on his campaign, and helped conclude the peace of 1514. In the same year he was made bishop of Lincoln and then archbishop of York. In 1515 he became a cardinal and lord chancellor of England, and in 1518 he was created papal legate. From 1514 to 1529 Wolsey virtually controlled domestic and foreign policy for the young Henry VIII. In 1518 he engineered a treaty of universal peace embracing all the principal European states, which was meant to establish England as the mediator of European politics. This was followed by a dramatic display of amity between England and France on the FIELD OF THE CLOTH OF GOLD (1520). After attempting (1521) unsuccessfully to avert war between France and the Holy Roman Empire, he allied England with Emperor Charles V in 1522, but after Charles's defeat of the French at Pavia (1525), Wolsey again inclined his favor to France. His attempts to secure for England the role of arbiter in the Hapsburg-Valois rivalry finally failed when England became diplomatically isolated in 1529. The cardinal was twice a candidate for the papacy, but the thesis that his diplomacy was shaped largely by his ambition to become pope has been seriously questioned. Internally, Wolsey centralized the administration and extended the jurisdiction of the conciliar courts, particularly STAR CHAMBER. However, his policy of raising money for England's wars by forced loans aroused considerable resentment. So too did his blatant ecclesiastical pluralism, enormous wealth, and lavish living. Wolsey's enemies at court, jealous of his power over the king, used the divorce of KATHARINE OF ARAGÓN as a means to bring about his ruin. At Henry's urging, he procured from the pope permission to try the issue in England. He presided at the trial with Cardinal CAMPEGGIO, who delayed and temporized and finally adjourned the case to Rome. He incurred Henry's anger for this failure to secure a quick and favorable decision and the enmity of Anne Boleyn for urging a French marriage on the king. In Oct., 1529, he lost the chancellorship and all his honors and privileges except the archbishopric of York. He turned to his diocese, which he had never previously visited, and ruled it well for a few months. However, in Nov., 1530, he was arrested on false charges of treason and died at Leicester on his way to London. The classic biography by George Cavendish was first published in 1641. See also biographies by Mandell Creighton (1888), A. F. Pollard (1929, repr. 1966), and C. W. Ferguson (1958, repr. 1965).

Wolverhampton (wo͝ol'vərhămp"tən), county borough (1971 pop. 268,847), Staffordshire, W central England, in the Black Country. The area of the borough was greatly enlarged in 1966. It is highly industralized; its products include automobiles, hardware, rayon, tires, and chemicals. St. Peter's Church in Wolverhampton dates mostly from the 13th and 15th cent. Its grammar school was established in 1512. There are two teacher-training schools and a technical school. In 1974, Wolverhampton became part of the new metropolitan county of West Midlands.

wolverine or **glutton,** largest member of the WEASEL family, *Gulo gulo,* found in the northern parts of North America and Eurasia, usually in high mountains near the timberline or in tundra. It is a heavy, short-legged animal, somewhat bearlike in appearance, 3 to 3½ ft (91–106 cm) long, including the 8-in. (20-cm) tail, and weighing 35 to 60 lb (16–27 kg). The tail is bushy and the paws large, with heavy claws. The long, dark brown fur is banded on the flank with chestnut or yellowish white. Extremely strong and fierce, the wolverine hunts a wide variety of animals, and will drive animals larger than itself away from a kill. It has been known to attack nearly every animal except man. It robs traps of bait and victims and steals food supplies in camps; however, its reputation for gluttony is exaggerated. Its fur does not hold moisture and for this reason is highly prized by the Eskimos as a frost-proof trim for hoods and cuffs. Wolverines are classified in the phylum CHORDATA, subphylum Vertebrata, class Mammalia, order Carnivora, family Mustelidae.

Wolyn: see VOLHYNIA, USSR.

Woman's Christian Temperance Union (WCTU), organization that seeks to upgrade the moral life of all people, especially through abstinence from alcohol. The National WCTU of the United States was founded (1874) in Cleveland, Ohio, as a result of the Woman's Temperance Crusade that spread through the Midwest at that time. Frances WILLARD, the group's second president (1879–98), was responsible for the organization (1883) of the World WCTU, which now has branches in approximately 70 countries. The organization has worked for public education against the use of alcohol and for legislation to prohibit its sale. It has also supported research and education concerning tobacco, narcotics, and other potentially dangerous drugs. As of 1972, the National WCTU had 250,000 members. Its official organ is the weekly *Union Signal.*

Woman's Medical College of Pennsylvania, in Philadelphia; chartered and opened 1851 as the Female Medical College of Pennsylvania; renamed 1867. It was the first woman's medical college in the world. Only women are accepted as candidates for the doctor of medicine degree, but there are male students in the graduate, intern, and resident programs.

woman suffrage, the right of women to vote. Throughout the latter part of the 19th cent. the issue of women's voting rights was an important phase of FEMINISM; it was first seriously proposed in the United States at Seneca Falls, N.Y., July 19, 1848, in a general declaration of the rights of women prepared by Elizabeth Cady STANTON, Lucretia MOTT, and several others. The early leaders of the movement in the United States—Susan B. ANTHONY, Elizabeth Cady Stanton, Lucretia Mott, Lucy STONE, Abby Kelley FOSTER, the GRIMKÉ sisters, and others—were usually also advocates of temperance and of the abolition of slavery. When, however, after the close of the Civil War, the Fifteenth Amendment (1870) gave the franchise to newly emancipated black men, but not to the women who had helped win it for them, the suffragists for the most part confined their efforts to the struggle for the vote. The National Woman Suffrage Association, led by Susan B. Anthony and Elizabeth Cady Stanton, was formed in 1869 to agitate for an amendment to the Federal Constitution. Another organization, the American Woman Suffrage Association, led by Lucy Stone, was organized the same year to work through the state legislatures. These differing approaches—i.e., whether to seek a Federal amendment or to work for state amendments—kept the woman suffrage movement divided until 1890, when the two societies were united as the National American Woman Suffrage Association. Later leaders included Anna Howard SHAW and Carrie Chapman CATT. Several of the states and territories (with Wyoming first, 1869) granted suffrage to the women within their borders; when in 1913 there were 12 of these, the National Woman's party, under the leadership of Alice Paul, Lucy Burns, and others, resolved to use the voting power of the enfranchised women to force a suffrage resolution through Congress and secure ratification from the state legislatures. In 1920 the Nineteenth Amendment to the Constitution granted nation-wide suffrage to women. The movement in Great Britain began with CHARTISM, but it was not until 1851 that a resolution in favor of female suffrage was presented in the House of Lords by the earl of Carlyle. John Stuart Mill was the most influential of the British advocates; his *Subjection of Women* (1869) is one of the earliest, as well as most famous, arguments for the right of women to vote. Among the leaders in the early British suffrage movement were Lydia Becker, Barbara Bodichon, Emily DAVIES, and Dr. Elizabeth Garrett Anderson; Jacob Bright presented a bill for woman suffrage in the House of Commons in 1870. Local societies united in 1897 into the National Union of Women's Suffrage Societies, of which Millicent Garrett Fawcett was president until 1919. In 1903 a militant suffrage movement emerged under the leadership of Emmeline PANKHURST and her daughters; their organization was the Women's Social and Political Union. The militant suffragists were determined to keep their objective prominent in the minds of both legislators and the public, which they did by heckling political speakers, by street meetings, and in many other ways. The leaders were frequently imprisoned for inciting riot; many of them used the HUNGER STRIKE. When World War I broke out, the suffragists ceased all militant activity and devoted their powerful organization to the service of the government. After the war a limited suffrage was granted; in 1928 voting rights for men and women were equalized. On the Continent, Finland (1906) and Norway (1913) were the first countries to grant woman suffrage; in France, women voted in the first election (1945) after World War II. Belgium granted suffrage to women in 1946. Among the Commonwealth nations, New Zealand granted suffrage in 1893, Australia in 1902, Canada in 1917 (except in Quebec, where it was postponed until 1940). In Latin American countries, woman suffrage was granted in Brazil (1934), Salvador (1939), the Dominican Republic (1942), Guatemala (1945), and Argentina and Mexico (1946). In the Philippines women have voted since 1937, in Japan since 1945, in mainland China since 1947, and in the Soviet Union since 1917. Women have been enfranchised in most of the countries of the Middle East, with the exception of Saudi Arabia, Jordan, Kuwait, and Yemen. In Africa, women were often enfranchised at the same time as men—e.g., in Liberia (1947), in Uganda (1958), and in Nigeria (1960). In Switzerland, women were denied the vote in federal elections until 1971. One of the first aims of the United Nations was to extend suffrage rights to the women of member nations, and in 1952 the General Assembly adopted a resolution urging such action; by the 1970s, most member nations were in compliance with it. See *The History of Woman's Suffrage* (ed. by E. C. Stanton et al., 6 vol., 1881–1922); Emmeline Pankhurst, *My Own Story* (1914, repr. 1970); Millicent Fawcett, *What I Remember* (1925); Aileen Kraditor, *The Ideas of the Woman Suffrage Movement, 1890–1920* (1965, repr. 1971); William Severn, *Free but Not Equal* (1967); David Morgan, *Suffragists and Democrats* (1972).

wombat, shy MARSUPIAL of Australia and Tasmania, related to the koala. The wombat is a thick-set animal with a large head, short legs (giving it a shuffling gait), and a very short tail. It is about 3 ft (91.5 cm) long. Its snout is either naked, as in the species *Vombatus ursinus,* or furred, as in *Lasiorhinus latifrons.* Its incisors, the only teeth, grow continually, like those of rodents. Wombats are native to savanna forests and grasslands. They are solitary, nocturnal animals that feed chiefly on grass, roots, and bark and have been known to gnaw down large trees. They are powerful burrowers, digging tunnels by lying on their sides and pushing out soil with their feet. Their burrows, which may be 100 ft (31.5 m) long, terminate in grassy nests. A single infant is carried by its mother in a marsupial pouch for a period of 6 to 12 months. Extinct wombats as large as hippopotamuses are known from fossil evidence. Wombats are classified in the phylum CHORDATA, subphylum Vertebrata, class Mammalia, order Marsupialia, family Vombatidae.

Women's Army Corps: see WAC.

women's clubs, groups that offer social, recreational, and cultural activities for adult females. Particularly strong in the United States, they became an important part of American town and village life in the latter part of the 19th cent. One of the earliest clubs was Sorosis, organized (1868) in New York City. In 1890 a convention called in New York by Sorosis resulted in the General Federation of Women's Clubs. The federation presently has about 11 million members in over 50 countries. The entry of women into public life has been reflected in the programs of their clubs, which show an increasing interest in questions of social welfare and international concern. Many town libraries, later supported by taxes, were started by women's clubs, and many health and welfare reforms have been initiated by them. The feminist movement also influenced women's clubs, especially by spurring the establishment of groups such as the NATIONAL ORGANIZATION FOR WOMEN (founded 1966), which are explicitly devoted to the expansion of women's rights.

women's movement: see FEMINISM; WOMAN SUFFRAGE.

Wonders, Seven: see SEVEN WONDERS OF THE WORLD.

Wonju (wŭn'jo͞o'), city (1970 pop. 111,972), N South Korea. It is an agricultural center and a former subcapital of the Silla dynasty (see KOREA).

Wonsan (wŭn'săn), Jap. *Gensan,* city (1967 est. pop. 300,000), capital of Kangwon prov., SE North Korea, on the Sea of Japan. It is a major port and naval base, with a natural harbor protected by a line of islands. The city has important fish and fish-processing industries. Oil refining, rice processing, and the manufacture of locomotives, textiles, and leather goods are also important. Opened to foreign trade in 1883, Wonsan became a Japanese naval base in World War II. It suffered heavy damage during the Korean War.

Wood or **à Wood, Anthony,** 1632-95, English antiquary. His painstaking researches into the history of Oxford resulted in two great works, *The History and Antiquities of the University of Oxford* (in Latin, 1674; in English, tr. by him but not published until 1792-96), and *Athenae Oxoniensis* (1691-92; rev. and enl. ed., 1721) containing biographies of noted Oxford graduates. The second work included statements about the 1st earl of Clarendon that were adjudged libelous and for which he was expelled from Oxford. Wood's own *Life and Times* (comp. from his papers by Andrew Clark, 5 vol., 1891-1900) was abridged by Llewelyn Powys (1932).

Wood, Clement, 1888-1950, American writer, b. Tuscaloosa, Ala., grad. Univ. of Alabama, 1909, LL.B. Yale, 1911. Among his many works are books on the craft of poetry; biographies, including a critical one of Amy Lowell (1926); novels; and a rhyming dictionary (1943). His most famous poem is the title piece of his collected poems, *The Glory Road* (1936).

Wood, Edward Frederick Lindley: see HALIFAX, EDWARD FREDERICK LINDLEY WOOD, 1ST EARL OF.

Wood, Fernando, 1812-81, American politician, b. Philadelphia. He became a successful shipping merchant in New York City and a leader of Tammany Hall. Wood was elected mayor in 1854 and was reelected in 1856, but he displeased the other Tammany leaders in dispensing patronage and was ousted in 1857. He formed Mozart Hall, a rival organization, and won reelection in 1859. Pro-South, Wood suggested in Jan., 1861, that New York establish itself as an independent city. He was defeated for reelection in that year. During the Civil War he was a leading Peace Democrat. As a Congressman (1841-43, 1863-65, 1867-81) he reflected the views of the city's moneyed interests. See biography by S. A. Pleasants (1948).

Wood, Grant, 1891-1942, American painter, studied at the Art Institute of Chicago and in Paris. In Munich in 1928 he was decisively influenced by German and Flemish primitive painting. Subsequently in the 1930s he created his "American scene" works in which stern people and stylized landscapes offer rigid, decorative images of the rural Midwest. He taught at the State Univ. of Iowa and was director of WPA art projects in Iowa. His *American Gothic* (Art Inst., Chicago) and *Daughters of Revolution* have been many times reproduced; other works include *Stone City* (Joslyn Art Mus., Omaha, Nebr.) and a series of murals at Iowa State Univ. See Darrell Garwood, *Artist in Iowa* (1944, repr. 1971).

Wood, Mrs. Henry, 1814-87, English novelist whose maiden name was Ellen Price. Her melodramatic and sensational novel *East Lynne* (1861) was dramatized and became a permanent stock piece for more than a generation. Most of her work appeared first in the magazine *Argosy,* which she bought in 1867.

Wood, Jethro, 1774-1834, American inventor, b. either in Dartmouth, Mass., or in Washington co., N.Y. In 1814, while a farmer in Cayuga co., N.Y., he patented a cast-iron plow in which he later embodied improvements (patented 1819). He used in the improved model replaceable cast-iron parts and a curved plate called a moldboard from which the shape of the modern moldboard is derived. Litigation concerning his patent rights impoverished him. See biography by Frank Gilbert (1882).

Wood, John, 1704-1754, English architect, called Wood of BATH. When he went (1727) to Bath from Yorkshire to begin his career as a road surveyor, the city was at its height as a center of fashion. Foreseeing the possibilities of a spacious architectural setting for this gay life, Wood devised civic layouts on a grand scale and succeeded in finding financial support for his project. His executed schemes exhibit entire streets and terraces formally arranged in continuous rows, curves, or circles. He designed Queen's Square, North and South Parade, and the Circus. Wood of Bath also designed the mansion of Prior Park, near Bath, his most handsome detached building. His work, by its charm and imagination, set a standard for the architects who later worked at Bath, and it remains an inspiration for modern city planners. His son, **John Wood, Jr.,** 1728-81, completed the Circus and also built the Royal Crescent and the Assembly Rooms.

Wood, Leonard, 1860-1927, American general and administrator, b. Winchester, N.H. After practicing medicine briefly in Boston, he entered the army in 1855 and was made an assistant surgeon; in 1891 he was promoted to captain. At the outbreak of the Spanish-American War he joined with his friend Theodore Roosevelt in organizing a volunteer cavalry unit—the Rough Riders—and as their commander he participated in the attack on Santiago de Cuba. He was military commander of Santiago (1898-99), and as military governor (1899-1902) of Cuba until the republic was formed, he cooperated in improving sanitary conditions on the island. Sent (1903) to the Philippines as governor of Moro prov., he was promoted (1903) to major general. He helped crush the opposition to U.S. occupation there, although he was criticized for his ruthlessness. From 1906 to 1908 he commanded U.S. military forces in the Philippines. Returning to the United States, he served (1910-14) as U.S. army chief of staff. He was commander (1914-17) of the Dept. of the East and after the outbreak of World War I in Europe led the movement for preparedness in America. He advocated the creation of civilian training camps, which brought him into conflict with the neutralist position of President Wilson, and incurred the President's displeasure. After the U.S. entry into World War I, Wood was refused a commission on the European front. He failed to win the Republican nomination for President in 1920, but he was appointed (1921) governor general of the Philippines. Distrusting the natives' capacity for self-government, he reversed the lenient policy of his predecessor, F. B. Harrison. Wood liquidated the economic enterprises of the Philippine government, assumed wide powers of control, allowed little prerogative to the legislature, and surrounded himself with military advisers. Until Wood died in 1927, unrest was widespread among the Filipinos, and in 1925 the Philippine senate unanimously voted to hold a plebiscite on independence. The report of the Thompson Commission, sent to the islands in 1926, sharply criticized Wood's rule. See biography by Hermann Hagedorn (1931, repr. 1969).

Wood, Robert Williams, 1868-1955, American physicist, b. Concord, Mass., grad. Harvard (B.A., 1891). After studying abroad he became associated with Johns Hopkins Univ. as professor of experimental physics in 1901, professor emeritus in 1938, and later research professor. Internationally known for his work in optics and spectroscopy, he made important researches in resonance radiation and in the use of absorption screens in astronomical photography and devised a vastly improved diffraction grating. He also developed a color-photography process, originated the method of thawing street mains by passing an electric current through them, and studied the biological and physiological effects of high-frequency sound waves. He wrote *Physical Optics* (1905) and *Researches in Physical Optics* (2 parts, 1913-19). Wood was also the author of *The Man Who Rocked the Earth* (with Arthur Train, 1915) and nonsense verse, *How to Tell the Birds from the Flowers* (rev. ed. 1917). See biography by William Seabrook (1941).

wood, botanically, the xylem tissue that forms the bulk of the stem of a woody plant. Xylem conducts sap upward from the roots to the leaves, stores food in the form of complex carbohydrates, and provides support; it is made up of various types of cells specialized for each of these purposes. Among them are tracheids, elongated conduction and support cells; parenchyma (food storage) cells, some of which form rays for transverse conduction; xylem vessels, formed of hollow cells joined end to end; and fiber cells which reinforce these tubes. The xylem is formed in the growing season by the CAMBIUM; in temperate regions the cells formed in the spring are larger in diameter than those formed in the summer, and this results in the annual rings observable in cross section. The new cells lose their protoplasm as they form the various tissues; the older, nonfunctional cells become plugged up, darken in color, and often accumulate bitter or poisonous substances (tannins, dyes, resins, and gums). This inner wood (the heartwood, as opposed to the functional sapwood) is valued for outdoor construction because of its resistance to moisture and to decay-producing organisms. In the conifers the xylem is made up mainly of tracheids, thus presenting a uniform, nonporous appearance; their wood is called softwood. Deciduous trees have more complex xylem, permeated by vessels, and are called hardwoods, although the description is sometimes inaccurate. Freshly cut wood contains much moisture and tends to warp and split as it dries. Lumber is therefore seasoned before use—dried either slowly in the sun and air or more quickly by artificial means (kiln drying). Seasoning increases wood's buoyancy, strength, elasticity, and durability. Although synthetic materials have supplanted wood in many of its former uses, it is still widely employed for furniture, floors, railway ties, paper manufacture, and innumerable other purposes. Wood distillation yields methyl alcohol, wood tar, acetic acid, acetone, and turpentine; charcoal is made by burning wood in insufficient air to consume it. The wood of

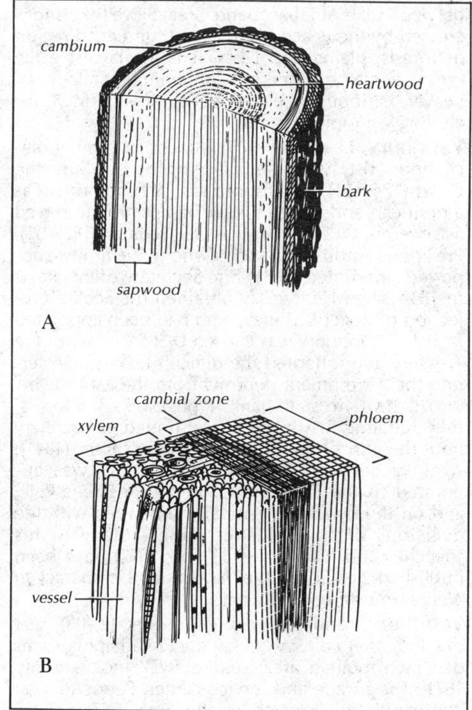

Wood

A. *Cross section of a woody stem*

B. *Enlarged view, showing xylem, phloem, and, cambium*

different species of trees varies considerably in weight, strength, and appearance. Softwood is normally uniform in grain (texture) and color; hardwood, in which the rays are more prominent and the arrangement of tissues is variable, produces lumber in which the grain may run vertically or horizontally and be coarse or smooth. The manner in which a log is cut results in lumber with thin or wide ray markings. A log cut horizontally shows the concentric annual rings; lengthwise cuts through the center are marked by thin vertical ray lines; and lengthwise cuts through the outer sections show the wood's characteristic wavy grain and wider ray markings, prized for their beauty. The rarer decorative woods may be cut in thin layers and glued to other wood structures (see VENEER). PLYWOOD, made of thin layers of wood glued so that the grains alternate in direction, makes an especially strong construction material. See H. P. Brown et al., *Textbook of Wood Technology* (Vol. I, 3d ed. 1970; Vol. II, 1952); F. H. Titmuss, *Commercial Timbers of the World* (3d. ed. 1965).

wood alcohol: see METHANOL.

Woodberry, George Edward, 1855-1930, American poet, critic, and teacher, b. Beverly, Mass., grad. Harvard 1877. He was professor of English at the Univ. of Nebraska (1880-82) and at Columbia (1891-1904). Typical of his work as a minor poet is *The Ideal Passion: Sonnets* (1917). Besides much literary criticism, he wrote scholarly biographies of Poe and Hawthorne. See his *Selected Letters* and *Selected Poems* (both: 1933).

woodbine, name for several vines, among them HONEYSUCKLE and VIRGINIA CREEPER.

Woodbridge, Frederick James Eugene, 1867-1940, American philosopher, b. Windsor, Ont., grad. Amherst, 1889, and Union Theological Seminary, 1892, and studied (1892-94) at the Univ. of Berlin. He taught philosophy at the Univ. of Minnesota (1894-1902) and at Columbia (1902-37), where he was dean of the faculties of political science, philosophy, pure science, and fine arts (1912-1929). He was editor of *Archives of Philosophy* and the *Journal of Philosophy, Psychology, and Scientific Methods.* Among his many books are *The Purpose of History* (1916), *The Realm of Mind* (1926), *Nature and Mind* (1937), and *An Essay on Nature* (1940), which sums up his philosophy that "Nature is the domain in which both knowledge and happiness are pursued." He had great influence as a teacher. See study by H. S. Pyun (1972).

Wood Buffalo National Park, 17,300 sq mi (44,807 sq km), in NE Alta., Canada, extending into S Mackenzie dist. of the Northwest Territories; est. 1922 to protect the only remaining herd of buffalo. It lies between Lake Athabasca and Great Slave Lake and is crossed by the Peace River. A vast, unfenced region of forests, plains, and lakes, it is the largest game preserve in North America, containing buffalo, bear, beaver, caribou, moose, and varied waterfowl, including whooping cranes.

Woodbury, Levi, 1789–1851, American cabinet officer and jurist, Associate Justice of the U.S. Supreme Court (1845–51), b. Hillsboro, co., N.H. Important as a politican and jurist in New Hampshire, he served as governor (1823–24) and as U.S. Senator (1825–31). President Andrew Jackson, whom he firmly supported, appointed (1831) him Secretary of the Navy. In 1834 when Henry Clay obtained the Senate's rejection of Roger B. Taney, who had been appointed in 1833, Woodbury was chosen U.S. Secretary of the Treasury and inherited the difficult task of transferring the government deposits from the BANK OF THE UNITED STATES to state banks ("pet banks"). Successfully fulfilling his duties he continued as Secretary until the end of President Van Buren's term (1841). Again a Senator (1841–45), Woodbury was appointed to the Supreme Court by President Polk, and on the bench he generally concurred with the decisions of Chief Justice Taney. Many of his speeches and his writings (3 vol., 1852) have been published. See D. B. Cole, *Jacksonian Democracy in New Hampshire* (1970).

Woodbury, residential city (1970 pop. 12,408), seat of Gloucester co., SW N.J., in the Philadelphia-Camden metropolitan area; settled 1683, inc. as a city 1871. It is a trade and service center. Petrochemical companies are located in the area. Originally a Quaker settlement, Woodbury attempted to stay aloof from the Revolutionary War, but the armies of both sides occupied the town and many battles were fought in the vicinity. The city's 18th-century buildings include the Cooper House, where Cornwallis stopped in 1777, and a Friends' meetinghouse. The county historical society has collections in the John Lawrence House (1765). A national park is nearby.

wood carving, as an art form, includes any kind of sculpture in wood, from the decorative bas-relief on small objects to life-size figures in the round, furniture, and architectural decorations. The woods used vary greatly in hardness and grain. The most commonly employed woods include boxwood, pine, pear, walnut, willow, oak, and ebony. The tools are simple gouges, chisels, wooden mallets, and pointed instruments. Although they were universally one of the earliest art media, wood carvings have withstood poorly the vicissitudes of time and climate. A few ancient examples have been preserved in the dry climate of Egypt, e.g., the wooden statue of Sheik-el-Beled (Cairo) from the Old Kingdom. The carving of wooden masks and statuettes was common to the African tribes (see AFRICAN ART), and totem poles were used for the basic religious rites of the tribes of the Northwest Coast of America (see NORTH AMERICAN INDIAN ART). The wooden objects of Oceania include animated designs, incised and in relief, on canoes and large standing figures (see OCEANIC ART). In Japan and China wooden carvings have long been used to decorate temples and private dwellings (see CHINESE ARCHITECTURE; JAPANESE ARCHITECTURE). The Muslim countries of North Africa abound in intricate architectural carvings. In Europe wood carving was highly developed in Scandinavia, and examples have been preserved of 10th- and 11th-century work. In England the Gothic period produced extremely fine carving, especially on choir stalls (see MISERICORDS) and rood screens. Although the Puritans destroyed much of this, enough has been preserved to show its beautiful workmanship. In France wood carving was also a part of religious art, and there the carved altarpieces were especially notable. Italian wood carving flourished during the Gothic period in Pisa, Siena, and Florence, as well as in the southern monasteries; during the Renaissance it remained an adjunct of Italian artistic development. Many of the 15th- and 16th-century artists in Germany worked in wood, creating monumental sculptures and altarpieces; among the greatest were Hans Multscher, Michael Pacher, Veit Stoss, and Tilman Riemenschneider. Fine retables were also created in Flanders and Spain. After the Renaissance wood carving went into a slight decline. It had a revival in the early 18th cent. when Grinling Gibbons in London carved for Sir Christopher Wren's buildings. In colonial America fine ships' FIGUREHEADS were executed in wood. The 20th cent. has seen a resurgence of interest in the medium of wood. Notable modern sculptors who have used wood include Archipenko, Barlach, Henry Moore, and the Finnish Tapio Virkkala. An appreciation of the basic material—the grain and texture of wood—has led many artists including William Zorach, Chaim Gross, Robert Laurent, and José de Creeft to work with wood. Louise Nevelson has made large, intricate sculptural compositions of carved wood forms. See D. Z. Meilach, *Contemporary Art with Wood* (1968); C. C. Carstenson, *The Craft and Creation of Wood Sculpture* (1971); M. V. Hayes, *Artistry in Wood* (1972); E. J. Tangerman, *The Modern Book of Whittling and Woodcarving* (1973).

woodchuck or **groundhog,** common name of a North American species of MARMOT, *Marmota monax.* This large RODENT is found in open woods and ravines throughout most of Canada and the NE United States. Its heavyset body is about 2 ft (60 cm) long, excluding the 6 in. (15 cm) tail, and is covered with thick, coarse, brownish hair. A terrestrial, day-active animal, it feeds on green vegetation. It has benefited by the clearing of forests for cultivation, and, despite the attacks of farmers, its numbers have increased. It nests in a burrow of many compartments, where it also hibernates in winter. According to an old superstition the groundhog leaves its burrow on Feb. 2, Groundhog Day, and returns underground for six weeks if it sees its shadow; thus, a sunny Feb. 2 supposedly means six more weeks of winter. Woodchucks are classified in the phylum CHORDATA, subphylum Vertebrata, class Mammalia, order Rodentia, family Sciuridae.

Woodcock, Leonard Freel, 1911–, American labor leader; b. Providence, R.I. In 1933 he went to work as a machine assembler at the Detroit Gear and Machine Co., where he joined a union that became a local of the United Auto Workers (UAW) a few years later. He served (1947–55) as regional director for UAW in Michigan, and from 1955 to 1970 he was vice president of the union, in charge of the General Motors and aerospace departments. In 1970 he succeeded Walter Reuther as president of UAW, the second largest union in the United States, with a membership of 1,600,000.

woodcock: see SNIPE.

woodcreeper or **woodhewer,** common names for woodpeckerlike birds of tropical forest and brush, constituting about 50 species in the family Dendrocolaptidae. Supported by their stiff tails, they cling vertically to tree trunks, progressing upward in short hops, circling the tree while exploring crevices for spiders and small insects, especially carpenter ants. When they reach the branches, they fly off to begin their curious climb from the base of another tree. Exception to this behavior is shown by the great rufous woodcreeper (*Xiphocolaptes major*) of N Argentina, a ground feeder, and the ocherous-billed woodcreeper (*Dendrocincla meruloides*) of Trinidad, noted for following columns of marching ants. Woodcreepers resemble the woodpeckers in form, having short legs with powerful, sharply clawed feet, stiff-shafted tail feathers, and moderately long, woodpeckerlike bills. Woodcreeper bills vary, however, from the long scimitar-shaped beak of the scythebill (*Campylorhaphus falcularius*), half as long as the bird itself, to the short beak of the wedgebill (genus *Glyphorhynchus*), with its slightly upcurved lower mandible. Found from Mexico to all but southernmost South America, woodcreepers are typically olive-plumaged with reddish wings and tail and striped heads and underparts. They range in body length from 5 to 15 in. (13–38 cm). They typically lay their two to three plain white or whitish eggs in leaf-lined tree holes, which, unlike true woodpeckers, they do not excavate for themselves. They usually take over the abandoned nests of other cavity nesters, such as the woodpecker. Woodcreepers are classified in the phylum CHORDATA, subphylum Vertebrata, class Aves, order Passeriformes, family Dendrocolaptidae.

woodcut and **wood engraving,** prints made from designs cut in relief on wood, in contrast to copper or steel ENGRAVING and ETCHING (which are INTAGLIO). The term *woodcutting* is loosely included within the wood-engraving process, from which, however, it can be distinguished. Woodcutting, the oldest method of printmaking, is accomplished using soft wood with a knife employed along the grain. Wood engraving, which developed in the 18th cent., is a technique using hard, end-grained wood worked with a graver or burin. Woodcuts were used in ancient Egypt and Babylonia for impressing intaglio designs into unpressed bricks and by the Romans for stamping letters and symbols. The Chinese used wood blocks for stamping patterns on textiles and for illustrating books. Woodcuts appeared in Europe at the beginning of the 15th cent., when they were used to make religious pictures for distribution to pilgrims, on playing cards and simple prints, and for the BLOCK BOOK which preceded printing. At that time the artist and the craftsman were one, the same man designing the cut and carving the block. One of the first dated European woodcuts is a *St. Christopher* of 1423. After the invention of the printing press, woodcuts, being inked in the same way as type, lent themselves admirably to book illustration. Albrecht Pfister first put them to this use c.1460. Other early woodcut illustrations are in the Bibles of the late 15th cent. and in the French Lyons edition (1493) of the works of Terence. The first Roman book with woodcuts appeared in 1467, but Venice became the center of Italian wood engraving. In the 16th cent. in France woodcuts frequently served to illustrate BOOKS OF HOURS. The actual cutting was often performed by a specialist rather than by the designer. In Germany, Dürer and Hans Holbein, the younger, were the most eminent woodcut designers of the Renaissance. Dürer's *Life of the Virgin* (1509–10) and *Great Passion* (1510–11) and Holbein's *Dance of Death* (1523–26) are among the best-known works of these masters. Lucas Cranach, the elder, Albrecht Altdorfer, and Hans Baldung also worked in wood engraving, employing a chiaroscuro technique originated by Jobst de Negker of Augsburg. There was a decline in woodcutting with the increasing versatility and popularity of line engraving on metal; even in the Netherlands, where woodcuts lasted longest, they were almost obsolete by the 18th cent. In England, however, Thomas Bewick popularized wood engraving. He brought to perfection the technique of white-line engraving, in which lines print white on a black background. Gustave Doré was the best-known French master in this medium in the 19th cent. William Blake also made wood engravings for some of his best book illustrations (e.g., for Thornton's *Vergil;* 1821). The Victorian weeklies used numerous wood-engraved drawings as illustrations. Most famous of English wood engravers were John Swain and the Dalziel brothers. In the United States wood engraving was practiced from the 19th cent. by such masters as Alexander Anderson, William James Linton, and Timothy Cole. The advances in photography and photographic processes slowly replaced woodcut as a means of book illustration and wood engraving for reproduction of oil paintings. In the 1890s in France a revival of woodcutting to produce original prints was initiated by Paul Gauguin, Edvard Munch, and Felix Vallotton, who cut their blocks themselves. Their influence on 20th-century expression in this medium was enormous. Derain, Dufy, and Maillol also made notable woodcuts. After World War II many artists in the United States, such as Leonard Baskin, Sue Fuller, and Seong Moy, began to explore new formal and technical possibilities in the medium of woodcutting. See A. M. Hind, *An Introduction to a History of Woodcut* (1935, repr. 1963); D. P. Bliss, *A History of Wood-Engraving* (rev. ed. 1964); A. H. Mayor, *Prints and People* (1971).

woodhewer: see WOODCREEPER.

woodhoopoe: see HOOPOE.

Woodhull, Victoria (Claflin), 1838–1927, and **Tennessee Claflin,** 1846–1923, American journalists and lecturers, b. Ohio, noted for their beauty and wildly eccentric behavior. As children they traveled throughout Ohio with their parents, giving spiritualist demonstrations. At 15, Victoria married Dr. Canning Woodhull but continued to tour as a clairvoyant with Tennessee. Victoria divorced Woodhull in 1864 and two years later probably married Col. James Blood (there is some doubt as to the validity of the marriage). Tennessee married John Bartels but retained her maiden name. The sisters went back to New York City in 1866 and were backed in a stock brokerage venture by Cornelius Vanderbilt, who was interested in spiritualism. In 1870, Victoria and Tennessee, with the financial support of Col. Blood, became proprietors of *Woodhull and Claflin's Weekly,* a sensational journal that supported such controversial issues as woman suffrage, free love, and socialism. The paper published an article containing rumors of an alleged love affair between Rev. Henry Ward BEECHER and the wife of Theodore TILTON, which provoked a national scandal. In 1872 the journal published the first English translation of

The Communist Manifesto. In the same year Victoria became the first woman candidate for President, running on the People's party ticket with Frederick DOUGLASS as her running mate. The two sisters moved to England in 1877. Victoria, having divorced Blood, married John Biddulph Martin, a wealthy banker. Tennessee, also divorced, married Francis Cook, an English art collector who became a baronet in 1886. Both women became well-known philanthropists. See biographies by Johanna Johnston (1967) and M. M. Marberry (1967).

Woodin, William Hartman (wo͝od'ən), 1868–1934, American cabinet officer, b. Berwick, Pa. After studying engineering at Columbia, he entered (1892) the railroad-equipment firm founded by his grandfather and became its president in 1899. President of the American Car and Foundry Company after 1916, he steadily expanded his industrial holdings. Although a Republican, Woodin supported Franklin Delano Roosevelt for President in 1932 and became Roosevelt's Secretary of the Treasury in 1933. He helped restore the nation's financial activities during the banking crisis of March, 1933. He resigned the post in Nov., 1933, because of ill health.

Woodland, city (1970 pop. 20,677), seat of Yolo co., N central Calif., in a rich farm area yielding tomatoes, rice, sugar beets, and alfalfa; inc. 1871. It is a center for the manufacture of mobile homes, with numerous plants and related warehousing operations. The city has many historic homes and is the site of a state historical farm.

Woodlawn, uninc. town (1970 pop. 28,811 including Woodmoor), Baltimore co., N Md., a residential suburb of Baltimore.

wood louse: see CRUSTACEAN.

Woodmere, uninc. residential town (1970 pop. 19,831), Nassau co., SE N.Y., on Long Island.

woodpecker, common name for members of the Picidae, a large family of climbing birds found in most parts of the world. Woodpeckers typically have sharp, chisellike bills for pecking holes in tree trunks, and long, barbed, extensible tongues with which they impale their insect prey. Their spiny tail feathers act as a prop in climbing, resting, and drilling. Usually the male has a red or orange patch on its head and barred and spotted black or brown plumage with light underparts. Among the North American woodpeckers are the sociable downy woodpecker, *Picus pubescens* (about 6½ in./17 cm long); the similar but larger hairy woodpecker, *P. villosus,* the red-crested pileated woodpecker, or logcock, *Hylotomus pileatus* (about 17 in./44.3 cm long), which is similar to the nearly extinct IVORY-BILLED WOODPECKER; the redheaded and three-toed woodpeckers, genus *Picoides;* and the California woodpecker, genus *Colaptes,* which makes small holes in trees for storing acorns. The flickers, genus *Melanerpes,* the only brown-backed woodpeckers, sometimes capture insects on the ground. The yellow-shafted flicker is known by many local names (e.g., high hole and yellowhammer) and interbreeds with the red-shafted flicker. The sapsuckers (e.g., the red-breasted and yellow-bellied sapsuckers) may damage or kill trees by girdling them with small holes through which they eat some of the cambium and drink sap; they also feed on ants and wild fruit. The PICULETS are tiny (3–5 in./7.6–12.7 cm long) Old and New World woodpeckers. The woodpecker family also includes the Old World WRYNECK, which does not peck wood. Woodpeckers are classified in the phylum CHORDATA, subphylum Vertebrata, class Aves, order Piciformes, family Picidae.

wood pulp: see PAPER.

wood rat: see PACK RAT.

Woodridge, village (1970 pop. 11,028), Du Page co., NE Ill.; inc. 1959. It is a residential community W of Chicago in a wooded and farm area.

Wood River, city (1970 pop. 13,186), Madison co., SW Ill., on the Mississippi River just above its junction with the Missouri; inc. 1923. It has oil refineries and pipeline terminals.

Woodruff, Lorande Loss, 1879–1947, American zoologist, b. New York City, grad. Columbia (B.A., 1901; Ph.D., 1905). He taught at Yale from 1907. In his research on the life history of protozoans, he maintained a race of paramecia for eight years through more than 20,000 generations to demonstrate the vitality of asexually reproduced individuals. He collected rare scientific works and wrote *Foundations of Biology* (1922, 6th ed. 1941) and edited *Development of the Sciences* (1923; 2d series 1941).

Woods, Leonard, 1774–1854, American Congregational theologian, b. Princeton, Mass. He was prominent in upholding orthodox Calvinistic views in the controversy over Unitarianism as presented by William Ellery Channing, Henry WARE, and others. He was professor of theology at Andover Theological Seminary (1808–46) and published (1885) a history of that institution. Among his works are *A Reply to Dr. Ware's Letter to Trinitarians and Calvinists* (1821) and *Remarks on Dr. Ware's Answer* (1822).

Woods, Robert Archey, 1865–1925, American social worker, b. Pittsburgh, grad. Amherst, 1886. After six months at Toynbee Hall, London, he helped found (1891) the South End House, Boston, which he headed until his death. He lectured on social ethics at the Episcopal Theological School, Cambridge, Mass. (1896–1914), was president of the Boston School Union (1908–25), and aided the development of the National Federation of Social Settlements, of which he was secretary from 1911 to 1923 and president for the two succeeding years. Woods wrote *English Social Movements* (1891) and *The Neighborhood in Nation Building* (1923). See biography by E. H. Woods (1929).

Woods Hole, village and seaport in the town of Falmouth, Barnstable co., SE Mass., at the southwestern extremity of Cape Cod. It is the site of an important marine biology laboratory and of the Oceanographic Institution, which maintains the research ship *Atlantis.* Tides, currents, and marine life are studied. A U.S. fish hatchery is also there.

Woods Hole Oceanographic Institution, at Woods Hole, Mass.; est. 1930. In addition to oceanographic research, it conducts important work in meteorology, biology, geology, and geophysics. Its facilities include laboratories and several ocean-going research vessels. Woods Hole is also the site of the U.S. Marine Biological Laboratory and the U.S. Bureau of Commercial Fisheries Biological Laboratory and Aquarium.

wood sorrel: see OXALIS.

Woodstock. 1 Town (1971 pop. 4,846), W N.B., Canada on the St. John River. Formerly a lumbering center, it is now a market for the surrounding agricultural region. It was founded by UNITED EMPIRE LOYALISTS. **2** City (1971 pop. 26,173), S Ont., Canada, SW of Hamilton. An industrial center with manufactures of furniture, textiles, and other products, it is the seat of St. Alphonsus Seminary. The surrounding country has mixed farming, dairying, and stock raising.

Woodstock. 1 City (1970 pop. 10,226) seat of McHenry co., NE Ill.; inc. 1845. Its manufactures include typewriters and business machines, metal products, and dairy items. **2** Town (1970 pop. 5,714), Ulster co., SE N.Y., in the foot hills of the Catskill Mts. There is an artists' colony (founded 1902), which sponsors a gallery. The Art Students League of New York also has a summer school there. In 1969 the town was overwhelmed by thousands of youths attending a summer rock music festival.

Woodsworth, James Shaver, 1874–1942, Canadian politician. Having done social welfare work while serving as a Methodist minister, he later gave up the ministry to devote himself wholly to labor and welfare causes. Supported by the Independent Labour party, he entered the Canadian House of Commons in 1921, remaining a member until his death. When the Co-operative Commonwealth Federation (see NEW DEMOCRATIC PARTY) was founded (1932) he became chairman of its national council and its parliamentary leader. See biographies by Grace MacInnis (1953) and K. W. McNaught (1959).

Woodville, Elizabeth, 1437–92, queen consort of EDWARD IV of England. She was the daughter of Richard Woodville (later the 1st Earl RIVERS). Her first husband, Sir John Grey, was killed fighting on the Lancastrian side at the battle of St. Albans (1461) in the Wars of the Roses. By him she had two sons, Thomas, 1st marquess of Dorset, and Richard. Edward IV married her in secret in 1464, partly because the powerful Richard Neville, earl of WARWICK, had other marriage plans for him and partly because of Elizabeth's Lancastrian connections. The marriage was soon made public, however, and Elizabeth's large family received numerous royal favors. At the death (1483) of Edward IV, Richard, duke of Gloucester (later RICHARD III), seized custody of the young EDWARD V, Elizabeth's eldest son by the late king, and destroyed the power of the Woodvilles (Elizabeth's brother the 2d Earl Rivers and son Richard Grey were executed). The queen mother again took sanctuary in Westminster and soon surrendered her second son by Edward, Richard, duke of York, to Gloucester. He then placed both boys in the Tower of London and declared them illegitimate, asserting that Elizabeth's marriage to Edward was voided by a precontract of marriage on Edward's part. (The boys were subsequently murdered.) After Henry VII seized the throne from Richard, he married (1486) Elizabeth's eldest daughter, who was also named Elizabeth. See biography by David MacGibbon (1938).

Woodville, Richard Caton, 1825–55, American genre painter, b. Baltimore. He turned from medical studies to painting and in 1845 studied in Düsseldorf. He spent most of his brief working life in Europe, but his popular paintings, which exhibit a relish for varied characterizations and interior detail, were widely distributed in the United States in prints. Among his works are *War News From Mexico* (National Acad. of Design, New York City) and *The Sailor's Wedding* (Walters Art Gall., Baltimore).

Woodward, Comer Vann, 1908–, American historian, b. Vanndale, Ark. He received his Ph.D. from the Univ. of North Carolina in 1937 and taught at several schools, most notably Johns Hopkins (1946–61) and Yale (1961–). An outstanding historian of the American South and of race relations in the United States, Woodward wrote *Tom Watson, Agrarian Rebel* (1938), *Origins of the New South, 1877–1913* (1951), *Reunion and Reaction: The Compromise of 1877 and the End of Reconstruction* (1951, rev. ed. 1956), *The Strange Career of Jim Crow* (1955, rev. ed. 1974), *The Burden of Southern History* (1960), and *American Counterpoint* (1971).

Woodward, Robert Burns, 1917–, American chemist and educator, b. Boston, grad. Massachusetts Institute of Technology (B.S., 1936; Ph.D., 1937). He taught at Harvard from 1938, becoming Donner professor of science there in 1960. He was one of the first to determine the structure of such organic chemical compounds as penicillin (1945), strychnine (1947), terramycin (1952), and aureomycin (1952). Woodward is best known for his chemical synthesis of the organic substances quinine (1944), patulin (1950), cholesterol (1951), cortisone (1951), strychnine, lysergic acid, lanosterol (1954), reserpine (1956), chlorophyll (1960), and tetracycline (1962). For this work in organic synthesis he was awarded the 1965 Nobel Prize in Chemistry. He has received many other awards in chemistry, as well as many honorary degrees.

woodwind instrument: see WIND INSTRUMENT.

woodwork: see CARPENTRY; CARVING; FURNITURE; INTARSIA; MARQUETRY; VENEER; WOOD CARVING.

Woodworth, Samuel, 1784–1842, American author, b. Scituate, Mass. He edited (1823–24) the *New York Mirror* and was author of the song "The Old Oaken Bucket." His comedy *The Forest Rose* (1825) was one of the most popular American plays before the Civil War.

woody plant: see HERBACEOUS PLANT.

woof: see WEAVING.

Wool, John Ellis, 1784–1869, American general, b. Newburgh, N.Y. He served in the War of 1812 and distinguished himself at Queenston Heights and Plattsburgh. By 1841 he had risen to the rank of brigadier general, and for his services in the Mexican War under Gen. Zachary Taylor, particularly at Buena Vista (1847), he was brevetted major general. At the beginning of the Civil War, Wool held Fort Monroe, Va., for the Union. He was promoted to major general in 1862 and retired in 1863.

wool, fiber from the fleece of the domestic sheep. It consists of the cortex, overlapping scales (sharper and more protruding than those of hair) that may expand at their free edges causing fibers to intermesh; elasticum, the inner layer; and a core. When soaked, the elasticum and core contract, shrinking the fiber. Elasticity resulting from the molecular structure of wool and resiliency from its crimp make wool fabrics crease resistant. Fine wool will stretch one third its length. Wool is warm because its fibers are nonconductors of heat and its crimp permits it to enmesh still air. It is highly absorbent and releases moisture slowly. Its tensile strength is one fourth greater than that of cotton. A protein compound of complex chemical composition, it is soluble in hot caustic soda. No known wild sheep are wool bearing. The supposed ancestors of the domestic sheep had long hair and a soft, downy undercoat, which under domestication gradually became wool, while the long hair disappeared. In this development, breeding, feed, climate, and protection were influential, as shown by an atavistic return of neglected sheep to long hair and rudimentary wool. Wool was probably the first fiber to be woven into a textile, as herding flocks was the first step upward from primitiveness. In the tombs and ruins of Egypt, Nineveh, and Babylon, in the barrows of early Britons, and among the relics of the Peruvians, fragments of woolen fabrics are found. The Romans as early as 200 B.C. began to improve their flocks, which became the progenitors of the famed Spanish MERINO SHEEP. The Britons kept sheep and wove wool long before the Roman invasion, but the establishment by the Romans of a factory at Winchester probably improved their methods. William the Conqueror brought into England skilled Flemish weavers. Henry II encouraged wool industries by laws, cloth fairs, and guilds of weavers. Edward III brought weavers, dyers, and fullers from Flanders. England became the great wool-producing country of Europe, and wool was the staple of its industry until cotton began to overshadow it in the 18th cent. In the American colonies, sheep raising started in Jamestown. Stringent English laws against exporting wool in the attempt to force upon the colonies the use of English cloth, early drove the settlers to the raising of sheep. George Washington imported sheep and brought spinners and weavers from England. Early in the 19th cent. imported Merinos greatly improved the existing stock. Spinning and weaving were early established in New England, at first in homes, later in small factories. The first factory in America using water power to weave wool was established (1788) at Hartford, Conn., and was encouraged by tax exemption and a bounty on each yard woven. The United States now produces a substantial amount of the world's wool, chiefly in Texas, Montana, Wyoming, Utah, Oregon, Idaho, New Mexico, Colorado, California, and Ohio. Woolen cloth manufacture is largely centered in New England. Other important wool producers include Australia, Argentina, New Zealand, the Soviet Union, the Republic of South Africa, Uruguay, Great Britain, China, and India. Wool is classed as: fine, usually short-staple wool of Merino fineness and including Delaine Merino, combable fibers 2 in. (5.1 cm) or more in length; medium, or mutton, 2½ to 6 in. (6.4–15.2 cm) long, e.g., Cheviot and Southdown; long-staple, 10 to 15 in. (25.4–38.1 cm) long, loosely crimped, e.g., the Lincoln and the Cotswold; and carpet, 1 to 15 in. (2.5–38.1 cm) long, strong, coarse, and usually blended for uniformity. For industrial purposes the fiber of the CAMEL, Angora goat (see MOHAIR), Kashmir goat, llama, alpaca, and VICUÑA is classed as wool. Sheep are sheared with mechanical clippers. The fleece is classed as: lamb's wool, or first clip; hog wool, clipped from sheep 12 to 14 months old; wether wool, from older animals; taglocks, the ragged, discolored portion; and pulled wool, usually weakened when recovered by sweating or chemical processes from sheep slaughtered for mutton. The wool is sorted as to fineness, crimp, length of fiber, and felting qualities. Dirt, suint (dried perspiration), and lanolin are removed by a soap-alkali scouring; by the expensive naphtha solvent method, which retains the full strength and softness of the fiber; or by freezing and shaking. Wool may be carbonized to remove vegetable matter. It is bleached and dyed as raw stock, yarn, or in the piece; it is oiled to withstand processing and is often blended. Woolen goods are woven from carded short-staple fibers into soft yarns adapted to fulling and napping. Worsted fabrics such as whipcord, gabardine, and serge have a hard, smooth texture. Originally made only from long-staple fibers, worsted yarn is now spun also from medium or short fibers. The fibers are carded, the resulting sliver gilled to straighten the fibers and double them for uniformity; subjected to successive combings to remove nails (short ends) and lay the fibers parallel; then drawn into roving and spun, usually by the rapid, continuous ring method, and twisted. Although the twill weave is usual for worsteds, the same weaves may be used as for woolens without the pattern being obscured by the napping, fulling, and shearing processes commonly employed in finishing woolens. In the United States, by the Wool Products Labeling Act of 1939, the term *wool* may be applied only to fabrics made entirely of new wool; the term *reprocessed wool*, to wool recovered from unused articles and waste; and *reused wool*, to wool reclaimed from used articles. The trade designates fleece wool as virgin wool, salvaged wool as shoddy. Salvaged wool may legitimately be used to add strength to soft new wool or to produce a cheaper product. Numerous synthetic fibers have been developed as wool imitations and for blending with wool. See W. J. Onions, *Wool: An Introduction to Its Properties, Varieties, Uses, and Production* (1962); Werner von Bergen, ed., *Wool Handbook* (2 vol., 3d ed. 1963–70); H. S. Bell, *Wool: An Introduction to Wool Production and Marketing* (1970).

Woolf, Virginia (Stephen), 1882–1941, English novelist and essayist; daughter of Sir Leslie Stephen. A successful innovator in the form of the novel, she is considered a significant force in 20th-century fiction. She was educated at home from the resources of her father's huge library. In 1912 she married Leonard Woolf, a critic and writer on economics, with whom she set up the Hogarth Press in 1917. Their home became a gathering place for a circle of artists, critics, and writers known as the BLOOMSBURY GROUP. As a novelist Woolf's primary concern was to represent the flow of ordinary experience. Her emphasis was not on plot or characterization but on a character's consciousness, his thoughts and feelings, which she brilliantly illuminated by the STREAM OF CONSCIOUSNESS technique. She did not limit herself to one consciousness, however, but slipped from mind to mind, particularly in *The Waves*, probably her most experimental novel. Her prose style is poetic, heavily symbolic, and filled with superb visual images. Woolf's early works, *The Voyage Out* (1915) and *Night and Day* (1919), were traditional in method, but she became increasingly innovative in *Jacob's Room* (1922), *Mrs. Dalloway* (1925), *To the Lighthouse* (1927), and *The Waves* (1931). Other experimental novels are *Orlando* (1928), *The Years* (1937), and *Between the Acts* (1941). She was a master of the critical essay, and some of her finest pieces are included in *The Common Reader* (1925), *The Second Common Reader* (1933), *The Death of the Moth and Other Essays* (1942), and *The Moment and Other Essays* (1948). *A Room of One's Own* (1929) and *Three Guineas* (1938) are feminist tracts. Her biography of Roger Fry (1940) is a careful study of a friend. Some of her short stories from *Monday or Tuesday* (1921) appear with others in *A Haunted House* (1944). Virginia Woolf suffered mental breakdowns in 1895 and 1915; she drowned herself in 1941 because she feared another breakdown from which she might not recover. Most of her posthumously published works were edited by her husband. See her *Writer's Diary*, ed. by Leonard Woolf (1953) and *Correspondence with Lytton Strachey*, ed. by Leonard Woolf and James Strachey (1956); J. R. Noble, ed., *Recollections of Virginia Woolf* (1972); biography by Quentin Bell (2 vol., 1972); studies by E. M. Forster (1942), Joan Bennett (2d ed. 1964), and Harvena Richter (1971). See also the autobiography of her husband, Leonard Sidney Woolf (5 vol., 1960–69).

Woollcott, Alexander, 1887–1943, American author and critic, b. Phalanx, N.J., grad. Hamilton College, 1909. Woollcott's flamboyant personality combined sharpness of wit with sentimentality. He was one of the best-known journalists of his time and exerted great influence on popular literary and theatrical tastes. From 1914 to 1922 he was drama critic for the New York *Times* and later, from 1925 to 1928, for the New York *World*. He also had a weekly radio show, the "Town Crier" (1929–42). His gossipy essays were collected in *While Rome Burns* (1934), *Long Long Ago* (1943), and others. Woollcott was the model for Sheridan Whiteside, the central character in *The Man Who Came to Dinner*, a play by George S. Kaufman and Moss Hart; he portrayed Whiteside in a road company production of the play. See his letters (1944); biography by E. P. Hoyt (rev. ed. 1973).

Woolley, Sir Charles Leonard, 1880–1960, English archaeologist. His early work included excavations at Carchemish (1912–14) and the Egyptian site of Tel-el-Amarna (1921–22). He was then chosen to direct the joint British Museum and Univ. of Pennsylvania Expedition at Ur in Mesopotamia (1922–34), where his findings did much to further the study of Middle Eastern archaeology and history. Later excavations led by him were those of the Syrian sites of Al-Mina (1936) and Tell Atchana (1937–39 and 1946–49). His writings include *The Sumerians* (1928), *Digging Up the Past* (1930), *Ur of the Chaldees* (1938, rev. ed. 1952), *A Forgotten Kingdom* (1953, rev. ed. 1959), and *Excavations at Ur* (1954).

Woolley, Mary Emma, 1863–1947, American educator, b. South Norwalk, Conn. After teaching at Wheaton Seminary (1886–91), she attended college and became the first woman to receive (1894) a B.A. from Brown Univ. She then taught biblical history and literature at Wellesley College (1895–1900) and from 1901 to her retirement in 1937 was president of Mt. Holyoke College. She was active also in the cause of world peace and was appointed (1931) a delegate to the Disarmament Conference that met in Geneva in 1932. She wrote several historical monographs, including *Early History of the Colonial Post Office* (1894), and magazine articles on current affairs.

Woolman, John, 1720–72, American Quaker leader, b. near Mt. Holly, N.J. In early life a tailor and shopkeeper, Woolman was recorded a minister (1743) by the Burlington, N.J., Meeting. Thereafter he made many journeys throughout the colonies, preaching and teaching. He died at York on a visit to England. He was keenly aware of social injustice and his was one of the first voices raised against Negro slavery. Among his published works is *Some Considerations on the Keeping of Negroes* (1754, 1762). Woolman is best remembered for his journal (1774; ed. by J. G. Whittier, 1871, and P. P. Moulton, 1971). See studies by Janet Whitney (1942), C. O. Peare (1954), E. H. Cady (1965), Paul Rosenblatt (1969), and A. D. Moulton (1973).

Woolworth, Frank Winfield, 1852–1919, American merchant, b. Rodman, N.Y. He established in 1879 a five-cent store at Utica, N.Y., which failed, and the same year he started a successful five-and-ten-cent store at Lancaster, Pa. Woolworth opened many others and soon extended business throughout the United States and to several foreign countries. In 1911 the F. W. Woolworth Company was incorporated with ownership of over 1,000 five-and-tens, and Woolworth became director of various financial firms. He had the Woolworth Building erected in New York City in 1913, the highest building in the world (792 ft/241.4 m) at that time. See J. K. Winkler, *Five and Ten* (1940, repr. 1970); J. P. Nichols, *Skyline Queen and the Merchant Prince* (1973).

Woomera-Maralinga (wo͝o'mərə-mâr'əlĭng'gə), town (1971 pop. 4,069), in the state of South Australia, S Australia, near Lake Torrens. It is the site of a missile-testing range used by Australia and its allies. Australia's first earth satellite was launched there in 1967. Nearby is a U.S. space tracking station.

Woonsocket (wo͝onsŏk'ĭt, wo͝on-), city (1970 pop. 46,820), Providence co., N R.I., on both sides of the Blackstone River; settled c.1666, set off from Cumberland 1867, inc. as a city 1888. The demise of the textile industry, which long shaped the city, has hurt its economy. Worsted weaving and package dyeing are still carried on; new manufactures are electronic equipment, plastics, and sporting goods. The inhabitants are primarily Franco-Americans whose forebears came from Canada. Of interest are the river falls in the center of the city and the unusual potholes worn by swirling stones in the river bed. Also in Woonsocket are a library in which Abraham Lincoln spoke (1860) and the John Arnold House (1712).

Wooster, David (wo͝os'tər), 1711–77, American Revolutionary officer, b. Fairfield co., Conn. He served as an officer in the British army during the last of the French and Indian Wars. Wooster resigned his commission upon the outbreak of the American Revolution, was one of the promoters of the Ticonderoga expedition (1775), and was made brigadier general in the Continental army. He led Connecticut troops in the Quebec campaign. After the death of Richard Montgomery, Wooster was put in command (1776) of American forces at Quebec, but he was soon recalled by the Continental Congress because of his ineptitude. Wooster, commanding the Connecticut militia, was mortally wounded in battle near Danbury, Conn., against Tory raiders.

Wooster (wo͝os'tər), city (1970 pop. 18,703), seat of Wayne co., N central Ohio, in a farm area; inc. 1817. Paper, brass, food and rubber products, and camera equipment are made. A state agricultural research and development station is nearby. The city is the seat of The College of Wooster, which was chartered in 1866 and opened in 1870.

Wooster, College of, at Wooster, Ohio; United Presbyterian; coeducational; chartered 1866, opened 1870.

Worcester, Charles Somerset, 1st earl of (wo͝os'tər), 1460?–1526, English nobleman. An illegitimate son of Henry Beaufort, 3d duke of Somerset, he rose rapidly in the service of Henry VII. He was admiral of a fleet in 1488, was sent on embassies to France in 1498 and 1502, and in 1506 was created Baron Herbert of Raglan. He became lord chamberlain under Henry VIII and in 1514 was created earl of Worcester. In 1525 he took part in arranging the treaty between France and England after the battle of Pavia.

Worcester, Edward Somerset, 6th earl and 2d marquess of, 1601?–1667, English soldier and inventor. Known as Lord Herbert after 1628, he received the title earl of Glamorgan in 1644 and succeeded as earl and marquess of Worcester in 1646. Sent to raise royalist troops in Ireland, Glamorgan, himself a Roman Catholic, exceeded his instructions when he signed (1645) on behalf of Charles I a treaty with the Irish Roman Catholics that would have given them freedom of worship. This treaty proved so offensive to the Protestant royalists that Charles repudiated it. Worcester went to France in 1648 and was imprisoned for two years on his return to England (1652). Most of his estates were returned to him at the Restoration (1660). He was interested in mechanical experiments, which he described in a long treatise, and is said to have invented a steam engine.

Worcester, Elwood, 1862?-1940, American Episcopal clergyman, b. Massillon, Ohio, grad. Columbia, 1886, Ph.D. Univ. of Leipzig, 1889. He was professor of philosophy and psychology and chaplain at Lehigh Univ. (1890-96). He then became rector of St. Stephen's Church, Philadelphia (1896-1904), and later of Emmanuel Church, Boston (1904-29). In Boston he initiated, with Samuel McComb, the Emmanuel movement, which was an attempt to combine psychotherapy with medicine. Worcester's books include *Religion and Medicine* (1908, with McComb and I. H. Coriat) and *Body, Mind, and Spirit* (1931).

Worcester, John Tiptoft, earl of, 1427?-1470, English nobleman. He studied at Oxford and was created earl of Worcester in 1449. He served as treasurer of the exchequer (1452-55) and lord deputy of Ireland (1456-57). In 1457 he went on a pilgrimage to the Holy Land and on the return journey stayed in Italy for two years. There he studied under GUARINO DA VERONA and acquired a considerable reputation as a Latin scholar. He was one of the first Englishmen to become familiar with the learning of the Italian Renaissance. On his return to England, Worcester, who was a brother-in-law of the powerful Richard Neville, earl of WARWICK, became (1462) constable of England under EDWARD IV. In this capacity he tried and sentenced to death many of the Lancastrian leaders. He again became (1467) lord deputy of Ireland and had the earl of Desmond executed—and, it is claimed, Desmond's two sons as well. He was appointed constable again in March, 1470, but when Warwick restored Henry VI to the throne in October, Worcester fled. He was captured, condemned by John de Vere, earl of Oxford (whose father and brother Worcester had sentenced to death in 1462), and executed. Hated by the Lancastrians, he was called "the butcher of England." His translation of Cicero's *De amicitia* was printed by William Caxton in 1481. See biography by R. J. Mitchell (1938).

Worcester, Noah, 1758-1837, American Congregational clergyman, b. Hollis, N.H. He was pastor (1787-1810) at Thornton, N.H. From 1813 to 1818 he was the first editor of the *Christian Disciple,* a Unitarian periodical. He is, however, best remembered for his work in behalf of peace. His *Solemn Review of the Custom of War* (1814), under the pseudonym Philo Pacificus, had world-wide circulation and led to the establishment of peace societies. Worcester was secretary of the Massachusetts Peace Society (founded 1815), and he founded and edited (1819-28) a magazine, *The Friend of Peace.*

Worcester, Thomas Percy, earl of, c.1344-1403, English nobleman; brother of Henry Percy, 1st earl of NORTHUMBERLAND. He served with considerable success in the wars in France and Spain, especially as admiral of the fleet of the north, a position to which he was appointed in 1378. He also served on several diplomatic missions, heading the English embassy to France to treat for peace in 1392. He was created earl of Worcester by Richard II in 1397. He accompanied Richard to Ireland in 1399 as admiral, but upon their return to England he joined his brother and his nephew, Sir Henry PERCY, in supporting the seizure of the throne by Henry IV. Henry confirmed Worcester's past privileges and in 1401 appointed him seneschal (steward), lieutenant of South Wales, and tutor to the prince of Wales (1402). In July, 1403, Worcester surprised the king by joining his kinsmen in open revolt against the crown. Captured in the subsequent battle of Shrewsbury, Worcester was beheaded.

Worcester (wo͝os'tər), county borough (1971 pop. 73,445), county town of Worcestershire, W central England, on the Severn River. The making of porcelain, gloves, and sauce are long-established industries; recently metal goods and machines have also been manufactured. The site became the seat of a bishopric c.680. The present cathedral is chiefly 14th cent., with a Norman crypt and tombs; in it are held, alternately with Hereford and Gloucester, the Festivals of the Three Choirs. There are several old parish churches and timbered houses. The Commandery, restored in 1954, was a hospital in the 11th cent. In the English civil war Worcester was the scene of Cromwell's final victory with the complete rout of Charles II and the Scots in 1651. There are two very old public schools: Royal Grammar School (13th cent.) and King's School (1541). In 1974, Worcester became part of the new nonmetropolitan county of Hereford and Worcester.

Worcester, town (1970 pop. 40,610), Cape Prov., SW South Africa. It produces wine and liquor and processes the fruits and vegetables of the surrounding farm region. There are also textile and metal industries. Worcester's large thermoelectric station powers the electrified railroad that runs through the nearby Hex River Mts. The town was founded in 1820 and was named for the Marquess of Worcester, governor of Cape of Good Hope Colony. A technical college and the Drostdy (1825), which is a national monument and the home of the Afrikaner Museum, are in Worcester.

Worcester, industrial city (1970 pop. 176,572), seat of Worcester co., central Mass., on the Blackstone River; inc. 1722. The canalization (1828) of the Blackstone River marked the beginning of Worcester's rapid industrial development. A port of entry, its manufactures now include machinery, metal goods, chemicals, plastics, pharmaceuticals, electrical equipment, textiles, shoes, and abrasives. There is also a printing and publishing industry. Settled in 1673, the city suffered Indian attacks in 1675 and 1683. In Shays's Rebellion the courthouse was besieged (1786) by insurgents. The first woman's suffrage national convention was held (1850) in Worcester. Edward Everett Hale was pastor there from 1842 to 1856. Worcester is the seat of Clark Univ., Worcester Polytechnic Institute, Worcester State College, College of the Holy Cross, and several junior colleges. It has a number of notable museums, two zoos, and an annual music festival (inaugurated in 1858). Also of interest is a huge three-level shopping center with a Plexiglas dome. In 1953 a severe tornado struck the city, causing the loss of many lives and extensive property damage. Lake Quinsigamond and two state parks are in the vicinity.

Worcestershire (wo͝os'tərshĭr,-shər), county (1971 pop. 692,605), 704 sq mi (1,823 sq km), W central England. The county town is WORCESTER. DUDLEY and WARLEY are also county boroughs. Worcestershire is largely hilly, with all or part of the Malvern, Cotswold, Clent, and Lickey hills within the county. The area is watered by the Severn and Avon rivers; the valley of the Avon is known as the Vale of Evesham. The county is famous for its orchards, and grains and hops are grown. There is dairy farming and sheep and cattle raising. The northern part of the county, formerly rich in iron and coal deposits, verges into the industrial Midlands area known as the Black Country. Metal products are manufactured there with imported metals. Other manufactured products are carpets (at Kidderminster) and porcelain (at Worcester). Worcestershire became an administrative unit in 1041 and was a monastic center in the Middle Ages. In 1974, Worcestershire became part of the new nonmetropolitan county of Hereford and Worcester.

Worcester ware, ceramic ware, first manufactured in 1751, when the Lowdin pottery was moved from Bristol to Worcester. Soft paste was employed, and tea services, vases, armorial mugs, and portrait plaques with underglaze decoration became popular. Modeled and painted floral and medallion motifs, Chinese landscapes, and the transfer print in blue, black, or purple were modes of ornamenting early Worcester ware. A more florid treatment, with grounds of color (especially blue) and gilt as foils for birds of brilliant plumage, was effected in 1768 by artists formerly at Chelsea factories; after 1783 deterioration in design was noticeable.

Worde, Wynkyn de: see WYNKYN DE WORDE.

Worden, John Lorimer (wûr'dən), 1818-97, American naval officer, b. Westchester co., N.Y. Appointed midshipman in 1834, he saw varied service before the Civil War. Worden was captured (April, 1861) by the Confederates and held prisoner for seven months. Shortly after his exchange, he assumed command of the new ironclad *Monitor.* In the famous battle of MONITOR AND MERRIMACK, Worden was wounded in the face and temporarily blinded. Later he saw service with the South Atlantic Blockading Squadron (1862-63). Promoted to rear admiral in 1872, Worden was (1869-74) superintendent of Annapolis and commanded (1875-77) the European squadron.

Wordsworth, Christopher, 1774-1846, English clergyman, educator, and writer; youngest brother of William Wordsworth. He was master of Trinity College, Cambridge, from 1820 to 1841. Most noted of his books is *Ecclesiastical Biography* (6 vol., 1810). His second son, **Charles Wordsworth,** 1806-92, became a prelate in Scotland. From 1847 to 1854 he was warden of Trinity College, Glenalmond, Perthshire. In 1853 he was consecrated bishop of St. Andrews, Dunkeld, and Dunblane. He was deeply interested in reuniting the churches of England and Scotland. His many books include *Shakespeare's Knowledge and Use of the Bible* (1864). See his *Annals of My Early Life, 1806-46* (1891) and *Annals of My Life, 1847-56* (ed. by W. E. Hodgson, 1893). **Christopher Wordsworth,** 1807-85, English prelate and scholar, was the youngest son of Christopher Wordsworth. Ordained a priest in 1835, he was headmaster (1836-44) of Harrow and thereafter canon and then archdeacon of Westminster until in 1869 he was consecrated bishop of Lincoln. He wrote *Athens and Attica* (1836) and other works of classical scholarship, but he is most noted for his editing of the entire Bible, with commentaries—the New Testament (1856-60) and the Old Testament (1864-70). See biography by J. H. Overton and Elizabeth Wordsworth (1888).

Wordsworth, William, 1770-1850, English poet, b. Cockermouth, Cumberland. One of the great English poets, he was a leader of the romantic movement in England. In 1791 he graduated from Cambridge and traveled abroad. While in France he fell in love with Annette Vallon, who bore him a daughter, Caroline, in 1792. Although he did not marry her, it seems to have been circumstance rather than lack of affection that separated them. Throughout his life he supported Annette and Caroline as best he could, finally settling a sum of money on them in 1835. The spirit of the French Revolution had strongly influenced Wordsworth, and he returned (1792) to England imbued with the principles of Rousseau and republicanism. In 1793 were published *An Evening Walk* and *Descriptive Sketches,* written in the stylized idiom and vocabulary of the 18th cent. The outbreak of the Reign of Terror prevented Wordsworth's return to France, and after receiving several small legacies, he settled with his sister Dorothy in Dorsetshire. Wordsworth was extraordinarily close to his sister. Throughout his life she was his constant and devoted companion, sharing his poetic vision and helping him with his work. In Dorsetshire, Wordsworth became the intimate friend of Samuel Taylor COLERIDGE and, probably under his influence, a student of David Hartley's empiricist philosophy. Together the two poets wrote *Lyrical Ballads* (1798), in which they sought to use the real language of ordinary men in poetry; it included Wordsworth's poem "Tintern Abbey." The work introduced romanticism into England and became a manifesto for romantic poets. In 1799 he and his sister moved to the Lake District of England, where they lived the remainder of their lives. A second edition of the *Lyrical Ballads* (1800), which included a critical essay outlining Wordsworth's poetic principles, in particular his ideas about poetic diction and meter, was unmercifully attacked by critics. In 1802 he married Mary Hutchinson, an old school friend; the union was evidently a happy one, and the couple had four children. *The Prelude,* his long autobiographical poem, was completed in 1805, though it was not published until after his death. His *Poems in Two Volumes* (1807) included the "Ode to Duty," the "Ode: Intimations of Immortality," and a number of famous sonnets. Thereafter Wordsworth's creative powers diminished; some notable poems, however, were produced after this date, including *The Excursion* (1814), "Laodamia" (1815), "White Doe of Rylstone" (1815), *Memorials of a Tour of the Continent, 1820* (1822), and "Yarrow Revisited" (1835). In 1842 he was given a civil list pension, and the following year, having long since put aside radical sympathies, he was named poet laureate. Wordsworth's personality, as well as his poetry, was deeply influenced by his love of nature, especially by the actual sights and scenes of the Lake Country, in which he spent most of his mature life. A profoundly earnest and sincere thinker, he displayed a high seriousness comparable, at times, to Milton's but tempered with tenderness and love of simplicity. His earlier work shows the poetic beauty of commonplace things and people as in "Margaret," "Peter Bell," "Michael," and "The Idiot Boy"; his use of the language of ordinary speech was heavily criticized, but it helped to rid English poetry of the more artificial conventions of 18th-century diction. Among his other well-known poems are "Lucy" ("She dwelt among the untrodden ways"), "The Solitary Reaper," "Resolution and Independence," "Daffodils," "The Rainbow," and the sonnet "The World Is Too Much with Us." Although Wordsworth was venerated in the 19th cent., by the early 20th cent. his reputation had declined. He was criticized for the uneven merit of his poetry, for his rather marked capacity for bathos, and for his transformation from an open-minded liberal to a cramped conservative; he was even subjected to psychoanalysis. In recent years, however, Wordsworth has again been recognized as a great English poet—a profound, original thinker who created a new tradition of poetry. See his poetical works, ed. by Ernest de Selincourt and Helen Darbishire (5 vol., 1940–49); his prose works, ed. by W. J. B. Owen and J. W. Smyser (3 vol., 1974); correspondence with his sister, ed. by Ernest de Selincourt (rev. ed. 1967); biography by Mary Moorman (2 vol., 1965); studies by Mark Reed (1967) and F. E. Halliday (1970); Graham McMaster, *William Wordsworth: A Critical Anthology* (1973). Wordsworth's sister, **Dorothy Wordsworth,** 1771–1855, is known principally for her poems and for her journals, which have proved invaluable for later biographies and studies of the poet. These journals, the first of which was started in 1798, are written in delicate, exquisite diction, describing the Wordsworth household, friends, and travels. For the last 20 years of her life Dorothy Wordsworth was an invalid, suffering from an obscure illness that made her prematurely senile. See her journals, ed. by Helen Darbishire (2 vol., 1958); biography by Ernest de Selincourt (1933); A. M. Ellis, *Rebels and Conservatives: Dorothy and William Wordsworth and Their Circle* (1967); Elizabeth Hardwick, *Seduction and Betrayal* (1974).

Work, Hubert, 1860–1942, American cabinet officer, b. Marion Center, Pa. A practicing physician in Colorado, he became prominent in state and then in national Republican politics. He was Postmaster General (1922–23) under President Harding; then, after the exposure of Albert B. Fall in the Teapot Dome Scandal, succeeded him (1923) as Secretary of the Interior and reorganized the department. He resigned in 1928 and, as Republican national chairman (1928–29), managed Herbert Hoover's successful campaign for the presidency.

work, in physics and mechanics, transfer of energy by a force acting against a resistance or a body and resulting in displacement. Work is equal to the product of the force and the distance through which it produces movement. Although both FORCE and displacement are VECTOR quantities, having both magnitude and direction, work is a scalar quantity, having only magnitude. If the force acts in a direction other than that of the motion of the body, then only that component of the force in the direction of the motion produces work. Thus when a 5-lb (22.4-newton) force pulls a body 10 ft (3 m), it does 50 foot-pounds (67.2 meter-newtons) of work. If a force acts on a body constrained to remain stationary, no work is done by the force. Even if the body is in motion, the force must have a component in the direction of motion. Thus, any centripetal force, such as the sun's gravitational pull on the earth, does no work because it acts at right angles to the motion and has no component in that direction (see CENTRIPETAL FORCE AND CENTRIFUGAL FORCE). Work, being a form of ENERGY, can be converted into other forms of energy. When there is no FRICTION and a force acts on a body, the work done by the force is equal to the increase of the kinetic and potential energy of the body, since all the energy expended by the agency exerting the force must be gained by the body. If frictional forces are present, then some of the work must go to overcome friction and appears finally in the form of heat energy. A simple MACHINE is a device for converting one form of work into another. For example the jackscrew converts an input of work done on the machine to raise the load. The efficiency of a machine, which is defined as the ratio of the work output to the work input, is always less than one, since some of the input is invariably wasted in overcoming friction. The element of time does not enter into the computation of work; the time rate of doing work is called POWER. One HORSEPOWER is an expenditure of 33,000 foot-pounds per minute. Some of the units used to measure work are the foot-pound, the ERG, and the JOULE.

workers' education: see VOCATIONAL EDUCATION.

workhouse: see POOR LAW.

working dog, classification used by breeders and kennel clubs to designate dogs raised by man to herd cattle and sheep, as draft animals, as message dispatchers in wartime, in police and rescue work, as guardians of persons and property, or as guides (see GUIDE DOG) for the blind. The following 29 breeds are designated working dogs by the American Kennel Club: ALASKAN MALAMUTE, BELGIAN MALINOIS, BELGIAN SHEEPDOG, BELGIAN TERVUREN, BERNESE MOUNTAIN DOG, BOUVIER DES FLANDRES, BOXER, BRIARD, BULL MASTIFF, CARDIGAN WELSH CORGI, COLLIE, DOBERMAN PINSCHER, GERMAN SHEPHERD, GREAT DANE, GREAT PYRENEES, KOMONDOR, KUVASZ, MASTIFF, NEWFOUNDLAND, OLD ENGLISH SHEEPDOG, PEMBROKE WELSH CORGI, PULI, ROTTWEILER, SAMOYED, SCHNAUZER (giant and standard), SHETLAND SHEEPDOG, SIBERIAN HUSKY, and ST. BERNARD. See DOG.

Workington, municipal borough (1971 pop. 28,414), Cumberland, NW England, at the mouth of the Derwent River. Workington has a good harbor. Coal mines are in the vicinity, and there are clothing and carpet industries, engineering works, steel mills, and tanneries. In 1974, Workington became part of the new nonmetropolitan county of Cumbria.

workmen's compensation, payment by employers for some part of the cost of injuries, or in some cases of occupational diseases, received by employees in the course of their work. The degree of responsibility varies in different countries and in different states of the United States. The relationship that developed under English common law whereby the employee was assumed to agree to run all ordinary risks of the employment, including those due to the negligence of fellow employees, is no longer in effect in most countries. Most modern workmen's compensation systems consist of legislation requiring the employer to furnish a reasonably safe place to work, suitable equipment, rules and instructions when they are reasonably necessary, and reasonably competent foremen and superintendents. The employer is liable for his own or employees' acts of negligence, for his own gross negligence, and for extraordinary risks of work. In most cases the employer is not liable for accidents occurring outside the place of work, or for those which have not arisen directly from employment. Workmen's compensation legislation was first passed in Germany, Austria, and Great Britain in the late 1800s. Such legislation came later in the United States, but by 1920 all but six states had passed some form of it. At present all states have legislation, but nearly one in five workers is not covered, the major exceptions being merchant seamen and railroad employees, who are covered by other legislation. Private insurance companies offer employers' compensation insurance; some states have made such insurance compulsory, and a few have created state insurance funds to secure payments even when the employer is insolvent. Most states similarly provide for public employees, although some limit this coverage to workers engaged in dangerous occupations. In Great Britain the payment of compensation is required for almost all industrial accidents. In France all noninsured employers are taxed for a state fund that guarantees compensation payments. In the United States, as well as in other countries, benefits usually cover medical expenses, cash payments in the case of temporary or permanent incapacity, and increasingly, vocational rehabilitation. See E. F. Cheit, ed., *Occupational Disability and Public Policy* (1963); H. E. Blair, *Reference Guide to Workmen's Compensation* (1968).

Work Projects Administration (WPA), former U.S. government agency, established in 1935 by executive order of President Franklin Delano Roosevelt as the Works Progress Administration; it was renamed the Work Projects Administration in 1939, when it was made part of the Federal Works Agency. Created when unemployment was widespread, the WPA—headed by Harry L. Hopkins until 1938—was designed to increase the purchasing power of persons on relief by employing them on useful projects. WPA's building program included the construction of 116,000 buildings, 78,000 bridges, and 651,000 mi (1,047,000 km) of road and the improvement of 800 airports. Also a part of WPA's diversified activities were the Federal Art Project, the Federal Writers' Project, and the Federal Theatre Project. Close to 10,000 drawings, paintings, and sculptured works were produced through WPA, and many public buildings (especially post offices) were decorated with murals. The experiments in theatrical productions were highly praised and introduced many fresh ideas. Musical performances under the project averaged 4,000 a month. The most notable product of writers in WPA was a valuable series of state and regional guidebooks. WPA also conducted an education program and supervised the activities of the NATIONAL YOUTH ADMINISTRATION. At its peak WPA had about 3.5 million persons on its payrolls. Altogether WPA employed a total of 8.5 million persons, and total Federal appropriations for the program amounted to almost $11 billion. There was sharp criticism of the WPA in a Senate committee report in 1939; the same year the WPA appropriation was cut, several projects were abolished, and others were curtailed. A strike of thousands of WPA workers to prevent a cut in wages on building projects was unsuccessful. Steadily increasing employment in the private sector, much speeded just before and during World War II, caused further drastic cuts in WPA appropriations and payrolls. In June, 1943, the agency officially went out of existence. See D. S. Howard, *WPA and Federal Relief Policy* (1943).

Worksop (wûrk'səp, wûr'–), municipal borough (1971 pop. 36,034), Nottinghamshire, central England. The borough contains a portion of Sherwood Forest. It is a coal-mining center with many industries, including foundries, chemical works, glassworks, and breweries. There are remains of an Augustinian priory founded in 1103.

Works Progress Administration: see WORK PROJECTS ADMINISTRATION.

work-week: see LABOR, HOURS OF.

World Bank: see INTERNATIONAL BANK FOR RECONSTRUCTION AND DEVELOPMENT.

World Council of Churches, an international, interdenominational organization of Protestant and Orthodox Eastern churches. It was formally constituted at an assembly at Amsterdam in 1948. The idea of a world fellowship of churches took concrete form in 1937, when two ecumenical conferences—on life and work and on faith and order—elected a joint committee to formulate plans for a world council of churches. This provisional committee met at Utrecht in 1938, but it was not until after World War II that the constitution of its drafting was formally ratified at the first international assembly of the World Council of Churches in 1948. The governing body of the council is the assembly, which meets roughly every six years; the second assembly was held (1954) at Evanston, Ill., the third (1961) at New Delhi, India, and the fourth (1968) at Uppsala, Sweden. The assembly appoints a central committee of 120 members, which meets once a year; within that committee is a 26-member executive committee. The council also has six presidents. The headquarters of the council and its permanent secretariat are at Geneva, Switzerland. The council, which has no legislative power over its member churches, provides an opportunity for its constituents to act together in matters of common concern, such as missions (in 1961 the International Missionary Council was incorporated into the World Council as the Commission and Division of World Mission and Evangelism), interchurch aid and reconstruction, the study of religious and social issues, international affairs, the enlargement of opportunities in church life for women and young people, and the growth of ecumenical consciousness in church members. At the Uppsala assembly a resolution was passed inviting the Roman Catholic Church to join the council, and Catholic members were appointed to the Commission on Faith and Order. In 1969, Pope Paul VI visited the council's headquarters in Geneva. In 1973 the World Council had a membership of 263 churches, from 90 countries and territories. See ECUMENICAL MOVEMENT. See bulletins and publications of the World Council of Churches; G. K. A. Bell, *The Kingship of Christ: The Story of the World Council of Churches* (1954); Edward Duff, *The Social Thought of the World Council of Churches* (1956); D. P. Gaines, *The World Council of Churches* (1966); Norman Goodall, *The Ecumenical Movement* (3d ed. 1966) and *Ecumenical Progress 1961–1971* (1972).

World Court, popular name of the Permanent Court of International Justice, established pursuant to Article 14 of the Covenant of the League of Nations. The protocol establishing it was adopted by the Assembly of the League in 1920 and ratified by the requisite number of states in 1921. By the time of its dissolution in 1945 (when its functions were transferred to the newly created INTERNATIONAL COURT OF JUSTICE), the court had 59 member states. Established at The Hague, the court was empowered to render judgments in disputes between states that were voluntarily submitted to it and to give advisory opinions in any matters referred to it by the Council or the Assembly of the League. Its functions, thus, were judicial rather than, as in the case of the older HAGUE TRIBUNAL, purely arbitral and diplomatic. It also differed from the Hague Tribunal in having a permanent group of judges instead of a panel from which judges might be selected to hear a particular dispute. The court originally had 11 judges and 4 deputy judges, but in 1931 its composition was changed to 15 regular judges. Judges were elected for nine-year terms by the Council and the Assembly concurrently; they were selected from a list of nominees of the Hague Tribunal regardless of nationality, except that not more than one citizen of a country might sit on the bench at any one time. Although the United States never joined the court (because the Senate refused to ratify the protocol), there was always an American jurist on the bench. To assure impartiality, the judges were paid salaries and were forbidden to engage in governmental service or in any legal activity except their judicial work. In the course of its existence, the court rendered 32 judgments and 27 advisory opinions. An important judgment was that which affirmed (1933) Danish sovereignty over the N coast of Greenland and disallowed Norway's claim. The advisory opinions of the court were important in developing international law. A notable opinion declared (1931) that the proposed customs union of Germany and Austria would violate Austria's pledge to remain independent. The court virtually ceased to function after the German occupation of the Netherlands in 1940. See Manley O. Hudson, *The Permanent Court of International Justice, 1920–1942* (rev. ed. 1943, repr. 1972); D. F. Fleming, *The United States and the World Court* (1945, repr. 1968).

World Cup: see SOCCER.

World Health Organization (WHO), specialized agency of the United Nations, established in 1948, with its headquarters at Geneva. WHO admits all sovereign states (including those that do not belong to the United Nations) to full membership, and it admits territories that are not self-governing to associate membership. In 1973 there were 138 full members and 2 associate members. WHO is governed by the World Health Assembly, consisting of representatives of the entire membership, which meets at least once a year; an executive board elected by the World Health Assembly; and a secretariat headed by a director general. Technical committees and regional organizations have been established to further the purpose of WHO, namely, "the attainment by all peoples of the highest possible level of health." In 1973 there were regional organizations in Africa, the E Mediterranean, SE Asia, Europe, the W Pacific, and the Americas. WHO has made notable strides in checking polio, leprosy, cholera, malaria, and tuberculosis, among other diseases; it has also authorized studies of mental health, of the standardization of health statistics, and of other problems of world-wide scope. WHO has drafted important conventions concerning sanitary and quarantine requirements and other measures for preventing the international spread of disease. It has also sponsored medical research and given attention to the problems of environmental pollution. See M. C. Morgan, *Doctors to the World* (1958); C. F. Brockington, *World Health* (1958); catalogue (1965) and bibliography (1969) of WHO publications.

World Meteorological Organization (WMO), specialized agency of the United Nations; established in 1951 with headquarters at Geneva. It replaced the International Meteorological Organization, which was established in 1878. WMO aims at promoting international cooperation between the world's meteorological stations, standardizing meteorological observations, encouraging research and training, and extending the use of meteorological findings to different fields. The launching of satellites to obtain meteorological data and the study of the meteorological aspects of the peaceful uses of atomic energy have greatly widened WMO's scope of activities. WMO operates through the World Meteorological Congress (which meets at least every four years) with delegates from its entire membership, an executive committee, a technical commission, a secretariat, and six regional meteorological associations in Africa, Asia, South America, North and Central America, SW Pacific, and Europe.

World's Columbian Exposition, held at Chicago, May–Nov., 1893, in commemoration of the 400th anniversary of the discovery of America by Christopher Columbus. Authorized (1890) by Congress, it was planned and completed by a commission headed by Thomas W. Palmer (1830–1913), and the grounds along the Lake Michigan shore were dedicated Oct. 12, 1892. The exposition, known as the White City, comprised 150 buildings of Romanesque, Greek, and Renaissance architecture constructed of staff, a material resembling marble. Among the architects were Charles F. McKim, William R. Mead, and Stanford White, who designed the Agricultural Building; Richard M. Hunt, who designed the Administration Building; and Dankmar Adler and Louis H. Sullivan, who initiated functional architecture with the Transportation Building. Daniel H. Burnham supervised the design and construction; Frederick Law Olmsted, the landscaping. Popularly called the Chicago Fair, the exposition covered 600 acres (243 hectares), attracted exhibitors from 72 countries, and drew over 27 million visitors. It produced an unparalleled surge of creative energy that had an important influence not only in architecture but also on the cultural values of the nation.

world's fair: see EXPOSITION.

world soul, Lat. *anima mundi,* in philosophy, term denoting a universal spirit or soul that functions as an organizing principle. While many early Greek philosophers saw the world as of one principle, Plato was the first to state that this concept held the same relation to the world as the human soul did to the body. Friedrich Wilhelm Josef von Schelling used the term as a unifying principle, coordinating the organic and the inorganic in life. World soul is prominent in Oriental philosophy. Hinduism is a religion whose theoretical basis is a world soul, called Brahman (see UPANISHADS; VEDANTA).

World's View, granite hill, SW Rhodesia, c.30 mi (50 km) S of Bulawayo. It was designated by Cecil Rhodes as the resting place for those who served Great Britain well in Africa. Rhodes and Sir Leander Starr Jameson are buried there.

World War I, 1914–18, also known as the Great War, conflict, chiefly in Europe, among most of the great Western powers. The largest war the world had yet seen was immediately precipitated by the assassination of Archduke Francis Ferdinand of Austria-Hungary by a Serbian nationalist in 1914. There were, however, many factors that had led toward war. Prominent causes were the imperialistic, territorial, and economic rivalries that had been intensifying from the late 19th cent., particularly among Germany, France, Great Britain, Russia, and Austria-Hungary. Of equal importance was the rampant spirit of nationalism, especially unsettling in the empire of Austria-Hungary and perhaps also in France. Nationalism had brought the unification of Germany by "blood and iron," and France, deprived of Alsace and Lorraine by the Franco-Prussian War of 1870–71, had been left with its own nationalistic cult seeking revenge against Germany. While French nationalists were hostile to Germany, which sought to maintain its gains by militarism and alliances, nationalism was creating violent tensions in the AUSTRO-HUNGARIAN MONARCHY; there the large Slavic national groups had grown increasingly restive, and Serbia as well as Russia fanned Slavic hopes for freedom and PAN-SLAVISM. Imperialist rivalry had grown more intense with the "new imperialism" of the late 19th and early 20th cent. The great powers had come into conflict over spheres of influence in China and over territories in Africa; and the EASTERN QUESTION, created by the decline of the Ottoman Empire, had produced several disturbing controversies. Particularly unsettling was the policy of Germany. It embarked late but aggressively on colonial expansion under Emperor WILLIAM II, came into conflict with France over MOROCCO, and seemed to threaten Great Britain by its rapid naval expansion. These issues, imperialist and nationalist, resulted in a hardening of alliance systems in the TRIPLE ALLIANCE AND TRIPLE ENTENTE and in a general armaments race. Nonetheless, a false optimism regarding peace prevailed almost until the onset of the war, an optimism stimulated by the long era in which major wars had been avoided, by the close dynastic ties and cultural intercourse of Europe, and by the advance of industrialization and economic prosperity. Many Europeans counted on the deterrent of war's destructiveness to preserve the peace. The Austrian annexation (1908) of BOSNIA AND HERCEGOVINA created an international crisis, but war was avoided. The BALKAN WARS (1912–13) remained localized but increased Austria's concern for its territorial integrity, while the solidification of the Triple Alliance made Germany more yielding to the demands of Austria, now its one close ally. The assassination (June 28, 1914) of Archduke FRANCIS FERDINAND at Sarajevo set in motion the diplomatic maneuvers that ended in war. The Austrian military party, headed by Count BERCHTOLD, won over the government to a punitive policy toward Serbia. On July 23, Serbia was given a nearly unacceptable ultimatum. With Russian support assured by Sergei SAZONOV, Serbia accepted some of the terms but rejected those infringing upon its sovereignty and hedged on others. Austria-Hungary, supported by Germany, rejected the British proposal of Sir Edward Grey (later Lord GREY OF FALLODON) and declared war (July 28) on Serbia. Russian mobilization precipitated a German ultimatum (July 31) that, when unanswered, was followed by a German declaration of war on Russia (Aug. 1). Convinced that France was about to attack its western frontier, Germany declared war (Aug. 3) on France and struck out for France through Belgium and Luxembourg. Germany had hoped for British neutrality, but German violation of Belgian neutrality gave the British government the pretext and popular support necessary for entry into the war. In the following weeks Montenegro and Japan joined the Allies (Great Britain, France, Russia, Serbia, and Belgium) and the Ottoman Empire joined the Central Powers (Germany and Austria-Hungary). The war had become general. Whether or not it might have been avoided or localized and which persons or nations were most responsible for its outbreak are questions still debated by historians.

From the Marne to Verdun. The German strategy, planned by Alfred von Schlieffen (who did not contemplate a two-front war), called for an attack on the weak left flank of the French army by a massive German force approaching through Belgium. The Schlieffen plan was weakened from the start when the German commander Helmuth von MOLTKE detached forces from the all-important German right wing, which was supposed to smash through Belgium, in order to reinforce the left wing in Alsace-Lorraine. Nevertheless, the Germans quickly occupied most of Belgium and advanced on Paris. In Sept., 1914, the first battle of the Marne (see MARNE, BATTLE OF THE) took place. For reasons still controversial, a general German retreat was ordered after the battle, and the Germans entrenched themselves behind the Aisne River. The Germans then advanced toward the Channel ports but were stopped in the first battle of Ypres (see YPRES, BATTLE OF); grueling TRENCH WARFARE began along the entire Western Front. For the next three years the battle line remained virtually stationary. It ran, approximately, from Ostend past Armentières, Douai, Saint-Quentin, Rheims, Verdun, and Saint-Mihiel to Lunéville. Meanwhile, on the Eastern Front, the Russians invaded East Prussia but were decisively defeated (Aug.–Sept., 1914) by the Germans under generals Hindenburg, Ludendorff, and Mackensen at TANNENBERG and the MASURIAN LAKES (see under MASURIA). The Germans advanced on Warsaw, but further south a Russian offensive drove back the Austrians. However, by the autumn of 1915 combined Austro-German efforts had driven the Russians out of most of Poland and were holding a line extending from Riga to Chernovtsy. The Russians counterattacked in 1916 in a powerful drive directed by General BRUSILOV; by the year's end, however, the offensive had collapsed and had cost Russia many thousands of lives. Soon afterward the RUSSIAN REVOLUTION eliminated Russia as an effective participant in the war. Although the Austro-Hungarians were unsuccessful in their attacks on Serbia and Montenegro in the first year of the war, these two countries were overrun in 1915 by the Bulgarians (who had joined the Central Powers in Oct., 1915) and by Austro-German forces. Another blow to the Allied cause was the failure in 1915 of the GALLIPOLI CAMPAIGN, an attempt to force Turkey out of the war and to open a supply route to S Russia. The Allies, however, won a diplomatic battle when Italy, after denouncing its partnership in the Triple Alliance and after being promised vast territorial gains, entered the war on the Allied side in May, 1915. Austro-Italian fighting along the Isonzo River was inconclusive until late 1917, when the rout of the Italians at Caporetto made Italy a liability rather than an asset to the Allies. Except for the conquest of most of Germany's overseas colonies by the British and Japanese, the year 1916 opened with a dark outlook for the Allies. The stalemate on the Western Front had not been affected in 1915 by the second battle of Ypres, in which the Germans used POISON GAS for the first time on the Western Front, nor by the French offensive in Artois, in which a slight advance of the French under Henri PÉTAIN was paid for with heavy losses, nor by the offensive of Marshal JOFFRE in Champagne, nor by the British advance toward Lens and Loos. In Feb., 1916, the Germans tried to break the deadlock by massing a huge assault on Verdun (see VERDUN, BATTLE OF). The French, rallying with the cry, "They shall not pass!" held fast despite enormous losses, and in July the British and French took the offensive along the SOMME River where tanks were used for the first time by the British. By November they had gained a few thousand yards and lost thousands of men. By December, a French counteroffensive at Verdun had restored the approximate positions of Jan., 1916. Yet, despite signs of exhaustion on both sides, the war went on, drawing ever more nations into the maelstrom. Portugal and Rumania joined the Allies in 1916; Greece, involved in the war by the Allied SALONICA CAMPAIGNS on its soil, declared war on the Central Powers in 1917.

American Intervention and Allied Victory. The neutrality of the United States was seriously imperiled after the sinking of the LUSITANIA (1915). At the end of 1916, Germany, whose surface fleet had been bottled up since the indecisive battle of Jutland (see JUTLAND, BATTLE OF), announced that it would begin unrestricted submarine warfare in an effort to break British control of the seas. In protest the United States broke off relations with Germany (Feb., 1917), and on April 6 it entered the war. American participation meant that the Allies now had at their command almost unlimited industrial and manpower resources, which were to be decisive in winning the war. It also served from the start to rouse Allied morale, and the insistence of President Woodrow Wilson on a "war to make the world safe for democracy" was to weaken the Central Powers by encouraging revolutionary groups at home. The war on the Western Front continued to be bloody and stalemated. But in the Middle East the British, who had stopped a Turkish drive on the Suez Canal, proceeded to destroy the Ottoman Empire; T. E. LAWRENCE stirred the Arabs to revolt, Baghdad fell (March, 1917), and Field Marshal ALLENBY took Jerusalem (Dec., 1917). The first troops of the American Expeditionary Forces (AEF), commanded by General PERSHING, landed in France in June, 1917, when they were rushed to the CHÂTEAU-THIERRY area to help stem a new German offensive. A unified Allied command in the West had been created in April, 1918; it was headed by Marshal FOCH, but under him the national commanders (Sir Douglas HAIG for Britain, King ALBERT I for Belgium, and General Pershing for the United States) retained considerable authority. However, the Central Powers had gained new strength through the Treaty of BREST-LITOVSK (March, 1918) with Russia; the resources of the Ukraine seemed at their disposal, thus enabling them to balance to some extent the effects of the Allied blockade; most important of all, their forces could now be concentrated on the Western Front. The critical German counteroffensive, known as the second battle of the Marne, was stopped just short of Paris (July-Aug., 1918). At this point Foch ordered a general counterattack that soon pushed the Germans back to their initial line (the so-called Hindenburg Line). The Allied push continued, with the British advancing in the north and the Americans attacking through the Argonne region of France. While the Germans were thus losing their forces on the Western Front, Bulgaria, invaded by the Allies under General FRANCHET D'ESPEREY, capitulated on Sept. 30, and Turkey concluded an armistice on Oct. 30. Austria-Hungary, in the process of disintegration, surrendered on Nov. 4 after the Italian victory at VITTORIO VENETO. German resources were exhausted and German morale collapsed. President Wilson's FOURTEEN POINTS were accepted by the new German chancellor, MAXIMILIAN, PRINCE OF BADEN, as the basis of peace negotiations, but it was only after revolution had broken out in Germany that the armistice was at last signed (Nov. 11) at Compiègne. Germany was to evacuate immediately all territory W of the Rhine, and the Treaty of Brest-Litovsk was declared void. Thus the war ended without a single truly decisive battle having been fought, and Germany lost the war while its troops were still occupying territory from France to the Crimea. This paradox became important in later German history, when nationalists and militarists sought to blame the defeat on traitors on the home front rather than on the utter exhaustion of the German war machine and war economy.

Aftermath. World War I and the resulting peace treaties (see VERSAILLES, TREATY OF; SAINT-GERMAIN, TREATY OF; TRIANON, TREATY OF; NEUILLY, TREATY OF; SÈVRES, TREATY OF) radically changed the face of Europe and precipitated political, social, and economic changes. By the Treaty of Versailles Germany was forced to acknowledge the guilt for the war. Later, prompted by the Bolshevik publication of the secret diplomacy of the czarist Russian government, the warring powers gradually released their own state papers, and the long historical debate on war guilt began. It has with some justice been claimed that the conditions of the peace treaties were partially responsible for World War II. Yet when World War I ended, the immense suffering it had caused gave rise to a general revulsion to any kind of war, and a large part of mankind placed its hopes in the newly created LEAGUE OF NATIONS. Warfare itself had been revolutionized (see AIR POWER; CHEMICAL WARFARE; MECHANIZED WARFARE; TANK). To compute the total losses caused by the war is impossible. About 10 million dead and 20 million wounded is a conservative estimate. Starvation and epidemics raised the total in the immediate postwar years. There is a tremendous amount of general and specialized literature on World War I. Classic accounts of the war are S. B. Fay, *The Origins of the World War* (rev. ed. 1930, repr. 1966) and B. E. Schmitt, *The Coming of the War, 1914* (1930, repr. 1966). Two short guides to the military history are B. H. Liddell Hart, *The Real War* (1930, repr. 1963) and H. W. Baldwin, *World War I* (1962). See Winston S. Churchill, *The World Crisis* (6 vol., 1923-31, repr. 1970); B. H. Liddell Hart, *A History of the World War, 1914-1918* (1934); C. R. M. F. Cruttwell, *A History of the Great War, 1914-1918* (1934, repr. 1961); C. B. Falls, *The Great War* (1959, repr. 1961); Lawrence LaFore, *The Long Fuse* (1965); Fritz Fischer, *Germany's Aims in the First World War* (tr. 1967); G. P. Hayes, *World War I: A Compact History* (1972).

World War II, 1939-45, worldwide conflict involving every major power in the world. The two sides were generally known as the Allies and the AXIS. This second global conflict resulted from the rise of totalitarian, militaristic regimes in Germany, Italy, and Japan, a phenomenon stemming in part from the GREAT DEPRESSION that swept over the world in the early 1930s and from the conditions created by the peace settlements (1919-20) following World War I. After World War I defeated Germany, disappointed Italy, and ambitious Japan were anxious to regain or increase their power; all three eventually adopted forms of dictatorship (see NATIONAL SOCIALISM and FASCISM) that made the state supreme and called for expansion at the expense of neighboring countries. These three countries also set themselves up as champions against Communism, thus gaining at least partial tolerance of their early actions from the more conservative groups in the Western democracies. Also important was a desire for peace, on the part of the democracies reflected in their military unpreparedness. Finally, the LEAGUE OF NATIONS, weakened from the start by the defection of the United States, was unable to promote disarmament (see DISARMAMENT CONFERENCE), while the long economic depression sharpened national rivalries, increased fear and distrust, and made the masses susceptible to the promises of demagogues. The failure of the League to stop the Second SINO-JAPANESE WAR in 1931 was followed by a rising crescendo of treaty violations and acts of aggression. Adolf HITLER, coming to power (1933) in Germany, recreated the German army and prepared it for a war of conquest; in 1936 he remilitarized the Rhineland. In 1935-36, Benito MUSSOLINI conquered Ethiopia for Italy; and from 1936 to 1939 the SPANISH CIVIL WAR raged, with Germany and Italy helping the fascist forces of Francisco FRANCO to victory. In March, 1938, Germany annexed Austria, and in Sept., 1938, the British and French policy of appeasement toward the Axis reached its height with the sacrifice of much of Czechoslovakia to Germany in the MUNICH PACT. When Germany occupied (March, 1939) all of Czechoslovakia, and when Italy seized (April, 1939) Albania, Great Britain and France abandoned their policy of appeasement and set about creating an "antiaggression" front, which included alliances with Turkey, Greece, Rumania, and Poland, and speeding rearmament. Germany and Italy signed (May, 1939) a full military alliance, and after the Soviet-German nonaggression pact (August, 1939) removed German fear of a possible two-front war, Germany was ready to launch an attack on Poland. World War II began on Sept. 1, 1939, when Germany, without a declaration of war, invaded Poland. Britain and France declared war on Germany on Sept. 3, and all the members of the British Commonwealth, except Ireland, rapidly followed suit. The fighting in Poland was brief. The German *Blitzkrieg* [lightning war], making use of new techniques of air warfare and armored forces, crushed the Polish defenses, and the conquest was almost complete when Soviet forces entered (Sept. 17) E Poland. While this campaign ended with the partition of Poland and while the USSR defeated Finland in the FINNISH-RUSSIAN WAR (1939-40), the British and the French behind the MAGINOT LINE spent an inactive winter, content with blockading Germany, by sea.

From Norway to Moscow. The inactive period ended with the surprise invasion (April 9, 1940) of Denmark and Norway by the Germans. Denmark offered no resistance; Norway was conquered by June 9. On May 10, German forces overran Luxembourg and invaded the Netherlands and Belgium; on May 13 they outflanked the Maginot Line. Their armored columns raced to the English Channel and cut off Flanders, and the Allied forces were evacuated from DUNKIRK (May 26-June 4). General WEYGAND had replaced General GAMELIN as supreme Allied commander, but was unable to stop the Allied debacle in the "battle of France." On June 22, France signed an armistice with Germany, followed by an armistice with Italy, which had entered the war on June 10. The VICHY government was set up in France under Marshal PÉTAIN. Britain, the only remaining Allied power, resisted, under the inspiring leadership of Winston CHURCHILL, the German attempt to bomb it into submission. While Germany received its first setback in the BATTLE OF BRITAIN, fought entirely in the air, the theater of war was widened by the Italian attack on the British in Africa (see NORTH AFRICA, CAMPAIGNS IN), by the Italian invasion (Oct. 28, 1940) of Greece, and by the German submarine warfare in the Atlantic Ocean. Hungary, Rumania, and Bulgaria joined the Axis late in 1940, but Yugoslavia resisted German pressure, and on April 6, 1941, Germany launched an attack on Yugoslavia and Greece and won a rapid victory. In May, Crete fell. Great Britain gained a new ally on June 22, 1941, when Germany (joined by Italy, Rumania, Hungary, Slovakia, and Finland), invaded the Soviet Union. By December, 1941, German mechanized divisions had destroyed a large part of the Soviet army and had overrun much of European Russia. However, the Russian winter halted the German sweep, and the drive on Moscow was foiled by a Soviet counteroffensive.

The War Comes to the United States. Though determined to maintain its neutrality, the United States was gradually drawn closer to the war by the force of events. To save Britain from collapse the Congress voted LEND-LEASE aid early in 1941; in Aug., 1941, President Franklin Delano ROOSEVELT met Churchill on the high seas, and together they formulated the ATLANTIC CHARTER as a general statement of democratic aims. To protect its shipping from attacks by German submarines, the United States occupied (April, 1941) Greenland and later shared in the occupation of Iceland; despite repeated warnings the attacks continued. While relations with Germany thus became increasingly strained, the aggressive acts of Japan in China, Indo-China, and Thailand provoked protests from the United States. Efforts to reach a peaceful settlement were ended on Dec. 7, 1941, when Japan without warning attacked PEARL HARBOR, the Philippines, and Malaya. War was declared (Dec. 8) on Japan by the United States, the British Commonwealth of Nations (except Ireland), and the Netherlands. Within a few days Germany and Italy declared war on the United States. The first phase of the war in the Pacific was disastrous for the Allies. Japan swiftly conquered the Philippines (where strong resistance ended at Corregidor), Malaya, Burma, Indonesia, and many Pacific islands, destroyed an Allied fleet in the Java Sea, and reached, by mid-1942, its furthest points of advance in the Aleutian Islands and New Guinea. Australia became the chief Allied base for the countermoves against Japan, directed by Gen. Douglas MACARTHUR, Admiral NIMITZ, and Admiral HALSEY. The first Allied naval successes against Japan were scored in the battles of Coral Sea and Midway. On land the Allies took the offensive on New Guinea and landed (Aug. 7, 1942) on GUADALCANAL in the Solomon Islands.

The Turning Point. Despite the slightly improved position in the Pacific, the late summer of 1942 was perhaps the darkest period of the war for the Allies. In North Africa, the Axis forces under Field Marshal ROMMEL were sweeping into Egypt; in Russia, they had penetrated the Caucasus and launched a gigantic offensive against Stalingrad (see VOLGOGRAD). In the Atlantic, even to the shores of the United States and in the Gulf of Mexico, German submarines were sinking Allied ships at an unprecedented rate. Yet the Axis war machine showed signs of wear, while the United States was merely beginning to put its potential into motion and while Russia still had huge reserves and was receiving U.S. lend-lease aid through Iran and Murmansk. The first decisive blow, however, was leveled at the Axis by Britain, when General MONTGOMERY routed Rommel at ALAMEIN in

North Africa (Oct., 1942). The next blow was the American invasion of Algeria (Nov. 8, 1942); the Americans and British were joined by Free French forces of General DE GAULLE and by regular French forces that had passed to the Allies after the surrender of Admiral DARLAN. After heavy fighting in Tunisia, Africa was cleared of Axis forces by May 12, 1943. Meantime, in the Soviet Union the stand of Stalingrad and a Russian counteroffensive resulted in the surrender (Feb. 2, 1943) of the German 6th Army and was followed by a nearly uninterrupted Russian offensive under the leadership of Premier STALIN. In the Mediterranean, the Allies followed up their African victory by the conquest of Sicily (July-Aug., 1943) and the invasion of Italy, which surrendered on Sept. 8. However, the German army in Italy fought bloody rearguard actions, and Rome fell (June 4, 1944) only after the battles of MONTE CASSINO and ANZIO. In the Atlantic, the submarine threat was virtually ended by the summer of 1944. Throughout German-occupied Europe, underground forces, largely supplied by the Allies, began to wage war against their oppressors. The Allies, who had signed (Jan. 1, 1942) the UNITED NATIONS declaration, were drawn, militarily, more closely together by the CASABLANCA CONFERENCE, at which they pledged themselves to continue the war until the unconditional surrender of the Axis, and by the MOSCOW CONFERENCES, the QUEBEC CONFERENCE, the CAIRO CONFERENCE, and the TEHERAN CONFERENCE. The invasion of German-held France was decided upon, and Gen. Dwight D. EISENHOWER was put in charge of the operation.

Allied Victory in Europe. By the beginning of 1944 air warfare had turned overwhelmingly in favor of the Allies, who wrought unprecedented destruction on many German cities and on communications and industries throughout German-held Europe. This air offensive prepared the way for the landing (June 6, 1944) of the Allies in N France (see NORMANDY CAMPAIGN) and a secondary landing (Aug. 15) in S France. After heavy fighting in Normandy, Allied armored divisions raced to the Rhine, clearing most of France and Belgium of German forces by Oct., 1944. The use of V-1 and V-2 rockets by the Germans proved as futile an effort as their counteroffensive in Belgium under General von RUNDSTEDT (see BATTLE OF THE BULGE). On the Eastern Front Soviet armies swept (1944) through the Baltic States, E Poland, Belorussia, and the Ukraine and forced the capitulation of Rumania (Aug. 23), Finland (Sept. 4), and Bulgaria (Sept. 10). Having evacuated the Balkan Peninsula, the Germans resisted in Hungary until Feb., 1945, but Germany itself was pressed. The Russians entered East Prussia and Czechoslovakia (Jan., 1945) and conquered E Germany to the Oder. On March 7 the Western Allies—whose chief commanders in the field were Omar N. BRADLEY and Montgomery—crossed the Rhine after having smashed through the strongly fortified Siegfried Line and overran W Germany. German collapse came after the meeting (April 25) of the Western and Russian armies at Torgau in Saxony, and after Hitler's death amid the ruins of Berlin, which was falling to the Russians under marshals ZHUKOV and KONEV. The unconditional surrender of Germany was signed at Rheims on May 7 and was ratified at Berlin on May 8.

Allied Victory in the Pacific. After the completion of the campaigns in the Solomon Islands (late 1943) and New Guinea (1944), the Allied advance moved inexorably in two lines that converged on Japan through scattered island groups—the Philippines, the Marianas Islands, Okinawa, and Iwo Jima. Japan, with most of its naval units sunk, staggered beneath these blows. At the YALTA CONFERENCE, the USSR secretly promised its aid against Japan, which, however, still refused to surrender after the Allied appeal made at the POTSDAM CONFERENCE in return for territorial concessions. On Aug. 6, 1945, the United States first used the ATOMIC BOMB and devastated HIROSHIMA; on Aug. 9, the second bomb was dropped on NAGASAKI. The USSR had already invaded Manchuria. On Aug. 14, Japan announced its surrender, formally signed aboard the U.S. battleship *Missouri* in Tokyo Bay on Sept. 2.

The Reckoning. Although hostilities came to an end in Sept., 1945, the new world crisis caused by the postwar conflict between the USSR and the United States—the two chief powers to emerge from the war—made settlement difficult. By March, 1950, peace treaties had been signed with Italy, Rumania, Hungary, Bulgaria, and Finland; in 1951, the Allies (but not including the USSR) signed a treaty with Japan, and, in 1955, Austria was restored to sovereignty. Germany, however, remained divided between the Western powers and the USSR. Despite the birth of the UNITED NATIONS, the world remained politically unstable and only slowly recovered from the incalculable physical and moral devastation wrought by the largest and most costly war in mankind's history. Civilians and soldiers had suffered alike in bombings that had wiped out entire cities. Modern methods of warfare, together with the attempt of Germany to exterminate whole racial groups (particularly the JEWS), famines, and epidemics, had brought death to tens of millions and made as many more homeless. The suffering and degradation of the war's victims were of proportions that passed the understanding of those who had been spared. The conventions of warfare had been violated on a large scale (see WAR CRIMES), and the technique of warfare itself was revolutionized by the use of nuclear weapons. Political consequences included the reduction of Britain and France to powers of lesser rank, the emergence of the Common Market, the independence of many former colonial countries in Asia and Africa, and, perhaps most important, the beginning of the COLD WAR between the Western powers and the Communist-bloc nations. There is a vast amount of literature on World War II, particularly official publications and memoirs. Among notable accounts are Dwight D. Eisenhower, *Crusade in Europe* (1948, repr. 1951); Omar H. Bradley, *A Soldier's Story* (1951, repr. 1970); Winston S. Churchill, *The Second World War* (6 vol., 1948–54); Harry S. Truman, *Memoirs* (2 vol., 1955–6); Field Marshal Montgomery, *Memoirs* (1958); Charles de Gaulle, *Complete War Memoirs* (1964, repr. 1967); Douglas MacArthur, *Reminiscences* (1964); Albert Speer, *Inside the Third Reich* (1970). See also H. R. Trevor-Roper, *The Last Days of Hitler* (1956); W. L. Shirer, *The Rise and Fall of the Third Reich* (1960); A. J. P. Taylor, *Origins of the Second World War* (1961, repr. 1963); S. E. Morison, *Two-Ocean War* (1963); A. R. Buchanan, *The United States and World War II* (1964); Alan Bullock, *Hitler: A Study in Tyranny* (rev. ed. 1964); Basil Collier, *The Second World War* (1967, repr. 1969) and *The War in the Far East, 1941–1945* (1969); B. H. Liddell Hart, *History of the Second World War* (1970); Peter Calvocoressi and Guy Wint, *Total War* (1972); Marie Fourcade, *Noah's Ark* (tr. 1974); Henri Michel, *The Second World War* (tr. 1974).

worm, common name for various unrelated invertebrate animals with soft, often long and slender bodies. Members of the phylum PLATYHELMINTHES, or the flatworms, are the most primitive; they are generally small, flat-bodied, and sluggish, and include the free-living PLANARIANS (of the class Turbellaria) as well as the parasitic FLUKES (class Trematoda) and TAPEWORMS (class Cestoda). The nemertines, or RIBBON WORMS (phylum NEMERTINEA), are colorful marine carnivores with an extensible proboscis. The smallest species are only a fraction of an inch (less than 2.5 cm) long, while giants of the group range up to 90 ft (27 m) and are the longest of all invertebrates. Several rather dissimilar classes of worms are grouped together in the phylum ASCHELMINTHES, although some authorities consider each of these groups to be a different phylum. Of these, the largest class is the nematodes, which includes some of the most numerous multicellular animals. Also called roundworms and threadworms, the nematodes include widespread free-living species as well as parasites, such as the HOOKWORM. Other parasitic nematodes include *Filaria,* the cause of filariasis, which may result in ELEPHANTIASIS; *Trichinella,* the cause of TRICHINOSIS; *Ascaris,* an intestinal parasite of man, horses, and pigs; the PINWORM, a parasite common in children; the Guinea worm of central Africa and Asia, which burrows into human flesh; and various other species that are agricultural pests. Like the nematodes, the hairworms, or horsehair worms, are unsegmented, but they are grouped separately in the class Nematophora. The larvae are parasitic, first in the bodies of aquatic insects and then within grasshoppers or beetles. The adult is about 6 in. (15 cm) long and covered with brown chitin, giving it a stiff appearance; since the worms were frequently found in watering troughs, superstition had it that they developed from horsehairs. The remaining classes of Aschelminthes contain species that are either quite small or microscopic. One of these, the freshwater rotifers (class Rotifera), can be observed in great numbers when a drop of pond water is placed under a microscope. The annelid worms (phylum ANNELIDA) have segmented bodies, distinct heads, digestive tubes, circulatory systems, and brains. Appendages on each segment are used for walking or swimming. They include the EARTHWORM, of the class Oligochaeta, the LEECH (class Hirudinea), and the marine annelids of the class Polychaeta. The SEA MOUSE, the clam worm, and the feather duster worm belong to the latter group. The SHIPWORM is a type of clam. The larvae of many insects are popularly called worms. Moth and butterfly larvae can be distinguished from adult animals called worms by the presence of several pairs of fleshy appendages at the rear end of the body (see CATERPILLAR). However, other insect larvae are completely legless, while still others are equipped with six pairs of legs, as in adult insects (see LARVA). Insect larvae known as worms include the ARMYWORM, BAGWORM, CUTWORM, and INCHWORM.

worm lizard, partially or entirely limbless burrowing lizard of the family Amphisbaenidae. All worm lizards lack hind limbs and most species lack forelimbs as well. Except for their size, they are very similar in appearance to earthworms, with cylindrical bodies ringed by shallow grooves. Their eyes and ears are covered by skin. Most are about a foot (30 cm) long. Members of many species remain underground most of their lives, feeding on earthworms, spiders, and insects. Worm lizards are found in tropical and warm temperate areas of Africa, SW Asia, S Europe, and the Americas. The only species found in the United States is the Florida worm lizard, *Rhineura floridana,* of N and central Florida, which attains a length of 11 in. (28 cm). Worm lizards are classified in the phylum CHORDATA, subphylum Vertebrata, class Reptilia, order Squamata, family Amphisbaenidae.

Worms (vôrms), city (1970 pop. 76,697), Rhineland-Palatinate, S central West Germany, on the Rhine River. It is an industrial city and a leading wine trade center. Manufactures include leather goods, chemicals, and machinery. One of the most venerable historic centers of Europe, Worms was originally a Celtic settlement called Borbetomagus. It was captured and fortified by the Romans under Drusus in 14 B.C. and was known as Civitas Vangionum. It became the capital of the first kingdom of Burgundy in the 5th cent.; much of the *Nibelungenlied* is set in Worms at the Burgundian court. The city was an early episcopal see, and its bishops ruled some territory on the right bank of the Rhine as princes of the Holy Roman Empire until 1803, when the bishopric was secularized and passed to Hesse-Darmstadt. The city itself, however, early escaped episcopal control; in 1156, it was created a free imperial city. Numerous important meetings, including about 100 imperial diets, were held there. The best known of these meetings were the episcopal synod of 1076, which declared Pope Gregory VII deposed; the conference that led in 1122 to the Concordat of Worms; the diet of 1495 (see MAXIMILIAN I, emperor); and the diet of 1521 (see WORMS, DIET OF). The City suffered heavy damage in the Thirty Years War (1618–48). It was annexed by France in 1797 and passed to Hesse-Darmstadt at the Congress of Vienna (1814–15). Worms was occupied (1918–30) by French troops after World War I. The city was more than half destroyed in World War II, but was reconstructed after 1945. Worms had one of the oldest Jewish settlements in Germany. Its Romanesque-Gothic synagogue, founded in 1034, was destroyed by the Nazis in 1938 but was rebuilt after the war and reopened in 1961. Of note is the city's Romanesque cathedral (11th–12th cent.). Near Worms is the Liebfrauenkirche (13th–15th cent.), a church surrounded by vineyards, which gave its name to the area's noted white wine, Liebfraumilch.

Worms, Concordat of, 1122, agreement reached by Pope Calixtus II and Holy Roman Emperor Henry V to put an end to the struggle over INVESTITURE. By its terms the emperor guaranteed free election of bishops and abbots and renounced the right to invest them with ring and staff, the symbols of their spiritual duties. The pope granted Henry the right, in Germany, to be present at elections and to invest those elected with their lay rights and obligations before their consecration. In Burgundy and Italy his right was confined to investiture with those rights and obligations after consecration. The compromise between spiritual and temporal power that this concordat achieved remained essentially the basis of all subsequent concordats.

Worms, Diet of, 1521, most famous of the imperial diets held at Worms, Germany. It was opened in Jan., 1521, by Holy Roman Emperor CHARLES V. After disposing of other business, notably the question of the REICHSREGIMENT, the diet took up the question of the recalcitrant behavior of Martin LUTHER. Charles was induced to summon Luther, who arrived at Worms under a safe-conduct on April 16. At the diet Luther was asked if he would retract his teachings condemned by the pope. After a day's meditation he refused. For a week various theologians argued with him, but he would not retire from his ground. According to tradition Luther ended his defense on April 18 with the words, "Here I stand. I cannot do otherwise. God help me. Amen." Finally, on April 26, the emperor, seeing that the dispute was fruitless, ordered Luther to leave the city. He was formally declared an outlaw in the Edict of Worms (May 25); the lines of the Reformation were thereby hardened.

wormwood, Mediterranean perennial herb or shrubby plant (*Artemisia absinthium*) of the family Compositae (COMPOSITE family), often cultivated in gardens and found as an escape in North America. It has silvery gray, deeply incised leaves and tiny yellow flower heads. Wormwood oil has been utilized since ancient times as an insect repellent, particularly for moths; until recently it was used for intestinal worms and for other medicinal purposes. It was also employed in brewing but is best known for its bitter principle which is an important ingredient of ABSINTHE. Because of its bitter taste the common wormwood has long symbolized any rancor felt by man and is often so represented in the Bible. Other artemisias, some American, are also called wormwood; still others include southernwood (*A. abrotanum*), TARRAGON, silver king artemisia (*A. albula),* old woman, or dusty miller *(A. stelleriana*), Roman wormwood *(A. pontica*), SAGEBRUSH, and the Levant wormseed *(A. cina*), which yields santonin. Wormwood is classified in the division MAGNOLIOPHYTA, class Magnoliopsida, order Asterales, family Compositae.

worsted: see WOOL.

Worth, Charles Frederick: see under FASHION.

Worth, William Jenkins, 1794-1849, American army officer, b. Hudson, N.Y. He served with distinction on the Niagara frontier in the War of 1812 and later became commandant of cadets and instructor of infantry tactics at West Point (1820-28), even though he was not a West Point man. Promoted to colonel in 1838, he was brevetted brigadier general for his service against the Seminole Indians. In the Mexican War, Worth first fought under Gen. Zachary Taylor in the northern campaign that ended with the capture of Monterrey. Later under Gen. Winfield Scott he further distinguished himself in the victorious advance from Veracruz to Mexico City. He was the first to enter Mexico City, receiving the surrender of the capital. In 1848 he was given command of the Dept. of Texas, but his career was cut short by cholera. Although he was an excellent commander in battle, Worth injured his reputation by his ungrateful and insubordinate conduct toward Scott, who had been his benefactor. Fort Worth, Texas, was named for him. See biography by E. S. Wallace (1953).

Worth, village (1970 pop. 11,999), Cook co., NE Ill., a suburb of Chicago; inc. 1914.

Wörther See, lake, Austria: see MARIA WÖRTH.

Worthing (wûr'thĭng), municipal borough (1971 pop. 88,210), West Sussex, S England. It is a seaside resort. Protected by the South Downs, the area has an unusually warm climate. Fruits, vegetables, and flowers are cultivated. There are many prehistoric and Roman ruins (including the largest earthwork in England), relics of which are found in the Worthing museum.

Worthington (wûr'thĭngtən), city (1970 pop. 15,326), Franklin co., central Ohio, a suburb of Columbus; settled 1803, inc. 1835. It is the seat of The Pontifical College Josephinum. Historic buildings in the city include the Orange Johnson House (1816). A railway museum is nearby.

Wotan: see WODEN.

Wotton, Sir Henry, 1568-1639, English poet and diplomat, b. Kent. He was secretary to the earl of Essex and later became a favorite of James I, who knighted him and appointed him ambassador to Venice. He was provost of Eton from 1624 until his death. His poetic fame rests largely on two poems, "Character of a Happy Life" and his tribute to Elizabeth, queen of Bohemia, beginning, "You meaner beauties of the night," which was first printed with music in East's *Sixth Set of Books* (1624). Wotton also wrote a number of prose tracts. His biography (1651) was written by his friend Izaak Walton.

Wotton, William, 1666-1727, English scholar. He is best known for his *Reflections upon Ancient and Modern Learning* (1694), a defense of contemporary learning written in response to an essay by Sir William TEMPLE. Both Wotton and Temple were satirized by Swift in *Battle of the Books* (1704).

Wounded Knee, creek, rising in SW S. Dak. and flowing NW to the White River; site of the last major battle of the INDIAN WARS. After the death of Sitting Bull, a band of Sioux Indians, led by Big Foot, fled into the badlands, where they were captured by the 7th Cavalry on Dec. 28, 1890, and brought to the creek. These Indians, adherents of the GHOST DANCE religion of the prophet WOVOKA, wore "bulletproof" ghost shirts. On Dec. 29, the Indians were ordered disarmed; but when a medicine man threw dust into the air, a warrior pulled a gun and wounded an officer. The U.S. troops opened fire, and within minutes almost 200 men, women, and children were shot. The soldiers later claimed that it was difficult to distinguish the Sioux women from the men.

Wouwerman, Philips (fē'lĭps vou'vərmän), 1619-68, Dutch painter of Haarlem. He is best known for his spirited scenes of battles, encampments, cavalry skirmishes, and hunts. Of these he painted several hundred, of varying excellence but all characterized by brilliant color, vivacity, and excellent composition. Figures and landscape are given almost equal prominence and are skillfully combined. He is represented in many important European galleries. His brothers Pieter Wouwerman (1623-82) and Jan Wouwerman (1629-66) imitated his style, Pieter with considerable success.

Wovoka (wōvō'kə), c.1858-1932, Paiute Indian, prophet of a messianic religion sometimes called the GHOST DANCE religion. Also known as Jack Wilson, he was influenced by his father (a mystic), as well as by the Christian family for whom he worked and the revivalistic Shaker religion popular at the time. Wovoka claimed that during an eclipse of the sun (Jan. 1, 1889) he had had a vision in which God had given him a message—the time was coming when the earth would die and come alive again; all whites would disappear from the earth's surface, and all Indians, living and dead, would be reunited to live a life free from death, disease, and misery. In order to bring this about, however, the Indians would have to follow Wovoka's doctrine of pacifism and practice the sacred dance he taught them. To make his message more convincing, Wovoka proved his supernatural powers by simple tricks, one of which, the supposedly bulletproof ghost shirt, was to play a tragic part in the massacre of the Sioux at WOUNDED KNEE. Before long his stature grew from Paiute prophet to Indian Messiah, and his religion, which spread rapidly through the Western Indians, took on warlike overtones never intended by its founder. The great popularity of Wovoka's ghost dance waned, however, as his prophecy failed to materialize and as his Indian converts were forced onto reservations. See biography by Paul Bailey (1957, repr. 1970).

WPA: see WORK PROJECTS ADMINISTRATION.

WPB: see WAR PRODUCTION BOARD.

Wrangel, Wrangell, or **Vrangel, Baron Ferdinand Petrovich von** (all: răng'gəl, Rus. fyĕrdyĕnänt' pĕtrō'vĭch vôn vrän'gĭl), 1796-1870, Russian naval officer, arctic explorer, and government administrator. He traveled around the world (1817-19) before he commanded a Russian naval expedition (1820-24) that explored the arctic regions. He led another Russian expedition around the world (1825-27) and was the first governor of the Russian colonies in Alaska (1829-35), director of the Russian-American company (1840-49), and minister of the navy (1855-57). He was highly critical of the sale of Alaska to the United States in 1867. Several islands are named for him. His diaries of his arctic expedition have been translated into German and English.

Wrangel, Friedrich Heinrich Ernst, Graf von (frē'drĭkh hīn'rĭkh ĕrnst gräf fən vräng'əl), 1784-1877, Prussian field marshal. He fought in the Napoleonic Wars. In 1848 he commanded the German federal army sent to aid the primarily German provinces of Schleswig and Holstein in their revolt against Danish rule. In the same year he suppressed the revolutionists in Berlin. He commanded the Austro-Prussian troops in the first months of the war with Denmark in 1864.

Wrangel, Karl Gustaf (kärl go͝o'stäf vrän'gĕl), 1613-76, Swedish general and admiral. After distinguishing himself in land campaigns in the THIRTY YEARS WAR, he succeeded to command of the fleet at Fehmarn and defeated (1644) the Danes. In 1646 he became field marshal, succeeded Torstensson as commander in chief of the Swedish army in Germany, and overran Bavaria with the French general, Turenne. Wrangel was created count of Salmis and Solvesborg in 1651. During the reign of CHARLES X he commanded in the Polish wars as admiral and general and successfully invaded (1657-58) Denmark. After the peace of 1660, he was presented with honors and was made regent of Charles XI.

Wrangel, Baron Piotr Nikolayevich (pyô'tər nyĭkəlī'əvĭch vrän'gĭl), 1878-1928, Russian general. After serving in the Russo-Japanese War (1904-5) and in World War I, he joined (late 1917) the anti-Bolshevik armies in S Russia. After the rout in early 1920 of the Denikin forces, Wrangel succeeded Denikin in command and soon whipped the demoralized remains of the White Army into shape. He also tried to win popular support with a program for land reform. He was successful for a while on the Crimean front, but the Russian armistice with Poland, with which it was at war from April to Oct., 1920, enabled the Communists to concentrate larger forces against him. Wrangel was forced back into the Crimea, and in Nov., 1920, he had to evacuate his forces to Constantinople. The Russian civil war thus came to an end. Wrangel died in exile at Brussels. See his memoirs (1924, Am. ed. 1957).

Wrangel Island or **Wrangell Island** (răng'gəl), Rus. *Ostrov Vrangelya,* island, 1,740 sq mi (4,507 sq km), in the Arctic Ocean, between the East Siberian Sea and the Chukchi Sea, off NE USSR. It is separated from the mainland by Long Strait. Generally barren, frozen, and rocky, it has an arctic station and a permanent settlement. The island is a breeding ground for polar bears, polar foxes, seals, and lemmings. During the summer it is visited by numerous varieties of birds. The island was sought by Russian Baron Ferdinand von Wrangel during his arctic expedition of 1820-24; he had heard of it from Siberian natives, but he did not succeed in finding it. It was finally discovered by Thomas Long, captain of an American whaling ship, who named it for Wrangel. Later George W. De Long, an American explorer, discovered that it was a small island and not a part of the mainland, as at first believed. In 1911 a group of Russians made a landing on the island, and in 1921 Vilhjalmur Stefansson, the Canadian explorer, sent a small party to Wrangel with a view to claiming it for Great Britain. In 1926 the Soviet government established the first permanent colony there, ousting the few of Stefansson's Eskimo settlers who had remained. The Soviet freighter *Chelyuskin*, trying to discover (1933) whether an ordinary cargo ship could navigate the Northeast Passage, was crushed in the ice off Wrangel Island. The party was marooned on the island but was later rescued.

Wrangell, Baron Ferdinand Petrovich von: see WRANGEL, BARON FERDINAND PETROVICH VON.

Wrangell Island (răng'gəl), 30 mi (48 km) long and 5 to 14 mi (8.1-22.5 km) wide, off SE Alaska in the Alexander Archipelago, south of the mouth of the Stikine River. It was occupied in 1834 by Russians, who named it for Baron Ferdinand von Wrangel. The city of Wrangell, on the northern coast, grew around a fort built to prevent encroachment by the Hudson's Bay Company traders. From 1867 to 1877 it was a U.S. military post, and later it became an outfitting point for hunters and explorers as well as for miners using the Stikine River route to the Yukon. Lumbering, fishing, mining, and fur farming are now pursued.

Wrangell Mountains, S Alaska, extending c.100 mi (160 km) SE from the Copper River to the Canadian border, where they meet the St. Elias Mts. Mt. Blackburn (16,523 ft/5,036 m) is the highest peak. There is a cosmic radiation observatory on Mt. Wrangell (14,006 ft/4,269 m).

wrasse (răs), common name for a member of the large family Labridae, brilliantly colored fishes found among rocks and kelp in tropical seas. Wrasses, related to the parrotfishes, feed on mollusks and are equipped with shell-crushing teeth in both the mouth and throat. The lips are fleshy, and some wrasses are able to extend the mouth and jaws forward to engulf their prey. Well known on the N Atlantic coast are the cunners (about 1 ft/30 cm long), which are useful scavengers. The tautog, or blackfish, an important food fish of the S New England coast, is a sluggish fish that hibernates in cold weather. Southern wrasses, found off the West Indies and Florida coasts, include the hogfish, a large, showy red fish with a piglike snout, and the puddingwife. The California redfish, or Pacific sheepshead, is a large wrasse reaching up to 3 ft (91 cm) and 30 lb (13.5 kg) and most abundant S of Monterey. The female is a dull red and the male is boldly patterned in crimson and black. The flesh of wrasses is sometimes poisonous to human consumers (see CIGUATERA). Most wrasses belong to the genus *Labrus.* Wrasses are classified in the phylum CHORDATA, subphylum Vertebrata, class Osteichthyes, order Perciformes, family Labridae.

Wrath, Cape, promontory, Sutherlandshire, northwestern extremity of the Scottish mainland. The headland, 368 ft (112 m) high, has a lighthouse.

Wray, John: see RAY, JOHN.

wreck, in law, goods washed ashore as distinguished from goods found at sea, i.e., FLOTSAM, JETSAM, AND LIGAN. In England the king had title to wreck not claimed by the owner within a year and a day. English law limited wreck to goods washed up on the seashore or on the shores of tidal rivers. In the United States, however, the term is also applied to goods washed upon the shores of inland lakes and rivers. U.S. law respecting the title to wreck varies. Subject always to a prompt claim by the owner, title is variously in the holder of the land on which the goods come to rest, in the state, or in the finder. See SALVAGE; SHIPWRECK.

Wrede, Karl Philipp von (kärl fē'lĭp fən vrā'də), 1767–1838, Bavarian general. He helped reorganize the Bavarian army, commanded part of the Bavarian troops fighting with the French against Austria in 1805 in the Napoleonic Wars, and led the Bavarian corps that aided Napoleon's victory at Wagram (1809). Just before the battle of Leipzig (1813) he negotiated the Treaty of Ried between Austria and Bavaria and fought with the allies against Napoleon. Created (1814) prince and field marshal, Wrede represented Bavaria at the Congress of Vienna.

Wren, Sir Christopher, 1632–1723, English architect. He was professor of astronomy at Gresham College, London, from 1657 to 1661, when he became Savilian professor of astronomy at Oxford. Though now known chiefly as an architect, Wren was a celebrated mathematician in his time. In 1665 he spent six months in Paris studying architecture. After the great fire of 1666 he prepared a masterly plan for the reconstruction of London, never executed. He designed, however, many new buildings, the greatest being SAINT PAUL'S CATHEDRAL. From 1670 to 1711 he executed 52 London churches, most of which still stand, notable for their varied and original designs and for their fine spires. They include St. Stephen, Walbrook; St. Martin, Ludgate; St. Bride, Fleet Street; and St. Mary-le-Bow, the latter manifesting the type of spire in receding stages generally associated with Wren's name. Among his numerous secular works are the Sheldonian Theatre and Queen's College library, both at Oxford; the library of Trinity College, Cambridge; the garden facade of Hampton Court Palace; Chelsea Hospital; portions of Greenwich Hospital; and the buildings of the Temple, London. Wren also built residences in London and in the country, and these, as well as his public works, received the stamp of his distinguished style. His buildings exhibit a remarkable elegance, order, clarity, and dignity. His influence was considerable on church architecture in England and abroad. In 1675, Wren was knighted. He was buried in the crypt of St. Paul's. See studies by Geoffrey Webb (1937), E. F. Sekler (1956), Viktor Fürst (1956), J. N. Summerson (new ed. 1965), and Margaret Whinney (1972).

wren, small, plump perching songbird of the family Troglodytidae. There are about 60 wren species, and all except one are restricted to the New World. The plumage is usually brown or reddish above and white, gray, or buff, often streaked, below. Wrens are similar to sparrows but have longer, slender bills and usually perch with their tails cocked straight up. They are valuable insect destroyers. Among the best singers are the canyon, Carolina, and winter wrens. Most wrens nest in natural holes and cavities; house wrens, which range over most of the United States and S Canada, will nest in boxes built for them and in crannies about dwellings. Also found in North America are the cactus, rock, and marsh wrens. The common European wren is a winter wren. Wrens are classified in the phylum CHORDATA, subphylum Vertebrata, class Aves, order Passeriformes.

wrentit: see BABBLER.

wrestling, sport in which two unarmed opponents grapple with one another. The object is to secure a fall, i.e., to pin the opponent's shoulders to the floor, through the use of body grips, strength, and adroitness. One of the most primitive and universal sports, wrestling probably was known to prehistoric man. In ancient Greece wrestlers were rated second only to discus throwers as popular Olympic heroes. The Greeks practiced two forms of wrestling—upright and ground. Wrestling also was included in the PENTATHLON and the pancratium (combined with boxing); the most famous Greek wrestler was MILO of Crotona. Homer's account of the match between Ajax and Ulysses (*Iliad*, XXIII) is one of the world's greatest wrestling stories. Wrestling tournaments were held in medieval Europe, and the sport has remained popular throughout history. Distinctly different styles of wrestling exist today. Greco-Roman wrestling, most popular in continental Europe, permits no tripping and no holds below the waist, and takes place mostly on the ground. It has no relation to classical wrestling, despite its name, but derives from French wrestling schools. Freestyle wrestling is most popular in the United States, Great Britain, and other parts of the world. This form permits tackling, tripping, leg holds, and other rough features and is a legitimate descendant of ancient Greek wrestling. Two different wrestling styles are popular in Japan—sumo and jujitsu. Sumo is quasi-religious in nature and involves much ritual. Most of its participants weigh 300 to 400 lb (135–180 kg). The earliest organized wrestling in the United States was in Greco-Roman style. Freestyle wrestling developed rapidly in popularity among professional wrestlers, but by the end of the 1930s professional wrestling had deteriorated into exhibitions of feigned competition and histrionic performances rather than legitimate athletic contests. Amateur wrestling, however, has maintained excellent standards. Olympic (initiated 1896) and annual world championships decide international titles in Greco-Roman and freestyle wrestling, while in the United States the Amateur Athletic Union and National Collegiate Athletic Association hold competitions annually. In amateur wrestling contestants are classified by weight. The contest itself is conducted on a mat 24 ft (7.32 m) square with a circle 10 ft (3.05 m) in diameter drawn in the center. Three periods of 3 min each compose a match. A fall (pinning both shoulders to the mat for 2 sec) ends the match. Points are scored during the match for certain maneuvers, and the highest accumulated total wins if there is no fall. See D. N. Camaione, *Wrestling Methods* (1968); Clayton Thompson, *Introduction to Wrestling* (1970).

Wrexham (rĕk'səm), municipal borough (1971 pop. 63,185), Denbighshire, NE Wales. It lies in the coal field of N Wales. Besides mining, Wrexham's industries include engineering and the manufacture of steel, rayon, plastics, and leather goods. There are livestock markets. Since 1946, Wrexham has been a "development area," in which the government has been attempting to stimulate industry. It is the seat of the Roman Catholic bishopric of Menevia, which includes all of Wales except Glamorganshire. St. Giles's Church was rebuilt in 1472 after a fire, and most of the present structure dates from the 16th cent. Elihu Yale is buried in the churchyard. In 1974, Wrexham became part of the new nonmetropolitan county of Clwyd.

Wright, Sir Almroth Edward, 1861–1947, British pathologist. He was professor of pathology (1892–1902) at the Army Medical School, Netley, and professor of experimental pathology, Univ. of London, and principal of the Institute of Pathology and Research (1902–46), St. Mary's Hospital, London. In 1906 he was knighted. An authority on vaccine therapy, he developed a system of antityphoid inoculation and a method of measuring protective substances in human blood (opsonins). His works include *Pathology and Treatment of War Wounds* (1942), *Researches in Clinical Physiology* (1943), and *Studies on Immunization* (2 vol., 1943–44).

Wright, Carroll Davidson, 1840–1909, American statistician, b. Dunbarton, N.H. His varied experience included a term (1872–73) in the Massachusetts senate. As U.S. commissioner of labor he organized the Bureau of Labor Statistics and stimulated objective research on labor problems. From 1902 until his death he was president of Clark College at Worcester, Mass. His books include *The Industrial Evolution of the United States* (1887) and *Battles of Labor* (1906). See James Leiby, *Carroll Wright and Labor Reform: The Origin of Labor Statistics* (1960).

Wright, Elizur (ĭlī'zər), 1804–85, American actuary and antislavery leader, b. near Canaan, Conn., grad. Yale, 1826. He taught (1829–33) mathematics at Western Reserve College. In 1833 he became corresponding secretary of the American Anti-Slavery Society, a post he left (1839) to assume editorship of the *Massachusetts Abolitionist*. While editing (1846–52) the Boston *Weekly Chronotype* he became interested in life insurance reform and began lobbying in the Massachusetts legislature. Through his efforts an act was passed (1858) compelling insurance companies to hold reserve funds to be applied against policies. Two later rulings—the nonforfeiture law of 1861 forbidding a company to appropriate the reserve funds and the legislation (1880) that requires companies to pay in cash the value of lapsed policies—were also directly due to Wright. He served (1858–66) as state supervisor for insurance legislation before taking positions as a private actuary. His vigorous campaigning in this field as well as his development of actuarial tabulations earned him the title "father of life insurance." See biography by P. G. Wright and E. Q. Wright (1937).

Wright, Frances (Fanny Wright), 1795–1852, Scottish-American reformer, later known as Mme Darusmont, b. Dundee, Scotland. After her first tour (1818–20) of the United States she wrote an enthusiastic account of her travels, *Views of Society and Manners in America* (1821). In 1824 she returned to the United States. Influenced by Robert Dale Owen, she founded NASHOBA, a colony for free Negroes, near Memphis, Tenn. After its failure she devoted herself to lecturing and publishing. She advocated equal rights for women, universal education, religious freedom, abolition, and birth control. In 1831 she married William P. Darusmont (or D'Arusmont); the marriage was dissolved in 1835. See biographies by W. R. Waterman (1924) and A. J. G. Perkins and Theresa Wolfson (1939).

Wright, Frank Lloyd, 1869–1959, American architect, b. Richland Center, Wis. After studying civil engineering at the Univ. of Wisconsin, he worked for seven years in the office of Dankmar Adler and Louis H. Sullivan in Chicago. Wright's first independent commission was the Winslow residence (1893). Establishing himself in Oak Park, Ill., he built a series of residences with low horizontal lines and strongly projecting eaves which echoed the rhythms of the surrounding landscape; it was termed his prairie style. The most famous examples are located in Chicago and its suburbs; they include the Willitts house (1900?–1902), Highland Park; the Coonley house (1908), Riverside; and the Robie house (1909), Chicago. From the beginning he practiced radical innovation both as to structure and aesthetics, and many of his methods have since become internationally current. At a time when poured reinforced concrete and steel cantilevers were generally confined to commercial structures, Wright did pioneer work in integrating machine methods and materials into a true architectural expression. He was the first architect in the United States to produce open planning in houses, in a break from the traditional closed volume, and to achieve a fluidity of interior space by his frequent elimination of confining walls between rooms. For the Millard house (1923) at Pasadena, Calif., he worked out a new method, known as textile-block slab construction, consisting of double walls of precast concrete blocks tied together with steel reinforcing rods set into both the vertical and the horizontal joints. The Larkin Office Building (1904; destroyed 1950), Buffalo, and Oak Park Unity Temple (1906), near Chicago, were early monumental works that exerted wide influence. Among other notable works are the Imperial Hotel (1916–22), Tokyo, Japan, which withstood the effects of the 1923 earthquake; the Midway Gardens (1914; destroyed 1923), Chicago; and Wright's own residence "Taliesin" (1911; twice burned and rebuilt) at Spring Green, Wis. Among his later projects were "Taliesin West" (1936–59), Scottsdale, Ariz. (which has continued since his death as a school of architecture under the supervision of his widow); the Johnson administration building (1936–39; research tower, 1950), Racine Wis.; and the Kaufmann house "Falling Water" (1936–37), Bear Run, Pa., which is dramatically cantilevered over a waterfall. After World War II, Wright continued a large and ever-inventive practice until his death. He created dynamic interior spaces with spiral ramps for the V. C. Morris Gift Shop (1948–49), San Francisco, and for the Solomon R. Guggenheim Museum (1946–59), New York City. Other notable later buildings include a Unitarian church (1947), Madison, Wis.; the Price Tower (1955), Bartlesville, Okla.; and Beth Sholom Synagogue (1959), Elkins Park, Pa. He left numerous unrealized projects, including one for a mile-high skyscraper ("The Illinois") for Chicago. Wright's architectural philosophy was expressed in his lectures and writings. Among them are *On Architecture* (1941); *When Democracy Builds* (1945); *Genius and the Mobocracy* (1949), an evaluation of the work of Sullivan; *The Future of Architecture* (1953); *An American Architecture* (1955); and *A Testament* (1957). His influence can be seen in Europe, particularly in the Netherlands. Volumes illustrative of his works were published there—and in France and Germany—as early as 1910. See his autobiography (rev. ed. 1943); biographies by his daughter, Iovanna Lloyd Wright (1962), his wife, Olgivanna Lloyd

Wright (rev. ed. 1970), and R. C. Twombly (1973); studies by V. Scully (1960), P. Blake (rev. ed. 1964), and H. A. Brooks (1972); catalog of his buildings by W. A. Storrer (1974).

Wright, Henry, 1878-1936, American architect and community planner, b. Lawrence, Kansas, studied architecture at the Univ. of Pennsylvania. He was widely recognized as a leader in the movement for better site planning and housing and for the building of better communities. His early professional years were spent in Kansas City, Mo., and in St. Louis, where he took part in the landscaping for the Louisiana Purchase Exposition (1904) and helped organize (1909-10) the St. Louis City Plan Association. He served (1918) as town planner for the Housing Division of the U.S. Emergency Fleet Corporation. Among the housing projects which he helped design were Sunnyside, L.I., and Radburn, N.J. He was consultant to the New York state commission of housing and regional planning. He wrote *Rehousing Urban America* (1935).

Wright, Horatio Gouverneur, 1820-99, Union general in the American Civil War, b. Clinton, Conn., grad. West Point, 1841. Chief engineer of a division at the first battle of Bull Run and of the Port Royal expedition, he led the campaign in Florida in 1862. In May, 1863, he joined the Army of the Potomac as a divisional commander. In the Wilderness Campaign he became major general of volunteers (May, 1864) and commander of the corps that defended (July) Washington, D.C. He later fought under Gen. Philip H. Sheridan in the Shenandoah valley. Wright was promoted to brigadier general and chief of engineers in the regular army in 1879.

Wright, James, 1927–, American poet, b. Ohio. He studied at Kenyon College and the Univ. of Washington and now teaches at the Univ. of Minnesota. The master of an elegant, beautifully controlled style, Wright often writes about the terror of existence and about various moral questions. His works include *The Green Wall* (1957), *Shall We Gather at the River?* (1968), *Collected Poems* (1971), and *Two Citizens* (1973).

Wright, Joseph: see under WRIGHT, PATIENCE L.

Wright, Judith, 1915–, Australian poet. After graduating from the Univ. of Sydney, she worked variously as a clerk, secretary, and statistician. She is regarded as one of the most important Australian writers of the 20th cent. Her lyric poetry is marked by sensitivity of interpretation and absolute mastery of technique. Among her volumes of poetry are *The Moving Image* (1946), *The Gateway* (1953), *City Sunrise* (1964), and *Collected Poems, 1942-1970* (1971). She has also published books for children; biographies of the Australian writers Charles Harpur and Charles Lawson; and the critical work, *Preoccupations in Australian Poetry* (1965).

Wright, Orville, 1871-1948, and **Wilbur Wright,** 1867-1912, American airplane inventors, brothers. Orville was born in Dayton, Ohio, and Wilbur near New Castle, Ind. Their interest in aviation was aroused in the 1890s by the German engineer Otto Lilienthal's glider flights. Both excellent mechanics, the Wrights used the facilities of the bicycle repair shop and factory which they operated (1892-1904) at Dayton for the construction of their early aircraft. By experimenting with movable portions of the wing assembly, rather than shifts in bodily weight, as a means of correcting the aircraft's position in flight they made an important improvement in aircraft design. During this period they drew up valuable tables of wind pressure and drift. Orville designed an engine, which they constructed and attached to their improved glider. On Dec. 17, 1903, they made near Kitty Hawk, N.C., the first controlled, sustained flights in a power-driven AIRPLANE. Of their four flights on that day, the first, made by Orville, lasted 12 sec, and the fourth, by Wilbur, covered 852 ft (259 m) in 59 sec. The brothers continued their experiments at Dayton and built several biplanes. Record-breaking flights in 1908 by Orville in the United States and by Wilbur in France brought them worldwide fame. In 1909 the U.S. government accepted the Wright machine for army use, and the brothers established the Wright Company. The house where Orville was born and the bicycle-shop laboratory have been restored and were moved to Greenfield Village, Mich. See their papers, ed. by M. W. McFarland (2 vol., 1953); bibliography ed. by A. G. Renstrom (1968); C. P. Graves, *The Wright Brothers* (1973).

Wright, Patience Lovell, 1725-86, American sculptor, b. Bordentown, N.J. Her portraits, modeled in wax, were the earliest recorded attempts at sculptural expression in the American colonies. They were highly praised there and in England, where she lived after 1772 and where she modeled likenesses of the king, the queen, and other notables. It is said that in the Revolution she rendered service to the Americans by reporting British plans and preparations. Her full-length likeness of William Pitt was placed in Westminster Abbey. The painter John Hoppner was her son-in-law. A son, **Joseph Wright,** 1756-93, b. Bordentown, N.J., was a portrait painter. He studied under Benjamin West in London, where he painted the prince of Wales (later George IV). Wright worked briefly in Paris, where he knew Franklin, whose letters of recommendation enabled him to obtain a sitting from General and Mrs. Washington on his return to America. He also painted a portrait of John Jay (N.Y. Historical Society) and a group portrait of his own family (Pa. Acad. of the Fine Arts). In 1792 he was made diesinker at the U.S. Mint, Philadelphia; the nation's first official coins and medals are probably Wright's work.

Wright, Richard, 1908-60, American author. A Negro born on a Mississippi plantation, Wright struggled through a difficult childhood and worked to educate himself. In the 1930s he joined the Federal Writers' Project in Chicago and wrote *Uncle Tom's Children* (1938), a collection of four novellas that deal with Southern racial problems. His novel *Native Son* (1940), which many consider Wright's most important work, concerns the victimized Negro fighting against the complicated political and social conditions of Chicago in the 1930s. In 1932, Wright joined the Communist party but later left it in disillusionment. After World War II, Wright moved to Paris. His other works include *Twelve Million Black Voices* (1941), a folk history of the American Negro; *Black Boy* (1945), an autobiography; *The Outsider* (1953) and *The Long Dream* (1958), two novels; *Black Power* (1954), an account of his trip to the African Gold Coast; and *Eight Men* (1961), a collection of stories published posthumously. See biographies by Constance Webb (1968) and Michel Fabre (tr. 1973); studies by Dan McCall (1969), Kenneth Kinnamon (1973), and David Ray and R. M. Farnsworth, ed. (1973).

Wright, Russel, 1905–, American industrial designer, b. Lebanon, Ohio. Wright is notable for introducing modern functional forms in furniture and ceramics. He was largely responsible for the popularity of light-colored wood for furniture and for the use of aluminum as a decorative material. His simple, sturdy forms in china were widely used and imitated. See his *Easier Living* (1951).

Wright, Sewall, 1889–, American geneticist, b. Melrose, Mass., B.S. Lombard College, 1911, M.S. Univ. of Illinois, 1912, D.Sc. Harvard, 1915. From 1915 to 1925 he worked in the bureau of animal industry of the U.S. Dept. of Agriculture. He then taught (1926–54) at the Univ. of Chicago and was professor of genetics (1955-60) at the Univ. of Wisconsin. He has conducted fundamental genetic studies, using the guinea pig as an experimental animal. He is best known for his research on statistical patterns of heredity and evolution.

Wright, Silas, 1795-1847, American political leader, b. Amherst, Mass. He was admitted (1819) to the bar and began practicing law at Canton, N.Y. Becoming involved in state politics, in the 1820s he put up much opposition to the faction headed by De Witt Clinton and soon become one of the leaders of the ALBANY REGENCY. Having served (1824-27) in the state senate, he became (1827) a member of the U.S. House of Representatives and was (1829-33) comptroller of New York state. In the U.S. Senate (1833-44), Wright consistently supported President Andrew Jackson, voted for the annexation of Texas, upheld the Independent Treasury System, and opposed slavery. In 1844 the Democratic convention chose him as its vice presidential candidate, but Wright refused the nomination, ran for governor of New York instead, and defeated Millard FILLMORE in a close contest. Wright vetoed a canal improvement bill, opposed calling the constitutional convention of 1846, and used the militia in the antirent riots. See biography by J. A. Garraty (1949, repr. 1970).

Wright, Wilbur: see WRIGHT, ORVILLE.

Wright, Willard Huntington, pseud. **S. S. Van Dine,** 1888–1939, American art critic and mystery story writer, b. Charlottesville, Va. He attended college in California and later studied art in Paris and Munich. Wright was literary critic for the Los Angeles *Times* and several periodicals and was editor (1912-14) of the *Smart Set.* Before 1923 he wrote nine books, chiefly art criticism, including *Modern Painting* (1915), *The Creative Will* (1916), and *The Future of Painting* (1923). After suffering a breakdown of health, he began writing highly successful detective stories under his pseudonym, modeling the erudite detective, Philo Vance, after himself. The best of these works include *The Benson Murder Case* (1926), *The Canary Murder Case* (1927), and *The Bishop Murder Case* (1929).

Wright Brothers National Memorial: see NATIONAL PARKS AND MONUMENTS (table).

Wright-Patterson Air Force Base, U.S. military installation, 8,023 acres (3,247 hectares), W Ohio, NE of Dayton; est. 1917. One of the largest airport installations in the world, it is the air force's main research and development base, and the headquarters of the Air Force Logistics Command (national center for defense activities). The Aerospace Medical Laboratory and the Air Force Museum are also on the base.

Wriothesley, Henry: see SOUTHAMPTON, HENRY WRIOTHESLEY, 3D EARL OF.

Wriothesley, Thomas: see SOUTHAMPTON, THOMAS WRIOTHESLEY, 1ST EARL OF; SOUTHAMPTON, THOMAS WRIOTHESLEY, 4TH EARL OF.

writ, in law, written order issued in the name of the sovereign or the state in connection with a judicial or an administrative proceeding. Usually the writ requires the person to whom the command is issued to report at a fixed time (the return day) with proof of compliance or a justification for disobedience. Apparently the exchequer was the first royal office in England to issue writs in transacting its business. The common-law courts, which administered justice for the king, found their required authorization to take a case in the original writ issued out of the chancery. The original writ (or original process) was essentially an order to the defendant to satisfy the plaintiff's demand or stand trial. Orders issued in the course of the trial (e.g., to produce a witness) were writs of mesne (middle) process. At the end of the case the successful plaintiff would be awarded a writ of execution (a type of final process) to carry the judgment into effect. The original writs were extremely limited in number. The Statute of Westminster (1285), which permitted the chancery to vary the terms of the existent writs slightly but forbade the issuance of new writs, in time worked great hardships. However, the principle, "no writ, no right" was at least partially overcome by the development of EQUITY as a separate system of justice. By the 18th cent. the use of original writs fell into disuse and cases were initiated by service of a summons. Several of the prerogative writs (writs issued as a matter of sovereign right) still survive, notably HABEAS CORPUS and MANDAMUS. The term *writ* usually is not applied to other types of compulsory process in current use.

writing, the visible recording of LANGUAGE peculiar to the human species. Writing enables the transmission of ideas over vast distances of time and space and is a prerequisite of complex civilization. Where, and by whom writing was first developed remains unknown, but scholars place the beginning of writing at 6,000 B.C. The norm of writing is phonemic; i.e., it attempts to symbolize all significant sounds of the language and no others (see PHONETICS). When the goal is established as one letter for one phoneme (and vice versa), the result is a complete ALPHABET. Few alphabets attain this phonemic ideal, but some ancient ones (e.g., Sanskrit) and some modern new ones (e.g., Finnish) have been very successful. The contemporary important writing not of alphabetic type is that in Chinese characters, in which thousands of symbols are used, each representing a word or concept, and Japanese, where each character represents a syllable. The Chinese system is so distant from the language that the same characters are used in writing mutually unintelligible dialects, e.g., Cantonese and Mandarin. In some languages, as in English and French, the modern freezing of spelling has removed the writing more and more from pronunciation and has resulted in the need to teach spelling and the growth of fallacies like the "silent" letter (a letter is really either the symbol of a sound or it is unnecessary). Writing was developed independently in Egypt (see HIEROGLYPHIC), Mesopotamia (see CUNEIFORM), China, and among the MAYA in Central America. There are some areas where the question as to whether writing was adopted or independently developed is in doubt, as at Easter Island. Ancient writing, at first pictographic in nature, is best known from stone and clay INSCRIPTIONS, but the use of perishable materials, mainly palm leaf, papyrus, and paper, began in ancient times. See ACCENT; CALLIGRAPHY; PUNCTUATION; PALEOGRAPHY. See Ignace J. Gelb, *The Study of Writing* (rev. ed. 1963); J. Hambleton Ober, *Writing: Man's Great Invention* (1965); Oscar Ogg, *The 26 Letters* (rev. ed. 1971).

Wrocław (vrôts'läf), Ger. *Breslau,* city (1970 pop. 523,318), capital of Wrocław prov., SW Poland, on the Oder (Odra) River. A railway center and river port, the city is also an industrial center with manufactures of machinery, iron goods, textiles, railroad equipment, and food products. Wrocław probably was a Slavic settlement when it was made (c.1000) an episcopal see subordinate to the archbishop of Gniezno. It became (1163) the capital of the duchy of Silesia, ruled by a branch of the Polish PIAST dynasty. Sacked by the Mongols in 1241, the city was rebuilt by German settlers and developed as a trade center. Passing (1335) to Bohemia, it became a member (1368–1474) of the Hanseatic League. It was ceded to the Hapsburgs in 1526 and to Prussia in 1742. The city grew considerably in the 19th cent., both in commercial and industrial importance, and was the site of two large semiannual trade fairs. Its university was founded in 1811, when it absorbed the university formerly at Frankfurt-an-der-Oder. Wrocław was badly damaged during a Soviet siege in World War II. After 1945 the German inhabitants were expelled and replaced by Poles. Historic buildings include a 13th-century cathedral, several Gothic churches, and a Gothic town hall that houses a historical museum.

Wrong, George MacKinnon, 1860–1948, Canadian historian. He was professor of history at the Univ. of Toronto from 1894 until his retirement in 1927. He was the author of many works on early colonial American and Canadian history, including *The Conquest of New France* (1910), *The Fall of Canada* (1914), *Washington and His Comrades in Arms* (1921), *The Rise and Fall of New France* (2 vol., 1928), and *Canada and the American Revolution* (1935). With H. H. Langton he edited *Chronicles of Canada* (32 vol., 1914–16).

wrought iron: see IRON.

wryneck, common name for a primitive, unspecialized bird of the genus *Jynx.* The name is said to derive from their habit of twisting their necks when disturbed. Unlike other members of the family Picidae, which includes the WOODPECKERS and piculets, wrynecks neither climb nor drill, but rather perch horizontally and feed aground. Their bills are weaker and more rounded than those of true woodpeckers, and their long tongues are smooth, lacking the barbs and bristles of the other members of the group. They are thus thought to be ancestral to the more specialized members of the family. Two species of wrynecks are recognized: the migratory Eurasian wryneck (*J. torquilla*), and the tropical African wryneck (*J. ruficollis*). Both are solitary birds with soft, cryptically mottled plumage of grays, blacks, and browns. They feed on a number of insects but especially prefer ants. Like the other members of the family, they nest in unlined tree holes, where they lay their glossy, pure white eggs. The young are blind and featherless at birth. Wrynecks are classified in the phylum CHORDATA, subphylum Vertebrata, class Aves, order Piciformes, family Picidae.

Wu-ch'ang or **Wuchang** (both: wōō-chäng), former city, since 1950 part of WU-HAN, E Hupeh prov., China, on the right bank of the Yangtze River at the mouth of the Han. It is an administrative and cultural center, with diverse industries. The oldest of the three Wu-han cities, it dates from the Han dynasty (200 B.C.–A.D. 200). The first outbreak of the Revolution of 1911, which led to the formation of the Chinese republic, occurred there on Oct. 10. The day is celebrated as the Double Tenth, the tenth day of the tenth month. The city's numerous institutions of higher learning include Wu-han Univ.

Wu-chou (wōō-jō), city (1970 est. pop. 150,000), E Kwangsi Chuang Autonomous Region, S China, a port on the Hsi River at the mouth of the Kwei River. It is an important trade and shipping center on the Kwangsi-Kwangtung border. Industries include sugar-refining, food-processing, and the manufacture of chemicals and wood products. A former treaty port, it was the site of a major U.S. air force base in World War II.

Wu-han or **Wuhan** (both: wōō-hän), city (1970 est. pop. 4,250,000), capital of Hupeh prov., central China, at the junction of the Han and Yangtze rivers. The great industrial, commercial, and transportation center of central China, Wu-han comprises (since 1950) the former cities of HAN-K'OU, HAN-YANG, and WU-CH'ANG. Situated in the heart of China, virtually equidistant from Peking, Shanghai, Canton, and Ch'eng-tu, it is an air, river, and rail hub dominating the middle Yangtze plain; China's main north-south railroad runs through the city. The Yangtze is there spanned by a mile-long bridge that accommodates both trains and motor vehicles. The busy port on the Yangtze, although about 600 mi (970 km) from the sea, handles large oceangoing vessels. Wu-han is one of the most important industrial centers in China; it has the country's largest integrated iron-steel complex. Also in the city are railroad shops, automotive works, textile mills (Wu-han has the country's largest cotton mill), food-processing establishments, and plants making heavy machinery, glass, cement, fertilizer, pharmaceuticals, and paper products. The many institutions of higher learning include Hupeh Univ., Wu-han Univ., and a medical college. A bridge across the Han River links Hank'ou and Han-yang.

Wu-hsi or **Wusih** (both:wōō-shē), city (1970 est. pop. 900,000), S Kiangsu prov., China, on the Grand Canal and the north bank of T'ai lake. It is a silk-producing center. Foods (especially grains) are processed, and machine tools, paper products, fertilizer, and motor vehicles are also made. Wu-hsi has long been famous for its little figurines of opera and drama characters, still being produced today. A small walled city in the early 19th cent., Wu-hsi rapidly replaced Su-chou as the economic center of the T'ai lake basin. It is on a railroad connecting Shanghai with much of N China. The city's name, which is translated as "without tin," refers to the tin mines in the area that were exhausted during the Han dynasty.

Wuhsien: see SU-CHOU, China.

Wu-hu or **Wuhu** (both: wōō-hōō), city (1970 est. pop. 300,000), E central Anhwei prov., China. It is a deepwater port on the Yangtze River, linked by rail with Nanking and Shanghai. It is a commercial center, a major rice market, and the distribution and processing point for the agricultural products of the region.

Wulfila: see ULFILAS.

Wulfstan, d. 1023, English churchman, archbishop of York (1003–1023) and bishop of Worcester, whose Latin name was Lupus. He is buried at Ely. Homilies are attributed to him, but most of them are doubtful; from them as from those of Ælfric written for Wulfstan, many details of English law were derived. A homily on the millennium in English alliterative prose, styled *Lupi sermo ad Anglos* [Wulfstan's address to the English], is usually ascribed to him.

Wu-lu-mu-ch'i (wōō-lōō-mōō-chē) or **Urumchi** (ōōrōōm'chē), city (1970 est. pop. 500,000), capital of Sinkiang Uigur Autonomous Region, NW China, in the Dzungarian basin. Wu-lu-mu-ch'i is an administrative and commercial center at the junction of several caravan routes from the USSR, Lan-chou (Kansu prov.), and Kashgar. Since 1963 it has been linked to the Chinese rail network via Lan-chou. The main industrial center of Sinkiang, Wu-lu-mu-ch'i has iron and steel works, tanneries, cotton mills, food-processing establishments, and plants manufacturing motor vehicles, agricultural machinery, chemicals, machine tools, and cement. Coal, tin, and silver mines are nearby. The population is mostly Uigur with minorities of Mongols, Chinese, and Kazakhs. Chinese influence began as early as about 122 B.C. when Emperor Wu Ti of the Han dynasty conquered E Sinkiang. Wu-lu-mu-ch'i is the seat of Sinkiang Univ., a medical college, and several technical institutes. The city was officially called Tihwa until 1954.

Wundt, Wilhelm Max (vĭl'hĕlm mäks vōōnt), 1832–1920, German physiologist and psychologist. From 1875 he was professor at Leipzig, where in 1878 he founded the first laboratory for experimental psychology. While his doctrines have been superseded, his experimental method remains a permanent contribution. His works include *Elements of Folk Psychology* (1912, tr. 1916), *Introduction to Psychology* (1911, tr. 1912), and *Principles of Physiological Psychology* (1874, tr. 1904).

Wuorinen, Charles (wûr'ĭnən), 1938–, American composer, b. New York City. Wuorinen studied with Jack Beeson, Otto Luening, and Vladimir Ussachevsky at Columbia and taught there from 1964 to 1971. He has also worked as a piano accompanist, a countertenor, and a recording engineer. His works include three symphonies, pieces for electronic media alone and with traditional instruments, and a concerto for electronic violin.

Wupatki National Monument: see NATIONAL PARKS AND MONUMENTS (table).

Wu P'ei-fu (wōō pā'-fōō), 1874–1939, Chinese general and political leader. He had a distinguished military career under the Ch'ing dynasty and was an important figure in the republic. For the most part Wu supported Yüan Shih-k'ai during his presidency. After Yüan's death (1916) Wu, as leader of the Chihli military faction, almost continuously warred with other military leaders, notably Chang Tso-lin, for the control of N China and the Peking government. In 1926 he was defeated by the NORTHERN EXPEDITION armies.

Wupper (vōōp'ər), river, c.65 mi (100 km) long, W central West Germany. It is formed by several headstreams and winds in a tortuous course N and SW past Wuppertal, Remscheid, and Solingen into the Rhine River. Its middle course is heavily industrialized. The river is used to generate power.

Wuppertal (vōōp'ərtäl), city (1970 pop. 418,454), North Rhine-Westphalia, W West Germany, on the Wupper River. It is an industrial center, formed in 1929 by the merger of Barmen, Elberfeld, Vohwinkel, and several smaller towns. Manufactures include textiles, metal goods, chemicals, pharmaceuticals, and paper. Barmen was first mentioned in the 11th cent. and Elberfeld in the 12th cent. Elberfeld pioneered in legislation for poor relief by a system that it adopted in the mid-19th cent. and that was widely imitated (see POOR LAW). As a major production center of ball bearings and chemicals in World War II, the city was heavily damaged by Allied bombing raids. Noteworthy buildings include the city hall (1912–22) and the opera house (1956). There is a museum of the history of clocks and watches.

Wurster, William Wilson, 1895–1973, American architect, b. Stockton, Calif. Wurster is a major designer of town and country dwellings in the roomy and comfortable West Coast aesthetic termed "Bay Region style." His buildings are carefully integrated with the surrounding environment. Wurster taught at Harvard and was dean of the School of Architecture and Planning at Massachusetts Institute of Technology (1944–50) and dean of the Univ. of California Architecture School at Berkeley (1950–59). His major works include the Golden Gateway Redevelopment Project and Ghirardelli Square, both in San Francisco, Cowell College of the Univ. of California at Santa Cruz, and a number of office buildings.

Württemberg (vür'təmbĕrk"), former state, SW Germany. In 1952 it was incorporated into the new state of BADEN-WÜRTTEMBERG. Stuttgart was the capital. The former state bordered on Baden in the northwest, west, and southwest, on Hohenzollern and Switzerland (from which it was separated by the Lake of Constance) in the south, and on Bavaria in the east and northeast. It included the Swabian Jura in the south, part of the Black Forest in the west, and the cities of Ulm, Esslingen, Heilbronn, Tübingen, and Friedrichshafen. The southern part of Württemberg was the core of the medieval duchy of SWABIA; Württemberg N of Stuttgart was part of Franconia. Franconia broke up into numerous fiefs in the 10th cent., and Swabia suffered the same fate in the 13th cent. when the house of Hohenstaufen became extinct. Among the local lords who obtained immediacy under the Holy Roman Empire were the counts of Württemberg, whose original domains, established by the 11th cent., were centered around Esslingen. In the following centuries the counts considerably expanded their territory, but aside from Stuttgart they held no important towns, most of the Swabian cities (e.g., Ulm, Hall, Gmünd, Esslingen, and Rottweil) being independent as free imperial cities. They also acquired (1397) the principality of MONTBÉLIARD in France and several places in Alsace. The various territories were subdivided among the branches of the family, but in 1482 Count Eberhard V declared the indivisibility of the holdings. Württemberg was raised to ducal rank in 1495. In 1519, however, the SWABIAN LEAGUE of cities, fearing the rising power of Württemberg, expelled Duke Ulrich I from his domains, and in 1520 it sold the duchy to the newly elected emperor Charles V. Ulrich, a turbulent individual, never ceased in his attempts to recover his lands. In 1524 he helped the rebelling peasants in the great PEASANTS' WAR, and in 1525 he invaded Württemberg with an army of Swiss mercenaries. The Swiss cantons, however, soon summoned their troops home, and Ulrich had to flee again. A Protestant convert, Ulrich secured (1534) the help of Philip of Hesse, a leading defender of the Reformation, and, through Philip, of Francis I of France; at the same time the peasants of Württemberg were rising against the unpopular government of King (later Emperor) Ferdinand I. At the battle of Lauffen (1534), Ulrich and Philip routed Ferdinand's troops. Ferdinand was obliged to restore Württemberg to Ulrich, although nominally Ulrich was to hold the duchy as a fief from Austria. Immediacy under the empire was restored only in 1599. With Ulrich's return, Lutheranism was introduced. However, large parts of S Württemberg remained in the hands of the house of Hapsburg and of a number of powerful abbeys; these territories were incorporated into Württemberg only later. As a result, a large minority of the present population is Roman Catholic. Württemberg was repeatedly the scene of fighting in the wars of the 17th and 18th cent. Duke Frederick II (1754–1816), through his alliance with Napoleon I, obtained the rank of elector in 1803 and became king of Württemberg as Frederick I in 1806, after joining the Confederation of the Rhine. Between 1802 and 1810 the territories of Württemberg were more than doubled and reached their final frontiers. Frederick retained both his royal title and his lands at the Congress of Vienna, after having passed (1813) from the French to the Allied camp. WILLIAM I, his successor, granted a liberal constitution in 1819. During the reign (1864–91) of King Charles, Württemberg sided against Prussia in the Austro-Prussian War of 1866, joined Prussia's side in the Franco-Prussian War of 1870–71, and became (1871) a member of the German Empire. Charles's successor, William II, abdicated in 1918, and Württemberg joined (1919) the Weimar Republic. After World War II, N Württemberg was a part of the temporary state of Württemberg-Baden, and S Württemberg was a part of the temporary state of Württemberg-Hohenzollern until the state of Baden-Württemberg was formed in 1952. Württemberg was formerly also spelled Würtemberg and Wirtemberg.

Württemberg-Baden (vür'təmbĕrk-bä'dən), former state, c.6,060 sq mi (15,700 sq km), SW West Germany. Stuttgart was the capital. The state was formed after 1945 and comprised the northern parts of the former states of Baden and Württemberg. In 1952 it became part of BADEN-WÜRTTEMBERG.

Württemberg-Hohenzollern (vür'təmbĕrk"-hō"-əntsôl'ərn), former state, c.4,020 sq mi (10,410 sq km), SW West Germany. Tübingen was the capital. Formed after 1945, the state comprised S Württemberg, the former Prussian province of Hohenzollern, and the former district of Lindau, Bavaria. In 1952 it became part of BADEN-WÜRTTEMBERG.

Wurtz, Charles Adolphe (shärl ädôlf' vürts), 1817–84, French chemist. He was professor at the Sorbonne (1852–75), at the Faculty of Medicine, Paris (1853–75), and at the Faculty of Sciences, Paris (from 1875). Noted for his research in organic chemistry, he discovered methyl and ethyl amines (1849), glycol (1856), and aldol condensation (1872). He developed (1855) a method of synthesizing hydrocarbons by treating alkyl halides with sodium (Wurtz reaction) that was adapted by the German chemist Rudolf Fittig to the preparation of mixed aliphatic and aromatic hydrocarbons (Wurtz-Fittig reaction). Wurtz also invented a bulbed fractionating column known as the Wurtz column. He wrote influential works in support of the atomic theory and on medical and biological chemistry and the noted *Dictionaire de chimie pure et appliquée* (3 vol., 1868–78; supplement, 1880–86).

Würzburg (vürts'bo͝ork), city (1970 pop. 117,147), capital of Lower Franconia, Bavaria, S central West Germany, on the Main River. It is an industrial city and the center of a wine-producing region. Manufactures include printing presses, machine tools, chemicals, textiles, and beer. Würzburg was originally a Celtic settlement and was made an episcopal see by St. Boniface in 741. After the breakup (10th cent.) of the duchy of Franconia, its bishops ruled a vast territory on both sides of the Main as princes of the Holy Roman Empire. In 1168 the bishops assumed the title of dukes of Eastern Franconia, of which they held a major part. During the Peasants' War the bishop of Würzburg temporarily lost (1524–25) his territory to the rebels, but he held out at his fortress of Marienberg against Götz von Berlichingen. Later, the splendor-loving prince-bishops transformed (17th–18th cent.) the city into one of the finest residences of Europe and founded (1582) the Univ. of Würzburg, where the anthropologist and pathologist Rudolf Virchow and the physicist Wilhelm Roentgen taught in the 19th cent. Secularized after the Treaty of Lunéville (1801), Würzburg passed (1803) to Bavaria; was made (1805) a separate electorate in favor of Ferdinand, the dispossessed grand duke of Tuscany; and reverted (1815) to Bavaria. The city was severely damaged during World War II. Noteworthy landmarks include the baroque former episcopal residence (1720–44; designed by B. Neumann); the Romanesque cathedral (11th–13th cent.), containing works by the sculptor Tilman Riemenschneider; the Marienkapelle (1377–1479), a late Gothic chapel; the Old Main Bridge; and Marienberg fortress (the episcopal residence from the mid-13th to the 18th cent.).

Wusih: see WU-HSI, China.

Wu-su or **Wusu** (both: wo͞o-so͞o), town and oasis, N Sinkiang Uigur Autonomous Region, China, in the Dzungarian basin. It is an oil-producing center in the great Karamai oil fields.

Wu-t'ai Shan (wo͞o-tī shän), mountain range, extending c.150 mi (240 km) across NE Shansi and NW Hopeh prov., NE China. The mountains, rising to c.11,500 ft (3,510 m), are sacred to the Mongols and contain lamaseries frequented by pilgrims.

Wu Ti (wo͞o dē), posthumous temple name of the 5th emperor (140 B.C.–87 B.C.) of the HAN dynasty. Wu Ti [Chin.,=martial emperor] ruled directly through a palace secretariat. During his vigorous reign he incorporated the native states of S China into the empire, drove the nomadic Hsiung-nu out of the Ordos region on the northern frontier, and extended Chinese rule to the Tarim basin of Central Asia (modern Sinkiang prov.). Wu Ti was the first Chinese monarch to extend court patronage to CONFUCIANISM, although contemporary Confucian scholars emphasized cosmology and magic rather than ethics.

Wutsin: see CH'ANG-CHOU, China.

Wyandot Indians: see HURON INDIANS.

Wyandotte (wī'ăndŏt), industrial city (1970 pop. 41,061), Wayne co., SE Mich., a suburb of Detroit on the Detroit River; inc. as a city 1867. Salt deposits there supply the city's extensive chemical industry. Other manufactures include automobile parts and barrels. Bessemer steel was first commercially produced in the city in 1864 by W. F. Durfee. A Wyandot Indian village was there in the 19th cent.; of interest is a totem pole depicting Wyandot history.

Wyandotte Cave, one of the largest natural caverns in the United States, S Ind., W of New Albany; discovered in 1798. There are 23 mi (37 km) of passages and several large and beautiful chambers on five levels. Saltpeter was mined there until the middle of the 19th cent.

Wyant, Alexander Helwig (wī'ənt), 1836–92, American landscape painter, b. Tuscarawas co., Ohio, studied in Cincinnati and in Germany. He was influenced by Inness, who became his friend. Wyant achieved distinction for his subtle, delicate treatment of scenes in the Adirondacks and Catskills and of peaceful rural landscapes. He is best represented in the Metropolitan Museum, which has several paintings.

Wyatt, Benjamin Dean: see under WYATT, JAMES.

Wyatt, Sir Francis, 1588–1644, English colonial governor of Virginia. Married to a niece of Sir Edwin SANDYS of the London Company, he went to Virginia as governor in 1621, taking with him the first written constitution for an English colony. In 1622 he had to face a disastrous Indian attack that took the lives of some 350 settlers. Virginia became a royal colony in 1624, but Wyatt, at the crown's request, stayed on as governor until 1626, when Sir George YEARDLEY, whom he had succeeded, resumed the office. He was governor again from 1639 until 1642, when he was replaced by Sir William Berkeley.

Wyatt, James, 1746–1813, English architect. He worked in many styles but is best known as one of the originators of the GOTHIC REVIVAL. Appointed surveyor at Westminster Abbey in 1776, he did cathedral restorations at Salisbury, Durham, and elsewhere and completed (1776–94) the Radcliffe Observatory, Oxford. He designed many residences in various parts of England. Fonthill Abbey, Wiltshire, built for William Beckford, was notable for its huge Gothic tower, which collapsed several times. Wyatt was also known for his interior decoration in the manner of Robert Adam. See studies on James Wyatt by Reginald Turnor (1950) and Antony Dale (1956). His son and pupil, **Benjamin Dean Wyatt,** 1775–1850?, succeeded him as surveyor (1813–27) at Westminster Abbey. He began the rebuilding of Drury Lane Theatre and wrote *Observations on the Design for the Theatre Royal, Drury Lane* (1813).

Wyatt, Sir Thomas, 1503–42, English poet and statesman. He served in various capacities under Henry VIII and was knighted in 1536. It is generally agreed he was the lover of Anne Boleyn before her marriage to the king. Greatly influenced by the works of the Italian love poets, Wyatt produced the first group of sonnets in English, modeled chiefly after Petrarch. The major theme throughout his poems is his ill-treatment at the hands of his mistress. Besides sonnets, he wrote lyrics, rondeaus, satires, and a paraphrase of the penitential psalms. See his collected poems edited by Kenneth Muir (1949). His son, **Sir Thomas Wyatt,** d. 1554, was a famous conspirator. In Jan., 1554, when Queen Mary's intention to marry Philip II of Spain was announced, Wyatt joined a group of gentlemen who were planning an insurrection against the queen. His allies in other parts of the country were arrested or dispersed, but Wyatt raised a small army in Kent. Troops were sent against him at Rochester, but most of them deserted to Wyatt's side. He set out for London and arrived early in February, but defections and the loyalty of Londoners to Queen Mary prevented him from capturing her and taking the city. He surrendered and was hanged as a traitor. It was supposed that Princess Elizabeth was involved, but Wyatt's last statement exonerated her. See study by Edmund K. Chambers (1933, repr. 1965).

Wycherley, William (wĭch'ərlē), 1640?–1716, English dramatist, b. near Shrewsbury. His first comedy, *Love in a Wood* (1671), was a huge success and won him the favor of the duchess of Cleveland, mistress of Charles II. His next play, *The Gentleman Dancing-Master* (1672), was followed by his two masterpieces, *The Country Wife* (1674?) and *The Plain Dealer* (1676). Although he has been considered the most vicious and licentious of the Restoration comic dramatists, his brilliant wit and satire give him a prominent place in the history of English drama. He lost court favor by his marriage (c.1680) to the countess of Drogheda, and after her death he spent several years in prison for debt. With the accession of James II he was released from prison and given a pension. The publication of his *Miscellany Poems* in 1704 led to a friendship with young Pope, who revised many of the elder poet's verses. See his complete plays, ed. by Gerard Weales (1966); biography by Willard Connely (1930, repr. 1969); study by Rose Zimbardo (1965).

Wyclif, Wycliffe, Wickliffe, or **Wiclif, John** (all: wĭk'lĭf), c.1328–1384, English reformer. A Yorkshireman by birth, Wyclif studied and taught theology and philosophy at Oxford. He was later made rector at Fillingham (1361), at Ludgershall (1368), and at Lutterworth (1374). His belief in the doctrine that Christ is man's only overlord and that power should depend on a state of grace made him a champion of the people against the abuses of the church. He early associated himself with the anticlerical party in the nation and in 1374 was sent to Bruges to represent the English crown in negotiations over payment of tribute to the Holy See. From 1377 he made many vigorous attacks in both Latin and English on orthodox church doctrines, especially that of transubstantiation. Through his own preaching in the vernacular at Oxford and London and the itinerant teaching of his "poor priests," he spread the doctrine that the Scriptures are the supreme authority and that the good offices of the church are not requisite to grace. He was condemned as a heretic in 1380 and again in 1382, and his followers were persecuted, but he was not disturbed in his retirement at Lutterworth, where he died in 1384. The Wyclif Bible is a great landmark in the history of the BIBLE and of the English language. This first and literal translation of the Latin Vulgate Bible into English was mainly the work of his followers, notably Nicholas Hereford; the smoother revision of c.1395 was directed by Wyclif's follower John Purvey. In England the Lollards (see LOLLARDRY) formed the link between Wyclif and the Protestant Reformation; on the Continent he was a chief forerunner of the Reformation, through his influence on Jan HUSS, the Bohemian reformer, and through Huss on Martin Luther and the Moravians. See editions of most of his works by the Wyclif Society; biography by H. B. Workman (1926); G. M. Trevelyan, *England in the Age of Wycliffe* (new ed. 1972); K. B. McFarlane, *John Wycliffe and the Beginnings of English Nonconformity* (1953); John Stacey, *John Wyclif and Reform* (1964).

Wye, river, c.130 mi (210 km) long, rising on Plynlimon Mt., W Wales, and flowing generally SE past Builth Wells, Wales, and Hereford and Monmouth, in England, to the estuary of the Severn River. It is noted for its beautiful valley, especially the part that forms the Gloucestershire-Monmouthshire boundary. Reservoirs on the Elan River, a tributary, provide water for Birmingham.

Wyeth, Andrew Newell (wī'əth), 1917–, American painter, b. Chadds Ford, Pa. Wyeth's work has gained enormous popular and critical acclaim since his first one-man show in 1937. He was trained by his father, the noted illustrator N. C. WYETH. The places and people of Chadds Ford and Cushing, Maine, are his principal subjects. Portrayed in a meticulous, naturalistic style, they are so intensely and immediately rendered as to appear surreal. The best-known of Wyeth's paintings, *Christina's World* (1948), is at the Museum of Modern Art, New York City. See Richard Meryman, *The Work of Andrew Wyeth* (1968); W. M. Corn, ed., *The Art of Andrew Wyeth* (1973).

Wyeth, Nathaniel Jarvis, 1802–56, American explorer and trader in the far West, b. Cambridge, Mass. A businessman in Boston, he was fired with a desire to go to Oregon by the eloquence of Hall J. KELLEY. When Kelley's plans for an expedition were long delayed, Wyeth formed one of his own and in 1832 crossed the continent, at the same time sending a ship around Cape Horn. The vessel, carrying all the supplies and some of his party, was never heard from, and after spending the winter at Fort Vancouver Wyeth returned to Boston. In 1834 he outfitted a new expedition, with grandiose plans for establishing fur-trading posts, a salmon fishery, a colony, and other developments. He founded FORT HALL (July, 1834) and built Fort William on the Columbia River; although his ship reached the Columbia and was used in trade, he was unsuccessful in competition with Dr. John McLoughlin of the Hudson's Bay Company. In 1836 he returned to the East, discouraged. His journals and letters have been edited by F. C. Young (1899).

Wyeth, Newell Convers, 1882–1945, American painter and illustrator, b. Needham, Mass., studied with Howard Pyle. Among his many well-known murals are those in the Missouri state capitol and the altar panels for the National Episcopal Cathedral, Washington, D.C. He also illustrated numerous adventure stories, histories, and classics for children. He taught his son, the painter Andrew WYETH. See his letters, ed. by B. J. Wyeth (1971); Douglas Allen and Douglas Allen, Jr., *N. C. Wyeth: The Collected Paintings, Illustrations and Murals* (1973).

Wykeham, William of: see WILLIAM OF WYKEHAM.

Wylie, Elinor (Hoyt), 1885–1928, American poet and novelist, b. Somerville, N.J. She was famous during her life almost as much for her ethereal beauty and personality as for her melodious, sensuous poetry. Her first notable collection of poems, *Nets to Catch the Wind* (1921) was followed by *Black Amour* (1923), *Trivial Breath* (1928), and the posthumously published sonnet sequence, *Angels and Earthly Creatures* (1929). Her highly polished, articulate, and deeply emotional verse shows the influence of the METAPHYSICAL POETS. Her novels, which are delicately wrought and filled with ironic fancy, include *Jennifer Lorn* (1923); *The Venetian Glass Nephew* (1925), *The Orphan Angel* (1926), and *Mr. Hodge and Mr. Hazard* (1928). After an unhappy marriage, she eloped to England with Horace Wylie in 1910; following her first husband's death she married Wylie, and although they were later divorced, she continued to write under the name Elinor Wylie. In 1923 she married William Rose Benét, poet and editor, who edited her collected poems (1932) and collected prose (1933) and wrote a study of her work (1934, 2d ed. 1971). See biography by her sister, Nancy Hoyt (1935); study by T. A. Gray (1969).

Wynants or **Wijnants, Jan** (both: yän vī'nänts), c.1625–84, Dutch landscape painter. A follower of Ruisdael, he worked chiefly in Haarlem. The little figures in his paintings are the work of others, often of his pupil Adriaen van de Velde. He is represented in many European galleries.

Wynkyn de Worde (wĭng'kĭn də wôrd, wûrd), d. 1535, English printer, whose original name was Jan van Wynkyn. He was born at Wörth in Alsace and probably accompanied William CAXTON to England in 1476. He assisted in the work of Caxton at Westminster and after Caxton's death took over his business. His independent work began in 1491 and continued until his death. At first he used only typefaces that Caxton had used, but to these he later added other styles. Wynkyn de Worde printed more than 700 books, including the first English example of music printed from moving type, Higden's *Polychronicon* (1495). See H. R. Plomer, *Wynkyn de Worde and His Contemporaries* (1925).

Wyoming (wīō'mĭng), state (1970 pop. 333,611), 97,914 sq mi (253,597 sq km), W United States, admitted as the 44th state of the Union in 1890. CHEYENNE is the capital and largest city; CASPER and LARAMIE are the second and third largest cities. The state, exactly rectangular in shape, is bounded on the north by Montana, on the east by South Dakota and Nebraska, on the south by Colorado and Utah, and on the west by Utah, Idaho, and Montana. Wyoming is traversed by the Rocky Mts., which angle across the state from the northwest. East of the mountains is the rolling country of the Great Plains, actually a mile-high region covered with grasses, cactus, and sage and interrupted by the upward thrust of mountain ranges. Only in the central section of the state is the sweep of plain unbroken, and across this stretch the wagon trains rolled westward over the Oregon Trail. In the extreme northeast the low, wooded Black Hills give way to eroded badlands extending west to the banks of the Powder River, which wanders through some of the most famous cattle country in the United States. West beyond the Powder is the tall grass country that was the hunting ground of the Crow Indians until the Sioux, following the buffalo, pushed the Crow into the mountains. The Sioux fell in turn before the relentless advance of the white man, and today farms and ranches occupy this fertile and beautiful plains area. In SE Wyoming the higher tablelands are interrupted by the Laramie and Medicine Bow ranges. Across this region travelers to the Pacific coast made their way when the Indian wars of the 1860s endangered treks on the regular Oregon Trail. The railroad followed the wagons and coaches as the Union Pacific laid its tracks along this southerly course. In SW Wyoming is the natural gateway through the Rockies: the broad, grassy South Pass. Immediately north

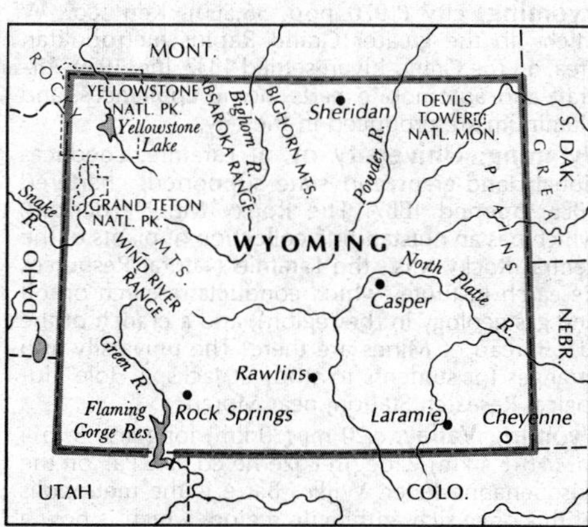

of the pass is the Wind River Range, reaching the highest altitude in the state at Gannett Peak (13,785 ft/4,202 m). Still farther north rise the Gros Ventre and Absaroka ranges, and to the west, near the Idaho line, the glorious Tetons loom above a lake and valley country of incomparable beauty. From the mountain heights snows melt to feed a number of rivers; the Snake begins its long, winding journey into Idaho and on to the Columbia, the Yellowstone travels north and east into the Missouri, and the Green River flows south to join the Colorado. This wealth of surface water supplements the scant rainfall, and water is impounded for irrigation, flood control, and in some cases hydroelectric power. Generous sunshine intensifies the growing season in the high altitudes. Dry farming, producing hay, wheat, and barley, is supplemented by the more diversified yield (especially sugar beets and dry beans) of the irrigated fields. Most of the inhabitants of the state derive their livelihood directly or indirectly from farming or ranching. The most valuable farm commodities, in terms of cash receipts, are cattle, sheep, sugar beets, dairy products, and wool. Sparse grasses over much of the region necessitate a large grazing area for each animal; sheep graze in places unfit for cattle, and both sheep and cattle range by permit in the national forests. Cooperative grazing tracts are on the increase. Horses, a prized essential of ranching, are carefully raised and trained. Oil wells were first drilled in the 1860s, and today petroleum is the state's most important mineral, followed by natural gas, sodium salts, and uranium. In 1970, Wyoming ranked first in the production of sodium carbonate and second in uranium. Low-grade coal is also abundant, and considerable amounts of gold, iron, copper, and various clays are mined. The production of petroleum and petroleum products, centered in Casper, comprises the state's leading industry. Other important manufactures are processed foods and clay, glass, and wood products. Wyoming has millions of acres of forest. The state's natural beauty draws hundreds of thousands of visitors annually, making tourism a major source of revenue. Wyoming has two spectacular national parks: Grand Teton, which embraces the most stunning portion of the Teton Range, and Yellowstone, which occupies the entire northwest corner of the state and is the oldest and largest of all the national parks (see NATIONAL PARKS AND MONUMENTS, table). Its geysers and hot springs are world famous, as is the breathtaking Grand Canyon of the Yellowstone. Wyoming is also prime hunting and fishing country. The nation's largest herds of elk and antelope are there; deer, moose, and bear are plentiful, and the rivers, lakes, and streams teem with fish. Also in the state are Devils Tower and Fossil Butte national monuments and two national recreational areas, Bighorn Canyon and Flaming Gorge. In addition, the multitude of rodeos, annual roundups, frontier celebrations, and dude ranches are drawing an increasingly large number of vacationers every year. Portions of present Wyoming were at one time claimed by Spain, France, and England; the acquisition of the territory by the United States was completed through five major annexations—the Louisiana Purchase in 1803, the Treaty of 1819 with Spain, cession by the republic of Texas in 1836 and partition from Texas after it was annexed in 1845, the Treaty of Guadalupe Hidalgo (1848) after the Mexican War, and the international agreement (1846) with Great Britain concerning the Columbia River country (see OREGON). The early development of Wyoming was closely linked with the fur trade and the great westward migrations. French trappers and explorers may have reached the area in the middle to late 18th cent., but the first authentic accounts of the region were provided by John Colter, who, trapped in the Wyoming mountains for several years, returned to St. Louis in 1810 with fantastic accounts of the steaming geysers and great canyons of the Yellowstone. Colter returned west, and other fur traders made their way into Wyoming. The overland party on its way to found ASTORIA on the Columbia River went through Teton Pass in 1811. The following year Robert Stuart, returning from Astoria, crossed South Pass and followed much of the route that was to be the Oregon Trail. Only the hardiest and most self-sufficient could survive the Indian attacks and the rugged isolation of the country. With the expeditions of William H. Ashley, the MOUNTAIN MEN entered the country, and some of the most famous of those early explorers—Thomas Fitzpatrick, James Bridger, and Jedediah S. Smith—crossed and recrossed the land. Attracted by the fur trade, Capt. B. L. E. de Bonneville organized a sizable expedition, and his were the first wagons to go (1832) through South Pass. The first permanent trading post was Fort William (1834), famous under its later name, Fort Laramie. In 1843, Fort Bridger (now in a state park) was built. The area also aroused the interest of John C. Frémont, who made an expedition in 1842. By the 1840s the route west through Wyoming was in steady use by caravans headed toward Oregon, and fur-trading posts became stations on the Oregon Trail. As the fur trade declined, many former trappers and mountaineers settled along the trail, furnishing horses and other supplies to the migrants and purchasing debilitated stock to be put to pasture and sold the following year. Mormons trekking to Utah (Brigham Young led the first party in 1847) and forty-niners rushing to the gold fields of California joined the many thousands traversing the mountain passes of Wyoming. A number of Mormons settled for a time in W Wyoming. The death of Mormon pioneers in a blizzard (1856) and the thousands of graves along the Oregon Trail give an indication of the toll taken by disease, starvation, Indian attacks, and winter snows. Despite the hardships, telegraph stations (1861) and stagecoach and freight lines were established, and in 1860–61 pony express riders heroically crossed Wyoming on their route between St. Joseph, Missouri, and Sacramento, California. Indian trouble in the early 1860s forced the rerouting of stagecoaches to the south, along the OVERLAND TRAIL. The Indians, displaced from their former homes in the east and west, and waging internecine warfare for control of the rich buffalo ranges, feared encroachment by the whites on their hunting grounds, especially after the opening (1864) of the Bozeman Trail. Treaties were made and broken by both sides, and wars with the Sioux persisted, particularly in the Powder River valley. Meanwhile, S Wyoming was relatively free of Indian attacks, and a gold rush, stimulated by the discoveries at South Pass (1867), brought the first heavy influx of settlers to that region; the flow was increased by the uncovering of vast coal deposits in SW Wyoming. Probably the greatest stimulus to settlement was the completion (1868) of the Wyoming sector of the Union Pacific RR. Towns, including Cheyenne, sprang up beside the tracks, and trade thrived on the demands of the road crews and the new settlers. In 1868 the region became the Territory of Wyoming, with Cheyenne as its capital. Wyoming pioneered in political equality when, in 1869, the first territorial legislature granted the vote to women. The territory continued to advance economically as huge herds of cattle were driven up over the Texas or Long Trail. Indian rebellions had been quelled by the late 1870s. The Arapaho Indians were placed on the Wind River Reservation with their former enemies, the Shoshone Indians, and cattlemen safely moved their herds to grasslands throughout Wyoming. But the days of dangerous living were not over. Cattle rustling became so common that the authorities could not control it, and juries grew fearful of returning just verdicts against criminals. The Wyoming Stock Growers Association was organized in 1873 to protect cattle owners, and members frequently formed vigilante groups to administer their own justice. The struggle reached its height in the Johnson county cattle war of 1892. Lawlessness was also exemplified by the Hole-in-the-Wall gang, which broadened its activities to include bank and train robberies as well as cattle theft. Gradually, vast areas were fenced in and winter pastures were established. The influx of sheep in the late 1890s, however, brought new violence. Cattlemen made frantic efforts to exclude the sheep from close grazing on the precious grasslands. Homesteaders were also unwelcome, and many left when they realized that the country was unsuited for small acreage cultivation. However, population increase was steady, advancing from about 9,000 in 1870 to over 90,000 in 1900. With expanding population came development in other ways: eager frontiersmen rapidly (and somewhat chaotically) established schools, and in 1887 the Univ. of Wyoming was founded. Statehood was achieved in 1890, and in keeping with its frontier ideals, Wyoming adopted a liberal state constitution that included the secret ballot. The Carey Act of 1894, providing for the reclamation and settlement of land, stimulated further agrarian development and, in addition, pointed out the need for conservation and efficient use of water. The establishment of national parks protected the timberlands and extensive grazing areas, and water power was harnessed to furnish electricity for farms and industries. In politics, the progressive movement found numerous adherents in Wyoming; in 1915, after one of the most bitter fights in the state's history, progressive forces triumphed over the railroad and related interests with the establishment of a state utilities commission. A workmen's compensation law was passed in 1915, and in that year also the legislature authorized the Univ. of Wyoming to accept Federal grants for agricultural experiments and demonstrations. Thus were begun the state's outstanding and widespread services for agrarian improvement. In 1924, Wyoming became the first state to elect a woman governor, Nellie Taylor Ross. By then the state ranked fourth in the nation in the production of crude oil, but the valuable finds at TEAPOT DOME are probably remembered best as the symbol of corruption in the administration of President Warren Harding. Under the New Deal, Wyoming was well served by the national soil conservation programs, which benefited dry farmers who had extended operations into semiarid regions and had suffered severely in the drought years beginning in the late 1920s. The cooperative movement in agriculture also gained ground in this period and has since continued to grow. One of the most important events in the state since World War II has been the discovery of uranium. New oil finds have also helped to offset economic losses resulting from a disastrous four-year-long drought in the 1950s. In politics, Wyoming has remained predominantly Republican since World War II. The state still operates under its first constitution, adopted in 1890. The executive branch is headed by a governor elected for a four-year term. Stanley K. Hathaway, a Republican, was elected to his second term in 1970. In 1974, Ed Herschler, a Democrat, was elected governor. Wyoming's bicameral legislature has a senate with 30 members elected for four-year terms and a house of representatives with 61 members elected for two years. The state sends two Senators and one Representative to the U.S. Congress and has three electoral votes. See H. H. Trachsel and R. M. Wade, *The Government and Administration of Wyoming* (1953); A. S. Mercer, *The Banditti of the Plains* (1954); M. H. Scott, *The Oregon Trail Through Wyoming* (1958); T. A. Larson, *History of Wyoming* (1966); *The Historical Encyclopedia of Wyoming*, pub. by the Wyoming Historical Institute (2 vol., 1970); L. M. Woods, *The Wyoming Country Before Statehood* (1971); Federal Writers' Project, *Wyoming: A Guide to Its History, Highways, and People* (1941, repr. 1973).

Wyoming, city (1970 pop. 56,560), Kent co., W Mich., in the greater Grand Rapids metropolitan area, on the Grand River; settled 1832, inc. 1959. Aircraft and automobile parts, home appliances, and aluminum are produced in the city.

Wyoming, University of, at Laramie; coeducational; land-grant and state supported; chartered 1886, opened 1887. The Rocky Mt. Herbarium, which has an outstanding collection of plants of the central Rocky Mts., the Laramie Natural Resources Research Institute (which conducts research on oil and gas geology in the region), and a branch of the U.S Bureau of Mines are there. The university also arranges for students to study at Jackson Hole Biological Research Station, near Moran.

Wyoming Valley, c.20 mi (30 km) long and 3 to 4 mi (4.8-6.4 km) wide, in Luzerne co., NE Pa., on the Susquehanna River. Wilkes-Barre is the metropolis of this once rich anthracite region, which is now a major manufacturing area. The valley was the scene of a long contest between Connecticut and Pennsylvania over conflicting land claims based on 17th-century charters. After the SUSQUEHANNA COMPANY purchased (1754) land there from the Indians at the Albany Congress, a temporary settlement of the region in 1762-63 led to the first permanent settlement in 1769 and the building soon after of Forty Fort. The First Pennamite War (1769-71) between the Connecticut and Pennsylvania settlers ensued, but rapid settlement of the area continued. In 1774, Connecticut set up the town of Westmoreland, from which representatives were sent to the Connecticut legislature. In 1778, during the American Revolution, the Connecticut settlers, under Zebulon Butler, were defeated by John Butler and a party of Tories and Indians; the massacre that followed is described in Thomas Campbell's poem, *Gertrude of Wyoming* (1809). The land quarrel continued and came before the Continental Congress. When a court of arbitration decided in favor of Pennsylvania in 1782, the Connecticut settlers refused to leave, and the Second Pennamite War (1784) ensued. Finally, through the Compromise Act of 1799, the Pennsylvania legislature secured a means of settlement with the Connecticut claimants, and Connecticut yielded to Pennsylvania's claims. The Connecticut settlers, however, contributed greatly to bringing civilization to the valley. They introduced free schools and gave Wyoming Valley a New England air that persisted, making it distinct from the rest of Pennsylvania.

Wyspiański, Stanisław (stänēs'läf vĭspyä'nyəskē), 1869-1907, Polish poet, dramatist, and painter. As a painter Wyspiański created numerous murals, stained-glass windows, and theatrical costumes. He is considered the founder of modern Polish drama; his plays, which are richly imaginative and often allegorical, generally treat the history or contemporary life of Poland, as in *The Legion* (1900), *The Wedding* (1901), *Liberation* (1903), and *November Night* (1904). Other plays are drawn from Greek themes, e.g., *Return of Odysseus* (tr. 1966). Wyspiański's dominant concern was Polish independence and individual freedom.

Wyss, Johann David (yō'hän dä'vĭt vēs), 1743-1818, Swiss author. His *Swiss Family Robinson* (1813), an internationally popular classic for children, relates the adventures of a shipwrecked family. It is based on *Robinson Crusoe*. The first English translation was published (1814) in a small edition by Mary Jane Godwin. Authorship is often wrongly attributed to Wyss's son **Johann R. Wyss,** 1781-1830, who edited the book. He was professor of philosophy at Berne and author of the Swiss national anthem.

Wyszynski, Stefan (stĕ'fän vĭzĭn'skē), 1901-, Polish prelate, cardinal of the Roman Catholic Church. Ordained in 1924, he received a doctorate in sociology and canon law from the Catholic Univ. of Lublin in 1929. He was active in the resistance during World War II. In 1946 he was consecrated bishop of Lublin. Pope Pius XII made Wyszynski archbishop of Gniezno and Warsaw and primate of Poland in 1949 and then a cardinal in 1953. A fierce opponent of the Polish Stalinist government's efforts to limit church influence, he was arrested and imprisoned (1953-56). In 1956, Wyszynski was restored to his functions by the new anti-Stalinist first secretary of the Communist party, Władysław Gomułka. A church-state agreement restoring religious education in state schools followed. Despite periodic setbacks, he subsequently enjoyed a considerable amount of personal and pastoral liberty. In 1962 he served as president of the Second Vatican Council.

Wythe, George (wĭth), 1726-1806, American jurist, signer of the Declaration of Independence, b. Elizabeth City co., Va. Admitted to the bar in 1746, Wythe was a member (1754-55, 1758-68) and clerk (1769-75) of the house of burgesses. An opponent of British colonial policy, he drafted a remonstrance against the Stamp Act (1765) and was a delegate to the Continental Congress (1775-76). Wythe, aided by Thomas Jefferson and Edmund Pendleton, revised (1776) the laws of Virginia, and was influential in getting Virginia to ratify the Constitution. Perhaps his greatest contribution was as professor of law (1779-90) at the College of William and Mary; his teachings influenced many men, including John Marshall, Thomas Jefferson, James Monroe, and Henry Clay. Wythe was one of the greatest early U.S. lawyers. He served as judge (1778-88) in the Virginia chancery court and as sole chancellor (1788-1801).

X

X, 24th letter of the ALPHABET. In English it has no peculiar sound, but stands for the combination *ks* as in *fox*, or *gz* as in *exempt*, or, initially, for the sound of *z* as in *xenia*. In words from Greek, x transliterates the 14th Greek letter, xi, a letter perhaps quite unrelated to the Roman x in form. The formal Greek correspondent of x was chi, hence it is used in phonetics to represent a velar fricative like *ch* in *loch*. As the initial of the name *Christ*, X has become a symbol for it, e.g., in Xmas and in the monogram XP (chi rho). In Roman numerals X stands for 10.

X, Malcolm: see MALCOLM X.

Xánthi or **Xanthe** (both: ksän'thē), city, capital of Xánthi prefecture, NE Greece, in Thrace. Tobacco is produced. The city has a sizeable Muslim minority.

Xanthus (zăn'thəs), ancient city of Lycia, W Asia Minor, in present Turkey. On the Xanthus River, it was besieged and taken by the Persians (c.546 B.C.) and centuries later (c.42 B.C.) by the Romans. Both times the inhabitants destroyed their city before surrendering. Sir Charles Fellows excavated the ruins. Many works of art from Xanthus, such as the archaic sculptured reliefs and the Nereid monument, are now in the British Museum.

Xauen: see CHECHAOUÈN, Morocco.

Xavier, Saint Francis: see FRANCIS XAVIER, SAINT.

Xe, chemical symbol of the element XENON.

Xenakis, Yannis (yăn'ĭs zănä'kĭs), 1922–, Greek composer, b. Brăila, Rumania. Xenakis was a composition pupil of Arthur Honegger, Darius Milhaud, and Olivier Messiaen. He also studied architecture with Le Corbusier. Xenakis has used both Greek folk elements and 12-tone technique in his music. He has also developed a "probabilistic" technique of composition, based on the mathematical probability of the recurrence of notes and rhythms. His works include *Métastasis* (1955) for orchestra, *Pithoprakta* (1957) for strings, and *Achorripsis* (1958) for 21 instruments. In 1958, Xenakis collaborated with Edgar Varèse on the *Poème Electronique*. Xenakis has written several treatises explaining his theories.

Xenia (zē'nēə), city (1970 pop. 25,373), seat of Greene co., SW Ohio; inc. 1814. It is a trade and industrial center in a farm area. Rope, twine, monuments and markers, plastics, potato chips, valves, and hydraulic lifts are among its manufactures. The county historical museum is there. A tornado destroyed about half of the city on April 3, 1974.

Xenocrates (zĭnŏk'rətēz), 396–314 B.C., Greek philosopher, b. Chalcedon, successor of Speusippus as head of the ACADEMY. He was a disciple of Plato, whom he accompanied to Sicily in 361 B.C. His ascetic life and noble character greatly influenced his pupils. He was the first to divide philosophy into dialectic (or logic), physics, and ethics, the latter two being his principal themes. He held that mathematical objects and the Platonic Ideas are both substances, and both identical, causing Aristotle to say of him that he "made ideal and mathematical number the same." His Platonic ethics taught that virtue produces happiness, although external goods can contribute. Only fragments of his work survive.

xenon (zē'nŏn) [Gr.,=strange], gaseous chemical element; symbol Xe; at. no. 54; at. wt. 131.30; m.p. −111.9°C; b.p. −108.1°C; density 5.89 grams per liter at STP; valence usually 0. Xenon is a rare, colorless, odorless, tasteless, chemically unreactive gas. It is one of the INERT GAS elements found in group 0 of the PERIODIC TABLE. Xenon was long considered incapable of chemical reaction, but in 1962 Neil Bartlett, a Canadian chemist, reported synthesis of xenon hexafluoroplatinate, $XePtF_6$, a true compound. Since that time a number of other xenon compounds have been reported. Xenon is present in the atmosphere in extremely low concentration (about one part in 20 million). It is obtained commercially from liquid air. Xenon is used in certain photographic flash lamps, in high-intensity arc lamps for motion picture projection, and in high-pressure arc lamps to produce ultraviolet light. It is used in numerous instruments for radiation detection, e.g., neutron and X-ray counters and bubble chambers. It has found some use in medicine, e.g., as an experimental anesthetic. Naturally occurring xenon is a mixture of 9 stable isotopes; 16 short-lived radioactive isotopes are also known. A mixture of stable and unstable isotopes of xenon is produced in nuclear reactors during neutron fission of uranium; one of these, xenon-135, is a very good neutron absorber and must be removed since it poisons the reaction. Xenon was discovered spectroscopically in 1898 by William Ramsay and M. W. Travers, who obtained it by fractional distillation of an impure sample of krypton.

Xenophanes (zĕnŏf'ənēz), c.570–c.480 B.C., pre-Socratic Greek philosopher of Colophon. Although thought by some to be the founder of the ELEATIC SCHOOL, his thought is only superficially similar to that of PARMENIDES. Xenophanes opposed the anthropomorphic representation of the gods common to the Greeks since Homer and Hesiod. Instead he asserted there is only one god, eternal and immutable but intimately connected with the world. Although interpretations of his thought vary, it was probably a form of pantheism. He was a singer of elegies, a poet, and a satirist who exhorted his hearers to virtue. See G. S. Kirk and J. E. Raven, *The Presocratic Philosophers* (1957).

Xenophon (zĕn'əfən), c.430 B.C.–c.355 B.C., Greek historian, b. Athens. He was one of the well-to-do young disciples of Socrates before leaving Athens to join the Greek force (the Ten Thousand) that was in the service of CYRUS THE YOUNGER of Persia. These troops served Cyrus at the disastrous battle of CUNAXA (401 B.C.). When Cyrus was killed, the Ten Thousand were forced to flee or surrender to the Persians. They retreated by fighting their way through an unknown and hostile land, harried by Tissaphernes. After the Greek generals had been treacherously killed by the Persians, Xenophon was chosen as one of the leaders of the heroic retreat. He tells the story in the most celebrated of his works, the ANABASIS (see tr. by W. H. D. Rouse, 1947). After his return Xenophon, a great admirer of the military, disciplined, and aristocratic life of the Spartans, was in the service of Sparta. He accompanied Agesilaus II on the campaign that ended (394 B.C.) in victory over the Athenians and Thebans at Coronea. The Athenians passed a sentence of banishment on him. Sparta gave him an estate at Scillus in the region of Elis, where he spent years in writing. Among his works other than the *Anabasis* are the *Hellenica*, a continuation of the history of Thucydides to 362 B.C.; works on Socrates (*Memorabilia, Oeconomicus*, a dialogue between Socrates and Critobulus on managing a household and a farm; the *Apology*, on the death of Socrates; and the *Symposium*) presenting a prudent and practical picture of Socrates in contrast to Plato's philosophical portrait; a eulogy of Agesilaus; the *Hieron*, a dialogue on despotism, named after Hiero I of Syracuse; the *Cyropaedia*, a romantic and didactic account of the education of Cyrus the Great; and essays on hunting, horsemanship, the ideal cavalry officer, and the constitutional practices of Sparta. See study by J. K. Anderson (1974); Leo Strauss, *Xenophon's Socratic Discourse* (1970) and *Xenophon's Socrates* (1972).

xerography (zərŏg'rəfē"), method of dry photocopying in which the image is transferred by using the attractive forces of electric charges. A beam of light is made to strike the original material, e.g., a white page with black lettering. Light rays are reflected off the white areas onto a plate over which electric charges have been spread. Charges are erased from the areas struck by the rays. Since no light rays are reflected from the lettering, charges are retained on the plate in areas corresponding to the lettered areas of the original. A plastic powder called toner is introduced that sticks to the charged areas, making them visible. A sheet of paper is then passed between the plate and another charged object that draws the powder from the plate to the paper, forming an image of the original; the powder is fused to the paper with heat. The process has image resolution that is sufficient for printed or written materials, and certain pictorial materials are fairly well reproduced. As the image in this process is a projected one rather than one made by contact printing, it is not difficult to produce a copy that is smaller or larger than the original. In comparison with other photocopying methods, xerography can be said to produce an image of good quality and good long-term stability at fairly low cost. Its chief disadvantage is its complexity and the high cost of the necessary equipment.

Xerxes I (Xerxes the Great) (zûrk'sēz), d. 465 B.C., king of ancient Persia (486–465 B.C.). His name in Old Persian is Khshayarsha, in the Bible AHASUERUS. He was the son of Darius I and Atossa, daughter of Cyrus the Great. After bringing (484 BC.) Egypt once more under Persian rule, Xerxes prepared for an invasion of Greece (see PERSIAN WARS) by constructing a bridge of boats across the Hellespont and cutting a canal through the isthmus of Athos. Setting out from Sardis, he marched through Thrace and Macedonia and, despite the bravery of LEONIDAS and his 300 Spartans, overthrew (480) the Lacedaemonians at THERMOPYLAE. He then occupied and pillaged Athens. In the same year his fleet was destroyed at Salamis. Leaving an army under his general, Mardonius, he retired into Asia. He was slain by the captain of his bodyguard and was succeeded by his son ARTAXERXES I. See Peter Green, *Xerxes at Salamis* (1970).

Xerxes II, d. 424 B.C., king of ancient Persia (424 B.C.), son of Artaxerxes I. After a reign of 45 days he was murdered by his half brother Sogdianus.

Ximenes. For Spaniards thus named, see JIMÉNEZ.

Xingu (zĭng-gōō', Port. shēng-gōō'), river, 1,230 mi (1,979 km) long, rising in central Mato Grosso state, Brazil, and winding north across Pará state into the Amazon River at the head of the Amazon delta. The Xingu, with many rapids and falls, passes through wild, partly unexplored country, and only in its lower course is it navigable. Pioneers have pushed into the area and have settled farms in the forest.

Xochimilco (sōchēmēl'kō), town (1970 pop. 117,083), a suburb of Mexico City. Mainly a commercial and tourist center, it is famous for its canals lined with poplars and flowers (*Xochimilco* is an Indian word meaning "plantation of flowers"). The Indians established soil-covered rafts (*chinampas*) in Lake Xochimilco; the rafts became islands rooted to the lake bottom and continued to supply vegetables and flowers to Mexico City. Boating on the canals is popular among tourists and city residents. A recent decline in the water supply has threatened Xochimilco. Colonial landmarks in the area include a 16th-century church.

X ray, invisible, highly penetrating ELECTROMAGNETIC RADIATION of much shorter wavelength (higher frequency) than visible light. The wavelength range for X rays is from about 10^{-8} m to about 10^{-11} m, or from less than a billionth of an inch to less than a trillionth of an inch; the corresponding frequency range is from about 3×10^{16} Hz to about 3×10^{19} Hz (1 Hz = 1 cps). X rays were discovered in 1895 by W. C. Roentgen, who called them X rays because their nature was at first unknown; they are sometimes also called Roentgen, or Röntgen, rays. Today X rays are commonly produced in a highly evacu-

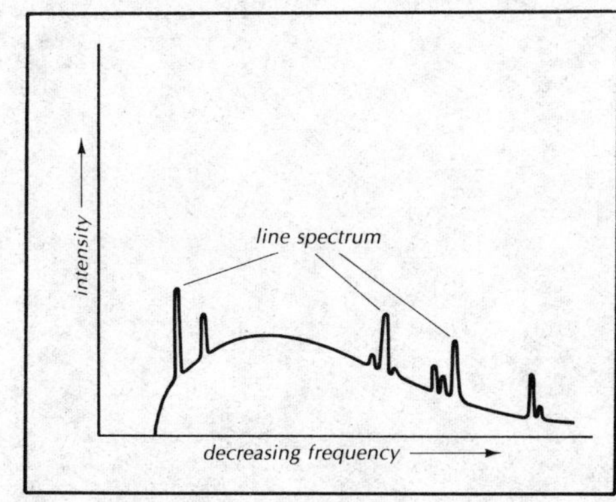

Typical X-ray composite spectrum (intensity as a function of frequency)

X Y Z

ated glass bulb, called an X-ray tube, that contains essentially two electrodes—an anode made of platinum, tungsten, or another heavy metal of high melting point, and a cathode. When a high voltage is applied between the electrodes, streams of electrons (cathode rays) are accelerated from the cathode to the anode and produce X rays as they strike the anode. Two different processes give rise to radiation of X-ray frequency. In one process radiation is emitted by the high-speed electrons themselves as they are slowed or even stopped in passing near the positively charged nuclei of the anode material. This radiation is often called *brehmsstrahlung* [Ger.,= braking radiation]. In a second process radiation is emitted by the electrons of the anode atoms when incoming electrons from the cathode knock electrons near the nuclei out of orbit and they are replaced by other electrons from outer orbits. The SPECTRUM of frequencies given off with any particular anode material thus consists of a continuous range of frequencies emitted in the first process, and superimposed on it a number of sharp peaks of intensity corresponding to discrete frequencies at which X rays are emitted in the second process. The sharp peaks constitute the X-ray line spectrum for the anode material and will differ for different materials. X-ray line spectra were used by H. G. J. Moseley in his important work on atomic numbers (1913) and also provided further confirmation of the QUANTUM THEORY of atomic structure. Also important historically is the discovery of X-ray DIFFRACTION by Max von Laue (1912) and its subsequent application by W. H. and W. L. Bragg to the study of crystal structure. Most applications of X rays are based on their ability to pass through matter. This ability varies with different substances; e.g., wood and flesh are easily penetrated, but denser substances such as lead and bone are more opaque. The penetrating power of X rays also depends on their energy. The more penetrating X rays, known as hard X rays, are of higher frequency and are thus more energetic, while the less penetrating X rays, called soft X rays, have lower energies. X rays that have passed through a body provide a visual image of its interior structure when they strike a photographic plate or a fluorescent screen; the darkness of the shadows produced on the plate or screen depends on the relative opacity of different parts of the body. Photographs made with X rays are known as radiographs or skiagraphs. Radiography has applications in both medicine and industry, where it is valuable for diagnosis and nondestructive testing of products for defects. Fluoroscopy is based on the same techniques, with the photographic plate replaced by a fluorescent screen (see FLUORESCENCE; FLUOROSCOPE); its advantages over radiography in time and cost are balanced by some loss in sharpness of the image. Another use of radiography is in the examination and analysis of paintings, where studies can reveal such details as the age of a painting and underlying brushstroke techniques that help to identify or verify the artist. X rays are used in several techniques that can provide enlarged images of the structure of opaque objects. These techniques, collectively referred to as X-ray microscopy or microradiography, can also be used in the quantitative analysis of many materials. One of the dangers in the use of X rays is that they can destroy living tissue and can cause severe skin burns on human flesh exposed for too long a time. This destructive power is used in X-ray therapy to destroy diseased cells. See A. R. Bleich, *The Story of X-rays, from Röntgen to Isotopes* (1960); Joseph Selman, *The Fundamentals of X-ray and Radium Physics* (1965).

X-ray astronomy, study of celestial objects by means of the X rays they emit. All stars emit X rays along with visible light, but only extremely hot objects can be strong sources. The ultimate sources of the X rays are at present a subject of conjecture, but most theories attribute X rays to superdense objects, either WHITE DWARFS, NEUTRON STARS, or black holes (see GRAVITATIONAL COLLAPSE). Because the earth's atmosphere absorbs nearly all radiation at short wavelengths, X-ray observations must be made at high altitude from rockets or artificial satellites. The first X-ray object studied was the sun, a weak but very close source. Of particular interest was the discovery that the center of our galaxy is a strong source of X rays. Powerful emissions were also found from the CRAB NEBULA and from a position located in the constellation Scorpius. The Scorpius source, known as Sco X-1, is the single most powerful source of X rays in the sky, although no visible object has been correlated with its position. A few recently discovered sources emit X rays in regularly timed bursts, thus qualifying as X-ray PULSARS.

Xuthus (zo͞o'thəs): see CREUSA **1**; HELLEN.

xylem (zī'ləm): see STEM; WOOD.

xylene (zī'lēn) or **dimethylbenzene** (dī''-mĕthəlbĕn'zēn), $C_6H_4(CH_3)_2$, colorless, oily, liquid aromatic HYDROCARBON, used extensively as a solvent, obtained from coal tar, wood tar, and sometimes from petroleum. It is a mixture of three isomers that differ structurally from one another in the location of the two methyl groups that have replaced hydrogen atoms in the BENZENE molecule. *Ortho*-xylene is 1,2-dimethylbenzene; it melts at −25°C and boils at 144°C. *Meta*-xylene is 1,3-dimethylbenzene; it melts at −48°C and boils at 139°C. *Para*-xylene is 1,4-dimethylbenzene; it melts at 13°C and boils at 138°C. The separation of these three isomers from one another by fractional distillation is difficult because their boiling points are so close together. The *ortho* and *para* isomers are converted to *meta*-xylene by treatment with aluminum trichloride and hydrochloric acid at about 80°C. The xylenes are often used in the synthesis of other compounds, e.g., the xylidenes that are amino derivatives used in the synthesis of azo dyes and other compounds.

Xylocaine (zī'lōkān), trade name for the drug lidocaine, used as a local anesthetic (see ANESTHESIA). It is used in dentistry and surgery, in the treatment of some forms of heart irregularity, and in ointment or aerosol form to relieve the discomfort of skin disorders such as bites and burns.

xylophone (zī'ləfōn) [Gr.,=wood sound], musical instrument having graduated wooden slabs that are struck by the player with small, hard mallets. The slabs are usually arranged like a keyboard, and the range varies from two to four octaves. Since the 1920s the xylophone has been equipped with tubular resonators and thus is essentially identical with the marimba. The latter, however, is deeper and larger, is often played by two or more players, and is struck with soft mallets.

XYZ Affair, name usually given to an incident (1797-98) in Franco-American diplomatic relations. The United States had in 1778 entered into an alliance with France, but after the outbreak of the French Revolutionary Wars was both unable and unwilling to lend aid. The anti-French Federalists gained the upper hand in the United States, and there was considerable antagonism toward France, particularly after the Genêt (see GENÊT, EDMUND CHARLES EDOUARD) affair. The conclusion (1795) of Jay's Treaty with England, which partially vitiated the agreements with France, aroused French anger. Numerous American ships were seized by French privateers, and the countries drifted into a mutually hostile attitude. President Washington sent Charles Cotesworth Pinckney as minister to France, but the French government refused to receive him. Shortly afterward John Adams, the new President, sent (1797) John Marshall and Elbridge Gerry to join Pinckney on a peace mission to France. This three-man commission was immediately confronted by the refusal of French foreign minister Charles Maurice de Talleyrand to receive it officially. Indirect suggestions of loans and bribes to France were made to the commissioners through Mme de Villette, a friend of Talleyrand. Negotiations were carried on through her with Jean Conrad Hottinguer and Lucien Hauteval, both Swiss, and a Mr. Bellamy, an American banker in Hamburg; the three were designated X, Y, and Z in the mission's dispatches to the United States. The proposal that the Americans pay Talleyrand about $250,000 before the French government would even deal with them created an uproar when it was released in the United States, where the pro-British party welcomed the chance to worsen Franco-American relations. The U.S. representatives made no progress and the mission broke up, Marshall coming home, Pinckney taking a sick daughter to S France, and Gerry, a Republican and Francophile, remaining in France temporarily. Meanwhile, an undeclared naval war ensued between France and the United States. Both Talleyrand and President Adams wished to avoid a declaration of war. In 1799 Adams, to the intense disgust of the Federalist leader, Alexander Hamilton, named William Vans Murray the U.S. minister to France and assigned Oliver Ellsworth and William Richardson Davie to accompany him. The result was the Treaty of Mortefontaine (Sept. 30, 1800), known as the Convention of 1800, a commercial agreement that improved relations between the two nations. The XYZ Affair contributed to American patriotic legend in the reply Pinckney is supposed to have made to a French request for money, "Millions for defense, sir, but not one cent for tribute." This reply was certainly not made, but a better case can be made for the alternate version, "No, no, not a sixpence."

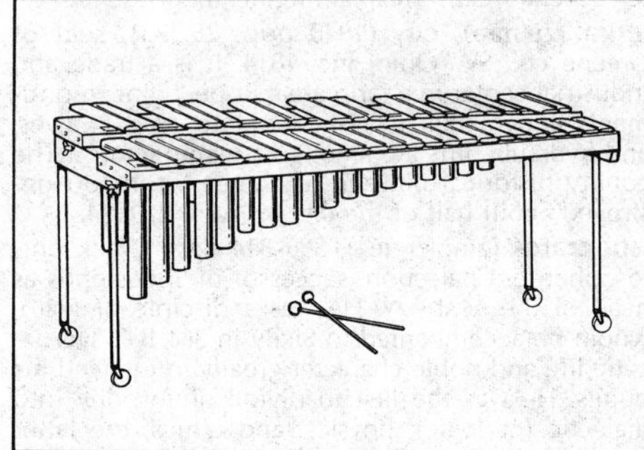

Xylophone

Y

Y, 25th letter of the ALPHABET. It was a Latin importation of the eastern Greek upsilon (see U), which was pronounced like *ü;* the Romans used it for Greek words. In English *y* mainly represents the semivowel occurring in words such as *yet;* the same semivowel is the second member of the diphthongs *ā, ē, ī,* and *oi.* The modern ignorant use of *y* in *ye* for *the* (as in "Ye Olde Shoppe") is based on a misreading of an old sign for *th.* In chemistry Y is the symbol for the element YTTRIUM.

Ya-an or **Yaan** (both: yä-än), city (1970 est. pop. 100,000), SW Szechwan prov., China, on a tributary of the Min River. It is a tea center for W Szechwan and a highway hub for the E Tibetan Plateau. From 1950 to 1955 it was the capital of Sikang prov. An agricultural institute is there.

Yablonovy Range (yä'blənəvē), mountain chain, in Transbaykalia, SE Siberian USSR. Forming part of the watershed between the Arctic and Pacific oceans, it extends c.700 mi (1,130 km) from the Mongolian border in the southwest to the Olekma River in the northeast. It is crossed by the Trans-Siberian RR at Chita. Sokhondo, c.8,230 ft (2,510 m) is the highest point.

yacht: see MOTORBOATING; SAILING.

Yacine, Kateb (kä'tăb yä'sēn), 1929–, Algerian author. In 1945 he moved to Paris. His most famous work is the novel *Nedjma* (1957, tr. 1961), a symbolic story of the love of four men for one woman. The work is notable for its carefully constructed, multilevel plot. His other works include a volume of poetry, *Soliloquies* (1946); the novel *La Polygone Étoile* (1966); and two anthologies of plays, *Le cercle des représailles* (1959) and *L'Homme aux sandales de caoutchouc* (1970).

Yadkin, river, N.C.: see PEE DEE, river.

Yahata: see KITAKYUSHU, Japan.

Yahweh (yä'wĕ), modern reconstruction of YHWH, the ancient Hebrew ineffable name for GOD. Other forms are Yahve, Yahveh, and Yahwe.

Yahya Khan, Agha Muhammad (ä'gä mo͞ohäm'-mäd yä'yä khän), 1917–, Pakistani general and president (1969–71). Fighting with the British, he saw action on several fronts in World War II and after Pakistan became independent in 1947 held increasingly important positions in the army. While chief of the general staff (1957–62) he helped to bring General AYUB KHAN to power. Yahya Khan performed well during the 1965 war with India and in 1966 became commander in chief of the army. Economic problems and disputes between East and West Pakistan led to Ayub Khan's resignation and his replacement as president by Yahya Khan in 1969. The imposition of martial law failed to curb domestic unrest, and civil war between East and West Pakistan broke out in 1971. The defeat of Pakistan's army and the ultimate success of Bangladesh (see INDIA-PAKISTAN WARS) caused him to resign in late 1971. He was succeeded by Zulfikar Ali BHUTTO.

Yaila Mountains: see CRIMEA, USSR.

Yajur-Veda: see VEDA.

yak, bovine mammal, *Bos grunniens,* of Tibet and adjacent regions. It is oxlike in build, with short, thick legs, humped shoulders, large upcurved horns, and a thick coat that hangs down to the ankles. Wild yaks were formerly found from Kashmir to W China, but were so extensively hunted for meat and hides that they now survive only in isolated highlands at elevations above 14,000 ft (4,300 m). They live in herds numbering from 10 to 100 animals, mostly females and young led by a few old bulls; males are mostly solitary. Yaks have been domesticated in Tibet for centuries, and the domestic form has been introduced into other parts of central Asia. The wild yak may attain a shoulder height of 65 in. (165 cm) and have horns 3 ft (90 cm) long; its coat is dark brown. The domesticated yak is smaller, with short horns; its coat, which may be long enough to reach the ground, may be black, brown, reddish, piebald, or albino. Yaks can live on vegetation so sparse that it cannot support other domesticated animals. The domestic yak is a source of milk, butter, meat, hair (for cloth), and leather and is also much used as a beast of burden. Yaks are classified in the phylum CHORDATA, subphylum Vertebrata, class Mammalia, order Artiodactyla, family Bovidae.

Yakima (yăk'əmô, –mə), city (1970 pop. 45,588), seat of Yakima co., S central Wash., on the Yakima River just below its confluence with the Naches; inc. 1886. It is the trade and shipping center of a great irrigated agricultural valley noted for its fruit, hops, and mint. It has several fruit canneries and plants that manufacture lumber products, blue jeans, and aircraft equipment and parts. Located in Yakima are a junior college, a school of nursing, a state fish hatchery, the central Washington fairgrounds, and a race track. A state park is to the east, and an Indian reservation is in the vicinity.

Yakima, river, 203 mi (327 km) long, rising in the Cascade Range, central Wash., and flowing SE past Yakima to the Columbia River near Kennewick. The U.S. Bureau of Reclamation's Yakima project (begun in 1906) utilizes the Yakima and its tributaries to irrigate c.460,000 acres (186,160 hectares) and has helped make the river valley an important farming and fruit-growing region. A major unit of the project is the Keechelus Dam (completed 1917).

Yakima Indians, North American Indians whose language belongs to the Sahaptin-Chinook branch of the Penutian linguistic stock (see AMERICAN INDIAN LANGUAGES). In the early 19th cent. they lived along the Columbia and the Yakima rivers, in central Washington. They then numbered some 1,200. In 1855 an attempt by the United States to place the Yakima on a reservation resulted in a war. Under a capable leader, Kamiakin, the Yakima continued warfare until 1859, when they were placed on a reservation in Washington. The culture of the Yakima was of the Plateau cultural area; they subsisted on salmon, roots, berries, and nuts. Today about 7,000 of them live on the Yakima Reservation, where the main income is derived through forestry. See Click Relander, *Strangers on the Land* (1962).

Yakub I (yäko͝ob'), 1160?–1199, ruler of Morocco (1184–99) and Moorish Spain. He was known as Yakub al-Mansur [the victorious] after his victory over Alfonso VIII of Castile at Alarcos (1195). One of the most powerful of the ALMOHADS, he encouraged art and literature and constructed many public buildings in both Spain and Morocco, notably the Giralda at Seville, the Koutoubiya tower at Marrakesh, and numerous edifices at Rabat. Yakub was a patron of AVERROËS.

Yakutat Indians: see TLINGIT INDIANS.

Yakut Autonomous Soviet Socialist Republic (yəko͞ot'), or Yakutia, autonomous division (1970 pop. 664,000), c.1,200,000 sq mi (3,108,000 sq km), NE Siberian USSR. YAKUTSK is the capital. The Soviet Union's largest administrative division except for the Russian Republic (RSFSR), Yakutia is bounded in the N by the Laptev and East Siberian seas of the Arctic Ocean, in the S by the Stanovoy Range, in the W by the Central Siberian Uplands, and in the E by the Verkhoyansk Range. It also encompasses the New Siberian and Lyakhov islands in the Arctic Ocean. The terrain is largely plain, with tundra in the north and taiga elsewhere. More than 40% of the territory lies inside the Arctic Circle. The Lena, Yana, Indigirka, and Kolyma rivers cross the republic, which includes virtually the entire Lena basin. There are many lakes in the lowlands. The rivers are used for navigation (during the summer) and for flotage and have great hydroelectric potential. The Yakutsk-Skovorodino highway is the chief overland route. Yakutia has no railroads. Air transport and winter sledge are widespread. One of the world's coldest inhabited regions, the republic has extremely severe winters and short summers; temperatures of -103°F (-75°C) have been recorded in some cities. Agriculture is possible only in the south, along the Lena and its tributaries. Wheat, barley, rye, and leaf and root vegetables are grown. Diamond mining is the republic's main industry; it is centered in Mirny, which has one of the world's largest diamond-processing plants. There is extensive gold mining in the Aldan district. Lumbering, fishing, hunting, fur breeding and trapping, livestock raising (especially horses), and reindeer herding are also important economic activities. Much lumber is exported. Yakutia has printing works, food-processing plants, and factories that produce cement and other building materials, clothing, and leather footwear. Bone carving has long been a noted art among the Yakut, who make up about half of the republic's population; most of the remainder are Russians, and there are small Evenki, Eveny, and Chukchi minorities. About half the people are urban dwellers. The Yakut, who speak a Turkic language with Mongolian influence, settled around the Lena River between the 13th and 15th cent. Russian colonization began after the establishment of a fort at Yakutsk in 1632. Many Yakut were converted to Orthodox Christianity, but shamanism is still practiced. Gold mining started in the middle of the 19th cent. The autonomous republic was organized in 1922. Yakutia has a university and a branch of the Siberian section of the Soviet Academy of Sciences.

Yakutsk (yəko͞otsk'), city (1970 pop. 108,000), capital of Yakut Autonomous Republic, E Siberian USSR, a port on the Lena River. It is also a highway center and has tanneries, sawmills, and brickworks. Yakutsk was founded in 1632. It has a university (founded 1956) and the Yakutsk branch of the Soviet Academy of Sciences.

Yale, Elihu, 1649–1721, English merchant, b. Boston. The family moved to England c.1652, and Yale was educated in London. He went to Madras in the service of the British East India Company c.1670 and rose in the ranks of the company. He was appointed governor of Fort St. George at Madras in 1687. Because of scandals concerning his administration, he was removed in 1692 and returned to London in 1699. While in the East he had amassed a large fortune through private trade. In 1718, Cotton Mather wrote Yale suggesting that the Collegiate School at Saybrook, Conn., might be named for him in return for financial support. Yale donated a parcel of goods, which when sold brought £562—the largest single gift to the college before 1837. The college, later moved to New Haven, took the name of Yale. See F. B. Dexter, *A Selection from the Miscellaneous Historical Papers of Fifty Years* (1918); biography by Hiram Bingham (1939, repr. 1968).

Yale University, at New Haven, Conn.; coeducational. Chartered as a collegiate school in 1701 largely as a result of the efforts of James Pierpont, it opened at Killingworth (now Clinton) in 1702, moved (1707) to Saybrook (now Old Saybrook), and in 1716 was finally moved to its permanent location in New Haven. Its name was changed to Yale College in 1718 in honor of Elihu YALE, who had been persuaded by Cotton MATHER and Jeremiah DUMMER to contribute to the college. Its present charter was drawn up in 1745. In the 19th cent. extensive changes were made in the college. Numerous schools were added, such as medicine (1813), divinity (1822), law (1824), a graduate school (1847), and art and architecture (1865), and as a result in 1887, under Timothy DWIGHT, the college was renamed Yale Univ. Later, other schools were added—music (1894), forestry (1900), the Sheffield school of engineering (undergraduate; 1932), and drama (1955). Further expansion included the founding of the Institute of Far Eastern Languages. The university library, one of the largest in the nation, houses a large number of important manuscript and book collections. Also notable are the Peabody Museum of Natural History and the well-known Yale art gallery. The Yale Univ. Press was established in 1908. See Edwin Oviatt, *The Beginnings of Yale* (1916, repr. 1969); Janet Lever and Pepper Schwartz, *Women at Yale* (1971); B. M. Kelley, *Yale: A History* (1974).

Yalta (yŏl'tə, Rus. yäl'tə), city (1970 pop. 62,000), SW European USSR, in S Crimea, on the Black Sea. Picturesquely situated near the seashore, Yalta is the largest resort in the Crimea. There are many hotels, sanatoriums, and tourist and rest homes—many of which were built as villas by the nobility before the Russian Revolution. Churchill, Roosevelt, and Stalin met in Yalta in Feb., 1945. Yalta is on the site of an ancient Greek colony. Nearby is the town and palace of LIVADIYA.

Yalta Conference, meeting (Feb. 4-11, 1945), at Yalta, Crimea, USSR, of British Prime Minister Winston Churchill, U.S. President Franklin Delano Roosevelt, and Soviet Premier Joseph Stalin. Most of the important decisions made remained secret until the end of World War II for military or political reasons; the complete text of all the agreements was not disclosed until 1947. The Yalta conferees confirmed the policy adopted at the CASABLANCA CONFERENCE of demanding Germany's unconditional surrender. Plans were made for dividing Germany into four zones of occupation (American, British, French, and Russian) under a unified control commission in Berlin, for war crimes trials, and for a study of the reparations question. Agreement was also reached on reorganizing the Polish Lublin government (supported by Stalin) "on a broader democratic basis" that would include members of Poland's London government-in-exile, which the Western Allies had supported. The conferees decided to ask China and France to join them in sponsoring the founding conference of the United Nations to be convened in San Francisco on April 25, 1945; agreement was reached on using the veto system of voting in the projected Security Council. Future meetings of the foreign ministers of the "Big Three" were planned. The USSR secretly agreed to enter the war against Japan within three months of Germany's surrender and was promised S Sakhalin, the Kurile Islands, and an occupation zone in Korea. The secret agreement respecting the disposal of Japan's holdings also provided that the port of Talien (Dairen) should be internationalized, that Port Arthur should be restored to its status before the 1904-5 Russo-Japanese War as a Soviet naval base, and that the Manchurian railroads should be under joint Chinese-Soviet administration. China later protested that it was not informed of these decisions concerning its territory and that its sovereignty was infringed. The United States and Great Britain also agreed to recognize the autonomy of Outer Mongolia, and it was decided to admit the Ukraine and Belorussia to the United Nations as full members. The Yalta agreements were disputed even before the POTSDAM CONFERENCE later in 1945. The subsequent outbreak of the cold war and Soviet successes in Eastern Europe led to much criticism in the United States of the Yalta Conference and of Roosevelt, who was accused of delivering Eastern Europe to Communist domination. See Diane Clemens, *Yalta* (1970); A. G. Theoharis, *The Yalta Myths* (1970); R. F. Fenno, ed., *The Yalta Conference* (2d ed. 1972).

Yalu (yä'lo͞o'), river, c.500 mi (800 km) long, rising in the Ch'ang-pai mts. in Kirin prov., NE China, and flowing SW to the Bay of Korea at Tan-tung; forms part of the China-North Korea border. In places it is navigable for shallow-draft vessels, but its chief commercial use is for floating timber to sawmills. Several railroad bridges span the river. The Supung Dam above Sinuiju, North Korea, one of the largest dams in Asia, supplies hydroelectric power to China and North Korea. Chinese troops entered the Korean War by crossing the Yalu.

Ya-lung (yä-lo͝ong), river, c.800 mi (1,290 km) long, rising in the Kunlun mts., S Tsinghai prov., W China, and flowing S across W Szechwan prov. to the Yangtze River at the Yünnan line. It flows through deep gorges and is one of the Yangtze's longest tributaries.

yam, common name for some members of the Dioscoreaceae, a family of tropical and subtropical climbing herbs or shrubs with starchy rhizomes often cultivated for food. The largest genus, *Dioscorea,* is commercially important in the Far East and in tropical America. The thick rhizomes, often weighing 30 lb (13.6 kg) or more, are used for human consumption and for feeding livestock. In the United States, cultivation of yams for food is restricted to the South, but the wild yam (sometimes used medicinally) is indigenous farther north, and another species, the cinnamon vine, is cultivated as a decorative plant. The sweet potato, which belongs to the morning glory family, is sometimes erroneously called yam. The S African elephant's-foot (*Testudinaria elephantipes*), also called Hottentot bread and tortoise plant, is sometimes grown in greenhouses; its large rootstock was formerly eaten by the natives. Yams are classified in the division MAGNOLIOPHYTA, class Liliatae, order Liliales, family Dioscoreaceae.

Yamagata, Aritomo (ärē'tōmō yämä'gätä), 1838-1922, Japanese soldier and statesman, chief founder of the modern Japanese army. A samurai of Choshu, he took part in the Meiji restoration. He studied military science in Europe and returned in 1870 to head the war ministry. Strongly influenced by Prussian military and political ideas and favoring military expansion abroad and authoritarian government at home, he supported Japanese military control of Taiwan, Korea, and Manchuria. As home minister (1883-87) he dissolved the new political parties and repressed the agrarian movement. In 1900, while premier, he ruled that only an active military officer could serve as war or navy minister, a rule that gave the military control over any cabinet. From 1900 to 1910 he opposed Hirobumilto, leader of the civilian party, and exercised influence through his protégé, Taro Katsura. As president of the privy council from 1909 to 1922, he was the power behind the throne and the leading advocate for higher military appropriations. See R. F. Hackett, *Yamagata Aritomo in the Rise of Modern Japan, 1838-1922* (1971).

Yamagata, city (1970 pop. 204,127), capital of Yamagata prefecture, N Honshu, Japan. It is a silk-reeling center. Agricultural production is also important. The city has a university. Yamagata prefecture (1970 pop. 1,255,678), 3,607 sq mi (9,342 sq km), yields high quality rice.

Yamaguchi (yämä'go͞ochē), city (1970 pop. 101,037), capital of Yamaguchi prefecture, SW Honshu, Japan. A great castle city from the 14th to 16th cent. and the site of many Buddhist temples and a mission established (1550) by St. Francis Xavier, it is now a commercial center. Yamaguchi prefecture (1970 pop. 1,511,425), 2,347 sq mi (6,079 sq km), has good lumber resources, and stock-raising is important.

Yamalo-Nenets National Okrug (yəmäl'ō-nyĕ'-nyĭts), administrative division (1970 pop. 80,000), c.290,000 sq mi (751,000 sq km), NW Siberian USSR, on both sides of the Gulf of Ob and including the Yamal peninsula. The area has frozen ground (permafrost) and tundra, forest tundra, and taiga vegetation. Reindeer raising, fishing, and fur trapping are the chief occupations. There are deposits of iron ore, coal, natural gas, and peat in the region. SALEKHARD is the capital and Novy Port is a regular supply point on the Northern Sea route. The population consists of Russians, Nentsy, Khanty, and Komi. The area was organized as an okrug in 1930. The Soviet government maintained forced labor camps in the area.

Yamamoto, Gombei (gōm'bā yämä'mōtō), 1852-1933, Japanese admiral. He was navy minister (1898-1906) during the Russo-Japanese War. Yamamoto was later (1913-14, 1923-24) prime minister. His first cabinet was involved in a scandal concerning the construction of battleships.

Yamamoto, Isoroku (ēsō'rōko͞o''), 1884-1943, Japanese admiral in World War II. He headed the combined fleet in 1941 and was the mastermind behind Japan's attack on Pearl Harbor. After he was killed in action in 1943, he became a national hero. Throughout his career he worked to build an integrated air-surface arm for the navy.

Yamanashi (yämä'näshē), prefecture (1970 pop. 762,029), central Honshu, Japan. KOFU is the capital. The mountainous region is drained by the Fuji River. Yamanashi is a major producer of raw silk and grapes. Fuji Hakone Izu National Park is there.

Yamasaki, Minoru (mĭnō'ro͞o yämäsä'kē), 1912-, American architect, b. Seattle. Yamasaki worked for prominent architectural firms in New York City from 1937 until 1949, when he formed his own company. In 1951 he designed the Lambert-St. Louis Municipal Air Terminal, an impressive concrete groin-vault construction. In his design (1954) for the U.S. consulate general in Kobe, Japan, Yamasaki adapted elements of the Japanese aesthetic. His interest in ornament and sculptural form is revealed in buildings for the American Concrete Institute, the Reynolds Metal Company, and the McGregor Memorial Community Conference Center, Wayne Univ., all in Detroit. Yamasaki's design for the U.S. science pavilion at the Seattle Exposition, 1962, is famed for its soaring arches and Gothic tracery. His other major works include the Plaza Hotel, Los Angeles (1966), and the Eastern Airlines Unit Terminal, Boston (1968). He is a chief designer of the vast World Trade Center complex, New York City.

Yamasee Indians, Yamasi Indians (both: yăm'əsē, yăm'-, yĕm'-), or **Yemasee Indians,** North American Indians whose language belongs to the Muskogean branch of the Hokan-Siouan linguistic stock (see AMERICAN INDIAN LANGUAGES). In the late 16th cent., when Spanish missions were established among them, the Yamasee lived in S Georgia and N Florida. They remained under Spanish rule until 1687, when they revolted and fled to South Carolina. The Yamasee were initially friendly toward the English, but in 1715 war broke out and they massacred over 200 settlers. Driven out of South Carolina, the Yamasee returned to Florida, where they became allies of the Spanish against the English. In 1727 their village near St. Augustine was attacked and destroyed by the English. Their population declined, and eventually they assimilated with the Seminole and the Creek.

Yamashita, Tomoyuki (tōmō'yo͞okē yämä'shētä), 1888-1946, Japanese general. He studied military science in Germany. He commanded (1941) the Malayan campaign and forced Singapore to surrender (Feb., 1942). In March, 1942, he assumed command in the Philippines and took Bataan and Corregidor. He also commanded during the unsuccessful defense (Oct., 1944-Aug., 1945) of the Philippines against the invading Allies under Douglas MacArthur. In Sept., 1945, he surrendered. He went on trial before a military commission in Manila for atrocities committed by soldiers under his command. He was found guilty and hanged (1946).

Yambol or **Jambol** (both: yäm'bôl), city (1968 est. pop. 67,900), SE Bulgaria. It is a commercial center and produces cotton textiles, machinery, and cement. There are mineral springs nearby. Dating from Roman times, Yambol was a residence of Turkish beys in the 15th to 18th cent. It has an 18th-century church and several Turkish mosques.

Yamburg: see KINGISEPP, USSR.

Yameogo, Maurice (mōrēs' yämä'ōgō), 1921-, president of Upper Volta (1960-66). A member of the Mossi tribe, he became active in African politics in the 1940s and was a founder of the interterritorial African Democratic Rally. Elected to Parliament (1957), he became prime minister (1958) and then president until his overthrow by Sangoulé Lamizana. In 1969 he was convicted of embezzling $3 million while president and was imprisoned until 1970.

Yamuna, river, India: see JUMNA.

Yancey, William Lowndes, 1814-63, American leader of SECESSION, b. Warren co., Ga. Admitted (1834) to the bar in Greenville, S.C., he soon moved to Alabama. There he became an outstanding lawyer, was elected to the state house of representatives (1841) and the state senate (1843), and served in Congress (1844-46). In response to the WILMOT PROVISO, Yancey wrote (1848) the Alabama Platform, which demanded of Congress the positive protection of slavery in the territories. Yancey's doctrine was adopted by several Southern states under his militant leadership and soon became the creed of the whole South. As extreme a "fire-eater" as William Lloyd Garrison was an abolitionist, he even advocated the reopening of the African slave trade. After the Compromise of 1850 he retired into the background, but the events of 1860 once more brought him to the fore. At the national convention of the Democratic party in Charleston, he expressed the Southern demands in one of his greatest speeches, and when the Northern delegates, led by Stephen A. Douglas, refused to accept the "Yancey platform," practically all his Southern colleagues followed him out of the convention. Yancey wrote the Alabama ordinance of secession. After the organization of the Confederacy, Jefferson Davis, then only provisional president, sent Yancey, a potential rival for the permanent office, to Europe as a Confederate commissioner. Failing to secure recognition from England and France, he returned in 1862, was elected to the Confederate senate, and served there until his death. See biography by J. W. DuBose (1892).

Yáñez, Agustín (ägo͞ostēn' yä' nyās), 1904-, Mexican novelist and critic. Yáñez's writings include works about Indian myths and the Spanish colonial era. His first work was a group of fanciful tales, *Archipiélago de mujeres* (1943). *Al filo del agua* (1947, tr. 1963), in which he uses a complex narrative technique, is his best-known work. Yáñez's later works include the novels *La creación* (1959), *La tierra pródiga* (1960), *The Lean Lands* (tr. 1968), and *Edge of the Storm* (tr. 1971).

Yang, Chen Ning (chĕn nĭng yäng), 1922-, American physicist, b. China, Ph.D. Univ. of Chicago, 1948. Chen Ning Yang was a member of the Institute for Advanced Study at Princeton, N.J. from 1949 to 1955, and a professor of physics there from 1955 to 1965. In 1965 he was appointed Albert Einstein Professor of Physics of the State University of New York at Stony Brook. He is known for his researches in statistical mechanics and meson physics. With American physicist T. D. Lee he shared the 1957 Nobel Prize in Physics for research refuting the law of parity, which stated that, at the subatomic level, nature does not distinguish between left-and right-handed configurations: if a nuclear reaction or decay occurs in nature, then so does its mirror image and with equal frequency.

Yang-chou or **Yangchow** (both: yăng-chou, yăng-jō), city (1970 est. pop. 210,000), N Kiangsu prov., China, on the Grand Canal. It is an agricultural market center with fertilizer and machine-tool industries. An ancient walled city, Yang-chou was in the 6th cent. one of the three capitals of the Sui dynasty and was later an important cultural center under the T'ang dynasty. It was a center of Nestorian Christianity and was governed by Marco Polo from 1282 to 1285. It is famous for its storytellers (who still perform today) as well as for its historic buildings and former palaces. The city was formerly known as Kiangtu.

Yangchow: see YANG-CHOU, China.

Yang-ch'üan (yäng-chüän), city, E central Shansi prov., China, on the highway and railroad linking T'ai-yüan with Hopeh prov. The center of an important coal-producing area, it is a growing industrial city. Iron is also mined nearby.

Yangku: see T'AI-YÜAN, China.

Yang Kuei-fei (yäng gwē-fā), 719–56, concubine of the T'ang emperor HSÜAN TSUNG. The most famous beauty in Chinese history, in legend she is blamed for demoralizing and corrupting the T'ang court. She is said to have persuaded Hsüan Tsung to place her corrupt and inefficient relatives in high positions, thus paving the way for the rebellion of AN LU-SHAN (755). While Hsüan Tsung was fleeing before the armies of An Lu-shan, discontented soldiers forced him to execute Yang Kuei-fei and the heart-broken emperor soon abdicated. See Wu Shu-chiung, *Yang Kuei-fei, The Most Famous Beauty of China* (1924).

Yangtze (yăng'sē', yăng'dzŭ'), Mandarin *Ch'ang Chiang*, longest river of China and of Asia, c.3,450 mi (5,550 km) long, rising in the Tibetan Highlands, SW Tsinghai prov., W China, and flowing generally E through central China into the East China Sea at Shanghai. The Yangtze and its tributaries drain more than 750,000 sq mi (1,942,500 sq km). The river passes through one of the world's most populated regions and has long been used as a major east-west trade and transportation route in China. The Yangtze's turbulent upper course, called the Chin-sha or Kinsha (1,600 mi/2,575 km long), flows south-east through forested, steep-walled gorges 2,000–4,000 ft (610–1,220 m) deep. After receiving the Ya-lung River, the first of its great tributaries, at the Szechwan-Yünnan province border, the Yangtze turns NE toward the Szechwan basin. At I-pin, on the western edge of the Szechwan basin, the river becomes the Yangtze proper and is joined by the "four rivers of Szechwan" (the Min, T'o, Fou, and Chai-ling). There is a hydroelectric power plant at Chungking, on the basin's eastern edge. Leaving the Szechwan basin, the Yangtze receives the Wu River and flows through the spectacular Yangtze gorges that extend from Feng-chieh to I-ch'ang; there the river is a serious hazard and at times navigation is impossible. Temples and pagodas are perched on prominent hills along the gorges. East of I-ch'ang, the Yangtze enters the lake-studded middle basin of Hupeh, Hunan, and Kiangsi provs., a rich agricultural and industrial region; Wu-han, at the confluence of the Han and Yangtze, is the principal city. The huge Tung-t'ing and P'o-yang lakes, which receive the Yüan, Tzu, and Hsiang rivers and the Kan River, respectively, are linked by numerous channels with the Yangtze and serve as natural overflow reservoirs. Now shallow because of sedimentation, the lakes are less effective as regulators of the Yangtze's flow. Dikes protect large areas of the river's middle basin from flood waters. Although the Yangtze does not often experience the devastating floods that characterize the Huang Ho (Yellow River), it has occasionally caused wide damage; great floods occurred in 1931 and 1954. The fertile middle basin is China's most productive agricultural region; rice is the main crop. The river enters the East China Sea through the extensive, ever-expanding delta region of Anhwei and Kiangsu provs. Dikes have been built to reclaim coastal marshes and create additional farmland. The Yangtze carries its greatest volume during the summer rainy season. It is navigable for ocean liners to Wu-han, c.600 mi (970 km) upstream; during the summer high-water period, I-ch'ang, c.1,000 mi (1,610 km) upstream, is the head of navigation. Smaller craft can sail to I-pin, c.1,500 mi (2,410 km) from the sea.

Yankee, term used by Americans generally in reference to a native of New England and by non-Americans, especially the British, in reference to an American of any section. The word is most likely from the Dutch and was apparently derived either from *Janke*, diminutive of *Jan*, or from *Jankees*, a combination of *Jan* and *kees* [cheese], thus signifying *John Cheese*. As early as 1683, *Yankey* was a common nickname among the pirates of the Spanish Main; always, however, it was borne by Dutchmen. There is no satisfactory explanation of how it came to be applied to the Englishmen of colonial America and particularly to New Englanders. By 1765 it was in use as a term of contempt or derision, but by the opening of the American Revolution, New Englanders were proud to be called Yankees. The popularity of the marching song *Yankee Doodle* probably had much to do with the term's subsequent wide usage. In the Civil War it was applied disparagingly by the Confederates to Union soldiers and Northerners generally, and with Southern hatred for the North rekindled by the Reconstruction period it survived long after the war was over. In World War I, the English began calling American soldiers, both Southerners and Northerners, Yankees. At that time too the shortened form *Yank* became popular in the United States, with George M. Cohan's war song "Over There" contributing largely to its increased usage. However, *Yank*, too, was known in the 18th cent., as early as 1778, and the Confederates also used that form in the Civil War. *Yankee* and *Yank* were again popular designations for the American soldier in World War II. In Latin America the term *Yanqui* is applied to U.S. citizens, often—especially after the Fidel Castro revolution in Cuba—with a note of hostility.

Yankton, city (1970 pop. 11,919), seat of Yankton co., extreme SE S.Dak., on the Missouri River; inc. 1869. A railroad and trade center in a farm and livestock region, it has grain elevators, creameries, and plants manufacturing a great variety of products, including elevators, trailers, and aircraft and electronic components. Settled 1858 as a fur-trading post, Yankton was the Dakota territorial capital from 1861 to 1879; the old capitol building still stands. Yankton College, Mount Marty College, and a state mental hospital are there. Nearby Lewis and Clark Lake, formed by Gavins Point Dam (completed 1956), is part of the Missouri River basin project.

Yankton Indians and **Yanktonnai Indians:** see SIOUX INDIANS.

Yannina, Greece: see IOÁNNINA.

Yaoundé (yäōōndā'), city (1970 est. pop. 178,000), capital of the United Republic of Cameroon. It is the country's administrative, financial, and communications center. Manufactures include cigarettes, dairy products, clay and glass goods, and lumber. Yaoundé is a regional trade center for coffee, cacao, copra, sugarcane, and Para rubber. The city is at a highway junction and is on Cameroon's main railroad. Yaoundé was founded in 1888 by German traders as a base for tapping the ivory trade. It was occupied by Belgian troops during World War I and after the war was (except for 1940-46) the capital of French Cameroon. Yaoundé is the site of the Univ. of Cameroon (1962), which includes schools of teaching and agriculture. The city has many other educational and research institutes, including a school of administration and law (1960) and a school of journalism (1970).

Yap (yăp, yäp), island group (1970 pop. 2,856), c.25 sq mi (60 sq km), in the W CAROLINE ISLANDS (see also PACIFIC ISLANDS, TRUST TERRITORY OF THE), W Pacific. A communications center, Yap is the principal cable station of the Pacific and an important radio transmitting point. It consists of 4 large and 10 small islands surrounded by a coral reef. Discovered by the Spanish in 1791, Yap was sold to Germany in 1899. It became part of the Japanese-mandated area of the Pacific under the League of Nations in 1920 and fell to U.S. forces in 1945 during World War II. Yap is known for the stone disks used as money by the Micronesian natives.

yapok: see OPOSSUM.

Yaqui Indians (yä' kē), people of Sonora, Mexico, settled principally along the Yaqui river. Their language is of Uto-Aztecan stock. They engage in weaving and agriculture; many work in the cotton regions of Sonora and S Arizona. The Yaqui have proved to be warlike and have opposed encroachments on their lands. In the late 19th cent. under the Mexican dictator Porfirio Díaz they were ruthlessly persecuted and many were deported to plantations at Yucatán and Quintana Roo, over 2,000 mi (3,219 km) away. Some escaped and returned on foot to Sonora. The Mexican government attempted to control resistance by further resettlement, and many Yaqui emigrated to Arizona to escape subjugation. Later, efforts were made to improve their lot. There are several thousand Yaqui today in Mexico and the United States. See E. H. Spicer, *Potam, a Yaqui Village in Sonora* (1954); R. W. Giddings, *Yaqui Myths and Legends* (1959); Rosalio Moisés, *The Tall Candle* (1971).

Yaqut al-Hamawi (yäkōōt' äl-hämäwē'), 1179–1229, Arab geographer. Born in Byzantium, he was bought as a slave by a merchant, al-Hamawi. He was freed on the death of his master and traveled extensively in Egypt, Syria, Iraq, and Persia. His *Mujam al-Buldan*, a geographical dictionary that includes much biographical, historical, and cultural data, is a primary source in Arabic scholarship.

yard, abbr. yd, basic unit of length in the customary system of ENGLISH UNITS OF MEASUREMENT; all other units in the English system, such as the inch, foot, rod, and mile, are derived from it. Since 1893 the yard has been defined in terms of the METER, the basic unit of length in the METRIC SYSTEM. For a long time the yard was held to equal 3600/3973 of a meter; it has since been recalculated so that 1 yd equals 0.9144 m. In the United States results of geodetic surveys are still expressed in feet based on the former definition of the yard; this is known as the U.S. Survey Foot, defined as 1200/3937 of a meter.

Yarkand (yärkănd'), Mandarin *So-chü*, river, c.500 mi (800 km) long, rising in the Karakorum range, Sinkiang Uigur Autonomous Region, NW China, and flowing northeast to join with the Kashgar (K'a-shih-ka-erh) to form the Tarim River. The city of **Yarkand,** the largest settlement in the Tarim Basin, forms an oasis at the western end of the Takla Makan desert; it is the main trade center for goods traveling from Sinkiang to the USSR and India. The city, mainly inhabited by Turkic-speaking Muslims, has more than 120 mosques. Marco Polo visited Yarkand in 1271 and in 1275; the city was on the important Silk Road between China and Europe. A treaty signed there in 1874 opened Yarkand to trade with India.

Yarmouth (yär'məth), city (1971 pop. 8,516), SW N.S., Canada, on the Atlantic Ocean. It is a port, with exports of lumber, fish, berries, and Irish moss. Manufactures include wood products, iron castings, and cotton fabric. Yarmouth is a summer resort and tourist center. The region was visited (1604) by Champlain, who named it Cap Fourchu, and it became a French fishing settlement. In 1759 a few settlers came to the site of the city from Yarmouth, Mass., and called it after their former home. The city was founded in 1761, when a larger group of settlers came from Sandwich, Mass. They were followed by Acadians (1767) from the Grand Pré district and by UNITED EMPIRE LOYALISTS (1785).

Yarmouth. 1 Parish, Isle of Wight, S England. It is a small port and resort. The castle there was built by Henry VIII. **2** Officially **Great Yarmouth,** county borough (1971 pop. 52,152), Norfolk, E England, a port on a long, narrow peninsula between the North Sea and Breydon Water. It is a resort and fishing port. The Yarmouth bloater (prepared herring) is famous. There are engineering and textile industries. The Church of St. Nicholas was founded early in the 12th cent. The Tolhouse (14th cent.), now a museum, is one of the oldest municipal buildings in Great Britain. Although heavily bombed during World War II, the older part of the town retains many of the "rows," narrow lanes from 29 in. to 6 ft (73.7 cm–1.8 m) wide.

Yarmouth, resort town (1970 pop. 12,033), Barnstable co., SE Mass., on the south shore of Cape Cod; settled and inc. 1639. The main street of this picturesque town is lined with well-preserved old houses. Of special interest is the Thacher House (1680). The Yarmouth port is a historic district.

Yarmuk (yärmōōk'), river, c.50 mi (80 km) long, rising near the Jordan-Syria border and flowing generally W to the Jordan River, S of the Sea of Galilee. One of the larger rivers of Jordan, it is extensively used for hydroelectricity and irrigation. The East Ghor Canal branches from the Yarmuk and irrigates c.30,000 acres (12,140 hectares) in the E Ghor region of the Jordan valley.

yarn, fibers or filaments formed into a continuous strand for use in weaving textiles or for the manufacture of thread. A staple FIBER, such as cotton, linen, or wool, is made into yarn by CARDING, COMBING (for fine, long staples only), drawing out into roving, then SPINNING. Continuous filaments, such as silk, rayon, and nylon, may be formed directly into yarn or may be cut into short lengths and prepared like staple fibers. Yarns are twisted to give them strength and smoothness; a clockwise twist is known as the Z twist and a counterclockwise twist is known as the S twist. Two or more strands twisted together form ply yarns. In slub yarns areas are left untwisted to vary the diameter for ornamental effects. Complex yarns, such as bouclé and ratiné, are made by twisting together yarns of different tensions or diameters. The relation between the weight of the raw fiber of staple yarns and the yarn length is expressed by the yarn number; the finer the yarn, the higher the number. In filament yarns the yarn number, expressed in deniers, increases with the coarseness of the yarn.

Yaroslav (Yaroslav the Wise) (yərəsläv'), 978–1054, grand duke of Kiev (1019–54); son of Vladimir I. Designated by his father to rule in Novgorod, he became grand duke of Kiev after defeating his older brother Sviatopolk, who succeeded Vladimir I. A shrewd statesman, he consolidated the power and prestige of Kiev. He regained W Galicia from the Poles (who had obtained it in return for supporting Sviatopolk), crushed (1036) the Pechenegs (nomadic invaders), and suppressed rebellions by Lithuanian and Finnish tribes. In 1043 he organized the last Russian campaign against Constantinople, in which his troops were routed. At home he encouraged learning, codified laws, erected magnificent buildings and churches, including the famous Cathedral of St. Sophia, and founded (1039) a patriarchate in Kiev. Yaroslav was in close contact with European dynasties; his daughters were married to Harold III of Norway, Andrew I of Hungary, and Henry I of France. Before his death Yaroslav divided his kingdom among his heirs, designating the oldest, Iziaslav, as grand duke of Kiev; the others were told to obey Iziaslav as they had their father. Yaroslav's sons did not follow his advice, however, and civil war ensued.

Yaroslavl (yərəslä'vəl), city (1970 pop. 517,000), capital of Yaroslavl oblast, E European USSR, on the upper Volga River. It is a river port, a major rail junction, and an industrial and commercial center. Yaroslavl has linen and leather factories dating from the 17th cent. and textile mills dating from the 18th. Other industries include oil refining, food and tobacco processing, printing, shipbuilding, and the manufacture of machinery and diesel engines. According to tradition, the city was founded by Yaroslav the Wise of Kievan Russia in 1010, although it was not mentioned in the chronicles until 1071. In 1218 it became the capital of the independent Yaroslavl principality, which was absorbed by Moscow in 1463. The city flourished during the 16th and 17th cent. as a commercial center on the Moscow-Arkhangelsk route from the White Sea to the Middle East. During the "Time of Troubles" (see RUSSIA), Yaroslavl served briefly (March–July, 1612) as Russia's capital. In 1564 the first modern Russian ships were built at Yaroslavl, and in 1722 it became the site of Russia's first cloth factory. It was a major Russian manufacturing city by the 18th cent., notably for textiles. F. G. Volkov (1729–63), regarded as the founder of the Russian theater, organized his first dramatic performance in Yaroslavl in 1750. Until the construction of the Moscow-Volga Canal in 1937, the city served as Moscow's Volga port. Yaroslavl's landmarks include the 12th-century Spaso-Preobrazhenski Monastery, several 17th-century churches, and the Volkov theater (1911).

Yarra, river, 115 mi (185 km) long, rising in the Great Dividing Range, S Victoria, Australia, and flowing generally westward through Melbourne to Port Phillip Bay. It is navigable 5 mi (8 km) below Melbourne by small steamers. There are recreational facilities along the river.

yarrow, a plant of the genus *Achillea,* perennial herbs of the family Compositae (COMPOSITE family), native to north temperate regions. Several species are cultivated as ornamentals for their flat-topped clusters of flowers and scented foliage. The common yarrow (*A. millefolium*), also called milfoil, has white flowers in the wild, but there are also pinkish varieties in cultivation. Yarrow was a love charm of high repute, and in Greek mythology Achilles (hence the generic name) used the plant to heal the wounds of his soldiers and to stop bleeding. American Indians also used the plant medicinally, particularly as a treatment for earache. The continued use of yarrow in folk medicine is based on its apparent anti-inflammatory and coagulatory properties. Some yarrows are among the plants imparting a disagreeable taste to milk when grazed by cows. Water milfoils are unrelated freshwater aquatic perennials of the genus *Myriophyllum,* sometimes grown in aquariums and ponds. Yarrow is classified in the division MAGNOLIOPHYTA, class Magnoliopsida, order Asterales, family Compositae.

Yasnaya Polyana (yä'snīə pəlyä'nə), village, central European USSR, just S of Tula. It was the birthplace and residence of Leo Tolstoy, who is buried at his estate there. The writer's home was looted during German occupation of the village in 1941, but it has since been restored and is a museum and literary shrine.

Yass-Canberra: see AUSTRALIAN CAPITAL TERRITORY.

Yates, Richard, 1815–73, American political leader, b. Warsaw, Ky. He studied law and became a lawyer and Whig politician in Jacksonville, Ill. A state legislator (1842–46, 1848–50) and U.S. Congressman (1851–55), he failed to win reelection because of his adherence to the new Republican party. As governor of Illinois (1861–65), Yates was active in raising troops (he gave Ulysses S. Grant his first Civil War commission) and managed to hold in check the powerful pro-Southern group in Illinois. In the U.S. Senate from 1865 to 1871, he supported the radical Republican program.

Yatsushiro (yätsōō'shĭrō), city (1970 pop. 101,866), Kumamoto prefecture, W Kyushu, Japan, on Yatsushiro Bay and the Kuma River estuary. It is a major commercial and fishing port and industrial center with chemical and foodstuffs industries.

Yauco (you'kō), town (1970 pop. 12,922), SW Puerto Rico, on the Yauco River. It is the trade and processing center of a sugar, coffee, tobacco, and cotton area. Yauco produces textiles and other light manufactures.

Yavapaí Indians (yävəpī'), North American Indians whose language belongs to the Yuman branch of the Hokan-Siouan linguistic stock (see AMERICAN INDIAN LANGUAGES). They were a nomadic tribe of the Southwest area, mainly in W Arizona. They were encountered by Spanish explorers in 1582, when their population was estimated at 1,500. In the historic period they were under the protection of the Apache, and the Yavapaí were sometimes called the Mohave Apache. There are today some 800 Yavapaí on three reservations in Arizona. See E. W. Gifford, *The Southwestern Yavapai* (1932) and *Northeastern and Western Yavapai* (1936).

Yavarí, river, Peru: see JAVARI.

yaw, in aviation: see AIRPLANE; AIRFOIL.

Yawata: see KITAKYUSHU, Japan.

yawl, sailing vessel, usually fore-and-aft rigged, with a large mainmast forward. It carries a mainsail and jibs and a much smaller mizzenmast abaft the rudder post. In the United States yawls are in wide use as yachts.

yaws, tropical infection of the skin caused by a spirochete (*Treponema pertenue*) closely related to that causing syphilis. Yaws, however, is not a venereal disease, i.e., it is not contracted by sexual contact; transmission is through ordinary contact with infected persons or their clothing and by insects. An ulcerating lesion ("mother yaw") appears at the site of contact. The second stage of the disease begins 6 to 12 weeks later, when similar ulcerating lesions appear all over the body. If the disease is not treated, the third stage develops several years later, nodular and ulcerating lesions affecting the soles of the feet and penetrating the bones with destructive changes. The first and second stages of yaws are easily treated with penicillin and other antibiotics. Yaws is rarely fatal; however, it can lead to chronic disfigurement and disability.

Yaxartes: see SYR DARYA, river, USSR.

Yazd (yäzd), city (1971 est. pop. 98,000), Esfahan prov., central Iran, in a desert region. The city is a trade center for cotton, carpets, pistachios, and opium. Textiles and felt goods are the chief manufactures. It is at the junction of several roads and caravan routes and is served by a railroad. An old city, Yazd was an important Zoroastrian center in Sassanid times. It was conquered by the Arabs in 642, and in the 13th cent., when Marco Polo visited Yazd, it was a large, flourishing city. Shah Ismail annexed it to Persia in the 16th cent. Yazd is a picturesque city, with narrow, winding streets and several fine medieval mosques, religious schools, and tombs. Its Zoroastrian community, the largest in Iran, erected a modern fire temple in 1942. There is an elaborate underground water system. The city is also known as Yezd.

Yazoo (yăz'ōō), river, 188 mi (303 km) long, formed in W central Miss. by the confluence of the Tallahatchie and Yalobusha rivers. Prevented by natural levees from joining the Mississippi River sooner, the Yazoo parallels the Mississippi for c.175 mi (280 km), meandering southwest along the eastern edge of the Mississippi's flood plain before entering it near Vicksburg. The Yazoo is navigable for shallow-draft vessels. Although subject to flooding, the fertile plain between the two rivers, called the Delta, is a major cotton growing region. In the spring of 1973 about 2,800 sq mi (7,250 sq km) of the Yazoo basin were inundated by water backed up because of floods on the Mississippi River; parts of the Delta region were saturated for as long as four months, causing a delay in spring plantings. The Yazoo River is exemplary of a stream of deferred junction, and the term *yazoo* is generally applied to any stream that has a belated confluence with the main river. See F. E. Smith, *The Yazoo River* (1954).

Yazoo City, city (1970 pop. 10,796), seat of Yazoo co., W central Miss., on the Yazoo River; inc. 1830. It is a trade, processing, and industrial center in a cotton, cattle, and soybean area. Oil is refined, and clothing and fertilizer are the leading manufactures. In the Civil War the ironclad ram C.S.S. *Arkansas* was built in a Confederate navy yard there. Union troops occupied the city in May, 1864, and burned many of its buildings.

Yazoo land fraud, name given to the sale in 1795 by an act of the Georgia legislature of vast holdings in the Yazoo River country to four land companies following the wholesale bribery of the legislators; the territory comprised most of present Alabama and Mississippi. The companies involved were the Georgia, Georgia Mississippi, Upper Mississippi, and Tennessee companies. Spain's acceptance, in the same year, of lat. 31°N as the northern boundary of West Florida (see WEST FLORIDA CONTROVERSY) enhanced the value of the lands, which had formerly been claimed by Spain, and the companies set about reselling them. However, the corruption that accompanied the passage of the act was soon detected, and in 1796 a newly elected legislature rescinded it. Georgia offered to restore the purchase price to the companies, but large numbers of investors declined to accept payment and pressed their land claims. In 1802, Georgia ceded all its lands W of the Chattahoochee River to the United States for $1,250,000. By the terms of the cession agreement the Yazoo claimants were to receive 5,000,000 acres (2,025,000 hectares) or the money received from their sale, an arrangement they rejected. The Yazoo frauds came to be a vexing issue in national politics. Congress, prodded by John Randolph, declined to give the speculators any relief. But in 1810 the U.S. Supreme Court, in FLETCHER VS. PECK, held that their land claims were valid since the Yazoo act of 1795 constituted a contract binding on Georgia even though it was conceived in fraud. Bolstered by this decision, the speculators were later awarded more than $4,000,000 by Congress. See C. H. Haskins, *The Yazoo Land Companies* (1891); C. P. Magroth, *Yazoo* (1966).

Yb, chemical symbol of the element YTTERBIUM.

Yeadon (yē'dən), borough (1970 pop. 12,136), Delaware co., SE Pa., a suburb of Philadelphia; inc. 1894.

year, TIME required for the earth to complete one orbit about the sun. The solar or TROPICAL YEAR is measured relative to the sun and is equal to 365 days, 5 hr, 48 min, 46 sec of MEAN SOLAR TIME. The SIDEREAL YEAR, measured relative to the stars, is longer than the tropical year by about 20 min. The CALENDAR year is used for practical purposes and always contains a whole number of days, the ordinary year being 365 days and the leap year 366 days.

Yeardley, Sir George (yärd'lē), c.1587–1627, British colonial governor of Virginia (1618–21, 1626–27). He was shipwrecked (1609) in the Bermudas but managed to reach Virginia in 1610. In 1616–17 he was acting governor of Virginia and then returned to England, where in 1618 he was appointed governor and knighted. Under Yeardley, acting on instructions of the London Company, the first English colonial representative assembly in the New World was convened (1619) at Jamestown. This and other improvements made him exceptionally popular among the colonists. Relieved at his own request in 1621, he remained in Virginia. In 1626 he replaced Sir Francis Wyatt, who had succeeded him, and governed until his death.

yeast, name applied specifically to a certain group of microscopic FUNGI and to commercial products consisting of masses of dried yeast cells or of yeast mixed with a starchy material and pressed into yeast cakes. Although a number of fungi are sometimes called yeasts, the true yeasts are unicellular, consist of oval or round cells, and reproduce chiefly by budding. Under certain conditions some yeast cells secrete a thickened wall, and the cytoplasm of the single cell within divides to form four or eight cells, or spores, known as ascospores, which emerge when the wall ruptures. In a few species two cells fuse before undergoing spore formation. Yeasts, especially those of the genus *Saccharomyces,* have long been of commercial importance because they are the chief agents in alcoholic FERMENTATION. Because of this they are essential to the making of BEER, wine, and industrial alcohol. Wild yeasts, those found in nature and probably carried by insects from the soil to fruits, are frequently active in the fermentation process. In breadmaking the yeasts act upon the carbohydrates in the dough, forming carbon dioxide and alcohol, which are driven off in the baking process; the escaping carbon dioxide causes the bread to rise. Since early times yeast has been used in treating various ailments. Brewer's yeast has a high content of thiamine and other vitamins of the B-complex group. There is some evidence that the human body benefits by these vitamins when active dry yeast is eaten but that the vitamin-B content of fresh baker's yeast is not available to the human body. Fungi of the genus *Torula* are among those often called yeasts, although they are not true yeasts. *Torula utilis* is used in the production of protein foods by fermentation of wood-waste and otherwise unusable carbohydrates. Yeasts are classified in the division FUNGI, class Ascomycetes.

Yeats, Jack Butler (yāts), 1871–1957, Irish painter, son of the painter John Butler Yeats and brother of the poet William Butler Yeats. He began his career as an illustrator and produced his first oils in 1915, choosing literary subjects. His Irish seascapes and landscapes are notable for their loose, spontaneous brush work.

Yeats, William Butler, 1865–1939, Irish poet and playwright, b. Dublin. The greatest lyric poet that Ireland has produced and one of the major figures of 20th-century literature, Yeats was the acknowledged leader of the IRISH LITERARY RENAISSANCE. Son of the painter John Butler Yeats, William studied painting in Dublin (1883–86). As a boy he attended school in London and spent vacations in Co. Sligo, Ireland, which was the setting for many of his poems. He became fascinated by the legends of Ireland and by the occult. His first work, the drama *Mosada* (1886), reflects his concern with magic, but the long poems in *The Wanderings of Oisin* (1889) reflect the intense nationalism of the Young Ireland movement. Yeats's poetry can be divided into two periods, the first, lasting from 1886 to about 1900. The verse of this period indicates Yeats's debt to Spenser, Shelley, and the Pre-Raphaelites. It centers on Irish mythology and themes and is mystical, slow-paced, and lyrical. Among the best-known poems of the period are "Falling of Leaves," "When You Are Old," and "The Lake Isle of Innisfree." Yeats's efforts to foster Irish nationalism were inspired for years by Maud Gonne, an Irish patriot for whom he had a hopeless passion. In 1898 with Lady Augusta Gregory, George Moore, and Edward Martyn he founded the Irish Literary Theatre in Dublin; their first production (1899) was Yeats's *The Countess Cathleen* (written 1889–92). Yeats helped produce plays and collaborated with Lady Gregory on the comedy *The Pot of Broth* (1929) and other plays. The Irish Literary Theatre produced several of Yeats's plays including *Cathleen Ni Houlihan* (1902), and—after the ABBEY THEATRE was opened—*The Hour Glass* (1904), *The Land of Heart's Desire* (1904), and *Deirdre* (1907). In the meantime Yeats had been writing prose tales, collected in *The Celtic Twilight* (1893) and in the symbolic *Secret Rose* (1897). He edited William Blake's works in 1893, and his own *Poems* were collected in 1895. Yeats's poetry improved as he grew older. In the verse of his middle and late years he renounced his early transcendentalism; his poetry became stronger, more physical and realistic. A recurring theme is the polarity between extremes such as the physical and the spiritual, the real and the imagined. Memorable poems from this period include "The Second Coming," "The Tower," and "Sailing to Byzantium." Yeats initiated his second period in such volumes as *In the Seven Woods* (1903) and *The Green Helmet and Other Poems* (1910). In 1917 he married Georgie Hyde-Lees, and his occultism was encouraged by his wife's power of automatic writing. His prose work *A Vision* (1937; privately printed 1926) is the basis of much of his poetry in *The Wild Swans at Coole* (1917) and *Four Plays for Dancers* (1921). He became a respected public figure, a member (1922–28) of the Irish senate, and winner of the 1923 Nobel Prize in Literature. Some of his best work was his last, *The Tower* (1928) and *Last Poems* (1940). All of Yeats's work shows interesting and important revisions from earlier to later versions (see *The Variorum Edition* of his poems, ed. by Peter Allt and Russell R. Alspach, 1957). *A Bibliography of the Writings of W. B. Yeats* was prepared by Allan Wade (2d rev. ed. 1957). See Yeats's *Autobiography* (3 vol. in one, 1938), *Letters* (ed. by Allan Wade, 1954), *Memoirs* (ed. by Denis Donoghue, 1973), *Collected Poems* (enl. ed. 1951), *Collected Plays* (enl. ed., reissued 1952), *Mythologies* (1959), *Senate Speeches* (ed. by D. R. Pearce, 1960), and *Essays and Introductions* (1961); biography by Harold Bloom (1970); studies by T. F. Parkinson (1951 and 1964), Richard Ellmann (2d ed. 1964), A. N. Jeffares (1966), P. L. Marcus (1970), and J. R. Moore (1971).

Yeddo or **Yedo:** see TOKYO, Japan.

Yegorevsk (yĭgô'ryəfsk), city (1970 pop. 67,000), W central European USSR. It is a cotton-milling and textile center and also produces machine tools and asbestos.

Yehoash: see BLOOMGARDEN, SOLOMON.

Yelets (yĭlyĕts'), city (1970 pop. 101,000), E central USSR, on the Sosna River, a tributary of the Don. A rail junction in a black-earth agricultural district, the city exports livestock and grain. Yelets has been famed for its lace since the 19th cent. Other industries include food processing, leather tanning, and the manufacture of machinery and hydroelectric equipment. First mentioned in 1146, Yelets was a frontier fortress protecting the duchy of Ryazan from Polovtsian (Cuman) attacks. It was taken by Tamerlane in 1395. Virtually abandoned after a Tatar raid in the 15th cent., the city revived in the 17th cent. and became an important commercial center.

Yelgava (yĕl'gävä), Ger. *Mitau,* city (1969 est. pop. 51,000), W European USSR, in Latvia, on the Lielupe River. It is a major rail hub and a trade center for grain and timber. The city has textile plants and sugar mills, as well as industries that manufacture machinery, linen, leather, and metal products. The city grew around a fortress established by the Livonian Knights in the 13th cent. but was destroyed by the Lithuanians in 1345. In 1561, Yelgava became the residence of the dukes of Courland; it passed to Russia with the duchy in 1795. German troops held Yelgava during World War I. In 1919, during the struggle for Latvian independence, the city was occupied in turn by Soviet forces, by German free corps, and by the Latvians. Part of independent Latvia from 1920 to 1940, Yelgava was then seized by the USSR, held by the Germans from 1941 to 1944, and liberated by Soviet troops. City landmarks include the 16th-century Trinity Church and the 18th-century ducal palace. It is also spelled Jelgava.

Yellow Book, English illustrated quarterly published (1894–97) in book form in London. Henry HARLAND was literary editor, and Aubrey BEARDSLEY, whose exotic and provocative drawings brought immediate attention to the publication, was art editor until 1896. The *Yellow Book* was a miscellany of short stories, articles, poetry, and drawings. It was able to draw material from writers with wide differences of style and viewpoint, but its emphasis was on the bizarre, the "modern," and the aesthetic. It included among its contributors Oscar Wilde, Max Beerbohm, John Davidson, Richard Le Gallienne, William Butler Yeats, Ernest Dowson, and Arnold Bennett. See Holbrook Jackson, *The Eighteen Nineties* (1927); E. L. Casford, *The Magazines of the 1890's* (1929); Norman Denny, ed., *The Yellow Book: A Selection* (1949); K. L. Mix, *A Study in Yellow: The Yellow Book and its Contributors* (1960, repr. 1969).

yellow daisy: see BLACK-EYED SUSAN.

Yellow Emperor, Mandarin *Huang Ti,* legendary Chinese ruler and culture hero; tradition holds that he reigned from 2697 B.C. to 2597 B.C. He is one of the mythical prehistoric emperors who supposedly created the basic elements of Chinese civilization. His wife is said to have developed silk production. Along with the semimythical LAO-TZE, he was associated in the traditional Chinese folk culture with the founding of Taoism.

yellow fever, acute infectious disease endemic in tropical Africa and many areas of South America. Epidemics have extended into subtropical and temperate regions during warm seasons; the last epidemic in the United States occurred in New Orleans in 1905. Yellow fever is caused by a filterable virus transmitted by the bite of the female *Aedes aegypti* mosquito, which breeds in stagnant water near human habitations. A form of the disease called sylvan yellow fever is transmitted in tropical jungles by other species of mosquitoes that live in trees. At the turn of the century yellow fever was highly prevalent in the Caribbean area, and a way of controlling it had to be found before construction of the Panama Canal could be undertaken. In 1900 a commission headed by Walter Reed and including James Carroll, Jesse Lazear, and Aristides Agramonte proved in Havana the theory of C. J. Finlay that yellow fever was a mosquito-borne infection. W. C. Gorgas, an army physician and sanitation expert, succeeded in controlling the disease in the Panama Canal Zone and other areas in that part of the world by mosquito-eradication measures. The later development of an immunizing vaccine and strict quarantine measures against ships, planes, and passengers coming from known or suspected yellow-fever areas further aided control of the disease. Yellow fever begins suddenly after an incubation period of three to five days. In mild cases only fever and headache may be present. The severe form of the disease commences with fever, chills, bleeding into the skin, rapid heartbeat, headache, back pains, and extreme prostration. Nausea, vomiting, and constipation are common. Jaundice usually appears on the second or third day. After the third day the symptoms recede, only to return with increased severity in the final stage, during which there is a marked tendency to hemorrhage internally; the characteristic "coffee ground" vomitus contains blood. The patient then lapses into delirium and coma, often followed by death. During epidemics the fatality rate was often as high as 85%. Although the disease still occurs, it is usually confined to sporadic outbreaks.

yellowhammer: see WOODPECKER.

Yellowhead Pass, 3,711 ft (1,131 m) high, in the Rocky Mts., on the boundary between Alta. and British Columbia, Canada, and W of Jasper, Alta. It is used by the Canadian National Railways.

yellow jacket: see WASP.

Yellowknife, town (1971 pop. 6,122), capital of the Northwest Territories, S Mackenzie dist., Northwest Territories, Canada, on the north shore of Great Slave Lake, at the mouth of the Yellowknife River. The town was founded (1935) after the discovery of rich deposits of gold. It is the largest town in the Northwest Territories and a mining, supply, and transportation center, with an airport, radio and meteorological stations, a public school, a post of the Royal Canadian Mounted Police, and regional offices of other federal agencies. Mining production began in 1938. Another mine was discovered in 1944 and a new townsite was established the next year. Yellowknife, named after an Indian tribe, became capital of the Northwest Territories in 1967.

yellow poplar: see MAGNOLIA.

Yellow River, China: see HUANG HO.

Yellow Sea or **Hwang-hai** (hwäng-hī), Mandarin *Huang-hai* [yellow sea], arm of the Pacific Ocean, between China and Korea. It has a maximum depth of 500 ft (152 m). Po Hai, Korea Bay, and the Liaotung Gulf are its major inlets. The Huang Ho, Huai, Liao, and Yalu rivers empty into it. South of the Korean peninsula, it becomes the East China Sea.

Yellowstone, river, 671 mi (1,080 km) long, rising in NW Wyo., and flowing NE through Mont. to enter the Missouri River near the N.Dak. line; it drains c.70,400 sq mi (182,340 sq km). The Yellowstone receives the Bighorn, Powder, Tongue, and many smaller rivers. The most scenic aspects of the river are found in Yellowstone National Park in NW Wyoming. There, the river feeds and drains Yellowstone Lake, 139 sq mi (360 sq km), the largest high-altitude (alt. 7,331 ft/2,234 m) lake in North America. After leaving the lake, the river drops 109 ft (33 m) at Upper Falls, then 308 ft (94 m) at Lower Falls, before entering the deep and spectacular Grand Canyon of the Yellowstone (19 mi/31 km long); Tower Falls, 132 ft (40 m) high, is at the northern end of the canyon. The river's waters have been used for irrigation since the late 1860s. The U.S. Bureau of Reclamation operates several projects on the Yellowstone that are used for irrigation, flood control, power production, and recreation. These include the Huntley project near Billings, Mont., the Buffalo Rapids project near Glendive, Mont., and the Savage unit of the Missouri River basin project.

Yellowstone National Park, first (est. 1872) and largest (2,221,773 acres/899,152 hectares) national park in the United States, NW Wyo., extending into Montana and Idaho. It lies mainly on a broad plateau in the Rocky Mts., on the Continental Divide, c.8,000 ft (2,440 m) above sea level, surrounded by mountains from 10,000 to 14,000 ft (3,048–4,267 m) high. Most of the plateau is formed from once molten lava; volcanic activity is still evidenced by nearly 10,000 hot springs, 200 geysers, and many vents and hot-mud pots. The more prominent geysers are unequaled in size, power, and variety of action. **Old Faithful,** the best known although not the largest geyser, erupts at an average interval of 64.5 min and shoots c.11,000 gal (41,640 liters) of water some 150 ft (46 m) high. Mammoth Hot Springs, a series of five terraces with reflecting pools, continues to grow, as residue from the mineral-rich steaming water is deposited. The park's other natural wonders include petrified forests, lava formations, and the "black glass" Obsidian Cliff. Eagle Peak, 11,370 ft (3,466 m), is the highest point in the park. Yellowstone Lake, the Grand Canyon of the Yellowstone, and waterfalls are notable features on the Yellowstone River, which crosses the park. Evergreen forests cover 90% of the park, and a great variety of flowers and other plant life are found. Bears, mountain sheep, elk, bison, moose, many smaller animals, and more than 200 kinds of birds make their homes in Yellowstone Park, which is one of the world's largest wildlife sanctuaries. See Ann and Myron Sutton, *Yellowstone* (1972).

yellowwood, common name for any species of the genus *Cladrastis,* leguminous trees of the family Leguminosae (PULSE family). Three of the four species are native to China and Japan. The other, *C. lutea,* is native to the SE United States and is cultivated as far north as Massachusetts, chiefly as an ornamental for the bright green leaves and the fragrant white blossoms. A dye is obtained from the yellow heartwood. The name yellowwood is used also for several unrelated trees yielding yellow lumber, e.g., *Podocarpus thunbergii* and *P. elongata,* conifers of S Africa used in construction; *Schaefferia frutescens* of S Florida and the West Indies, sometimes also called boxwood and used in engraving as a substitute for true boxwood; and West Indian satinwood. *Cladrastis* is classified in the division MAGNOLIOPHYTA, class Magnoliopsida, order Rosales, family Leguminosae.

Yemasee Indians: see YAMASEE INDIANS.

Yemen (yĕm'ən), officially Yemen Arab Republic, republic (1970 est. pop. 6,500,000), 75,290 sq mi (195,000 sq km), SW Asia, at the southwestern tip of the Arabian Peninsula. SANA is the capital. Yemen is bordered on the north and northeast by Saudi Arabia, on the southeast by Southern Yemen (People's Democratic Republic of Yemen), and on the west by the Red Sea. The Arabic name, Al-Yaman, probably means the right hand and describes the country's position as one stands before the Kaaba in Mecca facing east. Because it was confused with another Arabic word meaning happiness, the name was rendered Arabia Felix [happy or fortunate Arabia] by European geographers. In classical times, however,

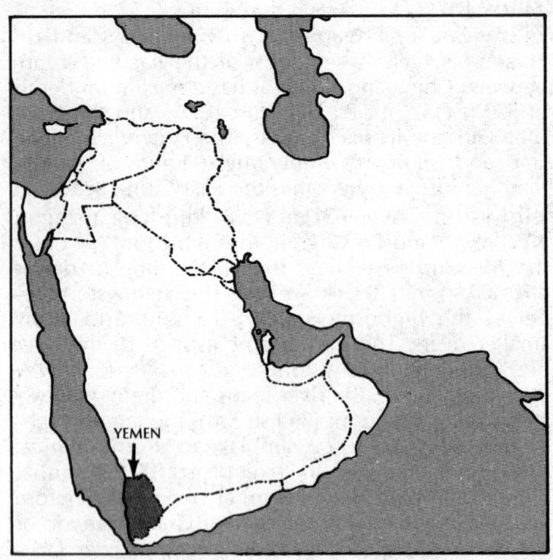

the name was applied to a much larger area than the present Yemen. The country consists of a narrow, coastal plain, the interior highlands, and the eastern desert. The coastal plain, or Tihamah, which is about 20 to 50 mi (30–80 km) wide, extends along the length of W Yemen. It is a hot and virtually rainless region with high humidity and is composed of alluvial and talus material carried down from the highlands; there is little vegetation. The interior highlands, which are actually a section of the upturned Arabian plateau, are the highest part (rising to more than 12,000 ft/3,660 m) of the Arabian Peninsula. The highlands receive an annual average rainfall of c.20 in. (50 cm), making them also the wettest part of the peninsula; most of the precipitation occurs during the summer rainy season. Vegetation is of the subtropical variety and varies with altitude. Numerous wadis radiate from the highlands, but Yemen has no permanent streams; oases and springs provide local water needs. The eastern side of the highlands, which is in a rain shadow, slopes eastward into the great sandy expanses of the Rub al Khali desert. The great majority of the people of Yemen are Arabs; most of those living on the Tihamah are of mixed Arab and African stock. About 60% of the population are Sunni Muslims, while the remainder are Zaidi Muslims. Between 1948 and 1950 about 50,000 Yemeni Jews emigrated to Israel. Arabic is the nation's principal language. Yemen has an overwhelmingly rural population, with most of the people engaged in agricultural activities. The nation's per capita income is among the world's lowest. In addition to Sana, Yemen's important cities include HODEIDA, the nation's chief port, and TAIZZ, a commercial center. The present literacy rate of Yemen is very low, although the region was once known for its centers of learning. Overland communication within Yemen is difficult since there are few roads and no railroads; air traffic is important. Except for salt, Yemen has no commercially exploitable minerals. The moist and fertile highlands are the country's (and the peninsula's) chief agricultural region. A variety of grains, as well as vegetables, fruits, cotton, coffee, and qat (a narcotic shrub) are raised there. In the Tihamah irrigated cotton and dates are grown; however, this area is primarily a livestock-raising region in which sheep, goats, and camels are raised. Manufacturing, which is largely based on agricultural products, has been generally increasing but provides the country with little revenue. Handicrafts play an important role in the economy. Agricultural products provide about 70% of Yemen's exports, with cotton, coffee, qat, salt, and hides and skins the leading commodities. Yemen's chief imports are machinery, oil, and textiles. Its main trading partners are the USSR, China, Japan, and Southern Yemen. The country receives a good portion of its foreign exchange from money sent home by Yemeni nationals working abroad, principally in Saudi Arabia. Yemen is governed by the constitution of 1970 and has a republican form of government. The chairman (president) of the presidential council, which has three members, is the head of state and has the most power. The consultative council, the legislative body, is composed of 179 members, of which 20 are appointed by the president. The earliest recorded civilizations of S Arabia were the Minaean and Sabaean. The Sabaean kingdom (see SHEBA) flourished from c.750 B.C. to c.115 B.C., with MARIB (located E of Sana) the capital after c.600 B.C. Sabaean society was highly developed technically, as witnessed by the remains of a great dam at Marib that was the center of a large irrigation system. The Himyarites, who followed the Sabaeans, were invaded by the Romans (1st cent. B.C.) and were occupied by the Ethiopians (A.D. c.340–378). During the second Himyarite kingdom Christianity and Judaism took root in Yemen. Ethiopia again conquered the country in 525. After a Persian period (575–628), Islam came to Yemen, which was soon reduced to a province of the Muslim caliphate. After the breakup of the caliphate, Yemen came under the control of the rising Rassite dynasty, imams of the Zaidi sect who built the theocratic political structure of Yemen that lasted until 1962. The Fatamid caliphs of Egypt occupied most of Yemen from c.1000 until c.1175, when it fell to the Ayyubids, who ruled until c.1250. By 1520, Yemen formed part of the Ottoman Empire, which exercised at least nominal sovereignty until the end of World War I. A turbulent wave of Wahabism, a puritanical sect of Islam, swept across the Arabian Peninsula at the opening of the 19th cent. and drove out the Zaidi imams. Ibrahim Pasha of Egypt, acting in the name of the Turkish sultan, drove out the Wahabis in 1818, and the Egyptians remained until 1840. The Turks then replaced the Egyptians, giving the imam full autonomy in the interior. After the Turkish evacuation (1918), Imam Yahya moved to expand Yemen's territory, but his only gain was the port and surrounding area of Hodeida. In 1934, after a brief Saudi Arabian invasion and skirmishes with Great Britain (which had the protectorate of Aden), Yemen's boundaries were fixed by treaty with Saudi Arabia and Great Britain. However, clashes on the Aden border continued sporadically. Modifying its traditional policy of isolation, Yemen became more active in foreign affairs after World War II; it joined the Arab League in 1945 and the United Nations in 1947 and established diplomatic relations with other nations. However, the imam, as both king and spiritual leader, continued to rule along theocratic lines. Dissatisfaction, hitherto rapidly suppressed, grew, and in 1948 a palace revolt broke out, and the old Imam Yahya was assassinated. Crown Prince Ahmad drove out the insurgents and succeeded as imam. The new ruler accepted technical and economic assistance from both the West and the Communist bloc. From 1958 to 1961, Yemen joined with the United Arab Republic (Egypt and Syria) to form the United Arab States, which in reality was a paper alliance. Disorders broke out in 1959, and Imam Ahmad survived an assassination attempt in 1961. After his death in 1962, Imam Ahmad was succeeded by Crown Prince Muhammad al-Bahr (later Imam Mansur Billah Muhammad), who favored a neutralist foreign policy. Soon afterward a revolt headed by pro-Egyptian army officers deposed the imam, but he escaped and led royalist tribes against the new government. The ruling junta, commanded by Col. Adallah al-Salal, proclaimed a republic, and the army contained the imam's forces. Yemen then became an international battleground, with Egypt supporting the republicans and Saudi Arabia and Jordan the royalists. The Yemeni republicans split into opposing factions on the issue of Egyptian support. In an administrative reorganization in 1966, the independent government of Premier Hassan al-Amri was ousted by a strongly pro-Egyptian regime, with al-Salal assuming the office of premier. Many of al-Amri's supporters were arrested or removed from office. In 1967 by mutual agreement, Egyptian troops were withdrawn from Yemen, and Saudi Arabian aid to the royalists was halted. In Nov., 1967, al-Salal's government was overthrown while he was abroad, and a three-man republican council was formed with Qadi Abd al-Rahman al-Iryani (one of the anti-Egyptian leaders) as chairman; al-Amri resumed the premiership. Fighting between the republicans and the royalists continued until 1970, when Saudi Arabia formally recognized the republican regime and stopped all aid to the royalists. Between 1967 and 1972 there were frequent border clashes between Yemen and Southern Yemen until an accord was signed (1972) to merge the two countries. However, by 1974 the agreement had not been implemented and friction continued between the two states. On June 12, 1974, Chairman al-Iryani resigned after a period of internal political tension, and the next day a group of army officers led by Col. Ibrahim al-Hamidi staged a nonviolent coup d'etat. The officers established a command council to govern the country and suspended the constitution, pledging to reestablish civilian rule as soon as possible. See Claudie Fayein, *A French Doctor in the Yemen* (tr. 1957); Thorkild Hansen, *Arabia Felix* (1964); W. H. Ingrams, *The Yemen: Imams, Rulers, and Revolutions* (1964); M. W. Wenner, *Modern Yemen, 1918–1966* (1967); Eric Macro, *Yemen and the Western World Since 1571* (1968); D. A. Schmidt, *Yemen: The Unknown War* (1968); Edgar O'Ballance, *The War in the Yemen* (1971).

Yemen, Southern, officially People's Democratic Republic of Yemen, republic (1973 est. pop. 1,400,000), 111,074 sq mi (287,683 sq km), SW Asia, at the southern edge of the Arabian Peninsula. ADEN is the capital. Southern Yemen is bordered on the north by Saudi Arabia, on the east by Oman, on the south by the Gulf of Aden and the Arabian Sea, and on the west by the Yemen Arab Republic. The islands of Karaman, in the Red Sea, PERIM, in the Bab el Mandeb, and SOCOTRA and the Kuria Maria islands, in the Arabian Sea, are part of Southern Yemen. The country consists of a coastal plain, a belt of mountains, and a portion of the Arabian plateau. The coastal plain, which is very narrow and stretches more than 700 mi (1,130 km) along the southern edge of the Arabian Peninsula, is a hot and virtually rainless region with high humidity and sparse vegetation (mainly thorn bushes). In the western part of the country are low mountains that are actually part of the edge of the Arabian plateau. The ranges increase in height from east to west, with the western portion also being the wettest part of the country. The mountains lead up to the level of the plateau, which, in the east, rises from the coastal plain. In N Southern Yemen the plateau slopes down into the barren, sandy expanses of the Rub al Khali desert. The mountains and the plateau, both of which have an arid, rocky, and rugged environment, are cut by numerous wadis that usually carry water only during the summer rainy season, and then mainly in the form of floods. Wadi Hadhramaut, in the central

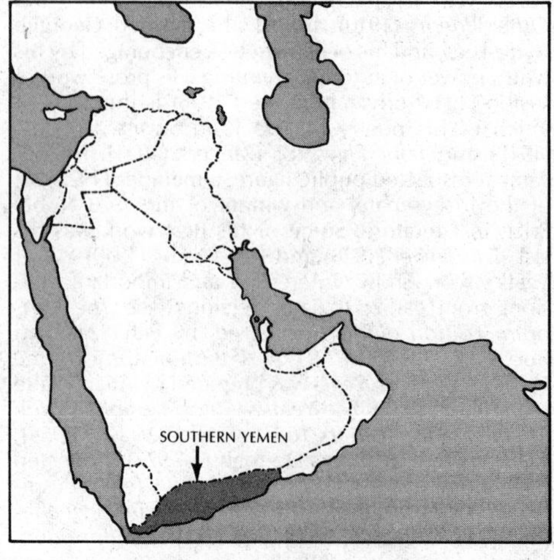

part of the country, is the largest wadi. Its wide upper and middle portions have alluvial soil and moisture from intermittent streams and are the country's best farmlands; the lower portion is dry and uninhabited. The majority of the people of Southern Yemen are Arabs; those on Socotra are of mixed European, African, and Arab descent. The tribal social structure is still prevalent in the country, although its importance diminishes along the coast, where there has been long contact with foreigners. Only the tribes in the north are entirely nomadic. Islam is the principal religion and Arabic the official language; Himyaritic, a form of Arabic, is spoken in the eastern part of the country and on Socotra. Overland transportation in Southern Yemen is difficult. There are few paved roads and no railroads, and camels remain a major form of transport. Southern Yemen is one of the world's poorest nations and relies heavily on foreign aid. Its economy was greatly damaged during the time that the Suez Canal was closed following the 1967 Arab-Israeli war. Agriculture is the mainstay of the economy, even though it is primarily of a subsistence nature and only a fraction of the land is arable. Modern methods of irrigation have increased the amount of tilled land. The principal farming areas are Wadi Hadhramaut, which produces coffee and tobacco; wadis Bana and Tibban, N of Aden, which produce cotton; and the moist highland region in the west, which produces grains and dates. Pastoralism is important throughout the country, and fishing is a major economic activity along the coast. Nearly all of Southern Yemen's industry is located in or near Aden. Petroleum refining is the most important industry, and petroleum products and ships' fuel account for nearly three quarters of the country's exports. Several light industries produce domestically consumed goods such as soap, cigarettes, and textiles. Cotton, fish products, and hides and skins are major exports. The region has also been a major supplier of incense. Southern Yemen's chief imports are food, textiles, and crude petroleum. Its main trading partners are Kuwait, Iran, Japan, and Great Britain. The country is governed under the constitution of 1970, which vests power in a three-man presidential council. The president is the head of state and the prime minister the head of government, and there is a 101-member supreme people's council. The National Liberation Front is the only legal political party. Southern Yemen was once part of a larger region called Al-Yaman, the Arabia Felix of early European geographers. A number of empires, including the Minaean, Sabaean, and Himyarite, flourished there. The region came under Muslim influence in the 7th cent. In the 16th cent. it became part of the Ottoman Empire and came under the suzerainty of the imams of Yemen. (For a more detailed history see ARABIA; YEMEN.) The British presence in Southern Yemen began in 1839, when forces of the British East India Co. occupied Aden. In 1854 and 1857 the Kuria Maria and Perim islands were ceded to the British and other mainland areas were purchased by them. Between 1886 and 1914, Britain signed a number of protectorate treaties with local rulers. In 1937 the area, which by then consisted of 24 sultanates, emirates, and sheikhdoms, was designated the Aden Protectorate and was divided for administrative purposes into the East Aden protectorate and the West Aden protectorate. In 1959, 6 small states of the West Aden protectorate formed the Federation of the Emirates of the South; it was later enlarged to 10 members. Despite considerable opposition from its population, the Aden colony proper was made part of the federation (1963), which was then renamed the Federation of South Arabia (see SOUTH ARABIA, FEDERATION OF). By 1965, 16 tribal states had joined the federation. However, nationalist groups in Aden remained adamantly opposed to the federation and began a terrorist campaign against the British. Two rival nationalist groups emerged: the National Liberation Front (NLF) and the Front for the Liberation of Occupied South Yemen (FLOSY). Although Britain had promised to withdraw from the region by 1968, the NLF, which had emerged as the dominant group by 1967, forced the collapse of the federation after taking control of the governments of all the component states. Britain accelerated its withdrawal, and Southern Yemen became independent in Nov., 1967, with Qahtan al-Shaabi of the NLF the first president. In 1970 the country received a new constitution and was renamed the People's Democratic Republic of Yemen. Since independence there have been border disputes with Oman and the Yemen Arab Republic; some of which have led to armed clashes. An accord was signed with the Yemen Arab Republic in 1972 calling for the end of fighting and the merger of the two countries. However, by 1974 the agreement had not yet been implemented. In April, 1972, the government of Southern Yemen suffered a severe blow when 25 of its top officials were killed in an airplane crash. See Tom Little, *South Arabia* (1968).

Yen, James Y. C. (yĕn), Mandarin *Yen Yang-chu,* 1893–, b. Szechwan prov., China, educator, educated at Yale (B.A., 1918) and Princeton (M.A., 1920) universities. Yen devised a simplified form of Chinese writing consisting of 1,000 characters and suitable for instructing adult illiterates. He became prominent for his work with the national association for mass education, which was organized to reduce illiteracy and encourage modern methods of farming and agricultural marketing.

Yenakiyevo (yĕnəkē'yəvə), city (1970 pop. 92,000), SE European USSR, in the Ukraine, on the Bulavin River. It is a large center for coal, iron and steel, and chemicals in the Donets Basin. Yenakiyevo was founded in 1883 as a coal-mining settlement.

Yen-an or **Yenan** (both: yĕn-än), city (1971 est. pop. 45,000), N Shensi prov., China, on the Yen River. Now a market and tourist center, it is famed as the terminus of the long march and the de facto capital (1936–47, 1948–9) of the Chinese Communists, who established arsenals, several colleges, and a military academy (now a museum) there. The city's many loess caves served as homes and air raid shelters during World War II. As a hallowed site of the revolution, Yen-an attracts thousands of pilgrims. Points of interest include the former homes of Mao Tse-tung and Chou En-lai, and a nine-story pagoda built during the Sung dynasty (960–1279) and now made into a monument to the revolution. Many people still live in cave dwellings. Oil is produced at nearby Yen-ch'ang. See Edgar Snow, *Red Star Over China* (1938, repr. 1961) and *Red China Today: The Other Side of the River* (rev. ed. 1971); Jan Myrdal, *Report from a Chinese Village* (tr. by M. Michael, 1965).

Yenikale Strait: see KERCH STRAIT, USSR.

Yenisei (yĕnĭsā', Rus. yĕnyĭsyā'), chief river of Siberia, c.2,500 mi (4,020 km) long, central Siberian USSR. It is formed at Kyzyl, Tuva Autonomous Oblast, by the junction of the Bolshoi Yenisei and Maly Yenisei rivers, which rise in the E Sayan Mts. along the USSR–Mongolian border. It flows westward, then generally north, past Minusinsk, Krasnoyarsk, Yeniseisk, and Igarka to enter the Kara Sea through a c.250 mi (400 km) long estuary composed of Yenisei Bay and Yenisei Gulf. The Angara, Stony Tunguska, and Lower Tunguska rivers are the Yenisei's chief tributaries. The river is frozen during the winter months. In the spring ice in the upper Yenisei melts before that in the lower river, causing extensive flooding as water backs up behind the frozen portion of the river. The Yenisei's upper course is turbulent, with many rapids, and has a great hydroelectric generating potential; there is a large hydroelectric station at Krasnoyarsk. The river's middle course widens and is navigable for steamers. Lumber, grain, and construction materials are transported along the Yenisei. Igarka on the lower river is the region's chief lumber-loading port. There is fishing for sturgeon and salmon in the river's lower reaches. The Ob River is joined to the Yenisei by a canal system.

Yen Li-pen (yŭn lē-bŭn), d. 673, Chinese painter, foremost master of the T'ang dynasty. He became the most celebrated court painter of the 7th cent. and held several high public offices. Although probably none of his original works survives today, records tell us that he was most renowned for his paintings of Buddhist and Taoist themes and also as the painter of historical personages and events. The superb scroll painting *Portraits of Thirteen Emperors* in the Museum of Fine Arts, Boston, has been attributed to him but may be a copy. It represents the peak of early T'ang art.

Yenping: see NAN-P'ING, China.

Yen-t'ai (yŭn-tī) or **Chefoo** (chē'fo͞o'), city (1970 est. pop. 180,000), N Shantung prov., China. It is Shantung's largest fishing port. The city also has fruit orchards, and wine and brandy are produced. Yen-t'ai was opened to foreign trade in 1862. By the Chefoo Convention, signed there in 1876, many new treaty ports were established. A rail line, built in 1955, links Yen-t'ai with Ch'ing'-tao and Chi-nan.

yeoman (yō'mən), class in English society. The term has always been ill-defined, but generally it means a freeholder of a lower status than gentleman who cultivates his own land. With the breakdown of medieval systems of tenure the numbers of this class increased and formed the basis for a rural middle class. Certain retainers of a fairly high rank in noble households were also called yeomen, and thus the name was given to specific branches of the royal household, e.g., yeomen of the horse or YEOMEN OF THE GUARD. The yeoman foot soldiers of the Hundred Years War were the troops most personally in the service of the king. The more modern military use of the term dates from the 18th cent., when voluntary cavalry units called the yeomanry were used to suppress riots. From 1794 they were organized into regiments. Their service in the South African War (1899–1902) earned them the name Imperial Yeomanry, and in 1907 they became a part of the Territorial Army.

Yeomen of the Guard, bodyguard, now ceremonial in function, of the sovereign of England. When the guard was originated by Henry VII in 1485, its members had numerous duties as defenders of the king's person and household functionaries. Until 1743 (the last time a British monarch appeared on the battlefield) they accompanied the king in battle. For a time purchased by civilians, positions in the corps were restricted in 1848 to veterans of the army and marines. Sometimes called the Beefeaters because of their fine physiques, the Yeomen of the Guard still wear the scarlet and gold uniform of the 15th cent. and carry halberds.

Yeotmal (yā'ōtmäl), town (1971 pop. 64,829), Maharashtra state, central India. Yeotmal, located c.1,500 ft (460 m) above sea level, is a district administrative center, a cattle-breeding town, and a market for peanuts, cotton, and timber.

Yeovil (yō'vĭl), municipal borough (1971 pop. 25,492), Somerset, SW England, on the Yeo River. It is a market town and a leather-making center. Glove making has been a local specialty since the 16th cent.; helicopters and processed foods are also produced. The Perpendicular Church of St. John (late 14th cent.) is sometimes called the "Lantern of the West." There are a number of picturesque old houses.

yerba buena (yĕr'bə bwā'nə), trailing evergreen perennial (*Micromeria chamissonis*) of the family Labiatae (MINT family). It is native to W North America and especially common to woodland areas along the Pacific coast. Its aromatic leaves were gathered by the Indians of California for use in a medicinal tea. Yerba buena is classified in the division MAGNOLIOPHYTA, class Magnoliopsida, order Lamiales, family Labiatae.

Yerba Buena Island, 300 acres (121 hectares), W Calif., in San Francisco Bay. It is the midpoint of the San Francisco-Oakland Bay Bridge, which crosses the island through a tunnel. On the island are several government installations, including a lighthouse service and a naval training station.

yerba maté: see MATÉ.

Yerevan (yĕrĕvän'), Rus. *Erivan,* city (1970 pop. 767,000), capital of the Armenian Soviet Socialist Republic, SE European USSR, on the Razdan River. One of the USSR's oldest towns and a leading industrial, cultural, and scientific center, Yerevan is also a rail junction and carries on a brisk trade in agricultural products. The city's industries produce metals, machine tools, electrical equipment, chemicals, textiles, and food products. Archaeological evidence indicates that the fortress of Yerbuni stood on Yerevan's site in the 8th cent. B.C. The city, known in the 7th cent. A.D., was the capital of Armenia under Persian rule and became historically and strategically important as a crossroads of the caravan routes between Transcaucasia and India. After the downfall (15th cent.) of Tamerlane's empire, to which Yerevan belonged, the city passed back and forth between Persia and Turkey. In 1440 it became the center of East Armenia. During the 17th cent. Yerevan was a frontier fort and a caravan trading point. It became the capital of the Yerevan khanate of Persia in 1725. Taken by Russia in 1827, the city was formally ceded by the Treaty of Turkmanchai (1828). Yerevan was the center of independent Armenia from 1918 to 1920, when it became the capital of the newly formed Armenian SSR. Educational and cultural facilities include a university, the Armenian Academy of Sciences, a state museum, and several libraries. There are ruins of a 16th-century Turkish fortress.

Yerkes, Charles Tyson (yûr'kēz, -kəs), 1837–1905, American financier, b. Philadelphia. He began his business career as a clerk in a Philadelphia grain commission house. He became a broker in 1858 and prospered, but in 1871 he was convicted of misappropriating city funds and was imprisoned. He regained his financial position through stock-market activities and became interested in the Philadelphia street railway system. He moved (1881) to Chicago, where by 1886 he had gained control of, and developed, the city transportation system. Later he went to London to participate in the development of the underground railway system of that city. In 1892, Yerkes furnished the Univ. of Chicago with the funds for the Yerkes Observatory, established (1897) at Williams Bay, Wis., near the Wisconsin-Illinois line.

Yerkes, Robert Mearns (yûr'kēz), 1876–1956, American psychologist, b. Bucks co., Pa., grad. Harvard (B.A. 1898; Ph.D. 1902). He taught (1901–17) at Harvard, served (1919–24) on the National Research Council, and from 1924 to 1944 was professor of psychobiology at Yale. He also founded and directed the Yale Laboratories of Primate Biology (renamed the Yerkes Laboratories of Primate Biology in 1942) at Orange Park, Fla. He is known for his work in comparative psychology, the experimental study of animal behavior (especially of anthropoids), and psychobiology. His works include *Introduction to Psychology* (1911), *The Mental Life of Monkeys and Apes* (1916), *The Mind of a Gorilla* (2 parts, 1926–27), and *The Great Apes* (with Ada Yerkes, 1929).

Yerkes Observatory, astronomical OBSERVATORY located in Williams Bay, Wis., on the shore of Lake Geneva. It was founded in 1892 with funds provided by C. T. Yerkes, and its first director was G. E. Hale. The observatory is administered by the Univ. of Chicago. The principal instrument is a 40-in. refracting TELESCOPE, completed in 1897, the largest of its type in the world; its size is very near the practical limit for a refractor because of distortions that may be caused by the weight of the lens itself. Other equipment includes a 41-in. and two 24-in. reflecting telescopes and a number of specialized instruments. Principal programs include astrometry, radio, infrared, and X-ray astronomy, and studies of comets, galaxies, and the interstellar medium. In 1932 the Univ. of Chicago joined with the Univ. of Texas in founding the MCDONALD OBSERVATORY at Fort Davis, Texas, and the two observatories often participate in joint programs of research.

Yermak or **Ermak** (both: yĕrmăk'), d. 1584?, Russian conqueror of Siberia. The leader of a band of independent Russian Cossacks, he spent his early career plundering the czar's ships on the Volga and later entered the service of a merchant family, the Stroganovs. They sent Yermak on an expedition to protect their lands in W Siberia from attack by local tribes. Advancing in river boats, Yermak and his band crossed the Urals and with the superior force of firearms conquered (1582) the capital of the Tatar khanate of SIBIR; he placed the conquered territory under the protection of Czar Ivan IV and asked him for aid. Yermak was killed in an encounter with the Tatars, and his troops were forced to retreat. However, Russian troops retook the territory in 1586.

Yersin, Alexandre Émile Jean (ălĕksäN'drə āmēl' zhän yĕrsăN'), 1863–1943, French bacteriologist, of Swiss descent. He studied with Pasteur and worked on diphtheria antitoxin with P. P. E. Roux at the Pasteur Institute, Paris. Yersin discovered (1894) the bacillus of bubonic plague (independently of Kitasato) and prepared a serum to combat the disease. He was director of the Pasteur Institute at Nhatrang (SE Annam) and inspector general of the Pasteur Institutes at Saigon, at Hanoi, and at Dalat (S of Nhatrang).

Yesenin, Sergei Aleksandrovich (syĭrgā' əlyĭksän'drəvĭch yĭsyä'nĭn), 1895–1925, Russian poet. Yesenin was the most popular poet of the early revolution and the object of a considerable cult. He belonged to the imaginist school, advocating absolute independence for the artist. Yesenin is known for his simple lyrics about village life and the Russian landscape. His epic *Pugachev* (1922) is a verse tragedy concerning the peasant rebellion of 1773–75. After welcoming the revolution, he rejected the policies of the Bolshevik regime. In 1922 Yesenin married Isadora DUNCAN and toured the United States and Europe. After they separated he married a granddaughter of Leo Tolstoy. At 30 he committed suicide. His name also appears as Esenin.

Yeshiva University, in New York City; mainly coeducational; begun 1886 as Yeshiva Eitz Chaim, a Jewish theological seminary, chartered 1928 as Rabbi Isaac Elchanan Theological Seminary and Yeshiva College; renamed 1945. Yeshiva, the oldest and largest university under Jewish auspices in the United States, maintains three campuses in New York. Noteworthy programs at Yeshiva include the well-known Albert Einstein College of Medicine, the Talmudic and Israel research institutes, and the graduate school of mathematical studies. Its library houses an outstanding collection of Hebraica and Judaica.

Yeşil Irmak (yĕshĕl' ərmäk'), anc. *Iris,* river, c.260 mi (418 km) long, rising NE of Sivas, N Turkey. It flows NW, then NE, past Tokat and Amasya into the Black Sea near Samsun.

Yesso: see HOKKAIDO, Japan.

yeti: see ABOMINABLE SNOWMAN.

Yevpatoriya (yĕfpətô'rēə), city (1969 est. pop. 75,000), S European USSR, in the Ukraine, in the Crimea. It is a Black Sea port, a rail hub, and a vacation and health resort. Fishing, food processing, wine making, limestone quarrying, weaving, and the manufacture of building materials, machinery, and furniture are the chief industries. Yevpatoriya stands on the site of the ancient Greek colony of Kerkinitida, founded in the 6th cent. B.C. In the 1st cent. B.C. the area was captured by the Pontian king Mitridat Evpator, for whom the city is named. Changing hands many times, Yevpatoriya came under the control of the Turko-Tatars in the 13th cent.; they later became vassals of Turkey, which took the city in 1478. Russia annexed Yevpatoriya along with the rest of the Crimea in 1783, and during the Crimean War it was occupied (1854) by British, French, and Turkish troops. Historic landmarks include a 16th-century mosque and the ruins of the Tatar fortress (15th cent.). The name of the city is sometimes spelled Evpatoriya or Eupatoria.

Yevtushenko, Yevgeny Aleksandrovich (yĕv"-tōōshĕng'kō, Rus. yĭvgā'nyē əlyĭksän'drəvĭch yĭvtəshĕn'kō), 1933–, Soviet poet. Yevtushenko's first book of poems was published in 1952. He soon became the most popular spokesman of the young generation of poets who refused to adhere to the doctrine of SOCIALIST REALISM. *Yevtushenko: Selected Poems* (1962) contains three of his most famous poems: "Talk," an indictment of Soviet hypocrisy, "Babi Yar," protesting Soviet anti-Semitism, and "Zima Junction," an autobiographical work. Yevtushenko has frequently been criticized for his nonconformist attitude. In 1963 the publication in Paris of his *Precocious Autobiography* (tr. 1963) brought him severe official censure. Despite this he has made several reading tours abroad. His later volumes of poetry include *Power Station of Bratsk* (1965, tr. 1967), *Poetry of Yevgeny Yevtushenko* (rev. ed. 1967), *Flowers and Bullets and Freedom to Kill* (tr. 1970), and *Stolen Apples* (1971; adaptations by James Dickey et al.). His name is also spelled Evtushenko.

yew, name for evergreen trees or shrubs of the genus *Taxus,* somewhat similar to hemlock but bearing red berrylike fruits instead of true cones. Of somber appearance, with dark green leaves, the yew since antiquity has been associated with death and funeral rites. The English yew (*T. baccata*) was used for the longbows of English archers. The wood of several yews is still employed in making bows and for cabinetwork. In North America the most common species is a low, spreading shrub (*T. canadensis*), called also ground hemlock, which is native to Canada and to the NW United States. Yews are often trimmed into hedges. Several related evergreen species are also cultivated for ornament, e.g., the plum-yews, of the Oriental genus *Cephalotaxus.* Yew is classified in the division PINOPHYTA, class Pinopsida, order Coniferales, family Taxaceae.

Yezd, Iran: see YAZD.

Yezo: see HOKKAIDO, Japan.

Yggdrasill (ĭg'drəsĭl, yōōg'-), in Norse mythology, the great tree of the world. Its branches and roots extended through all the universe—the heavens, the earth, and the underworld. At its top sat an eagle, at its bottom twined a serpent, and between them ran a squirrel breeding discord. It was prophesied that at the doom of the gods the tree would be destroyed. See GERMANIC RELIGION.

Yiddish language (yĭd'ĭsh), member of the West Germanic group of the Germanic subfamily of the Indo-European family of languages (see GERMANIC LANGUAGES; GERMAN LANGUAGE). Although it is not a national language, Yiddish is spoken as a first language by about 4 million Jews all over the world, especially in Argentina, Canada, France, Israel, Mexico, Rumania, the United States, and the USSR. Before the annihilation of 6 million Jews by the Nazis, it was the tongue of more than 11 million people. Growing out of a blend of a number of medieval German dialects, Yiddish arose c.1100 in the ghettos of Central Europe. From there it was taken to Eastern Europe by Jews who began to leave German-speaking areas in the 14th cent. as a result of persecution. By the 18th cent., Yiddish was almost universal among the Jews of Eastern Europe. It has generally accompanied Yiddish-speaking Jews in their migrations to other parts of the world. Phonetically, Yiddish is closer to Middle High German than is modern German. Although the vocabulary of Yiddish is basically German, it has been enlarged by borrowings from Hebrew, some Slavic and Romance languages, and English. Written from right to left like Hebrew, Yiddish also uses the Hebrew alphabet with certain modifications. In 1925 the Yiddish Scientific Institute (YIVO) was established in Vilna, Lithuania. It served as an academy to oversee the development of the language. Later its headquarters were transferred to New York City, where in time it became the Yivo Institute for Jewish Research. Coping with the problem of dialects, this institute has done much to bring about a standardization of Yiddish. In the eyes of many, Yiddish has significance both as the language of an important literature and as an expression of the Jewish people. See Leo Rosten, *The Joys of Yiddish* (1968); Marvin I. Herzog et al., ed., *The Field of Yiddish: Studies in Language, Folklore, and Literature* (1969); L. M. Feinsilver, *The Taste of Yiddish* (1971); and Maurice Samuel, *In Praise of Yiddish* (1971).

Yin, dynasty of China: see SHANG.

Yin-ch'uan or **Yinchwan** (both: yĭn-chwän), city, capital of Ninghsia Hui Autonomous Region, China, on the Huang Ho (Yellow River). It is a shipping point for the products of the fertile Ninghsia plain. Textiles are manufactured, and coal is mined in the area. Marco Polo visited Yin-ch'uan in the 13th cent. Ninghsia Univ. is in the city.

Ying-k'ou or **Yingkow** (both: yĭng-kou, yĭng-kō), city (1970 est. pop. 215,000), S Liaoning prov., China, on the Liao River near its mouth on the Po Hai. It is on the South Manchurian RR in an area producing rice, cotton, and oakleaf silk. It has fishing and lumbering industries and plants making textiles, petrochemicals, machinery, automotive parts, and paper products. From 1836 to 1900, Yink-k'ou was the chief port of Manchuria.

ylang-ylang (ē'läng-ē'läng), perfume oil obtained by distillation of the fragrant flowers of *Cananga odorata,* a large tropical Asiatic tree of the custard-apple family. The oil is highly valued for soaps, cosmetics, and expensive perfumes, particularly in what are known as Oriental blends.

Ymir (ē'mĕr), in Norse mythology, primeval giant and progenitor of a race of giants. Odin and his brothers slew Ymir; from his skull they fashioned the sky, from his flesh the earth, from his bones the mountains, and from his blood the sea.

yodel or **yodle** (both: yō'dəl), type of wordless singing, joyous in nature, usually associated with the Swiss. It is, in fact, practiced throughout the Alps and, as an importation, in the mountains of Kentucky. It is characterized by sudden shifts from the natural singing voice to FALSETTO.

yoga (yō'gə) [Skt.,=union; cognate with English *yoke*], general term for spiritual disciplines in both HINDUISM and BUDDHISM that are directed to the attainment of higher consciousness and liberation from ignorance, suffering, and rebirth. More specifically it is the name of one of the six orthodox systems of INDIAN PHILOSOPHY. Both Vedic and Buddhist literature discuss the doctrines of wandering ascetics in ancient India who practiced various kinds of austerities and meditation. The basic text of the philosophical school of Yoga, the *Yoga Sutras* of Patanjali (2d cent. B.C.), is a systematization of one of these older traditions. Patanjali divides the practice of yoga into eight stages. *Yama,* or restraint from vice, and *niyama,* or observance of purity and virtue, lay a moral foundation for practice and remove the disturbance of uncontrolled desires. *Asana,* or posture, and *pranayama,* or breath control, calm the physical body, and *pratyahara,* or withdrawal of the senses, detaches the mind from the external world. Internal control of consciousness is accomplished in the three stages of *dharana,* or concentration, *dhyana,* or meditation, and SAMADHI. Through such practices, yogis acquire miraculous powers, which, however, must be renounced if the highest state is to be achieved. In *samadhi* the subject-object distinction and the consciousness of the personal self is lost in a state usually described as one of supreme peace, bliss, and illumination. One-pointed concentration on a chosen object, which may be a part of the body, the breath, a MANTRA, a diagram, a deity, or an idea is a common feature of different types of yoga. Hindu tradition in general recognizes three main kinds of yoga: *jnana* yoga, the path of wisdom and discrimination, BHAKTI yoga, the path of love and devotion to a personal God, and *karma* yoga, the path of selfless action. Other classifications exist. Patanjali's yoga is known as *raja,* or "royal," yoga. *Hatha* yoga emphasizes physical control and postures and is widely practiced in the West. *Kundalini* yoga, especially associated with TANTRA, is based on the physiology of the "subtle body," according to which seven major centers of psychic energy, called *chakras*, are located along the spinal column. At the base of the spine is located the *kundalini*, or "coiled" energy in latent form. When the *kundalini* is activated by yogic methods, it rises up the spine through the main subtle artery of the *sushumna*, "opening" each *chakra* in turn. When the *kundalini* reaches the topmost *chakra* in the brain, *samadhi* is attained. Yoga is usually practiced under the guidance of a guru, or spiritual teacher. Contemporary systems of yoga, such as those of Sri Aurobindo GHOSE and Sri Chinmoy GHOSE, stress the attainability of spiritual realization without the withdrawal from the world characteristic of the older traditions. See Surendranath Dasgupta, *Yoga as Philosophy and Religion* (1924, repr. 1973); I. K. Taimni, *The Science of Yoga* (1967); Ernest Wood, *Yoga* (1967); Phulgenda Sinha, *Yoga* (1970).

Yogacara (yō"gəkär'ə) [Skt.,=yoga practice], philosophical school of Mahayana BUDDHISM, also known as the *Vijnanavada* or Consciousness School. The founders of this school in India were Maitreya (270–350), his disciple Asanga (c.375–430), and Asanga's younger half-brother Vasubandhu (c.400–480), who was also the greatest systematizer of the ABHIDHARMA type of Buddhist philosophy. The school held that consciousness (*vijnana*) is real, but its objects are constructions and unreal. The school's teachings are thus often characterized by the phrase "consciousness-only" (*citta-matra*) or "representation-only" (*vijnapti-matra*). The content of consciousness is produced not by independently existing objects but by the inner modifications of consciousness itself. A theory of eight kinds of consciousness was formed to explain how this process functions. The deepest level of consciousness is the "store-consciousness" (*alaya-vijnana*), which is both individual and universal and contains the seeds or traces of past actions, which are projected into manifestation through the "defiled mind" and the six sense-consciousnesses (the five physical senses plus mind or thought). The school was transmitted to China as the Fa-hsiang. It eventually syncretized with the MADHYAMIKA school. See D. T. Suzuki, *Studies in the Lankavatara Sutra* (1930); Sarvepalli Radhakrishman and C. A. Moore, *A Sourcebook in Indian Philosophy* (1957); A. K. Chatterjee, *The Yogacara Idealism* (1962); C. L. Tripathi, *The Problem of Knowledge in Yogacara Buddhism* (1972).

Yogananda (Paramahamsa Yogananda) (pärämhäN'sä yōgänän'dä), 1893–1952, Indian mystic. He was born in Gorakhpur, India, of a Kshatriya (warrior caste) family. While attending Calcutta Univ. he met his guru, Sri Yukteswar, and after graduating (1914) he became a monk in the order of Shankara. In 1917 he founded the Yogoda Sat-sang school for boys in Calcutta. In 1920 he went to the United States where he lectured widely, teaching a secret technique of meditation, which he called *kriya yoga*. He founded (1935) the Self-Realization Fellowship to carry on his work and lived in the United States until his death. His organization, which has its headquarters in Los Angeles, has centers throughout the world. See his *Autobiography of a Yogi* (1946).

yogurt: see FERMENTED MILK.

Yoho National Park (yō'hō), 507 sq mi (1,313 sq km), SE British Columbia, Canada, in the Rocky Mts. at the Alta. border; est. 1886. It lies W of the Continental Divide, adjoining Banff and Kootenay national parks, and contains lakes, glaciers, waterfalls, and high mountains, with a number of peaks more than 10,000 ft (3,048 m) high. Park headquarters are at Field, which is a center for mountain climbing.

Yokkaichi (yōk-kī'chē), city (1970 pop. 229,234), Mie prefecture, W Honshu, Japan, a port on Ise Bay. It is a manufacturing center that produces banko ware (a kind of porcelain), cotton textiles, tea, vegetable oil, and cement.

Yokohama (yō"kōhä'mä), city (1971 pop. 2,279,483), capital of Kanagawa prefecture, SE Honshu, Japan, on the western shore of Tokyo Bay. Japan's third largest city and one of its leading seaports, Yokohama belongs to the extensive urban-industrial belt around Tokyo. Among its industries are shipyards, steel mills, oil refineries, chemical plants, and factories that produce transportation equipment, electrical apparatus, automobiles, machinery, primary metals, and textiles. In 1854, U.S. Commodore Matthew C. Perry visited Yokohama, which was then a small fishing village. In 1859 it became a port for foreign trade and the site of a foreign settlement that enjoyed extraterritorial rights. Known especially for its exports of raw silk, Yokohama also handled canned fish and other local products. Foreign trade led to the rapid growth of Yokohama, which served during the last half of the 19th cent. as Tokyo's outer port. The capital has since expanded the facilities and operations of its own port; but Yokohama is still important in the export of machinery, iron, and steel, as well as in its traditional staple of raw silk. Japan's first railroad linked Yokohama with Tokyo in 1872. Yokohama formally became a city in 1889. Extraterritoriality was abolished in 1899. Virtually destroyed by an earthquake and fires in 1923, Yokohama was quickly rebuilt; the city was modernized, and extensive improvements were made in its harbor. Yokohama suffered heavy bombardment during World War II, but it revived and prospered. The city has four universities, a variety of Christian churches, Shinto shrines, and temples, and numerous parks and gardens, notably Nogeyama Park, which was created after the earthquake. The filling in of shallow areas of the bay for port facilities and industrial use has continued.

Yokosuka (yōkō'sōōkä), city (1970 pop. 347,568), Kanagawa prefecture, E central Honshu, Japan. It has an important naval base (founded 1868), shipyards, arsenals, and ironworks. Yokosuka is also known for the tomb of William Adams, first Englishman to visit Japan.

Yokut Indians (yō'kōōt), North American Indians of S California. Their culture was essentially that of the California cultural area, and their basketry and pictographs are notable. In the late 18th cent. the Yokut population was about 18,000; today they number about 500. The Yokut, or Mariposan, languages are a branch of the Penutian linguistic family (see AMERICAN INDIAN LANGUAGES). See H. F. Hughes, *The Valley of the Yokuts* (1940).

Yola (yō'lä), city, E Nigeria, a port on the Benue River. Cotton, groundnuts, hides, and skins are shipped from Yola. The city is a road junction and has an airport; there is ferry service across the Benue. Yola was founded in 1841 as the capital of a Muslim FULANI state. The British captured Yola in 1901.

Yom Kippur: see ATONEMENT, DAY OF.

Yonge, Charlotte Mary (yŭng), 1823–1901, English novelist. Her writing as well as her life was restricted by the rigid High Church tenets of her upbringing. In spite of their religiosity her books were long popular because of the excellence of their characterization and dialogue. *The Heir of Redclyffe* (1853), a novel, and *The Daisy Chain* (1856), a book for girls, are best known. She edited the *Monthly Packet* from 1851, and many of her stories first appeared there. See biography by Georgina Battiscombe (1943).

Yonkers (yŏng'kərz), city (1970 pop. 204,370), Westchester co., SE N.Y., on the east bank of the Hudson, in a hilly region just N of the Bronx (New York City); inc. 1855. Its elevator works date from 1852. Other manufactures are aerosol valves, sugar, seafood cocktails, chemicals, cable, wire, telephone parts, art supplies, and electronic duplicators. The area was included in the land grant given (1646) by the Dutch West India Company to the New Netherland lawyer Adriaen Van der Donck. It was a trading center in colonial days. Water power from the Nepperhan River attracted early industries, such as the elevator works and several carpet mills. Today Yonkers is the seat of Sarah Lawrence College, St. Joseph's Seminary, a junior college, and the Boyce Thompson Institute for Plant Research. Also in the city are Philipse Manor, built in the 17th cent. by Frederick Philipse; the Hudson River Museum and Space Planetarium; and Yonkers raceway.

Yonne (yôn), department (1968 pop. 283,376), N central France. AUXERRE is the capital.

Yorba Linda (yôr'bə lĭn'də), city (1970 pop. 11,856), Orange co., S Calif.; inc. 1967. Richard M. Nixon was born there.

Yorck von Wartenburg or **York von Wartenburg, Ludwig, Graf** (both: lōōt'vĭkh gräf yôrk fən vär'tənbōōrkh), 1759–1830, Prussian army officer. He commanded the Prussian auxiliary corps that had been sent to aid in the campaign of the French emperor Napoleon I against Russia (1812). When he realized that the expedition was doomed to failure he withdrew on his own responsibility from the fighting and concluded the Convention of Tauroggen with the Russians (see TAURAGE). His action was lauded by the nationalistic Prussians, desirous of escaping from their virtual vassalage to France, which had been imposed by the treaty of Tilsit in 1807 following Prussia's defeat by France. King Frederick William III of Prussia subsequently approved his act, and Prussia entered the coalition against Napoleon. Yorck defeated (1813) a French force at Wartenburg in Saxony, thus earning his title.

Yoritomo (Yoritomo Minamoto) (yōrē'tōmō mēnä'mōtō), 1148–99, Japanese warrior and dictator. After a prolonged struggle he led his clan, the Minamoto, to victory over the Taira in 1185. He became (1192) the first SHOGUN, established his capital at Kamakura, and rewarded his followers with estates strategically located throughout the country. These fiefs later became the basis of the power of the DAIMYO. Aided by scholars drawn from the imperial court, which Yoritomo controlled, he set up an administrative network that soon became the only effective central government. His reign marked the beginning of a vigorous period in Japanese history. Zen Buddhism was officially sponsored, and the military virtues of BUSHIDO were cultivated. Foreign commerce prospered, Japanese piracy off China and Korea increased, and the arts flourished. Yoritomo's system of centralized feudalism ended a long period of civil wars and endured for nearly 150 years.

York, Alvin Cullum, 1887–1964, American soldier known as Sergeant York, b. Fentress co., Tenn. He was reared on a back-country farm in Tennessee. A conscientious objector at the beginning of World War I, he later agreed to fight and was credited with killing 25 German soldiers, capturing 132 others, and taking a hill in an engagement (Oct. 8, 1918) in the Argonne Forest. York received the highest decorations of the American and French governments and became a popular hero. He later founded a school in the Tennessee mountains. See his autobiography (1928); biography by T. J. Skeykill (1930).

York, Cardinal: see STUART, HENRY BENEDICT MARIA CLEMENT.

York, Edmund of Langley, duke of, 1341–1402, fifth son of Edward III of England. He was made (1362) earl of Cambridge, served on expeditions to Spain and France, and married (1372) Isabel, daughter of Peter the Cruel, king of Castile. He became (1377) a member of the council of regency for his nephew Richard II and in 1381–82 made a fruitless expedition to help Ferdinand I of Portugal against John I of Castile. He served against the Scots in 1385, and in that year he was created duke of York. He acted as regent when Richard II went to Ireland in 1394–95 and again in 1399. When Henry of Lancaster landed in England in 1399, to claim the throne, Edmund opposed him halfheartedly and finally veered to his support. After Henry's coronation as Henry IV, York retired from court. The royal house of YORK takes its name from his creation as duke of York.

York, Edward, duke of, 1373?–1415, English nobleman; elder son of Edmund of Langley, duke of York. In 1390, Edward was made earl of Rutland, and in 1394 he was created earl of Cork while with his cousin RICHARD II in Ireland. He acted for the king in the marriage negotiations for the hand of Isabella of France. For his help in the proceedings (1397) against the lords appellant, Richard gave him the lands of the attainted Thomas of Woodstock, duke of Gloucester, and the title duke of Aumâle (Albemarle). He espoused the cause of Henry of Lancaster (HENRY IV) against Richard in 1399, but he was accused in Parliament of complicity in the murder of Gloucester and lost his dukedom. He was soon restored to favor, however, and in 1402 he succeeded his father as duke of York. He was appointed (1403) lieutenant of South Wales, but discontent over lack of funds led him to join in an unsuccessful plot to kidnap and make king the captive Edmund de MORTIMER, 5th earl of March. York was imprisoned (1405) but was later released and made a privy councilor. Subsequently he served Henry IV in Wales and France and was killed while fighting for Henry V at Agincourt. He was succeeded as duke of York by his nephew, Richard.

York, Frederick Augustus, duke of, 1763–1827, second son of George III of England. In the French Revolutionary Wars he commanded (1793–95) the unsuccessful English forces in Flanders. Despite his incompetence in the field, he became a field marshal (1795) and commander in chief of the army (1798) and set about reforming army abuses at home. He led another disastrous expedition to the Netherlands in 1799. He resigned his command in 1809 after he was accused of selling army commissions through his mistress, Mary Anne Clarke. He was cleared and reappointed in 1811.

York, Richard, duke of, 1411–60, English nobleman, claimant to the throne. He was descended from Edward III through his father, Richard, earl of Cambridge, grandson of that king, and also through his mother, Anne Mortimer, great-granddaughter of Lionel, duke of Clarence, who was the third son of Edward III. Richard was brought up as a royal ward, having become duke of York on the death of his uncle Edward in 1415. He inherited (1425) the vast estates of another uncle, Edmund de Mortimer, 5th earl of March, which made him the richest landholder in England. He served in the retinue of HENRY VI in France (1431) and was lieutenant general of France and Normandy (1436-37). In 1438 he married Cecily Neville, daughter of the earl of Westmoreland. He served again as lieutenant general in France from 1441 to 1445 but became increasingly discontented with the English government, which diverted men and funds from his operations to those of John Beaufort, 1st duke of Somerset. The death of the king's uncle Humphrey, duke of Gloucester, in 1447 made York heir presumptive to the throne, and the government, to get him out of the way, promptly ordered him to Ireland as lieutenant. He did not go until 1449 and returned in 1450 to struggle against the growing power of Queen MARGARET OF ANJOU and Edmund Beaufort, 2d duke of SOMERSET. In 1453 a son born to Henry VI displaced York as heir to the throne, but the onset of the king's insanity enabled York to secure control of the government as protector (1454). Dismissed when the king recovered, York resorted to arms (see ROSES, WARS OF THE) and, with the help of his wife's relatives, most notably Richard Neville, earl of WARWICK, won the first battle of St. Albans (1455), in which Somerset was killed. After this victory York once more became protector, but by 1456 the queen's faction had regained power. Forced to flee to Ireland in 1459, York returned after the victory of his supporters at Northampton (1460) and for the first time laid claim to the throne. A compromise was arranged by which York was recognized as protector and heir apparent to the throne, but Margaret (whose own son had thus been disinherited) gathered her forces and defeated the Yorkists at the battle of Wakefield, in which York was slain. His son, Edward of York, however, was to secure the throne as Edward IV. See E. F. Jacob, *The Fifteenth Century* (1961).

York, Ont.: see TORONTO, Ont., Canada.

York, county borough (1971 pop. 104,513), Yorkshire, N England, at the confluence of the Ouse and Foss rivers. It is located at the junction of the three ridings of Yorkshire. York is especially noted for the manufacture of cocoa, chocolate, and confectionery and is a great rail center. Instrument making, printing, and light engineering are among its other industries. York was a British settlement occupied by the ancient tribe of Brigantes. As Eboracum, it was an important military post of the British province of the Roman Empire. Emperor Hadrian visited York in 120 and built an earthen rampart to keep out the Picts and the Celts. The emperors Septimus Severus (211) and Constantius I (306) died there and Constantine I was proclaimed emperor at York in 306. York became an important center in the Kingdom of Northumbria. In the 7th cent. St. Paulinus, the first archbishop of York, was consecrated. The archbishopric of York is the ecclesiastical center of the N of England, second only to Canterbury in importance. In the 8th cent. York was one of the most famous centers of education in Europe. Alcuin was born there and became the headmaster of St. Peter's School, now one of the oldest public schools in England. In the Middle Ages, York was a busy wool market. The Cathedral of St. Peter, commonly known as York Minster, occupies the site of the wooden church in which King Edwin was baptized by St. Paulinus on Easter Day in 627. The present edifice dates partly from the Norman period. There are many other notable medieval structures in York. The ancient city is enclosed by walls dating in part from Norman times, but mainly from the 14th cent. Four of the gates, including Micklegate and Monk Bar, remain. The Univ. of York was founded in 1963; there is also a teacher-training school. York has several important museums. The York Plays (see MIRACLE PLAY) reached their height in the 15th cent. and were revived at the Yorkshire Festival of 1951. In 1974, York became part of the new nonmetropolitan county of North Yorkshire.

York, city (1970 pop. 50,335), seat of York co., SE Pa., on Codorus Creek, in a fertile agricultural area; laid out 1741, inc. as a city 1887. It is a market, trade, processing, and distribution center in the Pennsylvania Dutch country. In addition to food and related products, its factories make air conditioners, turbines, chains, and textile and paper products. York was a meeting place (1777-78) of the Continental Congress. During the Civil War it was occupied briefly (1863) by Confederates. It is the seat of York College of Pennsylvania and of a branch of Pennsylvania State Univ. Several Colonial houses remain. A fair is held there annually.

York, Cape, NW Greenland, in N Baffin Bay, W of Melville Bay. The Cape York meteorites were discovered by U.S. explorer Robert E. Peary, who brought the largest (c.100 tons) to the American Mus. of Natural History, New York City. In 1932 a monument to Peary was erected at Cape York.

York, house of, royal house of England, deriving its name from the creation of Edmund of Langley, fifth son of Edward III, as duke of York in 1385. The claims to the throne of Edmund's grandson, Richard, duke of York, in opposition to Henry VI of the house of Lancaster (see LANCASTER, HOUSE OF), resulted in the Wars of the Roses (see ROSES, WARS OF THE), so called because the badge of the house of York was a white rose, and a red rose was later attributed to the house of Lancaster. Richard's claim to the throne came not only from direct male descent from Edmund, but also through his mother Anne Mortimer, great-granddaughter of Lionel, duke of Clarence, who was the third son of Edward III. The royal members of the house of York were EDWARD IV, EDWARD V, and RICHARD III. The marriage of the Lancastrian Henry VII to Elizabeth, eldest daughter of Edward IV, united the houses of York and Lancaster. Henry was the first of the Tudor kings.

York College: see NEW YORK, CITY UNIVERSITY OF.

Yorke Peninsula, 160 mi (257 km) long and 35 mi (56 km) wide, SE South Australia state, Australia, between Spencer Gulf and Gulf St. Vincent. It is a farming area in which wheat and barley are raised.

Yorker Brethren: see RIVER BRETHREN.

York Factory, fur-trading post, NE Man., Canada, on Hudson Bay, at the mouth of the Hayes River, just east of the mouth of the Nelson River. The name was used for several early (late-17th-cent.) posts in the area, which changed hands during the struggle between England and France for control of the rich fur trade. The British gained final control after the Peace of Utrecht (1713). The present post (built 1788-93) was a major warehouse for the Hudson's Bay Company. It was closed in 1957.

York Plays: see MIRACLE PLAY.

Yorkshire (yôrk'shĭr), county, 6,148 sq mi (15,923 sq km), N England. Largest of the English counties, it is divided into three administrative counties, or ridings: East Riding (1971 pop. 542,565), 1,188 sq mi (3,077 sq km), with BEVERLEY as its county town; North Riding (1971 pop. 724,463), 2,151 sq mi (5,571 sq km), with Northallerton as its county town; West Riding (1971 pop. 3,780,539), 2,798 sq mi (7,247 sq km), with WAKEFIELD as its county town. The city of YORK is located at the junction of the ridings and is independent of them. The county borders on the North Sea between the Humber River and estuary on the south and the Tees River on the north. It extends westward almost to the Irish Sea. The Pennine Chain in the west rises to 2,591 ft (790 m) in Mickle Fell; the great fertile Yorkshire plain lies to the east of the mountains. The moors and the sea coast have much austere beauty. The principal rivers are the Ouse, the Derwent, the Aire, and their tributaries. There are rich coal deposits in West Riding and elsewhere. West Riding is part of the great English industrial area that extends into neighboring Lancashire, Derbyshire, and Nottinghamshire. The cities of this district, such as SHEFFIELD, LEEDS, and BRADFORD, have extensive iron and steel industries, textile mills, chemical plants, coal mines, and limestone quarries. The availability of water power aided industrialization. HULL, on the Humber, is one of England's chief ports. In the less industrialized areas of the county, grain cultivation, dairy farming, and sheep raising are significant. Yorkshire figures prominently in British history. There are numerous prehistoric remains, including barrows and huge monoliths. The city of York (Eboracum) was an important Roman post in N Britain. After the Roman withdrawal in the 5th cent. and the Saxon invasions, the region became a part of the kingdom of Northumbria. In the Middle Ages, Yorkshire was the center of British monastic life; by the early 16th cent. there were more than 100 abbeys, priories, nunneries, and friaries. In this period Yorkshire had a large woolen-cloth industry. The dissolution of the religious houses under Henry VIII was met with great resistance, notably in the PILGRIMAGE OF GRACE (1536). There are beautiful remains of the Cistercian houses of Rievaulx, Fountains, Jervaulx, Kirkstall, and Byland, as well as Benedictine establishments at Selby, Whitby, and St. Mary's, York. Cædmon, first of the Anglo-Saxon poets, lived in Yorkshire. Robin Hood's legendary exploits are recalled by many place names. The county was the home of Laurence Sterne and the Brontë sisters. In 1974, Yorkshire was reorganized; most of East Riding became part of the new nonmetropolitan county of Humberside, most of North Riding and West Riding became part of the new nonmetropolitan county of North Yorkshire, an area of West Riding became part of the new metropolitan county of West Yorkshire, and an area of North Riding became part of the new nonmetropolitan county of Cleveland.

Yorkshire terrier, breed of small, spirited TOY DOG originated and developed in Yorkshire, England, in the mid-19th cent. It stands about 9 in. (22.8 cm) high at the shoulder and weighs from 4 to 7 lb (1.8-3.2 kg). Its long, straight, glossy coat is finely textured and is dark steel blue and tan in color. Although the Yorkshire is a "man-made" breed, precisely what dogs were used in its creation remains largely a matter of speculation since no breeding records were kept and the Yorkshire area contained many popular toy and terrier types that could have been used for crossbreeding. However, the general consensus is that the Yorkshire represents the bred-down issue of crosses between Skye terrier and Manchester terrier. Today, as in the past, the Yorkshire is a very popular companion and house pet. See DOG.

Yorkton, city (1971 pop. 13,430), SE Sask., Canada, NE of Regina. It is a railroad center and has large stockyards, warehouses, a flour mill, brick and cement plants, and a farm-implement plant.

Yorktown, historic town (1970 est. pop. 300), seat of York co., SE Va., on the York River 10 mi (16 km) from its mouth on Chesapeake Bay; settled 1631, laid out 1691. It is included in the Colonial National Historical Park (see NATIONAL PARKS AND MONUMENTS, table). The town, once an important tobacco port, reached its zenith c.1750. The YORKTOWN CAMPAIGN (1781) brought to a close the American Revolution; the battlefield surrounds the town. In the Civil War, Yorktown was besieged (April-May, 1862) by McClellan in the PENINSULAR CAMPAIGN, and the city was taken by Union troops on May 4. Places of interest in Yorktown include the customhouse (c.1706; restored 1929); Grace Church (1697); the Moore House (c.1725), in which the terms of Cornwallis's surrender were negotiated; and the Yorktown Monument (1881), commemorating the victory of 1781. See Burke Davis, *The Campaign That Won America: The Story of Yorktown* (1970); C. F. Trudell, *Colonial Yorktown* (1938, repr. 1971).

Yorktown campaign, 1781, the closing military operations of the American Revolution. After his unsuccessful CAROLINA CAMPAIGN General Cornwallis moved into Virginia to join British forces there. His lieutenant, Banastre Tarleton, engaged American forces under the marquis de Lafayette, Baron von Steuben, and Gen. Anthony Wayne in several minor actions as the British retreated down the York peninsula. Cornwallis fortified Yorktown and waited for reinforcements to come from Sir Henry Clinton in New York. While he was there, late in August, a French fleet under Admiral de GRASSE arrived from the West Indies, blockaded Chesapeake Bay, and defeated (September) the British naval forces under Admiral Graves. Leaving a force to harry Clinton in New York, Gen. George Washington and General ROCHAMBEAU rushed south, with many French troops. Cornwallis, unaware of Washington's advance, remained more or less idle. Lafayette and Steuben distinguished themselves as commanders of the holding troops and did so even more after the reinforcements arrived. By mid-September an overwhelming Franco-American force had gathered. Cornwallis tried to escape, but his attempts failed. On Oct. 17, 1781, he asked for surrender terms, which he accepted Oct. 19, 1781. See H. P. Johnston, *The Yorktown Campaign* (1881, repr. 1971); T. J. Fleming, *Beat the Last Drum* (1963); Burke Davis, *The Campaign That Won America* (1970).

York University, at Downsview, Ont., Canada; nondenominational; coeducational; founded 1959 as an affiliate of the Univ. of Toronto, became independent 1965. It has faculties of administrative studies, environmental studies, arts, education, science, fine arts, and graduate studies and a school of law.

York von Wartenburg, Ludwig, Graf: see YORCK VON WARTENBURG, LUDWIG, GRAF.

Yoruba (yō'rōōbä), people of SW Nigeria, numbering about 13 million. The Yoruba are unusual in Africa in their tendency to form urban communities. Today many of the large cities in Nigeria (including LAGOS, IBADAN, and ABEOKUTA) are in Yorubaland. The old Yoruba kingdom of Oyo was traditionally one of the largest states of W Africa. It dominated both Benin and Dahomey, but after 1700 its power slowly waned. At the beginning of the 19th cent.,

Fulani invasions, slave raids from Dahomey, and the growing contact with Europeans divided the Yoruba into a number of small states. In the second half of the 19th cent. the Yoruba gradually fell under British control, and they were under direct British administration from 1893 until 1960. Yoruba religion includes a variety of gods. Vestiges of Yoruba culture are also found in Brazil and Cuba, where Yoruba were imported as slaves. See G. J. A. Ojo, *Yoruba Culture* (1967); Eva Krapf-Askari, *Yoruba Towns and Cities* (1969); R. S. Smith, *Kingdoms of the Yoruba* (1969); Harold Courlander, *Tales of Yoruba Gods and Heroes* (1973).

Yosai, Kikuchi (kēko͝o'chē yō'sī), 1788–1878, Japanese painter, known for his depiction of historical subject matter. Although he was well trained in the Chinese and Western painting styles, he advocated a revival of the medieval style of Japanese painting.

Yosemite National Park (yōsĕm'ĭtē), 761,320 acres (308,106 hectares), E central Calif.; est. 1890 as a result of the efforts of conservationist John Muir. Located in the Sierra Nevada, it is a glacier-scoured area of great beauty; Mt. Lyell (13,114 ft/3,997 m) is the highest peak. Enclosed within the park is the famed Yosemite Valley (alt. c.4,000 ft/1,200 m), surrounded by cliffs and pinnacles; Half Dome, which reaches a height of c.4,800 ft (1,460 m) above the valley and El Capitan, which rises perpendicularly c.3,600 ft (2,000 m) above the valley, are the highest of the surrounding peaks. The world's three largest monoliths of exposed granite are found in the park. There are also many beautiful lakes, rivers, streams, and waterfalls, the most noted of which is Yosemite Falls, the highest in North America, with a drop of 2,425 ft (739 m) in two segments; Ribbon Falls has a 1,612-ft (491-m) drop. Three groves of sequoias are within the park's limits, which also include fine growths of other trees and more than 1,000 varieties of flowering plants. In the scenic Hetch Hetchy Valley is the reservoir that supplies water to San Francisco.

Yoshida, Shigeru (shēgä'ro͞o yō'shēdä), 1878–1967, Japanese statesman. He was until 1954 the most powerful political figure in postwar Japan. He was ambassador to Italy (1930–32) and to Great Britain (1936–39). He was arrested late in 1944 for championing peace but returned to the government after the surrender in 1945 and became head of the Liberal party. He was prime minister five times between 1946 and 1954. During his administration a new constitution was promulgated, land reforms instituted, and the occupation ended. The unresolved problems of trade with mainland China, rearmament, the alliance with the United States, and economic rehabilitation finally forced him from office. See his memoirs (tr. 1961, repr. 1973).

Yoshihito: see TAISHA.

Yoshkar-Ola or **Ioshkar-Ola** (both: yəshkär"əlä'), city (1970 pop. 166,000), capital of the Mari Autonomous Soviet Socialist Republic, E central European USSR. Manufactures include pharmaceuticals and agricultural machinery. The city was founded in 1578 as a Russian outpost.

Yosu (yŭ'so͞o'), city (1970 est. pop. 114,000), S South Korea, on the Korea Strait. It is a trading port and fishing base and the site of South Korea's major oil refinery. Yosu also has an important thermal power plant. There is a large canning industry.

Youlou, Fulbert (yo͞o'lo͞o), 1917–72, first president (1960–63) of the Republic of the Congo (now People's Republic of the Congo). Originally a Roman Catholic priest, he entered politics, founded the country's strongest political party, and in 1956 was elected mayor of Brazzaville. Public reaction to his efforts to create a one-party state, coupled with the nation's economic failures, led to his forced resignation. He was replaced by Alphonse MASSAMBA-DEBAT.

Youmans, Vincent, 1898–1946, American composer, b. New York City. He first began composing while in the navy during World War I. After Youmans had held jobs as a "song-plugger" and rehearsal pianist, his first musical, *Two Little Girls in Blue,* with lyrics by Ira Gershwin, opened (1921) on Broadway. It was followed by such successes as *Wildflower* (1923), *No, No, Nanette* (1925), and *Hit the Deck* (1927). His last score was for the revue *Take a Chance* (1932), after which he retired.

Young, Arthur, 1741–1820, English agriculturist. His writings hastened the progress of scientific farming. He traveled widely, always observing techniques of farming. In 1784, Young founded the periodical *Annals of Agriculture* and edited it through 1808. Among his other works are three accounts of tours in England (1768–71) and *Travels during the Years 1787, 1788, 1789, and 1790* (1792–94). See his autobiography (1898), biography by J. G. Gazley (1973).

Young, Brigham (brĭg'əm), 1801–77, American Mormon, leader of the Church of Jesus Christ of Latter-Day Saints, b. Whitingham, Vt. Brigham Young was perhaps the greatest molder of Mormonism, his influence having a greater effect even than that of Joseph Smith in shaping the formation of the Mormon church. He was a painter and glazier in Mendon, Monroe co., N.Y., when he was first attracted to the new religion. He was not baptized until 1832. He led a group to the Mormon community at Kirtland, Ohio, and in 1835 he became one of the Council of Twelve (the Apostles). He did not, however, become important in the church until the Mormons were persecuted in their new Missouri Zion. He was one of the few Mormon leaders not placed under arrest, and his abilities as an organizer came to the fore. He was one of the chief figures in the move to Nauvoo, Ill. Sent as missionary to England, he converted many to Mormonism and started the movement that resulted in bringing many English immigrants to strengthen the new church. After Joseph Smith's assassination (1844), Young was the chief factor in maintaining the unity of the church in the Council of Twelve. From that time forward he was the dominant man in Mormonism. He led the great migration west in 1846–47 and was the director of the settlement at Salt Lake City. The Mormon state in Utah revolved around him. He exercised supreme control in the cooperative theocracy, and to his genius as much as anything else was due the phenomenal growth of a prosperous community. He headed the church, and after the creation of the U.S. provisional government he was also territorial governor and superintendent of Indian affairs. He built up Salt Lake City and the surrounding Mormon communities. When trouble arose between the United States and the Mormons, out of the general outcry elsewhere against the Mormon practice of polygamy and a general fear and hatred of Mormon power, he defied the U.S. government, especially in the vain and fruitless military expedition against the Mormons called the UTAH WAR, or the Mormon campaign (1857–58). He lost his post as governor, but through his able statesmanship he avoided a real break with the United States. In his old age he was arrested on charges of polygamy and murder, but he was acquitted and his influence increased rather than diminished until his death. His name was known not only throughout the United States, but also abroad. The number of his wives and the extent of his fortune were the objects of curiosity and idle rumor everywhere. The exact number of his wives is still a matter of argument. He seems to have been married in the course of his life to 27 women, although never to that many at the same time; he was survived by 17 wives. Nevertheless, the accusations of sensuality leveled against him by people who were ignorant of the basic principles of Mormon doctrine were not justified. The most serious charge that can be brought against him is that of condoning the massacre at MOUNTAIN MEADOWS. He did not instigate that crime, but it seems probable that he did protect its perpetrators. See Susa Young Gates (his daughter) and Leah E. Widtsoe, *The Life Story of Brigham Young* (1930); M. R. Werner, *Brigham Young* (1939); R. B. West, Jr., *Kingdom of Saints* (1957); M. R. Hunter, *Brigham Young, the Colonizer* (1973).

Young, Charles Augustus, 1834–1908, American astronomer, b. Hanover, N.H., grad. Dartmouth, 1853. He discovered the reversing layer of the solar atmosphere and proved the gaseous nature of the sun's corona. He was a pioneer in the study of the spectrum of the sun and experimented in photographing solar prominences in full sunlight. He was professor (1857–66) of astronomy, natural philosophy, and mathematics at Western Reserve College (now Case Western Reserve Univ.), professor of astronomy and natural philosophy at Dartmouth College (1866–77), and professor of astronomy at Princeton (1877–1905). His works include *The Sun* (1881, rev. ed. 1896), *Lessons in Astronomy* (1891, rev. ed. 1918), and *The Elements of Astronomy* (1890, rev. ed. 1919).

Young, Cy (Denton T. Young), 1867–1955, American baseball player, b. Gilmore, Ohio. He played with the Canton (Ohio) club of the Tri-State League before he pitched (1890–98) for the Cleveland Indians, then in the National League. He later hurled for the St. Louis Cardinals (1899–1900) of the National League, the Boston Red Sox (1901–8) and the Cleveland Indians (1909–11) of the American League, and the Boston Braves (1911) of the National League. In 22 years of major league baseball he pitched in 906 games. Young, known for his excellent control and his ability to outwit batters, won the most games (511), including 76 shutouts, and pitched three no-hit games. In 1904 he pitched baseball's first perfect game—no-hit, no-run, no opposing batter reaching first base. He retired from active play at the age of 44. He was elected to the National Baseball Hall of Fame in 1937.

Young, Edward, 1683–1765, English poet and dramatist. After a disappointing political life he took holy orders about 1724, serving for a time as the royal chaplain before becoming rector of Welwyn in 1730. He achieved great renown in his own time, both in England and on the Continent, for his long didactic poem *The Complaint, or Night Thoughts on Life, Death, and Immortality* (1742–45). Besides writing a series of satires, *The Universal Passion* (1725–28), he was the author of three bombastic tragedies, *Busiris* (1719), *The Revenge* (1721), and *The Brothers* (1753). His last important work was his prose *Conjectures on Original Composition* (1759). See his correspondence, ed. by Henry Pettit (1972); biography by Isabel S. Bliss (1969).

Young, Ella Flagg, 1845–1918, American educator, b. Buffalo, N.Y. She was identified with the Chicago public school system for 53 years, as teacher, principal, and superintendent of schools (1909–15). From 1899 to 1905 she was professor of education at the Univ. of Chicago and from 1905 to 1909 principal of the Chicago Normal School (later Chicago Teachers College). She was a leader in woman suffrage work, first woman president (1910–11) of the National Education Association, and author of monographs setting forth educational theories developed with John Dewey. She collaborated with Jane Addams in social work. See J. T. McManis, *Ella Flagg Young and a Half-Century of the Chicago Public Schools* (1916).

Young, Geoffrey Winthrop, 1876–1958, English writer, an authority on mountaineering. He was educated at Cambridge and later studied in Switzerland and France. Before 1914 he made an impressive record of new and difficult ascents in the Alps. In World War I he commanded British ambulance units in Belgium, France, and Italy and was several times decorated. Though he lost a leg, he continued mountain climbing. He wrote *Mountain Craft* (1920, 7th ed. 1949). He also wrote poetry. See his autobiography, *On High Hills* (1927), and *The Grace of Forgetting* (1953).

Young, John Russell, 1840–99, American journalist, b. Ireland. He started his newspaper career with the Philadelphia *Press* and by 1862 was its managing editor. From 1866 to 1869 he was managing editor of the New York *Tribune.* Young was sent abroad in the 1870s on missions for the government and for the New York *Herald.* He reported one of his trips in *Around the World with General Grant* (1879). Later he was minister to China (1882–85), and he played an important role in the negotiations that resulted in the French protectorate over Indochina. In 1897 he was made Librarian of Congress. See his *Men and Memories* (1901).

Young, Lester Willis, 1909–59, American jazz musician, b. Woodville, Miss. He played the tenor saxophone with various bands (1929–40), including those of Fletcher Henderson and Count Basie, with whom he first recorded in 1936. After 1946 alcoholism and emotional disturbances increasingly affected his work, especially in the last three years of his life. Young and Coleman Hawkins are considered the major influences on tenor-saxophone playing, and Young's style was important in the development of progressive, or cool, jazz, which arose in the late 1940s. He won several jazz polls and made a number of records, including a series with Billie Holiday, who gave him his nickname, "President," later shortened to "Pres" or "Prez."

Young, Mahonri Mackintosh (məhŏn'rē), 1877–1957, American sculptor, painter, and etcher, b. Salt Lake City, studied at the Art Students League and at Julian's Academy, Paris; grandson of Brigham Young. His statuettes of laborers, cowboys, and prizefighters and his larger works show strength and simplicity and fine workmanship. In the Metropolitan Museum are the bronzes *Stevedore* and *Man with Pick.* He also made the *Sea Gull Monument* in Salt Lake City, Utah, and a statue of Brigham Young for the Capitol rotunda in Washington, D.C.

Young, Owen D., 1874–1962, American lawyer and corporation official, b. Herkimer co., N.Y., grad. St. Lawrence Univ., 1894, and Boston Univ. law school, 1896. He lectured at Boston Univ. (1896–1903) and practiced law in Boston. He moved to New York City in 1913, became general counsel for the General Electric Company, and later served (1922–39) as chairman of the board. The creation of the Radio Corp. of America was chiefly the result of his efforts, and he was associated with other large corporations. With Charles G. Dawes he was a U.S. representative at the reparations conference of 1924. As chairman of the reparations conference of 1929, he forwarded the YOUNG PLAN, which made reparations a financial, rather than a purely political, matter. See biography by Ida M. Tarbell (1932).

Young, Thomas, 1773–1829, English physicist, physician, and Egyptologist. He established (1799) a medical practice in London and was elected (1811) to the staff of St. George's Hospital there. His lectures while professor of natural philosophy (1801–3) at the Royal Institution, London, published as *A Course of Lectures on Natural Philosophy and the Mechanical Arts* (1807), introduced the modern physical concept of energy. An authority on the mechanism of vision and on optics, he stated (1807) a theory of color vision now known as the Young-Helmholtz theory, studied the structure of the eye, and described the defect called astigmatism. He is especially noted for reviving the wave theory of light as opposed to the corpuscular theory, advancing as proof a demonstration based upon the principle of interference of light, which he first formulated in 1801. He applied (1809) the wave theory to refraction and dispersion phenomena. Young's versatility is evidenced by his contributions to the theory of tides, his participation in the deciphering of the Rosetta stone (see under ROSETTA), which provided a key to understanding Egyptian hieroglyphic writings, his explanation (1804) of capillarity (independently set forth by Laplace in 1805), and his establishment of a coefficient of elasticity, YOUNG'S MODULUS. See biographies by H. B. Williams (1930) and Alexander Wood (1954).

Younger, Cole (Thomas Coleman Younger), 1844–1916, American outlaw, b. Jackson co., Mo. After the Civil War he joined the outlaw band of Jesse James, with whom he had served as a Confederate guerrilla under William C. Quantrill. He became a trusted and influential member of the gang. With two of his brothers, James and Robert, Cole was captured after an unsuccessful attempt to rob the bank at Northfield, Minn. (1876), and all three were sentenced to life imprisonment. Largely through the efforts of Capt. Warren C. Bronaugh, a Confederate veteran, who alleged that the brothers had been driven into crime by persecution of their family during the Civil War, Cole and James were paroled in 1901. Robert had died in prison in 1889. James committed suicide in 1902, but Cole Younger, completely pardoned in 1903, returned to Missouri, where he lectured, traveled with a wild West show, and worked peacefully at various jobs. See his autobiography (1903, repr. 1955); W. C. Bronaugh, *The Youngers' Fight for Freedom* (1906); Homer Croy, *Last of the Great Outlaws* (1956); C. W. Breihan, *The Younger Brothers* (1961).

Young-Helmholtz theory: see VISION.

Younghusband, Sir Francis Edward, 1863–1942, British explorer, b. India. He explored Manchuria in 1886. The following year he journeyed from China to India, crossing the Gobi desert and the Mustagh Pass (alt. c.19,000 ft/5,791 m) of the Karakorum range. Lord Curzon, the British viceroy in India, sent Younghusband with a military expedition into Tibet in 1904, where he forced a treaty upon the Dalai Lama, opening Tibet to Western trade. Later he surveyed the Brahmaputra and Sutlej rivers and the upper reaches of the Indus. He three times tried and failed to scale Mt. Everest. His books include *Heart of a Continent* (1898), *India and Tibet* (1912), and *Everest: the Challenge* (1936). See biography by George Seaver (1953); Peter Fleming, *Bayonets to Lhasa* (1961).

Young Men's Christian Association (YMCA), organization having as its objective the improvement of conditions and opportunities for young men. Concerned primarily with spiritual and social well-being, it is also devoted to physical and intellectual development. Membership is not limited to Christians. The first association was launched (1844) in London by Sir George Williams among young men in business. In 1851 the movement took root in North America. Following the lead of Montreal and Boston, a number of other cities soon formed their own YMCAs, and in 1854 the first convention of North American associations took place in Buffalo. A world conference in Paris (1855), attended by delegates from eight nations, led to the formation of the World Alliance of Young Men's Christian Associations in the same year. The organization now has branches on every continent. Local YMCA chapters generally sponsor Bible study groups and other religious activities and provide libraries and reading rooms, classes, lectures, and social activities, as well as housing facilities and summer camps. Physical training is another prominent part of the association's program. As early as 1858, YMCA organizations for students were formed, the first of these being at the Univ. of Michigan and the Univ. of Virginia. Special provision for work among boys, now an essential part of YMCA endeavor, was first made in 1869 in Salem, Mass. Training for teachers, community recreation leaders, and other association workers is furnished in colleges founded for the purpose in Springfield, Mass. (1885), and Chicago (1890), as well as in various other centers, where summer sessions are held. During the Civil War several branches of the association organized the U.S. Christian Commission for the welfare of soldiers in camps and hospitals. Since that time the YMCA has taken an active part in social service in every war. In World War I it cared for prisoners, provided recreation and guidance for the armed forces, and cooperated with the Red Cross in relief work; since World War II it has combined with the Young Women's Christian Association and other agencies to form the United Service Organizations for recreation and welfare activities. See *Yearbook* of the association; G. M. Fisher, *Public Affairs and the Y.M.C.A.* (1948); C. H. Hopkins, *History of the Y.M.C.A. in North America* (1951); M. N. Zald, *Organizational Change* (1970).

Young Plan, program for settlement of German REPARATIONS debts after World War I. It was presented by the committee headed (1929–30) by Owen D. YOUNG. After the DAWES PLAN was put into operation (1924), it became apparent that Germany could not meet the huge annual payments, especially over an indefinite period of time. The Young Plan—which set the total reparations at $26,350,000,000 to be paid over a period of 58½ years—was thus adopted by the Allied Powers in 1930 to supersede the Dawes Plan. Designed to substitute a definite settlement under which Germany would know the exact extent of German obligations and to reduce the payments appreciably, the Young Plan divided the annual payment, set at about $473 million, into two elements—an unconditional part (one third of the sum) and a postponable part (the remainder). The annuities were to be raised through a transportation tax and from the budget. No sooner had the plan gone into effect than Germany felt the full impact of economic depression, and a moratorium was called for the fiscal year 1931–32. After Adolf Hitler took over Germany, he repudiated the unpaid reparations debt, and no further payments were ever made.

Young Pretender: see STUART, CHARLES EDWARD.

Young's modulus [for Thomas Young], number representing (in pounds per square inch or dynes per square centimeter) the ratio of stress to strain for a wire or bar of a given substance. According to Hooke's law the strain is proportional to stress, and therefore the ratio of the two is a constant that is commonly used to indicate the ELASTICITY of the substance. Young's modulus is the elastic modulus for tension, or tensile stress, and is the force per unit cross section of the material divided by the fractional increase in length resulting from the stretching of a standard rod or wire of the material. See STRENGTH OF MATERIALS.

Youngstown, city (1970 pop. 139,788), seat of Mahoning co., NE Ohio, near the Pa. line, in an extensive coal and iron region; founded 1797, inc. 1849. It is one of the largest iron and steel centers in the country. Rubber goods, electric lamps, machinery, plant equipment, aluminum extrusions, automobiles and parts, rolling mill equipment, and sprinkler systems are also produced. Discovery of iron ore, coal, and limestone led to the construction of the first iron furnace in 1803. The city's growth was spurred by the opening of the Pennsylvania and Ohio Canal (1839), the arrival of the railroad (1853), and the establishment of steel plants in the 1890s. It is the seat of Youngstown State Univ. and Butler Art Institute.

Youngstown State University, at Youngstown, Ohio; coeducational; est. 1908 as a department of the Youngstown Association School sponsored by the Young Men's Christian Association. In 1921 the school became the Youngstown Institute of Technology, changing its name in 1928 to the Youngstown College. The school gained university status in 1955 and adopted its present name in 1967 when it joined the Ohio system of higher education. In 1968 a graduate school and technical and community college were added to the university's college of arts and sciences and its schools of business administration, education, engineering, and music.

Young Turks: see OTTOMAN EMPIRE.

Young Women's Christian Association (YWCA), organization designed to promote the welfare of women and girls by offering opportunities for their development spiritually, socially, intellectually, and physically. The movement is nondenominational. It grew out of the homes for young women and female prayer unions established throughout Great Britain during the mid-19th cent., most notable of which was the London boardinghouse created (1855) by Lady Kinnaird, generally taken to be the first YWCA. In 1877 a number of these organizations merged officially to form the Young Women's Christian Association. The movement spread to the British colonies and to the Continent. Meanwhile, in New York City, a prayer group known as the Ladies' Christian Union, generally considered the first YWCA in the United States, had been organized in 1858 by Mrs. Marshall O. Roberts. In Boston, another group formed (1866) the first U.S. association officially to call itself the Young Women's Christian Association. The movement spread rapidly, and a national body, the Young Women's Christian Associations of the United States, was established in 1906. National headquarters have been in New York City since 1912. In 1894, a World's Young Women's Christian Association was formed; its headquarters are in Geneva, Switzerland, and about 65 national YWCA's belong to the organization. In the United States, the unit of organization is the local association in cities, towns, rural communities, and student centers. There are YWCA buildings in all cities of appreciable size, and most chapters place strong emphasis on vocational training. The main object is the building of a better society by interpreting Christianity in terms adequate to life today. The programs of activities are broad and varied, to meet the many-sided needs of all groups of women and girls. A subsidiary group, the Y-teens, sponsors activities for girls 12 to 17 years old. Males may participate in YWCA programs as associate members. See *YWCA Directory;* M. S. Sims, *The Natural History of a Social Institution* (1936) and *The Purpose Widens, 1947–1967* (1969).

Youskevitch, Igor (ē'gər yōōskā'vĭch), 1912–, Russian ballet dancer. In 1938, Youskevitch joined the Ballet Russe de Monte Carlo and became premier danseur; that year he made his New York debut with the company. Youskevitch danced with the Ballet Theatre in New York from 1946 to 1955, thereafter returning to the Ballet Russe de Monte Carlo as artistic director and dancer, and then retiring to teach in the 1960s. Often considered the greatest male dancer of his time, he was noted for his classic style and his elevation. His interpretation of *Afternoon of a Faun* was particularly celebrated.

Youth Aliyah: see HADASSAH.

youth-and-old-age: see ZINNIA.

Ypres, John Denton Pinkstone French, 1st earl of: see FRENCH, JOHN DENTON PINKSTONE, 1ST EARL OF YPRES.

Ypres (ē'prə), Flemish *Ieper,* town (1970 pop. 20,825), West Flanders prov., SW Belgium, near the French border. It is an agricultural market and an industrial center. Manufactures include textiles, textile-making machinery, and processed food. During the Middle Ages, Ypres was one of the most powerful towns of Flanders, with a flourishing cloth industry that rivaled those of Ghent and Bruges. However, political and social unrest and foreign wars led to the decline of this industry. A center of resistance to Spanish rule, the town was taken (1584) and sacked by Alessandro Farnese. It was held by France from 1678 to 1716 and from 1792 to 1814. In World War I, Ypres was the scene of three great battles. Ypres was completely destroyed during the war and was later rebuilt. Among the city's restored buildings are the Gothic Cathedral of St. Martin and the magnificent cloth-workers hall (both originally built in the 13th cent.). On the ramparts of the fortifications built (late 17th cent.) by Vauban is a British memorial gate designed by Sir Reginald Blomfield, and outside the town's walls are some 40 military cemeteries.

Ypres, battles of, three major engagements of WORLD WAR I fought in and around the town of Ypres in SW Belgium. The first battle of Ypres (Oct.–Nov., 1914) was the last of the series of engagements referred to as "the race for the sea." The German thrust toward the Channel ports of Dunkirk and Calais was stopped by the British at Ypres, but in the process the British Expeditionary Force of 100,000 was reduced to half its original size. The second battle began on April 22, 1915, when the Germans, using poison gas for the first time in the war, launched another massive assault on the salient at Ypres. The attack was unsuccessful and was broken off in May. The third battle of Ypres, popularly known as Passchendaele, began on July 31, 1917, and continued until November. The British sought to break the German line, but, bogged down by mud and rain, they advanced only 5 mi (8 km) at a cost of 300,000 lives. See Anthony Farrar-Hockley, *Death of an Army* (1967); E. N. Gladden, *Ypres, 1917* (1967).

Ypsilanti or **Hypsilanti** (both: ĭp"sĭlăn'tē), prominent Greek family of Phanariots (see under PHANAR). An early distinguished member, **Alexander Ypsilanti,** c.1725–c.1807, was dragoman (minister) of the Ottoman emperor and hospodar (governor) of Walachia (1774–82, 1796–97) and of Moldavia (1786–88). Captured (1790) by the Austrians in the Russo-Turkish War of 1787–92, he was imprisoned for two years in the Spielberg at Brno (Brünn). He was executed by the sultan for an alleged conspiracy. His son, **Constantine Ypsilanti,** 1760–1816, was hospodar of Moldavia (1799–1801) and became hospodar of Walachia in 1802. He was deposed in 1806 for his pro-Russian sympathies, but he was restored (1807) to the government of Walachia by the Russians, who had occupied that principality in their war with Turkey. Constantine Ypsilanti encouraged the anti-Turkish rebellion in Serbia and was raising an army to free Greece when the Treaty of Tilsit (1807) between Russia and France cut short his plans. He took refuge in Russia, where he died. His elder son, **Alexander Ypsilanti,** 1792–1828, accompanied his father into exile and became a general in the Russian army. He accepted the leadership of the Philike Hetairia, a secret organization that sought Greek independence and raised (1821) a revolt at Jassy (now Iaşi), the capital of Moldavia, proclaiming the independence of Greece. The Phanariot hospodar of Moldavia and the Greeks in Walachia and Moldavia rallied to him, but the Rumanian population, which had suffered long enough under Phanariot rule, refused to support the movement. Russia, on the pressure of the Austrian foreign minister, Prince von Metternich, disavowed Ypsilanti, who was disastrously defeated by the Turks. He sought asylum in Austria, but was imprisoned there until 1827. He died at Vienna. Ypsilanti's uprising marked the end of the rule of Moldavia and Walachia by Greek hospodars, who were replaced by native Rumanian princes. At the same time it helped in the success of the simultaneous Greek rebellion in the Peloponnesus by diverting the Turkish forces, and it thus marked the beginning of the Greek War of Independence. Alexander's younger brother, **Demetrios Ypsilanti,** 1793–1832, was to play a prominent role in that war. Like his brother, he had served in the Russian army, and took part in Alexander Ypsilanti's uprising at Jassy in 1821. In the same year he left Moldavia for Morea, as the Peloponnesus was then called, and helped the insurgent Greeks in the capture (1821) of Trípolis (then called Tripolitza), the chief Turkish fortress in Morea. He stubbornly resisted the forces of Ibrahim Pasha in 1825 and in 1828 was made commander of the Greek forces in E Greece. His differences with the Greek president, Count Capo d'Istria, led to his resignation in 1830.

Ypsilanti (ĭpsĭlăn'tē), city (1970 pop. 29,538), Washtenaw co., SE Mich., on the Huron River; inc. 1832. It is a residential, commercial, and farm-trade center and an industrial city where automobiles and automobile parts are manufactured. Indian trails crossed this site and an Indian village and a French trading post (1809–c.1819) were there. Eastern Michigan Univ. is in the city.

Ysaÿe, Eugène (ōzhĕn' ēzä'ē), 1858–1931, Belgian violinist, considered one of the foremost violinists of his time; pupil of Wieniawski and Vieuxtemps. He became professor of music at the Brussels Conservatory in 1886. He made his American debut in 1894, and the following year he founded the Société des Concerts Ysaÿe, which he also conducted. He was conductor (1918–20) of the Cincinnati Symphony Orchestra. See biography by Antoine Ysaÿe and Bertram Ratcliffe (1947).

Yser (ēzĕr'), river, c.50 mi (80 km) long, rising in N France and flowing generally NE through NW Belgium and into the North Sea at Nieuwpoort. It connects a network of canals. It was the scene of heavy fighting in World War I.

Yseult: see TRISTRAM AND ISOLDE.

Yssel: see IJSSEL, river, Netherlands.

Ystad (ü'städ), city (1970 pop. 14,164), Malmöhus co., S Sweden, a seaport on the Baltic Sea. It is a commercial and industrial center and a popular summer resort. At Ystad in 1799, Gustavus IV issued his declaration of war against Napoleon I.

ytterbium (ĭtûr'bēəm) [for Ytterby, a town in Sweden], metallic chemical element; symbol Yb; at. no. 70; at. wt. 173.04; m.p. about 825°C; b.p. about 1400°C; sp. gr. about 7.0; valence +2 or +3. Ytterbium is a soft, malleable, ductile, lustrous silver-white metal. Although it is one of the RARE-EARTH METALS of the LANTHANIDE SERIES in group IIIb of the PERIODIC TABLE, in some of its chemical and physical properties it more closely resembles calcium, strontium, and barium. It exhibits ALLOTROPY; at room temperature a face-centered cubic crystalline form is stable. The metal tarnishes slowly in air and reacts slowly with water but rapidly dissolves in mineral acids. It forms numerous compounds, some of which are yellow or green. The oxide (ytterbia, Yb_2O_3) is colorless. It is widely distributed in a number of minerals, e.g., gadolinite, and is recovered from monazite but has no commercial uses. Its discovery is credited to J. C. G. de Marignac, who in 1878 separated a substance he called ytterbia. In 1907, Georges Urbain showed that this substance contained lutetium in addition to ytterbium. At about this same time C. A. von Welsbach independently discovered ytterbium and called it aldebaranium.

yttrium (ĭt'rēəm) [for Ytterby, a town in Sweden], metallic chemical element; symbol Y; at. no. 39; at. wt. 88.905; m.p. about 1500°C; b.p. about 3000°C; sp. gr. about 4.45; valence +3. Yttrium is a highly crystalline iron-gray metal. Usually considered a RARE-EARTH METAL, it is found above lanthanum in group IIIb of the PERIODIC TABLE. Yttrium is fairly stable in air but oxidizes readily when heated. It reacts with water and mineral acids. The largest use of the element is as its oxide yttria, Y_2O_3, which is used in making red phosphors for color television picture tubes; it also has other uses. Yttrium metal has found some use alloyed in small amounts with other metals. Yttrium is not found uncombined in nature, but occurs in many minerals, e.g., gadolinite, euxenite, and xenotime. It is recovered commercially from monazite and bastnasite. In 1794, Johan Gadolin isolated impure yttria from the mineral gadolinite. In 1843, C. G. Mosander isolated pure yttria as well as two impure fractions that he called erbia and terbia. The metal was first isolated in 1828 by Friedrich Wöhler.

Yüan (yüän), Mongolian dynasty of China that ruled from 1260 to 1368. It was a division of the great empire conquered by the MONGOLS. KUBLAI KHAN, who founded the dynastic line, swept down from N China and in 1279 accomplished the final defeat of the Sung dynasty. In its early period the Yüan dynasty developed a fine postal system and an extensive network of roads and canals reaching to the distant Mongol domains of Turkistan, Persia, and S Russia. There was continuous overland contact with the West and exchange of products, and in this period gunpowder and printing seem to have been introduced to Europe from China. Of the occasional European travelers attracted to the Yüan country and its great capital at Cambuluc (now Peking) the best known is Marco POLO. From the early years of Mongol occupation some Chinese administrators were used by the Yüan rulers, but their influence never became dominant. The traditional Confucian ideals of Chinese government were also discouraged by the suspension (until 1315) of the system of civil service examinations. Since scholarship was unremunerative its place was partly taken by much writing of novels and plays. The Yüan dynasty, without the support of either the Chinese masses or the literati, speedily collapsed under the impact of revolts in Mongolia and in S China, civil war among the Mongol princes, and the debauches of the Yüan court. The native Ming dynasty followed. See J. W. Dardess, *Conquerors and Confucians* (1973).

Yüan, river, 540 mi (869 km) long, rising in S Kweichow prov. and flowing generally NE to Tung-t'ing lake, Hunan prov., SE China. Navigation above Ch'ang-te is limited by rapids to small craft. The Yüan valley, a major north-south trade route, yields tungsten, iron ore, and tung yu (wood oil).

Yüan Shih-kai (yüän' shē'-kī'), 1859–1916, president of China (1912–16). From 1885 to 1894 he was the Chinese resident in Korea, then an imperial dependency. He supported the dowager empress, Tz'u Hsi, against the reform movement (1898) of Emperor Kuang Hsü, and she rewarded him with the highest imperial honor, the viceregency of Chihli (now Hopeh). He built the strongest military force in China. Yüan was entrusted with defending the empire against the revolution of 1911, but on his advice the abdication of Emperor Hsüan T'ung (Henry Pu Yi) was procured on Feb. 12, 1912. A few days later, SUN YAT-SEN, who had been elected the first president of China two months earlier, resigned in Yüan's favor. Opposition to Yüan's dictatorial methods soon developed, and he had to suppress several revolts. In 1914 he dissolved the parliament and on Jan. 1, 1916, he assumed the title of emperor. A rebellion in Yünnan forced him almost immediately to abandon his imperial plans. See biography by Jerome Ch'en (2d ed. 1972).

Yuba City (yo͞o'bə), town (1970 pop. 13,986), seat of Sutter co., N central Calif., on the Feather River; founded 1849 during the gold rush; inc. 1908. It is a processing center for fruits, nuts, and vegetables. Beale Air Force Base is in the vicinity.

Yucatán (yo͞okətăn'), state (1970 pop. 774,011), 14,868 sq mi (38,508 sq km), SE Mexico, occupying most of the northern part of the Yucatán peninsula. It lies between Campeche and Quintana Roo. It became a state when Mexico won independence (1821) but seceded from 1839 to 1843. There were severe Indian uprisings in 1847 and in 1910. The principal industry is the cultivation and preparation of henequen—mostly exported to the United States. Roads and rail lines connect many of the larger towns with the capital, MÉRIDA.

Yucatán, peninsula, c.70,000 sq mi (181,300 sq km), mostly in SE Mexico, separating the Caribbean Sea from the Gulf of Mexico. It comprises the states of Yucatán and Campeche and the territory of Quintana Roo, Mexico; British Honduras; and part of Petén, Guatemala. The peninsula is largely a low, flat, limestone tableland rising to c.500 ft (150 m) in the south. To the north and west the plain continues as the Campeche Bank, stretching under shallow water c.150 mi (240 km) from the low, sandy shore line. The eastern coast rises in low cliffs in the north and is indented by bays and paralleled by islands and cays in the south; Cozumel is the largest island. Short ranges of hills cross the peninsula at scattered intervals. The only rivers are those flowing E and NW from Petén. In the northern half of the tableland, rainfall is light and is absorbed by the porous limestone. Water for the inhabitants, who are predominantly the modern descendants of the Maya, and for livestock comes from underground rivers and wells (*cenotes*) from which it is often pumped by windmills, and from surface pools (*aguadas*). The land has tropical dry and rainy seasons, but generally in the north the climate is hot and dry and in the south hot and humid. Most of the northern half, although covered with only a few inches of subsoil, is one of the most important henequen-raising regions of the world; the uncultivated area is under a dense growth of scrub, cactus, sapote wood, and mangrove thickets. Subsistence crops, tobacco, and cotton also are grown. Magnificent forests of tropical hardwoods in SW Campeche, Petén, and British Honduras provide the basis for a lumber industry. This area teems with tropical life, including the jaguar, the armadillo, the iguana, and the Yucatán turkey. Fishing is important along the Yucatán coast. The peninsula's fine beaches are being developed as tourist resorts. With limited access to the outside world (one main highway and a railroad), aircraft have become Yucatán's best means of transportation. Mérida and Campeche, Mexico, and Belize, British Honduras, are the chief cities of Yucatán. Centuries before the arrival of the Spanish, Yucatán was the seat of a great civilization (see MAYA). Probably the first white men to arrive were the two survivors of a Spanish shipwreck (1511)—Gonzalo de Guerrero, who joined the Maya, and Gerónimo de Aguilar, who was rescued by Cortés in 1519 and became his interpreter. Later (1524–25) Cortés made an epic march across the base of the peninsula to Honduras. Francisco Fernández de Córdoba had in 1517 already skirted the coast, and in the following year Juan de Grijalva had explored the same coast. The conquest of the Maya was begun in 1527 by Francisco de Montejo but was not completed until 1546, when his son, Francisco de Montejo the younger, crushed the revolt of a coalition of Mayan tribes. See Robert S. Chamberlain, *The Conquest and Civilization of Yucatan, 1517–50* (1949); F. F. Blom, *The Conquest of Yucatan* (1971); R. L. Roys, *The Indian Background of Colonial Yucatan* (new ed. 1972).

yucca (yŭk'ə), any plant of the genus *Yucca,* stiff-leaved stemless or treelike succulents of the family Liliaceae (LILY family), native chiefly to the tablelands of Mexico and the American Southwest but found also in the E United States and the West Indies. Yuccas in flower produce a large stalk of white or purplish blossoms. They are pollinated by the yucca moth, and in its absence they rarely fruit—a striking example of interdependence, since the moth, which lays its eggs during pollination and whose larvae feed on some of the developing seeds, cannot reproduce without the yucca. The leaves are usually stiff and spearlike, often with marginal threads. Several species are known as Adam's-needle, particularly those that are hardy and are cultivated in the North, most common of which is *Y. filamentosa.* The Joshua tree (*Y. brevifolia*) is a picturesque treelike species of desert regions. Mormons crossing the California deserts are said to have so named it because the grotesquely angular branches looked like the outstretched arms of a Joshua leading them out of the wilderness. The Spanish bayonet (*Y. aloifolia*) is another that is treelike in form, and the Spanish dagger (*Y. gloriosa*) is stemless or has a short trunk. The fruits and sometimes the flowers of several species of yucca were used as food by Indians. Certain species, particularly *Y. baccata* and *Y. glauca,* are called *soap plant* because of the use of their roots for soap. The fibers of some kinds have been utilized, and the wood of several of the arborescent types, while light, is tough and desirable for splints. A yucca is the state flower of New Mexico. Yuccas are classified in the division MAGNOLIOPHYTA, class Liliatae, order Liliales, family Liliaceae.

Yucca House National Monument: see NATIONAL PARKS AND MONUMENTS (table).

Yudenich, Nikolai Nikolayevich (nyĭkəlī´ nyĭkəlī´əvĭch yŏŏdyā´nyĭch), 1862–1933, Russian general. He served in the Russo-Japanese War and in World War I and after the Bolshevik Revolution in 1917 he took command of an anti-Bolshevik army in the Baltic states. In Oct., 1919, with some British support, Yudenich led his army against Petrograd (now Leningrad), but he was driven back into Estonia. He died in exile at Paris.

Yugoslavia (yōō″gōslä´vēə), Serbo-Croatian *Jugoslavija,* federal republic (1971 pop. 20,504,516), 98,766 sq mi (255,804 sq km), SE Europe, largely in the Balkan Peninsula. BELGRADE is the capital. Yugoslavia is bounded by Italy and the Adriatic Sea on the west, by Austria and Hungary on the north, by Rumania and Bulgaria on the east, and by Greece and Albania on the south. The country is a federation of six people's republics; in descending order of size, they are SERBIA (with Belgrade as the capital), which includes the autonomous provinces of KOSSOVO and VOJVODINA; CROATIA (with ZAGREB as capital); BOSNIA AND HERCEGOVINA (SARAJEVO); MACEDONIA (SKOPJE); SLOVENIA (LJUBLJANA); and MONTENEGRO (TITOGRAD). All the republics except Bosnia and Hercegovina are organized roughly on an ethnic basis and correspond to historic divisions. The Adriatic coast, known as DALMATIA, is dotted with numerous ports (notably PULA, RIJEKA [Fiume], ZADAR, ŠIBENIK, SPLIT, and DUBROVNIK), and there are many islands (e.g., KRK, BRAČ, CRES, HVAR, PAG, and KORČULA). About four fifths of Yugoslavia is mountainous, with an average altitude of 1,500 to 2,000 ft (457–610 m). The chief mountain chain, the Dinaric Alps, runs parallel to the Adriatic coast. In the northwest, the Julian Alps culminate at 9,396 ft (2,864 m) in the Triglav. Yugoslavia is traversed, in the northeast, by the Danube, and its main rivers—the Drava, the Sava, the Morava, the Timok, and the Tisza (Serb. *Tisa*)—are Danubian tributaries. Since World War II, Yugoslavia has become the most heavily industrialized nation in the Balkans. It is rich in mineral resources, notably lignite, petroleum, iron, copper, lead, zinc, bauxite, antimony, chrome, and manganese. Metal processing is the most important manufacturing industry; others produce textiles, chemicals, and processed food. Industries are located throughout the country, but the most important industrial area is the Sava valley between Belgrade and Zagreb. The country has great hydroelectric potential. Despite industrialization, nearly half the labor force is still engaged in agriculture. Livestock raising is important. Leading crops are corn, wheat, fruits, sugar beets, potatoes, and rye. The country has extensive vineyards. Metal products and foodstuffs are the leading exports, and machinery, transportation equipment, and other manufactured goods are the chief imports. The main trade partners are West Germany, Italy, and the USSR. Yugoslavia entered into a trade agreement with the Common Market in 1970. Tourism is increasing; the Adriatic coast has numerous resorts, and there are many mineral spas throughout the country. All major industrial enterprises have been nationalized. While there are state and cooperative farms, most productive land remains privately owned. To a significant extent the Yugoslav planned economy has been decentralized in an attempt to foster the production of consumer goods. The Yugoslav (i.e., South Slav) people consists of five ethnic nationalities —Serbs, Croats, Slovenes, Macedonians, and Montenegrins—the remainder being Yugoslavs with undeclared nationality (chiefly in Bosnia and Hercegovina) and nationals of neighboring countries. Linguistically the five groups are very closely related, but historical and cultural factors have kept them separate. The Croats and Slovenes, long associated with Hungary and with Austria, use the Roman rather than the Cyrillic alphabet and constitute the vast majority of the Roman Catholics (who are about 30% of the population) in Yugoslavia. The rest of the Yugoslavs mostly belong to the Orthodox Eastern Church (about 40%) and to Islam (about 10%); the majority of the Muslims live in Bosnia and Hercegovina. Higher education is centered at the universities of Belgrade, Zagreb, Ljubljana, Sarajevo, Skopje, Niš, and Novi Sad.

Creation of the State. Yugoslavia came into existence as a result of World War I. (The earlier histories of its six component republics are treated separately, under their respective names.) In 1914 only Serbia (which included the present Yugoslav republic of Macedonia) and Montenegro were independent states; Croatia, Slovenia, and Bosnia and Hercegovina belonged to the AUSTRO-HUNGARIAN MONARCHY. The movement for unification (see PAN-SLAVISM) was led by Serbia and was a major cause of World War I. In 1915, Serbia and Montenegro were overrun by the Central Powers, but the Serbian troops eventually were evacuated to Allied-held Corfu, Greece. There the representatives of the South Slavic peoples proclaimed (July, 1917) their proposed union under the Serbian king, PETER I. Montenegro adhered to the union in Nov., 1918, and in Dec., 1918, the "Kingdom of the Serbs, Croats, and Slovenes" was formally proclaimed. Its name was changed to Yugoslavia (sometimes spelled Jugoslavia) only in 1929. The Paris Peace Conference (see NEUILLY, TREATY OF; SAINT-GERMAIN, TREATY OF; TRIANON, TREATY OF) recognized the new state and enlarged its territory at the expense of Austria and Hungary. King ALEXANDER, who had been regent from 1918 for his invalid father, ascended the throne on Peter I's death (1921). In order to protect itself against Hungarian and Bulgarian demands for treaty revisions, Yugoslavia entered (1920, 1921) into alliances with Czechoslovakia and Rumania, the three states forming the LITTLE ENTENTE in close cooperation with France. With its western neighbor, Italy, relations were strained from the first over the Fiume question (see RIJEKA). Although this was settled in 1924 with Fiume given to Italy, Italian nationalists continued to entertain hopes of appropriating part or all of Dalmatia, which had been secretly promised to Italy in 1915 by the Allies in exchange for joining them in World War I. Yugoslav nationalists, on the other hand, claimed parts of Venezia Giulia on ethnic grounds, and relations remained tense. Internal problems were still more acute. Late in 1920 the Serbian PAŠIĆ became premier and obtained enactment of the centralized constitution of 1921. The Croats, led by RADIĆ, demanded autonomy. In 1928 Radić was shot and killed in parliament. After the Croats had set up (1928) a separate parliament at Zagreb, King Alexander in 1929 proclaimed a dictatorship, dissolved the parliament, and changed the name of the kingdom to Yugoslavia. The royal dictatorship officially ended in 1931, but the new parliamentary constitution provided for an electoral procedure that insured victory for the government party. Troubles with Croatian and Macedonian nationalists culminated (1934) in Alexander's assassination at Marseilles, France. His son, PETER II, succeeded under the regency of Alexander's cousin, Prince Paul. The Croatian problem had been eagerly exploited by Hungary and Italy, which encouraged particularist movements against the Serbian centralists. Prince Paul's gradual rapprochement with the AXIS powers thus had the paradoxical effect of leading to the restoration (1939) of a more democratic government and the establishment of Croatian autonomy. In March, 1941, Yugoslavia adhered to the Axis Tripartite Pact. Two days later a bloodless military coup d'etat ousted the regent. The new government proclaimed a policy of neutrality, but in April, 1941, German troops, assisted by Bulgarian, Hungarian, and Italian forces, invaded Yugoslavia. Striking swiftly, the Germans joined with the Italians in Albania; a week later organized resistance was over. A Croatian puppet state was proclaimed under the leadership of Ante Pavelić, chief of the Ustachi (a Croatian terrorist organization; see CROATIA). Dalmatia, Montenegro, and Slovenia were divided among Italy, Hungary, and Germany; Serbian Macedonia was awarded to Bulgaria. Serbia was set up as a puppet state under German control. Atrocities were committed by the Axis occupation forces and by the Ustachi. While Peter II established a government in exile in London, many Yugoslav troops continued to resist in their mountain strongholds. There were two main resistance groups: the *chetniks* under MIHAJLOVIĆ and an army under the Communist TITO. In 1943 civil war broke out between the two factions, of which the second was more uncompromising in its opposition to the Axis. Tito was supported by the USSR, and he won the support of Great Britain as well. King Peter was forced to transfer the military command from Mihajlović to Tito. By late Oct., 1944, the Germans had been driven from Yugoslavia. The Soviet army entered Belgrade. Tito's council of national liberation was merged (Nov., 1944) with the royal government. In March, 1945, Tito became premier. Lacking real power, the non-Communist members of the government resigned and were arrested. In Nov., 1945, national elections—from which the opposition abstained—resulted in victory for the government. The constituent assembly proclaimed a federal republic.

The Communist State. The constitution of 1946 gave wide autonomy to the six newly created republics, but actual power remained in the hands of Tito and the Communist party. The Allied peace treaty (1947) with Italy awarded Yugoslavia the eastern part of VENEZIA GIULIA and set up TRIESTE as a free territory; conflict with Italy over Trieste ended in a partition agreement (1954). Within Yugoslavia a vigorous program of socialization was inaugurated. Opposition was crushed or intimidated, and Mihajlović was executed. Close ties were maintained with the USSR and the COMINFORM until 1948, when a breach between the Yugoslav and Soviet Communist parties occurred and Yugoslavia was expelled from the Cominform. The Tito government began to pursue an independent course in foreign relations. Economic and military assistance was received from the West. In 1954, Yugoslavia concluded a military defense pact (independent of NATO) with Greece and Turkey. More cordial relations with the USSR were resumed in 1955, but new rifts occurred because of Soviet intervention in Hungary (1956) and Czechoslovakia (1968). Domestically Yugoslavia's "national communism" or "Titoism" included the abandonment of agricultural collectivization (1953) and the centralization of administrative and economic controls. Important economic power was given to workers' councils, and the republics were subdivided into communes. In 1966, Aleksander Ranković, the vice president and Tito's longtime associate, was purged for having maintained a network of secret agents and for opposing reform. Friction with the Roman Catholic Church ended with an accord with the Vatican in 1966. Yugoslavs possessed greater freedom than the inhabitants of any other Eastern European country. Intellectual freedom was still restricted, however, as the jailings and harassment of Milovan DJILAS and Mihaljo Mihaljov showed. Agitation among the nationalities revived, particularly among the Croats, and controls over intellectual life were stiffened in the early 1970s. Yugoslavia is governed under a constitution adopted in 1974. The bicameral parliament is made up of the 220-member federal chamber (30 delegates from each republic and 20 delegates from each province) and the 88-member chamber of the republics and provinces (12 delegates from each republic and 8 delegates from each province); members of both bodies are elected to four-year terms. The country's executive is composed of the nine-member collective presidency, made up of one representative from each republic and province and the president of the presidency (who is selected by parliament). The members of the presidency usually serve nonrenewable five-year terms; in May, 1974, Tito was elected president for life by parliament. The president is head of state, chief of the armed forces, and president of the League of Communists (since 1953 the name of the Yugoslav Communist party); he is the most powerful person in the country. A personal account of Yugoslavia is Rebecca West, *Black Lamb and Grey Falcon* (1941, repr. 1968). See J. B. Hoptner, *Yugoslavia in Crisis, 1934-1941* (1962); A. W. Palmer, *Yugoslavia* (1964); Stephen Clissold, ed., *A Short History of Yugoslavia* (1968); W. S. Vucinich, *Contemporary Yugoslavia* (1969); F. W. Deakin, *The Embattled Mountain* (1971); L. F. Edwards, *Yugoslavia* (1971); John Alexander, *Yugoslavia before the Roman Conquest* (1972); W. R. Roberts, *Tito, Mihailović and the Allies, 1941-1945* (1973).

Yugoslav literature, writings of the South Slavs in the Serbo-Croatian, Slovenian, and, especially since World War II, Macedonian languages. The Serbian and Croatian literary languages are similar, but the Serbs use the Cyrillic alphabet, while the Croatians and Slovenians use the Roman. Ecclesiastical works in OLD CHURCH SLAVONIC were produced in the Middle Ages, but under Turkish and later Austrian domination the development of a unique Yugloslav culture was suppressed. Nevertheless, a large body of orally transmitted folk poetry of great richness developed. The remarkable 16th-century flowering of learning and literature in the Adriatic trading city of Dubrovnik was a reflection of the Italian Renaissance, spread by commercial contacts and by Slavic youths educated at Padua. It reached its apogee in *Osman,* the Croatian epic by Ivan GUNDULIĆ, and in the plays of Marin Držić (1508?-67) and Junije Palmotić (1606-57). Yugoslav creative literature suffered a decline in the 18th cent., when Dubrovnik's political independence was crushed, and a slavish imitation of foreign writings took hold. However, the writing of history and biography were gaining prominence. Academies flourished, and the epic poems of the academician Ignat Dordić (1675-1737) were notable. The first national bard, Anora Kačić Miošić (1702-60), wrote his poems in ballad and folk style, while the moralist-philosopher Dositej Obradović (1742-1811) introduced fable writing into Yugoslav literature. The Yugoslavs experienced the general European nationalist upsurge in the late 18th and early 19th cent. In Slovenia this nationalism, which received much of its impetus from Germany, was weakened by a conflict between religious and secular writers. In Croatia the writers looked to Italy for inspiration, in Serbia, to Russia. Yugoslav intellectuals everywhere responded with enthusiasm to the Pan-Slavism of the Slovak Jan KOLLÁR. Among the Croatians a cultural movement known as Illyrianism (named after the state established by Napoleon after the defeat of Austria at Wagram in 1809) acted as a stimulant to literature. Illyrianism was suffused with romanticism and nationalism; the latter theme expressed itself throughout the 19th cent. partly in terms of antagonism to Austro-Hungarian rule. The groundwork for a popular, integrated Yugoslav literature was laid by three early romantic leaders—the Croat Ljudevit Gaj (1809-72), the Slovene Jernej Kopitar (1780-1844), and the Serb Vuk Stefanović KARADŽIĆ; they developed a literary language based on popular speech. Karadžić was also a great folklorist whose collections helped stimulate Yugoslav national poetry and delineate its development. Benefiting from these beginnings, by mid-century the Serbian lyric poet Branko Radičević (1824-53), the Slovene poet and political satirist Stanko Vraz (1810-51), and the Croatian Ivan Mažuranić (1814-90)—whose epic *The Death of Smail-Aga* (1846, tr. 1925) tells of Christian-Muslim conflict in Turkish-ruled Hercegovina—had made important contributions to the romantic-nationalist movement. More technically perfect were the poems of France Prešeren (1800-1849), a disciple of Byron, and Petar PRERADOVIĆ, who cultivated medieval traditions. Considered far superior was the prince-bishop Petar Petrović Njegoš (1813-51), whose verse drama *The Mountain Wreath* (1847, tr. 1930) earned him the designation of the Montenegrin Shakespeare. Later romanticism is represented by Djura Jaksić (1832-78), writer of heroic, nationalistic dramas and poems, and Jovan Jovanović-Zmaj (1833-1903), a lyrical poet. The rise of realism in the latter part of the 19th cent. furthered the development of the novel by such writers as the Serbs Simo Matavulj (1852-1908) and Jakov Ignatović (1824-88), whose penetrating studies portrayed the varied social classes of his region; the Croatian Evgenij Kumičić (1850-1904); and the Slovenes Josip Stritar (1836-1925) and Josip Jurcić (1844-81), both of whom portrayed Slovene society. Many novelists of the period also wrote poetry and drama. Outstanding for versatility and abundant production were the popular Croatian writer August Šenoa (1838-81), who revealed Croat social decay and criticized German influence, and the greatest of all Slovenian writers, Ivan Cankar (1876-1918). The late 19th cent. saw a growing interest in the psychology of motives and morals—a trend chiefly inspired by the writings of Dostoyevsky and Tolstoy. The best known of the psychological novelists was the Croatian Ksaver Šandor Gjalski (1854-1935), who in a series of some 20 novels depicted the whole range of contemporary Croatian life. In the drama, historical themes had predominated, as in the works of the Croatian Ivo Vojnović (1857-1929). In Croatia and in Slovenia 20th-century dramatists broke with the cult of history and concerned themselves with psychology. Among these writers are the Croatians Milan Begović (1876-1948) and Josip Kosor and the Slovenian Anton Medved (1869-1911). Serbian drama, however, long remained primarily romantic in the manner of its founder Jovan Sterija-Popović (1806-56), although contemporary problems were treated in the comedies of Branislav Nusić (1864-1938), who was also a noted novelist, story writer, and essayist. During the first quarter of the 20th cent., the modernists sought to assimilate literary trends imported from France and Germany. Anton Aškerc (1856-1912) wrote historical poems of social revolt, but Vojislav Ilić (1862-94), Aleksa Santić (1868-1924), and Silvije Strahimir Kranjčević (1865-1908) were influenced by the Parnassians. The symbolists numbered not only the Serbs Jovan Dučić (1874-1943) and Milan Rakić (1876-1938), but also Oton Župančić (1878-1949), the greatest Slovene poet of this century, and Vladimir Nazor (1876-1949), Croatia's 20th-century literary giant. Outstanding critics were the Serbs Bogdan Popović (1863-1944) and Jovan Skerlić (1877-1914) and the Croatian Milan Marjanović (1879-1955). During the 1930s socially conscious literature with local-color settings predominated. The Serbs Jovan Popović (1903-52) and Cedomir Minderović were among the more successful writers of this period. In Slovenia the epic novel has flourished under such writers as Jus Kozak, Anton Ingolić, and Prezihov Voranc. World War II produced a number of partisan poets, and war themes predominated in post-war writing. Since Macedonian was recognized in 1944 as one of the official languages of the country, writers have sought to develop a literature based on Macedonia's rich folk heritage. Although the Communist regime imposed severe restrictions on writers, freedom from Soviet influence since 1949 and the cultural independence of several regions have resulted in some innovation. Among the more recent notable Yugoslav writers are Mladen Horvat; Marko Ristić; the Serbian poets Miloš Crnjanski and Rastko Petrović; the Macedonian poet Koca Racin; the Bosnian novelist Ivo ANDRIĆ, who was awarded the 1961 Nobel Prize in Literature; the Croatian poet and dramatist Miroslav Krleža; the Slovenian prose writer France Bek; the fabulist Miodrag Bulatović; and the political writer Milovan DJILAS. See Antun Barac, *A History of Yugoslav Literature* (tr. 1955); Sveta Lukić, *Contemporary Yugoslav Literature* (1968, tr. 1972).

Yukawa, Hideki (hē'dĕkē yōōkä'wä), 1907-, Japanese physicist, grad. Kyoto Univ., 1929, Ph.D. Osaka Univ., 1938. He was professor of physics at Kyoto Univ. from 1939 to 1970. He received the 1949 Nobel Prize in Physics for predicting (1935) the existence of the MESON. After further developing the meson theory of nuclear forces, he began (1947) work on his "nonlocal field" theory for elementary particles. In 1948 he came to the United States, where he spent a year at the Institute for Advanced Study and was (1949-53) visiting professor at Columbia.

Yukon (yōō'kŏn), river, c.2,000 mi (3,220 km) long, rising in Atlin Lake, NW British Columbia, Canada, and receiving numerous headwater streams; one of the longest rivers of North America. It flows generally northwest, past Dawson and across the Alaska border, to Fort Yukon, thence generally southwest through central Alaska until, in a wide swing north, it enters Norton Sound of the Bering Sea through a delta that is 60 mi (97 km) wide. Its chief tributaries are the Teslin, Pelly, White, Stewart, Porcupine, Tanana, and Koyukuk rivers. The river is incised in the Yukon Plateau; marshy land borders much of its upper course. The Yukon is navigable for river boats three months of the year to Whitehorse, c.1,775 mi (2,860 km) upstream. The Yukon basin is one of the most sparsely populated and least developed regions of North America. Much of its history, exploration, and development centers on the river system. Its lower reaches were explored (1836-37, 1843) by Russians, and in 1843 Robert Campbell of the Hudson's Bay Company explored the upper course. During the Klondike gold rush (1897-98) the Yukon was a major route to the gold fields. Greater development of the basin occurred in the mid-1900s due to its strategic location, and several military installations were later built. The Yukon River is a major salmon-spawning ground, and salmon fishing is an important seasonal activity. The Yukon is used to generate hydroelectricity, but it remains one of the greatest undeveloped hydroelectric resources in North America. On the river's banks are fur-trading posts, missions, Eskimo villages, and towns with modern airports serving vast areas.

Yukon Territory, territory (1971 pop. 18,388), 207,076 sq mi (536,327 sq km), NW Canada. The capital and largest town is WHITEHORSE. Next in importance is DAWSON. The triangle-shaped territory is bordered on the N by the Beaufort Sea of the Arctic Ocean, on the E by the Mackenzie dist., Northwest Territories, on the S by British Columbia and Alaska, and on the W by Alaska. The highest point in the Yukon is Mt. Logan, 19,850 ft (6,050 m) high, part of the Coast Ranges in the southwest. Although most of the territory is a watershed for the Yukon River and its tributaries, the northern and southeastern regions drain into the Mackenzie River system. Immediately south of the desolate arctic coast the country is uninhabited and generally unknown. The other parts of the territory have great natural beauty, with snow-fed lakes backed by perpetually white-capped mountains and forests and streams abounding with wildlife. Winters are long and cold, with low humidity. During the short summers the longer day and surprisingly warm sun bring a profusion of wild flowers and enable the hardier grains and vegetables to mature. The few settlements are situated on the riverbanks. Transportation facilities are limited, and for many years the Yukon River system was the main artery. The White Pass and Yukon Railway from Whitehorse to Skagway, Alaska, was constructed during the Klondike gold rush of the 1890s. Air transportation now plays a vital role, and there is an international airport at Whitehorse. The Alaska Highway and other all-weather roads have been built since World War II. The leading industry in the territory is mining; asbestos, copper, silver, zinc, lead, and gold are the principal minerals. Fur trapping is the oldest industry but has declined in recent decades. Manufacturing and fishing are relatively unimportant, but tourism is gaining in importance. The territory's history began with the explorations in the 1840s of Robert Campbell and John Bell, fur traders for the Hudson's Bay Company. Several trading posts were built on the Yukon River, and before long prospectors began to search for treasure. After the famous gold strikes in the Klondike River region in the 1890s more than 30,000 people pushed across the icy barriers in search of gold. This colorful period has been recorded in the writings of Robert Service and Jack London. The Canadian government acquired the Yukon from the Hudson's Bay Company in 1870 and administered it as part of the Northwest Territories. To meet the need for local

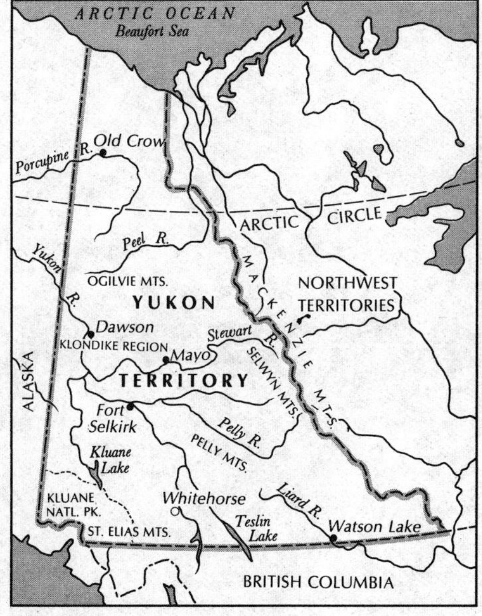

government created by the influx of gold prospectors, the Yukon was made a separate district (1895) and then a separate territory (1898) with Dawson as capital. Whitehorse became the capital in 1952. The government consists of a federally appointed governor and an elected legislative council of seven members. The territory elects one delegate to the Canadian Parliament. About 2,000 Indians and Eskimo are included in the population. Kluane National Park (est. 1972) is in the St. Elias Mts. See A. C. Hinton and P. H. Godsell, *The Yukon* (1955); W. R. Hamilton, *The Yukon Story* (2d ed. 1967); K. J. Rea, *The Political Economy of the Canadian North* (1968); E. A. McCourt, *The Yukon and Northwest Territories* (1969); J. R. Lotz, *Northern Realities: The Future of Northern Development in Canada* (1970).

Yuma (yo͞o' mə), city (1970 pop. 29,007), seat of Yuma co., extreme SW Ariz., on the eastern bank of the Colorado River near the confluence of the Gila River; founded 1854, inc. as a city 1914. It is a major trade center of an extensive farm area irrigated by the Yuma project. The project has turned more than 100,000 acres (40,470 hectares) of desert into a fertile farm region known for its cattle, citrus fruits, melons, winter vegetables, grains, and cotton. Two nearby military installations contribute to the city's economy—the sprawling Yuma Proving Grounds and a U.S. marine corps air station. Yuma is also a growing resort center because of its mild climate. Early missions were built in the area by Fathers Eusebio Kino and F. T. H. Garcés, but there was no white settlement until after Fort Yuma was built (1850) to protect overlanders on the route to California. After 1858, Yuma was a river port and the center of a gold-mining boom. Points of interest in the area include Fort Yuma (on the west bank of the river), the territorial prison (built 1875; now a museum), St. Thomas Mission (16th cent.), three dams on the Colorado River, and the California sand dunes. Yuma has a junior college.

Yuma Indians, North American Indians whose language belongs to the Yuman branch of the Hokan Siouan linguistic stock (see AMERICAN INDIAN LANGUAGES). They formerly lived in SW Arizona. The Yuma suffered much in warfare with the Maricopa, the Pima, and other Indians. In 1853 the Yuma numbered some 3,000. A reservation was created for them in 1883, but the next year they were removed to the California side of the Colorado River; they formally surrendered their lands to the United States in 1886. Today the remainder of the group lives on the Fort Yuma reservation in California and Arizona; they number some 1,200. See A. L. Kroeber, *Yuman Tribes of the Lower Colorado* (1920); Jack Forbes, *Warriors of the Colorado* (1965).

Yuman (yo͞o'mən), branch of American Indian languages belonging to the Hokan-Siouan linguistic stock, or family, of North America (including Mexico) and Central America. See AMERICAN INDIAN LANGUAGES.

Yü-men or **Yümen** (both: yü-mŭn), city (1970 est. pop. 325,000), NW Kansu prov., China. It is China's leading petroleum center, with oil fields and refineries. Yü-men, on the Old Silk Road to Sinkiang, is named for an ancient gateway in the nearby Great Wall. It is on the railroad that connects Lan-chou and Sinkiang.

yungas (yo͞ong'gäs), region of lowland valleys in the eastern piedmont of the Andes Mts., 5,000–8,000 ft (1,524–2,438 m) high, extending from the Peru-Bolivia border SE into central Bolivia. They receive excessive rainfall and are warm and humid. Although isolated and very difficult of access, the yungas assumed economic importance in the early 20th cent. as a major source of rubber and quinine. Coca, coffee, tobacco, and fruit are grown there. With improved communications the region's economy has grown, especially in the more accessible valleys close to La Paz, Bolivia, which have been developed as resorts.

Yung Lo (yo͞ong lô), 1359–1424, reign title of the 3d emperor (1403–24) of the Chinese MING dynasty, whose personal name was Chu Ti. He rose to power in N China after being delegated by his father, the Ming founding emperor Hung Wu (reigned 1368–98), to lead the fight against the retreating Mongols. He usurped the throne from his nephew, Emperor Chien Wen (reigned 1399–1402), after a devastating civil war. Under his reign six maritime expeditions led by the Muslim eunuch Cheng Ho sailed as far as Arabia and E Africa, and tributary relations were established with many kingdoms in SE Asia. Yung Lo focused his energy, however, on securing defense in the north. As emperor he personally led five vast military campaigns far across the steppe to subdue the Mongol tribes. The importance of the north was confirmed when in 1421 he moved the capital from Nanking to Peking, just S of the Great Wall.

Yünnan or **Yün-nan** (both: yün'nän) [south of the clouds], province (1968 est. pop. 23,000,000), c.162,000 sq mi (419,600 sq km), SW China. It borders Burma on the west and Laos and North Vietnam on the south. K'UN-MING is the capital. The average altitude is c.6,500 ft (1,980 m). The eastern half of the province is a limestone plateau with karst scenery and unnavigable rivers flowing through deep mountain gorges; the western half is characterized by mountain ranges and rivers running north and south. These include the Salween and the Mekong. The rugged, vertical terrain produces a wide range of flora and fauna, and the province has been called a natural zoological and botanical garden. It has a mild climate with balmy and fair weather, but although the growing period is long, there is little arable land. Agriculture is restricted to the few upland plains, open valleys, and terraced hillsides. Rice is the main crop; corn, wheat, sweet potatoes, soybeans (as a food crop), tea, sugarcane, and tobacco are also grown. Cotton is being developed. On the steep slopes in the west livestock is raised and timber is cut (teak in the southwest). However, Yünnan's chief source of wealth lies in its vast mineral resources. It is the country's leading tin producer; other deposits include iron, coal, lead, copper, zinc, gold, mercury, silver, antimony, and sulfur. Road and railroad traffic has been recently improved and K'un-ming is now a transportation center; an important railroad runs from K'un-ming to Hanoi, North Vietnam, while transportation to Burma is maintained by the Burma Road. There are many minority groups in Yünnan. From ancient times the Chinese invaders gradually pushed the aboriginal tribes into mountain localities, where today, retaining their distinct languages and culture, they populate eight autonomous districts. The Miao, Yao, Lolo, Lao, Shan, Thai, and Lisu are some of the larger tribes; there is also a considerable Tibetan minority. Separated by rugged mountains from the central authority in N China, Yünnan for centuries remained independent. In 1253 it was conquered by the Mongols of the Yüan dynasty, which destroyed the Thai kingdom of Nan Chao established there. Yünnan passed to the Manchus in 1659 and became a province of China under the control of the central government. It was the scene of a great Muslim revolt (1855–72). It was a major center of Chinese resistance in World War II, and in 1950 it passed to Communist control. Yünnan Univ. is in K'un-ming.

Yünnanfu: see K'UN-MING, China.

Yurok Indians (yo͝or'ŏk), North American Indians who in the mid-19th cent. occupied NW California, particularly the area around the Klamath River. They were of the California cultural area but had some Pacific Northwest Coast culture traits; they subsisted on salmon and acorns, and for money they used the dentalium shell, which they received from tribes living farther north. Their property laws were unique among Indians, pertaining only to the realm of the individual; the Yurok recognized no public claim to property. By 1855 a reservation was set aside for them. They then numbered some 2,500. Presently the Yurok live on the Hoopa Reservation in California and number about 140, although another 750 live off the reservation. The Yurok and their southern neighbors, the Wiyot, speak languages of the Ritwan group that belong to the Algonquian-Wakashan linguistic stock and possibly to the Algonquian branch of this stock (see AMERICAN INDIAN LANGUAGES).

Yusuf ibn Tashfin (yo͞osŏŏf' ĭ'bən täshfēn'), d. 1106, ruler in the dynasty of the ALMORAVIDS (c.1059–1106). A Muslim, he led the Berbers in N Africa, continued the conquest of Morocco, took Algeria, and founded (1062) Marrakesh, which became his capital. When the petty Moorish kings of Spain appealed for help against the Christians, he entered S Spain and with the help of the local kings decisively defeated (1086) ALFONSO VI of León and Castile. In 1090 he again invaded Spain. Turning conqueror (as Tarik had done in 711), he annexed all the Moorish territories of Spain except Zarogoza. His empire was inherited by his son Ali.

Yuzovka: see DONETSK, USSR.

Yvelines (ēvlēn'), department (1968 pop. 853,386), N central France, W of Paris. VERSAILLES is the capital.

Yverdon (ēvĕrdôN'), Ger. *Iferten*, town (1970 pop. 20,538), Vaud canton, W Switzerland, at the south end of the Lake of Neuchâtel. It is an old spa with Roman ruins. Typewriters are manufactured in the town. Heinrich Pestalozzi held (1805–25) his experimental classes in Yverdon's 13th-century castle.

Z

Z, 26th and last letter of the ALPHABET, representing the voiced correspondent of voiceless *s,* as in the English *zebra.* Its original is the Greek zeta, which the Romans borrowed and added to their alphabet.

Zaanaim (zā″ənā′ĭm), same as ZAANANNIM.

Zaanan (zā′ənăn), town, perhaps the same as ZENAN. Micah 1.11.

Zaanannim (zā″ənăn′ĭm). **1** Unidentified place, N Palestine. Joshua 19.33. **2** Place near Megiddo. Judges 4.11.

Zaandam (zändäm′), municipality (1971 pop. 65,981), North Holland prov., W Netherlands, near Amsterdam. Manufactures include food products, chemicals, lumber, and machinery. Peter I of Russia stayed at Zaandam in 1697 to learn shipbuilding, which at the time was a flourishing industry of the city.

Zaavan (zā′əvăn), grandson of Seir the Horite. Gen. 36.27. Zavan: 1 Chron. 1.42.

Zab (zăb, zäb), name applied to the two principal tributaries of the Tigris River. The **Great Zab,** 265 mi (426 km) long, rises in SE Turkey and flows generally S through Iraq to the Tigris. The **Little Zab,** 250 mi (402 km) long, rises in NW Iran and flows SW through Iraq to the Tigris. Both rivers are extensively used for irrigation, flood control on the Tigris, and hydroelectricty. Bekhme Dam on the Great Zab and Dokan Dam on the Little Zab are among the world's highest dams.

Zabad (zā′băd). **1, 2** Two of David's chief men. 1 Chron. 2.36; 11.41. They are perhaps the same person; ZABUD may be also. **3** Ephraimite. 1 Chron. 7.21. **4** See JOZACHAR. **5, 6, 7** Israelites who had married foreign wives. Ezra 10.27,33,43.

Zabbai (zăb′ī, zəbā′ī). **1** Israelite with a foreign wife. Ezra 10.28. **2** Father of BARUCH **3.**

Zabbud (zăb′əd), one who returned with Ezra from the Captivity. Ezra 8.14.

Zabdi (zăb′dī). **1** David's vintager. 1 Chron. 27.27. **2** Grandfather of Achan. Joshua 7.1,17,18. Zimri: 1 Chron. 2.6. **3** Benjamite. 1 Chron. 8.19. **4** Levite. Neh. 11.17. Apparently the same as ZICHRI **1.**

Zabdiel (zăb′dēĕl). **1** Father of JASHOBEAM. **2** Official under Nehemiah. Neh. 11.14.

Zabrze (zäb′zhĕ), Ger. *Hindenburg,* city (1970 pop. 197,214), S Poland. It is a railway junction in the KATOWICE mining and industrial region. Local coal deposits form the basis of Zabrze's coke and chemical industries. Founded in the 13th cent., Zabrze passed to Prussia in 1742. The city was renamed in 1915 in honor of German Field Marshal von Hindenburg; its old name was restored when it was ceded to Poland in 1945.

Zabud (zā′bəd), priest under Solomon, perhaps the same as ZABAD **1** or **2.** 1 Kings 4.5.

Zabulon (zăb′yo͝olən), same as ZEBULUN.

Zacatecas (säkätā′käs), state (1970 pop. 949,663), 28,125 sq mi (72,844 sq km), N central Mexico. ZACATECAS is the capital. Lying on the central plateau, Zacatecas is a state of semiarid plains and mountains. The Sierra Madre Occidental dominates the western half, and a transverse spur (often over 10,000 ft/3,048 m high) of the same range, crossing the state from west to east, divides it. Rainfall is light and vegetation scanty. The absence of large rivers to support irrigation makes the state relatively unimportant agriculturally. Extensive grazing lands make cattle raising a major activity, but the greatest industry is mining. With gold, silver, mercury, copper, iron, zinc, lead, bismuth, antimony, and salt, Zacatecas is second only to Guanajuato in mineral wealth produced. After the territory, which at first also included AGUASCALIENTES, had been opened (1530) but not colonized, it became a refuge for the Indians defeated in the MIXTÓN WAR. Their depredations on NUEVA GALICIA led to an expedition in 1546 to conquer them. The discovery of silver shortly afterward caused a silver rush that all but depopulated Nueva Galicia. The state is known for its numerous examples of baroque architecture.

Zacatecas, city (1970 pop. 56,829), capital of Zacatecas state, N central Mexico. With an altitude of more than 8,000 ft (2,438 m), it is situated in a deep ravine surrounded by arid hills. The climate is temperate. The city is characterized by old colonial buildings and narrow, tortuous, steep cobbled streets, frequently broken by stone steps. Zacatecas is a distributing center for the mining country and has industries making fine serapes and other items. Founded in 1848, the strategically located city was a key point in the Mexican wars and revolutions of the 19th and early 20th cent. Its cathedral was heavily pillaged during these struggles.

Zacatecoluca (säkätäkōlo͞o′kä), city (1971 est. pop. 57,001), S central El Salvador. Baskets, cotton products, and lumber are made. The city was heavily damaged by earthquake in 1932.

Zaccai (zăk′āī, zəkā′ī), family that returned from the Exile. Ezra 2.9; Neh. 7.14.

Zacchaeus or **Zaccheus** (both: zăkē′əs) [Gr.,= Heb. ZACCAI], publican of Jericho, short of stature, who climbed a tree to see Jesus. Luke 19.1-10.

Zacchur (zăk′ər), Simeonite. 1 Chron. 4.26.

Zaccur (zăk′ər). **1** Father of a spy sent into Canaan. Num. 13.4. **2** Leader of temple singers. 1 Chron. 25.2,10; Neh. 12.35. **3** Signer of the Covenant. Neh. 10.12. Additional mention of this name is in 1 Chron. 24.27; Neh. 3.2; 13.13. These passages may, in one or two cases, refer to the same person.

Zachariah (zăk″ərī′ə) [Heb.,= ZECHARIAH]. **1** King of Israel, son and successor of Jeroboam II. After ruling six months he was murdered by Shallum, who seized the throne. 2 Kings 14.29; 15.8-12. **2, 3** Same as ZECHARIAH **2** and **5,** respectively.

Zacharias (zăkərī′əs) or **Zachary, Saint** (zăk′ərē), pope (741-52), a Calabrian Greek; successor of St. Gregory III. He was the first pope after Gregory the Great not to seek confirmation of his election from the Byzantine emperor. By his personal prestige he forced Luitprand, king of the Lombards, to restore some towns he had taken from the pope. He sanctioned the assumption by PEPIN THE SHORT of the Frankish crown, thus beginning the cordial relations between Pepin's house and the papacy. St. Zachary's correspondence is extant; the letters to St. Boniface confirming the ecclesiastical settlements in Germany are notable. An illustrious pope, he did much to strengthen the authority of the Holy See. He was succeeded by Stephen II. Feast: March 22.

Zacharias [Gr. from Heb. ZECHARIAH] or **Zachary** [Eng. from Heb.]. **1** Priest to whom an angel appeared and foretold the birth of his son, John the Baptist. Luke 1.5-80. He and Elizabeth, his wife, are saints of the Roman Catholic Church; their day is Nov. 5. **2** Martyr prophet, the same as ZECHARIAH **2.** **3** Book of the Old Testament, often called ZECHARIAH.

Zacher (zā′kər), Benjamite. 1 Chron. 8.31. Zechariah: 1 Chron. 9.37.

Zacynthus, Greece: see ZÁKINTHOS.

Zadar (zä′där), Ital. *Zara,* city (1971 pop. 107,610), W Yugoslavia, in Croatia, on the Dalmatian coast of the Adriatic Sea. A seaport and a tourist center, it has industries that produce liqueur, tobacco, and jute. It is the seat of a Roman Catholic archbishop and has a branch of the Univ. of Zagreb. Founded by the Illyrians in the 4th cent. B.C., Zadar became a Roman colony in the 2d cent. B.C. It passed to the Byzantine Empire in 553 and was settled by the South Slavs in the 7th cent. Although disputed by Venice, Hungary, and Croatia, it remained under Byzantine protection until 1001, when Emperor Alexius I transferred it to Venice. At the end of the 11th cent. it was seized by Hungary, but the leaders of the Fourth Crusade, persuaded by the doge Enrico Dandolo, reconquered it for Venice in 1202. After a five-day siege the Crusaders sacked the city, an act for which they were condemned by Pope Innocent III. Hungary continued to dispute Zadar with Venice, which obtained permanent possession of the city only in 1409. The Treaty of Campo Formio (1797) gave it to Austria, where, from 1815 to 1918, it was the capital of the crownland of Dalmatia. Zadar passed to Italy by the Treaty of Saint-Germain (1919), was occupied (1945) by Yugoslav forces at the end of World War II, and was formally ceded to Yugoslavia by the Italian peace treaty of 1947. The city has several Roman monuments and medieval churches and palaces.

Zadkine, Ossip (ōsēp′ zädkēn′), 1890-1967, Russian sculptor who worked in France. Joining the cubists in 1914, Zadkine developed a powerful, original style. He exerted considerable influence upon contemporary sculptors after World War II. Among his best-known works is the public monument *The Destruction of Rotterdam* (1954).

Zadok (zā′dŏk). **1** Founder of a prominent priestly family. 2 Sam. 8.17; 1 Kings 2.35; 1 Chron. 6.8,53; 9.11; 18.16; Ezra 7.2; Neh. 11.11. **2** One of David's men. 1 Chron. 12.28. **3** Grandfather of Jotham. 2 Kings 15.33. **4** Sealer of the Covenant. Neh. 10.21. **5** High priest. 1 Chron. 6.12. **6, 7** Builders of the wall. Neh. 3.4,29. **8** Scribe. Neh. 13.13. The last two may be the same.

zadruga, village community of the South Slavs. The zadruga, a large family or clan organized on a patrilineal basis, lived together in one dwelling and held all land, livestock, and money in common. The oldest able member of the community was usually its ruler, responsible for allotting tasks to the members. This system, which was common to all the South Slavs, existed in Serbia into the 20th cent.

Żagań (zhä′gänyə), Ger. *Sagan,* town (1970 est. pop. 21,500), W Poland, on the Bóbr River. It has lignite mines, textile mills, and glassmaking industries. Founded in the 12th cent., Żagán was the capital of a principality that passed to the Hapsburgs in the 16th cent. and to Prussia in 1745. The town was incorporated into Poland after World War II.

Zagazig: see ZAQAZIQ, AZ, Egypt.

Zaghlul Pasha, Saad (säd zäglo͞ol′ päshä′), c.1850-1927, Egyptian nationalist leader, founder of the WAFD party. He suffered both arrest (1882) and exile (1919) for his attempts to end foreign domination in Egypt. Having founded (1919) the Wafd party, he became premier in 1924, but the opposition of Great Britain and the Egyptian court soon forced him to resign. The last year of his life he served as president of the Egyptian parliament.

Zagorsk (zəgôrsk′), city (1969 est. pop. 87,000), central European USSR. It is a rail terminus and a handicraft center known for wood carvings and toys. Manufactures include farm machinery, lacquers and paints, concrete pipes, automobile components, textiles, and furniture. The city developed from a settlement around the Troitse-Sergiyeva Lavra, one of Russia's most famous monasteries (founded 1340). The original wooden church, built by the monk Sergius, was destroyed in a Tatar raid in 1391. The Lavra contains the Troitski Cathedral (15th cent.); the Uspenski Cathedral (16th cent.), with the tomb of Boris Godunov; and a treasure chamber with rich tapestries and many objects of liturgical art. The monastery, long a place of pilgrimage, was made into a museum in 1920.

Zagreb (zä′grĕb), Ger. *Agram,* Hung. *Zágráb,* city (1971 pop. 602,058), capital of Croatia, NW Yugoslavia, on the Sava River. The second largest city in Yugoslavia and a major industrial and financial center, it has industries that produce machinery, machine tools, metal products, and chemicals. It is also a cultural center, with the Yugoslav Academy of Arts and Sciences (founded 1861), a university (founded 1669), an institute of nuclear physics, an observatory, and several fine museums and art galleries. Zagreb is the seat of a Roman Catholic archbishop, an Orthodox Eastern archbishop, a Protestant bishop, and a grand rabbi. The city was originally a suburb of the ancient Roman town of Andautonia. It was made an episcopal see of the Western church in 1903. Invaded by Mongols in 1242, it became in the second half of the 13th cent. the chief city of Croatia and Slavonia, which were then provinces of Hungary. The city was merged in 1557 with nearby Gradec, which had been a free royal city under the Hungarian crown. The part of Croatia in which Zagreb is situated escaped Turkish domination. During the 19th cent. Zagreb was a center of the Yugoslav nationalist movement. With the formation of the dual Austro-Hungarian Monarchy in 1867, the city became the capital of an autonomous Croatia. A fine modern city, Zagreb has its historic center in the old Kaptol dist., with the Catholic cathedral (begun 1093) and the Catholic archiepiscopal palace (18th cent.).

Zagros (zăg'rōs), mountain system of W Iran, extending c.1,100 mi (1,770 km) from the Turkish-Soviet frontier SE to the Strait of Hormuz, forming the western and southern border of the central Iranian plateau; rises to Mt. Sabalan, 15,592 ft (4,752 m) high. The Zagros vary from the rugged, forested, and snowcapped mountains of the northwest, with numerous volcanic cones and large basins (e.g., Lake Rezaiyeh), to the parallel ridge and valley system of the central portion, with lowland salt marshes, and the low, irregular southwest region, characterized by bare rock and sand dunes. The northern half of the Zagros is heavily populated, and the fertile valleys support agriculture. In the uplands of the central range, tribal pastoralism predominates. In the SE Zagros, dates and cereals are grown at oases. Kurds, Lurs, Bakhtiaris, Kashkais, and other nomads inhabit the mountains; some of the groups, especially the Kurds, are now sedentary. Iran's great oilfields lie along the western foothills of the central Zagros, where salt domes have trapped huge amounts of oil. In antiquity the Zagros formed the boundary between Assyria and Media.

Zaham (zā'hăm), son of Rehoboam and Abihail. 2 Chron. 11.19.

Zaharias, Babe Didrikson: see DIDRIKSON, BABE.

Zaharoff, Sir Basil (Basileios Zacharias) (zä'hərôf"), 1850–1936, international financier and munitions manufacturer, b. Anatolia, Turkey, probably of Greek-Russian parents, educated in England. His name is best known in connection with the Vickers-Armstrong munitions firm, of which he was director and chairman. For his services to the Allies during World War I, Zaharoff was knighted by George V and decorated by the French government. He was, however, popularly known as the "mystery man of Europe" and was accused of fomenting warfare and of secret political intrigue through his association with European statesmen, notably Lloyd George, and through his reputed holdings in Krupp, Skoda, and other munitions firms.

Zahedan (zähädän'), city (1971 est. pop. 42,000), capital of Seistan and Baluchistan prov., SE Iran, near the borders with Pakistan and Afghanistan. It is a road junction and the terminus of a railroad that runs into Pakistan.

Zähringen (tsĕr'ĭng-ən), noble German family. It took its name from a now ruined castle near Freiburg im Breisgau, Baden, and can be traced to the 10th cent. The family held extensive fiefs in Baden and W Switzerland, and Duke Berthold V, one of the most powerful nobles of his era, founded many towns, notably BERN. His death (1218) deprived the family of its Swiss holdings; his domains passed largely to the related KYBURG and HAPSBURG families. A younger branch continued in N Baden and split (16th cent.) into the branches of Baden-Baden and Baden-Durlach, reunited in 1771. In 1806, Charles Frederick of Baden was raised to grand ducal rank. Grand Duke Frederick II abdicated in 1918.

zaibatsu (zī'bätsōō) [Jap.,=money clique], the great family-controlled banking and industrial combines of modern Japan. The leading zaibatsu are Mitsui, Mitsubishi, Sumitomo, and Yasuda. They gained a position in the Japanese economy with no exact parallel elsewhere. Although the Mitsui were powerful bankers under the shogunate, most of the other zaibatsu developed after the Meiji restoration (1868), when, by subsidies and a favorable tax policy, the new government granted them a privileged position in the economic development of Japan. Later they helped finance strategic semiofficial enterprises in Japan and abroad, particularly in Taiwan and Korea. In the early 1930s the military clique tried to break the economic power of the zaibatsu but failed. In 1937 the four leading zaibatsu controlled directly one third of all bank deposits, one third of all foreign trade, one half of Japan's shipbuilding and maritime shipping, and most of the heavy industries. They maintained close relations with the major political parties. After Japan's surrender (1945) in World War II, the breakup of the zaibatsu was announced as a major aim of the Allied occupation, but by 1948 the old zaibatsu had reemerged. They still wield great economic power, but the growth of new business concerns in recent years has somewhat decreased their dominance.

Zaïmis, Alexander (zä'ēmēs), 1855–1936, Greek statesman. The son of Thrasyboulos Zaïmis, twice premier of Greece, he entered politics as a young man and joined (1890) the cabinet of his uncle as minister of justice. At the end of the disastrous war with Turkey, he became premier for the first time (1897–99). He was again premier in 1901–2 and 1904–6, was high commissioner in Crete (1906–11), and was premier three times during World War I between 1915 and 1917. He pursued a policy of "armed neutrality" in the war, did not interfere with the Allied landing at Salonica, and made way for Eleutherios VENIZELOS on the abdication of King Constantine I, when the neutrality policy had become untenable. Zaïmis headed (1926–28) a coalition cabinet and in 1929 was elected president of Greece; he was reelected in 1934. His presidency was marked by the struggle between the republicans and the royalists, whose respective leaders, Venizelos and Panayoti TSALDARIS, alternated as premiers. In 1935, General Kondylis, who had put down the Venizelist uprising, ousted Tsaldaris and held a plebiscite that resulted in the recall of King George II. Zaïmis died in exile at Vienna.

Zaindeh Rud: see ZAYANDEH RUD.

Zair (zā'ĭr), place, associated with Joram's campaign against Edom. 2 Kings 8.21.

Zaïre (zīēr', zäēr'), formerly Democratic Republic of the Congo, republic (1973 est. pop. 23,825,000), c.905,000 sq mi (2,344,000 sq km), central Africa, bordering on Angola in the southwest and west, on Cabinda and the Congo Republic in the west, on the Central African Republic and Sudan in the north, on Uganda, Rwanda, Burundi, and Tanzania in the east, and on Zambia in the southeast. KINSHASA is its capital and largest city; other cities include BOMA, BUKAVU, KALEMI, KAMINA, KANANGA, KISANGANI, KOLWEZI, LIKASI, LUBUMBASHI, MATADI, MBANDAKA, and MBUJI-MAYI. The country is divided into eight regions (Bandundu, Bas-Zaïre, Équateur, HAUT-ZAÏRE, Kasai-Occidental, Kasai-Oriental, KIVU, and SHABA) and a federal district (which includes Kinshasa). Zaïre lies astride the equator, and virtually all of the country is part of the vast CONGO (Zaïre) River drainage basin. North central Zaïre is made up of a large plateau (average elevation: c.1,000 ft/300 m), which is covered with equatorial forest and has numerous swamps. The plateau is bordered on the east by mountains, which rise to the lofty Ruwenzori Mts. (located on the border with Uganda). The Ruwenzori include Margherita Peak (16,763 ft/5,109 m), the country's highest point; they are situated in the western or Albertine branch of the Great Rift Valley, which runs along the entire eastern border of Zaïre and also takes in lakes Albert (Mobutu Sese Seko), Edward (Idi Amin Dada), Kivu, and Tanganyika. In S Zaïre are highland plateaus (average elevation: c.3,000 ft/910 m; highest elevation: c.6,800 ft/2,070 m), which are covered with savanna. The high Mitumba Mts. in the southeast include Lake Mweru (situated on the border with Zambia). Virtually the entire population of Zaïre is made up of black Africans, the great majority of whom speak Bantu languages. In addition, there are Nilotic speakers in the north near Sudan and scattered groups of Pygmies (especially in the Ituri Forest in the northeast). The principal Bantu-speaking ethnic groups are the Kongo, Mongo, Luba, Lulua, Lunda, and Bwaka. The Alur and Zande are the main Nilotic speakers. Many of the ethnic groups spill over into neighboring countries. In the late 1960s about 80% of the population was classified as rural. French is Zaïre's official language, but it is spoken by relatively few persons; Swahili is widely used in the east, and Lingala is widely spoken in the west. Most of the inhabitants of Zaïre follow traditional religious beliefs; in addition, about 25% are Roman Catholic, and a substantial number belong to independent black African Protestant groups. There are also small Baha'i and Muslim communities. In the early 1970s, Zaïre's economy was still based on agriculture, with about half the workers engaged as subsistence farmers; but the country's considerable mineral and energy resources had helped to create substantial modern mining and manufacturing sectors. The economy's growth spurted under Belgian control in the 1950s, slowed considerably during the country's post-independence troubles in the early 1960s, and accelerated again in the later 1960s when political stability returned. Less than 5% of Zaïre's land area is cultivated or used as pasture. The sown land falls into three categories—that used for growing food crops, that used for growing cash crops on a small scale, and that used for growing cash crops on plantations. The principal food crops are cassava, yams, maize, millet, rice, groundnuts, plantains, and pulses. Rubber, coffee, cotton, and palm products are produced commercially in limited quantities on small farms. The main plantation commodities are palm products, coffee, tea, cacao, sugarcane, and rubber. The plantations were mostly controlled by foreigners (mainly Belgians) until 1973, when a large-scale nationalization program was instituted. Substantial numbers of goats, sheep, and cattle are raised. Mining is centered in the Shaba, Kivu, and Kasai-Oriental regions. The products of Shaba include copper (the country's leading mineral product in terms of value), cobalt, zinc, manganese, uranium, cassiterite (tin ore), coal, gold, and silver. Tungsten, tantalum, silver, and gold are extracted in Kivu. Kasai-Oriental is by far the world's leading source of industrial diamonds (12.4 million carats in 1972), and some gem diamonds (1 million carats in 1972) are also found there. The extraction and processing of minerals is run largely by foreign-controlled firms, but in the early 1970s the government of Zaïre announced that it planned to nationalize the mining industry by 1980. In 1967 the government had nationalized the large Belgian copper-mining company Union Minière du Haut-Katanga (now known as the Société Générale Congolaise des Mines, or GECOMINES). There are major deposits (as yet unexploited) of petroleum and natural gas (methane) in NE Zaïre; in addition, modest offshore deposits of petroleum were discovered near the mouth of the Congo River in 1973. In 1974 a state-owned company was created to take over the distribution of oil petroleum products. Approximately 40% of Zaïre is covered with forest; considerable amounts of ebony and teak are produced annually as well as less valuable woods. Kinshasa and Lubumbashi are the country's most important industrial centers. The principal manufactures of Zaïre are processed copper, zinc, and cassiterite; refined petroleum; basic consumer goods such as processed food, beverages, clothing, and footwear; iron and steel; cement; and chemicals. The

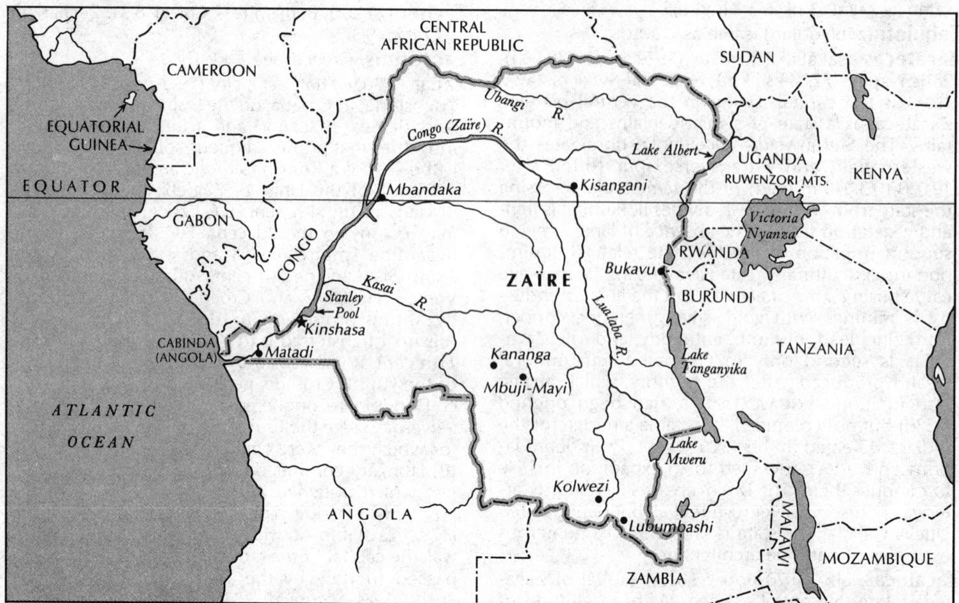

numerous rivers of Zaïre give it an immense potential for producing hydroelectricity, a small but significant percentage of which has been realized. The chief hydroelectric facilities are situated in Shaba and produce power for the mining industry; also, a major project (the first stage of which was completed in 1972) is located at Inga, on the Congo River near Kinshasa. Rivers form the backbone of Zaïre's transportation network; unnavigable parts of the Congo (e.g., Kinshasa-Matadi and Kisangani-Ubundi) are bridged by rail lines. Matadi, Boma, and Banana can handle oceangoing vessels. Shaba is connected by rail with the seaports of Lobito, Angola and Beira, Mozambique; E Zaïre is linked (via Lake Tanganyika) by rail with the seaport of Dar es Salaam, Tanzania. The annual value of Zaïre's exports is usually slightly higher than the cost of its imports; the country's export earnings come almost entirely from sales of primary products, which are vulnerable to sudden changes in world prices. About two thirds of the value of exports is contributed by copper; other important exports are diamonds, coffee, cobalt, palm products, cassiterite, and rubber. The leading imports are machinery, motor vehicles, foodstuffs, metals, and textiles and clothing. The principal trade partners are Belgium, Luxembourg, the United States, Italy, and France.

History. The earliest inhabitants of the region of Zaïre were probably Pygmies, who lived in small numbers in the equatorial forests of the north and northeast. By the end of the 1st millennium B.C. small numbers of black Africans had migrated into Zaïre from the northwest (present-day Nigeria and Cameroon) and settled in the savanna regions of the south. Scholars believe that the Bantu language family was started by some of these people in present-day SE Shaba around the start of the 1st millennium A.D. Aided by their knowledge of iron technology and agriculture, the Bantu-speakers migrated to other parts of Zaïre and Africa, at the same time developing new, related languages. (The Bantu languages are linked primarily by a common grammar and to a lesser extent by common words, prefixes, and suffixes.) From about 700 the copper deposits of S Shaba were worked by the Bantu and traded over wide areas. By about 1000 the Bantu had settled most of Zaïre, forcing the Pygmies into small, scattered areas. By the early 2d millennium the Bantu had increased considerably in number and were coalescing into states, some of which governed large areas and had complex administrative structures. Most of the states were ruled by a divine monarch, whose authority, although considerable, was checked by a council of high civil servants and elders. Notable among the states were the kingdom of the KONGO (founded in the 13th cent.), centered in modern N Angola but including extreme W Zaïre; a Luba empire (founded in the early 16th cent.), centered around lakes Kisale and Upemba in central Shaba; the Lunda kingdom of Mwata Yamwo (founded in the 16th cent.), centered in SW Zaïre; the Kuba kingdom of the Shongo people (established in the early 17th cent.), located in the region of the Kasai and Sankuru rivers in S Zaïre; and the Lunda kingdom of Mwata Kazembe (founded in the 18th cent.), located near the Luapula River (which forms part of the present Zaïre-Zambia boundary). Through intermarriage and other contacts the Luba transmitted political ideas to the Lunda, and numerous small Luba-Lunda states (in addition to those of Mwata Yamwo and Mwata Kazembe) were established in S Zaïre. The Kuba kingdom was noted for its sculpture and decorative arts. In 1482, Diogo Cão, a Portuguese navigator, became the first European to visit Zaïre when he reached the mouth of the Congo and sailed a few miles upstream. Soon thereafter the Portuguese established ties with the king of Kongo, and in the early 16th cent. they established themselves on parts of the coast of modern Angola, especially at the court of the king of Ndongo (a vassal state of Kongo). The Portuguese had little influence on Zaïre until the late 18th cent., when they backed black African and mulatto traders (called *pombeiros*) who traveled far inland (including to the kingdom of Mwata Kazembe). From the early 19th cent., Swahili and Nyamwezi traders from present-day Tanzania penetrated into SE Zaïre, where they exchanged cloth, beads, cowrie shells, and other goods for copper, salt, and ivory. Some of the traders established states with considerable power. Msiri (a Nyamwezi) established himself near Mwata Kazembe in 1856, soon enlarged his holdings (mainly at the expense of Mwata Kazembe), and was a major force until 1891, when he was killed by the Belgians. From the 1860s to the early 1890s, Muhammad bin Hamad (known as Tippu Tib), a Swahili trader from Zanzibar, ruled a large portion of E Zaïre NW of Lake Tanganyika. In the 1870s, on the eve of the scramble for African territory among the European powers, the territory of Zaïre had no political unity. However, beginning in the late 1870s the territory was unified by the efforts of Leopold II, king of the Belgians (reigned 1865–1909). Leopold believed that Belgium needed colonies to ensure its prosperity, and sensing that the Belgians would not support colonial ventures, he privately set about to establish a colonial empire. Between 1874 and 1877, Henry M. Stanley made a great journey across central Africa during which he discovered the course of the Congo River. Intrigued by Stanley's findings (especially that the region had considerable economic potential), Leopold engaged him in 1878 to establish the king's authority in the Congo basin, and between 1879 and 1884, Stanley founded a number of stations along the middle Congo River, and signed treaties with several African rulers giving the International Association of the Congo (as Leopold's cover organization was known) sovereignty in their areas. At the Conference of Berlin (1884–85) the European powers recognized the International Association's claim to the Congo basin, and in a ceremony (1885) at Banana, Leopold announced the establishment of the Independent State of the Congo, headed by himself. The announced boundaries of the state were roughly the same as those of present-day Zaïre, but it was not until the mid-1890s that Leopold's control was established in most parts of the state. In 1891–92, Shaba was conquered, and between 1892 and 1894, E Zaïre was wrested from the control of E African Arab and Swahili traders (including Tippu Tib, who for a time had served as an administrator of the Congo). Because he did not have sufficient funds to develop the Congo, Leopold sought and received loans from the Belgian parliament in 1889 and 1895, in return for which Belgium was given the right to annex the Congo in 1901. At the same time Leopold declared all unoccupied land (including cropland lying fallow) to be owned by the state, and unauthorized private traders were not permitted to operate there; instead, the state gained control of the lucrative trade in rubber and ivory. Much of the land was given to concessionaire companies, which in return were to build railroads or (as in the case of the Katanga Company) to effectively occupy a specified part of the country or merely to give the state a percentage of their profits. In addition, Leopold maintained a large estate in the region of Lake Leopold II (NE of Kinshasa). Private companies were also established to exploit the mineral wealth of Shaba and Kasai; a notable example was Union Minière du Haut-Katanga, chartered in 1905. The Belgian parliament did not exercise its right to annex the Congo in 1901, but reports starting in 1904 (particularly by Roger CASEMENT and E. D. Morel) about the brutal treatment of the black Africans in the Congo (especially those forced to collect rubber for concessionaire companies) led to a popular campaign for Belgium to take over the Congo from Leopold. After exhaustive parliamentary debates, Belgium in 1908 annexed the Congo, thus establishing the Belgian Congo. Under Belgian rule the worst excesses (such as forced labor) of the Independent State were ended, but the Congo was still regarded almost exclusively as a field for European investment, and little was done to give the black Africans a significant role in the government or economy of the colony. Economic development was furthered by the construction of railroads and other transportation facilities. European concerns established more large plantations, and vast mining operations were set up. Black Africans formed the labor pool for these operations, and Europeans were the managers. By the end of the 1920s, mining (especially of copper and diamonds) was the mainstay of the economy, having far outdistanced agriculture; in 1901 rubber had accounted for almost 90% of exports, but in 1930 it made up only about 1%. Some of the mining companies built cities for their workers, and there was a considerable movement of black Africans from the countryside to urban areas, especially from the 1930s. Between 1938 and 1955, Kinshasa's population increased from approximately 40,000 to about 325,000. Christian missionaries (the great majority of whom were Roman Catholic) were very active in the Congo, and they were the chief agents for raising the educational level of the black Africans and for improving medical services. The literacy level was raised considerably by the missionaries, but virtually no black Africans were educated beyond the primary level until the mid-1950s, when two universities were opened. A noteworthy indigenous religious movement was that of Simaon Kimbangu, who, educated by Protestant missionaries, around 1920 established himself as a prophet and healer. He soon gathered a large following, and although not explicitly anti-Belgian, was jailed in 1921 by the colonial government, which feared that his movement would undermine its authority. The Belgians outlawed the movement, but it continued clandestinely and became increasingly antiwhite. In the late 1930s, Simon-Pierre Mpadi organized a major Kimbanguist revival and was forced by the Belgians to flee the Congo. Kimbangu himself died in 1951 while still in jail. In 1955, when demands by blacks in Africa for independence were mounting, Antoine van Bilsen, a Belgian professor, published a "30-Year Plan" for granting the Congo increased self-government. The plan was accepted enthusiastically by most Belgians, who assumed that Belgian rule in the Congo would continue for a long period, but who wanted to improve the status of the black Africans. Events proved otherwise. Congolese nationalists, notably Joseph KASAVUBU (who headed ABAKO, a party based among the Kongo people) and Patrice LUMUMBA (who led the leftist Mouvement National Congolais), became increasingly strident. They were impressed greatly by the visit in late 1958 of French president Charles de Gaulle to neighboring Moyen-Congo (now the Congo Republic) where he offered the black Africans the opportunity to vote in a referendum for continued association with France or for full independence. In Jan., 1959, there were serious nationalist riots in Kinshasa, and thereafter the Belgians steadily lost control of events in the Congo. They panicked and lost the desire to hold onto the colony. At a round-table conference (which included Congolese nationalists) at Brussels in Jan.–Feb., 1960, it was decided that the Belgian Congo would become fully independent on June 30, 1960. Following elections, Lumumba in June became prime minister and Kasavubu head of state. However, shortly after independence began on June 30, the Republic of the Congo (as the nation was called) began to disintegrate as ethnic and personal rivalries came to the fore. On July 4, the Congolese army mutinied, and on July 11, Moïse TSHOMBE declared Katanga (now called Shaba), of which he was provisional president, to be independent. There were attacks on Belgian nationals living in the Congo, and Belgium sent troops to the country to protect its citizens and also its mining interests. However, most Belgian civil servants left the country, thus crippling the government. On July 14, the UN Security Council voted to send a force to the Congo to help establish order; under the UN Charter (as interpreted by Secretary-General Dag Hammarskjöld), the force was not allowed to intervene in internal affairs and thus it could not act against the Katanga secession. Therefore, Lumumba turned to the USSR for help against Katanga, but on Sept. 5 he was dismissed as prime minister by Kasavubu and replaced by Joseph Ileo. On Sept. 14, Col. Joseph MOBUTU, the head of the army, seized power and dismissed both Kasavubu and Ileo. On Dec. 1, Lumumba, who probably had the largest national following of any Congo politician, was arrested by the army; he was murdered while allegedly trying to escape imprisonment in Katanga in mid-Feb., 1961. By the end of 1960 the Congo was divided into four quasi-independent parts: Mobutu held the west, including Kinshasa (then called Léopoldville); Antoine Gizenga, the self-styled successor to Lumumba, controlled the east from Kisangani (then called Stanleyville); Albert Kalonji controlled S Kasai; and Tshombe headed Katanga, aided by Belgian and other foreign soldiers. The secession of Katanga, with its great mineral resources, particularly weakened the national government. In Feb., 1961, Ileo again became prime minister, with Kasavubu as head of state. In April, Tshombe was arrested by the central government, but was freed in June after agreeing to end the Katanga secession. By July, however, Tshombe was again proclaiming the independence of Katanga. In the same month Cyrille ADOULA became prime minister. In August the UN forces began to take an active role in Congo affairs by disarming Katangese soldiers; on Sept. 18, Secretary-General Hammarskjöld was killed in an air crash while on his way to a meeting with Tshombe. In November, Mobutu launched an attack on Katanga aimed at ending the secession, and in December, UN and Katangese forces became engaged in battle. A cease-fire was soon arranged, but throughout 1962, Tshombe maintained his independent position and in Dec., 1962, renewed UN-Katanga fighting broke out. Tshombe quickly was forced to give in, and in Jan., 1963, agreed to end Katanga's secession. However, the national scene remained confused; Adoula failed to command much support, the government's finances were weak, and there was considerable agitation by the followers of Lumumba. At the end of June, 1964, the last UN troops were withdrawn from the country. In desperation, Kasavubu appointed Tshombe prime minister in July, 1964, but this move resulted in large-scale rebellions. With the help of U.S. arms, Belgian troops, and white mercenaries, the central government gradually regained control of the country; in Nov., 1964, U.S. planes landed Belgian troops in Kisangani. National politics remained turbulent, highlighted by a clash between Kasavubu and Tshombe. In mid-1965, Kasavubu appointed Evariste Kimba prime minister. In Nov., 1965, Mobutu again intervened, dismissing Kasavubu and proclaiming himself president; Tshombe fled to Spain. (In 1967, Tshombe was kidnapped and taken to Algeria; he died in 1969.) In 1966 and 1967 there were several short-lived rebellions (notably in Kisangani and Bukavu), and in 1966 an attempted coup d'etat by Kimba was defeated. In late 1966, Mobutu abolished the office of prime minister, establishing a presidential form of government; this move was confirmed in a new constitution approved in a referendum in mid-1967. In 1966, Léopoldville, Stanleyville, and Elisabethville were given African names (Kinshasa, Kisangani, and Lubumbashi, respectively), thus in effect beginning the campaign for "African authenticity" that became a major policy of Mobutu in the early 1970s. (In 1971 the country was renamed Zaïre, as was the Congo River; in 1972, Katanga was renamed Shaba—largely in an attempt to destroy the region's past association with secession—and Mobutu dropped his Christian names and called himself Mobutu Sese Seko, while advising other Zaïreans to follow suit.) By the end of the 1960s, the country enjoyed political stability, although there was intermittent student unrest. The government was firmly guided by Mobutu, who headed the sole (from 1970) political party, the Popular Movement of the Revolution (MPR). In 1970, Mobutu was elected to a new seven-year term as president. In the early 1970s he centralized the administration of the nation (reducing the role of regional government), encouraged the participation of foreign firms in the economic development of the country, improved relations with neighboring black African-ruled countries, and maintained good relations with the West (especially the United States) while establishing (1972) full diplomatic relations with China. In 1973, Mobutu nationalized many foreign-owned firms in the attempt to reduce unemployment. Zaïre remained dependent on volatile world copper prices (which were high during 1969–71, but fell considerably in 1972); Mobutu hoped to double the country's output of copper by 1980. See Ruth Slade, *Belgian Congo* (2d ed. 1961) and *King Leopold's Congo* (1962); Robert Cornevin, *Histoire du Congo* (3d rev. ed. 1970); René Lemarchand, *Political Awakening in the Congo* (1964); Crawford Young, *Politics in the Congo: Decolonization and Independence* (1965); Catherine Hoskyns, *The Congo since Independence, January 1960–December 1961* (1965); Roger Anstey, *King Leopold's Legacy: The Congo under Belgian Rule, 1908–1960* (1966); W. R. Louis and Jean Stengers, ed., *E. D. Morel's History of the Congo Reform Association* (1968); J. C. Williame, *Patrimonialism and Political Change in the Congo* (1972); Marvin D. Markowitz, *Cross and Sword: The Political Role of Christian Missions in the Belgian Congo, 1908–1960* (1973).

Zaïre, river, Africa: see CONGO, river.

Zakarpatskaya Oblast (zəkərpät'skəyə) or **Transcarpathian Oblast,** administrative division (1970 pop. 1,057,000), 4,981 sq mi (12,901 sq km), SW European USSR, in the Ukraine, on the southwestern slopes of the Carpathian Mts. Uzhgorod (the capital), Mukachevo, and Khust are the chief cities. The oblast is bordered by Rumania to the south, Hungary to the southwest, Czechoslovakia to the west, and Poland to the northwest. It is thickly forested and largely agricultural. The plain in the southwest, which is drained by the Tisza River and its tributaries, supports crops of wheat, corn, tobacco, sugar beets, and potatoes. There are vineyards, fruit orchards, and walnut groves in the foothills. The oblast's mineral resources include brown coal, rock salt, fire clays, marble, limestone, and some iron, crude oil, and natural gas. Forests occupy nearly half the area of the oblast, and lumbering, along with the production of such items as wood chemicals, furniture, and cartons, is a leading industry. Among other industries are mining, food processing, brewing, wine making, tanning, and the manufacture of bricks, tiles, footwear, clothing, and textiles. The majority of the population is Ukrainian, with Hungarian, Russian, and Slovak minorities. Inhabited by Slavic tribes from the 8th cent., the region was part of the Kievan state in the 10th and 11th cent. but was conquered by the Magyars, who ruled it until 1918. It has been variously known as Ruthenia or the Carpathian Ukraine, or by its Czech name of *Podkarpatská Rus* [Subcarpathian Ruthenia] or its Ukrainian name of *Zakarpatska Ukraina* [Transcarpathian Ukraine]. Its inhabitants were historically called Ruthenians. Until the early 20th cent. the region was among the most economically and culturally backward areas of the world. Hungarian absentee landlords owned virtually the entire country. The peasantry was mired in abysmal poverty, ignorance, and superstition; the Jews, who formed a large element of the urban population, were economically better off but also lived under quasi-medieval conditions (the so-called wonder rabbis held their sway in this region). After World War I the National Ruthenian councils of Uzhgorod, Khust, and Presov jointly called for the region's union with newly independent Czechoslovakia, which incorporated Transcarpathia in May, 1919. Although a guarantee of provincial autonomy embodied in the Treaty of St. Germain (Sept., 1919) did not materialize, the region fared better under Czechoslovak than under Magyar control. Economic modernization began, and the peasants were freed from their nearly servile status, but agrarian reform failed to break up all the large estates. In the wake of the Munich Pact (1938), the reorganized state of Czecho-Slovakia was pressured by Germany to grant autonomy to Transcarpathia. After Czecho-Slovakia was dismembered in March, 1939, the region proclaimed its independence; but it was shortly occupied by and annexed to Hungary. Transcarpathia was reconquered late in 1944 by Soviet troops and local guerrillas, and in 1945, Czechoslovakia agreed to cede the area to the USSR. The oblast was formed in 1946.

Zákinthos (zä'kĭnthôs) or **Zante** (zăn'tē), Lat. *Zacynthus*, island (1971 pop. 30,180), c.157 sq mi (407 sq km), W Greece, in the Ionian Sea; one of the IONIAN ISLANDS. The chief town is Zákinthos, a port and trade center and the capital of Zákinthos prefecture. Wine, currants, citrus fruits, and olive oil are produced on the fertile, intensively cultivated island. According to tradition, the island was settled by persons led by Zacynthus, son of the Arcadian chief Dardanus.

Zakopane (zäkôpä'nĕ), town (1970 pop. 27,039), S Poland, at the foot of the Tatra Mts. A leading health resort and winter sports center, Zakopane was the site of the world skiing championship competitions in 1929 and 1939.

Zalaph (zā'lăf), father of a worker on the wall of Jerusalem. Neh. 3.30.

Zaleucus (zəlo͞o'kəs), fl. c.650 B.C., Greek lawgiver of Locris, in Italy. According to tradition, his was the earliest codification of Greek law. References to Zaleucus' code, which was widely adopted in Italy, indicate that it embodied the *lex talionis* [law of retaliation, i.e., an eye for an eye] and other severe features exemplified in the later Greek code of DRACO.

Zalew Wiślany, inlet: see VISTULA LAGOON, Poland.

Zalmon. 1 See ILAI. **2** Hill near Shechem. Judges 9.48. This is probably the place referred to in Ps. 68.14 as Salmon.

Zalmonah (zălmō'nə), encampment place of the Israelites in the wilderness. Num. 33.41.

Zalmunna (zălmŭn'ə), Midianite king, conquered by Gideon. Judges 8.1–21.

Zama (zā'mə), ancient town near the northern coast of Africa, in present Tunisia. Although there was more than one town named Zama, tradition says that in 202 B.C. Scipio Africanus Major defeated Hannibal there in the decisive and final battle of the Second Punic War (see PUNIC WARS). There is good reason for believing the actual battle was fought at some nearby place.

Zambezi (zămbē'zē), river, c.1,700 mi (2,740 km) long, rising in NW Zambia, S central Africa, and flowing in an S-shaped course generally E through E Angola, along the Zambia-Rhodesia border, and through central Mozambique to the Mozambique Channel of the Indian Ocean, near Chinde. The upper Zambezi flows over part of the great basalt plateau of Africa; the middle Zambezi is entrenched in the plateau (VICTORIA FALLS and Kariba Gorge are there); and the lower Zambezi flows through a wide valley. Many rapids interrupt the river's flow, making it unsuited for navigation; however, its navigable stretches are used for local traffic. Kariba Lake, impounded by KARIBA DAM, is one of the world's largest man-made lakes. The Zambezi's banks are fertile and well populated. The river has a great hydroelectricity-generating potential; there is a small power plant at Victoria Falls, and the one at Kariba Dam is one of the largest in Africa.

Zambia (zăm'bēə), formerly **Northern Rhodesia** (rōdē'zhə), republic (1971 est. pop. 4,396,000), 290,584 sq mi (752,614 sq km), central Africa, bordering on Zaïre in the north, on Tanzania in the northeast, on Malawi and Mozambique in the east, on Rhodesia, Botswana, and South West Africa in the south, and on Angola in the west. LUSAKA is the capital; other cities include CHINGOLA, KABWE, KITWE, LIVINGSTONE, LUANSHYA, MUFULIRA, Nchanga, NDOLA, and Nkana. The country is divided into eight provinces. Zambia is largely made up of a highland plateau, which rises in the east. The elevation there ranges from c.3,000 to 5,000 ft (915–1,520 m), and higher altitudes are attained in the Muchinga Mts. and on the Nyika plateau (adjacent to Malawi), where Zambia's highest point (c.7,120 ft/2,170 m) is located. Also in E Zambia are Lake Bangweulu, parts of lakes Mweru and Tanganyika, and the Luangwa and Chambeshi rivers. The Zambezi River drains much of the western part of the country (where the elevation is c.1,500–3,000 ft/460–910 m) and forms a large part of Zambia's southern boundary. The impressive

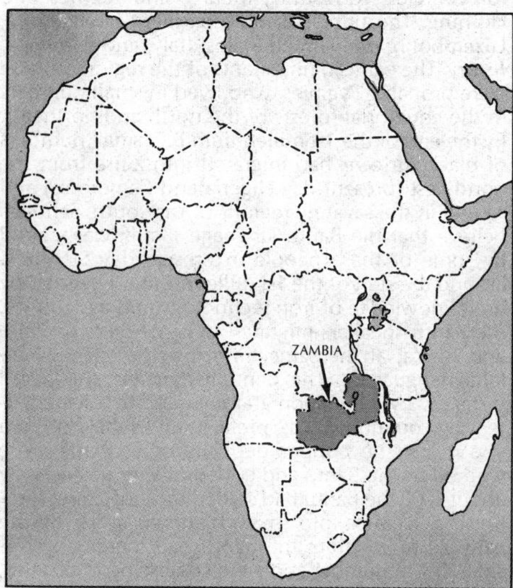

Victoria Falls and the huge Lake Kariba (formed by Kariba Dam), both on the border with Rhodesia, are part of the Zambezi in the south. The Kafue River drains W central Zambia, including the COPPERBELT in the north. About 98% of the country's population is made up of Bantu-speaking black Africans, of which the Bemba, Cewa, Lozi, and Tonga are the chief subgroups. The remainder of the inhabitants are Europeans and Asians. English is the country's official language. About half the population is Christian (equally divided between Roman Catholics and Protestants), and the rest follow traditional beliefs. Zambia's economy is divided into a poor traditional sector and an affluent modern sector, dominated by the copper industry. Most Zambians work the country's relatively infertile soil as subsistence farmers; commercial agriculture is mostly confined to a small number of large farms. The leading crops are maize, sorghum, millet, beans, groundnuts, tobacco, and cotton. Large numbers of poultry, cattle, sheep, goats, and pigs are raised, and there is a small fishing industry. The mining and refining of copper constitutes by far the largest industry in the country and is concentrated in the cities of the Copperbelt. Zambia is among the world's five leading producers of copper; coal, zinc, lead, gold, silver, and cobalt are also mined. Other manufactures include food products, beverages, textiles and clothing, construction materials, iron and steel, forest products, and plastics. Most of Zambia's energy is supplied by hydroelectric plants, especially the one at Kariba Dam. The annual value of Zambia's exports is usually considerably higher than the value of its imports, with copper normally accounting for more than 90% of the former; but world prices for copper tend to fluctuate widely, raising or lowering Zambia's income accordingly. The principal imports are machinery, transport equipment, manufactured consumer goods, petroleum and petroleum products, foodstuffs, and chemicals. The leading trade partners are Great Britain, Japan, Italy, and West Germany.

History. Parts of Zambia were probably inhabited by man about one million years ago, and subsequently Stone Age and Iron Age cultures flourished in the country. Some Bantu-speaking peoples (probably including the Tonga) reached the region by A.D.

c.1200, but the ancestors of most of modern Zambia's ethnic groups arrived from present-day Angola and Zaïre between the 16th and 18th cent. By the late 18th cent. traders (including Arabs, Swahilis, and black Africans) had penetrated the region from both the Atlantic and Indian Ocean coasts; they exported copper, wax, and slaves. In 1835 the Ngoni, a warlike group from S Africa, entered E Zambia. At about the same time the Kololo penetrated W Zambia from the south, and they ruled the Lozi kingdom of Barotseland (see WESTERN PROVINCE) from 1838 to 1864. The Scots explorer David Livingstone first visited Zambia in 1851; he discovered Victoria Falls in 1855, and in 1873 he died near Lake Bangweulu. In 1890 agents of Cecil Rhodes's British South Africa Company signed treaties with several African leaders, including Lewanika, the Lozi paramount chief, and proceeded to administer the region. It was divided into the protectorates of Northwestern and Northeastern Rhodesia until 1911, when the two were joined to form Northern Rhodesia. In the late 1890s company troops moved against several African peoples in the east (including the Ngoni and the Bemba) who had refused to recognize foreign rule. The mining of copper and lead began in the early 1900s, and by 1909 the central railroad from Livingstone to Ndola had been completed and about 1,500 Europeans had settled in the country. In 1924 the British took over the administration of the protectorate. In the late 1920s massive copper deposits were discovered in what soon became known as the Copperbelt, and by 1937 about 4,000 skilled Europeans and about 20,000 unskilled black African laborers were working there. The Africans protested the discrimination and ill-treatment to which they were subjected by staging strikes in 1935, 1940, and 1956. They were not allowed to form unions but did organize self-help groups that brought together persons of diverse ethnic backgrounds. In 1946, delegates from these groups met in Lusaka and formed the Federation of African Welfare Societies, the first protectorate-wide black African movement, and in 1948 this organization was transformed into the Northern Rhodesia African Congress. Under the leadership of Harry Nkumbula in the early 1950s, it fought strenuously, if unsuccessfully, against the establishment of the Federation of RHODESIA AND NYASALAND (1953-63), which joined Northern Rhodesia, Southern Rhodesia (now Rhodesia), and Nyasaland (now Malawi). The booming copper industry had attracted about 72,000 whites to Northern Rhodesia by 1958, and the blacks there experienced increasing European domination, similar to that in Southern Rhodesia. Kenneth Kaunda, a militant former schoolteacher, took over the leadership of the Africans from the more moderate Nkumbula and in 1959 formed a new party, the United National Independence Party (UNIP). Following a massive civil disobedience campaign in 1962, black Africans were given a larger voice in the affairs of the protectorate. On Oct. 24, 1964, Northern Rhodesia became independent as the Republic of Zambia, with Kaunda as its first president; he was reelected in 1968 and 1973. Zambia remained a member of the Commonwealth of Nations. The main problems faced by Kaunda in the first decade of independence were uniting Zambia's diverse peoples, reducing European control of the economy, and coping with white-dominated Southern Rhodesia (which unilaterally declared its independence as Rhodesia in Nov., 1965). In the mid-1960s, Kaunda overcame the resistence to central control of the Lozi (who had enjoyed considerable autonomy under the protectorate) and of the fanatical quasi-Christian Lumpa church (led by Alice Lenshina), centered in N Zambia; separatist sentiment among the Bemba, however, continued into the 1970s. European economic control was reduced by increasing the number of trained Zambians, by diversifying the country's economy, and (from 1969) by the government's acquisition of a 51% interest in most major firms (especially mining and banking companies) operating in the country. Zambia joined Great Britain and other countries in applying economic sanctions against Rhodesia. Zambia discontinued transportation of the bulk of its overseas trade to the seaport of Beira, Mozambique, via the rail link through Rhodesia and thus had to find an alternate outlet; in addition, the country halted imports of coal (used especially in the copper industry) and other goods from Rhodesia. From late 1965 trade items were transported to and from the seaport of Dar es Salaam, Tanzania, by plane and by truck (via the Great North Road). A petroleum pipeline between Dar es Salaam and Ndola was opened in 1968, and, with the help of Communist China, construction of the Great Uhuru (Tanzam) Railway connecting Dar es Salaam and Zambia was begun in 1970 (scheduled to be completed in 1975). Coal was mined in increasing quantities in S Zambia, and by the early 1970s it supplied most of the country's needs. Altogether, Zambia suffered considerably from the action taken against Rhodesia; for instance, it was not until 1969 that the 1965 level of copper production was again attained. From the late 1960s Kaunda faced formidable opposition from political and student groups protesting the growing concentration of power in his hands. In early 1972 the influential United Progressive party, led by Simon Kapwepwe, was banned, and later in the year all political parties except the UNIP were outlawed, as Zambia became a one-party state. In the early 1970s there were also border incidents with Mozambique and Rhodesia. See R. I. Rothberg, *The Rise of Nationalism in Central Africa* (1966); D. C. Mulford, *Zambia: The Politics of Independence, 1957-1964* (1967); B. M. Fagan, *Iron Age Cultures in Zambia* (2 vol., 1967-69) and *A Short History of Zambia* (1968); L. H. Gann, *A History of Northern Rhodesia: Early Days to 1953* (1969); Irving Kaplan et al., *Area Handbook for Zambia* (1969); N. H. Pollock, *Nyasaland and Northern Rhodesia* (1971); D. H. Davies, ed., *Zambia in Maps* (1971); Mark Bostock and Charles Harvey, ed., *Economic Independence and Zambian Copper* (1972).

Zamboanga (sām''bōäng'gä), city (1970 pop. 199,901), Zamboanga del Sur prov., SW Mindanao, the Philippines, at the tip of the Zamboanga peninsula, on Basilan Strait. One of the chief cities of Mindanao and a busy seaport, it is the hub of a major iron-producing and lumbering area, which has large-scale rubber cultivation, plywood mills, and resin plants. The city is situated at the foot of high mountains and is known for its delightful climate, beautiful parks, and nearby beaches. Most of the inhabitants are Muslims. Tourist attractions include a 16th-century Spanish fort and the mosque at Talangkusay, a famous Moro ceremonial center.

Zamojski or **Zamoyski, Jan** (both:yän zämoi'skē), 1542-1605, Polish statesman, general, and author. He championed the rights of the lesser nobility; after the extinction (1572) of the Jagiello dynasty, he used his influence to restrict the royal power with constitutional limitations, thus transforming Poland into a royal republic. A humanist, he supported art and learning and founded both the city and the university of ZAMOŚĆ. His *De senatu Romano* (1563) showed great admiration of ancient Rome, and he sought to apply constitutional principles of republican Rome to the Poland of his time. As a result of his reforms, Poland avoided the trend toward absolutism that characterized the other states of Europe. Always opposing the candidacy and influence of the Hapsburgs, Zamojski secured the election (1573) of Henry of Valois (later Henry III of France) as king of Poland; in 1575 he supported STEPHEN BATHORY, whose chancellor he became in 1576; in 1587 he succeeded in putting SIGISMUND III on the throne. Appointed (1580) commander in chief, he distinguished himself against Russia, Sweden, the Crimean Tatars, and the hospodar [governor] of Moldavia. During his last years his relations with Sigismund III were strained because of the king's pro-Hapsburg policy.

Zamora, Niceto Alcalá: see ALCALÁ ZAMORA, NICETO.

Zamora (thämō'rä), city (1970 pop. 49,029), capital of Zamora prov., NW Spain, in León, on the Duero River. It is a communications and agricultural marketing and processing center. Because of its strategic position, control of the city was contested during the Middle Ages, first between the Christians and Moors, then between León and Castile. Parts of the medieval fortifications are still preserved. There is a fine 12th-century Romanesque cathedral.

Zamość (zä'môstsyə), Rus. *Zamostye,* town (1970 pop. 106,171), SE Poland, on the Wieprz River. It is a commercial center, trading mainly in agricultural products. The town's chief industries are metalworking and the manufacture of furniture and clothing. Zamość was founded in 1579 by a Polish chancellor, Jan Zamojski, who also established a college there. The town defended itself against a Cossack invasion in 1648 and against the Swedish king Charles X in 1656. The city passed to Austria in 1772 and to Russia in 1815; it reverted to Poland after World War I.

Zampieri, Domenico: see DOMENICHINO.

Zamzam: see MECCA, Saudi Arabia.

Zamzummims (zămzŭm'ĭmz), Ammonite name for the REPHAIMS. Deut. 2.20.

Zanardelli, Giuseppe (jōōzĕp'pā dzänärdĕl'lē), 1826-1903, Italian politician and premier (1901-3). As minister of justice (1881-83, 1887-91) he prepared a new penal code, which was approved in 1890 and remained in force until 1931. A liberal, he tried as premier to introduce social reforms and to protect the labor movement. Relations with France improved during his premiership.

Zancle: see MESSINA, Italy.

Zane, Ebenezer, 1747-1812, American pioneer and land speculator, b. near what is now Moorefield, W. Va. (then Virginia). With his brothers Silas and Jonathan, he went west in 1769 and established the settlement at Wheeling, of which he became the leader. The Zanes distinguished themselves in warfare with the Indians in the American Revolution, defending Fort Henry in the Wheeling region from attacks in 1777 and 1782. It was in one of these attacks that a sister, Elizabeth Zane, is supposed to have displayed great heroism under fire. In 1796, Ebenezer obtained from Congress permission to blaze a trail through Ohio to Kentucky. With Jonathan Zane and John McIntire (Ebenezer's son-in-law), he opened the famous Zane's Trace from Wheeling to Maysville, Ky., and started settlements along the trace. In 1799, McIntire and Jonathan Zane began the settlement of Zanesville, Ohio.

Zanesville, city (1970 pop. 33,045), seat of Muskingum co., central Ohio, on the Muskingum River at its junction with the Licking; inc. 1815. It is a trade and industrial center manufacturing pottery, glassware, and electrical equipment. The area has deposits of clay, oil, natural gas, sand, limestone, and iron ore. The site was selected by Ebenezer Zane, surveyor of Zane's Trace, the gateway to the Northwest Territory. Zane's great-great-grandson, Zane Grey, was born in the city. A two-year interval as state capital (1810-12) and the city's location on waterways and the National Road spurred its growth. The rivers there, which are spanned by a notable "Y" bridge, are connected to the Ohio by 10 hand-operated locks and a 1-mi-long (1.6-km) canal. An art institute and a branch of Ohio Univ. are in the city. Of interest are the National Road-Zane Grey museum, several early homes of Federal design, and the nearby Ohio ceramics center. A state park is at Dillon Reservoir to the northwest.

Zangwill, Israel, 1864-1926, English author, b. London. He became a journalist and founded *Ariel,* a humorous paper. Zangwill wrote *Children of the Ghetto* (1892), later dramatized and performed in England and America, and *Dreamers of the Ghetto* (1898), a series of biographical studies. His other well-known works are *Merely Mary Ann* (1893) and *The Melting Pot* (1914), both dramatized. A prominent Zionist (see ZIONISM), he wrote *The Principle of Nationalities* (1917) and *Chosen Peoples* (1918). Uneven in value, Zangwill's novels attempt to portray modern Jewish life. See biography by Joseph Leftwich (1957).

Zanjan (zänjän'), city (1971 est. pop. 60,000), Gilan prov., NW Iran, on the Zanjanchal River. It is the trade center for an agricultural region where grain and fruit are grown. Manufactures include rugs and metalwork. It is served by roads and a railroad.

Zankoff or **Zankov:** see TSANKOV.

Zanoah (zənō'ə). **1** Town, SW Palestine, W of Bethlehem. Joshua 15.34; Neh. 3.13; 11.30. **2** Town, Palestine, near Hebron. Joshua 15.56. In 1 Chron. 4.18 Jekuthiel is called the father (or founder) of Janoah.

Zante, Greece: see ZÁKINTHOS.

Zanzibar (zăn'zĭbär, zănzĭbär'), region (1967 pop. 190,494), 950 sq mi (2,461 sq km), United Republic of Tanzania, E Africa, consisting of the coral islands of Zanzibar and Tumbatu, in the Indian Ocean. The main towns are ZANZIBAR, Chwaka, Kizimkazi, and Koani. The region is subdivided into three administrative districts. The islands are low-lying, with a maximum elevation of about 390 ft (120 m). About 80% of the population are black Africans, the majority of whom belong to the Bantu-speaking Hadimu ethnic group. Other black Africans include the Tumbatu (who live on Tumbatu and in the northern part of Zanzibar) and migrants from the E African mainland and from the Comoro Islands. In addition, about 10% of the inhabitants are of Arab descent and 7% are of Indian, Pakistani, or Goan background. Most Zanzibaris are Sunni Muslims; some of the black Africans follow traditional beliefs, and there are also small numbers of Christians and Hindus. Swahili is widely spoken. The economy of Zanzibar is almost exclusively agricultural; fertile soil is limited to the western half of the island. The chief commodities produced are cassava, sweet potatoes, rice, maize, plantains, citrus fruit, cloves (with nearby PEMBA island, Zanzibar is the world's main source of this spice), coconuts, and cacao. There is a sizable fishing industry. The islands' few manufactures include clove oil and woven goods. Handicraftsmen make objects of wood, ivory, and metal. Lime is the only mineral resource. The main imports are foodstuffs and fuel; the principal exports are cloves and copra.

History. The first permanent residents of Zanzibar seem to have been the ancestors of the Hadimu and Tumbatu, who began arriving from the E African mainland A.D. c.1000. They had belonged to various mainland ethnic groups, and on Zanzibar they lived in small villages and did not coalesce to form larger political units. Because they lacked central organization, they were easily subjected by outsiders. Traders from Arabia, the Persian Gulf region of modern Iran (especially Shiraz), and W India probably visited Zanzibar as early as the 1st cent.; they used the monsoon winds to sail across the Indian Ocean and landed at the sheltered harbor located on the site of present-day Zanzibar town. Although the islands had few resources of interest to the traders, they offered a good point from which to make contact with the towns of the E African coast. Traders from the Persian Gulf region began to settle in small numbers on Zanzibar in the late 11th or 12th cent.; they intermarried with the black Africans and eventually a hereditary ruler (known as the Mwenyi Mkuu or Jumbe), of mixed Shirazi-black African descent, emerged among the Hadimu. A similar ruler, called the Sheha, was set up among the Tumbatu. Neither rulers had much power, but they helped solidify the ethnic identity of their respective peoples. The first European to visit Zanzibar was the Portuguese navigator Vasco da Gama in 1499; by 1503 the Portuguese had gained control of Zanzibar, and soon they held most of the E African coast. The Portuguese established a trading station and a Roman Catholic mission on Zanzibar, but their cultural impact was minimal. In 1698, Arabs from Oman ousted the Portuguese from E Africa, including Zanzibar. The Omanis gained nominal control of the islands, but until the reign of Sayyid Said (1804–56) they took little interest in them. Said recognized the commercial value of E Africa and increasingly turned his attention to Zanzibar and Pemba, and in 1841 he permanently moved his court to Zanzibar town. Said brought many Arabs with him, and they gained control of Zanzibar's fertile soil, forcing most of the Hadimu to migrate to the eastern part of the island. The Hadimu were also obligated to work on the clove plantations. Said controlled much of the E African coast, and Zanzibar became the main center of the E African ivory and slave trade. Some of the slaves were used on the clove plantations, and others were exported to other parts of Africa and overseas. Zanzibar's trade was run by Omanis, who organized caravans into the interior of E Africa; the trade was largely financed by Indians resident on Zanzibar, many of whom were agents of Bombay firms. On Said's death in 1856 his African and Omani holdings were separated, with his son Majid becoming sultan of Zanzibar. Majid was succeeded as sultan by Barghash in 1870, by Khalifa in 1888, by Ali ibn Said in 1890, by Hamid ibn Thuwain in 1893, by Hamoud ibn Muhammad in 1896, by Ali in 1902, by Khalifa ibn Naroub in 1911, by Abdullah ibn Khalifa in 1960, and by Jamshid ibn Abdullah in 1963. From the 1820s, British, German, and U.S. traders were active on Zanzibar. As early as 1841 the representative of the British government on Zanzibar was an influential adviser of the sultan, and this was especially the case under Sir John Kirk, the British consul from 1866 to 1887. In a treaty with Great Britain in 1873, Barghash agreed to halt the slave trade in his realm. During the scramble for African territory among European powers, Great Britain gained a protectorate over Zanzibar and Pemba by a treaty with Germany in 1890. The sultan's mainland holdings were incorporated in German East Africa (later Tanganyika), British East Africa (later Kenya), and Italian Somaliland. The British considered Zanzibar an essentially Arab country and maintained the prevailing power structure. The office of sultan was retained (although stripped of most of its power), and Arabs, almost to the exclusion of other groups, were given opportunities for higher education and were recruited for bureaucratic posts. The chief government official during the period 1890 to 1913 was the British consul general, and from 1913 to 1963 it was the British resident. From 1926 the resident was advised by a legislative assembly. After World War II political activity in Zanzibar increased. In the 1950s three main political parties were established—the Zanzibar Nationalist party (ZNP) and its offshoot the Zanzibar and Pemba People's party (ZPPP), both of which principally represented the Arabs, and the Afro-Shirazi party (ASP), whose followers were black Africans. In 1957 popularly elected representatives sat on the legislative council for the first time, and in 1961, they were given a majority of seats. In June, 1963, Zanzibar gained internal self-government, and a ZNP-ZPPP coalition emerged victorious in elections held in July. On Dec. 10, 1963, Zanzibar (together with Pemba) became independent, with Sultan Jamshid ibn Abdullah as head of state and Prime Minister Muhammad Shamte Hamadi, also an Arab, as the leader of government. On Jan. 12, 1964, this arrangement was overthrown in a violent leftist revolt of the black Africans led by John Okello. A republic was declared, with Abeid Karume of the ASP as its president and as head of the Revolutionary Council (the country's chief governmental body). The sultan was forced into exile, all land was nationalized, the ZNP and ZPPP were banned, and numerous Arabs were imprisoned. Subsequently, many other Arabs and some Indians left the country. On April 27, 1964, Zanzibar and Tanganyika agreed to merge, and the resulting republic was renamed TANZANIA in Oct., 1964. Zanzibar has retained considerable independence in internal affairs, but its foreign relations and defense are handled by the central government in Dar es Salaam. Zanzibar's president serves as the first vice president of Tanzania. See Sir John M. Gray, *History of Zanzibar from the Middle Ages to 1856* (1962); Norman R. Bennett, *Studies in East African History* (1963); Michael F. Lofchie, *Zanzibar: Background to Revolution* (1965).

Zanzibar, city (1967 est. pop. 95,000), capital of Zanzibar Mjini region, Tanzania, on the west coast of ZANZIBAR island, separated by a 22-mile (35-km) wide channel from the mainland of E Africa. It is the island's chief commercial center and seaport. Cloves and copra are the main exports. Founded in the 16th cent. as a Portuguese trade depot, the city remained insignificant until the 19th cent., when the sultan of Oman transferred (1841) his court there. It flourished as a major center of the E African ivory and slave trade and was regularly visited by U.S., British, and German trading vessels. In 1890 it became the capital of the British protectorate of Zanzibar, and in 1963 it was made the capital of the independent republic of Zanzibar. When Zanzibar merged with Tanganyika in 1964 to form Tanzania, the city of Zanzibar continued as the seat of the island's government. It is a picturesque, cosmopolitan city, with winding streets, colorful bazaars, and interesting architecture. Of note are several mosques, the former sultan's palace, and Anglican and Roman Catholic cathedrals.

Zapata, Emiliano (āmēlyä'nō säpä'tä), c.1879–1919, Mexican revolutionary, b. Morelos. Zapata was almost pure Indian. A tenant farmer, he occupied a social position between the peon and the ranchero, but he was a born leader who felt keenly the injustices suffered by his people. About 1908, because of his attempt to recover village lands taken over by a rancher, he was impressed into a brief service in the army. Late in 1910, as MADERO rose against Porfirio Díaz, Zapata took up arms with the cry of "land and liberty." With an army of Indians recruited from plantations and villages, he began to seize the land by force. Zapata supported Madero until he thought that land reform had been abandoned, then he turned and formulated his own agrarian program. This program, outlined in the Plan of Ayala (Nov., 1911), called for the return of the land to the Indian. In defense of his plan, Zapata held the field against successive federal governments under Madero, Victoriano HUERTA, and Venustiano CARRANZA. The peasants rallied to Zapata's support, and by the end of 1911 he controlled most of Morelos; later he enlarged his power to cover Guerrero, Oaxaca, Puebla, and at times even the Federal District. After the overthrow of Madero, Zapata in the south and Carranza, OBREGÓN, and VILLA in the north were the chief leaders against Huerta. When Carranza seized the executive power, Zapata and Villa warred against him. Zapata's forces occupied Mexico City three times in 1914–15 (once with the followers of Villa), but finally retired to Morelos, where Zapata resisted until he was treacherously killed by an emissary of Carranza. To his enemies, Zapata was the apotheosis of nihilism, and his movement was only large-scale brigandage. To the Indians, he was a savior and the hero of the revolution. Although his attacks at times seemed to be mere banditry, his objective was not loot; he was single in purpose. His movement, *zapatismo,* was the Mexican agrarian movement in its purest and simplest form, and the agrarian movement was one of the chief aims and chief results of the revolution. As *zapatismo* became synonymous with *agrarismo,* so it did with *indianismo,* the Indian cultural movement which is the basis of nationalism in Mexico. Although illiterate and in command of illiterate men, Zapata was one of the most significant figures in Mexico during the period 1910 to 1919. Even while he lived he became legendary, celebrated in innumerable tales and ballads. His grave is revered by the Indians of S Mexico. See biographies by R. P. Millon (1969) and John Womack, Jr. (1968); Frank Tannenbaum, *The Mexican Agrarian Revolution* (1929); H. H. Dunn, *The Crimson Jester* (1934); E. N. Simpson, *The Ejido* (1937).

Zaphnath-paaneah (zăf'năth-pā"ənē'ə), Egyptian name of JOSEPH 1.

Zaphon (zā'fŏn), unidentified place, E of the Jordan. Joshua 13.27.

Zapolya, John: see JOHN I, king of Hungary.

Zapolya, John Sigismund: see JOHN II, king of Hungary.

Zápolya, Stephen (zä'pôlyŏ), d. 1499, palatine (regent) of Hungary (1492–99), of a noble Hungarian family. An able general of King Matthias Corvinus of Hungary, he fought against the Turks from 1479 to 1481; from 1481 to 1485 he conquered the archduchy of Austria for Matthias, who then appointed him its governor. After Matthias's death in 1490, he supported the claims of Ladislaus II, king of Bohemia, who became king of Hungary as Uladislaus II. Zápolya's son became king of Hungary as John I.

Zapopan (zäpōpän'), city (1970 pop. 182,934), Jalisco state, SW Mexico; est. 1541. Its economy is rural; cattle raising is the chief occupation, and maize is grown. Manufactures include fertilizers, textiles, and the products of local artisans. Stone quarries are nearby. The sanctuary of Our Lady of Zapopan, who is said to have brought peace by a miraculous intervention in the Mixtón War (1539–42), makes the city a pilgrimage point as well as a tourist spot.

Zaporozhye (zəpərôzh'yə), Ukr. *Zaporizhzhya,* city (1970 pop. 658,000), capital of Zaporozhye oblast, S European USSR, in the Ukraine, a port on the Dnepr River, opposite the island of Khortitsa. It is a major rail junction and industrial center and the site of the Dneproges dam and power station, one of the USSR's largest hydroelectric plants. Large quantities of grain are exported. The city has steel mills, coking plants, aluminum and magnesium works, and factories that produce farm machinery, transformers, automobiles, tractors, chemicals, soap, and other items. Well supplied with electricity, Zaporozhye forms, together with the adjoining Donets Basin and the Nikopol manganese and Krivoy Rog iron mines, one of Ukraine's leading industrial complexes. The city, founded in 1770 on the site of the Zaporozhye Cossack camp, consists of old Zaporozhye (called Aleksandrovsk before 1921) and the new industrial Zaporozhye, which developed during the 1930s and adjoins the Dneproges installations and the port of Lenin. The island of Khortitsa, in the Dnepr, was headquarters (*sich*) of the Zaporozhye Cossacks from the 16th to 18th cent. (The word *Zaporozhye* means "beyond the rapids," i.e., of the Dnepr.) The Zaporozhye Cossacks played an important role in the history of the Ukraine. For nearly three centuries they served as the rallying point for the Ukrainians' struggle against social, national, and religious oppression. In the 17th cent. the Cossacks founded an independent state, organized along republican lines and ruled by a hetman. It occupied most of S Ukraine except the Black Sea littoral, a possession of the Crimean khans. After the union of Poland and Lithuania in 1569, the Ukraine came under Polish rule; but the Poles were too weak to defend Ukraine from frequent devastating Tatar raids. The need for self-defense led at the end of the 15th cent. to the rise of the Ukrainian Cossacks, who by the mid-16th cent. had formed a state along the lower and middle Dnepr. Although they formally recognized the sovereignty of the Polish kings, the Cossacks, for all practical purposes, enjoyed complete political independence. By the end of the 16th cent., however, Poland sought fuller control over the Ukraine and the Zaporozhye Cossacks. Persecution of the Ukrainian Orthodox Church after 1596 provoked repeated outbreaks among the Ukrainians, and the Cossacks, as staunch adherents of the Orthodox faith, participated actively in the rebellions. In 1648 the Zaporozhye Cossacks, led by Hetman Bohdan CHMIELNICKI, began a series of campaigns that eventually defeated the Poles and freed the Ukraine from Polish domination. Chmielnicki's forces suffered defeat in 1651, however, and were forced at Belaya Tserkov to accept a treaty unfavorable to the Ukraine. In 1654, Chmielnicki persuaded the Cossacks to transfer their allegiance to the Russian czars. By the Treaty of Andrusov in 1667, the left bank of the Dnepr and Kiev were ceded to Russia. The Russians proceeded to encroach upon Cossack privileges much as the Poles had, thus engendering revolts in what was left of the Zaporozhye territory. When Hetman Ivan MAZEPA joined Charles XII of

Sweden against Russia in the NORTHERN WAR, he shared in the Swedish defeat at POLTAVA (1709). At that time, Czar Peter I virtually ended Cossack independence in Ukraine. Many Zaporozhye Cossacks fled to the khanate of Crimea, but in 1734 they were allowed to return to their old territory and to establish a new Cossack headquarters. Russia, however, continued to view the Cossacks with suspicion; and in 1775 the Russian army, on orders from Catherine II, destroyed the Zaporozhye camp, thus completely abolishing the last stronghold of Ukrainian independence. Most of the Zaporozhye Cossacks then moved to Turkish territory at the mouth of the Danube, where they founded a new community. In 1828-29, however, they returned to the Ukraine and settled along the shores of the Sea of Azov. When the Russians tried in the 19th cent. to settle them in the newly conquered N Caucasus, the Cossacks rebelled and were disbanded (1865). Those Zaporozhye Cossacks who had remained in the Ukraine were allowed in 1787 to settle along the Black Sea shores between the Dnepr and Bug rivers; they became known as the Black Sea Cossacks. In 1792 they were resettled in the Kuban region and after 1860 became known as the Kuban Cossacks.

Zapotec (zä'pətĕk, sä'-), Indian people of Mexico, primarily in S Oaxaca and on the Isthmus of Tehuantepec. Little is known of the origin of the Zapotec. Unlike most Indians of Middle America, they had no traditions or legends of migration, but believed themselves to have been born directly from rocks, trees, and jaguars. The early Zapotec were a sedentary, agricultural, city-dwelling people who worshiped a pantheon of gods headed by the rain-god, Cosijo—represented by a fertility symbol combining the earth-jaguar and sky-serpent symbols common in Middle American cultures. A priestly hierarchy regulated religious rites, which sometimes included human sacrifice. The Zapotec worshiped their ancestors and, believing in a paradisaical underworld, stressed the cult of the dead. They had a great religious center at MITLA and a magnificent city at MONTE ALBÁN, where a highly developed civilization flourished possibly more than 2,000 years ago. In art, architecture, hieroglyphics, mathematics, and calendar the Zapotec seem to have had strong cultural affinities with the OLMEC, with the ancient MAYA, and later with the TOLTEC. Coming from the north, the MIXTEC replaced the Zapotec at Monte Albán and then at Mitla; the Zapotec captured Tehuantepec from the Zoquean and Huavean Indians of the Gulf of Tehuantepec. By the middle of the 15th cent. both Zapotec and Mixtec were struggling to keep the AZTEC from gaining control of the trade routes to Chiapas and Guatemala. Under their greatest king, Cosijoeza, the Zapotec withstood a long siege on the rocky mountain of Giengola, overlooking Tehuantepec, and successfully maintained political autonomy by an alliance with the Aztec until the arrival of the Spanish. The Zapotec today are mainly of two groups, those of the southern valleys in the mountains of Oaxaca and those of the southern half of the Isthmus of Tehuantepec; together they number some 300,000. The social fabric of Zapotec life—customs, dress, songs, and literature—though predominantly Spanish, still retains strong elements of the Zapotec heritage, particularly in the present-day state of Juchitán. See Helen Augur, *Zapotec* (1954); Michael Kearney, *The Winds of Ixtepeji* (1972); Beverly Chinas, *The Isthmus Zapotecs* (1973).

Zaqaziq, Az (äz zäkäzēk') or **Zagazig** (zägäzēg'), city (1970 est. pop. 173,000), capital of Sharqiyah governorate, N Egypt, in the Nile River delta. It is Egypt's leading cotton market, as well as a trade center for grain and a rail and canal junction. Az Zaqaziq was established as a transportation and market center in the mid-19th cent., when cotton cultivation was spreading in the delta. Nearby are the ruins of the ancient city of BUBASTIS.

Zara or **Zarah** (both: zā'rə), same as ZERAH **1**.

Zara: see ZADAR, Yugoslavia.

Zaragoza (thärägō'thä) or **Saragossa** (sâr"əgŏ'sə), city (1970 pop. 479,845), capital of Zaragoza prov. and leading city of Aragón, NE Spain, on the Ebro River. An important commercial and communications center, it is situated in a fertile, irrigated agricultural region. Among the manufactures are wood products, foodstuffs, and paper. It is an archiepiscopal see and has a university (founded 1474). Of ancient origin, it was named Caesarea Augusta by Emperor Augustus. It fell to the Goths (5th cent.) and to the Moors (8th cent.), under whom it became (1017) the capital of an independent emirate. Charlemagne tried to take it but was defeated by the Moors (778). The CID fought for a time in the service of the Moorish ruler of Zaragoza. The city was conquered (1118) by Alfonso I of Aragón, who made it the capital of his kingdom. The most notable event in the later history of Zaragoza was its heroic resistance, under the leadership of Palafox, against the French in the Peninsular War. The city resisted the first siege (1808), surrendering only after some 50,000 defenders had died in the second siege (1808-9). Zaragoza is a cultural center and is rich in works of art, many of which show Moorish influence. There are two cathedrals—La Seo (12th-16th cent.), formerly a mosque, and El Pilar (17th cent.), named after the sacred pillar near which the Virgin is said to have appeared in the vision of St. James the Greater. El Pilar contains frescoes by Velázquez and Goya. Also noteworthy are the Church of San Pablo, the Moorish castle of Aljafería (residence of the emirs and later the kings of Aragón), the *lonja* (exchange building), and a 15th-century stone bridge across the Ebro. The modern church of San Antonio de Padua contains the remains of Italian soldiers killed in the civil war (1936-39).

Zarathushtra or **Zarathustra:** see ZOROASTER.

Zareah (zārē'ə), variant of ZORAH.

Zared (zā'rĕd): see ZERED.

Zarephath (zâr'ēfăth) or **Sarepta** (sərĕp'tə), town, ancient SW Syria, on the coast about one third of the distance from Sidon to Tyre. It is the modern Sarafand, Lebanon. Elijah stayed at Zarephath in the drought. 1 Kings 17.8-24; Luke 4.26.

Zaretan (zâr'ētăn), **Zartanan** (-tăn'-), or **Zarthan** (zär'thăn), unlocated place in the valley of the Jordan, associated with the crossing of the Jews. Variants, all probably referring to the same place, are Zartanah, Zereda, Zeredathah, and Zererath. Joshua 3.16; Judges 7.22; 1 Kings 4.12; 7.46; 11.26; 2 Chron. 4.17.

Zareth-shahar (zā'rĕth-shā'här), unlocated place, E of the Dead Sea. Joshua 13.19.

Zarhite, patronymic of the family of ZERAH **1**.

Zaria (zä'rēə), city (1969 est. pop. 193,000), N Nigeria. It is the ginning center for Nigeria's main cotton-growing region. Cottonseed, groundnut, and sheanut oil are produced, bicycles are assembled, and cigarettes are manufactured. The city is on a major north-south railroad and highway and has an airport. First known as Zazzau, it was founded about 1000 and was one of the seven HAUSA city-states. The city was captured by the FULANI in 1805 and included in the SOKOTO caliphate. In 1901 British forces led by Frederick LUGARD took the city. Zaria is the seat of Ahmadu Bello Univ. (1962) and an agricultural school. The old part of the city is surrounded by walls.

Zarqa or **Zerka** (both: zär'kä), river, 80 mi (129 km) long, rising in the hills W of Amman, N Jordan, and flowing generally north, then west, to the Jordan River; it is the ancient Jabbok. On its southern bank Jacob wrestled with the angel. Gen. 32.22; Num. 21.24; Deut. 2.37, 3.16; Joshua 12.2; Judges 11.12, 22.

Zartanah (zärtăn'ə), **Zereda** (zĕr'ēdə, zērē'-), **Zeredathah** (zērĕd'əthə), and **Zererath** (zĕr'ērăth, zērē'-), variant forms of ZARETAN.

Žatec (zhä'tĕts), Ger. *Saaz,* city (1970 pop. 15,725), NW Czechoslovakia, in Bohemia. It is the center of a famous hop-growing region. Žatec was founded in the 11th cent. The city was captured and burned by the Swedes in 1639, during the Thirty Years War.

Zatthu (zăth'yo͞o) or **Zattu** (zăt'-), family returned from Exile. Ezra 2.8; Neh. 7.13. Married foreign wives. Ezra 10.27. Sealers of the Covenant. Neh. 10.14.

Zavan (zā'văn), variant of ZAAVAN.

Zawiercie (zävyĕr'chĕ), city (1970 pop. 39,410), S Poland, on the Warta River. Its industries produce iron and steel, machinery and machine tools, chemicals, metals, glass, and textiles. Lignite and iron ore are mined nearby. Zawiercie passed to Prussia in 1795, to Russia in 1815, and to Poland after World War I.

Zayandeh Rud (zīyändĕ' ro͞od) or **Zaindeh Rud** (zīndĕ'), river, c.250 mi (400 km) long, rising in the Zagros mts., W central Iran, and flowing southeast through an agricultural district to a swamp W of Yazd; used for irrigation along its entire length. The Kuh-Rang Dam (built 1953) diverts water from the upper course of the Karun River through a 2-mi (3.2-km) tunnel into the Zayandeh Rud, where it is used to supplement irrigation in the Esfahan area.

Zayas, Alfredo (älfrā'thō sä'yäs), 1861-1934, president of Cuba (1921-25). He was one of the leaders of the Liberal party from the founding of the republic and was vice president (1909-13) under José Miguel Gómez. He was defeated for the presidency in 1912 and 1916 by Mario G. MENOCAL. He and Gómez quarreled violently, and it was with Menocal's help that Zayas defeated Gómez for the presidency in 1920. The election was denounced as fraudulent, and the United States intervened to prevent civil war. In the chaotic conditions following the collapse of the sugar market, Enoch J. Crowder, representing the United States, restored financial order. However, as soon as some balance was attained Zayas entered on an administration that was almost universally criticized as weak, wasteful, and corrupt. When he failed to get the presidential nomination in 1924, he supported Gerardo MACHADO.

Zayinda Rud: see ZAYANDEH RUD.

Zaysan, Lake (zīsän'), freshwater lake, c.700 sq mi (1,810 sq km), SE Kazakhstan, in the Altai Mts. It is crossed by the Irtysh River. The lake abounds in fish.

Zaza (zā'zə), Jerahmeelite. 1 Chron. 2.33.

Zea, Francisco Antonio (fränsēs'kō äntō'nyō sā'ä), 1770-1882, Colombian botanist and revolutionist. He was associated with MUTIS in botanical studies. Zea, like Antonio Nariño, was arrested (1795) for distributing copies of *The Declaration of the Rights of Man* and was for a time imprisoned in Spain. He returned to aid Bolívar in the liberation of South America. After becoming (1819) vice president of Venezuela, he resigned and accepted the presidency of the Congress of Angostura (see CIUDAD BOLÍVAR) and was later vice president of Greater Colombia. Appointed special diplomatic agent to Europe, he was not highly successful; he negotiated disadvantageous loans and gained recognition of his country only from the United States. He died in Bath, England. Zea wrote a history of Colombia and works on botany.

Zea, Greece: see KÉA.

Zealand: see SJAELLAND, Denmark.

Zealots (zĕl'əts), Jewish faction traced back to the revolt of the Maccabees (2d cent. B.C.). The name was first recorded by the Jewish historian Josephus as a designation for the Jewish resistance fighters of the war of A.D. 66-73. This term applied to them because of their fervent veneration of the Torah and detestation of heathens. The Zealots were organized as a party during the reign (37 B.C.-4 B.C.) of Herod the Great, whose idolatrous practices they resisted. Later (A.D. c.6), when Cyrenius, the Roman governor of Syria, attempted to take a census, the Zealots, under JUDAS OF GALILEE and the priest Zadok, arose in revolt against what they considered a plot to subjugate the Jews. Thereafter the Zealots expressed their opposition by sporadic revolts and by violence against Jews who conformed to Roman ways. In time certain elements of the Pharisees joined them. The Zealots disappeared from history after the unsuccessful revolt in which Jerusalem was destroyed (A.D. 70). One of the Twelve Disciples, St. Simon, was a Zealot; and it has been suggested that JUDAS ISCARIOT may have been connected with an extremist wing of the Zealots called the Sicarii [Lat.,=assassins].

Zebadiah (zĕb"ədī'ə). **1** Ally of David at Ziklag. 1 Chron. 12.7. **2** Officer of David. 1 Chron. 27.7. **3** Teacher of the Law. 2 Chron. 17.8. **4** High official of Jehoshaphat. 2 Chron. 19.11. Additional mention of this name is in 1 Chron. 8.15,17; 27.7; Ezra 8.8; 10.20.

Zebah (zē'bə), Midianite king conquered by Gideon. Judges 8; Ps. 83.11.

Zebaim (zēbā'ĭm), qualifier of the name Pochereth. Ezra 2.57; Neh. 7.59.

Zebedee (zĕb'ədē) [Gr., for ZEBADIAH], father of James and John. His wife Salome attended Jesus. Mat. 4.21; 20.20; 27.56; Mark 15.40.

Zebina (zēbī'nə), Israelite who married a foreign wife. Ezra 10.43.

Zeboiim (zēboi'ĭm) or **Zeboim** (zēbō'ĭm), one of the Cities of the Plain. See SODOM.

zebra, herbiverous hoofed African mammal of the genus *Equus,* which also includes the HORSE and the ass. It is distinguished by its striking pattern of black or dark brown stripes alternating with white. In size and body form it is intermediate between the larger horse and the smaller ass. It has a heavy head, stout body, short, stiff mane, and tufted tail. There are three living zebra species; a fourth species, the QUAGGA, became extinct in the last century. All zebras inhabit open plains or brush country; they congregate near water holes in herds of as many as 1,000, often mixed with other grazing animals, such as antelopes. They are swift runners, achieving speeds of up to 40 mi (60 km) per hr. Some authorities believe that the stripes, by breaking up the body outline and simulating patterns of light and shadow, provide camouflage in brush and grass. The zebra's natural enemies are the lion and the leopard. The common zebra, or bontequagga, *Equus burchelli,* is found throughout Africa S of the Sahara. It stands about 4 ft (120 cm) tall at the shoulder and has small ears. It has very broad stripes, which vary greatly in their pattern among the several races of the species, as well as among individuals of the same race. Grevy's zebra, *E. grevyii*, is a large, horselike zebra found in E Africa. It stands 4½ to 5 ft (140–150 cm) at the shoulder and weighs about 600 lb (270 kg). It has large, rounded ears and numerous very narrow stripes. Most distinctive is the mountain zebra, *E. zebra*, with a donkeylike build, long ears, and a characteristic stripe pattern. Unlike any other member of the genus *Equus*, it has a dewlap on its throat. The more numerous race of this species (Hartmann's mountain zebra), found in the arid mountains and coastal plains of SW Africa, has been declining in numbers in recent years, at least partly because of game fences that prevent its migrations in search of water. In 1967 the population of this race was thought to be only about 7,000. The other race (Cape mountain zebra) is now scarcely found outside a protected area in Cape Province, South Africa. Zebras have been hunted extensively for their flesh and skins, but the common zebra and Grevy's zebra are still numerous. Zebras have been crossed with horses in an attempt to produce a draft animal, but the offspring are sterile and have not proved reliable. Zebras are classified in the phylum CHORDATA, subphylum Vertebrata, class Mammalia, order Perissodactyla, family Equidae.

zebu (zē'byōō), domestic animal of the CATTLE family, *Bos indicus*, found in parts of E Asia, India, and Africa. The zebu characteristically has a large fatty hump (sometimes two humps) over the withers. It is usually fawn, gray, black, or bay. An inferior source of milk and meat, it has great endurance and comparatively long legs and has been used in India as a riding and draft animal. Zebus were first introduced into the United States, where they are called BRAHMAN CATTLE, in the 19th cent. They are used in Central and South America and are well established in the Gulf states, where they are interbred with domestic cattle to produce an animal that has greater resistance to heat and to ticks than the ordinary domestic cattle and better flesh than the zebu. Zebus are classified in the phylum CHORDATA, subphylum Vertebrata, class Mammalia, order Artiodactyla, family Bovidae.

Zebudah (zēbyōō'də, zĕb'yōō-), wife of Josiah and mother of Jehoiakim. 2 Kings 23.36.

Zebul (zē'bəl), ruler of Shechem, supporter of Abimelech. Judges 9.28–41.

Zebulun (zĕb'yōōlən), son of Jacob and Leah, eponymous ancestor of the 12 tribes of Israel. Its allotment was in N Palestine W of Mt. Carmel. The judge Elon was from this tribe. Apart from their bravery in the battle against Sisera, the Zebulunites played a minor part in Israel's history. Gen. 30.20; 46.14; Num. 26.26; Deut. 33.18,19; Joshua 19.10; Judges 5.14,18. Zabulon: Mat. 4.13,15; Rev. 7.8.

Zechariah (zĕk"ərī'ə). **1** Prophet and author of the book of ZECHARIAH. **2** Prophet who, with the connivance of King Jehoash, was stoned to death for his public rebuke of idolatry. 2 Chron. 24.20–22. In Mat. 23.35 and Luke 11.51 it is apparently this martyred Zechariah (NT Zacharias) to whom Jesus referred. See also BERECHIAH **7**. **3** Prophet in the reign of Uzziah. 2 Chron. 26.5. **4** King, the same as ZACHARIAH **1**. **5** Maternal grandfather of King Hezekiah. 2 Chron. 29.1. Zachariah: 2 Kings 18.2. **6** Priest in David's time. 1 Chron. 15.24. **7** One of Isaiah's witnesses. Isa. 8.2. **8** Prince of King Jehoshaphat. 2 Chron. 17.7. **9** Son of Jehoshaphat. 2 Chron. 21.2. **10** Ruler of the Temple. 2 Chron. 35.8. **11** Father of IDDO **1**. **12** Korahite doorkeeper. 1 Chron. 9.21; 26.2, 14. **13** Merarite doorkeeper. 1 Chron. 26.11. **14** Musician under David. 1 Chron. 15.18,20. **15** Chief man in the Exile. Ezra 8.16. **6** Father of JAHAZIEL **2**. **17, 18** Kohathites. 1 Chron. 24.25; 2 Chron. 34.12. **19** Reubenite. 1 Chron. 5.7. **20, 21** Heads of families that returned from the Exile. Ezra 8.3, 11. **22, 23** Asaphites. 2 Chron. 29.13; Neh. 12.35. **24** Priest in the return. Neh. 12.41. **25** Grandfather of ATHAIAH. **26** Ancestor of ASAIAH **4**. **27** Ancestor of ADAIAH **4**. **28** One who had a foreign wife. Ezra 10.26. **29** Same as ZACHER. Zacharias, Zachariah, and Zachary are forms of the name Zechariah.

Zechariah (zĕk"ərī'ə) or **Zacharias** (zăk"ərī'əs), book of the Old Testament, 38th in the order of the Authorized Version, 11th of the books of the Minor Prophets, dated in 519 and 517 B.C. at Jerusalem. The prophet was associated with Haggai in a movement to restore the Temple (Ezra 5.1; 6.14). The book, after an introduction (1.1–6), proceeds with eight visions (1.7–6.8), prophetic of the restitution of Israel, and a symbolic crowning of the high priest (6.9–15). A sermon follows (7–8) on the observance of the commandments and the rewards for so doing. The rest of the book (9–14), very different in tone, consists of prophecies of trouble and eventual redemption for Jerusalem. Scholars assign the latter portion of the book to a later date. See studies by David Baron (1918, repr. 1972) and F. A. Tatford (1971); see also bibliography under OLD TESTAMENT.

Zedad (zē'dăd), unidentified landmark on the northern boundary of Palestine. Num. 34.8; Ezek. 47.15.

Zedekiah (zĕd"əkī'ə). **1** Last king of Judah. He was the third son of Josiah to occupy the throne, the others being Jehoahaz and Jehoiakim. Zedekiah, whose name was originally Mattaniah, succeeded Jehoiachin. He was set on the throne as the puppet of NEBUCHADNEZZAR, but he allowed the patriot party to sway him into allying himself with the Egyptian pharaoh Apries (Hophra). This violated an agreement with Nebuchadnezzar, and the Chaldaeans came to Palestine and destroyed the kingdom of Judah. Zedekiah was carried with his people into captivity in Babylonia. JEREMIAH was contemporary with Zedekiah. 2 Kings 24.17–20; 25.2–7; 1 Chron. 3.15; 2 Chron. 36.10–13; Jer. 38; 39; 51.59; 52. **2** False prophet of Ahab. 1 Kings 22.11,24; 2 Chron. 18.10. **3** Hebrew false prophet in Babylonia. Jer. 29.21,22. **4** Prince of Judah. Jer. 36.12.

zedoary (zĕd'ōĕr"ē), name for a perennial herb *(Curcuma zedoaria)* of the Zingiberaceae (GINGER family) and for a spice consisting of its dried and pulverized aromatic rhizome. The plant, related to turmeric and to the East Indian arrowroot, is native to and principally cultivated in India. It is used as a condiment, as a flavoring for liqueurs and bitters, in perfumery, and medicinally as a carminative and stimulant. Zedoary is classified in the division MAGNOLIOPHYTA, class Liliatae, order Zingiberales, family Zingiberaceae.

Zeeb (zē'ĕb), one of the two Midianite princes killed while invading Israel. Judges 7.25; 8.3; Ps. 83.11.

Zeebrugge (zā'brŭ"gə), outer port of Bruges, West Flanders prov., NW Belgium, on the North Sea. Zeebrugge was developed c.1900 to replace the silted-up port of Bruges; it is connected to Bruges by a 6-mi (9.7-km) canal (opened 1907). Zeebrugge has coke and glass factories and oil-storage facilities. It is connected with Harwich, England, by a rail ferry. Used as a German submarine base in World War I, its harbor was sealed (April, 1918) by a British naval force under Sir Roger J. B. Keyes.

Zeeland, Paul van: see VAN ZEELAND, PAUL.

Zeeland (zē'lənd, Dutch zā'länt), province (1971 pop. 310,300), c.650 sq mi (1,680 sq km), SW Netherlands, bordering on Belgium in the south and the North Sea in the west. The main cities are Middelburg, which is the capital, and Vlissingen. The province consists of a strip of Flanders that is adjacent to Belgium and various former islands located in the Scheldt estuary; the chief islands are WALCHEREN, North and South BEVELAND, Schouwen-Duiveland, and Tholen. Much of the land is below sea level and is protected by dikes. Agriculture, dairying, and fishing are the chief occupations; there is some industry, notably shipbuilding. Zeeland, a part of Holland from the 10th cent., later became a separate county, but it continued to be ruled by the counts of Holland, and its history was largely identical with that of HOLLAND. In 1579, Zeeland joined the Union of Utrecht as one of the United Provinces of the Netherlands. The province was badly damaged by flooding in 1953.

Zeeman, Pieter (pē'tər zā'män), 1865–1943, Dutch physicist. He was professor of physics at the Univ. of Amsterdam from 1900 and director of the Physical Institute, Amsterdam, from 1908. In 1896 he discovered the ZEEMAN EFFECT. He shared the 1902 Nobel Prize in Physics with H. A. Lorentz. His works include *Researches in Magneto-Optics* (1913).

Zeeman effect, splitting of a single spectral line (see SPECTRUM) into a group of closely spaced lines when the substance producing the single line is subjected to a uniform magnetic field. The effect was discovered in 1896 by the Dutch physicist Pieter Zeeman. In the so-called normal Zeeman effect, the spectral line corresponding to the original frequency of the light (in the absence of the magnetic field) appears with two other lines arranged symmetrically on either side of the original line. In the anomalous Zeeman effect (which is actually more common than the normal effect), several lines appear, forming a complex pattern. The normal Zeeman effect was successfully explained by H. A. Lorentz using the laws of classical physics (Zeeman and Lorentz shared the 1902 Nobel Prize in Physics). The anomalous Zeeman effect could not be explained using classical physics; the development of the QUANTUM THEORY and the discovery of the electron's intrinsic spin led to a satisfactory explanation. According to the quantum theory all spectral lines arise from transitions of electrons between different allowed energy levels within the atom, the frequency (and therefore the wavelength) of the spectral line being proportional to the energy difference between the initial and final levels. Because of its intrinsic spin, the electron has a magnetic field associated with it. When an external magnetic field is applied, the electron's magnetic field may assume only certain alignments. Slight differences in energy are associated with these different orientations, so that what was once a single energy level becomes three or more. Practical applications based on the Zeeman effect include spectral analysis and measurement of magnetic field strength. Since the separation of the components of the spectral line is proportional to the field strength, the Zeeman effect is particularly useful where the magnetic field cannot be measured by more direct methods.

Zefat (zĕf'ät), town, NE Israel. It is a hot-weather resort and has a thriving artists' colony and many museums and old synagogues. Ceramics and handicrafts are produced in the town. Founded A.D. c.70, Zefat is referred to as Tzefiya in the TALMUD. Flavius Josephus, a Jewish historian and soldier, built fortifications that later formed the foundations of a 12th-century Crusader castle built by the Knights Templars; its ruins still stand. After the expulsion of the Jews from Spain in 1492, many learned Jews moved to Zefat and made the town an important center of rabbinical and cabalistic (see CABALA) studies, which it remained through the 17th cent. Joseph Caro, the last great codifier of rabbinic law, lived in Zefat from 1536 to 1575 and wrote the *Shulhan Aruk* there. In 1563 the first Hebrew printing press in the Holy Land was established in Zefat; its books were much in demand worldwide. Largely destroyed by an earthquake in 1769, Zefat was repopulated by Russian Hasidim in 1776. The Arabs forced most Jews to leave Zefat in 1929, but Jews returned after the 1948 Arab-Israeli war. The name also appears as Safad and Safed.

Zeffirelli-Cosi, Franco (fräng'kō zäf-fērĕl'lē-kô'sē), 1923–, Italian opera, stage, and film director and designer. Zeffirelli had his first successes as assistant to the director Luchino Visconti in the films *Troilus and Cressida* and *The Three Sisters*. His first opera production was *La Cenerentola* for Milan's La Scala, after which he became known chiefly for his opulent opera productions. He mounted productions of *Falstaff* (1964) and *Antony and Cleopatra* (1966) for the Metropolitan Opera Company. Zeffirelli's films include *The Taming of the Shrew* (1966), *Romeo and Juliet* (1968), and *Brother Sun, Sister Moon* (1973).

Zehsis: see CESIS, USSR.

Zeisberger, David (zīs'bərgər), 1721–1808, American Moravian missionary, b. Moravia. While a youth, he lived in Holland and later in London, where he met Graf von ZINZENDORF, who enabled him to join (1739) a Moravian colony in Georgia. Zeisberger moved (c.1740) to Pennsylvania with the colony and entered on missionary service. His assistant was J. G. E. HECKEWELDER. Zeisberger helped ally the Iroquois with the English against French aggressions on the continent. He worked effectively among the Pennsylvania Indians. His mission (est. 1772) at Schoenbrunn, Ohio (see SCHOENBRUNN VILLAGE STATE MEMORIAL) was destroyed (1777) during the American Revolution, and in 1781 the British temporarily imprisoned him. Zeisberger later set up other missions in Ohio and one in Canada. His numerous writings include a spelling book, an Indian grammar and dictionary, and a history of the Indians.

Zeist (zīst), municipality (1971 pop. 56,187), Utrecht prov., central Netherlands, near Utrecht. It is largely residential; manufactures include pharmaceuticals and furniture. A settlement of the Moravian Brethren was established there in 1746.

Zeitz (tsīts), city (1970 pop. 46,736), Halle dist., S East Germany, on the White Elster River. Manufactures include machinery, chemicals, furniture, and beer. Of note in the city are the late-Gothic Church of St. Michael and a castle (17th cent.), whose church contains the tomb of the 16th-century scientist Georg Agricola.

Zela (zē'lə), ancient city of Pontus, NE Asia Minor. There Mithridates VI defeated Triarius c.67 B.C., and in 47 B.C. Julius Caesar defeated Pharnaces, king of Pontus, recording the victory in his famous dispatch "Veni, vidi, vici" [I came, I saw, I conquered]. It is the modern Zile, Turkey.

Zelah (zē'lə), unidentified town, central Palestine. The family tomb of Saul was there. Joshua 18.28; 2 Sam. 21.14.

Zelaya, José Santos (hōsā' sän'tōs sälä'yä), 1853–1919, president of Nicaragua (1894–1909). Although a leader of the Liberal party, he kept power by playing the Liberal and Conservative parties against each other and established an unswerving dictatorship. Zelaya developed railroad and steamer transportation, coffee growing, and education, but nevertheless he drained Nicaragua's resources for his own profit. He seized (1894) the MOSQUITO COAST by force, thus ending British control. He fomented revolutions in neighboring countries and tried to re-establish the CENTRAL AMERICAN FEDERATION with himself as head. His ambitions created intense opposition, which led to the Washington Conference of 1907 and the establishment of the Central American Court of Justice. The United States was highly antagonistic to him, and the presence of U.S. cruisers helped rebel forces to overthrow and exile him.

Zelek (zē'lĕk), one of David's guard. 2 Sam. 23.37; 1 Chron. 11.39.

Zelophehad (zēlŏf'ēhăd), Manassite who had no sons and whose daughters received his inheritance, thus establishing a legal precedent. Num. 26.33; 27.1-7; 36.2; Joshua 17.3; 1 Chron. 7.15.

Zelotes (zēlō'tēz) [Gr.,=zealot], name of St. SIMON.

Zelzah (zĕl'zə), unlocated place, between Jerusalem and Bethlehem. 1 Sam. 10.2.

Zemaraim (zĕm"ərā'ĭm), town and highland, Palestine, probably N of Jerusalem. Joshua 18.22; 2 Chron. 13.4.

Zemarite (zĕm'ərīt), Canaanite tribe living in the city of Zemar. Gen. 10.18; 1 Chron. 1.16.

Zemgale: see LATVIA, USSR.

Zemira (zēmī'rə), descendant of Benjamin. 1 Chron. 7.8.

zemstvo (zĕmst'vō) [Rus., from *zemlya*=land], local assembly that functioned as a body of provincial self-government in Russia from 1864 to 1917. The introduction of the zemstvo system was one of the major liberal reforms in the reign of Alexander II. Each district elected representatives, who had control over education, public health, roads, and aid to agriculture and commerce. The district zemstvos elected executive committees and delegates to the provincial assemblies, which in turn elected an executive committee for the province. A similar system was introduced (1870) for town governments. Representation in the zemstvo was proportional to land ownership, and the electorate was divided into three groups—private landowners, urban population, and peasant communes. Although landowners predominated over the peasants and townspeople under the electoral system, the zemstvos accomplished imposing progress in the fields of education and health within the half century of their existence. The zemstvo was the stronghold of the Russian liberals and constitutionalists, who after the February Revolution of 1917 democratized the electoral system and sought to make the zemstvos the basis of the new regime. When the Bolsheviks came to power in Nov., 1917 (Oct., 1917, O.S.), the functions of the zemstvo were taken over by the SOVIET.

Zenan (zē'nən), town, SW Palestine. Joshua 15.37. See ZAANAN.

Zenas (zē'năs), lawyer and follower of Paul. Titus 3.13.

Zen Buddhism, Buddhist sect of Japan and China. The name of the sect (Chin. *Ch'an,* Jap. *Zen*) derives from the Sanskrit word *dhyana* [meditation]. In early China the school was known for making the practice of meditation its central tenet, rather than adherence to a particular scripture or doctrine. The founder of Zen in China was the legendary Bodhidharma, who came to China from India in the late 5th cent. A.D. He taught the practice of "wall-gazing" and espoused the teachings of the *Lanka-Vatara Sutra* (whose chief doctrine is that of "consciousness-only;" see YOGACARA), which he passed on to his successor Hui-k'o (487-593). Little is known of the early development of Zen, but according to tradition, Hui-neng (638-713) became the sixth patriarch of Chinese Zen by superseding his rival in the intuitive grasp of the truth of enlightenment, although he was illiterate. *The Platform Sutra,* attributed to Hui-neng, defines enlightenment as the direct seeing of one's own "original Mind" or "original Nature," which is Buddha, and this teaching has remained characteristic of Zen up to the present. A number of teaching lineages arose after Hui-neng, all claiming descent from him, and teaching the method of "sudden enlightenment" best known in the West by the term *satori.* In its formative period Zen received both Taoist influences and elements of Prajna-Paramita Buddhism (see SUNYATA). The 8th and 9th cent. were the "golden age" of Zen, producing such great masters as Ma-tsu, Nan-chuan, Huang-po, Lin-chi, and Chao-chou. The unique Zen teaching style was developed, stressing oral instruction and using nonrational forms of dialogue, from which the later KOAN was derived. In some cases even physical violence was used to jolt the student out of dependence on ordinary forms of thought and into the enlightened consciousness. Scholarly knowledge, ritual, and the performance of good deeds were considered of comparatively little spiritual value. After the great persecution of Buddhism in 845, Zen emerged as the dominant Chinese sect, due partly to its innate vitality and partly to its isolation in mountain monasteries away from centers of political power. Two main schools of Zen, the Lin-chi (Jap. Rinzai) and the Ts'ao-tung (Jap. Soto), flourished and were transmitted to Japan in the 14th cent. The Rinzai sect placed greater emphasis on the use of the koan and effort to attain sudden enlightenment, while in Soto the patriarch Dogen (1200–53) emphasized sitting in meditation (*zazen*) without expectation and with faith in one's own intrinsic state of enlightenment or Buddha-nature. The austere discipline and practical approach of Zen made it the Buddhism of the medieval Japanese military class. Zen monks occupied positions of political influence and became active in literary and artistic life. Zen monasteries, especially the main temples of Kyoto and Kamakura, were educational as well as religious centers. The Zen influence on Japanese aesthetics ranges from poetry, calligraphy, and painting to tea ceremony, flower arrangement, and landscape gardening, particularly the distinctive rock-and-sand temple gardens. Japanese Zen declined in the 16th and 17th cent., and its traditional forms were revived by the great Hakuin (1686-1769) from whom all present-day Rinzai masters trace their descent. Zen thought was made known in the West by the writings of D. T. SUZUKI, and since World War II the practice of Zen meditation has attracted interest, resulting in the establishment of Zen monastic centers in California and on the East Coast of the United States. See Alan Watts, *The Spirit of Zen* (1958, repr. 1960); Chang Ch'eng-chi, *The Practice of Zen* (1959, repr. 1970; Sohaku Ogata, *Zen for the West* (1959, repr. 1973); Erich Fromm, ed., *Zen Buddhism and Psychoanalysis* (1960, repr. 1970); N. W. Ross, ed., *The World of Zen* (1960); Paul Reps, ed., *Zen Flesh, Zen Bones* (1961, repr. 1968); D. T. Suzuki, *Essays in Zen Buddhism* (new ed., 3 vol., 1971), *A Manual of Zen Buddhism* (1950, repr. 1960), *An Introduction to Zen Buddhism* (2d ed. 1957), and *Essentials of Zen Buddhism* (1962, repr. 1973); Van Meter Ames, *Zen and American Thought* (1962); Kosho Uchiyama, *Approach to Zen* (1973).

Zend (zĕnd), term formerly used for the language of the *Avesta* (see ZOROASTRIANISM).

Zener diode: see DIODE.

Zenger, John Peter (zĕng'ər), 1697-1746, American journalist, b. Germany. He emigrated to America in 1710 and was trained as a printer by William BRADFORD (1663-1752). Zenger began publication of the New York *Weekly Journal* in 1733, an opposition paper to Bradford's New York *Gazette* and to the policies of Gov. William Cosby. Zenger's newspaper, backed by several prominent lawyers and merchants, truculently attacked the administration. Although most of the articles were written by Zenger's backers, Zenger was legally responsible and was arrested on libel charges and imprisoned (1734). In the celebrated trial that followed (1735) Zenger was defended by Andrew HAMILTON, who established truth as a defense in cases of libel. The trial, which resulted in the publisher's acquittal, helped to establish freedom of the press in America. Zenger later became public printer for the colonies of New York (1737) and New Jersey (1738). See biography by Livingston Rutherford (1904, repr. 1970); Vincent Buranelli, ed., *The Trial of Peter Zenger* (1957).

zenith, in astronomy, the point in the sky directly overhead; more precisely, it is the point at which the CELESTIAL SPHERE is intersected by an upward extension of a plumb line from the observer's location. Its position in the sky thus depends on the direction of the earth's gravitational field at the observer's location. The zenith is a reference point in the HORIZON COORDINATE SYSTEM; its altitude above the celestial horizon is 90°. The angular distance from the zenith to a celestial body is called the zenith distance. The nadir, directly opposite the zenith, has a zenith distance of 180°; the celestial horizon has a zenith distance of 90°.

Zeno (zē'nō), d. 491, Roman emperor of the East (474-491). An Isaurian, he succeeded his son Leo II and was the son-in-law of Leo I. During his reign he suppressed several revolts. He was driven from his throne for a period of 20 months (475-76) by the usurper BASILISCUS. One of his first acts was to conclude (476) a peace with the Vandal king GAISERIC. He supported orthodox Christianity and attempted to reconcile the Monophysites to the decrees of the Council of Chalcedon through his *Henotikon* (482), a compromise, which only provoked fresh controversy. Zeno was forced to recognize the de facto rule of ODOACER in Italy and to grant him the title of patrician. He freed the East from the raids of the OSTROGOTHS by encouraging the invasion of Italy by THEODORIC THE GREAT (488). Zeno was succeeded by Anastasius I.

Zenobia (zĭnō'bēə), d. after 272, queen of PALMYRA. She was of Arab stock and was the wife of Septimius ODENATHUS. He was murdered, probably through her contrivance, and she obtained rule of his lands in the name of her son. She expanded the territories further to rule E Asia Minor, Syria, N Mesopotamia, and even Egypt. Her ambition outran her prudence, and after she had dared to call her son emperor, the Romans under AURELIAN marched against her, took (272) Palmyra, and captured her. She was brought to Rome and exhibited at Aurelian's triumph. Later she was pensioned and lived in retirement at Tibur. By her beauty and intelligence, Zenobia attracted much admiration and sympathy, but her name has also been a symbol of ruthless arrogance.

Zeno of Citium (zē'nō, sĭsh'ēəm), c.334–c.262 B.C., Greek philosopher, founder of STOICISM. He left Cyprus and went to Athens, where he studied under the Cynics, whose teachings left an important impression on his own thought. Although his works have not survived, it is known that Zeno divided philosophy into logic, physics, and ethics, and taught that the first two must serve the last. He attempted to base his stern ethical system on the metaphysical and scientific teachings of Heraclitus, Aristotle, and others, and to forge from these elements a consistent philosophy. Zeno taught in Athens at the Stoa Poecile [Gr.,=painted porch]; his followers therefore came to be known as "Stoics," and his school as "the Porch."

Zeno of Elea (ē'lēə), c.490–c.430 B.C., Greek philosopher of the ELEATIC SCHOOL. He undertook to support in his only known work, fragments of which are extant, the doctrine of PARMENIDES by demonstrating that motion and multiplicity are logically impossible. The substance of his argument against multiplicity was that a whole must be composed of ultimate indivisible units, or it must be divisible ad infinitum. If the whole is divisible ad infinitum, there is a contradiction involved in the assumption that an infinite number of parts can be added up to a finite total. The essence of his argument against motion was that a moving body can never come to the end of a line, as it must first cover half the line, then half the remainder, and so on ad infinitum. The thrust of these arguments was to demonstrate, through logical reasoning, the error of commonsense notions of time and space. According to Aristotle, Zeno was the first to employ the dialectical method. Contemporary philosophers and mathematicians have taken renewed interest in Zeno's problems. See Adolf Grunbaum, *Modern Science and Zeno's Paradoxes* (1967).

Zephaniah (zĕf"ənī'ə). **1** Prophet, author of the book of ZEPHANIAH. **2** Father of HEN. **3** Father of JOSIAH **2**. **4** Singer. 1 Chron. 6.36. **5** Important priest at the time of the Captivity. 2 Kings 25.18; Jer. 21.1; 29.25; 52.24-27.

Zephaniah (zĕf"ənī'ə) or **Sophonias** (sōfōnī'əs), book of the Old Testament, 36th in the order of the Authorized Version, ninth of the books of the Minor Prophets. The prophet, who lived in the reign (c.640-608 B.C.) of King Josiah of Judah, traces his genealogy back to one Hizkiah (Hezekiah), thought by some to be King Hezekiah. The book consists of a denunciation of Judah for idolatry and wealth and a judgment of other nations; it ends with a prediction of salvation and the return from captivity of a remnant of Israel. Some scholars regard the last chapter, especially the last part (3.14-20) as a post-exilic addition. See H. E. Freeman, *Nahum, Zephaniah, Habakkuk* (1973).

Zephath (zē'făth), original name of HORMAH.

Zephathah (zĕf'əthə), valley, Palestine, of unknown location. 2 Chron. 14.10.

Zephi (zē'fī) or **Zepho** (-fō), duke of Edom. Gen. 36.11,15; 1 Chron. 1.36.

Zephon (zē'fŏn), son of Gad. Num. 26.15. Ziphion: Gen. 46.16.

Zephyr or **Zephyrus:** see EOS.

Zeppelin, Ferdinand, Graf von (zĕp'əlĭn, Ger. fĕr'-dēnänt gräf fən tsĕp''əlēn'), 1838-1917, German army officer and AIRSHIP inventor and builder. He entered the Prussian army in 1858 and served in the Seven Weeks War and in the Franco-Prussian War. He was an observer with the Union army during the American Civil War. In 1891 he retired from the Prussian army to devote himself to the building of motor-driven airships. He invented the first rigid airship in 1900, and in 1906 built one that had a speed of 30 mi (48 km) per hr. In 1908 he established at Friederichshafen the Zeppelin Foundation for the development of aerial navigation and the manufacture of airships.

Zer (zŭr), unidentified fortified city, SW of the Sea of Galilee. Joshua 19.35.

Zerah (zē'rə). **1** Younger of the twin sons of Judah and his daughter-in-law Tamar. Num. 26.20; 1 Chron. 2.6; 9.6; Neh. 11.24. Zarah: Gen. 38.30; 46.12. Zara: Mat. 1.3. The following patronymics are apparently derived from his name: Zarhite (Num. 26.13,20; Joshua 7.17; 1 Chron. 27.11); Izrahite (1 Chron. 27.8); Ezrahite (1 Kings 4.31 and in titles of Pss. 88 and 89). **2** Duke of Edom. Gen. 36.13,17; 1 Chron. 1.37. **3** Father of an Edomite king. Gen. 36.33; 1 Chron. 1.44. **4** Same as ZOHAR **2**. **5** Levite. 1 Chron. 6.21,41. **6** Leader of an Ethiopian invasion of Judah defeated by King Asa. 2 Chron. 14. He is not otherwise known in history.

Zerahiah (zĕr''ərī'ə). **1** Priestly ancestor of Ezra. 1 Chron. 6.6,51; Ezra 7.4. **2** Companion of Ezra in the Captivity. Ezra 8.4.

Zeravshan (zyĕrəfshän'), river, c.460 mi (740 km) long, rising in the Turkestan Range of the Pamir-Alai mountain system, S Central Asian USSR, in Tadzhikstan. It flows westward through the agricultural Zeravshan valley, then into Uzbekistan, past Samarkand and Bukhara, and disappears in the desert near the Amu Darya, N of Chardzhou. The valley, irrigated by the Katta-Kurgan reservoir, is one of the chief oases of Central Asia and is on the site of the ancient Sogdiana. The **Zeravshan Mountains,** forming the southern watershed of the river, rise to c.18,480 ft (5,630 m). The range has coal and ore deposits.

Zered (zē'rĕd) or **Zared** (zā'-), unidentified stream, E of the Dead Sea. Num. 21.12; Deut. 2.13.

Zeresh (zē'rĕsh), Haman's wife. Esther 5.10,14; 6.13.

Zereth (zē'rĕth), descendant of Judah. 1 Chron. 4.7.

Zeri (zē'rī), temple musician: see IZRI.

Zerka, river, Jordan: see ZARQA.

Zermatt (tsĕrmät'), village (1970 pop. 3,101), Valais canton, S Switzerland. Near the Matterhorn, Zermatt is a popular resort.

zero, that number which, when added to any number, leaves the latter unchanged; its symbol is 0. The introduction of zero into the DECIMAL SYSTEM was the most significant achievement in the development of a number system in which calculation with large numbers was feasible. Without it, modern astronomy, physics, and chemistry would have been impossible. The lack of such a symbol was one of the serious drawbacks of Greek mathematics. Its existence in the West is probably due to the Arabs, who, having obtained it from the Hindus, passed it on to European mathematicians in the latter part of the Middle Ages. The Maya of Central America and probably the Babylonians also invented zero. With the extension of the number system to negative as well as positive numbers, zero became the name for that position on the scale of integers between −1 and +1. It is used in this sense in speaking of zero degrees on the Fahrenheit and Celsius temperature scales; "absolute zero" is a term used by physicists and chemists to indicate the theoretically lowest possible temperature—a use reminiscent of zero as a symbol for nothing. Unlike other numbers, zero has certain special properties in connection with the four fundamental operations. By definition zero added to or subtracted from any number leaves the number unchanged. Any number multiplied by zero gives zero. Zero multiplied by or divided by any number (other than zero) is still zero. But division by zero is undefined; i.e., there is no number that is the value of a number divided by zero.

Żeromski, Stefan (stĕ'fän zhĕrôm'skē), 1864-1925, Polish writer. Family tragedies and emotional troubles contributed to the pessimistic strain evident in his revolutionary idealism. Among his novels are *The Homeless People* (1900), which won a national prize, *Ashes* (1904, tr. 1928), which dealt with cynicism and brutality in the Napoleonic era, and *Faithful River* (1912). Most of his works are intensely nationalistic. Much of Żeromski's life was spent in exile.

Zeror (zē'rôr), ancestor of Saul. 1 Sam. 9.1.

Zeruah (zēryo͞o'ə), mother of Jeroboam. 1 Kings 11.26.

Zerubbabel (zērŭb'əbəl), prince of Judah of the house of David, a governor of Jerusalem. He led a company returning from exile after the favorable edict of Cyrus. He was a contemporary of Haggai and Zechariah, under whose stimulating encouragement he finished the rebuilding of the Temple. He was an ancestor of St. Joseph. Ezra 2.2; 3.2,8; Hag. 1-2; Zech. 4.9,10. Zorobabel: Mat. 1.12,13; Luke 3.27. Some consider him identical with SHESHBAZZAR.

Zeruiah (zēro͞oī'ə), sister of David and mother of Joab. 2 Sam. 2.13,18; 1 Chron. 2.16.

Zesen, Philipp von (fē'lĭp fən tsā'zən), 1619-89, German poet and novelist. Zesen was a major champion of the purification of the German language. His works include *Deutscher Helikon* [German Helicon] (1640) and a phonetic orthography. Named poet laureate by Ferdinand III, he also wrote emotionally sensitive and philosophically interesting novels, including *Adriatische Rosemund* (1645), *Assenat* (1670), and the allegory *Simson* [Samson] (1679).

Zetham (zē'thăm), descendant of Gershom. 1 Chron. 23.8; 26.22.

Zethan (zē'thăn), descendant of Benjamin. 1 Chron. 7.10.

Zethar (zē'thər), chamberlain of King Ahasuerus. Esther 1.10.

Zethus (zē'thəs): see ANTIOPE **1**.

Zetkin, Klara (klä'rä tsĕt'kĭn), 1857-1933, German Communist leader and feminist. A teacher, she early joined the Social Democratic party and together with Rosa Luxemburg, became prominent in its radical wing. She was a founder and theoretician of the Socialist woman's movement, and established the party's paper for women, *Gleichheit*, which she edited until 1916. A member of the Spartacus party, in 1919 she was one of the chief founders of the German Communist party. She was a leader of the right-wing, Russophile element of the party, and was (1920-32) a Communist member of the Reichstag. During that period she spent much of her time in Russia. Zetkin was a profound student of Marxist thought; she wrote several works on socialism and on woman's rights. Her *Reminiscences of Lenin* was translated in 1929.

Zetland, Scotland: see SHETLAND.

Zeus (zo͞os), in Greek religion, son and successor of Cronus as supreme god. His mother, Rhea, immediately after his birth concealed him from Cronus, who, because he was fated to be overthrown by one of his children, ate all his offspring. Rhea gave him a stone wrapped in swaddling clothes which he devoured immediately, not suspecting that the infant Zeus still lived. Later, Zeus tricked Cronus into disgorging his brothers and sisters and led them in a successful revolt against their father (see TITAN). When lots were cast to divide the universe, the underworld went to Hades, the sea to Poseidon, and the heavens and earth to Zeus. Zeus was an amorous god. His first mate was probably Dione, but his official consort was his sister, Hera, who bore him Ares and Hebe. Zeus also loved Themis, Eurynome, Demeter, Mnemosyne, Leto, and Maia and fathered many gods. Famous among his mortal loves were Danaë, Leda, Semele, Thetis, Io, and Europa. His sons sired from mortal wives include Hercules, Dardanus, and Amphitryon. He was also the father of Athena, who was said to have sprung from his head. Supreme among the gods, Zeus, ruling from his court on Mt. Olympus, was the symbol of power, rule, and law. As the father god and the upholder of morality, he rewarded the good and punished the evil. The root meaning of Zeus is "bright" or "sky," and in this sense he was god of weather and fertility. Thus he was worshiped in connection with almost every aspect of life. The most famous weapon of Zeus was the thunderbolt, but, according to some legends, he also possessed the AEGIS. The Romans equated Zeus with their own supreme god, Jupiter (or Jove). See A. B. Cook, *Zeus* (3 vol., 1914-40).

Zeuss, Johann Caspar (yō'hän käs'pär tsois), 1806-56, German philologist. Zeuss's principal scholarly achievement was his establishment of the basis for the study of Celtic in his *Grammatica celtica* (1853, in Latin). Totally ignored by the academic world, he was still teaching in a high school when he died.

Zeuxis (zo͝ok'sĭs), fl. 5th cent. B.C., Greek painter. According to tradition he settled in Ephesus, was an intimate (possibly a pupil) of Apollodorus, and aided in developing a technique for painting light and shadow. Although none of his paintings survives, they are known through ancient writings. Pliny speaks of his competing with Parrhasius for realistic illusion.

Zeven: see KLOSTER-ZEVEN, CONVENTION OF.

Zeya (zā'ä, Rus. zyā'ə), river, c.800 mi (1,290 km) long, rising in the Stanovoy Range, Far Eastern USSR, and flowing south to join the Amur River at Blagoveshchensk. It carries gold in its upper reaches, and its basin has gold, graphite, and lignite deposits. The lower course flows through the rich agricultural Zeya-Bureya Plain.

Zeyer, Julius (yo͞o'lĭo͞os zā'ĕr, tsī'ər), 1841-1901, Czech writer. Restless, nostalgic, and mystical, Zeyer wrote ornate, almost decadent epic poetry based on ancient and medieval legends of many lands. His semi-autobiographical novel *Jan Maria Plojhar* (1880) deals with the tragic nature of the artist. His dramas, including *Raduz and Mahulena* (1898, tr. 1923), are celebrated as lyric poetry but are theatrically unsuccessful.

Zgierz (zgyĕsh), city (1970 pop. 42,838), E central Poland. A textile center, it also manufactures chemicals, textile machinery, and metals. Chartered about 1300, Zgierz grew after the textile industry was established there in 1818.

Zgorzelec, Poland: see GÖRLITZ, East Germany.

Zhdanov, Andrei Aleksandrovich (əndrā' əlyĭksän'drəvĭch zhdä'nôf), 1896-1948, Soviet Communist leader and general. A loyal supporter of Stalin, he was made (1934) secretary of the Leningrad Communist party and in 1939 became a full member of the politburo, the ruling body of the Communist party of the Soviet Union. He was a general in the Finnish-Russian War (1939-40), and in World War II he participated in the defense of Leningrad. After the war he was instrumental in formulating an aggressive, anti-Western foreign policy, and he organized (1947) the Cominform (Communist Information Bureau), aimed at better coordination of Communist efforts in Europe. Zhdanov was largely responsible for the extreme nationalism and strict political control of intellectuals in the postwar period. In Jan., 1953, a group of Jewish doctors was tried for the alleged murder of Zhdanov and other leading Soviet figures. The accusations, which reflected both intraparty struggles and anti-Semitism, were retracted after Stalin's death in March, 1953.

Zhdanov, city (1970 pop. 417,000), S European USSR, in the Ukraine, on the Sea of Azov and at the mouth of the Kalmius River. A seaport and railroad terminus, Zhdanov is also a large iron and steel center with machine plants, chemical works, and shipyards. Coal, salt, and grain are the chief exports. Founded in 1779 by Crimean Greeks, Zhdanov is on the site of an ancient Slavic settlement. It was called Mariupol until 1948.

Zhigatse: see JIH-K'A-TSE, China.

Zhiguli Mountains (zhēgo͞olyē'), wooded range, E European USSR, in the Samara bend of the Volga River at Kuybyshev. They rise to c.2,220 ft (680 m) and are rich in oil, which is piped to Kuybyshev. The mountains supply water for the Kuybyshev hydroelectric station.

Zhitomir (zhĭtô'mĕr), Ukr. *Zhytomyr,* city (1970 pop. 161,000), capital of Zhitomir oblast, SW European USSR, in the Ukraine, on the Teterev River, a tributary of the Dnepr. It is a road and rail junction in an agricultural area. Industries include lumber milling, food processing, granite quarrying, metalworking, and the manufacture of building materials. An old city on the trade route from Scandinavia to Constantinople, Zhitomir was known in 1240. It was part of the Kievan state and later passed to Lithuania (1320) and Poland (1569). Returned to Russia with the second partition of Poland (1793), it became an important provincial and trade center before the Bolshevik Revolution.

Zhivkov, Todor (tô'dôr zhĭvkôf'), 1911-, Bulgarian statesman. A Communist party member from 1932, he rose to prominence as a partisan leader during World War II and headed the coup against the monarchy in Sept., 1944. After the war, he became (1948) a member of the Communist party central committee. His steady rise culminated in 1954 when he became first secretary of the Communist party. He served (1962-71) as premier before assuming (1971) the post of president of Bulgaria. Although maintaining close relations with the Soviet Union during the 1960s, he sought to promote friendship with other Balkan nations, especially Turkey. He also stimulated Bulgarian economy through increased tourism, trade, and industry.

Zhukov, Georgi Konstantinovich (gēôr'gē kənstəntyē'nəvĭch zho͞o'kôf), 1896-1974, Soviet marshal.

He fought in the October Revolution (1917) and in the civil war (1918–20), which brought the Bolsheviks to power, and saw action against the Japanese on the Manchurian border (1938–39) and in the Finnish-Russian War. Promoted to full general in 1940, he was briefly (1941) chief of the general staff. In Oct., 1941, he replaced Semyon Timoshenko as commander of the central front and conducted the defense of Moscow. Made commander (1942) on the southwestern front, Zhukov defeated the Germans at Stalingrad (1943) and, with Marshal Voroshilov, lifted the siege of Leningrad. He led the offensive of 1944 and the final assault on Germany in 1945, capturing Berlin (April) and becoming commander of the Russian occupation zone in Germany. In 1946 Zhukov received command of the Russian ground forces, but in 1947 he was demoted to command the Odessa military district. After Stalin's death, Zhukov became deputy defense minister (1953) and defense minister (1955). He supported Nikita KHRUSHCHEV against the "anti-party faction" that tried to oust him in 1957, and was named (June, 1957) a full member of the central committee of the Communist party. In Oct.,1957, he was relieved of his ministry and dropped from the central committee by Khrushchev. After Khrushchev was deposed (1964) Zhukov began to appear in public again. See his memoirs (tr. 1971); *Marshal Zhukov's Greatest Battles*, ed. by H.E. Salisbury (tr. 1969); biography by O. P. Chaney, Jr. (1971).

Zhukovsky, Vasily Andreyevich (vəsē'lyē əndrā'əvĭch zho͝okôf'skē), 1783–1852, Russian poet and translator. Zhukovsky wrote fine lyrics and odes, including the patriotic poem "The Bard in the Camp of the Russian Warriors" (1812), but is important chiefly for his translations. He introduced into Russia the works of English, French, and German poets and also gave Russian verse a new quality of flexibility, subtlety, and grace. Zhukovsky was tutor to the future Czar Alexander II, who was influenced by his liberal ideas.

Zia (zī'ə), descendant of Gad. 1 Chron 5.13.

Ziba (zī'bə), servant of Saul. 2 Sam. 9; 16.1–4; 19.17,29.

Zibeon (zĭb'ēən). **1** Grandfather of Esau's wife Aholibamah. Gen. 36.2. **2** Son of Seir and father of Anah. Gen. 36.20,24; 1 Chron. 1.38,40. They may be the same person.

Zibia (zĭb'ēə), descendant of Benjamin. 1 Chron. 8.9.

Zibiah (zĭb'ēə), mother of Joash of Judah. 2 Kings 12.1; 2 Chron. 24.1.

Zichri (zĭk'rī). **1** Levite. 1 Chron. 9.15. Apparently the same as ZABDI **4**. **2** Ephraimite hero. 2 Chron. 28.7. **3** Priest after the return to Jerusalem. Neh. 12.17. **4, 5, 6, 7, 8, 9, 10, 11, 12** Israelites mentioned once only in genealogies. Ex. 6.21; 1 Chron. 8.19,23,27; 26.25; 27.16; 2 Chron. 17.16; 23.1; Neh. 11.9.

Ziddim (zĭd'ĭm), unlocated city, W of the Sea of Galilee. Joshua 19.35.

Zidkijah (zĭdkī'jə), sealer of the Covenant. Neh. 10.1.

Ziegfeld, Florenz (flôr'ənz zēg'fĕld), 1869–1932, American theatrical producer, b. Chicago. In 1907 he first produced the *Ziegfeld Follies,* for 24 years an annual revue famous for its extraordinarily elaborate staging, variety of performers, and chorus of beautiful girls. Anna HELD, Billie Burke, Fannie Brice, Eddie Cantor, Will Rogers, and W. C. Fields were among his stars. His other spectacular productions included *Sally, Rio Rita, Rosalie, Show Boat,* and *Bitter Sweet.* He was married to Anna Held from 1897 to 1913 and in 1914 married Billie Burke. See Marjorie Farnsworth, *The Ziegfeld Follies* (1956).

Ziegler, Karl (tsē'glər), 1898–1973, German chemist. Educated at the Univ. of Marburg, he taught at Heidelberg and Halle and for a short period at the Univ. of Chicago. He became director of the Max Planck Institute for Coal Research at Mülheim an der Ruhr in 1944. He shared the 1963 Nobel Prize in Chemistry with Giulio Natta for developing a system to control polymerizing, or uniting, of simple hydrocarbons into large molecule substances with important commercial uses, especially in the development of plastics.

Zielona Gora (zhĕlô'nä go͞o'rä), Ger. *Grünberg,* city (1970 pop. 73,156), capital of Zielona Gora prov., W Poland. It is a railroad junction and has lignite mines. Famous for its wines, the city also produces railroad cars, woolen textiles, machinery, and foodstuffs. Founded in the 13th cent., Zielona Gora became a prominent town on the trade route from Berlin to Upper Silesia. The city retains a 13th-century church and a 14th-century town hall.

ziggurat (zĭg'o͝orăt), form of temple common to the Sumerians, Babylonians and Assyrians. The earliest examples date from the end of the 3d millenium B.C., the latest from the 6th cent. B.C. The ziggurat was a pyramidal structure, built in receding tiers upon a rectangular, oval, or square platform, with a shrine at the summit. The core of the ziggurat was of sun-baked bricks, and the facings were of fired bricks, often glazed in different colors, which are thought to have had cosmological significance. Access to the summit shrine was provided by a series of ramps on one side or by a continuous spiral ramp from base to summit. The number of tiers ranged from two to seven. Notable examples are the ruins at Ur and Khorsabad in Mesopotamia. Similar structures were built by the Mayan cultures of Central America.

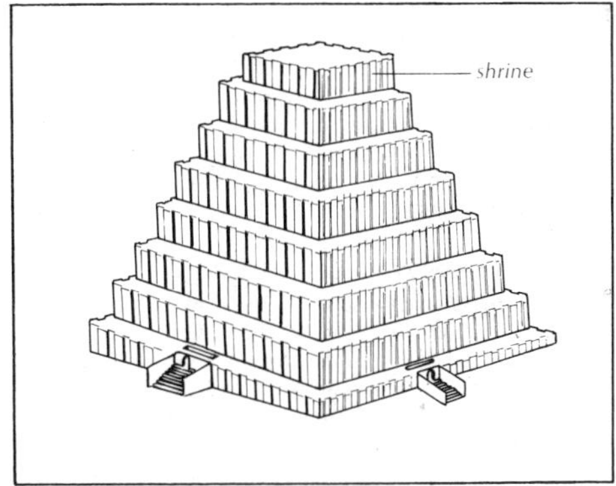

Ziggurat

Ziguinchor (zēgăNshôr'), city (1967 est. pop. 46,000), SW Senegal, a port on the Casamance River. Located in a rice-growing region, the city produces peanut oil, frozen fish, and orange juice and is an outlet to the sea for the shipment of peanuts and other products of the southern hinterlands. Ziguinchor was occupied by the French in 1888. The city has a mechanical training and crafts school and is the seat of a Roman Catholic bishopric.

Ziha (zī'hə), Nethinim family. Ezra 2.43; Neh. 7.46; 11.21.

Ziklag (zĭk'lăg), place of ancient Palestine, probably S of Beersheba, given to David by a Philistine ruler when he was in flight from Saul. David stayed there a while. Joshua 15.31; 19.5; 1 Sam. 27.6; 30.14,26; 2 Sam. 1.1; 4.10; 1 Chron. 12.1,20; Neh. 11.28.

Zillah (zĭl'ə), a wife of Lamech. Gen. 4.19–24.

Zillertal Alps (tsĭl'ərtäl"), range of the E Alps astride the Austro-Italian border and extending 35 mi (56 km) NE into the Tyrol. The range rises to 11,555 ft (3,522 m) in the Hockfeiler, on the international line. The Brenner Pass forms the divide between the Zillertal Alps and the Ötztal Alps. The Zillertal is noted for its magnificent scenery.

Zilpah (zĭl'pə), Leah's maid, mother of two of Jacob's sons. Gen. 30.9–13.

Zilthai (zĭl'thī, zĭlthā'ī). **1** Descendant of Benjamin. 1 Chron. 8.20. **2** Captain who came to David at Ziklag. 1 Chron. 12.20.

Zimbabwe (zĭmbäb'wā) [Bantu,=stone houses], ruined city, SE Rhodesia, near Fort Victoria. It was discovered by European explorers c.1870, and some believed it the biblical Ophir, where King Solomon had his mines. From 1890 to 1900 some 100,000 gold mining claims were staked out there, but all proved barren. Modern archaeological evidence has shown that Zimbabwe was first occupied by the earliest Iron Age people in the 3d cent. It was abandoned sometime thereafter until it was reoccupied in the late 9th cent. or early 10th cent. The remaining ruins include a massive wall, constructed in the 11th cent., a strong fortress, nearby dwellings, and an elliptically shaped enclosure, commonly called the Temple. The buildings were once richly decorated with stone carvings and gold and copper ornaments. Archaeologists believe that the city was constructed by a local African culture with little outside influence. See Gertrude Caton-Thompson, *The Zimbabwe Culture* (1970).

Zimbalist, Efrem (ĕ'frəm zĭm'bəlĭst), 1889–1970, Russian-American violinist. Zimbalist was a pupil of Leopold Auer at the St. Petersburg Conservatory. He made his debut in Berlin in 1907, toured Europe, and made his American debut in 1911. His concert career was enormously successful; he did much to revive interest in early violin music. In 1914 he married Alma GLUCK. He joined the faculty of the Curtis Institute of Music, Philadelphia, in 1928 and from 1941 to 1961 was its director. In 1943 he married Mary Louise Curtis Bok, founder of the institute. He has composed music for violin, piano, and orchestra.

Zimmah (zĭm'ə), Levitical family. 1 Chron. 6.20,42; 2 Chron. 29.12.

Zimmermann note, secret telegram sent on Jan. 16, 1917, by German foreign secretary Arthur Zimmermann to Count Johann von Bernstorff, the German ambassador to the United States. In it Zimmermann said that in the event of war with the United States, Mexico should be asked to enter the war as a German ally. In return, Germany promised to restore to Mexico the lost territories of Texas, New Mexico, and Arizona. British intelligence intercepted and deciphered the telegram and sent it to President Woodrow Wilson, who released it on March 1, 1917, to the press. The Zimmermann note helped turn U.S. public opinion against Germany during World War I and strengthened the advocates of U.S. entry into the war. See B. W. Tuchman, *The Zimmermann Telegram* (1966).

Zimmern, Sir Alfred Eckhard (ĕk'härt, zĭm'ərn), 1879–1957, English historian. He wrote *The Greek Commonwealth* (1911), a masterly study of the social history of ancient Athens. Also prominent in international affairs, he assisted the League of Nations in official capacities and later helped organize UNESCO. He was professor of international relations at Oxford (1930–44) and director of the School of International Studies at Geneva (1925–39). He wrote numerous works on international relations and Greek history.

Zimran (zĭm'răn), son of Abraham and Keturah. Gen. 25.2; 1 Chron. 1.32.

Zimri (zĭm'rī). **1** King of Israel for a few days. He was one of Elah's generals; he killed the king and held the throne until OMRI rebelled. 1 Kings 16.8–19. **2** Israelite killed with COZBI. **3** Same as ZABDI **2**. **4** Descendant of Saul. 1 Chron. 8.36; 9.42. **5** In an obscure passage the name, apparently, of a tribe. Jer. 25.25.

Zin, wilderness through which the Israelites wandered, SW of the Dead Sea. Num. 13.21; 20.1; 27.14; 33.36; 34.3,4; Deut. 32.51; Joshua 15.1,3.

Zina (zī'nə), variant of ZIZAH.

zinc, metallic chemical element; symbol Zn; at. no. 30; at. wt. 65.37; m.p. 419.58°C; b.p. 907°C; sp. gr. 7.133 at 25°C; valence +2. Zinc is a lustrous bluish-white metal. It is found in group IIb of the PERIODIC TABLE. It is brittle and crystalline at ordinary temperatures, but when heated to between 110°C and 150°C it becomes ductile and malleable; it can then be rolled into sheets. It is a fairly reactive metal. Although it is not abundant in nature, it is of great commercial importance. It is used principally for GALVANIZING iron, but is also important in the preparation of certain alloys, e.g., BABBITT METAL, BRASS, GERMAN SILVER, and sometimes BRONZE. It is used for the negative plates in certain electric batteries and for roofing and gutters in building construction. Since the metal reacts with dilute mineral acid to liberate hydrogen, it is often used for this purpose in the laboratory. Zinc compounds are numerous and are widely used. Perhaps most important is ZINC OXIDE, or zinc white, a versatile compound with many uses. Other zinc compounds include zinc chloride, used as a wood preservative, in soldering fluxes, as a mordant in dyeing textiles, and in adhesives and cements; and zinc sulfide, used in making LITHOPONE as well as television screens and X-ray apparatus. The chromate, zinc yellow, serves as a pigment; sodium zincate, as a water softener and as a flocculating agent in water purification. The crystalline sulfate is known commonly as white vitriol. Zinc is essential to the growth of many kinds of organisms, both plant and animal. It is a constituent of insulin, which is used in the treatment of diabetes. Chief sources of zinc are the sulfide ore, zinc blende, or SPHALERITE (called also blende or "black Jack"); zincite, an oxide; calamine, a silicate; and smithsonite, the zinc carbonate. Zinc ores are widely and abundantly distributed throughout the world. The United States is the leading producer. The metallurgy of zinc depends upon the ore used. The sulfide ore is roasted to the oxide, then mixed with coal and heated to 1,200°C. The zinc vaporizes and is condensed outside the reaction chamber and cast into blocks called spelter. In another method the ore is processed by flotation, filtering, roasting, and leaching; the resulting solution is filtered and the zinc removed by electrolysis.

zinc oxide, chemical compound, ZnO, that is nearly insoluble in water but soluble in acids or alkalies. It occurs as white hexagonal crystals or a white powder commonly known as zinc white. Zinc white is used as a pigment in paints; less opaque than LITHO-

PONE, it remains white when exposed to hydrogen sulfide or ultraviolet light. It is also used as a filler for rubber goods and in coatings for paper. Chinese white is a special grade of zinc white used in artists' pigments. Because it absorbs ultraviolet light, zinc oxide can be used in ointments, creams, and lotions to protect against sunburn. Crystalline zinc oxide exhibits the piezoelectric effect, is luminescent, and is light sensitive. Zinc oxide occurs in nature as the mineral zincite. Zinc peroxide, $ZnO_2 \cdot \frac{1}{2}H_2O$, is a white to yellow powder used in antiseptic ointments.

zinc sulfate, chemical compound $ZnSO_4$, a very water soluble, transparent, colorless, crystalline compound. It is commonly used as the heptahydrate, $ZnSO_4 \cdot 7H_2O$, and is commonly called white vitriol; it occurs naturally as the mineral goslarite, and can be prepared by reacting zinc with sulfuric acid. It is used to supply zinc in animal feeds, fertilizers, and agricultural sprays; in making LITHOPONE; in coagulation baths for rayon; in electrolyte for zinc plating; as a mordant in dyeing; as a preservative for skins and leather; and in medicine as an astringent and emitic.

zinc white: see ZINC OXIDE.

Zinder (zĭn'dər), town (1970 est. pop. 24,000), S Niger. It is the trade center for an agricultural region where grains, manioc, and peanuts are grown, and cattle and sheep are raised. Manufactures include millet flour, beverages, and tanned goods. Zinder was situated on an old trans-Saharan caravan route that connected N Nigeria with the African coast as early as the 11th cent. The walled town was the capital of a Muslim state controlled by BORNU from the 16th to the mid-19th cent. Zinder was conquered by the French in 1899 and during World War I was the scene of an unsuccessful TUAREG uprising against French control. The town grew after 1920, when nomads began settling there in large numbers, and from 1922 to 1926 it served as the capital of the French Niger colony. Parts of the old city wall and the 19th-century palace of the ruler of Zinder still stand.

Zinjanthropus (zĭnjăn'thrəpəs): see AUSTRALOPITHECUS.

zinnia, any species of the genus *Zinnia* of the family Compositae (COMPOSITE family), native chiefly to Mexico, though some range as far north as Colorado and as far south as Guatemala. The common zinnia of gardens (*Z. elegans*), called also youth-and-old-age, is a rather coarse, easily cultivated annual, popular as a cut flower for its warm colors—ranging from white and yellow to red and purple—and for its bold, stiff aspect. There are various forms in cultivation, including dwarfed, curled, and double varieties. The zinnia is the state flower of Indiana. Zinnias are classified in the division MAGNOLIOPHYTA, class Magnoliopsida, order Asterales, family Compositae.

Zinoviev, Grigori Evseyevich (grĭgô'rē yĭfsyā'əvĭch zēnô'vēĕf), 1883–1936, Russian Communist leader, originally named Radomyslsky. He joined the Russian Social Democratic Labor party in 1901 and sided with Vladimir Lenin's Bolshevik faction after 1903 (see BOLSHEVISM AND MENSHEVISM). He conducted agitation in St. Petersburg (now Leningrad) during the 1905 revolution and was elected to the central committee of the party in 1907. After a brief period in jail, he went abroad in 1908. Zinoviev was one of Lenin's closest collaborators in exile (1909–17) and returned to Russia with him after the February, 1917, revolution. He and Lev KAMENEV opposed Lenin's plan for the Bolshevik seizure of power in Nov., 1917 (Oct., 1917, O.S.), which they regarded as premature, but they were outvoted and abided by the majority decision. After the Bolshevik takeover, Zinoviev served as head of the COMINTERN (1919-26) and as a member of the Communist party politburo (1921-26). On Lenin's death (1924), Zinoviev, Kamenev, and Joseph STALIN formed a ruling triumvirate. Zinoviev led the triumvirate's attack on Leon TROTSKY, calling for his expulsion from the party. After an initial victory over Trotsky (1924), Stalin, in an effort to consolidate his own power, turned against Zinoviev and Kamenev, defeating them and their so-called left opposition in 1925. Zinoviev and Kamenev then allied themselves with Trotsky (1926), but to no avail. Zinoviev was removed from his party posts in 1926 and expelled from the party in 1927. He recanted and was readmitted in 1928 but wielded little influence. Many features of the Zinoviev-Kamenev program, emphasizing rapid industrialization and collectivization, were incorporated (1928) in Stalin's first FIVE-YEAR PLAN. In 1935, Zinoviev was sentenced to 10 years' imprisonment purportedly for giving his encouragement to the assassins of Sergei KIROV. Accused (1936) of conspiring to overthrow the government, he was the chief defendant in the first of the trials held by Stalin, which resulted in Zinoviev's execution along with Kamenev and 13 other old Bolsheviks. The so-called ZINOVIEV LETTER was published (1924) in the British press. It was allegedly written by Zinoviev in his capacity as Comintern chief and contained instructions for Communist revolution in England. Although almost certainly a forgery, the Zinoviev letter helped to defeat Britain's first Labour government in elections that year.

Zinovievsk: see KIROVOGRAD, USSR.

Zinsser, Hans (zĭns'ər), 1878–1940, American bacteriologist, b. New York City, grad. Columbia (B.A., 1899; M.D., 1903). He was professor of bacteriology at Stanford (1911–13), Columbia (1913–23), and Harvard medical school (from 1923). A noted epidemiologist, he was a leader in combating typhus and served with the American Red Cross sanitary commission during the 1915 typhus epidemic in Serbia and with the League of Nations sanitary commission (1923) in the USSR. Zinsser isolated the germ of the European type of typhus, and with his colleagues at Harvard, he developed (1940) a method for mass production of the vaccine. He wrote a popular work on typhus, *Rats, Lice, and History* (1935); several textbooks, including *Infection and Resistance* (1914; 4th ed. rev., *Resistance to Infectious Disease,* 1931; 5th ed. rev., *Immunity,* 1939); and the autobiographical *As I Remember Him* (1940).

Zinzendorf, Nikolaus Ludwig, Graf von (nē'kōlous lo͞ot'vĭkh gräf fən tsĭn'tsəndôrf), 1700–1760, German churchman, patron and bishop of the refounded Moravian Church, b. Dresden. Reared under Pietistic influences, he was early in sympathy with the persecuted and almost extinct Moravian Brethren (often called Bohemian Brethren), to whom he offered refuge (1722) on his Saxony estates. The colony was called Herrnhut. Zinzendorf wanted the Herrnhutters to be a group within the Lutheran Church, influencing others toward deeper religious experience, but he yielded to their insistence upon refounding the ancient Moravian Brethren. He was ordered (1736) to leave Saxony because of his religious activities, and for many years thereafter he traveled about, spreading the views of the reorganized Moravian Church, of which he became bishop in 1737. In London he was cordially received (1737) by John Wesley. In America (1741–43) he was active in the noted Moravian settlement at Bethlehem, Pa., and in establishing congregations in other places in E Pennsylvania. He made attempts to gather the German sects of that colony into a unified church. In 1747, Zinzendorf was allowed to return to Herrnhut. He preached (1749–55) in England and then returned again to Herrnhut, where he spent his last years in pastoral work. His emphasis on the role of emotion in religion profoundly influenced 19th-century Protestant theology, especially the work of Friedrich Schleiermacher. See Williston Walker, *Great Men of the Christian Church* (1908); biography by J. R. Weinlick (1956); study by A. J. Lewis (1962).

Zion (zī'ən) or **Sion** (sī'ən), part of JERUSALEM. It is defined in the Bible as the City of David. 2 Sam. 5.7. Christian tradition names the southwestern hill of the city as Zion, but there is controversy about the identity. Originally the name referred to the Jebusite fortress conquered by David, on the southeastern hill of Jerusalem. 1 Kings 8.1. The name is symbolic of Jerusalem, of the Promised Land, of Israel's hope of returning to Palestine (hence the term *Zionism*), and, among Christians, of heaven.

Zion, city (1970 pop. 17,268), Lake co., extreme NE Ill., on Lake Michigan; inc. 1902. Television sets, clothing, metal fittings, and food products are made, and there is a printing and publishing house. Zion was founded in 1901 by John Alexander Dowie of the Christian Catholic Church. Until 1935 it was a communal society with a theocratic government; all property was owned by the Church. Today the Christian Catholic Church is still a dominant force in the community. Of interest are the Zion Hotel (1902), and Shiloh House, the mansion built (1902) for the Dowie family. A nuclear-power plant is in the city, and Illinois Beach State Park is nearby.

Zionism, movement for reconstituting a Jewish national state in Palestine. From the time of the destruction of their state by Rome in A.D. 70, the Jews always wished to be restored to Palestine. The persecutions they endured combined with their sense of religious identity to keep them a distinct group wherever they settled. The faith that the Messiah would deliver Israel from its exile remained fresh, and Jews repeatedly followed false Messiahs, such as SABBATAI ZEVI. While some colonies of scholars had always lived in Palestine on the charity of Jews abroad, the bulk of Jewry took no practical steps to return to Palestine. The growth of a liberal attitude towards Jews in the 18th and 19th cent. led to some degree of assimilation with European national cultures, but this process was limited by rising nationalist feeling in Western Europe in the 19th cent. The larger number of Eastern European Jews had even less inducement to assimilate with the national cultures in view of the poverty and persecution that they suffered under the Austrian and Russian empires. The Zionist movement was largely cultural until Theodor HERZL began to organize a movement for the formation of a Jewish nation state as a solution to the Jewish problem and to ANTI-SEMITISM. In 1897 he called the first World Zionist Congress at Basel. The meeting set up Zionist organizations in most countries where there were large Jewish populations. The first issue to split the Zionist movement was whether Palestine was essential to a Jewish state. A majority of the delegates to the 1905 congress felt that it was essential and rejected the British offer of a homeland in Uganda. The opposition, the Territorialists led by Israel Zangwill, withdrew on the grounds that an immediate refuge for persecuted Jews was needed. The Zionist movement, now largely under the leadership of Chaim WEIZMANN, obtained few concessions from the Turkish sultan, who ruled Palestine; but it did achieve a signal success in 1917, when Great Britain was at war with Turkey as one of the Central Powers. The British government issued the Balfour Declaration (see BALFOUR, ARTHUR JAMES), which promised to help establish a national home for the Jewish people in Palestine. Great Britain was given a mandate of Palestine in 1920, in part to implement the Balfour Declaration. Jewish colonization vastly increased in the early years of the mandate (see PALESTINE for the period up to 1945), but soon the British limited its interpretation of the declaration, mainly because of Arab pressure. There were disputes in the Zionist movement on how to counter the British position. The Revisionists, led by Vladimir JABOTINSKY, favored large-scale immigration to Palestine to force the creation of a Jewish state. The most conciliatory faction was the General Zionists (representing the original national organizations), who generally remained friendly to Great Britain. After World War II the Zionist movement intensified its activities. The sufferings of the European Jews at the hands of the Germans demanded the opening of a refuge; the stiffening opposition of the Arabs increased the urgency. At this time the World Zionist Congress was divided, the Revisionists demanding all Palestine and the General Zionists reluctantly accepting the United Nations plan to partition Palestine (see ISRAEL). After the Jewish state was proclaimed (May 14, 1948) the World Zionist Congress was separated entirely from the Israeli government. This gave Israel absolute sovereignty and answered the criticism of those who maintained that Israel was a country to which Zionists throughout the world owed allegiance. The Zionist movement today facilitates immigration to Israel and supports cultural and educational activities outside of Israel. See Chaim Weizmann, *Trial and Error* (1949, repr. 1972); Israel Cohen, *A Short History of Zionism* (1951); Ben Halpern, *The Idea of the Jewish State* (2d ed. 1969); Walter Laqeur, *A History of Zionism* (1972).

Zionites: see CHRISTIAN CATHOLIC CHURCH.

Zion National Park, 147,035 acres (59,505 hectares), SW Utah; est. 1919. The park is noted for its many scenic trails and its vividly colored cliffs, rock formations, and deep canyons. The fingerlike, box-shaped Koblob Canyons have sheer 1,500-ft (457-m) walls. Zion Canyon, the park's main attraction, is a 15 mi (24 km) long, .5 mi (.8 km) deep, multicolored gorge cut by the Virgin River. Vegetation in the park ranges from desert type in the canyons to forests on the mesas. Small animals thrive in the area, and mule deer are common.

Zior (zī'ôr), hill town, S Palestine, the modern Siir (Jordan), NE of Hebron. Joshua 15.54.

Ziph (zĭf). **1** Judahite. 1 Chron. 4.16. **2** Unidentified city, S Palestine. Joshua 15.24. **3** City, S Palestine, the modern Khirbat Zif (Jordan), SSE of Hebron. David hid at Ziph in his flight from Saul. Joshua 15.55; 1 Sam. 23.14,15,19,24; 26.1,2; title of Ps. 54.

Ziphah (zī'fə), son of Jehaleleel. 1 Chron. 4.16.

Ziphion (zĭf'ēŏn), variant of ZEPHON.

Ziphron (zĭf′rŏn), unlocated landmark, extreme N Palestine. Num. 34.9.

Zippor (zĭp′pôr), father of Balak, king of Moab. Num. 22.2.

Zipporah (zĭp′ərə), daughter of Jethro and wife of Moses. Ex. 2.16-22; 4.18-26; 18.1-6.

zirconium (zərkō′nēəm), metallic chemical element; symbol Zr; at. no. 40; at. wt. 91.22; m.p. about 1850°C; b.p. about 3600°C; sp. gr. 6.5 at 20°C; valence +2, +3, or +4. Zirconium is a very strong, malleable, ductile, lustrous silver-gray metal. At ordinary temperatures it has a hexagonal close-packed crystalline structure. Its chemical and physical properties are similar to those of titanium, the element above it in group IVb of the PERIODIC TABLE. Zirconium is extremely resistant to heat and corrosion. It forms a number of compounds, among them zirconate (ZrO_3^{-2}) and zirconyl (ZrO^{+2}) salts. The most important compound is the oxide zirconia (ZrO_2), used extensively as a refractory material in furnaces and crucibles, in ceramic glazes, and, formerly, in gas mantles. It occurs in nature as the silicate ($ZrSiO_4$) and is used as a gemstone; it may be clear or colored, and is usually called zircon or HYACINTH. Zirconium compounds also have minor uses as catalysts, in the dye, textile, plastics, and paint industries, and in pharmaceuticals such as poison ivy lotions. The metal also has many uses, among them in photographic flashbulbs and surgical instruments, in the removal of residual gases from electronic vacuum tubes, and as a hardening agent in alloys, especially steel. A major use of the metal is in NUCLEAR REACTORS. It is employed in tubes for cladding URANIUM oxide fuel. It is well suited for this purpose because it is corrosion resistant and does not readily absorb thermal neutrons. It is specially purified to remove hafnium, which absorbs neutrons much more readily. It is usually alloyed with other metals to make it more corrosion resistant for these uses. Zirconium is a fairly abundant element and is widely distributed in minerals but is never found uncombined in nature. It always occurs with hafnium, which has almost identical chemical properties. The chief ore is zircon (the silicate); baddeleyite (the oxide) also has some importance. Zircon is recovered (along with monazite, ilmenite, and rutile) from certain beach sands in New South Wales, Australia, and near Jacksonville, Fla. The metal is produced by the Kroll process. The zircon is treated with carbon in an electric furnace to form a cyanonitride, which is in turn treated with chlorine gas to form the volatile tetrachloride. The tetrachloride is carefully purified by sublimation in an inert atmosphere and is then chemically reduced to metal sponge by reaction with molten magnesium. The spongy metal is cleaned and further processed into ingots. Special care is taken to exclude hydrogen, nitrogen, and oxygen, which make the metal brittle. If the metal is too brittle to be worked, it can be further purified by the Van Arkel-de Boer process, in which the crude metal is reacted with iodine to form volatile iodides that are thermally decomposed on a hot wire, resulting in pure crystalline zirconium. The commercial metal usually contains between 1% and 3% hafnium; for nuclear reactor use the hafnium is usually removed by solvent extraction from the tetrachloride. Zirconium was discovered as the oxide zirconia in the mineral zircon by M. H. Klaproth in 1789 and was first isolated in impure form by J. J. Berzelius in 1824.

Ziro (zĭr′ō), town (1973 pop. 99,982), Arunachal Pradesh union territory, extreme NE India, in the Himalayas near the Tibetan border.

Zita (zē′tə, Ger. tsē′tä), 1892–, last empress of Austria and queen of Hungary. The daughter of Duke Robert of Parma, she was married (1911) to Archduke Charles Francis, who in 1916 became emperor as CHARLES I. She exercised great influence over her husband and was blamed for Charles's letters to her brother, SIXTUS OF BOURBON-PARMA, during World War I that corroborated French claims to Alsace-Lorraine. She was also blamed for Charles's attempts to regain his throne after the war. After her husband's death (1922), Zita brought up her large family in Belgium. She never renounced her ambition to see Archduke OTTO, her son, crowned king of Hungary and possibly emperor of Austria. From 1940 to 1949 Zita lived in the United States and in Canada; she later lived in Switzerland.

zither (zĭth′ər), stringed musical instrument, derived from the PSALTERY and the DULCIMER. It has a flat sound box over which are stretched from 30 to 45 strings; these are plucked with the fingers and a plectrum. In the 18th cent. one or both sides began to be curved to produce greater sonority. In the baroque era the zither was generally used by the peasants of Central Europe, and it remains the most popular instrument in the Tyrol. The term *zither* is

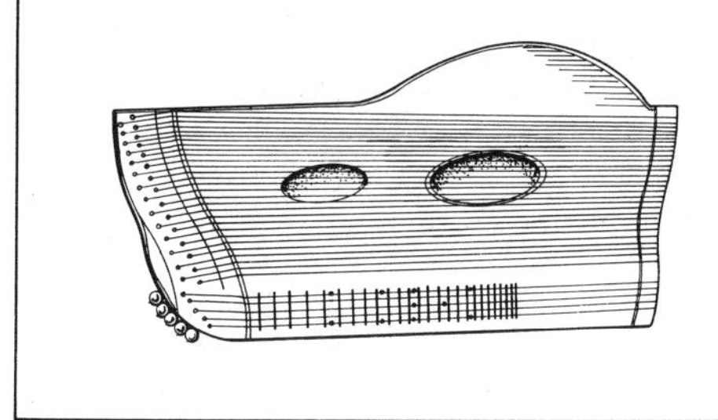

Zither

also used generically for various instruments, including the dulcimer, the psaltery, and several Oriental instruments. The dulcimer in use in the Kentucky mountains is, in fact, a zither.

Zittau (tsĭt′ou), city (1970 pop. 43,087), Dresden district, SE East Germany, on the Lusatian Neisse River, near the Polish and Czechoslovak borders. Manufactures include textiles, chemicals, machinery, and motor vehicles. An old Slavic settlement, Zittau was chartered in the 13th cent. In 1346 it joined the Lusatian League. It passed to Saxony in the early 17th cent. There are several medieval churches in the city.

Zituni: see LAMIA, Greece.

Ziz, pass or wadi, through which an allied army moved from the Dead Sea toward Jerusalem to attack Jehoshaphat. 2 Chron. 20.16.

Ziza (zī′zə). **1** Simeonite who participated in a raid on the pasturelands of Gedor. 1 Chron. 4.37. **2** Son of Rehoboam and Maachah. 2 Chron. 11.20.

Zizah (zī′zə), descendant of Gershom. 1 Chron. 23.11. In verse 10 he is called Zina.

Zizka, John (zĭs′kə), Czech *Jan Žižka* (yän zhĕsh′kä), d. 1424, Bohemian military leader and head of the Hussite forces during the anti-Hussite crusades of Holy Roman Emperor SIGISMUND. Before the HUSSITE WARS, which gave his military genius the opportunity to develop fully, Zizka served under various lords; he fought (1410) on the Polish side in the battle of Tannenberg, in which the Teutonic Knights were defeated. When the Hussite Wars broke out in 1420, Zizka was about 60 years old and blind in one eye. Having joined the Taborites (the radical Hussite wing), Zizka made TÁBOR in Bohemia into an almost impregnable fortress and led (July, 1420) the Taborite troops in their victory over Sigismund at Visehrad (now a part of Prague). In the following years he successfully withstood the anti-Hussite crusades and took one Catholic stronghold after another, continuing to command in person although he had become totally blind in 1421. He did not agree with the extreme religious views of the Taborites, and in 1423 formed his own Hussite wing, which, however, remained in close alliance with the Taborites. In the same year the tension between the Taborites and the moderate Utraquists, whose stronghold was at Prague, flared into open conflict, and late in 1424, Zizka led his army against Prague in order to compel that city to adhere to his uncompromising anti-Catholic policy. An armistice averted the outbreak of civil war between the two Hussite parties, which then decided on a joint expedition into Moravia under Zizka's command. Zizka died suddenly during the campaign. Although Zizka's fame is overshadowed by that of other commanders, he ranks with the great military innovators of all time. The bulk of his army consisted of peasants and townspeople, untrained in arms. Zizka did not attempt to make them adopt the conventional armament and tactics of the time, but let them make use of such weapons as iron-tipped flails and armored farm wagons, surmounted by small cannons of the howitzer type. His armored wagons, when used for offense, easily broke through the enemy lines, firing as they went, and thus enabled him to cut superior forces into pieces. When used for defense, the wagons were arranged into an impregnable barrier surrounding the foot soldiers; they also served to transport his men. Zizka thus fully anticipated modern motorized and tank warfare. It is only in recent times, however, that his military genius has been fully appreciated.

Zlatoust (zlətəo͞ost′), city (1970 pop. 181,000), E European USSR, on the Ai River in the S Urals. It is a rail terminus and an old metallurgical center. Besides steel mills, the city has metal-engraving works and factories that manufacture farm machinery, instruments, precision castings, small arms, abrasives, and clocks and watches. Zlatoust was founded in 1754 as one of Russia's first iron industry settlements.

Zlin: see GOTTWALDOV, Czechoslovakia.

Zn, chemical symbol of the element ZINC.

Znojmo (znoi′mō), Ger. *Znaim,* city (1970 pop. 26,538), S central Czechoslovakia, in Moravia. It is the center of an horticultural region; the city's industries produce ceramics, alcohol, textiles, and furniture. Chartered in 1226, it has several fine churches and a 15th-century town hall. At Znojmo, in 1809, an armistice was signed by the Austrians and the French after the French victory at Wagram.

Zoan: see TANIS, Egypt.

Zoar (zō′ər), at first named **Bela** (bē′lə), the only one of the Cities of the Plain (see SODOM) to escape destruction. Lot and his daughters took refuge here. It is probably now submerged in the southern end of the Dead Sea. Gen. 14.2,8; 19.19-30; Isa. 15.5; Jer. 48.34.

Zoar (zôr, zō′ər), village (pop. 228), Tuscarawas co., E central Ohio, on the Tuscarawas River; founded 1817, inc. 1884. It was founded by a group of Separatists from S Germany who fled religious persecution and, under the leadership of Joseph Michael Bimeler, emigrated to America. The Quakers received them kindly in Philadelphia and assisted them in obtaining land in Ohio. The village of Zoar was laid out, a communistic system was adopted to solve economic difficulties, and a strict moral and religious life was maintained. Flour and textile mills and other small industries were established, and the commune flourished. The Zoarites aided in the building of the Ohio and Erie Canal. After Bimeler's death (1853), the society declined, and in 1898 the communistic mode of life was abandoned. See Ohio Historical Society, *Zoar* (1970); E. O. Randall, *History of the Zoar Society* (1899), 3d ed. 1904, repr. 1972).

Zoba or **Zobah** (both: zō′bə), Aramaean state, NE of Palestine, at the time of Saul, David, and Solomon. It waged war on Israel. 1 Sam. 14.47; 2 Sam. 8.12; 10.6,8; 1 Chron. 18.3-9; Hamath-zobah: 2 Chron. 8.3. Aram-zobah in title of Ps. 60.

Zobebah (zōbē′bə), descendant of Judah. 1 Chron. 4.8.

zodiac (zō′dēăk) [Gr. *zoion*=animal], in astronomy, zone of the sky that includes about 8° on either side of the ECLIPTIC. The apparent paths of the sun, the moon, and the major planets all fall within this zone. The zodiac is divided into 12 equal parts of 30° each, each part being named for a constellation, each of which is represented by a sign and many of which have animal names. The constellations and their corresponding signs and dates are listed in the

Aries	*The Ram*	♈	*March 21–April 19*
Taurus	*The Bull*	♉	*April 20–May 20*
Gemini	*The Twins*	♊	*May 21–June 21*
Cancer	*The Crab*	♋	*June 22–July 22*
Leo	*The Lion*	♌	*July 23–Aug. 22*
Virgo	*The Virgin*	♍	*Aug. 23–Sept. 22*
Libra	*The Balance*	♎	*Sept. 23–Oct. 23*
Scorpio	*The Scorpion*	♏	*Oct. 24–Nov. 21*
Sagittarius	*The Archer*	♐	*Nov. 22–Dec. 21*
Capricornus	*The Goat*	♑	*Dec. 22–Jan. 19*
Aquarius	*The Water Bearer*	♒	*Jan. 20–Feb. 18*
Pisces	*The Fishes*	♓	*Feb. 19–March 20*

Signs of the zodiac

accompanying table. The zodiac serves as a convenient means of indicating the positions of the heavenly bodies. When the constellations of the zodiac were named about 2,000 years ago, the vernal equinox coincided with the beginning of the constellation Aries. For this reason, the first 30° section of the zodiac is called Aries; it extends eastward 30° from the vernal EQUINOX, which is therefore called the first point of Aries. However, because of the PRECESSION OF THE EQUINOXES, the vernal equinox has moved westward about 30° and now lies in the constellation Pisces; the zodiacal constellations thus no longer correspond to the segments of the zodiac represented by their signs. The constellations will again coincide with the sections of the zodiac in about 25,800 years. The zodiac probably had its origins among the Assyrians or Chaldaeans, although it may have originated among the Babylonians as early as 2000 B.C. It is of importance in ASTROLOGY.

zodiacal light, faint band of light sometimes seen in the western sky just after sunset, extending up from the horizon at the point where the sun has just set. It is caused by reflection of sunlight from tiny dust particles concentrated in the plane of the ECLIPTIC and thus appears in the region of the sky called the ZODIAC. Near the equator the zodiacal light sometimes seems to stretch completely across the sky.

Zoë (zō'ē), c.978–1050, Byzantine empress (1028–50), daughter and successor of Constantine VIII. Zoë was first married when she was 50 years old at the request of her father to insure stability in the empire. Her husband, ROMANUS III, soon neglected her and in 1034 was found murdered, probably by Zoë and her lover Michael. The same evening she married Michael, and he became Emperor Michael IV. He proved a capable ruler and eliminated Zoë from state affairs. Much of the government was exercised by his elder brother John, a eunuch of the court and a thoroughly corrupt man, but an able administrator and diplomat. On Michael's death (1041), his nephew, Michael V, became joint ruler with Zoë. He promptly sent his uncle John into exile and in 1042 banished Zoë to a convent. In response the people rose in rebellion, Zoë was recalled, and Michael was blinded and banished. At the same time Zoë's younger sister, Theodora, was crowned joint empress. A few months later (June, 1042), Zoë married Constantine IX, of a distinguished Byzantine family, who ruled jointly with the two sisters until Zoë's death. Under their rule the Byzantine court was a source of scandal but nontheless of intellectual brilliance. The chief event of the period was the final schism between the Eastern Church and the Western Church, brought about by the attacks of Michael Cerularius, patriarch of Constantinople, on the papacy and by the attacks of the legates of Pope Leo IX on the patriarchate. This resulted in mutual excommunication (1054). After Zoë's death in 1050, Constantine continued to rule jointly with Theodora; he died in 1055, and Theodora in 1056; Michael VI, a Byzantine nobleman who was chosen her successor, was forced to abdicate in 1057 in favor of Isaac I, founder of the Comnenus dynasty.

Zoffany, Johann (yō'hän zŏf'ənē), 1735–1810, English painter. After 12 years of study in Italy, Zoffany settled in England. He frequently painted conversation pieces, domestic tableaux filled with detailed, animated figures (see PORTRAITURE), that were influenced by Hogarth. His major full-length portraits include *Mrs. Oswald* (National Gall., London).

Zog (zôg), 1895–1961, king of Albania. Originally Ahmad Zogu, he came from a Muslim family and served in the Austrian army in World War I. He became Albanian minister of the interior in 1920, minister of war in 1921, and premier in 1922. A revolution in 1924 led to his flight, but he returned with Yugoslav backing and became (Jan., 1925) president of the Albanian republic. A constitution placed power in his hands, and opposition was soon crushed. In 1925, Zog turned to Italy for financial aid. The Treaty of Tirana (1926) gave Italian loans in return for Albanian concessions; a defensive military alliance followed one year later. In 1928, Zog was proclaimed king as Zog I. Albania's economy advanced during his reign, and a modern legal system was introduced. Zog attempted to avoid further Italian encroachment, but the appearance (1934) of an Italian fleet at Durazzo forced him into submission. In April, 1939, Italy invaded and quickly subdued Albania. Zog, who had married the Hungarian-American countess Geraldine Apponyi in 1938, fled to London with his queen and two-day-old son. Victor Emmanuel III, of Italy, was proclaimed king. He abdicated in 1943, but a Communist government gained control of Albania and proclaimed it (1946) a people's republic. Zog remained in exile in Egypt and in France, where he died.

Zohar (zō'här). **1** Father of the owner of the cave of MACHPELAH. **2** Son of Simeon. Gen. 46.10; Ex. 6.15. Zerah: 1 Chron. 4.24. For the book of Zohar, see CABALA.

Zoheleth (zōhē'lĕth), commemorative or sacred stone near EN-ROGEL. 1 Kings 1.9.

Zoheth (zō'hĕth), son of Ishi. 1 Chron. 4.20.

Zoilus (zō'ĭləs), c.400–c.320 B.C., Greek rhetorician and philosopher of Amphipolis. He is called Homeromastix [scourge of Homer], because of his denunciations of Homer as a purveyor of fables. He also criticized Isocrates and Plato, and his name has come to signify a carping critic.

zoisite: see TANZANITE.

Zola, Émile (āmēl' zôlä'), 1840–1902, French novelist. He was a professional writer and earned his living through journalism and his novels. About 1870 he became the apologist and most typical exponent of French naturalism. This literary school held that the novel should be scientific in a strict sense. Inspired by his readings in social history and medicine, Zola decided to apply scientific techniques and observations to the depiction of French society under the Second Empire. He composed a vast series of novels in which the characters and their social milieus are presented in minute and often sordid detail. Of his many novels, those considered most important are among the 20 that constitute the series *Les Rougon-Macquart* (1871–93), an account of the decay of a family as the result of heredity and environment, with special emphasis on alcoholism, disease, and degeneracy. Perhaps the best-known of these are *L'Assommoir* (1877, tr. *The Dram-Shop*), on lower-class life in Paris; *Nana* (1880); and *Germinal* (1885, tr. 1901), a "proletarian" novel on coal mining in N France. He also began the socialistic *Quatre Évangiles* [four gospels], of which he finished *Fécondité* (1899, tr. *Fruitfulness*, 1900), *Travail* (1901, tr. *Labor*, 1901), and *Vérité* (1903, tr. *Truth*, 1903). Zola had an ardent zeal for social reform. He was anti-Catholic and wrote many diatribes against the clergy and the Church. His part in the DREYFUS AFFAIR (notably his article, "J'accuse," 1898) was his most conspicuous public action, and he became the special object of the hatred of the anti-Dreyfus party. Prosecuted for libel (1898), he escaped to England, where he remained a few months until an amnesty enabled his return to France. He was accidentally asphyxiated in his bedroom after inhaling fumes from a blocked chimney. See studies by F. W. J. Hemmings (2d ed. 1966) and Angus Wilson (1952, repr. 1973).

Zollverein (tsôl'fərīn') [Ger.,=customs union], in German history, a customs union established to eliminate tariff barriers. Friedrich LIST first popularized the idea of a combination to abolish the customs barriers that were inhibiting trade among the numerous states of the GERMAN CONFEDERATION. In 1818, Prussia abolished internal customs and formed a North German Zollverein, which in 1834 became the German Zollverein after merging with two similar unions, the South German Zollverein and the Central German Trade Union, both founded in 1828. Customs barriers of member states were leveled, and a uniform tariff was instituted against nonmembers. The customs at foreign frontiers were collected on joint account, and the proceeds were distributed in proportion to the population and resources of the member states. A rival customs union, the Steuerverein of central Germany, was also organized in 1834. A series of treaties (1851–54) joined it to the Zollverein, which then comprised nearly all the German states except Austria, the two Mecklenburgs, and the Hanseatic towns. Prussia, despite the insistence of several states, was unwilling to admit Austria to the union, but the two countries negotiated a separate tariff treaty. After the AUSTRO-PRUSSIAN WAR (1866) a new agreement was reached by the members of the union. The newly formed NORTH GERMAN CONFEDERATION entered the Zollverein in a body, and the other German states also negotiated customs treaties with victorious Prussia. The constitution (1867) of the new Zollverein provided for a federal council of customs (*Zollbundesrat*), comprised of personal representatives of the several rulers, and for an elected customs parliament *(Zollparlament)*. In both bodies Prussia exercised predominant influence. In 1871 the laws and regulations of the Zollverein passed into the legislation of the newly created German Empire. Alsace-Lorraine entered the imperial customs area in 1872, and the Hanseatic cities joined in 1888. The Zollverein promoted the economic unification of Germany. See studies by J. R. MacDonald (1903, repr. 1972), W. O. Henderson (2d ed. 1959), and E. N. Roussakis (1968).

Zomba (zŏm'bə), town (1971 est. pop. 20,000), S Malawi, in the Shire Highlands. Until 1966 it was the national capital. European planters founded the town c.1880. It is the commercial center for a region growing cotton, coffee, and tobacco; tung oil is produced, and there is a hydroelectric power plant nearby. Zomba Plateau (c.7,000 ft/2,130 m high) is a popular summer resort.

zombi (zŏm'bē), in VOODOO, a person believed to have been raised from the grave by a *houngan* [sorcerer] for purposes of enslavement. The zombi is used by his master to perform heavy manual labor and to implement his evil schemes.

zone [Gr.,=girdle], in geography, area with a certain physical unity that distinguishes it from other areas. The division of the earth into five climatic zones probably originated (5th cent. B.C.) with Parmenides, who recognized a torrid zone (see TROPICS) and north and south temperate zones and postulated north and south frigid (or arctic) zones; his classification was adopted by Aristotle and is still in use. The zones are based on latitude: the torrid zone lies between 23½°N and 23½°S, the temperate zones between these parallels and the polar circles, and the frigid zones from the polar circles to the poles. Later geographers, recognizing that climate is affected by such conditions as altitude, distance from water, prevailing winds, and ocean currents, have used other bases for zoning. Most geographers today recognize five major climatic groups, based mainly on the work of the German meteorologist Wladimir Köppen. Two of these groups—the rainy tropics and the dry tropics, which encompass four different climates—together correspond roughly to the former torrid zone. Two humid climate groups of the Köppen system, encompassing six climates, together correspond roughly to the former temperate zones. Köppen's two polar climates correspond roughly to the two former frigid zones. In addition to the five groups encompassing twelve climates, geographers also recognize a series of highland zones where many of the other climates of the world are duplicated.

Zonguldak (zông"gŏŏldäk'), city (1970 pop. 72,688), capital of Zonguldak prov., N Turkey, a port on the Black Sea. It is the center of the major coal-producing region of Turkey.

zoning, legislative regulations by which a municipal government seeks to control the use of buildings and land within the municipality. It has become, in the United States, a widespread method of controlling urban and suburban construction and removing congestion and other defects of existing plans. Great Britain, Germany, and Sweden preceded the United States in zoning for the purpose of controlling building in new areas adjoining cities. The zoning resolution adopted by New York City in 1916 was the first in the United States and has profoundly affected New York architecture, while the standard it set has been followed by other cities. By this law (often amended since 1916) New York City is divided into use districts, area districts, and height districts. Use districts are of four classes: residential, business, retail, and unrestricted. Such zoning has made it possible to control the character of neighborhoods and to maintain residential sections free from objectionable encroachments. The area districts establish minimum dimensions for yards and courts and maximum areas of buildings relative to the areas of their sites. The height and area limitations serve to insure light and air for the occupants of city buildings. In the United States the state legislatures hold the power to authorize zoning, within which the separate cities enact their own zoning ordinances. To accomplish more than the mere amelioration of conditions, zoning is typically closely integrated with a CITY PLANNING program. See S. J. Makielski, Jr., *The Politics of Zoning: The New York Experience* (1966); Norman Williams, *The Structure of Urban Zoning, and Its Dynamics in Urban Planning and Development* (1966); S. I. Toll, *Zoned America* (1969); Irving Schiffman, *The Politics of Land-Use Planning and Zoning* (1970); R. B. Andrews, ed., *Urban Land Use Policy: The Central City* (1972).

zoological garden, public or private park where living animals are kept for exhibition and study. The menageries and aviaries of China, Egypt, and Rome were famous in ancient times. From the late medieval period many rulers had private menageries, some of which later formed the nucleus of public exhibits. Nearly all large cities now have zoological reserves. Notable ones include those of London (Regent's Park), Paris (Jardin des Plantes and Jardin d'Acclimatation, Bois de Boulogne), Berlin (Tiergarten), New York City (Bronx Park), Chicago (Lincoln Park and Brookfield), Cincinnati, Detroit, Philadelphia, St. Louis, and San Diego (Balboa Park). Although some of the exotic animals exhibited are born in captivity, most are captured in their native habitats. Some zoos, in order to save animal species faced with extinction, are trying to breed them in captivity. Modern trends are the exhibition of animals in enclosures simulating their natural habitat rather than in cages and the education of the public about principles of ecology.

zoology, branch of BIOLOGY concerned with the study of animal life. From earliest times animals have been vitally important to man; cave art demonstrates the practical and mystical significance animals held for prehistoric man. Early efforts to classify animals were based on physical resemblance, habitat, or economic use. Although Hippocrates and Aristotle did much toward organizing the scientific thought of their times, systematic investigation declined under the Romans and, after Galen's notable contributions, came to a virtual halt lasting through the Middle Ages (except among the Arab physicians). With the Renaissance direct observation of nature revived; landmarks were Vesalius' anatomy and Harvey's demonstration of the circulation of blood. The invention of the microscope and the use of experimental techniques expanded zoology as a field and established many of its branches, e.g., cytology and histology. Studies in embryology and morphology revealed much about the nature of growth and the biological relationships of animals. The system of binomial nomenclature (see CLASSIFICATION) was devised to indicate these relationships; Linnaeus was the first to make it consistent and apply it systematically. Paleontology, the study of fossil organisms, was founded as a science by Cuvier c.1812. Knowledge of physiological processes expanded greatly when physiology was integrated with the chemical and other physical sciences. The establishment of the cell theory in 1839 and the acceptance of protoplasm as the stuff of life 30 years later gave impetus to the development of genetics. Lamarck, Mendel, and Darwin presented concepts that revolutionized scientific thought. Their theories of evolution and of the physical basis of heredity prompted research into all life processes and into the relationships of all organisms. The classic work of Pasteur and Koch opened up bacteriology as a field. Modern zoology has not only concentrated on the cell, its parts and functions, and on expanding the knowledge of cytology, physiology, and biochemistry, but it has also explored such areas as psychology, anthropology, and ecology.

zooplankton: see MARINE BIOLOGY.

zootoxin: see VENOM.

Zophah (zō'fə), Asherite. 1 Chron. 7.35,36.

Zophai (zō'fī), variant of ZUPH **1**.

Zophar (zō'fär), comforter of Job. Job. 2.11.

Zophim, Field of (zō'fĭm), place, near Mt. Pisgah, associated with Balaam. Num. 23.14.

Zoppot: see SOPOT, Poland.

Zorach, William (zŏr'äk), 1887–1966, American sculptor, b. Lithuania. His family emigrated to the United States when he was four and settled near Cleveland. After studying at the Cleveland School of Art and the National Academy of Design, New York City, Zorach spent two years in France. Shortly after his return to the United States he took up permanent residence in New York. In 1922 he turned from painting to sculpture. Without formal training in this field he evolved a personal and monumental style that placed him among the foremost sculptors of his day. Carving mainly in stone and in wood, he is known for the simplicity and solidity of his forms. His works are in many private and public collections. In New York the Whitney Museum owns his *Pegasus* and *Future Generation;* the Radio City Music Hall has his *Spirit of the Dance.* Zorach taught at the Art Students League. See his *Zorach Explains Sculpture* (1960) and *Art Is My Life* (1967); study by J. I. H. Baur (1959).

Zorah (zō'rə) or **Zoreah** (zōrē'ə), town, Palestine, the modern Zora (Israel), W of Jerusalem. Zorah was the home of Samson. The town was also called Zareah, and its inhabitants were known as Zorathites or Zareathites. Joshua. 15.33; 19.41; Judges 13.25; 16.31; 18.2,8,11; 1 Chron. 4.2; 2 Chron. 11.10; 1 Chron. 2.53; Neh. 11.29.

zorilla, small, carnivorous, nocturnal mammal, *Ictonyx striatus,* of the WEASEL family, found in dry regions of Africa. It is also called striped weasel and striped polecat. Although it strongly resembles the North American SKUNK, a member of the same family, it is more closely related to the true POLECAT of Eurasia. The zorilla has thick fur with black and white markings, and a long, bushy tail. Its anal glands secrete a pungent fluid that can be ejected as a defense against predators. It is avoided by other animals. It lives in rocky crevices and hunts by night, feeding on small reptiles and rodents. Other African members of the weasel family, also called striped weasels, are more weasellike in appearance, with long, slender bodies. Zorillas are classified in the phylum CHORDATA, subphylum Vertebrata, class Mammalia, order Carnivora, family Mustelidae.

Zorites (zō'rīts), unidentified name, perhaps a reference to the natives of Zorah. 1 Chron. 2.54.

Zorn, Anders Leonhard (än'dərs lā'o͝onärd sôrn), 1860–1920, Swedish painter, etcher, and sculptor. Zorn's early and phenomenal popularity was sustained throughout his career as a portrait painter of eminent persons in all fields. He was admired for the charm and freshness of his work, which also included genre and landscape subjects. He traveled throughout Europe and in 1903 visited the United States but he always returned to his native Mora, Sweden. Zorn's works are in many European and American collections; his *Mora* (Worcester, Mass., Art Mus.) is a fine example. Since his death, his virtuoso etching style has been esteemed more than his work in oils. See studies by Karl Asplund (1921) and E. M. Lang (1923).

Zoroaster (zōr'ōăs"tər), c.628 B.C.–c.551 B.C., religious teacher and prophet of ancient Persia, founder of Zoroastrianism. Zoroaster, the name by which he is ordinarily known, is derived from the Greek form of Zarathushtra (or Zarathustra) [camel handler?], his Persian name. Zoroaster is believed to have been born in NW Persia. His youthful studies were crowned at the age of 30 by the first of a series of revelations of a new religion. His attempts to proselytize at home failed, and he fled east to ancient Chorasmia (now largely Persian Khorasan), where he converted King Vishtaspa (who may have been Hystaspes, the father of Darius). The religion then spread rapidly through Vishtaspa's domain. The circumstances of Zoroaster's death are not known. See Ernst Herzfeld, *Zoroaster and His World* (1947); R. C. Zaehner, *The Dawn and Twilight of Zoroastrianism* (1961).

Zoroastrianism (zô"rōăs'trēənĭzəm), religion founded by Zoroaster, but with many later accretions. Its scriptures are the *Avesta* or the *Zend Avesta* [Pahlavi *avesta*=law, *zend*=commentary]. The Avesta consists of fragmentary and much-corrupted texts; it is written in old Iranian, a language similar to Vedic Sanskrit. The major sections of the *Avesta* are four—the *Yasna,* a liturgical work that includes the *Gathas* ("songs"), probably the oldest part of the *Avesta* and perhaps in part written by Zoroaster himself; the *Vispered,* a supplement to the *Yasna;* the *Yashts,* hymns of praise, including the *Khurda* ("little") *Avesta;* and the *Videvdat,* a detailed code of ritual purification, often erroneously called the *Vendidad.* Other sources of Zoroastrianism are Achaemenid inscriptions, the writings of Herodotus, Strabo, and Plutarch, and the commentaries on the *Avesta* written (6th cent. A.D.) in Pahlavi, a Persian dialect used as a priestly language, under the Sassanids. In its origins Zoroastrianism appears to have been the religious expression of the peaceful, sedentary communities of N Iran as opposed to the animistic polytheism of their enemies, the nomadic horsemen. Zoroaster consistently contrasts these two peoples as the People of Righteousness (*asha*) and the People of the Lie (*druj*). The religion was concerned with increasing the harvest and with protecting and treating kindly the domestic animals whose labors accomplished the production of food. Gradually certain practices that Zoroaster appears to have deplored, such as the use of haoma (a narcotic intoxicant) in prayer and the sacrifice of bulls in connection with the cult of the god Mithra (a lesser god in Zoroastrianism), became features of the religion. It is not surprising, however, that former customs should be thus revived, because Zoroaster appears to have incorporated in his religion the old Persian pantheon, although very much refined. Instead of tolerating the worship of all the deities, however, he divided them into those who were beneficent and truthful and those whose malevolence and falseness made them abhorrent. Heading the good spirits was Ahura Mazdah (also Ormazd or Ormuzd) [sovereign knowledge], in primitive Zoroastrianism the only god. Six attendant deities, the Amesha Spentas, surround him. These abstract representations, formerly the personal aspects of Ahura Mazdah, are Vohu Manah [good thought], Asha Vahista [highest righteousness], Khshathra Vairya [divine kingdom], Spenta Armaiti [pious devotion], Haurvatat [salvation], and Ameretat [immortality]. In time the Amesha Spentas became archangelic in character and less abstract. Opposing the good *ahuras* were the evil spirits, the *daevas* or *divs,* led by Ahriman. The war between these two supernatural hosts is the subject matter of the fully developed cosmogony and eschatology of Zoroastrianism. The entire history of the universe, past, present, and future, the religion teaches, is divided into four periods, each of 3,000 years. In the first period there was no matter; the second preceded the coming of Zoroaster; and in the third his faith is propagated. The struggle between good and evil rages during the first nine millennia, and humans help Ahura Mazdah or Ahriman according to whether their conduct is good or evil. Each person after death crosses the Chinvato Peretav [bridge of the separator], which spans hell. If he is reprobate, the bridge narrows and he tumbles to perdition, but if he is worthy of salvation he finds a wide road to the realm of light. In the fourth period of the universe a savior, Saoshyant, will appear, the dead will rise for their final reward or punishment, and good will reign eternally. Zoroastrianism should be regarded as quasi-dualistic, rather than (as sometimes described) wholly dualistic, since it predicts the ultimate triumph of Ahura Mazdah. This god may be represented in the form of the pure natural substances that he has created, notably fire but also water and earth. The special veneration shown to fire and its use in religious ceremonies has led to the erroneous belief that the Zoroastrians were fire worshippers. The care taken to avoid contaminating these natural substances led to great elaboration of the purification ritual. The priests, successors to the pre-Zoroastrian MAGI, acquired great power by their command of the techniques of purification. The priests also had great influence on the government in the first period of Zoroastrianism, that under the Achaemenids, when it was for a time the state religion. Alexander's conquest of Persia and the collapse of the Achaemenids destroyed the privileged position of Zoroastrianism. Little is known of the religion for the next 500 years, except that an offshoot, Mithraism (stemming from the worship of MITHRA), was taking hold farther west. Zoroastrianism reemerged (A.D. c.226) under ARDASHIR I, who established the Sassanian dynasty and fostered a general revival of Achaemenian culture. For four centuries Zoroastrianism was the state religion of the Sassanids, and it successfully met the challenge of nascent Christianity and, later, of heretical MANICHAEISM. In the mid-7th cent. Persia fell to Islam, and Zoroastrianism virtually disappeared. Aside from the PARSIS of India, fewer than 10,000 persons (concentrated in Yezd and Kerman, Iran) practice the religion today. Zoroastrianism has affected Judaism (particularly during the time of the Captivity) and, through GNOSTICISM, Christianity. The *Manual of Discipline* in the Dead Sea Scrolls is believed to reflect Zoroastrian influence. See M. N. Dhalla, *Zoroastrian Theology* (1914, repr. 1972) and *History of Zoroastrianism* (1938, repr. 1963); R. C. Zaehner, *The Dawn and Twilight of Zoroastrianism* (1961). See also bibliography under ZOROASTER.

Zorobabel (zōrŏb'əbəl), variant of ZERUBBABEL.

Zorrilla y Moral, José (hōsā' thôrē'lyä ē mōräl'), 1817–93, Spanish poet and dramatist. His works and life epitomized the brief period of Spanish romanticism. One of the most honored of Spanish writers, he was nevertheless continually impoverished. Among his many plays *Don Juan Tenorio* (1844) is a Spanish favorite, as is *El zapatero y el rey* [the shoemaker and the king] (1840–42). He gathered and reconstructed many legends in *Cantos del trovador* (1841), *Granada* (1852), and other volumes of verse and also wrote an interesting autobiography (1880–83).

zorro: see FOX.

Zoshchenko, Mikhail Mikhailovich (mēkhəyēl mēkhī'ləvĭch zô'shchənkô), 1895–1958, Soviet humorist. Zoshchenko was born in Poltava, but spent most of his life in St. Petersburg where he attended the university. His first collection of short stories (1922) was a major success, and he became one of the most popular Soviet writers of the 1920s and 30s, poking fun at everything, while maintaining his artistic independence. His longer works, *Youth Restored* (1933) and *The Blue Book* (1936), combine fiction and nonfiction. *Before Sunrise* (1943) is autobiographical. A victim of the 1946 literary purge, Zoshchenko was expelled from the Union of Soviet Writers and his works were banned. His stories were not published again until 1956. See his *Scenes from the Bathhouse,* ed. by Sidney Monas and Marc Slonim (tr. 1961), *Nervous People and Other Satires,* ed. by Hugh McLean (tr. 1963), and *The Woman Who Could Not Read* (tr. 1940, repr. 1973).

Zr, chemical symbol of the element ZIRCONIUM.

Zrenjanin (zrĕnyä'nĕn), city (1971 pop. 129,846), NE Yugoslavia, in the Vojvodina region of Serbia, on the Begej River. A river port and a railway center, it has industries that produce foodstuffs, beer, textiles, and agricultural machinery. It was known as Nagybecskerek until its transfer (1918; confirmed 1920) from Hungary to Yugoslavia, and it was subsequently named Veliki Bečkerek (until the 1930s) and Petrovgrad (until 1947).

Zrinyi (zrĭn'yē), noble Hungarian family of Croatian origin. **Nicholas Zrinyi,** 1508–66, distinguished himself in the defense of Vienna (1529) against Sultan Sulayman I, took part in the campaign of Ferdinand I of Austria (later Holy Roman emperor) against John Zapolya, who claimed the Hungarian crown as JOHN I, and was appointed (1542) governor of Croatia. He is famous for his defense of Szigetvar against the army of Sulayman I and was killed there while attempting a sortie. His great-grandson **Nicholas Zrinyi,** 1616–64, was made governor of Croatia in 1647. He campaigned successfully against the Turks and was the acknowledged national leader of the Hungarians when he died in a hunting accident. He was a distinguished poet, one of the first to use Hungarian as a literary language. Besides lyric poetry, he also wrote an epic poem on the defense of Szigetvar by his ancestor and several prose works on political subjects, modeled on the style of Machiavelli. His brother, **Peter Zrinyi,** 1621–71, became governor of Croatia in 1665. Disappointed by the absolutist policy of the Hapsburgs, who owed their success in Hungary largely to the Zrinyi family, he joined (1671) with several other Hungarian magnates in a conspiracy against Holy Roman Emperor Leopold I. The plot, backed by Louis XIV of France, was ill organized and easily suppressed. Zrinyi was executed. His daughter, **Helen Zrinyi,** d. 1703, married Francis I RÁKÓCZY and, after Rákóczy's death, Imre THÖKÖLY. She was the mother of the Hungarian national hero, Francis II Rákóczy.

Zuar (zo͞o'är), father of an Issacharite chief. Num. 1.8; 2.5; 7.18,23; 10.15.

Zuccarelli, Francesco (fränchĕs'kō tso͞ok-kärĕl'lē), 1702–88, Florentine landscape painter and decorator. He twice visited London, where he decorated the Opera House and was well known through popular engravings of his scenes on the Thames. He was a charter member of the Royal Academy. His facile paintings of landscapes with ruins and small figures are best seen in Windsor Castle and in the Academy, Venice.

Zuccaro (tso͞ok'kärō), **Zuccari** (tso͞ok'kärē), or **Zucchero** (tso͞ok'kārō), Italian painters, two brothers, who were leading exponents of the late mannerist style in Rome. **Taddeo Zuccaro,** 1529–66, won recognition by his decorative paintings in the Mattei Palace, Rome. He became painter to Popes Julius III and Paul IV. Together with his brother Federigo, he painted some delightful mythological and historical scenes for the Caprarola Palace of Cardinal Farnese. They also painted frescoes in the Vatican. Among Taddeo's other works in Rome are the *Dead Christ* (Borghese Gall.) and the *Conversion of St. Paul* (Doria Gall.). He is buried in the Pantheon close to the tomb of Raphael. See John Gore, *Taddeo Zuccaro* (1969). **Federigo Zuccaro,** 1543–1609, was associated with his brother for years, but led a more picaresque life. He traveled to Venice, Holland, and England, where he painted portraits of Queen Elizabeth and Mary Stuart. Returning to Rome, he worked on the decoration of the Pauline Chapel, which had been started by Michelangelo. In Florence he completed the *Last Judgment* begun by Vasari in the dome of the cathedral. Subsequently he sojourned in Spain, where he executed some work in the Escorial for Philip II. Again in Rome, Federigo designed parts of several buildings. He constructed the Zuccari Palace and adorned the interior with allegorical scenes. As president (1593–94) of St. Luke's Academy, Federigo was one of the first to develop lectures and theoretical discussions on art. See Anthony Blunt, *Artistic Theory in Italy* (1956), and Nikolaus Pevsner, *Academies of Art, Past and Present* (1940).

Zucchi, Antonio (äntô'nyō tso͞ok'kē), 1726–95, Venetian painter. Robert and James Adam made Zucchi's acquaintance in Venice, traveled with him in Italy, and persuaded him (c.1766) to come to England to collaborate in their architectural works. Zucchi executed many wall and ceiling decorations for their interiors, notably at Syon House. He was elected associate of the Royal Academy in 1770. In 1781 he married the Swiss painter Angelica KAUFFMANN and moved with her to Italy, where he spent the rest of his life.

Zuckmayer, Carl (kärl tso͞ok'mīər), 1896–, German dramatist. Zuckmayer devoted himself to writing after the success of his comedy *Der fröhliche Weinberg* (1925). During World War II he lived in the United States. His popular plays include *Der Hauptmann von Köpenick* (1931; tr. *The Captain of Köpenick,* 1932), satirizing German militarism, and *Des Teufels General* (1946; tr. *The Devil's General,* 1950), portraying the dilemma of an anti-Nazi German army officer. Both have been adapted as films. Zuckmayer's expressionistic style exhibits a controlled sentimentality. His best-known film script is *Der blaue Engel* [the blue angel] (1930). Zuckmayer's other works include poems, the espionage novel *Das kalte Licht* (1955, tr. 1958), and two autobiographies (1940, in English; and 1966, tr. 1970).

Zug (tso͞ok), canton (1970 pop. 67,996), 93 sq mi (241 sq km), N central Switzerland. The smallest canton in Switzerland, it is a forested and mountainous region with orchards, meadows, and pastures in the valleys. Cattle breeding is a main occupation. Its inhabitants are mainly German-speaking and Catholic. Owned by the counts of Kyburg and later (after 1273) by the Hapsburg family, Zug joined the Swiss Confederation in 1352 and again in 1364, after a return to Hapsburg domination. In 1845 the canton joined the Catholic SONDERBUND. Its capital, **Zug** (1970 pop. 22,972), is on the Lake of Zug (15 sq mi/ 39 sq km). It has manufactures of metalware, electrical equipment, textiles, and kirsch. Zug retains a medieval flavor. Its Church of St. Oswald is one of the most splendid late-Gothic churches in Switzerland.

Zugspitze (tso͞ok'shpĭt'sə), mountain, 9,721 ft (2,963 m) high, in the Bavarian Alps and on the West German-Austrian border; highest peak of West Germany. A cog-and-pinion railroad connects the popular resort of Garmisch-Partenkirchen, at its foot, with the summit.

Zuhair (zo͞ohīr'), fl. 6th cent., Arabian poet. Zuhair is often considered the greatest writer of Arabic poetry in pre-Islamic times. His work is represented in the MUALLAQAT. Zuhair's poems deal with raids and other subjects of nomadic desert life. There are several European translations of his works.

Zuider Zee (zī'dər zē, zā, Du. zoi'dər zā), former shallow inlet of the North Sea, c.80 mi (130 km) long, indenting NE Netherlands. Once a lake, it was joined to the North Sea by a great flood in the 13th cent. A vast drainage project, begun in 1920, split the old Zuider Zee into the IJSSELMEER, S of the IJsselmeer dam, and the Waddenzee, between the dam and the West Frisian Islands. Much of the IJsselmeer has since been reclaimed for farm lands and urban expansion.

Zuloaga, Ignacio (ēgnä'thyō tho͞olōä'gä), 1870–1945, Spanish painter. He was the son of a celebrated Basque goldsmith. Zuloaga lived chiefly in Paris after 1889, but his subjects were usually Spanish. His figures, often Basque peasants or bullfighters, are usually richly colored against a somber background. Among his paintings are *Uncle David and His Family* (Mus. of Fine Arts, Boston); a self-portrait and *The Family of a Gypsy Bullfighter* (Hispanic Society, New York City.) There is a museum of his work in Madrid.

Zululand (zo͞o'lo͞olănd''), historic region and home of the Zulu, c.10,000 sq mi (25,900 sq km), NE Natal prov., Republic of South Africa. Zululand is bordered by the Indian Ocean on the east, by Mozambique on the north, and by Swaziland on the west. The terrain rises from a low coastal plain to the foothills of the Drakensberg range. There are several game and forest reserves. The Zulu, who belong to the southern branch of the Nguni-speaking peoples, constitute the majority of the population, and Zulu is the chief language. Although some maize is grown, the Zulu economy depends primarily on cattle raising. Zululand's two major commercial crops, sugarcane and cotton, are generally cultivated on European-owned coastal plantations. Sugar milling and some paper making are virtually the region's only industries. There is also considerable exploitation of wattle and eucalyptus. Most Zulu live as members of an extended family in a fenced compound (kraal), headed by the oldest man. Members of the family occupy beehive-shaped huts in the enclosure of the kraal, within which the cattle are kept penned. The prolonged absence of a majority of the men, many of whom are employed in the distant cities and mines of South Africa has, however, weakened Zulu society. The name Zulu originally denoted a small tribe that, migrating southward, reached the area around the Tugela River in the late 17th cent. The Zulu became historically important in the early 19th cent. under CHAKA, whose conquests reduced many tribes to vassalage and caused others to flee. His warlike successors soon encountered the Boer settlers migrating north into Natal as part of the Great Trek (see TREK). The Zulu chief Dingaan ambushed and slaughtered about 500 Boers in 1838. In revenge about 3,000 Zulu were killed by the forces of Andries PRETORIUS in the Battle of Blood River. Subsequent Boer intervention in Zulu domestic affairs led in 1840 to the overthrow of Dingaan and the crowning of Mpanda, who became a vassal of the Boer republic of Natal. The British, who succeeded the Boers as rulers of Natal in 1843, encountered the hostility of Mpanda's son, CETEWAYO. After he ignored an ultimatum that he submit to British rule, Great Britain launched an attack on Zululand in 1878 and, although suffering several grave defeats, finally triumphed in July, 1879. Faced with continuing Zulu rebellions, the British annexed Zululand in 1887; it became part of Natal in 1897. The Bantustan (black African homeland) designated by the government of South Africa, in accordance with the Bantu Self-Government Act of 1959, to be the Zulu homeland has been named Kwazulu [land of the Zulu]; it is 12,140 sq mi (31,444 sq km) in area and is made up of isolated tracts of land, only some of which were part of historical Zululand. It is, therefore, neither geographically unified nor territorially homogeneous. The area north of the Tugela River, where the largest tracts of Zulu territory lie, forms the hub of Kwazulu. Ulundi is the capital. Slightly more than half of South Africa's Zulu population lives in Kwazulu, which also has Xhosa, Sotho, and Swazi minorities.

Zumalacárregui, Tomás de (tōmäs' dā so͞o''-mäläkär'rāgē), 1788–1835, Spanish Carlist general. A professional soldier, he fought against the French in the Peninsular War (1808–14) and supported the absolutist cause during the disturbances of 1820–23. When King Ferdinand VII died (1833), Zumalacárregui supported the claim of Ferdinand's brother Don Carlos to the throne (see CARLISTS). Put in command of the Carlist army in 1834, he proved himself master of both regular and irregular warfare. He was undefeated until his death in the siege of Bilbao (1835).

Zumárraga, Juan de (hwän dā tho͞omä'rägä), 1468–1548, Spanish churchman, first bishop of Mexico, a Franciscan. Going to Mexico in 1528, he became prominent in governmental affairs and opposed Nuño de GUZMÁN and the AUDIENCIA. He was officially made protector of the Indians and exerted strenuous efforts to convert them and to end human sacrifice. In his zeal to bring Spanish civilization to the Indians, however, he destroyed valuable Indian manuscripts and remains. He was important in founding the college of Santa Cruz de Tlaltelolco for the education of the Indians. A close friend and assistant of Viceroy Antonio de MENDOZA, he helped to improve conditions in New Spain. Zumárraga was instrumental in bringing the first printing press to the New World and wrote religious manuals that were among the early products of the press.

Zungaria: see DZUNGARIA, China.

Zuñi (zo͞o'nyē, zo͞o'nē), pueblo (1970 pop. 3,958), McKinley co., W N.Mex., in the Zuñi Indian Reservation; built c.1695. Its inhabitants are Pueblo Indians of the Zuñian linguistic family. They are a sedentary people, who farm irrigated land and are noted for basketry, pottery, turquoise jewelry, and weaving, and for their ceremonial dances. The original seven Zuñi villages are usually identified with the mythical Seven Cities of Cibola, which were publicized by Marcos de Niza. In 1540, Francisco Vásquez de Coronado attacked the villages, thinking that they had vast stores of gold. The villages were abandoned in the Pueblo revolt of 1680. The present pueblo was built on the site of one of the original seven villages. Despite many attempts to Christianize the Zuñi, they have held to their ancient religion. Their chief festival, held in late November or early December, is the Shalako Festival, in which masked dancers represent Zuñi deities in the act of blessing new homes. See Aileen Nusbaum, *The Seven Cities of Cibola* (1926); *The Zuñis: Self-Portrayals,* by the Zuñi People (tr. by Alvina Guam, 1972).

Zunser, Eliakum (ĕl'yōko͞om tso͞on'zər), 1846–1913, Lithuanian folk poet and singer who wrote in Yiddish. The most popular Jewish folk singer of his time, he appeared at weddings all over Russia, delivering sermons and extemporizing songs. A collection of his poems, *Shrim Khadoshim,* was published in 1861. After the pogroms of 1880–81, he became an adherent of Zionism. In 1889 he emigrated to the United States, settling in New York City and opening a print shop.

Zunz, Leopold (lā'ōpôlt tso͞onts'), 1794–1886, German Jewish scholar. His critical research on Judaism became one of the cornerstones of the "science of Judaism," the modern approach of studying Judaism and Jewry in the context of the general history of mankind, particularly in its progress. Part II of his *Synagogale Poesie des Mittelalters* (1855) was translated as *The Sufferings of the Jews during the Middle Ages* (1907). See the letters of Leopold and Adelbeid Zunz, ed. by N. N. Glatzer (1958).

Zuph (zo͞of). **1** Ancestor of Samuel. 1 Sam. 1.1; 1 Chron. 6.35. Zophai: 1 Chron. 6.26. **2** District, near RAMATHAIM-ZOPHIM, inhabited by the clan of Zuph. 1 Sam. 9.5.

Zur (zûr). **1** Prince of Midian killed by the Jews. Num. 25.15; 31.8; Joshua 13.21. **2** Son of Jehiel. 1 Chron. 8.30; 9.36.

Zurbarán, Francisco de (frănthēs'kō thā tho͝orbärän'), 1598–1664, Spanish baroque painter, active mainly at Llerena, Madrid, and Seville. He worked mostly for ecclesiastical and royal patrons. His early paintings, including *Crucifixion* (1627; Art Inst., Chicago), *St. Michael* (Metropolitan Mus.), and *St. Francis* (City Art Museum, St. Louis), often suggest the austere simplicity of wooden sculpture. The figures, placed close to the picture surface, are strongly modeled in dramatic light against dark backgrounds, indicating the influence of Caravaggio. In the 1630s the realistic style seen in his famous *Apotheosis of St. Thomas Aquinas* (1631; Seville) yields to a more mystical expression in works such as the *Adoration of the Shepherds* (1638; Grenoble); in this decade he was influenced by Ribera's figural types and rapid brushwork. After c.1640 the simple power of Zurbarán's work lessened as Murillo's influence on his painting increased (e.g., *Virgin and Child with St. John,* Fine Arts Gall., San Diego, Calif.). There are works by Zurbarán in the Hispanic Society of America, New York City; the National Gallery, Washington, D.C.; and the Philadelphia Museum of Art. See study by M. S. Soria (repr. 1955).

Zürich (tsü'rĭkh), canton (1970 pop. 1,107,788), 668 sq mi (1,730 sq km), N Switzerland. Zürich is bounded in part by the Lake of Zürich in the south and West Germany in the north. It is a fertile agricultural region with orchards, meadows, and forests. Among the rivers that flow through the canton are the Rhine and the Thur. Machinery and other metal goods as well as textiles are manufactured. Its inhabitants are chiefly German-speaking and Protestant. In the canton there are numerous towns and a few industrial cities, notably WINTERTHUR and the capital, **Zürich** (1970 pop. 422,640). The largest Swiss city, Zürich is the country's commercial and economic center as well as the intellectual center of German-speaking Switzerland. Its industrial products include machine tools, radios, clothes, paper, and textiles. It is the hub of a printing and publishing industry and has many banking and financial institutions. Occupied as early as the Neolithic period by lake dwellers, the site of Zürich was settled by the Helvetii. It was conquered (58 B.C.) by the Romans, and after the 5th cent. passed successively to the Alemanni, the Franks, and to Swabia. It became a free imperial city after 1218, accepted a corporative constitution in 1336, and joined the Swiss Confederation in 1351. Its claim to the TOGGENBURG led to a ruinous war (1436–50) with the other confederates. In the 16th cent. Zürich, under the influence of Ulrich Zwingli, became the leading power of the Swiss Reformation and once more provoked a civil war. The Roman Catholic victory at Kappel (1531) ended Zürich's political leadership. In 1799 the city was the scene of two battles of the French Revolutionary Wars (see HELVETIC REPUBLIC). Zürich developed as a cultural and scientific center in the 18th and 19th cent. It has the largest Swiss university (founded 1833), a world-famous polytechnic school (est. mid-19th cent.), and many museums. The Romanesque Grossmünster (11th–13th cent.), where Zwingli preached, the Fraumünster (12th and 15th cent.), the 17th-century town hall, and numerous old residences contrast harmoniously with many fine modern structures. The educational reformer Heinrich Pestalozzi was born in the city, and James Joyce is buried there. The city is beautifully situated on the Limmat and Sihl rivers and at the northern end of the Lake of Zürich.

Zürich, Lake of, Ger. *Zürichsee,* narrow, elongated lake, 34 sq mi (88 sq km), 25 mi (40 km) long, N Switzerland. It has a maximum depth of c.470 ft (140 m). The lake is connected to the Lake of Wallenstadt (Walensee) by the Linth Canal and also receives water from the Linth River. It is drained by the Limmat River. The gently sloping shores of the lake are covered with vineyards, orchards, and woods; houses and villas dot the slopes. A causeway crosses the lake between Rapperswil and Hurden. The city of Zürich is located at the northern end of the lake.

Zuriel (zo͞o'rēĕl, zo͞orī'əl), chief Merarite. Num. 3.35.

Zurishaddai (zo͞o''rĭshăd'āī), father of a Simeonite chief. Num. 1.6; 2.12; 7.36,41; 10.19.

Zutphen (zŭt'fən), city (1971 pop. 27,871), Gelderland prov., E central Netherlands, on the IJssel River. It is an administrative, industrial, and commercial center. Zutphen was chartered in 1191 and was an important Spanish stronghold during the Dutch struggle for independence (16th cent.). Sir Philip Sidney died (1586) in a skirmish at the city's walls while aiding his uncle, the earl of Leicester, in an unsuccessful attempt to take Zutphen from the Spanish. The city was captured by the Dutch under Maurice of Nassau in 1591. Notable structures there include a 12th-century Gothic church and many fine buildings of the 17th and 18th cent.

Zuzims (zo͞o'zĭmz), unknown people. Gen. 14.5.

Zweibrücken (tsvī''brü'kən), Fr. *Deux-Ponts,* city (1970 pop. 32,764), Rhineland-Palatinate, W West Germany, near the Saarland border. Zweibrücken is a transportation center and has ironworks, steelworks, and factories that produce leather goods, machines, and textiles. It is also a noted horse-breeding center. Zweibrücken was chartered in 1352 and passed (1385) to the PALATINATE branch of the Bavarian house of Wittelsbach. In 1410 it became the seat of the counts (later dukes) palatine of Zweibrücken under a cadet line of the Palatinate branch. Charles X of Sweden was the nephew of John II, duke palatine of Zweibrücken; his son, Charles XI of Sweden, inherited Zweibrücken in the late 17th cent., and the duchy remained in personal union with Sweden from 1697 until the death (1718) of Charles XII. The Zweibrücken line continued in Sweden until the death (1741) of Ulrica Leonora, sister of Charles XII, and in Zweibrücken until 1731, when the related Palatinate-Birkenfeld line acceded. On the death (1799) of Elector Charles Theodore of Bavaria, who had reunited all the Wittelsbach lands except Zweibrücken, the duke palatine of Zweibrücken, his next of kin, succeeded him as elector of Bavaria, thus completing the reunion of the family territories; as Maximilian I he became (1806) the first king of Bavaria. However, the duchy of Zweibrücken itself had been annexed (1797) to France. It was restored to Bavaria at the Congress of Vienna (1814–15) and since then has shared the history of the Rhenish Palatinate.

Zweig, Arnold (är'nôlt tsvīk), 1887–1968, German novelist and dramatist. A Zionist, he was denationalized under National Socialism and went to Palestine. There he wrote about the plight of German Jews in *Insulted and Exiled* (1933, tr. 1937). After 1948 he returned to live in East Germany. Zweig's realistic novels are characterized by profound humanity and ironic style; the best known, which form a trilogy, are *Education before Verdun* (1935, tr. 1936), *The Case of Sergeant Grischa* (1927, tr. 1927), and *The Crowning of a King* (1937, tr. 1938). His powerful fictional study of life in Germany in 1937, *The Axe of Wandsbek,* appeared in 1947 (tr. 1947). Among his later works are *Five Romances* (tr. 1959). His reminiscences were published in 1967. See his correspondence with Sigmund Freud, ed. by E. L. Freud (1970).

Zweig, Stefan (shtĕf'än), 1881–1942, Austrian biographer, poet, and novelist. Born in Vienna of a well-to-do Jewish family, he was part of the humanitarian, pan-European cultural circle that included Hugo von Hofmannsthal and Richard Strauss. Zweig's first works were poetry and a poetic drama, *Jeremias* (1917, tr. 1929), which expressed his passionately anti-war feelings. Under National Socialism he went into exile in 1934, emigrating first to England. In 1941 he and his second wife went to Brazil, where they committed suicide. Zweig's best-known works of fiction are *Ungeduld des Herzens* (1938, tr. *Beware of Pity,* 1939) and *Schachnovelle* (1944, tr. *The Royal Game,* 1944), but his most outstanding accomplishments were his many biographies, which were based on psychological interpretation. The subjects of these include Marie Antoinette, Erasmus, Mary Queen of Scots, Magellan, Balzac, and Verlaine. Zweig's historical perception is best evident in *Sternstunden der Menschheit* (1928, tr. *The Tide of Fortune,* 1940). See his autobiography, *The World of Yesterday* (1943); biographies by D. A. Prater (1972) and Elizabeth Allday (1972).

Zwickau (tsvĭk'ou), city (1970 pop. 127,000), Karl-Marx-Stadt district, S East Germany, on the Mulde River. It is an industrial city and the center of a coal mining region. Manufactures include machinery, tractors, textiles, mining equipment, and motor vehicles. Zwickau was chartered in the early 13th cent., and it was a free imperial city from 1290 to 1323, when it passed to the margraves of Meissen. The city was (1520–23) the center of the Anabaptist movement of Thomas Münzer. It was repeatedly plundered during the Thirty Years War (1618–48). Noteworthy buildings include a basilica (12th–15th cent.), the Church of St. Catherine (14th cent.), and the city hall (15th cent.). Robert Schumann was born (1810) in Zwickau, and there is a Schumann museum there.

Zwicky, Fritz (tsvĭk'ē), 1898–1974, Swiss-American astrophysicist, b. Bulgaria, educated at Zürich. Associated with the California Institute of Technology after his arrival in the United States in 1925, he became professor of astrophysics in 1942 and emeritus professor in 1972. He discovered a number of supernovas and novas and suggested an explanation for their occurrence. He is also known for his study of jet propulsion, cosmic rays, crystals, and slow electrons and ions in gases.

Zwingli, Huldreich or **Ulrich** (ho͝old'rĭkh tsvĭng'lē, o͝ol'rĭkh), 1484–1531, Swiss Protestant reformer. Zwingli received a thorough classical education in Basel, Bern, and Vienna, and was considerably influenced by the humanist precepts of Erasmus. His devotion to learning and his passion for individual freedom, developed through contact with the self-governing Swiss cantons, were important influences in his life. In 1506 he was ordained and appointed pastor of Glarus; he also served (1513, 1515) as chaplain to Swiss mercenaries in Italy. In 1516 he became people's vicar at Einsiedeln. While there Zwingli began to formulate those ideas that were to lead him to renounce the church of Rome. Unlike Martin Luther, Zwingli experienced no acute religious crisis—he became a reformer through his studies. Later he was to adopt Luther's doctrine of justification by faith alone, but Zwingli's independent study of Scriptures had already led him to question the teaching of the Roman Catholic Church. When he became vicar at the Gross-Münster of Zürich in 1518 he found the democratic institutions of the community amenable to his beliefs. In 1519 he successfully opposed the dispensing of indulgences in the city and soon was preaching against clerical celibacy, monasticism, and many other church practices. The real beginning of the Reformation in Switzerland was Zwingli's lectures on the New Testament in 1519. Armed with Erasmus' 1516 edition of the Greek text he discarded scholastic commentaries and proclaimed the sole authority of the word of God as revealed in Scriptures. With his expression of opposition to Lenten observances in 1522 the Reformation in Zürich was well under way. In the same year, with the publication of *Architeles,* he made clear his belief in freedom from the control of the Roman hierarchy. A public disputation with a papal representative was held before the general council at Zürich in 1523; Zwingli presented his doctrines in 67 theses. The council approved the Zwinglian position and instructed all priests in the canton to comply. The new practices were rapidly put into effect—organs were destroyed, images were removed from churches, priests were allowed to marry, monasticism was abolished, the liturgy was simplified, and the sacrament of communion reduced to a commemorative feast. In 1524, Zwingli publicly celebrated his marriage, which he had illegally contracted two years previously. In 1525 the Catholic Mass was replaced by a reformed service at Zwingli's church in Zürich. He became embroiled with the Lutherans in a doctrinal dispute concerning the nature of the Eucharist (see LORD'S SUPPER). Philip of Hesse endeavored to reconcile these differences within the Protestant ranks by calling the disputants together at the Marburg Colloquy (1529). Zwingli and Johannes OECOLAMPADIUS and Luther and Philip Melanchthon were present, but no agreement was reached. Although Bern adopted Zwingli's reforms in 1528, and Basel and St. Gall soon after, he faced agitation by the Anabaptists, who wanted even more radical reform, and the armed resistance of the Forest Cantons that had remained loyal to Rome. When Zürich imposed a trade embargo on these cantons they retaliated with war (1531), and at the battle of Kappel, Zwingli was killed. Zwingli's work in Zürich was carried on by his colleague and son-in-law, Heinrich BULLINGER, but the Reformation in Switzerland passed into the hands of John Calvin. Calvin built his comprehensive theological system partly on the groundwork laid by Zwingli, but he resisted Zwingli's more radical teaching on baptism and the Lord's Supper. The Consensus Tigurinus (1549) marks the departure of the Swiss Reformation from Zwinglian to Calvinist doctrine. See biographies by J. H. Rilliet (tr. 1964) and Oskar Farner (tr. 1952, repr. 1968). For a selection of his writings, see G. W. Bromiley, ed., *Zwingli and Bullinger* (Library of Christian classics, XXIV, 1953).

Zwolle (zwôl'ə), municipality (1971 pop. 77,047), capital of Overijssel prov., N central Netherlands, on the Zwartewater River. It is an administrative, transportation, and industrial center. Notable buildings include the 15th-century town hall and the Church of St. Michael, a 15th-century Gothic structure. Nearby was the monastery where Thomas à Kempis lived (15th cent.).

Zworykin, Vladimir Kosma (zwô'rĭkĭn), 1889-, American physicist, b. Russia, educated in Russia, at the Collège de France, and at the Univ. of Pittsburgh (Ph.D., 1926). He became an American citizen in 1924. On the staff of the Radio Corp. of America after 1929, he became vice president and technical consultant of the corporation in 1947 and honorary vice president and consultant in 1954. In recognition of his many achievements he was awarded the National Medal of Science in 1967. His important researches in electronics enabled him to develop with his co-workers the iconoscope, a scanning tube for the television camera, and the kinescope, a cathode-ray tube in the television receiving apparatus. A group under his direction produced (1939) an electron microscope. Zworykin is coauthor of *Photocells and Their Application* (1930, rev. ed. 1934), *Television* (1940), *Electron Optics and the Electron Microscope* (1945), *Photoelectricity and Its Application* (1949), and *Television in Science and Industry* (1958).

zygote: see REPRODUCTION.

Żyrardów (zhĭrär'do͞of), city (1970 pop. 33,196), E central Poland. It is a textile center, known especially for its woolens. Leather goods are also manufactured in the city.

Zyrians: see KOMI.